Indicateurs de champs sémantiques et abréviations utilisés dans le texte

English	Abbr	French
mathematics	**Math**	mathématiques
medicine	**Med, Méd**	médecine
carpentry	**Menuis**	menuiserie
meteorology	**Met, Météo**	météorologie
metallurgy	**Metal, Métal**	métallurgie
masculine and feminine noun	**mf**	nom masculin et féminin
military	**Mil**	militaire
mining	**Min**	mines
mineralogy	**Miner, Minér**	minéralogie
marketing	**Mktg**	marketing
masculine plural	**mpl**	masculin pluriel
music	**Mus**	musique
mythology	**Myth**	mythologie
noun	**N**	nom
we	**n.**	nous
swimming	**Natation**	
nautical, naval	**Naut**	nautique, naval
negative	**neg, nég**	négatif
feminine noun	**NF**	nom féminin
feminine plural noun	**NFPL**	nom féminin pluriel
masculine noun	**NM**	nom masculin
masculine plural noun	**NMPL**	nom masculin pluriel
plural noun	**NPL**	nom pluriel
nuclear	**Nucl**	nucléaire
numeral	**NUM**	numéral
obstetrics	**Obst**	obstétrique
occasionally	**occ**	parfois
	Old-fashioned	vieilli
optics	**Opt**	optique
computing	**Ordinat**	ordinateurs, informatique
ornithology	**Orn**	ornithologie
occasionally	**parfois**	
parliament	**Parl**	parlement
fishing	**Pêche**	
pejorative	**Pej, Péj**	péjoratif
personal	**PERS**	personnel
petroleum industry	**Petr, Pétr**	industrie pétrolière
pharmacy	**Pharm**	pharmacie
philosophy	**Phil**	philosophie
philately	**Philat**	philatélie
past historic	**p hist**	passé simple
photography	**Phot**	photographie
physics	**Phys**	physique
physiology	**Physiol**	physiologie
plural	**pl**	pluriel
politics	**Pol**	politique
possessive	**POSS**	possessif
past participle	**pp**	participe passé
present tense	**pr**	présent
prefix	**PREF, PRÉF**	préfixe
preposition	**PREP, PRÉP**	préposition
present indicative	**pr ind**	présent de l'indicatif
pronoun	**PRON**	pronom
proverb	**Prov**	proverbe
present participle	**prp**	participe présent
present subjunctive	**pr sub**	présent du subjonctif

English	Abbr	French
psychology, psychiatry		
past tense		
something		
somebody		
registered trademark	**®**	marque déposée
	qn	quelqu'un
	Radio	
railways	**Rail**	chemin de fer
regionalism	**Région**	régionalisme
relative	**REL**	relatif
religion	**Rel**	religion
somebody	**sb**	quelqu'un
school	**Sch, Scol**	école
Scottish English	**Scot**	anglais d'Écosse
	see	voir
	Sewing	couture
singular	**sing**	singulier
skiing	**Ski**	
slang	**Sl**	argot
often	**souvent**	
	Sport	
specialist term	**Spec, Spéc**	terme de spécialiste
Stock Exchange	**St Exch**	Bourse
something	**sth**	quelque chose
subjunctive	**sub**	subjonctif
suffix	**SUFF**	suffixe
Swiss French	**Suisse**	français de Suisse
superlative	**superl**	superlatif
surgery	**Surg**	chirurgie
especially	**surtout**	
	Swimming	natation
technical	**Tech**	technique
telecommunications	**Tel, Tél**	télécommunications
textiles	**Tex**	textiles
theatre	**Theat, Théâtre**	
very colloquial	**très Fam**	
knitting	**Tricot**	
television	**TV**	télévision
typography, printing	**Typ**	typographie, imprimerie
European Union	**UE**	Union européenne
university	**Univ**	université
usually	**usu**	généralement
verb	**v**	verbe
you	**v.**	vous
veterinary medicine	**Vet, Vét**	médecine vétérinaire
intransitive verb	**VI**	verbe intransitif
old-fashioned	**Vieilli**	
see	**voir**	
pronominal verb	**VPR**	verbe pronominal
transitive verb	**VT**	verbe transitif
inseparable transitive verb	**VT INSEP**	verbe transitif jamais séparé
separable transitive verb	**VT SEP**	verbe transitif séparable
vulgar	**Vulg**	vulgaire
zoology	**Zool**	zoologie
gloss	**=**	glose
cultural equivalent	**≃**	équivalent culturel

HARRAP'S SHORTER

DICTIONARY
English–French / French–English

DICTIONNAIRE
Anglais–Français / Français–Anglais

HARRAP

This 7th edition first published in 2004
by Chambers Harrap Publishers Ltd
7 Hopetoun Crescent, Edinburgh EH7 4AY, UK

The previous (6th) edition of the *Harrap's Shorter Dictionary* was first published
in 2000 and reprinted 2000, 2001, 2002

ISBN 0245 60727 7 (UK)
ISBN 0245 50564 4 (France)

Dépôt légal: décembre 2003

www.chambersharrap.co.uk
www.harrap.com

Designed and typeset by Chambers Harrap Publishers Ltd, Edinburgh
Printed and bound in Italy by La Tipografica Varese SPA

Contributors to 7th edition/Ont participé à la 7ᵉ édition

Project editors/Directeurs de projet

Georges Pilard
Anna Stevenson

with/avec

Bérangère Chevalier
Nadia Cornuau
Pat Dunn
Isabelle Elkaim
Stuart Fortey
Alexandra Jaton
Laurence Larroche
Kate Nicholson
Liam Rodger
Rachel Skeet

Illustrations

Glen McBeth

Prepress/Prépresse

Clair Cameron
Sharon McTeir
David Reid
Kirsteen Wright

Publishing manager/Direction éditoriale

Patrick White

Acknowledgements/Remerciements

Acknowledgements

The publisher would like to acknowledge the contribution made by the previous editorial teams who worked on the Harrap's Shorter and in particular that made by the team managed by Peter Terrell in the making of the fifth edition of this dictionary.

Remerciements

Les éditions Harrap tiennent à remercier tous les rédacteurs qui ont participé aux précédentes éditions du Harrap's Shorter, et tout particulièrement Peter Terrell qui dirigea la cinquième édition de cet ouvrage.

Trademarks

Words considered to be trademarks have been designated in this dictionary by the symbol ®. However, no judgement is implied concerning the legal status of any trademark by virtue of the presence or absence of such a symbol.

Marques déposées

Les termes considérés comme des marques déposées sont signalés dans ce dictionnaire par le symbole ®. Cependant, la présence ou l'absence de ce symbole ne constituent nullement une indication quant à la valeur juridique de ces termes.

Structure of entries/Structure des entrées

Headwords are presented in blue in this dictionary and appear in alphabetical order. Homographs are numbered.

Les entrées du dictionnaire apparaissent en bleu et sont classées par ordre alphabétique. Les homographes sont numérotés.

The different senses of a word are numbered.

Les différents sens des mots sont numérotés.

The grammatical classification of an entry is marked in blue small capital letters (ADJ, ADV, N, etc). All the abbreviated labels included in the list of abbreviations on the inside front and back covers of the dictionary letters (ADJ, ADV, N, etc).

Les différentes catégories grammaticales sont indiquées en bleu et en petites capitales (ADJ, ADV, N, etc). La liste des abréviations des indicateurs de catégories grammaticales figure en début et en fin de dictionnaire.

Nuances of senses, or semantic splits required to show different translations for the same sense, are shown within the same sense category by using indicating material in brackets.

Les nuances et les distinctions sémantiques qui nécessitent des traductions différentes au sein d'une même catégorie sont signalées par des indicateurs de sens qui apparaissent entre parenthèses.

In instances where a term is given two translations, one technical and the other non-technical, the technical translation is placed second and the word preceded by the label *Spec* on the French-English side of the dictionary and *Spec* on the English-French side. The technical translation has been given in addition to the neutral one where the word being translated can be used in both technical and non-technical contexts.

Dans le cas où un mot de la langue source comporte deux traductions, l'une de registre technique et l'autre qui s'utilise dans la langue de tous les jours, la traduction technique est placée en seconde position et précédée de l'abréviation Spec du côté français-anglais et Spec du côté anglais-français. La traduction technique est fournie en plus de la traduction habituelle lorsque le mot traduit s'utilise dans des contextes techniques et non techniques.

The full form of abbreviations and acronyms is systematically given after the headword for greater ease of use.

Pour une plus grande facilité d'utilisation la forme développée des abréviations et acronymes est donnée systématiquement à la suite du mot de tête.

A term will frequently have no exact translation equivalent in the other language. In such cases a cultural equivalent (preceded by the ≈ sign) with similar connotations in the target language may be given.

Il n'est pas rare qu'un terme ne dispose pas d'une traduction exacte dans l'autre langue. Dans ce cas on optera parfois pour un équivalent culturel aux connotations comparables (précédé du signe ≈).

American spelling variants are given in translations on the French-English side.

Les variantes orthographiques américaines figurent au niveau des traductions du côté français-anglais.

---

calcul¹ [kalkyl] NM **1** (*compte*) calculation, reckoning, computation; **faire un c.** to make a calculation; **faux c., erreur de c.** miscalculation; *Ordinat* **calculs très rapides** number crunching **2** *Scol* **le c.** arithmetic, number work; **faible en c.** bad at sums or arithmetic; **apprendre le c.** to learn (how) to count; **enseigner le c.** to teach arithmetic; **3** (*prévision*) calculation; **agir par c.** to act from selfish or ulterior motives; **ça a été un bon c. de notre part** it was a good move on our part, we did the right thing; **un mauvais c.** a miscalculation; **faire un bon c.** to calculate correctly; **faire un mauvais c.** to miscalculate; **selon nos calculs** according to our calculations
▸▸ *Math* **c. différentiel** differential calculus; *Math* **c. intégral** integral calculus; **c. mental** mental arithmetic; **c. des probabilités** theory of probability

calcul² NM *Méd* (*dans la vésicule*) stone, *Spec* calculus; **avoir des calculs** to have stones in the bladder; (*aux reins*) to have kidney stones; **c. biliaire** gall stone; **c. rénal** kidney stone

calculateur, -trice [kalkylatœr, -tris] ADJ (*personne, politique*) calculating
▸▸ N (*personne*) **c'est un bon c.** he's good at or with figures

calculatrice NF calculator

calculer [kalkyle] VT (*compter*) (*prix, surface*) to work out, to calculate; (*conséquences*) to calculate; (*d'un triangle etc*) to work out, to calculate; (*comportement, réflexions etc*) to plan, to calculate; **c. qch de tête** to work sth out or calculate sth in one's head; **tout bien calculé** taking everything into account; **c. ses chances de réussite** to calculate or to weigh up one's chances of success; **c. ses dépenses au plus juste** to work out or calculate one's expenses to the nearest penny
▸▸ VI to calculate; *Péj* (*économiser*) to count every penny; **c. vite et bien** to be quick and accurate at or with figures; **machine à c.** adding machine, (desk) calculator

calculatrice (*machine*) (desktop) calculator; **calculatrice de bureau** desktop calculator; **calculatrice imprimante** print-out calculator; **calculatrice de poche** pocket calculator

calculateur NM 1 (*machine*) (desktop) calculator; **c.** (*electronique*) computer 2 (*de poche*) (pocket) calculator

calibre [kalibr] NM **1** (*d'arme à feu, tuyau etc*) calibre, *Am* caliber; (*de balle etc*) calibre, (*d'œufs, de fruits etc*) grade; **fusil de c. 8 mm** *Mil* 8-mm calibre rifle; *Sport* 8-mm **c.** heavy gun; **canon de gros c.** heavy gun, large-bore gun; *Fig* **sa sœur est d'un autre c.** his sister is of quite a different calibre, *Fam* his sister is in a different league; **il n'est pas de ce c.-là** he's not a man of that calibre; **j'ai rarement vu une bêtise de ce c.!** I've rarely seen stupidity on such a scale!

CAO [sao] NF *Ordinat* (*abrév* **conception assistée par ordinateur**) CAD

CAPES [kapɛs] NM *Univ* (*abrév* **certificat d'aptitude au professorat de l'enseignement secondaire**) = postgraduate teaching certificate

CCP [sesep] NM (*abrév* **compte courant postal, compte chèque postal**) ≈ Giro account

Préface à la 7e édition

Quatre ans déjà se sont écoulés depuis la dernière édition du *Harrap's Shorter*. Quatre ans pendant lesquels le monde a vécu bien des bouleversements, continuant à se transformer à un rythme soutenu, que ce soit dans le domaine de la politique internationale, de la société, et bien entendu dans le domaine technique. Comme toujours, l'ambition du *Harrap's Shorter* est de se faire le fidèle reflet de ces changements sur le plan linguistique afin de proposer à l'utilisateur un outil à la mesure de ses besoins, tant au niveau de la compréhension que de l'expression. Une fois encore, lors de la rédaction du *Shorter*, les maître-mots de notre équipe éditoriale furent "clarté, fiabilité et exhaustivité".

C'est pourquoi cette nouvelle édition s'enrichit de milliers de nouveaux termes issus de nos bases de données, tels que **weapons of mass destruction** ou **WMD**, **rogue state**, **antiglobalization**, **top-up card** pour le côté anglais, et **altermondialisation**, **biovigilance**, **chimiquier**, **biopuce** et **urgentiste** pour le côté français.

Les notes d'aide à la traduction concernant les faux amis et les termes souvent confondus, déjà présentes dans la précédente édition, ont été révisées et augmentées, offrant une aide encore plus précieuse à l'utilisateur pour une meilleure compréhension de la langue et une plus grande facilité d'expression. Par ailleurs, les grammaires anglaise et française situées en milieu d'ouvrage ont été entièrement revues et corrigées et le système de renvois depuis les entrées de dictionnaire vers les grammaires a été amélioré pour une aisance d'utilisation accrue.

D'autre part, cette édition du *Harrap's Shorter* voit l'inclusion de dizaines d'encadrés culturels de part et d'autre du dictionnaire. Ces encadrés proposent des informations complémentaires au lecteur sur des sujets tels que la "devolution" et le "shadow cabinet" du côté anglais, et sur "l'exception française" et les "grandes écoles" du côté français. Notons au passage que conformément à une tradition bien établie aux éditions Harrap, les canadianismes, helvétismes et belgicismes sont très bien représentés, ainsi que les termes et expressions originaires des Etats-Unis, d'Australie, d'Ecosse et d'Irlande.

Pour cette nouvelle mouture de notre ouvrage, l'accent a été mis sur l'aisance d'utilisation et la clarté de la présentation. Ainsi le texte est désormais présenté sur trois colonnes et les mots de tête apparaissent en bleu pour une plus grande lisibilité. De plus, les mots composés sont maintenant présentés alphabétiquement en fin d'article et sont facilement repérables grâce à un double triangle bleu. Autre innovation, les entrées longues et complexes sont dotées, en tête d'article, d'un "menu" où figurent les principales traductions du terme, accompagnées du numéro de catégorie où ce sens est traité. Ce système évite à l'utilisateur de devoir parcourir l'intégralité de l'article pour trouver le sens recherché et la consultation s'en trouve considérablement facilitée.

Enfin, pour le plaisir du lecteur et pour ne pas oublier la dimension ludique de la langue, cette nouvelle édition du *Harrap's Shorter* est agrémentée d'un supplément sur les expressions idiomatiques à connaître en anglais et en français, accompagné de nombreuses illustrations humoristiques en couleurs.

Preface to the 7th edition

Four years have passed since the last edition of the *Harrap's Shorter*, and in that short time the world has seen many changes – politically, socially, and technologically. The aim of the *Shorter* has always been to reflect how these changes influence the language and hence serve as a practical reference tool for its users in the two basic look-up functions: "decoding" (looking up foreign words to understand their meaning) and "encoding" (expressing oneself in the foreign language). As before, the watchwords of the editorial team on this seventh edition have been "clarity, reliability and comprehensiveness".

This new edition thus benefits from the addition of thousands of new words, such as **weapons of mass destruction (WMD)**, **rogue state**, **antiglobalization** and **top-up card** on the English-French side, and **altermondialisation**, **biovigilance**, **chimiquier**, **biopuce** and **urgentiste** on the French-English side.

The notes on false friends and easily confused words that featured in the previous edition have been revised and expanded, making them even more helpful for both decoding and encoding users. The English and French grammars in the centre of the book have also been completely updated, and the system of links from dictionary entries to these grammars has been changed to make it easier to use.

This new edition additionally sees the inclusion of a large number of boxed cultural notes on both sides of the dictionary. These notes give further information on subjects such as "devolution" and "shadow cabinet" on the English side and "exception française" and "grandes écoles" on the French side. It should also be mentioned that, in keeping with a long-standing tradition in Harrap dictionaries, Canadian, Swiss and Belgian French is very well represented in the *Shorter*, as is American, Australian, Scottish and Irish English.

The main thrust of this new edition has, however, been to improve ease of use and the clear presentation of information. The text is therefore now in three columns and headwords are in blue to make it easier to find the word you are looking for. In addition, compounds have been reorganized and are now presented in alphabetical order at the end of an entry, clearly signposted with a blue double arrowhead. A further innovation is the introduction of "menus" at the head of long or complex entries. These menus summarize the main translations of the word and indicate the sense number where that translation appears, thus making it easier for users to find the sense they are looking for without having to read through the whole entry.

Lastly, as an entertaining and informative extra, this new edition of the *Harrap's Shorter* also features a supplement of 400 essential French and English idioms, illustrated with many full-colour humorous cartoons.

Contents/Table des matières

chacal, -als [ʃakal] NM *aussi Fig* jackal

chahut [ʃay] NM *Fam* racket, din; **faire du c.** to make a din, to kick up a din or a racket or a rumpus, to create an uproar; **les élèves ont fait un c. pour protester contre la décision** the pupils kicked up a racket to show their disapproval of the decision

When a French noun has an irregular plural, this is shown immediately after the headword.
Du côté français-anglais, le pluriel irrégulier des noms est indiqué juste après l'intitulé de l'entré.

chat-huant, *pl* **chats-huants** [ʃayɑ̃] NM tawny owl, brown owl

The plural of hyphenated French nouns is always given, unless the noun does not change its form in the plural, in which case it is marked *inv.*
Le pluriel des noms composés avec trait d'union est donné systématiquement. Pour les noms invariables la mention inv figure juste après l'abréviation qui indique la catégorie grammaticale.

chauffe-assiettes NM INV plate warmer

chicaner [ʃikane] VI to quibble (**sur** over, about); *Jur* to chicane, to pettifog; **c. sur les frais** to haggle or quibble over the expense
VT **c. qn** to wrangle with sb (**sur** about); **c. qch** to haggle over sth
VPR **se chicaner** to squabble

Prepositions that commonly collocate with a particular term are given in brackets immediately after the translation.
Les prépositions les plus couramment employées avec un terme donné figurent entre parenthèses juste après la traduction.

circoncire [sirkɔ̃sir] VT (*prp* circoncisant; *pp* conconcis; *pr ind* je circoncis; *pr sub* je circoncise; *p hist* je circoncis; *fu* je circoncirai) to circumcise

On the French-English side of the dictionary, information about verb conjugations is detailed at the beginning of an entry.
Du côté français-anglais des informations sur la conjugaison des verbes sont données au début des entrées.

ciseau, -eaux [sizo] NM **1 (paire de) ciseaux** (pair of) scissors; (*de jardin*) shears, clippers; **ciseaux à bouts ronds** blunt- or round-ended scissors; **ciseaux à ongles** nail scissors; **ciseaux de couturière** dressmaking scissors; *Couture* **ciseaux à denteler** pinking shears; **coup de ciseaux** snip (of the scissors); **donner des coups de ciseaux dans qch** to snip away at sth with a pair of scissors; *Fig* **donner des coups de ciseaux dans un texte** to cut down or prune a text VOIR GRAMMAIRE A10 **2** *Sport* **c., saut en ciseaux** scissors (jump); *Gym* **faire des ciseaux** to do the scissors **3** *Tech* chisel

Pronunciation information has been given using the International Phonetic Alphabet (IPA). Pronunciation information is not given for headwords that are composed of two or more separate words, as long as each of the parts of such headwords appear as headwords in their own right.
La prononciation des entrées est donnée en alphabet phonétique international (API), cependant elle ne figure pas après les entrées composées dont les éléments sont traités séparément.

cohabitation [koabitasjɔ̃] NF cohabitation, living together; *Pol* **sous le régime de la c.** during the period of cohabitation

This dictionary contains a practical supplement consisting of English and French grammars which can be found in the centre of the book. A system of cross-references within the dictionary text directs the user to relevant explanations in the supplement.
Ce dictionnaire comprend un supplément pratique consacré à la grammaire anglaise et à la grammaire française situé en milieu d'ouvrage. En outre, un système de renvois intégré au texte oriente le lecteur vers des explications concernant des points de grammaire donnés.

Cohabitation
Originally, this term referred to the period (1986–1988) during which the socialist President (François Mitterrand) had a right-wing Prime Minister (Jacques Chirac), following the victory of the RPR in the legislative elections and Mitterrand's decision not to resign as President. It has since been used to refer to the similar situation which arose following the 1993 elections (with Édouard Balladur as Prime Minister) and more recently the 1997 elections (with the left-wing government of Lionel Jospin co-ruling with the President Jacques Chirac).

The *Harrap's Shorter* contains about two hundred notes on cultural topics, providing extra information in addition to the translation.
*Le **Harrap's Shorter** contient environ deux cents encadrés intégrés au texte qui portent sur des points de culture, de société, de politique ou d'histoire. Ils donnent un complément d'information lorsqu'une traduction ou une glose ne suffisent pas.*

Coton-Tige®, *pl* **Cotons-Tiges** NM cotton bud, *Am* cotton swab

When a French term has different translations in British and American English, the American variant translation is clearly indicated.
Lorsqu'un terme français se traduit différemment en anglais britannique et en anglais américain, la traduction américaine est clairement indiquée.

cru[1] [kry] ADJ **1** (*viande, poisson, légumes*), *Tex* (*tissus, soie etc*) raw; (*lait*) unpasteurized; (*cuir*) untreated, raw; (*couleur, lumière*) crude, garish; *Fig* (*réponse, langage, personne*) blunt; **il mange sa viande crue** he eats his meat raw; *Fig* **dans le jour c.** in the full light of day **2** (*licencieux*) crude, coarse; **cette plaisanterie est un peu crue** that's a rather coarse or crude joke **3** *Belg, Can, Suisse* (*temps, bâtiment*) damp and cold
ADV **je vous le dis tout c.** I'm not mincing my words, I'm telling you straight (out); **j'ai envie de l'avaler tout c.** I could eat or gobble him (all) up; (*je suis en colère*) I could strangle him; **manger c.** to eat raw food; **être chaussé à c.** to wear shoes without any socks; **monter à c.** to ride bareback

Numerous Canadian, Swiss and Belgian terms are given with the labels *Can, Suisse* and *Belg* respectively.
Les nombreux canadianismes, helvétismes et belgicismes sont indiqués par les étiquettes Can, Suisse et Belg.

Structure of entries/Structure des entrées

Compounds of two or more words have been presented under the entry for the first word of the compound. They appear in alphabetical order in a block at the end of the entry. The block is introduced by the symbol ▸▸
Les noms composés de deux éléments ou plus apparaissent dans l'article consacré au premier élément du mot composé. Ils sont présentés à la fin de l'article et sont classés par ordre alphabétique. La section des mots composés est signalée par le symbole ▸▸

Terms in Scottish English are clearly indicated.
Les termes d'anglais d'Ecosse sont clairement indiqués.

A term will frequently have no exact translation equivalent in the other language. In such cases an explanation (preceded by the = sign) may be given.
Il n'est pas rare qu'un terme ne dispose pas d'une traduction exacte dans l'autre langue. Dans ce cas on optera parfois pour une explication (précédée du signe =).

The *Harrap's Shorter* features a vast number of specialized items of vocabulary. A full list of the abbreviated field labels used to mark these terms is to be found on the inside front and back covers of the book.
Le Harrap's Shorter comporte un très grand nombre de termes techniques. La liste complète des abréviations des domaines de spécialité utilisés dans le dictionnaire figure en début et en fin d'ouvrage.

The register of all words and phrases in the source language is clearly indicated. Register labels are used to indicate the level of language – whether formal (*Fml*), informal (*Fam*), slang (*Sl/Arg*) or vulgar (*Vulg*) – and also to indicate usage, showing whether a word is, for example, pejorative, ironic or euphemistic (*Pej/Péj, Iron* and *Euph*).
Le registre de toutes les expressions et tous les mots donnés en langue source est clairement indiqué. Des indicateurs de registre sont donnés pour préciser le niveau de langue, qu'il soit soutenu (Fml), familier (Fam), argotique (Sl/Arg), ou vulgaire (Vulg). Les nuances sont également indiquées lorsqu'un terme est employé en tant qu'euphémisme ou de façon péjorative ou ironique (Euph, Pej/Péj et Iron).

American variant spellings are cross-referred to the corresponding entry in British English.
Les mots orthographiés à l'américaine sont renvoyés à l'entrée britannique correspondante.

American spelling variants are clearly shown at headword level.
Les variantes orthographiques américaines sont clairement indiquées au niveau du libellé de l'entrée.

Menus appear at the beginning of many long entries. The aim of these menus is twofold: (i) to summarize the main translations of an entry; (ii) to make use of the knowledge the user already has to help them find the sense they are looking for more quickly.
Des "menus" apparaissent en tête des articles longs pour faciliter la recherche de l'utilisateur. L'utilité de ces menus est double: 1/ ils présentent en résumé les traductions d'un terme suivant ses différentes acceptions 2/ ils permettent au lecteur de repérer facilement le sens qu'il recherche.

The plural of French compounds is given when these terms are translations on the English-French side of the dictionary.
Le pluriel des mots composés français figure également ces termes sont donnés comme traductions du côté anglais-français.

Register labels can occur in various combinations. For example, a word can be either archaic or literary, old-fashioned or humorous.
Un terme peut comporter plusieurs indicateurs de registre. À titre d'exemple, un mot archaïque peut également être utilisé pour ses accents littéraires, et l'on peut choisir d'employer un terme vieilli et familier de façon à produire un effet humoristique.

---

cabbage ['kæbɪdʒ] N **1** chou *m*, *pl* choux; **red c.** chou rouge **2** *Fam (person)* légume *m*; **the accident left him a c.** l'accident en a fait un légume, il est à l'état végétatif depuis l'accident
▸▸**c. lettuce** laitue *f* pommée; **c. palm** *(tree)* palmiste *m*; **c. rose** rose *f* centfeuilles; **c. white** *(butterfly)* piéride *f* du chou

caber ['keɪbər] N *Scot Sport* **tossing the c.** = concours *m* de lancer d'un tronc d'arbre *(dans les jeux des Highlands)*

cable ['keɪb(ə)l] N **1** *Naut* câble *m*; **c.('s) length** *(measure)* encâblure *f* **2** *Elec* câble *m*; **to lay a c.** poser un câble; **overhead/underground/submarine c.** câble aérien/souterrain/sous-marin; **twin c.** câble à deux conducteurs **3** *Tel* câble *m*, câblogramme *m* **4** *(cable TV)* câble *m*; **it's only available on c.** ça n'existe que sur le câble **5** *Knitting* torsade *f*
VT *Tel (message)* câbler; **to c. sb** câbler à qn, envoyer un câble à qn; **to c. sth to sb** câbler qch à qn
VI *Tel* câbler; **to c. to sb** envoyer un câble à qn
▸▸ *Tel* **c. address** adresse *f* télégraphique; *TV* **c. broadcasting** télédiffusion *f* par câble; **c. car** téléphérique *m*; *TV* **c. company** câblo-opérateur *m*, *pl* câblo-opérateurs; *TV* **c. distribution** câblodistribution *f*, distribution *f* par câble; *Comput* **c. modem** modem-câble *m*, *pl* modems-câble; *Knitting* **c. needle** aiguille *f* à torsades; *TV* **c. network** réseau *m* câblé; *TV* **C. News Network** = réseau d'information américain par câble et satellite; *TV* **c. operator** câblo-opérateur; **c. railway** funiculaire *m*; *Phot* **c. release** déclencheur *m*; *Tel, Naut* **c. ship** câblier *m*; *Knitting* **c. stitch** point *m* de torsade; *TV* **c. television** télévision *f* par câble; *Aut* **c. terminal** cosse *f*, **c. transfer** *(of money)* virement *m* télégraphique

cahoots [kə'huːts] NPL *Fam* **to be in c. (with sb)** être de mèche (avec qn)

caliber ['kælɪbər] N *Am* = **calibre**

calibre, *Am* **caliber** ['kælɪbər] N *(of firearm)*, *Fig (of person)* calibre *m*; **a man of your c.** un homme de votre calibre ou envergure; **a very high c. translator** un traducteur de très grande envergure

CALL [kɔːl]

N	appel **1, 2, 4** ▪ visite **5**
VT	appeler **1–6** ▪ réveiller **3**
VI	appeler **1** ▪ passer **3** ▪ s'arrêter **3**

camper ['kæmpər] N *(person)* campeur, -euse; *(vehicle)* camping-car *m*, *pl* camping-cars
▸▸**c. van** camping-car

campfire ['kæmpfaɪər] N feu *m* de camp

camphor ['kæmfər] N camphre *m*
▸▸**c. oil** essence *f* de camphre; **c. tree** camphrier *m*

camphorated ['kæmfəreɪtɪd] ADJ *(oil etc)* camphré

camping ['kæmpɪŋ] N camping *m*; **to go c.** faire du camping
▸▸**c. equipment, c. gear** matériel *m* ou équipement *m* de camping; **c. ground** terrain *m* de camping; **c. holiday** vacances *fpl* (en) camping; **c. site** (terrain de) camping; **c. stove** camping-gaz® *m inv*

carousal [kə'raʊz(ə)l] N *Old-fashioned, Hum* beuverie *f*

carouse [kə'raʊz] VI *Old-fashioned, Hum* faire la fête *ou Fam* la bombe

cellphone ['selfəʊn] N téléphone *m* cellulaire, radiotéléphone *m*; *Am (mobile phone)* (téléphone *m*) portable *m*, Belg GSM *m*, Suisse Natel® *m*, Can cellulaire *m*

> Belgian, Canadian and Swiss variant translations are shown as appropriate.
> *Des traductions en français de Belgique, du Canada et de Suisse sont fournies lorsque nécessaire.*

chandelier [ʃændə'lɪər] N lustre *m*

Note that the French word **chandelier** is a false friend and is never a translation for the English word **chandelier**. Its most common meaning is **candlestick** or **candelabra**.

> The *Harrap's Shorter* contains hundreds of usage notes to facilitate translation, including a large number which warn the user about the pitfalls presented by false friends.
> *Le* **Harrap's Shorter** *propose des centaines de notes d'aide à la traduction dont une large proportion renseignent l'utilisateur sur les difficultés de traduction présentées par les faux amis.*

cheer [tʃɪər] N **1** *(shout)* hourra *m*; **cheers** acclamations *fpl*, bravos *mpl*; **to give three cheers** pousser trois hourras; **three cheers for Mary!** un ban pour Mary!, vive Mary! **2** *Fam* **cheers!** *(toast)* (à votre) santé!; *Br (at parting)* à bientôt!; *Br (thanks)* merci! **3** *Lit (good spirits)* bonne disposition *f* (d'esprit); **be of good c.!** prenez courage!; **we were of good c.** nous étions de bonne humeur
> VT **1** *(shout for)* acclamer **2** *(encourage, make happier)* remonter le moral à
> VI *(shout)* pousser des hourras ou des acclamations

▶ **cheer on** VT SEP *(support)* encourager
▶ **cheer up** VI *(become more cheerful)* s'égayer, devenir plus gai; **the weather's cheered up** le temps s'est arrangé; **c. up!** courage!
> VT SEP **1** *(make more cheerful)* réjouir, remonter le moral à **2** *(make brighter) (room etc)* égayer

> Phrasal verbs are listed alphabetically after the main entry and are clearly indicated by a blue triangle.
> *Les verbes à particule sont classés alphabétiquement à la suite de l'entrée principale et sont facilement repérables grâce à un triangle bleu.*

chiseller ['tʃɪz(ə)lər] N *Sl* **1** *(swindler)* escroc *m* **2** *Ir (child)* gosse *mf*, môme *mf*

> Terms in Irish English are clearly indicated.
> *Les termes d'anglais d'Irlande sont clairement indiqués.*

chook [tʃuːk] N *Austr Fam (chicken)* poulet *m*

> Terms in Australian English are clearly indicated.
> *Les termes d'anglais d'Australie sont clairement indiqués.*

churchman, *pl* **churchmen** ['tʃɜːtʃmən] N *Rel* **1** *(clergyman)* homme *m* d'église **2** *(member of a church)* membre *m* d'une église

> English irregular plurals are given after the headword.
> *Les pluriels irréguliers anglais apparaissent à la suite du mot de tête*

cling [klɪŋ] VI *(pt, pp* **clung** [klʌŋ]*) (of child)* s'accrocher, se cramponner (**to sth/sb** à qch/qn); *Fig Pej* coller (**to sb** qn); *(of plant) (to wall)* s'accrocher (**to** à); **to c. to the figure** *(of garment)* mouler le corps; **he clung to the rope for dear life** il s'agrippa à la corde de toutes ses forces; **the two children were clinging to each other** les deux enfants étaient serrés l'un contre l'autre; *Fig* **to c. (on) to one's children/wife/ideas** s'accrocher à ses enfants/sa femme/ses idées; **to c. to an opinion** persister dans une opinion; **to c. to a hope** se raccrocher à un espoir
▶▶ **c. peach** pavie *f*

> Irregular forms of English verbs are given after the headword.
> *La forme irrégulière des verbes anglais est donnée après le mot de tête.*

> In examples, when the word in question corresponds to the exact form of the headword, only the initial letter of the word is given.
> *Dans les exemples, seule l'initiale du mot traité apparaît quand il correspond à la forme du mot de tête.*

confidant, *f* **confidante** [kɒnfɪ'dænt] N confident, -ente

Attention: ne pas confondre avec l'adjectif anglais **confident**.

> Words which are often confused are clearly marked.
> *Les termes susceptibles d'être confondus sont clairement indiqués.*

consume [kən'sjuːm] VT *(food, drink, fuel etc)* consommer; *(exhaust)* épuiser; *(of fire) (building etc)* consumer, dévorer; **the discussion consumed many hours** la discussion a pris de nombreuses heures; **to be consumed with** *(desire)* brûler de; *(jealousy, envy, curiosity)* être en proie à

When translating **to consume**, note that the French verbs **consommer** and **consumer** are not interchangeable. **Consommer** always refers to consumer activity, while **consumer** is used to describe the process of being eaten up or destroyed, especially by fire.

> Numerous usage notes warn the user against common translation errors.
> *De nombreuses notes d'usage mettent en garde contre des fautes de traduction communément commises.*

Pour indiquer la prononciation anglaise, nous avons utilisé dans ce dictionnaire les symboles de l'API (Alphabet phonétique international). Pour chaque son anglais, vous trouverez dans le tableau ci-dessous des exemples de mots anglais, suivis de mots français présentant un son similaire. Une explication est donnée lorsqu'il n'y a pas d'équivalent en français.

Caractère API	Exemple en anglais	Exemple en français
Consonnes		
[b]	**b**abble	**b**é**b**é
[d]	**d**ig	**d**ent
[dʒ]	**g**iant, **j**ig	**j**ean
[f]	**f**it, **ph**ysics	**f**ace
[g]	**g**rey, bi**g**	**g**a**g**
[h]	**h**appy	h aspiré : à quelques rares exceptions près, il est toujours prononcé en anglais
[j]	**y**ellow	**y**aourt
[k]	**c**lay, **k**ick	**c**ar
[l]	**l**ip, pi**ll**	**l**i**l**as
[m]	**m**u**mm**y	**m**a**m**an
[n]	**n**ip, pi**n**	**n**é
[ŋ]	si**ng**	parki**ng**
[p]	**p**i**p**	**p**a**p**a
[r]	**r**ig, w**r**ite	Pas d'équivalent français : se prononce en plaçant le bout de la langue au milieu du palais
[r]		Seulement prononcé en cas de liaison avec la voyelle qui suit comme dans : fa**r** away; the ca**r** is blue
[s]	**s**ick, **sc**ience	**s**ilen**c**e
[ʃ]	**sh**ip, na**ti**on	**ch**èvre
[t]	**t**ip, bu**tt**	**t**ar**t**ine
[tʃ]	**ch**ip, ba**tch**	a**tch**oum
[θ]	**th**ick	Son proche du [s] français, il se prononce en plaçant le bout de la langue entre les dents du haut et celles du bas
[ð]	**th**is, wi**th**	Son proche du [z] français, il se prononce en plaçant le bout de la langue entre les dents du haut et celles du bas
[v]	**v**ague, gi**v**e	**v**ie
[w]	**w**it, **wh**y	**w**hisky
[z]	**z**ip, phy**s**ics	ro**s**e
[ʒ]	plea**s**ure	**j**e
[χ]	lo**ch**	Existe seulement dans certains mots écossais. Pas d'équivalent français : se prononce du fond de la gorge, comme Ba**ch** en allemand ou la 'jota' espagnole.
Voyelles		
[æ]	r**a**g	n**a**tte
[ɑː]	l**ar**ge, h**al**f	p**â**te
[e]	s**e**t	[e] moins ouvert que le [ɛ] français
[ɜː]	c**ur**tain, w**e**re	h**eu**re
[ə]	utt**er**, **a**bout	ch**e**val

Caractère API	Exemple en anglais	Exemple en français
[ɪ]	b**i**g, w**o**men	[i] bref, à mi-chemin entre les sons [ɛ] et [i] français (plus proche de 'n**e**t' que de 'v**i**te')
[iː]	l**ea**k, w**ee**	[i] plus long que le [i] français
[ɒ]	l**o**ck	b**o**nne – mais plus ouvert et prononcé au fond du palais
[ɔː]	w**a**ll, c**o**rk	b**au**me – mais plus ouvert et prononcé au fond du palais
[ʊ]	p**u**t, l**oo**k	Son à mi-chemin entre un [u] bref et un [ɔ]
[uː]	m**oo**n	Son [u] prolongé
[ʌ]	c**u**p	À mi-chemin entre un [a] et un [ɛ]

Diphtongues : Elles sont rares en français et sont la combinaison de deux sons.

[aɪ]	wh**y**, h**igh**, l**ie**	**aï**e
[aʊ]	h**ow**	mi**aou**, **aoû**tat – mais se prononce comme un seul son
[eə]	b**ear**, sh**are**, wh**ere**	fl**air**
[eɪ]	d**ay**, m**a**ke, m**ai**n	merv**eille**
[əʊ]	sh**ow**, g**o**	Combinaison d'un [o] et d'un [u]
[ɪə]	h**ere**, g**ear**	Combinaison d'un [i] long suivi d'un [ɛ] bref
[ɔɪ]	b**oy**, s**oi**l	langue d'**oï**l
[ʊə]	s**ure**	Combinaison d'un son [u] suivi d'un [ɛ] bref

French pronunciation is shown in this dictionary using the symbols of the IPA (International Phonetic Alphabet). In the table below, examples of French words using these sounds are given, followed by English words which have a similar sound. Where there is no equivalent in English, an explanation is given.

IPA symbol	French example	English example
Consonants		
[b]	**b**é**b**é	**b**ut
[d]	**d**onner	**d**oor
[f]	**f**orêt	**f**ire
[g]	**g**are	**g**et
[ʒ]	**j**our	plea**s**ure
[k]	**c**arte	**k**itten
[l]	**l**ire	**l**onely
[m]	**m**a**m**an	**m**at
[n]	**n**i	**n**ow
[ŋ]	parki**ng**	si**ng**ing
[ɲ]	campa**gn**e	can**y**on
[p]	**p**atte	**p**at
[r]	**r**a**r**e	Like an English [r] but pronounced at the back of the throat
[s]	**s**oir	**s**it
[ʃ]	**ch**ose	**sh**am
[t]	**t**able	**t**ap
[v]	**v**aleur	**v**alue
[z]	**z**éro	**z**ero
Vowels		
[a]	ch**a**t	c**a**t
[ɑ]	**â**ge	g**a**sp
[e]	**é**t**é**	b**ay**
[ɛ]	p**è**re	b**e**d
[ə]	l**e**	**a**mend
[ø]	d**eu**x	Does not exist in English: [e] pronounced with the lips rounded
[œ]	s**eu**l	c**ur**tain
[i]	v**i**te	b**ee** – not quite as long as the English [i:]
[ɔ]	d**o**nner	c**o**t – slightly more open than the English [ɒ]
[o]	ch**au**d	d**au**ghter – but higher than its English equivalent
[u]	t**ou**t	y**ou** – but shorter than its English equivalent
[y]	voit**u**re	Does not exist in English: [i] with lips rounded
[ã]	**en**f**an**t	Nasal sound pronounced lower and further back in the mouth than [ɔ̃]
[ɛ̃]	v**in**	Nasal sound: [a] sound pronounced letting air pass through the nose
[ɔ̃]	b**on**jour	Nasal sound: closed [o] sound pronounced letting air pass through the nose
[œ̃]	**un**	Nasal sound: like [ɛ̃] but with lips more rounded

IPA symbol	French example	English example
Semi-vowels		
[w]	v**oi**r	**w**eek
[j]	**y**oyo, pai**ll**e	**y**ard
[ɥ]	n**ui**t	Does not exist in English: the vowel [y] elided with the following vowel

ENGLISH–FRENCH

ANGLAIS–FRANÇAIS

A, a¹ [eɪ] **N 1** *(letter)* A, a *m*; **two a's** deux a; **the car's old, but it gets me from A to B** c'est une vieille voiture mais elle me permet de me déplacer; **the train is the best way of getting from A to B** le train c'est le meilleur moyen de se déplacer d'un endroit à un autre; **the roads are so crowded that it takes forever to get from A to B** les routes sont si encombrées que le moindre trajet prend une éternité; **the numbering system helps the user get from A to B** le système de numérotation permet à l'utilisateur de s'y retrouver; **an A to Z of gardening** le jardinage de A à Z; **an A to Z of London** un plan de Londres; **we've been through all the details from A to Z** nous avons étudié tous les détails un par un; **51A** *(house number)* 51 bis
2 *Mus* la *m*; **in A flat** en la bémol
3 *Sch (grade)* **to get an A** avoir une très bonne note, ≃ avoir entre 16 et 20 sur 20; *Am Sch, Univ* **he got straight A's** *(top marks)* il a eu de très bonnes notes partout
4 *Br Cin Formerly* = mention *f* accompagnant les films interdits aux enfants de moins de 14 ans non accompagnés par un adulte (remplacé par "PG")

A², *before vowel sound* **an** [ə, ən; *stressed* eɪ, æn] **INDEF ART** VOIR GRAMMAIRE A5–6; B4–5 **1** un, une; **a man** un homme; **an old man** un vieillard; **a hill** une colline; **a hotel** [əhəʊ'tel], *Old-fashioned* **an hotel** [ənəʊ'tel] un hôtel; **an hour** [ən'aʊər] une heure; **a unit** [ə'juːnɪt] une unité; **an uncle** [ən'ʌŋk(ə)l] un oncle; **an MP** [ən'em'piː] un député; **a man and (a) woman** un homme et une femme; **a wife and mother** *(same person)* une épouse et mère
2 *(definite article in French)* **to have a red nose** avoir le nez rouge; **I have a sore throat/back/knee** j'ai mal à la gorge/au dos/au genou; **to have a taste for sth** avoir le goût de qch; *Iron* **a fine excuse!** la belle excuse!; **a computer is a useful machine** les ordinateurs sont des machines bien utiles
3 *(distributive)* **£5 a kilo** 5 livres le kilo; **five euros a head** cinq euros par tête; **three times a week/a year** trois fois par semaine/par an; **fifty kilometres an hour** cinquante kilomètres à l'heure
4 *(a certain)* **I know a doctor who …** je connais un médecin qui …; **in a sense** dans un sens
5 *(the same)* **to come in two at a time** entrer deux par deux; **of a size** de la même grandeur *ou* taille
6 *(a single)* **I haven't understood a word** je n'ai pas compris un seul mot; **I couldn't see a thing** je n'y voyais rien du tout; **there wasn't a book to be found in the house** il n'y avait pas un seul livre dans la maison; **not a chance!** aucune chance!; **we haven't a hope of finishing in time** il n'y a aucun espoir pour que nous terminions à temps
7 *(omitted in French)* **he is an Englishman/a father/a barrister** il est anglais/père/avocat;

to put an end to sth mettre fin à qch; **to make a fortune** faire fortune; **what a man!** quel homme!; **what a pity!** quel dommage!; **as a rule** en règle générale; **within a short time** en peu de temps
8 *(before nouns in apposition)* **Caen, a large town in Normandy** Caen, ville importante de Normandie; **forty years a sailor and he still gets seasick!** il a beau être marin depuis quarante ans, il lui arrive toujours d'avoir le mal de mer!

AA [eɪ'eɪ] **N 1** *(abbr* **anti-aircraft)** DCA *f*; **AA fire/guns** tir *m*/canons *mpl* de DCA
2 *(abbr* **Automobile Association)** = société *f* de dépannage pour les automobilistes, ≃ Touring Club *m* de France
3 *(abbr* **Alcoholics Anonymous)** AA *mpl*; **an AA meeting** une réunion des Alcooliques anonymes
4 *(abbr* **Advertising Association)** = organisme *m* britannique dont le rôle est de veiller à la qualité des publicités et de défendre les intérêts des annonceurs et des agences de publicité
5 *Br Cin Formerly* = mention *f* accompagnant les films interdits aux moins de 14 ans

AAA [θriː'eɪz] **N 1** *Formerly abbr* **Amateur Athletics Association 2** *abbr* **American Automobile Association**

A1 ['eɪ'wʌn] **ADJ** de première qualité; **in A1 condition** *(car, house)* en parfait état; *(person)* en parfaite santé

A3 ['eɪ'θriː] **N, ADJ** A3 *m*

A4 ['eɪ'fɔːr] **N, ADJ** A4 *m*; **an A4 sheet** une feuille A4; **A4 paper tray** bac *m* de papier A4

Aachen ['ɑːkən] **N** Aix-la-Chapelle

AAI [eɪeɪ'aɪ] **N** *Br TV (abbr* **Audience Appreciation Index)** = indice *m* de mesure de satisfaction du public

AAU [eɪeɪ'juː] **N** *(abbr* **Amateur Athletic Union)** = organisme *m* chargé de superviser les manifestations sportives aux États-Unis, en particulier dans les universités

AB [eɪ'biː] **N 1** *Naut (abbr* **able(-bodied) seaman)** matelot *m* de deuxième classe **2** *Am (abbr* **Artium Baccalaureus)** = BA

ABA [eɪbiː'eɪ] **N 1** *abbr* **Amateur Boxing Association 2** *abbr* **American Bar Association**

aback [ə'bæk] **ADV to be taken a.** en rester déconcerté *ou* interdit; **this remark rather took me a.** cette remarque m'a quelque peu décontenancé

abacus, *pl* **abaci, abacuses** ['æbəkəs, -saɪ, -kəsɪz] **N 1** *Math* boulier *m* (compteur) **2** *Archit* abaque *m*, tailloir *m*

abaft [ə'bɑːft] *Naut* **ADV** sur l'arrière, vers l'arrière
PREP a. the mast sur l'arrière du mât

abalone [æbə'ləʊnɪ] **N** *(shellfish)* ormeau *m*

abandon [ə'bændən] **VT 1** *(leave) (car, building, one's family)* abandonner; *Naut* **to a.**

ship abandonner *ou* évacuer le navire; **to a. to the insurer** délaisser à l'assureur **2** *(give up) (plan, principle)* renoncer à, abandonner; *Comput (file, routine)* abandonner; *Sport* **to a. play** *(temporarily)* interrompre la partie; *(permanently)* annuler la partie; **to a. all hope** abandonner tout espoir (**of doing sth** de faire qch); **to a. oneself to sth** s'abandonner à qch
N with reckless a. avec inconscience; *Hum* **with gay a.** avec une joyeuse désinvolture

abandoned [ə'bændənd] **ADJ 1** *(car, settlement, outpost)* abandonné; **the building had an a. look** le bâtiment avait l'air abandonné **2** *Old-fashioned (unrestrained) (behaviour, woman)* dévergondé

abandonment [ə'bændənmənt] **N** abandon *m*

abase [ə'beɪs] **VT** *Arch, Lit* abaisser, humilier; **to a. oneself** s'abaisser, s'humilier

abasement [ə'beɪsmənt] **N** *Lit* humiliation *f*

abash [ə'bæʃ] **VT** *(usu in passive)* **to be** *or* **feel abashed at** *or* **by sth** rester tout interdit de qch

abate [ə'beɪt] **VI** *(of storm, fear, anger, pain)* se calmer, s'apaiser; *(of flood)* baisser; *(of noise)* diminuer; **the wind abated** le vent est tombé

abatement [ə'beɪtmənt] **N** diminution *f*, affaiblissement *m*; *(of storm)* apaisement *m*; *(of flood)* abaissement *m*

> Note that the French word **abattement** is a false friend and is never a translation for the English word **abatement**. Its most common meaning is **despondency**.

abattoir ['æbətwɑːr] **N** abattoir *m*

abbess ['æbɪs] **N** abbesse *f*

abbey ['æbɪ] **N 1** abbaye *f* **2 Westminster A.** l'abbaye *f* de Westminster
▸▸ **a. church** *(église f)* abbatiale *f*

abbot ['æbət] **N** abbé *m*

abbreviate [ə'briːvɪeɪt] **VT** *(word)* abréger; **abbreviated dialling** numérotation *f* abrégée

abbreviation [əbriːvɪ'eɪʃən] **N** *(of word)* abréviation *f*

ABC, abc [eɪbiː'siː] **N 1** *(alphabet)* ABC *m*, abc *m*; **to know one's A.** connaître son alphabet; **it's as easy as A.** c'est facile comme bonjour
2 *Fig (rudiments)* b.a.-ba *m inv*
3 *TV (abbr* **American Broadcasting Company)** = chaîne *f* de télévision américaine
4 *TV (abbr* **Australian Broadcasting Corporation)** = chaîne *f* de télévision australienne
5 *Br Journ (abbr* **Audit Bureau of Circulation)** *(company)* ≃ Bureau *m* de vérification de la publicité; **the ABCs** *(statistics)* = statistiques *fpl* établies par le "Audit Bureau of Circulation" portant sur le tirage des journaux et magazines de la presse britannique

abdicate ['æbdɪkeɪt] **VT** *(throne, one's responsibilities)* abdiquer; *(right, position)* renoncer à
VI abdiquer

abdication [æbdɪ'keɪʃən] **N** *(of throne)* abdication *f*; *(of right, responsibilities)* renonciation *f*

abdomen ['æbdəmən] **N** abdomen *m*; *(general area)* ventre *m*

abdominal [æb'dɒmɪn(ə)l] **ADJ** abdominal, -aux

abduct [əb'dʌkt] **VT** *Law* enlever, kidnapper

abduction [əb'dʌkʃən] **N** *Law* enlèvement *m*, rapt *m*, kidnapping *m*

abductor [əb'dʌktər] **N 1** *(of person)* ravisseur, -euse, kidnappeur, -euse **2** *Anat (muscle m)* abducteur *m*
ADJ *Anat (muscle)* abducteur

abeam [ə'biːm] **ADV** *Aviat, Naut* par le travers

abed [ə'bed] **ADV** *Arch* au lit

aberrant [æ'berənt] **ADJ** aberrant, anormal

aberration [æbə'reɪʃən] **N** aberration *f*, déviation *f*, *Astron, Math, Opt etc* aberration; **a temporary a. on his part** *(in behaviour)* un écart de conduite de sa part; **mental a.** égarement *m* (de l'esprit), aberration, confusion *f* mentale; **in a moment of a.** dans un moment de folie

abet [ə'bet] **VT** (-tt-) *(crime)* encourager; **to a. sb in a crime** encourager *ou* pousser qn à un crime

abetting [ə'betɪŋ] **N** *Law* **(aiding and) a.** *(before or during a crime)* complicité *f*

abeyance [ə'beɪəns] **N** *(of law)* suspension *f*; **the matter is still in a.** la question est toujours en suspens; *Law* la question est toujours pendante; **the law is in temporary a.** la loi a momentanément cessé d'être appliquée; **to fall into a.** tomber en désuétude; *Law* **estate in a.** succession *f* vacante

abhor [əb'hɔːr] **VT** (-rr-) abhorrer, avoir en horreur; **nature abhors a vacuum** la nature a horreur du vide

abhorrence [əb'hɒrəns] **N** horreur *f* (**of** de); **his a. of flying** le fait qu'il a horreur de prendre l'avion; **to hold sth in a.** avoir qch en horreur; **such actions are held in a. by all decent people** de tels actes seront odieux à tous les gens convenables

abhorrent [əb'hɒrənt] **ADJ** odieux, répugnant (**to** à); **such things are a. to the rational mind** de telles choses répugnent à l'esprit rationnel

abide [ə'baɪd] (*pt & pp* abided) **VT** *(tolerate)* **I can't a. him** je ne peux pas le supporter *ou* le sentir; **I can't a. that sound/dishonesty** je ne supporte pas ce bruit/la malhonnêteté; **I can't a. it when you talk to me like that** je ne supporte pas que tu me parles comme ça
VI 1 *esp Lit (of thing)* demeurer; **those memories will a. with me as long as I live** ces souvenirs me resteront *ou* m'accompagneront jusqu'à ma mort **2** *Arch, Lit (of person)* rester, demeurer (**with sb** avec qn)
▸ **abide by VT INSEP** *(promise)* rester fidèle à, tenir; *(rule, decision, law)* se conformer à, se soumettre à, respecter; **I a. by my decision/what I said** je maintiens ma décision/ce que j'ai dit

abiding [ə'baɪdɪŋ] **ADJ** permanent; *(impression)* durable; **an a. sense of gratitude** un sentiment de gratitude éternelle

ability [ə'bɪlɪtɪ] **N 1** *(to do sth)* capacité *f*, *(skill)* habileté *f*, capacité, compétence *f*; **an a. to do sth** une capacité à faire qch; **a man of considerable a.** un homme très doué; **she shows artistic a.** elle manifeste des dons artistiques; **to do sth to the best of one's a.** faire qch de son mieux; **the needs and abilities of each student** les besoins et les aptitudes de chaque étudiant **2** *Law (to inherit)* habilité *f*, *(to make a will)* capacité *f* légale

abject ['æbdʒekt] **ADJ 1** *(miserable)* misérable; **a. poverty** misère *f* effroyable **2** *(despicable)* bas, *f* basse, vil, abject **3** *(servile) (apology, letter)* servile

abjectly ['æbdʒektlɪ] **ADV 1** *(miserably)* misérablement **2** *(despicably)* bassement, vilement, abjectement **3** *(to apologize)* servilement

abjure [əb'dʒʊər] **VT** *(one's religion)* abjurer; *(one's faith)* renier

ablative ['æblətɪv] *Gram* **N** ablatif *m*; **in the a.** à l'ablatif
ADJ *(case)* ablatif
▸ ▸ **a. absolute** ablatif absolu

ablaze [ə'bleɪz] **ADV, ADJ PRED** en feu, en flammes; **to be a.** être en feu *ou* en flammes, flamber; **to set sth a.** embraser qch; **a. with light** resplendissant de lumière; **her eyes were a. with anger** ses yeux étaient enflammés de colère; **the speaker set the audience a. with enthusiasm for reform** l'orateur avait empli le public d'un enthousiasme ardent en faveur d'une réforme

able ['eɪb(ə)l] **ADJ 1** *(person)* compétent, capable; **to be a. to do sth** *(know how to)* savoir faire qch, être capable de faire qch; *(be physically capable)* pouvoir faire qch; *(succeed in doing)* réussir à faire qch; **I shan't be a. to come** je ne pourrai pas venir; **someone else will be better a. to help you** quelqu'un d'autre sera plus à même de vous aider; **I'll do it if I'm a.** je le ferai si je le peux; **an a. piece of work** un travail compétent *ou* bien fait; **your a. assistance** votre aide efficace **2** *Law (to bequeath, succeed)* apte, habile
▸ ▸ *Naut* **a. seaman** matelot *m* breveté

able-bodied **ADJ** fort, robuste; *Mil* bon pour le service; **every a. person helped in the search** toute personne en état de le faire a participé aux recherches
▸ ▸ *Naut* **a. seaman** matelot *m* breveté

ablution [ə'bluːʃən] **N** ablution *f*, *Fam Hum* **to perform one's ablutions** faire ses ablutions

ably ['eɪblɪ] **ADV** avec compétence; **she performed a. in the 100 metres** elle s'est bien comportée dans le 100 mètres; **a. assisted by** efficacement assisté par

abnegation [æbnɪ'geɪʃən] **N** *(of belief etc)* renoncement *m* (**of** à)

abnormal [æb'nɔːm(ə)l] **ADJ** anormal
▸ ▸ *Psy* **a. psychology** psychopathologie *f*

abnormality [æbnɔː'mælɪtɪ] **N 1** *(abnormal character, state etc)* caractère *m* anormal, anormalité *f* **2** *(anomaly)* anomalie *f*, aberration *f*

abnormally [æb'nɔːm(ə)lɪ] **ADV** anormalement; *Hum* **he was late but not a. late** il était en retard mais pas plus que d'habitude; **he was a. shy** il était d'une timidité maladive

Abo, abo ['æbəʊ] **N** *Austr Offensive Sl (abbr* Aborigine*)* Aborigène *mf*

aboard [ə'bɔːd] **ADV** à bord; **to go a.** monter à bord; **to take sth a.** embarquer qch; **all a.!** *Naut* embarquez!; *Rail* en voiture!; **welcome a.!** *Aviat, Naut* bienvenue à bord!; *Fig* bienvenue dans l'équipe!
PREP *(train, bus, plane)* dans; *Aviat, Naut* à bord de; **a. ship** à bord (du navire)

abode [ə'bəʊd] **N** *Lit (home)* demeure *f*, *Fam* **welcome to my humble a.** bienvenu dans mon petit chez-moi; *Law* **place of a.** domicile *m*; **of no fixed a.** sans domicile fixe

abolish [ə'bɒlɪʃ] **VT** *(custom, committee etc)* abolir, supprimer; *(law)* abroger

abolition [æbə'lɪʃən] **N** *(of custom, committee etc)* abolition *f*, suppression *f*, *(of law)* abrogation *f*, **a. of slavery/the death penalty** abolition de l'esclavage/de la peine de mort

A-bomb **N** bombe *f* A

abominable [ə'bɒmɪnəb(ə)l] **ADJ** abominable
▸ ▸ **the a. snowman** l'abominable homme *m* des neiges

abominably [ə'bɒmɪnəblɪ] **ADV** *(to behave)* abominablement; **it's a. hot** il fait abominablement chaud

abominate [ə'bɒmɪneɪt] **VT** abominer, détester, avoir en abomination

abomination [əbɒmɪ'neɪʃən] **N** abomination *f*, **to hold in a.** avoir en abomination; *Fam* **this coffee's an a.** ce café est abominable

aboriginal [æbə'rɪdʒɪn(ə)l] **ADJ 1** *(culture, legend)* aborigène, des aborigènes **2** *Bot, Zool* aborigène **3 A.** *(relating to Australian Aborigenes)* aborigène, des aborigènes
N A. aborigène *mf* (d'Australie)

aborigine [æbə'rɪdʒɪnɪ] **ADJ** aborigène, des aborigènes
N 1 *(original inhabitant)* aborigène *mf* **2 A.** aborigène *mf* (d'Australie)

abort [ə'bɔːt] **VI 1** *Obst (of woman) (have termination)* avorter; *(miscarry)* faire une fausse couche; *(of foetus)* ne pas tenir **2** *Fig (of project)* avorter
VT 1 *Obst (woman)* faire avorter; **the foetus was aborted** la grossesse a été interrompue **2** *Fig (project)* faire avorter **3** *Comput (program)* suspendre l'exécution de, abandonner
N 1 *Aviat, Mil etc* mission *f* non accomplie; **launch a.** terminaison *f* prématurée d'un/du lancement **2** *Comput (of program)* suspension *f* d'exécution, abandon *m*

abortion [ə'bɔːʃən] **N 1** *Obst* avortement *m*, interruption *f* de grossesse; **to have an a.** se faire avorter; **to perform an a.** faire un avortement; **the a. debate** le débat sur l'avortement; **a. on demand** avortement libre **2** *Fig (of project)* avortement *m* **3** *Fam (person, animal)* avorton *m*, monstre *m*
▸ ▸ **a. clinic** clinique *f* d'avortement; **a. law** loi *f* sur l'avortement

abortionist [ə'bɔːʃənɪst] **N** *Pej* avorteur, -euse

abortive [ə'bɔːtɪv] **ADJ** *(plan, mission)* avorté, manqué; *(attempt)* manqué

abound [ə'baʊnd] **VI** abonder, foisonner; **to a. in** *or* **with sth** abonder en qch, regorger de qch; **the forest abounds with deer** la forêt regorge de daims

ABOUT [ə'baʊt]

PREP autour de **1**	■ en **2** ■ dans **2**
■ sur **4** ■ à propos de **4** ■ au sujet de **4**	
ADV de part et d'autre **1** ■ là **1**	
■ environ **5**	

PREP VOIR GRAMMAIRE A67 **1** *(around)* autour de; **the hills (round) a. the town** les collines autour *ou* à l'entour de la ville; **the people a. us** les gens auprès de nous, les gens qui nous entourent; **look a. you** regarde autour de toi; **it's good to have a few new faces a. the place** c'est bien de voir de nouvelles têtes par ici; **keep your wits a. you** garde ta présence d'esprit; *Fml* **to have sth a. one's person** avoir qch sur soi

2 *(in various parts of)* **to wander a. the town/the streets** se balader en ville/dans les rues

3 *(characteristic of)* **there is something unusual a. him** il y a chez lui quelque chose de pas ordinaire; **she found something amusing a. the situation** elle a trouvé que la situation avait quelque chose d'amusant;

there's something a. a horse that ... il y a chez le cheval un je ne sais quoi qui ...

4 *(on the subject of)* sur, à propos de, au sujet de; **a book a. France** un livre sur la France; **to speak a. sth** parler de qch; **to argue a. sth** se disputer à propos de *ou* au sujet de qch; **to quarrel a. nothing** se quereller à propos de rien; **what are they talking a.?** de quoi parlent-ils?; **what are you talking a.? of course I remembered!** qu'est-ce que tu racontes? bien sûr que j'y ai pensé!; **what's it all a.?** de quoi s'agit-il?; **how** *or* **what a. a game of bridge/going to Paris?** si on faisait un bridge/allait à Paris?; **well, what a. it? shall we go?** alors, qu'est-ce qu'on fait? on y va?; **what a. my bath?** et mon bain?; **what a. us?** et nous, alors?; **what a. the children?** *(what's to be done with them?)* et les enfants?; **what a. money?** *(have you got enough?)* tu as de l'argent?; **you remember that book? – what a. it?** tu te souviens de ce livre? – et alors?

5 *(active in, engaged in)* **to go a. one's work/business** vaquer à son travail/ses affaires; **while you're a. it** pendant que vous y êtes; **be quick a. it!** *(in irritation)* dépêchez-vous!; **you were long enough a. it!** ça vous aura pris assez de temps!

    ADV 1 *(in different directions)* de part et d'autre; **to stroll a.** se promener de-ci de-là *ou* de part et d'autre; **he looked a. to see if anyone was waiting for him** il a regardé autour de lui pour voir si quelqu'un l'attendait; **to follow sb a.** suivre qn partout; **to wave one's arms a.** agiter ses bras en tous sens; **there were clothes all a.** il y avait des vêtements un peu partout; **don't leave those papers lying a.** ne laissez pas traîner ces papiers

2 *(in the general area)* là; **is Jack a.?** est-ce que Jack est là?; **he must be somewhere a.** il doit être quelque part (par là), il doit être dans les parages; **there was nobody a.** il n'y avait personne (de visible); **there's never a policeman a. when you need one** il n'y a jamais un seul agent de police dans les parages quand on en a besoin; **there weren't many people a.** il n'y avait pas grand monde

3 *(active)* **to be up and a. again** *(after illness)* être de nouveau sur pied; **she's usually up and a. by 7 o'clock** elle est généralement debout à 7 heures; **to be a. early** être matinal; **there's a lot of flu a. at the moment** il y a beaucoup de cas de grippe actuellement

4 *(in opposite direction, order)* **the other way a.** en sens inverse, dans le sens contraire; **to turn a.** faire demi-tour, se retourner; *Mil* **a. turn!,** *Am* **a. face!** demi-tour!

5 *(approximately)* environ; **there are a. thirty** il y en a environ trente, il y en a une trentaine; **she's a. my age** elle a à peu près mon âge; **it will cost a. a hundred euros** ça coûtera dans les cent euros; **a. one o'clock** vers une heure; **he's a. as tall as you** il est à peu près de ta taille; **you've got a. as much intelligence as a two-year-old!** tu es à peu près aussi futé qu'un gamin de deux ans!; **that's a. right** c'est à peu près ça *ou* cela; **it's a. time** il serait *ou* est temps; **I've had (just) a. enough of you!** je commence à en avoir assez de toi!

6 *(ready, intending)* **to be a. to do sth** être sur le point de faire qch; **what were you a. to say?** qu'est-ce que vous alliez dire?; **he is a. to leave** il est sur le départ, il est sur le point de partir; *esp Am* **I'm not a. to pay 5,000 euros for that** je n'ai pas l'intention de payer cela 5000 euros; **he's not a. to change his ways just because of that** il n'y a pas de risque qu'il change ses manières de faire rien que pour ça VOIR GRAMMAIRE A52

about-face, about-turn N demi-tour *m, pl* demi-tours; *(of opinion, in policy)* revirement *m*; **to do an a.** *(turn around)* faire demi-tour; *(change one's mind)* changer complètement d'avis *ou* d'opinion

---

ABOVE [ə'bʌv]

| **PREP** au-dessus de **1, 2** ▪ plus de **4** |
| ▪ en amont de **5** ▪ au nord de **6** |
| **ADV** au-dessus **1** ▪ ci-dessus **2** |
| **ADJ** ci-dessus |
| **N** ci-dessus |

PREP 1 au-dessus de; **the water reached a. their knees** l'eau leur montait jusqu'au-dessus des genoux; **a. sea level** au-dessus du niveau de la mer; **his voice was heard a. the shouting** on entendait sa voix par-dessus le tumulte; **temperature a. normal** température supérieure à *ou* au-dessus de la normale; **that's a. me** *(beyond my understanding)* cela me dépasse; **they value friendship a. all else** ils placent l'amitié par-dessus tout; **over and a. that** en plus de cela VOIR GRAMMAIRE A67

2 *(morally or intellectually superior to)* **to be a. suspicion** être au-dessus de tout soupçon; **a. criticism** au-dessus de toute critique; **I am a. doing that** je me respecte trop pour faire cela; **she's not a. telling the occasional lie** il lui arrive de mentir de temps en temps; **he thinks he's a. all that** il pense qu'il est au-dessus de tout ça; *Fam* **to get a. oneself** se donner des airs

3 *(in rank)* **he is a. me (in rank)** il est mon supérieur (hiérarchique)

4 *(in degree, quantity)* **a. $100** plus de 100 dollars; **a. all** surtout; **a. twenty** plus de vingt; **the temperature didn't rise a. 10°C** la température n'a pas dépassé 10°C

5 *(upstream from)* **the Seine a. Paris** la Seine en amont de Paris

6 *(north of)* **a. this latitude** au nord de cette latitude

    ADV 1 au-dessus; **the tenants (of the flat) a.** les locataires du dessus; *esp Lit* **the sky a. was clear** au-dessus de moi/nous/*etc* le ciel était clair; **a view from a.** une vue plongeante; **a policy imposed from a.** une politique imposée d'en haut; **women aged 18 and a.** les femmes âgées de 18 ans et plus

2 *(in book, document etc)* ci-dessus; **the paragraph a.** le paragraphe ci-dessus; **as a.** comme ci-dessus

    ADJ *(in book etc)* **the a. quotation** la citation ci-dessus

    N the a. is a quotation from Hamlet le passage ci-dessus est une citation de Hamlet

aboveboard [ə'bʌv'bɔːd] **ADJ** franc, *f* franche; **his conduct was completely a.** il a agi en tout bien (et) tout honneur

aboveground [ə'bʌv'graʊnd] **ADJ 1** *(literal usage)* en surface **2** *Am Fig (income, earnings)* déclaré

above-mentioned,   **above-named** [-'menʃənd, -'neɪmd] **ADJ, N** susmentionné, -ée, susdit, -ite

above-the-line N *Mktg* publicité *f* média
    ADJ *Acct* au-dessus de la ligne
  ▸▸ *Acct* **a. accounts** comptes *mpl* de resultats courants; *Mktg* **a. advertising** publicité média; **a. costs** *Acct* coûts *mpl* au-dessus de la ligne; *Mktg* **a. expenditure** *Acct* dépenses *fpl* au-dessus de la ligne; *Mktg* dépenses média

abracadabra [æbrəkə'dæbrə] **INT** abracadabra

abrasion [ə'breɪʒən] N **1** *(of surface)* *(by rope)* usure *f* par frottement; *Tech* abrasion *f* **2** *(on skin)* écorchure *f*, éraflure *f*

abrasive [ə'breɪsɪv] **ADJ** *(surface, substance)* abrasif; *Fig (person)* caustique
    N abrasif *m*

abreast [ə'brest] **ADV** de front; **three/four a.** trois/quatre de front; **to march two a.** marcher par deux; **to march four a.** marcher par rangs de quatre; *Naut* **(in) line a.** en ligne

---

de front; **to come a. of a car** arriver à la hauteur d'une voiture; **to keep a. of a science** suivre les progrès d'une science; **I try to keep a. of the latest theories** j'essaie de me tenir au courant des dernières théories

abridge [ə'brɪdʒ] **VT** *(talk)* abréger; *(book, chapter)* raccourcir, abréger

abridged [ə'brɪdʒd] **ADJ** *(version)* abrégé

abridg(e)ment [ə'brɪdʒmənt] N **1** *(action)* abrégement *m* **2** *(result)* abrégé *m*, résumé *m*

abroad [ə'brɔːd] **ADV 1** à l'étranger; **to live a.** vivre à l'étranger; **our colleagues from a.** nos collègues étrangers **2** *(in every direction)* de tous côtés; **the news got a.** la nouvelle s'est répandue; **when it got a. that ...** quand la nouvelle s'est répandue que ... **3** *Arch (outside)* **to venture a.** sortir (de la maison)

abrogate ['æbrəgeɪt] **VT** *Fml (law)* abroger

abrogation [æbrə'geɪʃən] N *Fml (of law)* abrogation *f*

abrupt [ə'brʌpt] **ADJ 1** *(person, manner, tone)* abrupt; *(style)* heurté, saccadé **2** *(sudden) (drop in sales)* brusque; *(departure)* brusque, précipité; *(change)* brutal, -aux; **the evening came to an a. end** la soirée s'acheva brusquement; **there was an a. change in the weather** le temps a changé brutalement **3** *(steep) (slope, incline)* abrupt, raide, escarpé; *(rise)* ardu, raide

abruptly [ə'brʌptlɪ] **ADV 1** *(to interrupt, refuse, speak)* brusquement **2** *(to come to an end, decline)* brusquement **3** **to fall away a.** *(of cliff)* descendre à pic *ou* en pente raide

abruptness [ə'brʌptnɪs] N **1** *(of person, manner)* brusquerie *f*, manières *fpl* abruptes; *(of style)* caractère *m* heurté *ou* saccadé **2** *(suddenness) (of departure)* précipitation *f* **3** *(steepness) (of slope, incline)* raideur *f*

ABS [eɪbiː'es] N *(abbr* **anti-lock braking system)** ABS *m*
  ▸▸ **A. system** système *m* ABS

abs [æbz] **NPL** *Fam (abdominal muscles)* abdos *mpl*

abscess ['æbses] N abcès *m*

abscond [əb'skɒnd] **VI** *Law (run away)* s'enfuir; *(from prison)* s'enfuir, s'évader (**from** de); **to a. from justice** se soustraire à la justice **2** *Fam (make off)* décamper, filer

absconder [əb'skɒndər] N *Law* fugitif, -ive; *(prisoner)* évadé, -ée

absconding [əb'skɒndɪŋ] N *Law* évasion *f*, fuite *f*

▸ **abseil down** ['æbseɪl] **VI** *Sport* descendre en rappel

abseiling ['æbseɪlɪŋ] N *Sport* rappel *m*

absence ['æbsəns] N **1** *(state, instance of being away)* absence *f* (**from** de); **during one of his absences abroad** lors d'un de ses voyages à l'étranger; **in the a. of the manager** en l'absence du directeur; *Prov* **a. makes the heart grow fonder** = l'éloignement renforce l'affection; *Law* **sentenced in one's a.** condamné par contumace; *Admin* **leave of a.** congé *m*; *Mil* **a. without leave** absence illégale **2** *(lack)* absence *f*; **the a. of a tail in human beings** l'absence de queue chez l'être humain; **in the a. of definite information** faute de *ou* à défaut de renseignements précis **3** **a. of mind** distraction *f*

absent [1] ['æbsənt] **ADJ 1** *(not present)* absent (**from** de); **to a. friends!** *(toast)* à tous nos amis absents!; *Mil* **a. without leave** porté manquant **2** *(lacking)* absent **3** *(expression, look etc)* absent

absent [2] [æb'sent] **VT** **to a. oneself** *(for a few moments)* s'absenter (**from** de); **to a. oneself from a meeting** *(not attend)* être absent à une réunion

absentee [æbsən'tiː] N *(someone not pre-*

sent) absent, -ente; *(regularly)* absentéiste *mf*, *(from roll call)* manquant, -ante
▶▶ *Law* **a. landlord** propriétaire *m* absentéiste

absenteeism [æbsən'ti:ɪz(ə)m] N absentéisme *m*

absently ['æbsəntlɪ] ADV distraitement

absentminded [æbsənt'maɪndɪd] ADJ distrait

absentmindedly [æbsənt'maɪndɪdlɪ] ADV *(to say, listen)* distraitement; **she a. left it on the train** elle l'a laissé dans le train par distraction

absentmindedness [æbsənt'maɪndɪdnɪs] N distraction *f*

absinth(e) ['æbsɪnθ] N absinthe *f*

absolute ['æbsəlu:t] ADJ *Gram, Math etc* absolu; **case of a. necessity** cas *m* de nécessité absolue *ou* de force majeure; **it's an a. disgrace** c'est un véritable scandale; **he's an a. fool** c'est un parfait imbécile; **it would be a. madness** ce serait de la folie pure
N *Phil* **the a.** l'absolu *m*
▶▶ *Mktg* **a. frequency** fréquence *f* absolue; *Pol* **a. majority** majorité *f* absolue; **a. monarch** monarque *m* absolu; **a. power** pouvoir *m* absolu; *Math* **a. value** valeur *f* absolue; *Phys* **a. zero** zéro *m* absolu

absolutely [æbsə'lu:tlɪ] ADV absolument; **you're a. right** vous avez absolument *ou* tout à fait raison; **that's ridiculous – a.** c'est ridicule – (oui,) tout à fait; **do you support him? – a./a. not** vous le soutenez? – absolument/absolument pas; **I a. refuse** je refuse catégoriquement; **I a. insist that you attend the meeting** je tiens absolument à ce que vous soyez présent à la réunion; **it is a. forbidden** c'est absolument *ou* formellement interdit; *Gram* **a verb used a.** un verbe employé absolument

absolution [æbsə'lu:ʃən] N *Rel* absolution *f*, **to give sb a.** donner l'absolution à qn

absolutism ['æbsəlu:tɪz(ə)m] N *Pol* absolutisme *m*

absolve [əb'zɒlv] VT *(person)* absoudre (**from, of** de); **she was absolved from** *or* **of all blame** il fut reconnu qu'elle n'était aucunement responsable; **he felt he had been absolved from** *or* **of blame** il s'estimait complètement innocenté

absorb [əb'sɔ:b, -'zɔ:b] VT 1 *(liquid, heat etc)* absorber; *(shock, sound)* amortir; *(costs)* se charger de; *(loss)* essuyer; *(information)* enregistrer, assimiler; *Com (company)* racheter; **to a. a deficit** résorber un déficit; **to a. debts** éponger des dettes; **these units were absorbed into the new army** ces unités furent intégrées dans le nouveau corps d'armée **2** *(interest, occupy)* *(person)* absorber; **to be/become absorbed in sth** s'absorber dans qch; **to listen with absorbed interest** écouter avec un intérêt profond

absorbency [əb'sɔ:bənsɪ, -'zɔ:b-] N capacité *f* d'absorption

absorbent [əb'sɔ:bənt, -'zɔ:b-] ADJ, N absorbant *m*

absorber [əb'sɔ:bər, -'zɔ:b-] N *Aut etc (of shock etc)* amortisseur *m*

absorbing [əb'sɔ:bɪŋ, -'zɔ:b-] ADJ *(subject, article, discussion)* passionnant; *(work)* absorbant, prenant

absorption [əb'sɔ:pʃən, -'zɔ:p-] N 1 *(of liquid)* absorption *f*, *(of sound, impact etc)* amortissement *m*, *Com (of company)* rachat *m* **2** *(interest)* absorption *f*, **her a. in the book was so great that ...** elle était tellement absorbée dans son livre que ...

abstain [əb'steɪn] VI 1 *(refrain)* s'abstenir; **to a. from (doing) sth** s'abstenir de (faire) qch; **to a. from meat** s'abstenir de manger de la

viande **2** *Pol (in vote)* s'abstenir

abstainer [əb'steɪnər] N 1 *(from drinking)* **to be a total a.** ne pas boire d'alcool; **he's become a total a.** il a complètement arrêté de boire **2** *(in vote)* abstentionniste *mf*

abstemious [əb'sti:mɪəs] ADJ *(person)* sobre; *(diet, eating habits)* frugal, -aux; **you're being very a.!** tu t'es mis à la diète!

abstemiously [əb'sti:mɪəslɪ] ADV sobrement; *(to eat)* frugalement

abstemiousness [əb'sti:mɪəsnɪs] N sobriété *f*

abstention [əb'stenʃən] N 1 *(from action)* abstention *f* (**from** de); **their a. from making any comment** le fait qu'ils se soient abstenus de tout commentaire **2** *Pol (in vote)* abstention *f*

abstinence ['æbstɪnəns] N abstinence *f* (**from** de); *Rel* **day of a.** jour *m* d'abstinence; **total a.** abstinence complète

abstract¹ ['æbstrækt] ADJ 1 *(number, noun, art)* abstrait **2** *(obscure)* abstrait, abstrus
N 1 **the a.** l'abstrait *m*; **in the a.** dans l'abstrait **2** *(work of art)* œuvre *f* abstraite **3** *(summary)* résumé *m*, abrégé *m*
▶▶ *Art* **a. artist** artiste *m* abstrait, abstrait *m*

abstract² [æb'strækt] VT 1 *Fml (remove)* sortir, extraire (**sth from sth** qch de qch); *esp Hum (steal)* subtiliser (**sth from sb** qch à qn); *Chem* extraire (par distillation) **2** *(text)* résumer, abréger **3** *Phil (quality)* abstraire, faire abstraction de

abstracted [æb'stræktɪd] ADJ distrait

abstractedly [æb'stræktɪdlɪ] ADV distraitement, d'un air distrait

abstraction [æb'strækʃən] N 1 *Fml (theft)* subtilisation *f*, *Chem, Ind* extraction *f* (par distillation) **2** *(abstract idea)* abstraction *f*, idée *f* abstraite **3** *(distraction)* distraction *f*, **in a moment of a.** dans un moment d'inattention **4** *Phil* abstraction *f*

abstractly ['æbstræktlɪ] ADV abstraitement

abstruse [əb'stru:s] ADJ abstrus

abstruseness [əb'stru:snɪs] N caractère *m* abstrus

absurd [əb'sɜ:d] ADJ absurde
N *Phil* **the a.** l'absurde *m*

absurdity [əb'sɜ:dɪtɪ] N absurdité *f*, **the a. of paying people not to work** l'absurdité consistant à payer des gens à ne pas travailler

absurdly [əb'sɜ:dlɪ] ADV absurdement; **rather a., I seem to have forgotten your name** c'est absurde, mais je crois bien que j'ai oublié votre nom; *Fam* **she's a. rich** elle est ridiculement riche

ABTA ['æbtə] N *(abbr Association of British Travel Agents)* association *f* des agents de voyage britanniques

abundance [ə'bʌndəns] N 1 abondance *f*, **in a.** en abondance, à profusion; **they had an a. of musical talent** ils avaient un immense talent musical **2** *Biol etc (of species etc)* abondance *f* **3** *Cards (in solo whist)* abondance *f*

abundant [ə'bʌndənt] ADJ abondant (**in** en); *(in wheat etc)* fertile; **to be a. in natural resources** abonder en ressources naturelles; **there is a. evidence that ...** il y a de nombreuses preuves démontrant que ...

abundantly [ə'bʌndəntlɪ] ADV 1 *(in abundance)* abondamment, en abondance **2** *(obvious)* largement; **they made their feelings a. clear** ils exprimèrent leurs sentiments tout à fait clairement; **I think that's a. clear** je pense que c'est limpide; **is that clear? – a.** c'est clair? – limpide

abuse¹ [ə'bju:s] N 1 *(misuse)* abus *m* (**of** de); *(of facilities)* usage *m* abusif *(of term etc)* emploi *m* abusif; *Law* **a. of authority** abus

d'autorité *ou* de pouvoir; *Parl* **a. of privilege** abus de droit; **a. of trust** abus de confiance; **alcohol a.** l'abus *ou* l'excès *m* d'alcool **2** *(insults)* injures *fpl*, insultes *fpl*; **term of a.** injure *f*, **to shower a. on sb** accabler qn d'injures **3** *(of child etc)* mauvais traitement *m*; **sexual a.** sévices *mpl* sexuels

abuse² [ə'bju:z] VT 1 *(misuse)* *(one's authority, sb's trust, patience etc)* abuser de; *(one's power)* mésuser de, abuser de; **a much abused word** un mot employé abusivement **2** *(insult)* injurier, insulter **3** *(ill-treat)* maltraiter; *(sexually)* faire subir des sévices à; **abused child** *(sexually)* enfant *mf* victime de sévices

> Note that the French verb **abuser** never means **to insult**.

abusive [ə'bju:sɪv] ADJ 1 *(use)* abusif **2** *(words)* injurieux; *(person)* grossier; **he got** *or* **became a.** il devint grossier; **a. language** des grossièretés *fpl*

abusively [ə'bju:sɪvlɪ] ADV *(to speak)* injurieusement; **an a. worded letter** une lettre aux termes injurieux

▶ **abut on, abut against** [ə'bʌt] VT INSEP (**-tt-**) *(field, river etc)* confiner à; *Constr (partition)* s'appuyer *ou* buter contre; *(wall)* s'arcbouter contre

abutment [ə'bʌtmənt] N *Archit, Constr (of defensive wall)* arc-boutant *m*, *pl* arcsboutants; *(of wall)* contrefort *m*; *(of bridge)* butée *f*, culée *f*, *(of arch)* piédroit *m*

abysmal [ə'bɪzm(ə)l] ADJ 1 *(extreme)* *(stupidity, ignorance)* profond **2** *Fam (bad)* abominable, épouvantable

abysmally [ə'bɪzm(ə)lɪ] ADV atrocement; **the area is a. lacking in good restaurants** le quartier est absolument dépourvu de bons restaurants; **a. ignorant** d'une ignorance profonde

abyss [ə'bɪs] N *Geog, Fig* abîme *m*, gouffre *m*; *(in ocean)* abysse *m*, zone *f* abyssale

abyssal [ə'bɪs(ə)l] ADJ *(depths)*, *Geol* abyssal, -aux

Abyssinia [æbɪ'sɪnɪə] N Abyssinie *f*

Abyssinian [æbɪ'sɪnɪən] ADJ abyssinien, abyssin; *(cat)* abyssin
N 1 Abyssinien, -ienne **2** *Ling* abyssinien *m*

AC [eɪ'si:] N 1 *Elec (abbr* **alternating current**) CA *m* **2** *abbr* **air conditioning**

A/C, a/c *Com (abbr* **account**) c.

.ac [dɒteɪ'si:] *Comput* = abréviation *f* désignant les universités et les sites éducatifs dans les adresses électroniques britanniques

acacia [ə'keɪʃə] N *Bot* acacia *m*; **false a.** faux acacia

academia [ækə'di:mɪə] N *Univ* milieu *m* universitaire

academic [ækə'demɪk] ADJ 1 *(of school)* scolaire; *(of university)* universitaire; **the a. year** l'année *f* scolaire/universitaire; **we aim for a. excellence** notre objectif est l'excellence de notre enseignement; **her a. achievements are impressive** elle a fait de brillantes études; **the first a. study of ...** la première étude faite par un universitaire de ...
2 *(intellectual)* *(subjects)* d'enseignement général; *(person)* studieux, doué pour les études
3 *Pej (theoretical)* **an a. discussion** une discussion abstraite; **of purely a. interest** qui n'est intéressant qu'au point de vue théorique; **that's a. now** c'est hors de propos à présent, ça n'a plus d'importance; **I know this is a bit a., but why exactly ...?** je sais que ma question n'a qu'un intérêt théorique, mais pourquoi exactement ...?
4 *Art (painting etc)* académique

Nuniversitaire *mf*

academically [ækə'demɪklɪ] ADVacadémiquement; **to be a. gifted** être doué intellectuellement; **she's not very a. inclined** elle n'est pas très douée pour les études; **the school doesn't have a tremendous reputation a.** l'école n'est pas fabuleusement cotée pour la qualité de son enseignement

academician [əkædə'mɪʃən] N académicien, -ienne; *Br* **Royal A.** = membre *m* de l'Académie royale des beaux-arts

academicism [ækə'demɪsɪz(ə)m], **academism** [ə'kædəmɪz(ə)m] N *Art esp Pej* académisme *m*

academy [ə'kædəmɪ] N 1 académie *f*, *Br* **the Royal A. (of Arts)** = l'Académie *f* royale des beaux-arts; **a. of music** conservatoire *m*; **fencing a.** salle *f* d'escrime; **military a.** école *f* militaire 2 *(school) Scot* ≃ lycée *m*; *Br*, *Am* ≃ collège *m* (privé) 3 *Cin* **the A. (of Motion Picture Arts and Sciences)** l'Académie *f* des arts et des sciences cinématographiques *(association américaine de professionnels du cinéma, répartis selon leur métier)*
▸▸ *Cin* **A. Award** oscar *m*; **A. leader** amorce *f*, **A. ratio** écran *m* de format standard

acanthus [ə'kænθəs] N 1 *(shrub)* acanthe *f* 2 *Archit* (feuille *f* d')acanthe *f*

a cappella [a:kə'pelə] *Mus* ADJ a cappella; **a. singing** chant *m* a cappella
ADV a cappella

ACAS ['eɪkæs] N *(abbr* **Advisory, Conciliation and Arbitration Service)** = organisme *m* britannique indépendant d'arbitrage des conflits du travail

accede [æk'si:d] VI 1 **to a. to the throne** monter sur le trône 2 *Fml (assent)* **to a. to** *(treaty)* donner son adhésion à; *(request, demand)* accéder à

accelerant [ək'selərənt] N *Chem* accélérateur *m*

accelerate [ək'seləreɪt] VT *(one's pace, progress)* accélérer; *(movement)* presser, accélérer; *(events)* précipiter; *(computer)* augmenter la vitesse de
VI *Aut* accélérer; *(of motion etc)* s'accélérer

accelerated [ək'seləreɪtɪd] ADJ *(pace, process, rhythm)* accéléré
▸▸ *Acct* **a. depreciation** amortissement *m* dégressif, amortissement accéléré; *Phys* **a. motion** accéléré *m*

acceleration [əkselə'reɪʃən] N accélération *f*, **negative a.** accélération retardatrice *ou* négative; *Aut* **the car has good a.** cette voiture a une bonne accélération; *Phys* **uniform a.** vitesse *f* uniformément accélérée
▸▸ *Fin* **a. clause** clause *f* accélératrice; *Aut* **a. lane** voie *f* d'accélération; *Fin* **a. premium** prime *f* de rendement; *Com* **a. principle** principe *m* d'accélération

accelerator [ək'seləreɪtər] N 1 *Aut* accélérateur *m*; **to step on the a.** accélérer 2 *Comput*, *Phys* accélérateur *m*
▸▸ *Comput* **a. card** carte *f* accélératrice; *Aut* **a. heel point** point *m* talon; *Aut* **a. pedal** pédale *f* d'accélérateur

accent¹ ['æksənt] N 1 *(pronunciation)* accent *m*; **to have a Liverpool a.** avoir l'accent de Liverpool; **to have a German a.** avoir un accent allemand; **she speaks French with/without an a.** elle parle français avec un/sans accent 2 *Lit* **in broken accents** d'une voix brisée *ou* entrecoupée; **to speak in accents of doom** se montrer très pessimiste 3 *(sign)* accent *m*; **acute/grave a.** accent aigu/grave 4 *(stress)* accent *m*; **the a. is on the final syllable** l'accent est sur la dernière syllabe; *Fig* **we're putting the a. on efficiency** nous mettons l'accent sur l'efficacité; **fashion with the a. on youth** mode qui met l'accent sur la jeunesse

accent² [æk'sent] VT *(syllable etc)* accentuer

accented [æk'sentɪd] ADJ accentué; *Ling* accentuel
▸▸ *Ling* **a. character** caractère *m* accentué

accentuate [æk'sentʃʋeɪt] VT *(detail)* accentuer, faire ressortir; *(contrast)* accuser; **to a. the need for sth** accentuer la nécessité de qch

accentuated [æk'sentʃʋeɪtɪd] ADJ accentué; *(limp, stutter)* fortement marqué; *Mus* **the offbeat is a.** le temps faible est accentué

accentuation [æksentʃʋ'eɪʃən] N *(of vowel, detail etc)* accentuation *f*

accept [ək'sept] VT 1 *(take when offered) (gift, invitation, offer)* accepter; **please a. my apologies** je vous prie de bien vouloir accepter mes excuses; **the machine won't a. foreign coins** cette machine n'accepte pas la monnaie étrangère 2 *Fin* **to a. a bill** accepter un effet; *Com* **to a. (delivery of) goods** réceptionner des marchandises 3 *(recognize as valid) (reasons)* admettre; *(treaty)* donner son adhésion à; **while we a. that this may be more expensive ...** tout en admettant que ceci puisse être plus cher ...; **I cannot a. that you knew nothing of this** je n'arrive pas à croire que vous n'ayez rien su de ceci; **to a. responsibility for sth** prendre *ou* accepter la responsabilité de qch; **to a. no responsibility** décliner toute responsabilité; **it is generally accepted that ...** il est généralement admis que ...; **contrary to accepted opinion, ...** contrairement à l'idée communément admise, ...; **the accepted custom** *(socially approved)* l'usage *m* admis; **to be accepted** *(socially etc)* être accepté 4 *(resign oneself to)* accepter; **she just accepts these hardships** elle accepte tout bonnement ces épreuves
VI accepter; **they offered me a contract and I accepted** ils m'ont proposé un contrat que j'ai accepté

acceptability [əkseptə'bɪlɪtɪ] N acceptabilité *f*

acceptable [ək'septəb(ə)l] ADJ 1 *(admissible)* acceptable; **behaviour of this sort is not a.** un comportement de la sorte est inacceptable *ou* inadmissible; **I trust these terms will be a. to you** j'espère que ces conditions vous seront acceptables; **just about a.** juste passable 2 *(welcome, satisfactory)* bienvenu; **a most a. gift** un cadeau des plus bienvenus; **your cheque was most a.** votre chèque était fort apprécié
▸▸ *Comput* **A. Use Policy** = code *m* de conduite défini par un fournisseur d'accès à l'Internet

acceptance [ək'septəns] N 1 *(of gift, invitation, apology etc)* acceptation *f*; *(of candidate)* admission *f*, **to find a.** trouver créance; **to gain a.** *(of views, theory etc)* être accepté; **she's got two provisional acceptances** *(for university)* elle a été provisoirement admise dans deux universités 2 *Com, Ind (of goods)* réception *f*, *Fin (of bill of exchange)* acceptation *f*, *Fin (document)* effet *m* accepté, effet à payer; *Fin* **to present a bill for a.** présenter une traite à l'acceptation 3 *(of one's fate, circumstances)* acceptation *f*; **his unquestioning a. of this explanation** le fait qu'il ait accepté cette explication sans sourciller
▸▸ *Am Banking* **a. bank** banque *f* d'acceptation; *Fin* **a. bill** effet *ou* traite *f* contre acceptation; *Fin* **a. fee** commission *f* d'acceptation; **a. speech** discours *m* de réception; **a. test** essai *m* de réception *ou* de recette

acceptation [æksep'teɪʃən] N *Fml* acception *f*, **in the full a. of the word** dans toute l'acception du mot

accepting house [ək'septɪŋ] N *Banking* maison *f* d'acceptation

acceptor [ək'septər] N *Chem, Com etc* accepteur *m*

access ['ækses] N 1 *(to person, place)* accès *m* (**to** à); **there is easy a. to the beach** on accède facilement à la plage; **to have a. to sth/sb** avoir accès à qch/auprès de qn; **to give sb a. to sth/sb** donner à qn accès à qch/auprès de qn; *Aut* **a. only** *(sign)* accès interdit (sauf aux riverains); **the burglars gained a. through a window** les cambrioleurs sont passés *ou* entrés par une fenêtre; **we must not give terrorists a. to the media** nous ne devons pas donner l'accès aux médias aux terroristes; *Fml* **difficult of a.** d'un accès *ou* d'une approche difficile; *Comput* **to have a. to the Internet** avoir accès à l'Internet; *Comput* **to have a. to a file** avoir accès à un fichier; *Comput* **a. denied** *(DOS message)* accès refusé; *Comput* **up to 56K a.** accès jusqu'à 56 Kbit/s; **her ex-husband has unlimited a. to the children** son ex-mari a un droit de visite illimitée auprès de ses enfants; **a.-authorized person** personne *f* autorisée d'accès
2 *(of rage etc)* accès *m*; *often Iron (of enthusiasm, generosity)* élan *m*
VT *Comput (data)* accéder à, avoir accès à
▸▸ *Comput* **a. authorization code** code *m* d'autorisation d'accès; **a. barrier** barrière *f* d'accès; *TV* **a. broadcasting** télévision *f* ouverte; *TV* **a. channel** canal *m* d'accès; *Comput* **a. code** code d'accès; *Comput* **a. control** contrôle *m* d'accès; *Comput* **a. level** *(in network)* niveau *m* d'accès; *TV* **a. prime-time** accès *m* prime-time, période *f* précédant les heures de grande écoute; *Comput* **a. privileges** droits *mpl* d'accès; *Comput* **a. provider** fournisseur *m* d'accès; **a. ramp** bretelle *f* d'accès; *Law* **a. rights** *(to child)* droits de visite; **a. road** *(in general)* route *f* d'accès; *(to motorway)* bretelle d'accès *ou* de raccordement; *Comput* **a. speed** vitesse *f* d'accès; *TV* **a. television** télévision ouverte; *Comput* **a. time** temps *m* d'accès

accessary [ək'sesərɪ] N = **accessory** N 3

accessibility [əksesɪ'bɪlɪtɪ] N accessibilité *f*

accessible [ək'sesəb(ə)l] ADJ *(place, novel, style etc)* accessible (**to** à); *(person) (easy to talk to)* abordable, facile à aborder; *(easy to have a meeting with etc)* accessible; **she has a very a. manner** elle est d'un abord très facile; **information a. to everyone** connaissances à la portée de tout le monde

accession [ək'seʃən] N 1 *(to post, power etc)* accession *f* (**to** à); *(to throne)* avènement *m*, accession (**to** à) 2 *(to treaty)* accession *f*, adhésion *f* (**to** à); *(to demand)* accession 3 *(increase)* accroissement *m* (par addition); *(addition to collection)* addition *f*
▸▸ **a. book, accessions book** *(in library)* registre *m* des additions; **a. number** *(of book)* numéro *m* de catalogue

accessory [ək'sesərɪ] ADJ accessoire (**to** à)
N 1 *(item)* accessoire *m*; **car/camera accessories** accessoires d'automobile/d'appareilphoto 2 *(clothing) (usu pl)* **accessories** accessoires *mpl* 3 *Law* complice *mf*; **a. to a crime** complice d'un crime; **a. before the fact** complice par instigation *ou* par assistance; **a. after the fact** complice par aide après coup
▸▸ *Bot* **a. bud, a. shoot** prompt-bourgeon *m*, *pl* prompts-bourgeons

accident ['æksɪdənt] N accident *m*; *Law* cas *m* fortuit; **by a.** *(by chance)* par hasard, accidentellement; **I'm sorry, it was an a.** je suis

désolé, c'était un accident; **an a. in the home/at work** un accident domestique/du travail; **to have an a.** avoir un accident; **car a.** accident de voiture; **road a.** accident de la route; **the victims of the a.** les victimes de l'accident, les accidentés *mpl*; *Prov* **accidents will happen** on ne peut pas parer à tout; **it was an a. waiting to happen** c'est un accident qui devait arriver; **it's no a. that she made the film here** ce n'est pas par hasard si elle a tourné le film ici; **that was no a.** ce n'est pas le fait du hasard; **their last child was an a.** leur dernier enfant est un accident
▸▸ **a. blackspot** point *m* noir; *Br* **a. and emergency unit** *(in hospital)* service *m* des urgences, urgences *fpl*; **a. insurance** assurance *f* (contre les) accidents; **a. victim** victime *f* d'un/de l'accident, accidenté *m*

accidental [æksɪˈdent(ə)l] ADJ **1** *(chance)* accidentel, fortuit; *(meeting)* fortuit; **I gave him the a. impression that ...** sans le vouloir je lui ai donné l'impression que ... **2** *(incidental)* accessoire, subsidiaire
N *Mus* accident *m*, signe *m* accidentel
▸▸ *Law* **a. death** mort *f* accidentelle

accidentally [æksɪˈdent(ə)lɪ] ADV **1** *(by chance)* par hasard, accidentellement **2** *(not deliberately)* accidentellement, par mégarde; *Hum* **a. on purpose** comme par hasard, exprès

accident-prone ADJ prédisposé aux accidents; **he's a.** il lui arrive toujours des malheurs

acclaim [əˈkleɪm] N to meet with great critical **a.** être salué par la critique; **the a. of his peers** la reconnaissance de ses pairs; **I had never anticipated such wild a.** je ne m'attendais pas à de telles louanges
VT **1** acclamer; **to be acclaimed by the critics** être acclamé des critiques; **he was acclaimed as the new Caruso** il fut acclamé et proclamé le nouveau Caruso; **her acclaimed portrayal of Cleopatra** sa représentation acclamée de Cléopâtre **2** *(proclaim)* **Charlemagne was acclaimed emperor** Charlemagne fut acclamé *ou* proclamé empereur

acclamation [ækləˈmeɪʃən] N acclamation *f*; **carried by a.** adopté par acclamation

acclimate [əˈklaɪmeɪt, ˈæklɪmeɪt] VT *Am* = **acclimatize**

acclimation [æklɪˈmeɪʃən] N *Am* = **acclimatization**

acclimatization [əklaɪmətaɪˈzeɪʃən] N acclimatement *m* (**to** à); *Fig* acclimatation *f*

acclimatize [əˈklaɪmətaɪz] VT acclimater; *(plant etc)* naturaliser; **to become acclimatized to a new environment** s'acclimater à un nouvel environnement; **to a. oneself to sth** s'acclimater à qch
VI s'acclimater

accolade [ˈækəleɪd] N accolade *f*; **the ultimate a.** la consécration suprême

accommodate [əˈkɒmədeɪt] VT **1** *(provide room for) (specific number of people)* loger, recevoir; **restaurant that can a. 50 people** restaurant qui peut recevoir *ou* servir 50 personnes **2** *(satisfy)* satisfaire; **we will try to a. you** nous essaierons de vous satisfaire; **to do sth to a. sb** faire qch pour arranger qn **3** *(provide)* **to a. sb with sth** donner *ou* fournir qch à qn; **to a. sb with a loan** faire un prêt à qn **4** *(adapt)* accommoder; *(opinions, differences)* concilier; **to a. oneself to circumstances** s'adapter aux circonstances
VI *Physiol (of eye)* accommoder

> Note that the French verb **accommoder** is a false friend and is rarely a translation for the English verb **to accommodate**.

accommodating [əˈkɒmədeɪtɪŋ] ADJ complaisant, obligeant

accommodation [əkɒməˈdeɪʃən] N **1** *(Am usu* **accommodations**) logement *m*; *(in hotel)* chambre(s) *f(pl)* (d'hôtel); **to look for a.** *(flat to rent)* chercher un logement; *(hotel room)* chercher une chambre (d'hôtel); **a. only** logement sans restauration; **the huts were meant for short-term a.** les cabanes étaient destinées à servir de logement à court terme; **furnished/unfurnished a.** chambres garnies *ou* meublées/non meublées; **hotel a.** hébergement *m* en hôtel; **there is a. in this hotel for 50 people** cet hôtel peut loger 50 personnes VOIR GRAMMAIRE A11
2 *(adaptation)* ajustement *m*, adaptation *f* (**to** à); *Physiol (of eye)* accommodation *f*
3 *esp Fml (of argument)* arrangement *m*; **to come to an a.** arriver à un compromis; **to come to an a. with one's creditors** parvenir à un arrangement avec ses créanciers
4 *Fin (of money)* prêt *m*
▸▸ *Br* **a. address** adresse *f* (*utilisée uniquement pour la correspondance)*; **a. allowance** indemnité *f* de logement; *Fin* **a. bill** traite *f ou* effet *m* de complaisance; **a. capacity** *(of hotel)* capacité *f* d'accueil; **a. department** service *m* hébergement; **a. industry** industrie *f* de l'hébergement; *Naut* **a. ladder** échelle *f* de coupée; **a. package** forfait *m* hébergement; **a. shortage** capacités d'hébergement insuffisantes; **a. unit** unité *f* d'hébergement

accompaniment [əˈkʌmpənɪmənt] N **1** *Mus* accompagnement *m* (**on** à) **2** *Culin* accompagnement *m*

accompanist [əˈkʌmpənɪst] N *Mus* accompagnateur, -trice

accompany [əˈkʌmpənɪ] VT **1** accompagner; **to be accompanied by sb** être accompagné de qn; **she accompanied me to the door** elle m'a raccompagné jusqu'à la porte; **the hot weather is often accompanied by afternoon thunderstorms** la chaleur s'accompagne souvent d'orages dans l'après-midi; **fever accompanied by** *or* **with delirium** fièvre accompagnée de délire; **a meal accompanied with wine** un repas accompagné de vin **2** *Mus* accompagner (**on the piano** au piano); **he accompanied himself on the guitar** il s'accompagna à la guitare
▸▸ **accompanied baggage** bagages *mpl* accompagnés

accompanying [əˈkʌmpənɪɪŋ] ADJ **the a. documents** les documents ci-joints; **children will not be allowed in without an a. adult** l'entrée est interdite aux enfants non accompagnés

accomplice [əˈkɒmplɪs, -ˈkʌm-] N complice *mf*; **his accomplices in crime** les complices de ses crimes

accomplish [əˈkɒmplɪʃ, -ˈkʌm-] VT *(task)* accomplir, mener à bonne fin, venir à bout de; *(journey, crossing)* effectuer; **to a. one's object** atteindre son but

accomplished [əˈkɒmplɪʃt, -ˈkʌm-] ADJ **1** *(completed)* achevé **2** *(dancer, pianist, performance etc)* accompli
▸▸ **a. fact** fait *m* accompli

accomplishment [əˈkɒmplɪʃmənt, -ˈkʌm-] N **1** *(of task etc)* accomplissement *m*; *(of project)* réalisation *f* **2** *(feat, achievement)* prouesse *f*, exploit *m*; **that's quite an a.** c'est un véritable exploit, c'est une véritable prouesse **3** *(talent)* talent *m*; **one of his many accomplishments** un de ses nombreux talents

accord [əˈkɔːd] N **1** *(agreement)* accord *m*, consentement *m*; **with one a.** d'un commun accord; **this was in a. with their policy** ceci était en accord avec leur politique **2** *(pact)* accord *m*; **to reach an a.** parvenir à un accord **3** *(initiative)* **to do sth of one's own a.** faire qch de son plein gré; **the table seemed to be moving of its own a.** la table avait l'air de bouger toute seule
VI s'accorder, concorder (**with** avec); **this accords with her earlier statement** ceci concorde avec sa première déclaration
VT *Fml* accorder, concéder (**to** à); *(significance, status)* accorder; **a privilege/title accorded him by the Crown** un privilège/un titre qui lui a été concédé par la Couronne

accordance [əˈkɔːdəns] N accord *m*, conformité *f*; **in a. with** conformément à; **this is in a. with the rules** ceci est conforme au règlement; **his statement is not in a. with the facts** sa déclaration ne concorde pas avec les faits

according to [əˈkɔːdɪŋ] PREP ADV **1** *(depending on)* **a. how it is done** suivant la façon dont on le fait; **a. whether one is rich or poor** selon qu'on est riche ou pauvre; **a. which method you use** selon la méthode employée
2 *(in conformity with)* **a. instructions** selon *ou* suivant *ou* d'après les ordres; **a. age** par rang d'âge; **a. plan** conformément au plan; **a. our means** selon nos moyens
3 *(citing a source)* **a. him** selon lui, d'après lui, à ce qu'il dit; **the Gospel a. St Luke** l'Évangile selon saint Luc; **a. what I've heard** d'après ce que j'ai entendu dire

accordingly [əˈkɔːdɪŋlɪ] ADV **1** *(to act, dress etc)* en conséquence **2** *(therefore)* donc; **a., I wrote to him** je lui ai donc écrit, par conséquent je lui ai écrit

accordion [əˈkɔːdɪən] N *Mus* accordéon *m*; **piano a.** accordéon à touches
▸▸ **a. fold** *(in publishing)* pliure *f* en accordéon; **a. player** accordéoniste *mf*; **a. pleats** *(in garment, fabric)* plis *mpl* en accordéon

accordionist [əˈkɔːdɪənɪst] N *Mus* accordéoniste *mf*

accost [əˈkɒst] VT *(person)* accoster, aborder; *(of prostitute)* racoler

account [əˈkaʊnt] N **1** *Acct, Fin, Com, Banking* compte *m*; **to open an a.** *(in bank)* ouvrir un compte; **to pay money into one's a.** verser de l'argent sur son compte; **to overdraw an a.** mettre un compte à découvert; **to have an a. with Lloyds** avoir un compte à la Lloyds; **to have an a. with a shop/Marks & Spencer** avoir un compte dans un magasin/chez Marks & Spencer; **put it on** *or* **charge it to my a.** inscrivez-le *ou* mettez-le à mon compte; **to pay a sum on a.** payer une somme en acompte *ou* à compte ou à valoir; **to settle an a.** régler une note *ou* un compte; **cash or a.?** vous payez *ou* réglez comptant ou est-ce que vous avez un compte chez nous?; *Fig* **to settle accounts** régler ses comptes (**with sb** avec qn); **that should settle accounts with him** ça devrait régler mes comptes avec lui; **to keep (an) a. of sth** *(record)* tenir un compte de qch
2 *(in advertising, PR)* budget *m*, compte-client *m*, *pl* comptes-clients; **one of our major accounts** un de nos plus gros clients; **we lost the Guinness a.** nous avons perdu la clientèle de Guinness *ou* le budget Guinness **3** *St Exch* **the A.** la liquidation (mensuelle); **dealings for the a.** négociations *fpl* à terme
4 *Acct, Fin, Com (of expenses)* état *m*, note *f*; *(of transactions)* exposé *m*; **as per** *or* **to a. rendered** *(on statement)* suivant compte *ou* relevé remis
5 *Comput (with Internet service provider)* abonnement *m* (**with** auprès de); **to set up an a. with sb** s'abonner auprès de qn
6 *(advantage)* parti *m*; **to turn sth to a.** tirer parti *ou* avantage de qch, mettre qch à profit; **to turn sth to good a.** tirer un bon parti de qch

7 to call sb to a. demander une explication *ou* des comptes à qn (**for sth** de qch); **to be brought to a.** devoir rendre des comptes; **to give a good a. of oneself** bien se comporter **8** *(importance)* **of no a.** *(person, matter)* insignifiant, de peu d'importance; **to take sth into a., to take a. of sth** tenir compte de qch, faire entrer qch en ligne de compte; **taking everything into a.** tout bien calculé; **to leave out of a., to take no a. of** ne pas tenir compte de; *(circumstance)* négliger **9** *(because)* **on a. of sth** en raison de qch; *(esp in negative context)* à cause de qch; **I did it on your a.** je l'ai fait pour vous; **I did it on a. of you** *(reproaching)* je l'ai fait à cause de vous; **the road was closed on a. of the accident** la route était barrée à cause *ou* en raison de l'accident; **he can't play football on a. of his health** il ne peut pas jouer au football en raison de sa santé; **on no a., not on any a.** en aucun cas; **I don't want to talk to her on any a.** je ne veux lui parler en aucun cas *ou* sous aucun prétexte; **you're not on any a. to ...** tu ne dois en aucun cas *ou* sous aucun prétexte ... **10** *(responsibility)* **to act on one's own a.** agir de sa propre initiative ou de soi-même; **to set up in business on one's own a.** s'établir à son compte **11** *(report) (of events)* récit *m*; *(of facts, actual situation)* exposé *m*; *(in newspaper)* compte rendu *m*; **to give an a. of sth** faire le récit de qch; **an interesting a. of his travels** un récit intéressant de ses voyages; **his a. of the siege of Gerona** le récit qu'il fait/faisait du siège de Gérone; **his latest book contains an amusing a. of how he learned to drive** son dernier livre relate de façon amusante la manière dont il a appris à conduire; **her a. (of the events) was slightly different** son exposé des événements était légèrement différent; **on any a.** à tous points de vue; **by all accounts** au dire de tout le monde

VT *Fml* **to a. sb guilty** tenir qn pour coupable

▸▸**a. balance** *(status)* situation *f* de compte; *Acct (after audit)* reliquat *m* de compte; *Acct* **a. book** livre *m* de comptes, registre *m* de comptabilité; **a. card** *Fin (record of charges)* fiche *f* de compte *ou* de facture; *Com (for use in department store)* carte-clients *f, pl* cartes-clients; **a. charges** frais *mpl* de tenue de compte; **a. commission** commission *f* de compte; **a. credit** avoir *m* de compte; *St Exch* **a. day** *(jour m de)* liquidation *f*, (jour de) règlement *m*; *Com* **a. director** *(in advertising, marketing, PR)* directeur, -trice des comptes-clients; *Am St Exch* **a. executive** agent *m* de change; **a. fee** commission de compte; *Com* **a. handler** *(in advertising, marketing, PR)* responsable *mf* des comptes-clients; **a. handling fee** commission de tenue de compte; *Banking* **a. holder** titulaire *mf*; *Banking* **a. management charges** frais de tenue de compte; **a. manager** *Banking, Fin* chargé, -ée de compte; *Com (in advertising, marketing, PR)* responsable de budget; *Banking* **a. number** numéro *m* de compte; *Acct* **a. payable** compte créditeur, dette *f* fournisseur; *Acct* **accounts payable** dettes fournisseurs; *Acct* **accounts payable book, accounts payable ledger** livre des créanciers; *Banking* **a. position** situation de compte; *Acct* **a. receivable** compte client, compte débiteur; *Acct* **accounts receivable** créances *fpl*, créances clients; **accounts receivable book, accounts receivable ledger** livre des débiteurs; **a. statement** relevé *m ou* état *ou* bordereau *m* de compte

▸ **account for** VT INSEP **1** *(one's behaviour, expense) (explain)* rendre compte de; *(justify)* justifier; *(circumstance)* expliquer; **that accounts for his interest in baseball** voilà qui

explique son intérêt pour le base-ball; **I can't a. for it** je ne me l'explique pas; **five people have still not been accounted for** *(after accident etc)* cinq personnes n'ont toujours pas été retrouvées; **there is no accounting for taste** chacun son goût **2** *(constitute)* constituer; **oil accounts for 10 per cent of exports** le pétrole constitue 10 pour cent des exportations; **all my time is already accounted for** mon temps est *ou* je suis déjà complètement pris **3** *(destroy) (plane)* abattre; *(submarine)* couler; *(troops)* tuer; *Fig* **he accounted for three batsmen** il a renversé le guichet de trois batteurs; **that accounts for him** *(striking sb off list etc)* son compte est réglé, à celui-là

accountability [əkaʊntə'bɪlɪtɪ] N responsabilité *f* (**to** envers); **local government a. is an important issue** la nécessité pour les municipalités de rendre compte de leurs actions est une question d'actualité

accountable [ə'kaʊntəb(ə)l] ADJ **to be a. to sb for sth** être responsable de qch envers qn; **to hold sb a.** tenir qn (pour) responsable (**for sth** de qch); **to be a. for a sum of money** être redevable d'une somme d'argent; **I am a. to no one** je n'ai de comptes à rendre à personne; **the police must be made more a. for their actions** la police doit rendre davantage compte de ses actions; **a. government/police force** gouvernement *m*/police *f* responsable

▸▸**a. marketing** marketing *m* responsable

accountancy [ə'kaʊntənsɪ] N *Acct* comptabilité *f*, expertise *f* comptable; *Fam* compta *f*

accountant [ə'kaʊntənt] N *Acct* comptable *mf*; **chief a.** chef *m* de (la) comptabilité; **chartered a.,** *Am* **certified public a.** ≃ expert-comptable *m, pl* experts-comptables

accounting [ə'kaʊntɪŋ] N *Acct* comptabilité *f, Fam* compta *f*

▸▸**a. clerk** commis *m* aux écritures; **a. control** contrôle *m* de la comptabilité; **a. day** journée *f* comptable; **a. entry** écriture *f* comptable; **a. entry form, a. entry sheet** bordereau *m* de saisie; **a. firm** cabinet *m* d'expertise comptable *ou* d'expert-comptable; **a. method** méthode *f* de comptabilité, procédé *m ou* mode *m* comptable; **a. period** exercice *m* (financier), période *f* comptable; **a. policy** politique *f* comptable; **a. procedure** pratique *f* comptable; **a. records** états *mpl* comptables; **a. system** système *m ou* plan *m* comptable; **a. year** exercice (financier), année *f* comptable

accounts [ə'kaʊnts] NPL comptabilité *f*, comptes *mpl*; *(department)* (service *m* de la) comptabilité; **to keep the a.** tenir les livres *ou* les écritures *ou* les comptes; **to enter sth in the a.** comptabiliser qch; **who does your a.?** qui est-ce qui fait votre comptabilité?

▸▸**a. clerk** employé, -ée aux écritures; **a. department** (service de la) comptabilité; **a. ledger** grand livre *m* des comptes; *Comput* **a. software** logiciel *m* de comptabilité

accoutrements [ə'ku:trəmənts], *Am* **accouterments** [ə'ku:təmənts] NPL *(equipment)* équipement *m*; **all the a. of her profession** tout l'attirail propre à sa profession

accredit [ə'kredɪt] VT **1** *(attribute)* attribuer (**to** à) **2** *(appoint, authorize) (ambassador, journalist)* accréditer (**to** auprès de)

accreditation [əkredɪ'teɪʃən] N accréditation *f*

accredited [ə'kredɪtɪd] ADJ *(person)* accrédité, autorisé; *(journalist)* accrédité

▸▸**a. college** école *f* reconnue (par l'État)

accretion [ə'kri:ʃən] N accroissement *m*; *(of skills)* accumulation *f*; **an a. of fungus** une accumulation de moisissures

accrual [ə'kru:əl] N *Fin* accumulation *f*, *Acct*

accruals *(accrued expenses)* charges *fpl* à payer; *(accrued income)* produits *mpl* à recevoir

▸▸*Acct* **a. accounting** comptabilité *f* d'engagements; **accruals concept** principe *m* d'indépendance des exercices *ou* de rattachement à l'exercice; **a. rate** taux *m* d'accumulation *ou* d'accroissement

accrue [ə'kru:] VI **1** *Fin (of interest)* s'accumuler; **interest accrues (as) from the 5th of the month** les intérêts courent à partir du 5 du mois **2** *(of moneys, land etc)* **to a. to sb** revenir à qn

VT *(interest)* produire

▸▸**accrued benefits** *(under pension scheme)* points *mpl* de retraite; **accrued charges** effets *mpl* à payer; **accrued dividends** dividendes *mpl* accrus; **accrued expenses** frais *mpl* cumulés *ou* accumulés; **accrued income** produit *m* à recevoir; **accrued interest** intérêts *mpl* courus

accruing interest [ə'kru:ɪŋ] N *Fin* intérêts *mpl* à échoir

accumulate [ə'kju:mjʊleɪt] VT *(fortune etc)* accumuler, amasser; *(objects)* amonceler, entasser; *(heat, electricity etc)* emmagasiner; *(dust)* ramasser

VI s'accumuler

accumulated [ə'kju:mjʊleɪtɪd] ADJ ATTRIB accumulé

▸▸*Fin* **a. depreciation** amortissement *m* cumulé

accumulation [əkju:mjʊ'leɪʃən] N **1** *(act)* accumulation *f*, *(of objects)* amoncellement *m*, entassement *m*; *(of heat, electricity etc)* emmagasinage *m* **2** *(result) (of objects, sand etc)* amas *m*, tas *m*; *(of facts, evidence)* accumulation *f*

accumulative [ə'kju:mjʊlətɪv] ADJ qui s'accumule; *Fin* cumulatif

accumulator [ə'kju:mjʊleɪtər] N **1** *Tech, Constr, Elec* accumulateur *m* **2** *Horseracing* pari *m* avec report **3** *(person)* **he's an a. of useless gadgets** il accumule les gadgets inutiles

▸▸*Horseracing* **a. bet** pari avec report

accuracy ['ækjʊrəsɪ] N *(of calculation, forecast)* exactitude *f*, *(of firearm, shot, meter)* précision *f*; *(of report, statement, scales)* justesse *f*; *(of translation, portrayal)* fidélité *f*

accurate ['ækjʊrət] ADJ *(calculation, forecast)* correct, exact; *(firearm, shot, meter)* précis; *(report, statement, scales)* juste; *(translation, portrayal)* fidèle; **my typing is much more a.** ma frappe est beaucoup plus précise; **to be (strictly) a. ...** pour être tout à fait exact ...

accurately ['ækjʊrətlɪ] ADV *(to calculate, forecast)* exactement; *(to measure, aim, report)* avec précision; *(to translate, portray)* fidèlement; *(to draw)* correctement; **very a. measured/predicted** calculé/prédit avec une grande précision; **he a. predicted that ...** il a justement prédit que ...

accurateness ['ækjʊrətnɪs] N exactitude *f*, précision *f*

accursed [ə'kɜːsɪd] ADJ *Lit* maudit

accusation [ækjʊ'zeɪʃən] N accusation *f*; **to bring an a. against sb** porter *ou* déposer plainte contre qn; **an a. of bribery was made against him** on l'a accusé de corruption; **to make an a.** lancer une accusation; **he made some wild accusations about my having bugged his telephone** il m'a absurdement accusé d'avoir mis son téléphone sur écoute

accusative [ə'kju:zətɪv] *Gram* N *(cas m)* accusatif *m*; **in the a.** à l'accusatif

ADJ *(case)* accusatif

accusatory [ə'kju:zətrɪ, ækjʊ'zeɪtərɪ] ADJ accusateur, -trice

accuse [ə'kju:z] VT accuser (**sb of sth** qn de

qch; **of doing sth** de faire qch); **you stand accused** vous êtes inculpé; *Iron* **no one could a. her of being punctual** on ne peut pas l'accuser d'être ponctuelle

accused [ə'kju:zd] N *Law* **the a.** l'inculpé, -ée; *(of offence)* le prévenu, la prévenue; *(of crime)* l'accusé, -ée

accuser [ə'kju:zər] N accusateur, -trice

accusing [ə'kju:zɪŋ] ADJ ATTRIB *(look, finger etc)* accusateur, -trice; **she pointed an a. finger at him** elle dirigea vers lui un doigt accusateur; *Fig* elle l'a mis en cause

accusingly [ə'kju:zɪŋlɪ] ADV *(to ask)* d'une manière accusatrice; *(to look, stare)* d'un air *ou* d'un œil accusateur

accustom [ə'kʌstəm] VT habituer, accoutumer (**sb to sth** qn à qch; **to do sth** à faire qch); **to a. oneself to** *(new job, country, climate etc)* s'habituer *ou* se faire *ou* s'accoutumer à; **to a. oneself to doing/being sth** s'habituer à faire/être qch

accustomed [ə'kʌstəmd] ADJ **1 I am a. to getting up early** j'ai l'habitude de me lever de bonne heure; **they weren't a. to strangers/politeness** ils n'étaient pas habitués aux étrangers/à la politesse; **to get** *or* **grow a. to sth/to doing sth** s'habituer à qch/à faire qch; **her eyes had got a. to the dark** ses yeux s'étaient accoutumés à l'obscurité **2** *(habitual)* habituel, coutumier

AC/DC ['eɪsi:'di:si:] N *Elec (abbr* **alternating current/direct current)** CA/CC *m*; *Fig Fam* **to be A.** *(bisexual)* marcher à voile et à vapeur

ace [eɪs] N **1** *Cards* as *m*; **a. of spades** as de pique; *Fam* **to have an a. up one's sleeve** avoir un atout en réserve **2** *Tennis* **(service) a. ace** *m* **3** *Fam (expert)* as *m*; **flying a.** as de l'aviation; *esp Am* **a. reporter** journaliste *mf* d'élite **4 within an a. of sth** à deux doigts de qch

ADJ *Sl (very good)* extra *inv*

VT *Am Sl* **to a. an exam** réussir un examen les doigts dans le nez

acerbic [ə'sɜ:bɪk] ADJ *(fruit, taste)* aigre; *Fig (person, comment)* acerbe, mordant

acerbity [ə'sɜ:bɪtɪ] N aigreur *f*, acerbité *f*

acetate ['æsɪteɪt] N *Chem, Typ* acétate *m*
▸▸**a. foil** feuille *f* d'acétate

acetic [æ'si:tɪk, -'set-] ADJ *Chem* acétique
▸▸**a. acid** acide *m* acétique

acetone ['æsɪtəʊn] N *Chem* acétone *f*

acetylene [æ'setɪli:n] N *Chem* acétylène *m*
▸▸**a. lamp** lampe *f* à acétylène; **a. torch** torche *f* à acétylène; **a. welding** soudure *f* autogène

acetylsalicylic acid [æsɪtaɪlsælɪ'sɪlɪk] N *Pharm* acide *m* acétylsalicylique

ACH [eɪsi:'eɪtʃ] N *Banking (abbr* **automated clearing house)** chambre *f* de compensation automatisée

ache [eɪk] N mal *m*, douleur *f*, *Spec* algie *f*; **stomach a.** mal de ventre; **to have (a) stomach a.** avoir mal au ventre; **she's always telling people about all her aches and pains** elle n'arrête pas de se plaindre de ses maux à tout le monde; **I've just got a few aches and pains, that's all** j'ai quelques douleurs, c'est tout; *Fig esp Lit* **I have an a. in my heart** j'ai de la peine

VI **my head aches** j'ai mal à la tête; **it makes my head a.** cela me donne mal à la tête; **I'm aching all over** j'ai mal partout; *Fig* **it makes my heart a.** cela me serre le cœur; **he was aching to join in the fight** il brûlait de prendre part au combat

achieve [ə'tʃi:v] VT **1** *(accomplish) (aim, goal)* atteindre, arriver à; **to a great deal** *(in life)* accomplir beaucoup de choses; *(in task)* réussir à faire beaucoup de choses; **to**

a. very little *(in life, task)* ne pas faire grand-chose; **to a. one's purpose** *or* **ends** parvenir *ou* en venir à ses fins; **to a. the impossible** réussir l'impossible; **to a. success** réussir; **we achieved what we set out to do** nous avons rempli nos objectifs; **I feel that we have achieved something** j'ai le sentiment que nous sommes arrivés à quelque chose; **he will never a. anything** il n'arrivera jamais à rien; **this policy achieved very little** cette politique n'a pas donné de grands résultats; **what will that a.?** *(of suggestion etc)* qu'est-ce que ça fera de plus?, pour en venir à quoi? **2** *(gain) (honour, notoriety)* acquérir; *(reputation)* se faire
▸▸**achieved room rate** prix *m* total des chambres

> Note that the French verb **achever** is a false friend and is never a translation for the English verb **to achieve**. Its most common meaning is **to complete**.

achievement [ə'tʃi:vmənt] N **1** *(feat)* exploit *m*, haut fait *m*; **their real a. lay in ...** leur véritable prouesse résida dans ...; **getting him to talk about anything is quite an a.** arriver à le faire parler de quoi que ce soit relève vraiment d'un exploit; **a lasting a.** une réalisation durable; **her many achievements** ses nombreux succès **2** *(successful completion)* accomplissement *m*, réalisation *f*

> Note that the French word **achèvement** is a false friend and is never a translation for the English word **achievement**. It means **completion**.

achievement-orient(at)ed [-'ɔ:rient(eɪt)ɪd] ADJ **to be a.** mettre l'accent sur la réussite; *Pej* être obsédé par la réussite

achiever [ə'tʃi:vər] N homme *m*/femme *f* performant(e), battant, -ante

Achilles [ə'kɪli:z] N Achille
▸▸*Myth* **A. heel** talon *m* d'Achille; *Fig* **gambling is his A. heel** le jeu est son point faible; **A. tendon** tendon *m* d'Achille

aching ['eɪkɪŋ] ADJ *(tooth, head etc)* qui vous/me/*etc* fait mal; *(leg, shoulder etc)* endolori; **to have an a. heart** avoir une peine de cœur; **her death left an a. void in his life** sa mort a laissé un vide douloureux dans sa vie

achromatic [ækrə'mætɪk] ADJ *Opt* achromatique

achromatous [ə'krəʊmətəs], **achromous** [ə'krəʊməs] ADJ *Phot* achrome

achy ['eɪkɪ] ADJ courbaturé; **I feel rather a.** j'ai mal un peu partout; **I have an a. feeling in my joints** mes jointures sont douloureuses

acid ['æsɪd] ADJ **1** acide **2** *(tone, reply)* acerbe
N **1** acide *m* **2** *Fam (LSD)* acide *m*
▸▸**a. bath** bain *m* acide; **a. drop** *(sweet)* bonbon *m* acidulé; *Ecol* **a. rain** pluies *fpl* acides; *Chem* **a. solution** solution *f* acide; **a. test** épreuve *f* à la pierre de touche; *Fig* épreuve décisive; *Acct* **a. test ratio** ratio *m* de liquidité immédiate

acidic [ə'sɪdɪk] ADJ *Chem* acide; *Fig (comment etc)* acerbe

acidification [ə'sɪdɪfɪ'keɪʃən] N acidification *f*

acidify [ə'sɪdɪfaɪ] VT acidifier

acidity [ə'sɪdɪtɪ] N **1** *Chem* acidité *f*, *Med* aigreurs *fpl*; **excessive a. in the stomach** une acidité gastrique excessive **2** *Fig (of reply)* aigreur *f*

acidly ['æsɪdlɪ] ADV aigrement

acidosis [æsɪ'dəʊsɪs] N *Med* acidose *f*

acidulous ['æsɪdjʊləs] ADJ acidulé

ack-ack ['æk'æk] N *Mil Old-fashioned (weapon)* artillerie *f* antiaérienne; *(system)* ≃ Défense *f* contre avions, DCA *f*
▸▸**a. fire** tir *m* de DCA

acknowledge [ək'nɒlɪdʒ] VT **1** *(recognize) (mistake, debt etc)* reconnaître; *(service)* reconnaître, se montrer reconnaissant de, exprimer sa reconnaissance de; *TV, Cin (in credits)* mentionner; **to a. sth as a fact** faire la constatation de qch; **acknowledged as the** *or* **to be the best Chinese restaurant in the city** reconnu comme le meilleur restaurant chinois de la ville; **to a. oneself beaten, to a. defeat** s'avouer *ou* se reconnaître vaincu; **she acknowledged my presence** elle m'a fait signe qu'elle m'avait vu; **he didn't even a. my presence** il m'a complètement ignoré; **she never acknowledges me** *(greets)* elle fait toujours comme si elle ne me voyait pas **2** *(reply to) (courtesy, greeting etc)* répondre à; **to a. (receipt of) a letter** accuser réception d'une lettre; *Naut* **to a. a signal** faire l'aperçu
▸▸*Comput* **a. character** *(in datacomms)* caractère *m* d'accusé de réception

acknowledged [ək'nɒlɪdʒd] ADJ ATTRIB *(fact)* reconnu, avéré; *(expert etc)* qui fait autorité; **an a. thief** un voleur reconnu

acknowledg(e)ment [ək'nɒlɪdʒmənt] N **1** *(of mistake, service etc)* reconnaissance *f*, *(of fact)* constatation *f*, *Comput (in datacomms)* accusé *m* de réception; **I waved/smiled at him, but received no a.** je lui ai fait signe/ai souri mais il ne m'a pas répondu; **in a. of** pour témoigner ma/sa/*etc* reconnaissance de; **acknowledgments** *(in book)* remerciements *mpl*, *(in credits)* mentions *fpl* (au générique), remerciements; **to quote an author without a.** citer un auteur sans mentionner son nom; **to give some a. to the fact that ...** reconnaître le fait que ...; **there's not enough a. of the debt he owes to Goldstein** il ne rend pas suffisamment hommage à Goldstein; **a. of debt** reconnaissance de dette **2** *(of payment)* reçu *m*, quittance *f*, **a. (of receipt)** *(of letter)* accusé *m* de réception; **a. of reservation** confirmation *f* de réservation

acme ['ækmɪ] N *Lit (of perfection, politeness)* comble *m*

acne ['æknɪ] N *Med* acné *f*

acolyte ['ækəlaɪt] N *Rel, Fig* acolyte *m*

Acorn® ['eɪkɔ:n] N *Mktg (abbr* **A Classification of Residential Neighbourhoods)** = classement *m* des différents types de quartiers résidentiels existant en Grande-Bretagne en 39 catégories, utilisé par les entreprises pour mieux cibler leurs clients potentiels lors de campagnes commerciales

acorn ['eɪkɔ:n] N gland *m* (de chêne)

acoustic [ə'ku:stɪk] ADJ acoustique
▸▸*Comput, Tel* **a. coupler** coupleur *m* acoustique; **a. engineer** acousticien, -ienne; **a. feedback** effet *m* Larsen, rétroaction *f* acoustique, bouclage *m* acoustique; *Mus* **a. guitar** guitare *f* sèche; **a. hood** capot *m* antibruit; *Anat* **a. nerve** nerf *m* acoustique *ou* auditif; **a. screen** écran *m* acoustique; **a. signal** signal *m* sonore; *Constr* **a. tile** carreau *m* acoustique

acoustically [ə'ku:stɪk(ə)lɪ] ADV acoustiquement

acoustics [ə'ku:stɪks] N acoustique *f*; **the a. in the hall are good, the hall has good a.** cette salle a une bonne acoustique VOIR GRAMMAIRE A10

ACPO ['ækpəʊ] N *(abbr* **Association of Chief Police Officers)** = syndicat *m* d'officiers supérieurs de la police britannique

acquaint [ə'kweɪnt] VT **1** *esp Fml* **to a. sb with sth** *(his duties, situation, fact)* mettre qn au courant de qch, informer qn de qch; **to a. sb with the controls** instruire qn sur le fonctionnement des commandes; **a stay in the jungle had acquainted him with these dangers** un séjour dans la jungle l'avait familiarisé avec ces dangers; **to a. oneself with the facts/the situation** se mettre au courant des faits/de la situation; **the doctor acquainted himself with her case history** le médecin s'est informé de ses antécédents médicaux

2 to be acquainted with sb connaître qn; **to be acquainted with sth** connaître qch, être au fait *ou* au courant de qch; **to become** *or* **get acquainted** (*of two people*) faire connaissance; **to become** *or* **get acquainted with sb** faire *ou* lier connaissance avec qn; **we soon became** *or* **got acquainted** nous avons vite fait connaissance; **I got acquainted with him later** j'ai fait sa connaissance plus tard; **to become acquainted with the facts** prendre connaissance des faits

acquaintance [əˈkweɪntəns] **N 1** (*person*) connaissance *f*; **he is an a. (of mine)** c'est quelqu'un que je connais; **a casual a. (of mine)** quelqu'un que je connais de loin; **to have a wide circle of acquaintances** avoir des relations très étendues **2 a. with** (*person, fact, language*) connaissance *f* de; **to make sb's a.** faire la connaissance de qn; **during our brief a.** pendant la courte période où nous avons été en contact; **his apparent lack of a. with the facts** son ignorance apparente des faits

acquiesce [ækwɪˈes] **VI** acquiescer, donner son assentiment (**in, to** à); **to a. in an arrangement** accepter un arrangement

acquiescence [ækwɪˈes(ə)ns] **N** assentiment *m*, consentement *m*, acquiescement *m* (**in, to** à)

acquiescent [ækwɪˈes(ə)nt] **ADJ** consentant

acquire [əˈkwaɪər] **VT** (*house, knowledge, experience etc*) acquérir; (*habit*) prendre, contracter; (*friend*) se faire; (*overtones*) prendre; **to a. a taste for sth** prendre goût à qch; **he acquired a stoop** son dos s'est voûté; **to a. an accent** prendre un accent; **we seem to have acquired some friends** (*are being followed etc*) on dirait que nous avons de la compagnie; **we seem to have acquired a cat** il semble qu'on ait hérité d'un chat

acquired [əˈkwaɪəd] **ADJ** acquis; **gin/Proust is an acquired taste** le gin c'est quelque chose/Proust est un auteur qu'on apprend à aimer
▸▸*Psy* **a. characteristic** caractère *m* acquis; *Med* **a. immune deficiency syndrome** syndrome *m* immunodéficitaire acquis

acquirement [əˈkwaɪəmənt] **N** acquisition *f* (**of** de)

acquisition [ækwɪˈzɪʃən] **N 1** (*act*) acquisition *f* (**of** de) **2** (*object, person*) acquisition *f*, **she could be a useful a.** elle pourrait se révéler être une acquisition utile
▸▸*Acct* **a. accounting** = base *f* de préparation des comptes consolidés où une société a pris le contrôle d'une autre; *Acct* **a. cost** coût *m* d'acquisition

acquisitive [əˈkwɪzɪtɪv] **ADJ** thésauriseur, -euse; **an a. nature** une nature avide

acquit [əˈkwɪt] **VT** (-tt-) **1** *Law* (*person accused of a crime*) acquitter; **to a. sb of sth** (*mistake*) absoudre qn de qch; (*of charge*) décharger qn de qch **2** *Fin* (*debt*) acquitter, s'acquitter de, régler **3 to a. oneself with distinction** s'en sortir très honorablement; **he acquitted himself well/badly** il s'en est bien/mal acquitté; **how did he a. himself?** comment s'en est-il sorti?

acquittal [əˈkwɪt(ə)l] **N 1** *Law* (*of defendant*) acquittement *m*, décharge *f*; (*of debt*) acquittement **2** (*of duty*) exécution *f*, accomplissement *m*

acquittance [əˈkwɪtəns] **N** *Fin* (*of debt*) acquittement *m*, décharge *f*, quittance *f*

acre [ˈeɪkər] **N** acre *f* (= 0,4 *hectare*), ≃ arpent *m*, demi-hectare *m*; **vast acres** des terres *fpl* étendues; **acres of forest** des hectares *mpl* de forêts; *Fig Fam* **acres of ...** des tas de ...; **acres of room** énormément de place

acreage [ˈeɪkərɪdʒ] **N** superficie *f* (*en mesures agraires*)

acrid [ˈækrɪd] **ADJ 1** (*taste, smoke*) âcre **2** *Fig* (*style*) mordant; (*criticism*) acerbe

acrimonious [ækrɪˈmoʊnɪəs] **ADJ** acrimonieux; (*person*) acariâtre; **the discussion was becoming a.** la discussion s'envenimait

acrimoniously [ækrɪˈmoʊnɪəslɪ] **ADV** avec acrimonie

acrimony [ˈækrɪmənɪ], **acrimoniousness** [ækrɪˈmoʊnɪsnɪs] **N** acrimonie *f*, (*of tone, character*) aigreur *f*, **the tone of a. in his voice** l'aigreur qu'il y avait dans sa voix

acrobat [ˈækrəbæt] **N** acrobate *mf*

acrobatic [ækrəˈbætɪk] **ADJ** acrobatique; **an a. feat** une acrobatie

acrobatics [ækrəˈbætɪks] **N** acrobatie *f* **VOIR GRAMMAIRE A10**

acronym [ˈækrənɪm] **N** sigle *m*

Acropolis [əˈkrɒpəlɪs] **N** Acropole *f*

ACROSS [əˈkrɒs] **ADV, PREP 1** (*from one side to the other*) en travers (de); **line drawn a. the page** ligne tirée en travers de la page; **with his arms folded a. his chest** les bras croisés sur la poitrine; **they talked to each other a. the table** ils se parlaient de part et d'autre de la table; **there was no bridge a. the river** aucun pont n'enjambait la rivière; **to find a way a. the mountain** trouver un chemin pour traverser la montagne; **a. country** à travers champs; **from a. the entire range** de toute la gamme

2 (*of motion*) **to walk a. (a street)** traverser (une rue); **we helped him a. the road** nous l'avons aidé à traverser la rue; **to swim a. a river** traverser une rivière à la nage; **to go a. a bridge** passer (sur) un pont, franchir un pont; **they got the barrel a. the river/road** ils ont fait passer le tonneau de l'autre côté de la rivière/rue; **is he a. the river/road yet?** est-ce qu'il a enfin traversé la rivière/la rue?; **she threw it a. the room/courtyard** elle l'a balancé en travers de *ou* de l'autre côté de la pièce/de la cour; **we cut a. the park** nous avons coupé à travers le parc; **to get** *or* **come a.** (*of play*) passer la rampe; **to get sth a. to sb** (*make understand*) faire comprendre qch à qn; **he doesn't come a. as an aggressive person** il ne donne pas l'impression de quelqu'un d'agressif

3 (*of distance*) **2 km a.** 2 km de large; **he is broad a. the shoulders** il est large d'épaules; **the distance a.** (*width*) la distance en largeur; (*of crossing*) la longueur de la traversée; **it's too far a.** c'est trop loin

4 (*on the other side*) **a. the street** de l'autre côté de la rue; **the woman from a. the street** la femme d'en face; **there's a supermarket just a. the road from us/our house** il y a un supermarché juste en face/en face de notre maison; **just a. the border** de l'autre côté *ou* au-delà de la frontière; **from a. the sea** par-delà la mer

5 (*in crossword*) horizontalement

across-the-board **ADJ** général, -aux; **an a. wage increase** une augmentation générale des salaires; **a. cuts** réduction linéaire générale
ADV de façon générale; **this applies a.** ceci s'applique à tous les niveaux

acrostic [əˈkrɒstɪk] **N** *Liter* acrostiche *m*

acrylic [əˈkrɪlɪk] **ADJ** (*fibre, paint etc*) acrylique; (*garment*) en acrylique

N 1 (*resin*) résine *f* acrylique **2** (*material*) acrylique *m*, fibre *f* acrylique **3** (*garment*) vêtement *m* en acrylique **4** (*paint*) peinture *f* acrylique

ACT [ækt]

N	acte **1, 2** ▪ numéro **3** ▪ loi **4**
VT	jouer
VI	agir **1, 2** ▪ jouer **3**

N 1 (*of justice, kindness etc*) acte *m*; (*deed*) action *f*, **an a. of folly** une folie; **an a. of despair** un acte désespéré; **the a. of a criminal/madman** l'action d'un criminel/fou; **to catch sb in the (very) a.** prendre qn sur le fait *ou* en flagrant délit; **she was caught in the a. of taking the money** on l'a surprise en train de voler l'argent

2 (*in play*) acte *m*; **A. I, scene 1** Acte I, scène 1; **a one-a. play** une pièce en un acte

3 (*in cabaret, circus etc*) numéro *m*; **circus a.** numéro de cirque; **to put on an a.** (*pretend*) jouer la comédie; **it's all an a.** (*pretence*) c'est du cinéma; *Fig* **to get in on the a.** se mettre dans le mouvement; *Fig* **to be/to let sb in on the a.** être/mettre qn dans le coup; *Fam* **to have got one's a. together** (*professionally*) bien connaître son affaire; (*personally*) être un homme/une femme accompli(e); *Fam* **get your a. together!** (*professionally*) vous ne pourriez pas vous secouer, un peu!; (*personally*) prends ta vie en main!; *Am Fam* **to queer the a.** tout faire foirer

4 *Law, Pol* loi *f*; **Companies A.** = loi sur les sociétés; **factory a.** législation *f* industrielle; **land a.** loi agraire

VT (*play, character*) jouer; (*role*) jouer, tenir; **to a. Hamlet** jouer Hamlet; *Fig* **to a. the fool** faire l'imbécile; **to a. a part** jouer un rôle; *Fig* jouer la comédie, feindre; **to a. the part of an honest man** se conduire *ou* agir en honnête homme

VI 1 (*take action*) agir; **it is time to a.** il est temps d'agir; **to a. out of fear/greed/selfishness** agir sous l'emprise de la peur/par cupidité/par égoïsme; **I acted for the best** j'ai fait pour le mieux; **to a. for sb** agir au nom de qn; (*of lawyer*) représenter qn; **I'm acting for her** j'agis en son nom; **the police refused to a.** la police a refusé d'intervenir; **to a. as secretary** exercer les fonctions de secrétaire; **the stick acted as a tent pole** le bâton servit de montant pour la tente; **the smell acts as a warning to other animals** les autres animaux sont avertis par l'odeur; **the engine acts as a brake** le moteur fait fonction de frein; **to a. as a warning** servir d'avertissement; **to a. as a motivation** constituer une motivation

2 (*behave*) se comporter, agir; **they a. as if nothing had happened** ils se comportent *ou* ils font comme si rien ne s'était passé; **he acts as if he were** *or* *Fam* **like he was the boss** il se comporte comme si c'était lui le patron; **stop acting like a child!, a. your age!** arrête de faire l'enfant!

3 *Theat, Cin* jouer; (*pretend*) jouer la comédie; **he can't a.** c'est un mauvais acteur; **I always wanted to a.** j'ai toujours voulu être acteur; **to a. in a film** tourner dans un film; **to a. stupid/all innocent** faire l'idiot/l'innocent
▸▸*Bible* **the Acts of the Apostles** les Actes des Apôtres; *Rel* **a. of faith** acte de foi; **a. of God** cas *m* de force majeure; **A. of Parliament** loi, décret *m*; **a. of war** acte de guerre
▸ **act on VT INSEP 1** (*affect*) influer sur, agir sur; (*of remedy etc*) agir sur; **acid acts on metal** l'acide agit sur le métal; *Med* **to a. on the brain/the bowels** exercer une action sur *ou* agir sur le cerveau/l'intestin; **the rumours acted on their fears** les rumeurs ont joué sur leurs craintes

2 (*respond to*) (*advice*) agir d'après, suivre;

(order) exécuter; *(letter)* donner suite à; **acting on my lawyer's advice** conformément aux conseils de mon avocat; **the police acted on the information** la police a agi après avoir reçu l'information
▸ **act out** VT SEP **to a. out a fantasy** vivre un fantasme; **local people a. out scenes from the town's history** les gens du coin jouent des scènes de l'histoire de leur ville; **she acts out our deepest fears** elle exprime nos peurs les plus profondes
▸ **act up** VI *Fam (of child)* se conduire mal; *(of machine)* marcher mal; **the car's acting up again** la voiture recommence à faire des siennes; **don't start acting up!** conduis-toi bien!; **my knee/back is acting up again** mon genou/dos recommence à me faire souffrir
▸ **act upon** VT INSEP = **act on**

acting ['æktɪŋ] ADJ ATTRIB *(temporary)* suppléant, intérimaire
 N *Theat, Cin (of actor)* jeu *m*, interprétation *f*, *(profession)* métier *m* d'acteur; **she's done some a.** elle a fait du théâtre/du cinéma; **the a. is marvellous** le jeu des acteurs est merveilleux

ACTION ['ækʃən]

action 1–3, 5, 7	▪ acte 1 ▪ mécanisme
4 ▪ procès 5	▪ combat 6

N 1 *(of person, remedy etc)* action *f*, *(single act)* action, acte *m*, fait *m*; *Br* **(industrial) a.** mouvement *m* de revendication; *(strike)* grève *f*; **the a. of water** *(on river bank etc)* le travail des eaux, l'action de l'eau; **we want a. not words** nous voulons des actes non des paroles; **to take a.** agir; *(intervene)* intervenir; *Br (go on strike)* se mettre en grève; **their quick a. prevented more deaths** leur action rapide a évité d'autres morts; **course** *or* **line of a.** ligne *f* de conduite; **a man of a.** un homme d'action; **sphere of a.** sphère *f* d'activité; *Br* **day of a.** journée *f* d'action; **to put a plan into a.** mettre un projet à exécution; **to come into a.** entrer en action *ou* en jeu; **in a.** *(of machine)* en marche; *(of sportsman)* à l'œuvre; *Fam* **she destroys interviewers, you should see her in a.** elle anéantit les interviewers, tu l'as vue à l'œuvre!; **out of a.** *(machine, vehicle etc)* hors de service, hors d'usage; *(person)* hors de combat; **to put a machine out of a.** détraquer une machine; **the flu put** *or* **kept him out of a. for a month** la grippe l'a mis hors de combat pendant un mois; **impulsive a.** action irréfléchie, coup *m* de tête; **she's not responsible for her actions** elle n'est pas responsable de ses actes; *Prov* **actions speak louder than words** les actes en disent plus long que les paroles
 2 *Theat, Cin, TV, Liter (of play, novel etc)* action *f*; **the a. takes place in …** l'action se passe à …; *Cin* **a.!** on tourne!, action!
 3 *(movement) (of player)* action *f*, *(of horse)* allure *f*, **a song with actions** une chanson mimée
 4 *Tech (of watch, clock)* mécanisme *m*; *(of pump, lock)* jeu *m*
 5 *Law* action *f*, **a. at law, legal a.** action en justice; *(trial etc)* procès *m*; **a. for libel** procès *ou* plainte *f* en diffamation; **a. for damages** action en dommages et intérêts; **to bring an a. against sb** intenter une action *ou* un procès à *ou* contre qn
 6 *Mil etc* combat *m*, engagement *m*; **naval a.** engagement naval, opération *f* navale; **to go into a.** entrer en action, engager le combat; **ready for a.** prêt à combattre; **to send troops into a.** faire intervenir *ou* faire donner des troupes; **to see a.** *(of soldier)* combattre; **to put a gun/plane/***etc* **out of a.** *(destroy)* mettre un canon/avion/*etc* hors de combat; *(disable)* mettre un canon/un

avion/*etc* hors de service *ou Fam* de cause; **killed in a.** tué à l'ennemi; **as a result of enemy a.** à la suite de l'action ennemie; **a. stations!** tout le monde à son poste!; *Fig* vingt-deux!
 7 *Fam (excitement)* action *f*, **there's plenty of a. in the movie** il y a plein d'action dans ce film; **they were looking for some a.** *(nightlife etc)* ils cherchaient un peu d'animation; **where's the a. around here?** où est-ce que ça bouge par ici?
 8 *Sl* **they want a piece** *or* **slice of the a.** *(profits)* ils veulent une part du gâteau
▸▸ *Cin* **a. film, a. movie** film *m* d'action; *Art* **a. painting** peinture *f* gestuelle; **a. plan** plan *m* d'action; **a. programme** plan d'action, plan de manœuvre; **a. replay** reprise *f*, *(in slow motion)* ralenti *m*

actionable ['ækʃənəb(ə)l] ADJ *Law (remarks, action)* qui expose à des poursuites

action-packed ADJ *(film, novel, match)* plein d'action; *(day, morning etc)* bien rempli

activate ['æktɪveɪt] VT 1 *(put into operation) (mechanism, alarm)* déclencher 2 *Chem* activer 3 *Phys* rendre radioactif
▸▸ *Chem* **activated carbon** charbon *m* actif *ou* activé

activation [æktɪ'veɪʃən] N activation *f*, *(of alarm)* déclenchement *m*

active ['æktɪv] ADJ 1 *(person)* actif; *(mind)* éveillé; *(imagination)* vif; **to be still a.** *(of elderly person)* être encore alerte *ou* actif; **to be/become a.** *(of volcano)* être/entrer en activité; **she's very a. in the party** elle est très active au sein du parti; **he was very a. in seeing that the measure was passed** il a contribué très activement à l'approbation de cette mesure; **to take an a. part in sth** prendre une part active *ou* effective à qch; **to take an a. dislike to sb** se prendre d'une vive aversion contre qn; *Mil* **on a. service** en service actif; **to see a. service** *(fight)* combattre; *Mil* **to be on the a. list** être en activité
 2 *Gram (voice)* actif
 N *Gram* actif *m*, voix *f* active; **verb in the a.** verbe *m* à l'actif *ou* à la voix active VOIR GRAMMAIRE A40
▸▸ *Comput* **a. desktop** bureau *m* actif; *Comput* **a. file** fichier *m* actif; *Comput* **a. matrix** matrice *f* active; *Comput* **a. matrix screen** écran *m* à matrice active; *Banking, Fin* **a. money** monnaie *f* circulante; *Fin, Com* **a. partner** *(in company)* associé, -ée gérant(e), commandité, -ée; *Comput* **a. program** programme *m* en cours d'exécution; *Comput* **a. window** fenêtre *f* active *ou* activée

actively ['æktɪvlɪ] ADV activement; **they were a. seeking peace** ils cherchaient activement à faire la paix; **to a. dislike sb** avoir une vive aversion pour qn

activist ['æktɪvɪst] N *Pol* activiste *mf*, **anti-nuclear/peace activists** activistes antinucléaires/en faveur de la paix

activity [æk'tɪvɪtɪ] N activité *f*, **economic a.** activité économique; **this week has seen a lot of a. on the Stock Market** la Bourse a été très active cette semaine; **his numerous activities leave him little leisure** ses nombreuses occupations lui laissent peu de loisirs; **activities** *(at holiday camp)* animation *f*
▸▸ *Acct* **a. accounting** comptabilité *f* par centres de responsabilité; **a. book** livre-jeu *m*, *pl* livres-jeux; **a. break** (courtes) vacances *fpl* actives; **a. centre** centre *m* aéré; **a. chart** graphique *m* des activités; *Br* **a. holiday** vacances actives; **a. indicator** indicateur *m* d'activité; **a. rate** taux *m* d'activité; *Acct* **a. ratio** ratio *m* *ou* coefficient *m* d'activité, ratio de gestion

actor ['æktər] N *Theat* acteur *m*, comédien *m*; *Cin, Fig* acteur; **to be an a.** *Theat* faire du théâtre, être acteur *ou* comédien; *Cin* faire du cinéma, être acteur

actress ['æktrɪs] N *Theat* actrice *f*, comédienne *f*; *Cin* actrice; *Br Fam Hum* **he's got a huge one… as the a. said to the bishop** il en a une énorme, si j'ose dire

actual ['æktʃʊəl] ADJ *(concrete)* réel, véritable; *(case)* concret, -ète; **to give the a. figures** donner les chiffres mêmes; *Fam* **in a. fact** en fait; **her a. words were …** ce qu'elle a dit en fait, c'est …; **this is the a. house where she was born** voici en fait la maison où elle est née; *Br Fam* **the a. managing director visited us today** le directeur général nous a rendu visite en personne aujourd'hui; **the actual ceremony doesn't start until 10.30** la cérémonie même ne commence pas avant 10 h 30
▸▸ *Acct, Fin* **a. cost** prix *m* de revient *ou* d'achat; *Acct, Fin* **a. costs** coûts *mpl* constatés; **a. demand level** niveau *m* de demande réelle; **a. dollars** dollars *mpl* courants; **a. operating costs** coûts réels d'exploitation; **a. size** grandeur *f* réelle, vraie grandeur; *Cin, Radio, TV* **a. sound** son *m* direct; **a. value** valeur *f* réelle

> Note that the French adjective **actuel** is a false friend and is never a translation for the English adjective **actual**. It means **current**.

actuality [æktʃʊ'ælɪtɪ] N *Fml* 1 *(reality)* réalité *f* 2 **a play that lacks a.** une pièce qui n'a aucun rapport avec la vie d'aujourd'hui

actually ['æktʃʊəlɪ] ADV 1 *(really)* réellement, en fait, en réalité; **what a. happened?** que s'est-il passé au juste?; **what he a. means is …** ce qu'il veut vraiment dire, c'est …; **I didn't a. see it myself** en réalité, je ne l'ai pas vu de mes propres yeux; **the piano's just for decoration, no one a. plays it** le piano fait partie du décor, en fait personne n'en joue; **we haven't a. decided yet** on n'a pas encore vraiment décidé; **yes, but what will the government a. do?** oui, mais que va vraiment faire le gouvernement?
 2 *(even, surprisingly)* **he a. swore** il est (même) allé jusqu'à lâcher un juron; **she a. said good morning to me** à mon grand étonnement elle m'a dit bonjour; **he was a. on time for once** pour une fois il était à l'heure
 3 *(in fact)* en fait; **a., yes, I do mind, very much!** à vrai dire, oui, ça m'ennuie beaucoup!; **I'm not sure, a.** je n'en suis pas certain, en fait; **what do you do? – I'm a lawyer, a.** que faites-vous? – je suis avocat; **a., I rather like it** à vrai dire, ça me plaît assez; **he's not a very nice person, a.** il n'est pas très gentil à vrai dire

> Note that the French adverb **actuellement** is a false friend and is never a translation for the English adverb **actually**. It means **at present**.

actuals ['æktʃʊəlz] NPL 1 *Acct, Fin (real figures)* chiffres *mpl* réels; **to compare budgeted amounts with a.** comparer les prévisions budgétaires et les résultats obtenus 2 *St Exch* livraisons *fpl* physiques, marchandises *fpl* livrées au comptant

actuarial [æktʃʊ'eərɪəl] ADJ actuariel
▸▸ **a. tables** tables *fpl* de mortalité

actuary ['æktʃʊərɪ] N actuaire *mf*

actuate ['æktʃʊeɪt] VT 1 *(machine etc)* mettre en action, faire marcher 2 *(person)* faire agir; **actuated by jealousy** poussé par la jalousie

actuation [æktʃʊ'eɪʃən] N *(of machine etc)* mise *f* en action

actuator ['æktʃʊeɪtər] N actionneur *m*

acuity [ə'kjuːɪtɪ] N *Fml (of mind, comment)* acuité *f*, **visual a.** acuité visuelle

acumen ['ækjʊmən] N pénétration *f*, finesse *f* (d'esprit), perspicacité *f*; **he's got plenty of business a.** il a un très bon sens des affaires

acupressure ['ækjʊpreʃər] N *Med* acupressing *m*

acupuncture ['ækjʊpʌŋktʃər] N *Med* acupuncture *f*, acuponcture *f*

acupuncturist ['ækjʊpʌŋktʃərɪst] N *Med* acupuncteur, -trice, acuponcteur, -trice

acute [ə'kjuːt] ADJ **1** *(pain)* aigu, *f* aiguë, intense, vif; *(disease, crisis, shortage)* aigu; **to become more a.** *(of anxiety etc)* s'aviver; **a. appendicitis** appendicite *f* aiguë; **a. remorse** remords *mpl* cruels; **to suffer a. embarrassment** être vivement embarrassé; **the problem was made more a.** le problème a été intensifié **2** *(mind)* fin, perspicace; *(hearing, sense of smell)* fin; *(vision)* perçant; **an a. observer** un observateur pénétrant; **she has an a. awareness of their problems** elle a une perception pénétrante de leurs problèmes **3** *Math (angle)* aigu, *f* aiguë **4** *Ling (accent)* aigu, *f* aiguë ▸ N *Ling* accent *m* aigu ▸▸ *Med* **a. care** soins *mpl* médicaux de courte durée

acute-angled ADJ à angle(s) aigu(s)

acutely [ə'kjuːtlɪ] ADV **1** *(to feel)* vivement; **he felt the loss a.** il ressentit cette perte intensément; **we are a. aware** *or* **conscious of that** nous en sommes extrêmement conscients **2** *(with perspicacity)* finement, avec perspicacité

acuteness [ə'kjuːtnɪs] N **1** *(of pain)* acuité *f*, intensité *f*; *(of remorse, emotion, attack of illness)* intensité *f*; *(of mind)* pénétration *f*, perspicacité *f*; *(of hearing, judgement)* finesse *f*; *(of vision, sense of smell)* acuité *f*

AD¹ [eɪ'diː] ADV *(abbr* **anno Domini***)* après Jésus-Christ; *(written form)* apr. J.-C.; **in 1066 AD** en 1066 apr. J.-C.

AD² N *Cin (abbr* **artistic director***)* directeur, -trice artistique

ad [æd] N *Fam* annonce *f*, *TV*, *Radio* pub *f*, **small ads** petites annonces; **while the ads are on** pendant la pub ▸▸ **ad agency** agence *f* publicitaire; **ad break** page *f* de publicité

adage ['ædɪdʒ] N adage *m*

adagio [ə'dɑːʒɪəʊ, ə'dɑːdʒ-] ADV, N *Mus* adagio *m*

Adam ['ædəm] N Adam *m*; *Hum* **I don't know him from A.** je ne le connais ni d'Ève ni d'Adam ▸▸ *Hum* **A.'s ale** flotte *f*, château-la-pompe *m*; **A.'s apple** pomme *f* d'Adam

adam ['ædəm] N *Sl (ecstasy)* ecstasy *f*, exta *f*

adamant ['ædəmənt] ADJ inflexible, intransigeant; **he is a. on this point** sur ce point il ne transige pas; **she is a. that she saw him** elle affirme l'avoir vu et ne veut pas en démordre; **they are a. in their conviction** ils ne veulent pas en démordre

adamantly ['ædəməntlɪ] ADV inflexiblement, d'une manière intransigeante; **they a. refused** ils refusèrent catégoriquement

adapt [ə'dæpt] VT *(machine, vehicle etc)* adapter; **to a. a novel for the stage** adapter un roman à la scène; **the play was adapted for television** la pièce a été adaptée pour la télévision; **text adapted from Cicero** texte d'après Cicéron; **to a. oneself to circumstances/new surroundings** s'adapter aux circonstances/à un nouvel environnement ▸ VI *(of person, species)* s'adapter (**to** à); **failure to a.** incapacité *f* à s'adapter

adaptability [ədæptə'bɪlɪtɪ] N faculté *f* d'adaptation; **a. to the environment** adaptabilité *f* au milieu

adaptable [ə'dæptəb(ə)l] ADJ **1** *(adjustable)* adaptable, ajustable (**to** à) **2** *(person)* souple, qui s'adapte facilement; *(species)* qui s'adapte facilement

adaptation [ædæp'teɪʃən] N **1** adaptation *f* (**of sth to sth** de qch à qch); **a. for the stage** adaptation à la scène **2** *(novel, play)* adaptation *f* **3** *Biol* adaptation *f*, finalité *f*

adapted [ə'dæptɪd] ADJ *(novel etc)* adapté (**for the stage** à la scène); **a telephone a. for use by people with hearing difficulties** un téléphone adapté à l'usage des malentendants; **a. to sth** approprié à qch, fait pour qch

adapter [ə'dæptər] N **1** *Elec (plug)* adaptateur *m*; *(with several sockets)* prise *f* multiple **2** *Tech (connecting pipes)* raccord *m* **3** *Phot (for camera)* parquet *m* d'adaptation; **lens a.** bague *f* porte-objectif **4** *(for record)* centreur *m* **5** *(writer)* adaptateur, -trice ▸▸ *Comput* **a. card** carte-adaptateur *f*, *pl* cartes-adaptateurs

adaptive [ə'dæptɪv] ADJ *Biol (mechanism)* adaptif ▸▸ *Aut* **a. engine controls** commandes *fpl* adaptatives moteur

adaptor [ə'dæptər] N = **adapter**

ADC [eɪdiː'siː] N **1** *Mil abbr* aide-de-camp **2** *(abbr* **analogue-digital converter***)* CAN *m*

add [æd] VT **1** ajouter (**to** à); **this book adds little to the debate** ce livre n'apporte pas grand-chose au débat; **have you anything you would like to a.?** aimeriez-vous ajouter quelque chose?; **it'll a. another hour to the journey** ça allongera le trajet d'une heure **2** *Math* additionner; **to a. six to eight** additionner six et huit, ajouter six à huit; **a. these numbers (together)** additionnez ces nombres, faites l'addition de ces nombres; *Math* **to a. a zero** apposer un zéro ▸ VI *(perform addition)* faire des additions

▸ **add in** VT SEP *(salt etc)* ajouter

▸ **add on** VT SEP *(conservatory etc)* ajouter; **should we a. on something as a tip?** est-ce qu'il faut laisser un pourboire?

▸ **add to** VT INSEP *(increase) (building)* faire une addition à, agrandir; *(difficulty, surprise etc)* augmenter, ajouter à; *(beauty of sth)* rehausser; *(crisis)* accentuer; **the news added to their despondency** cette nouvelle ajouta à leur abattement; **this will a. to the cost** ceci va venir s'ajouter au prix; **to a. to my misfortune** pour mettre le comble à mon malheur; **to a. to what we were saying yesterday …** pour compléter ce que nous disions hier …

▸ **add up** VI **1** *(calculate)* additionner; **that boy can't a. up** ce garçon ne sait pas additionner **2** *(give correct total)* faire le compte; **the accounts don't a. up** ces comptes ne tombent pas juste **3** *(make sense)* **the facts don't a. up** les faits ne riment à rien; **it just doesn't a. up!** ça ne rime à rien!; **it's beginning to a. up** ça devient plus clair ▸ VT SEP *(figures etc)* additionner; **when you a. it all up, it was quite cheap** si on fait le total, c'était assez bon marché; **you've added this up wrong** tu t'es trompé dans l'addition

▸ **add up to** VT INSEP **1** *(of figures)* s'élever à, se chiffrer à; **it adds up to £22** cela s'élève à 22 livres **2** *(amount to)* **is that all you've done? it doesn't a. up to much** est-ce que c'est tout ce que tu as fait? ça ne fait pas beaucoup; **it all adds up to an enjoyable day out** cela nous/vous/*etc* fait une agréable journée de sortie

add-back N *Acct* réintégration *f*

added ['ædɪd] ADJ ATTRIB supplémentaire; **a. enjoyment was provided by a jazz band** un orchestre de jazz a aussi contribué à notre/leur/*etc* plaisir; **no a. sugar** sans ajout de sucre; **a. ingredients** *(on food package)* autres ingrédients; **no a. preservatives** sans conservateurs ▸▸ *Com*, *Mktg*, *Acct* **a. value** valeur *f* ajoutée

addendum, *pl* **addenda** [ə'dendəm, -ə] N *(to book etc)* addenda *m inv*, addition *f*

adder ['ædər] N *(snake)* vipère *f*

addict¹ ['ædɪkt] N **1** *Med* intoxiqué, -ée; **(drug) a.** toxicomane *mf*; **heroin a.** héroïnomane *mf* **2** *Fig* fana *mf*; **I'm a coffee a.** je suis accro au café; **I never miss an episode, I'm a complete a.** je ne rate jamais un épisode, je suis complètement accro

addict² [ə'dɪkt] VT *(used in passive)* **to be/become addicted to** *(alcohol, opium etc)* s'adonner à, *Fam* être/devenir accro à; *(a TV programme, aerobics)* ne pas pouvoir se passer de, *Fam* être/devenir accro à; **to become** *or* **get addicted to drugs/heroin** devenir toxicomane/héroïnomane; **you can easily get addicted to coffee** c'est facile de devenir accro au café

addiction [ə'dɪkʃən] N *(to drugs)* dépendance *f*, *(to chocolate, the cinema etc)* goût *m* immodéré (**to** pour); **a. to drugs** la dépendance envers la drogue, la toxicomanie; **my earlier a. to Italian cinema** ma passion dévorante d'autrefois pour le cinéma italien; **coffee at 4 o'clock had become something of an a. with her** elle ne pouvait plus se passer du café de quatre heures

addictive [ə'dɪktɪv] ADJ *Med (drug)* qui cause un phénomène de dépendance, *Spec* toxicomanogène; *Fig* **soap operas are very a.** on a du mal à se passer des feuilletons, on devient vite accro aux feuilletons; **it could become a.** on prend vite l'habitude

adding ['ædɪŋ] N addition *f* ▸▸ **a. machine** calculatrice *f*, machine *f* à calculer; **a. up** addition

Addis Ababa ['ædɪs'æbəbə] N Addis-Abeba

addition [ə'dɪʃən] N **1** *(adding)*, *Math* addition *f*; **the a. of three more musicians** l'adjonction *f* de trois musiciens supplémentaires; **in a.** en outre, de plus; **in a. to sth** en plus de qch; **in a. to that sum** en plus de cette somme; **in a. to these misfortunes** par surcroît de malheur; **to pay something in a.** payer un supplément VOIR GRAMMAIRE A77; B59 **2** *(something added)* addition *f*, *(to building)* extension *f*, rajout *m*; **additions to the staff** adjonction *f* de personnel; **he has just had an a. to his family** sa famille a grandi; **where is the latest a.?** *(baby)* où est le petit dernier/la petite dernière?; **an important a. to our collection** une nouvelle pièce de choix à notre collection; **she will be a valuable a. to the staff** sa contribution sera fort appréciable; **the east wing is an eighteenth-century a.** l'aile est a été ajoutée au dix-huitième siècle

additional [ə'dɪʃən(ə)l] ADJ supplémentaire; **70p for each a. 50 grams** *(in list of postal rates)* 70 pence par 50 grammes supplémentaires; **a. information can be found on page 28** se référer à la page 28 pour des informations complémentaires; **this will require a. investment** cela nécessitera un investissement supplémentaire ▸▸ **a. charge** supplément *m* de prix; **for** *or* **at no a. charge** sans supplément; **a. expenditure** surcroît *m* de dépenses; **a. expenses** dépenses *fpl* supplémentaires; *Fin* **a. payment** supplément *m*; **a. postage** surtaxe *f* postale; **a. premium** surprime *f*; **a. security** contre-caution *f*, *pl* contre-cautions; *Admin* **a. tax** impôt *m* additionnel; *(because of underpayment)* supplément d'imposition *(payé volontairement)*; *Fin* **a. voluntary contribution** supplément de cotisation retraite *(payé volontairement)*

additionally [ə'dɪʃ(ə)nəlɪ] ADV en plus, en outre

additive ['ædɪtɪv] N additif *m*

addled ['æd(ə)ld] ADJ **1** *Old-fashioned (egg)* pourri, gâté **2** *an a. mind* un esprit confus

add-on N *Comput* produit *m* supplémentaire *ou* complémentaire, extension *f*
ADJ ATTRIB additionnel
► ► *Comput* **a. board** carte *f* d'extension; **a. fare** supplément *m*

address [ə'dres, *Am* 'ædres] N **1** *(of person, letter)* adresse *f*; **what is your a.?** quelle est ton adresse?; *(of no (known)* a. sans domicile connu; **home** *or* **private/business a.** adresse privée *ou* personnelle/de bureau; **a Glasgow a.** une adresse à Glasgow; **not known at this a.** *(on returned letter)* inconnu à cette adresse; **she no longer lives at that a.** elle n'habite plus à cette adresse VOIR GRAMMAIRE A77
2 *(speech)* discours *m*, allocution *f*
3 *(title)* form of a. titre *m*; **what's the correct form of a. for a bishop?** comment doit-on s'adresser à un évêque?
4 *Comput* adresse *f*
5 *Fml, Arch (skill)* habileté *f*, doigté *m*; **she showed considerable a. in her handling of the situation** elle fit preuve d'une grande habileté dans la façon dont elle traita l'affaire
6 *Arch* **to pay one's addresses to a lady** faire la cour à une femme
VT **1** *(letter, postcard, parcel)* adresser (**to sb** à qn); **it's addressed to you** ça t'est adressé; **stamped addressed envelope** enveloppe *f* timbrée avec son adresse; **it's incorrectly addressed** l'adresse est incorrecte
2 *(direct) (reproaches, criticism etc)* adresser (**to sb** à qn)
3 *(speak to) (person, crowd etc)* s'adresser à; **to a. sb** *(start to speak to)* adresser la parole à qn; **he addressed her as 'Your Majesty'** il l'a appelée 'Votre Majesté'; **to a. a meeting** prendre la parole à une réunion
4 *(tackle) (question, problem etc)* aborder; *Fml* **to a. oneself to a task** entreprendre une tâche
5 *Comput* adresser, accéder à
6 *Golf (ball)* viser
► ► **a. book** carnet *m* d'adresses; *Comput* **a. bus** bus *m* d'adresse; *Comput* **a. file** fichier *m* d'adresses; **a. label** étiquette *f* d'adresse; **a. line** ligne *f* d'adressage; **a. list** fichier d'adresses; **a. space** cadre-adresse *m*, *pl* cadres-adresse

addressable [ə'dresəb(ə)l] N *Comput* adressable
► ► *Mktg* **a. audience** audience *f* utile; *Mktg* **a. market** marché *m* utile

addressee [ædre'siː] N destinataire *mf*

addressing [ə'dresɪŋ] N adressage *m*
► ► **a. machine** machine *f* à adresser

adduce [ə'djuːs] VT *Fml (reasons, evidence etc)* alléguer, apporter; *(authority)* invoquer, citer

adduct [ə'dʌkt] VT *Physiol (muscle etc)* déterminer l'adduction de

adduction [ə'dʌkʃən] N *Physiol* adduction *f*

adductor [ə'dʌktər] N, ADJ *Med (muscle)* adducteur *m*

adenoidal [ædɪ'nɔɪd(ə)l] ADJ adénoïde; *(voice)* nasillard

adenoids ['ædɪnɔɪdz] NPL *Med* végétations *fpl* (adénoïdes)

adept ADJ [ə'dept] expert, habile (**in sth** à qch; **at doing sth** à faire qch)
N ['ædept] expert, -erte (**in** en)

adequacy ['ædɪkwəsɪ] N *(of arrangements, skills etc)* caractère *m* adéquat; *(of person)* compétence *f*, capacité *f*; *(of theory)* adéquation *f*; **they had doubts as to the a. of the pay/ration** ils doutaient que la paye/ration soit suffisante; **they doubted her a. as a mother** ils doutaient de ses capacités de mère

adequate ['ædɪkwət] ADJ *(in quantity)* suffisant; *(appropriate, good enough)* adéquat; **the money we were given was more than a.** l'argent que l'on nous avait donné était plus que suffisant; **a room of a. size** une pièce d'une grandeur raisonnable; **a. to the task** *(of tool)* approprié à la tâche; **an a. supply** *(of meat etc)* une quantité suffisante; **a. training for the job** *(enough)* une formation suffisante pour le poste; *(right quality)* une formation adéquate pour le poste; **a. remuneration for the work carried out** rémunération proportionnée *ou* correspondant au travail accompli; **to be given a. warning** être suffisamment averti; **a. time to do sth** suffisamment de temps pour faire qch

adequately ['ædɪkwətlɪ] ADV *(in quantity)* suffisamment; *(suitably)* convenablement

ADF [eɪdiː'ef] N *Comput (abbr* **automatic document feeder**) dispositif *m* d'alimentation automatique

ADHD [eɪdiːeɪtʃ'diː] N *Med (abbr* **attention deficit hyperactivity disorder**) thada *m*

adhere [əd'hɪər] VI adhérer
► **adhere to** VT INSEP **1** *(stick to)* adhérer à **2** *(rule etc)* observer; *(one's decision)* persister dans, s'en tenir à, maintenir; *(plan)* s'en tenir à, se conformer à; **to a. to a party** adhérer *ou* donner son adhésion à un parti; **I don't a. to that philosophy at all** je n'adhère pas du tout à cette philosophie

adherence [əd'hɪərəns] N **1** *(of label etc)* adhérence *f* (**to** à) **2** *(to party, position)* adhésion *f* (**to** à); *(to rule etc)* observation *f* (**to** de)

adherent [əd'hɪərənt] N *(of party, belief etc)* adhérent, -ente; *(of doctrine)* partisan, -ane

adhesion [əd'hiːʒən] N **1** *(of label, road wheels etc)* adhérence *f* **2** *(of person)* adhésion *f* (**to** à)

adhesive [əd'hiːsɪv] ADJ *(tape etc)* adhésif; *(label)* gommé
N colle *f*, adhésif *m*
► ► *Med* **a. plaster**, *Am* **a. tape** sparadrap *m*

adhesiveness [əd'hiːsɪvnɪs] N adhérence *f*

ad hoc ['æd'hɒk] ADV, ADJ ad hoc; *(committee)* ad hoc, spécial, -aux; **we prefer to decide things on an a. basis** nous préférons prendre des décisions à mesure que les circonstances l'exigent; **it's all a bit a.** tout est un peu improvisé

ad hominem [æd'hɒmɪnem] ADV, ADJ ad hominem

adieu, *pl* **adieus** *or* **adieux** [ə'djuː, -z] *Arch Lit* INT adieu!
N **to bid sb a.** dire adieu à qn, faire ses adieux à qn

ad infinitum ['ædɪnfɪ'naɪtəm] ADV à l'infini; *Fam* **he went on talking a.** il parlait à n'en plus finir; **and so on a.** et ainsi de suite ad infinitum

adipose ['ædɪpəʊs] ADJ *Biol (tissue)* adipeux

adjacent [ə'dʒeɪsənt] ADJ *(angle, plot of land)* adjacent, contigu, *f* -uë, attenant (**to** à); *(country)* limitrophe (**to** de); **a. rooms** pièces *fpl* contiguës; **the two rooms are a.** les deux pièces sont contiguës; **in an a. street** dans une rue adjacente

adjectival [ædʒɪk'taɪv(ə)l] ADJ *Gram* adjectif, adjectival, -aux
► ► **a. clause** proposition *f* adjectivale

adjectivally [ædʒɪk'taɪv(ə)lɪ] ADV *Gram* adjectivement; **present participle used a.** participe présent adjectival

adjective ['ædʒɪktɪv] ADJ, N *Gram* adjectif *m*
VOIR GRAMMAIRE A17–19; B8–12

adjoin [ə'dʒɔɪn] VT *(place)* être contigu à, toucher à, attenir à; **our garden adjoins theirs** notre jardin est contigu au leur; **Kansas adjoins Colorado** le Kansas est un état limitrophe du Colorado

VI **the two houses a.** les deux maisons sont contiguës

adjoining [ə'dʒɔɪnɪŋ] ADJ contigu, *f* -uë; *(state, country)* limitrophe; **the a. room** la pièce voisine *ou* à côté; **a. rooms** pièces *fpl* attenantes; *(bedrooms)* chambres *fpl* attenantes

adjourn [ə'dʒɜːn] VT ajourner, remettre, reporter (**for a week** à huitaine); **the trial was adjourned until the next day** le procès fut ajourné au lendemain; **the judge adjourned the hearing** le juge a suspendu l'audience
VI **1** *(of person) (close session)* lever la séance; *(interrupt session)* suspendre la séance; **to a. to the drawing room** *(after dinner etc)* passer au salon; **shall we a.?** *(after dinner etc)* on passe au salon? **2** *(of meeting etc) (be closed)* être levé; *(be interrupted)* être suspendu (**until** jusqu'à)

adjournment [ə'dʒɜːnmənt] N *(of trial etc)* ajournement *m*; *(of meeting, matter etc)* renvoi *m*, remise *f*; **a. for a week** remise à huitaine; *Law* **an a.** une suspension d'audience

adjudge [ə'dʒʌdʒ] VT **1** **to a. sb guilty** déclarer qn coupable; **to a. sb the winner** déclarer qn vainqueur **2** *(prize, reward)* adjuger, décerner (**to sb** à qn); **to a. damages** adjuger *ou* accorder des dommages-intérêts

adjudicate [ə'dʒuːdɪkeɪt] VT *(issue)* juger, décider; *(prize)* adjuger, décerner; *Law* **to a. sb bankrupt** déclarer *ou* mettre qn en faillite
VI **1** *(act as referee)* arbitrer; **who is adjudicating?** *(in competition)* qui sont les membres du jury? **2** *(announce decision)* se prononcer (**on** sur)

adjudication [ədʒuːdɪ'keɪʃən] N jugement *m*, décision *f*, arrêt *m*
► ► *Law* **a. of bankruptcy** déclaration *f* de faillite

adjudicator [ə'dʒuːdɪkeɪtər] N **1** *(in dispute)* arbitre *m* **2** *(in competition etc)* membre *m* du jury

adjunct ['ædʒʌŋkt] N **1** *(person)* adjoint, -ointe (**to** de), auxiliaire *mf* **2** *(thing)* accessoire *m* (**to** de) **3** *Gram (of verb etc)* complément *m*

adjust [ə'dʒʌst] VT **1** *(scales, instrument, pressure, watch etc)* régler, ajuster; *(microscope, engine)* mettre au point; *(mechanism, brakes)* régler; *(valve)* tarer; *Naut (compass)* compenser, corriger; **to a. the sights of a rifle** ajuster le tir d'une arme à feu; **to a. the controls of a device** mettre au point le réglage d'un appareil; **to a. the picture on a TV set** régler l'image d'un téléviseur; **she adjusted the seat belt to the correct length** elle régla la ceinture de sécurité à la bonne longueur; **the seat can be adjusted for height** la hauteur du siège est réglable
2 *(reformulate)* ajuster; *(figures, salaries)* rajuster; *(in accounts)* régulariser; **the figures have been seasonally adjusted** les chiffres sont les données corrigées des variations saisonnières; **pensions have been adjusted upwards/downwards** les pensions ont été augmentées/diminuées; *Fin* **income adjusted for inflation** revenu réel compte tenu de l'inflation; **the terms of the contract have been adjusted** les termes du contrat ont été modifiés; *Fin* **to a. prices** ajuster les prix; **to a. an average** *(in insurance)* répartir une avarie; **to a. a claim** *(of insurance company)* régler une demande d'indemnité
3 *(one's hat, collar, tie)* arranger, rajuster; *Euph* **to a. one's clothing** *(do up flies)* remonter la braguette
4 *(adapt) (one thing to another)* ajuster (**to** à); **to a. oneself to sth** s'adapter à qch; **his eyes adjusted themselves to the light** ses yeux s'accommodèrent à la lumière
VI **1** *(of person)* s'adapter (**to sth** à qch); **he**

found it difficult to a. after his wife died il eut des difficultés à se faire à la mort de sa femme
2 *(of device)* se régler, s'ajuster; **the seat adjusts for height** la hauteur du siège est réglable

adjustable [ə'dʒʌstəb(ə)l] **ADJ** *(chair, height, speed)* ajustable, réglable; *(shape, size)* ajustable, adaptable; **the seat is a. for height** la hauteur du siège est réglable
▸▸ *Typ* **a. line space** interligne *f* réglable; *Br* **a. spanner** clef *f* anglaise, clef à molette

adjusted [ə'dʒʌstɪd] **ADJ** *(person)* **well a.** (bien) équilibré; **badly a.** pas équilibré
▸▸ **a. frequency** *(in audio)* fréquence *f* réglée

adjuster [ə'dʒʌstər] **N 1** *Fin* **average a.** dispacheur *m*, expert-répartiteur *m*, *pl* eperts-répartiteurs **2** *(device)* appareil *m* de réglage; *Aut (on brake)* régleur *m*
▸▸ *Tech* **a. nut** écrou *m* de réglage; *Tech* **a. screw** vis *f* de réglage

adjusting [ə'dʒʌstɪŋ] **N = adjustment**
▸▸ *Acct* **a. entry** écriture *f* de régularisation; *Tech* **a. screw** vis *f* de réglage

adjustment [ə'dʒʌstmənt] **N 1** *(of scales, instrument, pressure, watch etc)* réglage *m*, ajustement *m*; *(of mechanism, brakes)* réglage; *(of microscope etc)* mise *f* au point; *Naut (of compass)* compensation *f*, correction *f*; **fine a.** réglage de précision; **out of a.** déréglé; **to make an a. to sth** régler qch, ajuster qch; **a slight a. improved the picture** une légère mise au point a amélioré l'image
2 *(of figures, salaries)* rajustement *m*; *(of prices)* ajustement *m*; **no a. was made for seasonal variation** il n'y a pas eu de corrigé des variations saisonnières; **we had to make some adjustments to our plans** nous avons dû modifier quelque peu nos projets; **some adjustments had been made to the text** des modifications avaient été apportées au texte; **average a.** *(in insurance)* répartition *f* d'avarie, dispache *f*
3 *(adapting)* adaptation *f* (**to** à); **period of a.** période *f* d'adaptation
▸▸ *Acct* **a. account** compte *m* collectif

adjutant ['ædʒətənt] **N 1** *Mil (rank)* capitaine *m*, adjudant *m* major; *(assistant)* officier *m* adjoint **2** *(bird)* marabout *m* des Indes, *Fam* adjudant *m*
▸▸ **a. bird** marabout des Indes, *Fam* adjudant; *Mil* **a. general** adjudant général

ad-lib ['æd'lɪb] **ADV to speak a.** improviser
VT & VI (**-bb-**) improviser
N improvisation *f*
ADJ improvisé; **most of his speech was a.** la plus grande partie de son discours était improvisée

ad-libbing [æd'lɪbɪŋ] **N** improvisation *f*

ad(-)man, *pl* **ad(-)men** ['ædmæn, -men] **N** *Fam* publicitaire *m*

admass ['ædmæs] **N** *Br Fam* le grand public

admin ['ædmɪn] **N** *Fam (work)* travail *m* administratif; *(department)* administration *f*; **are you sales or a.?** vous êtes au service des ventes ou à l'administration?; **a. tasks** tâches *fpl* administratives

administer [əd'mɪnɪstər] **VT 1** *(manage)* *(territory, region)* administrer; *(business, property)* administrer, gérer; *(laws)* appliquer **2** *(give)* *(last sacraments, medication)* administrer (**to** à); *(reprimand)* faire, adresser (**to** à); **to a. justice** rendre la justice; *Law* **to a. an** *or* **the oath to sb** faire prêter serment à qn, assermenter qn

administration [ədmɪnɪ'streɪʃən] **N 1** *(of business, fortune etc)* administration *f*, business a. gestion *f* administrative
2 *(administrative work)* travail *m* administratif; *(department)* service *m* administratif

3 *(of justice, sacraments, remedy)* administration *f*, *(of oath)* prestation *f*, *Law* **letters of a.** lettres *fpl* d'administration
4 *esp Am* **the A.** le gouvernement; **the Bush A.** le gouvernement Bush
▸▸ **a. costs** frais *mpl* d'administration, frais de gestion; **a. department** service administratif; **a. fee** frais de dossier

administrative [əd'mɪnɪstrətɪv] **ADJ** administratif; *(error)* d'administration; **for a. convenience** pour faciliter le travail administratif
▸▸ **a. costs** frais *mpl* d'administration, frais de gestion; **a. expenses** frais d'administration, frais de gestion; *Br* **the a. grade** *(in civil service)* les fonctionnaires *mpl* supérieurs; **a. headquarters** siège *m* administratif; **a. skills** compétences *fpl* administratives; **a. staff** personnel *m* administratif; **a. unit** unité *f* administrative; **a. work** travail *m* administratif

administratively [əd'mɪnɪstrətɪvlɪ] **ADV** administrativement; **more convenient a.** plus commode d'un point de vue administratif

administrator [əd'mɪnɪstreɪtər] **N 1** administrateur, -trice **2** *Law (of minor's property etc)* curateur, -trice; *(of succession)* administrateur, -trice

admirable ['ædmərəb(ə)l] **ADJ** admirable

admirably ['ædmərəblɪ] **ADV** admirablement; **she succeeded a.** elle a admirablement bien réussi

admiral ['ædmərəl] **N 1** *Naut* amiral *m*; **a. of the fleet, fleet a.** vice-amiral *m* d'escadre, *pl* vice-amiraux d'escadre **2** **red a.** *(butterfly)* vulcain *m*

admiralty ['ædmərəltɪ] **N** *Naut, Hist* amirauté *f*, *Br* **the A.** ≃ le ministère de la Marine; *Br* **First Lord of the A.** ≃ ministre *m* de la Marine; **court of A.** tribunal *m* maritime
▸▸ *Br* **A. Board** = division *f* navale du ministère de la Défense; *Geog* **A. Islands** îles *fpl* de l'Amirauté

admiration [ædmə'reɪʃən] **N** admiration *f* (**of, for** pour); **I have great a. for doctors** j'ai beaucoup d'admiration pour les médecins; **their roads are the a. of the world** leurs routes font l'admiration du monde entier

admire [əd'maɪər] **VT** admirer; **I a. her as a leader** je l'admire en tant que dirigeante; **they a. him for sticking to his principles** ils l'admirent de s'en tenir à ses principes; **to a. oneself in a mirror** s'admirer dans une glace; **you can't help admiring his cheek!** on ne peut qu'admirer son culot!

admirer [əd'maɪərər] **N 1** admirateur, -trice; **I'm a great a. of people who speak their mind** j'admire énormément les gens qui disent ce qu'ils pensent **2** *Old-fashioned (suitor)* soupirant *m*; *Hum* **is that a letter from one of your admirers?** est-ce que c'est une lettre de l'un de tes admirateurs?

admiring [əd'maɪrɪŋ] **ADJ** *(look, tone etc)* admiratif

admiringly [əd'maɪrɪŋlɪ] **ADV** avec admiration

admissibility [ədmɪsɪ'bɪlɪtɪ] **N** *(of argument etc)* admissibilité *f*, *Law (of appeal, testimony)* recevabilité *f*

admissible [əd'mɪsɪb(ə)l] **ADJ 1** *Law (appeal)* recevable **2** *(idea)* acceptable; *(behaviour, error)* admissible, acceptable

admission [əd'mɪʃən] **N 1** *(to school)* admission *f*, accès *m*; *(to career)* accès; *(to museum, exhibition)* entrée *f*; **to gain a.** *(to a society)* se faire recevoir (**to** au sein de); *(to somebody)* trouver accès (**to** auprès de); *(to college etc)* se faire admettre (**to** au sein de); **a. free** entrée gratuite; **a. £2** entrée 2 livres; **a. is by ticket only** entrée sur présentation d'un billet seulement

2 *(price)* prix *m* *ou* droit *m* d'entrée
3 *(of argument, evidence)* admission *f*, acceptation *f*, *Law (of allegation)* reconnaissance *f*, *(of crime)* confession *f*, *(of guilt)* aveu *m*; **by** *or* **on his own a.** de son propre aveu
4 *Tech, Aut (of steam, gas etc)* admission *f*, adduction *f*, entrée *f*, *(of water)* injection *f*
▸▸ **a. fee** droit d'entrée

admit [əd'mɪt] **VT** (**-tt-**) **1** *(person to place, air, light)* laisser entrer; *(to university, institution etc)* admettre; **children not admitted** les enfants ne sont pas admis; **a. one** *(on ticket)* entrée pour une personne; **he was admitted to hospital** il a été admis à l'hôpital
2 *(truth, excuses)* admettre; *(fact)* consentir; *(principle, mistake)* reconnaître; **it must be admitted that ...** il faut (bien) reconnaître que ...; **to a. one's guilt** se reconnaître *ou* s'avouer coupable; **I a. (that) I was wrong** j'ai eu tort, j'en conviens *ou* je le reconnais; **it was hot, I must a.** je dois admettre qu'il a fait chaud; **I had to a. to myself that ...** j'ai dû m'avouer à moi-même que ...; **he admitted lying** il reconnut qu'il avait menti
▸ **admit of VT INSEP** *Fml (allow of)* permettre, admettre; **the remark admits of several interpretations** cette remarque admet plusieurs interprétations; **his conduct admits of no excuse/explanation** sa conduite est sans excuse/est inexplicable
▸ **admit to VT INSEP** *(confess)* admettre; **I must a. to having felt more than a little nervous** je dois avouer *ou* admettre que je me sentais assez nerveux

admittance [əd'mɪtəns] **N 1** permission *f* d'entrer; *(to place, somebody)* accès *m*; **to gain a. to a place** parvenir à entrer dans un lieu; **to refuse sb a.** refuser de laisser entrer qn; **no a.** entrée interdite, défense d'entrer **2** *Elec* admittance *f*

admittedly [əd'mɪtɪdlɪ] **ADV** de l'aveu général; **a. he's right, but ...** il faut reconnaître qu'il a raison, mais ...; **they got there, two hours late a., but ...** ils sont arrivés là-bas, avec deux heures de retard, j'en conviens, mais ...; **the car's old, a.** il faut reconnaître que la voiture est vieille; **although an a. problematic case, ...** il s'agit d'un cas problématique, certes, mais ...

admixture [əd'mɪkstʃər] **N 1** *(mixture)* mélange *m*; **there was an a. of sarcasm in his comments** il y avait une part de sarcasme dans ses remarques **2** *Pharm* (ad)mixtion *f*, **water with an a. of alcohol** eau additionnée d'alcool

admonish [əd'mɒnɪʃ] **VT 1** *(reprimand)* admonester, réprimander, faire des remontrances à; **he admonished them for their cowardice** il leur a fait des remontrances pour leur manque de courage **2** *Fml (warn)* **to a. sb against sth** mettre qn en garde contre qch **3** *Fml (exhort)* **to a. sb to do sth** exhorter qn à faire qch

admonition [ædmə'nɪʃən] **N 1** *(reprimand)* remontrance *f*, réprimande *f*, *Rel* admonition *f* **2** *(warning)* mise *f* en garde **3** *(exhortation)* exhortation *f* (**to** à)

ad nauseam ['æd'nɔːzɪæm] **ADV** à n'en plus finir

ado [ə'duː] **N** agitation *f*, bruit *m*, embarras *m*; **without (any) more a., without further a.** sans plus de façons *ou* de cérémonie *ou* d'embarras; **to make much a. about nothing** faire beaucoup de bruit pour rien

adobe [ə'dəʊbɪ] **N** *(house)* adobe *m*

adolescence [ædə'lesəns] **N** adolescence *f*

adolescent [ædə'lesənt] **ADJ** adolescent; **in his a. years** quand il était adolescent; **stop being so a. about it!** ton attitude est vraiment trop puérile!
N adolescent, -ente

Adonis [ə'dəʊnɪs] N *Myth, Fig* Adonis *m*

adopt [ə'dɒpt] VT **1** *(child, custom)* adopter; **a stray cat adopted us** un chat abandonné nous a adoptés **2** *(guideline, plan, product)* adopter; *(career)* choisir, embrasser; *(measures, method)* adopter, instaurer; *(opinion)* se rallier à; *(advice)* suivre; *Pol (sb as a candidate)* sélectionner; **to a. a patronizing tone** prendre un ton protecteur; **don't you a. that attitude with me!** ne prends pas cette attitude avec moi! **3** *(minutes of meeting)* approuver

adopted [ə'dɒptɪd] ADJ ATTRIB *(child, word)* adopté; *(son, daughter)* adoptif; **my a. country** mon pays d'adoption

adoption [ə'dɒpʃən] N **1** *(of child, custom, country)* adoption *f*; **I am an American by a.** je suis américain d'adoption; **they have two children of their own and another by a.** ils ont deux enfants à eux et un enfant adopté; **have you considered a.?** *(adopting a child)* avez-vous songé à l'adoption?; *(having your child adopted)* avez-vous songé à le/la faire adopter? **2** *(of law, plan, product)* adoption *f*, *(of career)* choix *m*; *(of measures, method)* instauration *f*; *Pol (of sb as candidate)* sélection *f*

adoptive [ə'dɒptɪv] ADJ *(child, parent)* adoptif

adorable [ə'dɔːrəb(ə)l] ADJ adorable

adorably [ə'dɔːrəblɪ] ADV adorablement; **a. beautiful** beau à ravir

adoration [ædə'reɪʃən] N adoration *f*

adore [ə'dɔːr] VT *(person, god)* adorer; *Fam* **I a. those cakes** j'adore ces gâteaux-là; **don't you a. the way he smiles?** est-ce que tu ne trouves pas son sourire adorable?

adorer [ə'dɔːrər] N adorateur, -trice

adoring [ə'dɔːrɪŋ] ADJ ATTRIB *(eyes, look)* plein d'adoration; *(expression)* d'adoration; **her a. grandfather** son grand-père qui l'adore/l'adorait

adoringly [ə'dɔːrɪŋlɪ] ADV avec adoration

adorn [ə'dɔːn] VT orner, parer (**with** de)

adornment [ə'dɔːnmənt] N **1** *(act)* ornementation *f* **2** *(object)* ornement *m*, parure *f*; **without a.** sans ornements

ADP [eɪdiː'piː] N **1** *Comput (abbr* **automatic data processing***)* traitement *m* automatique des données **2** *Chem (abbr* **adenosine diphosphate***)* ADP *f*

ADR [eɪdiː'ɑːr] N **1** *Fin (abbr* **American Depositary Receipt***)* certificat *m* américain de dépôt **2** *Cin, TV (abbr* **Automatic Dialogue Replacement, Additional Dialogue Recording***)* postsynchronisation *f*

adrenal [ə'driːn(ə)l] *Anat* ADJ surrénal, -aux N surrénale *f*
▸▸ **a. gland** surrénale *f*

adrenalin(e) [ə'drenəlɪn] N adrénaline *f*; *Fig* **it gets the a. going** ça fait monter l'adrénaline; *Fig* **he runs on a.** il marche à l'adrénaline; *Fig* **once the a. gets going** quand l'adrénaline commence à monter

Adriatic [eɪdrɪ'ætɪk] ADJ, N **the A.** la mer Adriatique, l'Adriatique *f*
▸▸ **the A. Sea** la mer Adriatique, l'Adriatique

adrift [ə'drɪft] ADV, ADJ PRED *Naut* à la dérive; **to run** *or* **go a.** *(of ship)* aller à la dérive, dériver; **they were a. for days** ils dérivèrent pendant plusieurs jours; **to break a.** rompre ses amarres, partir à la dérive; **to turn a vessel a.** abandonner *ou* laisser aller un navire à la dérive; *Fig* **young people a. in the big city** des jeunes à la dérive dans la grande ville; *Fig* **to turn sb a.** abandonner qn; *Fig* **to cut oneself a. from sb** rompre avec qn; **to come a.** *(of rope etc)* se détacher, se défaire; *Fig (of plan etc)* tomber à l'eau

adroit [ə'drɔɪt] ADJ adroit, habile; **to be a. at doing sth** être habile à faire qch

adroitly [ə'drɔɪtlɪ] ADV adroitement, habilement

adroitness [ə'drɔɪtnɪs] N adresse *f*, habileté *f* (**in doing** à faire)

ADSL [eɪdiːes'el] N *Tel, Comput (abbr* **Asynchronous Digital Subscriber Line***)* ADSL *f*, *Can* LNPA *f*

adulation [ædjʊ'leɪʃən] N adulation *f*

adulatory [ædjʊ'leɪt(ə)rɪ] ADJ adulateur, -trice

adult ['ædʌlt, ə'dʌlt] N adulte *mf*; **an a. lion** un lion adulte
▸▸ **a. education** enseignement *m* pour adultes; **a. fare** tarif *m* adulte; **a. movie** film *m* érotique

adulterate [ə'dʌltəreɪt] VT *(substance)* dénaturer; *(wine)* frelater; *(language)* corrompre

adulteration [ədʌltə'reɪʃən] N *(of substance)* dénaturation *f*, *(of wine)* frelatage *m*; *(of language)* corruption *f*

adulterer [ə'dʌltərər] N adultère *m (personne)*, homme *m* adultère

adulteress [ə'dʌltərɪs] N adultère *f*, femme *f* adultère

adulterous [ə'dʌltərəs] ADJ adultère

adulterously [ə'dʌltərəslɪ] ADV par adultère; *(to live)* en état d'adultère; *(to lust)* dans une passion adultère

adultery [ə'dʌltərɪ] N adultère *m*; **numerous adulteries** de nombreuses infidélités *fpl*; **to commit a.** commettre l'adultère

adulthood ['ædʌlthʊd] N âge *m* adulte; **to reach a.** devenir adulte, atteindre l'âge adulte

adults-only ADJ *(film)* classé X

adumbrate ['ædʌmbreɪt] VT *Fml* esquisser

ad valorem ['ædvæ'lɔːrem] ADJ proportionnel, ad valorem
▸▸ *Com, Fin* **a. duty** droit *m* sur la valeur, droit ad valorem

advance [əd'vɑːns] N **1** *(forward movement)* avance *f*; **with the a. of old age** avec l'âge; **a. towards sth** acheminement *m* vers qch; *Mil* **in their a. on the city** au cours de leur avance sur la ville; **in a.** *(to go)* en avant; *(to arrive)* en avance; **well/months in a.** largement/des mois à l'avance; **to know in a.** savoir à l'avance; **in a. of the others** avant les autres; **to be in a. of one's time** être en avance sur son temps, devancer son époque; **to pay in a.** payer d'avance; **to pay a sum in a.** *(part payment)* verser un acompte; *(total payment)* avancer un paiement; **thanking you in a.** *(in letter)* en vous remerciant à l'avance, avec mes remerciements anticipés
  2 *(progress) (of science etc)* progrès *m*, développement *m*, avancement *m*; **great advances in medicine** des progrès *ou* développements importants dans le domaine de la médecine; **some advances were made** on a fait des progrès
  3 *(sexual or business overture)* **to make advances to sb** faire une avance *ou* des avances à qn
  4 *Com, Fin (of funds)* avance *f*; **an a. on a contract** une avance *ou* un acompte sur un contrat; **an a. of £200 on his salary** une avance de 200 livres sur son salaire
  5 *(increase at auction)* **any a.?** qui dit mieux?; **any a. on a hundred?** cent, qui dit mieux?
  VT **1** *(one's foot, chesspiece, date of meeting etc)* avancer; *(troops)* faire avancer; **to a. the ignition** donner de l'avance à l'allumage **2** *(science, knowledge etc)* faire progresser, faire avancer; *(growth, development etc)* ac-

célérer; **this discovery has advanced our research by months** cette découverte nous fait gagner plusieurs mois de recherches
  3 *(idea, opinion, observation)* avancer, mettre en avant; *(pretext)* alléguer
  4 *Fin (money)* avancer (**to** à); **sums advanced** avances *fpl*, provisions *fpl*
  5 *(counter on photocopier etc)* faire progresser; *(magnetic tape)* faire défiler; *(paper in printer)* faire avancer
  6 *(promote) (person)* élever, donner de l'avancement à
  VI **1** *(move forward)* s'avancer (**towards** vers); *(of troops)* se porter en avant; **to a. on a town/enemy positions/etc** avancer sur une ville/des positions ennemies/etc; **the night is advancing** la nuit s'avance; **to a. two steps** *or* **paces** faire deux pas en avant **2** *(progress) (in age, one's studies)* avancer; *Biol etc* évoluer; **the work is advancing** l'ouvrage avance *ou* progresse
  3 *(be promoted)* recevoir de l'avancement, monter (en grade)
  4 *Fin (of shares etc)* augmenter; **prices are advancing** les prix sont à la hausse
▸▸ *Fin* **a. account** compte *m* d'avances; **a. booking** réservation *f* à l'avance; **a. booking charter** achat *m* de bloc-sièges; **a. copy** *(of book)* exemplaire *m* de lancement; *(of speech)* texte *m* distribué à l'avance; *Fin* **a. dividend** dividende *m* anticipé; *Cin* **a. funding** préfinancement *m*; *Mil* **a. guard** avant-garde *f*, *pl* avant-gardes; **a. notice** préavis *m*, avertissement *m*; **a. party** groupe *m* de reconnaissance; *Mil* détachement *m* précurseur; *Fin* **a. payment** paiement *m* anticipé, paiement par anticipation; **a. publicity** publicité *f* d'amorçage; **A. Purchase Excursion** = tarif *m* (aérien) spécial sujet à des restrictions de délai d'achat; **a. reservations office** bureau *m* des réservations; *Journ* **a. story** avant-papier *m*, *pl* avant-papiers; **a. warning** avertissement; *Aut* **a. warning triangle** triangle *m* de présignalisation

advanced [əd'vɑːnst] ADJ **1** *(studies, students, opinions, civilization)* avancé; *(economy)* développé; *(country)* développé, industrialisé; *(course)* supérieur; **she's very a. for two** elle est très avancée *ou* en avance pour une enfant de deux ans; **she's very a. for her age** elle est très en avance pour son âge; **to hold a. ideas** avoir des idées avancées; **the night was far a.** il était tard dans la nuit; **he died at an a. age** il est mort très vieux **2** *Tech (model, engine, reactor)* perfectionné; *(technique)* avancé **3** *Mil (post)* avancé
▸▸ **a. check-in** enregistrement *m* anticipé; *Nucl* **a. gas-cooled reactor** réacteur *m* à gaz avancé; **a. mathematics** mathématiques *fpl* supérieures; *Rail* **a. passenger train** train *m* à grande vitesse, TGV *m*

advancement [əd'vɑːnsmənt] N **1** *(of science)* avancement *m*, progrès *m*; **economic a.** essor *m* économique **2** *(of person)* avancement *m*, promotion *f*; **there is little scope for a.** il y a peu de possibilités d'avancement **3** *(of counter on photocopier etc)* progression *f*, *(of paper, tape)* avancement *m*, défilement *m*

advancing [əd'vɑːnsɪŋ] ADJ ATTRIB *(storm)* qui approche/approchait, qui s'avance/s'avançait; *(army)* qui avance/avançait

advantage [əd'vɑːntɪdʒ] N **1** avantage *m*; **to have/gain the a. over sb** avoir/remporter l'avantage sur qn; **it has the a. of being cheap** ça a l'avantage d'être bon marché; **in this sport, size is an a.** dans ce sport, c'est un avantage d'être grand; *Old-fashioned* **you have the a. of me** je n'ai pas l'honneur de vous connaître; **you will find it an a. to …** vous aurez avantage à …; **to take a. of sth**

profiter de qch, tirer avantage *ou* profit de qch; **to take a. of the situation** profiter de l'occasion (**to do** pour faire); **to take a. of an offer/opportunity** profiter d'une proposition/occasion; **they'll only take a.** (*of your generosity etc*) ils ne feront qu'en profiter; **that would be taking a.!** ce serait abuser!; **to take a. of sb** abuser de la crédulité *ou* de la bonne volonté de qn; (*sexually*) abuser de qn; **it is to their a. to keep quiet** c'est dans leur intérêt de se taire; **that would be to your competitor's a.** cela avantagerait votre concurrent; **the recession/weather worked to their a.** la récession/le temps les a avantagés *ou* a travaillé pour eux; **to turn sth to a.** tirer parti de qch, mettre qch à profit; **to turn out to sb's a.** (*of event*) tourner à l'avantage de qn, profiter à qn; **to show sth off to a.** faire valoir qch, mettre qch en valeur **2** *Tennis* avantage *m*; **a. Hewitt** avantage Hewitt
VT avantager, favoriser
▸▸*Sport* **a. rule** règle *f* de l'avantage

advantageous [ædvən'teɪdʒəs] **ADJ** avantageux (**to** pour)

advantageously [ædvən'teɪdʒəslɪ] **ADV** avantageusement

Advent ['ædvənt] **N** *Rel* l'Avent *m*; **the Second A.** le second Avènement
▸▸**A. calendar** calendrier *m* de l'Avent; **A. Sunday** le premier dimanche de l'Avent; **A. wreath** couronne *f* de l'Avent

advent ['ædvənt] **N** (*of spring, rainy season etc*) arrivée *f*; (*of era, computer age*) avènement *m*; (*of railways, the motorcar, computerization*) introduction *f*; **with the a. of McDonald as editor** avec l'arrivée de McDonald au poste de rédacteur en chef

Adventist ['ædvəntɪst] **N** *Rel* **Seventh-day A.** adventiste *mf* du septième jour

adventitious [ædven'tɪʃəs] **ADJ** *Fml* (*chance*) accidentel, fortuit; *Bot* (*roots*) adventif

adventure [əd'ventʃər] **N** aventure *f*; **after many adventures** après bien des péripéties; **the adventures of Tintin** les aventures de Tintin; **life of a.** vie *f* d'aventure, vie aventureuse; **where's your sense of a.?** où est ton sens de l'aventure?
▸▸**a. film** film *m* d'aventures; **a. holiday** = vacances *fpl* organisées avec des activités sportives; *Br* **a. playground** aire *f* de jeux; **a. story** récit *m* d'aventures; (*novel*) roman *m* d'aventure(s)

adventurer [əd'ventʃərər] **N** *Pej* aventurier *m*

adventuresome [əd'ventʃəsəm] **ADJ** (*person*) aventureux; *Pej* téméraire

adventuress [əd'ventʃərɪs] **N** *Pej* aventurière *f*

adventurous [əd'ventʃərəs] **ADJ** (*life, journey*) aventureux; (*person, child*) aventureux, hardi; **we had an a. trip** nous avons eu un voyage plein d'aventures; **be a., try the curry** sois un peu plus aventureux et essaie le curry

adventurously [əd'ventʃərəslɪ] **ADV** aventureusement

adventurousness [əd'ventʃərəsnɪs] **N** hardiesse *f*, audace *f*; (*liking adventure*) esprit *m* d'aventure

adverb ['ædvɜːb] **N** *Gram* adverbe *m* VOIR GRAMMAIRE A19–24; B12–14

adverbial [əd'vɜːbɪəl] **ADJ** *Gram* adverbial, -aux
▸▸**a. phrase** locution *f* adverbiale

adverbially [əd'vɜːbɪəlɪ] **ADV** adverbialement

adversary ['ædvəs(ə)rɪ] **N** adversaire *mf*

adverse ['ædvɜːs] **ADJ 1** (*direction*) contraire,

opposé; (*wind*) contraire; *Fin* **the stock markets had an a. reaction to the Chancellor's budget** les différentes places financières ont mal réagi au budget annoncé par le Chancelier de l'Échiquier **2** (*hostile*) hostile (**to** à, envers); **a. fortune** fortune *f* adverse **3** (*comments, criticism*) défavorable; *Fin* (*balance, budget*) déficitaire

> Attention: ne pas confondre avec le mot anglais **averse**.

adversely ['ædvɜːslɪ] **ADV to influence sb a.** exercer une influence défavorable sur qn; **to report a.** faire un rapport défavorable (**on** sur); **a. affected** affecté

adversity [əd'vɜːsɪtɪ] **N** adversité *f*; **in a.** dans l'adversité

advert ['ædvɜːt] **N** *Fam* **1** (*publicity*) pub *f*, réclame *f*; **you're a walking a. for Gap** tu as l'air tout droit sorti d'une pub pour Gap **2** (*for job, accommodation etc*) annonce *f*

advertise ['ædvətaɪz] **VT 1** (*announce*) (*in newspaper*) (*event*) annoncer; (*job*) mettre une annonce pour; (*on poster*) (*sale etc*) afficher; **the job as advertised** le poste tel que décrit dans l'offre d'emploi; **house advertised for sale** (*in newspaper*) maison dont la mise en vente est annoncée; (*at estate agent's*) maison dont la mise en vente est affichée; **the job was advertised in the paper/in a shop window** il y avait une annonce pour cet emploi dans le journal/dans une vitrine
2 (*do publicity for*) (*product, service*) faire de la réclame *ou* de la publicité pour; **as advertised** conforme à la spécification publicitaire; **as advertised on TV** vu à la télé
3 *Fig* **you needn't a. the fact** vous n'avez pas besoin de le crier sur les toits; **you needn't a. your ignorance** ce n'est pas la peine d'étaler ton ignorance; **he didn't want to a. his presence** il ne voulait pas se faire remarquer
VI (*place advertisement*) insérer *ou* mettre une annonce; (*do publicity*) faire de la publicité *ou* réclame; **they a. on television** ils font de la publicité à la télévision; **it pays to a.** la publicité paie; **to a. for sb/sth** chercher qn/qch par voie d'annonce; **they advertised for an accountant/a nanny** ils ont passé une annonce pour trouver un comptable/une bonne d'enfants

> Note that the French verb **avertir** is a false friend and is never a translation for the English verb **to advertise**. It means either **to inform** or **to warn**, according to the context.

advertised ['ædvətaɪzd] **ADJ ATTRIB** *Rail etc* **the a. time of departure** l'heure *f* prévue pour le départ; **the a. programme** (*on TV*) le programme annoncé

advertisement [əd'vɜːtɪsmənt] **N 1** (*publicity*) publicité *f*, réclame *f*, *Fam* pub *f*, *TV etc* spot *m* publicitaire; **an a. for toothpaste, a toothpaste a.** une publicité pour du dentifrice; **bad a.** contrepublicité *f*, *Fig* **you're not a good a. for your school** vous ne faites pas honneur à votre école **2** (*in newspaper*) annonce *f* (**for** pour); **to reply to** *or* **answer an a.** répondre à une annonce; **classified advertisements** petites annonces **3** (*on wall etc*) affiche *f*

> Note that the French word **avertissement** is a false friend and is never a translation for the English word **advertisement**. It means **warning**.

advertiser ['ædvətaɪzər] **N** annonceur *m*

advertising ['ædvətaɪzɪŋ] **N** (*publicity, profession*) publicité *f*, *Fam* pub *f*; **she works in a.** elle travaille dans la publicité

▸▸**a. agency** agence *f* de publicité; **a. agent** agent *m* de publicité; **A. Association** = organisme *m* britannique dont le rôle est de veiller à la qualité des publicités et de défendre les intérêts des annonceurs et des agences de publicité; *Mktg* **a. awareness** notoriété *f* publicitaire; *Comput* **a. banner** (*on web page*) bandeau *m* publicitaire; **a. brochure** plaquette *f* publicitaire; **a. budget** budget *m* publicitaire; **a. campaign** campagne *f* publicitaire *ou* de publicité; **a. concept** idée *f* publicitaire; **a. consultant** conseil *m* en publicité; **a. copy** texte *m* publicitaire; **a. department** service *m* de la publicité; **a. director** directeur, -trice de la communication *ou* de la publicité; *Mktg* **a. effectiveness** efficacité *f* publicitaire; **a. executive** chef *m* de la publicité; **a. expenditure** dépenses *fpl* publicitaires; **a. gift** cadeau *m* publicitaire; **a. gimmick** gadget *m* publicitaire; **a. insert** encart *m* publicitaire; **a. jingle** jingle *m*, sonal *m*; **a. manager** directeur, -trice de la communication *ou* de la publicité; **a. market** marché *m* publicitaire; **a. material** matériel *m* publicitaire; **a. medium** média *m* *ou* support *m* publicitaire; **a. message** message *m* publicitaire; **a. paper** journal *m* de petites annonces; **a. rates** tarif *m* des insertions; **a. revenue** recettes *fpl* publicitaires; **a. sales agency** régie *f* publicitaire; **a. schedule** programme *m* des annonces; **a. space** espace *m* publicitaire; **a. spot** spot *m* publicitaire; **a. standards** normes *fpl* publicitaires; *Br* **A. Standards Authority** ≃ Bureau *m* de vérification de la publicité; **a. strategy** stratégie *f* publicitaire

advertorial [ædvə'tɔːrɪəl] **N** publireportage *m*

advice [əd'vaɪs] **N 1** conseil(s) *m(pl)*, avis *m*; **piece of a.** conseil; **that's good a.** c'est un bon conseil; **to ask** *or* **seek sb's a.** demander conseil à qn; **when I want your a., I'll ask for it!** quand j'aurai besoin de tes conseils, je saurai te les demander!; **to give sb a.** donner des conseils à qn; **to take sb's a.** suivre le conseil *ou* les conseils de qn; **take my a. and don't have anything to do with them** suis mon conseil et ne te mêle pas de leurs affaires; **if you take my a., you'll not have anything to do with them** suis mon conseil, ne te mêle pas de leurs affaires; **my a. (to you) would be to buy a new car** mon conseil serait que tu achètes une nouvelle voiture; **to take medical/legal a.** consulter un médecin/un avocat; **on sb's a.** sur l'avis *ou* le conseil de qn; **the magazine is a useful source of a.** le magazine est une source utile de conseils
2 *Com* (*notice*) avis *m*; **as per a.** suivant avis; **until further a.** jusqu'à nouvel avis
▸▸**a. column** (*agony column*) courrier *m* du cœur; (*for practical advice*) rubrique *f* pratique; *Fin* **a. note** lettre *f* d'avis

> Attention à l'orthographe: ne pas confondre avec le verbe **to advise** et ses dérivés, qui prennent un **s** et non un **c**.

advisability [ədvaɪzə'bɪlɪtɪ] **N** (*of course of action, policy*) bien-fondé *m*, *pl* bien-fondés; **I'm wondering about the a. of this** je doute que ce soit à recommander

advisable [əd'vaɪzəb(ə)l] **ADJ PRED** recommandé, judicieux; **it is a. to book early** il est recommandé de réserver à l'avance; **I'm going in my old car – is that a.?** j'y vais dans ma vieille voiture – est-ce que c'est bien prudent?; **it would be a. to ...** il serait prudent de ...; **it might be a. to ...** peut-être conviendrait-il de ...; **if you consider** *or* **think it a.** si bon vous semble

advise [əd'vaɪz] **VT 1** (*person*) conseiller; (*caution*) recommander, conseiller; **to a. sb**

to do sth conseiller à qn de faire qch; **I strongly a. you to …** je vous recommande instamment de …; **customers are advised to book early** il est recommandé *ou* conseillé aux clients de réserver à l'avance; **what do you a. me to do?** que me conseillez-vous?; **you'd be well advised to take an umbrella** vous feriez bien de prendre un parapluie; **they were well advised to go by air** ils ont bien fait de prendre l'avion; **they are advising taking a different route** ils conseillent de prendre un itinéraire différent

2 *Fml (inform)* avertir, prévenir, instruire (**of** de); **to a. sb that …** avertir *ou* prévenir qn que …

VI *(of person)* être conseiller (**in, on** en)

▸ **advise against** VT INSEP *(thing, course of action)* déconseiller; **to a. sb against sth** déconseiller qch à qn; **to a. sb against doing sth** déconseiller à qn de faire qch; **I would strongly a. against it** je le déconseille fortement

> Attention à l'orthographe: ne pas confondre avec le nom **advice**, qui prend un **c** et non un **s**.

advisedly [əd'vaɪzɪdlɪ] ADV *(to say sth)* en connaissance de cause; *(to use a word, an expression)* délibérément, de propos délibéré

adviser [əd'vaɪzər] N conseiller, -ère

advising bank [əd'vaɪzɪŋ] N *Fin* banque *f* notificatrice

advisor [əd'vaɪzər] N = **adviser**

advisory [əd'vaɪzərɪ] ADJ *(council, committee)* consultatif; **in an a. capacity** en tant que conseiller
▸▸ **a. service** service *m* de renseignements

advocacy ['ædvəkəsɪ] N *(of cause)* plaidoyer *m*

advocate[1] ['ædvəkət, -eɪt] N **1** *Scot Law* avocat, -ate; **the Lord A.** ≃ le Procureur général **2** *(supporter)* avocat, -ate; *(of cause, doctrine etc)* défenseur *m*; **the advocates of free trade** les partisans *mpl* du libre-échange; *Rel, Fig* **to be** *or* **play devil's a.** se faire l'avocat du diable

advocate[2] ['ædvəkeɪt] VT *(cause)* soutenir; *(use of sth, method of proceeding)* préconiser, conseiller, plaider en faveur de; **she advocates leniency** elle préconise l'indulgence

adware ['ædweər] N *Comput* logiciel *m* publicitaire, adware *m*

adze, *Am* **adz** [ædz] N (h)erminette *f*; *(of ice axe)* sape *f*

A&E [eɪən'diː] N *Br Med (abbr* **accident and emergency***)* service *m* des urgences, urgences *fpl*

AEA [eɪiː'eɪ] N *Br (abbr* **Atomic Energy Authority***)* ≃ Commissariat *m* à l'énergie atomique

Aegean [ɪ'dʒiːən] ADJ *Antiq* égéen
N **1 the A.** la mer Égée **2** *Antiq* Égéen, -enne
▸▸ **the A. sea** la mer Égée

aegis, *Am* **egis** [iːdʒɪs] N égide *f*; **under the a. of …** sous l'égide de …

aegrotat ['aɪɡrəʊtæt] N *Br Univ* dispense *f* (d'examen) *(accordée pour cause de maladie)*

Aeneas [ɪ'niːəs] N Énée *m*

Aeneid [ɪ'niːɪd] N Énéide *f*

aeolian [iː'əʊlɪən] ADJ éolien
▸▸ *Mus* **a. harp** harpe *f* éolienne

aeon, *Am* **eon** ['iːɒn] N éternité *f*; **for aeons upon aeons** pendant des siècles *ou* des éternités; **aeons ago** il y a une éternité

aerate ['eəreɪt] VT **1** *(inject with air)* aérer **2** *Physiol (blood)* artérialiser **3** *Old-fashioned (water, mineral water)* gazéifier

aerated [eə'reɪtɪd] ADJ **1** *(with air)* aéré **2** *Old-fashioned (water)* gazeux **3** *Old-fashioned Fam (excited, upset)* **to be/get a. about sth** être énervé/s'énerver à cause de qch

aeration [eə'reɪʃən] N **1** *(injecting with air)* aération *f* **2** *Physiol (of blood)* artérialisation *f*

aerial ['eərɪəl] ADJ **1** aérien **2** *Bot* aérien; *(orchid etc)* aéricole
N *Radio, TV* antenne *f*; **transmitting/receiving a.** antenne d'émission/réceptrice
▸▸ **a. acrobatics** voltige *f* aérienne; **a. curtain** rideau *m* d'antennes; **a. dish** antenne parabolique; *Electron, TV* **a. engineer** antenniste *mf*; **a. photograph** photographie *f* aérienne; *Bot* **a. root** racine *f* aérienne; *Cin* **a. shot** prise *f* de vue aérienne; **a. walkway** passerelle *f*; *Mil* **a. warfare** combat *m* aérien

aerie ['eərɪ, 'ɪərɪ] N *esp Am* aire *f (d'un aigle)*

aerobatics [eərəʊ'bætɪks] N *Aviat* acrobaties *fpl* aériennes, voltige *f* aérienne VOIR GRAMMAIRE A10
▸▸ **a. display** démonstration *f* aérienne

aerobics [eə'rəʊbɪks] N aérobic *m*; **to do a.** faire de l'aérobic; **are you going to a. tonight?** est-ce que tu vas au cours d'aérobic ce soir? VOIR GRAMMAIRE A10
▸▸ **a. class** cours *m* d'aérobic; **a. teacher** professeur *m* d'aérobic

aerodrome ['eərədrəʊm] N aérodrome *m*

aerodynamic [eərəʊdaɪ'næmɪk] ADJ aérodynamique; **the car has a very a. shape** la voiture a une forme très aérodynamique
▸▸ **a. drag** résistance *f* de l'air; **a. noise** bruit *m* aérodynamique

aerodynamically [eərəʊdaɪ'næmɪklɪ] ADV aérodynamiquement

aerodynamics [eərəʊdaɪ'næmɪks] N VOIR GRAMMAIRE A10 **1** *(with sing verb) (science)* aérodynamique *f* **2** *(with pl verb) (quality)* aérodynamisme *m*

aero-engine ['eərəʊ-] N moteur *m* d'avion

aerofoil ['eərəʊfɔɪl], *Am* **airfoil** ['eəfɔɪl] N *Aviat* plan *m* à profil d'aile, surface *f* portante *ou* sustentrice; *(on car)* aileron *m*

aerogram ['eərəɡræm] N aérogramme *m*
▸▸ **a. form** aérogramme

aeromodeller, *Am* **aeromodeler** ['eərəʊ-ˌmɒd(ə)lər] N aéromodéliste *mf*

aeromodelling, *Am* **aeromodeling** ['eərəʊ'mɒd(ə)lɪŋ] N aéromodélisme *m*

aeronaut ['eərənɔːt] N aéronaute *mf*

aeronautic(al) [eərə'nɔːtɪk, -ɪk(ə)l] ADJ aéronautique

aeronautics [eərə'nɔːtɪks] N aéronautique *f* VOIR GRAMMAIRE A10

aeroplane ['eərəpleɪn] N *esp Br* avion *m*

aerosol ['eərəsɒl] N **1** *(container)* (bombe *f*) aérosol *m* **2** *(suspension system)* **available in a. form** existe en atomiseur; **a. deodorant** déodorant *m* en atomiseur; **a. paint** peinture *f* aérosol
▸▸ **a. can** (bombe) aérosol; **a. spray** atomiseur *m*

aerospace ['eərəspeɪs] N *Ind* aérospatiale *f*; **a. industries** industries *fpl* aérospatiales

aesthete, *Am* **esthete** ['iːsθiːt] N esthète *mf*

aesthetic, *Am* **esthetic** [iːs'θetɪk, ɪs-] ADJ esthétique; **in a. terms** en termes d'esthétique

aesthetically, *Am* **esthetically** [iːs'θetɪklɪ, ɪs-] ADV esthétiquement

aestheticism, *Am* **estheticism** [iːs'θetɪ-sɪz(ə)m, ɪs-] N esthétisme *m*

aesthetics, *Am* **esthetics** [iːs'θetɪks, ɪs-] N esthétique *f* VOIR GRAMMAIRE A10

aetiological, *Am* **etiological** [iːtɪə'lɒ-dʒɪk(ə)l] ADJ *Med, Phil* étiologique

aetiology, *Am* **etiology** [iːtɪ'ɒlədʒɪ] N *Med, Phil* étiologie *f*

afar [ə'fɑːr] ADV *usu Lit* **from a.** de loin

AFC [eɪef'siː] N *(abbr* **automatic frequency control***) (in audio)* correcteur *m* automatique de fréquence

afear(e)d [ə'fɪəd] ADJ *Arch* effrayé, apeuré; **to be a. of sb/sth** être effrayé par *ou* avoir peur de qn/qch

A-feature N *Cin* film *m* projeté en exclusivité *(lors d'une séance où deux longs métrages sont projetés)*

affability [æfə'bɪlɪtɪ] N affabilité *f*, courtoisie *f* (**towards** envers, avec)

affable ['æfəb(ə)l] ADV affable, courtois (**to** envers; **with** avec)

affably ['æfəblɪ] ADV avec affabilité, avec courtoisie

affair [ə'feər] N **1** *(matter, concern)* affaire *f*; **the a. in hand** l'affaire qui nous occupe; **that's my a.!, stick to your own affairs!** occupe-toi donc de tes affaires!; **what he does in private is his own a.** sa vie privée ne regarde que lui; **to put one's affairs in order** mettre de l'ordre dans ses affaires; **in the present state of affairs** dans l'état actuel des choses; *Iron* **that's a nice** *or* **fine state of affairs!** en voilà du propre!, c'est du joli!; **affairs of state** les affaires de l'État; **foreign affairs** les affaires étrangères; **our home affairs correspondent** notre spécialiste des affaires intérieures; *Arch* **a. of honour** affaire d'honneur, duel *m*; **the Watergate a.** l'affaire du Watergate

2 *(sexual)* liaison *f*; **to have an a. with sb** avoir une liaison avec qn; **they're having an a.** ils ont une liaison; **an a. of the heart** une affaire de cœur

3 *(event)* **the meal will be a lavish a.** le repas sera un véritable festin; **the festival was a dull a.** le festival était dépourvu d'intérêt; **it was one of those cheese and wine affairs** c'était une de ces soirées vin et fromage; **what kind of a. was it?** c'était comment?

4 *Fam (thing)* **the cake's one of those fresh-cream affairs** c'est un de ces gâteaux à la crème fraîche; **the house is a three-storey a.** il s'agit d'une maison à trois étages; **this workbench is an ingenious a.** cet établi est vraiment ingénieux

> Note that the French word **affaire** is never used to refer to a sexual relationship between two people.

affect[1] [ə'fekt] VT **1** *(have effect on) (person)* atteindre, toucher; *(organ etc)* affecter; *(decision)* influer sur; *(one's health)* altérer; *(smooth running, smooth traffic flow)* entraver; **roads have been seriously affected by the flooding** les routes ont été fortement touchées par l'inondation; **the economic crisis which is affecting the country at present** la crise économique qui frappe le pays en ce moment; **it affects me personally** cela me touche personnellement; **the strike didn't a. us** nous n'avons pas été touchés par la grève; **pensioners are not affected by this law** les retraités ne sont pas concernés par cette loi; **those most directly affected** les premiers intéressés; **how will this a. the traffic?** quelles seront les conséquences sur la circulation?

2 *(move) (person)* affecter, toucher; **to be deeply affected by sth** être très affecté par qch

VT **1** *(fake) (indifference, interest)* affecter, feindre, simuler; *(pain)* simuler; **to a. an accent** prendre un accent; **he affects to know a lot about …** il prétend savoir beaucoup de choses sur …

2 *(wear, use)* **he affects drab colours** il a un penchant pour les couleurs ternes

affect[2] ['æfekt] N *Psy* affect *m*

affectation [æfek'teɪʃən] N *Pej* **1** *(of interest, indifference etc)* affectation *f*, simulation *f* **2** *(affectedness)* affectation *f*, manque *m* de naturel; **his working-class accent was clearly an a.** clairement, son accent prolétaire était affecté

affected[1] [ə'fektɪd] ADJ **1** *Med* atteint; **to be a. with a disease** être atteint d'une maladie; **the lung is a.** le poumon est atteint *ou* touché; **apply to the a. part** appliquer sur la partie malade **2** *(emotionally)* ému, touché

affected[2] ADJ *Pej* **1** *(artificial) (person)* affecté, maniéré; *(manners)* affecté, apprêté; *(style)* maniéré, recherché, apprêté **2** *(indifference etc)* simulé

affectedly [ə'fektɪdlɪ] ADV avec affectation, d'une manière affectée

affectedness [ə'fektɪdnɪs] N *(no pl)* affectation *f*, manque *m* de naturel

affecting [ə'fektɪŋ] ADJ *(sight, scene etc)* touchant, attendrissant

affection [ə'fekʃən] N **1** affection *f*, tendresse *f*; **to show sb a.** montrer de l'affection *ou* de la tendresse pour qn; **to feel a. for sb** avoir de l'affection *ou* de la tendresse pour qn; **a rare display of a.** une rare manifestation d'affection *ou* de tendresse; **to have an a. for sb** ressentir de l'affection pour qn; **I have a great deal of a. for you** j'ai beaucoup d'affection pour toi; **with much a.** *(in letter)* (bien) affectueusement; **he is held in great a.** il est très aimé; **to gain** *or* **win sb's a.** gagner l'affection de qn; **this town has a special place in my affections** j'aime tout particulièrement cette ville **2** *Med (of chest, skin etc)* affection *f*

affectionate [ə'fekʃənət] ADJ affectueux (**towards** avec, envers); **an a. hug** une étreinte affectueuse; *Old-fashioned* **your a. nephew** *(in letter)* votre dévoué neveu

affectionately [ə'fekʃənətlɪ] ADV affectueusement; **yours a.** *(in letter)* bien affectueusement

affective [ə'fektɪv] ADJ affectif

affidavit [æfɪ'deɪvɪt] N *Law* déclaration *f* par écrit et sous serment; **to swear an a.** certifier sous serment une déclaration (écrite)

affiliate [ə'fɪlɪeɪt] VT *(of society etc) (members etc)* s'affilier; **to a. oneself to** *or* **with a society** s'affilier à une société
▸ VI **to a. to** *or* **with a society** s'affilier à une société
▸ N *(person)* affilié, -ée; *(company)* filiale *f*
▸▸ **affiliated company** société *f* affiliée; **affiliated member** affilié, -ée

affiliation [əfɪlɪ'eɪʃən] N **1** *(to society)* affiliation *f*, **political affiliations** attaches *fpl* politiques **2** *Law* procédure *f* en recherche de paternité
▸▸ *Law* **a. order** = injonction *f* au père putatif de verser une pension pour subvenir aux besoins de son enfant

affinity [ə'fɪnɪtɪ] N **1** *(liking, attraction)* affinité *f*, **to have an a. with sb/sth** avoir des affinités avec qn/qch; **there are many affinities between the two regions** les deux régions ont énormément de choses en commun **2** *(relationship)* lien *m* **3** *Math, Biol* affinité *f* (**with, to** avec; **between** entre); *Chem* **a. for a body** affinité pour un corps

affirm [ə'fɜːm] VT **1** affirmer, soutenir (**that** que); **to a. sth to sb** affirmer qch à qn; **to a. one's intention to do sth** affirmer qu'on a l'intention de faire qch **2** *Law (verdict)* confirmer, homologuer
▸ VI *Law* faire une affirmation *ou* déclaration solennelle

affirmation [æfə'meɪʃən] N **1** affirmation *f*, assertion *f* **2** *Law* déclaration *f* ou affirma-

tion *f* solennelle *(tenant lieu de serment)* **3** *Law (of verdict)* confirmation *f*, homologation *f*

affirmative [ə'fɜːmətɪv] ADJ *(answer)* affirmatif; *Am* **to take a. action** prendre des mesures antidiscriminatoires
▸ N **to answer in the a.** répondre affirmativement *ou* par l'affirmative; **the answer is in the a.** la réponse est affirmative
▸ INT **a., captain** affirmatif, mon capitaine

affirmatively [ə'fɜːmətɪvlɪ] ADV affirmativement

affix[1] ['æfɪks] N *Ling* affixe *m*

affix[2] [ə'fɪks] VT attacher (**to** à); *(seal, stamp, one's signature)* apposer (**to a document** à un document); **affixed to the wall** fixé au mur

afflict [ə'flɪkt] VT affliger; **to be afflicted with rheumatism** être affligé de rhumatismes; **he was afflicted by psoriasis** il souffrait de psoriasis; **she was afflicted by acute feelings of guilt** elle était accablée d'un fort sentiment de culpabilité; *Iron* **the family I'm afflicted with** la famille dont je suis affligé; *Fig* **the economic problems that a. the nation** les problèmes économiques qui accablent le pays

afflicted [ə'flɪktɪd] ADJ affligé; *(parts, area) (by illness)* atteint
▸ NPL **the a.** les affligés *mpl*; **don't mock the a.** ne te moque pas de moi/lui/*etc*; *Hum* **he can't help being stupid, don't mock the a.** ce n'est pas de sa faute s'il est bête, le pauvre

affliction [ə'flɪkʃən] N **1** *(suffering)* affliction *f*; **the afflictions of old age** les infirmités *fpl* de la vieillesse **2** *Fig (misfortune)* calamité *f*, revers *m*; **in her a.** dans sa détresse

affluence ['æfluəns] N *(wealth)* abondance *f*, richesse *f*; **to live in a.** vivre dans l'abondance

affluent ['æfluənt] ADJ *(wealthy)* riche
▸▸ **a. society** société *f* d'abondance

affluently ['æfluəntlɪ] ADV *(to live)* dans l'abondance

afford [ə'fɔːd] VT **1** *(usu with* **can***) (financially)* avoir les moyens (**to do sth** de faire qch; **sth** d'acheter qch); **I can't a. it** mes moyens ne le permettent pas; **we can't a. a new car** nous ne pouvons pas nous offrir une nouvelle voiture; **we could easily a. another car** nous avons largement les moyens d'acheter une autre voiture; **I can a. to eat out twice a week** je peux me permettre d'aller au restaurant deux fois par semaine; **give what you can a.** donnez selon vos possibilités; **it's more than we can a.** c'est au-dessus de nos moyens; **an extravagance I could ill a.** une extravagance qui n'était guère dans mes moyens
2 *(usu with* **can***) (non-financial use)* **I can a. to wait** je peux attendre; **can you a. the time?** est-ce que vous avez le temps?; **I cannot a. to create a bad impression/not to go** je ne peux pas me permettre de faire une mauvaise impression/de ne pas y aller; **I can't a. not to** je n'ai pas vraiment le choix **3** *Lit (give)* fournir, offrir; **to a. sb the opportunity to do sth** donner *ou* fournir à qn l'occasion de faire qch; **the trees afforded us very little shelter** les arbres ne nous fournissaient qu'un piètre abri; **it affords me great pleasure** cela me fait grand plaisir; **kind heaven a. him everlasting rest** que Dieu dans sa miséricorde lui donne le repos éternel

affordable [ə'fɔːdəb(ə)l] ADJ *(price, rent)* abordable; *(house, trip etc)* (d'un prix) abordable

afforest [ə'fɒrɪst] VT *(piece of land)* boiser

afforestation [əfɒrɪ'steɪʃən] N boisement *m*

affray [ə'freɪ] N *esp Law* bagarre *f*, rixe *f*

affreightment [ə'freɪtmənt] N *Com* affrètement *m*

affront [ə'frʌnt] N affront *m*, offense *f* (**to** à)
▸ VT offenser, faire (un) affront à; **he was affronted by the suggestion that he should help** il a été très vexé quand on lui a fait remarquer qu'il pourrait aider

Afghan ['æfgæn] ADJ afghan
▸ N **1** Afghan, -ane **2** *Ling* afghan *m* **3** *Am* couverture *f* de laine tricotée (au crochet)
▸▸ *Am* **a. blanket** couverture de laine tricotée (au crochet); **A. hound** lévrier *m* afghan

Afghanistan [æf'gænɪstɑːn] N Afghanistan *m*

AFI [eɪef'aɪ] N *Cin (abbr* **American Film Institute***)* American Film Institute *m (cinémathèque américaine dont le quartier général se trouve à Washington)*

aficionado [əfɪʃjə'nɑːdəʊ] N aficionado *m*; **he's become quite an a.** c'est devenu un vrai aficionado

afield [ə'fiːld] ADV **far/farther a.** très/plus loin; **she rarely ventures farther a. than the next village** elle s'aventure rarement au-delà du village voisin; **from as far a. as ...** de contrées aussi reculées que ...

afire [ə'faɪər] ADV, ADJ PRED *Arch, Lit* en feu; *Fig* enflammé; **a. with enthusiasm** brûlant d'enthousiasme

aflame [ə'fleɪm] ADV, ADJ PRED *Lit* embrasé; **the trees were a. with colour** les arbres étaient flamboyants

AFL-CIO [eɪefelsɪaɪ'əʊ] N *abbr* **American Federation of Labor and Congress of Industrial Organizations**

afloat [ə'fləʊt] ADV, ADJ PRED **1** à flot, sur l'eau; **the biggest ship a.** le plus gros navire à flot; **to be a.** *(of ship)* être à flot; **to keep a ship a.** maintenir un navire à flot; **to keep a.** *(of person, boat)* flotter; *Fig (of company)* se maintenir à flot; *Fig* **to keep sb a. (financially)** renflouer qn; *Fin* **to keep bills a.** faire circuler des effets; **to be a. in space** planer dans l'espace; **life a.** la vie en mer **2** *(flooded)* inondé; **the kitchen was a.** la cuisine était inondée

aflutter [ə'flʌtər] ADJ excité; **my heart was all a.** mon cœur battait la chamade; **to set sb's heart a.** faire battre le cœur de qn

AFM [eɪef'em] N *TV (abbr* **assistant floor manager***)* régisseur *m* de plateau adjoint

afoot [ə'fʊt] ADV **a plan is a. to ...** on projette de ..., on a formé un projet pour ...; **there's something a.** il se prépare *ou* se trame quelque chose; **there was trouble a.** des ennuis se préparaient

afore [ə'fɔːr] ADV, PREP, CONJ *Arch, Dial* = **before**

aforementioned [ə'fɔːmenʃənd] ADJ ATTRIB, N *esp Law* susmentionné, -ée, susdénommé, -ée

aforesaid [ə'fɔːsed] ADJ ATTRIB, N *esp Law* susdit, -ite

aforethought [ə'fɔːθɔːt] ADJ *esp Law* **with malice a.** avec préméditation, avec intention criminelle; **I know it wasn't done with malice a.** *(non-legal context)* je sais que ce n'était pas intentionnel

a fortiori [ɑː'fɔːtɪɔːrɪ] ADV a fortiori

afoul [ə'faʊl] ADV **to run a. of the law** avoir des ennuis *ou* maille à partir avec la police; **he ran a. of the chairman's new policy** il s'est heurté à la nouvelle politique du président

afraid [ə'freɪd] ADJ PRED **1** *(scared)* pris de peur; **to be a. of sb/sth** avoir peur de qn/qch; **don't be a.** n'ayez pas peur, ne craignez rien; **he felt a.** il avait peur; **if you're not a. of hard work** si le travail intensif ne vous fait pas peur; **there's nothing to be a. of** il n'y a pas de raison d'avoir peur *ou* de quoi avoir peur; **that's (exactly) what I was a. of!** c'est bien ce que je craignais!; **he was a. to open his mouth** il n'osait pas dire un mot

2 *(worried)* **to be a. that …** avoir peur *ou* craindre que + *sub* …; **I was a. you would ask me that question** je craignais *ou* j'avais peur que vous me posiez cette question; **I was a. that might happen** c'est bien ce que je craignais qu'il arrive; **I am a. he'll die** je crains qu'il ne meure

3 *(regretful)* **I'm a. so/not** je crains que oui/non; **I'm a. she's out** je regrette mais elle est sortie; **I can't help you, I'm a.** je suis désolé, je crois que je ne peux rien faire pour vous; **I'm a. that's it, we've no more money** j'ai bien peur que ça y soit, cette fois, nous n'avons plus d'argent

afresh [ə'freʃ] ADV de nouveau, à nouveau; **to start sth a.** recommencer qch; **to look at a problem a.** jeter un nouveau regard sur un problème

Africa ['æfrɪkə] N Afrique *f*, **in A.** en Afrique

African ['æfrɪkən] ADJ africain

N Africain, -aine

▸▸ **A. American** Noir américain, *f* Noire américaine; **A. American culture** la culture noire américaine; **A. elephant** éléphant *m* d'Afrique; **A. Union** Union *f* africaine; *Bot* **A. violet** saintpaulia *m*

Afrikaaner [æfrɪ'kɑːnər] ADJ afrikaner, afrikaander

N Afrikaner *mf*, Afrikaander *mf*

Afrikaans [æfrɪ'kɑːns] N *Ling* afrikaans *m*

Afro ['æfrəʊ] ADJ *(hairstyle)* afro *inv*

N *(hairstyle)* coiffure *f* afro

Afro-American ADJ afro-américain

N Afro-américain, -aine, *pl* Afro-américains, -aines

aft [ɑːft] ADV *Naut, Aviat* à l'arrière; **to go a.** aller à l'arrière; **a. of the mast** sur l'arrière du mât; **to have the wind dead a.** avoir le vent en poupe

AFTER ['ɑːftər]	
ADV après	
PREP après **1–4** ▪ sur **3** ▪ d'après **5**	
CONJ après (que)	
ADJ à venir	

ADV après; **to come a.** venir après *ou* à la suite; **he was ill for months a.** il en est resté malade pendant des mois; **soon/long a.** peu/longtemps après; **the night/the week a.** la nuit/la semaine d'après; **a year a.** un an après *ou* plus tard; **the day a.** le lendemain

PREP **1** *(of place)* après; **to run a. sb** courir après qn; **close the door a. you** fermez la porte derrière vous; **I called a. him to …** je lui ai crié de …; *Fam* **to be a. sb/sth** *(searching for)* être en quête de qn/qch, chercher qn/qch; **the police are a. you** la police est à vos trousses; *Fam* **what's he a.?** *(what does he want?)* qu'est-ce qu'il a en tête *ou* derrière la tête?; *(what is he looking for?)* qu'est-ce qu'il cherche?; **are you a. my job?** est-ce que tu veux me prendre ma place?; **she's a. a full-time job** elle cherche un travail à temps plein; **they are a. some fun** ils veulent s'amuser

2 *(of time)* après; **to reign a. sb** régner après qn; **a. three days** trois jours après *ou* plus tard; **a. dinner** après dîner; **a. this date** passé cette date; **a. all** *(all things considered)* après tout; *(in spite of everything)* finalement; **she's only young, a. all** elle est jeune, après tout; **so you went to the party a. all?** alors, finalement, vous êtes allés à la soirée?; **a. all we've done for you!** après tout ce que nous avons fait pour toi!; **the day a. the battle** le lendemain de la bataille; **the day a. tomorrow** après-demain; **it is a. five**

(o'clock) il est cinq heures passées; *Am* **twenty a. four** quatre heures vingt; **one a. the other** l'un après l'autre, les uns après les autres; **a. dinner speech** discours *m* d'après-dîner; **a. tax** après imposition, après impôt

3 he read page a. page il lut page sur page; **day a. day** jour après jour; **year a. year** tous les ans; **there was street a. street of apartment blocks** rue après rue, les immeubles se succédaient; **mile a. mile** mil(l)e après mil(l)e

4 *(of order)* après; **a. you** *(going through door, at a meal etc)* après vous; **I put Milton a. Dante** je mets Milton au-dessous de Dante; **a. her, he is the best** après elle, c'est lui le meilleur

5 *(of manner)* d'après; **landscape a. Turner** paysage d'après *ou* à la (manière de) Turner

6 *(about)* **to ask** *or* **inquire a. sb** demander des nouvelles de qn; **Mrs Smith asked a. you** Mme Smith a demandé de tes nouvelles

7 *Ir* **to be a. doing sth** *(in the middle of)* être en train de faire qch; *(inclined to)* être disposé à faire qch

CONJ *(when subject changes)* après que + *ind ou Fam sub*; *(when subject stays the same)* après + *inf*; **a. I came a. he had gone** je suis arrivé après qu'il est *ou Fam* soit parti; **a. I had seen him, I went out** après l'avoir vu, je suis sorti; **a. doing sth** après avoir fait qch

ADJ **1** *(yet to come)* à venir; **in a. years** plus tard (dans la vie)

2 *Naut* arrière

▸▸ *Naut* **a. cabin** cabine *f* sur l'arrière; *Naut* **a. hold** cale *f* arrière

---

afterbirth ['ɑːftbɜːθ] N *Obst* placenta *m*

afterburner ['ɑːftbɜːnər] N dispositif *m* de postcombustion

aftercare ['ɑːftəkeər] N *(after treatment)* postcure *f*, *(after giving birth)* soins *mpl* post-natals; *(after operation)* soins postopératoires; *(of convalescent, delinquent etc)* surveillance *f*

afterdeck ['ɑːftədek] N *Naut* plage *f* arrière

aftereffect ['ɑːftərɪfekt] N *(of drug)* effet *m* secondaire; *Fig (of remark, coup etc)* répercussion *f*, contrecoup *m*; **I'm still feeling the aftereffects of last night's drinking** je ne me suis toujours pas remis de ce que j'ai bu hier soir

afterglow ['ɑːftəgləʊ] N **1** *(of the setting sun)* dernières lueurs *fpl*, derniers reflets *mpl*; *Fig* **he was basking in the warm a. of his triumph** il savourait le sentiment de volupté dans lequel son triomphe l'avait laissé **2** *Comput (on screen)* rémanence *f*

after-hours ADJ *(after closing time)* qui suit la fermeture; *(after work)* qui suit le travail; **an a. bar** un bar de nuit

ADV *(after closing time)* après la fermeture; *(after work)* après le travail

▸▸ *St Exch* **a. dealing** transactions *fpl* hors Bourse; *Br* **a. drinking** = verres *mpl* servis après l'heure de fermeture légale des pubs; *St Exch* **a. market** marché *m* hors Bourse; *St Exch* **a. trading** transactions hors Bourse

afterimage ['ɑːftərɪmɪdʒ] N *TV* rémanence *f* à l'extinction

afterlife ['ɑːftəlaɪf] N **1** *Rel* au-delà *m*, vie *f* après la mort; **we shall meet in the a.** nous nous retrouverons dans l'au-delà **2** *(later life)* **in a.** plus tard dans la vie

aftermarket ['ɑːftəmɑːkɪt] N *St Exch* marché *m* secondaire

aftermath ['ɑːftəmæθ, -mɑːθ] N **1** *(of event)* suites *fpl*; **the a. of war** *(aftereffects)* les répercussions *fpl ou* le contrecoup de la guerre; *(period)* l'après-guerre *m*; **in the immediate a. of the accident** immédiatement après l'accident **2** *Agr (second mowing or crop)* regain *m*

aftermost ['ɑːftəməʊst] ADJ *Naut* le plus en arrière, le plus à l'arrière

afternoon [ɑːftə'nuːn] N après-midi *m ou f inv*; **this a.** cet(te) après-midi; **in the a.** *(pendant)* l'après-midi; **early/late (on) this a.** en début/en fin d'après-midi; **on a sunny a.** par un(e) après-midi ensoleillé(e); **on Tuesday a.** mardi après-midi; **on the a. of Wednesday 22 March** *(dans)* l'après-midi du mercredi 22 mars; **at two o'clock in the a.** à deux heures de l'après-midi; **good a.!**, *Fam* **a.!** *(hello)* bonjour!; *(goodbye)* au revoir!; **to work afternoons** travailler l'après-midi

ADV *esp Am* **afternoons** *(pendant)* l'après-midi

▸▸ *Cin, Theat* **a. performance** matinée *f*, **a. tea** = thé *m* pris avec une légère collation dans le cours de l'après-midi

afterpains ['ɑːftəpeɪnz] NPL *Obst* tranchées *fpl*

afters ['ɑːftəz] NPL *(with sing or pl verb) Br Fam* dessert *m*; **what's for a.?** qu'est-ce qu'il y a comme dessert?; **there was ice cream for a.** il y avait de la glace en dessert *ou* pour le dessert

aftersales ['ɑːftəseɪlz] ADJ *Com* après-vente *inv*

▸▸ **a. department** service *m* après-vente; **a. marketing** marketing *m* après-vente, MAV *m*; **a. service** service après-vente

aftershave ['ɑːftəʃeɪv] ADJ *(lotion)* après-rasage *inv*

N *(lotion f)* après-rasage *m*, *pl* après-rasages

aftershock ['ɑːftəʃɒk] N *(of earthquake)* réplique *f*

aftersun ['ɑːftəsʌn] N *(crème f)* après-soleil *m*, *pl* après-soleils

▸▸ **a. cream** crème après-soleil

aftertaste ['ɑːftəteɪst] N arrière-goût *m*, *pl* arrière-goûts

afterthought ['ɑːftəθɔːt] N réflexion *f* après coup; **to be an a.** *(of sth added)* être un rajout de dernière minute; *Fam Hum* **Susan was an a.** Susan est arrivée bien plus tard; **as an a.** après coup; **as an a., why not go twice?** pourquoi ne pas y aller deux fois?; **it's just an a., but why …?** ce n'est qu'une idée qui me vient maintenant, mais pourquoi …?

afterward ['ɑːftəwəd] ADV *esp Am* = **afterwards**

afterwards ['ɑːftəwədz] ADV *esp Br* après, ensuite; **a. they went home** ensuite *ou* après ils sont rentrés chez eux; **I regretted it a.** par la suite, je l'ai regretté; **a long time a.** longtemps après; **soon** *or* **shortly a.** peu de temps après

afterworld ['ɑːftəwɜːld] N au-delà *m inv*

Aga® ['ɑːgə] N = cuisinière *f* en fonte à l'ancienne

AGAIN [ə'gen]	
de nouveau **1** ▪ encore **1**	
▪ de plus **2** ▪ d'ailleurs **2** ▪ en outre **2**	
▪ d'un autre côté **3**	

ADV **1** de nouveau, encore; **once a.** encore une fois, une fois de plus; **hello, it's me a.!** bonjour, c'est encore moi!; *Fam* **not you a.!** non, encore toi!; *Fam* **not spaghetti a.!** pas encore des spaghettis!; **don't do it a.!** ne recommencez pas!; **never a.!** *(after bad experience)* plus jamais!; *Lit, Fml* **never a. will a king rule this land** plus jamais un roi ne régnera dans ce pays; **I'm not going to that shop a.** je ne remettrai jamais les pieds dans ce magasin; **a. and a., time and (time) a.** maintes et maintes fois; **I have told you so a. and a.** je vous l'ai dit vingt fois *ou* cent fois; **now and a.** de temps en temps, de temps à autre; **as much a.** deux fois autant; **half as much a.** moitié plus; **different a.** encore différent; **she was wearing something different a.** elle était encore habillée différemment; **to begin a.** recommencer; **to come a.** revenir; **he never came back a.** il n'est plus jamais revenu; **I've seen him a.** je l'ai revu; **I hope I shall find it a.** j'espère bien le retrouver; *Fam* **what was your name a.?** rappelez-moi votre nom; **what was that a.?** *(could you say that again)* comment?

2 *(rhetorical)* de plus, d'ailleurs, en outre; **a., I am not sure that …** d'ailleurs, je ne suis pas sûr que …

3 *(on the other hand)* **(then) a.** d'un autre côté; **then a., he may have forgotten** par ailleurs, il se peut qu'il ait oublié; **then a., others may disagree** d'un autre côté, certains peuvent ne pas être d'accord

AGAINST [ə'genst, *occ* ə'geɪnst] **PREP 1** *(in opposition to)* contre; **to fight a. sb** se battre contre qn; **to fight a. sth** *(against crime, cancer)* lutter contre qch; **to march a. the enemy** marcher à l'ennemi; **she was a. the idea** elle était opposée à l'idée; **to be a. abortion/nationalization** être contre l'avortement/la nationalisation; **to be a. sb** être contre qn, être opposé à qn; **what have you got a. him/going to Paris?** qu'est-ce que tu as contre lui/le fait d'aller à Paris?; **to have nothing a. sth** ne rien avoir contre qch; **the war set brother a. brother** la guerre a opposé des hommes à leurs frères; **a. my will** contre mon gré; **it was a. my instincts/principles** ça allait à l'encontre de mes instincts/principes; **to act a. the law** agir illégalement; **it's a. the law** c'est illégal *ou* contraire à la loi; **a. the rules** contraire au règlement; **conditions are a. us** les conditions nous sont défavorables; **there is no law a. it** il n'y a pas de loi qui s'y oppose; *Tex* **a. the nap** à rebrousse-poil; **it goes a. nature** c'est contre nature; **it was a race a. time** ça a été une véritable course contre la montre; **to be insured a. fire/theft** être assuré contre les incendies/le vol; **a. all risks** contre tous les risques

2 *(as protection from)* **to warn sb a. sb/sth** mettre qn en garde contre qn/qch; **protected a. the cold** protégé contre le froid; **a. this eventuality** pour parer à cette éventualité; **to vaccinate sb a. smallpox/malaria** vacciner qn contre la variole/la malaria

3 *(in contact with)* **leaning a. the wall** appuyé contre le mur; **to place sth a. a wall** adosser qch à un mur; **he banged his head a. the wall** il s'est cogné la tête contre le mur; **a cross is placed a. each name** *(beside)* une croix est placée à côté de chaque nom

4 *(in comparison)* **three deaths this year (as) a. thirty in 2002** trois morts cette année contre trente en 2002; **a. this must be set their extreme youth** en contrepartie il faut tenir compte de leur extrême jeunesse; **to check sth a. a list** vérifier qch d'après une liste; **to rise/fall a. the dollar** augmenter/chuter par rapport au dollar

5 *(in contrast to)* **to show up a. a background** se détacher sur un fond; **she was silhouetted a. the sky** sa silhouette se détachait sur le ciel; **the red stood out a. the grey** le rouge contrastait avec le gris; **a. the light** à contre-jour

6 *Fin* en contrepartie de; **to issue a ticket a. payment of …** remettre un ticket en contrepartie du paiement de …

---

agape [ə'geɪp] **ADV**, **ADJ** bouche bée; **to stand a.** rester bouche bée; **with mouth a.** bouche bée

agar(-agar) ['eɪgə('reɪgə)r] **N** agar-agar *m*, gélose *f*

agaric ['ægərɪk] **N** *(toadstool)* agaric *m*; **fly a.**

(amanite *f*) tue-mouches *m inv*, fausse oronge *f*

agate ['ægət] **N** *Miner* agate *f*; **an a. brooch** une broche en agate

agave [ə'gɑːvɪ] **N** *(plant)* agave *m*

AGC [eɪdʒiː'siː] **N** *(abbr Automatic Gain Control)* *(in audio)* antifading *m*

AGE [eɪdʒ] **N 1** âge *m*; **to be past middle a.** être sur le retour; **twenty years of a.** âgé de vingt ans; **what a. is she?, what's her a.?** quel âge a-t-elle?; **children of their own a.** des enfants de leur âge; **he's your a.** il a ton âge; **she's the same a. as me** *or* **as I am** elle a le même âge que moi; **they're the same a., they're of an a.** ils sont du même âge, ils ont le même âge; **when I was your a.** quand j'avais votre âge; **when you're my a.** quand vous aurez mon âge; **he doesn't look his a.** il ne fait pas son âge; *Fam* **act** *or* **be your a.!** ne fais pas l'enfant!; **at your a. you should know** à ton âge, tu devrais savoir; **at that a. children need a lot of attention** c'est un âge où les enfants demandent beaucoup d'attention; **fifteen is the worst a.** quinze ans est l'âge le plus difficile; **at the a. of thirty-three** à l'âge de trente-trois ans; **I'm at an a. where I question things more** je suis arrivé à un âge où l'on se pose davantage de questions; **to be of an a. to marry** être en âge de se marier; **people of all ages** des gens de tout âge; **people over the a. of fifty** les gens de plus de cinquante ans

2 *(old)* **a.** vieillesse *f*; **wisdom comes with a.** la sagesse vient avec l'âge; **a. has not been kind to her** elle est marquée par l'âge; **the house is falling to pieces with a.** la maison tombe de vieillesse *ou* de vétusté; **a tree of great a.** un très vieil arbre; **the car's beginning to show its a.** la voiture commence à donner des signes de vieillesse; **you're showing your a.!** *(remembering things like that etc)* tu es d'un autre âge!; *(you've lost touch)* tu te fais vieux!; *Hum* **a. before beauty** c'est le privilège de l'âge

3 *(adulthood)* **to be of a.** être majeur; **to come of a.** atteindre sa majorité; **coming of a.** entrée *f* en majorité; **to be under a.** *Law* être mineur; *(not old enough to buy alcohol etc)* ne pas avoir l'âge

4 *(era)* âge *m*, époque *f*, siècle *m*, ère *f*; **the a. we live in** notre siècle, le siècle où nous vivons; **in our a.** à notre époque; **in an earlier a. this wouldn't have been tolerated** il fut un temps où on n'aurait pas toléré cela; **she is the product of an earlier a.** elle est d'un autre temps; **in this a. of consumerism** en cette ère de consumérisme; **through the ages** à travers les âges *ou* les siècles; **the A. of Steam/the Dinosaurs** l'ère de la vapeur/des dinosaures

5 *Fam (a long time)* **it's ages** *or* **an a. since I saw him, I haven't seen him for ages** il y a une éternité que je ne l'ai pas vu; **I've been waiting (for) ages** cela fait une éternité que j'attends; **you'll be here for ages yet** tu en as encore pour un bon bout de temps; **it takes them ages to get dressed** ils mettent *ou* ça leur prend une éternité pour s'habiller; **it's expensive, but it lasts for ages** c'est cher, mais ça dure très longtemps

VI *(*aged [eɪdʒd]*, ageing, aging* ['eɪdʒɪŋ]*)* vieillir, prendre de l'âge; **to a. ten years** vieillir de dix ans; **he had aged beyond recognition** il avait tellement vieilli qu'on ne le reconnaissait plus

VT 1 *(of clothes etc)* vieillir; **the years had aged him** il avait beaucoup vieilli

2 *Ind etc (wine, whisky, wood)* vieillir

▸▸**a. of consent** = âge légal auquel on peut se marier ou avoir des rapports sexuels; **a. group** tranche *f ou* classe *f* d'âge; **the 15-to-20 a. group** le groupe *ou* la classe des 15-20 ans; **a. limit** limite *f* d'âge;

a. mix éventail *m* d'âges; *Hist* **A. of Reason** siècle des Lumières; **a. ring** *(on tree)* cerne *m*

aged¹ ['eɪdʒɪd] **ADJ** *Lit* âgé, vieux, *f* vieille; **an a. man** un vieillard
NPL the a. les personnes *fpl* âgées
▸▸**a.** *Acct* **creditor** créancier *m* âgé; *Acct* **a. debt** créance *f* âgée

aged² ['eɪdʒd] **ADJ PRED 1** *(of the age of)* **a. twenty** âgé de vingt ans **2** *(older)* **I found him greatly a.** je l'ai trouvé bien vieilli

ageing ['eɪdʒɪŋ] **ADJ 1** *(person, population)* vieillissant; *(industry)* déclinant; *(car)* qui prend/prenait de l'âge **2** *(making sb look older) (clothes)* qui vieillissent
N *(of person, wine etc)* vieillissement *m*; *(of person)* sénescence *f*
▸▸**a. process** processus *m* de vieillissement

ageism ['eɪdʒɪz(ə)m] **N** âgisme *m*

ageist ['eɪdʒɪst] **ADJ** *(policy etc)* âgiste, qui défavorise les personnes âgées; **or would that be a.?** ou est-ce que ce serait de la discrimination contre les personnes âgées?

ageless ['eɪdʒlɪs] **ADJ 1** sans âge; *(young-looking)* toujours jeune **2** *(eternal)* éternel

agency ['eɪdʒənsɪ] **N 1** *Com* agence *f*; **to have the sole a. for a firm** être le représentant exclusif d'une maison; **aid a.** association *f* d'aide aux pays en voie de développement; **news** *or* **press a.** agence de presse **2** *(action)* action *f*, opération *f*; **the a. of water** l'action de l'eau; **through sb's a.** par l'entremise *ou* l'intermédiaire de qn **3** *esp Am (government department)* organisme *m* gouvernemental
▸▸*Com* **a. agreement** accord *m* de représentation; *Com* **a. contract** contrat *m* d'agence; **a. copy** *(from press agency)* dépêche *f* d'agence; **a. fee** frais *mpl* d'agence; *Banking* commission *f* de gestion; **a. work** travail *m* pour une agence

agenda [ə'dʒendə] **N** *(of meeting)* ordre *m* du jour, programme *m*; **question on the a.** question *f* à l'ordre du jour; **what's on the a. for today?** qu'est-ce qu'il y a à l'ordre du jour?; *Fig* qu'est-ce qu'il y a de prévu aujourd'hui?; **to have a full a.** avoir un programme très chargé; *Fig* **drugs are back on the a.** la drogue revient à la une de l'actualité; **the problem of the homeless doesn't come very high on the government's a.** le problème des sans-abri ne figure pas parmi les priorités du gouvernement; **hidden a.** des projets *mpl* secrets
▸▸**a. setting** fonction *f* d'agenda

Note that the French word **agenda** is a false friend and is never a translation for the English word **agenda**. It means **diary**.

agent ['eɪdʒənt] **N 1** *Com* agent *m*, représentant, -ante; *(of actor, writer etc)* agent; **a. for the firm of …** représentant, -ante de la maison …; **sole a.** agent exclusif; *Pol* **(election) a.** directeur, -trice de campagne électorale. **2** *(secret)* **a.** agent *m* secret; **double a.** agent double **3** *(instrument)* agent *m*; **to be the a. of sth** être le moteur *ou* la cause de qch; **the a. of change was the revolution** la révolution était le moteur du changement; **she was the a. of her own downfall** elle a été l'artisan de sa propre perte **4** *(chemical, therapeutic etc)* agent *m* **5** *Comput (software)* logiciel *m* client
▸▸**a. middleman** agent intermédiaire; **a. provocateur** *(agent)* provocateur *m*

age-old **ADJ ATTRIB** *(custom etc)* séculaire

agglomerate¹ [ə'glɒmərət] **ADJ** *Fml* aggloméré
N *Geol* agglomérat *m*

agglomerate² [ə'glɒməreɪt] **VT** agglomérer

VI s'agglomérer

agglomeration [əglɒmə'reɪʃən] **N** agglomération *f*

agglutinate [ə'glu:tɪneɪt] *Physiol, Biol, Ling* **VT** agglutiner

VI s'agglutiner

agglutination [əglu:tɪ'neɪʃən] **N** agglutination *f*

aggrandize [ə'grændaɪz] **VT** *(state)* agrandir; *(one's importance, role)* grossir, grandir

aggrandizement [ə'grændɪzmənt] **N** *(of state etc)* agrandissement *m*; **they're doing it purely for their own a.** ils ne font cela que pour se grandir aux yeux des autres

aggravate ['ægrəveɪt] **VT 1** *(mistake, difficulty, situation)* aggraver; *(evil)* empirer; *(wound, quarrel)* envenimer; *(indignation, pain)* augmenter **2** *Fam (annoy, anger)* (person) agacer, exaspérer

aggravating ['ægrəveɪtɪŋ] **ADJ 1** *(circumstance)* aggravant **2** *Fam (exasperating)* exaspérant, agaçant; **I've had a very a. day** j'ai passé une journée atroce; **it's very a.** c'est vraiment agaçant

aggravation [ægrə'veɪʃən] **N 1** *(of situation, crime, illness)* aggravation *f*, *(of wound, quarrel)* envenimement *m* **2** *Fam (of person)* exaspération *f*, agacement *m*; **he does nothing but cause a.** il ne fait qu'embêter le monde; **I don't want to give** *or* **cause any more a.** je ne veux plus embêter qui que ce soit **3** *Fam (cause of aggravation)* circonstance *f* aggravante

aggregate¹ ['ægrɪgət] **ADJ ATTRIB 1** collectif; *Econ* global, -aux; **for an a. period of three years** pendant trois ans en tout **2** *Bot, Geol* agrégé

N 1 *(total)* ensemble *m*, total *m*; **world aggregates** totaux mondiaux; **a complex a. of forces** un assemblage complexe de forces; **in the a.** dans l'ensemble; *esp Sp* **on a.** au total; **Milan won on a.** c'est Milan qui a totalisé le plus de points **2** *Phys* masse *f*, assemblage *m*, agrégation *f*; *Chem, Miner* agrégat *m* **3** *Constr* granulat *m*

►► *Fin* **a. amount** montant *m* global; *Com, Econ* **a. economic activity** ensemble *m* des activités économiques; *Fin* **a. figure** chiffre *m* global; *Com* **a. output** production *f* globale

aggregate² ['ægrɪgeɪt] **VT 1** *Phys* agréger **2** *(group together) (various categories)* rassembler, regrouper

VI *Phys* s'agréger

aggregation [ægrɪ'geɪʃən] **N 1** *Phys* agrégation *f*, agglomération *f* **2** *Miner* agrégat *m*

aggression [ə'greʃən] **N 1** *(attack)* agression *f*; **an act of a.** une agression; **war of a.** guerre *f* d'agression **2** *(aggressiveness)* agressivité *f*

aggressive [ə'gresɪv] **ADJ 1** *(violent etc)* agressif (**towards** envers) **2** *(management, sales policy)* énergique, dynamique; *(chess player)* qui attaque

►► *Psy* **a. impulse** impulsion *f* agressive

aggressively [ə'gresɪvlɪ] **ADV 1** *(to behave)* d'une manière agressive; *(to say)* d'un ton agressif; *(to look at)* d'un air agressif **2** *(to sell)* énergiquement, avec dynamisme; *(to push sth through)* avec vigueur, vigoureusement; **to play a.** avoir un jeu offensif

aggressiveness [ə'gresɪvnɪs] **N 1** *(violent nature)* agressivité *f* **2** *(of management style, sales policy)* dynamisme *m*

aggressor [ə'gresər] **N** agresseur *m*

►► **a. nation** pays *m* agresseur

aggrieved [ə'gri:vd] **ADJ** *(expression, tone)* vexé; **to be** *or* **feel a.** se sentir lésé (**at, by** de); *Law* **the a. party** la partie lésée

aggro ['ægrəʊ] **N** *Br Fam* **1** *(hassle)* enquiquinement *m*; **it's not worth the a.** ça ne vaut pas le coup de s'enquiquiner; **there's a. with her all the time** on s'accroche tout le temps avec elle; **don't give me any more a.** arrête de m'enquiquiner; **can you do this for once without any a.?** est-ce que pour une fois tu pourrais faire ça sans m'embêter? **2** *(fighting)* bagarre(s) *f(pl)*, grabuge *m*; **to look for some a.** chercher la bagarre; **there was a bit of a. at the pub last night** il y a eu du grabuge *ou* ça a chauffé au pub hier soir

aghast [ə'gɑ:st] **ADJ** horrifié (**at** de); **to stand a.** en rester *ou* en être tout pantois; **they watched a. as ...** horrifiés, ils regardaient ...

agile ['ædʒaɪl] **ADJ** *(person, mind, limbs, movement)* agile

agilely ['ædʒaɪllɪ] **ADV** *(to move, jump)* agilement, avec agilité; *(to argue)* adroitement

agility [ə'dʒɪlɪtɪ] **N** agilité *f*

aging ['eɪdʒɪŋ] **ADJ, N** = **ageing**

agio ['ædʒɪəʊ] **N** *Fin* **1** *(price)* agio *m* **2** *(business)* commerce *m* du change

agitate ['ædʒɪteɪt] **VT** *(liquid, mind)* agiter

VI **to a. for/against sth** mener une campagne en faveur de/contre qch

agitated ['ædʒɪteɪtɪd] **ADJ** *(water, person)* agité; **now don't get a.!** allons, ne t'agite pas comme ça!

agitatedly ['ædʒɪteɪtɪdlɪ] **ADV** *(to act)* de manière agitée; *(to say)* avec agitation, d'une voix agitée

agitation [ædʒɪ'teɪʃən] **N** *(of air, sea, person)* agitation *f*; *Pol* agitation, troubles *mpl*; **the a. for a change in the law** la campagne en faveur d'un changement de la loi; **in a state of a.** agité; **they arrived in a state of considerable a.** ils étaient fort agités quand ils sont arrivés

agitator ['ædʒɪteɪtər] **N 1** *(person)* agitateur, -trice; *(for sth)* contestataire *mf* **2** *(machine)* agitateur *m*

agitprop ['ædʒɪtprɒp] **N** *Pol* agit-prop *f inv*

aglitter [ə'glɪtər] **ADJ PRED** brillant; **her eyes were a. with mischief** ses yeux pétillaient de malice

aglow [ə'gləʊ] **ADJ PRED** enflammé, embrasé; **the sky was a.** le ciel était embrasé; **to be a. with colour** briller de vives couleurs; *Fig* **face a. with delight** visage rayonnant de joie *ou* tout épanoui; *Fig* **a. with health** resplendissant de santé

AGM [eɪdʒi:'em] **N** *(abbr* **annual general meeting)** AGA *f*, AG *f*

agnostic [æg'nɒstɪk] **ADJ, N** agnostique *mf*

agnosticism [æg'nɒstɪsɪz(ə)m] **N** agnosticisme *m*

ago [ə'gəʊ] **ADV** **ten years a.** il y a dix ans; **he arrived an hour a.** il est arrivé il y a une heure; *(in this place)* il est là depuis une heure; **a little while a., a short time a.** tout à l'heure; **long a.** il y a longtemps; **long, long a.** il y a très, très longtemps; **not long a.** il n'y a pas longtemps; **not so long a.** il n'y a pas si longtemps; **no longer a. than the last century** pas plus loin qu'au siècle dernier; **how long a. is it since ...?** combien de temps y a-t-il que ...?, depuis combien de temps ...?; **as long a. as 1840** déjà en 1840, dès 1840; **I knew her long a.** je l'ai connue dans le temps; **that was years a.** ça fait des années de cela; **how long a. was that?** il y a combien de temps de cela?

agog [ə'gɒg] **ADV, ADJ** **to be all a. (with excitement)** être agité *ou* en émoi (**about sth** à cause de qch); **everyone was a.** tout le monde était en émoi; **he was a. to hear the latest news** il brûlait d'impatience d'apprendre les dernières nouvelles; **she was a. at

the news** elle était stupéfiée par cette nouvelle

agonize ['ægənaɪz] **VI 1** *(worry)* se ronger les sangs, se tourmenter; **to a. over the smallest details** se tourmenter à propos du moindre détail; **you shouldn't a. so much about these decisions** tu ne devrais pas te ronger les sangs comme ça à propos de ces décisions **2** *Lit (suffer)* être au supplice *ou* au martyre

> Note that the French verb **agoniser** is a false friend and is never a translation for the English verb to **agonize**. It means **to be dying**.

agonized ['ægənaɪzd] **ADJ** *(cry)* d'angoisse; **with an a. expression (on her face)** le visage déchiré par l'angoisse; **an a. look** un regard angoissé *ou* plein d'angoisse

agonizing ['ægənaɪzɪŋ] **ADJ** *(pain, worry, death)* atroce; *(sight)* navrant, angoissant; *(situation, silence, wait)* angoissant; *(decision, choice, dilemma)* pénible

N angoisse *f*; **to come to a decision without any a. over the consequences** parvenir à une décision sans se tourmenter sur ses conséquences; **why all this a. about something that can't be helped?** pourquoi se tourmenter à propos de quelque chose qu'on ne peut pas changer?

agonizingly ['ægənaɪzɪŋlɪ] **ADV** *(painful, difficult)* atrocement; **a. slow** d'une lenteur insupportable

agony ['ægənɪ] **N 1** *(anguish)* angoisse *f*; **in an a. of fear** saisi d'une peur atroce; **to be in an a. of suspense** attendre avec angoisse; **to be in an a. of doubt** être en proie à un doute terrible; **the a. of homelessness** le calvaire des sans-abri; **the a. of watching a child die** la douleur insoutenable de voir mourir un enfant; **to suffer agonies, to be in a.** être au supplice *ou* au martyre; *Fam* **it's a. walking in these shoes** c'est un véritable supplice de marcher avec ces chaussures; *Fam* **to pile** *or* **put on the a.** forcer la dose; **it was a. to watch them lose** c'était atroce de les voir perdre **2** *Lit (death)* agonie *f*

►► *Br* **a. aunt** = responsable *mf* du courrier du cœur; **a. column** courrier *m* du cœur

> Note that the French word **agonie** is a false friend. It means **death throes**.

agoraphobia [æg(ə)rə'fəʊbɪə] **N** *Psy* agoraphobie *f*; **to have a.** souffrir d'agoraphobie

agoraphobic [æg(ə)rə'fəʊbɪk] **ADJ, N** *Psy* agoraphobe *mf*; **to be (an) a.** souffrir d'agoraphobie, être agoraphobe

agrarian [ə'greərɪən] **ADJ** *(law, measure)* agraire; *(party)* agrarien

N *Pol* agrarien, -ienne

agree [ə'gri:] **VT 1** *(reach agreement on)* *(price, conditions etc)* s'accorder *ou* se mettre d'accord sur; **to be agreed** *(date)* à convenir; *(price)* à débattre; **(are we) agreed?** (nous sommes) d'accord?; **unless otherwise agreed** sauf arrangement contraire; **to a. to do sth** se mettre d'accord pour faire qch; **as agreed** comme convenu

2 *(concur)* **I a. that's expensive, but ...** c'est cher, j'en conviens, mais ...; **I a. that he was mistaken, but ...** j'admets qu'il s'est trompé, mais ...; **don't you a. that ...?** ne croyez-vous pas que ...?; **everyone agrees that he's the best singer** tout le monde s'accorde à dire que c'est le meilleur chanteur

3 *(consent)* **to a. to do sth** accepter *ou* convenir de faire qch, consentir à faire qch; **to a. to differ** accepter ses différences (**on** *or* **about sth** sur qch); **everyone agrees that ...** tout le monde accepte que ...; **it is generally agreed that ...** il est généralement admis que …; **he agreed to let us go home** il nous a permis de rentrer à la maison

4 *(accept, approve) (statement, plan)* accepter; *Acct* **to a. the accounts** *or* **the books** faire accorder les livres; **the figures were agreed between the accountants** les chiffres ont été acceptés (d'un commun accord) par les experts-comptables

VI 1 *(be of same opinion, concur)* être d'accord (**about** sur); *(after discussion)* se mettre d'accord (**about** sur); **I quite** *or* **entirely a.** je suis entièrement d'accord; **everyone agrees** tout le monde est d'accord; **I'm afraid I can't a.** *(with you, him etc)* j'ai bien peur de ne pas être du même avis; **I think it's too expensive, and Peter agrees** je pense que c'est trop cher, et Peter est d'accord avec moi *ou* est du même avis; **in the end she agreed** *(that it was too expensive)* elle a fini par l'admettre; **it's expensive, I a., but …** c'est cher, j'en conviens *ou* je suis d'accord, mais …; **I couldn't a. more!** je suis tout à fait d'accord!

2 *(match) (of statements, totals, facts etc)* s'accorder, concorder; *(of ideas, opinions)* concorder, coïncider; *Gram* s'accorder

3 *(accept)* consentir (**to** à); **she'll never a.** elle n'acceptera jamais *ou* ne sera jamais d'accord; **how did he get them to a.?** comment a-t-il fait pour qu'ils acceptent?; *Mktg* **to a. and counter** approuver et contre-argumenter

▶ **agree on VT INSEP 1** *(of people) (point)* être d'accord sur; *(after discussion)* se mettre d'accord sur; *(date)* se mettre d'accord sur, convenir de; **we a. on the need for research** nous concordons sur la nécessité de faire des recherches; *Law* **conditions agreed on** conditions *fpl* acceptées d'un commun accord **2** *(of books, versions etc) (point)* s'accorder sur

▶ **agree to VT INSEP** *(accept) (condition, proposal)* accepter; **to a. to sth being done** accepter que qch se fasse; **they have agreed to your visiting us** ils ont accepté que *ou* ils veulent bien que tu viennes nous voir

▶ **agree upon VT INSEP = agree on**

▶ **agree with VT INSEP 1** *(be of same opinion as) (person)* être du même avis que, être d'accord avec; **he entirely agrees with you** il est entièrement d'accord avec vous, il est entièrement de votre avis; **they a. with each other** ils sont du même avis; *Fam* **I couldn't a. with you more!** tu l'as bien dit!; **to a. with a theory** accepter une théorie; **to a. with a decision** approuver une décision; *Fam* **I don't a. with all this violence on television** je n'approuve pas toute cette violence à la télé **2** *(suit)* convenir à, réussir à; *(of food)* réussir à; **the climate doesn't a. with him** le climat ne lui convient pas *ou* ne lui réussit pas **3** *(coincide with) (what person said)* concorder avec, être en accord avec; *Gram* **the verb agrees with the subject in number** le verbe s'accorde en nombre avec le sujet

agreeable [ə'griːəb(ə)l] **ADJ 1** *(pleasant)* agréable (**to** à); *(person)* aimable (**to** envers); **if that is a. to you** si cela vous convient **2** *(willing)* **to be a. to sth/to doing sth** consentir à qch/à faire qch, accepter qch/de faire qch; **I am (quite) a.** je veux bien

agreeably [ə'griːəblɪ] **ADV** agréablement

agreed [ə'griːd] **ADJ** *(price, time etc)* convenu **INT** entendu!, soit!, d'accord!; **it was expensive, a., but …** c'était cher, soit *ou* d'accord, mais …

▶▶ **a. statement** *(in the media)* déclaration *f* commune

agreement [ə'griːmənt] **N 1** *(contract) (between people, countries)* accord *m* (**on, about** sur); **collective (wage)** convention *f* collective (des salaires); **to enter into** *or* **conclude an a. with sb** passer un accord *ou* un contrat avec qn; **to have an a. with sb**

avoir conclu *ou* passé un accord avec qn; **to hold sb to an a.** faire respecter un accord à qn; **our a. was that …** nous avions convenu que …; **to come to** *or* **arrive at** *or* **reach an a. with sb** se mettre d'accord avec qn; *(compromise)* s'accommoder *ou* s'arranger avec qn; **to work out an a.** parvenir à un accord; et Peter se mettre d'accord avec qn; **to sign a legal agreement (to do sth)** s'engager (par) devant notaire (à faire qch); **an a. has been concluded between the two parties** un accord est intervenu entre les deux parties; *Com* **as per a.** comme (il a été) convenu; **by mutual a.** d'un commun accord; **marketing a.** accord de commercialisation

2 the proposal met with unanimous a. la proposition a été reçue à l'unanimité; **to be in a. with sb** être d'accord avec qn; **to be in a. with a decision** approuver une décision; **there was a. on all sides that a change would be welcome** de toute part on convenait de l'opportunité d'un changement

3 *(match), Gram* accord *m* (**with** avec); **to be in a. with** *(facts)* concorder avec; *(rules)* être conforme à, être en conformité avec; **a. of adjectives** accord des adjectifs [SEE GRAMMAR B9; B38]

> Note that the French word **agrément** is a false friend. Its most common meaning is **pleasure.**

agribusiness ['ægrɪbɪznɪs] **N** agro-alimentaire *m*

agrichemical [ægrɪ'kemɪk(ə)l] **N** *esp Am* = **agrochemical**

agricultural [ægrɪ'kʌltʃər(ə)l] **ADJ** agricole; **East Anglia is very a.** l'East Anglia est une région très agricole

▶▶ **a. college** = école *f* supérieure d'agriculture et d'agronomie; **a. economy** économie *f* du secteur agricole; **a. engineer** ingénieur *m* agronome; **a. labourer** ouvrier, -ière agricole; **a. tourism** tourisme *m* agricole; **a. worker** ouvrier, -ère agricole

agriculturalist [ægrɪ'kʌltʃərəlɪst] **N** = **agriculturist**

agriculture ['ægrɪkʌltʃər] **N** agriculture *f*

agriculturist [ægrɪ'kʌltʃərɪst] **N** agriculteur, -trice

agritourism ['ægrɪtʊərɪz(ə)m] **N** tourisme *m* agricole

agrochemical [ægrəʊ'kemɪk(ə)l] **N** *Agr* produit *m* agrochimique

agronomic [ægrə'nɒmɪk] **ADJ** agronomique

agronomist [ə'grɒnəmɪst] **N** agronome *mf*

agronomy [ə'grɒnəmɪ] **N** agronomie *f*

aground [ə'graʊnd] **ADV** *Naut* échoué; **to run a.** *(of ship)* (s')échouer; *Fig (of policy, project etc)* échouer

ague ['eɪgjuː] **N** *Med, Arch* fièvre *f* (paludéenne)

ah [ɑː] **INT** ah!, ha!; **ah, yes, now you come to mention it** euh, oui, maintenant que tu m'en parles

aha [ə'hɑː] **INT** ah! ah!

AHEAD [ə'hed] **ADV 1** devant; **to send sb a.** envoyer qn en avant; **what lies a. for us?** qu'est-ce qui nous attend?, qu'est-ce que l'avenir nous réserve?; **to get a.** *(of person, car etc)* prendre de l'avance; *Fig (in career)* avancer (dans sa carrière); **to draw a.** *(of runner, cyclist etc)* décoller, prendre de l'avance; *Sport* **to be a. on points** avoir des points d'avance; **to be a. of sb** *(in space)* être en avant de qn; **to be a. of the bunch** mener le peloton; **to be a. of one's competitors** devancer ses concurrents; **to go on a.** prendre les devants; **to get a. of sb** dépasser qn; **to be two hours a. of sb** avoir deux heures d'avance sur qn; *Sch* **he is a. of his**

class il est en avance sur sa classe; **to be a. of one's time** être en avance sur son temps; **to be a. of time** *(of person)* arriver/avoir fini/etc avant l'heure; **you've got your best years a. of you** vous avez vos meilleures années devant vous; **to look a.** *(in front)* regarder devant soi; *(to the future)* penser à l'avenir; **to plan a.** faire des projets; **you have to plan a. for a big wedding** il faut s'organiser à l'avance pour un grand mariage; **how far a. should one book?** combien de temps à l'avance faut-il retenir?

2 *Naut* **to be a.** *(of ship)* être sur l'avant *ou* en avant *(du navire)*; **the ship was right a.** le navire était droit devant; **to go a.** aller de l'avant; **full speed a.!** en avant toute!; **wind a.** vent debout; **line a.** en ligne de file, en colonne; **single line a.** ligne de file

ahem [ə'hem] **INT** hum!

ahoy [ə'hɔɪ] **INT** *Naut* **boat/ship a.!** oh(é) du canot/du navire!; **land a.!** terre!

AI [eɪ'aɪ] **N 1** *Comput (abbr artificial intelligence)* IA *f* **2** *Biol abbr* artificial insemination **3** *Pol abbr* Amnesty International

AID [eɪaɪ'diː] **N 1** *Biol (abbr artificial insemination by donor)* IAD *f* **2** *Am Pol abbr* Agency for International Development

aid [eɪd] **N 1** *(help)* aide *f*, assistance *f*, secours *m*; *(to developing countries, for disaster relief)* aide; **with** *or* **by the a. of sb** avec l'aide de qn; **with** *or* **by the a. of sth** à l'aide de qch; **to go to sb's a.** aller *ou* se porter au secours de qn; **collection in a. of …** quête *f* au profit de …; *Fam* **what's (all) this in a. of?** c'est en quel honneur?; *Fam* **what's all this wiring in a. of?** ça sert à quoi tous ces fils?; *Fam* **what's all this noise in a. of?** qu'est-ce que c'est que tout ce bruit?; **mutual a.** entraide *f*, **mutual-a. society** société *f* de secours mutuels *ou* d'assistance mutuelle; **medical a.** soins *mpl* médicaux

2 *(device)* **beauty aids** produits *mpl* de beauté; **hearing** *or* **deaf a.** audiophone *m*; *Sch* **audio-visual aids** matériel *m* audiovisuel; **to act as an a. to international understanding** contribuer à la compréhension entre les nations

VT *(person, company)* aider, venir en aide à; *(sb's recovery)* contribuer à; *(digestion)* faciliter; **to a. one another** s'aider les uns les autres, s'entraider; *Law* **to a. and abet sb** être le complice de qn

▶▶ *Admin* **a. organization** organisme *m* d'aide; **a. worker** *(voluntary)* volontaire *mf*; *(paid)* employé, -ée d'une organisation humanitaire

AIDA [aɪ'iːdə] *Mktg (abbr attention-interest-desire-action)* AIDA

aide [eɪd] **N** aide *mf*, assistant, -ante; *(to president etc)* conseiller, -ère

aide-de-camp, *pl* **aides-de-camp** ['eɪd-də'kɒm] **N** *Mil* aide *m* de camp

aided recall ['eɪdəd] **N** *Mktg* notoriété *f* assistée

aide-mémoire ['eɪdmem'wɑːr] **N** aide-mémoire *m inv*

aiding ['eɪdɪŋ] **N** *Law* **a. and abetting** complicité *f*

AIDS, Aids [eɪdz] **N** *Med* sida *m*; **A.-related** lié au sida

▶▶ **A. clinic** clinique *f* spécialisée dans le traitement du sida; **A. sufferer** sidéen, -enne, malade *mf* atteint(e) du sida; **the A. virus** le virus du sida

aikido [aɪ'kiːdəʊ] **N** *Sport* aïkido *m*

ail [eɪl] **VT** *Arch* **what ails you?** qu'avez-vous? **VI** être souffrant

aileron ['eɪlərɒn] **N** *Aviat* aileron *m*

ailing ['eɪlɪŋ] **ADJ** *(person)* souffrant; *Fig (company, economy)* en mauvaise passe;

the a. state of the economy/country la mauvaise passe dans laquelle se trouve l'économie/le pays

ailment ['eɪlmənt] N mal *m*; childish ailments maladies *mpl* infantiles

AIM [eɪaɪ'em] N *Br St Exch* (*abbr* Alternative Investment Market) = marché *m* hors-cote rattaché à la Bourse de Londres

aim [eɪm] N 1 (*action*) action *f* de viser; to miss one's a. (*with firearm etc*) manquer la cible *ou* son coup; *Fig* frapper à faux; to take a. at sb/sth viser qn/qch; to take a. mettre en joue, viser; he took careful a. il visa avec soin; *Mil* take a.! en joue!; her a. was good elle visait bien
2 (*goal*) but *m*, dessein *m*, visées *fpl*; his a. was to ... son but était de ..., il avait pour but de ...; with the a. of doing sth dans le but *ou* le dessein de faire qch
VT 1 (*stone*) lancer (at à); (*blow*) porter, allonger (at à)
2 (*gun etc*) pointer (at sur); to a. a gun at sb/sth coucher qn/qch en joue avec un fusil, pointer un fusil sur qn; to a. a camera cadrer (at sur)
3 (*remarks, TV programme*) destiner (at à); to a. a criticism at sb adresser une critique à qn; these measures are aimed at reducing unemployment ces mesures visent une réduction du chômage
VI 1 (*with gun etc*) to a. at sb/sth viser qn/qch, mettre *ou* coucher qn/qch en joue; I aimed at the tyres j'ai visé (dans) les pneus
2 *Fig* to a. at becoming sth, to a. to become sth aspirer *ou* viser à devenir qch; what are you aiming at? (*what do you hope to do?*) quel but poursuivez-vous?; (*what do you mean?*) où voulez-vous en venir?; to a. high viser haut; *Fam* I a. to go (*intend*) j'ai l'intention d'y aller; we're aiming for a six a.m. start nous comptons partir à six heures du matin

aiming ['eɪmɪŋ] N *Mil* pointage *m*

aimless ['eɪmlɪs] ADJ sans but, sans objet; (*violence*) gratuit; an a. sort of life une vie désœuvrée; a few a. remarks quelques remarques en l'air

aimlessly ['eɪmlɪslɪ] ADV sans but, sans objet; to wander about a. aller *ou* errer à l'aventure

aimlessness ['eɪmlɪsnɪs] N the a. of their existence leur existence sans but

ain't [eɪnt] *Arch, Sl* CONTR 1 = am not, is not, are not, *see* be 2 = have not, *see* have

AIO [eɪaɪ'əʊ] *Mktg* (*abbr* activities, interests and opinions) AIO
▸▸ A. research étude *f* AIO

air [eər] N 1 air *m*; a change of a. will do me good un changement d'air me fera du bien; we need a change of a. nous avons besoin de changer d'air; in the open a. en plein air, au grand air, à ciel ouvert; high up in the a. très haut dans le ciel; in the a. en l'air, dans les airs; to throw sth (up) in the a. lancer qch en l'air; to fly through the a. voler *ou* voltiger en l'air; war in the a. guerre *f* aérienne
2 *Fig* I can't live on fresh a. je ne vis pas de l'air du temps; to walk on a. être aux anges; to be in the a. (*of rumour*) circuler; (*of idea*) être dans l'air; (*of project*) être encore vague; everything's up in the a. (*uncertain*) rien n'a été décidé pour l'instant; the date is still up in the a. la date n'a pas encore été fixée; our plans are up in the a. again et voilà nos projets qui retombent à l'eau; *Fam* to go up in the a. (*explode*), *Fig* (*in anger*) exploser; there's something in the a. il y a quelque chose dans l'air; *Fam* it's all hot a. c'est du vent; to melt *ou* vanish into thin a. s'évanouir, disparaître
3 *Naut, Lit* (*wind*) brise *f*, vent *m*; there was

no a. il n'y avait pas de vent
4 *Mil, Aviat* (*attack, base, defence etc*) aérien; by a. par avion
5 *Radio, TV* to be on the a. (*of person*) être à l'antenne; (*of programme*) être diffusé; (*of station*) émettre; we're going on the a. in two minutes nous sommes à l'antenne dans deux minutes; you're on (the) a. vous êtes à l'antenne; the station goes off the a. at midnight les programmes finissent à minuit; to put a play on the a. mettre une pièce en ondes *ou* sur les ondes
6 *Mus* air *m*
7 (*look*) air *m*, mine *f*, apparence *f*; he has an a. about him il en impose; to give oneself *or* to put on airs (and graces) se donner des airs
VT 1 (*room*) aérer, ventiler; (*clothing, bedding, duvet etc*) aérer, mettre à l'air
2 *Fig* (*one's opinions, differences*) exposer; (*one's knowledge*) faire parade de, faire étalage de; (*one's feelings*) donner libre cours à
3 *Radio, TV* (*programme*) passer, donner
VI 1 s'aérer
2 *Radio, TV* (*of programme*) passer
▸▸ a. bed matelas *m* pneumatique; *Br Fam Hum* a. biscuit (*fart*) perle *f*, prout *m*; a. brake frein *m* pneumatique; a. broker courtier *m* de l'air; a. cargo fret *m* aérien; a. carrier transporteur *m* aérien; *Br Mil* a. commodore ≃ général *m* de brigade aérienne, *Can* ≃ brigadier-général *m*, *pl* brigadiers-généraux; a. compressor compresseur *m* d'air; *Mil, Aviat* a. cover couverture *f* aérienne; *Tech* a. duct conduite *f* d'air, amenée *f* d'air; a. fare tarif *m* aérien; a. filter ≃ filtre *m* à air; A. Force Armée *f* de l'air, Aviation *f*; a. freshener désodorisant *m* (*pour la maison*); *Tech* a. gauge micromètre *m* pneumatique; a. gun fusil *m* à air comprimé; a. hostess hôtesse *f* de l'air; a. inclusive tour voyage *m* à forfait (par avion) a. injection injection *f* d'air; a. intake prise *f* d'air; *Aviat* a. link liaison *f* aérienne; *Aviat* a. mile mille *m* marin; *Hist* A. Ministry ≃ ministère *m* de l'Air; *Tech* a. passage conduit *m* aérifère; *Bot* a. plant plante *f* aéricole, (plante) épiphyte *m*; a. pocket *Met, Aviat* (*affecting plane*) trou *m* d'air; *Tech* (*in pipe*) poche *f* d'air; *Ecol* a. pollution pollution *f* atmosphérique; *Mil, Aviat* a. power puissance *f* aérienne; *Aviat* a. rage = comportement *m* agressif de certains passagers d'avion; *Mil* a. raid attaque *f* aérienne, raid *m* aérien; *Tech* a. rifle carabine *f* à air comprimé; *Aviat* a. route route *f* aérienne; *Aviat* a. service liaison aérienne; a. show *Com* (*exhibition*) salon *m* de l'aéronautique; *Aviat* (*display*) meeting *m* aérien; a. strikes frappes *fpl* aériennes; *Mil* a. supremacy suprématie *f* aérienne; *Met* a. temperature température *f* ambiante; *Aviat* a. terminal aérogare *f*, *Aviat* a. ticket billet *m* d'avion; *Aviat* a. traffic circulation *f* aérienne, trafic *m* aérien; *Aviat* a. transport transport *m* aérien *ou* par avion; *Aviat* a. travel voyages en avion; *Tech* a. valve soupape *f* (*pour l'air*); a. vent aérateur *m*, buse *f* de ventilation, diffuseur *m*; *Com* a. waybill lettre *f* de transport aérien, connaissement *m* aérien

airbag ['eəbæg] N Air Bag® *m*, sac *m* gonflable

airborne ['eəbɔːn] ADJ 1 (*particles, seeds etc*) en suspension dans l'air; (*disease*) présent dans l'air 2 (*aircraft*) en vol; (*balloon*) en l'air; to become a. (*of aircraft*) décoller; once we are a. une fois que nous aurons décollé 3 *Mil* (*troops, unit*) aéroporté 4 *Aviat* (*equipment, radar*) de bord
▸▸ *Mil* a. attack attaque *f* exécutée par des troupes aéroportées, assaut *m* vertical

airbrush ['eəbrʌʃ] *Art, Phot* N aérographe *m*, pistolet *m* vaporisateur

VT retoucher à l'aérographe
▸ airbrush in VT SEP *Art, Phot* ajouter à l'aérographe
▸ airbrush out VT SEP *Art, Phot* effacer à l'aérographe

airbrushing ['eəbrʌʃɪŋ] N *Art, Phot* peinture *f ou* retouchage *m* à l'aérographe

air-bubble N bulle *f* d'air

airburst ['eəbɜːst] N explosion *f* (en plein ciel)

Airbus® ['eəbʌs] N aérobus *m*, Airbus® *m*

aircon ['eəkɒn] N *Fam* (*abbr* air-conditioning) clim *f*

air-conditioned [-kən'dɪʃənd] ADJ climatisé, à air conditionné

air-conditioning [-kən'dɪʃənɪŋ] N climatisation *f*, *Fam* clim *f*

air-cooled [-kuːld] ADJ refroidi par air
▸▸ *Aut* a. engine moteur *m* à refroidissement par air

air-cooling N refroidissement *m* par air

aircraft ['eəkrɑːft] N INV avion *m*
▸▸ *Naut, Mil* a. carrier porte-avions *m inv*; *Aviat* a. engineering ingénierie *f* aéronautique; a. factory usine *f* d'aviation; a. grounding interdiction *f* de vol; a. identification code code *m* d'identification d'avion; a. manufacturer constructeur *m* d'avions, avionneur *m*

aircraftman, *pl* **aircraftmen** ['eəkrɑːftmən] N *Br* = soldat *m* de la Royal Air Force; leading a. = caporal *m* de la Royal Air Force

aircraftwoman, *pl* **aircraftwomen** ['eəkrɑːftwʊmən, -wɪmɪn] N *Br* = femme *f* soldat de la Women's Royal Air Force; leading a. = femme *f* caporal de la Women's Royal Air Force

aircrew ['eəkruː] N *Aviat* équipage *m*

airdrome ['eədrəʊm] N *Am* aérodrome *m*

airdrop ['eədrɒp] N *Aviat* largage *m* (de charges)

Airedale ['eədeɪl] N (chien *m*) airedale *m*

airer ['eərər] N (*for clothes*) séchoir *m*

airfield ['eəfiːld] N champ *m ou* terrain *m* d'aviation, aérodrome *m*

airflow ['eəfləʊ] N *Tech* écoulement *m* d'air; smooth/turbulent a. écoulement régulier/ turbulent
▸▸ *Am Aut* a. body carrosserie *f* aérodynamique; a. meter débitmètre *m* d'air

airfoil ['eəfɔɪl] N *Am* = aerofoil

airframe ['eəfreɪm] N *Aviat* cellule *f* d'avion, fuselage *m*

air-freight N fret *m* aérien; send it by a. envoyez-le par avion *ou* par air
VT expédier par fret aérien
▸▸ a. consignment note récépissé *m* aérien; a. consolidator groupeur *m* de fret aérien; a. container conteneur-avion *m*, *pl* conteneurs-avions; a. forwarding agent groupeur *m* de fret aérien; a. services messageries *fpl* aériennes

air/fuel mixture N mélange *m* air/ carburant

airhead ['eəhed] N *Sl* tête *f* de linotte, tête en l'air

airhole ['eəhəʊl] N trou *m* de ventilation *ou* d'aération

airily ['eərɪlɪ] ADV avec désinvolture; (*to say*) d'un ton dégagé *ou* désinvolte

airiness ['eərɪnɪs] N 1 (*of building, flat*) caractère *m* spacieux 2 (*casualness*) désinvolture *f*

airing ['eərɪŋ] N 1 (*of room etc*) ventilation *f*, aération *f*; give the room a good a. aère bien la pièce
2 (*of clothes*) give the clothes an a. outside mets ces habits à l'air dehors
3 (*of new car etc*) présentation *f*; they gave

the project/the matter an a. ils ont eu une première discussion à propos du projet/de la question; **to give one's grievances/feelings an a.** exposer ses griefs/ses sentiments

4 *Radio, TV (of programme)* diffusion *f*, transmission *f*

5 *Arch (walk)* (petite) promenade *f*; **to take an a.** prendre l'air

▸▸ **a. cupboard** = placard *m* chauffé où l'on fait sécher le linge

air-kiss vi = faire semblant de faire la bise

airless ['eəlɪs] ADJ **1** *(room, house etc)* privé d'air, qui sent le renfermé **2** *Tech* sans air **3** *(evening etc)* sans air, lourd

airlessness ['eəlɪsnɪs] N **1** *(of room)* manque *m* d'air *ou* d'aération **2** *(of weather)* lourdeur *f*

airlift ['eəlɪft] N pont *m* aérien
▸ vt *(supplies)* transporter par avion; **to a. in/out** *(supplies)* amener/emporter par avion; *(refugees)* amener/évacuer par avion

airline ['eəlaɪn] N **1** *Aviat* ligne *f ou* compagnie *f* aérienne, compagnie d'aviation; **to be an a. pilot** être pilote de ligne **2** *(of diver)* voie *f* d'air
▸▸ *Aviat* **a. club** = programme *m* de fidélisation de la clientèle d'une compagnie aérienne; *Aviat, Com* **a. operator** compagnie aérienne; *Aviat* **a. passenger** passager, -ère des compagnies aériennes; **a. ticket** billet *m* d'avion

airliner ['eəlaɪnər] N avion *m* de ligne

airlock ['eəlɒk] N **1** *Constr (of caisson)* écluse *f ou* sas *m* pneumatique *ou* à air; *Naut, Astronaut* sas **2** *(in pipe)* poche *f* d'air

airmail ['eəmeɪl] ADJ *(paper, envelope)* avion
▸ ADV par avion
▸ N *(service)* poste *f* aérienne, service *m* postal aérien; *(letters etc)* courrier *m* par avion; **by a.** par avion
▸ vt *(letter etc)* envoyer par avion
▸▸ **a. edition** = édition *f* imprimée sur papier très fin; **a. letter** *(letter sent by airmail)* lettre *f* par avion; *(bought at post office)* aérogramme *m*; **a. paper** papier *m* avion; **a. sticker** étiquette *f* par avion

airman, *pl* **airmen** ['eəmən] N **1** *(in general)* aviateur *m* **2** *Am Mil, Aviat* = soldat *m* de la United States Air Force
▸▸ *Am Mil, Aviat* **a. basic** = soldat de la United States Air Force

airpass ['eəpɑːs] N carte *f* d'abonnement de transport aérien

airplane ['eəpleɪn] N *esp Am* avion *m*

airplay ['eəpleɪ] N *Radio* diffusion *f*; **to get** *or* **receive a.** *(of record etc)* passer sur les ondes; **that record is getting a lot of a.** on entend souvent ce disque à la radio

airport ['eəpɔːt] N *Aviat* aéroport *m*; **Geneva A.** l'aéroport de Genève
▸▸ *Mktg* **a. advertising** publicité *f* dans les aéroports; **a. apron** aire *f* de stationnement (des avions); **a. of departure** aéroport de départ; **a. of destination** aéroport de destination; **a. hotel** hôtel *m* d'aéroport; *Fin* **a. landing tax** taxe *f* d'atterrissage; **a. lounge** hall *m* d'aéroport; **a. service charge** taxe d'aéroport; **a. shop** boutique *f* d'aéroport; *Fin* **a. tax** taxe d'aéroport; **a. taxi** taxi *m* desservant l'aéroport

airprox ['eəprɒks] N quasi-collision *f* aérienne

airscrew ['eəskruː] N *Aviat Old-fashioned* hélice *f*

air-sea rescue N sauvetage *m* aéromaritime, sauvetage aérien en mer

airship ['eəʃɪp] N dirigeable *m*

airsick ['eəsɪk] ADJ **to be a.** avoir le mal de l'air

airsickness ['eəsɪknɪs] N mal *m* de l'air

airspace ['eəspeɪs] N *Aviat* espace *m* aérien

airspeed ['eəspiːd] N *Aviat (of plane)* vitesse *f*

airstream ['eəstriːm] N courant *m* d'air

airstrike ['eəstraɪk] N *Mil* raid *m* aérien, attaque *f* aérienne

airstrip ['eəstrɪp] N *Aviat* bande *f ou* piste *f* d'atterrissage

airtight ['eətaɪt] ADJ *(seal)* hermétique; *(container etc)* hermétique, étanche (à l'air)

airtime ['eətaɪm] N **1** *Radio, TV (length of programme)* temps *m* d'antenne; **the subject didn't get much a.** *(during programme)* on n'a pas consacré beaucoup de temps au sujet pendant l'émission **2** *Radio, TV (starting time)* heure *f* où commence l'émission; **five minutes to a.** on est à l'antenne dans cinq minutes **3** *Tel* temps *m* de communication
▸▸ *Tel* **a. provider** société *f* de téléphonie mobile

air-to-air ADJ *Mil (missile etc)* air-air *inv*

air-to-ground ADJ *Mil (missile etc)* air-sol *inv*, air-terre *inv*

air-to-surface ADJ *(missile etc) Mil* air-sol *inv*, *Naut* air-surface *inv*

airwaves ['eəweɪvz] NPL *Radio, TV* ondes *fpl*, ondes hertziennes; **the best DJ on the a.** le meilleur DJ sur les ondes *ou* ondes hertziennes

airway ['eəweɪ] N **1** *Aviat (route)* route *f ou* ligne *f ou* voie *f* aérienne **2** *Med* bronches *fpl* **3** *Am Radio, TV* chaîne *f*
▸▸ *Aviat* **a. marker** balise *f* d'entrée de piste

airwoman, *pl* **airwomen** ['eəwʊmən, -wɪmɪn] N aviatrice *f*

airworthiness ['eəwɜːðɪnɪs] N *Aviat* tenue *f* en l'air, navigabilité *f*; **certificate of a.** certificat *m* de navigabilité

airworthy ['eəwɜːðɪ] ADJ *(aircraft)* en état de prendre l'air, en bon état de vol *ou* de navigabilité; *(certified)* muni d'un certificat de navigabilité; **to be a.** tenir l'air

airy ['eərɪ] ADJ **1** *(room, house)* clair et spacieux **2** *(dress, material)* léger; **the cake was light and a.** le gâteau était très léger **3** *(person, attitude)* insouciant, désinvolte **4** *(promises)* vain, illusoire

airy-fairy ADJ *Fam (person, idea)* farfelu

aisle [aɪl] N **1** *(between seats)* passage *m*; *(in plane)* couloir *m*; *(in bus etc)* couloir central; *(at cinema, theatre, in supermarket)* allée *f*; **he had them rolling in the aisles** il les faisait mourir de rire **2** *(in church)* allée *f*, *Fig* **to walk up the a.** se marier (à l'église)
▸▸ *Mktg* **a. end display** tête *f* de gondole; **a. seat** *(in train, plane)* siège *m* côté couloir

aitch [eɪtʃ] N *(letter)* h *m*; **to drop one's aitches** ne pas prononcer (correctement) les h

ajar [ə'dʒɑːr] ADV, ADJ PRED *(door, window)* entrouvert, entrebâillé; **to swing a.** s'entrouvrir, s'entrebâiller

aka [eɪkeɪ'eɪ] ADV *(abbr also known as)* alias

akimbo [ə'kɪmbəʊ] ADV **with arms a.** les (deux) poings sur les hanches

akin [ə'kɪn] ADJ **a. to sb/sth** apparenté à qn/qch; **feeling a. to fear** sentiment voisin de la peur; **this is a. to treachery** cela s'apparente à la traîtrise

alabaster ['æləbɑːstər, -bɑː-] N albâtre *m*
▸ ADJ ATTRIB **1** *(figurine, vase etc)* en albâtre **2** *Fig (complexion, hands etc)* d'albâtre

à la carte [ælə'kɑːt] ADJ, ADV à la carte

alacrity [ə'lækrɪtɪ] N empressement *m*, promptitude *f*; **he accepted with a.** il a accepté avec enthousiasme, il s'est empressé d'accepter

Aladdin [ə'lædɪn] N Aladin *m*; **the shop is an A.'s cave** *(full of wonderful things)* cette bou-

tique est une véritable caverne d'Ali Baba

alarm [ə'lɑːm] N **1** *(signal)* alarme *f*, alerte *f*, **false a.** fausse alerte; **to raise** *or* **give the a.** donner l'éveil *ou* l'alerte *ou* l'alarme
2 *(fright, anxiety)* alarme *f*, frayeur *f*, **there's no cause for a.** il n'y a aucune raison de s'alarmer; **he hid in a.** effrayé, il s'est caché
3 *(warning device)* avertisseur *m*, alarme *f*, *Fig* **to set (the) a. bells ringing** déclencher l'alerte; *(give rise to suspicion)* mettre la puce à l'oreille de qn
4 *(on clock)* sonnerie *f*, *(clock)* réveil *m*, réveille-matin *m inv*; **to set the a. for six o'clock** mettre le réveil à six heures; **the a. went off at six o'clock** le réveil a sonné à six heures
5 *(of bird etc)* cri *m* d'alarme
▸ vt *(frighten)* effrayer; **to be alarmed at sth** s'alarmer *ou* s'effrayer de qch, être alarmé de qch; **don't be alarmed** ne vous effrayez pas; **there's no need to feel alarmed** inutile de s'alarmer; **the parents looked alarmed** les parents semblaient très inquiets
▸▸ **a. call** *(to wake sleeper)* réveil téléphonique; *(in hotel)* appel *m* de réveil; **a. clock** réveil, réveille-matin; **a. signal** signal *m* d'alarme

alarming [ə'lɑːmɪŋ] ADJ *(news etc)* alarmant, inquiétant

alarmingly [ə'lɑːmɪŋlɪ] ADV d'une manière alarmante *ou* très inquiétante; **the shots were coming a. close** les tirs se rapprochaient dangereusement; **to develop a. fast** se développer à une vitesse alarmante

alarmist [ə'lɑːmɪst] ADJ, N alarmiste *mf*; **don't be such an a.** ne sois pas aussi alarmiste

Alas *abbr* Alaska

alas [ə'læs] INT *Lit, Fml* hélas!

Alaska [ə'læskə] N Alaska *m*; *Culin* **baked A.** omelette *f* norvégienne

alb [ælb] N *Rel* aube *f*

Albania [æl'beɪnɪə] N Albanie *f*

Albanian [æl'beɪnɪən] ADJ albanais
▸ N **1** Albanais, -aise **2** *Ling* albanais *m*

albatross ['ælbətrɒs] N *(bird)* albatros *m*; *Fig* **to be an a. around sb's neck** être un boulet pour qn; **this issue has become an a. around the government's neck** ce problème est devenu un gros handicap pour le gouvernement

albeit [ɔːl'biːɪt] CONJ quoique, bien que; **a brilliant, a. slipshod, writer** un écrivain brillant, bien que négligent

albinism ['ælbɪnɪz(ə)m] N *Biol* albinisme *m*

albino, *pl* **albinos** [æl'biːnəʊ, -əʊz] ADJ *(person)* albinos
▸ N albinos *mf*; **a. rabbit** lapin *m* albinos *ou* russe

Albion ['ælbɪən] N *Lit (England)* Albion *f*, **perfidious A.** la perfide Albion

album ['ælbəm] N **1** *(for photos, comic book)* album *m* **2** *(record)* album *m*

albumen ['ælbjʊmɪn, æl'bjuːmɪn] N **1** *(in egg)* albumen *m* **2** *(in blood)* albumine *f*

albumin ['ælbjʊmɪn, æl'bjuːmɪn] N *Chem* albumine *f*

alchemist ['ælkəmɪst] N alchimiste *m*

alchemy ['ælkəmɪ] N alchimie *f*

alcohol ['ælkəhɒl] N *(drink), Chem* alcool *m*; **I never touch a.** je ne bois jamais d'alcool; **low in a.** à faible teneur en alcool; **to have an a. problem** boire trop
▸▸ **a. abuse** abus *m* d'alcool; **a. content** teneur *f* en alcool

alcoholic [ælkə'hɒlɪk] ADJ alcoolique; **a. drink** boisson *f* alcoolisée
▸ N *(person)* alcoolique *mf*
▸▸ **Alcoholics Anonymous** Alcooliques *mpl* anonymes

alcoholism ['ælkəhɒlɪz(ə)m] N alcoolisme m

alcopop ['ælkəʊpɒp] N prémix m

alcove ['ælkəʊv] N alcôve f; (in wall) niche f; **dining a.** coin m des repas, coin salle à manger

aldehyde ['ældɪhaɪd] N Chem aldéhyde m

alder ['ɔːldər] N (tree) aune m, aulne m

alderman, pl **aldermen** ['ɔːldəmən] N Am (for city) conseiller m municipal; Br (for county) conseiller général

Alderney ['ɔːldənɪ] N Aurigny m

ale [eɪl] N bière f anglaise (légère), ale f; **pale/brown a.** bière blonde/brune

Alec(k) ['ælɪk] N Fam **a smart A.** un(e) je-sais-tout; **I've had enough of his smart A. re-marks** j'en ai assez de ses remarques dé-sobligeantes; **who's the smart A. who forgot to switch it off?** quel est le malin qui a oublié de l'éteindre?

alehouse ['eɪlhaʊs] N Arch taverne f, caba-ret m

alert [ə'lɜːt] N alerte f; **to be on the a.** être sur le qui-vive, être en état d'alerte; **police were on the a. for an escaped prisoner** la police était en état d'alerte à la suite de l'évasion d'un prisonnier; **to be on the a. against an attack** veiller en prévision d'une attaque; **the navy has been put on full a.** l'alerte gé-nérale a été déclarée dans la marine; **they're always on the a. for interesting sto-ries** ils sont toujours à l'affût d'histoires in-téressantes

ADJ **1** (temporarily) alerté, vigilant, éveillé; **to be a. to a danger** être conscient d'un dan-ger **2** (naturally) actif, vif, preste; **a. mind** es-prit m vif ou éveillé

VT alerter; **troops have been alerted** les troupes sont en état d'alerte; **to a. sb to a danger** avertir qn d'un danger; **a noise aler-ted her to the presence of an intruder** un bruit l'avertit de la présence d'un intrus

alertness [ə'lɜːtnɪs] N **1** (of sentry etc) vigi-lance f **2** (of mind) vivacité f

A-level N (in England, Wales and Northern Ireland) **A-levels, A. exams** ≃ baccalauréat m; **he teaches A. physics** ≃ il est professeur de physique en terminale; **he has an A. in maths** il a un diplôme de maths niveau bac; **to take one's A-levels** ≃ passer son bac

> **A-levels**
> Cet examen, qui ouvre l'accès aux étu-des supérieures en Grande-Bretagne, est beaucoup plus spécialisé que le baccalauréat français; il ne comprend que deux ou trois matières (exceptio-nellement quatre). D'autre part, les mentions sont très importantes pour pouvoir choisir l'université où l'on sou-haite faire ses études. En Écosse l'exa-men équivalent aux **A-levels** s'appelle le "Higher" ou "Higher Grade".

Alexander [ælɪg'zɑːndər] N
▸▸**A. the Great** Alexandre le Grand; Med **A. technique** technique f Alexander (visant à limiter les tensions exercées sur le corps en travaillant sur le maintien et les mouve-ments)

Alexandria [ælɪg'zɑːndrɪə] N Alexandrie f

alexandrine [ælɪg'zɑːndraɪn] ADJ, N Liter alexandrin m

alfalfa [æl'fælfə] N (plant) luzerne f

alfresco [æl'freskəʊ] ADJ, ADV en plein air; **a. meal** repas m en plein air

alga, pl **algae** ['ælgə, 'ældʒiː] N Bot algue f

algal ['ælg(ə)l] ADJ des algues

algebra ['ældʒɪbrə] N algèbre f

algebraic(al) [ældʒɪ'breɪɪk, -ɪk(ə)l] ADJ (sign, calculation etc) algébrique

Algeria [æl'dʒɪərɪə] N Algérie f

Algerian [æl'dʒɪərɪən] ADJ algérien
N Algérien, -ienne

Algiers [æl'dʒɪəz] N Alger m

ALGOL ['ælgɒl] N Comput algol m

algorithm ['ælgərɪð(ə)m] N algorithme m

algorithmic [ælgə'rɪðmɪk] ADJ algorithmi-que

alias ['eɪlɪəs] ADV alias
N (pl aliases ['eɪlɪəsɪz]) nom m d'emprunt, faux nom; Comput alias m

aliasing ['eɪlɪəsɪŋ] N Comput aliassage m, crénelage m

alibi ['ælɪbaɪ] N Law alibi m; **to produce an a.** produire ou fournir un alibi; **to establish an a.** prouver ou établir son alibi; **they're using the economic crisis as an a. for their own incompetence** ils se servent de la crise éco-nomique pour déguiser leur propre incompétence
VT trouver un alibi pour

alien ['eɪlɪən] N **1** Law étranger, -ère (non naturalisé, -ée); **illegal a.** clandestin, -ine **2** (from outer space) extra(-)terrestre mf, pl ex-tra(-)terrestres
ADJ **1** Law étranger **2** (from outer space) ex-tra(-)terrestre **3** Fig (foreign) (land, territory, concept) étranger; **a. to** contraire à; **an ac-tion entirely a. to her nature** une action en-tièrement contraire à sa nature; **such thoughts are a. to her** de telles pensées lui sont étrangères

alienable ['eɪlɪənəb(ə)l] ADJ Law (property) aliénable

alienate ['eɪlɪəneɪt] VT **1** (supporters, elec-torate, readers) éloigner; **she has alienated many of her colleagues** elle s'est aliéné beaucoup de ses collègues; **to a. sb from his friends** détacher ou éloigner qn de ses amis; **to a. oneself from sb** se détacher ou s'éloigner de qn; **these young people feel alienated from society** ces jeunes gens se sentent en marge de la société; **to be** or **feel alienated by sb's manner** être rebuté par les manières de qn **2** Law (property etc) aliéner **3** Fin (money) détourner

alienation [eɪlɪə'neɪʃən] N **1** désaffection f **2** Law (of property) aliénation f **3** Psy mental a. aliénation f mentale
▸▸ Theat **a. effect** distanciation f

alight¹ [ə'laɪt] ADJ PRED en feu; **to keep a flame/fire a.** maintenir une flamme/un feu; **to catch a.** prendre feu; **to set sth a.** mettre le feu à qch; Fig **his face was a. with joy** son visage resplendissait de joie; Fig Fam **to set the world a.** faire sensation

alight² VI **1** Fml (from train, car etc) descen-dre (**from** de) **2** (of bird, eyes, glance) se po-ser (**on** sur)

align [ə'laɪn] VT **1** (objects, soldiers etc) ali-gner, mettre en ligne; (paper in printer) met-tre bien droit; Comput, Typ (characters, graphics) aligner, cadrer; Tech (axes) faire coïncider; Aut (wheels) régler le parallé-lisme de; **to a. sth with sth** aligner qch avec qch; Aut **the wheels were badly aligned** les roues n'étaient pas centrées **2** Fin (of coun-try) (one's currency) aligner (**on** sur) **3** to a. oneself with sb s'aligner sur qn; **they align-ed themselves against the President/this policy** ils se sont ligués contre le président/cette politique
VI **1** s'aligner, se mettre en ligne; Fig **to a. with sb** s'aligner sur qn **2** (of shafts etc) coïncider

alignment [ə'laɪnmənt] N **1** alignement m; (of railway etc) tracé m; Comput, Typ (of char-acters, graphics) alignement, cadrage m; Aut (of wheels) parallélisme m; **out of a.** désali-gné; Constr hors d'œuvre; Typ sortant; **in a. aligné; to bring sth into a. with the new re-**

gulations aligner qch sur la nouvelle régle-mentation; **this is not in a. with current practice** ceci n'est pas conforme à ce qui se pratique actuellement **2** Fin **a. of currencies** alignement m des monnaies

alike [ə'laɪk] ADJ PRED semblable, pareil; **they are very much a.** ils se ressemblent beaucoup; **no two are a.** il n'y en a pas deux de pareils; **you are all a.!** vous êtes tous les mêmes!; **they're very a. in dress/their tastes** leur façon de s'habiller/leurs goûts se res-semble(nt) beaucoup
ADV (to dress, treat etc) de la même façon ou manière, pareillement, de même; **we don't think a.** nous ne sommes pas d'accord, nous n'avons pas le même point de vue; **every day, summer and winter a.** tous les jours, été comme hiver; **old and young a.** les vieux comme les jeunes; **the problem affects all of us a.** ce problème nous touche tous sans exception

aliment ['ælɪmənt] N Scot Law = alimony

alimentary [ælɪ'mentərɪ] ADJ alimentaire
▸▸ Anat **a. canal** tube m digestif

alimony ['ælɪmənɪ] N Law pension f alimentaire

A-list ADJ (star, celebrity, guest) très en vue; **all the A. stars were at the première** toutes les grandes stars étaient à la pre-mière

alive [ə'laɪv] ADJ PRED **1** (person, animal, plant) **to be (still) a.** être (encore) vivant ou en vie, vivre (encore); **to keep sb a.** mainte-nir qn en vie; **to come a. again** (after appar-ent death) revenir à la vie; (after real death) ressusciter; **to stay a.** survivre; **to be burnt a.** être brûlé vif; **to be buried a.** être enterré vivant; **to be a. and well** bien se porter; **no one got out of the build-ing a.** personne n'est sorti vivant de l'im-meuble; **Mr Evans was last seen a. on 21 June** c'est le 21 juin qu'on a vu M. Evans vivant pour la dernière fois; Fam **to be a. and kicking** être plein de vie; **it feels good to be a.!** il fait bon vivre!; **dead or a.** mort ou vif; **when your father was a.** du vivant de votre père; **no one a.** personne au monde; **the oldest man a.** l'homme le plus vieux au monde

2 (memory, hope, custom) **in parts of the country her memory/this custom is still very much a.** dans certaines régions, son souvenir/cette coutume est encore très vivant(e); **to keep sth a.** (memory, custom) garder ou entretenir qch; (conversation) en-tretenir qch, ne pas laisser languir qch; **to keep a religion a.** entretenir la pratique d'une religion

3 (aware) **to be fully a. to sth** avoir pleine-ment conscience de qch; **I am a. to the fact that …** je n'ignore pas que …; **she's very a. to the latest developments in the industry** elle est très au courant des derniers déve-loppements dans le secteur; **she's very a. to the world around her** elle est très ouverte au monde qui l'entoure

4 (full of vitality) vif, éveillé; **I've never felt so a.** je ne me suis jamais senti aussi plein de vie; **he came a. when someone men-tioned food** il s'est réveillé quand quelqu'un a parlé de manger; **the evening came a. when the musicians arrived** la soirée s'est animée à l'arrivée des musiciens; **look a.!** remuez-vous (donc)!

5 the cheese was a. with maggots le fro-mage grouillait de vers; **the street was a. with people** la rue fourmillait ou grouillait de monde

6 esp Am Elec **the wire was a.** le fil était sous tension

alkali ['ælkəlaɪ] N Chem alcali m
▸▸ **a. metal** métal m alcalin

alkaline ['ælkəlaɪn] ADJ *Chem* alcalin

alkaloid ['ælkəlɔɪd] ADJ, N *Chem* alcaloïde *m*

alky ['ælkɪ] N *Fam* **1** (*abbr* **alcoholic**) alcolo *mf* **2** *Am* (*abbr* **alcohol**) gnôle *f*

ALL [ɔːl] VOIR GRAMMAIRE A36; B15–16 ADJ tout, *f* toute, *mpl* tous, *fpl* toutes; **a. France** toute la France; **a. men** tous les hommes; **a. the others** tous les autres; **a. four of them** tous les quatre; **to be a. things to a. men** être tout à tous; **to be a. heart** être plein de bonnes intentions; **he's a. man, isn't he?** quel homme, hein?; **a. day** toute la journée; (**with**) **a. her life** toute sa vie; (**with**) **a. my love** (*at end of letter*) bien affectueusement; **the people/ books had a. disappeared** les gens/les livres avaient tous disparus; **they are a. smokers** ce sont tous des fumeurs; **a. the way** (*of journey*) tout le long du chemin; (*of course of action*) jusqu'au bout; **he leaves the door open a. the time** il laisse tout le temps la porte ouverte; **people have been phoning a. the time you've been out** le téléphone n'a pas arrêté de sonner pendant que tu étais sorti; **I've been here a. the time** je n'ai pas bougé d'ici; **is that a. the luggage you're taking?** c'est tout ce que vous emportez comme bagages?; **for a. his wealth** en dépit de *ou* malgré sa fortune; **with a. speed** au plus vite, à toute vitesse; **by a. accounts they've had a most successful year** tout semble indiquer qu'ils ont eu une excellente année; **at a. hours** à toute heure; **in a. sorts of ways** de toutes les façons; **in a. honesty/ sincerity** pour être honnête/sincère; in a. frankness en toute franchise; *Fml* **with a. due care (and attention)/dispatch** avec tout le soin requis/toute la promptitude requise; *Fml* **with a. due respect** avec tout le respect qui vous est dû; **what's a. that noise?** qu'est-ce que c'est que tout ce bruit?; **a. that's nonsense** tout ça, c'est des bêtises; **for a. that they say he's a genius, I think …** ils ont beau dire que c'est un génie, moi, je pense …; *Fam* **and a. that** et tout cela, et tout le reste; **you're not as ill as a. that** vous n'êtes pas aussi *ou* si malade que ça; **it's not a. that pleasant** ce n'est pas tellement agréable; **of a. the stupid things to say/do!** de toutes les idioties possibles!; **of a. times to phone!** il a bien choisi son heure pour téléphoner!; **you, of a. people, should know what I mean** toi au moins tu devrais savoir ce que je veux dire

PRON **1** (*with pl*) tous, *f* toutes; **a. are agreed that …** tous sont d'accord que …; **a. of us** nous tous; **we a. love him** nous l'aimons tous; **a. of them are blue, they are a. blue** ils sont tous bleus, tous sont bleus; **a. together** tous à la fois, tous ensemble; **a. but he** *or* **him** tous sauf *ou* excepté lui; **a. and sundry** tous sans exception

2 (*everything*) tout; **I want a. of it** je le veux en entier; **almost a.** presque tout; **I did a. I could** j'ai fait tout ce que j'ai pu; *Prov* **a. that glitters is not gold** tout ce qui brille n'est pas de l'or; *Iron* **Hum a.** is forgiven tout est pardonné; **I know it a.** (*of news etc*) je sais tout cela; (*of poem etc*) je le sais en entier; **best/ worst of a.,** … le mieux/pire, c'est que …; **most of a.** surtout, en particulier; **take it a.** prenez le tout; **in the middle of it a.** au milieu de tout cela; **for a. he may say** en dépit de ce qu'il dit, quoi qu'il en dise; **that's a.** c'est tout, voilà tout; **is that a.?** c'est tout?; *Iron* **ce n'est que ça?; if that's a.** si ce n'est que cela; **that's a. well and good** tout cela est bien joli; **a.'s well** tout va bien; **a.'s well that ends well** tout est bien qui finit bien; **I think that's about a.** je crois que c'est tout; **a. I said was 'good morning'** tout ce que j'ai dit a été 'bonjour'; **that's a. they ever do, complain** c'est tout ce qu'ils savent faire, se

plaindre; **it was a. I could do not to laugh** j'avais le plus grand mal à ne pas rire; **when** *or* **after a.'s said and done** en fin de compte; *Fam* **he must be a. of sixty** il doit avoir au moins soixante ans; *Fam Iron* **it cost a. of £2** ça a coûté 2 livres et pas moins

3 once and for a. une fois pour toutes; **for a. I know** autant que je sache; **for a. I care** pour (tout) ce que cela me fait; **it's a. the same to me** ça m'est égal; **thirty men in a.** trente hommes en tout; **above a.** surtout; **most of a.** surtout, le plus; **when I was busiest of a.** au moment où j'étais le plus occupé

4 *Sl* (*everything else*) **and a.** et (tout) le reste; **I know he's been very kind and a., but …** je sais bien qu'il a été très gentil et tout, mais …

5 *Br Sl* (*nothing*) **damn** *or* **bugger** *or* **sod a.** rien du tout, que dalle; **I've done damn a. today** je n'ai rien fichu aujourd'hui

ADV **1** (*entirely*) tout; **she is a. alone** elle est toute seule; **a. on one's own** tout seul; **to be (dressed) a. in black** être habillé tout en noir *ou* tout de noir; **she is a. ears/impatience/ smiles** elle est tout oreilles/impatience/ sourires; **a. (a)round the room** dans toute la pièce; **I forgot a. about the meeting** j'ai complètement oublié qu'il y avait une réunion; **a. in one piece** tout d'une pièce; **are you still a. in one piece?** (*after accident*) est-ce que tu es encore en un seul morceau?; **she is a. for accepting this offer** elle est tout en faveur d'accepter cette offre; **my wife was a. for calling in a doctor** ma femme voulait à toute force *ou* à tout prix appeler un médecin; **I'm a. for it** je suis entièrement d'accord *ou* pour; **to be a. in favour of sth** être entièrement favorable à qch; **he's not a. bad** il n'est pas entièrement mauvais; **that's a. to the good!** tant mieux!; **a. the better/worse (for me)** tant mieux/pis (pour moi); **you will be a. the better for it** vous vous en trouverez (d'autant) mieux; **a. the harder** encore plus dur; **the time came a. too soon** l'heure n'arriva que trop tôt; **a. along** depuis le début; **a. at once** (*suddenly*) tout à coup, subitement; (*everything together*) tout d'un coup, tous à la fois; **a. round** (*in general*) à tous points de vue; **a. of a sudden** tout à coup, soudain; **a. over** partout; **a. over the floor/pavement** partout par terre/sur le trottoir; *Fig* **the team was a. over the place** l'équipe faisait n'importe quoi; **she was a. over him at the party** elle n'a pas arrêté de lui tourner après à la soirée; **an a. girl band** un groupe composé uniquement de femmes; **an a. new outfit** un ensemble tout neuf; **a. ready** fin prêt; **to be a. indignant about sth** être fou d'indignation à propos de qch; **it's a. mine!** c'est tout à moi!; *Fam* **to be a. in** être complètement crevé; *Fam* **he's gone a. red** il est devenu tout rouge; *Fam* **the dress was a.** torn la robe était toute déchirée; *Fam* **he's not a. there** il est un peu simplet; **to go a. out** ne pas s'épargner; **to go a. out to pass one's exams** faire son maximum pour réussir ses examens; *Fam* **a. that** (*excellent*) super, génial; *Fam* **she thinks she's a. that** elle ne se prend pas pour n'importe qui

2 (*almost*) **a. but** presque; **it's a. but done** c'est pour ainsi dire fini, c'est presque fini *ou* fait

3 (*in the slightest*) **at a.** du tout; **do you know him at a.?** est-ce que vous le connaissez (un peu)?; **I didn't speak at a.** je n'ai pas parlé du tout; **I'm not at a. astonished** je n'en suis aucunement étonné; **not at a.** pas du tout, *Fam* du tout; (*when thanked*) je vous en prie; **if he comes at a.** s'il vient; **it seemed to worry him very little, if at a.** ça n'a pas eu l'air de l'inquiéter le moins du monde; **if it is at a. cold** s'il fait un (tant soit) peu froid; **if it is at a. possible** si c'était possible; **why do it at a.?** pourquoi se donner la peine de le

faire?

4 (*altogether*) **in a.** en tout; (**taking it**) **a. in a.** à tout prendre

5 (*in games*) *Ftbl etc* **five a.** cinq à cinq, cinq partout; *Tennis* **four (games) a.** quatre (jeux) partout; *Tennis* **fifteen a.** quinze à

N tout *m*, totalité *f*; **to stake one's a.** risquer le tout pour le tout; **I would give my a. to see her** je donnerais tout ce que j'ai pour la voir; **he was really giving his a. in the last aria** il a vraiment tout donné dans la dernière aria

all-absorbing ADJ absorbant, passionnant; **of a. interest** fascinant

Allah ['ælə] N Allah *m*

all-American ADJ cent pour cent américain

all-around ADJ *Am* (*athlete*) complet; (*man*) universel

allay [ə'leɪ] VT **1** (*storm, anger*) apaiser, calmer **2** (*fear*) calmer; (*suspicions*) endormir, dissiper **3** (*pain*) alléger, calmer, soulager; (*thirst, hunger, temperature*) apaiser

all-clear N (*signal m de*) fin *f* d'alerte; **to give the a.** *Mil* sonner la fin de l'alerte; (*for project etc*) donner le feu vert; **he gave us the a.** (*no one was watching*) il nous a fait signe que la voie était libre

all-conquering ADJ (*love etc*) qui triomphe de tout

all-consuming [-kən'sjuːmɪŋ] ADJ (*passion, ambition*) dévorant

all-day ADJ ATTRIB qui dure toute la journée

allegation [ælɪ'geɪʃən] N allégation *f*; **to make an a.** alléguer *ou* avancer quelque chose

allege [ə'ledʒ] VT alléguer, prétendre (**that** que); **the words alleged to have been spoken by …** les propos qui auraient été tenus par …; **he was alleged to be dead** on le prétendait *ou* disait mort; **it is alleged that …** on prétend que …

alleged [ə'ledʒd] ADJ ATTRIB (*attack, motive etc*) allégué; **the a. thief** le voleur présumé

allegedly [ə'ledʒɪdlɪ] ADV prétendument; **a. he's the greatest violinist since Paganini** on dit de lui qu'il est le plus grand violoniste depuis Paganini

allegiance [ə'liːdʒəns] N fidélité *f*, obéissance *f* (**to** à); **to owe a. to a party** devoir fidélité à un parti; **to renounce one's a. to a party** se détacher d'un parti; **to owe a. to a king** devoir fidélité et obéissance à un roi; **to take an oath of a.** prêter serment d'allégeance

allegorical [ælɪ'gɒrɪk(ə)l] ADJ allégorique

allegorically [ælɪ'gɒrɪklɪ] ADV allégoriquement

allegory ['ælɪgərɪ] N allégorie *f*

allegretto [ælɪ'gretəʊ] ADV, N *Mus* allegretto *m*

allegro [ə'legrəʊ, -'leɪ-] ADV, N *Mus* allegro *m*

alleluia [ælɪ'luːjə] INT, N *Rel* alléluia *m*

all-embracing [-ɪm'breɪsɪŋ] ADJ (*love*) qui embrasse tout; (*category*) hétéroclite; **a. knowledge** vaste érudition *f*

allen key ['ælən] N clé *f* allen

allergen ['ælədʒen] N *Med* allergène *m*

allergenic [ælə'dʒenɪk] ADJ allergisant

allergic [ə'lɜːdʒɪk] ADJ *Med* allergique (**to** à); *Fig* **I'm a. to him/rap music** il/le rap me hérisse

allergy ['ælədʒɪ] N *Med, Fig* allergie *f* (**to** à)

alleviate [ə'liːvɪeɪt] VT (*pain*) alléger, soulager; (*grief*) adoucir; (*thirst*) apaiser; (*problem*) alléger, modérer

alleviation [əliːvɪ'eɪʃən] N (*of pain*) allègement *m*, soulagement *m*; (*of grief*) adoucissement *m*; (*of thirst*) apaisement *m*; (*of* *problem)* allègement

all-expenses paid ADJ tous frais payés

all-expense tour N voyage *m* à forfait

alley ['ælɪ] N **1** *(narrow street)* ruelle *f*; **I wouldn't like to meet him in a dark a.!** je n'aimerais pas le rencontrer au coin d'un bois! **2** *Sport* bowling *m*. bowling *m*
▸▸ **a. cat** chat *m* de gouttière

alleyway ['ælɪweɪ] N *(street)* ruelle *f*

alliance [ə'laɪəns] N **1** alliance *f*; **to enter into an a.** s'allier (**with** avec); **electoral a.** apparentement *m*, alliance électorale; **to make a political a. with a party** s'allier à un parti; **in a. with a German firm** en association avec une firme allemande **2** *(by marriage)* alliance *f*

allied ['ælaɪd] ADJ **1** allié (**to** à; **with** avec); *(consideration, issue)* du même ordre, de la même nature; *(subjects, disciplines, sciences)* voisin; **the A. Powers** les Puissances *fpl* alliées; **closely a. industries** industries *fpl* connexes **2** *Biol, Med etc* du même ordre, de la même nature; *Biol (species)* voisin

alligator ['ælɪgeɪtər] N **1** *(animal)* alligator *m* **2** *(skin)* crocodile *m*; **a. handbag** sac *m* en crocodile *ou* *Am Fam* en croco
▸▸ **a. clip** pince *f* alligator; **a. pear** (poire *f* d')avocat *m*

all-important ADJ capital, -aux; **speed is a.** la vitesse est capitale *ou* est de la plus grande importance

all-in ADJ *(price, tariff)* net, tout compris, forfaitaire
ADV *Com* tout compris; **the holiday costs £500 a.** les vacances coûtent 500 livres tous frais compris
▸▸ **a. policy** *(in insurance)* police *f* tous risques; *Sport* **a. wrestler** catcheur *m*; *Sport* **a. wrestling** lutte *f* libre, catch *m*

all-inclusive ADJ *(price)* tout compris, forfaitaire; *(theory)* universel

alliteration [əlɪtə'reɪʃən] N allitération *f*

alliterative [ə'lɪtərətɪv, -reɪt-] ADJ allitératif

all-night ADJ *(party, session etc)* qui dure toute la nuit; **to maintain an a. vigil** veiller toute la nuit
▸▸ *Mil* **a. pass** permission *f* de (la) nuit; *Admin etc* **a. service** permanence *f* de nuit; *Cin* **a. showing** = projection *f* ininterrompue durant toute la nuit

all-nighter [-'naɪtər] N **it turned into another a.** finalement, ça a encore duré toute la nuit

allocate ['æləkeɪt] VT allouer, assigner (**to** à); **to a. duties** attribuer des fonctions (**to** à); **to a. a sum to sth** affecter *ou* assigner une somme à qch; **more money was allocated to defence** on a affecté plus d'argent à la défense; **in the time allocated** dans le temps *ou* les délais imparti(s); **you'll need to a. your time carefully** il va falloir que tu répartisses ton temps avec précaution; **allocated budget** allocation *f* budgétaire, budget *m* alloué

allocation [ælə'keɪʃən] N **1** *(action) (of sum of money)* allocation *f*, affectation *f*; *(of expenses, means etc)* répartition *f*; *(of capital)* affectation *f*; *(of duties)* attribution *f*; *Fin* **a. to lowest tender** adjudication *f* au mieux-disant **2** *(share)* part *f* assignée *ou* allouée; *(money)* somme *f* assignée *ou* allouée; **my a.** la part/somme qui m'est assignée *ou* allouée

allograft ['æləʊgrɑːft] N *Med* allogreffe *f*

allopathic [ælə'pæθɪk] ADJ *Med* allopathique

allopathy [æ'lɒpəθɪ] N *Med* allopathie *f*

all-or-none order N *St Exch* ordre *m* 'tout ou rien'

allot [ə'lɒt] VT (**-tt-**) **1** *(assign)* attribuer, assigner (**to sb** à qn); **to a. sth to a purpose** affecter *ou* destiner qch à un but; **in the allotted time** dans le temps imparti; **allotted budget** enveloppe *f* budgétaire **2** *(distribute) (tasks, seats)* répartir, distribuer; *(shares)* attribuer, répartir

allotment [ə'lɒtmənt] N **1** *Br (land)* jardin *m* (ouvrier) **2** *(distribution) (of rooms etc)* distribution *f*; *(of tasks)* partage *m*, répartition *f*; *(of property)* lotissement *m*; *St Exch (of shares)* attribution *f*; *St Exch* **letter of a.** (lettre *f* d')avis *m* de répartition **3** *(share)* portion *f*, part *f*; *(of airplane seats)* bloc-sièges *m inv*
▸▸ *St Exch* **a. right** droit *m* d'attribution

all-out *Fam* ADJ ATTRIB *(effort, resistance)* suprême, maximum; *(attack)* tous azimuts; *(strike, war)* total, -aux
ADV **to go a.** y aller tous azimuts *ou* à fond; **to go a. for gold** y aller tous azimuts pour avoir la médaille d'or; **we're going a. for the end of the month** on fait le maximum pour y arriver avant la fin du mois

all-over ADJ ATTRIB *(tan)* intégral, -aux; **with an a. pattern** dont le motif couvre toute la surface; **it gives a. relief** cela vous apportera un soulagement total

allow [ə'laʊ] VT **1** *(permit)* permettre; **to a. sb sth** permettre qch à qn; **to a. sb to do sth** permettre à qn de faire qch; **to a. sb home** laisser qn rentrer chez lui; **is he allowed sweets/help?** est-ce qu'il a le droit de manger des sucreries/de recevoir de l'aide?; **gambling is not allowed** les jeux d'argent sont interdits; **no conferring is allowed** il est interdit *ou* il n'est pas permis de se consulter; **she isn't allowed alcohol** elle n'a pas le droit de boire d'alcool; **to be allowed to compete** etre admis à concourir; **I am allowed to do it** on me permet *ou* il m'est permis de le faire; **a. me!** permettez(-moi)!; **a. me to …** permettez-moi de …; **passengers are not allowed on the bridge** la passerelle est interdite aux voyageurs; **as soon as circumstances a.** dès que les circonstances le permettront; **to a. oneself to be led/deceived/persuaded** se laisser mener/tromper/convaincre; **I will not a. you to be ill-treated** je ne vous laisserai pas maltraiter **2** *(accept) (request, claim)* faire droit à; *(petition)* admettre; *Sport (penalty, goal)* accorder **3** *(grant, allocate)* accorder; **to a. sb £5,000 a year** accorder *ou* allouer à qn une rente de 5000 livres; **to a. a debtor time to pay** accorder un délai à un débiteur; **how much time/money are we allowed?** de combien de temps/d'argent disposons-nous?; **they haven't allowed enough time** ils n'ont pas laissé assez de temps; *Com, Fin* **to a. sb a discount** consentir *ou* accorder un escompte *ou* une remise à qn; **the bank allows 5% interest on deposits** la banque alloue ou attribue 5% d'intérêt sur les dépôts; **at the end of the six months allowed** à l'expiration du délai de six mois; **a. 20 minutes to get to the airport** comptez 20 minutes pour aller à l'aéroport **4** *(admit)* admettre (**that** que) **5** *Am Fam (maintain)* juger, opiner, affirmer (**that** que)
▸ **allow for** VT INSEP tenir compte de; *(difficulties, delay etc)* prévoir; **after allowing for** *(discount, expenses etc)* déduction faite de; **to a. for some wastage** prévoir plus large; **a. two litres for wastage** comptez deux litres de pertes en plus; **to a. so much for carriage** compter tant pour le transport; **you must a. for his being ill** il faut tenir compte de ce qu'il est malade; **has that been allowed for in your figures?** en avez-vous tenu compte dans vos estimations?
▸ **allow in** VT SEP laisser entrer; **no one is al-**

lowed in personne n'a le droit d'entrer
▸ **allow of** VT INSEP *Fml* permettre, admettre; **the facts a. of only one interpretation** les faits n'admettent qu'une seule interprétation
▸ **allow out** VT SEP **to a. sb out** permettre à qn de sortir; **no one is allowed out after dark** personne n'a le droit de sortir après la tombée de la nuit; **some prisoners are allowed out at weekends** certains détenus ont la permission de sortir le weekend

allowable [ə'laʊəb(ə)l] ADJ **1** *(permissible)* admissible **2** *Com (claim)* recevable; *(expense)* déductible

allowance [ə'laʊəns] N **1** *(money given)* pension *f*, *Am (pocket money)* argent *m* de poche; **his parents stopped** *or* **cut off his a.** ses parents ont arrêté de lui verser de l'argent régulièrement; *(while he was living away from home)* ses parents ont arrêté sa pension **2** *Admin etc (compensation)* allocation *f*; **cost-of-living a.** indemnité *f* de vie chère; *Br Formerly* **family a.** allocations familiales; **supplementary allowances** majorations *fpl* de pension; *Fin* **personal a.** abattement *m* personnel (sur l'impôt); **entertainment a.** frais *mpl* de représentation; **travel** *or* **travelling a.** indemnité *f* de déplacement; **allowances in kind** prestations *fpl* en nature **3** *(free)* **luggage a.** *(on plane, coach etc)* bagages *mpl* en franchise; **there is an a. of one item of luggage per passenger** chaque passager a droit à un bagage; **what's the duty-free a.?** qu'est-ce qu'on a droit de ramener hors taxe?; *Sport* **time a.** rendement *m* de temps; *Horseracing* **weight a.** décharge *f* **4** *Com, Fin (discount)* remise *f*, rabais *m*; **to make an a. on an article** faire un rabais sur un article **5** **to make allowances** *or* **an a. for sth** tenir compte de qch; *(delays)* prévoir qch; **to make allowances for sb** avoir de l'indulgence pour qn; **some a. must be made for shrinkage** il faut tenir compte du rétrécissement **6** *Tech* tolérance *f*

alloy [1] ['ælɔɪ] N alliage *m*
▸▸ *Metal* **a. steel** acier *m* allié *ou* spécial; **a. wheel** jante *f* (en) alliage

alloy [2] [ə'lɔɪ] VT *(metals)* allier
VI *(of metals)* s'allier (l'un avec l'autre)

alloyed [ə'lɔɪd] ADJ *(metal etc)* allié (**with** à, avec)

all-pervading, **all-pervasive** ADJ *(stench)* envahissant, qui se répand partout; *(fear, corruption, influence)* omniprésent

all-powerful ADJ tout-puissant, toute-puissante, *pl* tout-puissants, toutes-puissantes

all-purpose ADJ *(glue, cleaner)* universel; *(vehicle)* tous usages; *(building, room)* polyvalent

all right ADJ **everything's a.** tout va très bien; **it's a.** *(there's no need to worry)* tout va bien, ne vous inquiétez pas; *(to person apologizing)* je vous en prie!; **a.!** *(expressing agreement)* bien!, entendu!; *Am (expressing great enthusiasm)* génial!!; **a., a., I'm coming** *(expressing irritation)* d'accord, d'accord, j'arrive; **are you a.?** *(are you well?)* est-ce que vous allez bien?; *(did you hurt yourself?)* vous ne vous êtes pas blessé?; *Iron* tu ne te sens pas bien?; **I'm a. again now** *(after being ill)* je suis tout à fait remis maintenant; **I'm a. until Monday** *(financially)* ça ira jusqu'à lundi; **are you a. for cash/cigarettes?** tu as assez de liquide/de cigarettes?; **it's a. for you to laugh!** ça vous va bien de rire!; **any more?** – no, **I'm a.,** thanks tu n'en veux encore? – non, ça va, merci; **I'm a. at algebra** en algèbre je me débrouille *ou* je ne me défends pas trop mal; **it was a.** *(film, party etc)* ce n'était pas mal; **he's/she's a.** *(a good sort)* c'est un bon type; *Fam* **to be a bit of a.** *(of woman)* être une jolie fille; *(of man)* être un beau mec

all-risks insurance N assurance *f* tous risques

all-round ADJ ATTRIB **1** *(athlete etc)* complet, -ète; *(education)* général, -aux; *(expert)* dans tous les domaines; **a. improvement** amélioration *f* générale *ou* sur toute la ligne **2** *Aut* **car with a. vision** voiture *f* à carrosserie panoramique

all-rounder [-'raʊndər] N homme *m* universel, femme *f* universelle; *(athlete)* athlète *mf* complet(ète); *Sch* **a good a.** un élève complet, une élève complète; **she's quite an a.** elle est douée pour tout

all-seater stadium N *Sport* = stade *m* ayant uniquement des places assises

All-Share Index N *Br St Exch* = indice *m* du Financial Times et de l'Institut des actuaires britannique

allspice ['ɔːlspaɪs] N *Bot, Culin* poivre *m* de la Jamaïque

all-star ADJ ATTRIB *Theat etc* **an a. cast** une distribution prestigieuse; **a. performance** spectacle *m* à la distribution prestigieuse

all-terrain ADJ *Aut* tout-terrain *inv*

all-time ADJ ATTRIB *Fam (record)* sans précédent, inouï; **a. high/low** record le plus élevé/bas; **the a. greats of rock music** les plus grands du rock; **one of the a. hits** un des plus grands succès

allude [ə'luːd] VI **to a. to sb/sth** *(of person)* faire allusion à qn/qch; *(of phrase)* avoir trait à *ou* se rapporter à qn/qch; **I am not alluding to anybody in particular** je ne vise personne

allure [ə'lʊər] N attrait *m*; **it holds no a. for me** ça ne m'attire pas du tout
VT attirer, séduire

> Note that the French word **allure** is a false friend. It means **pace**, **speed** or **appearance**, depending on the context.

alluring [ə'lʊərɪŋ] ADJ attrayant, attirant, séduisant

allusion [ə'luːʒən] N allusion *f*; **to make an a. to sth** faire allusion à qch; **in a. to sth** par allusion à qch

allusive [ə'luːsɪv] ADJ allusif

alluvial [ə'luːvɪəl] *Geol* ADJ *(terrain)* alluvial, -aux; **a. deposits** alluvions *fpl*, dépôts alluvionnaires
N *Austr* alluvions *fpl* aurifères
> **a. plain** plaine *f* alluviale

alluvium [ə'luːvɪəm] N *Geol* limon *m*

all-weather ADJ *Aviat etc (plane, landing strip)* tous temps; *(clothes), Sport (pitch)* pour tous les temps

all-wheel drive N quatre roues *fpl* motrices

ally[1] ['ælaɪ] N *(country, person etc)* allié, -ée; *Hist* **the Allies** les Alliés *mpl*; **to become allies** s'allier (ensemble), se coaliser

ally[2] [ə'laɪ] VT allier (**to** à; **with** avec); **the country has allied itself with its neighbour** le pays s'est allié à *ou* avec l'état voisin; **we must a. ourselves with other unions** nous devons nous allier à *ou* nous associer avec d'autres syndicats; **this newspaper is allied with another** ce journal est associé avec un autre

alma mater ['ælmə'meɪtər, -'mɑːtər] N = l'université *f* ou l'école *f* où l'on a fait ses études

almanac ['ɔːlmənæk, 'æl-] N almanach *m*

almighty [ɔːl'maɪtɪ] ADJ ATTRIB *(omnipotent)* tout-puissant, toute-puissante, *pl* tout-puissants, toutes-puissantes; *Fam (scandal etc)* monstrueux, terrible; *Fam* **an a. row** *or* **din** un fracas de tous les diables

N **the A.** le Tout-Puissant, le Très-Haut
ADV *Am Fam* très; **he's a. stubborn** il est têtu comme une mule

almond ['ɑːmənd] N amande *f*; **sweet/bitter a.** amande douce/amère; **ground almonds** amandes pilées; **a.(-shaped) eyes** yeux *mpl* en amande
> *Culin* **a. essence** essence *f* d'amande; **a. grove** amandaie *f*, amandraie *f*; **a. oil** huile *f* d'amande; *Culin* **a. paste** pâte *f* d'amande; **a. tree** amandier *m*

almoner ['ɑːmənər, 'æl-] N **1** *Br (in hospital)* assistant, -ante social(e) **2** *Hist (distributor of alms)* aumônier *m*

almost ['ɔːlməʊst] ADV presque; **it's a. six (o'clock)** il est presque six heures; **a. nothing** presque rien; **a. blind** presque *ou* quasi aveugle; **he a. fell/missed the bus** il a failli tomber/rater l'autobus; **we're a. there** nous sommes presque arrivés; **you're a. there** *(in answering question)* tu y es presque; **I a. didn't see you** j'ai failli ne pas vous voir

alms [ɑːmz] NPL aumône *f*; **to give a. to sb** donner *ou* faire l'aumône à qn, faire la charité à qn
> *Hist* **a. box** tronc *m* (pour les pauvres)

almshouse ['ɑːmzhaʊs] N hospice *m*

aloe ['æləʊ] N **1** *(plant)* aloès *m* **2** *Pharm* **aloes** aloès *mpl*; **bitter aloes** amer *m* d'aloès

aloft [ə'lɒft] ADV **1** *Naut* dans la mâture **2** *(in sky)* en haut, en l'air

alone [ə'ləʊn] ADJ PRED, ADV **1** *(in isolation)* seul; **he lives (all) a.** il vit (tout) seul; **I like being a.** j'aime la solitude *ou* être seul; **I want to speak to you a.** je voudrais vous parler seul à seul; **a. at last!** enfin seul(s)!; **he was left a. when his wife died** il s'est retrouvé seul quand sa femme est morte; **we are not a. in thinking that …** nous ne sommes pas seuls à penser que …; **you a. can help me** vous êtes le seul qui puissiez m'aider, vous seul pouvez m'aider; **he a. knows …** lui seul sait …; **I did it a.** je l'ai fait tout seul; *Fam* **to go it a.** faire cavalier seul; *Bible* **man does not live by bread a.** l'homme ne vit pas que de pain; **my salary a. isn't enough** mon salaire à lui seul *ou* mon seul salaire ne suffit pas; **his shoes a. must have cost what I earn in a week** rien que ses chaussures ont dû coûter ce que je gagne en une semaine; **with that charm which is his a.** avec ce charme qui lui est propre

2 *(undisturbed)* **to let** *or* **leave sb a.** *(not touch, not disturb)* laisser qn tranquille *ou* en paix; *(not interfere with)* laisser qn en paix; **leave me a.!** laissez-moi tranquille!, *Fam* fichez-moi la paix!; **leave her a. to get on with it** laisse-la se débrouiller toute seule; **to let** *or* **leave sth a.** *(not get involved)* ne pas se mêler de qch; **leave these things a.** *(don't touch)* ne touchez pas à tout ça; **a subject better left a.** un sujet qu'il vaut mieux ne pas aborder; **your work is all right, leave it a.** votre travail est bien, n'y touchez plus; **let a. …** encore moins …; **the soup wasn't even warm, let a. hot!** la soupe ne risquait pas d'être chaude, elle était à peine tiède!

ALONG [ə'lɒŋ] PREP le long de; **to walk a. the shore** se promener le long de la plage, longer la plage; **to go a. a street** suivre une rue; **to look a. the street/corridor** regarder dans la rue/le couloir; **to sail a. the coast** longer *ou* suivre la côte; **to crawl a. the ground** ramper à la surface du sol; *Fig* **victorious all a. the line** victorieux sur toute la ligne; **all a. the street** tout le long de la rue; **trees a. the river** arbres qui bordent la rivière; **they live somewhere a. this street** ils habitent quelque part dans cette rue; **it's somewhere a. here** c'est quelque part dans cette direction *ou* par là; **somewhere a. the way** en route, en chemin

ADV **to move a.** avancer; **move a. so I can sit down** *(in row of seats etc)* pousse-toi que je puisse m'asseoir; **to stride a.** avancer à grandes enjambées; **come a. with me** venez avec moi; *Fam* **come a. now!** *(be reasonable)* allons, sois raisonnable!; **he'll be a. in ten minutes** il va arriver dans dix minutes; **there'll be another one a. in a minute** *(of bus)* il en passera un autre dans une minute; **bring a tent a. (with you)** apportez une tente; **can I bring a friend a.?** est-ce que je peux amener un ami?; **a. with Mozart, Haydn is my favourite composer** avec Mozart, Haydn est mon compositeur favori; *Sl* **get a. (with you)!** *(go away)* allez!, filez!; *(expressing astonishment, disbelief)* allons donc!; *Am* **a. about four o'clock** vers quatre heures; *Am* **the afternoon was well a.** l'après-midi tirait à sa fin; **all a.** *(all the time)* depuis toujours; **I knew that all a.** je le savais dès *ou* depuis le commencement, je l'ai toujours su; **I said so all a.** c'est ce que j'ai toujours dit; **he was lying all a.** il n'a fait que mentir, il a menti du début à la fin

alongside [ə'lɒŋ'saɪd] PREP *esp Naut (boat, quay)* accosté à, le long de; **to come a. (of) a ship** accoster *ou* aborder un navire; **the police car pulled up a. us** la voiture de police s'est arrêtée à côté de nous; **to walk a. sb** marcher côte à côte avec qn *ou* à côté de qn; **read these instructions a. the illustrations** lisez ces instructions en accompagnement des illustrations; **if you look at it a. his earlier work** si vous le comparez à ses travaux plus anciens; **a. what others have done** par rapport à ce que *ou* à côté de ce que d'autres ont fait
ADV *Naut* **to come a.** accoster; **a police car pulled up a.** une voiture de police nous/les/ *etc* a accostés

aloof [ə'luːf] ADV **to keep a.** se tenir à l'écart *ou* à distance (**from sth** de qch); **to stand a. from** se tenir à l'écart de
ADJ *(person, manner)* distant; *(emphasizing coldness)* froid et distant

aloofness [ə'luːfnɪs] N attitude *f* distante, réserve *f*

alopecia [æləʊ'piːʃə] N *Med* alopécie *f*

aloud [ə'laʊd] ADV à haute voix, (tout) haut; **to read a.** lire à haute voix; **I was thinking a.** je pensais tout haut; **he says a. what others only dare to whisper** il dit tout haut ce que les autres pensent tout bas

alp [ælp] N *Geog* **1** *(pasture)* alpe *f*, pâturage *m* de montagne **2 the Alps** les Alpes *fpl*

alpaca [æl'pækə] N **1** *(animal)* alpaga *m* **2** *Tex* alpaga *m*; **a. coat/jacket** manteau *m*/ veste *f* en alpaga *ou* d'alpaga; **a. wool** laine *f* d'alpaga

alpenhorn ['ælpənhɔːn] N *Mus* cor *m* des Alpes

alpha ['ælfə] N alpha *m*; *Br (mark)* A *m*; *Lit, Fig* **the a. and omega** l'alpha et l'oméga
> *Zool* **a. male** mâle *m* alpha; *Fig* **he's the a. male of the group** c'est lui qui domine le groupe; *Phys* **a. rays** rayons *mpl* alpha

alphabet ['ælfəbet] N alphabet *m*
> **a. soup** *Culin* soupe *f* aux petites pâtes en forme de lettres; *Fig (speech, writing)* = charabia *m* bourré de sigles et d'abréviations

alphabetic(al) [ælfə'betɪk, -ɪk(ə)l] ADJ alphabétique; **in a. order** par ordre *ou* dans l'ordre alphabétique; **a. filing** classement *m* par ordre alphabétique

alphabetically [ælfə'betɪklɪ] ADV alphabétiquement, par ordre alphabétique

alphabetize ['ælfəbətaɪz] VT classer par ordre alphabétique; **to a. sth on sth** trier qch par ordre alphabétique sur la base de qch

alphanumeric(al) [ælfənjuːˈmerɪk, -ɪk(ə)l] **ADJ** *Comput* alphanumérique
▶▶ **a. code** code *m* alphanumérique; **a. field** champ *m* alphanumérique; **a. filing** classement *m* alphanumérique; **a. keyboard, a. keypad** clavier *m* alphanumérique

alphasort [ˈælfəsɔːt] *Comput* **N** tri *m* alphabétique; **to do an a. on sth** trier qch par ordre alphabétique
VT trier par ordre alphabétique

alphatest [ˈælfətest] *Comput* **N** alpha-test *m*, *pl* alpha-tests, essai *m* préliminaire
VT conduire les alpha-tests sur, conduire les essais préliminaires sur

alpine [ˈælpaɪn] **N** *(plant)* plante *f* alpine *ou* alpestre
ADJ *(skiing)* alpin; *(site, landscape, climate)* alpestre; *(plant)* alpin, alpestre
▶▶ **a. range** chaîne *f* de montagnes alpine

alpinism [ˈælpɪnɪz(ə)m] **N** alpinisme *m*

alpinist [ˈælpɪnɪst] **N** alpiniste *mf*

already [ɔːlˈredɪ] **ADV** déjà; **ten o'clock a.!** déjà dix heures!; **you've eaten enough a.** tu as déjà assez mangé

alright [ɔːlˈraɪt] **ADJ** = **all right**

Alsatian [ælˈseɪʃən] **ADJ** alsacien; *(wine)* d'Alsace
N 1 Alsacien, -ienne **2** *Br (dog)* berger *m* allemand

also [ˈɔːlsəʊ] **ADV** aussi; **he a. saw it, he saw it a.** *(didn't only hear it)* il l'a vu aussi; *(as well as other people)* lui aussi, il l'a vu, il l'a vu, lui aussi; *esp Am* **I study French a.** *(as well as other subjects)* j'étudie également le français; **not only … but a. …** non seulement … mais encore … *ou* mais aussi …; **it's very efficient and a. very cheap** c'est très efficace et, de plus, très bon marché; *Horseracing* **a. ran** non classé, ont couru aussi

also-ran **N** *Horseracing* concurrent, -ente non classé(ée); *Fam (unsuccessful person, thing)* non-valeur *f*, *pl* non-valeurs

alt [ɔːlt] **N** *Comput (key)* touche *f* alt
▶▶ **a. key** touche alt

Alta *abbr* **Alberta**

altar [ˈɔːltər] **N** autel *m*; **to lead sb to the a.** conduire qn à l'autel; *Fig* **they were sacrificed on the a. of the party's interests** ils ont été sacrifiés dans l'intérêt du parti; **high a.** maître-autel *m*, *pl* maîtres-autels
▶▶ **a. boy** enfant *m* de chœur; **a. cloth** nappe *f* d'autel; **a. rail(s)** cancel *m*; **a. screen** retable *m*

altarpiece [ˈɔːltəpiːs] **N** retable *m*

alter [ˈɔːltər] **VT 1** *(thing, person)* changer; *(design, one's opinion etc)* modifier; *(garment etc)* faire des retouches à; **that alters the case/the situation** voilà qui change les choses/la situation; **that doesn't a. the fact that …** cela ne change rien au fait que …; **this has not altered our determination to …** ceci n'a pas altéré notre détermination à …; *Naut* **to a. course** changer de route **2** *Am*, *Austr Fam (castrate)* châtrer
VI *(of person, situation)* changer; **her whole outlook has altered** elle a complètement changé d'horizon
▶▶ **a. ego** alter ego *m*

alteration [ɔːltəˈreɪʃən] **N** changement *m*, modification *f* (**to** apporté(e) à); *(to garment)* retouche *f* (**to** à); **subject to a.** *(programme, timetable etc)* susceptible de révisions, sauf modifications; **marginal alterations** *(written)* corrections *fpl* en marge

altercation [ɔːltəˈkeɪʃən] **N** *Fml* altercation *f*, querelle *f*; **to have an a.** se quereller

alternate[1] [ɔːlˈtɜːnət] **ADJ 1** alterné, alternant; **she comes on a. days** elle vient tous les deux jours *ou* un jour sur deux; **they**

come on a. days *(one after the other)* ils viennent en alternance un jour sur deux; **on a. afternoons/Wednesdays** un après-midi/mercredi sur deux; **a. layers of stone and timber** couches alternées de pierre et de bois; **a. periods of calm and distress** des périodes de calme alternant avec des périodes d'angoisse; **a. airfield** aérodrome *m* de dégagement; *Aviat etc* **a. route** parcours *m* de rechange
2 *Math, Bot (angle, leaf)* alterne
3 *Liter (rhyme)* croisé
4 *Am* = **alternative**
N *esp Am* remplaçant, -ante

Attention: ne pas confondre avec **alternative**.

alternate[2] [ˈɔːltəneɪt] **VT** *(methods)* employer tour à tour *ou* alternativement; *(jackets etc)* mettre tour à tour *ou* alternativement; **… alternating the tomato and cucumber slices** … en faisant alterner les rondelles de tomates et de concombre; *Agr* **to a. crops** alterner les récoltes
VI alterner (**with** avec); **he alternated with his friend on watches throughout the night** son ami et lui se sont relayés toute la nuit pour monter la garde; **they alternated between welcoming his help and resenting his intrusion** tantôt ils lui étaient reconnaissants de son aide, tantôt ils lui en voulaient de son intrusion; **rain and sunshine alternated all afternoon** la pluie et le soleil se sont succédés tout l'après-midi

alternately [ɔːlˈtɜːnətlɪ] **ADV** alternativement, tour à tour, en alternance; **boys and girls were seated a.** les garçons et les filles étaient assis en alternance; *Bot* **leaves placed a.** feuilles *fpl* alternes

Attention: ne pas confondre avec **alternatively**.

alternating [ˈɔːltəneɪtɪŋ] **ADJ 1** alternant, alterné **2** *Elec (current)* alternatif; *Tech (movement)* alternatif, de va-et-vient

alternation [ɔːltəˈneɪʃən] **N** alternance *f*

alternative [ɔːlˈtɜːnətɪv] **ADJ ATTRIB 1** *(plan, route, course of action)* alternatif; **an a. site will have to be found** il faudra trouver un autre endroit; **we'll find you a. employment** nous vous emploierons à autre chose; **to make a. arrangements** s'arranger autrement **2** *(not conventional)* parallèle, alternatif
N *(choice)* alternative *f*; **there is no a.** il n'y a pas d'alternative; **they were given the a. of a fine or a month's imprisonment** on leur a donné le choix entre une amende et un mois de prison; **the a. would be to …** une autre solution serait de …; **to have no a.** ne pas avoir le choix; **he had no a. but to obey** il n'a pu faire autrement que d'obéir; **there are alternatives to nuclear power** le nucléaire n'est pas la seule solution possible; **the a. was starvation** c'était ça ou mourir de faim
▶▶ **a. comedy** nouvelle comédie *f*; *Br St Exch* **A. Investment Market** = marché *m* horscote rattaché à la Bourse de Londres; *Med* **a. medicine** médecines *fpl* douces *ou* parallèles; **a. tourism** tourisme *m* vert

Attention: ne pas confondre avec **alternate**.

alternatively [ɔːlˈtɜːnətɪvlɪ] **ADV** *(on the other hand)* ou bien; *(in a different way) (employed etc)* autrement; **a., we could go to the beach** ou bien nous pourrions aller à la plage; **he's probably in the library, a. you might try the squash courts** il est sûrement à la bibliothèque, sinon, vous pouvez essayer les courts de squash

Attention: ne pas confondre avec **alternately**.

alternator [ˈɔːltəneɪtər] **N** *Elec* alternateur *m*

although [ɔːlˈðəʊ] **CONJ** quoique, bien que + *sub*; **a. I am a father** tout père que je suis; **Paul, a. rich, was not mean** Paul, bien que riche, n'était pas avare; **a. not beautiful, she was attractive** sans être belle, elle plaisait; **it's not possible … a. …** *(considering, changing mind)* cela n'est pas possible … à moins que …

altimeter [ˈæltɪmiːtər] **N** *Aviat* altimètre *m*; **radio a.** radiosonde *f*

altitude [ˈæltɪtjuːd] **N 1** altitude *f*; **at these altitudes** à cette altitude **2** *Astron, Geom (of star, triangle)* hauteur *f*
▶▶ *Tech* **a. recorder** enregistreur *m* d'altitude; **a. sickness** mal *m* d'altitude

alto [ˈæltəʊ] **N** *Mus* **1 to sing a.** chanter la partie alto **2** *(male voice)* haute-contre *f*, *pl* hautes-contre; *(female voice)* contralto *m*, alto *f*, **I'm an a.** je suis haute-contre/alto **3** *(viola)* alto *m* (à cordes); **a. trombone/saxophone** trombone *m*/saxophone *m* alto
▶▶ **a. clef** clef *f* d'ut

altocumulus [æltəʊˈkjuːmjələs] **N** altocumulus *m*

altogether [ɔːltəˈgeðər] **ADV 1** *(entirely)* entièrement, tout à fait; **to change sth a.** changer qch de fond en comble *ou* radicalement; **it's a. out of the question** c'est absolument impossible; **I was not a. pleased** ça ne me faisait pas exactement plaisir
2 *(in total)* en tout; **a. the bill came to £63** au total ça a fait 63 livres; **how much is that a.?** ça fait combien en tout?; **a., it was a memorable occasion** somme toute, ce fut un événement mémorable; **taking things a.** à tout prendre
N *Fam Hum* **in the a.** complètement nu, en tenue d'Adam/d'Ève

altostratus [æltəʊˈstraːtəs] **N** altostratus *m*

altruism [ˈæltrʊɪz(ə)m] **N** altruisme *m*

altruist [ˈæltrʊɪst] **N** altruiste *mf*

altruistic [æltrʊˈɪstɪk] **ADJ** altruiste

ALU [eɪelˈjuː] **N** *Comput (abbr* arithmetic and logic unit*)* unité *f* arithmétique et logique

alum [ˈæləm] **N** alun *m*
▶▶ *Phot* **a. bath** bain *m* aluné

alumina [əˈluːmɪnə] **N** *Miner* alumine *f*

aluminium [æljʊˈmɪnɪəm], *Am* **aluminum** [əˈluːmɪnəm] **N** aluminium *m*; *Metal* **a. alloy** alliage *m* d'aluminium; **a. saucepan** casserole *f* en aluminium
▶▶ **a. foil** papier *m* aluminium; *Chem* **a. oxide** alumine *f*

aluminize [əˈluːmɪnaɪz] **VT 1** *Metal* combiner avec de l'aluminium; **aluminized steel** acier *m* à l'aluminium **2** *Tech (mirror)* aluminer **3** *Chem* aluminer; *(in dyeing)* aluner

aluminum [əˈluːmɪnəm] **N** *Am* = **aluminium**

alumna, *pl* **alumnae** [əˈlʌmnə, -iː] **N** *esp Am (of school)* ancienne élève *f*; *(of university)* ancienne étudiante *f*

alumnus, *pl* **alumni** [əˈlʌmnəs, -aɪ] **N** *esp Am (of school)* ancien élève *m*; *(of university)* ancien étudiant *m*; **a. association** association *f* des anciens

alveolus, *pl* **alveoli** [ælˈvɪələs, -laɪ] **N** *Anat* alvéole *f* pulmonaire

always [ˈɔːlwəz, -wɪz, *stressed* -weɪz] **ADV 1** *(all the time)* toujours; **nearly** *or* **almost a.** presque toujours; **the office is a. open** le bureau est toujours ouvert *ou* est ouvert en permanence; **he's a. complaining** il se plaint tout le temps, il n'arrête pas de se plaindre; **I'll a. remember you!** je ne t'oublierai jamais! VOIR GRAMMAIRE A21

2 (as alternative) toujours; **I can a. try** je peux toujours ou quand même essayer; **there's a. the old age pension** il y a toujours la retraite

alyssum ['ælɪsəm] **N** alysse f

Alzheimer's, Alzheimer's disease ['æltshaɪməz] **N** Med maladie f d'Alzheimer

AM ['eɪ'em] **N** (abbr **amplitude modulation**) AM f

am[1] [æm] see **be**

am[2]**, a.m.** ['eɪ'em] **ADV** (abbr ante meridiem) avant midi; **five am** cinq heures du matin; **we're leaving at six – am or pm?** nous partons à six heures – du matin ou de l'après-midi? VOIR GRAMMAIRE A80

AMA ['eɪ'em'eɪ] **N1** Med (abbr **American Medical Association**) = ordre m américain des médecins **2** Mktg (abbr **American Marketing Association**) = institut m américain de marketing

amalgam [ə'mælgəm] **N** Metal, Fig amalgame m

amalgamate [ə'mælgəmeɪt] **VT** Metal amalgamer; Fig (ideas) amalgamer; (companies, industries), Fin (shares) fusionner
VI (of metals, ideas) s'amalgamer; (of companies) fusionner

amalgamation [əmælgə'meɪʃən] **N** (of metals) amalgamation f, (of two companies), Fin (of shares) fusionnement m; (collection) (of evidence etc) accumulation f

amaryllis [æmə'rɪlɪs] **N** (plant) amaryllis f (belle-dame)

amass [ə'mæs] **VT** (wealth, objects, information etc) amasser, accumuler

amateur ['æmətər, -tjʊər, æmə'tɜːr] **N1** (non-professional) amateur m; **a. painter/musician** peintre m/musicien m amateur; **he paints as an a.** il peint en amateur ou en dilettante; Pej **he's a real a.** ce n'est qu'un amateur, c'est un amateur; **they did a rather a. job** ils ont fait du travail d'amateur **2** Sport amateur m; **a. championship** championnat m amateur; Horseracing **a. rider** gentleman rider m; **a. sport** sport m d'amateur

amateurish ['æmətərɪʃ, æmə'tɜːrɪʃ] **ADJ** Pej (piece of work etc) d'amateur; (actor, singer etc) amateur

amateurishly ['æmətərɪʃlɪ] **ADV** Pej en amateur; (presented, written) avec amateurisme

amateurism ['æmətərɪz(ə)m] **N1** (in arts) dilettantisme m, Pej amateurisme m **2** Sport amateurisme m

amatory ['æmət(ə)rɪ] **ADJ** Lit, Hum (sentiment, conquests) amoureux; (letter) d'amour; (intentions, ambitions) galant; (poem) érotique

amaze [ə'meɪz] **VT** ébahir, stupéfier; **his courage amazed me** son courage m'a stupéfié; **I was amazed at or by the price** le prix m'a ébahi, j'étais très étonné par le ou du prix; **I was amazed to learn that** ça m'a ébahi ou stupéfié de l'apprendre; **it amazes me that he could have done such a thing** je suis stupéfait qu'il ait pu faire une telle chose; **you a. me sometimes** (are exasperating) tu es incroyable quelquefois; **you never cease to a. me** tu m'étonneras toujours; Iron **you a. me!** non, vraiment?; Iron **go on, a. me!** vas-y, surprends-moi!

amazement [ə'meɪzmənt] **N** stupéfaction f, stupeur f, grand étonnement m; **to listen in a.** écouter avec stupeur; **to our a.** à notre grand étonnement, à notre stupéfaction; **I heard with a. that …** j'ai été stupéfait d'apprendre que …

amazing [ə'meɪzɪŋ] **ADJ** stupéfiant, étonnant; (dexterity) prestigieux; **it's a.!** je n'en

reviens pas!; **it's a. that no one was hurt** c'est étonnant que personne n'ait été blessé; **you've been a.** tu as été formidable

amazingly [ə'meɪzɪŋlɪ] **ADV** étonnamment; **a. quickly** à une vitesse stupéfiante ou étonnante; **we were a. lucky** nous avons eu une chance formidable; **a., no one was hurt** c'est étonnant mais personne n'a été blessé; **he's doing a. well** (in business) il réussit à merveille; (recovering quickly) il se remet merveilleusement bien

Amazon ['æməz(ə)n] **N1 the** (river) **A.** l'Amazone f **2** Myth Amazone f, Fig femme f forte et athlétique
▸▸ **the A. basin** le bassin amazonien; **the A. rainforest** la forêt tropicale (humide) amazonienne

Amazonian [æmə'zəʊnɪən] **ADJ 1** Geog de l'Amazone, amazonien **2** Myth d'Amazone; Fig (woman) fort et athlétique; Fig **I like the A. type** j'aime les femmes fortes et athlétiques

ambassador [æm'bæsədər] **N** (diplomat), Fig ambassadeur m, ambassadrice f, **the French A. to Japan** l'ambassadeur de France au Japon

ambassadorial [æmbæsə'dɔːrɪəl] **ADJ** (duties etc) d'ambassadeur

ambassadress [æm'bæsədrɪs] **N** (diplomat), Fig ambassadrice f

amber ['æmbər] **N** (colour, stone) ambre m; **yellow a.** ambre jaune; **he crossed on a.** (traffic light) il a traversé à l'orange
ADJ 1 (necklace) d'ambre, en ambre; **a. varnish** vernis m au succin **2 a.(-coloured)** ambré
▸▸ **a. light** feu m orange; Br, Austr Fam Hum **a. nectar** bière f, mousse f

ambergris ['æmbəgriːs] **N** ambre m gris

ambidextrous [æmbɪ'dekstrəs] **ADJ** ambidextre

ambience, ambiance ['æmbɪəns] **N** ambiance f

ambient ['æmbɪənt] **ADJ** Tech, Cin (temperature, noise, light etc) ambiant
▸▸ **a. sound** son m d'ambiance

ambiguity [æmbɪ'gjuːɪtɪ] **N 1** (ambiguousness) ambiguïté f **2** (instance) équivoque f, **his speech was full of ambiguities** son discours a été très ambigu

ambiguous [æm'bɪgjʊəs] **ADJ** ambigu, f -uë, équivoque

ambiguously [æm'bɪgjʊəslɪ] **ADV** d'une manière ambiguë ou équivoque; **an a. worded reply** une réponse formulée de façon ambiguë

ambiguousness [æm'bɪgjʊəsnɪs] **N** ambiguïté f

ambit ['æmbɪt] **N** Fml (of law, investigations) portée f, **that does not come within our a.** cela n'entre pas dans nos compétences

ambition [æm'bɪʃən] **N** ambition f, **the a. to succeed** l'ambition de réussir; **to have great ambitions** avoir de grandes ambitions ou de hautes visées; **it's my a. to …, my a. is to …** j'ambitionne de …; **my parents had great ambitions for me** mes parents avaient de grands projets pour moi

ambitious [æm'bɪʃəs] **ADJ** (person, project etc) ambitieux; **to be a. to do sth** ambitionner de faire qch; **they're very a. for their children** ils sont très ambitieux en ce qui concerne leurs enfants

ambitiously [æm'bɪʃəslɪ] **ADV** ambitieusement; **they planned a.** ils ont fait des projets ambitieux

ambitiousness [æm'bɪʃəsnɪs] **N** (of project, design) caractère m ambitieux; (of person) ambition f

ambivalence [æm'bɪvələns] **N** ambivalence f

ambivalent [æm'bɪvələnt] **ADJ** ambivalent

amble ['æmb(ə)l] **N** (of horse) amble m; (of person) pas m ou allure f tranquille; **to walk at an a.** (of horse) aller l'amble, ambler
VI (of horse) aller (à) l'amble, ambler; **to make a horse a.** mettre un cheval à l'amble; **he ambled up to us** (of person) il s'est avancé vers nous d'un pas tranquille; **I'll just a. down to the corner shop** je vais faire un saut à l'épicerie du coin; **he just ambles in at ten o'clock** il arrive à dix heures les mains dans les poches ou en se baladant
▸ **amble along VI** (of horse) aller à l'amble; (of person) aller ou marcher d'un pas tranquille; (without destination) flâner

ambrosia [æm'brəʊzɪə] **N** Myth ambroisie f

ambrosial [æm'brəʊzɪəl] **ADJ** ambrosiaque

ambulance ['æmbjʊləns] **N** ambulance f
▸▸ Am Fam Pej **a. chaser** = avocat m qui ne s'occupe que d'affaires de demandes de dommages et intérêts pouvant rapporter gros; **a. crew** ambulanciers mpl; **a. man** (driver) ambulancier m; (nurse) infirmier m d'ambulance; (stretcher carrier) brancardier m; **a. plane** avion m sanitaire; **a. post** poste m d'ambulance; **a. ship** navire m hôpital; **a. train** train m sanitaire; **a. woman** (driver) ambulancière f, (nurse) infirmière f d'ambulance; (stretcher carrier) brancardière f

ambulant ['æmbjʊlənt] **ADJ** Med ambulatoire

ambulatory ['æmbjʊlətərɪ] **ADJ 1** ambulant, mobile **2** Med (treatment, sick person) ambulatoire
N promenoir m, préau m; Archit (in church) déambulatoire m

ambush ['æmbʊʃ] **N** embuscade f, guet-apens m, pl guets-apens; **to lie in a.** se tenir en embuscade; Fig être à l'affût; **to lay or set an a. for sb** tendre une embuscade à qn; **troops lying in a.** troupes embusquées; **they were caught in an a.** ils sont tombés dans une embuscade ou un guet-apens
VT (enemy) attirer dans une embuscade; **to be ambushed** tomber dans une embuscade

ameba, amebic Am = amoeba, amoebic

ameliorate [ə'miːlɪəreɪt] Fml **VT** améliorer
VI s'améliorer

amelioration [əmiːlɪə'reɪʃən] **N** Fml amélioration f

amen ['ɑːmen, 'eɪmen] **INT** Rel amen, ainsi soit-il; Fig certes; **and we all say a. to that** c'est ce que nous souhaitons tous

amenable [ə'miːnəb(ə)l] **ADJ** (subject) sujet (**to** à); (person) (to law, discipline) soumis; (to advice) docile; (child) soumis, docile; **a. to reason** raisonnable, disposé à entendre raison; **to prove a. to a suggestion** se ranger à une suggestion; **the case is not a. to ordinary rules** ce cas n'est pas sujet aux règles ordinaires; **to be a. to treatment** (of illness) pouvoir être traité

amend [ə'mend] **VT** (change) modifier, amender; Pol (bill) amender; (correct) rectifier, corriger; **amended invoice** facture f rectificative
VI s'amender

amendment [ə'mendmənt] **N** (change) modification f, Pol (of bill) amendement m; (correction) rectification f, correction f, (of mistake) redressement m, correction; Pol **to move an a.** proposer un amendement (**to a bill** à un projet de loi); Am **the third A.** (to the Constitution) le troisième amendement

amends [ə'mendz] **NPL to make a.** faire amende honorable; **nothing could make a. for what they had done** rien ne pouvait réparer ce qu'ils avaient fait; **to make a. to sb for sth** dédommager qn de qch

amenity [ə'miːnɪtɪ] **N 1** (usu pl) **amenities** (in town, city) facilités fpl, aménagements *mpl*; *(at sports centre, campsite etc)* équipements *mpl*; **close to all amenities** *(in accommodation advertisement)* proximité tous commerces **2** *Fml, Arch (of place)* agrément *m*

amenorrhoea, *Am* **amenorrhea** [eɪmenəˈrɪə] N *Med* aménorrhée *f*

America [əˈmerɪkə] N **1** *(continent)* Amérique *f*; **North/South A.** Amérique du Nord/Sud; **in A.** en Amérique; **the Americas** les Amériques **2** *(United States)* États-Unis *mpl* (d'Amérique)

American [əˈmerɪkən] ADJ **1** *(continental)* américain **2** *(of United States)* américain N **1** Américain, -aine; **Native A.** Amérindien, -ienne **2** *Ling* américain *m*
▸▸ **A. Automobile Association** = société *f* de dépannage pour les automobilistes, ≃ Touring Club *m* de France; **A. breakfast** petit déjeuner *m* américain; *Tex* **A. cloth** toile *f* cirée; *Fin* **A. depository receipt** certificat *m* américain de dépôt; **A. English** (anglais *m*) américain; **A. Express**® American Express®; **to pay by A. Express**® payer par American Express®; **A. Express**® **card** carte *f* American Express®; *Br* **A. football** football *m* américain; **A. Indian** Indien, -ienne d'Amérique, Amérindien, -ienne; *Mus* **A. organ** harmonium *m*; *Am* **A. plan** pension *f* complète; **A. service** service *m* à l'américaine *ou* à l'assiette; *Cin* **A. shot** plan *m* américain

Americanism [əˈmerɪkənɪz(ə)m] N *Ling* américanisme *m*

Americanize [əˈmerɪkənaɪz] VT américaniser; **to become Americanized** s'américaniser

American-style option N *St Exch* option *f* américaine

Amerind [ˈæmərɪnd], **Amerindian** [æməˈrɪndɪən] ADJ amérindien N Amérindien, -ienne

amethyst [ˈæmɪθɪst] N améthyste *f*

Amex [ˈæmeks] N **1** *(abbr* American Express®) Amex® carte *f* Amex® **2** *(abbr* American Stock Exchange) = deuxième place *f* boursière des États-Unis

amiability [eɪmɪəˈbɪlɪtɪ] N amabilité *f* (**to** envers)

amiable [ˈeɪmɪəb(ə)l] ADJ aimable (**to** envers); **to be very a.** être très aimable *ou* d'une grande amabilité

> Attention: ne pas confondre avec **amicable**.

amiably [ˈeɪmɪəblɪ] ADV aimablement, avec amabilité

amicability [æmɪkəˈbɪlɪtɪ] N nature *f* *ou* disposition *f* amicale; **the a. of his nature** sa nature amicale

amicable [ˈæmɪkəb(ə)l] ADJ *(manner, relationship, chat etc)* amical, -aux; *(separation, agreement)* à l'amiable
▸▸ *Law* **a. settlement** arrangement *m* à l'amiable

> Attention: ne pas confondre avec le terme anglais **amiable**.

amicably [ˈæmɪkəblɪ, əˈmɪk-] ADV amicalement; *(to part)* bons amis; *(to divorce, settle issue)* à l'amiable; **to live a. together** vivre en harmonie

AMICUS [ˈæmɪkəs] N = syndicat *m* industriel britannique né de la fusion de l'AEEU et du MSF

amid [əˈmɪd] PREP au milieu de; **the news came a. revelations of corruption** la nouvelle survint en plein milieu *ou* au moment des révélations de corruption; **the meeting ended a. some confusion** la réunion s'est terminée dans une certaine confusion

amide [ˈæmaɪd] N *Chem* amide *m*

amidships [əˈmɪdʃɪps] ADV *Naut* au milieu du navire; **cabin a.** cabine *f* par le travers; **to put the helm a.** mettre la barre droite; **helm a.!** barre à zéro!, zéro (la barre)!

amidst [əˈmɪdst] PREP = **amid**

amino-acid [æˈmiːnəʊ-] N *Chem* amino-acide *m*

amiss [əˈmɪs] ADV, ADJ PRED **1** *(badly)* **to take sth a.** prendre qch de travers, mal prendre qch; **he took it very much a.** il a très mal pris la chose **2** *(out of place)* malvenu; **a cup of coffee wouldn't come** *or* **go a.** une tasse de café serait bienvenue; **a few more women presenters on TV wouldn't go a.** ce ne serait pas un mal *ou* une mauvaise chose s'il y avait plus de présentateurs femmes à la télévision; **something is a.** il y a quelque chose qui ne va pas *ou* *Fam* qui cloche; **there was nothing a. when I last saw him** tout allait bien la dernière fois que je l'ai vu

amity [ˈæmɪtɪ] N *Fml (between countries)* amitié *f*, concorde *f*, bons rapports *mpl*; **to live in a. with sb** vivre en bonne intelligence avec qn

ammeter [ˈæmiːtər] N *Elec* ampèremètre *m*

ammo [ˈæməʊ] N *Fam* munitions *fpl*

ammonia [əˈməʊnɪə] N *Chem* ammoniac *m*, gaz *m* ammoniac

ammoniac [əˈməʊnɪæk] ADJ ammoniac, -iaque; **sal a.** sel *m* ammoniac N **(gum) a.** gomme *f* ammoniaque

ammonite [ˈæmənaɪt] N *(fossil)* ammonite *f*

ammonium [əˈməʊnɪəm] N *Chem* ammonium *m*
▸▸ **a. carbonate** carbonate *m* d'ammonium; **a. sulphate** sulfate *m* d'ammonium

ammunition [æmjʊˈnɪʃən] N *Mil* munitions *fpl*; *Fig* **the scandal provided the opposition with useful a.** le scandale a procuré à l'opposition un bon moyen d'offensive; *Fig* **protesters used the report as a.** les manifestants ont utilisé le rapport comme argument; **blank a.** munitions à blanc; **dummy a.** fausses munitions; **live a.** munitions réelles *ou* pour tir réel
▸▸ *Mil* **a. box** coffre *m* à munitions; *Mil* **a. depot, a. dump** dépôt *m* de munitions; *Mil* **a. train** train *m* de munitions

amnesia [æmˈniːzɪə] N *Med* amnésie *f*; **to suffer from a.** être amnésique *ou* souffrir d'amnésie

amnesiac [æmˈniːzɪæk], **amnesic** [æmˈniːzɪk] N, ADJ amnésique *mf*

amnesty [ˈæmnɪstɪ] N amnistie *f* VT amnistier

amniocentesis [æmnɪəʊsenˈtiːsɪs] N *Med* amniocentèse *f*

amoeba, *Am* **ameba,** *pl* **amoebas, amoebae** [əˈmiːbə, -əz, -iː] N *Biol* amibe *f*

amoebic, *Am* **amebic** [əˈmiːbɪk] ADJ *Med* amibien
▸▸ **a. dysentery** dysenterie *f* amibienne

amok [əˈmɒk] ADV **to run a.** *(of gunman)* faire des ravages; *(of rioters, editor)*, *Fam (children)* se déchaîner

among [əˈmʌŋ], **amongst** [əˈmʌŋst] PREP parmi; **a house standing a. trees** une maison située au milieu des arbres *ou* entourée d'arbres; **to wander a. the ruins** errer parmi les ruines; **a. the crowd** au milieu de la foule, parmi la foule; **to live a. savages** vivre au milieu des sauvages; **we are a. friends** nous sommes entre amis; **this expression is current a. young people** cette expression est courante chez les jeunes; **a. the guests were ...** au nombre des invités *ou* parmi les invités se trouvaient ...; **that cake won't go far a. twelve** ce gâteau ne donnera pas grand-chose, divisé entre douze person-

nes; **the orchestra is a. the finest in Europe** l'orchestre est l'un des meilleurs d'Europe; **not one a. them** pas un d'entre eux *ou* parmi eux; **a. other things, he said that ...** il a dit, entre autres, que ...; **a. ourselves** entre nous; **they quarrel a. themselves** ils se disputent entre eux

amoral [eɪˈmɒrəl] ADJ amoral, -aux

amorous [ˈæmərəs] ADJ *Lit, Hum (look, advances, adventures)* amoureux; **to be of an a. disposition** être romantique; **he became quite a.** il a commencé à me/lui/*etc* faire des avances

amorously [ˈæmərəslɪ] ADV amoureusement

amorphous [əˈmɔːfəs] ADJ **1** *Chem* amorphe **2** *(mass, lump)* amorphe; *Fig (opinions, project)* vague

amortizable [əmɔːˈtaɪzəb(ə)l] ADJ *Com, Fin (debt)* amortissable

amortization [əmɔːtɪˈzeɪʃən] N *Com, Fin (of debt)* amortissement *m*

amortize [əˈmɔːtaɪz] VT *Com, Fin (debt)* amortir

amount [əˈmaʊnt] N **1** *Com (sum of money)* somme *f*; *(total) (of bill etc)* montant *m*, total *m*; **please tender the exact a.** *(on bus etc)* on est prié de faire l'appoint; **(up) to the a. of ...** jusqu'à concurrence de ...; *Acct* **a. carried forward** report *m* à nouveau; **no a. (of money) could make up for what I've lost** rien ne pourrait compenser ce que j'ai perdu; **a. exclusive of VAT** montant hors TVA
2 *(quantity)* quantité *f*; **a massive a. of time** énormément de temps; **a massive a. of effort** des efforts énormes; **a certain a. of discomfort/comfort** un certain manque de confort/un certain confort; **the a. of work that an engine will do** la somme de travail que peut fournir une machine; **in small amounts** par petites quantités; **no a. of persuasion would make her stay** il n'y avait pas moyen de la persuader de rester; **a dwindling a. of funds** des fonds en quantité décroissante; **varying amounts of enthusiasm** des expressions d'enthousiasme inégales; *Fam* **he has any a. of money/friends/books** il a de l'argent/des amis/des livres tant et plus
▸ **amount to** VT INSEP **1** *(of money etc)* s'élever à, se monter à; **transactions amounting to several million pounds** opérations qui se chiffrent par plusieurs millions de livres; **I don't know what my debts a. to** j'ignore le montant de mes dettes, j'ignore à combien se montent *ou* s'élèvent mes dettes
2 *(be equivalent to)* équivaloir à, se réduire à, revenir à; **these conditions a. to a refusal** ces conditions équivalent à un refus; **it amounts to the same thing** cela revient au même; **all that amounts to very little/to nothing** tout cela se réduit à peu de chose/à rien; **he'll never a. to much/to anything** il ne fera jamais grand-chose/rien

amour [əˈmʊər] N *Lit, Arch* intrigue *f* amoureuse, liaison *f*

A-movie N *Cin* film *m* projeté en exclusivité *(lors d'une séance où deux longs métrages sont projetés)*

amp [æmp] N **1** *Elec (abbr* ampere) ampère *m*; **13-a. plug** fiche *f* de 13 ampères **2** *Mus Fam (abbr* amplifier) ampli *m*

ampere [ˈæmpeər] N *Elec* ampère *m*

ampersand [ˈæmpəsænd] N *Typ* esperluette *f*

amphetamine [æmˈfetəmɪn] N *Pharm* amphétamine *f*; **to be on amphetamines** *(of drug addict)* prendre des amphétamines

amphibia [æmˈfɪbɪə] NPL *Zool* amphibiens *mpl*

amphibian [æmˈfɪbɪən] ADJ amphibie N **1** *Zool* amphibie *m* **2** *(tank)* char *m* amphibie; *(vehicle)* voiture *f* amphibie

amphibious [æm'fɪbɪəs] ADJ *(animal, plane etc)* amphibie

amphitheatre, *Am* **amphitheater** ['æmfɪθɪətər] N *Archit, Theat etc* amphithéâtre *m*

amphora, *pl* **amphorae** ['æmfərə, -iː] N *Antiq* amphore *f*

ample ['æmp(ə)l] ADJ **1** *(garment)* ample, large; *(bag, stomach, bosom)* gros; **man of a. proportions** homme *m* corpulent **2** *(plentiful)* abondant; **this will be a.** ceci sera amplement suffisant, ceci suffira amplement; **to have a. means** avoir de gros moyens; **a. proof** de nombreuses preuves; **there are a. supplies of fish this week** *(in shops)* il y a de gros arrivages de poisson cette semaine; **the money we have is a. for our needs** nous avons largement assez d'argent pour subvenir à nos besoins; **to have a. time** avoir largement le temps (**to do** de faire); **you'll be given a. warning** vous serez averti longtemps à l'avance; **he was given a. opportunity to explain his actions** il a eu de nombreuses occasions d'expliquer ses actes; **you'll have a. opportunity to practise your backhand this summer** tu auras largement l'occasion de pratiquer ton revers cet été

amplification [æmplɪfɪ'keɪʃən] N **1** *(expansion)* augmentation *f*, extension *f*; **if I could say something in a. of …** si je pouvais dire quelque chose pour développer … **2** *(of power, current, volume etc)* amplification *f* **3** *Opt (using lens etc)* grossissement *m*

amplifier ['æmplɪfaɪər] N **1** *(for sound system)* amplificateur *m, Fam* ampli *m* **2** *Phot* (lentille *f*) amplificatrice *f*
▸▸ **a. circuit** circuit *m* d'amplification

amplify ['æmplɪfaɪ] VT **1** *(expand) (essay, remarks etc)* développer; *(report etc)* ajouter des détails à **2** *(current, power, volume etc)* amplifier

amplitude ['æmplɪtjuːd] N *Fml (of dimensions, resources etc)* ampleur *f*, *(of space)* étendue *f*, *Astron (of star)* amplitude *f*, *Phys (of oscillations, vibrations)* amplitude; *Phys* **magnetic a.** déclinaison *f* magnétique
▸▸ **a. modulation** modulation *f* d'amplitude

amply ['æmplɪ] ADV amplement; **a. proportioned** aux dimensions généreuses; **a. rewarded** largement récompensé

ampoule ['æmpuːl] N *Med (for hypodermic injection)* ampoule *f*

amputate ['æmpjʊteɪt] VT *(leg etc)* amputer; **his right leg was amputated** il a été amputé de la jambe droite
VI amputer

amputation [æmpjʊ'teɪʃən] N amputation *f*

amputee [æmpjʊ'tiː] N amputé, -ée

Amtrak ['æmtræk] N = société *f* des chemins de fer interurbains des États-Unis

amuck [ə'mʌk] ADV = **amok**

amulet ['æmjʊlet] N amulette *f*

amuse [ə'mjuːz] VT amuser, divertir, faire rire; **it amused her to do it** ça l'a amusée de le faire; **is something amusing you?** quelque chose vous amuse?; **to a. oneself** s'occuper, passer le temps; **to a. oneself by** *or* **with doing sth** *(have fun)* s'amuser à faire qch *ou* en faisant qch; *(pass the time)* s'occuper en faisant qch; **to a. oneself with sth** s'amuser avec qch; **to keep sb amused** *(occupied)* occuper qn; *(entertained)* amuser qn

amused [ə'mjuːzd] ADJ amusé; **to be a. at** *or* **by sth** s'amuser de qch, trouver qch drôle; **she wasn't at all a.** elle n'a pas du tout trouvé ça drôle; **a. smile** sourire *m* amusé

amusedly [ə'mjuːzɪdlɪ] ADV d'un air amusé

amusement [ə'mjuːzmənt] N **1** amusement *m*; **source of a.** source *f* d'amusement; **smile of a.** sourire *m* amusé; **to the great a. of the**

children au grand amusement des enfants; **much to everyone's a.** au grand amusement de la compagnie **2** *(occupation, pastime)* amusement *m*, divertissement *m*, distraction *f*; **we have few amusements here** nous avons peu de distractions ici; **it offered** *or* **provided little a. for them** cela ne les amusait guère; **place of a.** lieu *m* de divertissement
▸▸ **a. arcade** salle *f* de jeux électroniques; **a. park** parc *m* d'attractions

amusing [ə'mjuːzɪŋ] ADJ *(person)* amusant, drôle; *(book, film)* amusant, drôle, divertissant; **what an a. woman/idea** quelle femme/quelle idée amusante

amusingly [ə'mjuːzɪŋlɪ] ADV d'une manière amusante; **a. worded** drôle, amusant

amylase ['æmɪleɪz] N *Biol, Chem* amylase *f*

an *see* a²

ANA [eɪen'eɪ] N *Journ (abbr* **American Newspaper Association)** = syndicat *m* américain de la presse écrite

anabaptist [ænə'bæptɪst] ADJ, N *Rel, Hist* anabaptiste *mf*

anabolic [ænə'bɒlɪk] ADJ *Chem* anabolisant
▸▸ *Pharm* **a. steroid** stéroïde *m* anabolisant

anachronism [ə'nækrənɪz(ə)m] N anachronisme *m*; **she's an a.** c'est un véritable anachronisme

anachronistic [ənækrə'nɪstɪk] ADJ anachronique

anaconda [ænə'kɒndə] N *(snake)* anaconda *m*

anaemia, *Am* **anemia** [ə'niːmɪə] N anémie *f*; **to suffer from a.** souffrir d'anémie, faire de l'anémie

anaemic, *Am* **anemic** [ə'niːmɪk] ADJ *Med* anémique; *Fig* faible, mou, *f* molle; **to become a.** s'anémier

anaesthesia, *Am* **anesthesia** [ænəs'θiːzɪə] N anesthésie *f*; **general/local a.** anesthésie générale/locale; **spinal a.** anesthésie rachidienne

anaesthetic, *Am* **anesthetic** [ænəs'θetɪk] N *(product)* anesthésique *m*; *(procedure)* anesthésie *f*; **under a.** sous anesthésie; **under the a.** sous l'effet de l'anesthésie
ADJ anesthésique

anaesthetist, *Am* **anesthetist** [ə'niːsθətɪst] N anesthésiste *mf*

anaesthetize, *Am* **anesthetize** [ə'niːsθətaɪz] VT *Med, Fig* anesthésier

anagram ['ænəgræm] N anagramme *f*

anal ['eɪn(ə)l] ADJ *Anat* anal, -aux

analeptic [ænə'leptɪk] N, ADJ *Pharm* analeptique *m*

analgesia [ænəl'dʒiːzɪə] N *Med* analgésie *f*

analgesic [ænəl'dʒiːsɪk, -zɪk] ADJ, N *Med* analgésique *m*; *Pharm* antalgique *m*

analog ['ænəlɒg] ADJ *Comput* analogique
N *Am* = **analogue**

analogical [ænə'lɒdʒɪk(ə)l] ADJ analogique

analogically [ænə'lɒdʒɪklɪ] ADV analogiquement, par analogie; **a. speaking** analogiquement parlant

analogous [ə'næləgəs] ADJ analogue (**to, with** à)

analogously [ə'næləgəslɪ] ADV d'une manière analogue

analogue, *Am* **analog** ['ænəlɒg] N analogue *m*; **this is an a. of what happens on a national level** ceci est analogue à ce qui se passe au niveau national
ADJ *(clock, watch)* (à affichage) analogique
▸▸ **a. computer** calculateur *m* analogique; **a. network** réseau *m* analogique

analogy [ə'nælədʒɪ] N analogie *f* (**to, with** avec; **between** entre); **by a. with …** par analogie avec …; **to draw an a.** faire une analogie; **on the a. of …** en comparant avec …

analyse, *Am* **analyze** ['ænəlaɪz] VT *(text, events),* Chem, Math analyser, faire l'analyse de; *(feelings, attitude)* analyser; *Gram (sentence)* faire l'analyse logique de; *Psy (person)* psychanalyser

analysis, *pl* **analyses** [ə'næləsɪs, -iːz] N *(of text),* Chem, Phys analyse *f*, *Gram (of sentence)* analyse logique; *Psy* psychanalyse *f*; **nothing abnormal showed up under a.** l'analyse n'a rien révélé d'anormal; **our a. is that …** notre analyse démontre que …; **to hold up under** *or* **withstand a.** résister à l'analyse; *Psy* **to be in a.** *(of patient)* être en analyse; **in the final** *or* **last a.** *(ultimately)* en fin de compte, au bout du compte
▸▸ *Acct* **a. ledger** journal *m* analytique

analyst ['ænəlɪst] N analyste *mf*; *Psy* (psych)analyste *mf*

analytic(al) [ænə'lɪtɪk, -ɪk(ə)l] ADJ analytique; **a. mind** esprit *m* d'analyse
▸▸ **a. psychology** psychologie *f* introspective

analyze ['ænəlaɪz] VT *Am* = **analyse**

analyzer ['ænəlaɪzər] N *Comput* analyseur *m*

anamorphic [ænə'mɔːfɪk] ADJ *Cin, TV* anamorphique
▸▸ **a. format** format *m* anamorphique; **a. lens** objectif *m* anamorphoseur

anarchic [æ'nɑːkɪk] ADJ anarchique

anarchist ['ænəkɪst] ADJ, N anarchiste *mf*

anarchy ['ænəkɪ] N anarchie *f*

anastigmatic [ænəstɪg'mætɪk] ADJ *Opt* anastigmat(ique)

anastomosis [ənæstə'məʊsɪs] N *Med* anastomose *f*

anathema [ə'næθəmə] N *Rel, Fig* anathème *m*; **his name is a.** son nom est tabou; *Fig* **it's/he's a. to me** c'est ma bête noire; **such theories were pronounced a.** l'anathème a été jeté sur ces théories; **their ideas were a. to him** leurs idées l'horripilaient

anathematize [ə'næθəmətaɪz] VT *Arch, Fml* frapper d'anathème

anatomical [ænə'tɒmɪk(ə)l] ADJ anatomique; **a. specimen** pièce *f* d'anatomie, préparation *f* anatomique

anatomically [ænə'tɒmɪklɪ] ADV anatomiquement

anatomist [ə'nætəmɪst] N anatomiste *mf*

anatomy [ə'nætəmɪ] N **1** *(of human, animal)* anatomie *f* **2** *(science)* anatomie *f*, *(textbook)* cours *m* d'anatomie; **human a.** anatomie humaine **3** *Fig* analyse *f*, anatomie *f*

ANC [eɪen'siː] N *(abbr* **African National Congress)** ANC *m*

ancestor ['ænsestər] N ancêtre *m*, *Lit* aïeul *m*, *pl* aïeux
▸▸ **a. worship** culte *m* des ancêtres

ancestral [æn'sestr(ə)l] ADJ **1** ancestral, -aux, héréditaire, de famille; **it's an a. right** c'est un droit ancestral; **his a. home** la demeure de ses ancêtres **2** *Biol* ancestral, -aux

ancestress ['ænsestrɪs] N ancêtre *f*, *Lit* aïeule *f*

ancestry ['ænsestrɪ] N **1** *(descent)* ascendance *f*; **both families were of French a.** les deux familles étaient d'ascendance française; **this custom is of more recent a.** cette coutume est d'apparition plus récente **2** *(no pl) (ancestors)* ancêtres *mpl*, ascendants *mpl*, aïeux *mpl*

anchor ['æŋkər] N **1** *Naut etc* ancre *f*, *Fig* planche *f* de salut; **to let go** *or* **to drop the a.** jeter *ou* mouiller l'ancre; **to weigh a.** lever l'ancre, appareiller; **to lie** *or* **ride at a.** être à l'ancre, mouiller; **at a.** au mouillage; **to slip the a.** filer (sa chaîne) par le bout; **to drag**

her a. *(of ship)* chasser sur son ancre *ou* sur ses ancres

2 *TV (presenter)* présentateur, -trice principal(e)

VT1 *Naut (ship)* ancrer, mouiller

2 *(fix firmly) Constr* affermir par des ancres; *Naut etc (mast etc)* hauban(n)er; *Fig* **to be anchored to the spot** *(by indecision, terror)* être cloué sur place

3 *TV (programme)* présenter

VI *Naut* jeter l'ancre, mouiller

▸▸*Naut* **a. buoy** bouée *f* de mouillage *ou* d'ancre; *Constr* **a. iron** grappin *m*; *Constr* **a. plate** plaque *f* d'ancrage; *Constr* **a. stay** câble *m* d'ancrage; *Am* **a. store** magasin-phare *m*, *pl* magasins-phares; *Constr* **a. tie** grappin

anchorage ['æŋkərɪdʒ] **N1** *Naut (act, place)* mouillage *m*; **to leave the a.** dérader **2** *Naut (fee)* droits *mpl* d'ancrage *ou* de stationnement **3** *Constr* ancrage *m*; *(of tie beam)* point *m* d'attache

▸▸**a. point** *(of seatbelt)* point d'ancrage

anchored ['æŋkəd] **ADJ** *Naut* ancré, mouillé, à l'ancre; *Fig* **firmly a. faith** foi *f* solidement ancrée

anchoring ['æŋkərɪŋ] **N** *Naut* ancrage *m*, mouillage *m*

anchorite ['æŋkəraɪt] **N** *Rel* anachorète *m*

anchorman, *pl* **anchormen** ['æŋkəmən] **N1** *Sport (of team)* dernier coureur *m* **2** *Radio, TV* présentateur *m* principal

anchorwoman, *pl* **anchorwomen** ['æŋkəwʊmən, -wɪmɪn] **N** *Radio, TV* présentatrice *f* principale

anchovy ['æntʃəvɪ, æn'tʃəʊvɪ] **N** anchois *m*

▸▸**a. butter** beurre *m* d'anchois; **a. paste** pâte *f* d'anchois

ancient ['eɪnʃənt] **ADJ** ancien; *(monument)* historique; *(oak)* centenaire; *Fam (person)* très vieux, *f* vieille, décrépit; *Fam (car, TV etc)* antique, antédiluvien; *Fam* **this car is getting pretty a.** cette voiture est une vraie antiquité

NPL the ancients les anciens *mpl*

▸▸*also Fig* **a. history** histoire *f* ancienne; **A. Rome** la Rome antique; **the a. world** le monde antique

ancillary [æn'sɪlərɪ] **ADJ** subordonné (**to** à); *(assisting)* auxiliaire

N *(helper)* auxiliaire *mf*; *(in hospital)* auxiliaire de service

▸▸**a. equipment** matériel *m* annexe *ou* d'appoint, accessoires *mpl*; **a. rights** droits *mpl* dérivés; **a. staff** personnel *m* auxiliaire; *(in hospital)* personnel des services auxiliaires; *(in school)* personnel auxiliaire, auxiliaires; **a. worker** *(in hospital)* auxiliaire de service

AND [ænd] **N** *Comput*

▸▸**A. circuit** circuit *m* ET; **A. element** élément *m* ET

AND [ænd, *unstressed* ənd, ən, n] **CONJ 1** *(connecting words)* et; **a./or** et/ou; **a knife a. fork** un couteau et une fourchette; **my father a. mother are out** mon père et ma mère sont sortis; **four a. five make(s) nine** quatre plus cinq font neuf; **ham a. eggs** des œufs au jambon; **now a. then** de temps en temps; **he came without pencils a. paper** il est venu sans crayons ni papier; **he speaks English, a. very well too** il parle anglais et même très bien; **a. (what about) the invalids?** et les malades?; **the water was nice a. warm** l'eau était bien chaude; **good a. ready** fin prêt; **a. what if I am going?** et si j'y allais?

2 *(connecting clauses)* et; **he could read a. write** il savait lire et écrire; **move (an inch) a. you're a dead man** un pas et tu es mort; *esp Br* **go a. look for it** allez le chercher; **a. see me** venez me voir; **try a. help me** essaie de m'aider; **to look for sth a. not see it**

chercher qch sans le voir; **I waited an hour a. he still hadn't turned up** j'ai attendu une heure et il n'était toujours pas là; **they started taking drugs, so I came home – a. a good thing too!** ils ont commencé à prendre de la drogue, alors je suis rentré – tu as bien fait!

3 *(with numerals)* **two hundred a. two** deux cent deux; **four a. a half** quatre et demi; **four a. three-quarters** quatre trois quarts; **an hour a. twenty minutes** une heure vingt minutes; *Old-fashioned* **five a. twenty** vingt-cinq; *Br Arch* **three a. sixpence, three a. six** trois shillings six pence

4 *(repetition)* et; **for miles a. miles** pendant des kilomètres et des kilomètres, sur des kilomètres; **better a. better** de mieux en mieux; **smaller a. smaller** de plus en plus petit; **I knocked a. knocked (again)** j'ai frappé tant et plus; **over a. over again** maintes et maintes fois

5 *(contrast)* et; **there are doctors a. (there are) doctors** il y a médecins et médecins

6 a. so on, a. so forth, a. so on a. so forth et ainsi de suite

Andalusia [ændə'luːsɪə, -zɪə] **N** Andalousie *f*

andante [æn'dæntɪ] **ADV, N** *Mus* andante *m*

andantino [ændæn'tiːnəʊ] **ADV, N** *Mus* andantino *m*

Andean ['ændɪən] **ADJ** andin, des Andes

Andes ['ændiːz] **NPL the A.** les Andes *fpl*, la Cordillère des Andes

andiron ['ændaɪən] **N** chenet *m*

Andorra [æn'dɔːrə] **N** (république *f* d')Andorre *f*; **A. (City)** Andorre-la-Vieille

Andorran [æn'dɔːrən] **ADJ** andorran

N Andorran, -ane

androgen ['ændrədʒən] **N** *Biol* androgène *m*

androgynous [æn'drɒdʒɪnəs] **ADJ** androgyne

androgyny [æn'drɒdʒɪnɪ] **N** androgynie *f*

anecdotal [ænɪk'dəʊt(ə)l] **ADJ** anecdotique

anecdote ['ænɪkdəʊt] **N** anecdote *f*

anemia, anemic *Am* = **anaemia, anaemic**

anemometer [ænɪ'mɒmɪtər] **N** *Met* anémomètre *m*

anemone [ə'nemənɪ] **N** *(flower)* anémone *f*

aneroid ['ænərɔɪd] **ADJ** *Phys (barometer)* anéroïde *m*

anesthesia, anesthetic *etc Am* = **anaesthesia, anaesthetic** *etc*

anesthesiologist [ænəsθiːzɪ'ɒlədʒɪst] **N** *Am Med* anesthésiste *mf*

aneurism, aneurysm ['ænjʊrɪz(ə)m] **N** *Med* anévrisme *m*, anévrysme *m*

anew [ə'njuː] **ADV 1** *(again)* de nouveau; **to begin a.** recommencer **2** *(from beginning)* à nouveau; **to create sth a.** créer qch à nouveau

angel ['eɪndʒ(ə)l] **N1** ange *m*; **the a. of death** l'ange de la mort; **fallen a.** ange déchu; *Fam* **you a.!, you're an a.!** tu es un ange *ou* un amour!; *Fam* **be an a.** sois gentil **2** *Fam (financial backer)* bailleur *m* de fonds **3** *Aviat Fam* écho *m* radar non identifié

▸▸*Culin* **a. cake** gâteau *m* de Savoie; *Sl* **a. dust** poudre *f* d'ange; **a. face** visage *m* d'ange *ou* angélique; *Culin* **a. food cake** gâteau de Savoie

angelfish ['eɪndʒəlfɪʃ] **N** ange *m* de mer, angelot *m*

angelic [æn'dʒelɪk] **ADJ** angélique

angelica [æn'dʒelɪkə] **N** *Bot, Culin* angélique *f*

angelically [æn'dʒelɪklɪ] **ADV** comme un ange

angelus ['ændʒələs] **N** *Rel* angélus *m*

anger ['æŋgər] **N** colère *f*; **in a fit** *or* **moment of a.** dans un accès de colère; **to speak in a.** parler sous le coup de la colère; **the cannon was never fired in a.** on ne s'est jamais servi de ce canon en temps de guerre

VT mettre en colère, irriter; **he is easily angered** il se met facilement en colère, il est irascible; **to be slow to a.** ne pas se mettre facilement en colère; **these remarks have angered Christians** ces commentaires ont exaspéré la communauté chrétienne; **he is angered by suggestions that he took bribes** cela le met en colère qu'on suggère qu'il ait pu accepter des pots-de-vin

angina [æn'dʒaɪnə] **N** *Med* angine *f* de poitrine; **to have a.** avoir une angine de poitrine

▸▸**a. pectoris** angine de poitrine

angiology [ændʒɪ'ɒlədʒɪ] **N** *Med* angiologie *f*, angéiologie *f*

angioplasty ['ændʒɪəplæstɪ] **N** *Med* angioplastie *f*

angiosperm ['ændʒɪəʊspɜːm] **N** angiosperme *f*

Angle ['æŋg(ə)l] **N** *Hist* Angle *mf*

angle¹ ['æŋg(ə)l] **N 1** *Math, Fig* angle *m*; *(viewpoint)* point *m* de vue; *(of newspaper article etc)* perspective *f*; **at an a. of …** formant un angle de …; **at an a.** de biais; **the house stands at an a. to the street** la maison fait angle sur la rue; **from a different a.** sous un angle différent, sous un autre angle; **seen from this a.** vu sous cet angle; **to study a problem from every a.** *or* **all angles** étudier un problème sur toutes ses faces *ou* sous tous les angles; **we need a new a.** *(on story)* il nous faut un éclairage *ou* un point de vue nouveau; *Fig* **what's your a. on this?** qu'est-ce que vous pensez de ceci?; **visual** *or* **viewing a.** angle de vision, angle visuel

2 *Mil* angle *m*

3 *Aviat* **critical a. (of attack), stalling a.** angle *m* critique; **listing a.** angle de gîte

4 *Constr (of room)* coin *m*, encoignure *f*, angle *m*; **cutting a.** angle de coupe

5 *Elec, Electron* angle *m*; **phase a.** angle de phase

VT1 *(set at angle) (light beam)* orienter, diriger (**on, to** sur); **to a. a lamp onto one's book** orienter *ou* diriger le faisceau de sa lampe sur son livre; *Tennis* **to a. a shot** envoyer la balle en diagonale

2 *(report)* orienter; *(facts)* présenter d'une manière tendancieuse *ou* partiale; **it's angled towards the 16-18 age range** cela vise les 16-18 ans, c'est destiné aux 16-18 ans; **studies are angled towards exams** les études sont très axées sur les examens

▸▸*Mil* **a. of altitude** angle de hausse *ou* de tir positif; *Aviat* **a. of ascent** *(of plane, projectile)* angle de montée; *Aviat* **a. of attack** angle d'attaque; *Constr* **a. bar** cornière *f*, équerre *f*; *Constr* **a. brace** *(tool)* foret *m* à angle; *Typ* **a. bracket** crochet *m* en chevron; **a. of climb** *(of plane, projectile)* angle de montée; *Mil* **a. of deflection** angle de dérive; *Mil* **a. of elevation** angle de hausse *ou* de tir positif; **a. gauge** goniomètre *m*; *Naut* **a. of heel** *(of ship)* angle de gîte; *Phys* **a. of incidence** angle d'incidence; *Constr* **a. iron** cornière, équerre; *Naut* **a. of list** *(of ship)* angle de gîte; *Constr* **a. plate** cornière, équerre; *Cin* **a. shot** prise *f* de vue oblique; *Mil* **a. of sight** angle de mire *ou* de visée; *Constr* **a. of torque** angle de torsion; **a. of vision** angle de vision, angle visuel

angle² **VI** *(fish)* pêcher à la ligne

▸**angle for VT INSEP** *(fish)* pêcher; *Fig (compliments)* chercher; **to a. for promotion** chercher à être promu; **to a. for an invitation** chercher à se faire inviter

angled ['æŋg(ə)ld] **ADJ 1** **acute-a.** acutangle,

aux angles aigus **2** *(report etc)* partial, -aux, tendancieux
▸▸ *Sport* **a. shot** coup *m* en diagonale

Anglepoise® ['æŋg(ə)lpɔɪz] N
▸▸ **A. lamp** lampe *f* d'architecte

angler ['æŋglər] N **1** *(person)* pêcheur, -euse (à la ligne) **2** baudroie *f*, crapaud *m* de mer
▸▸ **a. fish** baudroie *f*, crapaud *m* de mer

Anglican ['æŋglɪkən] *Rel* ADJ anglican
N Anglican, -ane
▸▸ **the A. Church** l'Église *f* anglicane

Anglicanism ['æŋglɪkənɪz(ə)m] N *Rel* anglicanisme *m*

anglicism ['æŋglɪsɪz(ə)m] N anglicisme *m*

Anglicist ['æŋglɪsɪst] N angliciste *mf*

anglicization [æŋglɪsaɪ'zeɪʃən] N anglicisation *f*

anglicize ['æŋglɪsaɪz] VT angliciser

angling ['æŋglɪŋ] N *(fishing)* pêche *f* à la ligne

Anglo ['æŋgləʊ] N *Am* Américain, -aine d'ascendance européenne

Anglo-American ADJ anglo-américain
N Anglo-Américain, -aine, *pl* Anglo-Américains, -aines

Anglo-Catholic ADJ, N *Rel* anglo-catholique *mf*, *pl* anglo-catholiques

Anglo-French ADJ franco-britannique
N *Ling* anglo-normand *m*

Anglo-Indian ADJ anglo-indien
N **1** *(person of mixed ancestry)* métis *m*, -isse *f* d'origine anglaise et indienne **2** *(Briton who has lived in India)* Anglo-Indien, -ienne, *pl* Anglo-Indiens, -iennes

Anglo-Irish ADJ anglo-irlandais
NPL **the A.** les Anglo-Irlandais *mpl*

anglophile ['æŋgləʊfaɪl] ADJ, N anglophile *mf*

anglophobe ['æŋgləʊfəʊb] ADJ, N anglophobe *mf*

anglophobia ['æŋgləʊ'fəʊbɪə] N anglophobie *f*

Anglophone ['æŋgləfəʊn] ADJ, N anglophone *mf*

Anglo-Saxon ADJ anglo-saxon
N **1** *(person)* Anglo-Saxon, -onne, *pl* Anglo-Saxons, -onnes **2** *Ling* anglo-saxon *m*

Angola [æŋ'gəʊlə] N Angola *m*

Angolan [æŋ'gəʊlən] ADJ angolais
N Angolais, -aise

angora [æŋ'gɔːrə] N **1** *(animal)* angora *m* **2** *Tex* angora *m*; **a. jumper** pull *m* en angora; **a. wool** laine *f* angora
▸▸ **a. cat** chat *m* angora; **a. goat** chèvre *f* angora; **a. rabbit** lapin *m* angora

angostura [æŋgəs'tjʊərə] N *Pharm etc* angusture *f*
▸▸ **A. bitters®** bitter *m* à base d'angusture

angrily ['æŋgrɪlɪ] ADV *(to answer etc)* avec colère

angry ['æŋgrɪ] ADJ *(person)* en colère (**at sb** contre qn; **about sth** à cause de qch), fâché, irrité (**with** *or Am* **at sb** contre qn; **about sth** de qch); *(voice)* irrité; *(speech, letter)* furieux, virulent; **he was a. at being kept waiting** il était irrité qu'on le fît attendre; **to be a. with oneself** *(for not doing better)* être mécontent de soi; *(for giving offence, causing pain etc)* s'en vouloir; **to get a.** se mettre en colère, se fâcher, s'irriter; **to get a. with sb** se fâcher *ou* se mettre en colère contre qn; **to make sb a.** exaspérer qn, mettre qn en colère; **it makes me very a. when I hear people say that** ça m'exaspère d'entendre dire ça; **a. words were exchanged** il y eut un échange assez virulent; *Lit* **the a. sea** la mer courroucée *ou* en courroux; **a. sky** *(stormy)* ciel *m* orageux *ou* menaçant; *Med* **a. sore** plaie *f* irritée *ou* enflammée
▸▸ **a. young man** jeune *m* contestataire

angst [æŋst] N angoisse *f*

angstrom ['æŋstrəm] N *Phys* angström *m*

angsty ['æŋstɪ] ADJ *Fam* stressé

anguish ['æŋgwɪʃ] N **1** *(great anxiety)* angoisse *f*, douleur *f*; **to be in a.** être dans l'angoisse *ou* angoissé, être au supplice; **to cause sb a.** mettre qn dans l'angoisse, angoisser qn **2** *Med* angoisse *f*

anguished ['æŋgwɪʃt] ADJ angoissé

angular ['æŋgjʊlər] ADJ **1** *(rock, face)* anguleux; *(body)* maigre, osseux **2** *(movement)* saccadé **3** *Math, Phys (velocity etc)* angulaire

anhydride [æn'haɪdraɪd] N *Chem* anhydride *m*

anhydrous [æn'haɪdrəs] ADJ *Chem* anhydre

aniline ['ænɪlaɪn] N *Chem* aniline *f*
▸▸ **a. dye** colorant *m* d'aniline

animal ['ænɪm(ə)l] [VOIR GRAMMAIRE A27] N animal *m*, -aux; **to behave like an a.** se comporter comme un animal; *Fig* **he's an a.** c'est une brute; *Fig* **she's not a political a.** elle n'est pas portée sur la politique; *Fig* **that's an entirely different a.** c'est tout à fait autre chose; *Fam* **there ain't no such a.** ça n'existe pas
ADJ **1** *(fat, kingdom etc)* animal, -aux **2** *(instinct, need)* animal, -aux
▸▸ **a. husbandry** élevage *m*; **a. painter** animalier, -ière; **a. rights** droits *mpl* des animaux

animalcule [ænɪ'mælkjuːl] N *Zool* animalcule *m*

animate¹ ['ænɪmət] ADJ *(alive)* vivant, animé, doué de vie; **to become a.** s'animer

animate² ['ænɪmeɪt] VT *(person, party, conversation, film)* animer

animated ['ænɪmeɪtɪd] ADJ *(discussion)* animé; **to become a.** *(of person, discussion)* s'animer
▸▸ **a. cartoon** dessin *m* animé; **a. film** film *m* d'animation; *Comput* **a. GIF** (fichier *m*) GIF *m* animé

animatedly ['ænɪmeɪtɪdlɪ] ADV *(to say)* d'un ton animé; *(to discuss, speak, gesture)* avec animation

animatic [ænɪ'mætɪk] N *(storyboard)* animatique *f*

animation [ænɪ'meɪʃən] N **1** *(of person)* animation *f*, entrain *m*; *(of style)* chaleur *f*; *(of orator)* feu *m*, véhémence *f* **2** *(act)* stimulation *f* **3** *Cin* animation *f*

animator ['ænɪmeɪtər] N *Cin* animateur, -trice

animatronic [ænɪmə'trɒnɪk] ADJ *Cin, TV* animé électroniquement

animatronics [ænɪmə'trɒnɪks] N *Cin, TV* animatronique *f*

animism ['ænɪmɪz(ə)m] N *Phil* animisme *m*

animist ['ænɪmɪst] ADJ, N *Phil* animiste *mf*

animosity [ænɪ'mɒsɪtɪ] N animosité *f*; **to feel a. against** *or* **towards sb** ressentir de l'animosité contre qn; **there was considerable a. towards this idea** cette idée soulevait une grande hostilité

animus ['ænɪməs] N *Fml* **1** *(hostility)* animosité *f* **2** *(motive, stimulus)* stimulation *f*

anion ['ænaɪən] N *Phys, Elec* anion *m*

anise ['ænɪs] N *(plant)* anis *m*; **star a.** anis étoilé

aniseed ['ænɪsiːd] N *Bot, Culin* (graine *f* d')anis *m*
▸▸ **a. ball** bonbon *m* à l'anis; **a. cake** gâteau *m* à l'anis

anisette [ænɪ'zet] N *(liqueur)* anisette *f*

ankle ['æŋk(ə)l] N cheville *f*; **a.-length dress** robe *f* qui descend jusqu'à la cheville; **to be a.-deep in water/mud** avoir de l'eau/de la boue jusqu'aux chevilles
▸▸ **a. bone** astragale *m*; **a. boot** bottine *f*; **a.**

chain bracelet *m* de cheville; **a. joint** articulation *f* du pied; **a. sock** socquette *f*; **a. strap** bride *f*; **a. support** chevillière *f*

ankle-biter N *Fam (child)* gosse *mf*

anklet ['æŋklət] N **1** *(ornament)* bracelet *m*/anneau *m* de cheville **2** *Am (sock)* socquette *f*

ankylose ['æŋkɪləʊz] *Med* VT ankyloser
VI s'ankyloser

ankylosis [æŋkɪ'ləʊsɪs] N *Med* ankylose *f*

annalist ['ænəlɪst] N annaliste *mf*

annals ['æn(ə)lz] NPL annales *fpl*

Anne [æn] N Anne; *Hist* **A. of Austria** Anne d'Autriche

anneal [ə'niːl] VT *Tech (glass)* recuire, adoucir; *(metal)* détremper, recuire, adoucir

annealing [ə'niːlɪŋ] N *Tech (of glass)* recuit *m*, recuite *f*; *Metal (of metal)* adoucissement *m*, recuit, recuite; **box** *or* **close a.** recuit en vase clos
▸▸ **a. furnace** four *m* à recuire

annex¹ ['æneks] N *Am* = annexe

annex² [æ'neks] VT **1** *(take possession of) (province)* annexer **2** *(attach)* annexer (**sth to sth** qch à qch)

annexation [ænek'seɪʃən] N annexion *f* (**of** de)

annexe, *Am* annex ['æneks] N **1** *(of building)* annexe *f* **2** *(to document)* annexe *f*

annihilate [ə'naɪəleɪt] VT *(fleet, army)* anéantir, réduire à néant; *Fam* **his opponent annihilated him** son adversaire l'a pulvérisé *ou* anéanti

annihilation [ənaɪə'leɪʃən] N **1** *(of fleet, people)* anéantissement *m* **2** *Nucl* annihilation *f*; *(of electron and positron)* dématérialisation *f*

anniversary [ænɪ'vɜːs(ə)rɪ] N anniversaire *m*; **it's our wedding a.** c'est l'anniversaire de notre mariage; **on the a. of …** le jour (de l')anniversaire de …; **an a. dinner** un dîner d'anniversaire; **golden/silver/ruby (wedding) a.** noces *fpl* d'or/d'argent/de rubis

anno Domini ['ænəʊ'dɒmɪnaɪ, -niː] ADV en l'an du Seigneur *ou* de grâce

annotate ['ænəteɪt] VT *(book etc)* annoter; **annotated draft** brouillon *m* annoté

annotation [ænə'teɪʃən] N annotation *f*

annotator ['ænəteɪtər] N annotateur, -trice

announce [ə'naʊns] VT annoncer; **the Prime Minister has announced his cabinet** le Premier ministre a fait connaître *ou* a annoncé la composition de son cabinet; **to a. the birth/marriage/death of sb** faire part de la naissance/du mariage/du décès de qn

announcement [ə'naʊnsmənt] N annonce *f*; *(statement)* déclaration *f*; *(of birth, marriage etc)* faire-part *m inv*; *Journ* **a. of death** avis *m* de décès; **here is a passenger a.** avis voyageurs; **here is a staff a.** appel de service

announcer [ə'naʊnsər] N annonceur, -euse; *Radio, TV* speaker *m*, speakerine *f*
▸▸ **a. booth** cabine *f* de présentation; **a. studio** studio *m* d'annonceur

annoy [ə'nɔɪ] VT *(person)* ennuyer, embêter; *(stronger)* agacer, énerver; *(by going against sb's wishes etc)* contrarier; **you're really annoying me!** ce que tu peux m'embêter!; **is the light/noise annoying you?** est-ce que la lumière/le bruit t'ennuie *ou* te dérange?; **is this man annoying you?** est-ce que cet homme vous importune?

Note that the French verb **ennuyer** often means **to bore**.

annoyance [ə'nɔɪəns] N énervement *m*, agacement *m*, *Fam* embêtement *m*; **look of a.** air *m* contrarié *ou* ennuyé; **much to his a.** à son grand déplaisir *ou* mécontentement;

source of a. désagrément *m*, cause *f* d'ennuis; **petty annoyances** petits ennuis *mpl*, petites contrariétés *fpl*; **to cause a. to everyone** énerver tout le monde; *(by going against wishes etc)* contrarier tout le monde; **she failed to hide her a. at his words** elle n'a pas réussi à cacher l'énervement *ou* l'agacement que lui inspiraient ses paroles

annoyed [ə'nɔɪd] **ADJ**, *Fam* embêté (**at, about** par, à cause de); *(stronger)* agacé, énervé (**at, about** par, à cause de); *(because sb has gone against one's wishes)* contrarié; **to be a. with sb/oneself** être en colère contre qn/soi-même; **to get a. with sb/sth** se mettre en colère *ou* s'énerver contre qn/qch; **promise you won't get a.** promets-moi que tu ne vas pas te mettre en colère *ou* t'énerver

annoying [ə'nɔɪɪŋ] **ADJ** ennuyeux, agaçant; *(habits)* agaçant; **the a. thing about it is that ...** ce qu'il y a d'ennuyeux là-dedans c'est que ...; **how a.!** que c'est ennuyeux *ou Fam* embêtant!

annoyingly [ə'nɔɪɪŋlɪ] **ADV** *(irritatingly) (to behave)* d'une façon agaçante *ou* énervante; **a., he was late** il était en retard, ce qui était ennuyeux; **she's a. punctual** elle est agaçante à être aussi ponctuelle; **it's getting a. unreliable** il/elle devient de moins en moins fiable au point que c'en est agaçant; **he's so a. knowledgeable** il sait tellement de choses que c'en devient agaçant

annual ['ænjʊəl] **ADJ** *(holiday, payment, report etc)* annuel; **he has an a. salary of £50,000** il gagne 50 000 livres par an
▸ **N 1** *Bot* plante *f* annuelle **2** *(publication)* publication *f* annuelle; *(for children)* album *m* (annuel)
▸▸ *Acct, Fin* **a. accounts** bilan *m* annuel, comptes *mpl* de clôture *ou* de fin d'exercice; *Fin* **a. budget** budget *m* annuel; *Fin* **a. contribution** *(to pension scheme)* cotisation *f* annuelle; *Acct* **a. depreciation** dépréciation *f* annuelle, amortissement *m* annuel; *Fin* **a. earnings** *(of company)* recette(s) *f(pl)* annuelle(s); *(of person)* revenu *m* annuel; *Com* **a. general meeting** assemblée *f* générale (annuelle); **a. guaranteed salary** salaire *m* annuel garanti; **a. income** revenu annuel; **a. instalment** annuité *f*, *Admin* **a. leave** congé *m* annuel; *Fin* **a. percentage rate** taux *m* effectif global; **a. profit** profit *m* annuel; *Fin* **a. returns** déclarations *fpl* annuelles; **a. revenue** recette annuelle; **a. ring** *(of tree)* couche *f* annuelle; *Com* **a. sales figures** chiffre *m* d'affaires annuel; **a. spend** dépenses *fpl* annuelles; *Acct, Fin* **a. turnover** chiffre d'affaires annuel; *Acct* **a. writedown** dépréciation annuelle, amortissement annuel

annually ['ænjʊəlɪ] **ADV** *(in a year)* par an, annuellement; *(every year)* tous les ans

annuity [ə'njuːɪtɪ] **N** *Fin* rente *f* (annuelle); **government a.** rente sur l'État; **perpetual a.** rente perpétuelle, rente en perpétuel; **life a.** rente viagère, pension *f* viagère; **to buy an a.** placer son argent en viager *ou* à fonds perdu; **to pay sb an a.** servir *ou* faire une rente à qn; **a. in redemption of debt** annuité *f*

annul [ə'nʌl] **VT** (**-ll-**) *Law (contract)* annuler, résilier; *(bill)* annuler, casser; *(treaty)* dénoncer; *(marriage, will, agreement)* annuler, casser, déclarer nul; *(law)* abroger; *(decision)* infirmer

annular ['ænjʊlər] **ADJ** *(eclipse, finger)* annulaire

annulment [ə'nʌlmənt] **N** *Law (of contract etc)* annulation *f*, résiliation *f*; *(of will, marriage, bill)* annulation, cassation *f*; *(of law)* abrogation *f*; *(of decree)* abolition *f*; **decree of a.** décret *m* abolitif

annunciation [ənʌnsɪ'eɪʃən] **N** *Rel* **the A.** l'Annonciation *f*

anode ['ænəʊd] **N** *Elec* anode *f*, électrode *f* positive

anodyne ['ænəʊdaɪn] **N** *Med* calmant *m*, analgésique *m*
▸ **ADJ 1** *Med* antalgique, analgésique **2** *(remark, topic)* anodin

anoint [ə'nɔɪnt] **VT** oindre (**with** de); **to a. sb king/bishop** sacrer qn roi/évêque

anointing [ə'nɔɪntɪŋ] **N** onction *f*, *(of king etc)* sacre *m*

anomalous [ə'nɒmələs] **ADJ** anormal, -aux, irrégulier

anomaly [ə'nɒmælɪ] **N** anomalie *f*

anon[1] [ə'nɒn] **ADV** *Arch, Hum* **1** *(later)* plus tard; **more of this a.** je reviendrai sur cela **2** *(soon)* tout à l'heure, bientôt; **see you a.** à bientôt; **I'll be with you a.** je vous rejoins tout de suite

anon[2] **ADV** *abbr* **anonymous**

anonymity [ænə'nɪmɪtɪ] **N** anonymat *m*; **to preserve one's a.** garder l'anonymat, préserver son anonymat

anonymous [ə'nɒnɪməs] **ADJ 1** *(gift, letter etc)* anonyme; **to remain a.** garder l'anonymat, préserver son anonymat **2** *(building, face)* anonyme
▸▸ *Mktg* **a. buyer** acheteur, -euse anonyme; *Comput* **a. FTP** protocole *m* de transfert anonyme; *Comput* **a. remailer** service *m* de courrier électronique anonyme

anonymously [ə'nɒnɪməslɪ] **ADV** anonymement; **to write a.** écrire sous (le couvert de) l'anonymat

anopheles mosquito [ə'nɒfɪliːz] **N** anophèle *m*

anorak ['ænəræk] **N 1** *(garment)* anorak *m* **2** *Br Fam Pej (person)* ringard *m*

anorexia [ænə'reksɪə] **N** *Med* anorexie *f*
▸▸ **a. nervosa** anorexie *f* mentale

anorexic [ænə'reksɪk] **ADJ**, **N** *Med* anorexique *mf*; **you look a.** tu n'as plus que la peau sur les os

another [ə'nʌðər] **ADJ, PRON** VOIR GRAMMAIRE A36–7; 815–16 **1** *(one more)* encore un(e); *(second)* un(e) autre, un(e) deuxième, un(e) second(e); **we're thinking of getting a. car** *(in addition to the one we have)* nous pensons acheter une deuxième voiture; **a. cup of tea** encore une tasse de thé; **a. fifty years** encore cinquante ans; **in a. ten years** dans dix ans (d'ici); **a. hour/20 miles and we'll be there** encore une heure/une vingtaine de mil(l)es et nous y serons; **I don't want to see a. fish as long as I live** je ne veux plus voir un seul poisson de toute ma vie; **without a. word** sans (un mot de) plus; **have a. (drink)!** encore un(e)?; **this is not just a. small car** ce n'est pas seulement une petite voiture parmi d'autres; **he is a. Picasso** c'est le nouveau Picasso; **the situation could become a. Vietnam** la situation pourrait tourner en un autre Vietnam
2 *(different one)* un(e) autre; **we're thinking of getting a. car** *(to replace the car we have)* nous pensons acheter une nouvelle voiture *ou* changer de voiture; **take this cup away and bring me a. (one)** enlevez cette tasse et apportez-m'en une autre; **a. of the passengers** un autre passager; **that's (quite) a. matter** c'est (tout) autre chose; **science is one thing, art is a.** la science est une chose, l'art en est une autre; *Lit* **he loves a.** il en aime une autre; **she now has a. husband** elle a maintenant un nouveau mari; **a. athlete would have played safe** un autre athlète aurait joué la prudence; **a. time** une autre fois; **let's do it a. way** faisons autrement; *Fam* **tell me a.!** *(you're exaggerating)* ce n'est pas vrai!, à d'autres!; **one way or a.** d'une façon

ou d'une autre; **taking one thing with a., we just manage** l'un dans l'autre, on arrive à joindre les deux bouts; **what with one thing and a., I forgot** avec tout ça, j'ai oublié
3 *(reciprocal)* **one a.** l'un l'autre; *(more than two people)* les uns les autres; **to help one a.** s'entraider; **love one a.** aimez-vous les uns les autres; **to help one a.** s'entraider; **he and his wife adore one a.** lui et sa femme s'adorent; **they give one a. presents** ils se donnent des cadeaux

Ansaphone® ['ɑːnsəfəʊn] **N** *Tel* répondeur enregistreur *m*

ANSI ['ænsiː] **N** *Am* *(abbr American National Standards Institute)* = association *f* américaine de normalisation
▸▸ **A. character** caractère *m* ANSI

answer ['ɑːnsər] **N 1** *(to question, letter)* réponse *f*; *(to criticism)* réponse, réplique *f*; **she made no a.** elle n'a pas répondu; **I knocked but there was no a.** j'ai frappé mais personne n'a répondu; *Tel* **there's no a.** ça ne répond pas; **he has an a. to everything** il a réponse à tout; **you think you know all the answers, don't you?** tu crois que tu sais tout, c'est ça?; **his only a. was to burst into tears** pour toute réponse il a fondu en larmes; **Scotland's a. to Pelé** le Pelé écossais; **they had no a. to this/this new scrum half** ils ne savaient pas quoi faire contre ça/ce nouveau demi de mêlée; **there's no a. to that!** comment répondre à ça!; **it's the a. to the government's prayers** c'est exactement ce dont le gouvernement avait besoin; **she's the a. to all his prayers** c'est la femme de ses rêves; *Fml* **in a. to your letter** en réponse à votre lettre; *Law etc* **a. to a charge** réfutation *f* à une accusation SEE GRAMMAR B64
2 *Math, Fig (to problem)* solution *f*; **the a. is 624** la réponse est 624
▸ **VT** *(person, question, letter)* répondre à; **what did he a.?** qu'a-t-il répondu?; **letters to be answered** courrier *m* en cours; **letters answered** lettres *fpl* auxquelles on a répondu; **the question is not easy to a.** c'est une question à laquelle il n'est pas facile de répondre; **to a. the bell/the telephone** répondre à un coup de sonnette/au téléphone; **to a. the door** *(go)* aller ouvrir; *(come)* venir ouvrir; **to a. a prayer** exaucer une prière; *Law* **to a. a charge** répondre à *ou* réfuter une accusation; **to a. a description** répondre à un signalement; **to a. the helm** *(of ship)* obéir à la barre; **to a. a need** répondre à un besoin; **this should a. the purpose quite nicely** ceci fera très bien l'affaire; **it should a. the purposes of both students and translators** ce devrait être utile aux étudiants comme aux traducteurs; **that will a. my purpose** cela fera mon affaire
▸ **VI** répondre; **it's not answering** *(phone)* ça ne répond pas
▸▸ *Tel* **a. mode** mode *m* réponse; *Tel* **a. tone** tonalité *f* de réponse
▸ **answer back** **VI** *(be impertinent)* répondre; **don't a. back!** ne réponds pas!
VT SEP *(be impertinent to)* répondre à
▸ **answer for** **VT INSEP** répondre de; *(sb's integrity)* se porter garant de; **to a. for one's actions** prendre la responsabilité de ses propres actes; **to a. for one's crimes** payer pour ses crimes; **he/the motor car has a lot to a. for** il/la voiture est responsable de bien des problèmes
▸ **answer to** **VT INSEP 1** *(be accountable to)* être responsable envers, rendre compte à; **you'll have me to a. to** *(if you do that)* c'est à moi que vous devrez rendre des comptes; **to a. to sb for sth** être responsable de qch envers qn **2** *(correspond to) (description)* répondre à **3 the dog answers to the name of Rover** le chien répond au nom de Rover

answerable ['ɑːnsərəb(ə)l] **ADJ 1** garant, responsable (**to sb for sth** de qch envers qn); **to be a. to an authority** relever d'une autorité; **he is a. to nobody** il n'a de comptes à rendre à personne **2** *(accusation)* réfutable

answerback ['ɑːnsəbæk] N *Comput (in datacomms)* réponse f en retour

answering ['ɑːnsərɪŋ] ADJ **an a. cry** un cri jeté en réponse
▸▸ *Tel* **a. machine** répondeur *m* (automatique *ou* téléphonique); *Tel* **a. service** *(manned)* permanence f téléphonique; *(unmanned)* répondeur téléphonique

answerphone ['ɑːnsəfəʊn] N *Tel* répondeur *m* (automatique *ou* téléphonique)

ant [ænt] N fourmi f, *Fig Fam* **to have ants in one's pants** ne pas tenir en place, avoir la bougeotte
▸▸ **a. bear** tamanoir *m*; **a. colony** colonie f de fourmis; **a. hill** fourmilière f, **a. lion** fourmilion *m*, fourmi-lion *m*, *pl* fourmis-lions

antacid [ænt'æsɪd] ADJ, N *Med* antiacide *m*

antagonism [æn'tægənɪz(ə)m] N hostilité f (**to, towards** envers); *(between two people)*, *Physiol* antagonisme *m*

antagonist [æn'tægənɪst] N antagoniste *mf*, adversaire *mf*

antagonistic [æntægə'nɪstɪk] ADJ *(opposed)* opposé, contraire (**to** à); *(person, attitude)* hostile; *(parties)* antagonique; *Anat (muscle)* antagoniste

antagonize [æn'tægənaɪz] VT éveiller l'hostilité de; **to a. the public** ranger l'opinion contre soi; **don't a. him** ne te le mets pas à dos; **she only succeeded in antagonizing him further** elle n'a réussi qu'à le rendre encore plus hostile

Antarctic [æn'tɑːktɪk] ADJ antarctique
N **the A.** l'Antarctique *m*

Antarctica [æn'tɑːktɪkə] N Antarctique *m*

ante ['æntɪ] *Cards* N *(at poker)* première mise f, **to raise** *or* **up the a.** *Cards* lever la mise; *Fig (in dispute)* placer la barre plus haut
VI faire une mise
▸ **ante up** VI *Am Fam (pay)* casquer

anteater ['ænti:tər] N fourmilier *m*; **great a.** tamanoir *m*; **scaly a.** pangolin *m*; **spiny a.** échidné *m*

antebellum [æntɪ'beləm] ADJ d'avant la guerre; *Am* d'avant la guerre Civile

antecedence [æntɪ'siːd(ə)ns] N **1** *(precedence)* antériorité f **2** *(priority)* priorité f

antecedent [æntɪ'siːd(ə)nt] ADJ antérieur (**to** à)
N **1** *Gram, Math* antécédent *m* VOIR GRAMMAIRE A32–3; B22–3 **2 antecedents** *(of person)* *(past)* antécédents *mpl*; *(ancestors)* ancêtres *mpl*; *(of society etc)* origines *fpl*

antechamber ['æntɪtʃeɪmbər] N **1** *(room)* antichambre f **2** *(in engine)* préchambre f, **diesel engine with a.** moteur *m* diesel à chambre de précombustion

antedate [æntɪ'deɪt] VT *(precede)* précéder

antediluvian [æntɪdɪ'luːvɪən] ADJ antédiluvien

antelope ['æntɪləʊp] N *(pl* **antelopes, antelope)** antilope f

ante meridian ADV *Fml* du matin

antenatal [æntɪ'neɪt(ə)l] ADJ prénatal, -als, anténatal, -als; **an a. clinic** un cours de préparation à l'accouchement

antenna [æn'tenə] N **1** *(pl* **antennae** [-i:]) *(of insect, crustacean)* antenne f, *(of mollusc)* tentacule *m*; *(of snail)* corne f **2** *(pl usu* **antennas** [-əz]) *esp Am Radio, TV* antenne f

antepenultimate [æntɪpə'nʌltɪmət] ADJ antépénultième; **the a. syllable** l'antépénultième f (syllabe f)

anterior [æn'tɪərɪər] ADJ **1** antérieur, -eure

(**to** à) **2** *Gram past a.* passé *m* antérieur **3** *Anat (muscle)* antérieur

anteroom ['æntɪruːm] N antichambre f, vestibule *m*

anthem ['ænθəm] N *Rel* motet *m*; *Lit (song of joy)* chant *m* d'allégresse; **national a.** hymne *m* national; **the party's a.** l'hymne du parti

anther ['ænθər] N *Bot* anthère f

anthologist [æn'θɒlədʒɪst] N anthologue *mf*

anthology [æn'θɒlədʒɪ] N anthologie f

anthracite ['ænθrəsaɪt] N *Min* anthracite *m*

anthrax ['ænθræks] N charbon *m*, anthrax *m*

anthropoid ['ænθrəpɔɪd] N *Zool (ape)* (singe *m*) anthropoïde *m*
ADJ **1** *(person) (apelike)* simiesque **2** *(ape) (resembling man)* anthropoïde

anthropological ['ænθrəpə'lɒdʒɪk(ə)l] ADJ anthropologique

anthropologist [ænθrə'pɒlədʒɪst] N anthropologue *mf*

anthropology [ænθrə'pɒlədʒɪ] N anthropologie f

anthropometry [ænθrə'pɒmɪtrɪ] N anthropométrie f

anthropomorphic [ænθrəpə'mɔːfɪk] ADJ anthropomorphe

anthropomorphism [ænθrəpə'mɔːfɪz(ə)m] N anthropomorphisme *m*

anthropomorphous [ænθrəpə'mɔːfəs] ADJ anthropomorphe

anthropophagous [ænθrə'pɒfəgəs] ADJ anthropophage

anthropophagy [ænθrə'pɒfədʒɪ] N anthropophagie f

anti ['æntɪ, *Am* 'æntaɪ] PREP anti; **she was a. the idea** elle était contre cette idée; **he's a. everything** rien ne lui plaît; **she's a. anything which involves spending money** elle est contre tout ce qui entraîne des dépenses
N opposant, -ante

anti- ['æntɪ, *Am* 'æntaɪ] PREF anti-; **anti-American** anti(-)américain

anti-abortionist N adversaire *mf* de l'avortement

anti-aircraft ADJ *(gun, defence etc)* antiaérien

anti-aliasing N *Comput* anti-crénelage *m*, anti-aliassage *m*

anti-apartheid ADJ anti(-)apartheid

antibacterial [æntɪbæk'tɪərɪəl] ADJ *Med* antibactérien

antiballistic [æntɪbə'lɪstɪk] ADJ *Mil* antibalistique, antimissile
▸▸ **a. missile** engin *m* *ou* fusée f antimissile

antibiotic [æntɪbaɪ'ɒtɪk] ADJ antibiotique
N antibiotique *m*; **to be on antibiotics** être sous antibiotiques

antibody ['æntɪbɒdɪ] N *Physiol* anticorps *m*

anti-burst lock N serrure f renforcée

Antichrist ['æntɪkraɪst] N Antéchrist *m*

antichristian [æntɪ'krɪstʃən] ADJ antichrétien

anticipate [æn'tɪsɪpeɪt] VT **1** *(expect) (possibility, reaction)* prévoir; *(difficulty, pleasure etc)* s'attendre à, envisager; **we don't a. any objections** nous n'envisageons pas d'objections; **we do not a. any delays** aucun retard n'est prévu; **to a. that ...** prévoir que ...; **to a. the worst** s'attendre au pire
2 *(enjoy, count on in advance) (events)* anticiper sur; *(pleasure)* savourer d'avance; *(result, vote)* escompter; **to a. one's salary** anticiper sur son salaire; *Fin* **anticipated profit** profit *m* espéré
3 *(act in advance of) (person, sb's orders)* devancer, prévenir, aller au-devant de; **you must a. your opponent's moves/other drivers' intentions** il faut que vous anticipiez

les mouvements de votre adversaire/les intentions des autres conducteurs; **her writing anticipated later developments in English fiction** son style présageait des développements futurs de la fiction anglaise; **don't a. me** *(in telling story)* attends la suite, laisse-moi finir
VI anticiper

anticipation [æntɪsɪ'peɪʃən] N **1** *(foresight)* prévision f, **in a. of trouble** en prévision de troubles; **thanking you in a.** en vous remerciant d'avance; **Brian showed great a.** *(in game)* Brian a très bien anticipé **2** *(expectation)* anticipation f, **they awaited his arrival with eager a.** ils l'attendaient avec beaucoup d'impatience

anticipatory pricing [æn'tɪsɪpeɪt(ə)rɪ] N fixation f des prix par anticipation

anticlerical [æntɪ'klerɪk(ə)l] ADJ anticlérical, -aux

anticlericalism [æntɪ'klerɪk(ə)lɪz(ə)m] N anticléricalisme *m*

anticlimax [æntɪ'klaɪmæks] N *(disappointment)* déception f, **the party itself was a bit of an a.** la soirée a été plutôt décevante; **after all the waiting, the news almost felt like an a.** après toute cette attente, la nouvelle n'a pas produit tout l'effet escompté

anticline ['æntɪklaɪn] N anticlinal *m*

anticlockwise [æntɪ'klɒkwaɪz] ADV, ADJ *Br* **a., in an a. direction** dans le sens inverse des aiguilles d'une montre; **clockwise or a.?** dans le sens des aiguilles d'une montre ou l'inverse?

anticoagulant [æntɪkəʊ'ægjʊlənt] ADJ, N *Med* anticoagulant *m*

anticolonialism [æntɪkə'ləʊnɪəlɪz(ə)m] N anticolonialisme *m*

anticonstitutional [æntɪkɒnstɪ'tjuːʃ(ə)l] ADJ anticonstitutionnel

anti-corrosion ADJ anti-corrosion
▸▸ **a. guarantee** garantie f anti-corrosion; **a. primer** apprêt *m* anti-corrosion

antics ['æntɪks] NPL bouffonneries *fpl*, singeries *fpl*; **he's up to his a. again** le voilà qui fait de nouveau des siennes

anticyclone [æntɪ'saɪkləʊn] N anticyclone *m*

anti-dazzle ADJ anti-aveuglant; *(headlights)* anti-éblouissant

anti-democratic ADJ antidémocratique

antidepressant [æntɪdɪ'presənt] ADJ, N *Pharm* antidépresseur *m*

anti-dieselling valve [-'diːz(ə)lɪŋ] N *Aut* thermovalve f

anti-dive geometry N *Aut* géométrie f anti-plongée

antidote ['æntɪdəʊt] N *Med, Fig* antidote *m* (**to** contre), contrepoison *m* (**to** à)

anti-dumping ADJ *(laws, legislation)* anti-dumping *inv*

anti-establishment ADJ anticonformiste

antifascism [æntɪ'fæʃɪz(ə)m] N *Pol* antifascisme *m*

antifascist [æntɪ'fæʃɪst] ADJ, N antifasciste *mf*

antifebrile [æntɪ'fiːbraɪl] N, ADJ *Pharm* antipyrétique *m*, fébrifuge *m*

antifreeze ['æntɪfriːz] N *Aut* antigel *m*

antigen ['æntɪdʒen] N *Med* antigène *m*

anti-glare ADJ anti-aveuglant; *(headlights)* anti-éblouissant
▸▸ **a. mirror** rétroviseur *m* jour/nuit; **a. screen** écran *m* antireflets

antiglobalization [æntɪgləʊbəlaɪ'zeɪʃən] N antimondialisation f

Antigua [æn'tiːgə] N Antigua *m*

anti-hero N *Liter* antihéros *m inv*

anti-heroine N *Liter* antihéroïne *f*

antihistamine [æntɪ'hɪstəmɪn] ADJ, N *Med* antihistaminique *m*

anti-icing N *Aut* antigel *m*; *Aviat* antigivrant *m*
ADJ antigivre *inv*

anti-imperialist N, ADJ anti-impérialiste *mf*

anti-inflammatory ADJ, N *Med* anti-inflammatoire *m*

anti-inflationary ADJ *(measures, policy)* anti-inflationniste

anti-knock ADJ, N *Aut* antidétonant *m*

Antilles [æn'tɪliːz] NPL **the A.** les Antilles *fpl*

anti-lock ADJ
▸▸ **a. brakes** anti-blocage *m* des freins; **a. braking system** système *m* anti-blocage des freins

antilogarithm [æntɪ'lɒɡərɪð(ə)m] N *Math* antilogarithme *m*

antimacassar [æntɪmə'kæsər] N têtière *f*

antimalarial [æntɪmə'leərɪəl] N, ADJ *Pharm* antipaludique *m*, antipaludéen *m*

antimatter ['æntɪmætər] N antimatière *f*

antimilitarism [æntɪ'mɪlɪtərɪz(ə)m] N antimilitarisme *m*

anti-missile ADJ antimissile

antimony [æn'tɪmənɪ] N antimoine *m*

antinazi [æntɪ'nɑːtsɪ] ADJ, N *Pol* antinazi, -ie

anti-nuclear ADJ antinucléaire

antiparticle ['æntɪpɑːtɪk(ə)l] N *Nucl* antiparticule *f*

antipathetic(al) [æntɪpə'θetɪk, -ɪk(ə)l] ADJ antipathique; **a. to** qui a de l'aversion pour

antipathy [æn'tɪpəθɪ] N antipathie *f*; **to feel a. for sb** avoir de l'antipathie pour *ou* contre qn

antipersonnel [æntɪpɜːsə'nel] ADJ *(bomb)* antipersonnel

antiperspirant [æntɪ'pɜːspɪrənt] ADJ, N déodorant *m*

antiphon ['æntɪfɒn] N *Rel* antienne *f*

antipodean [æntɪpə'diːən] ADJ 1 *Geog* des antipodes 2 *Br (from Australia and/or New Zealand)* d'Australie/de Nouvelle-Zélande; *Hum* **our a. cousins** nos cousins d'Australie/ de Nouvelle-Zélande; **the kangaroo and other a. animals** le kangourou et les autres animaux australiens
▸▸ **A. day** jour *m* méridien

antipodes [æn'tɪpədiːz] NPL *Geog* **the a.** les antipodes *mpl*; **at the a.** aux antipodes; *Br* **the A.** l'Australie *f* et/ou la Nouvelle-Zélande

anti-pollution ADJ anti-pollution

antiproton [æntɪ'prəʊtɒn] N *Nucl* antiproton *m*

antipyretic [æntɪpaɪ'retɪk] N, ADJ *Pharm* antipyrétique *m*, fébrifuge *m*

antiquarian [æntɪ'kweərɪən] ADJ *(book)* ancien; **a. bookseller/bookshop** libraire *mf*/librairie *f* spécialisé(e) dans les éditions anciennes; **a. collection** collection *f* d'antiquités
N *(dealer)* antiquaire *mf*; *(collector)* amateur *m* d'antiquités; *(scholar)* historien, -ienne

antiquary ['æntɪkwərɪ] N *(collector)* amateur *m* d'antiquités; *(dealer)* antiquaire *mf*; *(scholar)* historien, -ienne

antiquated ['æntɪkweɪtɪd] ADJ *(outmoded) (method)* désuet, *f* -ète, suranné, *f* -ète; *(car, tools)* vieillot; **an a. kitchen range** une cuisinière (à charbon) d'autrefois

antique [æn'tiːk] ADJ antique, ancien; **a. furniture** meubles *mpl* anciens; *Fam* **she's got an a. gas cooker** sa cuisinière à gaz est une véritable antiquité
N *(ancient object, piece of furniture)* antiquité *f*; **a. shop** magasin *m* d'antiquités; **be**

careful with that, it's an a. fais attention, c'est ancien; *Fam* **that television's an a.** cette télévision est une antiquité
▸▸ **a. dealer** antiquaire *mf*

antiquity [æn'tɪkwɪtɪ] N 1 *(of custom)* ancienneté *f* 2 *Hist (Greek, Roman)* antiquité *f*; **the works of art of classical a.** les antiquités; **women in a.** la femme dans le monde ancien 3 **Roman antiquities** *(remains)* monuments *mpl* romains

anti-rabies ADJ antirabique

antiracism [æntɪ'reɪsɪz(ə)m] N antiracisme *m*

antiracist [æntɪ'reɪsɪst] ADJ antiraciste

antiraid precautions [æntɪ'reɪd] N *St Exch* barrières *fpl* antiraid

anti-roll bar N *Aut* barre *f* antiroulis

antirrhinum [æntɪ'raɪnəm] N *(plant)* muflier *m*

anti-run-on valve N *Aut* thermovalve *f*

anti-rust ADJ antirouille *inv*; **a. treatment** traitement *m* antirouille

anti-Semite N antisémite *mf*

anti-Semitic ADJ antisémite

anti-Semitism [-'semɪtɪz(ə)m] N antisémitisme *m*

antisepsis [æntɪ'sepsɪs] N *Med* antisepsie *f*

antiseptic [æntɪ'septɪk] ADJ *Med* antiseptique; *Fig (atmosphere)* aseptisé; *(person)* froid, peu amical, -aux
N *Med* antiseptique *m*

antiserum ['æntɪsɪərəm] N *Med* antisérum *m*

antislavery [æntɪ'sleɪvərɪ] ADJ antiesclavagiste

antisocial [æntɪ'səʊʃəl] ADJ 1 *(behaviour, element, vandalism)* asocial, -aux; *(bill, measure, policy)* antisocial, -aux 2 *(unsociable) (sort of person)* qui fait bande à part, sauvage; **he's being very a.** en ce moment il n'est pas très sociable; **I don't want to be a., but ...** *(I'd rather be alone)* désolé de faire bande à part, mais ...; *(I have to leave, you have to leave)* je m'en voudrais de gâcher l'ambiance, mais ...

antispasmodic [æntɪspæz'mɒdɪk] N, ADJ *Pharm* antispasmodique *m*

antistatic [æntɪ'stætɪk] ADJ antistatique

anti-submarine ADJ anti-sous-marin

anti-tank ADJ *Mil* antichar(s)

anti-terrorist ADJ antiterroriste

anti-theft ADJ *(lock)* antivol *inv*; **a. device** antivol *m inv*

antithesis *pl* **antitheses** [æn'tɪθɪsɪs, -iːz] N 1 *(opposite)* antithèse *f*, opposé *m* (**of** de) 2 *Phil (in dialectic)* antithèse *f* (**between** entre; **to, of** de)

antithetical [æntɪ'θetɪk(ə)l] ADJ antithétique

antitoxin [æntɪ'tɒksɪn] N *Med* antitoxine *f*

antitrust [æntɪ'trʌst] ADJ *Econ* antitrust

antitussive [æntɪ'tʌsɪv] N, ADJ *Pharm* antitussif *m*

antivirus ['æntɪvaɪrəs] N *Comput* antivirus *m*
▸▸ **a. check** vérification *f* antivirale; **a. program** programme *m* antivirus

antivivisectionist [æntɪvɪvɪ'sekʃənɪst] N antivivisection(n)iste *mf*

antler ['æntlər] N *(of stag)* andouiller *m*; **the antlers** les bois *mpl*

antonym ['æntənɪm] N antonyme *m*

antsy ['æntsɪ] ADJ *esp Am (nervous)* agité, nerveux; *(irritable)* à cran

Antwerp ['æntwɜːp] N Anvers *m*

anus ['eɪnəs] N *Anat* anus *m*

anvil ['ænvɪl] N *(of blacksmith, in ear)* enclume *f*

anxiety [æŋ'zaɪətɪ] N 1 *(worry, concern)* inquiétude *f*; **deep a.** anxiété *f*, angoisse *f*; **to cause sb great a.** donner de grandes inquiétudes *ou* bien des soucis à qn; **there is no cause for a.** il n'y a pas de quoi s'inquiéter; **to feel a.** s'inquiéter, être anxieux (**about** à propos de); **to be full of a.** être anxieux 2 *(individual concern)* souci *m*; **the report failed to remove their anxieties** le rapport ne leur a pas ôté leurs inquiétudes 3 *(desire)* désir *m*, souci *m* (**for sth** de qch); **a. to help sb/please sb** désir *ou* souci d'aider qn/de plaire à qn; **in her a. not to offend** dans son souci de n'offenser personne 4 *Psy* anxiété *f*
▸▸ *Psy* **a. attack** crise *f* d'angoisse

anxious ['æŋkʃəs] ADJ 1 *(worried)* inquiet, *f* -ète, soucieux (**about** sur, de, au sujet de); **what are you so a. about?** pourquoi es-tu aussi inquiet *ou* soucieux?; **very** *or* **extremely a.** angoissé; **he was a. that all his work might come to nothing** il craignait que tout son travail n'ait servi à rien; **the a. faces of relatives** le visage angoissé des membres de la famille; **to be a. for sb/sb's safety** être inquiet *ou* s'inquiéter pour qn/la sécurité de qn; **I am a. about his health** sa santé me préoccupe, je m'inquiète de sa santé 2 *(worrying)* inquiétant; **an a. moment** un moment d'anxiété; **it was an a. time for us** ça a été une période de grande inquiétude pour nous 3 *(eager)* désireux; **to be a. to do sth** tenir à faire qch, être désireux de faire qch; **why are you so a. to go?** *(impatient)* pourquoi êtes-vous si impatient de partir?; *(eager)* pourquoi tenez-vous tant à y aller? 4 *Psy* anxieux

anxiously ['æŋkʃəslɪ] ADV 1 *(worriedly)* anxieusement, avec inquiétude, avec anxiété 2 *(with concern)* avec sollicitude 3 *(with impatience)* avec impatience

ANY ['enɪ]   VOIR GRAMMAIRE A34; B5; B66–7

ADJ	du, de la, de l', des **1** ▪ aucun **2** ▪ n'importe quel **3** ▪ tout **4**
PRON	n'importe quel
ADV	ne... plus **1**

ADJ 1 *(some, one)* **have you a. milk/books?** avez-vous du lait/des livres?; **have you a. more milk?** avez-vous encore du lait?; **is there a. hope?** y a-t-il de l'espoir?; *(stressed)* y a-t-il aucun espoir?; **if you had a. sense (at all)** si tu avais ne serait-ce qu'un peu de bon sens
2 *(in neg sentences or with implied negation)* **not a.** ne ... aucun; **he hasn't a. reason to complain** il n'a aucune raison de se plaindre; **he hasn't a. more money** il n'a plus d'argent; **without a. help** sans aucune aide; **she is forbidden to do a. work** tout travail lui est interdit; **it is difficult to find a. explanation for it** il est difficile d'y trouver une quelconque explication; **complaining won't do a. good** se plaindre n'avancera à rien
3 *(no particular)* n'importe quel; **come a. day (you like)** venez n'importe quel jour; **a. man, woman or child** qui que ce soit, homme, femme, ou enfant; **a. doctor will tell you that** n'importe quel médecin vous le dira; **that may happen at a. time** cela peut arriver n'importe quand; **I expect him a. moment now** je l'attends d'un instant à l'autre; **take a. two cards** prenez deux cartes quelconques; *Fam* **a. old thing** n'importe quoi; *Fam* **a. old book** n'importe quel livre; **I don't want just a. (old) wine** je ne veux pas n'importe quel vin
4 *(every)* **a. pupil who forgets his books will be punished** tout élève qui oubliera ses livres sera puni; **at a. rate, in a. case** en tout cas

PRON I haven't got a. je n'en ai pas; **I haven't seen a.** je n'en ai pas vu; **have you a.?** en avez-vous?; **is there a. more?** y en a-t-il encore?; **I/you/etc needn't say a. more** pas besoin d'en dire davantage; **they won't take a. less** ils n'accepteront pas moins; **few, if a., can read** peu, si ce n'est aucun, savent lire; **he has no money and no prospect of a.** il est sans argent et sans l'espoir d'en avoir; **take a. of the bottles** prends n'importe laquelle des bouteilles; **a. of us** n'importe qui d'entre nous; **I don't think a. of the guests have arrived yet** je ne pense pas qu'aucun des invités soit encore arrivé; **there was no paper in a. of the boxes** il n'y avait de papier dans aucune des boîtes

ADV 1 *(with comparative)* **I'm not a. better** je ne vais pas mieux; **I can't go a. further** je ne peux pas aller plus loin; **the weather couldn't be a. worse** le temps ne pourrait pas être pire *ou* plus mauvais; **I don't see him a. longer** *or* **more** je ne le vois plus; **I didn't do it a. more than you did** je ne l'ai pas fait plus que vous; **I don't like her a. more than you do** je ne l'aime pas plus que tu ne l'aimes

2 *Fam* **that didn't help us a.** cela ne nous a été d'aucun secours; **her attitude didn't help a.** son attitude n'a rien arrangé; **a. old how** n'importe comment

ANYBODY [ˈenɪbɒdɪ], **anyone** [ˈenɪwʌn]

> quelqu'un **1** ▪ personne **2** ▪ n'importe qui **3**

PRON *(no pl)* *(NOTE in examples where one of the forms is preferred, the word has been printed in full)* **1** *(indeterminate)* quelqu'un; *(expecting answer 'no')* personne; **can you see a. over there?** est-ce que vous voyez quelqu'un là-bas?; **does a. mind if I close the window?** est-ce que cela gêne quelqu'un si je ferme la fenêtre?; **would a. like some more cake?** est-ce que quelqu'un voudrait reprendre du gâteau?; **does a. dare to say so?** y a-t-il personne qui ose le dire?; **he knows French if a. does** il sait le français comme pas un; **she'll know, if a. does** si quelqu'un le sait, c'est bien elle VOIR GRAMMAIRE A34; B67

2 *(in neg sentences)* **not a.** ne ... personne; **there isn't a. here** il n'y a personne ici; **there was hardly a.** il n'y avait presque personne; **don't speak to a.** ne parlez à personne, ne parlez pas à qui que ce soit VOIR GRAMMAIRE A34; B67

3 *(no particular person)* n'importe qui, tout le monde; **a. will tell you so** le premier venu *ou* n'importe qui *ou* tout le monde vous le dira; **a. would think he was mad** on le croirait fou; **a. but me** tout autre que moi; **you're not just a.** tu n'es pas n'importe qui; **a. with any sense** quiconque a un peu de bon sens; **bring along a. you like** amenez qui vous voudrez; **I challenge a. to ...** je défie qui que ce soit de ...; **I haven't met a. else** je n'ai rencontré personne d'autre; *Sport* **it's a.'s match** n'importe qui peut gagner, n'importe qui peut remporter la victoire; **it's a.'s guess!** qui sait?; *Hum Fam* **one drink and he's anybody's** un verre et il est prêt à repartir avec n'importe qui

4 *Fam (person with status)* **is he anybody?** est-ce que c'est quelqu'un d'important?; **he'll never be anybody** il n'arrivera jamais à rien

anyhow [ˈenɪhaʊ] **ADV 1** = **anyway 2** *Fam (carelessly)* **to do sth (all) a.** faire qch n'importe comment; **the clothes had been thrown on the bed just a.** les vêtements avaient été jetés n'importe comment *ou* en pagaille sur le lit

anyone *see* **anybody**

anyplace [ˈenɪpleɪs] **ADV** *Am Fam* = **anywhere**

ANYTHING [ˈenɪθɪŋ]

> **PRON** quelque chose **1** ▪ rien **2** ▪ n'importe quoi **3** ▪ tout **3**

PRON VOIR GRAMMAIRE A34; B67 **1** quelque chose; *(with implied negation)* rien; **can I do a. for you?** est-ce que je peux faire quelque chose pour vous (aider)?; **is there a. I can do (to help)?** puis-je faire quelque chose?; **have you a. to write with?** avez-vous de quoi écrire?; **is there a. more pleasant than ...?** est-il rien de plus agréable que ...?; **will there be a. else, madam?** *(in shop)* désirez-vous autre chose, madame?, et avec cela, madame?; **a. bigger than that won't go through a letterbox** quelque chose de plus volumineux que ça ne passera pas par une boîte aux lettres; **have you a. smaller?** *(in different size)* est-ce que vous avez la taille en-dessous?; *(money)* vous n'avez pas plus petit?; **if a. should happen to me** s'il m'arrivait quelque chose; **do you see a. of your friend?** voyez-vous quelquefois votre ami?; **is (there) a. the matter?** y a-t-il quelque chose qui ne marche pas?

2 *(in neg sentences)* **not a.** ne ... rien; **he doesn't do a.** il ne fait rien; **I shan't give you a. at all** je ne vous donnerai rien du tout; **hardly a.** presque rien; **it doesn't mean a.** cela ne veut rien dire

3 *(no matter what)* n'importe quoi, tout; **he eats a.** il mange de tout; **a. you like** tout ce que vous voudrez; **a. will do** n'importe quoi fera l'affaire; **I love a. French** j'aime tout ce qui est français; **he would do a. for me** il ferait tout *ou* n'importe quoi pour moi; **I would have given a. not to go** j'aurais tout donné *ou* j'aurais donné n'importe quoi pour ne pas y aller; **he's a. but mad** il est loin d'être fou; **he's not mad, a. but** il n'est pas fou, loin de là

4 *Fam (adv phrase, intensive)* **as easy/funny/strong as a.** facile/drôle/fort comme tout; **to work like a.** travailler comme un fou; **it's raining like a.** il pleut à verse; **it's not that you were wrong or a.** ce n'est pas du tout que vous ayez tort; **I don't want to cause a problem or a., but ...** je ne veux surtout pas causer de problème, mais ...

ADV she doesn't look a. like her sister elle ne ressemble pas du tout *ou* en rien à sa sœur; **is it a. like Chinese food?** est-ce que ça ressemble un peu à de la cuisine chinoise?; **it didn't cost a. like £500** *(less)* ça a coûté bien moins de 500 livres; **the weather wasn't a. like as bad as I'd expected** le temps était loin d'être aussi mauvais que ce à quoi je m'attendais; **if the food's a. like as good as it was at the last party** si on mange ne serait-ce qu'aussi bien qu'à la soirée précédente

anyway [ˈenɪweɪ] **ADV** en tout cas, de toute façon; **a., it's too late** en tout cas *ou* de toute façon, il est trop tard; **a., you can always try** vous pouvez toujours essayer; **a., let's get back to what we were saying** enfin *ou* bon, revenons à ce que nous disions

anywhere [ˈenɪweər] **ADV** SEE GRAMMAR B67 **1** *(no matter where)* n'importe où; **put it a.** mettez-le n'importe où; **I'd know him a.** je le reconnaîtrais entre mille; **a. else** n'importe où (ailleurs); **it's miles from a.** c'est en pleine cambrousse; **this could be a. in Europe** ce pourrait être n'importe où en Europe; **has he a. near finished?** est-ce qu'il a bientôt terminé?

2 *(in negative clauses)* **not a.** nulle part; **I've never been a.** je ne suis jamais allé nulle part; **you won't find a better curry a.** vous ne trouverez de meilleur curry nulle part; **I can't find it a.** je ne le trouve nulle part; *Fig*

we're not getting a. nous n'arrivons à rien, nous n'avançons pas

3 *(somewhere)* quelque part; **can you see it a.?** est-ce que vous le voyez?; **have you found a. to live?** avez-vous trouvé à vous loger?

AOB [eɪəʊˈbiː] *(abbr* **any other business)** divers

A-OK [eɪəʊˈkeɪ] **ADJ** *Am Fam* excellent; **everything's A.** tout baigne; **he's A.** c'est un type bien

ADV parfaitement; **to go A.** se passer vachement bien

AOR [eɪəʊˈɑːr] **N** *(abbr* **adult-orientated rock)** rock *m* pour adultes

aorta [eɪˈɔːtə] **N** *Anat* aorte *f*

aortic [eɪˈɔːtɪk] **ADJ** *Anat* aortique

AP [eɪˈpiː] **N** *Journ (abbr* **Associated Press)** AP *f*

apace [əˈpeɪs] **ADV** *Arch, Lit* vite, rapidement

Apache [əˈpætʃɪ] **N** Apache *mf*

apart [əˈpɑːt] **ADV 1** *(at a distance)* à l'écart; **to hold oneself** *or* **stand a.** se tenir à l'écart **(from** de); **the house was set a little way a. from the others** la maison était un peu à l'écart des autres; **the garage stands a. from the house** le garage est séparé de la maison

2 *(separated)* **they are a mile a.** ils sont à un mil(l)e l'un de l'autre; **lines 10 centimetres a.** lignes espacées de 10 centimètres; **to stand with one's feet a.** se tenir les jambes écartées; **they consider themselves in a class a.** ils se considèrent au-dessus des autres; **place set a. for worship** endroit réservé au culte; **cities as far a. as New York and Tokyo** des villes aussi éloignées que New York et Tokyo; **children born two years a.** des enfants nés à deux ans d'intervalle; **the boys and girls were kept a.** on tenait séparés les garçons et les filles; **they're never a.** ils ne se séparent jamais; **they're living a.** *(because of circumstances)* ils n'habitent pas ensemble; *(because of divorce, split-up)* ils sont séparés, ils vivent séparément; **it is difficult to tell them a.** il est difficile de les distinguer l'un de l'autre; **this problem cannot be treated a.** c'est un problème qu'on ne peut pas considérer séparément

3 *(to pieces)* **to take a machine a.** démonter *ou* désassembler une machine; **my dress is coming a. at the seams** ma robe est en train de se découdre; *Fam* **to take a room a.** fouiller une pièce à fond

4 a. from à part, sauf; **a. from the fact that ...** indépendamment du fait que ..., outre (le fait) que ...; **a. from a few mistakes** à part *ou* sauf quelques erreurs; **a. from him, there is nobody who can do it** à part lui, personne ne peut le faire; **I don't know anyone a. from you** je ne connais personne à part toi

apartheid [əˈpɑːtaɪt, -eɪt] **N** *Pol* apartheid *m*

apartment [əˈpɑːtmənt] **N 1** *Am* appartement *m* **2** *(room)* pièce *f*; **state apartments** grands appartements *mpl*, salons *mpl* d'apparat; **(furnished) apartments to let** chambres *fpl* (meublées) à louer
▸ ▸ **a. block, a. building** immeuble *m* d'habitation; **a. hotel** résidence *f* hôtelière, résidence de tourisme

apathetic [æpəˈθetɪk] **ADJ** apathique; **to be a. about sth** être indifférent à qch; **the response to the appeal has been a.** l'appel a été reçu dans l'apathie générale

apathetically [æpəˈθetɪklɪ] **ADV** avec apathie *ou* indifférence; **to smile a.** sourire mollement *ou* sans grande conviction

apathy [ˈæpəθɪ] **N** apathie *f*, indifférence *f*; **an air of a.** un air apathique; **their a. about the issue** leur indifférence à l'égard de ce problème

ape [eɪp] N grand singe m (sans queue); **the higher apes** les primates mpl; Fig **he's a big a.** c'est une grande brute; Sl **to go a.** (become angry) piquer une crise (**over sb/sth** à propos de qn/qch); (enthuse) s'emballer (**over sb/sth** pour qn/qch); **VT** (imitate) singer

apelike ['eɪplaɪk] ADJ (face, appearance, creature) simiesque; (noises) de singe

Apennines (the) [ðiː'æpənaɪnz] NPL les Apennins mpl

aperient [ə'pɪərɪənt] ADJ, N Med laxatif m

aperitif [əperɪ'tiːf] N apéritif m

aperture ['æpətʃər] N orifice m; (of lens, diaphragm) ouverture f

apeshit ['eɪpʃɪt] ADV Sl **to go a.** (get angry) piquer une crise

APEX ['eɪpeks] N (abbr **Advance Purchase Excursion**) APEX m
▸▸ **A. fare** tarif m APEX

apex, pl **apexes, apices** ['eɪpeks, -ɪz, 'eɪpɪsiːz] N (of triangle, building, mountain) sommet m; Fig (of career) apogée m, sommet; Br Sl Hum **to fall arse over a.** tomber cul par-dessus tête

aphasia [ə'feɪzɪə] N Med aphasie f

aphasic [ə'feɪzɪk] ADJ, N Med aphasique mf

aphid ['eɪfɪd, 'æfɪd] N = **aphis**

aphis, pl **aphides** ['eɪfɪs, 'æfɪs, -ɪdiːz] N (insect) aphis m, puceron m

aphorism ['æfərɪz(ə)m] N aphorisme m

aphoristic [æfə'rɪstɪk] ADJ aphoristique

aphrodisiac [æfrəʊ'dɪzɪæk] ADJ, N aphrodisiaque m

API [eɪpiː'aɪ] N Journ (abbr **American Press Institute**) = association f de journalistes américains

apiarist ['eɪpɪərɪst] N apiculteur, -trice

apiary ['eɪpɪərɪ] N rucher m

apiculture ['eɪpɪkʌltʃər] N apiculture f

apiculturist [eɪpɪ'kʌltʃərɪst] N apiculteur, -trice

apiece [ə'piːs] ADV chacun; **to cost £10 a.** (of things) coûter 10 livres (la) pièce; **he gave them 5 euros a.** (to each of them) il leur donna 5 euros chacun

aplenty [ə'plentɪ] ADV en abondance

aplomb [ə'plɒm] N aplomb m; **with great a.** avec un aplomb formidable

apnoea, Am **apnea** [æp'niːə] N Med apnée f

apocalypse [ə'pɒkəlɪps] N Rel, Fig apocalypse f; **the four horsemen of the A.** les quatre cavaliers mpl de l'Apocalypse

apocalyptic [əpɒkə'lɪptɪk] ADJ apocalyptique

Apocrypha (the) [ðiːə'pɒkrɪfə] NPL Bible les livres mpl deutérocanoniques; (not in Protestant Bible) les apocryphes mpl

apocryphal [ə'pɒkrɪfəl] ADJ apocryphe; **the story's a.** je doute que l'histoire soit vraie

apogee ['æpədʒiː] N (of career, fame) apogée m

apolitical [eɪpə'lɪtɪk(ə)l] ADJ apolitique

Apollo [ə'pɒləʊ] N Myth Apollon m

apologetic [əpɒlə'dʒetɪk] ADJ 1 (tone) d'excuse; (voice, smile) désolé, contrit; **to be very a.** se confondre en excuses; **she was quite a. about it** elle a fait beaucoup d'excuses; **he was most a. about the whole affair** il était vraiment désolé de toute cette histoire 2 (book etc) apologétique

apologetically [əpɒlə'dʒetɪklɪ] ADV (in regret) pour s'excuser, en s'excusant; **she looked/smiled at me a.** elle me regarda/sourit d'un air contrit

apologize [ə'pɒlədʒaɪz] VI s'excuser (**for sth** de qch); **to a. for doing sth** s'excuser

d'avoir fait qch; **to a. to sb for sth** s'excuser de qch auprès de qn, faire ou présenter des ou ses excuses à qn pour qch; **I was wrong, I a.** j'ai eu tort, excusez-moi ou je m'excuse; **I a. for having kept you waiting** excusez-moi de vous avoir fait attendre; **we a. for any inconvenience** veuillez nous excuser pour les désagréments occasionnés; **I had to a. for you or your behaviour** j'ai dû demander qu'on excuse ta conduite; **it's him you should be apologizing to** c'est à lui qu'il faut demander pardon, c'est auprès de lui que tu dois t'excuser; **there's no need to a.** vous n'avez pas à vous excuser

apology [ə'pɒlədʒɪ] N 1 excuses fpl; **to make/offer an a.** faire/présenter des excuses; **to make/send one's apologies** faire/envoyer ses excuses; **I owe you an a.** je vous dois des excuses; **by way of an a. (for having …)** pour s'excuser/m'excuser/etc (d'avoir …); **will you accept this gift by way of an a.?** accepterez-vous ce cadeau avec mes excuses?; **I got a very handsome a. from them** ils se sont gracieusement excusés; **did you get an a.?** est-ce qu'il s'est/ils se sont/etc excusé(s)?; **letter of a.** lettre f d'excuses; Fig **an a. for a …** un/une … lamentable; **an a. for a dinner** un semblant de dîner
2 Lit (defence) apologie f, justification f (**for** de)

> Note that the French word **apologie** is a false friend. Its most common meaning is **eulogy**.

apoplectic [æpə'plektɪk] ADJ (person) apoplectique; (attack) d'apoplexie; **to be a. (with rage)** s'étrangler de rage; **she was a. when I told her** elle a failli avoir une attaque quand je le lui ai dit

apoplexy ['æpəpleksɪ] N Med apoplexie f

apostasy [ə'pɒstəsɪ] N apostasie f

apostate [ə'pɒstət] ADJ, N apostat, -ate

apostatize [ə'pɒstətaɪz] VI apostasier

apostle [ə'pɒs(ə)l] N (disciple), Fig apôtre m
▸▸ **the Apostles' Creed** le Symbole des Apôtres; **a. spoon** cuiller f avec figurine d'apôtre

apostolic(al) [æpəs'tɒlɪk, -ɪk(ə)l] ADJ Rel (benediction etc) apostolique
▸▸ **a. succession** succession f apostolique

apostrophe [ə'pɒstrəfɪ] N Gram apostrophe f

apostrophize [ə'pɒstrəfaɪz] VT Liter apostropher

apothecary [ə'pɒθɪkərɪ] N Arch apothicaire m

apotheosis, pl **apotheoses** [əpɒθɪ'əʊsɪs, -'əʊsiːz] N apothéose f

app [æp] N Comput Fam (abbr **application**) application f

appal, Am **appall** [ə'pɔːl] VT (Br **appals,** Am **appalls;** Br, Am **appalled, appalling**) consterner; (stronger) choquer, révolter; **to be appalled at or by sb's behaviour** être choqué par le comportement de qn; **it appals me to think that …** je suis horrifié à la pensée que …; **I'm appalled!** ça me scandalise!

Appalachian [æpə'leɪtʃɪən] ADJ, N **the A. Mountains, the Appalachians** les (monts mpl) Appalaches mpl

appalling [ə'pɔːlɪŋ] ADJ (behaviour, conditions, smell etc) épouvantable, effroyable; **to make an a. row** faire un bruit de tous les diables

appallingly [ə'pɔːlɪŋlɪ] ADV 1 (badly) épouvantablement, effroyablement; (to cook, play) effroyablement mal; **he speaks French quite a.** son français est épouvantable ou effroyable; **he's a. badly behaved** il se tient tellement mal que c'en est consternant; **to treat sb a.** se conduire épouvantablement

mal envers qn **2** (very) (ugly, boring, rude etc) effroyablement; **he's a. stupid** il est d'une stupidité effroyable ou extraordinaire

apparatchik [æpə'rɑːtʃɪk] N Pol Fam apparatchik m

apparatus, pl **apparatuses** [æpə'reɪtəs, -əsɪz] N (usu no pl) appareil m, dispositif m; **breathing a.** appareil respiratoire; **a piece of a.** un appareil; Fig **the a. of the state** l'appareil de l'État; Liter critical a., **a. criticus** (of text) appareil ou apparat m critique; Physiol **the digestive a.** l'appareil digestif; **laboratory a.** appareils de laboratoire; **mental a.** cellules fpl grises
▸▸ Gym **a. work** (gymnastique f ou exercices mpl aux) agrès mpl

apparel [ə'pærəl] N Arch, Lit, Am vêtement(s) m(pl)

apparent [ə'pærənt] ADJ 1 (clear, obvious) apparent, manifeste, évident; **to make sth a.** indiquer qch clairement; **his indifference was a.** son indifférence était manifeste; **the truth became a. to her** la vérité lui apparut; **it was a. to me that …** pour moi, il était évident que …; **as will soon become a.** comme on le verra bientôt **2** (seeming) apparent; **with a. ease** avec une facilité apparente; **in spite of his a. indifference** malgré son air d'indifférence
▸▸ Econ **a. consumption** consommation f apparente

apparently [ə'pærəntlɪ] ADV apparemment; **he's a. going to Venice** il paraît qu'il va aller à Venise; **a. not** il paraît que non

apparition [æpə'rɪʃən] N (ghost, vision, appearance) apparition f

appeal [ə'piːl] N 1 (call) appel m (**for** à); **to make or issue an a. for help** lancer un appel au secours; **to make an a. to sb** (for help, support, money) lancer un appel auprès de qn; **the president's a. for calm** l'appel au calme du président; **to make an a. to sb's generosity** faire appel à la générosité de qn; **an a. for donations** une demande de contributions; **a charity a.** un appel de la part d'une œuvre de bienfaisance
2 Law appel m (**against** de); **without a.** sans appel; **notice of a.** intimation f (d'appel); **to lodge an a.** se pourvoir en appel; **acquitted on a.** acquitté en seconde instance; **Court of A.** cour f d'appel; **Supreme Court of A.** cour de cassation; **military a. court** conseil m de révision
3 (attraction) attrait m, attraction f; **to have or hold little a. for sb** ne guère attirer qn; **to have great a.** (of thing) être très attrayant; (of person) avoir beaucoup de charme; **to have a narrow a.** (of music, politician etc) plaire à peu de gens; **their music has a wide a.** leur musique plaît à toutes sortes de gens; Com **sales a.** attraction commerciale

VI 1 (make a plea) **to a. (to sb) for help/money** demander de l'aide/de l'argent (à qn); **I a. to you to …** je vous supplie de …; **to a. to sb's generosity** faire appel à la générosité de qn
2 (attract, interest) **this appealed to his imagination** cela parlait à son imagination; **the plan/idea appeals to me** ce projet/cette idée me plaît; **it doesn't a. to me** cela ne me dit rien; **the idea did not a. to him** l'idée ne l'enchantait guère; **to a. to the emotions/ the senses** faire appel aux sentiments/aux sens; **styles that a. to the young** modes qui plaisent aux jeunes
3 Law etc interjeter appel; **to a. against a judgment** faire appel d'un jugement; **to a. to another court** en appeler à un autre tribunal, introduire un recours devant un autre tribunal; **to a. against a decision** réclamer contre une décision; Law faire appel d'une décision

vt *Law* (*decision*) faire appel de
▶▶ *Law* **A. Court** cour d'appel

> Note that the French verb **appeler** is a false friend. Its most common meaning is **to call**.

appealing [ə'piːlɪŋ] **ADJ 1** (*imploring*) (*look, tone*) suppliant **2** (*attractive*) (*personality, person, smile*) sympathique; (*idea, prospect*) séduisant, attrayant; **there's something very a. about him/puppies** il y a quelque chose de très attirant chez lui/les chiots

appealingly [ə'piːlɪŋlɪ] **ADV 1** (*beseechingly*) (*to say*) d'un ton suppliant; (*to look*) d'un air suppliant **2** (*attractively*) de façon attrayante

appear [ə'pɪər] **vi 1** (*come into view*) paraître, apparaître, se montrer; (*in accounts, on a list etc*) figurer; **a head appeared at the window** un visage a paru ou est apparu ou s'est montré à la fenêtre; **a huge lorry suddenly appeared out of the fog** un gros camion a surgi tout à coup du brouillard; **she appeared to him in a dream** elle lui est apparue en rêve; **she only appears at meal times** elle n'apparaît qu'au moment des repas; **where did you a. from?** d'où est-ce que tu sors?; **to a. from nowhere** sortir de nulle part
2 *Law* comparaître, paraître; **to a. before a court** comparaître devant un tribunal; **to fail to a.** faire défaut; **failure to a.** défaut *m* de comparution; **to a. for sb** représenter qn; (*of counsel*) plaider pour qn
3 *Theat, Cin* paraître; **to a. on the stage** (*make entrance*) entrer en scène; (*act*) faire du théâtre; **to a. on TV** passer à la télé; *Fig* **that was when I appeared on the scene** c'est à ce moment que je suis arrivé
4 (*of book, newspaper etc*) paraître, sortir
5 (*seem*) sembler, paraître; **he appeared to hesitate** il paraissait ou semblait hésiter, il avait l'air d'hésiter; **she appears to have a lot of friends** elle semble avoir beaucoup d'amis; **there appears to be a mistake** il semble(rait) qu'il y ait erreur; **it appears not** il semble que non; **it appears to us that the situation is worse** la situation nous semble pire; **to make it a. that ...** faire croire que ...; **to a. to be lost** avoir l'air d'être perdu; **to a. sad** paraître *ou* sembler triste, avoir l'air triste
6 (*become apparent*) **it appeared later that ...** on a vu par la suite *ou* plus tard que ...; **as appears from these records** comme il ressort de ces pièces

appearance [ə'pɪərəns] **N 1** (*arrival etc*) apparition *f*, arrivée *f*; **they were startled by the a. of a teacher** ils ont été surpris par l'arrivée d'un professeur; **with the a. of fast-food restaurants** avec l'apparition *ou* l'arrivée des fast-foods; **to put in an a.** passer; *Iron* faire acte de présence
2 (*of actor*) entrée *f* en scène; *Sport* (*of athlete*) entrée sur le terrain de jeu; **first a. of Miss Kane** (*as an actress*) début *m* de Mlle Kane; **to make one's first a.** débuter, faire ses débuts; **her Olympic a.** sa participation aux jeux Olympiques
3 *Law* (*in court*) comparution *f*
4 (*of book, newspaper etc*) parution *f*
5 (*looks, demeanour*) apparence *f*, aspect *m*, air *m*; **she had the a. of somebody who had not slept well** elle avait l'air de quelqu'un qui a mal dormi; **from his a. one would say ...** à son air *ou* son extérieur on dirait ...; **you should not judge by appearances** il ne faut pas juger selon les apparences; **his beard gave him the a. of a sailor** avec sa barbe il avait l'air d'un marin; **they gave every a. of being bored** ils ont donné tous les signes possibles de l'ennui; **an a. of gaiety** un air de gaieté; **it is like a mushroom in a.**

ça ressemble à un champignon; **at first a.** à première vue; **it has all the appearances of a conspiracy** ça a toutes les apparences d'une conspiration; **appearances are against him** les apparences sont contre lui; **appearances can be deceptive** les apparences peuvent être trompeuses; **to all appearances** selon toute apparence, apparemment; **to keep up appearances** sauver les apparences

appease [ə'piːz] **vt** apaiser; *Pej* endormir; (*anger, hunger*) apaiser

appeasement [ə'piːzmənt] **N 1** (*of person*) apaisement *m*; (*of nation*) conciliation *f* (**of** avec); **to aim at the a. of terrorists/one's enemies** chercher à endormir les terroristes/ses ennemis; **policy of a.** politique *f* de conciliation **2** (*of anger, hunger etc*) assouvissement *m*

appellant [ə'pelənt] **ADJ**, **N** *Law* appelant, -ante

appellate [ə'pelət, -leɪt] **ADJ** *Law* (*court*) d'appel

appellation [æpe'leɪʃən] **N** *Fml* appellation *f*, nom *m*

append [ə'pend] **vt** (*attach*) (*document*) joindre (**to** à); (*in writing*) (*one's signature*) apposer (**to** à); (*notes, comments*) ajouter; *Comput* (*to database*) ajouter; **to a. a document to a file** annexer *ou* joindre un document à un dossier
▶▶ *Comput* **a. mode** mode *m* ajout

appendage [ə'pendɪdʒ] **N** *Anat, Biol* appendice *m*; **the concert was just an a. to the main events of the day** le concert n'était qu'un prolongement des principaux événements de la journée; **I will not be treated as a mere a. of my husband** je n'existe pas qu'en fonction de mon mari, j'existe aussi par moi-même

appendectomy [æpen'dektəmɪ], **appendicectomy** [æpendɪ'sektəmɪ] **N** *Surg* appendicectomie *f*

appendicitis [əpendɪ'saɪtɪs] **N** *Med* appendicite *f*

appendix, *pl* **appendixes**, **appendices** [ə'pendɪks, -ɪksɪz, -ɪsiːz] VOIR GRAMMAIRE **A14 1** *Anat* appendice *m*; **to have one's a.** (**taken**) **out** se faire enlever l'appendice; **have you had your a. out?** tu as encore ton appendice?; *Med* **grumbling a.** appendicite *f* chronique **2** (*of report etc*) annexe *f*, (*of book*) appendice *m*

appertain [æpə'teɪn] **vi** *Fml* **1** (*belong*) appartenir (**to** à); **lands appertaining to the Crown** terres *fpl* appartenant à *ou* dépendant de la Couronne **2** (*of duties, responsibilities*) incomber (**to** à)

appetite [æpɪtaɪt] **N 1** (*for food*) appétit *m* (**for** pour); **to have a good a.** avoir bon appétit; **to have a poor a.** ne pas avoir beaucoup d'appétit; **to have a big a.** avoir un gros *ou* solide appétit; **to have a small a.** avoir un petit appétit, avoir peu d'appétit; **to take away** *ou* **spoil sb's a.** couper l'appétit *ou* la faim à qn; **to give sb an a.** donner de l'appétit à qn, mettre qn en appétit; **the walk gave him an a.** la marche lui a ouvert l'appétit; **loss of a.** manque *m* d'appétit; *Med* inappétence *f*
2 *Fig* (*for knowledge*) soif *f*, (*for travel, Chinese music etc*) goût *m*; (*for doing sth*) envie *f*, **that whetted his a. for travel** cela a aiguisé son goût des voyages; **a. for revenge** soif de vengeance; **she had an enormous a. for books** elle avait une immense soif de lecture, elle était avide de lecture; **to have little a. for a fight** être peu enclin à une querelle *ou* à se disputer; **sexual a.** appétit *m* sexuel

appetizer [æpɪtaɪzər] **N** *Culin, Fig* amuse-gueule *m*, *pl* amuse-gueule(s)

appetizing [æpɪtaɪzɪŋ] **ADJ** (*food, smell*) appétissant, alléchant; *Fig* **he doesn't look very a.** il n'est pas ragoûtant

appetizingly [æpɪtaɪzɪŋlɪ] **ADV** d'une façon appétissante

applaud [ə'plɔːd] **vt** (*performer, decision*) applaudir; **to a. sb's efforts** applaudir les efforts de qn
vi (*of audience etc*) applaudir

applause [ə'plɔːz] **N** applaudissements *mpl*; *Fig* (*approval*) approbation *f*; **to meet** *or* **be greeted with a.** (*of performance, decision etc*) être applaudi, soulever les applaudissements; **to win a.** (*of performance, decision etc*) être applaudi (**from** par, de)
▶▶ *TV* **a. meter** applaudimètre *m*

apple [æp(ə)l] **N** pomme *f*, **eating** *or* **dessert a.** pomme à couteau *ou* à dessert; **cooking a.** pomme à cuire; **baked a.** pomme cuite (au four); *Prov* **an a. a day keeps the doctor away** = mangez une pomme par jour et vous resterez en bonne santé; *Fig* **his son is the a. of his eye** il tient à son fils comme à la prunelle de ses yeux; *Fam* **the Big A.** = la ville de New York
▶▶ **a. core** trognon *m* de pomme; **a. green** (*colour*) vert *m* pomme; **a. juice** jus *m* de pomme; **a. orchard** pommeraie *f*, **a. pie** (*covered*) tourte *f* aux pommes; (*open*) tarte *f* aux pommes; *Am Fam* **a. polisher** lèche-bottes *mf inv*; *Am* **a. sauce** compote *f* de pommes; **a. tart** tarte aux pommes; **a. tree** pommier *m*

applecart [æp(ə)lkɑːt] **N** *Fig* **to upset the a.** tout chambouler

applejack [æp(ə)ldʒæk] **N** *esp Am* ≃ calvados *m*

apple-pie **ADJ** *Fam* **in a. order** admirablement rangé, parfaitement en ordre
▶▶ *Br* **a. bed** lit *m* en portefeuille

applet [æplət] **N** *Comput* appelette *f*, appliquette *f*

appliance [ə'plaɪəns] **N 1** (*machine*) appareil *m*; **mechanical a.** engin *m* mécanique; **electrical/household appliances** appareils électriques/ménagers **2** (*fire engine*) auto-pompe *f*, pompe *f* à incendie

applicable [ə'plɪkəb(ə)l, æplɪkəb(ə)l] **ADJ** applicable (**to** à); **not a.** (*on form*) sans rapport; **delete where not a.** rayer les mentions inutiles

applicant [æplɪkənt] **N 1** (*for job*) candidat, -ate (**for** à), postulant, -ante; (*for loan, funding, patent*) demandeur, -euse (**for** de); *Fin* (*for shares*) souscripteur, -trice (**for** de) **2** *Law* demandeur, -deresse, requérant, -ante

application [æplɪ'keɪʃən] **N 1** (*putting on*) application *f* (**of sth to sth** de qch à *ou* sur qch); *Aut, Tech Fml* **a. of the brake** freinage *m*
2 (*thing applied*) application *f*, (*of paint*) couche *f*, enduit *m*
3 (*use*) (*of theory, principle, discovery etc*) application *f*, **practical applications of a process** applications d'un procédé
4 (*assiduousness*) assiduité *f*, application *f*, **to show a lot of a.** faire preuve d'une grande application *ou* assiduité; **a. to a task** application à un travail
5 (*for help, patent*) demande *f* (**for** de); (*for job*) candidature *f*, **to submit an a.** (*for help*) faire une demande; (*for job*) présenter sa candidature; **to make an a. for sth** formuler une demande pour obtenir qch; **full details on a.** informations complètes sur demande; *St Exch* **a. for shares** demande de titres en souscription; **to make an a. for shares** souscrire (à) des actions
6 *Comput* application *f*
▶▶ **a. form** (*for grant, benefits*) formulaire *m* de demande; (*for membership*) demande d'inscription; (*detailed*) dossier *m* de candi-

dature; *Univ* dossier d'inscription; *St Exch (for shares)* bulletin *m* de souscription; *Comput* **a. program** programme *m* d'application; *Comput* **a. software** logiciel *m* d'application

Note that the French word **application** is a false friend. It never means **request**.

applicator ['æplɪkeɪtər] N *(for glue, eyeshadow, tampon)* applicateur *m*

applied [ə'plaɪd] ADJ *(maths etc)* appliqué; *(sciences)* expérimental, -aux
►► **a. psychology** psychotechnique *f*

appliqué [æ'pli:keɪ] N *Sewing (decoration)* application *f*, *(decorative work)* travail *m* d'application

apply [ə'plaɪ] VT **1** *(put on) (paint, lotion, bandage)* appliquer (**to** sur); *(brake)* actionner; **to a. the brake** freiner; **to a. pressure** exercer une pression; **to a. pressure on sb** faire pression sur qn
2 *(use) (system, theory, experience)* appliquer (**to** à), mettre en application; *(rule)* appliquer (**to** à); **to a. one's mind to sth** s'appliquer à qch; **to a. oneself to one's work** travailler avec application; **he would like to a. his experience in IT to industry** il voudrait utiliser ses compétences en informatique dans le domaine de l'industrie
VI **1 to a. to sb for sth** s'adresser *ou* recourir à qn pour obtenir qch; **to a. for a job** faire une demande d'emploi, poser sa candidature à un emploi, *Fml* solliciter *ou* postuler un emploi; **to a. for a loan** demander un prêt; **to a. for a grant** faire une demande de bourse; **a. within** s'adresser ici; **to a. in writing** écrire; **to a. in person** se présenter; *St Exch* **to a. for shares** souscrire (à) des actions
2 *(of law, rule, order)* s'appliquer (**to** à); **that applies to all of you!** *(what I've just said)* cela s'adresse à vous tous!

appoint [ə'pɔɪnt] VT **1** *(director etc)* nommer; *(committee)* constituer, nommer; *(heir)* instituer; **to a. sb to a post** nommer *ou* désigner qn à un poste; **to a. sb to do sth** désigner qn pour faire qch; **to a. sb (to be) manager** nommer qn directeur; **newly appointed officials** fonctionnaires *mpl* entrants *ou* nouvellement nommés **2** *Fml (time, place)* fixer, désigner; *(day)* arrêter

appointed [ə'pɔɪntɪd] ADJ **1** *(official)* nommé; *(agent)* attitré **2** *Fml (agreed) (place, hour)* convenu, dit; **on the a. day** le jour convenu *ou* dit **3 a well a. house** une maison bien montée *ou* bien agencée *ou* bien installée

appointee [əpɔɪn'tiː] N personne *f* nommée; **she was an a. of the President** elle avait été nommée par le Président

appointment [ə'pɔɪntmənt] N **1** *(meeting) (at doctor's etc)* rendez-vous *m*; *(for business)* rendez-vous, entrevue *f*; **to make an a. with sb** *(for oneself)* donner rendez-vous à qn; *(for sb else)* fixer un rendez-vous avec qn; **I've made an a. with the doctor for you** je t'ai pris un rendez-vous chez le docteur; **please telephone if you cannot make** *or* **keep your a.** veuillez téléphoner s'il vous est impossible de venir à votre rendez-vous; **she didn't keep our** *or* **the a.** elle n'est pas venue au rendez-vous; **I've got an a. with the doctor** j'ai rendez-vous chez le médecin; *(announcing arrival to receptionist)* j'ai rendez-vous avec le médecin; **to meet sb by a.** rencontrer qn sur rendez-vous; **by a. only** sur rendez-vous seulement; **have you got an a.?** avez-vous un rendez-vous?; *Admin* êtes-vous convoqué?; **appointments diary** carnet *m* de rendez-vous, agenda *m*
2 *(of sb to job)* nomination *f*, *Admin (of sb for task)* désignation *f*, *Mil, Naut (of sb to unit, ship)* affectation *f*; **he is a popular a.** tout le

monde est content de sa nomination *ou* qu'il ait été nommé; **by a. to His/Her Majesty** *(of company, shop etc)* fournisseur breveté *ou* attitré de Sa Majesté; *Journ* **appointments** offres *fpl* d'emploi
3 *Fml* **appointments** *(of house)* aménagement *m*

Note that the French word **appointements** is a false friend and is never a translation for the English word **appointments**. It means **salary**.

apportion [ə'pɔːʃən] VT *(expenses, praise)* répartir; *(property)* lotir; **to a. sth to sb** assigner qch à qn; **to a. (out) a sum among several people** partager *ou* distribuer une somme entre plusieurs personnes; **to a. blame** dégager les responsabilités de chacun

apportionment [ə'pɔːʃənmənt] N *(of taxes, expenses etc)* répartition *f*, partage *m*; *(of rations etc)* allocation *f*, *(of shares, property)* distribution *f*, *(of blame)* répartition

apposite ['æpəzɪt] ADJ approprié (**to** à); *(remark)* (fait) à propos, pertinent; *(observation)* juste

apposition [æpə'zɪʃən] N *Gram, Bot etc* apposition *f*, **words in a.** mots *mpl* apposés *ou* en apposition VOIR GRAMMAIRE A6; B5

appraisal [ə'preɪzəl] N *(of standards, personnel)* évaluation *f*, *(of object for insurance purposes etc)* estimation *f*, appréciation *f*, *(before auction)* prisée *f*, **to carry out an a.** conduire une expertise; **official a.** *(of object)* expertise *f*; **self a.** autocritique *f*

appraise [ə'preɪz] VT estimer, évaluer (**at so much** à tant); *(situation)* évaluer; *(damage)* faire l'expertise de; **to a. the value of sth** estimer *ou* apprécier la valeur de qch; **with an appraising eye** d'un œil critique

appreciable [ə'priːʃəb(ə)l] ADJ *(difference, variation, amount, distance)* appréciable, notable; *(change, improvement)* sensible

appreciably [ə'priːʃəblɪ] ADV *(changed, improved, better)* sensiblement

appreciate [ə'priːʃeɪt, -ʃɪeɪt] VT **1** *(know the value of, attach importance to) (person, thing)* apprécier; **she was never appreciated properly** elle n'a jamais été appréciée à sa juste valeur; **no one appreciates me** personne ne m'apprécie à ma juste valeur; **to a. the value of sb/sth** reconnaître la valeur de qn/qch
2 *(be grateful for)* être reconnaissant de, être sensible à; **I greatly a. your kindness** je suis très sensible à votre gentillesse; **I a. your having done this** je vous suis reconnaissant d'avoir fait cela; *esp Am (thanks)* je vous en remercie
3 *(grasp, understand)* comprendre, se rendre compte de; **I fully a. (the fact) that ...** je me rends bien compte que ...; **he doesn't a. his good fortune** il ne se rend pas compte à quel point il a de la chance; **while I a. your predicament ...** tout en comprenant bien votre situation difficile ...; **we a. the risks/difficulties involved** nous sommes conscients des risques que cela implique/des difficultés que cela comporte; **I hadn't appreciated you needed one** je ne savais pas qu'il vous en fallait un
VI *(of goods, investment etc)* prendre de la valeur; *(of value)* augmenter; *(of currency)* s'apprécier; **the euro has appreciated in terms of other currencies** l'euro s'est apprécié par rapport aux autres monnaies

appreciation [əpriːʃɪ'eɪʃən, əpriːsɪ-] N **1** *(gratitude)* gratitude *f*, reconnaissance *f*, **as a sign of our a.** en témoignage de notre gratitude *ou* reconnaissance; **I should like to express my a. of your kindness** j'aimerais

vous dire combien je suis sensible à votre gentillesse; **in a. of her years of loyal service** pour témoigner de ma/notre/leur/*etc* reconnaissance pour ses années de bons et loyaux services; **the audience showed its a. of the performance by cheering** le public a acclamé le spectacle
2 *(understanding)* compréhension *f*, **she has no a. of what is involved** elle ne se rend pas compte de ce que ça implique
3 *Fin (increase)* accroissement *m ou* hausse *f* de valeur; **a. of assets** plus-value *f* d'actif
4 *(review)* critique *f*, **to write an a. of a new play** faire la critique d'une nouvelle pièce
5 *(evaluation) (of object)* appréciation *f*, estimation *f*, *literary* **a.** explication *f* de texte; **musical a.** appréciation musicale; **a literary/wine a. society** une société d'amateurs de littérature/de vin

appreciative [ə'priːʃɪətɪv, -sɪətɪv] ADJ **1** *(grateful)* reconnaissant; **I'm very a. of all you've done for me** je vous suis reconnaissant de tout ce que vous avez fait pour moi; **she's a very a. sort of person** c'est une personne qui sait faire preuve de reconnaissance *ou* de gratitude; **in a few a. words** avec quelques mots de reconnaissance
2 *(review, audience)* favorable; *(praising)* élogieux
3 *(showing liking etc)* **I gave him the present, but he wasn't very a.** je lui ai donné le cadeau, mais il n'a pas beaucoup aimé; **to be a. of music** apprécier la musique
4 *(showing understanding, awareness)* **to be a. of sth** comprendre l'importance de qch, être sensible à qch; **he was very a. of their problems** il s'est montré très sensible à leurs problèmes

appreciatively [ə'priːʃɪətɪvlɪ, -sɪətɪvlɪ] ADV **1** *(gratefully)* avec reconnaissance
2 *(showing understanding, praising) (to review etc)* en termes élogieux, favorablement; *(to listen)* avec appréciation; **they clapped a.** ils applaudirent pour montrer leur enthousiasme; **she smiled a. at his joke** elle a aimé l'histoire qui l'a fait sourire; **she smiled a.** *(approving of point made)* elle eut un sourire approbateur; **'a superb brandy,' she said a.** 'un cognac exceptionnel,' dit-elle en connaisseuse; **the performance was received a.** le spectacle a été bien *ou* favorablement reçu
3 *(showing liking)* **'excellent coffee,' he said a.** 'excellent café,' dit-il avec plaisir

apprehend [æprɪ'hend] VT **1** *Law (arrest)* appréhender **2** *Fml (understand) (facts)* comprendre; **as far as I a. it** si je comprends bien **3** *Arch, Lit (fear) (danger etc)* appréhender, craindre

apprehension [æprɪ'henʃən] N **1** *(fear)* appréhension *f*, **to give cause for a.** motiver des craintes **2** *Law (arrest)* appréhension *f*, arrestation *f*

apprehensive [æprɪ'hensɪv] ADJ *(look, smile etc)* timide, craintif; **to be a. for sb/sth** craindre pour qn/pour la sûreté de qn; **to be a. about sth/doing sth** appréhender qch/de faire qch; **there's nothing to be a. about** il n'y a aucune raison de s'inquiéter; **I'm feeling a bit a.** je me sens un peu nerveux

apprehensively [æprɪ'hensɪvlɪ] ADV avec appréhension

apprentice [ə'prentɪs] N apprenti, -ie; **carpenter's/plumber's a., a. carpenter/ plumber** apprenti menuisier/plombier; **sorcerer's a.** apprenti sorcier
VT **to a. sb to sb** placer *ou* mettre qn en apprentissage chez qn

apprenticed [ə'prentɪst] ADJ en apprentissage (**to sb** chez qn)

apprenticeship [ə'prentɪʃɪp] N apprentissage *m*; **to serve an a.** faire un apprentissage; *Fig* **to serve one's a.** faire ses débuts

apprise [ə'praɪz] *VT Fml* **to a. sb of sth** apprendre qch à qn, prévenir *ou* informer qn de qch; **we were not apprised of his arrival** nous n'avons pas été informés de son arrivée

appro ['æprəʊ] *N Com Fam* **on a.** à l'essai

approach [ə'prəʊtʃ] *N* **1** *(coming) (of person)* approche *f*, *(of spring)* venue *f*, *(of night)* tombée *f*, *(of death)* approche(s); **I could hear his a.** je l'entendais s'approcher; *Aviat* **a. end of the runway** entrée *f* de piste, seuil *m* de la piste
2 *(method)* méthode *f*, démarche *f*; **let's try a different a.** essayons une autre méthode; **her a. to the problem** sa façon d'aborder le problème; **I don't like her a.** je n'aime pas sa façon de s'y prendre
3 *Fig (to person)* avance *f*, ouverture *f*, *(for business purposes)* proposition *f*, ouverture; **to make an a. to sb** faire une proposition à qn
4 *(point of entry)* voie *f* d'accès; **the a. to a town** les abords *mpl ou* les approches *fpl* d'une ville; **all approaches to the town have been sealed off** tous les abords de la ville ont été bouclés; **a. to a harbour** atterrage *m*, accès *m* d'un port
5 *(approximation)* **a. to an apology/a smile** semblant *m* d'excuse/de sourire; **it is the nearest a. to perfection** c'est ce qui s'approche le plus de la perfection
VI approcher, s'approcher; **Christmas/spring is approaching** Noël/le printemps approche
VT 1 *(get nearer to)* approcher; *(place)* approcher de; **the town can only be approached from the north** on ne peut accéder à *ou* gagner la ville que par le nord; **I'm approaching 45** je vais sur mes 45 ans; **the wind was approaching gale force** le vent soufflait presque en tempête; **something approaching a feeling of relief** un sentiment proche du soulagement
2 *(go up to) (person)* s'approcher de, aborder, approcher; *(of company, group, team)* pressentir, faire des propositions *ou* des ouvertures à; **I was approached by a man in the street** j'ai été abordé par un homme dans la rue; **to a. sb on the subject of …** approcher qn au sujet de …; **to be easy/difficult to a.** avoir l'abord facile/difficile
3 *(question)* aborder, s'attaquer à; **she approaches the issue from the angle of …** elle aborde la question du point de vue de …
▸▸ *Aviat* **a. aids** moyens *mpl* d'approche; **a. shot** *Tennis* coup *m* d'approche; *Golf* approche

approachable [ə'prəʊtʃəb(ə)l] *ADJ* **1** *(person)* d'un abord facile, abordable **2** *(building, place)* accessible

approaching [ə'prəʊtʃɪŋ] *ADJ (death)* prochain; *(storm)* qui arrive; **the a. war …** la guerre qui approche/approchait …; **the a. car** *(from opposite direction to one's own)* la voiture qui vient/venait en sens inverse

approbation [æprə'beɪʃən] *N* approbation *f*, **smile of a.** sourire *m* approbateur

appropriate[1] [ə'prəʊprɪət] *ADJ (suitable, fitting)* approprié (**to** à); *(word, expression)* juste; *(clothes)* convenable (**for** pour); *(name, site)* bien choisi; *(music)* de circonstance; *(moment)* opportun; **to take a. action** prendre les mesures indiquées; **he could have chosen a more a. time and place** il aurait pu choisir un moment et un endroit plus appropriés (**to** pour); **it seemed a. that she should have died in a theatre** cela semblait être dans l'ordre des choses qu'elle soit morte dans un théâtre

appropriate[2] [ə'prəʊprɪeɪt] *VT* **1** *(take)* s'approprier, s'emparer de; *(keep for oneself)*

s'attribuer, se réserver; **to a. sb's ideas** s'approprier les idées de qn **2** *(set aside) (money, funds)* affecter, destiner (**to** à); **£4,000 has been appropriated to upgrading computers** 4000 livres ont été affectées à l'augmentation de mémoire des ordinateurs

appropriately [ə'prəʊprɪətlɪ] *ADV (suitably)* de manière appropriée; *(properly)* convenablement, proprement; **a. dressed** en tenue convenable

appropriateness [ə'prəʊprɪətnɪs] *N (of behaviour)* correction *f*, bienséance *f*, *(of remarks)* justesse *f*, à-propos *m inv*

appropriation [əprəʊprɪ'eɪʃən] *N* **1** *(taking)* appropriation *f*, prise *f* de possession (**of** de) **2** *(setting aside) (of money for specific purpose)* application *f*, affectation *f* **3** *Fin* affectation *f* de fonds; *(of sum)* attribution *f*, *Pol* crédit *m* (budgétaire)

approval [ə'pruːv(ə)l] *N* **1** approbation *f*, assentiment *m*, *Fml* agrément *m*, *(of dealer, distributor)* agrément; **to meet with sb's a.** recevoir *ou* obtenir l'approbation de qn; **to submit sth for a. (by sb)** soumettre qch à l'approbation (de qn); **gesture** *or* **sign of a.** geste *m ou* signe *m* d'approbation; **to nod a.** approuver d'un signe de (la) tête; **subject to a.** soumis à l'approbation
2 *Com* **on a.** à condition, à l'essai; **a book sent on a.** un livre envoyé à l'examen; *Am* **approvals** *(goods)* marchandises *fpl* envoyées à l'essai
3 *(of document, proposal)* ratification *f*, homologation *f*, **for (your) a.** *(of draft letter)* pour approbation
▸▸ **a. rating** *(of politician)* cote *f* de popularité; *Mktg (of product)* score *m* d'agrément

approve [ə'pruːv] *VT (action)* approuver, sanctionner; *(decision, proposal)* ratifier, homologuer; *(contract, dealer, distributor)* agréer; **read and approved** lu et approuvé; **approved by the government** agréé par l'État
VI être d'accord; **I told her what I had done and she seemed to a.** je lui ai dit ce que j'avais fait et elle a eu l'air de m'approuver
▸ **approve of** *VT INSEP* approuver; **I don't a. of your friends** tes amis ne me plaisent pas; **I don't a. of the plan** je ne suis pas d'accord avec ce projet; **she doesn't a. of them smoking** ça ne lui plaît pas qu'ils fument

approved [ə'pruːvd] *ADJ* approuvé, agréé; *Admin* **(officially) a.** homologué
▸▸ **a. dealer** concessionnaire *m* agréé; *Formerly* **a. school** = nom anciennement donné en Grande-Bretagne à un centre d'éducation surveillé (aujourd'hui appelé "community home"); **a. stallion** étalon *m* autorisé

approving [ə'pruːvɪŋ] *ADJ (look, smile)* approbateur, -trice

approvingly [ə'pruːvɪŋlɪ] *ADV (to look)* d'un air approbateur; *(to say)* d'un ton approbateur; **to react a.** approuver

approx *abbr* **approximately**

approximate[1] [ə'prɒksɪmɪt] *ADJ* **1** *(calculation etc)* approximatif, approché SEE GRAMMAR B59 **2** *Biol, Phys* rapproché, proche, voisin
▸▸ **a. value** valeur *f* approximative

approximate[2] [ə'prɒksɪmeɪt] *VT* **to a. sth in size/cost** se rapprocher de qch par les dimensions/le prix
VI **to a. in size/cost to sth** se rapprocher de qch par les dimensions/le prix; **to a. to the truth** se rapprocher de la vérité

approximately [ə'prɒksɪmətlɪ] *ADV* approximativement, à peu près; **5 miles are a. 8 kilometres** 5 mil(l)es équivalent à peu près à 8 kilomètres; **his income is a. £15,000** son revenu est d'environ 15 000 livres

approximation [əprɒksɪ'meɪʃən] *N* approximation *f*, **his statement was no more than an a. of the truth** sa déclaration n'avait qu'un lointain rapport avec la réalité

appurtenance [ə'pɜːtɪnəns] *N (usu pl)* **appurtenances** accessoires *mpl*, *Law* **a house with all its appurtenances** un immeuble avec ses appartenances et dépendances

APR [eɪpiː'ɑːr] *N Fin (abbr* **annual percentage rate)** TEG *m*

Apr *abbr* **April**

après-ski [æpreɪ'skiː] *N* = distractions *fpl* après une séance de ski

> Note that the French word **après-ski** is a false friend and is never a translation for the English word **après-ski**. It means **snowboot**.

apricot ['eɪprɪkɒt] *N* **1** abricot *m*; **a. yoghurt/ice cream** yaourt *m*/glace *f* à l'abricot **2** *(colour)* abricot *m inv*; **a. dress** robe *f* (couleur) abricot
▸▸ **a. jam** confiture *f* d'abricots; **a. tart** tarte *f* aux abricots; **a. tree** abricotier *m*

April ['eɪprɪl] *N* VOIR GRAMMAIRE A81–2; B61 avril *m*; **in A.** en avril, au mois d'avril; **(on) the first/the seventh of A.** le premier/le sept avril
▸▸ **A. fool** *(person)* = personne *f* à qui l'on a fait un poisson d'avril; *(trick)* poisson *m* d'avril; **A. fool!** poisson d'avril!; **A. Fool's Day** le premier avril; **A. showers** ≃ giboulées *fpl* de mars

April Fool's Day
En Grande-Bretagne, le premier avril est l'occasion de farces en tous genres; en revanche, la tradition du poisson en papier n'existe pas.

a priori ['eɪpraɪ'ɔːraɪ, ɑːprɪ'ɔːrɪ] *ADV, ADJ* a priori

apron ['eɪprən] *N* **1** *(clothing)* tablier *m*; *Fig* **to be tied to one's mother's a. strings** être pendu aux jupons de sa mère **2** *Theat* avant-scène *f*, *pl* avant-scènes **3** *Aviat* aire *f* de manœuvre *ou* de stationnement; *(for plane maintenance and repair)* tablier *m*, aire en dur
▸▸ *Theat* **a. stage** avant-scène

apropos ['æprəpəʊ] *ADJ (remark)* opportun, pertinent
PREP **a. (of)** à propos de

APS [eɪpiː'es] *ADJ, N Phot (abbr* **advanced photo system)** APS *m*
▸▸ **A. camera** appareil *m* photo APS

apse [æps] *N (in church)* abside *f*

apt[1] [æpt] *ADJ* **1** *(word)* juste; *(expression)* heureux, qui convient; *(description)* parlant; **it is very a. that it should end in this way** il est tout à fait approprié que cela se termine de cette manière **2** **to be a. to do sth** *(of person, thing)* avoir tendance à faire qch **3** *(student etc)* intelligent, doué; **to be a. at languages** être doué en *ou* pour les langues

apt[2] *Am (abbr* **apartment)** appt

aptitude ['æptɪtjuːd] *N* aptitude *f* (**for** à, pour); **to show great a.** montrer de grandes dispositions; **to have an a. for science** avoir une aptitude pour la science, avoir des dispositions scientifiques; **to have no a. for French** n'avoir aucune facilité pour le français
▸▸ **a. test** test *m* d'aptitude

aptly ['æptlɪ] *ADV (to say, comment)* avec justesse, à propos; *(described)* justement; **a. chosen name** nom *m* bien choisi

aptness ['æptnɪs] *N* **1** *(appropriateness) (of expression, quotation etc)* justesse *f*, à-propos *m inv* **2** *(tendency)* tendance *f* (**to do sth** à faire qch)

aqualung ['ækwəlʌŋ] N scaphandre *m* autonome

aquamarine [ækwəmə'ri:n] N *(gem)* aigue-marine *f*, *pl* aigues-marines
ADJ *(dress etc)* bleu vert *inv*

aquanaut ['ækwənɔ:t] N aquanaute *mf*

aquaplane ['ækwəpleɪn] N *Sport* aquaplane *m*
VI *Sport* faire de l'aquaplane; *Aut* faire de l'aquaplaning

aquaplaning ['ækwəpleɪnɪŋ] N *Sport* aquaplane *m*; *Aut* aquaplaning *m*, effet *m* d'hydroglisseur

aquarelle [ækwə'rel] N *Art* aquarelle *f*

aquarium, *pl* **aquariums, aquaria** [ə'kweərɪəm, -ɪəmz, -ɪə] N aquarium *m*

Aquarius [ə'kweərɪəs] N *Astrol* le Verseau; **to be (an) A.** être (du) Verseau

aquarobics ['ækwə'rəʊbɪks] N aquagym *f*

aquatic [ə'kwætɪk] ADJ *(plant etc)* aquatique
▸▸**a. display** numéro *m* aquatique; **a. sports** sports *mpl* nautiques

aquatics [ə'kwætɪks] NPL sports *mpl* nautiques VOIR GRAMMAIRE A10

aquatint ['ækwətɪnt] N aquatinte *f*

aqueduct ['ækwɪdʌkt] N aqueduc *m*

aqueous ['eɪkwɪəs] ADJ aqueux
▸▸*Anat* **a. humour** humeur *f* aqueuse; *Chem* **a. solution** soluté *m*

aquilegia [ækwɪ'li:dʒɪə] N *(plant)* aquilégie *f*

aquiline ['ækwɪlaɪn] ADJ aquilin; *(nose)* aquilin, busqué, en bec d'aigle

A&R [eɪən'dɑ:r] N *(abbr* **artists and repertoire**) = service *m* d'une maison de disques chargé de recruter de nouveaux artistes
▸▸**A. man** = personne *f* qui recrute de nouveaux artistes

Arab ['ærəb] VOIR GRAMMAIRE A19 ADJ **1** arabe; **the A. world** le monde arabe **2** *(horse)* arabe
N**1** *(person)* Arabe *mf* **2** *(horse)* arabe *m*
▸▸*Pol* **the A. League** la Ligue arabe

Arab

En anglais le mot "Arab" désigne l'ensemble des ressortissants des pays de culture arabe, et surtout de l'Arabie Saoudite. Il n'a pas le sens restreint de "Maghrébin" que l'on rencontre souvent en français: "the firm was bought by a wealthy Arab family".

---

arabesque [ærə'besk] ADJ *Art (decoration)* de style arabe
N**1** *(usu pl) Art* arabesque *f* **2** *(in ballet)* arabesque *f*

Arabia [ə'reɪbɪə] N Arabie *f*

Arabian [ə'reɪbɪən] VOIR GRAMMAIRE A19 ADJ arabe
N *(from Arabia)* Arabe *mf*
▸▸**the A. Gulf** le golfe Arabique; *Liter* **the A. Nights** les Mille et Une Nuits; **the A. Peninsula** la péninsule d'Arabie

Arabic ['ærəbɪk] VOIR GRAMMAIRE A19 ADJ *(language, literature)* arabe; **A. scholar** arabisant, -ante
N *Ling* arabe *m*
▸▸**A. numerals** chiffres *mpl* arabes

Arabist ['ærəbɪst] N arabisant, -ante

arable ['ærəb(ə)l] ADJ *(land)* arable

arachnid [ə'ræknɪd] N *Zool* arachnide *m*

Aramaic [ærə'meɪɪk] ADJ, N *Ling* araméen *m*

arbiter ['ɑ:bɪtər] N *(of fashion etc)* arbitre *m*; **a. of taste** arbitre des élégances

---

arbitrage ['ɑ:bɪtrɑ:ʒ] N *Fin, St Exch* arbitrage *m*

arbitrager ['ɑ:bɪtrɑ:ʒər] N *Fin, St Exch* arbitragiste *mf*

arbitrarily ['ɑ:bɪtreərəlɪ] ADV arbitrairement

arbitrariness ['ɑ:bɪtrərɪnɪs] N *(of decision etc)* caractère *m* arbitraire

arbitrary ['ɑ:bɪtrərɪ] ADJ *(decision etc)* arbitraire

arbitrate ['ɑ:bɪtreɪt] VT *(dispute)* arbitrer, trancher
VI arbitrer (**between** entre)

arbitration [ɑ:bɪ'treɪʃən] N arbitrage *m*; **to go to a.** *(of union)* soumettre le différend à l'arbitrage; *(of dispute)* être soumis à l'arbitrage; **to refer a question to a.** soumettre une question à un arbitrage
▸▸**a. board** commission *f* d'arbitrage; **a. clause** clause *f* compromissoire; **a. committee** commission d'arbitrage; **a. court** instance *f* chargée d'arbitrer les conflits sociaux, tribunal *m* arbitral; **a. ruling** décision *f* arbitrale; **a. tribunal** instance chargée d'arbitrer les conflits sociaux, tribunal arbitral

arbitrator ['ɑ:bɪtreɪtər] N médiateur, -trice; *Law* arbitre *m*

arbor N *Am* = **arbour**

arboreal [ɑ:'bɔ:rɪəl] ADJ **1** *(relating to trees)* d'arbre(s) **2** *(living in trees) (animal)* arboricole; *(existence)* dans les arbres

arboriculture ['ɑ:bərɪkʌltʃər] N arboriculture *f*

arbour, *Am* **arbor** ['ɑ:bər] N berceau *m* de verdure, charmille *f*; *(on trellis)* tonnelle *f*; **vine a.** treille *f*

arbutus [ɑ:'bju:təs] N *(shrub)* arbousier *m*

arc [ɑ:k] N *Math etc (of circle etc)* arc *m*; **to describe an a.** décrire un arc; *Mil* **a. of fire** *(of cannon etc)* champ *m* de tir
VI (**arcing** ['ɑ:kɪŋ], **arced** [ɑ:kt]) *Elec* faire jaillir un arc, amorcer l'arc
▸▸**a. lamp, a. light** lampe *f ou* projecteur *m* à arc

arcade [ɑ:'keɪd] N *(covered passageway)* passage *m* (couvert); *(for shopping)* galerie *f* (marchande)

Arcadia [ɑ:'keɪdɪə] N Arcadie *f*

Arcadian [ɑ:'keɪdɪən] ADJ arcadien
N Arcadien, -ienne

arcane [ɑ:'keɪn] ADJ mystérieux, ésotérique; *(knowledge, practice, ritual)* secret, -ète
N **the a.** le mystérieux

arch[1] [ɑ:tʃ] N**1** *Archit, Constr* voûte *f*, arc *m*; *Constr (of bridge, viaduct)* arche *f*; **a. of a vault** arceau *m* d'une voûte **2** *Anat (of foot)* cambrure *f*, voûte *f* plantaire; **to have fallen arches** avoir les pieds plats
VT *(one's back)* arquer, courber; **the cat arched its back** le chat a fait le dos rond
VI former une voûte
▸▸*Archit* **a. stone** claveau *m*, voussoir *m*; **a. support** *(in shoes)* cambrure

arch[2] ADJ *(mischievous)* espiègle, malicieux

arch[3] ADJ *(great)* grand
PREF archi-
▸▸**a. enemy** adversaire *m ou* ennemi *m* numéro un; **a. traitor** traître *m* insigne

archaeological, *Am* **archeological** [ɑ:kɪə'lɒdʒɪk(ə)l] ADJ archéologique

archaeologically, *Am* **archeologically** [ɑ:kɪə'lɒdʒɪklɪ] ADV archéologiquement

archaeologist, *Am* **archeologist** [ɑ:kɪ'ɒlədʒɪst] N archéologue *mf*

archaeology, *Am* **archeology** [ɑ:kɪ'ɒlədʒɪ] N archéologie *f*

archaic [ɑ:'keɪɪk] ADJ archaïque

archaism [ɑ:keɪɪz(ə)m] N archaïsme *m*

---

archangel ['ɑ:keɪndʒ(ə)l] N archange *m*

archbishop [ɑ:tʃ'bɪʃəp] N archevêque *m*; **a.'s palace** palais *m* archiépiscopal

archbishopric [ɑ:tʃ'bɪʃəprɪk] N archevêché *m*

archdeacon [ɑ:tʃ'di:k(ə)n] N archidiacre *m*

archdiocese [ɑ:tʃ'daɪəsɪs, -si:z] N archidiocèse *m*, archevêché *m*

archduchess [ɑ:tʃ'dʌtʃɪs] N archiduchesse *f*

archduchy [ɑ:tʃ'dʌtʃɪ] N archiduché *m*

archduke [ɑ:tʃ'dju:k] N archiduc *m*

arched [ɑ:tʃt] ADJ *Archit (roof)* voûté
▸▸**a. window** *(semicircular)* fenêtre *f* cintrée; *(pointed)* fenêtre en arc brisé

archeological, archeologically etc *Am* = **archaeological, archaeologically** etc

archer ['ɑ:tʃər] N *Mil, Sportort* archer *m*

archery ['ɑ:tʃərɪ] N tir m à l'arc

archetypal [ɑ:kɪ'taɪp(ə)l] ADJ **the a. English village** l'archétype *m* du village anglais

archetype ['ɑ:kɪtaɪp] N archétype *m*

archiepiscopal [ɑ:kɪɪ'pɪskəp(ə)l] ADJ archiépiscopal, -aux

Archimedes [ɑ:kɪ'mi:di:z] N Archimède
▸▸*Phys* **A.' principle** principe *m* d'Archimède; **A.' screw** vis *f* d'Archimède

archipelago, *pl* **archipelagos, archipelagoes** [ɑ:kɪ'pelǝgǝʊ, -ǝʊz] N *Geog* archipel *m*

architect ['ɑ:kɪtekt] N *also Fig* architecte *mf*; **naval a.** ingénieur *m* des constructions navales *ou* du génie maritime; **to be the a. of one's own downfall** être l'artisan de sa propre ruine

architectural [ɑ:kɪ'tektʃər(ə)l] ADJ architectural, -aux

architecturally [ɑ:kɪ'tektʃǝrǝlɪ] ADV du point de vue de l'architecture

architecture ['ɑ:kɪtektʃər] N *Constr, Comput* architecture *f*

architrave ['ɑ:kɪtreɪv] N *Archit* architrave *f*

archive ['ɑ:kaɪv] N *(usu pl)* **archives** archives *fpl*; **we'll be showing film from the archives** nous présenterons des extraits d'archives
VT mettre aux archives; *Comput* archiver
▸▸*Comput* **a. copy** copie *f* archivée; *TV* **a. footage** extraits *mpl* d'archives; **a. librarian** archiviste *mf*; **a. material** matériel *m* d'archives; *Comput* **a. site** site *m* FTP

archiving ['ɑ:kaɪvɪŋ] N archivage *m*
▸▸*Comput* **a. facility** fonction *f* d'archivage

archivist ['ɑ:kɪvɪst] N archiviste *mf*

archly ['ɑ:tʃlɪ] ADV d'un air espiègle *ou* malicieux; *(to say)* d'un ton espiègle *ou* malicieux

archness ['ɑ:tʃnɪs] N espièglerie *f*, malice *f*

archway ['ɑ:tʃweɪ] N *(entry)* porte *f* cintrée, voûte *f* d'entrée

arctic ['ɑ:ktɪk] ADJ *(territory, circle, expedition etc)* arctique
N **the A.** l'Arctique *m*; **an expedition to the A.** une expédition dans l'Arctique
▸▸**a. fox** isatis *m*

arc-weld VT *Tech* souder à l'arc (électrique)

arc-welding N *Tech* soudure *f* à l'arc

ardent ['ɑ:d(ə)nt] ADJ *(desire, love)* passionné, ardent; *(admirer, believer)* fervent

ardently ['ɑ:d(ə)ntlɪ] ADV ardemment

ardour, *Am* **ardor** ['ɑ:dər] N *(of passion, desire)* ardeur *f*, *(religious)* ferveur *f*

arduous ['ɑ:djʊəs] ADJ *(path, task)* ardu, pénible

arduously ['ɑ:djʊəslɪ] ADV péniblement

arduousness ['ɑ:djʊəsnɪs] N difficulté *f*

are [ɑ:r] *see* **be**

area ['eərɪə] N**1** *(of circle, field, room etc)* superficie *f*, aire *f*; *(of floor)* surface *f*; **the room**

has an a. of 24 square metres *or* is 24 square metres in a. la pièce a une superficie de 24 mètres carrés, la superficie de la pièce est de 24 mètres carrés; **surface a.** surface

2 *(region)* territoire *m*, région *f*; *(of town)* zone *f*, quartier *m*; *(of lung, brain, disk, surface)* zone; *(part of office, hall, playground etc)* espace *m*; *(of influence etc)* périmètre *m*; *Fig (of knowledge, research)* domaine *m*; **a. of competence** domaine de compétence; **a. of coverage** *(of satellite)* zone de couverture; **a. of expertise** domaine de compétence; **a. of operations** branche *f* d'activité; **residential a.** *(in town)* quartier résidentiel; **industrial/suburban a.** zone industrielle/suburbaine; **houses were searched over a wide a.** on a fouillé les maisons sur un large périmètre; **cotton (growing)/mining a.** région du coton/minière; **customs a.** territoire douanier; **currency a.** zone monétaire; **the Manchester a.** la région de Manchester; **the Greater London a.** l'agglomération *f* londonienne, le grand Londres; **a. of agreement** terrain *m* d'entente; *Fig* **problem a.** domaine problématique; **growth a.** secteur *m* de croissance; *Mil etc* **forward a.** zone de l'avant, zone avancée; **prohibited *or* restricted a.** zone prohibée; *Comput* **storage a.** zone de mémoire; *Aut* **parking a.** parking *m*; **service a.** *(on motorway)* relais *m* d'autoroute; **play a.** *(in park)* aire *f* de jeu; **dining a.** *(in living room)* coin *m* salle à manger; *(in kitchen)* coin-repas *m*, *pl* coins-repas

▸▸ *Mil* **a. bombing** bombardement *m* sur zone; *Com* **a. manager** directeur, -trice régional(e); **A. of Outstanding Natural Beauty** = zone naturelle protégée; *Am* **a. rug** tapis *m*, *Can* carpette *f*; *Mktg* **a. sample** échantillon *m* par zone; *Mktg* **a. sampling** échantillonnage *m* par zone

areaway ['ɛərɪəweɪ] N *Am (courtyard)* cour *f* d'entrée en sous-sol

▸▸ **a. steps** escalier *m* de service *(du sous-sol)*

areca ['ærɪkə] N

▸▸ **a. nut** noix *f* d'arec; **a. palm (tree)** aréquier *m*

arena, *pl* **arenas** [ə'riːnə, -əz] N *(bullring etc)* arène *f*, *Fig (economic, international etc)* scène *f*, *Fig* **the political a.** l'arène politique; *Fig* **to enter the a.** entrer dans l'arène

aren't [ɑːnt] CONTR **1** = are not, *see* be **2** a. I? = am I not?, *see* be

Argentina [ɑːdʒən'tiːnə] N Argentine *f*

Argentine ['ɑːdʒəntaɪn] ADJ argentin N **1** *Old-fashioned* **the A.** l'Argentine *f* **2** *(person)* Argentin, -ine

Argentinian [ɑːdʒən'tɪnɪən] ADJ argentin N Argentin, -ine

argon ['ɑːgɒn] N *Chem* argon *m*

Argonaut ['ɑːgənɔːt] N **1** *Myth* Argonaute **2** a. *(mollusc)* voilier *m*, argonaute *m*

argot ['ɑːgəʊ] N argot *m*

arguable ['ɑːgjʊəb(ə)l] ADJ **1** *(open to discussion)* discutable, contestable; **that's a.** c'est discutable; **it is a. whether it would have made any difference** on peut se demander si cela aurait changé quelque chose **2** *(capable of being maintained)* *(theory)* défendable; **it is a. that they didn't need our help** on pourrait soutenir qu'en fait ils n'avaient pas besoin de notre aide

arguably ['ɑːgjʊəblɪ] ADV **it's a. the city's best restaurant** on peut dire que c'est le meilleur restaurant de la ville

argue ['ɑːgjuː] VT **1** *(debate)* discuter; *(question)* débattre; **she argued the case well** elle a bien débattu la question; **he argued the case for lower taxes** il a plaidé en faveur d'une baisse des impôts

2 *(put a case)* **to a. that ...** soutenir *ou* maintenir que ... + *ind*

3 *Fig (of fact etc) (existence of ancient civilization etc)* témoigner de, révéler

VI **1** *(debate)* discuter (**with sb about sth** avec qn de qch); *(quarrel)* se disputer (**with sb about sth** avec qn à propos de qch); **I'm not going to a. about it** *(I refuse to discuss it)* je ne veux pas en discuter; **to a. about politics** discuter (de) politique; **those two are always arguing** ces deux-là sont toujours à se disputer; **he's always arguing** c'est un argumentateur; **don't a.!** pas de discussion!; **they're always arguing about whose turn it is to do the washing-up** ils sont toujours à se disputer pour savoir qui va faire la vaisselle

2 *(put a case)* plaider; **all this argues in his favour** tout ceci plaide *ou* témoigne en sa faveur

▸ **argue against** VT INSEP plaider contre

▸ **argue away** VT SEP *(make disappear)* nier l'importance de

VI **they've been arguing away for hours** *(quarrelling)* ils se disputent depuis des heures; *(discussing)* ils discutent depuis des heures

▸ **argue for** VT INSEP plaider pour *ou* en faveur de

▸ **argue out** VT SEP *(settle by argument)* résoudre par le débat; **I'll leave you to a. it out between you** je vous laisse résoudre la question *ou* le problème entre vous

arguing ['ɑːgjuːɪŋ] N argumentation *f*; **that's enough a.** assez discuté; *Fam* **and no a.!** pas de discussion!

argument ['ɑːgjʊmənt] N **1** *(debate)* discussion *f*, débat *m*; *(quarrel)* dispute *f*; **to have an a. about sth** *(debate)* discuter de *ou* sur qch; *(quarrel)* se disputer à propos de qch; **I don't want to have an a. about it** je ne veux pas qu'on se dispute pour ça; **to get into an a.** se disputer (**with sb** avec qn; **about sb/sth** à propos de qn/qch); **to get the best of an a.** l'emporter dans une discussion; **to obey without a.** obéir sans discuter

2 *(reasoning, case)* argument *m* (**for** en faveur de; **against** contre); **that is another a. for dismissing him** c'est une raison de plus pour le congédier; **to follow sb's (line of) a.** suivre le raisonnement de qn; **suppose for a.'s sake that ...** supposons à titre d'exemple que ... + *sub*

3 *Lit (of work)* argument *m*

argumentative [ɑːgjʊ'mentətɪv] ADJ *(person)* raisonneur, disposé à argumenter *ou* à disputailler; *(tone)* polémique, agressif; **don't be so a.** arrête de faire le raisonneur

Argy ['ɑːdʒɪ] N *Br Offensive Sl* Argentin, -ine

argy-bargy ['ɑːdʒɪ'bɑːdʒɪ] N *Br Fam* chamailleries *fpl*

aria ['ɑːrɪə] N *Mus* aria *f*

arid ['ærɪd] ADJ *(land, subject)* aride

aridity [ə'rɪdɪtɪ], **aridness** ['ærɪdnɪs] N aridité *f*

Aries ['eəriːz] N *Astrol* le Bélier; **to be (an) A.** être (du) Bélier

aright [ə'raɪt] ADV *Arch, Lit* bien, juste; **to put *or* set things a.** redresser la situation

arise [ə'raɪz] VI (**arose** [ə'rəʊz]; **arisen** [ə'rɪz(ə)n]) **1** *(come about) (of situation, deficit)* se produire; *(of problem)* surgir, survenir, se présenter; *(of storm)* se lever; **if complications a.** s'il survient des complications; **if the need arises** si besoin est; **the question has not yet arisen** la question ne s'est pas encore posée; **should the occasion a.** le cas échéant

2 *(result)* émaner, provenir, résulter (**from** de); **obligations that a. from a clause** obligations qui émanent d'une clause

3 *Lit (of person)* s'élever; **a prophet arose** un prophète surgit *ou* se révéla; **a., Sir John!** *(in knighthood ceremony)* relevez-vous, Sir

John!; *Bible* **to a. from the dead** ressusciter (des morts)

aristocracy [ærɪs'tɒkrəsɪ] N *(nobility)* aristocratie *f*, *Fig* **the a. of the fashion world** le gratin de la mode

aristocrat ['ærɪstəkræt, ə'rɪs-] N aristocrate *mf*

aristocratic [ærɪstə'krætɪk] ADJ aristocratique

aristocratically [ærɪstə'krætɪklɪ] ADV aristocratiquement

Aristotelian [ærɪstɒ'tiːlɪən] ADJ *Phil* aristotélicien

Aristotle ['ærɪstɒt(ə)l] N Aristote

arithmetic [ə'rɪθmətɪk] N *(calculations)* calcul *m*; *(subject)* arithmétique *f*; **my a. is absolutely appalling** je suis nul en calcul; **your a. is spot on** tes calculs tombent pile; **it's a simple question of a.** les chiffres parlent d'eux-mêmes; **the a. is against a Labour victory** mathématiquement, les Travaillistes ont peu de chances de gagner; *Sch* **a. book** livre *m* d'arithmétique VOIR GRAMMAIRE A77; B59

arithmetic(al) [ærɪθ'metɪk, -ɪk(ə)l] ADJ arithmétique; **a. mistakes** *or* **errors** des erreurs *fpl* de calcul

arithmetically [ærɪθ'metɪklɪ] ADV arithmétiquement

Ariz *abbr* Arizona

Ark *abbr* Arkansas

ark [ɑːk] N **1** arche *f*, *Fam* **it looked like it had come out of the a.** il avait l'air vieux comme Hérode **2** *Rel* **the A. of the Covenant** l'Arche *f* d'alliance

arm¹ [ɑːm] N **1** *(of person)* bras *m*; **upper a.** haut du bras; **to carry a child in one's arms** porter un enfant dans ses bras; **to hold sb in one's arms** tenir qn dans ses bras; **to carry sth under one's a.** porter qch sous le bras; **to carry a basket over** *or* **on one's a.** porter un panier au bras; **with a girl on his a.** une fille à son bras; **to walk a. in a.** marcher bras dessus bras dessous; **give me your a.** donne-moi le *ou* ton bras; **to hold out one's arms** *(in front)* tendre les bras; *(to sides)* lever les bras; **to receive sb with open arms** recevoir qn à bras ouverts; **to keep sb at a.'s length** tenir qn à distance

2 *(of dress etc)* manche *f*, *(of chair)* accoudoir *m*, bras *m*; *(of sea, river, lever)* bras; **(pick-up) a.** *(on record player)* bras de lecture; *Fig* **the secular a.** le bras séculier; *Fig* **the long a. of the law** l'autorité *f* de la loi, *Fam* le représentant de la loi **3** *Mil (branch)* arme *f*

arm² VT **1** *(person, regiment, fortified place)* armer; **to a. oneself with an umbrella** se munir d'un parapluie; *Lit* **to a. oneself with patience** s'armer de patience **2** *(bomb, rocket, torpedo, mine)* armer

VI s'armer, prendre les armes; **the country was arming for war** le pays s'armait pour la guerre

armada [ɑː'mɑːdə] N **1** *Hist* **the (Spanish) A.** l'Invincible Armada *f* **2** *(any fleet of warships)* armada *f*

armadillo [ɑːmə'dɪləʊ] N *(animal)* tatou *m*

Armageddon [ɑːmə'ged(ə)n] N *Bible, Fig* Armageddon

armament ['ɑːməmənt] N *(weapons) (of ship, tank, plane)* artillerie *f*; **armaments** *(weapons)* armement *m*, armes *fpl*

armature ['ɑːmətʃər] N **1** *Zool* armure *f* **2** *Elec* armature *f* **3** *Constr, Art* armature *f*

armband ['ɑːmbænd] N brassard *m*; *(for swimmers)* manchon *m*; **black a.** brassard de deuil

armchair ['ɑːmtʃeər] N fauteuil *m*; **a. strategist/traveller** stratège *m*/voyageur *m* en chambre

armed [ɑ:md] ADJ *(person, conflict, torpedo, fuse)* armé; **a. to the teeth/with a gun** armé jusqu'aux dents/d'un fusil; **to offer a. resistance** résister par les armes, se défendre les armes à la main
▸▸ *Mil* **a. forces** forces *fpl* armées; *Law* **a. robbery** vol *m* ou attaque *f* à main armée; **a. truce** suspension *f* d'armes; **a. warfare** conflit *m* armé

Armenia [ɑ:ˈmiːnɪə] N Arménie *f*

Armenian [ɑ:ˈmiːnɪən] ADJ arménien
N **1** Arménien, -ienne **2** *Ling* arménien *m*

armful [ˈɑ:mfʊl] N brassée *f*; **to bring armfuls of flowers** *or* **flowers by the a.** apporter des fleurs à pleins bras, apporter des brassées de fleurs

armhole [ˈɑ:mhəʊl] N *Sewing* emmanchure *f*

armistice [ˈɑ:mɪstɪs] N armistice *m*
▸▸ **A. Day** l'Armistice *m*

armless [ˈɑ:mlɪs] ADJ sans bras

armlet [ˈɑ:mlɪt] N **1** *(bracelet)* bracelet *m* *(porté au-dessus du coude)* **2** *(armband)* brassard *m*

armor etc Am = **armour** etc

armorial [ɑ:ˈmɔ:rɪəl] ADJ armorial, -aux
▸▸ **a. bearings** armoiries *fpl*

armour, Am **armor** [ɑ:mər] N *(no pl)* **1** *Naut (of ship)* cuirasse *f*, cuirassement *m*, blindage *m*; *Mil (of vehicle, tank etc)* blindage **2** *Mil (units, vehicles)* blindés *mpl* **3** *Hist (of knight etc)* armure *f*; **suit of a.** armure complète; **in full a.** armé de pied en cap
VT *Naut (ship)* cuirasser; *Mil (train etc)* blinder

armoured, Am **armored** [ˈɑ:məd] ADJ *Naut (ship)* cuirassé; *Mil (vehicle, train)* blindé
▸▸ **a. car** voiture *f* blindée; *Mil* engin *m* blindé de reconnaissance; *(for cash, gold etc)* fourgon *m* bancaire; *Am Mil* **a. corps** blindés *mpl*; *Mil* **a. personnel carrier** véhicule *m* blindé de transport de troupes; *Mil* **a. troops** blindés

armourer, Am **armorer** [ˈɑ:mərər] N *Ind, Mil, Naut* armurier *m*

armour-piercing, Am **armor-piercing** ADJ *(shell)* perforant, de rupture

armour-plated, Am **armor-plated** ADJ *Naut* cuirassé, blindé; *Mil* blindé

armour-plating, Am **armor-plating** N blindage *m*

armoury, Am **armory** [ˈɑ:mərɪ] N **1** *(store room)* magasin *m* d'armes; *(in barracks)* armurerie *f*; *(in museum etc)* salle *f* d'armes **2** *Am (factory)* fabrique *f* d'armes; *(workshop)* armurerie *f*

armpit [ˈɑ:mpɪt] N aisselle *f*, *Fam Pej* **the a. of the universe** *(place)* un coin paumé, un trou

armrest [ˈɑ:mrest] N accoudoir *m*, appuie-bras *m inv*

arms [ɑ:mz] NPL **1** *(weapons)* armes *fpl*; **side a.** armes blanches; **small a.** armes portatives; **call to a.** appel *m* aux armes; **nation in a.** nation *f* en armes; **100,000 men under a.** 100 000 hommes sous les drapeaux; **to take up a.** prendre les armes, s'armer *(against* contre); **to rise up in a.** se dresser en armes *(against sb/sth* contre qn/qch); *Fig* **to be up in a. about sth** s'insurger contre qch **2** *Her* armoiries *fpl*, armes *fpl*
▸▸ *Mil* **a. dealer** armurier *m*; **a. embargo** embargo *m* sur les armes; *Pol* **a. limitation talks** négociations *fpl* pour la limitation des armements; **a. manufacturer** fabricant *m* d'armes, armurier *m*; *Mil* **a. race** course *f* aux armements; **the a. trade** le commerce d'armes; **a. trader** trafiquant *m* d'armes

arm's-length ADJ *Com (relationship)* impartial, -aux; *(price)* réaliste

army [ˈɑ:mɪ] N VOIR GRAMMAIRE A11 *Mil, Fig (of ants, civil servants etc)* armée *f*, *(of people)* foule *f*, multitude *f*; **he joined the A. not the Air Force** il est entré dans l'armée de terre et non pas dans l'armée de l'air; **to be in the a.** être dans l'armée, être militaire; **to go into** *or* **join the a.** *(volunteer)* s'engager, s'enrôler; *(be conscripted)* partir au régiment ou à l'armée; **there was enough food for an a.** il y avait assez de nourriture pour un régiment; **standing** *or* **regular a.** armée permanente ou active; **professional a.** armée de métier
▸▸ *Entom* **a. ant** fourmi *f* légionnaire; **a. barracks** caserne *f*, baraquement *m* militaire; **a. corps** corps *m* d'armée; *Br Mil* **A. List** annuaire *m* militaire ou des officiers de carrière *(de l'armée de terre)*; **a. lorry** camion *m* militaire; **a. officer** officier *m* de l'armée de terre

arnica [ˈɑ:nɪkə] N *Bot, Pharm* arnica *f*

A-road N *Br Aut* ≃ route *f* nationale

aroma [əˈrəʊmə] N arôme *m*

aromatherapy [ərəʊməˈθerəpɪ] N aromathérapie *f*

aromatic [ærəʊˈmætɪk] ADJ *(herb, tea, smell)* aromatique
N **1** aromate *m* **2** *Chem* **aromatics** carbures *mpl* aromatiques ou à noyau

AROUND [əˈraʊnd]

ADV	autour **1**
PREP	autour de **1** ▪ environ **3**

ADV **1** autour; **all a.** tout autour, de tous côtés; **the woods (all) a.** les bois d'alentour; **for miles a.** à des kilomètres à la ronde; **people came from miles a.** les gens sont venus de partout ou de très loin; **the trunk was over two metres a.** le tronc faisait plus de deux mètres de circonférence
2 *(in different directions, places)* **to walk a.** marcher par-ci par-là; **I try to get a. as much as I can** j'essaie de me déplacer le plus possible; **to run a.** courir dans tous les sens; **to throw things a.** jeter des choses dans tous les sens; **swivel it a. a little** fais-le pivoter un peu; **he's now able to get a. again** il est de nouveau sur pied; *Fam* **she's been a.** *(is mature)* elle n'est pas née d'hier; *(sexually)* elle a des kilomètres au compteur, elle a des heures de vol
3 *(in existence, in the area etc)* **this product has been a.** *for a long time* ce produit existe ou est en circulation depuis longtemps; **I still see her a.** il m'arrive encore de la voir; **I haven't seen him a.** *for ages* ça fait longtemps que je ne l'ai vu dans les parages; **are you a. this weekend?** tu es là ce weekend?; **there aren't many good translators a.** les bons traducteurs ne courent pas les rues; **is he still a.?** *(in the area)* est-ce qu'il est encore dans les parages ou là?; *(alive)* est-ce qu'il est encore de ce monde?; **it's the best value a.** c'est ce qu'il y a de meilleur marché
4 *(in circular motion)* **to turn a.** se retourner; **to spin** *or* **whirl** *or* **wheel a.** faire volte-face; **he was waving his arms a.** il gesticulait dans tous les sens
PREP **1** autour de; **his arms were a. her neck** il avait les bras autour de son cou; **she had her family a. her** elle a été entourée de sa famille; **the people a. him** les gens qui l'entourent; **we walked a. the lake** nous avons fait le tour du lac en marchant
2 *(in different parts)* **to travel a. the country** parcourir le pays; **there were books all a. the room** il y avait des livres dans toute la pièce; **a. town** en ville
3 *(in the region of)* environ; **at a. four o'clock** vers quatre heures, sur les quatre heures; **it cost a. £200** ça a coûté dans les 200 livres ou environ 200 livres

4 *(near)* **somewhere a. here** quelque part par ici; **is there anywhere a. here I can sleep?** est-ce que je peux trouver où dormir par ici?

arousal [əˈraʊz(ə)l] N *(from sleep)* éveil *m*, réveil *m*; *(of interest, suspicion)* éveil; *(of anger)* soulèvement *m*; *(sexual)* excitation *f*

arouse [əˈraʊz] VT *(person) (wake)* réveiller, éveiller; *(stir up) (from laziness, torpor)* secouer; *(sexually)* exciter; *(feeling)* exciter, éveiller; *(passions)* soulever; *(jealousy)* piquer, éveiller, provoquer; *(curiosity)* éveiller, chatouiller; *(sb's suspicion, interest)* éveiller; *(pity, enthusiasm)* inspirer; **they aroused her from her sleep** ils l'ont réveillée; **the crowd was aroused** la foule était agitée; **once (their anger was) aroused, ...** une fois leur colère éveillée, ...

arpeggio [ɑ:ˈpedʒɪəʊ] N *Mus* arpège *m*

arr *(abbr* **arrives)** *(on timetables etc)* arrive

arrack [ˈærək] N *(drink)* arac(k) *m*

arraign [əˈreɪn] VT **1** *Law* poursuivre en justice; **to a. sb before a court** traduire qn en justice ou devant un tribunal **2** *Lit (criticize) (declaration, action etc)* attaquer, critiquer violemment

arraignment [əˈreɪnmənt] N *Law* **1** *(of person)* mise *f* en accusation ou en jugement **2** *(charges)* acte *m* d'accusation

arrange [əˈreɪndʒ] VT **1** *(put in an order) (furniture etc)* disposer, arranger; *(flowers)* disposer; **the chairs were arranged in a circle** les chaises étaient disposées en cercle; **they arranged themselves around the room** ils se sont répartis dans la pièce
2 *(organize) (wedding)* arranger; *(concert, meeting etc)* organiser; *(date, time)* fixer; **an arranged marriage** un mariage de convenance; **everything is arranged** tout est en ordre; **it was arranged that ...** il fut convenu que ...; **try to a. it** tâchez d'arranger la chose; **that can be arranged** cela peut s'arranger; **a. it among yourselves** arrangez cela entre vous, entendez-vous là-dessus; **the meeting arranged for tomorrow** la réunion prévue pour demain; **at the time arranged** à l'heure prévue; **I've got nothing arranged** je n'ai rien de prévu; **have you arranged what to do if ...?** as-tu pris tes dispositions pour le cas où ...?; **what have you arranged?** *(with him)* qu'est-ce que vous avez prévu?; **to a. one's affairs** mettre ses affaires en ordre; *Mktg* **arranged interview** entretien *m* organisé
3 *Mus (piece)* adapter, arranger *(for (the) piano* pour piano)
VI *(organize)* **to a. to do sth** *(make preparations)* s'arranger ou prendre ses dispositions pour faire qch; *(with sb else)* convenir de faire qch; **to a. for sth to be done** s'arranger ou prendre des dispositions ou prendre des mesures pour que qch se fasse; **I had arranged to ...** j'avais prévu de ...; **we arranged to meet** nous avons prévu de nous rencontrer; **I think I'll a. to be out when he comes** je crois que je m'arrangerai pour être sorti quand il viendra; **can you a. to have it finished by Friday?** est-ce que vous pouvez vous arranger pour qu'il soit terminé vendredi?; **to a. to have sth delivered** faire le nécessaire pour que qch soit livré; **they arranged for a taxi to meet me** ils se sont arrangés pour qu'un taxi vienne me chercher

arrangement [əˈreɪndʒmənt] N **1** *(preparation)* disposition *f*, aménagement *m* *(of* de); **to make arrangements** prendre des dispositions ou des mesures, faire des préparatifs *(for sth/to do sth/for sth to be done* pour qch/pour faire qch/pour que qch se fasse); **to make arrangements for a journey** faire ses préparatifs pour un voyage; **I've made all the arrangements** j'ai tout arrangé

2 *(agreement)* arrangement *m*, accord *m*; *Fin (with creditors)* accommodement *m*; *Law* transaction *f*, *Com etc* **to make an a.** *or* **to come to an a. with sb** prendre un arrangement avec qn; **to come to an a. with one's creditors** parvenir à un accord avec ses créanciers; **the a. was that …** *(I or you etc would do)* on avait prévu que …; **price by a.** prix à débattre; **by prior a.** sur accord préalable

3 *Mus* arrangement *m*, adaptation *f* (**for (the) piano** pour piano)

arranger [əˈreɪndʒər] **N** *Mus* arrangeur, -euse

arrant [ˈærənt] **ADJ ATTRIB** *(rogue, fool)* fini; *(liar)* fieffé; **don't talk such a. rubbish** comment est-ce que tu peux dire des bêtises pareilles?; **this is a. folly** c'est de la folie pure

array [əˈreɪ] **N 1** *(display)* étalage *m*, collection *f*; **a bewildering a. of salads** un étalage de salades stupéfiant; **an imposing a. of tools** une imposante collection d'outils

2 *Mil* rangs *mpl*; **in close a.** en rangs serrés; **in battle a.** en ordre de bataille

3 *Math (of figures)* tableau *m*; *Comput* matrice *f*, tableau

4 *Lit (fine clothing)* parure *f*, appareil *m*; **in rich a.** paré de ses plus beaux atours

VT 1 *(troops etc) (in battle formation)* disposer, déployer; **his medals were arrayed across his chest** ses médailles étaient étalées sur sa poitrine

2 *Lit (clothe)* revêtir, parer (**sb in sth** qn de qch)

arrears [əˈrɪəz] **NPL** arriéré *m*, arrérages *mpl*; **I'm £100 in a.** j'ai 100 livres d'arriérés; **rent a.** arriéré de loyer; **to be in a. with the rent, to let one's rent fall into a.** être en retard pour payer son loyer; **I'm a month in a.** j'ai (pris) un retard d'un mois, je suis en retard d'un mois; **to get into a.** s'arriérer; **to be getting into a. with the repayments** prendre du retard pour payer *ou* avec les versements; **work in a.** travail *m* en retard; **to be paid monthly in a.** être payé à la fin du mois; **to be in a. with one's correspondence** avoir du retard dans sa correspondance

arrest [əˈrest] **N 1** *(of wrongdoer)* arrestation *f*, *Mil*, *Naut* arrêts *mpl*; **to put sb/to be under a.** mettre qn/être en état d'arrestation; *Mil*, *Naut* mettre qn/être aux arrêts; **you're under a.!** vous êtes en état d'arrestation!; **several arrests were made** plusieurs personnes ont été arrêtées; **to make an a.** *(of police officer)* procéder à une arrestation; *Mil*, *Naut* **open a.** arrêts simples; *Mil*, *Naut* **close a.** arrêts forcés *ou* de rigueur

2 *(of movement, progress etc)* arrêt *m*, suspension *f*

3 *Law* **a. of judgment** sursis *m* à l'exécution d'un jugement

VT 1 *(capture) (person)* arrêter; *Scot*, *Naut (property, ship)* saisir

2 *(stop) (movement, sb's progress, thing)* arrêter; **arrested growth** *(of person)* arrêt *m* dans la croissance; *(of thing)* arrêt dans le développement

3 *Law* **to a. judgment** suspendre l'exécution d'un jugement

4 *(attention)* retenir, arrêter, fixer

► ► *Law* **a. warrant** mandat *m* d'arrêt

arrester [əˈrestər] **N** *Tech* intercepteur *m*, séparateur *m*; **spark a.** pare-étincelles *m inv*

► ► **a. gear** *Aviat (on runway)* dispositif *m* d'arrêt; *Aviat*, *Naut (on carrier deck)* dispositif d'appontage

arresting [əˈrestɪŋ] **ADJ 1** *(spectacle etc)* frappant, qui retient l'attention **2** *Law* **the arresting officer** le policier qui a effectué/qui effectue l'arrestation

N 1 *Law* arrestation *f* **2** *Tech etc* arrêt *m*

► ► *Tech* **a. device** dispositif *m* d'arrêt

arrhythmia [əˈrɪðmɪə] **N** *Med* arythmie *f*

arrival [əˈraɪv(ə)l] **N 1** arrivée *f*, *Com (of goods)* arrivage *m*; *Naut (of ship)* entrée *f*; *(of passengers)* débarquement *m*; **port of a.** port *m* d'arrivée; **on a.** à l'arrivée; *(of passengers)* au débarquement; **arrivals and departures** arrivées et départs; **to await a.** *(on letter)* ne pas faire suivre

2 *(person)* arrivant, -ante; **a new a.** un nouveau venu, une nouvelle venue; *(baby)* un nouveau-né, une nouveau-née, *pl* nouveau-nés, -ées; *(book)* une dernière parution; **late arrivals** retardataires *mpl*

► ► **a. form** fichette *f* d'arrivée; **arrivals list** liste *f* des arrivées; **arrivals lounge** salle *f* d'arrivée; **a. quay** quai *m* d'arrivée; **a. time** heure *f* d'arrivée

arrive [əˈraɪv] **VI 1** arriver (**at** à; **in** dans); **she has just arrived** elle arrive à l'instant, elle vient d'arriver; **the baby arrived at 4.37 a.m.** le bébé est né à 4 h 37 du matin; **he is expected to a. next week** on attend son arrivée pour la semaine prochaine; **as soon as he arrived** dès son arrivée; **to a. unexpectedly** survenir, arriver à l'improviste; **to a. at the age of sixty** atteindre *ou* parvenir à *ou* arriver à l'âge de soixante ans; **to a. at a decision** arriver à *ou* en venir à *ou* aboutir à une décision; **we arrived at a situation where** *or* **in which …** nous en sommes arrivés à *ou* nous avons abouti à une situation dans laquelle …; **to a. at a price** *(of seller)* calculer *ou* fixer un prix; *(of seller and buyer)* convenir d'un prix

2 *Fam (achieve recognition) (of person)* réussir, arriver, faire son trou; **you know you've really arrived when …** on sait qu'on a vraiment réussi le jour où …; **that was before the telephone had really arrived** c'était avant l'avènement du téléphone; **notebook computers have arrived in a big way** on voit des notebooks partout maintenant

arrogance [ˈærəɡəns] **N** arrogance *f*

arrogant [ˈærəɡənt] **ADJ** arrogant

arrogantly [ˈærəɡəntlɪ] **ADV** avec arrogance; **to a. assume that …** avoir l'arrogance de présumer que …

arrogate [ˈærəɡeɪt] **VT** *Law*, *Lit* **1** *(appropriate)* **to a. sth to oneself** s'arroger qch **2** *(attribute wrongly)* attribuer injustement (**to sb** à qn)

arrow [ˈærəʊ] **N 1** *(missile)* flèche *f*; **to shoot** *or* **let fly an a.** lancer *ou* décocher une flèche; **to fly straight as an a.** voler droit comme une flèche; **as swift as an a.** vif comme l'éclair **2** *(indicating direction) (on sign etc)* flèche *f*; *(of surveyor)* fiche *f* **3** *Br Fam* **arrows** *(darts)* fléchettes *fpl*

VT marquer d'une flèche; *(route, direction)* flécher

► ► *Comput* **a. key** touche *f* fléchée, touche de direction; **a. slit** *(in building)* arbalétrière *f*

► **arrow in VT SEP** *(insertion)* marquer d'une flèche

arrowhead [ˈærəʊhed] **N 1** *(on missile)* tête *f ou* fer *m ou* pointe *f* de flèche **2** *(plant)* sagittaire *f*, flèche *f* d'eau

arrowroot [ˈærəʊruːt] **N 1** *(plant)* marante *f* **2** *Culin* arrow-root *m*

arse [ɑːs] *Br Vulg* **N 1** cul *m*; **a kick up the a.** un coup de pied dans le cul; **to talk out of one's a.** raconter des conneries; **he fell** *or* **went a. over tit** *or* **tip** *or* **apex** il est tombé cul par-dessus tête; **get your a. in gear!** remuez-vous le cul!; **get your a. in here right now!** rapplique tout de suite!, ramène ta fraise!; **get your a. over to the town hall!** file à la mairie!; **it's my a. that's on the line** ça risque de me retomber sur la gueule; **he's**

been sitting on his a. all day il a rien foutu de la journée; **to make an a. of sth** saloper qch; **he doesn't know his a. from his elbow** il est complètement nul; **to make an a. of oneself** se ridiculiser; **to do sth a.-backwards** faire qch à l'envers *ou* n'importe comment; **my a.!** *(I don't believe you)* mon cul!

2 *(idiot)* connard *m*, connasse *f*

VT I couldn't be arsed doing it myself ça m'a fait chier de le faire moi-même; **why don't you come with us? – I can't be arsed** tu viens avec nous? – non, j'ai trop la flemme

► **arse about, arse around VI** *Br Vulg* déconner

► **arse up VT SEP** *Br Vulg* foirer

arsehole [ˈɑːshəʊl] **N** *Br Vulg* **1** *(anus)* trou *m* du cul; *Fig* **the a. of the universe** *(ugly town etc)* le trou du cul du monde **2** *Fig (stupid person)* connard *m*, connasse *f*; *(nasty person)* salaud *m*, salope *f*; **don't be such an a.!** arrête de faire/dire des conneries!; *(nasty person)* ne fais pas le salaud!

arseholed [ˈɑːshəʊld] **ADJ** *Br Vulg (drunk)* bourré comme un coing, complètement pété

arse-licker [-lɪkər] **N** *Br Vulg* lèche-cul *mf inv*

arse-licking N *Br Vulg* **they're sick of his a.** ils en ont marre de ce lèche-cul

arsenal [ˈɑːsən(ə)l] **N** arsenal *m*, -aux

arsenic [ˈɑːs(ə)nɪk] **N** arsenic *m*

arsewipe [ˈɑːswaɪp] **N** *Br Vulg (person)* raclure *f*

arsey [ˈɑːsɪ] **ADJ** *Br Vulg (stupid)* débile; *(unfashionable)* ringard; **that was a bit of an a. thing to say** c'est un peu débile de dire un truc pareil

arson [ˈɑːs(ə)n] **N** incendie *m* criminel *ou* volontaire; **to commit a.** provoquer (volontairement) un incendie; **to be charged with a.** être accusé d'avoir provoqué un incendie; **police suspect a.** la police suspecte un incendie criminel

arsonist [ˈɑːsənɪst] **N** incendiaire *mf*

art¹ [ɑːt] **N 1** art *m*; **the (fine) arts** les beaux-arts *mpl*; **arts and crafts** artisanat *m*; **a. for a.'s sake** l'art pour l'art

2 *Univ* arts lettres *fpl*; **faculty of arts** faculté *f* de lettres (et sciences humaines)

3 *(technique)* art *m*; **the a. of war** l'art militaire, l'art de la guerre; **it's an a. in itself** c'est tout un art; **there's an a. to doing that** c'est tout un art que de faire cela; **to get** *or* **have sth down to a fine a.** maîtriser qch jusque dans les moindres détails; **she's got time-saving down to a fine a.** elle est passée maître dans l'art de gagner du temps; **a dying a.** un art en voie de disparition; **the black arts** la magie noire

4 *Typ (illustrations)* iconographie *f*, illustrations *fpl*

5 *Pej (trick)* stratagème *m*, ruse *f*

► ► **a. cinema** cinéma *m* d'art et d'essai; **a. class** cours *m* de dessin; **a. critic** critique *mf* d'art; **a. department** service *m* création; **a. desk** bureau *m* de dessin; **a. direction** direction *f* artistique; **a. director** directeur, -trice artistique; **a. editor** rédacteur, -trice artistique; **a. exhibition** exposition *f* d'art; *Univ* **arts faculty** faculté *f* de lettres (et sciences humaines); **arts festival** festival *m* culturel; **a. form** moyen *m* d'expression artistique; **a. gallery** *(museum)* musée *m* d'art; *(shop)* galerie *f* d'art; **a. nouveau** art *m* nouveau, modern style *m*; **a. nouveau furniture** meubles *mpl* de style art nouveau; **a. object** objet *m* d'art; *Comput* **a. package** logiciel *m* de dessin; **a. paper** papier *m* couché classique; **arts programme** programme *m* culturel; **a. reviewer** critique d'art; **a. school** ≃ école *f* des Beaux-Arts; **a. student** étudiant, -ante en art; **arts student** étudiant, -ante en lettres (et sciences humaines); **a. teacher** professeur *m* de dessin

art² *Bible, Arch (2nd pers sing pr of* be) thou **a. good** tu es bon

artefact ['ɑːtɪfækt] N **1** *Archeol* objet *m* (fabriqué *ou* façonné) **2** *(side-effect)* conséquence *f*; **to be a mere a. of sth** être simplement la conséquence de qch, découler simplement de qch

arterial [ɑːˈtɪərɪəl] ADJ *Anat, Med etc (blood etc)* artériel
▶▶ *Br Transp* **a. road** route *f ou* voie *f* à grande circulation

arteriole [ɑːˈtɪərɪəʊl] N *Anat* artériole *f*

arteriosclerosis [ɑːˌtɪərɪəʊsklə'rəʊsɪs] N *Med* artériosclérose *f*

artery ['ɑːtərɪ] N **1** *Anat* artère *f* **2** *(road, river etc)* artère *f*; **main arteries** grandes voies *fpl* de communication, grandes artères

artesian [ɑːˈtiːzɪən, -ˈtiːʒən] ADJ
▶▶ **a. well** puits *m* artésien

artful ['ɑːtfʊl] ADJ **1** *(person)* rusé, astucieux, malin, *f* -igne; **a. as a monkey** malin comme un singe **2** *(solution, device)* ingénieux; **an a. dodge** un truc ingénieux

artfully ['ɑːtfʊlɪ] ADV ingénieusement

artfulness ['ɑːtfʊlnɪs] N **1** *(of person)* habileté *f* (**in doing** à faire) **2** *(of thing, reply)* ingéniosité *f*

arthouse ['ɑːthaʊs] ADJ
▶▶ **a. cinema** cinéma *m* d'art et d'essai; **a. film** film *m* d'art et d'essai

arthritic [ɑːˈθrɪtɪk] ADJ, N *Med* arthritique *mf*

arthritis [ɑːˈθraɪtɪs] N *Med* arthrite *f*

arthropod ['ɑːθrəpɒd] N *Zool* arthropode *m*

arthrosis [ɑːˈθrəʊsɪs] N *Med* arthrose *f*

Arthurian [ɑːˈθjʊərɪən] ADJ *Liter, Myth (cycle etc)* d'Arthur; *(novel)* arthurien

artic ['ɑːtɪk] N *Br Sl (lorry)* semi-remorque *m, pl* semi-remorques

artichoke ['ɑːtɪtʃəʊk] N **(globe) a.** artichaut *m*
▶▶ **a. hearts** cœurs *mpl* d'artichauts

article ['ɑːtɪk(ə)l] N **1** *(object)* objet *m*; **a. of clothing** vêtement *m*; **toilet articles** produits *mpl* de toilette **2** *Journ etc (in newspaper, magazine)* article *m* **3** *Com, Law (in agreement, treaty)* article *m*, clause *f*; *Naut* **ship's articles** contrat *m* d'engagement, conditions *fpl* d'embarquement **4** *Gram* **definite/indefinite a.** article *m* défini/indéfini VOIR GRAMMAIRE A5–8; B3–5
VT *Law etc* **to a. sb to an attorney/an architect** placer qn (comme élève) chez un avoué/un architecte; **articled clerk** clerc *m* d'avoué lié par un contrat d'apprentissage
▶▶ *Law* **articles of apprenticeship** contrat d'apprentissage; *Law* **articles of association** statuts *mpl* de société; *Rel* **a. of faith** article *m* de foi; **articles of war** *Mil* code *m* (de justice) militaire; *Naut* code de justice maritime

articulate¹ [ɑːˈtɪkjʊlət] ADJ **1** *(speech)* net, distinct; **to be a.** *(of person)* s'exprimer facilement *ou* avec facilité; **try to be more a.** essaie d'être plus clair; **the child gave a very a. account** l'enfant a fait un compte rendu très clair **2** *Zool* articulé

articulate² [ɑːˈtɪkjʊleɪt] VT **1** *(pronounce clearly) (word etc)* articuler; **he doesn't a. his words** il n'articule pas **2** *(express clearly) (one's thoughts, idea)* exprimer clairement
VI **1** *Anat* s'articuler; **a bone that articulates or is articulated with another** un os qui s'articule *ou* est articulé avec un autre **2** *(in speaking)* articuler

articulated [ɑːˈtɪkjʊleɪtɪd] ADJ *Anat, Ling etc* articulé

▶▶ *Aut* **a. lorry** semi-remorque *m, pl* semi-remorques

articulately [ɑːˈtɪkjʊlətlɪ] ADV **1** *(to express oneself, argue)* clairement; **as you so a. put it** comme vous l'avez si bien exprimé **2** *(to speak)* distinctement

articulateness [ɑːˈtɪkjʊlətnɪs] N **1** *(of speaker)* facilité *f* d'expression; *(of writing, speech)* clarté *f* **2** *(clarity of sound)* articulation *f* nette, netteté *f* d'énonciation

articulation [ɑːˌtɪkjʊˈleɪʃən] N **1** *Biol, Ling etc* articulation *f* **2** *(of thought)* expression *f*; **you've heard his a. of the new theory** vous avez entendu sa présentation de la nouvelle théorie

artifact ['ɑːtɪfækt] N = **artefact**

artifice ['ɑːtɪfɪs] N **1** *(trick)* artifice *m*, ruse *f*, stratagème *m*; **a. of war** ruse *ou* artifice de guerre **2** *(skill)* habileté *f*, adresse *f*

artificial [ɑːtɪˈfɪʃəl] ADJ **1** *(conditions, light, distinction, situation)* artificiel **2** *(behaviour, person)* affecté; *(style)* factice, recherché; **she is very a.** elle manque de naturel
▶▶ **a. fibres** fibres *fpl* synthétiques; *Astron* **a. horizon** horizon *m* artificiel; **a. insemination** insémination *f* artificielle; *Comput* **a. intelligence** intelligence *f* artificielle; **a. limb** prothèse *f*, membre *m* artificiel; **a. manure** engrais *mpl* chimiques; *Med* **a. respiration** respiration *f* artificielle; **to give sb a. respiration** faire la respiration artificielle à qn; *Cin* **a. sunlight** sunlight *m*; **a. sweetener** édulcorant *m* (de synthèse)

artificiality [ɑːtɪfɪʃɪˈælɪtɪ] N **1** *(of product etc)* nature *f* artificielle **2** *(of person, smile)* manque *m* de naturel; *(of behaviour, manner)* affectation *f*

artificially [ɑːtɪˈfɪʃəlɪ] ADV artificiellement; **to behave a.** avoir un comportement affecté, manquer de naturel; **a. coloured** *(on packet etc)* contient un colorant artificiel

artillery [ɑːˈtɪlərɪ] N artillerie *f*; **heavy/light a.** artillerie lourde/légère; **to lay down an a. barrage** déployer un barrage d'artillerie
▶▶ **a. fire** tir *m* d'artillerie; **a. regiment** régiment *m* d'artillerie; **a. shell** obus *m*

artilleryman, *pl* **artillerymen** [ɑːˈtɪlərɪmən, -men] N artilleur *m*

artisan [ɑːtɪˈzæn] N artisan, -e *m*

artist ['ɑːtɪst] N *(painter)* artiste *mf*; **he is an a.** *(painter)* il est artiste, il est peintre; *(footballer etc)* c'est un véritable artiste

Note that the French word **artiste** is not restricted to the contexts of painting or drawing and is used to describe someone who practises any kind of art.

artiste [ɑːˈtiːst] N *Theat, Cin, TV* artiste *mf*

artistic [ɑːˈtɪstɪk] ADJ *(style, taste, temperament, arrangement)* artistique; **she came from an a. family** elle venait d'une famille d'artistes; **she's the a. one in the family** c'est l'artiste de la famille; **I'm not at all a.** je n'ai aucune inclination artistique, je n'ai pas la fibre artistique
▶▶ **a. adviser** conseiller, -ère artistique; *Cin, Theat* **a. director** directeur, -trice artistique

artistically [ɑːˈtɪstɪklɪ] ADV avec art, artistiquement, artistement; **to be a. gifted/inclined** avoir des dons/la fibre artistique(s); **a. speaking** du point de vue artistique

artistry ['ɑːtɪstrɪ] N *(of painter, footballer)* art *m*; *(of painting, sb's game)* qualité *f* artistique; **his goal was sheer a.** son but, c'était du grand art

artless ['ɑːtlɪs] ADJ **1** *(natural)* naturel, sans artifice **2** *(naive)* naïf, ingénu

artlessly ['ɑːtlɪslɪ] ADV **1** *(naturally)* natu-

rellement, sans artifice **2** *(naively)* naïvement, ingénument

artlessness ['ɑːtlɪsnɪs] N **1** *(naturalness)* naturel *m*, simplicité *f* **2** *(naivety)* naïveté *f*, ingénuité *f*

artwork ['ɑːtwɜːk] N *Art (in book production) (illustrations)* illustrations *fpl*; *(layout)* mise *f* en page; *(made-up page for printing)* document *m* d'exécution; **to use sth as a.** utiliser qch dans la maquette

arty ['ɑːtɪ] ADJ *Fam (person, style, job, furniture)* artistique; *(existence)* bohème; *Pej (person)* qui donne dans le genre artiste; *(furniture etc)* qui se veut artistique; **he's an a. type** c'est le genre artiste; **the a. set** le milieu artiste

arty-crafty ADJ *Fam Hum Pej* bohème

arty-farty [-'fɑːtɪ], *Am* **artsy-fartsy** ['ɑːtsɪ'fɑːtsɪ] ADJ *Fam Pej* aux prétentions artistiques, soi-disant artistique; **it's a lot of a. rubbish** c'est un tas d'idioties prétendument artistiques

arum ['eərəm] N *Bot* arum *m*
▶▶ **a. lily** calla *f*

arvo ['ɑːvəʊ] N *Austr Fam (afternoon)* après-midi *m ou f* inv, aprème *m ou f*

Aryan ['eərɪən] *Ling etc* ADJ aryen
N Aryen, -enne

AS [əz, *stressed* æz]

PREP	comme
CONJ	comme **1, 2, 4** ■ puisque **2** ■ que **6** ■ aussi … que *(as … as)* **8**
ADV	comme **1** ■ quant à *(as for)* **2** ■ aussi, en plus *(as well)* **3** ■ en plus de *(as well as)* **3** ■ comme si *(as if)* **4**

PREP *(manner, function, role, condition)* comme; **they rose as one man** ils se levèrent comme un seul homme; **to acknowledge sb as an expert/one's equal** reconnaître qn en tant qu'expert/comme son égal; **to consider sb as a friend** considérer qn comme un ami; **to treat sb as a stranger** traiter qn en étranger; **to treat sth as a joke** tourner qch à la plaisanterie; **to recognize sb as one's son** reconnaître qn comme son fils; **I intended it as a compliment** j'ai dit ça en bien; **she was often ill as a child** enfant elle était souvent malade, elle était souvent malade dans son enfance; **to use sth as a flag** se servir de qch comme drapeau *ou* en guise de drapeau; **to send sth as a present** envoyer qch comme cadeau; *Theat* **Olivier as Hamlet** Olivier dans le rôle de Hamlet; **to act as interpreter** servir d'interprète; **I acted in my capacity as a magistrate** j'ai agi en ma qualité de magistrat; **to be dressed as a boy** être habillé en garçon; **as a very old friend of your father's** en tant que vieil ami de votre père; **the novel as social history** le roman comme témoin de l'histoire de la société; **my rights as a mother** mes droits de mère; **as one doctor to another** soit dit entre médecins; **as someone new to the place** en tant que nouveau venu; **as revenge for …** pour se venger de …
CONJ VOIR GRAMMAIRE B74–6; B58 **1** *(time)* **as I was opening the door** au moment où *ou* comme j'ouvrais la porte; **he went out (just) as I came in** il est sorti au moment (même) où *ou* comme j'entrais; **as I spoke, I could see …** tandis que je parlais, je voyais …; **as you get older** en vieillissant; **he's probably trying to contact us as we sit here** il essaie probablement de nous contacter en ce moment même; **one day as I was sitting …** un jour que j'étais assis …; **she drew back as I advanced** à mesure que j'avançais, elle reculait; **it's the last one as you come from the station** c'est le dernier en venant de la gare; **as and when required** à discrétion; **as and**

when I want à mon bon plaisir; **as (and when) is necessary** quand c'est nécessaire

2 *(reason)* puisque, comme; **as he has now left** puisqu'il *ou* comme il est maintenant parti

3 *(concessive)* **ignorant as he is** tout ignorant qu'il est; **late as it was** malgré l'heure tardive; **try as she might, she couldn't open it** elle avait beau essayer, elle n'arrivait pas à l'ouvrir; **hard as it may be to believe, ...** c'est peut-être difficile à croire, mais ...; **much as I like her** quelle que soit mon affection pour elle; **be that as it may** quoi qu'il en soit

4 *(manner)* comme; **do as you like** faites comme vous voulez *ou* voudrez; **it happened as I told you** cela s'est passé comme je vous l'ai dit; **as Mrs Smith remarked ...** comme Mme Smith l'a fait remarquer ...; **covered with dust as he was**, he didn't want to come in couvert qu'il était de poussière, il ne voulait pas entrer; **as they say, ...** comme on dit, ...; **why should I do as he says?** pourquoi devrais-je faire ce qu'il dit?; **as often happens** comme il arrive souvent, ainsi qu'il arrive souvent; **leave it as it is** laissez-le tel quel, laissez-le tel qu'il est; **as it is, we must ...** les choses étant ainsi, il nous faut ...; **there are too many cars as it is** il y a déjà trop de voitures; **as it were** pour ainsi dire; *Mil, Gym* **as you were!** revenez!, au temps!; **as a man lives, so he dies** comme on a vécu, ainsi l'on meurt; **as is** tel quel; *Fam* **the Apollo theatre as was** *(it now has another name)* le théâtre de l'Apollo comme on l'appelait; *(it now has another function)* l'ancien théâtre de l'Apollo

5 *(result, purpose)* **he is not so foolish as to believe it** il n'est pas assez stupide pour le croire; **put on your gloves so as to be ready** mettez vos gants pour être prêt *ou* de manière à être prêt

6 **mother is well, as are the children** maman va bien, de même que les enfants; **beasts of prey, such as the lion or tiger** les bêtes fauves, telles que *ou* comme le lion ou le tigre; **he was a foreigner, as they noticed from his pronunciation** il était étranger, ce qui se remarquait à sa prononciation; **it's the same one as I was telling you about** c'est celui-là même dont je vous parlais

7 *Eng Dial* **it was her as told me** c'est elle qui me l'a dit

8 *(in comparisons) (also adv)* **as ... as ...** aussi ... que ...; **not as ... as ...** pas aussi *ou* si ... que ...; **you are as tall as he (is)** *or* **as him** vous êtes aussi grand que lui; **you are not as** *or* **not so tall as he (is)** *or* **as him** vous n'êtes pas aussi grand que lui; **I'm not as rich as I was** je ne suis pas aussi riche que je l'ai été; **is it as high as that?** est-ce si *ou* aussi haut que ça?; **I came down as fast as I could** je suis descendu aussi vite que possible; **I worked as hard as I could** j'ai travaillé autant que j'ai pu; **as many as you want** autant que tu veux; **he's not such a fool as he looks** il n'est pas si bête qu'il en a l'air; **a house twice as large (as this)** une maison deux fois plus grande (que celle-ci); **as white as a sheet** blanc comme un linge; **as recently as last week** pas plus tard que la semaine dernière; **as much for your sake as for mine** tant pour vous que pour moi; **she doesn't enjoy it as much as I do** elle n'aime pas ça autant que moi; **I don't know why I like her as much as I do** je ne sais pas pourquoi elle me plaît à ce point; **as soon/as much as possible** aussitôt/autant que possible; **we could go as high as 5,000, but no higher** nous pourrions monter jusqu'à 5000, mais pas au-delà

ADV **1** *(form, manner, kind)* **as per advice** suivant avis; **as per invoice** selon facture; **as promised** comme promis; **as ordered** conformément à la commande; **as reques-**

ted comme il a été requis; **as advertised on TV** vu à la télé; **as recommended** comme il est recommandé; **the GR241, as recommended by leading experts** le GR241, modèle recommandé par les plus grands experts; **ready to use as delivered** livré prêt à fonctionner; **if used as intended** s'il est utilisé selon les recommandations; **we didn't arrive at lunch time as intended** nous ne sommes pas arrivés à l'heure du déjeuner, comme cela avait été notre intention; **as noted/discussed above** comme il est mentionné/démontré plus haut; **B as in Bombay** B comme Bombay

2 *(switching or identifying topic)* **as for that, as to that, as regards that** quant à cela, pour cela; **as for you** quant à vous; **as for money, I can lend you some** pour ce qui est de l'argent, je peux t'en prêter; **to question sb as to his/her motives** interroger qn sur ses motifs

3 as well aussi; **I don't want trouble from you as well** je ne veux pas que toi aussi tu me causes des problèmes; **as well as the rent, there was the heating to consider** en plus du loyer, il fallait penser au chauffage; **you can't expect me to cook as well as do the dishes** tu ne peux pas me demander de faire la cuisine et la vaisselle en plus; **by day as well as by night** le jour comme la nuit, de jour comme de nuit

4 as if comme si; **it was as if ...** on aurait dit que ...; **he winked as if** *or* **though to say ...** il fit un clin d'œil, comme pour dire ...; **we can't go on as if** *or* **though nothing had happened** nous ne pouvons pas continuer comme si de rien n'était; **it isn't as if** *or* **though I haven't tried** ce n'est pourtant pas manque d'avoir essayé; **it isn't as if** *or* **though it's difficult** ce n'est pourtant pas difficile; **he made as if** *or* **though to go** il a fait mine de partir; **he looked as if** *or* **though he was about to go out** on aurait dit qu'il était sur le point de sortir; **as if you didn't know!** comme si tu ne le savais pas!

ASA [eɪesˈeɪ] N *Phot (abbr* **American Standards Association)** ASA *f*; **A./DIN exposure index** graduations *fpl* ASA/DIN; **an A. 100 film, a 100 A. film** une pellicule 100 ASA

asap [eɪeseɪˈpiː] ADV *(abbr* **as soon as possible)** le plus tôt possible, dans les plus brefs délais; **we need to reply a.** il faut qu'on réponde dès que possible

asbestos [æsˈbestəs] N amiante *m*
▸▸ **a. dust** poudre *f* d'amiante

asbestosis [æsbesˈtəʊsɪs] N *Med* asbestose *f*

ascend [əˈsend] VI *Fml* monter
VT **1** *(ladder)* monter à; *(stairs)* monter, gravir; *(mountain)* gravir, faire l'ascension de; *(throne)* monter sur **2** *(river)* remonter

ascendancy, ascendency [əˈsendənsɪ] N *Fml* ascendant *m* (**over sb** sur qn); **to gain (the) a. over sb** prendre de l'ascendant sur qn

ascendant, ascendent [əˈsendənt] ADJ **1** *Astrol, Astron, Math etc* ascendant; *(power, faction)* dominant **2** *Bot (stalk)* montant
N *Astrol* ascendant *m*; **to be in the a.** être à l'ascendant; *Fig* avoir le dessus, s'affirmer; **his star is in the a.** son étoile est à l'ascendant; **his fortunes are once more in the a.** ses finances commencent à mieux se porter
▸▸ *Astrol* **a. star** astre *m* ascendant

ascender [əˈsendər] N *Typ (of character)* hampe *f* (montante), ascendante *f*

ascending [əˈsendɪŋ] ADJ **1** *Astrol, Astron, Math etc* ascendant; *Met (current)* ascendant; **in a. order** en ordre croissant; **steeply a. path** sentier *m* raide **2** *Bot (stalk)* montant
▸▸ *Law* **a. line** ascendance *f*, ligne *f* ascendante; *Mus* **a. scale** gamme *f* ascendante *ou* montante; **a. series** progression *f* crois-

sante; *Comput* **a. sort** tri *m* en ordre croissant

ascension [əˈsenʃən] N ascension *f*; **her a. to the throne** son élévation *f* sur le trône
▸▸ *Rel* **A. Day** jour *m ou* fête *f* de l'Ascension; **A. Island** île *f* de l'Ascension

ascent [əˈsent] N **1** *(of mountain)* ascension *f*; **first a.** première *f* (ascension); **balloon a.** ascension en ballon; **to make an a.** faire une ascension; *Fig* **the a. of man** le progrès de l'humanité; **his a. to power** son ascension jusqu'au pouvoir **2** *Tech (of piston etc)* montée *f*, remontée *f* **3** *(slope)* montée *f*, pente *f* **4** *Law* line of a. ascendance *f*

> Attention: ne pas confondre avec **assent**.

ascertain [æsəˈteɪn] VT *(fact)* déterminer; *(truth about sth)* s'assurer de; **to a. sth from sb** s'informer de qch auprès de qn; **I ascertained from his report that ...** j'ai déduit de son rapport que ...; **are we to a. from this that ...?** devons-nous en déduire que ...?

ascertainable [æsəˈteɪnəb(ə)l] ADJ *(information, fact)* qui peut être déterminé; *(truth)* vérifiable; **that's as much detail as is a. from this distance** c'est tout ce qu'on peut distinguer avec certitude à cette distance

ascertainment [æsəˈteɪnmənt] N *Fml (of fact)* détermination *f*; *(of truth)* vérification *f*

ascetic [əˈsetɪk] ADJ USU ATTRIB *(life etc)* ascétique; **a thin a. face** un maigre visage d'ascète
N *esp Rel* ascète *mf*; **he led the life of an a.** il menait une vie d'ascète, il vivait en ascète

ascetically [əˈsetɪklɪ] ADV ascétiquement; *(to live)* en ascète

asceticism [əˈsetɪsɪz(ə)m] N ascétisme *m*

ASCII [ˈæskiː] N *Comput (abbr* **American Standard Code for Information Interchange)** ASCII *m*
▸▸ **A. code** code *m* ASCII; **A. file** fichier *m* ASCII; **A. text** texte *m* ASCII

ascorbic [əˈskɔːbɪk] ADJ *Chem (acid etc)* ascorbique

ascribable [əˈskraɪbəb(ə)l] ADJ PRED attribuable (**to** à); *(of sth negative)* imputable (**to** à); **certain parts of the text are easily a.** l'origine de certaines parties du texte est facile à déceler

ascribe [əˈskraɪb] VT attribuer (**to** à); *(sth negative)* imputer (**to** à)

ascription [əˈskrɪpʃən] N *Fml* attribution *f* (**of sth to sth** de qch à qch); *(of sth negative)* imputation *f* (**of sth to sth** de qch à qch)

asdic [ˈæzdɪk] N *Naut* asdic *m*

ASEAN [ˈæziæn] N *(abbr* **Association of South East Asian Nations)** ANASE *f*

asepsis [eɪˈsepsɪs] N *Med* asepsie *f*

aseptic [eɪˈseptɪk] ADJ *Med* aseptique; *Fig (smile, charm)* aseptisé

asexual [eɪˈseksjʊəl] ADJ *Biol, Fig* asexué; *(flower)* neutre
▸▸ *Biol* **a. reproduction** reproduction *f* asexuée

ash [æʃ] N *(tree, wood)* frêne *m*; **a. furniture** meubles *mpl* en *ou* de frêne
▸▸ **a. tree** frêne *m*

ash² N **1** *(from fire etc)* cendre(s) *f(pl)*; *Ind etc* escarbilles *fpl*; **cigar a.** cendre de cigare; **to drop a. on the carpet** laisser tomber des cendres sur la moquette; **to reduce** *or* **burn sth to ashes** réduire qch en cendres; **volcanic a.** cendres volcaniques; *Lit* **to rake over the ashes of the past** tisonner les cendres du passé; **to rise from the ashes** renaître de ses cendres; **ashes** *(of dead)* cendres *fpl*; **ashes to ashes, dust to dust** *(from funeral service)* tu es poussière, et tu retourneras en poussière; *Cr* **the Ashes** = le trophée que se disputent les équipes anglaises et australiennes se disputent

2 (colour) cendré m, gris cendré m inv
ADJ (in colour) gris cendré inv
▸▸ **a. cloud** (above volcano) nuée f de cendres; **a. heap** crassier m; Rel **A. Wednesday** mercredi m des Cendres

ashamed [əˈʃeɪmd] ADJ USU PRED honteux, confus; **to be a. of sb/sth** avoir honte de qn/qch; **I am a. of you** vous me faites honte; **to feel a.** être honteux ou confus; **you make me feel a.** (of myself, you) vous me faites honte; **I am a. to say that …** j'avoue à ma grande honte que …; **a. though I am to admit it, I have never been there** j'ai honte de l'avouer, mais je n'y suis jamais allé; **I'm not a. to admit it** je l'admets sans honte; **you ought to be a. of yourself** vous devriez avoir honte; **there is nothing to be a. of** il n'y a pas de quoi avoir honte; **… he said, with an a. look on his face** … dit-il, l'air confus

A-share N St Exch action f ordinaire sans droit de vote

ash-blond(e) ADJ (hair) blond cendré inv N (person) **she's an a.** elle a les cheveux blond cendré

ashcan [ˈæʃkæn] N Am boîte f à ordures, poubelle f

ashen [ˈæʃən] ADJ (colour) cendré; (face) pâle comme la mort; **his face turned a.** il devint blême, son visage blêmit

ashen-faced [ˈæʃənˈfeɪst] ADJ pâle comme la mort

ashlar [ˈæʃlər] N Constr, Archit **1** (stone) pierre f de taille **2** (facing) parements mpl, revêtement m

ashore [əˈʃɔːr] ADV Naut **1** (on land) à terre; **to go a.** aller ou descendre à terre, débarquer; **to set** or **put sb a.** débarquer qn **2** (to the shore) (to swim etc) jusqu'au rivage, jusqu'à la rive; **to be driven a.** (of ship) être jeté à la côte; **to run a.** (of ship) s'échouer, faire côte

ashpan [ˈæʃpæn] N (for stove) cendrier m

ashtray [ˈæʃtreɪ] N cendrier m

ashy [ˈæʃɪ] ADJ **1** cendreux, couvert de cendres **2** (in colour) cendré, couleur de cendre

Asia [ˈeɪʒə] N Asie f
▸▸ **A. Minor** Asie f Mineure

Asian [ˈeɪʒən] ADJ asiatique; (Indian) indien; (Pakistani) pakistanais
N Asiatique mf, (Indian) Indien, -ienne; (Pakistani) Pakistanais, -aise
▸▸ Fam **A. babe** Indienne f/Pakistanaise f/ Orientale f super belle; Med **A. flu** grippe f asiatique

---

Asian
Pour les Britanniques, "Asian" désigne le plus souvent les habitants de l'Inde et des pays limitrophes: ainsi, l'expression "the Asian community in Edinburgh" fait référence aux personnes d'origine indienne, pakistanaise et bangladaise qui habitent Edimbourg.

Asiatic [eɪsɪˈætɪk] ADJ asiatique
N Asiatique mf

aside [əˈsaɪd] ADV **1** de côté, à l'écart, à part; **to pull a.** (curtain etc) écarter; **to lay** or **put sth a.** mettre qch de côté; **to put sth a. for sb** (in shop) mettre qch de côté pour qn; **stand a.!** écartez-vous!; **to turn a.** se détourner (**from** de); **I took** or **drew him a.** je le pris à part ou à l'écart ou en particulier; **(leaving) politics a., I think …** si on laisse de côté la politique, je pense …; **injuries to my vanity a., it hasn't caused me much trouble** à part quelques blessures d'amour-propre, ça ne m'a pas vraiment causé de problèmes; **joking a.** blague à part; Theat **(words spoken) a.** (paroles dites) en aparté

2 esp Am **a. from** à part; (except for) excepté, sauf; **a. from my own interest** mon propre intérêt à part; **a. from being frightened, I was unhurt** j'en ai été quitte pour la peur
N Theat, Fig aparté m (**to sb** avec qn); (purely) **as an a.** soit dit entre nous

A-side N (of record) face f A

asinine [ˈæsɪnaɪn] ADJ **1** (stupid) stupide, sot **2** (like an ass) asinien

ask [ɑːsk] (asked [ɑːskt]) VT **1** demander; **to a. sb sth** demander qch à qn; **a. him his name/how old he is** demandez-lui son nom/son âge; **to a. the time** demander l'heure; **to a. (sb) the way** demander son chemin (à qn); **to a. (sb) a question** poser une question (à qn) (**about** sur); **it may be asked whether …** on peut se demander si …; **I've often asked myself whether …** je me suis souvent demandé si …, je me suis souvent posé la question de savoir si …; Fam **if you a. me** à mon avis; Fam **I a. you!** je vous demande un peu!

2 (request) demander; **to a. sb for sth** demander qch à qn; **to a. a favour of sb, to a. sb a favour** demander une faveur à qn; **if it isn't asking too much** si ce n'est pas trop vous demander; **to a. sb's permission to do sth** demander à qn la permission de faire qch; **to a. to do sth** demander à faire qch, demander la permission ou l'autorisation de faire qch; **to a. to be excused** s'excuser de partir; (in class) demander la permission de sortir; **to a. sb to do sth** demander à qn de faire qch; **a. him to wait/to come in** priez-le d'attendre/d'entrer

3 (charge) **to a. 600 euros for sth** demander 600 euros pour ou de qch; **how much** or **what are you asking for it?** combien en voulez-vous?

4 (question) (person) interroger (**about** sur); **he asked me all about my work** il m'a interrogé longuement sur mon travail

5 (invite) inviter; **to a. sb to lunch** inviter qn à déjeuner; **I have asked him to come for the weekend** je l'ai invité à passer le week-end chez nous; **can I a. a friend along?** est-ce que je peux inviter un ami à se joindre à nous?

VI **1** (inquire) se renseigner (**about** sur); **if you don't mind me** or **my asking** si vous permettez que je vous le demande; **the police were asking about you** la police a posé des questions à votre sujet
2 (request) **all you have to do is a.!** il n'y a qu'à demander!
▸▸ St Exch **a. price** cours m offert, cours vendeur

▸ **ask after** VT INSEP (show concern for, ask for news of) (person, sb's health) demander des nouvelles de

▸ **ask around** VI (enquire) demander autour de soi, se renseigner; **some odd people have been asking around after you** il y a des drôles de types qui te cherchent

▸ **ask back** VT SEP (invite to one's home) inviter à la maison; (invite again) réinviter; **do you want to a. them back for a drink?** tu veux les inviter à boire un verre à la maison?

▸ **ask for** VT INSEP **1 to a. for sb** demander à voir qn; (on the telephone) demander à parler à qn; **to a. for sth** demander qch; **to a. for something to eat/to drink** demander (quelque chose) à manger/à boire; **to a. for more** en redemander; **to a. for sth back** (that has been lent) redemander qch; **when I want your opinion, I'll a. for it** lorsque j'aurai besoin de ton avis, je te le demanderai; **to be asking for trouble** aller au-devant des ennuis; Fam **he's been asking for it!** il l'a bien cherché!, il ne l'a pas volé!; **that's asking for a cold** tu/il/etc cherche(s) vraiment à

tomber malade!; Fam **you asked for that!** tu l'as cherché! **2** esp Scot = **ask after**

▸ **ask in** VT SEP (invite in) inviter à entrer; **I would a. you in for tea, but …** je vous inviterais bien à (entrer) prendre le thé, mais …

▸ **ask out** VT SEP (on a date etc) inviter à sortir

▸ **ask round** VT SEP (invite to one's home) inviter; **why don't we a. them round for dinner one night?** pourquoi ne pas les inviter à dîner un soir?

▸ **ask up** VT SEP (invite up) inviter à monter; **they asked us up to their flat** ils nous ont invités à monter dans leur appartement ou chez eux

askance [əˈskæns, -ˈɑːns] ADV Fig **to look a. at sb/sth** regarder qn/qch de travers ou avec méfiance; **she looked rather a. when I suggested Burger King** elle a fait un drôle d'air quand j'ai suggéré Burger King

askew [əˈskjuː] ADV de biais, de travers; (to put one's hat on) de guingois; Fig **his calculations were slightly a.** il s'était un peu trompé dans ses calculs; **I don't want anything going a.** je tiens à ce que rien n'aille à travers

asking [ˈɑːskɪŋ] N **it's yours for the a.** il n'y a qu'à (le) demander; **it was theirs for the a.** ils n'ont eu qu'à demander
▸▸ **a. price** Fin prix m de départ, prix demandé; Am St Exch cours m offert, cours vendeur

aslant [əˈslɑːnt] ADV obliquement, de travers, de biais
PREP en travers de

asleep [əˈsliːp] ADJ PRED endormi; **to be a.** dormir; **to fall a.** s'endormir; **they lay a. on the floor** ils s'étaient endormis par terre; **to be fast** or **sound a.** être profondément endormi ou plongé dans le sommeil; **my foot is a.** j'ai le pied engourdi

ASLEF [ˈæzlef] N Br abbr Associated Society of Locomotive Engineers and Firemen

ASM [eɪesˈem] N **1** Mil abbr air-to-surface missile **2** Theat abbr assistant stage manager

as-new ADJ comme neuf

asocial [eɪˈsəʊʃəl] ADJ asocial, -iaux

asp [æsp] N (snake) (vipère f) aspic m

asparagus [əˈspærəgəs] N (no pl) Culin asperges fpl; **a piece** or **spear of a.** une asperge; **a. soup** soupe f aux asperges
▸▸ **a. fern** asparagus m; **a. tips** pointes fpl d'asperges

aspect [ˈæspekt] N **1** (of problem, subject etc) aspect m; **the worrying a. of the situation is …** ce qu'il y a d'inquiétant dans cette situation c'est …; **there were amusing aspects to the situation** la situation avait des côtés amusants
2 Fml (appearance) air m; **a man of serious a.** un homme à l'air sérieux
3 (outlook) (of house etc) exposition f, orientation f; **to have a northern a.** être exposé au nord; **flats with southern a.** appartements mpl orientés au sud
4 Astrol (of planets) aspect m
5 Gram aspect m VOIR GRAMMAIRE A39
▸▸ Cin **a. ratio** rapport m hauteur/largeur, format m de l'image

aspen [ˈæspən] N (tree) (peuplier m) tremble m
▸▸ **a. leaf** feuille f de tremble

asperity [æˈsperɪtɪ] N (of climate) rigueur f, sévérité f; (of character, voice) aspérité f, rudesse f; (of reproach) âpreté f; (of style) aspérité

aspersion [əˈspɜːʃən] N Fml, Hum calomnie f; **to cast aspersions on sb/sth** calomnier qn/ qch; **to cast aspersions on sb's honour** porter atteinte à l'honneur de qn

asphalt [ˈæsfælt] N Miner, Constr asphalte m,

bitume *m*; **a. roadway** chaussée *f* asphaltée
VT *Constr (road etc)* asphalter, bitumer

asphalting ['æsfæltɪŋ] **N** asphaltage *m*, bitumage *m*

asphyxia [æs'fɪksɪə] **N** asphyxie *f*; **it led to a.** cela a provoqué l'asphyxie *ou* une asphyxie

asphyxiate [æs'fɪksɪeɪt] **VT** asphyxier
VI mourir d'asphyxie

asphyxiation [æsfɪksɪ'eɪʃən] **N** asphyxie *f*

aspic ['æspɪk] **N** *Culin* gelée *f*; **eggs in a.** œufs *mpl* en gelée; **chicken/salmon in a.** aspic *m* de volaille/de saumon; *Fig* **preserved in a.** mis sous verre

aspidistra [æspɪ'dɪstrə] **N** *(plant)* aspidistra *m*

aspirant ['æspɪrənt] **N** candidat, -ate

aspirate¹ ['æspɪrət] **ADJ** *Ling* aspiré

aspirate² ['æspɪreɪt] **VT 1** *Ling (vowel, h)* aspirer **2** *Tech (gas, liquid)* aspirer; **aspirating filter** filtre *m* à vide

aspiration [æspɪ'reɪʃən] **N 1** *Ling, Med etc* aspiration *f* **2** *(ambition)* aspiration *f*; **to have aspirations to greater things/to become a doctor** aspirer à de grandes choses/à devenir médecin; **to have political aspirations** avoir des aspirations politiques; **to have presidential aspirations** aspirer à la présidence

aspirational [æspɪ'reɪʃən(ə)l] **ADJ** *Mktg (product)* qui fait chic; *(consumer)* qui achète des produits de prestige; *(advertising)* qui joue sur le prestige d'un produit
▸▸ **a. group** groupe *m* de référence

aspirator ['æspɪreɪtər] **N** *Phys, Med* aspirateur *m*

aspire [ə'spaɪər] **VI** aspirer; **to a. to** *or* **after sth** aspirer *ou* prétendre *ou* viser à qch, ambitionner qch; **to a. to do sth** aspirer à *ou* ambitionner de faire qch; **they aspired to greatness** ils aspiraient à la gloire

aspirin ['æsprɪn] **N** *(drug)* aspirine *f*; *(pill)* comprimé *m* d'aspirine

aspiring [ə'spaɪərɪŋ] **ADJ ATTRIB** *(artiste etc)* en herbe; **to be an a. doctor/dancer** aspirer à devenir médecin/danseur

ass¹ [æs] **N 1** *(animal)* âne *m*; **she a.** ânesse *f*; **a.'s milk** lait *m* d'ânesse; **wild a.** onagre *m* **2** *(idiot)* âne *m*, idiot, -ote; **don't be a silly a.** ne fais pas l'imbécile *ou* l'idiot; **to make an a. of oneself** se ridiculiser; *(make an exhibition of oneself)* se donner en spectacle

ass² **N** *esp Am Vulg (buttocks)* cul *m*; **she's got a great little a. on her** elle a un beau petit cul; **a nice piece of a.** *(woman)* un beau cul, une belle pépée; *see also* **arse, arse about** *etc*
▸ **ass about, ass around** **VI** *Am Sl* déconner

ass³ **N** *abbr* assistant

assail [ə'seɪl] **VT** *Fml (enemy)* assaillir, attaquer; *Fig* **to a. sb with questions** accabler *ou* assaillir qn de questions; **assailed with doubts** saisi de doutes

assailant [ə'seɪlənt] **N** assaillant, -ante, agresseur *m*

assassin [ə'sæsɪn] **N** *(of head of state etc)* assassin *m*; *Hist* **Assassins** Assassins, Ismaïliens *mpl*

assassinate [ə'sæsɪneɪt] **VT** assassiner

assassination [əsæsɪ'neɪʃən] **N** assassinat *m*; **character a.** diffamation *f*
▸▸ **a. attempt** attentat *m* *(contre quelqu'un)*

assault [ə'sɔːlt] **N 1** *Law* tentative *f* de voie de fait; *(attempted rape)* tentative *f* de viol; *(rape)* viol *m*; **unprovoked a.** agression *f*; **a. and battery** voies *fpl* de fait, coups *mpl* et blessures *fpl*; **criminal a.** agression *f* **2** *Mil* assaut *m*; *Fig (on government, person's beliefs etc)* attaque *f* *(on* contre); **to take** *or* **carry a**

town by a. prendre une ville d'assaut; **to make an a. on sth** donner l'assaut à qch; *Fig (on problem, correspondence)* s'attaquer à qch
VT 1 *(attack) (person)* agresser, attaquer; *Law* se livrer à des voies de fait sur; *(sexually)* violenter; **to be assaulted** être victime d'une agression; *(sexually)* être victime d'un attentat à la pudeur **2** *Mil (town, position etc)* attaquer, assaillir, donner l'assaut à; *Fig (senses)* agresser
▸▸ *Mil* **a. course** parcours *m* du combattant; *Mil* **a. craft** engin *m* d'assaut; **a. rifle** fusil *m* d'assaut

assay [ə'seɪ] **N** *Metal (of precious metal, mineral)* essai *m*; *Chem* dosage *m*
VT 1 *Metal (precious metal, mineral)* essayer, titrer, analyser; *(metal)* faire l'essai de; *(gold, silver)* coupeller **2** *Lit (attempt)* tenter
▸▸ **a. office** laboratoire *m* d'essais

assaying [ə'seɪɪŋ] **N** *Metal (of mineral etc)* essai *m*, titrage *m*, analyse *f*; *(of gold, silver)* coupellation *f*

assemblage [ə'semblɪdʒ] **N 1** *Tech (of pieces of woodwork etc)* assemblage *m* **2** *(of objects)* collection *f*; *(of individuals)* assortiment *m*

assemble [ə'semb(ə)l] **VT 1** *(people)* rassembler, réunir; *(documents, evidence)* réunir; *(insurgents etc)* ameuter; *(parliament)* convoquer; *Mil (troops)* rassembler; **he addressed the assembled schoolchildren** il s'est adressé à l'ensemble des élèves réunis **2** *Tech (in joinery)* assembler; *(machine)* ajuster, assembler, monter; *(watch etc)* habiller
VI *(of people)* s'assembler, se rassembler, se réunir; *(of insurgents etc)* s'ameuter

assembler [ə'semblər] **N** *Ind* monteur, -euse; *Comput* assembleur *m*

assembly [ə'semblɪ] **N 1** *(gathering)* réunion *f*, *Br Sch etc* rassemblement *m*; **place of a.** lieu *m* de réunion; *Law* **unlawful a.** attroupement *m*; **right of a.** droit *m* à la liberté de réunion **2** *Pol etc* assemblée *f*; **the National A.** l'Assemblée nationale **3** *Ind, Cin etc (assembling)* montage *m*, assemblage *m* **4** *(group of components)* assemblage *m*
▸▸ *Mil* **a. area** zone *f* d'attente; **a. hall** = hall *m* où les enfants se réunissent le matin avant d'entrer en classe; **a. instructions** instructions *fpl* de montage *ou* d'assemblage; *Comput* **a. language** langage *m* d'assemblage; *Comput* **a. language program** programme *m* en assembleur; *Ind* **a. line** chaîne *f* de montage; *Ind* **a. plant** usine *f* de montage; **a. rooms** salle *f* des fêtes, salle de danse; *Ind* **a. shop** salle *f* de montage

assent [ə'sent] **N** assentiment *m*; *Law* agrément *m*; **to withhold one's a. from a proposal** refuser son assentiment à une proposition; **he acted with the full a. of his colleagues** il a agi avec l'approbation totale de ses collègues; **to gain the a. of sb** *or* **sb's a.** obtenir l'assentiment de qn; **the royal a.** le consentement du souverain; **by common a.** du consentement de tous
VI donner son assentiment (**to** à); **to a. to a bill** *(of sovereign)* sanctionner une loi

Attention: ne pas confondre avec **ascent**.

assert [ə'sɜːt] **VT 1** *(one's rights, point of view etc)* faire valoir; **to a. oneself** s'imposer, se faire entendre; **you must a. your authority** il vous faut imposer votre autorité **2** *(declare) (one's innocence etc)* protester de; **to a. that ...** affirmer *ou* prétendre *ou* soutenir que ... + *ind*

assertion [ə'sɜːʃən] **N 1** *(of right)* revendication *f* **2** *(claim)* assertion *f*, affirmation *f*; **her a. that she had never seen him was un-**

convincing elle prétendait de façon peu convaincante qu'elle ne l'avait jamais vu

assertive [ə'sɜːtɪv] **ADJ** *(tone, person, manner etc)* assuré; **don't be too a.** ne te montre pas trop autoritaire; **he's not a. enough** il n'a pas assez d'autorité, il ne s'affirme pas assez

assertiveness [ə'sɜːtɪvnɪs] **N** assurance *f*
▸▸ **a. training** stage *m* d'affirmation de soi

assess [ə'ses] **VT 1** *(value of sth)* estimer; *(quality of product)* juger de; **to a. the damage** évaluer les dégâts; *Naut* évaluer l'avarie; *Law* **to a. the damages** fixer les dommages et intérêts; *Admin* **to a. sb at so much** imposer *ou* taxer qn à tant; **to a. a property (for taxation)** évaluer une propriété; **if we a. this speech at its true worth** si nous estimons ce discours à sa juste valeur; **to a. the situation** évaluer la situation; **how do you a. the team's chances?** à votre avis, quelles sont les chances de l'équipe?, quelles chances accordez-vous à l'équipe?; **to a. the chances of sth happening** évaluer les chances que qch a de se produire **2** *Admin (tax)* répartir, établir **3** *Sch, Univ* évaluer; **students are continuously assessed** le niveau des étudiants est évalué par un contrôle continu

assessment [ə'sesmənt] **N 1** *(of value of sth)* estimation *f*; *(for insurance or tax purposes)* évaluation *f*; *Law* **a. of damages** fixation *f* de dommages et intérêts; *Sch* **continuous a.** contrôle *m* continu; **they gave their a. of the situation** ils ont donné leur avis sur la situation, ils ont dit ce qu'ils pensaient de la situation; **what is your a. of their chances?** à votre avis, quelles sont leurs chances?, quelles chances leur accordez-vous? **2** *Admin (for tax) (of municipality, building)* imposition *f*; *(of taxpayer)* cotisation *f*; *(amount)* cote *f*, taxe *f* officielle; **basis of a.** assiette *f* des impôts; **notice of a.** avis *m* de contributions; **year of a.** année *f* d'imposition; **a. on landed property** cote foncière; **a. on income** impôt *m* sur le revenu **3** *Admin (of tax)* répartition *f*, assiette *f*

assessor [ə'sesər] **N 1** *(of tax)* répartiteur, -trice **2** *(for insurance)* expert *m* **3** *Law* assesseur *m*, juge *m* assesseur

asset ['æset] **N 1** *(advantage)* avantage *m*, atout *m*; **she is a great a. to the firm** c'est un grand atout pour l'entreprise **2** *Fin etc (usu pl)* **assets** actif *m*, avoir(s) *m(pl)*; *(personal)* patrimoine *m*; *Law (of inheritance, company)* masse *f*; *(on liquidation after bankruptcy)* masse active; **capital assets** actif immobilisé; **frozen assets** fonds *mpl* bloqués *ou* non liquides
▸▸ *Fin* **a. allocation** répartition *f* des actifs; *Fin* **a. management** gestion *f* de biens, gestion de capital; *(of individual's wealth)* gestion de patrimoine; *Fin* **a. swap** swap *m* d'actifs; *Fin* **a. turnover** rotation *f* des capitaux

asset-strip **VT** démembrer les actifs de

asset-stripper **N** = personne *f* spécialisée dans le démembrement d'actifs

asset-stripping [-'strɪpɪŋ] **N** démembrement *m* des actifs *(suite au rachat d'une société)*

asseverate [ə'sevəreɪt] **VT** *Fml (one's innocence)* protester de; **to a. that ...** affirmer (solennellement) que ... + *ind*

asshole ['æʃəʊl] **N** *Am Vulg* **1** *(anus)* trou *m* du cul **2** *Fig (idiot)* connard *m*, connasse *f*; *(nasty person)* fumier *m*, salaud *m*, salope *f*; **don't be such an a.** ne sois pas si con

assiduity [æsɪ'djʊɪtɪ] **N** assiduité *f* (**in doing sth** à faire qch)

assiduous [ə'sɪdjʊəs] **ADJ** assidu; **she was a. in her attention to detail** elle portait une attention assidue aux détails

assiduously [ə'sɪdjʊəslɪ] ADV assidûment

assign [ə'saɪn] VT 1 *(allocate) (task, equipment, time, function)* assigner (**to** à); *(funds)* affecter (**to** à); **to a. sb to a task** assigner une tâche à qn; **they had been assigned to guard duty** on leur avait assigné la garde; **responsibilities haven't yet been assigned** les responsabilités n'ont pas encore été réparties *ou* assignées; **to a. sb to do sth** charger qn de faire qch
2 *(ascribe)* attribuer; **to a. a reason for sth** donner la raison de qch; **to a. a meaning to a word** attribuer un sens à un mot
3 *Law (property)* céder, transférer; *(lawsuits, patent)* transmettre (**to sb** à qn)

assignation [æsɪg'neɪʃən] N **1** *Old-fashioned (meeting)* rendez-vous *m* secret; *(with lover)* rendez-vous galant; **to have an a. with sb** avoir un rendez-vous avec qn
2 *Law* = **assignment 3**
3 *Fml (allocation etc)* = **assignment 1**

assignee [æsaɪ'niː] N cessionnaire *mf*

assignment [ə'saɪnmənt] N **1** *(of task, equipment, function)* assignation *f*, *(of funding)* affectation *f*, allocation *f*, *(of duties, responsibilities)* attribution *f*, *(sharing out)* répartition *f*; **a. of sb to a post** affectation de qn à un poste; *Mil* **he was on a. to headquarters** il était affecté au quartier général;
2 *(task) Sch etc* devoir *m*; *Journ (of individual reporter)* reportage *m* assigné; **dangerous a.** tâche *f* dangereuse; *Journ* **to be on a.** être en reportage
3 *Law etc (of property, debts etc)* cession *f*, transfert *m*; **deed of a.** acte *m* attributif, acte de transfert
▸▸ *Acct* **a. of accounts receivable** transfert de créances; *Comput* **a. table** table *f* d'affectation

assimilate [ə'sɪmɪleɪt] VT *(food, facts, immigrants etc)* assimiler
VI **1** *(become absorbed)* s'intégrer, être assimilé; *(of people)* s'intégrer **2** *(become similar)* **to a. to** *or* **with sth** s'assimiler à qch

assimilation [əsɪmɪ'leɪʃən] N *(of food, ideas, immigrants etc)* assimilation *f*

Assisi [ə'siːzɪ, ə'siːsɪ] N Assise *f*; **St Francis of A.** saint François d'Assise

assist [ə'sɪst] VT *(person)* aider, prêter son assistance à; *(in their work)* seconder, prêter (son) concours à; *(process)* faciliter; *(sth's growth, development)* contribuer à; **to a. sb in doing sth** aider qn à faire qch; **economic growth was assisted by lower interest rates** des taux d'intérêts plus faibles ont contribué à la croissance économique
VI **1** *(help)* aider **2** *(be present) (at ceremony etc)* assister
▸▸ **assisted suicide** suicide *m* assisté

assistance [ə'sɪstəns] N aide *f*, secours *m*, assistance *f*; **to give sb a.** prêter son aide *ou* assistance à qn; *(in work, task)* prêter (son) concours à qn; **to come to sb's a.** venir en aide à qn; **with the a. of sth/sb** à l'aide de qch/avec l'aide de qn; **can I be of any** *or* **some a.?** puis-je être utile à quelque chose?, est-ce que je peux vous aider?; **to be of as much a. as one can** prêter toute l'assistance possible; **this theatre receives financial a. from the state** ce théâtre reçoit des subventions de l'État; *Br Admin Arch* **National A.** ≃ aide sociale

assistant [ə'sɪstənt] N **1** aide *mf*, adjoint, -ointe; **(shop) a.** vendeur, -euse; **laboratory a.** laborantin, -ine **2** *Sch* assistant, -ante; **French a.** assistant, -ante de français
▸▸ **a. accountant** aide-comptable *mf*, *pl* aides-comptables; **a. cameraman** aide-opérateur, -trice, *pl* aides-opérateurs, -trices; **a. director** sous-directeur, -trice, *pl* sous-directeurs, -trices; *Cin* assistant-réalisateur *m*, assistante-réalisatrice *f*, *pl* assistants-

réalisateurs, assistantes-réalisatrices; **a. editor** *TV* assistant monteur *m*; *Cin* monteur, -euse adjoint(e); *Journ* rédacteur, -trice en chef adjoint(e); *TV* **a. floor manager** régisseur *m* de plateau adjoint; **a. housekeeper** *(in hotel)* assistante gouvernante *f*, aide-gouvernante *f*, *pl* aides-gouvernantes; *Br Univ* **a. lecturer** ≃ maître-assistant, -ante, *pl* maîtres-assistants, -antes, *Can* ≃ professeur *m* adjoint; *Com* **a. manager** sous-directeur, -trice, *pl* sous-directeurs, -trices, directeur, -trice adjoint(e); **a. producer** producteur, -trice adjoint(e); *Am Univ* **a. professor** ≃ maître-assistant, -ante, *pl* maîtres-assistants, -antes, *Can* ≃ professeur *m* adjoint; *Ftbl* **a. referee** juge *m* de touche

assize [ə'saɪz] N *Law* **1** *(usu pl)* **(court of) assizes** (cour *f* d')assises *fpl*; **to be brought before the assizes** être traduit en cour d'assises **2** *Scot (trial)* jugement *m* par jury; *(jury)* jury *m*
▸▸ **a. court** (cour d')assises

associate¹ [ə'səʊʃɪət, -sɪət] N *(in business)* associé, -ée, partenaire *mf*; *(in criminal venture)* complice *mf*; *(of society of letters, science etc)* membre *m* correspondant, associé, -ée
ADJ associé
▸▸ *Com* **a. company** société *f* affiliée; *Cin* **a. director** assistant-réalisateur *m*, assistante-réalisatrice *f*, *pl* assistants-réalisateurs, assistantes-réalisatrices; *Journ* **a. editor** rédacteur, -trice associé(e); **a. membership** *(members)* membres *mpl* associés; *(participation)* adhésion *f* en tant que membre associé; **a. producer** producteur, -trice associé(e); *Am Univ* **a. professor** ≃ maître *m* de conférences, *Can* professeur *m* agrégé

associate² [ə'səʊʃɪeɪt, -sɪeɪt] VT **1** *(mentally)* associer (**with sb** avec qn; **with sth** à qch); **I don't a. the two things** pour moi, les deux choses sont indépendantes
2 *(in partnership etc)* **to a. oneself** s'associer (**with sb** avec qn); **to be associated with sb in an undertaking** s'associer avec qn pour une entreprise; **to be associated with sth** *(with project, research etc)* participer à qch, *(with company etc)* avoir des liens avec qch, travailler avec qch; **we are not associated in any way with that company** nous n'avons absolument rien à faire *ou* voir avec cette société
VI **1** *(frequent)* **to a. with sb** fréquenter qn; **to a. with undesirable companions** avoir de mauvaises fréquentations
2 *(join)* **to a. with sb in sth/doing sth** s'associer *ou* s'unir avec qn pour qch/pour faire qch

associated [ə'səʊʃɪeɪtɪd] ADJ associé
▸▸ *Com* **a. company** société *f* affiliée; *Journ* **A. Press** Associated Press *f (agence de presse dont le siège est à New York)*

association [əsəʊsɪ'eɪʃən] N **1** *(mental)* association *f*, **a. of ideas** association d'idées; **a land full of historic associations** un pays fertile en souvenirs historiques; **the name has unfortunate associations for her** ce nom lui évoque des pensées désagréables; **the associations of the name** ce qu'on associe à ce nom
2 *(of people)* fréquentation *f* (**with sb** de qn); **through long a. with ...** à force de fréquenter ...; **in a. with ...** associé à ...; **to do sth in a. with sb** faire qch en association avec qn; **I have no a. with that company** je n'ai pas de liens avec cette société; **it has only a tenuous a. with its original purpose** cela n'a plus qu'un rapport lointain avec l'idée de départ; **my a. with the company has now ended** ma collaboration avec cette société est maintenant terminée
3 *(organization)* association *f*, société *f*, *(of*

teachers etc) amicale *f*; **to form an a.** constituer une société; **trade a.** association professionnelle; **Young Men's/Women's Christian A.** Union *f* chrétienne de jeunes gens/de jeunes femmes; *Law* **deed of a.** acte *m* d'association
▸▸ *Br* **a. football** football *m* association; *Psy* **a. test** test *m* d'association

associative [ə'səʊsɪətɪv] ADJ *Psy* associatif

assonance ['æsənəns] N *Ling* assonance *f*

assorted [ə'sɔːtɪd] ADJ **1** *(sweets, screws etc)* assorti; *(colours)* varié; **an audience of a. academics and businessmen** un public très varié, composé d'universitaires et d'hommes d'affaires **2** *(matched)* assorti; **well a. couple** époux bien assortis

assortment [ə'sɔːtmənt] N *(of sweets, tools etc)* assortiment *m*; **I did it for an a. of reasons** je l'ai fait pour des raisons diverses; **quite an a. of people** des gens de toutes sortes

asst *abbr* **assistant**

assuage [ə'sweɪdʒ] VT *Lit (anger, hunger)* apaiser

assume [ə'sjuːm] VT **1** *(believe without proof)* présumer, supposer; **we can't a. anything** nous ne pouvons présumer de rien; **if we a. there will be no problems, ...** en supposant qu'il n'y aura aucun problème, ...; **I a. that he will come** je présume qu'il viendra; **he was assumed to be rich** on le supposait riche; **in the absence of proof, he must be assumed to be innocent** en l'absence de preuves, il doit être présumé innocent; **don't a. that people will like you because you are rich** ne crois pas que les gens t'aimeront parce que tu es riche; **let us a. that ...** mettons *ou* supposons que ...; **assuming that the story is true** en supposant *ou* en admettant que l'histoire soit vraie; **to a. the worst** mettre les choses au pis
2 *(take over) (responsibility)* prendre sur soi, assumer; *(duty)* se charger de; *(power, command)* prendre; *(running of hotel, company etc)* prendre en main
3 *(adopt) (right, title etc)* s'attribuer, s'arroger, s'approprier; *(name)* adopter, emprunter; *Law* **to a. ownership** faire acte de propriétaire
4 *(take on) (air, appearance, tone)* prendre, se donner; *(shape, character)* affecter, revêtir; *(of problem) (importance, vast proportions)* prendre; **his voice assumed a tone of authority** sa voix prit un ton autoritaire
5 *(feign) (indifference)* feindre, simuler

> Note that the French verb **assumer** is a false friend. It never means **to suppose** or **to adopt**.

assumed [ə'sjuːmd] ADJ ATTRIB *(identity)* faux; *(cause of death, motive, rate of increase)* présumé; **with a. nonchalance** avec une nonchalance feinte
▸▸ **a. load** *(on bridge etc)* surcharge *f* hypothétique; **a. name** nom *m* d'emprunt; *(of author)* pseudonyme *m*

assumption [ə'sʌmpʃən] N **1** *(supposition)* supposition *f*, hypothèse *f*, *Phil* postulat *m*; **it's a fair a. that ...** on peut facilement supposer que ...; **I am going on the a. that ...** je me fonde sur l'hypothèse que ...; **to work on the a. that ...** se fonder sur l'hypothèse que ...; **the assumptions on which society is based** les idées de base qui servent de fondement à la société **2** *(of power, responsibility etc)* prise *f*; **a. of office** entrée *f* en fonctions; **his a. of the role of chairman** *(after nomination)* son entrée en fonctions en tant que président; *(without consent)* le fait qu'il s'arroge la fonction de président **3** *Rel (of Virgin)* assomption *f*; **Feast of the A.** fête *f* de l'Assomption

assurance [ə'ʃʊərəns] N **1** (promise) promesse f(formelle); **I can give you an a. that ...** je peux vous assurer ou vous affirmer que ...; **he gave us any number of assurances that ...** il nous a assuré maintes et maintes fois que ...; **based on their a. that delivery would be within two days** en considération de leur promesse d'une livraison dans les deux jours **2** (affirmation) affirmation f; **a. to the contrary** affirmation contraire **3** (confidence) assurance f; **I have every a. that he will help us** j'ai la ferme assurance qu'il nous aidera **4** (self-confidence) assurance f, confiance f en soi; **to lack a.** (of person, answer) manquer d'assurance; **to answer with a.** (self-confidently) répondre d'un ton assuré ou avec assurance **5** Br (insurance) assurance f; **life a.** assurance sur la vie f, assurance-vie f, pl assurances-vie ►► Br **a. company** compagnie f d'assurances

assure [ə'ʃʊər] VT **1** (person) assurer; **to a. sb of the truth of sth** assurer qn de la vérité de qch; **to a. sb of a fact** assurer ou affirmer un fait à qn; **he assures me that it is true** il me certifie que c'est vrai; **he assured me he was coming** il m'a assuré qu'il viendrait; **he will do it, I (can) a. you!** il le fera, je vous assure! **2** (ensure) (peace, sb's happiness etc) assurer **3** Br (insure) (sb's life) assurer; **to a. one's life** s'assurer (sur la vie)

assured [ə'ʃʊəd] ADJ **1** (certain) (success etc) assuré; **they are a. of victory** ils sont certains de gagner; **she is a. a place in the finals** elle est certaine d'aller en finale; **you're a. of a warm welcome** on vous garantit un accueil chaleureux **2** (self-confident) (person) sûr de soi; (manner, performance) plein d'assurance, assuré **3** (in insurance) **the sum a.** la valeur assurée

N (in insurance) **the a.** l'assuré, -ée, plles assurés, -ées

assuredly [ə'ʃʊərɪdlɪ] ADV Fml assurément, sans aucun doute; **when she returns, as she a. will, ...** quand elle reviendra, ce qui ne laisse aucun doute, ...

Assyria [ə'sɪrɪə] N Antiq Assyrie f

Assyrian [ə'sɪrɪən] Antiq ADJ assyrien N **1** Assyrien, -ienne **2** Ling assyrien m

AST [eɪes'tiː] N Am abbr **Atlantic Standard Time**

aster ['æstər] N (flower) aster m; **China a.** aster de Chine, reine-marguerite f, pl reines-marguerites

asterisk ['æst(ə)rɪsk] N astérisque m VT (word etc) marquer d'un astérisque

astern [ə'stɜːn] Naut ADV à l'arrière, sur l'arrière; **two guns a.** deux canons à l'arrière ou en poupe; **to go/come a.** (of ship) faire machine ou marche arrière; **full speed a.!** en arrière à toute vitesse!, en arrière toute!; **to make a boat fast a.** amarrer un canot derrière; **to fall** or **drop a.** (of another ship) rester en arrière; **ship right a.** navire droit derrière PREP **a. of a ship** derrière un navire, sur l'arrière d'un navire; **to pass a. of a ship** passer sur l'arrière d'un navire

asteroid ['æstərɔɪd] N Astron astéroïde m

asthma ['æsmə] N asthme m; **to have a.** avoir de l'asthme; **a. sufferer** asthmatique mf

asthmatic [æs'mætɪk] ADJ, N asthmatique mf

astigmatic [æstɪg'mætɪk] ADJ, N Opt astigmate mf

astigmatism [ə'stɪgmətɪz(ə)m] N Opt astigmatisme m

astir [ə'stɜːr] ADJ PRED Old-fashioned **1** (out of bed) debout, levé **2** (in motion) animé; **the whole town was a.** toute la ville était en émoi

ASTMS ['æztems] N Br abbr **Association of Scientific, Technical and Managerial Staffs**

astonish [ə'stɒnɪʃ] VT stupéfier, étonner; **you a. me** vous m'étonnez; **it never fails to a. me that ...** ça m'étonnera toujours de voir que ...; **to be astonished at seeing sth** être étonné ou s'étonner de voir qch; **I was astonished at** or **by the price** j'ai été étonné du prix; **I am continually astonished by her audacity** son audace ne cesse de m'étonner; **I am astonished that ...** cela m'étonne que ... + sub; **she had an astonished look on her face** elle avait l'air étonné(e) ou stupéfait(e)

astonishing [ə'stɒnɪʃɪŋ] ADJ étonnant, surprenant; **it is a. to me that ...** je m'étonne que ... + sub

astonishingly [ə'stɒnɪʃɪŋlɪ] ADVétonnamment; **a. enough, he arrived** chose étonnante, il est arrivé

astonishment [ə'stɒnɪʃmənt] N étonnement m, stupéfaction f; **look of a.** regard m étonné ou stupéfait; **I fell back in a.** j'ai failli en tomber à la renverse; **to my a.** à mon grand étonnement; **to everyone's a.** à la stupéfaction générale

astound [ə'staʊnd] VTabasourdir, frapper de stupeur, stupéfier; **I was astounded by it** j'en ai été stupéfait; **you a. me!** c'est stupéfiant!

astounding [ə'staʊndɪŋ] ADJ abasourdissant, renversant; **a., but true!** incroyable, mais vrai!

astrakhan [æstrə'kæn] N(fur) astrakan m; **a. coat** manteau m d'astrakan

astral ['æstrəl] ADJ Astron (body etc) astral, -aux ►► **a. projection** projection f astrale

astray [ə'streɪ] ADV, ADJ PRED (lost) égaré; (morally) dévoyé; **to go a.** (of person, letter etc) s'égarer; (morally) se dévoyer, se détourner du droit chemin; **my pen seems to have gone a.** j'ai égaré mon stylo; **to come a.** (of hair) se détacher; (of wires) se débrancher; **to lead sb a.** (with false information) égarer qn, induire qn en erreur; (morally) dévoyer qn, détourner qn du droit chemin

astride [ə'straɪd] ADV Horseriding à califourchon; **to ride a.** monter à califourchon PREP **to stand a. sb/sth** enjamber qn/qch; **to sit a. sth** être à cheval ou à califourchon sur qch

astringency [ə'strɪndʒənsɪ] N virulence f, acrimonie f

astringent [ə'strɪndʒənt] ADJ Med astringent; Fig (person, voice etc) caustique N Med astringent m

astringently [ə'strɪndʒəntlɪ] ADV (to say) d'une voix péremptoire; **a. worded** virulent

astrologer [ə'strɒlədʒər] Nastrologue mf

astrological [æstrə'lɒdʒɪk(ə)l] ADJ astrologique

astrology [ə'strɒlədʒɪ] Nastrologie f

astronaut ['æstrənɔːt] Nastronaute mf

astronautics [æstrə'nɔːtɪks] N astronautique f VOIR GRAMMAIRE A10

astronomer [ə'strɒnəmər] Nastronome mf

astronomic(al) [æstrə'nɒmɪk, -ɪk(ə)l] ADJ (year, unit etc) astronomique; Fig **an a. price** un prix astronomique; **an a. failure/disaster** un échec/désastre aux proportions astronomiques

astronomically [æstrə'nɒmɪklɪ] ADVastronomiquement; Fig (to increase) de façon astronomique; **it's a. expensive** ça coûte les yeux de la tête

astronomy [ə'strɒnəmɪ] Nastronomie f

astrophysicist [æstrəʊ'fɪzɪsɪst] N astrophysicien, -ienne

astrophysics [æstrəʊ'fɪzɪks] N astrophysique f VOIR GRAMMAIRE A10

Astro Turf® ['æstrəʊtɜːf] N pelouse f artificielle

astute [ə'stjuːt] ADJ (shrewd) astucieux; (person) astucieux, malin, fmaligne

astutely [ə'stjuːtlɪ] ADV astucieusement, avec finesse; **she realized a. that ...** elle a eu la finesse de se rendre compte que ...

astuteness [ə'stjuːtnɪs] Nastuce f, finesse f

asunder [ə'sʌndər] ADV Arch, Lit (to pieces) **to tear sth a.** mettre qch en pièces; **the family had been torn a. by war** la famille avait été déchirée par la guerre; **to break a.** se casser en deux

asylee [æsaɪˈliː] N= personne fqui a obtenu l'asile politique

asylum [ə'saɪləm] N **1** (shelter) (lieu m de) refuge m; (in church etc) asile m (inviolable); **to seek a.** chercher asile; **he was granted/refused a.** on lui a accordé/refusé l'asile; **the right to** or **of a.** le droit d'asile; **political a.** asile politique **2** Arch (hospital etc) hospice m; (for lunatics) asile m d'aliénés

asylum-seeker N demandeur, -euse d'asile

asymmetric(al) [eɪsɪ'metrɪk, -ɪk(ə)l] ADJ asymétrique; **a charmingly a. room** une pièce dont l'asymétrie fait le charme

asymmetry [eɪ'sɪmɪtrɪ] Nasymétrie f

asymptomatic [eɪsɪmptə'mætɪk] ADJ Med asymptomatique

asymptote ['æsɪmptəʊt] N Math asymptote f

asynchronous [eɪ'sɪŋkrənəs] ADJ Comput, Cin, TVasynchrone ►► **a. data transmission** transmission f de données asynchrone

AT [æt, unstressed ət]

à **1–3, 9** ▪ dans la direction de **7** ▪ en **6**

PREP VOIR GRAMMAIRE A68; B54 **1** (place) à; **at the centre/the top** au centre/sommet; **at table/church/school/the station** à table/l'église/l'école/la gare; **at my side** à mes côtés, à côté de moi; **at hand** sous la main; **at Oxford** à l'université d'Oxford; **at sea** en mer; **at home** à la maison, chez soi; **at my uncle's/the dentist's** chez mon oncle/le dentiste; **to sit at the window** être assis près de la fenêtre **2** (time) à; **at six o'clock** à six heures; **at present** à présent; **at that time** (period) à cette époque, en ce temps-là; **at all times** tout le temps; **at the weekend** (pendant ou durant) le week-end; **at a time when ...** à un moment où ...; **two at a time** deux par deux, deux à la fois; **at the beginning of the year** au début de l'année; **at night** la nuit, le soir; **at (the age of) 20** à 20 ans **3** (price, speed, height etc) à; **at two euros a pound** à deux euros la livre; **at 30 mph** à 30 mil(l)es l'heure; **at an altitude of 10,000 feet** à une altitude de 10 000 pieds; **at 5 feet 2 inches, he was too short** avec ses 5 pieds 2 pouces, il était trop petit; **at minus 13°** à moins 13°; **at a rate of 2 cm a year** à un rythme de 2 cm par an **4** (state, condition) **to be at war/peace** être en guerre/paix; **she's not at her best in the morning** le matin, elle n'est pas au mieux de sa forme; **Skye is at its most beautiful in early June** c'est au début juin que Skye est la plus belle; **at all events** en tout cas; **we'll leave it at that for today** nous en resterons là pour aujourd'hui **5** (resulting from) **at my request/invitation** sur ma demande/mon invitation; **at a word from her, he left the room** il a suffi qu'elle prononce un mot pour qu'il quitte la pièce

6 *(skill)* **quick at repartee** prompt à la repartie; **to be good/bad at mathematics** être fort/faible en mathématiques; **to be good at games** être sportif; **she's very good at making people feel welcome** elle est très douée pour mettre les gens à l'aise

7 *(direction)* vers, dans la direction de; **to look at sb/sth** regarder qn/qch; **to aim at sb** viser qn; **to throw sth at sb/sth** jeter qch sur qn/qch; **to laugh at sb** se moquer de qn; **to swear at sb** jurer contre qn; **to shout at sb** crier après *ou* contre qn; *Fam* **she is always (on) at him** elle est toujours après lui, elle lui casse tout le temps les pieds; *Fam* **he's been on at me to do it** il me casse les pieds pour que je le fasse; **at him!** *(to dog)* attaque!

8 *(cause)* **to be surprised/delighted at sth** être étonné/enchanté de qch; **to be angry at sb** être fâché contre qn; **I'm very excited at the idea of going to Rome** je suis très content à l'idée d'aller à Rome

9 *(activity)* **to be at work** être au travail; **to be hard at work on a project** travailler dur sur un projet; **schoolchildren at play** élèves en récréation; **he's at his beekeeping again** le revoilà à s'occuper de ses abeilles; **I've been at this all morning** je suis là-dessus depuis ce matin; **to keep sb at it** faire trimer qn; **keep at it!** continue!; **she's at it again!** voilà qu'elle recommence!, la voilà qui recommence!; **they're at it again!** *(arguing, having sex)* ils remettent ça!; **they're always at it over something** ils sont toujours à se disputer pour une chose ou pour une autre; **while we are at it** pendant que nous y sommes; **it's an old idea and a rather poor one at that!** cette idée est démodée, et d'ailleurs elle n'est pas très bonne!

10 *Fam* **where are we at?** *(situation, in book etc)* où en sommes-nous?; **where's he at politically?** *(what are his views)* politiquement, il se situe où?; **Paris is where it's at!** c'est à Paris que ça se passe!; **that's not where I'm at** *(not my style)* ce n'est pas mon genre; **jazz is not really where I'm at** le jazz, ce n'est pas vraiment mon trip; **that's where I was at musically** c'est ce que j'écoutais (à l'époque)

11 *Comput (in e-mail address)* arobase *f*, a commercial; **gwilson at transex, dot, co, dot, uk** gwilson, arobase, transex, point, co, point, uk

atavism ['ætəvız(ə)m] N atavisme *m*

atavistic [ætə'vıstık] ADJ atavique

ataxia [ə'tæksıə], **ataxy** [ə'tæksı] N *Med* ataxie *f*; **locomotor a.** ataxie locomotrice progressive, tabes *m* dorsalis

ate PT *see* eat

atheism ['eıθıız(ə)m] N athéisme *m*

atheist ['eıθııst] N athée *mf*

atheistic(al) [eıθı'ıstık, -ık(ə)l] ADJ athée

Athenian [ə'θi:nıən] ADJ athénien, d'Athènes
N Athénien, -ienne

Athens ['æθənz] N Athènes *f*
▸▸ *Naut* **A. Convention** Convention *f* d'Athènes

athlete ['æθli:t] N athlète *mf*; *Med* **a.'s foot** pied *m* d'athlète, mycose *f*

athletic [æθ'letık] ADJ athlétique; **she's very a.** c'est une sportive; **an a.-looking young man** un jeune homme à l'allure sportive; **I don't do anything very a.** je ne fais pas beaucoup de sport

athletically [æθ'letıklı] ADV de façon athlétique

athletics [æθ'letıks] NPL *(usu with sing verb)* athlétisme *m*
▸▸ **a. club** société *f* d'athlétisme

at-home N réception *f*, *(in evening)* soirée *f*

athwart [ə'θwɔ:t] *Naut* ADV en travers, par le travers
PREP en travers de

atishoo [ə'tı∫u:] INT *(sneeze)* atchoum!

Atlantic [ət'læntık] N **the A.** l'(océan *m*) Atlantique *m*
ADJ *(coast etc)* atlantique
▸▸ *Naut* **A. liner** transatlantique *m*; **the A. Ocean** l'(océan) Atlantique; **A. Standard Time** = heure *f* d'hiver des Provinces Maritimes du Canada et d'une partie des Caraïbes

Atlantis [ət'læntıs] N *Myth* Atlantide *f*

Atlas ['ætləs] N *Myth* Atlas
▸▸ *Geog* **the A. Mountains** l'Atlas *m*

atlas ['ætləs] N **1** *(book)* atlas *m* **2** *Anat* atlas *m* **3** *Archit (pl* **atlantes** [ət'lænti:z]*)* atlante *m*, télamon *m*

ATM [eıti:'em] N **1** *Banking (abbr* **automated teller machine***)* DAB *m* **2** *Tel (abbr* **asynchronous transfer mode***)* ATM *m*

atmosphere ['ætməsfıər] N *(of earth, air)*, *Phys* atmosphère *f*; *Fig* atmosphère, ambiance *f*; *Fig* **there was a bit of an a. in the office** l'atmosphère était plutôt tendue au bureau; *Fig* **there was a great a.** il y avait une de ces ambiances; *Fig* **the place has no a.** l'endroit est impersonnel

atmospheric [ætməs'ferık] ADJ *(pressure, condition etc)* atmosphérique; *Fig (novel)* plein d'atmosphère; *(lighting, music)* qui met dans l'ambiance; **the music was very a.** la musique vous mettait complètement dans l'ambiance

atmospherics [ætməs'ferıks] NPL *Radio etc (interference)* (parasites *mpl*) atmosphériques *fpl*

ATOL ['ætɒl] N *(abbr* **air travel organizer's licence***)* licence *m* d'organisateur de voyages par avion

atoll ['ætɒl] N *Geog* atoll *m*

atom ['ætəm] N *Phys* atome *m*; *Fig* **not an a. of common sense** pas un grain de bon sens; **smashed to atoms** réduit en miettes *ou* en poudre
▸▸ *Mil, Nucl* **a. bomb** bombe *f* atomique

atomic [ə'tɒmık] ADJ *(energy, war, weapon, explosion)* atomique, nucléaire; *Phys (weight, number etc)* atomique; **the a. age** l'ère *f* ou l'âge *m* atomique
▸▸ *Mil, Nucl* **a. bomb** bombe *f* atomique; **a. physicist** atomiste *mf*; **a. reactor** réacteur *m* nucléaire

atomization [ætəmaı'zeı∫ən] N *(of fuel)* atomisation *f*, pulvérisation *f*

atomize ['ætəmaız] VT *(matter)* atomiser; *(fuel)* atomiser, pulvériser; *(in spray, liquid)* vaporiser

atomized ['ætəmaızd] ADJ *(life, society)* fragmenté

atomizer ['ætəmaızər] N atomiseur *m*; **an a. spray** un atomiseur, un vaporisateur

atonal [eı'təʊn(ə)l] ADJ *Mus* atonal, -aux

▸ **atone for** [ə'təʊn] VT INSEP *(sin, crime)* expier; *(mistake, behaviour)* racheter, réparer

atonement [ə'təʊnmənt] N *(for sin, crime)* expiation *f*, *(for mistake, behaviour)* réparation *f* *(for* de); **in a. for a wrong** en réparation d'un tort; *Rel* **to make a.** expier; *Jewish Rel* **Day of A.** Fête *f* du Grand Pardon

atop [ə'tɒp] PREP *esp Lit* en haut de, au sommet de; **sitting a. a suitcase** assis sur une valise

ATP [eıti:'pi:] N *Chem (abbr* **adenosine triphosphate***)* ATP *m*

at-risk ADJ **an a. group** un groupe *ou* une population à risque

atrium ['eıtrıəm] N **1** *Archit* atrium *m* **2** *Anat* oreillette *f*

atrocious [ə'trəʊ∫əs] ADJ **1** *Fam (very bad)* *(pun, weather, journey etc)* atroce, exécrable; *(hat etc)* affreux; *(behaviour, manners, mess)* ignoble; *(injuries)* atroce; **his French is a.** son français est très mauvais; **his singing is a.** il chante atrocement *ou* affreusement mal **2** *(crime)* atroce; **a. act** atrocité *f*

atrociously [ə'trəʊ∫əslı] ADV **1** *Fam (very badly)* exécrablement; **a. bad** atroce, exécrable **2** *(cruelly)* atrocement

atrociousness [ə'trəʊ∫əsnıs] N **1** *(of crime)* atrocité *f* **2** *Fam (of pun, weather etc)* caractère *m* exécrable *ou* atroce; **we could scarcely believe the a. of the weather** nous avions peine à croire qu'il faisait un temps aussi exécrable *ou* atroce

atrocity [ə'trɒsıtı] N **1** *(act)* atrocité *f* **2** *(of crime)* atrocité *f*

atrophied ['ætrəfıd] ADJ atrophié

atrophy ['ætrəfı] N atrophie *f*
VT atrophier
VI s'atrophier

at-sign N *Typ* arobase *f*

attaboy ['ætəbɔı] INT *Fam* bravo!

attach [ə'tæt∫] VT **1** *(join)* attacher, fixer *(to* à); *(two things)* attacher; *(document)* annexer, joindre; **the climbers were attached to each other by a rope** les alpinistes étaient reliés *ou* accrochés les uns aux autres par une corde; **the attached letter** la lettre ci-jointe; **please find attached ...** *(in letter)* veuillez trouver ci-joint ...; *(in e-mail)* veuillez trouver ci-joint ..., veuillez trouver en annexe ...,; **the two pieces of paper weren't attached** *(to each other)* les deux feuilles de papier étaient indépendantes; *(enclosed)* les deux feuilles n'étaient pas jointes; **house with garage attached** maison avec garage attenant; **the kitten attached himself to her** *(followed her)* le chaton l'a adoptée

2 *(assign)* *(importance)* prêter, attacher *(to* à); *(blame)* imputer *(to* à); **official attached to another department** fonctionnaire détaché à un autre service; **to be attached to a unit** être affecté à une unité

3 *Law (property, salary)* mettre une saisie-arrêt sur

4 *Comput (file)* joindre *(to* à); **to a. a file to an e-mail** joindre un fichier à un message électronique

VI **1 to a. to** *(fix on to)* s'accrocher à; *(of appliance, shelves)* *(to wall)* se fixer à; *(of rope, hook)* être relié à

2 no blame attaches to the crew l'équipage n'est nullement à blâmer

attaché [ə'tæ∫eı] N attaché *m*; **military a.** attaché militaire
▸▸ **a. case** mallette *f*, attaché-case *m*, *pl* attachés-cases

attached [ə'tæt∫t] ADJ **1 to be a. to sb/sth** *(fond of)* être attaché à qn/qch; **she became very a. to the dog** elle s'est beaucoup attachée au chien **2 the only woman not a.** *(not married)* la seule femme qui soit libre; **is he a. (to anyone) at the moment?** est-ce qu'il a quelqu'un en ce moment?

attachment [ə'tæt∫mənt] N **1** *(for machine)* accessoire *m*; **lathe with drilling a.** tour *m* avec accessoire pour foret

2 *(act)* *(of object)* fixation *f* *(to* à); *(of document)* annexation *f* *(to* à)

3 *(fastener)* attache *f*, lien *m*; **attachments of a muscle** attaches d'un muscle

4 *(secondment)* rattachement *m*, stage *m*; **to serve an a. with the French army** faire un stage dans l'armée française; **to be on a. to a department** être détaché à un service

5 *(fondness)* attachement *m* *(for sb* pour qn; **to sth** à qch), affection *f* *(for* pour); **to form an a. for sb** s'attacher à qn, se prendre d'affection pour qn; **because of his a. to the**

idea à cause de l'attachement qu'il portait à cette idée

6 *Law* arrêt *m*, saisie *f*, saisie-arrêt *f*, *pl* saisies-arrêts; **a. of real property** saisie immobilière

7 *Comput (of e-mail)* fichier *m* joint

attack [ə'tæk] **N 1** *Mil, Sport* attaque *f*; **combined a.** attaque combinée; **to be/come under a. from sb** être attaqué par qn; **to launch an a.** lancer une attaque; **a. is the best form of defence** l'attaque est la meilleure forme de défense

2 *(on person)* agression *f*, attaque *f* (**on** contre); *Pol* attentat *m*

3 *(strong criticism)* attaque *f* (**on sb** contre qn; **on sth** de *ou* contre qch); **an a. on freedom of speech/on the right to strike** une atteinte à la liberté d'expression/au droit de grève

4 *Med (of asthma etc)* attaque *f*, crise *f*; *(of fever)* poussée *f*; **a. of nerves** *(nervousness)* trac *m*; *(hysteria)* crise de nerfs; **to have an a. of the shakes** être pris de tremblements; **to have an a. of giddiness** être pris de vertiges; **an a. of self-doubt** une crise de doute

5 *Mus (of note)* attaque *f*

VT 1 *Mil, Sport* attaquer; **to be attacked** subir une attaque, être attaqué; *Fig* **the government is attacking our rights** le gouvernement porte atteinte à nos droits

2 *(person) (in street etc)* agresser, attaquer

3 *(criticize) (person, project etc)* attaquer; *(abuse of sth etc)* s'attaquer à

4 *(set about with energy) (task, problem etc)* s'attaquer à

5 *(of disease) (person, organ etc)* s'attaquer à, atteindre; *(of rust) (metal)* attaquer, s'attaquer à, ronger; *(of fear, doubts)* assaillir

VI attaquer

▸▸ **a. dog** chien *m* d'assaut

attacker [ə'tækər] **N** attaquant, -ante, agresseur *m*, assaillant, -ante; *Sport* attaquant, -ante; **could you describe your a.?** pourriez-vous décrire votre agresseur?

attacking [ə'tækɪŋ] **ADJ** attaquant; *(game, play)* d'attaque

attagirl [ˈætəgɜːl] **INT** *Fam* bravo!

attain [ə'teɪn] **VT** *(great age, one's ends, success etc)* atteindre, parvenir à, arriver à; *(high rank, position)* s'élever jusqu'à, parvenir à; *(knowledge)* acquérir; *(ambition)* réaliser; *(happiness)* atteindre; **to a. a reputation** se faire une réputation (**for** de)

VI *Fml* **to a. to perfection** atteindre la perfection; **to a. to power** arriver au pouvoir

attainable [ə'teɪnəb(ə)l] **ADJ** *(dream, ambition etc)* réalisable

attainment [ə'teɪnmənt] **N 1** *(no pl) (achieving) (of goal, ambition)* réalisation *f*; *(of independence)* obtention *f*; *(of happiness)* conquête *f*; **for the a. of his purpose** pour atteindre ses fins, pour arriver à ses fins **2** *(skill, achievements) (usu pl)* attainments *(knowledge)* connaissance(s) *f(pl)*; *(skills)* talents *mpl*; **a man of considerable attainments** un homme qui a beaucoup d'instruction *ou* d'acquis; **her linguistic attainments** sa connaissance des langues

attempt [ə'tempt] **N 1** *(effort)* tentative *f*, essai *m*; **an a. at a smile** l'esquisse *f* d'un sourire; **was that an a. at an apology?** est-ce que c'était censé être une excuse?; **her feeble a. to justify herself** la piètre tentative qu'elle a faite pour se justifier; **without (making) any a. at concealment** sans chercher à se cacher; **they made no a. to help** ils n'ont pas essayé d'aider; **a. to escape** tentative d'évasion; **to make an a. at (doing) sth** *or* **to do sth** essayer *ou* tâcher de faire qch; **he made an a. at 'War and Peace'** il a essayé de lire 'Guerre et paix'; **to make an a. on a record** *or* **to beat a record** essayer de battre

un record; **to make an a. on Everest** tenter l'ascension de l'Everest; **first a.** coup *m* d'essai, première tentative; **it wasn't bad for a first a.** ce n'était pas mal pour une première tentative *ou* un premier essai; **at the first a.** du premier coup; **at the fourth a.** à la quatrième tentative, au quatrième coup; **to make another a.** renouveler ses tentatives, revenir à la charge; **to give up the a.** y renoncer; **he died in the a.** il est mort en essayant

2 *(attack)* attentat *m*; **a. on sb's life** tentative *f* d'assassinat; **to make an a. on sb's life** attenter à la vie de qn

VT **to a. to do sth** essayer *ou* tenter de faire qch, chercher à faire qch; **he attempted to get up** il essaya *ou* tenta de se lever; **he attempted a smile** il s'efforça de sourire; **to a. a piece of work** entreprendre un travail; **candidates must a. five questions** les candidats doivent traiter cinq questions; **to a. the impossible** tenter l'impossible; **attempted murder/theft** tentative *f* d'assassinat/de vol

attend [ə'tend] **VI 1** *(be present)* être présent; **two delegates did not a.** deux délégués étaient absents

2 *(pay attention)* faire attention

3 *Fml (serve)* **to a. on sb** servir qn, être au service de qn

VT 1 *(go to) (church, school, funeral)* aller à; *(be present at) (conference, meeting)* assister à; *(course)* suivre; **the lectures are well attended** les cours sont très suivis; **the celebrations were well attended** les cérémonies ont attiré beaucoup de monde

2 *(of doctor) (sick person)* soigner, donner des soins à

3 *Lit Fml (accompany)* accompagner; **success attended my efforts** mes efforts furent couronnés de succès; **it was attended by considerable publicity** cela s'est accompagné d'une vaste publicité

4 *Fml (serve)* **we were attended by three waiters** nous étions servis par trois garçons; **to a. a prince** suivre *ou* accompagner un prince

▸ **attend to VT INSEP 1** *(deal with) (matter)* s'occuper de; *(one's business)* vaquer à; *(one's interests)* veiller à; *(one's health, appearance)* soigner; *(order)* exécuter; **I shall a. to it** je m'en occuperai, je m'en chargerai **2** *(customer etc)* s'occuper de; **are you being attended to?** est-ce qu'on s'occupe de vous? **3** *(pay attention to)* faire *ou* prêter attention à; **a. to what I'm saying** écoutez attentivement ce que je dis

attendance [ə'tendəns] **N 1** *(presence) (at meeting)* présence *f*; **regular a.** assiduité *f*; **school a.** fréquentation *f* scolaire; **church attendances have fallen** le nombre de personnes qui vont à l'église a baissé; **his a. has been good/bad** il a été/il n'a pas été assidu; **poor a.** manque *m* d'assiduité

2 *(people present)* assistance *f*; **there was a good a. at the meeting** il y avait une assistance nombreuse à la réunion; **there was a record a. at the final** la finale a attiré un nombre record de spectateurs; **the evening class had to be cancelled because of poor a.** le cours du soir a dû être annulé pour manque d'élèves

3 to be in a. on *(of doctor) (sick person)* donner des soins à; *(of courtier) (king etc)* être de service auprès de; **with six bodyguards in a.** accompagné de six gardes du corps; **in close a.** à proximité

▸▸ *Br* **a. allowance** = allocation *f* pour les handicapés; **a. list** *(for meetings)* liste *f* de présence; **a. register** registre *m* de présence; **a. sheet** *(for meetings)* feuille *f* de présence

attendant [ə'tendənt] **N 1** *(official)* surveillant, -ante; *(in public lavatory, cloakroom*

etc) préposé, -ée; *(in museum, car park etc)* gardien, -ienne; *(in theatre)* ouvreuse *f*, **(petrol-)pump a.** pompiste *mf*; **swimming pool a.** maître *m* nageur **2** *(usu pl)* **attendants** *(of king etc)* gens *mpl*, suite *f*

ADJ *Fml* **a. on sb/sth** qui accompagne qn/qch; **famine and its a. diseases** la famine et les maladies dont elle s'accompagne

▸▸ *Law* **a. circumstances** *(of crime etc)* circonstances *fpl* concomitantes

attending [ə'tendɪŋ] **ADJ** *Med* **the a. physician** le médecin traitant

attention [ə'tenʃən] **N 1** *(concentration, thought)* attention *f* (**to** à); **a. to details** attention portée aux détails; **a. to truth** souci *m* de vérité; **to pay a. to sth** faire attention à qch; **to pay a.** *or* **give one's a. to sb** prêter attention à qn; **she didn't pay a. in class** elle n'a pas été attentive en cours; **to give sb/sth one's full a.** consacrer toute son attention à qn/qch; **you have my undivided a.** je suis tout à vous; **the report will receive our full a.** nous prêterons une attention toute particulière à ce rapport; **your a. please, ladies and gentlemen** mesdames et messieurs, votre attention s'il vous plaît; **particular a. should be given to posture** surveillez tout particulièrement votre attitude; *Admin, Com* **for the a. of Mr Green** à l'attention de M. Green; **to turn one's a. to sth** diriger son attention vers qch, porter son attention sur qch; **she constantly switched her a. between the two conversations** elle passait sans cesse d'une conversation à l'autre; **to call** *or* **attract** *or* **draw (sb's) a. to sth** attirer l'attention (de qn) sur qch, faire remarquer qch (à qn); **to draw a. to oneself** se faire remarquer; *Fml* **it has been brought to our a. that …** il a été porté à notre connaissance que …, on nous a fait savoir *ou* remarquer que …; **to catch sb's a.** attirer *ou* capter l'attention de qn; **to attract everybody's a.** fixer tous les regards; **to hold** *or* **engage sb's a.** retenir l'attention de qn; **to get a.** *(of application, plan etc)* être considéré; **the child doesn't get much a.** on ne s'occupe pas beaucoup de cet enfant chez lui; **he gets all the a.** il n'y en a que pour lui; **he just does it to get a.** il ne fait ça que pour se faire remarquer; **she likes being the centre of a.** elle aime être le centre du monde; *(at party)* elle aime se faire remarquer

2 *(maintenance)* soins *mpl*, entretien *m*; **the engine needs** *or* **requires some a.** le moteur a besoin d'être entretenu *ou* d'être entretenu; **the batteries require daily/monthly a.** les accus exigent un entretien journalier/mensuel; **the bathroom looks as if it needs some a.** la salle de bains a besoin d'être un peu retapée

3 *Old-fashioned* **attentions** *(acts of affection)* attentions *fpl*, prévenances *fpl*, empressement *m*; **he was always paying his wife little attentions** il était toujours plein d'attentions *ou* de prévenances pour sa femme; **to pay one's attentions to a lady** faire la cour à une dame

4 *Mil* **a.!** garde-à-vous!; **to come to a.** se mettre au garde-à-vous; **to stand at a.** être *ou* se tenir au garde-à-vous

▸▸ *Med* **a. deficit** déficit *m* de l'attention, déficit attentionnel; *Med* **a. deficit hyperactivity disorder** syndrome *m* hyperkinétique de l'enfant, syndrome de l'enfant hyperactif; **a. span** capacité *f* de concentration

attention-seeking [-siːkɪŋ] **N** **it's just a.** il/elle/*etc* ne cherche qu'à attirer l'attention sur lui/elle/*etc*

ADJ **her a. behaviour** son besoin constant de se faire remarquer

attentive [ə'tentɪv] **ADJ 1** *(pupil, listener, audience etc)* attentif (**to** à); *(in one's work)* soigneux; **she is very a. to detail** elle porte une grande attention aux détails **2** *(anxious to please, considerate)* prévenant, empressé, attentionné; **to be very a. to sb** être très attentionné pour qn, être très empressé auprès de qn; **she was a. to his every need** elle était aux petits soins pour lui; *esp Fml* **thank you, most a.** merci, c'est très aimable à vous

---

When translating **attentive**, note that **attentif** and **attentionné** are not interchangeable. **Attentif** refers to someone who pays attention and **attentionné** to someone who is considerate.

---

attentively [ə'tentɪvlɪ] ADVattentivement

attentiveness [ə'tentɪvnɪs] N **1** *(concentration)* attention *f* **2** *(anxiety to please)* prévenances *fpl*, empressement *m* (**to sb** auprès de qn); **to look after sb with a.** être plein de prévenances pour qn

attenuate [ə'tenjʊeɪt] VT **1** *(seriousness of sth etc)* atténuer; **attenuating circumstances** circonstances *fpl* atténuantes **2** *Tech (gas etc)* raréfier
▪ VI *Tech* s'atténuer, diminuer

attenuation [ətenjʊ'eɪʃən] N atténuation *f*

attenuator [ə'tenjʊeɪtər] N *TV etc* atténuateur *m*

attest [ə'test] VT **1** *(affirm, prove) (fact)* attester; **to a. that …** attester que …; **the document attests the fact that …** le document atteste que …; *Agr* **attested herd** troupeau *m* tuberculiné **2** *(of witness) (thing)* affirmer sous serment; *(signature)* légaliser; **attested copy** copie *f* certifiée **3** *Law (person)* assermenter
▪ VI **to a. to sth** *(be evidence of)* témoigner de qch; *(give evidence of)* attester qch

attestation [æte'steɪʃən] N *Law* **1** *(of witness)* déposition *f*, témoignage *m* **2** *(of fact)* attestation *f* **3** *(of signature)* légalisation *f* **4** *(oath-taking)* prestation *f* de serment

at-the-money option N *St Exch* option *f* au cours, option à la monnaie

attic ['ætɪk] N grenier *m*
▪▪ **a. room** mansarde *f*; **a. window** fenêtre *f* en mansarde; *(skylight)* lucarne *f*

Attica ['ætɪkə] N *Hist Lit* Attique *f*

attire [ə'taɪər] *Fml, Hum (clothing)* tenue *f*
▪ VT *Arch, Lit (usu passive or reflexive)* vêtir, parer; **attired in black/silk** vêtu de noir/soie

attitude ['ætɪtjuːd] N **1** *(of mind)* attitude *f*; **what's your a. to people who say that?** que pensez-vous des gens qui disent cela?; **what's your a. to abortion?** que pensez-vous de l'avortement?, quelle est votre attitude face à l'avortement?; **old-fashioned attitudes** des idées *fpl* démodées; **their a. is that …** leur point de vue est que …; **she takes the a. that …** elle considère que …; **his whole a. is 'I don't care'** tout lui est égal; **I don't like your a.** je n'aime pas ton attitude; **well, if that's your a.** très bien, si c'est comme ça que tu le prends; **she's got an a. problem** elle n'est pas du tout coopérative; *Fam* **she's got a.** elle a du caractère; *Fam* **a car with a.** une voiture qui a du caractère **2** *(pose)* attitude *f*, pose *f*; **to strike an a.** prendre une attitude dramatique, poser **3** *Mktg (of consumer to product)* attitude *f* **4** *Aviat etc (of plane, missile etc on its trajectory)* attitude *f*
▪▪ *Mktg* **a. research** enquête *f* d'attitudes; **a. scale** échelle *f* d'attitudes; **a. survey** enquête *f* d'attitudes

attn *abbr* attention

attorney [ə'tɜːnɪ] N *Law* **1** *Am (lawyer)* avocat, -ate; *Am* **District A.** ≃ procureur *m* de la République **2** *(legal agent)* procureur *m*, fondé *m* de pouvoir(s)
▪▪ **A. General** *(in England, Wales and North-*

---

ern Ireland) = principal avocat *m* de la couronne; *(in US)* ≃ ministre *m* de la Justice; *(in Canada)* procureur général

attract [ə'trækt] VT *(of magnet, person, advert etc)* attirer (**to** à, vers); **he is not attracted to her** elle ne lui plaît pas, *Fam* elle ne lui dit rien; **I was sexually attracted to her** elle m'attirait physiquement; **what really attracts me to him is his sense of humour** ce qui me plaît chez lui, c'est son sens de l'humour; **the prospect of a week in London doesn't a. me** ça ne me dit rien d'aller passer une semaine à Londres; **how does that a. you?** qu'est-ce que tu dis de ça?

attraction [ə'trækʃən] N **1** *(act, power)* attraction *f*, attirance *f* (**to** vers); **wealth has no a. for her** elle n'est pas attirée par la richesse; **the prospect holds little/no a. for me** cette perspective ne me dit pas grand-chose/rien du tout; **I can't** *or* **don't see the a. of it** je n'en vois pas l'intérêt; **his a. to her** son attirance pour elle **2** *(thing, person)* attraction *f*; **the chief a.** *(at fair)* la grande attraction; *(in show etc)* le clou; **tourist a.** attraction pour touristes; **it's the main a. of the job** c'est ce que cet emploi a de plus attrayant **3** *(of person) (usu pl)* **physical attractions** charmes *mpl* physiques; **that's one of my attractions** cela fait partie de mes charmes

attractive [ə'træktɪv] ADJ **1** *(person, offer, manner, prospect etc)* attrayant, attirant, séduisant; *(house, town, region)* beau, *f* belle; *(village)* coquet; *(price)* intéressant, attrayant, attractif; **do you find him a.?** il te plaît?, tu le trouves séduisant?; **in an a. shade of blue** dans une jolie teinte de bleu **2** *(magnet, properties)* attractif, attirant

attractively [ə'træktɪvlɪ] ADV d'une manière attrayante *ou* séduisante; **a. bound in red leather** élégamment relié de cuir rouge; **an a. laid out garden** un jardin qui est un plaisir pour les yeux; **a. priced** à un prix attrayant *ou* attractif

attractiveness [ə'træktɪvnɪs] N attrait *m*; **the a. of their prices/offer** leurs prix attrayants/leur offre attrayante

attributable [ə'trɪbjʊtəb(ə)l] ADJ *(words, success, work of art)* attribuable (**to** à); *(crime, fault etc)* imputable (**to** à)
▪▪ *Acct* **a. profit** bénéfices *mpl* nets

attribute[1] ['ætrɪbjuːt] N **1** *(quality)* attribut *m* **2** *Gram* épithète *f* VOIR GRAMMAIRE A17 **3** *Comput* attribut *m*

attribute[2] [ə'trɪbjuːt] VT *(work of art, success etc)* attribuer (**to** à); *(quality, words)* prêter, attribuer (**to** à); *(mistake, error, crime etc)* imputer (**to** à)

attribution [ætrɪ'bjuːʃən] N *(of words, work of art etc)* attribution *f* (**to** à); *(of crime, fault etc)* imputation *f* (**to** à)

attributive [ə'trɪbjʊtɪv] *Gram* VOIR GRAMMAIRE A17 ADJ épithète
N épithète *f*
▪▪ **a. adjective** épithète *f*

attributively [ə'trɪbjʊtɪvlɪ] ADV *(word used)* avec valeur d'épithète VOIR GRAMMAIRE A17

attrition [ə'trɪʃən] N **1** *(wearing away)* usure *f* par le frottement; **policy of a.** politique *f* d'usure; **war of a.** guerre *f* d'usure **2** *Econ, Ind* attrition *f*, départs *mpl* volontaires

attune [ə'tjuːn] VT accorder, harmoniser (**to** avec); **ear attuned to every sound** oreille exercée à saisir tous les sons; **to a. oneself** *or* **become attuned to sth** se faire à qch, s'accoutumer à qch

ATW [eɪtiː'dʌb(ə)ljuː] *(abbr* **around the world)** autour du monde

atypical [eɪ'tɪpɪk(ə)l] ADJ atypique

aubergine ['əʊbəʒiːn] N *Br Culin* aubergine *f*

---

auburn ['ɔːbən] ADJ *(hair)* châtain roux, auburn *inv*

auction ['ɔːkʃən] N **1** *Com (sale by)* a., **a. sale** vente *f* aux enchères; *(for fish, vegetables etc)* (vente à la) criée *f*, **car a.** vente aux enchères de voitures; **to sell by a.** *or* **at a.** vendre aux enchères; *(fish etc)* vendre à la criée; **to put sth up for a.** mettre qch aux enchères; **the estate is up for a.** le domaine va être mis *ou* vendu aux enchères **2** *Cards* enchère *f*
▪ VT *(put up for auction)* mettre aux enchères; *(sell)* vendre aux enchères; *(foodstuffs, building by legal authority)* vendre à la criée
▪▪ *Cards* **a. bridge** bridge *m* aux enchères; **a. room** salle *f* des ventes; *(for fish, vegetables etc)* chambre *f* des criées
▪ **auction off** VT SEP vendre aux enchères

auctioneer [ɔːkʃə'nɪər] N commissaire-priseur *m*, *pl* commissaires-priseurs; *(at fish or vegetable market etc)* crieur, -euse

audacious [ɔː'deɪʃəs] ADJ **1** *(daring) (attempt, neckline)* audacieux, hardi **2** *(insolent)* effronté, hardi

audaciously [ɔː'deɪʃəslɪ] ADV **1** *(bravely)* audacieusement, avec audace **2** *(insolently)* effrontément

audacity [ɔː'dæsɪtɪ] N **1** *(bravery)* audace *f*, intrépidité *f*, hardiesse *f* **2** *(nerve)* audace *f*, effronterie *f*; **to have the a. to do sth** avoir l'audace de faire qch

audibility [ɔːdɪ'bɪlɪtɪ] N perceptibilité *f*, audibilité *f*

audible ['ɔːdɪb(ə)l] ADJ *(sound)* perceptible (à l'oreille); *(speech, voice)* audible; **he was scarcely a.** on l'entendait à peine
▪▪ *Phys* **a. frequency** fréquence *f* audible

audibly ['ɔːdɪblɪ] ADV *(to speak)* de façon à être entendu; *(to yawn, purr)* bruyamment

audience ['ɔːdɪəns] N **1** *(spectators, listeners)* assistance *f*, *Theat* spectateurs *mpl*, auditoire *m*, public *m*; *Radio* auditeurs *mpl*; *TV* téléspectateurs *mpl*; *Mktg (for product, advertisement)* public; **the whole a. applauded** toute la salle applaudit; **do we have any Americans in the a.?** y a-t-il des Américains dans la salle?; **to perform before a large a.** se produire devant un nombreux public VOIR GRAMMAIRE A11 **2** *Fml (with king, pope etc)* audience *f*; **to grant sb an a.** donner audience *ou* accorder une audience à qn; **to hold an a.** tenir une audience
▪▪ **a. chamber** salle *f* d'audience; *Mktg* **a. exposure** exposition *f* au public; *Radio, TV* **a. figures** indice *m* d'écoute; *Radio, TV* **a. measurement** mesure *f* de l'audience; **a. participation** participation *f* de l'assistance (à ce qui se passe sur la scène); *Radio, TV* **a. rating** indice d'écoute; *Mktg* **a. research** études *fpl* d'audience; *Radio, TV* **a. share** part *f* d'audience; *Radio, TV* **a. show** émission *f* en public; *Mktg* **a. size** audience *f* cumulée; *Mktg* **a. study** étude *f* d'audience

---

Note that the French word **audience** is rarely a translation for the English word **audience**.

---

audio ['ɔːdɪəʊ] ADJ ATTRIB sonore
N son *m*
▪▪ **a. book** livre *m* audio; **a. cassette** cassette *f* audio; **a. cassette recorder** magnétophone *m* à cassette; **a. CD** CD *m* audio; **a. (control) console** pupitre *m* son; **a. equipment** équipement *m* acoustique; **a. feedback** effet *m* Larsen, bouclage *m*; *Phys* **a. frequency** audiofréquence *f*; **a. library** sonothèque *f*, phonothèque *f*; **a. logo** logo *m* audio; **a. recording** enregistrement *m* sonore; **a. response** réponse *f* acoustique; **a. signal** signal *m* audio, signal son; **a. system** système *m* audio; **a. tape** bande *f* magné-

tique audio; **a. tape recorder** magnéto-phone à bande; **a. track** piste *f* son

audioconference ['ɔːdɪəʊkɒnfərəns] **N** au-dioconférence *f*

audiometer ['ɔːdɪəʊmiːtər] **N** *Tech* audio-mètre *m*

audiotyping ['ɔːdɪəʊtaɪpɪŋ] **N** audiotypie *f*

audiotypist ['ɔːdɪəʊtaɪpɪst] **N** audiotypiste *mf*

audiovisual [ɔːdɪəʊ'vɪzjʊəl] **ADJ** audiovi-suel
  ►►**a. archives** archives *fpl* audiovisuelles; **a. equipment** équipement *m* audiovisuel, matériel *m* audiovisuel

audit ['ɔːdɪt] **N** *Fin* audit *m* (comptable), vé-rification(s) *f(pl)* comptable(s), apurement *m*; *Econ* **internal a.** contrôle *m* interne
  VT 1 *Fin (accounts)* vérifier, apurer, examiner **2** *Am Univ (course)* assister en auditeur libre à
  ►►*Admin* **A. Office** ≃ Cour *f* des Comptes; **a. trail** *Comput* protocole *m* de vérification *ou* de contrôle; *Fin* vérification *f* à rebours

auditing ['ɔːdɪtɪŋ] **N** vérification *f* et certifi-cation *f* des écritures, apurement *m*

audition [ɔː'dɪʃən] **N** *Theat, Mus etc* audi-tion *f*; **I've got an a.** je vais passer une audi-tion; **she didn't even get an a.** elle n'a même pas obtenu d'audition
  VT & VI *Theat, Mus etc* auditionner (**for a part** pour un rôle)

auditor ['ɔːdɪtər] **N 1** *Admin* vérificateur, -trice des comptes **2** *Com, Fin* audit *m*, audi-teur, -trice; *(of company)* commissaire *m* aux comptes; *(of insurance company)* censeur *m*; **firm of auditors** cabinet *m* d'audit, cabinet comptable **3** *(at conference, lecture etc)* audi-teur, -trice; *Am Univ* auditeur, -trice libre
  ►►**auditors' report** rapport *m* des vérificateurs

auditorium [ɔːdɪ'tɔːrɪəm] **N** auditorium *m*; *(of theatre, concert hall)* salle *f*; *(lecture theatre)* amphithéâtre *m*

auditory ['ɔːdɪtrɪ] **ADJ** *Anat (nerve etc)* au-ditif; **the a. organ** l'organe *m* de l'ouïe

AUEW [eɪjuːiː'dʌb(ə)ljuː] **N** *Br Formerly abbr* **Amalgamated Union of Engineering Workers**

Aug *abbr* **August**

Augean [ɔː'dʒiːən] **ADJ** *Myth* **the A. Stables** les écuries *fpl* d'Augias

auger ['ɔːgər] **N** *Carp* tarière *f*

aught [ɔːt] **N** *Arch, Lit* quelque chose *m*, quoi que ce soit; **for a. I know** (pour) autant que je sache

augment [ɔːg'ment] **VT** *Fml* augmenter, ac-croître (**with, by** de); *Mus* **augmented inter-val** intervalle *m* augmenté; *Mktg* **augmented product** produit *m* augmenté
  VI *Fml* augmenter, s'accroître

augmentation [ɔːgmen'teɪʃən] **N** *(of for-tune etc)* augmentation *f*, accroissement *m*

augur ['ɔːgər] *Lit* **VT** augurer, présager, pré-dire; **it augurs no good** cela ne présage *ou* n'annonce rien de bon
  VI it augurs well/ill c'est de bon/de mauvais augure (**for** pour); **it doesn't a. well for the future** cela ne présage *ou* n'annonce rien de bon
  N *(prophet)* augure *m*

augury ['ɔːgjʊrɪ] **N 1** *Fml (sign)* augure *m*, présage *m* **2** *(practice)* science *f* des augu-res, science augurale

August ['ɔːgəst] VOIR GRAMMAIRE A81–2; B61–2
août *m*; **in A.** au mois d'août, en août; **(on) the first/the seventh of A.** le premier/le sept août

august [ɔː'gʌst] **ADJ** *(assembly)* auguste; *(bearing, figure)* imposant, majestueux

Augustinian [ɔːgə'stɪnɪən] **ADJ** *Rel, Hist* au-gustinien, de saint Augustin; **A. monk** *or* **friar** Augustin *m*
  N *Rel* Augustin, -ine

Augustus [ɔː'gʌstəs] **N** Auguste

auk [ɔːk] **N** *(bird)* alque *f*; **great a.** grand pin-gouin *m*

auld [ɔːld] **ADJ** *Scot* vieux, *f* vieille
  ►►*Mus* **A. Lang Syne** = chanson *f* sur l'air de "ce n'est qu'un au revoir" que l'on chante à minuit le soir du 31 décembre en Grande-Bretagne

aunt [ɑːnt] **N** tante *f*
  ►►*Br* **A. Sally** *(at fairground)* ≃ jeu *m* de massacre; *Fig (person)* tête *f* de Turc

auntie, aunty ['ɑːntɪ] **N 1** *Fam* tatie *f*, tata *f*, tantine *f*; **A. Julia** tatie *ou* tata Julia **2** *Br Sl* **Auntie** = surnom *m* affectueux de la BBC, perçue comme une vieille tante détentrice des valeurs morales

AUP [eɪjuː'piː] **N** *Comput (abbr* **Acceptable Use Policy)** = code *m* de conduite défini par un fournisseur d'accès à l'Internet

au pair [əʊ'peər] **N** (jeune fille *f*) au pair *f*; **she's working as an a.** elle travaille au pair
  ADV she's staying with them a. elle est chez eux au pair
  VI travailler *ou* être au pair

aura ['ɔːrə] **N 1** aura *f*, *(of place)* atmosphère *f*, **he's got an a. of …** une aura de … émane de lui **2** *Med* aura *f*, **epileptic a.** aura épileptique

aural ['ɔːrəl] **ADJ** auditif, sonore
  ►►**a. comprehension** compréhension *f* orale; *Radio etc* **a. reception** réception *f* du son; **a. specialist, a. surgeon** auriste *mf*

> Attention: ne pas confondre avec l'adjec-tif anglais **oral**.

aureola [ɔː'riːələ], **aureole** ['ɔːrɪəʊl] **N 1** *Art (of saint)* auréole *f* **2** *Astron (of sun)* auréole *f*

auricle ['ɔːrɪk(ə)l] **N** *Anat* **1** *(of heart)* auri-cule *f* **2** *(external ear)* pavillon *m*

auricular [ɔː'rɪkjʊlər] **ADJ** *Anat* auriculaire
  ►►*Rel* **a. confession** confession *f* auricu-laire

aurochs ['ɔːrɒks] **N** *(animal)* aurochs *m*

Aurora [ɔː'rɔːrə] **N** *Myth* Aurore

aurora [ɔː'rɔːrə] **N** aurore *f*
  ►►**a. australis** aurore australe; **a. borealis** aurore boréale

auscultate ['ɔːskəlteɪt] **VT** *Med* ausculter

auscultation [ɔːskəl'teɪʃən] **N** *Med* auscul-tation *f*

auspices ['ɔːspɪsɪz] **NPL** auspices *mpl*; **fa-vourable a.** d'heureux auspices; **under the a. of the United Nations** sous l'égide des Na-tions unies

auspicious [ɔː'spɪʃəs] **ADJ** *(wind etc)* pro-pice, favorable; *(sign)* de bon augure; *(age)* heureux, prospère; **an a. start to a career** des débuts prometteurs dans une carrière; **on this a. occasion** en ce jour mémorable

auspiciously [ɔː'spɪʃəslɪ] **ADV** sous d'heu-reux auspices, favorablement; **to begin a.** bien commencer

auspiciousness [ɔː'spɪʃəsnɪs] **N** *(of begin-ning)* aspect *m* prometteur; **the a. of this omen** cet heureux auspice

Aussie ['ɒzɪ] *Fam* **ADJ** australien
  N 1 Australien, -ienne **2** *Ling* anglais *m* australien

austere [ɒ'stɪər] **ADJ** *(life, style, person etc)* austère; *(home)* sans luxe, d'un goût sévère, austère

austerely [ɒ'stɪəlɪ] **ADV** austèrement, avec austérité; *(to live)* dans l'austérité, austère-ment; *(furnished)* sans luxe, de façon dépouillée

austerity [ɒ'sterɪtɪ] **N** *(of life, style, person, home etc)* austérité *f*
  ►►*Econ* **a. measures** mesures *fpl* d'austérité

Australasia [ɒstrə'leɪʒə, -'leɪʃə] **N** Australa-sie *f*

Australasian [ɒstrə'leɪʒən, -'leɪʃən] **ADJ** australasien
  N Australasien, -ienne

Australia [ɒ'streɪlɪə] **N** Australie *f*

Australian [ɒ'streɪlɪən] **ADJ** australien
  N 1 Australien, -ienne **2** *Ling* anglais *m* australien

Austria ['ɒstrɪə] **N** Autriche *f*

Austria-Hungary **N** *Hist* Autriche-Hon-grie *f*

Austrian ['ɒstrɪən] **ADJ** autrichien
  N Autrichien, -ienne

Austro-Hungarian ['ɒstrəʊ-] **ADJ** *Hist* aus-tro-hongrois; **the A. Empire** l'empire *m* d'Au-triche-Hongrie

autarchy ['ɔːtɑːkɪ] **N** autarchie *f*

autarky ['ɔːtɑːkɪ] **N** autarcie *f*

auteur [əʊ'tɜːr] **N** *Cin* auteur *m*

authentic [ɔː'θentɪk] **ADJ** *(document, fact, story etc)* authentique

authentically [ɔː'θentɪklɪ] **ADV** authen-tiquement

authenticate [ɔː'θentɪkeɪt] **VT 1** *(prove genuine), Law* authentifier **2** *Mil, Radio (cor-respondent)* identifier

authenticity [ɔːθen'tɪsɪtɪ] **N** authenticité *f*

author ['ɔːθər] **N** *(of book, plan etc)* auteur *m*; **to be an a.** être écrivain; *Lit* **to be the a. of one's own misfortunes** être l'artisan de ses malheurs; *Typ* **a.'s correction** correction *f* d'auteur

authoress [ɔː'θə'res] **N** *Old-fashioned* femme *f* auteur, écrivain *m*

authoritarian [ɔːθɒrɪ'teərɪən] **ADJ, N** auto-ritaire *mf*

> Attention: ne pas confondre avec **authoritative**.

authoritative [ɔː'θɒrɪtətɪv] **ADJ** *(statement, book, document etc)* qui fait autorité; **to have sth from an a. source** avoir qch de source autorisée *ou* de bonne source

> Attention: ne pas confondre avec **authoritarian**.

authoritatively [ɔː'θɒrɪtətɪvlɪ] **ADV 1** *(commandingly)* autoritairement; *(to look)* d'un air autoritaire **2 I can state a. that …** je puis affirmer de source sûre que …

authority [ɔː'θɒrɪtɪ] **N 1** *(power)* autorité *f*; **those in a.** les autorités; **in a position of a.** en position d'autorité; **to be in** *or* **have** *or* **exer-cise a. over sb** *(officially)* avoir *ou* exercer une autorité sur qn; *(have power)* avoir de l'ascendant sur qn; **an air of a.** un air auto-ritaire
  2 *(authorization)* autorisation *f*, mandat *m*; **to have a. to act** avoir qualité pour agir; **to give sb a. to do sth** autoriser qn à faire qch; **they had the full a. of the law** ils ont agi avec la pleine autorité de la loi; **to act on sb's a.** agir sur l'autorité de qn; **to do sth on one's own a.** faire qch de sa propre autorité; **on what a./on whose a. did they search the house?** avec quelle autorisation/avec l'au-torisation de qui ont-ils perquisitionné la maison?
  3 *(of person, book)* **to be an a.** être expert dans la matière; **to be an a. on sth** faire au-torité en matière de qch; **to have sth on good a.** tenir *ou* savoir qch de bonne part *ou* de bonne source *ou* de source autorisée; **to quote sb as one's a.** se réclamer de qn; **to quote one's authorities** citer ses sources *ou*

ses auteurs; **she spoke with a.** elle a parlé avec autorité

4 *Admin* **the authorities** les autorités *fpl*; *(government)* l'administration *f*; **the health authorities** les services *mpl* de santé; **the military authorities** les autorités militaires

authorization [ɔ:θərаɪˈzeɪʃən] N autorisation *f* (**to do sth** de faire qch); *(given to official)* pouvoir *m*, mandat *m*; **to give sb/to be given a. to do sth** donner à qn/recevoir l'autorisation de faire qch

authorize [ˈɔ:θəraɪz] VT *(person, thing)* autoriser (**to do sth** à faire qch); **to be authorized to act on sb's behalf** avoir qualité pour agir au nom de qn; **to a. a payment** ordonnancer un paiement; **to a. a price** homologuer un prix

authorized [ˈɔ:θəraɪzd] ADJ autorisé; *(supplier etc)* agréé; *Mil etc* réglementaire; **a. to sign** habilité à signer
▸▸*Com* **a. agent** mandataire *mf*, agent *m* mandataire; *Fin* **a. capital** capital *m* autorisé *ou* social *ou* nominal; *Admin* **a. charges** prix *mpl* homologués; **a. distributor** distributeur *m* agréé; *Banking* **a. overdraft facility** autorisation *f* de découvert; *Com* **a. representative** mandataire, agent mandataire; *St Exch* **a. share capital** capital autorisé; **a. signatory** signataire *mf* autorisé(e) *ou* accrédité(e); *Rel* **the A. Version** = la traduction anglaise de la Bible de 1611

authorship [ˈɔ:θəʃɪp] N *(of book, plan etc)* paternité *f*; **to establish the a. of a book** identifier l'auteur d'un livre; **a manuscript of unknown a.** un manuscrit d'un auteur anonyme

autism [ˈɔ:tɪz(ə)m] N *Med* autisme *m*

autistic [ɔ:ˈtɪstɪk] *Med* ADJ autistique, autiste
N autiste *mf*

auto [ˈɔ:təʊ] N *Am Fam* auto(mobile) *f*, voiture *f*; **a. accident** accident *m* de voiture

auto- [ˈɔ:təʊ] PREF auto-

auto-addresser [-ədresər] N *(on laser printer)* adressage *m* automatique

auto-answer N *Comput (in datacomms)* réponse *f* automatique

auto-antigen [-ˈæntɪdʒən] N *Med* auto-antigène *m*

autobank [ˈɔ:təʊbæŋk] N distributeur *m* automatique de billets

autobiographic(al) [ɔ:təʊbaɪəˈgræfɪk, -ɪk(ə)l] ADJ autobiographique

autobiography [ɔ:təʊbaɪˈɒgrəfɪ] N autobiographie *f*

autocade [ˈɔ:təʊkeɪd] N *Am* cortège *m* de voitures

autocorrect [ˈɔ:təʊkərekt] VT *Comput* corriger automatiquement

autocracy [ɔ:ˈtɒkrəsɪ] N autocratie *f*

autocrat [ˈɔ:təkræt] N autocrate *m*

autocratic(al) [ɔ:təˈkrætɪk, -ɪk(ə)l] ADJ *(government, policies)* autocratique; *(person)* autocrate; *(character)* absolu

autocratically [ɔ:təˈkrætɪklɪ] ADV autocratiquement

autocue [ˈɔ:təʊkju:] N *TV* téléprompteur *m*

autodial [ˈɔ:təʊdaɪəl] N numérotation *f* automatique

autodialler [ˈɔ:təʊdaɪələr] N numéroteur *m* automatique

autodidact [ˈɔ:təʊˈdaɪdækt] N *Fml* autodidacte *mf*

auto-dissolve N *TV, Cin* fondu *m* enchaîné automatique

autoerotic [ˈɔ:təʊɪˈrɒtɪk] ADJ autoérotique

autoexec. bat [ɔ:təʊeksekˈbæt] N *Comput* **a. (file)** fichier *m* autoexec. bat

autofocus [ˈɔ:təʊfəʊkəs] N *Phot* autofocus

m; **a. camera, camera with a.** appareil *m* autofocus

autogenous [ɔ:ˈtɒdʒɪnəs] ADJ *Biol, Metal* autogène

autogiro [ɔ:təʊˈdʒaɪrəʊ] N *Aviat* autogyre *m*

autograft [ˈɔ:təgrɑ:ft] N *Med* autogreffe *f*

autograph [ˈɔ:təgrɑ:f] N autographe *m*
VT *(book, photo, programme etc)* signer, dédicacer
▸▸**a. album** album *m* de signatures; **a. collector, a. hunter** collectionneur, -euse d'autographes

autogyro [ɔ:təʊˈdʒaɪrəʊ] = **autogiro**

auto-ignition N auto-allumage *m*

autoload [ˈɔ:təʊləʊd] VI *Comput* se charger automatiquement

automat [ˈɔ:təmæt] N *Am Old-fashioned* cafétéria *f* à distributeurs automatiques

automatable [ˈɔ:təmeɪtəb(ə)l] ADJ automatisable

automate [ˈɔ:təmeɪt] VT automatiser

automated [ˈɔ:təmeɪtɪd] ADJ automatisé
▸▸*Banking* **a. clearing house** chambre *f* de compensation automatisée; **a. reservation** réservation *f* télématique; *Banking* **a. teller machine** distributeur *m* automatique (de billets); **a. ticket** billet *m* informatisé; *Banking* **a. withdrawal** retrait *m* automatique

automatic [ɔ:təˈmætɪk] ADJ **1** automatique; **fully a.** entièrement automatique **2** *(movement)* automatique, inconscient, machinal, -aux
N **1** *Aut* (voiture *f*) automatique *f*; **a Renault®** **a.** une Renault® (avec boîte de vitesses) automatique **2** *(pistol)* automatique *m*
▸▸*Comput* **a. backup** sauvegarde *f* automatique; *Comput* **a. data processing** traitement *m* automatique des données; *Tel* **a. dialling** composition *f* automatique de numéros; *Comput* **a. feed** avance *f* automatique; *Radio, Elec* **a. gain control** antifading *m*; *Comput* **a. line break** coupure *f* automatique de fin de ligne; *Comput* **a. pagination** séparation *f* automatique des pages; *Aviat* **a. pilot** pilote *m* automatique; *Fig* **to do sth on a. pilot** faire qch mécaniquement *ou* machinalement; **a. pistol** pistolet *m* automatique, automatique; **a. search** *(on cassette player)* recherche *f* automatique (de séquences musicales); **a. ticket distributor** distributeur *m* automatique de titres de transport; **a. ticket machine** billetterie *f* automatique; *Banking* **a. transfer** virement *m* automatique; *Aut* **a. transmission** transmission *f* automatique; *Radio, Elec* **a. volume control** antifading

automatically [ɔ:təˈmætɪklɪ] ADV **1** automatiquement; **a. renewable** renouvelable automatiquement **2** *(without thinking)* sans réfléchir, automatiquement

automation [ɔ:təˈmeɪʃən] N automatisation *f*

automatization [ɔ:tɒmətaɪˈzeɪʃən] N automatisation *f*

automaton, *pl* **automatons, automata** [ɔ:ˈtɒmətən, -ɒnz, -ə] N automate *m*

automobile [ˈɔ:təməʊbi:l] N *Am* automobile *f*, voiture *f*
▸▸**A. Association** = société *f* de dépannage pour les automobilistes, ≃ Touring Club *m* de France; **a. club** club *m* automobile; **the a. industry** l'industrie *f* automobile; **a. manufacture** fabrication *f* d'automobiles; **a. workers** ouvriers *mpl* de l'industrie automobile

automotive [ˈɔ:təˈməʊtɪv] ADJ **1** *(self-propelled)* automoteur, -trice **2** *Aut* automobile
▸▸*Am* **a. engineering** technique *f* automobile; **a. parts** pièces *fpl* d'automobile

autonomous [ɔ:ˈtɒnəməs] ADJ autonome

autonomy [ɔ:ˈtɒnəmɪ] N autonomie *f*

autopilot [ˈɔ:təʊpaɪlət] N *Aviat* pilotage *m* automatique; **to be on a.** *(of aircraft)*, *Fig (person)* être en pilotage automatique

autopsy [ˈɔ:tɒpsɪ] N autopsie *f*; **to carry out an a.** faire une autopsie; *esp Pol, Fig* faire une analyse
VT autopsier

auto-redial N renumérotation *f* automatique

auto-refresh N *Comput* autorafraîchissement *m*

autoresponder [ɔ:təʊrɪˈspɒndər] N *Comput* fonction *f* de réponse automatique

autoreverse [ɔ:təʊrɪˈvɜ:s] N autoreverse *m*, inversion *f* automatique du sens de défilement

autosave [ˈɔ:təʊseɪv] N *Comput* sauvegarde *f* automatique

autosome [ˈɔ:təsəʊm] N *(in genetics)* chromosome *m* somatique

autostart [ˈɔ:təʊstɑ:t] N *Comput* démarrage *m* automatique

autosuggestion [ɔ:təʊsəˈdʒestʃən] N *Psy* autosuggestion *f*

autoswitch [ˈɔ:təʊswɪtʃ] N *Comput* commutateur *m* automatique

autowinder [ˈɔ:təʊwaɪndər] N *Phot* avance *f* automatique du film

autumn [ˈɔ:təm] N automne *m*; **in a.** en automne; **a. colours** couleurs *fpl* automnales *ou* de l'automne; **a. leaves** feuilles *fpl* d'automne; **a. plants** plantes *fpl* automnales; **a. evening** une soirée d'automne; *Lit* **he was in the a. of his years** il était à l'automne de sa vie VOIR GRAMMAIRE A81; B61
▸▸*Bot* **a. crocus** safran *m* cultivé

autumnal [ɔ:ˈtʌmn(ə)l] ADJ automnal, -aux, d'automne; **there was an a. feeling in the air, it was a.** il y avait de l'automne dans l'air; **a. shades** teintes *fpl* automnales
▸▸*Astron* **a. equinox** équinoxe *m* d'automne

auxiliary [ɔ:gˈzɪlɪərɪ, -zɪlərɪ] ADJ *(staff, troops etc)* auxiliaire; *(machine etc)* auxiliaire, de secours; *(heating, lighting)* d'appoint VOIR GRAMMAIRE A38–9; A57–61; B26–8; B39–40
N auxiliaire *mf*; *Gram* (verbe *m*) auxiliaire *m*; *Mil* **auxiliaries** (troupes *fpl*) auxiliaires *mpl*; **nursing a.** infirmier, -ière auxiliaire
▸▸*Aut* **a. driving lamps** feux *mpl* facultatifs; *Gram* **a. verb** (verbe) auxiliaire VOIR GRAMMAIRE A38–9; A57–61; B26–8; B39–40

AV [eɪˈvi:] **1** *(abbr* **Authorized Version)** = traduction *f* anglaise de la Bible de 1611 **2** *(abbr* **audiovisual)** audiovisuel

Av *(abbr* **avenue)** av.

avail [əˈveɪl] N of no a., without a. sans effet; **to be of little a.** être peu utile *ou* peu avantageux; **to no a.** sans résultat; **to work to little** *or* **no a.** travailler sans (grand) résultat; **their efforts were all to no a.** leurs efforts n'ont produit aucun résultat
VT **to a. oneself of sth** *(of guidebook, map)* se servir *ou* s'aider de qch; *(of offer)* profiter de qch; *(of right)* user *ou* faire usage de qch; *(of sb's services)* faire appel à qch; **to a. oneself of the opportunity to do sth** saisir l'occasion de faire qch
VI *Lit* **nothing availed against the storm** contre la tempête nous ne pouvions/il ne pouvait/*etc* rien

availability [əveɪləˈbɪlɪtɪ] N *(of materials, people etc)* disponibilité *f*; **offer subject to a.** dans la limite des stocks disponibles; *(of tickets)* dans la limite des places disponibles

available [əˈveɪləb(ə)l] ADJ *(worker, room, theatre seat etc)* disponible; **they used the time a. to evacuate the area** ils ont utilisé le temps dont ils disposaient pour évacuer le secteur; **capital that can be made a.** capitaux *mpl* mobilisables; **a. to download from our web site** peut être téléchargé à partir de notre site Web; **a. on CD-ROM/DVD** existe en CD-ROM/DVD; **a. for work** disponible; **when are you a. to start work?** à partir de quand pouvez-vous commencer à travailler?; **a. for delivery** livraison immédiate; *Com* **a. in all bookshops** en vente *ou* disponible chez tous les libraires; *Com* **also a. in white** existe également en blanc; *Com* **we regret that this offer is no longer a.** nous avons le regret de vous annoncer que cette offre n'est plus valable; **drugs are readily a. in the town** on se procure facilement de la drogue dans cette ville; **legal aid should be a. to everyone** l'assistance juridique devrait être accessible à tous; **I'm catching the first a. flight** je prends le premier avion; **they're not readily a.** il est difficile de s'en procurer; **a. means** moyens *mpl* disponibles; **to try every a. means** essayer tous les moyens possibles

▸▸ *Fin* **a. assets** actif *m* disponible *ou* liquide; *Fin* **a. balance** solde *m* disponible; **a. bed capacity** capacité *f* d'accueil; *Fin* **a. capital** capitaux disponibles; *Fin* **a. cash flow** cash-flow *m* disponible; *Fin* **a. funds** fonds *mpl* liquides *ou* disponibles, disponibilités *fpl*; *Phot* **a. light** lumière *f* naturelle; *Mktg* **a. market** marché *m* effectif; *Comput* **a. memory** mémoire *f* disponible

aval [æ'væl] N *Banking* aval *m* bancaire

avalanche ['ævəlɑːntʃ] N *(of snow)*, *Fig (of congratulations, mail etc)* avalanche *f*; **an a. of tourists** une nuée de touristes

avalize ['ævəlaɪz] VT *Banking* avaliser

avant-garde [ævɒŋ'gɑːd] N avant-garde *f*, *pl* avant-gardes

ADJ d'avant-garde, avant-gardiste; **a. films** films *mpl* d'avant-garde

avarice ['ævərɪs] N cupidité *f*

avaricious [ævə'rɪʃəs] ADJ cupide

avariciously [ævə'rɪʃəslɪ] ADV *(to behave)* cupidement

avast [ə'vɑːst] INT *Naut Old-fashioned* tiens bon!, tenez bon!, baste!

AVC [eɪviː'siː] N *(abbr* **additional voluntary contribution***)* supplément *m* de cotisation retraite *(payé volontairement)*

Ave[1] ['ɑːvɪ] N

▸▸ **A. Maria** Ave (Maria) *m inv*

Ave[2] *(abbr* **avenue***)* av.

avenge [ə'vendʒ] VT *(person, crime)* venger; **to a. oneself for an insult/on sb** se venger d'une injure/de qn

avenger [ə'vendʒər] N vengeur *m*, vengeresse *f*

avenging [ə'vendʒɪŋ] ADJ *(angel etc)* vengeur, *f* vengeresse

avenue ['ævɪnjuː] N **1** allée *f*, *(with trees)* avenue *f*, *Fig* **to explore every a.** explorer toutes les voies; **this opens up another a. of investigation** ceci ouvre une nouvelle voie de recherche; **an a. to fame/wealth** un moyen de parvenir à la gloire/fortune **2** *(in street name)* avenue *f* **3** *esp Am (wide street)* boulevard *m*

aver [ə'vɜːr] VT *(-rr-)* *Lit* déclarer, affirmer *(***that** que)

average ['ævərɪdʒ] N **1** moyenne *f*; **on a.** en moyenne; **to work out the a.** établir la moyenne; **that gives an a. of 6** ça fait une moyenne de 6; **above (the) a.** au-dessus de la moyenne; **to spend an a. of £85 per week** dépenser en moyenne 85 livres par semaine

2 *(in marine insurance)* avarie(s) *f(pl)*
3 *St Exch* indice *m*

ADJ *(price, time, weight etc)* moyen; **the a. Englishman** l'Anglais *m* moyen; **of a. height**

de taille moyenne; **the food is better than a.** la nourriture est au-dessus de la moyenne; **no better than a.** pas si bien que ça; **far from a.** exceptionnel; **in an a. week** dans une semaine ordinaire; **how was your day? – a.** comment s'est passée ta journée? – moyen; *Fam* **a very a. singer** un chanteur de qualité très moyenne

VT **1** *(amount to on average)* **to a. 500** atteindre une moyenne de 500; **sales a. a thousand copies a year** la vente moyenne *ou* la moyenne des ventes est de mille exemplaires par an; **to a. eight hours' work a day** travailler en moyenne huit heures par jour; **to a. 85 kph** rouler en moyenne à 85 km/h; **household spending averages £120 per week** les dépenses des ménages sont de *ou* atteignent les 120 livres par semaine en moyenne

2 *(calculate average of) (results, sales etc)* calculer *ou* faire la moyenne de

▸▸ **a. adjuster** dispacheur *m*, expert-répartiteur *m*, *pl* experts-répartiteurs; **a. adjustment** dispache *f*; *Fin* **a. cost** coût *m* moyen; *Radio* **a. listening time** durée *f* d'écoute par auditeur, DEA *f*; *Fin* **a. revenue** produit *m* moyen; *Fin* **a. unit cost** coût moyen unitaire; *TV* **a. viewing time** durée d'écoute par téléspectateur, DET *f*; *Fin* **a. yield** rendement *m* moyen

▸ **average out** VT SEP *(calculate average of)* **I've averaged out how much I spend a week** j'ai calculé combien je dépense en moyenne par semaine

VI **how does it a. out per week?** combien ça fait en moyenne par semaine?; **it'll a. out over a month** sur un mois ça s'équilibrera

▸ **average out at** VT INSEP *(amount to as an average)* équivaloir en moyenne à; **what does it a. out at?** ça fait combien en moyenne?

averse [ə'vɜːs] ADJ opposé *(***to** à); **to be a. to sth** *(to task, job)* répugner à qch; *(to criticism, change etc)* détester qch; **to be a. to doing sth** répugner à faire qch; **why are you so a. to the idea of helping?** pourquoi l'idée d'apporter ton aide te répugne-t-elle tant?; **he is not a. to a glass of beer** il prend volontiers un verre de bière

> Attention: ne pas confondre avec le mot anglais **adverse**.

aversion [ə'vɜːʃən] N **1** *(feeling)* aversion *f*; **to feel** *or* **have an a. to sb** ressentir de l'aversion pour *ou* envers qn; **to feel** *or* **have a great a. to sth/to doing sth** avoir horreur *f* de qch/de faire qch **2** *(thing)* objet *m* d'aversion; **my pet a.** ma bête noire

avert [ə'vɜːt] VT **1** *(eyes, one's gaze, thoughts)* détourner *(***from** de) **2** *(suspicion, danger, misfortune)* écarter, éloigner, prévenir; *(catastrophe, accident, war)* éviter, parer à, conjurer; *(blow)* détourner

aviary ['eɪvɪərɪ] N volière *f*

aviation [eɪvɪ'eɪʃən] N aviation *f*; **a. history** histoire *f* de l'aviation

aviator ['eɪvɪeɪtər] N *Old-fashioned* aviateur, -trice

aviculture ['eɪvɪkʌltʃər] N aviculture *f*

avid ['ævɪd] ADJ passionné, fervent *(***for** de); **to be a. for sth** être avide de qch; **a. reader** lecteur, -trice passionné(e)

avidity [ə'vɪdɪtɪ] N avidité *f* *(***for** de, pour)

avidly ['ævɪdlɪ] ADV avidement, avec avidité

avionics [eɪvɪ'ɒnɪks] N avionique *f* VOIR GRAMMAIRE A10

avocado [ævə'kɑːdəʊ] N *(fruit)* avocat *m*; *(tree)* avocatier *m*

▸▸ **a. pear** avocat

Avogadro's number [ævəʊ'gædrəʊz] N *Chem* nombre *m* d'Avogadro

avoid [ə'vɔɪd] VT *(person, thing)* éviter; *(punishment etc)* se soustraire à; *(sb's attentions, blow, difficulty)* esquiver; *(truth, fact)* nier; **you've been avoiding me** tu m'évites; **to a. doing sth** éviter de faire qch; **I could not a. speaking to him** je ne pouvais faire autrement que de lui parler; **to a. (paying) tax** échapper à *ou* se soustraire à l'impôt; **to a. sb like the plague** fuir qn comme la peste; **to a. sth like the plague** éviter qch à tout prix; **he avoided doing his homework until the last possible minute** il a reculé le moment de faire ses devoirs jusqu'à la dernière minute; **the comparison is hard to a.** la comparaison est difficile à éviter; **to a. sb's eye** fuir le regard de qn; **to a. the issue** éviter *ou* contourner le problème; *Pej (be devious)* esquiver la question

avoidable [ə'vɔɪdəb(ə)l] ADJ évitable

▸▸ *Fin* **a. costs** coûts *mpl* évitables

avoidance [ə'vɔɪdəns] N **a. of taxes** évasion *f* fiscale; **a. of payment** non-paiement *m*

avoirdupois [ævədə'pɔɪz] N **1** poids *m* du commerce; **ounce a.** once *f* avoirdupois **2** *Hum (stoutness)* excès *m* de poids, embonpoint *m*

avow [ə'vaʊ] VT *Fml* **1** *(declare)* **to a. oneself a socialist** se déclarer socialiste **2** *(admit) (mistake)* avouer, admettre; **to a. oneself beaten** s'avouer vaincu

avowal [ə'vaʊəl] N déclaration *f*

avowed [ə'vaʊd] ADJ *(enemy, believer etc)* déclaré; **a. atheist** athée *mf* de son propre aveu

avowedly [ə'vaʊɪdlɪ] ADV de son propre aveu

avuncular [ə'vʌŋkjʊlər] ADJ paternel

AWACS ['eɪwæks] N *Mil (abbr* **Airborne Warning and Control System***)* AWACS *m*

await [ə'weɪt] VT *Lit* attendre; *Com* **awaiting your instructions** dans l'attente de vos instructions; **soldiers awaiting discharge** soldats en instance de libération; *Com* **parcel awaiting delivery** colis en souffrance; *Com* **awaiting collection** en souffrance; *Law* **to be awaiting trial** être en instance de jugement

awake [ə'weɪk] ADJ PRED éveillé; **to stay a.** rester éveillé; **he lay a. for hours worrying** l'inquiétude l'a tenu éveillé pendant des heures; **I was a.** je ne dormais pas; **drink some coffee, and that will keep you a.** bois du café, ça te tiendra éveillé; **that noise is keeping me a.** ce bruit m'empêche de dormir; **to be a. to** *(aware of) (possibility)* avoir conscience de; *(danger, fact etc)* se rendre compte de, avoir conscience de; *(careful of) (one's interests)* veiller à

VI *(pt* **awoke** [ə'wəʊk]; *pp* **awoken** [ə'wəʊkən]*)* s'éveiller, se réveiller; **to a. from a deep sleep** se réveiller d'un profond sommeil; **I awoke to the sound of birds singing** à mon réveil j'ai entendu chanter les oiseaux; *Fig* **to a. to** *(danger, fact etc)* se rendre compte de, prendre conscience de; *(possibility)* prendre conscience de; **to a. from** *(illusion, dream etc)* revenir de; *(trance, unconsciousness)* sortir de

VT *(person, sb's remorse)* éveiller, réveiller; *(curiosity, suspicions, interest)* éveiller; *(hope, passion)* faire naître; *Fig* **to a. sb to sth** faire prendre conscience de qch à qn

awaken [ə'weɪk(ə)n] VT & VI = **awake** VT & VI

awakening [ə'weɪk(ə)nɪŋ] N réveil *m*

award [ə'wɔːd] N **1** *(for writer, actor etc)* prix *m*; *Mil etc* distinction *f* honorifique; *Sch etc* récompense *f*; **to make/be given an a.** décerner/recevoir un prix/une récompense; **the annual awards ceremony** la cérémonie annuelle de remise des prix; **the Oscar**

awards ceremony la cérémonie de remise des Oscars **2** *Law (money)* dommages-intérêts *mpl*; *(decision)* décision *f* (arbitrale), adjudication *f*; *(of contract)* adjudication; **to make an a.** rendre un jugement (arbitral)

VT *(prize)* décerner, adjuger; *(medal)* décerner, remettre; *(contract)* adjuger; *(high office)* conférer; *(pay increase, grant, free kick)* accorder; **she was awarded first prize** on lui a décerné le premier prix; *Law* **to a. sb a sum as damages** allouer *ou* attribuer une somme à qn à titre de dommages-intérêts

award-winning ADJ *(film, book etc)* primé; *(writer, actor)* à qui on a décerné un prix; **his a. performance** son interprétation qui lui a valu un prix

aware [ə'weər] ADJ **1 to be a. of sth** *(fact)* avoir connaissance *ou* conscience de qch, être au courant de qch; **I wasn't a. of him** je ne m'étais pas aperçu qu'il était là; **I am a. of all the circumstances** je connais tous les détails; **I am well** *or* **fully a. that …** je n'ignore pas que …, j'ai pleinement conscience que …; **were you a. that your husband owed money?** saviez-vous que votre mari était endetté?; **not that I am a. of** pas que je sache; **as far as I'm a.** autant que je sache; **to become a. of** *(fact)* prendre connaissance de; **I became a. of a smell of burning/a presence** j'ai senti une odeur de brûlé/une présence **2** *(well-informed)* **socially/environmentally a.** au courant *ou* informé des questions sociales/de l'environnement; **politically a.** politisé

awareness [ə'weənɪs] N *(of something)* conscience *f*; **he has little a. of the situation** il n'a guère conscience de la situation
▶▶ *Mktg* **a. rating** taux *m* de notoriété; *Mktg* **a. study** étude *f* de notoriété

awash [ə'wɒʃ] ADJ **1** *Naut (of submarine etc)* à fleur d'eau; **rocks a. at high tide** roches couvertes d'eau à marée haute **2** *(flooded)* inondé; *Fig* **to be a. with money** crouler sous l'argent; **his desk was a. with complaints** son bureau croulait sous les lettres de réclamation

AWAY [ə'weɪ] ADV **1** *(in opposite direction)* **to turn (one's face) a. from sth** détourner la tête de qch; **to look a.** détourner son regard; **the signpost pointed a. from the village** le bras du poteau indiquait une direction opposée à celle du village; **to go a.** partir, s'en aller; **to walk/drive a.** partir (à pied/en voiture); **to run/fly a.** s'enfuir/s'envoler **2** *(at a distance)* **far a.** dans le lointain, au loin; **a. in the distance** tout au loin; **the town is five miles a.** la ville est à (une distance de) cinq mil(l)es; **it's less than five minutes' walk a.** c'est à moins de cinq minutes à pied; **the church was set a. from the road** l'église était située en retrait par rapport à la route; **to hold sth a. from sth** tenir qch éloigné *ou* loin de qch **3** *(absent)* **a. from home** absent (de chez soi); **he is a.** *(from home, school etc)* il est absent; **she is a. on business** elle s'est absentée pour affaires; *Sport* **to play a.** jouer à l'extérieur **4** *(disappearance)* **to melt a.** *(of snow)* fondre; **to boil a.** s'évaporer; **to fade** *or* **die a.** *(of sound)* s'éteindre; *(of protests)* se taire; **to fritter a.** *(one's money, time)* gaspiller; **put that knife a.!** range ce couteau! **5** *(continuity)* **to work a.** travailler beaucoup *ou* *(stronger)* sans relâche; **he was coughing a.** il toussait beaucoup; **to laugh/hoot a.** ne pas s'arrêter de rire/klaxonner **6** *(elliptical)* **a. with you!** *(don't be silly)* arrête!; *esp Arch, Lit* **a. with him!** emmenez-le!; *Arch, Lit* **we must a.** il nous faut partir **7** *(in motion)* **and they're a.!** *(at beginning of* race etc*)* et ils sont partis!; *Fam* **a couple of drinks and he's a.** *(talking, doing sth)* deux verres et il est parti; *Fam* **well a.** *(progressing)* bien en train; *(drunk)* soûl **8** *(without delay)* **to do sth right** *or* **straight a.** faire qch tout de suite *ou* sur-le-champ **9** *(time)* **I knew him a. back in 1980** je l'ai connu dès 1980; **that was a. back** c'était il y a longtemps; **it's two weeks a.** c'est dans deux semaines; **Christmas is only two weeks a.** il n'y a que deux semaines jusqu'à Noël, nous ne sommes qu'à deux semaines de Noël
▶▶ *Sport* **a. game** match *m* à l'extérieur; *Sport* **a. ground** terrain *m* adverse; *Sport* **a. match** match *m* à l'extérieur; *Sport* **the a. team** l'équipe *f* qui joue à l'extérieur, les visiteurs *mpl*

AWB [eɪdʌb(ə)lju:'bi:] N *Com (abbr* **air way-bill)** LTA *f*

awe [ɔ:] N *(fear)* crainte *f*; *(respect)* respect *m*, révérence *f*; **to strike sb with a.** *(of person)* imposer à qn un respect mêlé de crainte; *(of object, phenomenon)* faire une forte impression à qn; **to be in a. of sb/sth, to hold sb/sth in a.** *(fear)* craindre *ou* redouter qn/qch; *(respect)* avoir une crainte respectueuse de qn/qch
VT *Fml (frighten)* remplir de crainte; *(make respect)* intimider, impressionner; **the children were awed by the cathedral/the tone of her voice** les enfants ont été terriblement impressionnés par la cathédrale/le ton de sa voix; **they were awed into silence** ils tombèrent dans un silence respectueux

aweigh [ə'weɪ] ADV *Naut* **with anchor a.** l'ancre dérapée; **anchors a.!** levez l'ancre!

awe-inspiring ADJ imposant, impressionnant

awesome ['ɔ:səm] ADJ **1** *(awe-inspiring)* *(height, strength)* imposant, impressionnant; *(responsibility, task)* imposant; *(prospect)* effrayant; **the a. silence of the desert** le silence imposant du désert **2** *Am Fam (wonderful)* super

awe-struck, awe-stricken ADJ *(frightened)* terrifié; *(respectful)* intimidé, impressionné; **to be a. by sb/sth** être terriblement impressionné par qn/qch

awful ['ɔ:fʊl] ADJ **1** horrible, effroyable; **to die an a. death** mourir d'une mort horrible; **that's the a. part of it** c'est cela le plus terrible; **an a. silence** un silence effroyable **2** *Fam (very bad)* horrible, affreux, abominable; **it's simply a.** c'est affreux *ou* horrible; **she's an a. woman** c'est une femme épouvantable; **what a. weather!** quel temps abominable!; **he's an a. fool** il est bien bête; **an a. lot of people** énormément de gens; **I don't care an a. lot** ça ne me fait pas grand-chose
ADV *Fam* terriblement; **I'm a. glad to see you** je suis rudement content de vous voir; **an a. long time** terriblement longtemps

awfully ['ɔ:flɪ] ADV **1** terriblement, effroyablement **2** *Fam (very)* énormément; **a. funny** amusant *ou* drôle comme tout; **I'm a. sorry** je regrette infiniment *ou* énormément; **I'm a. glad** je suis rudement content; *esp Old-fashioned* **thanks a.!** merci mille fois!; **he's an a. good player** il joue affreusement *ou* terriblement bien; *Fam Hum* **a. a.** = maniérisme *m* utilisé pour décrire les manières et l'accent de la haute bourgeoisie britannique

awfulness ['ɔ:fʊlnɪs] N **1** *(of situation)* horreur *f* **2** *Fam* **the a. of the weather/this place** le temps/cet endroit abominable

awhile [ə'waɪl] ADV *Am, Lit* un moment, un peu

awkward ['ɔ:kwəd] ADJ **1** *(clumsy)* *(move-* ment, person*)* gauche, maladroit, balourd; *(sentence etc)* maladroit; **to be a. with one's hands** ne pas être habile de ses mains **2** *(embarrassed)* embarrassé, gêné **3** *(embarrassing)* embarrassant; **it would be a. if we met** une rencontre serait embarrassante; **an a. silence** un silence gêné; **to arrive at an a. moment** arriver mal à propos; **to ask a. questions** poser des questions embarrassantes **4** *(difficult, not straightforward)* incommode, peu commode; *(tool)* peu maniable; *(bend)* difficile, dangereux; **the switch is in an a. place** l'interrupteur est situé à un endroit peu accessible; **their house is a. to get to** leur maison est d'un accès difficile; **I'm sorry to be a.** *(but that doesn't suit me)* je suis désolé d'être peu accommodant; **they're just trying to be a.** ils font ça pour compliquer les choses; **the a. age** l'âge *m* ingrat; *Fam* **he's an a. customer** c'est un type difficile, il n'est pas commode

awkwardly ['ɔ:kwədlɪ] ADV **1** *(clumsily)* gauchement, maladroitement; **to put sth a.** mal tourner qch, dire qch d'une façon maladroite **2** *(showing embarrassment)* d'une manière embarrassée; *(to speak)* d'un ton embarrassé *ou* gêné **3** *(causing embarrassment)* d'une façon embarrassante **4** *(inconveniently)* **the lever is a. placed** le levier est mal placé; **their house is a. situated** leur maison est mal située

awkwardness ['ɔ:kwədnɪs] N **1** *(clumsiness)* gaucherie *f*, maladresse *f*; *(lack of grace)* balourdise *f* **2** *(embarrassment)* embarras *m*, gêne *f*; **a moment of a.** un moment de gêne **3** *(inconvenience)* *(of situation etc)* difficulté *f*, incommodité *f*

awl [ɔ:l] N alêne *f*, poinçon *m*, perçoir *m*

awn [ɔ:n] N *Bot (of barley etc)* barbe *f*

awning ['ɔ:nɪŋ] N *(of shop etc)* store *m*, banne *f*; *(of cart)* bâche *f*; *(of theatre, hotel etc)* marquise *f*; *Naut* tente *f*, tendelet *m*; *(on deck of boat)* cabane *f*; **rain a.** taud *m*, taude *f*
▶▶ **a. blind** store à l'italienne; **a. deck** pont-abri *m*, *pl* ponts-abris

AWOL ['eɪwɒl] ADJ *Mil Fam (abbr* **absent without leave) to go A.** s'absenter sans permission; **to have gone A.** être absent sans permission

awry [ə'raɪ] ADV, ADJ de travers, de guingois; **to go all a.** *(of plans etc)* aller tout de travers; **services were thrown a. by the strike** les services ont été perturbés par la grève

axe, *Am* **ax,** *pl* **axes** [æks, 'æksɪz] N **1** hache *f*; **ice a.** piolet *m*; *Fig* **to have an a. to grind** agir dans un but intéressé **2** *Fam* **to get the a.** *(of project etc)* être abandonné; *(of employee etc)* être mis à la porte; *(of department etc)* être supprimé; **500 threatened with a.** *(newspaper headline)* 500 personnes menacées de chômage **3** *Mus Sl (guitar)* gratte *f*, râpe *f*
VT *Fam (person, worker)* renvoyer, mettre à la porte; *(project)* abandonner (pour des raisons d'économie); *(job)* supprimer; **to a. public expenditure** tailler dans les dépenses publiques
▶▶ **a. handle** manche *m* de hache; **a. head** fer *m* de hache

axial ['æksɪəl] ADJ *Geom* axial, -aux

axil ['æksɪl] N *Bot (of leaf)* aisselle *f*

axiom ['æksɪəm] N axiome *m*

axiomatic [æksɪə'mætɪk] ADJ **1** axiomatique **2** *(self-evident)* évident

axis, *pl* **axes** ['æksɪs, 'æksiːz] N **1** *Geom, Geol etc (of sphere, plant, crystal)* axe *m*; **a. of the**

earth axe de la terre; **a. of revolution** axe de révolution **2** *Anat (of neck)* axis *m* **3** *Hist* **the A.** l'Axe *m*

axle [ˈæks(ə)l] **N 1** *(of vehicle)* essieu *m*; *Rail* **driving a.** essieu moteur; *Aut* **front/rear a.** essieu *ou* pont *m* avant/arrière **2** *(of wheel)* tourillon *m*, arbre *m*, axe *m*
▸▸ **a. box** boîte *f* de l'essieu; **a. shaft** arbre *m* d'essieu; **a. tramp** rebond *m* de l'essieu; **a. tree** essieu

ay(e) [aɪ] **INT** *esp Scot* oui, mais oui; *Naut*

a. a., sir! oui, commandant/lieutenant/*etc*! **N** *(in voting)* ayes and noes voix *fpl* pour et contre; **the ayes have it** les voix pour l'emportent

azalea [əˈzeɪlɪə] **N** *(plant)* azalée *f*

Azerbaijan [æzəbaɪˈdʒɑːn] **N** Azerbaïdjan *m*

Azerbaijani [æzəbaɪˈdʒɑːnɪ], **Azeri** [əˈzeərɪ] **ADJ** azerbaïdjanais, azéri
N Azerbaïdjanais, -aise, Azéri, -ie

AZERTY keyboard [əˈzɜːtɪ-] **N** clavier *m* AZERTY

azimuth [ˈæzɪməθ] **N** *Astron etc* azimut *m*

Azores (the) [ðəəˈzɔːz] **NPL** les Açores *fpl*

AZT [eɪzedˈtiː] **N** *Pharm (abbr* **azidothymidine***)* AZT *m*

Aztec [ˈæztek] *Hist* **ADJ** aztèque
N 1 Aztèque *mf* **2** *Ling* aztèque *m*

azure [ˈæʒər, ˈeɪʒər] **N** *Her, Lit* azur *m*
ADJ d'azur, azuré

B, b¹ [biː] N **1** *(letter)* B, b *m*; **two b's** deux b; **51B** *(house number)* 51 ter; *Mil* **B company** deuxième compagnie *f* **2** *Mus* si *m*; **in B flat** en si bémol **3** *Sch (grade)* **to get a B** avoir une bonne note, ≃ avoir 14 ou 15 sur 20 **4** *Med* **B cell** lymphocyte *m* B
▸▸ *Br* **B road** route *f* secondaire; **B side** *(of record)* face *f* B

b² *(abbr* **born)** né

BA [biːˈeɪ] N *Univ (abbr* **Bachelor of Arts) to have a BA in history** ≃ avoir une licence en histoire; **John Smith, BA** ≃ John Smith, licencié ès lettres/en droit/*etc*

baa [baː] N bêlement *m*; **b.!** bêê!; **b.-lamb** *(in children's language)* petit agneau *m*
VI (**baaed, baa'd** [baːd]) bêler

baba [ˈbaːbaː] N *Culin* **rum b.** baba *m* au rhum

babble [ˈbæb(ə)l] N **1** *(incoherence)* brouhaha *m*; **the b. of voices coming from downstairs** le brouhaha qui parvenait d'en bas; **his speech was full of the usual b. about ...** son discours était le verbiage habituel sur … **2** *(of stream)* murmure *m*
VI **1** *(tell secrets)* bavarder, jaser **2** *(chatter incoherently) (of baby)* babiller, gazouiller; *(of adult)* bafouiller **3** *(of stream)* murmurer, gazouiller
▸ **babble away, babble on** VI bavarder, papoter; **you were babbling away in your sleep last night** tu n'as pas arrêté de bredouiller des choses incompréhensibles dans ton sommeil cette nuit; **what are you babbling on about?** qu'est-ce que tu bafouilles encore?

babbler [ˈbæblər] N **1** *(who tells secrets)* bavard, -arde **2** *(incoherent talker)* **she's a b.** elle bafouille

babbling [ˈbæb(ə)lɪŋ] ADJ **1** *(incoherent)* bafouilleur; **I felt like a b. idiot** j'avais l'impression que je racontais n'importe quoi **2** *(stream)* murmurant
N = **babble** N

babe [beɪb] N **1** *Lit* petit enfant *m*, bambin *m*; **a b. in arms** un bébé; *Fig* un naïf, une naïve; **his mother died when he was still a b. in arms** il était encore au berceau quand sa mère mourut **2** *Fam (attractive woman)* canon *m*; **hi, b.!** salut, poupée!

Babel [ˈbeɪb(ə)l] N **the Tower of B.** la Tour de Babel; *Fig* **b. of voices** brouhaha *m*

baboon [bəˈbuːn] N *(animal)* babouin *m*; *Fig* singe *m*

baby [ˈbeɪbɪ] N **1** bébé *m*; **when I was a b.** quand j'étais bébé; **b. brother/sister** petit frère/petite sœur; **a b. boy/girl** un petit garçon/une petite fille; **b. carrots/aubergines** carottes *fpl*/aubergines *fpl* naines; **b. elephant/chimpanzee** bébé éléphant/chimpanzé; **the b. of the family** le benjamin; **you're such a b.!** tu es un vrai bébé!; **don't be such a b.** arrête de faire le bébé; **I'm not**

a b.! je ne suis plus un bébé!; **my b. pictures** *(of me)* des photos de moi bébé; *Fig* **to throw the b. out with the bath water** jeter le bébé avec l'eau du bain; *Fig* **to leave sb holding the b.** refiler le bébé à qn; *Fig* **the dictionary is his b.** le dictionnaire est son bébé
2 *Am Fam (girlfriend)* jeune fille *f*, nana *f*; *(boyfriend)* mec *m*; *(as form of address)* chéri, -ie; *(thing)* machin *m*; *(machine)* merveille *f*
VT (**babied**) *(person) Pej (treat as baby)* materner; *(give love and attention to)* dorloter
▸▸ **b. boom** baby boom *m*; **b. boomer** enfant *m* du baby boom; **b.'s breath** *(flower)* gypsophile *f*, *Am* **B. Buggy®** landau *m*, voiture *f* d'enfant; *Am* **b. carriage** voiture d'enfant, landau; *Mus* **b. grand** *(piano m)* demi-queue *m*, *pl* demi-queues; **b. scales** pèse-bébé *m*, *pl* pèse-bébés; *Aut* **b. seat** siège *m* auto pour bébé, siège enfant; **b. snatcher** kidnappeur, -euse; **b. snatching** enlèvement *m* ou rapt *m* d'enfant, kidnapping *m*; **b. talk** langage *m* enfantin ou de bébé; **b. tooth** dent *f* de lait

baby-changing area N nurserie *f*, point-bébé *m*

baby-face N visage *m* poupin; **he's a real b.** il a le visage poupin

baby-faced [-feɪst] ADJ au visage poupin

Babygro® [ˈbeɪbɪɡrəʊ] N grenouillère *f*

babyhood [ˈbeɪbɪhʊd] N petite enfance *f*

babyish [ˈbeɪbɪɪʃ] ADJ *Pej* de bébé

baby-listening service N service *m* de surveillance à distance des bébés, service babyphone

Babylon [ˈbæbɪlɒn] N *Antiq* Babylone *f*

Babylonia [bæbɪˈləʊnɪə] N *Antiq* Babylonie *f*

Babylonian [bæbɪˈləʊnɪən] *Antiq* ADJ babylonien
N Babylonien, -ienne

baby-minder N nourrice *f*

babyproof [ˈbeɪbɪpruːf] VT *(house, room)* sécuriser *(pour éviter qu'un bébé ne se blesse)*

baby-sit VI (**-sat, -sitting**) faire du baby-sitting, garder des/les enfants

baby-sitter N baby-sitter *mf*, *pl* baby-sitters, *Can* gardienne *f*

baby-sitting N baby-sitting *m*, garde *f* d'enfants

baby-walker N trotteur *m*

baccalaureate [bækəˈlɔːrɪət] N *Univ Am* ≃ licence *f*, *Can* baccalauréat *m*

baccara(t) [ˈbækəraː] N *Cards* baccara *m*; **to play b.** jouer au baccara

bacchanal [ˈbækən(ə)l] *Lit* ADJ bachique
N *(orgy)* bacchanale *f*, débauche *f* bachique

bacchanalia [bækəˈneɪlɪə] NPL *Lit* bacchanales *fpl*

bacchanalian [bækəˈneɪlɪən] ADJ *Lit* bachique

baccy [ˈbækɪ] N *Old-fashioned Fam* tabac *m*

bachelor [ˈbætʃələr] N **1** célibataire *m*; **b. uncle** oncle *m* non marié **2** *Univ* ≃ licencié, -ée; *Fam* **b.'s** ≃ licence *f*; **to have a b.'s (degree) in French** ≃ avoir une licence de français; *Univ* **B. of Arts** *(person)* ≃ titulaire *mf* d'une licence de lettres; *(qualification)* licence de lettres; **B. of Laws** ≃ licencié, -ée en droit *Univ* **B. of Science** *(person)* = titulaire d'une licence de sciences; *(qualification)* licence de sciences **3** *Hist* bachelier *m* *(aspirant à la chevalerie)*; **knight b.** chevalier *m*
▸▸ *Univ* **b.'s degree** ≃ licence; **b. flat** garçonnière *f*, **b. girl** célibataire *f*

bachelorhood [ˈbætʃələhʊd], **bachelordom** [ˈbætʃələdəm] N célibat *m*, vie *f* de garçon

bacillary [bəˈsɪlərɪ] ADJ *Biol* bacillaire

bacillus, *pl* **bacilli** [bəˈsɪləs, -aɪ] N *Biol, Med* bacille *m*

BACK [bæk]

N	dos **1, 2** ▪ fond **3** ▪ arrière **2, 4**
ADJ	arrière **1** ▪ de derrière **1**
ADV	en arrière **1** ▪ re + *verb* **2, 3**
VT	financer **1** ▪ parier sur **2**
	▪ reculer **3**
VI	reculer

N **1** *(of person, animal)* dos *m*; *(of chair etc)* dossier *m*; **mind your backs!** attention, s'il vous plaît!; *Fig* **to be at sb's back** *(chase, harry)* poursuivre qn; **he had two policemen at his b.** il avait deux policiers à ses trousses; **with an army at his b.** *(supporting him)* soutenu par une armée; **to do sth behind sb's b.** faire qch dans le dos de qn; **he laughs at you behind your b.** il se moque de vous quand vous avez le dos tourné; **to talk about sb behind their b.** dire du mal de qn dans son dos; **to turn one's b. on sb** tourner le dos à qn; *Fig* abandonner qn; **when my b. was turned** quand j'avais le dos tourné; **to sit/stand with one's b. to sb** tourner le dos à qn; **to sit with one's b. to the engine** s'asseoir dans le sens contraire à la marche; **sitting with one's b. to the light** assis à contre-jour; **he was sitting with his b. to the wall** il était assis, dos au mur; *Fig* **our backs were to the wall** nous étions au pied du mur; **to be glad to see the b. of sb/sth** être content d'être débarrassé de qn/qch; **I saw him only from the b.** je ne l'ai vu que de dos; **to be on one's b.** *(lying down)* être étendu sur le dos; *Fam (ill)* être alité; *Fam* **I spent three months (flat) on my b.** j'ai passé trois mois au lit; *Fam* **the boss was on my b. all day** j'ai eu le patron sur le dos toute la journée; *Fam* **get off my b.!** fiche-moi la paix!; **to live off the backs of the poor/the Third World** vivre sur le dos des pauvres/du tiers-monde; **to put** *or* **get sb's b. up** mettre qn en colère; *Fig* **to put one's b. into it** s'y mettre énergiquement; **b. pain** mal *m* de dos; **to have b. problems** avoir des problèmes de dos; **to break one's b.** se casser les reins; *Fam* **he won't break his b.** working il ne se casse pas au travail; **to break the b. of the work** faire le plus dur *ou* le plus gros du travail; **to break her b.** *(of ship)* se briser en deux, se casser

2 *(reverse)* *(of knife, book, envelope, cheque etc)* dos *m*; *(of fabric)* envers *m*; *(of page)* verso *m*; *Mus* *(of violin etc)* table *f* du fond; *(of medal)* revers *m*; *(of hand)* revers, dos; *(of house, clock, wardrobe etc)* arrière *m*; *also Fig* **to be at the b. of sth** être derrière qch; **outside agitators were at the b. of the trouble** des agitateurs extérieurs étaient à l'origine des troubles; *Fam* **I've parked the car round the b.** j'ai garé la voiture derrière; *Fam* **you'll feel the b. of my hand in a minute!** tu vas en prendre une!; **there was an advert on the b. of the bus** il y avait une publicité à l'arrière du bus; *Br Fam* **to have a face like the b. of a bus** être moche comme un pou; **carriage at the b. of the train** voiture en queue de *ou* du train; **the house has a garden at the b.** *or Am* **in b.** il y a un jardin derrière la maison; **the dress fastens at the b.** *or Am* **in b.** la robe s'agrafe dans le dos; **the worry was always there at the b. of his mind** ce souci lui trottait constamment dans la tête; **it was always there at the b. of his mind that …** l'idée ne le quittait pas que …; **it's something to keep at the b. of your mind** c'est quelque chose à ne pas oublier; **you have your sweater on b. to front** tu as mis ton pullover sens devant derrière *ou* à l'envers; *Fig* **she knows the system (inside out and) b. to front** elle connaît le système par cœur; **he knows London like the b. of his hand** il connaît Londres comme sa poche

3 *(rear, furthest away part)* *(of cupboard, room, stage)* fond *m*; **b. of the mouth** arrière-bouche *f*, *pl* arrière-bouches; **b. of the throat** arrière-gorge *f*, *pl* arrière-gorges; **to sit in the b.** *or Am* **in b.** *(of car)* monter à l'arrière; **to sit at the b.** *(of bus)* s'asseoir à l'arrière; *(of church, hall etc)* s'asseoir dans le *ou* au fond; **at the b. of the book** à la fin du livre; *Fam* **b. of beyond** le bout du monde; *Fam* **to live at the b. of beyond** habiter un trou perdu; **b. of the house** *(hotel services)* emplois *mpl* fonctionnels

4 *Sport* arrière *m*; **(full) b.** arrière; **right/left b.** arrière droit/gauche; *Rugby* **the backs** les arrières; *(three quarters)* les trois quarts *mpl*

ADJ 1 *(part, wheel, axle etc)* arrière; *(door, garden etc)* de derrière; *Fig* **to put sth on the b. burner** remettre qch à plus tard

2 *(in opposite direction)* *(movement)* inverse

ADV 1 *(of place)* en arrière; **to step b. a pace** faire un pas en arrière; **he left him three miles b.** il l'a laissé à trois mil(l)es d'ici; **far b.** *(seated)* dans les derniers rangs; **the house stands b. from the road** la maison est en retrait par rapport à la route; *Am* **b. of sth** derrière qch

2 *(in return, retaliation)* **if somebody hits you, hit them b.** si quelqu'un te frappe, rends-lui ses coups; **if you kick me, I'll kick you b.** si tu me donnes un coup de pied, je te le rendrai; **to get one's own b.** prendre sa revanche (**on sb** sur qn); **that's her way of getting b. at you** c'est sa façon de prendre sa revanche sur toi; **to call sb b.** *(shout, telephone)* rappeler qn

3 *(to original starting point)* **to come b.** revenir; **to arrive b.** rentrer; **to go b.** *(return)* retourner (**to** à); **to go** *or* **turn b.** *(retrace footsteps)* rebrousser chemin; **to make one's way b.** s'en retourner; **I'll be b. on Friday** je serai de retour vendredi; **I'll be b.** *(threat)* vous me reverrez; **I expect him b. tomorrow** j'attends son retour pour demain; **as soon as I am** *or* **get b.** dès mon retour; **he's just b. from a trip** il arrive de voyage; **b. home** chez

nous/lui/*etc*; **she's b. at work** elle a repris son travail; **a few pages b.** quelques pages plus haut; **b. in Britain** en Grande-Bretagne

VOIR GRAMMAIRE A21

4 *(of time)* **a few years b.** il y a (déjà) quelques années; **way b. in the Middle Ages** il y a bien longtemps au Moyen Âge; **as far b. as 1914** déjà en 1914, dès 1914; **b. in 1992** en 1992; **b. when I was young** quand j'étais jeune

VT 1 *(support)* *(person)* soutenir, appuyer; *(in an argument)* donner raison à; *Com etc* *(person, project etc)* financer; *Fin (bill)* avaliser, endosser

2 *Sport etc* *(gamble money on)* *(team)* parier *ou* miser sur; *(horse)* jouer, parier *ou* miser sur; **a well-backed horse** un cheval très coté; *Horseracing, Fig* **to b. a winner** parier *ou* miser sur le gagnant; *Horseracing, Fig* **to b. the wrong horse** parier *ou* miser sur le mauvais cheval

3 *(move)* *(cart)* reculer; *(horse)* faire reculer; *(train)* refouler; **to b. one's car into the garage** entrer en marche arrière dans le garage; **to b. one's car into a lamppost/another car** rentrer dans un lampadaire/une autre voiture en reculant; *Naut* **to b. the oars, to b. water** ramer à rebours, déramer

4 *(put backing on)* *(picture)* rentoiler

5 *Mus (person)* accompagner

VI *(of car, lorry)* faire marche arrière, reculer; *(of horse)* reculer; **to b. into sb** *(of person)* rentrer dans qn; *Aut* **to b. into the garage** entrer dans le garage en marche arrière; **I backed into my neighbour's car** je suis rentré dans la voiture de mon voisin en reculant; **to b. into the station** *(of train)* arriver dans la gare en marche arrière

▸▸ *Tech* **b. boiler** = ballon *m* d'eau chaude situé derrière un foyer; *Comput* **b. button** bouton *m* Précédente; *Journ* **b. copy** vieux numéro *m*; *Austr* **b. country** campagne *f*, arrière-pays *m inv*; **b. door** *(of building)* porte *f* de derrière; *Fin* financement *m* déguisé; **b. entrance** entrée *f* située à l'arrière; *Ling* **b. formation** dérivation *f* régressive; *Fin* **b. interest** arrérages *mpl*, intérêts *mpl* arriérés; *Journ* **b. issue** vieux numéro; *Cin, TV* **b. light** décrochage *m*; **b. list** *(of publisher)* = liste *f* des titres disponibles et régulièrement réimprimés; *Cin* **b. lot** plateau *m* extérieur d'un studio; **b. matter** *(in book)* annexes *fpl*; *Journ* **b. number** vieux numéro; *Banking* **b. office** back-office *m*, *pl* back-offices; *Banking* **b. office staff** personnels *mpl* de back-office; *Com* **b. orders** commandes *fpl* en souffrance; **b. page** dernière page *f*, *Ftbl* **b. pass** passe *f* en retrait; **b. passage** *Anat* rectum *m*; *(alley)* ruelle *f*; **b. pay** rappel *m* de salaire; *Aut* **b. plate** *(for brakes)* plaque-support *f*, *pl* plaques-support; *Cin, Theat* **b. projection** rétroprojection *f*; **b. rent** arriéré *m* de loyer; **b. rest** *(of seat)* dossier *m*; **b. road** petite route *f*; **b. room** *(in house)* pièce *f* de derrière; *(in shop)* arrière-boutique *f*, *pl* arrière-boutiques; *(for research)* laboratoire *m* de recherche secret; **b. seat** siège *m* arrière; **b. shelf** *(of car)* tablette *f* arrière; **b. shift** *(people)* = équipe *f* du soir; *Ling* **b. slang** ≃ verlan *m*; **b. slapping** *(friendly behaviour)* démonstrations *fpl* d'amitié un peu exubérantes; *(congratulatory)* félicitations *fpl* un peu exubérantes; *Sport* **b. straight** *(on athletics track)* ligne *f* (droite) d'en face; *Horseracing, Fig* **b. stretch** *(on race course)* ligne d'en face; **b. yard** *(of building)* arrière-cour *f*, *pl* arrière-cours

▸ **back away** VI *(in fear)* reculer (**from** devant)

▸ **back down** VI **1** *Fig (in argument)* admettre qu'on est dans son tort; *(in conflict)* faire marche arrière

2 *(from ladder etc)* descendre à reculons

▸ **back off** VI **1** *(move away)* reculer

2 *Am Fig* = **back down (a)**

▸ **back on to** VT INSEP *(of building)* **the colleges b. on to the river/garden** les collèges donnent sur la rivière/le jardin à l'arrière

▸ **back out** VI **1** *(of person etc)* sortir à reculons; *Aut* sortir en marche arrière

2 *Fig (withdraw)* retirer sa promesse, se dédire; *(of a responsibility)* se défiler; **to b. out of an undertaking** se dédire d'un engagement; **he's trying to b. out (of it)** il voudrait se dédire

VT SEP *(car)* sortir en marche arrière

▸ **back up** VT SEP **1** *(support)* *(person, story, version of events)* soutenir, appuyer; **to b. sb up in an argument** donner raison à qn

2 *(car etc)* faire reculer; **the accident has backed traffic up all the way to the service station** l'accident a créé un ralentissement jusqu'à la station-service

3 *Comput (data, file)* sauvegarder (**to** sur)

VI 1 *(of car)* reculer, faire marche arrière

2 *Comput* sauvegarder (**to** sur)

3 *(of drains)* être obstrué

backache ['bækeɪk] N mal *m* de dos; **to have b.** avoir mal au dos

backbench ['bæk'bentʃ] N **1** *Br Parl (usu pl)* **backbenches** = banc *m* des députés qui n'occupent pas de poste officiel dans le gouvernement ou dans l'opposition; **discontent on the backbenches** mécontentement parmi les députés de base; **she got b. support** elle a eu le soutien des députés de base; **b. MPs** = députés *mpl* qui n'occupent pas de poste officiel dans le gouvernement ou dans l'opposition **2** *Journ* équipe *f* de soutien; *(night desk)* équipe de nuit

backbencher ['bæk'bentʃər] N *Br Parl* député *m* de base *(qui n'occupe pas de poste officiel dans le gouvernement ou dans l'opposition)*

> **Backbencher**
> Les "backbenchers" sont assis aux derniers rangs de la Chambre des communes, tandis que les rangs de devant sont réservés aux ministres et aux membres du "**shadow cabinet**" (voir la note à l'entrée 'shadow').

backbite ['bækbaɪt] VI médire; **VT** *(person)* médire de

backbiting ['bækbaɪtɪŋ] N médisance *f*

backboard ['bækbɔːd] N *(in basketball)* panneau *m*

backbone ['bækbəʊn] N **1** *(of person, animal)* épine *f* dorsale, colonne *f* vertébrale; *(of fish)* grande arête *f*, *Fig* **English to the b.** anglais jusqu'au bout des ongles; **he's got no b.** il n'a rien dans le ventre *ou Fam* les tripes; **he hasn't got the b. to do it** il n'a pas les tripes pour le faire; **she is the b. of the movement** c'est elle qui mène le mouvement; **tourism is the b. of the economy** le tourisme est le pivot de l'économie **2** *Comput* épine *f* dorsale

backbreaking ['bækbreɪkɪŋ] ADJ *(work etc)* éreintant

backburn ['bækbɜːn] *Austr* N *(to control forest fire)* contre-feu *m*, *pl* contre-feux; **VI** allumer un contre-feu

backchat ['bæktʃæt] N *Br Fam (impudence)* impertinence *f*; **none of your b.!** ne réponds pas!

backcloth ['bækklɒθ] N *Br* = **backdrop**

backcomb ['bækkəʊm] VT *(hair)* crêper

backdate ['bækdeɪt] VT antidater; **an increase backdated to 1st July** une augmentation avec effet rétroactif au 1er juillet; **will it be backdated?** est-ce qu'il aura effet rétroactif?

backdrop ['bækdrɒp] N **1** *Theat* toile *f* de fond; *(with perspective)* découverte *f* **2** *Fig (background)* toile *f* de fond, arrière-plan *m*, *pl* arrière-plans; **against a b. of continuing violence** avec, comme arrière-plan *ou* toile de fond, un climat de violence permanente

-backed ['bækt] SUFF **broad-b.** *(person)* qui a le dos large; **a high-b. chair** une chaise à haut dossier

back-end load N *Am St Exch* frais *mpl* de sortie

backer ['bækər] N **1** *Horseracing* parieur, -euse **2** *Pol etc* partisan *m*; *Com* commanditaire *mf*; *Fin (of bill)* donneur *m* d'aval; *Theat etc* **we need a b.** il nous faut un mécène; **financial b.** bailleur, -eresse de fonds

backfill ['bækfɪl] *Constr* N *(of trench)* remplissage *m*
VT *(trench)* remplir
VI remplir

backfire [bæk'faɪər] N **1** *(of engine)* retour *m* de flamme; *(noise)* pétarade *f* **2** *Am (to control forest fire)* contre-feu *m*, *pl* contre-feux
VI **1** *Aut* avoir des retours de flamme, pétarader, avoir un raté (d'allumage); *Fig* **the plan backfired on them** le projet leur est retombé sur le dos **2** *Am (to control forest fire)* allumer un contre-feu

backgammon ['bækgæmən] N backgammon *m*
▶▶ **b. board** damier *m* de backgammon

background ['bækgraʊnd] N **1** *(position)* fond *m*, arrière-plan *m*, *pl* arrière-plans; *Comput* arrière-plan; **b. of mountains** fond de montagnes; **in the b.** dans le fond, à l'arrière-plan; *Comput* en arrière-plan; **b. colour** couleur *f* de fond; **music was playing in the b.** il y avait de la musique en bruit de fond; **there's a lot of noise in the b.** il y a beaucoup de bruit de fond; *Comput* **the program works in the b.** le programme est exécuté en arrière-plan; **against a dark b.** sur (un) fond sombre; *Fig* **the protests took place against a b. of repression** les manifestations se sont inscrites dans un climat de ou sur fond de répression; **to keep (oneself) or to stay in the b.** s'effacer; *Fig* **she stays very much in the b.** elle est très effacée; **to push sb into the b.** mettre *ou* reléguer qn au second plan; *(outshine)* prendre le pas sur qn; *Fig* **to fade/melt into the b.** disparaître/se fondre dans l'arrière-plan; **he's rather faded into the b. since then** on n'entend plus tellement parler de lui depuis **2** *(social class)* origines *fpl*, *(education)* formation *f*, *(experience)* expérience *f*; *(to event)* contexte *m* historique (**to** de); *(to problem)* contexte (**to** de); **a young man of good b.** un garçon de bonne famille; **to come from a middle-class/deprived b.** venir d'un milieu bourgeois/défavorisé; **what's his professional b.?** quelle expérience professionnelle a-t-il?; **he's been given a b. briefing** on lui a fait un briefing sur l'historique de l'événement; **I need a bit more b. (information)** j'ai besoin de plus de données ▶▶ *Comput* **b. job** tâche *f* de fond; **b. light** éclairage *m* d'ambiance; *Comput* **b. mode printing** impression *f* en arrière-plan; **b. music** musique *f* d'ambiance *ou* de fond; *Cin, Theat* fond *m* sonore; **b. noise** bruit *m* de fond; *Comput* **b. printing** impression en arrière-plan; *Comput* **b. processing** traitement *m* de données en tâches de fond; *Phys* **b. radiation** rayonnement *m* naturel; **b. reading** lectures *fpl* complémentaires; *TV etc* **b. sound** fond sonore; *Comput* **b. task** tâche d'arrière-plan

backhand ['bækhænd] N **1** *Tennis* revers *m*; **her b. is weak** son revers manque de puissance **2** *(writing)* écriture *f* renversée *ou* penchée à gauche

backhanded [bæk'hændɪd] ADJ *(blow)* de revers; *Fig (compliment)* équivoque

backhander ['bækhændər] N *Fam* **1** *(blow)* revers *m*; *Fig (attack)* attaque *f* indirecte **2** *(bribe)* pot-de-vin *m*, *pl* pots-de-vin

backing ['bækɪŋ] N **1** *(support) (for person)* soutien *m*, appui *m*; *(for picture)* entoilage *m*; **financial b.** *(for person, project etc)* financement *m*; **to give financial b. to sth** financer qch **2** *Horseracing (bets)* paris *mpl* **3** *(movement) (of car, horse, cart)* recul *m* **4** *(providing with back) (of picture)* rentoilage *m* **5** *Mus* accompagnement *m*
▶▶ *Mus* **b. track** piste *f* de fond

backlash ['bæklæʃ] N **1** *Fig (of event)* contrecoup *m*; *(political etc)* réaction *f*, retour *m* de manivelle (**against** contre) **2** *Aut (gearing)* jeu *m* entre-dents

backless ['bæklɪs] ADJ *(dress)* dos nu; *(seat etc)* sans dossier

backlighting ['bæklaɪtɪŋ] N *Cin, TV* éclairage *m* en contre-jour

backlit ['bæklɪt] ADJ **1** *Cin, TV* éclairé en contre-jour **2** *Comput (screen)* rétro-éclairé

backlog ['bæklɒg] N *(of work)* retard *m*; *Com* **b. of orders** commandes *fpl* non exécutées; **to have a b. of correspondence/work** avoir du retard dans son courrier/travail, avoir du courrier/travail en retard; **to clear a b.** se mettre à jour

backpack ['bækpæk] N sac *m* à dos
VI faire de la randonnée

backpacker ['bækpækər] N randonneur, -euse

backpacking ['bækpækɪŋ] N randonnée *f*; **to go b.** aller faire de la randonnée

back-pedal VI (-ll-, *Am* -l-) *(on bicycle)* rétropédaler; *Fig* faire marche arrière; **to b. on a promise** revenir sur une promesse

back-pedalling, *Am* **back-pedaling** ['bækped(ə)lɪŋ] N *(on bicycle)* rétropédalage *m*; *Fig* marche *f* arrière

back-pressure N *Aut* contre-pression *f*, *pl* contre-pressions

backscratcher ['bækskrætʃər] N gratte-dos *m inv*

backscratching ['bækskrætʃɪŋ] N *Fig* échange *m* de faveurs

back-seat ['bæksiːt] ADJ **I don't want any b. driving** je n'ai pas besoin de conseils pour conduire
▶▶ *Pej* **b. driver** *(in car)* = personne *f* qui donne toujours des conseils au conducteur; *(interfering person)* donneur, -euse de leçons; **b. passenger** passager, -ère arrière

backsheesh, backshish ['bækʃiːʃ] N bakchich *m*

backside [bæk'saɪd] N *Fam* derrière *m*, postérieur *m*

backsight ['bæksaɪt] N *(on rifle)* hausse *f*

backslash ['bækslæʃ] N *Comput* barre *f* oblique inversée
▶▶ **b. key** touche *f* barre oblique inversée

backslide ['bækslaɪd] VI (**backslid** ['bækslɪd]) récidiver

backsliding ['bækslaɪdɪŋ] N récidive *f*

backspace ['bækspeɪs] N espacement *m* arrière, touche *f* d'espacement arrière
VI *(on keyboard)* revenir en arrière d'un caractère; **b. twice** revenir en arrière de deux caractères
▶▶ **b. character** caractère *m* de retour arrière; **b. command** commande *f* de retour arrière; **b. key** espacement arrière, touche d'espacement arrière

backstage [bæk'steɪdʒ] ADV *Theat* derrière la scène, en coulisse, dans les coulisses; *Fig* en coulisse; *Theat* **to help b.** aider en coulisse(s)

ADJ ATTRIB *Theat (area, activity)* de derrière la scène; *Fig* en coulisse
▶▶ **b. worker** personne *f* qui travaille dans les coulisses

backstairs [bæk'steəz] N *(for servants etc)* escalier *m* de service; *(hidden)* escalier dérobé
▶▶ **b. gossip** commérages *mpl* (des domestiques); **b. influence** influence *f*

backstitch ['bækstɪtʃ] *Sewing* N point *m* de piqûre
VI coudre au point de piqûre

backstreet ['bækstriːt] N petite rue *f*; **he was brought up in the backstreets** il a été élevé dans les quartiers populaires
▶▶ **b. abortion** avortement *m* clandestin; **b. abortionist** faiseur, -euse d'anges, *Pej* avorteur, -euse

backstroke ['bækstrəʊk] N **1** *Swimming* dos *m* crawlé; **the 100 metres b.** le 100 mètres dos **2** *Tech (of piston etc)* course *f* arrière, course de retour

backtalk ['bæktɔːk] N *Am* = **backchat**

back-to-back ADJ *(seats, people)* dos à dos; *Br* **a row of b. houses** une rangée de maisons adossées les unes aux autres; *Sport* **to play two games b.** jouer deux parties l'une à la suite de l'autre
N *Br (house)* **a row of little back-to-backs** une rangée de petites maisons adossées les unes aux autres
▶▶ *Fin* **b. credit** crédit *m* dos-à-dos; *Fin* **b. loan** opération *f* de face à face; *Fin* **b. operation** opération de face à face

backtrack ['bæktræk] VI revenir sur ses pas; *Fig* faire marche arrière; **to b. on a promise/decision** revenir sur une promesse/une décision

backup ['bækʌp] N **1** *(support)* soutien *m*, appui *m*; *Mil etc* renfort *m*; *Med* soins *mpl* supplémentaires; **to ask for b.** *(of police etc)* demander des renforts; **we have a generator as b.** nous avons un générateur de secours **2** *Comput* sauvegarde *f*; **to do the b.** faire la sauvegarde; **the b. has failed** la sauvegarde a échoué
▶▶ **b. car** voiture *f* de rechange; *Comput* **b. copy** copie *f* de sauvegarde; *Comput* **b. device** unité *f* de sauvegarde; *Comput* **b. disk(ette)** disquette *f* de sauvegarde; *Comput* **b. drive** unité de sauvegarde; *Comput* **b. file** fichier *m* de sauvegarde; *Comput* **b. system** *(for doing the backup)* système *m* de sauvegarde; *(auxiliary system)* système de secours; **b. team** *(which provides support)* équipe *f* de soutien; *(which acts as replacement)* équipe de remplacement; *Mil* **b. troops** renforts *mpl*

back-up ADJ
▶▶ *Am Aut* **b. lights** feux *mpl* de recul

backward ['bækwəd] ADJ **1** *also Fig (movement, glance, step etc)* en arrière; **b. and forward motion** mouvement *m* de va-et-vient **2** *(child)* retardé, attardé; *(area, region)* moins développé; *(people)* attardé; **the b. state of the country** le retard dont souffre le pays; **to be b. in doing sth** être lent à faire qch; *Br Fam* **he isn't b. in coming forward** il n'a pas peur de se mettre en avant; **he isn't b. in coming forward with his ideas** il n'a pas peur de mettre ses idées en avant; **he isn't b. in coming forward to complain** il n'est jamais le dernier à se plaindre
ADV = **backwards**
▶▶ *Econ* **b. integration** intégration *f* en amont; *Mktg* **b. invention** invention *f* en amont; *(simplification of product)* invention rétrograde; **b. pricing** rajustement *m* des prix; *Comput* **b. search** recherche *f* arrière

backwardation [bækwə'deɪʃən] N *Fin* déport *m*

backward-compatible ADJ *Comput* compatible avec les versions antérieures

backwardness ['bækwədnɪs] N *(mental)* arriération *f* mentale, retard *m*; **b. in doing sth** hésitation *f* à faire qch

backwards ['bækwədz] ADV *(to jump, lean)* en arrière; *(to go, walk)* à reculons; *(to fall)* à la renverse; *(to say, read sth)* à l'envers; **to look b.** jeter un coup d'œil en arrière; *(in time)* remonter dans le passé; **to flow b.** *(of water)* couler à contre-courant; *Fig* **to know sth b.** connaître qch parfaitement; *also Fig* **a step b.** un pas en arrière; **to walk b. and forwards** aller et venir; **movement b. and forwards** mouvement *m* de va-et-vient; **to go b. and forwards** faire la navette *(entre deux endroits)*

backwash ['bækwɒʃ] N remous *m*; *Fig* conséquences *fpl* néfastes; **in the b. of the civil war** dans les remous qui ont suivi la guerre civile

backwater ['bækwɔːtər] N *(tributary)* bras *m* de décharge *(d'une rivière)*; *Fig, often Pej* **to live in a b.** habiter un trou perdu; **a secluded b.** un coin tranquille

backwoods ['bækwʊdz] NPL *esp Am* forêts *fpl* de l'intérieur; *Fig* **to live in the b.** habiter un trou perdu *ou* un bled

backwoodsman, *pl* **backwoodsmen** [bæk'wʊdzmən] N *Fam* **1** *Am (uncouth man)* rustre *m*, rustaud *m* **2** *Br Pol* = membre *m* de la Chambre des lords qui ne fait acte de présence que lorsqu'il s'intéresse à un vote

baclava [bə'klɑːvə] N *Culin* baklava *m*

bacon ['beɪkən] N bacon *m*; **b. and eggs** œufs *mpl* au bacon; **streaky b.** ≃ petit salé *m*; *Fig* **to save sb's b.** sauver la peau de qn; *Fig* **to bring home the b.** *(provide material support)* faire bouillir la marmite; *(be successful)* réussir

BACS [bæks] N *(abbr* **bankers' automated clearing services)** système *m* électronique de paiement; **to pay by B.** payer par virement automatique

bacteria [bæk'tɪərɪə] NPL bactéries *fpl*

bacterial [bæk'tɪərɪəl] ADJ bactérien

bacteriological [bæktɪərɪə'lɒdʒɪk(ə)l] ADJ bactériologique

▸▸*Biol, Mil* **b. warfare** guerre *f* bactériologique

bacteriologist [bæktɪərɪ'ɒlədʒɪst] N bactériologiste *mf*, bactériologue *mf*

bacteriology [bæktɪərɪ'ɒlədʒɪ] N bactériologie *f*

bacterium, *pl* **bacteria** [bæk'tɪərɪəm, -ɪə] N bactérie *f*

Bactrian camel ['bæktrɪən] N chameau *m* (bactrien)

BAD [bæd]

ADJ	mauvais **1–3** ▪ grave **2**
N	mauvais

ADJ *(* **worse** [wɜːs], **worst** [wɜːst]*)* **1** *(of poor quality)* mauvais, de mauvaise qualité; *(unfortunate, incorrect)* mauvais; **it's not b.** ce n'est pas mal; **the pay's not b.** ça ne paie pas mal; **things are not as b. as all that** ça ne va pas si mal que ça; *Br Fam* **it's not half b.** ce n'est pas mal du tout; **he's/she's not b. looking** il/elle n'est pas mal; **it was a b. buy** ce n'était pas un bon investissement; **to go b.** *(of food)* se gâter, s'avarier; **to speak b. French** parler mal le français; **b. at maths** nul en maths; **he's b. at keeping a secret** il ne sait pas garder un secret; **he's b. at helping about the house** il n'aide pas souvent aux tâches ménagères; **to have a b. effect on sth** avoir un effet néfaste sur qch; **to be** *or* **have a b. influence on sb** avoir une mau-

vaise influence sur qn; **to get into b. habits** *or* **ways** prendre de mauvaises habitudes; **b. light stopped play** *(at cricket match)* la partie a été remise à cause d'un manque de lumière; **is this a b. time to ask for leave?** peut-être n'est-ce pas le moment de demander des congés?; **am I phoning at a b. time?** je vous dérange?; **to be in a b. way** *(of person)* aller mal; **he'll come to a b. end** il finira mal; **to have a b. name** avoir (une) mauvaise réputation; **it wouldn't be a b. thing** *or* **plan** *or* **idea to …** cela ne serait pas une mauvaise idée de …; **things are going from b. to worse** les choses vont de mal en pis; **a b. apple** une pomme pourrie; *Fig* une brebis galeuse; *Fig* **one b. apple spoils the barrel** il ne faut qu'une brebis galeuse pour gâter un troupeau; *Fig* **there's b. blood/feeling between them** il y a du ressentiment *ou* de la rancune entre eux; *Fam* **he's always turning up like a b. penny** on n'arrive jamais à se débarrasser de lui; **don't worry, he'll turn up like a b. penny** ne t'en fais pas, tu sais bien qu'il revient toujours; *Fam* **I'm having a b. hair day** *(my hair's a mess)* je n'arrive pas à me coiffer aujourd'hui; *(I'm having a bad day)* aujourd'hui c'est un jour sans

2 *(unpleasant, serious)* *(news, smell, mood etc)* mauvais; *(cold)* gros; *(headache)* violent; *(accident, mistake etc)* grave; **it's a b. business** c'est une mauvaise affaire; **is the pain b.?** est-ce que cela fait très mal?; *Fig* **she's b. news** elle ne te/lui/*etc* apportera que des ennuis; **b. weather** mauvais temps *m*; *Naut* **to be on b. terms with sb** être mal *ou* en mauvais termes avec qn; **it's (really) too b.!, that's too b.!** c'est vraiment dommage!; *Old-fashioned* **it's too b. of him!** ce n'est vraiment pas bien de sa part!; **if you don't like it, that's just too b.** si cela ne te plaît pas, tant pis pour toi

3 *(not healthy)* **to be b. for sb/sth** ne rien valoir à qn/pour qch; **all that whisky is b. for him** tout ce whisky ne lui vaut rien; **smoking is b. for you** *or* **your health** le tabac est mauvais pour la santé; **because of my b. leg** parce que ma jambe me fait souffrir; **I have a b. heart/back** j'ai le cœur/le dos fragile; **I'm not so b.** *(I'm well)* je ne vais pas trop mal; **how's business? – not so b.** comment vont les affaires? – pas trop mal

4 *(wicked)* méchant; *Fam* **he's a b. lot** c'est un vaurien

ADV *Fam* **that looks b.** *(of injury, accident etc)* ça a l'air grave; *(in eyes of other people)* c'est mal vu; *(augurs ill)* c'est mauvais signe; **to feel b. about sth** *(regret)* avoir du remords au sujet de qch; **I feel b. about firing him but I'll have to** cela m'embête d'avoir à le renvoyer, mais il faudra bien que je le fasse; **I feel b. about not having told him sooner** je m'en veux de ne pas lui avoir dit plus tôt; *Fam* **she was taken b. yesterday** *(became ill)* elle est tombée malade hier; *Fam* **to have it b.** *(be in love)* être mordu

N **to take the b. with the good** accepter la mauvaise fortune aussi bien que la bonne; *Fam* **to go to the b.** *(of person)* mal tourner; *(of business)* être en mauvaise passe; **to be £500 to the b.** en être de 500 livres (de sa poche); *Fam* **to be in b. with sb** être en mauvais termes avec qn; *Am Fam* **my b.!** c'est ma faute!

▸▸**b. breath** mauvaise haleine *f*; *Banking* **b. cheque** chèque *m* sans provision; *Comput* **b. command** commande *f* erronée; *Fin* **b. debt** créance *f* irrécouvrable *ou* douteuse; *Fin* **b. debtor** créance *f* irrécouvrable *ou* douteuse; *Comput* **b. file name** nom *m* de fichier erroné; **b. language** gros mots *mpl*; *Comput* **b. sector** secteur *m* endommagé

badass ['bædæs] *Am Sl* N *(person)* dur *m* (à cuire)

ADJ **1** *(intimidating, tough)* **to be b.** être un dur à cuire **2** *(excellent)* super, génial, -aux; **her new sneakers are so b.** ils sont super, ses nouveaux tennis

baddie, **baddy** ['bædɪ] N *Fam* méchant, -ante

bade PT *see* **bid** VT & VI

badge [bædʒ] N **1** *(metal, plastic)* badge *m*; *Mil, Sch* écusson *m*; *(to indicate membership of club)* insigne *m* **2** *Fig* symbole *m*, signe *m*

▸▸**b. of office** insigne de fonction

badger ['bædʒər] N *(animal)* blaireau *m*

VT *(person)* harceler; **to b. sb with sth/to do sth** harceler qn avec qch/pour qu'il fasse qch; **to b. sb into granting a favour, to b. a favour out of sb** obtenir une faveur de qn à force de harcèlement

▸▸**b. baiting** déterrage *m* du blaireau

badinage ['bædɪnɑːʒ] N *Fml, Lit* badinage *m*

badly ['bædlɪ] ADV *(* **worse** [wɜːs], **worst** [wɜːst]*)* **1** *(poorly)* *(informed, dressed, behave, explain sth etc)* mal; **to do b., to come off b.** mal réussir; **he didn't do b.** il ne s'en est pas trop mal tiré; **to be very b. off** *(financially)* être dans la gêne; *Fig* **I'm very b. off for clothes** je ne suis pas riche en vêtements; **to speak English b.** parler mal l'anglais; **he took it very b.** il a très mal pris la chose; **they get on b.** (with each other) ils ne s'entendent pas; **I get on b. with him** je ne m'entends pas bien avec lui

2 *(seriously)* *(damaged, scratched)* très; **his arm was b. broken** il a eu une mauvaise fracture au bras; **he was b. disabled in the accident** il a été sérieusement handicapé dans l'accident; **b. wounded** gravement *ou* grièvement blessé

3 *(greatly)* **to want sth b.** avoir très envie de qch; **if you want it b. enough, you'll get it** quand on veut, on peut; **I need it b.** j'en ai bien *ou Fml* grand besoin; *Sport etc* **b. beaten** battu à plate(s) couture(s); **he's b. in need of a haircut** il a bien besoin de se faire couper les cheveux

bad-mannered ADJ mal élevé

badminton ['bædmɪntən] N badminton *m*

▸▸**b. court** terrain *m* de badminton; **b. player** joueur, -euse de badminton

bad-mouth VT *esp Am (person)* déblatérer sur, dire du mal de

badness ['bædnɪs] N **1** *(of cooking, writing etc)* mauvaise qualité *f* **2** *(of person)* méchanceté *f*

bad-tempered ADJ *(person)* grincheux; *(reply)* désagréable; **to be b.** *(temporarily)* être de mauvaise humeur; *(permanently)* avoir mauvais caractère

baffle ['bæf(ə)l] N **1** *Tech* chicane *f*, déflecteur *m* **2** *Radio (of loudspeaker)* écran *m*, baffle *m*

VT **1** *(mystify)* *(person)* laisser perplexe; **to b. the imagination** dépasser l'imagination; **it baffles the imagination why she agreed** Dieu sait pourquoi elle a accepté!; **a mystery that has baffled all investigators** un mystère qui a déjoué toutes les recherches; **the police admit they are baffled** la police admet qu'elle est perplexe; **I'm baffled as to why she said that** je ne comprends vraiment pas pourquoi elle a dit ça; **to b. definition** échapper à toute définition **2** *(foil)* *(plot, attempt)* déjouer

▸▸*Radio* **b. board** *(of loudspeaker)* écran, baffle; *Tech* **b. plate** plaque-chicane *f*, *pl* plaques-chicanes

baffling ['bæf(ə)lɪŋ] ADJ *(behaviour)* déconcertant; *(mystery etc)* inexplicable

BAFTA ['bæftə] N *(abbr* **British Academy of Film and Television Arts)** **B. (award)** = prix *m* récompensant les meilleurs films et émissions de télévision en Grande-Bretagne

bag [bæg] **N 1** *(container)* sac *m*; *(handbag)* sac à main; **travel(ling) b.** sac de voyage; *Old-fashioned, Lit* **b. and baggage** avec armes et bagages; **to pack one's bags** faire ses bagages; *Fam* **we've bags of time** on a tout le temps; *Fam* **they've bags of money** ils sont pleins aux as; *Fam* **there's bags of room** la place ne manque pas; *esp Am Sl* **that's not my b.** *(I'm not good at it)* ce n'est pas mon fort; *(I'm not interested in it)* ce n'est pas mon genre; *Fam* **bags under the eyes** poches *fpl* sous les yeux; **to let it out of the b.** vendre la mèche; *Fam* **b. of bones** sac *m ou* tas *m* d'os

2 *Br Sl Pej (woman)* **old b.** vieille toupie *f*
3 *(in hunting)* **the b.** le tableau; **to make a good b.** faire un grand abattis de gibier; *Fig (of fighter pilot)* avoir un beau tableau de chasse; *Fam* **it's in the b.** l'affaire est dans le sac
4 *Br Old-fashioned Fam* **bags** *(trousers)* pantalon *m*

VT (**-gg-**) **1** *Fam (take)* s'emparer de, mettre la main sur; *(best seats)* accaparer; *Br* **bags I go first!** c'est moi le premier!; *Br* **bags I sit in front!** c'est moi qui monte devant!
2 *(pack) (coal, potting compost)* mettre en sac; *(apples, sweets)* ensacher; *Am (purchases) (in supermarket)* emballer
3 *(kill) (game)* abattre, tuer; *Aviat Fam (enemy aircraft)* abattre

VI *(of garment)* bouffer, avoir trop d'ampleur; **trousers that b. at the knees** pantalon qui fait des poches aux genoux
▸▸ *Fam* **b. lady** clocharde *f*

bagatelle [bægə'tel] **N** *(trifle)*, *Mus* bagatelle *f*

bagel ['beɪg(ə)l] **N** *Culin* = petit pain *m* en forme de couronne, *Can* bagel *m*

baggage ['bægɪdʒ] **N 1** *(luggage)* bagages *mpl*; **one piece of b.** un bagage; *Fig* **to have a lot of (emotional) b.** avoir accumulé les échecs sentimentaux **2** *Old-fashioned (cheeky girl)* coquine *f* **3** *Mil* bagage *m*
▸▸ **b. allowance** franchise *f* de bagages; *Am* **b. car** fourgon *m* (*d'un train*); **b. check** *(inspection)* contrôle *m* des bagages; *Am (ticket)* ticket *m* d'enregistrement; **b. claim** retrait *m* des bagages; **b. claim area** zone *f* de livraison des bagages; **b. claim sticker** étiquette *f* autocollante d'identification de bagage; **b. container** conteneur *m* à bagages; **b. conveyor belt** tapis *m* de livraison de bagages; **b. cover** *(lid, hood)* cache-bagage *m inv*; *(insurance)* assurance *f* bagage(s); **b. handler** bagagiste *m*; **b. lift** ascenseur *m* à bagages; **b. reclaim** retrait des bagages; *Am* **b. room** consigne *f*, *Am* **b. tag** bulletin *m* de consigne; **b. waggon** fourgon à bagages

baggy ['bægɪ] **ADJ** *(sweater, trousers) (deliberately so)* ample, large; *(out of shape)* déformé

Baghdad [bæg'dæd] **N** Bagdad

bagpipe(s) ['bægpaɪp(s)] **NPL** cornemuse *f*
▸▸ **b. player** joueur, -euse de cornemuse

bah [bɑː] **INT** bah!

Bahama [bə'hɑːmə] **N** **the Bahamas, the B. Islands** les (îles *fpl*) Bahamas *fpl*, l'archipel *m* des Bahamas VOIR GRAMMAIRE A12

Bahrain [bɑː'reɪn] **N** Bahreïn

Bahraini [bɑː'reɪnɪ] **ADJ** bahreïni
N Bahreïni, -ie

bail¹ [beɪl] *Law* **N** *(system)* cautionnement *m*; *(money)* caution *f*, **to go** *or* **stand b. for sb** se porter garant *ou* caution de qn, fournir une caution pour qn *(pour sa libération pro-*

visoire); **to grant sb b.** *(of judge)* libérer qn sous caution; **released on b.** libéré sous caution; **to be (out) on b.** être en liberté provisoire (sous caution); *Fam* **to jump b.** se dérober à la justice *(alors qu'on jouit de la liberté provisoire)*

VT *(person) (of judge)* libérer sous caution; *(of lawyer, family member etc)* se porter caution pour

bail² **N** *Cr* **bails** barrettes *fpl*, bâtonnets *mpl*

bail³ **N** *Naut (bucket)* écope *f*
▸ **bail out** **VT SEP 1 to b. sb out** *Law* se porter garant *ou* caution pour qn; *Fig* tirer qn d'affaire; *Fig* **to b. out a company** renflouer une entreprise **2** *(boat, water)* écoper, vider
VI écoper

bailer ['beɪlər] **N** *Naut (bucket)* écope *f*

Bailey ['beɪlɪ] **N the Old B.** = le tribunal principal de Londres
▸▸ *Mil* **B. bridge** pont *m* Bailey

bailiff ['beɪlɪf] **N 1** *Law* huissier *m* **2** *(of estate, farm)* régisseur *m*; **water b.** garde-pêche *m*, *pl* gardes-pêche **3** *Br Hist (sovereign's representative)* bailli *m*

bailiwick ['beɪlɪwɪk] **N** *Law* baillage *m*; *Fig (territory)* territoire *m*; *Fig* **it's not my b.** *(field, area of expertise)* ce n'est pas mon rayon

bairn [beən] **N** *Scot* enfant *mf*

bait [beɪt] **N** *(for fish)* amorce *f*, appât *m*; *Fig* appât, leurre *m*; **ground b.** amorce de fond; **to rise** *to or* **swallow** *or* **take the b.** *(of fish)*, *Fig* mordre à l'hameçon
VT 1 *(tease) (animal)* harceler; *(person)* harceler, tourmenter **2** *(put bait on) (hook, trap etc)* amorcer (**with** avec); *(line)* mettre l'appât à

baiting ['beɪtɪŋ] **N 1** *(teasing) (of animals, person)* harcèlement *m*; *(of badger)* déterrage *m* **2** *(of hook, trap etc)* amorçage *m*

baize [beɪz] **N** feutre *m*; **green b.** tapis *m* de billard; **green b. door** porte *f* recouverte de feutre vert

bake [beɪk] **VT** *Culin* (faire) cuire au four; *Tech (bricks, porcelain etc)* cuire; **to b. bread** faire cuire le pain; **earth baked by the sun** sol durci *ou* desséché par le soleil; *Fam* **I'm baked** je crève de chaleur, je cuis
VI *(of bread etc)* cuire; *(of person) (make cakes)* faire de la pâtisserie *ou* des gâteaux; *(make bread)* faire du pain; *Fam* **I'm baking** je crève de chaleur

baked [beɪkt] **ADJ** cuit au four
▸▸ *Culin* **b. Alaska** omelette *f* norvégienne; **b. beans** *Br (in tomato sauce)* haricots *mpl* blancs à la sauce tomate; *Am (dish)* haricots au lard, *Can* fèves *fpl* au lard; **b. potato** pomme *f* de terre en robe de chambre *ou* en robe des champs

baker ['beɪkər] **N** boulanger, -ère; **b.'s (shop)** boulangerie *f*
▸▸ **b.'s dozen** treize à la douzaine

bakery ['beɪkərɪ] **N** boulangerie *f*

Bakewell tart ['beɪkwel] **N** *Br Culin* = fond *m* de tarte, fourré au biscuit de Savoie, à la confiture et à la pâte d'amandes

baking ['beɪkɪŋ] **ADJ** *Fam* **b. hot** *(food, container)* brûlant; *(day)* torride; **it's b. in here** on étouffe ici; **the b. streets** les rues écrasées de chaleur
N 1 *(of bread etc)* cuisson *f*, *(of bricks etc)* cuisson, cuite *f*, **I'll do a** *or* **some b. tomorrow** demain, je ferai de la pâtisserie **2** *(batch) (of bread, cakes)* fournée *f*, *(of bricks etc)* cuite *f*
▸▸ **b. powder** levure *f* (chimique); **b. sheet** plaque *f* (de four), tôle *f*, **b. soda** bicarbonate *m* de soude; **b. tin** moule *m* à gâteau

baklava [bə'klɑːvə] **N** *Culin* baklava *m*

baksheesh ['bækʃiːʃ] **N** bakchich *m*

Balaclava [bælə'klɑːvə] **N** passe-montagne *m*, *pl* passe-montagnes
▸▸ **B. helmet** passe-montagne

balalaika [bælə'laɪkə] **N** *Mus* balalaïka *f*

BALANCE ['bæləns]

| **N** équilibre 1 ▪ solde, reste 2 ▪ balance 2, 3 |
| **VT** mettre en équilibre 1 ▪ balancer, solder 2 ▪ équilibrer 2 |
| **VI** s'équilibrer 2 ▪ être en équilibre 3 |

N 1 *(steadiness)* équilibre *m*; **there's a good b. of funny and serious articles** il y a une proportion égale d'articles amusants et sérieux; **to keep** *or* **maintain one's b.** garder l'équilibre; **to lose one's b.** perdre l'équilibre; *Fig* **to catch sb off b.** prendre qn au dépourvu; *Fig* **to throw sb off b.** faire perdre l'équilibre à qn; *Fig* **to be off b.** être déséquilibré; **to put out of b.** *(scales, machine)* dérégler; *Fig* **to strike a b.** *(between two things)* trouver le juste milieu; *Pol* **the b. of power** l'équilibre des forces; *Pol* **the Liberals hold the b. of power** les Libéraux ont le pouvoir de faire pencher l'Assemblée d'un côté ou de l'autre; **while the b. of his mind was disturbed** alors qu'il n'était pas dans son état normal

2 *(remainder)* reste *m*, *Com, Fin (of account)* solde *m*; *Acct* balance *f*, bilan *m*; **credit/debit b.** solde créditeur/débiteur; *Fig* **on b.** tout bien considéré

3 *Tech (for weighing)* balance *f*, *Astron* **the B.** la Balance; *Fig* **the b. of evidence** l'ensemble *m* des preuves; *Fig* **to swing the b. (in sb's favour)** faire pencher la balance (du côté de qn); *Fig* **to hang in the b.** être en jeu

VT 1 *(object)* mettre *ou* maintenir en équilibre; *Aut, Naut* équilibrer; *(counteract weight of)* faire contrepoids à; **to b. sth on one's head** mettre qch en équilibre sur sa tête; **women balancing pots on their heads** des femmes portant des pots sur la tête; **one thing balances another** une chose compense l'autre

2 *Com, Fin (account)* balancer, solder, aligner; *(debt)* compenser; *(budget)* équilibrer; **to b. the books** balancer les livres

VI 1 *(of scales)* équilibrer; **the two things b.** les deux choses s'équilibrent

2 *Com, Fin (of accounts)* s'équilibrer; **account that balances** compte *m* en balance; **I can't get the accounts to b.** je n'arrive pas à équilibrer les comptes

3 *(remain in stable position)* se maintenir en équilibre; *(be in stable position)* être en équilibre; **to b. on one foot** se tenir en équilibre sur un pied; **books balancing on the desk** des livres en équilibre sur le bureau
▸▸ *Gym* **b. beam** poutre *f*, *Acct* **b. brought forward** solde reporté; *(on balance sheet)* report *m*; *Acct* **b. carried forward** solde à reporter; *(on balance sheet)* report à nouveau; *Acct, Fin* **b. due** solde dû; *Econ* **b. of payments** balance des paiements; *Econ* **b. of payments deficit** déficit *m* de la balance des paiements, déficit extérieur; *Acct* **b. sheet** bilan *m*; *Acct* **b. sheet auditing** contrôle *m* du bilan; *Acct* **b. sheet consolidation** consolidation *f* de bilan; *Acct* **b. sheet item** poste *m* de bilan; *Acct* **b. sheet value** valeur *f* bilantielle *ou* d'inventaire; *Econ* **b. of trade** balance commerciale; *Tech* **b. wheel** balancier *m*; *(of clock)* roue *f* de rencontre
▸ **balance against** **VT SEP** **to b. one thing against another** comparer les avantages d'une chose par rapport à une autre; **you have to b. the advantages against the disadvantages** il faut peser le pour et le contre

► **balance out** VI *(of figures)* correspondre VT SEP *(match) (something)* compléter; **they b. each other out** *(because of their respective skills)* ils se complètent bien

> Note that the French word **balance** is a false friend. Its most common meaning is **scales**.

balanced ['bælənst] ADJ **1** *(in weight)* équilibré, compensé; *Fig (judgment)* pondéré; *(report, account)* objectif; **to be well b.** *(of person)* être équilibré; **a (well-)b. diet** un régime *(alimentaire)* équilibré **2** *(in strength, value)* égal, -aux; *Fin (budget)* équilibré; **the two parties are pretty well b.** les deux parties sont à peu près égales

balancer shaft ['bælənsər] N *Aut* arbre *m* d'équilibrage

balancing ['bælənsɪŋ] N **1** mise *f* en équilibre; *Aut (of wheels)* équilibrage *m*; *Art (of elements in a painting)* balancement *m* **2** *Com, Fin* **b. of accounts** solde *m ou* alignement *m* des comptes **3** *(of two things)* ajustement *m*; *(of sth by sth)* compensation *f*
> ► **b. act** numéro *m* d'équilibriste; **b. pole** *(of tightrope walker)* contrepoids *m*

balcony ['bælkənɪ] N **1** *(on house)* balcon *m*; **on the b.** sur le balcon **2** *Theat, Cin* balcon *m*; **we always sit in the b.** nous prenons toujours des places au balcon; **there are two b. seats left** il reste deux places au balcon

bald [bɔːld] ADJ **1** *(person)* chauve; *(tyre)* lisse; *Fig (hillside)* nu; **his b. head** son crâne chauve; **he is going b.** il commence à perdre ses cheveux *ou* à devenir chauve; **to go b. as a coot** *or* **an egg** chauve comme un œuf *ou* une boule de billard **2** *Fig (style etc)* dépouillé, sec, *f* sèche; **a b. statement of the facts** une simple exposition des faits
> ► **b. eagle** pygargue *m* à tête blanche; **b. patch** tonsure *f*

balderdash ['bɔːldədæʃ] *Old-fashioned Fam* N bêtises *fpl*, balivernes *fpl*; **to talk b.** dire des bêtises *ou* des balivernes; **the book is utter b.** le livre est complètement nul
> INT balivernes!

bald-headed ADJ chauve; *Fig Fam* **to go b. into** *or* **at sth** foncer tête baissée dans qch

balding ['bɔːldɪŋ] ADJ **a b. fifty-year-old** un homme de cinquante ans avec une calvitie naissante; **he's b.** il commence à perdre ses cheveux, il devient chauve

baldly ['bɔːldlɪ] ADV *Fig (to write)* d'un style dépouillé *ou* sec; *(to say)* sèchement; **b. worded** *(reply)* sec; *(statement)* bref; **to put it b.** pour parler clairement; **you didn't have to put it so b.!** tu n'avais pas besoin d'être aussi brutal!

baldness ['bɔːldnɪs] N **1** *(of person)* calvitie *f*, premature b. calvitie précoce **2** *Fig (of style etc)* sécheresse *f*

bale[1] [beɪl] N *Com (of goods)* balle *f*, ballot *m*; *(of hay, straw)* botte *f*, **b. of paper** ballot de dix rames de papier
> VT *(goods)* mettre en ballot; *(hay, straw)* botteler

bale[2] N *Naut* = **bail**[3]
► **bale out** VI *Aviat* sauter en parachute d'un avion en perdition; **he baled out over the Atlantic** il s'est éjecté de l'avion au-dessus de l'Atlantique
> VT SEP = **bail out** VT SEP **2**

Balearic [bælɪˈærɪk] ADJ **the B. Islands, the Balearics** les *(îles fpl)* Baléares *fpl*

baleen ['beɪliːn] N *(of whale)* fanon *m* de baleine

baleful ['beɪlfʊl] ADJ *Lit* sinistre, maléfique

balefully ['beɪlfʊlɪ] ADV sinistrement

---

baler[1] ['beɪlər] N **1** *Agr (machine)* botteleuse *f* **2** *(person)* emballeur, -euse

baler[2] N *Naut (bucket)* écope *f*

Bali ['bɑːlɪ] N Bali

Balinese [bɑːlɪˈniːz] ADJ balinais

baling ['beɪlɪŋ] N *(of goods)* mise *f* en balles, paquetage *m*
> ► *Agr* **b. machine** botteleuse *f*

balk [bɔːk] VT *Fml (person's plans)* déjouer, contrarier; *(person)* contrarier
> VI *(of horse)* refuser, (se) dérober; **to b. at a fence** refuser un obstacle; *Fig* **to b. at** *(difficulty, expense)* s'arrêter *ou* reculer *ou* hésiter devant

Balkan ['bɔːlkən] ADJ **the B. States** les États *mpl* balkaniques; **the B. Peninsula** la péninsule des Balkans
> NPL **the Balkans** *(region, mountains)* les Balkans *mpl*

Balkanization [bɔːlkənaɪˈzeɪʃən] N balkanisation *f*

Balkanize ['bɔːlkənaɪz] VT *(country)* balkaniser

ball[1] [bɔːl] N **1** *(for playing football, rugby, basketball etc, of child)* ballon *m*; *(for cricket, tennis, golf)* balle *f*; *(for croquet, bowling)* boule *f*; *(for billiards)* bille *f*; *(of wool, string)* pelote *f*; *Culin (of dough etc)* boulette *f*; **to wind wool into a b.** mettre de la laine en pelote; **to roll sth (up) into a b.** mettre qch en boule; **b. of earth** motte *f*; **b. of fire** boule de feu; *Fig* **to be a b. of fire** déborder d'énergie; *Tennis* **to knock the b. about** faire des balles; **to kick a b. about** s'amuser avec un ballon; *Cr* **no b.** balle nulle; **to play b.** jouer à la balle *ou* au ballon; *Am (baseball)* jouer au baseball; *Fig* coopérer, jouer le jeu; *Fig* **to be on the b.** *(quick-witted)* avoir de la présence d'esprit; *(knowledgeable)* connaître son affaire; *Fig* **to keep one's eye on the b.** rester très vigilant; *Fig* **to keep the b. rolling** *(in conversation)* soutenir la conversation; *Fig* **to start** *or* **get the b. rolling** faire démarrer les choses, mettre les choses en route; *Fig* **the b. is in your court** c'est à vous de jouer; *Fig* **to have the b. at one's feet** avoir la partie belle

2 *Vulg (testicle)* **balls** couilles *fpl*; *Fig (courage)* courage *m*; *(nonsense)* conneries *fpl*; **balls!** *(rubbish)* quelles conneries!; **to talk a lot** *or* **a load of balls** dire beaucoup de conneries; **balls to him!** qu'il aille se faire foutre!; *Fig* **they've got us by the balls** ils nous ont à leur merci; *Fig* **to have balls** *(courage)* avoir des couilles; **that type of thing takes balls** il faut avoir des couilles pour faire ce genre de truc

3 *Anat (of foot)* plante *f*; *(of eye)* globe *m*; *(of thumb)* partie *f* charnue, gras *m*
> VT **1 to b. one's fist** serrer le poing **2** *Am Vulg (have sex with)* **to b. sb** se faire qn
> ► *Tech* **b. bearing** bille de roulement; *Sport* **b. boy** ramasseur *m* de balles; **b. cock** robinet *m ou* soupape *f* à flotteur; **b. game** *(with small ball)* jeu *m* de balle; *(with large ball)* jeu de ballon; *(baseball)* match *m* de baseball; *Sport* **b. girl** ramasseuse *f* de balles; **b. joint** *Anat* articulation *f* à emboîtement *ou* à trois axes; *Tech* joint *m* à rotule, articulation à genouillère; *Met* **b. lightning** éclair *m* en boule; *Tech* **b. peen hammer** marteau *m* à panne ronde *ou* sphérique; **b. race** piste *f* des billes, chemin *m* de roulement des billes; **b. ramp** plan *m* incliné, rampe *f*, **b.-and-socket joint** *Anat* articulation à emboîtement *ou* à trois axes; *Tech* joint *m* à rotule, articulation à genouillère; *Tech* **b. valve** robinet *m* à tournant sphérique
► **ball up** VT SEP *Am Vulg* = **balls up**

> When translating **ball**, note that **balle** and **ballon** are not interchangeable.

---

ball[2] N *(dance)* bal *m*, *pl* bals; *Fam* **to have (oneself) a b.** s'éclater; **how was the party? – an absolute b.!** et la soirée, c'était comment? – génial!
> ► ► **b. dress, b. gown** robe *f* de bal

ballad ['bæləd] N **1** *Mus* romance *f* **2** *Liter* ballade *f*

ballast ['bæləst] N **1** *Naut, Aviat* lest *m*; **ship in b.(-trim)** navire *m* sur lest; **to take in b.** faire son lest; **to discharge b.** se délester, jeter du lest; *Fig* **I'm carrying a bit too much b.** j'ai un peu de poids en excédent; *Fig* **to act** *or* **serve as b.** apporter un équilibre **2** *Constr* pierraille *f*, cailloutage *m*; *Rail* ballast *m*, empierrement *m*
> VT **1** *Naut, Aviat* lester **2** *Constr* empierrer, caillouter; *Rail* ballaster
> ► ► **b. bed** *(of railway track)* coffre *m*, empierrement; *(of road)* encaissement *m*; *Rail* **b. car** wagon *m* de terrassement; *Naut* **b. tank** *(of submarine)* ballast *m*; *Rail* **b. truck** wagon de terrassement

ballerina [bæləˈriːnə] N ballerine *f*

ballet ['bæleɪ, *esp Am* bæˈleɪ] N danse *f* classique, ballet *m*; **I'm going to the b. this evening** je vais voir un ballet *ou* un spectacle de danse classique ce soir; **the Bolshoi b.** le ballet Bolchoï
> ► ► **b. dancer** danseur, -euse de ballet; **b. lesson** cours *m* de danse classique; **b. school** école *f* de danse classique; **b. shoe** chausson *m* de danse

ballistic [bəˈlɪstɪk] ADJ balistique; *Fam* **to go b.** *(get angry)* piquer une crise, grimper aux rideaux
> ► ► *Mil* **b. missile** missile *m* balistique

ballistics [bəˈlɪstɪks] N balistique *f* VOIR GRAMMAIRE A10

balloon [bəˈluːn] N **1** *(toy)* ballon *m*; *Aviat* ballon *(dirigeable)*, montgolfière *f*; *Fig* **when the b. goes up** quand il va y avoir du grabuge; *Fig* **to go down like a lead b.** *(of suggestion, joke)* tomber complètement à plat **2** *(in cartoons, comic strips)* bulle *f*, phylactère *m*
> VI *(of skirt, sail etc)* ballonner; *(of cheeks)* gonfler; **to b. (up)** *(of arm, leg etc)* enfler; **she ballooned out in the last months of her pregnancy** elle avait un ventre énorme durant les derniers mois de sa grossesse
> ► ► *Chem* **b. flask** ballon *m*; **b. glass** verre *m* ballon; *Comput* **b. help** bulles *fpl* d'aide; *Psy* **b. test** test *m* de la bulle *ou* de frustration

ballooning [bəˈluːnɪŋ] N **1** *(sport)* ballon *m*, montgolfière *f*; **to go b.** faire du ballon *ou* de la montgolfière **2** *(of skirt, sail etc)* ballonnement *m*

balloonist [bəˈluːnɪst] N aérostier *m*

ballot ['bælət] N **1** *(process)* tour *m* de scrutin; *(vote)* scrutin *m*, vote *m*; **to vote by b.** voter par *(voie de)* scrutin; **to put sth to the b.** soumettre qch à un vote; **second b.** deuxième tour de scrutin; **to cast one's b. for sb** voter pour qn **2** *St Exch (when shares are oversubscribed)* allocation *f* d'actions par tirage au sort
> VT *Pol* appeler à voter; **union members will be ballotted on Tuesday** les membres du syndicat décideront par voie de scrutin mardi
> VI **1** *Pol* voter par *(voie de)* scrutin; **to b. for/against sb** voter pour/contre qn **2** *Arch (draw lots)* tirer au sort; **to b. for a place** tirer une place au sort
> ► ► **b. box** *(for ballot papers)* urne *f*, *Fig* système *m* électoral *ou* démocratique; **b. box stuffing** fraude *f* électorale *(consistant à ajouter des bulletins dans les urnes)*; **b. paper** bulletin *m* de vote; **b. rigging** fraude électorale

balloting ['bælətɪŋ] N **1** *Pol* scrutin *m* **2** *Arch (drawing of lots)* tirage *m* au sort

ballpark ['bɔːlpɑːk] N Am terrain m de base-ball; Fig **you're not even in the b.!** tu es loin du compte!; Fig **are we in the same b.?** est-ce qu'on est sur la même longueur d'ondes? ►► Fig **b. figure** estimation f, approximation f

ballplayer ['bɔːlpleɪər] N Am Sport joueur m de base-ball

ballpoint ['bɔːlpɔɪnt] N stylo m (à) bille ►► **b. pen** stylo (à) bille

ballroom ['bɔːlruːm] N salle f de bal, salle de danse
►► **b. dancing** danse f de salon; **to go b. dancing** aller danser; **b. dancing championship** championnat m de danses de salon

► **balls up** [bɔːlz] Br Vulg VT SEP foutre la merde ou le merdier dans; **don't b. things up again!** ne recommence pas à foutre la merde!
VI merder

balls-up N Br Vulg merdier m; **to make a (right) b. of sth** foutre la merde ou le merdier dans qch

ballsy ['bɔːlzɪ] ADJ Am Sl Fam culotté

ballup ['bɔːlʌp] N Am Vulg = **balls-up**

bally ['bælɪ] ADJ Old-fashioned Br Fam sacré, satané

ballyhoo [bælɪ'huː] N Fam Pej **1** (publicity) battage m (publicitaire) **2** (fuss) blabla m; **to see through the b.** ne pas être dupe; **what's all the b. about?** pourquoi tout ce remue-ménage?
VT esp Am Fam (book, show) faire du battage (publicitaire) pour promouvoir

balm [bɑːm] N Pharm, Fig baume m; **b. to the soul** baume au cœur

balminess ['bɑːmɪnɪs] N **1** (mildness) **the b. of the evening air** l'air embaumé du soir **2** Br Fam = **barminess**

balmoral [bɑːl'mɒrəl] N (shoe) balmoral m

balmy ['bɑːmɪ] ADJ **1** (air, weather) doux, f douce; **the air was b. with the scent of roses** l'air était embaumé du parfum des roses **2** Br Fam = **barmy**

balneotherapy [bælnɪəʊ'θerəpɪ] N balnéothérapie f

baloney [bə'ləʊnɪ] N Am (sausage) saucisse f bolognaise; Fam **it's all b.** (nonsense) c'est des bêtises; **the film/book is a load of b.** le film/livre est complètement nul; **the usual b. from the government** les boniments habituels du gouvernement; **don't give me that b.!** à d'autres!
INT ne dites pas de bêtises!

balsa ['bɔːlsə] N balsa m
►► **b. wood** balsa m; **b. wood raft** radeau m en bois de balsa

balsam ['bɔːlsəm] N **1** (substance) baume m **2** (plant) balsamine f
►► Bot **b. fir** sapin m baumier

balsamic vinegar [bɔːl'sæmɪk] N vinaigre m balsamique

balti ['bɔːltɪ] N Br Culin (container) = récipient m métallique utilisé dans la cuisine indienne; (food) = plat m épicé préparé dans un balti

Baltic ['bɔːltɪk] N **the B.** la (mer) Baltique
ADJ **1** (state) balte, baltique **2** Br Fam **it's b.** (very cold) il fait un froid de canard
►► **B. port** port m balte; **the B. Sea** la mer Baltique; **the B. States** les pays mpl baltes

baluster ['bæləstər] N balustre m; **balusters** rampe f d'escalier

balustrade [bælə'streɪd] N balustrade f

bamboo [bæm'buː] N bambou m; **b. chair** chaise f en bambou
►► **b. cane** bambou m; **B. Curtain** rideau m de bambou; **b. shoots** pousses fpl de bambou

bamboozle [bæm'buːz(ə)l] VT Fam (person) embobiner; **you've been bamboozled** tu t'es fait embobiner; **to b. sb out of sth** (cheat) refaire qn de qch; (trick) soutirer qch à qn; **to b. sb into doing sth** embobiner qn pour qu'il fasse qch

ban [bæn] N interdiction f, Hist (banishment) ban m, bannissement m, proscription f, Rel interdit m; **atomic test b.** interdiction des essais nucléaires; **to put** or **impose a b. on sth** interdire qch; **to lift the b. on sth** lever l'interdiction qui porte sur qch; **is there a b. on smoking?** est-il interdit de fumer?
VT (-nn-) interdire; **b. the bomb!** non à la bombe atomique!; **to be banned from driving** se voir retirer son permis de conduire; **he should be banned for life** (from driving) on devrait lui retirer son permis de conduire à vie; **dogs have been banned from the beach** les chiens sont interdits sur la plage; **to be banned from a club** être exclu d'un club; **he's been banned from the restaurant/bar** il n'a plus le droit de rentrer dans ce restaurant/bar

banal [bə'nɑːl] ADJ banal, -als, ordinaire

banality [bə'nælɪtɪ] N banalité f

banana [bə'nɑːnə] N banane f, Fam **to go bananas** (become excited) déjanter; (become angry) grimper aux rideaux; Fam **you're bananas!** (crazy) tu es cinglé!; Fig Fam **top b.** grand chef m
►► **b. boat** bananier m (bateau); **b. plantation** bananeraie f, Fam **b. republic** république f bananière; **b. skin** peau f de banane; Culin **b. split** banana split m; **b. tree** bananier m

bancassurance ['bæŋkəʃʊərəns] N Banking bancassurance f

band¹ [bænd] N **1** (round hat) ruban m; (round cigar) bague f
2 (stripe) (of colour) bande f, raie f, Radio **bands of the spectrum** bandes du spectre
3 Radio bande f de fréquence
4 (range) tranche f; **children in the 10–15 age b.** les enfants dans la tranche des 10–15 ans
5 Tech etc bande f, courroie f
6 Rel, Law **bands** (on collar) rabat m
7 (wedding ring) alliance f, **b. of gold** alliance en or
►► Ind **b. conveyor** tapis m roulant; Tech **b. saw** scie f à ruban

band² N **1** Mus (jazz) orchestre m, groupe m; (rock music) groupe m; **to be** or **play in a b.** faire partie d'un orchestre/un groupe **2** (group) bande f, troupe f, Pej clique f
► **band together** VI (unite) se liguer (**to do** pour faire)

bandage ['bændɪdʒ] N Med bandage m, bande f, (blindfold) bandeau m; **to have** or **wear a b. on one's arm, to have one's arm in a b.** avoir le bras bandé; **to put a b. on sb/sth** bander qn/qch
VT (person, wound, leg) bander, panser
► **bandage up** VT SEP (person) bander, panser; **I'll by this up for you** je vais te faire un bandage; **I bandaged her up with towels** je lui ai fait un bandage avec des serviettes de toilette

bandaging ['bændɪdʒɪŋ] N **1** (bandages) bandage m, pansement m **2** (action) pansement m

Band-Aid® ['bændeɪd] N esp Am sparadrap m; Fig **a b. solution/measure** une solution/ une mesure d'attente ou provisoire

bandan(n)a [bæn'dænə] N bandana m

bandbox ['bændbɒks] N Old-fashioned Fig **she looks as if she's just stepped out of a b.** elle est tirée à quatre épingles

banded ['bændɪd] ADJ (striped) rayé
►► Com **b. pack** lot m; Com **b. pack selling** vente f par lot

bandit ['bændɪt] N bandit m, brigand m

banditry ['bændɪtrɪ] N brigandage m

bandmaster ['bændmɑːstər] N Mil etc chef m de musique; (of brass band) chef de fanfare

bandoleer, bandolier [bændə'lɪər] N cartouchière f (portée en bandoulière)

bandsman, pl **bandsmen** ['bændzmən] N (in military band) musicien m; (in brass band) fanfariste m

bandstand ['bændstænd] N kiosque m à musique

bandwagon ['bændwæg(ə)n] N char m des musiciens (en tête de la cavalcade); Fig **to climb** or **jump on the b.** prendre le train en marche

bandwidth ['bændwɪdθ] N Radio largeur f de bande; (of computer monitor) bande f passante

bandy¹ ['bændɪ] VT (witticisms, insults etc) échanger; (statistics) se renvoyer; **they were bandying words** (quarrelling) ils se chamaillaient; **don't b. words with me, young man!** ne venez pas me faire la leçon, jeune homme!

bandy² ADJ aux jambes arquées; **to be b.** avoir les jambes arquées
►► **b. legs** jambes fpl arquées; **to have b. legs** avoir les jambes arquées
► **bandy about, bandy around** VT SEP her name was being bandied about as a possible candidate son nom est revenu plusieurs fois parmi ceux des candidats possibles; **I don't like the papers bandying my name about** je n'aime pas que mon nom revienne à tout propos dans les journaux; **decentralization is a word the government bandies about a lot** la décentralisation est un mot que le gouvernement a souvent à la bouche

bandy-legged ADJ aux jambes arquées

bane [beɪn] N Lit plaie f, **she is the b. of pretentious authors** elle est la bête noire des auteurs prétentieux; Fam **he's the b. of my life** il m'empoisonne l'existence

baneful ['beɪnfʊl] ADJ Lit funeste; (influence) néfaste

banefully ['beɪnfʊlɪ] ADV funestement

bang¹ [bæŋ] N **1** (blow) coup m (violent); **she got a bad b. on the head** elle a reçu un mauvais coup sur la tête
2 (noise) (of rifle etc) détonation f, (of door) claquement m; **the door shut with a b.** la porte s'est refermée en claquant; **to shut the door with a b.** claquer la porte; **to shut the windows/cupboard with a b.** fermer les fenêtres/les portes du placard en les faisant claquer; **to go off with a b.** (of firework) détoner; Fam Fig **to go (off)** or Am **over with a b.** être une réussite; **to end with a b.** finir en beauté
3 Am Sl (pleasure) **to get a b. from doing sth** prendre son pied à faire qch; **she gets a real b. out of her grandchildren** elle retire beaucoup de plaisir de ses petits-enfants
4 Sl (of heroin) shoot m d'héroïne
5 Vulg (sexual intercourse) baise f
VI **1** (make noise) (of door, shutter) claquer, battre; (of gun) retentir; **the door banged shut** la porte s'est refermée en claquant; **to b. at** or **on the door** frapper à la porte à grands coups; **to b. on the table with one's fist** taper du poing sur la table
2 Sl (of heroin addict) se shooter
VT **1** (strike) frapper (violemment); **to b. one's head** se cogner la tête; Fig **to b. one's head against a brick wall** perdre son temps; Fig **to b. a few heads together** taper du poing sur la table
2 (make noise with) (door, window) (faire) claquer
3 Vulg (have sex with) baiser

INT pan!, v'lan!, boum!; *Br Fam* **b. went fifty pounds!** et vlan! cinquante livres se sont envolées; *Br Fam* **b. went my hopes of a quiet weekend** pour le week-end tranquille c'était râpé

ADV to go b. éclater; **he crashed b. into the tree** il est rentré en plein dans l'arbre; *Fam* **to fall b. in the middle** tomber en plein milieu; *Fam* **b. on time** pile à l'heure; *Fam* **it's b. on** c'est au poil; *Fam* **b. up to date** *(equipment etc)* à la pointe de la technologie; *(reference book etc)* vraiment à jour; **to be b. up-to-date on sth** être vraiment à jour pour ce qui est de qch; *Br Fam* **to be caught b. to rights** être pris la main dans le sac

▸ **bang about, bang around** VI faire du potin

▸ **bang away** VI **1** *(with hammer)* donner des coups, taper; *(with gun)* tirer, donner des coups de feu; **to b. away at a typewriter/piano** taper sur un clavier de machine à écrire/piano **2** *(criticize)* **they've been banging away at the government for months** cela fait des mois qu'ils s'acharnent sur le gouvernement à jour; *Fam (have sex)* baiser

▸ **bang down** VT SEP *(lid)* refermer violemment; **he banged the book down on the table** il a fait claquer le livre sur la table

▸ **bang into** VT INSEP *(collide with)* foncer dans

▸ **bang on** VI *Sl* **he's always banging on about it** il n'arrête pas de bassiner tout le monde avec ça; **if I have to listen to him banging on one more time about it** s'il se remet à me casser les oreilles avec ça

▸ **bang out** VT SEP *(tune)* jouer tant bien que mal

▸ **bang up** VT SEP *Br Sl* **1** *(imprison)* boucler; **to be banged up** être en taule **2** *(make pregnant) (usu passive)* **to get banged up** se faire mettre en cloque

bang² N *(also* **bangs***) (hair)* frange *f*; **to have bangs, to wear one's hair in a b.** avoir une frange

banger ['bæŋər] N *Br* **1** *Fam (sausage)* saucisse *f*; **bangers and mash** purée *f* avec des saucisses **2** *(firework)* pétard *m* **3** *Fam (car)* **old b.** vieux tacot *m*, vieille guimbarde *f*

Bangladesh [bæŋglə'deʃ] N Bangladesh *m*

Bangladeshi [bæŋglə'deʃɪ] N Bangladais, -aise

ADJ *(government, representative etc)* bangladais

bangle ['bæŋg(ə)l] N *(for wrist)* bracelet *m* rigide; *(for ankle)* anneau *m* attaché autour de la cheville

bang-up ADJ *Br Fam (excellent)* super, génial, - aux; **she did a b. job of throwing a good party** elle avait organisé une super soirée

banish ['bænɪʃ] VT **1** *(exile) (person)* bannir, exiler, proscrire **2** *Fig (drive away) (fear, care, idea)* chasser; **to b. sth from one's thoughts** chasser qch de ses pensées; **you can b. all thoughts of a holiday** ce n'est plus la peine de compter sur des vacances

banishment ['bænɪʃmənt] N bannissement *m*, exil *m*; **to go into b.** partir pour l'exil; **to be sent into b.** être banni *ou* exilé

banisters ['bænɪstəz] NPL rampe *f* (d'escalier); **to slide down the b.** glisser le long de la rampe d'escalier

banjax ['bændʒæks] VT *Scot, Ir Fam (break)* bousiller

banjo, *pl* **banjos, banjoes** ['bændʒəʊ, -əʊz] N *Mus* banjo *m*

banjoist ['bændʒəʊɪst] N joueur, -euse de banjo, banjoiste *mf*

bank¹ [bæŋk] N **1** *(of river, canal)* berge *f*, bord *m*, rive *f*; *(of lake)* bord, rive; **the banks of the Thames** les berges de la Tamise **2** *(on side of road etc)* talus *m*; *(man-made)*

terrasse *f*, levée *f* de terre; *Constr* banquette *f*, remblai *m*; *Rail* rampe *f*; *Horseracing* banquette (irlandaise)

3 *(mass) (of fog, cloud, sand)* banc *m*; **banks of flowers** des multitudes *fpl* de fleurs; *Geog* **the Banks of Newfoundland** les Bancs de Terre-Neuve

4 *Aviat* inclinaison *f*, *(turn)* virage *m* incliné

VT 1 *(river)* contenir par des berges; *Constr* **to b. a road** surhausser *ou* relever un virage; **banked corner** virage *m* relevé **2** *(mass, form)* **to be banked** *(of clouds, snow)* être tassé

VI *(of road)* être incliné; *Aviat* s'incliner sur l'aile; *(turn)* virer (sur l'aile)

▸ **bank up** VT SEP *(earth etc)* remblayer, terrasser; *(fire)* remettre du bois/du charbon dans

VI *(of snow, clouds, mist etc)* s'entasser, s'accumuler

bank² N **1** *Com, Fin* banque *f*, *(for coins)* tirelire *f*; **is there a b. nearby?** y a-t-il une banque par ici?; **could you tell me where the nearest Barclays® b. is?** pouvez-vous me dire où se trouve la Barclays® la plus proche?

2 *(in game)* banque *f* (de celui qui tient le jeu); **to break the b.** faire sauter la banque; *Fig* **it won't break the b.** *(of expenditure)* ça ne va pas me/nous/*etc* ruiner

3 *(store) (for blood, sperm, information)* banque *f*

VT *(money)* mettre *ou* déposer en banque

VI to b. with sb avoir un compte en banque chez qn; **who do you b. with?** à quelle banque êtes-vous?; **do you b. with us?** avez-vous un compte chez nous?

▸▸ **b. account** compte *m* en banque; **b. accounting** comptabilité *f* bancaire; **b. advice note** avis *m* de la banque; **b. balance** solde *m* bancaire; **b. base rate** taux *m* de base bancaire; **b. borrowings** emprunts *mpl* bancaires, concours *m* bancaire; **b. branch code** code *m* guichet; **b. buying rate** taux de change à l'achat; **b. card** carte *f* (d'identité) bancaire; **b. charges** frais *mpl* bancaires *ou* de banque; **b. cheque** chèque *m* bancaire; **b. clerk** employé, -ée de banque; **b. commission** commission *f* bancaire; **b. credit** avoir *m* en banque, crédit *m* bancaire; **b. debts** dettes *fpl* bancaires; **b. details** relevé *m* d'identité bancaire, RIB *m*; **b. discount** escompte *m* de banque, escompte en dehors; **b. discount rate** escompte officiel; **b. draft** traite *f* bancaire; **the B. of England** la Banque d'Angleterre; **the B. of France** la Banque de France; **b. guarantee** garantie *f* bancaire, caution *f* de banque; **b. holiday** *(in UK)* jour *m* férié; *(in US)* jour de fermeture des banques; **b. interest** intérêt *m* bancaire; **b. ledger** livre *m ou* journal *m* de banque; **b. lending** concours bancaire; **b. loan** *(money lent)* prêt *m* bancaire; *(money borrowed)* emprunt *m* bancaire; **b. manager** directeur, -trice de banque; **b. money** monnaie *f* de banque, monnaie scripturale; **b. notification** avis *m* de la banque; **b. overdraft** découvert *m* bancaire; **b. rate** taux d'escompte *ou* de l'escompte, taux bancaire; **b. reconciliation** rapprochement *m* bancaire; **b. references** références *fpl* bancaires; **b. reserves** réserves *fpl* bancaires; **b. robber** cambrioleur, -euse de banque; **b. selling rate** taux de change à la vente; *St Exch* **b. shares** valeurs *fpl* bancaires; **b. sort code** code guichet; **b. statement** relevé de compte; **b. transactions** transactions *fpl* bancaires; **b. transfer** virement *m* bancaire; **b. treasurer** trésorier, -ière de banque

▸ **bank on** VT INSEP compter sur; *(event)* miser sur; **to b. on success** escompter un succès; **I wouldn't b. on her being there** ça

m'étonnerait qu'elle soit là; **don't b. on it** ne comptez pas là-dessus

bank³ N **1** *(group, series) (of switches, dials, of cylinders)* rangée *f*; *Cin (of projectors)* rampe *f*, *(of speakers, transformers etc)* groupe *m*, batterie *f*; *Comput (of chips)* banc *m* **2** *Naut (of rowers)* banc *m*; *(of oars)* rang *m*; *(of seats)* travée *f*

bankable ['bæŋkəb(ə)l] ADJ *Fin* bancable; *Fig* **to be b.** *(of film star etc)* être une valeur sûre; *Fig* **a b. idea** une idée qui vaut de l'or

bankbook ['bæŋkbʊk] N *(of account holder)* livret *m ou* carnet *m* de compte *ou* banque; *(for accounting)* journal *m ou* livre *m* de banque

banker ['bæŋkər] N **1** *Fin* banquier, -ière **2** *(in game)* banquier, ière; **to be b.** tenir la banque

▸▸ *Fin* **b.'s acceptance** acceptation *f* bancaire; *Fin* **Bankers' Automated Clearing System** système *m* électronique de paiement; *Fin* **b.'s card** carte *f* bancaire; *Fin* **b.'s cheque** traite *f* bancaire *ou* de banque; *Fin* **b.'s draft** chèque *m* bancaire *ou* de banque; *Fin* **b.'s order** ordre *m* de transfert permanent

banking¹ ['bæŋkɪŋ] N **1** *Constr* remblayage *m*; *(of bend)* surhaussement *m*, relèvement *m* **2** *Aviat* inclinaison *f*, *(turning)* virage *m* incliné

banking² N **1** *(business)* affaires *fpl ou* opérations *fpl* de banque; **electronic b.** bancatique *f* **2** *(profession)* profession *f* de banquier, la banque; **she's in b.** elle travaille dans la banque

▸▸ *Am* **b. account** compte *m* en banque, compte bancaire; **b. centre** place *f* bancaire; **b. consortium** consortium *m* de banques; **b. controls** contrôle *m* bancaire; **b. hours** heures *fpl* d'ouverture des banques; **b. law** droit *m* bancaire; **b. network** réseau *m* bancaire; **b. products** produits *mpl* bancaires; **b. profession** métier *m* de banquier; **b. regulator** régulateur *m* bancaire; **b. secrecy** secret *m* bancaire; **b. services** services *mpl* bancaires; **b. terms** conditions *fpl* de banque

banknote ['bæŋknəʊt] N billet *m* de banque

bankroll ['bæŋkrəʊl] VT *Am Fam (person, project)* financer

bankrupt ['bæŋkrʌpt] N *(person)* failli, -ie; **fraudulent b.** banqueroutier, -ière

ADJ failli; **to go b.** *(of person, business)* faire faillite; *(fraudulently)* faire banqueroute; **to be b.** être en faillite; **to declare sb b.** déclarer *ou* mettre qn en faillite; *Fig* **to be morally b.** avoir perdu toute crédibilité

VT *(person)* mettre en faillite, *Fam* ruiner

bankruptcy ['bæŋkrəptsɪ] N faillite *f*; **fraudulent b.** banqueroute *f*; **to present** *or* **file one's petition for bankruptcy** déposer son bilan; **to bring sb to the verge of b.** amener qn au bord de la ruine

▸▸ *Br Law* **b. court** ≃ tribunal *m* de commerce; *Hum* **you'll have me in the b. court!** tu veux ma ruine!; **b. proceedings** procédure *f* de faillite

banner ['bænər] N *(flag)* bannière *f*; *Comput, Mktg (for advertising on Internet)* bandeau *m*, bannière publicitaire; **the Star-Spangled B.** la bannière étoilée

ADJ *Am (year etc)* excellent

▸▸ *Journ* **b. heading, b. headline** manchette *f*

bannisters ['bænɪstəz] NPL = **banisters**

banns [bænz] NPL bans *mpl*; **to read** *or* **publish the b.** = (faire) publier les bans

banoffee pie, banoffi pie [bə'nɒfɪ] N *Culin* = gâteau *m* à la banane et au caramel

banquet ['bæŋkwɪt] N banquet *m*; **b. facilities** *(notice in hotel etc)* possibilité d'organiser des banquets

VT *(person)* offrir un banquet à

VI banqueter

▸▸**b. hall** salle *f* de banquet; **b. room** salle de banquet

banqueting [ˈbæŋkwɪtɪŋ] N
▸▸**b. hall** salle *f* de banquet; **b. manager** responsable *mf* des banquets; **b. room** salle de banquet

banquette [bæŋˈket] N *esp Am (seat)* banquette *f*

banshee [bænˈʃiː] N *Myth* fée *f* de la mythologie irlandaise, qui hurle pour annoncer une mort imminente; **to wail like a b.** hurler comme un sauvage

bantam [ˈbæntəm] N **1** *(chicken)* = poulet *m* de petite taille **2** *Boxing* = **bantamweight**

bantamweight [ˈbæntəmweɪt] N poids *m* coq; **b. champion** champion *m* poids coq

banter [ˈbæntər] N *(jokes)* badinage *m*; *(teasing)* taquineries *fpl*

bantering [ˈbæntərɪŋ] ADJ *(tone etc)* taquin

Bantu [ˈbæntuː] ADJ bantou
N **1** Bantou, -oue **2** *Ling* bantou *m*

banyan [ˈbænjən] N *(tree)* banian *m*

BAOR [biːeɪəʊˈɑːr] *abbr* **British Army of the Rhine**

bap [bæp] N *Br Culin* petit pain *m* rond au lait

baptism [ˈbæptɪz(ə)m] N baptême *m*; *Fig* **b. of fire** baptême du feu

baptismal [bæpˈtɪzm(ə)l] ADJ *(register)* baptistaire; *(name)* de baptême
▸▸**b. font** fonts *mpl* baptismaux

Baptist [ˈbæptɪst] N *Rel* baptiste *mf* **2** (St) **John the B.** saint Jean-Baptiste
ADJ baptiste
▸▸**B. doctrine** doctrine *f* baptiste, baptisme *m*

baptist(e)ry [ˈbæptɪstrɪ] N baptistère *m*

baptize [bæpˈtaɪz] VT *(person, ship etc)* baptiser; **to be baptized a Catholic/(in the name of) John** être baptisé catholique/du nom de Jean

BAR¹ [bɑːr]
▪ N barre **1, 4, 7, 9** ▪ obstacle **2**
▪ interdiction **3** ▪ le barreau **5**
▪ bar **6, 8**
▪ **VT** barrer **1** ▪ interdire **2** ▪ exclure **2**
▪ mettre des barreaux à **3**

N **1** *(of iron, gold etc)* barre *f*, *(of chocolate)* tablette *f*, *(smaller)* barre; *(of electric fire)* résistance *f*, *(of medal)* barrette *f*, *(in gym)* barre; **with b.** *(medal)* ≃ avec palme; **bars** *(of window, cage, prison)* barreaux *mpl*; **to be behind (prison) bars** être derrière les barreaux
2 *(obstacle)* empêchement *m*, obstacle *m*; *(in river, harbour)* barre *f* (de sable), traverse *f*; **to be a b. to sth** faire obstacle à qch; **a colour b. anywhere is illegal** il est illégal de faire de la discrimination raciale où que ce soit
3 *(ban)* interdiction *f*; **there is a b. on bringing drink into the club** il est interdit d'introduire de l'alcool au sein du club
4 *Br Law (in court)* barre *f*; **the prisoner at the b.** l'accusé, -ée; *Fig* **to be judged at the b. of public opinion** être jugé par l'opinion publique
5 *Law (profession)* **the B.** l'Ordre *m* des avocats, le barreau; **to read for the B.** faire son droit; **to be called to the B.** être reçu au barreau, être reçu avocat
6 *(pub)* bar *m*, café *m*, *Fam* bistro *m*; *(counter)* comptoir *m*, bar; *Fam* **he's always propping up the b.** c'est un vrai pilier de bar *ou* de bistro
7 *(line)* barre *f*; *Mus* mesure *f*; *Mus* **double b.** double barre
8 *Met* bar *m*
9 *Comput (menu bar)* barre *f*
VT **(-rr-) 1** *(obstruct) (the way)* barrer; **to b.**

sb's way barrer la route à qn, être dans le chemin de qn; **he's been barred from the club** il a été exclu du club
2 *(forbid) (action)* défendre, prohiber, interdire; *(subject of conversation)* exclure; **to b. sb from doing sth** défendre à qn de faire qch; **she's been barred from playing** elle a été interdite de jeu
3 *(put bars on) (window)* mettre des barreaux à
4 *Old-fashioned (lock) (door etc)* barrer; **to b. the door against sb** barrer la porte à qn
▸▸**b. chart** histogramme *m*; **b. code** code-barres *m*, *pl* codes-barres; **b. code reader** lecteur *m* de code-barres; **b. diagram** histogramme; **b. food** = repas *mpl* simples servis dans les bars; **b. graph** histogramme; *Mus* **b. line** barre; *Rel* **b. mitzvah** bar-mitsva *f inv*; **b. staff** personnel *m* de bar

> When translating **bar**, note that **barre** and **barreau** are not interchangeable.

bar² PREP *(except)* sauf, excepté, à l'exception de; **we've decided everything b. the time** nous avons tout prévu sauf l'heure; **we've finished all of them b. one** nous les avons tous terminés sauf un; **the finest/the quickest b. none** sans conteste le meilleur/le plus rapide; **it's all over b. the shouting** les jeux sont faits

barb [bɑːb] N **1** *(on fish-hook)* barbillon *m*, dardillon *m*; *(on arrow)* barbillon; *(of barbed wire)* picot *m* **2** *(on fish, animal)* barbillon *m*; *Bot* arête *f*, *(on feather)* barbe *f* **3** *Fig (gibe)* pique *f*, remarque *f* acerbe

Barbados [bɑːˈbeɪdɒs] N Barbade *f*

barbarian [bɑːˈbeərɪən] ADJ, N barbare *mf*

barbaric [bɑːˈbærɪk] ADJ barbare

barbarism [ˈbɑːbərɪz(ə)m] N **1** *(of person, behaviour)* barbarie *f* **2** *Gram, Ling* barbarisme *m*

barbarity [bɑːˈbærɪtɪ] N **1** *(cruelty)* barbarie *f*, cruauté *f* **2** *(action)* acte *m* de barbarie, atrocité *f*

barbarize [ˈbɑːbəraɪz] VT **to b. sb** faire de qn un monstre; **to b. the language** estropier la langue

barbarous [ˈbɑːbərəs] ADJ barbare

barbarously [ˈbɑːbərəslɪ] ADV cruellement

Barbary [ˈbɑːbərɪ] N
▸▸**b. ape** singe *m* de Barbarie, magot *m*; **B. horse** cheval *m* barbe; **the B. States** la Barbarie, les États *mpl* barbaresques

barbecue [ˈbɑːbɪkjuː] N *(fireplace, party)* barbecue *m*; **to cook sth on the b.** faire cuire qch au barbecue; **to have a b.** faire un barbecue
VT *(food)* (faire) griller au barbecue; **barbecued chicken** poulet *m* rôti *ou* grillé au barbecue
▸▸**b. sauce** sauce *f* barbecue

barbed [bɑːbd] ADJ **1** barbelé **2** *Fig (comment etc)* acerbe **3** *Bot* hameçonné
▸▸**b. arrow** flèche *f* à barbelures; **b. wire** (fil *m* de fer) barbelé *m*

barbel [ˈbɑːb(ə)l] N **1** *(fish)* barbeau *m* (commun) **2** *(on fish)* barbillon *m*

barbell [ˈbɑːbel] N *Gym* haltère *m*

barber [ˈbɑːbər] N coiffeur *m* pour hommes, *Old-fashioned* barbier *m*; **I'm going to the b.'s** je vais chez le coiffeur

barbershop [ˈbɑːbəʃɒp] N *Am* salon *m* de coiffure *(pour hommes)*
▸▸*Mus* **b. harmony** chants *mpl* à quatre voix d'hommes; *Mus* **b. quartet** = quatuor *m* d'hommes chantant en harmonie étroite

barbican [ˈbɑːbɪkən] N *(fortification)* barbacane *f*

Barbie® [ˈbɑːbɪ] N *(poupée f)* Barbie® *f*
▸▸**B. doll** *(poupée)* Barbie®

barbie [ˈbɑːbɪ] N *Br, Austr Fam* barbecue *m*

barbiturate [bɑːˈbɪtjʊrət] N *Chem* barbiturique *m*
▸▸*Med* **b. poisoning** barbiturisme *m*

barbituric [bɑːbɪˈtjʊərɪk] ADJ barbiturique

barbwire [bɑːbˈwaɪər] N *Am* = **barbed wire**

barcarol(l)e [ˈbɑːkərəʊl] N *Mus* barcarolle *f*

Barcelona [bɑːsɪˈləʊnə] N Barcelone *f*

bard¹ [bɑːd] N **1** *Arch (poet)* poète *m*; *Lit* **B. (of Avon)** Shakespeare **2** *(Celtic)* barde *m*

bard² *Culin* N barde *f*
VT barder

bardic [ˈbɑːdɪk] ADJ *(poetry)* des bardes

bardolatry [bɑːˈdɒlətrɪ] N *Hum Pej* = admiration *f* sans bornes pour Shakespeare et ses œuvres

bare [beər] ADJ **1** *(without covering, unadorned) (head, leg, chest, room etc)* nu; *(cupboard, shelf)* vide; *(tree)* dénudé, dépouillé; *(country)* nu, dénudé; *Elec (wire)* dénudé; **to strip a house b.** *(remove contents)* dévaliser une maison; **they stripped the car b.** *(removed wheels etc)* ils n'ont laissé que la carcasse de la voiture; **the wind stripped the tree b.** le vent a dénudé l'arbre; **the room was b. of furniture/pictures** la pièce ne comportait aucun meuble/tableau; **at this time of year, the garden is b. of flowers** à cette époque de l'année, le jardin n'a plus de fleurs; **to fight with b. hands** se battre à mains nues; **I'll kill him with my b. hands** je le tuerai de mes propres mains; **in one's b. feet** pieds nus; **to lie** *or* **sleep on the b. boards** coucher sur la dure; **the b. facts** les faits bruts; **the b. bones of the case are ...** les grandes lignes de cette affaire sont ...; **to lay b.** *(surface, mistakes, one's heart)* mettre à nu, exposer; *(secret, fraud)* dévoiler; *(foundations, roots etc)* déchausser
2 *attrib (just sufficient)* **to earn a b. living** gagner tout juste *ou* à peine de quoi vivre; **the b. minimum** le strict minimum; **the b. necessities (of life)** le strict nécessaire; *Sch* **he got a b. pass** il a eu son examen en ayant juste la moyenne; **a b. pass isn't good enough in my father's eyes** pour mon père, réussir un examen de justesse n'est pas suffisant; **b. majority** faible majorité *f*
VT mettre à nu; **to b. one's head** se découvrir; **to b. one's teeth** montrer les dents; **to b. one's heart** *or* **soul** ouvrir son cœur, mettre son âme à nu

bareback [ˈbeəbæk] ADV **to ride b.** monter (un cheval) à nu *ou* à cru; *Sl Hum (have unprotected sex)* faire l'amour sans capote
▸▸**b. rider** cavalier, -ière qui monte à cru

barefaced [ˈbeəfeɪst] ADJ ATTRIB *Fam Pej (lie, liar etc)* éhonté, effronté

barefoot(ed) [ˈbeəfʊt, -ɪd] ADJ aux pieds nus
ADV nu-pieds, pieds nus; **she goes b.** elle marche pieds nus

barehanded [beəˈhændɪd] ADJ aux mains nues
ADV les mains nues

bareheaded [beəˈhedɪd] ADJ à la tête nue
ADV nu-tête, (la) tête nue

bare-legged ADJ aux jambes nues
ADV (les) jambes nues

barely [ˈbeəlɪ] ADV *(just)* à peine, tout juste; **b. know her** je la connais à peine; **he can b. read and write** c'est tout juste s'il sait lire et écrire; **you've b. got here and you're leaving** tu viens à peine d'arriver et tu es déjà reparti; **a b. furnished room** *(lacking furniture)* une pièce avec très peu de meubles

bareness [ˈbeənɪs] N **1** *(of room)* aspect *m* dépouillé; *(of hillside, wall)* nudité *f* **2** *(of style etc)* dépouillement *m*

barf [bɑːf] VI *esp Am Fam* vomir
▸▸**b. bag** sac *m* pour vomir

barfly ['bɑːflaɪ] N *Am Fam* pilier *m* de bar

bargain ['bɑːgɪn] N **1** *(deal)* marché *m*, affaire *f*; **a good/bad b.** une bonne/mauvaise affaire; **to make** *or* **strike a b. with sb** conclure *ou* faire un marché avec qn; **I'll make a b. with you** on fait un marché; **I thought we had a b.** je croyais qu'on s'était mis d'accord; **you haven't kept your side** *or* **part of the b.** vous n'avez pas respecté notre accord; **to drive a hard b.** ne pas faire de cadeaux; **it's a b.!** c'est entendu!; **into the b.** par-dessus le marché, en plus **2** *(good buy)* occasion *f*, affaire *f*
   VI négocier (**with** avec); *(in market place)* marchander (**with** avec)
   ▸▸**b. basement** *(in shop)* = sous-sol *m* où sont regroupés les articles en solde et autres bonnes affaires; **b. break** séjour *m* discompté; **b. counter** rayon *m* des soldes; **b. hunter** chineur, -euse; **b. hunting** chasse *f* aux affaires; **b. offer** promotion *f*, offre *f* exceptionnelle; **b. price** prix *m* avantageux; **b. sale** soldes *mpl* exceptionnels; **b. store** magasin *m* bon marché
▸ **bargain away** VT SEP brader
▸ **bargain for** VT INSEP *(reaction, question)* s'attendre à, compter sur; **he got more than he bargained for** il ne s'attendait pas à cela; **you might get more than you bargained for** tu auras peut-être du fil à retordre; **I didn't b. for that** je ne m'attendais pas à cela, je ne comptais pas là-dessus
▸ **bargain on** VT INSEP s'attendre à, compter sur; **I hadn't bargained on him being there** je ne m'attendais pas à ce qu'il soit là, je n'avais pas compté qu'il serait là

bargaining ['bɑːgɪnɪŋ] N *(in market)* marchandage *m*; *Ind* négociations *fpl*; **to be in a good b. position, to have a lot of b. power** être dans une bonne position pour négocier; **this has reduced their b. power** cela a affaibli leur position dans les négociations; **to use sb/sth as a b. chip** utiliser qn/qch comme monnaie d'échange
   ▸▸*Ind* **b. table** table *f* des négociations; **b. unit** unité *f* de négociation

barge [bɑːdʒ] N *(for transporting goods)* péniche *f*, barge *f*, chaland *m*; *(for living on)* péniche; *(ceremonial)* bateau *m* d'apparat
   VT *(goalkeeper, player)* écarter d'un coup d'épaule; **to b. sb out of the way** écarter qn d'un geste brusque; **there's a lot of barging going on** *(in race)* on joue beaucoup des épaules
▸ **barge in** VI **1** *(enter abruptly)* faire irruption **2** *(interrupt)* intervenir mal à propos; **don't keep barging in with questions** arrête de me/nous/*etc* interrompre avec tes questions
▸ **barge into** VT INSEP **1** *(collide with)* *(person, lamppost etc)* rentrer dans; **you nearly barged into me!** tu as failli me rentrer dedans! **2** *(enter abruptly)* *(room)* faire irruption dans
▸ **barge through** VT INSEP **to b. through a door** passer une porte en trombe; **to b. through a crowd** se forcer un passage à travers la foule
   VT SEP **just b. your way through** force le passage

bargee [bɑː'dʒiː], *Am* **bargeman** ['bɑːdʒmən] N marinier *m*

bargepole ['bɑːdʒpəʊl] N *(for propelling barge)* gaffe *f*; *Fig* **I wouldn't touch it with a b.** *(it's disgusting)* ça me dégoûterait d'y toucher; *(it's risky for me)* je ne veux rien avoir à faire avec ça; *(it's risky for you)* si j'étais vous, je ne m'en mêlerais pas

barhop ['bɑːhɒp] VI *Am Fam* faire la tournée des bars

baritone ['bærɪtəʊn] N *Mus (voice, singer, instrument)* baryton *m*

barium ['beərɪəm] N *Chem* baryum *m*
   ▸▸*Med* **b. meal** bouillie *f* barytée

bark[1] [bɑːk] N **1** *(of tree)* écorce *f*; **to strip the b. off a tree** écorcer un arbre **2** *(for tanning)* tan *m*
   VT *(tree)* écorcer; *Fig* **to b. one's shins** s'écorcher *ou* s'érafler les jambes (**on** sur)

bark[2] N *(of dog)* aboiement *m*; *(of fox)* glapissement *m*; *Fig* **his b. is worse than his bite** il aboie plus qu'il ne mord
   VI *(of dog)* aboyer (**at** après, contre, à); *(of fox)* glapir; *Fig (of person)* crier (**at** sur); *Fig* **to be barking up the wrong tree** faire fausse route
   VT *(of person)* dire en aboyant; **to b. an order** aboyer un ordre

bark[3] N *Naut (three-master)* trois-mâts *m inv*; *Lit (any boat)* barque *f*
▸ **bark out** VT SEP *(something)* aboyer

barkeep(er) ['bɑːkiːp, -ər] N *Am* barman *m*

barker[1] ['bɑːkər] N *(at fair)* aboyeur *m*

barker[2] N *(machine)* écorceuse *f*

barking ['bɑːkɪŋ] ADJ **1** *(dog)* aboyeur; *(fox)* glapissant **2** *Fam (cough)* sec, *f* sèche **3** *Sl* **b. (mad)** complètement cinglé
   N *(of dog)* aboiement *m*; *(of fox)* glapissement *m*

barley ['bɑːlɪ] N orge *f*
   ▸▸*Culin* **b. sugar** sucre *m* d'orge; *Br* **b. water** = sirop *m* à base d'orge généralement parfumé au citron ou à l'orange

barleycorn ['bɑːlɪkɔːn] N grain *m* d'orge

barm [bɑːm] N *(of beer)* levure *f*; *(yeast)* levain *m*

barmaid ['bɑːmeɪd] N *Br* serveuse *f*, *(in a bar)*, barmaid *f*

barman, *pl* **barmen** ['bɑːmən] N barman *m*

barminess ['bɑːmɪnɪs] N *Br Fam* folie *f*

barmy ['bɑːmɪ] ADJ *Br Fam (crazy)* toqué, cinglé

barn [bɑːn] N grange *f*; *(for cows)* étable *f*; *(for horses)* écurie *f*; *Fam* **they live in an old b. of a house** ils habitent dans un vrai hangar; *Hum* **were you born in a b.?** on ne t'a jamais appris à fermer tes portes?; **he couldn't hit a b. door** *(he's a poor shot)* c'est un mauvais tireur
   ▸▸**b. dance** = bal *m* de campagne où l'on danse des quadrilles; **b. owl** (chouette *f*) effraie *f*, chouette des clochers

barnacle ['bɑːnək(ə)l] N *(mollusc)* bernacle *f*
   ▸▸**b. goose** *(bird)* bernache *f* (nonnette)

barnet ['bɑːnɪt] N *Br Sl (hair)* tifs *mpl*

barney ['bɑːnɪ] N *Br Fam (argument)* prise *f* de bec, dispute *f*; **I had a bit of a b. with the bus driver** j'ai eu une prise de bec avec le conducteur du bus; *Hum* **I had a bit of a b. with a bus** *(of car driver)* j'ai eu un accrochage avec un bus; **we've had a b.** nous nous sommes disputés; **to get into a b. with sb** se disputer avec qn

barnstorm ['bɑːnstɔːm] VI **1** *Br Theat* faire une tournée théâtrale **2** *Am Pol* faire une tournée électorale

barnstormer ['bɑːnstɔːmər] N *Am Pol* orateur, -trice électoral(e)

barnstorming ['bɑːnstɔːmɪŋ] ADJ *(speech, performance)* plein de brio

barnyard ['bɑːnjɑːd] N basse-cour *f*, *pl* basses-cours
   ▸▸**b. humour** humour *m* au ras des pâquerettes

barometer [bə'rɒmɪtər] N *(instrument)*, *Fig* baromètre *m*
   ▸▸**b. reading** hauteur *f* barométrique

barometric [bærə'metrɪk] ADJ *(pressure etc)* barométrique

baron ['bærən] N *(nobleman)* baron *m*; *Fig* **press/oil b.** magnat *m* de la presse/du pétrole; *Culin* **b. of beef** double aloyau *m*

baroness ['bærənes] N baronne *f*

baronet ['bærənet] N baronnet *m*

baronetcy ['bærənɪtsɪ] N dignité *f* de baronnet; **to be given a b.** être élevé au rang de baronnet

baronial [bə'rəʊnɪəl] ADJ baronnial, -aux
   ▸▸**b. hall** demeure *f* seigneuriale

barony ['bærənɪ] N *(domain)* baronnie *f*

baroque [bə'rɒk] ADJ, N *Archit, Art, Mus* baroque *m*

barque [bɑːk] N *Naut* = **bark**[3]

barrack[1] ['bærək] N **1** *Mil (usu pl) (with sing or pl verb)* **barracks** caserne *f*, quartier *m*; **to be confined to barracks** être consigné **2** *Pej Fam (house)* maison *f* grande et laide
   VT *Mil (troops)* caserner
   ▸▸*Mil* **b. square** cour *f* de caserne

> Note that the French word **baraque** is a false friend. Its most common meaning is **shack**.

barrack[2] VT *Br Fam (jeer at) (person)* se moquer de

barracking ['bærəkɪŋ] N *Br Fam* mauvais accueil *m*; **to get** *or* **be given a b.** se faire malmener

barrackroom ['bærəkruːm] N chambrée *f*
   ▸▸**b. language** langage *m* de corps de garde *ou* de caserne; **b. lawyer** chicanier, -ière

barracuda [bærə'kjuːdə] N barracuda *m*, bécune *f*

barrage ['bærɑːʒ] N *(dam)*, *Mil* barrage *m*; *Fig (of questions, insults)* torrent *m*
   VT **to b. sb with** *(questions, offers of help etc)* assaillir qn de
   ▸▸*Mil* **b. balloon** ballon *m* de barrage

barred [bɑːd] ADJ *(locked) (door)* barré; *(with bars on) (window)* muni de barreaux

barrel ['bær(ə)l] N **1** *(container) (for wine etc)* tonneau *m*, barrique *f*, fût *m*; *(for oil)* baril *m*; *(for herring etc)* caque *f*, baril; *Fam* **to have sb over a b.** avoir qn à sa merci; **they've got us over a b.** nous sommes coincés, nous sommes à leur merci
   2 *Fam (large amount)* grande quantité *f* (**of** de); **she's a b. of fun** *or* **laughs** c'est une sacrée boute-en-train; **he's not exactly a b. of fun** *or* **laughs** il n'est pas franchement très marrant; **it wasn't a b. of laughs** *(interview, project)* ça n'a pas été une partie de plaisir; *(film, show)* ce n'était pas très rigolo
   3 *(cylinder, tube)* cylindre *m*, partie *f* cylindrique; *(of gun, lock, key)* canon *m*; *(of pump)* corps *m*, barillet *m*; *(of lock)* cylindre, barillet; *(of capstan, winch)* fusée *f*, mèche *f*, tambour *m*; *Mil (of artillery piece)* tube *m*
   VT (**-ll-**, *Am* **-l-**) mettre en fût
   ▸▸*Mus* **b. organ** orgue *m* de Barbarie; *Aviat* **b. roll** tonneau *m* en spirale; *Archit* **b. vault** voûte *f* en berceau
▸ **barrel along** VI *Fam (in car etc)* foncer

barren ['bær(ə)n] ADJ *(land)* stérile; *(hillside)* sans végétation; *Old-fashioned (woman)* stérile; *Lit Fig (subject)* maigre; **the area is b. of interest for the art-lover** la région ne présente aucun intérêt pour les amateurs d'art; **he's going through a b. period** *(of author)* il n'a pas beaucoup d'inspiration ces temps-ci
   NPL *Am* **barrens** lande(s) *f(pl)*
   ▸▸**b. lands** lande(s)

barrenness ['bærənnɪs] N stérilité *f*

barrette [bə'ret] N *esp Am* barrette *f*

barricade ['bærɪkeɪd, bærɪ'keɪd] N barricade *f*
   VT barricader
▸ **barricade in** VT SEP *(person)* barricader dans une pièce *etc*; **they barricaded themselves in** ils se sont barricadés
▸ **barricade off** VT SEP *(street)* barrer

barrier ['bærɪər] N barrière f, Fig barrière (**between** entre), obstacle m (**to** à); **to break down the barriers** abattre les barrières; **language b.** barrière linguistique
▶▶**b. cream** crème f protectrice; **b. ice** banquise f; **b. method** (of contraception) méthode f de contraception locale; **b. reef** barrière de corail

barring ['bɑːrɪŋ] N **1** (of door etc) barrage m **2** (of action) interdiction f, (of person) exclusion f
PREP (except) excepté, sauf; **b. accidents** sauf accident, sauf imprévu; **b. a miracle** à moins d'un miracle

barrister ['bærɪstər] N Br Law ≃ avocat, -ate

barrow[1] ['bærəʊ] N (in garden etc) brouette f, esp Br (handcart) voiture f ou charrette f à bras; Rail diable m
▶▶Br **b. boy** marchand m ambulant

barrow[2] N Archeol tumulus m, tertre m (funéraire)

Bart abbr baronet

bartender ['bɑːtendər] N Am barman m

barter ['bɑːtər] N troc m
VT troquer; **to b. sth for sth** troquer qch contre qch
VI faire du troc
▶▶**b. society** société f vivant du troc

Bartholomew [bɑː'θɒləmjuː] N Hist the Massacre of St B. le Massacre de la Saint-Barthélemy

basal ['beɪsəl] ADJ basal, -aux

basalt ['bæsɔːlt] N basalte m

basaltic [bə'sɔːltɪk] ADJ basaltique

bascule ['bæskjuːl] N Constr bascule f
▶▶**b. bridge** pont m à bascule

base[1] [beɪs] N **1** (foundation), Fig base f, (of column, statue) socle m; (of machine tool etc) sole f, embase f, Elec (of lamp) culot m **2** Math, Chem etc base f, Ling base, racine f **3** Mil etc (of operations, supplies) base f, **Glasgow is a good b. from which to explore the Highlands** Glasgow est un point idéal pour partir à la découverte des Highlands **4** Sport (in baseball, rounders) base f, Fig **you won't even get to first b. with the chairman if you don't play golf** tu n'arriveras à rien avec le président si tu ne joues pas au golf; **he didn't even get to first b. with her** (girlfriend) il n'est parvenu à rien avec elle; **to be (way) off b.** (mistaken) être (complètement) à côté de la plaque; Am Fam (crazy) être fou ou cinglé; Am Fam **to touch b. with sb** contacter qn; **I just thought I would call and touch b.** je me suis dit que j'appellerais pour prendre des nouvelles
VT **1** (found) (calculation, hope) baser, fonder (**on** sur); (novel, film) baser (**on** sur); (opinion) asseoir, fonder (**on** sur); **what are your accusations based on?** sur quoi tes accusations sont-elles fondées?; **to b. oneself on sth** se baser sur qch **2** (have as headquarters) **to be based in Bath** être basé à Bath
▶▶Mil **b. camp** camp m de base; **b. coat** (of paint) première couche f, Fin **b. date** date f de base; Sport **b. jumping** = saut m en chute libre à partir d'un pont, d'une falaise ou d'une montagne, avec parachute plié que l'on ouvre le plus tard possible; Banking **b. rate** taux m de base (bancaire) (utilisé par les banques pour déterminer leur taux de prêt); TV, Radio **b. station** station f de base; TV, Radio **b. studio** studio m de base; Banking **b. year** année f de référence

base[2] ADJ Fml (ignoble) (man, accusations etc) vil; (reason) bas, f basse, indigne; (action) ignoble, indigne
▶▶**b. coin, b. coinage** (counterfeit) fausse monnaie f; **b. metals** métaux mpl vils

baseball ['beɪsbɔːl] N Sport base-ball m, pl base-balls
▶▶**b. game** match m de base-ball; **b. player** joueur m de base-ball

baseboard ['beɪsbɔːd] N Am plinthe f
▶▶**b. heater** plinthe électrique

Basel ['bɑːz(ə)l] N Bâle f

baseless ['beɪslɪs] ADJ sans fondement

baseline ['beɪslaɪn] N Tennis ligne f de fond; Art ligne de fuite; Comput ligne de base
▶▶Com **b. sales** ventes fpl de base

basely ['beɪslɪ] ADV Fml de façon ignoble

basement ['beɪsmənt] N (in house, shop) sous-sol m, pl sous-sols; **in the b.** au sous-sol
▶▶**b. flat** (appartement m en) sous-sol

baseness ['beɪsnɪs] N Fml (of action, accusation etc) bassesse f

bash [bæʃ] Fam N **1** (blow) coup m; (with fist) coup de poing, gnon m; Br Fam **to have a b. at sth** (attempt) essayer qch; **I'll have a b. at mending it** je vais essayer de le réparer **2** (dent) bosse f, gnon m **3** (party) fête f, soirée f
VT **to b. one's head** se cogner la tête
▶**bash about, bash around** VT SEP Br Fam (beat) (person) battre, maltraiter, rudoyer; (handle roughly) (suitcase, toys etc) maltraiter; **the parcel's been** or **got a bit bashed about** le colis a été un peu abîmé
▶**bash down** VT SEP Br Fam (smash) (door) enfoncer
▶**bash in** VT SEP Br Fam (smash) (door) enfoncer; **I'll b. your face in** je vais te défoncer la tête
▶**bash into** VT INSEP Br Fam (person, object) rentrer dans
▶**bash on** VI Br Fam continuer
▶**bash up** VT SEP Br Fam (person) tabasser; (car) esquinter

bashful ['bæʃfʊl] ADJ **1** (timid) modeste, timide; **b. lover** amoureux m transi **2** (modest) modeste, pudique

bashfully ['bæʃfʊlɪ] ADV **1** (timidly) modestement, timidement **2** (modestly) pudiquement

bashfulness ['bæʃfʊlnɪs] N **1** (timidity) modestie f, timidité f **2** (modesty) pudeur f

bashing ['bæʃɪŋ] N Fam volée f de coups, rossée f, Mil, Sport etc **to take** or **get a b.** prendre une raclée ou une peignée; **queer-/Paki-b.** persécution f des homosexuels/des Pakistanais; Fig Clinton-/union-b. acharnement m contre Clinton/les syndicats

BASIC ['beɪsɪk] N Comput BASIC m

basic ['beɪsɪk] ADJ (elementary) (understanding, vocabulary, agreement etc) de base; (fundamental) (principle etc) fondamental, -aux; (truth, problem) premier; (rudimentary) (furniture, accommodation, skills) rudimentaire; **to learn some b. French** apprendre les bases du français; **my French is a bit b.** mon français est plutôt rudimentaire; **I've got the b. idea** je vois de quoi il s'agit en gros; **trust is b. to any human relationship** la confiance est la base des relations humaines; **these facts are b. to an understanding of the problem** ces faits sont essentiels pour comprendre le problème
NPL basics choses fpl essentielles, essentiel m; (of a language, science etc) bases fpl, rudiments mpl; **let's get down to basics** allons à l'essentiel; **to get back to basics** (important things in life) retourner aux choses essentielles; Pol back to basics = expression f qui suggère un retour aux valeurs traditionnelles en matière d'éducation ou de moralité, lancée par les Conservateurs comme argument de renouveau politique au début des années 90
▶▶Am TV **b. cable** câble m de base; Econ **b.**

commodity denrée f de base; Mktg **b. consumer goods** denrées de consommation courante; Ins **b. cover** assurance f de garantie de base; **b. offer** offre f de base; Fin **b. pay** salaire m de base; **b. population** population-mère f, Br Fin **b. rate** taux m de base; Br Fin **b. salary** salaire de base, traitement m de base; Fin **b. wage** salaire de base

basically ['beɪsɪklɪ] ADV (different, sound, right etc) fondamentalement; **b., I think you're right** au fond, je pense que tu as raison; **I think it's b. a question of experience** je pense qu'en fait c'est une question d'expérience; **b., what he said was ...** en gros, ce qu'il a dit c'est que ...

basil ['bæz(ə)l, Am 'beɪz(ə)l] N Bot, Culin basilic m

basilica [bə'zɪlɪkə] N Archit basilique f

basilisk ['bæzɪlɪsk] N Myth basilic m; Fig Lit **a b. stare** un regard assassin

basin ['beɪs(ə)n] N **1** (bowl) (for washing up etc) bassine f, cuvette f, (of fountain) vasque f, coupe f, (wash-)hand **b.** lavabo m **2** (of river) bassin m; **the Paris B.** le Bassin parisien; **coal b.** bassin houiller **3** Naut (for mooring) bassin m; (in canal, river) garage m

basinful ['beɪs(ə)nfʊl] N (of soup) plein bol m, bolée f, (of water) pleine cuvette f, Sl **to have had a b.** (enough) en avoir ras le bol, en avoir marre

basing fare ['beɪsɪŋ] N tarif m de référence

basing point N (for establishing air fares) point m de référence

basis, pl bases ['beɪsɪs, -iːz] N **1** (of talks etc) base f, (of opinion etc) fondement m; (of tax) assiette f, **on the b. of ...** sur la base de ...; **I will be taking part on an unofficial b.** je participerai à titre non officiel; **on the b. of what you told me** d'après ce que tu m'as dit; **the rumours have no b. in fact** ces rumeurs ne sont fondées sur aucun fait; Acct **b. for depreciation** base amortissable; **b. of calculations** base de calcul **2** Math matrice f de base

bask [bɑːsk] VI **to b. in the sun** se chauffer (au soleil), Fam lézarder; Fig **to b. in sb's favour** jouir de la faveur de qn

basket ['bɑːskɪt] N (with or without handles) corbeille f, (with handles) panier m; (carried on back) hotte f, (for coal etc) banne f, manne f, (plaited shopping basket) cabas m, couffin m; (for carrying baby) couffin; (in basketball) panier; Fin **b. of currencies** panier de monnaies; St Exch **b. of shares** panier d'actions; Old-fashioned Br Fam **(you) silly b.!** espèce d'idiot!
▶▶Fam **b. case** (nervous wreck) paquet m de nerfs; (mad person) cinglé, -ée, barjo mf; Am (invalid) grand (e) invalide mf; **she's turning into a b. case** elle est en train de devenir cinglée; **economic b. case** pays m invalide sur le plan économique; **b. chair** chaise f en osier; **b. hilt** (of sword) (garde f en) coquille f, **b. maker** vannier m; **b. making** vannerie f

basketball ['bɑːskɪtbɔːl] N basket-ball m, pl basket-balls; Fam basket m
▶▶**b. player** basketteur, -euse

basketful ['bɑːskɪtfʊl] N plein panier m

basketry ['bɑːskɪtrɪ], **basketwork** ['bɑːskɪtwɜːk] N vannerie f

basking shark ['bɑːskɪŋ] N pèlerin m

Basle [bɑːl] N Bâle

basmati rice [bæs'mætɪ] N Culin riz m basmati

Basque [bɑːsk] ADJ basque; **the B. Country** le Pays basque
N **1** Basque mf **2** Ling basque m

basque [bɑːsk] N (bodice) guêpière f, (of jacket) basque f

bas-relief ['bæsrɪliːf] N bas-relief *m, pl* bas-reliefs; **in b.** en bas-relief

bass[1] [bæs] N *(fish) (freshwater)* perche *f* commune; *(saltwater)* bar *m*; **striped b.** bar rayé

bass[2] [beɪs] N *(voice, singer, instrument)* basse *f*; *(on amplifier)* basses; *(double bass)* contrebasse *f*; **he sings b.** il chante dans les basses; **deep b.** basse profonde
ADJ ATTRIB *Mus (voice, part)* de basse; **b. tones** sons *mpl* graves
▸▸*Mus* **b. clef** clef *f* de fa; **b. drum** grosse caisse *f*; **b. guitar** guitare *f* basse

bass[3] [bæs] N *(material)* tille *f*, filasse *f*

basset ['bæsɪt] N basset *m*
▸▸**b. hound** basset

bassinet(te) [bæsɪ'net] N *Old-fashioned* **1** *(cradle)* moïse *m* **2** *(pram)* voiture *f* d'enfant

bassist ['beɪsɪst] N *Mus* contrebassiste *mf*

basso profundo [bæsəuprn'fʊndəu] N *Mus* (voix *f* de) basse *f* profonde

bassoon [bə'suːn] N *Mus* basson *m*; **double b.** contrebasson *m*

bassoonist [bə'suːnɪst] N *Mus* basson *m*, bassoniste *mf*

bast [bæst] N = **bass**[3]

bastard ['bɑːstəd] N **1** bâtard, -arde; *Law* enfant *mf* naturel(le) **2** *Sl (person)* salaud *m*; **you b.!** espèce de salaud!; **he's a stupid b.!** c'est un pauvre con!; **you lucky b.!** sacré veinard(e)!; **the poor b.** le pauvre vieux; **it's a b. of a book to translate** ce livre est vachement dur à traduire; **I can't get the b. thing to work** j'arrive pas à faire marcher cette saloperie; **a b. of a job** une saloperie de travail; **it's a b.** *(of work, problem)* c'est vachement difficile
ADJ *(child)* bâtard

bastardize ['bɑːstədaɪz] VT **1** *(debase)* corrompre **2** *Arch (child)* déclarer illégitime

bastardy ['bæstədɪ] N *Arch* bâtardise *f*

baste[1] [beɪst] VT *Sewing* bâtir, faufiler

baste[2] VT *Culin (roast)* arroser de sa graisse/de son jus

basting[1] ['beɪstɪŋ] N *Sewing (action)* faufilage *m*, faufilure *f*; *(stitching)* bâti *m*, faufilure
▸▸**b. thread** fil *m* à faufiler

basting[2] N *Culin (of roast)* arrosage *m*

bastion ['bæstɪən] N *(fortification)*, *Fig* bastion *m*

bat[1] [bæt] N *Zool* chauve-souris *f*, *pl* chauves-souris; *Fig* **like a b. out of hell** comme un bolide; *Fam* **to have bats in the belfry** avoir une araignée au plafond

bat[2] N **1** *(for cricket, baseball etc)* batte *f*; *(for ping-pong)* raquette *f*; **he's a good b.** il manie bien la batte; *Fam* **to do sth off one's own b.** faire qch de sa propre initiative; *esp Am* **to do sth right off the b.** faire qch tout de suite; *esp Am* **to go to b. for sb** *(intercede for)* intervenir *ou* intercéder pour *ou* en faveur de qn **2** *Am* **to go on a b.** se soûler
VI **(-tt-)** *(use bat) (in cricket, baseball etc)* manier la batte; *Cr (be at wicket)* être au guichet; *Sl* **to b. for the other side** *or* **team** *(of gay man)* en être, être pédé; *(of lesbian)* être gouine; *Sl* **to b. for both sides** *or* **teams** *(of bisexual)* marcher à voile et à vapeur

bat[3] VT *(one's eyelids)* battre; *Fig* **he didn't b. an eyelid** il n'a pas sourcillé *ou* tiqué

batch [bætʃ] N *(of bread)*, *Fam (of people)* fournée *f*; *(of letters)* tas *m*, paquet *m*; *(of goods etc)*, *Comput (of data)* lot *m*; *(of cement, concrete)* gâchée *f*; **in batches of 20** *(people)* par groupes de 20; *(of files etc)* par lots de 20
▸▸*Comput* **b. command** commande *f* séquentielle; *Comput* **b. file** fichier *m* de commandes; *Comput* **b. processing** traite-

ment *m* par lots; *Ind* **b. production** production *f* par lots

bated ['beɪtɪd] ADJ **with b. breath** *(to wait, watch)* en retenant son souffle

bath, *pl* **baths** [bɑːθ, bɑːðz] N **1** *(washing)* bain *m*; **to take** *or* **have a b.** prendre un bain; **to give a child a b.** baigner *ou* donner un bain à un enfant; *Br Old-fashioned* **(public) baths** *(for washing)* bains publics; *(for swimming)* piscine *f*; *Br* **the Order of the B.** l'Ordre *m* du Bain **2** *(tub)* baignoire *f*; **he's in the b.** il est dans son bain; **hip b., sitz b.** bain *m* de siège **3** *(bathroom)* salle *f* de bain(s) **4** *Phot etc* cuvette *f*; *(liquid)* bain *m*
VT baigner, donner un bain à
VI prendre un bain
▸▸**b. mat** tapis *m* de bain; **b. pearls** perles *fpl* de bain; **b. rail** barre *f* de soutien; **b. salts** sels *mpl* de bain; **b. sheet** drap *m* de bain; **b. towel** serviette *f* de bain; **b. water** eau *f* du bain

bathcap ['bæθkæp] N *Am* bonnet *m* de bain

bathe [beɪð] N *Old-fashioned* bain *m* (de rivière/de mer), baignade *f*; **to go for a b.** (aller) se baigner
VT *(wash) Med (wound)* laver; *Am (child)* baigner; **to b. one's face** se passer de l'eau sur le visage; **a face bathed in tears** un visage baigné de larmes; **bathed in perspiration** trempé de sueur, en nage; **bathed in light** baigné de lumière
VI **1** *Old-fashioned (swim)* se baigner, prendre un bain (de rivière/de mer) **2** *Am (have bath)* prendre un bain

bather ['beɪðər] N *Old-fashioned* baigneur, -euse

bathers ['beɪðəz] NPL *Austr Fam (swimming costume)* maillot *m*

bathing ['beɪðɪŋ] N **1** *esp Old-fashioned (swimming)* bains *mpl* (de rivière/de mer), baignade *f*; **b. is prohibited** la baignade est interdite, il est interdit de se baigner; **the water is too cold for b.** l'eau est trop froide pour se baigner **2** *Med (of wound etc)* lavage *m*
▸▸**b. cap** bonnet *m* de bain; **b. costume** maillot *m* de bain; **b. place** baignade; **b. suit** maillot *m* de bain; *Br* **b. trunks** maillot de bain

bathos ['beɪθɒs] N *Liter* chute *f* du sublime au ridicule

bathrobe ['bɑːθrəub] N peignoir *m*

bathroom ['bɑːθruːm] N **1** *(with bath)* salle *f* de bain(s) **2** *Am (toilet)* toilettes *fpl*; **to go to the b.** aller aux toilettes
▸▸**b. scales** pèse-personne *m*, *pl* pèse-personnes

bathtime ['bɑːθtaɪm] N l'heure *f* du bain

bathtub ['bɑːθtʌb] N baignoire *f*

batik ['bætɪk, bə'tiːk] N batik *m*; **b. skirt** jupe *f* en batik

batman, *pl* **batmen** ['bætmən] N *Mil* ordonnance *mf*

baton ['bætən] N **1** *(of official)* bâton *m*; *Sport (in relay race)* témoin *m*; *Mus (of conductor)* baguette *f*, bâton; **orchestra under the b. of Jonathan Butcher** orchestre sous la direction de Jonathan Butcher **2** *Br (of policeman)* bâton *m*
▸▸*Sport* **b. change** passage *m* de témoin; **b. charge** charge *f* à la matraque; **b. mike** micro *m* tenu à la main; **b. round** balle *f* en plastique

bats [bæts] ADJ *Br Old-fashioned Fam* loufoque; **to be b. about sb/sth** être fou de qn/qch; **I'm not exactly b. about the idea** je ne raffole pas de cette idée

batsman, *pl* **batsmen** ['bætsmən] N *Cr* batteur *m*

battalion [bə'tæljən] N *Mil* **1** bataillon *m*;

tank b., armoured b. bataillon de chars **2** *Am* groupe *m* d'artillerie
▸▸**b. commander** commandant *m* de bataillon

batten ['bæt(ə)n] N *Carp (for joint)* couvre-joint *m, pl* couvre-joints; *(lathe)* latte *f*, liteau *m*; *(in floor)* planche *f*
VT **1** *Carp* latter, voliger **2** **to b. down the hatches** *Naut* condamner les panneaux; *Fig* se préparer à affronter la crise/la situation
▸**batten on** VT INSEP *(live off)* vivre aux crochets de
▸**batten onto** VT INSEP *(person)* mettre le grappin sur; *(idea)* se mettre dans la tête; **once he battens onto you** une fois qu'il vous a mis le grappin dessus

batter[1] ['bætər] N *Cr, Baseball* batteur *m*

batter[2] N *Culin* pâte *f* à frire; **pancake b.** pâte à crêpes

batter[3] VT **1** *(child, wife etc)* battre **2** *Mil (town)* bombarder
VI **to b. at** *or* **on a door** marteler une porte; **the waves battered against the coast** les vagues s'abattaient le long de la côte
▸**batter down** VT SEP *(door etc)* abattre, démolir; *(wall)* battre en brèche
▸**batter in** VT SEP *(door etc)* enfoncer; **the victim's skull was battered in** la victime a eu le crâne défoncé

battered ['bætəd] ADJ **1** *(face)* meurtri **2** *(furniture, car, house etc)* délabré; *(hat, pan)* cabossé
▸▸**b. baby, b. child** enfant *mf* maltraité(ée), enfant martyr(e); **b. wife** femme *f* battue

battering ['bætərɪŋ] N *(of child, wife)* mauvais traitements *mpl*; **that's not the first b. he's given her** ce n'est pas la première fois qu'il la bat; *Fig* **his confidence took a b.** sa confiance en soi en a pris un coup; *Fig* **to give sb a b.** *(defeat)* mettre une raclée à qn; *Fig* **to take a b.** se prendre une raclée
▸▸**b. ram** bélier *m*

battery ['bæt(ə)rɪ] N **1** *Elec (for calculator, watch etc)* pile *f*; *(for car)* batterie *f*; **(storage) b.** accumulateur *m*; *Fam* **to be b. operated** *or* **powered** *(of radio, toy)* fonctionner sur piles; **batteries not included** *(on packaging)* piles non fournies **2** *Mil* batterie *f*; *Fig* **a b. of criticism** un feu roulant de critiques **3** *(set, group) (of furnaces, tests)* batterie *f* **4** *Law* voie *f* de fait **5** *(for poultry)* batterie *f* **6** *Sport (in baseball)* **the b.** le lanceur et le receveur
▸▸*Elec* **b. back-up** alimentation *f* de secours par batterie; *Elec* **b. cable** câble *m* de batterie; *Elec* **b. charger** chargeur *m*; *Elec* **b. compartment** compartiment *m* réservé à la batterie/aux piles; *Agr* **b. farming** élevage *m* intensif *ou* en batterie; *Agr* **b. hen** poule *f* de batterie; *Elec* **b. life** durée *f* de vie de la batterie/des piles; *Elec* **b. pack** boîtier *m* d'alimentation par pile

batting ['bætɪŋ] N *Cr etc* maniement *m* de la batte

battle ['bæt(ə)l] N *Mil, Fig* bataille *f*, combat *m*; *(against poverty, disease etc)* lutte *f* (**against** contre); **to fight/win a b.** livrer/gagner une bataille; **killed in b.** tué au combat; **to do b. with sb** livrer bataille à qn; **to join b. with sb** entrer en lutte avec qn, livrer bataille à qn; *Fig* **that's half the b.** c'est déjà ça de gagné; **understanding the instructions is half the b.** quand on a compris les instructions, la partie est déjà à moitié gagnée; **a b. of words** une altercation; *(argument)* dispute *f* violente
VI se battre, lutter (**with sb for sth** contre qn pour qch); **to b. with** *or* **against a fire** combattre *ou* lutter contre un incendie
VT **to b. one's way through difficulties** surmonter les difficultés; **I had to b. my way to**

the top il a fallu que je me batte pour arriver au sommet
▸▸ *Hist* **the B. of Britain** la bataille d'Angleterre; *Mil, Naut* **b. cruiser** croiseur *m* cuirassé; *Mil* **b. cry** cri *m* de guerre; **b. fleet** flotte *f* de ligne *ou* de combat; **b. royal** *(fight)* bagarre *f*, *(argument)* querelle *f*, *Mil* **b. zone** zone *f* de bataille *ou* d'engagement

battle-axe N hache *f* d'armes; *Pej Fig (woman)* virago *f*, mégère *f*

battledore ['bæt(ə)ldɔːr] N *Hist, Sport* raquette *f*; **to play at b. and shuttlecock** jouer au volant

battledress ['bæt(ə)ldres] N *Mil* tenue *f* de campagne

battlefield ['bæt(ə)lfiːld], **battleground** ['bæt(ə)lgraʊnd] N *Mil, Fig* champ *m* de bataille

battle-hardened ADJ aguerri

battlements ['bæt(ə)lmənts] NPL remparts *mpl*

battle-scarred [-skɑːd] ADJ *(town)* qui porte les traces de combats violents; *(soldier)* qui porte encore les traces de ses blessures; *Fig (politician)* qui en a vu de rudes

battleship ['bæt(ə)lʃɪp] N *Naut* cuirassé *m*; *Hist* bâtiment *m* de ligne

batty ['bætɪ] ADJ *Fam* toqué, timbré

batwing ['bætwɪŋ] ADJ en forme d'aile de chauve-souris
▸▸ **b. sleeves** manches *fpl* chauve-souris

bauble ['bɔːb(ə)l] N babiole *f*, colifichet *m*

baud [bɔːd] N *Comput* baud *m*; **at 2,400 b.** à (une vitesse de) 2400 bauds
▸▸ **b. rate** débit *m* en bauds

baulk [bɔːk] VT & VI = **balk**

bauxite ['bɔːksaɪt] N *Miner* bauxite *f*

Bavaria [bə'veərɪə] N Bavière *f*

Bavarian [bə'veərɪən] ADJ bavarois
N Bavarois, -oise

bawdiness ['bɔːdɪnɪs] N *(of conversation)* grivoiserie *f*, *(of humour, joke, poetry)* paillardise *f*, grivoiserie

bawdy ['bɔːdɪ] ADJ *(conversation)* grivois; *(humour, joke, poetry etc)* paillard, grivois

bawdyhouse ['bɔːdɪhaʊs] N *Arch* maison *f* de passe

bawl [bɔːl] VI **1** *(shout)* hurler, brailler, *Fam* beugler; **to b. at sb** hurler après qn **2** *Fam (weep)* brailler
VT *(order)* gueuler
▸ **bawl out** VT SEP **1** *(shout) (order)* gueuler **2** *Fam (scold)* engueuler

bawling ['bɔːlɪŋ] N **1** *(shouting)* hurlements *mpl*, braillements *mpl* **2** *Fam (weeping)* braillement(s) *m(pl)*; **stop that b.** arrête de brailler
▸▸ *Fam* **b. out** *(reprimand)* engueulade *f*

bay¹ [beɪ] N *(shrub)* **sweet b.** laurier *m* commun, laurier des poètes
▸▸ **b. laurel** laurier commun, laurier des poètes; **b. leaf** feuille *f* de laurier; **b. tree** laurier; **b. wreath** couronne *f* de laurier(s)

bay² N *Geog* baie *f*, *(small)* anse *f*, **Hudson B.** la baie d'Hudson
▸▸ **the B. of Biscay** le golfe de Gascogne

bay³ N *(alcove)* enfoncement *m*, renfoncement *m*
▸▸ **b. window** *Archit* fenêtre *f* en saillie; *Am Fam (stomach)* gros bide *m*

bay⁴ N **to keep** *or* **hold at b.** *(the enemy)* tenir en échec; *(assailant)* tenir en respect; *(creditors, persistent caller etc)* tenir tête à; **Fam I'm managing to keep my cold at b.** jusqu'ici j'ai réussi à combattre le rhume; **to bring a stag to b.** mettre un cerf aux abois, forcer *ou* acculer un cerf; **to be at b.** *(of stag), Fig* être aux abois
VI *(of hound)* aboyer, donner de la voix; **to b. at the moon** hurler *ou* aboyer à la lune

bay⁵ ADJ, N *(horse)* bai *m*

baying ['beɪɪŋ] N *(of hound)* aboiement *m*

bayonet ['beɪənɪt] N *Mil* baïonnette *f*; **with fixed bayonets** baïonnette au canon
VT *(-t-) (person)* passer à la baïonnette
▸▸ *Mil* **b. charge** charge *f* à la baïonnette; *Elec* **b. holder** *(of light-fitting)* douille *f* à baïonnette; *Tech* **b. joint** joint *m* à baïonnette; *Elec* **b. socket** *(of light-fitting)* douille à baïonnette

bayou ['baɪjuː] N *Am Geog* bayou *m*

bazaar [bə'zɑːr] N **1** *(in Middle East)* bazar *m* **2** *(in aid of charity)* vente *f* de charité

bazooka [bə'zuːkə] N *Mil* bazooka *m*

B & B [biːən'biː] N *Br (abbr* **bed and breakfast)** bed and breakfast *m*

BBC [biːbiː'siː] N *(abbr* **British Broadcasting Corporation)** what's on B./on BBC1? qu'est-ce qu'il y a sur la BBC/sur BBC 1?; **B. programme** émission *f* de la BBC
▸▸ **B. English** = l'anglais *m* tel qu'il était parlé sur la BBC et qui servait de référence pour la "bonne" prononciation; **B. World Service** = émissions *fpl* radiophoniques de la BBC diffusées dans le monde entier

BBQ *abbr* = **barbecue** N

BBS [biːbiː'es] N *Comput (abbr* **bulletin board system)** serveur *m* télématique

BC [biː'siː] *abbr* ADV *(before Christ)* avant Jésus-Christ; **in (the year) 25 BC** en (l'an) 25 av. J.-C.
N *Geog* **(British Columbia)** C.-B. *f*

BCE [biːsiː'iː] N *(abbr* **Board of Customs and Excise)** = douane *f* britannique

BCG [biːsiː'dʒiː] N *Med (abbr* **bacille Calmette-Guérin)** BCG *m*

BE [biː'iː] N *Fin (abbr* **Bank of England)** Banque *f* d'Angleterre

---

BE [biː] *(pr ind am* [æm], *are* [ɑːr], *is* [ɪz], *pl are; past ind was* [wɒz], *were* [wɜːr], *was, pl were; pr sub be; past sub were; prp being* ['biːɪŋ], *pp been* [biːn], *imp be;* **I am, he is, she is, it is, we are, you are, they are** *can be shortened into* **I'm, he's, she's, it's, we're, you're, they're; is not, are not, was not, were not** *into* **isn't, aren't, wasn't, weren't)**

VI être **1, 2, 4, 5** ▪ aller **2** ▪ voici, voilà **2** ▪ avoir **3** ▪ faire **3** ▪ coûter **2** ▪ il y a *(there is/are)* **4** ▪ aller, venir **5**
V AUX être **1–3, 5, 7** ▪ *in tag questions* **6**

VI 1 *(specifying attribute)* être; **Mary is pretty** Marie est jolie; **the sky was blue** le ciel était bleu; **time is money** le temps, c'est de l'argent; **he's a bit odd, is Bob** c'est un drôle de garçon que Bob; **his father is a doctor** son père est médecin; **he is an Englishman** il est anglais, c'est un Anglais; **are they English?** sont-ils anglais?; **if I were you** à votre place, si j'étais vous; **as it is, we must go** les choses étant ce qu'elles sont, il nous faut partir; **unity is strength** l'union fait la force; **three and two are five** trois et deux font cinq; **money isn't everything** l'argent n'est pas tout dans la vie; **you be Robin Hood and I'll be …** tu seras Robin des Bois et moi je serai …; *(kids playing)* on dirait que tu es Robin des Bois et moi je suis … VOIR GRAMMAIRE A55; B66

2 *(specifying location, time, health, price)* **the books are on the table** les livres sont *ou* se trouvent sur la table; **I was at the meeting** j'ai assisté *ou* j'étais à la réunion; **where am I?** où suis-je?; **I don't know where I am** *(I am lost)* je ne sais pas où je suis; *(I have lost my place)* je ne sais pas où j'en suis; **where was I?** *(after digression when talking)* où en étais-je?; **you never know where you are with him** avec lui on ne sait jamais à quoi s'en tenir; **here I am** me voici; **ah, there you are!** ah, vous voilà!; **how are you?** comment allez-vous?; **I am better** je vais mieux; **how much is that?** combien cela coûte-t-il?, c'est combien?; **how far is it to London?** combien y a-t-il d'ici à Londres?; **when is the concert?** quand est-ce que le concert a lieu?; **today is the tenth, it is the tenth today** nous sommes (aujourd'hui) le dix (du mois); **tomorrow is Friday** demain, c'est vendredi; **it is six o'clock** il est six heures; **it is late** il est tard; **it is a fortnight since I saw him** il y a quinze jours que je ne l'ai pas vu; **it is my birthday tomorrow** demain, c'est mon anniversaire

3 to be cold/hot *(of person)* avoir froid/chaud; *(of water etc)* être froid/chaud; **it is fine/cold** il fait beau *(temps)*/froid; **to be ashamed of sb/sth** avoir honte de qn/qch; **to be hungry/thirsty** avoir faim/soif; **to be right/wrong** avoir raison/tort; **my hands are cold** j'ai froid aux mains; **to be twenty (years old)** avoir vingt ans; **the wall is six metres high** le mur fait six mètres de haut; **he was so foolish as to do it** il a eu la sottise de le faire

4 *(exist, remain)* **to be or not to be** être ou ne pas être; **business is not what it was** les affaires ne sont plus ce qu'elles étaient; **that may be** cela se peut; **to see things as they are** voir les choses comme elles sont; **be that as it may** quoi qu'il en soit; **let me be!** laissez-moi tranquille!; **there is, there are** *(impersonal)* il y a; **there is a man in the garden** il y a un homme dans le jardin; **what is there to see?** qu'est-ce qu'il y a à voir?; **there will be dancing** on dansera; **there were a dozen of us** nous étions une douzaine

5 *(go, come)* **I have been to see David** j'ai été *ou* je suis allé voir David; **I have been to the museum** j'ai visité le musée, je suis allé au musée; **I have never been to Venice** je n'ai jamais été *ou* je ne suis jamais allé à Venise; **he was into the room like a flash** il est entré en trombe dans la pièce; **where have you been?** où étais-tu?; **has anyone been?** est-ce que quelqu'un est venu *ou* passé?; **has the postman been?** est-ce que le facteur est passé?; *Br Sl* **(now) you've been and gone and done it!** vous en avez fait une belle!; **be off (with you)!** va-t'en!

6 *(with impers subject)* **it is easy to do it** il est facile de le faire; **it is right that …** il est juste que + *sub*; **it is said that …** on dit que …; **it is for you to decide** c'est à vous de décider; **what is it?** *(what do you want?)* que voulez-vous?; *(what is wrong?)* qu'est-ce qu'il y a?; **as it were** pour ainsi dire, en quelque sorte; *Fam* **what's it to be?** *(in pub, bar)* qu'est-ce que vous prenez?; *(make up your mind)* décidez donc!

V AUX 1 *(forming continuous tenses)* **I am/was doing sth** je fais/faisais qch; *(be in the process of)* je suis/j'étais en train de faire qch; **they are always laughing** ils sont toujours à rire; **the house is being built** la maison est en construction; **I have been waiting for a long time** il y a longtemps que j'attends, j'attends depuis longtemps VOIR GRAMMAIRE A49–50; A51

2 *(with a few intransitive verbs as aux of perfect)* **the sun is set** le soleil est couché; **the guests were all gone** les invités étaient tous partis

3 *(forming passive)* **he was killed** il a été tué; **she is respected by all** elle est respectée de tous; **he was always being laughed at** on se moquait toujours de lui; **she is to be pitied** elle est à plaindre; **what's to be done?** que faire? VOIR GRAMMAIRE A40; A54–5; B39

4 *(denoting future)* **I am to see them tomorrow** je dois les voir demain; **he was never to see them again** il ne devait plus les revoir; **and in July 2002 when the government announced there was to be an election …** et en juillet 2002 quand le gouvernement annonça qu'il y aurait des élections ...; **there was to be an election next year but it's been cancelled** il devait y avoir des élections l'année prochaine mais elles ont été annulées; **am I to do it or not?** *(obligation)* est-ce qu'il faut que je le fasse ou non? VOIR GRAMMAIRE A51–2

5 I am all for reform je suis pour *ou* je suis partisan de la réforme; **I'm all for staying here** je ne demande qu'à rester ici; **what are you?** que faites-vous?

6 *(in tag questions)* **so you're back, are you?** alors, vous voilà de retour?; **she is beautiful, isn't she?** elle est belle, n'est-ce pas?; **they're big, aren't they?** ils sont grands, n'est-ce pas? VOIR GRAMMAIRE A40

7 *(elliptical)* **John's very stupid – I know he is/no he isn't** John est un imbécile – je le sais bien/non, ce n'est pas un imbécile

8 *(imperatives)* **be quiet!** tiens-toi tranquille!; **don't be ridiculous!** ne sois pas ridicule! VOIR GRAMMAIRE A40; B34

beach [biːtʃ] **N** plage *f*; **to go to the b.** aller à la plage; *Fig* **he's not the only pebble on the b.** un de perdu, dix de retrouvés

VT *(ship)* *(run aground)* échouer; *(pull up on to beach)* tirer à sec; **to b. itself** *(of whale)* s'échouer; **a beached whale** une baleine échouée

▸▸ **b. buggy** buggy *m*; **b. chair** chaise *f* longue; **b. hotel** hôtel *m* de plage; **b. hut** cabine *f* (de bains *ou* de plage); **b. tent** tente *f* de plage; **b. wear** vêtements *mpl* de plage

beachball ['biːtʃbɔːl] **N** ballon *m* de plage

▸▸ *Comput* **b. pointer** pointeur-balle *m, pl* pointeurs-balles

beachcomber ['biːtʃkəʊmər] **N 1** *(person)* personne *f* qui ramasse les objets échoués ou laissés sur la plage **2** *(wave)* vague *f* déferlante

beachhead ['biːtʃhed] **N** *Mil (for landing)* tête *f* de pont

beacon ['biːk(ə)n] **N 1** *Naut, Aviat (lighthouse)* phare *m*; *(marking channel, runway)* balise *f*; *(light, signal)* feu *m*; *(at crossing)* signal *m* lumineux; *Fig* phare; **radar b.** balise radar, radar *m* de radionavigation **2** *Arch (fire)* feu *m* (pour donner l'alarme); *(location)* tour/colline *f* où un feu est allumé pour donner l'alarme

▸▸ **b. light** balise

bead [biːd] **N 1** *(of glass, enamel etc)* perle *f*; **(string of) beads** collier *m*; **beads of dew** perles de rosée; **there were beads of perspiration on his forehead** la sueur perlait sur son front

2 *(for prayers)* grain *m*; **to tell one's beads** égrener *ou* dire son chapelet

3 *(on sparkling wine etc)* bulle *f*

4 *Architc, Carp (moulding)* baguette *f*

5 *(on gun)* guidon *m*, mire *f*

6 *Metal* cordon *m* de soudure

7 *Aut (on tyre)* bourrelet *m*

VT 1 couvrir *ou* orner de perles **2** *Archit, Carp* appliquer une baguette sur

VI *(of liquid)* perler

▸▸ *Aut* **b. apex** bord *m* de talon (de pneu); **b. curtain** rideau *m* de perles; *Aut* **b. wire** armature *m* de bourrelet

beaded ['biːdɪd] **ADJ** *(material)* perlé

▸▸ *Archit, Carp* **b. strip** chapelet *m*

beading ['biːdɪŋ] **N 1** *(decoration)* garniture *f* de perles **2** *Archit, Carp* baguette *f* **3** *(of tyre)* talon *m*, bourrelet *m*

beadle ['biːd(ə)l] **N** bedeau *m*

beady ['biːdɪ] **ADJ** *(eyes)* petits et brillants; **a b.-eyed shopkeeper** un commerçant qui tient ses clients à l'œil dans sa boutique; *Br Fam* **I've got my b. eye on you** je t'ai à l'œil

beagle ['biːg(ə)l] **N** beagle *m*, briquet *m*

beagling ['biːglɪŋ] **N** chasse *f* au briquet

beak [biːk] **N 1** *(of bird, tortoise, jug, vase etc)* bec *m*; *Fam Hum (of person)* tarin *m*, blair *m* **2** *Br Sl (judge)* juge *m*; *(headmaster)* dirlo *m*

beaked [biːkt] **ADJ** *(animal)* à bec; *(nose)* crochu

▸▸ **b. whale** hyperodon *m*

beaker ['biːkər] **N 1** *(container)* gobelet *m*, timbale *f* **2** *Chem* vase *m* à bec

be-all and end-all **N** *Fam (aim)* but *m* suprême, fin *f* des fins; **it's not the b. if it doesn't work** ce n'est pas la fin du monde si ça ne marche pas; *Hum Pej* **he thinks he's the b.** il ne se prend pas pour n'importe qui; **she thinks her son's the b.** elle pense que son fils est une petite merveille

beam [biːm] **N 1** *Constr* poutre *f* (en bois), solive *f*, madrier *m*; *(small)* poutrelle *f*; **ceiling b.** doubleau *m*

2 *Gym (balance)* **b.** poutre *f* horizontale

3 *(width)* **(breadth of) b.** *(of ship)* largeur *f*, broad in the b. *(ship)* à larges baux; *Fam (person)* large de hanches

4 *(of ship)* travers *m*; **on the port/starboard b.** par le travers bâbord/tribord

5 *(of light, sun)* rayon *m*; *(of headlamp etc)* faisceau *m*; *Fig (smile)* grand *ou* large sourire *m*; **the headlights were on full b.** la voiture était en pleins phares

6 *Elec* faisceau *m*; **electronic/radar b.** faisceau électronique/radar; **radio b.** faisceau hertzien; *Aviat* **radio landing b.** axe *m* balisé d'atterrissage; *Fam* **you're way off b.** *(mistaken)* tu es complètement à côté de la plaque; **the calculations are way off b.** les calculs sont archifaux

VT 1 *TV (pictures)* transmettre; *Tel (message)* transmettre par ondes dirigées; *Aviat* **to be beamed in on Orly** *(of aircraft)* être dirigé sur Orly **2** *TV (of person)* **she beamed her thanks** elle a fait un grand sourire en guise de remerciement

VI *(of sun)* rayonner; *(of person)* faire un grand sourire; **beaming with health** resplendissant de santé; **she beamed with pride** *(smiled)* elle a eu un sourire de fierté; **she is beaming with pride** *(radiating pride)* elle rayonne de fierté

▸▸ *Aut* **b. deflector** déflecteur *m* de faisceau, traverse *f*

beam-ends **NPL** *(of ship)* baux *mpl*; **to be on her b.** *(of ship)* être sur le flanc; *Fig* **to be on one's b.** être *ou* se trouver à bout de ressources

beaming ['biːmɪŋ] **ADJ** *(sun, face)* rayonnant, radieux; *(smile)* radieux

bean [biːn] **N 1** *(vegetable)* haricot *m*; **broad b.** fève *f*; **French b.,** *Am* **string b.** haricot vert, *Can* fève verte; **runner b.** haricot d'Espagne; *Br* **butter b.,** *Am* **Lima b.** haricot de Lima; **kidney b., haricot b.** *(red)* haricot rouge; *(white)* haricot de Soissons; **soya b.** graine *f* de soja; *Culin* **dried beans** haricots secs; *Fam* **to be full of beans** être en pleine forme; *Fam* **it isn't worth a b.** ça ne vaut pas un radis; *Fam* **he hasn't a b.** il n'a pas un radis; *Am Fam* **not to know beans about sth** savoir que dalle sur qch; *Am Fam* **she knows how many beans make five** elle n'est pas née d'hier, c'est un vieux renard; *Old-fashioned* **old b.** *(form of address)* mon vieux

2 *(of coffee)* grain *m*; *(of cocoa)* graine *f*, fève *f*

3 *Am Sl (head)* caboche *f*

4 *Am Offensive Sl* métèque *mf* (d'origine latino-américaine)

▸▸ *Culin* **b. curd** pâte *f* de soja; **b. sprout** germe *m* de soja

beanbag ['biːnbæg] **N 1** *(bag)* balle *f* lestée **2** *(cushion, chair)* fauteuil *m* poire

bean-counter **N** *esp Am Fam Pej* comptable *mf*

beanery ['biːnərɪ] **N** *Am* = petit restaurant *m* pas cher

beanfeast ['biːnfiːst] **N** *Br Fam (festive occasion)* bombe *f*

beanie hat ['biːnɪ] **N** bonnet *m*

beano ['biːnəʊ] **N** *Br Fam* = **beanfeast**

beanpole ['biːnpəʊl] **N** rame *f* pour haricots; *Fig (person)* échalas *m*, perche *f*

beanstalk ['biːnstɔːk] **N** tige *f* de haricot

bear¹ [beər] **N 1** *(animal)*, *Fig* ours *m*; **to be like a b. with a sore head** être d'une humeur massacrante; **the Great B. Lake** le grand lac de l'Ours; *Astron* **the Great/Little B.** la Grande/Petite Ourse; **she b.** ourse *f* **2** *St Exch* baissier, -ière, joueur, -euse à la baisse; **to go a b.** spéculer à la baisse; **to sell a b.** vendre à découvert

VT **(-r)** *St Exch* **to b. the market** chercher à faire baisser les cours

VI *St Exch* spéculer à la baisse

▸▸ *St Exch* **b. closing** arbitrage *m* à la baisse; **b. cub** ourson *m*; **b. garden** *Hist* fosse *f* aux ours; *Fig* pétaudière *f*; *St Exch Fam* **b. hug** = communiqué *m* d'information annonçant une OPA imminente; **to give sb a b. hug** serrer qn très fort dans ses bras; *St Exch* **b. market** marché *m* à la baisse *ou* baissier; *Zool* **b. pit** fosse aux ours; *St Exch* **b. speculation** spéculation *f* à la baisse; *St Exch* **b. spread** spread *m* baissier; *St Exch* **b. trading** spéculation à la baisse

BEAR² *(pt* **bore** [bɔːr]; *pp* **borne** [bɔːn]*)* **VT 1** *(burden, arms, name, date, signature)* porter; *Lit* **to b. gifts** apporter des cadeaux; **I still b. the scars** *(of attack etc)* j'en porte encore les cicatrices; *Fig* j'en garde encore les cicatrices; **to b. all the marks of sth** être caractéristique de qch; **the murder bore all the marks of a mafia killing** le meurtre avait tout d'un crime mafieux; **to b. sth in mind** *(remember)* se souvenir de qch; *(take into account)* tenir compte de qch; **b. us in mind if ever you want to sell it** pensez à nous si jamais vous décidez de le vendre; **it bears no relation/resemblance to ...** cela n'a aucun rapport/aucune ressemblance avec ...; **his account bears no relation to the truth** sa version n'a rien à voir avec ce qui s'est vraiment passé; **he bore himself with dignity** il est resté très digne; **to be borne backwards/along** être refoulé/emporté; **to b. the costs** supporter *ou* assumer les frais; **we will b. the costs** nous prendrons les frais en charge; **to b. the responsibility for sth** être responsable de qch; **I refuse to b. the responsibility for that** je décline toute responsabilité à ce sujet; **she bears a heavy responsibility** elle porte une lourde responsabilité; **to b. one's troubles with patience** supporter ses malheurs avec courage

2 *(tolerate)* *(weight)* supporter, soutenir; *(suffering, consequences, pain)* supporter; **he can't b. being beaten** il ne supporte pas d'être battu; **he could b. it no longer** il ne pouvait plus tenir; **I can't b. this** je ne peux pas supporter ça; **his language does not b. repeating** il a été si grossier que je n'ose même pas répéter ce qu'il a dit; **I can't b. (the sight of) him** je ne peux pas le supporter; **I can't b. the idea of it** je ne peux pas en supporter l'idée; **it doesn't b. thinking about** l'idée en est insupportable

3 *Lit, Arch (give birth to)* *(see also* **born***)* donner naissance à; **she has borne him three sons** elle lui a donné trois fils

4 *(yield)* **to b. interest** porter intérêt; **to b. fruit** *(of tree)* donner des fruits; *Fig (of work etc)* porter ses fruits; **my enquiries bore fruit** mes recherches ont été couronnées de succès *ou* ont porté leurs fruits

VI 1 *(move, lie)* **to b. (to the) right/left** *(of person)* tourner à droite/à gauche, prendre à droite/à gauche; *(of road)* tourner à droite/à gauche

2 pressure has been brought to b. on a exercé une pression sur lui/elle/*etc*

▸ **bear away** VT SEP *(thing)* emporter

▸ **bear down** VI *(of woman in labour)* pousser

VT SEP *Lit (usu passive)* **to be borne down by poverty** être accablé par la misère

▸ **bear down on, bear down upon** VT INSEP *(person, enemy, boat etc)* foncer sur

▸ **bear on** VT INSEP **1** *(weigh)* **to bring all one's strength to b. on a lever** s'appuyer de toutes ses forces sur un levier; **to bring all one's energies to b. on sth** apporter *ou* consacrer toute son énergie à qch; **to bring one's mind to b. on sth** porter son attention sur qch; **to bring influence/pressure to b. on sb** exercer une influence/une pression sur qn; **it was gradually borne in on him that …** peu à peu il s'est rendu compte que …

2 *(be relevant to)* avoir un rapport avec; **I don't see how that bears on what I'm doing** je ne vois pas le rapport que ça a avec ce que je fais

▸ **bear out** VT SEP *(confirm) (assertion)* confirmer; **to b. sb out, to b. out what sb has said** confirmer *ou* corroborer ce que qn a dit; **I feel – and I'm sure Peter will b. me out on this – …** j'estime – et je suis sûr que Peter confirmera *ou* corroborera ce point – …

▸ **bear up** VI **1** *(of person)* **to b. up under misfortune** faire face au malheur; **she's bearing up remarkably well** elle tient drôlement bien le coup; **b. up!** tenez bon!, du courage!; *Br Fam* **how are you? – bearing up** comment ça va? *ou* ça va? – on fait aller

2 *(of results)* tenir

▸ **bear upon** VT INSEP = **bear on**

▸ **bear with** VT INSEP **1** *(tolerate) (sb's bad mood etc)* supporter

2 *(be patient with)* **if you'll b. with me, I'll explain** si vous patientez un instant, je vais vous expliquer; **b. with me while I finish this** je termine ceci et je suis à vous; **I won't be a minute, if you could b. with me** je suis à vous dans une minute

bearable ['beərəb(ə)l] ADJ supportable

bearably ['beərəblɪ] ADV d'une façon supportable; **it was hot but b. so** il faisait chaud mais c'était supportable

bear-baiting N combat *m* d'ours et de chiens

beard [bɪəd] N **1** *(of man, animal), Bot (of ear of barley etc)* barbe *f*; **to have a b.** porter la barbe; **to grow a b.** se laisser pousser la barbe; **a week's b.** une barbe de huit jours **2** *Sl (woman going out with gay man)* = femme *f* que fréquente un homosexuel de façon à dissimuler son homosexualité

VT *(person)* braver, défier; *Fig* **it was very brave of you to b. the lion in his den** c'est très courageux de ta part d'avoir été l'affronter

bearded ['bɪədɪd] ADJ *(man)* barbu

▸▸ **b. lady** femme *f* à barbe

-bearded ['bɪədɪd] SUFF **black-/white-b.** à la barbe noire/blanche

beardless ['bɪədlɪs] ADJ imberbe

bearer ['beərər] N *(of news, letter, cheque)* porteur, -euse; *(of passport)* titulaire *mf*; **bearers** *(at funeral)* les porteurs

▸▸ *Fin* **b. bill** effet *m ou* billet *m* au porteur; *St Exch* **b. bond** titre *m* au porteur; *Fin* **b. cheque** chèque *m* au porteur; *Fin* **b. paper** papier *m* au porteur; *St Exch* **b. share** action *f* au porteur

bearing ['beərɪŋ] ADJ *(axle etc)* porteur

N **1** *(of arms)* port *m*

2 *(deportment)* port *m*, maintien *m*, allure *f*; **because of her dignified b. throughout** parce qu'elle est restée digne jusqu'au bout

3 *Tech* palier *m*; **self-lubricating b.** palier graisseur; **ball/roller/needle b.** roulement *m* à billes/à rouleaux/à aiguilles

4 *(direction)* orientation *f*, *(in surveying)* gisement *m*, azimut *m*; *Naut, Aviat* relèvement *m*, position *f*; **true b.** *(in surveying)* azimut *ou* gisement géographique; *Naut, Aviat* relèvement vrai; **compass b.** relèvement au compas; **to take the ship's bearings** faire le point; *Naut* **to take one's bearings** s'orienter, se repérer; **to lose one's bearings** *Naut* perdre sa direction *ou* sa route; *Fig* ne plus s'y retrouver; **to get one's bearings** *Naut* retrouver sa direction *ou* sa route; *Fig* s'y retrouver

5 *(connection)* rapport *m* (**on a question** avec une question); **it has no b. on the matter** *(of fact etc)* cela n'a aucun rapport avec l'affaire

▸▸ **b. surface** *(of beam)* surface *f* d'appui; *(of joist)* tablette *f*, *Tech* surface portante *ou* de portage; **b. wall** mur *m* d'appui

-bearing ['beərɪŋ] SUFF **fruit-b.** fructifère, qui porte des fruits; **interest-b. capital** capital *m* qui rapporte; **silver-b.** argentifère; **wool-b.** lanifère

bearish ['beərɪʃ] ADJ **1** *Fig (manners)* d'ours; *(person)* bourru **2** *St Exch (market)* à la baisse, baissier; **to be b.** spéculer *ou* jouer à la baisse

▸▸ *St Exch* **b. tendency** tendance *f* à la baisse

bearskin ['beəskɪn] N **1** peau *f* d'ours **2** *Mil (helmet)* bonnet *m* à poil

▸▸ **b. rug** peau d'ours

beast [biːst] N **1** bête *f*, **wild b.** *(not domesticated)* bête sauvage; *(fierce)* bête féroce; *Lit* **the king of the beasts** le roi des animaux; **b. of prey** carnassier *m*; *Lit* **b. of burden** *(ass etc)*, *Fig* bête de somme; *Bible* **the B.** l'Antéchrist *m*; **beasts** *(on farm)* bétail *m*, bestiaux *mpl* **2** *Fig (brute)* brute *f*, *Fam (unkind person)* vache *f*, peau *f* de vache; **the little b.** le petit diable; **he's a perfect b.!** c'est une peau de vache!; **it was a b. of a day** *(bad weather)* il a fait un temps abominable *ou* un temps de chien; **I've had a b. of a day** *(full of problems)* j'ai eu une journée affreuse; **a b. of a job** *(task)* un travail pénible

beastliness ['biːstlɪnɪs] N *esp Old-fashioned* **the b. of his behaviour** sa conduite ignoble

beastly ['biːstlɪ] *Fam* ADJ *(person)* affreux; *(place, smell, taste)* dégoûtant; **a b. job** *(task)* un travail pénible; **what b. weather!** quel sale temps!

ADV bigrement, vachement

BEAT [biːt] N **1** *(stroke, blow) (of heart, clock, drum)* battement *m*; *Mus* mesure *f*, temps *m*; **music with a strong b.** musique avec un fort rythme

2 *Br (of policeman)* ronde *f*; **a policeman on the b.** un agent qui fait sa ronde; *Fig Fam* **it's off my b. altogether** cela ne relève pas de ma compétence, ce n'est pas de mon ressort

VT *(pt* **beat;** *pp* **beaten** ['biːt(ə)n]*)* **1** *(hit) (person, rug, eggs, wood for game birds etc)* battre; **to b. sb with a stick** donner des coups de bâton à qn; **to b. one's breast** se frapper la poitrine; **to b. a drum** battre du tambour; **the world is beating a path to her door** tout le monde se rue sur elle; *Fam* **b. it!** *(go away)* file!, fiche le camp!; *Vulg* **to b. one's meat** se branler; **to b. its wings** *(of bird)* battre des ailes

2 *(defeat, conquer) (enemy)* battre, vaincre; *(record)* battre; *(get ahead of)* battre, devancer; **to b. sb at chess** battre qn aux échecs; *Fam* **that beats me!** ça me dépasse!; *Fam* **it beats me why he did it** je ne pige vraiment pas pourquoi il a fait ça; *Fam* **that beats everything!** ça c'est le comble *ou* le

bouquet!; *Fam* **you can't b. a good book** rien de tel qu'un bon livre; *Fam* **I got up early to b. the traffic** je me suis levé tôt pour éviter les embouteillages; *Fam* **he b. me to it** *(arrived, telephoned before me etc)* il m'a devancé; *Prov* **if you can't b. them, join them** mieux vaut s'allier aux gens que l'on ne peut pas vaincre

3 *Am Sl (cheat, get the better of)* rouler, refaire; **to b. the customs** frauder la douane

VI **1** *(of heart, rain)* battre; **the waves are beating against the shore** les vagues déferlent sur le rivage

2 *Naut* **to b. to windward** louvoyer

3 *Fig* **to b. about** *or Am* **around the bush** tourner autour du pot

ADJ *Fam* **1 you've got me b.** *(defeated)* je m'avoue vaincu; *(unable to answer)* je sèche; **I think Hingis has got Williams b.** je pense que Hingis a déjà battu Williams; **this crossword's got me b.** je sèche sur ces mots croisés; **it's got** *or* **it has me b. why she did it** je ne comprends pas pourquoi elle a fait ça

2 *(very tired)* crevé; **dead b.** complètement crevé

▸ **beat back** VT SEP *(people, enemy troops, flames)* repousser

▸ **beat down** VT SEP *(door)* enfoncer; *(nettles, grass etc with stick)* rabattre; *(earth)* damer; *Fig* **to b. down the price of sth** *(by bargaining)* faire baisser le prix de qch; **to b. sb down** faire baisser le prix à qn

VI *(of rain)* tomber à verse; *(of sun)* taper; **the rain was beating down on the tin roof** la pluie s'abattait sur le toit en tôle; **the sun is beating down on our heads** le soleil nous tape sur la tête

▸ **beat in** VT SEP *(door etc)* défoncer

▸ **beat off** VT SEP *(person, assault)* repousser

VI *Am Vulg (masturbate)* se branler

▸ **beat out** VT SEP **1** *(extinguish) (flames)* étouffer

2 *(flatten) (sheet metal)* battre, aplatir; *(gold etc)* marteler; *(bodywork)* débosseler; **to b. out the dents in a car door** débosseler une porte de voiture

3 *Mus* **to b. out the rhythm,** *Fam* **to b. it out** marquer le rythme

4 *Fam* **I'll b. your brains out!** je vais te démolir!; *Fig* **to b. one's brains out** se creuser la tête *ou* la cervelle

5 **to b. the dust out of sth** battre qch pour en faire sortir la poussière

▸ **beat up** VT SEP **1** *(person)* tabasser

2 *(eggs)* battre

3 *(game)* rabattre, traquer

VI *Naut* louvoyer *ou* gagner vers la terre

▸ **beat up on** VT INSEP *esp Am Fam (hit)* battre, tabasser; **stop beating up on yourself** arrête de culpabiliser

beat-'em-up N = film *m* ou jeu *m* vidéo comportant de nombreuses bagarres

beaten ['biːt(ə)n] ADJ **1** *(gold, metal)* battu, martelé; *(earth)* battu; *Fig* **off the b. track** *(house, to live)* à l'écart; **let's go somewhere a bit more off the b. track** sortons un peu des sentiers battus **2** *(enemy)* battu, vaincu

beater ['biːtər] N **1** *(person)* batteur, -euse; *(in hunting)* rabatteur, -euse **2** *(device) (for eggs)* fouet *m*

beatific [biːə'tɪfɪk] ADJ *Lit (vision)* béatifique; *(smile)* béat

beatifically [biːə'tɪfɪklɪ] ADV *Lit* d'un air béat

beatification [biːætɪfɪ'keɪʃən] N *Rel* béatification *f*

beatify [biː'ætɪfaɪ] VT *Rel* béatifier

beating ['biːtɪŋ] ADJ *(heart)* battant, palpitant; *(rain)* battant

N **1** *(of wings, heart etc)* battement *m*; *(of game)* rabattage *m*, rabat *m*; *(of wood for game)* traque *f* **2** *(thrashing)* raclée *f*, rossée *f*, **to give sb a b.** donner une raclée à qn, rosser qn **3** *(in match etc)* défaite *f*, *Fam* raclée *f*, **to get a good b.** être battu à plate(s) couture(s); *Fam* recevoir une bonne raclée **4** *Naut* louvoyage *m*

beatitude [biː'ætɪtjuːd] N béatitude *f*; *Bible* **the Beatitudes** les Béatitudes

beatnik ['biːtnɪk] N beatnik *mf*

beat-up ADJ *Fam (car, chair etc)* déglingué

beau, *pl* **beaus, beaux** [bəʊ, bəʊz] N **1** *Arch (dandy)* élégant *m*, dandy *m* **2** *Arch, Am (of young girl)* prétendant *m*, galant *m*

beaut [bjuːt] *Fam* N **what a b.!** quelle merveille!; **what a b. of a car!** quelle voiture! ADJ *Austr* super, génial, -aux

beautician [bjuː'tɪʃən] N esthéticien, -ienne; *(make-up artist)* visagiste *mf*

beautiful ['bjuːtɪfʊl] ADJ **1** *(person, place, face etc)* (très) beau, (très) belle; **the b. people** le beau monde **2** *(dinner, weather etc)* magnifique

beautifully ['bjuːtɪfʊlɪ] ADV *(intensifier)* admirablement, à merveille; **b. dressed** merveilleusement bien habillé

beautify ['bjuːtɪfaɪ] VTembellir

beauty ['bjuːtɪ] N **1** *(appearance)* beauté *f*, **the beauties of nature** les beautés de la nature; **that's the b. of it** c'est ça qu'il y a de bien; *Prov* **b. is in the eye of the beholder** ce qu'on aime est toujours beau **2** *(person, object)* **she was a b. in her day** c'était une beauté dans son temps; **B. and the Beast** la Belle et la Bête; **Sleeping B.** la Belle au bois dormant; *Fam* **isn't it a b.?** *(of flower)* n'est-ce pas qu'elle est belle?; *(of car)* n'est-ce pas qu'elle est super?; *(of mistake)* elle est bonne celle-là!; *Br Fam* **(you) b.!** super!; *Fam* **he fetched him a b. on the chin** il lui a flanqué un coup magnifique *ou* formidable au menton; *Fam* **that black eye is a real b.** c'est un bel œil au beurre noir
▶▶**b. contest** concours *m* de beauté; **b. parlour** institut *m* de beauté; **b. products** produits *mpl* de beauté; **b. queen** reine *f* de beauté; **b. salon** institut de beauté; **b. sleep** sommeil *m* avant minuit *(considéré comme le plus réparateur)*; **b. spot** *(on skin)* grain *m* de beauté; *(artificial)* mouche *f*; *(scenic place)* site *m* touristique; **b. treatment** soins *mpl* esthétiques

beaver ['biːvər] N **1** *(animal, fur)* castor *m*; *Fam* **to work like a b.** travailler d'arrache-pied; **b. coat/jacket** manteau *m*/veste *f* de castor **2** *Am Vulg (female genitals)* chatte *f*
▶▶**b. lamb** mouton *m* doré
▶ **beaver away** VI travailler d'arrache-pied *(* at *à)*

becalmed [bɪ'kɑːmd] ADJ *(ship)* encalminé

became PT see become

because [bɪ'kɒz, -kəz] CONJ parce que; **I eat b. I'm hungry** je mange parce que j'ai faim; **I was all the more astonished b. I had been told that …** j'en fus d'autant plus étonné qu'on m'avait assuré que …; **b. he dashed off a sonnet, he thinks himself a poet** il se prend pour un poète simplement parce qu'il a torché un sonnet; **why? – just b.** pourquoi? – parce que
PREP **b. of sth** à cause de qch; **b. of his illness** à cause de *ou* en raison de sa maladie

béchamel ['beʃəmel] N *Culin* béchamel *f*
▶▶**b. sauce** sauce *f* (à la) béchamel

beck¹ [bek] N **to have sb at one's b. and call** avoir qn à ses ordres *ou* à sa disposition; **to be at sb's b. and call** obéir aux moindres volontés de qn, être aux ordres de qn

beck² N *Dial* ruisseau *m* de montagne

beckon ['bekən] VT & VI faire signe (**to sb** à qn); **to b. sb in** faire signe à qn d'entrer; *Fig* **the bright lights of the city beckoned** les lu-

mières de la ville étaient une tentation; **I can't stay, work beckons** il faut que je m'en aille, j'ai du travail; **and fame beckoned** et les portes de la gloire lui étaient ouvertes; **to b. sb** faire signe à qn de s'approcher

become [bɪ'kʌm] *(pt* **became** [bɪ'keɪm]; *pp* **become)** VI **1** *(a priest, an adult, sb's enemy etc)* devenir; **to b. king/a doctor** devenir roi/médecin; **to b. old/thin** vieillir/maigrir; **to b. suspicious of sb** commencer à avoir des soupçons à propos de qn, devenir soupçonneux à l'égard de qn; **the murmurs became louder** les murmures se faisaient plus forts; **to b. accustomed/attached/interested** s'accoutumer/s'attacher/s'intéresser; **to b. known** *(of person)* commencer à être connu; **it will soon b. clear that …** il sera bientôt évident que …
2 what has b. of Tom? qu'est devenu Tom?; **what will b. of him?** que va-t-il devenir?; **I don't know what has b. of her** je ne sais pas ce qu'elle est devenue
VT *esp Fml (person) (of behaviour etc)* être digne de; *(of clothes, colour etc)* aller bien à

becoming [bɪ'kʌmɪŋ] ADJ **1** *(proper) (behaviour)* convenable, bienséant **2** *(colour, clothes)* seyant; **red is very b. to her** le rouge lui va très bien *ou* lui sied; **green looks very b. on you** le vert te va très bien; **you look very b. in that dress** cette robe te va très bien

becquerel [bek(ə)'rel] N *Phys* becquerel *m*

BEd [biː'ed] N *Univ abbr* **Bachelor of Education**

bed [bed] N **1** lit *m*; **to be in b.** *(to rest)* être couché, être au lit; *(through illness)* être alité, garder le lit; **to keep sb in b.** garder qn au lit; **to read in b.** lire au lit; **to get out of b.** se lever; **to get out of b. on the wrong side** se lever du pied gauche; **I'm sorry to get you out of b.** je suis désolé de vous tirer du lit; *Hum* **I wouldn't kick her out of b.** si elle voulait de moi, je ne dirais pas non; **to go to b.** se coucher; *Journ* **the paper has gone to b.** le journal est bouclé; **I'm going home to b.** je vais rentrer me coucher; **to keep to one's b.** garder le lit; *Fam* **to go to b. with a man/woman** coucher avec un homme/une femme; *Fig* **to be in b. with sb** être allié avec qn de façon officieuse; **to put a child to b.** coucher un enfant, mettre un enfant au lit; *Journ* **to put a paper to b.** boucler un journal; **she always takes her teddy to b. with her** elle emmène toujours son ours au lit avec elle; **it's time for b.** c'est l'heure d'aller au lit *ou* d'aller se coucher; **to make the b.** faire le lit; *Fig* **you've made your b. and now you must lie in it** comme on fait son lit, on se couche; **to sleep in separate beds** faire lit à part
2 *(of river, sea)* lit *m*; *(of billiard table)* fond *m*; **filter b.** lit de filtrage; **place the roast on a b. of vegetables** placez le rôti sur un lit de légumes
3 *(in garden) (for vegetables)* carré *m*; *(for flowers)* parterre *m*; **oyster b.** banc *m* d'huîtres; *(on oyster farm)* parc *m* à huîtres
4 *Geol* assise *f*, couche *f*; *Miner* gisement *m*
5 *Constr etc (of concrete)* assise *f*, lit *m*; *(of stone)* assise; *Rail* infrastructure *f*
6 *Tech (of lathe)* banc *m*
VT **(-dd-)** *Fam (woman)* coucher avec
▶▶**b. and board** pension *f* complète; **b. and breakfast** *(establishment)* chambre *f* d'hôte; chambre et petit déjeuner; *St Exch* **b. and breakfasting** aller et retour *m*; **b. head** chevet *m*, tête *f* (de lit); *Br* **b. jacket** liseuse *f*; **b. linen** draps *mpl* de lit (et taies *fpl* d'oreiller); **b. occupancy** occupation *f* des lits; **b. settee** convertible *m*, canapé-lit *m*, *pl* canapés-lits; **b. sheet** drap *m*
▶ **bed down** VI *(of animal)* se gîter; *Fam (of person)* se coucher
VT SEP *(horses)* faire la litière à
▶ **bed out** VT SEP *(plants)* repiquer

bedbug ['bedbʌg] N punaise *f*

bedchamber ['bedtʃeɪmbər] N *Arch* chambre *f* à coucher

bedclothes ['bedkləʊðz] NPL couvertures *fpl* et draps *mpl*; **to turn down the b.** ouvrir le lit

beddable ['bedəb(ə)l] ADJ *Fam Hum* baisable

bedding ['bedɪŋ] N **1** *(for bed)* literie *f* **2** *(for animals)* litière *f*
▶▶**b. out** *(of plants)* dépotage *m*, dépotement *m*; **b. plants** plants *mpl* à repiquer

bedevil [bɪ'dev(ə)l] VT **(-ll-,** *Am* **-l-) 1** *(torment)* tourmenter **2** *(cause difficulties or problems for)* **industrial relations bedevilled by politics** rapports entre patrons et ouvriers empoisonnés par la politique; **the project is bedevilled by problems** le projet est en proie à de nombreux problèmes; **the strikes which had bedevilled the industry** les grèves qui avaient affligé l'industrie; **to be bedevilled by complaints** être assailli de réclamations

bedfellow ['bedfeləʊ] N compagnon *m*/compagne *f* de lit; *Fig* **they make strange bedfellows** c'est une association inattendue, c'est un couple disparate

bedlam ['bedləm] N **1** *Fig* bazar *m*; **the meeting was absolute b.** la réunion était un véritable bazar **2** *Arch (asylum)* maison *f* de fous *ou* d'aliénés

bed-night N nuitée *f*

Bedouin ['beduɪn] ADJ bédouin
N *(pl* **Bedouin)** Bédouin, -ine

bedpan ['bedpæn] N bassin *m*

bedpost ['bedpəʊst] N colonne *f* de lit

bedraggled [bɪ'dræg(ə)ld] ADJ *(muddy)* crotté, taché de boue; *(wet)* trempé; **you look a bit b.** tu es dans un piteux état

bedridden ['bedrɪd(ə)n] ADJ alité, cloué au lit; *(permanently)* grabataire

bedrock ['bedrɒk] N *Geol* roche *f* de fond; *Fig (of one's belief etc)* fondement *m*; *Fig* **to get down to b.** parler des choses sérieuses

bedroll ['bedrəʊl] N *Am* matériel *m* de couchage

bedroom ['bedruːm] N chambre *f* (à coucher); **spare b.** chambre d'ami; **b. curtains** rideaux *mpl* de chambre
▶▶*Theat* **b. farce** comédie *f* légère, vaudeville *m*; **b. furniture** meubles *mpl* de chambre; **b. slippers** pantoufles *fpl*

-bedroom, -bedroomed ['bedruːm(d)] SUFF **a two/three-bedroom(ed) house** une maison à deux/trois chambres

Beds *abbr* **Bedfordshire**

bedside ['bedsaɪd] N chevet *m*; **to have a good b. manner** *(of doctor)* être agréable avec les malades; **I didn't think much of his b. manner** je ne l'ai pas trouvé très agréable
▶▶**b. lamp** lampe *f* de chevet; **b. rug** descente *f* de lit; **b. table** table *f* de nuit *ou* de chevet

bedsit ['bedsɪt], **bed-sitter, bed-sitting-room** N *Br* chambre *f* meublée

bedsock ['bedsɒk] N chausson *m* de nuit

bedsore ['bedsɔːr] N escarre *f*

bedspace ['bedspeɪs] N *(in hotels etc)* capacité *f* d'accueil

bedspread ['bedspred] N dessus-de-lit *m inv*

bedstead ['bedsted] N châlit *m*, bois *m* de lit

bedtick ['bedtɪk] N *Am (bug)* punaise *f*

bedtime ['bedtaɪm] N heure *f* du coucher; **b.!** c'est l'heure d'aller au lit *ou* de se coucher; **when is your b.?** à quelle heure vous couchez-vous?; **it's past your b.** vous devriez déjà être couché; **it's long past my b.** je devrais être couché depuis longtemps;

they were allowed to stay up past their b. on leur a permis de se coucher plus tard que d'habitude; **to tell sb a b. story** raconter une histoire à qn avant qu'il ne s'endorme

bed-wetter [-wetər] N (child) enfant mf qui fait pipi au lit; **he's a b.** il fait pipi au lit

bed-wetting [-wetɪŋ] N énurésie f nocturne; **if b. is a problem for your child** si votre enfant fait pipi au lit

bee [bi:] N **1** abeille f; **bees' nest** nid m d'abeilles; **to keep bees** élever des abeilles; Fig **to be a busy b.** être très actif; Fig **to have a b. in one's bonnet** avoir une idée fixe; **he's got a b. in his bonnet about it** c'est pour lui une idée fixe; **he's got a b. in his bonnet about burglars** les cambrioleurs, c'est une idée fixe chez lui; Br Fam **she thinks she's the b.'s knees** elle ne se prend pas pour n'importe qui; Br Fam **she thinks he's the b.'s knees** elle le trouve formidable **2** Am (meeting) réunion f (pour travaux en commun); **spelling b.** concours m (oral) d'orthographe
▸▸ Bot **b. balm** monarde f d'Amérique; Bot **b. orchid** ophrys f abeille

Beeb [bi:b] N Fam **the B.** la BBC

beech [bi:tʃ] N (tree) hêtre m; **b. furniture** meubles mpl en hêtre
▸▸ Bot **b. mast** faines fpl (tombées par terre); **b. wood** bois m de hêtre

beechnut ['bi:tʃnʌt] N faîne f, faînes fpl

bee-eater N (bird) guêpier m (d'Europe)

beef [bi:f] N **1** (no pl) Culin bœuf m; Fig **to have plenty of b.** (muscles) avoir du muscle, être costaud; **give it some b.!** fais un petit effort!; **the team's a bit short of b.** l'équipe manque un peu de muscle **2** Am (animal) (pl **beeves** [bi:vz]; **beefs** [bi:fs]) bœuf(s) m(pl) à l'engrais; **a b.** un bœuf, une vache **3** Fam (complaint) (pl **beefs**) plainte f, grief m; **he enjoys a good b.** il aime ronchonner ou rouspéter; **what's your b.?** qu'est-ce que tu as à ronchonner?; **my main b. is that ...** ce qui m'énerve le plus, c'est que ...
VI Fam ronchonner, rouspéter
▸▸ Agr **b. cattle** bœufs mpl de boucherie; **b. farm** élevage m de bœufs; **b. farmer** éleveur m de bœufs; **b. stew** ragoût m de bœuf, bœuf mode; **b. tea** bouillon m de bœuf; **b. tomato** ≃ marmande f
▸ **beef up** VT SEP Fam (text, character in play etc) étoffer, donner plus de consistance à; (army) renforcer; **we need to b. up our coverage of Latin America** il faut que nous couvrions l'Amérique latine davantage

beefburger ['bi:fbɜ:gər] N hamburger m

beefcake ['bi:fkeɪk] N Fam beaux hommes mpl musclés

Beefeater ['bi:fi:tər] N Fam = hallebardier m de service à la Tour de Londres

beefing ['bi:fɪŋ] N Fam (moaning) ronchonnements mpl, rouspétances fpl

beefsteak ['bi:fsteɪk] N Culin bifteck m
▸▸ **b. tomato** ≃ marmande f

beefy ['bi:fɪ] ADJ Fam **1** (muscular) musclé, costaud **2** (fleshy) bien en chair

beehive ['bi:haɪv] N **1** (for bees) ruche f **2** (hairstyle) coiffure f toute en hauteur, choucroute f

beekeeper ['bi:ki:pər] N apiculteur, -trice

beekeeping ['bi:ki:pɪŋ] N apiculture f

beeline ['bi:laɪn] N Fig **to make a b. for sth** aller droit ou directement vers qch

Beelzebub [bɪ'elzɪbʌb] N Bible Belzébuth

beemer ['bi:mər] N Fam (BMW) BM f

been PP see be

beep [bi:p] N (of satellite, computer, watch etc) bip m; signal m ou bip sonore; (of car) coup m de klaxon; Aut **to give the horn a b.** klaxonner; Aut **to give sb a b.** klaxonner qn
VI (of satellite, computer, watch etc) faire bip,

émettre un signal ou bip sonore; (of car driver) klaxonner; **to b. at sb** klaxonner qn
VT **1** Aut **to b. the horn** klaxonner **2** (person) (on pager) appeler au récepteur d'appel; **I'm being beeped** (of doctor etc) on m'appelle

beeper ['bi:pər] N récepteur m d'appels

beeping ['bi:pɪŋ] N (of satellite, computer, watch etc) bip-bip m, pl bips-bips; **a sudden b. of car horns** des coups de klaxon brutaux

beer [bɪər] N bière f; **to go for a b.** aller boire une bière; **will you join me in a b.?** est-ce que tu prends une bière aussi?; Fig **life's not all b. and skittles** la vie n'est pas qu'une partie de rigolade
▸▸ **b. barrel** tonneau m à bière; Fam **b. belly** brioche f, bide m; **b. bottle** canette f ou bouteille f de bière; **b. cellar** (bar) brasserie f, **b. garden** = jardin m d'un pub, où l'on peut prendre des consommations; **b. glass** verre m à bière; Fam **b. gut** brioche, bide; **b. mat** sous-bock m inv; **b. pump** pompe f à bière

beery ['bɪərɪ] ADJ **1** (atmosphere etc) qui sent la bière **2 b. voice** voix f avinée

beeswax ['bi:zwæks] N cire f d'abeilles
▸▸ **b. polish** cire d'abeilles

beet [bi:t] N **1** betterave f; **fodder b.** betterave fourragère **2** Am = **beetroot**
▸▸ **b. industry** industrie f betteravière; **b. sugar** sucre m de betterave

beetle¹ ['bi:t(ə)l] N (insect) coléoptère m; Aut Fam (Volkswagen) B. coccinelle f
▸ **beetle along** VI Fam (hurry along) se dépêcher, se presser; **I must be beetling along now** il faut que je mette les bouts
▸ **beetle away, beetle off** VI Fam décamper

beetle² N (for beating, pounding) (large) masse f (en bois); (small) maillet m; (for paving) hie f, demoiselle f

beetle³ VI (of cliff) surplomber

beetle-browed [-'braʊd] ADJ (with overhanging eyebrows) aux sourcils proéminents; (with bushy eyebrows) aux sourcils touffus

beetle-crusher [-krʌʃər] N Fam écrase-merde m, pl écrase-merdes

beetling ['bi:tlɪŋ] ADJ (cliff, rock etc) surplombant, en surplomb

beetroot ['bi:tru:t] N Bot, Culin betterave f (potagère)
ADJ (colour) rouge foncé; **he turned b.** il est devenu rouge comme une tomate
▸▸ **b. red** rouge foncé

befall [bɪ'fɔ:l] VT (conj like fall; used only in third person) Lit, Arch (person) arriver à, survenir à

befit [bɪ'fɪt] VT (-tt-) Lit (used only in third person) convenir à; **as befits her position** comme il convient à son rang; **it does not b. a man to ...** ce n'est pas le fait d'un homme de ...

befitting [bɪ'fɪtɪŋ] ADJ convenable, seyant (for sb/sth à qn/qch), digne (of sb de qn); **with b. modesty/generosity** avec la modestie/générosité qui convient

BEFORE [bɪ'fɔ:r]

ADV	avant **1**	▪ devant **2**
PREP	devant **1**	▪ avant **2, 3**
CONJ	avant de, avant que **1**	▪ plutôt que de **2**

ADV 1 (of time) auparavant, avant; **two days b.** deux jours avant ou auparavant, l'avant-veille f, pl avant-veilles; **the day b.** la veille; **the year b.** l'année d'avant, un an auparavant; **she had come two years b.** elle était venue deux ans auparavant; **a moment b.** un instant plus tôt; **I have seen him b.** je l'ai déjà vu; **I have never seen him b.** je ne l'ai jamais vu (de ma vie); **we've met b.** nous nous sommes déjà rencontrés; **I've told**

you b. je te l'ai déjà dit; **you should have told me so b.** vous auriez dû me le dire plus tôt; **she gave me the same advice as b.** elle m'a redonné le même conseil; **to go on as b.** faire comme avant

2 (of place) devant; Lit **to go on b.** (at front of procession) marcher en tête; (in advance) partir devant; **this page and the one b.** cette page et la précédente

PREP 1 (of place) devant; **b. my (very) eyes** sous mes (propres) yeux; **b. God and man** devant Dieu et les hommes; **to appear b. the judge** comparaître devant le juge; **that is the task b. us** c'est là la tâche qui nous incombe

2 (of time) avant; **b. that, she was a teacher** auparavant ou avant ça, elle était professeur; **where did you go b. that?** où est-ce que vous êtes allé avant ça?; **not b. Easter** pas avant Pâques; **it ought to have been done b. now** ce devrait déjà être fait; **to arrive an hour b. time** arriver avec une heure d'avance ou une heure à l'avance; Fam **it's not b. time, and not b. time** ce n'est pas trop tôt; **I got here b. you** je vous ai devancé; je suis arrivé avant vous; **you were b. me** (in queue) vous étiez avant moi; **the day b. the battle** la veille de la bataille; **two days b. Christmas** l'avant-veille de Noël; **b. answering/leaving** avant de répondre/partir; **b. tax** hors taxe, HT; (income) avant impôt

3 (of order) **b. anything else, I must have ...** il me faut avant tout ...; **death b. dishonour** plutôt la mort que le déshonneur; **ladies b. gentlemen** les dames d'abord; **this word should come b. that one** ce mot devrait être placé devant celui-là; **the welfare of the country comes b. everything** le bien de la patrie prime tout; **she puts family b. friends** pour elle, la famille est plus importante que les amis

CONJ 1 (of time) avant que (ne) + sub; **come and see me b. you leave** venez me voir avant de partir ou avant votre départ; **I saw him the day b. he died** je l'ai vu la veille de sa mort; **don't come in b. I call you** n'entrez pas avant que je vous appelle; **it was long b. he came** (it happened before that) c'était longtemps avant qu'il arrive; **how long will it be b. you hear?** quand est-ce que tu sauras?; **b. long** avant longtemps, sous peu; Fam **b. you know where you are, b. I/he/etc knew where I/he/etc was** en moins de rien; **b. I forget, they expect you this evening** avant que je n'oublie, il faut que je te dise qu'ils comptent sur toi ce soir

2 (of order) **I will die b. I yield** je préfère mourir plutôt que de céder

3 (or else) avant que (ne) + sub; **get out b. I throw you out** sortez avant que je vous jette dehors; **tell me, b. I die of curiosity** dis-le moi, je n'en peux plus de curiosité; **give it to her b. she cries** donne-le-lui avant qu'elle ne se mette à pleurer

beforehand [bɪ'fɔ:hænd] ADV à l'avance, au préalable; **to come an hour b.** venir une heure à l'avance; **I must tell you b. that ...** il faut vous dire d'avance ou au préalable que ...; **if I come I'll let you know b.** si je viens je vous préviendrai; **we should make sure b.** nous ferions mieux de nous en assurer au préalable

befriend [bɪ'frend] VT (make friends with) se lier d'amitié avec; **I was befriended by a stray dog** un chien perdu s'est attaché à moi

befuddle [bɪ'fʌd(ə)l] VT **1** (confuse) embrouiller; **his mind is befuddled with drink** l'alcool lui a embrouillé l'esprit **2** (make drunk) griser; **befuddled (with drink)** éméché

beg [beg] (-gg-) VI (for money) mendier; (plead) supplier; **to sit up and b.** (of dog) faire le beau; **to b. for mercy** demander grâce; **I b. of you!** je vous en prie!; **these jobs are going begging** ce sont des emplois qui trouvent peu d'amateurs; **there's a piece of cake going begging** il reste un morceau de gâteau

vt to b. sb to do sth supplier qn de faire qch; **to b. a favour of sb** demander instamment un service à qn; **she begged to be sent back to school** elle supplia qu'on la renvoie à l'école; *Fml* **I b. to inform you that ...** j'ai l'honneur de vous faire savoir que ...; **I b. your pardon** je vous demande pardon; **to b. forgiveness** implorer le pardon; **I b. to differ** permettez-moi d'être d'un autre avis; *Fml* **to b. leave to do sth** demander la permission de faire qch; **to b. the question** *(evade the issue)* ne pas aborder la question; *(in logic)* faire une pétition de principe; **wanting to climb Mount Everest rather begs the question 'why'** on serait enclin à se demander pourquoi quelqu'un aurait envie d'escalader le mont Everest

▸ **beg off** **vi** *(from a meeting, party etc)* demander à être excusé

beget [bɪ'get] **vt** *(pt* **begot** [bɪ'gɒt]*, Bible* **begat** [bɪ'gæt]*; pp* **begotten** [bɪ'gɒt(ə)n]*)* **1** *Bible, Lit* engendrer; **Abraham begat Isaac** Abraham engendra Isaac; *Bible* **the only begotten Son of the Father** le Fils unique du Père **2** *Lit Fig* engendrer, causer

beggar ['begər] **N 1** *(in street)* mendiant, -ante; *Prov* **beggars can't be choosers** il ne faut pas être difficile quand on n'a pas le choix **2** *esp Br Fam (person)* **poor b.!** pauvre diable!; **lucky b.!** chançard!, veinard!; **you little b.!** petit coquin!, petit espiègle!

vt *(* **beggared** ['begəd]*)* **1 to b. sb** réduire qn à la mendicité; **they are beggaring themselves doing it** en faisant cela, ils vont tout droit à la ruine **2** *Fig* **to b. description** être indescriptible

beggarly ['begəlɪ] **ADJ** *(very poor)* minable, misérable; *(wage)* dérisoire, minable

beggar-my-neighbour **N** *Cards* bataille *f*

beggary ['begərɪ] **N** mendicité *f*

begging ['begɪŋ] **N** mendicité *f*; **to live by b.** vivre d'aumône

▸ ▸ **b. bowl** sébile *f (de mendiant)*; **b. letter** lettre *f* de requête *(demandant de l'argent)*

BEGIN [bɪ'gɪn] **vt & vi** *(pt* **began** [bɪ'gæn]*; pp* **begun** [bɪ'gʌn]*)* commencer; *(piece of work, new chapter)* commencer, entamer; **b. at the beginning** commencez par le commencement; **before winter begins** avant le début de l'hiver; **the day began well/badly** la journée commença bien/mal; **to b. to do sth, to b. doing sth** commencer à faire qch, se mettre à faire qch; **to b. to laugh/cry, to b. laughing/crying** se mettre à rire/à pleurer; **he soon began to complain** il ne tarda pas à se plaindre; **we began** *or* **we were beginning to get hungry** nous commencions à avoir faim; **it doesn't b. to compare with ...** cela est loin d'être comparable à ...; **I couldn't (even) b. to explain/describe it to you** c'est presque impossible à t'expliquer/ de te le décrire; **to b. by doing sth** commencer par faire qch; **the play begins with a prologue** la pièce commence *ou* débute par un prologue; **to b. again** recommencer

▸ **begin with** **vi** **to b. with** *(in the first place)* premièrement, pour commencer; *(at first)* au départ

vt INSEP commencer par; **what did you have to b. with?** *(in restaurant etc)* par quoi avez-vous commencé?

beginner [bɪ'gɪnər] **N 1** *(novice)* débutant, -ante, novice *mf*; **English for beginners** anglais pour débutants; **b.'s class** cours *m* de débutants; **(it's just) b.'s luck** aux innocents les mains pleines; **she just had b.'s luck** elle

n'y connaît rien, elle a simplement eu de la chance; **complete** *or* **absolute b.** grand débutant **2** *Theat* **beginners please!** en scène!

beginning [bɪ'gɪnɪŋ] **N** *(of speech, career etc)* commencement *m*, début *m*; *(of the world etc)* origine *f*, naissance *f*; **in the b.** au commencement, au début; **from the b.** dès le commencement *ou* le début; **from b. to end** depuis le commencement jusqu'à la fin; **at the b. of the week** au début de la semaine; **at the b. of term** à la rentrée (des classes); **the first beginnings of civilization** l'aube *f* de la civilisation; **I have the beginnings of a cold** je couve un rhume, j'ai un début de rhume; **to make a b.** commencer, débuter; **the b. of the end** le début de la fin; **to have one's beginnings in sth** avoir qch pour origine

begone [bɪ'gɒn] **vi** *Arch, Lit (used as imp)* va-t'en!, allez-vous-en!

begonia [bɪ'gəʊnɪə] **N** bégonia *m*

begrudge [bɪ'grʌdʒ] **vt 1** *(be unwilling to give)* donner à contrecœur; **you don't b. me the money do you?** tu ne me donnes pas cet argent à contrecœur, n'est-ce pas?; **they b. him his food** ils le nourrissent à contrecœur; **to b. doing sth** faire qch à contrecœur; **I b. spending so much money** c'est à contrecœur que je dépense une telle somme; **I b. the money I spent on that dress** je regrette d'avoir eu à payer autant pour cette robe; **he begrudged every moment spent away from his wife** chaque minute passée loin de sa femme lui était pénible **2** *(be envious of)* **to b. sb sth** envier qch à qn; **I don't b. him his success** je ne lui en veux pas d'avoir réussi

beguile [bɪ'gaɪl] **vt** *Lit* **1** *(charm)* enjôler, séduire; **to b. sb with promises** bercer qn de promesses; **to b. sb into doing sth** séduire qn pour qu'il fasse qch **2** *(while away)* **to b. the time** faire passer le temps

beguiling [bɪ'gaɪlɪŋ] **ADJ** *(smile)* enjôleur, séduisant

begum ['beɪgəm] **N** bégum *f*

behalf [bɪ'hɑːf] **N on** *or Am* **in b. of sb** au nom de qn, de la part de qn; *(to sign)* au nom de qn, pour qn; **he is acting on my b.** il agit pour moi *ou* pour mon compte; **don't be uneasy on my b.** ne vous inquiétez pas à mon sujet; **speaking on my own b.** *or* **on b. of myself** en mon (propre) nom; **on b. of my husband and myself** de la part de mon mari et moi; **she accepted the award on his b.** elle a reçu le prix en son nom *ou* pour lui

behave [bɪ'heɪv] **vi 1** se comporter, se conduire; *(well)* bien se comporter, bien se conduire; **to b. well/badly to(wards) sb** bien/mal agir *ou* se comporter envers qn; **what a way to b.!** quelles manières!; **to know how to b.** savoir vivre; **I'll teach him how to b.!** je lui apprendrai la politesse!; **b. yourself!** *(to husband etc)* tiens-toi comme il faut *ou* bien!; *(to child)* sois sage!, tiens-toi comme il faut *ou* bien!

2 to b. (itself) *(of machine, clock etc)* marcher, fonctionner; **the television hasn't behaved properly since** la télévision ne marche pas bien depuis

-behaved [bɪ'heɪvd] **SUFF** **well-b.** sage, qui se conduit *ou* se tient bien; **badly-b.** qui se conduit *ou* se tient mal

behaviour, *Am* **behavior** [bɪ'heɪvjər] **N 1** *(of person)* comportement *m* **(towards** envers**)**; *(of pupil)* conduite *f* **(to(wards)** sb avec *ou* envers qn**)**; **good b.** bonne conduite; **to be on one's best b.** se tenir (particulièrement bien) **2** *(of machine, car)* fonctionnement *m*

▸ ▸ *Psy* **b. pattern** type *m* de comportement; *Mktg* **b. segmentation** segmentation *f* comportementale

behavioural, *Am* **behavioral** [bɪ'heɪvjər(ə)l] **ADJ** de comportement

▸ ▸ **b. analysis** étude *f* de comportement; **b. pattern** type *m* de comportement; **b. scientist** behavioriste *mf*; **b. study** étude *f* de comportement

behaviourism, *Am* **behaviorism** [bɪ'heɪvjərɪz(ə)m] **N** *Psy* behaviorisme *m*

behaviourist, *Am* **behaviorist** [bɪ'heɪvjərɪst] **N, ADJ** *Psy* behavioriste *mf*

behead [bɪ'hed] **vt** décapiter

beheading [bɪ'hedɪŋ] **N** décapitation *f*

behemoth [bɪ'hiːmɒθ] **N** *Lit* monstre *m*

behest [bɪ'hest] **N** *Lit* commandement *m*, ordre *m*; **at whose b.?** sur l'ordre de qui?

BEHIND [bɪ'haɪnd]

ADV derrière ▪ en retard	
PREP derrière ▪ en retard sur	
N derrière	

ADV derrière; **to attack sb from b.** attaquer qn par-derrière; **to stay** *or* **remain b.** *(be at the back)* rester *ou* demeurer en arrière; *(not leave)* ne pas partir; **I'll stay b. and wait for them** je resterai derrière pour les attendre; **the teacher kept him b.** *or* **made him stay b.** le professeur l'a retenu *ou* l'a mis en retenue; **I left my umbrella b.** *(at home)* j'ai oublié mon parapluie à la maison; *(at sb else's home)* j'ai oublié mon parapluie (chez lui/eux/etc); **to be b. with** *or* **in one's work** être en retard dans son travail; **to be b. with the rent** être en retard pour payer son loyer; **to get** *or* **fall b. in one's work** prendre du retard dans son travail; *Sport* **they are only three points b.** ils ne sont qu'à trois points; **to follow close b.** suivre de très près

PREP derrière; **he hid b. it** il s'est caché derrière; **look b. you** regardez derrière vous; **I'm right b. you** *(at your back)* je suis juste derrière toi; *Fig (I support you)* je suis avec toi; **to walk** *or* **follow close b. sb** suivre qn de près; *Fig* **he has the minister b. him** il a le ministre derrière *ou* avec lui, il est protégé par le ministre; *Fig* **to be b. sth** être derrière qch; **the reasons b. sth** les raisons de qch; **to be b. schedule** avoir du retard; **she's ten minutes b. the leaders** *(in race)* elle a dix minutes de retard sur le peloton de tête; **she is b. the other pupils** elle est en retard sur les autres élèves; *Fig* **to put sth b. one** ne plus penser à qch, oublier qch (volontairement); **let's put it all b. us** oublions tout cela, n'y pensons plus; **it's all b. me now** tout ça, c'est du passé; **b. the times** *(country)* arriéré, attardé; **you're b. the times** *(old-fashioned)* tu n'es pas à la page; *(not aware of latest developments)* tu as un métro de retard

N *Fam (buttocks)* derrière *m*; **to kick sb's b.** botter le derrière à qn; **get up off your b. and find yourself a job!** remue-toi un peu et trouve du boulot!

behindhand [bɪ'haɪndhænd] **ADV** en retard; **to be b. with the rent/with one's work** être en retard pour payer le loyer/dans son travail; **I've got awfully b.** j'ai pris énormément de retard

behind-the-scenes **ADJ** en coulisse

behold [bɪ'həʊld] **vt** *(pt, pp* **beheld** [bɪ'held]*)* *Lit, Arch* voir; **b.!** voyez!

beholden [bɪ'həʊld(ə)n] **ADJ** *Fml* **to be b. to sb** être redevable à qn **(for** de**)**

beholder [bɪ'həʊldər] **N** *Prov* **beauty is in the eye of the b.** il n'y a point de laides amours

behove [bɪ'həʊv], *Am* **behoove** [bɪ'huːv] **v IMPERS** *Arch* incomber à; **it ill behoves her to criticize** ça lui va mal de critiquer

beige [beɪʒ] **ADJ, N** *(colour)* beige *m*

Beijing [beɪˈʒɪŋ] N Beijing

being [ˈbiːɪŋ] N **1** *(existence)* existence f; **to come into b.** prendre forme, prendre naissance; **the company is still in b.** la société existe toujours; **my entire b. rebels at the idea** tout mon être se révolte à cette idée; **I loathe him with all my b.** je le hais de tout mon être **2 (human) b.** être m humain; **human beings** le genre humain, les (êtres) humains mpl; **the Supreme B.** l'Être suprême; **a b. from another planet** un être venu d'une autre planète
ADJ **for the time b.** pour le moment

Beirut [beɪˈruːt] N Beyrouth

bejewelled, *Am* **bejeweled** [bɪˈdʒuːəld] ADJ paré de bijoux

belabour, *Am* **belabor** [bɪˈleɪbər] VT *(beat)* rouer de coups; **to b. sb with insults** accabler *ou* abreuver qn d'injures; *Fig* **to b. a point** insister lourdement sur un point

Belarus [beləˈruːs] N Biélorussie f

belated [bɪˈleɪtɪd] ADJ *(information, invitation etc)* tardif; *(guest, traveller etc)* en retard; **to wish you a b. happy birthday** pour te souhaiter un bon anniversaire avec un peu de retard

belatedly [bɪˈleɪtɪdlɪ] ADV *Fml* en retard, avec du retard, tardivement; **he apologized, somewhat b., for his conduct** il s'est excusé de sa conduite, mais un peu tard

belay [bɪˈleɪ] VT **1** *Naut (line)* amarrer **2** *(mountaineer)* assurer

belaying [bɪˈleɪɪŋ] N **1** *Naut* amarrage m; **b. pin** *or* **cleat** cabillot m, taquet m **2** *(in mountaineering)* assurance f, assurage m

belch [beltʃ] N éructation f, *Fam* rot m; **he gave a b.** il a fait un rot
VI éructer, *Fam* roter; **he belched all through the meal** il a roté pendant tout le repas
VT *Fig* **the house was belching smoke and flames** la maison crachait de la fumée et des flammes
▸ **belch forth, belch out** VT SEP *(flames, smoke etc)* vomir, cracher
VI **smoke and flames were belching out of the house** la maison crachait de la fumée et des flammes

beleaguer [bɪˈliːgər] VT *(city)* assiéger; *Fig* critiquer; *(project, ideology etc)* s'attaquer à; **she was beleaguered by problems** elle croulait sous les problèmes

beleaguered [bɪˈliːgəd] ADJ *(city)* assiégé; *Fig (project, ideology)* très critiqué; *(government, politician)* assailli de toutes parts; *(parents, look, manner)* accablé

belfry [ˈbelfrɪ] N beffroi m, clocher m

Belgian [ˈbeldʒən] ADJ belge; *(history, ambassador)* de Belgique
N Belge mf

Belgium [ˈbeldʒəm] N Belgique f

belie [bɪˈlaɪ] VT *(prp* **belying** [bɪˈlaɪɪŋ]) *(image, feelings)* s'opposer à, être en contradiction avec; *(wealth)* être en contradiction avec; **his appearance belies it** il n'en a pas l'air; **his looks b. his age** il ne fait pas son âge

belief [bɪˈliːf] N **1** conviction f, *Rel* croyance f; **b. in ghosts** croyance aux revenants; **b. in God** croyance en Dieu; **she did it in the b. that ...** elle l'a fait en étant persuadée que ...; **it is beyond b.** c'est incroyable; **to the best of my b.** autant que je sache; **it is my b. that ...** je suis convaincu que ..., j'ai la conviction que ... **2** *(trust)* foi f, confiance f *(in* on)

believable [bɪˈliːvəb(ə)l] ADJ *(story, account)* croyable, crédible; *(character in novel, person)* crédible; **far from b.** pas du tout crédible

BELIEVE [bɪˈliːv] VT *(person, news, rumour etc)* croire; **I b. that it is true** je crois que c'est vrai; **I b. (that) I am right** je crois avoir raison; **I b. him to be alive** je le crois vivant; **she is believed to be in Paris** on la croit à Paris; **the house was believed to be haunted** on croyait la maison hantée; **he believes himself to have been unfairly treated** il se croit (la) victime d'une injustice; **I b. not** *(I don't think so)* je crois que non; **I b. so** *(I think so)* je crois que oui; **I don't b. a word of it** je n'en crois rien *ou* pas un mot; **I don't know what to b.** je ne sais que croire; **I could scarcely** *or* **hardly b. my eyes** j'en croyais à peine mes yeux; **you can't b. everything you read in the papers** il ne faut pas croire tout ce qu'on lit dans les journaux; **to make sb b. that ...** faire croire à qn que ...; **I can well b. it** je suis prêt à le croire, je veux bien le croire; **b. it or not, he fell for her!** tu le croiras si tu veux, il s'est épris d'elle!; **would you b. it!** vous vous rendez compte!; **if he is to be believed** à l'en croire, s'il faut l'en croire; **she's a smart one, b. me!** *or Fam* **b. you me!** c'est une maligne, crois-moi!; **I wouldn't have believed it of you** je n'aurais pas cru ça de toi; *Fam* **I don't b. it!** c'est pas vrai!; *Fam* **don't you b. it!** n'en croyez rien! VOIR GRAMMAIRE A47-8
VI **to b. in (one) God** croire en (un seul) Dieu; **to b. in ghosts** croire aux revenants; **I b. in his innocence** je crois en son innocence; **to b. in sth** *(support)* être partisan de qch, être pour qch; **I don't b. in making promises** je ne fais jamais de promesses; **to b. in sb/oneself** croire en qn/soi; **I don't b. in doctors** je ne fais pas confiance aux médecins

believer [bɪˈliːvər] N *Rel* croyant, -ante; **to be a b. in sth** croire à qch; *(supporter of)* être partisan de qch, être pour qch; **I'm a great b. in newborn babies being breast-fed** je suis très en faveur de l'allaitement au sein pour les nouveau-nés

Belisha beacon [bəˈliːʃə] N *Br Formerly* = sphère f orange lumineuse (indiquant un passage clouté)

belittle [bɪˈlɪt(ə)l] VT *(person)* rabaisser; *(person's merits, efforts)* déprécier, amoindrir; **to b. oneself** *(disparage)* se déprécier; *(demean)* se déconsidérer *(aux yeux de qn, auprès de qn)*; **a belittling remark** une remarque désobligeante

Belize [beˈliːz] N Belize m

bell[1] [bel] N **1** cloche f, *(small)* clochette f, *(on door)* sonnette f, *(on bicycle)* sonnette, timbre m; *(for cattle etc)* clochette, clarine f, *(for cat)* grelot m; *Br Fam* **to give sb a b.** *(telephone)* passer un coup de fil à qn; **electric b.** sonnerie f *(électrique)*; **set of bells** *(in church)* sonnerie; **great b.** *(of a church)* bourdon m; **there's the b.** *(on door)* on sonne; *(in school)* la cloche sonne; **to ring the b.** *(on door)* sonner; *(handbell)* agiter la sonnette; *Fig* **that rings a b.** cela me rappelle *ou* me dit quelque chose; *Naut* **six bells** six coups *(de cloche)* **2** *(of flower)* calice m; *(of trumpet etc)* pavillon m; *(of blast furnace)* cône m, cloche f
VT *Fig* **to b. the cat** attacher le grelot
▸ *Naut* **b. buoy** bouée f à cloche; *Am* **b. captain** chef m chasseur; *Tech* **b. crank lever** levier m coudé; *Bot* **b. heather** bruyère f cendrée; *Chem* **b. jar** cloche de verre; **b. pull** *(in room)* cordon m de sonnette; **b. push** bouton m de sonnette; **b. tent** tente f conique; **b. tower** clocher m
▸ **bell out** VI *(of tube etc)* s'évaser

bell[2] N *(cry) (of stag)* bramement m, brame m
VI *(of stag)* bramer

belladonna [beləˈdɒnə] N *Bot, Pharm* belladone f

bell-bottomed [-bɒtəmd] ADJ **b. trousers = bell-bottoms**

bell-bottoms [-bɒtəmz] NPL pantalon m (à) pattes d'éléphant

bellboy [ˈbelbɔɪ] N *Am* groom m

belle [bel] N beauté f; **the b. of the ball** la reine du bal

bellflower [ˈbelflaʊər] N campanule f

bellhop [ˈbelhɒp] N *Am Fam* groom m

bellicose [ˈbelɪkəʊs] ADJ belliqueux

bellicosity [belɪˈkɒsɪtɪ] N *(of speech, behaviour)* caractère m belliqueux, agressivité f; *(of person)* humeur f belliqueuse

-bellied [-ˈbelɪd] SUFF round-/swollen-/etc **b.** au ventre rond/enflé/etc

belligerence [beˈlɪdʒərəns] N agressivité f

belligerent [beˈlɪdʒərənt] ADJ **1** *(aggressive) (person, tone of voice, attitude etc)* agressif, belliqueux **2** *(at war) (country)* belligérant
N belligérant, -ante

bellow [ˈbeləʊ] N *(of bull)* beuglement m, mugissement m; *(of person)* braillement m
VI *(of bull)* beugler, mugir; *(of person)* brailler; **to b. with pain** hurler de douleur; **to b. at sb** *(with rage)* brailler dans les oreilles de qn; **I bellowed at him but he was too far away to hear** j'ai crié dans sa direction mais il était trop loin pour m'entendre
VT *(order)* brailler; *Fam (song)* beugler
▸ **bellow out** VT SEP **= bellow** VT

bellowing [ˈbeləʊɪŋ] N *(of animal)* beuglement m, mugissement m; *(of person)* braillement m

bellows [ˈbeləʊz] NPL **1** *(for fire)* **(pair of) b.** soufflet m VOIR GRAMMAIRE A10 **2** *Mus (of organ)* soufflerie f

bell-ringer N carillonneur, -euse

bell-ringing N *(sound)* carillonnement m; *(art)* art m du carillonnement

bell-shaped ADJ en forme de cloche

bellwether [ˈbelweðər] N *(sheep)* mouton m qui mène le troupeau; *Fig* chef m de file

belly [ˈbelɪ] N **1** *(of person)* ventre m, *Fam* bedaine f, *(large)* panse f, *(of animal)* panse f; *Culin* **b. of pork** poitrine f de porc; **to have an empty b.** avoir l'estomac vide; **to have a full b.** avoir le ventre plein; **his eyes are bigger than his b.** il a les yeux plus gros que le ventre; **to do a b. flop** *(of diver)* faire un plat; *Fig Fam* **to go b. up** *(of company)* faire faillite **2** *(of plane, ship, jug etc)* ventre m **3** *Mus (of violin etc)* table f d'harmonie **4** *Naut (of sail)* creux m, renflement m
VT *(of wind) (sail)* enfler, gonfler
VI *(of sail)* faire (le) sac, s'enfler, se gonfler
▸▸ **b. band** *(around book)* bande f publicitaire; **b. dance** danse f du ventre; **b. dancer** danseuse f du ventre *ou* orientale; *Aviat* **b. landing** atterrissage m sur le ventre; *Fam* **b. laugh** gros rire m
▸ **belly out** VT SEP, VI **= belly** VT & VI

bellyache [ˈbelɪeɪk] N *Fam* mal m au ventre
VI ronchonner, rouspéter, râler; **he's always bellyaching about something** il faut toujours qu'il rouspète après qch

bellyacher [ˈbelɪeɪkər] N *Fam* râleur, -euse; **to be a b.** être un râleur

bellyaching [ˈbelɪeɪkɪŋ] N *Fam* rouspétance f, jérémiades fpl; **I don't want any b.** je n'accepterai aucune rouspétance; **your constant b. is driving me up the wall** tes jérémiades incessantes me fatiguent

bellybutton [ˈbelɪbʌt(ə)n] N *Fam* nombril m

belly-flop VI *Fam (of diver)* faire un plat

bellyful [ˈbelɪfʊl] N *Fig Fam* **to have had a b.** en avoir ras le bol, en avoir marre; **I've had a** *or* **my b. of him** j'en ai marre *ou* plein le dos de lui

bellyland ['belɪlænd] VI *Aviat* atterrir sur le ventre

belong [bɪ'lɒŋ] VI **1** *(be property of)* **to b. to** appartenir à; **that book belongs to me** ce livre m'appartient *ou* est à moi; **to b. to the Crown** *(of land etc)* dépendre de la Couronne

2 *(be connected to)* **what category do they b. to?** à quelle catégorie appartiennent-ils?; **to b. to a society** faire partie d'une société; **do you b. to this club?** êtes-vous membre de ce cercle?; **I b. here** *(come from)* je suis d'ici; *(feel at ease)* je me sens chez moi ici; **to feel that one doesn't b.** ne pas se sentir à sa place

3 *(usually go)* **this is where the spoons b.** c'est ici qu'on range les cuillers; **where does this book b.?** où *va ou* se range ce livre?; **things that b. together** choses qui vont ensemble; **to put things back where they b.** remettre les choses à leur place

belonging [bɪ'lɒŋɪŋ] N **to feel** *or* **have a sense of b.** se sentir chez soi *ou* à sa place

belongings [bɪ'lɒŋɪŋz] NPL affaires *fpl*

beloved ADJ [bɪ'lʌvd] bien-aimé; **b. by all** aimé de tous; **the b. wife of ...** l'épouse bien-aimée de ...

N [bɪ'lʌvɪd] bien-aimé, -ée, *pl* bien-aimés, -ées, chéri, -ie; **my b.** mon bien-aimé, ma bien-aimée; *Rel* **dearly b.** mes bien chers frères

below [bɪ'ləʊ] ADV en bas, (en-)dessous; **voices from b.** des voix qui venaient d'en bas; **the tenants (of the flat) b.** les locataires du dessous; **on the floor b.** à l'étage d'en-dessous; *Fam* **it's ten (degrees) b.** il fait moins dix; **here b.** *(on earth)* ici-bas; *Naut* **all hands b.!** tout le monde en bas!; **the passage quoted b.** *(immediately afterwards)* le passage cité ci-dessous; *(further on)* le passage cité plus loin *ou* ci-après

PREP au-dessous de; **b. the knee** au-dessous du genou; **b. (the) average** au-dessous de la moyenne; **people b. the age of 65** les gens âgés de moins de 65 ans; *Fam* **I'm feeling a bit b.** par je ne suis pas dans mon assiette; **temperature b. normal** température inférieure à la normale; **ten degrees b. zero** dix degrés au-dessous de zéro; **b. sea level** au-dessous du niveau de la mer; **b. the surface** sous la surface; **b. the bridge** *(downstream)* en aval du pont

below-the-line N *Mktg* publicité *f* hors-média

ADJ *Acct* au-dessous de la ligne; *Mktg* hors-média

▸▸ *Acct* **b. accounts** comptes *mpl* de résultats exceptionnels; *Mktg* **b. advertising** publicité hors-médias; **b. costs** *Acct* coûts *mpl* au-dessous de la ligne; *Mktg* coûts hors-média; **b. expenditure** *Acct* dépenses *fpl* au-dessus de la ligne; *Mktg* dépenses hors-média; *Mktg* **b. promotion** promotion *f* hors-média

belt [belt] N **1** *(round waist)* ceinture *f*, *Mil* ceinturon *m*; **to tighten one's b.** serrer sa ceinture; *Fig* se serrer la ceinture; *Fam* **I'm a b. and braces type** *(very cautious)* je suis du genre à penser que deux précautions valent mieux qu'une; **to be a brown/black b.** *(in martial arts)* être ceinture marron/noire; *Boxing* **to hold the b.** être le champion; *Boxing* **a blow beneath the b.** un coup bas; *Fig* **to hit sb beneath** *or* **below the b.** donner à qn un coup en traître *ou* un coup bas; **that was a bit beneath** *or* **below the b.** *(of joke, remark)* c'était un coup bas; *Fig* **to have sth under one's b.** *(move, project)* en avoir fini avec qch; *(driving licence, degree)* avoir qch en poche; **once you've got a few years' experience under your b.** une fois que tu as quelques années d'expérience à ton actif

2 *Tech* courroie *f*, **b. driven** entraîné par courroie

3 *(area)* région *f*, zone *f*

4 *Fam (blow) (with hand)* gifle *f*, *(with bat, stick)* coup *m*; **he gave the ball a terrific b.** il a tapé un grand coup dans la balle; **to give sb a b. in the face** flanquer un gnon *ou* un pain dans la tronche à qn

VT *Fam (hit with belt)* donner des coups de ceinture à; *(hit with hand)* gifler; *(hit with bat, stick) (ball)* frapper dans, taper dans; *(person)* frapper; **less of your cheek or I'll b. you one!** ne sois pas insolent ou je t'en mets une!

VI *Fam* **to b. down the stairs** descendre l'escalier quatre à quatre; **she belted out of the house** elle est sortie de la maison en courant

▸▸ **b. buckle** boucle *f* de ceinture; *Tech* **b. conveyor** transporteur *m* à courroie *ou* à ruban *ou* à bande; *Tech* **b. drive** transmission *f* par courroie; **b. loop** passant *m* *(de ceinture)*

▸ **belt along** VI *Fam* courir/aller/conduire à toute vitesse

▸ **belt out** VT SEP *Fam (order etc)* vociférer, gueuler; *(song)* gueuler, brailler

▸ **belt up** VI **1** *Br Sl* se taire; **b. up!** ta gueule! **2** *Aut Fam (put on seatbelt)* attacher sa ceinture de sécurité

belted ['beltɪd] ADJ ceinturé

▸▸ *Aut* **b. tyre** pneu *m* à ceinture

belter ['beltər] N *Br Fam* **a b. of a film** un super film; **that last song was a b.** la dernière chanson était super

belting ['beltɪŋ] N **1** *Tech (belts)* courroie(s) *f(pl)*; *(material)* matériau *m* à courroies **2** *Fam* **to give sb a (good) b.** *(spanking)* donner une bonne fessée à qn; *(beating-up)* donner une bonne raclée à qn; *(in match, competition etc)* mettre la pâtée à qn

beltway ['beltweɪ] N *Am* périphérique *m*

beluga [bə'lu:gə] N *(fish)* béluga *m*; *(whale)* béluga, dauphin *m* blanc; *(caviar)* caviar *m* de béluga

belvedere ['belvɪdɪər] N *Archit* belvédère *m*

bemoan [bɪ'məʊn] VT pleurer; **to b. the loss of sth** se lamenter de *ou* pleurer la perte de qch; **to b. one's fate** pleurer son sort; **she was bemoaning the fact that they had no money** elle se lamentait de ce qu'ils n'avaient pas d'argent

bemuse [bɪ'mju:z] VT *Lit (confuse)* rendre perplexe, dérouter

bemused [bɪ'mju:zd] ADJ perplexe

ben [ben] N *Scot Geog* sommet *m*, mont *m*

▸▸ **B. Nevis** = point *m* culminant de la Grande-Bretagne, en Écosse (1343m)

bench [bentʃ] N **1** *(seat) (in park, garden)* banc *m*; *(upholstered)* banquette *f*, *(in lecture hall, amphitheatre)* gradin *m*; *Sport* banc *(pour les joueurs qui ne sont pas sur le terrain)*; *Law (for judge, magistrates)* siège *m*; *Br Law* **the B.** *(magistrates)* la magistrature; *(court)* la Cour; **to be on the B.** *(as a magistrate)* être magistrat; *(as a judge)* siéger au tribunal; **to retire from the B.** prendre sa retraite; *Sport* **to be on the b.** *(waiting to play)* être remplaçant; *(as punishment)* avoir été renvoyé du terrain **2** *Tech (worktable) (for carpenter)* établi *m*; *(for fitter)* banc *m*, marbre *m*; *(in greenhouse)* tablette *f*, *Chem etc* **laboratory b.** paillasse *f*

▸▸ **b. seat** *(in vehicle)* banquette *f*; **b. test** essai *m* au banc

benchmark ['bentʃmɑːk] N *Comput, Fig* référence *f*, *Com* point *m* de repère; *(in surveying)* repère *m* *(de nivellement)*

VT comparer

▸▸ *Mktg* **b. market** marché *m* de référence; *Can Admin* **b. position** poste-repère *m*, *pl* postes-repères; *Comput* **b. program** programme *m* d'évaluation des performances;

Comput **b. test** test *m* d'évaluation (de programme)

benchmarking ['bentʃmɑːkɪŋ] N évaluation *f* de performances, benchmarking *m*

benchtest ['bentʃtest] N essai *m* au banc

VT faire passer au banc d'essai

BEND¹ [bend] N **1** *(curve)* courbure *f*, *(in road)* tournant *m*, virage *m*; *(in pipe)* coude *m*; *(in river)* courbe *f*, **bends for 3 kilometres** *(road sign)* virages sur 3 kilomètres; *Aut* **to take a b. at speed** prendre un virage à toute vitesse; *Fam* **to be round the b.** être fou *ou* cinglé; *Fam* **you're driving me** *or* **sending me round the b.** tu me rends dingue *ou* fou

2 *Med Fam* **the bends** maladie *f* des caissons; **to have the bends** souffrir de la maladie des caissons

3 *(action) (of body)* inclination *f*

VT *(pt bent* [bent]; *pp bent, Arch bended) (knee, arm etc)* plier; *(head)* baisser; *(of age) (the back)* courber; *(pipe, rail)* cambrer, cintrer; *(wood, iron) (into a specific shape)* cambrer, arquer; *(metal) (of strong man in circus)* tordre; *(bow, spring)* tendre, bander; *Phys (light) (ray)* infléchir; *Fig (law, rule etc)* faire une entorse à; **to b. one's head over a book** pencher la tête sur un livre; **to b. sb to one's will** plier qn à sa volonté; **to b. a rod/a key (out of shape)** tordre une barre de fer/une clef; *Br Fam* **to b. the elbow** *(drink)* lever le coude; *Br Fam* **to b. sb's ear** casser les oreilles à qn; **thanks for letting me b. your ear** merci de m'avoir laissé m'épancher

VI *(of rod, branch etc)* plier, ployer; *(of person)* se pencher; *(of road, river)* tourner; **to b. under the strain** *(of wood, iron)* arquer; *(of steel plate etc)* s'envoiler; *(of rod, wheel)* se voiler; **an old man bending under a heavy load** un vieillard courbé sous un pesant fardeau; *Fig* **to b. (to pressure)** céder (à la pression); *Fig Lit* **to b. to sb's will** se plier à la volonté de qn; *Fig* **to b. before the wind** plier

▸ **bend back** VT SEP **to** recourber; *(to original straight position)* détordre; *(to original bent position)* replier; *(light)* infléchir

VI *(of person)* se pencher en arrière; *(of light)* s'infléchir

▸ **bend down** VT SEP *(branch)* courber, ployer; **the tree was bent down by the weight of the fruit** l'arbre penchait sous le poids des fruits

VI *(of person)* se courber, se baisser

▸ **bend forward** VI se pencher en avant

▸ **bend over** VI *(of person)* se pencher; *Fig* **to b. over backwards** se mettre en quatre (**to do** pour faire)

VT INSEP **to b. over sb** se pencher sur qn

VT SEP *(steel plate etc)* plier

bend² N *Naut (knot)* nœud *m*

bended ['bendɪd] ADJ *Lit* **on one's b. knees, on b. knee** *(ask for sth)* à genoux; **to go down on b. knee** *or* **knees** *(kneel down)* se mettre à genoux, s'agenouiller; *Fig* **to go down on one's b. knees to sb** *(beg)* supplier qn

bender ['bendər] N **1** *Fam (drinking session)* soûlerie *f*, **to go on a b.** se soûler **2** *Sl (homosexual)* pédale *f*, tantouze *f*

bending ['bendɪŋ] N **too much b. is bad for the back** il est mauvais pour le dos de se pencher trop souvent

▸▸ *Tech* **b. moment** moment *m* de flexion, moment fléchissant; *Tech* **b. strength** résistance *f* à la flexion; *Tech* **b. test** essai *m* *ou* épreuve *f* de ployage *ou* de flexion

beneath [bɪ'ni:θ] ADV dessous, au-dessous; **from b.** de dessous

PREP sous; **b. contempt** parfaitement méprisable; **to marry b. one** faire une mésalliance; **she thinks everybody's b. her** elle s'imagine que tout le monde lui est inférieur; **he would consider it b. him to**

complain il considère qu'il serait indigne de lui de se plaindre; **to be b. sb's dignity** *(of behaviour etc)* ne pas être digne de qn; **the plank gave way b. me** la planche a cédé sous mon poids

Benedictine [benɪˈdɪktɪn] N **1** *Rel* Bénédictin, -ine **2** *(also* [-tiːn]*) (liqueur)* Bénédictine *f* ADJ *Rel* bénédictin

benediction [benɪˈdɪkʃən] N bénédiction *f; (at meals)* bénédicité *m*

benefaction [benɪˈfækʃən, ˈbenɪ-] N *Lit* **1** *(kindness)* bienfaisance *f* **2** *(act of kindness)* bienfait *m; (donation)* don *m* charitable

benefactor, benefactress [ˈbenɪfæktər, ˈbenɪfæktrɪs] N bienfaiteur, -trice

benefice [ˈbenɪfɪs] N *Rel, Hist* bénéfice *m*

beneficence [bɪˈnefɪs(ə)ns] N *Lit* **1** *(kindness)* bienfaisance *f* **2** *(act of charity)* œuvre *f* de bienfaisance

beneficent [bɪˈnefɪsənt] ADJ *Lit* bienfaisant

beneficial [benɪˈfɪʃəl] ADJ *(doing good)* bon, bénéfique; **b. to** *(the health, business)* bon pour
▸▸*Law* **b. owner, b. occupant** usufruitier, -ière

beneficiary [benɪˈfɪʃərɪ] ADJ, N *Law* bénéficiaire *mf*, ayant droit *m*, *pl* ayants droit; *(of family allowance)* allocataire *mf*; *Fig* **the main beneficiaries of the new law will be working mothers** ce sont les mères qui travaillent qui bénéficieront le plus de la nouvelle loi

benefit [ˈbenɪfɪt] N **1** *(advantage)* avantage *m*; **to derive b. from sth** profiter de qch, tirer profit de qch; **in order to derive full b. from the medicine** de façon à tirer tout le profit de ce médicament; **it's no b. to me, I get or gain no b. from it** je n'en retire aucun avantage; **a performance for the b. of the blind** une représentation au profit des aveugles; **for the b. of the others** à l'intention des autres; **that remark was for my b.** cette remarque était à mon intention ou m'était destinée; **I'm not doing this for my own b. or Fam for the b. of my health** je ne fais pas ça pour moi; **for the b. of one's health** dans l'intérêt de sa santé; **to give sb the b. of the doubt** accorder à qn le bénéfice du doute; **she hasn't had the b. of a university education** elle n'a pas eu la chance d'aller à l'université; **to offer sb the b. of one's experience** faire profiter qn de son expérience; **b. in kind** avantage en nature; *Fin* **benefits (package)** *(to employee)* avantages sociaux

2 *Theat (performance)* représentation *f* de bienfaisance; *Sport* **a b. match to raise money for the victims' families** un match organisé au bénéfice des familles des victimes

3 *Br Admin (allowance)* indemnité *f*, allocation *f*; **social security benefits** prestations *fpl* sociales; **to be on b.** toucher l'aide sociale; **child b.** = allocations familiales; **housing b.** allocation logement; **maternity b.** allocation de maternité; **sickness b.** indemnité de maladie; **unemployment b.** allocation de chômage

VT être avantageux à, profiter à; **a steady exchange rate benefits trade** un change stable est avantageux pour le commerce ou favorise le commerce; **who(m) does it b.?** qui en bénéficie; **it will b. mankind** c'est l'humanité toute entière qui en profitera; **to b. the cause of disarmament** favoriser le désarmement

VI **to b. by** or **from sth** bénéficier de qch, profiter de qch, tirer avantage de qch; **you will b. by a holiday** un congé vous fera du bien; **who benefits most from his death?** à qui sa mort profite-t-elle le plus?; **to b. from a rise in prices** profiter ou tirer profit d'une hausse des prix
▸▸*Theat* **b. performance** représentation de

bienfaisance; *Mktg* **b. segmentation** segmentation *f* par avantages recherchés

Benelux [ˈbenɪlʌks] N *Pol* Bénélux *m*
▸▸**the B. countries** les pays *mpl* du Bénélux

benevolence [bɪˈnevələns] N **1** *(kindness)* bienveillance *f*, bonté *f* **2** *(charitableness)* bienfaisance *f*

benevolent [bɪˈnevələnt] ADJ **1** *(kindly disposed)* bienveillant (**to** envers) **2** *(charitable)* bienfaisant, charitable (**to** envers)
▸▸*Hist* **b. despotism** despotisme *m* éclairé; *Fin* **b. fund** fonds *m* de prévoyance; *Admin* **b. society** association *f* de bienfaisance

benevolently [bɪˈnevələntlɪ] ADV avec bienveillance

BEng [biːˈeŋ] N *Univ abbr* **Bachelor of Engineering**

Bengal [beŋˈgɔːl] N Bengale *m*

Bengali [beŋˈgɔːlɪ], **Bengalese** [beŋgəˈliːz] ADJ bengali, bengalais
N **1** Bengali *mf*, Bengalais, -aise **2** *Ling* bengali *m*

benighted [bɪˈnaɪtɪd] ADJ *Lit (country etc)* plongé dans (les ténèbres de) l'ignorance

benign [bɪˈnaɪn] ADJ *(smile, look etc)* bienveillant; *(climate)* doux, *f* douce
▸▸*Med* **b. tumour** tumeur *f* bénigne

Benin [beˈniːn] N Bénin *m*

Benjamin [ˈbendʒəmɪn] N *Arch* **the B. of the family** le benjamin de la famille

benny [ˈbenɪ] N *Sl (drug)* (comprimé *m* de) benzédrine *f*

bent [bent] PT, PP *see* bend[1]
ADJ **1** *(branch)* courbé, plié; *(axle, lever)* coudé; *(back)* voûté; *(out of shape) (aerial, coathanger)* tordu; **to become b.** *(with age)* se voûter; *Am Fig Fam* **b. out of shape** *(angry, upset)* dans tous ses états **2** *Sl (corrupt) (politician, police officer etc)* malhonnête, pourri **3** *Sl (homosexual)* homosexuel, inverti; **as b. as a nine-bob note** or **as a three-pound note** pédé comme un phoque **4** *(determined)* déterminé, résolu; **(up)on doing sth** à faire qch); **he is b. on seeing me** il veut absolument me voir; **the government is b. on eliminating dissent** le gouvernement est résolu à éliminer toute opposition

bentwood [ˈbentwʊd] ADJ *(chair)* en bois courbé

benumbed [bɪˈnʌmd] ADJ *Fml* engourdi

benzene [ˈbenziːn] N *Chem* benzène *m*

benzin(e) [ˈbenziːn, benˈziːn] N *Chem, Ind* benzine *f*

benzodiazepine [benzəʊdaɪˈeɪzəpiːn] N *Pharm* benzodiazépine *f*

benzol [ˈbenzɒl] N *Chem* benzol *m*

bequeath [bɪˈkwiːð] VT léguer (**to** à)

bequest [bɪˈkwest] N legs *m*; **it was a b. from my grandmother** je l'ai hérité de ma grand-mère; **she made a b. of £2,000 to her favourite charity** elle a légué 2000 livres à l'œuvre de bienfaisance qu'elle préférait

berate [bɪˈreɪt] VT *Fml (person)* réprimander; *(plan, intention)* condamner

Berber [ˈbɜːbər] ADJ berbère
N **1** Berbère *mf* **2** *Ling* berbère *m*

bereave [bɪˈriːv] VT *(pt, pp usu* **bereft** [bɪˈreft]*)* **he has been bereaved** *(by a death)* il est en deuil

bereaved [bɪˈriːvd] ADJ en deuil; *(family, parents etc)* du défunt, de la défunte; **the entire nation feels b.** le pays tout entier est en deuil
NPL **the b.** la famille du défunt/de la défunte

bereavement [bɪˈriːvmənt] N deuil *m*; **owing to a recent b.** en raison d'un deuil récent; **she has suffered a b.** elle a été affligée par un deuil
▸▸*Br* **b. counsellor** = conseiller *m* qui pro-

pose une assistance psychologique aux personnes qui ont perdu un être cher

bereft [bɪˈreft] ADJ *Fml* **to be b. of sth** être privé de qch; **b. of all hope** ayant perdu tout espoir; **to leave sb b. of speech** rendre qn muet; **she collapsed into a chair, her face b. of colour** elle s'effondra sur une chaise, le visage livide

beret [ˈbereɪ, ˈberɪ] N béret *m*; *Mil* **the blue berets** les casques *mpl* bleus; **the red berets** les bérets rouges, les parachutistes *mpl*

berg [bɜːg] N *Fam (iceberg)* iceberg *m*

bergamot [ˈbɜːgəmɒt] N *(plant)* bergamote *f*

beriberi [berɪˈberɪ] N *Med* béribéri *m*

berk [bɜːk] N *Br Sl* andouille *f*, con *m*, conne *f*; **to make a complete b. of oneself** se conduire comme une andouille ou un con; **to feel a right b.** se sentir con ou *f* conne

Berks [bɑːks] *abbr* **Berkshire**

Berlin [bɜːˈlɪn] N Berlin; *Formerly* **East/West B.** Berlin Est/Ouest; **the B. airlift** le pont aérien de Berlin; **the B. Wall** le mur de Berlin

Berliner [bɜːˈlɪnər] N Berlinois, -oise

berm(e) [bɜːm] N **1** *(fortification)* berme *f* **2** *(path)* berme *f*, banquette *f*

Bermuda [bəˈmjuːdə] N les Bermudes *fpl*; *Fam* **bermudas** bermuda *m*
▸▸*Am* **B. Plan** tarif *m* chambre avec petit déjeuner anglais; *Naut* **B. rig** gréement *m* Marconi; **B. shorts** bermuda; **the B. Triangle** le triangle des Bermudes

Bern(e) [bɜːn] N Berne

Bernese [bɜːˈniːz, ˈbɜː-] ADJ bernois
N Bernois, -oise
▸▸**the B. Alps** l'Oberland *m* bernois

berried [ˈberɪd] ADJ **1** *Bot* à baies, couvert de baies **2** *Zool (lobster etc)* œuvé

berry [ˈberɪ] N **1** *(fruit)* baie *f*; **to go b. picking** aller cueillir des baies **2** *Zool (of crustacean)* œuf *m*; **lobster in b.** homard *m* œuvé
VI **to go berrying** aller cueillir des baies

berserk [bəˈzɜːk] ADJ *Fam* fou furieux, *f* folle furieuse; **to go b.** devenir fou furieux; **to send sb b.** rendre qn fou furieux

berth [bɜːθ] N **1** *Naut, Rail* couchette *f*, *Fam* **I can give you a b. for the night** tu peux pieuter ici cette nuit si tu veux **2** *Naut (for ship)* poste *m* à quai; **she left her b. this morning** il est sorti du quai ce matin; **(anchoring) b.** poste de mouillage ou d'amarrage **3** *(distance) Naut* **to give a ship a wide b.** éviter ou parer un navire, passer au large d'un navire; *Fig* **to give sb a wide b.** éviter qn **4** *Fam (job)* boulot *m*; **to find a soft** or **an easy b.** trouver un emploi pépère
VT *(ship) (of helmsman)* faire accoster le long du quai, amener ou amarrer à quai; *(of port official)* donner ou assigner un poste à; **where is she berthed?** à quel quai se trouve-t-il?
VI **1** *(of ship)* aborder à quai, se ranger à quai; **when do we b.?** quand accostons-nous? **2** **to b. forward/aft** *(of passengers, crew)* coucher à l'avant/à l'arrière

berthing [ˈbɜːθɪŋ] N *(of ship)* abordage *m* à quai

beryl [ˈberɪl] N *Miner* béryl *m*

beryllium [beˈrɪlɪəm] N *Chem* béryllium *m*

beseech [bɪˈsiːtʃ] VT *(pt, pp* **besought** [bɪˈsɔːt]*) Lit* implorer, supplier, conjurer (**sb to do sth** qn de faire qch); **help me, I b. you** aidez-moi, je vous en supplie ou conjure

beseeching [bɪˈsiːtʃɪŋ] ADJ *(air, ton)* suppliant

beset [bɪˈset] *(pt, pp* **beset**; *prp* **besetting**) VT *Fml usu passive (of misfortunes, temptations etc)* assaillir; **b. with dangers/difficulties** environné ou entouré de dangers/de difficultés; **to be b. by doubts** être assailli de doutes *ou* par le doute

besetting [bɪˈsetɪŋ] ADJ ATTRIB *Fml (idea, thought etc)* obsédant; **it's his b. sin** c'est son plus grand défaut

beside [bɪˈsaɪd] PREP **1** *(place) (person)* à côté de, auprès de; *(object)* à côté de; **seated b. me** assis à côté de *ou* auprès de moi, assis à mes côtés; **a house b. the lake** une maison au bord du lac
2 *(comparison)* à côté de; **b. him, everyone else appears slow** à côté de lui, tous les autres paraissent lents; **I feel very underdressed b. you** par rapport à toi *ou* à côté de toi, je ne me sens pas assez habillée
3 *(in addition to)* en dehors de; **other people b. ourselves** d'autres (personnes) que nous
4 *(wide of)* **that is b. the point** cela n'a rien à voir (avec l'affaire en question); **whether you arrrived or not is b. the point** que tu sois arrivé ou non n'est pas le problème; **b. oneself (with joy/anger)** fou de joie/colère; **b. oneself with enthusiasm** débordant d'enthousiasme

Attention: ne pas confondre avec **besides**.

besides [bɪˈsaɪdz] ADV **1** *(in addition)* en outre, en plus; **many more b.** encore bien d'autres; **and many more people b.** et bien d'autres gens encore **2** *(moreover)* d'ailleurs, du reste, (et) en outre
PREP *(in addition to)* excepté, hormis; **ten of us, b. myself** (nous sommes/serons/*etc*) dix, sans me compter; **there are others b. him** il y en a d'autres que lui; **have you got it in anything b. black?** est-ce que vous l'avez dans d'autres couleurs qu'en noir?; **what else can you do b. type?** que savez-vous faire en dehors de *ou* à part taper à la machine?; **b. watching television, I did nothing all night** à part regarder la télévision, je n'ai rien fait de la soirée; **b. his grandmother, he was the only one with blue eyes** à part sa grand-mère, il était le seul de la famille à avoir les yeux bleus; **b. being an excellent singer, she also plays the violin** c'est une excellente chanteuse, et en plus elle joue du violon; **b. which, he was unwell** sans compter qu'il était indisposé

Attention: ne pas confondre avec **beside**.

besiege [bɪˈsiːdʒ] VT *(city)* assiéger; *Fig (building)* faire le siège de; *(person)* assaillir; **we have been besieged with requests to …** nous avons été assaillis de demandes de …; **the public besieged the tourist office with complaints** l'office du tourisme fut inondé de plaintes de la part du public

besmirch [bɪˈsmɜːtʃ] VT *Lit* salir, tacher; *Fig (sb's memory)* salir, entacher, ternir

besom [ˈbiːzəm] N **1** *(broom)* balai *m* (de jonc) **2** *Pej (woman)* bonne femme *f*

besotted [bɪˈsɒtɪd] ADJ **1** *(in love)* entiché (**with sb** de qn); **to be b. with sth** *(car, computer etc)* adorer qch; **she was b. with the idea of going to Mexico** l'idée d'aller au Mexique l'obsédait **2** *(with drink)* abruti par l'alcool

bespatter [bɪˈspætər] VT éclabousser; **bespattered with mud** tout couvert de boue

bespeak [bɪˈspiːk] VT *Fml (be sign of)* témoigner de

bespectacled [bɪˈspektək(ə)ld] ADJ qui porte des lunettes, à lunettes

bespoke [bɪˈspəʊk] ADJ USU ATTRIB *esp Br (clothing)* (fait) sur mesure; **b. tailor/shoemaker** tailleur *m*/cordonnier, -ière à façon

besprinkle [bɪˈsprɪŋk(ə)l] VT saupoudrer (**with** de)

Bess [bes] N *(dimin* of **Elizabeth)** *(in English*

history) **Good Queen B.** = la reine Élisabeth Iʳᵉ d'Angleterre

BEST [best]

| ADJ meilleur |
| N le meilleur **1, 3, 4** ▪ le mieux **1, 3, 4** ▪ pour le mieux *(for the best)* **7** |
| ADV mieux **1** ▪ au mieux *(at best)* **2** |

ADJ VOIR GRAMMAIRE A25; A41 *(superl of* **good)** meilleur; **the b. man on earth** le meilleur homme du monde; **may the b. man win** que le meilleur gagne; **my b. dress** ma plus belle robe; **to be dressed in one's b. clothes** être sur son trente et un; **to be on one's b. behaviour** bien se conduire; **I am acting in your b. interests** j'agis au mieux de vos intérêts; **with the b. will in the world** avec la meilleure volonté du monde; **the b. part of the year** *(most of)* la plus grande partie de l'année; **I waited for the b. part of an hour** j'ai attendu presque une heure; **the b. at biology** *(it's my strongest subject)* la biologie, c'est mon point fort; *(better than others)* je suis le meilleur en biologie; **it is b. to …** le mieux, c'est de …; **the b. thing you can do** *or* **the b. course to take is to …** ce qu'il y a de mieux à faire, c'est de …; **it would be b. to …, the b. plan would be to …** le mieux serait de …; **to know what is b. for sb** savoir ce qui va *ou* convient le mieux à qn; **I only want what's b. for you** je ne veux que ce qu'il y a de mieux pour toi; **I thought it (would be) b. to stay** j'ai pensé qu'il valait mieux rester; **b. before … (on packaging)** à consommer/utiliser avant le …; **the b. years of one's life** les meilleures années de sa vie; **to put one's b. foot forward** *(do one's best)* faire de son mieux; *(make an effort)* faire un petit effort; *Fam Hum* **it's the b. thing since sliced bread** c'est ce qu'on a inventé de mieux depuis le fil à couper le beurre

N **1** *(maximum, peak)* le meilleur, la meilleure; **this is the b. there is** voici ce qu'il y a de meilleur *ou* de mieux; **I am in the b. of health** je me porte à merveille, je suis en excellente santé; **to do sth to the b. of one's ability** faire qch de son mieux; **to the b. of my belief/knowledge** à ce que je crois/autant que je sache; **the b. of it is that …** le plus beau de l'affaire, c'est que …; **to have** *or* **get the b. of both worlds** gagner sur les deux tableaux; **he can sing with the b. (of them)** il chante comme un dieu *ou* divinement; **she's up there with the b. of them** elle peut rivaliser avec les meilleurs; **we are the b. of friends** nous sommes les meilleurs amis du monde; **he was undemonstrative at the b. of times** même dans ses meilleurs moments, il était peu démonstratif; **let's make it the b. of five** le premier qui remporte trois jeux *ou* parties sur cinq a gagné; *Sch Old-fashioned Br Fam* **six of the b.** une correction magistrale; **to be dressed in one's Sunday b.** porter ses habits du dimanche; **I keep it for b.** *(of dress, suit etc)* je le garde pour des occasions spéciales
2 *(good wishes) Fam* **the b. of luck!** bonne chance!; *Fam* **all the b.** *(spoken)* toutes mes amitiés; *(written)* amitiés; **my brother sends his b.** mon frère vous dit bien des choses *ou* vous prie d'accepter toutes ses amitiés
3 *(optimum performance)* **I did my b.** j'ai fait de mon mieux; **your b. wasn't good enough** tu as peut-être fait de ton mieux, mais ça n'a pas suffi; **to do one's b.** *or* **the b. one can to …** faire de son mieux pour …; **I did my b. to comfort her** je l'ai consolée du mieux que j'ai pu, j'ai fait de mon mieux pour la consoler; **he did his b. to smile** il s'efforça de sourire; **I am doing my (level) b.** or **the b. I can for you** je fais tout ce que je peux pour vous; **that's the b. I can offer** c'est ce que je peux vous offrir de mieux; **is that the b. you can do?**

vous ne pouvez pas faire mieux?; **do the b. you can** *(given the circumstances)* arrangez-vous; *(in exam)* faites de votre mieux; **to bring out the b. in people** faire ressortir les bons côtés des gens; **to get the b. out of sb** tirer le maximum de qn; **to get the b. out of sth** tirer le meilleur parti de qch
4 *(appearance, condition)* **to look one's b.** être *ou* paraître à son avantage; **to be at one's b.** être en grande forme *ou* au meilleur de sa forme; **I am not at my b. in the morning** je ne suis pas au mieux de ma forme le matin; **you haven't seen the house at its b.** tu n'as pas vu la maison sous son meilleur jour; **that is Dickens at his b.** voilà du meilleur Dickens
5 *(advantage)* **to get** *or* **have the b. of it** *or* **of the bargain** faire une bonne affaire; **to have the b. of an argument** l'emporter dans une discussion; **to get the b. of sb in an argument** l'emporter sur qn dans une discussion
6 *(compromise)* **to make the b. of sth** s'accommoder de qch; **you'll just have to make the b. of it** il faudra t'y faire; **to make the b. of things** *or* **a bad job** faire avec ce qu'on a, faire contre mauvaise fortune bon cœur
7 *(result, outcome)* **to act for the b.** agir pour le mieux; **I did it for the b.** j'ai fait pour le mieux; **it's all for the b.** tout est pour le mieux; **I meant it for the b.** cela partait d'une bonne intention; **to hope for the b.** ne pas désespérer, avoir bon espoir; **we must hope for the b.** il faut être optimiste; **only the b. will do** ne fera l'affaire que ce qu'il y a de meilleur; **your parents only want the b. for you** tes parents ne veulent que ce qu'il y a de mieux pour toi

ADV *(superl of* **well) 1 he does it b.** c'est lui qui le fait le mieux; **I comforted her as b. I could** je la consolai de mon mieux; **I got down as b. I could** je suis descendu comme j'ai pu; **you know b.** c'est vous (qui êtes) le mieux placé pour en juger; **mother knows b.** maman a raison; **he's b. able to decide** il est le plus à même de décider; **do as you think b.** faites comme bon vous semble(ra); **he had b. agree** il ferait mieux d'accepter; **the b. dressed man** l'homme le mieux habillé; **the b. kept secret of the war** le secret le mieux gardé de la guerre; **the b. known book** le livre le mieux *ou* le plus connu; **the b.-looking women** les femmes les plus jolies; **to come off b.** *(in argument, discussion)* l'emporter, avoir l'avantage, avoir le dessus; **I like beef b.** je préfère le bœuf; **what goes down b. with the public is …** ce que le public préfère, c'est …; **these things are b. left to the police** il vaut mieux laisser à la police le soin de s'occuper de ces choses-là
2 at b. au mieux; **at b., he will get 2,000 votes** au mieux, il aura 2000 voix; **your article is at b. unhelpful, at worst obstructive** au mieux, votre article n'apporte rien d'utile, au pire il constitue un obstacle
VT *(in argument etc)* l'emporter sur, battre; **she is rarely bested in an argument** il est rare qu'elle soit battue *ou* qu'on l'emporte sur elle dans un débat
▸▸ *TV, Cin* **b. boy** aide-électricien *m, pl* aides-électriciens; *Br Culin* **b. end** *(of lamb)* = filet *m*; *Br Culin* **b. end of neck** carré *m*; **b. man** *(at wedding)* garçon *m* d'honneur; *Com* **b. practice** meilleure pratique *f*

Best Man

Dans les pays anglo-saxons, le garçon d'honneur présente l'alliance au marié et prononce un discours lors de la réception de mariage.

best-before date N date *f* limite de consommation

bestial [ˈbestɪəl] ADJ bestial, -aux

bestiality [bestɪˈælɪtɪ] N bestialité f

bestially [ˈbestɪəlɪ] ADV avec bestialité, bestialement

best-in-class N Mktg chef m de file

bestir [bɪˈstɜːr] VT (-rr-) Fml **to b. oneself** se démener, s'activer

best-of-breed N Mktg nec plus ultra m inv

bestow [bɪˈstəʊ] VT Lit accorder, donner **(sth (up)on sb)** qch à qn); **to b. a favour on sb** accorder une faveur à qn

bestowal [bɪˈstəʊəl] N octroi m

bestride [bɪˈstraɪd] VT Fml (pt **bestrode** [bɪˈstrəʊd]; pp **bestridden** [bɪˈstrɪd(ə)n]) **1** (straddle) être à cheval ou à califourchon sur **2** (cross) (ditch etc) enjamber

bestseller [bestˈselər] N (book, record) best-seller m, pl best-sellers; **to be a b.** (of book, record) être un best-seller; (of author, musician etc) être un auteur/un musicien/etc à succès; **the month's bestsellers** les meilleures ventes du mois; **this book is the year's b.** ce livre est le plus gros succès de l'année; **it's been on the b. list for months** il est au palmarès des meilleures ventes depuis des mois

best-selling ADJ (book, author) à succès; **this is our b. item** c'est l'article que nous vendons le mieux; **it's been on the b. list for months** il est au palmarès des ventes depuis des mois

bet [bet] N pari m (**on** sur); **to win/lose a b.** gagner/perdre un pari; **to make** or **lay a b.** parier, faire un pari; Fam **your best b. would be to ...** ce que vous avez de mieux à faire, c'est de ...; **I'd take a b. on it** je serais prêt à le parier; Fam **it's my b.** or **my b. is that he'll come** je parie qu'il viendra; **all bets are off** les paris sont annulés
▪ VT (pt **bet**; pp **bet**, occ **betted**) (sum of money) parier; **I'll b. you that ...** je vous parierais que ..., parions que ...; **to b. ten to one that ...** parier à dix contre un que ...; Fam **I'll b. you anything (you like) that ...** je te parie tout ce que tu veux que ..., j'en donnerais ou mettrais ma tête à couper que ...; Fam **I b. you don't!** chiche (que tu ne le feras pas)!; Fam **I b. you I will!** chiche (que je le fais)!; Fam **you b. I will/you did/etc!** bien sûr que oui!; **you b. I won't/you didn't/etc!** bien sûr que non!
▪ VI **to b. on a horse** miser sur ou jouer un cheval; **to b. with sb** parier avec qn; **to b. on sth** parier sur qch; **I never b. on a sure thing** ce serait un pari perdu d'avance; **do you want to b.?** (as challenge) tu paries?; **b.!** (expressing disbelief) sûrement!; **you b.!** bien sûr

beta-blocker [ˈbiːtəblɒkər] N (drug) bêta-bloquant m

Betamax® **cassette** [ˈbiːtəmæks] N Betamax® f

beta test [ˈbiːtə] Comput N bêta-test m, pl bêta-tests, essai m approfondi
▪ VT conduire les bêta-tests sur, conduire les essais approfondis sur

beta testing N Comput béta-tests mpl

betel [ˈbiːt(ə)l] N (for chewing), Bot bétel m
▪ ▸ **b. nut** noix f d'arec; **b. nut palm, b. palm** arec m, aréquier m

Bethlehem [ˈbeθlɪhem, -lɪəm] N Bethléem m ou f

betide [bɪˈtaɪd] VT Arch, Lit, Hum (used only in) **woe b. him/you/etc** malheur ou gare à lui/à toi/etc

betimes [bɪˈtaɪmz] ADV Arch de bonne heure

betoken [bɪˈtəʊkən] VT Fml dénoter

betray [bɪˈtreɪ] VT **1** (be disloyal to) (person, one's country, faith etc) trahir; **to b. sb's trust**

trahir la confiance de qn **2** (disclose) (secret, one's ignorance, emotion) révéler, trahir

betrayal [bɪˈtreɪəl] N **1** (disloyalty) trahison f (**of** de); **b. of trust** abus m de confiance **2** (disclosure) (of one's ignorance, secret etc) révélation f

betrayer [bɪˈtreɪər] N **1** (of country) traître, -esse; **she attacked her b. with a knife** elle attaqua avec un couteau celui/celle qui l'avait trahie **2** (of secret) dénonciateur, -trice

betrothal [bɪˈtrəʊðəl] N Fml fiançailles fpl

betrothed [bɪˈtrəʊðd] ADJ, N Fml, Arch fiancé, -ée

BETTER¹ [ˈbetər]

ADJ	meilleur ▪ mieux
N	le meilleur **2**
ADV	mieux
VT	améliorer

ADJ (comp of **good**) meilleur; **you will find no b. hotel** vous ne trouverez pas mieux comme hôtel; **he's a b. man than you** (morally) il est mieux que vous; **you're b. than I am** (at maths etc) vous êtes plus fort que moi; **she's b. at tennis than her brother** elle est meilleure que son frère au tennis; **he's b. at maths than me** il est meilleur que moi en math; **fruit juice is b. for you than coffee** le jus de fruit est meilleur pour la santé que le café; **he is no b.** (of patient) il ne va pas mieux; **he is no b. than his brother** il ne vaut pas mieux que son frère; Old-fashioned, Hum **she's no b. than she should be** elle n'a rien d'une sainte; **to appeal to sb's b. feelings** faire appel aux bons sentiments de qn; **I had hoped for b. things** j'avais espéré mieux; **to get b.** (of patient) se remettre, se rétablir; (at doing sth) faire des progrès; (of weather, situation etc) s'améliorer; (of wine etc) se bonifier; **the weather is b.** il fait meilleur; **to be b.** (in health) aller ou se porter mieux; **I hope you will soon be b.** j'espère que vous serez bientôt rétabli; **is your cold any b.?** ton rhume va mieux?; **is your headache any b.?** tu as encore mal à la tête?; **is your foot any b.?** est-ce que tu as moins mal au pied?; **it's b. that way** c'est mieux comme ça; **it's b. to do without it** mieux vaut ou il vaut mieux s'en passer; **it would be b. for you to go** (to that place) il vaudrait mieux que vous y alliez; **that's b.** voilà qui est mieux; **it would be b. if you called me tomorrow** ce serait ou il vaudrait mieux que tu m'appelles demain; **nothing could be b., it couldn't be b.** cela ne peut pas être mieux, c'est on ne peut mieux; **b. luck next time!** tu feras mieux la prochaine fois!; **for the b. part of the day** pendant la plus grande partie de la journée; Br Fam **my b. half** la (chère) moitié, ma légitime; (man) mon homme; Br **to go one b. than sb**, Am **to go sb one b.** (r)enchérir ou surenchérir ou faire une surenchère sur qn VOIR GRAMMAIRE A25; A41

N **1 I expected b. of you** je m'attendais à mieux de ta part; **one's betters** (socially) ceux qui sont d'un rang social plus élevé; **one's elders and betters** ses aînés **2** (superior of two) le meilleur, la meilleure; **which is the b. of the two?** lequel des deux est le meilleur?; **what do you think of this wine? – I've tasted b.** comment trouvez-vous ce vin? – j'en ai bu de meilleurs; **change for the b.** changement m en bien; (in state of health) amélioration f; **he has changed for the b.** (his character has improved) il a changé à son avantage; **things are taking a turn for the b.** les choses prennent meilleure tournure; **to get the b. of sb** l'emporter sur qn, prendre le dessus sur qn; **to get the b. of** (obstacle etc) surmonter, vaincre; (one's

anger etc) maîtriser; **his anger/shyness got the b. of him** sa colère/timidité a eu raison de lui; **to be (all) the b. for doing sth** se trouver mieux d'avoir fait qch; **I'm all the b. for seeing you** ça me fait du bien de te voir; **I'd feel all the b. for a holiday** je partirais volontiers en vacances; **you will be all the b. for it** vous vous en trouverez (d'autant) mieux; **I think all the b. of you for it** je vous en estime d'autant plus; **all the b.!** tant mieux!

ADV (comp of **well**) mieux; **so much the b.** tant mieux; **to take sb for b. or for worse** (in marriage ceremony) s'unir à qn pour le meilleur comme pour le pire; **b. and b.** de mieux en mieux; **I know that b. than you** je sais cela mieux que vous; **I am feeling b.** je me sens mieux; **you are looking b.** tu as meilleure mine; **to know sb b.**, **to get to know sb b.** mieux connaître qn; **the more I know him, the b. I like him** plus je le connais, plus je l'aime; **I can understand it all the b. because ...** je le conçois d'autant mieux que ...; **you'd b. stay** il vaut mieux que vous restiez; **I'd b. begin by ...** je ferais bien de commencer par ...; **we'd b. be going back** il est temps de rebrousser chemin; **you'd b. not** il ne vaudrait mieux pas; **hadn't you b. phone first?** est-ce qu'il ne vaudrait pas mieux que tu appelles avant?; **to think b. of it** changer d'opinion, se raviser; **to think b. of sb for doing sth** estimer qn davantage d'avoir ou pour avoir fait qch; **that's b. still** (what you have done) c'est encore mieux; **b. still, you could come tomorrow** mieux encore, tu pourrais venir demain, ce qui serait mieux, c'est que tu viennes demain; **b. dressed** mieux habillé; **b. known** plus connu; **b. looking** (more attractive) plus beau ou joli; **he's b. tempered than his brother** il est plus agréable que son frère; **I hope you're a bit b. tempered tomorrow!** j'espère que tu seras de meilleure humeur demain!; **to be b. off** (wealthier) être plus aisé; (well situated) se trouver dans de meilleures conditions; **he's b. off where he is** il est bien mieux où il est; **you're b. off without him** tu es bien mieux sans lui; **the children of b.-off parents** les enfants dont les parents sont aisés

VT **1** (improve) améliorer; **to b. oneself** améliorer sa condition **2** (surpass) (exploit, piece of work) surpasser; Sport (time) améliorer; **the company has bettered the competition for the second year running** c'est la deuxième année consécutive que l'entreprise a fait mieux que la concurrence; **can you b. that?** pouvez-vous faire mieux que cela?

---

better² N (person who bets) parieur, -ieuse

betterment [ˈbetəmənt] N Fml amélioration f

betting [ˈbetɪŋ] N (bets) paris mpl; (price) cote f; **the b. ran high on a pretty gros**; **the b. is twenty to one** la cote est à vingt contre un; **the b. is that ...** il y a fort à parier que ...; **what's the b. he doesn't turn up?** combien tu paries qu'il ne viendra pas?; **if I were a b. man** si j'étais homme à parier
▪ ▸ **b. book** carnet m de paris; **b. shop** bureau m de paris (appartenant à un bookmaker); **b. slip** bulletin m de pari

bettor [ˈbetər] N = **better²**

BETWEEN [bɪˈtwiːn] PREP entre; **a table stood b. him and the door** une table le séparait de la porte; **to stand b. two opponents** s'interposer ou intervenir entre deux adversaires; **no one can come b. us** personne ne peut nous séparer; **to be b. life and death** être entre la vie et la mort; **to be something b. ... and ...** tenir autant de ... que de ...; **b. eight and nine o'clock** entre huit et neuf heures; **b. now and Monday** d'ici (à) lundi; **b. twenty and thirty** de vingt à trente; **you must**

choose b. them il faut choisir entre eux; to distinguish b. A, B and C distinguer entre A, B et C; b. the two/the three of them à eux deux/trois; they scored 1,500 b. them (of two people) ils ont marqué 1500 à eux deux; (of more than two people) ils ont marqué 1500 à tous; we bought it b. us nous l'avons acheté à nous deux/à nous trois/*etc*; they shared the loot b. them ils se sont partagé le butin; b. ourselves ... entre nous ...; this is strictly b. ourselves *or* b. you and me que cela reste entre nous; *Fam* b. you (and) me and the gatepost (soit dit) entre nous; b. one thing and another ... d'une chose à l'autre ...; there's no love lost b. them ils ne peuvent pas se souffrir *ou* se sentir
ADV (in) b. entre les deux; (*in the intervening time*) dans l'intervalle

between-decks *Naut* **ADV** dans l'entrepont
N entrepont *m*

betweentime(s) [bɪ'twiːntaɪm(z)], **betweenwhile, betweenwhiles** [bɪ'twiːnwaɪl(z)] **ADV** dans l'intervalle, entre-temps

betwixt [bɪ'twɪkst] **ADV** *Fam* it's b. and between c'est entre les deux

bevel ['bev(ə)l] **N** biseau *m*
VT (-ll-, *Am* -l-) biseauter, chanfreiner, tailler en biseau
VI aller en biseau
▸▸ *Mining* b. cut fausse coupe *f*; *Carp* b. edge biseau *m*; *Tech* b. gear engrenage *m* conique; b. rule, b. square fausse équerre *f*

bevelled, *Am* **beveled** ['bevəld] **ADJ** (*edge*) biseauté, en biseau, en chanfrein

bevelling, *Am* **beveling** ['bev(ə)lɪŋ] **N** biseautage *m*, chanfreinage *m*

beverage ['bevərɪdʒ] **N** boisson *f*
▸▸ *Can* b. room bar *m*

bevvied ['bevɪd] **ADJ** *Br Fam* bourré, beurré; to get b. se cuiter, prendre une cuite

bevvy ['bevɪ] **N** *Br Fam* **1** (*alcohol*) alcool *m* **2** (*alcoholic drink*) to have a b. boire un coup **3** (*drinking session*) beuverie *f*; to go on the b. aller se cuiter

bevy ['bevɪ] **N 1** (*group*) bande *f*, troupe *f*; b. of girls bande de filles **2** (*of larks, quail*) volée *f*

bewail [bɪ'weɪl] **VT** pleurer; (*one's fate*) se lamenter sur

beware [bɪ'weər] **VI** (*used only in inf and imp*) (*of sb*) se méfier, *Lit* se défier (of de); (*of sth*) se méfier (of de), prendre garde (à); b.! prenez garde!; b. of pickpockets attention aux pickpockets; b. of the dog (*sign*) ≃ chien méchant; to b. of doing sth se garder de faire qch

bewhiskered [bɪ'wɪskəd] **ADJ** *Lit, Hum* qui porte des rouflaquettes

bewilder [bɪ'wɪldər] **VT 1** (*puzzle*) désorienter, dérouter **2** (*confuse*) ahurir, abasourdir

bewildered [bɪ'wɪldəd] **ADJ 1** (*puzzled*) désorienté; (*air*) perplexe **2** (*confused*) ahuri, abasourdi

bewildering [bɪ'wɪldərɪŋ] **ADJ 1** (*puzzling*) (*problem, question*) déroutant **2** (*confusing*) (*number, variety*) ahurissant

bewilderingly [bɪ'wɪldərɪŋlɪ] **ADV** the problem is b. complex le problème est d'une complexité déroutante; even more b., ... chose encore plus ahurissante, ...; b. varied/frequent d'une variété/fréquence ahurissante

bewilderment [bɪ'wɪldəmənt] **N 1** (*puzzlement*) perplexité *f* **2** (*confusion*) ahurissement *m*

bewitch [bɪ'wɪtʃ] **VT** ensorceler, jeter un sort sur; *Fig* captiver

bewitching [bɪ'wɪtʃɪŋ] **ADJ** ravissant

bey [beɪ] **N** bey *m*

beyond [bɪ'jɒnd] **ADV** au-delà, par-delà; the next century and b. le siècle à venir et au-delà
PREP 1 (*of place*) au-delà de, par-delà; the house is b. the church la maison est au-delà de *ou* plus loin que l'église; b. the seas par-delà les *ou* au-delà des mers
2 (*of time*) b. a certain date passé une certaine date
3 (*surpassing*) to live b. one's means vivre au-dessus de ses moyens; it's b. me cela me dépasse, je n'y comprends rien; it's b. me how they can do it je ne comprends vraiment pas comment ils peuvent le faire; circumstances b. our control circonstances indépendantes de notre volonté; what you're asking is b. my power ce que vous demandez me dépasse *ou* dépasse mes attributions; it's b. my power to save him je ne peux rien pour le sauver; b. my reach hors de ma portée; I'm b. caring what they do next peu m'importe ce qu'ils feront ensuite; frankly, I'm b. caring franchement, ça m'est complètement égal; b. belief incroyable, à ne pas y croire; b. doubt hors de doute, sans le moindre doute; *Fml* b. measure outre mesure, sans mesure; b. praise au-dessus de tout éloge; b. reach inaccessible, hors de portée; b. repair irréparable; b. question indiscutablement, incontestablement; to be b. question être indiscutable *ou* incontestable; it is a fact b. doubt *or* question c'est un fait avéré; that's (going) b. a joke cela dépasse les bornes (de la simple plaisanterie); she is b. recovery (*of sick person*) elle est perdue; the agreement is b. saving l'accord est à l'eau
4 (*except*) he has nothing b. his wages il n'a rien que son salaire
N the b. l'au-delà *m inv*

bezel ['bezəl] **N 1** (*of cut gem*) biseau *m*, bezel *m* **2** (*of ring*) chaton *m*

BF [biː'ef] **N** *Br Sl abbr* bloody fool

B-feature **N** *Cin* film *m* de série B

BFI [biːef'aɪ] **N** *Cin* (*abbr* British Film Institute) = organisme *m* britannique de promotion du cinéma (aide à la réalisation notamment)

bhp [biːeɪtʃ'piː] **N** (*abbr* brake horsepower) ch *mpl*, CV *mpl*

Bhutan [buː'taːn] **N** Bhoutan *m*

bi [baɪ] **ADJ** *Fam* (*abbr* bisexual) bi

bi-annual **ADJ** semestriel

bi-annually **ADV** deux fois par an

bias ['baɪəs] **N 1** préjugé *m*, parti *m* pris (against contre; in favour de); to be without b. être sans parti pris; the b. in his remarks was obvious il était clair à ses remarques qu'il était de parti pris **2** *Sewing* biais *m*; material cut on the b. étoffe coupée en *ou* de biais
VT (*pt, pp* bias(s)ed) rendre partial, influencer, prévenir (towards, in favour of en faveur de; against contre)
▸▸ *Sewing* b. binding biais *m* (ruban); *Aut* b. tyre pneu *m* à structure diagonale

bias(s)ed ['baɪəst] **ADJ 1** (*person*) partial; you're b. in her favour tu as un parti pris pour elle; b. opinion opinion *f* préconçue **2** (*bowling ball*) décentré
▸▸ b. error (*in statistics*) erreur *f* systématique; b. sample (*in statistics*) échantillon *m* biaisé *ou* avec erreur systématique

bib [bɪb] **N 1** (*child's*) bavette *f*, bavoir *m* **2** (*of apron*) bavette *f*; *Old-fashioned Fam* in one's best b. and tucker sur son trente et un

bible ['baɪb(ə)l] **N** bible *f*; the B. la Bible; *Fig* this dictionary is his b. il fait de ce dictionnaire sa bible
▸▸ the B. Belt = États *mpl* du sud des États-

Unis où l'évangélisme est très répandu; B. class (*in school, church*) classe *f* d'instruction religieuse; (*in Catholic church*) catéchisme *m*; B. stories histoires *fpl* tirées de la Bible

Bible-basher [-bæʃər] **N** *Fam Pej* grenouille *f* de bénitier

Bible-bashing **N** *Fam Pej* B. preacher évangéliste *m* zélé

Bible-thumper [-θʌmpər] **N** *Fam Pej* = Bible-basher

Bible-thumping **N** *Fam Pej* = Bible-bashing

biblical ['bɪblɪk(ə)l] **ADJ** biblique

bibliographer [bɪblɪ'ɒgrəfər] **N** bibliographe *mf*

bibliographical [bɪblɪə'græfɪk(ə)l] **ADJ** bibliographique

bibliography [bɪblɪ'ɒgrəfɪ] **N** bibliographie *f*

bibliophile ['bɪblɪəfaɪl] **N** bibliophile *mf*

bibulous ['bɪbjʊləs] **ADJ** *Fml, Hum* (*person*) qui s'adonne à la boisson; (*celebration*) bien arrosé

bicameral [baɪ'kæmərəl] **ADJ** *Pol* bicaméral, -aux
▸▸ b. system bicaméralisme *m*, bicamérisme *m*

bicarb [baɪ'kaːb] **N** *Fam* bicarbonate *m* de soude

bicarbonate [baɪ'kaːbəneɪt] **N** (*of soda etc*) bicarbonate *m*

bicentenary [baɪsen'tiːnərɪ], *Am* **bicentennial** [baɪsen'tenɪəl] **ADJ, N** bicentenaire *m*; the b. celebrations les cérémonies *fpl* du bicentenaire

biceps ['baɪseps] **N** *Anat* (*muscle m*) biceps *m*

bicker ['bɪkər] **VI** se chamailler, se quereller

bickering ['bɪkərɪŋ] **N** chamailleries *fpl*, querelles *fpl*

bickie ['bɪkɪ] **N** *Br Fam* biscuit *m*

bicolour(ed), *Am* **bicolor, bicolored** ['baɪkʌlər, -ləd] **ADJ** bicolore

bicultural [baɪ'kʌltʃərəl] **ADJ** *esp Am* biculturel

bicycle ['baɪsɪk(ə)l] **N** bicyclette *f*, vélo *m*; to go by b. aller à *ou Fam* en bicyclette *ou* vélo; to ride a b. faire de la bicyclette *ou* du vélo; to know how to ride a b. savoir monter à bicyclette *ou* à vélo, savoir faire du vélo; he was riding his b. il était à bicyclette *ou* à vélo
VI (*for exercise*) faire de la bicyclette *ou* du vélo; (*travel*) aller à bicyclette *ou* à vélo (to à)
▸▸ b. chain chaîne *f* de vélo; (*for securing bike*) antivol *m inv*, b. clip pince *f* à vélo; b. club club *m* de cyclistes; *Ftbl* b. kick retourné *m* bicyclette; b. path piste *f ou* bande *f* cyclable; b. race course *f* de bicyclette; b. rack (*on pavement*) ratelier *m* à bicyclettes *ou* à vélos; (*on car*) porte-vélos *m inv*; b. track piste cyclable

BID [bɪd] **N 1** (*offer*) (*at auction*) enchère *f*; higher *or* further b. offre *f* supérieure, surenchère *f*; lowest/highest b. offre la plus basse/forte; to make a b. faire une offre, enchérir
2 (*attempt*) tentative *f* (for sth de qch; to do sth pour faire qch); to make a b. for sth tenter d'obtenir qch; to make a b. for power (*legally*) viser le pouvoir; (*illegally*) tenter un coup d'État; she failed in her b. to beat the record elle a échoué dans sa tentative de battre le record
3 *Cards* (*in bridge*) annonce *f*; (*in solo whist*) demande *f*; b. of two diamonds ouverture de deux carreaux; no b.! je passe!, parole!
4 (*in takeover*) offre *f*; (*tender*) soumission *f*;

to make a b. soumissionner; **to put a b. in on a flat** faire une offre pour un appartement
VT & VI (*pt* **bade** [bæd, beɪd], **bid**; *pp* **bidden** [bɪd(ə)n], **bid**) **1** (*pt, pp* **bid**) (*offer*) **to b. for sth** faire une offre pour qch; **what am I b. for this table?** qu'est-ce que vous m'offrez pour cette table?; **to b. ten pounds** faire une offre de dix livres
2 *Cards* **to b. three diamonds** enchérir de trois carreaux
3 (*in call for tenders*) faire une soumission (**on sth** pour qch)
4 *Fml* (*greet*) **to b. sb welcome/good day** souhaiter la bienvenue/le bonjour à qn; **to b. sb goodbye** faire ses adieux à qn
5 *Arch, Fml* (*seem probable*) **the weather bids fair to be fine** *or* **to improve** le temps s'annonce beau; **he bids fair to become … il** promet de devenir …
6 *Arch, Lit* (*order*) commander, ordonner (**sb (to) do sth** à qn de faire qch); **to b. sb be silent** ordonner à qn de se taire, commander le silence à qn
▸▸ *Fin* **b. bond** caution *f* d'adjudication *ou* de soumission; *St Exch* **b. price** cours *m* acheteur
▸ **bid up** VT SEP *Fin* **to b. up the price of goods** enchérir sur le prix des marchandises

biddable ['bɪdəb(ə)l] ADJ (*child etc*) obéissant, docile

bidder ['bɪdər] N (*at sale*) enchérisseur, -euse; (*at cards*) demandeur, -euse; **there were no bidders** il n'y a pas eu de preneurs; **the highest b.** le plus offrant

bidding ['bɪdɪŋ] N **1** (*at auction*) enchères *fpl*; **the b.** les enchères; **to start the b. at £5,000** commencer les enchères à 5000 livres; **to open the b.** ouvrir les enchères; **the b. is against you** est-ce que vous voulez surenchérir? **2** *Fml* (*order*) **at sb's b.** sur l'ordre de qn; **to do sb's b.** exécuter les ordres de qn; **he needed no second b.** il n'a pas eu besoin qu'on lui répète cet ordre
▸▸ *Am St Exch* **b. price** cours *m* acheteur

bide [baɪd] VT (*pt* **bided**) **to b. one's time** attendre le bon moment

bidet ['bi:deɪ] N bidet *m*

bidirectional [baɪdɪ'rekʃən(ə)l] ADJ bidirectionnel
▸▸ *Typ* **b. printing** impression *f* bidirectionnelle

biennial [baɪ'enɪəl] ADJ **1** (*event*) biennal, -aux **2** (*plant*) bisannuel
N *Bot* plante *f* bisannuelle

biennially [baɪ'enɪəlɪ] ADV tous les deux ans

bier [bɪər] N (*for coffin, body*) bière *f*

biff [bɪf] N *Sl* baffe *f*
INT v'lan!, pan!
VT *Sl* (*hit*) flanquer une baffe à

bifocal [baɪ'fəʊk(ə)l] *Opt* ADJ bifocal, -aux, à double foyer
NPL **bifocals** verres *mpl* bifocaux *ou* à double foyer

bifurcate ['baɪfəkeɪt] VI *Fml* bifurquer

bifurcation [baɪfə'keɪʃən] N *Fml* bifurcation *f*

BIG [bɪg]

| ADJ | grand **1–3** ▪ gros **1–3** ▪ important **2** |

ADJ (**bigger** ['bɪgər], **biggest** ['bɪgɪst]) **1** (*object*) (*large, tall*) grand; (*bulky*) gros; **a b. hotel** un grand hôtel; **a b. drop in prices** une forte baisse des prix; **to be doing a b. trade** faire de grosses affaires; *Fam* **you've got a b. mouth** (*you let the secret out*) tu n'es pas capable de la fermer; *Fam* **a b. A** un A majuscule; **to give sb a b. hand** applaudir qn bien fort

2 (*serious, important*) (*problem, explosion, argument, difference*) gros; (*mistake*) grave; (*decision*) important; **this is our b. day** c'est le grand jour pour nous; **you've got a b. day ahead of you tomorrow** tu as une journée importante devant toi demain; **you want to look your best on the b. day** tu veux être la plus belle possible le grand jour; *Fam* **he had b. ideas** il voyait grand; **don't get any b. ideas about doing this yourself** ne crois pas que tu vas pouvoir faire ça tout seul; *Fam* **I've got b. plans for you** j'ai de grands projets pour toi; **b. budget film** superproduction *f*, *Fam* **b. money** *or Am* **bucks** fric *m*; *Fam* **to earn b. money** gagner beaucoup d'argent; *Fam* **I'm talking b. money here** je te parle de beaucoup d'oseille; **a b. eater** un gros mangeur; **the b. names in the theatre world** les grands noms du théâtre; **she's a b. noise in publishing** c'est quelqu'un d'important dans le monde de l'édition; **they'll need to bring in the b. guns from New York on this one** il faudra qu'ils amènent les experts de New York sur ce coup-là; *Theat, Cin* **the b. battle scene** la grande scène de bataille; **this is your b. scene** (*of main character*) la scène est à toi; (*of minor character*) c'est ta scène
3 (*person*) (*tall*) grand et fort; (*fat*) gros; *Fam* (*important*) important; **you're a b. girl/boy now** tu es une grande fille/un grand garçon maintenant; **she's b. enough to look after herself** elle est assez grande pour se défendre; *Fam* **he's getting too b. for his boots** *or Am* **britches** il ne s'en ressent plus; **my b. brother** mon grand frère; **to get big(ger)** (*taller*) grandir; (*fatter*) grossir; **you're the biggest fool of the lot!** c'est toi le plus bête de tous!; *Arch Lit* **to be b. with child** être sur le point d'enfanter
4 (*idioms*) **she goes for Frenchmen in a b. way** elle se pâme devant les Français; **he goes in for office memos in a b. way** il envoie des quantités de mémos; **we don't celebrate Christmas in a b. way** nous ne faisons pas tellement la fête à Noël; **you really do things in a b. way** tu ne fais pas les choses à moitié; **they've decided to get into exports in a b. way** ils ont décidé de se lancer à fond dans les exportations; *also Iron* **that was b. of you** c'était vraiment généreux de votre part; *Fam* **to be b. on sth** (*keen*) aimer beaucoup qch; **reality TV was b. last year** la télé réalité a eu un succès fou l'année dernière; *Fam* **to be in the b. time, to have made the b. time** être en haut de l'échelle, être le dessus du panier, être arrivé; *Fam* **to hit** *or* **make the b. time** réussir; *Fam* **once they've had a taste of the b. time** une fois qu'ils ont goûté au succès; *Fam* **to be into sb/sth b. time** *or* **in a b. way** être dingue de qn/qch; *Fam* **he's been doing drugs b. time** *or* **in a b. way** depuis quelque temps il n'arrête pas de se droguer; *Fam* **he messed up his driving test b. time** il s'est planté dans les grandes largeurs au permis
ADV *Fam* **to talk b.** (*boast*) se vanter, faire l'important; **to think b.** voir grand; **to go over** *or* **down b.** avoir un succès fou; **the last song went down b. with the audience** la dernière chanson a fait un tabac auprès du public; **to make it b.** réussir
▸▸ *Fam* **the B. Apple** = surnom *m* donné à la ville de New York; **the B. Bang** *Br St Exch Fam* = déréglementation *f* de la Bourse de Londres en octobre 1986; *Astron* le big bang; **b. bank** grande banque *f*, enseigne *f* bancaire; *Comput* **B. Blue** = surnom de la société IBM; *Am St Exch* **the b. board** = la Bourse de New York; **B. Brother** Big Brother; *Com* **b. business** les grandes entreprises *fpl*; *Zool* **b. cat** fauve *m*, grand félin *m*; *Fam Fig* **b. cheese** gros bonnet *m*; *Br Aut* **b. end** tête *f* de bielle; **b. game** gros gibier *m*; *Br Fam Hum* **b. girl's blouse** (*wimp*) femmelette *f*, *Fam* **b. hair** =

coiffure *f* volumineuse et apprêtée; *Am Fam* **b. house** (*prison*) taule *f*, placard *m*; *Br Journ* **The B. Issue** = hebdomadaire *m* vendu au profit des sans-logis par ces derniers, ≃ le Réverbère; *Sport* **b. match** grand match *m*; *Fam* **the b. screen** le grand écran; *Fam Fig* **b. shot** gros bonnet; **b. spender** = personne *f* qui dépense beaucoup d'argent; **he's a b. spender when it comes to clothes** il dépense beaucoup d'argent en vêtements; *Iron* **you know what he's like, the last of the b. spenders!** tu le connais, toujours à faire des frais!; *Anat* **b. toe** gros orteil *m*; **b. top** (*tent*) grand chapiteau *m*; (*circus*) cirque *m*; **b. wheel** grand roue *f*, *Fig Fam* gros bonnet
▸ **big up** VT SEP *Fam* faire du battage à propos de; **to b. oneself up** se faire mousser; **all the radio stations are bigging up his new album** toutes les stations de radio font un sacré battage autour de son dernier album

> **Big Ben**
> Nom de la cloche de la Tour de l'horloge à Westminster, souvent donné à tort à la tour elle-même. Elle est considérée comme un des monuments principaux de Londres.

bigamist ['bɪgəmɪst] N bigame *mf*

bigamous ['bɪgəməs] ADJ bigame; **b. marriage** bigamie *f*, **to enter into a b. marriage** se rendre coupable de bigamie

bigamy ['bɪgəmɪ] N bigamie *f*, **to commit b.** être coupable de bigamie

big-bellied [-'belɪd] ADJ (*fat*) ventru, pansu; **she's b.** (*of pregnant woman*) elle a un gros ventre

big-boned ADJ fortement charpenté

biggie ['bɪgɪ] N *Fam* **that's a b.** (*fish, car etc*) c'en est un(e) gros(se); **it's gonna be a b.** (*book, film, record*) il va faire un malheur; **there's a storm coming and it's a b.** il y a un orage qui se prépare, j'te dis pas

biggish ['bɪgɪʃ] ADJ (*tall, large*) assez grand; (*fat*) assez gros

bighead ['bɪghed] N *Fam* crâneur, -euse

bigheaded [bɪg'hedɪd] ADJ *Fam* crâneur

bigheadedness [bɪg'hedɪdnɪs] N *Fam* suffisance *f*, prétention *f*

big-hearted [-'hɑːtɪd] ADJ **to be b.** avoir le cœur; *also Iron* **in his usual b. way** le cœur sur la main, comme à son habitude

bight [baɪt] N *Geog* (*in coastline*) renfoncement *m*; **the Great Australian B.** la Grande Baie Australienne, le Grand Golfe Australien *ou* de l'Australie

bigness ['bɪgnɪs] N (*of person*) (*tallness*) grande taille *f*, (*fatness*) grosseur *f*, (*of thing*) grandes dimensions *fpl*; **his b. made him self-conscious** il était complexé parce qu'il était si gros

bigot ['bɪgət] N sectaire *mf*, fanatique *mf*

> Note that the French word **bigot** is a false friend. It is used to describe an excessively religious person but has no overtones of sectarianism.

bigoted ['bɪgətɪd] ADJ sectaire (**against** à l'égard de); **don't be so b.** ne sois pas si borné

bigotry ['bɪgətrɪ] N sectarisme *m*; (*religious*) bigoterie *f*

big-ticket ADJ *Am* (*expensive*) cher

big-time ADJ *Fam* **a b. lawyer/executive** un avocat/cadre qui a réussi; **b. actor** acteur *m* de premier plan; **b. operator** gros trafiquant *m*

bigwig ['bɪgwɪg] N *Fam Hum, Pej* gros bonnet *m*, grosse légume *f*

bijou ['biːʒuː] ADJ **b. flat** or **residence** petit appartement m ravissant

bike [baɪk] Fam N (bicycle) vélo m; (motorbike) moto f; Br Sl **on your b.!** (go away) tiretoi!; (hurry up) magne-toi!; (I don't believe you, don't talk rubbish) à d'autres!, tu charries!

▪ VT (send by motorcycle courier) envoyer par coursier; **to b. sth round to sb** envoyer qch à qn par coursier

▪ VI faire du vélo; (on motorbike) faire de la moto; **we biked there** nous y sommes allés à ou en vélo/moto

▸▸**b. carrier** porte-vélo m, pl porte-vélos; **b. lane** piste f cyclable; **b. shed** cabane f ou remise f à vélos

biker ['baɪkər] N cycliste mf; (on motor bike), Pej motard, -arde; (courier) coursier, -ière

bikini [bɪˈkiːnɪ] N bikini® m

bilabial [baɪˈleɪbɪəl] ADJ, N Ling (consonne f) bilabiale f

bilateral [baɪˈlætər(ə)l] ADJ bilatéral, -aux

bilaterally [baɪˈlætər(ə)lɪ] ADV bilatéralement

bilberry ['bɪlbərɪ] N airelle f, myrtille f

bile [baɪl] N Physiol bile f; Fig Fml **to be full of b.** (bad-tempered) être plein de hargne

▸▸Anat **b. duct** canal m biliaire

bilestone ['baɪlstəʊn] N calcul m biliaire

bilge [bɪldʒ] N Naut (hold) fond m de cale; (water) eau f de cale; Fam **to talk a lot of b.** dire des bêtises; **b.!** sottises!

▸▸Naut **b. pump** pompe f de drain ou de cale; **b. water** eau de cale

bilharzia [bɪlˈhɑːtsɪə] N Med **1** (disease) bilharziose f **2** (parasite) bilharzia f, bilharzie f

biliary ['bɪlɪərɪ] ADJ Physiol biliaire

bilingual [baɪˈlɪŋgwəl] ADJ bilingue

▸▸**b. secretary** secrétaire mf bilingue

bilingualism [baɪˈlɪŋgwəlɪz(ə)m] N bilinguisme m

bilious ['bɪlɪəs] ADJ **1** Physiol bilieux; **he looks rather b.** on dirait qu'il va nous faire une crise de foie; **b. attack** crise f de foie; Fig **b. yellow/green** jaunâtre/verdâtre **2** Fig (bad-tempered) colérique

biliousness ['bɪlɪəsnɪs] N Med affection f bilieuse; Fig hargne f

bilk [bɪlk] VT Old-fashioned Fam (cheat) avoir; **he bilked her (out) of all her money** il lui a extorqué tout son argent; **you've been bilked** tu t'es fait avoir

Bill [bɪl] N Br Fam **the (Old) B.** (police) les flics mpl, les poulets mpl

bill¹ [bɪl] N **1** (notice of payment due) Com facture f; (for gas, electricity) facture, note f; (in hotel) note; Br (in restaurant) addition f; **to pay a b.** payer ou régler une facture; **to foot the b.** payer la note ou les dépenses; **to make out a b.** dresser ou rédiger une facture; **can I/we have the b., please?** (in restaurant) l'addition, s'il vous plaît; **put it on my b.** (in hotel) mettez-le sur ma note

2 Am (banknote) billet m de banque; **five-dollar b.** billet de cinq dollars

3 Com, Fin effet m (de commerce); **bills** valeurs fpl, papier m (bancable); **long(-dated)/short(-dated) bills** effets à longue/courte échéance

4 Theat etc (poster) affiche f; (for political party) affiche, placard m; **(stick) no bills!** défense d'afficher; **to head** or **top the b.** (of actor) être en tête d'affiche; Fam **that will fill** or **fit the b.** cela fera l'affaire

5 Fig **the doctor gave me a clean b. of health** le docteur m'a trouvé en parfaite santé; **the investigators gave the engine a clean b. of health** les enquêteurs ont conclu que le moteur était en parfait état

6 Pol projet m de loi; (private) proposition f de loi; **to pass/reject a b.** adopter/repousser un projet de loi

▪ VT **1** (invoice) envoyer une facture à (for pour) **2** Theat **she is billed to play Ophelia** elle est à l'affiche dans le rôle d'Ophélie; Fig **he is billed as America's greatest actor** on dit que c'est le meilleur acteur américain

▸▸Fin **b. made out to bearer** effet m au porteur; Fin **b. book** livre m d'échéance; Fin **bills for collection** effets à l'encaissement; Fin **bills for collection form** formulaire m d'encaissement; **b. of entry** déclaration f d'entrée (en douane); Fin **b. of exchange** lettre f de change, effet de commerce; Fin **bills of exchange statement** lettre de change relevé, LCR f; **b. of fare** carte f (du jour); **b. of lading** Com connaissement m; Am Rail feuille f d'expédition; Acct **bills payable** effets à payer; Acct **bills payable ledger** livre ou journal m des effets à payer; Constr **b. of quantities** devis m; Acct **bills receivable** effets à recevoir; Acct **bills receivable ledger** livre ou journal m des effets à recevoir; Hist **the B. of Rights** (in UK) = loi f de 1689 déterminant les droits du citoyen anglais; (in US) = les dix premiers amendements mpl à la Constitution américaine garantissant, entre autres droits, la liberté d'expression, de religion et de réunion; **b. of sale** acte m ou contrat m de vente; Fin **b. 'without protest'** traite f 'sans frais'

bill² [bɪl] N **1** (of bird) bec m **2** Geog bec m, promontoire m

▪ VI (of birds) se becqueter; Fam **to b. and coo** (of couple) se faire des mamours

billboard ['bɪlbɔːd] N esp Am panneau m ou support m d'affichage

▸▸**b. advertising** publicité f sur panneaux; **b. site** emplacement m d'affichage

billet ['bɪlɪt] N **1** Mil (requisition) billet m de logement **2** Mil (accommodation) (in sb's house) logement m; (in town) cantonnement m; (of evacuee) logement **3** Old-fashioned Br Fam (job) situation f

▪ VT (-t-) (troops, evacuee) loger (**on sb** chez qn); **to b. troops on** or **in a town** cantonner des troupes dans une ville

▪ VI loger (**with** chez)

billeting ['bɪlɪtɪŋ] N Mil (in private house) logement m chez l'habitant; (on town) cantonnement m

▸▸**b. officer** officier m de cantonnement

billfold ['bɪlfəʊld] N Am (wallet) portefeuille m

billhook ['bɪlhʊk] N (for pruning, chopping) serpe f, (small) serpette f

billiard ['bɪljəd] N **1** (usu pl with sing verb) **billiards** (jeu m de) billard m; **to play billiards** jouer au billard; **to have** or **play a game of billiards** faire ou disputer une partie de billard; **bar billiards** billard russe **2** Am (shot) carambolage m

▸▸**b. ball** boule f de billard; **b. cue** queue f de billard; **b. room** salle f de billard; **b. table** (table f de) billard m

billing ['bɪlɪŋ] N **1** Theat, Cin affichage m; **to get** or **to have top/second b.** (of actor) être en tête d'affiche/en deuxième place à l'affiche **2** Fin facturation f

▸▸Fin **b. date** date f de facturation; Fin **b. machine** caisse f (enregistreuse); Fin **b. office** bureau m de facturation

billion ['bɪljən] N (one thousand million) milliard m; Br Old-fashioned (one million million) billion m VOIR GRAMMAIRE A76

billionaire [bɪljəˈneər] N milliardaire mf

billionth ['bɪljənθ] ADJ milliardième

N **1** (ordinal) milliardième mf **2** (fraction) milliardième m

billow ['bɪləʊ] N Lit (large wave) lame f; Lit **the billows** les flots mpl; **billows of smoke** nuages mpl de fumée

▪ VI (of sea) se soulever en vagues; (of crowds, smoke etc) ondoyer; **the sails billowed in the wind** les voiles se gonflaient au vent

billowy ['bɪləʊɪ] ADJ (sea) houleux

billposter ['bɪlpəʊstər], **billsticker** ['bɪlstɪkər] N afficheur, -euse, colleur, -euse d'affiches; **billposters will be prosecuted** ≃ défense d'afficher

billposting ['bɪlpəʊstɪŋ], **billsticking** ['bɪlstɪkɪŋ] N affichage m

billy, pl **billies** ['bɪlɪ, -z] N **1** Austr, New Zealand (can) gamelle f; **to boil the b.** faire du thé **2** (club) gourdin m; Am (for police) matraque f

▸▸**b. club** gourdin m

billycan ['bɪlɪkæn] N = **billy 1**

billy-goat N bouc m

billy-o(h) N Old-fashioned Br Fam **it's raining like b.** il pleut à verse; **to run like b.** courir très vite ou à toutes jambes

BIM [biːaɪˈem] N (abbr British Institute of Management) = organisme m britannique dont la fonction est de renseigner et de conseiller les entreprises en matière de gestion, ainsi que de promouvoir l'enseignement de cette discipline

bimbo ['bɪmbəʊ] N Pej minette f, jolie sotte f; **she's a real b.** elle n'a rien dans la tête

bimedia [baɪˈmiːdɪə] ADJ bi-média; **to be a b. reporter** être journaliste à la radio et à la télévision

bimetallic [baɪmɪˈtælɪk] ADJ Econ (system) bimétallique

▸▸**b. strip** bilame m

bimetallism [baɪˈmetəlɪz(ə)m] N Econ bimétallisme m

bimonthly [baɪˈmʌnθlɪ] ADJ **1** (every two months) bimestriel; **to appear on a b. basis** paraître tous les deux mois **2** (twice a month) bimensuel; **to appear on a b. basis** paraître deux fois par mois

N (magazine) (every two months) bimestriel m; (twice monthly) bimensuel m

ADV **1** (every two months) tous les deux mois **2** (twice a month) deux fois par mois

bin [bɪn] N coffre m, huche f, bac m; (dustbin) poubelle f; **wine b.** casier m à bouteilles, porte-bouteilles m inv; Sl **the b.** la maison de fous

▪ VT Fam (throw in the bin) mettre à la poubelle

▸▸**b. bag** sac m poubelle; Br **b. end** (wine) fin f de série; Br **b. liner** sac poubelle

binary ['baɪnərɪ] ADJ Math etc binaire

N Astron binaire f

▸▸**b. code** code m binaire; **b. number** nombre m binaire; Comput **b. search** recherche f binaire ou dichotomique; Astron **b. star** binaire; Mil **b. weapon** arme f binaire; Comput **b. word** mot m binaire

bind [baɪnd] (pt, pp bound [baʊnd]) VT **1** (attach) (object) attacher, lier (**to** à); (sheaf of corn) lier; (prisoner) attacher, ligoter; **to b. sb hand and foot** lier pieds et poings à qn; Fig **to be bound hand and foot** (powerless) avoir les mains liées; **they are bound together by a close friendship** ils sont unis par les liens de l'amitié; **they are very much bound up with each other** (of lovers) ils sont très attachés l'un à l'autre; (of friends) ils sont très liés; **the present is bound up with the past** le présent est étroitement lié au passé; **to b. one's skis** fixer ses skis

2 (dress) (wound) bander, panser

3 (cover) (book) relier; **bound in boards** cartonné; **bound in cloth** relié toile

4 (cause to cohere) (sand etc) lier, agglutiner, agglomérer; **stones bound together with cement** pierres liées avec du ciment; **b. the mixture with egg white** liez le mélange avec du blanc d'œuf

5 *usu passive (of obligation, promise etc)* lier, engager; **to be bound to do sth** *(obliged)* être obligé *ou* tenu de faire qch; **to be bound by an oath** être lié par un serment; **to b. sb to pay a debt** astreindre *ou* obliger qn à payer une dette; **to b. oneself to do sth** s'engager à faire qch
6 *Sewing (coat, hat)* border; *(buttonhole)* brider
vi *(of gravel etc)* se lier, s'agglomérer, s'agglutiner
n *Fam (nuisance)* plaie *f*; **what an awful b.!** quelle plaie *ou* barbe!; **to be in a b.** *(difficult situation)* être dans une mauvaise passe; **I'm in a bit of a b.** j'ai un petit problème, je suis un peu coincé
▸ **bind over** VT SEP *Law* **to b. sb over to keep the peace** exiger de qn sous caution qu'il ne se livrera à aucune voie de fait; **to be bound over** être sommé d'observer une bonne conduite
▸ **bind up** VT SEP **1** *(tie) (sheaf of corn)* lier **2** *(wound)* bander, panser

binder ['baɪndər] N **1** *(for papers)* classeur *m* **2** *(of books)* relieur, -ieuse **3** *Agr (machine) (for sheaves of corn)* lieuse *f*, *(for hay)* botteleuse *f* **4** *(on sewing machine)* ourleur *m* **5** *Culin (for sauce)* liant *m*; *Constr* matériau *m* d'agrégation; *(for road surface)* liant, agglomérant *m*

bindery ['baɪnd(ə)rɪ] N atelier *m* de reliure

binding ['baɪndɪŋ] ADJ **1** *Constr (agent)* agglomérant, agglutinant **2** *(contract etc)* obligatoire; **upon sb** pour qn), qui engage; **agreement b. (up)on sb** contrat *m* qui lie qn; **decision b. on all parties** décision *f* obligatoire pour tous **3** *Med* constipant
N **1** *Sport (on ski)* fixation *f*; **safety (release) bindings** fixations de sécurité **2** *(of book)* reliure *f* **3** *Constr* agglutination *f*, agrégation *f*, *(of road surface)* liant *m*, agglomérant *m* **4** *(of dress etc)* bordure *f*, liseré *m*
▸▸ **b. machine** *(for book)* brocheuse *f*, *Constr* **b. material** matière *f* agglomérante *ou* d'agrégation

bindweed ['baɪndwiːd] N *(plant)* liseron *m*

binge [bɪndʒ] *Fam* N **to go on a b.** *(of drinking)* prendre une cuite; *(of eating)* se gaver; *(of shopping)* faire une razzia; **b. drinking** excès *mpl* de brisson
vi *(drink a lot)* prendre une cuite; *(eat a lot)* s'en mettre plein la lampe, se gaver; **he binged on chocolate** il s'est gavé de chocolat

bingo ['bɪŋɡəʊ] N bingo *m*; *Br Fam* **to go to the b.** aller jouer au bingo
INTet voilà!
▸▸ **b. hall** salle *f* de bingo

Bingo
Ce jeu d'argent très populaire en Grande-Bretagne et aux États-Unis consiste à tirer des numéros et à les cocher sur une carte jusqu'à ce qu'elle soit remplie; il est souvent pratiqué dans d'anciens cinémas ou des salles municipales.

BinHex [bɪn'heks] N *Comput (abbr* **Binary Hexadecimal**) BinHex

binman, *pl* **binmen** ['bɪnmæn, -men] N *Br* éboueur *m*

binnacle ['bɪnək(ə)l] N *Naut* habitacle *m*

binocular [bɪ'nɒkjʊlər, baɪ-] ADJ *(vision etc)* binoculaire

binoculars [bɪ'nɒkjʊləz] NPL jumelles *fpl*, **to look at sth through b.** regarder qch avec des jumelles VOIR GRAMMAIRE A10

binomial [baɪ'nəʊmɪəl] *Math (factor etc)* binôme; **the b. theorem** le binôme de Newton, le théorème de Newton
N binôme *m*

bint [bɪnt] N *Br Sl Pej (woman)* grognasse *f*

biochemical [baɪəʊ'kemɪk(ə)l] ADJ biochimique; **b. oxygen demand** demande *f* biochimique en oxygène

biochemist [baɪəʊ'kemɪst] N biochimiste *mf*

biochemistry [baɪəʊ'kemɪstrɪ] N biochimie *f*

biodegradability [baɪəʊdɪɡreɪdə'bɪlɪtɪ] N biodégradabilité *f*

biodegradable [baɪəʊdɪ'ɡreɪdəb(ə)l] ADJ biodégradable

biodiversity [baɪəʊdaɪ'vɜːsɪtɪ] N biodiversité *f*

bioethanol [baɪəʊ'eθanɒl] N *Chem* bioéthanol *m*

bioethics [baɪəʊ'eθɪks] N bioéthique *f*; **b. debate** débat *m* sur la bioéthique VOIR GRAMMAIRE A10

biogenesis [baɪəʊ'dʒenɪsɪs] N biogenèse *f*

biographer [baɪ'ɒɡrəfər] N biographe *mf*

biographical [baɪə'ɡræfɪk(ə)l] ADJ biographique
▸▸ **b. novel** biographie *f* romancée

biography [baɪ'ɒɡrəfɪ] N biographie *f*

biological [baɪə'lɒdʒɪk(ə)l] ADJ biologique
▸▸ **b. clock** horloge *f* interne *ou* biologique; **my b. clock is ticking (away)** *(of woman)* si je veux des enfants il va falloir que je commence à y penser sérieusement; **my b. clock is ticking and I don't even have a boyfriend** le temps passe et je n'ai toujours pas d'enfant ni même de petit ami; **b. control (of insects)** élimination *f* des insectes par des méthodes biologiques; *Mil* **b. warfare** guerre *f* bactériologique

biologically [baɪə'lɒdʒɪklɪ] ADV biologiquement

biologist [baɪ'ɒlədʒɪst] N biologiste *mf*

biology [baɪ'ɒlədʒɪ] N biologie *f*

biomass ['baɪəʊmæs] N biomasse *f*

biomaterial [baɪəʊmə'tɪərɪəl] N biomatériau *m*

biometrics [baɪəʊ'metrɪks] N biométrie *f* VOIR GRAMMAIRE A10

bionic [baɪ'ɒnɪk] ADJ bionique

bionics [baɪ'ɒnɪks] N bionique *f* VOIR GRAMMAIRE A10

biophysics [baɪəʊ'fɪzɪks] N biophysique *f* VOIR GRAMMAIRE A10

biopic ['baɪəʊpɪk] N *Cin Fam* film *m* biographique

biopiracy [baɪəʊ'paɪrəsɪ] N biopiratage *m*

biopsy ['baɪɒpsɪ, baɪ'ɒpsɪ] N biopsie *f*

biorhythm ['baɪəʊrɪð(ə)m] N rythme *m* biologique, biorythme *m*

BIOS ['baɪɒs] N *Comput (abbr* **basic input/ output system**) BIOS *m*

bioscope ['baɪəskəʊp] N *Cin* **1** *Old-fashioned (projector)* bioscope *m* **2** *(in South Africa) (cinema)* cinéma *m*

biosphere ['baɪəsfɪər] N biosphère *f*

biosynthesis [baɪəʊ'sɪnθɪsɪs] N biosynthèse *f*

biotechnology [baɪəʊtek'nɒlədʒɪ], *Fam* **biotech** ['baɪəʊtek] N biotechnologie *f*

biotope ['baɪətəʊp] N *Biol* biotope *m*

bipartisan [baɪ'pɑːtɪzæn] ADJ *Pol etc* bipartite, biparti

bipartite [baɪ'pɑːtaɪt] ADJ **1** *Biol* bipartite, biparti **2** *Law (document)* rédigé en double **3** *(agreement)* bipartite, biparti

biped ['baɪped] ADJ, N bipède *m*

biplane ['baɪpleɪn] N *Aviat (avion m)* biplan *m*

bipolar [baɪ'pəʊlər] ADJ *Elec, Physiol etc* bipolaire

birch [bɜːtʃ] N **1** *(tree)* bouleau *m*; *(wood)* (bois *m* de) bouleau; *(rod)* verge *f* **2 to give sb the b.** donner le fouet à qn, fouetter qn
VT donner le fouet à, fouetter
▸▸ **b. rod** verge; **b. wood** (bois de) bouleau

birching ['bɜːtʃɪŋ] N correction *f* *(au fouet)*; **to give sb a b.** fouetter qn

bird [bɜːd] N **1** oiseau *m*; **(farmyard) b.** volaille *f*; *Fam* **told me** mon petit doigt me l'a dit; *Lit* **a b. of ill omen** un oiseau de mauvais augure; **to eat like a b.** avoir un appétit d'oiseau; *Fam* **to give sb the b.** *(hiss)* huer *ou* siffler qn; *(send packing)* envoyer qn paître; *Am (make fun of)* se foutre de la gueule de qn; *(gesture at)* faire un doigt d'honneur à qn; *Fam* **to get the b.** être hué *ou* sifflé; *Prov* **a b. in the hand is worth two in the bush** un tiens vaut mieux que deux tu l'auras; *Fig* **the b. has flown** l'oiseau s'est envolé; *Prov* **birds of a feather flock together** qui se ressemble s'assemble; **you and your father are birds of a feather** toi et ton père, vous ne valez pas mieux l'un que l'autre, toi et ton père, je vous mets dans le même sac; *Euph* **it's time you talked to him about the birds and the bees** *(facts of life)* il serait temps de lui expliquer que les bébés ne naissent pas dans les choux; *Fam* **it's (strictly) for the birds** c'est de la roupie de sansonnet
2 *Br Sl (woman)* nana *f*; **who's the b. in the corner?** qui est la fille au coin?
3 *Br Sl (time in prison)* taule *f*, tôle *f*; **to do b.** faire de la taule
4 *Fam (fellow)* type *m*, individu *m*; **he's a queer b.** c'est un drôle d'oiseau; **a home b.** un casanier, une casanière; *Fig* **night b.** noctambule *mf*
▸▸ *Fam Pej* **b. brain** tête *f* de linotte, écervelé, -ée; **b. call** cri *m* d'oiseau; *(device)* appeau *m*, pipeau *m*; *Br* **b. fancier** *(interested in birds)* ornithologue *mf* amateur; *(breeder)* aviculteur, -trice; **b.'s nest** nid *m* d'oiseau; *Culin* **b.'s nest soup** soupe *f* aux nids d'hirondelles; **b. of paradise** *(bird, flower)* oiseau de paradis; **b. of passage** oiseau de passage; **I'm just a b. of passage** je ne suis que de passage; **b. of prey** oiseau de proie, rapace *m*; **b. sanctuary** réserve *f* *ou* refuge *m* d'oiseaux; **b. shot** cendrée *f*, **b. strike** collision *f* d'un avion avec un oiseau; **b. table** *(in garden)* mangeoire *f*

birdbath ['bɜːdbɑːθ] N vasque *f* pour les oiseaux

bird-brained [-breɪnd] ADJ *Fam Pej* écervelé; **to be b.** avoir une cervelle d'oiseau *ou* de moineau

birdcage ['bɜːdkeɪdʒ] N cage *f* (à oiseaux); *(large)* volière *f*

birdcatcher ['bɜːdkætʃər] N oiseleur, -ière

bird-dog VT *Am Fam* surveiller de près

bird-house N *(aviary)* volière *f*

birdie ['bɜːdɪ] N *Fam* **1** *Golf* birdie *m* **2** *(in children's language)* gentil petit oiseau *m*; *Phot Fam* **watch the b.!** attention, le petit oiseau va sortir!

birdlike ['bɜːdlaɪk] ADJ *(appetite)* d'oiseau; **b. movements/features** mouvements *mpl*/ traits *mpl* semblables à ceux d'un oiseau

birdlime ['bɜːdlaɪm] N glu *f*

bird-nesting N **to go b.** = rechercher des nids pour y prendre les œufs

birdseed ['bɜːdsiːd] N graines *fpl* pour oiseaux

bird's-eye ['bɜːdzaɪ] N *Bot* véronique *f*
▸▸ **b. mahogany** acajou *m* moucheté; **b. maple** érable *m* madré *ou* à broussin; **b. shot** *Phot* photographie *f* aérienne oblique; *Cin* *(prise f de vue en)* plongée *f*, **b. view** vue *f* aérienne; *Fig* **a b. view of the situation** une vue d'ensemble de la situation

bird-watcher N ornithologue *mf* amateur

bird-watching [-wɒtʃɪŋ] N observation f des oiseaux *(dans leur milieu naturel)*; **to go b.** aller observer les oiseaux

biretta [bɪˈretə] N *Cathol* barrette f

Biro® [ˈbaɪrəʊ] N *Br* stylo m (à) bille

birth [bɜːθ] N **1** *(of child, nation, industry)* naissance f; *Fig (of idea etc)* genèse f; **date/ place/country of b.** date f/lieu m/pays m de naissance; **to give b. to a child** mettre un enfant au monde, donner naissance à un enfant; **she has given b. to a daughter** elle a donné naissance à une fille; **at b.** à la naissance; *Hum Fam* **he should have been drowned at b.!** on aurait dû le noyer à la naissance!; **will the father be present at the b.?** le père assistera-t-il à l'accouchement *ou* à la naissance?; **it was a difficult b.** cela a été un accouchement difficile; **Irish by b.** Irlandais de naissance; **from b.** *(to be blind, deaf etc)* de naissance; *(to be delicate)* dès *ou* depuis la naissance **2** *(of animal)* mise f bas; **to give b. to a litter** mettre bas une portée ►► *Admin* **b. certificate** *(original)* acte m de naissance; *(copy)* extrait m de naissance; *Astrol* **b. chart** thème m astral; *Journ* **births column** carnet m rose; **b. control** *(contraception)* contraception f; *(family planning)* contrôle m des naissances; **b. rate** (taux m de) natalité f; **b. statistics** statistiques fpl de natalité

birthday [ˈbɜːθdeɪ] N *(anniversary)* anniversaire m; *(day of birth)* jour m de naissance; **she was 42 on her last b.** elle a 42 ans; *Fam Hum* **to be in one's b. suit** être dans le *ou* en costume d'Adam/d'Ève, être dans le plus simple appareil; **let me buy the b. girl a drink** laisse-moi te payer un verre pour ton anniversaire ►► **b. card** carte f d'anniversaire; **b. cake** gâteau m d'anniversaire; **the B. Honours** = titres mpl honorifiques et autres distinctions décernés chaque année le jour de l'anniversaire officiel du souverain britannique; **b. present** cadeau m d'anniversaire; **b. party** fête f d'anniversaire

birthing [ˈbɜːθɪŋ] N ►► *Br* **b. pool** piscine f d'accouchement; **b. room** salle f d'accouchement

birthmark [ˈbɜːθmɑːk] N tache f de naissance, envie f

birthplace [ˈbɜːθpleɪs] N lieu m de naissance; *Fig (of religion etc)* berceau m

birthright [ˈbɜːθraɪt] N *(something to which one is entitled)* droit m de naissance, droit du sang; *(of first-born)* droit d'aînesse; *(inheritance)*, *Fig* patrimoine m; *Fig* **clean air is everyone's b.** tout le monde a le droit de vivre dans un endroit non pollué

birthstone [ˈbɜːθstəʊn] N *Astrol etc* pierre f porte-bonheur, pl pierres porte-bonheur

biryani [bɪrɪˈɑːnɪ] N *(Indian dish)* biriani m

Biscay [ˈbɪskeɪ] N **the Bay of B.** le golfe de Gascogne

biscuit [ˈbɪskɪt] N **1** *Br* biscuit m; *Am (scone)* petit pain m; **ship's b.** biscuits de mer; **dog b.** biscuit pour chien; *Fam* **that (really) takes the b.!** ça, c'est le bouquet! **2** *Cer* biscuit m **3** *(colour)* marron m clair ►► **b. barrel** boîte f à biscuits; **b. factory** biscuiterie f; *Cer* **b. ware** biscuit

bisect [baɪˈsekt] VT *Geom (line, angle)* couper *ou* diviser en deux parties égales VI *(of road etc)* bifurquer

bisection [baɪˈsekʃən] N *Geom* bissection f

bisector [baɪˈsektər] N *Geom* bissectrice f, ligne f de bissection

bisexual [baɪˈseksjʊəl] ADJ *(attracted to both sexes)* bisexuel; *(having characteristics of both sexes)* bisexué N bisexuel, -elle; **to be a b.** être bisexuel

bishop [ˈbɪʃəp] N **1** *Rel* évêque m; **b.'s palace** palais m épiscopal, évêché m **2** *Chess* fou m

bishopric [ˈbɪʃəprɪk] N *(office, diocese)* évêché m

bismuth [ˈbɪzməθ] N *Miner, Pharm* bismuth m

bison [ˈbaɪsən] N bison m

bisque¹ [biːsk] N *Cer* biscuit m

bisque² N *Culin (lobster etc)* bisque f

bistre [ˈbɪstər] ADJ, N bistre m

bistro [ˈbiːstrəʊ] N petit resto m

bisulphite [baɪˈsʌlfaɪt] N *Chem* bisulfite m; **sodium b.** bisulfite de sodium *ou* de soude

bisync [baɪˈsɪŋk], **bisynchronous** [baɪˈsɪŋkrənəs] ADJ *Comput* bisynchrone

bit¹ [bɪt] N **1** *(on bridle)* mors m; **to champ at the b.** *(of horse)* mâcher son mors; *(of person)* ronger son frein; **to take the b. between one's teeth** *(of horse, person)* prendre le mors aux dents **2** *(for brace)* mèche f, *(for drill)* foret m

BIT²

morceau **1, 2** ▪ bout **1** ▪ un peu **3** ▪ pièce **4**

N **1** *(piece) (of bread, cake etc)* morceau m; *(of paper, string, old carpet etc)* bout m; *(of straw etc)* brin m; **a b. of news** une nouvelle; **a b. of luck** une chance; **a (little) b. of hope** un petit brin d'espoir

2 *(part)* partie f, morceau m; *(of book, film, report etc)* passage m; **to tear sth to bits** déchirer qch en morceaux; **smashed to bits** brisé (en mille morceaux); **to take sth to bits** démonter qch; **to come to bits** *(dismantle)* se démonter; *(break)* tomber en morceaux; *Fig* **to go to bits** *(of person)* s'effondrer, craquer; **in bits** en morceaux; **he has eaten every b.** il a tout mangé; **this is the difficult b.** c'est là où ça se complique; **made of bits and pieces** *or Fam* **bits and bobs** fait de bric et de broc; *Fam* **my bits and pieces** *or* **bobs** mes affaires

3 *(little)* **a b.** un peu (**of** de); **a tiny** *or* **little b.** un tout petit peu; **I'm a b. late** je suis un peu en retard; **I'm a b. hungry** j'ai un peu faim, *Fam* j'ai un petit creux; **she's a b. of an artist** *(paints, draws)* elle est artiste à ses heures perdues; **it was a b. of a nuisance** c'était vraiment ennuyeux; **quite a b. of sun/rain/ trouble** pas mal de soleil/de pluie/d'ennuis; **I've had quite a b. to drink** j'ai un peu trop bu; *Fam* **he's a b. of a lad** *(likes a good time)* il aime faire la bringue; *(runs after women)* c'est un coureur (de jupons); **we got a b. of a shock** ça nous a fait un choc; **to give you a b. of an idea** pour te donner une petite idée; **it was a b. too much of a coincidence** c'était un peu fort comme coïncidence; **b. by b.** peu à peu, petit à petit; **not a b. (of it)!** pas du tout!; **I don't care a b.** cela m'est bien *ou* complètement égal; **it's not a b. of use** cela ne sert absolument à rien; **hold on** *or* **wait a b.!** attendez un peu *ou* un instant!; *Fam* **in a b.** dans quelques minutes; *Fam* **after a b.** quelques minutes après; **that takes a b. of doing** ça, c'est bien difficile; **a good b. older/colder** nettement plus âgé/froid; **every b. as good/interesting as** aussi bon/intéressant que; *Fam* **it's a b. much!** ça, c'est vraiment trop fort!; **we all had to do our b.** nous avons dû tous nous y mettre, nous avons dû tous y mettre du nôtre; **I did my b. too, you know** moi aussi j'ai fait ma part, tu sais; *Fam* **to make quite a b.** *(earn money)* gagner pas mal d'argent *ou* de fric; **to have a b. put away** avoir un petit pécule; **that must be worth quite a b.!** ça doit valoir pas mal d'argent!; *Fam* **she's a nice b. of stuff** *or* **skirt** c'est un beau brin de fille; **he's a b. of all right** c'est un beau mec, il est pas mal

4 *Fam (coin)* pièce f, *Br Arch* **threepenny b.** pièce de trois pence; *Am* **two bits** vingt-cinq cents

5 *Am Fam (term of imprisonment)* peine f de prison; **he did a b. in Fort Worth** il a fait de la taule à Fort Worth ►► *Cin, Theat* **b. part** petit rôle m; *Cin, Theat* **b. player** acteur, -trice qui joue des petits rôles

bit³ N *Comput* bit m; **bits per second** bits par seconde ►► **b. command** commande f binaire; **b. rate** débit f binaire

bit⁴ PT *see* **bite** VT & VI

bitch [bɪtʃ] N **1** *(dog)* chienne f, *(fox etc)* femelle f, **terrier b.** terrier m femelle **2** *Sl Pej (woman)* garce f **3** *Sl* **a b. of a job** un travail de chien; **life's a b.!** quelle *ou* cette chienne de vie!; **I've had a b. of a day!** j'ai eu une putain de journée! VI **1** *Sl (complain)* rouspéter; *Br (say nasty things)* déblatérer; **stop bitching about the weather** arrête de rouspéter après le temps; **bitching session** séance f de défoulement

bitchin [ˈbɪtʃɪn] ADJ *Am Sl* super, génial, -aux

bitchy [ˈbɪtʃɪ] ADJ *Sl (woman)* garce, vache; *(remark etc)* vache; **that was a b. thing to do!** quelle vacherie!, quel sale coup!; **to be b.** *(of woman)* être garce *ou* vache; *(of man)* être vache

BITE [baɪt] N **1** *(of person)* coup m de dent; *(in dentistry)* articulé m dentaire; *esp Am Sl* **to put the b. on sb** *(extort money from)* gruger qn; *(borrow money from)* taper qn

2 *(in fishing)* touche f, **I haven't had a b. all day** je n'ai pas eu une seule touche de toute la journée

3 *(of dog etc)* morsure f, *(of insect)* piqûre f, morsure f; **the dog had given him a playful b. on the arm** le chien lui avait mordu le bras en jouant

4 *Fam (of food)* bouchée f, morceau m; **would you like a b. to eat?** voulez-vous manger quelque chose?; **I could do with a b. to eat** je mangerais bien quelque chose; **I haven't had a b. all day** je n'ai rien mangé de la journée; **come over for a b. of supper** viens manger un morceau à la maison ce soir; **can I have a b.?** *(of apple, chocolate bar)* je peux en avoir un peu?; **to take a (big) b. out of sth** mordre dans qch (à pleines dents); *Fig* **the repairs took a big b. out of our savings** les réparations ont fait un trou dans nos économies; *Fig* **you don't get two bites (at the cherry)** l'occasion ne se présente qu'une fois

5 *(of mustard, spice)* piquant m; *Fig* **your speech needs more b.** ton discours manque de mordant

VT *(pt bit* [bɪt], *pp bitten* [ˈbɪtən]) *(of animal, person)* mordre, donner un coup de dent à; *(of insect)* piquer; **the dog bit him in the leg** le chien l'a mordu à la jambe; **to b. one's lips** se mordre les lèvres; **to b. one's nails** se ronger les ongles; *also Fig* **to b. one's tongue** se mordre la langue; **to b. the dust** mordre la poussière; *Prov* **once bitten twice shy** chat échaudé craint l'eau froide; *Fig* **to b. the bullet** serrer les dents; **let's b. the bullet and give him what he wants** faisons contre mauvaise fortune bon cœur et donnons-lui ce qu'il veut; **to get bitten** *(by dog)* se faire mordre; *(by insect)* se faire piquer; *Fam* **what's biting/bitten him?** quelle mouche l'a piqué?; *Fam* **he got bitten by the skiing/ chess bug at the age of six** il se passionne pour le ski/les échecs depuis l'âge de six ans; *Fig* **to bite the hand that feeds you** cracher dans la soupe; *Am Sl* **b. me!** va te faire voir!

VI **1** *(of fish)* mordre (à l'hameçon); *(of in-*

sect) piquer; **does the dog b.?** est-ce que ce chien mord?; **he bit into the apple** il a mordu dans la pomme; **are they** *or* **the fish biting (today)?** alors, ça mord?; *Fig* **don't worry, I don't b.!** n'ayez pas peur, je ne mords pas!; *Fig* **sanctions are beginning to b.** l'effet des sanctions commence à se faire sentir

2 *(of screw, file)* mordre **(on** sur); *(of tool)* mordre, s'engager; *(of anchor)* mordre, prendre fond; **a screw that won't b.** une vis qui foire

▶ **bite back** VT SEP *(reply)* ravaler

▶ **bite off** VT SEP enlever *ou* détacher d'un coup de dent(s); *Fam* **to b. sb's head off** rembarrer qn; *Fig* **to b. off more than one can chew** tenter quelque chose au-dessus de ses forces

biter ['baɪtər] N **it's a case of the b. bit** c'est l'arroseur arrosé

biting ['baɪtɪŋ] ADJ *(cold)* âpre, perçant; *(wind)* cinglant; *(style, wit, irony)* mordant, caustique

▸▶ *Aut* **b. point** *(of clutch)* point *m* d'attaque

bitmap ['bɪtmæp] *Comput* N bitmap *m*
ADJ pixélisé, bitmap
▸▶ **b. font** police *f* pixélisée *ou* bitmap

bitmapped ['bɪtmæpt] ADJ *Comput (image)* pixélisé, bitmap
▸▶ **b. font** police *f* pixélisée *ou* bitmap

bit-slice processor N *Comput* processeur *m* en tranches

bitten ['bɪtən] PP *see* **bite** VT & VI

bitter ['bɪtər] ADJ *(taste)*, *Fig (person, tears, experience, disappointment)* amer; *(words)* acerbe; *(wind)* glacial, -als *ou* -aux; *(weather)* rigoureux; *(cold)* glacial, cinglant; *(enemy, hatred)* implacable; *(conflict, opposition, resistance)* âpre; *(tone)* aigre, âpre; **not being promoted was a b. pill for him to swallow** ça a été dur à avaler pour lui de ne pas être promu; **to feel** *or* **be b. about sth** ressentir de l'amertume à propos de qch; **she's very b. about it** elle en est très amère, *Fam* elle l'a pas digéré; *Fig* **to go on/resist to the b. end** aller/résister jusqu'au bout

N **1** *Br (beer)* bière *f* brune **2** **bitters** bitter(s) *m(pl)*, amer(s) *m(pl)*
▸▶ *Pharm* **b. aloes** aloès *m* (médicinal); **b. lemon** Schweppes® *m* au citron; *Bot* **b. orange** orange *f* amère

bitterly ['bɪtəlɪ] ADV *(to say)* amèrement, avec amertume; *(to cry)* amèrement; *(to argue)* aigrement; **b. disappointed** amèrement déçu; **it was b. cold** il faisait un froid de loup *ou* de canard; **I've regretted it b. ever since** je n'ai cessé de le regretter amèrement; **to be b. opposed to sth** être farouchement opposé à qch

bittern ['bɪtən] N *(bird)* butor *m*

bitterness ['bɪtənɪs] N *(of drink, pain, person)* amertume *f*, *(of weather)* rigueur *f*, *(of reproach)* âpreté *f*, *(of words, quarrel)* aigreur *f*, acrimonie *f*

bittersweet ['bɪtəswiːt] ADJ *also Fig* doux-amer
N *(plant)* douce-amère *f*, *pl* douces-amères

bitty ['bɪtɪ] ADJ *Fam (book etc)* (d'un style) décousu

bitumen ['bɪtjəmɪn] N **1** *Chem, Miner* bitume *m* **2** *Austr Fam (road)* route *f* goudronnée

bituminous [bɪ'tjuːmɪnəs] ADJ bitumineux; **b. coal** houille *f* grasse *ou* collante

bivalent [baɪ'veɪlənt] ADJ *Chem* bivalent

bivalve ['baɪvælv] ADJ, N *(mollusc)* bivalve *m*

bivouac ['bɪvʊæk] N bivouac *m*
VI **(bivouacked; bivouacking)** bivouaquer

biweekly [baɪ'wiːklɪ] ADJ **1** *(every two weeks)* bimensuel **2** *(twice a week)* bihebdomadaire

ADV **1** *(every two weeks)* tous les quinze jours **2** *(twice a week)* deux fois par semaine

bizarre [bɪ'zɑːr] ADJ bizarre

bizarrely [bɪ'zɑːlɪ] ADV bizarrement

bizarreness [bɪ'zɑːnɪs] N bizarrerie *f*

bizzies ['bɪzɪz] NPL *Br Sl* **the b.** *(the police)* les flics *mpl*

B/L, b/l *Com (abbr* **bill of lading)** connt

blab [blæb] *Fam* VI **(-bb-) 1** *(betray secret)* vendre la mèche **2** *(prattle)* jaser, bavarder
VT *(secret)* divulguer, laisser échapper
N = **blabber**
▶ **blab out** VT SEP = **blab** VT

blabber ['blæbər] *Fam* N bavard, -arde, jaseur, -euse
VI jacasser

blabbermouth ['blæbəmaʊθ] N grande langue *f*, bavard, -arde

Black [blæk] N Noir *m*, Noire *f*, **B.-on-B. violence** violence *f* des Noirs sur les Noirs

BLACK [blæk] ADJ **1** *(colour) (coffee, dress, hair, Africa, music etc)* noir; *(cloud, sky etc)* sombre; **as b. as night** noir comme la nuit; **a b. man/woman** un Noir/une Noire; **b. with age** noirci par le temps; **it** *or* **the night was pitch b.** il faisait noir comme dans un four; **his hands were b.** il avait les mains toutes noires; *Fig* **to be in sb's b. books** être mal vu de qn; *Hum* **little b. book** *(of addresses)* carnet *m* d'adresses; *(of wrongdoers)* liste *f* noire; **is it b. tie?** *(at dinner etc)* est-ce que la tenue habillée est de rigueur?

2 *Fig (gloomy, sombre) (mood, thought)* noir; **to look as b. as thunder** avoir l'air furieux; **to give sb a b. look** jeter un regard noir à qn; **things are looking b.** les affaires prennent une mauvaise tournure; **to paint things blacker than they are** noircir la situation; **she's not as b. as she's painted** elle n'est pas si mauvaise qu'on le dit; **he's in one of his b. moods** il est dans un de ses mauvais jours; **it's a b. day for Britain** c'est un mauvais jour pour la Grande-Bretagne

3 *Fig (sinister, malevolent)* malveillant; **b. hearted** malveillant

4 *Fig (macabre) (humour)* noir
N **1** noir *m*; **she always wears b.** elle porte toujours du noir, elle est toujours en noir; **to work in b. and white** *(of artist)* faire du dessin à l'encre *ou* au crayon noir; **I have his consent in b. and white** j'ai son consentement par écrit; **I should like to have it in b. and white** je voudrais avoir cela noir sur blanc; **she sees everything in b. and white** pour elle, c'est tout l'un ou tout l'autre; **she would swear that b. is white to help him** elle serait prête à tout pour l'aider; **he'll swear b. is white for the price of a couple of drinks** il est prêt à jurer n'importe quoi en échange d'un verre ou deux

2 *Fin Fam* **to be in the b.** être en crédit; **to get back into the b.** sortir du rouge

3 *Sport* **the b.** *(in roulette)* le noir; *(in snooker)* la bille *ou* boule noire
VT **1** *(blacken)* **to b. one's face** se noircir le visage; **to b. sb's eye** pocher l'œil à qn
2 *Ind (boycott)* mettre à l'index
3 *(polish) (shoes)* cirer
▸▶ **b. art** sciences *fpl* occultes; **b. belt** *Sport* ceinture *f* noire; *Am* **b.** = zone *f* habitée par des Noirs; *Aviat* **b. box** boîte *f* noire; *Culin* **b. bread** pain *m* de seigle; *Scot Culin* **b. bun** = sorte de pain au raisin consommé au Nouvel An; *Br Law, Hist* **the b. cap** = bonnet noir *(que coiffait le juge en prononçant une condamnation à mort)*; **b. comedy** comédie *f* noire; *Br* **the B. Country** région *f* de Birmingham; *Hist* **B. Death** peste *f* noire; *Com* **b. economy** économie *f* noire; **b. eye** œil *m* poché *ou* au beurre noir; **b. flag** drapeau *m* noir; **the B. Forest** la Forêt noire; *Astron* **b. hole** trou *m* noir; **b. ice** verglas *m*; *St Exch* **b.**

knight chevalier *m* noir; **b. magic** magie *f* noire; *Fam* **B. Maria** panier *m* à salade *(fourgon)*; **b. mark** mauvais point *m*; *Com* **b. market** marché *m* noir; *Com* **b. marketeer** vendeur, -euse au marché noir; **B. Mass** messe *f* noire; **b. money** *(earned on black market)* argent *m* du marché noir; *(undeclared)* argent non déclaré au fisc; *Culin* **b. pudding** boudin *m* (noir); *Parl* **B. Rod** = huissier *m* chargé par la Chambre des lords britannique de convoquer les Communes; **the B. Sea** la mer Noire; **b. sheep** brebis *f* galeuse; *Br Fig* **b. spot** point noir; **b. swan** cygne *m* noir; **b. and tan** *(drink)* = mélange *m* de bière et de porter; *Hist* **the B. and Tans** = forces *fpl* armées britanniques envoyées en Irlande en 1920 pour lutter contre le Sinn Fein; **b. velvet** *(cocktail)* = cocktail *m* de champagne et de stout; **b. widow** *(spider)* veuve *f* noire

▶ **black out** VI *(faint)* perdre connaissance, s'évanouir; *(lose memory)* avoir un trou (de mémoire)
VT SEP **1** *(house etc) (completely)* éteindre les lumières dans, faire le black-out dans; *(partially)* voiler *ou* masquer les lumières dans; *Theat* **to b. out the stage** faire l'obscurité sur scène

2 *Radio, TV* **industrial action has blacked out this evening's programmes** un mouvement de grève a interrompu les programmes de la soirée

3 *(delete)* rayer *(d'un gros trait noir)*
▶ **black up** VI *Theat* se maquiller la peau en noir, se noircir le visage

black-and-blue ADJ **to beat sb b.** rosser qn, couvrir qn de bleus; **to be b. all over** être couvert de bleus, être tuméfié

black-and-tan ADJ
▸▶ **b. terrier** chien *m* noir et feu *inv*

black-and-white N *(photograph)* photo *f* noir et blanc
ADJ *(photograph, television)* noir et blanc; **b. film** film *m* en noir et blanc

blackball ['blækbɔːl] VT blackbouler

blackballing ['blækbɔːlɪŋ] N blackboulage *m*

blackbeetle ['blækbiːt(ə)l] N *Fam (insect)* blatte *f*, cafard *m*, cancrelat *m*

blackberry ['blækb(ə)rɪ] N mûre *f*
▸▶ **b. bush** mûrier *m*; **b. jam** confiture *f* de mûres; **b. tart** tarte *f* aux mûres

blackberrying ['blækberɪŋ] N **to go b.** aller cueillir des mûres, aller à la cueillette des mûres

blackbird ['blækbɜːd] N **1** merle *m* (noir) **2** *Am* (variété *f* d')étourneau *m*

blackboard ['blækbɔːd] N tableau *m* noir

black-bordered [-'bɔːdəd] ADJ à bordure noire

blackcock ['blækkɒk] N *(bird)* tétras-lyre *m*, *pl* tétras-lyres, coq *m* des bouleaux

blackcurrant [blæk'kʌrənt] N *(bush, fruit)* cassis *m*

blacken ['blæk(ə)n] VT *(wall)*, *Fig (sb's reputation)* noircir; *(sky)* obscurcir; *(paper, glass) (with smoke)* enfumer; *Fig* **to b. sb's character** calomnier qn
VI noircir, devenir noir; *Fig (of face)* s'assombrir

blackening ['blæk(ə)nɪŋ] N noircissement *m*

black-eyed pea N dolique *m*

blackfly ['blækflaɪ] N *Fam (insect)* mouche *f* noire

blackguard ['blægɑːd] N *Arch* fripouille *f*, canaille *f*

blackhead ['blækhed] N *(on face)* point *m* noir

blackheaded gull ['blækhedɪd] N mouette *f* rieuse

blacking ['blækɪŋ] N 1 *Ind (of ship, company)* mise f à l'index 2 *Arch (for shoes)* cirage m

blackish ['blækɪʃ] ADJ noirâtre, tirant sur le noir

blackjack ['blækdʒæk] N 1 *Am (weapon)* nerf m de bœuf 2 *Cards* vingt-et-un m inv VT *Am* frapper avec un nerf de bœuf

blacklead ['blækled] VT *Old-fashioned (stove etc)* passer à la mine de plomb

blackleg ['blækleg] *Ind Fam Pej* N jaune m, briseur m de grève VI (-gg-) briser une grève, être un briseur de grève

blacklist ['blæklɪst] N liste f noire VT *(person, company etc)* inscrire ou mettre sur la liste noire

blackmail ['blækmeɪl] N chantage m; **emotional b.** chantage aux sentiments VT soumettre à un chantage, *Fam* faire chanter; **to be blackmailed** être victime d'un chantage; **I'm being blackmailed for £5,000** je suis victime d'un chantage, on me réclame 5000 livres; **to b. sb into resigning** faire chanter qn pour qu'il démissionne

blackmailer ['blækmeɪlər] N maître chanteur m, pl maîtres chanteurs

blackness ['blæknɪs] N *(of hair, sky etc), Fig* noirceur f

blackout ['blækaʊt] N 1 *(during war)* blackout m inv; *Fig* **to impose a news b.** interdire la divulgation d'une information; *(in general)* imposer le black-out sur l'information 2 *Elec* panne f d'électricité 3 *Theat* obscurcissement m de la scène 4 *(loss of consciousness)* évanouissement m; *(memory lapse)* trou m de mémoire

Blackshirt ['blækʃɜːt] N *Pol* chemise f noire

blacksmith ['blæksmɪθ] N forgeron m; *(who shoes horses)* maréchal-ferrant m, pl maréchaux-ferrants

blackthorn ['blækθɔːn] N 1 *(shrub)* épine f noire, prunier m épineux, prunellier m 2 *(stick)* gourdin m (en épines)

blacktop ['blæktɒp] N *esp Am* 1 *(substance)* bitume m 2 *(road)* route f bitumée

blackwater ['blækwɔːtər] ADJ ► ► *Med* **b. fever** hématurie f

bladder ['blædər] N 1 *(for urine)* vessie f; **to have a full b.** avoir la vessie pleine 2 *(sac)* vésicule f; **air b.** *(of fish)* vésicule aérienne; *(of seaweed)* vésicule aérocyste 3 *(of ball)* vessie f

bladdered ['blædəd] ADJ *Br Fam (drunk)* bourré, pété

bladderwort ['blædəwɜːt] N *(plant)* utriculaire f

bladderwrack ['blædəræk] N *(seaweed)* goémon m jaune vésiculeux

blade [bleɪd] N 1 *(of knife, sword, skate)* lame f, *(of guillotine)* couperet m; *(of saw)* feuille f, lame 2 *(of propeller)* pale f, *(of oar)* pelle f, pale; *(of ventilator, turbine)* ailette f, *(of waterwheel)* aube f, *(of spade)* fer m; *Aut (of windscreen wiper)* balai m, raclette f 3 *(of grass)* brin m 4 *Sl (knife)* lame f, surin m 5 *Arch (sword)* sabre m, épée f 6 *Arch, Hum* **a young b.** un jeune gaillard

bladed ['bleɪdɪd] ADJ à lame(s)/à pales; **three-b.** *(penknife)* à trois lames; *(propeller)* à trois pales

blag [blæg] *Br Fam* N *(robbery)* braquage m VT 1 *(steal)* piquer 2 *(con)* **to b. oneself sth** obtenir qch au culot; **to b. one's way in** resquiller

blah(-blah) ['blɑː(blɑː)] N *Fam* bla-bla m inv, baratin m; **the usual b.** le baratin habituel

blame [bleɪm] N 1 *(reproof)* reproches mpl; **to deserve b.** mériter des reproches;

to be free from b. être irréprochable 2 *(responsibility)* responsabilité f, faute f; **to lay** or **put the b. (for sth) on sb, to lay the b. (for sth) at sb's door** rejeter ou faire retomber la responsabilité ou la faute (de qch) sur qn; **to bear** or **take the b.** endosser la responsabilité (**for sth** de qch); **why is it always me that gets the b.?** pourquoi est-ce que tout retombe toujours sur moi?; **I got the b. for breaking the window** c'est moi qu'on a accusé d'avoir cassé la fenêtre; **to shift the b. onto sb** rejeter la responsabilité sur qn; **where does the b. lie?** à qui la faute?; **the b. lies with her** c'est (de) sa faute VT *(person)* rendre responsable; **to b. sb for sth** reprocher qch à qn; *(hold responsible for)* rendre qn responsable de qch, attribuer à qn la responsabilité de qch; **he can't be blamed for the accident** on ne peut pas le rendre responsable de l'accident; **to b. sth on sb** rejeter la faute ou la responsabilité de qch sur qn; **the accident was blamed on the bad weather** on a dit que le mauvais temps était la cause de l'accident; **to b. sb for doing sth** reprocher à qn de faire ou d'avoir fait qch; **he can't be blamed for trying** on ne peut pas lui reprocher d'avoir essayé; **I have nothing to b. myself for** je n'ai rien à me reprocher; **I b. the parents** pour moi, ce sont les parents qui sont responsables; **I b. myself** je me sens responsable, c'est (de) ma faute; **don't b. me!** ne me mets pas ça sur le dos!; **don't b. me if you're late** tu ne viendras pas dire que c'est de ma faute si tu es en retard; **I wouldn't b. you if you left me** si tu me quittais, je ne te le reprocherais pas; **I wouldn't b. you if you left him** je te comprendrais si tu le quittais; **she's leaving him and who can b. her?** elle le quitte et on la comprend bien; **to have only oneself to b., to have nobody to b. but oneself** n'avoir à s'en prendre qu'à soi-même; **he is to b.** c'est de sa faute; **she was in no way to b.** elle n'était en aucun cas responsable; **the bad weather was to b.** c'était à cause du mauvais temps

blamed [bleɪmd] ADJ *esp Am Euph* sacré

blameless ['bleɪmlɪs] ADJ irréprochable, *Lit* irréprehensible; **to lead a b. life** avoir une vie irréprochable; **none of us is b.** nous sommes tous responsables

blamelessly ['bleɪmlɪslɪ] ADV de façon irréprochable

blameworthy ['bleɪmwɜːðɪ] ADJ *Fml (person)* coupable, blâmable; *(action, behaviour)* répréhensible

blanch [blɑːntʃ] VT *(vegetables, almonds)* blanchir; **blanched almonds** amandes fpl émondées VI *(of person)* blêmir, pâlir

blancmange [bləˈmɒnʒ] N *Culin* blanc-manger m, pl blancs-mangers

bland [blænd] ADJ 1 *(person, speech)* *(insipid)* insipide; *(suspiciously smooth)* doucereux, mielleux; *(smile)* de politesse 2 *(without flavour)* *(food, drink)* fade; *Fig (music, film)* insipide

blandish ['blændɪʃ] VT amadouer

blandishments ['blændɪʃmənts] NPL cajoleries fpl; **to resist sb's b.** ne pas se laisser amadouer par qn

blandly ['blændlɪ] ADV *(to reply, smile)* mielleusement

blank [blæŋk] ADJ 1 *(empty, with nothing on it)* *(paper)* blanc, f blanche; *(page)* blanc, vierge; *(tape, cassette)* vierge; *(wall)* aveugle; *(cartridge)* à blanc; *Comput (disk, screen)* vide; *(unformatted)* vierge; *Comput* **the screen suddenly went b.** soudain tout a disparu de l'écran; **to leave b.** *(part of form etc)* laisser blanc, ne pas remplir; **leave the other side of the paper b.** ne rien écrire sur

l'envers de la feuille; *Cards* **to be b. in clubs** ne pas avoir de trèfles dans son jeu 2 *(vacant)* *(look)* vide, sans expression; **my mind went b.** je me suis senti la tête vide, j'ai eu un trou; **to look b.** avoir l'air complètement déconcerté ou ahuri; **a look of b. astonishment** un air ébahi 3 *(absolute, complete)* *(impossibility, refusal)* absolu N 1 *(in document etc)* blanc m, vide m; *Am (for telegram etc)* formulaire m, formule f; *Mil* cartouche f à blanc; *(on target)* blanc; **to fire blanks** tirer à blanc; *Fam Hum* **to shoot blanks** *(of man)* être stérile; **to leave blanks** laisser des blancs; **his mind is a b.** *(he has lost his memory)* il ne se souvient de rien; **I'm sorry, my mind is a b.** je suis désolé, j'ai un trou; **the rest is a b.** après cela, c'est le vide; *Cards* **to have a b. in clubs** ne pas avoir de trèfles dans son jeu 2 *(in dominoes)* blanc m; *Fig* **to draw a b.** *(be unsuccessful in search)* faire chou blanc; *Am (be unable to remember)* avoir un trou de mémoire 3 *(metal disc)* *(in minting coins)* flan m; *Metal, Tech* flan, masselotte f, galette f 4 *Typ (to replace swearword etc)* tiret m VT *Fam (ignore)* *(person)* ignorer; **he blanked me** il a fait comme s'il ne me voyait pas ► ► *Fin* **b. cheque** chèque m en blanc; *Fin* **b. credit** crédit m en blanc; *Fin* **b. endorsement** endossement m en blanc; **b. space** blanc, espace m vide; *Comput* **b. unformatted disk** disquette f vierge; *Literature* **b. verse** vers mpl blancs ou sans rime
► **blank out** VT SEP *(parts of text, tape etc)* effacer; **her face had been blanked out** *(on negative)* on avait effacé son visage; *(on print)* on avait caché son visage; **she's blanked out the memory** elle a effacé cet événement de sa mémoire VI *(lose consciousness)* tomber dans les pommes

blank-endorse VT *Fin* endosser en blanc

blanket ['blæŋkɪt] N 1 *(for bed, horse)* couverture f, *Fig (of fog, mist)* manteau m; *(of snow)* couche f, *Old-fashioned Fam* **he was born on the wrong side of the b.** c'est un enfant naturel 2 *Typ* blanchet m ADJ ATTRIB *(general)* *(acceptance)* général, -aux, global, -aux VT **the mountain was blanketed in fog/snow** la montagne était couverte d'un manteau de brouillard/de neige ► ► *Com* **b. agreement** accord-cadre m, pl accords-cadres; **b. bath** grande toilette f *(d'un malade alité)*; **b. contract** contrat m global; *Radio, TV* **b. coverage** *(of event)* reportage m *(très)* complet; *Sewing* **b. stitch** point m de feston; **b. term** terme m général

blanking ['blæŋkɪŋ] N *TV* suppression f de faisceau; *(erasing)* effacement m

blankly ['blæŋklɪ] ADV *(to look at sb)* *(without expression)* sans expression, avec l'air de ne rien comprendre; *(in confusion)* d'un air déconcerté; **to stare b. into space** avoir le regard perdu dans le vide

blankness ['blæŋknɪs] N 1 *(of person)* air m confus ou décontenancé 2 *(of eyes, expression)* vacuité f

blare [bleər] N *(of trumpet)* beuglement(s) m(pl); *(of radio)* braillement(s) m(pl); **the b. of the brass band** le son éclatant de la fanfare; **the b. of car horns** le son discordant des klaxons de voiture VI *(of trumpet)* sonner; *(of car horn)* retentir; *(of radio)* beugler, *Fam* gueuler, brailler; **the band blared** le son de la fanfare retentit de façon discordante
► **blare away** VI *(of radio etc) Fam* gueuler
► **blare out** VI *(of trumpet)* sonner; *(of voice)* résonner (de façon discordante) VT SEP *(of loudspeaker, band)* faire retentir

Blarney ['blɑːnɪ] N *Fam* **to have kissed the B. Stone** avoir le don pour embobiner les gens

blarney ['blɑːnɪ] N boniments *mpl*; **don't give me any of your b.** arrête tes boniments ▸ VT *Fam* embobiner; **to b. sb into doing sth** faire faire qch à qn en l'embobinant; **to b. one's way out of trouble/into a job** se sortir d'embarras/obtenir un emploi grâce à son bagou(t)

blasé ['blɑːzeɪ] ADJ blasé

blaspheme [blæs'fiːm] VT & VI blasphémer

blasphemer [blæs'fiːmər] N blasphémateur, -trice

blasphemous ['blæsfəməs] ADJ *(person)* blasphémateur, -trice; *(words etc)* blasphématoire

blasphemously ['blæsfəməslɪ] ADV de façon blasphématoire; **to speak b.** blasphémer

blasphemy ['blæsfəmɪ] N blasphème *m*

blast [blɑːst] N 1 *(gust of wind)* coup *m ou* rafale *f* de vent; **b. of heat** bouffée *f* de chaleur; **b. of steam** jet *m* de vapeur 2 *(of whistle, siren)* coup *m*; **b. on the trumpet** sonnerie *f* de trompette; **to give a b. on the whistle** donner un coup de sifflet 3 *Fig* **to be** *or* **be working at full b.** être en pleine activité, travailler à plein rendement; *Fam* **to turn the radio up full b.** faire gueuler *ou* brailler la radio 4 *(shock wave) (from explosion etc)* souffle *m*; **a lot of people were killed by the b.** beaucoup de gens ont été tués par l'explosion 5 *(explosion)* explosion *f* 6 *Am Fam (thrill)* **to get a b. out of doing sth** prendre son pied *ou* s'éclater en faisant qch 7 *Fam* **a b. from the past** *(song)* un vieux tube; **that's a real b. from the past** *(fashion, behaviour etc)* c'est comme autrefois; *(brings back memories)* ça me ramène des années en arrière ▸ INT mince (alors)!, zut (alors)! ▸ VT 1 *Min (with dynamite etc)* faire sauter 2 *(of frost) (plant)* brûler, flétrir; *(of lightning) (tree etc)* foudroyer; **to b. sb's hopes** anéantir les espoirs de qn 3 *Fam* **b. it!** zut alors!; **b. you/her!** je te/la maudis!; **b. this computer!** maudit ordinateur! 4 *Fam (criticize)* démolir ▸ VI *(of brass instrument)* sonner; *(of radio etc)* hurler, brailler ▸▸ **b. furnace** *Tech* haut-fourneau *m*, *pl* hauts-fourneaux; *Mil* fourneau *m* de mine; *Min* **b. hole** pétard *m*, trou *m* de mine ▸ **blast away** VI 1 *(of radio etc)* hurler, brailler 2 *(with gun, rifle etc)* tirer en rafales ▸ **blast off** VI *(of rocket, missile)* décoller

blasted ['blɑːstɪd] ADJ ATTRIB 1 *(heath)* désolé; *(tree)* foudroyé 2 *Fam (intensifier)* sacré; **you b. idiot!** espèce d'idiot!; **it's a b. nuisance!** c'est vraiment casse-pieds! 3 *Fam (drunk)* bourré, beurré; *(on drugs)* défoncé

blasting ['blɑːstɪŋ] N 1 *Min* travail *m* aux explosifs; **beware of b.!** attention aux coups de mine! 2 *Fam (severe criticism)* critique *f* féroce *ou* violente; *(reprimand)* savon *m*; **her latest novel got a b. from reviewers** son dernier roman a été démoli par les critiques *ou* la critique

blastoderm ['blæstəʊdɜːm] N *Biol* blastoderme *m*

blastoff ['blɑːstɒf] N *(of rocket)* décollage *m*; **b. is at two o'clock** la fusée décollera à deux heures

blatancy ['bleɪtənsɪ] N *(of injustice, crime etc)* caractère *m* flagrant

blatant ['bleɪtənt] ADJ *(injustice)* criant; *(lie, prejudice, disregard)* flagrant, manifeste; a

b. liar un fieffé menteur, un menteur éhonté; **don't be so b.** *(in your approach)* sois un peu plus diplomate; **it was a b. attempt to win him over** c'était une tentative évidente de s'assurer ses faveurs

blatantly ['bleɪtəntlɪ] ADV *(to lie etc)* d'une manière flagrante; **it's b. obvious that …** il est évident que …; **yes, that's b. obvious** oui, évidemment

blather ['blæðər] N, VI = **blether**

blaxploitation [blæksplɔɪ'teɪʃən] N *Cin* = genre *m* de cinéma qui exploitait les stéréotypes associés à l'identité noire américaine au cinéma, au cours des années 70

blaze[1] [bleɪz] N 1 *(fire)* flamme(s) *f(pl)*, feu *m*; *(in fireplace)* flambée *f*; *Fig (of sun)* flamboiement *m*; *(of colours, diamonds etc)* éclat *m*; **many people died in the b.** beaucoup de gens ont péri dans les flammes; **in a b.** en feu, en flammes; *Fig* **b. of anger** éclat de colère; **in a b. of anger** enflammé de colère; **the street was a b. of light** la rue était tout illuminée; **the garden was a b. of colour** le jardin était resplendissant de couleur; **he married her in a b. of publicity** il l'a épousée sous le feu des médias; **the film was released in a b. of publicity** la sortie du film a été accompagnée d'une publicité monstre; **in a b. of glory** *(to die, retire, return)* plein de gloire 2 *Old-fashioned Fam* **go to blazes!** allez au diable!; **what the blazes does he want/is he doing?** mais qu'est-ce qu'il veut/fait, bon sang?; **to work like blazes** travailler comme un forcené; **to run like blazes** courir comme un dératé ▸ VI 1 *(of fire etc)* flamber; **they had left all the lights blazing** ils avaient laissé toutes les lumières allumées; **the house was blazing** *(on fire)* la maison flambait; **the house was blazing with lights** la maison était tout illuminée; **his eyes were blazing with anger/passion** ses yeux lançaient des éclairs de colère/passion 2 *(of sun, colours)* flamboyer ▸ **blaze away** VI 1 flamboyer 2 *(with gun)* = **blast away** 2 ▸ **blaze down** VI *(of sun)* taper; **the sun was blazing down on the beach** le soleil dardait ses rayons sur la plage ▸ **blaze up** VI *(of fire)* s'embraser, s'enflammer; *Fam (in anger) (of person)* s'emporter

blaze[2] N 1 *(on face of horse, ox)* marque *f* allongée blanche 2 *(on tree)* blanchis *m*, griffe *f* ▸ VT *(tree)* griffer, blanchir; **to b. a trail** tracer un chemin; *Fig* faire œuvre de pionnier, montrer la voie; *(in science etc)* poser des jalons ▸▸ **b. mark** *(on tree)* blanchis, griffe

blazer ['bleɪzər] N *(clothing)* blazer *m*

blazing ['bleɪzɪŋ] ADJ USU ATTRIB 1 *(on fire)* en feu, enflammé; *(ship)* embrasé 2 *Fig (fire, sun)* ardent 3 *Fam* **a b. row** une dispute violente 4 *Fam (angry)* fou de rage; **he was b.** il fulminait, il était fou de rage

blazon ['bleɪzən] N *Her (arms)* blason *m* ▸ VT 1 *Fig* **his name was blazoned over the front pages of all the newspapers** son nom s'étalait en grosses lettres à la une de tous les journaux 2 *Her* blasonner ▸ **blazon abroad** VT SEP *Fml (news)* annoncer à son de trompe ▸ **blazon out, blazon forth** VT SEP *Fml* annoncer *ou* proclamer à son de trompe

bldg *abbr* **building**

bleach [bliːtʃ] N *(for hair)* décolorant *m*; **(household) b.** eau *f* de Javel ▸ VT *(clothes)* passer à l'eau de Javel; *(hair)* décolorer; **hair/sheets bleached by the sun** cheveux/draps décolorés par le soleil; *Phot* **to b. out** blanchir ▸ VI *Tex etc* blanchir; *Chem etc* se décolorer;

do not b. *(washing instruction)* Javel interdite; **the colours had bleached out** les couleurs étaient passées

bleachers ['bliːtʃəz] NPL *Am Sport* gradins *mpl*

bleaching ['bliːtʃɪŋ] N *Tex etc* blanchiment *m*; *(of hair)*, *Chem* décoloration *f* ▸▸ **b. agent** produit *m* blanchissant, décolorant *m*; *Chem* décolorant

bleak [bliːk] ADJ 1 *(weather)* morne, triste; *(terrain)* exposé au vent; *(wind)* froid 2 *Fig (future)* lugubre; *(smile)* pâle; **the prospects are b.** les perspectives sont peu encourageantes

bleakly ['bliːklɪ] ADV *(to smile, stare)* d'un air affligé *ou* désolé; *(to reply, answer)* d'un ton affligé *ou* désolé

bleakness ['bliːknɪs] N *(of weather, landscape)* aspect *m* morne, tristesse *f*; *Fig (of future, room)* caractère *m* lugubre

blearily ['blɪərɪlɪ] ADV *(to look at sb)* les yeux troubles

bleary ['blɪərɪ] ADJ *(eyes)* trouble

bleary-eyed ADJ aux yeux troubles; **to be b. with lack of sleep** avoir des petits yeux (à cause du manque de sommeil)

bleat [bliːt] N *(of sheep)* bêlement *m*; *Fig (complaint)* plainte *f* ▸ VI *(of sheep)* bêler; *(of ram)* blatérer; *(of goat, old man etc)* chevroter; *Fig (complain)* se plaindre; **what's he bleating about?** de quoi se plaint-il?

bleating ['bliːtɪŋ] ADJ *(voice)* chevrotant ▸ N *(of sheep)* bêlement *m*; *Fig (complaining)* plaintes *fpl*

bleed [bliːd] *(pt, pp* **bled** [bled]*)* VI 1 saigner; **his nose is bleeding** il saigne du nez; **to b. to death** saigner à mort; *Iron* **my heart bleeds for you** tu me fends le cœur 2 *(of tree etc)* pleurer, perdre sa sève 3 *(of colour) (on washing)* couler ▸ VT 1 *Med* saigner; *Fam* **to b. sb white** *or* **dry** saigner qn à blanc 2 *Tech (brakes, pipes, radiator etc)* purger ▸ N *Typ* fond *m* perdu ▸▸ *Tech* **b. nipple** téton *m* de purge; *Tech* **b. screw** vis *f* de purge; *Tech* **b. valve** soupape *f* de purge

bleeder ['bliːdər] N 1 *Br Sl Pej* salaud *m*; **poor b.** pauvre type *m*; **you lucky b.!** sacré veinard! 2 *Tech* dispositif *m* de drainage, purgeur *m*

bleeding ['bliːdɪŋ] ADJ 1 saignant, qui saigne 2 *Br Sl (intensifier)* sacré; **you b. liar!** sacré menteur!; **what a b. nuisance!** quelle saloperie! 3 *Typ* à fond perdu ▸ N 1 saignement *m*, hémorragie *f*; *Bot* écoulement *m* de sève; **b. from the nose** saignement de nez 2 *Med, Hist (blood-letting)* saignée *f* 3 *Tech (of brakes, radiator)* purge *f* ▸▸ **b. heart** *Pej (person)* sentimental *m*; *Bot* cœur-de-Jeannette *m*, *pl* cœurs-de-Jeannette; *Lit* **with a b. heart** le cœur brisé

bleeding-heart ADJ **b. liberals** = des libéraux *mpl* au cœur tendre

bleep [bliːp] N *(of electronic device)* bip *m* ▸ VI *(of electronic device)* faire bip ▸ VT 1 *(with pager)* appeler au moyen d'un bip; **I'm being bleeped** on m'appelle 2 *Radio, TV* **to b. words (out)** masquer des paroles (par un bip)

bleeper ['bliːpər] N bip *m*, récepteur *m* d'appel *ou* de poche, Alphapage® *m*

bleeping ['bliːpɪŋ] N *(of electronic device)* bip-bip *m*, *pl* bips-bips

blemish ['blemɪʃ] N *(mark)* tache *f*; **there's not a b. on it** *(on piece of furniture etc)* il/elle n'a pas le moindre défaut; *Fig* **there's not a b. on her record** il n'y a rien à redire à ses états de service; **a reputation without b.** une ré-

putation sans tache; **the case left her without a b. on her reputation** le procès se termina sans que sa réputation soit entachée
vt *(work of art etc)* abîmer, gâcher; *Fig (reputation etc)* entacher, ternir; **blemished fruit** fruits *mpl* tachés

> Note that the French verb **blêmir** is a false friend and is never a translation for the English verb **to blemish**. It means **to go pale.**

blench [blentʃ] **vi** *(turn pale)* blêmir; **to b. with terror** pâlir de terreur

blend [blend] **n** *(of teas, whiskies, tobaccos etc)* mélange *m*
vt *(teas, coffees, whiskies etc)* mélanger; **to b. sth with sth** mélanger qch à *ou* avec qch; **to b. one colour with another** *(mix)* mélanger une couleur avec une autre; *(harmonize)* allier *ou* marier deux couleurs; **to b. one colour into another** *(in painting)* fondre une couleur dans une autre
vi se mêler, se mélanger, se confondre (**into** en); *(of voices etc)* se marier harmonieusement; *(of colours, flavours)* s'allier, se marier; *(of ideas etc)* fusionner; **oil does not b. with water** l'huile ne se mélange pas à l'eau; **the colours b. well** les couleurs se marient bien *ou* vont bien ensemble; **the new building blends into the background** le nouveau bâtiment se fond dans son environnement; *Fig* **she tends to b. into the background** elle a tendance à se fondre dans les décors
▸ **blend in vi** *(harmonize)* s'harmoniser, se marier (**with** avec); *(of person)* s'intégrer; **that new building doesn't b. in with its surroundings** ce nouveau bâtiment ne se marie pas bien *ou* ne va pas bien avec ce qui l'entoure
vt sep *(mix) (flour etc)* incorporer

blender ['blendər] **n** *(kitchen appliance)* mixer *m*, mixeur *m*

blending ['blendɪŋ] **n** *(of teas, tobaccos etc)* mélange *m*; *(of two characteristics)* alliance *f*; *(in wine-making)* coupage *m*

bless [bles] **vt** *[pt, pp* **blessed** [blest], *pp Arch* **blest** [blest]*)* **1** *(of God, priest) (people)* bénir; *(bell)* consacrer, bénir; **I b. the day I learnt to swim** béni soit le jour où j'ai appris à nager; **God b. you!** que Dieu vous bénisse!; **b. you!** *(when sb sneezes)* à vos souhaits!; *Fam* **b. you for doing the washing-up** merci bien d'avoir fait la vaisselle; **Mary, b. her, has agreed to do it** Mary, Dieu soit loué, a accepté de le faire; **b. her (heart)!** quel ange!
2 *usu passive (be fortunate in possessing)* **to be blessed with sth** jouir de qch, avoir le bonheur de posséder qch; **to be blessed with a cheerful disposition** être doté d'un heureux caractère; **they have been blessed with two fine children** ils ont deux enfants adorables; *Iron* **they are blessed with eight children** ils ont huit enfants sur les bras; *Fam* **he hasn't a penny to b. himself with** il n'a pas le sou
3 *(glorify)* **to b. God** bénir *ou* adorer Dieu
4 *Old-fashioned (expressing surprise)* **b. me!, (God) b. my soul!** mon Dieu!; **well, I'm blest!** par exemple!; **I'm blest if I know** que le diable m'emporte si je le sais

blessed ['blesɪd] **adj 1** *Rel (Sacrament, Virgin etc)* saint; **the late king of b. memory** le feu roi, d'heureuse mémoire; *Bible* **b. are the poor in spirit** heureux les pauvres d'esprit **2** *Fam (intensifier)* **every b. day** tous les jours que Dieu fait; **the whole b. day** toute la sainte journée; **the whole b. lot** tout le bazar, tout le bataclan; **it's a b. nuisance having to ...** quelle barbe d'avoir à ...; **I can't see a b. thing** je n'y vois rien

blessedly ['blesɪdlɪ] **adv** parfaitement; **the speech was b. short** Dieu merci, le discours fut bref

blessedness ['blesɪdnɪs] **n** félicité *f, Rel* béatitude *f*

blessing ['blesɪŋ] **n 1** *(divine sanction, favour)* bénédiction *f;* **to give** *or* **pronounce the b.** donner la bénédiction; **to ask** *or* **say a b.** *(at meal)* dire le bénédicité; **the blessings of God** les grâces *fpl* de Dieu; **to give a plan one's b.** donner sa bénédiction à un projet; **it's a b. no one was hurt** c'est une bénédiction que personne n'ait été blessé
2 *(benefit, advantage)* **the blessings of civilization** les bienfaits *mpl* de la civilisation; **it turned out to be a b. in disguise** à la longue, j'ai/il a *etc* pu m'en/s'en/*etc* féliciter; **losing my job was a b. in disguise** finalement, ça a été une bonne chose de perdre mon travail; **to count one's blessings** s'estimer heureux avec ce qu'on a; **count your blessings** ne te plains pas, estime-toi heureux

blest [blest] **adj** bienheureux
npl *Rel Arch* **the B.** les bienheureux *mpl*, les saints *mpl* du Paradis

blether ['bleðər] *Fam* **n 1** *(nonsense)* paroles *fpl* en l'air, bêtises *fpl* **2** *(person)* = personne *f* qui parle à tort et à travers *ou* qui dit des bêtises
vi parler à tort et à travers, dire des bêtises; **blethering idiot** espèce *f* d'idiot

blight [blaɪt] **n 1** *Agr (on cereals)* rouille *f, (on potatoes)* brunissure *f, (on peaches etc)* cloque *f* **2** *Fig* influence *f* néfaste; **his arrival cast a b. over the company** son arrivée a jeté un froid sur l'assistance
vt *Agr (wheat)* rouiller; *(of wind)* flétrir; *Fig* **to b. sb's hopes** anéantir les espoirs de qn; *Fig* **a marriage blighted by money problems** un mariage assombri par des problèmes d'argent

blighter ['blaɪtər] **n** *Old-fashioned Br Fam* **1** *(fellow)* individu *m*, type *m*; **poor b.** pauvre type; **(you) lucky b.!** veinard! **2** *Pej (despicable person)* salaud *m*; **the little b.** le petit coquin

Blighty ['blaɪtɪ] **n** *Br Mil, Hist Fam (Britain)* Grande-Bretagne *f*, le pays; *(wound)* = pendant la Première Guerre mondiale, une blessure suffisamment grave pour qu'elle nécessite un rapatriement en Grande-Bretagne

blimey ['blaɪmɪ] **int** *Br Sl* mince alors!

blimp [blɪmp] **n 1** *Aviat* (petit) dirigeable *m* de reconnaissance **2** *Br Fig (reactionary)* réactionnaire *m* endurci; **a real Colonel B.** une vraie culotte de peau, un scrogneugneu

blind [blaɪnd] **adj 1** *(person)*, *Fig (obedience, faith, hatred)* aveugle; **b. from birth** aveugle de naissance; **b. in one eye** borgne; **a b. man/woman** un/une aveugle; **to be struck b.** être frappé de cécité; **I'm b. without my glasses** je ne vois rien sans mes lunettes; **he's as b. as a bat** il est myope comme une taupe; **to turn a b. eye on** *or* **to sth** fermer les yeux sur qch; **to be b. to sb's faults** ne pas voir les défauts de qn, être aveugle aux défauts de qn; *Prov* **love is b.** l'amour est aveugle; *Fam* **he didn't take a b. bit of notice** il n'a pas fait la moindre attention; *Fam* **in a b. stupor** *(drunk)* bourré
2 *(bend)* masqué, sans visibilité
3 *(without exit) (window, door)* feint, aveugle
adv to fire b. tirer au jugé; *Aviat* **to fly b.** voler à l'aveuglette; *Culin* **bake b. for five minutes** cuire le fond de tarte cinq minutes; *Fam* **to go at sth b.** se lancer à l'aveuglette dans qch; **she swore b. that ...** elle a juré ses grands dieux que ...; **b. drunk** complètement ivre *ou* soûl
vt *(person)* aveugler, rendre aveugle; *(temporarily) (of tears)* aveugler; *(dazzle)* aveugler, éblouir; **blinded ex-servicemen** aveugles *mpl* de guerre; **blinded by passion**

aveuglé par la passion; **love blinded her to his faults** aveuglée par l'amour, elle n'a pas vu ses défauts; *Fig* **don't b. me with science** pas la peine de m'éblouir avec ta science
n 1 *Br (at window)* store *m; Aut (on radiator)* rideau *m;* **shop b.** *(over pavement)* banne *f* **2** *Fig (pretext)* prétexte *m*
npl the b. les aveugles *mp*
▸▸ *Br* **b. alley** impasse *f*, cul-de-sac *m*, *pl* culs-de-sac; *Fig* impasse; **b. date** *(meeting)* rendez-vous *m inv* ou rencontre *f* arrangé(e) *(avec quelqu'un qu'on ne connaît pas); (person)* inconnu, -ue *(avec qui on a rendez-vous); Aviat* **b. flying** vol *m* sans visibilité, vol en PSV; **b. man's buff** *(game)* colin-maillard *m, pl* colin-maillards; *Old-fashioned Fam* **b. school** école *f* pour aveugles *ou* pour non-voyants; **b. side** *Sport (in rugby)* côté *m* fermé; *Aut* angle *m* mort; **b. spot** *Aut (in mirror)* angle mort; *(in road)* endroit *m* sans visibilité; *Med* point *m* aveugle; *Fig (weak area)* côté faible, faiblesse *f, Mktg* **b. test** test *m* aveugle; *Mktg* **b. testing** tests aveugles

blinder ['blaɪndər] **n 1** *Br Sl* **to go on a b.** *(get very drunk)* se bourrer (la gueule) **2** *Sport Fam (outstanding feat)* **he played a b.** *(of a game)* il a eu un jeu spectaculaire; **the first goal was a b.** le premier but a été spectaculaire **3** *Am (for horse)* œillère *f*

blindfold ['blaɪndfəʊld] **adj** les yeux bandés
adv *(to enter into an undertaking)* aveuglément; *Chess (to play)* sans voir l'échiquier; **I can do it b.** *(I am very familiar with the task)* je pourrais le faire les yeux fermés
n bandeau *m* sur les yeux; **they put a b. over my eyes** ils m'ont mis un bandeau sur les yeux
vt to b. sb bander les yeux à *ou* de qn, couvrir les yeux de qn avec un bandeau; **to be blindfolded** avoir les yeux bandés, avoir un bandeau sur les yeux

blinding ['blaɪndɪŋ] **adj 1** *(dazzling)* aveuglant; **b. headache** mal *m* de tête effroyable; **it was a b. revelation** ça a été une véritable révélation; **the b. intensity of his criticism** l'intensité affolante de ses critiques **2** *Br Fam (excellent)* super *inv,* génial, -aux
n aveuglement *m*; *(by headlights, light etc)* éblouissement *m*

blindingly ['blaɪndɪŋlɪ] **adv** **it's b. obvious** c'est tout à fait évident, cela saute aux yeux (**that** que)

blindly ['blaɪndlɪ] **adv 1** *(to look at sth, sb)* sans le/la/*etc* voir; *(to grope)* à l'aveuglette **2** *Fig (to obey)* aveuglément; *(to follow)* aveuglément, sans réfléchir

blindness ['blaɪndnɪs] **n** cécité *f, Fig* aveuglement *m*; **b. to the facts** refus *m* d'envisager *ou* de voir les faits

blindworm ['blaɪndwɜːm] **n** orvet *m*

bling (bling) ['blɪŋ('blɪŋ)] *Sl* **n** *(jewellery)* bijoux *mpl*, quincaillerie *f*
adj *(ostentatious)* tape-à-l'œil; **that car is so b.!** cette voiture est vraiment tape-à-l'œil

blink [blɪŋk] **n 1** *(of eyes)* battement *m ou* clignement *m* de paupières **2** *(of light)* lueur *f* momentanée **3** *Br Sl* **to be on the b.** *(of television set etc)* être en panne, faire des siennes
vi 1 *(of person)* battre *ou* cligner des paupières, clignoter; *Fig without blinking (calmly, without surprise)* sans sourciller; *Fig* **he was the first to b.** *(in confrontation)* c'est lui qui a cédé le premier; **to b. at sb/sth** regarder qn/qch en clignant des yeux; **she blinked at the sight in astonishment** elle regardait en croyait pas ses yeux; *Fig* **to b. at the fact that ...** *(pretend not to see)* nier le fait que ...; *Fig* **to b. at the facts** fermer les yeux sur

la vérité **2** *(of light, cursor)* clignoter
VT to b. one's eyes cligner des yeux
▸ ▸ *Comput* **b. rate** *(of cursor)* vitesse *f* de clignotement
▸ **blink away VT SEP** *(tears)* refouler d'un battement de paupières

blinker ['blɪŋkər] **N 1** *(for horse)*, *Fig* œillère *f*
2 *(at airfield)* phare *m* à éclats; *Aut* clignotant *m*
VT *(horse)* mettre des œillères à; *Fig* **they are very blinkered, that's very blinkered thinking on their part** ils ont des œillères

blinking ['blɪŋkɪŋ] **ADJ 1** *(eyes)* qui clignotent **2** *(light)* clignotant, papillotant **3** *Old-fashioned Br Fam* **what a b. nuisance!** quelle barbe!; **b. idiot!** espèce d'idiot!; **a b. good meal** un repas sacrément bon; **I b. well did see her there** je l'y ai vue de mes propres yeux
N 1 *(of eyes)* clignotement *m* **2** *(of light)* papillotage *m*

blintz(e) [blɪnts] **N** *Am Culin* crêpe *f* fourrée *(au fromage, aux fruits etc)*

blip [blɪp] **N** *(of radar)* *(on screen)* spot *m*; *(noise)* top *m* d'écho; *Fig Fam* *(in statistics)* écart *m* momentané; **the company suffered a b. in February when it lost that contract** l'entreprise a subi un contretemps en février lorsqu'elle a perdu ce contrat

bliss [blɪs] **N** grand bonheur *m*, béatitude *f*; **breakfast in bed, what b.!** le petit déjeuner au lit, quel bonheur!; **it was b. to plunge into the water** c'était un bonheur de plonger dans l'eau; **it's sheer b.!** c'est le bonheur total!; **isn't it b. not having your mother here!** quel bonheur de ne plus avoir ta mère ici, hein?

blissful ['blɪsful] **ADJ** *(person)* (bien)heureux; *(holiday, weekend etc)* plein de bonheur; **we had a b. time in France** nous avons passé un merveilleux séjour en France; **... she said with a b. sigh** ... dit-elle en soupirant de bonheur; **he was in b. ignorance of what was happening** il n'avait pas la moindre idée de ce qui se passait; **I'd rather remain in b. ignorance** j'aime autant ne pas savoir

blissfully ['blɪsful] **ADV** **... she said b.** ... dit-elle, au comble du bonheur; **he smiled b.** il eut un grand sourire de bonheur; **b. happy** au comble du bonheur; **to be b. ignorant of sth** ne pas se douter le moins du monde de qch; **to be b. unaware that ...** ne pas se douter le moins du monde que ...; **the house is b. quiet without the children** la maison est merveilleusement calme sans les enfants

B-list ADJ *(star, celebrity, guest)* pas parmi les plus connus; **there were only B. stars among the guests** il n'y avait aucune vedette de stature internationale parmi les invités

blister ['blɪstər] **N 1** *(on skin)* ampoule *f*, cloque *f* **2** *(in paint)* cloque *f*, boursouflure *f*; *(in glass)* bulle *f*; *Metal* soufflure *f*
VT *(hand etc)* provoquer des ampoules sur
VI 1 *(of heel etc)* se couvrir d'ampoules **2** *(of paint)* cloquer
▸ ▸ *Br* **b. pack** *(for light bulb, pens)* blister *m*; *(for pills)* plaquette *f*

blistered ['blɪstəd] **ADJ** couvert d'ampoules

blistering ['blɪstərɪŋ] **ADJ** *(sun, heat)* brûlant, ardent; *Fig (attack)* foudroyant; **she's setting a b. pace** elle mène un train d'enfer
N 1 *(on skin)* ampoules *fpl*; **b. is inevitable** la formation d'ampoules est inévitable **2** *(of paint)* cloquage *m*

blisteringly ['blɪstərɪŋlɪ] **ADV** **it was a b. hot day** c'était une journée d'une chaleur étouffante; **it was b. hot** il faisait une chaleur étouffante

blithe ['blaɪð] **ADJ** joyeux, allègre; *(irresponsible)* *(disregard, attitude, response etc)* désinvolte

blithely ['blaɪðlɪ] **ADV** joyeusement, allègrement; *(irresponsibly)* avec désinvolture; **she b. ignored him** elle l'a ignoré avec une complète désinvolture; **he was b. unaware of the danger** il ne se doutait pas le moins du monde du danger qu'il courait

blithering ['blɪðərɪŋ] **ADJ** *Fam* sacré; **b. idiot!** espèce d'idiot!

BLitt [biː'lɪt] **N** *Univ* *(abbr* **Bachelor of Letters***)* *(diploma)* licence *f* ès lettres; *(person)* licencié, -ée ès lettres

blitz [blɪts] **N** *Mil* blitz *m*, bombardement *m* aérien; *Hist* **the B.** le Blitz; *Fig* **to have a b. on sth** s'attaquer à qch; *Fig* **the b. of holiday advertisements starts immediately after Christmas** dès que les fêtes sont finies, on est bombardé de publicité par les agences de voyages
VT bombarder; **the house was blitzed** la maison a été endommagée/détruite par un bombardement; *Fig Fam* **to b. sb with letters/complaints** bombarder qn de lettres/plaintes

blitzed [blɪtst] **ADJ** *Sl (drunk)* bourré; *(on drugs)* défoncé

blizzard ['blɪzəd] **N** tempête *f* de neige; *(in North America)* blizzard *m*

bloat [bləʊt] **VT** boursoufler, bouffir
VI bouffir

bloated ['bləʊtɪd] **ADJ** bouffi, boursouflé; *Fig (estimate, bill)* salé; **to feel b.** *(because of water retention, overeating)* se sentir ballonné *ou* gonflé; **he suffers from a b. ego** sa suffisance n'a pas de limites; **b. with pride** bouffi d'orgueil

bloater ['bləʊtər] **N** *(herring)* hareng *m* bouffi

blob [blɒb] **N** *(of colour)* tache *f*, *(of ink)* pâté *m*

bloc [blɒk] **N** *Pol etc* bloc *m*

BLOCK [blɒk] **N 1** *(slab)* *(of marble, paper etc)* bloc *m*; *(of wood)* tronçon *m*; *(of chocolate)* grosse tablette *f*; *(for chopping)* billot *m*; *(for getting on horse)* montoir *m*; *(for athletes)* bloc de départ; **like a b. of stone** *(transfixed)* immobile; *(unfeeling)* dur; *(not speaking)* silencieux, muet; *Am* **to be on the b.** *(up for auction)* être mis aux enchères; **blocks** *(for children)* *(jeu m de)* cubes *mpl*, *Fam* **to have been around the block a few times** ne plus être de la première jeunesse
2 *esp Am (buildings between two streets)* pâté *m* de maisons; *(Austr (plot of land)* lot *m*; **he lives two blocks from us** il habite à deux rues de nous; **it's two blocks north/south of here** c'est à deux rues d'ici vers le nord/sud; **we live on the same b.** nous habitons dans le même pâté de maisons; **to walk round the b.** faire le tour du pâté de maisons; *Br* **b. of flats** immeuble *m*
3 *(obstruction)* **traffic b.** embouteillage *m*; **mental b.** blocage *m* psychologique; **I have a mental b. about computers** je fais un blocage psychologique avec les ordinateurs; *Fin* **to put a b. on an account** bloquer un compte
4 *Sl (head)* caboche *f*, **I'll knock your b. off!** je vais te casser la gueule!
5 *(of rooms)* contingent *m*; **to book a b. of four weeks** réserver quatre semaines consécutives; **b. of seats** bloc-sièges *m inv*; *Fin* **b. of shares** paquet *m* d'actions
6 *Aut* **(engine) b.** bloc-moteur *m*, *pl* blocs-moteurs; **to put a car up on blocks** mettre une voiture sur cales
7 *Comput* bloc *m*
8 *(in engraving) (wood)* planche *f*, bois *m*
9 *Tech (pulley)* poulie *f*, **b. and tackle** palan *m*

VT 1 *(passage etc)* bloquer, obstruer; *(wheel)* bloquer, enrayer; *(flow of traffic)* entraver, gêner; *(progress)* arrêter; *Fin (cheque, account)* bloquer; **to b. sb's way** barrer le passage *ou* le chemin à qn; **to b. the view** cacher la vue; *Parl* **to b. a bill** faire obstruction à un projet de loi
2 *Sport (ball)* bloquer; *Ftbl etc (opponent)* gêner; **the goalkeeper blocked the shot** le gardien arrêta le tir; *Tennis* **she blocked the serve magnificently** elle fit un superbe retour de service
3 *Comput (text)* sélectionner; **to b. text** sélectionner un bloc de texte; **to b. and copy** sélectionner et copier
4 *(room)* retenir, bloquer
5 *(actors)* = faire prendre leurs marques aux acteurs; *(scene, play)* prendre les marques pour
▸ ▸ **b. association** association *f* de riverains; **b. booking** *(of theatre tickets etc)* réservation *f* *ou* location *f* de groupe; *Typ* **b. capital** *(caractère m)* majuscule *f*; **in b. capitals**; *Comput* **b. copy** copie *f* de bloc; **b. diagram** *Comput*, *Geog* bloc-diagramme *m*, *pl* blocs-diagrammes; *Electron* schéma *m* *(de principe)*; *Typ* **b. letter** *(caractère m)* majuscule; **in b. letters** en majuscules; *Comput* **b. marker** délimiteur *m* de bloc; *Comput* **b. structure** *(of file)* structure *f* de bloc; *Pol, Ind* **b. vote** = mode *m* de scrutin utilisé par les syndicats britanniques par opposition au mode de scrutin "un homme, une voix"
▸ **block in VT SEP** *esp Aut (person)* empêcher de sortir, bloquer le passage à; **I'm blocked in** je suis coincé
▸ **block off VT SEP** *(street)* barrer
▸ **block out VT SEP 1** *(prevent entry of)* empêcher d'entrer *ou* de passer; **those trees b. out all the sun** ces arbres empêchent le soleil de passer; **to b. out the memory of sb/sth** refouler le souvenir de qn/qch; **it's impossible to b. that music out** il est impossible d'ignorer cette musique
2 *(draft) (book, project)* ébaucher, esquisser
▸ **block up VT SEP 1** *(close) (hole)* boucher; *(door, window)* boucher, murer
2 *(clog) (pipe etc)* obstruer, engorger; *(sink)* boucher

blockade [blɒ'keɪd] **N** *Mil, Pol* blocus *m*; **to impose/break a b.** imposer/forcer un blocus; **to raise** *or* **lift a b.** lever un blocus; *Hist* **to run the b.** forcer le blocus
VT 1 *(town, port)* bloquer, faire le blocus de; *(fortified place)* faire le blocus de **2** *Am (flow of traffic)* *(street)* encombrer
▸ ▸ *Hist* **b. runner** forceur *m* de blocus

blockage ['blɒkɪdʒ] **N** *(of pipe, artery etc)* obstruction *f*, *(in street)* embouteillage *m*

blockbuster ['blɒkbʌstər] **N** *Fam (film)* superproduction *f*, *(book)* best-seller *m*, *pl* best-sellers

blocked [blɒkt] **ADJ** *(account, cheque, market)* bloqué; **b. up** bouché; **b. space** *(reserved)* espace *m* réservé

blockhead ['blɒkhed] **N** *Fam* lourdaud *m*

blockhouse ['blɒkhaʊs] **N** *Mil* blockhaus *m*

blocking ['blɒkɪŋ] **N 1** *(of street)* encombrement *m*, embouteillage *m*; *(of port)* blocus *m* **2** *Elec (of current)* blocage *m* **3** *(in bookbinding)* gaufrage *m*, frappe *f*
▸ ▸ *Comput* **b. software** logiciel *m* de filtrage

block-oriented ADJ *Comput* orienté bloc

blog [blɒg] **N** *Comput (abbr* **weblog***)* blog *m*

bloke [bləʊk] **N** *Br Fam (man)* type *m*

blokeish ['bləʊkɪʃ] **ADJ** *Br Fam* = typique d'un style de vie caractérisé par de fréquentes sorties entre copains, généralement copieusement arrosées, et un goût prononcé pour le sport et les activités de groupe

blond, f **blonde** [blɒnd] ADJ, N blond, f blonde

blood [blʌd] N sang m; **to give b.** (of donor) donner du sang; **his b. will be on your hands** tu porteras la responsabilité de sa mort; Fig **his b. is up** il est furieux; **it makes my b. boil/ run cold** cela me fait bouillir/me glace le sang; **to commit a crime in cold b.** commettre un crime de sang-froid; Fig **the committee needs new** or **fresh b.** le comité a besoin d'être rajeuni; **to shed** or **spill b.** verser le sang; Fig **it's not worth shedding** or **spilling b. over** inutile de se battre pour ça; Fig **to be out for b.** chercher à se venger; Fig **to be after** or **out for sb's b.** vouloir se venger de qn, en vouloir à qn; Fig **the boss is after your b.** le patron en a après toi; Prov **it's like trying to get b. out of a stone** c'est comme si on se heurtait à un mur; **the theatre is in her b.** elle a le théâtre dans le sang; Prov **b. is thicker than water** la famille passe avant tout; **prince of the b.** prince m du sang; **warm the milk until it is at b. temperature** chauffe le lait jusqu'à ce qu'il atteigne la température du corps

VT (first-time hunter) initier (en l'aspergeant du sang de la bête morte); (hounds) donner le goût du sang à **2** esp Sp Fig initier

▸▸ Med **b. bank** banque f du sang; **b. bath** carnage m, massacre m; **b. blister** pinçon m; **b. brother** frère m de sang; Anat **b. cell** cellule f sanguine, globule m (du sang); Med **b. count** numération f globulaire; Med **b. donor** donneur, -euse de sang; **b. doping** = transfusion f sanguine utilisée comme méthode de dopage; Med **b. group** groupe m sanguin; **b. horse** pur-sang m inv; **b. money** prix m du sang; **b. orange** (orange f) sanguine f; Biol **b. plasma** plasma m sanguin; Med **b. poisoning** septicémie f; Med **b. pressure** tension f (artérielle); Med **b. product** dérivé m du sang; Culin **b. pudding** boudin m (noir); **b. red** (colour) rouge sang m inv; **b. relation** parent, -ente par le sang; Med **b. sample** prise f de sang; Culin **b. sausage** boudin (noir); Med **b. serum** sérum m sanguin; **b. sports** chasse f, Med **b. test** analyse f de sang

blood-and-thunder ADJ (film, novel etc) sensationnel, mélodramatique

bloodcurdling ['blʌdkɜ:dlɪŋ] ADJ (story, scream) à vous tourner les sangs, à (vous) figer le sang

-blooded ['blʌdɪd] SUFF hot-/cold-b. à sang chaud/froid

bloodhound ['blʌdhaʊnd] N (dog), Fig (detective) limier m

bloodiness ['blʌdɪnɪs] N état m sanglant; (of battle) sauvagerie f

bloodless ['blʌdlɪs] ADJ **1** (victory etc) sans effusion de sang **2** (pale) exsangue, pâle **3** (lifeless) sans vitalité

bloodlessly ['blʌdlɪslɪ] ADV sans effusion de sang

blood-letting N **1** (violent feud, bloodshed) effusion f de sang **2** Med, Hist saignée f

blood-red ADJ rouge sang inv

bloodshed ['blʌdʃed] N **1** effusion f de sang; **without b.** sans verser de sang **2** (slaughter) carnage m

bloodshot ['blʌdʃɒt] ADJ (eye) injecté de sang; **to become b.** (of eye) s'injecter

bloodstain ['blʌdsteɪn] N tache f de sang

bloodstained ['blʌdsteɪnd] ADJ taché ou souillé de sang, ensanglanté

bloodstock ['blʌdstɒk] N pur-sang mpl

bloodstone ['blʌdstəʊn] N Miner jaspe m sanguin

bloodstream ['blʌdstri:m] N Physiol sang m

bloodsucker ['blʌdsʌkər] N Zool sangsue f, Fig Fam sangsue, parasite m

bloodsucking ['blʌdsʌkɪŋ] ADJ ATTRIB Zool hématophage; Fig Fam vampirique

bloodthirsty ['blʌdθɜ:stɪ] ADJ (person) sanguinaire; (film, book) très violent

bloody ['blʌdɪ] ADJ **1** (stained with blood) ensanglanté, taché de sang; (revolution, battle etc) sanglant; **he came home with a b. nose** il est rentré en saignant du nez; Fig **to give sb a b. nose** donner une raclée à qn **2** Br Sl (intensifier) sacré; **a b. liar** un sacré menteur; **(you) b. fool!** espèce d'imbécile!; **b. hell!** merde, bon sang!; **he wouldn't even tell me his b. name!** il n'a même pas voulu me dire son nom, cet animal!; **politicians are all the b. same!** ces foutus hommes politiques sont tous les mêmes!

ADV Br Sl **it's b. hot!** on crève de chaleur!; **he can b. well do it himself!** il n'a qu'à se démerder tout seul!; **I b. well am going out** j'ai bien l'intention de sortir (et personne ne m'en empêchera); **I'm b. tired** je suis complètement crevé; **not b. likely!** il n'y a pas de danger!; **I wish he'd b. stop it!** quand est-ce qu'il va s'arrêter, merde!

VT (pt, pp bloodied) (one's hands etc) ensanglanter, souiller de sang; Fig **to b. one's hands** se salir les mains

▸▸ **B. Mary** Hist (queen) = surnom m de la reine Marie Tudor, donné par les protestants qu'elle persécuta; (cocktail) bloody mary m inv

bloody-minded ADJ Br Sl **he's just b.** c'est un mauvais coucheur; **don't be so b.** arrête d'emmerder le monde

bloody-mindedness ['-maɪndɪdnɪs] N Br Sl **it's sheer b.** ce n'est rien que pour emmerder le monde; **the b. of the decision is unbelievable** la décision, prise uniquement pour emmerder le monde, est incroyable; **I admire her b.** j'admire la façon qu'elle a d'emmerder le monde

bloom [blu:m] N **1** (flower) fleur f; **to come** or **burst into b.** fleurir; **flower in b.** fleur éclose; **the roses are in b.** les roses sont ouvertes; **in full b.** épanoui; Lit **in the b. of youth** à ou dans la fleur de l'âge; **the constant arguing soon took the b. off their marriage** les disputes perpétuelles firent rapidement perdre son charme à leur mariage **2** (on grape, peach etc) velouté m, pruine f, duvet m; (of cheeks) éclat m; Chem **cobalt/zinc b.** fleur f de cobalt/zinc

VI (of plant) fleurir, être en fleur; Fig (of child) être éclatant ou resplendissant de santé

bloomer ['blu:mər] N Br Fam (mistake) bourde f, (in social circumstances) gaffe f

bloomers ['blu:məz] NPL culotte f bouffante (de femme)

blooming ['blu:mɪŋ] ADJ **1** (flower) éclos; Fig florissant; **b. with health** resplendissant de santé **2** Br Fam (intensifier) **you b. idiot!** espèce d'idiot!; **it's a b. lie!** ça, pour un mensonge!; **the woman's a b. genius** cette femme, c'est vraiment un génie

ADV Br Fam **I b. well will go!** et moi, je te dis que j'irai!

N floraison f, fleuraison f

blooper ['blu:pər] N Am Fam = bloomer

blootered ['blu:təd] ADJ Scot Fam (drunk) pété, bourré

blossom ['blɒs(ə)m] N (of trees) fleur f, **tree in b.** arbre m en fleur(s); **apple/cherry/ orange b.** fleur de pommier/de cerisier/ d'oranger; **to come into b.** fleurir

VI (of tree) fleurir; Fig (of friendship, relationship) s'épanouir; **she had blossomed into a charming young woman** elle était devenue une charmante jeune femme

▸ **blossom out** VI = blossom VI

blossoming ['blɒsəmɪŋ] N fleuraison f, floraison f, Fig épanouissement m

ADJ qui commence à fleurir; Fig (friendship, partnership) en herbe

blot [blɒt] N tache f, (of ink) pâté m; Fig **a b. on sb's honour/reputation** une tache faite à l'honneur/la réputation de qn; Fig **to be a b. on the landscape** (of building) gâcher le paysage

VT (-tt-) **1** (stain) tacher, souiller; (with ink) faire des pâtés sur; Fig **to b. one's copybook (with sb)** se faire mal voir (de qn) **2** (letter etc) passer un buvard sur; (lipstick) passer un Kleenex® sur

VI (of blotting paper) boire l'encre

▸ **blot out** VT SEP (obliterate) (memory etc) effacer; (word) rayer, barrer; (of fog etc) (feature of landscape etc) cacher, masquer

blotch [blɒtʃ] N **1** (of ink, paint) tache f, éclaboussure f **2** (on skin) tache f, marbrure f

VT (skin) couvrir de taches; **cold blotches the skin** le froid marbre la peau; **her face was blotched with tears** son visage portait des traces de larmes

VI **this pen blotches** ce stylo fuit

blotchy ['blɒtʃɪ] ADJ tacheté; (complexion) brouillé, couperosé

blotter ['blɒtər] N **1** (for ink) (paper) buvard m; (desk pad) sous-main m inv; (with handle) tampon m buvard **2** Com Old-fashioned brouillard m, main f courante

blotting ['blɒtɪŋ] N séchage m au papier buvard

▸▸ **b. pad** (bloc m) buvard m; (large) sous-main m inv, **b. paper** (papier m) buvard

blotto ['blɒtəʊ] ADJ Br Sl (drunk) bourré

blouse [blaʊz] N **1** (woman's) chemisier m, corsage m **2** Am (sailor's etc) vareuse f

Note that the French word **blouse** is a false friend. Its most common meaning is **overall**.

BLOW[1] [bləʊ]

N souffle **1** ▪ coup **2**	
VI souffler **1, 2**	
VT faire bouger **1** ▪ souffler **2** ▪ jouer de **3** ▪ faire sauter **6** ▪ gâcher **7** ▪ claquer **8**	

N **1** (through mouth) souffle m; **give your nose a good b.** (to child) mouche-toi bien **2** (of whistle) coup m **3** Br Sl (cannabis) shit m; Am Sl (cocaine) coke f, neige f, (heroin) héro f, blanche f

VI (pt blew [blu:], pp blown [bləʊn]) **1** (of wind) souffler; **the wind's blowing from the west** le vent souffle de l'ouest; **it was blowing a gale** le vent soufflait en tempête; **the wind was blowing down the chimney** le vent s'engouffrait dans la cheminée; **my papers blew out of the window** mes papiers se sont envolés par la fenêtre; **the door blew open** le vent a ouvert la porte

2 (of person, animal) souffler; (of whale) rejeter l'eau par les évents; (of whistle) retentir, se faire entendre; **to b. on one's fingers** souffler dans ses doigts; Fam **to b. into town** arriver en ville à l'improviste; **when did you b. into town?** quand est-ce que tu es arrivé?

3 Am Fam (boast) se vanter

4 (of fuse) sauter; (of boiler etc) exploser

5 Fam **b.!** zut!

VT **1** (of wind) faire bouger; **the wind is blowing the rain against the windows** le vent pousse la pluie contre les vitres; **to b. a ship ashore** (of wind) pousser un navire à la côte; **to be blown out to sea** être poussé au large; **he was nearly blown off his feet** (by wind, explosion) il a failli être emporté

2 (of person) souffler; **to b. one's nose** se moucher; **he blew the dust off the book** il

a soufflé sur le livre pour enlever la poussière; **to b. sb a kiss** envoyer un baiser à qn **3** *(musical instrument)* jouer de; **to b. a whistle** donner un coup de sifflet; **he blew the whistle** il donna un coup de sifflet; *Fig* **to b. the whistle on sb** balancer qn; **to b. the dust off sth** souffler sur qch pour enlever la poussière; **to b. the horn** sonner du cor; *Fig* **to b. one's own trumpet** chanter ses propres louanges, se faire mousser **4** *(soap bubbles)* faire; *(glass)* souffler; *(egg)* vider **5** *(horse etc)* essouffler **6** *(fuse, gasket, safe)* faire sauter; *Fam* **the Grand Canyon blew my mind** j'ai vraiment été époustouflé par le Grand Canyon!; *Fam* **the prices blew my mind** les prix m'ont affolé **7** *Fam (ruin, spoil)* gâcher, bousiller; *(opportunity)* louper; **that's blown it!** ça a tout gâché *ou* bousillé, ça a tout fait louper **8** *Fam (money)* claquer (**on** dans) **9** *Fam* **b. the expense!** au diable l'avarice!; **I'll be blowed if ...** je veux bien être pendu si ...; **well, I'm blowed!** ça, par exemple!; **b. it!** zut!
▸▸*Vulg* **b. job** *(oral sex)* pipe *f*; **to give sb a b. job** tailler une pipe à qn
▸ **blow about** *vi (of leaves etc)* voler çà et là *vt sep* agiter, faire voler; *(leaves etc)* disperser
▸ **blow away** *vt sep* **1** *(of wind etc)* emporter **2** *Am Sl (kill)* descendre, flinguer
vi (of papers etc) s'envoler; **his hat blew away in the wind** son chapeau s'est envolé à cause du vent; **all my cares have blown away** tous mes soucis se sont évanouis *ou* envolés
▸ **blow down** *vt sep (of wind) (fence etc)* abattre, renverser; *(tree)* abattre; *Old-fashioned Fam* **well b. me down!** c'est pas Dieu possible!
vi (of fence etc) s'abattre, se renverser; *(of tree)* s'abattre
▸ **blow in** *vt sep* **1** *(of explosion, wind etc)* *(window, door)* enfoncer **2** *(of person)* souffler; **b. some more air in** souffle un peu plus d'air dedans
vi **1** *(of window etc)* s'enfoncer **2** **the dust is blowing in** le vent fait entrer la poussière **3** *Fam (of person)* arriver à l'improviste; **when did you b. in?** quand est-ce que tu es arrivé?
▸ **blow off** *vt sep* **1** *(of wind) (hat, slates)* emporter; **the wind blew the papers off my desk** le vent a fait s'envoler les papiers qui étaient sur mon bureau **2** *(of person) (dust etc)* enlever en soufflant dessus **3** *(with gun, explosives)* faire sauter; **the gunman threatened to b. their heads off** l'homme au pistolet a menacé de leur faire sauter la cervelle; **she got her hand blown off** sa main a été arrachée dans l'explosion
vi (of hat etc) s'envoler
▸ **blow out** *vt sep* **1** *(candle)* souffler **2** *(air)* chasser, expulser; *(one's cheeks)* gonfler; **to b. one's brains out** se faire sauter la cervelle; **to b. sb's brains out** faire sauter la cervelle à qn; **to b. itself out** *(of storm)* se dissiper, se calmer
vi **1** *(of candle)* s'éteindre **2** *Aut etc (of gasket)* sauter; *(of tyre)* éclater; *Elec (of fuse)* sauter
▸ **blow over** *vt sep (of wind) (table etc)* renverser
vi **1** *(fall down)* se renverser **2** *(come to an end) (of storm)* se calmer, se dissiper; *Fig (of argument)* se calmer; **the scandal soon blew over** le scandale a été vite oublié
▸ **blow up** *vi (of mine)* éclater, sauter; *(of boiler etc)* crever, exploser; *Fig (of person)* piquer une colère (**at sb** contre qn); **the ar-**

gument blew up out of nowhere la dispute a commencé sans raison; **to b. up into a crisis** *(of situation)* prendre les proportions d'une crise; **there's a gale blowing up** il se prépare une tempête; *Fig* **to b. up in sb's face** *(go wrong)* se retourner contre qn
vt sep **1** *(bomb, booby-trapped car etc)* faire sauter; *(explosion)* faire sauter; *(building)* faire sauter **2** *(tyre, balloon etc)* gonfler **3** *Phot* agrandir; **I'd like this photograph blown up** j'aimerais un agrandissement de cette photo **4** *Fam (exaggerate) (incident etc)* exagérer; **you're blowing this up out of all proportion** tu en fais un drame

blow² N *(with fist etc)*, *Fig (of fate)* coup *m*; **at the first b.** du premier coup; **at a (single) b.** d'un (seul) coup; **to strike a b.** asséner *ou* donner un coup; *Fig* **to strike a b. for/ against sth** remporter une bataille en faveur de/contre qch; **to come to blows, to exchange blows** en venir aux coups *ou* aux mains; **to return b. for b.** rendre coup pour coup; **his death is a sad b. to his family** sa mort est un rude coup pour sa famille; **b. to sb's pride** atteinte *f* (faite) à l'amour-propre de qn

blowback ['bləʊbæk] N *Aut* retour *m* de flamme

blow-by N *Aut* fuite *f* de gaz

blow-by-blow ADJ *(account)* minutieux, détaillé

blowcock ['bləʊkɒk] N robinet *m* d'extraction *ou* de vidange

blowdart ['bləʊdɑːt] N petite flèche *f*

blow-dry N *(at hairdresser's)* brushing *m*
vt (one's hair) sécher (avec un séchoir); **to b. sb's hair** faire un brushing à qn

blow-drying N **too much b. can damage your hair** à force d'être séchés au séchoir, les cheveux s'abîment

blower ['bləʊər] N **1** *Br Fam (telephone)* bigophone *m*; **on the b.** au bigophone; **to get on the b. to sb** passer un coup de fil à qn **2** *(in ventilation system)* turbine *f* de ventilation; *(supercharger)* soufflante *f*

blowfly, *pl* **blowflies** ['bləʊflaɪ, -flaɪz] N mouche *f* de la viande, mouche bleue

blowgun ['bləʊɡʌn] N *Am (for darts)* sarbacane *f*

blowhard ['bləʊhɑːd] N *Fam (boaster)* vantard, -arde, crâneur, -euse

blowhole ['bləʊhəʊl] N **1** *Zool (of whale)* évent *m* **2** *(in ice)* = trou *m* où un phoque etc vient respirer **3** *(in tunnel)* bouche *f* d'aération

blowing ['bləʊɪŋ] N **1** *(of wind)* souffle *m*; **he could hear the b. of the wind outside** il entendait le vent souffler dehors **2** *(of glass)* soufflage *m*

blowlamp ['bləʊlæmp] N **1** *(for welding, brazing)* chalumeau *m*, lampe *f* à souder *ou* à braser **2** *(for removing paint)* brûloir *m*

blown [bləʊn] ADJ **1** *(person)* essoufflé, hors d'haleine **2** *Elec* **b. fuse** fusible *m* fondu, plomb *m* sauté
▸▸ **b. glass** verre *m* soufflé

blowout ['bləʊaʊt] N **1** *Sl (large meal)* gueuleton *m*, grande bouffe *f*; **we had a b. last night** on a fait un gueuleton hier soir **2** *Aut etc (of tyre)* éclatement *m* **3** *Min etc (of gas, oil etc)* éruption *f* au cours d'un sondage

blowpipe ['bləʊpaɪp] N **1** *(for darts)* sarbacane *f* **2** *Chem, Metal* chalumeau *m*; *(of glassblower)* fêle *f*

blowtorch ['bləʊtɔːtʃ] N *Am* = **blowlamp**

blow-up N **1** *(argument)* dispute *f*, bagarre *f*; *(tantrum)* accès *m* de fureur; **we had a b. last night** on s'est bagarrés *ou* disputés hier soir **2** *Phot* agrandissement *m*

blow-valve N *(on steam boiler)* reniflard *m*

blowy ['bləʊɪ] ADJ *(day, weather)* de (grand) vent

blowzy ['blaʊzɪ] ADJ *(woman)* négligé

blub [blʌb] VI *Fam* (**-bb-**) = **blubber²**

blubber¹ ['blʌbər] N *(of whale)* graisse *f*, lard *m*; *Fam (of person)* graisse

blubber² VI *Fam* chialer, pleurer comme un veau *ou* une madeleine (**over** sur)

blubbering ['blʌbərɪŋ] N larmoiements *mpl*

bludge [blʌdʒ] VI *Austr Fam* **1** *(shirk responsibilities)* se défiler **2** *(cadge)* quémander **3** *(live off the State)* vivre en parasite de la société

bludgeon ['blʌdʒən] N gourdin *m*, matraque *f*
vt matraquer; **he was bludgeoned to death** il a été matraqué à mort; *Fig* **to b. sb into doing sth** forcer qn à faire qch par des méthodes brutales

bludger ['blʌdʒər] N *Austr Fam* **1** *(shirker)* tire-au-flanc *m inv* **2** *(cadger)* pique-assiette *mf inv*; parasite *m* **3** *(who lives off the State)* parasite *m* de la société

blue¹ [bluː] ADJ **1** *(dress, sky etc)* bleu; **to go** *or* **turn b.** *(of sky, litmus paper)* virer au bleu; *(of person)* devenir violacé *ou* bleu; **to go** *or* **turn b. with cold** devenir bleu de froid; **her face was b. with cold** elle avait le visage violacé par le froid *ou* bleu de froid; *Fam* **I've told you until I'm b. in the face** je me tue à te le dire; *Fam* **she can complain until she's b. in the face** elle peut se plaindre autant qu'elle veut; *Fam* **to be in a b. funk** avoir une trouille bleue; *Fam* **to scream** *or* **yell b. murder** crier comme un putois, hurler comme un damné; **once in a b. moon** tous les trente-six du mois; *Fig* **to take a b. pencil to sth** censurer qch; *Am* **to talk a b. streak** tchatcher **2** *Fam (depressed)* triste, déprimé; **to feel b.** avoir le cafard **3** *Fam (indecent) (joke)* grivois, paillard; **to tell b. jokes** en dire de vertes, en raconter des vertes et des pas mûres **4** *Pol* conservateur, -trice
N **1** *(colour)* bleu *m*; *Fig* **a bolt from the b.** un événement imprévu; **her resignation was** *or* **came like a bolt from the b.** sa démission a été une véritable surprise; **he arrived out of the b.** il est arrivé à l'improviste; **his resignation came out of the b.** personne ne s'attendait à ce qu'il démissionne; **you can't just fire him out of the b. like that** tu ne peux pas le renvoyer du jour au lendemain comme ça **2 the blues** *Mus* le blues; *Fam (depression)* le cafard; **to sing the blues** chanter le blues; *Am Fig (complain)* pleurnicher; **to have (a fit of) the blues, to get the blues** avoir le cafard; **this kind of weather gives me the blues** ce temps me donne le cafard **3** *Pol* conservateur, -trice; **a true b.** *(patriot)* un(e) patriote; *Pol* un conservateur, une conservatrice **4** *Sport* **Oxford/Cambridge b.** membre *m* d'une équipe sportive de l'université d'Oxford/de Cambridge **5** *Mil* **the Blues** *Br* la Cavalerie de la Maison du Souverain; *Am Hist* l'armée *f* du Nord
▸▸ *Med* **b. baby** enfant *mf* bleu(e); **b. blood** sang *m* bleu *ou* noble; **b. cheese** (fromage *m*) bleu; **b. chip** *St Exch (stock)* valeur *f* de père de famille *ou* de premier ordre; *Fin (investment)* placement *m* de bon rapport; **b. film** film *m* porno; **b. fox** *(animal)* isatis *m*, renard *m* bleu; *(fur)* renard bleu; **b. movie** film porno; **b. ribbon** *(first prize)* premier prix *m*; **b. rinse** rinçage *m* à reflets bleus; *Zool* **b. whale** baleine *f* bleue

blue² VT *Br Fam* **to b. one's money** claquer

son argent (**on** dans); **don't tell me you've blued the lot!** ne me dis pas que tu as tout claqué!

blue-arsed fly [-ɑːst-] **N** *Br Sl* **to run about** *or* **around like a b.** courir dans tous les sens

Bluebeard ['bluːbɪəd] **N** Barbe-Bleue *m*

bluebell ['bluːbel] **N** *(flower)* jacinthe *f* sauvage *ou* des bois; *Scot (harebell)* campanule *f*

blueberry ['bluːb(ə)rɪ] **N** *(shrub, fruit)* airelle *f*, myrtille *f*, *Can* bleuet *m*

bluebird ['bluːbɜːd] **N** rouge-gorge *m* bleu, *pl* rouges-gorges bleus

blue-black **ADJ** *(hair, plumage)* noir aux reflets bleus; *(sky)* bleu (de) nuit; *(ink, coat)* bleu-noir *inv*

bluebottle ['bluːbɒt(ə)l] **N 1** *(insect)* mouche *f* de la viande **2** *Old-fashioned Br Fam (policeman)* flic *m*

blue-chip **ADJ** *St Exch*
▸▸ **b. company** affaire *f* de premier ordre; **b. stocks, b. shares** valeurs *fpl* de père de famille *ou* de tout repos

blue-collar **ADJ**
▸▸ **b. union** syndicat *m* ouvrier; **b. worker** col *m* bleu

blue-eyed **ADJ** aux yeux bleus; *Br Fam* **his mother's b. boy** le chouchou de sa maman, le petit chéri de sa maman; **the boss's b. boy** le chouchou du patron

bluegrass ['bluːgrɑːs, -æs] **N 1 the B. state** Kentucky **m 2** *Mus* folklore *m* du Kentucky

blue-green **ADJ** bleu-vert *inv*

blueness ['bluːnɪs] **N** bleu *m*

blue-pencil **VT** *Old-fashioned (article)* censurer

blueprint ['bluːprɪnt] **N** plan *m*, *Spec* épure *f*; *Fig* **a b. for success** une recette *ou* une garantie de succès

blue-ribbon **ADJ**
▸▸ *Am* **b. committee** comité *m* constitué par des personnalités; *Sport* **b. event** épreuve *f* phare; *Law* **b. jury** jury *m* d'experts

bluestocking ['bluːstɒkɪŋ] **N** *Pej (woman)* bas-bleu *m*, *pl* bas-bleus

Bluetooth ['bluːtuːθ] **N** *Tel* Bluetooth *m*

bluff[1] [blʌf] **ADJ 1** *(cliff, coast)* escarpé, à pic **2** *(person)* carré et sincère
N *(cliff)* cap *m ou* falaise *f* à pic, à-pic *m inv*

bluff[2] **N 1** *(at poker)* bluff *m*; **to call sb's b.** *(at poker)* inviter qn à mettre cartes sur table; *Fig* prendre qn au mot **2** *(deception)* bluff *m*
VT *Cards etc* bluffer; *Fig* **he bluffed her into agreeing** il a bluffé pour le lui faire accepter
VI bluffer, faire du bluff; *Cards* bluffer
▸ **bluff out** **VT SEP** *(use cleverness)* **to b. one's way out of a tricky situation** se tirer d'affaire par un coup de bluff; **we'll just have to b. it out** nous n'aurons qu'à bluffer

bluffer ['blʌfər] **N** bluffeur, -euse

blunder ['blʌndər] **N** bévue *f*, *Fam* gaffe *f*
VI faire une bévue *ou Fam* une gaffe; **to b. along** avancer d'un pas maladroit; *(in task)* progresser tant bien que mal; **she was blundering about the room** elle avançait dans la pièce en se cognant contre tout ce qu'elle rencontrait; **to b. against** *or* **into sth** heurter qch, se heurter contre *ou* à qch; **to b. against** *or* **into sb** heurter qn; **she blundered into a situation she knew nothing about** elle s'est trouvée prise dans une situation dont elle ignorait tout; **he managed to b. through** il s'en est tiré tant bien que mal; **to b. on the truth/the solution** tomber sur la vérité/la solution par accident

blunderbuss ['blʌndəbʌs] **N** *Hist* tromblon *m*

blunderer ['blʌndərər] **N** gaffeur, -euse

blundering ['blʌndərɪŋ] **ADJ** maladroit
N maladresse *f*

blunt [blʌnt] **ADJ 1** *(knife, cutting edge etc)* émoussé; *(pencil)* mal taillé; *Law (instrument)* contondant **2** *Fig (person)* brusque, carré; *(question)* brusque; *(reply)* carré; *(fact)* brutal, -aux; *(refusal)* net, carré; **to be b., ...** pour parler franchement, ...
VT 1 *(knife etc)* émousser; *(pencil)* épointer **2** *Fig (sb's feelings, anger)* émousser

bluntly ['blʌntlɪ] **ADV** *(to ask)* brusquement; *(to reply)* carrément, brutalement; **to put it b., ...** (pour parler) franchement, ...; **to speak b.** parler net *ou* carrément

bluntness ['blʌntnɪs] **N 1** *(of knife, sword etc)* manque *m* de tranchant; **because of the b. of the pencil** parce que le crayon n'avait pas de pointe **2** *Fig (of person)* brusquerie *f*; *(of question, manner, attitude)* rudesse *f*

blur [blɜːr] **N** *(vague shape)* forme *f* confuse; *Phot* flou *m*; **without my glasses, everything is a b.** sans mes lunettes, je suis complètement dans le brouillard; *Fig* **it's all a b. now** *(of past events)* ce n'est plus qu'un vague souvenir; **her memories were a b.** ses souvenirs étaient très vagues; **the first years of her marriage had gone by in a b.** les premières années de son mariage étaient passées à toute vitesse; **when travelling at such speeds, the countryside is little more than a b.** quand on avance à une telle vitesse, le paysage n'est qu'une suite de formes confuses
VT (-rr-) **1** *(make hazy)* brouiller, troubler; **eyes blurred with tears** yeux voilés *ou* brouillés de larmes; **the haze has blurred the outline of the mountain** la brume a estompé les contours de la montagne; **time had blurred the memory** le souvenir était devenu confus avec le temps **2** *(smear)* *(with ink etc)* barbouiller; *Typ* maculer, mâchurer
VI 1 *(become hazy)* **her memories had blurred with time** ses souvenirs s'étaient estompés avec le temps **2** *(smear) (of ink)* s'estomper

blurb [blɜːb] **N** notice *f* publicitaire; *(on book)* promotion *f* (en quatrième de couverture); *(on front page of paper etc)* accroche *f*

blurred [blɜːd] **ADJ** *(photograph)* flou; *(contours)* indécis, flou, estompé; *(memories)* confus, vague
▸▸ *Med* **b. vision** vue *f* trouble; **to have b. vision** voir trouble

blurring ['blɜːrɪŋ] **N** *Phot* flou *m*

▸ **blurt out** [blɜːt] **VT SEP** *(secret)* lâcher étourdiment, laisser échapper; **'he's dead,' she blurted out** 'il est mort,' a-t-elle lâché

blush [blʌʃ] **N 1** *(of shyness, shame)* rougeur *f*; **a b. rose to her cheeks** le sang lui est monté au visage; **to hide one's blushes** baisser les yeux d'embarras; **to bring a b. to sb's cheeks** faire rougir qn; *Lit* **the first b. of dawn** les premières rougeurs de l'aube **2** *Fml* **at first b.** à l'abord, au premier abord
VI *(of person)* rougir; **he blushed at the thought** il rougit à cette pensée; **to b. for** *or* **with shame** rougir de honte; **to b. crimson** devenir cramoisi; **to b. to the roots of one's hair** rougir jusqu'à la racine des cheveux; *Fig* **to b. to admit sth** rougir de devoir admettre qch
▸▸ **b. wine** vin *m* rosé très léger

blusher ['blʌʃər] **N** *(for face)* blush *m*, fard *m* à joues

blushing ['blʌʃɪŋ] **ADJ** *(person)* rougissant; **the b. bride** la mariée
N rougissement *m*

bluster ['blʌstər] **N** *(of storm)* fureur *f*, fracas *m*; *Fig* **I wasn't impressed by his b.** ses grands cris ne m'impressionnaient pas; **his threats were no more than b.** ses menaces fulminantes n'étaient en fait que du vent

VI *(of wind)* souffler en rafales; *Fig (speak aggressively)* fanfaronner
▸ **bluster out** **VT SEP** **to b. one's way out of a situation** se sortir d'une situation en fanfaronnant; **to b. it out** s'en sortir en fanfaronnant

blustering ['blʌstərɪŋ] **ADJ** *(wind)* violent; *Fig (person, tone)* fanfaron
N fanfaronnade(s) *f(pl)*

blustery ['blʌst(ə)rɪ] **ADJ** *(wind)* violent; *(day)* de (grand) vent

blvd *(abbr* **boulevard***)* boul, bd

BMA [biːemˈeɪ] **N** *(abbr* **British Medical Association***)* ≃ ordre *m* des médecins

B-movie **N** film *m* de série B; **he was a B. actor** c'était un acteur de série B

BO [biːˈəʊ] **N** *Fam (abbr* **body odour***)* = odeur *f* corporelle; **to have BO** sentir (la transpiration), sentir mauvais

boa ['bəʊə] **N** *(snake)* boa *m*; **feather b.** *(scarf)* boa
▸▸ *Zool* **b. constrictor** (boa) constricteur *m*

boar [bɔːr] **N** *(animal)* verrat *m*; **wild b.** sanglier *m*; *(young)* marcassin *m*
▸▸ *Culin* **b.'s head** hure *f* de sanglier; **b. hunting** chasse *f* au sanglier

board [bɔːd] **N 1** *(plank)* planche *f*; *(thick)* madrier *m*; *(for bread)* planche à (couper le) pain; *(for notices)* panneau *m* de publicité *ou* d'affichage; *(inscribed with information)* écriteau *m*; *Sch* **to write sth on the b.** écrire qch au tableau; *Theat Old-fashioned, Hum* **the boards** les planches
2 *Admin etc* conseil *m*, comité *m*, commission *f*; **b. (of directors)** *(of company)* conseil d'administration; **to be on the b.** *(of company)* faire partie *ou* être membre du conseil d'administration; **advisory b.** comité consultatif; **disciplinary b.** conseil de discipline; **medical b.** conseil de santé
3 *(table)* table *f*; *(food)* table, nourriture *f*; **b. and lodging** pension *f* complète; **full b.** pension complète; *Fig* **to sweep the b.** faire table rase
4 *(for draughts)* damier *m*; *(for chess)* échiquier *m*
5 *Aviat, Naut* **on b.** à bord; **to take goods on b.** embarquer des marchandises; *Fig* **to take on b.** *(work, responsibility)* accepter; *(problem)* assumer; *(comments)* prendre note de; **to go on b.** monter à bord, s'embarquer; *Fig* **to go by the b.** *(of plan, hopes etc)* être abandonné; *(of reputation)* être perdu; *Fig* **to let sth go by the b.** abandonner qch, laisser tomber qch
6 *(in bookbinding) (cardboard)* carton *m*; **the boards** *(of book)* les plats *mpl*; **in paper boards** cartonné; **limp boards** cartonnage *m* souple
7 *Am TV etc* console *f*
8 *Comput (in PC)* carte *f*, *(in mainframe)* panneau *m*; **on b.** installé
VT 1 *(of passengers) (ship, plane)* aller *ou* monter à bord de; *(train, bus)* monter dans; *Naut (come alongside)* aborder, accoster; *Admin (ship) (for inspection)* arraisonner
2 *(book)* cartonner
VI 1 *(lodge)* être en pension; **I b. at Mrs Brown's** *or* **with Mrs Brown** je suis en pension chez Mme Brown; *Sch* **he'll start boarding when he's twelve** à douze ans, il ira en pension
2 *Aviat* **flight 123 is now boarding** l'embarquement a commencé pour le vol 123
▸▸ **b. of enquiry** commission d'enquête; **b. of examiners** jury *m* d'examen; **b. game** jeu *m* de société; *Com* **b. meeting** réunion *f* du conseil d'administration; *Com* **b. member** membre *m* du conseil d'administration; *Com* **the B. of Trade** *(in UK)* le ministère du Commerce; *(in US)* la chambre de

commerce; **b. of trustees** conseil de gestion; *TV* **b. test** animatique *f*
▸ **board in** VT SEP = **board up**
▸ **board out** VT SEP *(children)* mettre en pension
▸ **board up** VT SEP *(door, window)* condamner

boarder ['bɔːdər] N **1** *(lodger)* pensionnaire *mf*; *Sch* interne *mf*; **she takes in boarders** elle prend des pensionnaires **2** *Naut* abordeur *m*

boarding ['bɔːdɪŋ] N **1** *Naut, Aviat* embarquement *m*; *Naut (for inspection)* arraisonnement *m*; *Naut (by pirates, enemy)* abordage *m*; **flight 123 is now ready for b.** le vol 123 est maintenant prêt pour l'embarquement; *Aviat* **in preparation for b., please extinguish all cigarettes** veuillez éteindre vos cigarettes en vue de l'embarquement **2** *Sch* pensionnat *m*
▸ ▸ *Aviat* **b. bridge** (pré-)passerelle *f*; *Aviat* **b. card** carte *f* d'embarquement; *Aviat* **b. gate** porte *f* d'embarquement; **b. house** pension *f*; *Sch* internat *m*; **b. kennels** *(for dogs)* = chenil *m* où l'on peut faire garder les chiens pendant les vacances; **b. party** *Naut (for inspection)* détachement *m* de visite; *(of pirates, enemy)* détachement d'abordage; *Aviat* **b. pass** carte d'embarquement; **b. school** internat, pensionnat *m*

Boarding Schools
Les "boarding schools", traditionnellement réservées à la progéniture de la haute bourgeoisie, existent en Grande-Bretagne depuis des siècles et furent pendant très longtemps caractérisées par une discipline stricte et un confort rudimentaire. Aujourd'hui, même si les "boarding schools" prônent toujours des valeurs traditionnelles elles ont dû s'adapter à la société moderne. Elles sont maintenant très souvent mixtes et acceptent des pensionnaires d'origine sociale un peu plus variée ainsi qu'un nombre croissant d'internes à la semaine.

---

boardroom ['bɔːdruːm] N salle *f* de réunion *(du conseil d'administration)* ; **there is uncertainty in boardrooms across the country** l'incertitude règne au sein des conseils d'administration de toutes les entreprises du pays; **to be promoted to the b.** être promu au conseil d'administration

boardwalk ['bɔːdwɔːk] N *Am* = passage *m* ou trottoir *m* fait de planches de bois (au bord de la mer); **on the b.** sur les planches

boast [bəʊst] N vantardise *f*; **it is their b. that ...** ils se vantent que ...; **it was her proud b. that she had read ...** elle se vantait d'avoir lu ...; **it turned out to be no more than an empty b.** finalement, ce n'était que des fanfaronnades
▸ VI se vanter (*of* or *about* sth de qch); **without wishing to b., I ...** sans vouloir me vanter, je ...; **that's nothing to b. about** il n'y a pas de quoi se vanter
▸ VT **1** *(to claim)* **he boasted that he could beat me** il s'est vanté de pouvoir me battre **2** *(to take pride in)* **the school boasts a fine library** l'école est fière de posséder une belle bibliothèque; **the entire town boasts just one pub** il n'y a qu'un seul pub dans toute la ville

boaster ['bəʊstər] N vantard, -arde, fanfaron, -onne

boastful ['bəʊstfʊl] ADJ vantard, fanfaron

boastfully ['bəʊstfʊlɪ] ADV avec vantardise

boasting ['bəʊstɪŋ] N vantardise *f*

boat [bəʊt] N **1** *Naut* bateau *m*; *(small)* canot *m*, embarcation *f*; **I came by b.** je suis venu en bateau *ou* par (le) bateau; *Fig* **we're all in the same b.** nous sommes tous dans le

---

même cas *ou* logés à la même enseigne; **b. stations!** à vos postes d'abandon! **2** *(for sauce, gravy)* saucière *f*
▸ VI se promener en bateau; *(in rowing boat etc)* canoter, faire du canotage
▸ ▸ *Naut* **b. deck** pont *m* des embarcations; *Naut* **b. drill** manœuvres *fpl* d'évacuation; **b. neck** *(on dress, jumper)* encolure *f* bateau; *Hist* **b. people** boat people *mpl*; **b. race** *(event)* course *f* d'avirons; *Naut* régates *fpl*; *Br Sl (face)* visage *m*; **b. train** = train *m* qui assure la correspondance avec un bateau

boatbuilder ['bəʊtbɪldər] N constructeur *m* de bateaux

boater ['bəʊtər] N *(hat)* canotier *m*

boathook ['bəʊthʊk] N gaffe *f*

boathouse ['bəʊthaʊs] N hangar *m* à bateaux

boating ['bəʊtɪŋ] N canotage *m*; **to go b.** faire du canotage
▸ ▸ **b. accident** accident *m* de bateau; **b. holiday** vacances *fpl* en bateau; **b. song** barcarolle *f*

boatload ['bəʊtləʊd] N *(of wood, cars, fruit etc)* cargaison *f*; **six boatloads of refugees** six bateaux pleins de réfugiés; **to arrive by the b.** arriver par bateaux entiers

boatman, *pl* **boatmen** ['bəʊtmən, -men] N **1** *(operator)* passeur *m* **2** *(renter)* loueur *m* de canots

boatswain ['bəʊs(ə)n] N *Naut* maître *m* d'équipage, maître principal de manœuvre, bosco *m*

boatyard ['bəʊtjɑːd] N chantier *m* de construction pour canots et bateaux de plaisance

Bob [bɒb] N *Fam* **and B.'s your uncle!** et ça y est!, et voilà (le travail)!

bob¹ [bɒb] N **1** *(sudden movement)* petit coup *m* **2** *(curtsey)* petite révérence *f* **3** *(on pendulum)* lentille *f*, *(on plumb line)* plomb *m*; *(on end of kite tail)* poids *m*; *(on fishing line)* bouchon *m*
▸ VT **to b. a curtsey** faire une petite révérence
▸ VI s'agiter; **bobbing for apples** = à Hallowe'en, jeu *m* consistant à essayer d'attraper avec les dents des pommes flottant dans une bassine d'eau; **to b. down** se baisser subitement; **to b. up** surgir brusquement; *Fig* réapparaître d'une façon inattendue; **to b. up and down** *(in one's seat)* s'agiter; **to b. up and down in the water** danser sur l'eau; **to b. under** *(of fisherman's float)* plonger

bob² N *(hairstyle)* (coupe *f* au) carré *m*; **to wear one's hair in a b.** avoir les cheveux coupés au carré; **to have a b.** avoir une coupe au carré, avoir un carré
▸ VT (-bb-) **to have one's hair bobbed** se faire couper les cheveux au carré

bob³ N INV *Br Old-fashioned Fam (shilling)* shilling *m*; **that must cost a few b.** ça ne doit pas être donné; **he's not short of a b. or two** il n'est pas dans l'indigence, il a de quoi

bob⁴ N *Sport (sleigh)* bob(sleigh) *m*

bobbin ['bɒbɪn] N **1** *Tex (for shuttle)* bobine *f*, *(for lace)* fuseau *m* **2** *Elec* corps *m* de bobine
▸ ▸ *Tex* **b. frame** bobinoir *m*; *Tex* **b. winder** bobineuse *f*

bobble ['bɒb(ə)l] N *Fam (on hat etc)* pompon *m*

bobby ['bɒbɪ] N *Old-fashioned Br Fam (policeman)* flic *m*; **we need more bobbies on the beat** il nous faut plus de policiers dans le quartier
▸ ▸ *Am* **b. pin** pince *f* à cheveux; **b. socks** socquettes *fpl*

bobby-dazzler [-'dæzlər] N *Old-fashioned Br Fam (girl)* jolie fille *f*; **his new car's a b.** sa nouvelle voiture est vraiment extra

---

bobbysoxer ['bɒbɪsɒksər] N *Old-fashioned Am Fam* = jeune fille *f* portant socquettes et jupe ample, à la mode des années 50

bobcat ['bɒbkæt] N *Am (animal)* lynx *m* rufus

bobo ['bəʊbəʊ] N *Fam (abbr* **bohemian bourgeois**) bobo *mf*

bobsled ['bɒbsled], **bobsleigh** ['bɒbsleɪ] N bobsleigh *m*, *Fam* bob *m*
▸ VI faire du bobsleigh *ou Fam* du bob
▸ ▸ **b. race** course *f* de bobsleigh

bobtail ['bɒbteɪl] N **1** *(of horse, dog)* queue *f* écourtée **2** *(dog)* bobtail *m*

bock [bɒk] N *(glass)* bock *m*; *Am (beer)* bière *f* brune (allemande)
▸ ▸ *Am* **b. beer** bière brune (allemande)

bod [bɒd] N **1** *Br Fam (fellow)* type *m*; **any old b. can do it** n'importe quel péquenaud peut le faire **2** *Fam (body)* corps *m*; **what a great b. he's got!** il est vachement bien (foutu)!

bode [bəʊd] VI **to b. well/ill** être de bon/de mauvais augure (*for* pour)
▸ VT *Arch, Lit* présager

bodge [bɒdʒ] VT *Fam (piece of work)* bousiller, saboter; **to b. sth up** *(make temporary or unskilful repair)* rafistoler qch, faire une réparation de fortune sur qch

bodice ['bɒdɪs] N *(of dress)* corsage *m*
▸ ▸ **b. ripper** = roman *m* grivois à trame historique

-bodied ['bɒdɪd] SUFF **a large-/slender-b. man** un homme au corps gros/svelte; **a full-b. wine** un vin robuste

bodily ['bɒdɪlɪ] ADJ corporel, physique; **to be in b. fear of sb** craindre d'être attaqué par qn
▸ ADV **1** *(forcibly)* **he was carried b. to the door** on l'a saisi (à bras-le-corps) et transporté jusqu'à la porte; **they hurled him b. through the window** ils le saisirent à bras-le-corps et le firent sortir par la fenêtre sans ménagement **2** *(as whole)* entièrement, en masse
▸ ▸ **b. functions** fonctions *fpl* corporelles; **b. needs** besoins *mpl* matériels; **b. strength** force *f* physique

bodkin ['bɒdkɪn] N *(for threading)* passe-lacet *m*, *pl* passe-lacets; *(for piercing)* poinçon *m*

body ['bɒdɪ] N **1** *(of person, animal)* corps *m*; *(dead body)* cadavre *m*, corps; *Fig* **to throw oneself b. and soul into sth** se jeter corps et âme dans qch; *Fig* **to have just enough to keep b. and soul together** avoir tout juste de quoi vivre; *Fam* **(it'll be) over my dead b.!** plutôt crever!; **if he comes into this house, it'll be over my dead b.!** il faudra qu'il me passe sur le corps s'il veut rentrer dans cette maison!; **this obsession with the b. beautiful** cette obsession que tout le monde a d'avoir un corps parfait
  2 *(of wine)* corps *m*; *(of hair)* volume *m*; *Mus* **to give b. to the tone** nourrir le son
  3 *(group)* corps *m*; *(organization)* organisme *m*; *(of laws)* recueil *m*; *(of water)* étendue *f*, **large b. of people** foule *f* nombreuse, assistance *f* nombreuse; **there is a large b. of support for the policy** un grand nombre de personnes sont en faveur de cette politique; **b. of troops** troupe *f* armée; **the main b.** *(of employees, refugees etc)* la majeure partie; *Mil* le gros des troupes; **to come in a b.** venir en masse; *Old-fashioned* **learned b.** corps savant; **public b.** corporation *f*
  4 *(main part)* *(of document, building etc)* corps *m*; *(of church)* nef *f*; *(of musical instrument)* coffre *m*; *(of plane)* fuselage *m*; *(of pram)* nacelle *f*; *Law* **the b. of evidence** l'ensemble *m* des preuves
  5 *Aut* carrosserie *f*

6 *Phys etc* corps *m*; *Astron* **heavenly b.** corps céleste, astre *m*
7 *(underwear)* body *m*
►► **b. bag** sac *m* mortuaire; *Boxing* **b. blow** coup *m* dur; **to be a real b. blow to sb's hopes** être un véritable coup porté aux espoirs de qn; *Sport* **b. builder** culturiste *mf*; *Sport* **b. building** culturisme *m*; **b. clock** horloge *f* interne *ou* biologique; *Pol* **b. corporate** personne *f* morale; **b. count** pertes *fpl* en vies humaines; *Cin* **b. double** doublure *f*, *Psy* **b. dysmorphic disorder** dysmorphophobie *f*, **b. language** attitude *f*, **b. lotion** lait *m* corporel; **b. odour** odeur *f* corporelle; *Aut* **b. panel** panneau *m* de carrosserie; **b. part** *Aut* pièce *f* de carrosserie; *(of person)* partie *f* de corps humain; **b. piercing** piercing *m*; *Aut* **b. platform** plate-forme *f*, *pl* plates-formes; *Pol* **b. politic** corps politique; **b. popper** smurfer, -euse; **b. popping** smurf *m*; *Aut* **b. repair centre** atelier *m* (de réparation) de carrosserie; *Aut* **b. roll** roulis *m* de la caisse, mouvement *m* de caisse; **b. scrub** produit *m* exfoliant pour le corps; *Typ* **b. setting** composition *f* (des caractères); **b. shop** *Aut (for vehicles)* atelier *m* de carrosserie; *Am Fam (gym)* club *m* de gym; *Typ* **b. size** taille *f* de corps; *Hist* **b. snatcher** déterreur, -euse de cadavres; **b. stocking** body; **b. swerve** feinte *f*, **b. warmer** gilet *m* matelassé

bodycheck ['bɒdɪtʃek] **N** *Sport (in ice hockey)* interception *f*, *(in wrestling)* coup *m* de bélier
VT *Sport (in ice hockey, football)* intercepter

bodyguard ['bɒdɪgɑːd] **N 1** *(individual)* garde *m* du corps, *Fam* gorille *m* **2** *(no pl) (group)* gardes *mpl* du corps

bodylock ['bɒdɪlɒk] **N** *Aut* **b. seat restraint** blocage *m* de maintien du corps

bodyshell ['bɒdɪʃel] **N** *Aut* caisse *f*, coque *f*, carcasse *f*

body-surf **VI** body-surfer

body-surfer **N** body-surfe(u)r, -euse, *pl* body-surfe(u)rs, -euses

body-surfing **N** body-surfing *m*

bodywork ['bɒdɪwɜːk] **N** *Aut* **1** *(structure)* carrosserie *f* **2** *(repairs)* travail *m* de carrosserie

Boer [bɔːr] **ADJ** boer; **the B. War** la guerre des Boers
N Boer *mf*

boffin ['bɒfɪn] **N** *Br Fam Hum* savant *m*

bog [bɒg] **N 1** *(marsh)* marécage *m*; **peat b.** tourbière *f* **2** *Br Fam (lavatory)* chiottes *fpl*, gogs *mpl*, gogues *mpl*
►► *Br Fam* **b. brush** brosse *f* à chiottes; *Br Fam* **b. paper** PQ *m*; *Br Fam* **b. roll** *(roll)* rouleau *m* de PQ; *(paper)* PQ; *Br Fam* **b. seat** cuvette *f* des chiottes
► **bog down** **VT SEP** *(usu passive)* **to get bogged down** *(of car etc)* s'embourber, s'enliser, s'enfoncer dans une fondrière; *Fam (of person, discussion etc)* s'enliser; **don't let's get bogged down in details** ne nous perdons pas dans les détails
► **bog off** **VI** *Br Sl* dégager; **oh, b. off!** *(go away)* dégage!; *(expressing contempt, disagreement)* va te faire voir!

bogey ['bəʊgɪ] **N 1** *(source of fear)* spectre *m*, hantise *f*, **unionization is the b. of the company** la syndicalisation est la hantise de la société **2** *Fam (source of bad luck)* chose *f* qui porte malheur; *(cause of worry)* bête *f* noire **3** *Fam (in nose)* crotte *f* de nez **4** *Golf* bogey *m* **5** *(spirit)* fantôme *m*, spectre *m* *(effrayant)*; *Arch (devil)* diable *m*
VT *Golf* **to b. a hole** jouer un trou en un coup au-dessus du par

bogeyman, *pl* **bogeymen** ['bəʊgɪmæn, -men] **N** **the b.** le croque-mitaine, *pl* croque-mitaines, le Père fouettard; **the b. will get you** le Père fouettard va venir te chercher

boggle ['bɒg(ə)l] **VI 1 to b. at doing sth** rechigner à faire qch **2 the mind boggles** ça laisse rêveur
VT it boggles the mind *or* **the imagination** ça laisse rêveur

boggy ['bɒgɪ] **ADJ** marécageux

bogie ['bəʊgɪ] **N** *Rail* bog(g)ie *m*

bog-standard **ADJ** *Br Fam* tout simple

bog-trotter **N** *Sl* **1** *Offensive (Irish person)* Irlandais, -aise **2** *(country bumpkin)* plouc *m*, péquenaud *m*

bogus ['bəʊgəs] **ADJ 1** *(fake)* faux, *f* fausse; **he's completely b.** *(not genuine in feelings etc)* c'est un faux jeton **2** *Am Sl (unfashionable)* ringard
►► *Com* **b. company** société *f* fantôme

Bohemia [bəʊ'hiːmɪə] **N 1** *Geog* Bohême *f* **2** *(unconventional life)* (vie *f* de) bohème *f*

Bohemian [bəʊ'hiːmɪən] **ADJ 1** *Geog* bohémien **2** *Fig (life etc)* de bohème
N 1 *Geog* Bohémien, -ienne **2** *(unconventional person)* bohème *mf*, *(gipsy)* bohémien, -ienne

boil [bɔɪl] **N to come to the b.** *(of water etc)* commencer à bouillir, arriver à ébullition; **let the water come to a** *or* **the b.** attendre que l'eau arrive à ébullition; **the water is on the b.** l'eau bout; **to bring the water to the b.** amener l'eau à l'ébullition; *Fig* **their romance has gone off the b.** leur histoire tourne au ralenti, leur histoire ne marche plus très fort; **to go off the b.** *(of athlete, actor etc)* perdre son entrain
VI 1 *(of liquid)* bouillir; *(violently)* bouillonner; **to begin to b.** arriver à ébullition; *Culin* **allow to b. gently** laissez mijoter; **to let the kettle b. dry** laisser évaporer complètement l'eau de la bouilloire; **the kettle's boiling** l'eau bout dans la bouilloire; **are the potatoes boiling?** est-ce que les pommes de terre bouillent?; *Fam* **to keep the pot boiling** *(bring in enough money)* faire bouillir la marmite; **it makes me** *or* **my blood b.!** ça me met hors de moi!; **to b. with rage** bouillir de colère; *Fam* **I'm boiling!** *(very hot)* je crève de chaleur *ou* de chaud! **2** *Lit (of sea)* bouillonner
VT 1 *(liquid)* faire bouillir; *Culin (potatoes, vegetables, meat)* faire cuire à l'eau; *(sugar)* cuire; **to b. the kettle** *(by gas)* mettre la bouilloire sur le feu; *(by electricity)* brancher la bouilloire; **to b. an egg** faire cuire un œuf à la coque; *Hum* **he can't b. an egg** *(does not know how to cook)* il n'est même pas capable de faire cuire un œuf; *Sl* **go (and) b. your head!** va te faire cuire un œuf! **2** *(in papermaking) (fibres)* décreuser
► **boil away** **VI 1** *(go on boiling)* continuer à bouillir **2** *(evaporate)* s'évaporer
► **boil down** **VT SEP** *(solution)* réduire; *(syrup etc)* (faire) réduire; *Fig (article)* condenser
VI *(of sauce etc)* se réduire
► **boil down to** **VT INSEP** *Fam* se ramener *ou* se résumer *ou* revenir à; **what her story boils down to is that ...** ce à quoi se résume son histoire, c'est que ...; **this is what it all boils down to** voilà à quoi cela revient *ou* se résume
► **boil over** **VI 1** *(of liquid)* déborder, *Fam* se sauver; *(of pot)* déborder **2** *Fam (become angry)* exploser (de colère) **3** *(worsen)* empirer; **the dispute is in danger of boiling over into a strike** le conflit risque de virer à la grève
► **boil up** **VT SEP** *(water, milk)* faire bouillir
VI *(of water, milk)* monter

boil² **N** *Med* furoncle *m*

boiled [bɔɪld] **ADJ** bouilli; *Culin* cuit à l'eau
►► *Culin* **b. egg** œuf *m* à la coque; *Culin* **b. ham** jambon *m* blanc; *Culin* **b. potatoes** pommes *fpl* de terre à l'eau *ou* bouillies; *Br* **b. sweet** bonbon *m* à sucer

boiler ['bɔɪlər] **N 1** chaudière *f*, *Culin* **double b.** bain-marie *m*, *pl* bains-marie **2** *Culin* poule *f* (à la casserole) **3** *Sl Pej* **(old) b.** *(woman)* vieille peau *f*
►► **b. maker** chaudronnier *m*; **b. room** *(in building)* salle *f* des chaudières, chaufferie *f*, *Naut (in boat)* chaufferie, chambre *f* de chauffe; *Am Fin* = organisation *f* qui vend illégalement au public des produits financiers très spéculatifs ou sans valeur; *Br Ind* **b. suit** *(for work)* bleu(s) *m(pl)* (de travail); *(fashion garment)* salopette *f*

boilerman, *pl* **boilermen** ['bɔɪləmən, -men] **N** chauffeur *m*

boiling ['bɔɪlɪŋ] **ADJ 1** *(water)* bouillant **2** *Lit (sea)* bouillonnant
ADV *Fam* **b. hot** bouillant; *Fam* **it's been a b. hot day** il a fait une chaleur à crever aujourd'hui; *Fam* **I'm b. hot** je crève de chaleur *ou* de chaud
N bouillonnement *m*, ébullition *f*
►► **b. point** point *m* d'ébullition

boiling-water reactor **N** *Nucl* réacteur *m* à eau bouillante

boil-in-the-bag **ADJ** *Culin (rice etc)* en sachet de cuisson

boink [bɔɪŋk] *Am Fam* **N to have a b.** *(have sex)* faire une partie de jambes en l'air
VT s'envoyer en l'air avec
VI faire une partie de jambes en l'air

boisterous ['bɔɪst(ə)rəs] **ADJ** *(person) (noisy)* bruyant, tapageur; *(unruly)* turbulent; *(wind)* violent; *(sea)* tumultueux; **b. spirits** gaieté *f* débordante *ou* tapageuse

boisterously ['bɔɪst(ə)rəslɪ] **ADV** bruyamment

boisterousness ['bɔɪst(ə)rəsnɪs] **N** turbulence *f*, agitation *f*

bold [bəʊld] **ADJ 1** *(fearless, confident)* hardi; *(tone, look)* assuré, confiant; *(audacious) (move, plan, thinker)* audacieux; **to put on a b. front** *or* **face, to put a b. front** *or* **face on it** faire bonne figure
2 *(impudent)* impudent, effronté; *Old-fashioned, Hum* **if I may be** *or* **make so b.** si je puis me permettre; **she made so b. as to ask what my salary was** elle a eu l'effronterie de me demander combien je gagnais; *Fam* **as b. as brass** *(to do sth)* avec un culot pas possible; **he's as b. as brass** il a un culot pas possible
3 *(strong, distinctive) (style, brushstrokes)* nerveux, vigoureux; **b. colours** couleurs *fpl* vives; **b. features** traits *mpl* accusés
4 *Typ* gras
N *Typ* **in b.** en gras
►► *Typ* **b. character** caractère *m* gras; *Typ* **b. face** caractères gras; *Typ* **b. italics** caractères italiques gras; *Typ* **b. print, b. type** caractères gras

boldly ['bəʊldlɪ] **ADV 1** *(confidently, fearlessly)* hardiment; *(audaciously)* audacieusement; **to state sth b.** affirmer qch avec assurance; **to deal with sth b.** *(subject, problem etc)* traiter qch de façon directe **2** *(impudently)* effrontément, avec impudence **3** *Art* avec vigueur

boldness ['bəʊldnɪs] **N 1** *(fearlessness)* hardiesse *f*, *(audacity)* audace *f* **2** *(impudence)* effronterie *f*, impudence *f* **3** *Art (of style, brushstrokes)* nervosité *f*, vigueur *f*

bole [bəʊl] **N** *(of tree)* fût *m*, tronc *m*

bolero [bə'leərəʊ] **N 1** *(dance, music)* boléro *m* **2** *(also* ['bɒlərəʊ]*) (jacket)* boléro *m*

boletus [bə'liːtəs] **N** *(fungus)* bolet *m*

Bolivia [bə'lɪvɪə] **N** Bolivie *f*

Bolivian [bə'lɪvɪən] **ADJ** bolivien
N Bolivien, -ienne

boll [bəʊl] **N** *Bot (of cotton, linen)* capsule *f* *(du cotonnier)*
►► *Entom* **b. weevil** anthonome *m* *(du cotonnier)*

bollard [ˈbɒlɑːd] N **1** *Naut (for mooring)* bitte *f* **2** *Br (in road)* borne *f*

bollocking [ˈbɒləkɪŋ] N *Sl (reprimand)* engueulade *f*; **he got a b. from the boss** il s'est fait engueuler par le patron

bollocks [ˈbɒləks] NPL *Vulg* couilles *fpl*; **b.!** c'est des conneries!; **oh, b., I've got no money on me!** quelle merde *ou* quelle connerie, je n'ai pas d'argent sur moi!
► **bollocks up** VT SEP *Vulg* bousiller

Bollywood [ˈbɒlɪwʊd] N *Cin* = appellation *f* humoristique de l'industrie du film en Inde, formée à partir de Bombay (où sont produits la plupart des films) et Hollywood

Bologna [bəˈlɒnjə] N Bologne

Bolognese [bɒləˈniːz, -eɪz] ADJ bolognais N Bolognais, -aise

boloney [bəˈləʊnɪ] N = baloney

Bolshevik [ˈbɒlʃəvɪk], **Bolshevist** [ˈbɒlʃəvɪst] ADJ, N bolchevik *mf*, bolcheviste *mf*

Bolshevism [ˈbɒlʃəvɪz(ə)m] N bolchevisme *m*

bolshie, bolshy [ˈbɒlʃɪ] *Fam* ADJ **he's b.** c'est un mauvais coucheur; **he turned b.** il a commencé à râler; **she's in a b. mood** elle est de très mauvais poil; **she was a bit b. about going to school** elle a un peu rechigné pour aller à l'école
N *Pol Old-fashioned* rouge *mf*

bolster [ˈbəʊlstər] N *(pillow)* traversin *m*
VT *(strengthen)* **to b. sb's confidence** redonner de la confiance à qn; **it bolstered his ego** ça a fait du bien à son amour-propre; **to b. one's courage** se donner du courage
► **bolster up** VT SEP *Fig (regime, government)* appuyer, soutenir; *(theory)* étayer; **he bolstered himself up with a few drinks** il a bu quelques verres pour se donner du courage; **bolstered up by recent successes** fort de ses récents succès; *Fin* **to b. up the pound** soutenir la livre

bolt [bɒlt, bəʊlt] N **1** *(closing device) (for door etc)* verrou *m*; *(of lock)* pêne *m*
2 *Tech (for nut)* boulon *m*
3 *Fam (rush)* **to make a b. for it** décamper, déguerpir; **he tried to make a b. for it** il a essayé de se tailler; **she made a b. for the door** elle s'est précipitée vers la porte
4 *Met* **a b. of lightning** la foudre; *Fig* **it was** *or* **came like a b. from the blue** ce fut comme un coup de foudre
5 *(roll)* **a b. of cloth** une coupe de tissu
6 *Arch (of crossbow)* carreau *m*; *Fig* **he's shot his b.** *(is exhausted)* il est épuisé; *(of politician etc)* il a joué sa dernière carte
VT **1** *(close) (door etc)* verrouiller **2** *Tech (join)* boulonner, cheviller; **to be bolted to the floor** être fixé au sol par des boulons **3** *Fam (eat quickly) (one's dinner etc)* avaler à toute vitesse, engloutir
VI **1** *(of door etc)* se verrouiller **2** *(of horse)* s'emballer, prendre le mors aux dents; *Fam (of person)* décamper, déguerpir **3** *(of plant)* monter en graine
ADV **b. upright** droit comme un piquet
► ► **b. hole** abri *m*, refuge *m*
► **bolt down** VT INSEP *(stairs, street)* dévaler
VT SEP **to b. down one's food** *or* **a meal** manger avec un lance-pierres; **don't b. your food down** ne mange pas si vite
► **bolt in** VI *(enter quickly)* entrer comme un bolide
VT SEP *(lock in)* enfermer (au verrou)
► **bolt out** VI *(leave quickly)* sortir comme un bolide; **they bolted out of the door** ils sont sortis comme des bolides
VT SEP *(lock out)* enfermer dehors

bomb [bɒm] N *Mil etc* bombe *f*; **the b.** *(atom bomb)* la bombe atomique; **to release** *or* **drop a b.** lâcher *ou* larguer une bombe; *Fam* **this room looks as if a b.'s hit it** cette pièce est un véritable champ de bataille; *Br Fam* **to go like a b.** *(of car)* être une vraie fusée; *(of party)* être génial; *(of play, show etc)* casser la baraque, marcher très bien; *Am* **it's a b.** *(of musical, play etc)* c'est un fiasco *ou* un flop; *Fam* **it costs a b.** ça coûte les yeux de la tête; *Fam* **to make a b.** se faire un fric fou
VT **1** *(town etc)* bombarder, lancer des bombes sur; *Sl* **to b. the hell** *or* **shit out of a place** pilonner un endroit **2** *Am Fam (fail) (test)* se planter complètement à
VI *Am Fam (of play etc)* faire un flop; *(of student)* se planter complètement
► ► **b. attack** bombardement *m*; *Aviat* **b. bay** soute *f* à bombes; **b. crater** entonnoir *m*, cratère *m*; *Mil* **b. disposal** déminage *m*; *Mil* **b. expert** démineur *m*; **b. hoax** fausse alerte *f* à la bombe; **b. scare** alerte à la bombe; **b. threat** menace *f* d'attentat à la bombe
► **bomb along** *Fam* VI *(of car, driver)* bomber
VT INSEP **to b. along the road** bomber sur la route
► **bomb down** VT INSEP *Fam (of car, driver)* **to b. down the road at 100 mph** foncer à 160 (km/h)
► **bomb out** VT SEP **1** **they have been bombed out of their homes** ils sont à la rue parce que leurs maisons ont été bombardées; **the whole street had been bombed out** toute la rue avait été détruite par les bombardements **2** *Br Fam (fail to keep appointment with)* **to b. sb out** poser un lapin à qn

bombard [bɒmˈbɑːd] VT *Mil etc* bombarder; *Fig* **to b. sb with questions** bombarder qn de questions

bombardier [bɒmbəˈdɪər] N **1** *Aviat* bombardier *m* **2** *Br Mil* brigadier *m*

bombardment [bɒmˈbɑːdmənt] N *Mil* bombardement *m*

bombast [ˈbɒmbæst] N emphase *f*

bombastic [bɒmˈbæstɪk] ADJ *(style)* ampoulé, emphatique

bombastically [bɒmˈbæstɪklɪ] ADV dans un style ampoulé *ou* emphatique

Bombay mix [bɒmˈbeɪ] N *Culin* = mélange *m* apéritif épicé composé de cacahouètes et de lentilles

bombazine [ˈbɒmbəziːn] N *Tex* bombasin *m*

bombe [bɒm] N *(ice cream)* bombe *f* glacée

bombed out [bɒmd] ADJ *Sl* **1** *(exhausted)* crevé, nase **2** *(very crowded)* plein à craquer **3** *(drunk)* bourré; *(on drugs)* défoncé

bomber [ˈbɒmər] N **1** *(aircraft)* bombardier *m* **2** *(person) Aviat* bombardier *m*; *(terrorist)* poseur, -euse de bombe(s)
► ► **b. jacket** blouson *m* d'aviateur

bombing [ˈbɒmɪŋ] N attentat *m* à la bombe; *Aviat* bombardement *m*
► ► **b. campaign** campagne *f* d'attentats à la bombe; **b. raid** bombardement aérien; **b. run** course *f* de visée

bombproof [ˈbɒmpruːf] ADJ à l'épreuve des bombes
► ► **b. shelter** abri *m* blindé

bombshell [ˈbɒmʃel] N **1** *Mil* obus *m*; *Fig* **the news came as a b. (to us)** cette nouvelle nous a fait l'effet d'une bombe; **to drop a b.** faire part d'une nouvelle qui fait l'effet d'une bombe **2** *Fam (attractive woman)* beauté *f*

bombsight [ˈbɒmsaɪt] N *Aviat* viseur *m ou* collimateur *m* de bombardement

bombsite [ˈbɒmsaɪt] N zone *f* bombardée; **to look like a b.** ressembler à un champ de bataille

bombthrower [ˈbɒmθrəʊər] N **1** *(device)* lance-bombes *m inv* **2** *(person)* lanceur, -euse de bombes

bona fide [ˈbəʊnəˈfaɪdɪ] ADJ *(excuse, contract, reason, agreement)* valable; *(offer)* sérieux, sincère; *(agent)* agréé; *(charity)* vrai; **are you sure he was a b. salesman?** es-tu sûr que c'était vraiment un vendeur?
N **one's bona fides** [-faɪdɪz] sa bonne foi

bonanza [bəˈnænzə] N *Min* riche filon *m*; *Fig* aubaine *f*; **the tourist industry has had a bit of a b.** l'industrie touristique a fait de bonnes affaires; **to strike a b.** *Min* rencontrer un riche filon; *Fig* faire une affaire en or
ADJ **b. year** année *f* exceptionnelle

Bonapartist [ˈbəʊnəpɑːtɪst] N, ADJ *Hist* bonapartiste *mf*

bonbon [ˈbɒnbɒn] N bonbon *m*

bonce [bɒns] N *Br Fam (head)* caboche *f*

bond [bɒnd] N **1** *(tie)* lien *m*; *Lit* bonds *(chains)* fers *mpl*, liens; *Fig* **the bonds of friendship/marriage** les liens de l'amitié/du mariage; **there is a very close b. between us** nous sommes très liés
2 *Chem* liaison *f*, *(of glue)* adhérence *f*, *Constr etc* attache *f*
3 *(commitment)* engagement *m*, contrat *m*; *Law* obligation *f*, *Fml* **my word is my b.** *(you can trust me)* je vous donne ma parole d'honneur; *(I cannot back out)* j'ai donné ma parole d'honneur
4 *Fin* bon *m*, obligation *f*, **registered b.** bon nominatif; **mortgage b.** titre *m* hypothécaire
5 *Law (for bail)* caution *f*
6 *Com (warehouse)* dépôt *m*; **to be in b.** être à l'entrepôt *ou* en dépôt; **to take goods out of b.** dédouaner des marchandises
7 *(paper)* papier *m* à lettres (de luxe)
VT **1** *(metals etc)* coller; *Constr (stones)* liaisonner **2** *Com (goods)* entreposer, mettre en dépôt *ou* à l'entrepôt **3** *Fig* **hardship had bonded them together** les privations qu'ils avaient endurées avaient créé un lien très fort entre eux
► ► *Fin* **b. equivalent yield** = rendement *m* équivalent à celui d'une obligation; *Fin* **b. holder** détenteur, -trice d'obligations; *Fin* **b. investment** placement *m* obligataire; *Fin* **b. issue** emprunt *m* obligataire; **to make a b. issue** émettre un emprunt; *Fin* **b. market** marché *m* obligataire *ou* des obligations; *Fin* **b. note** titre d'obligation; **b. paper** papier *m* à lettres (de luxe); *Fin* **b. yield** rendement de l'obligation

bondage [ˈbɒndɪdʒ] N **1** *Lit (slavery)* esclavage *m*, asservissement *m* **2** *Hist (serfdom)* servage *m* **3** *(sexual practice)* bondage *m*, = pratique *f* sexuelle où l'un des partenaires est attaché

bonded [ˈbɒndɪd] ADJ **1** *Constr (masonry)* en liaison **2** *Com (goods)* en dépôt, en entrepôt **3** *Fin (debt)* garanti par obligations
► ► *Com* **b. warehouse** entrepôt *m* sous douane

bonder [ˈbɒndər] N *Com* entrepositaire *m*

bonding [ˈbɒndɪŋ] N **1** *Constr (of stones)* liaison *f* **2** *(of metals)* collage *m* **3** *Com (of goods)* entreposage *m* **4** *(emotional attachment)* lien *m* affectif; **the b. process** la formation de liens affectifs; **male b.** la formation de liens affectifs entre hommes
► ► *Chem* **b. agent** agent *m* de collage *ou* d'adhésivité; **b. scheme** *(with tour operator)* agrément *m*

bondholder [ˈbɒndhəʊldə(r)] N *Fin* obligataire *mf*, détenteur, -trice *ou* porteur, -euse d'obligations

bondstone [ˈbɒndstəʊn] N *Constr* parpaing *m*

bone [bəʊn] N **1** *(of human, animal)* os *m*; *(of fish)* arête *f*, **the handle was made from b.** le manche était en os; **to be as dry as a b.** *or* **b. dry** *(of earth)* être desséché; *(of well)* être à sec; *(of washing)* être complètement sec; *Old-fashioned* **he won't make old bones** il ne fera pas de vieux os; **chilled** or **frozen to the b.** gelé ou transi jusqu'à la moelle; **to cut expenses to the b.** réduire les dépenses au minimum; **to work one's fingers to the b.** se tuer au travail; **to be b. idle** or **lazy** être paresseux comme une couleuvre; **I feel it in my bones** je le sens; Fam **to have a b. to pick with sb** avoir un compte à régler avec qn; **to make no bones about doing sth** ne pas hésiter à faire qch; **he made no bones about it** il y est allé carrément, il n'y est pas allé par quatre chemins; **she made no bones about her displeasure** elle n'a pas caché son mécontentement; **near** or **close to the b.** (joke etc) douteux, limite

2 (of corset) baleine f

3 bones (of the dead) ossements mpl

VT 1 (meat) désosser; (fish) ôter les arêtes de **2** (corset) garnir de baleines **3** Am Vulg (have sex with) tringler

▸▸ Cer **b. china** porcelaine f tendre; **b. of contention** sujet m de dispute; Anat **b. marrow** moelle f; Med **b. marrow transplant** greffe f de moelle; Agr **b. meal** engrais m (de cendres d'os); **b. structure** ossature f

▸ **bone up** VT INSEP Sl (study) potasser

boned [bəʊnd] ADJ **1** (meat) désossé; (fish) sans arêtes **2** (corset) baleiné

bone-dry ADJ (earth) desséché; (well) à sec; (washing) complètement sec

bonehead ['bəʊnhed] N Fam (stupid person) idiot, -ote; (stubborn person) tête f de bois

boneless ['bəʊnlɪs] ADJ (meat) sans os; (from which bones have been removed) désossé; (fish) sans arêtes

boner ['bəʊnər] N **1** Am Fam (mistake) gaffe f; **I made a real b.!** j'ai fait une de ces gaffes! **2** Vulg (erection) **to have a b.** avoir le gourdin ou la trique

boneshaker ['bəʊnʃeɪkər] N Fam esp Hum **1** (car) vieux clou m, vieille guimbarde f **2** Arch (bicycle) vélocipède m

bonfire ['bɒnfaɪər] N (with fireworks) feu m de joie; (for burning leaves etc) feu de jardin; **to make** or **build a b.** (with wood, leaves etc) faire un feu

▸▸ Br **B. Night** le 5 novembre (commémoration de la tentative de Guy Fawkes de faire sauter le Parlement en 1605)

bong [bɒŋ] N (of bell, drum) coup m

bongo ['bɒŋgəʊ] N bongo m; **a set of bongos** un bongo

bonhomie [bɒnɒ'miː] N bonhomie f

bonito [bə'niːtəʊ] N (fish) bonite f

bonk [bɒŋk] Fam N Br **to have a b.** tirer un coup

VT 1 Br (have sex with) **to b. sb** se faire qn **2** (hit) taper; **he got bonked on the head by a tennis ball** il s'est pris une balle de tennis sur la tête

VI Br (have sex) tirer un coup, s'envoyer en l'air (**with sb** avec qn)

bonkers ['bɒŋkəz] ADJ Br Sl cinglé; **it's driving me b.!** ça me rend dingue!

bonnet ['bɒnɪt] N **1** (hat) bonnet m **2** Br Aut capot m; **to have a look under the b.** jeter un coup d'œil sous le capot

▸▸ Aut **b. release** déverrouillage m du capot; Aut **b. strut** tige f (de maintien) de capot, béquille f de capot

bonny ['bɒnɪ] ADJ esp Scot joli

bonsai ['bɒnsaɪ] N bonsaï m

bonus, pl **bonuses** ['bəʊnəs, -əsɪz] N (esp at work) prime f; St Exch (on shares) dividende m supplémentaire, bonification f; **to work on a b. system** travailler à la prime; **cost-of-living b.** indemnité f de vie chère ou de cherté de vie; Com etc **Christmas b.** gratification f de fin d'année; Fig **the hot weather was an unexpected b.** le beau temps fut vraiment bienvenu étant donné qu'on ne

s'y attendait pas; **it's a real b. having a theatre close by** le fait qu'il y ait un théâtre tout près constitue vraiment un plus

▸▸ Br St Exch **b. issue** émission f d'actions gratuites; **b. number** (in lottery) numéro m complémentaire; Mktg **b. pack** prime produit en plus; Br St Exch **b. share** action f gratuite ou donnée en prime

bony ['bəʊnɪ] ADJ **1** (person, body, face) osseux; (knees, shoulders) anguleux; (fingers, arms) squelettique; (meat) plein d'os; (fish) plein d'arêtes **2** (like bone) osseux

bonzer ['bɒnzər] Austr Fam ADJ vachement bien, super, génial, -aux

INT super!, génial!

bonzo ['bɒnzəʊ] N Am Fam cinglé, fêlé

boo [buː] INT hou!; Fam **he wouldn't say b. to a goose** c'est un timide

N huée f, **her arrival was greeted with boos** elle s'est fait huer à son arrivée

VT & VI to b. (at) sb huer qn; **to be booed off the stage** quitter la scène au milieu des huées

boob [buːb] Fam N **1** (fool) idiot, -ote, crétin, -ine **2** Br (mistake) gaffe f **3** (breast) nichon m; **to have a b. job** se faire refaire les nichons

VI Br faire une gaffe

▸▸ Fam **b. tube** (strapless top) bustier m moulant; Am (television) télé f

boo-boo N Fam (blunder) gaffe f, bourde f, **to make a b.** faire une gaffe ou une bourde

booby ['buːbɪ] N **1** Old-fashioned (fool) idiot, -ote, crétin, -ine, nouille f **2** (bird) fou m

▸▸ **b. hatch** Naut écoutillon m; Am Fam (mental hospital) asile m de dingues; Sport **b. prize** prix m de consolation (attribué par plaisanterie au dernier); **b. trap** Mil objet m piégé; (practical joke) traquenard f

booby-trap VT (car etc) piéger

booger ['buːgər] N Am Fam crotte f de nez

boogie ['buːgɪ] VI **1** Mus (dance) danser, guincher; (party) faire la fête **2** Am (leave) mettre les bouts, s'arracher; **let's b. on out of here** on met les bouts, on s'arrache

N Mus boogie m; **to have a b.** danser, guincher

▸▸ Sport **b. board** boogie board m

boogie-woogie [-'wuːgɪ] N Mus boogie-woogie m, pl boogie-woogies

booing ['buːɪŋ] N huées fpl

BOOK [bʊk]

| **N** livre **1** ▪ registre **2** ▪ pari **2** |
| ▪ carnet **3** |
| **VT** réserver **1** ▪ engager **1** |
| **VI** réserver **1** |

N **1** (for reading) livre m; (of opera) livret m, libretto m; (of songs, prayers etc) recueil m; Tel annuaire m; Tel **I'm in the b.** (listed in directory) je suis dans l'annuaire; **a b. on** or **about gardening** un livre de jardinage; **old books** vieux bouquins mpl; (antiquarian) vieilles éditions fpl; **not published in b. form** inédit en librairie; **her articles have now been published in b. form** ses articles ont maintenant été publiés sous forme de livre; Fig **by** or **according to the b.** selon les règles; **to do things** or **go by the b.** suivre les règles; **to be a closed b. to sb** (of subject) être du chinois pour qn; **she's a closed b. to me** (I don't understand her) cette fille est un mystère pour moi; **she's an open b.** (her feelings etc are obvious) elle ne peut rien cacher, elle est transparente; **to read sb like an open b.** lire à livre ouvert dans la pensée de qn; **in my b.** (to my mind) d'après moi; **that doesn't suit my b.** ça ne me convient pas; Old-fashioned **the good B.** la Bible; **to swear on the B.** prêter serment sur la Bible

2 (for writing in) Com, Fin etc registre m; Sch

cahier m; **account b.** livre m de comptes; **to keep the books of a firm** tenir les comptes d'une entreprise; Fig **he's on our books** (member of our team etc) c'est un de nos membres; (player in our team) c'est un de nos joueurs; (employee) il est dans nos fichiers; **to be in sb's good books** être dans les petits papiers de qn, être bien vu par qn; **to be in sb's bad books** être mal vu par qn; **to bring sb to b. for sth** forcer qn à rendre compte de qch; Fam **to throw the b. at sb** (tell off) passer un savon à qn; (punish) donner le maximum à qn; Horseracing **to make a b.** faire un pari; **we've opened a b. on how late he'll be** les paris sont ouverts sur le retard qu'il va avoir

3 b. of stamps/tickets carnet m de timbres/billets; **b. of matches** pochette f d'allumettes

VT 1 (seat, room, table) réserver, retenir; Rail, Aviat (ticket, seat) réserver; Theat etc (performer) engager; **I've booked you on the next flight** je vous ai réservé une place sur le prochain vol; **fully booked** (theatre, flight) complet; **I'm booked for this evening** (have engagement) je suis pris ce soir

2 (of policeman) (motorist) dresser une contravention à; (of referee) (player) donner un avertissement à; **I was booked for speeding yesterday** hier j'ai eu une contravention pour excès de vitesse; **have you booked him?** (in police station) tu as pris tous ses renseignements?

3 Am Fam **to b. it** (leave) mettre les bouts, s'arracher

VI 1 Rail, Aviat, Theat réserver une place; (in restaurant, hotel) réserver; **to b. through to Nice** prendre tous les billets nécessaires pour Nice

2 Am Fam (leave) mettre les bouts, s'arracher; (move quickly) foncer

▸▸ **b. club** club m du livre; Acct **b. debts** comptes mpl fournisseurs, dettes fpl compte; **b. end** serre-livres m inv; Acct **b. entry** écriture f comptable; Acct **b. entry transfer** transfert m de compte à compte; **b. fair** salon m du livre; (secondhand) foire f aux livres; **b. matches** allumettes fpl plates; Acct **b. of original entry** livre-journal m, pl livres-journaux; **b. review** revue f littéraire; **b. reviewer** critique mf littéraire; Br **b. token** bon m d'achat de livres, chèque-livre m, pl chèques-livres; **the b. trade** l'industrie f du livre, la librairie; Fin **b. value** valeur f comptable, valeur de bilan

▸ **book in** VI (of hotel guest) se faire inscrire sur le registre

VT SEP (of receptionist) inscrire au registre

▸ **book into** VT INSEP **to b. into a hotel** prendre une chambre d'hôtel

VT SEP **I've booked myself into the best hotel in town** (in advance) j'ai réservé une chambre dans le meilleur hôtel de la ville; (on the spur of the moment) j'ai pris une chambre dans le meilleur hôtel de la ville

▸ **book out** VI (of hotel guest) quitter un/l'hôtel

VT SEP (find other hotel for) trouver un autre hôtel pour; **I booked them out at noon** (they left) ils ont réglé leur note à midi

▸ **book up** VI (make reservations) réserver; **have you booked up for your holiday?** est-ce que vous avez réservé pour vos vacances?

VT SEP (usu passive) **the hotel is all booked up** l'hôtel est complet; **I'm booked up for this evening** (have engagement) je suis pris ce soir

bookable ['bʊkəb(ə)l] ADJ Theat etc (seat) qui peut être réservé à l'avance

bookbinder ['bʊkbaɪndər] N relieur, -ieuse

bookbinding ['bʊkbaɪndɪŋ] N reliure f

bookcase ['bʊkkeɪs] N bibliothèque f

booker ['bʊkər] N *(for model, actor etc)* agent *m*

bookie ['bʊkɪ] N *Horseracing Fam* bookmaker *m*, book *m*

booking ['bʊkɪŋ] N **1** *(of order)* enregistrement *m*, inscription *f* **2** *(of room, seat etc)* réservation *f*, *(of seats, tickets)* location *f*; *Theat etc (of performer)* engagement *m*; **to make a b.** *(for theatre, plane seat etc)* réserver une place; *(for restaurant)* réserver (une table); **I have a b. in the name of Smith** *(to hotel clerk)* j'ai réservé au nom de Smith
▸▸ **b. agency** agence *f* de réservation; **b. clerk** préposé, -ée aux réservations; **bookings diary** agenda *m* de réservation; **b. fee** frais *mpl* de réservation; **b. form** feuille *f ou* fiche *f* de réservation; **b. office** bureau *m* de location; **b. status** état *m* de la réservation

bookish ['bʊkɪʃ] ADJ **1** *(studious)* studieux **2** *Pej (person, style)* pédant

book-keeper N *Com* comptable *mf*

book-keeping N *Com* comptabilité *f*

book-learning N érudition *f*, *Pej* savoir *m* livresque

booklet ['bʊklɪt] N *(pamphlet)* brochure *f*, *(small book)* plaquette *f*

booklover ['bʊklʌvər] N bibliophile *mf*

bookmaker ['bʊkmeɪkər] N *Horseracing* bookmaker *m*

bookmark ['bʊkmɑːk] N *also Comput* signet *m*
VT *Comput (web page)* créer un signet sur; **don't forget to b. this page** n'oublie pas de créer un signet sur cette page
▸▸ *Comput* **b. list** liste *f* de signets

bookmobile ['bʊkməbiːl] N *Am* bibliobus *m*

bookplate ['bʊkpleɪt] N ex-libris *m inv*

bookrest ['bʊkrest] N lutrin *m*

bookseller ['bʊkselər] N libraire *mf*; **second-hand b.** bouquiniste *mf*

bookselling ['bʊkselɪŋ] N librairie *f*, commerce *m* du livre

bookshelf, *pl* **bookshelves** ['bʊkʃelf, -ʃelvz] N rayon *m*, étagère *f*

bookshop ['bʊkʃɒp] N librairie *f*

bookstall ['bʊkstɔːl] N **1** *(selling second-hand books)* étalage *m* de livres **2** *(in station)* kiosque *m* à journaux

bookstore ['bʊkstɔːr] N *Am* librairie *f*

bookworm ['bʊkwɜːm] N **1** *(person)* mordu, -ue de lecture **2** *(insect)* anobion *m*, ptine *m*

Boolean ['buːlɪən] ADJ booléen
▸▸ **B. algebra** algèbre *f* booléenne; **B. function** fonction *f* booléenne; **B. operator** opérateur *m* booléen; **B. search** recherche *f* booléenne

boom[1] [buːm] N **1** *(at harbour mouth)* barrage *m* flottant, barre *f ou* estacade *f* flottante **2** *Naut (for jib)* bout-dehors *m*, *pl* bouts-dehors; **derrick b.** mât *m* de charge; **swinging b.** tangon *m* **3** *(of crane)* flèche *f*; *Cin, TV (for microphone)* perche *f*, *Fam* girafe *f*
▸▸ *Cin, TV* **b. microphone** micro *m* sur perche; *Cin, TV* **b. operator** perchiste *mf*

boom[2] N *(sound)* (of cannon, thunder, waves) grondement *m*; (of wind) mugissement *m*; (of organ) ronflement *m*; (of bells) bourdonnement *m*; *Aut (of engine)* ronflement, grondement; **the b. of his voice** les éclats *mpl* de sa voix
VI *(of thunder, waves)* gronder; *(of wind)* mugir; *(of guns)* gronder, tonner; *(of organ)* ronfler; *(of bells)* résonner sourdement; *(of voice)* retentir; **'stop!' he boomed** 'arrête!' dit-il de sa voix retentissante
▸ **boom out** VI *(sound loudly)* résonner
VT SEP *(utter loudly)* *(order)* hurler

boom[3] N *Com, Fin etc* boom *m*

VI *(of trade, business etc)* être florissant
▸▸ *Econ* **b. town** ville *f* en plein essor, ville-champignon *f*, *pl* villes-champignons; *(prosperous)* ville prospère

boomerang ['buːməræŋ] N *(for throwing)*, *Fig* boomerang *m*
VI *Fig* faire boomerang; **the joke boomeranged on him** la plaisanterie lui est retombée dessus

booming ['buːmɪŋ] ADJ *(wind)* mugissant; *(thunder, voice)* retentissant

boon [buːn] N **1** *(useful item)* avantage *m*; **I found it a great b.** cela m'a rendu grand service **2** *Arch Lit (favour)* faveur *f*
▸▸ **b. companion** bon compère *m*; **they're b. companions** ils sont inséparables

boondocks ['buːndɒks], **boonies** ['buːnɪz] NPL *Am Fam* (grande) banlieue *f*; **to live in the boonies** habiter à Perpète(-les-Oies)

boondoggle ['buːndɒg(ə)l] VI *Am Fam* flemmarder, peigner la girafe

boor [bɔːr] N rustre *m*, rustaud *m*

boorish ['bɔːrɪʃ] ADJ *(manners, behaviour, person)* rustre, grossier

boorishly ['bɔːrɪʃlɪ] ADV grossièrement, de façon rustre

boorishness ['bɔːrɪʃnɪs] N grossièreté *f*

boost [buːst] N **1** **to give a b. to** *(industry, production, exports, sales etc)* relancer; *(morale)* remonter; *(product)* faire du battage pour; *Fam* **to give sb a b.** *(morally)* regonfler qn; *(in finding a job)* donner un coup de pouce à qn; *(over a wall)* soulever qn; **to give sb's confidence a b.** redonner confiance à qn; **to give sb's morale a b.** remonter le moral à qn; **that win will have given her ego a b.** cette victoire aura regonflé son amour-propre **2** *Elec* survoltage *m*; *Aviat* surpression *f*
VT **1** *(industry, production, exports etc)* relancer; *(recruitment, numbers etc)* augmenter; *(morale)* remonter; *(product)* faire du battage pour; *Fam (person) (morally)* regonfler; *(in finding job)* donner un coup de pouce à; **to b. sb's hopes/confidence** redonner de l'espoir/de la confiance à qn **2** *(speed, energy, pressure of sth)* augmenter; *Elec* survolter; *(engine)* suralimenter **3** *Am Fam (steal)* piquer, faucher; *(break into)* cambrioler

booster ['buːstər] N **1** *Elec* survolteur *m* **2** *(of missile)* propulseur *m* auxiliaire de départ, booster *m* **3** *Aviat* démarreur *m* auxiliaire, accélérateur *m* (de décollage) **4** *(supercharger)* compresseur *m*; *(on heater)* ventilateur *m*; *(for brakes)* servofrein *m* **5** *Electron* suramplificateur *m*, booster *m* **6** *Chem* renforçateur *m*
▸▸ **b. cushion** *(in car)* rehausseur *m*; *Med* **b. dose** (dose *f* de) rappel *m*; *Med* **b. injection** (injection *f* de) rappel; **b. rocket** fusée *f* de démarrage; **b. seat** *(in car)* (siège *m*) rehausseur, siège de rehausse; **b. station** *Tel* station *f* relais; *Tech* station auxiliaire de pompage

boot[1] [buːt] N **1** *(footwear)* botte *f*, *(short)* bottine *f*, *(for football, rugby)* chaussure *f*; **walking** *or* **climbing boots** chaussures de marche; **riding boots** bottes de cheval *ou* de cavalier; **... or you'll feel (the toe of) my b. up your backside** ... sinon tu vas recevoir un bon coup de pied au derrière; *Fam* **to put** *or* **stick the b. in** *(kick someone)* flanquer des coups de pied à; **they really put the b. in** *(kicked him)* ils l'ont vraiment bourré de coups de pied; *Fig* **you really know how to put the b. in!** tu es vraiment doué pour enfoncer le couteau dans la plaie!; *Fig* **the b.'s on the other foot** les rôles sont renversés *ou* inversés; *Fig* **you can bet your boots that ...** je te fiche mon billet que ...; *Fig Fam* **to give sb (the order of) the b.** *(from job)* mettre *ou* flanquer qn à la porte; *(from relationship)* plaquer qn; *Fig* **to get the b.** *(from job)* être

mis à la porte; *(from relationship)* se faire plaquer; *Fam* **as tough as old boots** *(meat)* dur comme de la semelle; *(plant)* très résistant; **to die with one's boots on** *(in battle)* mourir les bottes aux pieds; *Fig* rester fidèle au poste jusqu'à la mort; *Fig Fam* **to be too big for one's boots** avoir les chevilles qui enflent, avoir la grosse tête
2 *Br Aut* coffre *m*
3 *(kick)* coup *m* de pied; **to give a ball a b.** donner un coup de pied dans un ballon; **he needs a b. up the backside** il a besoin d'un bon coup de pied au derrière
4 *Br Fam Pej (ugly woman)* boudin *m*, cageot *m*
VT *Fam* flanquer des coups de pied à; **to b. sb out** *(dismiss)* flanquer qn à la porte; **her parents booted her out of the house** ses parents l'ont mise à la porte
VI *(of computer)* s'amorcer
▸▸ *Fam* **b. camp** *Am Mil* = camp *m* d'entraînement pour nouvelles recrues; *Br (centre for young offenders)* = centre *m* de redressement *(pour jeunes délinquants)*; *Comput* **b. disk** *(hard)* disque *m* de démarrage; *(floppy)* disquette *f* de démarrage; *Br Aut* **b. light** éclaireur *m* de coffre; *Br* **b. sale** = sorte de marché aux puces où des particuliers apportent dans leur voiture les objets de brocante qu'ils souhaitent vendre; *Comput* **b. sector** secteur *m* d'initialisation; *Comput* **b. track** piste *f* d'amorçage
▸ **boot up** *Comput* VI *(of computer)* s'amorcer, démarrer; *(of person)* démarrer
VT SEP *(computer)* amorcer, faire démarrer

boot[2] N *(only in the phrase)* **to b.** en sus, par-dessus le marché; **and a liar/a thief to b.** et par-dessus le marché c'est un menteur/un voleur

bootable ['buːtəb(ə)l] ADJ *Comput* amorçable

bootblack ['buːtblæk] N cireur, -euse, de chaussures

bootee [buː'tiː] N **1** *(short boot)* bottillon *m* **2** *(baby's)* chausson *m*

booth [buːð, buːθ] N *(at fair)* baraque *f*, *Am (at exhibition)* stand *m*; *Tel* cabine *f*, *(in restaurant)* alcôve *f*

bootjack ['buːtdʒæk] N tire-botte *m*, *pl* tire-bottes

bootlace ['buːtleɪs] N lacet *m* (de botte)

bootleg ['buːtleg] N *(cassette, video)* cassette *f* pirate
ADJ *(whisky)* de contrebande; *(record, video)* pirate
VT *(-gg-)* *(alcohol)* *(produce)* produire illégalement; *(transport)* transporter illégalement; *(sell)* vendre illégalement; *(video, tape)* pirater
VI *(deal)* *(in alcoholic drinks)* trafiquer, faire de la contrebande; *(in videos, software etc)* faire du piratage
▸▸ **b. trousers** = pantalon *m* légèrement évasé que l'on porte avec des bottes

bootlegger ['buːtlegər] N *(of videos, software etc)* personne *f* qui se livre au piratage; *Hist (of alcohol)* bootlegger *m*

bootlegging ['buːtlegɪŋ] N *(of videos, software)* piratage *m*; *(of alcohol)* contrebande *f*

bootlicker ['buːtlɪkər] N *Fam* lèche-bottes *mf inv*

bootlicking ['buːtlɪkɪŋ] N *Fam* lèche-bottes *m*; **b. is his speciality** il est spécialiste du lèche-bottes

bootloader ['buːtləʊdər] N *Comput* chargeur-amorce *m*, *pl* chargeurs-amorces

bootmaker N bottier *m*

bootstrap ['buːtstræp] N **1** *(on boot)* languette *f*, *Fig* **to pull oneself up by one's bootstraps** se faire tout seul **2** *Comput* amorce *f*, programme *m* d'amorcement

▶▶ *Comput* **b. loader** chargeur-amorce *m, pl* chargeurs-amorces, chargeur *m* initial; *Comput* **b. routine** routine *f* d'amorçage

booty ['bu:tɪ] N **1** *(loot)* butin *m* **2** *Am Sl (buttocks)* cul *m*, derche *m*; **to get some b.** *(have sexual intercourse)* s'envoyer en l'air

booze [bu:z] *Fam* **vi** boire, picoler; **he's gone out boozing** il est allé picoler
N boisson *f* (alcoolique); **there's no more b.** il n'y a plus rien à boire; **to go on the b.** se mettre à boire; **I'm (staying) off the b.** j'ai arrêté de boire

boozehound ['bu:zhaʊnd] N *Am Sl* poivrot, -ote

boozer ['bu:zər] N *Sl* **1** *(drunkard)* poivrot, -ote **2** *Br (pub)* pub *m*; **down the b.** au pub

booze-up N *Br Sl* bringue *f*; **we're having a b. on Friday** on fait une bringue vendredi

boozily ['bu:zɪlɪ] ADV *Fam* **to look at sb b.** regarder qn à travers les vapeurs de l'alcool; **to say sth b.** dire qch d'une voix avinée

boozy ['bu:zɪ] ADJ *Fam (breath)* qui sent l'alcool; *(voice)* aviné; *(look, manner)* d'ivrogne; **a b. evening** une soirée bien arrosée; **a b. old man** un vieil ivrogne

bop¹ [bɒp] N **1** *Mus* bop *m* **2** *Fam (at disco)* danse *f*; **to go for a b.** aller danser
vi *Fam (at disco)* danser

bop² *Fam* N *(blow)* léger coup *m*
vt *(hit)* donner un léger coup à

bo-peep [bəʊ-] N *Fam* cache-cache *m inv*

boracic [bə'ræsɪk] ADJ *Chem (acid)* borique; **b. ointment** pommade *f* boriquée

borage ['bɒrɪdʒ] N *Bot, Culin* bourrache *f*

borax ['bɔ:ræks] N *Chem etc* borax *m*

bordeaux [bɔ:'dəʊ] N *(wine)* bordeaux *m*

border ['bɔ:dər] N **1** *(of rug, plate, picture) also Comput* bordure *f*
2 *(edge) (of path)* bord *m*; **there were flowers along the b. of the path** il y avait des fleurs sur le bord du chemin
3 *(between two countries)* frontière *f*; **to cross the b.** passer la frontière; **north of the B.** *(from viewpoint of England)* en Écosse; *(from viewpoint of the US)* au Canada; **south of the B.** *(from viewpoint of Scotland)* en Angleterre; *(from viewpoint of Canada)* aux États-Unis; *(from viewpoint of the US)* au Mexique; **the Borders** *(in Britain)* = région *f* vallonnée du sud-est de l'Écosse
4 *(hem)* bordure *f*
5 *(flowerbed)* plate-bande *f, pl* plates-bandes
vt **1** *(be adjacent to) (lake, garden)* border; *(country)* confiner à *ou* avec; **the countries that b. the Mediterranean** les pays qui sont en bordure de la Méditerranée **2** *Sewing* lisérer
▶▶ **b. controls** contrôles *mpl* aux frontières; **b. crossing** passage *m* de frontière; *Mil* **b. guard** garde-frontière *m, pl* gardes-frontières; **b. post** poste-frontière *m, pl* postes-frontières; **b. region** région frontalière; **b. town** ville *f* frontière *ou* frontalière
▶ **border on vt insep 1** *(of territory) (another country)* confiner à; **the two countries b. on each other** les deux pays se touchent *ou* ont une frontière commune; **his estate borders on mine** ses terres touchent les miennes **2** *(be almost equivalent to) (madness, cruelty etc)* approcher de, être voisin de; **to b. on rudeness/a lie/the absurd** friser l'impolitesse/le mensonge/l'absurde; **he was bordering on sixty** il frisait la soixantaine; **emotion bordering on terror** émotion voisine de la terreur

borderer ['bɔ:dərər] N *Br* habitant, -ante des "Borders"

bordering ['bɔ:dərɪŋ] ADJ *(country)* contigu, -uë, limitrophe

borderland ['bɔ:dəlænd] N pays *m* frontalier *ou* limitrophe; *Fig* **the b. between sleeping and waking** l'état de demi-sommeil

borderline ['bɔ:dəlaɪn] N *(between two categories etc)* distinction *f*; *(between two countries)* frontière *f*, *Fig* **the b. between sanity and insanity** la limite entre le bon sens et la folie; **she's on the b.** c'est un cas limite
ADJ **a b. case** un cas limite; **it's b.** c'est un cas limite

bore¹ ['bɔ:r] N **1** *(person)* personne *f* ennuyeuse, *Fam* raseur, -euse; **what a (crashing) b. (he is)!** ce qu'il est barbant *ou* rasoir!; **he's a real b. on the subject of gardening** il est vraiment barbant quand il se met à parler de jardinage **2** *(thing)* chose *f* ennuyeuse; **the film was a bit of a b.** le film était un peu ennuyeux; **I know it's a b. but it's got to be done** je sais que ce n'est pas marrant mais il faut le faire; **what a b.!** quelle barbe!
vt ennuyer, *Fam* raser, *Fam* barber; *Fam* **it/ he bores me rigid** *or* **stiff** *or* **to death** *or* **to tears** ça/il m'ennuie à mourir; *Fam* **to b. the pants off sb** ennuyer qn à mourir; **I won't b. you with the details** je vous passe les détails

bore² N **1** *(diameter)* calibre *m*; *(of pipe etc)* alésage *m*; *(of firearm)* calibre **2** *(cylinder) (of firearm)* âme *f*, **smooth/rifled b.** âme lisse/rayée **3** *Min (hole)* trou *m* de sonde, sondage *m*, forage *m*
vt *(well)* foncer; *(hole)* forer, creuser; *(cylinder)* aléser
vi **to b. into wood** *(of insect)* creuser un trou *ou* une galerie dans le bois; **to b. through sth** percer qch; *Min* **to b. for water/minerals** faire un sondage *ou* sonder pour trouver de l'eau/des minéraux

bore³ N *(wave)* mascaret *m*

bore⁴ pt *see* bear²

Boreal ['bɔ:rɪəl] ADJ *(forest)* boréal, -als *ou* -aux

bored [bɔ:d] ADJ *(look, sigh etc)* d'ennui; *(person)* qui s'ennuie; **you look b.** tu as l'air de t'ennuyer; **to be** *or* **get b.** s'ennuyer; **I'm never b.** je ne m'ennuie jamais; **she is b. with him/it** elle en a assez de lui/elle en a assez; **he's a bit b. with his job** il s'ennuie un peu dans son travail; **I'm getting b. with this conversation** j'en ai assez de cette conversation; *Fam* **to be b. rigid** *or* **to tears** *or* **out of one's mind** s'ennuyer à mourir

boredom ['bɔ:dəm] N ennui *m*

borehole ['bɔ:həʊl] N *Min (exploratory)* trou *m* de sonde, sondage *m*; *(for mine)* trou de mine

borer ['bɔ:rər] N *(device) (for wood, metal)* foret *m*; *Min (of well)* sonde *f*

boric ['bɔ:rɪk] ADJ *Chem (acid etc)* borique

boring¹ ['bɔ:rɪŋ] ADJ *(tedious)* ennuyeux, *Fam* barbant, *Fam* rasant, *Fam* rasoir

boring² ADJ *(insect)* térébrant
N *(of hole)* percement *m*; *Tech* forage *m*, perçage *m*; *(of cylinder)* alésage *m*; *Min* sondage *m*, forage
▶▶ *Tech* **b. machine** *(for wood)* perceuse *f*, *(for metal)* alésoir *m*

born [bɔ:n] *(pp of* bear² *used in formation of passive verb)* **to be b.** naître; **I was b. in London/in 1977** je suis né à Londres/en 1977; **my mother died when I was b.** ma mère est décédée en me mettant au monde; **Queen Victoria was still on the throne when I was b.** la reine Victoria régnait toujours quand je suis né; **the house where I was b.** ma maison natale; **he is French b.** il est français de naissance; **to be b. deaf/blind** être sourd/aveugle de naissance; **to be b. lucky** être né coiffé; *Fam* **I wasn't b. yesterday** je ne suis pas né d'hier *ou* tombé de la dernière pluie; *Hum* **were you b. in a barn** *or* **a stable?**

on ne t'a jamais appris à fermer les portes?; *Fig* **it was a decision b. of necessity** cette décision était dictée par les circonstances; ... **he said, with a cynicism b. of experience** ... dit-il avec le cynisme que lui conférait l'expérience
ADJ **a b. storyteller/linguist** un conteur/linguiste né; **she's a b. liar** elle ment comme elle respire; **a b. loser** un raté irrécupérable; **a Londoner b. and bred** un vrai Londonien de Londres; **in all my b. days** de toute ma vie

born-again ADJ *Rel, Hum* régénéré; *Fig* **b. vegetarian** personne *f* devenue végétarienne (et qui essaye de convaincre les autres)
▶▶ **b. Christian** chrétien, -ienne régénéré(e)

borne pp *see* bear²

Borneo ['bɔ:nɪəʊ] N Bornéo *m*

borough ['bʌrə] N *Br* **1** *(British town)* = ville *f* représentée à la Chambre des communes par un ou plusieurs députés **2** *(in London)* = une des 32 subdivisions administratives de Londres **3** *(in New York)* = une des cinq subdivisions administratives de New York
▶▶ **b. council** = conseil *m* municipal d'un "borough"

borrow ['bɒrəʊ] vt emprunter (**from** à); **to b. money from sb** emprunter de l'argent à qn, faire un emprunt à qn; **can I b. the car?** est-ce que je peux prendre la voiture?; **to b. an idea from sb** emprunter une idée à qn; **this word was borrowed from Latin** ce mot est un emprunt au latin
vi emprunter; **to b. from sb** *(money)* faire un emprunt à qn, emprunter de l'argent à qn
▶ **borrow against vt insep** *Fin* emprunter sur; **the company borrowed against its assets** l'entreprise a emprunté de l'argent en utilisant son actif comme garantie

borrowed ['bɒrəʊd] ADJ **the doctors say he's living on b. time** *(close to death)* les médecins disent qu'il n'en a plus pour longtemps; **the company is living on b. time** les jours de l'entreprise sont comptés; **my grandfather is living on b. time** *(is very old)* mon grand-père a de la chance d'être encore en vie; **he'd been living on b. time since he was caught stealing from his employer** *(his job was in danger)* il était en sursis depuis qu'on l'avait pris à voler son employeur
▶▶ *Fin* **b. capital** capitaux *mpl* empruntés *ou* d'emprunt

borrower ['bɒrəʊər] N emprunteur, -euse

borrowing ['bɒrəʊɪŋ] N *(action, money)* emprunt *m*; **financed by b.** financé par des emprunts
▶▶ **b. capacity** capacité *f* d'endettement, capacité à emprunter; **b. limit** maximum *m* d'emprunt, limite *f* d'endettement; **b. power** capacité de crédit *ou* d'emprunt *ou* d'endettement; **b. rate** taux *m* d'intérêt des emprunts; **b. requirements** besoins *mpl* d'emprunt

borsch [bɔ:ʃ] N *Culin* bortsch *m*

borstal ['bɔ:st(ə)l] N *Br Formerly* maison *f* de redressement *(pour jeunes délinquants âgés de 15 à 21 ans)*
▶▶ **b. boy** jeune délinquant *m*

borzoi ['bɔ:zɔɪ] N *(dog)* lévrier *m* russe, barzoï *m*

bosh [bɒʃ] *Old-fashioned Fam* N bêtises *fpl*, blagues *fpl*
INT n'importe quoi!, sottises!

bos'n ['bəʊs(ə)n] N = boatswain

Bosnia ['bɒznɪə] N Bosnie *f*, **B.-Herzegovina** Bosnie-Herzégovine *f*

Bosnian ['bɒznɪən] N Bosniaque *mf*
ADJ bosniaque

bosom ['bʊzəm] N *(of woman)* seins *mpl*, *Old-fashioned, Lit (of person)* poitrine *f*; *Fig*

in the b. of one's family au sein de sa famille; in the b. of the Church dans le giron de l'Église
▸▸b. friend ami, -ie intime; they're b. friends ils sont grands amis

bosomy ['bʊzəmɪ] **ADJ** (woman) à la poitrine opulente; she was a b. lady elle avait une poitrine opulente

Bosp(h)orus (the) [ðə'bɒsfərəs, ðə'bɒspərəs] **N** le Bosphore

boss[1] [bɒs] Fam **N** (person in charge) patron, -onne, chef m; Am (of political party) chef; the trade-union bosses les gens mpl à la tête du syndicat; show them who's (the) b. montre-leur qui commande ici; to be one's own b. être son propre patron
ADJ esp Am (excellent) épatant, merveilleux
VT (person) donner des ordres à; Fig to b. the show faire la loi
▸ boss about, boss around **VT SEP** donner des ordres à; stop bossing me about! j'en ai assez que tu me donnes des ordres!

boss[2] **N 1** (knob) protubérance f, Archit, Metal, Zool etc bosse f, (on furniture) capiton m **2** Tech mamelon m, portée f, Aviat (of propeller) moyeu m; Aut (centre of steering wheel) bossette f, centre b. (of wheel, crank) tourteau m

boss-eyed **ADJ** Br Fam qui louche; to be b. avoir un œil qui dit merde à l'autre

bossily ['bɒsɪlɪ] **ADV** Fam de façon autoritaire

bossiness ['bɒsɪnɪs] **N** Fam (of person, manner) façons fpl autoritaires

bossy ['bɒsɪ] **ADJ** Fam autoritaire; don't be so b., don't be such a b. boots arrête de jouer au petit chef

Boston matrix ['bɒstən] **N** Mktg matrice f BCG

bosun ['bəʊs(ə)n] **N** = boatswain

bot [bɒt] **N** Comput robot m

botanical [bə'tænɪk(ə)l] **ADJ** botanique
▸▸b. garden(s) jardin m botanique

botanist ['bɒtənɪst] **N** botaniste mf

botanize ['bɒtənaɪz] **VI** herboriser

botany ['bɒtənɪ] **N** botanique f
▸▸Tex b. wool laine f mérinos

botch [bɒtʃ] Fam **N** travail m mal fait ou salopé; you've made an awful b. of it tu as complètement salopé le boulot; to make a b. of an interview/speech rater complètement un entretien/un discours; she made a terrible b. of putting up the shelves elle a mis les étagères n'importe comment
VT (job) saloper; (interview, speech) rater; he botched the shelves il a mis les étagères n'importe comment
▸ botch up **VT SEP** (job) saloper; (interview, speech) rater

botched [bɒtʃt] **ADJ** Fam a b. attempt at suicide une tentative de suicide ratée; his b. apology only made matters worse ses excuses minables n'ont fait qu'empirer la situation; a b. job un travail de sagouin

botcher ['bɒtʃər] **N** Fam bousilleur, -euse

botch-up **N** = botch **N**

botel ['bəʊtel] **N** bateau-hôtel m, pl bateaux-hotels; (on barge) péniche-hôtel f, pl péniches-hôtels

both [bəʊθ] **ADJ**, **PRON** les deux, tous (les) deux, toutes (les) deux; b. brothers, b. (of) the brothers les deux frères; b. (of them) are dead ils sont morts tous (les) deux; b. of us saw it nous l'avons vu tous les deux; he has two houses, b. of which are vacant il a deux maisons, qui sont vides toutes les deux; she kissed him on b. cheeks elle l'a embrassé sur les deux joues; to hold sth in b. hands tenir qch à deux mains; on b. sides des deux côtés; b. alike l'un comme l'autre;

look b. ways (when crossing street) regarde des deux côtés; you can't have it b. ways on ne peut pas avoir le beurre et l'argent du beurre; Naut stop b. engines stoppez partout VOIR GRAMMAIRE A5; A37
ADV b. you and I vous et moi; b. you and I know it's not that simple vous savez comme moi que cela n'est pas aussi simple; she is b. intelligent and beautiful elle est à la fois intelligente et belle

bother ['bɒðər] **N 1** (trouble) ennui m; to be having a bit or a spot of b. avoir quelques ennuis (with avec); it's such a b. having to take it back c'est tellement embêtant d'avoir à le ramener; to be in b. with the police avoir des ennuis avec la police; if it's not too much b. si cela ne vous dérange pas trop; I hope I haven't put you to a lot of b. j'espère que je ne vous ai pas trop dérangé; it's a lot of b. to go to ça représente beaucoup de dérangement pour pas grand-chose; I hate to be a b., but … je suis désolé de vous déranger, mais …; it's no b. at all ça ne m'ennuie pas du tout; it's not worth the b. cela ne vaut pas la peine; to go to the b. of doing sth se donner la peine de faire qch **2** Br Sl (fighting) bagarre f; there was a bit of b. in the pub il y a eu un peu de bagarre dans le pub
VT 1 (annoy) ennuyer; (disturb) déranger; (be in the way of) gêner; does the light b. you? est-ce que la lumière vous gêne ou dérange?; my back's still bothering me (giving pain) j'ai toujours des problèmes de dos; his old wound bothers him in damp weather sa vieille blessure le fait souffrir par temps humide; I hate to b. you, but … je suis désolé de vous déranger, mais …; he didn't even b. to apologize il n'a même pas pris la peine de s'excuser; don't b. me! laissez-moi tranquille!; I can't be bothered (to do it) ça ne me dit rien (de le faire); b. (it)! zut!; b. the man! qu'il aille au diable!
2 (worry) inquiéter; to be bothered about sth s'inquiéter de qch, se faire du mauvais sang pour qch; don't b. yourself or your head about me ne vous inquiétez pas pour moi; Fam I'm not bothered cela m'est égal
VI 1 (take trouble) s'occuper (with de); prendre ou se donner la peine (to do sth de faire qch); don't b. to ring me up/to turn the lights off ce n'est pas la peine de me téléphoner/d'éteindre la lumière; don't b. with the dishes just now ne t'embête pas à faire la vaisselle maintenant; I'll call you next week – don't b.! (I can get on without you) je t'appellerai la semaine prochaine – te fatigue pas!
2 (worry) s'inquiéter (about de); he doesn't b. about anything il ne s'inquiète de rien

botheration [bɒðə'reɪʃən] **INT** Old-fashioned Fam zut!

bothersome ['bɒðəsəm] **ADJ** gênant

bottle ['bɒt(ə)l] **N 1** bouteille f, (small) (for perfume etc) flacon m; (wide-mouthed) bocal m; (for baby) biberon m; Med urinal m, Fam pistolet m; bring your own b. (on invitation) chacun doit amener une bouteille; (notice in restaurant) = les clients peuvent apporter leur vin (étant donné que le restaurant n'a pas de licence); he drank the whole b. il a bu toute la bouteille; brought up on the b. (baby) élevé au biberon; Fam to be fond of the b. aimer la bouteille; Fam to be on the b. boire; Fam to hit or take to the b. commencer à picoler; Fam he's been hitting the b. a lot recently il picole beaucoup ces temps-ci
2 Br Sl (courage, nerve) cran m; to have a lot of b. avoir beaucoup de cran; to lose one's b. se dégonfler; (permanently) perdre son assurance
VT (wine etc) mettre en bouteilles; (jam etc)

mettre en bocal; autumn is the best time for bottling fruit l'automne est la meilleure saison pour faire des conserves de fruits
▸▸b. bank = conteneur m pour la collecte du verre usagé; Fam Pej b. blonde blonde f décolorée; b. green vert m bouteille; b. opener ouvre-bouteilles m inv, décapsuleur m; Br b. party = soirée f où chacun des invités apporte à boire
▸ bottle out **VI** Br Sl (be too frightened) se dégonfler; he bottled out of the fight il s'est dégonflé au dernier moment et a refusé de se battre; he bottled out of telling her the truth finalement il a eu la trouille de lui dire la vérité
▸ bottle up **VT SEP** (one's feelings) étouffer; (one's anger) refouler, ravaler

bottlebrush ['bɒt(ə)lbrʌʃ] **N 1** (for cleaning) goupillon m **2** (plant) callistemon m

bottled ['bɒt(ə)ld] **ADJ** (wine, beer, gas etc) en bouteille(s); b. fruit fruits mpl en bocaux; b. water eau f minérale

bottle-fed **ADJ** nourri au biberon

bottle-feed **VT** (baby, lamb etc) nourrir au biberon

bottle-feeding **N** alimentation f au biberon

bottleful ['bɒt(ə)lfʊl] **N** a b. of sth une pleine bouteille de qch; by the b. à pleine bouteille

bottleneck ['bɒt(ə)lnek] **N 1** goulot m (de bouteille) **2** Fig (in road) rétrécissement m de la chaussée; (traffic jam) embouteillage m, bouchon m; (in production etc) goulet m ou goulot m d'étranglement **3** Mus (guitar style) bottleneck m

bottlenosed dolphin ['bɒtlnəʊzd] **N** grand dauphin m, dauphin à gros nez

bottle-washer **N** (person) laveur, -euse de bouteilles; (machine) rince-bouteilles m inv

bottling ['bɒt(ə)lɪŋ] **N** (of wine etc) mise f en bouteille(s); (of fruit) mise en bocaux

BOTTOM ['bɒtəm] **N 1** Fam (of person) derrière m
2 bottoms (of pyjamas, tracksuit) pantalon m, bas m
3 (of hill, stairs, page) bas m; (of well, box, sea) fond m; at the b. of the garden/of my bag au fond du jardin/de mon sac; he's at the b. of the class il est le dernier de sa classe; at the b. of the page au ou en bas de la page; to send a ship to the b. envoyer un bâtiment par le fond; to go to the b. (of ship) couler; to strike or touch b. (of ship) toucher le fond; to touch b. (of swimmer) Fig toucher le fond; from the b. of one's heart du fond du cœur; to get to the b. of sth (solve) tirer qch au clair; to get to the b. of things aller au fond des choses; to be at the b. of sth (be instigator) être derrière qch, être l'instigateur de qch; (be cause) être la cause de qch; at b. au fond, dans le fond
4 (of chair) siège m; Naut (of ship) carène f, fond m; the b. of my glass/plate (inside) le fond de mon verre/assiette; (outside) le dessous de mon verre/assiette; to put sth b. up(wards) mettre qch sens dessus dessous; a box with a false b. une boîte à double fond; to knock the b. out of (box etc) défoncer; Fig (argument) démolir; the b. has fallen out of the market le marché s'est effondré; Fam bottoms up! (empty your glass) cul sec!; (cheers) à votre santé!; Billiards to put b. on a ball faire de l'effet à revenir ou de l'effet rétrograde
5 Aut (gear) première f
ADJ b. half partie f inférieure; it's on the b. shelf il se trouve sur l'étagère du bas; the b. book in the pile le livre qui est en bas de la pile; b. end of the table bout m de la table; b. stair (going up) première marche f, (going

down) dernière marche; *Aut* **in b. gear** en première; *Fam* **you can bet your b. dollar that ...** vous pouvez être sûr que ...

▸▸ *Tech* **b. dead centre** point *m* mort bas; *Br* **b. drawer** *(trousseau)* trousseau *m*; **b. feeder** *(fish)* poisson *m* de fond; *Fam Fig Pej (unsuccessful person)* raté, -ée; *(team, company)* ratés *mpl*; **b. fishing** pêche *f* à la ligne de fond; *Acct, Fin* **b. line** résultat *m* net *ou* final, solde *m* final; *Fig* **the b. line is that we can't afford it** le fait est que nous ne pouvons pas nous le permettre; *Typ* **b. margin** marge *f* du bas; **b. price** prix *m* plancher

▸ **bottom out** vi *(of inflation, unemployment, prices)* atteindre son niveau le plus bas; *(of recession)* atteindre son plancher

bottomless ['bɒtəmlɪs] ADJ **1** *(well etc)* sans fond **2** *(resources, reserves)* inépuisable

▸▸ *Fig* **b. pit** gouffre *m*; **it's like pouring money into a b. pit** c'est comme jeter de l'argent par les fenêtres; **he's a b. pit** *(always hungry)* c'est un crevard

bottommost ['bɒtəmməʊst] ADJ ATTRIB *(shelf)* le plus bas, d'en bas; **the b. book in the pile** le livre qui se trouve tout en bas de la pile; *Lit* **the b. depths** le tréfonds

bottom-of-the-range N modèle *m* de base

ADJ bas de gamme

botty ['bɒtɪ] N *Fam* fesses *fpl*

botulism ['bɒtjʊlɪz(ə)m] N *Med* botulisme *m*

bouclé ['bu:kleɪ] ADJ, N *Tex* bouclé *m*; **b. sweater** pull *m* en bouclette; **b. wool** bouclette *f*

boudoir ['bu:dwɑ:r] N *Old-fashioned* boudoir *m*

bouffant ['bu:fɒn] ADJ *(hair, sleeve, skirt)* bouffant

bougainvillea [bu:gən'vɪlɪə] N *(plant)* bougainvillée *f*

bough [baʊ] N *(of tree)* branche *f*, rameau *m*

bought PT, PP *see* buy

▸▸ *Acct, Fin* **b. ledger** cahier *m ou* livre *m* des achats

bouillon ['bu:jɒn] N *Culin* bouillon *m*, consommé *m*

▸▸ *Am* **b. cube** cube *m* de bouillon; *Am* **b. cup** tasse *f* à bouillon *ou* à consommé

boulder ['bəʊldər] N *(gros)* bloc *m* de pierre

boulevard ['bu:ləvɑ:d] N **1** *(street)* boulevard *m* **2** *Am (on road)* terre-plein *m* *(central)*, *pl* terre-pleins *(centraux)*

bounce [baʊns] N **1** *(of ball)* rebond *m*; **you get a better b. on grass** cela rebondit mieux sur l'herbe; **to catch the ball on the b.** prendre la balle au bond; *Am Fam* **to get the b.** *(from job)* se faire virer; **she gave him the b.** *(from relationship)* elle l'a plaqué; *Br Fam* **on the b.** *(consecutively)* de suite; **they won three games on the b.** ils ont gagné trois matchs de suite

2 *Fam (of person)* entrain *m*; **a shampoo to put the b. back in your hair** un shampooing qui redonnera de la vitalité à vos cheveux

VI **1** *(of ball)* rebondir; *(of breasts)* ballotter; **to b. (up and down) on a bed/trampoline** sauter sur un lit/trampoline; **the epaulettes bounced (up and down) on his shoulders** les épaulettes dansaient sur ses épaules; **to b. up and down** *(not sit still)* s'agiter; **to b. into/out of a room** *(of person)* entrer dans une/sortir d'une pièce en coup de vent *ou* en trombe; *Fam* **the cheque bounced** le chèque a été refusé (parce qu'il était sans provision)

2 *Comput (of e-mail)* revenir à l'expéditeur

VT **1** *(ball)* faire rebondir; *Fig* **to b. a few ideas around** explorer quelques idées; **to b. a baby on one's knee** faire sauter un bébé sur ses genoux; *Fam* **to b. a cheque** *(of bank)* refuser un chèque sans provision

2 *Am Fam (person) (from job, nightclub etc)* flanquer à la porte

▸ *Comput* **b. message** = message *m* électronique non délivré revenu à l'expéditeur

▸ **bounce back** vi *(of ball)* rebondir; *Fig (of actor etc) (after failure)* faire son retour; *(from illness, disappointment)* se remettre; *(of Stock Exchange)* reprendre, remonter; *Fin* **the pound has bounced back against the dollar** la livre a regagné du terrain par rapport au dollar

▸ **bounce off** vt sep **to b. a ball off a wall/off the ground** faire rebondir une balle contre un mur/sur le sol; *Fig* **to b. an idea off sb** soumettre une idée à qn (pour voir sa réaction)

VT INSEP *(of ball, rain, bullets etc) (window, houses)* rebondir contre; *(roof, pavement)* rebondir sur; *Fig* **criticism bounces off him** *(does not penetrate)* les critiques ne l'atteignent pas

bouncer ['baʊnsər] N **1** *Fam (in nightclub etc)* videur *m* **2** *Sl (cheque)* chèque *m* sans provision *ou Fam* en bois **3** *Cr* balle *f* qui rebondit en hauteur

bouncing ['baʊnsɪŋ] ADJ *(ball)* rebondissant; *Fig (baby)* plein de vie et de santé

bouncy ['baʊnsɪ] ADJ **1** *(ball)* qui rebondit; *(hair)* plein de vigueur **2** *Fig (person)* plein d'entrain

▸▸ **b. castle** château *m* gonflable

bound¹ [baʊnd] N *(usu pl) (limit)* limite(s) *f(pl)*, bornes *fpl*; **out of bounds** interdit; *Mil etc* consigné; **to go beyond the bounds of reason** dépasser les bornes de la raison; **it is not beyond the bounds of possibility** c'est dans le domaine du possible; **my fury knew no bounds** je n'ai (pas) pu contenir ma fureur; **his ambition knows no bounds** son ambition ne connaît pas de bornes; **to keep within bounds** ne pas exagérer; **to keep one's imagination within (reasonable) bounds** mettre un frein à son imagination; **to keep one's spending within (reasonable) bounds** modérer *ou* limiter ses dépenses

VT *(usu passive) (area of town)* limiter, délimiter; *(country, region)* être limitrophe de; **France is bounded by Spain in the south** l'Espagne est limitrophe de la France au sud; **an area bounded by Smith Street on the west, James Avenue on the south** une zone délimitée par Smith Street à l'ouest et James Avenue au sud

bound² N *(jump)* bond *m*, saut *m*; **at one b.** d'un (seul) bond, d'un saut

VI *(of person, dog)* bondir; *(of ball etc)* rebondir; **he bounded across the room to greet them** il a traversé la pièce d'un bond pour venir les saluer

bound³ ADJ **1** *Naut* **a ship b. for America** *(still in port)* un navire en partance pour l'Amérique; *(under way)* un navire en route pour l'Amérique; **a plane b. for Paris** un avion à destination de Paris; **the plane which was b. for Paris crashed** l'avion qui volait à destination de Paris s'est écrasé; **where are you b. for?** où allez-vous?

2 *(sure)* **he's b. to come** il ne peut pas manquer de venir, il viendra sûrement; **it's b. to rain tomorrow** il pleuvra sûrement demain; **it's b. to happen** c'est fatal; *Fam* **he'll come, I'll be b.** il viendra, j'en suis sûr *ou* je vous le promets; *Am* **he's b. (and determined) to come and see you** il veut absolument venir vous voir

3 *Com* **b. by contract** lié par contrat

▸▸ *Ling* **b. morpheme** morphème *m* lié

bound⁴ PT, PP *see* bind

boundary ['baʊnd(ə)rɪ] N limite *f*; *Fig (between private and professional life etc)* frontière *f*; *Cr* **to hit** *or* **score a b.** envoyer la balle jusqu'aux limites du terrain; **the boundaries**

of human knowledge les limites de la connaissance humaine

(of parliamentary constituency) = modification *f* des limites d'une circonscription; **b. line** *(between properties)* limite; *Fig* frontière; *Sport* ligne *f* du jeu; **to form the b. line between two estates** marquer la limite entre deux domaines; **b. stone** borne *f*, pierre *f* de bornage

bounden ['baʊndən] ADJ *Lit* **b. duty** devoir *m* impérieux

bounder ['baʊndər] N *Old-fashioned Fam* goujat *m*

boundless ['baʊndlɪs] ADJ sans bornes, illimité

bounteous ['baʊntɪəs] ADJ *Lit* **1** *(harvest etc)* abondant **2** *(person)* libéral, -aux, généreux

bounteousness ['baʊntɪəsnɪs] N *Lit* **1** *(of harvest etc)* abondance *f* **2** *(of person)* bonté *f*, générosité *f*

bountiful ['baʊntɪfʊl] ADJ *Lit* **1** *(harvest, supply etc)* abondant **2** *(person)* généreux

bounty ['baʊntɪ] N **1** *(reward)* récompense *f* **2** *Lit (of person)* bonté *f*, générosité *f*; **the b. from one's garden** les fruits *mpl ou* produits *mpl* de son jardin

▸▸ **b. hunter** chasseur *m* de primes

bouquet N **1** [bəʊ'keɪ, bu:-] *(of flowers)* bouquet *m* *(composé par un fleuriste)*; *TV* **b. of channels** bouquet de chaînes **2** [bu:'keɪ] *(of wine)* bouquet *m*

Bourbon ['bʊəb(ə)n] N *Hist* Bourbon *mf*

▸▸ *Br* **b. biscuit** = biscuit *m* au chocolat fourré de crème au chocolat

bourbon ['bɜ:b(ə)n] N *(whiskey)* bourbon *m*

bourdon ['bʊəd(ə)n] N *Mus (of organ, bagpipes)* bourdon *m*

bourgeois ['bʊəʒwɑ:] ADJ, N *usu Pej* bourgeois, -oise

bourgeoisie [bʊəʒwɑ:'zi:] N *usu Pej* bourgeoisie *f*

bout [baʊt] N **1** *(in boxing, wrestling)* combat *m* **2** *(brief attack) (of malaria, rheumatism, bronchitis etc)* accès *m*; *(of fever)* accès, poussée *f*; *(of coughing)* quinte *f*, *(of self-pity)* crise *f*, *(of depression, intense activity)* période *f*, **she had a bad b. of flu** elle a eu une mauvaise grippe; **a b. of drinking** une période d'excès de boisson

boutique [bu:'ti:k] N boutique *f* de mode; *(in department store)* boutique

bovine ['bəʊvaɪn] ADJ *Zool* bovin; *Fig Pej (person)* lourd; **b. expression** *or* **look** regard *m* bovin; **b. stupidity** lourdeur *f*

▸▸ *Vet* **b. spongiform encephalopathy** encéphalite *f* bovine spongiforme

bovver ['bɒvər] N *Br Sl (hooliganism, rowdiness)* **to go out looking for b.** chercher la bagarre

▸▸ **b. boots** brodequins *mpl*, rangers *mpl*; **b. boys** voyous *mpl*

bow¹ [bəʊ] N **1** *(of archer)* arc *m*; **to draw a b.** bander *ou* tendre un arc; *Fig* **to have more than one string to one's b.** avoir plus d'une corde à son arc **2** *Mus (for violin etc)* archet *m*; *(movement)* coup *m* d'archet **3** *(in ribbon, shoelace)* nœud *m*

VT *Mus* jouer (avec l'archet); **bowed instrument** instrument *m* à archet

VI *Mus* jouer (de l'archet)

▸▸ **b. legs** jambes *fpl* arquées; **b. tie** nœud *m* papillon; *Br Archit* **b. window** fenêtre *f* en saillie, oriel *m*, bow-window *m*, *pl* bow-windows

bow² [baʊ] N *(as greeting etc)* salut *m*; *(from waist)* révérence *f*; **to make a deep** *or* **low b. to sb** saluer qn bien bas; **to take a b.** *(of performer)* saluer; **to take one's final b.** *(retire from stage etc permanently)* faire ses adieux

VI 1 *(as greeting etc)* s'incliner (**to** devant); *Pej* **to b. and scrape** faire des salamalecs *ou* des courbettes **2** *(to sb's will, decision etc)* se soumettre (**to** à); **to b. to the inevitable** s'incliner devant les faits; **I bowed to her (greater) wisdom** je me suis incliné devant tant de sagesse

VT *(head)* incliner, baisser; *(knee)* fléchir; *(sb's back, shoulders)* courber, voûter; **to become bowed** se voûter

▸ **bow down** **VI** *(incline one's head)* s'incliner; **to b. down before sb** faire des courbettes devant qn; *(very deeply)* se prosterner devant qn; *Fig* **the teachers b. down before the headmaster** les professeurs s'écrasent devant le directeur

VT SEP *(of poverty etc)* accabler; **he is bowed down by worry** il est accablé par les soucis

▸ **bow out** **VI** *Fam (leave job, relationship etc voluntarily)* tirer sa révérence

bow³ **N 1** *Naut (often pl)* avant *m*, étrave *f*, bossoir *m*; **on the port/starboard b.** par le bossoir bâbord/tribord; **to cross the bows of a ship** couper la route d'un navire **2** *(oarsman)* nageur *m* de tête *ou* de l'avant
▸▸ **b. oar** aviron *m* de l'avant; **b. rope** amarre *f* de bout *ou* de l'avant; **b. wave** lame *f* d'étrave

bowdlerize ['baʊdləraɪz] **VT** *(literary work)* expurger, couper; *Fig* **a bowdlerized version of the party** une version tronquée de la soirée

bowed [baʊd] **ADJ** **with b. head** la tête inclinée; *(with shame etc)* la tête baissée; **b. with age** courbé par le fardeau des ans

bowel ['baʊəl] **N** *Anat* intestin *m*; **bowels** intestins; **b. complaint** affection *f* intestinale; *Lit* **the bowels of the earth** les entrailles *fpl ou* le sein de la terre
▸▸ **b. movement** selles *fpl*; **have you had a b. movement today?** est-ce que vous êtes allé (à la selle) aujourd'hui?

bower ['baʊər] **N 1** *(in wood, garden)* berceau *m* de verdure, charmille *f*; *(made of trelliswork)* tonnelle *f* **2** *Lit Arch (lady's boudoir)* appartement *m*, boudoir *m*

bowerbird ['baʊəbɜːd] **N** oiseau *m* à berceau

bowfronted [baʊ'frʌntɪd] **ADJ** *(piece of furniture)* pansu; *(house)* à la façade arrondie

bowhead ['baʊhed] **N** *(whale)* baleine *f* boréale

bowing¹ ['baʊɪŋ] **N** *(as greeting etc)* saluts *mpl*; *Pej* **b. and scraping** courbettes *fpl*, salamalecs *mpl*

bowing² ['bəʊɪŋ] **N** *Mus* coups *mpl* d'archet; **her wonderful b.** son jeu magnifique à l'archet

bowl¹ [bəʊl] **N 1** *(for soup, cereal etc)* bol *m*; *(made of crystal etc)* coupe *f*; *(for washing hands, dishes)* cuvette *f*, bac *m* (d'évier); *(plastic)* bassine *f*; *(of toilet)* cuvette **2** *(of tobacco pipe)* fourneau *m*, godet *m*; *(of spoon)* cuilleron *m*; *(of stemmed glass)* coupe *f*, *(of scales)* plateau *m* **3** *Geog* cuvette *f*, bassin *m* **4** *Am (for concerts etc)* amphithéâtre *m*

bowl² **N** *Sport* boule *f*; **bowls** *(game)* *(on grass)* boules; *(in bowling alley)* bowling *m*; **to play (at) bowls** jouer aux boules/au bowling VOIR GRAMMAIRE A10
VT 1 *(hoop)* faire rouler **2** *Sport (ball)* lancer, rouler **3** *Cr (ball)* lancer, servir; *(player)* renverser le guichet à
VI 1 *(play bowls) (on grass)* jouer aux boules; *(in bowling alley)* jouer au bowling **2** *Cr* lancer *ou* servir la balle; **well bowled!** bien lancé!
▸ **bowl along** **VI** *(in car, train)* rouler rapidement
▸ **bowl out** **VT SEP** *Cr* renverser le guichet de

▸ **bowl over** **VT SEP 1** *(knock down)* *(skittles, person etc)* renverser **2** *Fam (astound)* époustoufler; **I was bowled over by her beauty** sa beauté m'a époustouflé, j'ai été époustouflé par sa beauté; **I was bowled over by winning first prize** j'ai été sidéré *ou* époustouflé de gagner le premier prix

bowlegged [baʊ'legɪd] **ADJ** aux jambes arquées

bowler¹ ['baʊlər] **N 1** *(in bowls)* *(on grass)* joueur, -euse de boules, bouliste *mf*; *(in bowling alley)* joueur, -euse de bowling **2** *Cr* lanceur, -euse, serveur, -euse

bowler² **N** *(chapeau m)* melon *m*
▸▸ **b. hat** *(chapeau)* melon

bowlful ['baʊlfʊl] **N** *(of milk, soup etc)* plein bol *m*; *(of washing-up water)* cuvette *f*

bowline ['baʊlɪn] **N** *Naut* **1** *(rope)* bouline *f* **2** *(knot)* nœud *m* de chaise *ou* d'agui

bowling ['baʊlɪŋ] **N 1** *(game)* *(on grass)* jeu *m* de boules; *(tenpin)* bowling *m* **2** *(action)* lancement *m* de la boule; *Cr* lancement de la balle
▸▸ **b. alley** *(building)* bowling *m*; *(single lane)* piste *f* de bowling; **b. ball** boule *f* de bowling; **b. green** terrain *m* de boules *(sur gazon)*

bowman, *pl* **bowmen** ['baʊmən] **N** *Hist* archer *m*

bowsaw ['baʊsɔː] **N** *(tool)* scie *f* à archet *ou* à arc *ou* à chantourner

bowser ['baʊzər] **N** *Petr* camion-citerne *m*, *pl* camions-citernes

bowsprit ['baʊsprɪt] **N** *Naut* beaupré *m*

bowstring ['baʊstrɪŋ] **N** corde *f* d'arc

bow-wow ['baʊ'waʊ] **INTERJ** oua-oua!
N *Fam (dog in children's language)* toutou *m*

box¹ [bɒks] **N 1** *(container)* *(small)* boîte *f*, *(large)* coffre *m*, caisse *f*, *Gym (for vaulting)* plinth *m*; *(casing of computer)* boîte; **a b. of cigars/chocolates** une boîte de cigares/chocolats; **jewel b.** coffret *m* à bijoux; **safety deposit b.** coffre-fort *m*, *pl* coffres-forts; **Christmas b.** *(gratuity)* ≃ étrennes *fpl*; *Fig* **in a pine** *or* **wooden b.** *(coffin)* dans un cercueil; *Br Sl* **to be out of one's b.** *(extremely drunk)* être complètement pété, être plein comme une barrique
2 *(postal)* **b. number 12** référence 12; **write to b. number 12** *(in newspaper advertisement)* écrire en rappelant la référence 12
3 *Fam* **the b.** *(television)* la télé; **on the b.** à la télé
4 *(enclosed space)* *(in stables)* stalle *f*, *Theat* loge *f*, *(on ground floor)* baignoire *f*, *Tel* cabine *f* téléphonique; *Ftbl (for penalties)* surface *f* de réparation; **my flat is a bit of a b.** mon appartement est à peu près grand comme un mouchoir de poche
5 *Tech (of axle, brake)* boîte *f*, *(of wheel)* moyeu *m*; *(of lock)* palâtre *m*, palastre *m*
6 *(printed, drawn) (to fill in on form etc)* case *f*, *(boxed text)* pavé *m*, encadré *m*; *(frame around article)* cadre *m*; *(on screen)* boîte *f*, case; *(that can be drawn)* encadré; **to draw a b. round sth** encadrer qch
VT *(goods)* mettre en carton
▸▸ *Phot* **b. camera** appareil *m* photographique rudimentaire; *Am Geog* **b. canyon** cañon *m ou* canyon *m* encaissé; **b. file** boîte archive; *Constr* **b. girder** poutre-caisson *f*, *pl* poutres-caissons; *Br* **b. junction** carrefour *m* *(matérialisé sur la chaussée par des bandes croisées)*; **b. kite** cerf-volant *m* cellulaire, *pl* cerfs-volants cellulaires; *Cin*, *Theat* **b. office** *(office)* bureau *m* de location; *(window)* guichet *m* (de location); *Sewing* **b. pleat** pli *m* creux; **b. spanner** clef *f* à douille; **b. spring** sommier *m* à ressort; **b. wrench** clef à douille
▸ **box in** **VT SEP 1** *(surround)* *(person)* coincer;

the defence seem to have him boxed in la défense semble l'avoir coincé **2** *(enclose)* *(bath, washbasin etc)* encastrer; **don't you feel boxed in in such a small room?** tu ne te sens pas un peu à l'étroit dans une pièce aussi petite?; **to be boxed in** *(by other cars)* être coincé par d'autres voitures

box² **N** *(blow)* **b. (on the ear)** gifle *f*, claque *f*, taloche *f*; **to give sb a b. on the ear** gifler qn
VT **to b. sb's ears** gifler qn, *Fam* flanquer une gifle *ou* une claque *ou* une taloche à qn
VI *Sport* boxer, faire de la boxe; *(of two opponents)* combattre

box³ **N 1** *(tree)* buis *m* **2** *(wood)* (bois *m* de) buis *m*
▸▸ **b. tree** buis

box-calf **N** *(leather)* box-calf *m*, *pl* box-calfs, *Fam* box *m*

boxcar ['bɒkskɑːr] **N** *Am Rail* wagon *m*, fourgon *m*

boxed [bɒkst] **ADJ 1** *Com etc* en boîte; *(jewellery)* en écrin; *(person) (surrounded)* coincé; *(confined)* à l'étroit; **b. in** *(bath etc)* encastré **2** *(text)* encadré; **b. article** encadré *m*

Boxer ['bɒksər] **N** *Hist* Boxer *m* (chinois)
▸▸ **the B. Rebellion** la révolte des Boxers

boxer ['bɒksər] **N 1** *(fighter)* boxeur, -euse; *Fam* **boxers** *(underwear)* caleçon *m* **2** *(dog)* boxer *m*
▸▸ *Aut* **b. engine** moteur *m* à cylindres à plat, boxer *m*; **b. shorts** caleçon

boxful ['bɒksfʊl] **N** *(small)* pleine boîte *f*, *(large)* plein coffre *m*, pleine caisse *f*

Boxing Day **N** *Br* = le 26 décembre

boxing ['bɒksɪŋ] **N** *Sport* boxe *f*; **he loves b.** il adore la boxe
▸▸ **b. glove** gant *m* de boxe; **b. match** match *m* de boxe; **b. ring** ring *m*

box-pleated **ADJ** à plis creux *ou* ronds

boxroom ['bɒksruːm] **N** débarras *m*

boxwood ['bɒkswʊd] **N** (bois *m* de) buis *m*

boy [bɔɪ] **N 1** garçon *m*; **boys will be boys** les hommes et les garçons sont comme ça et on ne les changera pas
2 *Sch* élève *m*; **day b.** externe *m*
3 *Fam (man)* **a new b.** *(in company)* un nouveau; **the race was won by a local b.** c'est un jeune de la région qui a gagné la course; **a nice old b.** un vieux monsieur sympathique; *Br Old-fashioned* **I say, old b.!** dis, mon vieux!; **one of the boys** un joyeux vivant; **he's having a night out with the boys** il est sorti avec ses copains; **come on, boys!** allons-y les gars!; *Br Fam* **the boys in blue** *(police)* = la police; *Sl* **he threatened to send the boys round** il a menacé d'envoyer ses gars; *Sl* **the big boys** *(important men)* les grosses légumes *fpl*; *Fig* **to play with the big boys** jouer dans la cour des grands; *esp Am* **oh b.!** ben alors!, dis donc!; *esp Am* **b., am I glad to be home!** dis donc, qu'est-ce que je suis content d'être rentré à la maison!
4 *(employee) (in Africa)* boy *m*; **office b.** garçon *m* de bureau
▸▸ **b. band** boys band *m*; *Br Fam* **b. racer** jeune conducteur *m* imprudent; **b. scout** scout *m*; **b. wonder** petit génie *m*

boycott ['bɔɪkɒt] **N** boycott *m*, boycottage *m*; **to put under a b.**, **to put a b. on** *(goods, company, event etc)* boycotter
VT *(person, company, event etc)* boycotter

boyfriend ['bɔɪfrend] **N** *(of girl, woman)* (petit) ami *m*, *Can Fam* chum *m*

boyhood ['bɔɪhʊd] **N** *(when very young)* enfance *f*, première jeunesse *f*, *(in teens)* adolescence *f*; **b. friends** amis *mpl* d'enfance

boyish ['bɔɪʃ] **ADJ 1** *(hopes, enthusiasm)* d'enfant, enfantin **2** *(charm)* juvénile; *(tomboyish) (clothes, figure, face)* de garçon; **b. good looks** *(of man)* air *m* de beau gosse;

(of woman) air de joli garçon; **b. haircut** coupe *f* de cheveux à la garçonne **3** *(manners)* de garçon

boyishly [ˈbɔɪɪʃlɪ] **ADV** *(to smile, laugh)* comme un enfant; *(tomboyishly)* comme un garçon

boyishness [ˈbɔɪɪʃnɪs] **N** manières *fpl* de garçon *ou* de jeune homme

boy-meets-girl **ADJ** **b. story** *(book, film)* banale histoire *f* d'amour

bozo [ˈbəʊzəʊ] **N** *Am Sl (stupid man)* débile *m*, abruti *m*

bps [biːpiːˈes] **N** *Comput (abbr* **bits per second)** bps

BR [biːˈɑːr] **N** *Formerly (abbr* **British Rail)** = service *m* national des chemins de fer britannique

bra [brɑː] **N** soutien-gorge *m*, *pl* soutiens-gorge
▸▸**b. top** brassière *f*

brace [breɪs] **N 1** *Constr etc* étai *m*; **cross or diagonal b.** écharpe *f*, diagonale *f*
2 *Med (on teeth)* appareil *m* dentaire; *(on leg)* armature *f* orthopédique; *(on torso)* corset *m*; **neck b.** minerve *f*
3 *Br* **braces** *(for trousers)* bretelles *fpl*
4 *(pair) (of partridges, pheasants etc)* couple *m*; *(of pistols etc)* paire *f*, **two b. of partridges** deux couples de perdrix
5 *(drill)* **b. (and bit)** vilebrequin *m* (et sa mèche); *Aut* **wheel b.** vilebrequin (à roues)
6 *Typ (bracket)* accolade *f*
VT 1 *Constr etc (construction, wall, roof)* étayer; *Aviat (wing)* croisillonner
2 *(tense) (bow)* tendre, bander; **to b. (the skin of) a drum** tendre la peau d'un tambour, bander un tambour; **the passengers braced themselves for the impact** les passagers se raidirent avant le choc; **she braced herself between two rocks** elle s'arc-bouta entre deux rochers; **b. yourself!** *(hold tight)* tiens bon!; *(be brave)* courage!; **b. yourself for a shock** prépare-toi à recevoir un choc
3 *(strengthen) (body)* fortifier; *(nerves)* tonifier; **a whisky to b. myself** un whisky pour me donner du courage; **to b. oneself to do sth** rassembler ses forces pour faire qch, s'armer de courage pour faire qch

bracelet [ˈbreɪslɪt] **N 1** *(jewellery)* bracelet *m*; **chain b.** gourmette *f* **2** *Fam* **bracelets** *(handcuffs)* bracelets *mpl*; **put the bracelets on him** passe-lui les bracelets
▸▸**b. watch** montre-bracelet *f* pour femme, *pl* montres-bracelets

bracer [ˈbreɪsər] **N** *Fam* (petit verre *m* de) remontant *m*

brachial [ˈbrækɪəl, ˈbreɪk-] **ADJ** *Anat* brachial, -aux

brachiopod [ˈbrækɪəpɒd] **N** *(mollusc)* brachiopode *m*

brachycephalic [brækɪsɪˈfælɪk] **ADJ** brachycéphale

bracing [ˈbreɪsɪŋ] **ADJ** *(air, climate etc)* vivifiant, tonifiant; *Fig (effect)* stimulant
▸▸ *Constr* **b. strut** jambe *f* de force

bracken [ˈbræk(ə)n] **N** *(plant)* fougère *f*

bracket [ˈbrækɪt] **N 1** *Constr, Tech (for fixing or supporting)* tasseau *m*, équerre *f*; *(for holding part)* support *m*; *(for lamp)* applique *f*; *Archit* corbeau *m* **2** *Typ etc (square)* crochet *m*; *(round)* parenthèse *f*, *(connecting two lines)* accolade *f*; **in brackets** entre parenthèses/crochets/accolades **3** *Admin (level of income, tax)* tranche *f*; *(of salaries)* fourchette *f*; **the 15-to-20 age b.** le groupe *ou* la classe des 15 à 20 ans; **people in the upper income brackets** les gens dans les tranches de revenu les plus élevées; **what tax b. are you in?** dans quelle tranche d'imposition es-tu?
VT (-t-) 1 *(words etc)* mettre entre parenthè-

ses; *(in square brackets)* mettre entre crochets; *(in a vertical list)* réunir par une accolade **2** *Fig (two ideas)* associer; *(two candidates)* placer ex aequo; **bracketed together** *(candidates)* classé ex aequo; **his name has often been bracketed with hers** son nom a souvent été associé au sien; **he didn't want to be bracketed (together) with them** il ne voulait pas qu'on le mette dans le même sac
▸▸**b. lamp** (lampe *f* d')applique

bracketing [ˈbrækɪtɪŋ] **N** *(action)* mise *f* entre parenthèses; *(with square brackets)* mise entre crochets; *(in a vertical list)* réunion *f* par une accolade

brackish [ˈbrækɪʃ] **ADJ** *(water)* saumâtre

bract [brækt] **N** *Bot* bractée *f*

brad [bræd] **N** *(nail)* clou *m* de tapissier, semence *f*

bradawl [ˈbrædɔːl] **N** *(tool)* alêne *f* plate, poinçon *m*

bradycardia [brædɪˈkɑːdɪə] **N** *Med* bradycardie *f*

brae [breɪ] **N** *Scot* colline *f*

brag [bræg] **N 1** *(boast)* vantardise *f*, forfanterie *f* **2** *Cards* = sorte *f* de poker
VI (-gg-) *(boast)* se vanter (**of, about** de); **it's not something to b. about!** il n'y a pas de quoi s'en vanter!; **you've got nothing to b. about** tu n'as pas de quoi te vanter
VT to b. that one has done sth se vanter d'avoir fait qch; **he bragged that he would win** il s'est vanté de pouvoir gagner

braggadocio [brægəˈdəʊtʃɪəʊ] **N** *Lit* vantardise *f*

braggart [ˈbrægət] **N** *Old-fashioned* vantard, -arde, hâbleur, -euse

bragging [ˈbrægɪŋ] **ADJ** vantard, hâbleur, -euse
N vantardise *f*, hâblerie *f*

Brahman [ˈbrɑːmən] **N** brahmane *mf*

Brahmanism [ˈbrɑːmənɪz(ə)m] **N** brahmanisme *m*

Brahmin [ˈbrɑːmɪn] **N 1** *(in India)* brahmane *mf* **2** *Am Fam (intellectual)* intellectuel, -elle; *(member of the upper classes)* membre *m* de la haute

braid [breɪd] **N 1** *esp Am (of hair)* tresse *f*, natte *f*, **she wears her hair in braids** elle porte *ou* se fait des nattes **2** *(on cushion, clothing etc)* galon *m*, passepoil *m*; **gold b.** *(on officer's uniform)* galon
VT 1 *(straw)* tresser; *esp Am (hair)* tresser, natter **2** *(clothing)* galonner, soutacher; *(edge of chair etc)* passementer

braiding [ˈbreɪdɪŋ] **N 1** *esp Am (of hair)* tressage *m*, nattage *m* **2** *(decoration) (on cushion, clothing)* galon *m*, passepoil *m*

Braille [breɪl] **N** braille *m*; **to read B.** lire le braille; **in B.** en braille
▸▸**B. alphabet** alphabet *m* braille

brain [breɪn] **N 1** *(organ)* cerveau *m*; *Culin* **brains** cervelle *f*; **to blow sb's brains out** faire sauter la cervelle à qn; *Fam* **to have money on the b.** être obsédé par l'argent; *Fam* **to have a tune on the b.** avoir un air dans la tête; **to be b. dead** *Med* être en coma dépassé; *Fam Fig (extremely stupid)* ne rien avoir dans la cervelle; **she had a b. scan** on lui a fait un scanner du cerveau
2 *(intelligence)* **brains** intelligence *f*, **he has brains** *or* **a good b.** il est intelligent; **I haven't the brains to become a doctor** je ne suis pas assez intelligent pour devenir médecin; **anyone with half a b.** n'importe qui d'un tant soit peu intelligent; **he's the brains of the family** c'est lui le plus intelligent de la famille; **she's the brains of the business** c'est elle le cerveau de l'entreprise; **use your brains** fais marcher ta cervelle

3 *Fam (intelligent person)* cerveau *m*; **to call in the best brains** faire appel à tous les talents; **she's a real b. at maths** c'est une tête en maths
VT *Sl (hit over head)* assommer; **I brained myself on the cupboard door** je me suis cogné contre la porte du placard
▸▸ *Med* **b. damage** lésions *fpl* cérébrales; *Med* **b. death** mort *f* cérébrale; **b. disease** maladie *f* cérébrale; *Fam* **the b. drain** l'exode *m ou* la fuite des cerveaux; *Old-fashioned* **b. fever** fièvre *f* cérébrale; *Anat* **b. stem** pédoncule *m* cérébral; *Med* **b. surgeon** neurochirurgien, -ienne; *Med* **b. surgery** neurochirurgie *f*, *Am* **b. trust**, *Br* **brains trust** brain-trust *m*, *pl* brain-trusts; *Med* **b. tumour** tumeur *m* au cerveau; *Br Fam* **b. wave** idée *f* de génie, idée lumineuse

> When translating **brain**, note that **cerveau** and **cervelle** are not interchangeable. **Cerveau** refers to the organ, whereas generally **cervelle** refers to brain matter.

brainbox [ˈbreɪnbɒks] **N** *Sl* **1** *Old-fashioned (skull)* boîte *f* crânienne **2** *(intelligent person)* tête *f*; **she's a real b.** c'est une sacrée tête

brainchild [ˈbreɪntʃaɪld] **N** *Fam* trouvaille *f*

brainless [ˈbreɪnlɪs] **ADJ** *Fam (stupid)* stupide; **he's a b. idiot** c'est un idiot sans pareil

brainpower [ˈbreɪnpaʊər] **N** intelligence *f*

brainstorm [ˈbreɪnstɔːm] **N 1** *Br* **I must have had a b.** j'ai dû avoir un moment d'égarement **2** *Am Fam (brilliant idea)* idée *f* de génie

brainstorming [ˈbreɪnstɔːmɪŋ] **N** brainstorming *m*, remue-méninges *m inv*; **b. session** réunion *f* de remue-méninges; **we had a b. session** nous avons eu un brainstorming

brain-teaser **N** casse-tête *m inv*

brainwash [ˈbreɪnwɒʃ] **VT** faire un lavage de cerveau à; **to b. sb into doing sth** faire un lavage de cerveau à qn pour qu'il fasse qch; *Fig* **they've been brainwashed into believing that ...** on leur a mis dans la tête que ...; **I won't be brainwashed into buying things I don't need** je refuse de me laisser manipuler pour acheter des choses dont je n'ai pas besoin

brainwashing [ˈbreɪnwɒʃɪŋ] **N** lavage *m* de cerveau

brainwork [ˈbreɪnwɜːk] **N** travail *m* intellectuel

brainy [ˈbreɪnɪ] **ADJ** *Fam (person)* intelligent; *(idea)* génial, -aux; **she's really b.** il y en a là-dedans; **I can't cope with b. stuff like that** c'est trop compliqué pour moi

braise [breɪz] **VT** *Culin* braiser, cuire à l'étouffée; **braised beef** bœuf *m* braisé; **braised chicken** poulet *m* en cocotte

braising [ˈbreɪzɪŋ] **N** *Culin* cuisson *f* à l'étouffée
▸▸**b. beef** bœuf *m* à braiser

brake¹ [breɪk] **N** *(on car, train etc)* frein *m*; **to apply the brake(s)** *(in traffic)* freiner; **to put the b. on** *(after parking)* mettre ou serrer le frein; **to slam on the brakes** écraser la pédale de frein, *Fam* piler; **to release the brake(s)** desserrer le frein; *Fig* **to put a b.** *or* **the brakes on a project** donner un coup de frein à un projet; *Fig* **b. on growth** frein à l'expansion
VI *Aut (in traffic)* freiner; **to b. hard** freiner brusquement, écraser la pédale de frein, *Fam* piler
▸▸ *Aut* **b. adjuster spanner** clé *f* de réglage des freins; *Aut* **b. block** sabot *m ou* patin *m* de frein; *Aut* **b. fade** fading *m*; *Aut* **b. fluid** liquide *m* de freins, Lockheed® *m*; *Aut* **b. horsepower** puissance *f* au frein; *Aut, Tech* **b. lever** frein à main; *Aut* **b. light** feu *m* de stop; *Aut* **b. lining** garniture *f* de frein; *Aut* **b.**

pad plaquette *f* de frein; *Aut* **b. pedal** pédale *f* de frein; *Aut* **b. shoe** mâchoire *f* de frein; *Br Rail* **b. van** fourgon *m* à frein

brake² N *(undergrowth)* fourré *m*, hallier *m*

brake³ N *(vehicle)* = **break²**

braked trailer ['breɪkt] N remorque *f* freinée

brakelight function ['breɪklaɪt] N *Am TV, Radio* signal *m* de fin de temps de parole

brakesman, *Am* **brakeman,** *pl* **brakesmen** ['breɪk(s)mən] N *Rail etc* garde-frein(s) *m*, *pl* gardes-frein(s)

braking ['breɪkɪŋ] N *(in traffic)* freinage *m*; *(abrupt)* coup *m* de frein
▸▸ **b. distance** distance *f* de freinage

bramble ['bræmb(ə)l] N 1 *(shrub)* ronce *f ou* mûrier *m* des haies; **brambles** *(thorns)* ronces 2 *(fruit)* mûre *f* (de ronce), mûre sauvage
▸▸ **b. jelly** gelée *f* de mûres

brambly ['bræmblɪ] ADJ plein *ou* couvert de ronces

bran [bræn] N *(of oats, wheat)* son *m*
▸▸ **b. flakes** son en flocons; *Br* **b. mash** son *ou* bran *m* mouillé; *Br* **b. tub** pêche *f* miraculeuse *(jeu)*

branch [brɑːntʃ] N 1 *(of tree)* branche *f*, rameau *m*; **the branches** le branchage, les branches
2 *(of road)* embranchement *m*; *(of river)* bras *m*; *(of candlestick, family, science, industry etc, of artery)* branche *f*
3 *Admin, Com (of shop)* succursale *f*; *(of company)* agence *f*, succursale; *(of bank)* agence, succursale, guichet *m*; **where's the nearest b. of Harvey Nicks?** où se trouve le Harvey Nicks le plus proche?
4 *Mil (of armed forces)* division *f*; *(in administration)* branche *f*
5 *Comput* branchement *m*
VI 1 *(of road etc)* bifurquer; **at the point where the road branches** à l'endroit où la route bifurque 2 *(of tree)* faire des branches
▸▸ **b. banking** banque *f* à réseau; *Rail* **b. line** ligne *f* secondaire; **b. manager** *(of bank)* directeur, -trice d'agence; *(of shop)* directeur, -trice de succursale; **b. office** *(of company)* succursale; *(of bank)* agence, succursale
▸ **branch off** VI *(of road)*, *Fig (in conversation etc)* bifurquer; *Fig* **then I branched off into quantum mechanics** puis j'ai bifurqué vers la mécanique quantique
▸ **branch out** VI *(of person, organization etc)* étendre ses activités, se diversifier; **to b. out into …** étendre ses activités à …; **I'm going to b. out on my own** je vais faire cavalier seul

branched [brɑːntʃt] ADJ 1 *Bot* branchu, rameux 2 *(candlestick)* à (plusieurs) branches

branchia, *pl* **branchiae** ['bræŋkɪə, -iː] N branchie *f*

branchiate ['bræŋkɪət] ADJ *Zool* branchié

brand [brænd] N 1 *Com, Mktg* marque *f* (de fabrique); *Fig* **he has his own b. of humour** il a un humour un peu particulier; **a good b. of cigars** une bonne marque de cigares 2 *(on cattle)* marque *f* au fer rouge; *Hist (on criminal)* flétrissure *f*, marque au fer rouge; *(branding iron)* fer *m* rouge; **the cattle have his b. on them** le bétail porte sa marque 3 *(burning wood)* brandon *m*, tison *m*
VT *(with branding iron) (person, animal, goods)* marquer au fer rouge; *Hist (criminal)* flétrir, marquer au fer rouge; *(slave)* marquer; **to b. sb (as) a liar/coward/etc** coller à qn une étiquette de menteur/lâche/*etc*; *Fig* **to be branded on sb's memory** *(of sight, scene)* être gravé dans la mémoire de qn; **the experience branded them for life** l'expérience les a marqués à vie
ADV **b. new** tout neuf, flambant neuf
▸▸ *Mktg* **b. advertising** publicité *f* de

marque, publicité sur la marque; **b. awareness** mémorisation *f* de la marque, notoriété *f* de la marque; **b. beliefs** croyances *fpl* vis-à-vis d'une marque; **b. competition** concurrence *f* entre marques; **b. concept** concept *m* de marque; **b. extension** extension *f* de la marque; **b. familiarity** connaissance *f* de la marque; **b. identifier** identificateur *m* de marque; **b. image** image *f* de marque; **b. imitation** imitation *f* de marque; **b. leader** marque dominante; **b. life-cycle** cycle *m* de vie de la marque; **b. loyalty** fidélité *f* à la marque; **b. manager** chef *m* de marque; **b. mapping** carte *f* perceptuelle des marques, carte des positions de marques; **b. mark** emblème *m* de marque; **b. name** marque (de fabrique); **b. name recall** mémorisation de la marque; **b. positioning** positionnement *m* de la marque; **b. preference** préférence *f* pour une marque; **b. recognition** identification *f* de la marque; **b. sensitivity** sensibilité *f* aux marques; **b. switching** changement *m* de marque

branded ['brændɪd] ADJ 1 *(cattle, criminal etc)* marqué au fer rouge 2 *(product)* de marque

branding ['brændɪŋ] N 1 *(of cattle)* marquage *m* au fer rouge 2 *Mktg* marquage *m*
▸▸ **b. iron** fer *m* à marquer

brandish ['brændɪʃ] VT *(weapon etc)* brandir

brand-led ADJ *Mktg* conditionné *ou* piloté par la marque

brand-loyal ADJ *Mktg* fidèle à la marque

brandy ['brændɪ] N *(cognac)* cognac *m*; *(clear spirit)* eau-de-vie, *pl* eaux-de-vie; **b. and soda** = cognac à l'eau de Seltz
▸▸ *Br Culin* **b. butter** = beurre *m* mélangé avec du sucre et parfumé au cognac; **b. glass** verre *m* à cognac; *Br Culin* **b. snap** cigarette *f* russe au gingembre

brash [bræʃ] ADJ *(person) (impudent)* effronté, présomptueux, impudent; *(showing off)* exubérant; *(manner)* présomptueux; *(colour)* cru

brashly ['bræʃlɪ] ADV *(with impudence)* effrontément, présomptueusement, impudemment; *(when showing off)* avec exubérance

brashness ['bræʃnɪs] N *(impudence)* effronterie *f*, impudence *f*; *(showing off)* exubérance *f*

brass [brɑːs] N 1 *(metal)* laiton *m*; *Fig* **to get down to b. tacks** en venir aux faits; *Br* **I haven't got a b. farthing** *(any money)* je n'ai pas un rond; *Br* **it's not worth a b. farthing** ça ne vaut pas un clou; *Mil Fam* **the top b.** les huiles *fpl*; *Br Sl* **it's a bit b. monkeys today** *(very cold)* on se les caille 2 *(item) (in church)* plaque *f* tombale en cuivre; **brass(es)** *(household objects etc)* cuivres *mpl*; **to do** *or* **clean the b.** *or* **brasses** faire les cuivres; **the b.** *(in band, orchestra)* les cuivres 3 *Br Fam (money)* argent *m*, galette *f* 4 *Br Fam (cheek, nerve)* culot *m*; **to have the b. to do sth** avoir le culot de faire qch
▸▸ *Mus* **b. band** fanfare *f*, orchestre *m* de cuivres; **b. foundry** fonderie *f* de cuivre; *Br Fam Fig* **b. hat** gros bonnet *m*; *Mus* **b. instrument** cuivre *m*; *Br Fam* **b. neck** *(cheek, nerve)* culot; **to have a b. neck** avoir du culot, être culotté; *Can* avoir du front tout le tour de la tête; **what a b. neck!** quel culot!; **b. plate** plaque de cuivre; *(of doctor, lawyer etc)* plaque; *Art* **b. rubbing** *(picture)* décalque *m*; *(action)* décalquage *m* par frottement
▸ **brass off** VT SEP *Br Fam (usu passive)* **to be brassed off** en avoir marre, en avoir ras le bol; **I'm brassed off with waiting** j'en ai marre *ou* ras le bol d'attendre; **I'm brassed off with their complaints** j'en ai plein le dos de leurs récriminations

brasserie ['bræsərɪ] N *(restaurant, bar)* brasserie *f*

brassic ['bræsɪk] ADJ *Br Fam (poor)* fauché, à sec, sans un

brassica ['bræsɪkə] N *Bot* brassica *m*

brassie ['bræsɪ] N *Golf* brassie *m*

brassière ['bræzɪər, *Am* brə'zɪər] N soutien-gorge *m*, *pl* soutiens-gorge

brassiness ['brɑːsɪnɪs] N 1 *(of piece of music)* sons *mpl* cuivrés 2 *Fam (insolence)* culot *m*

brassware ['brɑːsweər] N dinanderie *f*

brasswork ['brɑːswɜːk] N dinanderie *f*, chaudronnerie *f* d'art

brassy ['brɑːsɪ] N *Golf* brassie *m*
ADJ 1 *Pej (yellow, blonde)* artificiel; *(cheap jewellery)* qui fait toc 2 *(sound)* cuivré 3 *Pej Fam (person)* effronté

brat [bræt] N *Pej* gamin, -ine, morveux, -euse
▸▸ *Cin* **the B. Pack** = terme désignant les jeunes acteurs américains populaires des années 80

bravado [brə'vɑːdəʊ] N bravade *f*

brave [breɪv] ADJ courageux; **be b. for a little bit longer** courage, c'est presque fini; **as b. as a lion** courageux comme un lion; **to put a b. face on it** faire bonne contenance; **to make a b. effort to smile** s'efforcer bravement de sourire; **it was a b. effort, nonetheless** néanmoins, c'était un bel effort; *Fig* **a b. new world for small business** un paradis pour les petites entreprises
N *(American Indian warrior)* brave *m*
VT *(person)* braver, défier; *(danger etc)* braver, affronter

---

Note that the French adjective **brave** is a false friend. Its most common meaning is **kind**.

---

bravely ['breɪvlɪ] ADV courageusement, vaillamment

bravery ['breɪvərɪ] N courage *m*, bravoure *f*; **she was decorated for b.** elle a été décorée pour son courage

bravo [brɑː'vəʊ] INT bravo!

bravura [brə'vʊərə] N *Mus* morceau *m* de bravoure

brawl [brɔːl] N rixe *f*, bagarre *f*; **drunken b.** querelle *f* d'ivrognes
VI *(of people)* se bagarrer

brawler ['brɔːlər] N bagarreur, -euse

brawling ['brɔːlɪŋ] N rixes *fpl*, bagarres *fpl*

brawn [brɔːn] N 1 *Fam* muscles *mpl*; **to have plenty of b.** avoir du biceps; **he's got more b. than brains** il a du muscle mais pas grand-chose dans la tête 2 *Br Culin* fromage *m* de tête

brawny ['brɔːnɪ] ADJ *(arm)* fort, musculeux; *(person)* musclé, bien bâti

bray [breɪ] N *(of donkey)* braiment *m*
VI *(of donkey)* braire

braze [breɪz] VT *Tech (using solder)* braser; *(using brass)* souder au laiton

brazen ['breɪz(ə)n] ADJ 1 *(shameless)* effronté, impudent; **I wish they weren't so b. about it** ils pourraient au moins faire ça discrètement; **b. lie** mensonge *m* éhonté; **a b. hussy** une effrontée 2 *Lit (made of brass)* *(vase, pot etc)* d'airain 3 *Mus* cuivré
▸ **brazen out** VT SEP **to b. it out** s'en tirer au culot

brazen-faced [-feɪst] ADJ effronté, impudent

brazenly ['breɪz(ə)nlɪ] ADV effrontément, impudemment

brazenness ['breɪz(ə)nnɪs] N effronterie *f*

brazier ['breɪzɪər] N brasero *m*

Brazil [brə'zɪl] N Brésil *m*

brazil [brə'zɪl] N noix *f* du Brésil
▸▸ **b. nut** noix du Brésil

Brazilian [brə'zɪlɪən] **ADJ** brésilien
 N 1 (person) Brésilien, -ienne **2** (wax) épilation f maillot brésilien

breach [briːtʃ] **N 1** (of regulations etc) infraction f, contravention f; (of law, professional secrecy etc) violation f (**of** de); (of discipline) manquement m (**of** à); (of contract) rupture f (**of** de); **the company is in b. of the law** la société enfreint la législation; **the company is suing him for b. of contract** la société lui fait un procès pour rupture de contrat; **b. of good manners** manque m de savoir-vivre; **to commit a b. of etiquette** manquer au protocole
 2 (between two friends etc) brouille f
 3 (in wall), Mil (in defences) brèche f; Fig **they found a b. in his defences** ils ont trouvé sa faille; Mil **to stand in the b.** monter sur la brèche; **to make a b. in the enemy's lines** percer les lignes de l'ennemi; Fig **to step into the b.** intervenir au pied levé; **it was very good of you to step into the b.** c'est très aimable à vous de l'avoir remplacé(e)
 VT 1 (violate) (contract, agreement, treaty) rompre **2** (make hole in) (dam, wall) ouvrir une brèche dans; Mil (wall) battre en brèche; (enemy lines) percer; **to b. the surface of the water** apparaître à la surface de l'eau; (of rocks) pointer à la surface de l'eau
 VI (of whale) sauter au-dessus de la surface de l'eau
 ▸▸ **b. of faith** manquement à sa parole; Law **b. of the peace** atteinte à l'ordre public; Parl **b. of privilege** atteinte f aux privilèges parlementaires; **b. of promise** manque de parole; (of marriage) violation de promesse de mariage; **b. of trust** abus m de confiance; Law (by trustee etc) violation d'un des devoirs d'un mandataire

bread [bred] **N 1** pain m; **a loaf of b.** un pain; **b. and butter** pain beurré; **a slice of b. and butter** une tartine de beurre, une tartine beurrée; Fig **poetry doesn't earn you your b. and butter** la poésie ne nourrit pas son homme; Fig **the customers are our b. and butter** les clients sont notre gagne-pain; **to be on b. and water** être au pain (sec) et à l'eau; Rel **give us this day our daily b.** donne-nous aujourd'hui notre pain de ce jour; Fig **to earn one's (daily) b.** gagner sa vie ou son pain; Fig **to take the b. out of sb's mouth** enlever le pain de la bouche de qn; Fig **to put b. on the table** (of person) faire bouillir la marmite; **we want policies that will put b. on the table** nous voulons des politiques qui nous permettent de gagner notre pain; Fig **he knows which side his b. is buttered on** il sait où est son avantage ou son intérêt; Fig **b. and circuses** du pain et des jeux
 2 esp Am Old-fashioned Sl (money) blé m, avoine f, galette f
 VT (fish etc) passer à la chapelure
 ▸▸ **b. bin** (horizontal) boîte f à pain; (vertical) huche f à pain; **b. cutter** coupe-pain m inv; **b. knife** couteau m à pain; Culin **b. pudding** gâteau m de pain; **b. roll** petit pain; Br Culin **b. sauce** sauce f à la mie de pain; **b. slicer** coupe-pain

bread-and-butter **ADJ**
 ▸▸ **b. issues** problèmes mpl essentiels, questions fpl essentielles; Fam **b. letter** lettre f de remerciements; Culin **b. pudding** pain perdu m (cuit au four)

breadbasket ['bredbɑːskɪt] **N 1** corbeille f à pain; esp Am Fig **the b. of the world** la principale région productrice de céréales panifiables dans le monde **2** Old-fashioned Sl (stomach) estomac m, bedaine f

breadboard ['bredbɔːd] **N 1** planche f à pain
 2 Electron etc montage m expérimental

breadcrumb ['bredkrʌm] **N** miette f (de pain); Culin **breadcrumbs** chapelure f; **fried** **in breadcrumbs** pané; **to coat fish with breadcrumbs** passer du poisson à la chapelure
 VT (fish etc) passer à la chapelure

breaded ['bredɪd] **ADJ** pané

breadfruit ['bredfruːt] **N** (fruit) fruit m à pain
 ▸▸ **b. tree** arbre m à pain

breadline ['bredlaɪn] **N** = file f d'attente pour toucher des bons de pain ou recevoir de la nourriture gratuite; Fig **on the b.** indigent, sans ressources

breadth [bredθ] **N 1** (width) largeur f; (of material) largeur, lé m **2** Fig (of thought, mind, views etc) largeur f; (of style, sound) ampleur f; **her b. of understanding** l'ampleur de ses connaissances

breadthwise ['bredθwaɪz], **breadthways** ['bredθweɪz] **ADV** dans le sens de la largeur

breadwinner ['bredwɪnər] **N** soutien m de famille

BREAK¹ [breɪk]

N cassure, brisure **1** ▪ fracture **1**		
▪ trouée **2** ▪ interruption **2** ▪ rupture		
3 ▪ pause **4** ▪ évasion **5** ▪ chance **6**		
VT casser **1** ▪ briser **1, 4**		
▪ rompre **1–3** ▪ couper **1** ▪ amortir **3**		
▪ enfreindre **5**		
VI se casser **1** ▪ se briser **1** ▪ se		
fracturer **1**		

N 1 (in china, glass) cassure f, brisure f; (in wood) cassure, rupture f; (fracture) (in limb) fracture f; **b. in the voice** Physiol (at puberty) mue f; (caused by emotion) altération f de la voix; Lit **b. of day** point m du jour
 2 (interruption) (in hedge, wall etc) trouée f, percée f, brèche f; (in clouds) trouée; Elec (in circuit) rupture f; (in series, line) interruption f; Typ (in word) césure f; (in pagination) fin f de page; Radio, TV **(commercial) b.** page f de publicité; Radio, TV **b. (in transmission)** interruption; **b. or of continuity** interruption, solution f de continuité; **b. in the journey** arrêt m; **b. in the weather** changement m du temps; **there will be a b. in the weather tomorrow** le temps va changer demain; **without a b.** sans s'arrêter
 3 (breach) (between countries, spouses) rupture f; (between two friends) brouille f; **b. with a tradition** rupture avec une tradition; **in a b. with tradition** en rupture avec la tradition; **to make a b. with the past** rompre avec son passé
 4 (rest), Mus pause f; Sch (between classes) récréation f; (holiday) vacances fpl; **an hour's b. for lunch** une heure de pause pour le déjeuner; **a weekend in the country makes a pleasant b.** un week-end à la campagne fait du bien; **a much needed b.** un repos indispensable; **give us a b.!** (talk about something else) change de disque!; **give me a b.!** (stop nagging) fiche-moi la paix!; (don't talk nonsense) arrête ton char; **give work/ tennis a b. for a while** tu devrais arrêter un peu de travailler/de jouer au tennis
 5 Fam (escape) évasion f; **to make a b. for it** s'évader; Fig **to make the b.** larguer les amarres
 6 Fam (chance) chance f; **a good/bad b.** une bonne/mauvaise chance; **this could be your big b.** ça pourrait être la chance de ta vie; **she's never had an even b. in her life** rien n'a jamais été facile dans sa vie; **we had a lucky b.** nous avons eu de la veine; **give him a b.** donne-lui une chance; (he won't do it again) donne-lui une seconde chance
 7 Billiards etc (opening shot) acquit m; (series of shots) série f, suite f (de coups gagnants); Tennis (of opponent's service) break m; **she had a b. of serve** (lost her serve) elle a perdu son service; (won her op-

ponent's serve) elle a gagné le service de son adversaire; Tennis **to have two b. points** avoir deux balles de break
 8 Mus (solo jazz passage) solo m; (pause) break m
 VT (pt **broke** [brəʊk], pp **broken** ['brəʊk(ə)n])
 1 (fracture, shatter, sever) (glass) casser, briser; (egg, toy etc) casser; (window, ties of friendship etc) briser; (rope), Naut (moorings etc) rompre; (stick) casser, rompre; (skin) entamer; Law (seals) (illegally) briser; (legally) lever; Elec (current) interrompre; (circuit) couper; Aviat (sound barrier) franchir; **to b. sth into pieces** mettre qch en morceaux; **to b. one's arm/neck** se casser le bras/le cou; **to b. a branch off a tree** détacher une branche d'un arbre; Lit Arch **to b. bread with sb** rompre le pain avec qn; Constr **to b. ground** donner les premiers coups de pioche; Fig **to b. (new or fresh) ground** faire œuvre de pionnier, innover; Fig **to b. the ice** rompre ou briser la glace; **to b. a ten-pound note** entamer un billet de dix livres; **to get broken** se casser
 2 (interrupt) (silence, fast etc) rompre; Typ (page) couper; **to b. step** rompre le pas; **to b. ranks** rompre les rangs; **to b. the thread of a story** interrompre le fil d'une narration; **to b. one's journey** s'arrêter en route, faire une étape; Naut faire escale; Aviat **to b. one's journey in Singapore** faire (une) escale à Singapour
 3 (weaken impact of) (fall, force of sth) amortir; (wind) arrêter; (current) rompre; **to b. the force of a blow** amortir un coup
 4 (overcome, destroy) (strike, person's resistance) briser; (person's pride) abattre, dompter; (person's health) ruiner; (alibi) écarter; (record) battre; (horse) dresser, entraîner; (bad habit) corriger; **to b. sb into the work** rompre qn au travail; **to b. sb of a habit** corriger ou guérir qn d'une habitude; **to b. one-self of a habit** se corriger ou se défaire d'une habitude; **to b. sb** (financially) ruiner qn; (of grief etc) briser qn; **to b. the bank** (when gambling) faire sauter la banque; Hum **one night out won't b. the bank** une sortie ne va pas me/vous/etc ruiner; Tennis **to b. one's opponent's service** gagner le service de son adversaire; **to b. sb's heart/spirit** briser le cœur à qn/le courage de qn
 5 (fail to respect) (law, regulation, ceasefire) enfreindre, ne pas observer; (one's word, appointment etc) manquer à; (contract, agreement, treaty) rompre; **to b. one's word to sb** manquer à sa parole envers qn; **to b. a promise** ne pas tenir sa promesse; **to b. gaol** s'évader de prison; **to b. cover** (of animal) débucher; Mil, Sch **to b. bounds** violer la consigne; **his insolence has broken all bounds** son insolence a passé les bornes
 6 (reveal, disclose) **to b. the news of sth to sb** apprendre qch à qn; **to b. a piece of bad news gently to sb** apprendre une mauvaise nouvelle doucement à qn
 7 Physiol **to b. wind** lâcher un vent
 VI 1 (fracture, shatter etc) (of glass) se casser, se briser; (of egg, toy etc) se casser; (of window) se briser; (of wood, rope) se rompre; (of limb) se fracturer, se casser; (of wave) se briser, déferler; (of heart) se briser, se fendre; **my waters have just broken** (of pregnant woman) je suis en train de perdre les eaux; **to b. with sb/a tradition** rompre avec qn/ une tradition; **to b. in two/into pieces** se casser en deux/en morceaux; **the sea was breaking against the rocks** les vagues se brisaient sur les rochers
 2 (collapse, give way) (of health) s'altérer; **to b. under torture** s'effondrer sous la torture
 3 (change) (of weather) changer; (of heatwave) passer, prendre fin; (of voice) Physiol muer; (with emotion) se briser, s'étrangler
 4 (start) (of storm) éclater, se déchaîner; (of

news, scandal) éclater; **we bring you the stories as they b.** nous transmettons les événements au fur et à mesure qu'ils arrivent; **day was beginning to b.** le jour commençait à se lever

5 *Billiards* donner l'acquit

6 *Boxing (move away from each other)* se séparer; **b.!** break!, stop!

7 *Typ (in paginating)* faire une coupure de page

8 to b. free of one's bonds briser ses liens

▸▸ *Comput* **b. character** caractère *m* d'interruption; *Comput* **b. key** touche *f* d'interruption; *Typ* **b. line** *(of paragraph)* dernière ligne *f*; *Elec* **b. switch** disjoncteur *m*, interrupteur *m*

▸ **break away** **VT SEP** détacher (**from** de)

VI 1 *(escape)* s'évader; *Sport* se détacher; **she broke away from the guards** elle a échappé à la surveillance de ses gardiens

2 *(cut ties with)* se dégager, se détacher (**from** de); *(of province) (from State)* se séparer; **when did you b. away from your family?** quand est-ce que tu as coupé les ponts avec ta famille?; *Pol* **to b. away from a party** abandonner un parti; **the year France broke away from NATO** l'année où la France a quitté l'OTAN

3 *(come off)* se détacher (**from** de)

▸ **break back** **VI** *Tennis* = gagner le service de son adversaire après avoir perdu son propre service

▸ **break down** **VT SEP 1** *(destroy) (door)* enfoncer; *(wall etc)* abattre, démolir

2 *(overcome) (resistance)* briser; *(prejudice)* vaincre, surmonter; **to b. down all opposition** vaincre toute opposition

3 *(separate into parts)* *Fin etc (account, figures)* décomposer, ventiler; *(statistics)* analyser; *(bill, estimate)* détailler; *Chem (substance)* décomposer; *(molecules)* dissocier; *Com* **to b. down bulk** ventiler un lot; **we need to b. the figures down a bit further** il faut que nous décomposions *ou* ventilions les chiffres un peu plus; **we can b. the problem down into three parts** le problème peut se décomposer en trois parties; **the story can be broken down into two parts** on peut diviser l'histoire en deux parties

VI 1 *(fail) (of health)* se détériorer, s'altérer; *(of car, train, machinery)* tomber en panne; *(of ship)* subir une avarie; **that's where your argument breaks down** c'est là que ton argument s'effondre *ou* ne tient plus debout

2 *(collapse) (of negotiations)* échouer; *(of resistance)* s'effondrer; *(of person) (have nervous breakdown)* faire une dépression nerveuse; *(burst into tears)* éclater en sanglots, fondre en larmes; *(confess)* faire des aveux complets, passer aux aveux; **their marriage is breaking down** leur mariage se désagrège

3 *(separate)* se décomposer (**into** en)

▸ **break even** **VI** *(financially) (of person, company)* rentrer dans ses frais

▸ **break in** **VT SEP 1** *(destroy) (door etc)* enfoncer

2 *(accustom to being used) (horse)* dresser; *(pipe)* culotter; *(new shoes)* faire, briser; *Am (car)* roder; **to b. sb/oneself in to sth** rompre qn/se rompre à qch; **I'm getting these shoes broken in at last** ces chaussures commencent enfin à se faire

VI 1 *(interrupt)* interrompre; **to b. in on sb/a conversation** interrompre qn/une conversation; **I really must b. in at this point** il faut vraiment que je vous interrompe ici

2 *(enter premises) (of burglar)* s'introduire *ou* entrer *ou* pénétrer par effraction; **I'd lost my front-door key so I had to b. in** j'avais perdu la clé de ma porte d'entrée et donc j'ai dû forcer la porte; **the police broke in through a window** la police est entrée par la fenêtre

▸ **break into** **VT INSEP 1** *(house) (illegally)* en-

trer *ou* pénétrer par effraction dans; *(desk, safe)* forcer; **I had to b. into my flat through a window** j'ai dû forcer une fenêtre pour entrer chez moi; **they've been broken into three times** ils se sont fait cambrioler trois fois

2 *(begin suddenly)* **to b. into laughter** éclater de rire; **to b. into a song** se mettre à chanter; **to b. into a trot/run/sprint** se mettre au trot/à courir/à sprinter; **her face broke into a smile** son visage s'éclaira d'un sourire

3 *(use part of) (stocks, large-denomination bank note, savings)* entamer

4 *(interrupt) (conversation)* interrompre

▸ **break loose** **VI** *(from bonds)* se dégager; *(escape)* s'évader (**from** de); *(of ship)* partir à la dérive

▸ **break off** **VT SEP 1** *(remove)* casser, rompre, détacher (**from** de); **I've broken the handle off a cup** j'ai cassé l'anse d'une tasse

2 *(end) (temporarily)* interrompre; *(permanently)* abandonner; *(negotiations)* rompre; **to b. off relations with** *(person)* cesser tout contact avec; *(country)* rompre les relations avec

3 *(romantic relationship)* rompre; **to b. it off** rompre (**with sb** avec qn)

VI 1 *(become detached)* se casser net, se détacher net, se détacher (**from** de); **the handle broke off in my hand** l'anse m'est restée dans la main

2 *(stop)* **to b. off for ten minutes** prendre dix minutes de pause; **to b. off for lunch** s'arrêter pour déjeuner; **shall we b. off for the rest of the day?** on s'arrête là pour aujourd'hui?

3 *(stop talking)* s'interrompre, se taire; **to b. off in the middle of a speech** s'arrêter *ou* s'interrompre au milieu d'un discours

▸ **break open** **VT SEP** *(door)* enfoncer; *(lock, safe, till)* forcer; *Fam (bottle of wine etc)* ouvrir, déboucher; **to b. a desk open** ouvrir un bureau en forçant la serrure, forcer un bureau

VI *(of box etc)* s'ouvrir

▸ **break out** **VI 1** *(escape) (from prison etc)* s'échapper, s'évader (**of** de)

2 *(start) (of argument, war, riots)* éclater; *(of fire, epidemic)* se déclarer; **panic broke out in the cinema when ...** ce fut la panique dans le cinéma lorsque ...

3 *(develop)* **to b. out into a sweat** se mettre à transpirer; **to b. out in spots** *(of face etc)* se couvrir de boutons; **the baby is breaking out into a rash** le bébé est en train de faire une éruption; **to b. out in a laugh** éclater de rire

VT INSEP 1 *Fam (bottle of wine etc)* ouvrir, déboucher

2 *Am (prepare for use)* sortir; *(flag)* déployer

▸ **break through** **VT INSEP** *(barrier, police cordon etc)* enfoncer; *(wall)* faire une brèche dans; *Aviat (sound barrier)* franchir; *(of sun) (clouds)* percer; **to b. through sb's reserve** vaincre la réserve de qn

VI *(of sun)* percer

▸ **break up** **VT SEP 1** *(reduce to pieces)* mettre *ou* briser en morceaux; *(building, ship etc)* démolir; *(property)* morceler; *(empire)* dissoudre; *(crowd, family)* disperser; *Com (conglomerate, trust)* scinder, diviser; *(coalition)* rompre; *Chem (compound)* résoudre; *Agr (earth)* ameublir; **to b. a word up into syllables** décomposer un mot en syllabes

2 *(bring to an end) (marriage)* détruire; *(meeting)* dissoudre; *(conference)* mettre fin à; **to b. up a fight** séparer des combattants; *Fam* **b. it up!** la paix!

VI 1 *(disintegrate) (of ship)* se briser; *(of empire)* se dissoudre; *(of road surface)* se désagréger; *(of thawing ice)* se briser; *(of crowd, group etc)* se disperser; *(of clouds)* se

dissiper, se disperser; *Fig Fam* **I just broke up (with laughter)** j'ai été pris d'un fou rire

2 *(end) (of party, celebration etc)* se terminer; *Sch* être en vacances; **the meeting broke up in disorder** la réunion s'est terminée dans la pagaille; *Sch* **we b. up on the 4th** nos vacances commencent le 4, nous sommes en vacances le 4; **the schools will be breaking up for summer soon** les écoles vont bientôt fermer pour l'été; **their marriage has broken up** ils se sont séparés

3 *(end relationship)* se séparer, rompre; **they're breaking up** ils se séparent

4 *(of weather)* se gâter

break² **N 1** *(carriage)* break *m* **2** *Aut* shooting **b.** break *m* (de chasse)

breakable ['breɪkəb(ə)l] **ADJ** cassable, fragile

NPL breakables objets *mpl* fragiles

breakages ['breɪkɪdʒɪz] **NPL** have there been any **b.**? *(was anything broken?)* est-ce qu'il y a eu de la casse?; **to pay for b.** payer la casse

breakaway ['breɪkəweɪ] **N 1** sécession *f* (**from** de); **b. union/party** syndicat *m*/parti *m* dissident **2** *Ftbl (of winger etc)* échappée *f*

break-dance **VI** danser le smurf

break-dancer **N** danseur, -euse de smurf

break-dancing **N** smurf *m*

breakdown ['breɪkdaʊn] **N 1** *(failure) (of efforts)* échec *m*; *(in negotiations, communications)* rupture *f*; *(of marriage)* échec; *(of system)* écroulement *m*; *(of service)* arrêt *m* complet

2 *(collapse) (of health)* délabrement *m*; **(nervous) b.** dépression *f* (nerveuse); **she's had a b.** *(and has not yet recovered)* elle fait une dépression; *Hum* **I'm going to have a b.** je vais craquer; **mental b.** dépression nerveuse

3 *Aut, Rail etc (mechanical)* panne *f*; **I've had a b.** je suis tombé en panne

4 *(into component parts) (of statistics etc)* analyse *f*; *(of account, figures etc)* décomposition *f*, ventilation *f*; *(of bill, costs)* détail *m*; *(of population) (by class, age etc)* répartition *f*, classement *m*; *(of script)* prédécoupage *m*; *(for recording)* dépouillement *m*; *Banking* **b. of charges/interest** décompte *m* d'agios/ d'intérêts

5 *Chem* dissociation *f*

▸▸ *Aut* **b. gang** équipe *f* de dépannage; *Aut* **b. and recovery service** service *m* de remorquage et de dépannage; *Aut* **b. service** service de dépannage; *TV, Cin* **b. sheet** *(artistic)* fiche *f* artistique; *(technical)* fiche technique; **b. truck, b. van** dépanneuse *f*, camion *m* de dépannage

breaker ['breɪkər] **N 1** *(of horses)* dresseur, -euse **2** *(wave)* (vague *f*) déferlante *f* **3** *Aut* rupteur *m*

▸▸ **b.'s yard** *(for cars, boats etc)* chantier *m* de démolition

breakeven ['breɪkiːv(ə)n] **ADJ ATTRIB N** seuil *m* de rentabilité; *Acct* point *m* mort; **to reach b.** atteindre le seuil de rentabilité

▸▸ *Fin* **b. analysis** analyse *f* du point mort; **b. point** seuil de rentabilité; **b. prices** prix *mpl* permettant de rentrer dans ses frais

breakfast ['brekfəst] **N** petit déjeuner *m*; **to have (one's) b.** déjeuner, prendre le *ou* son (petit) déjeuner; **while we were at b.** pendant que nous déjeunions; **what do you want for b.?** qu'est-ce que tu veux pour le petit déjeuner?; *Fam* **to have sb for breakfast** ne faire qu'une bouchée de qn **VOIR GRAMMAIRE A7**

VI déjeuner (le matin)

▸▸ **b. buffet** buffet *m* du petit déjeuner; **b. cereals** céréales *fpl* (en flocons); **b. chef** chef *m* de petit déjeuner; **b. cook** cafetier *m*; **b.**

meeting réunion *f* pendant le petit déjeuner; **b. room** salle *f* du petit déjeuner; **b. television** télévision *f* du matin; **b. tray** plateau *m* petit déjeuner

break-in N 1 (by burglar etc) effraction *f* 2 Tech, Am Aut rodage *m*

breaking ['breɪkɪŋ] N 1 (of window etc) bris *m*; (of silence etc) rupture *f*; (of journey) interruption *f*; Aviat (of sound barrier) franchissement *m*; Law **b. and entering** (into house) entrée *f* par effraction; Law **b. of seals** (illegal) bris *m* des scellés; (legal) levée *f* des scellés; **b. of new** or **fresh ground** Agr défrichage *m*; Fig (in research, science etc) œuvre *f* de pionnier 2 (disintegration) (of waves) déferlement *m*; Med (of bone etc) fracture *f*; **b. of the voice** Physiol mue *f*; (with emotion) altération *f* de la voix 3 (of horse) dressage *m* 4 (of fall, force of sth) amortissement *m* 5 (of strike, sb's heart) action *f* de briser 6 (of law, treaty etc) violation *f*; (of promise) rupture *f*
ADJ (news) de dernière minute
▸▸ Com **b. bulk** fractionnement *m* d'un lot; **b. point** point *m* de rupture; (of resistance) limite *f* critique; Fig (of strength etc) limite; **she has reached b. point** elle est au bout du rouleau, elle est à bout; **their marriage has reached b. point** leur mariage a atteint le point critique; **to try sb's patience to b. point** pousser à bout la patience de qn; Tech **b. strain** tension *f* de rupture

breakneck ['breɪknek] ADJ **at b. speed** à une vitesse ou allure folle

break-out N (from prison etc) évasion *f*

breakpoint ['breɪkpɔɪnt] N Typ point *m* de césure

breakthrough ['breɪkθruː] N 1 Mil (of enemy lines) percée *f* 2 (advance, discovery, in market) percée *f*; (in negotiations) progrès *m*; **their latest b. in computing technology** leur dernière découverte en technologie informatique; **to make a b.** (discovery) faire une percée; (in negotiations) progresser; **the b. came only after a week of deadlock** la situation ne s'est débloquée qu'après une semaine

break-up N 1 (of empire, meeting) dissolution *f*; (of company) scission *f*; (of marriage etc) échec *m*; (of ship etc) dislocation *f*; **they still saw one another after the b.** ils ont continué à se voir après leur séparation 2 (of ice) débâcle *f*
▸▸ Fin **b. price** prix *m* de liquidation; Com **b. value** valeur *f* de liquidation

breakwater ['breɪkwɔːtər] N 1 (wall) brise-lames *m inv*; môle *m*; (jetty) jetée *f* 2 (of bridge) éperon *m*

bream [briːm] N (fish) brème *f*; **sea b.** dorade *f*

breast [brest] N 1 (of woman) sein *m*; **a child at the b.** un(e) enfant au sein 2 (chest) (of person) poitrine *f*; (of horse) poitrail *m*; (of bird) gorge *f*; (of shirt etc) devant *m*; Culin (of chicken) blanc *m*; **to make a clean b. of it** tout avouer; **b. high** or **deep** (water etc) jusqu'à la poitrine
VT Lit (storm) affronter; (hill) atteindre le sommet de; **to b. the waves** (of swimmer) fendre la lame; Sport **to b. the tape** être le premier à franchir la ligne d'arrivée
▸▸ **b. cancer** cancer *m* du sein; **b. enlargement** augmentation *f* mammaire; **b. pocket** poche *f* de poitrine; **inside b. pocket** poche poitrine intérieure, poche portefeuille; **b. pump** tire-lait *m inv*; **b. reduction** réduction *f* mammaire

breastbone ['brestbəʊn] N (of person, animal, bird) sternum *m*

breastfeed ['brestfiːd] (pt, pp **breastfed** [-fed]) VT (baby) nourrir au sein, allaiter
VI allaiter

breastfeeding ['brestfiːdɪŋ] N allaitement *m* maternel

breastplate ['brestpleɪt] N (armour) cuirasse *f*

breaststroke ['bres(t)strəʊk] N (in swimming) brasse *f*; **I can only do** or **swim b.** je ne sais nager que la brasse

breastwork ['brestwɜːk] N Mil parapet *m*

breath [breθ] N (smelt) haleine *f*; (breathed) souffle *m*; **his b. smelt of onions** son haleine sentait l'oignon; **to have bad b.** avoir mauvaise haleine; **I felt his b. on my neck** j'ai senti son souffle dans mon cou; **to draw b.** respirer; **give me time to draw b.** donnez-moi le temps de souffler; **to draw** or **take a deep** or **long b.** respirer profondément ou à pleins poumons; **to pause for b.** (when speaking) s'arrêter pour reprendre sa respiration; **to draw one's last** or **dying b.** rendre le dernier soupir; **the b. of life** le souffle vital ou de la vie; Fig **music is the very b. of life to me** je ne pourrais pas vivre sans musique; **(all) in the same b.** tout d'une haleine; **he agreed and disagreed (all) in the same b.** il a dit qu'il était d'accord puis il est immédiatement revenu sur ce qu'il avait dit; **but in the next b. he said the opposite** mais quelques secondes plus tard il a dit le contraire; **they are not to be mentioned in the same b.** on ne saurait les comparer; **to hold one's b.** retenir son souffle; Fam **I wouldn't hold my b.!** je ne compterais pas trop là-dessus!; **to gasp for b.** haleter; **to waste one's b.** perdre son temps en discours inutiles, perdre sa salive; **I'm wasting my b.** je perds mon temps, je me fatigue pour rien; **save your b.** ne te fatigue pas; **to be short of b.** être essoufflé, avoir la respiration coupée; **out of b.** à bout de souffle, hors d'haleine, essoufflé; **to get** or **run out of b.** s'essouffler; **to take sb's b. away** couper la respiration ou le souffle à qn; Fig couper le souffle à qn; **to get one's b. (back), to recover** or **catch one's b.** reprendre haleine; **under one's b.** (to talk) d'une voix très basse, à voix basse; (to swear) entre ses dents; **the first b. of spring** le premier souffle du printemps; **a b. of wind/of air** un souffle de vent/d'air; **to go out for a b. of (fresh) air** sortir prendre l'air; Fig **it's/she's like a b. of fresh air** c'est/elle est comme une bouffée d'air frais; **a b. of scandal** l'ombre *f* d'un scandale
▸▸ **b. freshener** purificateur *m* d'haleine, spray *m* buccal; **b. test** Alcootest® *m*

breathalyse, Am **breathalyze** ['breθəlaɪz] VT faire subir l'Alcootest® à; **he was breathalysed** on l'a fait souffler dans le ballon

breathalyser, Am **breathalyzer** ['breθəlaɪzər] N Alcootest® *m*
▸▸ **b. test** Alcootest®

breathe [briːð] VI 1 respirer; **to b. hard** haleter; **to b. heavily** (noisily) respirer bruyamment; (with difficulty) respirer péniblement; **you can't b. in here** (it's too hot) on ne peut pas respirer ici; **I feel as if I can't b.** je me sens oppressé; **I need room to b.** (in relationship) j'ai besoin d'espace, il faut que je respire; **to b. (easily) again** (with relief) respirer de nouveau; **to b. on one's fingers** souffler dans ses doigts; Fam **to b. down sb's neck** (supervise) être sur le dos de qn; (look over their shoulder) regarder par-dessus l'épaule de qn; Fam **he's breathing down my neck for this translation** il me casse les pieds à propos de cette traduction; Fam **the police are breathing down our necks** (very close to arresting us) la police nous talonne; Fam **there's a police car breathing down our necks** on a une voiture de police aux fesses

2 (of voice, instrument, wind) soupirer, souffler doucement; **open the bottle to let the wine b.** ouvre la bouteille pour permettre au vin de respirer
VT 1 (air) respirer 2 (sigh) exhaler, laisser échapper; (prayer) murmurer; **to b. a sigh of relief** pousser un soupir de soulagement; Lit **to b. one's last** rendre le dernier soupir, rendre l'âme; **don't b. a word (of it)!** n'en soufflez (pas un) mot!; **to b. fire** (be very angry) cracher des flammes; **to b. new life into sth** insuffler une force nouvelle à qch; **he was breathing whisky fumes all over me** il me soufflait des relents de whisky en pleine figure 3 Ling (sound, consonant) aspirer
▸ **breathe in** VT SEP (smoke, fumes) inhaler
VI inspirer
▸ **breathe out** VI expirer

breathed [briːðd] ADJ Ling (unvoiced) sourd, non voisé

breather ['briːðər] N 1 Fam (rest) pause *f*; **to give sb a b.** laisser souffler qn, laisser un moment de répit à qn; **to go out for a b.** aller respirer un peu d'air, sortir prendre l'air; **to take a b.** faire une pause 2 Fam (person) **heavy b.** (on telephone) = homme *m* qui donne des coups de téléphone anonymes
▸▸ Aut **b. pipe** (tuyau *m* de) reniflard *m*; Tech **b. port** orifice *m* de reniflard

breathing ['briːðɪŋ] N (of person) respiration *f*; **heavy b.** (noisy) respiration bruyante; (difficult) respiration pénible
▸▸ Tech **b. apparatus** (for fireman, miner etc) masque *m* à oxygène; (for diver) scaphandre *m*; **b. space** moment *m* de répit; Fig **I need some b. space** (in relationship) j'ai besoin de respirer ou d'espace

breathless ['breθlɪs] ADJ 1 (person) (out of breath) à bout de souffle, hors d'haleine, essoufflé; **b. from running** essoufflé d'avoir couru; **he was b. with excitement** l'exultation lui avait coupé le souffle 2 (very fast) (chase, speed) fou 3 Fig **to have sb b.** (of film etc) tenir qn en haleine; **b. silence** or **hush** silence *m* absolu; **b. calm** calme *m* plat; **b. suspense** suspense *m* total

breathlessly ['breθlɪslɪ] ADV 1 (out of breath) tout essoufflé 2 (to wait, listen) en retenant son souffle

breathlessness ['breθlɪsnɪs] N essoufflement *m*; (of patient) manque *m* de souffle, oppression *f*

breathtaking ['breθteɪkɪŋ] ADJ (beauty, imagination, audacity etc) à vous couper le souffle; **with a b. lack of tact** avec un manque de tact incroyable; **it's b.** (view) c'est à vous couper le souffle; (stupidity etc) c'est sidérant

breathtakingly ['breθteɪkɪŋlɪ] ADV (beautiful) extraordinairement; (stupid, tactless etc) incroyablement

breath-test VT faire subir l'Alcootest® à

breathy ['breθɪ] ADJ Mus (voice) qui manque d'attaque; **b. voice** voix *f* haletante

breech [briːtʃ] N Obst (accouchement *m* par le) siège *m* 2 (of firearm) culasse *f*, tonnerre *m*; **b. action** or **mechanism** mécanisme *m* de culasse
▸▸ Obst **b. birth, b. delivery** (accouchement par le) siège; Obst **b. presentation** présentation *f* par le siège

breeches ['brɪtʃɪz] NPL (knee-length) haut-de-chausses *mpl*, culotte *f*; (full-length) pantalon *m*; **knee b.** culotte
▸▸ Naut **b. buoy** bouée-culotte *f*, *pl* bouées-culottes

breed [briːd] N (of people, animals) race *f*; Fig **she is one of the new b. of executives** elle fait partie de la nouvelle race ou génération de cadres; **a new b. of modems** une nou-

velle génération de modems; **thatchers are a dying b.** les couvreurs de toits en chaume sont une race en voie de disparition
VT (*pt, pp* **bred** [bred]) **1** (*give birth to*) (*children, offspring*) produire, procréer; *Fig* engendrer, donner naissance à; **dirt breeds disease** la saleté entraîne des maladies; **all these rumours are breeding insecurity** toutes ces rumeurs engendrent l'insécurité **2** (*raise*) (*cattle, rabbits etc*) élever; **they're specially bred for racing** ils sont élevés spécialement pour la course; **to be town/country bred** (*of person*) avoir été élevé à la ville/à la campagne; *Prov* **what's bred in the bone will come out in the flesh** bon chien chasse de race
VI **1** (*of animals*) se multiplier, se reproduire; (*of people*) se reproduire **2** (*of animal breeder*) faire de l'élevage

breeder ['briːdər] N **1** (*animal*) reproducteur, -trice **2** (*person*) (*of animals*) éleveur, -euse; **poultry b.** aviculteur, -trice
▸▸ *Nucl* **b. reactor** surgénérateur *m*, surrégénérateur *m*, *Fam* couveuse *f*

breeding ['briːdɪŋ] N **1** (*reproduction*) reproduction *f*, multiplication *f* **2** (*raising*) (*of domestic animals etc*) élevage *m*; **animal kept for b. purposes** animal (*m*) reproducteur *m*; **sheep b.** élevage des moutons **3** (*education*) (*of child etc*) éducation *f*, **(good) b.** bonne éducation, bonnes manières *fpl*, savoir-vivre *m inv*; **to lack b.** manquer de savoir-vivre *ou* d'éducation
▸▸ **b. ground** = lieu *m* de reproduction de certains animaux; *Fig* foyer *m*, terrain *m* propice; **a b. ground of anarchists** un foyer d'anarchistes; **a b. ground of crime/violence** un terrain propice au crime/à la violence; **damp areas are a b. ground for germs** les zones humides sont des foyers de microbes *ou* constituent un terrain propice aux microbes; **b. stock** animaux *mpl* élevés en vue de la reproduction

breeze[1] [briːz] N (*wind*) brise *f*, **gentle or light b.** petite *ou* légère brise; *Naut* **strong or stiff b.** vent *m* frais; **fresh b.** bonne brise; *Fam* **it was a b.** (*easy*) c'était simple comme bonjour, c'était un jeu d'enfant
▸ **breeze in** VI (*quickly*) entrer en coup de vent; (*casually*) entrer d'une façon désinvolte
▸ **breeze out** VI (*quickly*) sortir en coup de vent; (*casually*) sortir d'une façon désinvolte
▸ **breeze through** VI (*pass exam with ease*) réussir les doigts dans le nez
VT INSEP (*exam*) réussir les doigts dans le nez; **to b. through life** se laisser vivre

breeze[2] N
▸▸ **b. block, b. brick** parpaing *m*

breezeway ['briːzweɪ] N *Am* passage *m* couvert (*souvent entre la maison et le garage*)

breezily ['briːzɪlɪ] ADV (*in lively fashion*) avec verve; (*casually*) avec désinvolture

breezy ['briːzɪ] ADJ **1** (*day, place etc*) venteux **2** *Fam* (*pleasant*) jovial, -aux; (*casual*) désinvolte; (*speech*) plein de verve

brekky ['brekɪ] N *Br Fam* petit déj *m*

Bremen ['breɪmən] N Brême

Bren [bren] N *Mil* fusil-mitrailleur *m*, *pl* fusils-mitrailleurs
▸▸ **B. carrier** chenillette *f* porte-fusil-mitrailleur, *pl* chenillettes porte-fusil(s)-mitrailleur(s); **B. gun** fusil-mitrailleur

brent [brent] N bernache *f* cravant
▸▸ **b. goose** bernache *f* cravant

brethren ['breðrɪn] NPL *esp Rel* frères *mpl*; **my dearly beloved b.** mes très chers frères

Breton ['bretɒn] ADJ breton
N **1** Breton, -onne **2** *Ling* breton *m*

breve [briːv] N **1** (*accent*) brève *f* **2** *Mus* double ronde *f*
▸▸ *Mus* **b. rest** double pause *f*

breviary ['briːvɪərɪ] N *Rel* bréviaire *m*

brevity ['brevɪtɪ] N **1** (*of style*) brièveté *f*, concision *f*; (*of expression*) laconisme *m*; *Prov* **b. is the soul of wit** le secret d'un bon mot d'esprit réside dans sa concision **2** (*of life etc*) brièveté *f*, courte durée *f*

brew [bruː] N **1** (*of beer*) cuvée *f*, **home b.** bière *f*/cidre *m* de ménage; *Fig* **the book is a heady b. of ...** le livre est un mélange formidable de ... **2** (*tea*) thé *m* **3** *Am Fam* (*beer*) mousse *f*
VT **1** (*beer*) brasser; **home brewed** (*beer, cider*) de ménage, (fait à la) maison **2** (*tea*) faire (infuser)
VI (*of tea*) infuser; *Met, Fig* **there's a storm brewing** il y a de l'orage dans l'air; *Fig* **there's something brewing** il se trame quelque chose, il y a quelque chose qui se prépare; **there's trouble brewing** il va y avoir du grabuge
▸ **brew up** VI *Br Fam* faire du thé

brewer ['bruːər] N brasseur, -euse; **b.'s yeast** levure *f* de bière; *Br Sl Hum* **b.'s droop** = impuissance *f* due à l'alcool; **to have b.'s droop** ne pas pouvoir bander après un excès d'alcool

brewery ['bruːərɪ] N brasserie *f*

brewing ['bruːɪŋ] N **1** (*of beer*) brassage *m*; **the b. industry** la brasserie **2** (*of tea*) infusion *f*

brewski ['bruːskɪ] N *Am Fam* (*beer*) mousse *f*

brew-up N *Br Fam* **to have a b.** faire du thé

briar[1] ['braɪər] N **1** (*shrub*) bruyère *f* **2** (*pipe*) pipe *f* de bruyère

briar[2] N = **brier**[1]

briarroot ['braɪəruːt], **briarwood** ['braɪəwʊd] N racine *f* de bruyère

bribable ['braɪbəb(ə)l] ADJ corruptible

bribe [braɪb] N pot-de-vin *m*, *pl* pots-de-vin; **to take bribes** toucher des pots-de-vin
VT soudoyer, acheter; *Fam* graisser la patte à; **to b. sb into silence** acheter le silence de qn; **to b. sb into doing sth** soudoyer *ou* acheter *ou Fam* graisser la patte à qn pour qu'il/elle fasse qch; *Fig* **I bribed her with some chocolate to go to bed** je lui ai donné du chocolat pour qu'elle aille se coucher

bribery ['braɪbərɪ] N corruption *f*; **open/not open to b.** corruptible/incorruptible; **b. and corruption** corruption; *Hum* **that's b. and corruption!** c'est une tentative de corruption!

bribing ['braɪbɪŋ] N corruption *f*, *Fam* graissage *m* de patte; *Law* (*of witnesses*) subornation *f*

bric-a-brac ['brɪkəbræk] N (*no pl*) bric-à-brac *m*

brick [brɪk] N **1** brique *f*, **air b.** brique perforée; *Fig* **to invest in bricks and mortar** investir dans la pierre; *Prov* **you cannot make bricks without straw** on ne peut pas faire de miracles; *Fam* **to come down on sb like a ton of bricks** tomber sur le dos à qn; *Fig* **to drop a b.** faire une bourde *ou* une gaffe; **box of (building) bricks** (*toys*) jeu *m* de cubes *ou* de construction; *Com, Comput* **a bricks-and-clicks shop** une société qui vend ses produits en magasin et sur Internet **2** *Old-fashioned Br Fam* **he's a b.** c'est un chic type **3** (*of ice cream*) pain *m*; (*of tea*) brique *f*
VT *Br Fam* **to b. it** (*be scared*) avoir la trouille, avoir les jetons
▸▸ **b. kiln** four *m* à briques; **b. red** rouge *m* brique *inv*; **he went b. red** il est devenu tout rouge; **b. wall** mur *m* de brique; *Fig* **to come up against a b. wall** se heurter à un obstacle infranchissable; **to knock one's head against a b. wall** se démener en pure perte;

it's like knocking your head against a b. wall c'est peine perdue; **it's like talking to a b. wall** (*he or she etc won't listen*) c'est comme parler à un mur *ou* à un sourd
▸ **brick up, brick in** VT SEP (*window, doorway etc*) murer

brickbat ['brɪkbæt] N *Fig* **she got a lot of brickbats for her performance** son interprétation lui a valu beaucoup de critiques; **the government has been receiving more brickbats than bouquets** le gouvernement a été plus critiqué qu'applaudi

brickfield ['brɪkfiːld] N briqueterie *f*

bricklayer ['brɪkleɪər], *Br Fam* **brickie** ['brɪkɪ] N maçon *m*

bricklaying ['brɪkleɪɪŋ] N briquetage *m*

brickmaker ['brɪkmeɪkər] N briquetier *m*

brickwork ['brɪkwɜːk] N briquetage *m*, maçonnerie *f* de brique

brickworks ['brɪkwɜːks] N (*place*) briqueterie *f*

brickyard ['brɪkjɑːd] N briqueterie *f*

bridal ['braɪd(ə)l] ADJ ATTRIB nuptial, -aux, de noce(s)
▸▸ **the b. party** la noce (*les invités*); **b. suite** suite *f* nuptiale; **b. veil** voile *m* de mariée

bride [braɪd] N (*about to be married*) future mariée *f*, (*married*) jeune mariée; **the b. and (bride)groom** (*about to be married*) les futurs époux *mpl*; (*married*) les jeunes mariés *mpl*; **with his young b.** avec sa jeune épouse; **his b. of four months** la femme avec qui il est/était marié depuis quatre mois

bridegroom ['braɪdgruːm] N (*about to be married*) futur marié *m*; (*married*) jeune marié

bridesmaid ['braɪdzmeɪd] N demoiselle *f* d'honneur

bride-to-be N future mariée *f*

bridge[1] [brɪdʒ] N **1** (*across river etc*) pont *m*; *Fig* **we'll cross that b. when we get or come to it** chaque chose en son temps
2 (*in wrestling*) pont *m*; **to make a b.** ponter
3 (*in billiards etc*) chevalet *m*
4 (*on ship*) passerelle *f*
5 (*of nose*) arête *f*, (*of violin*) chevalet *m*; (*of spectacles*) arcade *f*
6 (*on teeth*) bridge *m*
7 *Cin, TV* (*shot*) transition *f*, (*piece of music*) pont *m* sonore
VT (*river etc*) construire un pont sur; **to b. a gap** relier les bords d'une brèche; *Fig* (*in knowledge etc*) combler une lacune; (*of snack*) boucher un trou; **to b. the gap between two groups** réduire l'écart qui existe entre deux groupes; *Com* **to b. the gap** (*for supplies*) faire la soudure
▸▸ **b. building** construction *f* de ponts; *Fig* réconciliation *f*; *Am Fin* **b. loan** prêt-relais *m*, *pl* prêts-relais

bridge[2] N *Cards* bridge *m*; **to play b.** jouer au bridge; **game of b.** (partie *f* de) bridge
▸▸ *Cards* **b. partner** partenaire *mf* au bridge; *Cards* **b. player** bridgeur, -euse; *Br* **b. roll** petit pain *m* (au lait)

bridgehead ['brɪdʒhed] N *Mil, Fig* tête *f* de pont

bridgework ['brɪdʒwɜːk] N *esp Am* (*on teeth*) bridge *m*

bridging ['brɪdʒɪŋ] N **1** *Constr* **the b. of the river took several months** la construction du pont sur la rivière a pris plusieurs mois; **2** *Fig* (*of gap*) comblement *m* **3** *Elec, Electron* shuntage *m*
▸▸ *Elec* **b. connection** montage *m* en pont; *Br Fin* **b. loan** prêt-relais *m*, *pl* prêts-relais; *Constr* **b. party** équipe *f* de pontonniers; *Constr* **b. piece** entretoise *f*, *Cin* **b. title** titre *m* de liaison

bridle ['braɪd(ə)l] **N** *(for horse)* bride *f*, *Fig (restraint)* frein *m*
VT *(horse)* brider; *Fig (one's passions)* maîtriser, mettre un frein à; **to b. one's tongue** tenir sa langue
VI *(of horse)* redresser la tête; *Fig (of person)* s'indigner, se scandaliser; *Fig* **she bridled at the implication** elle s'est indignée en entendant l'insinuation
▸▸**b. bit** mors *m* de bride; **b. path** piste *f* cavalière

brief [bri:f] **ADJ** *(letter, interval etc)* court; *(pause)* petit; *(discussion, explanation etc)* bref, succinct, concis; *(account, report)* sommaire, bref; *(stay etc)* bref, de courte durée; **we exchanged a few b. words** nous avons échangé quelques mots; **give me a b. idea of what happened** donne-moi une petite idée de ce qui s'est passé; **I caught a b. glimpse of her** je n'ai fait que l'entrevoir; **a very b. pair of shorts** un short très court; **for a b. period** pendant peu de temps, pendant une courte période; **in b.** en bref; **to be b., ...** *(in short)* bref, ...; **please be b.** soyez bref, s'il vous plaît
NPL briefs *(for man, woman)* slip *m*; **bikini briefs** slip de bikini
N 1 *Law* dossier *m*; *Am* **b. (of argument)** conclusions *fpl (présentées à la cour avant l'audience)*; **to take a b.** accepter un dossier; **to hold a b.** être chargé d'un dossier; **to hold a b. for sb** représenter qn en justice; **to hold a watching b. for sb** veiller (en justice) aux intérêts de qn; *Fig* **I don't hold any** *or* **I hold no b. for him** ce n'est pas mon affaire de plaider sa cause; *Fig* **I hold no b. for this policy** je n'adhère absolument pas à cette politique **2** *(instructions) (of committee etc)*, *Pol* mission *f* **3** *Br Sl Eng Law (lawyer)* avocat *m*
VT 1 *Eng Law (lawyer)* confier une cause à **2** *Aviat, Com etc (inform)* donner des informations à (**about** sur), faire l'exposé à (**about** de); *(instruct)* donner *ou* fournir des instructions *ou* des directives à; **have you been briefed?** *(brought up to date)* est-ce que vous avez été mis au courant?; *(given instructions)* est-ce qu'on vous a donné vos instructions?; **was the Prime Minister briefed?** est-ce que le Premier ministre a été renseigné sur la question?

briefcase ['bri:fkeɪs] **N** serviette *f*, *(for carrying under arm)* porte-documents *m inv*

briefing ['bri:fɪŋ] **N 1** *Eng Law* **b. of a barrister** ≃ constitution *f* d'avoué **2** *(orders) (for mission)* instructions *fpl*, directives *fpl*; *(meeting)* réunion *f* d'information, *Fam* briefing *m*; *Aviat* briefing; **they gave me a final b.** ils m'ont donné les dernières directives
▸▸**b. room** salle *f* de réunion

briefly ['bri:flɪ] **ADV 1** *(in a few words)* brièvement, en peu de mots, en bref **2** *(for a short time) (to work, stay)* brièvement; *(to pause, smile etc)* un court instant; **we spoke b. on the telephone** nous avons échangé quelques mots au téléphone

Attention: ne pas confondre avec **shortly**.

briefness ['bri:fnɪs] **N** *(of time, visit)* brièveté *f*, *(of speech)* concision *f*

brier¹ ['braɪər] **N 1** *(wild rose)* églantier *m*; **wild b.** églantier commun, rosier *m* sauvage; **sweet b.** églantier odorant **2** *briers (thorny bushes)* ronces *fpl*
▸▸**b. rose** églantine *f*

brier² **N** = **briar¹**

brierroot ['braɪəru:t], **brierwood** ['braɪəwʊd] **N** = **briarroot, briarwood**

Brig [brɪg] **N** *Mil abbr* **Brigadier**

brig [brɪg] **N** *Naut* **1** *(ship)* brick *m* **2** *esp Am (prison)* prison *f*, cellule *f* (à bord d'un navire)

brigade [brɪ'geɪd] **N** *Mil* brigade *f*, *Fig Hum Pej (group of people)* bande *f*, **infantry b.** régiment *m* d'infanterie; *Am* **artillery b.** brigade d'artillerie; *Fig* **one of the old b.** un vieux de la vieille

brigadier [brɪgə'dɪər] **N** *Mil* général *m* de brigade
▸▸**b. general** général de brigade

brigand ['brɪgənd] **N** *Old-fashioned* brigand *m*, bandit *m*

brigandage ['brɪgəndɪdʒ] **N** *Old-fashioned* brigandage *m*

bright [braɪt] **ADJ 1** *(star, metal, gem etc)* brillant; *(sun)* éclatant; *(fire, light etc)* vif, *f* vive; *(eyes)* lumineux, brillant; *(day, weather, sound)* clair; *(colour)* vif, éclatant; *Met* **it'll be brighter tomorrow** le temps sera plus clair demain; *Met* **to become brighter** s'éclaircir; *Met* **b. intervals** éclaircies *fpl*; **b. red** *(colour)* rouge *m* vif; **to go b. red** *(blush)* devenir tout rouge *ou* rouge comme une tomate; **b. red socks** des chaussettes rouge vif; **the company's future looks b.** cette société est très prometteuse; **it was the only b. spot in the day** c'était la seule chose positive de la journée; **the only b. spot in the play was her acting** son jeu était le seul intérêt de la pièce; **brighter days** *(happier)* des jours plus heureux; **the unemployment situation is looking a bit brighter** la situation de l'emploi commence à s'améliorer; **b. future** avenir *m* brillant *ou* qui promet; **to look on the b. side (of things)** prendre les choses du bon côté; *Fig* **the b. lights** *(big city)* la ville; **as soon as he could, he headed for the b. lights of the city** dès qu'il a pu, il est allé s'installer en ville **2** *(cheerful, lively)* vif, animé, sémillant; *(face, smile)* gai **3** *(clever)* intelligent; **a b. idea** une idée lumineuse; **she's a real b. spark** c'est une vraie lumière; *Iron* **some b. spark has locked the door** il y a un gros malin qui a fermé la porte à clef; **he's not very b.** ce n'est pas une lumière, il n'est pas très futé *ou* malin; *Iron* **that's b.!** c'est vraiment intelligent!
ADV to get up/leave b. and early se lever/partir de bonne heure
NPL *Am Aut* **brights** pleins phares *mpl*; **put the brights on** mets en (pleins) phares

brighten ['braɪt(ə)n] **VT** *(colour)* aviver; *Fig (room, person)* égayer
VI *(of person, face)* s'épanouir; *(of eyes)* s'allumer, briller; *(of weather)* s'éclaircir; *(of future)* s'éclaircir, devenir moins sombre; *(of prospects)* s'améliorer; **their mood brightened** ils se sont déridés
▸ **brighten up VT SEP, VI = brighten**

brightening ['braɪt(ə)nɪŋ] **N 1** *(of sky, weather)* éclaircissement *m*; *Fig* **there was a momentary b. of her mood** elle s'est égayée un moment **2** *(of colours)* avivage *m*

bright-eyed **ADJ** aux yeux brillants; *Fig (eager)* enthousiaste; *Fam* **b. and bushy-tailed** *(eager)* très enthousiaste; *(alert)* en pleine forme

brightly ['braɪtlɪ] **ADV 1** *(coloured, to sparkle)* vivement; **the sun was shining b.** le soleil était éclatant; **to burn b.** *(of fire)* être vif; **b. lit** *(street, shop window etc)* bien éclairé; **b. polished** reluisant **2** *(to say)* gaiement, gaîment

brightness ['braɪtnɪs] **N** *(of sun, light, sound)* éclat *m*; *(of lighting)* intensité *f*, *(of surface)* luminosité *f*, *(of day, sound, room)* clarté *f*, *(of colour)* vivacité *f*, *(of child etc)* intelligence *f*, *(of steel)* brillant *m*, éclat; *TV* luminosité *f*
▸▸*TV* **b. control** dispositif *m* de réglage de la luminosité

brill¹ [brɪl] **N** *(fish)* barbue *f*

brill² **ADJ** *Br Fam (abbr* **brilliant)** super *inv*

brilliance ['brɪljəns], **brilliancy** ['brɪljənsɪ] **N 1** *(of sun)* éclat *m*; *(of shine)* brillant *m*, lustre *m*; *(of sound)* netteté *f*, *Opt etc* luminance *f* **2** *(intelligence) (of person)* intelligence *f* remarquable; *(of mind, style, acting etc)* génie *m*; *(of plan, scheme)* ingéniosité *f*, *(skill) (of surgeon etc)* habileté *f* remarquable

brilliant ['brɪljənt] **ADJ 1** *(lighting)* intense, brillant; *(sun)* brillant, éclatant; *(smile)* radieux **2** *(painter, scientist, actor etc)* excellent, brillant; *(speech)* remarquable; *(future, career)* brillant; *(idea)* lumineux; *(success)* éclatant; **she was b. in her last film** elle était formidable dans son dernier film; **you were b.!** tu étais formidable *ou* magnifique!; **he's not b.** il n'est pas brillant; *Fam* **I'm not feeling too b.** *(I feel ill)* je ne suis pas dans mon assiette
N *(diamond, cut)* brillant *m*

brilliantine ['brɪljənti:n] **N** *(for hair)* brillantine *f*

brilliantly ['brɪljəntlɪ] **ADV 1** *(coloured)* vivement; **the sun was shining b.** le soleil était éclatant; **b. lit** très bien éclairé **2** *(performed, played)* brillamment; **b. intelligent** d'une intelligence brillante; *Mus* **to play b.** jouer avec brio

brim [brɪm] **N** *(of glass, hat etc)* bord *m*; **to fill a glass to the b.** remplir un verre à ras bord
VI (-mm-) **eyes brimming with tears** yeux noyés de larmes; **to be brimming with ideas** *(of person)* déborder d'idées
▸ **brim over VI** déborder, regorger (**with sth** de qch); *Fig* **brimming over with health/life/ideas** débordant de santé/de vie/d'idées

brimful ['brɪmfʊl] **ADJ** *(glass etc)* plein jusqu'au bord; **to fill a glass b.** remplir un verre à ras bord; **b. of health/of life/of ideas** débordant de santé/de vie/d'idées

brimless ['brɪmlɪs] **ADJ** *(chapeau)* sans bord(s)

-brimmed [brɪmd] **SUFF broad/narrow-b.** à larges bords/à bords étroits

brimstone ['brɪmstəʊn] **N 1** *Arch (sulphur)* soufre *m* (brut) **2** *(butterfly)* citron *m*
▸▸**b. butterfly** citron

brindled ['brɪnd(ə)ld] **ADJ** moucheté, tacheté

brine [braɪn] **N 1** *Culin* saumure *f*, **tuna in b.** thon *m* mariné **2** *(seawater)* eau *f* de mer; *Lit* **the b.** *(the sea)* la mer, l'océan *m*

BRING [brɪŋ]

amener **1**	apporter **1**
provoquer **2**	rapporter **4**

VT *(pt, pp* **brought** [brɔ:t]) **1** *(lead, carry) (person, animal)* amener; *(object, letter, news etc)* apporter; **b. your friend** amenez votre ami; **she brought a lot of luggage (with her)** elle a apporté beaucoup de bagages; **what brings you to London?** qu'est-ce qui vous amène à Londres?; **to b. sth onto the market** introduire qch sur le marché; **to b. a child into the world** mettre un enfant au monde; *Law* **to b. before a court** *(person)* faire comparaître devant un tribunal; *(case)* soumettre *ou* déférer à un tribunal; *Law* **to b. an action** introduire une action en justice; *Law* **to b. an action against sb** intenter un procès contre *ou* à qn; *Law* **to b. an accusation** *or* **a charge against sb** porter une accusation contre qn
2 *(lead to, cause)* provoquer; **to b. sb (good) luck/bad luck** porter bonheur/malheur à qn; **the announcement brought an angry reaction** la nouvelle a suscité la colère; **production has been brought to a standstill** la production a été paralysée; **to b. new hope to sb** redonner de l'espoir à qn; **you've brought it on yourself** vous l'avez cherché;

to b. tears to sb's eyes faire venir les larmes aux yeux de qn; **to b. discord into a family** semer la discorde dans une famille; **it has brought me great happiness** cela m'a apporté un grand bonheur

3 *(cause to come to a particular condition)* **to b. sb to his senses** ramener qn à la raison; **to b. sb into the conversation** *(involve)* mêler qn à la conversation; **to b. sb's name into the conversation** mentionner le nom de qn dans la conversation; **to b. water to the boil** faire bouillir de l'eau; **to b. sth into question** mettre qch en question; **to b. sth into disrepute** discréditer qch; **to b. sth to sb's attention** attirer l'attention de qn sur qch; **to b. sth to mind** rappeler qch; **to b. to light** *(old artefacts, manuscripts etc)* déterrer; *(crime, secret)* révéler; **to b. sth to an end** mettre fin à qch; **to b. sth to a successful conclusion** faire aboutir qch; **to b. oneself to do sth** se résoudre *ou* se décider à faire qch; **he cannot b. himself to speak about it** il lui est trop pénible d'en parler

4 *(be sold for)* **the house won't b. very much** la maison ne rapportera pas beaucoup

▸ **bring about** VT SEP **1** *(cause)* amener, causer, occasionner; *(reconciliation)* amener; *(person's downfall)* entraîner; *(accident etc)* provoquer, causer; *(change)* provoquer

2 *Naut (boat)* retourner, faire virer

▸ **bring along** VT SEP *(person)* amener; *(object)* apporter

▸ **bring away** VT SEP *(carry)* *(object)* rapporter; *(memories, impressions)* garder; **I brought away a lot of happy memories from my stay** j'ai gardé de mon séjour le souvenir de beaucoup de moments heureux

▸ **bring back** VT SEP **1** *(carry)* *(object)* rapporter; *(lead)* *(person)* ramener; **crying won't b. him back** pleurer ne le fera pas revenir; *Law* **to b. a case back before the court** ressaisir le tribunal d'un dossier

2 *(of letter, song etc)* *(memories)* rappeler; **it brings back my childhood to me** cela me rappelle mon enfance

3 *(restore)* *(freedom, discipline, monarchy etc)* rétablir; *(confidence)* ramener; **the electors will decide whether the government should be brought back** les électeurs décideront si le gouvernement doit être maintenu; **a couple of days in bed will b. him back to normal** quelques jours au lit le remettront d'aplomb; **to b. sb back to health** rendre la santé à qn; **to b. sb back to life** ramener qn à la vie

▸ **bring down** VT SEP **1** *(destroy)* *(tree, game bird, plane, wall etc)* abattre; *Fam* **her performance brought the house down** son interprétation lui a valu des applaudissements à tout rompre; *Fam* **the audience brought the house down** les spectateurs ont applaudi à tout rompre

2 *(cause to fall)* *(adversary)* terrasser; *(government)* faire tomber

3 *(lead, carry)* *(person)* faire descendre; *(object)* descendre (**from** de); **what brings you down to the fourth floor?** qu'est-ce qui t'amène au quatrième étage?

4 *(reduce)* *(price, costs, temperature)* faire baisser; *(currency)* déprécier, avilir; *(birth rate, inflation, unemployment, swelling)* réduire

5 *(land)* *(plane)* faire atterrir

6 *(cause to appear)* *(esp a person in authority)* attirer; **stop making so much noise or you'll b. the headmaster down on us** ne fais pas tant de bruit, tu vas attirer l'attention du proviseur sur nous

▸ **bring forth** VT SEP **1** *Arch, Lit (young)* mettre au monde; *(of animal)* mettre bas; *(of plant)* *(fruit)* produire

2 *Fig (idea)* faire naître; *(suggestion)* donner lieu à; *(condemnation, objections)* provoquer; *(of research, investigations)* générer

▸ **bring forward** VT SEP **1** *(carry, lead)* *(chair etc)* avancer; *(person)* amener, faire avancer, faire approcher; *(witness, evidence)* produire, présenter; *(argument)* avancer, présenter

2 *(in time)* *(meeting etc)* avancer

3 *Com (sum of money)* reporter; **brought forward** report *m*

▸ **bring in** VT SEP **1** *(lead, carry)* *(person)* introduire, faire entrer; *(object)* rentrer; **b. him in** faites-le entrer; **to b. in the harvest** rentrer la moisson; **to b. sb in for questioning** emmener qn au poste de police pour l'interroger

2 *(introduce)* *(fashion etc)* introduire, lancer; *(bill)* déposer, présenter; **to b. in new measures** instaurer des mesures; **new legislation will be brought in next year** une nouvelle loi prendra effet l'an prochain

3 *(involve)* *(person)* faire intervenir, faire appel à; **the company is bringing consultants in** la société fait appel à des experts-conseils

4 *(earn)* **to b. in interest** rapporter, porter intérêt; **investment that brings in 10%** placement qui rapporte 10%; **this land brings her in an income of £5,000** cette terre lui procure un revenu de 5000 livres; **how much money is he bringing in?** *(earning)* combien est-ce qu'il gagne?

5 *Law* **to b. in a verdict** rendre un verdict

6 **to b. in the New Year** *(celebrate it)* fêter le Nouvel An

▸ **bring off** VT SEP **1** *(person)* *(from ship)* débarquer; **the injured men will be brought off by helicopter** les blessés seront évacués en hélicoptère

2 *(complete successfully)* réussir; **they brought it off** ils ont réussi

3 *Vulg (bring to orgasm)* **to b. sb/oneself off** branler qn/se branler

▸ **bring on** VT SEP **1** *(cause to appear)* *(illness, asthma attack)* causer, provoquer; *Hum* **what brought this on?** *(why are you offering to help with dishes etc)* qu'est-ce que tu me caches?

2 *(of sun etc)* *(plants)* faire pousser; *(of teacher, trainer)* *(person)* faire faire des progrès à

3 *Theat (person, animal)* amener sur la scène; *(object)* apporter sur la scène; **please b. on our next contestant** faites entrer le concurrent suivant

4 **I brought it on myself** *(it was my own fault)* c'est entièrement de ma faute

▸ **bring out** VT SEP **1** *(extract, lead)* *(object)* sortir; *(person)* faire sortir; *Fig* **to b. sb out (of his/her shell)** *(make less shy)* faire sortir qn de sa réserve

2 *(cause to appear)* *(meaning of sth)* révéler, faire ressortir; *(colour, detail etc)* faire ressortir; *(publish)* *(book)* publier, sortir; **to b. out the best/the worst in sb** faire ressortir les qualités/les défauts de qn; **the sun has brought out the roses** le soleil a fait s'épanouir les roses; **strawberries b. her out in a rash** les fraises lui donnent de l'urticaire

▸ **bring over** VT SEP *(lead, carry)* *(person)* amener, faire venir; *(object)* amener, apporter

▸ **bring round** VT SEP **1** *(lead, carry)* *(person)* amener; *(object)* amener, apporter; **b. her round to meet us some time** amène-la un jour, qu'on puisse faire sa connaissance

2 *(restore to consciousness)* faire reprendre connaissance à, ranimer

3 *(restore to good mood)* rendre sa bonne humeur à

4 *(persuade)* convertir (**to an opinion** à une opinion)

5 *(steer)* *(conversation)* (r)amener (**to a subject** sur un sujet)

6 *Naut (ship)* faire virer

▸ **bring through** VT SEP *(cure with success)* guérir; *(lead with success)* conduire à la réussite; **his faith, which had brought him through the crisis** sa foi, qui l'avait aidé à surmonter la crise; **she brought all of us through the exam** grâce à elle, nous avons tous réussi l'examen

▸ **bring to** VT SEP *(restore to consciousness)* faire reprendre connaissance à, ranimer

▸ **bring together** VT SEP *(people)* réunir; *(put in touch with each other)* mettre en contact; *(documents)* rassembler, réunir; **he brought them together again** *(for meeting)* il les a réunis; *(after quarrel)* il les a réconciliés; *Law* **to b. the parties together** mettre les parties en présence

▸ **bring up** VT SEP **1** *(carry, lead upstairs)* *(object)* monter; *(person)* faire monter; *(carry, lead forward)* *(object)* approcher; *(troops)* faire avancer; *(reinforcements, fresh supplies etc)* faire venir; **to be brought up before the magistrate** comparaître devant le tribunal; **to b. sb/sth up to professional standard** élever qn/qch à un niveau professionnel

2 *(vomit)* vomir; **to b. up one's food** vomir

3 *(rear)* *(children)* élever; **I was brought up to be polite** on m'a appris la politesse; **well/badly brought up child** enfant bien/mal élevé; **to b. sb up the hard way** élever qn à la dure

4 *(mention)* *(question)* soulever, mettre sur le tapis; **to b. sth up against sb** reprocher qch à qn

5 *(stop)* **to be brought up short by a road-block/an accident** *(of car)* s'arrêter brusquement à cause d'un barrage routier/d'un accident; **to be brought up short by sb's indifference** *(when talking)* être choqué par l'indifférence de qn

bring-and-buy (sale) N *Br* vente *f* de charité

Bring-and-Buy

Ces brocantes sont en général destinées à réunir des fonds pour une œuvre de charité. On y vend des articles d'occasion et des produits faits maison.

bringing-up ['brɪŋɪŋ-] N *(of child)* éducation *f*

brink [brɪŋk] N *(of precipice, river)* bord *m*; *Fig* **to be on the b. of** *(tears, war, success, starvation etc)* être au bord de; *(discovery)* être à la veille de; *(death)* être à deux doigts de; *(ruin)* être au bord *ou* à deux doigts de; *Fig* **I was on the b. of telling him/of doing it** j'étais à deux doigts de le lui dire/de le faire; *Fig* **to be on the b. of extinction** *(of animal)* être en voie de disparition; *Fig* **to stand shivering on the b.** hésiter à faire le plongeon

brinkmanship ['brɪŋkmənʃɪp] N *esp Pol* politique *f* de la corde raide; **he's a master in the art of b.** c'est un maître dans l'art de savoir jusqu'où il peut aller *ou* *Iron* jusqu'où il peut aller trop loin

briny ['braɪnɪ] ADJ saumâtre
N *Lit, Hum* **the b.** la grande bleue

briquette [brɪ'ket] N *(of coal)* briquette *f*

brisk [brɪsk] ADJ **1** *(person, attitude, tone)* vif; *(to the point of curtness)* sec, *f* sèche **2** *(movement)* vif; *Com (business, trade)* actif; *(demand)* fort; **at a b. pace** à vive allure; **to take a b. walk** aller se promener d'un bon pas; **business is b.** les affaires marchent bien; **to do a b. trade** *(of shop)* marcher à plein rendement; *(of street seller)* faire de bonnes affaires; **we're doing a b. trade in this particular item** cet article se vend très bien **3** *(air)* vivifiant; *(morning, wind, weather etc)* frais, *f* fraîche

brisket ['brɪskɪt] N *Culin* poitrine *f*

briskly ['brɪsklɪ] ADV **1** *(to say)* d'un ton vif;

(to the point of curtness) sèchement **2** *(to move)* vivement; **to step out b.** marcher d'un bon pas; **to sell b.** bien se vendre

briskness ['brɪsknɪs] N **1** *(of person, voice)* vivacité *f*; *(to the point of curtness)* brusquerie *f*; **the b. with which she goes about her job** l'extrême diligence avec laquelle elle fait son travail **2** *(of movement)* vivacité *f*; *(of business, trading)* dynamisme *m* **3** *(of air etc)* fraîcheur *f*

bristle ['brɪs(ə)l] N **1** *(of pig, caterpillar, badger)* soie *f*; *(of brush)* soie, poil *m*; *(of beard)* poil raide; **his face was covered with bristles** il avait une barbe de trois jours **2** *Bot* soie *f*, poil *m*

vi *(of animal, hair etc)* se hérisser; *Fig* **to b. (with anger)** se hérisser (**at** à)

▸ **bristle with** vt INSEP grouiller de; **the room was bristling with security men** la pièce grouillait d'agents de sécurité; **a situation bristling with difficulties** une situation hérissée de difficultés; **bristling with machine guns** *(fort, trench)* hérissé de mitrailleuses; **soldiers bristling with weapons** des soldats bardés d'armes

bristly ['brɪslɪ] ADJ **1** *(face)* couvert de poils raides; *(animal)* couvert de soies; *(moustache)* hérissé **2** *Bot* poilu, garni de soies

Bristol ['brɪst(ə)l] N *Naut, Fig* **(shipshape and) B. fashion** en bon ordre

▸▸ **B. board** bristol *m*

bristols ['brɪst(ə)lz] NPL *Br Old-fashioned Sl* *(breasts)* nichons *mpl*

Brit [brɪt] N *Fam* *(abbr* **Briton**) Britannique *mf*, Anglais, -aise, *Pej* rosbif *mf*

Britain ['brɪt(ə)n] N Grande-Bretagne *f*

Britannia [brɪ'tænɪə] N = nom *m* symbolique de la Grande-Bretagne

Britannic [brɪ'tænɪk] ADJ **His/Her B. Majesty** Sa Majesté britannique

Britart ['brɪtɑːt] N = appellation *f* collective des jeunes artistes britanniques qui ont fait de Londres, depuis la fin des années 1970, un important centre d'art contemporain

Briticism ['brɪtɪsɪz(ə)m] N *Ling* anglicisme *m*

British ['brɪtɪʃ] VOIR GRAMMAIRE A19 ADJ britannique, de la Grande-Bretagne; **B. goods** produits *mpl* ou marchandises *fpl* britanniques; **the B. consul** le consul de Grande-Bretagne

NPL **the B.** les Britanniques *mpl*, *Fam* les Anglais *mpl*

▸▸ **B. Columbia** Colombie-Britannique *f*, **B. Council** = organisme *m* chargé de promouvoir la langue et la culture anglaises; **B. English** anglais *m* britannique; **B. Isles** îles *fpl* Britanniques; **B. Standards Institution** = association *f* britannique de normalisation; **B. Summer Time** = heure *f* d'été en Grande-Bretagne; **B. thermal unit** = 1055,06 joules *mpl*

> **British Council**
> Le British Council est un organisme chargé de promouvoir la langue et la culture anglaises, et de renforcer les liens culturels avec les autres pays.

Britisher ['brɪtɪʃər] N *Am* Britannique *mf*, *Fam* Anglais, -aise

Briton ['brɪt(ə)n] N **1** Britannique *mf*, *Fam* Anglais, -aise VOIR GRAMMAIRE A19 **2** *Hist* *(Celt)* Breton, -onne *(de la Grande-Bretagne)*

Britpop ['brɪtpɒp] N = la musique pop britannique du milieu des années 90

Brittany ['brɪtənɪ] N Bretagne *f*

brittle ['brɪt(ə)l] ADJ fragile, cassant; *Fig (laugh)* un peu forcé; **to suffer from b. bones** souffrir d'ostéoporose; *Fig* **in a b. voice** *(brusque)* d'un ton cassant; *(strained)* d'une

voix tendue; **there is still a slightly b. air about the new coalition** la nouvelle coalition donne toujours une légère impression de fragilité; **a b. and rather unconvincing defence** une défense faible et peu convaincante

N = bonbon *m* croquant à base de mélasse et de noix

brittleness ['brɪt(ə)lnɪs] N *(of bones)* fragilité *f*; **the b. of his humour** son humour caustique

broach [brəʊtʃ] N *(for tapping cask)* perçoir *m*

VT *(cask)* percer; *Fig (question etc)* aborder; **I broached with your mother the subject of your leaving school** j'ai abordé la question de ton départ de l'école avec ta mère

broad [brɔːd] ADJ **1** *(wide)* large; **the road is 15 metres b.** la route a 15 mètres de large ou de largeur; **to make sth broader** élargir qch; **a b. smile** un large sourire; **to have a b. back** avoir une forte carrure; *Fig* avoir bon dos; **it was already b. daylight** il faisait déjà grand jour; **in b. daylight** en plein jour; *Fig* au grand jour, devant tout le monde; *Fig* **it's as b. as it's long** cela revient au même, c'est tout un, c'est bonnet blanc et blanc bonnet; **b. views** *or* **ideas** *or* **outlook** idées *fpl* larges; **b. humour** humour *m* de mauvais goût *ou* peu délicat; **b. joke** grosse plaisanterie *f*, **to have b. tastes in literature** avoir des goûts éclectiques en littérature; *Fig* **the party is a b. church** le parti rassemble de nombreux courants différents

2 *(general) (rule, implications)* général, -aux; *(distinction)* sommaire; **term used in its broadest sense** terme employé dans un sens (très) large; **b. outline** *(of project etc)* aperçu *m*; **the project has b. support** le projet bénéficie d'un large soutien; **to be in b. agreement** être d'accord dans les grandes lignes

3 *(accent)* prononcé; **to speak b. Scots/Yorkshire** parler avec un accent écossais/du Yorkshire prononcé

N **1 the b. of the back** le milieu du dos **2** *Br* **the Broads** la région des lacs du Norfolk **3** *esp Am Sl (woman)* gonzesse *f*

▸▸ **b. bean** fève *f*, *Am Sport* **b. jump** saut *m* en longueur; *Ling* **b. vowel** voyelle *f* large

broadband ['brɔːdbænd] *Tel, Comput* N connexion *f* à haut débit *ou* à large bande
ADJ à haut débit, à large bande

broad-brimmed ADJ *(hat)* à large bord

broadcast ['brɔːdkɑːst] VT *(pt, pp* **broadcast**) **1** *(programme etc)* *Radio* transmettre, (radio)diffuser; *TV* transmettre, diffuser; **the match will be b. live** le match sera diffusé en direct **2** *Agr (seed)* semer à la volée; *Fig (news)* répandre; **don't b. it!** ne le crie pas sur les toits!

VI **1** *(of person) (on radio)* parler/chanter/*etc* à la radio; *(on television)* passer à la télévision **2** *(of radio or TV authority)* émettre

N *Radio, TV* émission *f*; **simultaneous/recorded/live/outside b.** émission simultanée/en différé/en direct/hors studio

ADJ **1** *Radio* (radio)diffusé; *TV* télévisé **2** *Agr* semé à la volée

ADV *Agr* **to sow b.** semer à la volée

▸▸ *TV etc* **b. antenna** antenne *f* d'émission; **b. journalism** *Radio* journalisme *m* de radiodiffusion; *TV* journalisme de télévision; *TV etc* **b. master** copie *f* antenne; **b. network** réseau *m* de transmission; *TV etc* **b. satellite** satellite *m* de radiodiffusion; *Agr* **b. sowing** semis *m* à la volée; *Mktg* **b. sponsorship** parrainage *m* audiovisuel

broadcaster ['brɔːdkɑːstər] N *(reporter)* *Radio* reporter *m* radio; *TV* reporter de la télévision; *(who gives talks, speaks)* personne *f* qui fait de la radio/la télévision; *Radio, TV*

independent b. *(station)* station *f* de radio/chaîne *f* de télévision privée

broadcasting ['brɔːdkɑːstɪŋ] N **1** *Radio* radiodiffusion *f*; *TV* diffusion *f*; **she works in b.** *Radio* elle fait de la radio; *TV* elle fait de la télévision; **(television) b.** télévision *f*, **news b.** *Radio* reportage *m* (radio); *TV* téléreportage *m*, reportage (télévisé); **music/children's b.** émissions *fpl* musicales/pour les enfants; **this is the end of today's b.** voici la fin de nos émissions pour aujourd'hui **2** *Agr* semis *m* à la volée

▸▸ **b. centre** centre *m* de diffusion; **b. company** *TV* société *f* de télédiffusion; *Radio* société *f* de radiodiffusion; **B. House** = siège *m* de la BBC à Londres; **b. network** réseau *m* de diffusion; **b. rights** droits *mpl* de diffusion *ou* d'antenne; **b. station** station *f* émettrice

broadcloth ['brɔːdklɒθ] N *Tex* **1** *(for men's clothing)* drap *m* fin **2** *Am (poplin)* popeline *f*

broaden ['brɔːd(ə)n] VT élargir; **to b. sb's outlook** *or* **horizons** élargir l'horizon de qn; **travel broadens the mind** les voyages ouvrent de nouveaux horizons
VI s'élargir

▸ **broaden out** VI *(of river, road, valley)* s'élargir

broad-leaved ADJ *(tree)* à larges feuilles, *Spec* latifolié

broadloom ['brɔːdluːm] N moquette *f* grande largeur

▸▸ **b. carpet** moquette grande largeur

broadly ['brɔːdlɪ] ADV **1** *(widely)* largement; **smiling b.** avec un large sourire **2** *(generally)* généralement; **b. speaking** généralement parlant, d'une façon générale; **to b. agree** être d'accord sur les grandes lignes **3** *(to speak)* avec un accent prononcé

broad-minded ADJ tolérant; **to be b.** avoir l'esprit large, être tolérant, être large d'esprit; **she takes a b. attitude to that kind of thing** elle est très tolérante pour ce genre de choses

broad-mindedness [-'maɪndɪdnɪs] N largeur *f* d'esprit, tolérance *f*

broadness ['brɔːdnɪs] N **1** *(width)* largeur *f* **2** *(of accent)* **because of the b. of his Yorkshire accent** à cause de son accent du Yorkshire à couper au couteau

broadsheet ['brɔːdʃiːt] N **1** *(newspaper)* journal *m* grand format *(de qualité)* **2** *(pamphlet)* feuille *f* imprimée

▸▸ **b. format** plein format *m*; **the b. press** les journaux grand format

broad-shouldered [-'ʃəʊldəd] ADJ large d'épaules, aux larges épaules

broadside ['brɔːdsaɪd] N *Naut* **1** *(of ship)* flanc *m*, travers *m*; **collision b. on** abordage *m* par le travers **2** *(from guns)* bordée *f*, *Fig (attack)* attaque *f* virulente; **to fire a b.** *Naut* tirer une bordée; *Fig* lancer une attaque virulente (**at** contre)

broad-spectrum ADJ *(antibiotic)* au spectre d'action très large

broadways, **broadwise** ['brɔːdweɪz, -waɪz] ADV dans le sens de la largeur

brocade [brə'keɪd] *Tex* N brocart *m*; **b. curtains/skirt** rideaux *mpl*/jupe *f* en brocart
VT brocher; **brocaded gown** robe *f* de brocart

broccoli ['brɒkəlɪ] N brocoli *m*; **eat your b.** mange tes brocolis

brochure ['brəʊʃʊər, -ʃər] N brochure *f*, *(folding)* dépliant *m*

brogue¹ [brəʊg] N *(shoe)* = chaussure *f* basse, ornée de petits trous

brogue² N *(accent)* accent *m*

broil [brɔɪl] *Am* VT *Culin (under grill)* passer au gril; *(over fire)* griller, (faire) cuire sur le gril

VI *Fam* **we were broiling (hot)** on grillait; **a broiling hot day** un jour où il fait une chaleur à crever

broiler ['brɔɪlər] **N 1** *Am (grill)* gril *m*, rôtissoire *f*; **put it under the b.** passez-le au gril **2** *(fowl)* poulet *m* (à rôtir) **3** *Am Fam* **it's a real b. (of a day)** on crève de chaleur
▶▶ **b. fowl** poulet (à rôtir); **b. house** éleveuse *f* (de poulets)

broke [brəʊk] **PT** *see* **break**[1]
ADJ *Fam* fauché, à sec; **to go b.** *(of company)* faire faillite; **to be (stony** or **dead) b.** être sans le sou, être fauché, être à sec; *Sl* **to go for b.** jouer le tout pour le tout

broken ['brəʊk(ə)n] **PP** *see* **break**[1]
ADJ 1 *(limb, egg, stick, toy etc)* cassé; *(glass, window)* cassé, brisé; *(friendship)* brisé; *(rope), Naut (moorings etc)* rompu; *(stones)* (con)cassé **2** *(terrain)* accidenté; *(shoreline)* découpé; *(outline)* irrégulier **3** *(sleep)* interrompu; *(words)* entrecoupé; **we had rather a b. night** nous avons été réveillés plusieurs fois pendant la nuit; **a voice b. with sobs** une voix entrecoupée de sanglots; **in a b. voice** d'une voix brisée; **to speak b. English** parler un mauvais anglais **4** *(marriage, heart)* brisé; *(promise)* violé; **b. health** mauvaise santé *f*; **b. home** foyer *m* ou famille *f* désuni(e); **a b. man** *(financially)* un homme ruiné; *(by grief etc)* un homme brisé
▶▶ *Com* **b. lots** articles *mpl* dépareillés; **b. white line** *(on road)* ligne *f* discontinue

broken-down **ADJ** *(car etc)* en panne; *(mechanism)* détraqué; *(house, furniture)* délabré; *(horse)* fourbu; **a b. old man** un vieil homme usé

brokenhearted [brəʊk(ə)n'hɑːtɪd] **ADJ** au cœur brisé; **to die b.** mourir de douleur ou de chagrin

brokenly ['brəʊk(ə)nlɪ] **ADV** *(to speak)* de façon entrecoupée

broken-winded [-'wɪndɪd] **ADJ** *Vet (horse)* poussif

broker ['brəʊkər] **N 1** *Com (for insurance etc)* courtier, ière; **insurance b.** courtier d'assurances; **wine b.** négociant, -ante en vins **2** *St Exch* courtier, ière ou agent *m* de change; **outside b.** courtier libre; *St Exch* **b.'s commission** (frais *mpl* de) courtage *m*; **b.'s contract** courtage
VT *Fig* **to b. an agreement** négocier un accord en tant qu'intermédiaire

brokerage ['brəʊkərɪdʒ] **N** *Fin (fee)* (frais *mpl* de) courtage *m*
▶▶ **b. house** *(business)* maison *f* de courtage

broking ['brəʊkɪŋ] **N** *Fin (profession)* courtage *m*

brolly ['brɒlɪ] **N** *Br Fam (umbrella)* pépin *m*, pébroc *m*

bromeliad [brəʊ'miːlɪæd] **N** *Bot* broméliacée *f*

bromide ['brəʊmaɪd] **N 1** *Chem, Typ* bromure *m*; *Phot* papier *m* au gélatinobromure (d'argent); **potassium b.** bromure de potassium **2** *Fig (platitude)* banalité *f*
▶▶ *Phot* **b. paper** papier au gélatinobromure (d'argent)

bronchial ['brɒŋkɪəl] **ADJ** *Anat, Med (artery, asthma etc)* bronchique
▶▶ *Med* **b. pneumonia** broncho-pneumonie *f*, *pl* broncho-pneumonies; *Anat* **b. tubes** bronches *fpl*

bronchiole ['brɒŋkɪəʊl] **N** *Anat* bronchiole *f*

bronchitic [brɒŋ'kɪtɪk] **ADJ, N** *Med* bronchitique *mf*

bronchitis [brɒŋ'kaɪtɪs] **N** *Med* bronchite *f*; **she has b.** elle a une bronchite

bronchopneumonia [brɒŋkəʊnjuː'məʊ-

nɪə] **N** *Med* broncho-pneumonie *f*, *pl* broncho-pneumonies

bronchus, *pl* **bronchi** ['brɒŋkəs, -kiː] **N** *Med* bronche *f*

bronco ['brɒŋkəʊ] **N** cheval *m* sauvage *(dans l'ouest américain)*

broncobuster ['brɒŋkəʊbʌstər] **N** *Am* dresseur *m* de chevaux

brontosaurus [brɒntə'sɔːrəs] **N** brontosaure *m*

bronze [brɒnz] **N 1** *(metal)* bronze *m* **2** *Art (object)* (objet *m* en) bronze *m* **3** *Sport etc Fam (medal)* médaille *f* de bronze
ADJ 1 *(statue)* de ou en bronze **2** *(colour)* (couleur) bronze *inv*
VT bronzer
▶▶ **the B. Age** l'âge *m* de bronze; *Sport etc* **b. medal** médaille de bronze

bronzed [brɒnzd] **ADJ** *(skin)* bronzé

bronzing ['brɒnzɪŋ] **N** bronzage *m*

brooch [brəʊtʃ] **N** broche *f*

brood [bruːd] **N 1** *(of chicks)* couvée *f*, nichée *f* **2** *Fig (children)* enfants *mpl*, *Pej* marmaille *f*; **a member of the McGowan b.** un membre de la progéniture des McGowan **3** *Fig Pej (of scoundrels etc)* race *f*, engeance *f*
VI *(of hen)* couver; *Fig* broyer du noir; **to b. about** or **on** or **over** *(the past, mistakes)* remâcher; *(idea)* ruminer; **there's no point in brooding over what might have happened** ça ne sert à rien de ruminer en imaginant ce qui aurait pu se passer; **she's brooding about the exam** *(which she has sat)* elle repense à son examen; *(which she will sit)* elle n'arrête pas de penser à son examen; **stop brooding about what he said** arrête de ruminer ce qu'il a dit; **to b. about things** ruminer; *Lit* **night brooded over the castle** les ténèbres enveloppaient le château
▶▶ **b. cell** *(in beehive)* cellule *f* d'incubation; **b. hen** (poule *f*) couveuse *f*; **b. mare** (jument *f*) poulinière *f*

brooder ['bruːdər] **N 1** *(hen)* (poule *f*) couveuse *f* **2** *(enclosure)* couveuse *f* (artificielle) **3** *Fig (person)* **he's such a b.** il est toujours à ruminer

broody ['bruːdɪ] **ADJ** *(hen)* couveuse *f*, qui demande à couver; *Fig (person)* songeur, pensif; **to feel b.** *(of woman)* être en mal d'enfant

brook[1] [brʊk] **N** ruisseau *m*
▶▶ *Ich* **b. trout** saumon *m* de fontaine

brook[2] **VT** *Lit (used only in neg sentences)* tolérer, supporter; **the matter brooks no delay** l'affaire n'admet aucun retard; **he will b. no insolence** il ne supporte pas d'impertinence; **I will b. no refusal** je ne tolérerai pas que tu/il/etc refuse(s)

broom [bruːm] **N 1** *(shrub)* genêt *m* (à balai) **2** *(for sweeping)* balai *m*; *Fig* **new b.** = personne *f* nouvellement arrivée qui veut remanier l'organisation de l'entreprise; *Prov* **a new b. sweeps clean** = de nouveaux dirigeants mettent en œuvre de nouvelles méthodes

broomstick ['bruːmstɪk] **N** manche *m* à balai

Bros [brɒs] **Com** *(abbr* **Brothers)** Thomas B. maison *f* Thomas frères

broth [brɒθ] **N** *Culin (clear)* bouillon *m*; *(with vegetables etc)* potage *m*; **Scotch b.** soupe *f* (de mouton) avec orge et légumes

brothel ['brɒθ(ə)l] **N** maison *f* close, *Fam* bordel *m*
▶▶ *Br Fam* **b. creepers** chaussures *fpl* à semelles de crêpe; **b. keeper** tenancier, -ière de bordel

brother ['brʌðər] **N 1** *(sibling)* frère *m*; **older b.** frère aîné; **younger b.** (frère) cadet *m*; *Com* **Thomas Brothers** maison *f* Thomas frè-

res **2** *Rel (in community)* frère *m*; **B. John** Frère John **3** *(fellow member) (in guild)* confrère *m*; *Sl (fellow Black American)* frère; **brothers!** *(at union meeting etc)* camarades! **INT** *esp Am Fam* bon sang!
▶▶ **brothers in arms** frères d'armes; **b. officers** officiers *mpl* de la même brigade; *Mil* officiers du même régiment

brotherhood ['brʌðəhʊd] **N 1** *(relationship)* fraternité *f*; **the b. of man** la fraternité des hommes **2** *(organization)* fraternité *f*, *(religious)* confrérie *f* **3** *esp Am (trade union)* syndicat *m* ouvrier

brother-in-law, *pl* **brothers-in-law** **N** beau-frère *m*, *pl* beaux-frères

brotherliness ['brʌðəlɪnɪs] **N** *(of relation)* amour *m* fraternel

brotherly ['brʌðəlɪ] **ADJ** *(love etc)* fraternel

brought [brɔːt] **PP, PT** *see* **bring**

brouhaha [bruːhɑːhɑː] **N** brouhaha *m*

brow [braʊ] **N 1** *Anat* front *m*; **to knit one's brows** froncer les sourcils **2** *(of hill)* sommet *m*; **the b. of a hill** *(on road)* le haut d'une côte

browbeat ['braʊbiːt] **VT** intimider; **to b. sb into doing sth** intimider qn pour qu'il fasse qch

browbeaten ['braʊbiːt(ə)n] **ADJ** persécuté

browbeating ['braʊbiːtɪŋ] **N** intimidation *f*

brown [braʊn] **ADJ** *(coat, shoes)* marron *inv*; *(hair)* brun, châtain; *(eyes)* brun, marron; **light b. hair** cheveux châtain clair; **to be b.** *(tanned)* être bronzé; **to be as b. as a berry** *(tanned)* être tout bronzé ou noir
N marron *m*
VT 1 *(of sun)* brunir, bronzer; **a face browned by the sun** un visage bruni ou hâlé par le soleil **2** *Culin (fish, meat etc)* faire dorer; *(butter, sauce)* faire roussir; *(almonds)* praliner
VI 1 *(in sun)* brunir **2** *Culin* dorer
▶▶ **b. ale** bière *f* brune; **b. bear** ours *m* brun; **b. bread** pain *m* complet ou bis; *Com* **b. goods** = biens *mpl* de consommation de taille moyenne tels que téléviseur, radio ou magnétoscope; **B. Owl** *(in Brownies)* cheftaine *f*, **b. owl** chat-huant *m*, *pl* chats-huants, chouette *f* des bois, hulotte *f*, **b. paper** papier *m* d'emballage; **b. paper bag** sac *m* en papier kraft; *Zool* **b. rat** surmulot *m*; **b. rice** riz *m* complet; **b. sugar** *Culin* cassonade *f*, sucre *m* roux; *Sl (heroin)* héro *f*, **b. trout** truite *f* de rivière

brown-bag **VT & VI** *Am Fam* **to b. (it)** = apporter son déjeuner (sur son lieu de travail)
▶▶ *Am* **b. seminar** = séminaire *m* où les participants apportent leur déjeuner

brown-bagger [-'bægər] **N** *Am Fam* = personne *f* qui apporte son déjeuner sur son lieu de travail

browned-off [braʊnd-] **ADJ** *esp Br Fam* **to be b.** en avoir marre ou ras le bol; **I'm b. with always having to do the dishes** j'en ai marre de devoir toujours faire la vaisselle; **he's very b. with you** il en a vraiment marre de toi

brown-eyed **ADJ** aux yeux bruns ou marron

brownfield site ['braʊnfiːld] **N** terrain *m* à bâtir *(après démolition de bâtiments préexistants)*

brown-haired **ADJ** aux cheveux bruns ou châtains

brownie ['braʊnɪ] **N 1** *(elf)* lutin *m* (bienfaisant), farfadet *m* **2 B.** *(guide)* ≃ jeannette *f*; *Fig* **to win** or **get b. points** se faire bien voir **3** *Am Culin* brownie *m*

Browning ['braʊnɪŋ] **N** *(gun)* browning *m*

browning ['braʊnɪŋ] **N 1** *(by sun)* brunissement *m*, bronzage *m* **2** *Culin (of almonds)* pralinage *m*; **the b. of the meat is important**

c'est important de faire rissoler la viande **3** *Br Culin (substance)* colorant *m* brun (pour les sauces)

brownish ['braʊnɪʃ] **ADJ** brunâtre

brown-nose *Am Sl* **VI** faire du lèche-cul **VT** faire du lèche-cul à

brown-noser [-nəʊzər] **N** *Am Sl* lèche-cul *mf inv*

brownout ['braʊnaʊt] **N** *Am Elec* baisse *f* de tension

Brownshirt ['braʊnʃɜːt] **N** *Hist* Chemise *f* brune

browse [braʊz] **VT** *Comput* **to b. the Web** naviguer sur le Web; **to b. the contents of one's hard disk** parcourir le contenu du disque dur **VI 1** *(of animal)* brouter, paître; **to b. on leaves** brouter des feuilles; *Fig* **I'm just browsing, thank you** *(in shop)* je regarde, merci **2** *Comput* se promener
▸▸*Comput* **b. mode** mode *m* survol
▸**browse through** **VT INSEP 1** *Fig* **to b. through a book/magazine** feuilleter un livre/un magazine; **to b. through sb's books/ records** jeter un coup d'œil aux livres/disques de qn **2** *Comput* se promener dans, survoler

browser ['braʊzər] **N** *Comput* navigateur *m*, logiciel *m* de navigation

brucellosis [bruːsɪ'ləʊsɪs] **N** *Med, Vet* brucellose *f*

bruise [bruːz] **N** bleu *m*, contusion *f*, *Spec* ecchymose *f*, *(on fruit)* meurtrissure *f*, talure *f*; **she just has cuts and bruises** *(of accident victim)* elle n'a que quelques égratignures **VT 1** *(part of body)* meurtrir; *(fruit)* meurtrir, taler; **to b. one's arm** se faire un bleu au bras, se meurtrir le bras; **you've bruised my arm!** tu m'as fait un bleu au bras!; *Fig* **to b. sb's pride** blesser l'amour propre de qn **2** *(crush)* *(substance)* broyer, écraser, concasser **VI** *(of person)* se faire des bleus; *(of fruit etc)* s'abîmer; **he bruises easily** il se fait des bleus très facilement; *Fig* il est très sensible

bruised [bruːzd] **ADJ** meurtri; *Fig (pride)* blessé; **badly b.** couvert de bleus

bruiser ['bruːzər] **N** *Fam (boxer)* boxeur *m*; *(bully)* cogneur *m*; *Fam* **their baby's a real b.!** *(big)* leur bébé est vraiment costaud

bruising ['bruːzɪŋ] **N 1** *(on skin)* bleus *mpl*, meurtrissures *fpl*, contusions *fpl*, *Spec* ecchymoses *fpl*; *(on fruit)* meurtrissures, talures *fpl*, *Fig* **to take a b.** *(of ego, self-confidence etc)* en prendre un coup **2** *(of substance)* broyage *m*, écrasement *m*, concassage *m* **ADJ** *Fig (hurtful to emotions, self-confidence etc)* douloureux

brumbie, brumby ['brʌmbɪ] **N** *Austr Fam* cheval *m* sauvage *ou* non dressé

Brummie ['brʌmɪ] **N** *Br Fam* = personne *f* née à ou habitant Birmingham

brunch [brʌntʃ] **N** *Fam* brunch *m*

Brunei [bruː'naɪ] **N** Brunei *m*

brunette [bruː'net] **N** brune *f*; **she's a b.** elle est brune

brunt [brʌnt] **N** *(of blow etc)* choc *m*; **the car took the b. of it** c'est la voiture qui a tout pris; *Fig* **the b. of his argument** le point principal de sa thèse; **to bear the b. of** *(attack, storm etc)* soutenir le plus fort de; *(sb's anger)* soutenir le poids de; **to bear the b. of the expense** supporter la plus grande partie des frais

brush [brʌʃ] **N 1** *(undergrowth)* broussailles *fpl*, *(scrubland)* brousse *f*
2 *(for hair, clothes etc)* brosse *f*, *(for sweeping)* balai *m*; *(with dustpan)* balayette *f*; *(for paint, paste)* pinceau *m*; **flat b.** queue-de-morue *f*, *pl* queues-de-morue; **paste b.** pinceau à colle; **to paint with a full b.** *(of artist)* peindre dans la pâte

3 *(tail) (of fox)* queue *f*
4 *Elec* balai *m*; **(contact) b.** frotteur *m*
5 **to give sth a b.** *(clothes)* donner un coup de brosse à qch; *(floor)* donner un coup de balai à qch; **to give one's hair a b.** se donner un coup de brosse; **to give one's teeth a b.** se brosser les dents
6 *(encounter) (with enemy)* rencontre *f*, échauffourée *f*, *Fam (with boss)* prise *f* de bec; *Fam* **to have a b. with the police** avoir des ennuis avec la police; *Fig* **to have a b. with death** frôler la mort
7 *(light stroke)* effleurement *m*; **she felt the b. of his lips on her neck** elle a senti ses lèvres lui effleurer le cou
VT 1 *(clothes, carpet)* brosser; **to b. one's hair** se brosser les cheveux; **to b. one's teeth** se brosser *ou* se laver les dents; **to b. sth clean** nettoyer qch avec une brosse *ou* à la brosse **2** *(touch in passing) (surface)* effleurer, raser, frôler **3** *Tex (wool, nylon)* gratter
▸▸**b. fire** *(fire)* feu *m* de brousse, incendie *m* de broussailles; *Mil (minor war)* conflit *m* armé; **b. holder** porte-balai *m*, *pl* porte-balai(s)
▸**brush against** **VT INSEP** frôler, effleurer
▸**brush aside** **VT SEP** *(person, difficulty)* écarter; *(objection, problem)* mépriser
▸**brush away** **VT SEP 1** *(remove) (from clothes)* enlever d'un coup de brosse; *(from floor)* enlever d'un coup de balai; *(tears)* essuyer; **b. the leaves away from the path** balaye les feuilles qui sont sur le chemin **2** *(treat as unimportant) (person, difficulty)* écarter; **to b. away criticism** mépriser les critiques
▸**brush down** **VT SEP** *(person)* donner un coup de brosse à; *(horse)* brosser
▸**brush off** **VT SEP 1** *(remove) (from clothes)* enlever d'un coup de brosse; *(from floor)* enlever d'un coup de balai; **b. those flies off** chasse ces mouches **2** *Fam (reject)* envoyer promener; **he never brushes anyone off** il n'envoie jamais les gens promener; **to b. off pleas for help** rejeter des demandes d'aide
VI *(of dirt etc)* s'enlever à la brosse
▸**brush over** **VT SEP b. the varnish over the surface** badigeonner la surface de vernis **VT INSEP to b. over an issue** *(not treat in detail)* effleurer une question; *(ignore)* ignorer une question
▸**brush past** **VT INSEP** passer tout près de; **but he just brushed past me** mais il est passé à côté de moi sans s'arrêter
▸**brush up** **VT SEP 1** *(collect) (crumbs etc)* ramasser (avec une brosse) **2** *Fam (subject) (improve knowledge of)* se remettre à; *(for exam etc)* réviser; **to b. up one's French** *(improve)* se remettre au français, remettre son français à niveau

brushdown ['brʌʃdaʊn] **N to give sb a b.** donner un coup de brosse à qn; **to give a horse a b.** brosser *ou* panser un cheval

brushed [brʌʃt] **ADJ** *Tex (wool, nylon)* gratté

brushing ['brʌʃɪŋ] **N** *(of hair, carpet etc)* brossage *m*; *(of floor)* balayage *m*

brushoff ['brʌʃɒf] **N** *Fam* **to give sb the b.** envoyer promener qn

brush-up **N** coup *m* de brosse

brushwood ['brʌʃwʊd] **N 1** *(undergrowth)* broussailles *fpl* **2** *(worthless wood)* mortbois *m*, *pl* morts-bois; *(for fire etc)* menu bois *m*; *(twigs)* brindilles *fpl*

brushwork ['brʌʃwɜːk] **N** *Art (of artist)* touche *f*

brusque [bruːsk] **ADJ** *(manner)* brusque, rude; *(tone)* rude, bourru

brusquely ['bruːsklɪ] **ADV** *(to behave)* de façon brusque, avec rudesse; *(to answer)* avec rudesse

brusqueness ['bruːsknɪs] **N** brusquerie *f*, rudesse *f*; *(of tone)* rudesse

Brussels ['brʌs(ə)lz] **N** Bruxelles
▸▸**B. sprouts** choux *mpl* de Bruxelles

brutal ['bruːt(ə)l] **ADJ** brutal, -aux; **the b. truth** la vérité toute nue

brutality [bruː'tælɪtɪ] **N** brutalité *f*, *Law* sévices *mpl* (**to** envers)

brutalize ['bruːtəlaɪz] **VT 1** *(make brutal)* rendre brutal **2** *(ill-treat)* brutaliser, maltraiter

brutally ['bruːtəlɪ] **ADV** brutalement; **to be b. frank** *or* **honest with sb** être d'une franchise brutale avec qn

brute [bruːt] **N** *(animal)* bête *f*, brute *f*, *Fig (person)* brute; **you b.!** espèce de brute!; *Fam* **a b. of a job** un travail pénible **ADJ b. beast** bête *f*, brute *f*, *Fig* **b. strength** *or* **force** force *f* brutale; **by b. force** par la force; **you'll have to use b. force** il faudra user de la manière forte

brutish ['bruːtɪʃ] **ADJ** bestial, -aux; *Fig (stupid)* abruti; *(violent)* brutal, -aux

brutishly ['bruːtɪʃlɪ] **ADV** comme une brute

Brylcreem® ['brɪlkriːm] **N** = marque *f* de brillantine

bryony ['braɪənɪ] **N** *(plant)* bryone *f* couleuvrée

BS¹ [biː'es] **N** *(abbr British Standard)* = indique que le chiffre qui suit renvoie au numéro de la norme fixée par l'association britannique de normalisation

BS² *Am Sl (abbr bullshit)* conneries *fpl*

BSc [biːes'siː] **N** *Univ (abbr Bachelor of Science)* **to have a BSc** ≃ être licencié, -ée en sciences; **John Smith, BSc** ≃ John Smith, licencié ès sciences

BSE [biːes'iː] **N** *Vet (abbr bovine spongiform encephalopathy)* EBS *f*

B-share **N** *St Exch* action *f* ordinaire avec droit de vote, action à dividende prioritaire

BSI [biːes'aɪ] **N** *abbr* **British Standards Institution**

BST [biːes'tiː] **N** *abbr* **British Summer Time**

BT [biː'tiː] **N** *abbr* **British Telecom**

BTW *Comput (abbr* **by the way)** *(used in e-mails)* à propos

B2B ['biːtəbiː] **ADJ** *(abbr* **business to business)** B2B

B2C ['biːtəsiː] **ADJ** *(abbr* **business to consumer)** B2C

bubba ['bʌbə] **N** *Am Fam* **1** *(term of address)* mec *m*, vieux *m*; **hey b., gimme a smoke!** hé, vieux! file-moi une clope! **2** *Pej (redneck)* plouc *m (du sud des États-Unis)*

bubble ['bʌb(ə)l] **N** *(of air, soap, gas etc)* bulle *f*, *(in glass)* soufflure *f*, bulle; *Metal* boursouflure *f*; **to blow bubbles** faire des bulles de savon; *Fig* **to burst sb's b.** détruire les illusions de qn; **the economic b.** l'illusion d'un miracle économique
VI *(of boiling liquid etc)* bouillonner; *Chem, Ind (of gas through liquid)* barboter; *(of liquid poured)* faire glouglou, glouglouter
▸▸**b. bath** bain *m* moussant; *Br Aut* **b. car** = petite voiture *f* à trois roues; **b. economy** économie *f* de bulle; **b. gum** bubble-gum *m*; *Comput* **b. memory** mémoire *f* à bulles; **b. pack** *Com (for toy, batteries)* blister *m*, emballage *m* bulle; *(for pills)* plaquette *f*, *Br Culin* **b. and squeak** = plat *m* à base de pommes de terre et de choux, servi réchauffé; *Com* **b. wrap** bullpack® *m*
▸**bubble over** **VI** *(of soup, milk)* (bouillonner et) déborder; *(of champagne)* (mousser et) déborder; *Fig* **to b. over with vitality/ with high spirits** déborder de vie/de gaieté; **to b. over with joy** pétiller de joie; **he was bubbling over with laughter** il ne se retenait pas de rire

bubble-jet printer N imprimante f à bulles

bubbling ['bʌb(ə)lɪŋ] ADJ bouillonnant
N bouillonnement m; Chem, Ind barbotage m; (in paintwork) boursouflures fpl

bubbly ['bʌblɪ] ADJ plein de bulles; Fig (person) pétillant, plein d'entrain; (personality) plein de vitalité
N Fam (champagne) champagne m; (sparkling wine) vin m mousseux

bubonic [bjuː'bɒnɪk] ADJ
▸▸ b. plague peste f bubonique

buccal ['bʌk(ə)l] ADJ Anat buccal, -aux

buccaneer [bʌkə'nɪər] N boucanier m
VI faire le boucanier

Bucharest [bʊkə'rest] N Bucarest

buck¹ [bʌk] N 1 (male deer) daim m, chevreuil m (mâle)
2 (male reindeer, chamois etc) mâle m; to have b. teeth avoir des dents de lapin
3 esp Am Pej (young Black) (jeune) Noir m; (American Indian) (jeune) Indien m (d'Amérique)
4 Am Fam (dollar) dollar m; to make a fast or quick b. faire du fric
5 (sawhorse) chèvre f (de sciage); Gym cheval-d'arçons m, pl chevaux-d'arçons ou cheval-d'arçons
6 (jump) (of horse) saut m de mouton
VI 1 (of horse) faire le saut de mouton; (of aircraft) se cabrer 2 Am (of person) résister, regimber; to b. against or at sth résister à qch
VT 1 (of horse) to b. sb (off) désarçonner qn 2 Fig he bucked the odds by being chosen yet again contre toute attente, il a encore été choisi; you can't b. the odds tu ne peux pas forcer le destin; you can't b. the system on ne peut rien faire contre l'ordre établi; to b. a trend aller à l'encontre d'une tendance; to b. the question ne pas répondre à la question
▸▸ b.'s fizz = cocktail m fait à partir de champagne et de jus d'orange; b. rabbit lapin m (mâle)
▸ **buck for** VT INSEP Am Fam (strive to achieve) chercher à obtenir
▸ **buck up** Old-fashioned Fam VT SEP (of person) remonter le moral à; this whisky will b. you up ce whisky vous remontera; getting that job has really bucked her up ça lui a remonté le moral d'obtenir cet emploi; to b. one's ideas up se ressaisir, se prendre en mains
VI (become more cheerful) reprendre courage; (hurry) se grouiller, se remuer; b. up! (be cheerful) courage!; (hurry) remue-toi!, grouille-toi!

buck² N Fig to pass the b. (shift blame) rejeter la responsabilité sur quelqu'un d'autre; (make sb else decide) laisser la décision à quelqu'un d'autre; Fam the b. stops here (with me) en fin de compte, c'est moi qui en suis responsable ou c'est moi le responsable; (with you) en fin de compte, c'est toi qui en es responsable ou c'est toi le responsable

buckaroo ['bʌkəruː] N Am cow-boy m, pl cow-boys

bucked [bʌkt] ADJ Old-fashioned Fam enchanté; I was really b. to hear the news ça m'a fait vraiment plaisir d'apprendre la nouvelle

bucket ['bʌkɪt] N 1 seau m; a b. of water un seau d'eau; Br Fam it's coming down in or raining buckets il pleut à verse ou à seaux; Fam to cry or weep buckets pleurer à chaudes larmes; Sl to kick the b. (die) casser sa pipe 2 Min, Ind baluchon m, baquet m; (of crane) benne f; (of water wheel) auget m, auge f; (of dredger) godet m, louchet m
VI Br Fam 1 (move jerkily) cahoter; the car bucketed down the street la voiture avançait en cahotant dans la rue 2 (rain heavily) pleuvoir à verse ou à seaux
▸▸ b. chain = chaîne f de personnes qui se passent des seaux d'eau pour éteindre un incendie; Tech b. dredger drague f à godets; Tech b. elevator élévateur m à godets, noria f, Aut, Aviat b. seat baquet m, siège-baquet m, pl sièges-baquets, siège m cuve; b. shop Fin bureau m ou maison f de contrepartie, bureau de courtier marron; Br Com (travel agency) = organisme m de vente de billets d'avion à prix réduit; Tech b. wheel roue f à augets
▸ **bucket along** VI Br Fam (of car etc) aller à une vitesse folle
▸ **bucket down** VI Br Fam pleuvoir à verse ou à seaux

bucketful ['bʌkɪtfʊl] N (pl bucketsful or bucketfuls) plein seau m

bucking ['bʌkɪŋ] N (of horse) sauts mpl de mouton

buckle ['bʌk(ə)l] N 1 (fastener) (for strap, belt etc) boucle f 2 (deformation) (of wheel etc) gauchissement m, voile m
VT 1 (fasten) (suitcase, belt etc) boucler; (safety belt) attacher; to b. sth to sth attacher qch à qch (à l'aide d'une boucle) 2 (deform) (metal) gauchir; (wheel) voiler; (accumulator plate) tordre
VI (of wheel) se voiler; (of metal) gauchir; Fig (under attack) céder; (under criticism) se décomposer; the bridge buckled under the weight of traffic le pont s'est déformé sous le poids des véhicules; his knees buckled ses jambes cédèrent sous lui; Fig I'm buckling at the knees (exhausted) je suis sur les rotules
▸ **buckle down** VI (set to work) s'y mettre; to b. down to a task se mettre ou s'atteler à un travail; isn't it time you buckled down to your homework? il serait peut-être temps de faire tes devoirs, non?; he buckled down and finished cleaning the car il s'est armé de courage et a fini de nettoyer la voiture
▸ **buckle on** VT SEP (belt, sword) attacher; (armour) revêtir, mettre
▸ **buckle to** VI = buckle down
▸ **buckle up** VI 1 Aut attacher sa ceinture de sécurité 2 = buckle VI
VT SEP = buckle VT 1

buckled ['bʌk(ə)ld] ADJ 1 (fastened) (belt) bouclé 2 (deformed) (metal) déformé, gauchi; (wheel) voilé; (accumulator plate) tordu

buckling ['bʌk(ə)lɪŋ] N (of metal etc) déformation f, gauchissement m; (of wheel, sheet iron) voilure f

buckram ['bʌkrəm] N Tex bougran m

Bucks [bʌks] abbr Buckinghamshire

bucksaw ['bʌksɔː] N (tool) scie f à bûches

buckshee [bʌk'ʃiː] ADJ, ADV Br Fam gratis inv; we got in b. on est entré gratis ou sans payer

buckshot ['bʌkʃɒt] N (ammunition) chevrotine f

buckskin ['bʌkskɪn] N peau f de daim; b. breeches, buckskins culotte f de peau (de daim)

bucktoothed ['bʌktuːθt] ADJ (person) aux dents de lapin; he gave a b. grin il a souri en montrant ses dents de lapin

buckwheat ['bʌkwiːt] N Agr sarrasin m

bucolic [bjuː'kɒlɪk] ADJ (life, poetry, poet) bucolique
NPL Liter **bucolics** (poems) bucoliques fpl

bud¹ [bʌd] N (on shrub, tree) bourgeon m; (of flower) bouton m; to be in b. (of tree) bourgeonner
VI (-dd-) (of shrub, tree) bourgeonner; (of flower) être en bouton(s)

bud² INT Am Fam hey, b.! (to stranger) hep,

vous là-bas!; (to friend) salut, mon pote ou mon vieux!

Budapest [bjuːdə'pest] N Budapest

Buddha ['bʊdə] N Bouddha m

Buddhism ['bʊdɪz(ə)m] N bouddhisme m

Buddhist ['bʊdɪst] N bouddhiste mf
ADJ (priest, doctrine) bouddhiste; (art, temple) bouddhique

budding ['bʌdɪŋ] ADJ (shrub, tree) bourgeonnant; (flower) en bouton; Fig (artist, lawyer, genius etc) en herbe; (passion, talent) naissant
N (of plant, tree) bourgeonnement m

buddleia ['bʌdlɪə] N buddleia m

buddy ['bʌdɪ] N Fam copain m, copine f, pote m; hey b., what are you doing in my car? eh mec, qu'est-ce que tu fais dans ma bagnole?
▸▸ Am b. movie film m qui raconte les histoires de deux copains
▸ **buddy up** VI Am Fam former des groupes de deux; do you want to buddy up (with me)? tu veux te mettre avec moi?; Pej to b. up to sb faire de la lèche à qn

buddy-buddy ADJ esp Am (close, friendly) copain, f copine (with avec); those two are very b. ils sont très copain-copain

budge [bʌdʒ] VI 1 (move) bouger; if you (so much as) b. si vous faites le moindre mouvement; the door won't b. la porte est bloquée 2 (give way) céder, reculer; to refuse to b. refuser de céder
VT 1 (change mind of) I couldn't b. him il est resté inébranlable 2 (move) bouger; Fig I won't b. an inch je ne reculerai pas d'un centimètre
▸ **budge up, budge along** VI se pousser

budgerigar ['bʌdʒərɪgɑːr] N perruche f

budget ['bʌdʒɪt] N Fin etc budget m; (allocated ceiling) enveloppe f budgétaire; we are within b. (at the moment) nous n'avons pas dépassé le budget; the museum was finished within b. le musée a été fini sans dépasser le budget; it was finished well below or within b. c'est revenu bien moins cher que prévu; the project is already well over b. on a déjà largement dépassé le budget qui était alloué pour le projet; Fam I'm on a b. this month je fais des économies ce mois-ci; family/household b. budget familial/du ménage; Can to bring down the b. présenter le budget; Parl to pass the b. voter le budget
ADJ 1 (inexpensive) économique, bon marché; b. brand/fare marque f/tarif m économique; b. holiday des vacances fpl économiques ou pas chères; b. meals repas mpl bon marché; b. prices prix mpl raisonnables ou avantageux 2 Fin (relating to budgets) budgétaire
VI prévoir ses dépenses
VT (time, money) gérer
▸▸ b. account (with store) compte-crédit m, pl comptes-crédits; (with bank) ≃ compte m permanent; b. constraint contrainte f budgétaire; b. cuts coupes fpl budgétaires; Br B. Day = jour m de la présentation du budget par le Chancelier de l'Échiquier; b. deficit déficit m budgétaire; b. estimates prévisions fpl budgétaires; b. forecast prévisions budgétaires; b. planning planification f budgétaire; b. rate tarif économique; Br, Can b. speech = discours m à l'occasion de la présentation du budget au Parlement; b. surplus excédent m budgétaire
▸ **budget for** VT INSEP (allow for in accounts) porter ou inscrire au budget; (expense) prévoir, Spec budgétiser; we didn't b. for all these car repair bills nous n'avions pas prévu toutes ces dépenses pour la réparation de la voiture; I'm budgeting for my holidays

je surveille mes dépenses pour pouvoir partir en vacances

budgetary ['bʌdʒɪtərɪ] ADJ *Fin etc* budgétaire

budgeting ['bʌdʒɪtɪŋ] N *Fin etc* budgétisation *f*

budgie ['bʌdʒɪ] N *Fam (bird)* perruche *f*

Buenos Aires ['bwenɒs'aɪrɪz] N Buenos Aires

buff [bʌf] N **1** *(shine)* **to give sth a b.** faire briller qch **2** *(colour)* couleur *f* chamois **3** *Fam* **in the b.** tout nu **4** *(fan)* enthousiaste *mf*; **he's a film b.** c'est un cinéphile; **she's a history b.** elle est passionnée d'histoire; **computer b.** mordu, -ue *ou* passionné, -ée d'informatique
▮ADJ *(coloured)* de couleur chamois; *(envelope)* (en) kraft
▮VT *(car, shoes)* lustrer; *Metal (metal etc)* polir; **to b. one's nails** se polir les ongles
  ▸ ▸ **b. stick** polissoir *m*
▸ **buff up** VT SEP *(car, shoes)* lustrer, faire briller

buffalo, *pl* **buffaloes** *or inv* ['bʌfələʊ, -əʊz] N **1** buffle *m*; **water b.** karbau *m*; **young b.** bufflon *m* **2** *Am (bison)* bison *m*

buffer¹ ['bʌfər] N *Rail (at end of train)* tampon *m*; *(at end of line)* butoir *m*, heurtoir *m*; *Elec, Electron (circuit m)* *Comput* tampon *m*, mémoire *f* intermédiaire; *Fig* **to run into the buffers** tomber à l'eau; *Fam* **to act as a b.** *(between people)* faire tampon; *Mil* **recoil b.** frein *m*, amortisseur *m* de recul
  ▸ ▸ *Comput* **b. memory** mémoire tampon; *Radio* **b. stage** étage *m* tampon *ou* intermédiaire; *Pol* **b. state** état *m* tampon; *Com* **b. stock** stock *m* tampon; *Pol* **b. zone** région *f* tampon

buffer² N *Br Fam* **old b.** vieux *m*; *(fool)* vieille ganache *f*, vieux bonze *m*

buffer³ N *(for polishing)* polissoir *m*

buffering ['bʌfərɪŋ] N *Comput (storage)* stockage *m* en mémoire tampon; *(use)* utilisation *f* de mémoire tampon

buffet¹ ['bʌfɪt] N *(with fist)* coup *m*; *(slap)* gifle *f*
▮VT *(person)* bourrer de coups de poing; **buffeted by the waves/the wind** *(ship)* battu *ou* ballotté par les vagues/secoué par le vent; *Fig* **to be buffeted by events** être ballotté par les événements

buffet² N **1** ['bʌfɪt] *(piece of furniture)* buffet *m* **2** ['bʊfeɪ] *(meal, counter)* buffet *m*; **cold b.** *(on menu)* viandes *fpl* froides, assiette *f* anglaise; *(meal)* buffet froid; **b. lunch/supper** buffet
  ▸ ▸ *Rail* **b. car** wagon-restaurant *m*, *pl* wagons-restaurants; *Rail* **b. service** service *m* de restauration

buffeting ['bʌfɪtɪŋ] N succession *f* de coups *ou* de chocs; *(by waves)* ballottement *m*; *(by wind)* secousses *fpl*; **the ship took a b. in the storm** le navire a été violemment ballotté par la tempête; *Fig* **she's taken quite a b. in the past couple of months** elle a beaucoup enduré au cours de ces derniers mois

buffing ['bʌfɪŋ] N *Metal etc* polissage *m*
  ▸ ▸ **b. wheel** meule *f* à polir

buffoon [bə'fuːn] N bouffon *m*; **to act** *or* **play the b.** faire le pitre

buffoonery [bə'fuːnərɪ] N bouffonneries *fpl*

bug [bʌg] N **1** *(insect)* **(bed) b.** punaise *f* (des lits)
2 *esp Am (any insect)* insecte *m*
3 *Med Fam* virus *m*, microbe *m*; **to catch a b.** attraper un microbe; **there's a b. going round** il y a un virus qui traîne; **she's got a stomach b. of some kind** elle a des ennuis gastriques; *Fig* **to have** *or* **have been bitten by the skiing b.** avoir la passion *ou* la folie du

ski; *Fig* **the travel b.** la passion des voyages
4 *Comput* bogue *f*
5 *(concealed listening device)* micro *m* caché; **to plant a b.** cacher un micro
▮VT **1** *(room)* cacher des micros dans; *(telephone)* *(with hidden microphone)* cacher un micro dans; *(tap)* brancher sur table d'écoute; *(conversation)* enregistrer *(de façon clandestine)* **2** *Fam (annoy) (of thing, person)* taper sur les nerfs à, embêter, *Vulg* emmerder; **stop bugging me about it** arrête de m'embêter *ou Vulg* m'emmerder avec ça; **it really bugs me to think of her having all that money** ça m'énerve vraiment de savoir qu'elle a tout cet argent; **he's been bugging me to buy it** il n'arrête pas de m'embêter pour que je l'achète
▸ **bug off, bug out** VI *Am Fam (leave hurriedly)* ficher le camp

bugaboo ['bʌgəbuː] N *esp Am Fig* = **bugbear**

bugbear ['bʌgbeər] N *Fam (goblin)* croquemitaine *m*; *Fig (cause of fear)* épouvantail *m*; **maths is my b.** les maths, c'est mon cauchemar; **inflation is the government's chief b.** l'inflation est le grand cauchemar du gouvernement

bug-eyed ADJ *Fam* aux yeux exorbités; **to go b. at sth** ouvrir de grands yeux ébahis devant qch

bug-free ADJ **1** *Comput (program)* exempt d'erreurs *ou* de bogues **2** *(room) (without listening devices)* sans micros clandestins; *(having no insects)* d'où les insectes ont été chassés

bugger ['bʌgər] N **1** *Sl (unpleasant person)* salaud *m*; *(foolish person)* couillon *m*; **silly b.!** espèce d'idiot!; **poor b.** pauvre type; **a b. of a job** un travail pénible; **this recipe's a real b. to make** cette recette est vachement compliquée; **her house is a b. to find** sa maison est vachement dure à trouver; **b. all money/thanks** pas un sou/un merci; **she knows b. all about it** elle n'y connaît foutrement rien; **he doesn't care** *or* **give a b.** il s'en fout complètement **2** *Law (pederast)* pédéraste *m*
▮VT **1** *Sl* **b. (it)!** merde!; **I'll be buggered if I'm going to pay for it!** pas question que je paye!; **that's really buggered it!** *(spoilt things)* ça a tout gâché; *(broken it)* ça l'a complètement bousillé **2** *Law* sodomiser
▸ **bugger about, bugger around** *Sl* VI déconner; **to b. about** *or* **around with one's car** s'amuser avec sa voiture; **stop buggering about with my computer** arrête de tripoter mon ordinateur
▮VT SEP *(person)* emmerder, faire chier
▸ **bugger off** VI *Sl* se casser, foutre le camp; **b. off!** *(go away)* fous le camp!; *(leave me alone)* fous-moi la paix!
▸ **bugger up** VT SEP *Sl (spoil) (plan, holiday etc)* foutre en l'air; *(machine, TV etc)* bousiller; **having to work overtime buggered up my weekend** ça m'a foutu mon week-end en l'air de devoir faire des heures supplémentaires; **you've buggered the whole thing up** tu as tout foutu en l'air

buggeration [bʌgə'reɪʃən] INT *Br Sl* bordel!, putain!

buggered ['bʌgəd] ADJ PRED *Sl* **to be b.** *(exhausted)* être crevé; *(broken, in trouble)* être foutu; **if we don't get the money soon, we're b.** si on a pas l'argent rapidement, on est foutus

buggery ['bʌgərɪ] N **1** *Law* sodomie *f* **2** *Sl* **to run like b.** courir ventre à terre; **my plans have been shot to b.** ça a foutu mes projets en l'air

bugging ['bʌgɪŋ] N *(of room)* installation *f* de micros *(pour espionner)*; *(of telephone)* mise *f* sur table d'écoute

▸ ▸ **b. device** appareil *m* d'écoute *(clandestin)*

buggy¹ ['bʌgɪ] N **1** *(carriage)* boghei *m*, buggy *m*; **(beach) b.** buggy; **(moon) b.** jeep *f* lunaire **2** *Am (for baby)* landau *m*; *Br (pushchair)* poussette *f*

buggy² ADJ *Comput* plein de bogues

bughouse ['bʌghaʊs] *Am Sl* N *(for the insane)* maison *f* de fous
▮ADJ *(insane)* fou, *f* folle

bugle¹ ['bjuːg(ə)l] N *Mil* clairon *m*
  ▸ ▸ **b. call** sonnerie *f* de clairon

bugle² N *(plant)* bugle *f*

bugler ['bjuːglər] N *(sonneur m* de) clairon *m*

bugless ['bʌglɪs] ADJ *Comput* sans bogues

bug-ridden ADJ *Comput* plein de bogues

build [bɪld] VT *(pt, pp* built [bɪlt]) *(house etc)* construire, bâtir; *(ship, bridge, road etc)* construire; *(temple)* édifier; *(nest)* faire; **the walls were built of granite** les murs étaient *(construits ou* bâtis) en granit; **the house is being built** la maison est en construction; **to b. one's hopes on sth** fonder *ou* baser ses espoirs sur qch; *Mktg* **to b. a brand** créer une marque
▮VI **1** *Constr* construire, bâtir; **to b. on a piece of land** bâtir un terrain; *Fig* **to b. on sand** bâtir sur le sable; **to b. on one's success** mettre à profit sa réussite; **to b. on an opportunity** profiter d'une occasion **2** *(increase) (of pressure)*, *Fig (of excitement, tension)* augmenter
▮N *(of person)* carrure *f*; **a man of powerful b.** un homme à forte carrure; **of slight b.** fluet
▸ **build in** VT SEP *(incorporate)* intégrer, incorporer; *Constr (wardrobe, beam etc)* encastrer; **to b. in safety features** intégrer des dispositifs de sécurité
▸ **build into** VT SEP **to b. sth into a product** incorporer qch dans un produit
▸ **build on** VT SEP *(add to existing structure) (porch etc)* ajouter; **we've built on a garage** nous avons ajouté un garage; **the stables are built on to the house** les écuries sont attenantes à la maison
▸ **build up** VT SEP **1** *(increase) (demand)* développer; *Mil etc (reserves)* constituer; *(forces, reinforcements etc)* mettre sur pied; *(one's strength)* reprendre; **don't b. your hopes up** ne te fais pas trop d'illusions
2 *(create) (theory, system)* bâtir, échafauder, construire; *(business)* développer; *(reputation)* se faire; *(collection, library)* constituer; **to b. up custom** *or* **a clientele** *(of company)* se faire *ou* se constituer une clientèle; **his father built the company up from nothing** son père a créé la société à partir de rien; *Med etc* **to b. up an immunity** développer une immunité
3 *(strengthen)* **the children need vitamins to b. them up** les enfants ont besoin de vitamines pour se fortifier
4 *(usu passive)* **this area has been very much built up** on a beaucoup construit par ici
5 *(publicize) (film, book, actor etc)* dire du bien de; **the film wasn't as good as it had been built up to be** le film n'était pas aussi bon qu'on le prétendait
6 *(wall) (make higher)* rehausser; *(rebuild)* réparer
▮VI *(of pressure)* s'accumuler, augmenter; *(of tension)* augmenter, monter; *(of traffic)* devenir dense; *(of snow, clouds)* s'amonceler; *(of hurricane, storm)* se préparer

builder ['bɪldər] N *Constr* entrepreneur, -euse *en* bâtiment; *(of ships etc)* constructeur, -trice; *Fig (of empire etc)* créateur, -trice, fondateur, -trice

building ['bɪldɪŋ] N **1** *(house, factory etc)* bâtiment *m*, immeuble *m*; *(large)* édifice *m*; **public b.** édifice public **2** *(action)* construc-

tion *f*, *Fig* **the b. of better relations** l'établissement *m* de meilleures relations
▸▸ **b. block** *(toy)* cube *m*; *Fig* composante *f*; *Constr* **b. contractor** entrepreneur, -euse (en bâtiment *ou* construction); **b. materials** matériaux *mpl* de construction; **b. plot** terrain *m* à bâtir; **b. site** chantier *m* (de construction); **b. slip** *(for ship)* cale *f* de construction; *Br Fin* **b. society** ≃ société *f* de crédit immobilier; **the b. trade** le bâtiment; **b. worker** ouvrier, -ière du bâtiment

Building Societies
Les "building societies" fonctionnent comme des banques mais elles n'ont pas de système de compensation. Établissements consentant des prêts immobiliers aux particuliers, elles jouent un rôle important dans la vie en Grande-Bretagne. Au cours des dernières années, de nombreuses "building societies" ont abandonné leur statut de sociétés mutuelles pour devenir des banques cotées en Bourse.

build-up N **1** *(of pressure)* accumulation *f*, augmentation *f*; *(of tension)* augmentation *f*; **the b. of traffic on the motorway** la formation de bouchons sur l'autoroute; **traffic b.** bouchon *m*
2 *(of system etc)* élaboration *f*, développement *m*
3 *Mil (of forces, reinforcements etc)* mise *f* sur pied; *(of reserves of troops, supplies etc)* constitution *f*; **there has been a b. of troops along the border** on a envoyé du renfort aux troupes le long de la frontière
4 *(publicity)* battage *m* (publicitaire); **her latest book is getting a lot of b.** on fait beaucoup de battage autour de son dernier livre; **despite the big b., the film didn't do well** en dépit du battage dont il a fait l'objet, le film n'a pas bien marché
5 *(preparatory period)* **the b. to the match** la période d'avant le match; **in the b. to the election, there will be …** pendant la période qui précédera les élections, il y aura …

built [bɪlt] ADJ bâti; **British b.** de construction britannique; **a powerfully b. man** un homme à forte carrure *ou* charpente
▸▸ **b. attraction** *(in tourism)* centre *m* d'intérêt 'non-naturel'

built-in ADJ *(wardrobe, bath, beam)* encastré; *(device, safeguard)* intégré; *Comput* incorporé; *Fig (feature)* inné, ancré; *Comput* incorporé; *Fig* **a b. resistance to …** une opposition viscérale à …
▸▸ **b. obsolescence** obsolescence *f* programmée

built-to-order ADJ *Comput* construit sur mesure

built-up ADJ *(beam)* composé, rapporté; *(shoulders of garment)* rehaussé
▸▸ **b. area** agglomération *f* (urbaine); **b. shoes** chaussures *fpl* à semelles compensées

bulb [bʌlb] N **1** *(tulip etc)* bulbe *m*, oignon *m* **2** *Elec* ampoule *f* **3** *Phys (of thermometer)* réservoir *m*; *Chem (flask)* ballon *m*; *Culin (of baster)* poire *f* **4** *Anat* bulbe *m*

bulbous ['bʌlbəs] ADJ bulbeux; **b. nose** gros nez *m*

Bulgaria [bʌl'geərɪə] N Bulgarie *f*

Bulgarian [bʌl'geərɪən] ADJ bulgare
N **1** Bulgare *mf* **2** *Ling* bulgare *m*

bulge [bʌldʒ] N *(in wall, ceiling)* bombement *m*, renflement *m*; *(on face, body, caused by a growth etc)* protubérance *f*, *(in tyre)* hernie *f*, *Mil (of front)* saillant *m*; *Econ Fam (increase)* poussée *f*; **this dress shows all my bulges** cette robe révèle toutes mes rondeurs; **the gun made a b. in his pocket** le revolver faisait une protubérance dans sa poche

VI **to b. (out)** bomber, ballonner; *(stick out)* faire saillie; *(of wall, ceiling etc)* faire ventre; **his eyes were bulging** il avait les yeux exorbités; **a sack bulging with potatoes** un sac bourré de pommes de terre; **I knew from the way his pocket bulged** j'ai su à la protubérance que formait sa poche

bulging ['bʌldʒɪŋ] ADJ *(forehead, wall, ceiling)* bombé; *(stomach)* ballonné; *(eyes)* protubérant; *(cheeks)* bouffi; *(bag, wallet etc)* bourré, plein à craquer
N *(of wall etc)* bombement *m*, renflement *m*; *(of stomach)* ballonnement *m*

bulimia [bju:'lɪmɪə, bʊ'l-] N *Med* boulimie *f*

bulk [bʌlk] N **1** *(size)* masse *f*, volume *m*; *(of parcel)* encombrement *m* **2 the b.** *(greater part) (of people)* la masse, la plupart; *(of army)* le gros; *(of one's property, work, money etc)* la plus grosse partie **3** *Comput (of information)* volume *m*, masse *f* **4** *Com etc* **to buy in b.** acheter en gros *ou* par grosses quantités; **to sell in b.** vendre en gros
VI *Fig* **to b. large** occuper une place importante *(in sb's eyes* aux yeux de qn)
VT *Com (packages)* grouper; **to b. sth out** étoffer qch
▸▸ *Com* **b. buying** achat *m* par grosses quantités, achat en gros; **b. cargo** cargaison *f* en vrac; *Naut* **b. carrier** vraquier *m*, transporteur *m* de vrac; *Com* **b. discount** remise *f* quantitative; *Com* **b. order** grosse commande *f*, *Com* **b. rate** affranchissement *m* à forfait

bulkhead ['bʌlkhed] N *(on ship etc)* cloison *f*

bulkiness ['bʌlkɪnɪs] N **1** volume *m* excessif; *(of parcel)* encombrement *m* **2** *(of sweater)* épaisseur *f*

bulky ['bʌlkɪ] ADJ **1** *(parcel etc)* volumineux, encombrant; *(book)* épais **2** *(sweater)* gros, épais

bull¹ [bʊl] N **1** taureau *m*; *Astron* **the B.** le Taureau; *Fig* **to take the b. by the horns** prendre le taureau par les cornes; **like a b. in a china shop** comme un éléphant dans un magasin de porcelaine; **to go at sth like a b. at a gate** foncer tête baissée *ou* la tête la première dans qch
2 *(male) (elephant, whale etc)* mâle *m*
3 *Br Mil Sl (polishing)* fourbissage *m*
4 *Sl (nonsense)* conneries *fpl*; **he talks a lot of b.** il raconte beaucoup de conneries
5 *St Exch* spéculateur, -trice à la hausse, haussier, -ière
6 *(of target)* mouche *f*, mille *m*; **he got six bulls** il a fait mouche six fois, il a mis six fois dans le mille
7 *(dog)* bouledogue *m*; **b. bitch/pup** chienne *f*/chiot *m* de bouledogue
INT *Sl* foutaise!, quelle(s) connerie(s)!
VT *St Exch* **to b. the market** chercher à faire monter les cours
VI *St Exch (of person)* spéculer à la hausse; *(of stocks)* être en hausse
▸▸ *Aut* **b. bars** pare-buffles *m inv*; **b. calf** jeune taureau *m*, taurillon *m*; *St Exch* **b. market** marché *m* à la hausse *ou* haussier; **b. mastiff** = chien *m* issu d'un métissage entre le bouledogue et le mastiff; *St Exch* **b. spread** spread *m* haussier; **b. terrier** bull-terrier *m*, *pl* bull-terriers; *St Exch* **b. trading** spéculation *f* à la hausse; *St Exch* **b. transaction** opération *f* à la hausse

bull² N *Rel* bulle *f*; **papal b.** bulle papale

bulldog ['bʊldɒg] N bouledogue *m*; *Fig (tenacious person)* personne *f* très tenace; *Br Univ (official)* appariteur *m* du censeur *(aux universités d'Oxford et de Cambridge)*
▸▸ *Br St Exch* **b. bond** obligation *f* bulldog *(obligation d'un emprunteur étranger à la Bourse de Londres, libellée en sterling)*; **b. clip** pince *f* à dessin

bulldoze ['bʊldəʊz] VT *(land)* dégager *ou*

déblayer au bulldozer; *(house etc)* démolir au bulldozer; *Fig* **to b. sb into doing sth** forcer qn à faire qch; **I was bulldozed into it** on m'a forcé à le faire; **to b. sth through a committee** forcer une commission à adopter qch

bulldozer ['bʊldəʊzər] N *Constr* bulldozer *m*

bulldyke ['bʊldaɪk] N *Sl* lesbienne *f* à l'allure masculine

bullet ['bʊlɪt] N **1** *(from rifle, revolver)* balle *f*, *Fam* **to stop a b.** recevoir une balle **2** *Typ* puce *f*
▸▸ *Am Fin* **b. bond** obligation *f* remboursable en une seule fois; **b. hole** impact *m* de balle; *Typ* **b. point** puce *f*; *Rail* **b. train** train *m* à grande vitesse *(au Japon)*; **b. wound** blessure *f* par balle

bulleted list ['bʊlɪtɪd] N *Typ* liste *f* à puces

bullet-headed ADJ **1** à tête ronde **2** *Am Fig (obstinate)* entêté, têtu

bulletin ['bʊlɪtɪn] N bulletin *m*, communiqué *m*
▸▸ **b. board** *Am* tableau *m* d'affichage; *Comput* serveur *m* télématique, *Can* babillard *m*; *Comput* **b. board service** serveur télématique, *Can* babillard

bulletproof ['bʊlɪtpru:f] ADJ *(glass, car)* à l'épreuve des balles
▸▸ **b. vest** gilet *m* pare-balles

bullfight ['bʊlfaɪt] N course *f* de taureaux, corrida *f*

bullfighter ['bʊlfaɪtər] N torero *m*

bullfighting ['bʊlfaɪtɪŋ] N courses *fpl* de taureaux; *(as art)* tauromachie *f*

bullfinch ['bʊlfɪntʃ] N *(bird)* bouvreuil *m*

bullfrog ['bʊlfrɒg] N grenouille *f* taureau

bull-headed ADJ *Fam* **1** *(impetuous)* d'une impétuosité de taureau; **to go at sth b.** foncer la tête la première dans qch **2** *(obstinate)* entêté, têtu

bullhorn ['bʊlhɔ:n] N *Am* porte-voix *m inv*

bullion ['bʊljən] N INV *(gold)* or *m* en barres *ou* en lingot(s); *(silver)* argent *m* en lingot(s); *Fin* métal *m*
▸▸ **b. van** fourgon *m* bancaire

bullish ['bʊlɪʃ] ADJ **1** *St Exch (market, trend)* à la hausse, haussier; **to be b.** spéculer à la hausse **2** *Fig (optimistic)* optimiste *(about sth* au sujet de qch, à propos de qch)

bull-necked [-nekt] ADJ au cou de taureau

bullock ['bʊlək] N bœuf *m*; **young b.** bouvillon *m*
▸▸ **b. cart** char *m* à bœufs

bullpen ['bʊlpen] N *Am (in police station)* = grande cellule *f* commune

bullring ['bʊlrɪŋ] N arène *f*

bull's-eye N **1** *(of target)* mouche *f*, mille *m*; **to hit the** *or* **get a b.** *(in archery)* faire mouche, mettre dans le mille; *(at darts)* mettre dans le mille; *Fig* **to hit the b.** *(of remark)* faire mouche **2** *(in glass)* boudine *f* **3** *(sweet)* gros bonbon *m* à la menthe
▸▸ **b. panes** carreaux *mpl* à boudines *ou* en culs-de-bouteille

bullshitter ['bʊlʃɪtər] N *Vulg (smooth-talker)* baratineur, -euse; **he's a b.** *(talks nonsense)* il dit des conneries

bully[1] ['bʊlɪ] N tyran *m*; *Sch* petit tyran *(qui fait subir des brimades à ses camarades)*; **don't be such a b.** ne sois pas si tyrannique ▪ VT *(wife, employee)* brimer; *(classmates, little sister etc)* brimer, persécuter; **to b. sb into doing sth** faire faire qch à qn à force de menaces *ou* d'intimidations; **to b. sb into submission** faire céder qn à force de menaces
▸▸ *Old-fashioned Br Fam* **b. beef** singe *m (corned-beef)*

bully[2] INT *Old-fashioned Fam* **b. for you!** *(what luck)* vous avez de la chance!; *(well done)* bravo!

▸ **bully off** VI *(in hockey)* engager (le jeu)

bullyboy ['bʊlɪbɔɪ] N voyou *m*, dur *m*; **b. tactics** manœuvres *fpl* d'intimidation

bullying ['bʊlɪɪŋ] ADJ brutal, -aux ▪ N brimades *fpl*

bully-off N *(in hockey)* engagement *m* (du jeu)

bulrush ['bʊlrʌʃ] N *(plant)* jonc *m* des marais

bulwark ['bʊlwɜːk] N **1** *(fortification)*, *Fig* rempart *m* **2** *Naut* **bulwarks** bastingage *m*

bum[1] [bʌm] N *Br Fam (bottom)* derrière *m*
▸▸ *Br* **b. bag** banane *f*; **b. fluff** *(beard)* barbe *f* très peu fournie

bum[2] *esp Am Sl* ADJ moche, minable; **b. advice** des conseils *mpl* inutiles; **b. check** chèque *m* en bois
▪ N **1** *(worthless person)* fainéant, -ante; *(tramp)* clochard, -arde, trimardeur *m*; **to give sb the b.'s rush** *(from relationship, meeting)* virer qn avec perte et fracas; **to give a suggestion/an idea the b.'s rush** ne tenir aucun compte d'une suggestion/idée **2 to be on the b.** *(live off other people)* vivre aux crochets des autres; *(travel round country)* vagabonder
▪ VI (**-mm-**) *Am Sl (beg)* vivre aux crochets des autres, vivre en parasite
▪ VT *Sl* **to b. a cigarette from** *or* **off sb** taper une cigarette à qn; **to b. a ride** *(from stranger)* faire de l'auto-stop; **I managed to b. a ride from a lorry driver** je me suis fait prendre en auto-stop par un routier; **do you mind if I b. a ride to the station?** ça t'ennuierait de me déposer à la gare?
▸▸ **b. rap** *(false charge)* accusation *f* inventée de toutes pièces; *(unfair punishment)* punition *f* injuste; **b. steer** tuyau *m* percé

▸ **bum around** *Sl* VI glander, glandouiller; *(travel)* vadrouiller; **they spent three months bumming around in Mexico** ils ont passé trois mois à se balader au Mexique
▪ VT INSEP **to b. around Europe/Paris** vadrouiller en Europe/à Paris
▸ **bum around with** VT INSEP *Sl* traîner avec

bumble ['bʌmb(ə)l] VI *(be inefficient)* s'agiter et ne rien faire d'efficace

bumblebee ['bʌmb(ə)lbiː] N bourdon *m*

bumbler ['bʌmb(ə)lər] N *Fam* **an old b.** un vieux maladroit

bumbling ['bʌmb(ə)lɪŋ] ADJ **b. fool** *or* **idiot** andouille *f*

bumboat ['bʌmbəʊt] N *Naut* canot *m* d'approvisionnement

bumf [bʌmf] N **1** *Fam (useless paper)* paperasse *f* **2** *Sl (lavatory paper)* papier *m* cul

bumfreezer ['bʌmfriːzər] N *Br Sl* = veste *f* qui arrive au ras des fesses

bumhole ['bʌmhəʊl] N *Sl* trou *m* de balle

bummed [bʌmd] ADJ *Am Sl* **to be b.** l'avoir mauvaise

bummer ['bʌmər] N *Sl (something worthless)* fiasco *m*; **the film's a b.** ce film est nul; **I didn't get the job – what a b.!** je n'ai pas eu

le boulot – c'est con!; **it's a real b. when you find out …** ça en fiche un coup quand on découvre que …

bump [bʌmp] N **1** *(collision)* choc *m*, heurt *m*; *(jolt)* secousse *f*, cahot *m*; *(by boat in bumping race)* heurt *m*; **the boat hit the jetty with a b.** le bateau a cogné contre la jetée; **to sit down with a b.** s'asseoir brusquement
2 *(lump)* *(in path, road surface etc)* bosse *f*; *(on head)* *(as result of being hit)* bosse; *(in phrenology)* protubérance *f*, *Fam* bosse; *Hum* **she patted her b.** *(unborn baby)* elle a tapoté son ventre; **she's had a b. on the head** elle s'est cogné la tête; *Aut* **to hit a b.** passer sur une bosse
3 *Fam* **bumps and grinds** *(of stripper)* déhanchements *mpl*
4 *Aviat (air current)* trou *m* d'air
▪ VT **1** *(hit)* cogner, frapper; *(boat in front in bumping race)* heurter; **to b. one's head on** *or* **against sth** se cogner la tête contre qch **2** *Aviat Fam* **to be bumped** *(from a flight)* perdre sa place sur un vol *(pour cause de surréservation)*
▪ VI *Fam* **to b. and grind** *(of stripper)* se déhancher
▪ ADV, INT pan!, boum!; *Fam* **things that go b. in the night** des bruits étranges dans la nuit
▸▸ *Aut* **b. steer** réversibilité *f* de direction

▸ **bump along** VI *(in cart etc)* cahoter
▸ **bump into** VT INSEP **1** *(collide with)* *(of person)* se cogner *ou* se heurter *ou* buter contre; *(of vehicle)* heurter **2** *(meet)* rencontrer par hasard
▸ **bump off** VT SEP *Fam (kill)* supprimer, *Fam* faire la peau à
▸ **bump up** VT SEP *Fam (prices)* gonfler (d'une façon exagérée)

bumper ['bʌmpər] N **1** *Aut* pare-chocs *m inv*; bouclier *m*, pare-chocs bouclier; **front/rear b.** pare-chocs avant/arrière; **the cars were b. to b.** les voitures étaient pare-chocs contre pare-chocs **2** *(large measure of alcoholic drink)* rasade *f*
▪ ADJ **b. crop** *or* **harvest** récolte *f* magnifique *ou* exceptionnelle; **it's been a b. year for tourism** ça a été une année exceptionnelle pour le tourisme
▸▸ *Aut* **b. apron** tablier *m* de pare-chocs; *Aut* **b. guard** butoir *m* de pare-chocs; *Aut* **b. skirt** jupe *f* de pare-chocs

bumpety-bump ['bʌmpɪtɪ-] ADV *Fam* en cahotant; **my heart went b.** mon cœur a battu à tout rompre

bumph [bʌmf] N = **bumf**

bumping ['bʌmpɪŋ] N **1** *(collision)* heurt(s) *m(pl)*, choc(s) *m(pl)*; *(jolting)* cahotement *m* **2** *(of air passenger)* bumping *m*, refus *m* d'embarquer suite à surréservation
▸▸ **b. race** course-poursuite *f*, *pl* courses-poursuites *(dans laquelle chaque bateau doit rattraper le précédent et de son avant le heurter l'arrière)*

bumpkin ['bʌmpkɪn] N **(country) b.** rustre *m*, rustaud *m*

bump-start *Aut* N démarrage *m* poussé; **to give sb a b.** pousser la voiture de qn pour la faire démarrer
▪ VT **to b. a car** pousser une voiture pour la faire démarrer

bumptious ['bʌmpʃəs] ADJ orgueilleux, suffisant

bumpy ['bʌmpɪ] ADJ **1** *(road etc)* cahoteux, défoncé; **we had a b. flight** nous avons été secoués dans l'avion; *Fig* **we've got a b. road ahead of us** nous avons une période difficile devant nous; *Fig* **to give sb a b. ride** faire passer un mauvais moment à qn; **the proposals were given a b. ride** les propositions ont rencontré une vive opposition **2** *(forehead etc)* couvert de bosses

bun [bʌn] N **1** *Culin* petit pain *m* au lait; *Fig*

Fam **to have a b. in the oven** avoir un polichinelle dans le tiroir **2** *(in hair)* chignon *m*; **she wears her hair in a b.** elle se fait un chignon **3** *esp Am Sl* **buns** *(buttocks)* miches *fpl*; **a nice pair of buns** un beau cul, de belles miches
▸▸ *Br Fam Hum* **b. fight** *(gathering)* réception *f*

bunch [bʌntʃ] N **1** *(of flowers)* bouquet *m*; *(of radishes, carrots etc)* botte *f*; *(of grapes)* grappe *f*; *(of herbs)* touffe *f*; *(of feathers)* houppe *f*; *(of keys)* trousseau *m*; *(of bananas)* régime *m*; **to wear one's hair in bunches** porter des couettes **2** *(of people)* groupe *m*; *Am (of livestock)* troupeau *m*; **he's the best** *or* **the pick of the b.** c'est lui le meilleur (de la bande); **they're quite an intelligent b.** c'est un groupe plutôt intelligent; **the b. (of people) I work with** les gens avec qui je travaille; **what a stupid b.!** ce qu'ils peuvent être bêtes!; **they seem like a pretty nice b. of people** ils ont l'air très sympa; *Sport* **the b.** le peloton; *Am Fam* **thanks a b.** merci beaucoup; *Fam* **a whole b. of stuff** *or* **things** plein de trucs, tout un tas de choses; *Br Sl* **a b. of fives** un coup de poing
▪ VT *(flowers etc)* mettre en bouquet; *(radishes etc)* mettre en bottes
▸ **bunch together** VI *(of people)* se serrer
▪ VT SEP *(books etc on shelf)* serrer; **to be bunched together** *(of runners, horses etc)* être serrés
▸ **bunch up** VT **1** *(dress)* retrousser **2** *(books etc on shelf)* serrer; **to be bunched up** *(of runners, horses etc)* être serrés
▪ VI *(of material)* se retrousser

bundle ['bʌnd(ə)l] N tas *m*; *(secured, fastened in some way)* *(of washing etc)* paquet *m*, ballot *m*; *(of goods)* ballot *m*; *(of asparagus etc)* botte *f*; *(of canes, wires etc)* faisceau *m*; *(of banknotes, papers)* liasse *f*; *(of wood)* fagot *m*; *Am Fam* **to make a b.** *(lots of money)* faire son beurre; *Am Fam* **thanks a b.** merci beaucoup; *Am Fam* **to go a b. on sb/sth** *(like)* être fou de qn/qch; *Fam* **she's a b. of nerves** c'est un paquet de nerfs; *Fam* **my driving test wasn't exactly a b. of fun** passer mon permis de conduire n'a pas vraiment été une partie de plaisir; *Hum* **they came with their b. of joy** *(new baby)* ils sont venus avec leur bambin
▪ VT **1** *(make bundle of)* faire un paquet de; *(documents)* mettre en liasses; *(straw)* mettre en bottes; **she bundled the baby in a blanket** elle a enveloppé le bébé dans une couverture; *Mktg, Com* **to b. sth with sth** offrir qch en plus de qch; *Mktg, Com* **to come bundled with sth** être livré avec qch **2** *(put, lead hastily)* **to b. papers into a drawer** fourrer des papiers dans un tiroir; **to b. sb into a car** embarquer qn dans une voiture; **he bundled me down the stairs** il m'a fait descendre les escaliers en toute hâte
▸ **bundle off** VT SEP *(send hastily)* envoyer à la hâte *ou* sans attendre; **the baby was bundled off to hospital** le bébé a été envoyé à l'hôpital sans attendre; **they bundled me off the train** ils m'ont fait descendre du train en toute hâte **2** *Pej (get rid of)* se débarrasser de (sans cérémonie); **his father bundled him off to boarding school** son père l'a expédié en pension
▸ **bundle out** VT SEP faire sortir sans cérémonie *ou* ménagement
▸ **bundle up** VT SEP **1** *(make parcel of)* = **bundle** VT **1 2** *(collect)* *(one's things etc)* rassembler
▪ VI *(wear warm clothes)* s'emmitoufler

bundling selling ['bʌndlɪŋ] N *Com* vente *f* par lots

bung [bʌŋ] N **1** *(for cask)* bonde *f*, bondon *m* **2** *Br Sl (money given)* bakchich *m*
▪ VT **1** *(opening)* boucher **2** *Br Fam (put)* met-

tre, fourrer; **b. it in a drawer** fourre-le dans un tiroir; **b. it over** *(throw it)* balance-le; **I bunged him a tenner** je lui ai filé un billet de dix livres; **they bunged him in prison** ils l'ont jeté en prison

▸ **bung up** VT SEP *Fam (block) (drain)* boucher; **I'm** *or* **my nose is all bunged up** j'ai le nez complètement bouché

bungalow ['bʌŋgələʊ] N pavillon *m*; *(in India)* bungalow *m*

bungee ['bʌndʒɪ] N *(cord)* tendeur *m*
▸ ▸ **b. cord** tendeur *m*; **b. jump** saut *m* à l'élastique; **b. jumping** saut à l'élastique

bunghole ['bʌŋhəʊl] N *(in cask)* bonde *f*

bungle ['bʌŋg(ə)l] N gâchis *m*, ratage *m*, *Fam* bousillage *m*; **to make a b. of sth** gâcher *ou Fam* cochonner *ou Fam* saloper qch
VT *(piece of work)* gâcher, *Fam* cochonner, *Fam* saloper; *(hold-up, operation, escape attempt)* rater
VI s'y prendre maladroitement; **someone has bungled** quelqu'un a fait une bourde

bungler ['bʌŋglər] N incapable *mf*, bon *m* à rien, bonne *f* à rien

bungling ['bʌŋglɪŋ] ADJ **b. idiot** incapable *mf*, bon *m* à rien, bonne *f* à rien
N gâchis *m*, *Fam* bousillage *m*; **your b. has cost us the contract** tes bourdes nous ont fait perdre le contrat

bunion ['bʌnjən] N *Med* oignon *m*

bunk[1] [bʌŋk] N **1** *Naut, Rail etc* couchette *f* **2** *Old-fashioned Fam (sleeping place)* logement *m*; **I can give you a b. for the night** je peux te loger pour la nuit
VI *Naut* coucher (**forward** à l'avant)
▸ ▸ **b. beds** lits *mpl* superposés

bunk[2] N *Br Fam* **to do a b.** déguerpir, décamper
▸ **bunk down** VI *Fam* **1** *(go to bed)* aller se coucher **2** *(sleep)* passer la nuit (**with friends** chez des amis)
▸ **bunk off** VI *Fam* **1** *(leave without permission) (from work)* partir avant l'heure sans en avoir l'autorisation; *(from school)* faire l'école buissonnière **2** *(leave hurriedly)* filer
VT INSEP **to b. off school** faire l'école buissonnière

bunk[3] N *Old-fashioned Fam (nonsense)* bêtises *fpl*

bunker ['bʌŋkər] N **1** *(in home) (for coal)* coffre *m* à charbon; *Naut (for coal, oil etc)* soute *f*; *(for oil)* réservoir *m*; *Com* **b. adjustment factor** ajustement *m* fret **2** *Golf* banquette *f*, bunker *m* **3** *Mil* blockhaus *m*; **nuclear b.** abri *m* antiatomique
VT **1** *Naut (fuel)* mettre en soute **2** *Golf* **to be bunkered** se trouver dans le sable
VI *Naut* se ravitailler en charbon

bunkhouse ['bʌŋkhaʊs] N *Am (for lumberjacks etc)* baraquement *m* pourvu de couchettes

bunkum ['bʌŋkəm] N *Fam* foutaise(s) *f(pl)*, âneries *fpl*

bunny ['bʌnɪ] N *Fam (rabbit)* Jeannot lapin *m*, petit lapin
▸ ▸ **b. girl** = employée *f* de boîte de nuit play-boy (habillée en lapin); **b. rabbit** Jeannot lapin, petit lapin

Bunsen ['bʌns(ə)n] N
▸ ▸ *Chem etc* **B. burner** bec *m* Bunsen

bunt [bʌnt] *Am Sp* N coup *m* retenu
VT frapper doucement
VI frapper doucement la balle

bunting[1] ['bʌntɪŋ] N *(bird)* bruant *m*

bunting[2] N *(flags)* drapeaux *mpl*, fanions *mpl*; **decorated with b.** pavoisé

buoy [bɔɪ] N *Naut* bouée *f*
VT *Naut (channel)* baliser; *(wreck)* marquer
▸ **buoy up** VT SEP *Naut (object)* faire flotter; *Fig (person, currency)* soutenir, maintenir;

Fig **buoyed up with new hope** animé *ou* soutenu par un nouvel espoir

buoyancy ['bɔɪənsɪ] N **1** *Naut, Aviat etc (of object)* flottabilité *f*, **centre of b.** centre *m* de poussée **2** *Fig* entrain *m*, allant *m*; *St Exch* dynamisme *m*; *Com (of market)* fermeté *f*; *(of prices, currency)* stabilité *f*; **she has great b. mood** elle a un ressort incroyable
▸ ▸ **b. bag** ballonnet *m* de flottabilité; **b. tank** réservoir *m* de flottabilité

buoyant ['bɔɪənt] ADJ **1** *Naut, Aviat etc* qui flotte; **saltwater is more b. than fresh** l'eau salée porte mieux que l'eau douce **2** *Fig (person)* qui a du ressort; *Com (market)* soutenu, ferme; *(prices)* stable; **to be in a b. mood** être plein d'entrain; **a b. step** un pas élastique

buoyantly ['bɔɪəntlɪ] ADV avec entrain

BUPA ['buːpə] N *(abbr* British United Provident Association) = service *m* de santé privé

bur [bɜːr] N = **burr**[1] **1**

Burberry® ['bɜːbərɪ] N **1** *(raincoat)* imperméable *m* (de la marque Burberry®), Burberry® *m* **2** *(garment)* vêtement *m* de la marque Burberry®

burble ['bɜːb(ə)l] VI *(of stream)* murmurer; *Fig (of baby)* gazouiller; *(of person)* murmurer (des sons inarticulés); *Fam Pej (talk nonsense)* débiter des inepties
▸ **burble away, burble on** VI *Fam Pej* débiter des inepties

burbot ['bɜːbət] N *(fish)* lotte *f*, barbot *m*, barbot(e) *f*

burbs [bɜː(r)bz] NPL *Am Fam* **the b.** la banlieue

burden ['bɜːd(ə)n] N **1** fardeau *m*, charge *f*, **b. of taxation** poids *m* de la fiscalité *ou* des impôts; *Law* **b. of proof** charge de la preuve; **the b. of proof rests with him** c'est à lui qu'il incombe d'apporter des preuves; **I'm a b. to you** je suis un fardeau pour toi; **to make sb's life a b.** rendre la vie dure à qn **2** *Fml (theme, gist) (of speech, complaint, argument)* substance *f*, *Old-fashioned (of song)* refrain *m* **3** *Naut (of ship)* charge *f*, contenance *f*
VT accabler (**sb with sth** qn de qch); **to b. one's memory with useless facts** se charger *ou* s'encombrer la mémoire de faits inutiles; **I'm sorry to b. you with my worries** je suis désolé de vous accabler avec mes soucis; **a donkey burdened with wood** un âne chargé d'un fardeau de bois; **she is burdened with a retarded child** elle a un enfant handicapé à sa charge

burdensome ['bɜːd(ə)nsəm] ADJ *Fml* lourd

burdock ['bɜːdɒk] N *(weed)* bardane *f*, glouteron *m*

bureau, *pl* **bureaux** ['bjʊərəʊ, -əʊz] N **1** *(furniture)* bureau *m*; *(with roll top)* secrétaire *m*; *Am (chest of drawers)* commode *f* **2** *Am (government department)* bureau *m*, service *m*
▸ ▸ **b. de change** bureau de change

bureaucracy [bjʊə'rɒkrəsɪ] N *Pej* bureaucratie *f*

bureaucrat ['bjʊərəkræt] N *Pej* bureaucrate *mf*

bureaucratic [bjʊərə'krætɪk] ADJ *Pej* bureaucratique

burette, *Am* **buret** [bjʊ'ret] N *Chem* burette *f*, éprouvette *f* graduée

burg [bɜːg] N *Am Fam (village)* bled *m*; *(town)* ville *f*; **there's nothing happening in this b.** il ne se passe rien dans ce coin *ou* bled

burgeon ['bɜːdʒən] VI *Lit* fleurir

burgeoning ['bɜːdʒənɪŋ] ADJ *Lit, Fml (industry, population etc)* en expansion; **a b. talent** un talent en herbe; **the b. movement for independence** le mouvement naissant pour l'indépendance

burger ['bɜːgər] N *Fam* hamburger *m*

burgess ['bɜːdʒɪs] N **1** *Hist (in England)* citoyen *m* **2** *(in English history) (MP)* député *m (représentant une ville)* **3** *Am* = conseiller *m* municipal

burgher ['bɜːgər] N *Arch, Hum (citizen)* citoyen *m*

burglar ['bɜːglər] N cambrioleur, -euse; **b. proof** inviolable
▸ ▸ **b. alarm** alarme *f* antivol

burglarize ['bɜːgləraɪz] VT *Am* cambrioler

burglary ['bɜːglərɪ] N cambriolage *m*; *(breaking and entering)* vol *m* avec effraction

burgle ['bɜːg(ə)l] VT cambrioler; **it's the third time they've been burgled** c'est la troisième fois qu'ils se sont fait cambrioler

Burgundian [bɜː'gʌndɪən] ADJ bourguignon
N Bourguignon, -onne

Burgundy ['bɜːgəndɪ] N **1** *Geog* Bourgogne *f* **2** *(wine)* bourgogne *m*, vin *m* de Bourgogne **3** *(colour)* bordeaux *m*

burial ['berɪəl] N enterrement *m*, inhumation *f*, *Fig* **the b. of sb's hopes** la fin des espoirs de qn
▸ ▸ **b. chamber** caveau *m*; **b. ground** cimetière *m*; **b. mound** tumulus *m*; **b. place** (lieu *m* de) sépulture *f*, *(for radioactive substances)* dépôt *m* souterrain; **b. service** office *m* des morts

burin ['bjʊərɪn] N *(for engraving)* burin *m*

burk [bɜːk] N *Br Sl* **you (great) b.!** espèce d'idiot!

Burkina-Faso [bɜː'kiːnə'fæsəʊ] N Burkina *m*

burlap ['bɜːlæp] N *Tex* toile *f* d'emballage

burlesque [bɜː'lesk] ADJ burlesque
N **1** *(satire)* burlesque *m*; *(caricature)* parodie *f* **2** *Am Theat* revue *f* vulgaire
VT parodier, tourner en ridicule

burliness ['bɜːlɪnɪs] N **1** *(person's build)* forte *ou* solide charpente *f* **2** *Am (brusqueness)* brusquerie *f*

burly ['bɜːlɪ] ADJ **1** *(well-built)* bien bâti, *Fam* costaud **2** *Am (brusque)* brusque, bourru

Burma ['bɜːmə] N Birmanie *f*

Burmese [bɜː'miːz] ADJ birman
N **1** Birman, -ane **2** *Ling* birman *m*
▸ ▸ **B. cat** birmese *m*, chat *m* birman

BURN[1] [bɜːn] N **1** *Med etc* brûlure *f*, **the child suffered severe burns** l'enfant a subi de graves brûlures
2 *Astronaut* allumage *m*; *(of rocket)* poussée *f*, *Fig Fam* **I was doing a slow b.** la moutarde me montait au nez
VT *(pt, pp* **burnt** [bɜːnt], *occ* **burned)** **1** *(fuel, building)* brûler; **to b. coal/oil/gas** *(of boiler)* marcher au charbon/au mazout/au gaz; *Fig* **to b. one's boats** *or* **one's bridges** brûler ses vaisseaux; **to b. sth to ashes** réduire qch en cendres; **to b. sth to a cinder** *or* **a crisp** carboniser qch; *Old-fashioned Fam* **to be burnt** *(of police informer)* être grillé; **to be burnt alive, to be burnt to death** être brûlé vif; **the house was burned to the ground** la maison a été complètement brûlée; **to b. one's fingers** se brûler les doigts; *Fig* **he got his fingers burnt, he burnt his fingers over it** il s'est fait échauder (dans cette affaire); **to b. a hole in sth with a cigarette/the iron** faire un trou dans qch avec une cigarette/le fer à repasser; *Fig* **money burns a hole in his pocket** l'argent lui brûle les doigts; *Fig* **to have money to b.** avoir de l'argent à ne plus savoir quoi en faire; **acids b. into metal** les acides rongent le métal; **mustard burns the tongue** la moutarde pique *ou* brûle la langue; **I burned my tongue** je me suis brûlé la langue
2 *Ind (bricks, charcoal)* cuire; *(rubber)* vulcaniser, cuire

3 *Comput (CD)* graver
4 *Am Fam (swindle)* arnaquer
5 *Am Fam (anger)* foutre en rogne
▮**VI 1** *(of house, forest, fire, wood)* brûler; *Culin (of meat, toast etc)* brûler; *(of sauce, milk etc)* attacher; *(of wound, eyes)* brûler, piquer; **the smell of burning rubber** l'odeur de caoutchouc brûlé; **to b. low** *(of fire)* baisser; *Fig* **to b. with** *(impatience, passion, desire)* brûler de; *(anger, hatred)* bouillonner de; **his cheeks were burning with shame** il était rouge de honte
2 *(of mixture in engine)* exploser
▶ **burn down** VT SEP *(town, house etc)* brûler, incendier
▮**VI 1** *(of building etc)* être détruit par le feu *ou* par un incendie
2 *(of fire)* baisser
▶ **burn in** VT SEP *Comput* roder
▶ **burn off** VT SEP **1** *(remove by burning)* *(bracken, gas)* brûler; *(paint)* décaper au chalumeau; *(rust etc)* enlever au feu
2 *(consume, use up)* *(calories)* brûler; **to b. off some energy** se dépenser
▶ **burn out** VT SEP *Aut etc (brake linings or pads)* brûler; *Elec (coil)* brûler, court-circuiter; *(lamp)* griller; **the house was burnt out** le feu a complètement détruit l'intérieur de la maison; **to b. itself out** *(of fire)* s'éteindre; *Fig* **it'll b. itself out** *(of love affair)* une passion comme ça ne dure pas; *Fig* **to b. oneself out** s'épuiser (par excès de travail), se vider
▮**VI** *(of fire, oil lamp)* s'éteindre; *(of candle)* s'éteindre, brûler jusqu'au bout; *(of light bulb)* griller
▶ **burn up** VT SEP **1** *(consume)* brûler (entièrement), consumer; **to b. up energy** se dépenser; *Fam* **to b. up the miles** *or* **the motorway** avaler les kilomètres
2 *(of sun)* *(leaves etc)* griller, flétrir; *Fam (make angry)* mettre en pétard
▮**VI 1** *Fam (get angry)* se mettre en pétard; **to b. up inside** bouillir intérieurement
2 *(of rocket)* brûler, se consumer; *(of person with high temperature)* être brûlant; **the pavement was burning up** le trottoir était brûlant

burn² N *Scot (stream)* ruisseau *m*

burner ['bɜːnər] N **1** *(on stove)* brûleur *m*, feu *m* **2** *(in gas or acetylene lamp)* bec *m* **3** *Comput* graveur *m*

burn-in N *Comput (of machine)* rodage *m*

burning ['bɜːnɪŋ] ADJ *(fever, thirst, desire etc)* brûlant, ardent; *(coal)* embrasé, allumé, ardent; *(town, house)* incendié, enflammé, en feu; *(heat)* brûlant, torride; *(sun)* *Fig (question)* brûlant; *Fam* **I'm b. (hot)** je crève de chaleur
▮**N** *(of house etc)* incendie *m*; *Chem* combustion *f*; *Hist* **b. (at the stake)** supplice *m* du bûcher; **there's a smell of b.** ça sent le brûlé; **b. sensation** *(heat)* sensation *f* de chaleur (excessive); *(discomfort)* sensation de brûlure; *(pain)* douleur *f* cuisante
▶▶ **b. bush** *Bible* buisson *m* ardent; *(shrub)* fraxinelle *f*

burnish ['bɜːnɪʃ] N *(on metal)* bruni *m*, poli *m*
▮**VT** *(metal)* brunir, polir; *Phot (print)* satiner; *Lit* **her hair was like burnished gold** elle avait les cheveux d'un or cuivré

burnisher ['bɜːnɪʃər] N *Metal* **1** *(person)* brunisseur, -euse **2** *(instrument)* brunissoir *m*, polissoir *m*

burnishing ['bɜːnɪʃɪŋ] N brunissage *m*, polissage *m*

burnous(e) [bɜː'nuːs] N burnous *m*

burnout ['bɜːnaʊt] N *Fig* saturation *f*, épuisement *m*

burnt [bɜːnt] ADJ **1** *(person, object)* brûlé; *(smell, taste)* de brûlé, de roussi; **to be b. beyond recognition** être carbonisé; *Prov* **a**

b. child dreads *or* **fears the fire** chat échaudé craint l'eau froide **2** *(earth, clay)* cuit
▶▶ **b. offering** *Rel (sacrifice)* holocauste *m*; *Hum (food)* plat *m* calciné *ou* carbonisé

burnt-out ADJ **1** *(destroyed by fire)* incendié, brûlé **2** *Fam (person)* lessivé, vidé; **she was b. by thirty** elle était usée avant (l'âge de) trente ans **3** *Tech (bearings)* grippé; *Elec (coil, light bulb)* grillé

burp [bɜːp] N éructation *f*, *Fam* rot *m*
▮**VI** éructer, *Fam* roter
▮**VT** *(baby)* faire roter

burr¹ [bɜːr] N **1** *Bot (of burdock etc)* teigne *f*; *Fig* **to stick to sb like a b.** se cramponner *ou* s'accrocher à qn **2** *(on metal)* bavure *f*, barbe *f*; **to take the burrs off metal** ébarber le métal
▶▶ **b. walnut** ronce *f* de noyer

burr² N **1** *Ling* grasseyement *m*; **to speak with a b.** grasseyer **2** *(of machine)* ronflement *m*
▮**VI** **to b. one's r's** grasseyer
▮**VT** *(of machine etc)* ronfler

burro ['bʊrəʊ] N *Am* âne *m*

burrow ['bʌrəʊ] N terrier *m*
▮**VI** *(dig)* *(of rabbit, dog etc)* creuser (la terre); *Fig* **to b. into the archives** fouiller dans les archives; **to b. in one's pocket/bag** fourrager dans sa poche/son sac
▮**VT** *(hole)* creuser; **to b. one's way underground** creuser (un chemin) sous terre; **to b. the ground** *(of rabbits)* creuser *ou* fouir la terre

burrowing ['bʌrəʊɪŋ] ADJ *(animal)* fouisseur; *(insect)* fossoyeur, mineur

bursar ['bɜːsər] N *Sch (official in charge of finance)* économe *mf*, intendant, -ante

bursary ['bɜːsərɪ] N **1** *(office)* économat *m*, intendance *f* **2** *esp Scot (grant)* bourse *f* *(d'études)*; **b. student** boursier, -ière

bursitis [bɜː'saɪtɪs] N *Med* bursite *f*; **I have b. in my shoulder** j'ai une bursite à l'épaule

BURST [bɜːst]

N	éclatement **1** ▪ jaillissement **2** ▪ éclat **2**
VI	éclater ▪ crever
VT	faire éclater

N 1 *(of bomb, boiler etc)* éclatement *m*, explosion *f*
2 *(of flame)* jaillissement *m*, jet *m*; *(of gunfire, machine-gun)* rafale *f*; *(of laughter)* éclat *m*; *(of anger)* explosion *f*; *(of eloquence)* élan *m*; *(of applause)* salve *f*; *(of activity)* poussée *f*, *(of enthusiasm)* accès *m*; *Sport* **b. of speed** accélération *f*; **to put on a b. of speed** faire une accélération; *Sport* **final b.** sprint *m*
▮**VI** *(pt, pp burst)* *(of boiler, bomb etc)* éclater, exploser; *(of dam)* éclater, céder; *(of abscess, blister)* crever, percer; *(of bubble)* crever; *(of storm, paper bag)* éclater; *Hum* **he'll b. if he eats any more** il va éclater s'il mange davantage; *Fam* **to be bursting (for the toilet)** avoir terriblement envie d'aller aux toilettes; **we've got a b. pipe** *(in house)* nous avons un tuyau qui a éclaté; *Fig* **her heart was ready to b.** *(with sorrow)* elle avait le cœur brisé; *(with happiness)* elle débordait de joie; **to be bursting at the seams** *(of dress etc)* se découdre; *Fig (of building etc)* être plein à craquer; **to be bursting with pride** crever d'orgueil; **to be bursting with health** déborder de santé; **to be bursting with impatience** bouillir d'impatience; **I was bursting to tell him so** je mourais d'envie de le lui dire; **a cry b. from his lips** un cri s'échappa de ses lèvres; *Lit* **to b. upon sb's sight** se présenter aux yeux de qn; *Lit* **to b. upon sb's ears** *(of sound)* parvenir brusquement aux oreilles de qn

▮**VT** *(balloon, tyre, paper bag)* faire éclater; *(boiler)* faire éclater *ou* exploser; *Lit (one's bonds)* rompre; **to b. a blood vessel** se rompre un vaisseau sanguin; *Fig* **he nearly b. a blood vessel when I told him** il a failli attraper un coup de sang quand je le lui ai dit; **to b. its banks** *(of river)* sortir de son lit
▶▶ *Comput* **b. mode** mode *m* continu
▶ **burst in** VT SEP *(door)* enfoncer
▮**VI** *(of person)* faire irruption, entrer en trombe; **to b. in on sb** faire irruption chez qn/dans le bureau de qn; **to b. in on a conversation** interrompre brusquement une conversation
▶ **burst into** VT INSEP **1** *(enter noisily)* **to b. into a room** faire irruption dans une pièce
2 *(suddenly start)* **to b. into flame(s)** s'enflammer brusquement; **to b. into song** entonner une chanson; **to b. into blossom** *(of tree)* commencer à fleurir; **to b. into laughter/tears** éclater de rire/fondre en larmes
▶ **burst open** VT SEP *(door)* *(open suddenly)* ouvrir brusquement; *(smash open)* enfoncer, briser; *(cover, lock)* faire sauter
▮**VI** *(of door)* s'ouvrir brusquement
▶ **burst out** VI **1** *(say suddenly)* s'écrier; **to b. out laughing/crying** éclater de rire/fondre en larmes
2 *(leave noisily)* **to b. out of a room** sortir précipitamment d'une pièce
▶ **burst through** VT INSEP *(police cordon)* enfoncer; **to come bursting through the door** *(open it suddenly)* entrer précipitamment; *(smash it)* enfoncer la porte; **the sun b. through the clouds** le soleil creva les nuages

bursting ['bɜːstɪŋ] N *(of bomb, tyre etc)* éclatement *m*, explosion *f*; *(of dam)* rupture *f*

burton ['bɜːt(ə)n] N *Br Sl* **to have gone for a b.** *(be dead)* être mort; *(of hopes, plans etc)* être tombé à l'eau; *(be broken)* *(of plate etc)* être cassé; *(of iron, television etc)* être foutu; *(be lost)* *(of ball etc)* être perdu pour de bon; **there's another plate gone for a b.!** voilà une autre assiette de cassée!

Burundi [bə'rʊndɪ] N Burundi *m*

bury ['berɪ] VT *(pt, pp buried)* **1** *(body)* enterrer, inhumer, ensevelir; *(at sea)* immerger; *(object)* enterrer, enfouir; **to b. sb alive** enterrer qn vivant; **to b. itself** *(of animal)* se terrer, s'enfouir; **buried treasure** trésor *m* enterré *ou* enfoui; *Elec* **buried cable** câble *m* souterrain
2 *(of snow, landslide)* *(town, house)* ensevelir; **I found the letter buried under my papers** j'ai trouvé la lettre enfouie sous mes papiers; **to b. oneself in the country** s'enterrer à la campagne; **to b. oneself in one's work** se plonger *ou* s'absorber dans son travail; **to b. one's face in one's hands** se cacher la figure dans les mains; *Fig* **to b. one's head in the sand** pratiquer la politique de l'autruche; **she always has her head buried in a book** elle est toujours plongée dans un livre; **to be buried in thought** être absorbé dans ses pensées

burying beetle ['berɪɪŋ] N nécrophore *m*

bus, *pl* **buses**, *Am* **busses** [bʌs, 'bʌsɪz] N **1** bus *m*, autobus *m*; *(on long-distance services)* car *m*; **by b.** en bus; **to miss the b.** manquer *ou* rater le bus; *Fig Fam* manquer le coche; *Fam* **old b.** *(car)* vieille bagnole *f*, *(aircraft)* coucou *m*; **have you got enough money for your b. fare?** est-ce que tu as assez d'argent pour le bus? **2** *Comput, Electron* bus *m*
▮**VI** voyager en autobus
▮**VT 1** *(drive in a bus)* transporter en autobus/en car; **the children are bus(s)ed to school** les enfants sont emmenés à l'école en autobus; **are you bus(s)ing it?** tu y vas en autobus? **2** *Am (restaurant tables)* débarrasser
▶▶ **b. advertising** publicité *f* sur les auto-

bus; *Comput* **b. board** carte *f* bus; *Am* **b. boy** aide-serveur *m*, *pl* aides-serveurs; *Br* **b. conductor** receveur, -euse d'autobus; *Br* **b. conductress** receveuse *f* d'autobus; *Comput* **b. controller** contrôleur *m* de bus; **b. depot** dépôt *m* d'autobus; *(long-distance bus station)* gare froutière; **b. driver** conducteur, -trice d'autobus; **b. lane** voie *f* ou couloir *m* d'autobus; *Mktg* **b. mailing** publipostage *m* groupé, multipostage *m*; *Mktg* **b. phoning** télévente *f* groupée; **b. route** trajet *m* de bus; **are you on a b. route?** est-ce qu'il y a un bus qui passe près de chez toi?; **b. shelter** Abribus® *m*; **b. station** gare routière; **b. stop** arrêt *m* de bus; **b. ticket** ticket *m* de bus; *Comput* **b. structure** structure *f* de bus

busbar ['bʌzbɑːr] N *Electron* bus *m*

busby ['bʌzbɪ] N *Mil* bonnet *m* de hussard

bush[1] [bʊʃ] N **1** buisson *m*; **a great b. of red hair** une grosse tignasse rousse **2** *(in Africa, Australia)* **the b.** la brousse; **to take to the b., to go b.** *Austr* prendre la brousse **3** *Vulg (woman's pubic hair)* barbu *m*
▸▸ **b. hat** chapeau *m* de brousse; **b. jacket** saharienne *f*, *Am Sport* **b. league** = petite équipe *f* locale de baseball; *Aviat* **b. pilot** pilote *m* de ligne opérant dans une région peu habitée *ou* dans la brousse *ou* *Can* dans le Grand Nord; **b. shirt** saharienne; **b. telegraph** téléphone *m* de brousse; *Br Fig Hum (grapevine)* téléphone arabe

bush[2] *Tech* N bague *f*, douille *f*, manchon *m*; *(between bearing and shaft)* coussinet *m*
VT baguer, manchonner; *(bearing)* mettre un coussinet à

bushbaby ['bʊʃbeɪbɪ] N galago *m*

bushed [bʊʃt] ADJ *Fam* **1** *(exhausted)* fatigué, éreinté **2** *Can (confused)* rendu déséquilibré par un isolement prolongé **3** *Austr (lost)* perdu *ou* égaré dans la brousse; *Fig (bewildered)* désorienté

bushel ['bʊʃəl] N **1** *(unit of measurement)* boisseau *m* (= *approx 36 litres)*; *Fig* **to hide one's light under a b.** cacher son talent **2** *Am Fam (great amount)* grande quantité *f*

bushfire ['bʊʃfaɪər] N feu *m* de brousse

bushing ['bʊʃɪŋ] N *Tech (sleeve)* bague *f*, bague de culbuteur; *(between bearing and shaft)* coussinet *m*

Bushman, *pl* **Bushmen** ['bʊʃmən] *(in South Africa)* ADJ bochiman
N **1** Bochiman, -ane **2** *Ling* bochiman *m*

bushman, *pl* **bushmen** ['bʊʃmən] N broussard *m* *(en Australie)*

bushwhacker ['bʊʃwækər] N **1** *Am* = personne *f* qui vit dans des régions boisées et reculées; *Austr* broussard *m* **2** *Am (guerrilla)* guérillero *m*

bushy ['bʊʃɪ] ADJ **1** *(country, eyebrows)* broussailleux; *(beard)* fourni; *(hair)* touffu, embroussaillé **2** *(shrub)* épais, touffu

busily ['bɪzɪlɪ] ADV *(to prepare)* activement; *(to search)* d'un air affairé

BUSINESS ['bɪznɪs] N **1** *(affair, matter)* affaire *f*, **it's a bad** *or* **sad** *or* **sorry b.** c'est une bien triste affaire; **it's a bad** *or* **sad** *or* **sorry b. when you can't trust your own brother** c'est triste quand on ne peut même pas faire confiance à son propre frère; **I'm sick of the whole b.** j'en ai assez de toute cette affaire; **it's quite a b. finding a plumber** ce n'est pas une petite affaire que de trouver un plombier; **it was a real b. persuading him to come** j'ai/nous avons/*etc* eu beaucoup de mal à le persuader de venir; **what's your b. (with him)?** que (lui) voulez-vous?; **it's/it's not my b. to ...** c'est/ce n'est pas à moi de ...; **it's not your b., it's none of your b.** cela ne vous regarde pas, ce n'est pas votre affaire; **you have no b. (being) in here** vous n'avez rien à faire ici; **you had no b. telling her** ce n'était

pas à toi de le lui dire; **what b. is it of yours where she spent the night?** qu'est-ce que ça peut te faire où elle a passé la nuit?; **mind your own b.** occupez-vous de ce qui vous regarde *ou* de vos affaires; **I mind my own b.** je m'occupe de mes affaires; **I was just walking along, minding my own b., when ...** je marchais tranquillement dans la rue quand ...; **to go about one's b.** vaquer à ses occupations; *esp Fml* **I sent him about his b.** *(sent him away)* je l'ai envoyé promener; **to make it one's b. to do sth** prendre sur soi de faire qch; **... or I'll make it my b.** ... ou je vais m'en occuper personnellement; **let's get down to b.!** au travail!; **can we get down to b.?** est-ce qu'on peut commencer?, est-ce qu'on peut se mettre au travail?; **we got through a lot of b.** nous avons abattu de la besogne; **to mean b.** être sérieux; **the b. before a meeting** l'ordre *m* du jour; **(any) other b.** *(on agenda)* questions *fpl* diverses; **can we turn to the b. of who's going to be responsible?** est-ce que nous pouvons discuter de la question de qui sera responsable?; *Fam* **he can sing like nobody's b.** *(does it very well)* elle chante très bien; *Fam* **they're working like nobody's b.** *(very hard)* ils travaillent très dur; *Br Fam* **it's the b.** c'est impec'; *Euph* **has the dog done its b.?** est-ce que le chien a fait ses besoins?

2 *(dealings)* affaires *fpl*, *(commerce)* commerce *m*; **somebody in the antiques/restaurant b.** quelqu'un qui est dans les antiquités/la restauration; **to go into** *or* **to set up in b. as a grocer** s'établir épicier, ouvrir une épicerie; **to be in/go into b. on one's own** *or* **for oneself** être/s'établir *ou* s'installer à son compte; **to do b. with sb** faire affaire *ou* des affaires avec qn; **she's in b.** elle est dans les affaires; **the shop has been in b. for twenty years** le magasin existe depuis vingt ans; **they've been in b. together for twenty years** ils sont associés depuis vingt ans; *Fig* **now we're in b.** maintenant nous pouvons y aller; *Fig* **it looks as if we're back in b.** on dirait que les choses reprennent pour nous; **to go out of b.** fermer; **supermarkets have put many small shops out of b.** les supermarchés ont obligé beaucoup de petits magasins à fermer; **I've got some b. to discuss with him** il faut que je discute affaires avec lui; **they've put a lot of b. our way** ils nous ont donné beaucoup de travail; **to go to London on b.** aller à Londres pour affaires; **a profitable piece of b.** une affaire rentable *ou* qui rapporte; **to lose b.** perdre de la clientèle; **to do b. with sb** faire des affaires avec qn; **shop that does good b.** commerce qui marche bien; **it's good/bad for b.** c'est bon/mauvais pour les affaires; **how's b.?** comment vont les affaires?; **b. is b.** les affaires sont les affaires; **b. as usual** *(sign)* ouvert; **it's b. as usual in the town despite the floods** la vie continue dans la ville malgré les inondations; **this shop will be open for b. from tomorrow** ce magasin ouvrira demain; **hours of b.** *(sign)* heures d'ouverture; **to mix b. with pleasure** joindre l'utile à l'agréable; **you shouldn't mix b. with pleasure** il ne faut pas mélanger le travail et les loisirs; **b. before pleasure** le travail avant tout; **b. is slow** les affaires ne vont pas; **she has a good head for b.** elle a le sens des affaires; **to talk b.** parler affaires; **the tourist trade is big b.** le tourisme est une industrie qui rapporte beaucoup d'argent; **looking for b.?** *(said by prostitute)* tu viens, chéri?; **with b. experience** rompu aux affaires

3 *(company, firm)* affaire *f*, entreprise *f*, *(shop)* commerce *m*; **to run a b.** gérer une entreprise; **to carry on a b.** avoir une affaire/un commerce; **b. for sale** commerce à vendre; **a farm is a b. like any other** une ferme est une entreprise comme les autres

4 *(trade)* métier *m*; **what's his line of b.?, what b. is he in?** qu'est-ce qu'il fait (comme métier)?; **I'm not in this b. for the good of my health** je ne fais pas ce métier pour le plaisir; **I'm not in the b. of solving your problems** ce n'est pas à moi de résoudre tes problèmes; **the best in the b.** le meilleur de tous

5 *Theat* jeux *mpl* de scène
▸▸ **b. account** compte *m* professionnel *ou* commercial; **b. accounting** comptabilité *f* commerciale; **b. acumen** sens *m* des affaires; **b. address** adresse *f* professionnelle; **b. administration** gestion *f* commerciale; **b. assignment** mission *f* commerciale; **b. associate** associé, -ée; **b. bank** banque *f* d'affaires; **b. banking** operations *fpl* des banques d'affaires; **b. buyer** acheteur *m* industriel; **b. card** carte *f* de visite; **b. career** carrière *f* d'affaires; **b. centre** centre *m* des affaires; *Aviat* **b. class** classe *f* affaires; **b. computer** ordinateur *m* de bureau; **b. computing** informatique *f* de gestion; **b. concern** exploitation *f* commerciale; *Journ* **b. correspondent** correspondant, -ante financier(ière); **b. cycle** cycle *m* économique, temps *m* de cycle; *Fam* **b. end** *(of knife)* partie *f* coupante; *(of gun)* gueule *f*; **b. enterprise** entreprise commerciale; **b. environment** environnement *m* commercial; **b. ethics** déontologie *f* professionnelle; **b. expansion** extension *f* du commerce; **b. expenses** *(for individual)* frais *mpl* professionnels; *(for company)* frais généraux; **b. failure** défaillance *f* d'entreprise; **b. fare** tarif *m* affaires; *Comput* **b. graphics** graphiques *mpl* de gestion; **b. hotel** hôtel *m* d'affaires; **b. hours** *(of office)* heures *fpl* de bureau; *(of shop, public service)* heures d'ouverture; **b. incubator** pépinière *f* d'entreprises; *Comput* **b. intelligence system** réactive *f*, *Admin* **b. letter** lettre *f* commerciale; **b. lunch** déjeuner *m* d'affaires; **b. management** gestion d'entreprise *ou* des sociétés, direction *f* des entreprises; *(study)* économie *f* d'entreprise; **b. manager** *Com, Ind* directeur, -trice commercial(ale); *Sport* manager *m*; *Theat* directeur, -trice; **b. market** marché *m* industriel *ou* des entreprises; **b. meeting** rendez-vous *m inv* d'affaires; *Mktg* **b. mission** mission *f* d'activité *ou* de l'entreprise; **b. news** chronique *f* économique; **b. park** zone *f* d'activités; **b. plan** projet *m* commercial; **b. portfolio** portefeuille *m* d'activités; **b. premises** locaux *mpl* commerciaux; **b. relations** relations *fpl* d'affaires, relations commerciales; **b. reply envelope** enveloppe *f* préaffranchie; **b. school** école *f* de commerce; **b. section** *(of newspaper)* rubrique *f* des affaires; *Econ* **b. sector** secteur *m* tertiaire, secteur d'affaires; **b. services** services *mpl* du secteur tertiaire, services aux entreprises; **b. strategy** stratégie *f* d'entreprise; **b. studies** études *fpl* commerciales *ou* de commerce; **b. suit** complet *m* (-veston *m*), *pl* complets(-vestons); *Comput* **b. systems** logiciels *mpl* de bureautique; **b. tourism** tourisme *m* d'affaires; **b. travel** voyages *mpl* d'affaires; **b. traveller** = personne *f* qui voyage pour affaires; **b. trend** courant *m* d'affaires; **b. trip** voyage *m* d'affaires

businesslike ['bɪznɪslaɪk] ADJ *(person, manner)* sérieux; *(attitude, appearance)* professionnel; *(transaction)* régulier, sérieux

businessman, *pl* **businessmen** ['bɪznɪsmən] N homme *m* d'affaires; **big b.** homme d'affaires important

businesswoman, *pl* **businesswomen** ['bɪznɪswʊmən, -wɪmɪn] N femme *f* d'affaires; **she's a good b.** elle s'y connaît en affaires

busing ['bʌsɪŋ] N = **bussing**

busk [bʌsk] vi *esp Br* = chanter ou jouer d'un instrument dans les rues ou le métro

busker ['bʌskər] n *esp Br* musicien, -ienne ambulant(ante)

busman, *pl* **busmen** ['bʌsmən] n *Fam* **to take a b.'s holiday** faire la même chose pendant ses loisirs que pendant son travail; **that's a bit of a b.'s holiday** vous appelez ça des vacances!

bussing ['bʌsɪŋ] n *(of schoolchildren etc)* transport *m* par autobus *(surtout dans le cadre de la politique de déségrégation aux États-Unis)*

bust[1] [bʌst] n **1** *Anat (of woman)* poitrine *f*; **what (size) b. are you?** combien est-ce que vous faites de tour de poitrine?; **what b. is this dress?** combien cette robe fait-elle de tour de poitrine?; **to be small/big in the b.** avoir une petite/grosse poitrine; **it's too tight round the b.** c'est trop serré à la poitrine; **b. measurement** tour *m* de poitrine **2** *(by sculptor)* buste *m*

bust[2] *Fam* adj *(iron, radio etc)* foutu; **if it ain't b., don't fix it** le mieux est l'ennemi du bien; **to go b.** faire faillite
vt **1** *(break)* casser; *(balloon etc)* crever; *Am* **to b. sb's nose** donner un coup de poing à qn sur le nez; *FigFam* **to b. a gut** se décarcasser, se donner un mal de chien; *Am Vulg* **to b. one's ass doing sth** se crever le cul à faire qch
2 *(arrest) (thief etc)* coffrer; *(gang of traffickers)* démanteler; **he was busted for armed robbery** il s'est fait coffrer pour vol à main armée; **you're busted** tu es fait
3 *(raid) (bar etc)* faire une descente dans
4 *Am esp Mil (reduce in rank)* rétrograder; **he's been busted to private** il a été rétrogradé au rang de simple soldat
5 *Am (wild horses)* dresser

bust[3] n *Fam (by police) (of thief etc)* arrestation *f*; *(raid)* descente *f*, *(search)* perquisition *f*
► **bust out** vi *Fam* s'échapper
► **bust up** *Fam* vt sep **1** *(marriage, friendship etc)* casser; **to b. up a meeting** interrompre une réunion **2** *(damage, destroy) (bar, flat)* saccager
vi *(of spouses, lovers)* casser; **their marriage has b. up** ils ont cassé

bustard ['bʌstəd] n *(bird)* outarde *f*

buster ['bʌstər] n *Am Fam (child)* (petit) garçon *m*; *(man)* homme *m*, type *m*; **hi, b.!** *(as address)* salut, mon pote!; **now listen, b. ...** écoute, mec ...

bustle[1] ['bʌs(ə)l] n *(activity)* agitation *f*; **the b. in the streets** l'animation *f* des rues
vi **to b. (about)** s'activer, s'affairer; **the streets are bustling with people** les rues grouillent de monde
vt **to b. sb out of the house** faire sortir qn précipitamment

bustle[2] n *(of skirt)* tournure *f*

bustling ['bʌs(ə)lɪŋ] adj *(person)* très actif; *(street)* animé; **the b. crowds of shoppers** la foule animée des gens qui font leurs courses

bust-up n *Fam* **1** *(of marriage, relationship)* échec *m*; **their b. was quite a shock to me** leur séparation m'a fait un choc **2** *(quarrel)* engueulade *f*; **to have a b.** se brouiller **3** *(brawl)* bagarre *f*

busty ['bʌstɪ] adj *Fam (woman)* à la poitrine plantureuse

busy ['bɪzɪ] adj **(busier, busiest)** **1** *(person)* occupé; **not now, I'm b.** pas maintenant, je suis occupé; **you have been b.!** tu as été bien travaillé!; **my work keeps me b. all morning** mon travail m'occupe toute la matinée; **to keep (oneself) b.** s'occuper; **to be b. with sth** être occupé à qch; **to be b. doing sth** être

occupé à faire qch; **I suppose it's time I got b.** il est temps que je m'y mette; *Fam* **get b.!** grouille-toi!
2 *(day etc)* chargé; *Rail (line)* à grand trafic; *(street)* animé, passant; **it's a b. road** c'est une route à grande circulation; **the roads were very b. this morning** il y avait beaucoup de circulation sur les routes ce matin; **the train was very b.** il y avait beaucoup de monde dans le train; **the hotel industry is at its busiest in August** l'industrie hôtelière est au plus haut de son activité au mois d'août; **we're not b. at the moment** *(of business etc)* nous travaillons au ralenti en ce moment; **this is a b. time of year for us** *(of business etc)* nous travaillons beaucoup à cette période de l'année; **this is a b. time of year for gardeners** c'est une période de l'année où il y a beaucoup à faire pour les jardiniers
3 *esp Am Tel* occupé; **the line is b.** la ligne est occupée
4 *Comput (printer)* occupé
vt **to b. oneself with sth** s'occuper à qch; **to b. oneself (with) doing the housework/ironing the shirts** s'occuper en faisant le ménage/en repassant les chemises; **I can always find something to b. myself with** je trouve toujours à m'occuper; **to b. oneself with other people's problems** s'occuper des problèmes des autres
►► *Bot* **b. lizzie** balsamine *f*, impatiente *f*; *esp Am Tel* **b. signal** tonalité *f* occupée; **I keep getting the b. signal** ça sonne toujours occupé

busybody ['bɪzɪbɒdɪ] n curieux, -ieuse, indiscret, -ète; **he's an awful b.** il se mêle des affaires de tout le monde

---

BUT [bʌt]

CONJ	mais **1, 3**
ADV	ne ... que
PREP	sauf **1** ▪ sans **3**

conj **1** *(coordinating)* mais; **he is small b. strong** il est petit mais fort; **b. I tell you I saw it!** (mais) puisque je vous dis que je l'ai vu!; **he does nothing b. complain** il n'arrête pas de se plaindre
2 *(subordinating)* **I can't go out for a minute b. something happens** je ne peux pas sortir une minute sans qu'il se passe quelque chose; *Arch, Lit* **I cannot b. believe that ... I** m'est impossible de ne pas croire que ...; **what could I do b. invite him?** que pouvais-je faire d'autre que de l'inviter? VOIR GRAMMAIRE A76
3 *(intensive)* **not just once b. twice** pas une fois, mais deux; **nobody, b. nobody** personne, mais absolument personne
adv *(only)* ne ... que; *esp Lit* **had I b. known!** si j'avais su!; **I can b. try** je ne peux qu'essayer; **it seems b. yesterday** c'est comme si c'était hier; **it seems b. yesterday that she was here** on dirait qu'hier encore elle était ici; *Formal* **his resignation cannot b. confirm such suspicions** sa démission ne fait que confirmer de tels soupçons; **if I could b. see him!** si seulement je pouvais le voir!; **he's b. a boy** ce n'est qu'un garçon
prep **1** *(except)* **any day b. tomorrow** n'importe quel jour excepté *ou* sauf demain; *Arch, Lit* **all b. he** *or* **him** tous excepté *ou* sauf lui; *Arch, Lit* **none b. he** personne d'autre que lui; **nobody b. me** could have done something so stupid il n'y a que moi pour faire quelque chose d'aussi stupide; **nobody b. me knew about it** personne d'autre que moi n'était au courant; **anyone b. me** tout autre que moi; **I wish the prize had been won by anyone b. him** j'aurais voulu que n'importe qui d'autre remporte le prix plutôt que lui; **anything b. that** tout plutôt que cela; **he's anything b. a hero** c'est loin d'être un

héros; **he is anything b. happy** il n'est pas du tout heureux; **is she lazy? – anything b.!** est-ce qu'elle est paresseuse? – bien au contraire!; **it's nothing b. laziness** ce n'est que de la paresse; **there is nothing for it b. to obey** il n'y a qu'à obéir
2 **the last b. one** l'avant-dernier; **the next house b. one** la deuxième maison (à partir d'ici)
3 **b. for** sans; **b. for the rain I should have gone out** s'il n'avait pas plu je serais sorti; **he wouldn't have left b. for me** *(it was my fault for being there)* il serait resté si je n'avais pas été là; *(it was for my sake)* il ne serait pas parti si ça n'avait pas été pour moi; **b. for you I would have been killed** *(if you hadn't been there)* si vous n'aviez pas été là, j'aurais été tué
n **there is a b.** il y a un mais; **I don't want any buts!** il n'y a pas de mais!; **you're coming to dinner at our place and I don't want any buts** tu viens dîner chez nous, et je ne veux pas de discussions

---

butane ['bjuːteɪn] n *Chem* butane *m*

butch [bʊtʃ] adj *Fam (man, woman)* très masculin; *(haircut, clothes)* de mec

butcher ['bʊtʃər] n **1** *(for meat)* boucher, -ère; **to go to the b.'s** aller chez le boucher; **b.'s block** billot *m* de boucher; **b.'s boy** garçon *m* boucher; **b.'s shop/trade** boucherie *f* **2** *Pej (killer)* boucher *m* **3** *Fam (surgeon)* boucher *m*, charcutier *m*
vt **1** *(animal) (kill for meat)* abattre; *(cut up)* dépecer **2** *Pej (kill) (person)* massacrer; *Fam* **he butchered that song** il a massacré cette chanson **3** *Fam (of surgeon) (patient)* charcuter

butcher's ['bʊtʃəz] n *Br Sl* **to have a b. at sb/sth** viser *ou* mater qn/qch; **let's have a b. at the photos** laisse-moi voir les photos

butchery ['bʊtʃərɪ] n **1** *(trade)* boucherie *f* **2** *Pej (bloodshed)* boucherie *f*, massacre *m*

butler ['bʌtlər] n maître *m* d'hôtel; **b.'s pantry** office *m*

butt[1] [bʌt] n **1** *(cask)* barrique *f*, futaille *f* **2** *(for rainwater)* tonneau *m*

butt[2] n **1** *(of cigar etc)* mégot *m* **2** *esp Am Fam (buttocks)* derrière *m*; **get off your b. and do something!** remue-toi le cul et fais quelque chose!; **move your b.!** bouge-toi! **3** *(of tool)* gros bout *m*; *(of fishing rod)* gros brin *m*; *(of rifle)* crosse *f*, *Fig* **the b. end of the conversation** la fin de la conversation **4** *Billiards (of cue)* masse *f*, talon *m* **5** *Carp* about *m*
►► **b. end** *(of tool)* gros bout; *(of fishing rod)* gros brin; *(of rifle)* crosse; *Carp* about *mf*; **b. hinge** charnière *f*; *Tech* **b. joint** joint *m* abouté, soudure *f* bout à bout; **b. welding** soudure bout à bout

butt[3] n **1** *Mil (mound)* butte *f* (de tir); **the butts** le champ de tir **2** *(target)*, *Fig (of humour, joke)* cible *f*

butt[4] n *(with head)* coup *m* de tête *ou Fam* de boule; *(of ram etc)* coup de tête
vt *(of person)* donner un coup de tête *ou Fam* de boule à; *(of ram etc)* donner un coup de tête à
► **butt in** vi interrompre la conversation; **if I could just b. in here** permettez-moi d'intervenir
► **butt into** vt insep **to b. into the conversation** interrompre la conversation
► **butt out** vi *Fam* **b. out!** ne t'en mêle pas!; **I decided to b. out** j'ai décidé de rester en dehors de ça

butter ['bʌtər] n beurre *m*; *Fig* **b. wouldn't melt in her mouth** on lui donnerait le bon Dieu sans confession
vt **1** *(bread)* beurrer **2** *Culin (vegetables etc)* mettre du beurre dans

▸▸**b. bean** = sorte de haricot de Lima; **b. cream** crème *f* au beurre; **b. dish** beurrier *m*; **b. knife** couteau *m* à beurre; *EU* **b. mountain** montagne *f* de beurre
▸**butter up** *VT SEP Fam* passer de la pommade à

butterball ['bʌtəbɔːl] **N** *Am Fam (plump person)* personne *f* boulotte

buttercup ['bʌtəkʌp] **N** renoncule *f* des champs, *Fam* bouton-d'or *m*, *pl* boutons-d'or

butterfat ['bʌtəfæt] **N** *(of milk)* matière *f* grasse

butterfingered ['bʌtəfɪŋgəd] **ADJ** *Fam* maladroit, empoté; **to be b.** tout laisser tomber

butterfingers ['bʌtəfɪŋgəz] **N** *Fam* maladroit, -oite, empoté, -ée *(qui laisse tout tomber)*; **b.!** espèce de maladroit!

butterfly ['bʌtəflaɪ] **N 1** *(insect)* papillon *m* (diurne); *Fig (person)* papillon *m*; *Fam* **to have butterflies (in one's stomach)** avoir l'estomac noué, avoir le trac **2** *Swimming* (nage *f* ou brasse *f*) papillon *m*
▸▸**b. net** filet *m* à papillons; *Tech* **b. nut** papillon, écrou *m* à ailettes; *St Exch* **b. spread** spread *m* papillon; *Tech* **b. valve** (soupape *f* à) papillon; *Swimming* **b. stroke** (nage ou brasse) papillon

buttermilk ['bʌtəmɪlk] **N** babeurre *m*

butterscotch ['bʌtəskɒtʃ] **N** caramel *m* (dur) au beurre

buttery[1] ['bʌtərɪ] **N** *(esp in some English universities)* office *f*, dépense *f*, restaurant *m*
▸▸**b. hatch** passe-plats *m inv*

buttery[2] **ADJ** *(taste)* de beurre; **with a b. texture** avec la consistance du beurre; **b. fingers** doigts pleins de beurre

butthead ['bʌthed] **N** *Am Fam* crétin, -ine

butting ['bʌtɪŋ] **N** *(by person)* coups *mpl* de tête; *(by ram, goat)* coups de corne; **he was disqualified for b.** il a été disqualifié pour avoir donné un/des coup(s) de tête

buttock ['bʌtək] **N** fesse *f*, **the buttocks** les fesses, le derrière; **cross b.** *(in wrestling)* ceinture *f* arrière ou à rebours, tour *m* de hanche

button ['bʌtən] **N 1** *(on dress etc)* bouton *m*; **as bright as a b.** *(child)* vif, éveillé; *Am* **she's as cute as a b.** elle est trognon; *Fam* **it's not worth a b.** ça ne vaut pas un clou; *Fam* **I don't care a b.** je m'en fiche pas mal; **a b. nose** un petit nez; **chocolate buttons** *(sweets)* pastilles *fpl* de chocolat; *Br Old-fashioned* **buttons** *(pageboy)* groom *m*
2 *(for doorbell etc)* bouton *m*; *Comput (on mouse)* bouton; *(for menu selection)* case *f*, *Fam* **to be right on the b.** *(of answer)* tomber pile; *Fam* **you've hit it right on the b.** tu as mis en plein dans le mille
3 *Am (badge)* badge *m*
4 *(of foil)* bouton *m*, mouche *f*
VT 1 *(garment)* boutonner; *Fam* **b. your lip or it, keep your lip buttoned** ferme-la, la ferme, boucle-la **2** *Fencing (foil)* moucheter
VI *(of garment)* se boutonner; **a dress that buttons at the back/side** une robe qui se boutonne par derrière/sur le côté
▸▸**b. mushroom** champignon *m* de couche ou de Paris
▸**button up** *VT SEP* **1** *(fasten)* boutonner; **buttoned up** *(person)* boutonné jusqu'au menton **2** *Fig* **we've got the deal all buttoned up** l'affaire est dans le sac

button-down **ADJ** *(collar)* à pointes boutonnées; **b. shirt** chemise *f* à col boutonné

buttoned-up ['bʌtənd-] **ADJ** *Fam (taciturn)* constipé

buttonhole ['bʌtənhəʊl] **N 1** *(in garment)* boutonnière *f* **2** *Surg* boutonnière *f*, petite incision *f* **3** *(flower)* (fleur *f* portée à la) boutonnière *f*
VT *Fam* **to b. sb** coincer qn
▸▸*Sewing* **b. stitch** point *m* de boutonnière

button-through **ADJ** **b. dress** robe *f* chemisier; **b. skirt** jupe *f* boutonnée jusqu'en bas

buttress ['bʌtrɪs] **N** *Archit* contrefort *m*; *Fig* pilier *m*, *Lit* étai *m*
VT *Constr* arc-bouter, étayer; *Fig* étayer

butty ['bʌtɪ] **N** *Eng Dial* sandwich *m*

buxom ['bʌksəm] **ADJ** *(full-bosomed)* à forte poitrine; *(plump)* bien en chair, aux formes rebondies ou plantureuses

BUY [baɪ] **N** achat *m*; **a good/bad b.** un bon/mauvais achat, une bonne/mauvaise affaire
VT *(pt, pp bought* [bɔːt]*)* **1** acheter (**from** à); *(company)* racheter; **to b. sb sth** acheter qch à qn; **to b. sth for sb** acheter qch pour qn; **to b. sth cheap** acheter qch (à) bon marché; **money can't b. you love/health/happiness** l'amour/la santé/le bonheur ne s'achète pas; **a dearly bought advantage** un avantage chèrement payé; *Fam* **he's bought it,** *Am* **he's bought the farm** *(is dead)* il a passé l'arme à gauche; *Fig* **to b. time** gagner du temps
2 *Pej (bribe) (witness etc)* acheter
3 *Fam (believe)* gober, croire; **I won't b. that!** tu ne me feras pas gober ou croire ça!; **I'll b. that!** *(believe it)* je te/le/*etc* crois!; *(that's good, I agree)* d'accord!
VI *Fin* **to b. on credit** acheter à crédit ou à terme; **to b. forward** acheter à terme; **to b. on margin** acheter à découvert; **to b. spot** acheter au comptant
▸▸*St Exch* **b. order** ordre *m* d'achat
▸**buy back** *VT SEP (house etc)* racheter (**from** à)
▸**buy in** *VT SEP (supplies etc)* s'approvisionner en
▸**buy into** *VT INSEP (purchase share in) (business)* acheter une part de
▸**buy off** *VT SEP Fam* acheter; **she refused to be bought off** elle refusa de se laisser acheter
▸**buy out** *VT SEP* **1** *Com (partner etc)* (r)acheter la part de, désintéresser; **he was bought out for £50,000** on lui a (r)acheté sa part pour 50 000 livres
2 *Mil* racheter; **to b. oneself out** racheter son contrat avec l'armée
▸**buy up** *VT SEP (surplus grain, wine etc)* acheter; *(in anticipation of shortages)* rafler; *Fam* **you must have bought up the entire store** tu as dû dévaliser tout le magasin

buyback ['baɪbæk] **N** rachat *m*
▸▸**b. arrangement** accord *m* de reprise; **b. right** droit *m* de rachat

buyer ['baɪər] **N 1** *(consumer)* acheteur, -euse **2** *(for shop)* acheteur, -euse, responsable *mf* des achats; **head b.** acheteur principal
▸▸*Mktg* **b. behaviour** comportement *m* de l'acheteur; *Fin* **b. credit** crédit-acheteur *m*, *pl* crédits-acheteurs; *Fin* **b. credit guarantee** garantie *f* de crédit-acheteur; **b.'s market** marché *m* demandeur ou d'acheteurs

buyer-readiness **N** *Mktg* prédisposition *f* à l'achat

buying ['baɪɪŋ] **N** achat *m*; **b. and selling** l'achat et la vente
▸▸*Mktg* **b. behaviour** comportement *m* d'achat; **b. centre** centrale *f* d'achat; *Mktg* **b. decision** décision *f* d'achat; **b. department** service *m* (des) achats; **b. group** centrale d'achat; **b. office** centrale ou bureau *m* d'achat; *Fin* **b. power** pouvoir *m* d'achat; **b. ring** groupement *m* d'achat

buy-out **N** *Com (of company)* rachat *m*; *(of partner)* désintéressement *m*

buy-sell agreement **N** *Com, Law* protocole *m* ou accord *m* d'achat et de vente

buzz [bʌz] **N 1** *(of insect)*, *Fig (of conversation)* bourdonnement *m*; *(of plane)* vrombissement *m*; *Radio* ronflement *m*; **to give sb a b.** *Tel Fam* donner un coup de fil à qn; *Sl (thrill)* faire vibrer qn; *Sl being recognized gives him a b.* ça l'éclate d'être reconnu; *Sl* **there's nothing quite like the b. you get from skiing** rien ne vaut le frisson qu'on ressent en skiant; *Sl* **she gets a real b. out of those grandchildren of hers** elle prend beaucoup de plaisir à s'occuper de ses petits-enfants **2** *(rumour, gossip)* rumeur *f*, **the b. is that he's been fired** on murmure qu'il a été renvoyé
VI *(of insect, ears)* bourdonner; *(of aircraft)* vrombir; **the whole town was buzzing with excitement** la ville était en pleine agitation; **she is buzzing with ideas** elle a plein d'idées; **her head was buzzing with ideas** elle avait la tête bourdonnante d'idées
VT *Fam* **1** *Aviat (plane, ship)* frôler; *(building, town)* raser **2** *(call) (on telephone)* donner un coup de fil à; *(on intercom)* appeler (à l'Interphone®)
▸▸**b. word** mot *m* en vogue
▸**buzz about, buzz around** **VI** *(of bees, flies)* voler en bourdonnant; *Fam (of person)* s'activer; **I like to hear the bees buzzing about** j'aime entendre le bourdonnement des abeilles
▸**buzz off** **VI** *Br Fam* décamper; **b. off!** allez, file ou décampe!

buzzard ['bʌzəd] **N** buse *f*, busard *m*

buzzcut ['bʌzkʌt] **N** coupe *f* en brosse

buzzer ['bʌzər] **N** *(device)* sonnette *f*, *(sound)* sonnerie *f*, **there's the b.** *(on machine)* ça sonne; *(at door)* on sonne

buzzing ['bʌzɪŋ] **N** *(of insect), Med (of ears)* bourdonnement *m*; **a b. noise** un bourdonnement
ADJ *Fam (party, nightclub)* hyper animé; *(person)* speed, speedé

buzz-kill **N** *Am Fam* rabat-joie *mf inv*

BY [baɪ]

| **PREP** par **1, 3, 4, 11** ■ près de **2** ■ au bord de **2** ■ devant **5** ■ à **4, 11** ■ en **4** ■ de **10, 12, 15** |
| **ADV** près **1** ■ de côté **2** |

PREP 1 *(agent)* par; **to be punished by sb** être puni par qn; **to be loved by sb** être aimé de qn; **made by hand** fait à la main; **to have a child by sb** avoir un enfant de qn; **she has a daughter by her first marriage/husband** elle a une fille de son premier mariage/mari; *Lit* **to die by one's own hand** mourir de ses propres mains; **he took me by the arm/hand** il m'a pris le bras/la main; **to live by one's work** vivre de son travail; **what do you mean by that?** qu'entendez-vous par là?; **by force** de force; **by way of a joke** par plaisanterie; **by chance** par hasard; **by heart** par cœur
2 *(near) (person)* (au)près de, à côté de; *(thing)* près de, à côté de; *(in compass reading)* quart; **sitting by the fire** assis près du feu; **by the side of the road** au bord de la route; **by the sea** au bord de la mer; **north by east** nord quart nord-est
3 *(via)* par; **to go by the same road** aller par la même route; **by land and sea** par terre et par mer; **by land/sea** par (voie de) terre/mer
4 *(means of transport)* **to travel by rail** voyager en ou par le chemin de fer; **to come by car/motorcycle** venir en voiture/à motocyclette
5 *(past)* **he walked by the churchyard** il est passé devant le cimetière; **she drove by me** elle m'a dépassé *(en voiture)*
6 *(time: at or before)* **he will be here by three o'clock** il sera ici avant ou pour trois heures; **you will hear from us by Monday** vous aurez de nos nouvelles d'ici lundi; **he ought to be here by now** or **by this time** il

devrait être déjà ici; **I'll be gone by the time (that) you have finished** quand vous aurez fini, je serai parti; **you'll have it by tomorrow** vous l'aurez pour demain; **they were tired by the end of the day** ils étaient fatigués à la fin de la journée; **by 1990** *(talking about the past)* en 1990; **by 2025** *(talking about the future)* d'ici (à) 2025

7 *(during)* **by day** de jour, le jour; **by night** de nuit, la nuit; **by daylight** au jour, à la lumière du jour

8 by oneself (tout) seul; **to do sth (all) by oneself** faire qch (tout) seul

9 *(+ doing sth)* **to earn one's living by teaching** gagner sa vie en enseignant; **I shall gain/lose by (doing) it** j'y gagnerai/j'y perdrai; **to begin/end by laughing** commencer/finir par rire; **we shall lose nothing by waiting** nous n'avons rien à perdre en attendant

10 *(according to)* **to call sb by his name** appeler qn par son nom; **cheerful by nature** gai par nature, d'un naturel gai; **by my watch** à ma montre; **to set one's watch by the time signal** régler sa montre sur le signal horaire; **to judge sb by appearances** juger qn sur les apparences; **I can tell by your face** on le voit à votre visage; **he's a plumber by trade** il est plombier de son métier; **I know him by name/sight** je le connais de nom/vue

11 *(with numbers, measurements etc)* **to divide by three** diviser par trois; **three metres by two** trois mètres sur deux; **to sell sth by the pound/dozen** vendre qch à la livre/douzaine; **to rent a house by the year** louer une maison à l'année; **by degrees** par degrés; **by turns** chacun son tour, tour à tour; **they did it by turns** ils l'ont fait chacun leur tour; **he was happy and sad by turns** il était tour à tour heureux et triste; **one by one** un à un; **to come in by twos** *or* **two by two** entrer deux par deux; **little by little** peu à peu, petit à petit; **day by day** jour par jour, de jour en jour

12 *(to the extent of)* de; **longer by two metres** plus long de deux mètres; **by far** de loin; **they overcharged me by ten per cent**

ils m'ont compté dix pour cent en trop

13 *(in oaths)* **by God** au nom de Dieu; **to swear by all one holds sacred** jurer par tout ce qu'on a de plus sacré

14 *Mil* **by the right, quick march!** ≃ en avant, marche!

15 *(with regard to)* de; **to do one's duty by sb** faire son devoir envers qn; **she's Canadian by birth** elle est canadienne de naissance; **he's an actor by trade** *or* **profession** il est acteur de profession; *Fam* **it's all right by me!** ça (me) va!, d'accord!; *Fam* **if that's okay by you** si ça te va, si tu es d'accord

ADV 1 *(near)* près; **close by** tout près, ici près, tout à côté; **by and large** dans l'ensemble

2 *(aside)* **to lay** *or* **set** *or* **put sth by** mettre qch de côté; **to put** *or* **lay money by** mettre de l'argent de côté

3 to go *or* **pass by** *(elapse)* passer; **time goes by** le temps passe; **to come** *or* **stop by** *(to see sb, fetch sth)* passer

4 by and by *(soon)* bientôt, tantôt; *(in the immediate future)* tout à l'heure; **by the by(e)**, **by the way** à propos

---

bye[1] [baɪ] **N 1** *Cr* balle *f* passée **2** *Sport* **to have a b.** *(of player)* être exempt *(d'une épreuve, d'un match, dans un tournoi)* **3 by the b. ...** à propos ...

bye[2] **INT** *Fam* au revoir!, salut!; **b. for now!** à bientôt!

bye-bye *Fam* **INT** salut!, au revoir!
N *(in children's language)* **to go to b., to go bye-byes** aller faire dodo

bye-law **N =** bylaw

by-election **N** *Pol* élection *f* partielle

Byelorussia [bɪeləʊ'rʌʃə] **N** Biélorussie *f*

Byelorussian [bɪeləʊ'rʌʃən] **ADJ** biélorusse **N** Biélorusse *mf*

bygone ['baɪɡɒn] **ADJ** passé, ancien, d'autrefois; **in b. days** autrefois, dans l'ancien temps
NPL to let bygones be bygones oublier le passé

bylaw ['baɪlɔ:] **N** arrêté *m* municipal; *Am*

Law **bylaws** *(of company)* statuts *mpl* de société

by-line **N 1** *Journ* signature *f*, **a report under the b. of Mary Jones** un reportage signé Mary Jones **2** *Sport* limites *fpl* du terrain

BYO [bi:waɪ'əʊ] **N** *Austr* *(abbr* **bring your own)** = restaurant *m* qui ne sert pas d'alcool et où l'on peut apporter sa boisson

BYOB [bi:waɪəʊ'bi:] **ADJ** *Fam abbr* **bring your own bottle**

bypass ['baɪpɑːs] **N 1** *Aut* rocade *f*, **temporary b.** déviation *f* **2** *Med* pontage *m*; **she's had a b., she's had b. surgery** on lui a fait un pontage **3** *Tech* (conduit *m* de) dérivation *f* **4** *Elec* dérivation *f*
VT 1 *(town etc)* *(of motorist)* contourner, éviter; *(of road)* contourner; *Fig (middleman etc)* court-circuiter **2** *Tech (steam etc)* amener en dérivation **3** *Elec* mettre hors circuit
▸▸ *Aut* **b. filter** filtre *m* en dérivation; *Tech* **b. valve** soupape *f* *ou* clapet *m* de dérivation, clapet by-pass

by-play **N** *Theat etc (action)* jeu *m* accessoire, jeu de second plan; *(speech)* aparté *m* mimé, jeu muet

by-product **N** *Ind* sous-produit *m*, *pl* sous-produits, dérivé *m*; *Fig* effet *m* secondaire

byre ['baɪər] **N** *esp Scot* étable *f* à vaches

byroad ['baɪrəʊd] **N** petite route *f*

bystander ['baɪstændər] **N** spectateur, -trice

byte [baɪt] **N** *Comput* **(eight-bit) b.** octet *m*

byway ['baɪweɪ] **N** petite route *f*, *Fig* **byways of history** à-côtés *mpl* de l'histoire

byword ['baɪwɜːd] **N** *Arch* proverbe *m*, dicton *m*; *Fig* **to have become a b.** être devenu proverbial; **she is a b. for punctuality** elle est l'exemple même de la ponctualité; **she has become a b. for punctuality** sa ponctualité est devenue proverbiale

Byzantine [bɪ'zæntaɪn, baɪ-] **ADJ** *Hist, Fig* byzantin; **the B. Empire** l'Empire *m* byzantin **N** *Hist* Byzantin, -ine

Byzantium [bɪ'zæntɪəm, baɪ-] **N** *Antiq* Byzance *f*

C¹, c [siː] N **1** *(letter)* C, c *m*; **two c's** deux c **2** *Mus* do *m*, ut *m*; **in C sharp** en do dièse **3** *Sch (grade)* **to get a C** avoir une note moyenne, ≃ avoir entre 10 et 13 sur 20
▸▸ *Am Fam* **C note** billet *m* de cent dollars

C² *(abbr* **centigrade)** C.

c, ca *(abbr* **circa)** env.

CA [siːˈeɪ] N *Br Fin abbr* **chartered accountant**

C/A, c/a *Banking (abbr* **current** *or* **cheque** *or Am* **checking account)** C/C *m*, CCB *m*

CAA [siːeɪˈeɪ] N *Br Aviat, Admin (abbr* **Civil Aviation Authority)** = organisme *m* de réglementation de l'aviation civile

CAB *abbr* **Citizens' Advice Bureau**

cab [kæb] N **1** *(taxi)* taxi *m*; *Arch (horse-drawn)* fiacre *m*; **to call** *or* **hail a c.** appeler *ou* héler un taxi; **by c.** en taxi; **hansom c.** cab *m* **2** *(of truck, train, crane etc)* cabine *f*, **driver's c.** cabine *ou* poste *m* de conduite
▸▸ **c. driver** chauffeur *m* de taxi; **c. rank** station *f* de taxis

cabal [kəˈbæl] N *esp Pol, usu Pej* **1** *(plot)* cabale *f* **2** *(group)* coterie *f*

cabana [kəˈbænə] N *(room by beach/swimming pool)* cabine *f* de bain

cabaret [ˈkæbəreɪ] N **1** *(show)* spectacle *m* de music-hall *ou* de cabaret; **she's in c.** c'est une artiste de cabaret **2** *(nightclub, restaurant)* cabaret *m*
▸▸ **c. act** numéro *m* de cabaret; **c. artist** artiste *mf* de cabaret; **c. show** *(in nightclub)* spectacle de music-hall *ou* de cabaret

cabbage [ˈkæbɪdʒ] N **1** chou *m*, *pl* choux; **red c.** chou rouge **2** *Fam (person)* légume *m*; **the accident left him a c.** l'accident en a fait un légume, il est à l'état végétatif depuis l'accident
▸▸ **c. lettuce** laitue *f* pommée; **c. palm** *(tree)* palmiste *m*; **c. rose** rose *f* centfeuilles; **c. white** *(butterfly)* piéride *f* du chou

cab(b)alistic [kæbəˈlɪstɪk] ADJ cabalistique

cabbie, cabby [ˈkæbɪ] N *Fam* chauffeur *m* de taxi

caber [ˈkeɪbər] N *Scot Sport* **tossing the c.** = concours *m* de lancer d'un tronc d'arbre *(dans les jeux des Highlands)*

cabin [ˈkæbɪn] N **1** *(hut)* cabane *f*, case *f*, *Br Rail (signal box)* poste *m ou* cabine *f* d'aiguillage **2** *Naut* cabine *f*, *(on barge etc)* cabane *f*, *Aviat* cabine, habitacle *m* **3** *Aut (of passenger car)* habitacle *m*; *(of lorry)* cabine *f*
▸▸ *Aviat* **c. attendant** *(male)* steward *m*; *(female)* hôtesse *f* de l'air; *Aviat* **c. baggage** bagages *mpl* à main; *Naut* **c. boy** mousse *m*; *Aviat* **c. crew** personnel *m* de cabine; *Naut* **c. cruiser** cruiser *m*, yacht *m* de croisière; *Aviat* **c. staff** personnel *m* de cabine; **c. steward** steward *m*; **c. trunk** malle-cabine *f*, *pl* malles-cabine

cabinet [ˈkæbɪnɪt] N **1** *(piece of furniture)* meuble *m* à tiroirs; *(for TV)* meuble télé; *(for video)* meuble vidéo; *(for stereo system)* meuble hi-fi; **filing c.** classeur *m*; *(for index cards)* fichier *m*; **bathroom c.** armoire *f* de toilette *ou* de salle de bains; **medicine c.** armoire à pharmacie **2** *Pol* cabinet *m*, ministère *m*; **to form a c.** former un cabinet *ou* un ministère **3** *Arch (room)* cabinet *m*
▸▸ *Pol* **c. meeting** conseil *m* des ministres; *Pol* **c. minister** ministre *m* siégeant au cabinet; *Pol* **c. reshuffle** remaniement *m* ministériel

cabinet-maker N ébéniste *mf*

cabinet-making N ébénisterie *f*

cable [ˈkeɪb(ə)l] N **1** *Naut* câble *m*; **c.('s) length** *(measure)* encâblure *f* **2** *Elec* câble *m*; **to lay a c.** poser un câble; **overhead/underground/submarine c.** câble aérien/sous-terrain/sous-marin; **twin c.** câble à deux conducteurs **3** *Tel* câble *m*, câblogramme *m* **4** *(cable TV)* câble *m*; **it's only available on c.** ça n'existe que sur le câble **5** *Knitting* torsade *f*
▸ VT *Tel (message)* câbler; **to c. sb** câbler à qn, envoyer un câble à qn; **to c. sth to sb** câbler qch à qn
▸ VI *Tel* câbler; **to c. to sb** envoyer un câble à qn
▸▸ *Tel* **c. address** adresse *f* télégraphique; *TV* **c. broadcasting** télédiffusion *f* par câble; **c. car** téléphérique *m*; *TV* **c. company** câblo-opérateur *m*, *pl* câblo-opérateurs; *TV* **c. distribution** câblodistribution *f*, distribution *f* par câble; *Comput* **c. modem** modem-câble *m*, *pl* modems-câble; *Knitting* **c. needle** aiguille *f* à torsades; *TV* **c. network** réseau *m* câblé; *TV* **C. News Network** = réseau d'information américain par câble et satellite; *TV* **c. operator** câblo-opérateur; **c. railway** funiculaire *m*; *Phot* **c. release** déclencheur *m*; *Tel, Naut* **c. ship** câblier *m*; *Knitting* **c. stitch** point *m* de torsade; *TV* **c. television** télévision *f* par câble; *Aut* **c. terminal** cosse *f*; **c. transfer** *(of money)* virement *m* télégraphique

cabled [ˈkeɪb(ə)ld] ADJ câblé
▸▸ **c. network** réseau *m* câblé

cablegram [ˈkeɪb(ə)lgræm] N *Tel* câblogramme *m*

cableless [ˈkeɪb(ə)lɪs] ADJ sans câble

cableway [ˈkeɪb(ə)lweɪ] N téléphérique *m*

cabling [ˈkeɪb(ə)lɪŋ] N *Elec etc (cables)* câbles *mpl*, câblage *m*

cabman, *pl* **cabmen** [ˈkæbmən] N chauffeur *m* de taxi

caboodle [kəˈbuːd(ə)l] N *Fam* **the whole (kit and) c.** tout le bazar *ou* bataclan

caboose [kəˈbuːs] N **1** *Am Rail (of goods train)* fourgon *m* de queue **2** *Am Sl (jail)* tôle *f*, taule *f* **3** *Can (for loggers etc)* baraquement *m* mobile **4** *Naut (kitchen)* cuisine *f*, coquerie *f*

cabotage [ˈkæbəˈtɑːdʒ] N *Aviat, Naut* cabotage *m*
▸▸ **c. fare** tarif *m* de cabotage; **c. route** itinéraire *m* de cabotage

CAC 40 index [kæk] N *StExch* indice *m* CAC 40

cacao [kəˈkɑːəʊ, kəˈkeɪəʊ] N *Bot* **1** *(tree)* cacaotier *m*, cacaoyer *m* **2** *(bean)* (graine *f* de *ou* fève *f* de) cacao *m*
▸▸ **c. bean** (graine *ou* fève de) cacao; **c. pod** cabosse *f*; **c. tree** cacaotier, cacaoyer

cache [kæʃ] N **1** *(arms, drugs etc that have been hidden)* objets *mpl* cachés; **a c. of guns/drugs** une cache d'armes/de drogues; **the c. had a value of ...** les armes/drogues/*etc* cachées là avaient une valeur de ... **2** *(hiding place)* cache *f* **3** *Comput* antémémoire *f*, mémoire-cache *f*, *pl* mémoires-cache
▸ VT **1** *(hide)* cacher **2** *Comput (data)* mettre en antémémoire *ou* en mémoire-cache
▸▸ *Comput* **c. memory** antémémoire, mémoire-cache

cachet [ˈkæʃeɪ] N *Pharm, Fig* cachet *m*; *Mktg* label *m*; *Fig* **to have a certain c.** avoir un certain cachet

cack [kæk] *Br Sl* N **1** *(excrement)* caca *m* **2** *(nonsense)* conneries *fpl*; **don't talk c.!** arrête de raconter n'importe quoi! **3** *(worthless things)* camelote *f*; **the film was a load of c.** le film était nul
▸ ADJ *(bad)* nul; **her music is c.** sa musique est nulle
▸ VT **he was cacking himself** *(scared)* il faisait dans son froc

cack-handed [-ˈhændɪd] ADJ *Fam (clumsy)* maladroit

cackle [ˈkæk(ə)l] N **1** *(of hen)* caquet *m* **2** *Fig Fam (talking)* caquet *m*, jacassement *m*; *(laughter)* gloussement(s) *m(pl)*; **cut the c.!** la ferme!
▸ VI **1** *(of hen)* caqueter; *(of goose)* cacarder **2** *Fig Fam (talk)* caqueter, jacasser; *(laugh)* glousser

cacophonous [kəˈkɒfənəs] ADJ cacophonique

cacophony [kəˈkɒfənɪ] N cacophonie *f*

cactus, *pl* **cacti** [ˈkæktəs, -tiː, -taɪ] N cactus *m*

CAD N **1** [kæd] *Comput (abbr* **computer-assisted design)** CAO *f* **2** [siːeɪˈdiː] *Com (* **cash against documents)** comptant *m* contre documents

cad [kæd] N *Br Old-fashioned* mufle *m*, goujat *m*

cadaver [kəˈdævər] N *esp Am Med* cadavre *m*

cadaverous [kəˈdævərəs] ADJ **1** *(pale) (complexion etc)* cadavéreux, cadavérique **2** *(haggard) (appearance, face)* cadavérique

CAD/CAM [ˈkædkæm] N *Comput (abbr* **computer-assisted design/computer-assisted manufacture)** CFAO *f*

caddie ['kædɪ] *Golf* N caddie *m*
 ▸ vɪ **to c. for sb** servir de caddie à qn
 ▸▸**c. car, c. cart** chariot *m* (pour crosses de golf)

caddish ['kædɪʃ] ADJ *Br Old-fashioned (behaviour)* de mufle; *(person)* mufle; **a c. thing to do** une preuve de muflerie

caddy[1] ['kædɪ] N**(tea) c.** boîte *f* à thé

caddy[2] N, vɪ = **caddie**

cadence ['keɪdəns] N cadence *f*, rythme *m*; *Mus* cadence

cadenza [kə'denzə] N *Mus* cadence *f*

cadet [kə'det] N *Mil etc* élève *mf* d'une école militaire, élève officier; *Sch* élève de la préparation militaire
 ▸▸*Mil* **c. corps** peloton *m* d'instruction militaire; *(for police training)* corps *m* d'élèves policiers

cadge [kædʒ] *Fam, often Pej* vɪ mendier, quémander (**from, off** à); *(money, cigarette)* taxer, taper (**from, off** à); **can I c. a lift?** ça ne t'ennuierait pas de me déposer?
 ▸ vɪ mendier

cadger ['kædʒər] N *Fam Pej* quémandeur, -euse; *(of cigarette, money)* tapeur, -euse

Cadiz [kə'dɪz] N Cadix

cadmium ['kædmɪəm] N *Miner* cadmium *m*

cadre [kɑːdər] N *Mil, Pol* cadre *m*

CAE [siːeɪ'iː] N *Comput (abbr* **computer-aided engineering**) ingénierie *f* assistée par ordinateur

caecum, *pl* **caeca,** *Am* **cecum,** *pl* **ceca** ['siːkəm, -ə] N *Anat* cæcum *m*

Caesar ['siːzər] N César; **Julius C.** Jules César
 ▸▸*Culin* **C. salad** = salade *f* à base de romaine, de croûtons et d'une vinaigrette additionnée d'œuf

Caesarean, Caesarian [sɪ'zeərɪən] N1 *Obst* césarienne *f*; **it was a C.** *(of delivery)* on lui a fait une césarienne; **to be a C.** *(of baby)* être né par césarienne; **she has to have a C.** il va falloir lui faire une césarienne; **the baby was born by C.** l'enfant est né par césarienne 2 *Hist* Césarien, -ienne
 ADJ césarien
 ▸▸*Obst* **C. section** césarienne

caesura [sɪ'zjʊərə] N *Liter* césure *f*

café ['kæfeɪ] N*(in UK)* ≃ café-restaurant *m*, *pl* cafés-restaurants; *(in rest of Europe)* café *m*

> **Café**
> En Grande-Bretagne, le mot "café" désigne une sorte de snack où l'on peut prendre un repas léger et boire du thé ou du café.

cafeteria [kæfɪ'tɪərɪə] N*(in large store)* cafétéria *f*; *(for employees)* cantine *f* en self-service

caff [kæf] N *Br Sl* ≃ café-restaurant *m*, *pl* cafés-restaurants

caffeine ['kæfiːn] N caféine *f*

caffeine-free ADJ *(without caffeine)* sans caféine

caftan ['kæftæn] N caf(e)tan *m*

cage [keɪdʒ] N1 *(for birds, animals etc)* cage *f* 2 *(of lift)* cabine *f* 3 *Min* cage *f* d'extraction
 vɪ *(bird etc)* mettre en cage; **caged animal** animal *m* en cage; **I feel caged in** je me sens enfermé
 ▸▸**c. bird** oiseau *m* d'agrément *ou* d'appartement

cagey ['keɪdʒɪ] ADJ *Fam (careful)* prudent, circonspect; *(not frank)* cachottier; **to be c. about one's age** ne pas vouloir avouer son âge, rester vague concernant son âge

cagily ['keɪdʒɪlɪ] ADV *(carefully)* très prudemment; **to answer c.** *(deliberately vaguely)* donner une réponse vague

caginess ['keɪdʒɪnɪs] N *(carefulness)* prudence *f*, *(deliberate vagueness)* vague *m*; **there was a certain c. in her replies** elle évitait de répondre en restant dans le vague

cagoule [kə'guːl] N anorak *m* léger et long *(avec capuche)*

cahoots [kə'huːts] NPL *Fam* **to be in c. (with sb)** être de mèche (avec qn)

CAI [siːeɪ'aɪ] N *Comput (abbr* **computer-aided instruction**) IAO *f*

caiman ['keɪmən] N caïman *m*

Cain [keɪn] N *Bible* Caïn; *Fam* **to raise C.** *(make noise)* faire un bruit *ou* un fracas de tous les diables; *(make scene)* faire une scène monumentale

cairn [keən] N1 *(of stones)* cairn *m*, tumulus *m* de pierres 2 *(dog)* terrier *m* cairn
 ▸▸**c. terrier** terrier cairn

cairngorm [keən'gɔːm] N *(gem)* pierre *f* de cairngorm

Cairo ['kaɪrəʊ] N Le Caire

caisson ['keɪs(ə)n] N1 *Constr (for working underwater)* caisson *m* 2 *Naut (in dry dock)* bateau-porte *m*, *pl* bateaux-portes 3 *Mil (for ammunition)* caisson *m*
 ▸▸*Med* **c. disease** maladie *f* des caissons

cajole [kə'dʒəʊl] vɪ enjôler; **to c. sb into/out of doing sth** persuader/dissuader qn de faire qch

cajolery [kə'dʒəʊlərɪ] N cajolerie(s) *f(pl)*

Cajun ['keɪdʒən] ADJ *(language, music, recipe)* cajun *inv*
 N1 *(person)* Cajun *mf* 2 *Ling* cajun *m*

cake [keɪk] N *Culin* gâteau *m*; *(small)* pâtisserie *f*, **(small) cakes** (petits) gâteaux, pâtisseries; **fruit c.** cake *m*; *Am Fam* **that takes the c.!** ça c'est le comble *ou* le bouquet!; *Fig Fam* **it's a piece of c.** c'est simple comme bonjour, c'est du gâteau!; *Fam* **they're going** *or* **selling like hot cakes** ça se vend comme des petits pains; *Prov* **you can't have your c. and eat it** on ne peut pas avoir le beurre et l'argent du beurre; **a big c. of mud** un gros paquet de boue 2 *Old-fashioned (of soap)* pain *m*; *(of chocolate, paint)* tablette *f*
 vɪ *(solidify)* former une croûte; *(of mud)* sécher; *(of blood etc)* coaguler
 ▸▸**c. mix** préparation *f* (instantanée) pour gâteau; **c. shop** pâtisserie *f*; **c. stand** plat *m* à gâteaux; **c. tin** moule *m* à gâteau

caked [keɪkt] ADJ *(mud)* séché; *(blood)* coagulé; **c. with mud/blood** couvert de boue/sang séché(e)

cakehole ['keɪkhəʊl] N *Br Fam* bouche *f*, **shut your c.** ferme-la!, ferme ton clapet!

cakewalk ['keɪkwɔːk] N *(dance)* cake-walk *m*, *pl* cake-walks; *Am Fig Fam* **it was a c.** *(very easy)* c'était du gâteau

CAL [kæl] N *Comput (abbr* **computer-aided learning**) EAO *m*

Cal *abbr* **California**

calabash ['kæləbæʃ] N1 *(tree)* calebassier *m* 2 *(bottle)* calebasse *f*, gourde *f*
 ▸▸**c. gourd** calebasse, gourde; **c. tree** calebassier

calaboose ['kæləbuːs] N *Am Sl (prison)* taule *f*, tôle *f*; **ten days in the c.** dix jours de taule *ou* tôle

calamine ['kæləmaɪn] N calamine *f*
 ▸▸**c. lotion** lotion *f* calmante à la calamine

calamitous [kə'læmɪtəs] ADJ désastreux

calamity [kə'læmɪtɪ] N désastre *m*, calamité *f*
 ▸▸*Fam* **C. Jane** Miss Catastrophe *f*

calcareous [kæl'keərɪəs] ADJ *Geol etc* calcaire

calceolaria [kælsɪə'leərɪə] N *(plant)* calcéolaire *f*

calcification [kælsɪfɪ'keɪʃən] N calcification *f*

calcify ['kælsɪfaɪ] *Chem etc* vɪ calcifier
 vɪ se calcifier

calcium ['kælsɪəm] N *Chem* calcium *m*
 ▸▸**c. carbide** carbure *m* de calcium; **c. chloride** chlorure *m* de calcium; **c. deficiency** carence *f* en calcium

calculable ['kælkjʊləb(ə)l] ADJ calculable

calculate ['kælkjʊleɪt] vɪ *(sum, figure, amount, distance)* calculer 2 *(intend)* calculated to do sth fait pour faire qch; **the remark was calculated to shock** la remarque était délibérément choquante 3 *Am Fam (think)* croire, supposer (**that** que)
 vɪ *esp Am (rely)* **to c. on sth/on doing sth** compter sur qch/compter faire qch

calculated ['kælkjʊleɪtɪd] ADJ *(insolence etc)* délibéré, calculé; *(crime)* prémédité; **words c. to reassure us** paroles propres à nous rassurer
 ▸▸*Comput* **c. field** champ *m* calculé; **c. risk** risque *m* calculé

calculating ['kælkjʊleɪtɪŋ] ADJ 1 *Pej (person)* calculateur, -trice; **this was not the action of a c. murderer** ce n'était pas un meurtre prémédité 2 *(cautious)* prudent, mesuré
 ▸▸*Math* **c. machine** machine *f* à calculer

calculation [kælkjʊ'leɪʃən] N calcul *m*; *(estimate)* estimation *f*; **to make a c.** effectuer un calcul; **to upset sb's calculations** bouleverser les calculs de qn

calculator ['kælkjʊleɪtər] N1 *(machine)* calculatrice *f*, machine *f* à calculer; *(pocket)* calculatrice, calculette *f* 2 *(person)* calculateur, -trice

calculus ['kælkjʊləs] N *Math, Med* calcul *m*

Calcutta [kæl'kʌtə] N Calcutta

Caledonia [kælɪ'dəʊnɪə] N *Antiq, Lit (Scotland)* Calédonie *f*

Caledonian [kælɪ'dəʊnɪən] *Antiq, Lit* ADJ calédonien
 N Calédonien, -ienne

calendar ['kælɪndər] N *(of dates), Rel* calendrier *m*; *(of institution, university etc)* annuaire *m*; *Law (list of cases)* rôle *m* des causes; *(in criminal law)* rôle des assises; *Am (of Congress)* ordre *m* du jour; **I'll check my c.** je vais vérifier mon agenda; **c. of (forthcoming) events** calendrier des manifestations; **the club has a full c. this month** le club a un calendrier chargé ce mois-ci; **an important date in the publishing c.** une date importante dans le calendrier de l'édition
 ▸▸**c. month** mois *m* civil; **c. year** année *f* civile

calender ['kælɪndər] *Tech* N calandre *f*
 vɪ calandrer

calendered ['kælɪndəd] ADJ *(paper)* calandré, satiné

calends ['kælɪndz] NPL *Antiq* calendes *fpl*

calf[1], *pl* **calves** [kɑːf, kɑːvz] N1 *(animal)* veau *m*; **cow in** *or* **with c.** vache *f* pleine; **buffalo c.** bufletin *m*; **elephant c.** éléphanteau *m*; **sea c.** phoque *m* commun; **whale c.** baleineau *m* 2 *(leather)* veau *m* 3 *(broken off from iceberg)* glaçon *m*
 ▸▸**c. binding** *(of book)* reliure *f* en veau *ou* en vélin; **c. love** premières amours *fpl*

calf[2], *pl* **calves** N *(of leg)* mollet *m*; **c.-length boots** demi-bottes *fpl*

calfskin ['kɑːfskɪn] N *(cuir m* de*)* veau *m*; **c. wallet** portefeuille *m* en veau

caliber ['kælɪbər] N *Am* = **calibre**

calibrate ['kælɪbreɪt] vɪ *Tech (measuring instrument etc)* étalonner; *(bore)* calibrer; *(thermometer)* graduer; *Mil (piece of artillery)* vérifier le calibre de

calibration [kælɪ'breɪʃən] N *(of measuring instrument)* étalonnage *m*, *(of bore)* calibrage *m*

calibre, *Am* **caliber** ['kælɪbər] N *(of firearm)*, *Fig (of person)* calibre *m*; **a man of your c.** un homme de votre calibre *ou* envergure; **a very high c. translator** un traducteur de très grande envergure

calico ['kælɪkəʊ] N *Tex* calicot *m*; **printed c.,** *Am* **c.** calicot imprimé, indienne *f*
ADJ 1 *Tex* de calicot **2** *Am (cow)* tacheté; *(cat)* moucheté

California [kælɪ'fɔːnɪə] N Californie *f*

Californian [kælɪ'fɔːnɪən] **ADJ** californien
N Californien, -ienne

caliper ['kælɪpər] N **1** *Aut* étrier *m* (de frein à disque) **2** = **calliper**

caliph ['keɪlɪf] N calife *m*

caliphate ['keɪlɪfɪt] N califat *m*

calisthenics [kælɪs'θenɪks] N *esp Am* gymnastique *f* rythmique VOIR GRAMMAIRE A10

calk¹ [kɔːk] VT *Art etc* décalquer

calk² VT *(ship)* calfater, étouper

CALL [kɔːl]

N	appel **1, 2, 4** ▪ visite **5**
VT	appeler **1–6** ▪ réveiller **3**
VI	appeler **1** ▪ passer **3** ▪ s'arrêter **3**

N **1** *(shout)* appel *m*, cri *m*; *(of bird)* cri; **to give sb a c.** appeler qn

2 *(summons) (of person)* convocation *f*, *(of bugle)* sonnerie *f*, **c. for help** appel *m* au secours; **the President's c. for calm** l'appel au calme lancé par le Président; **to come at/ answer sb's c.** venir/répondre à l'appel de qn; **on c.** *(doctor)* de garde; *(interpreter, engineer etc)* disponible à tout moment; **to be within c.** être à portée de voix; **to give sb a c.** *(waken)* réveiller qn; *Euph* **to obey** *or* **answer a c. of nature** satisfaire un besoin naturel; **c. for tenders** appel d'offres

3 *Rel* vocation *f*, **he felt a c. (to the ministry)** il se sentait une vocation religieuse

4 *Tel* **(telephone) c.** coup *m* de téléphone *ou* *Fam* de fil, *Fml* appel *m* téléphonique; **to make a c.** passer un coup de téléphone *ou* *Fam* de fil; **to give sb a c.** téléphoner à qn, appeler qn (au téléphone), *Fam* passer un coup de fil à qn; **you have a c. from Canada** on vous appelle du Canada; **you had a c. from Pam** Pam t'a appelé; **there was a c. for you** il y a eu un coup de téléphone *ou* un appel pour toi; **he's on a c.** il est en ligne; **will you accept the c.?** *(when charges are reversed)* est-ce que vous prenez *ou* acceptez l'appel?; **to put a c. through** passer la communication; **to return sb's c.** rappeler qn; **local c.** appel local

5 *(visit)* visite *f*, *Com (of representative)* passage *m*; **to pay** *or* **make a c. on sb** rendre visite à qn; *Euph* **to pay a c.** *(go to toilet)* aller se laver les mains

6 *(demand)* demande *f*, **there's not much c. for …** il n'y a pas une forte demande de …; **there's not much c. for them** ce n'est pas un article très demandé

7 *(need)* besoin *m*; **there's no c. for rudeness!** pas besoin *ou* ce n'est pas la peine d'être impoli!

8 *Cards (at bridge)* appel *m*; *(at solo whist, boston)* demande *f*, **c. for trumps** invite *f* d'atout; **a c. of three diamonds** une annonce de trois carreaux

9 *Tennis, Cr (of umpire)* décision *f*

10 *Fin (for money)* demande *f*, appel *m* de fonds *ou* de versement; **c. for capital** appel de fonds; **payable at c.** remboursable sur demande *ou* à vue; **money at** *or* **on c.** prêts *mpl* au jour le jour, argent *m* à court terme

VT **1** *(attract attention of) (person)* appeler; **come quickly, he called** venez vite, a-t-il crié **2** *(say out loud)* **to c. sb's name** appeler qn;

---

to c. the banns publier les bans; **to c. a halt** faire halte; **to c. the roll** faire l'appel

3 *(summon) (person, fire brigade, lift)* appeler; *(meeting)* convoquer; *Law (case)* appeler; **to c. sb's attention to sth** attirer l'attention de qn sur qch; **to c. a strike** appeler à la grève; **to c. the doctor** faire venir le médecin, appeler le médecin; **I was called to the manager's office** j'ai été appelé dans le bureau du directeur; **c. me at six o'clock** *(wake me)* réveillez-moi à six heures; **to be called away on an emergency** être appelé en urgence; **she's been called away, her mother is ill** elle a dû s'absenter parce que sa mère est malade

4 *Tel (person)* téléphoner à, appeler; *(taxi)* appeler; **I called her house** j'ai téléphoné chez elle; **I got the impression it was a case of 'don't c. us, we'll c. you'** j'ai eu l'impression que ça voulait dire 'on vous écrira'

5 *(name)* appeler; **he is called Martin** *(that is his name)* il s'appelle Martin; *(by other people)* on l'appelle Martin; **c. me by my Christian** *or* **first name** appelez-moi par mon prénom; **to c. sb after sb** appeler qn comme qn; **she's called Margaret, after her grandmother** elle s'appelle Margaret, comme sa grand-mère; **to c. oneself a colonel** s'attribuer le titre de colonel; **c. yourself a carpenter!** et tu te prétends menuisier!; **and they c. themselves socialists!** et ils se disent socialistes!; **do you c. that clean?** c'est ce que tu appelles propre?; **to c. sb names** injurier qn, invectiver qn; **to c. sb a liar/a thief** traiter qn de menteur/de voleur; **we'll c. it three** mettons trois; **I c. that a dirty trick** voilà ce que j'appelle un sale tour

6 *Cards (two diamonds etc)* appeler, déclarer; **to c. spades** déclarer pique

7 *(call on)* **to c. a guarantee** faire jouer une garantie

VI **1** *(to attract attention)* **to c. to sb** appeler qn; **the bird was calling to its mother** l'oiseau appelait sa mère

2 *(summon)* **duty calls** le devoir m'appelle

3 *(visit, come to door etc)* passer; **has anyone called?** est-ce que quelqu'un est passé?; **I called at your house** je suis passé chez vous; **I must c. at the grocer's** il faut que je passe chez l'épicier; **to c. again** repasser; **the train calls at every station** le train s'arrête à toutes les gares; *Naut* **to c. at a port** *(of ship)* faire escale à un port

4 *Tel* appeler; **who's calling, please?, may I ask who's calling?** c'est de la part de qui, s'il vous plaît?; **to c. again** rappeler

5 *Cards* appeler (l'atout); *(at poker)* forcer l'adversaire à déclarer son jeu

▸▸ *Tel* **c. barring** interdiction *f* d'appels; **c. button** bouton d'appel; *Com* **c. centre** centre *m* d'appels; *Tel* **c. connection** établissement *m* d'appel; *Banking* **c. deposit** dépôt *m* à vue; *Tel* **c. diversion** transfert *m* d'appel; *Tel* **c. forwarding** redirection *f* d'appel; *Tel* **c. forwarding device** dispositif *m* de redirection d'appel; **c. girl** *(prostitute)* call-girl *f*, *pl* call-girls; *Tel* **c. holding** mise *f* en attente d'appels; *Tel* **c. key** touche *f* d'appel; *Am Radio* **c. letters** indicatif *m* d'appel *(d'une station de radio)*; *Fin* **c. money** prêts au jour le jour, argent à court terme; *St Exch* **c. option** option *f* d'achat, call *m*; *St Exch* **c. price** cours *m* du dont; *Tel* **c. screening** filtrage *m* d'appels; **c. sheet** *(in hotel etc)* feuille *f* des réveils; *Cin, TV* feuille de service; *Radio* **c. sign** indicatif d'appel *(d'une station de radio)*; *Tel* **c. waiting service** signal *m* d'appel

▸ **call back** VT SEP *(person) (summon again)*, *Tel* rappeler; *Theat (with applause)* rappeler sur scène; **to c. sb back from vacation** demander à qn de rentrer de vacances
VI **1** *(return)* repasser; **I'll c. back for it** je repasserai le prendre *ou* le chercher
2 *Tel* rappeler

▸ **call by** VI = **call round** VI **1**

▸ **call down** VT SEP **they called her down from upstairs** ils lui ont demandé de descendre; **to c. down God's wrath upon sb** appeler la colère de Dieu sur qn
VI **I called down after him** je l'ai appelé du haut de l'escalier/de la fenêtre/*etc*

▸ **call for** VT INSEP **1** *(summon) (person)* appeler, faire venir; *(thing)* faire apporter; *(drink etc)* commander; **to c. for help** crier au secours, appeler à l'aide
2 *(collect)* venir prendre, venir chercher; **to be called for** *(by messenger)* à remettre au messager; *(on envelope)* poste restante; *Rail* en gare
3 *(request, demand) (explanation, apology)* demander, exiger; **the opposition were calling for his resignation** l'opposition exigeait sa démission; **some union members are calling for industrial action** certains syndicalistes appellent à la grève; **the police are calling for tougher penalties** la police réclame des sanctions plus fermes; **to c. for volunteers** demander des volontaires
4 *(require) (attention, reform)* demander, réclamer, exiger; **situation that calls for tactful handling** situation qui demande à être gérée avec tact; **this calls for a celebration/ a drink!** il faut fêter/arroser ça!; **that sort of behaviour isn't called for** on se passe bien de ce genre de comportement; **that wasn't called for** ça n'était vraiment pas nécessaire

▸ **call in** VT SEP **1** *(person) (into building, office etc)* faire entrer; **c. Miss Smith in, please** faites entrer Mlle Smith, s'il vous plaît; **he called the children in** *(back into the house)* elle a fait rentrer les enfants
2 *(withdraw from circulation) (coin, book)* retirer de la circulation; *(of manufacturer) (defective product)* rappeler; **to c. in one's money** faire rentrer ses fonds; **to c. in a loan** *(of bank)* demander le remboursement d'un prêt
3 *(specialist, army) (for advice, help)* faire appel à
VI **1** *(visit)* rendre visite; **to c. in at sb's house/at the grocer's** passer chez qn/chez l'épicier; **to c. in to see sb** aller/venir voir qn; **I'll c. in on my way home** je passerai en rentrant chez moi
2 *(by telephone)* passer un coup de téléphone *ou* *Fam* de fil; **nurses called in and offered to help** des infirmières ont téléphoné pour offrir leur aide; **to c. in sick** téléphoner pour prévenir qu'on est malade

▸ **call off** VT SEP **1** *(cancel) (appointment, strike, match, holiday)* annuler; *(deal)* rompre, annuler; **they were going to get married, but they called it off** ils étaient sur le point de se marier mais ils ont tout annulé; **she called it off** elle a rompu
2 *(tell to come away) (dog)* rappeler

▸ **call on** VT INSEP **1** *(request)* **to c. on sb for sth** demander instamment qch à qn, réclamer qch à qn; **to c. on sb to do sth** demander instamment à qn de faire qch, prier instamment qn de faire qch; **I c. on the government to act** je demande instamment au gouvernement d'agir; **I now c. on Mr Stewart** *(to speak)* la parole est à M. Stewart; **the limited resources the police can c. on** les ressources limitées que la police peut mettre en œuvre; **to c. on the experts/sb's services** faire appel aux *ou* avoir recours aux experts/services de qn
2 *(person) (visit)* rendre visite à; *(drop in on)* passer voir
3 *(name of God)* invoquer

▸ **call out** VT SEP **1** *(summon) (person)* faire sortir, prier de sortir; *(fire brigade)* appeler; **to c. out workers (on strike)** donner l'ordre de grève à des ouvriers
2 *(shout)* crier; **she called out the winning number** elle a annoncé le numéro gagnant

VI 1 *(shout out)* appeler; **to c. out in anger/pain** crier de colère/douleur; **to c. out for sth** appeler pour demander qch
2 to c. out for *(urgently require)* nécessiter de façon urgente; **it's calling out for it!** c'est urgent de le faire!; *Fam* **this room is calling out for red velvet curtains** il faut à tout prix des rideaux de velours rouge dans cette pièce
▸ **call round VI 1** *(in person)* passer; **c. round when you're in the area** passez nous/me/*etc* voir quand vous serez dans la région
2 *(on telephone)* passer une série de coups de fil; **c. round and see if any of the local shops have any** téléphonez pour savoir si les boutiques du coin en ont
VT INSEP *(on phone)* **I've called round all her friends** j'ai appelé tous ses amis
▸ **call up VT SEP 1** *(summon)* *(person)* faire monter; *Mil etc (reinforcements)* appeler
2 *(evoke)* *(spirit)* invoquer; *(memory)* évoquer
3 *Tel (person)* téléphoner à, appeler (au téléphone)
4 *Mil, Naut (reservist)* mobiliser; *(for military service)* appeler; **to be called up** être mobilisé/appelé
5 *Fin* **called-up capital** capital *m* appelé
6 *Comput (help screen etc)* appeler
VI I called up after him je l'ai appelé du bas de l'escalier/l'échelle/*etc*

callable ['kɔːləb(ə)l] **ADJ** *Fin (bond, debt)* remboursable avant échéance
▸▸ **c. loan** crédit *m* révocable

callbox ['kɔːlbɒks] **N** cabine *f* téléphonique

callboy ['kɔːlbɔɪ] **N** *Theat etc* avertisseur *m*

caller ['kɔːlər] **N 1** *(visitor)* visiteur, -euse; **to be a frequent c. at sb's house** aller souvent chez qn **2** *Tel* personne *f* qui appelle (au téléphone); *Comput* appelant *m*; **did the c. say anything?** est-ce qu'il/elle a dit quelque chose?; **the vast majority of callers just need someone to talk to** la plupart des gens qui nous appellent ont juste besoin de parler; **one minute please, c.** un instant s'il vous plaît, monsieur/madame **3** *(in bingo hall)* celui/celle qui annonce les numéros gagnants
▸▸ *Tel* **c. display** présentation *f* du numéro de l'appelant; *Tel* **c. ID** identification *f* d'appel

calligrapher [kə'lɪɡrəfər] **N** calligraphe *mf*

calligraphy [kə'lɪɡrəfɪ] **N** calligraphie *f*

call-in N *Am Radio, TV* émission *f* à ligne ouverte

calling ['kɔːlɪŋ] **N 1** *(shouting)* appel *m*; **the stallholders' c. of their wares** les cris des marchands qui vantent leurs marchandises **2** *(of meeting etc)* convocation *f* **3** *(vocation)* vocation *f* (**for** pour); **I felt no/a c. for a religious life** je n'avais pas/j'avais la vocation **4** *(profession)* profession *f*, métier *m*
▸▸ *Am* **c. card** *(visiting card)* carte *f* de visite; *Tel* carte téléphonique; *Fin* **c. in** *(of debt, loan)* demande *f* de remboursement immédiat; *(of currency)* retrait *m*; **c. off** *(of appointment, meeting, match, holidays)* annulation *f*, *(of deal)* rupture *f*, *(of dog, attacker)* rappel *m*; **c. up** *(of memory)* évocation *f*, *(by telephone)* appel au téléphone; *Mil* appel (sous les drapeaux)

calliper ['kælɪpər] **N 1** *Tech* (**pair of**) **callipers** compas *m* de calibre *ou* à calibrer **2** *Med* attelle-étrier *f*, *pl* attelles-étriers
▸▸ *Tech* **c. compasses** compas de calibre *ou* à calibrer; *Med* **c. splint** attelle-étrier

callisthenics [kælɪs'θenɪks] **N** gymnastique *f* rythmique VOIR GRAMMAIRE A10

callosity [kæ'lɒsɪtɪ] **N** *Fml* callosité *f*

callous ['kæləs] **ADJ** *(person)* dur, sans cœur; *(treatment, behaviour)* dur, brutal, -aux; *(remark)* dur; **to be c. to sb** être dur avec qn; **the**

c. way in which the government has reacted la dureté de la réaction du gouvernement; **to show a c. indifference to sth** montrer une indifférence totale pour qch

calloused ['kæləst] **ADJ** *(skin, feet, hands)* calleux

callously ['kæləslɪ] **ADV** durement

callousness ['kæləsnɪs] **N** *(of person)* dureté *f*, insensibilité *f*, manque *m* de cœur; *(of treatment, behaviour)* dureté

callout ['kɔːlaʊt] **N** *(by maintenance man)* dépannage *m*
▸▸ **c. charge** (frais *mpl* de) déplacement *m*; **c. maintenance insurance** assurance *f* maintenance visite

callow ['kæləʊ] **ADJ** *(youth)* sans expérience

callowness ['kæləʊnɪs] **N** manque *m* d'expérience

call-up N *Mil* appel *m* (sous les drapeaux)
▸▸ **c. papers** ordre *m* d'incorporation; **to receive one's c. papers** être appelé sous les drapeaux

callus ['kæləs] **N** *(on skin)* cal *m*, *pl* cals, durillon *m*

calm [kɑːm] **N** *(peace)*, *Naut* calme *m*; *(of person)* tranquillité *f*, sérénité *f*; **the government appealed for c.** le gouvernement appela au calme; *Naut* **flat c.** calme plat; **period of c.** accalmie *f*, *Naut*, *Fig* **the c. before the storm** le calme avant la tempête
ADJ *(peaceful)* calme, tranquille; *(person)* calme, posé; *(sea)* calme; *(day)* sans vent; **to remain** *or* **keep c.** rester calme; **to grow calmer** se calmer
VT *(anger, people, storm of protest etc)* calmer, apaiser; *(pain)* calmer, atténuer; **this will c. your nerves** *or* **you** cela vous calmera; **c. yourself** calmez-vous!
▸ **calm down VI** *(of person, storm)* se calmer; *(of sea, wind)* calmir, se calmer; **things have calmed down** *(after crisis, busy spell etc)* les choses se sont calmées
VT SEP *(person)* calmer

calming ['kɑːmɪŋ] **ADJ** *(effect etc)* tranquillisant, calmant
N *(of waves, anger etc)* apaisement *m*; *(of pain)* atténuation *f*

calmly ['kɑːmlɪ] **ADV** calmement; **she c. shot him** elle lui tira dessus sans sourciller; **he just c. wrote out a cheque for £50,000** il a fait un chèque de 50 000 livres sans cérémonie

calmness ['kɑːmnɪs] **N** *(of person)* tranquillité *f*, calme *m*; *(of sea)* calme

Calor Gas® [kælə'ɡæs] **N** butane *m*

caloric [kə'lɒrɪk] **ADJ** *Phys* calorique

calorie ['kælərɪ] **N** *Phys* calorie *f*; **to be low/high in calories** *(of food)* être pauvre/riche en calories; **low-cal. diet**, **c. controlled diet** régime *m* hypocalorique *ou* basses calories *ou* faible en calories; **calories per serving** nombre *m* de calories par portion; *Fam* **to watch** *or* **count the calories** surveiller sa ligne

calorific [kælə'rɪfɪk] **ADJ** *Phys* calorifique
▸▸ *Phys* **c. value** valeur *f* calorifique

calumniate [kə'lʌmnɪeɪt] **VT** *Fml* calomnier

calumny ['kæləmnɪ] **N** calomnie *f*

Calvary ['kælvərɪ] **N 1** (**Mount**) **C.** le Calvaire **2** *Fig* **c.** calvaire *m*

calve [kɑːv] **VI** *(of cow)* vêler

calving ['kɑːvɪŋ] **N** *(of cow)* vêlage *m*, vêlement *m*; **at c. time** pendant le vêlement

Calvinism ['kælvɪnɪz(ə)m] **N** *Rel, Hist* calvinisme *m*

Calvinist ['kælvɪnɪst] **N, ADJ** *Rel* calviniste *mf*

calypso [kə'lɪpsəʊ] **N** *Mus* calypso *m*

calyx, *pl* **calyxes**, **calyces** ['keɪlɪks, -ɪksiːz, -ɪsiːz] **N** *Bot* calice *m*

CAM [kæm] **N** *Comput* (*abbr* **computer-assisted manufacture**) FAO *f*

cam [kæm] **N** *Tech etc* came *f*
▸▸ *Aut* **c. follower** poussoir *m*

camber ['kæmbər] **N** *(of road)* bombement *m*; *(of beam)* cambrure *f*, *Naut (of deck)* tonture *f*, *Aut (of wheel)* carrossage *m*; *Aviat (of wing)* flèche *f*
VT *(road surface)* bomber; *(beam)* cambrer
VI *(of road)* bomber; *(of beam)* cambrer

Cambodia [kæm'bəʊdɪə] **N** Cambodge *m*

Cambodian [kæm'bəʊdɪən] **ADJ** cambodgien
N 1 Cambodgien, -ienne **2** *Ling* cambodgien *m*

cambric ['kæmbrɪk, 'keɪm-] **N** *Tex* batiste *f*

Cambs [kæmz] *abbr* **Cambridgeshire**

camcorder ['kæmkɔːdər] **N** *Phot* caméscope® *m*

camel ['kæməl] **N 1** *(animal)* chameau *m*; **she-c.** chamelle *f* **2** *(colour)* chameau *m inv*
▸▸ *Mil* **the C. Corps** les compagnies *fpl* de méharistes; **c. driver** chamelier *m*

camelhair ['kæməlheər] **N** poil *m* de chameau; **c. brush** *(for watercolour painting)* pinceau *m* en petit-gris; **c. coat** manteau *m* en poil de chameau

camellia [kə'miːlɪə] **N** camélia *m*

cameo ['kæmɪəʊ] **N 1** *(gem)* camée *m*; **c. brooch** camée **2** *Theat, Cin (appearance)* brève apparition *f* *(par un acteur connu)*
▸▸ *Theat, Cin* **c. performance** brève apparition *(par un acteur connu)*; *Theat, Cin* **c. role** petit rôle *m* *(joué par un acteur connu)*

camera ['kæmərə] **N 1** *Phot* appareil *m* photo, *pl* appareils photos; *TV, Cin* caméra *f*; **I'm no good with a c.** je ne suis pas doué pour prendre des photos; *TV, Cin* **in front of the c.** devant les caméras; *TV* **on c.** à l'écran; **off c.** hors champ; **film c.** caméra *f* **2** *Law* **in c.** à huis clos; **the trial was held in c.** le procès a eu lieu à huis clos
▸▸ **c. angle** angle *m* de prise de vue; **c. assistant** assistant, -ante opérateur(trice); **c. blocking** *(rehearsal)* prise *f* de repères; **c. crew** équipe *f* de tournage; **c. cue** signal *m* caméra; **c. head** tête *f* de caméra; *TV, Cin* **c. loader** clapman *m*; *TV, Cin* **c. matte** cache *m* de caméra; *Opt* **c. obscura** chambre *f* noire; **c. operator** cadreur, -euse, opérateur, -trice de prise de vue; **c. platform** plateforme *f* de prise de vue; **c. script** liste *f* des mouvements de caméra; **c. test** essai *m* (de) caméra; **c. tower** échafaudage *m* pour caméra, tour *f*, *TV, Opt* **c. tube** tube *m* analyseur; **c. unit** unité *f* de tournage

cameraman, *pl* **cameramen** ['kæmərəmən] **N** *Cin, TV* cameraman *m*, *pl* cameramen; **assistant c.** opérateur *m*

camera-ready copy N *Typ* épreuves *fpl* bonnes à filmer

camera-shy ADJ **he is c.** il n'aime pas être pris en photo; *(doesn't like being filmed)* il n'aime pas être filmé

camerawork ['kæmərəwɜːk] **N** photographie *f*, *TV, Cin* prise(s) *f* (*pl*) de vues, photographie; *(document)* document *m* d'exécution

Cameroon [kæmə'ruːn] **N** **the Republic of C.** la République fédérale du Cameroun

camiknickers ['kæmɪnɪkəz] **NPL** = sous-vêtement *m* féminin comprenant une culotte et une chemise

camisole ['kæmɪsəʊl] **N** caraco *m*

camomile ['kæməmaɪl] **N** *Bot, Culin* camomille *f*
▸▸ **c. tea** infusion *f* de camomille

camouflage ['kæməflɑːʒ] **N** *Mil etc, Fig* camouflage *m*
VT *Mil etc* camoufler; *Fig (one's intentions etc)* dissimuler

▸▸ *Mil* **c. net(ting)** filet *m* de camouflage; **c. painting** peinture *f* de camouflage

camp[1] [kæmp] **N** camp *m*, campement *m*; **to break c.** lever le camp; *Fig* **to go over to the other c.** passer dans l'autre camp; *Fig* **to have a foot in both camps** avoir des intérêts dans les deux camps; **gipsy c.** camp *ou* campement de gitans; **(holiday) c.** camp de vacances; *(for children)* ≃ colonie *f* de vacances

VI camper

▸▸ **c. bed** lit *m* de camp; **c. chair** pliant *m*, chaise *f* pliante; **c. counsellor** moniteur, -trice; **c. follower** *Mil* = civil *m* qui accompagne une armée pour rendre des services; *(prostitute)* prostituée *f*, fille *f* à soldats; *Fig (supporter)* compagnon *m* de route; **c. site** camp; **c. stool** pliant, chaise pliante

▸ **camp out VI** camper

camp[2] *Fam* **ADJ 1** *(affected)* affecté; *(suggesting homosexuality)* efféminé; *(theatrical)* théâtral, -aux; *Hum* **he's as c. as a row of tents** il fait très grande folle **2** *(kitsch) (decor)* kitsch

VT to c. it up forcer la dose

campaign [kæmˈpeɪn] **N** campagne *f*, **on c.** en campagne; **to lead** *ou* **conduct a c. against sb** mener (une) campagne contre qn; **advertising c.** campagne publicitaire

VI *Mil* faire (une)/des campagne(s); *Pol* faire campagne; **she campaigned on an anti-drug platform** elle a axé sa campagne sur la lutte contre la drogue; **they campaigned for his release** ils ont mené une campagne pour sa libération; **campaigning journalism** journalisme *m* militant

▸▸ *Mil* **c. medal** médaille *f* commémorative

campaigner [kæmˈpeɪnər] **N** *(activist)* militant, -ante; **old c.** *Mil* vieux soldat *m*, vieux troupier *m*; *Fig* vétéran *m*

campanologist [kæmpəˈnɒlədʒɪst] **N** carillonneur, -euse

campanology [kæmpəˈnɒlədʒɪ] **N** art *m* du carillon

campanula [kæmˈpænjʊlə] **N** *(flower)* campanule *f*

camper [ˈkæmpər] **N** *(person)* campeur, -euse; *(vehicle)* camping-car *m*, *pl* camping-cars

▸▸ **c. van** camping-car

campfire [ˈkæmpfaɪər] **N** feu *m* de camp

camphor [ˈkæmfər] **N** camphre *m*

▸▸ **c. oil** essence *f* de camphre; **c. tree** camphrier *m*

camphorated [ˈkæmfəreɪtɪd] **ADJ** *(oil etc)* camphré

camping [ˈkæmpɪŋ] **N** camping *m*; **to go c.** faire du camping

▸▸ **c. equipment, c. gear** matériel *m ou* équipement *m* de camping; **c. ground** terrain *m* de camping; **c. holiday** vacances *fpl* (en) camping; **c. site** (terrain de) camping; **c. stove** camping-gaz® *m inv*

camping-caravanning **N** campage-caravanage *m*, camping-caravaning *m*

campion [ˈkæmpɪən] **N** *(plant)* lychnide *f*, lychnis *m*; **white c.** compagnon *m* blanc

campus [ˈkæmpəs] **N** campus *m* (universitaire); **they live on c.** *(of students)* ils vivent sur le campus

camshaft [ˈkæmʃɑːft] **N** *Tech* arbre *m* à came(s)

▸▸ **c. drive** entraînement *m* d'arbre à cames

can[1] [kæn] **N 1** *(for drink, esp American food)* boîte *f*

2 *(for petrol, oil, water etc)* bidon *m*; *(for milk, film)* boîte *f*; *Fig Fam* **to carry the c.** payer les pots cassés; *Fam* **I'm not carrying the c. for you** je ne vais pas payer les pots cassés pour toi; *Fam* **in the c.** *(of film)* en boîte; *Fig (of deal etc)* dans la poche; *Fig*

Fam **c. of worms** problème *m* insoluble; *Fig Fam* **don't let's open up that c. of worms** ne nous occupons pas de ce problème pour le moment; *Am* **trash** *or* **garbage c.** poubelle *f*, **watering c.** arrosoir *m*

3 *Fam* **cans** *(earphones)* casque *m*

4 *Sl (prison)* taule *f*, tôle *f*

5 *Am Sl (lavatory)* **the c.** les chiottes *fpl*

6 *Am Sl (buttocks)* fesses *fpl*; **to kick sb in the c.** botter les fesses à qn

VT (-nn-) **1** *(put in cans) (meat etc)* mettre en boîte *ou* en conserve; **canned fruit** fruits en conserve *ou* en boîte; *Am Sl* **c. it!** *(shut up!)* la ferme! **2** *Am Sl (dismiss) (person)* virer

▸▸ **c. opener** ouvre-boîtes *m inv*

CAN[2] *(stressed* [kæn], *unstressed* [k(ə)n]*)*

pouvoir **1, 3–6** ▪ savoir **2**

MODAL AUX V VOIR GRAMMAIRE A58–9; B39–40 *(pr* **can;** *neg* **cannot** [ˈkænɒt], *Am* **can not** [ˈkæn'nɒt]; *pt, cond* **could** [kʊd]; *no inf, prp, pp; defective parts are supplied from* **to be able to; cannot** *and* **could not** *are often contracted into* **can't** [kɑːnt], **couldn't** [ˈkʊdnt]) **1** *(be able to)* pouvoir; **I c. do it** je peux le faire; **we cannot** *or Am* **c. not possibly do it** nous ne pouvons absolument pas le faire; **I will come as soon/as often as I c.** je viendrai aussitôt/ aussi souvent que possible; **he will do what he c.** il fera ce qu'il pourra; **I will help you all I c., I will do all I c. to help you** je vous aiderai de mon mieux, je ferai tout mon possible pour vous aider; **I can't very well accept** il m'est difficile d'accepter; *Fam* **I'd like it finished by tomorrow – c. do!** j'aimerais que ce soit fini demain – aucun problème!; *Fam* **no c. do** c'est impossible; **(it) can't be helped!** tant pis!, on n'y peut rien!; **it can't be done** il est impossible de le faire; **how could he say that?** comment a-t-il pu dire cela?; **how c. you say that?** comment peux-tu dire une chose pareille?; **what c. it be?** qu'est-ce que cela peut bien être?; **c. it be true?** serait-ce vrai?; **(it) could be** c'est possible; **I never could understand maths** je n'ai jamais été capable de comprendre les maths; **what can I do?** qu'est-ce qu'il peut bien me/ nous/etc vouloir?; **how could you!** comment avez-vous pu faire une chose pareille?; **he could not have been kinder** il n'aurait pu être plus aimable

2 *(know how to)* savoir; **I c. swim** je sais nager; **a man who c. cook** un homme qui sait faire la cuisine; **she c. play the violin** elle sait jouer du violon

3 *(indicating possibility)* **you don't know how hot it c. get** vous ne savez pas à quel point il peut faire chaud; **the crossing c. be rough** il arrive que la traversée soit mauvaise; **adult animals c. grow to 20 feet** l'animal adulte peut mesurer jusqu'à 6 mètres; **you can't be serious!** tu plaisantes!

4 *(indicating permissibility)* pouvoir; **when c. I move in?** quand est-ce que je peux emménager?; **could you be quiet please?** pourriez-vous vous taire, s'il vous plaît?; **c. I ask you something?** est-ce que je peux vous demander quelque chose?; **you can't smoke in here** il est défendu de fumer ici

5 *(asking help)* pouvoir; **c. you help me?** peux-tu m'aider?; *(asking more politely)* pourrais-tu m'aider?; **could you get me some water?** pourriez-vous m'apporter de l'eau?

6 *(making suggestion)* pouvoir; **we could always telephone** nous pourrions toujours téléphoner; **you could go to the beach** tu pourrais aller à la plage; **I c. help if you like** je peux t'aider si tu veux

7 *(with 'see', 'hear' etc: not translated)* **I c. see nothing** je ne vois rien; **c. you see that hill?** est-ce que tu vois cette colline?; **I could hear them talking** je les entendais parler; **I c. see**

you don't believe me je vois bien que vous ne me croyez pas; **how c. you tell?** comment le savez-vous?

8 *(in conditional)* **he could have done it** il aurait pu le faire; **I could not have asked for anything better** je n'aurais pas désiré mieux; **I could weep/could have wept** j'ai/ j'avais envie de pleurer; **I could have smacked his face!** je l'aurais giflé!; **you could have warned me!** tu aurais pu me prévenir!

9 *(elliptically)* **I cannot but believe him** je suis bien forcé de le croire; **you c. but try** vous pouvez toujours essayer

Canada [ˈkænədə] **N** Canada *m*; **in C.** au Canada

▸▸ **C. Day** Fête *f* du Canada *(anniversaire de l'indépendance canadienne, le 1er juillet)*; *Orn* **C. goose** bernache *f* du Canada

Canadian [kəˈneɪdɪən] **ADJ** canadien

N Canadien, -ienne

▸▸ *Ling* **C. English** anglais *m* du Canada; *Ling* **C. French** français *m* du Canada

Canadianism [kəˈneɪdɪənɪz(ə)m] **N** canadianisme *m*

canal [kəˈnæl] **N 1** *(waterway)* canal *m*, -aux; **ship c.** canal maritime **2** *Anat etc* canal *m*, -aux; **auditory c.** conduit *m* auditif

▸▸ **c. barge** péniche *f*, **c. boat** péniche; *Geog* **the C. zone** la zone du canal de Panamá

canalization [kænəlaɪˈzeɪʃən] **N** canalisation *f*

canalize [ˈkænəlaɪz] **VT** *(river etc)*, *Fig* canaliser; **to c. one's efforts/energy into sth** canaliser ses efforts/son énergie dans qch

canapé [ˈkænəpeɪ] **N** *Culin* canapé *m*

canard [ˈkænɑːd, kəˈnɑːd] **N** *Lit* canard *m*, fausse nouvelle *f*

Canary [kəˈneəri] **N** **the C. Islands, the Canaries** les îles *fpl* Canaries

canary [kəˈneəri] **N** *(bird)* serin *m*, canari *m*

▸▸ *Bot* **c. seed** millet *m*; **c. yellow** jaune *m* canari

canasta [kəˈnæstə] **N** *Cards* canasta *f*

cancan [ˈkænkæn] **N** cancan *m*

▸▸ **c. dancer** danseuse *f* de cancan

cancel [ˈkæns(ə)l] (-ll-, *Am* -l-) **VT 1** *(meeting, reservation, message, cheque, debt)* annuler; *(order)* Com annuler; *Mil* lever; *(deal, contract)* annuler, résilier; *(train)* supprimer; *(stamp)* oblitérer; **to c. each other** *(of two book-keeping entries)* s'annuler; **500, no c. that, 350 …** 500, ou plutôt, 350 … **2** *Math (factors in fraction)* éliminer

VI 1 *(having made booking)* se décommander **2** *Comput* s'annuler; **press 'esc' to c.** appuyer sur 'Échap' pour annuler; **c. entry** *(command)* annulation d'entrée

▸▸ *Comput* **c. button** case *f* 'annuler'

▸ **cancel out VT SEP** *Math (term)* annuler; **to c. each other out** s'annuler; **inflation cancelled out the increase in salary** l'inflation a annulé la hausse des salaires

cancellation [kænsəˈleɪʃən] **N** annulation *f*, *Com (of order, sale, contract)* annulation, résiliation *f*, *(of stamp)* oblitération *f*, **there have been several cancellations** *(in restaurant, hotel)* il y a plusieurs réservations qui ont été annulées

▸▸ **c. charge** frais *mpl* d'annulation; **c. clause** clause *f* d'annulation *ou* de résiliation; **c. fee** frais d'annulation; **c. form** bon *m ou* bulletin *m* d'annulation; **c. holiday** = vacances *fpl* annulées et soldées

cancer [ˈkænsər] **N 1** *Med* cancer *m*; **to have c.** avoir un *ou* le cancer; **c. of the lung/skin, lung/skin c.** cancer du poumon/de la peau; **c. of the pancreas** cancer du pancréas; *Fig* **we must remove the c. of militarism** il faut enrayer le cancer du militarisme **2** *Astrol* **C. Cancer** *m*; **to be (a) C.** être (du) Cancer **3**

Geog **the Tropic of C.** le tropique du Cancer
▸▸**c. patient** cancéreux, -euse; **c. research** oncologie f, cancérologie f; **c. specialist** cancérologue mf, *Fam Hum* **c. stick** clope f

cancer-causing [-kɔ:zɪŋ] ADJ *(substance etc)* cancérigène

cancerous ['kæns(ə)rəs] ADJ cancéreux

candelabra, pl **candelabras** [kændɪ'lɑːbrə, -əz], **candelabrum**, pl **candelabra** [kændɪ'lɑːbrəm, -ə] N candélabre m

candid ['kændɪd] ADJ franc, f franche, sincère
▸▸**c. camera** caméra f invisible ou cachée; **c. camera shot** = photo f prise à l'insu de la personne photographiée

> Note that the French word **candide** is a false friend and is never a translation for the English word **candid**. It means **ingenuous**.

candida ['kændɪdə] N *Med* candidose f

candidacy ['kændɪdəsɪ] N candidature f

candidate ['kændɪdeɪt] N *(for job, office)* candidat, -ate (**for** à); **to stand as c. for sth** se présenter comme candidat à qch, poser sa candidature à qch; **presidential c.** candidat aux élections présidentielles; **successful candidates will have …** les candidats retenus auront …

candidature ['kændɪdətʃər] N *Br* candidature f

candidiasis [kændɪdɪ'eɪsɪs] N *Med* muguet m, candidose f

candidly ['kændɪdlɪ] ADV franchement, sincèrement

candidness ['kændɪdnɪs] N franchise f, sincérité f

candied ['kændɪd] ADJ *Culin* glacé, confit (au sucre)
▸▸**c. peel** zeste m confit

candle ['kænd(ə)l] N bougie f, *Old-fashioned* chandelle f, *(lit in church)* cierge m; *Fig* **to burn the c. at both ends** brûler la chandelle par les deux bouts; *Fig* **he can't hold a c. to you** il ne vous arrive pas à la cheville
▸▸**c. grease** suif m; **c. power** intensité f lumineuse

candlelight ['kænd(ə)laɪt] N lumière f de bougie; **by c.** à la chandelle, à la bougie

candle-lit ADJ *(room)* éclairé à la bougie; *(meal)* aux chandelles

Candlemas ['kænd(ə)ləməs] N *Rel* Chandeleur f

candlestick ['kænd(ə)lstɪk] N *(tall)* chandelier m; *(low)* bougeoir m

candlewick ['kænd(ə)lwɪk] N *Tex* candlewick m, chenille f de coton; **c. bedspread/dressing gown** dessus m de lit/robe f de chambre en chenille de coton **2** *(of candle)* mèche f de bougie ou de chandelle

can-do ADJ dynamique, entreprenant; **c. spirit** esprit m de battant ou de gagneur

candour, *Am* **candor** ['kændər] N franchise f, sincérité f

> Note that the French word **candeur** is a false friend and is never a translation for the English word **candour**. It means **ingenuousness**.

candy ['kændɪ] N **1** *(sugar)* **c.** sucre m candi; **stick of (sugar) c.** sucre d'orge **2** *Am (sweet)* bonbon m; *(sweets)* bonbons; *Fam* **it's like taking c. from a baby** c'est simple comme bonjour
VT *(sugar)* faire candir; *(fruit)* glacer
VI *(of sugar)* se candir, se cristalliser
▸▸*Am* **c. apple** pomme f d'amour; *Am* **c. bar** barre f chocolatée; *Am* **c. store** confiserie f

candyfloss ['kændɪflɒs] N *Br Culin* barbe f à papa

candy-striped ADJ *Tex* à raies (de deux couleurs)

candy-striper [-straɪpər] N *Am Med Fam* = bénévole mf

cane [keɪn] N **1** *Bot (of bamboo)* (canne f de) bambou m; *(of rattan)* rotin m; *(of raspberry bush)* tige f; **c. furniture** meubles mpl en rotin; **c. chair** siège m en rotin; **c.-seated chair** chaise f cannée **2** *(walking stick)* canne f **3** *(for punishment)* verge f, baguette f, badine f; **to get the c.** recevoir des coups de verge ou de baguette
VT **1** *(person, pupil)* **(beat)** donner des coups de verge ou de baguette à **2** *Sl (defeat)* démolir **3** *Br Fam* **to c. it** se bourrer ou se pinter la gueule **4** *(chair)* canner
▸▸**c. sugar** sucre m de canne

caned [keɪnd] ADJ *Br Fam (drunk)* bourré comme un coing

canine ['keɪnaɪn, 'kæ-] ADJ ATTRIB de chien; *(race, species)* canin; **c. devotion** dévotion f de chien
N **1** *Anat (tooth)* canine f **2** **canines** *(animals)* canidés mpl
▸▸*Anat* **c. tooth** canine

caning ['keɪnɪŋ] N **1** *(punishment)* coups mpl de verge ou de baguette *(comme châtiment corporel)* **2** *Sl* **to get a c.** *(be defeated)* se faire démolir **3** *(in furniture)* cannage m

canister ['kænɪstər] N boîte f (en fer blanc)

canker ['kæŋkər] N **1** *Med, Fig* chancre m **2** *Vet (in horse's hoof)* crapaud m; *(of dog etc)* gale f de l'oreille **3** *Bot* chancre m; *(in wood)* nécrose f

cankerworm ['kæŋkəwɜːm] N ver m rongeur *(des plantes)*

cannabis ['kænəbɪs] N cannabis m
▸▸**c. resin** résine f de cannabis

canned [kænd] ADJ **1** *TV, Cin (laughter, applause)* préenregistré; *(music)* enregistré, en conserve **2** *Sl (drunk)* soûl, beurré; **to get c.** se soûler, se beurrer

cannelloni [kænɪ'ləʊnɪ] N cannelloni mpl

cannery ['kænərɪ] N conserverie f

cannibal ['kænɪb(ə)l] N, ADJ cannibale mf

cannibalism ['kænɪbəlɪz(ə)m] N cannibalisme m

cannibalization [kænɪbəlaɪ'zeɪʃ(ə)n] N *Mktg, Aut* cannibalisation f

cannibalize ['kænɪbəlaɪz] VT *Tech, Aut etc (machine etc)* récupérer des pièces en bon état sur, cannibaliser; *Mktg (product)* cannibaliser; **cannibalized income** revenu m cannibalisé

cannily ['kænɪlɪ] ADV *esp Scot (cautiously)* prudemment, avec circonspection; *(cleverly)* avec ruse

canning ['kænɪŋ] N *(of food)* mise f en conserve
▸▸**c. factory** conserverie f, fabrique f de conserves; **c. industry** conserverie, industrie f de la conserve

cannon ['kænən] N **1** *(usu inv) Mil* canon m; *Am Fig* **he's a loose c.** on ne sait pas trop ce qu'il va faire **2** *Billiards* carambolage m; **c. off the cushion** bricole f
VI *Billiards* faire un carambolage, caramboler; **to c. off the cushion** *(of player)* jouer la bricole
▸▸*Mil* **c. fodder** chair f à canon; *Billiards* **c. shot** *(ball)* boulet m de canon
▸ **cannon into** VT INSEP se heurter à

cannonade [kænə'neɪd] N *Mil Old-fashioned* canonnade f

cannonball ['kænənbɔːl] N *Mil, Fig* boulet m de canon; *Tennis* **serve** service m boulet de canon

cannot ['kænɒt] *see* **can²**

cannula ['kænələ] N *Med* canule f

canny ['kænɪ] ADJ *esp Scot (cautious)* prudent, circonspect; *(aware)* avisé; *(clever)* rusé; *(thrifty)* économe; **c. answer** réponse f de Normand

canoe [kə'nuː] N canoë m; **(dugout) c.** pirogue f, *Fig* **to paddle one's own c.** mener seul sa barque
VI *(pp, pt canoed; prp canoeing)* faire du canoë; **to c. up the river** remonter la rivière en canoë

canoeing [kə'nuːɪŋ] N canoë m; **to go c.** faire du canoë; **c. holiday** raid m ou randonnée f en canoë-kayak; **c. trip** voyage m en canoë

canoeist [kə'nuːɪst] N canoéiste mf

canon¹ ['kænən] N **1** *Rel (of mass etc)* canon m **2** *Lit (rule)* canon m **3** *Liter (of author)* œuvre f; **the literary c.** les classiques mpl **4** *Mus* canon m
▸▸*Rel* **c. law** droit m canon

canon² N *Rel (priest)* chanoine m

canonical [kə'nɒnɪk(ə)l] ADJ **1** *Rel (right, epistle, residence etc)* canonique; *Fig (accepted)* autorisé, accepté **2** *Mus (passage)* en canon
NPL **canonicals** vêtements mpl sacerdotaux
▸▸**c. dress** vêtements sacerdotaux; **c. hours** *(Catholic)* heures fpl canoniales; *(Church of England)* = heures pendant lesquelles la célébration des mariages est autorisée *(entre 8 heures et 18 heures)*

canonization [kænənaɪ'zeɪʃən] N *Rel* canonisation f

canonize ['kænənaɪz] VT *Rel* canoniser

canoodle [kə'nuːd(ə)l] VI *esp Hum* se faire des mamours

canopy ['kænəpɪ] N *(over throne)* dais m; *(over bed)* baldaquin m; *(over fireplace)* hotte f, *(over doorway)* auvent m, marquise f, *(of parachute)* calotte f, voilure f, *Aviat (of cockpit)* verrière f, *Archit (of roof, over window)* gable m, gâble m; *Rel (above altar etc)* ciel m; *Fig* **c. of leaves** voûte f de feuillage ou de verdure

cant¹ [kænt] N **1** *(of thieves, beggars)* argot m **2** *(hypocritical talk)* langage m hypocrite; **c. phrase** cliché m
VI **1** *(of thieves, beggars etc)* parler en argot **2** *(talk hypocritically)* faire l'hypocrite

cant² N **1** *Carp, Constr etc (slope)* inclinaison f, dévers m; *Rail (of outer rail)* surélévation f, dévers; **to give sth a c.** incliner qch; **to have a c.** pencher **2** *Archit, Carp (edge)* chanfrein m, biseau m
VT **1** *(turn over)* renverser, retourner; *Naut (boat for repair)* chavirer **2** *(tilt) (beam, pillar)* dévoyer, incliner; *(barrel)* incliner, pencher; *Rail (outer rail)* surhausser **3** *Carp etc (edge)* biseauter, écorner
VI **1** *Carp, Constr etc* s'incliner **2** *(tilt)* se trouver incliné, pencher

can't [kɑːnt] *(abbr* cannot*) see* **can²**

Cantab ['kæntæb] *(abbr* **Cantabrigiensis**) de l'université de Cambridge

cantaloup(e) ['kæntəluːp] N *(melon)* cantaloup m

cantankerous [kæn'tæŋk(ə)rəs] ADJ *(bad-tempered)* revêche, acariâtre; *(irritable)* querelleur, -euse

cantata [kæn'tɑːtə] N *Mus* cantate f

canteen [kæn'tiːn] N **1** *(in school, factory etc)* cantine f **2** *Mil (shop)* magasin m à l'usage des soldats; *(water bottle)* bidon m; *(mess tin)* gamelle f **3** **c. of cutlery** ménagère f

canter ['kæntər] N *Horseriding* petit galop m; *Fig* **let's have a quick c. through tomorrow's agenda** revoyons rapidement l'emploi du temps de demain
VI *Horseriding* aller au petit galop; *Fig* **to c.**

through a speech *(do quickly)* expédier un discours; **to c. through an exam** *(do easily)* réussir un examen haut la main

VT *(horse)* faire aller au petit galop

Canterbury ['kæntəb(ə)rɪ] **N** Canterbury; *Hist* Cantorbéry

▸▸ **C. bell(s)** *(flower)* campanule *f*

canticle ['kæntɪk(ə)l] **N** cantique *m*

cantilever ['kæntɪliːvər] **N** *Archit* encorbellement *m; Aviat* cantilever *m*

▸▸ *Constr etc* **c. beam** poutre *f* en porte-à-faux; **c. bridge** pont *m* cantilever

canto ['kæntəʊ] **N** *Liter (of poem)* chant *m*

canton ['kæntɒn] **N** canton *m*

cantonal ['kæntən(ə)l] **ADJ** cantonal, -aux

Cantonese [kæntə'niːz] **ADJ** cantonais **N 1** Cantonais, -aise **2** *Ling* cantonais *m*

cantonization [kæntənaɪ'zeɪʃən] **N** morcellement *m*

cantonment [kæn'tuːnmənt] **N** cantonnement *m*

cantor ['kæntɔːr] **N** *Rel* chantre *m*

Canuck [kə'nʌk, kə'nʊk] **N** *Pej* Canadien, -ienne français(e)

canula ['kænələ] **N** *Med* canule *f*

canvas ['kænvəs] **N 1** *Tex* (grosse) toile *f, (for tapestry)* canevas *m; Mil etc* **under c.** sous la tente; **c. bucket** seau *m* en toile; **c. shoes** chaussures *fpl* de toile **2** *Art (material, painting)* toile *f* **3** *Boxing* tapis *m* **4** *(sails)* voile(s) *f(pl)* **under c.** sous voiles

> Attention: ne pas confondre avec le verbe **to canvass.**

canvass ['kænvəs] **VT 1** *Pol, Com (solicit) (votes, orders)* solliciter; **to c. sb** *(for vote)* solliciter la voix de qn *(en faisant du porte-à-porte), (for custom)* solliciter la clientèle de qn; *(for support in job application etc)* solliciter l'appui de qn; *Com* **to c. a client** démarcher un client; *Pol* **to c. a district** faire une tournée électorale dans une région **2** *(debate, discuss)* discuter **3** *(get opinion of)* sonder; **to c. opinions** sonder l'opinion *(on* à propos de) **4** *Am Pol (inspect) (votes)* pointer, vérifier

VI 1 *Pol* faire campagne, faire une tournée électorale; **candidates were out canvassing today** les candidats ont fait une tournée électorale aujourd'hui; **I'm canvassing on behalf of the Labour Party** je fais campagne pour le Parti travailliste **2** *Com* faire du démarchage; **to c. for customers** prospecter un quartier/une région en y recherchant la clientèle

N = canvassing

> Attention: ne pas confondre avec le nom **canvas.**

canvasser ['kænvəsər] **N** *Pol* = personne *f* qui sollicite les voix des électeurs en faisant du porte-à-porte; *Com* prospecteur, -trice; *(door-to-door)* représentant, -ante, démarcheur, -euse; **no canvassers** *(notice on door)* démarchage interdit

canvassing ['kænvəsɪŋ] **N** *Pol (of votes)* démarchage *m* électoral; *Com (of orders)* démarchage; *(for support in job application etc)* sollicitation *f* d'appui

canyon ['kænjən] **N** *Geog* canyon *m*, cañon *m*

canyoning ['kænjənɪŋ] **N** *Sport* canyoning *m*

CAP [siːeɪ'piː] **N** *EU (abbr* **Common Agricultural Policy)** PAC *f*

cap¹ [kæp] **N 1** *(headgear)* bonnet *m; (with peak)* casquette *f, (of university graduate, jockey)* toque *f,* **swimming c.** bonnet de bain; *Sport* **to win one's c.** être sélectionné dans l'équipe nationale; *Univ* **in c. and gown** en costume d'apparat; *Fig* **to come/go c. in hand** se présenter chapeau bas *ou* humblement *(* **to sb** devant qn); *Fig* **if the c. fits(, wear it)!** qui se sent morveux se mouche!; *Fig* **to put on one's thinking c.** réfléchir, méditer la question; *Old-fashioned Fam* **to set one's c. at sb** jeter son dévolu sur qn **2** *(cover) (of pen, tyre valve)* capuchon *m; (of pump)* calotte *f, (of bottle)* capsule *f, Phot (for lens)* capuchon, bouchon *m; Tech (protective)* chapeau *m; (of bearing, valve)* chapeau, couvercle *m; (for tooth)* couche *f* d'émail; **(Dutch) c.** *(contraceptive)* diaphragme *m* (contraceptif) **3** *(upper part) (of column)* chapiteau *m; (of mushroom)* chapeau *m* **4** *(for toy gun)* amorce *f,* capsule *f; Am Sl (bullet)* bastos *f,* **percussion c.** amorce **5** *Orn (of bird)* capuchon *m* **6** *(spending limit)* plafond *m*

VT (-pp-) **1** *(cover)* recouvrir (**sth with sth** qch de qch); *(bottle)* capsuler; **the mountain was capped with snow** le sommet de la montagne était recouvert de neige; **to c. a tooth** mettre une couche d'émail sur une dent **2** *(surpass, do better than)* surpasser; **to c. a quotation** renchérir sur une citation; **that caps everything** *or* **the lot** *or* **it all!** ça c'est le comble! *ou* le bouquet!; **c. that!** tu n'es pas cap de faire mieux! **3** *Scot, New Zealand Sch (candidate)* conférer un diplôme à **4** *Sport* **to be capped for England** être sélectionné dans l'équipe d'Angleterre **5** *Admin (impose limit on) (spending)* limiter; *(borough etc)* limiter les dépenses de **6** *Am Sl (shoot)* descendre

cap² **N** *Typ Fam* majuscule *f,* **put in small caps** à imprimer en petites capitales

capability [keɪpə'bɪlɪtɪ] **N** capacité *f* (**to do sth** de faire qch); **we have the military c. to …** nous avons les capacités militaires de …; **to have outstanding/limited capabilities** *(of person)* être très doué/avoir des moyens limités

capable ['keɪpəb(ə)l] **ADJ 1** capable (**of sth** de qch; **of doing sth** de faire qch); **to show what one is c. of** montrer ce dont on est capable; **c. of love** capable d'aimer; **the machine is c. of producing 300 items a minute** cette machine a une capacité de production de 300 pièces à la minute; **she's not c. of lying** elle est incapable de mentir; **that man's c. of anything** cet homme est capable de tout **2** *(competent)* capable, compétent; **the business is in c. hands** l'affaire est entre de bonnes mains **3** *Fml* **c. of improvement** susceptible d'amélioration *ou* d'être amélioré

capably ['keɪpəblɪ] **ADV** avec compétence, d'une manière compétente

capacious [kə'peɪʃəs] **ADJ** vaste, spacieux; *(clothing)* ample

capacitance [kə'pæsɪtəns] **N** *Elec* capacité *f*

capacitate [kə'pæsɪteɪt] **VT** *Law* donner pouvoir *ou* qualité à (**to act** pour agir)

capacitor [kə'pæsɪtər] **N** *Elec* condensateur *m*

capacity [kə'pæsɪtɪ] **N 1** *(of cylinder, tank, hotel, theatre, train, stadium etc)* capacité *f; (of barrel, drum, cask)* contenance *f;* **there was a c. crowd at the match** le stade était plein *ou* bondé pour le match; **we played to c. audiences** on a fait salle comble; **there was a c. audience at the theatre** le théâtre était comble; **the stadium has a c. of 50,000** le stade peut accueillir 50 000 personnes; *Theat, Sport etc* **to play to c.** jouer à guichets fermés; *Fam* **he has a remarkable c. for alcohol/beer** il peut absorber des quantités extraordinaires d'alcool/de bière **2** *Ind etc (output)* rendement *m;* **to work at (full) c.** travailler à plein rendement; **production c.** capacité *f* de production **3** *Elec* capacité *f* **4** *(aptitude)* **c. for work** capacité *f* de travail; **he has no c. for love** il est incapable d'aimer; **to be beyond sb's c.** dépasser les compétences de qn; **to be within sb's c.** être dans les possibilités de qn; **to the utmost of my c.** dans la mesure de mes moyens **5** *Law* **to have c./no c. to act** avoir/ne pas avoir capacité pour agir **6** *(position)* **in the c. of …** en qualité de …; **to act in one's official c.** agir dans le cadre de ses fonctions; **in my c. as chairwoman** en ma qualité de présidente

▸▸ **c. occupancy** *(of hotel etc)* occupation *f* maximale; *Ind etc* **c. utilization** rentabilisation *f*

caparison [kə'pærɪs(ə)n] *Hist* **N** caparaçon *m*

VT caparaçonner

cape¹ [keɪp] **N** *(cloak)* pèlerine *f,* cape *f, (small)* collet *m; (of priest)* camail *m,* *pl* camails

cape² **N** *Geog* cap *m,* promontoire *m*

▸▸ **C. Coloured** métis, -isse sud-africain(e); **the C. of Good Hope** le cap de Bonne-Espérance; **C. Town** Le Cap

caper¹ ['keɪpər] **N 1** *Bot, Culin (bud)* câpre *f* **2** *(plant)* câprier *m*

caper² **N 1** *(movement)* cabriole *f,* gambade *f;* **to cut a c.** faire des cabrioles **2** *(prank)* farce *f, Fam* bonne rigolade *f,* **I've had enough of his capers** j'en ai assez de ses bêtises; **what a c.!** *(fuss)* quel cirque! **3** *Sl (robbery)* hold-up *m inv*

VI **to c. (about)** *(about)* faire des cabrioles, cabrioler, gambader

capercaillie, capercailzie [kæpə'keɪlɪ] **N** *(bird)* grand tétras *m,* (grand) coq *m* de bruyère

capful ['kæpfʊl] **N** *(of liquid, disinfectant etc)* plein bouchon *m*

capillary [kə'pɪlərɪ] **ADJ** *(tube, pressure etc)* capillaire; *Anat* **the c. vessels** les vaisseaux *mpl* capillaires

NPL *Anat* **the capillaries** les capillaires *mpl*

capital ['kæpɪt(ə)l] **ADJ 1** *(principal)* capital, -aux; **a c. A** un A majuscule; *Fam* **he's lazy with a c. L** c'est un paresseux avec un grand P **2** *(important)* capital, -aux; **of c. importance** d'une importance capitale **3** *Old-fashioned Br Fam (excellent)* excellent

N 1 *Typ* capitale *f,* majuscule *f* **2** *(city)* capitale *f* **3** *Fin* capital *m,* capitaux *mpl,* fonds *mpl; (assets)* avoir *m;* **to live on one's c.** vivre sur son capital; *Fig* **to make c. out of sth** profiter *ou* tirer parti de qch; *Fig* **they're trying to make political c. out of the scandal** ils essaient de récupérer ce scandale **4** *Archit* chapiteau *m*

▸▸ *Fin* **c. assets** actif *m* immobilisé, immobilisations *fpl; Fin* **c. budget** budget *m* d'investissement; *Fin* **c. charge** intérêt *m* des capitaux (investis); **c. city** capitale *f; Fin* **c. contribution** apport *m* en capital, dotation *f* en capital, apport de capitaux; *Law* **c. crime** crime *m* capital *ou* puni de mort; *Acct* **c. employed** capital engagé, capitaux permanents; *Acct, Fin* **c. equipment** biens *mpl* d'équipement, capitaux fixes; **c. error** erreur *f* fatale; *Fin* **c. expenditure** mise *f* de fonds, investissements *mpl* (en immobilisations), dépenses *fpl* d'équipement; *Fin* **c. gain** plus-value *f* (en capital), *pl* plus-values; **to make a c. gain on sth** réaliser une plus-value sur qch; *Fin* **c. gains tax** impôt *m* sur les plus-values (en capital); *Fin* **c. goods** biens d'équipement *ou* d'investissement; *Fin* **c. grants** subventions *fpl* en capital; *Fin*

c. growth croissance *m* du capital; *Fin* **c. injection** injection *f* de capital, injection de capitaux; *Fin* **c. investment** mise de fonds; *Fin* **c. items** biens capitaux; **c. letter** (lettre *f*) capitale, (lettre) majuscule; *Fin* **c. levy** impôt *ou* prélèvement *m* sur le capital; *Fin* **c. loss** moins-value *f*, *pl* moins-values; *Fin* **c. market** marché *m* des capitaux; *Law* **c. offence** crime capital *ou* puni de mort; *Law* **c. punishment** peine *f* capitale, peine de mort; *Fin* **c. reserves** profits *mpl* mis en réserve, réserves *fpl* non distribuées; *Fin* **c. share** part *f* sociale; *Fin* **c. tax** impôt sur le capital; *Fin* **c. transfer** transfert *m* de capitaux; *Fin Formerly* **c. transfer tax** droits *mpl* de mutation; *Fin* **c. turnover** rotation *f* des capitaux

capital-intensive ADJ *(industry etc)* qui nécessite un investissement important

capitalism ['kæpɪtəlɪz(ə)m] N capitalisme *m*

capitalist ['kæpɪtəlɪst] N capitaliste *mf*

capitalist(ic) ['kæpɪtəlɪst, -'lɪstɪk] ADJ *(system, society etc)* capitaliste

capitalization [kæpɪtəlaɪ'zeɪʃən] N1 *Fin (of interest etc)* capitalisation *f* 2 *Typ* emploi *m* des majuscules; *(putting into caps)* mise *f* en majuscules
▸▸*Fin* **c. issue** attribution *f* d'actions gratuites; *Fin* **c. ratio** ratio *m* de capitalisation

capitalize ['kæpɪtəlaɪz] VT1 *Fin (income etc)* capitaliser; **capitalized value** valeur *f* capitalisée 2 *Typ (word) (first letter)* écrire avec une majuscule; *(entire word)* écrire en majuscules
▸ **capitalize on, capitalize upon** VT INSEP *Fig (something)* tourner à son avantage

capital-output ratio N ratio *m* capital-travail

capitation [kæpɪ'teɪʃən] N *Econ* capitation *f*
▸▸*Admin* **c. grant** allocation *f* par tête

Capitol (the) [ðəkæpɪtɒl] N *(of Rome, Washington etc)* le Capitole

Capitol Hill
Ce nom désigne, par extension, le Congrès américain. Par exemple, "The proposed bill is in danger of being rejected on Capitol Hill." ("La proposition de loi risque d'être rejetée par le Congrès américain.")

capitulate [kə'pɪtjʊleɪt] VI capituler (**to** devant)

capitulation [kəpɪtjʊ'leɪʃən] N *(surrender)* capitulation *f*

capon ['keɪpən] N *Culin* chapon *m*

capper ['kæpər] N *Am Fam* **that was the c.!** c'est la goutte d'eau qui a fait déborder le vase!

cappuccino [kæpʊ'tʃiːnəʊ] N cappucino *m*

caprice [kə'priːs] N1 *(whim)* caprice *m* 2 *Mus* caprice *m*

capricious [kə'prɪʃəs] ADJ capricieux

capriciously [kə'prɪʃəslɪ] ADV capricieusement

Capricorn ['kæprɪkɔːn] N1 *Astrol* Capricorne *m*; **to be (a) C.** être (du) Capricorne 2 *Geog* **the Tropic of C.** le tropique du Capricorne

caps [kæps] NPL *(abbr* **capital letters)** majuscules *fpl*, capitales *fpl*
▸▸*Comput* **c. lock** verrouillage *m* des majuscules; *Comput* **c. lock key** touche *f* de verrouillage des majuscules

capsicum ['kæpsɪkəm] N1 *Culin (hot)* piment *m*; *(mild)* poivron *m* 2 *(plant)* piment *m*; *(mild)* poivron *m*

capsize [kæp'saɪz] VI *(of boat)* chavirer; **we capsized** nous avons chaviré
VT *(boat)* faire chavirer

capstan ['kæpst(ə)n] N1 *Naut etc* cabestan *m* 2 *Tech (of lathe)* revolver *m*
▸▸*Tech* **c. lathe** tour *m* revolver

capsular ['kæpsjʊlər] ADJ *Biol etc* capsulaire

capsule ['kæpsjuːl] N capsule *f*; *Med (of drug)* gélule *f*, **space c.** capsule spatiale

Capt N *abbr* **Captain**

captain ['kæptɪn] N1 *Naut, Sport* capitaine *m*; *Aviat* commandant *m* de bord; *(in fire brigade)* capitaine; *(of quiz team etc)* leader *m*; *(in Girl Guides)* cheftaine *f*, *Am (in restaurant)* maître *m* d'hôtel; *Br* **c. of the school, school c.** = élève *mf* délégué(e) qui a certaines responsabilités et représente son établissement au cours de cérémonies officielles; *Fig* **captains of industry** capitaines d'industrie
2 *(officer, rank)* capitaine *m*; *Naut* capitaine de vaisseau; *(in American police force)* = officier *m* de police responsable d'un quartier; **c. of the fleet** capitaine de pavillon; **C. James Brown** *(in title)* le capitaine James Brown; **yes, c.!** oui, mon capitaine!
VT *Sport (team)* être capitaine de; *(expedition etc)* conduire, mener; *Sport* **he captained the side in the World Cup** c'était lui le capitaine de l'équipe pour la Coupe du monde

captaincy ['kæptɪnsɪ] N1 *Mil, Naut* grade *m* de capitaine; **to take over the c. of the ship** prendre le commandement du vaisseau 2 *Sport* fonction *f* de capitaine; **under** *or* **during his c.** quand il était capitaine

caption ['kæpʃən] N *(of cartoon, photograph, illustration)* légende *f*, *Cin (in silent film)* sous-titre *m*, *pl* sous-titres
VT *(illustration)* légender, écrire la légende de; *(film, television programme)* sous-titrer
▸▸*TV, Cin* **c. generator** générateur *m* de caractères

captious ['kæpʃəs] ADJ *Fml (reasoning)* captieux; *(person)* pointilleux, chicaneur, -euse

captivate ['kæptɪveɪt] VT *(of story, storyteller)* captiver; *(of smile, charm etc)* séduire

captivating ['kæptɪveɪtɪŋ] ADJ *(person, smile)* séduisant; *(personality)* captivant, fascinant; *(smile)* enchanteur, -eresse

captivation [kæptɪ'veɪʃən] N fascination *f*

captive ['kæptɪv] ADJ captif; **he was taken c.** il a été fait prisonnier; **he had a c. audience** le public était forcé de l'écouter
N captif, -ive, prisonnier, -ière
▸▸**c. audience** audience *f* captive; *Mktg* **c. market** clientèle *f* captive, marché *m* captif; *Mktg* **c. product** produit *m* lié; *Mktg* **c.-product pricing** fixation *f* du prix des produits liés; **c. state** état *m* de captivité

captivity [kæp'tɪvɪtɪ] N captivité *f*; **animals in c.** animaux en captivité

captor ['kæptər] N ravisseur, -euse

capture ['kæptʃər] N1 *(of ship, criminal, animal etc)* capture *f* 2 *Comput (of data)* saisie *f* 3 *(thing or person taken)* prise *f*
VT *(ship, criminal, animal etc)* capturer; *(town)* prendre, s'emparer de (**from** sur); *(sb's attention, imagination)* captiver; *(of artist, painting) (sb's likeness)* saisir; *(of film, book, director etc) (atmosphere)* rendre; *Comput (data)* saisir; **to c. the moment** *(of photographer, photograph)* saisir l'instant; **to c. sb/sth (on film)** immortaliser qn/qch *(sur la pellicule)*; *Com* **to c. a market** accaparer un marché

Capuchin ['kæpʊʃɪn] N *Rel* capucin, -ine

capuchin ['kæpʊʃɪn] N *(monkey)* capucin *m*

car [kɑːr] N1 *Aut* **(motor) c.** voiture *f*, automobile *f*; **to go by c.** aller en voiture 2 *Am Rail* voiture *f*, wagon *m*; **buffet** *or* **refreshment c.** voiture-bar *f*, *pl* voitures-bars 3 *(cabin) (of balloon)* nacelle *f*, *Am (of lift)* cabine *f*
▸▸**c. bomb** voiture piégée; *Br* **c. ferry** ferry-boat *m*, *pl* ferry-boats; **c. hire** location *f* de voitures; **c. hire company** société *f* de location de voitures; **c. industry** industrie *f* automobile; **c. insurance** assurance *f* auto; **c. manufacturer** constructeur *m* automobile; *Br* **c. park** parking *m*, parc *m* de stationnement; **c. phone** téléphone *m* de voiture; **c. radio** autoradio *f*, **c. rental** location de voitures; **c. theft** vols *mpl* de voiture

> Note that the French word **car** is a false friend and is never a translation for the English word **car**. It means **coach**.

carafe [kə'ræf, -'rɑːf] N carafe *f*, *(small)* carafon *m*

caramel ['kærəməl] N1 *Culin* caramel *m* 2 *(sweet)* caramel *m* 3 *(colour)* (couleur *f*) caramel *m inv*
▸▸*Culin* **c. cream** crème *f* caramel; *Culin* **c. custard** crème (renversée) au caramel

caramelize ['kærəməlaɪz] *Culin* VT caraméliser
VI se caraméliser

carapace ['kærəpeɪs] N *Zool* carapace *f*

carat ['kærət] N1 *(for gold)* carat *m* (de fin); **eighteen-c. gold** *or* *m* à dix-huit carats 2 *(for diamonds)* **metric c.** carat *m* (de 200 milligrammes)

caravan ['kærəvæn] N1 *Br (pulled by car)* caravane *f*, **c. holiday** vacances *fpl* en caravane 2 *(horse-drawn) (of gypsy, fair people)* roulotte *f* 3 *(in desert)* caravane *f*, **to travel in c.** voyager en convoi
▸▸**c. park** terrain *m* de caravaning; **c. route** piste *f* caravanière; *Br* **c. site** *(for campers)* camping *m* (pour caravanes); *(of gypsies)* campement *m*

caravanette [kærəvæ'net] N camping-car *m*, *pl* camping-cars

caravan(n)ing ['kærəvænɪŋ] N caravaning *m*; **to go c., to go on a c. holiday** faire du caravaning

caravanserai [kærə'vænsəraɪ] N caravansérail *m*

caraway ['kærəweɪ] N *(plant)* carvi *m*, cumin *m* des prés
▸▸**c. seeds** (graines *fpl* de) carvi

carb [kɑːb] N *Fam* 1 *Aut* carburateur *m* 2 *(carbohydrate)* glucide *m*

carbide ['kɑːbaɪd] N *Chem, Ind* carbure *m*

carbine ['kɑːbaɪn] N *Mil* 1 *Hist* carabine *f* 2 *Am (automatic)* mitraillette *f*

carbohydrate [kɑːbəʊ'haɪdreɪt] N1 *Chem* hydrate *m* de carbone 2 *(in food)* **carbohydrates** glucides *mpl*

carbolic [kɑː'bɒlɪk] ADJ *Chem* phénique
▸▸**c. acid** phénol *m*; **c. soap** ≃ savon *m* de Marseille

carbon ['kɑːbən] N1 *Chem* carbone *m* 2 *(copy, paper)* carbone *m*
▸▸**c. copy** *(of letter etc)* double *m ou* copie *f* (au carbone); *Fig* **she is a c. copy of her mother** c'est la copie conforme de sa mère; *Aut* **c. deposit** calaminage *m*; *Chem* **c. dioxide** gaz *m* carbonique, dioxyde *m* de carbone; **c. electrode** électrode *f* de charbon; *Chem, Tex* **c. fibre** fibre *f* de carbone; *Aut* **c. filter** filtre *m* au charbon; **c.(-14) dating** *(in archaeology)* datation *f* au carbone 14; *Chem* **c. monoxide** monoxyde *m* de carbone; **c. paper** (papier *m*) carbone; *Comput* **c. ribbon** ruban *m* de carbone; *Metal* **c. steel** acier *m* carburé

carbonaceous [kɑːbə'neɪʃəs] ADJ *Chem* carboné; *Geol* carbonifère

carbonate ['kɑːbəneɪt] N *Chem* carbonate *m*

carbonated ['kɑːbəneɪtɪd] ADJ gazéifié, gazeux
▸▸**c. water** eau *f* gazeuse

carbonic [kɑːˈbɒnɪk] ADJ *Chem* carbonique

Carboniferous [kɑːbəˈnɪfərəs] ADJ, N *Geol* carbonifère *m*

carboniferous [kɑːbəˈnɪfərəs] ADJ carbonifère

carbonization [kɑːbənaɪˈzeɪʃən] N *(of wood etc)* carbonisation *f*, *Aut etc* encrassement *m*, calaminage *m*

carbonize [ˈkɑːbənaɪz] VT *Chem* carboniser; *Ind (wood etc)* carboniser, charbonner VI *Aut etc* s'encrasser, se calaminer

car-boot sale N *Br* = vente *f* à la brocante où les vendeurs exposent leurs marchandises à l'arrière de leur voiture

Carborundum® [kɑːbəˈrʌndəm] N carborundum® *m*

carboy [ˈkɑːbɔɪ] N bonbonne *f*

carbuncle [ˈkɑːbʌŋk(ə)l] N **1** *Med* furoncle *m* **2** *(gem)* escarboucle *f*

carburation [kɑːbjʊˈreɪʃən] N carburation *f*

carburettor, *Am* **carburetor** [ˈkɑːbjʊretər] N *Aut* carburateur *m*
▸▸ **c. damper** amortisseur *m* de commande sur carburateur

carcass [ˈkɑːkəs] N **1** *(of animal)* cadavre *m*, carcasse *f* **2** *(of house, ship)* charpente *f* **3** *Fam Pej (of person) (corpse)* macchabée *m*; *Fam Hum (body)* carcasse *f*; **move** or **shift your c.!** pousse-toi de là!

carcinogen [kɑːˈsɪnədʒen] N *Med* substance *f* cancérigène

carcinogenic [kɑːsɪnəʊˈdʒenɪk] ADJ *Med* cancérigène, cancérogène

carcinoma [kɑːsɪˈnəʊmə] N *Med* carcinome *m*

card¹ [kɑːd] N **1** *Cards* **(playing) c.** carte *f* (à jouer); **to play cards** jouer aux cartes; **to win at cards** gagner aux cartes; **to play one's cards well** bien jouer ses cartes; *Fig* **to play one's cards right** bien se débrouiller, bien mener sa barque; **play your cards right and you could get promoted** si tu te débrouilles bien, tu peux avoir une promotion; *Fig* **to play one's last c.** jouer son va-tout; *Fig* **to hold all the (winning** or **best) cards** avoir tous les atouts dans son jeu ou en main; *Fig* **to keep one's cards close to one's chest** cacher son jeu; *Cards, Fig* **to put one's cards on the table** mettre cartes sur table; *Fig* **to have a c. up one's sleeve** avoir un atout dans son jeu; *Fig* **it is on** or *Am* **in the cards that** … il est bien possible que …, il se pourrait fort bien que …; **I don't think that's on the cards** je ne pense pas que ce soit possible; *Fig* **to throw in the** or **one's cards** abandonner; *Old-fashioned Fam* **he's a (real) c.** or **quite a c.** c'est un original
2 *(with printed information)* carte *f*, *(postcard)* carte (postale); *Golf* carte du parcours; *Sport (list of races)* programme *m* des courses; **here's my c.** voici ma carte; *Br Fam* **to get** or **be given one's cards** être renvoyé; **birthday/Christmas c.** carte d'anniversaire/de Noël
3 *(for card index)* fiche *f*
4 *(for holding wool, buttons)* carte *f*
5 *(cardboard)* carton *m*
6 *Comput* carte *f*
7 *(plastic)* carte *f*; **banker's c., cheque c.** carte (d'identité) bancaire; **smart c.** carte à puce
▸▸ **c. catalogue** fichier *m* (de bibliothèque); **c. file** fichier; **c. game** jeu *m* de cartes; **c. index** fichier; **c. key** carte-clé *f*, *pl* cartes-clés; **c. player** joueur, -euse de cartes; **c. reader** lecteur *m* de cartes; *Comput* **c. slot** emplacement *m* pour carte; **c. table** table *f* de jeu; **c. trick** tour *m* de cartes; *Br* **c. vote** vote *m* sur carte *(chaque voix représentant le nombre de voix d'adhérents représentés)*

card² *Tex* N *(tool)* carde *f*, peigne *m*
VT *(wool etc)* carder, peigner

cardamom [ˈkɑːdəməm] N cardamome *f*

cardan joint [ˈkɑːdən] N *Aut* joint *m* de cardans

cardboard [ˈkɑːdbɔːd] N carton *m*; *(thin)* bristol *m*
▸▸ **c. box** (boîte *f* en) carton *m*; *Fig* **c. character** *(in play, novel etc)* personnage *m* sans aucune profondeur; **c. city** quartier *m* des sans-abri; **c. cutout** personnage découpé dans du carton

card-carrying ADJ
▸▸ **c. member** adhérent, -ente *(of* à)

cardiac [ˈkɑːdɪæk] ADJ *Anat, Med* cardiaque
▸▸ **c. arrest** arrêt *m* cardiaque; **he suffered c. arrest** il a eu un arrêt cardiaque; **c. massage** massage *m* cardiaque

cardigan [ˈkɑːdɪgən] N cardigan *m*, gilet *m*

cardinal [ˈkɑːdɪn(ə)l] ADJ **1** *(importance, significance)* capital, -aux; **c. error** erreur *f* fondamentale [VOIR GRAMMAIRE A76; B58–9] **2** *(colour)* pourpre, rouge cardinal *inv* N *Rel* cardinal *m*, -aux
▸▸ **c. numbers** nombres *mpl* cardinaux; **the c. points** les (quatre) points *mpl* cardinaux; *Rel* **c. sin** péché *m* capital; **the c. virtues** les (quatre) vertus *fpl* cardinales

carding [ˈkɑːdɪŋ] N *Tex* cardage *m*, peignage *m*
▸▸ **c. machine** cardeuse *f*

cardiogram [ˈkɑːdɪəʊgræm] N *Med* cardiogramme *m*

cardiograph [ˈkɑːdɪəʊgrɑːf] N *Med* cardiographe *m*

cardiologist [kɑːdɪˈɒlədʒɪst] N *Med* cardiologue *mf*

cardiology [kɑːdɪˈɒlədʒɪ] N *Med* cardiologie *f*

cardiovascular [kɑːdɪəʊˈvæskjʊlər] ADJ *Med (disease)* cardio-vasculaire, *pl* cardio-vasculaires

card-operated lock N *(in hotel etc)* serrure *f* à carte perforée

cardphone [ˈkɑːdfəʊn] N *Tel* publiphone® *m* ou téléphone *m* à carte

cardsharp(er) [ˈkɑːdʃɑːp, -ər] N tricheur, -euse professionnel(elle)

cardy [ˈkɑːdɪ] N *Fam* = **cardigan**

CARE [keər]

N	souci **1** ▪ soin **2, 3**
VI	se soucier ▪ aimer
VT	vouloir **2**

N **1** *(worry)* souci *m*, inquiétude *f*; **to be full of cares** avoir beaucoup de soucis; **to be free of** or **from c.** être insouciant; **a life of c.** une vie pleine de soucis; **she doesn't have a c. in the world** elle n'a aucun souci; **cares of State** responsabilités *fpl* d'État
2 *(attention)* soin(s) *m(pl)*, attention *f*; **constant c.** soins continuels ou assidus; **to do sth with great c.** faire qch avec beaucoup de soin; **to put a lot of c. into sth** apporter beaucoup de soin à qch; **to put a lot of c. into doing sth** mettre beaucoup de soin à faire qch; **to drive without due c.** conduire de façon imprudente; **with c.** *(on parcel etc)* fragile; **they didn't receive the proper c. in hospital** ils n'ont pas reçu les soins appropriés à l'hôpital; **to take c. of** *(invalid, child, customer, problem etc)* s'occuper de; **he doesn't take c. of his bicycle** il ne prend pas soin de son vélo; **to take good c. of sb/sth** prendre bien soin de qn/qch; **to take c. of oneself** savoir se débrouiller tout seul; *(healthwise)* prendre soin de sa santé; **take c. of yourself** *(look after yourself)* soignez-vous bien; **to take c. of one's health** ménager sa santé; **to take c. of itself** s'arranger tout seul ou de soi-même; **this should take**

c. of that stain cela devrait venir à bout de cette tache; **to take c. to do sth** avoir (bien) soin ou prendre (bien) garde de faire qch; **take c. when you cross the road** fais attention en traversant la rue; **take c.!** *(look out!)* faites attention!, prenez garde!; **take c., bye** à bientôt
3 *(looking after) (of teeth, hair etc)* soin(s) *m(pl)*; *(of machine, shoes, clothes etc)* entretien *m*; *Br Admin* **children in c.** enfants confiés aux services sociaux; **to be in/go into c.** *(of child)* être/être confié à l'Assistance publique; **to put a child in c.** confier un enfant à l'Assistance publique; **to put sb/sth in sb's c.** confier qn/qch à qn; **to be in** or **under sb's c.** être sous la responsabilité de qn; **to be under a doctor's c.** se faire soigner par un médecin; **write to me c. of Mrs Smith** or **c/o Mrs Smith** or *Am* **in c. of Mrs Smith** écrivez-moi aux bons soins de Mme Smith ou chez Mme Smith
VI *(be concerned)* se soucier, se préoccuper *(about* de); **people who c.** des gens compatissants; **no one seems to c.** tout le monde s'en moque; **no one seems to c. about the environment/the elderly** personne ne semble se préoccuper ou se soucier de l'environnement/des personnes âgées; **to care about** or **for sb** aimer qn; **of course we c. about you!** mais bien sûr qu'on t'aime; **that's all he cares about** il n'y a que cela qui l'intéresse; **who cares?** qu'est-ce que ça peut faire?; **do you really c.?** *(how I am, what my feelings are etc)* est-ce que ça t'intéresse vraiment?; **she just doesn't c.** elle s'en moque complètement, *Fam* elle n'en a rien à faire; **for all I c.** pour ce que ça me fait; **I don't c.!** ça m'est égal!, je m'en fiche!; **as if I cared!, I couldn't c. less** je m'en fiche éperdument, je m'en fous; **couldn't-c.-less attitude** je-m'en-foutisme *m*
VT **1** *(mind)* **I don't c. what he says** peu m'importe ce qu'il dit; **what do I c.?** qu'est-ce que ça peut bien me faire?; **I don't c. whether he likes it or not** que cela lui plaise ou non, ça m'est parfaitement égal
2 *(like)* **would you c. to come with me?** voulez-vous m'accompagner?, aimeriez-vous m'accompagner?; **if you c. to join us** si vous voulez vous joindre à nous
▸▸ *Br Admin* **c. in the community** = système *m* de soins prodigués aux malades mentaux en dehors du milieu hospitalier; **c. label** *(on garment)* conseils *mpl* d'entretien; **c. parcel** *(for famine relief etc)* colis *m* d'aide humanitaire
▸ **care for** VT INSEP **1** *(tend) (patients, children)* soigner; **to look well cared for** *(of animal, child, hair etc)* avoir l'air soigné ou une apparence soignée; *(of car, garden etc)* avoir l'air bien entretenu
2 *(like)* **I don't c. for this music** je n'aime pas tellement cette musique; **he doesn't c. for her** elle ne lui plaît pas; **would you c. for some tea?** voulez-vous du thé?
3 *(love) (person)* aimer, tenir à

careen [kəˈriːn] VT *Naut* **1** *(make keel over) (boat)* abattre ou mettre en carène **2** *(clean)* caréner
VI **1** *Naut (of ship)* se coucher **2** *Am (of car etc)* pencher sur le côté

careening [kəˈriːnɪŋ] N *Naut (cleaning)* carénage *m*

career¹ [kəˈrɪər] N *(working life, profession)* carrière *f*; **his dancing c.** sa carrière de danseur; **a job with c. prospects** un emploi qui offre des perspectives; **it's a good/bad c. move** c'est bon/mauvais pour ta/sa/*etc* carrière
▸▸ **c. break** interruption *f* de carrière; **c. diplomat** diplomate *mf* de carrière; **careers officer** conseiller, -ère d'orientation; **careers service** service *m* d'orientation profession-

nelle; **c. woman** = femme *f* ambitieuse *ou* qui ne pense qu'à sa carrière

career[2] **vi** **to c. (along)** aller à toute vitesse; **to c. into a lorry** *(of vehicle)* foncer dans un camion; **the car careered off the road** la voiture a quitté la route à vive allure

careerist [kə'rɪərɪst] **N** *usu Pej* carriériste *mf*

carefree ['keəfriː] **ADJ** sans souci

careful ['keəfʊl] **ADJ** **1** *(taking pains)* soigneux *(of* de), attentif *(of* à); **a c. worker** un travailleur méticuleux; **c. speakers would avoid this usage** les gens qui parlent correctement éviteraient cet usage; **to be c. of** *(appearance)* être soucieux de; **be c. of his feelings** ne heurte pas ses sentiments; **to be c. with one's money** regarder à la dépense; **to be c. to do sth** avoir soin de faire qch, veiller à faire qch; **she was c. not to mention this** elle a fait bien attention de ne pas mentionner cela; **(be) c.!** faites attention!; **be c. you don't fall** *or* **not to fall** faites attention de ne pas tomber; **be c. what you say** faites attention à ce que vous dites; **we are very c. (about) who we employ** nous faisons très attention quand nous engageons quelqu'un; **c. consideration of a question** examen *m* attentif *ou* approfondi d'une question

2 *(prudent)* prudent, circonspect; **you can't be too c. these days** de nos jours, on n'est jamais trop prudent; **a c. answer** une réponse bien pesée *ou* réfléchie; **a c. driver** un conducteur prudent

carefully ['keəfʊlɪ] **ADV 1** *(painstakingly)* soigneusement, avec soin; *(to choose)* avec soin; *(to listen)* attentivement; **a c. worded document** un document aux termes choisis avec soin **2** *(to drive, approach sb)* prudemment

carefulness ['keəfʊlnɪs] **N 1** *(taking pains)* soin *m*, attention *f* **2** *(prudence)* prudence *f*

careless ['keəlɪs] **ADJ 1** *(negligent)* négligent; *(work)* négligé; *(error, moment)* d'inattention; **accused of c. driving** accusé d'imprudence au volant; **to be c. about one's appearance** être négligé de sa personne; **she's very c. about her things** elle n'est pas soigneuse avec ses affaires **2** *(unconcerned)* insouciant, peu soucieux *(of, about* de); *Fml* **to be c. of sb's feelings** manquer de délicatesse avec qn; **a c. remark** une observation inconsidérée *ou* irréfléchie; **with a c. wave of her hand** en faisant un léger geste de la main

carelessly ['keəlɪslɪ] **ADV 1** *(negligently)* négligemment, sans soin **2** *(casually)* avec insouciance; **he threw the towel c. over his shoulder** il balança nonchalamment la serviette sur son épaule

carelessness ['keəlɪsnɪs] **N 1** *(negligence)* négligence *f* **2** *esp Lit (lack of concern)* insouciance *f*, inattention *f*

carer ['keərər] **N** *(professional)* aide *mf* à domicile; *(relative)* = personne *f* s'occupant d'un parent malade ou âgé

caress [kə'res] **N** caresse *f*
   VT caresser

caret ['kærət] **N** *Typ* signe *m* d'insertion

caretaker ['keəteɪkər] **N** *(of building, school)* concierge *mf*, gardien, -ienne; *(of museum etc)* gardien, -ienne
   ▸▸*Pol* **c. government** gouvernement *m* intérimaire

careworn ['keəwɔːn] **ADJ** *(face etc)* rongé *ou* usé par les soucis

cargo, *pl* **cargoes** ['kɑːgəʊ, -əʊz] **N** *Naut, Aviat* cargaison *f*, chargement *m*; **full c.** plein chargement; **general** *or* **mixed c.** cargaison mixte
   ▸▸**c. afloat** cargaison flottante; **c. floor** *(of truck)* plancher *m* de chargement; **c. insur-**

ance assurance *f* sur facultés; **c. list** bordereau *m* de chargement; **c. plane** avion-cargo *m*, *pl* avions-cargos; **c. ship** cargo *m*; **c. space** espace *m* cargo; **c. vessel** cargo

Note that the French word **cargo** is a false friend and is never a translation for the English word **cargo**. It means **cargo ship**.

Caribbean [kærɪ'biːən, *Am* kə'rɪbɪən] **N the C.** *(area)* les Antilles *fpl*; *(sea)* la mer des Caraïbes *ou* des Antilles; **in the C.** dans les Caraïbes, aux Antilles
   ADJ des Caraïbes
   ▸▸**the C. islands** les Antilles; **the C. Sea** la mer des Caraïbes *ou* des Antilles

caribou ['kærɪbuː] **N** caribou *m*, *pl* -ous

caricature ['kærɪkətʃʊər] **N** caricature *f*
   VT caricaturer

caricaturist [kærɪkə'tjuːrɪst] **N** caricaturiste *mf*

caries ['keəriːz] **N** *Med* carie *f*

carillon [kə'rɪljən] **N** *Mus* carillon *m*

caring ['keərɪŋ] **ADJ** *(society)* humain; **she's a c. person** c'est une personne très humaine *ou* généreuse; **a c. family atmosphere** une atmosphère familiale chaleureuse; **the c. professions** = les professions *fpl* médicales et paramédicales

carjacking ['kɑːdʒækɪŋ] **N** = vol *m* de voiture sous la menace d'une arme

carless ['kɑːlɪs] **ADJ** sans voiture

carload ['kɑːləʊd] **N 1** *Aut* pleine voiture *f*; **a c. of people/furniture** une voiture pleine de passagers/de meubles; **to arrive by the c.** arriver par voitures entières **2** *Am Rail* plein wagon *m*

Carmelite ['kɑːməlaɪt] **N** *(nun)* carmélite *f*; *(friar)* carme *m*
   ADJ carmélite

carmine ['kɑːmaɪn] **N** carmin *m*
   ADJ carmin *inv*

carnage ['kɑːnɪdʒ] **N** carnage *m*

carnal ['kɑːn(ə)l] **ADJ** charnel
   ▸▸**c. knowledge** connaissance *f* charnelle; **to have c. knowledge of sb** *Bible, Lit* connaître qn; *Law* avoir des relations sexuelles avec qn; **c. sins** péchés *mpl* de la chair

carnation [kɑː'neɪʃən] **N 1** *(flower)* œillet *m* **2** *(colour)* incarnat *m*
   ADJ *(colour)* incarnat

carnet ['kɑːneɪ] **N** *Com (customs pass)* carnet *m* de passage en douanes

carnival ['kɑːnɪv(ə)l] **N 1** *(festive occasion)* carnaval *m*, -als, fête *f*; **during C.** pendant le Carnaval; **a c. atmosphere** une ambiance de fête *ou* de carnaval **2** *(funfair)* fête *f* foraine **3** *Rel (before Lent)* carnaval *m*, -als

carnivora [kɑː'nɪvərə] **NPL** *Zool* carnivores *mpl*

carnivore ['kɑːnɪvɔːr] **N** *(animal)* carnivore *m*

carnivorous [kɑː'nɪv(ə)rəs] **ADJ 1** *(animal)* carnivore, carnassier **2** *(person, plant)* carnivore

carob ['kærəb] **N 1** *(tree)* caroubier *m* **2** *Culin* caroube *m*

carol ['kær(ə)l] **N** chant *m*, chanson *f*; **(Christmas) c.** (chant de) Noël *m*; **to go c. singing** aller chanter des chants de Noël
   vi (-ll-, *Am* -l-) **1** *(sing carols)* chanter des chants de Noël **2** *Lit (sing)* chanter (joyeusement); *(of lark)* chanter
   vt chanter joyeusement; **I'll be with you in a minute, she carolled** je suis à vous dans un instant, lança-t-elle gaiement
   ▸▸**c. service** = office *m* religieux qui précède Noël; **c. singer** = personne *f* qui, à l'époque de Noël, va chanter et quêter au profit des bonnes œuvres

> ## Carol Service
> Le "Carol Service" se tient juste avant Noël et se compose surtout de chants de Noël et de lectures de la Bible.

Carolina [kærə'laɪnə] **N** Caroline *f*; **South/North C.** Caroline du Sud/du Nord; **the Carolinas** la Caroline du Sud et la Caroline du Nord

Carolingian [kærə'lɪndʒɪən] *Hist* **ADJ** carolingien
   N Carolingien, -ienne

carom ['kærəm] **N** *Am Billiards* carambolage *m*

carotid [kə'rɒtɪd] *Anat, Med* **ADJ** *(artery)* carotide; *(nerve, system)* carotidien
   N *(artère f)* carotide *f*
   ▸▸**c. artery** artère carotide

carousal [kə'raʊz(ə)l] **N** *Old-fashioned, Hum* beuverie *f*

carouse [kə'raʊz] **vi** *Old-fashioned, Hum* faire la fête *ou Fam* la bombe

carousel [kærə'sel] = **carrousel**

carp[1] [kɑːp] **N** *inv (fish)* carpe *f*

carp[2] **vi** se plaindre; **to c. about sb/sth** se plaindre de qn/qch

carpal ['kɑːp(ə)l] **ADJ** carpien
   N carpe *m*

Carpathian [kɑː'peɪðɪən] **ADJ, N the C. Mountains, the Carpathians** les (monts *mpl*) Carpates *mpl*

carpel ['kɑːp(ə)l] **N** *Bot* carpelle *m*, carpophylle *m*

carpenter ['kɑːpɪntər] **N** charpentier *m*, menuisier *m* en bâtiments; *(making smaller objects)* menuisier
   VT charpenter

carpentry ['kɑːpɪntrɪ] **N** *Constr* charpenterie *f*, *(for smaller items)* menuiserie *f*; **that's a nice piece of c.** *(chair, table, etc)* c'est un beau travail de menuiserie

carpet ['kɑːpɪt] **N 1** tapis *m*; *(fitted, in car)* moquette *f*, **to lay a c.** poser un tapis/une moquette; *Fig* **to sweep sth under the c.** enterrer qch; *Fig* **to be on the c.** *(of question)* être sur le tapis; *(of person)* être sur la sellette; *Fig* **to have** *or* **put sb on the c.** réprimander qn **2** *Fig (of flowers, leaves etc)* tapis *m*
   vt 1 *(floor)* recouvrir d'un tapis; *(with fitted carpet)* recouvrir d'une moquette; *(room)* moquetter; **all the rooms are carpeted** il y a de la moquette dans toutes les pièces; *Fig* **the pond was carpeted with weed** le bassin était tapissé d'algues **2** *Fam (person)* réprimander
   ▸▸*Mil* **c. bombing** bombardement *m* intensif; **c. cleaner** *(product)* produit *m* nettoyant pour moquette; *(machine)* shampouineuse *f*, **c. shampoo** shampooing *m* pour moquette; **c. slippers** pantoufles *fpl*; **c. tack** fixe-tapis *m inv*; **c. tile** carreau *m* de moquette

Note that the French word **carpette** is a false friend and is never a translation for the English word **carpet**. It means **small rug**.

carpetbagger ['kɑːpɪtbægər] **N 1** *esp Am Pol Fam* candidat, -ate étranger(ère) à la circonscription **2** *Am Hist* profiteur, -euse venu(e) d'un état nordiste *(après la guerre de Sécession)*

carpeting ['kɑːpɪtɪŋ] **N 1** *(laying of carpet)* pose *f* de(s) tapis/de(s) moquette(s) *(of* dans) **2** *(carpets)* moquette *f* **3** *Fam (severe reprimand)* réprimande *f*, **to give sb a c.** passer un savon à qn

carpet-sweeper **N** balai *m* mécanique

carping ['kɑːpɪŋ] ADJ *(person)* très critique, pointilleux; *(criticism)* malveillant
N critiques *fpl*

carport ['kɑːpɔːt] N *Aut* auvent *m* pour voitures

carpus ['kɑːpəs] N *Med* carpe *m*

carriage ['kærɪdʒ] N **1** *(vehicle)* voiture *f*; *(together with horses and driver)* équipage *m*; **open/closed c.** voiture découverte/fermée; **invalid c.** voiture d'infirme; **c. and pair** voiture à deux chevaux
2 *Br Rail* voiture *f*, wagon *m*
3 *Tech (of lathe, typewriter etc)* chariot *m*; *Mil* **gun c.** affût *m*
4 *(transport)* transport *m*; *Com (cost)* (frais *mpl* de) port *m*; **c. forward** (en) port dû, port avancé; **c. free** franc de port, franco; **c. insurance paid** port payé, assurance comprise; **c. paid** (en) port payé
5 *(bearing) (of person)* port *m*, maintien *m*
▸▸ *Br* **c. clock** pendulette *f (à boîtier rectangulaire muni d'une poignée)*; **c. entrance** porte *f* cochère; *Typ* **c. release arm** *(on typewriter)* levier *m* de dégagement du chariot; *Typ* **c. return** retour *m* de chariot; *esp Am* **the c. trade** la clientèle haut de gamme

carriageway ['kærɪdʒweɪ] N *Br Aut* chaussée *f*

carrier ['kærɪər] N **1** *Med etc (of disease, germs etc)* porteur, -euse
2 *Com (company)* transporteur *m*; *Law* voiturier *m*
3 *(container) (on bicycle etc) (basket)* panier *m*; *(behind the saddle)* porte-bagages *m inv*; *(for homing pigeon)* cartouche *f*
4 *Ind (mechanism)* transporteur *m*
5 **(aircraft) c.** porte-avions *m inv*
6 *Tel (fréquence f)* porteuse *f*
▸▸ **c. bag** sac *m* en plastique; **c. pigeon** pigeon *m* voyageur; *Comput* **c. signal** signal *m* de détection de porteuse; *Tel* **c. tone** tonalité *f*

carrier-based [-'beɪst] ADJ *Aviat, Naut* embarqué

carrion ['kærɪən] N *(no pl)* charogne *f*
▸▸ *Orn* **c. crow** corneille *f* noire

carrot ['kærət] N carotte *f*, *Fig* **a pay rise is the c. management is holding out to the unions** le patronat tente d'amadouer les syndicats en promettant une hausse des salaires; **the c. and the stick** la carotte et le bâton; *Fam* **carrots, c. top** *(hair)* cheveux *mpl* roux *ou* carotte; *(person)* rouquin, -ine, poil *m* de carotte

carroty ['kærətɪ] ADJ *Fam (person, hair)* roux, rousse

carrousel [kærə'sel] N **1** *(for slides)* magasin *m* **2** *(at airport)* carrousel *m* (pour bagages) **3** *Am (at fairground)* chevaux *mpl* de bois, manège *m*

CARRY ['kærɪ] *(pt & pp* **carried)**

VT porter **1, 2, 7, 8** ▪ transporter **1**	
▪ transmettre **1** ▪ adopter **5**	
▪ vendre **6** ▪ retenir **9**	
VI porter **1**	

VT 1 *(of person, wind) (burden, bag, child, scent etc)* porter; *(goods, passengers etc)* transporter; *Med (disease)* véhiculer; *(of wires etc) (sound etc)* conduire, transmettre; *(of pipes) (water etc)* amener, transporter; *(revolver, watch etc) (on one's person)* porter (sur soi); **I don't c. much money about** *or* **on me** je n'ai jamais beaucoup d'argent sur moi; **the current carried the raft out to sea** le courant a emporté le radeau au large; **rats c. diseases** les rats sont porteurs de maladies; **a memory that he will c. with him to the grave** un souvenir qu'il n'oubliera jamais; **the bus carried us to our destination** l'autobus nous a conduits jusqu'à notre des-

tination; **we were carrying livestock** *(of ship)* nous avions du bétail à bord; **to c. sth in one's head** avoir qch en mémoire; **to c. him** les autres membres de l'équipe doivent le porter; **he's being carried by the other members of the team** il se repose sur les autres membres de l'équipe; **his strong constitution carried him through his illness** sa forte constitution lui a permis de surmonter sa maladie; **to c. a child** *(be pregnant)* porter un enfant, être enceinte; **I can't c. a tune** je suis incapable de chanter sans faire de fausses notes
2 *(involve)* porter, comporter; **to c. (no) conviction** (ne pas) être convaincant; **to c. a guarantee** être garanti; **to c. a fine/penalty** être passible d'amende/d'une peine; **to c. a risk** comporter un risque; **to c. responsibility** comporter des responsabilités; **to c. weight/authority** *(of person, opinion)* avoir du poids/de l'autorité; **to c. significance (for sb/sth)** avoir de l'importance (pour qn/qch); **to c. interest** *(of money)* porter intérêt
3 *(take, lead, extend)* **to c. an argument to its logical conclusion** aller au bout d'un raisonnement; **to c. sth too far** pousser qch trop loin; **to c. the battle** *or* **fight into the enemy's camp** *Mil* faire du territoire ennemi le lieu du conflit; *Fig* attaquer l'ennemi sur son propre terrain
4 *(capture, win) (fortress)* enlever; *(position)* emporter d'assaut; **to c. all before one** *(be successful)* remporter tous les prix; *(win support, approval)* vaincre toutes les résistances, triompher sur toute la ligne; *Hum* **she carries all before her** *(has large bosom)* il y a du monde au balcon; **to c. the day** l'emporter; **to c. several states** l'emporter dans plusieurs états; **to c. one's point** établir la validité de son argument
5 *(proposal) (pass)* adopter; *(secure passage of)* faire adopter *ou* passer; **the bill was carried** le projet a été adopté
6 *Com (keep in stock) (article)* faire, vendre, avoir; *(goods)* avoir en magasin *ou* en dépôt; **to c. an advertisement/article** *(of newspaper etc)* comporter une publicité/un article; **do you c. bathroom accessories?** *(to sales assistant)* est-ce que vous vendez des accessoires pour salles de bain?
7 *(hold)* **to c. oneself well/badly** se tenir bien/mal; **to c. one's head high** porter la tête haute
8 *Archit, Constr (beam, vault)* porter, supporter
9 *Math* **c. two** je retiens deux, on retient deux

VI 1 *(of sound, gun etc)* porter; **her voice carries well** elle a une voix qui porte bien
2 *Sl (possess drugs)* avoir de la drogue sur soi; **he was arrested for carrying** il a été arrêté parce qu'il avait de la drogue sur lui

▸ **carry along** VT SEP emporter, entraîner; *(of stream etc) (mud etc)* charrier

▸ **carry away** VT SEP **1** *(take) (object)* emporter, enlever; *(person)* entraîner, emmener
2 *(make excited, over-enthusiastic)* **he let his enthusiasm c. him away** il s'est laissé emporter par son enthousiasme; **I got carried away** je me suis emballé; **don't get carried away!** ne te laisse pas emporter!; *Iron Fam* ne t'emballe pas!

▸ **carry back** VT SEP **1** *(bring) (object)* rapporter; *(person)* ramener
2 *(take) (object)* reporter; *(person)* remmener; **that carries me back to my youth** cela me ramène à l'époque de ma jeunesse

▸ **carry down** VT SEP **1** *(from upstairs etc) (person, thing)* descendre
2 *(pass passively) (tradition)* transmettre

▸ **carry forward** VT SEP *Acct* **to c. an item forward** reporter un article; **carried forward** reporté, à reporter; **carried forward from the**

previous year report de l'exercice précédent; **carried forward to the next year** report à l'exercice suivant

▸ **carry off** VT SEP **1** *(bring, take) (object)* emporter; *(person)* emmener
2 *(win) (prize)* remporter
3 *(be successful in) (sth unusual)* faire passer, faire accepter; **to c. it off** réussir le coup; **they managed to c. the robbery off** ils ont mené à bien le cambriolage; **it's a difficult role and he didn't quite c. it off** c'est un rôle difficile, et il n'a pas su se montrer à la hauteur
4 *Old-fashioned (of disease)* emporter

▸ **carry on** VT SEP *(task)* poursuivre, continuer; *(tradition)* continuer; *(business, trade)* exercer; *(correspondence)* entretenir; **they were carrying on a conversation** ils étaient en train de parler
VI 1 *(continue)* continuer; **to c. on doing sth** continuer à faire qch; **just c. on with what you were doing** continuez ce que vous étiez en train de faire; **c. on!** continuez!; *Mil* **c. on, sergeant!** vous pouvez disposer, sergeant; **I shall c. on to the end** j'irai jusqu'au bout; **will you be able to c. on during my absence?** *(assume responsibility)* pourras-tu prendre les choses en main pendant mon absence?
2 *Fam (behave)* se comporter; **I don't like the way she carries on** je n'aime pas ses façons; **from the way he carries on anyone'd think that …** vu la façon dont il se comporte, on croirait vraiment que …
3 *Fam (behave badly)* faire des scènes, s'emporter; **don't c. on like that!** ne vous emballez pas comme ça!
4 *Fam (have an affair)* avoir une liaison (**with** avec)

▸ **carry out** VT SEP **1** *(bring, take) (object)* porter dehors/hors de la salle/*etc*; *(person)* transporter dehors
2 *(do, execute) (plan, threat, decision)* mettre à exécution; *(experiment)* effectuer; *(instructions, order)* exécuter; *(idea, order etc)* donner suite à; *(wish)* satisfaire à; *(responsibilities)* assumer; *(job)* mener à bonne fin; *(task, duty)* s'acquitter de; **the police carried o** la police a effectué une perquisition; **to c. out a procedure** suivre une procédure

▸ **carry over** VT SEP *(take, bring)* transporter de l'autre côté; *Com, Math (figure, sum)* reporter; *(practice, tradition)* continuer; **to c. over one's holiday entitlement/tax allowance to the next year** reporter ses congés/son abattement fiscal sur l'année suivante; **that will have to be carried over to the next meeting** il faudra poursuivre ce point lors de la prochaine réunion
VI *(of effect, implications)* avoir des répercussions (**into** sur); **the right carries over to future owners** les futurs propriétaires conservent ce droit

▸ **carry through** VT SEP **1** *(complete) (undertaking)* mener à bien *ou* à bonne fin *ou* à bon terme; *(task)* exécuter
2 **his strong constitution carried him through** sa forte constitution lui a permis de s'en sortir

▸ **carry up** VT SEP monter

carryall ['kærɪɔːl] N *(sac m)* fourre-tout *m inv*

carrycot ['kærɪkɒt] N porte-bébé *m inv*

carrying ['kærɪɪŋ] ADJ
▸▸ *Tech* **c. axle** *(of locomotive)* essieu *m* porteur; **c. capacity** *(of vehicle)* charge *f* utile; *(of tourist attraction)* capacité *f* d'accueil; *Com* **c. charge** *Am (extra charge)* supplément *m* *(que l'on paye lorsqu'on achète à crédit)*; *Br (transport costs)* frais *mpl* de transport; *Acct* **c. forward** report *m*

carrying-on N *Fam (foolish behaviour) (of child)* cirque *m*; *(of unfaithful spouse, lover)* écart *m* de conduite

carry-on¹ N *Fam* cinéma *m*; **what a c. just to buy a ticket!** quelle histoire *ou* quel cinéma rien que pour acheter un billet!

carry-on² ADJ *(luggage)* à main

carry-out *Scot, Am* N *(meal)* repas *m* à emporter; *(restaurant)* restaurant *m* qui fait des plats à emporter; *(alcohol)* = alcool *m* acheté (surtout) dans un pub pour être consommé à l'extérieur
  ADJ ATTRIB *(meal, food)* à emporter
  ▸▸ **c. menu** liste *f* des plats à emporter

carryover ['kærɪəʊvər] N **it's a c. from my childhood** *(habit, tradition)* c'est une habitude qui vient de mon enfance; *(fear, phobia)* c'est une peur qui vient de mon enfance

carsick ['kɑːsɪk] ADJ **to be/get c.** avoir mal au cœur en voiture

carsickness ['kɑːsɪknɪs] N mal *m* de la route

cart¹ [kɑːt] N charrette *f* (*à deux roues*); *(small)* carriole *f*, *(with four wheels)* chariot *m*; *Fig* **to put the c. before the horse** mettre la charrue avant les bœufs
  VT **1** *Fam (carry)* trimballer **2** *(transport by cart)* charrier, voiturer
  ▸▸ **c. track** chemin *m* de terre
 ▸ **cart about, cart around** VT SEP *Fam (parcels etc)* trimbal(l)er
 ▸ **cart away, cart off** VT SEP *Fam (rubbish etc)* enlever, emporter; *(person)* emmener; **he was carted away** *or* **off to prison** ils sont venus le chercher pour l'emmener en prison

cart² N *(abbr* **cartridge**) cartouche *f*, cassette *f*
  ▸▸ **c. tape** bande *f* magnétique en cartouche

cartage ['kɑːtɪdʒ] N **1** *(transport)* *(in cart)* charroi *m*, charriage *m*; *(in lorry)* camionnage *m* **2** *(cost)* *(by cart)* (coût *m* de) charriage *m*; *(by lorry)* (coût de) camionnage *m*

carte blanche ['kɑːt'blɑ̃ʃ] N **to give sb c. (to do sth)** donner carte blanche à qn (pour faire qch)

cartel [kɑː'tel] N *Com* cartel *m*; **oil/steel c.** cartel du pétrole/de l'acier; **to form a c.** former un cartel
  ▸▸ **c. laws** lois *fpl* anti-trust

carter ['kɑːtər] N charretier *m*

Cartesian [kɑː'tiːzɪən] ADJ, N *Phil* cartésien, -ienne

carthorse ['kɑːθɔːs] N cheval *m* d'attelage

Carthusian [kɑː'θjuːzɪən] ADJ **1** *Rel* chartreux **2** *Br Sch* de l'école de Charterhouse
  N **1** *Rel* chartreux, -euse **2** *Br Sch* élève *m*/ ancien élève de l'école de Charterhouse

cartilage ['kɑːtɪlɪdʒ] N cartilage *m*

cartload ['kɑːtləʊd] N charretée *f*, voiturée *f* (**of** de); *(transported in tip cart)* tombereau *m*

cartographer [kɑː'tɒɡrəfər] N cartographe *mf*

cartographic(al) [kɑːtə'ɡræfɪk, -ɪk(ə)l] ADJ cartographique

cartography [kɑː'tɒɡrəfɪ] N cartographie *f*

cartomancy ['kɑːtəmænsɪ] N cartomancie *f*

carton ['kɑːtən] N **1** *(box)* (boîte *f* en) carton *m* **2** *(container)* *(for yoghurt, cream etc)* pot *m*; *(for milk, orange juice etc)* brick *m*; **a c. of cigarettes** une cartouche de cigarettes

cartoon [kɑː'tuːn] N **1** *(in newspaper etc)* dessin *m* humoristique *ou* satirique; *Cin* dessin animé; **(strip) c.** bande *f* dessinée, BD *f* **2** *(caricature)* caricature *f* **3** *Art (sketch)* carton *m*
  ▸▸ **c. character** personnage *m* de bande dessinée *ou* de dessin animé; **c. strip** bande dessinée, BD

cartoonist [kɑː'tuːnɪst] N **1** *(in newspaper etc)* dessinateur, -trice de dessins humoristi

ques *ou* satiriques; *(of strip cartoons)* dessinateur de bandes dessinées; *(for films)* dessinateur de dessins animés, animateur, -trice **2** *(caricaturist)* caricaturiste *mf*

cartridge ['kɑːtrɪdʒ] N **1** *Mil (for firearm)* cartouche *f* **2** *(container, unit)* *(of film, ink, fuse etc)* cartouche *f*; *(on record-player)* cellule *f* de lecture; *(for tape recorder)* cassette *f*; **3** *Phot* chargeur *m* (d'appareil photo)
  ▸▸ **c. belt** *(for hunter, soldier)* cartouchière *f*, *(for machine gun)* bande *f* (de mitrailleuse), bande-chargeur *f* souple *ou* articulée, *pl* bandes-chargeurs; **c. clip** chargeur *(d'une arme à feu)*; **c. paper** papier *m* à cartouche; **c. pen** stylo *m* à cartouche; **c. tape** bande *f* magnétique en cartouche

cartwheel ['kɑːtwiːl] N roue *f* de charrette; *Gym* **to turn cartwheels** faire la roue; **to do a c.** faire une roue

cartwright ['kɑːtraɪt] N charron *m*

carve [kɑːv] VT **1** *(wood, stone)* sculpter; *(design, name on marble etc)* graver, ciseler; **to c. a statue in** *or* **out of marble** sculpter une statue dans le marbre; **carved lion** lion *m* sculpté; *Fig* **carved in stone** *or* **tablets of stone** *(instructions, orders etc)* auquel on doit obéir à la lettre; **her recommendations are not carved in stone** il n'est pas nécessaire d'obéir à la lettre à ses recommandations **2** *(meat, poultry)* découper
  VI **1** *(sculpt)* sculpter (**in** dans) **2** *(of material)* **wood that carves well/badly** bois qui se prête bien/mal à la sculpture **3** *(at meal)* découper
 ▸ **carve out** VT SEP *(cut out)* *(piece of wood etc)* tailler, découper; *(sculpt)* *(statue etc)* sculpter; *Fig* **the company carved out a niche in the market** la société s'est taillé une place sur le marché; **to c. out a career for oneself** se faire une carrière
 ▸ **carve up** VT SEP **1** *(cut)* *(meat, poultry)* découper; *Fig Fam* **to c. sb up** *(disfigure)* défigurer qn; *Fig* **Europeans carved up the continent (among themselves)** les Européens se sont partagé le continent **2** *Aut Fam (overtake dangerously)* faire une queue de poisson à; **did you see how that idiot carved me up?** tu as vu la queue de poisson que m'a faite cet imbécile?

carver ['kɑːvər] N **1** *(sculptor)* sculpteur *m* **2** *(knife)* couteau *m* à découper **3** *Br (chair)* fauteuil *m* de table *(qu'occupe le chef de famille)*

carvery ['kɑːvərɪ] N grill *m*

carving ['kɑːvɪŋ] N **1** *Art (technique, object)* sculpture *f*; *(on wood, metal)* gravure *f*; *(on metal, stone)* ciselure *f*; **wood c.** sculpture sur bois **2** *(of meat)* découpage *m*
  ▸▸ **c. fork** fourchette *f* à découper; **c. knife** couteau *m* à découper; **c. set** service *m* à découper; **c. table** table *f* à découper

carwash ['kɑːwɒʃ] N *Aut* lave-auto *m*, *pl* lave-autos

caryatid [kærɪ'ætɪd] N *Archit* cariatide *f*

cascade [kæs'keɪd] N *(waterfall)*, *Fig* cascade *f*
  VI *(of water etc)*, *Fig (of balloons, hair)* tomber en cascade; **the tins came cascading down** les boîtes de conserve sont tombées les unes après les autres

cascading menu [kæs'keɪdɪŋ] N *Comput* menu *m* en cascade

CASE [keɪs] N *Comput (abbr* **computer-aided software engineering**) ingénierie *f* des systèmes assistée par ordinateur

CASE¹ [keɪs]

cas **1, 2, 4**	▪	affaire **3**	▪	arguments **3**

N **1** *(instance, situation)* cas *m*; **a c. in point** un cas d'espèce; **to put the c. clearly** exposer

clairement le cas *ou* la situation; **if that's the c.** dans ce cas-là, *Fml* s'il en est ainsi; **should that be the c.** le cas échéant; **it's a c. of now or never** il s'agit de saisir l'occasion *ou* de faire vite; **in c. of emergency/accident/ need** en cas d'urgence/d'accident/de besoin; **in c. he isn't there** au cas *ou* dans le cas où il n'y serait pas; **just in c.** à titre de précaution, *Fam* au cas où; **just in c. it rains I'll take an umbrella** je prends un parapluie, juste au cas où il pleuvrait; **I'll take an umbrella, just in c.** je prends un parapluie au cas où; **in any c.** en tout cas; *(besides)* de toute façon; **in that c.** dans ce cas; **in such a c., in such cases** en pareil cas, en pareille circonstance; **in these cases it's best to wait** dans de telles circonstances, il vaut mieux attendre; **in his c.** dans son cas; **let's take the c. of Mrs Smith** prenons le cas de Mme Smith; **or not, as the c. may be** ou non, suivant le cas; **in most cases** dans la plupart des cas; **it appears to be a c. of mistaken identity** il semble y avoir erreur sur la personne; **if it's a c. of not having enough money** si c'est une question d'argent; *Fam* **he's always on my c.** je l'ai tout le temps sur le dos; *Fam* **get off my c.!** lâche-moi les baskets!, oublie-moi!

2 *Med (of jaundice, scarlet fever etc)* cas *m*; *(patient)* malade *mf*; **heart c.** cardiaque *mf*; *Fam* **he's a c.** *(odd)* c'est un drôle de type

3 *Law etc* affaire *f*; **famous cases** causes *fpl ou* affaires célèbres; **the police are working on the c.** la police enquête sur cette affaire; **the c. will be heard on January 5th** l'audience aura lieu le 5 janvier; **to state** *or* **put one's c.** plaider sa cause; **to put the c. for the defence** présenter la défense du prévenu; **the c. for the Crown** *(in criminal trial)* l'accusation *f*; **there is no c. against you** vous êtes hors de cause; **the judge ruled that there was no c. to answer** le juge a rendu un non-lieu; *Fig* **the c. for sb/sth** les arguments *mpl* en faveur de qn/qch; **to put up a strong c. for sb** *(defend)* prendre le parti de qn, défendre qn; *(recommend)* recommander qn très chaudement; **divorce c.** procès *m* en divorce

4 *Gram* cas *m*
  ▸▸ *Gram* **c. ending** désinence *f*; **c. history** antécédents *mpl*; **c. law** jurisprudence *f*, droit *m* jurisprudentiel; *Law* **c. load** (nombre *m* de) dossiers *mpl* à traiter; **c. study** étude *f* de cas

case² N **1** *(large)* **(packing) c.** caisse *f*, boîte *f* (d'emballage); **c. of wine** caisse de vin

2 *(for specific object)* *(for spectacles, cigarettes, musical instrument etc)* étui *m*; *(for jewellery)* coffret *m*, écrin *m*; *(for pencils, geometry etc instruments)* trousse *f*, **(display** *or* **glass) c.** vitrine *f*; **record c.** mallette *f* porte-disques; **dressing c.** nécessaire *m* ou trousse *f* de toilette; **card c.** porte-cartes *m inv*

3 *(suitcase)* valise *f*; *(briefcase)* porte-documents *m inv*

4 *(outer part)* *(of piano)* coffre *m*, caisse *f*, *(of organ)* buffet *m*; *(of clock)* caisse; *(of watch etc)* boîtier *m*; *(of lock)* palastre *m*, coffre; *(of cartridge)* douille *f*, étui *m*; *(of engine cylinder)* chemise *f*, enveloppe *f*; *(of turbine)* bâche *f*; *Aut (of differential etc)* carter *m*

5 *(in bookbinding)* couverture *f* cartonnée

6 *Typ* casse *f*; **lower c.** bas *m* de casse; **lower-c. letter** minuscule *f*; **upper c.** haut *m* de casse; **upper-c. letter** (lettre *f*) majuscule *f*, (lettre) capitale *f*; *Comput* **c. insensitive** qui ne distingue pas les majuscules des minuscules; *Comput* **c. sensitive** qui distingue les majuscules des minuscules; **this e-mail address is c. sensitive** cette adresse électronique tient compte des majuscules

VT 1 (*put in box*) (*goods*) mettre en caisse(s) **2** (*put outer layer on*) envelopper (**with** de); (*boiler, cylinder*) chemiser; (*turbine*) bâcher **3** (*in bookbinding*) (*book*) cartonner **4** *Sl* **to c. the joint** (*before burglary*) examiner les lieux

casebook ['keɪsbʊk] **N 1** *Law* recueil *m* de jurisprudence **2** *Med* dossier *m* médical

casebound ['keɪsbaʊnd] **ADJ** (*book*) cartonné

cased [keɪst] **ADJ** (*edition*) cartonné

case-harden **VT** *Metal* (*steel*) tremper *ou* durcir à la surface

case-hardened **ADJ** *Metal* trempé à la surface; *Fam* (*person*) endurci

case-hardening **N** *Metal* (*of steel*) cémentation *f*

casein ['keɪsɪɪn] **N** *Chem, Ind* caséine *f*

casement ['keɪsmənt] **N** (*frame*) châssis *m* de fenêtre à deux battants
▸▸ **c. window** fenêtre *f* à battant *ou* battants, croisée *f*

casework ['keɪswɜːk] **N** *Med* traitement *m* individuel; (*social work*) assistance *f* individuelle

caseworker ['keɪswɜːkər] **N** assistant, -ante social(e)

cash [kæʃ] **N** (*no pl*) (*coins, banknotes*) argent *m*, liquide *m*; (*in commerce*) liquide, espèces *fpl*; *Fam* (*money*) argent, *Fam* fric *m*; **I haven't got any c.** (*no money*) je n'ai pas d'argent; (*no change*) je n'ai pas de monnaie; *Fam* **I'm short of c.** je suis à sec; **that's an awful lot of c.** c'est beaucoup d'argent *ou Fam* de fric; **to pay (in) c.** payer comptant; (*money not cheque*) payer en liquide *ou* en espèces; **will that be c. or shall I charge it to your account?** (*not credit*) vous payez comptant ou est-ce que je le mets sur votre compte?; (*money not cheque*) vous payez en liquide ou est-ce que je le mets sur votre compte?; **c. (purchases) only** (*notice at checkout*) paiements en liquide seulement; *Com* **c. against documents** comptant contre documents; *Acct* **c. at bank** avoir *m* en banque; **c. on delivery** paiement à la livraison; **c. in hand** fonds *mpl ou* espèces *ou* argent en caisse; **it's all c. in hand in this sort of work** dans cette branche, tout se paye de la main à la main; *Acct* **c. in till** encaisse *f*, *Acct* **c. on hand** argent en caisse; *Com* **c. with order** paiement *m* à la commande, envoi *m* contre paiement; **discount for c.** escompte *m* de caisse
▸▸ **c. account** compte *m* de caisse; **c. advance** avance *m* en numéraire; **c. balance** (*status*) situation *f* de caisse; (*amount remaining*) solde *m* actif, solde de caisse; *Acct* **c. basis accounting** comptabilité *f* de caisse *ou* de gestion; **c. benefits** avantages *mpl* en espèces; **c. bonus** prime *f* en espèces; **c. book** livre *m ou* journal *m* de caisse; **c. box** caisse *f*; **c. budget** budget *m* de trésorerie; **c. card** carte *f* de retrait; *Br* **c. and carry** libre-service *m* de gros, *pl* libres-services; *Acct* **c. contribution** apport *m* en numéraire *ou* en espèces; *Mktg* **c. cow** vache *f* à lait; *Agr* **c. crop** culture *f* de rapport *ou* commerciale; *Com* **c. deal** marché *m* au comptant; **c. deficit** déficit *m* de trésorerie; **c. deposit** versement *m* en espèces; **c. desk** caisse *f*; **c. discount** escompte de caisse; **c. dispenser** distributeur *m* (automatique) de billets, DAB *m*, *Suisse* bancomat *m*; **c. dividend** dividende *m* en espèces; *Acct* **c. expenditure** dépenses *fpl* de caisse; **c. incentive** stimulation *f* financière; *Acct* **c. inflow** rentrées *fpl* de fonds; *Acct* **c. ledger** journal *m* de caisse; *Banking* **c. machine** distributeur de

billets; **c. management** gestion *f* de trésorerie; *Acct* **c. order** ordre *m* au comptant; *Acct* **c. outflow** sorties *fpl* de trésorerie; *Acct* **c. overs** excédent *m* de caisse; **c. payment** (*immediate*) paiement comptant; (*in cash*) paiement en espèces *ou* en liquide; *Banking* **c. point** distributeur *ou* guichet *m* automatique; *Acct* **c. position** situation de caisse; **c. price** prix *m* comptant; **c. purchase** achat *m* au comptant, achat contre espèces; *Acct* **c. ratio** ratio *m* de trésorerie; *Com* **c. rebate** remboursement *m*; *Acct* **c. receipt** reçu *m* pour paiement en espèces, reçu d'espèces; *Acct* **c. received** (*balance sheet item*) entrée *f* d'argent; **c. register** caisse (enregistreuse); *Acct* **c. report (form)** situation de caisse; **c. reserves** réserves *fpl* en espèces; *St Exch* **c. settlement** liquidation *f* en espèces; *Fin* **c. shortage** insuffisance *f* de trésorerie; *Acct* **c. statement** état *m ou* relevé *m* de caisse; *Acct* **c. surplus** restant *m* en caisse; **c. transaction** transaction *f ou* opération *f* au comptant; *Mktg* **c. trap** poids *m* mort; *Acct* **c. unders** manque *m* de caisse; *Fin* **c. voucher** pièce *f* de caisse, PC *f*; **c. withdrawals** retraits *mpl* d'espèces
▸ **cash in** **VT SEP** *Fin* (*exchange for money*) **to c. in savings stamps** se faire rembourser des timbres-épargne; *Sl* **to c. in one's chips** *or* **checks** (*die*) casser sa pipe
▸ **cash in on** **VT INSEP** *Fam* (*derive benefit from*) profiter de, tirer profit de
▸ **cash up** **VI** *Br* faire les comptes

cashable ['kæʃ(ə)bl] **ADJ** (*bill etc*) encaissable

cashback ['kæʃbæk] **N** *Br* = espèces *fpl* retirées à la caisse d'un magasin lors d'un paiement par carte

cashew [kæ'ʃuː] **N** (*tree*) anacardier *m*; (*nut*) (noix *f* de) cajou *m*
▸▸ **c. nut** (noix de) cajou; **c. nut tree** anacardier

cashflow ['kæʃfləʊ] **N** *Fin* cash-flow *m*, *pl* cash-flows, trésorerie *f*; *Acct* (*in cashflow statement*) marge *f* brute d'autofinancement; *Fam* **I've got a c. problem** j'ai des problèmes d'argent
▸▸ **c. forecast** prévision *f* de trésorerie; **c. management** gestion *f* de trésorerie; *Acct* **c. statement** état *m* des mouvements de la trésorerie

cashier ¹ [kæ'ʃɪər] **N** caissier, -ière; *Am* **c.'s check** chèque *m* de banque; **c.'s desk** comptoir-caisse *m*, *pl* comptoirs-caisses; **c.'s office** bureau *m* du caissier

cashier ² **VT** *Mil, Naut* (*dismiss*) casser

cashless ['kæʃlɪs] **ADJ** **the c. society** la société où l'argent liquide n'est plus utilisé; **c. transaction** transaction *f* sans argent

cashmere ['kæʃmɪər] **N** *Tex* cachemire *m*; **c. shawl** (*châle m* de) cachemire; **c. sweater** pull *m* en cachemire

casing ['keɪsɪŋ] **N 1** (*process*) (*of goods*) encaissage *m*, mise *f* en caisses; (*of book*) cartonnage *m*; (*of mine shaft etc*) tubage *m*, cuvelage *m* **2** (*outer layer*) (*of pump etc*) enveloppe *f*, garniture *f*; (*of cylinder*) blindage *m*, chemise *f*; (*of turbine*) huche *f*, bâche *f* fermée; (*of machine*) cage *f*, coquille *f*; *Constr* (*for reinforced concrete*) coffrage *m*; *Aut* (*of differential*) carter *m*; (*of clutch*) boîte *f*, caisse *f*, carter; **tyre c.** enveloppe (extérieure) de pneu

casino [kə'siːnəʊ] **N** casino *m*

cask [kɑːsk] **N** fût *m*, tonneau *m*; *Com* **wine in the c.** vin *m* en fût

casket ['kɑːskɪt] **N 1** (*for jewellery*) coffret *m*, cassette *f*; (*for money*) cassette **2** *esp Am* (*coffin*) cercueil *m* **3** (*for ashes*) urne *f*

CASM ['kæz(ə)m] **N** *Comput* (*abbr* **computer-aided sales and marketing**) vente *f* et marketing *m* assistés par ordinateur

Caspian ['kæspɪən] **ADJ** caspien; **the C. Sea** la mer Caspienne

Cassandra [kə'sændrə] **N** *Myth* Cassandre *f*, *Fig* oiseau *m* de malheur

cassata [kə'sɑːtə] **N** *Culin* cassate *f*

cassava [kə'sɑːvə] **N** *Bot* cassave *f*, manioc *m*
▸▸ **c. flour** farine *f* de manioc

casserole ['kæsərəʊl] **N 1** *Br* (*pan*) cocotte *f* **2** (*food*) ragoût *m* en cocotte; **beef c.** ragoût de bœuf
VT (*meat etc*) cuire à la cocotte

> Note that the French word **casserole** is a false friend and is never a translation for the English word **casserole**. It means **saucepan**.

cassette [kə'set] **N 1** (*audio, video etc*) cassette *f* **2** *Phot* chargeur *m*
▸▸ **c. case** étui *m* de cassette; **c. deck** lecteur *m* de cassettes; *Comput* **c. drive** lecteur de cassettes; **c. head cleaner** cassette autonettoyante; **c. library** cassettothèque *f*, **c. player** lecteur de cassettes; **c. recorder** magnétophone *m* à cassettes

cassock ['kæsək] **N** *Rel* soutane *f*

cassowary ['kæsəweərɪ] **N** (*bird*) casoar *m*

CAST [kɑːst]

N	acteurs **1**	• coup **2**	• plâtre **3**
• moulage **3**			
VT	projeter **1**	• jeter **1**	• distribuer les
rôles de **3**	• mouler **5**		

N 1 *Theat, Cin, TV* distribution *f*, acteurs *mpl*; **the c. is Italian** tous les acteurs sont italiens; **the members of the c.** la distribution; **members of the c. include ...** parmi les comédiens il y a ...; *esp Radio* **other parts were played by members of the c.** les autres rôles étaient tenus par les comédiens déjà nommés; **he was in the c. of ...** il a joué dans ...; *Theat* **to have a c. of three** être joué par trois acteurs; *Cin* **a c. of thousands** des milliers d'acteurs; **c. and credits** générique *m* **2** (*of dice, net*) coup *m*; (*in fishing*) (*of line, fly, net*) lancer *m* **3** *Med* plâtre *m*; *Art, Metal etc* (*mould*) moule *m* en creux; (*item*) pièce *f* moulée; (*of plaster*) plâtre; **plaster c.** *Art* moulage *m* au plâtre; *Med* plâtre; **to take a c. of sth** mouler qch; **the dentist took a c. of my teeth** le dentiste a fait un moulage en plâtre de mes dents; **they took a c. of the footprints** ils ont relevé les empreintes de pas; **to have one's arm in a c.** avoir le bras dans le plâtre **4** (*squint*) **to have a c. in one's eye** avoir une coquetterie dans l'œil **5** *Lit* **a man of his c.** un homme de sa trempe; **c. of mind** mentalité *f* **6** (*of earthworm*) déjections *fpl* **7** (*skin of insect, snake*) dépouille *f* **8** (*regurgitated food*) pelote *f* régurgitée (*par les hiboux, les faucons*)

VT (*pt, pp* **cast**) **1** (*shadow*) porter, projeter; *Fml* (*stone etc*) jeter, lancer; (*net, line*) lancer; *Fml* **she c. her eyes over the letter** elle a parcouru la lettre; *Naut* **to c. anchor** jeter l'ancre; **to c. doubt on sth** jeter le doute sur qch; **this cast doubt on his ability** cela jeta un doute sur ses capacités; **to c. its skin** (*of reptile*) muer; **to c. a shoe** (*of horse*) perdre un fer; **to c. a spell over sb** ensorceler qn, envoûter qn **2** *Pol etc* **to c. a vote, to c. one's vote** voter (**for** pour); **the numbers of votes c. for ...** le nombre de voix pour ... **3** *Theat, Cin, TV* (*play, film*) distribuer les rôles de; **to c. sb for a part** attribuer un rôle à qn; **she was c. as** *or* **in the role of Desdemona** on lui a donné le rôle de Desdémone; *Fig* **to c. sb in the role of the villain** donner à qn le rôle du méchant

4 *(horoscope)* faire
5 *Art, Metal etc (metal)* fondre; *(cylinder etc)* mouler, couler; *(medal)* sabler; *(statue)* couler; **the statue had been cast in bronze** la statue avait été coulée dans le bronze; **cast in one piece** coulé en bloc
vi lancer; **to c. for fish** pêcher au lancer
ADJ *Art, Metal* coulé, fondu
▶▶**c. iron** fonte *f;* **c. list** *Cin, TV* générique; *Theat* distribution; **c. steel** acier *m* moulé; *Cer* **c. ware** pièces coulées
▶**cast about, cast around vi** chercher; **to c. around for sth** chercher qch
▶**cast aside vt sep** jeter sur le côté; *Fig (wife, friends, doubts)* abandonner, se défaire de; **to c. aside one's fears** oublier ses craintes; **to c. aside one's former life** changer de vie; **are you going to c. all this aside for a foolish dream?** est-ce que tu vas renoncer à tout ça pour une chimère?
▶**cast away vt sep** *Naut* **to be c. away** faire naufrage
▶**cast back vt sep** **to c. one's mind back** revenir en arrière; **to c. one's mind back to sth** se rappeler qch; **c. your mind back a year** souvenez-vous de *ou* rappelez-vous l'année dernière
▶**cast down vt sep 1** *(eyes)* baisser; *(weapons)* déposer
2 *Lit* **to be c. down** *(dejected)* être abattu *ou* découragé *ou* déprimé
▶**cast off vt sep 1** *(reject) (person)* rejeter
2 *(clothes)* enlever, se dépouiller de; *(bonds etc)* se défaire de, se libérer de; *Fig (shyness etc)* se débarrasser de
3 *Knitting (stitches)* arrêter
4 *Naut (moorings)* larguer
vi 1 *Naut (of ship)* larguer les amarres
2 *Knitting* arrêter les mailles
▶**cast on** *Knitting* **vt sep** *(stitches)* monter
vi monter les mailles
▶**cast out vt sep 1** *(reject) (person)* rejeter
2 *(exorcise) (evil spirits)* chasser, exorciser
▶**cast up vt sep 1 to c. sth up to sb** *(as reproach)* reprocher qch à qn
2 *(of sea)* rejeter

castanets [kæstə'nets] **NPL (pair of) c.** (paire *f* de) castagnettes *fpl*

castaway ['kɑːstəweɪ] **N** naufragé, -ée

caste [kɑːst] **N** caste *f;* **high/low-c.** de haute/basse caste; *Fig* **to lose c.** se discréditer

casteless ['kɑːstlɪs] **ADJ** sans caste

castellated ['kæstɪleɪtɪd] **ADJ** *Archit* crénelé; *(with turrets)* à tourelles

caster ['kɑːstər] **N 1** *Metal etc (machine)* fondeuse *f* **2** *(for sugar, cocoa)* saupoudroir *m*
▶▶*Aut* **c. action** *(of steering)* effet *m* de chasse; *Br* **c. sugar** sucre *m* en poudre

castigate ['kæstɪgeɪt] **vt 1** *Old-fashioned (punish) (person)* châtier, corriger **2** *Fml (criticize) (person, book etc)* critiquer sévèrement, étriller

castigation [kæstɪ'geɪʃən] **N 1** *Old-fashioned (punishment)* châtiment *m*, correction *f* **2** *Fml (criticism)* critique *f* sévère

Castile [kæ'stiːl] **N** Castille *f;* **New C.** Nouvelle-Castille *f*

Castilian [kæs'tɪlɪən] **ADJ** castillan
N 1 *(person)* Castillan, -ane **2** *Ling* castillan *m*

casting ['kɑːstɪŋ] **N 1** *(in fishing)* lancer *m* **2** *Art, Metal etc (process)* moulage *m*, fonte *f;* *(individual item)* pièce *f* coulée, pièce de fonte; **heavy castings** grosses pièces; **die c.** *(item)* pièce moulée sous pression; **sand c.** *(process)* coulée *f* en sable **3** *Cin, Theat* distribution *f* des rôles, casting *m;* *Fam* **she got the part through the c. couch** elle a eu le rôle parce qu'elle a couché avec le metteur en scène
▶▶*Cin, Theat* **c. director** directeur, -trice de

casting, régisseur *m* de distribution; *Fishing* **c. net** épervier *m;* *Knitting* **c. off** arrêt *m* (de mailles); *Knitting* **c. on** montage *m* (de mailles); **c. vote** voix *f* prépondérante; **the chairman has the c. vote** la voix du président est prépondérante

castle ['kɑːs(ə)l] **N 1** château *m;* *(fortress)* château fort; *Fig* **to build castles in the air** *or* **in Spain** bâtir des châteaux en Espagne **2** *Chess* tour *f*
vi *Chess* roquer

castling ['kɑːs(ə)lɪŋ] **N** *Chess* roque *f*

cast-off N 1 *(item of clothing)* vieux vêtement *m;* **I used to wear my brother's cast-offs** je portais les vieilles nippes de mon frère **2** *Fig (person) (male)* laissé-pour-compte *m, pl* laissés-pour-compte; *(female)* laissée-pour-compte *f, pl* laissées-pour-compte; **one of society's cast-offs** un laissé-pour-compte de la société; **the manager had built a team from other clubs' cast-offs** le directeur sportif avait formé une équipe avec les joueurs dont les autres équipes ne voulaient pas; **I'm not going out with one of his cast-offs** je ne veux pas sortir avec une copine dont il ne veut plus **3** *Typ (in printing)* calibrage *m*
ADJ dont personne ne veut; **c. clothing** vieux vêtements

castor ['kɑːstər] **N** *(on chair, bed etc)* roulette *f;* **the desk is on castors** le bureau est sur roulettes
▶▶**c. oil** huile *f* de ricin

castrate [kæs'treɪt] **vt** *(animal, man)* châtrer, castrer; *Fig (text etc)* mutiler, expurger

castration [kæs'treɪʃən] **N** *(of animal, man)* castration *f;* *Fig (of text etc)* mutilation *f*, expurgation *f*

castrato, *pl* **castrati** [kæ'strɑːtəʊ, -tiː] **N** *Mus* castrat *m*

casual ['kæʒjʊ(ə)l] **ADJ 1** *(remark)* en passant, désinvolte; *(glance)* au hasard; **it was just a c. remark** j'ai/il a etc dit ça en passant; **to engage in c. conversation** parler de choses et d'autres *ou* de la pluie et du beau temps; **to throw out a c. suggestion** suggérer quelque chose en passant; **to the c. observer** pour un observateur non-averti
2 *(relaxed) (person, manner, approach)* décontracté; **they were very c. about the danger** ils ne se sont pas souciés du danger
3 *(not serious, not taking sth seriously)* insouciant; **your attitude's too c.** tu es trop insouciant; **I found the police very c. about the whole situation** j'ai trouvé que la police a manqué de sérieux dans cette affaire
4 *(jacket etc)* sport *inv*, décontracté
5 *(employment, worker)* temporaire
6 *(encounter)* fortuit, accidentel
N *Br Fam (football supporter)* jeune supporter *m* de foot *(soucieux de sa mise et souvent responsable de violences)*
NPL casuals *(shoes)* mocassins *mpl*
▶▶**c. clothes** tenue *f* sport *inv ou* décontractée; **c. employment** *(temporary)* emploi *m* temporaire; *(without social benefits)* = emploi précaire sans avantages sociaux; **c. labour** main-d'œuvre *f* occasionnelle *ou* temporaire, *pl* mains-d'œuvre; **c. sex** rapports *mpl* sexuels de rencontre; **c. wear** tenue sport *ou* décontractée; **c. worker** *(temporary)* employé, -ée *ou* travailleur, -euse temporaire; *(without social benefits)* = employé qui ne bénéficie d'aucun avantage social

casualisation [kæʒjʊ(ə)laɪ'zeɪʃən] **N the c. of labour** la précarisation de l'emploi

casually ['kæʒjʊəlɪ] **ADV 1** *(to remark, suggest)* en passant
2 *(to walk, do sth)* avec décontraction; **she told him, quite c., that she had …** elle lui a dit, tout tranquille, qu'elle avait …

3 *(not seriously enough)* *(to treat sth)* avec trop de décontraction; **they're treating this far too c.** il y a un manque de sérieux
4 to dress c. s'habiller décontracté *ou Fam* décontract; **you're much too c. dressed to …** tu es habillé de façon bien trop décontractée pour …
5 *(to meet)* par hasard

casualness ['kæʒjʊ(ə)lnɪs] **N 1** *(of remark)* désinvolture *f* **2** *(of style of dress, approach)* décontraction *f* **3** *(lack of seriousness)* manque *m* de sérieux

casualty ['kæʒjʊəltɪ] **N 1** *(victim)* *(in accident, fire, earthquake etc)* victime *f;* *(in war)* blessé, -ée; *(in road accident)* blessé, accidenté, -ée; **to be a c. of sth** être la victime de qch; **there were no casualties** il n'y a pas eu de victimes; *Mil* **casualties** pertes *fpl;* *Fig* **the party had many casualties in the last election** le parti a perdu beaucoup de députés aux dernières élections; **freedom of speech was one of the first casualties** la liberté d'expression a été une des premières choses à disparaître; **these children are the casualties of divorce** ces enfants sont les victimes du divorce **2** *Br (hospital department)* urgences *fpl;* **she was taken to c.** elle a été emmenée aux urgences
▶▶*Br* **c. department** *(of hospital)* service *m* des urgences; *Mil* **c. list, c. return** état des pertes

casuist ['kæzjʊɪst] **N** casuiste *m*

casuistry ['kæzjʊɪstrɪ] **N** casuistique *f*

CAT [kæt] **N** *Med (abbr* **computerized axial tomography)** TDM *f*
▶▶**C. scan** scanographie *f*

cat [kæt] **N 1** *(male)* chat *m;* *(female)* chatte *f,* **tom c.** matou *m;* **ginger** *or Fam* **marmalade c.** chat roux tigré; **wild c.** chat sauvage; **the big cats** *(lions, tigers etc)* les grands félins *mpl;* **it smelled of cats** ça sentait le pipi de chat; *Fam* **that looks like something the c.'s brought in** ça, c'est dégoûtant; *Fam* **you look like something the c.'s brought in** tu es dans un état lamentable; **to fight like c. and dog** s'entendre comme chien et chat; *Fam* **c. got your tongue?** tu as perdu ta langue?; *Fam* **he thinks he's the c.'s whiskers** il se croit sorti de la cuisse de Jupiter; **to see which way the c. jumps** voir d'où vient le vent; **to play a c.-and-mouse game with sb** jouer au chat et à la souris avec qn; *Prov* **when the c.'s away the mice will play** quand le chat n'est pas là, les souris dansent; *Prov* **a c. may look at a king** = un chien regarde bien un évêque; *Fam* **to be like a c. on hot bricks** *or* **on a hot tin roof** ne pas tenir en place; *Fam* **to let the c. out of the bag** vendre la mèche; *Fam* **to put** *or* **set the c. among the pigeons** jeter un pavé dans la mare; *Fam* **there's no** *or* **there isn't enough room to swing a c.** on ne peut pas se tourner
2 *Pej (woman, girl)* sale vache *f*
3 *Am Sl (man)* type *m,* individu *m*
▶▶**c. burglar** monte-en-l'air *m inv;* **c.'s cradle** *(game)* = jeu *m* qui consiste à faire des figures avec une ficelle; *Aut* **c.'s eyes®** catadioptres *mpl,* cataphotes® *mpl,* yeux *mpl* de chat; **c. flap** chatière *f;* **c. litter** litière *f* (pour chats); **c. show** exposition *f* féline

cataclysm ['kætəklɪz(ə)m] **N** cataclysme *m*

cataclysmic [kætə'klɪzmɪk] **ADJ** cataclysmique

catacombs ['kætəkuːmz] **NPL** catacombes *fpl*

catafalque ['kætəfælk] **N** catafalque *m*

Catalan ['kætəlæn] **ADJ** catalan
N 1 *(person)* Catalan, -ane **2** *Ling* catalan *m*

catalepsy ['kætəlepsɪ] **N** *Med* catalepsie *f*

cataleptic [kætə'leptɪk] **ADJ, N** *Med* cataleptique *mf*

catalogue, *Am* **catalog** ['kætəlɒg] **N 1** *Com (book)* catalogue *m* **2** *(list) (of books, works etc)* catalogue *m*; *Fig* **the holiday was a c. of disasters** les vacances ont été une suite de catastrophes; **subject c.** catalogue thématique
VT cataloguer
▸ ▸ **c. number** référence *f*, *(for library book)* référence bibliographique; *Com* **c. price** prix *m* catalogue; *Com* **c. selling** vente *f* par catalogue

cataloguing, *Am* **cataloging** ['kætəlɒgɪŋ] **N** catalogage *m*

Catalonia [kætə'ləʊnɪə] **N** Catalogne *f*

catalysis [kə'tælɪsɪs] **N** *Chem* catalyse *f*

catalyst ['kætəlɪst] **N** *Chem, Fig* catalyseur *m*

catalytic [kætə'lɪtɪk] **ADJ** *Chem* catalytique; *Fig* catalyseur
▸ ▸ *Aut* **c. converter** pot *m* catalytique

catamaran [kætəmə'ræn] **N** *Naut* catamaran *m*

cataplasm ['kætəplæz(ə)m] **N** *Med* cataplasme *m*

catapult ['kætəpʌlt] **N 1** *Br (for stones etc)* fronde *f* **2** *(on aircraft carrier)* catapulte *f*
VT catapulter, projeter; *Tech (plane)* catapulter; **he catapulted the stone over the wall** il a lancé la pierre par-dessus le mur; *Fig* **these reforms catapulted the country into the 20th century** ces réformes ont propulsé le pays dans le vingtième siècle; **to c. sb to stardom** *(of film etc)* propulser qn vers la célébrité
VI entrer en trombe (**into a room** dans une pièce)

cataract ['kætərækt] **N** *(in river), Med* cataracte *f*

catarrh [kə'tɑːr] **N** *Med* catarrhe *m*; **bronchial c.** bronchite *f*

catarrhal [kə'tɑːr(ə)l] **ADJ** *(cough, person)* catarrheux

catastrophe [kə'tæstrəfɪ] **N** catastrophe *f*, **to head for/end in c.** aller vers la/se terminer en catastrophe

catastrophic [kætə'strɒfɪk] **ADJ** *(effect etc)* catastrophique

catastrophically [kætə'strɒfɪklɪ] **ADV** d'une façon catastrophique

catatonia [kætə'təʊnɪə] **N** *Med* catatonie *f*

catatonic [kætə'tɒnɪk] **N, ADJ** *Med* catatonique *mf*

catcall ['kætkɔːl] **N** *Theat etc* sifflet *m* de mécontentement; **there were catcalls from the audience** le public a sifflé en signe de mécontentement
VT *(actor)* siffler
VI *(of audience)* siffler (en signe de mécontentement)

CATCH [kætʃ]

N	prise **1** ▪ pêche **2** ▪ loquet **4** ▪ piège **5**
VT	attraper **1, 2, 6** ▪ saisir **3** ▪ attirer **4** ▪ se prendre **5**
VI	se prendre **4**

N 1 *(of ball etc)* prise *f* au vol; **that was a good c.** bien joué!; **to make an easy/a difficult c.** attraper une balle facile/difficile; **to play c.** *(of children)* jouer au ballon
2 *(in fishing)* pêche *f*, **to have a good c.** faire (une) bonne pêche; **the day's c.** la pêche de la journée
3 *(person as marriage partner)* parti *m*; **he's/she's no great c.** ce n'est pas un bon parti
4 *(fastening) (on door etc)* loquet *m*, loqueteau *m*; *(of window)* loqueteau; *(to permit dismantling, opening etc)* crochet *m*; *(to limit movement of mechanism, drawer etc)* taquet *m*
5 *(disadvantage)* piège *m*; **there's a c. in it** il y

a un truc *ou* un piège; **that's** *or* **there's the c.** voilà le hic;
6 **with a c. in one's voice** la voix pleine d'émotion
7 *Mus* canon *m*
8 *(in rowing)* attaque *f*
VT *(pt, pp* **caught** [kɔːt]*)* **1** *(ball etc)* attraper, saisir; *(fish, thief etc)* attraper, prendre; **c.!** *(when throwing sth to sb)* attrape!; **well caught!** bien joué!; *Ftbl* le beau blocage!; *(said by sports coach etc)* excellente réception de la balle!; *Naut* **to c. the wind** *(of sail etc)* prendre le vent; **I caught him as he fell** je l'ai retenu *ou* attrapé au moment où il tombait; **I caught him by the hand** je l'ai attrapé par la main; **to c. sb in the act** *or* **red-handed** prendre qn sur le fait *ou* la main dans le sac; **don't get caught!** ne te fais pas prendre!; **you'll be in trouble if your mother catches you** gare à toi si ta mère t'attrape; **caught you!** je t'y prends!; **to c. sb doing sth** surprendre qn en train de faire qch; *Fam* **you won't c. me doing that again** on ne m'y reprendra plus; **to be caught in a storm** être surpris par un orage; **you might c. her if you run** vous pouvez la rattraper si vous courez; **you're unlikely to c. her at home** je ne pense pas que tu la trouveras chez elle; **you caught me just as I was going into a meeting** tu m'as parlé au moment où j'allais en réunion; **we caught him in a good mood** il était de bonne humeur quand nous l'avons vu; **to c. sb napping** prendre qn au dépourvu; *Fam* **c. you later!** on se voit plus tard!
2 *(not miss) (train etc)* attraper, prendre; *Fam (manage to see) (film)* voir; *Fam (manage to hear) (radio programme)* écouter; *Fam* **c. this outstanding singer next month** ne manquez pas ce chanteur étonnant le mois prochain
3 *(perceive) (sounds)* saisir, percevoir; **to c. a glimpse of sth, to c. sight of sth** apercevoir qch; **I caught a few words** j'ai entendu *ou* j'ai saisi quelques mots; **I didn't c. what you were saying** je n'ai pas entendu ce que vous disiez; **I caught a hint of bitterness** *(in what she said)* j'ai senti un peu d'amertume dans ses paroles; **the author has caught the mood of the time** l'auteur a su rendre l'ambiance de l'époque
4 *(make impression on) (sb's attention)* attirer; **to c. sb's eye** attirer l'attention de qn; **nothing in the shop caught my fancy** je n'ai rien trouvé qui me plaisait dans la boutique; **their story caught the imagination of the public** leur histoire a passionné le public *ou* retenu l'attention du public
5 *(entangle)* **I caught my dress on a nail** j'ai fait un accroc à ma robe avec un clou; **he caught his foot on a root and fell** il s'est pris le pied dans une racine et il est tombé; **don't c. your fingers in the door!** ne te coince pas les doigts dans la porte!; **there's something caught in the door** il y a quelque chose de coincé dans la porte
6 *(contract) (illness)* attraper; *Fig (habit)* prendre; **to c. (a) cold** s'enrhumer, attraper un rhume; **I caught this cold from you** c'est toi qui m'as passé ce rhume; **to c. fire** *or* **light** prendre feu
7 *(of blow, object)* **the punch caught me in the chest** j'ai reçu le coup de poing en plein dans la poitrine; **the stone caught her on the arm** elle a reçu la pierre sur le bras; *Boxing* **he caught him with a left to the chin** il lui a porté un gauche au menton; *Fam* **you'll c. it!** ça va être ta fête!
8 **to c. the sun** *(of person)* prendre des couleurs; **the sun caught her hair/the drops of dew** le soleil brilla dans ses cheveux/les perles de rosée; **my bedroom catches the sun** le soleil donne dans ma chambre; **the garden really catches the sun in the afternoon** le jardin est très ensoleillé l'après-midi
9 *Fam (fool)* attraper, avoir; **you won't c. me!** ça ne prend pas (avec moi)!
VI 1 attraper; **(here) c.!** tiens, attrape!; **I'm**

hopeless at catching *(ball etc)* je n'arrive jamais à rien attraper
2 *(of gears)* s'enclencher
3 *(of fire)* prendre, s'allumer
4 *(become entangled) (in door, machinery etc)* se prendre; *(on thorn, nail etc)* s'accrocher; **my fingers caught in the drawer** je me suis coincé les doigts dans le tiroir
5 *Am* **to c. on fire** prendre feu
▸ ▸ *Agr* **c. crop** culture *f* dérobée; **c. question** question-piège *f*, *pl* questions-pièges, colle *f*, *Fig* **c. 22** cercle *m* vicieux
▸ **catch at VT INSEP** *(grab at)* essayer de saisir; *(hold on to)* s'accrocher à; **to c. at an opportunity** saisir une opportunité
▸ **catch on VI 1** *(of fashion etc)* avoir du succès; *(of tune)* accrocher; **the game never caught on in Europe** ce jeu n'a jamais pris en Europe *ou* eu de succès en Europe
2 *Fam (understand)* saisir, piger; **he still hasn't caught on** il n'est toujours pas; **to c. on quickly** comprendre vite
▸ **catch out VT SEP** *(trap) (by difficult question)* prendre, piéger; *(of circumstances)* surprendre; **the police caught her out when they asked her …** la police l'a piégée en lui demandant …; **to c. sb out in a lie** prendre *ou* surprendre qn à mentir; **a lot of investors got caught out when the stock market collapsed** beaucoup d'investisseurs se sont fait piéger quand la Bourse s'est effondrée; **we got caught out by the rain** nous avons été surpris par la pluie
▸ **catch up VI** *(close gap, get closer)* rattraper son retard; **to c. up with sb** rattraper qn; **we caught up with them at the lights** nous les avons rattrapés au feu rouge; **the runners behind are catching up** les coureurs qui sont derrière se rapprochent; **to c. up on** *or* **with one's work/sleep** rattraper du travail/du sommeil en retard; *Fam* **it will c. up with you (one of these days)** ça va te retomber sur le nez
VT SEP 1 *(reach) (person, car in front etc)* rattraper
2 *(entangle)* **I got caught up in a discussion** j'ai été entraîné dans une discussion; **she got really caught up in the electoral campaign** elle s'est laissé complètement absorber par la campagne électorale; **they were caught up in a traffic jam for hours** ils ont été bloqués dans un embouteillage pendant des heures; **to be caught up in a wave of enthusiasm** être entraîné dans un mouvement d'enthousiasme
3 *(snatch up) (object)* saisir; *(baby, child)* prendre au bras

catch-all **N** *Fam* fourre-tout *m inv*
▸ ▸ **c. category** catégorie *f* fourre-tout; **c. clause** clause *f* fourre-tout

catch-as-catch-can **N** *(wrestling)* catch *m*, lutte *f* libre

catcher ['kætʃər] **N 1** attrapeur, -euse *f*; **rat c.** *(person, dog)* preneur *m* de rats **2** *Baseball* attrapeur *m*, receveur *m*; **c.'s mitt** gant *m* de baseball

catching ['kætʃɪŋ] **ADJ** *(disease, habit etc)* contagieux; *(enthusiasm)* communicatif
N 1 *(of ball)* réception *f*; **I'm no good at c.** je ne suis pas doué pour rattraper les balles qu'on m'envoie **2** *(of toothed wheel)* engrenure *f*, *(of gearing)* enclenchement *m*

catchline ['kætʃlaɪn] **N** accroche *f*, *(identification for story)* intitulé *m*

catchment ['kætʃmənt] **N** *(of water)* captation *f*, captage *m*
▸ ▸ **c. area** *Geog (drainage area)* bassin *m* hydrographique; *Admin (for hospital)* = circonscription *f* hospitalière; *(for school)* secteur *m* de recrutement scolaire; *Geog* **c. basin** bassin hydrographique

catchpenny ['kætʃpenɪ] **ADJ** *(book, ornaments)* racoleur; **c. scheme** *or* **show** attrape-nigaud *m*, *pl* attrape-nigaud(s)

catchphrase ['kætʃfreɪz] N *(of comedian)* formule f *(comique); (political)* slogan m; *(in advertising)* accroche f

catchword ['kætʃwɜːd] N **1** *Pol* slogan m **2** *Theat (cue)* réplique f

catchy ['kætʃɪ] ADJ *(tune)* entraînant, facile à retenir; *(slogan)* facile à retenir

catechism ['kætəkɪz(ə)m] N catéchisme m

catechist ['kætəkɪst] N catéchiste mf

catechize ['kætəkaɪz] VT **1** *Rel* catéchiser **2** *Fig (question)* interroger, questionner

categoric(al) [kætɪ'gɒrɪk, -ɪk(ə)l] ADJ catégorique; *Phil* **categorical imperative** impératif m catégorique

categorically [kætɪ'gɒrɪklɪ] ADV *(to answer, refuse etc)* catégoriquement

categorization [kætɪgəraɪ'zeɪʃ(ə)n] N catégorisation f

categorize ['kætɪgəraɪz] VT classer par catégories; **I don't like being categorized** je n'aime pas qu'on me colle une étiquette

category ['kætɪgərɪ] N catégorie f
▸▸ *Mktg* **c. leader** *(product)* chef m de file dans sa catégorie

cater ['keɪtər] VT **to c. a party** fournir le repas d'une soirée; **we're having the meal catered** nous faisons fournir le repas
▸ **cater for** VT INSEP **1** *(provide with food) (people, function etc)* fournir les repas à, préparer les repas pour **2** *(provide with special requirement)* **parties catered for** *(notice in hotel etc)* = banquets, noces; **hotel that caters for English visitors** hôtel qui s'adresse surtout à la clientèle anglaise; **the hotel doesn't c. for children** l'hôtel ne prévoit pas d'aménagements pour les enfants; **to c. for all tastes** satisfaire tous les goûts; **I hadn't catered for that** *(allowed for)* je n'avais pas prévu ça
▸ **cater to** VT INSEP *(needs)* satisfaire à

cater-corner(ed) ADJ, ADV *Am* diamètralement opposé

caterer ['keɪtərər] N *Com* traiteur m

catering ['keɪtərɪŋ] N restauration f; *Aviat* service m traiteur; **who did the c. at your wedding?** qui a préparé le repas/le buffet à votre mariage?
▸▸ **c. company** société f de restauration; **c. contract** contrat m de restauration; **c. industry** industrie f de la restauration; **c. manager** chef m ou responsable mf de la restauration; **c. staff** personnel m de restauration

caterpillar ['kætəpɪlər] N **1** chenille f **2** *Tech* chenille f
▸▸ *Tech* **C®. track** chenille; **C®. tractor** tracteur m à chenilles; **C®. tread** chenille

caterwaul ['kætəwɔːl] VI **1** *(of cat)* feuler **2** *Fig (of person)* hurler

caterwauling ['kætəwɔːlɪŋ] N **1** *(of cats)* feulements mpl **2** *Fig (of person)* hurlements mpl

catfish ['kætfɪʃ] N **1** silure m, poisson-chat m, pl poissons-chats **2** *(wolffish)* blennie f

catgut ['kætgʌt] N **1** *Mus* corde f de boyau; **c. strings** *(for violin)* cordes en boyau de chat **2** *Med* catgut m

catharsis [kə'θɑːsɪs] N catharsis f

cathartic [kə'θɑːtɪk] ADJ cathartique

cathedral [kə'θiːdrəl] N cathédrale f
▸▸ **c. city** ville f épiscopale, évêché m

Catherine ['kæθrɪn] N *Hist* **C. the Great** la Grande Catherine
▸▸ **C. wheel** *(firework)* soleil m

catheter ['kæθɪtər] N *Med* cathéter m; **indwelling c.** sonde f intérieure ou à demeure; **he has to have a c.** il faut qu'on lui pose un cathéter

cathode ['kæθəʊd] N *Elec* cathode f; **photo-(electric) c.** cathode photoélectrique

▸▸ *Elec* **c. beam** faisceau m cathodique; *Elec* **c. rays** rayons mpl cathodiques; *Elec* **c. ray tube** tube m cathodique; *Elec* **c. ray tube monitor** moniteur m à tube cathodique; *Elec* **c. screen** écran m cathodique

Catholic ['kæθəlɪk] *Rel* ADJ catholique
N catholique mf; **she has become a C.** elle est devenue catholique

catholic ['kæθəlɪk] ADJ *(wide-ranging)* éclectique; *(broad-minded)* à l'esprit large; *(universal)* universel; **to be c. in one's tastes** avoir des goûts éclectiques

Catholicism [kə'θɒlɪsɪz(ə)m] N *Rel* catholicisme m

cathouse ['kæthaʊs] N *Am Sl (brothel)* bordel m

catkin ['kætkɪn] N *Bot* chaton m

catlick ['kætlɪk] N *Fam* **to give oneself** or **have a c.** se laver le bout du nez, faire une toilette de chat

catmint ['kætmɪnt] N *(plant)* cataire f, herbe f aux chats

catnap ['kætnæp] *Fam* N petite sieste f, somme m; **to take** or **have a c.** faire une petite sieste
VI (-pp-) faire une petite sieste ou un somme

catnip ['kætnɪp] N *(plant)* cataire f, herbe f aux chats

cat-o'-nine-tails N chat m à neuf queues

catspaw, cat's-paw ['kætspɔː] N *Old-fashioned* **to be sb's c.** être le pigeon de qn; **to be made a c. of** être dupé

catsuit ['kætsuːt] N combinaison f

catsup ['kætsəp] N *Am* = **ketchup**

cattery ['kætərɪ] N pension f pour chats

cattiness ['kætɪnɪs] N *Fam* vacherie f, rosserie f

cattle ['kæt(ə)l] N *(no pl)* bétail m, bestiaux mpl; **horned c.** bêtes fpl à cornes, bovins mpl; **we were herded onto trucks like c.** on nous a entassés dans des camions comme du bétail VOIR GRAMMAIRE A11
▸▸ **c. breeding** élevage m *(du bétail); Am* **c. car** wagon m à bétail ou bestiaux; **c. crossing** passage m de troupeaux; **c. market** marché m ou foire f aux bestiaux; **c. prod** aiguillon m électrique; **c. truck** wagon à bétail ou bestiaux

cattle-cake N tourteau m

cattle-grid N = grille f placée sur un fossé pour empêcher le passage du bétail

cattleman, pl **cattlemen** ['kæt(ə)lmən] N *Am* bouvier m

catty ['kætɪ] ADJ *Fam* **1** *(esp woman)* vache, rosse; **c. remark** vacherie f, rosserie f **2** *(like a cat)* **there's a c. smell** ça sent le pipi de chat

catty-corner(ed) ADJ, ADV *Am* diamètralement opposé

catwalk ['kætwɔːk] N passerelle f; *Naut* coursive f, *(for fashion models)* passerelle f de défilé de mode; **on the c.** *(model)* sur la passerelle du défilé

Caucasian [kɔː'keɪʒən, -'keɪzɪən] ADJ **1** *Geog, Ling* caucasien **2** *(in ethnology)* caucasien
N Caucasien, -ienne; *(white person)* blanc m, blanche f

Caucasus (the) [ðə'kɔːkəsəs] N le Caucase

caucus ['kɔːkəs] N *esp Pol* **1** *(group)* bloc m **2** *(meeting)* réunion f du bloc

caudal ['kɔːd(ə)l] ADJ *Zool* caudal, -aux
▸▸ **c. fin** *(nageoire f)* caudale f

caught PT, PP *see* **catch**

caul [kɔːl] N coiffe f *(de nouveau-né);* **born with a c.** né coiffé

cauldron ['kɔːldrən] N chaudron m

cauli ['kɒlɪ] N *Br Fam* chou-fleur m, pl choux-fleurs

cauliflower ['kɒlɪflaʊər] N chou-fleur m, pl choux-fleurs
▸▸ *Culin* **c. cheese** chou-fleur au gratin; **c. ear** oreille f en chou-fleur

caulk [kɔːk] VT *(boat)* calfater, étouper

caulking ['kɔːkɪŋ] N calfatage m
▸▸ **c. iron** calfait m, burin m

causal ['kɔːz(ə)l] ADJ causal, -als ou -aux

causality [kɔː'zælɪtɪ] N causalité f; **what's the c.?** quelles sont les causes?

causally ['kɔːzəlɪ] ADV **to be c. connected** avoir un rapport de cause à effet

causation [kɔː'zeɪʃən] N causalité f

causative ['kɔːzətɪv] ADJ *Gram (verb)* causatif

cause [kɔːz] N **1** *(origin)* cause f; **c. and effect** la cause et l'effet; **to be the c. of an accident** être la cause d'un accident
2 *(reason)* raison f, motif m, sujet m; **I have c. to be thankful** j'ai lieu d'être reconnaissant; **you've no c. to be indignant** vous n'avez pas lieu d'être indigné, vous n'avez pas de quoi être indigné; **to have good c. for doing sth** avoir de bonnes raisons de faire qch; **to give c. for complaint** susciter des plaintes; **his condition is giving c. for concern** son état est inquiétant; **and with good c.** et pour cause; **without c.** sans raison
3 *(purpose etc)* cause f; **to win sb over to one's c.** gagner qn à sa cause; **to make common c.** faire cause commune *(with* avec); **in the c. of justice** *(cause de)* la justice; **to work for a good c.** travailler pour une bonne cause; **it's for a good c.** c'est pour une bonne cause; *Fam* **it's all in a good c.** ce n'est pas du temps perdu
4 *Law* cause f; **to plead sb's c.** plaider la cause de qn
VT *(misfortune, delay etc)* causer, occasionner; *(accident)* provoquer, causer; *(mirth, quarrel, surprise)* provoquer; **to c. a fire** provoquer un incendie; **to c. grief** causer du chagrin; **to c. trouble** *(disturbance)* semer la perturbation; *(problems)* causer des ennuis; **to c. a sensation** faire sensation; **all the worry you've caused us** toute l'inquiétude que tu nous as causée; **to c. sb/sth to do sth** faire faire qch à qn/qch; **a dog caused him to swerve** un chien lui a fait faire une embardée; **to c. sb to be punished** faire punir qn; **to c. sth to be done** faire faire qch; **something caused him to change his mind** quelque chose l'a fait changer d'avis

causeway ['kɔːzweɪ] N *(over marshy area)* chaussée f

caustic ['kɔːstɪk] ADJ *(substance)* caustique; *Fig (humour, joke etc)* caustique, décapant
N *Chem, Med* caustique m
▸▸ *Chem* **c. soda** soude f caustique

cauterization [kɔːtəraɪ'zeɪʃən] N *Med* cautérisation f

cauterize ['kɔːtəraɪz] VT *Med* cautériser

caution ['kɔːʃən] N **1** *(prudence)* prudence f, précautions fpl; **with great c.** avec beaucoup de prudence ou de précautions; **c. is advised** on conseille la prudence **2** *(warning)* avis m, avertissement m; **c.! steep gradient/pressurized container** attention! descente rapide/récipient sous pression **3** *Law, Sport etc (reprimand)* réprimande f; **he has been let off with a c.** il s'en est tiré avec une réprimande; **to be given a c.** se faire réprimander **4** *Old-fashioned Fam (amusing person)* numéro m, phénomène m
VT **1** *(warn)* avertir, mettre en garde; *Sport (player, boxer)* mettre en garde; **to c. sb against sth** mettre qn en garde contre qch; **to c. sb against doing sth** déconseiller à qn de faire qch **2** *Law* **to c. a suspect** = prévenir un suspect que tout ce qu'il dira pourra être

utilisé contre lui lors du procès **3** *Law (reprimand)* réprimander

Note that the French word **caution** is a false friend and is never a translation for the English word **caution**. Its most common meaning is **deposit**, **guarantee**. Note also that the French verb **cautionner** is a false friend. It never means **to warn**.

cautionary ['kɔːʃənərɪ] **ADJ** a c. tale une histoire édifiante

cautious ['kɔːʃəs] **ADJ** circonspect; *(driver, remark)* prudent; **to be c. in doing sth** faire qch avec prudence *ou* précaution; **to play a c. game** jouer serré; **c. optimism** optimisme *m* prudent

cautiously ['kɔːʃəslɪ] **ADV** *(to proceed)* avec prudence *ou* précaution; *(to drive)* prudemment; **to be c. optimistic** faire preuve d'un optimisme prudent

cautiousness ['kɔːʃəsnɪs] **N** *(of driver, remark etc)* prudence *f*

cavalcade [kævəl'keɪd] **N** cortège *m*; *(on horseback)* cavalcade *f*

Cavalier [kævə'lɪər] **N** *(in English history)* royaliste *m*; **the Cavaliers and Roundheads** les Cavaliers *mpl* et les Têtes *fpl* rondes

cavalier [kævə'lɪər] **ADJ** *(attitude etc)* cavalier, désinvolte; **with a c. air** avec désinvolture

cavalry ['kævəlrɪ] **N** cavalerie *f*
▸▸*Mil* **c. officer** officier *m* de cavalerie

cavalryman, *pl* **cavalrymen** ['kævəlrɪmən] **N** *Mil* cavalier *m*, soldat *m* de cavalerie

cave[1] [keɪv] **N** caverne *f*, grotte *f*
VI *Sport* faire de la spéléologie
▸▸**c. art** art *m* rupestre; **c. dweller** *(in prehistory)* homme *m* des cavernes; *(troglodyte)* troglodyte *m*; **c. dwelling** maison *f* troglodyte; **c. paintings** peintures *fpl* rupestres
▸**cave in VI 1** *(of ground, structure etc)* céder, s'affaisser, s'effondrer **2** *Fam (of person, government)* céder, s'avouer vaincu; *(of team, defence)* s'effondrer

Note that the French word **cave** is a false friend and is never a translation for the English word **cave**. It means **cellar**.

cave[2] ['keɪvɪ, 'kɑːveɪ] **INT** *Br Sch Arch Fam* attention!, pet!

caveat ['kævɪæt] **N 1** *Fml* mise *f* en garde (**against** contre) **2** *Law* opposition *f* (**to** à)

cave-in **N** *(of ground, structure etc)* affaissement *m*, effondrement *m*; *Fam (of person, government)* capitulation *f*

caveman, *pl* **cavemen** ['keɪvmæn, -men] **N** *(prehistoric man)* homme *m* des cavernes; *Fig Hum* primitif *m*

caver ['keɪvər] **N** spéléologue *mf*

cavern ['kævən, -ɜːn] **N** caverne *f*

cavernous ['kævənəs] **ADJ** *(room etc)* immense et vide; *(yawn)* à se décrocher la mâchoire; **a monster with a c. mouth** un monstre à la gueule immense

caviar(e) ['kævɪɑːr] **N** caviar *m*; *Prov* **(it's) c. to the general** c'est donner de la confiture aux cochons

cavil ['kævɪl] **VI** (**-ll-**, *Am* **-l-**) *Fml* chicaner, ergoter (**at** *or* **about sth** sur qch)

caving ['keɪvɪŋ] **N** *Sport* spéléologie *f*

cavity ['kævɪtɪ] **N** cavité *f*, creux *m*; *Med (abdominal, thoracic)* cavité *f*; **(dental) c.** cavité dentaire
▸▸**c. wall** mur *m* creux *ou* à double paroi; **c. wall insulation** isolation *f* en murs creux

cavort [kə'vɔːt] **VI** faire des cabrioles; *Fig* batifoler

cavy ['keɪvɪ] **N** *(animal)* cobaye *m*, cochon *m* d'Inde

caw [kɔː] **VI** *(of crow etc)* croasser
N *(of crow etc)* croassement *m*

cawing ['kɔːɪŋ] **N** *(of crow etc)* croassement *m*

cayenne [keɪ'en] **N** cayenne *f*
▸▸**c. pepper** (poivre *m* de) cayenne

cayman ['keɪmən] **N** *(animal)* caïman *m*
▸▸**C. Islands** îles *fpl* Caïmans

CB [siː'biː] **N** *(abbr* **Citizens' Band)** CB *f*

CBC [siːbiː'siː] **N** *TV, Radio (abbr* **Canadian Broadcasting Corporation)** (société *f)* Radio-Canada *f*

CBE [siːbiː'iː] **N** *abbr* **Commander of the Order of the British Empire**

CBI [siːbiː'aɪ] **N** *Br (abbr* **Confederation of British Industry)** ≃ Medef *m*

CBS [siːbiː'es] **N** *abbr* **Columbia Broadcasting System**

CC [siː'siː] **N** *abbr* **County Council**

cc [siː'siː] **N 1** *(on memorandum) (abbr* **carbon copy)** copie **2** *(abbr* **cubic centimetres)** cm^3
VT envoyer une copie à

CCA [siːsiː'eɪ] **N** *Acct (abbr* **current cost accounting)** comptabilité *f* en coûts actuels

CCI [siːsiː'aɪ] **N** *(abbr* **Chamber of Commerce and Industry)** CCI *f*

CCTV [siːsiːtiː'viː] **N** *(abbr* **closed circuit television)** télévision *f* en circuit fermé

CD [siː'diː] **N 1** *Comput (abbr* **compact disc)** CD *m*; **on CD** sur CD **2** *Admin (abbr* **Corps Diplomatique)** CD *m*; **a car with CD plates** une voiture avec des plaques du Corps diplomatique
▸▸**CD burner** graveur *m* de CD; **CD library** CDthèque *f*; **CD player** lecteur *m* laser; **CD rewriter** graveur de CD réinscriptibles; **CD stacker** meuble *m* à CD; **CD system** chaîne *f* laser; **CD video** CD vidéo *m*; **CD writer** graveur de CD

CDI, CD-I [siːdiː'aɪ] **N** *Comput (abbr* **compact disc interactive)** CD-I *m*

CDR, CD-R [siːdiː'ɑːr] *Comput* **N 1** *(abbr* **compact disc recorder)** graveur *m* de disque compact **2** *(abbr* **compact disc recordable)** CD-R *m*

Cdr **N** *Mil abbr* **Commander**

Cdre **N** *Naut abbr* **Commodore**

CD-ROM [siːdiː'rɒm] **N** *Comput (abbr* **compact disc-read only memory)** CD-ROM *m*, CD-Rom *m*; **available on C.** existe en CD-ROM
▸▸**C. burner** graveur *m* de CD-ROM; **C. drive** lecteur *m* de CD-ROM, lecteur *m* de disque optique; **C. newspaper** journal *m* sur CD-ROM; **C. reader** lecteur de CD-ROM; **C. recorder** graveur de CD-ROM; **C. rewriter** graveur de CD-ROM réinscriptible; **C. writer** graveur de CD-ROM

CD-RW [siːdiːɑː'dʌb(ə)ljuː] **N** *Comput (abbr* **compact disc rewritable)** CD *m* réinscriptible
▸▸**C. drive** lecteur *m* de CD réinscriptible

CDT [siːdiː'tiː] **N** *(abbr* **Central Daylight Time)** = heure *f* d'été du centre des États-Unis

CDV [siːdiː'viː] **N** *Comput (abbr* **compact disc video)** vidéodisque *m*

cease [siːs] **N** *Fml* **without c.** sans cesse
VI cesser; **hostilities have ceased** les hostilités ont cessé; **they have ceased to exist** ils n'existent plus; **it never ceases to amaze me that** ... cela m'étonne toujours que ...; **without ceasing** sans arrêt; **we will not c. from campaigning for her release** nous ne cesserons pas de nous battre pour sa libération
VT cesser; **to c. doing sth** cesser de faire qch; *Mil* **to c. fire** cesser le feu; *Com* **to c. trading** cesser ses activités, cesser toute activité commerciale

cease-fire **N** cessez-le-feu *m inv*

ceaseless ['siːslɪs] **ADJ** incessant, continuel

ceaselessly ['siːslɪslɪ] **ADV** sans cesse, continuellement

cecum ['siːkəm] **N** *Am* = caecum

cedar ['siːdər] **N** *(tree)* cèdre *m*; **c. panelling** lambris *mpl* en cèdre
▸▸*Am* **c. closet** *(for protecting clothes etc against moths)* placard *m* en cèdre; **c. of Lebanon** cèdre du Liban; *Bot* **c. tree** cèdre

cede [siːd] **VT** *Law (property, province, debt)* céder (**to** à); **to c. a point** *(in argument)* concéder un point

cedilla [sɪ'dɪlə] **N** *Ling* cédille *f*

Ceefax® ['siːfæks] **N** *TV* Ceefax® *m*

ceilidh ['keɪlɪ] **N** = bal *m* folklorique écossais ou irlandais

ceiling ['siːlɪŋ] **N 1** *(of room etc)* plafond *m*; *Fam* **to hit the c.** *(become angry)* péter les plombs **2** *Econ etc* plafond *m*; *Fin* **to have a c. of** être plafonné à; **to reach a c.** *(of prices etc)* plafonner **3** *Aviat* plafond *m*; **to fly at the c.** plafonner **4** *Met* plafond *m* (nuageux)
▸▸**c. light** plafonnier *m*; *Fin* **c. price** prix *m* plafond; **c. tile** dalle *f* pour plafond

celadon ['selədɒn] **N** *(porcelain)* céladon *m*
▸▸**c. green** (vert *m)* céladon

celandine ['selədaɪn] **N** *(flower)* **greater c.** chélidoine *f*, grande éclaire *f*; **lesser c.** ficaire *f*, petite éclaire

celeb [sə'leb] **N** *Fam* célébrité *f*

celebrant ['selɪbrənt] **N** *Rel* célébrant *m*, officiant *m*

celebrate ['selɪbreɪt] **VT 1** *(mark with festivity) (event)* fêter, célébrer; **the city is celebrating the anniversary of its founding** la ville fête l'anniversaire de sa fondation; **to c. sb's birthday** fêter l'anniversaire de qn; **let's open a bottle of wine to c. the occasion** ouvrons une bouteille de vin pour fêter ça **2** *Rel (mass, wedding, feast)* célébrer
VI faire la fête; **let's c. with a new car/a weekend in Paris** achetons une nouvelle voiture/allons passer un week-end à Paris pour fêter ça; **will you be celebrating tonight?** tu vas arroser ça ce soir?; **let's c. with some champagne** on va arroser ça au champagne

celebrated ['selɪbreɪtɪd] **ADJ** célèbre (**for** sth par qch)

celebration [selɪ'breɪʃən] **N 1** *(party, drink etc)* fête *f*, festivités *fpl*; **the Independence Day celebrations** les festivités à l'occasion de l'anniversaire de l'Indépendance; **this calls for a c.!** il faut fêter ça!, ça s'arrose!; **a party in c. of sth** une fête pour célébrer qch **2** *Rel (of communion, feast)* célébration *f*

celebratory [selɪ'breɪtərɪ] **ADJ** *(dinner)* de fête; *(marking official occasion)* commémoratif; *(atmosphere, mood)* de fête, festif

celebrity [sɪ'lebrɪtɪ] **N 1** *(person)* célébrité *f*; **2** *(fame)* célébrité *f*, renommée *f*
▸▸**c. magazine** magazine *m* people

celeriac [sɪ'lerɪæk] **N** céleri-rave *m*, *pl* céleris-raves

celerity [sɪ'lerɪtɪ] **N** *Fml* célérité *f*

celery ['selərɪ] **N** céleri *m*; **head of c.** pied *m* de céleri; **stick of c.** branche *f* de céleri; **c. soup** soupe *f* au céleri

celestial [sɪ'lestɪəl] **ADJ** céleste

celiac ['siːlɪæk] **ADJ, N** *Am* = coeliac

celibacy ['selɪbəsɪ] **N** *(sexual abstinence)* abstinence *f* sexuelle, chasteté *f*; *(not being married)* célibat *m*; *Rel* **to take a vow of c.** faire vœu de chasteté

celibate ['selɪbət] **ADJ** *(person) (chaste)* qui n'a pas de rapports sexuels, chaste; *(life) (by choice)* de chasteté; *(forced)* sans rapports sexuels
N personne *f* qui n'a pas de rapports sexuels

Note that the French word **célibataire** is a false friend and is never a translation for the English word **celibate**. It means **unmarried**.

cell [sel] **N 1** *(in prison)* cellule *f*; **they spent a night in the cells** ils ont passé la nuit en cellule

2 *(of monk, hermit)* cellule *f*

3 *(in beehive)* cellule *f*, alvéole *m*

4 *Elec, Electron etc (of battery)* cellule *f*; **dry c.** pile *f* sèche; **wet c.** pile à liquide; **photoelectric/photovoltaic c.** cellule photoélectrique/photovoltaïque; **solar c.** pile solaire, photopile *f*

5 *Biol* cellule *f*; **blood c.** globule *m*; **cancer c.** cellule cancéreuse

6 *Pol* communist **c.** cellule *f* communiste

7 *Comput (on spreadsheet)* cellule *f*

8 *Am Fam (cellphone)* portable *m*, *Belg* GSM *m*, *Suisse* Natel® *m*, *Can* cellulaire *m*

▸▸ *Biol* **c. wall** paroi *f* cellulaire

cellar ['selər] **N** cave *f*; *(of wine merchant)* chai *m*; **to keep a good c.** avoir une bonne cave

Note that the French word **cellier** is a false friend. It means **storeroom**.

cellarman, *pl* **cellarmen** ['seləmən] **N** sommelier *m*

cellist ['tʃelɪst] **N** *Mus* violoncelliste *mf*

cello ['tʃeləʊ] **N** *Mus* violoncelle *m*

▸▸ **c. concerto** concerto *m* pour violoncelle

Cellophane ® ['seləfeɪn] **N** *Br* cellophane® *f*

cellphone ['selfəʊn] **N** téléphone *m* cellulaire, radiotéléphone *m*; *Am (mobile phone)* (téléphone *m*) portable *m*, *Belg* GSM *m*, *Suisse* Natel® *m*, *Can* cellulaire *m*

cellular ['seljʊlər] **ADJ** *Biol (structure etc)* cellulaire

▸▸ *Tex* **c. blanket** couverture *f* alvéolaire; **c. board** *(cardboard)* carton *m* ondulé; *Electron, Tel* **c. logic** logique *f* cellulaire; **c. phone** téléphone *m* cellulaire, radiotéléphone *m*

cellulite ['seljʊlaɪt] **N** cellulite *f*

Celluloid® ['seljʊlɔɪd] **N** *(no pl)* celluloïd® *m*; *Cin* **on c.** sur la pellicule

cellulose ['seljʊləʊs] **ADJ** celluleux **N** cellulose *f*

Celsius ['selsɪəs] **ADJ** Celsius; **ten degrees C.** dix degrés Celsius

▸▸ **C. thermometer** thermomètre *m* de Celsius

Celt [kelt] **N** Celte *mf*

Celtic ['keltɪk] *Ling* **ADJ** celtique, celte **N** *(ancient)* celtique *m*; *(modern)* langues *fpl* celtiques *ou* celtes

cement [sɪ'ment] **N 1** *Constr* ciment *m*; **Portland c.** ciment de Portland; **quick-setting c.** ciment à prise rapide; **c. path** allée *f* en ciment **2** *(for tooth)* amalgame *m* **3** *(glue)* colle *f*

VT 1 *(join) (stones, bricks), Fig (friendship)* cimenter **2** *(in dentistry)* obturer

▸▸ **c. mixer** bétonnière *f*; **c. powder** poudre *f* à ciment

cementation [si:men'teɪʃən] **N** cimentation *f*

cemetery ['semətrɪ] **N** cimetière *m*

cenotaph ['senətɑːf] **N** cénotaphe *m*

censer ['sensər] **N** *Rel* encensoir *m*

censor ['sensər] **N 1** *Admin, Mil* censeur *m*; **the film c.** la censure cinématographique; *Mil, Cin etc* **to get past the c.** échapper à la censure **2** *Antiq* censeur *m*

VT 1 *(ban) (book, film, article etc)* interdire, censurer; *(scene)* supprimer, couper; *(line, word)* supprimer **2** *(cut parts of) (film, article,*

newspaper) censurer; *(play, book, scenario)* censurer, expurger

▸▸ *TV, Radio* **c. bleep** bip *m* de censure

Attention: ne pas confondre avec le verbe **to censure**.

censoring ['sensərɪŋ] **N** censure *f*

censorious [sen'sɔːrɪəs] **ADJ** *Fml* sévère (**of** vis-à-vis de)

censorship ['sensəʃɪp] **N** censure *f*; **there is no longer any c.** of his films ses films ne sont plus censurés

▸▸ **c. laws** censure

censurable ['senʃərəb(ə)l] **ADJ** *Fml* censurable, blâmable

censure ['senʃər] *Fml* **N** critiques *fpl*; *Law* réprimande *f*; **he deserves c.** il mérite des reproches; *Pol* **vote of c.** motion *f* de censure

VT blâmer, critiquer

Note that the French verb **censurer** is a false friend and is never a translation for the English verb **to censure**. It means **to censor**.

Attention: ne pas confondre avec le verbe **to censor**.

census ['sensəs] **N** recensement *m*; **to take a c.** faire un recensement; **c. of population** recensement de la population

▸▸ *Am* **C. Bureau** Bureau *m* des statistiques; **c. return** formulaire *m* de recensement; **c. taker** agent *m* recenseur

cent [sent] **N** *(coin, sum)* cent *m*; *Fam (smallest amount of money)* sou *m*; **to pay to the last c.** payer jusqu'au dernier sou

centaur ['sentɔːr] **N** *Myth* centaure *m*

centenarian [sentɪ'neərɪən] **N** *(person)* centenaire *mf*

ADJ centenaire

centenary [sen'ti:nərɪ] **N** (anniversaire *m*) centenaire *m*; **c. celebrations** célébrations *fpl* du centenaire

ADJ centenaire

centennial [sen'tenɪəl] **ADJ** centenaire

N *Am* = **centenary N**

center, centerboard *etc Am* = **centre, centreboard** *etc*

centering ['sentərɪŋ] **N** *Typ* centrage *m*

centigrade ['sentɪgreɪd] **ADJ** centigrade; **ten degrees c.** dix degrés centigrades

▸▸ **c. thermometer** thermomètre *m* centigrade

centigramme, *Am* centigram ['sentɪgræm] **N** centigramme *m*

centilitre, *Am* centiliter ['sentɪliːtər] **N** centilitre *m*

centimetre, *Am* centimeter ['sentɪmiːtər] **N** centimètre *m*; **square/cubic c.** centimètre carré/cube

centipede ['sentɪpiːd] **N** mille-pattes *m* inv; *Spec* scolopendre *f*

central ['sentrəl] **ADJ 1** *(in location)* central, -aux; **in a c. position** situé au centre; **the office is very c.** *(in town)* le bureau est situé en plein centre **2** *(in importance)* central, -aux; **the c. character** le personnage central; **c. to the debate is the question of safety** la question de la sécurité se situe au cœur du débat; **of c. importance** d'une importance capitale

N *Am Tel Old-fashioned* central *m* (téléphonique)

▸▸ *Banking* **c. account** compte *m* centralisateur; **C. America** Amérique *f* centrale; **c. bank** banque *f* centrale; *Com* **c. buyer** acheteur, -euse principal(ale); *Com* **c. buying group** centrale *f* d'achat(s); **c. government** gouvernement *m* central; **c. heating** chauffage *m* central; *Br Parl* **C. Lobby** = hall *m* principal de la Chambre des communes;

Aut **c. locking** verrouillage *m* central; *Anat* **c. nervous system** système *m* nerveux central; *Admin* **C. Office of Information** = organisme *m* chargé d'organiser les campagnes d'information du gouvernement britannique; **c. point** centre *m*; *Comput* **c. processing unit** unité *f* centrale (de traitement), processeur *m* central; *Com* **c. purchasing** achats *mpl* centralisés; *Com* **c. purchasing department** *(in company)* centrale d'achat(s); *Com* **c. purchasing group** centrale d'achat(s); *Com* **c. purchasing office** centrale d'achat(s); *Br Aut* **c. reservation** *(with grass)* terre-plein *m* central, *pl* terre-pleins centraux, *Belg, Suisse* berme *f* centrale; *(with barrier)* bande *f* médiane; **c. reservations** réservations *fpl*; **c. reservations office** centrale de réservation; **C. Standard Time** heure *f* d'hiver du centre des États-Unis

centralize ['sentrəlaɪz] **VT** centraliser

centralized ['sentrəlaɪzd] **ADJ** *(power, planning etc)* centralisé

▸▸ *Comput* **c. data capture** saisie *f* centralisée; **c. management** gestion *f* intégrée; **c. purchasing** achats *mpl* centralisés; *Comput* **c. storage** mémoire *f* centrale

centrally ['sentrəlɪ] **ADV** centralement; **c. heated** avec chauffage central; **the flat is c. heated** l'appartement a le chauffage central; **c. situated** situé dans le centre, central, -aux

centre, *Am* center ['sentər] **N 1** *(of circle, earth, town etc)* centre *m*; *(of table etc)* milieu *m*; *(of wheel)* corps *m*, centre; *Med (of infection)* foyer *m*; **in the c.** au centre, au milieu; **the great urban centres** les grandes agglomérations *fpl* urbaines; **commercial/industrial c.** centre commercial/industriel; **civic/community c.** centre civique/social; **shopping c.** centre commercial; **sports c.** centre sportif; *Phys* **c. of gravity** centre de gravité; **c. of attraction** *Phys* centre d'attraction *ou* de gravitation; *Fig* centre d'attraction

2 *Pol* centre *m*; **the c. party** le parti du centre; **to be left/right of c.** être du centre gauche/droit

3 *Sport (player)* centre *m*

4 *Tech etc (of lathe)* pointe *f*; **out of c.** décentré; **ten centimetres c. to c.** dix centimètres centre à centre

VT 1 *(text, wheel, sth on lathe etc)* centrer **2** *Cin, Phot (image)* centrer, cadrer **3** *Ftbl etc (ball etc)* centrer

▸▸ *Ftbl* **c. forward** avant-centre *m*, *pl* avant(s)-centres; *Ftbl* **c. half** demi-centre *m*, *pl* demi-centres; *Journ* **c. page** page *f* centrale; *Tech* **c. punch** pointeau *m*; *Typ* **c. spread** double page centrale

▸ **centre on, centre round** **VT INSEP** être centré *ou* axé sur

VT SEP *(usu passive)* **to be centred on sb/sth** se concentrer sur qn/qch

centreboard, *Am* centerboard ['sentəbɔːd] **N** *Naut* dérive *f*

centrefold, *Am* centerfold ['sentəfəʊld] **N** *(in magazine, newspaper)* double page *f* centrale détachable; *(nude picture)* photo *f* de pin-up; **to do a c.** *(nude picture)* poser comme une pin-up; **c. girl** pin-up *f* inv

centrepiece, *Am* centerpiece ['sentəpiːs] **N** *(on table)* décoration *f* centrale d'une table; *Fig* pièce *f* de résistance

centre-point steering **N** *Aut* direction *f* à point milieu

centrifugal [sentrɪ'fjʊg(ə)l] **ADJ** *(force, pump etc)* centrifuge

centrifuge ['sentrɪfjuːdʒ] **VT** *(liquid)* centrifuger

N centrifugeur *m*, centrifugeuse *f*

centring, *Am* centering ['sent(ə)rɪŋ] **N 1** *(of*

sth on lathe, of text etc) centrage *m* **2** *Cin, Phot* cadrage *m*

▸▸**c. tool** centreur *m*

centripetal [sen'trɪpɪtəl] ADJ *(force etc)* centripète

centrist ['sentrɪst] *Pol* N centriste *mf* ADJ centriste

centuries-old ['sentʃərɪz-] ADJ vieux/*f* vieille de plusieurs siècles

century ['sentʃərɪ] N **1** siècle *m*; **in the nineteenth c.** au dix-neuvième siècle; **the wedding of the c.** le mariage du siècle; **trees centuries old** arbres *mpl* séculaires *ou* centenaires **2** *Cr (one hundred runs)* centaine *f*, série *f* de cent

▸▸*Am Fam* **c. note** billet *m* de cent dollars

CEO [si:i:'əʊ] N *Com (abbr* **chief executive officer)** ≃ directeur *m* général; **President and C.** ≃ président-directeur général *m*, P-DG *m*

cephalic [se'fælɪk] ADJ *(vein, index etc)* céphalique

ceramic [sə'ræmɪk] ADJ céramique

NPL **ceramics** céramique *f*

▸▸*Br* **c. hob** plaque *f* vitrocéramique; **c. tiles** carrelage *m*

cereal ['sɪərɪəl] N céréale *f*, **(breakfast) cereals** céréales

▸▸**c. bowl** assiette *f* creuse, bol *m* à céréales; **c. crops** céréales

cerebellum [serɪ'beləm] N *Anat* cervelet *m*

cerebral ['serɪbrəl, *Am* sə'ri:brəl] ADJ **1** *Anat* cérébral, -aux **2** *(intellectual)* cérébral, -aux

▸▸*Med* **c. death** mort *f* cérébrale; *Anat* **c. hemisphere** hémisphère *m* cérébral; *Med* **c. palsy** paralysie *f* cérébrale

cerebrospinal fluid [serebrəʊ'spaɪn(ə)l] N *Anat* liquide *m* céphalo-rachidien

cerebrum ['serɪbrəm] N *Anat* cerveau *m*

ceremonial [serɪ'məʊnɪəl] ADJ de cérémonie

N cérémonial *m*

ceremonially [serɪ'məʊnɪəlɪ] ADV en grande cérémonie

ceremonious [serɪ'məʊnɪəs] ADJ cérémonieux

ceremoniously [serɪ'məʊnɪəslɪ] ADV cérémonieusement, avec cérémonie

ceremony ['serɪmənɪ] N cérémonie *f*; **the marriage c.** la cérémonie du mariage; **with c.** avec cérémonie, cérémonieusement; **without c.** sans cérémonies; **we don't stand on c.** nous ne faisons pas de cérémonies

cert [sɜ:t] N *Fam (certainty)* **a dead c.** une certitude (absolue); *Horseracing* un gagnant sûr; **he's a dead c. for the job** à tous les coups, il a le poste; **if one thing's a c. it's that ...** s'il y a une chose qui est sûre c'est que ...

cert. N *Cin (abbr* **certificate)** certificat *m*; **a c. 18 film** un film interdit aux moins de 18 ans

certain ['sɜ:t(ə)n] ADJ **1** *(sure) (success, failure etc)* certain, assuré; *(cure, solution)* infaillible; **they face c. dismissal** ils seront renvoyés à coup sûr; **they face c. death** ils sont condamnés; **it's absolutely c.** c'est sûr et certain; **there is c. to be some opposition to the bill** il est sûr que la loi rencontrera une opposition; **he is c. to come** il viendra à coup sûr; **to my c. knowledge, they are ...** je sais pertinemment qu'ils sont ...; **in the c. belief that he was right** convaincu qu'il avait raison; **I am almost c.** j'en suis presque sûr; **I am c. that he will come** je suis certain *ou* sûr qu'il viendra; **to know sth for c.** être certain de qch; **I can't say for c.** je ne peux pas vous dire de façon certaine; **you'll have it tomorrow for c.** vous l'aurez demain sans faute; **to make c. that ...** *(find out, ensure)* s'assurer que ...; **I'd better make c.** je ferais mieux de m'en assurer; **to make c. of sth** *(find out)* s'assurer de qch; *(make sure to get*

sth) s'assurer qch; **I made c. of the date** je me suis assuré de la date; **to make c. of a seat** s'assurer une place; **don't worry, I made c. of that!** ne t'inquiète pas, j'ai pris toutes les dispositions!

2 *(particular)* certain; **women of a c. age** les femmes d'un certain âge; **a c. person** une certaine personne; **c. people** (de) certaines gens, certains *mpl*; **a c. Mr Thomas** un certain M. Thomas; **he used to write to me on a c. day** il m'écrivait à jour fixe

certainly ['sɜ:tənlɪ] ADV *(definitely)* certainement; *(admittedly)* certes; **she c. knows her facts** elle sait parfaitement de quoi elle parle; **you shall c. have it tomorrow** vous l'aurez demain sans faute; **it c. won't be ready tomorrow** ça ne sera jamais prêt pour demain; **may I? – c.!** *or* **you c. may!** vous permettez? – je vous en prie! *ou* certainement!; **will you tell him? – c. not!** tu vas lui dire? – certainement pas!; **did you tell him? – c. not!** tu lui as dit? – bien sûr que non!

┌─────────────────────────────────────┐
│ Note that the most common meaning of │
│ the French word **certainement** is │
│ **probably**.   │
└─────────────────────────────────────┘

certainty ['sɜ:təntɪ] N **1** *(sureness) (of future event)* certitude *f*; **there is no c. that we will win** il n'est absolument pas certain que nous gagnions **2** *(thing)* **I know it for a c.** je le sais parfaitement; **we now know for a c. that he was here last night** nous avons maintenant la preuve qu'il était là hier soir; **it's a dead c.** c'est une certitude absolue **3** *(conviction)* certitude *f*, conviction *f*; **she said it with some c.** elle a dit cela avec une certaine conviction

certifiable ['sɜ:tɪfaɪəb(ə)l] ADJ **1** *(insane) (person)* dont l'état nécessite l'internement psychiatrique; *Fam* **he's c.** il est fou à lier **2** *(document, fact etc)* que l'on peut certifier

certificate [sə'tɪfɪkət] N **1** certificat *m*; **birth/marriage/death c.** certificat de naissance/mariage/décès; *Fin etc* **bearer c.** titre *m* au porteur; **(government) savings c.** bon *m* d'épargne; *Aut* **test c.** = certificat de contrôle technique **2** *(professional, educational)* diplôme *m*; **teaching/nursing c.** diplôme d'enseignement/d'infirmière; **coaching/first aid c.** brevet *m* d'entraîneur/de secourisme; *Naut* **master's c.** brevet de capitaine **3** *Cin* visa *m* de censure

▸▸*Aviat* **c. of airworthiness** certificat de navigabilité; *Fin* **c. of deposit** certificat de dépôt; *Acct* **c. of dishonour** certificat de non-paiement; *Com* **c. of incorporation** certificat d'enregistrement de société; **c. of insurance** attestation *f* d'assurance; *Com* **c. of origin** certificat d'origine; *Com* **c. of quality** certificat de qualité; *Br Sch Formerly* **C. of Secondary Education** = ancien brevet de l'enseignement secondaire en Grande-Bretagne, aujourd'hui remplacé par le "GCSE", ≃ BEPC *m*; *Fin* **c. of transfer** acte *m* de cession; *Com* **c. of value** certificat de valeur

certificated [sə'tɪfɪkeɪtɪd] ADJ diplômé

certification [sɜ:tɪfɪ'keɪʃən] N certification *f*, authentification *f*; *(of product)* homologation *f*

certified ['sɜ:tɪfaɪd] ADJ **1** *(having certificate)* diplômé **2** *(guaranteed)* **c. by a notary** notarié **3** *(declared insane)* dont l'état nécessite l'internement psychiatrique

▸▸**c. accounts** comptes *mpl* approuvés; *Am Fin* **c. cheque** chèque *m* certifié; **c. copy** copie *f* certifiée conforme, copie authentique; *Com* **c. invoice** facture *f* certifiée; *Am* **c. letter** lettre *f* recommandée; *Am Sch* **c. public accountant** ≃ expert-comptable *m*, *pl* experts-comptables; *Am Sch* **c. teacher** *(in state school)* professeur *m* diplômé; *(in private school)* professeur habilité

certify ['sɜ:tɪfaɪ] VT **1** *(confirm)* certifier, attester; *(death)* constater; **to c. that sth is true** certifier que qch est vrai; **this is to c. that A. Gooch has ...** *(on certificate)* ce document certifie que A. Gooch a ...; **to c. sb insane** *(of doctor)* déclarer que l'état de santé de qn nécessite l'internement psychiatrique; *Fam* **you ought to be certified** tu es complètement fou **2** *(guarantee) (document)* authentifier, homologuer, légaliser; *Acct* **to c. the books** viser les livres de commerce

VI **to c. to sth** attester qch

certitude ['sɜ:tɪtju:d] N certitude *f*

cervical ['sɜ:vɪk(ə)l, sɜ:'vaɪk(ə)l] ADJ *Anat* **1** *(of the cervix)* du col de l'utérus **2** *(of the neck)* cervical, -aux

▸▸**c. cancer** cancer *m* du col de l'utérus; **c. collar** minerve *f*; **c. smear** frottis *m* vaginal; **c. vertebra** vertèbre *f* cervicale

cervix, *pl* **cervices** ['sɜ:vɪks, -vɪsi:z] N *Anat* **1** *(of uterus)* col *m* de l'utérus **2** *(neck)* cou *m*

▸▸**c. uteri** col de l'utérus

cessation [se'seɪʃən] N cessation *f*, arrêt *m*

cession ['seʃən] N *(of territory)* cession *f*, *Law (to creditors)* cession de biens

cesspit ['sespɪt] N = **cesspool**

cesspool ['sespu:l] N *(for sewage)* fosse *f* d'aisances; *Fig* cloaque *m*; **the district is a c. of drug-dealing and prostitution** le quartier est un cloaque où règnent le trafic de drogue et la prostitution

CET [si:i:'ti:] N *EU (abbr* **common external tariff)** tarif *m* externe commun

Ceylon [sɪ'lɒn] N *Hist Formerly* Ceylan *m*

C & F [si:ænd'ef] *Com (abbr* **cost and freight)** C et F

cf [si:'ef] *(abbr* **confer)** cf

CFC [si:ef'si:] N *(abbr* **chlorofluorocarbon)** CFC *m inv*

CFO [si:ef'əʊ] N *Am (abbr* **Chief Financial Officer)** chef *m* comptable, chef de la comptabilité

CFSP [si:efes'pi:] N *(abbr* **Common Foreign and Security Policy)** PESC *f*

cg *(abbr* **centigramme)** cg

CGI [si:dʒi:'aɪ] N *Comput* **1** *(abbr* **common gateway interface)** interface *f* commune de passerelle, CGI *f* **2** *(abbr* **computer-generated images)** images *fpl* créées par ordinateur

CH [si:'eɪtʃ] *(abbr* **central heating)** c. c., ch. c.

ch *(abbr* **chapter)** chapitre *m*

cha [tʃɑ:] N *Old-fashioned Br Fam (tea)* thé *m*

Chad [tʃæd] N Tchad *m*

chaebol ['tʃeɪbɒl] N *Econ* chaebol *m*

chafe [tʃeɪf] VT **1** *(make worn) (rope, collar)* user; *(make sore) (skin)* irriter; **the boots chafed her ankles** les bottes lui blessaient les chevilles; **apply to chafed skin** *(of lotion etc)* appliquer sur la peau irritée **2** *Fig (annoy)* irriter, agacer **3** *(warm) (sb's limbs etc)* frictionner

VI **1** *(of skin)* être irrité; **his skin chafed under the coarse material** sa peau était irritée à cause du tissu rugueux **2** *Fig (of person)* **to c. at** *or* **under sth** s'énerver contre qch, s'irriter de *ou* contre qch; **to c. under restraint** ronger son frein

chafed [tʃeɪft] ADJ *(rope, shirt)* usé; *(skin)* irrité

chaff[1] [tʃɑ:f] N **1** *Agr (husks)* balle *f*, *Fig* **the bulk of his collected poems is mere c.** la plupart de ses poèmes ne valent pas grand-chose **2** *Electron* ruban *m* métallique antiradar

chaff[2] VT *(tease)* taquiner

chaffinch ['tʃæfɪntʃ] N *(bird)* pinson *m*

chafing ['tʃeɪfɪŋ] N **1** *(of skin)* irritation *f* **2**

(warming) (of limbs) friction *f*
  ►► **c. dish** chauffe-plats *m inv*

chagrin [ˈʃægrɪn] N *Fml* dépit *m*; **much to my c.** à mon grand dépit
  VT *esp Lit* dépiter; **to be chagrined at sth** être contrarié par qch

chain [tʃeɪn] N **1** chaîne *f*; *(small) (for medallion etc)* chaînette *f*; **to put a dog on a c.** attacher un chien à une chaîne; **a prisoner in chains** un prisonnier enchaîné; *Fig* **to break** *or* **burst one's chains** rompre ses chaînes; *Fig* **to have nothing to lose but one's chains** n'avoir rien d'autre à perdre que ses chaînes; **to form a c.** *(to pass buckets of water etc)* former *ou* faire la chaîne; **to pull the c.** *(in WC)* tirer la chasse d'eau; **a c. of events** un enchaînement de faits; *Com* **c. of distribution** circuit *m* de distribution, réseau *m* de distribution; *Naut* **anchor c.** chaîne d'ancrage; **bicycle c.** chaîne de bicyclette; *Aut* **(snow) chains** chaînes
  2 *Geog (of mountains)* chaîne *f*
  3 *Com (of stores, restaurants)* chaîne *f*, **fast food c.** chaîne de restauration rapide
  4 *Phys, Chem etc* chaîne *f*
  5 *Arch (measurement)* = 20,12 m; **surveyor's c., measuring c.** chaîne f d'arpenteur *ou* d'arpentage
  VT *(door etc)* fermer avec une chaîne; **to c. sb** enchaîner qn (**to sth/sb** à qch/qn); **to c. sth to sth** attacher qch à qch avec une chaîne/des chaînes; **she chained herself to the railings** elle s'est enchaînée à la grille; *Fig* **chained to one's desk** rivé à son bureau; *Fig* **she's chained to the kitchen sink** elle ne sort pas de sa cuisine
  ►► **c. armour** mailles *fpl*, *(suit)* cotte *f* de mailles; *Tech* **c. drive** transmission *f* par chaîne; **c. gang** chaîne de forçats; **c. guard** caiter *m (de bicyclette)*; *Aut* **c. guide** guide *m* chaîne; **c. letter** lettre *f* faisant partie d'une chaîne; **c. link** chaînon *m ou* maillon *m* de chaîne; **c. mail** mailles *fpl*, *(suit)* cotte de mailles; *Phys, Chem, Fig* **c. reaction** réaction *f* en chaîne; **c. saw** tronçonneuse *f*, *Sewing* **c. stitch** point *m* de chaînette; **c. store** magasin *m* à succursales (multiples); *(individual store)* succursale *f*, *Aut* **c. tensioner** tendeur *m* de chaîne

► **chain down** VT SEP *(cargo on ship)* attacher avec des chaînes; *(person)* enchaîner; *Fig* **to be chained down by one's work** être esclave de son travail

► **chain up** VT SEP *(dog)* attacher à une chaîne; *(person)* enchaîner; *(bike, gate)* mettre une chaîne à; **I left it chained up** j'ai mis le cadenas

chaining [ˈtʃeɪnɪŋ] N *Comput* chaînage *m*

chain-smoke VT **he chain-smokes untipped cigarettes** il fume des cigarettes sans filtre du matin au soir; **he was chain-smoking Gitanes** il fumait Gitane sur Gitane
  VI fumer cigarette sur cigarette

chain-smoker N personne *f* qui fume cigarette sur cigarette

chair [tʃeər] N **1** chaise *f*, *(armchair)* fauteuil *m*; **folding c.** chaise pliante, pliant *m*; **easy c.** fauteuil; **invalid c., Old-fashioned bath c.** voiture *f* de malade, fauteuil roulant
  2 *Univ (of professor)* chaire *f*
  3 *(in meeting)* fauteuil *m* de président; *(chairperson)* président, -ente; **to be in the c.** présider (la séance); **to address the c.** s'adresser au président
  4 *Am Fam* **the c.** *(electric chair)* la chaise électrique; **to go to the c.** passer sur *ou* à la chaise électrique
  VT **1** *(preside over) (meeting)* présider **2** *(person) (after victory etc)* porter en triomphe
  ►► **c. attendant** *(in park etc)* loueur, -euse de chaises, chaisier, -ière

chairback [ˈtʃeəbæk] N dossier *m* de chaise
chaircover [ˈtʃeəkʌvə(r)] N housse *f* de fauteuil
chairlift [ˈtʃeəlɪft] N *Ski* télésiège *m*
chairman, *pl* **chairmen** [ˈtʃeəmən] N *(of committee, meeting)* président, -ente; *(of party)* secrétaire *m* général; *Com (of company)* président-directeur *m* général; **c. and managing director** président-directeur général, P-DG *m*; **c. of the board** Président du conseil; **to act as c.** présider (la séance); **Mr C.** Monsieur le Président; **Madam C.** Madame la Présidente

chairmanship [ˈtʃeəmənʃɪp] N *(of committee, meeting)* présidence *f*, *(of party)* secrétariat *m* général; **under the c. of Mr Stevens** sous la présidence de M. Stevens

chairperson [ˈtʃeəpɜːsən] N *(of committee, meeting)* président, -ente; *(of party)* secrétaire *mf* général(ale)

chairwoman, *pl* **chairwomen** [ˈtʃeəwʊmən, -wɪmɪn] N *(of committee, meeting)* présidente *f*, *(of party)* secrétaire *f* générale

chalet [ˈʃæleɪ] N chalet *m*
  ►► **c. girl** = jeune femme *f* qui s'occupe de l'entretien d'un chalet de sports d'hiver; **c. park** parc *m* résidentiel de loisirs

chalice [ˈtʃælɪs] N **1** *Rel* calice *m* **2** *Arch, Lit* coupe *f*

chalk [tʃɔːk] N *(for writing etc)*, *Geol, Billiards* craie *f*; **they are as different as c. and cheese** c'est le jour et la nuit; *Br Fam* **not by a long c.** loin s'en faut; *Br Fam* **by a long c.** de beaucoup; **a set of coloured chalks** un assortiment de craies de couleur; **c. hills/cliffs** collines *fpl*/falaises *fpl* crayeuses; *Sewing* **French c.** craie de tailleur
  VT *(mark)* marquer à la craie; *(write)* écrire (à la craie); *Carp etc* **to c. a line** tringler une ligne; *Billiards* **to c. one's cue** mettre de la craie sur sa queue de billard
  ►► **c. drawing** dessin *m* à la craie; **c. line** *(drawn)* trait *m* à la craie; *Carp (string)* cordeau *m*; *(made by string)* ligne *f* faite au cordeau

► **chalk up** VT SEP **1** *(write)* écrire à la craie **2 c. it up** *(give credit in shop)* mettez-le sur mon ardoise **3** *(put down to)* **you'll just have to c. it up to experience** maintenant, tu sauras; **they chalked their defeat up to lack of practice** ils ont mis leur défaite sur le compte du manque d'entraînement **4** *(achieve) (victory, success, points)* remporter

chalkboard [ˈtʃɔːkbɔːd] N *Am* tableau *m* (noir)

chalkdust [ˈtʃɔːkdʌst] N poussière *f* de craie

chalkpit [ˈtʃɔːkpɪt] N carrière *f* de craie, crayère *f*

chalky [ˈtʃɔːkɪ] ADJ **1** *(terrain, soil)* crayeux; *(deposit)* calcique **2** *(colour)* pâle, terreux; *(texture, taste)* plâtreux; **c. white** *(complexion, houses)* blanc, *f* blanche; *(because of illness, shock etc)* pâle comme un linge

challenge [ˈtʃælɪndʒ] N **1** défi *m*; *Sport* défi, challenge *m*; *Mil (by sentry)* interpellation *f*; **to throw down** *or* **issue a c.** lancer un défi; **to accept** *or* **take up a c.** relever un défi; *Pol* **a c. to his leadership** une tentative pour le supplanter à la tête du parti; **to enjoy a c.** aimer les défis; **I find the work a real c.** ce travail est une vraie gageure pour moi; **environmental problems are the major c. for our generation** les problèmes d'environnement constituent la principale gageure *ou* le principal défi de notre génération
  2 *Law (of jury member)* récusation *f*
  VT **1** **to c. sb** *(to a fight)* provoquer qn; **to c. sb to do sth** défier qn de faire qch; **to c. sb to single combat** provoquer qn en combat singulier; **to c. sb to a game of chess/to a game of tennis** proposer une partie d'échecs/de

tennis à qn; *(with serious intent to beat them)* défier qn aux échecs/au tennis
  2 *(statement etc)* protester contre, disputer; *(sb's word)* mettre en question *ou* en doute *ou* en cause; *(sb's qualifications, account, figures)* contester; **their position was challenged by younger artists** leur position a été remise en question par des artistes plus jeunes; **to c. sb's right to do sth** contester à qn le droit de faire qch
  3 *(stimulate)* **you need a job that will c. you** il te faut un travail stimulant
  4 *Mil (of sentry)* interpeller
  5 *Law (member of jury)* récuser
  ►► *Sport* **c. cup** coupe-challenge *f*, *pl* coupes-challenges; *Sport* **c. match** challenge

challenger [ˈtʃælɪndʒər] N *(to a fight)* provocateur, -trice; *Sport* challengeur *m*; *Mktg* challengeur, prétendant *m*

challenging [ˈtʃælɪndʒɪŋ] ADJ **1** *(look, remark etc)* provocateur, -trice; *(air)* de défi **2** *(job)* stimulant

chamber [ˈtʃeɪmbər] N **1** *(hall, room)* chambre *f*; *Pol (upper, lower)* Chambre
  2 *Law* **chambers** *(of barrister, judge)* cabinet *m*; **in chambers** en chambre du conseil; **to hear a case in chambers** juger une cause en référé
  3 *Metal (of furnace)* laboratoire *m*; *Phys (for ionization, expansion)* chambre *f*, *(of revolver)* chambre; **air c.** *(in pump)* chambre à air
  4 *Anat* cavité *f*
  5 *Arch, Lit (room)* salle *f*, *Lit* **(bed-)c.** chambre *f* (à coucher); **council c.** salle du conseil
  ►► **C. of Commerce** Chambre de commerce; **C. of Commerce and Industry** Chambre de commerce et d'industrie; **c. music** musique *f* de chambre; *Mus* **c. orchestra** orchestre *m* de chambre; **c. pot** pot *m* de chambre

chamberlain [ˈtʃeɪmbəlɪn] N chambellan *m*

chambermaid [ˈtʃeɪmbəmeɪd] N *(in hotel)* femme *f* de chambre

chameleon [kəˈmiːlɪən] N *(animal)*, *Fig* caméléon *m*

chamfer [ˈtʃæmfər] *Carp etc* N biseau *m*, chanfrein *m*
  VT *(beam etc)* biseauter, chanfreiner; *(cut grooves in) (column etc)* canneler

chammy [ˈʃæmɪ] N *Fam* = **chamois 2**

chamois N **1** [ˈʃæmwɑː] *(deer)* chamois *m* **2** [ˈʃæmɪ] *(cloth for washing car)* chamois *m*, peau *f* de chamois; **c. jacket** veste *f* en peau de chamois
  ►► **c. leather** *(for washing car)* chamois, peau de chamois

champ¹ [tʃæmp] N *Sport Fam* champion, -ionne

champ² VT *(of horse etc) (fodder)* mâcher bruyamment; *(bit)* ronger, mâcher, mâchonner
  VI *Fig Fam* **to c. at the bit** *(of person)* ronger son frein

champagne [ʃæmˈpeɪn] N **1** *(drink)* champagne *m* **2** *(colour)* champagne *m inv*
  ADJ *(colour)* champagne *inv*; **a c.-coloured sofa** un canapé couleur champagne
  ►► **c. flute** flûte *f* à champagne; **c. glass** *(tall)* flûte à champagne; *(broad)* coupe *f* à champagne; **c. reception** réception *f* avec champagne

champers [ˈʃæmpəz] N *Fam (champagne)* champ *m*

champion [ˈtʃæmpɪən] N **1** *Sport* champion, -ionne; **world c.** champion du monde; **a c. footballer** un champion du football **2** *(of cause)* champion, -ionne
  ADJ *Br Dial* formidable
  VT *(cause)* se faire le champion de; *(person)* soutenir

championship ['tʃæmpɪənʃɪp] N **1** *Sport etc* championnat *m* **2** *(of cause)* défense *f*
▸▸ *Sport* **c. match** match *m* de championnat

CHANCE [tʃɑːns]

N	chance **1, 3** ▪ hasard **1**
	▪ occasion **2** ▪ risque **4**
ADJ ATTRIB	fortuit
VT	risquer

N **1** *(luck)* hasard *m*, chance *f*; **by c.** par hasard; **somebody I met by c.** quelqu'un que j'ai rencontré par hasard; **do you by any c. know his address?** est-ce que par hasard tu connaîtrais son adresse?; **to leave nothing to c.** ne rien laisser au hasard; **to leave everything to c.** s'en remettre entièrement au hasard; *Fam* **to have an eye to** *or* **for the main c.** chercher à tirer profit de toutes les occasions; *Fam* **c. would be a fine thing!** ah, si seulement je pouvais!
2 *(opportunity)* occasion *f*; **now's your c.** c'est maintenant qu'il faut y aller; **it's your last c.** c'est ta dernière chance; **it's a c. in a million** c'est une occasion qui ne se présentera pas deux fois; **I had a c. to work in the States** j'ai eu l'occasion de travailler aux États-Unis; **I go to the theatre when I get the c.** je vais au théâtre quand j'en ai l'occasion; **can you translate this for me when you get a c.?** est-ce que tu pourras me traduire ça quand tu auras le temps?; **there are no second chances, there is no second c.** tu n'as pas droit à l'erreur; **to give sb a c.** *(in job)* mettre qn à l'essai; *(to do better)* donner une chance à qn; **give me another c.** donne-moi une autre chance; **you didn't give me a c.!** *(to tell you)* tu ne m'en as pas laissé le temps!; *Fam* **given half a c. she'd play tennis every day** si elle pouvait elle jouerait au tennis tous les jours
3 *(possibility)* **to have** *or* **stand a c.** *(of succeeding)* avoir des chances de succès; **he never had a c., the truck was coming straight at him** il n'avait aucune chance de s'en sortir, le camion est arrivé droit sur lui; **she stands a good c. of being chosen** elle a de bonnes chances d'être choisie; **he hasn't the slightest c.** *or Fam* **a c. in hell of succeeding** il n'a pas la moindre chance de réussir; **they have an even** *or* **a fifty-fifty c. of winning** ils ont une chance sur deux *ou* cinquante pour cent de chances de gagner; **there's little/no/a good c. of that happening** il y a peu de chance/aucune chance/de bonnes chances que cela se produise; *Fam* **do you think they'll win? – no c.!** est-ce que tu crois qu'ils vont gagner? – aucune chance!; *Fam* **can I stay the night? – no c.!** est-ce que je peux passer la nuit ici? – pas question!; **(the) chances are (that) he'll forget** il y a fort à parier qu'il oubliera
4 *(risk)* risque *m*; **she takes too many chances** elle prend trop de risques; **to take a c.** prendre un risque; **he took a c. on them not finding out** il a pris le risque en espérant qu'ils ne le découvrent pas; **I'll have to take a c. on that** j'en prends le risque; **I'm taking no chances** je ne veux pas prendre de risques; **to take a sporting c.** tenter le coup; **to take one's chances** tenter sa chance
ADJ ATTRIB c. customer client *m* imprévu; **c. discovery** découverte *f* accidentelle *ou* fortuite; **c. meeting** rencontre *f* fortuite
VI *Lit (happen)* **to c. to do sth** faire qch par hasard; **only when she chanced to visit him was the body discovered** c'est en passant chez lui par hasard qu'elle a découvert le corps
VT *(risk)* risquer; *Fam* **to c. it** *or* **one's luck** *or* **one's arm** risquer *ou* tenter le coup; **to c. doing sth** prendre le risque de faire qch

---

▸ **chance on, chance upon** VT INSEP *(find by accident)* tomber (par hasard) sur

> Note that the French noun **chance** is a false friend. Its most common meaning is **luck**.

chancel ['tʃɑːns(ə)l] N *Archit* chœur *m*
▸▸ **c. screen** jubé *m*
chancellery ['tʃɑːnsələrɪ] N chancellerie *f*
chancellor ['tʃɑːnsələr] N **1** *Univ, Rel* chancelier *m* **2** *Pol* **C.** chancelier *m*; *Br Pol* **C. (of the Exchequer)** Chancelier de l'Échiquier, = ministre *m* des Finances; *Br Law* **the Lord (High) C.** le Grand Chancelier, = le ministre de la Justice
chancer ['tʃɑːnsər] N *Br Sl (opportunist)* filou *m*; **he's a real c.** il n'en rate pas une
chancery ['tʃɑːnsərɪ] N **1** *Law Br* **(Court of) C.** cour *f* de la chancellerie; *Am* **(court of) c.** cour d'équité **2** *(of embassy)* chancellerie *f*
chancre ['ʃæŋkər] N *Med* chancre *m*
chancy ['tʃɑːnsɪ] ADJ *Fam* risqué
chandelier [ʃændə'lɪər] N lustre *m*

> Note that the French word **chandelier** is a false friend and is never a translation for the English word **chandelier**. Its most common meaning is **candlestick** or **candelabra**.

chandler ['tʃɑːndlər] N *Com* **ship('s) c.** fournisseur *m* de navires; **corn c.** marchand *m* de blé *ou* de grains

---

CHANGE [tʃeɪndʒ]

N	changement **1** ▪ monnaie **2**
VT	changer **1–4**
VI	changer **1, 3** ▪ se changer **2**

N **1** *(alteration) (of air, job etc)* changement *m*; *(in expression, voice)* altération *f*; *(modification)* modification *f*; **c. of address** changement de domicile *ou* d'adresse; **to have a c. of opinion** *or* **of heart** changer d'avis; **c. for the better/worse** *(of health etc)* amélioration *f*/détérioration *f*; **there's been a c. in the weather** il y a eu un changement de temps; **there's been a c. in the law** la loi a été modifiée; **sudden c. of fortune** revirement *m* de fortune; **there is no/little c. in the situation** il n'y a pas/il y a peu de changement dans la situation; **there are going to be some changes in this office!** il va y avoir du nouveau *ou* du changement dans ce bureau!; **some changes were made to the train timetable** il y a eu des changements *ou* des modifications dans les horaires de train; **you need a c.** tu as besoin de changer d'air; **the c. will do you good** le changement te fera du bien; *Prov* **a c. is as good as a rest** changer de décor fait autant de bien que partir en vacances; **this trip will be** *or* **make a bit of a c. for you** ce voyage vous changera un peu; **you must find it a bit of a c. living in the country** vous devez trouver un drôle de changement à vivre à la campagne; **he was early for a c.** pour une fois, il était en avance; **why don't you wash the dishes for a c.?** si tu faisais la vaisselle, pour une fois?; **it** *or* **that makes a c.** ça change un peu; **yes, it makes a (nice) c., doesn't it?** oui, ça change (un peu) (de l'ordinaire) n'est-ce pas?; **it was a c. from the old system** ça changeait du système précédent; **the c. of life,** *Fam* **the c. (of woman)** le retour d'âge; *Fam* **to go through the c. (of woman)** traverser la ménopause; *Mus* **chord c.** changement d'accord; *Theat* **scene c.** changement de décor; **c. of clothes** vêtements *mpl* de rechange
2 *(money)* monnaie *f*; **small** *or* **loose c.** petite *ou* menue monnaie; **to get c.** faire de la monnaie; **to get c. for £5** faire la monnaie de 5 livres; **have you got c. for a £10 note?** est-ce que tu as de la monnaie sur un billet de 10 livres?; **keep the c.** gardez la monnaie; **the machine doesn't give c.** cet appareil ne rend pas la monnaie; *Fam* **you won't get much c. out of £100** *(if you buy that)* il ne va pas te rester grand-chose sur tes 100 livres; *Fam* **he won't get much c. out of me** il en sera pour ses frais avec moi
3 *(in bell-ringing)* **to ring the changes** carillonner avec variations *ou* avec permutations; *Fig* **to ring the changes on** *(subject)* ressasser, rabâcher, broder des variations sur; *(menu, programme etc)* varier, introduire des changements dans
VT 1 *(alter) (one's plans, lifestyle etc)* changer, modifier; **to c. water into wine** changer l'eau en vin; **you can't c. a dictatorship into a democracy overnight** on ne transforme pas une dictature en démocratie en une nuit; **the witch changed him into a frog** la sorcière l'a transformé en crapaud; **to c. one's ways** *or* **habits** changer (ses habitudes); **to c. one's mind** *or* **opinion** changer d'avis; **to c. the subject** changer de sujet; **don't c. the subject!** ne détourne pas la conversation!; **to c. colour** changer de couleur
2 *(replace) (sheets)* changer; **to c. one's clothes** se changer; **to c. one's dress/one's shoes** changer de robe/de chaussures; **to c. the baby** changer le bébé; *Aut* **to c. a tyre** changer *ou* remplacer un pneu; *Aut* **to c. the oil** faire une *ou* une vidange; *Aut* **to c. gear** changer de vitesse; **to c. channels** *(on TV)* changer de chaîne; **to c. trains/one's seat** changer de train/de place; **I've changed doctors** j'ai changé de médecin
3 *(exchange)* **to c. one thing for another** changer une chose pour *ou* contre une autre; **to c. places** *or* **seats with sb** changer de place avec qn; *Fig* **I wouldn't (like to) c. places with him** je ne changerais pas avec lui; *Fig* **to c. sides** changer de camp, virer de bord; *Mil* **to c. the guard** relever la garde
4 *(money)* changer; **to c. a note into coins** faire de la monnaie sur un billet; **to c. dollars into euros** changer des dollars contre des euros *ou* en euros; **they won't c. pounds** ils ne changeront pas des livres
VI 1 *(alter)* changer; *(of moon)* changer de quartier; *(of luck, wind)* tourner; **she's changed since I last saw her** elle a changé depuis la dernière fois que je l'ai vue; **some things never c.** certaines choses ne changent jamais; **to c. for the better** changer en mieux, s'améliorer; *(of weather)* tourner au beau; **the situation has changed for the worse** la situation s'est détériorée; **to c. beyond recognition** être méconnaissable; **to c. into sth** *(by magic, through biological transformation)* se transformer en qch; **he changed into a psychopath** il est devenu psychopathe; **the country had changed from dictatorship to democracy overnight** en une nuit, le pays était passé de la dictature à la démocratie; **the lights changed from green to amber** les feux sont passés du vert à l'orange; **to c. from one system to another** passer d'un système à un autre
2 *(put on other clothes)* se changer; **to c. into another dress** changer de robe; **to c. into trousers** se mettre en pantalon; **to c. into something more comfortable/less formal** mettre un vêtement plus confortable/moins habillé; **to c. out of a wet shirt** enlever *ou* quitter une chemise mouillée
3 *Rail etc (of passenger)* changer; **we had to c. twice** nous avons eu deux correspondances; *(in underground)* nous avons eu deux changements; **all c.!** tout le monde descend!
4 *(of sentries, shifts)* se relever
▸▸ **c. machine** distributeur *m* de monnaie
▸ **change down** VI *Aut (use lower gear)* ré-

trograder; **to c. down (in)to second** passer en seconde

▶ **change over** VI **1** *(convert)* **the UK changed over to decimal currency in 1971** le Royaume-Uni est passé à la monnaie décimale en 1971; **we c. over next year** on passe au nouveau système l'an prochain

2 *(switch)* **let's c. over** *(exchange places etc)* on change?; *(exchange jobs, roles etc)* on échange?; *TV* **to c. over (to another channel)** passer sur une autre chaîne; *TV* **c. over for the news** change de chaîne pour regarder les informations; *TV* **why don't you c. over to ITV?** et si on mettait ITV?

3 *Sport (change ends)* changer de côté; *(in relay race)* passer le témoin

▶ **change up** VI *Aut (use higher gear)* passer à la vitesse supérieure; **to c. up (in)to third** passer en troisième

changeability [tʃeɪndʒə'bɪlɪtɪ], **changeableness** ['tʃeɪndʒəb(ə)lnɪs] N *(of weather etc)* variabilité f; *(of moods)* changements mpl

changeable ['tʃeɪndʒəb(ə)l] ADJ changeant; *(weather)* variable, instable; *(wind)* inégal, -aux; **c. character** caractère m changeant *ou* instable

changeless ['tʃeɪndʒlɪs] ADJ *(rituals, landscape)* immuable

changeling ['tʃeɪndʒlɪŋ] N = enfant mf que des fées ont substitué(ée) à un(e) autre

changeover ['tʃeɪndʒəʊvər] N **1** *(to new system)* changement m, passage m **2** *(after election etc)* relève f **3** *Sport* changement m de côté; *(in relay race)* passage m du témoin **4** *Cin* changement m de bobine

changing ['tʃeɪndʒɪŋ] ADJ *(nature, world, mood)* changeant

N changement m

▶ ▶ *Aut* **c. down** *(of gears)* rétrogradage m; **the C. of the Guard** la relève de la garde; *Br* **c. room** *(in sports centre, gym)* vestiaire m; *(in shop)* cabine f d'essayage; **c. table** table f à langer

channel ['tʃæn(ə)l] N **1** *(of river)* lit m; *(waterway)* chenal m; **the (English) C.** la Manche; **on the other side of the C.** outre-Manche

2 *(of distribution)* canal m, circuit m; *(for complaint, inquiry etc)* voie f; **to go through (official) channels** suivre la filière *ou* la voie hiérarchique; **through diplomatic channels** par voie diplomatique; **channels of communication** canaux de communication; **there were still channels of communication open** la communication n'était pas totalement interrompue; **channels of communication are still open** *(between us)* nous sommes toujours en relation, le dialogue continue

3 *TV* chaîne f; *Radio* station f

4 *Elec, Electron etc* voie f; *Comput* canal m; *(on stereo)* sortie f

5 *(for irrigation)* canal m

6 *(groove) (in wood)* rainure f, *(on column)* cannelure f

VT **(-ll-, Am -l-) 1** *(direct) (effort, energy, information)* canaliser *(towards* vers; *into* dans); *(resources, aid etc)* acheminer; **she channelled all her energy into charity work** elle a investi toute son énergie dans des œuvres de bienfaisance **2** *(cut channels in) (ground)* creuser des rigoles dans

▶ ▶ *Com* **c. of distribution** circuit de distribution, canal de distribution; **C. Four** = chaîne de télévision privée britannique à vocation culturelle; **the C. Islands** les îles fpl Anglo-Normandes; *Mktg* **c. management** gestion f du circuit de distribution; **C. port** port m sur la Manche; **the C. Tunnel** le tunnel sous la Manche

channel-hop VI *TV* zapper

channel-hopper N *TV* zappeur, -euse

channel-hopping N *TV* zapping m

chant [tʃɑːnt] N **1** *(of demonstrators)* slogans mpl (scandés); **the c. went up … on** commença à scander … **2** *Mus, Rel* psalmodie f; **Gregorian c.** chant m grégorien

VT **1** *(slogans, name etc)* scander **2** *Rel* psalmodier

VI **1** *(of demonstrators, crowd etc)* scander des slogans **2** *Rel* psalmodier

> Note that the French verb **chanter** is a false friend and is never a translation for the English verb **to chant**. It means **to sing**.

chantey ['tʃæntɪ] N *Am* chanson f de marin

chanting ['tʃɑːntɪŋ] ADJ *(voice etc)* monotone, traînant

N **1** *(of demonstrators)* slogans mpl (scandés) **2** *Rel* chants mpl, psalmodie f

chantry ['tʃɑːntrɪ] N *Rel Arch* chantrerie f, chanterie f

chaos ['keɪɒs] N chaos m; *(in filing system, sb's life)* pagaille f, *Fam* bordel m; **it'll be c. if you try to introduce these changes** ça va être la pagaille si tu fais ces changements; **the country is in a state of c.** le pays est dans un état de confusion totale; *Journ* **c. on roads as bus drivers strike** la grève des chauffeurs de bus entraîne le chaos sur les routes; **it was c. in the post office** c'était la pagaille au bureau de poste; **it's just c.!** c'est la confusion totale!

▶ ▶ **c. theory** théorie f du chaos

chaotic [keɪ'ɒtɪk] ADJ chaotique; *(office, filing system)* en désordre; **in a c. state** en pagaille; **a c. love life** une vie amoureuse chaotique

chaotically [keɪ'ɒtɪklɪ] ADV en pagaille; **clothes all c. piled into one drawer** des vêtements tous mis en pagaille dans un tiroir; **a c. disorganized life** une vie totalement chaotique

chap¹ [tʃæp] N *Fam (man)* type m, mec m; **a good c.** un type bien; **an odd c.** un drôle de type; **be a good c.** sois sympa; *Old-fashioned* **I say, old c.!** dis, mon vieux!

chap² N *(on skin)* gerçure f, crevasse f

VT *(-pp-)* *(skin)* gercer; **chapped lips** lèvres fpl gercées

VI se gercer

chapel ['tʃæp(ə)l] N **1** *(of school etc)* chapelle f, *(private)* oratoire m; *(in cathedral etc)* chapelle latérale **2** *Rel (protestant)* temple m; *Scot Cathol* **to go to c.** aller à la messe **3** *(of print union, NUJ)* branche f syndicale *(dans l'industrie du livre et de l'édition)*; **Father/ Mother of C.** président/présidente de la branche syndicale

▶ ▶ **c. of rest** = chambre f mortuaire dans une entreprise de pompes funèbres

chaperone ['ʃæpərəʊn] N *(for young girl)* Hum chaperon m; **to act as c.** servir de chaperon; **the foreign journalists had a c.** les journalistes étrangers étaient accompagnés partout où ils allaient

VT *(girl, young woman)* chaperonner

chaplain ['tʃæplɪn] N *Rel* aumônier m

chaplaincy ['tʃæplɪnsɪ] N aumônerie f

chappie ['tʃæpɪ] N *Fam (man)* type m, gus m; *(little boy, baby)* petit gars m

Chaps [tʃæps] N *Banking (abbr* **clearing house automated payment system)** Sit m

chapter ['tʃæptər] N **1** *(of book), Fig* chapitre m; *Fig* **to give c. and verse for sth** citer les références exactes de qch; **a new c. in East-West relations** un nouveau chapitre dans les relations est-ouest; **what a c. of accidents!** quelle série noire! **2** *Rel (of canons, monks)* chapitre m **3** *(of society etc)* groupe m; **a Hell's Angel c.** une bande de Hell's Angels

▶ ▶ *Rel* **c. house** salle f capitulaire

char¹ [tʃɑːr] *(-rr-)* VT *(wood, bones)* carboniser, réduire en cendres; **the charred remains of a building** les restes carbonisés d'un bâtiment

VI se carboniser

char² N *Br Sl (tea)* thé m

char³ *Br Fam* N *(charlady)* femme f de ménage

VI *(work as charlady)* faire des ménages

char⁴ N *(fish)* omble m (chevalier)

charabanc ['ʃærəbæŋ] N *Br Hist* char m à bancs; *Hum (sightseeing coach)* car m de touristes

character ['kærɪktər] N **1** *Liter, Theat etc* personnage m; **a c. straight out of a novel** un vrai personnage de roman; **Chaplin plays two different characters in 'The Great Dictator'** Chaplin joue deux rôles différents dans 'Le Dictateur'; **characters in order of appearance** *(in credits)* distribution par ordre d'entrée en scène

2 *(distinctive quality)* *(of person, race, book etc)* caractère m; **her face is full of c.** son visage a beaucoup de caractère; **to have c.** avoir du caractère; **this region has a c. of its own** cette région a un caractère particulier; **books of this c.** les livres de ce genre; **his behaviour/remark was in/out of c.** la façon dont il s'est conduit/la remarque qu'il a faite lui correspond bien/ne lui correspond pas

3 *(moral qualities)* caractère m; *(reputation)* réputation f; **a man of (strong) c.** un homme de caractère *ou* de volonté; **to be lacking in c.** manquer de caractère; *Fml* **a person of good c.** une personne honorable; **a place of very dubious c.** un endroit mal famé

4 *(person)* **a suspicious c.** un individu suspect *ou* louche; **he's quite a c.!** *(odd, remarkable)* c'est un sacré numéro!, c'est un personnage!

5 *Comput, Typ* caractère m; **in Greek characters** en caractères grecs; **special/binary c.** caractère spécial/binaire; **characters per inch** caractères par pouce; **characters per second** caractères par seconde

▶ ▶ *Cin, Theat* **c. actor** acteur m de genre; **c. assassination** diffamation f, *Comput* **c. code** code m de caractère; *Comput* **c. count** nombre m de caractères; **to do a c. count** compter les caractères; *Comput, Typ* **c. font** fonte f de caractère; *Comput* **c. generator** générateur m de caractères; *Comput* **c. insert** insertion f de caractère; *Mktg* **c. licensing** cession f de licence sur un personnage; *Comput* **c. map** tableau m des caractères; *Comput* **c. mode** mode m caractère; *Cin, Theat* **c. part** rôle m de composition; *Comput* **c. recognition** reconnaissance f de caractères; **c. reference** des références fpl; *Comput* **c. set** jeu m de caractères; **c. sketch** portrait m ou description f rapide; *Comput* **c. smoothing** lissage m de caractères; *Comput* **c. space** espace m; *Comput* **c. spacing** espacement m des caractères; *Comput* **c. string** chaîne f de caractères; *Law* **c. witness** témoin m de moralité

character-building, **character-forming** ADJ qui forme le caractère; **it's c.** ça forme le caractère

characteristic [kærɪktə'rɪstɪk] ADJ *(sign, taste etc)* caractéristique; **this attitude is c. of him** cette attitude lui correspond bien, c'est bien de lui

N **1** caractéristique f, trait m caractéristique **2** *Math (of logarithm)* caractéristique f

characteristically [kærɪktə'rɪstɪklɪ] ADV de façon caractéristique; **he was c. blunt / evasive** comme à son habitude, il a été abrupt/vague

characterization [kærɪktəraɪ'zeɪʃən] N **1** (description) caractérisation f **2** Cin, Liter, Theat représentation f ou peinture f des personnages

characterize ['kærɪktəraɪz] VT **1** (of writer) (person) caractériser; (century etc) dépeindre **2** (be characteristic of) être caractéristique de, caractériser; **the long pauses that c. his speech** les longs silences qui caractérisent son discours

characterless ['kærɪktəlɪs] ADJ sans caractère

charade [ʃə'rɑːd] N **1** (farce) mascarade f **2** (game) **to play charades** jouer aux charades mimées

> Note that the French word **charade** is a false friend. It is a type of word game.

charcoal ['tʃɑːkəʊl] N **1** charbon m de bois **2** Art fusain m
▸▸ **c. drawing** (dessin m au) fusain m; **c. filter** filtre m à charbon

charcoal-broiled [-'brɔɪld] ADJ (steak etc) grillé au charbon de bois

charcoal-burner N **1** (person) charbonnier m **2** (stove) réchaud m à charbon de bois

chard [tʃɑːd] N Bot, Culin Swiss **c.** bette f, blette f

CHARGE [tʃɑːdʒ] N **1** (cost) frais mpl; Admin droits mpl; Law privilège m, droit m; (to an account) imputation f; **list of charges** tarif m; **scale of charges** barème m des prix; **no c. for admission** (in museum etc) entrée gratuite; **there is no extra c. for installation** l'installation est comprise dans le prix; **to make a c. for sth** faire payer qch; **free of c.** gratis, (à titre) gratuit, à titre gracieux; Com, Banking exempt de frais, sans frais; esp Am **will that be cash or c.?** vous payez comptant ou vous le portez à votre compte?; **service c.** prestation f de service; **extra c.** supplément m (de prix); **bank charges** frais bancaires, agios mpl; **minimum c.** (in taxi) prise f en charge; (in café, restaurant) = prix m minimum à payer; Banking **c. over business assets** nantissement m de fonds de commerce

2 (accusation) accusation f; Law chef m d'accusation, acte m d'accusation; (by public prosecutor) réquisitoire m; **to bring** or **lay a c. against sb** porter une accusation ou porter plainte contre qn; **on a c. of having …** accusé d'avoir …; **what's the c.?** de quoi est-il/suis-je/etc accusé?; **he denies the c.** il nie les accusations

3 (responsibility) garde f, soin m; **to place sth in sb's c.** confier qch à qn ou à la garde de qn ou aux mains de qn; **to have c. of sth** avoir la garde de qch; **to take c. of sth/sb** se charger de qch/qn; **I'll take c. while the director is sick** je m'occupe de tout pendant que le directeur est malade; **to be in c. of** piloter; **Jane is in c. of sales** Jane est chargée ou responsable des ventes; **he is in overall c. of the project** il est responsable du projet dans son ensemble; **he was put in c. of 100 men** on a mis 100 hommes sous sa responsabilité; **who is in c.?** qui est le responsable?; **look, I'm in c. here!** écoute, c'est moi le patron ici!; **I want to speak to the person in c.** je veux parler au responsable ou à la personne responsable; **who was in c. of the vehicle?** (driving) qui était au volant?; Law **to take sb in c.** arrêter qn

4 (person, thing entrusted) f; chose f confiée à la garde de qn; **the nanny is out for a walk with her charges** la nourrice est partie se promener avec les enfants qu'elle garde ou dont elle a la charge

5 Mil (attack) attaque f, charge f; **to sound the c.** sonner la charge

6 Elec, Phys (of cartridge, bomb, battery) charge f; Fig **the word has an emotional c.** le mot a une charge affective; Am Fam Fig **to get a c. out of sth/doing sth** (thrill) s'éclater ou prendre son pied avec qch/en faisant qch

VT **1** (price) faire payer; Com, Fin (account) charger (**with** de); **he charged me £15** il m'a fait payer 15 livres; Fam **they charged me a fortune for this haircut** j'ai payé une fortune pour me faire couper les cheveux; **how much do you c. for an hour?** combien prenez-vous de l'heure?; Tel **calls charged for conversations** fpl taxées; **to c. the postage to the customer** faire payer les frais d'envoi au client; **commission charged by the bank** commission prélevée par la banque; **c. it to my account/the bill** mettez-le sur mon compte/la note

2 (accuse) accuser (**with sth** de qch; **with doing** de faire ou d'avoir fait); Law inculper (**with a crime** d'un crime); Am **to c. that …** alléguer que …

3 (entrust, order) **to c. sb to do sth** ordonner à qn de faire qch; **to c. sb with a task** confier une tâche à qn

4 (of troops, forwards, bull etc) charger

5 Elec (electrical conductor, battery etc) (re)charger (**with** de); Fig **a highly charged atmosphere** une atmosphère très tendue; **charged with emotion** chargé d'émotion

VI **1** Mil charger, faire une charge; (of animal) foncer; Fam (run heavily) (of person) se précipiter, foncer; Mil **c!** chargez!; **he charged in** il s'est précipité dans la maison/la pièce/etc; **the crowd charged across the square** la foule s'est ruée à travers la place; **stop charging around, you kids, this is a living room!** arrêtez de courir dans tous les sens, les enfants, ici c'est un salon!

2 (require payment) faire payer (**for sth** qch); **do you c. for delivery?** est-ce qu'il y a des frais de livraison?

3 (of battery) se (re)charger
▸▸ Am Com, Fin **c. account** compte m crédit d'achats, compte accréditif; Com, Fin **c. card** carte f de paiement; Br **c. hand** sous-chef m d'équipe, pl sous-chefs d'équipe; Br **c. nurse** infirmier, -ière en chef; Br Law **c. sheet** procès-verbal m, pl procès-verbaux (établi par la police avant le passage d'un prévenu devant un tribunal)

▸ **charge down** VT SEP Rugby (ball) contrer
▸ **charge off** VT SEP Am Fin (capital) amortir, imputer à l'exercice; **we were obliged to c. the whole operation** il a fallu imputer l'intégralité du coût de l'opération à l'exercice
▸ **charge up** VT SEP **1** (in shop etc) **to c. sth up to sb's account** mettre qch sur le compte de qn; **could you c. it up?** pourriez-vous le mettre sur mon compte?

2 (battery) (re)charger
VI (of battery) se (re)charger

chargeable ['tʃɑːdʒəb(ə)l] ADJ **1** Law (person) **we would be c. with fraud** on nous accuserait de fraude; **a c. offence** un délit **2** Com etc (to an account) imputable; **to be c. to sb** (payable by) être à la charge de qn, être pris en charge par qn; **is it c.?** est-ce qu'il y a des frais?; **a small fee is c. for delivery and installation** il y a quelques frais de livraison et d'installation; **who is it c. to?** c'est à la charge de qui?; **could you make that c. to …?** est-ce que vous pourriez facturer …?; **is this a c. expense?** est-ce que c'est frais facturable?
▸▸ **c. distance** (in taxi) distance f tarifaire; Fin **c. gain** bénéfice m imposable; Com **c. weight** poids m de taxation

charge-cooled [-kuːld] ADJ Aut (engine) suralimenté refroidi

chargé d'affaires [ʃɑːʒeɪdæ'feər] N chargé m d'affaires

charger ['tʃɑːdʒər] N **1** Elec (for battery) chargeur m **2** (horse) cheval m de bataille, destrier m

charily ['tʃeərɪlɪ] ADV (cautiously) avec précaution, avec prudence

chariot ['tʃærɪət] N char m

charioteer [tʃærɪə'tɪər] N conducteur m de char

charisma [kə'rɪzmə] N charisme m; **to have c.** avoir du charisme

charismatic [kærɪz'mætɪk] ADJ charismatique

charitable ['tʃærɪtəb(ə)l] ADJ **1** (person, action) charitable; Fig **the critics were not c.** les critiques n'ont pas été très tendres ou bienveillants **2** (organization) caritatif, de bienfaisance, de charité; (work) de bienfaisance, de charité
▸▸ **c. donation** don m à une œuvre de bienfaisance; **c. society** organisation f caritative; **c. status** statut m d'organisation caritative; **c. trust** fondation f d'utilité publique

charitably ['tʃærɪtəblɪ] ADV avec charité

charity ['tʃærɪtɪ] N **1** (money, food) charité f, aumônes fpl; **to live on c.** vivre d'aumônes; **I don't want your c.** je ne veux pas que tu me fasses la charité **2** (organization) organisation f caritative; **registered c.** œuvre f reconnue d'utilité publique; **we're not a c.!** nous ne sommes pas des philanthropes ou une organisation de bienfaisance! **3** (kindness) charité f; **out of c.** par charité; Prov **c. begins at home** charité bien ordonnée commence par soi-même
▸▸ **c. ball** bal m de bienfaisance; Br **the C. Commission** = commission f gouvernementale britannique contrôlant les associations caritatives; **c. organization** association f caritative, œuvre de bienfaisance; **c. run** = course f à pied au profit d'une œuvre de bienfaisance; **c. shop** = magasin m dont les employés sont des bénévoles et dont les bénéfices servent à subventionner une œuvre d'utilité publique; **c. work** bénévolat m

charlady ['tʃɑːleɪdɪ] N Br femme f de ménage

charlatan ['ʃɑːlət(ə)n] N charlatan m

charleston ['tʃɑːlstən] N (dance) charleston m

Charley, Charlie ['tʃɑːlɪ] N Br Fam **I felt a right** or **a proper C.** j'ai vraiment eu l'air bête

charley horse N Am Fam **to have a c.** avoir des crampes

charlie ['tʃɑːlɪ] N Sl (cocaine) coke f, neige f

charlotte ['ʃɑːlət] N Culin **apple c.** charlotte f aux pommes

charm [tʃɑːm] N **1** (attractiveness) charme m, agrément m; (of youth etc) charme, attrait m; **a film of great c.** un film plein de charme; **the village has a quiet c.** le village a un charme tranquille; **to be devoid of c.** manquer de charme; Fam **to turn on the c.** faire du charme; **(physical) charms** (of person) charmes, attraits; **the c. of this system is that it's so easy to use** ce qu'il y a de bien avec ce système, c'est qu'il est facile à utiliser; Iron **what c. school did you go to?** oh, comme tu parles bien!

2 (spell) charme m (**against** contre), sortilège m, sort m, enchantement m; **to be under a c.** être envoûté; Fam **it worked like a c.** ça a marché à merveille

3 (talisman) amulette f, fétiche m; **(lucky) c.** porte-bonheur m inv

VT (person) (delight) charmer, enchanter; (snake) charmer; **she charmed them into signing** elle a obtenu leur signature à force de charme; **he leads a charmed life** c'est un veinard
▸▸ **c. bracelet** bracelet m à breloques; **c. offensive** offensive f de charme

charmer ['tʃɑːmər] N charmeur, -euse f; **he's quite a c.** c'est un charmeur; **snake c.** charmeur de serpents

charming ['tʃɑːmɪŋ] ADJ *(person, child, village, story), Iron* charmant; **Prince C.** le Prince Charmant

charmingly ['tʃɑːmɪŋlɪ] ADV d'une façon charmante

charnel ['tʃɑːn(ə)l] N *(for corpses)* charnier m

▸ ▸ **c. house** *(for bones)* ossuaire m

charring ['tʃɑːrɪŋ] N carbonisation f

chart [tʃɑːt] N **1** *Math etc (graph)* graphique m; *(diagram)* diagramme m; *(table)* tableau m; *Med* **temperature c.** feuille f de température; *Com* **colour c.** nuancier m **2** *Mus* **(pop) charts** hit-parade m, pl hit-parades; **she's (got a record) in the charts** elle est au hit-parade; **it's number one in** *or* **it's top of the charts** c'est le numéro un au hit-parade **3** *Naut, Aviat (for navigation)* carte f

VT **1** *Naut (sea etc)* hydrographier, faire l'hydrographie de; *(rock etc)* porter sur une carte **2** *(patient's temperature etc)* porter sur la feuille; *(plot graph of) (series of readings etc)* établir le graphique de; **this graph charts sales over the last ten years** ce graphique montre l'évolution des ventes au cours des dix dernières années; *Fig* **the book charts the rise of the labour movement** ce livre retrace la montée du mouvement travailliste

VI *Mus Fam (of record)* être classé; **it charted at number 16** il a été classé 16ᵉ

▸ ▸ *Acct* **c. of accounts** plan m comptable général; **c. analyst** analyste mf sur graphiques; *Naut* **c. room** cabine f des cartes; *Mus* **c. topper** numéro m un

charter ['tʃɑːtər] N **1** *Hist, Law (of town, university etc)* charte f; *(of company)* statuts mpl; *Pol* **the Atlantic C.** la Charte de l'Atlantique **2** *(of plane, ship, bus)* affrètement m; **on c.** *(to company)* affrété

VT **1** *(hire) (ship, plane)* affréter, noliser; *(ship)* prendre à fret; *(coach)* affréter **2** *(company etc)* accorder une charte à

▸ ▸ **c. flight** *(vol m)* charter m; **c. plane** *(avion m)* charter

chartered ['tʃɑːtəd] ADJ **1** *(ship, plane)* affrété, nolisé; *(coach)* affrété **2** *(company, bank)* privilégié

▸ ▸ *Br* **c. accountant** expert-comptable m, pl experts-comptables; **c. surveyor** expert m immobilier

charterer ['tʃɑːtərər] N *Naut, Aviat* affréteur m

chartering ['tʃɑːtərɪŋ] N *(of plane, ship, coach)* affrètement m; *(of plane, boat)* nolisation f; *(at reduced rates)* chartérisation f

▸ ▸ **c. broker** courtier m d'affrètement

charwoman, pl **charwomen** ['tʃɑːwʊmən, -wɪmɪn] N *Br* femme f de ménage

chary ['tʃeərɪ] ADJ *(cautious)* prudent, circonspect; **to be c. of doing sth** hésiter à faire qch; **to be c. of praise** *(sparing with it)* être avare de compliments

chase¹ [tʃeɪs] N **1** *(pursuit)* chasse f, poursuite f; **to give c. to sb** se lancer à la poursuite de qn; **in c. of sb** à la poursuite de qn; **a car c.** une poursuite en voitures; **paper c.** rallye-paper m, pl rallye-papers **2** *Horse-racing* steeple m **3** **the c.** *(hunting)* la chasse à courre

VT **1** *(pursue) (thief, enemy etc)* poursuivre, donner la chasse à; *(hunt) (deer)* chasser; **to c. a dog away** chasser un chien; **to c. sb out of the house** chasser qn de la maison **2** *Fam (court) (man, woman)* courir après

VI **I've been chasing around all day** j'ai couru toute la journée; **the kids were chasing all over the house** les gosses passaient leur temps à courir partout dans la maison

▸ **chase after** VT INSEP *Fam (man, woman)* courir après; *(car, animal etc)* être à la poursuite de, poursuivre; **we've been all over**

town **chasing after that spare part** nous avons dû faire tout le tour de la ville pour trouver cette pièce détachée

▸ **chase away** VT SEP chasser

▸ **chase up** VT SEP **1** *(insistently contact or try to contact)* relancer; **I'll c. them up about those files** je vais leur réclamer ces fichiers; **to c. up a debtor** relancer un débiteur **2** *(payment)* réclamer; **I'll c. the matter up for you** je vais tenter d'activer les choses pour vous

> Note that the French verb **chasser** is a false friend. Its most common meaning is **to hunt**.

chase² VT **1** *(engrave) (gold, silver)* ciseler; **chased work** ouvrage m ciselé **2** *(emboss) (metal)* repousser; **chased silver** argent m repoussé

chaser ['tʃeɪsər] N *Fam* **1** *(drink)* = alcool m bu après une bière ou vice versa **2** **woman c.** coureur m de jupons

chasing ['tʃeɪsɪŋ] N **1** *(engraving) (of gold, silver)* ciselage m, ciselure f **2** *(embossing) (of metal)* repoussage m

chasm ['kæz(ə)m] N *(abyss)* abysse m, abîme m, gouffre m béant; *Fig (between two people)* abîme m; **the c. between their political viewpoints** l'abîme qui sépare leurs opinions politiques

chassis ['ʃæsɪ] N *Aut, Aviat etc, Sl (of woman)* châssis m; *Hum* **she's got a classy c.** elle est super bien balancée *ou* carrossée

▸ ▸ **c. number** numéro m de châssis

chassisless construction ['ʃæsɪlɪs] N *Aut* carrosserie f autoporteuse

chaste [tʃeɪst] ADJ **1** *(sexually)* chaste **2** *Lit (speech, taste, style)* sobre, simple

chastely ['tʃeɪstlɪ] ADV **1** *(in sexual sense)* chastement **2** *Lit (soberly)* sobrement

chasten ['tʃeɪs(ə)n] VT *esp Lit (of providence, suffering etc) (person)* éprouver; *(humble)* rabattre la présomption *ou* l'orgueil de; *(subdue)* assagir; **he was in a chastened mood** il était abattu; **my son returned from Bangladesh chastened by what he had seen** le voyage de mon fils au Bangladesh, et ce qu'il y a vu, lui a mis du plomb dans la tête

chasteness ['tʃeɪstnɪs] N *(sexual)* chasteté f

chastening ['tʃeɪs(ə)nɪŋ] ADJ salutaire; **it had a c. effect on her** ça l'a assagie

chastise [tʃæs'taɪz] VT **1** *(reprimand, criticize)* réprimander **2** *Old-fashioned, Fml (punish)* châtier; *(beat) (child)* corriger

chastisement ['tʃæs'taɪzmənt] N *Old-fashioned, Fml (punishment)* châtiment m; *(beating) (of child)* correction f

chastity ['tʃæstɪtɪ] N *(sexual)* chasteté f; **to take a vow of c.** faire vœu de chasteté

▸ ▸ **c. belt** ceinture f de chasteté

chasuble ['tʃæzjʊb(ə)l] N *Rel* chasuble f

chat [tʃæt] N petite conversation f, causette f; *Comput* bavardage m; **to have a c. with sb** bavarder avec qn; *(about a problem, their work performance etc)* dire un mot à qn; **it's time we had a little c.** il est temps que nous ayons une petite discussion; **the c. at work is all about cars** au travail, on ne discute que de voitures

VI (-tt-) causer, bavarder; *Comput* bavarder; **to c. with sb** bavarder avec qn, faire la causette avec qn; **to c. about one thing and another** parler de choses et d'autres

▸ ▸ *Comput* **c. room** site m de bavardage, salon m, *Can* bavardoir m; *Br TV* **c. show** causerie f télévisée, talk-show m, pl talk-shows; *Br TV* **c. show host** présentateur, -trice de talk-show

▸ **chat up** VT SEP *Fam (talk flirtatiously to)* ba-

ratiner, draguer; *Fig* **to c. up a client** baratiner un client

chattel ['tʃæt(ə)l] N *Law* bien m meuble, bien mobilier; **chattels** biens; **goods and chattels** biens et effets mpl

chatter ['tʃætər] N *(of people)* bavardage m; *(of birds)* caquet(age) m, jacasserie f; *(of monkeys)* babil m; *(of teeth)* claquement m; *(of machine-gun)* martèlement m

VI *(of person)* bavarder, jaser; *(of birds)* caqueter, jacasser; *(of monkeys)* babiller; *(of teeth)* claquer; **my teeth were chattering** je claquais des dents

chatterbox ['tʃætəbɒks] N *Fam* moulin m à paroles

chatterer ['tʃætərər] N = **chatterbox**

chattering ['tʃætərɪŋ] N *(of people)* bavardage m; *(of birds)* caquetage m; *(of monkeys)* babil m; *(of teeth)* claquement m; *(of machine-gun)* martèlement m

▸ ▸ *Pej* **the c. classes** les intellectuels mpl qui s'écoutent parler *(terme journalistique appliqué, dès le début des années 80, à une poignée de personnes qui pensent que leurs opinions ont de l'importance mais qui ne représentent guère l'opinion de la majorité)*

chatty ['tʃætɪ] ADJ *(person)* bavard; *(letter)* plein de bavardages; *(article etc)* écrit sur le ton de la conversation; **Mr Smith was very c.** *or* **in a very c. mood today** M. Smith était très bavard aujourd'hui; **the interview with the President was rather too c.** il y avait un peu trop de bavardage dans l'entretien avec le Président

chat-up line N *Fam* **that's his standard c.** c'est son baratin habituel quand il drague

chauffeur ['ʃəʊfər] N chauffeur m; **c.-driven** *(car)* avec chauffeur

VT *(person)* accompagner, conduire; *(car)* conduire; **we were chauffeured to the airport** on nous a conduits à l'aéroport

chauvinism ['ʃəʊvɪnɪz(ə)m] N *Pej* **1** *(patriotism)* chauvinisme m **2** **(male) c.** machisme m

chauvinist ['ʃəʊvɪnɪst] *Pej* N **1** *(patriot)* chauvin, -ine **2** *Fam* **(male) c.** macho m, machiste m

ADJ **1** *(patriotic)* chauvin **2** *Fam* **(male) c.** macho, machiste; **male c. pig** phallocrate m

> Note that the French word **chauvin** only refers to patriotism.

chauvinistic [ʃəʊvɪ'nɪstɪk] ADJ *Pej* **1** *(patriotic)* chauvin **2** *Fam (of male chauvinist)* macho, machiste

> Note that the French word **chauvin** only refers to patriotism.

cheap [tʃiːp] ADJ **1** *(inexpensive)* bon marché inv, pas cher; **it's c. to run** *(car)* elle est économique à l'entretien; **a cheaper model** un modèle moins cher *ou* meilleur marché; **it works out cheaper to take a whole bottle** cela revient moins cher de prendre la bouteille entière; **the cheapest** le meilleur marché, le moins cher; *Fam* **he's very c.** *(shopkeeper)* il n'est pas cher; **to do sth on the c.** *(at little cost)* faire qch à peu de frais; *(meanly)* faire qch chichement; **it's c. at the price** c'est une affaire; **c. and cheerful** sans prétentions

2 *Pej (of little worth)* de peu de valeur; *(emotion)* superficiel; **life is c. there** la vie a peu de valeur là-bas; **it's c. and nasty** c'est de la camelote; **a c. remark** une remarque facile; **that was a c. thing to do** ça n'était pas bien de faire ça; *Fam* **to feel c.** avoir honte; *Fam* **to make oneself c.** s'abaisser

3 *Pej (mean)* pingre

ADV **to go c.** se vendre bon marché; **he got off c.** il s'en est tiré à bon compte

►►*Br* **c. day return** = aller-retour *m* à tarif réduit valable une journée; **c. fare** tarif *m* réduit; *Fin* **c. money** argent *m* à bon marché; **c. rate** tarif tarif réduit

cheapen ['tʃiːp(ə)n] *VT* **1** *(degrade) (something)* diminuer la valeur de; **to c. oneself** s'abaisser **2** *(lower price of)* (ra)baisser *ou* faire baisser le prix de

cheapjack ['tʃiːpdʒæk] *Pej Fam* **N** camelot *m* ▸ *ADJ (goods)* de la camelote; *(solution)* facile; *(remark)* facile, mesquin

cheaply ['tʃiːplɪ] *ADV (to buy)* (à) bon marché, à bas prix; *(to do sth, to travel)* à peu de frais; **to eat out c.** manger dehors pour pas cher; **the room was c. furnished** *(at little cost)* la pièce avait été meublée à moindre frais; *(nastily)* le mobilier de la pièce était de mauvaise qualité

cheapness ['tʃiːpnɪs] **N 1** *(low price)* bas prix *m* **2** *Pej (low worth)* peu *m* de valeur, mauvaise qualité *f*; *(of remark)* bassesse *f*

cheapo ['tʃiːpəʊ] *Fam ADJ (inexpensive)* bon marché, pas cher
N it's a real c. c'est un truc pas cher

cheapskate ['tʃiːpskeɪt] *Pej Fam* **N** radin, -ine
▸ *ADJ (remark)* facile, mesquin

cheat [tʃiːt] **N 1** *(at games)* tricheur, -euse **2** *(dishonest person)* escroc *m* **3** *(deception)* triche *f*
▸ *VT (be dishonest to)* tromper, *Fam* rouler; *(defraud)* frauder; **I felt cheated** je me suis senti dupé; **to c. sb out of sth** escroquer qch à qn; **to c. sb into doing sth** faire faire qch à qn en le trompant; **I feel as if I've been cheated of my chance to represent my country** *(because of injury, illness)* j'ai l'impression d'avoir été privé de la possibilité de représenter mon pays
▸ *VI* **1** *(at games)* tricher **2** *(be dishonest)* tricher, frauder
▸ **cheat on** *VT INSEP* **1** *(be unfaithful to) (wife, husband)* tromper **2** *(be dishonest about) (expenses)* tricher sur

cheating ['tʃiːtɪŋ] **N 1** *(dishonesty)* tromperie *f* **2** *(in games)* tricherie *f*, *Fam* triche *f*; **that's c.!** c'est de la triche!

CHECK¹ [tʃek]

| **N** contrôle **1** ▪ coche **2** ▪ addition **3** |
| ▪ frein **7** ▪ échec **9** |
| **VT** vérifier **1** ▪ contrôler **2** |
| ▪ enregistrer **3** ▪ cocher **4** |
| **VI** vérifier **1** |

N 1 *(inspection)* contrôle *m*, vérification *f*; *(of accounts etc)* vérification; **to keep a c. on sth** contrôler qch; **to run a c. on sb/sth** enquêter sur qn/vérifier qch
2 *Am (tick)* coche *f*; **there's a c. mark against his name** son nom a été coché
3 *Am (bill in restaurant etc)* addition *f*, note *f*
4 *Am (for deposited item)* billet *m*, ticket *m*; *Rail etc* **luggage c.** bulletin *m* de bagages *ou* d'enregistrement; **cloakroom c.** bulletin de consigne
5 *Am (gambling chip)* jeton *m*
6 *Am Fin* = **cheque**
7 *(restraint)* frein *m*; **to keep** *or* **hold the enemy in c.** tenir l'ennemi en échec; **to keep one's feelings in c.** se contraindre, se contenir; *Pol* **a system of checks and balances** un système reposant sur l'équilibre des pouvoirs; **there is no effective c. on presidential power** il n'y a pas de limitation réelle du pouvoir du président
8 *(reversal)* revers *m*; **her plans had suffered a c.** ses projets avaient été contrariés
9 *Chess* échec *m*; **c.!** échec au roi!
▸ *VT* **1** *(verify, examine) (account, pressure etc)* vérifier; *(against the original) (document)* compulser sur l'original; *Typ (proofs)* (go

over) réviser; *(compare)* comparer; **I'll c. the arrival time/when they're supposed to arrive** je vérifierai l'heure d'arrivée/quand ils sont censés arriver; **to c. the names on a list** *(mark off)* pointer les noms sur une liste; *(by calling out)* faire l'appel des noms sur une liste; **to c. sth against sth** comparer qch à qch; **c. these names against the ones on the list** vérifie que ces noms sont les mêmes que ceux de la liste; *Sch* **c. your work before handing it in** relisez votre travail avant de le rendre; *Com* **to c. the books** pointer les écritures; **checked and double checked** vérifié et revérifié; **to c. that ...** vérifier *ou* s'assurer que ... + *ind*
2 *(officially inspect) (tickets)* contrôler
3 *Am (hand in) (baggage)* enregistrer; *(at restaurant etc) (hat, raincoat)* mettre au vestiaire; *(take in) (baggage)* enregistrer; *(hat, raincoat)* prendre; **checked baggage** bagages *mpl* enregistrés
4 *(mark with tick)* cocher; **c. the appropriate box** cocher la case appropriée
5 *(halt)* faire échec à, arrêter net; *(crisis, price rise)* enrayer; *(attack)* arrêter; **to c. inflation** juguler l'inflation
6 *(restrain) (tears, anger)* refouler, retenir; *(passion, emotion)* réprimer, refréner
7 *Chess (king)* mettre en échec; faire échec à
8 *Scot (reprimand)* réprimander
▸ *VI* **1** *(verify)* vérifier; **they usually have vacancies, but it's a good idea to c.** d'ordinaire, ils ont de la place, mais il vaut mieux s'en assurer *ou* vérifier; **we checked with the university** nous avons vérifié auprès de l'université; **you'd better c. with her** vous feriez mieux de lui demander
2 *(halt)* hésiter, s'arrêter (**at** devant)
3 *(match)* **that checks with what we were told** cela confirme ce qu'on nous a dit; *Am* **c.!** *(confirming data etc)* d'accord!
▸►*Comput* **c. bit** bit *m* de contrôle; *Comput* **c. box** case *f* de pointage, case d'option; *Comput* **c. byte** octet *m* de contrôle; **c. list** liste *f* de contrôle; *Aviat* **check-list** *f*, *pl* **check-lists**; *Mktg* **c. question** question *f* de contrôle, question filtre; *Mktg* **c. sample** échantillon *m* témoin
▸ **check in** *VI* **1** *(at hotel)* remplir la fiche d'entrée *ou* le registre; **have you checked in yet?** *(not said by receptionist)* est-ce que tu es passé à l'hôtel?
2 *(at airport)* se faire enregistrer
▸ *VT SEP* **1** *(of receptionist)* enregistrer l'arrivée de; **I checked them in myself** c'est moi-même qui les ai accueillis
2 *(make reservation for)* faire une réservation pour; **they checked the actress into a four-star hotel** ils ont fait une réservation pour l'actrice dans un hôtel quatre étoiles; **I've checked myself into a hotel for the night** je suis descendu dans un hôtel pour la nuit
3 *(at airport etc) (baggage)* enregistrer
▸ **check off** *VT SEP* **1** **to c. sth off (against sth)** vérifier qch (avec qch); *Com* **to c. off goods** recenser des marchandises
2 *Am (name etc)* cocher
▸ **check on** *VT INSEP* *(information etc)* vérifier, recouper; **to c. on sb** *(for security reasons etc)* enquêter sur qn, prendre des renseignements sur qn
▸ **check out** *VI* **1** *(leave hotel)* quitter l'hôtel; *Fam Euph (die)* caner
2 *Fam (of story, statement)* tenir debout; **it doesn't c. out** ça ne tient pas debout, ça ne marche pas
▸ *VT SEP* **1** *(investigate) (information etc)* vérifier, recouper; *(person) (for security reasons etc)* enquêter sur; *esp Am Fam* **there's a new club we could c. out** il y a une nouvelle boîte que nous pourrions essayer; *Fam* **c. it out!** regarde un peu ça!, *Fam* vise un peu ça!

2 *(of hotel receptionist)* **to c. sb out** encaisser la note de qn *(avant son départ)*
▸ **check over** *VT SEP (look over)* vérifier
▸ **check through** *VT SEP* **1** *(examine) (baggage etc)* contrôler, examiner
2 *(send by plane)* faire envoyer (par avion); **I'd like my luggage checked through to Los Angeles** je voudrais faire envoyer directement mes bagages à Los Angeles
▸ **check up** *VI (make sure)* vérifier
▸ **check up on** *VT INSEP* = **check on**

check² **N** *Tex* carreau *m*; **c. material/shirt** tissu *m*/chemise *f* à carreaux

checkbook ['tʃekbʊk] **N** *Am* = **chequebook**

check-control **N** *Aut* appareil *m* de signalisation des défauts

checked [tʃekt] *ADJ (material etc)* à carreaux, quadrillé

checker¹ ['tʃekər] **N** *(person)* contrôleur, -euse; *Comput* **grammar/spelling c.** correcteur grammatical/orthographique

checker² *VT Am* = **chequer**

checkerboard ['tʃekəbɔːd] **N** *Am* damier *m*

checkered ['tʃekəd] *ADJ Am* = **chequered**

checkers ['tʃekəz] *NPL Am* jeu *m* de dames
VOIR GRAMMAIRE A10

check-in **N** *Aviat* **1** *(of passengers)* enregistrement *m* **2** *(desk)* guichet *m* *ou* comptoir *m* d'enregistrement
▸►**c. desk** guichet *ou* comptoir d'enregistrement; **c. time** *(at airport, hotel)* heure *f* d'enregistrement

checking ['tʃekɪŋ] **N** *(verification, examination)* contrôle *m*, vérification *f*; *(more detailed)* pointage *m*
▸►*Am Banking* **c. account** compte *m* courant

checklist ['tʃeklɪst] **N** liste *f* de contrôle

checkmark ['tʃekmɑːk] **N** *Am* coche *f*

checkmate ['tʃekmeɪt] *Chess* **N** échec *m* et mat; *Fig* **it was c.** *(we won)* ce fut une victoire; *(we lost)* ce fut un échec
▸ *VT (king)* faire échec et mat à; *Fig* faire échec à; *(sb's plans)* contrecarrer, déjouer

checkout ['tʃekaʊt] **N 1** *(in supermarket)* caisse *f* **2** *(in hotel)* heure *f* de départ
▸►**c. desk** caisse; **c. display** devant *m* de caisse, nez *m* de caisse; **c. display item** article *m* de caisse; **c. girl** caissière *f*; **c. operator** caissier, -ière; **c. point** caisse; **c. time** heure de départ; **c. time is 12 noon** les clients doivent libérer la chambre avant midi

checkpoint ['tʃekpɔɪnt] **N** contrôle *m*

checkroom ['tʃekruːm] **N** *Am* vestiaire *m*
▸►**c. ticket** ticket *m* de vestiaire

checksum ['tʃeksʌm] **N** *Comput* somme *f* de contrôle

checkup ['tʃekʌp] **N 1** *Med* examen *m* médical (complet), bilan *m* de santé, check-up *m inv*; **to give sb a c.** faire le bilan de santé de qn; **to have a c.** faire faire un check-up; **it's just a c.** c'est juste une visite de routine **2** *(inspection)* vérification *f*, inspection *f*; *(of machinery)* révision *f*

cheddar ['tʃedər] **N** *(fromage m de)* cheddar *m*

cheek [tʃiːk] **N 1** *Anat* joue *f*; **to dance c. to c.** danser joue contre joue; *Fig* **c. by jowl with sb** coude à coude avec qn; *Fig* **to turn the other c.** tendre l'autre joue **2** *Fam (buttock)* fesse *f* **3** *Br Fam (impudence)* toupet *m*, culot *m*; **he's got a c.!** il est culotté *ou* gonflé!; **that's enough of your c.!** j'en ai assez de cette impertinence!; **the c. (of it)!**, **some c.!** quel culot *ou* toupet!
▸ *VT Br Fam* dire des impertinences à, faire l'insolent avec

cheekbone ['tʃiːkbəʊn] **N** pommette *f*, *Spec* os *m* malaire; **high/prominent cheekbones** pommettes hautes/saillantes

cheekily ['tʃiːkɪlɪ] ADV *Br Fam (to do sth)* d'une manière impertinente *ou* effrontée; *(to say)* d'un air impertinent *ou* effronté

cheekiness ['tʃiːkɪnɪs] N *Br Fam* effronterie f

cheeky ['tʃiːkɪ] ADJ *Br Fam* effronté, impertinent; **don't be c.!** pas d'impertinence!; **a c. little wine** un bon petit pinard

cheep [tʃiːp] N *(of bird)* piaulement m; *Fam* **you can't get a c. out of her** elle ne dit jamais mot
  VI *(of bird)* piauler

cheer [tʃɪər] N **1** *(shout)* hourra m; **cheers** acclamations fpl, bravos mpl; **to give three cheers** pousser trois hourras; **three cheers for Mary!** un ban pour Mary!, vive Mary! **2** *Fam* **cheers!** *(toast)* (à votre) santé!; *Br (at parting)* à bientôt!; *Br (thanks)* merci! **3** *Lit (good spirits)* bonne disposition f (d'esprit); **be of good c.!** prenez courage!; **we were of good c.** nous étions de bonne humeur
  VT **1** *(shout for)* acclamer **2** *(encourage, make happier)* remonter le moral à
  VI *(shout)* pousser des hourras *ou* des acclamations
  ▸ **cheer on** VT SEP *(support)* encourager
  ▸ **cheer up** VI *(become more cheerful)* s'égayer, devenir plus gai; **the weather's cheered up** le temps s'est arrangé; **c. up!** courage!
  VT SEP **1** *(make more cheerful)* réjouir, remonter le moral à **2** *(make brighter) (room etc)* égayer

cheerful ['tʃɪəfʊl] ADJ *(person)* gai, de bonne humeur; *(face)* souriant, riant; *(room)* gai, d'aspect agréable; *(conversation, music etc)* joyeux; *(news etc)* encourageant; **that's a c. thought!** ça c'est encourageant!; *Iron* comme vous êtes optimiste!; **you're (very) c. this morning** tu es de bonne humeur ce matin

cheerfully ['tʃɪəfʊlɪ] ADV **1** *(happily)* gaiement, avec entrain, allègrement **2** *(willingly)* de bon cœur, volontiers **3** *(without compunction)* sans remords; **she would c. leave the work for the others** elle laisserait sans remords le travail aux autres; **I could quite c. strangle him** je l'étranglerais volontiers

cheerfulness ['tʃɪəfʊlnɪs] N *(of person)* gaieté f, bonne humeur f; *(of room)* aspect m agréable

cheerily ['tʃɪərɪlɪ] ADV gaiement, avec gaieté

cheering ['tʃɪərɪŋ] N acclamations fpl, bravos mpl
  ADJ *(sight, display)* réjouissant; *(piece of news, conversation)* qui remonte le moral

cheerio [tʃɪərɪ'əʊ] INT *Br Fam (at parting)* salut!, ciao!; *(in drinking a toast)* à la vôtre/tienne!; **it's c. 2003** bye-bye 2003

cheerleader ['tʃɪəliːdər] N *Am* = majorette f qui stimule l'enthousiasme des supporters des équipes sportives, surtout aux États-Unis

cheerless ['tʃɪəlɪs] ADJ morne, triste, sombre

cheery ['tʃɪərɪ] ADJ *(person, smile, wave, colour)* joyeux, gai

cheese [tʃiːz] N **1** fromage m; **blue c.** (fromage) bleu m; **cream c.** fromage frais; **cottage c.** fromage blanc *(salé et grenu)*; **cauliflower/macaroni c.** chou-fleur m/macaronis mpl au gratin; **toasted c.** toast m au fromage; **c. sandwich/omelette** sandwich m/omelette f au fromage; **the c. industry** l'industrie f fromagère; *Phot Fam* **(say) c.!** souriez! **2** *(individual piece of cheese) (pl cheeses)* **a c.** un fromage (entier), une meule (de fromage)
  ▸▸ **c. biscuit** *(for cheese)* biscuit m salé;

(cheese-flavoured) biscuit au fromage; **c. grater** râpe f à fromage; **c. maker, c. manufacturer** fromager, -ère; **c. mite** mite f du fromage; **c. straw** allumette f au fromage
  ▸ **cheese off** VT SEP *(usu passive) Br Fam* **to be cheesed (off)** en avoir marre (**with** de)

cheeseboard ['tʃiːzbɔːd] N **1** *(for cutting cheese)* plateau m à fromage **2** *(as part of meal)* plateau m de fromages; **a selection from our** *or* **the c.** *(in restaurant etc)* une sélection de fromages

cheeseburger ['tʃiːzbɜːgər] N *Culin* cheeseburger m

cheesecake ['tʃiːzkeɪk] N **1** *Culin* cheesecake m **2** *(no pl) Fam Hum (attractive women)* belles nanas fpl; *(in photo)* pin-up f inv; *Br* **she's a real c.** elle est vraiment bien foutue

cheesecloth ['tʃiːzklɒθ] N *(for cheese)* gaze f, étamine f; *Tex* crépon m

cheeseparing ['tʃiːzpeərɪŋ] ADJ parcimonieux
  N économies fpl de bouts de chandelle

cheesy ['tʃiːzɪ] ADJ **1** *(in taste)* qui a un goût de fromage; *(in smell)* qui sent le fromage **2** *Am Fam (poor quality)* moche **3** *Fam* **a c. grin** un large sourire

cheetah ['tʃiːtə] N guépard m

chef [ʃef] N chef m (de cuisine)

chemical ['kemɪk(ə)l] ADJ chimique
  N produit m chimique
  ▸▸ **c. company** compagnie f de produits chimiques; **c. dependency** toxicodépendance f, **c. engineer** ingénieur m chimiste; **c. engineering** génie m chimique; **c. reaction** réaction f chimique; **c. toilet** W-C mpl chimiques; **c. warfare** guerre f chimique; **c. weapons** armes fpl chimiques

chemically ['kemɪk(ə)lɪ] ADV chimiquement

chemist ['kemɪst] N **1** *esp Br Com* pharmacien, -ienne; **c.'s (shop)** pharmacie f **2** *(scientist)* chimiste mf

chemistry ['kemɪstrɪ] N chimie f, **organic/inorganic c.** chimie organique/minérale; **industrial c.** chimie industrielle; *Fig* **there was a certain c. between the members of the band** il y avait une certaine affinité entre les musiciens; *Fig* **the c.'s right/wrong** ça passe bien/mal (entre nous/eux/etc); *Fig* **the c.'s missing** le courant ne passe pas, on n'a pas d'atomes crochus
  ▸▸ **c. set** panoplie f de chimiste

chemotherapy [kiːmə'θerəpɪ], *Fam* **chemo** ['kiːməʊ] N *Med* chimiothérapie f, **to have c.** suivre un traitement de chimiothérapie

cheque, *Am* **check** [tʃek] N *Fin* chèque m; **to pay by c.** payer par chèque; **to cash a c.** toucher un chèque; **to stop a c.** faire opposition à un chèque; **to write sb a c.** faire un chèque à qn; **who should I make the c. out to?** à quel ordre dois-je faire *ou* écrire le chèque?; **will you take a c.?** est-ce que vous acceptez les chèques?; **c. for £20** chèque de vingt livres; **c. made out to bearer** chèque au porteur; **c. without cover** chèque sans provision; *Fam* **dud c.** chèque en bois
  ▸▸ *Br* **c. account** compte m chèques; *Br* **c. guarantee card** carte f bancaire; **c. number** numéro m de chèque; **c. stub** talon m de chèque, souche f

chequebook, *Am* **checkbook** ['tʃekbʊk] N carnet m de chèques, chéquier m
  ▸▸ **c. account** compte m (de) chèques; **c. journalism** = dans les milieux de la presse, pratique qui consiste à payer des sommes importantes pour le témoignage d'une personne impliquée dans une affaire

chequer, *Am* **checker** ['tʃekər] VT *(variegate with colour)* diaprer, bigarrer

chequered, *Am* **checkered** ['tʃekəd] ADJ **1**

(pattern) quadrillé, à carreaux; *(two colours only)* en damier **2** *(variegated)* diapré, bigarré; *Fig (life)* plein de vicissitudes; **she's had a somewhat c. career** *(varied)* elle a fait toutes sortes de métiers; *(ups and downs)* elle a eu une carrière en dents de scie; **this text has had a fairly c. history** ce texte a eu une histoire assez compliquée

cherish ['tʃerɪʃ] VT **1** *(hope)* bercer, caresser; *(past, occasion, memory, possessions, gift)* chérir; *(idea, opinion)* nourrir, entretenir; **to c. illusions** se nourrir d'illusions; **his most cherished hopes** ses espérances les plus chères **2** *(love) (person)* chérir

cheroot [ʃə'ruːt] N petit cigare m

cherry ['tʃerɪ] N **1** *(fruit)* cerise f, *(tree)* cerisier m; *Fam* **you don't get two bites at the c.** il n'y a pas de deuxième chance; *Prov* **life is just a bowl of cherries** il faut voir la vie en rose **2** **wild c.** *(fruit)* merise f, *(tree)* merisier m **3** *(colour)* cerise f, **c.-red** rouge m cerise **4** *Sl (virginity)* **to lose one's c.** perdre sa fleur **5** *Am Fam (newcomer)* bleu m
  ADJ **1** cerise inv; **c.-red** rouge cerise inv **2** *Am Fam (in perfect condition)* en parfait état, impec
  ▸▸ **c. brandy** cherry m; **c. orchard** cerisaie f, **c. stone** noyau m de cerise; **c. tart** tarte f aux cerises; **c. tomato** tomate f cerise; **c. tree** cerisier

cherry-pick VT **to c. the best** sélectionner ce qu'il y a de meilleur

cherub, *pl* **cherubs,** *Bible* **cherubim** ['tʃerəb, -z, -əbɪm] N *Bible* chérubin m; *Art* angelot m, ange m joufflu; *Fig* **a little c.** *(child)* un petit ange

cherubic [tʃɪ'ruːbɪk] ADJ *Bible, Art* de chérubin; *Fig (smile, face etc)* d'ange

chervil ['tʃɜːvɪl] N *Bot, Culin* cerfeuil m

Ches abbr **Cheshire**

Cheshire ['tʃeʃər] N **to grin like a C. cat** sourire jusqu'aux oreilles
  ▸▸ *Culin* **C. cheese** fromage m de Chester, chester m

chess [tʃes] N échecs mpl; **a c. game, a game of c.** une partie d'échecs; **to play c.** jouer aux échecs
  ▸▸ **c. player** joueur, -euse d'échecs

chessboard ['tʃesbɔːd] N échiquier m

chessman, *pl* **chessmen** ['tʃesmən], **chesspiece** ['tʃespiːs] N pièce f (du jeu d'échecs)

chest [tʃest] N **1** *Anat* poitrine f, *(of horse)* poitrail m; *Fig* **to get it off one's c.** dire ce qu'on a sur le cœur **2** *(box)* coffre m, caisse f, **tea c.** caisse à thé **medicine c.** (coffret m de) pharmacie f
  ▸▸ **c. cold** rhume m de poitrine; **c. of drawers** commode f, **c. expander** extenseur m *(pour développer les pectoraux)*; **c. infection** infection f des voies respiratoires; **c. pains** douleurs fpl dans la poitrine; **c. size** tour m de poitrine; **what c. size are you?** quel est votre tour de poitrine?

chesterfield ['tʃestəfiːld] N *(sofa)* canapé m capitonné

chestnut ['tʃesnʌt] N **1** **(sweet** *or* **Spanish) c.** *(fruit)* châtaigne f, *(when cooked)* marron m; *(tree)* châtaignier m; **(horse) c.** *(fruit)* marron (d'Inde); *(tree)* marronnier m (d'Inde); *Fam* **an old c.** *(joke)* une plaisanterie usée; *Fig* **to pull sb's chestnuts out of the fire** tirer les marrons du feu à qn **2** *(wood)* châtaignier m **3** *(colour)* châtain m **4** *(horse)* alezan m
  ADJ **1** *(hair)* châtain **2** *(colour)* châtain **3** *(horse)* alezan
  ▸▸ **c. puree** purée f de marrons; **c. tree** châtaignier

chesty ['tʃestɪ] ADJ *Fam* **to be c.** être bronchitique; **a c. cough** une toux de poitrine

cheval glass [ʃə'væl] N psyché f

chevron ['ʃevrən] N *Her, Mil* chevron *m*

Chevvy ['ʃevɪ] N *Fam* Chevrolet® *f*

chew [tʃuː] N **1** *(action)* **to have a c. at sth** mâchonner qch **2** *(tobacco)* chique *f*, *(sweet)* bonbon *m*
▶ VT *(food)* mâcher, mastiquer; *(tobacco)* chiquer; *(cigar, end of pen etc)* mâchonner; **to c. one's nails** se ronger les ongles; **to c. the cud** *(of cow)* ruminer; *Fam* **to c. the rag** *or* **the fat** *(chat)* discuter le coup; *(complain)* ronchonner, râler
▶ VI *(food)* mâcher, mastiquer; **the rats had chewed through the rope** les rats avaient coupé la corde en la rongeant
▶ **chew on** VT INSEP **1** *(gnaw)* mâchouiller, ronger; **he chewed on his pipe** il mâchouillait sa pipe **2** *Fam (consider)* réfléchir sur; **how much longer do you need to c. on it?** combien te faut-il encore de temps pour réfléchir à la question?
▶ **chew out** VT SEP *Am Fam (reprimand)* engueuler
▶ **chew over** VT SEP *Fam (think over)* réfléchir à; *(discuss)* discuter de
▶ **chew up** VT SEP *(damage by chewing)* abîmer à force de mâchonner; *Fig (damage) (bank card, tape etc)* endommager; **the dog has chewed up the newspaper** le chien a mangé le journal; **his arm had been badly chewed up by the machinery** son bras avait été déchiqueté par la machine

chewing ['tʃuːɪŋ] N mastication *f*, mâchement *m*, mâchonnement *m*
▶▶**c. gum** chewing-gum *m*; **c. tobacco** tabac *m* à chiquer

chewy ['tʃuːɪ] ADJ **1** *Pej (meat etc)* difficile à mâcher **2** *(sweet)* mou, *f* molle, tendre

chiaroscuro [kɪɑːrə'skʊərəʊ] N *Art* clair-obscur *m*

chic [ʃiːk, ʃɪk] ADJ élégant, chic
▶ N chic *m*

chicane [ʃɪ'keɪn] N *Aut, Sport, Cards* chicane *f*

chicanery [ʃɪ'keɪnərɪ] N chicanerie *f*, chicane *f*

chicano [tʃɪ'kænəʊ] N *Am* citoyen, -enne d'origine mexicaine

chichi ['ʃiːʃiː] *Fam* ADJ prétentieux
▶ N prétention *f*

chick [tʃɪk] N **1** *(young bird)* oisillon *m*; *(of fowl)* poussin *m*; *Fig (child)* poussin **2** *Fam (young woman)* fille *f*, nana *f*
▶▶**c. flick** = film *m* qui plaît particulièrement aux femmes; **c. lit** = genre *m* romanesque destiné à un public de jeunes femmes et qui est censé réfléter leurs préoccupations

chickadee [tʃɪkə'diː] N *Am (bird)* mésange *f* (à tête noire)

chicken ['tʃɪkɪn] N **1** *(bird)* poulet *m*; *Prov* **don't count your chickens before they are hatched** il ne faut pas vendre la peau de l'ours avant de l'avoir tué; **prairie c.** *Am* tétras *m* cupidon, cupidon *m* des prairies, *Can* poule *f* des prairies **2** *Fam (coward)* lâche *mf*, froussard, -arde **3** *Am Fam (young person)* mineur, -eure, gamin, -ine; **she's no (spring) c.** elle n'est plus de la première jeunesse
▶ ADJ *Fam (cowardly)* lâche, froussard
▶▶**c. breast** blanc *m* (de poulet); **c. farm** élevage *m* de poulets, élevage avicole; **c. farmer** éleveur, -euse de volailles, aviculteur, -trice; *Am Sl* **c. hawk** pédophile *m*; **c. liver** foie *m* de volaille; **c. run** enclos *m* (d'un poulailler); **c. soup** *(clear)* potage *m* au poulet; *(creamy)* velouté *m* ou crème *f* de volaille; **c. wire** grillage *m*
▶ **chicken out** VI *Fam* se dégonfler; **she chickened out of going** elle s'est dégonflée; **she chickened out of her dental appointment** elle avait rendez-vous chez le dentiste mais elle s'est dégonflée

chickenfeed ['tʃɪkɪnfiːd] N nourriture *f* pour volaille; *Fig* **it's c.** c'est de la gnognote; **£2,000 is c.** 2 000 livres, c'est pas grand-chose

chickenhearted [tʃɪkɪn'hɑːtɪd], **chickenlivered** [tʃɪkɪn'lɪvəd] ADJ *Old-fashioned Fam* poltron, froussard

chickenpox ['tʃɪkɪnpɒks] N *Med* varicelle *f*; **to have c.** avoir la varicelle

chickenshit ['tʃɪkɪnʃɪt] ADJ *Am Vulg* dégonflé

chickpea ['tʃɪkpiː] N pois *m* chiche

chickweed ['tʃɪkwiːd] N *(plant)* mouron *m* des oiseaux, morgeline *f*

chicory ['tʃɪkərɪ] N **1** *(plant)* endive *f* **2** *(ground)* **c.** chicorée *f* (en poudre)

chide [tʃaɪd] VT *Arch, Lit* (*pt* chided ['tʃaɪdɪd] *or* chid [tʃɪd], *pp* chided *or* chidden ['tʃɪd(e)n]) réprimander, gronder

chief [tʃiːf] N (*pl* chiefs) *(of tribe, gang)* chef *m*; *Am* **fire/police c.** chef des pompiers/de la police; *Fam* **the c.** *(boss)* le patron; *Fig Fam* **he's the big white c.** c'est lui le grand patron; **in c.** en chef; *Mil, Naut* **commander-in-c.** commandant *m* en chef; **editor in c.** rédacteur *m* en chef; *Prov* **too many chiefs and not enough Indians** trop de gens qui donnent des ordres et pas assez pour les exécuter
▶ ADJ *(most important)* principal, -aux; *(in rank)* (en) chef; **my c. assistant** mon principal collaborateur; **the c. reason for doing sth** la raison majeure *ou* principale pour faire qch
▶▶*Am Pol* **the C. Executive** le président des États-Unis, le chef de l'exécutif; *Com, Ind* **c. executive officer** président-directeur *m* général, *pl* présidents-directeurs généraux; *Am* **C. Financial Officer** chef comptable, chef de la comptabilité; *Br* **C. Inspector** *(of police)* inspecteur *m* principal; **c. justice** président, -ente de la Haute cour de justice; *Am* juge *m* de la Cour suprême; **c. photographer** *(on newspaper)* photographe *mf* en chef; **c. reporter** grand reporter *m*; *Br Pol* **C. Secretary to the Treasury** ≃ ministre *m* du Budget; **c. of staff** *Mil* chef d'état-major; *Am (at White House)* secrétaire *m* général de la Maison Blanche

chiefly ['tʃiːflɪ] ADV principalement, surtout

chieftain ['tʃiːftən] N *(of clan)* chef *m*

chiffon ['ʃɪfɒn] N mousseline *f* de soie

chignon ['ʃiːnjɒn] N chignon *m*

chihuahua [tʃɪ'wɑːwɑː] N chihuahua *m*

chilblain ['tʃɪlbleɪn] N *Med* engelure *f*; **to have chilblains** avoir des engelures

child, *pl* **children** [tʃaɪld, 'tʃɪldrən] N enfant *mf*; **to treat sb like a c.** traiter qn en enfant; **I'm not a c.!** je ne suis pas un enfant!; *Old-fashioned* **come here, c.!** viens ici, (mon/ma) petit(e)!; **the c. in all of us** l'enfant qui est en chacun de nous; **ever since I was a c.** depuis mon enfance; *Old-fashioned* **I have known him from a c.** *(when he was a child)* je l'ai connu enfant; *(when I was a child)* je le connais depuis mon enfance; **it's c.'s play** *(easy)* c'est un jeu d'enfant; **our children's children** les enfants de nos enfants; **children's shoes/clothes** chaussures/vêtements pour enfants; **children's literature** littérature *f* enfantine *ou* pour enfants; **children's television** émissions *fpl* pour enfants; *Bible* **the children of Israel** les enfants d'Israël; **children's area** *(in restaurant etc)* coin *m* enfants
▶▶**c. abuse** mauvais traitements *mpl* à enfant; *(sexual)* abus *m* sexuel sur enfant; **c. abuser** = personne *f* coupable de mauvais traitements à enfant; *(sexual)* = personne

coupable d'abus sexuel sur enfant; **c. actor** acteur *m* enfant, actrice *f* enfant; *Br Admin* **c. benefit** allocation *f* familiale, allocations *fpl* familiales *(pour un enfant)*; *Aut* **c. booster cushion** réhausseur *m*; *Aut* **c. booster seat** siège *m* réhausseur; **c. bride** femme *f* enfant; **I was his c. bride** j'étais une enfant quand il m'a épousée; **c. labour** travail *m* des enfants; *Aut* **c. lock** sécurité-enfants *f*, *pl* sécurités-enfants; **I put the c. lock on** j'ai mis la sécurité; **c. poverty** pauvreté *f* des enfants, pauvreté infantile; *Aut* **c. restraint** dispositif *m* de retenue pour enfant, ceinture *f* pour enfant; **c. seat** siège-auto *m*, *pl* sièges-auto *(pour enfant)*; **c. welfare** protection *f* de l'enfance

child-bearing N maternité *f*; **after 20 years of c.** après 20 ans de maternités successives; **of c. age** en âge d'avoir des enfants; **past c. (age)** *(woman)* trop âgée pour avoir des enfants; **to have c. hips** avoir les hanches larges

childbirth ['tʃaɪldbɜːθ] N accouchement *m*; **to die in c.** mourir en couches

childcare ['tʃaɪldkeər] N **1** *(day care)* garde *f* d'enfants; **we haven't decided on c. arrangements yet** nous n'avons pas encore pris de décision quant à la garde des enfants **2** *Br Admin* protection *f* de l'enfance

child-friendly ADJ *(area, city)* aménagé pour les enfants; *(furniture, house)* pas dangereux pour les enfants

childhood ['tʃaɪldhʊd] N enfance *f*; **to be in one's second c.** être retombé en enfance
▶▶**c. memory** souvenir *m* d'enfance; **c. sweetheart** amour *m* d'enfance

childish ['tʃaɪldɪʃ] ADJ **1** *Pej (person, behaviour, remarks)* puéril; **don't be so c.** ne faites pas l'enfant, ne soyez pas aussi puéril **2** *(of children, childlike) (laughter, curiosity, innocence)* enfantin; *(ailment)* infantile; *(question)* naïf, *f* naïve; **c. games** jeux enfantins *ou* d'enfant

childishness ['tʃaɪldɪʃnɪs] N *Pej* enfantillage *m*, puérilité *f*

childless ['tʃaɪldlɪs] ADJ sans enfant(s); *(marriage)* stérile; **she died c.** elle est morte sans enfants

childlike ['tʃaɪldlaɪk] ADJ enfantin; *(question)* naïf, *f* naïve; *(smile)* d'enfant; **he was c. in his curiosity** il avait une curiosité enfantine *ou* d'enfant

child-minder N gardienne *f* d'enfants

child-minding ['tʃaɪldmaɪndɪŋ] N garde *f* d'enfants

childproof ['tʃaɪldpruːf] ADJ *(lock etc)* ne pouvant être ouvert par les enfants, de sécurité; *(not breakable)* ne pouvant être cassé par les enfants

children *see* **child**

Chile ['tʃɪlɪ] N Chili *m*

Chilean ['tʃɪlɪən] ADJ chilien
▶ N Chilien, -ienne

chili ['tʃɪlɪ] N *esp Am* = **chilli**

chill [tʃɪl] N **1** *Med* coup *m* de froid; **to catch a c.** prendre froid; **c. of fear** frisson *m* de peur; **his laugh sent a c. down my spine** son rire m'a fait froid dans le dos **2** *(of water, marble etc)* froideur *f*, fraîcheur *f*; **there's a c. in the air** le fond de l'air est frais; **to take the c. off** *(water)* (faire) tiédir; *(wine)* chambrer; *Fig* **to cast a c. over the company** jeter un froid sur l'assemblée
▶ ADJ froid, glacé; *(wind)* froid
▶ VT **1** *(of wind) (person, air)* refroidir, glacer; **chilled to the bone** gelé jusqu'aux os; *Fig* **chilled with fear** transi de peur **2** *(put in fridge) (wine, melon, dessert etc)* mettre au frais
▶ VI **1** *(food, drink)* refroidir **2** = **chill out**
▶▶**c. cabinet** armoire *f* réfrigérante

► **chill out** VI *Fam* se détendre; **I wish he'd c. out a bit** ça serait bien qu'il soit un peu plus cool; **he likes chilling out at home** il aime bien être chez lui, peinard; **c. out!** relax!, calmos!

chilled [tʃɪld] ADJ **1** *Culin* refroidi; **best served c.** *(on label)* servir glacé *ou* très frais; **c. meat** viande *f* réfrigérée *ou* frigorifiée; **c. products** produits *mpl* frigorifiés **2** *Fam (relaxed)* relax

chilli ['tʃɪlɪ] N *Culin (vegetable)* piment *m* (rouge); *(dish)* chili *m*
► ► **c. con carne** chili con carne; **c. pepper** piment (rouge); **c. powder** chili; **c. sauce** sauce *f* aux tomates et piments

chilliness ['tʃɪlɪnɪs] N *(of air)* froid *m*, froideur *f*, *Fig (of person, welcome)* froideur

chilling ['tʃɪlɪŋ] ADJ *(wind, welcome)* glacial, -als *ou* aux; *(story, events)* qui donne la chair de poule

chill-out room N *Fam (in nightclub)* espace *m* chill-out

chilly ['tʃɪlɪ] ADJ **1** *(cold) (weather etc)* frais, *f* fraîche; **to feel c.** *(of person)* avoir froid; **it's** *or* **it feels c. this morning** il fait frais *ou Fam* frisquet ce matin **2** *(person) (feels the cold a lot)* frileux **3** *Fig (person, manner, welcome)* froid; *(politeness)* glacial, -als *ou* aux

chime [tʃaɪm] N **c. (of bells)** carillon *m*; **the chimes of St. Mary's** le carillon de St. Mary; **to ring the chimes** carillonner; **(door) chimes** carillon de porte
VI *(of clock, bells)* carillonner
VT **1** *(bells)* sonner en carillon **2** *(of clock) (the hour)* sonner
► **chime in** VI *Fam* **1** *(intervene)* placer son mot, intervenir; **they all chimed in at once** ils sont tous intervenus en même temps **2** *(agree)* **his story chimes in with what we already know** sa version correspond à ce que nous savons déjà

chimera [kaɪ'mɪərə, kɪ-] N *Myth, Lit Fig* chimère *f*, *Lit Fig* **to pursue a c.** poursuivre des chimères

chiming ['tʃaɪmɪŋ] ADJ carillonnant; *(clock)* à carillon
N carillonnement *m*, carillon *m*

chimney ['tʃɪmnɪ] N **1** *(of house, factory)* cheminée *f*, *Fam* **to smoke like a c.** *(of person)* fumer comme un sapeur **2** *(in mountaineering)* cheminée *f* **3** *Geol* cheminée *f*
► ► **c. breast** manteau *m* de (la) cheminée; **c. corner** coin *m* du feu; **c. stack** *(of house)* tuyau *m* de cheminée; *(of factory)* cheminée (d'usine); **c. sweep** ramoneur *m*

Note that the French word **cheminée** also means **fireplace** and **mantelpiece**.

chimneypiece ['tʃɪmnɪpiːs] N *esp Br* (manteau *m* de) cheminée *f*

chimneypot ['tʃɪmnɪpɒt] N mitre *f*

chimpanzee [tʃɪmpæn'ziː, *Am* tʃɪm'pænziː], *Fam* **chimp** [tʃɪmp] N chimpanzé *m*

chin [tʃɪn] N menton *m*, *Fig* **to keep one's c. up** tenir bon, tenir le coup; *Fig* **to take sth on the c.** encaisser qch sans broncher; **she took the news on the c.** elle a écouté la nouvelle sans broncher
► ► **c. strap** *(on helmet)* jugulaire *f*

China ['tʃaɪnə] N Chine *f*
► ► **the C. Sea** la mer de Chine; **C. tea** thé *m* de Chine

china ['tʃaɪnə] N **1** *(no pl) (material)* porcelaine *f*, *(plates etc)* vaisselle *f* (de porcelaine); **made of c.** en porcelaine; **c. plate** assiette *f* en porcelaine; *Br Sl (friend)* pote *m*; **my old c.!** mon vieux!
► ► **c. clay** kaolin *m*; **c. doll** poupée *f* en porcelaine

Chinagraph® ['tʃaɪnəɡrɑːf] N *(pencil)* crayon *m* gras

Chinaman, *pl* **Chinamen** ['tʃaɪnəmən] N *Old-fashioned* Chinois *m*

Chinatown ['tʃaɪnətaʊn] N quartier *m* chinois; **in C.** dans le quartier chinois

chinaware ['tʃaɪnəweər] N porcelaine *f*

chinchilla [tʃɪn'tʃɪlə] N *(rodent, fur)* chinchilla *m*; **c. coat/jacket** manteau *m*/veste *f* en chinchilla

chin-chin INT *Fam (as a toast)* santé!, à la vôtre/la tienne!

chine [tʃaɪn] N *Anat, Culin* échine *f*

Chinese [tʃaɪ'niːz] ADJ chinois; **the C. Ambassador** l'ambassadeur *m* de Chine
N **1** Chinois, -oise **2** *Ling* chinois *m* **3** *Fam (food)* **I feel like a C. tonight** j'ai envie de manger chinois ce soir
► ► *Bot, Culin* **C. cabbage** chou *m* chinois; **C. checkers** dames *fpl* chinoises; *Bot, Culin* **C. gooseeberry** kiwi *m* *(fruit)*; **C. lantern** lanterne *f* vénitienne; *Bot, Culin* **C. leaves** chou chinois; **C. white** blanc *m* de Chine

Chink [tʃɪŋk] N *Offensive Sl (Chinese)* Chinetoque *mf*

chink¹ [tʃɪŋk] N *(gap) (in wall etc)* fente *f*, crevasse *f*, lézarde *f*, *(in door)* entrebâillement *m*; *Fig* **to have a c. in one's armour** avoir une faiblesse; **the c. in sb's armour** le talon d'Achille de qn

chink² N *(sound)* tintement *m*
VT *(money)* faire sonner *ou* tinter; *(glasses etc)* faire tinter
VI sonner (sec)

Chinky ['tʃɪŋkɪ] N *Offensive Fam* **1** *(restaurant)* (restaurant *m*) chinois *m*; *(meal)* repas *m* chinois **2** *(person)* Chinetoque *mf*

chinless ['tʃɪnlɪs] ADJ au menton fuyant
► ► *Br Fam Hum* **c. wonder** = individu *m* de bonne famille dépourvu de volonté et d'intelligence

chino ['tʃiːnəʊ] N *Tex* chino *m*; **chinos** *(trousers)* chinos *mpl*

chintz [tʃɪnts] N *Tex* chintz *m*, indienne *f*, **c. curtains** rideaux *mpl* de chintz

chinwag ['tʃɪnwæɡ] N *Br Fam* causette *f*, **to have a c.** tailler une bavette (**with** avec)

chip [tʃɪp] N **1** *(small piece) (of wood)* éclat *m*, copeau *m*; *(of marble)* écaille *f*, éclat; *(of chocolate)* pépite *f*; **diamond chips** semence *f* de diamants; *Fig* **he's a c. off the old block** c'est son père tout craché; *Fig* **to have a c. on one's shoulder** être aigri, en vouloir à tout le monde; **get rid of that c. on your shoulder** cessez d'en vouloir à tout le monde
2 *(piece missing) (in plate)* ébrechure *f*, *(in knife blade)* brèche *f*, **this cup has a c.** cette tasse est ébréchée
3 *Br Culin (French fry)* (pomme de terre *f*) frite *f*
4 *Am Culin (crisp)* chips *f inv*
5 *Cards etc* jeton *m*; *Fig* **when the chips are down** aux moments critiques; *Fig Fam* **he's had his chips** il est cuit *ou* fichu
6 *Comput* **(silicon) c.** puce *f*
7 *Sport (shot)* pichenette *f*
VT **(-pp-) 1** *(cut at)* tailler
2 *(damage) (knife, plate)* ébrécher; *(furniture)* écorner; *(enamel)* écailler; *(tooth)* casser
3 *Sport (ball)* prendre en dessous, donner une pichenette à; **he chipped the ball over the net** d'une pichenette, il a envoyé la balle au-dessus du filet
VI *(of stone, china)* s'ébrécher
► ► *Br* **c. basket** panier *m* à frites; *Br* **c. cutter** coupe-frites *m inv*; *Comput* **c. manufacturer** fabricant *m* de pastilles de silicium; *Br* **c. pan** friteuse *f*; *Br* **c. shop** = boutique foù l'on vend des frites ainsi que du poisson frit, des saucisses etc; *Comput* **c. technology** technologie *f* des puces

Note that the French word **chips** is a false friend for British English speakers. It means **crisps**.

► **chip away** VT SEP *(plaster etc)* décaper, enlever petit à petit
VI *(of plaster)* s'écailler

► **chip away at** VT INSEP **to c. away at the old paintwork** enlever la vieille peinture petit à petit; **to c. away at sb's authority** grignoter l'autorité de qn; **just keep chipping away at him until he changes his mind** continuez à le travailler au corps jusqu'à ce qu'il change d'avis

► **chip in** VI **1** *Fam (contribute) (in collection)* participer; *(in discussion)* intervenir; *Pej (interrupt)* s'emmêler, mettre son grain de sel; **they chipped in to buy her a present** ils ont tous participé à l'achat de son cadeau; **if everyone chips in with an idea** si chacun proposait une idée **2** *Cards* miser
VT SEP *Fam (contribute)* donner; **everyone chipped in £5** tout le monde a donné 5 livres

► **chip off** VI *(fall off, break off) (of paint etc)* s'écailler
VT SEP *(break off)* enlever; **somebody had chipped the nose off the statue** quelqu'un avait cassé le nez de la statue; **to c. a piece off a plate** ébrécher une assiette

chipboard ['tʃɪpbɔːd] N *Carp* aggloméré *m*; **a piece of c.** un panneau d'aggloméré

chipmunk ['tʃɪpmʌŋk] N tamia *m* rayé, écureuil *m* rayé, *Can* suisse *m* rayé *ou* barré

chipolata [tʃɪpə'lɑːtə] N *esp Br Culin* chipolata *f*
► ► **c. sausage** chipolata

chipped [tʃɪpt] ADJ *(knife, plate)* ébréché; *(furniture)* écorné; *(enamel)* écaillé; *(tooth)* cassé
► ► *Am Culin* **c. beef** ≃ éminçé *m* de bœuf; *Br Culin* **c. potatoes** (pommes de terre *fpl*) frites *fpl*

chipper ['tʃɪpər] ADJ *Fam (person)* gai, vif

chippings ['tʃɪpɪŋz] NPL *(of stone, marble)* éclats *mpl*; **(wood) c.** copeaux *mpl* (de bois); **loose c.** *(road sign)* gravillons *mpl*, *Can* gravelle *f*

chippy ['tʃɪpɪ] N *Br Fam* **1** *(fish and chip shop)* = boutique foù l'on vend des frites ainsi que du poisson frit, des saucisses, etc **2** *Old-fashioned (carpenter)* charpentier *m*

Chips [tʃɪps] N *Banking (abbr* **clearing house interbank payment system)** *Sit m*

chipset ['tʃɪpset] N *Comput* ensemble *m* de puces

chiromancer ['kaɪərəʊmænsər] N chiromancien, -ienne

chiromancy ['kaɪərəʊmænsɪ] N chiromancie *f*

chiropodist [kɪ'rɒpədɪst] N *Med* pédicure *mf*

chiropody [kɪ'rɒpədɪ] N *Med* pédicurie *f*

chiropractic [kaɪrə'præktɪk] N *Med* chiropraxie *f*

chiropractor ['kaɪrəpræktər] N *Med* chiropracteur *m*, chiropracticien, -ienne

chirp [tʃɜːp] N *(of birds)* pépiement *m*, gazouillement *m*, gazouillis *m*; *(of chick)* piaulement *m*; *(of grasshopper)* chant *m*
VT & VI **1** *(of bird)* pépier, gazouiller; *(of chick)* piauler; *(of grasshopper)* chanter **2** *(of person)* babiller

chirpily ['tʃɜːpɪlɪ] ADV *Fam* gaiement

chirpiness ['tʃɜːpɪnɪs] N *Fam* humeur *f* joyeuse

chirpy ['tʃɜːpɪ] ADJ *Fam* d'humeur joyeuse

chirrup ['tʃɪrəp] N, VT & VI = **chirp**

chisel ['tʃɪz(ə)l] N ciseau *m*, burin *m*; **wood**

c. ciseau à bois; **hollow c.** gouge *f*; **cold c.** ciseau à froid, burin

vt (**-ll-**, *Am* **-l-**) **1** *(wood, stone)* ciseler; *(metal)* buriner, ciseler; **to c. sth off** enlever qch au burin **2** *Sl (cheat)* rouler; **to c. sb out of sth** rouler qn de qch

chiselled ['tʃɪz(ə)ld] ADJ **delicately c. features** visage délicatement ciselé

chiseller ['tʃɪz(ə)lər] N *Sl* **1** *(swindler)* escroc *m* **2** *Ir (child)* gosse *mf*, môme *mf*

chit [1] [tʃɪt] N *Old-fashioned Fam (child)* mioche *mf*, gosse *mf*, gamin, -ine; *(girl)* jeune fille *f ou* femme *f*

chit [2] N *(note)* petit mot *m*, billet *m*; *(for money owed)* note *f*

chitchat ['tʃɪttʃæt] N *Fam* bavardage *m*, papotage *m*

chitterlings ['tʃɪtəlɪŋz], **chitlings** ['tʃɪtlɪŋz], **chitlins** ['tʃɪtlɪnz] NPL *Culin Old-fashioned* tripes *fpl*

chivalrous ['ʃɪvəlrəs] ADJ courtois; *Hist (worthy of a knight)* chevaleresque

chivalrously ['ʃɪvəlrəslɪ] ADV courtoisement; *Hist* chevaleresquement

chivalry ['ʃɪvəlrɪ] N **1** *(of medieval knight)* chevalerie *f*, **in the days of c.** aux temps de la chevalerie **2** *(courteous behaviour)* courtoisie *f*, *esp Hum* **it's nice to see c. is not dead** ça fait plaisir de voir que la galanterie n'a pas entièrement disparu

chives [tʃaɪvz] NPL ciboulette *f*, civette *f*

chiv(v)y ['tʃɪvɪ] VT *Br Fam (pester)* harceler; **to c. sb into doing sth** harceler qn jusqu'à ce qu'il fasse qch; **you'll have to c. them along** il faudra que tu les presses un peu; **go and c. them along** va leur dire de se dépêcher

chlamydia [klə'mɪdɪə] N *Med* chlamydia *f*

chloral ['klɔːr(ə)l] N *Chem* chloral *m*

chlorate ['klɔːreɪt] N *Chem* chlorate *m*

chloric ['klɔːrɪk] ADJ *Chem (acid etc)* chlorique

chloride ['klɔːraɪd] N *Chem* chlorure *m*
▸▸**c. of silver** chlorure d'argent

chlorinate ['klɒrɪneɪt] VT *(water)* chlo(ru)rer

chlorinated ['klɔːrɪneɪtɪd] ADJ *(water)* chloré

chlorination [klɒrɪ'neɪʃən] N chloration *f*
▸▸**c. plant** usine *f* de chloration; **c. works** usine de chloration

chlorine ['klɔːriːn] N *Chem* chlore *m*

chlorite ['klɔːraɪt] N **1** *Chem* chlorite *m* **2** *Miner* chlorite *f*

chlorofluorocarbon [klɒrəfluərəʊ'kɑːbən] N chlorofluorocarbone *m*

chloroform ['klɒrəfɔːm] N chloroforme *m*
vt chloroformer

chlorophyl(l) ['klɒrəfɪl] N *Chem, Bot* chlorophylle *f*

chloroquine ['klɔːrəʊkwiːn] N *Med* chloroquine *f*

choc [tʃɒk] N *Fam* **a box of chocs** une boîte de chocolats

chocaholic [tʃɒkə'hɒlɪk] N *Fam* accro *mf* du chocolat

choc-ice N esquimau® *m*

chock [tʃɒk] N *(under car wheel, door etc)* cale *f*; *Aviat* **to remove the chocks** enlever les cales; *Aviat* **chocks away!** enlevez les cales!
vt 1 *(barrel, wheel, door)* caler **2** *(in engineering etc) (part)* coincer

chock-a-block ADJ *Fam* plein à craquer, bourré (**with** de)

chock-full ADJ *Fam* bourré (**of** de)

chocolate ['tʃɒklət] N *(also drink)* chocolat *m*; **bar of c.** tablette *f* de chocolat; **white c.** chocolat blanc; **cooking c.** chocolat à cuire;

drinking c. *(drink)* chocolat; *(powder)* chocolat en poudre; **hot c.** chocolat chaud; **a c.** un chocolat; **c. biscuit/ice cream/cake** biscuit *m*/glace *f*/gâteau *m* au chocolat
ADJ **1** *(coloured)* chocolat *inv* **2** *(made of chocolate)* en chocolat; *(chocolate-flavoured)* au chocolat, chocolaté
▸▸**c. bar** barre *f* chocolatée; **c. brown** chocolat *m inv*; **c. chip cookie** biscuit *m* aux pépites de chocolat *ou Can* brisures de chocolat; **c. factory** chocolaterie *f*

choice [tʃɔɪs] N **1** *(act of choosing)* choix *m*; **to make** *or* **take one's c.** faire son choix, choisir; **a difficult/easy c.** un choix difficile/facile; **by** *or* **out of c.** par choix; **to do sth of one's own c.** faire qch volontairement
2 *(thing chosen)* choix *m*; **the red wine was her c.** c'est elle qui avait choisi le vin rouge; **Spain would be my c.** je choisirais l'Espagne
3 *(alternative)* choix *m*; **to have the c. of two evils** avoir le choix entre deux maux; **what c. did she have?** *(rhetorical)* qu'est-ce qu'elle pouvait faire d'autre?; **you have no c. in the matter** vous n'avez pas le choix
4 *(selection)* assortiment *m*, choix *m*; **available in a c. of colours** disponible en plusieurs couleurs; **there isn't much c.** il n'y a pas grand choix; **to have a wide c.** avoir amplement de quoi choisir
ADJ **1** *(well chosen)* bien choisi; **in a few c. sentences** en quelques phrases bien choisies; *Hum* **she used some c. language** elle a juré comme un charretier
2 *(of good quality) (article)* de choix; *(wine)* fin
▸▸*Mktg* **c. set** ensemble *m* de considérations, éventail *m* de choix

choir ['kwaɪər] N **1** *Mus* chœur *m*, chorale *f*; **male voice c.** chœur *ou* chorale d'hommes
VOIR GRAMMAIRE A11 **2** *Archit (of church)* chœur *m*
▸▸**c. practice** répétition *f* de la chorale; **c. school** maîtrise *f*, **c. screen** jubé *m*; **c. stall** stalle *f*

choirboy ['kwaɪəbɔɪ] N *Rel* jeune choriste *m*

choirmaster ['kwaɪəmɑːstər] N *Rel* maître *m* de chapelle *ou* de chœur

choke [tʃəʊk] N **1** *Aut* starter *m*; *(on carburettor)* buse *f*; **to pull out the c.** mettre le starter; **you've given it too much c.** tu as mis trop de starter **2** *(in voice)* étranglement *m* **3** *Elec (coil of wire)* bobine *f* d'impédance, self *f* **4** *(of artichoke)* foin *m*
vt 1 *(strangle)* étouffer, suffoquer; *(of weeds) (flowers)* étouffer; **voice choked with sobs** voix entrecoupée par les sanglots **2** *(block) (pipe etc)* obstruer, boucher (**with** de); **the streets were choked with traffic** les rues étaient congestionnées
vi 1 *(become stifled)* étouffer; **I choked on a bone** je me suis étranglé avec un os; **he was choking with anger** il suffoquait de colère; **to c. with laughter** s'étrangler de rire **2** *Sl (die)* clamser
▸▸**c. cable** câble *m* de starter; **c. chain** *(for dog)* collier *m* étrangleur; *Elec* **c. coil** bobine d'impédance, self
▸ **choke back** VT SEP *(suppress) (tears, words, anger)* refouler, ravaler
▸ **choke up** VT SEP *(block)* boucher, obstruer; **the drain is all choked up with leaves** la bouche d'égout est complètement obstruée par les feuilles; **she was all choked up** *(upset)* elle était bouleversée *ou* toute émue

choked [tʃəʊkt] ADJ *Br Fam (disappointed)* déçu; *(annoyed)* ennuyé

choker ['tʃəʊkər] N *(necklace)* collier *m* de chien

choking ['tʃəʊkɪŋ] ADJ étouffant, suffocant; **he made a c. sound** il a fait un bruit comme quelqu'un qui s'étouffe
N étouffement *m*, suffocation *f*

cholera ['kɒlərə] N choléra *m*; **to have c.** avoir le choléra

choleric ['kɒlərɪk, kə'lerɪk] ADJ *Fml* colérique, coléreux

cholesterol [kə'lestərɒl] N *Med* cholestérol *m*; **with a high/low c. content** riche/pauvre en cholestérol
▸▸**c. level** taux *m* de cholestérol

chomp [tʃɒmp] VT & VI mâcher bruyamment
N mâchonnement *m* bruyant

choo-choo ['tʃuːtʃuː] N *Br Fam (in children's language)* petit train *m*; **the train goes c.** le train fait tchou-tchou

chook [tʃʊk] N *Austr Fam (chicken)* poulet *m*

choose [tʃuːz] *(pt* **chose** [tʃəʊz], *pp* **chosen** ['tʃəʊz(ə)n]) VT choisir; **there is nothing to c. between them** l'un vaut l'autre, ils se valent; **I didn't c. to go there** je n'ai pas choisi d'y aller; **since you chose not to accept** puisque vous avez décidé de ne pas accepter; **well if you will c. to ignore my advice** bon, si tu préfères ne pas tenir compte de mes conseils
VI choisir; **c. for yourself** je vous laisse le choix; **to pick and c.** se montrer difficile, faire le/la difficile; **I'll do as I c.** je ferai comme il me plaît *ou* comme bon me semble; **to c. from** *or* **between several people** choisir entre *ou* parmi plusieurs personnes

chooser ['tʃuːzə(r)] N *Comput* sélecteur *m*

choosing ['tʃuːzɪŋ] N choix *m*; **it was none of my c.** ce n'est pas moi qui l'ai choisi; **the circumstances were not of his c.** les circonstances n'étaient pas de son fait

choosy ['tʃuːzɪ] ADJ *Fam* difficile; **I'm not c.** *(at this moment)* ça m'est égal; *(in general)* je ne suis pas difficile; **don't be so c.** ne fais pas le difficile; **he isn't too c. who he does business with** il n'est pas très difficile quant aux gens avec lesquels il traite

chop [1] [tʃɒp] N **1** *(blow) (with axe etc)* coup *m*; *Fam* **to get the c.** *(of person)* se faire saquer, être mis à la porte; *(of project)* être annulé; *(of chapter, part of text, film etc)* être supprimé **2** *Culin (pork, lamb)* côtelette *f* **3** *(in karate etc)* coup *m* porté avec le tranchant de la main
vt (**-pp-**) **1** *(wood)* couper, fendre; *(meat, vegetables etc)* couper en morceaux; **to c. sth in(to) pieces** couper qch en morceaux; **to c. sth finely** hacher qch menu; **to c. logic** couper les cheveux en quatre **2** *Tennis (ball)* couper
vi *Fam* **c., c.!** vite, vite!
▸▸*Culin* **c. suey** chop suey *m*
▸ **chop at** VT INSEP *(something) (with axe, knife etc)* donner des coups à; *(aim blow at)* tenter de porter un coup à
▸ **chop down** VT SEP *(tree etc)* abattre
▸ **chop off** VT SEP trancher, couper; **to c. sb's head off** trancher la tête à qn
▸ **chop up** VT SEP couper en morceaux, hacher

chop [2] VI **to c. and change** changer sans cesse; **he's always chopping and changing** *(changing his mind)* il change d'opinion à tout bout de champ; *(changing policy/approach)* il change de politique/méthode tout le temps

chophouse ['tʃɒphaʊs] N grill *m*

chopper ['tʃɒpər] N **1** *(tool)* couperet *m*, hachoir *m* **2** *(person) (of wood)* fendeur, -euse **3** *Fam (helicopter)* hélico *m* **4** *(motorcycle)* chopper *m*; *(bicycle)* vélo *m* cross **5** *Vulg (penis)* bite *f*

choppers ['tʃɒpəz] NPL *Fam (false teeth)* râtelier *m*; *(teeth)* ratiches *fpl*

chopping ['tʃɒpɪŋ] N *(of wood)* coupe *f*
▸▸**c. block** billot *m*; **c. board** planche *f* à découper; **c. knife** couperet *m*, hachoir *m*

choppy ['tʃɒpɪ] ADJ *(sea, lake)* agité

chops [tʃɒps] NPL *Fam* bajoues *fpl*; **he had a smile all over his fat c.** un large sourire lui couvrait la tronche; **to lick one's c.** se lécher les babines

chopsticks ['tʃɒpstɪks] NPL baguettes *fpl*

choral ['kɔːr(ə)l] ADJ *Mus* choral, -als
▸▸ **c. society** chorale *f*; **c. symphony** symphonie *f* avec chœur

choral(e) [kəˈrɑːl] N *Mus* **1** *(hymn)* choral *m*, *pl* -als **2** *Am (choir)* chorale *f*

chord[1] [kɔːd] N *Mus (group of notes)* accord *m*; **a c. sequence** une suite d'accords
▸▸ **c. progression** progression *f* harmonique

chord[2] N **1** *(of harp)* corde *f*, *Fig* **to strike a c., to strike the right c.** faire vibrer la corde sensible; **his words struck a c. with the audience** ses paroles ont trouvé un écho auprès du public **2** *Math (of arc)* corde *f*

chore [tʃɔːr] N **1** *(usu pl)* **chores** *(in household)* travaux *mpl* ménagers; **the daily chores** les travaux quotidiens; **to do the chores** faire le ménage **2** *(unwelcome task)* corvée *f*

choreograph ['kɒrɪəɡrɑːf] VT *(ballet, show)* faire la chorégraphie de

choreographer [kɒrɪˈɒɡrəfər] N chorégraphe *mf*

choreographic [kɒrɪəˈɡræfɪk] ADJ chorégraphique

choreography [kɒrɪˈɒɡrəfɪ] N chorégraphie *f*

chorister ['kɒrɪstər] N choriste *mf*

chortle ['tʃɔːt(ə)l] N gloussement *m* (de joie); **she gave a c.** elle a gloussé, elle a poussé un gloussement de joie
VI glousser (de joie), pousser un gloussement de joie
VT **oh, no, he chortled** ah non, dit-il dans un gloussement

chorus, *pl* **-uses** ['kɔːrəs, -əsɪz] N **1** *(of song)* refrain *m*; **to join in the c.** *(of several people)* chanter le refrain en chœur; *(of one person)* se joindre aux autres pour le refrain **2** *(group of singers, actors)* chœur *m*; **in the c.** *(of musical)* dans les chœurs VOIR GRAMMAIRE A11 **3 to sing in c.** chanter en chœur; **no!, they shouted in c.** non!, se sont-ils exclamés en chœur; **c. of praise** concert *m* de louanges; **a c. of criticism** une avalanche de critiques; **they greeted him with a c. of cheers** ils l'accueillirent avec des hourras
VT **-s-)** dire en chœur; *(song)* chanter en chœur; **yes please!, they chorused** volontiers, ont-ils répondu en chœur
▸▸ *Theat, Mus* **c. girl** girl *f*

chorusmaster ['kɔːrəsmɑːstər] N maître *m* de chant

chosen ['tʃəʊz(ə)n] PP *see* **choose**
ADJ choisi; **the c. people** les élus *mpl*; **the c. few** les heureux élus
NPL **the c.** les élus *mpl*

chough [tʃʌf] N *(bird)* crave *m* à bec rouge

choux [ʃuː] Culin N *(pastry)* pâte *f* à choux
▸▸ **c. bun** chou *m* à la crème; **c. pastry** pâte à choux

chow [tʃaʊ] N **1** *(dog)* chow-chow *m*, *pl* chows-chows **2** *Fam (food)* boustifaille *f*
▸ **chow down** VI *Am Fam* bouffer

chow-chow N *(dog)* chow-chow *m*, *pl* chows-chows

chowder ['tʃaʊdər] N *Culin* = potage *m* épais contenant du poisson ou des fruits de mer

Christ [kraɪst] N le Christ, Jésus-Christ *m*; **the C. Child** l'Enfant Jésus *m*
INT *Fam* bon Dieu!; **C. Almighty!** nom de Dieu!

christen ['krɪs(ə)n] VT **1** *(person, ship)* baptiser; *(nickname)* surnommer; **to c. a child George** baptiser un enfant Georges **2** *(use for first time)* étrenner

Christendom ['krɪs(ə)ndəm] N chrétienté *f*; **throughout C.** dans toute la chrétienté; **he's the biggest fool in C.** c'est l'homme le plus bête du monde

christening ['krɪs(ə)nɪŋ] N baptême *m*
▸▸ **c. ceremony** cérémonie *f* du ou de baptême; **c. robe** *(for baby)* robe *f* de baptême

Christian ['krɪstʃən] *Rel* N chrétien, -ienne; **to be a C.** être chrétien
ADJ **1** chrétien; **C. burial** sépulture *f* en terre sainte; **C. charity** charité *f* chrétienne **2** *(good, kind)* chrétien, de chrétien; **that wasn't very C. of you** ce n'était pas très aimable de ta part; **that's not a very C. attitude** ce n'est pas une attitude très chrétienne
▸▸ **the C. era** l'ère *f* chrétienne; **C. name** prénom *m*; **C. Scientist** scientiste *mf* chrétien, -ienne

Christianity [krɪstɪˈænɪtɪ] N christianisme *m*; **in a spirit of C.** en chrétien

Christianize ['krɪstʃənaɪz] VT christianiser, convertir au christianisme

Christmas ['krɪsməs] N Noël *m*; **at C.** à (la) Noël; **to spend C. at home** passer Noël chez soi; **Merry** *or* **Happy C.!** joyeux Noël!; **Father C.** le père Noël
▸▸ *Br* **C. box** étrennes *fpl (offertes à Noël)*; **C. cake** gâteau *m* de Noël *(cake décoré au sucre glace)*; **C. card** carte *f* de Noël; **C. carol** *(chant m de)* Noël; **C. Day** jour *m* de Noël; **on C.** le jour de Noël; **C. dinner** repas *m* de Noël; **C. Eve** veille *f* de Noël; **C. present** cadeau *m* de Noël; **C. pudding** pudding *m* de Noël, plum-pudding *m*, *pl* plum-puddings; *Bot* **C. rose** rose *f* de Noël; **C. stocking** = chaussette *f* que les enfants suspendent à la cheminée pour que le père Noël y dépose les cadeaux; **C. tree** sapin *m* de Noël

Christmassy ['krɪsməsɪ] ADJ *Fam* typique de Noël; **to be in a C. mood** être dans l'ambiance de Noël; **not in a C. mood** pas d'humeur à supporter Noël; **it all looks so C.** c'est tout décoré pour Noël

Christmastide ['krɪsməstaɪd] N *Old-fashioned* période *f* de Noël; **at C.** à la Noël

Christopher Columbus ['krɪstəfər] N Christophe Colomb

chromatic [krəʊˈmætɪk] ADJ *Mus, Phys* chromatique

chromatography [krəʊməˈtɒɡrəfɪ] N chromatographie *f*

chrome [krəʊm] N chrome *m*; *Br Fam Hum* **he's a c. dome** il a une casquette en peau de fesse
ADJ *(taps, handles etc)* chromé
▸▸ **c. nickel** nickel-chrome *m*; **c. steel** acier *m* chromé ou au chrome; **c. tape** bande *f* magnétique chromée; *Art* **c. yellow** jaune *m* de chrome

chromium ['krəʊmɪəm] N *Chem* chrome *m*
▸▸ **c. plating** chromage *m*

chromium-plated ADJ chromé

chromosome ['krəʊməsəʊm] N *Biol* chromosome *m*; **X-c.** chromosome X

chronic ['krɒnɪk] ADJ **1** *Med, Fig* chronique; **c. unemployment** chômage *m* chronique; **c. invalid** invalide *mf* chronique; **to suffer from c. ill health** être de santé fragile; *Fig* **a c. drunkard/liar** un buveur/menteur invétéré **2** *Br Fam (very bad)* atroce; **their singing was c.** ils chantaient atrocement mal; **my back was hurting something c.** mon dos me faisait un mal de chien
▸▸ *Med* **c. fatigue syndrome** encéphalomyélite *f* myalgique, syndrome *m* de fatigue chronique

chronically ['krɒnɪklɪ] ADV chroniquement

chronicity [krɒˈnɪsɪtɪ] N *Med* chronicité *f*

chronicle ['krɒnɪk(ə)l] N chronique *f*, *Fig* **a c. of disasters** une suite de catastrophes; *Bible* **(the Book of) Chronicles** les Chroniques *fpl*
VT **to c. events** faire la chronique d'événements

chronicler ['krɒnɪklər] N chroniqueur *m*

chronological [krɒnəˈlɒdʒɪk(ə)l] ADJ *(order etc)* chronologique

chronologically [krɒnəˈlɒdʒɪklɪ] ADV chronologiquement, par ordre chronologique

chronology [krəˈnɒlədʒɪ] N chronologie *f*

chronometer [krəˈnɒmɪtər] N chronomètre *m*

chronometry [krəˈnɒmɪtrɪ] N chronométrie *f*

chrysalid ['krɪsəlɪd], **chrysalis**, *pl* **chrysalises** ['krɪsəlɪs, 'krɪsəlɪsɪz] N *Entom* chrysalide *f*

chrysanthemum [krɪˈsænθəməm] N chrysanthème *m*

chub [tʃʌb] N *(fish)* chevesne *m*, meunier *m*

chubbiness ['tʃʌbɪnɪs] N *(of person)* apparence *f* potelée

chubby ['tʃʌbɪ] ADJ *(person)* potelé, boulot, dodu, grassouillet; *(hands)* potelé; *(face)* joufflu; *(cheeks)* rebondi; **c.-cheeked** aux joues rebondies
N **come on, c.!** allez, gros dodu!

chuck[1] [tʃʌk] VT **1** *Fam (throw) (stone etc)* balancer; **c. me that hammer** balance-moi le marteau; **to c. one's money about** *or* **around** gaspiller son argent
2 *Fam (finish with) (job)* lâcher, laisser tomber; *(girlfriend, boyfriend)* plaquer
3 *Fam (throw away)* balancer, foutre en l'air
4 *Br Fam* **c. it!** *(stop it!)* arrête!
5 **to c. sb under the chin** donner une petite tape à qn sous le menton
N **1** *Fam* **to give sb the c.** *(from job)* virer *ou* sa(c)quer qn; *(from relationship)* plaquer qn
2 *(under the chin)* petite tape *f*
3 *(steak)* morceau *m* de bœuf dans le paleron
▸▸ **c. steak** morceau *m* de bœuf dans le paleron; **c. wagon** cantine *f* ambulante *(pour les cow-boys)*
▸ **chuck away** VT SEP *Fam* balancer, flanquer *ou* foutre en l'air; **that's just chucking money away** ça, c'est flanquer l'argent par les fenêtres
▸ **chuck down** VT SEP *Br Fam* **it's chucking it down** *(raining)* il flotte vraiment
▸ **chuck in** VT SEP *Fam (finish with) (job)* lâcher, laisser tomber; *(person)* plaquer, virer; **he chucked it all in and bought a farm** il a tout plaqué pour acheter une ferme; **to c. one's hand in** *Cards* jeter ses cartes sur la table; *Fig (admit defeat)* s'avouer vaincu
▸ **chuck off** VT SEP *Fam* virer; **he was chucked off the team** il s'est fait virer de l'équipe
▸ **chuck on** VT SEP *Fam (clothes, aftershave)* mettre
▸ **chuck out** VT SEP *Fam* **1** *(throw away)* jeter **2** *(from pub, house etc)* flanquer à la porte, vider
▸ **chuck up** *Fam* VT SEP *(finish with) (job)* lâcher, laisser tomber; **she chucked everything up and became a nurse** elle a tout plaqué pour devenir infirmière
VI *esp Am (vomit)* vomir, rendre

chuck[2] N *Tech (for lathe, drill)* mandrin *m*

chucker-out ['tʃʌkər-] N *Br Fam (in disco etc)* videur *m*

chucking-out ['tʃʌkɪŋ-] N *Br Fam* **c. time** l'heure *f* de la fermeture (des pubs)

chuckle ['tʃʌk(ə)l] N rire *m* étouffé, petit rire; **to give a c.** lâcher un petit rire

vi rire tout bas *ou* en soi-même (**at, over** de)

chuff[1] [tʃʌf] **vi** *(of train)* haleter

chuff[2] **n** *Br Vulg* **1** *(vagina)* craquette *f*, fente *f*; **to be as tight as a nun's c.** *(miserly)* avoir des oursins dans le porte-monnaie, les lâcher avec des élastiques **2** *(anus)* trou *m* de balle

chuffed [tʃʌft] **adj** *Br Fam* tout content (**about sth**); **he's dead c. with his present** il est super content de son cadeau; **I'm really c. with myself** je suis tout content de moi

chuffing ['tʃʌfɪŋ] **adj** *Br Sl* foutu, sacré; **that c. idiot** ce sombre crétin

chug [tʃʌg] **n** *(of steam engine)* souffle *m* **vi** (**-gg-**) *(of steam engine)* souffler, haleter
► **chug along vi** *Fam (move slowly)* avancer doucement; **the guy in front was chugging along at 30 km/h** le type devant moi se traînait à 30 à l'heure

chum [tʃʌm] **n** *Fam* camarade *mf*, copain *m*, copine *f*
► **chum up with vt insep** (**-mm-**) *Fam* copiner avec

chummy ['tʃʌmɪ] **adj** *Fam* (bon) copain, *f* (bonne) copine; **she's quite c. with the boss** elle est assez copine avec le patron; **he's a c. sort of bloke** c'est un type sympa (et sociable); **he's a bit too c. for my liking** il est un peu trop familier à mon goût

chump [tʃʌmp] **n 1** *Fam (foolish person)* idiot, -ote **2** *Culin (end of mutton)* selle *f* d'agneau **3** *Fam (head)* **off one's c.** timbré, maboul
►► *Am Fam* **c. change** *(small amount of money)* cacahuètes *fpl*; *Br Culin* **c. chop** côtelette *f* d'agneau *(coupée dans le gigot)*

chunder ['tʃʌndər] **vi** *Br, Austr Sl (vomit)* dégueuler

chunk [tʃʌŋk] **n** *(of bread, cheese etc)* gros morceau *m*; *(of bread)* quignon *m*; *(of wood)* tronçon *m*

chunky ['tʃʌŋkɪ] **adj** *Fam* **1** *(person)* trapu **2** *(pullover)* gros; *(glass)* solide

Chunnel ['tʃʌn(ə)l] **n** *Fam* **the C.** le tunnel sous la Manche, l'Eurotunnel *m*
► **chunter away, chunter on** ['tʃʌntər] **vi** *Fam* papoter; **he's still chuntering away about it** il continue son baratin; **with those two chuntering away in the background** avec ces deux-là qui papotent/papotaient dans le fond

church [tʃɜːtʃ] **n** VOIR GRAMMAIRE A6–7 **1** *(building)* église *f*; *(French Protestant)* temple *m*; **to go to c.** aller à l'église; *(of Catholic)* aller à l'église *ou* à la messe; *(of French Protestant)* aller au temple; **I saw her in c. on Sunday** je l'ai vue à l'église dimanche **2** *(institution)* **the C.** l'Église *f*; **the Anglican C.** l'Église anglicane; **to go into the C.** *(take orders)* entrer dans les ordres; **to leave the C.** quitter l'église; **High C.** = section *f* de l'Église anglicane qui se rapproche du catholicisme en matière de rituel; **Low C.** = section de l'Église anglicane qui se distingue par la simplicité du rituel; **the (Roman) Catholic C.** l'Église catholique; **C. of England** Église anglicane
►► **C. Fathers** Pères *mpl* de l'Église; **c. hall** salle *f* paroissiale; **c. leader** chef *m* de l'église; **c. service** office *m*, culte *m*; **c. wedding** mariage *m* religieux

churchgoer ['tʃɜːtʃgəʊər] **n** *Rel* pratiquant, -ante; **an occasional c.** une personne qui va à l'église de temps en temps

churchgoing ['tʃɜːtʃgəʊɪŋ] *Rel* **adj** pratiquant; **the c. public** les gens qui vont à l'église **n** fréquentation *f* des églises; **c. is not regarded as an essential part of ...** aller à l'église n'est pas considéré comme une part essentielle de ...

Churchillian [tʃɜːˈtʃɪljən] **adj** churchillien

churchman, *pl* **churchmen** ['tʃɜːtʃmən] **n** *Rel* **1** *(clergyman)* homme *m* d'église **2** *(member of a church)* membre *m* d'une église

churchwarden [tʃɜːtʃˈwɔːd(ə)n] **n 1** *Rel* marguillier *m*, bedeau *m* **2** *(pipe)* longue pipe *f (en terre)*, pipe hollandaise
►► **c. pipe** longue pipe *(en terre)*, pipe hollandaise

churchwoman, *pl* **churchwomen** ['tʃɜːtʃwʊmən, -wɪmɪn] **n** *Rel* **1** *(clergywoman)* femme *f* d'église **2** *(member of a church)* femme *f* membre d'une église

churchy ['tʃɜːtʃɪ] **adj** *Fam* calotin, bondieusard

churchyard ['tʃɜːtʃjɑːd] **n** *(graveyard)* cimetière *m*; *(grounds)* enclos *m* d'église

churl [tʃɜːl] **n** rustre *m*

churlish ['tʃɜːlɪʃ] **adj** *(rude)* grossier; *(surly) (behaviour, person)* revêche; **it would be c. to refuse** ce serait mal élevé de refuser

churlishly ['tʃɜːlɪʃlɪ] **adv** *(rudely)* avec grossièreté; *(in a surly way)* de façon revêche

churlishness ['tʃɜːlɪʃnɪs] **n** *(rudeness)* grossièreté *f*; *(surliness)* attitude *f* revêche; **he agreed, but with his usual c.** il accepta, revêche comme à l'ordinaire

churn [tʃɜːn] **n 1** *Agr (for butter)* baratte *f* **2** *Agr (for milk)* bidon *m* à lait **3** *Mktg* perte *f* de clients passés à la concurrence **vt** *(milk, cream)* baratter; *(butter)* battre; **to c. water** *(of propellor etc)* faire des remous **vi** *(of sea)* bouillonner; *Fig* **my stomach's churning** *(with nerves, excitement)* j'ai l'estomac noué
► **churn out vt sep** *Fam (produce in large numbers) (books etc)* produire en série, *Fam* pondre en série; *(objects)* produire en série
► **churn up vt sep** *(mud)* remuer; **to c. up water** faire bouillonner l'eau; *Fig* **I felt all churned up** *(nervous)* j'étais tout retourné; *(excited)* j'étais tout excité

churning ['tʃɜːnɪŋ] **n** *(of cream)* barattage *m*

chute [ʃuːt] **n 1** *(for parcels etc)* glissière *f*; *(for coal)* déversoir *m*; **(rubbish** *or Am* **garbage) c.** vide-ordures *m inv* **2** *Sport (for sleds)* piste *f*; *(in swimming pool, playground)* toboggan *m* **3** *(waterfall)* chute *f* d'eau **4** *Fam (parachute)* parachute *m*

chutney ['tʃʌtnɪ] **n** *Culin* chutney *m*

chutzpah ['hʊtspə] **n** culot *m*

chyme [kaɪm] **n** *Med* chyme *m*

C & I [siːændˈaɪ] **n** *Com (abbr* **cost and insurance)** c et a

CIA [siːaɪˈeɪ] **n** *Am (abbr* **Central Intelligence Agency)** CIA *f*

ciborium, *pl* **ciboria** [sɪˈbɔːrɪəm, -ɪə] **n** *Rel (vessel)* ciboire *m*

cicada [sɪˈkɑːdə, -ˈkeɪdə] **n** *(insect)* cigale *f*

cicatrice ['sɪkətrɪs], **cicatrix** ['sɪkətrɪks] **n** *Fml* cicatrice *f*

Cicero ['sɪsərəʊ] **n** Cicéron

cicerone [sɪsəˈrəʊnɪ] **n** *Old-fashioned* cicérone *m*

CID [siːaɪˈdiː] **n** *Br (abbr* **Criminal Investigation Department)** ≃ PJ *f*; **Joanna Smith, C.** ≃ Joanna Smith, de la PJ

cider ['saɪdər] **n 1** *Br (alcoholic drink)* cidre *m* **2** *Am (apple juice)* jus *m* de pommes; **hard c.** cidre *m*
►► **c. apple** pomme *f* à cidre; **c. press** pressoir *m* à cidre; **c. vinegar** vinaigre *m* de cidre

cif ['siːaɪef] *Com (abbr* **cost, insurance and freight)** CAF

cigar [sɪˈgɑːr] **n** cigare *m*
►► **c. butt** mégot *m* de cigare; **c. case** étui *m* à cigares; **c. cutter** coupe-cigares *m inv*; **c. holder** fume-cigare *m inv*; **c. lighter** allume-cigare *m inv*

cigarette, *occ Am* **cigaret** [sɪgəˈret] **n** cigarette *f*
►► **c. advertising** publicité *f* pour les cigarettes; **c. ash** cendre *f* de cigarette; **c. butt** mégot *m* de cigarette; **c. card** = image *f* offerte autrefois avec chaque paquet de cigarettes; **c. case** étui *m* à cigarettes, porte-cigarettes *m inv*; **c. end** mégot *m*; **c. holder** fume-cigarette *m inv*; **c. lighter** briquet *m*; **c. machine** *(vending machine)* distributeur *m* automatique de cigarettes; *(for rolling cigarettes)* rouleuse *f*; **c. packet** paquet *m* de cigarettes; **c. paper** papier *m* à cigarettes; **c. smoke** fumée *f* de cigarette; **c. smoker** fumeur, -euse (de cigarettes)

ciggie ['sɪgɪ] **n** *Br Fam* tige *f*, clope *f*

CIM [siːaɪˈem] **n** *Comput (abbr* **computer-integrated manufacturing)** CFAO *f*

CIM waybill n *Com* lettre *f* de voiture CIM

C-in-C, C in C [siːɪnˈsiː] **n** *Mil, Naut (abbr* **Commander in Chief)** commandant *m* en chef

cinch [sɪntʃ] **n 1** *Fam (something very easy)* **it's a c.** c'est simple comme bonjour, c'est un jeu d'enfant **2** *Fam (certainty)* certitude *f*; **it's a c.** c'est certain *ou* couru **3** *Am (for horse)* sangle *f*, sous-ventrière *f*, *pl* sous-ventrières

cinder ['sɪndər] **n** cendre *f*; **burnt to a c.** *(meat, toast etc)* complètement carbonisé
►► *Am* **c. block** parpaing *m*; **c. track** (piste *f*) cendrée *f*

Cinderella [sɪndəˈrelə] **n** *Liter* Cendrillon *f*, *Fig* **poetry has always been the C. of the arts** la poésie a toujours été le parent pauvre des arts

Cinders ['sɪndəz] **n** *Fam* Cendrillon *f*

cine ['sɪnɪ] **pref** *Br*
►► **c. camera** caméra *f*; **c. film** film *m*; **c. projector** projecteur *m* de cinéma

cineaste, cineast ['sɪnɪæst] **n** cinéphile *mf*

cinema ['sɪnəmə] **n 1** *(art)* cinéma *m*; **French c.** le cinéma français **2** *esp Br (place)* cinéma *m*; **to go to the c.** aller au cinéma;
►► *Mktg* **c. advertising** publicité *f* au cinéma; *TV* **c. channel** chaîne *f* de cinéma

cinemagoer ['sɪnəməgəʊər] **n** cinéphile *mf*; **he's not much of a c.** ce n'est pas un grand amateur de cinéma

cinema-going n fréquentation *f* des salles de cinéma
adj **the c. public** les cinéphiles *mpl*

Cinemascope® ['sɪnəməskəʊp] **n** Cinémascope® *m*

cinematic [sɪnəˈmætɪk] **adj** cinématique; **the novel has a c. quality** le roman utilise des effets qui rappellent le cinéma

cinematograph [sɪnəˈmætəgræf] **n** *Br Old-fashioned* cinématographe *m*

cinematographer [sɪnəməˈtɒgrəfər] **n** directeur *m* de la photographie, chef opérateur *m*

cinematographic [sɪnəmætəˈgræfɪk] **adj** cinématographique

cinematography [sɪnəməˈtɒgrəfɪ] **n 1** *(technique)* cinématographie *f* **2** *(camerawork)* prises *fpl* de vue

cinephile ['sɪnɪfaɪl] **n** *Am* cinéphile *mf*

Cinerama® [sɪnəˈrɑːmə] **n** Cinérama® *m*

cineraria [sɪnəˈreərɪə] **n** *(plant)* cinéraire *f*

cinnabar ['sɪnəbɑːr] **n** *Miner* cinabre *m*

cinnamon ['sɪnəmən] **n 1** *Culin (spice)* cannelle *f* **2** *Bot (tree)* cannelier *m*
adj *(colour)* cannelle *inv*
►► **c. stick** bâton *m* de cannelle; *Bot* **c. tree** cannelier

cinq(ue)foil ['sɪŋkfɔɪl] **n 1** *(plant)* potentille *f* rampante, quintefeuille *f* **2** *Archit* quintefeuille *m*

cipher ['saɪfər] **n 1** *(secret writing)* chiffre *m*,

code *m*; *(message)* message *m* chiffré *ou* codé; **to write a message in c.** chiffrer un message; **2** *(monogram)* chiffre *m* **3** *Math* zéro *m*; *Fig* **he's a mere c.** c'est un zéro *ou* une nullité
  vt *(message)* chiffrer
  ▸▸ **c. clerk** chiffreur, -euse

circa ['sɜːkə] **PREP** *(of time)* aux alentours de; *(of amount)* environ

circadian [sɜː'keɪdɪən] **ADJ** circadien

circle ['sɜːk(ə)l] **N 1** *Math etc* cercle *m*; **to draw a c.** tracer un cercle; **to stand in a c.** *(of people)* se tenir en cercle; **the chairs were arranged in a c.** les chaises étaient disposées en cercle; *Fig* **to go round in circles** tourner en rond; **to have circles under one's eyes** avoir les yeux cernés, avoir des cernes sous les yeux; **Arctic/Antarctic C.** cercle (polaire) arctique/antarctique; *Gym* **to do a c. (on the horizontal bar)** faire le (grand) soleil; *Archeol* **stone c.** cercle de pierres
  2 *(movement) (of planet)* révolution *f*, orbite *f*; **to come full c.** *(of planet)* compléter son orbite; *(of argument, person walking)* revenir à son point de départ; *(of fashion, history)* revenir au même point
  3 *Theat* **first c.** (premier) balcon *m*, corbeille *f*; **upper c.** deuxième balcon
  4 *(group)* cercle *m*, groupe *m*; **a c. of friends** un cercle d'amis; **the family c.** le cercle familial; **in certain circles** dans certains milieux; **in theatrical circles** dans le monde du théâtre; **the inner c.** *(of friends)* le cercle intime
  vt 1 *(go round)* tourner autour de, faire le tour de
  2 *(surround)* entourer (**with** de)
  vi *(of plane, tiger around prey)* tourner; *(of birds)* tourner, tournoyer; **to c. round sth** tourner/tournoyer autour de qch; **the planes are circling overhead** les avions décrivent des cercles au-dessus de nos têtes; *Fig* **she circled round the issue** elle tournait autour du pot

circlet ['sɜːklɪt] **N** bandeau *m*

circlip ['sɜːklɪp] **N** *Tech* circlip *m*
  ▸▸ **c. pliers** pince *f* à circlip

circuit ['sɜːkɪt] **N 1** *Elec* circuit *m*; **in/out of c.** en/hors de circuit
  2 *(journey, movement around) (of sun)* révolution *f*; *(of assizes judge)* tournée *f*; **to make one c. of the track** faire un tour de circuit; **to make a c. of the estate** faire le tour du domaine; **to make a wide c.** faire un grand détour; *Law* **to go on c.** *(of judge)* aller en tournée
  3 *(route, places visited) (of assizes judge)* circonscription *f* de tournée, ressort *m*; *(series of venues etc)* circuit *m*; **the hottest act on the club c.** le meilleur numéro du circuit
  4 *Sport (in motor racing)* circuit *m*, parcours *m*
  ▸▸ *Elec* **c. board** plaquette *f* (de circuits imprimés); *Elec* **c. breaker** disjoncteur *m*; *Law* **c. court** = tribunal *m* en service dans les principales villes de province lors du passage du "circuit judge"; *Law* **c. judge** = juge *m* itinérant; *Sport* **c. training** programme *m* d'exercices en salle

circuitous [sə'kjuːɪtəs] **ADJ** *(route)* détourné, indirect; *(reasoning)* long et compliqué; **by c. means** par des moyens détournés *ou* indirects

circuitously [sə'kjuːɪtəslɪ] **ADV** *(to reach destination etc)* par le chemin le plus long; *(to reason etc)* avec beaucoup de circonvolutions; **the path winds c. to the summit** le chemin monte en lacets jusqu'au sommet

circuitry ['sɜːkɪtrɪ] **N** *(no pl) Electron* circuits *mpl*; **the c. on this board is really simple** le montage de cette plaquette est vraiment simple

circular ['sɜːkjʊlər] **ADJ** *(movement, argument)* circulaire

N *(letter f)* circulaire *f*, *(publicity material)* prospectus *m*; *Br Journ* **Court c.** rubrique *f* de la Cour *(décrivant les engagements de la famille royale)*
  ▸▸ *Econ* **c. flow of income** flux *m* circulaire des revenus; *Tech* **c. saw** scie *f* circulaire

circularity [sɜːkjʊ'lærɪtɪ] **N** circularité *f*

circularize ['sɜːkjʊləraɪz] **VT** *(customers etc) (letter)* envoyer une/des circulaire(s); *(publicity material)* envoyer un/des prospectus à

circulate ['sɜːkjʊleɪt] **VI** *(of rumour, person at party, money)* circuler
  VT 1 *(air, wine etc)* faire circuler **2** *(money)* mettre en circulation; *(news)* répandre, faire circuler

circulating ['sɜːkjʊleɪtɪŋ] **ADJ** circulant
  ▸▸ *Acct* **c. assets** actif *m* circulant; *Fin* **c. capital** capitaux *mpl* circulants; **c. library** *(mobile library)* bibliothèque *f* ambulante *ou* mobile; *Am (lending library)* bibliothèque de prêt

circulation [sɜːkjʊ'leɪʃən] **N 1** *(of air, liquid, news)* circulation *f*; **to put a book into c.** mettre un livre en circulation; **for private c.** *(in publishing)* hors commerce; **the memo was for internal c. only** c'était une note de service à usage interne uniquement; **newspaper with a large c.** journal à grand tirage; *Journ* **a c. of 500,000** un tirage de 500 000 exemplaires
  2 *Physiol (of blood etc)* circulation *f*; **to have poor** *or* **bad c.** avoir une mauvaise circulation; **to restore the c. in one's legs** se dégourdir les jambes
  3 *(of currency)* circulation *f* (de la monnaie); **to put forged notes into c.** mettre de faux billets en circulation; **notes in c.** billets en circulation; **to be in c.** être en circulation; *Fig* **to be in/out of c.** *(of person)* être/ne plus être dans le circuit; **to withdraw sth from c.** retirer qch de la circulation
  ▸▸ *Journ* **c. figures** chiffres *mpl* de diffusion

Note that the French word **circulation** also means **traffic**.

circulatory [sɜːkjʊ'leɪt(ə)rɪ, ˌsɜːkjʊlət(ə)rɪ] **ADJ** *Anat etc* circulatoire, de (la) circulation

circumcise ['sɜːkəmsaɪz] **VT** *(boy)* circoncire; *(girls)* exciser

circumcised ['sɜːkəmsaɪzd] **ADJ** *(boy)* circoncis; *(girl)* excisée

circumcision [sɜːkəm'sɪʒən] **N** circoncision *f*, **female c.** excision *f*, *Rel* **the C.** la (fête de la) Circoncision

circumference [sə'kʌmfərəns] **N** circonférence *f*, **to be thirty metres in c.** avoir trente mètres de circonférence

circumflex ['sɜːkəmfleks] *Gram* **N** accent *m* circonflexe
  ADJ *(accent)* circonflexe; **it's spelt with an "e" c.** ça s'écrit avec un "e" accent circonflexe

circumlocution [sɜːkəmlə'kjuːʃən] **N** circonlocution *f*, périphrase *f*, **without c.** sans ambages

circumlocutory [sɜːkəmlə'kjuːt(ə)rɪ] **ADJ** périphrastique

circumnavigate [sɜːkəm'nævɪgeɪt] **VT** faire le tour de *(par la mer)*

circumnavigation [sɜːkəmnævɪ'geɪʃən] **N** circumnavigation *f*

circumscribe ['sɜːkəmskraɪb] **VT 1** *(limit) (powers, field of operations)* limiter, restreindre **2** *Geom (circle etc)* circonscrire

circumscribed ['sɜːkəmskraɪbd] **ADJ 1** *(limited)* restreint, limité **2** *Geom (circle etc)* circonscrit

circumscription [sɜːkəm'skrɪpʃən] **N 1** *(limitation)* restriction *f*, limitation *f* **2** *Geom* circonscription *f*

circumspect ['sɜːkəmspekt] **ADJ** *(person,*

conduct) circonspect, avisé, prudent; *(speech etc)* mesuré

circumspection [sɜːkəm'spekʃən] **N** circonspection *f*

circumspectly ['sɜːkəmspektlɪ] **ADV** avec circonspection

circumstance ['sɜːkəmstəns] **N 1** *(situation) (usu pl)* **circumstances** circonstances *fpl*, **in** *or* **under the circumstances** dans ces circonstances, en de telles circonstances; **in** *or* **under no circumstances** en aucun cas, sous aucun prétexte; **it depends on the circumstances** cela dépend des circonstances, *Fam* c'est selon; **he was the victim of c.** *or* **circumstances** il a été la victime des circonstances; **due to circumstances beyond our control** en raison de circonstances indépendantes de notre volonté; **by force of circumstances** par la force des choses
  2 *(financial situation)* **in easy circumstances** à l'aise; **if his circumstances allowed** si ses moyens le permettaient
  3 **with pomp and c.** en grande cérémonie, en grand apparat

circumstantial [sɜːkəm'stænʃəl] **ADJ 1** *(incidental)* accidentel, fortuit; **it's all a bit c.** il n'y a rien de concret **2** *(detailed)* détaillé, circonstancié
  ▸▸ *Law* **c. evidence** preuves *fpl* indirectes

circumstantiate [sɜːkəm'stænʃɪeɪt] **VT** *Fml (report)* donner des détails circonstanciés sur

circumvent [sɜːkəm'vent] **VT** circonvenir; **to c. the law** contourner la loi

circumvention [sɜːkəm'venʃən] **N** *(of law etc)* contournement *m*

circus, *pl* **circuses** ['sɜːkəs, -əsɪz] **N** *(show, troupe), Antiq, Fig* cirque *m*; **to join a c.** entrer dans un cirque; *Aviat* **flying c.** parade *f* aérienne itinérante; **travelling c.** cirque forain
  ▸▸ **c. act** numéro *m* de cirque

cirrhosis [sɪ'rəʊsɪs] **N** *Med* cirrhose *f*, **c. of the liver** cirrhose du foie; **to have c.** avoir une cirrhose

cirrus, *pl* **cirri** ['sɪrəs, -raɪ] **N** *Met* cirrus *m*

CIS [siːaɪ'es] **N** *(abbr* **Commonwealth of Independent States)** CEI *f*

cisalpine [sɪs'ælpaɪn] **ADJ** cisalpin
  ▸▸ **C. Gaul** Gaule *f* cisalpine

cissy ['sɪsɪ] **N, ADJ** *Fam Pej* = **sissy**

Cistercian [sɪ'stɜːʃən] **N, ADJ** *Rel* cistercien, -ienne; **the C. Order** l'ordre *m* de Cîteaux

cistern ['sɪstən] **N** *(in attic)* réservoir *m* d'eau; *(in lavatory)* réservoir de chasse d'eau; *(underground)* citerne *f*, *(of pump)* réservoir

citadel ['sɪtədəl, -del] **N** citadelle *f*

citation [saɪ'teɪʃən] **N 1** *(from author)* citation *f* **2** *Mil* citation *f* (à l'ordre du jour) **3** *Law (summons)* citation *f* à comparaître

cite [saɪt] **VT 1** *(quote) (passage, author, example)* citer **2** *Mil (soldier for heroism)* citer **3** *Law* **to c. sb before a court** citer qn devant un tribunal

citizen ['sɪtɪzən] **N 1** *(of nation)* citoyen, -enne; *(of city, town)* habitant, -ante; **c. of the world** citoyen du monde; **a private c.** un simple particulier **2** *Am (as opposed to person in army, navy)* civil *m*
  ▸▸ *Br* **Citizens' Advice Bureau** = service *m* gratuit d'aide juridique; **c. army** armée *f* de citoyens; **c.'s arrest** = arrestation *f* effectuée par un individu en vertu du droit commun; **citizens' band (radio)** (radio *f* de la) citizen band *f*; **c. rights** droits *mpl* civiques

citizenry ['sɪtɪzənrɪ] **N** ensemble *m* des habitants

citizenship ['sɪtɪzənʃɪp] **N** *(of nation)* citoyenneté *f*, *(of city, town)* droit *m* de cité *ou* de bourgeoisie; **to be granted full c. of a**

country se voir accorder la citoyenneté d'un pays; **good c.** civisme *m*

citrate ['sɪtreɪt] N *Chem* citrate *m*

citric ['sɪtrɪk] ADJ *Chem (acid etc)* citrique

citron ['sɪtrən] N *(fruit)* cédrat *m*; *(tree)* cédratier *m*
▸▸**c. tree** cédratier

citronella [sɪtrə'nelə] N *(plant)* citronnelle *f*

citrus fruit ['sɪtrəs] Nagrume *m*

City ['sɪtɪ] N *Br* **the C.** *(district)* la Cité de Londres; *(financial world)* le monde de la finance
▸▸*Journ* **C. editor** rédacteur, -trice en chef pour les nouvelles financières; *Journ* **C. pages** pages *fpl* financières

> **City**
> La City, quartier financier de la capitale, est une circonscription administrative autonome de Londres ayant sa propre police.

city ['sɪtɪ] N (grande) ville *f*, *Lit* cité *f*; *Br* **cathedral c.** ville épiscopale, évêché *m*; **the Holy C.** la Ville sainte; **the Celestial C.** la Cité céleste; **the Eternal C.** la Ville éternelle; **the C. of Manchester** la ville de Manchester SEE GRAMMAR B7
▸▸**c. break** *(holiday)* court séjour *m* en ville; *Br* **c. centre** centre *m* de la ville, centre-ville *m*, *pl* centres-villes; **c. council** ≃ conseil *m* d'arrondissement; *Am Journ* **c. editor** rédacteur, -trice en chef pour les nouvelles locales; **c. fathers** édiles *mpl* locaux; *Am* **c. hall** hôtel *m* de ville; *Fig* **you can't win against c. hall** on ne peut pas gagner contre la bureaucratie; *Acct* **c. ledger** *(in hotels, business)* débiteurs *mpl* divers; **c. terminal** *(of airline)* terminal *m* urbain

cityscape ['sɪtɪskeɪp] N paysage *m* urbain

city-state Nétat-cité *m*, *pl* états-cités

civet ['sɪvɪt] N *(animal, scent)* civette *f*

civic ['sɪvɪk] ADJ *(authority, building)* municipal, -aux; *(duty, pride etc)* civique; **the c. authorities** les autorités *fpl* municipales
▸▸**c. centre** = centre *m* administratif d'une ville, parfois complété par des équipements de loisirs, ≃ cité *f* administrative; **c. rights** droits *mpl* civils

civics ['sɪvɪks] N *Sch* instruction *f* civique
VOIR GRAMMAIRE A10

civies ['sɪvɪz] NPL *Fam* vêtements *mpl* civils

civil ['sɪv(ə)l] ADJ **1** *(of community, non-military)* civil **2** *(polite)* poli, *Vieilli* civil; **he was very c. to me/to them** il s'est montré très aimable; **keep a c. tongue in your head!** soyez plus poli!; **that's very c. of you** c'est bien aimable (de votre part)
▸▸*Law* **c. action** action *f* civile; **c. aircraft** appareil *m* de l'aviation civile; **c. airline** compagnie *f* d'aviation civile; **c. aviation** aviation *f* civile; **c. commotion** agitation *f* sociale; *Mil* **c. defence** protection *f* civile; **c. engineer** ingénieur *m* des travaux publics; **c. engineering** génie *m* civil; **c. law** droit *m* civil; *Br* **C. List** liste *f* civile *(allouée à la famille royale britannique)*; *Law* **c. proceedings** action *f* civile; **c. rights** droits *mpl* civils *ou* civiques; *Admin* **c. servant** fonctionnaire *mf*; *Admin* **c. service** fonction *f* publique, administration *f*; **c. war** guerre *f* civile

civilian [sɪ'vɪljən] N civil, -ile
ADJ civil; **in c. life** dans le civil
▸▸**c. clothes** tenue *f* civile

civility [sɪ'vɪlɪtɪ] N courtoisie *f*, politesse *f*; **exchange of civilities** échange *m* d'amabilités

civilization [sɪvɪlaɪ'zeɪʃən] N civilisation *f*, *Fam* **it's miles from c.** c'est à des kilomètres de toute civilisation

civilize ['sɪvɪlaɪz] VT civiliser

civilized ['sɪvɪlaɪzd] ADJ *(life, people)* civilisé; **the little girl is really quite c.** la petite fille est très bien élevée; **they have real coffee in their office – very c.** ils ont du vrai café dans leur bureau – la classe!; **their divorce was a very c. affair** ils ont divorcé comme des gens civilisés; **let's be c. about this** restons civilisés; **you can't eat in a c. manner?** tu ne peux pas manger convenablement?

civilizing ['sɪvɪlaɪzɪŋ] ADJ **the c. influence of ...** l'influence civilisatrice de ...; **the new teacher has had a c. influence on them** le nouveau professeur semble les avoir calmés

civvies ['sɪvɪz] NPL *Fam* vêtements *mpl* civils

civvy ['sɪvɪ] ADJ *Fam* **to get back to c. street** rentrer dans le civil; **on c. street** dans le civil

CJD [siːdʒeɪ'diː] N *(abbr* **Creutzfeldt-Jakob disease)** MCJ *f*; **new variant C.** nouveau variant *m* de MCJ

cl *(abbr* **centilitre)** cl

clack [klæk] N *(sound)* bruit *m* sec, claquement *m*; **click-c.** clic-clac *m*
VI *(make sound)* cliqueter

clacking ['klækɪŋ] N *(noise)* claquement *m*

clad¹ [klæd] PT, PP *see* **clothe**

clad² VT *(-dd-) Tech (wall, metal plate etc)* revêtir (**with** de)

cladding ['klædɪŋ] N *Tech* revêtement *m*

claim [kleɪm] N **1** *(demand) (for damages, compensation etc)* revendication *f*, réclamation *f*, **to make** *or* **put in a c. for damages** demander une indemnité, réclamer des dommages-intérêts; **to put in a c.** *(in insurance)* demander à être indemnisé; **pay c.** revendications *fpl* salariales
2 *(right)* droit *m* (**to sth** à qch); **legal c. to sth** titre *m* juridique à qch; **to put in a c.** faire valoir ses droits; **to have a c. to sth** avoir droit à qch; **what is her c. to the throne?** quel est son titre à la couronne?; **they have no c. to the land** ils n'ont aucun droit sur le terrain; **to lay c. to** *(property etc)* prétendre à, revendiquer son droit à; *(skills)* s'attribuer; *Fig* **I have many claims on my time** je suis très pris; **his only c. to fame** la seule chose notable qu'il ait faite
3 *(assertion)* déclaration *f*, **she makes no c. to being original** elle ne prétend pas être originale; **exaggerated claims have been made for this medicine** on a exagéré l'efficacité de ce médicament
4 *Min* concession *f* (minière)
VT **1** *(demand as a right) (right, territory)* revendiquer; *(respect, attention)* exiger, demander; **to c. sth from sb** réclamer qch à qn; **to c. damages** réclamer des dommages et intérêts; **to c. a privilege** prétendre à un privilège; **have you claimed your allowance?** est-ce que tu as réclamé ton allocation?; **to c. the right to do sth** revendiquer le droit de faire qch; **to c. responsibility for an attack** *(of terrorist)* revendiquer un attentat
2 *(assert)* **to c. that ...** prétendre *ou* affirmer que ... + *ind*; **he claims knowledge of their plans** il prétend *ou* affirme qu'il connaît leurs projets; **to c. acquaintance with sb** prétendre connaître qn; **he claims to be an expert** il prétend être expert; **I don't c. to be an expert** je ne prétends pas être un expert
3 *(collect, take) (baggage)* récupérer; *(lost property)* réclamer; **has anyone arrived to c. her?** *(lost child)* est-ce que quelqu'un est venu la chercher?; **the sea claims many victims** la mer fait de nombreuses victimes
VI *(in insurance)* demander à être indemnisé

▸▸**claims adjuster** répartiteur *m*; **claims book** livre *m* des réclamations; **claims cover** garantie *f* de recours; **c. form** *(for insurance)* formulaire *m* de déclaration de sinistre; *(for expenses)* note *f* de frais
▸ **claim back** VT SEP *(expenses, cost)* se faire rembourser

claimant ['kleɪmənt] N *(for social security, insurance etc)* demandeur, -eresse; *(to throne)* prétendant, -ante; **rightful c.** ayant droit *m*, *pl* ayants droit

clairvoyance [kleə'vɔɪəns] N **1** *(second sight)* voyance *f*, don *m* de seconde vue **2** *(shrewdness)* clairvoyance *f*

clairvoyant [kleə'vɔɪənt] ADJ **1** doué de seconde vue **2** *(shrewd)* clairvoyant
N voyant, -ante, extra-lucide *mf*, *pl* extra-lucides

clam [klæm] N **1** *(mollusc)* palourde *f*, clam *m*; **to shut up like a c.** refuser de dire quoi que ce soit **2** *Am Fam (dollar)* dollar *m*
▸▸*Culin* **c. chowder** = potage *m* épais aux palourdes
▸ **clam up** VI *(-mm-) Fam* se fermer comme une huître; **don't c. up on me** parle-moi

clambake ['klæmbeɪk] N *Am (picnic)* = pique-nique *m* où l'on mange des fruits de mer; *Fam (noisy gathering)* grande réunion *f* tapageuse

clamber ['klæmbər] N **it was quite a c.** c'était une sacrée grimpette
VI escalader; **to c. up a wall** escalader un mur; **he clambered over the pile of bricks** il a escaladé le tas de briques; **they clambered out of the car** ils se sont extirpés de la voiture

clamminess ['klæmɪnɪs] N *(of skin)* moiteur *f* froide; *(of air)* humidité *f* froide

clammy ['klæmɪ] ADJ *(hands, skin)* moite; *(atmosphere)* froid et humide

clamor ['klæmər] N, VI *Am* = **clamour**

clamorous ['klæmərəs] ADJ *esp Lit* bruyant; *(crowd)* vociférant

clamorously ['klæmərəslɪ] ADV *esp Lit* bruyamment

clamour ['klæmər] N **1** *(noise)* clameur *f*, cris *mpl*, vociférations *fpl* **2** *(protest)* tollé *m*; **there was a great c.** ça a été un tollé général
VI vociférer, crier; **to c. for sth** réclamer *ou* demander qch à grands cris

clamp [klæmp] N **1** crampon *m*, presse *f*, *(of vice)* mordache *f*, *(for wire)* pince *f*, *Surg* clamp *m*; *Aut* **(wheel) c.** sabot *m* de Denver **2** *Agr (for potatoes)* silo *m* (temporaire)
VT **1** *(fasten)* cramponner; *(precision instrument)* bloquer; *Surg* clamper; **to c. two pieces of wood together** cramponner deux morceaux de bois **2** *(car)* mettre un sabot à **3** *Agr (potatoes)* mettre en silo
▸ **clamp down** VT SEP fixer par un crampon
VI *Fam (become stricter)* sévir (**on sb/sth** contre qn/qch); **the police are clamping down on illegal parking** la police sévit contre *ou* devient plus sévère avec les automobilistes en stationnement interdit

clampdown ['klæmpdaʊn] N renforcement *m* des mesures (de répression) (**on** contre); **as a result of the c.** suite au mesures de répression

clamping ['klæmpɪŋ] N *(of cars)* immobilisation *f* des voitures au moyen de sabots de Denver

clamshell ['klæmʃel] N *(mobile phone)* téléphone *m* portable avec couvercle

clan [klæn] N *Scot (of tribe)* clan *m*; *Fig* bande *f*, clique *f*; **the head of the c.** le chef de *ou* du clan; *Fig* **gathering of the clans** réunion *f* d'adhérents *ou* de partisans
▸▸**c. name** nom *m* du clan; **c. tartan** couleurs *fpl* du clan

clandestine [klæn'destɪn] ADJ clandestin

clandestinely [klæn'destɪnlɪ] ADV clandestinement

clang [klæŋ] N son *m* ou bruit *m* métallique VI retentir, résonner, rendre un son métallique; **the gate clanged shut** le portail s'est refermé avec un bruit métallique VT (*bell etc*) faire résonner; **she clanged the gate shut** elle ferma le portail bruyamment

clanger ['klæŋər] N *Br Fam* bourde *f*; **to drop a c.** faire une gaffe ou une boulette, gaffer

clank [klæŋk] N (*of chains etc*) bruit *m* métallique VI (*of chain, bucket*) rendre un bruit métallique

clannish ['klænɪʃ] ADJ *Pej* (*person*) qui a l'esprit de clan; (*group*) fermé

clansman, *pl* **clansmen** ['klænzmən, -mən] N = membre *m* d'un clan

clanswoman, *pl* **clanswomen** ['klænzwʊman, -wɪmɪn] N = membre *f* d'un clan

clap[1] [klæp] N (*with hands*) **to give sb a c.** applaudir qn; **to give sb a big c.** applaudir qn bien fort; **she got a c. for that** on l'a applaudie pour ça; **to give sb a c. on the back** donner une tape sur le dos de qn; **a c. of thunder** un coup de tonnerre VT (-pp-) **1 to c. one's hands** battre des mains; **to c. a performer** applaudir un artiste; **to c. sb on the back** donner à qn une tape sur le dos **2** (*put*) mettre, *Fam* coller; **to c. sb in irons** mettre qn aux fers; **to c. sb in prison** fourrer qn en prison; *Fam* **to c. eyes on sb/sth** voir qn/qch; *Fam* **I've never clapped eyes on her before** je ne l'ai jamais vue de ma vie VI (*of person, audience etc*) applaudir
▸ **clap on** VT SEP **he clapped his hat on** il a enfoncé son chapeau sur sa tête; *Naut* **to c. on more sail** augmenter de toile

clap[2] N *Sl* (*gonorrhoea*) chaude-pisse *f*; **he's got a dose of the c.** il a la chaude-pisse; **to give sb the c.** passer la chaude-pisse à qn

clapboard ['klæpbɔːd] N *Am Constr* planche *f* à clin; (*house*) maison *f* à clins; **c. house** maison à clins

Clapham ['klæpəm] N *Br* **the man on the C. omnibus** le citoyen lambda; **it's like C. Junction in here** c'est un vrai moulin ici

clapometer [klæ'pɒmɪtər] N *TV etc* applaudimètre *m*

clapped out [klæpt] ADJ *Br Fam* (*person*) crevé, éreinté; (*car, television etc*) pourri

clapper ['klæpər] N **1** (*of bell*) battant *m* **2** *Agr* (*for scaring birds*) moulin *m* à claquet; *Br Fam* **like the clappers** (*to work*) comme un enragé; (*to run*) comme un dératé; (*to drive*) comme un fou
▸▸ **c. valve** (soupape *f* à) clapet *m*

clapperboard ['klæpəbɔːd] N *TV, Cin* clap *m*, claquette *f*

clapping ['klæpɪŋ] N (*applause*) applaudissements *mpl*

claptrap ['klæptræp] N **1** *Fam* sottises *fpl*; **to talk c.** raconter des histoires; **what c.!** quel tissu d'âneries ou de sottises! **2** *TV, Cin* (*clapperboard*) clap *m*

claque [klæk] N *Theat* claque *f*

claret ['klærət] N **1** (*wine*) bordeaux *m* rouge **2** (*colour*) bordeaux *m inv* ADJ (*coloured*) bordeaux *inv*

clarification [klærɪfɪ'keɪʃən] N **1** (*further explanation*) clarification *f*, (*of question etc*) éclaircissement *m*, élucidation *f*; **to ask for c.** demander des éclaircissements **2** (*of butter, stock*) clarification *f*; (*of wine*) collage *m*

clarify ['klærɪfaɪ] VT **1** (*thinking*) clarifier; (*mind, views, opinions*) éclaircir; (*question*) élucider **2** (*butter, stock*) clarifier; (*wine*) coller

VI (*of liquid, one's thoughts*) se clarifier, s'éclaircir

clarinet [klærɪ'net] N clarinette *f*

clarinettist [klærɪ'netɪst] N clarinettiste *mf*

clarion ['klærɪən] N *Lit* clairon *m*; *Fig* **the speech was a c. call to ...** le discours était un appel à ...

clarity ['klærɪtɪ] N clarté *f*

clash [klæʃ] N **1** (*noise*) fracas *m*; (*of swords etc*) cliquetis *m*; (*of cymbals*) son *m* assourdissant **2** (*conflict*) (*of colours, styles*) discordance *f*, (*of opinions*) conflit *m*, choc *m*; (*of doctrines*) opposition *f*, (*between people*) affrontement *m*; (*between mobs*) échauffourée *f*, **a c. of interests** un conflit d'intérêts; **we had a slight c. of opinions** nous avons eu un léger désaccord; **clashes on the border** des affrontements à la frontière; **there was a c. (between them) over the methods to be used** il y a eu un conflit entre eux quant aux méthodes à utiliser; **c. of personalities, personality c.** incompatibilité *f* de caractères VI **1** (*of cymbals*) résonner (bruyamment); (*of swords etc*) s'entrechoquer **2** (*come into conflict*) entrer en conflit, s'affronter; **police clashed with protestors** il y a eu des heurts entre la police et les manifestants; **they clashed over how to solve the problem** ils sont entrés en conflit quant à la manière de résoudre le problème; **their personalities c.** leurs personnalités se heurtent, il y a incompatibilité entre leurs caractères **3** (*of colours*) jurer, détonner; (*of evidence, explanations etc*) ne pas correspondre; (*of literary styles*) être discordant; (*of events, appointments*) tomber le même jour/la même heure VT (*cymbals*) faire résonner

clashing ['klæʃɪŋ] ADJ **1** (*sound*) bruyant, retentissant **2** (*opinions*) opposé; (*colours, styles*) discordant

clasp [klɑːsp] N **1** (*fastener*) (*on brooch, medal etc*) agrafe *f*, (*on book, necklace, handbag*) fermoir *m*; **2** (*grip*) étreinte *f* VT **1** (*fasten*) (*bracelet etc*) fermer **2** (*grip*) (*in hand*) serrer; (*in arms*) (*person*) étreindre, enlacer; (*object*) prendre dans ses bras; **to be clasped in each other's arms** se tenir étroitement enlacés; **to c. sb's hand** serrer la main à qn; **to c. one's hands** joindre les mains; **to c. one's knees** entourer ses genoux de ses bras
▸▸ **c. knife** couteau *m* pliant

class [klɑːs] N **1** (*in social hierarchy*) classe *f* **2** *Fam* (*quality*) classe *f*; **to have c.** avoir de la classe **3** *Sch* (*lesson*) cours *m*; (*group of pupils*) classe *f*, **the French c.** le cours de français; **evening c.** cours du soir; **day release classes** scolarité *f* à temps partiel; **in c.** en classe **4** *Am Sch* (*students in year*) promotion *f*, **the c. of '89** la promotion 1989 **5** (*category*) catégorie *f*, classe *f*, *Rail, Aviat, Naut, Biol* classe; **to be in a c. of one's own, to be in a c. by oneself** (*of person, thing*) être unique, être de loin le/la meilleur(e); *Iron* être imbattable; **what c. are you travelling?** en quelle classe est-ce que vous voyagez?; *Br Univ* **what c. (of) degree did you get?** quelle mention est-ce que tu as eu (à ton diplôme)?; **of Olympic c.** digne de participer aux Jeux olympiques ADJ *Fam* (*excellent*) classe *inv*; **a c. car** une voiture classe; **a c. player** un joueur hors pair; **she's a real c. act** elle est vraiment classe VT classer; **to c. sb/sth with ...** assimiler qn/qch à ...; **classed first** classé premier
▸▸ *Am Law* **c. action** recours *m* collectif en justice; **c. distinctions** distinctions *fpl* entre les classes; **c. prejudice** préjugés *mpl* so-

ciaux; **c. struggle** lutte *f* des classes; **c. traitor** personne *f* qui renie ses origines sociales; **c. war** lutte des classes

class-conscious ADJ conscient des différences de classe

class-consciousness N conscience *f* des différences de classe

classic ['klæsɪk] ADJ classique; **c. records of the sixties** des classiques de la musique des années soixante; *Fam* **a c. example** un exemple classique ou typique N (*book etc*) classique *m*; *Horseracing* classique *f*, **a c. of romantic poetry** un classique de la poésie romantique; *Fam* **it was a c.!** ça payait!; **classics** (*usu with sing verb*) (*subject*) les langues *fpl* classiques, les humanités *fpl*; **a classics degree** une licence en latin et (en) grec
▸▸ *Horseracing* **c. race** course *f* classique

classical ['klæsɪk(ə)l] ADJ **1** (*civilization etc*) de l'antiquité; **the c. world** le monde de l'antiquité; **in c. times** dans l'antiquité; **c. Greece** la Grèce antique; **c. scholar** humaniste *mf* **2** *Mus, Art, Liter etc* classique
▸▸ *Econ* **c. economics** économie *f* classique

classically ['klæsɪk(ə)lɪ] ADV classiquement; **c. trained** (*pianist etc*) ayant reçu une formation classique

classicism ['klæsɪsɪz(ə)m] N **1** *Art, Liter, Archit etc* classicisme *m* **2** *Ling* tour *m* ou locution *f* emprunté(e) aux langues classiques

classicist ['klæsɪsɪst] N humaniste *mf*; (*advocate of classical studies*) partisan, -ane des études classiques

classification [klæsɪfɪ'keɪʃən] N **1** (*action*) (*of plants, animals*) classification *f*, (*of papers, competitors, books etc*) classement *m* **2** (*category*) classification *f*, classe *f*

classified ['klæsɪfaɪd] ADJ **1** (*arranged*) classé **2** (*secret*) (*document, information*) confidentiel
▸▸ *Journ* **c. advertisements** petites annonces *fpl*; *Sport* **c. results** résultats *mpl* et classements *mpl*

classifieds ['klæsɪfaɪdz] NPL *Journ* **the c.** les petites annonces *fpl*

classifier ['klæsɪfaɪər] N (*person*) classificateur, -trice

classify ['klæsɪfaɪ] VT **1** classer; **their music is classified as jazz** leur musique est classée comme étant du jazz **2** (*make secret*) (*document etc*) classer confidentiel

classless ['klɑːslɪs] ADJ (*society*) sans classes; (*accent*) neutre

classmate ['klɑːsmeɪt] N **1** *Sch* (*in same class*) camarade *mf* de classe **2** *Am Univ* (*in same year*) camarade *mf* de promotion

classroom ['klɑːsruːm] N *Sch* (salle *f* de) classe *f*

classy ['klɑːsɪ] ADJ *Fam* (*person*) qui a de la classe, classieux; (*restaurant*) chic *inv*, (*car, hotel*) de luxe

clatter ['klætər] N bruit *m*, vacarme *m*, fracas *m*; (*of typewriters*) claquement *m*; (*of machine*) ferraillement *m*; **the c. of dishes** les bruits de vaisselle VI faire du bruit; **we could hear him clattering about in the attic** on l'entendait qui faisait un bruit de tous les diables dans le grenier; **the old cart clattered by** le vieux chariot est passé en faisant du bruit; **to come clattering down** dégringoler avec fracas VT faire résonner; **don't c. your spoons!** ne faites pas de bruit avec vos cuillers!

Claudius ['klɔːdɪəs] N *Hist* Claude

clause [klɔːz] N **1** *Law* (*of treaty, law*) clause *f*, article *m*; (*of will*) disposition *f*, **c. of a/the contract** clause contractuelle **2** *Gram* proposition *f* VOIR GRAMMAIRE A4; B2

claused bill [klɔːzd] N *Com* connaissement *m* clausé

claustrophobia [klɔːstrəˈfəʊbɪə, klɒs-] N claustrophobie *f*

claustrophobic [klɔːstrəˈfəʊbɪk, klɒs-] ADJ *(person)* claustrophobe; **this room feels quite c.** cette pièce donne une impression de claustrophobie; **I feel c.** j'ai un sentiment de claustrophobie

clavichord [ˈklævɪkɔːd] N *Mus* clavicorde *m*

clavicle [ˈklævɪk(ə)l] N *Anat* clavicule *f*

claw [klɔː] N **1** *(of cat etc)* griffe *f*, *(of bird of prey)* serre *f*, *(of lobster)* pince *f*; **to sharpen its claws** *(of cat)* se faire les griffes; **to show its/one's claws** *(of cat), Fig* rentrer ses griffes; **to draw in its/one's claws** *(of cat), Fig* rentrer ses griffes, faire patte de velours; **c.-footed** *(table etc)* à pied de griffon; *Fig* **to get one's claws into sb** *(trap)* mettre le grappin sur qn; **she's got her claws in me** *(dislikes me)* elle a une dent contre moi **2** *Tech (of hammer)* panne *f* fendue
▪ VT *(scratch)* griffer, donner un coup de griffe à; *Fig* **to c. one's way to the top** arriver au sommet par tous les moyens
▪ VI **to c. at sth** *(of cat)* saisir qch avec ses griffes, s'accrocher à qch; *(grip)* s'accrocher à qch, agripper qch; *(try to grip)* essayer de s'accrocher à qch *ou* d'agripper qch; **she clawed at my face** *(scratched me)* elle m'a griffé au visage; *(tried to scratch me)* elle a essayé de me griffer au visage
▸ ▸ **c. hammer** marteau *m* à pied-de-biche, marteau fendu; **c. marks** griffures *fpl*
▸ **claw back** VT SEP **1** *Fin (expenditure)* récupérer **2** *(regain)* regagner péniblement; **she clawed her way back to a prominent position** à force de persévérance, elle a réussi à regagner une position influente

clawback [ˈklɔːbæk] N *Fin* récupération *f*

clay [kleɪ] N argile *f*, (terre-)glaise *f*, **(modelling) c.** pâte *f* à modeler; *Lit* **idol with feet of c.** idole aux pieds d'argile; *Lit* **mortal c.** le corps humain; *Tennis* **to play on c.** jouer sur terre battue; *Tennis* **to be good on c.** jouer bien sur la terre battue
▸ ▸ *Tennis* **c. court** court *m* en terre battue; **c. pigeon** pigeon *m* d'argile *ou* de ball-trap; *Am Fam Fig (sitting duck)* cible *f* facile; **c. pigeon shooting** ball-trap *m*, *pl* ball-traps; **c. pipe** pipe *f* de *ou* en terre; **c. pit** glaisière *f*; **c. soil** terre *f* glaise

clayey [ˈkleɪɪ] ADJ *(soil)* argileux, glaiseux

claymation [kleɪˈmeɪʃən] N *Br Cin, TV* = animation *f* de figurines en pâte à modeler

claymore [ˈkleɪmɔːr] N *Scot Hist* = sabre *m* écossais à deux tranchants

---

CLEAN [kliːn]

ADJ	propre **1** ▪ net **1, 2** ▪ pur **1**
ADV	complètement
N	nettoyage
VT	nettoyer ▪ vider
VI	se nettoyer **2** ▪ nettoyer **3**

ADJ 1 propre, net; *(clothes)* propre; *(water)* pur, propre; *(sheet of paper)* blanc, *f* blanche; *(break)* franc, net; *(wound)* pas infecté; *(joke)* décent; **to keep sth c.** tenir qch propre; *Fam* **keep it c.!** *(the joke, story etc)* pas de grossièretés!; *Fig Fam* **to be c.** *(innocent)* n'avoir rien à se reprocher; *(without incriminating material)* n'avoir rien sur soi; *(not carrying drugs)* ne pas avoir de drogue sur soi; *(not carrying weapons)* ne pas être armé; *(no longer addicted to drugs)* avoir décroché; **good c. fun** jeu *m* innocent; **to make a c. break** *(in relationship)* en finir une bonne fois pour toutes; *Fig* **to show sb a c. pair of heels** *(run away)* s'enfuir devant qn; **he's showing the other runners a c. pair of heels** il a pris une belle avance sur les autres

concurrents; **to make a c. copy of sth** mettre qch au net; **he made a c. sweep of the medals/prizes** il a raflé toutes les médailles/ tous les prix; **c. (driving) licence** permis *m* de conduire vierge; *Com* **c. on board** net de réserves à bord; **c. living** vie *f* saine; **the doctor gave him a c. bill of health** le docteur l'a trouvé en parfaite santé
2 *(sharp, well-defined)* **c. (out)lines** contours *mpl* nets; **car with c. lines** voiture aux lignes élégantes
3 *Sport Fam (honest) (player, boxer)* fair-play *inv*; **qui joue franc jeu**
▪ ADV *Fam (completely)* **I c. forgot** j'ai complètement oublié; **they got c. away** ils se sont échappés sans laisser de traces; **we're c. out of sugar** nous n'avons plus de sucre du tout; **to cut c. through sth** couper *ou* traverser qch de part en part; **to come c.** avouer, dire toute la vérité
▪ N nettoyage *m*; **to give sth a c.** nettoyer qch
▪ VT *(floor, house etc), Med (sore, ulcer)* nettoyer; *Culin (fish, poultry)* vider; *(boiler)* décrasser; **to c. one's teeth** se laver les dents; **to c. one's nails** se nettoyer *ou* se curer les ongles; **to c. the mud off one's shoes** enlever la boue de ses chaussures; **to c. one's plate** *(eat everything on it)* finir son assiette; *Am* **to c. house** faire le ménage
▪ VI **1** *(do the cleaning)* faire le ménage
2 *(of pan etc)* se nettoyer
3 *(of cleaning product, detergent)* nettoyer
▸ ▸ **c. bill** *Fin* effet *m* libre, traite *f* libre; *Com* connaissement *m* net; *St Exch* **c. float** taux *mpl* de change libres *ou* flottants; *Typ* **c. proof** *(with few corrections)* épreuve *f* peu chargée; *(final)* épreuve pour bon à tirer; **c. room** *Med* pièce *f* aseptisée; *Comput* salle *f* blanche
▸ **clean out** VT SEP **1** *(cupboard etc)* nettoyer; *(furnace, boiler)* curer, décrasser; *(ditch)* vidanger
2 *Fam (leave without money)* nettoyer, laisser sans un rond; **they cleaned out the safe** ils ont vidé le coffre; **cleaned out** *(penniless)* nettoyé (à sec), fauché
3 *(buy, take all of)* **to c. a shop out of sugar** dévaliser un magasin de son stock de sucre
▸ **clean up** VT SEP **1** *(dirt etc)* enlever; *(room etc)* nettoyer; *(make less polluting) (engine)* dépolluer; *Fig (television)* assainir; **to c. oneself up** se débarbouiller; *Fig* **to c. up a town** *(get rid of enemy, gangsters etc)* nettoyer une ville; **to c. up one's act** *(of lewd comedian)* rendre son spectacle moins choquant; *(of corrupt or inefficient organization)* faire le ménage; *(of unsatisfactory employee, pupil)* s'améliorer
2 *Am Sl (obtain)* **to c. up a thousand dollars** gagner *ou* ramasser mille dollars
▪ VI **1** *(in room, building etc)* nettoyer; *(wash oneself)* se débarbouiller
2 *(put back in order)* nettoyer, ranger, remettre tout en ordre; **he expects us to c. up after him** il compte sur nous pour nettoyer après lui
3 *(repair damage)* réparer les dégâts
4 *Fam (make a lot of money)* ramasser une fortune

clean-cut ADJ *(lines)* d'une grande netteté; *(man)* à l'apparence très soignée

cleaner [ˈkliːnər] N **1** *(person)* employé, -ée du service de nettoyage; *(in home)* personne *f* qui fait le ménage; *(woman)* femme *f* de ménage; **(dry) c.** teinturier, -ière; **to take sth to the c.'s** donner qch à nettoyer *ou* au nettoyage; *Fam* **to take sb to the c.'s** *(cheat)* nettoyer qn, plumer qn; *(defeat)* battre qn à plates coutures **2** *(device, machine)* **(vacuum) c.** aspirateur *m*; **pipe c.** cure-pipe *m*, *pl* cure-pipes **3** *(product)* produit *m* nettoyant *ou* pour nettoyer; *(for clothes)* détachant *m*

cleaning [ˈkliːnɪŋ] N nettoyage *m*; *(in household)* ménage *m*; *(of boiler)* décrassage *m*; *Culin (of fish)* vidage *m*
▸ ▸ **c. fluid** produit *m* nettoyant; **c. lady** femme *f* de ménage; **c. materials** produits *mpl* d'entretien; **c. staff** personnel *m* de nettoyage; **c. up** *(of room), Fig (of neighbourhood)* nettoyage *m*; *(of exhaust gases)* dépollution *f*; **c. woman** femme de ménage

clean-limbed [kliːnˈlɪmd] ADJ bien proportionné

cleanliness [ˈklenlɪnɪs] N propreté *f*; **c. of habit** habitudes *fpl* de propreté; *Prov* **c. is next to godliness** la propreté du corps s'apparente à la pureté de l'âme

clean-living ADJ *(person)* réglé, qui mène une vie réglée

cleanly[1] [ˈkliːnlɪ] ADV proprement, nettement; **to break c.** se casser net

cleanly[2] [ˈklenlɪ] ADJ *(person)* propre (par habitude)

cleanness [ˈkliːnnɪs] N *(of habits, language, apartment etc)* propreté *f*; *(of water)* pureté *f*; *(of lines)* netteté *f*, pureté

clean-out N nettoyage *m*; **to give a room a c.** nettoyer une pièce

clean-room clothing N *Comput* vêtements *mpl* de salle blanche

cleanse [klenz] VT *(face)* démaquiller; *(wound)* nettoyer; *(blood)* purifier; *(air)* épurer; *Arch, Lit (heart, soul)* purifier

cleanser [ˈklenzər] N *(for skin)* démaquillant *m*

clean-shaven ADJ *(man, face)* glabre

cleansing [ˈklenzɪŋ] N *(of face)* démaquillage *m*; *(of blood, soul)* purification *f*
▸ ▸ **c. cream** crème *f* démaquillante; *Br Admin* **c. department** service *m* du nettoyage; **c. lotion, c. milk** *(for skin)* lait *m* démaquillant; **c. pads** disques *mpl* démaquillants

cleanup [ˈkliːnʌp] N *(of room), Fig (town)* nettoyage *m*; **to give sth a c.** nettoyer qch

---

CLEAR [klɪər]

ADJ	clair **1–3** ▪ tranquille **1** ▪ net **2, 3, 5** ▪ évident **2** ▪ certain **4** ▪ libre **6**
VT	débarrasser **1** ▪ innocenter **2** ▪ franchir **6** ▪ autoriser **9** ▪ clarifier **11**
VI	s'éclaircir **1**

ADJ 1 *(sky, complexion, eye, sound etc)* clair; *(weather)* clair, dégagé; *(water)* clair, limpide; **on a c. day** par temps clair; *TV* **the picture was very c.** l'image était très nette; **to have c. skin** avoir la peau nette; **a c. conscience** une conscience tranquille; **my conscience is c.** j'ai la conscience tranquille; **c. voice** voix *f* claire *ou* nette
2 *(unmistakeable, manifest)* clair, net; *(sign)* évident; **a c. case of bribery** un cas manifeste de corruption; **the meaning of the sentence was c.** le sens de la phrase était clair; **to make one's meaning** *or* **oneself c.** se faire comprendre; **have I made myself c.?** est-ce que je me suis bien fait comprendre?; **to make it c. to sb that ...** faire bien comprendre à qn que ...; **she made it quite c. that ...** elle lui/nous/*etc* a bien fait comprendre que ...; **the letter doesn't make it c. when they will arrive** la lettre n'indique pas clairement quand ils vont arriver; **I want to be quite c. on this point** je tiens à ce qu'il n'y ait aucun malentendu sur ce point; **is that c.?** *(do you understand?)* c'est clair?; **it is c. that ...** il est clair *ou* évident que ...; **it was not c. who had won** on ne savait pas exactement qui avait gagné; **it is not yet c. whether ...** on ne sait pas encore si ...; **as c. as daylight** *or* **crystal** clair comme le jour *ou* comme de l'eau de roche

3 *(not confused)* *(description, explanation, argument, style)* clair, net; *(reasoning)* lucide, clair; *(instructions)* clair; **c. thinker/ mind** esprit *m* lucide; **c. thinking is essential** la clarté de pensée est essentielle; **to keep a c. head** garder les idées claires

4 *(certain)* **to be c. about sth** être certain de qch; **are you c. about what you have to do?** es-tu sûr de ce que tu as à faire?; **there's something I'm not c. about** il reste quelque chose dont je ne suis pas sûr; **I wasn't c. what she meant** je n'étais pas sûr de ce qu'elle voulait dire

5 *(unqualified)* **c. profit** bénéfice *m* net; **a c. ten thousand pounds a year** un revenu net de dix mille livres; **c. majority** majorité *f* absolue; *Sport* **c. winner** vainqueur *m* incontesté; **there wasn't a c. winner** on ne pouvait pas dire qui l'avait emporté; *Law* **three c. days** trois jours francs

6 *(unobstructed, free)* libre; *(view etc)* dégagé; **his latest X-rays are c.** ses dernières radios ne montrent rien d'anormal; **to be c. of sth** *(rid of)* être débarrassé de qch; **he was c. of all signs of the disease** il ne montrait aucun symptôme de la maladie; **we were c. of the last checkpoint** nous avions passé le dernier poste de contrôle; **the sea is c. of ice** la mer est libre; **the exhaust pipe is 30 cm c. of the ground** le tuyau d'échappement est à 30 cm du sol; *Aviat* **you are c. to take off** vous êtes autorisé à *ou* vous pouvez décoller; **all c.!** *(there's no traffic, no-one is watching)* vous pouvez y aller, la voie est libre; *Mil* fin d'alerte

ADV we could hear them c. across the valley on les entendait de l'autre bout de la vallée; **to jump five centimetres c. of the bar** franchir la barre avec cinq centimètres de reste; **to hang c. of the ground** être suspendu de manière à ne pas toucher le sol; **to stand c.** s'écarter (**of** de); **stand c. of the doors!** attention aux portes!; *Rail* ≃ attention au départ!; **to keep** *or* **steer c. of sth** éviter qch; *Naut* **to steer c. of a rock** passer au large d'un écueil; **they pulled him c. of the wreckage** ils l'ont dégagé de l'épave; **she was thrown c. of the car** elle a été éjectée de la voiture; **to get c. of sb** échapper à qn; **to get c.** s'échapper; *Sport* **to punch the ball c.** écarter le ballon d'un coup de poing

N 1 to be in the c. *(of person)* *(free from suspicion)* être lavé de tout soupçon; *(free from debt)* ne pas avoir de dettes; *(out of danger)* être hors de danger

2 *Mil etc* **despatch sent in c.** *(not coded)* dépêche *f* en clair

VT 1 *(free of obstacles)* *(road, area, entrance)* dégager; *(room etc)* débarrasser, désencombrer; *(forest)* défricher; *(streets, room)* *(of people)* faire évacuer; *(pipe)* déboucher; *Law* **to c. the court** faire évacuer la salle; **to c. one's conscience** décharger sa conscience; **to c. one's throat** se racler la gorge; **he cleared a space on the floor** il a dégagé un espace sur le sol; **they cleared 20 acres of forest** ils ont défriché 8 hectares de forêt; **to c. a way** *or* **a passage for sb** frayer un passage à qn; *Fig* **to c. the way for sth** ouvrir la voie pour qch; **to c. a way for oneself** se frayer un passage; **to c. the table** *(after meal)* débarrasser la table; **to c. one's desk** *(tidy)* débarrasser son bureau; *(complete pending tasks)* régler les affaires en suspens; *Naut* **to c. the decks for action** faire le branle-bas de combat; *Fig* **to c. the decks** déblayer le terrain; *Comput* **to c. the screen** vider l'écran; **the rain had cleared the streets** la pluie avait vidé les rues; **to c. slums** assainir des taudis; *Mil* **to c. an area of mines** déminer un terrain; **fresh air clears the head** un peu d'air frais vous éclaircit les idées; *Com* **to c. goods** *(in sale etc)* solder *ou* liquider des marchandises; *Rail* **to c. the line**

dégager la voie; *(after an accident)* déblayer la voie

2 *(exonerate)* disculper, innocenter; **he was cleared of all blame** il a été entièrement disculpé; **to c. oneself** se justifier; **to c. one's name** se disculper; **to clear sb's name** disculper qn

3 *(make less dense)* *(fog etc)* dissiper; **to c. the air** *(of thunderstorm)* rafraîchir l'air; *(of discussion etc)* mettre les choses au point

4 *(remove)* **to c. sth from** *or* **off sth** enlever qch de qch; **to c. all this out of here** débarrassez-moi de tout cela

5 *(empty)* **to c. the postbox** lever le courrier; *Med* **to c. the bowels** purger les intestins

6 *(go past, over etc without touching)* **to c. a barrier (by 10 centimetres)** franchir une barrière (avec 10 centimètres de marge); **to c. a ditch** sauter *ou* franchir un fossé; *Naut* **to c. the harbour** sortir du port, quitter le port; **the ship just cleared the bottom** le bateau a évité le fond de justesse

7 *(make a profit of)* **to c. 10%** faire un bénéfice net de 10%; **I cleared a hundred pounds** j'ai touché cent livres net

8 *Banking* *(cheque)* compenser, virer

9 *Admin* *(authorize)* *(ship)* expédier; *(goods through customs)* dédouaner; **to c. customs** être dédouané; **cleared through customs** dédouané; **to c. sb** *(for security purposes)* attribuer à qn un certificat de sécurité; **he's been cleared** l'enquête de sécurité a été favorable; **to c. sth with sb** *(obtain permission for)* obtenir de qn la permission de faire qch; **I'll need to c. it with the boss** il faut que j'obtienne la permission du patron; **to c. an article for publication** *(ask for authorization)* demander l'autorisation de publier un article; *(authorize)* autoriser la publication d'un article; **the plane was cleared for take-off** l'avion a été autorisé à décoller, l'avion a reçu l'autorisation de décoller

10 *Fin* *(debt)* acquitter; *(mortgage)* purger; *(account)* solder; **to c. one's property of debt** purger son bien de dettes

11 *(free from impurities)* *(liquid)* clarifier; *(blood)* purifier

12 *Sport* *(ball)* dégager; **to c. the ball with one's head** écarter le ballon d'un coup de tête

VI 1 *(of the weather)* s'éclaircir; *(of mist)* se dissiper; *(of sky)* se dégager; **her face cleared** son visage se détendit

2 *(of cheque)* être viré

3 *(of liquid)* se clarifier

4 *Sport* *(of goalkeeper, fullback)* dégager; **he cleared off the line with his head** il a écarté le ballon de la ligne des buts d'un coup de tête

▸ **clear away VT SEP** *(remove)* enlever, ôter; *(obstacle)* écarter; *(one's things)* ranger
VI *(of mist)* se dissiper

▸ **clear off VT SEP** *(remove)* retirer, enlever
VI *Br Fam* *(leave)* filer, déguerpir, se tirer; **my wife cleared off** ma femme s'est tirée; **c. off!** tire-toi!, casse-toi!, dégage!
VT INSEP dégager de; **he told them to c. off his land** il leur a dit de dégager de sa propriété

▸ **clear out VT SEP** *(empty)* *(cupboard)* vider; *(garage, shed)* débarrasser; *Fam* *(leave without money)* nettoyer
VI *Br Fam* *(leave building, room etc)* filer, déguerpir; *(leave home)* *(of spouse etc)* se tirer; **c. out!** filez!, dehors!

▸ **clear up VT SEP 1** *(tidy)* *(room)* (re)mettre en ordre; *(one's things)* ranger; **we had to c. up the mess** *(after party)* il a fallu tout ranger *ou* nettoyer; *Fig* il a fallu tout arranger

2 *(misunderstanding)* dissiper; *(mystery, doubt, problem)* éclaircir; *(difficulty)* résoudre; **to c. up a matter** tirer une affaire au clair

3 *(cure)* guérir

VI 1 *(of weather)* se (re)mettre au beau
2 *(of rash, headache etc)* disparaître
3 *(tidy up)* ranger; *(after flood, earthquake, bombing etc)* déblayer

---

clearance ['klɪərəns] **N 1 (slum)** c. assainissement *m* des taudis

2 *(of land)* défrichement *m*; *Hist* **the (Highland) Clearances** = l'expulsion *f* des habitants des Highlands aux XVIIIe et XIXe siècles pour faire paître les moutons

3 *Banking* *(of a cheque)* compensation *f*

4 *(authorization)* autorisation *f*; *(by customs)* dédouanage *m*, dédouanement *m*; **we got c. to inspect the documents** nous avons eu l'autorisation d'examiner les documents; *Aviat* **(flight) c.** autorisation de vol; *Admin, Mil* **(security) c.** autorisation

5 *Tech* *(space)* espace *m* *(libre)*; *(of piston etc)* jeu *m*; *Constr* *(under bridge, doorway etc)* hauteur *f* libre

6 *Ftbl* dégagement *m*

7 *Med* *(of kidneys)* clairance *f*

▸▸ *Com* **c. sale** liquidation *f*, soldes *mpl*

clear-cut ADJ *(outline, feature)* net; *(opinion)* bien défini, tranché, net; *(order)* précis; *(division, dividing line)* net; **it's not quite as c. as that** ce n'est pas aussi simple que ça

clear-headed ['klɪə'hedɪd] **ADJ** lucide

clearing ['klɪərɪŋ] **N 1** *(unblocking, freeing of obstacles)* *(of track)* dégagement *m*, déblaiement *m*; *(of ground)* défrichement *m*; *(of ditches)* curage *m*

2 *(removal)* *(of rubbish)* enlèvement *m*

3 *(emptying)* *(of room)* évacuation *f*

4 *Fin* *(of debts)* acquittement *m*

5 *Banking* compensation *f*, clearing *m*; **under the c. procedure** par voie de compensation

6 *(in forest)* clairière *f*

▸▸ *Banking, Fin* **c. account** compte *m* de compensation; *Br* **c. bank** banque *f* de compensation; **c. house** *Banking, Fin* chambre *f* de compensation; *(for information, materials)* bureau *m* central; *St Exch* **c. member** adhérent-compensateur *m*, *pl* adhérents-compensateurs, membre *m* de compensation; **c. price** cours *m* de compensation; *Mil* **c. station** *(for wounded)* centre *m* de triage *ou* d'évacuation; *Banking, Fin* **c. system** système *m* de compensation; **c. up** *(of house etc)* remise *f* en ordre; *(after earthquake, flood, bombing etc)* déblaiement *m*; **c. up operations have started** les opérations de déblaiement ont commencé

clearly ['klɪəlɪ] **ADV 1** *(to see)* clair; *(to explain, write, speak)* clairement, d'une manière claire; *(to hear)* distinctement; *(to distinguish)* clairement, nettement; **you're not thinking very c.** tu raisonnes de travers; **is that c. understood?** c'est bien compris?; **c. legible** bien lisible **2** *(obviously, plainly)* évidemment; **he is c. wrong** il est évident qu'il a tort; **they are c. different** il est évident qu'ils sont différents; **c., this can't be right** c'est faux, il n'y a aucun doute là-dessus; **c., we'll have to pay** nous devrons payer, c'est certain; **this is c. unacceptable** c'est tout à fait inacceptable; **c. not** manifestement pas

clearness ['klɪənɪs] **N 1** *(of water, atmosphere etc)* clarté *f*, limpidité *f* **2** *(of image)* netteté *f* **3** *(of ideas, explanations)* clarté *f*

clearout ['klɪəraʊt] **N this room needs a good c.** cette pièce a besoin d'un bon nettoyage par le vide; **to have a c.** faire le nettoyage par le vide; **to give the cupboards a c.** faire le nettoyage par le vide dans les placards; *Fig* **the party has had a c.** le parti s'est débarrassé de quelques-uns de ses membres

clear-sighted ADJ 1 *(having good judge-*

ment) lucide, clairvoyant **2** *(having good sight)* qui a une bonne vue

clear-sightedness [-'saɪtɪdnɪs] N *(good judgement)* lucidité *f,* clairvoyance *f*

clear-up N *(of room etc)* remise *f* en ordre; **this place needs a good c.** cet endroit a bien besoin d'être remis en ordre; **c. rate (for crimes)** pourcentage *m* d'affaires élucidées par la police

clearway ['klɪəweɪ] N *Br Aut* grande route *f* à stationnement interdit

cleat [kliːt] N *esp Naut* taquet *m (de tournage)*

cleavage ['kliːvɪdʒ] N **1** *(of woman)* décolleté *m;* **what a c.!** quel décolleté!; **it fell down her c.** c'est tombé dans son décolleté; **to show a lot of c.** *(of woman)* avoir un décolleté plongeant; *(of dress)* être très décolleté **2** *(split) (in party)* clivage *m* **3** *(splitting)* *Tech* fendage *m; Geol, Chem* clivage *m; Biol* division *f*

cleave [kliːv] *(pt* **cleaved, cleft** [kleft], *Lit* **clove** [kləʊv], *pp* **cleaved, cleft,** *Lit* **cloven** ['kləʊv(ə)n]) VT *Lit (wood, waters)* fendre
VI **1** *Lit* **to c. (asunder)** se fendre, se feuilleter **2** *(of crystals)* se cliver
▸ **cleave to** VT INSEP *(pt, pp* **cleaved)** *Lit (person, party, principle)* être fidèle à

cleaver ['kliːvər] N fendoir *m; (for meat)* couperet *m; (for wood)* merlin *m*

clef [klef] N *Mus* clef *f,* **bass c.** clef de fa; **C c.** clef d'ut

cleft [kleft] N fente *f,* fissure *f,* crevasse *f*
ADJ fendu
▸▸ *Med* **c. palate** palais *m* fendu; **c. stick** branche *f* fourchue; *Fig* **to be in a c. stick** se trouver dans une impasse

clematis ['klemətɪs, klə'meɪtɪs] N clématite *f*

clemency ['klemənsɪ] N **1** *(mercy)* clémence *f,* indulgence *f* **(to** envers); **to show c.** faire preuve de clémence **2** *(of weather)* douceur *f*

clement ['klemənt] ADJ *Fml* **1** *(person)* clément, indulgent **(to** envers, pour) **2** *(weather)* doux, clément

clementine ['kleməntiːn, -aɪn] N clémentine *f*

clench [klen(t)ʃ] VT *(teeth, fist)* serrer; **between clenched teeth** *(to say)* les dents serrées; **to c. sth in one's hand** serrer qch dans la main
VI *(of teeth, hands)* se serrer

Cleopatra [kliə'pætrə] N *Antiq* Cléopâtre
▸▸ **C.'s needle** l'Obélisque *m* de Cléopâtre

clerestory ['klɪəstɔːrɪ] N *Archit* claire-voie *f,* *pl* claires-voies

clergy ['klɜːdʒɪ] N *(no pl)* Rel clergé *m* VOIR
GRAMMAIRE A11

clergyman, *pl* **clergymen** ['klɜːdʒɪmən] N *Rel* ecclésiastique *m; (protestant)* pasteur *m; (catholic)* prêtre *m*

clergywoman, *pl* **clergywomen** ['klɜːdʒɪˌwʊmən, -wɪmɪn] N *Rel* femme *f* pasteur

cleric ['klerɪk] N *Rel* ecclésiastique *m*

clerical ['klerɪk(ə)l] ADJ **1** *(work)* d'écritures, de bureau; *(staff)* de bureau **2** *Rel* clérical, -aux; *(dress)* ecclésiastique
▸▸ **c. assistant** employé, -ée de bureau; **c. error** *(in document)* faute *f* de copiste; *(in accounting)* erreur *f* d'écriture

clericalism ['klerɪk(ə)lɪz(ə)m] N *Rel* cléricalisme *m*

clerk [klɑːk, *Am* klɜːrk] N **1** *(in office)* employé, -ée de bureau; *(of solicitor)* clerc *m;* **bank c.** employé, -ée de banque; **filing c.,** *Am* **file c.** employé, -ée au classement; **records c.** archiviste *mf;* **shipping c.** expéditionnaire *mf,* employé, -ée de l'expédition
2 *Am (in shop)* vendeur, -euse
3 *Am (receptionist)* réceptionniste *mf*

4 *Rel* **c. in holy orders** ecclésiastique *m*
VI *Am* **1** *(work in office)* travailler comme employé, -ée de bureau
2 *(in shop)* travailler comme vendeur, -euse
3 *Am Pol, Law* **to c. for a senator/a judge** être assistant d'un sénateur/d'un juge
▸▸ *Sport* **c. of the course** commissaire *m* de piste; **C. of the Court** greffier, -ière (du tribunal); *Constr* **c. of (the) works** conducteur *m* des travaux

clever ['klevər] ADJ **1** *(intelligent)* intelligent; *(plan, gadget)* ingénieux, astucieux; *Sch* **c. at mathematics** fort en mathématiques; **he was too c. for us** il s'est montré plus malin que nous; *Pej* **he's/she's too c. by half** il/elle est bien trop malin/maligne; **don't get c. with me** ne fais pas le malin avec moi; *Fam* **a c. Dick** un petit malin **2** *(skilful)* habile, adroit; **to be c. with one's hands** être adroit *ou* habile de ses mains; **c. at doing sth** habile à faire qch; *Fam* **to play it c.** jouer serré

cleverly ['klevəlɪ] ADV **1** *(intelligently)* avec intelligence, intelligemment; *(planned)* ingénieusement; **the dog had c. worked out how to ...** le chien avait astucieusement découvert comment ... **2** *(skilfully)* habilement, adroitement

cleverness ['klevənɪs] N **1** *(intelligence)* intelligence *f,* *(of invention etc)* ingéniosité *f* **2** *(with hands)* adresse *f,* dextérité *f*

cliché ['kliːʃeɪ] N cliché *m*

clichéd ['kliːʃeɪd] ADJ rebattu; **that's very c.** c'est un cliché

cliché-ridden ADJ bourré *ou* truffé de clichés

click [klɪk] N *(sound)* bruit *m* sec, déclic *m,* clic *m; (of camera)* déclic; *Comput (of keys, mouse)* clic; *(with tongue)* claquement *m* de langue; *Ling* clic; **he gave a c. of the tongue** il fit claquer sa langue; *Fig Fam* **something went c.** il y a eu comme un déclic, et puis ça a été le déclic
VI **1** *(make a sound)* faire un petit bruit sec; *Comput (with mouse)* cliquer; *Comput* **to c. on sth** cliquer sur qch; *Comput* **to c. and drag** cliquer et glisser; **she clicked along the pavement in her high heels** ses hauts talons faisaient de petits bruits secs sur le trottoir; **cameras were clicking** on entendait le déclic des appareils; **to c. together** *(of two parts)* s'emboîter *(avec un bruit sec);* **to c. shut** *(of door etc)* se refermer avec un bruit sec
2 *Fig (become clear)* faire tilt; **now it's clicked** *(of one thing)* ça a fait tilt; *(of something more complicated)* tout s'est mis en place; **it'll c. if you work at it** tu finiras par comprendre si tu t'y mets
3 *Fam (of two people)* **we clicked right away** nous nous sommes tout de suite entendus à merveille; **to c. with the public** *(of play, film)* avoir du succès auprès du public
VT **to c. one's heels** *(when saluting)* (faire) claquer les talons; **to c. one's tongue** claquer la langue
▸▸ *Ling* **c. language** langue *f* à clics; *Com, Comput* **clicks-and-mortar company** = société *f* qui vend ses produits en magasin et sur Internet
▸ **click away** VI *(take photos)* prendre sans cesse des photos; **the photographers were clicking away furiously** les photographes s'en donnaient à cœur joie
▸ **click on** VI *Br Fam (understand)* piger
VT INSEP *Comput* cliquer, cliquer sur

clickable ['klɪkəbəl] ADJ *Comput* cliquable
▸▸ **c. image** image *f* cliquable; **c. image map** image cliquable

clicking ['klɪkɪŋ] N *(noise)* cliquetis *m*

client ['klaɪənt] N *(of shop, lawyer)* client, -ente
▸▸ *Banking* **c. account** compte *m* client;

Com, Mktg **c. base** clientèle *f; Com, Mktg* **c. file** dossier *m* client, fichier *m* client; *Pej* **c. government** gouvernement *m* à la solde d'un autre; *Com, Mktg* **c. list** liste *f* de clients; *Pej* **c. state** état *m* à la solde d'un autre

clientele [kliːɒn'tel] N *(of shop, lawyer etc)* clientèle *f*

client-server ADJ *Comput* client-serveur *inv*
▸▸ **c. database** base *f* de données client-serveur; **c. model** modèle *m* client-serveur

cliff [klɪf] N falaise *f, (in mountains)* à-pic *m,* *pl* à-pics

cliffhanger ['klɪfhæŋər] N *(film, novel etc)* film *m*/roman *m*/etc à suspense; *(situation)* situation *f* qui vous tient en haleine; **it was a real c.** ça m'a/nous a/etc tenu en haleine jusqu'à la fin; **a real c. of an ending** une fin qui vous tient en haleine; **the election/race was a c.** le résultat de l'élection/de la course est resté incertain jusqu'à la dernière minute

climacteric [klaɪ'mæktərɪk] N climatère *m*

climactic [klaɪ'mæktɪk] ADJ *(scene)* qui constitue le paroxysme; **the c. moment of the film** le paroxysme du film

> Attention: ne pas confondre avec l'adjectif **climatic**.

climate ['klaɪmət] N *Met, Fig* climat *m*
▸▸ *Aut* **c. control (system)** climatiseur *m*

climatic [klaɪ'mætɪk] ADJ climatique

> Attention: ne pas confondre avec l'adjectif **climactic**.

climatologist [klaɪmə'tɒlədʒɪst] N climatologue *mf*

climatology [klaɪmə'tɒlədʒɪ] N climatologie *f*

climax ['klaɪmæks] N **1** *(highest point)* paroxysme *m; (of play, piece of music etc)* point *m* culminant; *(of career)* apogée *f,* point culminant; **the c. of the festivities** l'apogée des réjouissances; **to reach a c.** *(of music)* atteindre son point culminant; **to work up to a c.** *(in rhetoric)* procéder par gradation (ascendante); *Theat etc* corser l'action; **as a c. to the entertainment ...** comme bouquet de la fête ... **2** *(sexual)* orgasme *m*
VI **1** *(reach climax)* atteindre son paroxysme *ou* point culminant; **to c. in a firework display** finir en beauté par un feu d'artifice **2** *(have an orgasm)* jouir

climb [klaɪm] N *(of rock face)* montée *f,* ascension *f, (of mountain)* ascension, course *f, (steep slope) (of road etc)* côte *f,* montée *f; Fig* ascension; *Sport, Aut* **hill c.** course de côte; **to go for a c.** faire de l'escalade; *Aviat* **rate of c.** vitesse *f* ascensionnelle *ou* de montée; **a short c. takes you to the village** une petite montée vous mène au village
VI **1** grimper; **to c. on(to) the roof** monter *ou* grimper sur le toit; **to c. over the wall** escalader le mur; **to c. out of a hole** se hisser hors d'un trou; **to c. into bed** grimper dans son lit; *Fig* **to c. to power** gravir tous les échelons qui mènent au pouvoir; **to c. (socially** *or* **in the world)** s'élever (au-dessus de sa condition)
2 *Sport (go mountain climbing)* faire de l'alpinisme; *(go rock climbing)* faire de la varappe
3 *(rise) (of road)* monter; *(of prices)* monter, augmenter, *Fam* grimper
4 *Aviat* prendre de l'altitude, monter; **the plane climbed 200 feet** l'avion a pris 60 mètres d'altitude
VT *(tree)* grimper à *ou* dans; *(ladder)* monter *ou* grimper à; *(cliff, mountain)* escalader
▸ **climb down** VI **1** *(descend)* descendre; **to**

c. down out of a tree descendre d'un arbre **2** *Fig (in negotiations etc)* reculer
VT INSEP descendre
► **climb up VT INSEP** = **climb VT**

climb-down N *Fig* reculade *f*

climber ['klaɪmər] N **1** *(of mountain)* alpiniste *mf*; *(of rock face)* varappeur, -euse; *(leopard, koala etc)* grimpeur, -euse; *Fig Pej* **(social) c.** arriviste *mf* **2** *Bot* plante *f* grimpante

climbing ['klaɪmɪŋ] ADJ *(plant)* grimpant; *(animal)* grimpeur
N escalade *f*; *Sport* alpinisme *m*; **(rock) c.** varappe *f*; *Pej* **social c.** arrivisme *m*
► ► *Br* **c. frame** cage *f* à poules *(jeu)*; **c. irons** *(for mountaineer)* grappins *mpl*; *(on boots)* crampons *mpl*; *(for climbing trees, poles)* étriers *mpl*; *Sport* **c. wall** mur *m* d'escalade

clime [klaɪm] N *Lit (climate)* climat *m*; **they have gone to sunnier** *or* **warmer climes** ils sont partis sous des cieux plus cléments; **in these climes** sous ces climats

clinch [klɪntʃ] N **1** *Fam (embrace)* étreinte *f*; **to go into a c.** *(of lovers)* s'étreindre **2** *Boxing* clinch *m*; **to break a c.** briser un corps à corps; **to go into a c.** se prendre corps à corps
VT *(settle) (deal)* conclure, clore; *(argument)* confirmer; **that clinches it!** c'est terminé!; **that was what clinched it for me** c'est ce qui m'a décidé
VI 1 *Boxing* en venir aux prises, se prendre corps à corps **2** *Fam (of lovers)* s'étreindre

clincher ['klɪntʃər] N *Fam* **1** *(argument)* argument *m* irréfutable; **that was the c. for me** *(that realization, experience etc)* c'est ce qui m'a décidé **2** *Sport* but *m*/point *m* décisif

cling [klɪŋ] VI *(pt, pp* clung [klʌŋ]*) (of child)* s'accrocher, se cramponner *(* **to sth/sb** à qch/qn*)*; *Fig Pej* coller *(* **to sb** qn*)*; *(of plant) (to wall)* s'accrocher *(* **to** à*)*; **to c. to the figure** *(of garment)* mouler le corps; **he clung to the rope for dear life** il s'agrippa à la corde de toutes ses forces; **the two children were clinging to each other** les deux enfants étaient serrés l'un contre l'autre; *Fig* **to c. (on) to one's children/wife/ideas** s'accrocher à ses enfants/sa femme/ses idées; **to c. to an opinion** persister dans une opinion; **to c. to a hope** se raccrocher à un espoir
► ► **c. peach** pavie *f*

clingfilm ['klɪŋfɪlm] N *Br* film *m* alimentaire

clinging ['klɪŋɪŋ] ADJ *(plant)* qui s'accroche; *(garment)* collant, qui colle; *(material)* qui moule le corps; *(perfume)* tenace; *Fam (person)* collant; *(parent, boyfriend etc)* possessif
► ► *Am Fam Fig* **c. vine** pot *m* de colle

clingy ['klɪŋɪ] ADJ *Pej* collant; **she's so c.** *(child)* elle est toujours dans mes pattes; **he's the c. type** c'est le genre collant

clinic ['klɪnɪk] N *Med* **1** *(for outpatients)* dispensaire *m*, centre *m* médical **2** *Br (nursing home)* clinique *f*

clinical ['klɪnɪk(ə)l] ADJ **1** *Med* clinique **2** *Fig (analysis, approach)* froid
► ► *Med* **c. psychology** psychologie *f* clinique; *Med* **c. thermometer** thermomètre *m* médical

clinically ['klɪnɪklɪ] ADV **1** *Med* cliniquement; **c. dead** cliniquement mort **2** *Fig (coldly, in detached way)* froidement

clinician [klɪ'nɪʃ(ə)n] N clinicien, -ienne

clink¹ [klɪŋk] N *(sound)* tintement *m*
VI *(of glasses etc)* tinter
VT faire tinter; **to c. glasses** choquer les verres, trinquer

clink² N *Br Sl (prison)* taule *f*, tôle *f*; **to be in (the) c.** être en taule *ou* tôle

clinker ['klɪŋkər] N **1** *Constr (for tiling)* brique *f* hollandaise; *(vitrified)* brique vitrifiée, brique à four **2** *(cinders) (of forge etc)* mâchefer *m*

clinker-built ADJ *Naut* bordé à clin(s)

clip [klɪp] N **1** *(for attaching, holding)* pince *f*; *(brooch)* clip *m*; *(hair ornament)* barrette *f*; **(paper) c.** trombone *m*; **bicycle** *or* **trouser c.** pince à pantalon, pince-pantalon *m inv* **2** *Elec (of wire, cable)* cosse *f* **3** *(cut) (of dog etc)* tondage *m*; **to give a hedge a c.** couper *ou* tailler une haie; **to give one's nails a c.** se couper les ongles **4** *Fam (blow)* **c. (on the ear)** taloche *f* **5** *Cin (of film, programme etc)* extrait *m* **6** *Am (from newspaper)* coupure *f*
VT *(-pp-)* **1** *(fasten)* **to c. (together)** *(papers)* attacher *(avec un trombone)*; **to c. one document to another** attacher un document à un autre; **to c. a brooch on a blouse** accrocher une broche à un chemisier; **to c. a microphone to sb's tie** attacher *ou* fixer un micro à la cravate de qn **2** *(cut) (dog, lawn)* tondre; *(hedge)* couper, tailler; *(metal plate)* couper, cisailler; **to c. the wings of a bird** rogner les ailes à un oiseau; *Fig* **to c. sb's wings** rogner les ailes à qn; **to c. ten seconds off a record** améliorer un record de dix secondes **3** *Rail etc (ticket)* poinçonner **4** *(hit) Tennis* **to c. the line** *(of ball)* mordre la ligne; *Fam* **to c. sb's ear** flanquer une taloche à qn; **I just clipped the wall** j'ai effleuré le mur
► ► *Comput* **c. art** clipart *m*; *Fam* **c. joint** = boîte *f* de nuit où l'on pratique des prix excessifs; *TV, Radio* **c. mike** micro-cravate *m*, *pl* micros-cravates
► **clip on VT SEP** attacher
VI s'attacher

clipboard ['klɪpbɔːd] N **1** planchette *f* porte-papiers; *Comput* presse-papiers *m inv*; bloc-notes *m, pl* blocs-notes
► ► *Comput* **c. file** fichier *m* presse-papiers

clip-clop ['klɪpklɒp] N bruit *m* de sabots; **the horse went c. down the street** on entendit le bruit des sabots du cheval qui descendait la rue

clip-on ADJ qui s'attache avec une pince
N *(earring)* clip *m*
► ► **c. earring** clip *m*; **c. microphone** micro-cravate *m, pl* micros-cravates; **c. tie** cravate *f* à système

clipped [klɪpt] ADJ *(pronunciation, speech)* saccadé

clipper ['klɪpər] N *Naut* clipper *m*
► ► *Aviat* **c. class** classe *f* affaires

clippers ['klɪpəz] NPL *(for the hair etc)* tondeuse *f*; **(hedge) c.** taille-buissons *m inv*; **(nail) c.** coupe-ongles *m inv*

clippie ['klɪpɪ] N *Old-fashioned Br Fam* receveuse *f* (d'autobus)

clipping ['klɪpɪŋ] N **1** *(from newspaper)* coupure *f* de presse **2 clippings** *(from nails)* rognures *fpl*; *(from hair)* mèches *fpl (de cheveux coupés)*; *(from hedge)* bouts *mpl* de branches

clique [kliːk] N *Pej* coterie *f*, clique *f*

cliqu(e)y ['kliːkɪ], **cliquish** ['kliːkɪʃ] ADJ *Fam* qui a l'esprit de clique

clitoral ['klɪtərəl] ADJ clitoridien

clitoridectomy [klɪtərɪ'dektəmɪ] N clitoridectomie *f*

clitoris ['klɪtərɪs] N clitoris *m*

Cllr *abbr* Councillor

cloak [kləʊk] N *(grande)* cape *f*; *Fig Lit* **under the c. of night** sous le couvert de la nuit
VT couvrir *ou* revêtir d'une *(grande)* cape; *Fig* **cloaked in mystery** enveloppé de mystère

cloak-and-dagger ADJ *(film, novel)* de cape et d'épée; **it was all very c.** c'était très mystérieux; **what's all this c. stuff about?** qu'est-ce que c'est que tout ce mystère?

cloakroom ['kləʊkruːm] N *(for coats etc)* vestiaire *m*; *Br (lavatory)* toilettes *fpl*; *Br* **ladies' c.** *(lavatory)* toilettes des dames
► ► **c. attendant** préposé, -ée au vestiaire; *Br (in lavatory)* préposé, -ée aux cabinets de toilette

clobber¹ ['klɒbər] N *Br Fam* **1** *(clothes)* frusques *fpl*, fringues *fpl* **2** *(belongings)* bazar *m*, fourbi *m*

clobber² VT *Br Fam (hit)* tabasser; *(defeat heavily)* flanquer une raclée à; *(penalize)* écraser, accabler; **the new tax legislation will c. small businesses** les nouvelles lois fiscales vont saigner à blanc les petites entreprises

clobbering ['klɒbərɪŋ] N *Br Fam* **to get a c.** *(be beaten up)* prendre une dérouillée *ou* une raclée; *(be heavily defeated)* se prendre une pâtée; **to give sb a c.** *(beat up)* tabasser qn, flanquer une raclée à qn; *(defeat)* flanquer une raclée à qn

cloche [klɒʃ] N cloche *f*

clock [klɒk] N **1** horloge *f*; *(small)* pendule *f*; *Fam* **to watch the c.** *(of employee)* avoir les yeux rivés sur l'horloge, ne penser qu'à l'heure de la sortie; **I don't pay you to come in here and watch the c.** je ne vous paie pas pour que vous passiez votre temps à ne rien faire; **a full hour by the c.** une bonne heure d'horloge; **to work round the c.** travailler vingt-quatre heures sur vingt-quatre; **a race against the c.** une course contre la montre; **to beat the c.** arriver/finir avant l'heure; **to put** *or* **turn the clocks back** *(in autumn)* retarder les pendules; *Fig* **to put the c. back** revenir en arrière, *Pej* régresser; **the measures will turn the c. back to Victorian times** les mesures nous feront retourner à l'époque victorienne; *Aut* **dashboard c.** pendule de tableau de bord
2 *Aut (milometer)* compteur *m*; *(in taxi)* compteur horokilométrique, taximètre *m*; **15,000 miles on the c.** 15 000 mil(l)es au compteur
3 *Comput* horloge *f*
VT *Fam* **1** *Sport etc (measure speed of) (runner etc)* chronométrer **2** *(reach speed)* faire; *Aut* **to c. ninety** faire du 150 chrono; **the fastest time he's clocked this year** son meilleur temps cette année **3** *Br Sl (notice)* repérer; **she clocked him as soon as he walked in** elle l'a repéré dès qu'il est entré
► ► **c. golf** jeu *m* de l'horloge; *Comput* **c. rate** fréquence *f* d'horloge; *Comput* **c. speed** fréquence d'horloge; *Comput* **c. speed doubler** doubleur *m* de fréquence (d'horloge)
► **clock in VI 1** *Sport (have a time of)* **for the 100 metres she clocked in at nine seconds** elle a fait neuf secondes aux 100 mètres; **the last of the marathon runners clocked in at six hours** le dernier marathonien a effectué le parcours en six heures
2 *Ind (record arrival at work)* pointer *(en arrivant)*; **you clocked in 10 minutes late** vous avez pointé avec 10 minutes de retard
VT SEP *Ind* **to c. sb in** pointer pour qn
► **clock off** *Ind* VI *(record departure from work)* pointer *(en partant)*
VT SEP **to c. sb off** pointer pour qn
► **clock on** VI, VT SEP = **clock in** VI **2**, VT SEP
► **clock out** VI, VT SEP = **clock off**
► **clock up** VT SEP *(achieve)* *(parvenir à)* atteindre; **she has clocked up 700 kilometres in two days** elle a fait 700 kilomètres en deux jours

clock-doubled [-dʌb(ə)ld] ADJ *Comput* à fréquence d'horloge doublée

clocking-in ['klɒkɪŋ] N *Ind* pointage *m* à l'arrivée
▸ ▸ **c. card** fiche *f* de pointage

clocking-off N *Ind* pointage *m* à la sortie

clocking-on N *Ind* = **clocking-in**

clocking-out N *Ind* = **clocking-off**

clocklike ['klɒklaɪk] ADJ *(regularity)* d'horloge

clockmaker ['klɒkmeɪkər] N horloger, -ère

clock-watcher [-wɒtʃər] N *Fam* = employé, -ée qui ne pense qu'à l'heure de sortie

clockwise ['klɒkwaɪz] ADV, ADJ dans le sens des aiguilles d'une montre

clockwork ['klɒkwɜːk] N mouvement *m* d'horloge; *(in toy etc)* mécanisme *m* à ressort; **as regular as c.** réglé comme du papier à musique; **everything's going like c.** tout va *ou* marche comme sur des roulettes; **the hotel runs like c.** l'hôtel marche sans problème ◾ ADJ *(toy)* mécanique; *(mechanism)* qui se remonte; **everything is done with c. precision** tout est réglé comme du papier à musique; *Sl* **as queer as a c. orange** *(homosexual)* pédé comme un phoque

clod [klɒd] N **1** *(of earth)* motte *f* **2** *Fam (stupid person)* lourdaud, -e; **you great c.!** espèce de lourdaud!

clodhopper ['klɒdhɒpər] N *Fam* **1** *(person)* lourdaud, -aude **2 clodhoppers** *(shoes)* (grosses) godasses *fpl*

clog[1] [klɒg] N *(shoe)* gros brodequin *m* à semelle de bois; **(wooden) c.** sabot *m*; *Fam* **to pop one's clogs** *(die)* casser sa pipe
▸ ▸ **c. dance** = danse *f* où les participants marquent le rythme avec leurs sabots

clog[2] (**-gg-**) VT **1** *(block) (artery, pipe etc)* boucher, obstruer; *(firearm, machine)* encrasser; *(filter)* boucher, encrasser; **our boots got clogged with mud** nos bottes se sont crottées dans la boue **2** *(prevent from moving) (animal)* entraver; *Fig (enterprise etc)* entraver, gêner
◾ VI *(of artery, pipe etc)* se boucher, s'obstruer; *(of firearm, machine)* s'encrasser; *(of filter)* se boucher, s'encrasser
▸ **clog up** VT SEP, VI = **clog** VT **1**, VI

cloister ['klɔɪstər] N **1** *Archit (usu pl)* **cloisters** *(of convent, church etc)* cloître *m* **2** *Rel (monastery)* monastère *m*
◾ VT cloîtrer

cloistered ['klɔɪstəd] ADJ **1** *(life)* de cloître, cloîtré; *Fig* **a c. childhood** une enfance protégée; **to lead a very c. life** mener une vie très protégée **2** *Archit* entouré d'un cloître

clone [kləʊn] N *Bot, Biol, Comput etc* clone *m*; **a Tom Cruise/Marilyn Monroe c.** un sosie de Tom Cruise/Marilyn Monroe
◾ VT *Bot, Biol, Comput* cloner

cloner ['kləʊnər] N *Mktg* cloneur *m*

cloning ['kləʊnɪŋ] N *Bot, Biol, Comput* clonage *m*

CLOSE[1] [kləʊs]

ADJ	proche **1, 2** ◾ près **1** ◾ soutenu **3** ◾ lourd **5** ◾ serré **6, 7**
ADV	près

ADJ **1** *(in distance, time)* proche; *(to each other)* rapproché; *(ties)* étroit; **we must be c. now** nous devons être près maintenant; **our office is c. to the town hall** notre bureau est près de la mairie; **he was c.** *(of person guessing)* il brûlait; **in c. proximity to sth** dans le voisinage immédiat *ou* tout près de qch; **to be c. to tears** être au bord des larmes; **to be (very) c. to victory** être (tout) près de la victoire; **at c. intervals** à intervalles rapprochés; **I saw him at c. quarters** je l'ai vu de près; **to fire at c. range** tirer à bout portant

2 *(in relationship)* proche; **to be c. to sb** être proche de qn; **he and his brother are very c.** lui et son frère sont très proches; **Italian is c. to French** l'italien est proche du français; **to be in c. contact** être en contact étroit; **a c. friend** un ami intime; **a c. relative** un parent proche, un proche

3 *(careful) (attention)* soutenu; *(observer)* attentif; *(study)* minutieux; **on closer examination** en y regardant de plus près; **after c. consideration** après mûre réflexion; **to keep (a) c. watch on sb/sth** surveiller qn/qch de près; **a c. copy of sth** une bonne imitation de qch

4 *(secret)* intime; **to keep sth a c. secret** garder le secret absolu sur qch; **to keep sth c. (be secretive)** ne rien dire de qch; **to play a c. game** jouer serré

5 *(weather)* lourd; **it's c. in here** *(stuffy)* on étouffe ici; **it's c. today** il fait lourd aujourd'hui

6 *(dense)* serré, dense; *(thicket, woods)* épais, touffu; **c. grain** *(of metal, stone, wood etc)* grain *m* serré *ou* fin; **c. texture** *(of metal, stone etc)* (con)texture *f* serrée, tissu *m* serré; **Mil** **in c. order** *or* **ranks** en rangs serrés

7 *(contest)* serré; **c. election** élection *f* vivement contestée; *Sport* **c. finish** arrivée *f* serrée; **c. match** match *m* serré; **a c. shave** un rasage de près; *Fig* **that was a c. shave** *or* **thing** *or* **call** nous l'avons/ils l'ont/*etc* échappé belle; *Fam* c'était moins une *ou* cinq

8 *Fam* **to be c. with money** être près de ses sous

ADV *(near)* près, de près; **to be** *or* **follow c. behind sb** suivre qn de près; **to stand c. against a wall** se coller contre un mur; **houses c. together** maisons serrées les unes contre les autres; **to sit/stand c. together** être/se tenir serrés; **to keep c.** rester tout près; **it keeps c. to the original** cela reste proche de l'original; **c. to** *or* **by sb/sth** *(tout)* près de *ou* à proximité de qn/qch; **to keep c. to sb** se tenir tout près de qn; **he lives c. to here** il habite tout près *ou* à deux pas (d'ici); **to come** *or* **draw c./closer to sb** s'approcher/se rapprocher de qn; **it's brought us closer** ça nous a rapprochés; **put it closer to the door** mets-le plus près de la porte; **c. to the ground** au ras *ou* près du sol; **to cut c.** *(hair)* couper ras; **to keep c. to the text** rester près du texte; **she came c. to losing her job** elle a failli perdre son emploi; **to come c. to death** frôler la mort; **to come c. to the world record** frôler le record du monde; **c. at hand, c. by** tout près, tout contre; **c. on nine (o'clock)** tout près de neuf heures; **to be c. on fifty** *(age)* friser la cinquantaine

N **1** *Br (street)* impasse *f*, cul-de-sac *m*, *pl* culs-de-sac

2 *(of cathedral)* enceinte *f*
▸ ▸ *Mil* **c. combat** corps à corps *m*; *Mus* **c. harmony** tessiture *f* limitée; *Cin, TV* **c. shot** plan *m* rapproché; *Mktg* **c. substitute** substitut *m* rapproché

CLOSE[2] [kləʊz] N *(end)* fin *f*, conclusion *f*; *(of year)* fin; *(of meeting, session)* clôture *f*, levée *f*; *St Exch* **at c. of business** à la *ou* en clôture; *Lit* **at c. of day** à la tombée du jour; *Cr* **at c. of play** à la fin de la journée; **to draw to a c.** tirer à sa fin

VT **1** *(door, eyes, book, shop etc)* fermer; *(road)* barrer; **a road closed to motor traffic** une route interdite à la circulation automobile; **cold closes the pores** le froid resserre les pores; *Fig* **to c. ranks** serrer les rangs, faire bloc; **the party closed ranks around its leader** le parti a fait bloc autour de son leader

2 *(bring to an end) (matter)* conclure, terminer; *(meeting, session)* lever, clore; *(debate)* fermer; *(account)* fermer, clôturer; **to**

declare the discussion closed prononcer la clôture des débats

3 *(shut down) (factory, shop, railway line etc)* fermer (définitivement)

4 *(finalize) (sale)* conclure; *(deal)* arrêter

5 *Acct* **to c. the books** régler les livres; **to c. an account** arrêter un compte

6 *St Exch (operation)* liquider; *(position)* couvrir

VI **1** *(of door etc)* (se) fermer; *(of wound, hole etc)* se refermer; **the theatre will c. for a month** le théâtre fermera pendant un mois; **theatres c. on Good Friday** les théâtres font relâche le vendredi saint

2 *(end)* finir, se terminer; **I must c. now** *(in letter writing)* je dois vous quitter; **I will c. with a story** pour terminer, je vais vous raconter une histoire

3 *(shut down) (of factory, shop, railway line etc)* fermer (définitivement)

4 *St Exch* **the shares closed at £1.57** les actions ont clôturé à 1,57 livre; **the share index closed two points down** l'indice (boursier) a clôturé en baisse de deux points
▸ ▸ *Comput* **c. box** case *f* de fermeture; *Br* **c. season** *(in hunting)* fermeture *f* de la chasse; *(in fishing)* fermeture de la pêche; *Ftbl* intersaison *f*, *Ling* **c. vowel** voyelle *f* fermée

▸ **close down** VT SEP *(factory etc)* fermer (définitivement)
◾ VI **1** *(of factory, shop etc)* fermer (définitivement), fermer ses portes; *(of shopkeeper)* fermer boutique
2 *Radio, TV* terminer ses émissions

▸ **close in** VI **1** *(approach) (of night)* tomber; **the police/his creditors are closing in** l'étau de la police/de ses créanciers se resserre
2 *(get shorter) (of days)* raccourcir
◾ VT SEP *(enclose) (land etc)* clôturer

▸ **close in on** VT INSEP *(person)* encercler, cerner; **darkness closed in on us** la nuit nous enveloppa

▸ **close off** VT SEP fermer; *(road)* barrer; *Acct* **to c. off an account** arrêter un compte

▸ **close out** VT SEP *St Exch* **to c. a position** boucler *ou* clore *ou* fermer une position

▸ **close round** VT INSEP *(person)* cerner, se presser autour de

▸ **close up** VI **1** *(of aperture)* s'obturer; *(of wound, hole etc)* se refermer
2 *(of people)* se serrer, se tasser; *Mil etc* **c. up!** serrez (les rangs)!
3 *(of shopkeeper)* fermer
◾ VT SEP **1** *(seal) (opening etc)* boucher, obturer
2 *(shop, house)* fermer
3 *Typ (characters)* rapprocher; *Mil etc (ranks)* serrer; **the car accelerated to c. up the gap** la voiture accéléra pour réduire l'écart

▸ **close with** VT INSEP **1** *Com* **to c. with sb** conclure un/le marché avec qn
2 *(in fighting)* **to c. with sb** se battre avec qn

close-cropped [-'krɒpt] ADJ *(hair)* coupé ras; *(grass)* rasé, tondu ras

closed [kləʊzd] ADJ *(door, electrical circuit etc)* fermé; **c.** *(notice)* *Theat* relâche; *(on shop)* fermé; **behind c. doors** *(of official meeting etc)* à huis clos; **with eyes c.** les yeux fermés; **to have a c. mind** être hermétique aux idées des autres *ou* aux idées nouvelles; **it remains a c. book to me** je n'y comprends rien; **road c.** *(notice)* rue barrée
▸ ▸ **c. question** question *f* fermée; *Br* **c. season** *(in hunting)* fermeture *f* de la chasse; **c. set** *Math* ensemble *m* fermé; *Cin, TV* plateau *m* fermé; *Ind* **c. shop** *(practice)* = système *m* selon lequel une entreprise n'embauche que des travailleurs syndiqués; *(establishment)* = entreprise *f* qui n'embauche que des travailleurs syndiqués; **c. shop policy**

exclusivité *f* syndicale; *Comput* **c. user group** groupe *m* fermé d'utilisateurs

closed-circuit television N télévision *f* à *ou* en circuit fermé

closed-end ADJ
▸▸*Fin* **c. (investment) fund** société *f* d'investissement à capital fixe; **c. mortgage** prêt *m* hypothécaire à montant fixe

close-down N **1** *(of factory etc)* fermeture *f* **2** *TV, Radio* fin *f* des émissions

close-fisted [-ˈfɪstɪd] ADJ avare, pingre

close-fitting ADJ *(dress etc)* bien ajusté

close-knit ADJ *(community etc)* étroitement lié, très uni

closely [ˈkləʊslɪ] ADV **1** *(to examine, watch)* de près, attentivement; *(to listen)* attentivement; *(to resemble)* beaucoup; *(followed, observed)* de près; *(connected, guarded, related)* étroitement; **c. contested** très disputé; **c. cut** tondu ras **2** *(densely)* **a c. planted forest** une forêt très dense; **c. packed in a box** serré dans une boîte; **two c. written pages** deux pages d'une écriture serrée; **a c. printed book** un livre imprimé très petit; **a c. reasoned argument** une argumentation très détaillée; **c. packed** *(people)* entassé

closeness [ˈkləʊsnɪs] N **1** *(nearness)* proximité *f* **(to** de)
2 *(of relationship, contact etc)* intimité *f* **(to sb** avec qn)
3 *(of description)* exactitude *f*, *(of translation)* fidélité *f*, exactitude
4 *(stuffiness)* manque *m* d'air
5 *(of weather)* lourdeur *f*
6 *(reserve, secretiveness) (of person)* réserve *f*, caractère *m* réservé
7 *(meanness)* avarice *f*, pingrerie *f*

close-range ADJ
▸▸*Mil* **c. weapon** arme *f* à courte portée

close-run ADJ *(election, race)* serré; **we won in the end, but it was a c. thing** on a fini par gagner, mais il s'en est fallu d'un cheveu; **he may not be as boring as Thomas but it's a c. thing** il n'est peut-être pas aussi ennuyeux que Thomas, mais presque

close-set ADJ *(eyes)* rapproché

close-shaven ADJ rasé de près

closet [ˈklɒzɪt] N **1** *esp Am (cupboard)* placard *m*, armoire *f*; *Fam* **to come out of the c.** *(of homosexual)* se déclarer homosexuel, révéler (publiquement) qu'on est homosexuel; *Fam* **many economists are coming out of the c. as Keynesians** beaucoup d'économistes se révèlent keynésiens; *Fam* **many country music fans are now coming out of the c.** bien des fans de country avouent maintenant leur passion **2** *Arch (room)* cabinet *m* de travail, bureau *m* **3** *Old-fashioned* **(water) c.** waters *mpl*, cabinets *mpl*
ADJ *(secret) (discussions etc)* confidentiel; **c. homosexual** = homosexuel, -elle qui n'ose pas s'avouer
VT **(-t-) to be closeted with sb** être enfermé avec qn

close-up N *Cin, TV* gros plan *m*, plan serré; **in c.** en gros plan; *Fig* **the programme gives us a c. of life in prison** l'émission nous donne une vision en gros plan de la vie carcérale
ADJ *(shot, photograph, picture)* en gros plan
▸▸**c. lens** bonnette *f*

closing [ˈkləʊzɪŋ] ADJ *(final)* dernier, final, -als *ou* -aux; **the c. bid** la dernière enchère
N **1** *(shutting) (of shops, factory, theatre etc)* fermeture *f* **2** *(ending) (of meeting, session)* levée *f*, *(of conference)* clôture *f* **3** *Fin, Admin (of account)* arrêté *m*, règlement *m*; *(of bank account)* fermeture *f*; *St Exch* **c. of a position** clôture *f* d'une position
▸▸*Typ* **c. bracket** parenthèse *f* fermante; *Cin, TV* **c. credits** générique *f* de fin; **c. date**

(for applications) date *f* limite de dépôt; *(for project)* date de réalisation *(d'une opération)*; **c. down** *(of factory, shop, business)* fermeture *(définitive)*; *Acct* **c. entry** écriture *f* d'inventaire *ou* de clôture; **c. headlines** *(in news programme)* rappel *m* des titres; **c. off** *Acct (of accounts)* arrêté; *Comput (of bad sector)* fermeture; *Am* **c. out** *(of factory, shop, business)* fermeture *(définitive)*; *St Exch* **c. prices** cours *mpl* de clôture; *St Exch* **c. quotation** cotes *fpl* en clôture; **c. remarks** observations *fpl* finales *(à la fin d'une conférence etc)*; **c. speech** discours *m* de clôture; **c. time** heure *f* de fermeture; *St Exch* **c. trade** transactions *fpl* de clôture

closure [ˈkləʊʒər] N **1** *(of factory etc)* fermeture *f (définitive)*; *St Exch* **c. by repurchase** clôture *f* par rachat **2** *Parl* clôture *f*; **to move the c.** voter la clôture **3** *(of crisis, conflict)* résolution *f*; **it gave him a sense of c.** ça lui a permis de tourner la page

clot [klɒt] N **1** *(of blood)* caillot *m* **2** *Br Fam (stupid person)* patate *f*, andouille *f*
VI **(-tt-)** *(of blood)* (se) coaguler
VT *(cream)* caillebotter; *(blood)* coaguler

cloth, *pl* **cloths** [klɒθ, klɒθs] N **1** *(material)* étoffe *f*, *(linen, cotton)* toile *f*; **c. of gold** drap *m* d'or; *Br Fam* **hey, c. ears, didn't you hear me?** espèce de sourdingue, tu n'as pas entendu ce que j'ai dit?; *Fig* **to be cut from the same c.** être coulé dans le même moule **2** *(individual piece)* linge *m*; *(for cleaning)* chiffon *m*; *(tablecloth)* nappe *f*, *Theat* toile *f* (de décor) **3** *Rel Fam* **the c.** *(the clergy)* le clergé; **a man of the c.** un membre du clergé
▸▸**c. binding** reliure *f* en toile; **c. cap** casquette *f (symbole de la classe ouvrière britannique)*; **the Labour Party wants to get rid of its c. cap image** les travaillistes veulent se débarrasser de leur image 'prolo'

cloth-bound ADJ relié toile

clothe [kləʊð] VT *(pt, pp* **clad** [klæd], **clothed** [kləʊðd]*) (dress)* vêtir, habiller (**in,** with de); **three children to feed and c.** trois enfants à nourrir et à habiller; **warmly/lightly clad** chaudement/légèrement vêtu

cloth-eared ADJ *Br Fam (deaf)* dur de la feuille

clothes [kləʊðz] NPL vêtements *mpl*, habits *mpl*; **in one's best c.** (tout) endimanché; **to put on/take off one's c.** s'habiller/se déshabiller; **to go to bed with one's c. on** *or* **in one's c.** se coucher tout habillé; **with no c. on** (tout) nu; **dirty c.** *(washing)* linge *m* sale
▸▸**c. basket** panier *m* à linge; **c. brush** brosse *f* à habits; *Am* **c. closet** penderie *f*, **c. hanger** cintre *m*; **c. hook** patère *f*, **c. peg** pince *f* à linge; **c. pole** poteau *m* de corde à linge; **c. prop** perche *f* de corde à linge; *Am* **c. rack** séchoir *m*

clotheshorse [ˈkləʊðhɔːs] N séchoir *m* (à linge); *esp Am Fig Fam* **she's a c.** à part les fringues, rien ne l'intéresse

clothesline [ˈkləʊðzlaɪn] N corde *f* à linge

clothespin [ˈkləʊðzpɪn] N *esp Am* pince *f* à linge

clothier [ˈkləʊðɪər] N *Com* **1** *(clothes seller)* marchand, -ande de confections **2** *(cloth seller)* marchand, -ande de drap; *(cloth maker)* fabricant, -ante de drap

clothing [ˈkləʊðɪŋ] N *(no pl) (clothes)* habillement *m*, vêtements *mpl*; **warm c.** vêtements chauds; **articles of c.** vêtements; **the c. trade** l'industrie *f* du vêtement
▸▸**c. allowance** indemnité *f* vestimentaire

clotted [ˈklɒtɪd] ADJ
▸▸*Br Culin* **c. cream** = crème *f* très épaisse typique du sud-ouest de l'Angleterre

clotting [ˈklɒtɪŋ] N *(of blood)* coagulation *f*

cloud [klaʊd] N **1** *Met* nuage *m*, *Lit* nuée *f*, *Fig* **to have one's head in the clouds** être dans

les nuages *ou* dans la lune; *Fam* **to be on c. nine** être aux anges; *Prov* **every c. has a silver lining** à quelque chose malheur est bon; *Fig* **to be under a c.** *(suspected)* être *ou* faire l'objet de soupçons; *(out of favour)* être en défaveur; **he left the firm under a c.** il a quitté la société dans une atmosphère de scandale étouffé; **this was not enough to remove the c. of suspicion hanging over him** cela ne suffit pas à faire oublier la méfiance à son égard
2 *(of smoke, dust)* nuage *m*, voile *m*
3 *(swarm) (of locusts etc)* nuée *f*
VT *(liquid)* troubler, rendre trouble; *(mirror)* ternir; *(by breathing on it)* embuer; *(sb's happiness)* troubler; *(reputation)* ternir; **a clouded sky** un ciel plein de nuages; **eyes clouded with tears** yeux voilés de larmes; **to c. the issue** embrouiller la question
VI *(of sky)* se couvrir *ou* se voiler (de nuages)
▸▸*Met* **c. bank** banc *m* de nuages; *Nucl* **c. chamber** chambre *f* de détente *ou* d'ionisation

▸ **cloud over** VI *(of sky)* se couvrir *ou* se voiler (de nuages); *Fig (of face)* s'assombrir; **it clouded over in the afternoon** ça s'est couvert dans l'après-midi

▸ **cloud up** VI **it's clouding up** ça se couvre; **the mirror had clouded up** le miroir s'était couvert de buée
VT SEP *(windows)* embuer

cloudburst [ˈklaʊdbɜːst] N trombe(s) *f(pl)* d'eau, averse *f* violente

cloud-cuckoo-land N **you're living in c. if you think ...** tu te fais des idées *ou* tu rêves doucement *ou* Can tu rêves en couleurs si tu penses que ...; **that's c.** il rêve/tu rêves/etc

clouded [ˈklaʊdɪd] ADJ *(sky)* couvert (de nuages); *(liquid)* trouble; **to become c.** *(of sky)* se couvrir; *(of mind)* s'obscurcir

cloudiness [ˈklaʊdɪnɪs] N **1** *(of sky)* aspect *m* nuageux **2** *(of liquid)* turbidité *f*

cloudless [ˈklaʊdlɪs] ADJ *(sky)* sans nuages

cloudy [ˈklaʊdɪ] ADJ **1** *(weather)* couvert; *(sky)* nuageux; **it's c.** le temps est couvert; **a c. day** un jour nuageux **2** *(liquid)* trouble; *Med (urine)* chargé

clout [klaʊt] N **1** *Fam (influence)* influence *f*, *(power)* poids *m*; **to have (plenty of) c.** *(be powerful)* être puissant; *(be influential)* avoir de l'influence *ou* le bras long **2** *Fam (blow)* coup *m*, taloche *f*, **to give sb/sth a c.** flanquer une taloche à qn/qch **3** *Br Old-fashioned, Dial (cloth)* chiffon *m*
VT *Fam* flanquer une taloche à

clove[1] [kləʊv] N *Bot, Culin* **c. of garlic** gousse *f* d'ail

clove[2] N **1** *Bot, Culin* clou *m* de girofle; **oil of cloves** essence *f* de girofle **2** *Bot (flower)* œillet-giroflée *m*, *pl* œillets-giroflées, œillet *m* des fleuristes; *(tree)* giroflier *m*
▸▸*Bot* **c. pink** œillet-giroflée, *pl* œillets-giroflées, œillet des fleuristes; *Bot* **c. tree** giroflier

clove[3] PT *see* cleave
▸▸**c. hitch** demi-clef *f*, *pl* demi-clefs, nœud *m* de cabestan

cloven [ˈkləʊv(ə)n] ADJ fendu, fourchu
▸▸**c. foot, c. hoof** *(of ruminant)* sabot *m* fendu; *(of devil)* pied *m* fourchu

cloven-footed, cloven-hoofed [ˈkləʊv(ə)nˈfʊtɪd, -ˈhuːft] ADJ *(ruminant)* aux sabots fendus; *(devil)* aux pieds fourchus

clover [ˈkləʊvər] N *(plant)* trèfle *m*; *Fam* **to be** *or* **live in c.** être *ou* vivre comme un coq en pâte
▸▸**c. honey** miel *m* de trèfle

cloverleaf, *pl* **cloverleafs, cloverleaves** [ˈkləʊvəliːf, -liːfs, -liːvz] N *Bot* feuille *f* de trèfle; *Aut* croisement *m* *ou* carrefour *m* en trèfle

▸▸*Aut* **c. intersection** croisement *ou* carrefour en trèfle

clown [klaʊn] **N** *(in circus)*, *Fig* clown *m*; *Theat* bouffon *m*; **to act the c.** faire le clown; **to make a c. of oneself** se ridiculiser
VI = **clown about**
▸ **clown about, clown around VI** faire le clown *ou* le pitre

clowning ['klaʊnɪŋ] **N** *Theat*, *Fig* bouffonneries *fpl*, pitreries *fpl*

clownish ['klaʊnɪʃ] **ADJ**clownesque

cloy [klɔɪ] **VI** *Lit* **delights that never c.** plaisirs dont on ne se lasse pas

cloying ['klɔɪɪŋ] **ADJ** *(cake, taste etc)*, *Fig* écœurant

club [klʌb] **N1** *(political, literary, gentlemen's etc)* club *m*, cercle *m*; *(sporting)* club; **football/tennis/yacht c.** club de football/tennis/yachting; **I've got a cold – join the c.!** j'ai un rhume – on est deux!; *Fam* **to be in the (pudding) c.** *(pregnant)* avoir un polichinelle dans le tiroir
2 *(nightclub)* boîte *f* de nuit; **the London c. scene** les milieux nocturnes londoniens
3 *(weapon etc)* massue *f*, gourdin *m*; *Golf* club *m*, crosse *f*; *Gym* **(Indian) c.** massue de gymnastique
4 *Cards* trèfle *m*; **ace of clubs** as *m* de trèfle
VT (-bb-) *(hit)* frapper avec une massue *ou* avec un gourdin; **to c. sb to death** tuer qn à coups de gourdin
▸▸**c. chair** club; *Aviat* **c. class** classe *f* club, classe affaires; *Med* **c. foot** pied *m* bot; **c. sandwich** sandwich *m* mixte *(à trois étages)*; **c. tie** cravate *f* aux couleurs d'une association sportive
▸ **club together VI** se cotiser, mettre son argent en commun; **to c. together to buy sth** se cotiser pour acheter qch

> **Clubs**
> Les "clubs" britanniques sont des lieux de rencontre et de détente très fermés, qui jouent un rôle important dans la vie sociale des milieux aisés en Grande-Bretagne. Traditionnellement ces institutions (notamment les "gentlemen's clubs" londoniens, tels que l'Athenaeum ou le Carlton Club) étaient interdites aux femmes, mais récemment cette tendance a commencé à changer.

clubbable ['klʌbəb(ə)l] **ADJ** *Old-fashioned* sociable

clubber ['klʌbər] **N** *Fam* fêtard *m*, adepte *mf* des boîtes de nuit

clubbing ['klʌbɪŋ] **N** *Fam* **to go c.** aller en boîte

clubfooted ['klʌbfʊtɪd] **ADJ** *Med* qui a un pied bot

clubhouse ['klʌbhaʊs] **N** *Golf*, *Tennis etc* pavillon *m*

clubland ['klʌblənd] **N1** *(area of gentlemen's clubs)* = quartier *m* des alentours de Saint James où se trouvent la plupart des clubs sélects de Londres **2** *(nightclub area)* = quartier *m* des boîtes de nuit

cluck [klʌk] **N** *(of hens)* gloussement *m*
VI *(of hen)* glousser; *(of person)* faire claquer sa langue

clucking ['klʌkɪŋ] **N** *(of hens)*, *Fig* *(of scandalized person)* gloussement *m*

clue [kluː] **N1** *(indication, hint)* indication *f*, indice *m*; *(to crime)* indice; **to get** *or* **find the c. to sth** trouver *ou* découvrir la clef de qch; **her hat provides a c. to her profession** on devine sa profession à son chapeau; **to give sb a c.** donner un indice à qn, mettre qn sur la voie *ou* sur la piste; *Fam* **I haven't got a c.** je n'en sais absolument rien, je n'en

ai pas la moindre idée; *Fam* **he hasn't got a c. what he's doing** il fait n'importe quoi; *Fam* **when it comes to physics I haven't got a c.** je ne pige rien à la physique **2** *(in crossword)* définition *f*; **what's the c. to 13 down?** quelle est la définition du 13 vertical?
▸ **clue in VT SEP** *Fam* *(inform)* renseigner, mettre au courant *ou* au parfum
▸ **clue up VT SEP** *Fam* *(usu passive)* **I'm not very clued up on astrophysics** je ne suis pas très calé en astrophysique

clueless ['kluːlɪs] **ADJ** *Fam* **he's quite c.** il ne sait rien de rien

clump [klʌmp] **N1** *(cluster)* *(of trees)* groupe *m*, bouquet *m*; *(of bushes, flowers)* massif *m* **2** *(lump)* *(of earth)* motte *f* **3** *(sound)* bruit *m* de pas lourd(s); **the c. of his footsteps** le bruit lourd de ses pas
VI1 *(group)* se grouper en masse compacte **2** **to c.** *(about* or *around)* *(of person)* marcher lourdement; **with the neighbours clumping about upstairs** avec les voisins qui font du potin en haut
VT grouper en masse compacte; *(bushes, flowers)* planter en massif

clumsily ['klʌmzɪlɪ] **ADV1** *(to move)* maladroitement, gauchement **2** *(drawn)* grossièrement; **c. built** mal bâti **3** *(to break bad news etc)* maladroitement, gauchement, sans tact

clumsiness ['klʌmzɪnɪs] **N1** *(of person, movement etc)* maladresse *f*, gaucherie *f* **2** *(of shape)* grossièreté *f*, lourdeur *f*; *(of sentence)* lourdeur, maladresse *f* **3** *(lack of tact)* manque *m* de tact, maladresse *f*

clumsy ['klʌmzɪ] **ADJ1** *(person, movement etc)* maladroit, gauche; **these boots are really c.** ce sont de vrais godillots, ces bottes **2** *(heavy)* *(phrase)* maladroit, gauche; *(shape)* lourd, disgracieux; **3** *(tactless)* *(person, excuse, remark)* maladroit, gauche

clung **PT, PP** *see* **cling**

clunk [klʌŋk] **N** bruit *m* sourd

cluster ['klʌstər] **N** *(of flowers, cherries)* bouquet *m*; *(of grapes)* grappe *f*; *(of stars)* amas *m*; *(of people, islands, houses, diamonds)* groupe *m*; *Comput* cluster *m*, bloc *m* *(d'information sur disque)*; *(of terminals)* grappe
VI **to c. round sb/sth** *(of people)* se grouper *ou* se rassembler autour de qn/qch; **to c. together** *(of particles etc)* se conglomérer
▸▸*Mktg* **c. analysis** analyse *f* par segments; **c. bomb** bombe *f* à fragmentation; *Mktg* **c. sample** échantillon *m* aréolaire, échantillon par grappes; *Mktg* **c. sampling** échantillonnage *m* aréolaire, échantillonnage par grappes

clutch¹ [klʌtʃ] **N1** *Aut etc* embrayage *m*; **to let in the c.** embrayer; **to release** *or* **let out the c.** débrayer **2** *(action)* prise *f*, étreinte *f*; **to make a c. at sth** essayer de saisir qch **3** *(claw)* *(of animal)* griffe *f*; *(of bird of prey)* serre *f*; **to fall into sb's clutches** tomber sous la patte *ou* la griffe *ou* entre les griffes de qn; **to escape from sb's clutches** se tirer des pattes *ou* des griffes de qn
VT *(to hold tightly)* tenir fermement; *(to seize)* agripper; **to c. hold of sth** s'agripper *ou* se cramponner à qch
VI **to c. at sth** tenter de s'agripper *ou* se cramponner à qch; *Fig* **to c. at straws** se raccrocher à n'importe quoi
▸▸**c. bag** pochette *f*; *Aut* **c. cone** cône *m* d'embrayage; *Aut* **c. disc** disque *m* d'embrayage; *Aut* **c. fluid** fluide *m* d'embrayage; *Aut* **c. housing** carter *m* d'embrayage; *Aut* **c. pedal** pédale *f* d'embrayage *ou* de débrayage; *Aut* **c. plate** plateau *m* d'embrayage; *Am* **c. purse** pochette *f*; *Aut* **c. slip** patinage *m* de l'embrayage; *Aut* **c. start** démarrage *m* à l'embrayage

clutch² **N** *(of eggs, chicks)* couvée *f*

clutter ['klʌtər] **N** encombrement *m*, désordre *m*, *Fam* pagaille *f*, *Fam* pagaïe *f*; *(of furniture etc)* entassement *m*; **the Victorians loved c.** les Victoriens adoraient accumuler des objets dans leurs maisons; **among the c. on her desk** au milieu du désordre *ou Fam* de la pagaille qu'il y a sur son bureau; **everything's in a c.** tout est en désordre *ou Fam* en pagaille
VT *(room, desk)* encombrer (**with** de); **to c. one's mind with useless facts** s'encombrer la mémoire de faits inutiles
▸ **clutter up VT SEP** = **clutter VT**

cluttered ['klʌtəd] **ADJ** encombré (**with** de); **the c. appearance of the room** l'impression d'encombrement qui se dégageait de la pièce

cm *(abbr* **centimetre**) cm

Cmdr *abbr* **Commander**

CMOS ['siːmɒs] **ADJ** *Comput* *(abbr* **complementary metal oxide silicon**) CMOS

CMR waybill [siːem'ɑː] **N** *Com* lettre *f* de voiture CMR

CMYK [siːemwaɪ'keɪ] **N** *Typ*, *Comput* *(abbr* **cyan, magenta, yellow, black**) CMJN

CND [siːen'diː] **N** *Br* *(abbr* **Campaign for Nuclear Disarmament**) = mouvement *m* pour le désarmement nucléaire

CNN [siːen'en] **N** *TV* *(abbr* **Cable News Network**) = réseau *m* d'information américain diffusé par câble et satellite

CO [siː'əʊ] **N** *Mil* **1** *abbr* **Commanding Officer 2** *abbr* **conscientious objector**

Co, co [kəʊ] *Com* *(abbr* **company**) Cie; *Fig* **Jane and co** Jane et compagnie

.co [dɒt'kəʊ] *Comput* = abréviation *f* désignant les entreprises commerciales dans les adresses électroniques britanniques

c/o *(abbr* **care of**) aux bons soins de, chez

coach [kəʊtʃ] **N1** *Br* *(motor vehicle)* car *m* **2** *Rail* voiture *f*, wagon *m* **3** *(trainer)* *Sport* entraîneur, -euse, *Fam* coach *m*; *Sch* répétiteur, -trice **4** *(horse-drawn)* carrosse *m*; *Hist* *(stage)* diligence *f*; **c. and four** carrosse à quatre chevaux; *Fig* **to drive a c. and horses through sth** démolir qch (en le critiquant), tailler qch en pièces
VT *Sch* donner des leçons particulières à; *Sport* *(person, team)* entraîner; **to c. sb in French** donner des leçons particulières en français à qn; *Theat* **to c. sb for a part** faire répéter un rôle à qn; **the police coached the witness** la police a préparé le témoin à la déclaration; **he had been carefully coached in what to say** on lui avait bien expliqué quoi dire
▸▸*Am Aviat* **c. class** classe *f* économique; *Am Aviat* **c. fare** tarif *m* économique; **c. house** remise *f* *(pour carrosse ou voiture)*; **c. party** groupe *m* voyageant en autocar; **c. shuttle** autocar *m* navette; *Br* **c. station** gare *f* routière; **c. tour** circuit *m* (touristique) en car, voyage *m* en autocar; *(excursion)* excursion *f* en car; **c. tour operator** autocariste *m*; **c. trip** excursion en car

coachbuilder ['kəʊtʃbɪldər] **N** *Aut* carrossier *m*

coaching ['kəʊtʃɪŋ] **N** *Sport* entraînement *m*; *Sch* leçons *fpl* particulières
▸▸*Hist* **c. inn** relais *m*

coachman, pl coachmen ['kəʊtʃmən] **N** cocher *m*

coachwork ['kəʊtʃwɜːk] **N** *Aut* carrosserie *f*

coagulant [kəʊ'ægjʊlənt] **N** coagulant *m*

coagulate [kəʊ'ægjʊleɪt] **VT** coaguler
VI (se) coaguler

coagulation [kəʊægjʊ'leɪʃən] **N** coagulation *f*

coal [kəʊl] **N** charbon *m*; *(ore)* houille *f*; **a piece** *or* **lump of c.** un morceau de charbon;

the c. (mining) industry l'industrie *f* minière *ou* houillère; *Fig* to carry coals to Newcastle porter de l'eau à la rivière; *Fig* to haul sb over the coals réprimander qn vertement; live coals braise *f*, charbons *mpl* ardents

VT *Naut (ship)* approvisionner en charbon; to c. ship charbonner

VI *Naut* charbonner

▸▸ *Br* c. bunker coffre *m* à charbon; *Naut* soute *f* à charbon; c. cellar cave *f* à charbon; *Min* c. cutter *(person)* haveur *m*; *(machine)* haveuse *f*; c. gas gaz *m* de houille; c. merchant charbonnier, -ière, marchand, -ande de charbon; c. mine mine *f* de charbon *ou* de houille, houillère *f*; c. miner mineur *m*; c. mining exploitation *f* du charbon *ou* de la houille; c. scuttle seau *m* à charbon; c. shovel pelle *f* à charbon; c. strike grève *f* des mineurs; c. tar coaltar *m*, goudron *m* de houille

coal-black ADJ noir comme du charbon

coalesce [kəʊə'les] VI *(of parties, movements)* s'unir, fusionner; *Chem* se combiner

coalescence [kəʊə'lesəns] N union *f*, fusion *f*

coalface ['kəʊlfeɪs] N *Min* front *m* de taille

coalfield ['kəʊlfiːld] N *Min* bassin *m* houiller

coal-fired [-faɪəd] ADJ (alimenté) au charbon

coalition [kəʊə'lɪʃən] N coalition *f*; *Pol* to form a c. former une coalition, se coaliser; a c. government une coalition gouvernementale

coalman, *pl* coalmen ['kəʊlmən] N (petit) marchand *m* de charbon, charbonnier *m*

coalshed ['kəʊlʃed] N hangar *m* à charbon

coal-tar soap N savon *m* au coaltar

coaltit ['kəʊltɪt] N *(bird)* mésange *f* noire

coarse [kɔːs] ADJ **1** *(vulgar)* grossier, vulgaire; *(language, joke)* grossier **2** *(material)* gros, grossier; *(skin, hands)* rugueux, rêche; *(hair)* rêche; *(features)* grossier, lourd **3** *(food, drink)* ordinaire, commun; this is a fairly c. wine ce vin n'est pas très fin; c. red wine du gros rouge

▸▸ c. cut marmalade marmelade *f* avec des écorces d'orange; c. fish poisson *m* d'eau douce *(sauf truite et saumon)*; c. fishing pêche *f* à la ligne en eau douce; c. grain gros grain *m*; c. salt gros sel *m*; c. sandpaper papier de verre *m* épais; c. weave texture *f* grossière

coarsely ['kɔːslɪ] ADV **1** *(vulgarly)* grossièrement, vulgairement **2** *(ground)* grossièrement; *(chopped etc)* gros

coarsen ['kɔːs(ə)n] VT rendre (plus) grossier

VI devenir (plus) grossier

coarseness ['kɔːsnɪs] N **1** *(vulgarity)* grossièreté *f*, vulgarité *f* **2** *(roughness) (of skin, hair)* rudesse *f*, *(of material)* texture *f* grossière

coast [kəʊst] N *(of sea)* côte *f*, rivage *m*; *(extensive)* littoral *m*; *Br* the c. *(seaside)* la côte; from c. to c. d'un bout à l'autre du pays; the country's Caribbean c. la côte caraïbe du pays; two miles off the c. of France *or* the French c. à deux mil(l)es de la côte française; the country has no sea c. le pays n'est bordé par aucune mer; we took the c. road nous avons pris la route qui longe la mer; *Fig* the c. is clear le champ *ou* la voie est libre

VI *(on bicycle, in car etc)* avancer en roue libre; *(downhill)* descendre en roue libre; *(on sledge)* descendre en luge; *Fig* he coasted home *(in race)* il a gagné sans effort; she coasted through her exams elle a passé ses examens sans difficulté *ou Fam* les doigts dans le nez; *Fig* you're coasting *(not working hard)* tu te la coules douce

coastal ['kəʊst(ə)l] ADJ côtier, littoral, -aux

▸▸ c. defence défense *f* côtière; c. naviga-

tion navigation *f* côtière, cabotage *m*; c. resort station *f* balnéaire; c. waters eaux *fpl* littorales

coaster ['kəʊstər] N **1** *Naut (ship)* cabotier *m*, caboteur *m* **2** *(for wine bottle/carafe)* dessous *m* de bouteille/de carafe; *(for glass)* dessous de verre

coastguard ['kəʊstgɑːd] N **1** *(no pl) (force)* garde-côtes *mpl*; he's in the c. il est garde-côte; a c. official un garde-côte **2** *(person)* garde-côte *m*, *pl* garde-côtes

▸▸ c. cutter garde-côte; c. station bureau *m* de la gendarmerie maritime; c. vessel garde-côte

coastguard(s)man, *pl* -men [kəʊst-'gɑːd(z)mən] N garde-côte *m*, *pl* garde-côtes

coasting ['kəʊstɪŋ] N *Naut* navigation *f* côtière

▸▸ c. vessel caboteur *m*

coastline ['kəʊstlaɪn] N littoral *m*

coat [kəʊt] N **1** *(short)* veste *f*, *(long)* manteau *m*; *(for men)* manteau, pardessus *m*; *esp Am (of man's suit)* veston *m*; morning c. jaquette *f*, car c. manteau trois quarts; lab c. blouse *f* blanche

2 *(of dog, horse)* robe *f*, *(of big cat)* pelage *m*

3 *(of snow etc)* manteau *m*, couche *f*

4 *(of paint, varnish, tar etc)* couche *f*, application *f*

VT *(with paint, tar etc)* enduire, couvrir; *(with chocolate etc)* enrober; *(cable)* revêtir, armer (with de); *(paper)* coucher; to c. with sugar enrober de sucre; *(pill)* dragéifier; *(almonds)* recouvrir de sucre; to c. sth with dust couvrir qch de poussière

▸▸ *Her* c. of arms blason *m*, armoiries *fpl*; c. hanger cintre *m*; c. hook patère *f*, *Hist* c. of mail cotte *f* de mailles; c. rack portemanteau *m*

coated ['kəʊtɪd] ADJ *(with dust, mud)* (re)couvert (with de); *(with sugar, chocolate)* enrobé (with de); *(tongue)* chargé, pâteux; *(paper)* couché

coati [kəʊ'ɑːtɪ] N *Zool* coati *m*

coating ['kəʊtɪŋ] N *(of paint, varnish etc)* couche *f*, *(of chocolate)* couche, enrobage *m*

coat-tails NPL basques *fpl* *ou* pan *m* d'un habit; *(of tail coat)* queue-de-pie *f*, *Fig* to ride *or* hang on sb's c. profiter de l'influence de qn

co-author N coauteur *m*

VT *(book)* écrire en collaboration; a book co-authored by Marsh and Brown un livre écrit conjointement par Marsh et Brown

coax [kəʊks] VT *(person)* enjôler; to c. sb into doing sth amener qn à faire qch en l'enjôlant *ou* par les cajoleries; to c. sth out of sb obtenir qch de qn en l'enjôlant *ou* par les cajoleries

coaxial [kəʊ'æksɪəl] ADJ *Elec (cable etc)* coaxial, -aux

coaxing ['kəʊksɪŋ] ADJ *(tone etc)* cajoleur, enjôleur

N cajoleries *fpl*; he took a lot of c. il s'est bien fait tirer l'oreille; no amount of c. would get him to agree malgré les efforts pour l'enjôler, on n'a pas réussi à le faire accepter

cob [kɒb] N **1** *(horse)* cob *m*

2 *(swan)* cygne *m* mâle

3 *(hazelnut)* aveline *f*, grosse noisette *f*

4 *(corn)* c. *(with grain)* épi *m* de maïs; *(without grain)* rafle *f*, *Culin* corn on the c. maïs *m* en épi

5 *Br (type of loaf)* pain *m* rond, miche *f* de pain

▸▸ c. swan cygne mâle

cobalt ['kəʊbɔːlt] N **1** *Chem* cobalt *m* **2** *(colour)* bleu *m* de cobalt

▸▸ c. bloom fleur *f* de cobalt; c. blue bleu de cobalt; *Chem* c. bomb bombe *f* au cobalt

cobber ['kɒbə] N *Austr Fam* copain *m*, pote *m*

cobble ['kɒb(ə)l] N *(of roadway)* pavé *m*

VT 1 *(road etc)* paver **2** *Br Old-fashioned (shoes)* réparer

▸ **cobble together** VT SEP *(make hastily, get together) (bookcase, newspaper article, team etc)* bricoler

cobbled ['kɒb(ə)ld] ADJ *(path, street)* pavé

cobbler ['kɒblər] N **1** *Br (shoe repairer)* cordonnier, -ière; *(maker of shoes)* bottier *m* **2** *Am Culin* = dessert *m* chaud à base de fruits recouvert d'une génoise

cobblers ['kɒbləz] *Br Sl* NPL **1** *(rubbish)* conneries *fpl*; that's c. c'est des conneries tout ça **2** *Vulg (testicles)* couilles *fpl*

INT quelles foutaises!

cobblestone ['kɒb(ə)lstəʊn] N *(on roadway)* pavé *m*

cobloaf ['kɒbləʊf] N *Br* pain *m* rond, miche *f* de pain

cobnut ['kɒbnʌt] N aveline *f*, grosse noisette *f*

COBOL ['kəʊbɒl] N *Comput (abbr* Common Business-Oriented Language*)* Cobol *m*

cobra ['kəʊbrə] N cobra *m*

co-branding N *Mktg* alliance *f* de marque, co-branding *m*

cobweb ['kɒbweb] N *(web)* toile *f* d'araignée; *(thread)* fil *m* d'araignée; *Fig* to go for a walk to blow away the cobwebs prendre l'air pour se rafraîchir les idées; *Fig* to brush the cobwebs off sth ressortir qch

coca ['kəʊkə] N *Bot* coca *m or f*, *Pharm* coca *f*

cocaine [kə'keɪn] N cocaïne *f*, c. addict cocaïnomane *mf*

coccyx ['kɒksɪks] N *Anat* coccyx *m*, rachis *m* coccygien

cochineal ['kɒtʃɪniːl] N cochenille *f*

cock [kɒk] N **1** *(male fowl)* coq *m*; *(male bird)* *(oiseau m)* mâle *m*; fighting c. coq de combat; *Fig* c. of the walk *or* of the roost coq de village; at university he was the c. of the walk à l'université, c'était un vrai petit coq (de village)

2 *Vulg (penis)* bit(t)e *f*

3 *Tech etc (in plumbing)* robinet *m*

4 *(on firearm)* chien *m*; at full c. au cran de l'armé; *Fig* to go off at half c. rater; *(of person)* démarrer au quart de tour

5 *Br Sl (form of address)* watcher c.! salut, mon vieux!

VT 1 to c. one's eye at sb/sth donner un coup d'œil à qn/qch; to c. one's hat *(put on one side)* mettre son chapeau de côté

2 to c. (up) its ears *(of horse, dog)* dresser les oreilles

3 *(gun)* armer

▸▸ c. canary serin *m*; c. lobster homard *m* mâle; c. pheasant coq faisan *m*; c. sparrow moineau *m* mâle

▸ **cock up** *Br Sl* VT SEP bousiller

VI merder

cockade [kɒ'keɪd] N cocarde *f*

cock-a-doodle-doo ['kɒkəduːd(ə)l'duː] INT cocorico!

cock-a-hoop [kɒkə'huːp] ADJ jubilant; *(having done sth)* triomphant; all c. fier comme Artaban

cock-a-leekie [kɒkə'liːkɪ] N *Scot Culin* = bouillon *m* de volaille aux poireaux et à l'avoine

▸▸ c. soup = bouillon de volaille aux poireaux et à l'avoine

cock-and-bull N *Fam* balivernes *fpl*

▸▸ c. story histoire *f* à dormir debout

cockatoo [kɒkə'tuː] N cacatoès *m*

cockchafer ['kɒktʃeɪfər] N *(beetle)* hanneton *m*

cockcrow ['kɒkkrəʊ] N chant *m* du coq; to rise at c. se lever au (premier) chant du coq *ou* à l'aube

cocked [kɒkt] ADJ
▸▸**c. hat** chapeau *m* à cornes; *Fam* **to knock sb into a c. hat** *(defeat)* battre qn à plate(s) couture(s), démolir qn; *(be better than)* dépasser qn de très loin, *Fam* enfoncer qn; **as for cooking, she knocks me into a c. hat** pour ce qui est de la cuisine, je ne lui arrive pas à la cheville

cocker ['kɒkər] N *(dog)* cocker *m*
▸▸**c. spaniel** cocker

cockerel ['kɒk(ə)r(ə)l] N jeune coq *m*, coquelet *m*

cockeyed ['kɒkaɪd] ADJ *Fam* **1** *(absurd)* farfelu; *(story)* qui ne tient pas debout **2** *(person)* qui a un œil qui dit zut à l'autre

cockfight ['kɒkfaɪt] N combat *m* de coqs

cockfighting ['kɒkfaɪtɪŋ] N combats *mpl* de coqs

cockiness ['kɒkɪnɪs] N assurance *f* excessive; **because of his c.** parce qu'il était trop sûr de lui

cockle ['kɒk(ə)l] N *(mollusc)* coque *f*, fausse praire *f*, *Fig* **that will warm the cockles of your heart** voilà qui vous réchauffera le cœur

cockleshell ['kɒk(ə)lʃel] N **1** *(boat)* coquille *f* de noix **2** *(of mollusc)* coquille *f* de coque

Cockney ['kɒknɪ] ADJ cockney
N **1** *(person)* Cockney *mf (des quartiers de l'est de Londres)* **2** *(dialect)* cockney *m*

cockpit ['kɒkpɪt] N **1** *(of plane)* poste *m* de pilotage, cockpit *m*; *(of racing car)* cockpit *m* **2** *(in cockfighting)* arène *f* de combats de coqs

cockroach ['kɒkrəʊtʃ] N *(insect)* blatte *f*, cafard *m*

cockscomb ['kɒkskəʊm] N *(on bird)* crête *f* de coq

cocksure [kɒk'ʃʊər] ADJ trop sûr de soi

cocktail ['kɒkteɪl] N *(drink)*, *Fig* cocktail *m*
▸▸**c. bar** bar *m*; **c. cabinet** bar *(meuble)*; **c. dress** robe *f* de cocktail; **c. lounge** bar; **c. mixer** shaker *m*; **c. party** cocktail *(fête)*; **c. sausage** petite saucisse *f* (à apéritif); **c. shaker** shaker; **c. stick** pique *f* à apéritif

cockup ['kɒkʌp] N *Br Sl* connerie *f*, cagade *f*; **the mission was a complete c.** la mission a complètement merdé *ou* foiré; **to make a c. of sth** *(exam, interview, speech, relationship)* foutre qch en l'air

cocky ['kɒkɪ] ADJ *Fam* trop sûr de soi, culotté; **don't get c.!** ne prends pas tes airs supérieurs

cocoa ['kəʊkəʊ] N *(powder, drink)* cacao *m*
▸▸**c. bean** graine *f* de cacao; **c. butter** beurre *m* de cacao

coconut ['kəʊkənʌt] N *(noix f de)* coco *m*
▸▸**c. butter** beurre *m* de coco; **c. fibre** fibre *f* de coco, coir *m*; **c. matting** tapis *m* en fibres de noix de coco; **c. milk** lait *m* de coco; **c. oil** huile *f* de coco; **c. palm** cocotier *m*; **c. shy** jeu *m* de massacre *(où l'on essaie d'abattre des noix de coco)*; **c. tree** cocotier

cocoon [kə'ku:n] N *(of silkworm etc)* cocon *m*
VT envelopper (**in** dans); *Fig* **workers in the public sector have been cocooned from unemployment** les travailleurs du secteur public ont été protégés du chômage

cocooning [kə'ku:nɪŋ] N cocooning *m*

COD, cod [si:əʊ'di:] *Com (abbr* **cash** *or Am* **collect on delivery)** contre remboursement, paiement à la livraison

cod² [kɒd] N **1** *(fish)* morue *f*; **fresh c.** morue fraîche, cabillaud *m*; **dried c.** morue sèche, merluche *f*; **c.'s roe** œufs *mpl* de morue **2** *Br Sl (nonsense)* foutaises *fpl*

coda ['kəʊdə] N *Mus* coda *f*

coddle ['kɒd(ə)l] VT **1** *(spoil)* choyer, dorloter; **to c. oneself** se dorloter **2** *Culin (eggs)* à peine faire cuire; **coddled eggs** des œufs *mpl* à peine cuits

code [kəʊd] N **1** *Tel, Comput* code *m*; *Tel* **(dialling) c.** indicatif *m*; **the terrorist used a c. word** le terroriste a utilisé un code; *Comput* **computer c.** code machine
2 *(secret writing)* code *m*, chiffre *m*; **to write a message in c.** coder *ou* chiffrer un message; **the letter was in c.** la lettre était codée
3 *(rules etc)* code *m*; **c. of conduct** déontologie *f*, code de conduite; **c. of criminal procedure** code d'instruction criminelle; **c. of honour** code *ou* règles *fpl* de l'honneur; **c. of practice** règlements *mpl* et usages, déontologie
VT **1** *(message etc)* coder, mettre en code *ou* en chiffre **2** *Comput* coder
▸▸**c. book** *(for encoding)* code *ou* carnet *m* de chiffrement; *(for decoding)* code *ou* carnet de déchiffrement; **c. letter** lettre *f* code; **c. message** message *m* codé *ou* chiffré; **c. name** nom *m* de code; **c. translation** transcodage *m*
▸ **code up** VT SEP *Typ (text)* insérer les codes dans

coded ['kəʊdɪd] ADJ **1** *(message etc)* codé, chiffré **2** *Comput* codé
▸▸*Aut* **c. engine immobilizer** antidémarrage *m* codé, ADC *m*; **c. signal** *(in video)* signal *m* codé

co-defendant N *Law* coaccusé, -ée; *(in civil law)* codéfendeur, -eresse

codeine ['kəʊdi:n] N *Pharm* codéine *f*

coder ['kəʊdər] N *(device)* codeur *m*

code-sharing N partage *m* de code, code sharing *m*

codex, *pl* **codices** ['kəʊdeks, -ɪsi:z] N manuscrit *m* (ancien)

codger ['kɒdʒər] N *Br Fam* **an old c.** un vieux bonhomme

codicil ['kɒdɪsɪl] N *Law (of will)* codicille *m*

codification [kəʊdɪfɪ'keɪʃən] N codification *f*

codify ['kəʊdɪfaɪ] VT *(laws etc)* codifier

coding ['kəʊdɪŋ] N **1** *(putting into code)* codification *f*, codage *m* **2** *Comput (providing codes)* codage *m*; *(system of codes)* codes *mpl*
▸▸*Comput* **c. error** erreur *f* de codage; *Comput* **c. line** ligne *f* de programmation; *Comput* **c. sequence** séquence *f* programmée

co-director N codirecteur, -trice

cod-liver oil N huile *f* de foie de morue

codpiece ['kɒdpi:s] N braguette *f*

co-driver N *Sport* copilote *mf*

codswallop ['kɒdzwɒləp] N *Br Sl* foutaises *fpl*; **it's a load of (old) c.** c'est un tas de foutaises

co-ed ['kəʊ'ed] *Fam* ADJ *(school)* mixte; **to go c.** *(of school)* devenir mixte
N **1** *Br (school)* école *f* mixte **2** *Am (pupil)* élève *f* d'une école mixte

coeducation ['kəʊedjʊ'keɪʃən] N enseignement *m* mixte

coeducational ['kəʊedjʊ'keɪʃənəl] ADJ mixte

coefficient [kəʊɪ'fɪʃənt] N *Math, Phys* coefficient *m*

coelacanth ['si:ləkænθ] N cœlacanthe *m*

coeliac, *Am* **celiac** ['si:lɪæk] *Med* ADJ cœliaque
N = personne *f* atteinte de maladie cœliaque
▸▸**c. disease** maladie *f* cœliaque

coerce [kəʊ'ɜ:s] VT forcer, contraindre (**sb into doing sth** qn à faire qch)

coercion [kəʊ'ɜ:ʃən] N coercition *f*, contrainte *f*; *Law* coaction *f*; **to act under c.** agir sous la coercition; **to use c. to obtain a confession** utiliser la contrainte pour obtenir une confession

coexist ['kəʊɪg'zɪst] VI coexister (**with** avec)

coexistence ['kəʊɪg'zɪstəns] N coexistence *f* (**with** avec); *Pol* **peaceful c.** coexistence pacifique

coexistent ['kəʊɪg'zɪstənt] ADJ coexistant (**with** avec)

C of E [si:əv'vi:] ADJ *Rel (abbr* **Church of England)** anglican

coffee ['kɒfɪ] N **1** *(drink)* café *m*; **two coffees, please!** deux cafés, s'il vous plaît!; **black c.** café noir; *Br* **white c.**, *Am* **c. with milk** café crème, crème *m* **2** *(colour) (dark)* café *m inv*, *(light)* café au lait *inv*
ADJ *(colour) (dark)* café *inv*; *(light)* café au lait *inv*
▸▸*Br* **c. bar** café, cafétéria *f*; **c. bean** grain *m* de café; **c. break** pause-café *f*, *pl* pauses-café; **c. cream** *(chocolate)* chocolat *m* fourré au café; **c. cup** tasse *f* à café; **c. grinder** moulin *m* à café; **c. grounds** marc *m* de café; **c. machine** cafetière *f* électrique; *(in café)* percolateur *m*; *(drinks dispenser)* machine *f* à café; **c. mill** moulin à café; **c. pot** cafetière; **c. shop** *(small restaurant)* ≃ café-restaurant *m*, *pl* cafés-restaurants; *(shop selling coffee)* magasin *m* spécialisé dans le café; **c. spoon** cuillère *f ou* cuiller *f* à café, petite cuillère *ou* cuiller; *(smaller)* cuillère *ou* cuiller à moka; **c. table** table *f* basse; **c. tree** caféier *m*

coffee-coloured ADJ *(dark)* café *inv*; *(light)* café au lait *inv*

coffee-maker N cafetière *f* électrique

coffee-table book N = livre *m* de grand format abondamment illustré *(destiné à être feuilleté plutôt que véritablement lu)*

coffer ['kɒfər] N **1** *(chest)* coffre *m*; *Fig* **the coffers** *(of country, organization etc)* les caisses *fpl*; *Fig* **to swell the State coffers** renflouer les caisses de l'État **2** *Archit (of ceiling)* caisson *m* **3** *(in dam, lock etc)* chambre *f*, bassin *m*, sas *m* **4** = **cofferdam**
VT **1** *Min, Constr (well)* coffrer **2** *(ceiling)* diviser en caissons; **coffered ceiling** plafond *m* à caissons

cofferdam ['kɒfədæm] N *Tech* coffre *m*, batardeau *m*, caisson *m* hydraulique

coffering ['kɒfərɪŋ] N *Min etc* coffrage *m*

coffin ['kɒfɪn] N **1** cercueil *m*, bière *f*, *Fam* **that's another nail in his c.** *(he's closer to death)* c'est (pour lui) un pas de plus vers la tombe; *(he's closer to defeat, disaster etc)* c'est un autre coup funeste pour lui **2** *(of horseshoe)* cavité *f* du sabot
▸▸*Br Fam Pej* **c. dodger** *(old person)* croulant, -ante; *Fam Hum* **c. nail** *(cigarette)* clope *m ou f*, tige *f*

cofounder [kəʊ'faʊndər] N cofondateur, -trice

cog [kɒg] N **1** *(of cogwheel)* dent *f*; **the cogs** la denture; *Fig* **I'm only a c. in the machinery** je ne suis qu'un rouage de la machine **2** *(wheel)* pignon *m*, roue *f* dentée
▸▸**c. rail** crémaillère *f*, *Am* **c. railroad** chemin *m* de fer à crémaillère; *Br* **c. railway** chemin de fer à crémaillère

cogency ['kəʊdʒənsɪ] N force *f*, puissance *f*

cogent ['kəʊdʒənt] ADJ *(argument)* convaincant; *(reason)* valable, convaincant

cogently ['kəʊdʒəntlɪ] ADV avec force, puissamment

cogitate ['kɒdʒɪteɪt] VI *Fml* méditer, réfléchir (**on, over** sur)

cogitation [kɒdʒɪ'teɪʃən] N réflexion *f* (**on, over** sur)

cognac ['kɒnjæk] N cognac *m*

cognate ['kɒgneɪt] N **1** *Ling* mot *m* de même origine **2** *Law* cognat *m*
ADJ *Fml* apparenté; *Ling* de même origine

cognition [kɒg'nɪʃən] N cognition f, connaissance f

cognitive ['kɒgnɪtɪv] ADJ cognitif

cognizance ['kɒgnɪzəns, 'kɒnɪzəns] N 1 *Fml (knowledge)* connaissance f; **to take c. of sth** prendre connaissance de qch 2 *Law (of a court)* compétence f; **within** or **under the c. of a court** de la compétence ou du ressort d'une cour

cognizant ['kɒgnɪzənt, 'kɒnɪzənt] ADJ 1 *Fml* ayant connaissance (**of** de); **to be c. of a fact** être instruit ou avoir connaissance d'un fait 2 *Law* **court c. of an offence** tribunal m compétent pour juger un délit

cognoscenti [kɒnjəʊ'ʃentɪ, kɒgnə-] NPL connaisseurs mpl, spécialistes mpl

COGS [kɒgz] N *Acct (abbr* **cost of goods sold**) coût m des produits vendus

cogwheel ['kɒgwiːl] N roue f à dents ou dentée, roue d'engrenage

cohabit [kəʊ'hæbɪt] VI vivre maritalement (**with** avec)

cohabitation [kəʊhæbɪ'teɪʃən] N vie f maritale, union f libre (**with** avec)

cohabitee [kəʊhæbɪ'tiː] N compagnon m, compagne f

cohere [kəʊ'hɪər] VI *(of whole, of parts)* tenir ensemble; *(of argument, style)* se suivre (logiquement), être cohérent; **they don't c. as a team** ils ne forment pas une équipe unie

coherence [kəʊ'hɪərəns] N *(of argument, style)* suite f (logique), cohérence f

coherent [kəʊ'hɪərənt] ADJ *(whole)* cohérent; *(plan, speech, thinker etc)* cohérent, logique; *(argument)* qui se tient, logique; *Fam* **the man wasn't c.** il racontait n'importe quoi, il était incohérent

coherently [kəʊ'hɪərəntlɪ] ADV d'une manière cohérente, avec cohérence

cohesion [kəʊ'hiːʒən] N cohésion f
▸▸ *EU* **c. policy** politique f de cohésion

cohesive [kəʊ'hiːsɪv] ADJ cohésif; *Phys (force)* de cohésion

cohort ['kəʊhɔːt] N *Antiq, Mil* cohorte f, *Fig* **he was there with his cohorts** il était là avec toute une armée de suiveurs; **a c. of lawyers** une armée d'avocats

coiffure [kwaː'fjʊər] N coiffure f

coil [kɔɪl] N 1 *(roll) (of rope)* rouleau m; *(of wire)* rouleau, torque f
2 *(single loop) (of rope)* pli m, repli m; *(of snake)* anneau m; *(of hair)* boucle f
3 *(in hairdressing)* rouleau m (de cheveux), chignon m
4 *Med (contraceptive)* stérilet m
5 *Elec* bobine f
VT (en)rouler; *Elec (wire)* bobiner; **to c. sth around sth** enrouler qch autour de qch; **to c. itself up** *(of snake)* s'enrouler, se lover
VI serpenter; *(of snake)* se lover
▸▸ *Aut* **c. ignition system** circuit m d'allumage par bobine

coiled [kɔɪld] ADJ (en)roulé; *(spring)* en spirale; *(snake)* lové; *Fig* **like a c. spring** tendu, prêt à l'action

coin [kɔɪn] N 1 pièce f de monnaie; **a 10p c.** une pièce de 10 pence 2 *(no pl) (currency)* monnaie f, *Fig* **to pay sb back in their own c.** rendre à qn la monnaie de sa pièce
VT 1 **to c. money** frapper de la monnaie; *Fig Fam* **he's simply coining money** or **coining it** il fait des affaires en or 2 *(invent) (new word)* inventer, créer; **to c. a phrase** inventer une formule; *Iron* ..., **to c. a phrase** ... pour employer le cliché habituel

coinage ['kɔɪnɪdʒ] N 1 *(coins)* monnaie(s) f(pl), *Spec* numéraire m 2 *(coining) (of money)* frappe f 3 *(invention)* **the word is a recent c.** c'est un mot nouveau, c'est un néo-

logisme 4 *(currency) (of country)* système m monétaire

coincide [kəʊɪn'saɪd] VI 1 *(in space, time)* coïncider (**with** avec) 2 *(agree) (of interests, opinions etc)* coïncider, s'accorder (**with** avec)

coincidence [kəʊ'ɪnsɪdəns] N coïncidence f; **what a c.!** quelle coïncidence!; **it is no c. that** ... ce n'est pas une coïncidence si ...

coincidental [kəʊɪnsɪ'dent(ə)l] ADJ **it was more than merely c. that** ... ce n'était pas une coïncidence si ...; **this had the c. effect of** ... par coïncidence, cela a eu le résultat de ...; **any similarity with** ... **is purely c.** toute ressemblance avec ... ne serait que pure coïncidence

coincidentally [kəʊɪnsɪ'dentlɪ] ADV par (pure) coïncidence

coiner ['kɔɪnər] N *(of word, expression)* inventeur, -trice

coin-op N *Fam* laverie f automatique

coin-operated [-ɒpəreɪtɪd] ADJ automatique
▸▸ **c. laundry** laverie f automatique

co-insurance N coassurance f

co-insurer N coassureur m

coitus ['kɔɪtəs, 'kɔɪ-] N *Fml* coït m
▸▸ **c. interruptus** coït m interrompu

Coke® [kəʊk] N *Fam* Coca® m

coke¹ N *(fuel)* coke m; **c. oven** four m à coke
VT *(coal)* cokéfier, convertir en coke
VI *(of coal)* se cokéfier, se convertir en coke

coke² N *Fam (cocaine)* neige f, blanche f, coke f

cokehead ['kəʊkhed] N *Fam* **to be a c.** marcher à la coke

coking ['kəʊkɪŋ] ADJ *(coal)* cokéfiable
N cokéfaction f, coké(i)fication f

Col 1 *(abbr* **Colonel**) Col 2 *abbr* **Colombia** 3 *abbr* **Colorado**

col¹ [kɒl] N *Geog* col m

col² *(abbr* **column**) col

COLA ['kəʊlə] N *Am Admin (abbr* **cost-of-living adjustment** or *Can* **allowance**) = augmentation f de salaire indexée sur le coût de la vie, *Can* IVC f, indemnité f de vie chère

colander ['kʌləndər, 'kɒl-] N passoire f

cold [kəʊld] ADJ 1 *(weather, bath, meal, engine etc)* froid; **it's c.** *(ice-cream, food, object etc)* c'est froid; *(weather)* il fait froid; **to get** or **grow c.** se refroidir; **it's getting c.** *(weather)* le temps se refroidit, il commence à faire froid; **it's getting colder** *(weather)* la température baisse; **to be** or **feel c.** *(of person)* avoir froid; *Fam* **out c.** sans connaissance, inanimé; **to knock sb out c.** étendre qn raide; *esp Am* **you'll knock them c.!** *(with your performance)* tu vas faire un tabac!; **you're c.** *(in game)* tu gèles; **my hands are c.** j'ai les mains froides, j'ai froid aux mains; **my feet are as c. as ice** j'ai les pieds glacés; *Fig* **to have c. feet** avoir la frousse; **the scent had gone c.** *(in hunting)*, *Fig* on avait perdu sa/leur/etc trace
2 *Fig (person, manner, welcome etc)* froid; **to be c. with sb** se montrer froid avec qn; **to give sb the c. shoulder** tourner le dos à qn, snober qn; *Fam* **that leaves me c.** cela me laisse froid; *Fam* **he's a c. fish** c'est un pisse-froid
ADV 1 *Am Fam* **to turn sb down c.** envoyer promener qn 2 *(without preparation)* à froid; *Surg* **to operate c.** opérer à froid
N 1 *(of the weather etc)* froid m; **I feel the c.** je suis très frileux; *Fig* **to leave sb out in the c.** laisser qn à l'écart; *Fig* **to be left out in the c.** rester sur le carreau; *Fig* **to come in from the c.** rentrer en faveur ou en grâce
2 *Med* **(common) c.** rhume m; **to have a c.** être enrhumé, avoir un rhume; **a bad** or

heavy c. un gros rhume; **c. in the head, head c.** rhume de cerveau; **c. on the chest, chest c.** rhume de poitrine; **to catch (a) c.** s'enrhumer, attraper un rhume
▸▸ **c. buffet** buffet m froid; *Com, Mktg* **c. call** visite f à froid; *(on phone)* appel m à froid; *Com, Mktg* **c. calling** visites f à froid; *(on phone)* appels f à froid; *Tech* **c. chisel** ciseau m à froid; **c. cream** crème f de beauté, cold-cream m; *Am Culin* **c. cuts** viandes fpl froides; *(on menu)* assiette f anglaise; **c. drink** boisson f fraîche; *Met* **c. front** front m froid; *Culin* **c. meats** viandes froides; *(on menu)* assiette anglaise; **c. remedy** remède m contre le rhume; *Tech* **c. riveting** rivure f à froid; *Com, Mktg* **c. selling** vente f à froid; **c. snap** vague f de froid; **c. sore** bouton m de fièvre, *Can* feu m sauvage; *Aut, Comput* **c. start** démarrage m à froid; *Aut* **c. start protection** protection f de démarrage à froid; **c. storage** conservation f par le froid; **c. storage dock** dock m frigorifique; **c. store** *(room)* chambre f froide ou frigorifique; *(warehouse)* entrepôt m frigorifique; **c. tap** robinet m d'eau froide; *Fam* **c. turkey** *(drugs withdrawal)* manque m; *Pol* **c. war** guerre f froide; *Pol* **c. warrior** partisan, -ane de la guerre froide

cold-blooded [-'blʌdɪd] ADJ 1 *(animal)* à sang froid; **reptiles are c.** les reptiles sont des animaux à sang froid 2 *Fig (unemotional)* froid, insensible; *(murderer etc)* sans pitié; *(murder etc)* (commis) de sang-froid

cold-bloodedly [-'blʌdɪdlɪ] ADV *(unemotionally)* froidement; *(to murder)* de sang-froid, froidement

cold-bloodedness [-'blʌdɪdnɪs] N froideur f, insensibilité f

coldcock ['kəʊldkɒk] VT *Am Fam (knock out)* assommer, estourbir

cold-hearted [-'hɑːtɪd] ADJ *(person)* froid, insensible; *(words)* dur; *(action)* impitoyable; **that was a c. thing to do/say** c'était faire preuve d'insensibilité que de faire/dire ça

coldly ['kəʊldlɪ] ADV froidement; *(to look at sb, sth)* avec froideur

coldness ['kəʊldnɪs] N 1 *(of climate etc)* froideur f 2 *Fig (of welcome, person etc)* froideur f; **there is a c. between them** il y a un froid entre eux

cold-pressed ADJ embouti à froid; *(olive oil)* pressé à froid

cold-rivet VT *Tech* riveter à froid

cold-shoulder VT *(somebody)* tourner le dos à, snober, se montrer très froid avec; **the party continues to be cold-shouldered by the electorate** le parti est toujours boudé par les électeurs

coleslaw ['kəʊlslɔː] N *Culin* = salade f de chou blanc à la mayonnaise

colic ['kɒlɪk] N *Med, Vet* colique f

coliform bacteria ['kɒlɪfɔːm] NPL colibacilles mpl

colitis [kə'laɪtɪs] N *Med* colite f

collaborate [kə'læbəreɪt] VI *(in work)*, *Pej* collaborer (**with** avec; **on** à)

collaboration [kəlæbə'reɪʃən] N *(in work)*, *Pej* collaboration f; **in c. with** en collaboration avec

collaborator [kə'læbəreɪtər] N *(in work)*, *Pej* collaborateur, -trice

collage ['kɒlɑːʒ] N *Art* collage m

collagen ['kɒlədʒən] N collagène m

collapse [kə'læps] N 1 *(of building)* effondrement m, écroulement m; *(of land)* éboulement m; *Fig (of hopes, moral values, market, economy)* effondrement; *(of plan, institution)* effondrement, débâcle f; *(of prices)* effondrement, chute f subite; *(of the dollar etc)* effondrement, *Fam* dégringolade f

2 *Med (of lungs)* collapsus *m*; **she's had a c.** elle a perdu connaissance

VI 1 *(of building, institution etc)* s'écrouler, s'effondrer; *(of screen, bookshelf etc)* s'écrouler; *(of resistance, support, prices, economy)* s'effondrer; *(of bridge, axle etc)* s'effondrer, s'affaisser

2 *(of person)* s'effondrer, s'affaisser subitement; **I collapsed from the heat** je me suis évanoui tellement il faisait chaud; **he collapsed into an armchair** il s'effondra dans un fauteuil; **I feel like I'm about to c.** j'ai l'impression que je vais m'effondrer; *Med* **her lung has collapsed** elle a eu *ou* fait un collapsus pulmonaire

3 *(be collapsible)* se (re)plier

VT 1 *(table etc)* plier **2** *(merge) (paragraphs, entries)* mettre ensemble, fusionner

collapsed lung [kə'læpst] **N** *Med* collapsus *m* pulmonaire

collapsible [kə'læpsəb(ə)l] **ADJ** *(chair, boat etc)* pliant, repliable; *(handle etc)* rabattable; *Aut (steering column)* rétractile, rétractable
▸▸*Aut* **c. hood** capote *f* pliante *ou* rabattable

collar ['kɒlər] **N 1** *(of shirt etc)* col *m*; *(for dog)* collier *m*; **to seize** *or* **grab sb by the c.** prendre *ou* saisir qn au collet; *Fig* **to get hot under the c.** *(angry)* se mettre *ou Fam* se ficher en rogne; *(embarrassed)* se sentir gêné; **detachable c.** faux col **2** *Tech* bague *f*, *(of pipe)* collet *m* **3** *Zool (marking) (on bird, animal)* collier *m*
VT *(seize by the collar)* saisir *ou* prendre au collet; *Fig Fam (catch)* pincer

collarbone ['kɒləbəʊn] **N** clavicule *f*

collate [kə'leɪt] **VT 1** *(assemble) (documents, data)* rassembler; *Comput (documents)* interclasser; *(in bookbinding) (sheets)* assembler, collationner **2** *(compare) (text)* collationner (**with** avec)

collateral [kə'lætər(ə)l] **N** *Fin* nantissement *m*; **what can you provide as c.?** qu'est-ce que vous pouvez fournir en nantissement?
ADJ 1 *(secondary)* accessoire, subsidiaire **2** *(parallel)* parallèle; *(fact)* concomitant; *Law* collatéral, -aux **3** *(branch, family), Med (artery)* collatéral, -aux
▸▸*Mil* **c. damage** dégâts *mpl* collatéraux; *Fin* **c. loans** crédits *mpl* sur nantissement; *Fin* **c. security** nantissement *m*

collateralize [kə'lætərəlaɪz] **VT** *Banking* garantir

collation [kə'leɪʃən] **N 1** *(assembling) (of documents, data)* rassemblement *m*; *(in bookbinding) (of sheets)* assemblage *m*, collationnement *m* **2** *(comparing) (of texts)* collation *f* **3** *Culin Old-fashioned, Fml* collation *f*

collator [kə'leɪtər] **N** *(on photocopier)* interclasseuse *f*

colleague ['kɒliːg] **N** collègue *mf*, *(doctor, lawyer)* confrère *m*, consœur *f*

collect¹ [kə'lekt] **VT 1** *(as pastime) (stamps, books etc)* collectionner, faire collection de; **she has collected more than 2,000 records** elle a une collection de plus de 2 000 disques

2 *(gather) (crowd, one's belongings, material)* rassembler; *(friends, documents)* réunir; *(data, news)* recueillir; *(of post office) (letters)* faire la levée de; *Mil (wounded)* ramasser; **he had collected six parking fines** il avait ramassé six P.V.; **he collects parking fines** il collectionne les P.V.; **that tray is there to c. the drips** ce plateau sert à recueillir les gouttes

3 *Fig (one's thoughts, strength)* rassembler; **to c. oneself** se reprendre, se calmer

4 *(pick) (flowers)* cueillir; *(mushrooms)* ramasser

5 *Fin (salary)* toucher; *(debt)* recouvrer; **to c. taxes** percevoir *ou* lever des impôts

6 *(recover, call for) (luggage, ticket, car)* aller chercher, aller prendre; *(goods)* enlever; **I'll c. you at midday** je passerai vous prendre à midi

VI 1 *(of people)* s'assembler, se rassembler, se réunir; *(of things)* s'amasser **2** *(gather money)* faire la quête, quêter (**for** pour)
ADV *Am* **to send a telegram c.** envoyer un télégramme en port dû; *Tel* **to call (sb) c.** appeler (qn) en PCV, *Can* faire un appel à frais virés (à qn)
▸▸*Am Tel* **c. call** appel *m* en PCV, *Can* appel à frais virés

collect² ['kɒlekt] **N** *Rel (prayer)* collecte *f*

collectable [kə'lektəb(ə)l] **ADJ 1** *(sought-after)* prisé par les collectionneurs **2** *(debt)* recouvrable
N objet *m* de collection

collected [kə'lektɪd] **ADJ 1** *(assembled)* réuni; **the c. works of Jane Austen** les œuvres complètes de Jane Austen **2** *(calm)* plein de sang-froid; **to remain calm and c.** garder son sang-froid

collectible [kə'lektəb(ə)l] **ADJ, N** = **collectable**

collecting [kə'lektɪŋ] **N** **he does a lot of c. for the blind** il quête beaucoup *ou* il fait de nombreuses quêtes pour les aveugles
▸▸*Banking, Fin* **c. agency** banque *f* de recouvrement; *Banking, Fin* **c. bank** banque de recouvrement

collection [kə'lekʃən] **N 1** *(of stamps, butterflies etc)* collection *f*, *(of songs, poems)* recueil *m*; **spring c.** *(in fashion industry)* collection de printemps

2 *(act of collecting) (of sum of money, debts)* recouvrement *m*; *(of taxes)* perception *f*, *(of water, electric current)* captage *m*; *(of data)* collecte *f*, **c. times are 8.45 and 17.30** *(from letterbox)* les levées sont à 8h45 et 17h30; **c. and delivery** enlèvement *m* et livraison *m*; **c. of customs duties** perception douanière

3 *(group, accumulation) (of people)* assemblée *f*, rassemblement *m*; *(of things)* amas *m*; *(ordered)* assemblage *m*; **a c. of rubbish had built up outside the door** des ordures s'étaient amassées devant la porte

4 *(in church)* quête *f*, *(for charity etc)* collecte *f*, quête; **to take up a c.** faire la quête

5 *Fin (of bill)* encaissement *m*; **to send sth for c.** envoyer qch à l'encaissement

6 *(picking up) (of foods)* enlèvement *m*; **your watch will be ready for c. tomorrow** votre montre sera prête demain

7 *(removal) (of garbage)* ramassage *m*
▸▸**c. box** caisse *f*, *(in church)* tronc *m*; *Com* **c. charge** commission *f* d'encaissement; **c. department** service *m* de recouvrement; *Com* **c. fee** commission d'encaissement; **c. plate** *(in church)* corbeille *f*, *Fin* **c. rate** tarif *m* d'encaissement

collective [kə'lektɪv] **ADJ** collectif
N 1 *Gram* collectif *m* VOIR GRAMMAIRE A11; B8 **2** *(farm etc)* coopérative *f*
▸▸*Ind* **c. agreement** convention *f* collective; *Ind* **c. bargaining** = négociations *fpl* pour une convention collective; *Agr* **c. farm** ferme *f* collective; *Ling* **c. noun** collectif *m*; *Law* **c. ownership** propriété *f* collective; *(of building)* copropriété *f*, *Mktg* **c. promotion** communication *f* collective

collectively [kə'lektɪvlɪ] **ADV** collectivement; **c. owned** mis en commun; **c. owned building** immeuble *m* en copropriété

collectivism [kə'lektɪvɪz(ə)m] **N** collectivisme *m*

collectivist [kə'lektɪvɪst] **ADJ, N** collectiviste *mf*

collectivity [kɒlek'tɪvɪtɪ] **N** collectivité *f*

collectivization [kəlektɪvaɪ'zeɪʃən] **N** collectivisation *f*

collectivize [kə'lektɪvaɪz] **VT** collectiviser

collector [kə'lektər] **N 1** *(of paintings, stamps etc)* collectionneur, -euse; **c.'s item** pièce *f* de collection **2** *(for charity)* quêteur, -euse; **c. of taxes** percepteur *m* **3** *Tech etc (for oil, steam etc)* collecteur *m*; *(of overflow)* récepteur *m*

colleen ['kɒliːn] **N** *(in Ireland)* jeune fille *f*

college ['kɒlɪdʒ] **N 1** *(of further or higher education)* établissement *m* d'enseignement supérieur; *(technical)* IUT *m*, collège *m* technique; **to go to c., to be at c.** *(be a student there)* faire des études supérieures; **I've got to go off to c. now** il faut que j'aille en cours maintenant; **c. of art** école *f* des beaux-arts; *Br* **C. of Education** ≃ institut *m* de formation des maîtres; **c. of music** conservatoire *m* (de musique); **agricultural c.** institut *m* agronomique; **military/navy c.** école militaire/navale; **technical c.** collège technique VOIR GRAMMAIRE A6–7

2 *(part of British university)* collège *m* *(comme ceux d'Oxford)*; **the c. team** l'équipe du collège; **he played rugby for his c.** il a joué au rugby pour son collège *ou* dans l'équipe de son collège

3 *Rel* collège *m*

4 *Pol* **electoral c.** collège *m* électoral
▸▸**the C. of Cardinals** le Collège des cardinaux, le Sacré Collège; **c. education** études *fpl* supérieures; **c. student** étudiant, -ante

collegiate [kə'liːdʒɪət] **ADJ** *(system)* des collèges; *(life)* dans un collège/les collèges; *(university)* organisé en collèges
▸▸*Rel* **c. church** collégiale *f*

collide [kə'laɪd] **VI** *(of vehicles etc)* se heurter, se tamponner, entrer en collision; **to c. with** *(of vehicle)* heurter, tamponner, entrer en collision avec; *(ship)* aborder; **to c. with sb** *(of person)* se heurter à *ou* contre qn; *Fig* **the two countries have collided over the issue of human rights** les deux pays se sont heurtés sur la question des droits de l'homme

collie ['kɒlɪ] **N** *(dog)* colley *m*, chien *m* de berger écossais

collier ['kɒlɪər] **N 1** *(ship)* (navire *m*) charbonnier *m* **2** *Min (person)* mineur *m* (de charbon)

colliery ['kɒlɪərɪ] **N** *Min* houillère *f*, mine *f* de charbon

collision [kə'lɪʒən] **N 1** collision *f*, *(of ships)* abordage *m*, collision; *Fig (of interests etc)* conflit *m*; **to come into c. with sth** *(with moving object)* entrer en collision avec qch; *(with stationary object)* rentrer dans qch; *(of ship)* aborder qch; *Naut* **to be on a c. course** être sur un cap de collision; *Fig* **they are on a c. course** ils vont se rentrer dedans; *Fig* **to be on a c. course with sb** avoir toutes les chances de rentrer en conflit avec qn; *Fig* **to avoid a c. with sb** éviter les heurts avec qn **2** *Phys (of particles)* choc *m*, collision *f*
▸▸*Aut* **c. damage waiver** = suppression *f* de franchise pour les dommages causés aux véhicules

colloid ['kɒlɔɪd] **N** colloïde *m*

colloquial [kə'ləʊkwɪəl] **ADJ** familier, parlé

colloquialism [kə'ləʊkwɪəlɪz(ə)m] **N** expression *f* familière

colloquially [kə'ləʊkwɪəlɪ] **ADV** familièrement, en style familier; **known c. as …** communément appelé …

collude [kə'luːd] **VI** être de connivence (**with sb** avec qn)

collusion [kə'luːʒən] **N** collusion *f*, **to act in c. with sb** agir de connivence avec qn; **to do sth in c. with sb** faire qch de connivence avec qn; **to be in c. with sb** être d'intelligence *ou* de connivence avec qn

collywobbles ['kɒlɪwɒb(ə)lz] **NPL** *Fam* **to**

have the **c.** *(an upset stomach)* avoir mal au ventre; *(be nervous)* avoir la frousse; **he gives me the c.** il me fiche la frousse

Colo *abbr* Colorado

cologne [kə'ləʊn] **N** eau *f* de Cologne

Colombia [kə'lʌmbɪə] **N** Colombie *f*

Colombian [kə'lʌmbɪən] **ADJ** colombien **N** Colombien, -ienne

colon[1] ['kəʊlən] **N** *Anat* côlon *m*

colon[2] **N** *(punctuation mark)* deux-points *m inv*

colonel ['kɜːn(ə)l] **N** *Mil, Am Aviat* colonel *m*

colonial [kə'ləʊnɪəl] **ADJ** colonial, -aux; *Am Archit etc (style)* du dix-huitième siècle, colonial; **in c. times** au *ou* du temps des colonies **N** colonial, -ale

colonialism [kə'ləʊnɪəlɪz(ə)m] **N** colonialisme *m*

colonialist [kə'ləʊnɪəlɪst] **ADJ, N** colonialiste *mf*

colonic [kə'lɒnɪk] **ADJ** du côlon ▸▸ *Med* **c. irrigation** lavement *m*

colonist ['kɒlənɪst] **N** colon *m*

colonization [kɒlənaɪ'zeɪʃən] **N** colonisation *f*

colonize ['kɒlənaɪz] **VT** coloniser

colonizer ['kɒlənaɪzər] **N** colonisateur, -trice

colonnade [kɒlə'neɪd] **N** *Archit* colonnade *f*

colony ['kɒlənɪ] **N** *(also of animals, writers)* colonie *f*; **to live in the colonies** vivre aux colonies; *Hist* **the Colonies** les Colonies *fpl*; **the English c. in Paris** la colonie anglaise de Paris

colophon ['kɒləfən] **N** *Typ (of publisher, printer)* logo *m*

color, color-blind *etc Am* = **colour, colour-blind** *etc*

Colorado [kɒlə'rɑːdəʊ] **N** Colorado *m* ▸▸ **C. beetle** doryphore *m*, *Can* bête *f* à patates

coloration [kʌlə'reɪʃən] **N** coloration *f*, coloris *m*

coloratura [kɒlərə'tʊərə] **N** *Mus* colorature *f* ▸▸ **c. aria** air *m* de coloratura; **c. soprano** (soprano *f*) coloratura

colored *Am* = **coloured**

colossal [kə'lɒs(ə)l] **ADJ** colossal, -aux

colossus, *pl* **colossi, colossuses** [kə'lɒsəs, -aɪ, -əsɪz] **N** colosse *m*; **the C. of Rhodes** le colosse de Rhodes

colostomy [kə'lɒstəmɪ] **N** *Surg* colostomie *f*, **to have a c.** subir une colostomie ▸▸ **c. bag** poche *f*

colour, *Am* **color** ['kʌlər] **N** **VOIR GRAMMAIRE** **A7; B10 1** couleur *f*; **what c. is it?** de quelle couleur est-ce?; **it's the c. of a ripe cherry** ça a *ou* c'est de la couleur d'une cerise mûre; **a dark grey c.** une couleur gris foncé; **it's a sort of greenish c.** c'est d'une couleur un peu verdâtre; **local c.** couleur locale; **the political c. of a journal** la couleur politique d'un journal; **to give** *or* **lend c. to a story** rendre une histoire plus vivante; *Fig* **I've still to see the c. of his money** je n'ai pas encore vu la couleur de son argent

2 *Art etc (tones)* coloris *m*; **light colours** coloris clairs

3 *(pigment)* matière *f* colorante, couleur *f*; **box of colours** boîte de couleurs

4 *(complexion)* teint *m*, couleurs *fpl*; **she had a lot of c. in her cheeks** ses joues avaient de belles couleurs; **to lose c.** perdre ses couleurs; **a week in the country will bring the c. (back) to her cheeks** une semaine à la campagne, et elle reprendra des couleurs; **indignation brought the c. to his cheeks** l'indignation colorait ses joues; *Br*

to be off c. ne pas être dans son assiette; *Fig* **the joke was a bit off c.** la plaisanterie était d'un goût douteux

5 *(race)* couleur *f*; **to discriminate against sb on the basis of c.** faire de la discrimination contre qn en fonction de sa couleur de peau; **the c. problem** les problèmes *mpl* raciaux

6 colours *(insignia etc) (of party)* couleurs *fpl*; *Naut* pavillon *m*, couleurs; *Mil* **the (regimental) colours** le fanion du régiment; **to serve with the colours** servir sous les drapeaux; **with colours flying** (à) enseignes déployées; *Fig* **to pass with flying colours** *(in exam)* être reçu brillamment *ou* haut la main; **to sail under false colours** naviguer sous un faux pavillon; *Fig* **to show oneself in one's true colours** se révéler tel que l'on est; **to see sb in his/her true colours** voir qn sous son vrai jour; *Fig* **to nail one's colours to the mast** afficher ses opinions

7 *Sport, Horseracing* **colours** *(of jockey, team)* couleurs *fpl*; *Sport, Sch* **to get one's colours** recevoir une haute distinction sportive

VT 1 colorer; *(card, drawing)* colorier; *(etching)* enluminer; **to c. sth blue** colorer *ou* colorier qch en bleu

2 *(description) (exaggerate)* exagérer; *(enliven)* rendre plus vivant; *(with false details)* enjoliver

3 *(bias, distort) (fact, view of reality, judgement)* influencer; *(stronger)* déformer

VI *(of person) (become embarrassed)* rougir ▸▸ *Phot* **c. balance** équilibre *m* des couleurs; *Br* **c. bar** discrimination *f* raciale; **c. bearer** porte-drapeau *m*, *pl* porte-drapeaux; **c. blindness** daltonisme *m*; **c. chart** nuancier *m*; *Comput* **c. display** affichage *m* couleur; **c. film** *(for camera)* pellicule *f* (en) couleur; *(movie)* film *m* en couleur; *Phot* **c. filter** filtre *m* coloré; *Comput* **c. graphics** graphisme *m* en couleur; **c. line** discrimination *ou* ségrégation *f* raciale; *Comput* **c. monitor** moniteur *m* couleur; *Mil* **c. party** garde *f* du drapeau; **c. photocopying** photocopie *f* en couleurs; **c. photography** photographie *f* en couleur(s); *Typ* **c. plate** planche *f* en couleur; *Typ, Phot* **c. positive** positif *m* (en) couleur; *Typ* **c. print** reproduction *f* en couleurs; *Typ* **c. printer** imprimante *f* couleur; *Typ* **c. printing** impression *f* couleur; **c. scheme** palette *f* *ou* combinaison *f* de couleurs; *Comput* **c. screen** écran *m* couleur; *Typ* **c. separation** séparation *f* des couleurs, séparation quadrichromique; *Br Mil* **c. sergeant** ≃ sergent-chef *m*, *pl* sergents-chefs *(de la garde du drapeau)*; *Br Journ* **c. supplement** supplément *m* illustré; **c. television** télévision *f* couleur; *Art* **c. value** valeur *f* chromatique

▸ **colour in,** *Am* **color in VT SEP** *(add colour to black and white illustration)* colorier; *(film, photo)* coloriser

colour-blind, *Am* **color-blind ADJ** daltonien

colour-coded, *Am* **color-coded ADJ** repéré par des couleurs; **everything is c.** on classe tout par un système de couleurs

colour-coding, *Am* **color-coding N** système *m* de classement par couleurs; **what's their c.?** de quelle couleur sont-elles dans le classement?

Coloured, *Am* **Colored** ['kʌləd] **N (Cape) C.** *(in South Africa)* métis, -isse

coloured, *Am* **colored** ['kʌləd] **ADJ 1** coloré; *(drawing)* colorié; *(shirt)* de couleur; **gaily c. butterfly** papillon multicolore; **brightly c. clothing** des vêtements aux couleurs vives; *Fig* **highly c. narrative** récit *m* coloré **2** *(person etc)* de couleur

coloureds, *Am* **coloreds** ['kʌlədz] **NPL 1** *(clothes)* couleurs *fpl*; **separate whites and**

c. *(washing instruction)* lavez les couleurs et le blanc séparément **2** *(people)* gens *mpl* de couleur

colourful, *Am* **colorful** ['kʌləfʊl] **ADJ** *(sky etc)* coloré; *(style)* coloré, pittoresque; **a c. character** un original; **c. language** langage *m* coloré

colouring, *Am* **coloring** ['kʌlərɪŋ] **N 1** *(act)* coloration *f*, *(of children's pictures)* coloriage *m* **2** *(shade) (of painting, style)* coloris *m* **3** *(complexion) (of person)* teint *m* ▸▸ **c. book** album *m* à colorier

colouring-in, *Am* **coloring-in N** coloriage *m* ▸▸ **c. book** album *m* à colorier

colourist, *Am* **colorist** ['kʌlərɪst] **N** *Art* coloriste *mf*

colourization, *Am* **colorization** [kʌləraɪ'zeɪʃən] **N** *Cin* colorisation *f*

colourize, *Am* **colorize** ['kʌləraɪz] **VT** *Cin* coloriser

colourless, *Am* **colorless** ['kʌləlɪs] **ADJ 1** *(clear)* sans couleur, incolore **2** *(pale)* terne, incolore; *(face)* blême; *(complexion)* pâle, délavé; *(light)* pâle, falot **3** *Fig (dull) (style)* insipide, fade; *(voice)* terne; *(person)* sans caractère

colourlessness, *Am* **colorlessness** ['kʌləlɪsnɪs] **N 1** absence *f* de couleur; *(of complexion)* pâleur *f* **2** *Fig (of style)* fadeur *f*, *(of person)* manque *m* de personnalité

colourway, *Am* **colorway** ['kʌləweɪ] **N** coloris *m*

colt [kəʊlt] **N** *(horse)* poulain *m*, jeune cheval *m* mâle

coltish ['kəʊltɪʃ] **ADJ 1** *(immature)* sans expérience **2** *(playful)* folâtre

coltsfoot ['kəʊltsfʊt] **N** *(plant)* pas-d'âne *m inv*

Columbia [kə'lʌmbɪə] **N British C.** Colombie-britannique *f*, **(District of) C.** (District *m* fédéral de) Columbia *f*

Columbine ['kɒləmbaɪn] **N** *Theat* Colombine *f*

columbine ['kɒləmbaɪn] **N** *(plant)* ancolie *f*

Columbus [kə'lʌmbəs] **N (Christopher) C.** Christophe Colomb

column ['kɒləm] **N 1** *(of building, smoke, figures etc)* colonne *f*, **putting into columns** colonnage *m*; *Aviat* **control c.** levier *m* de commande

2 *Mil, Naut (formation)* colonne *f*, **to march in c./in two columns** marcher en colonne/ en deux colonnes; **supply/relief c.** colonne de ravitaillement/de secours

3 *Journ* colonne *f*, *(feature)* rubrique *f*, **six-c. page** page de six colonnes; **sports c.** rubrique *ou* chronique *f* sportive

4 *Comput, Typ* colonne *f* ▸▸ *Journ* **c. centimetre** *(for advertisement)* centimètre-colonne *m*, *pl* centimètres-colonne; *Aut* **c. change** levier *m* de vitesses sur colonne de direction; *Comput, Typ* **c. graph** histogramme *m*; *Comput, Typ* **c. header** en-tête *m* de colonnes, *pl* en-têtes; *Journ* **c. inch** = unité *f* de mesure des espaces publicitaires équivalant à une colonne sur un pouce, ≃ centimètre-colonne; **it got a lot of c. inches** *(of story)* on lui a consacré beaucoup d'espace dans le journal; *Comput, Typ* **c. mode** mode *m* colonne; *Comput, Typ* **c. printing** impression *f* en colonnes; *Journ* **c. space** colonnage *m*; *Comput, Typ* **c. spacing** espacement *m* des colonnes

columnist ['kɒləmnɪst] **N** *Journ* chroniqueur, -euse, courriériste *mf*, **sports c.** chroniqueur sportif, chroniqueuse sportive

colza ['kɒlzə] **N** *(plant)* colza *m* ▸▸ **c. oil** huile *f* de colza

COM [kɒm] **N** *Comput (abbr* **Computer Output Microfilm**)

▶▶**C. plotter** traceur *m* COM; **C. printer** imprimante *f* sur microfilm; **C. unit** unité *f* d'impression sur microfilm

.com [dɒt'kɒm] *Comput* = abréviation *f* désignant les entreprises commerciales dans les adresses électroniques

coma ['kəʊmə] N *Med* coma *m*; **to go into/be in a c.** entrer/être dans le coma

co-management N cogérance *f*

comatose ['kəʊmətəʊs] ADJ *Med* comateux; **to be c.** être dans le coma; *Fam (fast asleep)* en écraser

comb [kəʊm] N **1** *(for hair, wool etc)* peigne *m*; *(for horse)* étrille *f*, **to run a c. through one's hair, to give one's hair a c.** se donner un coup de peigne **2** *(of cock)* crête *f* **3** *(honeycomb)* rayon *m*; **honey in the c.** miel *m* en rayon
VT **1** *(sb's hair)* peigner; **to c. one's hair** se peigner; **to c. down a horse** étriller un cheval **2** *Tex etc (wool etc)* peigner, carder; **combed cotton** coton peigné **3** *(search thoroughly) (area, town etc)* ratisser, passer au peigne fin (**for sb** pour (re)trouver qn); **she combed the book for references to the crisis** elle a passé le livre au peigne fin *ou* au crible pour trouver des références à la crise
▶ **comb out** VT SEP **1** *(hair)* peigner; *(untangle)* démêler; **to c. the knots out of one's hair** démêler ses cheveux **2** *(wool)* peigner **3** *(remove) (fleas)* retirer avec un peigne

combat ['kɒmbæt] N combat *m*; **in c.** au combat; **single c.** combat singulier; **women are now used in a c. role** on envoie maintenant les femmes dans des situations de combat
VT (**-t-**) *(disease, prejudice, crime)* lutter contre, combattre
VI combattre (**against** contre)
▶▶**c. dress** tenue *f* de combat; *Psy* **c. fatigue** psychose *f* traumatique, syndrome *m* commotionnel; **c. jacket** veste *f* de treillis; **c. mission** mission *f* de combat; **c. troops** troupes *fpl* de combat; **c. trousers** battle-dress *m inv*; pantalon *m* multi-poches; **c. zone** zone *f* de combat

combatant ['kɒmbətənt] ADJ, N combattant, -ante

combative ['kɒmbətɪv] ADJ combatif

combi ['kɒmbɪ] N *Austr Fam* **c. (van)** camping-car *m*, *pl* camping-cars

combination [kɒmbɪ'neɪʃən] N **1** combinaison *f*, *(of circumstances)* concours *m*; *Chem* combiné *m*, combinaison; **nitrogen in c. with oxygen** l'azote combiné avec l'oxygène; **an interesting c. of flavours** un mélange intéressant de parfums **2** *(of people, workers etc)* association *f*; **to enter into a c. with …** s'associer avec … **3** *(for lock)* combinaison *f* **4** *Br Old-fashioned (clothing)* **(pair of) combinations** combinaison-culotte *f*, *pl* combinaisons-culottes
▶▶**c. lock** serrure *f* à combinaison; **c. rate** *(in advertising)* couplage *m*, tarif *m* couplage; **c. skin** peau *f* mixte; *Tech* **c. spanner** clé *f* mixte; *Med* **c. therapy** trithérapie *f*

combine¹ ['kɒmbaɪn] N **1** *Com, Fin* cartel *m* **2** *Agr* moissonneuse-batteuse *f*, *pl* moissonneuses-batteuses
▶▶*Agr* **c. harvester** moissonneuse-batteuse, *pl* moissonneuses-batteuses

combine² [kəm'baɪn] VT combiner (**with** à); *(qualities etc)* allier (**with** à); **to c. forces** joindre ses forces (**with** à); **to c. strength of body with strength of mind** allier la force du corps à celle de l'âme; **to c. business with pleasure** joindre l'utile à l'agréable; **the play combines drama and music** la pièce allie intrigue et musique
VI *(of people)* s'unir, s'associer, s'allier; *(ag-*

gressively) se liguer (**against** contre); *(of workers)* se syndiquer; *Pol (of parties)* s'allier; *(merge)* fusionner; *Chem (of elements)* se combiner; **everything combined to give me this impression** tout concourait à me donner cette impression

combined [kəm'baɪnd] ADJ *(efforts)* réuni; **the c. sound of a pneumatic drill and the traffic** le bruit d'un marteau-piqueur additionné à celui de la circulation
▶▶*Naut* **c. fleets** flottes *fpl* combinées; *Mil* **c. force** force *f* mixte; *Mil etc* **c. operation** *(by several nations)* opération *f* alliée; *(by forces of one nation)* opération interarmées; *Com* **c. transport bill of lading** connaissement *m* de transport combiné; **c. transport company** entrepreneur *m* de transport combiné, ETC *m*

combining [kəm'baɪnɪŋ] N combinaison *f*
▶▶*Gram* **c. form** affixe *m*

combo ['kɒmbəʊ] N **1** *Mus* petite formation *f* musicale **2** *Fam (combination)* combinaison *f*; *(mixture)* mélange *m*
▶▶*Comput* **c. box** équipement *m* de jonction

combust [kəm'bʌst] VI brûler

combustible [kəm'bʌstɪb(ə)l] ADJ combustible
N matière *f* inflammable; *(fuel)* combustible *m*

combustion [kəm'bʌstʃən] N combustion *f*
▶▶**c. chamber** chambre *f* de combustion; **c. gases** gaz *mpl* de combustion

COME [kʌm] VI (*pt* **came** [keɪm], *pp* **come**) **1** venir; *(arrive)* venir, arriver (**to** à; **from** de); **to c. from France/Edinburgh** venir de France/d'Édimbourg; **here c. the children** voici les enfants qui arrivent; **here he comes!** le voilà qui arrive!; **I'm coming with you** je viens avec vous, je vous accompagne; **she comes this way every week** elle vient par ici chaque semaine; **what way do you usually c.?** par où passes-tu d'habitude?; **they don't c. here often** ils ne viennent pas souvent ici; **we're coming to a crossroads** nous arrivons à un croisement; **c. here!** venez ici!, *Fam* **arrive ici!**; *(to dog)* **au pied!; coming!** j'arrive!; **ok ok, I'm coming!** d'accord, je viens!; **(are you) coming?** *(with me, us etc)* tu viens?; **c. and see/do** viens voir/faire; **to c. for sb/sth** venir chercher qn/qch; **to c. to sb for advice** venir demander conseil à qn; **you've c. to the wrong person** vous vous adressez à la mauvaise personne; **you've c. to the wrong place** vous vous êtes trompé de chemin, vous faites fausse route; **if you're looking for sun, you've c. to the wrong place** si c'est le soleil que vous cherchez, il ne fallait pas venir ici; **to c. to the end of sth** arriver à la fin de qch; **I was coming to the end of my stay** j'arrivais à la fin de mon séjour; **when you c. to the last coat of paint …** quand tu en seras à la dernière couche de peinture …; **to c. to the throne** monter sur le trône; **a crisis is coming** une crise se prépare; **the fireworks c. next** le feu d'artifice est après; **what comes after the performance?** qu'est-ce qu'il y a après la représentation?; **what are things coming to (when …)?** où allons-nous (si …)?; **letters came pouring in** ce fut une avalanche de lettres; **he has c. a long way** il vient de loin; *Fig* il a fait du chemin; **computers have c. a long way** les ordinateurs ont beaucoup évolué; *Fig* **they saw you coming (a mile off)** ils t'ont vu venir (de loin); **to c. and go** aller et venir; **the idea came to me that …** il m'est venu à l'esprit que …; **suddenly it came to me** *(I remembered)* tout d'un coup, je m'en suis souvenu; *(I had idea)* **the idea came to me one morning** l'idée m'est venue à l'esprit un matin; **a smile came to her lips** un

sourire parut sur ses lèvres *ou* lui vint aux lèvres; **c. now!, c., c.!** allons!, voyons!; *Fam* **she's as obstinate/intelligent as they c.** il n'y a pas plus têtue/intelligente qu'elle; *Fam* **he had it coming to him** il n'a eu que ce qu'il méritait; *Fig* **I don't know whether I'm coming or going** je perds la tête *ou Fam* les pédales; **c. summer (and) we'll all meet again** quand viendra l'été, on se retrouvera tous; **she'll be ten c. January** elle aura dix ans en janvier; **I've got £500 coming to me** je vais (bientôt) toucher 500 livres; **we mustn't let a small disagreement c. between us** nous n'allons pas nous disputer à cause d'un petit malentendu; **a woman came between them** ils se sont disputés à cause d'une femme; **she won't let anything c. between her and her work** son travail passe avant tout
2 *(happen)* **we must take things as they c.** il faut prendre les choses comme elles viennent; **c. what may, we'll get it finished** quoi qu'il arrive, nous finirons; **how did the door c. to be open?** comment se fait-il que la porte soit ouverte?; **c. how c.?** pourquoi?; *(how)* comment se fait-il?; **now that I c. to think of it** maintenant que j'y pense
3 *(originate)* venir; **word that comes from Latin** mot qui vient du latin; **that's surprising coming from him** cela étonne de sa part, venant de lui, c'est étonnant; **to c. from or of a good family** être issu *ou* venir d'une bonne famille
4 *(be)* **that comes easy/natural(ly) to him** cela lui est facile/naturel, ça lui vient facilement/naturellement; **it came as a shock/a relief to me** cela a été un choc/un soulagement pour moi; **gold watches don't c. cheap** les montres en *ou* ne sont pas données; **that doesn't c. within my duties** cela ne rentre pas dans mes fonctions
5 *(become)* **to c. undone/untied/loose** *(of tie, knot, bootlaces etc)* se dénouer/se délacer/se défaire
6 **in the years/days to c.** dans les années/les jours à venir; **that will not be for some time to c.** cela va prendre un peu de temps
7 *(of teeth)* sortir
8 *Fam* **that's coming it a bit strong** ça, c'est un peu fort; **don't c. the big boss with me** ne prends pas ce ton autoritaire avec moi; **don't c. it with me** *(don't pretend)* à moi, on ne me la fait pas!; *(as threat)* arrête!; **don't even think about coming it with me!** ne joue pas à ça avec moi!
9 *Fam (reach orgasm)* jouir; *(ejaculate)* prendre son pied, décharger
N *Fam (semen)* sperme *m*, *Vulg* foutre *m*
▶ **come about** VI **1** *(of event, occurrence etc)* arriver, se passer, se produire; **it came about that …** il arriva *ou* il advint que …
2 *(of ship)* virer de bord; *(of wind)* tourner
▶ **come across** VT INSEP *(find) (person)* rencontrer par hasard, tomber sur; *(object)* trouver par hasard, tomber sur
VI **1** *(make an impression)* **to c. across well/badly** *(at interview)* faire une bonne/mauvaise impression, bien/mal passer; *(on TV)* bien/mal passer; **they c. across as nice people** ils ont l'air gentils; **the story doesn't c. across so well on the screen** l'histoire ne rend pas très bien à l'écran; **how did her story c. across?** quelle impression est-ce que son histoire t'a faite *ou* laissée?
2 *Fam (pay up)* payer ce que l'on doit
▶ **come across with** VT INSEP *Fam (supply) (money)* cracher
▶ **come after** VT INSEP **1** *(chase)* poursuivre
2 *(follow)* venir *ou* être après, suivre; n **comes after k in the alphabet** le n vient après le k dans l'alphabet; **what comes after the dancing?** qu'est-ce qu'il y a après la danse?
VI *(follow)* suivre, venir après

► **come along** vi **1** c. along! *(hurry)* allons-y!; *(come here)* viens, viens par ici!

2 *(make progress)* how's the work coming along? comment ça avance, le travail?; the preparations are coming along fine les préparatifs avancent bien

3 *(arrive)* arriver; everything was peaceful until he came along tout était calme avant qu'il n'arrive; these things c. along when you least expect them ces choses-là arrivent quand on s'y attend le moins

4 *(come as well)* the children came along les enfants sont venus avec moi/nous *ou* aussi; would you like to c. along? tu voudrais venir?

► **come apart** vi *(fall to pieces)* tomber en morceaux; *Fig (of person)* craquer; *(of plans etc)* aller à la catastrophe; to c. apart at the seams *(of garment)* se défaire aux coutures

► **come at** vt insep **1** *(attack)* attaquer; criticisms/jibes were coming at me from all sides des critiques/quolibets arrivaient sur moi de tous côtés

2 *(approach)* to c. at a problem from a different angle aborder un problème sous un angle différent

► **come away** vi **1** *(leave)* partir, s'éloigner; why not c. away with us to Paris for the weekend? pourquoi ne pas venir avec nous à Paris ce week-end?; c. away from that cat éloigne-toi de ce chat

2 *(become detached)* se détacher; *(when glued)* se décoller, se détacher; *(when nailed)* se déclouer, se détacher; the handle came away in his hand l'anse lui est restée dans la main

► **come back** vi **1** *(return)* revenir; to c. back (home) rentrer; it's all coming back to me cela me revient (à la *ou* en mémoire); her name will c. back to me later son nom me reviendra plus tard; to c. back to what I was saying … pour en revenir à ce que je disais …

2 *(of fashion)* revenir; *(of long skirts etc)* revenir (à la mode)

3 *(from losing position etc)* revenir; to c. back from a defeat/setback revenir après une défaite/un échec

4 *Fam (retort)* répliquer, riposter

► **come by** vt insep *(acquire)* how did you c. by this camera/those bruises? comment as-tu fait pour avoir cet appareil-photo/ces bleus?; how did she c. by all that money? comment s'est-elle procuré tout cet argent?; how did you c. by your fortune? d'où vient ta fortune?; how did you c. by your Nordic looks? d'où vient que tu as l'air nordique?

vi *(go past, visit)* passer

► **come down** vi **1** *(descend) (from ladder, stairs)* descendre; *(from mountain etc)* descendre, faire la descente; *(of plane) (crash)* s'écraser; *(land)* atterrir; *(of rain)* tomber; to c. down to breakfast descendre déjeuner *ou* prendre le petit déjeuner; the plane came down in the sea *(crashed)* l'avion est tombé en mer; *(landed)* l'avion a amerri; hemlines are coming down this year les jupes rallongent cette année; *Fig* to c. down (in the world) déchoir; *Fig* to c. down to earth descendre des nues

2 *(decrease) (of temperature, prices)* baisser; he'll c. down a few pounds if you bargain il baissera son prix de quelques livres si tu marchandes

3 *(decide)* se décider; to c. down in favour of sb/sth se décider en faveur de qn/qch; to c. down on sb's side décider en faveur de qn

4 *(reach)* her hair came down to her waist les cheveux lui tombaient *ou* descendaient jusqu'à la taille; the curtains should c. right down to the floor les rideaux devraient tomber jusqu'au sol

5 *(be an inheritance)* être laissé en héritage *ou* légué (to sb à qn; from par); *(of tale, tra-*

dition) être transmis (from par); the necklace came down to her from her great-aunt elle tient ce collier de sa grand-tante; the tales that have c. down to us les contes qui nous sont parvenus

6 *(collapse) (of tree etc)* s'abattre; *(of structure)* s'écrouler

7 *(be removed)* être défait *ou* décroché; that wallpaper will have to c. down il va falloir enlever ce papier peint; the Christmas decorations are coming down today aujourd'hui, on enlève les décorations de Noël; that disgusting poster is coming down now! enlève-moi tout de suite cet affreux poster!; the tree will have to c. down *(be felled)* il faut abattre cet arbre; these houses are coming down soon on va bientôt démolir ces maisons

8 *(be a question of)* to c. down to se résumer *ou* se réduire à; the whole difficulty comes down to this question toute la difficulté se réduit à cette question; it all comes down to money ce n'est qu'une question d'argent

9 *Am Fam (to happen)* se préparer

vt insep *(stairs, street)* descendre

► **come down on** vt insep *Fam (criticize, punish)* tomber sur le dos de; one mistake and he'll c. down on you like a ton of bricks si tu fais la moindre erreur, il te tombera sur le dos; she came down on me for not having told her about it earlier elle m'est tombée dessus parce que je ne lui en avais pas parlé plus tôt

► **come down with** vt insep *(succumb to) (cold, flu etc)* attraper

► **come forward** vi *(present oneself)* se proposer; no one has c. forward with any alternative ideas personne n'a rien proposé d'autre; the police have appealed for witnesses to c. forward la police a demandé aux témoins de se faire connaître; to c. forward as a candidate poser sa candidature, se porter candidat; *Hum* he's not backward in coming forward il ne se gêne pas

► **come in** vi **1** *(enter)* entrer; to c. in again rentrer; c. in! entrez!; *(on radio)* répondez!; *Br Fam* Mrs Brown comes in twice a week *(to clean)* Madame Brown vient (faire le ménage) deux fois par semaine; Mr Jones isn't coming in today *(to office etc)* M. Jones n'est pas là aujourd'hui; *Cin, Fig* this is where we came in on a déjà vu ça; *Radio, TV* c. in Barry Stewart from New York *(begin to speak)* à vous, Barry Stewart à New York

2 *(of tide)* monter; *(of ship)* arriver; *Pol (of party)* arriver *ou* parvenir au pouvoir; *Cr (of batsman)* venir prendre son tour au guichet; we don't have much money coming in il n'y a pas beaucoup d'argent qui rentre; *Sport* to c. in first/second arriver premier/second; this fashion is coming in again cette mode revient *ou* reprend; reports of a coup are coming in on nous annonce qu'il y a eu un coup d'état

3 *(have a role) (in matter)* avoir un rôle à jouer; and where do I c. in? et moi, quel est mon rôle?; that's where I c. in *(to help)* voilà où je peux vous aider, voilà où j'interviens; to c. in useful *(to sb/for sth/for doing sth)* servir (à qn/à qch/à *ou* pour faire qch); extra money always comes in useful *ou* handy il est toujours utile d'avoir de l'argent en plus

4 *(join an enterprise etc)* to c. in with sb s'associer à qn; they were the founder members, the others didn't c. in till later ce sont les membres fondateurs, les autres ne s'y sont associés que plus tard

► **come in for** vt insep to c. in for praise être félicité; to c. in for criticism être critiqué, être en butte aux critiques; the government came in for a lot of criticism over its handling of the crisis le gouvernement a été très critiqué pour la façon dont il gère la crise; to

c. in for a share of sth avoir part à qch

► **come in on** vt insep *(be given a part in)* prendre part à; they let him c. in on the deal ils l'ont laissé prendre part à l'affaire

► **come into** vt insep **1** *(enter) (room)* entrer dans; to c. into the world venir au monde; to c. into power *(of party, person etc)* arriver *ou* parvenir au pouvoir; to c. into force *or* effect *(of law, ruling etc)* entrer en vigueur; when does the law c. into force *or* effect? quand la loi prend-elle effet *ou* entre-t-elle en vigueur?; to c. into possession of sth entrer en possession de qch; how did this painting c. into your possession? comment êtes-vous entré en possession de ce tableau?; to c. into sb's mind *(of idea)* venir à l'esprit de qn

2 *(inherit) (money, property etc)* hériter (de); *(inheritance)* entrer en possession de, recueillir; to c. into some money *(inherit it)* faire un héritage; *(win it)* gagner le gros lot

3 *(be involved in)* luck doesn't c. into it la chance n'a rien à voir là-dedans

► **come of** vt insep **1** *(result from)* what will c. of it? qu'en adviendra-t-il?, qu'en résultera-t-il?; no good will c. of it cela tournera mal; that's what comes of being too ambitious voilà ce qui arrive quand on est trop ambitieux

2 to c. of age *(reach legal status)* atteindre la *ou* sa majorité

► **come off** vi **1** *(become detached) (of button etc)* se détacher, sauter; *(of paint, stain etc)* s'enlever, partir; *(of paint, stain etc)* s'enlever, partir; *(become unstuck)* se décoller; does this bit c. off? est-ce que ça s'enlève?; the colour came off on my dress la couleur a déteint sur ma robe; the chain has c. off *(of bicycle)* la chaîne a sauté; the top of the pen had c. off le bouchon du stylo avait sauté

2 *(fall from horse, motorbike etc)* tomber

3 *(take place) (of meeting etc)* avoir lieu

4 *(succeed)* réussir, aboutir; did it c. off all right? ça s'est bien passé?; my little trip abroad didn't c. off mon petit voyage à l'étranger est tombé à l'eau; the experiment came off l'expérience a réussi

5 *(acquit oneself)* to c. off badly mal s'en tirer; you'll c. off worst tu auras le dessous

6 *Sl (reach orgasm)* jouir

vt insep **1** *(climb down from, leave) (wall, ladder etc)* descendre de; to c. off a ship/ plane débarquer d'un navire/d'un avion; I've just c. off the night shift *(finished work)* je viens de quitter l'équipe de nuit; *(finished working nights)* je viens de finir le travail de nuit

2 *(fall from) (horse, motorbike etc)* tomber de

3 *(become detached from)* the handle has c. off the knife le manche s'est détaché du couteau

4 *(be removed from)* that stain will never c. off the carpet cette tache sur le tapis ne partira jamais

5 *Fam* c. off it! arrête ton baratin!; c. off it, he's not 21! arrête de dire n'importe quoi, il n'a pas 21 ans!

► **come on** vi **1** c. on! *(with motion, encouraging, challenging)* vas-y!, allez!; *Fam (expressing incredulity)* tu rigoles!; c. on, hurry! allez, dépêche-toi!; c. on, let's have a game! allons! faisons une partie!; c. on Scotland! allez l'Écosse!

2 *(make progress) (of plants etc)* se développer; *(of people)* faire des progrès; Jackie's French is really coming on le français de Jackie s'améliore vraiment; Jackie is really coming on with her French Jackie fait de gros progrès en français; how's the work coming on? est-ce que le travail avance?; the building work is coming on fine la construction avance bien

3 *(start) (of winter etc)* venir, arriver; *(of*

night) tomber; (of symptoms) apparaître; **I feel a cold coming on** je sens que je suis en train de m'enrhumer; **I have a sore throat coming on** je commence à avoir mal à la gorge

4 Theat (appear) entrer en scène; Sport (on to field) (r)entrer

5 (be shown) (of film etc) passer; **the play/film is coming on next week** on va donner la pièce/le film va passer la semaine prochaine; **when does that programme c. on?** quand passe cette émission?; **the film's coming on** le film va commencer

6 Fam **to c. on to sb** (make sexual overtures to) draguer qn

7 Br Sl (start menstruating) avoir ses ragnagnas

▶ **come out** VI **1** (from room, prison, hospital etc) sortir; **to c. out of a place/a room** sortir d'un lieu/d'une pièce

2 (become detached) partir; (of screw) se dévisser; (of tooth) tomber; (of page) se détacher; **my filling has c. out** j'ai perdu mon plombage

3 esp Br Ind **to c. out (on strike)** se mettre en grève

4 (emerge) **to c. out of an affair badly/well** mal/bien se tirer d'une affaire; **they came out of the business looking rather foolish** à la suite de cette affaire, ils avaient l'air plutôt ridicule; Sch **to c. out first/second** sortir premier/second, être reçu premier/second

5 (appear) (of sun, stars) paraître; (of buds) éclore; (of pimple) sortir; (of rash) apparaître; **to c. out in a rash** (of person) se couvrir de boutons, avoir une éruption

6 (become known) (of the truth) être découvert; (of election, sports results etc) être révélé ou communiqué; **as soon as the news came out ...** dès qu'on a su la nouvelle ...; **it came out that ...** il s'avéra que ..., il se trouva que ...

7 (be published, issued) (of book, journal) paraître, sortir; (of record, film) sortir

8 (of photo) **he always comes out well** il est toujours bien sur les photos; **these photos have c. out well** ces photos sont bien sorties

9 (be removed) (of stain) s'enlever; (of colour, dye) déteindre; **when do your stitches c. out?** quand est-ce qu'on t'enlève les points?

10 Math (be solved) **I can't get this sum to c. out** je n'y arrive pas, la somme ne tombe pas juste; **it won't c. out** (of total etc) être de ..., se monter à ...; (of average) être de ...; **it comes out at ...** le résultat est de ...; Fig **everything will c. out (all) right in the end** tout finira par s'arranger

11 Br (of debutante) débuter, faire son entrée dans le monde

12 Fam (as gay or lesbian) se déclarer homosexuel

13 (decide) **to c. out strongly** se prononcer avec vigueur (**for** pour; **against** contre); **we've c. out against the idea of moving** nous avons renoncé à déménager; **the committee came out in her favour** le comité s'est décidé en sa faveur

14 Comput (exit) sortir; **to c. out of a document** sortir d'un document

▶ **come out with** VT INSEP (say) sortir, dire; (remark) sortir, faire; **I'm always wondering what he'll c. out with next** je me demande toujours ce qu'il va sortir; **she finally came out with what was bothering her** elle a fini par dire ce qui la tracassait

▶ **come over** VI **1** (travel, walk etc across) traverser; **a lot of Americans came over during the war** de nombreux Américains sont venus (en Europe) pendant la guerre; **friends are coming over from Canada** des amis arrivent du Canada; **some friends are coming over** (who live not far away) des amis viennent me/nous/etc voir; **c. over to-**

morrow passe demain; **he came over and spoke to me** il est venu me parler

2 (change allegiance) **to c. over to sb's side** passer dans le camp de qn ou du côté de qn; **to c. over to sb's way of thinking** se rallier à l'opinion de qn

3 (make impression) **how did she c. over?** quelle impression vous a-t-elle faite?; **he doesn't c. over well on television** il ne passe pas bien à la télévision, il n'est pas très médiatique; **her voice comes over well** sa voix passe ou rend bien; **he comes over as (being) rather pompous** il a l'air (d'être) assez solennel

4 Fam (suddenly become) **to c. over (all) funny** être pris d'un malaise

VT INSEP (affect) (of mood etc) (person) envahir, gagner; **a change has c. over him** il a bien changé; **what's c. over you?** qu'est-ce qui te prend?

▶ **come round** VI **1** (travel) faire le tour; **the road is blocked, I had to c. round by the village** la route est bloquée, j'ai dû faire un détour par le village

2 (visit) **c. round and see me one day** venez me voir un de ces jours

3 (arrive) **the weekend will soon c. round** ce sera bientôt le week-end; **birthdays seem to c. round more often after you're 40** les anniversaires semblent revenir plus souvent quand on a dépassé la quarantaine

4 (regain consciousness) reprendre connaissance, revenir à soi

5 (change one's mind) changer d'avis; **to c. round to sb's way of thinking** se ranger à l'avis de qn; **they soon came round to the idea** ils se sont faits rapidement à cette idée; **he's c. round** il a cédé

6 Naut (of ship) venir dans le vent; (of wind) remonter

▶ **come through** VI **1** (penetrate) (of tooth) percer; (of water) pénétrer

2 (survive) **he came through without a scratch** il s'en est tiré indemne

3 (arrive) (of message etc) arriver, parvenir; **my visa is taking a long time to c. through** mon visa met du temps à arriver ou à me parvenir

VT INSEP **1** (penetrate) **water is coming through the roof** l'eau s'infiltre par le toit; **the nail has c. through the wood** le clou a traversé le bois

2 (survive) survivre à; **he came through the war without a scratch** il a survécu à la guerre sans une égratignure; **I'm sure you will c. through this crisis** je suis sûr que tu te sortiras de cette crise; **she came through her exams with flying colours** elle a réussi brillamment (à) ses examens

▶ **come to** VI **1** = come round **4**

2 Naut (of ship) lofer, venir dans le vent

VT INSEP **1** (amount to) s'élever à; **the bill came to $80** la note s'éleva à 80 dollars; **how much does it c. to?** combien cela fait-il?; **the plan never came to anything** le projet n'a abouti à rien; **that nephew of yours will never c. to anything** ton neveu n'arrivera jamais à rien

2 (be a question of) **when it comes to ...** en ce qui concerne ...; **when it comes to music I haven't got a clue** je ne m'y connais absolument pas en musique; **c. to that, what are you doing here?** au fait, qu'est-ce que vous faites ici?; **if it comes to that ...** à ce compte-là ...; **let's hope it won't c. to that** espérons que nous n'en arrivions pas là; **when it comes to buying a car, find yourself a reputable dealer** si vous voulez acheter une voiture, adressez-vous à un concessionnaire de bonne réputation

3 (get as far as) en venir à; **I wish she'd c. to the point** si seulement elle en venait au fait; **if it comes to a fight, we outnumber them** si on en vient à se battre, nous sommes plus

nombreux qu'eux; **it's really c. to something when ...** si ce n'est pas malheureux que ...; **what is the world coming to?** où est-ce qu'on va!

▶ **come together** VI **1** (gather) s'assembler, se réunir; (of troops) opérer une jonction

2 (meet) se rencontrer; **the two roads c. together at this point** les deux routes se rejoignent à cet endroit

▶ **come up** VI **1** (by stairs, on ladder, up a hill etc) monter; **would you like to c. up for tea?** (to my room etc) vous voulez monter prendre un thé?; **a man came up from the office downstairs** un homme est monté du bureau d'en-dessous; **to c. up after a dive** revenir à la surface après un plongeon

2 Br **to c. up to town** venir en ville

3 (approach) **a man came up (to me) and started talking** un homme est venu vers moi ou s'est approché de moi et a commencé à me parler; **a police car came up alongside ours** une voiture de police s'est mise à la hauteur de la nôtre; **it's coming up to 10 o'clock** il est presque 10 heures; Tennis **to c. up to the net** monter au filet

4 (appear) apparaître; (of plant) sortir de terre, pousser; (of sun) se lever; **some words came up on the screen** quelques mots sont apparus sur l'écran; Naut **to c. up on the horizon** (of land etc) paraître à l'horizon; **there's a cabaret act coming up (next)** il y a un numéro de cabaret tout de suite après; **there are some interesting films coming up on television** il y a quelques films intéressants qui vont passer à la télévision; **one coffee, coming up!** (in café) un café, oui m'sieur/m'dame!

5 (arise) (of opportunity, question etc) se présenter; (of problem etc) survenir, surgir; **to deal with problems as they c. up** traiter les problèmes au fur et à mesure; **have any vacancies c. up recently?** est-ce que des postes se sont libérés récemment?; **I'll let you know if anything comes up** (if I find further information) s'il y a du nouveau, je vous tiendrai au courant; (anything that is suitable) je vous tiendrai au courant si je vois quelque chose qui vous convienne; **call me if something comes up that you can't handle** appelle-moi s'il y a quelque chose qui te pose problème; Law **to c. up before the court** comparaître (devant le tribunal); **the case comes up (for trial) tomorrow** la cause sera entendue demain; **two houses in our street are coming up for sale soon** dans notre rue, deux maisons seront bientôt à vendre; **the question has never yet c. up** cette question n'a encore jamais été soulevée; **the subject came up twice in the conversation** le sujet est revenu deux fois dans la conversation; **your name came up twice** on a mentionné votre nom deux fois

6 (shine, look clean) **the sideboard came up beautifully** le buffet a retrouvé toute sa splendeur

VT INSEP (stairs) monter; (street) remonter

▶ **come up against** VT INSEP **1** (encounter) se heurter à; **the reformers came up against some pretty strong opposition** les réformateurs se sont heurtés à une opposition plutôt violente; **who does she c. up against in the next round?** qui doit-elle affronter dans la prochaine manche?

2 (hit, come into contact with) rencontrer; **his hand came up against something cold** sa main rencontra quelque chose de froid; **the tunnellers came up against solid rock** les ouvriers qui creusaient le tunnel se sont retrouvés face à un mur de roche dure

▶ **come upon** VT INSEP (find) (person, object) tomber sur

▶ **come up to** VT INSEP **1** (reach) (something) atteindre; **the water came up to my knees** l'eau m'arrivait jusqu'aux genoux; **I only c.**

up to her shoulder je ne lui arrive qu'aux épaules; **we're coming up to the halfway mark** nous atteindrons bientôt la moitié **2** *(equal)* égaler; **to c. up to sb's expectations** répondre à l'attente de qn; **to c. up to standard** être au niveau

▸ **come up with** VT INSEP *(produce) (solution, money)* trouver; *(idea, theory)* proposer; *(suggestion)* faire; **unless someone comes up with a better idea** à moins que quelqu'un ait une meilleure idée

comeback ['kʌmbæk] N **1** *(return)* retour *m* (en vogue); *(of politician)* retour au pouvoir; *(of actor)* retour à la scène/à l'écran, comeback *m inv*; *(of sports person)* retour, comeback; **to make a c.** faire un come-back; **70's fashions are making a c.** la mode des années 70 revient **2** *Fam (reply)* réplique *f* **3** *(justification for complaint)* **to have no c.** n'avoir aucun recours

Comecon ['kɒmɪkɒn] N *(abbr* **Council for Mutual Economic Aid**) COMECON *m*

comedian [kə'miːdɪən] N comique *mf*; *Fig (amusing person)* comique; *(practical joker)* farceur, -euse

> Note that the French word **comédien** is a false friend and is never a translation for the English word **comedian**. It means **actor**.

comedienne [kəmiːdɪ'en] N actrice *f* comique

comedown ['kʌmdaʊn] N *Fam (loss of status)* déchéance *f*; **isn't that a bit of a c. for you?** c'est un peu la dégringolade pour toi, non?

comedy ['kɒmɪdɪ] N **1** *(genre)* comédie *f*, genre *m* comique **2** *(play, film)* comédie *f*; *TV* **(situation) c.** comédie de situation, sitcom *m ou f*; *Fig* **it was a c. of errors from start to finish** ce fut une farce grotesque du début à la fin; *Fig* **we weren't taken in by her little c.** sa petite comédie n'a pas pris

▸ **c. actor** acteur *m* de comédie; **c. actress** actrice *f* de comédie; **c. drama** comédie dramatique; **c. of manners** comédie de mœurs

come-hither ADJ *Fam (look)* aguichant

comely ['kʌmlɪ] ADJ *Lit (person)* avenant

come-on N *Fam* incitation *f*; **it was a c. to get buyers interested** c'était pour attirer les clients; **to give sb the c.** *(sexually)* faire du gringue à qn

comer ['kʌmər] N **open to all comers** ouvert à tous; **I'm ready to take on all comers** je suis prêt à me battre avec n'importe qui

comestible [kə'mestɪb(ə)l] ADJ *esp Am* comestible

NPL *Old-fashioned, Fml* **comestibles** comestibles *mpl*

comet ['kɒmɪt] N *Astron* comète *f*

come-to-bed ADJ **c. eyes** regard *m* aguichant *ou* suggestif

comeuppance [kʌm'ʌpəns] N *Fam* **he got his c.** il n'a eu que ce qu'il mérite

comfort ['kʌmfət] N **1** *(ease)* confort *m*; **to live in c.** être aisé; **the boots are furlined for extra c.** les bottes sont fourrées pour plus de confort; **to do sth in the c. of one's own home** faire qch confortablement chez soi

2 comforts commodités *fpl*; **tobacco was one of the soldiers' few comforts** le tabac était l'un des seuls plaisirs des soldats

3 *(consolation)* réconfort *m*, consolation *f*; **to give sb c.** réconforter qn; **to take c. from** *or* **in sth** trouver du réconfort *ou* de la consolation dans qch; **that's cold c.** c'est là une piètre consolation; **to get too close for c.** *(of ship, truck)* devenir trop dangereux; **the deadline's getting a bit too close for c.** la

date limite est un peu trop proche à mon goût; **it was a great c. to him** ça lui a été d'un grand réconfort, ça l'a beaucoup soulagé; *Iron* **some c. you are/that is!** tu parles d'une consolation!; **there was little c. in the news that the strike would continue** la nouvelle selon laquelle la grève allait continuer était peu réconfortante

VT *(console)* réconforter, consoler; *(of beverage etc)* réconforter; **they comforted the wounded** ils ont réconforté les blessés; **it comforted him to know she had had a decent burial** ça l'a réconforté de savoir qu'elle avait eu un enterrement décent

▸ ▸ **c. eating** = fait *m* de manger pour se remonter le moral; **c. food** = chose *f* que l'on mange pour se remonter le moral; *Am* **c. station** toilettes *fpl* publiques *(sur le bord d'une route)*

comfortable ['kʌmfətəb(ə)l] ADJ **1** *(bed, armchair, hotel, garment etc)* confortable; *(warmth, sensation)* agréable, doux, *f* douce; **you will be more c. in this armchair** vous serez mieux dans ce fauteuil; **to make oneself c.** se mettre à son aise; **to be c.** *(of person)* être à l'aise *ou* à son aise; **to feel c.** se sentir bien *ou* à son aise; **I wouldn't feel c. accepting that money** ça me mettrait mal à l'aise d'accepter cet argent; **he couldn't get c. in bed** il ne savait pas comment se mettre dans le lit pour être à l'aise; **she makes people feel c.** elle met les gens à l'aise

2 *(not in pain)* **to be c.** ne pas souffrir; **he had a c. night** il a passé une bonne nuit

3 *(substantial) (majority, lead, income)* confortable; **to be c. circumstances** mener une vie aisée; **two hours will give you a c. margin** en deux heures, tu auras largement le temps

comfortably ['kʌmftəblɪ] ADV **1** *(to sit etc)* confortablement; *(warm etc)* agréablement **2** *(in financial, material sense)* **to be c. off** être à l'aise; **to live c.** être à l'aise, vivre dans l'aisance **3** *(without difficulty) (to win)* facilement; **we can get there c. in an hour** une heure suffira amplement pour y aller

comforter ['kʌmfətər] N **1** *(person)* consolateur, -trice **2** *Am (quilt)* édredon *m* **3** *Br Old-fashioned (scarf)* cache-nez *m inv* **4** *(baby's dummy)* tétine *f*, sucette *f*

comforting ['kʌmfətɪŋ] ADJ réconfortant

comfortless ['kʌmfətlɪs] ADJ *(room etc)* sans confort, peu confortable; *(prospect, thought)* décourageant; **he was left alone and c.** il s'est retrouvé seul et sans réconfort

comfy ['kʌmfɪ] ADJ *Fam* = **comfortable 1**

comic ['kɒmɪk] ADJ *(song etc)* comique

N **1** *(performer) (man)* comique *m*; *(woman)* actrice *f* comique **2** *(magazine)* bande *f* dessinée, BD *f* **3** *Am Fam (in newspaper)* **comics** (page *f* des) bandes *fpl* dessinées

▸ ▸ **c. actor** acteur *m* comique; **c. actress** actrice comique; **c. book** bande dessinée, BD; **c. opera** opéra-comique *m, pl* opéras-comiques; **c. relief** *Theat* intervalle *m* comique; *Fig* moment *m* de détente (comique); **to provide some c. relief** décrisper l'atmosphère; **c. strip** bande dessinée

comical ['kɒmɪk(ə)l] ADJ comique, drôle; **what a c. idea!** quelle drôle d'idée!

comically ['kɒmɪklɪ] ADV de façon comique; **they tried, c., to distract her attention** ils essayaient de détourner son attention et c'était comique

coming ['kʌmɪŋ] ADJ *(year, week)* qui vient; *(trials, difficulties, elections)* à venir; *(storm)* qui approche

N *(of person)* venue *f*, arrivée *f*; *(of night)* approche *f*; *(of the Messiah)* avènement *m*, venue; *Rel* **the Second C.** le second avènement; **comings and goings** allées *fpl* et venues

comma ['kɒmə] N virgule *f*; **inverted commas** guillemets *mpl*; **to put a word in inverted commas** mettre un mot entre guillemets; *Comput* **c.-separated values format** format *m* valeurs séparées par des virgules

command [kə'mɑːnd] N **1** *(order)* ordre *m*, commandement *m*; **to give a c.** donner un ordre; **to do sth at sb's c.** faire qch sur les ordres de qn; **to be at sb's c.** être aux ordres de qn; **word of c.** commandement

2 *Mil (authority) (of army, expedition)* commandement *m* *(of* de; *over* sur); *(of fort, town etc)* gouvernement *m*; **he was given (the) c. of a division/fleet** on lui a confié le commandement d'une division/d'une flotte; **to be in c. of a battalion** avoir le commandement d'un bataillon, commander un bataillon; **it was my first c.** c'était la première fois que j'étais au commandement; **to be in c. of a pass** *(hold it)* commander un défilé; **c. of the seas** maîtrise *f* des mers; *Fig* **c. over oneself** maîtrise de soi; **who is in c.?** qui est-ce qui commande?; **to be first/second in c.** commander en premier/en second; **under (the) c. of ...** sous le commandement de ...

3 *Mil (troops)* **to be responsible for one's c.** être responsable de ses troupes; **they were my first c.** c'est la première section que j'ai commandée; **bomber/fighter c.** aviation *f* de bombardement/de chasse

4 *Mil (area)* **Scottish/Northern c.** région *f* militaire d'Écosse/du Nord; **air/naval c.** région aérienne/maritime

5 *(knowledge) (of language)* connaissance *f*, maîtrise *f*; **to have a c. of several languages** parler plusieurs langues couramment; **she has a good c. of English** *or* **of the English language** elle a une bonne maîtrise de l'anglais

6 *Comput* commande *f*; *(from menu options)* article *m*

VT **1** *(order)* ordonner, commander *(sth* qch; *sb to do sth* à qn de faire qch); **he did what** *or* **as I commanded him** il a fait ce que je lui ai demandé; **do as I c.!** fais ce que je te demande!; *esp Lit* **we are yours to c.** nous sommes à vos ordres

2 *Mil (be in command of) (ship, regiment)* commander

3 *(have at one's disposal)* avoir à sa disposition; **all the skill he could c.** toute l'habileté qu'il possédait

4 *(inspire) (respect, admiration)* inspirer; *(attention)* forcer; **to c. a high price** se vendre très cher

5 *(of fort etc) (town, entry to pass)* dominer; **window that commands a view over the valley** fenêtre qui donne sur la vallée

VI commander

▸ ▸ *Comput* **c. button** case *f* de commande; *Comput* **c. code** code *m* de commande; **c. economy** économie *f* planifiée; *Comput* **c. file** fichier *m* de commande; *Comput* **c. key** touche *f* de commande; *Comput* **c. language** langage *m* de commande; **c. line** ligne *f* de commande; **c. module** *(of spacecraft)* module *m* de commande; *Br Theat* **c. performance** = représentation *f* (d'un spectacle) à la requête du monarque; *Comput* **c. processor** interpréteur *m* de commandes; *Comput* **c. sequence** séquence *f* de commandes

commandant [kɒmənˈdænt] N *Mil (of camp etc)* commandant *m*

commandeer [kɒmənˈdɪər] VT *Mil* réquisitionner; *Fig* **the boss commandeered our photocopier** le patron a fait main basse sur notre photocopieuse

commander [kəˈmɑːndər] N *Mil (of army, company etc)* commandant *m*; *(of section)* chef *m*; *Aviat* chef de bord; *Naut* capitaine *m* de frégate; **one of the great commanders of history** un des grands chefs de l'histoire

commander-in-chief, *pl* **commanders-in-chief** N commandant *m* en chef

commanding [kəˈmɑːndɪŋ] ADJ **1** *(in command)* qui commande **2** *(tone)* d'autorité, impérieux; *(air)* imposant; *(beauty)* majestueux **3** *(position, height)* dominant; *(lead)* considérable
▸▸ *Mil* **c. officer** commandant *m*

commandment [kəˈmɑːndmənt] N *Rel* commandement *m*; **the Ten Commandments** les Dix Commandements *mpl*; **to keep the commandments** observer les commandements

commando [kəˈmɑːndəʊ] N *Mil* commando *m*

command-orientated [-ɔːrɪənteɪtɪd] ADJ *Comput (program)* orienté commande

commemorate [kəˈmeməreɪt] VT *(person, person's memory)* commémorer

commemoration [kəmeməˈreɪʃən] N commémoration *f*, **in c. of sb/sth** en commémoration de qn/qch

commemorative [kəˈmemərətɪv] ADJ commémoratif (**of** de); **c. issue of a stamp** émission *f* d'un timbre commémoratif

commence [kəˈmens] VT & VI *Am, Br Fml* commencer; **he commenced speaking** il commença à parler

commencement [kəˈmensmənt] N **1** *Fml (beginning)* commencement *m*, début *m* **2** *Univ (in US, Canada, at Cambridge, in Trinity College, Dublin)* remise *f* des diplômes
▸▸ *Univ* **C. Day** *(in US, at Cambridge)* jour *m* de la remise des diplômes

commend [kəˈmend] VT **1** *(praise) (person)* faire l'éloge de, louer; **to c. sb for bravery** faire l'éloge de la bravoure de qn
 2 *(recommend) (something)* recommander; **a course of action that did not c. itself to me** une façon de faire que je ne pouvais pas approuver; **the train journey has little to c. it** je ne vous recommande pas le voyage en train; **the hotel has little to c. it apart from the cooking** il n'y a pas grand-chose de bien à dire sur cet hôtel à part la cuisine
 3 *Lit (entrust)* **to c. sth to sb's care** recommander *ou* confier qch aux soins de qn; **to c. one's soul to God** recommander son âme à Dieu
 4 *Arch, Fml (remember)* **c. me to Dr Smith** rappelez-moi au bon souvenir du Docteur Smith

commendable [kəˈmendəb(ə)l] ADJ louable; *(action)* digne d'éloges; **with c. promptness** avec une rapidité digne d'éloges

commendably [kəˈmendəblɪ] ADV d'une manière louable

commendation [kɒmenˈdeɪʃən] N *(praise)* éloge *m* (**of** de); *(award in competition)* mention *f* spéciale; **worthy of c.** digne d'éloges

commensurable [kəˈmensərəb(ə)l, -ʃər-] ADJ **1** *Math* commensurable (**with, to** avec)
 2 = **commensurate 2**

commensurate [kəˈmensərət, -ʃər-] ADJ **1** *(of same proportions)* coétendu (**with** à) **2** *(proportionate)* proportionnel (**to, with** à); **the salary offered will be c. with experience** le salaire sera proportionnel à l'expérience; **there was no post c. with his abilities** aucun

poste ne correspondait à ses compétences; **of c. value** d'une valeur équivalente

comment [ˈkɒment] N observation *f*, commentaire *m*; **to make the observations sur qch; no c.** sans commentaire; **to refrain from c.** s'abstenir de faire des commentaires
 VT **to c. that ...** (faire) remarquer *ou* (faire) observer que … +*ind*
 VI **1** faire un/des commentaire(s); **I'd rather not c.** je préfère m'abstenir de tout commentaire; **to c. on sth** faire des observations *ou* des commentaires sur qch; **nobody commented on it** personne n'a fait de commentaire à ce sujet **2** *Liter* **to c. on a text** commenter un texte
▸▸ **c. card** fiche *f* d'observations

commentary [ˈkɒmənt(ə)rɪ] N **1** *Radio, TV* commentaire *m*; **with c. by Terry Davis** commenté par Terry Davis **2** *Liter (on text etc)* commentaire *m* **3** *(remarks)* commentaire *m*, observations *fpl*
▸▸ *Radio, TV* **c. booth** cabine *f* du commentateur; *Radio, TV* **c. box** tribune *f* des journalistes

commentate [ˈkɒmənteɪt] VI *Radio, TV* faire le commentaire; **to c. on an event** faire le commentaire d'un *ou* commenter un événement

commentator [ˈkɒmənteɪtər] N **1** *Radio, TV* commentateur, -trice; **(sports) c.** commentateur sportif, commentatrice sportive **2** *Journ* journaliste *mf (de la presse écrite);* **political c.** journaliste politique **3** *Liter (on text)* commentateur, -trice

commerce [ˈkɒmɜːs] N **1** *(trade)* commerce *m*; **Chamber of C.** Chambre *f* de commerce **2** *Fml (social relations)* relations *fpl*, rapports *mpl* (**between** entre)

commercial [kəˈmɜːʃəl] ADJ **1** commercial, -aux; *(port, tribunal etc)* de commerce; *(value)* marchand; **a course in c. French** un cours de français commercial **2** *also Pej (profit-orientated) (mind)* mercantile, commercial, -aux; *(record, music)* commercial; *(mainstream) (film)* grand public *inv*; **his films are terribly c.** ses films sont vraiment commerciaux **3** *(radio, television)* commercial, -aux
 N *Radio, TV* publicité *f*, pub *f*, spot *m* publicitaire
▸▸ **c. agency** agence *f* commerciale; **c. artist** graphiste *mf*; **c. attaché** attaché *m* commercial; **c. bank** banque *f* commerciale; *Fin* **c. bill** effet *m* de commerce; *Radio, TV* **c. break** page *f* de publicité; **c. channel** *Écon* circuit *m* commercial; *TV* chaîne *f* commerciale; **c. contract** contrat *m* commercial; **c. directory** annuaire *m* du commerce; **c. documents** papiers *mpl* d'affaires; **c. law** droit *m* commercial; **c. loan** prêt *m* commercial; *Fin* **c. paper** billet *m* de trésorerie; *Old-fashioned* **c. traveller** voyageur *m ou* représentant *m* de commerce, VRP *m*; **c. vehicule** véhicule *m* utilitaire, commerciale *f*

commercialism [kəˈmɜːʃəlɪz(ə)m] N esprit *m* commercial; *Pej (obsession with profit)* mercantilisme *m*

commercialization [kəmɜːʃəlaɪˈzeɪʃən] N *also Pej* commercialisation *f*

commercialize [kəˈmɜːʃəlaɪz] VT *Pej* commercialiser

commercially [kəˈmɜːʃəlɪ] ADV commercialement

commie [ˈkɒmɪ] N, ADJ *Fam Pej (communist)* coco *mf*, communiste *mf*

commis [ˈkɒmɪ] ADJ
▸▸ **c. chef** commis *m*, commis cuisinier, commis de cuisine; **c. waiter** commis

commiserate [kəˈmɪzəreɪt] VI **to c. with sb** être désolé pour qn

commiseration [kəmɪzəˈreɪʃən] N commisération *f*, compassion *f* (**with** pour); **commiserations are in order, I think** *(for you)* j'avoue que vous n'avez pas de chance

commissariat [kɒmɪˈseərɪət] N *Mil (department)* commissariat *m* de l'armée de terre, *Old-fashioned* intendance *f*

commissary [ˈkɒmɪsərɪ] N *Am Mil (store)* dépôt *m* de vivres; *(officer)* officier *m* d'intendance

Commission [kəˈmɪʃən] N *EU* Commission *f*

commission [kəˈmɪʃən] N **1** *Com (payment)* commission *f*, *(on exchange)* commission de change; **sale on c.** vente *f* à la commission; **three per cent c.** trois pour cent de commission; *Com* **c. only** rémunération *f* à la commission
 2 *Com etc (order)* commande *f*, mission *f*, **work done on c.** travail fait sur commande; **to carry out a c.** s'acquitter d'une commande
 3 *(investigating body)* commission *f*, **fact-finding c.** commission d'enquête
 4 *Naut etc (of ship)* armement *m*; **to put a ship into c.** armer un navire; **in c.** *(ship)* en commission; *(plane, factory)* en service; **out of c.** *(ship)* désarmé; *(car, machine)* hors service; **you'll be out of c. for six weeks** vous serez obligé de suspendre vos activités pendant six semaines
 5 *Mil* brevet *m* (d'officier); **to resign one's c.** démissionner, donner sa démission; **to get a or one's c.** être nommé officier
 6 *(of a crime)* perpétration *f*
 VT **1** *(order) (person)* commissionner (**to do sth** pour faire qch); *(book, painting)* commander; **to c. an artist to paint a portrait** commander un portrait à un artiste; **to be commissioned to do sth** être chargé de faire qch
 2 *(appoint)* préposer *ou* déléguer à une fonction; *Mil (officer)* nommer à un commandement; *Mil* **to be commissioned** être nommé officier
 3 *Naut etc (ship)* armer; *(plane, factory)* mettre en service
▸▸ *Com* **c. agent** commissionaire *mf*; *Acct* **c. note** note *f* de commission

commissionaire [kəmɪʃəˈneər] N portier *m*

commissioned [kəˈmɪʃənd] ADJ **1** *Naut (ship)* armé **2** *(operative)* en service
▸▸ *Mil* **c. officer** officier *m*

commissioner [kəˈmɪʃənər] N **1** *(member of a commission)* commissaire *m*, membre *m* d'une/de la commission **2** *(of police) Br* ≃ préfet *m* de police; *Am* ≃ (commissaire *m*) divisionnaire *m*
▸▸ *Law* **c. for oaths** = officier *m* ayant qualité pour recevoir les déclarations sous serment

commissioning [kəˈmɪʃənɪŋ] N **1** *Mil (of officer)* nomination *f* à un commandement **2** *Naut etc (of ship)* armement *m*; *(of new power plant etc)* mise *f* en service *ou* en exploitation
▸▸ **c. editor** directeur, -trice éditorial(e) *(chargé(e) notamment de commander de nouveaux ouvrages aux auteurs)*

commit [kəˈmɪt] VT (-tt-) **1** *(carry out) (crime)* commettre; **to c. suicide** se suicider
 2 *(promise)* **to c. oneself** s'engager; **to c. oneself to sth/to doing sth** s'engager à qch/à faire qch; **without committing myself** sans m'engager; **to c. sth to sth** *(funds to project etc)* engager qch dans qch; **he had committed 2,000 troops to the defence of the village** il avait assigné 2 000 soldats à la défense du village
 3 *(entrust)* confier, remettre (**sb/sth to sb's care** qn/qch aux soins *ou* à la garde de qn); **to c. sb's body to the earth/the deep** porter

un corps en terre/confier un corps aux flots; **to c. one's soul to God** rendre son âme à Dieu; **to c. sth to writing** coucher qch par écrit; **to c. sth to memory** apprendre qch par cœur

4 *(confine)* **she has been committed** *(to mental institution)* on l'a fait interner; **to c. sb (to prison)** envoyer qn en prison

5 *Law* **to c. sb for trial** mettre qn en accusation; *(send to assizes)* renvoyer qn aux assises

6 *Pol (bill)* renvoyer à une commission

commitment [kə'mɪtmənt] **N 1** *(obligation)* engagement *m*; **family commitments** obligations *fpl* familiales; **I cannot do it because of other commitments** d'autres obligations m'empêchent de le faire; **there are no teaching commitments attached to this job** ce poste ne comporte pas d'heures d'enseignement obligatoires; **my teaching commitments this term** les heures d'enseignement que je dois assurer ce trimestre; **without any c. on your part** sans aucun engagement de votre part

2 *(to a political party, union etc)* engagement *m* (**to** pour); **his c. to the proposed reform of the tax system** son soutien pour la réforme du système fiscal qui a été proposée; **so many men avoid c. in relationships** il y a tellement d'hommes qui refusent de s'investir dans les relations amoureuses; **I found her lacking in c.** je trouvais qu'elle ne s'investissait pas assez; **to make a c.** s'engager

3 *Law* emprisonnement *m*

4 *(act of entrusting) (of document to notary etc)* dépôt *m*
▸▸ *Banking* **c. fee** commission *f* d'engagement

committal [kə'mɪt(ə)l] **N 1** *Law* emprisonnement *m*, mise *f* en prison; *(of insane person)* internement *m* dans un hôpital psychiatrique **2** *(of corpse)* mise *f* en terre; **the c. of a body to the ground/the deep** la mise en terre/l'immersion *f* d'un mort
▸▸ *Law* **c. order** mandat *m* de dépôt; *Law* **c. proceedings** = mise en accusation afin de décider si une affaire doit être renvoyée devant un tribunal de plus grande instance; *Law* **c. for sentence** = fait de renvoyer une affaire devant un tribunal de plus grande instance pour une condamnation qui reflète la gravité du crime; *Law* **c. for trial** = fait de renvoyer une affaire devant un tribunal de plus grande instance

committed [kə'mɪtɪd] **ADJ** engagé (**to** dans); **a c. socialist** un socialiste engagé; **he didn't seem very c.** son engagement ne semblait pas être très ferme; **to be c. to an idea** être attaché à une idée
▸▸ *Acct* **c. costs** coûts *mpl* engagés

committee [kə'mɪtɪ] **N** comité *m*, commission *f*, *Parl* commission *f*; **to be** *or* **sit on a c.** être membre *ou* faire partie d'un comité *ou* d'une commission; **in c.** en commission; **standing c.** commission permanente **VOIR** GRAMMAIRE A11
▸▸ **c. meeting** réunion *f* de comité; **c. member** membre *m* d'un/du comité *ou* d'une/de la commission; *Br Parl* **c. stage** = stade *m* de discussion d'un projet de loi par une commission; *Br Parl* **C. of Ways and Means** commission *f* du budget

committeeman, *pl* **committeemen** [kə-'mɪtɪmæn, -men] **N** *esp Am* homme *m* membre d'un/de plusieurs comité(s)

committeeperson [kə'mɪtɪpɜːsən] **N** *esp Am* membre *m* d'un/de plusieurs comité(s)

committeewoman, *pl* **committee- women** [kə'mɪtɪwʊmən, -wɪmɪn] **N** *esp Am* femme *f* membre d'un/de plusieurs comité(s)

commode [kə'məʊd] **N 1** *(with drawers)* commode *f* **2** *(toilet)* chaise *f* percée

commodious [kə'məʊdɪəs] **ADJ** spacieux

commodity [kə'mɒdɪtɪ] **N** *Com, Econ* marchandise *f*, produit *m*; **primary** *or* **basic c.** produit de base
▸▸ *St Exch* **c. broker, c. dealer** courtier, -ière en matières premières; *St Exch* **c. futures** opérations *fpl* à terme sur matières premières; *St Exch* **c. market** marché *m* des matières premières; **c. money** monnaie *f* de marchandise; **c. tax** impôt *m* sur les denrées

commodore ['kɒmədɔːr] **N** *Naut* chef *m* de division; *(of convoy)* chef de convoi; *(in merchant navy)* capitaine *m* le plus ancien; *(of yacht club)* président *m*

common ['kɒmən] **ADJ 1** *(frequent, widespread)* ordinaire, courant; **mixed marriages are c. here** les mariages mixtes sont courants ici; **in c. use** d'usage courant; **it is c. (practice) to ...** il est courant de ...; **it is c. knowledge** tout le monde le sait; **the agreement is c. knowledge** l'accord est connu de tous; **c. or garden cabbage** chou *m* commun; *Hum* **I'm just a c. or garden journalist** je ne suis qu'un journaliste ordinaire *ou* un journaliste parmi tant d'autres; **you may think this just a c. or garden wristwatch but ...** tu as peut-être l'impression que c'est une montre ordinaire *ou* comme les autres mais ...; **c. prostitute** vulgaire prostituée *f*, **c. thief** vulgaire voleur *m*; **c. decency** les convenances *fpl* (sociales)

2 *(shared)* commun; **he was, by c. consent ...** il était, de l'avis de tous, ...; **by c. consent, it has been decided to ...** d'un commun accord, on a décidé de ...; *Law* **c. land** champs *mpl* communs; **c. ownership** copropriété *f*, **c. staircase** escalier *m* commun; **c. wall** mur *m* commun *ou* mitoyen; **to make c. cause with sb** s'allier à qn; **we have c. interests** nous avons des intérêts communs

3 *(average)* **the c. people** les gens *mpl* ordinaires; **the c. man** l'homme *m* de la rue; **he lacks the c. touch** il ne sait pas parler aux gens; **he's nothing but a c. criminal** ce n'est qu'un vulgaire criminel

4 *Pej (vulgar) (person, manners, language, style, joke)* vulgaire; *(accent)* populaire; **he's rather a c. little man** il est plutôt commun

N 1 to have sth in c. with sb/sth avoir qch en commun avec qn/qch; **they have nothing in c.** ils n'ont rien en commun

2 *(land)* terrain *m* communal; **the village c.** les terrains communaux, les communaux *mpl*

3 *Law* **(right of) c.** droit *m* de (vaine) pâture
▸▸ *EU* **C. Agricultural Policy** politique *f* agricole commune; **c. carrier** *(of goods)* transporteur *m* public, entreprise *f* de transport public; **c. cold** rhume *m*; *Math, Fig* **c. denominator** dénominateur *m* commun; *Math* **c. divisor** commun diviseur *m*; *EU* **c. external tariff** tarif *m* externe commun; *Math* **c. factor** facteur *m* commun; *EU* **C. Fisheries Policy** politique commune de la pêche; *Comput* **c. gateway interface** interface *f* commune de passerelle; **c. ground** *(in interests)* intérêt *m* commun; *(for discussion)* terrain *m* d'entente; *Fig* **there is no c. ground between them** il n'y a pas de terrain d'entente entre eux; **c. interest group** groupe *m* d'intérêt commun; **c. law** droit *m* coutumier, common law *f*, *EU* **the C. Market** le marché commun; **c. name** *(of plant)* nom *m* vulgaire; *Gram* **c. noun** nom *m* commun; *Aviat* **c. rated fare** tarif *m* commun; *Br Sch, Univ* **c. room** *(for students)* salle *f* commune; *(for staff)* salle des professeurs; **c. salt** sel *m* ordinaire; **c. sense** bon sens *m*, sens commun; *Am St Exch* **c. stock** actions *fpl* ordinaires; *Mus* **c. time** mesure *f* à quatre temps

commoner ['kɒmənər] **N 1** *(not noble)* rotu-

rier, -ière **2** *Law* usager, -ère du droit de vaine pâture **3** *Univ (at Oxford)* étudiant, -ante ordinaire *(qui ne reçoit pas de bourse)* **4** *Br Parl* député *m*, membre *m* de la Chambre des communes

common-law **ADJ** *Law* **c. husband** concubin *m*; **c. wife** concubine *f*, **c. marriage** concubinage *m*, union *f* libre; **the children of c. marriages** les enfants issus d'unions libres

commonly ['kɒmənlɪ] **ADV 1** *(frequently)* communément, ordinairement; **what is c. known as ...** ce qu'en langage courant on appelle ... **2** *Pej (vulgarly)* vulgairement, de façon vulgaire

commonness ['kɒmənnɪs] **N 1** *(frequency)* fréquence *f* **2** *Pej (vulgarity)* vulgarité *f*

commonplace ['kɒmənpleɪs] **N** *(thing)* banalité *f*, *(saying)* lieu *m* commun, platitude *f* **ADJ** banal, -als; **such operations are becoming c.** de telles opérations deviennent de plus en plus banales
▸▸ *Old-fashioned* **c. book** recueil *m* de pensées

commons ['kɒmənz] **NPL 1** *(people)* **the c.** le peuple; **the (House of) C.** la Chambre des Communes **2** *Old-fashioned (food)* **to be on short c.** faire maigre chère

commonweal ['kɒmənwiːl] **N** *Lit* bien *m* commun

Commonwealth ['kɒmənwelθ] **N 1 the (British) C. (of Nations)** le Commonwealth **2** *Br Hist* **the C.** = période *f* de l'histoire britannique de 1649 (mort de Charles I) à 1660 (rétablissement de la monarchie)
▸▸ **the C. of Australia** le Commonwealth d'Australie; **C. country** pays *m* du Commonwealth; *Br* **C. Development Group** = organisme *m* gouvernemental dont le rôle est de répartir l'aide aux pays en voie de développement; **the C. of Massachusetts** l'État *m* du Massachusetts; **the C. of Pennsylvania** l'État de Pennsylvanie

commotion [kə'məʊʃən] **N** *(noise)* agitation *f*, commotion *f*; **in a state of c.** en émoi; **to create a c.** faire du bruit; **what's all the c. about?** pourquoi toute cette agitation?

comms [kɒmz] **N** *Comput* communication *f*
▸▸ **c. package** logiciel *m* de communication; **c. port** port *m* de communication

communal ['kɒmjʊn(ə)l] **ADJ 1** *(shared) (bathroom, garden etc)* commun; *Law* **c. estate** communauté *f* (conjugale); **c. property** biens *mpl* en commun *ou* en copropriété **2** *(of community)* communautaire, collectif; **c. life** la vie commune *ou* communautaire; **c. violence** violence *f* entre communautés

communally [kə'mjuːnəlɪ] **ADV** en commun; **c. owned** en copropriété

commune[1] ['kɒmjuːn] **N 1** *(of hippies etc)* communauté *f*, *Hist* **the Paris C.** la Commune (de Paris) **2** *Admin (in France, Belgium, Italy etc)* commune *f*

commune[2] [kə'mjuːn] **VI 1** *Lit* communiquer (**with sb** avec qn); **to c. with nature** être en communion avec la nature **2** *Am Rel* communier

communicable [kə'mjuːnɪkəb(ə)l] **ADJ** *(disease)* transmissible; *(idea)* communicable

communicant [kə'mjuːnɪkənt] **N** *Rel* communiant, -ante

communicate [kə'mjuːnɪkeɪt] **VI 1** communiquer; **to c. with sb** communiquer avec qn; **to c. by letter** communiquer par lettre; **he finds it difficult to c.** il a du mal à communiquer; **we can't seem to c.** on ne se comprend pas; **we've stopped communicating** on a cessé toute communication; **to c. well/badly** avoir de grandes qualités relationnelles/ manquer de qualités relationnelles **2** *(connect) (of rooms)* communiquer; **rooms that**

c. with one another chambres qui communiquent **3** *Rel* communier, recevoir la communion
VT *(news etc)* communiquer, faire parvenir; *(illness)* passer; *(emotion, heat etc)* communiquer

communicating [kə'mjuːnɪkeɪtɪŋ] **ADJ** *(room)* communicant; *(door)* de communication

communication [kəmjuːnɪ'keɪʃən] **N 1** *(contact)* **to be in c. with ...** être en relation avec ...; **to be in close c. with one another** être en relation constante; **we haven't had any c. for six months** nous ne sommes plus en relation(s) depuis six mois; **to break off all c. with sb** rompre toutes relations avec qn; **communications between the two have broken down** ils ne sont plus en relation; **line of c.** lien *m*; *Mil* ligne *f* de communication
2 *(message etc)* communication *f*, **no official c. of his death has yet been received** on n'a encore reçu aucune communication officielle de sa mort
3 *(of information, feeling etc)* communication *f* (**to sb** à qn); **means of c.** moyens *mpl* de communication; **c. gap** manque *m* de communication; **c. problem** problème *m* de communication
4 communications *(technology)* communications *fpl*, *Mil (system)* transmissions *fpl*, liaison(s) *f(pl)*; **radio communications** liaison (par) radio
▸ ▸ *Br* **c. cord** sonnette *f* d'alarme *(dans les trains)*; **communications director** directeur, -trice de la communication, dircom *m*; **communications link** liaison *f* de communications; **communications manager** directeur, -trice de la communication, dircom; **c. network** réseau *m* de communication; **communications satellite** satellite *m* de communications; **communications sector** secteur *m* des communications; **c. skills** *(of person)* qualités *fpl* relationnelles; **to have good c. skills** avoir des talents de communication, être un bon communicateur; *Comput* **communications software** logiciel *m* de communication; *Mil* **c. trench** boyau *m*; *Br* **C. Workers Union** = syndicat *m* des travailleurs des postes et des télécommunications

communications-intensive **ADJ** utilisant intensivement les moyens de communication

communicative [kə'mjuːnɪkətɪv] **ADJ** communicatif; *(skills)* en matière de communication; *(she's not very c.* elle n'est pas très communicative

communion [kə'mjuːnjən] **N 1** *Rel* **(Holy) C.** sainte communion *f*; **to administer Holy C. to sb** administrer la sainte communion à qn; **to take (Holy) C.** communier; **the c. of saints** la communion des saints **2** *Lit* communication *f* (**with sb** avec qn)
▸ ▸ *Rel* **c. cup** calice *m*; *Rel* **c. wafer** hostie *f*; *Rel* **c. wine** vin *m* de messe

communiqué [kə'mjuːnɪkeɪ] **N** communiqué *m*

communism ['kɒmjʊnɪz(ə)m] **N** communisme *m*

communist ['kɒmjʊnɪst] **ADJ, N** communiste *mf*

Community [kə'mjuːnɪtɪ] **ADJ** *EU* communautaire
▸ ▸ **C. law** droit *m* communautaire

community [kə'mjuːnɪtɪ] **N 1** *(group)* communauté *f*; **the international c.** la communauté internationale; **the Greek c. in Paris** la communauté grecque de Paris
2 *(village etc)* communauté *f*; **a small mining c.** une petite communauté minière; **c. of 2,000** une communauté de 2 000 habitants

3 *Rel* communauté *f* *(religieuse)*
4 *(public)* **the c.** le public; **harmful to the c.** nuisible à la communauté
5 *(something shared)* *(of possessions, interests etc)* communauté *f*, *(of tastes)* communauté, identité *f*; **there's no c. of values between them** il n'y a pas de communauté de valeurs entre eux
▸ ▸ *Admin* **c. care** = système *m* britannique de soins et d'aide au niveau local; **c. centre** foyer *m* municipal, centre *m* social; *Am TV* **c. channel** = chaîne *f* du réseau câblé sur laquelle des particuliers peuvent diffuser leurs propres émissions; *Br Admin Formerly* **c. charge** = impôt *m* local; *Am Fin* **c. chest** fonds *m* commun *(à des fins sociales)*; **c. policing** ≃ îlotage *m*, *Can* services *mpl* de police communautaires, patrouille *f* pédestre de quartier; **c. radio** radio *f* communautaire; *Law* **c. service** ≃ travail *m* d'intérêt général; **c. singing** chansons *fpl* populaires *(reprises en chœur)*; **c. spirit** esprit *m* de groupe

commutable [kə'mjuːtəb(ə)l] **ADJ 1** *Law (sentence)* commuable **2** *(interchangeable)* permutable, interchangeable

commutation [kɒmjuː'teɪʃən] **N** commutation *f*, *Law* **c. of sentence** commutation de peine
▸ ▸ *Am* **c. ticket** *(for public transportation)* carte *f* d'abonnement

commutator ['kɒmjuːteɪtər] **N** *Elec* commutateur *m*

commute [kə'mjuːt] **VI** faire la navette entre sa résidence et son travail; **I c. here every day** je fais le trajet tous les jours; **to c. by train/car** se rendre à son travail en train/voiture
VT 1 *(exchange)* échanger (**for, into** pour, contre); **to c. an annuity into** *or* **for a lump sum** racheter une rente par un versement global **2** *Law* **to c. a penalty into** *or* **for another** commuer une peine en une autre **3** *(interchange)* interchanger **4** *Metal* transformer
N *Am* trajet *m* *(entre travail et domicile)*; **it's an easy c.** c'est un trajet commode

commuter [kə'mjuːtər] **N** *(from suburbs)* banlieusard, -arde *(qui fait la navette entre sa résidence et son travail)*, *Belg* navetteur, -euse; **I've been a c. for fifteen years** ça fait quinze ans que je fais la navette (entre chez moi et le travail); **the problems caused by c. traffic** les problèmes provoqués par l'utilisation de la voiture pour se rendre au travail; **c. traffic is very heavy this evening** la circulation en direction de la banlieue est très dense ce soir
▸ ▸ **c. airline** compagnie *f* d'aviation court-courrier; *Br* **the c. belt** la grande banlieue; *Rail* **c. line** ligne *f* de banlieue; **c. plane** commuter *m*; **c. town** cité-dortoir *f*, *pl* cités-dortoirs; **c. train** train *m* de banlieue

commuterland [kə'mjuːtəlænd] **N** = grande banlieue *f* considérée comme un pays à part, où l'on ne fait rien d'autre que dormir

commuting [kə'mjuːtɪŋ] **N** trajets *mpl* réguliers, migrations *fpl* quotidiennes *(entre le domicile, généralement en banlieue, et le lieu de travail)*; **I'm tired of c.** j'en ai assez de faire le trajet jusqu'à mon travail tous les jours

comp [kɒmp] **N 1** *Typ (compositor)* metteur *m* (en pages) **2** *(ticket)* exonéré *m*

compact[1] [kɒm'pækt, 'kɒmpækt] **ADJ 1** *(dense, closely packed)* *(snow, ground etc)* compact; *(style)* concis **2** *(small)* *(apartment, kitchen etc)* petit mais fonctionnel; *(telephone, computer, camera etc)* compact; *Am (car)* petit et économique; *(person)* trapu; **to have a c. build** être trapu
▸ ▸ **c. disc** *(disque m)* compact *m*, CD *m*; **c. disc interactive** CDI *m*; **c. disc player** platine *f* CD; **c. disc recorder** graveur *m* de disque

compact; **c. disc rewritable** CD réinscriptible; **c. disc video** CD vidéo *m*

compact[2] ['kɒmpækt] **N 1** *(for powder)* *(in handbag)* poudrier *m* **2** *Am Aut* voiture *f* petite et économique **3** *Fml (agreement)* convention *f*, accord *m*

compact[3] [kəm'pækt] **VT** rendre compact; *(snow)* tasser; *Constr* compacter

compacting [kəm'pæktɪŋ] **N** *Comput* compression *f*

compactly [kəm'pæktlɪ] **ADV** d'une manière compacte

compactness [kəm'pæktnɪs] **N 1** *(of earth, snow, muscles)* dureté *f*, *(of style)* concision *f* **2** *(smallness)* *(of computer, design, camera etc)* compacité *f*; **the c. of the kitchen** la cuisine petite mais fonctionnelle

Companies Act ['kɒmpənɪz] **N** *Law* Loi *f* sur les sociétés

Companies House **N** *Br Com* = institut *m* où sont enregistrées toutes les informations concernant les entreprises du pays

companion[1] [kəm'pænjən] **N 1** *(male)* compagnon *m*; *(female)* compagne *f*, **(lady) c.** dame *f* de compagnie; **c. in arms** compagnon d'armes; **a drinking/travelling c.** un compagnon de boisson/voyage **2** *(other of a pair)* *(of book etc)* pendant *m* (**of** à) **3** *(in titles)* compagnon *m*; **C. to English Literature** guide *m* de la littérature anglaise
▸ ▸ **c. fare** *(for additional person)* tarif *m* par personne supplémentaire

companion[2] **N** *Naut*
▸ ▸ **c. hatch** capot *m*; **c. ladder** échelle *f* de commandement

companionable [kəm'pænjənəb(ə)l] **ADJ** sociable

companionship [kəm'pænjənʃɪp] **N** compagnie *f*, *(comradeship)* camaraderie *f*, **the dog provides c. for her** le chien lui fait de la compagnie *ou* lui tient compagnie

companionway [kəm'pænjənweɪ] **N** *Naut* escalier *m* des cabines

company ['kʌmpənɪ] **N 1** *(companionship)* compagnie *f*, **in sb's c.** en compagnie de qn; **I like his c.** j'aime sa compagnie, j'aime être avec lui; **to keep sb c.** tenir compagnie à qn; **he's very good c.** c'est un compagnon agréable, il est de bonne compagnie; **it's nice to have c.** c'est agréable d'avoir de la compagnie; **she needs the c. of children of her own age** elle a besoin d'être avec des enfants de son âge; **to be fond of one's own c.** aimer être seul; *Prov* **two's c., three's a crowd** ≃ vous seriez/nous serions/*etc* mieux tous les deux; **to part c. with sb** *(split up)* se séparer de qn; *(disagree)* ne plus être d'accord avec qn
2 *(acquaintances)* compagnie *f*, société *f*; **I don't like the c. he keeps** je n'aime pas ses fréquentations; **to get into bad c.** avoir de mauvaises fréquentations
3 *(people present)* assemblée *f*, personnes *fpl* présentes; **to do sth in c.** faire qch en public; **present c. excepted** à part les personnes ici présentes; **the most intelligent of the c. were in agreement** les plus intelligentes des personnes présentes étaient d'accord
4 *(guests)* invités *mpl*; **are you expecting c.?** vous attendez de la visite?; *Fam* **we've got c.!** *(there's someone else here, we're being followed)* nous avons de la compagnie
5 *Com, Ind* entreprise *f*, société *f*; **to form** *or* **incorporate a c.** constituer une société; **insurance c.** compagnie *f* d'assurances; **(the firm of) Thomas and C.** (la maison) Thomas et Cie; **on** *or* **in c. time** *(to make telephone call etc)* pendant les heures de travail **VOIR GRAMMAIRE A11**
6 *Theat* compagnie *f*

7 *Naut* **the ship's c.** l'équipage *m (au complet, y compris les officiers)* **8** *Mil* compagnie *f* **9** *(of girl guides)* compagnie *f* **10** *(guild)* corporation *f* de marchands ▸▸**c. car** voiture *f* de fonction; **c. credit card** carte *f* de crédit professionnelle; **c. director** directeur, -trice; **c. doctor** *(medical)* médecin *m* du travail; *(businessperson)* redresseur *m* d'entreprises; **c. funds** fonds *m* social; **c. law** droit *m* des sociétés; **c. lawyer** avocat, -ate d'une/de l'entreprise *ou* d'une/ de la société; *Mil* **c. officer** officier *m* de compagnie; **c. policy** politique *f* de la maison *ou* de la société; **it isn't c. policy** ce n'est pas la politique de la maison *ou* de la société; **c. savings scheme** plan *m* d'épargne entreprise; **c. secretary** secrétaire *mf* général(e) *(d'une entreprise)*

comparability [kɒmpərə'bɪlɪtɪ] **N** comparabilité *f*

comparable ['kɒmpərəb(ə)l] **ADJ** comparable (**with** avec; **to** à)

comparative [kəm'pærətɪv] **ADJ 1** *(comparing)* comparatif; **c. rating scale** échelle *f* d'évaluation comparative; **c. methodology** méthodologie *f* comparative; **a c. study** une étude comparative **2** *(relative) (cost, comfort, wealth etc)* relatif; **he's a c. stranger to me** je ne le connais pratiquement pas
N *Gram* comparatif *m*; **in the c.** au comparatif VOIR GRAMMAIRE A24–7; B11; B13–14 ▸▸*Econ* **c. advantage** avantage *m* comparé; *Gram* **c. adverb** adverbe *m* de comparaison *ou* comparatif; *Am* **c. advertising** publicité *f* comparative; *Econ* **c. cost** loi *f* des avantages comparés; *Gram* **c. degree** le comparatif; **c. grammar** grammaire *f* comparée; **c. linguistics** linguistique *f* comparée; *Mktg* **c. test** test *m* comparatif

comparatively [kəm'pærɪtɪvlɪ] **ADV 1** *(in comparison)* comparativement, par comparaison **2** *(relatively) (easy, expensive etc)* relativement

compare VT *(facts, ideas)* comparer; **to c. sth to sth** *(liken)* comparer qch à qch; *(contrast)* comparer qch avec qch; **to c. sth with sth** *(contrast)* comparer qch avec qch; **compared with** *or* **to ...** en comparaison de ..., à côté de ..., par rapport à ...; **compared with last year's figures** par rapport aux chiffres de l'année dernière; **to c. notes** *(exchange impressions)* échanger ses impressions
VI être comparable (**with** à); **he can't c. with you** on ne peut pas le comparer à vous; **nothing compares to you** tu es unique; **other brands of washing powder just can't c.** les autres marques de lessive ne sont pas à la hauteur de celle-ci; **to c. favourably with sth** ne le céder en rien à qch; **the French car compares well with the Italian one** la voiture française supporte la comparaison avec l'italienne
N *Lit* **beyond c.** sans comparaison; **beauty without c.** beauté sans pareille

comparison [kəm'pærɪs(ə)n] **N** comparaison *f*; **to make** *or* **draw a c. between sth and sth** faire la comparaison de qch avec qch; **in** *or* **by c.** en comparaison; **in c. with ...** comparé à ...; **without c., beyond all c.** sans comparaison; **there is no c.** il n'y a pas de comparaison; **to stand** *or* **bear c.** supporter la comparaison; **that's a rather unfair c.** ce n'est pas très juste de me/le/*etc* comparer à lui/elle/*etc*; *Gram* **degrees of c.** degrés *mpl* de comparaison ▸▸*Mktg* **c. advertising** publicité *f* comparative; *Mktg* **c. shopping** achats *mpl* comparatifs

compartment [kəm'pɑːtmənt] **N 1** *Rail* compartiment *m*; **sleeping c.** compartiment

lit *(dans un wagon-lit)* **2** *(of a drawer etc)* case *f*, compartiment *m*

compartmentalize [kɒmpɑːt'ment(ə)laɪz] VT compartimenter

compass ['kʌmpəs] **N 1** *(in surveying), Naut etc (with moving needle)* boussole *f*, *(with moving card)* compas *m* **2** *Geom* **(pair of) compasses** compas *m* **3** *Fml (scope) (of knowledge, powers)* étendue *f*, *(of inquiry, reforms)* cadre *m*; *(of time)* espace *m*; *(of mind)* portée *f*, *Mus (of voice)* étendue, diapason *m*, registre *m*; **to be beyond the c. of the human mind** dépasser les limites de l'entendement humain ▸▸*Naut* **c. bearing** relèvement *m* au compas; **to take a c. bearing** prendre un relèvement au compas; *Naut* **c. card** rose *f* des vents; *Naut* **c. dial** rose des vents; *Naut* **c. error** erreur *f ou* variation *f* du compas

compassion [kəm'pæʃən] **N** compassion *f*, pitié *f*; **to arouse c.** faire pitié, exciter la compassion; **to show c.** montrer de la compassion; **you have no c.** tu n'as pas de pitié ▸▸**c. fatigue** = lassitude *f* du public à l'égard des nécessiteux

compassionate [kəm'pæʃənət] **ADJ** compatissant (**to** à; **towards** pour); **on c. grounds** pour des raisons personnelles *ou* familiales *(en cas de décès d'un proche etc)* ▸▸**c. leave** congé *m* exceptionnel; *Mil* permission *f* exceptionnelle *(pour raisons personnelles)*

compassionately [kəm'pæʃənətlɪ] **ADV** avec compassion

compatibility [kəmpætə'bɪlɪtɪ] **N** *(of people), Comput* compatibilité *f*

compatible [kəm'pætəb(ə)l] **ADJ** *(person), Comput* compatible (**with** avec); **IBM-c.** compatible IBM

compatibly [kəm'pætəblɪ] **ADV** d'une manière compatible (**with** avec)

compatriot [kəm'pætrɪət, -'peɪ-] **N** compatriote *mf*

compel [kəm'pel] VT (**-ll-**) contraindre, forcer, obliger (**to do sth** à faire qch); **to be compelled to do sth** être contraint *ou* obligé de faire qch; **don't feel compelled to do it** ne vous sentez pas obligé de le faire; **to c. sb's admiration/respect** forcer l'admiration/le respect de qn

compelling [kəm'pelɪŋ] **ADJ** *(force, curiosity, urge, desire etc)* irrésistible; *(film, performance)* captivant; **her book makes c. reading** son livre est captivant *ou* prenant; **a c. speaker** un orateur qui subjugue *ou* captive son auditoire

compellingly [kəm'pelɪŋlɪ] **ADV** irrésistiblement

compendium, *pl* **compendiums** [kəm'pendɪəm, -z] **N** *(summary)* abrégé *m*, précis *m*, compendium *m* ▸▸**c. of games** boîte *f* de jeux; *Law* **c. of laws** recueil *m* des lois

compensable [kəm'pensəb(ə)l] **ADJ** indemnisable ▸▸*Acct* **c. loss** perte *f* indemnisable

compensate ['kɒmpənseɪt] VT **1** *(make amends for/to)* dédommager, indemniser (**for** de) **2** *Tech (pendulum etc)* compenser; **to c. one another** *(of factors etc)* se compenser
VI **1** **to c. for sth** compenser qch; **experience may c. for lack of qualifications** l'expérience peut compenser le manque de qualifications **2** *Psy* compenser

compensated ['kɒmpənseɪtɪd] **ADJ** *Elec etc* compensé

compensating ['kɒmpənseɪtɪŋ] **ADJ** compensateur ▸▸**c. errors** erreurs *fpl* compensatoire

compensation [kɒmpən'seɪʃən] **N** compensation *f*, *(for loss, injury, damage)* dédommagement *m*, indemnisation *f*, **all of the victims will receive c.** toutes les victimes recevront une indemnité; **in c.** à titre compensatoire *ou* de compensation *ou* de dédommagement; **c. for loss of custom** indemnité *f* de clientèle; **c. for wrongful dismissal** indemnité de rupture abusive; **c. in lieu of notice** indemnité compensatrice de préavis ▸▸**c. package** *Br (for redundancy)* prime *f* de licenciement; *Am (when starting new job)* avantages *mpl* sociaux; *Com* **c. plan** mode *m* de rémunération

compensator ['kɒmpenseɪtər] **N** *Tech* ▸▸**c. arm** bras *m* compensateur; **c. valve** valve *f* de compensation

compensatory [kɒmpən'seɪt(ə)rɪ] **ADJ** compensatoire

compère ['kɒmpeər] *Theat, TV etc* **N** animateur, -trice, présentateur, -trice
VT *(programme)* présenter, animer

compete [kəm'piːt] VI rivaliser (**with sb** avec qn; **for sth** pour qch); *Com (of one company)* faire de la concurrence (**with** à); *(of two companies)* se faire concurrence; **we can't c.** *(are not competitive)* nous ne sommes pas concurrentiels; **children here aren't encouraged to c.** ici, les enfants ne sont pas encouragés à la compétition; **the player had competed for every point** le joueur s'était battu sur chaque point; **to c. with one another** se faire concurrence; *Sport* **to c. against sb** concourir avec qn; **France is competing against several countries for the contract** la France est en compétition avec plusieurs autres pays pour décrocher ce contrat; **to c. for a prize** concourir pour un prix; **to c. with sb for a prize** disputer un prix à qn; **her cooking can't c. with yours** sa cuisine ne peut pas rivaliser avec la tienne

competence ['kɒmpɪtəns] **N 1** *(ability)* compétences *fpl*, capacités *fpl* (**in** *or* **for sth** en qch; **in doing** pour faire) **2** *Fml (scope of functions) (of civil servant)* attributions *fpl*, *Law* compétence *f*; **to be within/beyond the c. of a court** être/ne pas être du ressort d'un tribunal

competency ['kɒmpɪtənsɪ] **N** = **competence**

competent ['kɒmpɪtənt] **ADJ 1** *(able) (doctor, worker etc)* compétent, capable; **a c. piece of work** du bon travail; **c. to do sth** capable de faire qch; *(qualified)* apte à faire qch, qualifié pour faire qch; **he's quite c. at French** il a un bon niveau de français; **c. knowledge of English** bonne connaissance *f* de l'anglais **2** *Law (tribunal)* compétent; **c. to inherit** habilité à succéder

competently ['kɒmpɪtəntlɪ] **ADV** avec compétence

competition [kɒmpɪ'tɪʃən] **N 1** *(rivalry)* rivalité *f*, concurrence *f*, **to be in c.** être en compétition; **to enter into c. with sb** concurrencer qn, faire concurrence à qn; **there was a lot of c. for the job** il y avait beaucoup de concurrence pour cette place **2** *(contest)* concours *m*; *Sport* compétition *f* *(sportive)*; **a poetry c.** un concours de poésie; **to win a prize in open c.** remporter un prix dans un concours ouvert à tous; **to take part in competitions** faire de la compétition; **that's him out of the c.** le voilà hors compétition

3 *Com, Econ* concurrence *f*, **free c.** libre concurrence

4 the c. *(rivals) Com* la concurrence; *Sport* les concurrents, -entes *ou* adversaires *mfpl*; *(for a job)* les autres candidats, -ates; **you're up against some tough c.** *(in race)* vous êtes en face d'adversaires de taille; *(for job, uni-*

versity) la concurrence est rude; **the company has to stay ahead of the c.** l'entreprise doit rester plus compétitive que les autres
▸▸ **c. car** *(in motor racing)* voiture *f* de compétition

competitive [kəm'petɪtɪv] **ADJ 1** *(person)* qui a l'esprit de compétition, qui aime la compétition; *(atmosphere, environment)* de compétition; **a c. school/society** une école/société où l'on met l'accent sur la compétition; **he's so c.** il a vraiment l'esprit de compétition **2** *Com, Econ (price)* concurrentiel, compétitif; *(product)* concurrent; *(firm, company, industry)* compétitif; **to offer c. terms** proposer des prix très compétitifs; **in a c. marketplace** dans un marché de concurrence; **industry must get more c.** l'industrie doit devenir plus compétitive
▸▸ *Com* **c. advantage** avantage *m* concurrentiel; *Com* **c. awareness** sensibilité *f* compétitive; *Com* **c. discounting** remise *f* compétitive; **c. edge** (léger) avantage concurrentiel; *Com* **c. equilibrium price** prix *m* d'équilibre concurrentiel; **c. examination** concours *m*; **c. position** position *f* concurrentielle; *Mktg* **c. positioning** positionnement *m* concurrentiel; **c. scope** domaine *m* concurrentiel, champ *m* concurrentiel; **c. spirit** esprit *m* de compétition; **c. sports** sports *mpl* de compétition; **c. strategy** stratégie *f* concurrentielle

competitively [kəm'petɪtɪvlɪ] **ADV** dans un esprit de compétition; *Com, Econ* **c. priced** à un prix concurrentiel *ou* compétitif

competitiveness [kəm'petɪtɪvnɪs] **N 1** compétitivité *f* **2** *Com, Econ (of product)* concurrence *f*, *(of firm, company)* compétitivité *f*

competitor [kəm'petɪtər] **N** *Sport, Com* concurrent, -ente

compilation [kɒmpɪ'leɪʃən] **N 1** *(activity)* compilation *f* **2** *(list)* compilation *f*
▸▸ **c. album** compilation *f*

compile [kəm'paɪl] **VT** compiler

compiler [kəm'paɪlər] **N** *(of dictionary etc)* compilateur, -trice, rédacteur, -trice; *Comput* compilateur

complacency [kəm'pleɪsənsɪ] **N** contentement *m* de soi; **there is no room for c.** il n'y a pas de quoi faire de l'autosatisfaction; **this is no time for c.** ce n'est pas le moment de faire de l'auto-satisfaction

complacent [kəm'pleɪsənt] **ADJ** *(person)* content de soi; *(look, remark)* très satisfait; **to be c. about sth** faire de l'auto-satisfaction à propos de qch; **we shouldn't become c. about unemployment just because of a few successes** nous ne devons pas relâcher notre effort dans la lutte contre le chômage sous prétexte que nous avons marqué quelques points

Attention: ne pas confondre avec l'adjectif anglais **complaisant**.

complacently [kəm'pleɪsəntlɪ] **ADV** *(to smile, reply)* d'un air suffisant; **some of our managers have been sitting c. behind their desks** certains de nos dirigeants se sont un peu trop reposés sur leurs lauriers

complain [kəm'pleɪn] **VI 1** se plaindre (**about** de; **to** à); *(officially)* se plaindre (**to** auprès de); **he's always complaining** il se plaint toujours; **to c. that …** se plaindre que *ou* de ce que … + *ind*; **don't come complaining to me about it** tu ne viendras pas te plaindre à moi; **I can't c.** je n'ai pas à me plaindre **2** *(of sore throat, headaches etc)* se plaindre (**of** de)

complainant [kəm'pleɪnənt] **N** *Law* plaignant, -ante

complaint [kəm'pleɪnt] **N 1** *(grievance)* plainte *f*, **I have no cause** *or* **grounds for c.** je n'ai aucun motif de plainte; **do you have any complaints about the company?** est-ce que vous avez à vous plaindre de l'entreprise?; **her latest c. was that …** la dernière chose dont elle s'est plainte a été que …; **I've got no c. against you** je n'ai rien à te reprocher **2** *(official)* plainte *f*, réclamation *f*, **to lodge** *or* **make a c. against sb** porter plainte contre qn **3** *(illness)* maladie *f*, **liver c.** maladie *ou* affection *f* du foie
▸▸ **complaints book** cahier *m* de réclamations; **complaints office** bureau *m* *ou* service *m* des réclamations

complaisance [kəm'pleɪzəns] **N** *Fml* complaisance *f*

complaisant [kəm'pleɪz(ə)nt] **ADJ** *Fml* complaisant

Attention: ne pas confondre avec l'adjectif **complacent**.

complement ['kɒmplɪmənt] **N 1** *(of bus etc)* *(passengers)* charge *f* complète; *Naut (crew etc)* effectif *m*; *Naut* **full c.** effectif complet; **have we got a full c.?** *(in office, team etc)* est-ce que nous sommes au complet? **2** *Math (of angle etc)* complément *m*; *Gram (of verb)* complément *m*; *(following 'to be', 'to seem' etc)* attribut *m*
VT compléter; *(of wine, sauce etc)* mettre en valeur; **they c. each other well** *(of two people)* ils se complètent parfaitement

complementary [kɒmplɪ'ment(ə)rɪ] **ADJ** *(angle, colour)* complémentaire
▸▸ **c. medicine** médecine *f* douce; *Comput* **c. MOS** MOS *m* complémentaire

complete [kəm'pliːt] **ADJ 1** complet, -ète, entier; *(surprise, failure)* total, -aux; **I need a c. break from teaching** j'ai besoin de vraies vacances où je ne penserai plus du tout à mes cours; **is the pack c.?** *(of cards)* le jeu est-il complet?; *Com* **c. with battery** livré avec pile; **my happiness is c.** mon bonheur est total, rien ne manque à mon bonheur; **a visit to Brussels would not be c. without a meal here** la visite de Bruxelles ne serait pas complète sans un repas ici; **to give a c. account** donner tous les détails; **a c. (and utter) failure** un échec total; **the operation has been a c. success** l'opération a pleinement réussi; **she is a c. fool** elle est complètement idiote; **he's a c. stranger** c'est un total inconnu
2 *(finished)* terminé, achevé
VT 1 *(finish)* *(job, task)* achever, terminer; *(training, apprenticeship)* accomplir **2** *(find missing parts of)* *(collection, number, tea service)* compléter **3** *(fill in)* *(form, questionnaire)* remplir

completely [kəm'pliːtlɪ] **ADV** complètement, totalement; **I c. understand your frustration** je comprends tout à fait ta frustration

completeness [kəm'pliːtnɪs] **N** état *m* complet; **there's a c. to it** *(to novel, film etc)* il a un caractère abouti; **they added a final volume for c.** ils ont ajouté un dernier volume pour que l'ensemble soit complet

completion [kəm'pliːʃən] **N** *(of work)* achèvement *m*; **in the process of c.** en (cours d')achèvement; **near c.** près d'être achevé; **to reach c.** *(of project etc)* s'achever; **occupation on c.** *(of contract)* *(of property)* prise *f* de possession des lieux à la signature du contrat
▸▸ **c. date** *(for building, repair work)* date *f* d'achèvement; *Com (for sale)* date d'exécution; **c. guarantee** caution *f* de bonne fin

complex ['kɒmpleks] **ADJ** *(question, phrase)* complexe
N 1 *(building(s))* complexe *m*; **industrial c.** complexe industriel; **shopping c.** centre *m*

commercial **2** *Psy* complexe *m*; *Fam* **he has a c. about his teeth** il fait un complexe à cause de *ou* pour ses dents; *Fam* **you'll give her a c.** tu vas lui donner un complexe
▸▸ *Math* **c. number** nombre *m* complexe

complexion [kəm'plekʃən] **N 1** teint *m*; **to have a dark/fair c.** avoir le teint mat/clair; **to have a good** *or* **clear c.** avoir une belle peau **2** *Fig* nature *f*, caractère *m*; **that puts a new** *or* **a different c. on it** voilà qui change la situation

complexity [kəm'pleksɪtɪ] **N** complexité *f*

compliance [kəm'plaɪəns] **N** observation *f* (**with** de); **in c. with your wishes** conformément à vos désirs
▸▸ *Com* **c. test** test *m* de conformité

compliant [kəm'plaɪənt] **ADJ 1** complaisant, accommodant **2** *Pej (submissive)* servile

complicate ['kɒmplɪkeɪt] **VT** compliquer (**with** de); **that complicates matters** cela complique les choses

complicated ['kɒmplɪkeɪtɪd] **ADJ** compliqué; **to become c.** *(of situation etc)* se compliquer

complication [kɒmplɪ'keɪʃən] **N** complication *f*; *Med* **if no complications set in** s'il ne survient pas de complications; **you're always creating complications!** tu compliques toujours les choses!

complicity [kəm'plɪsɪtɪ] **N** complicité *f* (**in** dans)

compliment ['kɒmplɪmənt] **N 1** compliment *m*; **to pay a c. to sb, to pay sb a c.** faire *ou* adresser un compliment à qn; **to return the c.** retourner le compliment; **my compliments to the chef** mes compliments au chef; **with the compliments of the chef** avec les compliments du chef; **compliments of the season** meilleurs vœux de fin d'année; **with compliments** avec nos compliments **2** *Old-fashioned (greetings)* **to pay one's compliments to sb** faire une visite (de politesse) à qn; **to present** *or* **send one's compliments to sb** se rappeler au bon souvenir de qn
VT complimenter, féliciter, faire des compliments à; **to c. sb on sth/on doing sth** féliciter qn de qch/d'avoir fait qch; **she complimented him on his English/haircut** elle l'a félicité *ou* elle lui a fait des compliments pour son anglais/sa coupe de cheveux
▸▸ **compliments slip** papillon *m* présentant les compliments de la société

complimentary [kɒmplɪ'ment(ə)rɪ] **ADJ 1** flatteur, -euse (**about** à l'égard de); **they weren't very c. about my paintings** ils ne se sont pas montrés très flatteurs à l'égard de mes tableaux; **c. remarks** compliments *mpl*, félicitations *fpl* **2** *(free)* gratuit, gracieux
▸▸ **c. copy** *(of book)* exemplaire *m* offert à titre gracieux; **c. ticket** billet *m* de faveur

comply [kəm'plaɪ] **VI** **to c. with** *(code, specifications, rule etc)* se conformer à; *(contract)* respecter; *(law)* se soumettre à; *(request)* accepter; *(wish)* satisfaire; *(order)* obéir à; **we asked them to move on but they did not c.** nous leur avons demandé de circuler mais ils n'ont pas obéi

component [kəm'pəʊnənt] **ADJ** composant, constituant
N *Ind, Phys, Chem* composant *m*; *Fig (of program, education, system etc)* élément *m*
▸▸ **c. part** *(of machine)* pièce *f* détachée; *(of theory)* composante *f*

comport [kəm'pɔːt] *Fml* **VT** **to c. oneself** se comporter
VI concorder (**with** avec)

comportment [kəm'pɔːtmənt] **N** *Fml* conduite *f*, comportement *m*

compose [kəm'pəʊz] **VT 1** *(poem, symphony etc)*, *Typ* composer **2** *(constitute)* composer,

constituer; **to be composed of sth** se composer *ou* être composé *ou* être constitué de qch **3** *Art (people in painting)* composer **4** *(calm) (mind)* calmer, tranquilliser; **to c. one's thoughts** mettre de l'ordre dans ses pensées; **she composed her features into a smile** elle réussit à esquisser un sourire; **c. yourself!** calmez-vous! **5** *Fml (settle) (difference)* régler
▸ *Vi Mus* composer

composed [kəm'pəʊzd] **ADJ** *(calm)* calme

composer [kəm'pəʊzər] **N** *Mus* compositeur, -trice

composing [kəm'pəʊzɪŋ] **N 1** *(of letter, musical or literary work)* composition *f*, création *f* **2** *Typ* composition *f*
▸▸ *Typ* **c. room** (salle *f* de) composition

composite ['kɒmpəzɪt] **ADJ** composite; *Bot* composé
N composé *m*; *Bot* composée *f*, *Pol* = proposition *f* discutée au niveau national; **my main character is a c. of several people** mon personnage principal est un mélange de plusieurs personnes
▸▸ *St Exch* **c. index** indice *m* composé *ou* composite; *Cin* **c. shot** impression *f* combinée

composition [kɒmpə'zɪʃən] **N 1** *(of symphony, poem etc)* composition *f*; **a sonata of his own c.** une sonate de sa composition **2** *(piece of music)* composition *f* **3** *(constitution) (of air, water, committee etc)* composition *f* **4** *Art (distribution of elements)* composition *f* **5** *(mixture)* mélange *m*, composé *m* **6** *Sch (essay)* dissertation *f*, rédaction *f*; *Old-fashioned* prose **c.** thème *m* **7** *Com (settlement) (with creditors)* arrangement *m*, accommodement *m*; *(on bankruptcy)* concordat *m* préventif; **to make a c.** composer

compositor [kəm'pɒzɪtər] **N** *Typ* compositeur, -trice, metteur *m* en pages

compos mentis ['kɒmpɒs'mentɪs] **ADJ** *Law* sain d'esprit; **to be c.** *(not drunk, not half asleep)* être en possession de toutes ses facultés; **I'm not c. yet** je suis encore à moitié endormi

compost ['kɒmpɒst] **N** *(for garden)* compost *m*, terreau *m*
VT *(treat with compost)* composter *(une terre)*; *(make compost from)* faire du compost à partir de
▸▸ **c. heap** tas *m* de compost

composure [kəm'pəʊʒər] **N** calme *m*, sang-froid *m*; **to regain** *or* **recover one's c.** retrouver son sang-froid, se calmer

compote ['kɒmpɒt] **N** *Culin* compote *f*

compound¹ ['kɒmpaʊnd] **VOIR GRAMMAIRE** **A14 ADJ** composé, combiné; *Gram (word, noun)* composé; *Mus (time)* composé; *Surg (fracture)* compliqué; *Math (number)* complexe
N 1 *(combination) Chem* (corps *m*) composé *m*; *Tech* composition *f*, mastic *m*; *Gram* mot *m* composé; *chemical* **c.** composé chimique **2** *(of palace etc)* enceinte *f*; *(of prison)* cour *f* **3** *(in South Africa) (for miners)* quartier *m* des noirs; *(for livestock)* parc *m* à bétail
▸▸ *Acct* **c. entry** *(in bookkeeping)* article *m* composé; *Biol* **c. eye** œil *m* composé *ou* à facettes; *Math* **c. fraction** fraction *f* composée; *Fin* **c. interest** intérêts *mpl* composés

compound² [kəm'paʊnd] **VT 1** *(worsen) (problem etc)* aggraver **2** *Chem, Pharm (elements)* combiner; *(drug)* préparer **3** *(settle) (difference)* régler, arranger; **to c. a debt** faire une transaction pour le règlement d'une dette
VI 1 *Fml* s'arranger, composer *(with sb* avec

qn) **2** *Com (with one's creditors)* arriver à un concordat

comprehend [kɒmprɪ'hend] **VT** *(understand, include)* comprendre

comprehensible [kɒmprɪ'hensəb(ə)l] **ADJ** compréhensible, intelligible

comprehensibly [kɒmprɪ'hensəblɪ] **ADV** d'une manière compréhensible *ou* intelligible

comprehension [kɒmprɪ'henʃən] **N 1** *(understanding)* compréhension *f*; **it is above** *or* **beyond my c.** cela dépasse mon compréhension **2** *Sch (of text etc)* compréhension *f*; **a reading/listening c.** un exercice de compréhension écrite/orale
▸▸ *Sch* **c. test** test *m* de compréhension

comprehensive [kɒmprɪ'hensɪv] **ADJ** *(wide-ranging) (answer, introduction, coverage, list etc)* complet, ète; *(study, view)* d'ensemble; *(defeat, victory)* écrasant; **c. knowledge** vastes connaissances *fpl*; **c. measures** mesures *fpl* d'ensemble
N *Br Sch* = établissement *m* secondaire d'enseignement général
▸▸ *Br* **c. insurance** assurance *f* tous risques; *Br* **c. policy** police *f* tous risques, police multirisque; *Br* **c. school** = établissement secondaire d'enseignement général; **c. site insurance** assurance tous-risques chantiers

---

Note that the French word **compréhensif** is a false friend and is never a translation for the English word **comprehensive**. Its most common meaning is **understanding**.

Comprehensive Schools

Les "comprehensive schools" ont été introduites en Grande-Bretagne dans les années 60 dans le but d'assurer l'égalité des chances pour tous les enfants, quel que soit leur origine sociale. Aujourd'hui 90 pour cent des élèves du secondaire fréquentent ce type d'établissement scolaire. Cependant l'insuffisance des crédits alloués à l'éducation ainsi que la persistance d'un système d'enseignement privé dont ne peuvent bénéficier que les classes aisées rendent très aléatoire la réalisation d'un projet de démocratisation de l'enseignement.

---

comprehensively [kɒmprɪ'hensɪvlɪ] **ADV** de façon complète; **c. beaten** *or* **defeated** battu à plate(s) couture(s)

comprehensiveness [kɒmprɪ'hensɪvnɪs] **N** *(of answer, treatment of subject)* caractère *m* complet

compress¹ ['kɒmpres] **N** *Med* compresse *f*

compress² [kəm'pres] **VT 1** *(gas, air, spring)* comprimer; *(of compressor) (air etc)* refouler; **to c. one's lips** serrer *ou* pincer les lèvres **2** *(speech, detail etc)* condenser; **to c. 3,000 years of history into a 45-minute video** condenser 3 000 ans d'histoire en une vidéo de 45 minutes **3** *Comput (file)* compresser
VI *Tech (of gas, spring etc)* se comprimer

compressed [kəm'prest] **ADJ** *(lips)* serré, pincé; *(style)* condensé
▸▸ **c. air** air *m* comprimé

compression [kəm'preʃən] **N 1** *(of gas, spring etc)* compression *f* **2** *(of thought, style etc)* concentration *f* **3** *Comput (of file)* compression *f*
▸▸ **c. chamber** chambre *f* de compression; *Aut* **c. ignition** allumage *m* par compression; **c. period** période *f* de compression; **c. pump** pompe *f* de compression; *Tech* **c. ratio** taux *m* de compression; *Tech* **c. stroke** *(in engine)* (temps *m* de) compression

compressive [kəm'presɪv] **ADJ** compressif, de compression
▸▸ *Tech* **c. strain** déformation *f* occasionnée par la compression; *Tech* **c. strength** résistance *f* à la compression; *Tech* **c. stress** contrainte *f* de compression

compressor [kəm'presər] **N** *Anat, Tech (of gas, air etc)* compresseur *m*
▸▸ *Comput* **c. program** programme *m* de compression

comprise [kəm'praɪz] **VT** être composé de, comprendre; **the flat is comprised of** *or* **comprises three rooms** l'appartement comprend trois pièces; **a meal comprising meat and vegetables** un repas composé de viande avec des légumes

compromise ['kɒmprəmaɪz] **N** compromis *m*; **to agree to a c.** accepter un compromis; **to make** *or* **reach** *or* **arrive at a c.** parvenir à un compromis *(with sb* avec qn); **policy of no c.** politique *f* intransigeante; **there must be no c.** il ne faut pas faire de compromis
VT *(person, one's principles)* compromettre; **to c. oneself with sb** se compromettre avec qn
VI transiger, composer *(with sb* avec qn); **if he agrees to c.** s'il accepte un compromis; **let's c.** faisons un compromis, transigeons

compromising ['kɒmprəmaɪzɪŋ] **ADJ** *(situation etc)* compromettant

comptroller [kən'trəʊlər] **N** *Admin* contrôleur, -euse; *(of accounts)* vérificateur, -trice

compulsion [kəm'pʌlʃən] **N 1** *(obligation)* contrainte *f*; **under c.** sous la contrainte; **to be under c. to do sth** être astreint à faire qch; **there's no c. to do it** il n'y a pas d'obligation à le faire **2** *Psy (urge)* compulsion *f*; **to feel a c. to do sth** avoir une envie irrésistible de faire qch

compulsive [kəm'pʌlsɪv] **ADJ** *Psy (behaviour)* compulsif; *(smoker, gambler, liar)* invétéré; **I am a c. eater** je suis boulimique; **c. eating is a sign of stress** la boulimie est un signe de stress; **I found it c. reading/viewing** j'ai trouvé que c'était absolument captivant *ou* prenant

compulsively [kəm'pʌlsɪvlɪ] **ADV** **to smoke/lie/talk c.** ne pas pouvoir s'empêcher de fumer/de mentir/de parler; **to eat c.** être boulimique; **it's c. readable/watchable** c'est passionnant

compulsorily [kəm'pʌlsərɪlɪ] **ADV** obligatoirement; *Admin* **to be retired c.** être mis à la retraite d'office

compulsory [kəm'pʌlsərɪ] **ADJ 1** *(obligatory)* obligatoire; **military service/Latin is c.** le service militaire/le latin est obligatoire; **c. school attendance** présence *f* obligatoire à l'école **2** *(coercive)* coercitif
▸▸ *Fin* **c. liquidation** liquidation *f* forcée; **c. powers** pouvoirs *mpl* coercitifs; **c. purchase** expropriation *f* pour cause d'utilité publique; **c. purchase order** ordre *m* d'expropriation; **c. redundancy** licenciement *m* sec; **c. retirement** mise *f* à la retraite d'office; *Law* **c. sale** adjudication *f* forcée; **c. schooling** scolarisation *f* obligatoire; *Pol* **c. voting** vote *m* obligatoire

compunction [kəm'pʌŋkʃən] **N** remords *m*, scrupule *m*; **without c.** sans remords *ou* scrupules

computation [kɒmpjʊ'teɪʃən] **N** *Fml* calcul *m*; **to make a c. of** faire le calcul de, calculer

computational [kɒmpjʊ'teɪʃən(ə)l] **ADJ** *Comput* de calcul
▸▸ **c. linguistics** linguistique *f* computationnelle

compute [kəm'pjuːt] **VT** calculer
VI faire des calculs; *Fam* **it doesn't c.** ce n'est pas logique

computer [kəm'pju:tər] N ordinateur *m*; **to be c. literate** avoir des connaissances en informatique; **she's in computers** elle est dans l'informatique; **to have sth on c.** avoir qch sur ordinateur; **to put sth on c.** mettre qch sur ordinateur; **analog/digital c.** calculateur *m* analogique/numérique; **to go on a c. course** suivre un cours d'informatique
▸▸ **the c. age** l'ère *f* des ordinateurs *ou* de l'informatique; **c. analyst** analyste *mf*; **c. animation** animation *f* par ordinateur; **c. art** dessin *m* par ordinateur; *Am* **c. camp** colonie *f* de vacances centrée sur l'informatique; **c. centre** centre *m* informatique, infocentre *m*; **c. code** code *m* d'ordinateur; **c. crime** fraude *f* informatique; **c. dating** = rencontres *fpl* sélectionnées par ordinateur; **c. dealer** revendeur *m* informatique; **c. department** service *m* informatique; **c. diagram** diagramme *m* réalisé par *ou* sur ordinateur; **c. engineer** ingénieur-informaticien, -ienne, *pl* ingénieurs-informaticiens, -iennes; **c. equipment** équipement *m* informatique; **c. expert** informaticien, -ienne; **c. fraud** fraude informatique; *Fam* **c. freak** (*enthusiast*) dingue *mf* d'informatique; **c. game** jeu *m* informatique; *Fam* **c. geek** allumé, -ée de l'informatique; **c. generation** génération *f* d'ordinateur; **c. genius** génie *m* de l'informatique; **c. graphics** graphiques *mpl*, (*technique*) infographie *f*; **c. hacker** pirate *mf* informatique; **c. hardware** matériel *m* informatique; **c. instruction** instruction *f* machine; **c. keyboard** clavier *m* d'ordinateur; **c. language** langage *m* de programmation; **c. link-up** liaison *f* informatique; **c. literacy** compétence *f* informatique; **c. manager** directeur, -trice informatique; **c. manufacturer** constructeur *m* informatique; **c. model** modèle *m* informatique; **c. modelling** réalisation *f* de modèles sur ordinateur; **c. network** réseau *m* informatique; **c. operator** opérateur, -trice (sur ordinateur); **c. output** sortie *f* d'ordinateur; **c. printout** sortie papier; (*continuous*) listing *m*, listage *m*; **c. processing** traitement *m* sur ordinateur; **c. program** programme *m* informatique; **c. programmer** programmeur, -euse; **c. programming** programmation *f*; **c. revolution** révolution *f* informatique; **c. room** salle *f* des ordinateurs; **c. science** informatique *f*; **c. scientist** informaticien, -ienne; **c. simulation** simulation *f* par ordinateur; **c. supplier** fournisseur *m* informatique; **c. system** système *m* informatique; **c. technician** technicien, -ienne en informatique; **c. terminal** terminal *m* informatique; **c. translation** traduction *f* par ordinateur; **c. typesetting** composition *f* par ordinateur; **c. virus** virus *m* informatique

computer-aided [-'eɪdɪd] ADJ assisté par ordinateur
▸▸ **c. design** conception *f* assistée par ordinateur; **c. engineering** ingénierie *f* assistée par ordinateur; **c. instruction** enseignement *m* assisté par ordinateur; **c. learning** enseignement assisté par ordinateur; **c. manufacturing** fabrication *f* assistée par ordinateur; **c. presentation** présentation *f* assistée par ordinateur; **c. sales and marketing** vente *f* et marketing *m* assistés par ordinateur; **c. trading** commerce *m* assisté par ordinateur; **c. translation** traduction *f* assistée par ordinateur

computer-assisted [-ə'sɪstɪd] ADJ assisté par ordinateur
▸▸ **c. interviewing** entretien *m* assisté par ordinateur

computer-controlled ADJ contrôlé par ordinateur
▸▸ **c. lock** serrure *f* électronique

computer-enhanced [-ɪn'hɑːnst] ADJ (*graphics etc*) amélioré par ordinateur

computer-generated [-'dʒenəreɪtɪd] ADJ généré par ordinateur
▸▸ **c. image** image *f* de synthèse

computer-integrated manufacturing N *Comput* fabrication *f* intégrée par ordinateur

computerizable [kəmpju:tə'raɪzəb(ə)l] ADJ informatisable

computerization [kəmpju:təraɪ'zeɪʃən] N (*of organization, records etc*) informatisation *f*

computerize [kəm'pju:təraɪz] VT (*organization, filing system etc*) informatiser

computerized [kəm'pju:təraɪzd] ADJ informatisé
▸▸ **c. accounts** compatabilité *f* informatisée; **c. banking** informatique *f* bancaire; **c. data** données *fpl* informatiques; **c. key** clé *f* magnétique; *St Exch* **c. trading system** système *m* informatique de cotation; **c. typesetting** composition *f* par ordinateur

computer-to-computer ADJ (*transmission*) d'ordinateur à ordinateur

computer-typeset VT & VI composer sur ordinateur

computing [kəm'pju:tɪŋ] N **1** (*calculating*) calcul *m* **2** (*science*) informatique *f*; **he works in c.** il travaille dans l'informatique
▸▸ **c. centre** centre *m* de calcul; **c. course** stage *m* d'informatique; **c. machine** machine *f* à calcul; **c. power** puissance *f* de calcul; **c. skills** connaissances *fpl* en informatique

comrade ['kɒmreɪd, -rəd] N camarade *mf*, compagnon *m*; *Pol* camarade; *Mil, Fig* **comrades in arms** compagnons d'armes; **Jones** le/la camarade Jones

comradeship ['kɒmreɪdʃɪp, -rəd-] N camaraderie *f*

COMSAT® ['kɒmsæt] N satellite *m* de communication

Con *Pol abbr* **Conservative**

con¹ [kɒn] *Fam* N (*trick*) arnaque *f*, escroquerie *f*; **what a c.!** quelle arnaque!
VT (-nn-) (*trick*) arnaquer, escroquer; **I've been conned** je me suis fait arnaquer; **they were conned out of £500** ils se sont fait arnaquer de cinq cents livres; **to c. sb into doing sth** persuader qn de faire qch par la ruse
▸▸ **c. artist** arnaqueur, -euse, escroc *m*; **c. man** arnaqueur, escroc; **c. woman** arnaqueuse *f*, **c. trick** arnaque, escroquerie

con² N **the pros and cons** le pour et le contre

con³ N *Sl* (*convict*) taulard *m*, tôlard *m*; **an ex-c.** un ancien taulard

con⁴ VT (-nn-) *Old-fashioned* (*study*) consulter

concatenated [kɒn'kætəneɪtɪd] ADJ *Comput* concaténé

concatenation [kɒnkætə'neɪʃən] N *Comput* enchaînement *m*

concave ['kɒnkeɪv] ADJ concave, incurvé

concavity [kɒn'kævɪtɪ] N concavité *f*

conceal [kən'si:l] VT (*object, intentions, truth etc*) cacher, dissimuler; (*thoughts*) cacher, voiler; **to c. oneself** se cacher; **to c. one's intentions** cacher *ou* déguiser ses intentions *ou* son jeu; **to c. sth from sb** (*hide, not tell*) cacher qch à qn

concealed [kən'si:ld] ADJ caché; (*bend*) masqué; (*lighting*) indirect; *Aut* **danger! c. entrance** (*notice*) danger! sortie de véhicules

concealment [kən'si:lmənt] N dissimulation *f*; **to keep sb in c.** cacher qn; **place of c.** cachette *f*; *Fin* **c. of assets** dissimulation d'actif

concede [kən'si:d] VT (*privilege, corner etc*) concéder; *Pol, Sport etc* **to c. defeat** s'avouer vaincu; **to c. that one is wrong** reconnaître qu'on a tort

conceit [kən'si:t] N **1** (*vanity*) vanité *f*, suffisance *f*, eaten up with c. pétri *ou* pourri de vanité **2** *Liter* métaphore *f* astucieuse

conceited [kən'si:tɪd] ADJ suffisant, vaniteux; **I don't want to sound c. but ...** je ne veux pas avoir l'air prétentieux mais ...; **he is unbearably c.** il est d'une suffisance insupportable

conceitedly [kən'si:tɪdlɪ] ADV avec suffisance, avec vanité; **he c. imagined that ...** il a eu la prétention d'imaginer que ...

conceivable [kən'si:vəb(ə)l] ADJ concevable, imaginable; **it is c.** cela se conçoit; **it is c. that ...** il est concevable que ... + *subj*; **by every c. means** par tous les moyens possibles et imaginables; **what c. reason could I have?** quelle raison pourrais-je bien avoir?

conceivably [kən'si:vəblɪ] ADV **she could c. have done it, it's c.** possible that she did it il n'est pas exclu qu'elle l'ait fait; **I don't see how it's c. possible** ce n'est pas concevable; **this is c. the best/worst ...** c'est peut-être le meilleur/pire ...; **is he capable of it? – c.** en est-il capable? – c'est fort possible

conceive [kən'si:v] VT **1** (*form*) (*plan*) concevoir; **to c. a dislike for sb** prendre qn en aversion **2** (*imagine*) **I cannot c. why ...** je n'arrive pas à imaginer pourquoi ...; **it is difficult to c. how ...** il est difficile de concevoir *ou* d'imaginer comment ... **3** (*child*) concevoir; **to be conceived** (*of child*) être conçu
VI (*become pregnant*) concevoir
▸ **conceive of** VT INSEP imaginer; **I can c. of him having done it** je peux très bien imaginer qu'il l'ait fait

concentrate ['kɒnsəntreɪt] N (*of tomatoes, orange juice etc*) concentré *m*; (*mineral*) minerai *m* concentré; **made from c.** (*orange juice etc*) fait à base de concentré
VT (*troops, attention, efforts*) concentrer (**on** sur); **the presence of danger helped to c. our minds** la présence du danger nous a aidés à nous concentrer; **with concentrated fury** avec une fureur intense; **industry is concentrated in the south** l'industrie est concentrée dans le sud
VI **1** (*mentally*) se concentrer; **to c. on sth** se concentrer sur qch; **to c. on doing sth** s'appliquer à faire qch **2** (*specialize*) **to c. on sth** se concentrer sur qch **3** (*group*) se concentrer, être groupé; **the population tends to c. in cities** la population tend à se concentrer dans les villes

concentration [kɒnsən'treɪʃən] N **1** (*mental*) concentration *f*, application *f*; **to lose one's c.** se déconcentrer; **the work requires c.** le travail demande de la concentration; **c. span** concentration; **she has a poor c. span** elle n'arrive pas à se concentrer très longtemps
2 (*specializing*) spécialisation *f*; **in view of their recent c. on other areas of the market** étant donné qu'ils se sont récemment concentrés sur d'autres secteurs du marché **3** (*grouping*) (*of troops etc*) concentration *f*; **there was a c. of cases of food poisoning in the area** il y a eu plusieurs cas d'intoxication alimentaire dans le quartier; **c. of effort** convergence *f* des efforts; *Chem* (**degree of**) **c.** (*of acid etc*) titre *m*; **the large urban concentrations** les grandes agglomérations *fpl* urbaines
▸▸ **c. camp** camp *m* de concentration

concentric [kən'sentrɪk] ADJ *Geom* concentrique

concept ['kɒnsept] N concept *m*; **this is a difficult c. for children** c'est un concept difficile à comprendre pour les enfants
▸▸ **c. car** concept-car *m*, *pl* concept-cars; *Mktg* **c. test** test *m* de concept

conception [kən'sepʃən] N **1** (*action*) (*of child, idea etc*) conception *f* **2** (*idea*) conception *f*, idée *f*; **to have a clear c. of sth** se représenter clairement qch par la pensée; **he has no c. of how long the work takes** il ne se rend absolument pas compte du temps que prend le travail

concept-testing N *Mktg* tests *mpl* de concept

conceptual [kən'septjʊəl] ADJ conceptuel

conceptualize [kən'septjʊəlaɪz] VT & VI conceptualiser

CONCERN [kən'sɜːn] N 1 *(interest)* intérêt *m* (**in** dans); **it's no c. of mine/yours** cela ne me/vous regarde pas; **this is a matter of public c.** c'est une affaire qui nous concerne tous 2 *(worry, compassion)* inquiétude *f*, souci *m*; *(stronger)* anxiété *f*; **to show c.** se montrer inquiet; **there is growing c. for her safety** on est de plus en plus inquiet à son sujet *ou* sur son sort; **there is growing c. that ...** on craint de plus en plus que ...; **my only c. has been to ensure that ...** ma seule préoccupation a été de m'assurer que ...; **there is no cause for c.** il n'y a pas de raison de s'inquiéter; **to express c. about sth** exprimer de l'inquiétude au sujet de qch; **thank you for your c.** tu es gentil de m'avoir posé la question/de me l'avoir proposé/*etc* 3 *Com, Ind* entreprise *f*, **a large publishing c.** une grande maison d'édition

VT 1 *(apply to, affect) (person, matter)* concerner, toucher; *(be the business of) (person)* regarder, être l'affaire de; **matters that c. the public** choses qui intéressent le public; **to whom it may c.** à qui de droit; **to c. oneself with** *or* **about sth** s'intéresser à qch, s'occuper de qch; **don't c. yourself with that for the moment** ne t'occupe pas de cela pour l'instant; **where work is/children are concerned** en ce qui concerne le travail/les enfants, pour ce qui est du travail/des enfants; **to be concerned with sth** s'occuper de qch; **the parties/people concerned** les intéressés *mpl*; *Com etc* **the department concerned** le service compétent; **as far as I am concerned** en ce qui me concerne, quant à moi; **as far as this question is concerned** en ce qui concerne cette question, pour ce qui est de cette question 2 *(be about)* traiter de; **the book is concerned with politics** ce livre traite de politique; **it concerns your mother** c'est au sujet de votre mère 3 *(usu passive) (worry)* **to be concerned about sb/sth** s'inquiéter *ou* être inquiet de qn/qch; **I am concerned for his health** son état de santé m'inquiète

concerned [kən'sɜːnd] ADJ *(smile, look)* inquiet, soucieux; **we feel very c. about this** cela nous préoccupe au plus haut point, cela nous inquiète beaucoup; **he didn't seem at all c.** il n'avait pas du tout l'air inquiet *ou* de s'inquiéter

concerning [kən'sɜːnɪŋ] PREP concernant, au sujet de; **information c. the crime** des informations au sujet du *ou* concernant le délit

concert[1] ['kɒnsət] N 1 *Mus* concert *m*; **Bob Dylan in c.** Bob Dylan en concert; **to give a c.** donner un concert; 2 *Fml (association)* concert *m*; **to act in c.** agir de concert (**with** avec)
▸▸ *Mus* **c. grand** piano *m* de concert; **c. hall** salle *f* de concert; *St Exch* **c. party** action *f* de concert; *Mus* **c. performer** concertiste *mf*; *Mus* **c. pianist** pianiste *mf* de concert; *Mus* **c. pitch** diapason *m* (de concert); *Mus* **c. tour** tournée *f*

concert[2] [kən'sɜːt] VT *(measures etc)* concerter

concerted [kən'sɜːtɪd] ADJ *(plan, effort etc)* concerté; **c. action** action *f* concertée *ou* d'ensemble

concertgoer ['kɒnsətgəʊər] N amateur, -trice de concerts

concertina [kɒnsə'tiːnə] N *Mus* concertina *m*
VI (**concertinaed** [-nəd]) *(of car etc in collision)* se plier en accordéon

concertmaster ['kɒnsətmɑːstər] N *Am (of orchestra)* premier violon *m*

concerto [kən'tʃɜːtəʊ] N *Mus* concerto *m*; **piano/violin c.** concerto pour piano/violon

concession [kən'seʃən] N 1 *(allowance)* concession *f*; **to make concessions** faire des concessions; **the only c. the film makes to reality is ...** la seule concession que le film fasse à la réalité est ... 2 *Com* concession *f*; **she has a c. in a department store** elle a une concession dans un grand magasin 3 *Min (mining)* **c.** concession *f* minière 4 *Br (reduction)* tarif *m* réduit; **price: £4.50 (concessions £3)** prix des billets: 4,50 livres (tarif réduit 3 livres); **we offer a 10% c. to retailers** nous accordons une remise de 10% aux détaillants
▸▸ *Com* **c. close** conclusion *f* par concession; *Br* **c. ticket** *(for theatre, cinema)* billet *m* à prix réduit

concessionary [kən'seʃən(ə)rɪ] *Com* ADJ *(company etc)* concessionnaire; *Br (fare, rate etc)* réduit
N = **concession(n)aire**

concession(n)aire [kənseʃə'neər] N *Com* concessionnaire *mf*

conch [kɒŋk, kɒn(t)ʃ] N *(mollusc)* conque *f*

conchie, conchy ['kɒntʃɪ] N *Old-fashioned Fam (abbr* **conscientious objector)** objecteur *m* de conscience

concierge [kɒnsɪ'eəʒ] N *(in hotel)* concierge *mf*; **c.'s desk** comptoir *m* du concierge

conciliate [kən'sɪlɪeɪt] VT 1 *(win over)* apaiser; **she refused to be conciliated** elle refusait la conciliation 2 *(reconcile) (theories, beliefs)* concilier, réconcilier
VI *Fml* **to c. between two people/countries** réconcilier deux peuples/pays

conciliation [kənsɪlɪ'eɪʃən] N conciliation *f*
▸▸ **c. board, c. service** *(in industrial dispute)* conseil *m* d'arbitrage, ≃ conseil des prud'hommes

conciliator [kən'sɪlɪeɪtər] N conciliateur, -trice; *(in industrial dispute)* médiateur, -trice

conciliatory [kən'sɪlɪət(ə)rɪ] ADJ conciliant; *(spirit)* de conciliation; *Law* conciliatoire

concise [kən'saɪs] ADJ concis; *(style)* concis, dense; *(dictionary)* abrégé

concisely [kən'saɪslɪ] ADV brièvement, avec concision

conciseness [kən'saɪsnɪs], **concision** [kən'sɪʒən] N concision *f*; **to aim at c.** *(in one's style)* essayer d'être concis

conclave ['kɒnkleɪv] N 1 *(meeting)* conseil *m*, réunion *f*; **to be in c. with sb** tenir conseil avec qn 2 *Cathol* conclave *m*

conclude [kən'kluːd] VT 1 *(finish) (speech, book, programme)* conclure, finir, achever; *(session)* clôturer; *(meal)* terminer 2 *(infer)* conclure; **from this I c. that ...** de ceci je conclus que ... 3 *(sign etc) (peace, treaty)* conclure; *(deal, contract)* arranger, régler
VI 1 *(of play, evening, book etc)* s'achever, se terminer (**with** avec) 2 *(at end of speech etc)* conclure; **to c. ...** en conclusion ..., pour conclure ...

concluding [kən'kluːdɪŋ] ADJ *(chapter, episode)* dernier; *(concert)* de clôture; **he made a few c. remarks** il a fait quelques remarques finales

conclusion [kən'kluːʒən] N 1 *(inference)* conclusion *f*; **to draw a c. from sth** tirer une conclusion de qch; **draw your own conclusions** tirez vos propres conclusions; **to come to** *or* **reach the c. that ...** conclure que ... + *ind*, (en) arriver à la conclusion que ... + *ind*; **without coming to any c.** sans arriver à une conclusion; **you're jumping to conclusions** tu tires une conclusion hâtive; **don't jump to conclusions!** réfléchis avant de conclure!; **he jumped to the wrong c.** il a tiré une conclusion erronée 2 *(end) (of essay, film)* conclusion *f*; *(of session)* clôture *f*, **in c.** pour conclure, en conclusion; **to bring a matter to a successful c.** mener une affaire à bonne fin 3 *(signing etc) (of treaty etc)* conclusion *f*

conclusive [kən'kluːsɪv] ADJ *(argument)* concluant, décisif; *(test)* probant

conclusively [kən'kluːsɪvlɪ] ADV *(to argue, show)* de façon concluante

concoct [kən'kɒkt] VT 1 *(make) (cocktail)* préparer; *(dish)* concocter 2 *(think up) (plan)* imaginer, élaborer, concocter; *(plot)* machiner

concoction [kən'kɒkʃən] N 1 *(action) (of food etc)* confection *f* 2 *(drink, dish etc)* mélange *m*, concoction *f* 3 *(of plan)* élaboration *f*, *(of plot)* machination *f*, **a c. of lies** un tissu de mensonges

concomitant [kən'kɒmɪtənt] *Fml* ADJ concomitant (**with** de)
N **the concomitants of old age/marriage** ce qui va de pair avec la vieillesse/le mariage

concord ['kɒŋkɔːd] N 1 *Fml (between people)* entente *f*, harmonie *f*; *Lit* **to live in c.** vivre en harmonie (**with** avec) 2 *Gram* concordance *f* 3 *Mus* accord *m* consonant

concordance [kən'kɔːdəns] N 1 *Fml* accord *m*, concordance *f* (**with** avec); **to be in c. with ...** être en accord avec ... 2 *Mus* consonance *f* 3 *Liter (of Bible)* index *m*, concordance *f*

concordant [kən'kɔːdənt] ADJ 1 en accord, concordant (**with** avec) 2 *Mus* consonant

concordat [kɒn'kɔːdæt] N concordat *m*

Concorde ['kɒnkɔːd] N *Aviat* Concorde *m*

concourse ['kɒnkɔːs] N 1 *(of railway station)* hall *m* 2 *Fml (gathering place)* lieu *m* de rassemblement 3 *Fml (crowd)* foule *f*, rassemblement *m*

concrete ['kɒnkriːt] N *Constr* béton *m*; **reinforced c.** béton armé
ADJ *(example, term, noun)* concret, -ète; *(suggestion, proposal)* concret, pratique
VT *Constr (wall etc)* bétonner
▸▸ *Fig* **c. jungle** univers *m* de béton; *Constr* **c. mixer** bétonnière *f*, **c. music** musique *f* concrète; **c. poem** calligramme *m*; **c. poetry** calligrammes *mpl*
▸ **concrete over** VT SEP *(garden, field etc)* bétonner

concreting ['kɒnkriːtɪŋ] N *Constr* bétonnage *m*

concretion [kən'kriːʃən] N *Med, Geol etc* concrétion *f*

concubinage [kɒn'kjuːbɪnɪdʒ] N concubinage *m*

concubine ['kɒŋkjʊbaɪn] N concubine *f*

concur [kən'kɜːr] VI (-rr-) 1 *(agree) (of person)* être d'accord (**with sb/sth** avec qn/qch), être du même avis (**with sb** que qn); **to c. with sb's views/opinions/conclusions** partager le point de vue/l'opinion/les conclusions de qn; **he proposed a different approach and she concurred** il a proposé une approche différente et elle a approuvé 2 *(of findings, results of experiment)* concorder (**with** avec) 3 *Fml (of events)* coïncider; **to c. in a result** concourir à un résultat

concurrence [kənˈkʌrəns] **N** *(agreement)* accord *m*; *(assent)* assentiment *m*, consentement *m* (**in** à); *Fml* **c. of events** concours *m* de circonstances

concurrent [kənˈkʌrənt] **ADJ 1** *(in time)* simultané; *Math* concourant **2** *(in agreement) (views etc)* qui concordent
▸▸ *Law* **c. cause** cause *f* contribuante; *Law* **c. sentences** confusion *f* des peines

concurrently [kənˈkʌrəntlɪ] **ADV** simultanément (**with** avec); *Law* **the two sentences to run c.** avec confusion des deux peines

concuss [kənˈkʌs] **VT** commotionner; **she was badly concussed in the accident** elle a subi de graves commotions lors de l'accident

concussion [kənˈkʌʃən] **N** commotion *f* cérébrale; **suffering from c.** souffrant de commotion cérébrale

condemn [kənˈdem] **VT 1** *(sentence)* condamner; **to c. sb to death** condamner qn à mort; **to be condemned to sth/to do sth** être condamné à qch/à faire qch; **she was condemned to a life of poverty** elle était condamnée à vivre dans la pauvreté **2** *(declare unsafe) (building)* déclarer inhabitable; **this meat has been condemned** cette viande a été jugée impropre à la consommation **3** *(censure) (person, policy, abuse etc)* condamner; **she condemned the remarks as pure prejudice** elle a condamné les remarques comme étant de purs préjugés

condemnation [kɒndemˈneɪʃən] **N 1** *(of prisoner)* condamnation *f* **2** *(of building)* condamnation *f* **3** *(censure)* condamnation *f*

condemned [kənˈdemd] **ADJ 1** *Law (sentenced)* condamné; **the c. man** le condamné **2** *(building)* condamné; *(meat)* jugé impropre à la consommation
▸▸ **c. cell** cellule *f* des condamnés

condensation [kɒndenˈseɪʃən] **N** *(of gas, liquid, text etc)* condensation *f*, *(on windows)* buée *f*

condense [kənˈdens] **VT** *(gas, liquid, text etc)* condenser; **to c. a chapter into a single paragraph** condenser un chapitre en un seul paragraphe
VI se condenser

condensed [kənˈdenst] **ADJ** concentré, condensé
▸▸ **c. book** livre *m* condensé; **c. milk** lait *m* concentré; *Comput* **c. mode** mode *m* condensé; *Comput, Typ* **c. print** impression *f* condensée; **in c. print** en caractères étroits

condenser [kənˈdensər] **N** *Elec* condensateur *m*; *(for condensing liquids)* condenseur *m*
▸▸ **c. microphone** microphone *m* électrostatique

condensing [kənˈdensɪŋ] **N** condensation *f*

condescend [kɒndɪˈsend] **VI 1** *(agree, accept with reluctance)* condescendre (**to do sth** à faire qch), daigner (**to do sth** faire qch) **2** *(be condescending)* se montrer condescendant (**to sb** envers qn)

condescending [kɒndɪˈsendɪŋ] **ADJ** condescendant

condescendingly [kɒndɪˈsendɪŋlɪ] **ADV** d'une manière condescendante, avec condescendance

condescension [kɒndɪˈsenʃən] **N** condescendance *f* (**to** envers, pour)

condiment [ˈkɒndɪmənt] **N** condiment *m*
▸▸ **c. set** poivrier *m* et salière *f*

condition [kənˈdɪʃən] **N 1** *(state)* état *m*; **in good c.** en bon état; **in bad c., in a poor c.** en mauvais état; **you're in no c. to drive** *(you're ill, tired, drunk)* tu n'es pas en état de

conduire; **in your c.** *(to pregnant woman)* dans ton état; **to keep oneself in c.** se maintenir en forme; **I'm out of c.** je n'ai pas la condition physique; **he's in excellent c.** sa condition physique est excellente

2 *(circumstance) (usu pl)* condition *f*, **working conditions** *(in factory etc)* conditions de travail; **normal operating conditions** *(of machine)* régime *m* de fonctionnement normal; **weather conditions** conditions météorologiques; **road** *or* **driving conditions** état *m* des routes; **drive with particular care as conditions on the roads are hazardous** soyez prudents sur les routes: le mauvais temps rend la circulation très dangereuse; **the human c.** la condition humaine

3 *(term)* condition *f*; **to impose conditions on sb** (im)poser des conditions à qn; **conditions of sale/carriage** conditions de vente/ transport; **conditions of a contract** stipulations *fpl* ou termes *mpl* d'un contrat; **on c. that …** à (la) condition que … + *subj*; **you can borrow the book, on one c.** tu peux emprunter le livre, à une condition; **it was a c. of the lease that …** l'une des stipulations du bail était que …; **under these conditions** dans ces conditions

4 *(illness) (of heart, liver etc)* maladie *f*, affection *f*, **to have a heart c.** avoir une maladie du cœur

VT 1 *Psy (subject)* conditionner (**to do** à faire); **a conditioned reflex** un réflexe conditionné

2 to c. one's hair utiliser de l'après-shampooing

3 *(subject to a condition) (usu pass)* déterminer; **to be conditioned by** dépendre de

conditional [kənˈdɪʃən(ə)l] **ADJ** *(offer, agreement), Gram (tense)* conditionnel; **c. on sth** dépendant de qch; **my promise was c.** j'ai promis sous certaines conditions
N *Gram* conditionnel *m*; **in the c.** *(verb)* au conditionnel VOIR GRAMMAIRE A52–3; B34
▸▸ **c. acceptance** acceptation *f* sous réserve; **c. access television** télévision *f* à accès conditionnel

conditionally [kənˈdɪʃən(ə)lɪ] **ADV** de façon conditionnelle

conditioner [kənˈdɪʃənər] **N air c.** climatiseur *m*; **(fabric) c.** adoucissant *m*; **(hair) c.** après-shampoing *m*, démêlant *m*

conditioning [kənˈdɪʃənɪŋ] **N** *Psy* conditionnement *m*

condo [ˈkɒndəʊ] **N** *Am Fam* = **condominium 2**

condole [kənˈdəʊl] **VI** *Fml* **to c. with sb** faire *ou* exprimer ses condoléances à qn

condolence [kənˈdəʊləns] **N** condoléances *fpl*; **to offer sb one's condolences** présenter ses condoléances à qn; **a letter of c.** une lettre de condoléances

condom [ˈkɒndəm] **N** préservatif *m*

condominium [kɒndəˈmɪnɪəm] **N 1** *(shared sovereignty)* condominium *m*; **the territory was made a c.** le territoire fut placé sous un régime de condominium **2** *Am (building)* immeuble *m* en copropriété; *(apartment)* appartement *m* dans un immeuble en copropriété; *(ownership)* copropriété *f*

condone [kənˈdəʊn] **VT** trouver des excuses pour, excuser; **I am not condoning the crime** je ne cherche pas à excuser le crime

condor [ˈkɒndɔːr] **N** condor *m*

conduce [kənˈdjuːs] **VI** *Fml (of action or thing)* contribuer (**to** à)

conducive [kənˈdjuːsɪv] **ADJ c. to sth** favorable à qch; **this weather is not c. to work** ce temps n'incite pas au travail

conduct¹ [ˈkɒndʌkt] **N 1** *(behaviour)* conduite *f* (**towards sb** à l'égard de *ou* avec *ou* envers qn) **2** *(management)* conduite *f*,

gestion *f*, **the lawyer's c. of the case** la manière dont l'avocat a mené l'affaire

conduct² [kənˈdʌkt] **VT 1** *(manage, direct) (business, operations, orchestra, religious service)* diriger; *(carry out) (campaign, survey)* mener; *(experiment)* effectuer; *Law* **to c. one's own case** plaider soi-même sa cause; **to c. the traffic** faire la circulation **2 to c. oneself** se comporter, se conduire **3** *(lead)* **to c. sb round a building/factory/ museum** faire visiter un bâtiment/une usine/un musée à qn; **conducted tours** visites *fpl* guidées; **to give sb a conducted tour** faire faire une visite guidée à qn **4** *Elec, Phys (heat, electricity)* conduire, être conducteur de
VI *Mus* diriger; *(work as conductor)* être chef d'orchestre; **who's conducting?** qui est le chef d'orchestre?, qui dirige?

conducting [kənˈdʌktɪŋ] **N** *Mus* direction *f* d'orchestre

conduction [kənˈdʌkʃən] **N** *Phys, Elec* conduction *f*

conductive [kənˈdʌktɪv] **ADJ** *Phys, Elec* conducteur, -trice

conductivity [kɒndʌkˈtɪvɪtɪ] **N** *Phys, Elec* conductivité *f*

conductor [kənˈdʌktər] **N 1** *Br (on bus)* receveur *m*; *Am Rail* chef *m* de train **2** *Mus* chef *m* d'orchestre **3** *Phys, Elec (of electricity etc)* conducteur *m*
▸▸ *Rail* **c. rail** rail *m* conducteur *ou* sous tension; **c. wire** fil *m* conducteur

> Note that the French word **conducteur** is not always a translation for the English word **conductor**.

conductress [kənˈdʌktrɪs] **N** *Br (on bus)* receveuse *f*

conduit [ˈkɒndjʊɪt] **N** *Tech (for fluid)* conduit *m*, canalisation *f*, *Elec* tube *m*; *Fig (for money)* intermédiaire *mf*

condyle [ˈkɒndɪl] **N** *Med* condyle *m*

cone [kəʊn] **N** *(of light, volcano, retina etc)* cône *m*; *(of pine)* pomme *f* de pin, cône; *(for ice cream)* cornet *m*; **(traffic) c.** cône *ou* balise *f* de signalisation
▸▸ *Aut* **c. clutch** embrayage *m* à cône
▸ **cone off VT SEP to c. off two lanes of a motorway** fermer la circulation sur deux voies d'une autoroute *(avec des cônes de signalisation)*

cone-bearing ADJ conifère

cone-shaped ADJ en forme de cône, conique

coney [ˈkəʊnɪ] **N** *Old-fashioned* lapin *m*; **c. skin** peau *f* de lapin

confab [ˈkɒnfæb] **N** *Fam (conversation)* discussion *f*, **to have a c. (about sth)** *(discuss)* discuter, (de qch), se consulter (sur qch)

confection [kənˈfekʃən] **N 1** *esp Am Culin (cake, sweet)* friandise *f* **2** *Fml (act)* confection *f*

confectioner [kənˈfekʃənər] **N** *(selling sweets)* confiseur, -euse; *(making, selling cakes)* pâtissier, -ière; **c.'s** confiserie *f*, **J. Smith bakers & confectioners** boulangerie-pâtisserie J. Smith
▸▸ **c.'s custard** crème *f* pâtissière; **c.'s shop** confiserie; *Am* **c.'s sugar** sucre *m* glace

confectionery [kənˈfekʃən(ə)rɪ] **N** *(sweets)* confiserie *f*

confederacy [kənˈfed(ə)rəsɪ] **N** *(alliance)* confédération *f*, *Am Hist* **the C.** les États *mpl* Confédérés

confederate¹ [kənˈfed(ə)rət] **ADJ** confédéré
N confédéré *m*; *(in crime)* complice *mf*
▸▸ *Hist* **the C. States** les États *mpl* Confédérés

confederate² [kənˈfedəreɪt] **VT** *(states)*

confédérer; **to c. oneself with ...** se liguer avec ...
VI *(join)* se confédérer (**with** avec); *(conspire)* conspirer (**with** avec; **against** contre)
confederation [kənfedə'reɪʃən] **N** confédération *f*
▸▸**C. of British Industry** = patronat *m* britannique, ≃ Medef *m*

confer [kən'fɜːr] (**-rr-**) **VT** *(title, rank, powers)* conférer (**on** à); *(degree, diploma)* remettre (**on** à)
VI s'entretenir (**with** avec; **on, about** sur); **contestants are not allowed to c.** les concurrents n'ont pas le droit de se consulter

conference ['kɒnfərəns] **N 1** conférence *f*, **press** *or* **news c.** conférence de presse; **to be in c.** *(with several people)* être en conférence (**with** avec); *(with one or two people)* être en réunion (**with** avec); **round-table c.** table *f* ronde; **we hope to get management to the c. table** nous espérons réunir la direction en table ronde **2** *(of professional association etc)* congrès *m*; *Pol* **Party C.** congrès annuel du parti
▸▸**c. call** téléconférence *f*; **c. centre** *(building)* centre *m* de congrès; *(town)* = ville *f* pouvant accueillir des congrès; **c. coordinator** responsable *mf* des congrès; **c. delegate** congressiste *mf*, *Naut,Com* **c. line** ligne *f* maritime de conférence; **c. organizer** organisateur, -trice de conférences *ou* de congrès; **c. pack** = dossier *m* offert aux conférenciers avec informations générales sur la conférence, petits cadeaux etc; **c. room** salle *f* de conférence; *Naut, Com* **c. ship** navire *m* de conférence

conferment [kən'fɜːmənt] **N** *(of rank, powers)* attribution *f*; *(of title, diploma)* remise *f*

confess [kən'fes] **VI 1** *(of criminal)* avouer, faire des aveux; **to c. to a crime** avouer un crime
2 *(admit)* **to c. to sth** avouer qch; **to c. to doing** *or* **having done sth** avouer avoir fait qch; **I c. to not liking her** j'avoue que je ne l'aime pas; **to c. to a liking for ...** avouer avoir un penchant *ou* un faible pour ...
3 *Rel* se confesser (**to sb** à qn, auprès de qn)
VT 1 *(admit)* *(fault)* avouer, confesser; **to c. that ...** avouer *ou* confesser que ... + *ind*; **I must c. that ...** je dois avouer que ..., je dois reconnaître que ...; **I was wrong, I c.** j'admets que j'ai eu tort; **I don't understand either, I must c.** je dois avouer que je ne comprends pas non plus; **medical experts c. themselves helpless** les médecins s'avouent impuissants
2 *Rel (of sinner)* *(sins)* confesser, se confesser de; *(of priest)* *(penitent)* confesser; **to c. oneself** se confesser (**to sb** à qn, auprès de qn)

confession [kən'feʃən] **N 1** *(admission)* aveu *m*, confession *f*; **to make a full c.** faire des aveux complets; **I have a c. to make** j'ai un aveu à faire; **on their own c.** de leur propre aveu; **that would be a c. of failure** cela reviendrait à s'avouer vaincu **2** *Rel* confession *f*, **to go to c.** aller se confesser; **to hear sb's c.** *(of priest)* entendre la confession de qn, entendre qn en confession, confesser qn; **c. of faith** confession de foi; **the seal of c.** le secret de la confession *ou* du confessionnal

confessional [kən'feʃən(ə)l] **ADJ** confessionnel
N *Rel* confessionnal *m*

confessor [kən'fesər] **N** *Rel (priest)* confesseur *m*; *(sinner)* personne *f* qui se confesse; *Hist* **Edward the C.** Édouard le Confesseur

confetti [kən'fetɪ] **NPL** confettis *mpl* **VOIR GRAMMAIRE A14**

confidant, *f* **confidante** [kɒnfɪ'dænt] **N** confident, -ente

> Attention: ne pas confondre avec l'adjectif anglais **confident**.

confide [kən'faɪd] **VT** *(secret)* confier (**to sb** à qn); **she confided to me that ...** elle m'a confié que ...; **to c. sth to sb's care** confier qch à la garde de qn
▸ **confide in VT INSEP** se confier à

confidence ['kɒnfɪdəns] **N 1** *(trust)* confiance *f* (**in** en); **to place** *or* **put one's c. in sb/sth** placer *ou* mettre sa confiance en qn/qch, faire confiance à qn/qch; **have a bit more c.!** *(in me)* fais-moi un peu plus confiance; **to win sb's c.** gagner la confiance de qn; **to have every c. in sb** faire entièrement confiance à qn, avoir toute confiance en qn; **I have every c. that ...** je ne doute pas un instant que ...; **she has no c. in her own ability** elle n'a aucune confiance en elle; **with complete c.** en toute confiance; **vote of c.** vote *m* de confiance; *Pol* **motion of no c.** motion *f* de censure
2 *(certainty)* confiance *f*; **because of their c. that it would work** parce qu'ils étaient sûrs que ça marcherait
3 *(self-assurance)* assurance *f*, confiance *f* en soi; **full of c.** *(person)* plein d'assurance *ou* de confiance en soi; *(performance)* plein d'assurance; *(letter, article)* qui dénote une grande assurance; **with c.** *(to act etc)* avec assurance
4 in c. confidentiellement, en confidence; **remarks made in c.** des remarques formulées confidentiellement; **to take sb into one's c.** se confier à qn; **to be in sb's c.** partager les secrets de qn
5 *(secret)* confidence *f*; **to exchange confidences** échanger des confidences
▸▸**c. trick** escroquerie *f*, abus *m* de confiance; **c. trickster** escroc *m*

> Note that the French word **confidence** never means **trust** or **self-assurance**.
>
> When translating **confidence**, note that the French words **confiance** and **confidence** are not interchangeable. **Confiance** means **trust** and **confidence** is only used in the sense of a **secret**.

confident ['kɒnfɪdənt] **ADJ** sûr (**of** de); *(self-assured)* sûr de soi, assuré; *(remark, performance)* plein d'assurance; **are you feeling c.?** tu te sens sûr de toi?; **we are c. that it will work** nous sommes sûrs *ou* persuadés que ça marchera; **I'm c. about this translation** je suis sûr que cette traduction est bonne; **c. of success** sûr de réussir; **be c.!** aie confiance en toi!

> Attention: ne pas confondre avec le nom anglais **confidant**.

confidential [kɒnfɪ'denʃəl] **ADJ 1** *(information, report, tone etc)* confidentiel; **keep it c.** n'en parlez à personne **2** *(attached to one person)* *(position)* de confiance; *(secretary)* particulier
▸▸**c. agent** homme *m* de confiance

confidentiality [kɒnfɪdenʃɪ'ælɪtɪ] **N** *(of information, report)* caractère *m* confidentiel, confidentialité *f*

confidentially [kɒnfɪ'denʃəlɪ] **ADV** *(to tell sb sth)* confidentiellement, en confidence; **c., I don't trust him** entre nous, je ne lui fais pas confiance

confidently ['kɒnfɪdəntlɪ] **ADV** *(with trust)* avec confiance, en toute confiance; *(with self-assurance)* avec assurance

confiding [kən'faɪdɪŋ] **ADJ** confiant

config. sys, config. sys file [kɒnfɪg'sɪs] **N** *Comput* fichier *m* config. sys

configurable [kən'fɪgjʊrəb(ə)l] **ADJ** *Comput* configurable, paramétrable

configuration [kənfɪgjʊ'reɪʃən] **N** *(shape)* configuration *f*, *Comput* configuration, paramétrage *m*

configure [kən'fɪgər] **VT** *Comput* configurer, paramétrer

confine [kən'faɪn] **VT 1** *(in prison etc)* enfermer; **to be confined to one's room** (être obligé de) garder la chambre; **confined to bed** alité; *Mil* **confined to barracks** consigné; **confined space** espace restreint **2** *(limit)* **to c. oneself to sth/to doing sth** se borner *ou* se limiter *ou* s'en tenir à qch/à faire qch; **let us c. ourselves to the question of ...** tenons-nous-en à la question de ...; **c. your answer to the matter in hand** limitez votre réponse au sujet qui nous occupe **3** *Obst Old-fashioned* **to be confined** accoucher

confinement [kən'faɪnmənt] **N 1** *(in prison)* emprisonnement *m* **2** *(limitation)* limitation *f*, restriction *f* (**to** à) **3** *Obst Old-fashioned* couches *fpl*, accouchement *m*

confines ['kɒnfaɪnz] **NPL** *Lit (of a place etc)* confins *mpl*; **within the c. of this subject** dans les limites de ce sujet; **within/beyond the c. of human knowledge** dans/au delà des limites de la connaissance humaine

confirm [kən'fɜːm] **VT 1** *(corroborate)* *(news, suspicions)* confirmer, corroborer; *(reservation)* confirmer; *Aviat* **flight confirmed** vol confirmé; **to be confirmed** *(notice)* *(concert, film etc)* à confirmer; **to c. that ...** confirmer que ... + *ind*
2 *(reinforce)* *(power)* raffermir, consolider; *(person's reputation, position)* consolider; **to c. sth as sth** confirmer qch comme étant qch; **to c. sb's fears** confirmer les craintes de qn
3 *(approve, validate)* *(treaty, result)* confirmer; *(nomination)* approuver; *(decision)* entériner; *(election)* valider
4 *Rel* confirmer, donner la confirmation à; **to be confirmed** recevoir la confirmation
VI confirmer; **please c. in writing** veuillez confirmer par écrit

confirmation [kɒnfə'meɪʃən] **N 1** *(of news, doubts, reservation etc)* confirmation *f*; **there has been no c. of the rumour** la rumeur n'a pas été confirmée; **in c. of** en confirmation de
2 *(reinforcement)* *(of person's authority)* raffermissement *m*, consolidation *f*
3 *(validation)* *(of treaty, result)* confirmation *f*, *(of nomination)* approbation *f*, *(of decision)* entérinement *m*; *(of election)* validation *f*; **c. of ...** *(booking)* pour confirmer ...; **she wrote in c. of her acceptance** elle a écrit pour confirmer qu'elle acceptait
4 *Rel* confirmation *f*
▸▸*Com* **c. of receipt** accusé *m* de réception

confirmed [kən'fɜːmd] **ADJ 1** *(habit, liar, womanizer etc)* invétéré; *(drunkard)* incorrigible, invétéré; **he's a c. bachelor** c'est un célibataire endurci **2** *Rel* confirmé
▸▸*Fin* **c. credit** crédit *m* confirmé; *Fin* **c. irrevocable letter of credit** lettre *f* de crédit irrévocable confirmé; **c. letter of credit** lettre de crédit confirmé; *Aviat* **c. seat** place *f* confirmée

confirming [kən'fɜːmɪŋ] **ADJ**
▸▸**c. bank** banque *f* confirmatrice; **c. house** organisme *m* confirmateur

confiscate ['kɒnfɪskeɪt] **VT** confisquer (**from sb** à qn)

confiscation [kɒnfɪs'keɪʃən] **N** confiscation *f*

confiscatory [kɒnfɪs'keɪtərɪ] **ADJ** *(power)* de confiscation

conflagration [kɒnflə'greɪʃən] **N** *Fml (fire)*, *Fig* conflagration *f*

conflate [kən'fleɪt] vt *(issues, reports)* amalgamer

conflation [kən'fleɪʃən] n fusion f

conflict[1] ['kɒnflɪkt] n *(between people, of feelings etc)* conflit m; **c. of interests** conflit d'intérêts; **a c. of interest situation** une situation présentant un conflit d'intérêts; **to come into/be in c.** entrer/être en conflit (**with** avec); **this was in c. with her principles** c'était en conflit *ou* en contradiction avec ses principes

conflict[2] [kən'flɪkt] vi être en conflit *ou* en désaccord (**with sth** avec qch); **this conflicts with his earlier statement** ceci est en contradiction avec sa déclaration précédente; **duties that c. with each other** charges incompatibles; **it conflicts with another appointment** j'ai/elle a *etc* un autre rendez-vous à cette heure

conflicting [kən'flɪktɪŋ] adj *(opinions)* opposé; *(advice, evidence)* contradictoire
▸▸**c. interests** des intérêts mpl qui s'opposent

confluence ['kɒnfluəns] n Geog *(place)* confluent m; *(action)* (of two rivers, glaciers) confluence f

conform [kən'fɔːm] vi se conformer (**to** *or* **with sth** à qch); **to c. to a standard** *(of equipment)* être conforme à *ou* répondre à une norme; **to c. to the law** obéir aux lois; **to c. (in shape) to another part** être identique à une autre pièce; **this conforms with what we were told/we expected** ceci est conforme à ce que l'on nous avait dit/nos attentes; **to c. to fashion** suivre la mode vtconformer (**sth to sth** qch à qch)

conformism [kən'fɔːmɪz(ə)m] n conformisme m

conformist [kən'fɔːmɪst] adj, n conformiste mf

conformity [kən'fɔːmɪtɪ] n conformité f (**to, with** à); **in c. with ...** conformément à ...; **their action was in c. with the law** ce qu'ils ont fait était en conformité avec la loi

confound [kən'faʊnd] vt 1 *(confuse, surprise)* confondre; **they were confounded by this news** cette nouvelle les a consternés; **he confounded his critics** il a fait mentir les gens qui le critiquaient 2 *(bring to nothing)* (sb's plans etc) renverser; (hopes) réduire à néant 3 Lit *(put in confusion)* mettre la confusion dans; **to c. sth with sth** confondre qch avec qch 4 Old-fashioned Fam *(curse)* **c. him!** la peste soit de lui!; **c. it!** la barbe!

confounded [kən'faʊndɪd] adj Old-fashioned Fam sacré; **you c. idiot!** espèce d'idiot!

confraternity [kɒnfrə'tɜːnɪtɪ] n association f

confront [kən'frʌnt] vt *(enemy, danger, problem, situation)* affronter, faire face à; **to c. the issue** faire face au problème; **to c. sb with** *(witness etc)* confronter qn avec; *(something)* mettre qn en face de; **she confronted him with his responsibilities** elle l'a mis face à ses responsabilités; **a difficult situation confronts them** ils doivent faire face à une situation difficile; **to be confronted by** *(somebody, something)* être en face de, se trouver en présence de; **to be confronted by** *or* **with a difficulty** se trouver face à une difficulté

confrontation [kɒnfrʌn'teɪʃən] n 1 *(of two people, armies etc)* affrontement m (**with** avec) 2 *(bringing into contact)* (of witnesses etc) confrontation f

confrontational [kɒnfrʌn'teɪʃən(ə)l] adj *(situation)* d'affrontement; *(policy)* de confrontation; *(management style)* agressif; **he's quite c.** il aime la confrontation

Confucian [kən'fjuːʃən] adj Phil confucéen, confucianiste

confuse [kən'fjuːz] vt 1 *(bewilder)* (person) embrouiller; *(animal)* troubler; **to get confused** s'embrouiller, s'y perdre 2 *(put into disorder)* **to c. the issue, to c. things** *or* **matters** compliquer les choses 3 *(mix up)* (dates, names etc) confondre; **he always confuses the two** il confond toujours les deux; **to c. sth/sb with** *or* **and sth/sb** confondre qch/qn avec qch/qn

confused [kən'fjuːzd] adj 1 *(person)* (because not understanding sth) embrouillé; (not knowing what to do) perdu; (after blow on head, anaesthetic etc) sonné, groggy; (mind) troublé; **to get c.** (of person) s'embrouiller; **I'm c.** (don't understand) je suis perdu, je n'y comprends rien; **I'm still a little c. as to why he did it** je ne comprends toujours pas très bien pourquoi il a fait cela; **the old lady's a bit c.** (mentally) la vieille dame ne sait plus trop où elle en est *ou* est un peu perdue 2 *(disordered)* (mass, speech, logic, reasoning) confus

---

Note that the most common meaning of the French word **confus** is **embarrassed**.

---

confusedly [kən'fjuːzɪdlɪ] adv confusément

confusing [kən'fjuːzɪŋ] adj *(unclear, causing lack of understanding)* embrouillé, confus; **it's very c.** on s'y perd; **it's too c. for the user** l'utilisateur s'y perdra; **I hope my explanation wasn't too c.** j'espère que mon explication ne vous a pas trop embrouillé; **there's a c. number of different makes** il y a tant de marques différentes qu'on s'y perd

confusingly [kən'fjuːzɪŋlɪ] adv *(unclearly, causing lack of understanding)* de manière embrouillée, confusément; **c., they both had the same name** ils avaient le même nom, ce qui provoquait souvent des confusions

confusion [kən'fjuːʒən] n 1 *(bewilderment)* confusion f, Med confusion f mentale; **in his c. he forgot his hat** dans sa confusion il a oublié son chapeau; **to add to the c. ...** pour ajouter à la confusion ...; **this news added to her c.** cette nouvelle a ajouté à sa confusion; **there's still some c. about the exact number killed** on ne connaît toujours pas le nombre de victimes; **it will only lead to c.** ce ne va faire qu'embrouiller les choses 2 *(disorder)* confusion f, désordre m; **everything was in c.** tout était en désordre, tout était pêle-mêle; **to spread c. everywhere** jeter partout le désordre *ou* la confusion
3 *(mixing up)* **c. of sth with** *or* **and sth** confusion f de qch avec qch
4 *(embarrassment)* confusion f, **to be covered in c.** être rempli de confusion

confute [kən'fjuːt] vt Fml *(disprove)* (argument, person) réfuter

conga ['kɒŋɡə] n conga f
vi danser la conga

congeal [kən'dʒiːl] vi *(of fat, oil)* se figer; *(of blood)* se coaguler, se figer
vt *(blood)* faire coaguler; *(oil)* faire figer

congenial [kən'dʒiːnɪəl] adj *(person, character)* sympathique, aimable; *(work)* agréable (**to** à); **I find his company c.** je le trouve d'une compagnie agréable; **an evening spent in c. company** une soirée passée en compagnie de gens sympathiques

congenital [kən'dʒenɪt(ə)l] adj *(defect, idiot etc)* congénital, -aux

congenitally [kən'dʒenɪtlɪ] adv congénitalement; **to be c. insane** souffrir de folie congénitale

conger ['kɒŋɡər] n congre m, anguille f de mer
▸▸**c. eel** congre, anguille f de mer

congest [kən'dʒest] vt 1 *(traffic, roads etc)* encombrer, embouteiller 2 Med *(with blood, mucus)* congestionner

congested [kən'dʒestɪd] adj 1 *(street, road, airport etc)* encombré; *(room)* (with furniture) encombré; *(with people)* plein; **the c. state of the roads** l'encombrement m des routes; **the traffic gets c. at ...** il y a des encombrements à ... 2 Med *(lungs)* congestionné; **I'm feeling really c.** j'ai les bronches très prises

congestion [kən'dʒestʃən] n 1 *(of traffic etc)* encombrements mpl, *(action, of grouping)* encombrements mpl; **the new road will relieve the c. in the town** la nouvelle route va décongestionner la ville 2 Med congestion f
▸▸**c. charge** taxe f anti-embouteillages

conglomerate[1] [kən'ɡlɒmərət] n Econ conglomérat m; Geol conglomérat, aggloméré m

conglomerate[2] [kən'ɡlɒməreɪt] vi Geol, Ind s'agglomérer

conglomeration [kənɡlɒmə'reɪʃən] n conglomération f, *(of rocks etc)* agrégat m; Fig **a c. of ideas** un mélange d'idées

Congo ['kɒŋɡəʊ] n **the (River) C.** le Congo; **the C.** *(state)* le Congo

Congolese [kɒŋɡə'liːz] n Congolais, -aise
adj congolais

congrats [kən'ɡræts] npl Br Fam = congratulations

congratulate [kən'ɡrætjʊleɪt] vt *(person)* féliciter (**on** de); **I c. you** je vous félicite, (je vous fais) mes compliments; **to c. oneself on sth/on having done sth** se féliciter de qch/d'avoir fait qch; **they are to be congratulated** ils méritent d'être félicités

congratulations [kənɡrætjʊ'leɪʃənz] npl félicitations fpl; **give her my c.** transmets-lui mes félicitations, félicite-la de ma part; **c.!** félicitations!; **c. on passing your exams** félicitations pour tes examens; **warmest c. on your promotion** (on card) toutes nos félicitations pour votre promotion; **c. are in order, I hear** au fait, félicitations!

congratulatory [kən'ɡrætjʊleɪtərɪ] adj *(letter etc)* de félicitation(s)

congregate ['kɒŋɡrɪɡeɪt] vi se rassembler, s'assembler

congregation [kɒŋɡrɪ'ɡeɪʃən] n 1 *(in church)* assemblée f des fidèles, assistance f; **I'm not a member of your c.** je ne fais pas partie de votre paroisse, je ne viens pas à l'église ici 2 *(group, action of grouping)* rassemblement m 3 Br Univ *(at Oxford, Cambridge)* (of professors etc) assemblée f générale

congregational [kɒŋɡrɪ'ɡeɪʃən(ə)l] adj Rel en assemblée; **the C. Church** l'Église f congrégationaliste; **c. worship** culte m public

Congress ['kɒŋɡres] n Am Pol Congrès m

Congress
Le Congrès, organe législatif américain, est constitué du Sénat et de la Chambre des représentants. Une proposition de loi doit obligatoirement être approuvée séparément par ces deux Chambres.

---

congress ['kɒŋɡres] n 1 *(conference)* congrès m 2 Fml *(sexual intercourse)* rapports mpl sexuels

Congressional [kən'ɡreʃən(ə)l] adj Am Pol *(committee, election)* du Congrès

Congressman, pl **Congressmen** ['kɒŋɡresmən] n Am Pol membre m du Congrès

Congresswoman, pl **Congresswomen** ['kɒŋɡreswʊmən, -wɪmɪn] n Am Pol membre f du Congrès

congruence ['kɒŋgruəns] N **1** *Fml* adéquation *f* (**with** avec) **2** *Geom* congruence *f* (**with** à)

congruent ['kɒŋgruənt] ADJ **1** *Fml* conforme (**with** à) **2** *Geom (triangle)* congruent

congruity [kɒŋ'gruːɪtɪ] N *Fml* = **congruence 1**

congruous ['kɒŋgruəs] ADJ *Fml* = **congruent 1**

conic ['kɒnɪk] ADJ *Geom* conique

conical ['kɒnɪk(ə)l] ADJ conique; **a c. paper hat** un chapeau pointu en papier
▸▸ **c. projection** *(in mapmaking)* projection *f* conique

conifer ['kɒnɪfər] N conifère *m*

coniferous [kə'nɪfərəs] ADJ conifère; *(forest)* de conifères

conjectural [kən'dʒektʃər(ə)l] ADJ conjectural, -aux

conjecture [kən'dʒektʃər] N conjecture *f*, **to hazard a c.** risquer une hypothèse *ou* une supposition; **it's a matter of c.** cela relève de l'hypothèse *ou* de la conjecture; **it's sheer c.** ce ne sont que des suppositions
VT supposer
VI faire des conjectures

conjoin [kən'dʒɔɪn] VT *Fml* unir, réunir

conjoint [kɒn'dʒɔɪnt] ADJ *Fml* conjoint, associé

conjointly [kɒn'dʒɔɪntlɪ] ADV *Fml* conjointement, ensemble

conjugal ['kɒndʒʊg(ə)l] ADJ conjugal, -aux

conjugate ['kɒndʒʊgeɪt] VT *Gram (verb)* conjuguer
VI *Gram, Biol* se conjuguer

conjugation [kɒndʒʊ'geɪʃən] N *Gram, Biol* conjugaison *f* SEE GRAMMAR B24–7

conjunction [kən'dʒʌŋkʃən] N **1** *(combination)* conjonction *f*, **in c. with sb** conjointement avec qn; **these factors, in c. with others, were responsible for …** ces facteurs combinés à d'autres furent responsables de … **2** *Gram* conjonction *f* VOIR GRAMMAIRE A73–6; B57–8 **3** *Astron* conjonction *f*, **in c.** *(planets)* en conjonction
▸▸ *Aviat* **c. tickets** billets *mpl* complémentaires

conjunctive [kən'dʒʌŋktɪv] ADJ *(tissue etc)* conjonctif

conjunctivitis [kəndʒʌŋktɪ'vaɪtɪs] N *Med* conjonctivite *f*, **to have c.** avoir de la conjonctivite

conjure ['kʌndʒər] VI faire des tours de passe-passe *ou* de prestidigitation; *Fig* **a name to c. with** un nom qui fait rêver
VT **1** *(produce)* **they conjured a bottle of wine out of nowhere** *or* **thin air** ils ont fait apparaître une bouteille de vin comme par enchantement **2** [kən'dʒʊər] *Fml (entreat)* conjurer (**sb to do sth** qn de faire qch)
▸ **conjure up** VT SEP **1** *(call to mind) (images, memories)* évoquer **2** *(call up) (spirit etc)* faire apparaître **3** *(produce)* **they conjured up some armchairs** ils ont déniché des fauteuils d'on ne sait où; **she conjured up an incredible meal out of almost nothing** elle a réussi à préparer un repas fantastique avec presque rien; **I'll c. something up** *(to eat)* je vais me débrouiller pour préparer quelque chose avec ce que j'ai; **I can't just c. extra staff up out of thin air!** je ne peux pas sortir du personnel supplémentaire de mon chapeau!

conjurer, conjuror ['kʌndʒərər] N prestidigitateur *m*, illusionniste *mf*

conjuring ['kʌndʒərɪŋ] N prestidigitation *f*
▸▸ **c. trick** tour *m* de passe-passe *ou* de prestidigitation

conk [kɒŋk] *Sl N Br (nose)* blair *m*, pif *m*
VT *(hit)* foutre un gnon à

▸ **conk out** VI *Fam* **1** *(of machine, television etc)* tomber en panne **2** *(lose consciousness)* tomber dans les pommes **3** *(go to sleep)* s'endormir, s'écrouler **4** *Am (die)* clamser, clamecer

conker ['kɒŋkər] N *Br Fam* marron *m* (d'Inde); **conkers** *(game)* = jeu *m* qui consiste à faire éclater le marron que son adversaire tient au bout d'une ficelle

Conn *abbr* **Connecticut**

connect [kə'nekt] VT **1** *(join) (something)* relier, rattacher (**to** à); *Tech etc (two shafts)* embrayer; *(pipes)* joindre; *Elec (circuits)* interconnecter; *(wires)* connecter; **a road connects the two cities, the two cities are connected by a road** une route relie les deux villes, les deux villes sont reliées par une route; **a corridor connects the room to the library** il y a un couloir qui relie la pièce à la bibliothèque; **we were connected with the studio by radio** nous étions en liaison radio avec le studio; **the telephone/electricity hasn't been connected** le téléphone/l'électricité n'a pas été branché(e); **c. this wire to the other terminal** connectez ce fil à l'autre borne **2** *Tel (caller)* mettre en ligne *ou* en communication (**with** avec); **will you c. me with reservations, please?** est-ce que vous pouvez me passer votre service des réservations?; **to c. two subscribers** mettre deux abonnés en communication **3** *(link, associate)* associer (**sb/sth with sb/sth** qn/qch avec qn/à qch); **there is nothing to c. the two crimes** il n'y a aucun lien entre les deux crimes; **at first I didn't c. the name with the face** au début je n'ai pas fait le lien *ou* le rapprochement entre le nom et le visage; **to be connected with …** *(of person)* avoir des relations *ou* un lien avec …; *(of thing)* se rattacher *ou* se rapporter à …; **the questions were connected with another subject** les questions étaient relatives *ou* se rapportaient à un autre sujet; **to be connected with** *or* **to a family** *(be related to)* avoir un lien de parenté avec une famille
VI **1** *(of wires)* être reliés (**with** à); *(of roads)* se rejoindre; *(of rooms)* communiquer (**with** avec); **this road connects with the motorway** cette route rejoint l'autoroute; **the tunnels don't c.** les deux tunnels ne sont pas reliés *ou* ne communiquent pas
2 to c. with a train/a flight *(of train, plane)* assurer la correspondance avec un train/un vol; *(of person)* prendre la correspondance **3** *Fam (of blow)* atteindre son but; *(of boxer)* frapper *ou* atteindre son adversaire; *(of tennis player, cricketer, racket, bat)* frapper la balle
N *Comput* connexion *f*
▸▸ *Comput* **c. time** durée *f* (d'établissement) de la connexion

▸ **connect up** VT SEP *(pipes)* raccorder; *(wires)* connecter; *Comput (to Internet)* connecter

connected [kə'nektɪd] ADJ *(linked) (facts, events etc)* connexe, lié; **to be well c.** *(of person)* avoir des relations

connecting [kə'nektɪŋ] ADJ *(cable, wire)* de connexion
▸▸ **c. door** porte *f* de communication; **c. flight** correspondance *f*, *Tech* **c. piece** pièce *f* de raccordement; *Tech* **c. pipe** tuyau *m* de raccordement *ou* de jonction; *Tech* **c. rod** bielle *f*, **c. rooms** *(in hotel)* pièces *fpl* communicantes; **c. time** *(for travel)* temps *m* de correspondance; **c. train** correspondance

connection [kə'nekʃən] N **1** *(link, association)* rapport *m*, lien *m* (**between** entre **with** avec); **I didn't make the c.** je n'ai pas fait le rapprochement; **in c. with …** à propos de …; **in this c.** à ce propos, à cet égard

2 *(personal relationship)* relations *fpl*, rapports *mpl*, **I have broken off all c. with him** j'ai cessé toutes relations avec lui; **to establish a business c. with a firm** établir des relations commerciales avec une entreprise **3** *(acquaintance)* relation *f*, *Sl (drug dealer)* dealer *m*; **she has important connections** elle a des relations en haut lieu; **I have some useful connections within the police** j'ai des relations très utiles dans la police **4** *(family relationship)* parenté *f*, **to form a c. by marriage with a good family** s'allier à *ou* avec une bonne famille; **there's no c. with the Yorkshire Smythes** il n'y a pas de lien de parenté avec les Smythe du Yorkshire; **my family has Scottish connections** il y a des Écossais dans ma famille **5** *Tech etc* connexion *f*, *(of pipes, wires etc)* assemblage *m*, raccordement *m*; *(of machine parts)* accouplement *m*, engrenage *m*; *Elec* raccordement, connexion, branchement *m*; *Comput* connexion, liaison *f*; *Tel* communication *f*; *Elec* **the c. is loose** il y a un faux contact; *Tel* **we had a very bad c.** la communication était très mauvaise **6** *Elec (connecting device)* **earth** or *Am* **ground c.** prise *f* de terre **7** *(in journey) (train, plane, boat etc)* correspondance *f*, **I missed my c.** j'ai manqué *ou* raté ma correspondance
▸▸ *Tech* **c. kit** kit *m* d'accès *ou* de connexion

connective [kə'nektɪv] ADJ *Gram (word, phrase)* conjonctif
N *Gram* conjonction *f* de coordination
▸▸ *Anat* **c. tissue** tissu *m* conjonctif

connectivity [kɒnek'tɪvɪtɪ] N *Comput* connectivité *f*

connector [kə'nektər] N *Elec* connecteur *m*; *Tech etc* raccord *m*
▸▸ *Tech* **c. kit** kit *m* d'accès *ou* de connexion

connexion [kə'nekʃən] N = **connection**

conning tower ['kɒnɪŋ] N *(of submarine)* kiosque *m*

conniptions [kə'nɪpʃənz] N *Am Fam* **to have c.** piquer une crise (**about sth** à propos de qch)

connivance [kə'naɪvəns] N connivence *f*, **c. at** *or* **in a crime** complicité *f* dans un crime; **to be in c. with sb** être de connivence avec qn

connive [kə'naɪv] VI *(scheme, plot)* être de connivence (**with** avec; **to do** pour faire); **to c. at** *(abuse, irregularity etc)* se rendre complice de

conniving [kə'naɪvɪŋ] ADJ ATTRIB malhonnête; **you c. bastard!** espèce de pourri!

connoisseur [kɒnə'sɜːr] N connaisseur, -euse (**of** en); **to be a c. of sth** s'y connaître en qch, être un connaisseur en matière de qch

connotation [kɒnə'teɪʃən] N *(of term)* connotation *f*

connote [kɒ'nəʊt] VT *Fml (of word) (notion, idea)* suggérer, comporter; **the word connotes courage** le mot suggère une idée de courage

connubial [kə'njuːbɪəl] ADJ *Fml* conjugal, -aux

conquer ['kɒŋkər] VT *(country, world, sb's heart, market)* conquérir; *(difficulty, one's shyness, fears)* vaincre, surmonter; *(inflation, illness)* vaincre; **Everest was conquered in 1953** l'Everest a été conquis en 1953

conquering ['kɒŋkərɪŋ] ADJ *(army, hero)* conquérant, victorieux

conqueror ['kɒŋkərər] N **1** *(of country)* conquérant *m*; *Hist* **(William) the C.** Guillaume le Conquérant **2** *(victor)* vainqueur *m*

conquest ['kɒŋkwest] N *(victory, prize)*, *Fig* conquête *f*; *Hist* **the (Norman) C.** la conquête de l'Angleterre; *Fig* **his many**

conquests ses nombreuses conquêtes; *Fig* **to make a c. of sb** faire la conquête de qn

conrod ['kɒnrɒd] N *Aut* bielle *f*

Cons *Pol abbr* Conservative

consanguinity [kɒnsæŋ'gwɪnɪtɪ] N *Fml* consanguinité *f*

conscience ['kɒnʃəns] N conscience *f*; **to have a clear** *or* **an easy c.** avoir la conscience tranquille; **to have a guilty** *or* **bad c.** avoir mauvaise conscience; **to have sth on one's c.** avoir qch sur la conscience; **it's on my c.** je l'ai sur la conscience; **it's on my c. that I left him alone** je l'ai laissé tout seul et j'ai mauvaise conscience; **I can't sleep with that on my c.** je ne peux pas dormir avec ça sur la conscience; **he had no c. about abandoning them to their fate** il n'avait aucun scrupule à les abandonner à leur sort; **a matter of c.** une affaire de conscience; **freedom of c.** liberté *f* de conscience; **one cannot in all c. believe that ...** on ne peut pas raisonnablement croire que ...
▸▸ **c. clause** clause *f* de conscience; **c. money** argent *m* restitué *(pour soulager sa conscience)*

conscience-stricken ADJ pris de remords

conscientious [kɒnʃɪ'enʃəs] ADJ *(worker, work)* consciencieux; **to be c. about timekeeping** être très ponctuel
▸▸ **c. objection** objection *f* de conscience; **c. objector** objecteur *m* de conscience

conscientiously [kɒnʃɪ'enʃəslɪ] ADV *(to work)* consciencieusement

conscientiousness [kɒnʃɪ'enʃəsnɪs] N minutie *f*, conscience *f*

conscious ['kɒnʃəs] ADJ **1** *Med* **to be c.** être conscient; **to become c.** reprendre connaissance; **he's not c. yet** il n'a pas encore repris connaissance; *Hum* **(he's still in bed)** il n'a pas encore fait surface
2 *(aware)* conscient; **to be c. of sth** avoir conscience de qch, être conscient de qch; **to become c. of sth** s'apercevoir de qch; **I wasn't c. of having annoyed you** je ne m'étais pas rendu compte que je t'avais énervé; **to be c. that ...** être conscient du fait que ...
3 *(intentional)* conscient; **it was not a c. decision** ce n'était pas une décision prise de façon consciente; **it required a c. effort to ...** il fallait se forcer pour ...
4 *Phil, Psy* conscient; **the c. mind** la conscience; **to have a c. dislike of sb** éprouver une aversion consciente pour qn
N *Phil, Psy* **the c.** le conscient

-conscious SUFF **fashion-c.** qui suit de près la mode; **clothes-c.** qui s'habille avec soin; **health-c.** qui se préoccupe de sa santé; **safety-c.** soucieux de sécurité

consciously ['kɒnʃəslɪ] ADV consciemment; *(deliberately)* sciemment

consciousness ['kɒnʃəsnɪs] N **1** *Med* conscience *f*, connaissance *f*; **to lose c.** perdre connaissance *ou* conscience; **to regain c.** reprendre connaissance, revenir à soi **2** *(awareness)* conscience *f* (of de); **the organization aims to raise people's c. of these problems** l'organisme a pour objet de sensibiliser les gens à ces problèmes **3** *Phil, Psy* conscience *f*
▸▸ **c. raising** sensibilisation *f*

conscript[1] ['kɒnskrɪpt] N *Mil* conscrit *m*
▸▸ **c. army** armée *f* de conscrits

conscript[2] [kən'skrɪpt] VT *Mil* enrôler, appeler (sous les drapeaux); **to be conscripted** être appelé (sous les drapeaux); *Fig* **I've been conscripted to do the dishes** on m'a enrôlé pour faire la vaisselle

conscription [kən'skrɪpʃən] N *Mil* conscription *f*

consecrate ['kɒnsɪkreɪt] VT **1** *Rel (church,*

communion bread) consacrer; *(king, bishop)* sacrer **2** *(dedicate)* consacrer; **to c. one's life to sth** consacrer sa vie à qch, se vouer à qch; **the day was consecrated to the memory of the country's dead** la journée a été dédiée à la mémoire des morts du pays

consecrated ['kɒnsɪkreɪtɪd] ADJ *Rel (church, bread)* consacré; **in c. ground** en terre sainte *ou* bénite

consecration [kɒnsɪ'kreɪʃən] N **1** *(of church, communion bread)* consécration *f*; *(of king, bishop)* sacre *m* **2** *(dedication)* **the c. of her life to helping the poor** le fait de consacrer sa vie à aider les pauvres

consecutive [kən'sekjʊtɪv] ADJ consécutif; **on three c. days** trois jours de suite, trois jours consécutifs

consecutively [kən'sekjʊtɪvlɪ] ADV **two days c.** deux jours de suite, deux jours consécutifs; **to deal with problems c.** traiter les problèmes l'un après l'autre

consensual [kən'sensjʊəl] ADJ consensuel

consensus [kən'sensəs] N *(of opinion, evidence etc)* consensus *m*; **to reach a c.** arriver à un consensus; **a c. was beginning to emerge** un consensus commençait à apparaître; **the c. was that the new road was unnecessary** l'opinion générale était que la nouvelle route n'était pas nécessaire; **what is the c. of opinion?** quelle est l'opinion générale?
▸▸ **c. management** gestion *f* par consensus; **c. politics** politique *f* de consensus

consent [kən'sent] N consentement *m*, accord *m*, assentiment *m*; **to give/withhold one's c. to sth** donner/ne pas donner son consentement à qch; **I'll never give my c.** je n'y consentirai jamais, je ne donnerai jamais mon accord; **do I have your c.?** est-ce que j'ai votre accord?; **by common c.** de l'aveu de tout le monde; **by mutual c.** de gré à gré; *(divorce)* par consentement mutuel; *Law* **age of c.** âge *m* nubile
VI **to c. to sth/to do sth** consentir à qch/à faire qch; **I c.** j'y consens

consenting [kən'sentɪŋ] ADJ *Law (adult)* consentant; *Hum* **she is a c. adult, after all** elle est majeure et vaccinée après tout

consequence ['kɒnsɪkwəns] N **1** *(result)* conséquence *f*, suites *fpl*; **the c. is that ...** il en résulte *ou* il s'ensuit que ...; **in c., as a c.** par conséquent; **in c. of ...** par suite de ...; **this decision had dire consequences for the region** cette décision a eu des conséquences terribles pour la région; **unforeseen consequences** conséquences imprévues; **to take the consequences** accepter les conséquences
2 *(importance)* importance *f*; **it is of no c.** cela n'a pas d'importance, cela ne fait rien; **it is of some c. to me** ça a de l'importance pour moi; **he is of no c.** il ne compte pas; **a woman of c.** une femme avec qui il faut compter
3 *Br* **consequences** *(game)* (jeu *m* des) petits papiers *mpl*

consequent ['kɒnsɪkwənt] ADJ **1** *(resulting)* résultant; **c. upon sth** qui est la conséquence de qch, qui résulte de qch; **a glut and the c. drop in prices** un surplus et la baisse des prix qui en résulte **2** *(in logic)* conséquent

consequential [kɒnsɪ'kwenʃəl] ADJ *(resulting)* conséquent, consécutif (to à); **c. effects** *(of action)* répercussions *fpl*
▸▸ *Law* **c. damages** dommages *mpl* indirects

consequently [kɒnsɪ'kwəntlɪ] ADV, CONJ par conséquent, donc

conservancy [kən'sɜːvənsɪ] N *Br (for protection of forest, river etc)* commission *f* de conservation

conservation [kɒnsə'veɪʃən] N **1** conservation *f*, *c.* **of energy** économies *fpl* d'énergie **2** *(of environment)* protection *f* de l'environnement; **c. expert** expert *m* de la protection de l'environnement
▸▸ **c. area** zone *f* protégée *(d'un point de vue architectural ou historique)*

conservationist [kɒnsə'veɪʃənɪst] N partisan, -ane de la protection de l'environnement

conservatism [kən'sɜːvətɪz(ə)m] N conservatisme *m*

conservative [kən'sɜːvətɪv] ADJ **1** conservateur, -trice; *(evaluation)* prudent; **at a c. estimate** au minimum, au bas mot **2** *Pol* conservateur, -trice
N *Pol* conservateur, -trice; **the Conservatives** les conservateurs
▸▸ *Br* **C. Central Office** = siège *m* du parti conservateur britannique; **the C. Party** le parti conservateur

conservatively [kən'sɜːvətɪvlɪ] ADV *(to dress)* de façon classique; **it was c. estimated at £5,000** selon des estimations prudentes, cela devrait coûter 5 000 livres

conservatoire [kən'sɜːvətwaːr] N *Mus* conservatoire *m*

conservatory [kən'sɜːvətrɪ] N **1** *(attached to house)* véranda *f* **2** = **conservatoire**

conserve[1] ['kɒnsɜːv] N *Culin (jam)* confiture *f*

conserve[2] [kən'sɜːv] VT *(ancient monument etc)* conserver, préserver; **to c. water/energy** faire des économies d'eau/d'énergie; **they had to c. their water supplies to get across the desert** il a fallu qu'ils économisent l'eau pour pouvoir traverser le désert

consider [kən'sɪdər] VT **1** *(reflect on, think over) (matter)* considérer; *(facts, proposal, offer)* étudier; **I'll c. it** j'y réfléchirai; **he was considering whether to go out when ...** il se demandait s'il allait sortir quand ...; **have you considered (buying) a larger model?** est-ce que vous avez envisagé d'acheter un modèle plus grand?; **the jury retired to c. its verdict** le jury se retira pour délibérer; **to c. sb for a job** envisager de donner un poste à qn
2 *(take into account) (sb's feelings)* avoir égard à; *(expense)* regarder à; *(possibility)* envisager; **she never considers anybody but herself** elle ne fait jamais attention aux autres; **when you c. that ...** quand on pense *ou* songe que ...; **c. the cost!** pensez au coût!; **you ought to have considered my feelings** tu aurais dû penser à moi; **all things considered** tout bien considéré, tout compte fait
3 *(regard)* considérer; **I c. him a friend** je le considère comme un ami; **c. it done** considérez cela comme fait; **c. yourself dismissed** tenez-vous pour congédié; **to c. oneself happy** s'estimer heureux; **I c. it my duty to ...** j'estime qu'il est de mon devoir de ...; **I would c. it an honour** ce serait pour moi un honneur; **we c. it likely that ...** nous estimons qu'il est probable que ...

considerable [kən'sɪdərə(ə)l] ADJ **1** *(great)* considérable; **a c. number of ...** un nombre considérable de ...; **the new car attracted c. attention** la nouvelle voiture a fait l'objet d'une attention considérable; **she only found the house after c. difficulty** elle n'a trouvé la maison qu'avec beaucoup de difficulté **2** *(worthy of attention)* digne d'attention; *(person)* notable, important

considerably [kən'sɪdərəblɪ] ADV considérablement

considerate [kən'sɪdərət] ADJ prévenant, plein d'égards (**towards, to** pour, envers); **it's very c. of you** c'est très aimable de votre part, c'est très gentil de ta part; **try to be more c.** essaie d'être un peu plus prévenant

considerately [kən'sɪdərətlɪ] ADV avec considération, avec prévenance

consideration [kənsɪdə'reɪʃən] N **1** *(deliberation)* **under c.** *(question, candidate etc)* à l'étude; **to give c. to a question** mettre une question à l'étude; **I'll give it some c.** j'y penserai; **after due c.** après mûre réflexion; **to take sth into c.** prendre qch en considération, tenir compte de qch, prendre qch en ligne de compte; **taking all things into c.** tout bien considéré; **taking her age into c.** si l'on tient compte de son âge; **to leave sth out of c.** ne pas tenir compte de qch

2 *(factor)* facteur *m*; **there is another c.** il y a autre chose dont il faut tenir compte; **money is always the first c.** la question d'argent vient toujours en premier; **on no c.** à aucun prix; **money is no c.** l'argent n'entre pas en ligne de compte

3 *(regard)* considération *f*; **to have no c. for anyone** n'avoir de considération pour personne; **show some c.!** fais preuve d'un peu de considération!; **out of c. for sb** par égard pour qn; **to treat sb with c.** traiter qn avec considération

4 *(payment)* compensation *f*, rémunération *f*; *Com etc* **for a c.** moyennant paiement; **he'll do it for a c.** il le fera si vous le payez; **in c. of your services** en récompense de vos services

▸▸*Mktg* **c. set** ensemble *m* de considérations

considered [kən'sɪdəd] ADJ **1** *(thought out)* **it is my c. opinion that …** après mûre réflexion je pense que …; **is that your c. opinion?** est-ce ainsi que vous voyez les choses? **2** *(thought of)* **to be highly** *or* **well c.** être très estimé

considering [kən'sɪdərɪŋ] PREP étant donné, vu; **c. his age/the circumstances** étant donné *ou* vu son âge/les circonstances

CONJ étant donné que, vu que; **c. (that) he is so young** étant donné son jeune âge

ADV *Fam* après tout, malgré tout; **it's not so bad, c.** ce n'est pas si mauvais après tout *ou* malgré tout

consign [kən'saɪn] VT **1** *(entrust)* confier, remettre (**sth to sb's care** à qn); **to c. a body to the grave** livrer un corps à la tombe **2** *Com (goods)* expédier (**to sb** à qn)

consignee [kɒnsaɪ'niː] N destinataire *mf*, réceptionnaire *mf*; *Com (of goods on consignment)* consignataire *mf*

consignment [kən'saɪnmənt] N *Com* **1** *(goods)* livraison *f*, *(incoming)* arrivage *m*, livraison **2** *(act) (of goods)* envoi *m*, expédition *f*; *Com* **on c.** en consignation; **to send sb goods on c.** livrer à qn une marchandise en dépôt permanent

▸▸**c. note** bordereau *m* d'expédition

consignor [kən'saɪnər] N *Com* expéditeur, -trice

▸ **consist in** [kən'sɪst] VT INSEP consister en; **to c. in doing sth** consister à faire qch

▸ **consist of** VT INSEP consister en, se composer de; **her inheritance consisted of a house** son héritage consistait en une maison

consistency [kən'sɪstənsɪ] N **1** *(of liquid etc)* consistance *f*; **to be the c. of sth** avoir la consistance de qch **2** *(internal logic)* cohérence *f*, *(in ideas)* logique *f*; **to lack c.** *(of statements, views etc)* manquer de suite *ou* de cohérence **3** *(staying the same) (of quality of work, ideas)* constance *f*, *(of athlete, performances)* régularité *f*, **4** *(compatibility)* concordance *f*

▸▸**c. check** contrôle *m* d'uniformité; *Acct* **c. concept** principe *m* de la permanence (des méthodes)

consistent [kən'sɪstənt] ADJ **1** *(having internal logic) (reasoning, behaviour, person)* conséquent, cohérent, logique; **she was c. in her choice of partners** elle a toujours fait preuve de cohérence dans le choix de ses partenaires

2 *(staying the same) (quality of work, ideas)* constant; *(refusal, failure)* persistant; *(athlete, performer)* régulier; **because of her c. denial of the accusation** du fait qu'elle a toujours nié être coupable

3 *(compatible)* compatible (**with** avec); **the results are c. with the theory** les résultats concordent avec la théorie; **this action is not c. with his character** cette action n'est pas en harmonie avec son caractère; **her behaviour is c. with a diagnosis of …** son comportement est caractéristique d'un diagnostic de …

> Note that the French word **consistant** is a false friend and is never a translation for the English word **consistent**. Its most common meaning is **substantial**.

consistently [kən'sɪstəntlɪ] ADV **1** *(with logic)* de manière cohérente *ou* conséquente **2** *(with regularity) (to play, perform, work)* avec régularité; *(to fail, maintain)* constamment; **she has c. denied the accusation** elle a toujours nié cette accusation; **he has been c. better than the others** il a constamment été meilleur que les autres

consistory [kən'sɪstərɪ] N *Rel (pontifical)* consistoire *m*

▸▸**C. Court** tribunal *m* ecclésiastique

consolation [kɒnsə'leɪʃən] N consolation *f*; **words of c.** paroles *fpl* consolatrices; **that's one c.** c'est déjà une consolation; **if it's any c. reflect that tomorrow was her birthday** c'était une piètre consolation de penser que son anniversaire était le lendemain

▸▸**c. prize** prix *m* de consolation

console¹ [kən'səʊl] VT consoler (**for** de); **c. yourself with the thought that it's Friday tomorrow** console-toi en pensant que demain c'est vendredi

console² ['kɒnsəʊl] N **1** *(control panel)* console *f*, pupitre *m*; *Aviat* tableau *m* de bord; *Comput* pupitre *m* de commande **2** *Radio, TV (cabinet)* meuble *m* (pour téléviseur, chaîne hi-fi) **3** *Mus (of organ)* console *f*

▸▸**c. table** console *f*

consolidate [kən'sɒlɪdeɪt] VT *(foundations)* consolider, renforcer; *Mil (position)* raffermir; *Fig (position, lead)* conforter; *Com (orders, deliveries)* grouper; *Fin (debt)* consolider; *St Exch (shares)* regrouper; **to c. one's power** asseoir son pouvoir; **the company has consolidated its position as the market leader** la société a conforté sa position de leader sur le marché

VI se consolider

consolidated [kən'sɒlɪdeɪtɪd] ADJ *Fin* consolidé; *Com (orders, deliveries)* groupé

▸▸*Acct* **c. accounts** comptes *mpl* consolidés; *Fin* **c. annuities** fonds *mpl* consolidés; *Acct* **c. balance sheet** bilan *m* consolidé; *Fin* **c. debt** dette *f* consolidée; *Acct* **c. entry** écriture *f* de consolidation; *Br Pol* **c. fund** = compte *m* du gouvernement à la Banque d'Angleterre, qui sert à régler toutes les dépenses publiques; *Br Fin* **c. funds** fonds consolidés; **c. loan** emprunt *m* consolidé; **c. subsidiary** filiale *f* consolidée

consolidation [kənsɒlɪ'deɪʃən] N **1** *(of foundations, power etc)* consolidation *f*, renforcement *m*; *(of public opinion)* raffermissement *m* **2** *Fin (of national debt)* consolidation *f*; *St Exch (of shares)* regroupement *m*; *Law (of laws)* unification *f* **3** *Com (of*

orders, deliveries) groupage *m*; **c. for export** groupement *m* à l'export

consolidator [kən'sɒlɪdeɪtər] N *Com* groupeur *m*

consoling [kən'səʊlɪŋ] ADJ consolateur, -trice

consols ['kɒnsəlz, kən'sɒlz] NPL *Br Fin* (fonds *mpl*) consolidés *mpl*

consonance ['kɒnsənəns] N **1** *Mus, Ling* consonance *f* **2** *Fml (of ideas etc)* accord *m*, conformité *f*

consonant ['kɒnsənənt] N *Ling* consonne *f*

ADJ *Fml* en accord; **to be c. with** *or* **to sth** être en accord avec qch

consort ['kɒnsɔːt] N *(spouse) (of ruler etc)* époux, -ouse; **prince c.** prince *m* consort

▸ **consort with** [kən'sɔːt] VT INSEP frayer avec, fréquenter

consortium [kən'sɔːtɪəm] N *Com, Fin* consortium *m*

conspicuous [kən'spɪkjʊəs] ADJ **1** *(easily visible)* bien visible, apparent, manifeste; *(monument, landmark)* bien visible; *(uniform etc)* voyant; **in a c. position** bien en évidence; **to make oneself c.** se faire remarquer (**by, through** par) **2** *(obvious) (failure, lack)* manifeste, évident; *(striking) (bravery, intelligence)* remarquable, frappant; **c. gallantry** acte *m* de bravoure insigne; **to be c. by one's absence** *(of person, quality)* briller par son absence

▸▸**c. consumption** consommation *f* ostentatoire

conspicuously [kən'spɪkjʊəslɪ] ADV **1** *(visibly)* visiblement, manifestement; **to be c. absent** briller par son absence **2** *(remarkably)* remarquablement; *(dressed)* de façon (un peu) ostentatoire

conspicuousness [kən'spɪkjʊəsnɪs] N **1** *(visibility)* caractère *m* bien visible; *(of uniform etc)* caractère voyant **2** *(striking nature) (of action)* caractère *m* insigne *ou* remarquable

conspiracy [kən'spɪrəsɪ] N conspiration *f*, conjuration *f*, complot *m*; *Law* association *f* de malfaiteurs; **c. of silence** conspiration du silence; **c. to obtain documents illegally** conspiration pour obtenir des documents de façon illégale; **there's a c. against me** il y a un complot contre moi; **it's a c.** c'est un complot

▸▸**c. theorist** partisan *m* de la thèse *ou* théorie du complot; **c. theory** thèse *f ou* théorie *f* du complot

conspirator [kən'spɪrətər] N conspirateur, -trice

conspiratorial [kənspɪrə'tɔːrɪəl] ADJ *(air)* de conspirateur; **she gave me a c. wink** elle m'a jeté un coup d'œil complice

conspire [kən'spaɪər] VI **1** *(of person)* conspirer (**against** contre; **with** avec); **to c. to do sth** comploter de faire qch **2** *(of events etc)* concourir, contribuer; **everything conspired to make him late** tout a contribué à le mettre en retard; **circumstances conspired against me** les circonstances se sont liguées contre moi

constable ['kʌnstəb(ə)l, 'kɒn-] N *Br (in police)* agent *m* de police; *(rural)* gendarme *m*; **good evening, c.** bonsoir, monsieur l'agent; **special c.** auxiliaire *m* de police; **chief c.** ≃ commissaire *m* divisionnaire

constabulary [kən'stæbjʊlərɪ] N *(no pl) Br* police *f*; **the Kent C.** la Gendarmerie du Kent

constancy ['kɒnstənsɪ] N *(of character, temperature)* constance *f*; *(of friend)* fidélité *f*; *(of wind etc)* régularité *f*

constant ['kɒnstənt] ADJ **1** *(unchanging) (temperature, price, pressure)* constant; *(friend)* fidèle; **to remain c.** *(of temperature,*

price) rester constant **2** *(unceasing) (attention)* continuel; *(doubts, questions, complaining)* incessant; *(care)* continuel, assidu, soutenu; **through c. repetition** à force de répéter; **there was c. pressure for reform** il y avait une pression continuelle pour qu'une réforme soit mise en œuvre; **a c. stream of insults** un flot d'injures ininterrompu
N *Math, Phys* constante *f*; **time c.** constante de temps

constantly ['kɒnstəntlɪ] **ADV** constamment, continuellement

constant-velocity joint N *Aut* joint *m* de cardan, joint homocinétique

constellation [kɒnstə'leɪʃən] **N** constellation *f*

consternation [kɒnstə'neɪʃən] **N** consternation *f*; **a look of c.** un air consterné; **they looked at each other in c.** ils se regardaient atterrés; **to our c.** à notre consternation

constipate ['kɒnstɪpeɪt] **VT** *Med* constiper

constipated ['kɒnstɪpeɪtɪd] **ADJ** *Med, Fig* constipé; *Fig* **his rather c. prose style** son style plutôt empesé *ou* guindé

constipation [kɒnstɪ'peɪʃən] **N** *Med* constipation *f*

constituency [kən'stɪtjʊənsɪ] **N** *Pol* **1** *(voters)* électeurs *mpl (d'une circonscription)* **2** *(district)* circonscription *f* électorale; *Br* **the c. party** la section locale du parti

constituent [kən'stɪtjʊənt] **ADJ** constitutif **N 1** *Pol (of MP)* électeur, -trice **2** *(part)* élément *m* constitutif, composant *m*; *Ling* constituant *m*
▸▸ *Pol* **c. assembly** assemblée *f* constituante

constitute ['kɒnstɪtjuːt] **VT 1** *(make up, form)* constituer; *(sb's happiness etc)* faire; **to c. a threat to** constituer une menace pour ...; **the countries that c. the EU** les pays qui constituent l'UE; **factors that c. an offence** éléments constitutifs d'un délit; **that, to me, constitutes happiness** pour moi, c'est ça le bonheur **2** *Fml (appoint)* **to c. sb arbitrator** constituer qn arbitre

constitution [kɒnstɪ'tjuːʃən] **N 1** *Pol (of state, organization)* constitution *f* **2** *(of person)* constitution *f*; **to have a strong/an iron c.** avoir une bonne constitution/une santé de fer **3** *(composition)* constitution *f*, composition *f*

constitutional [kɒnstɪ'tjuːʃən(ə)l] **ADJ 1** *Pol etc (monarchy, regime, reform)* constitutionnel; **the president's actions are not c.** les actions du président sont anticonstitutionnelles **2** *Med (disorder)* diathésique **N** *(short walk)* (petite) promenade *f*

constitutionally [kɒnstɪ'tjuːʃən(ə)lɪ] **ADV 1** *Pol (act)* constitutionnellement **2** *(by nature) (lazy, weak, strong)* de *ou* par nature

constitutive ['kɒnstɪtjuːtɪv] **ADJ** constitutif

constrain [kən'streɪn] **VT 1** *(compel) (person)* contraindre, forcer (**to do** à *ou* de faire); **to find oneself constrained to do sth** se voir contraint de faire qch **2** *(restrict movement of) (of clothing etc)* gêner; *(of person)* contenir; **she did not feel constrained by the conventions of her time** elle ne se sentait pas obligée d'obéir aux conventions sociales de son époque

constrained [kən'streɪnd] **ADJ** *(air)* contraint, gêné; *(voice)* forcé; *(smile)* contraint

constraint [kən'streɪnt] **N 1** *(compulsion, restriction)* contrainte *f*, *Law etc* coercition *f*; **to do sth under c.** faire qch sous la contrainte **2** *(of manner)* gêne *f*, contrainte *f* **3** *(self-control)* retenue *f*; **to speak about sth without c.** parler librement de qch

constrict [kən'strɪkt] **VT** *(opening)* resserrer,

rétrécir; *(of clothing) (movements)* entraver **VI** se resserrer

constricted [kən'strɪktɪd] **ADJ** *(opening, passage)* étroit

constriction [kən'strɪkʃən] **N** resserrement *m*, rétrécissement *m*; *Med* constriction *f*

constrictor [kən'strɪktər] **N** *Anat* (muscle *m)* constricteur *m*; **boa c.** boa *m* constricteur

construct [kən'strʌkt] **VT** *(building, machine, novel)* construire; *(phrase, play)* **well/badly constructed** bien/mal agencé *ou* construit

construct ['kɒnstrʌkt] **N** *Phil (idea)* concept *m*

construction [kən'strʌkʃən] **N 1** *(of building, ship, machine etc)* construction *f*; **under c.** en (cours de) construction **2** *(thing constructed)* construction *f* **3** *Gram* construction *f* **4** *(interpretation) (of action etc)* interprétation *f*; **to put a good/bad c. on sb's words/actions** interpréter en bien/en mal les paroles/actions de qn; **to put another c. on sth** interpréter qch d'une autre façon
▸▸ **the c. industry** le bâtiment; **c. set** jeu *m* de construction; **c. site** chantier *m* (de construction); **c. worker** ouvrier *m* du bâtiment

constructional [kən'strʌkʃən(ə)l] **ADJ** de construction; *(technique)* mécanique
▸▸ *Tech* **c. engineering** construction *f* mécanique

constructive [kən'strʌktɪv] **ADJ 1** *(criticism, remark)* constructif; *(mind)* créateur **2** *(relating to construction)* de construction
▸▸ *Ind* **c. dismissal** = démission *f* provoquée par la conduite de l'employeur

constructively [kən'strʌktɪvlɪ] **ADV** *(to criticize)* d'une manière constructive

constructor [kən'strʌktər] **N** constructeur, -trice

construe [kən'struː] **VT** *(interpret) (sb's words)* interpréter; **the phrase can be construed to mean two things** on peut interpréter l'expression de deux manières différentes

consul ['kɒns(ə)l] **N** *(diplomat)* consul *m*
▸▸ **c. general** consul *m* général

consular ['kɒnsjʊlər] **ADJ** consulaire
▸▸ *Com* **c. fees** frais *mpl* consulaires; *Com* **c. invoice** facture *f* consulaire

consulate ['kɒnsjʊlət] **N** *(office)* consulat *m*
▸▸ **c. general** consulat général

consult **VT** *(doctor, dictionary etc)* consulter (**on, about** sur)
VI consulter (**with sb** qn); **to c. together** se consulter
N *Fam* = **consultation**

consultancy [kən'sʌltənsɪ] **N 1** *(company)* cabinet *m* d'expert-conseil; *(advice)* assistance *f* technique; **to do c. work** être consultant **2** *Br Med (post)* poste *m* de médecin/chirurgien consultant
▸▸ **c. fees** frais *mpl* de conseil; **c. firm** cabinet *m* d'expert-conseil; **c. service** service *m* d'assistance technique

consultant [kən'sʌltənt] **N 1** *Com, Ind etc* consultant, -ante; **engineering c.** ingénieur *m* conseil; **beauty c.** esthéticien, -ienne; *(for face)* visagiste *mf*; **financial c.** conseiller, -ère financier(ière) **2** *Br Med* médecin *m*/chirurgien, -ienne spécialiste, consultant, -ante

consultation [kɒnsəl'teɪʃən] **N** *(of person, dictionary etc), Law* consultation *f*; *(as a group)* délibération *f*; **in c. with sb** en consultation avec qn; **to hold a c.** délibérer, conférer

consultative [kən'sʌltətɪv] **ADJ** *(committee)* consultatif; **to play a c. role** avoir un rôle de consultant *ou* de conseil

consulting [kən'sʌltɪŋ] **ADJ** *(doctor)* consultant; *(engineer)* conseil

▸▸ *Med* **c. room** cabinet *m* de consultation; **c. service** (service *m* de) conseil *m*

consumable [kən'sjuːməb(ə)l] **N** produit *m* ou article *m* ou bien *m* de consommation; *Comput* **computer consumables** petit matériel *m* informatique
ADJ consommable
▸▸ *Com, Econ* **c. goods** produits *mpl* de consommation

consume [kən'sjuːm] **VT** *(food, drink, fuel etc)* consommer; *(exhaust)* épuiser; *(of fire) (building etc)* consumer, dévorer; **the discussion consumed many hours** la discussion a pris de nombreuses heures; **to be consumed with** *(desire)* brûler de; *(jealousy, envy, curiosity)* être en proie à

> When translating **to consume**, note that the French verbs **consommer** and **consumer** are not interchangeable. **Consommer** always refers to consumer activity, while **consumer** is used to describe the process of being eaten up or destroyed, especially by fire.

consumer [kən'sjuːmər] **N** consommateur, -trice; **gas/electricity consumers** abonnés *mpl* au gaz/à l'électricité
▸▸ **c. advocate** défenseur *m* des intérêts des consommateurs; *Mktg* **c. behaviour** comportement *m* du consommateur; *Mktg* **c. benefit** bénéfice *m* consommateur; *Com, Mktg* **c. brand** marque *f* grand public; *Com, Mktg* **c. credit** crédit *m* à la consommation; *Com, Econ* **c. debt** endettement *m* des consommateurs; *Com, Mktg* **c. demand** demande *f* des consommateurs; *Com, Econ* **c. durables** biens *mpl* de consommation durables; **c. expenditure** dépenses *fpl* de consommation; **c. goods** biens de consommation durables; *Com, Econ* **c. industry** industrie *f* de consommation; **c. journalism** = journalisme *m* dans le cadre de la défense des consommateurs; **c. loan** prêt *m* à la consommation; **c. magazine** magazine *m* pour les consommateurs; *Com, Econ* **c. market** marché *m* de la consommation; *Com, Econ* **c. nondurables** biens de grande consommation; *Com* **c. organization** organisme *m* de défense des consommateurs; *Mktg* **c. panel** groupe-témoin *m*, *pl* groupes-témoins, panel *m* de consommateurs; *Com, Econ* **c. price index** indice *m* des prix à la consommation; *Com, Econ* **c. protection** défense *f* des consommateurs; **c. protection agency** bureau *m* d'accueil des consommateurs; *Mktg* **c. research** étude *f* de marché; *Mktg* **c. resistance** résistance *f* ou réticence *f* des consommateurs; **c. society** société *f* de consommation; *Mktg* **c. survey** étude auprès des consommateurs finaux; *Mktg* **c. welfare** intérêt *m* du consommateur

consumerism [kən'sjuːmərɪz(ə)m] **N** consumérisme *m*

consummate ['kɒnsəmɪt, kən'sʌmɪt] **ADJ** *(art)* consommé, achevé; *(liar)* fieffé; *(snob, hypocrite)* parfait; *(linguist, cook, musician etc)* de premier ordre; **she was c. in the art of concealing her feelings** elle était maître dans l'art de cacher ses sentiments; **to be a c. master of one's craft** connaître à fond son métier

consummate ['kɒnsjəmeɪt] **VT** *(marriage, relationship)* consommer

consummation [kɒnsə'meɪʃən] **N 1** *(of marriage, relationship)* consommation *f* **2** *(of ambition, career)* aboutissement *m*

consumption [kən'sʌmpʃən] **N 1** *(of goods, heat, coal, petrol etc)* consommation *f*; **unfit for human c.** impropre à la consommation; *Econ* **home c.** consommation intérieure; *Fig* **the president's remarks were strictly for domestic c.** les remarques du président ne s'adressaient qu'à son pays **2** *Med Old-fashioned* consomption *f*, phtisie *f*

▸▸*Econ* **c. expenditure, c. spending** dépenses *fpl* de consommation

consumptive [kən'sʌmptɪv] **ADJ, N** *Med Old-fashioned* phtisique *mf*

cont 1 *abbr* **contents 2** (*abbr* **continued**) suite

contact ['kɒntækt] **N 1** (*act of touching*) contact *m*; **to come into c. with** entrer en contact avec, toucher; **the substance must not come into c. with the air** la substance ne doit pas être exposée à l'air; **point of c.** (*of two curves etc*) point *m* de contact **2** (*between people*) rapport *m*, contact *m*; **to be in/come into c. with sb** être/entrer en contact *ou* en rapport avec qn; **are you still in c.?** (*of two people*) est-ce que vous êtes toujours en contact?; **the two leaders are in close c.** les deux dirigeants sont en contact étroit; **he didn't get in c. (with me/them/**etc**)** il n'est pas entré en contact (avec moi/eux/etc), il ne m'a/les a/etc pas contacté(s); **to put sb in c. with sb** mettre qn en rapport avec qn; **she hadn't come into c. with poverty** elle ne s'était pas trouvée au contact de la pauvreté; **anyone who has come into c. with the sick man** quiconque s'est trouvé au contact du malade; **to make c. with sb** (*by radio etc*) contacter qn, prendre contact avec qn; **after three days they made c. with civilization** après trois jours ils ont pris contact avec la civilisation; **to make eye c. with sb** rencontrer le regard de qn; **we made eye c.** nos regards se sont croisés; *Mil* **to establish c. with the enemy** prendre contact avec l'ennemi **3** (*contact lens*) verre *m ou* lentille *f* de contact; **to wear contacts** porter des lentilles de contact **4** *Med* (*person*) = personne *f* ayant approché un malade contagieux; **sexual c.** partenaire *mf* sexuel(elle) **5** (*acquaintance etc*) relation *f*, **I have a c. who may be able to help you** je connais quelqu'un qui pourrait vous aider; **who's our c. in Paris?** qui est notre contact à Paris? **6** *Elec etc* (*state, part*) contact *m*

VT se mettre en contact *ou* en rapport *ou* en relation avec, *Fam* contacter; **I can be contacted at this address** on peut me contacter à cette adresse

▸▸*Elec* **c. breaker** disjoncteur *m*; *Elec* **c. breaker plate** plateau *m* porte-rupteur; *Elec* **c. breaker points** contacts *mpl* rupteur; **c. lens** lentille *f* de contact; *Phot* **c. print** planche *f* contact, épreuve *f* par contact; **c. sport** sport *m* de contact

contactable [kɒn'tæktəb(ə)l] **ADJ** joignable

contagion [kən'teɪdʒən] **N** *Lit, Fig* contagion *f*

contagious [kən'teɪdʒəs] **ADJ** (*disease*) contagieux; *Fig* (*laughter*) communicatif, contagieux

contagiousness [kən'teɪdʒəsnɪs] **N** contagiosité *f*, *Fig* **the c. of laughter** la contagion du rire

contain [kən'teɪn] **VT 1** (*hold*) contenir **2** (*include*) (*of book, medicine etc*) contenir; **the ore contains a high percentage of iron** le minerai a une forte teneur en fer; **the document contains a reference to …** le document contient une référence à … **3** (*control*) (*rage, emotion, inflation*) contenir, maîtriser; *Mil* (*enemy*) contenir; (*epidemic, spread of an idea*) circonscrire; **he was unable to c. his laughter** il ne pouvait pas s'empêcher de rire; **I could no longer c. myself** je ne pouvais plus me contenir davantage

container [kən'teɪnər] **N 1** récipient *m* **2** (*for transport*) conteneur *m*

▸▸**c. depot** entrepôt *m* de conteneurs, dépôt *m* pour conteneurs; **c. lorry** = camion *m* adapté au transport des conteneurs; **c. port** port *m* pour conteneurs; **c. premium** prime *f* contenant; **c. ship** navire *m* porte-conteneurs, porte-conteneurs *m inv*; **c. terminal** terminal *m* à conteneurs; **c. truck** = camion *m* adapté au transport des conteneurs

containerization [kənteɪnəraɪ'zeɪʃən] **N** conteneurisation *f*, (*of port*) conversion *f* à la conteneurisation

containerize [kən'teɪnəraɪz] **VT** mettre en conteneur, conteneuriser; (*port*) convertir à la conteneurisation

containerized freight [kən'teɪnəraɪzd] **N** fret *m* par conteneur

containment [kən'teɪnmənt] **N 1** (*of disease, ideology*) action *f* de circonscrire; **a policy of c.** une politique d'endiguement **2** *Nucl* confinement *m*

contaminate [kən'tæmɪneɪt] **VT** contaminer; **contaminated air** air *m* vicié; *Fig* **he has been contaminated by contact with political activists** il a été contaminé au contact d'activistes

contamination [kəntæmɪ'neɪʃən] **N** (*bacterial, radioactive etc*) contamination *f*

contango, *pl* **contangoes** [kən'tæŋɡəʊ, -əʊz] **N** *Br St Exch* report *m*; (*percentage*) taux *m* du report

contd (*abbr* **continued**) suite; **c. on p.14** suite à la page 14; **to be c.** à suivre

contemplate ['kɒntempleɪt] **VT 1** (*look at*) contempler **2** (*think about, consider*) (*the universe, the past, one's life*) réfléchir à, méditer sur **3** (*envisage*) envisager; **to c. doing sth** envisager de *ou* songer à faire qch; **it's too awful to c.** c'est insupportable rien que d'y penser; **to c. suicide** songer au suicide; **that was never contemplated** il n'a jamais été question de cela

VI se recueillir, méditer

contemplation [kɒntem'pleɪʃən] **N 1** (*of painting, shop window etc*) contemplation *f* **2** (*thinking about*) **they sat in silent c. of …** ils méditaient en silence sur … **3** (*meditation*) contemplation *f*

contemplative [kən'templətɪv] **ADJ** *Rel* (*life, order*) contemplatif

contemporaneous [kəntempə'reɪnɪəs] **ADJ** contemporain (**with** de)

contemporaneously [kəntempə'reɪnɪəslɪ] **ADV** **c. with …** à la même période *ou* époque que …

contemporary [kən'temp(ə)rərɪ] **ADJ 1** (*of same time*) contemporain (**with** de) **2** (*present day*) contemporain, actuel, moderne

N **our contemporaries** nos contemporains *mpl*; **she and I are contemporaries** elle et moi sommes de la même génération; **a c. of mine at school** quelqu'un qui était dans la même année que moi à l'école

contempt [kən'tempt] **N** mépris *m*, dédain *m*; **to hold sb/sth in c.** mépriser qn/qch; **to treat sb/sth with c.** traiter qn/qch avec dédain *ou* mépris; **it is/he is beneath c.** c'est/il est tout ce qu'il y a de plus méprisable; **her c. for the law/our opinions** son mépris de la loi/nos opinions; **I have nothing but c. for him** je n'éprouve que du mépris pour lui; *Law* **c. of court** outrage *m* au tribunal, offense *f* à la cour

contemptible [kən'temptəb(ə)l] **ADJ** méprisable

contemptibly [kən'temptɪblɪ] **ADV** (*to say, to look at*) avec mépris; **a c. small amount** une quantité dérisoirement faible

contemptuous [kən'temptjʊəs] **ADJ** (*air, person*) méprisant; (*gesture, word*) de mépris, méprisant; **to be c. of sth** mépriser qch

contemptuously [kən'temptʊəslɪ] **ADV** avec mépris, avec dédain

contend [kən'tend] **VI** (*struggle*) affronter, lutter (**with, against** contre); (*argue*) se disputer (**with** avec; **about** sur); **the difficulties I have to c. with** les difficultés que je dois affronter; **they still had the perimeter fence to c. with** il leur restait encore à régler le problème de la clôture d'enceinte; **I have a lot to c. with** je dois faire face à beaucoup de problèmes; **several candidates were contending for the job** plusieurs candidats étaient en compétition pour le poste

VT (*maintain, argue*) **to c. that …** prétendre *ou* soutenir que …

contender [kən'tendər] **N** concurrent, -ente; (*in election*) candidat, -ate; *Sport etc* (*for title*) challenger *m* (**for sth** de qch); **he is the main c. in the battle for the leadership** c'est le grand favori dans la lutte pour la position de leader

contending [kən'tendɪŋ] **ADJ** **the c. parties** les concurrents *mpl*; **the c. armies** les armées *fpl* opposées

content¹ ['kɒntent] **N** VOIR GRAMMAIRE A10 **1** *Chem, Miner etc* teneur *f*; **gold/moisture c.** teneur en or/humidité; **high protein/fibre/fat c.** haute teneur en protéines/fibres/lipides; **peanut butter has a high protein c.** le beurre de cacahuètes est riche en protéines **2** (*of book, film, speech*) contenu *m*; (*meaning*) teneur *f*, fond *m*; **there is more emphasis on style than on c.** une plus grande importance est accordée au style qu'au fond

▸▸*Comput* **c. provider** fournisseur *m* de contenu

content² [kən'tent] **ADJ** content, satisfait (**with** de); **they were poor but c.** ils étaient pauvres mais heureux; **to be c. with sth** se contenter de qch; **he's quite c. to stay at home** il ne demande pas mieux que de rester à la maison; **she's never c. to just watch a film, she has to make comments** il ne lui suffit pas de regarder un film, il faut qu'elle fasse des commentaires; **not c. with having ruined our evening, he came round next day** non content d'avoir gâché notre soirée, il revint le lendemain

VT contenter, satisfaire; **to c. oneself with (doing) sth** se contenter de (faire) qch

N = contentment

contented [kən'tentɪd] **ADJ** content, satisfait (**with** de); (*smile*) de satisfaction; **he's a very c. baby** il est toujours content, ce bébé

contentedly [kən'tentɪdlɪ] **ADV** avec contentement; **to live c.** vivre heureux

contentedness [kən'tentɪdnɪs] **N** contentement *m*

contention [kən'tenʃən] **N 1** (*struggle*) lutte *f*, (*argument*) dispute *f* **2** (*competition*) **to be in c.** être en compétition (**for sth** pour qch); **the teams in c.** les équipes concurrentes *ou* rivales **3** (*opinion*) affirmation *f*, **my c. is that …** je soutiens que …

contentious [kən'tenʃəs] **ADJ 1** (*issue etc*) controversé **2** (*person, mood*) querelleur

contentment [kən'tentmənt] **N** contentement *m*; **a smile of c.** un sourire de satisfaction

contents ['kɒntents] **NPL** (*of box, drawer, house etc*) contenu *m*; **(table of) c.** (*of book*) table *f* des matières VOIR GRAMMAIRE A10

▸▸**c. insurance** assurance *f* mobilier; **c. list** liste *f* du contenu; **c. page** table des matières

contest¹ ['kɒntest] **N 1** (*competition*) concours *m*; *Sport* compétition *f*, *Boxing etc* combat *m*; *Pol* **presidential c.** élection *f* présidentielle; *Fig* **there's simply no c.** il n'y a aucune comparaison; **beauty c.** concours de beauté **2** (*struggle*) combat *m*, lutte *f* (**with**

avec, contre; **between** entre) **3** *Am Law* **no c.** pas de témoins à charge

contest² [kən'test] **VT 1** *(call into question) (right, ability, will, inheritance)* contester; **to c. sb's right to do sth** contester à qn le droit de faire qch; *Fin* **contested debt** créance *f* litigieuse **2** *Pol (seat in Parliament)* se porter candidat pour; **to c. an election** disputer *ou* se présenter à une élection; *Sport* **to c. a race** participer à une course; *Pol* **a hotly contested seat** un siège très disputé

contestant [kən'testənt] **N** concurrent, -ente; *(in boxing, wrestling etc)* combattant *m*

contestation [kɒntes'teɪʃən] **N** *Fml (of right etc)* contestation *f*

context ['kɒntekst] **N** contexte *m*; **in this c.** *(regard)* à ce propos; **in/out of c.** en/hors contexte; **she was quoted out of c.** on a cité ses paroles hors de leur contexte; **in the c. of** dans le contexte de; **to put sth into c.** replacer qch dans son contexte

context-dependent **ADJ** **to be c.** dépendre du contexte

context-sensitive **ADJ** *Comput (spell-checker)* contextuel

contextual [kən'tekstjʊəl] **ADJ** contextuel

contextualize [kən'tekstjʊəlaɪz] **VT** *(historical event, film etc)* placer dans son contexte; *(word, expression)* contextualiser, donner dans un contexte

contextually [kən'tekstjʊəlɪ] **ADV** *(to examine)* dans son contexte; **to be c. dependent** dépendre du contexte

contiguous [kən'tɪgjʊəs] **ADJ** *Fml* contigu, -uë (**to** à, avec)

continence ['kɒntɪnəns] **N 1** *Physiol (control of bladder, bowel)* continence *f* **2** *Fml (sexual)* chasteté *f*

continent¹ ['kɒntɪnənt] **N** *Geog* continent *m*; *Br* **the C.** l'Europe *f* continentale; *Br* **on the C.** en Europe (continentale)

continent² **ADJ 1** *(in control of bladder, bowel)* continent **2** *Fml (sexually)* chaste

continental [kɒntɪ'nent(ə)l] **ADJ 1** *Geog* continental, -aux **2** *Br (European)* de l'Europe continentale

▪ **N** *Br (European)* continental, -ale, habitant, -ante de l'Europe (continentale)

▸▸ **c. breakfast** petit déjeuner *m* à la française; *Geol* **c. drift** dérive *f* des continents; *Am* **c. plan** *(at hotel)* tarif *m* chambre avec petit déjeuner à la française; **c. quilt** couette *f*, duvet *m*; *Geol* **c. shelf** plateau *m* continental, plate-forme *f* continentale, *pl* plates-formes continentales

Continental Breakfast
Ce terme désigne un petit déjeuner léger, par opposition au breakfast anglais, beaucoup plus copieux et comportant un plat chaud.

contingency [kən'tɪndʒənsɪ] **N 1** *(unexpected event)* éventualité *f*; **to provide for every c.** parer à toute éventualité; **contingencies** *(item on balance sheet)* frais divers; **prepared for all contingencies** préparé à toutes les éventualités; **to allow for contingencies** parer aux imprévus **2** *Fml (uncertainty) (of events)* contingence *f*

▸▸ *Fin* **c. fund** fonds *mpl* de prévoyance; **c. plan** plan *m* d'urgence; **c. tax** impôt *m* imprévu

contingent [kən'tɪndʒənt] **ADJ 1** *(conditional)* conditionnel; **c. on sth** sous réserve de qch; **to be c. (up)on sth** *(of event)* dépendre de qch **2** *Phil* contingent

▪ **N** *Mil etc* contingent *m*; **a c. of holidaymakers** un contingent de vacanciers

▸▸ *Acct* **c. liability** passif *m* éventuel *ou* exigible; *St Exch* **c. order** ordre *m* conditionnel

continual [kən'tɪnjʊəl] **ADJ** continuel, incessant

Attention: ne pas confondre avec l'adjectif **continuous**.

continually [kən'tɪnjʊəlɪ] **ADV** continuellement, sans cesse

Attention: ne pas confondre avec l'adverbe **continuously**.

continuance [kən'tɪnjʊəns] **N 1** *(continuation)* continuation *f*; **the c. of these abuses is a scandal** il est scandaleux que ces abus puissent continuer **2** *Am Law* ajournement *m*

continuation [kəntɪnjʊ'eɪʃən] **N 1** *(action) (of work, project etc)* continuation *f*; *(of road)* prolongement *m* **2** *(result) (of wall, road etc)* prolongement *m*; *(of novel)* suite *f*, **to be a c. of ...** faire suite à ... *St Exch* report *m*

continue [kən'tɪnjuː] **VT 1** *(work, activity etc)* continuer, poursuivre; *(straight line)* prolonger; *(journey)* poursuivre; *(conversation)* continuer; *(after interruption)* reprendre; *(species, tradition)* perpétuer; **to c. one's studies** poursuivre ses études; *(later in life)* reprendre ses études; **to c. to do sth** *or* **doing sth** continuer à *ou* de faire qch; **after lunch we continued working** après le déjeuner nous avons repris notre travail; *Journ* **to be continued** à suivre; **continued on page 30** suite à la page 30

2 *Am Law (trial)* ajourner

▪ **VI 1** continuer; *(of line)* se prolonger; **the situation cannot c.** la situation ne peut pas durer; **the situation continued into the 1990s** la situation s'est prolongée jusque dans le courant des années 1990; **to c. in office** garder sa charge; *(of political party)* rester au pouvoir; **she will c. as director until December** elle gardera les fonctions de directrice jusqu'en décembre; **his bad luck continues** ses malheurs se poursuivent; **to c. on one's way** continuer son chemin; **they continued to Rome** ils ont poursuivi leur chemin jusqu'à Rome

2 *(resume talking)* continuer; **'and then', he continued** 'et puis', continua-t-il

continued [kən'tɪnjuːd] **ADJ** *(effort, interest)* soutenu

continuing [kən'tɪnjuːɪŋ] **ADJ** continu; *(interest)* soutenu; **the c. story of a small American town** *(TV serial etc)* l'histoire *f* d'une petite ville américaine

▸▸ **c. education** formation *f* permanente *ou* continue; **c. education class** cours *mpl* de formation permanente *ou* continue

continuity [kɒntɪ'njuːɪtɪ] **N 1** continuité *f*, **to ensure c.** assurer la continuité (**between** entre) **2** *Cin, TV* continuité *f*

▸▸ *TV, Radio* **c. announcement** annonce *f* de continuité; *TV, Radio* **c. announcer** speaker, -ine (de transition); *Cin, TV* **c. girl** scripte *f*, *Cin, TV* **c. man** scripte *m*

continuous [kən'tɪnjʊəs] **ADJ 1** *(uninterrupted)* continu, ininterrompu; *(unbroken)* continu **2** *Gram* progressif **VOIR GRAMMAIRE A49–51; B30**

▸▸ *Sch, Univ* **c. assessment** contrôle *m* continu; *Mktg* **c. innovation** innovation *f* continue; *Comput* **c. mode** mode *m* continu; *Comput* **c. paper** papier *m* (en) continu; *Cin* **c. performance** cinéma *m* permanent; *Comput* **c. stationery** papier (en) continu

Attention: ne pas confondre avec l'adjectif **continual**.

continuously [kən'tɪnjʊəslɪ] **ADV** continuellement, continûment, sans interruption

▸▸ *Aut* **c. variable transmission** transmission *f* à réglage continu, transmission CVT

Attention: ne pas confondre avec l'adverbe **continually**.

contort [kən'tɔːt] **VT** *(features etc)* tordre; **face contorted by pain** visage tordu par la douleur

▪ **VI** **his face contorted with rage/pain** il grimaçait de rage/de douleur

contortion [kən'tɔːʃən] **N** *(of features etc)* crispation *f*, *(of body)* contorsion *f*, *Fig* **he went through all sorts of contortions to justify this decision** il a fait des pieds et des mains pour justifier cette décision

contortionist [kən'tɔːʃənɪst] **N** contorsionniste *mf*; **a c. act** un numéro de contorsionnisme; **you have to be a c. to get into this car!** il faut faire toute une gymnastique *ou* tout un tas de contorsions pour monter dans cette voiture

contour ['kɒntʊər] **N** *(line)* courbe *f* de niveau, *(of object)* contour *m*; **the contours of the hill** les contours de la colline

▸▸ **c. line** *(on map)* courbe de niveau, courbe hypsométrique; **c. map** carte *f* topographique

Contra ['kɒntrə] **N** *Pol* Contra *m*

contra ['kɒntrə] **PREP** contre

▪ **N** *Acct* **per c.** par contre; **as per c.** en contrepartie, porté ci-contre

▪ **VT** *Acct* contrepasser

▸▸ *Acct* **c. account** compte *m* de contrepartie *ou* d'autre part; *Acct* **c. entry** article *m ou* écriture *f* inverse, contre-passation *f*, *pl* contre-passations

contraband ['kɒntrəbænd] **N** contrebande *f*, **c. goods** marchandises *fpl* de contrebande

contrabass ['kɒntrəbeɪs] **N** *Mus* contrebasse *f*

contrabassoon [kɒntrəbə'suːn] **N** *Mus* contrebasson *m*

contraception [kɒntrə'sepʃən] **N** contraception *f*, **method of c.** méthode *f* contraceptive *ou* de contraception

contraceptive [kɒntrə'septɪv] *Med* **N** contraceptif *m*

▪ **ADJ** contraceptif

▸▸ **c. advice** conseils *mpl* sur la contraception; **c. device** contraceptif; **c. method** méthode *f* contraceptive *ou* de contraception; **c. pill** pilule *f* contraceptive; **c. sponge** éponge *f* contraceptive

contract¹ ['kɒntrækt] **N** contrat *m*; *(of sale)* acte *m* de vente; **marriage c.** contrat de mariage; **to draw up a c.** dresser *ou* rédiger un contrat; **to bind oneself by c.** s'engager par contrat; **to sign a c.** signer un contrat; **to break one's c.** rompre son contrat; **that isn't in my c.** ce n'est pas dans mon contrat; **to be under c.** être sous contrat (**to** avec); **to enter into a c.** *(of person)* passer (un) contrat (**with** avec); **they were given a c. to build the new road** ils se sont vu attribuer le contrat pour construire la nouvelle route; **to put work out to c.** faire effectuer un travail en sous-traitance; **to tender for a c.** soumissionner à une adjudication; **conditions of c.** *(in tender)* cahier *m* des charges; **breach of c.** rupture *f* de contrat; **you are in breach of c.** vous violez *ou* vous ne respectez pas votre contrat; *Sl* **there was a c. out on him** *(he was to be murdered)* un tueur à gages avait été engagé pour le tuer

▸▸ *St Exch* **c. bond** garantie *f* d'exécution; *Cards* **c. bridge** bridge *m* contrat; **c. killer** tueur *m* à gages; **c. labour** main-d'œuvre *f* contractuelle; **c. law** droit *m* des contrats; *St Exch* **c. note** avis *m* d'exécution, avis d'opération sur titre; **c. staff** personnel *m* en contrat à durée déterminée *ou* en CDD;

(in public sector) contractuels *mpl*; **c. work** travail *m* en sous-traitant

contract² [kən'trækt] **VT 1** *(obligation, illness)* contracter; *(habit)* prendre; **to c. debts** s'endetter **2** *Com* **to c. to do sth** s'engager (par contrat) à faire qch; **she has contracted to make two films** elle a signé un contrat pour faire deux films **3** *(muscles)* contracter; *(features)* crisper; *Physiol (tissues)* resserrer; *Ling* **to c. 'shall not' into 'shan't'** contracter 'shall not' en 'shan't'

VI 1 *Com* **to c. for a supply of sth** s'engager à fournir qch; **to c. for work** entreprendre des travaux à forfait **2** *(of metal, muscle etc)* se contracter; *(of opening, material)* rétrécir; **the pupil contracts in bright light** la pupille se contracte à la lumière intense; *Ling* **'cannot' contracts into 'can't'** 'cannot' se contracte en 'can't' VOIR GRAMMAIRE A66

▸ **contract in** *VI Br (into insurance scheme)* souscrire; *Hist (into trade union)* s'inscrire au syndicat

▸ **contract out** *VI Br (out of insurance policy, pension plan)* arrêter de souscrire (**of** à); *(of hospital)* se retirer du service public; *Hist (of union member)* cesser de payer sa cotisation au syndicat

VT SEP *Com (work)* donner en sous-traitance (**to** à)

contract-awarding party [-əwɔːdɪŋ] **N** adjudicateur *m*

contracting [kən'træktɪŋ] **ADJ**
▸▸ **c. company** *(party to a contract)* contractant *m*; *(sub-contractor)* sous-traitant *m*, *pl* sous-traitants; **c. parties** contractants *mpl*

contraction [kən'trækʃən] **N 1** *(of metal, pupil etc)* contraction *f*, *(of muscle)* contraction, contracture *f*, *(of material)* rétrécissement *m*; *Physiol (of tissues)* resserrement *m*; *Obst* **contractions have begun** les contractions ont commencé **2** *Ling (of two words)* contraction *f*; *(word)* mot *m* contracté **3** *Fml* **c. of debts** endettement *m*

contractor [kən'træktər] **N 1** *(firm of builders)* entrepreneur *m* (en bâtiment); *(building worker)* ouvrier *m* en bâtiment; **the contractors haven't finished yet** les ouvriers n'ont pas encore fini **2** *(company, supplier)* **haulage c.** entreprise *f* de transports; **arms c.** fournisseur *m* d'armement **3** *(party to a contract)* entrepreneur *m*

contractual [kən'træktʃəl] **ADJ** *(agreement, obligations etc)* contractuel; **on the present c. basis** selon les stipulations actuelles du contrat
▸▸ *Acct* **c. allowance** indemnité *f* conventionnelle; **c. cover** *(in insurance)* garantie *f* conventionnelle; *Com, Fin* **c. date** date *f* contractuelle; *Com, Fin* **c. guarantee** garantie contractuelle; *Com, Fin* **c. liability** responsabilité *f* contractuelle; *Com, Fin* **c. price** prix *m* contractuel

contractually [kən'træktʃəlɪ] **ADV** *(bound, obliged)* par contrat; *(stipulated)* dans le contrat; **I'm c. forbidden to …** le contrat m'interdit de …

contradict [kɒntrə'dɪkt] **VT** *(person)* contredire; *(rumour)* démentir; **to c. oneself** se contredire; **the statements of the witnesses c. each other** les dépositions des témoins se contredisent

contradiction [kɒntrə'dɪkʃən] **N** contradiction *f*; **this was a c. of what they had previously said** c'était un démenti de ce qu'ils avaient dit auparavant; **in c. with** en contradiction avec; **it's a c. in terms** c'est parfaitement contradictoire, c'est une contradiction dans les termes; **he's full of contradictions** il est plein de contradictions

contradictory [kɒntrə'dɪktərɪ] **ADJ 1** *(statement etc)* contradictoire (**to** à) **2** *Fam (per-*

son) raisonneur; **don't be so c.** ne sois pas aussi raisonneur

contradistinction [ˈkɒntrədɪsˈtɪŋkʃən] **N** *Fml* **in c. to …** contrairement à …

contra(-)flow **N** *Br Aut* contre-courant *m*, *pl* contre-courants
▸▸ **c. system** système *m* de circulation à contre-sens

contraindication [ˈkɒntrəˌɪndɪˈkeɪʃən] **N** *Med* contre-indication *f*, *pl* contre-indications

contralto [kən'træltəʊ] *Mus* **N** contralto *m*
ADJ de contralto

contraption [kən'træpʃən] **N** *Fam* machin *m*, engin *m*, truc *m*

contrapuntal [ˌkɒntrə'pʌnt(ə)l] **ADJ** *Mus (piece, accompaniment etc)* en contrepoint

contrarily [kən'treərɪlɪ] **ADV** de façon contrariante

contrariness [kən'treərɪnɪs] **N** esprit *m* de contradiction

contrariwise [ˈkɒntrərɪwaɪz] **ADV 1** *(on the other hand)* au contraire **2** *(in the opposite direction)* dans le sens opposé **3** [kən'treərɪwaɪz] *(perversely)* par esprit de contradiction

contrary ['kɒntrərɪ] **N** contraire *m*; **on the c.** au contraire; **unless you hear to the c.** sauf avis contraire
ADJ 1 *(opposite)* contraire (**to** à); *(interests etc)* opposé (**to** à); **c. to nature** contre nature; **c. to reason** contraire à la raison; **c. to the terms of the contract** contraire aux termes du contrat **2** *Fml (winds)* contraire **3** [kən'treərɪ] *(person)* contrariant, qui a l'esprit de contradiction; *(remark)* formulé par esprit de contradiction
ADV contrairement (**to** à); **to act c. to instructions** contrevenir aux ordres reçus; **c. to my expectations** contre mon attente; **c. to what I was told** contrairement à ce qu'on m'a dit

contrast¹ ['kɒntrɑːst] **N** *(difference)*, *Comput, TV, Phot, Art* contraste *m* (**between** entre); **in c. with** *or* **to sth/sb** par contraste avec qch/qn; **by c. the president was almost optimistic** par contraste, le président était presque optimiste; **to form a c. to …** faire contraste avec …; **as a c. to …** comme contraste à …
▸▸ **c. button** bouton *m* de contraste; **c. control** réglage *m* du contraste

contrast² [kən'trɑːst] **VT** faire contraster, mettre en contraste (**with** avec); **it was impossible not to c. her attitude with her brother's** c'était impossible de ne pas comparer son attitude à celle de son frère
VI contraster (**with** avec); **to c. strongly** trancher (**with** sur)

contrasting [kən'trɑːstɪŋ] **ADJ** *(colours)* contrasté; *(opinion, attitude, temperament)* opposé; **the c. yellow on the wall opposite** le jaune qui fait contraste sur le mur d'en face

contrasty ['kɒntrɑːstɪ] **ADJ** *Phot* contrasté

contravene [kɒntrə'viːn] **VT** *(law etc)* transgresser, enfreindre; *(rule)* enfreindre, être en contravention avec

contravention [kɒntrə'venʃən] **N** *(of law)* infraction *f*; **to act in c. of the law** enfreindre la loi

contribute [kən'trɪbjuːt] **VT** donner; *(money)* donner, verser; **to c. one's time** donner de son temps; **to c. one's share** payer sa part; **she contributed \$50,000 to the cause** elle a versé 50 000 dollars au profit de la cause; **he didn't c. anything to the discussion** il n'a rien apporté à la discussion; **to c. an article to a newspaper** écrire un article pour un journal
VI 1 contribuer; **if everyone contributes**

we'll be able to get a bigger present si tout le monde participe, nous pourrons acheter un cadeau plus important; **he rarely contributes to discussions** il contribue rarement aux discussions; **to c. to a charity** donner à une œuvre de charité; **to c. to a newspaper** collaborer à un journal; **to c. to the success** contribuer au succès; **everything contributed to make him happy** tout contribuait à le rendre heureux **2** *(to pension scheme etc)* cotiser (**to** à)

contribution [kɒntrɪ'bjuːʃən] **N 1** contribution *f*; *(to meal, present etc)* contribution, participation *f*; **I've already made a c.** *(to sb collecting for charity)* j'ai déjà donné; **contributions welcome** *(to charity)* toutes les contributions sont les bienvenues; **their c. to the carnival was a brass band** leur participation au carnaval s'est concrétisée par une fanfare
2 *Journ (article)* article *m*
3 *Fin (to pension plan, NIC etc)* cotisation *f*
4 *Acct (in management accounting)* marge *f* (brute); **c. in kind** apport *m* en nature
▸▸ *Acct* **c. margin** marge sur les coûts variables

contributor [kən'trɪbjʊtər] **N 1** *(to charity)* donateur, -trice; **the contributors to the meal/the present** les personnes *fpl* qui ont contribué au repas/au cadeau **2** *Journ* collaborateur, -trice (**to a paper** d'un journal)

contributory [kən'trɪbjʊtərɪ] **ADJ** *(cause, factor etc)* concourant; **to be a c. factor in sth** contribuer à qch; **the weather may have had a c. effect, but …** le temps a peut-être joué un rôle mais …
▸▸ *Law* **c. negligence** imprudence *f*, faute *f* (avant un accident)

contrite [kən'traɪt, 'kɒntraɪt] **ADJ** contrit

contritely [kən'traɪtlɪ] **ADV** d'un air contrit, avec contrition

contrition [kən'trɪʃən] **N** contrition *f*, pénitence *f*

contrivance [kən'traɪvəns] **N 1** *(device)* appareil *m*, dispositif *m*, engin *m* **2** *esp Fml (invention)* *(of scheme, plan)* invention *f*; **I was fairly sure the scheme was of George's c.** j'étais presque certain que c'était un stratagème de George **3** *(inventiveness)* ingéniosité *f* **4** *Pej (scheme)* stratagème *m*

contrive [kən'traɪv] **VT** *(device etc)* inventer, concevoir; **to c. to do sth** trouver le moyen de faire qch; **she contrived to get herself mentioned in the article** elle a réussi à faire en sorte qu'on parle d'elle dans l'article

contrived [kən'traɪvd] **ADJ** forcé, qui manque de naturel

CONTROL [kən'trəʊl]

N contrôle **1, 2, 4**	▪ maîtrise **1**	
▪ direction **1**	▪ témoin **3**	
▪ commande **4**		
VT contrôler **1–3**	▪ diriger **1**	
▪ maîtriser **2**		

N 1 *(power)* contrôle *m*; *(over oneself)* maîtrise *f*, *(of country, organization)* direction *f*; **to take c.** prendre le contrôle (**of** de); **to have c. over sth/sb** avoir le contrôle de qch/qn; **the state has no c. over the media** l'état n'a aucun contrôle sur les médias; **she has no c. over the children** elle n'a aucune autorité sur les enfants; **to be in c. of sth/sb** avoir le contrôle de qch/qn; **the government is now firmly back in c.** le gouvernement a maintenant fermement repris le contrôle; **to have c. of a business** être à la tête d'une entreprise, diriger une entreprise; **things had got out of c.** les choses étaient/la situation était devenue(s) incontrôlable(s); **the children/the horses were out of c.** les enfants/les chevaux étaient incontrôlables; **she soon had the horse under c.** elle est vite parvenue à maîtriser le cheval; **to keep one's feelings under c.** contrôler ou maîtriser ses émotions; **everything is under c.** *(organized, in hand)* tout est en bonne voie; *(there's no need to panic)* tout va bien; **to bring under c.** *(fire etc)* maîtriser; *(illness)* enrayer; **circumstances beyond our c.** circonstances indépendantes de notre volonté; **these things are beyond our c.** ces choses-là ne dépendent pas de notre volonté; **to lose c. (of oneself)** ne plus être maître de soi; **to regain c. of oneself** se ressaisir; **to exercise strict c. over sth** exercer un contrôle strict sur qch; **to exercise strict c. over sb** tenir la bride serrée à qn

2 *Econ etc (of exchange rates, rents)* contrôle *m*; **to impose controls on rents/prices** contrôler les loyers/prix; **new government controls on financial practices** nouvelles réglementations *fpl* gouvernementales sur les pratiques financières

3 *(used in experiment)* témoin *m*

4 *(action) (of mechanism)* commande *f*; *(of power, volume)* réglage *m*; **to lose c. of one's car** perdre le contrôle de sa voiture; **the driver/pilot lost c.** le conducteur/pilote a perdu le contrôle; **the truck went out of c.** le chauffeur a perdu le contrôle de son camion; **the ship was out of c.** le navire n'était plus manœuvrable; **temperature c.** régulation *f* thermique; **automatic c.** réglage automatique; **dual c.** double commande; **remote c.** télécommande *f*, commande à distance

5 *Tech (device)* (organe *m* de) commande *f*; **the controls** les commandes; **to be at the controls** être aux commandes; *Aviat* **flying controls** commandes de vol; *Radio etc* **volume c.** bouton *m* de (réglage de) volume

VT 1 *(be in charge of, direct) (business, production) (of troops) (area etc)* contrôler; *(action of machine)* commander; **to c. the traffic** réglementer la circulation

2 *(master, restrain) (horse)* maîtriser; *(child, pupils, class)* avoir de l'autorité sur, tenir; *(one's passions)* dompter; *(one's reactions etc)* contrôler, maîtriser; *(one's tears)* retenir; *(price increases, inflation)* contenir, enrayer; *Med (diabetes etc)* équilibrer; *(vehicle)* maîtriser, garder le contrôle de; **to c. oneself** se contrôler, se maîtriser; **to try to c. oneself** faire un effort sur soi-même; **he can't c. his pupils** il ne tient pas ses élèves, il manque d'autorité sur ses élèves; **couldn't you c. that child a little better?** tu ne crois pas que tu pourrais avoir un peu plus d'autorité sur cet enfant?

3 *(check) (quality etc)* contrôler

▸▸ *Comput* **c. bit** bit *m* de contrôle; *Aut* **c. box** régulateur *m* de charge; *Comput* **c. bus** bus *m* de contrôle; *Comput* **c. character** caractère *m* de contrôle; *Comput* **c. code** code *m* de commande; **c. column** manche *m* à balai; **c. experiment** expérience *f* de contrôle; **c. freak** = personne *f* qui veut tout contrôler; *Tech* **c. gear** appareils *mpl* ou organes *mpl* de commande; **c. group** groupe *m* témoin; *Comput* **c. key** touche *f* contrôle; *Comput* **c. knob** molette *f* de réglage; *Mktg* **c. market** marché *m* témoin; **c. mechanism** appareil *m* de commande; *TV* **c. monitor** écran *m* de contrôle; **c. panel** *Aviat* tableau *m* de bord; *Comput* panneau *m* de configuration; *Sport, Aut* **c. point** contrôle; *Comput* **c. program** programme *m* de contrôle; *Mktg* **c. question** *(in market research)* question *f* de contrôle; *Nucl* **c. rod** barre *f* de contrôle; **c. room** salle *f* des commandes; *Naut* poste *m* de commande; *Radio, TV* (cabine *f* de) régie *f*; **c. tower** tour *f* de contrôle; *Comput* **c. unit** unité *f* de commande, contrôleur *m*; *Aut* **c. valve** valve *f* modulatrice

controllable [kən'trəʊləb(ə)l] **ADJ** *(speed, heat, brightness)* réglable; *(economic growth, inflation, mechanism)* qui peut être contrôlé; *(moods)* maîtrisable; **it's c. by the user** cela peut être réglé par l'utilisateur; **if you find that the class is just not c.** si vous trouvez que la classe est vraiment intenable; **the spread of the disease is c.** la progression de la maladie peut être maîtrisée *ou* enrayée; **the more easily c. aspects of the project** les aspects du projet les plus faciles à contrôler

controlled [kən'trəʊld] **ADJ** *(person)* qui sait se maîtriser *ou* se contrôler; *(market)* réglementé; *(experiment)* contrôlé; *Med (diabetes etc)* équilibré; **to remain c.** *(of person)* garder son sang-froid; **the transition to democracy must take place in a c. manner** le passage à la démocratie doit se faire dans l'ordre

▸▸ *Econ* **c. economy** économie *f* dirigée *ou* planifiée; **c. explosion** neutralisation *f (d'un explosif)*; **c. parking zone** zone *f* de stationnement réglementé; *Econ* **c. price** taxe *f*; **to sell goods at the c. price** vendre des marchandises à la taxe

controller [kən'trəʊlər] **N** *(person)* contrôleur, -euse; *Fin, Comput* contrôleur; *(of TV channel)* directeur, -trice d'antenne; *Aviat* **flight c.** contrôleur de vol; *Comput* **disk c.** contrôleur de disques

▸▸ *Comput* **c. card** carte *f* contrôleur

controlling [kən'trəʊlɪŋ] **ADJ** *(power)* dirigeant

▸▸ *Fin, Com* **c. factor** facteur *m* déterminant; *Fin* **c. interest, c. stake** *(in company)* participation *f* majoritaire

controversial [kɒntrə'vɜːʃəl] **ADJ** controversé; **he's trying to be c.** il cherche la controverse; **I only said that to be c.** je n'ai dit cela que pour provoquer la controverse

controversy ['kɒntrəvɜːsɪ, kən'trɒvəsɪ] **N** controverse *f*; **to avoid c.** éviter la controverse; **to court c.** inviter à la controverse; **to be the subject of c.** être sujet à controverse; **the decision was surrounded by c.** la décision a soulevé beaucoup de controverses

contumacious [kɒntjʊ'meɪʃəs] **ADJ** *Fml* désobéissant

contumacy ['kɒntjʊməsɪ, kɒn'tjuː-] **N 1** *Law* contumace *f* **2** *Fml (disobedience)* désobéissance *f*

contumely ['kɒntjuːmlɪ] **N** *Fml (scorn)* mépris *m*

contusion [kən'tjuːʒən] **N** *Med* contusion *f*

conundrum [kə'nʌndrəm] **N 1** *(riddle)* devinette *f* **2** *(mystery)* énigme *f*

conurbation [kɒnɜː'beɪʃən] **N** conurbation *f*

convalesce [kɒnvə'les] **VI** *Med* se remettre (d'une maladie); *(be resting)* être en convalescence

convalescence [kɒnvə'lesəns] **N** *Med* convalescence *f*

convalescent [kɒnvə'lesənt] *Med* **N** convalescent, -ente

ADJ convalescent

▸▸ **c. home** maison *f* de convalescence *ou* de repos

convection [kən'vekʃən] **N** *Phys, Elec* convection *f*

▸▸ **c. drier** séchoir *m* à convection; **c. drying** séchage *m* par convection; **c. heater** convecteur *m*, radiateur *m* à convection

convector [kən'vektər] **N** *(heater)* convecteur *m*, radiateur *m* à convection

convene [kən'viːn] **VT** *(meeting)* convoquer **VI** se réunir

convener [kən'viːnər] **N 1** *Br (of trade union)* délégué, -ée (syndical(e)) **2 he was the c. of the meeting** c'est lui qui a demandé la réunion

convenience [kən'viːnɪəns] **N 1** commodité *f*; **at your c.** quand cela vous conviendra; *Com* **at your earliest c.** dans les meilleurs délais; **at your own c.** à votre convenance; **for c. I use tinned fruit** j'utilise des fruits en conserves pour des raisons de commodité; **a bus service is provided for our customers' c.** un service d'autobus est à la disposition de nos clients; **marriage of c.** mariage *m* de convenance; *Naut* **flag of c.** pavillon *m* de complaisance **2** *(installation)* **(public) c.** W.-C. *mpl* (publics), toilettes *fpl*; **the rooms are fitted with all modern conveniences** les chambres ont tout (le) confort moderne

▸▸ *Com* **c. brand** marque *f* pratique; **c. food** aliments *mpl* prêts à consommer, plats *mpl* cuisinés; *Com* **c. goods** produits *mpl* d'achat courant, produits de consommation courante; **c. store** = supérette *f* de quartier qui reste ouverte tard le soir, *Can* dépanneur *m*

convenient [kən'viːnɪənt] **ADJ** commode, pratique; *(time)* opportun; **if it is c. for you** si cela vous convient, si vous n'y voyez pas d'inconvénient; **2 o'clock isn't very c. (for me)** 14 heures ne m'arrange pas; **a c. place to stop** un endroit commode pour s'arrêter; **to find a c. opportunity to do sth** trouver l'occasion de faire qch; **we climbed through a c. hole in the fence** un trou bien situé nous a permis de traverser la clôture; **the ticket collector wasn't there – how very c.!** le contrôleur n'était pas là – ça tombait très bien!; **the flat is very c. for the shops** l'appartement est bien situé pour les commerces

conveniently [kən'viːnɪəntlɪ] **ADV** commodément; *(to arrive)* opportunément, à propos; **the house is c. situated near the town centre** la maison est située près du centre-ville, ce qui est bien pratique; *Iron* **someone had c. forgotten to lock the door** *(accidentally)* quelqu'un avait oublié de fermer la porte, ce qui était bien pratique; *(deliberately)* comme par hasard, quelqu'un avait oublié de fermer la porte

convenor [kən'viːnər] **N** = **convener**

convent ['kɒnvənt] **N** *Rel* couvent *m*; **to enter a c.** entrer au couvent; **she went to c. school** elle est allée à l'école chez les sœurs

convention [kən'venʃən] **N 1** *(conference)* assemblée *f*, convention *f*, congrès *m*; *Am Pol* convention; **medical c.** congrès médical **2** *(agreement)* accord *m*; *(international)* convention *f* (**on** relative à) **3** *(established practice)* usage *m*; *Mus, Theat etc* convention *f*; **the c. is that …** la convention veut que …; **there is a c. that Ministers do not answer such questions** l'usage est que les ministres ne répondent pas à ce genre de questions; **to be a slave to c.** être l'esclave des usages **4** *(custom) (usu pl)* **conventions** convenances *fpl*; **to observe the conventions** respecter les convenances; **social conventions** conventions *fpl* sociales

▸▸ **c. centre** palais *m* des congrès

conventional [kən'venʃ(ə)l] **ADJ 1** *(normal) (person, upbringing)* conventionnel, *Pej* sans originalité; *(beauty, good looks)* classique **2** *(established, traditional) (method)* classique, traditionnel; **the c. wisdom is that …** la sagesse populaire veut que …

▸▸ *Constr* **c. material** matériau *m* traditionnel; *Comput* **c. memory** mémoire *f* conventionnelle; **c. propriety** les convenances *fpl*; *Mil* **c. warfare** guerre *f* conventionnelle; *Mil* **c. weapon** arme *f* conventionnelle

conventionality [kənvenʃə'nælɪtɪ] **N** *(of person, upbringing)* caractère *m* conventionnel *ou* ordinaire

conventionally [kən'venʃ(ə)lɪ] **ADV 1** *(in accepted fashion)* conventionnellement, *Pej* sans originalité; **she's not c. beautiful** elle n'est pas d'une beauté classique **2** *(traditionally)* d'une manière classique

conventioneer [kənvenʃə'nɪər] **N** *Am* congressiste *mf*

converge [kən'vɜːdʒ] **VI 1** *Opt, Phys* converger (**on** vers) **2** *(of people)* se diriger (**on** vers); **over a hundred had converged on the town** plus de cent s'étaient rassemblés dans la ville; **three armies were converging on Paris** trois armées convergeaient sur Paris

convergence [kən'vɜːdʒəns] **N** *(of lines, opinions), EU* convergence *f*, *Math* focalisation *f*

convergent [kən'vɜːdʒənt] **ADJ** convergent ▸▸ *Opt* **c. lens** lentille *f* convexe *ou* convergente

conversant [kən'vɜːsənt] **ADJ to be c. with sth** *(with French grammar, the law etc)* s'y connaître en qch; *(with type of engine etc)* connaître qch; *(with recent developments etc)* être au courant de qch

conversation [kɒnvə'seɪʃən] **N 1** conversation *f*; **to hold** *or* **have a c. with sb** avoir une conversation avec qn; **to get into c. (with sb)** entamer une conversation (avec qn); **she was just making c.** elle parlait par politesse; **from my c. with him I got the impression that ...** lorsque je me suis entretenu avec lui, j'ai eu l'impression que ...; **his c. was very dull** sa conversation était sans aucun intérêt; **I'm not good at (making) c.** je ne suis pas très doué pour faire la conversation **2** *Comput* dialogue *m* ▸▸ *Fam* **c. killer** = **c. stopper**; *Comput* **c. mode** mode *m* conversationnel *ou* dialogue; **c. piece** objet *m* qui suscite des commentaires; **the vase is quite a c. piece** le vase alimente bien des conversations; **c. skills** l'art *m* de la conversation; *Fam* **c. stopper** remarque *f*/sujet *m* qui arrête net les conversations; *Fam* **that was a c. stopper** cela a arrêté net la conversation

conversational [kɒnvə'seɪʃən(ə)l] **ADJ 1** *(tone, voice)* de la conversation; *(style)* familier; **in a c. tone** sur le ton de la conversation **2** *Comput (mode)* dialogue

conversationalist [kɒnvə'seɪʃənəlɪst] **N to be a c.** *(like talking)* aimer la conversation; *(be a good talker)* bien parler; **I'm not much of a c.** je ne suis pas brillant causeur

conversationally [kɒnvə'seɪʃən(ə)lɪ] **ADV** sur le ton de la conversation

converse[1] [kən'vɜːs] **VI** *Fml* converser (**on, about** sur), deviser (**on, about** de)

converse[2] ['kɒnvɜːs] **ADJ** *(results, theory etc)* contraire; *Math* réciproque
N inverse *m*, contraire *m*; *(in logic)* proposition *f* converse; *Math* proposition réciproque

conversely ['kɒnvɜːslɪ, kən'vɜːslɪ] **ADV** réciproquement, inversement

conversion [kən'vɜːʃən] **N 1** *Rel, Fig* conversion *f* (**to** à)
2 *(adaptation, alteration)* conversion *f* (**of sth into sth** de qch en qch); **the c. of a house into flats** l'aménagement *m* *ou* la transformation d'une maison en appartements
3 *(in American football, rugby)* transformation *f*
4 *(in converted building)* = appartement *m* aménagé dans un ancien hôtel particulier, entrepôt, atelier etc
5 *Law* conversion *f*, **improper c. of funds** détournement *m* de fonds
6 *(of bonds, securities, loan stock)* conversion *f*
▸▸ *Fin* **c. loan** emprunt *m* de conversion; *Fin* **c. order** ordre *m* de conversion; *Fin* **c. premium** prime *f* de conversion; *Fin* **c. price** prix *m* de conversion; *Comput* **c. program** pro-

gramme *m* de conversion; *Fin* **c. rate** taux *m* de conversion; *Fin* **c. right** droit *m* de conversion; *Comput* **c. software** logiciel *m* de conversion; **c. table** table *f* de conversion; *Comput* **c. utility** utilitaire *m* de conversion

convert[1] ['kɒnvɜːt] **N** *Rel, Fig* converti, -ie; **to become a c. to sth** se convertir à qch; **to make a c. of sb** convertir qn; **she's made another c.** elle a encore converti quelqu'un

convert[2] [kən'vɜːt] **VT 1** *Rel, Fig* convertir (**to** à); **to be converted to Christianity** se convertir au christianisme; *Fig* **she converted them to her way of thinking** elle les a amenés à voir les choses à sa manière
2 *(alter, adapt)* transformer, convertir (**sth into sth** qch en qch); **the car has been converted to run on unleaded petrol** la voiture a été modifiée pour rouler à l'essence sans plomb; **her studio was a converted barn** son studio était une grange aménagée; **to c. miles into kilometres** convertir les mil(l)es en kilomètres; *Fin* **to c. loan stock/securities** convertir un emprunt/des valeurs; *Fin* **converted share** action *f* convertie
3 *Rugby* **to c. a try** transformer un essai
4 *Law* **to c. funds to another purpose** affecter des fonds à un autre usage; **to c. funds to one's own use** détourner des fonds
VI 1 *Rel* se convertir (**to** à); *Fig* **she converted to a belief in capitalism** elle s'est mise à croire au capitalisme
2 *(of settee etc)* se transformer (**into a bed** en lit); **we've converted to electricity** nous sommes passés à l'électricité

converter [kən'vɜːtər] **N** *(person), Metal, Elec, Radio, Comput* convertisseur *m*; **steel c., Bessemer c.** convertisseur Bessemer; ▸▸ *Aut* **c. clutch** convertisseur-embrayage *m, pl* convertisseurs-embrayages; *Nucl* **c. reactor** réacteur *m* convertisseur

convertibility [kənvɜːtə'bɪlɪtɪ] **N** convertibilité *f*

convertible [kən'vɜːtəb(ə)l] **ADJ 1** *(thing)* convertible (**into** en); *(settee etc)* transformable **2** *Aut* décapotable **3** *Fin* *(bond, security, money)* convertible
N *Aut* (voiture *f*) décapotable *f*
▸▸ *Fin* **c. currency** monnaie *f* *ou* devise *f* convertible; **c. loan stock** emprunt *m* obligataire convertible; **c. money of account** monnaie de compte convertible

convex ['kɒnveks] **ADJ 1** *Phys* convexe **2** *(road, road surface)* bombé

convexity [kən'veksɪtɪ] **N** *Phys* convexité *f*

convey [kən'veɪ] **VT 1** *(communicate) (order)* transmettre, donner; *(one's thoughts, news)* transmettre, communiquer (**to** à); **please c. my good wishes to the young couple** veuillez transmettre tous mes vœux aux jeunes époux; **to c. one's meaning** communiquer sa pensée; **his writing conveys the mood of the country** sa manière d'écrire évoque l'atmosphère du pays; **does that name c. anything to you?** est-ce que ce nom vous dit quelque chose? **2** *(transport)* transporter; *(person)* transporter, (a)mener; *(of air)* *(sound, smell)* transmettre **3** *Law* faire cession de, transférer, céder (**to** à)

conveyance [kən'veɪəns] **N 1** *(transportation) (of goods)* transport *m* **2** *Old-fashioned, Fml (vehicle)* véhicule *m*, voiture *f*; **public c.** véhicule de transport(s) en commun **3** *Law* *(of property)* transfert *m*, cession *f*, disposition *f*, *(document)* acte *m* translatif de propriété, acte de cession

conveyancing [kən'veɪənsɪŋ] **N** *Law* **1** *(procedure)* procédure *f* translative de propriété **2** *(drawing up documents)* rédaction *f* des actes de cession *ou* des actes translatifs de propriété

conveyor [kən'veɪər] **N 1** *Ind* (appareil *m*)

transporteur *m*; *Min* convoyeur *m*; *(belt)* convoyeur, tapis *m* roulant; **bucket c.** transporteur à godets **2** *Fml (person) (of letter, parcel)* porteur, -euse
▸▸ **c. belt** tapis *m* roulant

convict[1] ['kɒnvɪkt] **N** *(convicted person)* détenu, -ue; *Old-fashioned (prisoner)* forçat *m*, bagnard *m*; **former c.** repris *m* de justice

convict[2] [kən'vɪkt] **VT to c. sb (of a crime)** déclarer qn coupable (d'un crime); **he was convicted** il fut reconnu coupable; **you stand convicted by your own words** vos propres paroles vous condamnent

> Attention: ne pas confondre avec le verbe **to convince**.

conviction [kən'vɪkʃən] **N 1** *Law* condamnation *f*; **previous convictions** condamnations antérieures; **c. for murder** condamnation pour meurtre **2** *(belief)* conviction *f*; **to act from c.** agir par conviction; **to have the courage of one's convictions** avoir le courage de ses opinions; **to carry c.** *(of voice, manner)* être convaincant; **to lack c.** *(of person, voice, manner)* manquer de conviction

convince [kən'vɪns] **VT** convaincre, persuader (**of** de; **that ...** que ...); **to allow oneself to be convinced** se laisser convaincre; **you'll never c. me of that** tu ne me feras jamais croire cela

> Attention: ne pas confondre avec le verbe **to convict**.

convinced [kən'vɪnsd] **ADJ** convaincu; **to be c. (that) ...** être convaincu que ... + *ind*; **I'm not c.** je ne suis pas convaincu

convincing [kən'vɪnsɪŋ] **ADJ** *(argument, theory, performance etc)* convaincant; *(victory)* décisif; **she wasn't very c. as Juliet** elle n'était pas convaincante dans le rôle de Juliette; **the battle scenes were very c.** les scènes de bataille étaient très réalistes

convincingly [kən'vɪnsɪŋlɪ] **ADV** d'une manière convaincante; *(to win)* d'une manière décisive

convivial [kən'vɪvɪəl] **ADJ** *(person)* bon vivant; *(atmosphere)* convivial, -aux, joyeux; **to have a c. evening** passer une soirée conviviale

conviviality [kənvɪvɪ'ælɪtɪ] **N** convivialité *f*, esprit *m* de société

convocation [kɒnvə'keɪʃən] **N 1** *(of meeting)* convocation *f* **2** *(meeting)* assemblée *f*, *Br Rel* assemblée, synode *m*

convoke [kən'vəʊk] **VT** *Fml (meeting)* convoquer

convoluted ['kɒnvəluːtɪd] **ADJ 1** *(complicated)* compliqué, *Fam* emberlificoté **2** *Biol* convoluté

convolution [kɒnvə'luːʃən] **N 1** *(complication) (of argument etc)* méandre *f* **2** *(twist)* circonvolution *f*, *Anat* **cerebral convolutions** circonvolutions cérébrales

convolvulus, *pl* **convolvuluses** [kən'vɒlvjʊləs, -əsɪz] **N** volubilis *m*, belle-de-jour *f*, *pl* belles-de-jour

convoy ['kɒnvɔɪ] *Mil, Naut, Aut* **N** convoi *m*; **ship under** *or* **in c.** bâtiment *m* convoyé *ou* en convoi; **to drive in c.** *(of lorries)* rouler en convoi; *(of private cars)* se suivre; **to be on c. duty** *(of ship)* assurer un convoi
VT convoyer, escorter

convulse [kən'vʌls] **VT 1** *(of sobs, spasms etc) (person)* secouer; *Fig (disrupt) (sb's life)* bouleverser; **to be convulsed with laughter/pain** se tordre de rire/douleur; **scene that convulses the audience** scène qui fait tordre de rire toute la salle **2** *Med (muscle)* convulsionner

VI *(of person)* avoir des convulsions; *(of face, body etc)* se contracter

convulsion [kən'vʌlʃən] **N** *Med (usu pl)* convulsions convulsions *fpl*; *Fam* **to be in convulsions** *(laughing)* se tordre de rire; *Fig* **political convulsions** bouleversements *mpl* politiques

convulsive [kən'vʌlsɪv] **ADJ** *(movement etc)* convulsif; *(transition)* brutal, -aux; **the most c. years in the country's history** les années les plus agitées dans l'histoire du pays

convulsively [kən'vʌlsɪvlɪ] **ADV** convulsivement

coo¹ [kuː] **INT** *Br Sl* tiens!, ça alors!

coo² **VI** *(of dove)* roucouler; *(of baby)* gazouiller; **the neighbours came to c. over the baby** les voisins sont venus s'extasier sur le bébé
▪ **VT** *(of person)* dire (d'un ton attendri); *(greeting, endearment etc)* murmurer, susurrer; **what a beautiful baby, he cooed** quel beau bébé, s'est-il extasié
▪ **N** *(of dove)* roucoulement *m*

cooing ['kuːɪŋ] **N** *(of dove)* roucoulement *m*; *(of baby)* gazouillement *m*; *(of person)* mots *mpl* attendris

cook [kʊk] **N** cuisinier, -ère; *Naut* coq *m*; **to be a good/bad c.** être bon/mauvais cuisinier; **head c.** chef *m* (de cuisine); *Fam Hum* **chief** *or* **head c. and bottlewasher** factotum *m*; *Prov* **too many cooks spoil the broth** on ne parvient jamais à rien quand tout le monde met son grain de sel
▪ **VT** *(meal)* faire, préparer; *(meat etc)* (faire) cuire; **half-cooked** demi-cuit, à moitié cuit; **the meat should be cooked all the way through** la viande doit être bien cuite; *Fig Fam* **to c. the accounts** *or* **the books** falsifier *ou* truquer les comptes
▪ **VI** *(of food)* cuire; *(of person)* faire la cuisine, cuisiner; **can you c.?** est-ce que tu sais faire la cuisine?; *Fig Fam* **what's cooking?** *(happening)* qu'est-ce qui se passe?; *Fig Fam* **to be cooking with gas** marcher très fort
▪ **cook up VT SEP** *Fam (fabricate) (excuse etc)* inventer, imaginer

cookbook ['kʊkbʊk] **N** livre *m* de cuisine

cook-chill **ADJ** cuisiné (et réfrigéré)

cooked [kʊkt] **ADJ** cuit; **c. breakfast** petit déjeuner *m* à l'anglaise; **I always have a c. meal in the evening** je mange toujours un repas chaud le soir

cooker ['kʊkər] **N 1** *(stove)* cuisinière *f*; **gas/electric c.** cuisinière à gaz/électrique; **pressure c.** cocotte-minute® *f*, *pl* cocottes-minute **2** *Br Fam (apple)* pomme *f* à cuire

cookery ['kʊkərɪ] **N** cuisine *f*
▪▪ **c. book** livre *m* de cuisine; **c. course** stage *m* de cuisine; **c. programme** émission *f* de cuisine

cookhouse ['kʊkhaʊs] **N** cuisine *f*

cookie ['kʊkɪ] **N 1** *esp Am (sweet biscuit)* biscuit *m*; *Fam* **that's the way the c. crumbles!** c'est la vie (que veux-tu)! **2** *esp Am Fam (person)* **a tough c.** un dur à cuire; **a smart c.** un petit malin **3** *Comput* cookie *m*, mouchard *m* électronique

cooking ['kʊkɪŋ] **N 1** *(process)* cuisson *f*, **method of c.** cuisson **2** *(style, activity)* cuisine *f*, **plain** *or* **home c.** cuisine bourgeoise; **my mother's c.** la cuisine de ma mère; **do you like c.?** est-ce que tu aimes faire la cuisine?; **to do the c.** faire la cuisine **3** *Fam (falsification)* **c. of the books** *or* **accounts** falsification *f* des comptes
▪▪ **c. apple** pomme *f* à cuire; **c. chocolate** chocolat *m* à cuire; **c. fat** matière *f* grasse pour la cuisine; **c. foil** papier *m* d'aluminium; **c. oil** huile *f* de cuisine; **c. time** temps *m* de cuisson; **c. utensils** batterie *f* de cuisine

cool [kuːl] **ADJ 1** *(wind, weather etc)* frais, *f*

fraîche; *(drink)* frais, rafraîchissant; *(coffee, bathwater etc)* tiède; **it's c.** *(weather)* il fait frais; **it's getting c.** *(weather)* le temps se rafraîchit; *Com etc* **keep in a c. place** tenir au frais
2 *(calm)* calme; **to keep c., calm and collected** rester calme, garder son sang-froid; **keep c.!** du calme!; **to keep a c. head** garder la tête froide, garder son sang-froid
3 *(unfriendly) (person, reception etc)* froid
4 *Fam (unruffled)* sans gêne; **I call that c.!** ça, c'est du toupet!; **well, you're a c. customer!** eh bien, vous avez du culot *ou* du toupet!
5 *Fam (of money)* **I lost a c. thousand** j'ai perdu mille livres bien comptées
6 *Fam (fashionable, sophisticated)* super *inv*; **you look c. in that jacket** tu es super avec cette veste; **he thinks he's so c.** il se croit vraiment super; **it's not c. to smoke** ce n'est pas cool de fumer
7 *Fam (nice, excellent)* sympa *inv*; **cool** *inv*; **my sister's c.** ma sœur est sympa *ou* cool
8 *Fam (allowed, acceptable)* **is it c. to smoke dope here?** est-ce que c'est OK de fumer de l'herbe ici?
▪ **N 1** fraîcheur *f*; **in the c. of the evening** dans la fraîcheur du soir **2** *Fam (calm)* **to keep/lose one's c.** garder/perdre son sang-froid
▪ **ADV** *Fam* **to play it c.** *(act calm)* jouer décontracté; *(be calm)* être décontracté
▪ **VT** *(water, air)* rafraîchir, refroidir; **to c. sb's ardour** refroidir l'ardeur de qn; *Fam* **c. it!** calme-toi!, on se calme!; **to c. one's heels** poireauter, faire le pied de grue; **he was put in jail overnight to c. his heels** on l'a gardé au poste pour la nuit histoire de le calmer
▪ **VI** *(of liquid)* se rafraîchir, (se) refroidir; *Fig (of friendship etc)* se refroidir; **his anger soon cooled** sa colère a vite passé
▪ **cool down VI 1** *(of person) (become calm)* s'apaiser, se calmer; **we'll talk about it when you've cooled down** nous en parlerons quand tu te seras calmé; **he still hasn't cooled down** il ne s'est pas encore calmé, il n'a pas encore décoléré **2** *(of weather)* se rafraîchir; *(of liquid)* (se) refroidir, se rafraîchir; *Fig* **things have cooled down between them** les relations se sont refroidies entre eux
▪ **VT SEP 1** *(make calm)* calmer, apaiser **2** *(of cold drink)* rafraîchir
▪ **cool off VI** *(of person) (by going for a swim etc)* se rafraîchir; *(of food)* refroidir; *Fig (of affection, enthusiasm)* se refroidir; *(of angry person)* se calmer

coolant ['kuːlənt] **N** *Tech* liquide *m* de refroidissement
▪▪ **c. inlet** arrivée *f* de liquide de refroidissement; **c. outlet** sortie *f* de liquide de refroidissement

cooler ['kuːlər] **N 1** *Am (refrigerator)* réfrigérateur *m* **2** *Tech (appareil m)* refroidisseur *m* **3** *Sl (prison)* taule *f*, tôle *f*

cool-headed [-'hedɪd] **ADJ** *(person)* calme, imperturbable

coolie ['kuːlɪ] **N** coolie *m*

cooling ['kuːlɪŋ] **ADJ** *(breeze, drink)* rafraîchissant; *Ind etc* réfrigérant
▪ **N** *(of temperature etc)* refroidissement *m*; **there had been a c. in their relationship** leurs relations s'étaient refroidies
▪▪ *Tech* **c. fan** ventilateur *m* de refroidissement; *Aut* **c. fin** ailette *f* de refroidissement; *Tech* **c. jacket** chemise *f* d'eau; *Fig* **c. off period** période *f* de réflexion; *Tech* **c. system** système *m* de refroidissement; *Tech* **c. tower** refroidisseur *m*; *Aut, Nucl* **c. water** eau *f* de refroidissement

coolly ['kuːlɪ] **ADV 1** *(calmly) (to act)* avec calme; **she walked c. out of the room** elle a calmement quitté la pièce **2** *Fam (impudently)* effrontément **3** *(to welcome)* froidement

coolness ['kuːlnɪs] **N 1** *(of air)* fraîcheur *f* **2** *(calm)* calme *m*, sang-froid *m* **3** *(of reception)* froideur *f*

coon [kuːn] **N 1** *Am Fam (raccoon)* raton *m* laveur **2** *Offensive Sl (Negro)* nègre *m*, négresse *f*

coonskin ['kuːnskɪn] **N** *Am Fam* peau *f* de raton laveur

coop [kuːp] **N** **(hen** *or* **chicken) c.** cage *f* à poules, poulailler *m*; *Fig* **to fly the c.** prendre la fuite, filer
▪ **coop up VT SEP** *(usu passive)* **to c. sb up** tenir qn enfermé; **we were cooped up for hours in a tiny room** nous sommes restés enfermés pendant des heures dans une pièce minuscule; **to feel cooped up** se sentir à l'étroit

co(-)op ['kəʊɒp] **N** coopérative *f*

cooper ['kuːpər] **N** tonnelier *m*

cooperage ['kuːpərɪdʒ] **N** tonnellerie *f*

co(-)operate [kəʊ'ɒpəreɪt] **VI** coopérer **(with sb in sth** avec qn à qch); **the two governments are co-operating in the drug war** les deux gouvernements coopèrent dans la lutte contre la drogue; **if you c. your sentence may be reduced** si vous coopérez, votre peine pourra être réduite

co(-)operation [kəʊɒpə'reɪʃən] **N** coopération *f*, **your c. would be appreciated** nous vous serions reconnaissants de votre coopération

co(-)operative [kəʊ'ɒpərətɪv] **ADJ 1** *(activity, work)* coopératif; **c. dairy** coopérative *f* laitière **2** *(person, attitude)* coopératif; **to be c.** se montrer coopératif
▪ **N** *Com (agricultural, viticultural etc)* coopérative *f*
▪▪ **c. advertising** publicité *f* coopérative *ou* associée; **c. credit society** coopérative de crédit; **c. exporting** exportation *f* collective; **c. group** coopérative de (consommateurs); **c. selling** vente *f* en coopération; **c. society** société *f* coopérative

co(-)opt [kəʊ'ɒpt] **VT 1** *(onto committee)* coopter **(onto** à) **2** *Fam (commandeer)* réquisitionner; **I've been co-opted to help with the spring cleaning** j'ai été réquisitionné pour le nettoyage de printemps

co(-)ordinate¹ [kəʊ'ɔːdɪnət] **ADJ** *Gram, Math* coordonné
▪ **N** *Math, Astron etc* coordonnée *f*
▪▪ *Gram* **c. clause** proposition *f* coordonnée

co(-)ordinate² [kəʊ'ɔːdɪneɪt] **VT** coordonner **(with** à, avec)

co(-)ordinated [kəʊ'ɔːdɪneɪtɪd] **ADJ** *(physically, in movements)* coordonné; **you look very c. for a change** pour une fois tu portes des couleurs qui vont bien ensemble *ou* qui ne jurent pas; **to give sth a more c. appearance** donner à qch une apparence plus harmonieuse

co(-)ordinates **NPL** *(clothes)* coordonnés *mpl*

co(-)ordinating [kəʊ'ɔːdɪneɪtɪŋ] **ADJ** coordinateur, -trice
▪▪ *Gram* **c. conjunction** conjonction *f* de coordination VOIR GRAMMAIRE A73-4; B57-8

co(-)ordination [kəʊɔːdɪ'neɪʃən] **N** coordination *f*, **you need good c. to play tennis** il faut avoir une bonne coordination pour jouer au tennis

co(-)ordinator [kəʊ'ɔːdɪneɪtər] **N** coordinateur, -trice

coot [kuːt] **N 1** *(bird)* **(common** *or* **bald) c.** foulque *f* (macroule), *Can* foulque noire **2** *Old-fashioned Fam (fool)* idiot, -ote

cooties ['kuːtɪz] **NPL** *Am Fam* poux *mpl*

co-owner ['kəʊ'əʊnər] **N** *(of building etc)* copropriétaire *mf*

co-ownership [ˈkəʊˈəʊnəʃɪp] N copropriété f

cooze [kuːz] N Am Vulg (female genitals) craquette f, fente f, (women) nanas fpl, cuisse f

cop [kɒp] N1 Fam (policeman) flic m; **speed c.** motard m; **to play cops and robbers** jouer aux gendarmes et aux voleurs **2** Br Sl (arrest) **it's a fair c.!** je suis fait **3** Br Sl **it's not much c.** (not very good) ça ne vaut pas grand-chose
  VT Sl (catch) (person) attraper, pincer; **c. this!** (listen) écoute-moi ça!; (look) regarde-moi ça!; **to get copped** (by police etc) se faire pincer; Br **to c. it** (be caught and punished) se faire pincer; (get injured) être blessé; (die) clamser; **to c. hold of sth** attraper qch; **to c. some zeds** or Am **zees** roupiller; Law **to c. a plea** plaider coupable (pour éviter une charge plus grave)
  ▸▸Fam **c. shop** (police station) poste m de police; TV Fam **c. show** série f policière
▸ **cop off** VI Br Sl **to c. off with sb** lever ou emballer qn; **did you c. off last night?** t'as réussi à lever quelqu'un hier soir?
▸ **cop out** VI Sl (avoid responsibility) se défiler; (choose easy solution) choisir la solution de facilité

co-partner [ˈkəʊˈpɑːtnər] N coparticipant, -ante, coassocié, -ée

co-partnership [ˈkəʊˈpɑːtnəʃɪp] N coparticipation f

cope¹ [kəʊp] N Rel chape f

cope² VT Constr (wall) chaperonner, mettre un couronnement à

cope³ VI se débrouiller, s'en tirer, s'en sortir; **to c. with** (situation, danger, job, debt) faire face à; (difficulty) venir à bout de; (troublemaker) se charger de; (look after) (children) s'occuper de; (put up with) (children, noise etc) supporter; **to be able to c. with a job** être à la hauteur d'une tâche; **I can't c. with her when she gets angry** je ne sais pas comment la prendre quand elle se met en colère; **the engine couldn't c. with the extra weight** le moteur n'était pas assez puissant pour supporter cette charge supplémentaire; **I just can't c.** je n'y arrive plus; **that's all right, thanks, I can c.** ça va, merci, j'y arriverai; **I'll c. with it** (take care of it) je m'en chargerai; **I'll c.** je me débrouillerai; **he seems to be coping** il a l'air de se débrouiller ou de s'en sortir

Copenhagen [kəʊpənˈheɪɡ(ə)n] N Copenhague

copiable [ˈkɒpɪəb(ə)l] ADJ Comput copiable

copier [ˈkɒpɪər] N1 (person) copiste mf **2** Pej (imitator) imitateur, -trice **3** (device) duplicateur m, copieur m; (photocopying machine) (photo)copieuse f

copilot [ˈkəʊpaɪlət] N Aviat copilote m

coping [ˈkəʊpɪŋ] N Constr (of wall etc) chaperon m
  ▸▸Tech **c. saw** scie f à découper ou à chantourner; Constr **c. stone** couronnement m, chaperon

copious [ˈkəʊpɪəs] ADJ copieux, abondant; **we drank c. amounts of beer** nous avons bu des quantités de bière

copiously [ˈkəʊpɪəslɪ] ADV abondamment

co-plaintiff [ˈkəʊˈpleɪntɪf] N Law codemandeur, -eresse

cop-out N Sl **1** (act) solution f de facilité; **that's a bit of a c.** c'est la solution de facilité **2** Am (person) personne f qui se défile

copper [ˈkɒpər] N1 (metal, colour) cuivre m **2** Br Fam (coin) sou m; **coppers** petite monnaie f, **to give a beggar a few coppers** donner quelques sous à un mendiant **3** Br (for washing) cuve f à lessive **4** Fam (policeman) flic m
  ADJ (colour, hair) cuivré

VT (in metalwork) cuivrer
  ▸▸Bot **c. beech** hêtre m pourpre; **c. wire** fil m de cuivre

copper-bottomed [-bɒtəmd] ADJ (pot, saucepan etc) à fond en cuivre; Fig (guarantee) sûr

copper-coloured ADJ cuivré

copperhead [ˈkɒpəhed] N (snake) trigonocéphale m

copperplate [ˈkɒpəpleɪt] N **1** Typ (plate) cuivre m **2** (plate) plaque f (de cuivre); (in engraving) taille-douce f, pl tailles-douces **3** (handwriting) écriture f moulée; **written in c.** calligraphié
  ▸▸**c. engraving** taille-douce

coppersmith [ˈkɒpəsmɪθ] N chaudronnier, -ière

copperware [ˈkɒpəweər] N ustensiles mpl en cuivre

coppery [ˈkɒpərɪ] ADJ (colour) cuivré

coppice [ˈkɒpɪs] N taillis m, hallier m

copra [ˈkɒprə] N Com copra(h) m

co-presenter [ˈkəʊprɪzentər] N coprésentateur, -trice

co-processor [kəʊˈprəʊsesər] N Comput coprocesseur m; **maths c.** coprocesseur arithmétique

coproduce [kəʊprəˈdjuːs] VT Cin etc coproduire

coproducer [kəʊprəˈdjuːsər] N Cin etc coproducteur, -trice

coproduction [kəʊprəˈdʌkʃən] N Cin etc coproduction f

copse [kɒps] N taillis m

copter [ˈkɒptər] N Aviat Fam hélico m

Coptic [ˈkɒptɪk] ADJ coptique, copte
  N Ling copte m

copula [ˈkɒpjʊlə] N Gram etc copule f

copulate [ˈkɒpjʊleɪt] VI copuler, s'accoupler (**with** avec)

copulation [kɒpjʊˈleɪʃən] N Physiol copulation f, coït m

copulative [ˈkɒpjʊlətɪv] ADJ Gram etc copulatif; Physiol, Anat copulateur, -trice

copy [ˈkɒpɪ] N **1** (reproduction) copie f, (of statue etc) reproduction f, copie; **this picture is only a c.** ce tableau n'est qu'une copie **2** (of handwritten letter, text) copie f, (of typewritten letter etc) double m; **rough c.** brouillon m; **fair c.** copie (au net); **certified c.** copie authentique; **true c.** copie conforme **3** (of book) exemplaire m; (of newspaper) numéro m; **5,000 copies of the book were printed** le livre a été tiré à 5000 exemplaires **4** Typ (written material for printing) manuscrit m, copie f, (in advertisement) texte m; Journ copie; **this would make good c.** voilà un bon sujet d'article; **he wrote some brilliant c.** (articles) il a écrit d'excellents articles ou Fam papiers
  5 Comput **c. and paste** copier-coller m inv
  VT **1** (work of art, drawing etc) copier, imiter **2** (model oneself on) copier; (sb's walk) copier, imiter; Art, Liter, Mus (sb's style) copier, pasticher
  3 (write out) (letter etc) (re)copier **4** Sch (in order to cheat) copier (**from sb** sur qn; **from sth** dans qch) **5** Comput copier; **to c. sth to disk** copier qch sur disquette; **to c. and paste sth** faire un copier-coller sur qch **6** (send copy to) envoyer une copie à; **to c. sb with sth** faire parvenir une copie de qch à qn
  VI Sch copier (**from another pupil** sur un autre élève)
  ▸▸Comput **c. block** copie de bloc; Comput **c. check** contrôle m par duplication; Comput **c. command** commande f de copie; Journ **c. deadline** tombée f, dernière heure f; Comput

c. disk disquette f de copie; **c. editor** Journ secrétaire mf de rédaction; (in publishing) préparateur, -trice de copie; Comput **c. protection** protection f contre la copie; **c. taster** premier lecteur m; Mktg **c. test** pré-test m publicitaire, pl pré-tests publicitaires; Mktg **c. testing** pré-tests mpl publicitaires; **c. typist** dactylographe mf, dactylo mf
▸ **copy out** VT SEP recopier; **to c. out a passage from a book** transcrire ou recopier un passage d'un livre

copybook [ˈkɒpɪbʊk] N cahier m d'écriture; Fig **to blot one's c.** ternir sa réputation (**with sb** auprès de qn); **he really blotted his c. when he suggested that ...** il a fait une vraie bourde lorsqu'il a proposé que ...; **a c. example** un exemple classique

copycat [ˈkɒpɪkæt] N Fam copieur, -euse; **they're just copycats** ce ne sont que des copieurs
  ▸▸**c. crime** crime m inspiré par un autre

copy-edit Typ VI corriger les épreuves
  VT (proofs) corriger

copy-editing N Typ correction f d'épreuves

copy-holder N (for keyboarder) porte-copies m, bras m porte-copies

copying [ˈkɒpɪɪŋ] N (imitation) imitation f, Sch (cheating) copiage m
  ▸▸**c. machine** duplicateur m; (photocopier) photocopieuse f, Comput **c. program** programme m de copie

copyist [ˈkɒpɪɪst] N copiste mf

copy-protect VT Comput protéger contre la copie

copy-protected ADJ Comput protégé contre la copie

copyreader [ˈkɒpriːdər] N secrétaire mf de rédaction, correcteur, -trice

copyright [ˈkɒpɪraɪt] N droit m d'auteur, copyright m; **it's still subject to c.** c'est toujours soumis au droit d'auteur; **breach** or **infringement of c.** violation f du droit d'auteur; **to hold the c.** or **to have c. on sth** avoir le droit d'auteur sur qch; **it's his c.** c'est lui qui détient les droits d'auteur; **c. Lawrence Durrell** copyright, Lawrence Durrell; **out of c.** (tombé) dans le domaine public
  ADJ (book) qui est protégé par des droits d'auteur; (article) dont le droit de reproduction est réservé; **c. (in all countries)** tous droits de reproduction et de traduction réservés (pour tous pays)
  VT (book) réserver les droits de
  ▸▸**c. library** bibliothèque f de dépôt légal; **c. notice** mention f de réserve

copyrighted [ˈkɒpɪraɪtɪd] ADJ (book, music) déposé

copytaker [ˈkɒpɪteɪkər] N Journ opérateur, -trice

copywriter [ˈkɒpɪraɪtər] N rédacteur, -trice publicitaire

copywriting [ˈkɒpɪraɪtɪŋ] N rédaction f publicitaire

coquetry [ˈkəʊkɪtrɪ, ˈkɒk-] N esp Lit coquetterie f

coquette [kəʊˈket, kɒk-] N esp Lit coquette f

coquettish [kəˈketɪʃ, kɒk-] ADJ **1** (woman) flirteuse **2** (smile etc) aguichant

cor¹ [kɔːr] N
  ▸▸Mus **c. anglais** cor m anglais

cor² INT Br Sl ça alors!

coracle [ˈkɒrək(ə)l] N (boat) coracle m

coral [ˈkɒr(ə)l] ADJ **1** (island) de corail, corallien; (necklace) de corail inv **2** (colour) corail
  N **1** corail m, -aux **2** (colour) corail
  ▸▸**c. red** rouge m corail; **c. reef** récif m de corail; **the C. Sea** la mer de Corail; Zool **c. snake** serpent m corail

corbel ['kɔːb(ə)l] N *Archit* corbeau *m*, console *f*

cord [kɔːd] N **1** *(string)* grosse ficelle *f*; *(for curtains)* cordon *m*; *(of pyjama trousers)* cordon, ficelle; *(of dressing gown)* ceinture *f* **2** *Anat* **(umbilical) c.** cordon *m* (ombilical) **3** *Tex (corduroy)* velours *m* côtelé; **(pair of) cords** *(trousers)* pantalon *m* en *ou* de velours côtelé **4** *Am Elec* cordon *m*, fil *m*

cordage ['kɔːdɪdʒ] N *Naut* cordage *m*

corded ['kɔːdɪd] ADJ *Tex* côtelé, à côtes

cordial ['kɔːdɪəl] ADJ cordial, -aux
  N *(drink)* cordial *m*, sirop *m*

cordiality [kɔːdɪˈælɪtɪ] N cordialité *f*, *Fml* **exchange of cordialities** échange *m* de cordialités

cordially ['kɔːdɪəlɪ] ADV cordialement; *Am* **c. yours** *(at end of letter)* bien cordialement

cordite ['kɔːdaɪt] N cordite *f*

cordless ['kɔːdlɪs] ADJ sans fil
  ▸▸ *Comput* **c. keyboard** clavier *m* sans fil; **c. mouse** souris *f* sans fil; **c. telephone** téléphone *m* sans fil

cordon ['kɔːd(ə)n] N **1** *(barrier)* cordon *m*; **police c.** cordon de police **2** *Bot (tree)* cordon *m*
  ▸▸ *Bot* **c. tree** cordon
  ▸ **cordon off** VT SEP *(close) (road)* barrer; *(area etc)* boucler; **the street was cordoned off by the police** *(they ordered it closed)* la police a barré la rue; *(they acted as a barrier)* on a isolé la rue par un cordon de police

cordon bleu [-blɜː] *Culin* N *(cookery, chef)* cordon bleu *m*
  ADJ de cordon bleu

corduroy ['kɔːdərɔɪ] N *Tex* velours *m* côtelé; **(pair of) corduroys** pantalon *m* en *ou* de velours côtelé
  ADJ de velours côtelé
  ▸▸ **c. road** chemin *m* de rondins

core [kɔːr] N **1** *(of mass)* centre *m*, partie *f* centrale; *(of apple etc)* trognon *m*, cœur *m*; *(of argument)* essentiel *m*; *(of organization)* noyau *m*, *Fig* **hard c.** noyau *m* dur; **selfish to the c.** d'un égoïsme foncier; *Fam* **he's rotten to the c.** il est pourri jusqu'à la moelle; **it shocked us to the c.** cela nous a complètement bouleversés; **the c. issue** la question centrale **2** *Geol (of the earth)* noyau *m* **3** *Tech (of cable)* mèche *f*, *Elec (of electromagnet)* noyau *m*; *Nucl (of reactor)* cœur *m*
  VT *(apple etc)* enlever le cœur de, évider
  ▸▸ *Com, Mktg* **c. brand** marque *f* phare; *Com* **c. business** activité *f* principale; **c. competence** principale compétence *f*; *Sch* **c. curriculum** tronc *m* commun; *Tech* **c. hole** *(in engine block)* trou *m* de coulée *ou* d'usinage; **c. hours** *(in flexitime scheme)* plage *f* fixe; *Mktg* **c. market** marché *m* principal, marché de référence; *Comput* **c. memory** mémoire *f* à tores (magnétiques); *(main memory)* mémoire centrale; *Com, Mktg* **c. message** *(in advertising)* message *m* principal; *Aut* **c. plug** obturateur *m* de trou de coulée *ou* de trou d'usinage; *Geol* **c. sample** carotte *f*; **c. time** *(in flexitime scheme)* plage fixe; **c. values** valeurs *fpl* principales; *Ling* **c. vocabulary** vocabulaire *m* de base

coreligionist [kəʊrɪˈlɪdʒ(ə)nɪst] N coreligionnaire *mf*

corer ['kɔːrər] N **(apple) c.** vide-pomme *m*, *pl* vide-pommes

co-respondent [kəʊrɪˈspɒndənt] N *Law (in divorce suit)* complice *mf*

Corfu [kɔːˈfuː] N Corfou *f*

corgi ['kɔːgɪ] N corgi *m*

coriander [kɒrɪˈændər] N *Bot, Culin* coriandre *f*
  ▸▸ **c. seeds** graines *fpl* de coriandre

Corinthian [kəˈrɪnθɪən] ADJ **1** *Geog* corin-

thien **2** *Archit (column etc)* corinthien
  N *Geog* Corinthien, -ienne

cork [kɔːk] N **1** *(material)* liège *m* **2** *(stopper)* bouchon; *Br Fam* **put a c. in it!** *(shut up)* la ferme!
  VT **1** *(bottle)* boucher **2** *(blacken)* **to c. one's face** se noircir le visage avec un bouchon brûlé
  ▸▸ **c. charge** *(in restaurant)* droit *m* de bouchon; *Bot* **c. oak** chêne-liège *m*, *pl* chênes-lièges
  ▸ **cork up** VT SEP **the genie had been corked up in the bottle for years** le génie avait été enfermé dans la bouteille pendant des années; *Fig* **to c. up one's feelings** refouler ses émotions

corkage ['kɔːkɪdʒ] N *(in restaurant)* droit *m* de bouchon

corked [kɔːkt] ADJ *(wine)* bouchonné, qui sent le bouchon; **the wine tasted c.** le vin était bouchonné

corker ['kɔːkər] N *Br Sl* **1** *(thing, action)* chose *f*/action *f* qui vous en bouche un coin; **that was a c. of a goal** c'était un super but; **that joke was a c.** elle était super cette blague!; **a c. of a lie** un énorme mensonge **2** *Old-fashioned (man)* type *m* épatant; *(pretty woman)* canon *m*; **when it comes to telling lies he's a c.** comme menteur il se pose là

corking ['kɔːkɪŋ] ADJ *Old-fashioned Br Sl (wonderful)* épatant, fameux

corkscrew ['kɔːkskruː] N tire-bouchon *m*, *pl* tire-bouchons
  VI **to c. (up/down)** *(of staircase)* monter/descendre en colimaçon; **the plane corkscrewed into the sea** l'avion est descendu en vrille et s'est écrasé dans la mer
  ▸▸ **c. curl** mèche *f* en tire-bouchon

cork-tipped ADJ *(cigarette)* à bout de liège

corkwood ['kɔːkwʊd] N liège *m*

corm [kɔːm] N *Bot* bulbe *m* (solide)

cormorant ['kɔːmərənt] N *(bird)* cormoran *m*

corn¹ [kɔːn] N **1** *(no pl) Br (cereal)* blé(s) *m(pl)*; **winter c.** semis *m* d'hiver **2** *esp Am (maize)* maïs *m*; **c. on the cob** maïs en épi **3** *(seed)* grain *m (de plante céréalière)* **4** *Fam (sentimentality)* mièvrerie *f*; *(lack of originality)* banalité *f*; **that film was pure c.** ce film était d'une mièvrerie affligeante; **his routine was pure c.** *(of comedian)* son spectacle manquait totalement d'originalité
  ▸▸ *Geog* **c. belt** plaines *fpl* du centre des Etats-Unis *(où est cultivé le maïs)*; **c. bread** pain *m* à la farine de maïs; *Orn* **c. bunting** bruant *m*; **c. chandler** marchand, -ande de blé *ou* de grains; **c. dolly** figurine *f* en paille tressée; **C. Exchange** halle *f* aux blés; **c. meal** farine *f* de maïs; **c. merchant** marchand, -ande de blé *ou* de grains; **c. oil** huile *f* de maïs; **c. poppy** coquelicot *m*; *Bot, Culin* **c. salad** mâche *f*; *Bot* **c. silk** barbe *f*; *Am* **c. whiskey** whisky *m* de maïs

corn² N *Med (on toe etc)* cor *m*; *Fig Fam* **to tread on sb's corns** froisser qn
  ▸▸ **c. plaster** pansement *m* (pour cors)

cornball ['kɔːnbɔːl] *Am Fam* **1** N personne *f* gnangnan
  ADJ cucul, gnangnan

corncob ['kɔːnkɒb] N épi *m* de maïs; *(pipe)* pipe *f* en épi de maïs
  ▸▸ **c. pipe** pipe en épi de maïs

corncockle ['kɔːnkɒk(ə)l] N *(plant)* nielle *f* des blés

corncrake ['kɔːnkreɪk] N *(bird)* râle *m* des genêts

cornea ['kɔːnɪə] N *Anat (of eye)* cornée *f*

corneal ['kɔːnɪəl] ADJ *Anat* cornéen
  ▸▸ *Med* **c. graft** greffe *f* de la cornée

corned [kɔːnd] ADJ
  ▸▸ *Culin* **c. beef** corned beef *m*

cornelian [kɔːˈniːlɪən] N *(gem)* cornaline *f*

CORNER ['kɔːnər]

> **N** coin **1–3, 6, 7** ▪ angle **3** ▪ virage **4** ▪ corner **5**
> **VT** coincer **1** ▪ accaparer **2**
> **VI** prendre un virage

N 1 *(of page, screen)* coin *m*; **to turn down the c. of a page** corner une page; **bottom left-hand c.** *(of page, photograph etc)* coin en bas à gauche

2 *(of room etc)* coin *m*; **the four corners of the earth** les quatre coins du monde; **to search every c. of the house** chercher dans tous les coins et recoins de la maison; **to put a child in the c.** mettre un enfant au coin; *Fig* **to drive sb into a c.** acculer qn, mettre qn au pied du mur; *Fig* **driven into a c.** acculé, au pied du mur; *Fig* **to be in a tight c.** être dans une mauvaise passe; *Fig* **to paint oneself into a c.** se mettre dans une impasse

3 *(on street)* coin *m*, angle *m*; **situated at** *or* **on the c.** situé au coin *ou* à l'angle; **the house on the c.** la maison qui fait l'angle, la maison au coin; **you'll find the grocer's round the c.** tournez au coin de la rue ou vous verrez l'épicerie; **it's just round the c.** c'est au coin de la rue; *Fig* **spring is just around the c.** ce sera bientôt le printemps; **with the elections just round the c.** avec les élections qui approchent; **another rise in mortgage rates is just round the c.** une autre augmentation des taux de prêt se prépare; **you never know what's around the c.** on ne sait jamais ce qui peut se produire; **to hang around street corners** traîner dans les rues; **to turn the c.** tourner le coin; *Fig (of economy, company)* passer le moment critique; *(of sick person)* commencer à se rétablir

4 *(bend in road)* tournant *m*; *Aut* virage *m*; *Aut* **to take a c.** prendre un virage; **to cut a c. (close)** couper un virage; *Fig* **to cut corners** *(economize excessively)* faire des économies exagérées; *(not follow rules)* contourner les règlements; **if you cut corners now you'll just have more work to do later on** si tu fais les choses trop vite maintenant, tu auras plus à faire plus tard; **we had to cut a few corners to get the job finished on time** il nous a fallu simplifier un peu les choses pour finir ce travail à temps

5 *Ftbl* corner *m*; **to take a c.** faire un corner **6** *(of eye)* coin *m*, *(of lips)* coin *m*, commissure *f*; **to look out of the c. of one's eye** regarder du coin de l'œil

7 a little c. of Normandy un petit coin de Normandie; **they had created a little c. of France in Rome** ils avaient recréé un petit coin de France à Rome
  VT **1** *(drive into a corner)* acculer, coincer; *Fig* coincer, mettre au pied du mur **2** *Com (market)* accaparer, *Belg* s'accaparer *(in de)*
  VI *Aut* prendre un virage; **the car corners well** cette voiture prend bien les virages
  ▸▸ **c. cupboard** armoire *f* de coin; *Sport* **c. flag** drapeau *m* de corner; *Ftbl* **c. kick** corner *m*; *Ftbl* **c. post** piquet *m* de corner; *Br* **c. shop** magasin *m* de quartier

cornered ['kɔːnəd] ADJ *(driven into a corner)* acculé, coincé; *Fig* coincé, au pied du mur; **you've got me c.** là, tu m'as coincé; **we've got him c.** *(criminal etc)* nous l'avons coincé

cornering ['kɔːnərɪŋ] N **1** *Com (of market)* accaparement *m* **2** *Aut (of driver)* façon *f* de prendre les virages; *(of car)* stabilité *f* dans les virages; **the car is good at c.** la voiture prend bien les virages

cornerstone ['kɔːnəstəʊn] N *Constr, Fig* pierre *f* angulaire

cornet ['kɔːnɪt, *Am* kɔːˈnet] N **1** *Mus (instru-*

ment) cornet *m* à pistons; *(player)* cornettiste *mf* **2** *(of paper)* cornet *m* (en papier) **3** *Br* **(ice-cream) c.** cornet *m* de glace

cornet(t)ist [kɔː'netɪst] N *Mus* cornettiste *mf*

cornfield ['kɔːnfiːld] N *Br* champ *m* de blé; *Am* champ de maïs

cornflakes ['kɔːnfleɪks] NPL *Culin* flocons *mpl* de maïs, cornflakes *mpl*

cornflour ['kɔːnflaʊər] N *Br Culin* farine *f* de maïs

cornflower ['kɔːnflaʊər] N **1** *(plant)* bleuet *m*, barbeau *m inv* **2** *(colour)* bleu *m* centaurée
ADJ *(colour)* bleu centaurée *inv*
▸▸ **c. blue** bleu centaurée

cornice ['kɔːnɪs] N *(of wardrobe, snow)*, *Archit* corniche *f*

Cornish ['kɔːnɪʃ] ADJ *Geog* cornouaillais
N *Ling* cornique *m*
▸▸ *Br Culin* **C. pasty** = chausson *m* à la viande et aux légumes

Cornishman, *pl* **Cornishmen** ['kɔːnɪʃmən] N Cornouaillais *m*

Cornishwoman, *pl* **Cornishwomen** ['kɔːnɪʃwʊmən, -wɪmɪn] N Cornouaillaise *f*

cornstarch ['kɔːnstɑːtʃ] N *Am Culin* farine *f* de maïs

cornucopia, *pl* **cornucopias** [kɔːnjʊ'kəʊpɪə, -əz] N *Myth, Fig* corne *f* d'abondance

Cornwall ['kɔːnw(ə)l] N Cornouailles *f*

corny ['kɔːnɪ] ADJ *Fam (poor) (joke)* nul; *(sentimental) (story, film, novel)* tarte; **don't be so c.** ne sois pas aussi tarte

corolla [kə'rɒlə] N *Bot* corolle *f*

corollary [kə'rɒlərɪ] N corollaire *m* (**of** à)

corona, *pl* **coronae** [kə'rəʊnə, -ɪ] N *Astron, Bot, Elec, Phys* couronne *m*;
▸▸ *Phys* **c. discharge** effluve *f* électrique; *Phys* **c. shielding** dispositif *m* anti-effluves

coronary ['kɒrən(ə)rɪ] *Med* ADJ coronarien
N infarctus *m* (du myocarde); **to have a c.** avoir un infarctus (du myocarde); *Fam* **I just about had a c. when I saw the bill** j'ai failli avoir une attaque quand j'ai vu l'addition
▸▸ **c. artery** artère *f* coronaire; **c. bypass** pontage *m* coronaire; **c. thrombosis** infarctus du myocarde, thrombose *f* coronarienne

coronation [kɒrə'neɪʃən] N couronnement *m*
▸▸ *Culin* **c. chicken** = morceaux *mpl* de poulet froid à la mayonnaise parfumée au curry; *Br* **c. mug** = tasse *f* haute fabriquée spécialement à l'occasion d'un couronnement et décorée sur ce thème

coroner ['kɒrənər] N *Law* coroner *m (officier civil chargé d'instruire, assisté d'un jury, en cas de mort violente ou subite)*; **c.'s inquest** enquête *f* du coroner

coronet ['kɒrənɪt] N (petite) couronne *f*; *(lady's)* diadème *m*

corp, Corp 1 *Com (abbr* **corporation)** Cie **2** *Mil abbr* **corporal**

corporal[1] ['kɔːpər(ə)l] ADJ corporel
▸▸ **c. punishment** châtiment *m* corporel

corporal[2] N *Mil (in infantry, air force)* caporal-chef *m, pl* caporaux-chefs; *(in cavalry, artillery)* brigadier-chef *m, pl* brigadiers-chefs

corporate ['kɔːp(ə)rət] ADJ **1** *Com (of a specific company)* corporatif, de société; *(of companies in general)* d'entreprise; *(taxation)* sur les sociétés; **I mean 'we' in the c. sense** par 'nous' j'entends la société; **we have a number of c. customers** certains de nos clients sont des entreprises; **to be a good c. citizen** *(of company)* avoir le sens des responsabilités civiques **2** *(forming a single body)* constitué (en corps), formant

(un) corps; *Law* **body c.** corps *m* constitué, corporation *f*, *(considered as an individual)* personne *f* morale **3** *(of a group of people)* de corporation, de corps; **c. feeling** esprit *m* de corps
▸▸ **c. advertising** publicité *f* institutionnelle, publicité d'entreprise; *Am* **c. apartments** = appartements *mpl* destinés au personnel d'une société; **c. banking** banque *f* d'entreprise; *Law* **c. body** corps constitué, corporation; *(considered as an individual)* personne morale; **c. budget** budget *m* de l'entreprise; **c. culture** culture *f* d'entreprise; **c. image** image *f* de marque de l'entreprise; **the company cares about its c. image** la société se préoccupe de son image; **our c. image demands that ...** notre image en tant que société exige que ...; **c. income** revenu *m* de société; **c. income tax** impôt *m* sur les bénéfices des sociétés; **c. law** droit *m* des sociétés *ou* des entreprises; **c. lawyer** juriste spécialisé(e) en droit des sociétés; *Fin* **c. lending** crédit *m* aux entreprises; **c. literature** = brochures *fpl* décrivant une société; **c. member** *(of association)* société-membre *f, pl* sociétés-membres; **c. name** raison *f* sociale; *St Exch* **c. raider** attaquant *m*; **c. sponsorship** sponsoring *m*, parrainage *m* d'entreprises; **c. strategy** stratégie *f* de l'entreprise; **c. tax** impôt sur les sociétés

corporation [kɔːpə'reɪʃən] N **1** *Com Am* société *f*, compagnie *f*; *Br* **public c.** entreprise *f* publique **2** *Br* **municipal c.** *(council)* conseil *m* municipal, municipalité *f* **3** *Law* personne *f* morale **4** *Old-fashioned Fam (paunch)* bedaine *f*, bedon *m*
▸▸ *Am Fin* **c. income tax** impôt *m* sur les sociétés; *Br Fin* **c. tax** impôt sur les sociétés

corporeal [kɔː'pɔːrɪəl] ADJ corporel, matériel

corps [kɔːr, *pl* kɔːz] N INV corps *m*; *Mil* corps d'armée; **the diplomatic c.** le corps diplomatique; **tank c.** blindés *mpl*

corpse [kɔːps] N cadavre *m*
▸▸ *Theat (of actor)* avoir le fou rire sur scène

corpulence ['kɔːpjʊləns] N corpulence *f*

corpulent ['kɔːpjʊlənt] ADJ corpulent

corpus ['kɔːpəs] N **1** *(of writings)* corpus *m* **2** *(main body)* corpus *m* **3** *Ling* corpus *m*
▸▸ *Cathol* **C. Christi** la Fête-Dieu; *Law* **c. delicti** corps *m* du délit

corpuscle ['kɔːpʌs(ə)l] N *Biol* corpuscule *m*; **red/white blood corpuscles** globules *mpl* rouges/blancs

corral [kɒ'rɑːl] N corral *m, pl* -als
VT *(livestock, horses etc)* renfermer dans un corral; *Fig (demonstrators)* isoler; **to c. sb into doing sth** amener qn à faire qch

correct [kə'rekt] VT **1** *(translation, homework, proofs)* corriger
2 *(rectify) (error, imbalance, oversteer)* rectifier, corriger; *(instrument setting)* modifier; **to c. a misunderstanding** dissiper un malentendu; **to c. a squint** *(of glasses)* corriger un strabisme
3 *(put right) (person)* reprendre, corriger; **he had the nerve to c. my grammar/ English/pronunciation** il a eu le culot de corriger *ou* de me reprendre sur ma grammaire/mon anglais/ma prononciation; **I said it was 2 o'clock but someone corrected me** j'ai dit qu'il était 2 heures mais quelqu'un m'a corrigé; **to c. oneself** se reprendre; **c. me if I'm wrong, but ...** reprenez-moi si je me trompe, mais ...; **I stand corrected** j'avais tort
4 *Old-fashioned (punish) (guilty person)* punir, infliger une correction à
ADJ **1** *(exact)* correct, exact, juste; **the c. time** l'heure exacte; **c. to a millimetre** exact à un millimètre près; **am I c.?** je ne me trompe pas?; **his prediction proved c.** sa pré-

diction s'est vérifiée; **you must be Mr Jones – that's c.** vous devez être M. Jones – c'est exact; **if my memory is c.** si j'ai bonne mémoire; **figures c. at time of going to press** chiffres exacts au moment de la publication
2 *(appropriate) (behaviour)* convenable, correct; *(person)* convenable, comme il faut; **it's the c. thing to send a letter of thanks** la politesse veut que l'on envoie une lettre de remerciements; **it's the c. thing to do** c'est ce qu'il convient de faire; **as is only c.** comme il se doit, comme il convient

correcting fluid [kə'rektɪŋ] N liquide *m* correcteur

correction [kə'rekʃən] N **1** *(of proofs, homework)*, *Tech* correction *f*, *(statement in newspaper)* mise *f* au point, rectificatif *m*; **to make corrections to a text** apporter des corrections à un texte; **subject to c.** sous toutes réserves **2** *Old-fashioned (punishment)* correction *f*, punition *f*, *Arch* **house of c.** maison *f* de correction *ou* de redressement
▸▸ **c. fluid** liquide *m* correcteur

corrective [kə'rektɪv] N rectificatif *m*, correctif *m*; *Med (for teeth)* appareil *m* dentaire; *(for deformed limb)* appareil orthopédique
ADJ *(action, measure)* rectificatif, correctif; *(exercises, treatment)* correctif; *(lens, make-up)* correcteur, -trice

correctly [kə'rektlɪ] ADV **1** *(to answer, report, predict)* correctement; **or (to put it) more c.** ou pour mieux dire **2** *(to behave)* correctement

correctness [kə'rektnɪs] N **1** *(of description, answer)* exactitude *f*, justesse *f* **2** *(of dress, behaviour)* correction *f*

correlate ['kɒrɪleɪt] VI correspondre (**with** à), être en corrélation (**with** avec)
VT corréler, mettre en corrélation (**with** avec); **poverty and ill-health are closely correlated** il y a une corrélation étroite entre la pauvreté et la maladie

correlation [kɒrɪ'leɪʃən] N corrélation *f* (**with** avec; **between** entre)

correlative [kɒ'relətɪv] ADJ corrélatif
N corrélatif *m*

correspond [kɒrɪ'spɒnd] VI **1** *(conform)* correspondre, être conforme (**with, to** à); **to c. with** *or* **to reality** correspondre à la réalité **2** *(be equivalent)* correspondre (**to** à), être l'équivalent (**to** de), équivaloir (**to** à); **the gendarmes roughly c. to our motorway police** les gendarmes sont à peu près l'équivalent de notre 'motorway police' **3** *(write letters)* correspondre (**with** avec); **they corresponded for many years** ils ont correspondu *ou* ils se sont écrit pendant des années

correspondence [kɒrɪ'spɒndəns] N **1** *(relationship)* correspondance *f* (**with, to** avec), rapport *m* (**with, to** entre) **2** *(letter writing)* correspondance *f*; **to be in c. with sb** être en correspondance avec qn; **they kept up a c. for many years** ils sont restés en correspondance pendant des années; **to do one's c.** faire sa correspondance **3** *(mail)* courrier *m*; **I don't get much c.** je ne reçois pas beaucoup de courrier
▸▸ *Journ* **c. column** courrier *m* des lecteurs; **c. course** cours *m* par correspondance; **c. tray** bac *m* à correspondance

correspondent [kɒrɪ'spɒndənt] N correspondant, -ante; *Journ* **our London c.** notre correspondant à Londres; **parliamentary c.** *Journ* rédacteur, -trice parlementaire; *TV* correspondant, -ante parlementaire; **special c.** envoyé, -ée spécial(e)
▸▸ **c. bank account** compte *m* de correspondant

corresponding [kɒrɪ'spɒndɪŋ] ADJ correspondant (**to** à); **as compared with the c. period last year** par rapport à la même période l'année dernière

▸▸**c. member** (of society, club) membre m correspondant

correspondingly [kɒrɪ'spɒndɪŋlɪ] ADV (to react, respond, adjust) en conséquence; (as a consequence) donc, par conséquent; **prices are c. more expensive** les prix sont proportionnellement plus élevés

corridor ['kɒrɪdɔːr] N couloir m, corridor m; Aviat (air) c. couloir aérien; Hist **the Polish C.** le couloir ou le corridor de Dantzig; Fig **the corridors of power** les hautes sphères fpl du pouvoir

▸▸**c. train** train m à couloir

corroborate [kə'rɒbəreɪt] VT (evidence, confession) corroborer, confirmer

corroboration [kərɒbə'reɪʃən] N corroboration f, confirmation f; **in c. of** ... à l'appui de ...

corroborative [kə'rɒb(ə)rətɪv] ADJ (evidence, statement) qui confirme ou corrobore

corrode [kə'rəʊd] VT (metal) corroder, attaquer; Fig (society) miner; (optimism) entamer
VI se corroder

corroded [kə'rəʊdɪd] ADJ corrodé, attaqué; **badly c. metal** métal très corrodé ou attaqué

corrosion [kə'rəʊʒən] N corrosion f

corrosion-resistant ADJ anti-corrosion inv

corrosive [kə'rəʊsɪv] ADJ, N corrosif m, corrodant m

corrugated ['kɒrʊgeɪtɪd] ADJ (cardboard, paper) ondulé

▸▸**c. cardboard** carton m ondulé; **c. iron** tôle f ondulée; **c. iron roof** toit m en tôle ondulée

corrupt [kə'rʌpt] ADJ **1** (dishonest) (official, politician) corrompu **2** (depraved) corrompu, dépravé; **c. morals** immoralité f **3** Comput (disk, file) corrompu, altéré, endommagé; **to go c.** s'endommager **4** Liter (text) corrompu, altéré
VT **1** (deprave) (youth) corrompre; **to c. sb's morals** dépraver qn; **to be corrupted by power** être corrompu par le pouvoir **2** Comput corrompre, altérer, endommager **3** Liter (text etc) corrompre, altérer

corruptible [kə'rʌptəb(ə)l] ADJ corruptible

corrupting [kə'rʌptɪŋ] ADJ dépravant, corrupteur, -trice; **c. influence** influence f corruptrice

corruption [kə'rʌpʃən] N **1** (giving and taking bribes) corruption f; **bribery and c.** corruption **2** (act of making depraved) corruption f, dépravation f **3** Comput corruption f, altération f, dommage m **4** Liter (of text) corruption f, altération f

corruptive [kə'rʌptɪv] ADJ corrupteur, -trice

corruptly [kə'rʌptlɪ] ADV d'une manière corrompue

corsage [kɔː'sɑːʒ] N **1** fleur f (portée au corsage, à la taille ou au poignet) **2** (bodice of dress) corsage m

corsair ['kɔːseər] N Hist (pirate, ship) corsaire m

corset ['kɔːsɪt] N corset m; **orthopaedic** or **surgical c.** corset orthopédique

Corsica ['kɔːsɪkə] N Corse f

Corsican ['kɔːsɪkən] ADJ corse
N **1** (person) Corse mf **2** Ling corse m

cortège [kɔː'teʒ] N cortège m; **funeral c.** convoi m ou cortège funèbre

cortex, pl **cortices** ['kɔːteks, -ɪsiːz] N Bot, Anat cortex m

corticosteroids [kɔːtɪkəʊ'sterɔɪdz] NPL Med corticoïdes mpl

cortisone ['kɔːtɪzəʊn] N Biol, Chem, Med cortisone f

corundum [kə'rʌndəm] N Miner corindon m

coruscate ['kɒrəskeɪt] VI Lit scintiller

coruscating ['kɒrəskeɪtɪŋ] ADJ Lit brillant, scintillant; Fig (wit) brillant, étincelant

corvette [kɔː'vet] N Naut corvette f

cos [kɒz] N Math (abbr **cosine**) cosinus m

cos² CONJ Fam = **because**

cos³ [kɒs] N Br (lettuce) (laitue f) romaine f
▸▸**c. lettuce** (laitue) romaine

cosh [kɒʃ] Br N matraque f
VT assommer, matraquer

cosignatory ['kəʊ'sɪgnətərɪ] N cosignataire mf (**to** de)

cosily ['kəʊzɪlɪ] ADV (warmly) confortablement, douillettement; **c. wrapped up** bien emmitouflé

cosine ['kəʊsaɪn] N Math cosinus m

cosiness ['kəʊzɪnɪs] N **1** (of armchair, room) confort m **2** Fig (of arrangement) caractère m combinard

cosmetic [kɒz'metɪk] N cosmétique m; **cosmetics** produits mpl de beauté, cosmétiques mpl; **the cosmetics industry/counter** l'industrie f/le rayon des cosmétiques ou des produits de beauté
ADJ **1** (for beautifying) cosmétique **2** (superficial) superficiel; **the policy change is c. rather than real** le changement de politique est plutôt un changement de forme que de fond; **the alterations they made to the translation are purely c.** les changements qu'ils ont apportés à la traduction sont très superficiels

▸▸**c. surgery** chirurgie f esthétique

cosmetician [kɒzmɪ'tɪʃən] N esthéticien, -ienne

cosmetologist [kɒzmə'tɒlədʒɪst] N cosmétologue mf

cosmetology [kɒzmə'tɒlədʒɪ] N cosmétologie f

cosmic ['kɒzmɪk] ADJ (ray, dust) cosmique; Fig gigantesque

cosmogony [kɒz'mɒgənɪ] N cosmogonie f

cosmology [kɒz'mɒlədʒɪ] N cosmologie f

cosmonaut ['kɒzmənɔːt] N cosmonaute mf

cosmopolitan [kɒzmə'pɒlɪt(ə)n] N cosmopolite mf
ADJ (city etc) cosmopolite

cosmos ['kɒzmɒs] N cosmos m

Cossack ['kɒsæk] ADJ cosaque
N Cosaque mf

cosset ['kɒsɪt] VT dorloter, choyer

cossie ['kɒzɪ] N Br, Austr Fam maillot m de bain

COST [kɒst] N **1** (price) coût m, frais mpl; Law **costs** frais d'instance, dépens mpl; Law **they were ordered to pay costs** ils ont été condamnés aux dépens; **at little/great c.** à peu de/à grands frais; **to sell at c.** vendre au prix coûtant; **for the c. of a room in a hotel you could ...** pour le prix d'une chambre à l'hôtel, vous pourriez ...; **the c. of money** le loyer de l'argent; **c., insurance and freight** coût, assurance, fret; **c. and freight** coût et fret; Acct **c. of goods purchased** coût d'achat; Acct **c. of goods sold** coût des ventes, coût des marchandises vendues; Mktg **c. per thousand** coût par mille, CPM m; Acct **c. of sales** coût des marchandises vendues
2 Fig **to count the cost(s) of sth** calculer le coût de qch; **at any c., at all costs** à tout prix, à n'importe quel prix, coûte que coûte; **I learnt it to my c.** je l'ai appris à mes dépens; **as I know to my c.** comme je l'ai appris à mes dépens; **at the c. of one's life** au prix de sa vie; **the c. in human life** (of disaster etc) le prix en vies humaines

VT **1** (pt, pp cost) coûter; **it costs $25** ça coûte 25 dollars; **it c. me £30 a night to stay here** ça m'a coûté 30 livres par nuit ici; **how much does it c.?** combien cela coûte-t-il?; **it costs nothing to join the library** l'inscription à la bibliothèque est gratuite; **that will c. him a great deal of money/trouble** cela lui coûtera beaucoup d'argent/de peine; **to c. a fortune** or **the earth** coûter une fortune, coûter les yeux de la tête; Br Fam **if you go by air it'll c. you** si tu y vas par avion, tu vas le sentir passer; **the attempt c. him his life** cette tentative lui a coûté la vie; **it must have c. her something to admit that** il a dû lui en coûter de l'avouer
2 (pt, pp costed) Com, Ind (estimate cost of) (article) établir le prix de revient de; (job) évaluer le coût de; **how much was it costed at?** (of work) à combien est-ce que le coût a été évalué?

▸▸**c. accounting** comptabilité f analytique ou d'exploitation; Acct **c. allocation** imputation f des charges; Fin **c. analysis** analyse f des coûts, analyse du prix de revient; **c. assessment** évaluation f du coût; **c. budget** budget m des charges; Acct **c. centre** m d'analyse; Fin **c. curve** courbe f des coûts; **c. equation** équation f de coût; **c. factor** facteur m coût; **c. of living** coût de la vie; Fin **c. management** gestion f des coûts; **c. overrun** dépassement m de coût; **c. price** prix m coûtant ou de revient; Acct **c. pricing** méthode f des coûts marginaux

▸ **cost out** VT SEP = **cost** VT **2**

Costa Brava ['kɒstə'brɑːvə] N Costa Brava f

Costa del Crime ['kɒstədel'kraɪm] N Br Fam Hum = appellation f humoristique de la Costa del Sol, par allusion au grand nombre de criminels britanniques qui y résident

Costa del Sol ['kɒstədelsɒl] N Costa del Sol f

co-star ['kəʊstɑːr] Cin N partenaire mf à l'écran
VI partager la vedette (**with** avec)
VT **the film co-stars Tom Cruise and Nicole Kidman** le film met en scène Tom Cruise et Nicole Kidman dans les rôles principaux ou vedettes; **co-starring Gwyneth Paltrow** (in credits) avec Gwyneth Paltrow

Costa Rica ['kɒstə'riːkə] N Costa Rica m

Costa Rican ['kɒstə'riːkən] ADJ costaricien
N Costaricien, -ienne

cost-benefit analysis N Fin analyse f coûts-bénéfices

cost/benefit ratio N Fin rapport m coût/profit

cost-competitive ADJ (product) à prix compétitif; **we're not c.** nos prix ne sont pas compétitifs

cost-conscious ADJ qui fait attention aux dépenses; **to be c.** contrôler ses dépenses

cost-cutting N réduction f des frais ou des dépenses; **further c. may be necessary** d'autres compressions ou réductions des coûts pourraient s'avérer nécessaires
ADJ de réduction des frais ou des dépenses; **c. measures** mesures fpl visant à réduire les frais ou les dépenses

cost-effective ADJ rentable; **the project must be made c.** il faut rentabiliser le projet

cost-effectiveness N Com rentabilité f

coster(monger) ['kɒstər, 'kɒstəmʌŋgər] N Br Old-fashioned marchand, -ande des quatre saisons

costing ['kɒstɪŋ] N Ind, Com (of article) établissement m du prix de revient; (of job) évaluation f du coût

costive ['kɒstɪv] ADJ Med constipé

costliness ['kɒstlɪnɪs] N cherté f; Fig **the c. of an error** les conséquences fpl d'une erreur

costly ['kɒstlɪ] **ADJ** cher, coûteux, onéreux; *Fig* it was a c. mistake c'est une erreur qui a coûté cher

cost-plus ADJ *Fin* à coût majoré
▸▸c. pricing fixation *f* du prix en fonction du coût

cost-push inflation N inflation *f* par les coûts

cost-reduce VT *Com* réduire le coût de

costume ['kɒstjʊm] **N 1** costume *m*; *Theat* to be (dressed) in c. porter un costume (de scène); national c. costume national; *Br* (bathing *or* swimming) c. maillot *m* de bain **2** *Old-fashioned (woman's suit)* tailleur *m*
▸▸*Theat* c. department, costumes department service *m* des costumes; c. designer costumier, -ière; c. drama dramatique *f* en costumes d'époque; c. jewellery bijoux *mpl* fantaisie; c. party bal *m* costumé

costum(i)er [kɒ'stjʊm(ɪ)ər] **N** costumier, -ière

cosy, *Am* **cozy** ['kəʊzɪ] **ADJ 1** *(room, pub)* confortable, douillet; to feel *or* be c. *(of person in room)* être confortablement *ou* douillettement installé; *(in coat, blankets etc)* être bien emmitouflé; it's c. here c'est confortable ici **2** *Fig* a c. little job *(undemanding)* un travail pépère; a c. little arrangement une bonne petite combine; at university it's all very c. à l'université, c'est pépère; the c. relationship between government and the employers les relations très privilégiées entre le gouvernement et le patronat; it's all a bit too c. for my liking *(of relationship between union and management etc)* c'est un peu trop copain-copain à mon goût
N (egg) c. couvre-œuf *m*, *pl* couvre-œufs; **(tea) c.** couvre-théière *m*, *pl* couvre-théières
▸**cosy up to VT INSEP** *(ingratiate oneself with)* se mettre dans les papiers de

cot [kɒt] **N** *(for child)* lit *m* d'enfant; *esp Am (folding bed)* lit d'enfant pliant; *(camp bed)* lit de camp; *Naut* cadre *m* à l'anglaise
▸▸*Br* c. death mort *f* subite du nourrisson

cotangent ['kəʊ'tændʒ(ə)nt] **N** *Math* cotangente *f*

cotel ['kɒtl] **N** *Am* auberge *f* de jeunesse

coterie ['kəʊtərɪ] **N** coterie *f*

co-trustee ['kəʊtrʌs'tiː] **N** *Law* co-administrateur, -trice

cottage ['kɒtɪdʒ] **N 1** petite maison *f* (à la campagne), cottage *m*; *Am (for holidays)* petite maison de vacances, *Can* chalet *m*; **(thatched) c.** chaumière *f* **2** *Br Sl (for homosexuals)* = toilettes *fpl* publiques utilisées comme lieu de rencontre par les homosexuels
▸▸c. cheese fromage *m* blanc (égoutté), cottage cheese *m*; *Br* c. flat = appartement *m* situé dans un pavillon; *Br* c. hospital petit hôpital *m* de campagne; c. industry industrie *f* artisanale; *(small-scale, at home)* industrie familiale; *Br* c. loaf = miche *f* de pain en forme de brioche; *Br* c. pie hachis *m* parmentier

cottager ['kɒtɪdʒər] **N 1** *Br (in countryside)* = habitant, -ante d'un cottage **2** *Am (in holiday resort)* = propriétaire *mf*/locataire *mf* d'une maison de campagne

cottaging ['kɒtɪdʒɪŋ] **N** *Br Sl* = relations *fpl* homosexuelles dans des toilettes publiques

cotter ['kɒtər] **N** *Tech (wedge)* goupille *f*, *(pin)* clavette *f*
▸▸c. pin clavette *f*

cotton ['kɒt(ə)n] **N 1** *(crop)* coton *m*; to pick c. cueillir le coton **2** *(cloth)* (toile *f* de) coton *m*; is this dress c.? *(made of cotton)* cette robe est-elle en coton?; c. goods cotonnades *fpl*; put it with the rest of the cottons *(garments made of cotton)* mets-le avec le reste du (linge en) coton **3** *(for sewing)* fil *m* à coudre

▸▸*Geog* **C. Belt** = région *f* du coton dans le sud des États-Unis; *Br* **c. bud** coton-tige® *m*, *pl* cotons-tiges; *Bot* **c. bush** cotonnier *m*; *Am* **c. candy** barbe *f* à papa; **c. field** champ *m* de coton; **c. growing** culture *f* du coton; **c. grass** linaigrette *f*, lin *m* des marais; **c. mill** filature *f* de coton; **c. picker** *(person)* cueilleur, -euse de coton; **c. plant** cotonnier; **c. plantation** plantation *f* de coton; *Am* **c. swab** coton-tige®; *Br* **c. wool** coton hydrophile, ouate *f*, **c. yarn** coton filé, fil de coton

▸**cotton on VI** *Fam (understand)* piger; to c. on to sth piger qch

▸**cotton to VT INSEP** *Am Fam* **1** *(take a liking to)* se prendre d'amitié pour **2** *(approve of) (person)* avoir à la bonne; *(behaviour, suggestion)* voir d'un bon œil; **I don't c. to that kind of behaviour** je n'approuve pas ce genre de comportement

cotton-picking [-'pɪkɪŋ] **ADJ** *Am Fam (intensifier)* sacré; that's a c. lie! ce n'est qu'un mensonge!; get your c. hands off me! enlève tes sales pattes!

cottonseed ['kɒt(ə)nsiːd] **N** graine *f* de coton
▸▸c. oil huile *f* de coton

cottontail ['kɒt(ə)nteɪl] **N** *Am* lapin *m* (de garenne)

cotyledon [kɒtɪ'liːd(ə)n] **N** *Bot* cotylédon *m*

couch [kaʊtʃ] **N** *(sofa)* canapé *m*, divan *m*, sofa *m*; *(in psychiatrist's office)* divan *m*, *Fig* to be on the c. *(in psychoanalysis)* être en analyse
VT *(express) (phrase, comment)* formuler, rédiger; the complaint was couched in very polite language la plainte avait été formulée très poliment
▸▸*Bot* c. grass chiendent *m*; *Fam* c. potato mollasson, -onne *(toujours affalé devant la télévision)*; he's a real c. potato il est toujours affalé devant la télé

couchette [kʊ'ʃet] **N** *Rail, Naut* couchette *f*
▸▸*Rail* c. car voiture-couchette *f*, *pl* voitures-couchettes

cougar ['kuːgər] **N** *(animal)* puma *m*

cough [kɒf] **N** toux *f*; I've got a c. je tousse; he gave a c. to warn me il toussota pour m'avertir; he cleared his throat with a c. il toussota pour s'éclaircir la voix *ou Fam* la gorge; dry c. toux sèche
VI *(of person, animal)*, *Fam (engine)* tousser; *(to warn sb)* avertir
▸▸c. drop pastille *f* contre la toux *ou* antitussive; c. lozenge pastille contre la toux *ou* antitussive; c. mixture sirop *m* antitussif *ou* contre la toux; c. sweet pastille contre la toux *ou* antitussive; c. syrup sirop contre la toux *ou* antitussif
▸**cough up VT SEP 1** *(produce by coughing)* cracher (en toussant), expectorer; to c. up phlegm/blood cracher des glaires/du sang **2** *Fam (pay)* sortir; I had to c. up £50 for the meal j'ai dû sortir 50 livres pour le repas
VI *Fam (pay)* casquer, cracher, raquer; come on, c. up! *(money owed me)* allez! filemoi mon argent!; *(pay your share)* allez! allonge!

coughing ['kɒfɪŋ] **N** toux *f*; fit of c., c. fit quinte *f* de toux; your c. woke me up tu m'as réveillé en toussant

could **PT** *See* **can²**

couldn't-care-less ['kʊd(ə)ntkeə'les] **ADJ** c. attitude laisser-aller *m*, *Fam* je-m'enfichisme *m*, *Fam* je-m'en-foutisme *m*

coulomb ['kuːlɒm] **N** *Elec* coulomb *m*, ampère-seconde *m*

council ['kaʊnsəl] **N 1** *(group of people)* conseil *m*; the UN Security C. le Conseil de sécurité des Nations unies
2 *Br Admin (elected local body) (people)* conseil *m*; *(government)* municipalité *f*; the c. sent a repairman la municipalité a envoyé

un réparateur; to be on the c. être au conseil municipal
3 *Rel* concile *m*
4 *(meeting)* conseil *m*; *Mil, Fig* to hold a c. of war tenir un conseil de guerre
▸▸*Am Pol* **C. of Economic Advisers** = groupe *m* de conseillers nommés par le président des États-Unis pour formuler la politique économique du pays; **c. estate** cité *f*, **C. of Europe** Conseil *m* de l'Europe; *Br* **c. flat** ≃ habitation *f* à loyer modéré, HLM *f*, *Br* **c. house** ≃ habitation à loyer modéré, HLM; **c. meeting** réunion *f* du conseil municipal; *EU* **C. of Ministers** Conseil des ministres; **c. offices** bureaux *mpl* de la municipalité

> Attention: ne pas confondre avec le nom **counsel**.

councillor, *Am* **councilor** ['kaʊnsɪlər] **N** conseiller, -ère, membre *m* du conseil; **C. John Smith** M. John Smith, membre du conseil

> Attention: ne pas confondre avec le nom **counsellor**.

councillorship, *Am* **councilorship** ['kaʊnsɪləʃɪp] **N 1** *(rank)* dignité *f* de conseiller **2** *(period in office)* période *f* d'exercice des fonctions de conseiller; during his c. pendant la période où il a exercé en tant que conseiller

counsel ['kaʊns(ə)l] **N 1** *Fml (advice)* conseil *m*, avis *m*; to take c. with sb consulter qn (about sur, au sujet de) **2** to keep one's (own) c. *(about one's plans, intentions)* garder ses projets pour soi; *(about one's opinions)* garder son opinion pour soi **3** *(no pl) Br Law (in court)* avocat *m*; *(adviser)* conseil *m* juridique; to be represented by c. être représenté par un avocat; to take the advice of c. suivre les conseils d'un avocat; c. for the defence défenseur *m*; *(in criminal law)* avocat de la défense; c. for the prosecution procureur *m*; King's/Queen's c. conseiller *m* du Roi/de la Reine, conseiller de la Couronne
VT *(-ll-, Am -l-) (patience, prudence)* conseiller; to c. sb to do sth conseiller à qn de faire qch

> Attention: ne pas confondre avec le nom **council**.

counselling [kaʊns(ə)lɪŋ] **N** *(activity, profession)* activité *f* de conseil; *(advice)* conseils *mpl*; he needs (professional) c. *(psychological)* il a besoin d'un soutien psychologique; to offer c. for alcoholics/people suffering from AIDS offrir un soutien psychologique et moral aux alcooliques/aux malades du SIDA

counsellor, *Am* **counselor** ['kaʊns(ə)lər] **N 1** *(diplomatic)* conseiller, -ère d'ambassade **2** *(social, psychological)* conseiller, -ère **3** *Am Law* avocat, -ate

> Attention: ne pas confondre avec le nom **councillor**.

COUNT¹ [kaʊnt] **N 1** *(act of counting)* compte *m*, comptage *m*; *(of votes)* dépouillement *m*; *(of people)* dénombrement *m*, comptage; to keep c. tenir le compte (of de); to lose c. perdre le compte; I've lost c. of how many times I've asked you to ... je t'ai demandé je ne sais combien de fois de ...; we'll have to do another c. il faudra qu'on recompte; a quick c. revealed that half were car owners un comptage rapide a révélé que la moitié étaient propriétaires de voitures; at the last c. au dernier comptage
2 *(total, result of count)* compte *m*, total *m*; what was the c.? quel était le total?; this is

short of the c. cela ne fait pas le compte
3 *Boxing* compte *m* (de dix secondes); **to take the c.** rester au tapis pour le compte, être knock-out; *Boxing, Fig* **to be out for the c.** être K.O.
4 *Law* chef *m* d'accusation; **not guilty on the first c.** non coupable au premier chef; *Fig* **I'm angry with them on both counts** je suis fâché avec eux pour les deux raisons; **to fail on a number of counts** (*of project etc*) échouer à plusieurs égards

VT 1 *(enumerate)* (*people, vehicles, animals etc*) dénombrer, compter; (*money*) compter; **to c. the votes** (*at election*) dépouiller le scrutin; **I counted three wrecked cars** j'ai compté trois voitures démolies; **to c. sheep** (*in order to go to sleep*) compter les moutons
2 *(include)* compter; **there were four of us, counting the dog** nous étions quatre en comptant le chien; **without** or **not counting … sans compter …
3 *(consider)* compter (**as** comme); **I don't c. him as a friend** je ne le considère pas comme un ami; **to c. sb among one's friends** compter qn parmi ses amis; **to be counted as a member** compter parmi les membres; **I c. it (as) one of my triumphs** je considère cela comme un de mes triomphes; **c. yourself lucky you weren't killed** estime-toi heureux de n'avoir pas été tué

VI 1 compter; **to c. on one's fingers** compter sur ses doigts; **to c. (up) to 100** compter jusqu'à 100; **to c. from 1 to 100** compter de 1 à 100; **counting from tomorrow** à compter de demain
2 *(be considered)* compter (**among** parmi); **he counts among my best friends** il compte parmi mes meilleurs amis; **two children c. as one adult** deux enfants comptent pour un adulte; **he's under five so he doesn't c.** il a moins de cinq ans, donc il ne compte pas; **marks in this exam c. towards your degree** les notes de cet examen comptent pour votre licence
3 *(be of importance)* compter; **I don't c. around here** je ne compte pas ici; **every vote counts** chaque voix compte; **every minute counts** il n'y a pas une minute à perdre; **experience counts for more than qualifications** l'expérience compte plus que les diplômes; **doesn't that c. for anything?** est-ce que ça ne compte pas, ça?
▸▸ *Gram* **c. noun** nom *m* comptable
▸ **count against** VT INSEP jouer contre
▸ **count down** VI (*for rocket launch*), *Fig* faire le compte à rebours
▸ **count in** VT SEP (*include*) compter; **c. me in!** je suis de la partie, *Fam* je suis partant
▸ **count on** VT INSEP **1** (*depend on*) compter sur; **we're counting on you to give a speech** nous comptons sur vous pour faire un discours; **you can always c. on him to be late** tu peux compter sur lui pour être en retard, tu peux être sûr qu'il sera en retard; **I wouldn't c. on the train arriving on time** je ne compterais pas sur le fait que le train soit à l'heure; **can we c. on your vote?** pouvons-nous compter sur votre voix?
2 (*expect*) compter; **I didn't c. on seeing you** je ne comptais pas te voir
▸ **count out** VT SEP **1** (*add up*) (*money*) compter; **he counted me out twenty £1 coins** il m'a compté vingt pièces d'une livre
2 (*exclude*) ne pas compter; **he's teetotal, so you can c. him out** il ne boit pas, donc ne le compte pas; **no thanks, c. me out!** non merci, ne comptez pas sur moi
3 *Boxing* **to be counted out** rester au tapis pour le compte, être (mis) knock-out
▸ **count up** VT SEP (*add up*) compter

count² N (*nobleman*) comte *m*

countable ['kaʊntəb(ə)l] *Gram* ADJ (*noun*) dénombrable, comptable VOIR GRAMMAIRE
A9–12

▸▸ **c. noun** nom *m* dénombrable *ou* comptable
countdown ['kaʊntdaʊn] N (*for rocket launch*) compte *m* à rebours; *Fig* **the c. to Christmas has begun** on commence à compter les jours qui nous séparent de Noël
countenance ['kaʊntɪnəns] N *esp Lit* **1** (*face*) (*expression f* du) visage *m*, mine *f*; **to lose c.** se décontenancer, perdre contenance; **to be out of c.** avoir perdu contenance, être décontenancé **2** (*support*) **to give** or **lend c. to sb/sth** apporter son appui *ou* son soutien à qn/qch, appuyer qn/qch
VT approuver, appuyer; **she wouldn't c. borrowing money** elle n'approuverait pas le fait d'emprunter de l'argent

counter¹ ['kaʊntər] N **1** (*in shop*) comptoir *m*; (*in supermarket*) rayon *m*; (*in bank etc*) guichet *m*; **you can get these drugs over the c.** on peut acheter ces médicaments sans ordonnance, ces médicaments sont en vente libre; *Fin* **to buy shares over the c.** acheter des actions sur le marché hors cote; **sold over the c.** (*not pre-packaged*) vendu au détail; **to sell under the c.** vendre sous le manteau
2 (*token in games*) (*square*) fiche *f*, (*round*) jeton *m*; **the hostage was being used as a bargaining c.** l'otage a été utilisé comme monnaie d'échange
3 *Comput etc* (*device*) compteur *m*
▸▸ *Br* **c. hand** vendeur, -euse; *Banking* **c. services** services *mpl* de caisse; *Banking* **c. staff** employés, -ées du guichet, guichetiers, -ières; *Banking* **c. transactions** opérations *fpl* de caisse

counter² N *Fencing, Boxing* contre *m*
ADJ **1** (*contrary*) contraire, opposé (**to** à) **2** (*in compounds*) contre-
ADV en sens inverse; **to act c. to one's orders** agir contrairement aux ordres (que l'on a) reçus; **to run c. to sth** aller à l'encontre de qch
VT (*person, thing*) aller à l'encontre de; (*sb's intentions*) contrecarrer; (*accusation, criticism*) répondre à; **measures have been taken to c. the threat of the disease** des mesures ont été prises pour lutter contre la menace que représente la maladie; *Boxing* **to c. a blow** contrer un coup; (*ward off*) parer un coup; **to c. that …** riposter *ou* rétorquer que … + *ind*
VI riposter, contre-attaquer; *Boxing, Fencing* contrer; (*ward off*) parer
▸▸ **c. declaration** contre-déclaration *f*, *pl* contre-déclarations; *Med* **c. indication** contre-indication *f*, *pl* contre-indications; **c. reaction** contre-réaction *f*, *pl* contre-réactions

counteract [kaʊntə'rækt] VT (*act against*) contrecarrer; (*neutralize*) (*influence, effects of drug*) neutraliser
counter-appraisal N *Am Com* contre-expertise *f*, *pl* contre-expertises
counterattack ['kaʊntərətæk] *Mil, Fig* N contre-attaque *f*, *pl* contre-attaques
VT & VI contre-attaquer
counterattraction ['kaʊntərə'trækʃən] N attraction *f* concurrente; (*on TV*) émission *f* concurrente
counterbalance¹ ['kaʊntəbæləns] N contrepoids *m*
counterbalance² [kaʊntə'bæləns] VT contrebalancer, faire contrepoids à
counterbid ['kaʊntəbɪd] N *Fin* suroffre *f*, surenchère *f*, (*during takeover*) contre-OPA *f inv*
counterblast ['kaʊntəblɑːst] N contre-attaque *f*, *pl* contre-attaques
countercharge ['kaʊntətʃɑːdʒ] N *Law*

contre-accusation *f*, *pl* contre-accusations, contre-plainte *f*, *pl* contre-plaintes
countercheck ['kaʊntətʃek] VT vérifier (une seconde fois)
counterclaim ['kaʊntəkleɪm] N demande *f* reconventionnelle
VI *Law* faire une demande reconventionnelle (*en dommages-intérêts*)
counterclockwise ['kaʊntə'klɒkwaɪz] ADV, ADJ *esp Am* en sens inverse des aiguilles d'une montre
counterculture ['kaʊntəkʌltʃər] N contre-culture *f*, *pl* contre-cultures
counterespionage [kaʊntər'espɪɑːnɑːʒ] N contre-espionnage *m*
counterfeit ['kaʊntəfɪt] ADJ (*banknote, document*) faux; (*piece of jewellery*) contrefait; *Fig* (*emotions*) feint
N (*banknote, document*) contrefaçon *f*, faux *m*; (*piece of jewellery*) faux
VT (*banknote, document, piece of jewellery*) contrefaire; *Fig* (*emotions*) feindre
counterfeiter ['kaʊntəfɪtər] N faussoire *mf*; (*of money*) faux-monnayeur *m*, *pl* faux-monnayeurs
counterfoil ['kaʊntəfɔɪl] N *Br* (*of cheque, receipt*) souche *f*, talon *m*
▸▸ **c. book** carnet *m* à souches
counter-guarantee N *St Exch* contre-garantie *f*, *pl* contre-garanties
counterinsurgency ['kaʊntərɪn'sɜːdʒənsɪ] N contre-insurrection *f*, *pl* contre-insurrections
counterintelligence ['kaʊntərɪn'telɪdʒəns] N contre-espionnage *m*
counterintuitive ['kaʊntərɪn'tjuːɪtɪv] ADJ qui va contre l'intuition
countermand ['kaʊntə'mɑːnd] VT (*order*) annuler
countermarketing ['kaʊntəmɑːkətɪŋ] N contremarketing *m*, contremercatique *f*
countermeasure ['kaʊntəmeʒər] N contre-mesure *f*, *pl* contre-mesures
countermove ['kaʊntəmuːv] N contre *m*
counteroffensive ['kaʊntərə'fensɪv] N *Mil* contre-offensive *f*, *pl* contre-offensives
counter-offer N contre-offre *f*, *pl* contre-offres
counterorder ['kaʊntərɔːdər] N contrordre *m*
counterpane ['kaʊntəpeɪn] N couvre-lit *m*, *pl* couvre-lits; (*quilted*) courtepointe *f*
counterpart ['kaʊntəpɑːt] N **1** (*person*) homologue *mf* **2** (*corresponding system*) équivalent *m*; (*of pair of works of art*) pendant *m*; (*piece that corresponds*) pièce *f* qui va de pair
counterparty risk ['kaʊntəpɑːtɪ] N *Banking* risque *m* de contrepartie
counterplot ['kaʊntəplɒt] N contre-ruse *f*, *pl* contre-ruses
counterpoint ['kaʊntəpɔɪnt] N *Mus* contrepoint *m*
counterpoise ['kaʊntəpɔɪz] N *also Fig* contrepoids *m*; **in c.** en équilibre; **his sense of organization served as a c. to …** son sens de l'organisation contrebalançait …
VT contrebalancer, faire contrepoids à
counterproductive ['kaʊntəprə'dʌktɪv] ADJ qui a des effets contraires; **that would be c.** cela irait à l'encontre du but recherché
counterproposal ['kaʊntəprə'pəʊz(ə)l] N contre-proposition *f*, *pl* contre-propositions
counterpurchase ['kaʊntəpətʃɪs] N contre-achat *m*, *pl* contre-achats
Counter-Reformation N *Rel, Hist* **the C.** la Contre-Réforme
counter-revolution N *Pol* contre-révolution *f*, *pl* contre-révolutions

counter-revolutionary *Pol* N contre-révolutionnaire *mf*, *pl* contre-révolutionnaires
ADJ contre-révolutionnaire

countersegmentation ['kaʊntəsegmen-'teɪʃən] N *Mktg* contre-segmentation *f*, stratégie *f* d'indifférenciation

countershaft ['kaʊntəʃɑːft] N *Aut (layshaft)* arbre *m* intermédiaire

countersign ['kaʊntəsaɪn] VT *(order etc)* contresigner, signer en second, viser

countersignature ['kaʊntə'sɪgnətʃər] N contreseing *m*

countersink ['kaʊntəsɪŋk] N **1** *(tool)* fraise *f* **2** *(for head of screw)* noyure *f*, *(of hole)* fraisure *f*
VT (*pt*, *pp* **countersunk**) *(head of screw)* noyer; *(hole)* fraiser
▸▸ **c. bit** *(tool)* fraise *f*

counterstroke ['kaʊntəstrəʊk] N *Mil, Fig* contre-offensive *f*, *pl* contre-offensives

countersunk ['kaʊntəsʌŋk] ADJ *(screw)* fraisé, noyé

countertenor ['kaʊntətenər] N *Mus (person)* haute-contre *m*, *pl* hautes-contre, contre-ténor *m*, *pl* contre-ténors

counterterrorism ['kaʊntə'terərɪz(ə)m] N contre-terrorisme *m*

counterterrorist ['kaʊntə'terərɪst] ADJ contre-terroriste

countertop ['kaʊntətɒp] N *Am* plan *m* de travail

countertrade ['kaʊntətreɪd] N commerce *m* d'échange, troc *m*

countertrading [kaʊntə'treɪdɪŋ] N troc *m*

countervailing [kaʊntə'veɪlɪŋ] ADJ ATTRIB *Fml* compensatoire
▸▸ *Econ* **c. duty** droit *m* compensateur

countervaluation ['kaʊntəvælju'eɪʃən] N contre-expertise *f*, *pl* contre-expertises

counterweight ['kaʊntəweɪt] N contrepoids *m*

countess ['kaʊntɪs] N comtesse *f*

counting ['kaʊntɪŋ] N compte *m*; *(of vote)* dépouillement *m*; *(of people)* compte, dénombrement *m*

countless ['kaʊntlɪs] ADJ innombrable, sans nombre

countrified ['kʌntrɪfaɪd] ADJ aux allures campagnardes; **it's very c. here** c'est comme la campagne ici

country ['kʌntrɪ] N **1** *(political entity)* pays *m*; **in this c.** dans ce pays; **the Prime Minister isn't in the c.** le premier ministre est à l'étranger; **to die for/love one's c.** mourir pour/aimer sa patrie; *esp Br Pol* **to go to the c.** *(call election)* se présenter aux suffrages des électeurs; **c. of destination** pays de destination VOIR GRAMMAIRE A12
2 *(opposed to town)* campagne *f*, **in the c.** à la campagne
3 *(opposed to capital)* province *f*, **a quiet little c. town** une petite ville tranquille de province
4 *(region)* pays *m*, région *f*, **rough c.** terrain *m* accidenté; **open c.** rase campagne *f*; **flat c.** pays *ou* terrain plat; **wheat-growing c.** région à blé; **this is Proust c.** c'est le pays de Proust
▸▸ *Fam Pej* **c. bumpkin** péquenaud, -aude, plouc *mf*; **c. club** = club *m* sportif ou de loisirs situé à la campagne; **the c. code** = code *m* de conduite à respecter lorsqu'on se promène dans la campagne, qu'on y pique-nique etc; *Pej* **c. cousin** cousin, -ine de province; **c. dancing** danse *f* folklorique; **c. gentleman** gentilhomme *m* campagnard; **c. house** = grande maison *f* de campagne, souvent historique; *Comput* **c. keyboard** cla-

vier *m* national; **c. life** vie *f* à la campagne; *Br* **c. park** parc *m* naturel; **c. seat** *(of noble family)* manoir *m*; *Mktg* **c. version** *(of a product)* version *f* nationale; *Mus* **c. and western** country *m ou f inv*

countryfolk ['kʌntrɪfəʊk] NPL gens *mpl* de la campagne

countryman, *pl* **countrymen** ['kʌntrɪmən] N **1** *(not living in town)* campagnard *m* **2** *(compatriot)* compatriote *m*

countryside ['kʌntrɪsaɪd] N campagne *f*, **beautiful c.** beau paysage *m*; **there's some beautiful c. around Bath** il y a de beaux paysages autour de Bath; **the voters in the c.** les électeurs des régions rurales

country-specific ADJ *Comput (keyboard)* particulier à un pays

country-style ADJ **c. cooking** cuisine *f* campagnarde

countrywoman, *pl* **countrywomen** ['kʌntrɪwʊmən, -wɪmɪn] N **1** *(not living in town)* campagnarde *f* **2** *(compatriot)* compatriote *f*

county ['kaʊntɪ] N **1** comté *m*; *Br* **the c. of Kent** le comté du Kent; *Am* **New York C.** le comté de New York **2** *(population)* habitants *mpl* du comté
ADJ *(rural upper class)* **the c. set** la noblesse campagnarde; **she's very c.** elle fait très femme de la noblesse campagnarde
▸▸ *Br* **c. council** ≃ conseil *m* général; *Br* **c. councillor** ≃ conseiller, -ère général(e); *Br* **c. cricket** = grands matches *mpl* de cricket disputés par les équipes du comté; *Am* **c. line** frontière *f* délimitant un/le comté; *Br* **c. society** l'aristocratie *f* et la haute bourgeoisie du comté; **c. town** *(in England)* chef-lieu *m* de comté, *pl* chefs-lieux de comté

coup [kuː] N **1** coup *m* (audacieux); **to bring off a c.** réussir un joli coup **2** *(overthrow of government)* coup *m* d'État
▸▸ **c. d'état** coup d'État

coupé ['kuːpeɪ] N *Aut* coupé *m*

couple ['kʌp(ə)l] N **1** **a c.** *(a few)* quelques-uns, *f* quelques-unes; *(two)* deux; **a c. of** *(a few)* quelques; *(two)* deux; **a c. of seconds** deux secondes; *Fam* **to have a c.** *(of drinks)* prendre un verre ou deux **2** *(two people, dancers)* couple *m*; **the married c.** les (deux) époux *mpl*; **the newly married c.** les nouveaux *ou* jeunes mariés *mpl*; **they make a lovely c.** ils font un beau couple; **a married c.** un couple marié
VT **1** *(bring together) (oxen)* (ac)coupler; *(male and female)* accoupler; *(names, ideas etc)* associer; **common sense coupled with intelligence** le bon sens allié à l'intelligence; **the course couples theory with practical work** le cours allie la théorie à la pratique **2** *(two engines, batteries)* accoupler; *Rail* **to c. (up) a carriage** atteler *ou* accrocher un wagon
VI *(of male and female)* s'accoupler

coupler ['kʌplər] N *Comput* coupleur *m*

couplet ['kʌplɪt] N *Liter* distique *m*; **rhyming couplets** distiques qui riment

coupling ['kʌp(ə)lɪŋ] N **1** *(bringing together)* accouplement *m*; *(of ideas, names)* association *f* **2** *Rail (of carriages)* attelage *m*; *(of batteries)* couplage *m* **3** *(static device)* raccord *m*, joint *m*; *Rail* attelage *m*; *(device for transmitting motion)* accouplement *m*, embrayage *m* **4** *(mating)* accouplement *m*
▸▸ *Aut* **c. bar** barre *f* d'accouplement

coupon ['kuːpɒn] N *(to be filled in)* coupon *m*; *(exchangeable voucher)* bon *m*; *Fin (on bearer bond)* coupon; *Br Admin* **petrol c.** bon *m* d'essence; *Br Sport* **football** *or* **pools c.** = formulaire de concours de pronostics de football
▸▸ *Fin* **c. bond** obligation *f* au porteur; *Com*

c. offer offre *f* de bon de réduction; *Fin* **c. yield** rendement *m* coupon

couponing ['kuːpənɪŋ] N *Mktg* couponing *m*, couponnage *m*

courage ['kʌrɪdʒ] N courage *m*; **to have the c. to do sth** avoir le courage de faire qch; **to take one's c. in both hands** prendre son courage à deux mains; **to restore sb's c.** redonner du courage à qn

courageous [kə'reɪdʒəs] ADJ courageux

courageously [kə'reɪdʒəslɪ] ADV courageusement, avec courage

courgette [kʊə'ʒet] N *Br* courgette *f*

courier ['kʊrɪər] N **1** *(messenger)* messager *m*; *Com* coursier *m*; **to send sth/arrive by c.** envoyer qch/arriver par coursier; **(motorcycle) c.** messager/coursier en moto; **she was a c. for drug dealers** elle transportait de la drogue pour le compte de trafiquants **2** *(in tourism)* accompagnateur, -trice

COURSE [kɔːs]

> N cours **1, 5** ▪ bien sûr *(of course)* **2**
> ▪ route **3** ▪ ligne de conduite **4**
> ▪ plat **7** ▪ terrain **8**

N **1** *(process) (of river, time, business, events etc)* cours *m*; *(of illness)* évolution *f*; **in the c. of conversation/the evening** au cours de la conversation/de la soirée; **in the c. of time** *(gradually)* à la longue; *(eventually)* finalement; **the building is in the c. of completion** le bâtiment est en cours d'achèvement; **to be in the c. of doing sth** être en train de faire qch; **in the ordinary** *or* **normal c. of things** *or* **events** normalement; **in due c.** en temps utile; **to let nature take its c.** laisser la nature faire les choses; **let things take** *or* **run their c.** laisser les choses suivre *ou* se faire leur cours; **it's best to let the fever run its c.** il vaut mieux laisser la fièvre évoluer normalement; **that is a matter of c.** cela va sans dire; **as a matter of c.** tout naturellement, automatiquement; **blood tests are carried out as a matter of c.** des examens sanguins sont effectués automatiquement

2 **of c.** bien sûr, bien entendu, naturellement; **of c. not!** bien sûr que non!; **of c. she was angry!** bien sûr qu'elle était fâchée!; **he forgot, of c.** bien entendu, il a oublié

3 *(route)* route *f*, direction *f*; **to keep one's c.** ne pas dévier de sa route; *Naut* maintenir son cap; **to change (one's) c.** changer de direction; *Naut* changer le cap; *Naut, Fig* **to be on c.** suivre le cap fixé; **to be driven off c.** *(of ship)* être dévié de son cap, dévier de son cap

4 **c. (of action)** ligne *f* de conduite; **to take a c. of action** adopter une ligne de conduite; **it is the only c. open to me** c'est la seule chose que je puisse faire; **there is no other c. open to us** nous n'avons pas d'autre solution; **the best c. would be to ...** la meilleure chose à faire *ou* le mieux serait de ...; **his best c. would be to ...** le mieux pour lui serait de ...; **the right c.** la bonne voie

5 *Sch, Univ* cours *m*; **to give a c. of lectures** donner une série de cours; **to take** *or* **follow** *or* **do a c. (in sth)** suivre un cours (de qch); **a degree c.** un cours de licence; **he has published a French c.** il a publié une méthode de français

6 *Med* **c. (of treatment)** traitement *m*; **a c. of injections** une série de piqûres

7 *(of meal)* plat *m*; **first c.** entrée *f*; **four-c. dinner** dîner *m* de quatre plats

8 *Sport etc (for races)* parcours *m*; *(for motor-racing)* circuit *m*; **(golf) c.** terrain *m* de golf, golf *m*; **to finish the c.** finir le course; *Fig* finir

9 *Constr (of bricks)* assise *f*

VI **1** *(of liquids)* ruisseler; **the blood coursed**

through her veins le sang courait dans ses veines; **tears were coursing down my face** j'avais le visage ruisselant de larmes **2** *(in hunting)* courir le lièvre **VT** *(hare)* courir

courseware ['kɔːsweər] N *Comput* didacticiel *m*

coursing ['kɔːsɪŋ] N **1** *(hunting)* chasse *f* à courre au lièvre **2** *(racing hounds)* = concours *m* de vitesse entre lévriers lâchés sur un lièvre en champ clos

court [kɔːt] N **1** *Law* cour *f*, tribunal *m*; *(courtroom)* auditoire *m* de tribunal; **civil/criminal c.** tribunal civil/criminel; *Br* **county c.** tribunal de grande instance; **International C. of Justice** Cour internationale de justice; **to go to c.** aller en justice; **to take sb to c.** faire un procès à qn; **are you prepared to say that in c.?** est-ce que vous seriez prêt à le jurer devant le tribunal?; **in open c.** en plein tribunal; **case before the c.** affaire *f* en cause; **to come before the c.** *(of person)* comparaître devant le tribunal; *(of case)* être jugé; **to settle a case out of c.** arranger une affaire à l'amiable; **we've decided to settle out of c.** nous avons décidé d'arranger ça à l'amiable; **tell the c. what you saw** veuillez dire à la cour ce que vous avez vu; **sale by order of the c.** vente *f* judiciaire; **this is a matter for the courts, not the government** c'est à la justice d'en décider, pas au gouvernement
VOIR GRAMMAIRE A6-7

2 *(for tennis, squash etc)* court *m*; **tennis c.** court (de tennis), tennis *m*; **grass c.** court sur gazon; **hard c.** court en dur; **he was on c. for three hours** il a été sur le court pendant trois heures

3 *(royal etc)* cour *f*; **to pay c. to the king** faire sa cour au roi; **to hold c.** *(of celebrity etc)* s'entretenir avec toute une cour d'admirateurs

4 *(courtyard)* cour *f*, *(in names of blocks of flats)* ≃ résidence *f*, *(in names of palaces)* château *m*, palais *m*

5 *Old-fashioned* **to pay c. to a woman** faire la cour à une femme
VT 1 *(seek)* *(sb's friendship)* (re)chercher, solliciter; *(sb's favour)* briguer; *(failure)* aller au-devant de; *(death)* braver; **to c. popularity** chercher à se faire bien voir; **(with** auprès de**)**; **to c. disaster** aller à la catastrophe; **to c. the electorate** chercher à gagner les voix des électeurs

2 *Old-fashioned (seek in marriage) (woman)* courtiser, faire la cour à; **they had been courting one another for nearly a year** ils se fréquentaient depuis presque un an
VI *Old-fashioned* **to be courting** *(of individual)* fréquenter; *(of couple)* se fréquenter; **courting couple** couple *m* d'amoureux
▸▸*Law* **C. of Appeal** cour d'appel; *Law* **c. appearance** *(of accused)* comparution *f* en justice; *EU* **C. of Auditors** Cour des comptes européenne; *Br Cards* **c. card** figure *f*, *Law* **c. case** procès *m*, affaire *f*, *Br Journ* **c. circular** = rubrique *f* d'un journal indiquant les engagements officiels de la famille royale; *Journ* **c. correspondent** correspondant, -ante à la cour royale; *Law* **c. of first instance** juridiction *f* de première instance; *Br* **c. of inquiry** *(body of people)* commission *f* d'enquête; *(investigation)* enquête *f*, **c. of law** tribunal; *Mil* **c. martial** cour martiale; *Law* **c. reporter** chroniqueur, -euse judiciaire; *Law* **c. ruling** décision *f* de justice; *Br* **c. shoe** escarpin *m*; *Am* **c. tennis** jeu *m* de paume

courteous ['kɜːtɪəs] ADJ courtois, poli (**to**, **towards** envers)

courteously ['kɜːtɪəslɪ] ADV courtoisement, poliment

courtesan [kɔːtɪ'zæn] N courtisane *f*

courtesy ['kɜːtəsɪ] N courtoisie *f*, politesse *f*; **common c.** la politesse la plus élémen-

taire; **he didn't have the c. to reply to my letter** il n'a pas eu la politesse de répondre à ma lettre; **by c. of ...** avec la gracieuse permission de ...; **exchange of courtesies** échange *m* de politesses
▸▸ **c. bus** navette *f* gratuite; **c. call** visite *f* de politesse; **to pay sb a c. call** faire une visite de politesse à qn; **c. car** *(from hotel)* voiture *f* de courtoisie; *(from garage)* voiture *f* de remplacement; *Aut* **c. light** plafonnier *m*, éclairage *m* intérieur; *Aut* **c. mirror** miroir *m* de courtoisie; *Br* **c. title** titre *m* de courtoisie

courthouse ['kɔːthaʊs] N *esp Am* palais *m* de justice, tribunal *m*

courtier ['kɔːtɪər] N courtisan *m*

courtly ['kɔːtlɪ] ADJ *(polite)* courtois, d'une politesse raffinée
▸▸ *Hist* **c. love** amour *m* courtois

court-martial VT *(-ll-, Am -l-) (soldier)* faire passer en cour martiale; **to be court-martialled** passer en cour martiale

court-ordered ADJ *(sale)* judiciaire

courtroom ['kɔːtruːm] N *Law* salle *f* d'audience; *(people)* auditoire *m* d'un/du tribunal; **his c. performances** ses performances *fpl* devant la cour
▸▸ *Cin, TV* **c. drama** drame *m* judiciaire

courtship ['kɔːtʃɪp] N *(of woman)* cour *f*, **during their c.** à l'époque où il lui faisait la cour
▸▸ *Zool* **c. display** parade *f* nuptiale

courtyard ['kɔːtjɑːd] N *(of house etc)* cour *f*

couscous ['kuːskuːs] N couscous *m*

co-user ['kəʊjuːzər] N *Comput* co-utilisateur *m*

cousin ['kʌz(ə)n] N cousin, -ine; **first c., full c.** cousin, -ine germain(e); **second c.** cousin, -ine issu(e) de germains; *Fig* **our American cousins** nos cousins américains; **a distant c. of the sparrow** un cousin éloigné du moineau

couth [kuːθ] ADJ *Br Hum* **he's not very c.** il n'est pas très raffiné

couture [kuː'tʊər] N couture *f*, **haute c.** haute couture

couturier, *f* **couturière** [kuː'tjʊərɪeɪ, -ɪeər] N (grand) couturier *m*, (grande) couturière *f*, *(head of company)* directeur, -trice d'une maison de haute couture

covalent [kəʊ'veɪlənt] ADJ *Chem* covalent

cove[1] [kəʊv] N *Geog* anse *f*, crique *f*

cove[2] N *Old-fashioned Br Fam (fellow)* type *m*; **a queer c.** un drôle de pistolet

coven ['kʌv(ə)n] N bande *f* ou réunion *f* de sorcières

covenant ['kʌvənənt] N **1** *Law* convention *f*, contrat *m* **2** *Pol* pacte *m*, traité *m* **3** *Bible (of Jews)* alliance *f*
VT *Law* promettre par contrat; **to c. to do sth** convenir de faire qch; **to c. a sum of money** s'engager par contrat à payer une somme d'argent
VI *Law* **to c. with sb for sth** convenir (par contrat) de qch avec qn

Coventry ['kɒvəntrɪ] N *Br Fam* **to send sb to C.** mettre qn en quarantaine

COVER ['kʌvər]

N couvercle **1**	▪ couvre-lit **2**	
▪ couverture **3, 8, 9**	▪ abri **5, 6**	
VT couvrir **1-10**	▪ recouvrir **2**	
▪ parcourir **6**	▪ marquer **12**	

N 1 *(lid) (for pot etc)* couvercle *m*
2 *(soft covering) (bedspread)* couvre-lit *m*, *pl* couvre-lits; *(for umbrella)* fourreau *m*; *(for car, boat, furniture, computer)* housse *f*, **covers** *(on bed)* couvertures *fpl*; *Met* **cloud c.** couverture nuageuse
3 *(of book, magazine)* couverture *f*, *(in*

bookbinding) plats *mpl*; **to read a book from c. to c.** lire un livre d'un bout à l'autre; **(front) c.** couverture; **hard/soft covers** couverture rigide/souple
4 *(envelope)* **under plain/separate c.** sous pli ordinaire/séparé
5 *(shelter from weather)* abri *m*; **to take c.** *(from the rain etc)* se mettre à l'abri; **the rocks gave us some c.** les rochers nous ont fourni un abri; **to be under c.** être à couvert *ou* à l'abri
6 *Mil etc (from gunfire etc)* couvert *m*, abri *m*; *(firing)* tir *m* de couverture *ou* de protection; **under c.** à couvert, à l'abri; **to take c.** se mettre à couvert, s'abriter; **to give sb c.** *(of aircraft, artillery etc)* couvrir qn; **the rocks provided c. for snipers** les rochers ont fourni des abris pour les tireurs isolés; **without c.** à découvert; **air/radar c.** couverture *f* aérienne/radar
7 *(in hunting)* couvert *m*, fourré *m*, gîte *m*, *Old-fashioned* remise *f*, **to take c.** se remiser; **to break c.** *(of game)* débusquer; *Fig (of person)* sortir de sa retraite
8 *(something that conceals)* voile *m*, masque *m*; *(for spy, police officer etc)* couverture *f*, **under the c. of** *(friendship etc)* sous le couvert *ou* le masque de; **under (the) c. of darkness** à la faveur de la nuit; **to go under c.** *(of police officer etc)* adopter une identité d'emprunt *(pour les besoins d'une enquête)*; **to blow sb's c.** *(in espionage, undercover police work)* démasquer qn
9 *(in insurance)* couverture *f*, provision *f*, **with c.** avec couverture; **without c.** à découvert; **full c.** garantie *f* totale
10 *(in restaurant)* couvert *m*
VT 1 *(person, object)* couvrir (**with, in** de); **covered in** *or* **with snow** couvert de neige *ou* par la neige; **to c. one's head** se couvrir (la tête); **to c. one's ears** *(so as not to hear)* se boucher les oreilles; **writing covered the page** la page était couverte d'écriture; **the scarf covered her mouth** l'écharpe lui couvrait la bouche; **to be well covered** *(warmly dressed)* être bien couvert; *Fam (plump, fat)* être bien en chair; **to c. oneself with glory** se couvrir de gloire; **to c. sb with ridicule** couvrir qn de ridicule; **covered with shame** couvert de honte
2 *(in order to protect)* recouvrir (**with** de); *(in bookbinding) (book)* couvrir; **a wire covered with plastic** un fil électrique recouvert de plastique
3 *(hide) (one's anxiety, confusion etc)* couvrir, dissimuler; **to c. one's tracks** brouiller les pistes
4 *Mil etc (protect)* protéger; *(person)* couvrir; **I've got you covered** *(I have a gun aimed at you)* j'ai mon fusil/revolver braqué sur toi
5 *(deal with, take into account)* couvrir; **the course covers the first half of the century** le cours couvre la première moitié du siècle; **to c. all eventualites** parer à toute éventualité; **that's not covered** ce n'est pas traité; **it's covered in some detail** c'est traité en détail
6 *(travel) (a distance)* couvrir, parcourir; **we covered 100 kilometres before breakfast** nous avons fait cent kilomètres avant le petit déjeuner; **to c. a lot of ground** *(travel great distance)* faire beaucoup de chemin; *(search etc over a wide area)* parcourir un champ très vaste; *Fig (of book, author etc)* couvrir de nombreux domaines; *(of meeting etc)* traiter bien des problèmes
7 *(in insurance) (risk)* couvrir; *Fin* **to be covered** *(of creditor)* être couvert; **we're not covered for** *or* **against theft** nous ne sommes pas couverts contre le vol; **to c. oneself** se couvrir (**against a risk** d'un risque); *Fig* **the president covered himself by saying that ...** le président s'est couvert en disant que ...
8 *(of money) (expenses, cost etc)* couvrir;

£100 won't c. the cost of a new carpet 100 livres ne couvriront pas le coût d'une moquette neuve; **to c. a deficit** combler un déficit; *Acct* **to c. a loss** couvrir un déficit; **to c. an overdraft** couvrir un découvert; **will that c. it?** est-ce que ça suffira?

9 *Journ, TV, Radio (sports event etc)* couvrir **10** *(in breeding) (female)* couvrir, saillir **11** *Mus* **to c. a song** faire une reprise d'une chanson

12 *Sport (mark) (player)* marquer

VI **paint that covers well** peinture qui couvre bien *ou* bien couvrante

▸▸**c. charge** *(in restaurant)* couvert; *Am (in bar)* entrée *f*, prix *m* d'entrée; **c. clause** clause *f* de garantie; **c. girl** cover-girl *f*, *pl* cover-girls; *Am* **c. letter** *(for job application)* lettre *f* de motivation; *(sent with invoice etc)* lettre d'accompagnement; **c. mount** = cadeau *m* offert avec un magazine; *Br* **c. note** *(in insurance)* attestation *f* provisoire; **c. page** *(of fax)* page *f* de garde; **c. price** *(of magazine)* prix; **c. sheet** *(of fax)* page de garde; *Journ* **c. story** article *m* principal (faisant la couverture); *Mus* **c. version** reprise *f*

▸**cover for** **VT INSEP** *(replace)* remplacer; *(provide excuses for)* couvrir; **I refuse to c. for you with the boss** je refuse de te couvrir auprès du patron

▸**cover in** **VT SEP** *(fill in) (trench)* remplir

▸**cover up** **VT SEP 1** *(conceal)* recouvrir; *(truth, illegal act)* dissimuler

2 *(with blanket etc)* couvrir, recouvrir; **keep the baby covered up** garde le bébé bien couvert; **they covered up the bodies** ils ont recouvert les corps; **that dress is a bit too low – c. yourself up a bit** cette robe est trop décolletée – couvre-toi un peu

VI *(conceal the truth)* cacher la vérité; **the government has been accused of covering up** on a accusé le gouvernement de vouloir étouffer l'affaire; **to c. up for sb** protéger qn; **architects and builders are covering up for each other** les architectes et les entrepreneurs se protègent les uns les autres

coverage ['kʌvərɪdʒ] **N 1** *Journ etc* couverture *f* (médiatique); **some people objected to XTV's c. of these events** certaines personnes ont protesté contre la manière dont XTV a traité ces événements; *TV* **there was no c. of the match** on n'a pas retransmis ce match; **the c. given to the elections was biased** le compte-rendu des élections était partial; **the book gives good c. of the coup** le livre décrit bien la façon dont le coup d'État s'est déroulé; **sports get too much c. on TV** la télé consacre trop de temps au sport

2 *(in insurance)* couverture *f*, provision *f* **3** *Tel (of mobile phone network)* couverture *f*

coverall(s) ['kʌvərɔːl, -z] **N(PL)** *Am* bleu(s) *m(pl)* (de travail)

covered ['kʌvəd] **ADJ 1** *(market, way etc)* couvert **2** *(by insurance policy) (risk)* couvert; *(person)* assuré

▸▸*St Exch* **c. position** position *f* couverte; *St Exch* **c. short position** position courte couverte; **c. wagon** chariot *m* (à bâche)

covering ['kʌvərɪŋ] **ADJ 1** *(document, note)* d'accompagnement **2** *Mil (forces, troops)* de couverture

N 1 *(protective) (for floor)* revêtement *m*; *(for plants, object in trailer)* bâche *f*, *(on furniture)* housse *f* **2** *(of snow, dust, chocolate)* couche *f*

▸▸*Mil* **c. fire** tir *m* de couverture; *Br* **c. letter** lettre *f* d'accompagnement; *(sent with job application)* lettre de motivation

coverlet ['kʌvəlɪt] **N** dessus-de-lit *m inv*

cover-line **N** *Journ* titraille *f*, titre *m* de rappel

covert ['kʌvət] **ADJ** *(threat etc)* caché, voilé;

(action etc) secret, clandestin

N *(in hunting)* couvert *m*, fourré *m*

covertly ['kʌvətlɪ] **ADV** secrètement

cover-up ['kʌvərʌp] **N** *(of irregularity etc)* dissimulation *f*; **the president denied there had been a c.** le président a nié qu'on ait tenté d'étouffer l'affaire; **in a c. attempt that went wrong** dans une tentative ratée pour étouffer l'affaire

covet ['kʌvɪt] **VT** (**-t-**) convoiter; **a highly coveted prize** un prix très convoité

covetous ['kʌvɪtəs] **ADJ** *(person)* avide (**of** de); *(gaze)* de convoitise; **to be c. of sb's property** convoiter les biens d'autrui

covetously ['kʌvɪtəslɪ] **ADV** avec convoitise

covetousness ['kʌvɪtəsnɪs] **N** *(greed)* cupidité *f*, avidité *f*; *(for particular thing)* convoitise *f*

covey ['kʌvɪ] **N** *(of partridges etc)* compagnie *f*, vol *m*

cow [kaʊ] **N 1** vache *f*, *Fig Fam* **till the cows come home** *(to wait)* jusqu'à la Saint-Glinglin; *(to argue, talk)* à n'en plus finir **2** *Pej Fam (woman)* peau *f* de vache; **old c.** vieille bique *f*, vieux chameau *m*; **silly c.** espèce *f* d'idiote; **poor c.!** la pauvre!; **lucky c.!** la veinarde! **3** *(female elephant)* éléphant *m* femelle, éléphante *f*; *(female seal)* phoque *m* femelle; *(female whale)* baleine *f* femelle

VT intimider; **to look cowed** avoir l'air d'un chien battu; **to c. sb into submission** intimider qn jusqu'à ce qu'il/elle se soumette

▸▸*Bot* **c. parsley** cerfeuil *m* sauvage

coward ['kaʊəd] **N** lâche *mf*, poltron, -onne; **I'm a terrible c. in the dark** j'ai très peur du noir; **he's a moral c.** c'est un lâche, il n'a pas le courage de ses opinions

cowardice ['kaʊədɪs], **cowardliness** ['kaʊədlɪnəs] **N** lâcheté *f*, poltronnerie *f*; **moral c.** lâcheté

cowardly ['kaʊədlɪ] **ADJ** lâche

cowbell ['kaʊbel] **N** clochette *f* (pour bétail)

cowboy ['kaʊbɔɪ] **N 1** cow-boy *m*, *pl* cow-boys; **to play cowboys and indians** jouer aux cow-boys et aux indiens **2** *Br Fam Pej (careless or dishonest workman)* fumiste *m*; **a bunch of cowboys, a c. outfit** des petits rigolos *mpl*; **what c. did this plumbing?** quel est le petit rigolo qui s'est occupé de la plomberie?

▸▸**c. boots** bottes *fpl* de cow-boy, santiags *fpl*; **c. film, c. movie** film *m* de cow-boys

cowcatcher ['kaʊkætʃər] **N** *Am Rail* chasse-pierres *m inv*

cower ['kaʊər] **VI** se tapir (à terre); **to c. before sb** *(show fear)* trembler devant qn

cowhand ['kaʊhænd] **N** vacher *m*

cowherd ['kaʊhɜːd] **N** vacher *m*, bouvier *m*

cowhide ['kaʊhaɪd] **N** peau *f ou* cuir *m* de vache

cowl [kaʊl] **N 1** *Rel (hood)* capuchon *m*; *(habit)* habit *m* à capuchon **2** *(on chimney)* capuchon *m*, abat-vent *m inv*; *Aviat, Naut (on engine, funnel)* capot *m*

▸▸**c. neck** *(on sweater)* col *m* cagoule *ou* boule

cowled [kaʊld] **ADJ** (en)capuchonné

cowlick ['kaʊlɪk] **N** *Fam* épi *m* (de cheveux)

cowling ['kaʊlɪŋ] **N** *(on chimney)* capuchonnement *m*; *Aviat (on engine)* capot *m*; *Aut* capot de ventilateur

cowman, *pl* **cowmen** ['kaʊmən] **N** vacher *m*; *Am (rancher)* propriétaire *m* d'un/du ranch

co-worker ['kəʊ'wɜːkər] **N** collègue *mf*

cowpat ['kaʊpæt] **N** bouse *f* de vache

cowpoke ['kaʊpəʊk] **N** *Am Fam* cow-boy *m*, *pl* cow-boys

cowpox ['kaʊpɒks] **N** *Vet* cowpox *m*, vaccine *f*

cowpuncher ['kaʊpʌntʃər] **N** *Am Fam* cow-boy *m*, *pl* cow-boys

cowrie, cowry ['kaʊrɪ] **N** *(mollusc)* porcelaine *f*, *(shell)* cauri *m*

cowshed ['kaʊʃed] **N** étable *f*

cowslip ['kaʊslɪp] **N** coucou *m*, primevère *f* commune

cox [kɒks] *Sp* **N** *(in rowing)* barreur, -euse **VT & VI** *(in rowing)* gouverner, barrer

coxless four [kɒkslɪs] **N** quatre *m* sans barreur

coxswain ['kɒks(ə)n] **N** barreur, -euse

coy [kɔɪ] **ADJ** *(shy)* timide; *Pej (affectedly shy)* qui fait la sainte-nitouche; *(seductive)* qui fait des mines; **a c. look** un air de sainte-nitouche; **to go all c.** *(of child)*, *Pej* faire le/la timide; **with a c. little smile** avec un petit sourire séducteur; **why be so c. about accepting?** pourquoi faire semblant d'hésiter?; **he was rather c. about the price** il était plutôt évasif quant au prix; **the rather c. treatment of the sex scenes** la façon un peu mièvre dont sont traitées les scènes de sexe

coyly ['kɔɪlɪ] **ADV** timidement; *Pej* en faisant le/la timide; **to reply c.** *(evasively)* faire une réponse évasive

coyness ['kɔɪnɪs] **N** *(shyness)* timidité *f*, *Pej (affected shyness)* fausse timidité; **... he said, with a certain c.** *(evasively and vaguely)* ... dit-il, restant dans le vague

coyote [kɔɪ'jəʊtɪ] **N** coyote *m*

coypu ['kɔɪpuː] **N** coypou *m*, ragondin *m*

coziness ['kəʊzɪnɪs] **N** *Am* = **cosiness**

cozy ['kəʊzɪ] **ADJ** *Am* = **cosy**

cp *(abbr* **compare**) comparer

CPA [siː'piː'eɪ] **N** *Am (abbr* **Certified Public Accountant** *)* expert-comptable *m*, *pl* experts-comptables

cpa [siː'piː'eɪ] **N** *(abbr* **critical path analysis**) analyse *f* du chemin critique

cpi [siː'piː'aɪ] *Comput (abbr* **characters per inch**) cpp

Cpl *Mil abbr* **Corporal**

CP/M [siː'piː'em] **N** *Comput (abbr* **control program/monitor**) CP/M *m*

cps [siː'piː'es] *Comput (abbr* **characters per second**) cps

CPU [siː'piː'juː] **N** *Comput (abbr* **central processing unit**) unité *f* centrale

CR [siː'ɑːr] **N** *Comput (abbr* **carriage return**) retour *m* chariot

crab¹ [kræb] **N 1** *(crustacean)* crabe *m* **2** *(louse)* morpion *m*; **to have crabs** avoir des morpions **3** *Astron* **the C.** *(constellation)* le Cancer; *(nebula)* le Crabe **4** *Cin, TV* travelling *m* latéral

VI 1 *esp Am Fam (grumble)* ronchonner (**about** contre) **2** *Cin, TV* faire un travelling latéral; **to c. right/left** faire un travelling latéral vers la droite/gauche

▸▸*Med* **c. louse** morpion *m*; *Culin* **c. paste** beurre *m* de crabe; **c. pot** casier *m* à crabes

crab² **N** *(apple)* pomme *f* sauvage

▸▸**c. apple** *(fruit)* pomme sauvage; *(tree)* pommier *m* sauvage

crabbed ['kræbɪd, kræbd] **ADJ 1** *(writing)* en pattes de mouche **2** *(grumpy)* maussade, grincheux

crabby ['kræbɪ] **ADJ** maussade, grincheux

CRACK [kræk]

N fente **1** ▪ fissure **1** ▪ fêlure **1** ▪ crevasse **1** ▪ craquement **3** ▪ claquement **3** ▪ coup **5** ▪ plaisanterie **6**
VT fêler **1** ▪ crevasser **1** ▪ faire craquer **2** ▪ faire claquer **2** ▪ assommer **3**
VI se fêler **1** ▪ se crevasser **1** ▪ craquer **3, 4** ▪ claquer **4**

N 1 *(split)* fente *f*, fissure *f*; *(in bone)* fêlure *f*; *(in skin)* crevasse *f*, gerçure *f*; *(in wall, ground)* crevasse, lézarde *f*; *(in varnish, enamel)* craquelure *f*; *(in glass, pottery, bell etc)* fêlure; *Fig (in policy, argument)* fissure, faiblesse *f*; **cracks were beginning to appear in the coalition** la coalition commençait à se fissurer

2 *(of door etc)* entrebâillement *m*; **open the window a c.** ouvrez la fenêtre un petit peu; *Fig* **at the c. of dawn** à la pointe du jour

3 *(sound) (of branches, ice etc)* craquement *m*; *(of whip)* claquement *m*; *(of rifle)* détonation *f*, claquement sec; *Fig Fam* **to get a fair c. of the whip** avoir toutes ses chances; *Fam* **to give sb a fair c. of the whip** donner toutes ses chances à qn

4 *Fig Fam (attempt)* **to have a c. at sth** s'essayer à qch; **I'll have a c. (at it)** je vais tenter le coup; **to give sb** *or* **let sb have a c. at sth** laisser qn essayer de faire qch

5 *Fam (blow)* **c. on the head** coup *m* sec sur la tête

6 *Fam (gibe)* plaisanterie *f*; **to make a c.** faire une plaisanterie, lancer une vanne; **a cheap c. about short people** une plaisanterie facile sur les gens de petite taille; **nasty c.** plaisanterie acerbe *ou* acérée

7 *Sl (drug)* crack *m*

8 *Ir Fam* **there was some good c.** on s'est bien marré

ADJ *Fam* d'élite; *Sport* **c. player** as *m*, crack *m*; **c. regiment** régiment *m* d'élite

INT crac!, clac!

VT 1 *(damage, break etc) (glass, plate, bone, tooth)* fêler; *(lip)* gercer; *(wall, earth)* lézarder, crevasser; *(stone etc)* fendre; *(varnish, paint, plastic)* fendiller, craqueler

2 *(make sound with) (whip)* faire claquer; *(one's fingers)* faire craquer

3 *Fam (hit)* **to c. sb over the head** assommer qn; **he cracked his head against the wall** il s'est cogné au mur

4 *(solve) (problem)* résoudre; *(code)* décrypter; **I think I've cracked it** je crois que j'y suis arrivé

5 *(break open) (safe)* percer; *(nut)* casser; *Com (market)* percer sur; *Fam* **to c. a bottle of wine (with sb)** boire une bouteille de vin (avec qn)

6 *(make)* **to c. a joke** raconter une blague; **it's not the sort of thing you can c. jokes about** ce n'est pas le genre de choses sur lequel on peut plaisanter; **where are you going, the North Pole?, he cracked** où est-ce que tu vas, au pôle Nord?, a-t-il plaisanté

7 *Ind (heavy oil)* fractionner

VI 1 *(become cracked) (of glass, plate, bone etc)* se fêler; *(of wall)* se crevasser, se lézarder; *(of skin, lips)* se gercer; *(of paint, varnish)* se fendiller, se craqueler

2 *(of voice)* se casser; *(at puberty)* muer

3 *(of person) (under pressure)* craquer; *(of resistance)* lâcher; *Hum* **the boss has finally cracked** *(gone mad)* le patron a fini par craquer

4 *(make sound)* craquer; *(of whip)* claquer; **a rifle cracked** un coup de fusil a claqué

► ► **c. house** = lieu *m* où l'on achète, vend et consomme du crack; **c. shot** tireur, -euse d'élite

► **crack down** **VI** sévir

► **crack down on** **VT INSEP** *(become stricter about)* prendre des mesures plus sévères *ou* énergiques contre; *(punish) (drunk driving etc)* sévir contre

► **crack up** **VI 1** *(break)* se briser en morceaux; **the ice is cracking up** la glace se brise

2 *Fam (of person) (have nervous breakdown)* craquer; *(of marriage, organization)* aller à la ruine

3 *Br Fam (be helpless with laughter)* s'écrouler (de rire); *(get angry)* péter les plombs

VT SEP 1 *Fam (cause to be helpless with laugh-*

ter) **it really cracked me up when I heard about it** je me suis vraiment écroulé de rire quand j'ai entendu parler de ça

2 *Fam (praise)* **it's not all it's cracked up to be** ce n'est pas tout ce qu'on en dit

crackbrained ['krækbreɪnd] **ADJ** *Fam (person)* fêlé, complètement dingue; *(idea, plan etc)* complètement dingue

crackdown ['krækdaʊn] **N** mesures *fpl* énergiques (**on** *sth* contre qch); **the government c. on reporting** the restrictions *fpl* gouvernementales concernant les reportages

cracked [krækt] **ADJ** *Fam (crazy)* dingue, cinglé

cracker ['krækər] **N 1** *(biscuit)* biscuit *m* salé, cracker *m*

2 *Br Fam (excellent thing)* merveille *f*; *(pretty woman)* canon *m*; **the first goal was an absolute c.** le premier but était une pure merveille; **she's an absolute c.** elle est canon; **it's a c. of a joke!** cette histoire est à se tordre!

3 *(firework)* pétard *m*; *(at Christmas)* diablotin *m*; **to pull a c.** faire éclater un diablotin

4 *(for nuts)* casse-noisette(s) *m inv*; casse-noix *m inv*

5 *Am Sl (poor white person)* blanc *m* pauvre *(du sud des États-Unis)*

6 *Comput* pirate *m* informatique

► ► *Am* **c. barrel** boîte *f* à biscuits

cracker-barrel **ADJ** *Am Fam (wisdom, philosophy etc)* populaire

crackers ['krækəz] **ADJ** *Br Fam* **he's c.** il est cinglé; **to go c.** perdre la boule

crackhead ['krækhed] **N** *Sl (drug addict)* drogué, -ée au crack, consommateur, -trice de crack

cracking ['krækɪŋ] *Fam* **ADJ** excellent, épatant; **to be in c. (good) form** être en super forme, avoir la pêche; **at a c. pace** à fond de train

ADV *Fam* **to get c.** s'y mettre; **they got c. with their work** ils se sont mis au travail; **get c.!** grouille-toi!

N 1 *(sound)* craquement *m*; *(of whip)* claquement *m* **2** *(of paint)* craquelure *f*, craquelage *m* **3** *Ind (of oil)* fractionnement *m*, craquage *m* **4** *Comput* piratage *m* informatique

crackle ['kræk(ə)l] **N 1** *(sound) (of dry leaves, twigs)* craquement *m*; *(of shots)* crépitement *m*, crépitation *f*; *(of something frying)* grésillement *m*; *(of fire)* crépitement, pétillement *m*; *Radio* crachotement *m*, crachements *mpl*; *Tel* **there's a bit of a c. on the line** il y a de la friture sur la ligne **2** *(finish) (of paint, porcelain)* craquelure *f*

VI *(of dry leaves, twigs etc)* craquer; *(of shots)* crépiter; *(of something frying)* grésiller; *(of fire)* crépiter, pétiller; *Radio* crachoter

► ► **c. finish** *(of porcelain)* craquelage *m*

crackleware ['kræk(ə)lweər] **N** *Cer* craquelé *m*

crackling ['kræklɪŋ] **ADJ** pétillant, crépitant

N 1 *Br Culin (of roast pork)* = peau *f* de porc grillée **2** *Old-fashioned Br Sl* **a nice bit of c.** *(woman)* une belle pépée

crackpot ['krækpɒt] *Fam* **N** fêlé, -ée, cinglé, -ée; **he's a c.** il est fêlé *ou* cinglé

ADJ *(idea, scheme)* dingue

crackup ['krækʌp] **N 1** *Fam (nervous breakdown)* dépression *f* nerveuse **2** *(of system)* débâcle *f*, *(of civilization)* effondrement *m*

cradle ['kreɪd(ə)l] **N 1** *(of child)*, *Fig (of civilization)* berceau *m*; **from the c.** dès le berceau; **from the c. to the grave** du berceau à la tombe; *Med* **to have c. cap** *(of baby)* avoir des croûtes de lait; *Fam* **he's/she's a c. snatcher** il/elle les prend au berceau *ou* au biberon

2 *Ind etc (of machine etc)* berceau *m*, cadre

m; *(for window cleaner)* nacelle *f*; *Constr, Min* pont *m* volant; *(for painter)* sellette *f*

3 *Med (over bed)* cerceau *m*, arceau *m*

4 *Tel (for receiver)* support *m*

VT 1 *(in cradle) (baby)* mettre *ou* coucher dans un berceau; *Fig* **cradled in luxury** bercé dans le luxe; **the village was cradled in a valley** le village était blotti au fond d'une vallée

2 *(in one's arms) (person)* bercer; *(object)* tenir délicatement; **to c. a child in one's arms** bercer un enfant dans ses bras; **he cradled the rifle in his arms** il serrait le fusil contre lui

cradlesong ['kreɪd(ə)lsɒŋ] **N** *Mus* berceuse *f*

cradle-to-grave **ADJ 1** *(health cover, welfare system)* qui prend l'individu en charge tout au long de sa vie **2** *(service, support)* de bout en bout; **c. management** *or* **control of toxic waste** gestion *f* de bout en bout des déchets dangereux

► ► *Mktg* **c. marketing** = type de marketing qui vise les enfants dès le plus jeune âge

craft [krɑːft] **N 1** *(art)* art *m*; *(occupation)* métier *m* (manuel); *(professional skill) (of teacher etc)* métier *m*; *Sch* travaux *mpl* manuels; **the c. of weaving** l'art du tissage; **painter who is master of his c.** peintre qui maîtrise parfaitement son art **2** *(skill)* habileté *f*, adresse *f*, *Pej (cunning)* ruse *f* **3** *Naut (pl craft)* embarcation *f*, petit navire *m*; **small c.** *(small boats)* canots *mpl*, petits bateaux *mpl*

► ► **c. centre** centre *m* d'artisanat; *Sch* **c. teacher** professeur *m* de travaux manuels

craftily ['krɑːftɪlɪ] **ADV** *(cleverly)* astucieusement, ingénieusement, *Pej* avec ruse *ou* roublardise

craftiness ['krɑːftɪnɪs] **N** ingéniosité *f*, *Pej* ruse *f*, roublardise *f*

craftsman, *pl* **craftsmen** ['krɑːftsmən] **N 1** *(artisan)* artisan *m* **2** *(artist)* artiste *m*; **this is the work of a real c.** c'est l'œuvre de quelqu'un qui s'y connaît

craftsmanship ['krɑːftsmənʃɪp] **N** *(skill)* habileté *f* (manuelle); *(knowledge, experience)* connaissance *f* du métier *m*; **a wonderful piece of c.** un chef-d'œuvre extraordinaire; **think of the c. that has gone into making this table!** songe à l'habileté qu'il a fallu pour faire cette table!

craftswoman, *pl* **craftswomen** ['krɑːftswʊmən, -wɪmɪn] **N** artisane *f*

craftwork ['krɑːftwɜːk] **N** artisanat *m*

crafty ['krɑːftɪ] **ADJ** astucieux, ingénieux, malin, *f* maligne; *Pej* rusé, roublard; **you c. old thing!** espèce de vieux renard!

crag [kræg] **N** rocher *m* ou flanc *m* de montagne escarpé, rocher à pic; **overhanging c.** rocher en surplomb

craggy ['krægɪ] **ADJ 1** *(rocky)* rocailleux **2** *(face)* anguleux, taillé à coups de serpe

cram [kræm] **(-mm-)** **VT 1** *(force)* fourrer, entasser (**sth into sth** qch dans qch); **they crammed 60 people into the bus** ils ont entassé 60 personnes dans le bus; **to c. food into one's mouth** se fourrer la nourriture dans la bouche, se gaver de nourriture, *Fam* s'empiffrer

2 *(fill)* bourrer (**sth with sth** qch de qch); **to c. sb with food** bourrer *ou* gaver qn de nourriture; **cupboards crammed with linen** armoires bourrées de linge; **at school they crammed our heads with facts** à l'école, ils nous ont bourré le crâne d'informations

3 *Sch Fam (candidate for exam)* faire bachoter; **to c. maths** *(of student)* potasser ferme les maths

4 *Agr (poultry)* appâter, gaver

VI 1 *(enter)* s'entasser; **we all crammed into the car** nous nous sommes tous entassés dans la voiture

2 *Sch Fam* potasser, se bourrer le crâne; **to c. for an exam** bachoter

▸ **cram in** VT SEP *(force in)* fourrer, entasser; **you certainly crammed a lot in in two weeks** *(did a lot)* vous avez fait des tas de choses en deux semaines

VI *(enter)* s'entasser; **100 people crammed in** 100 personnes se ou s'y sont entassées

cram-full ADJ *(train, room etc)* bondé; **the streets were c. of people** les rues grouillaient de monde

crammer ['kræmər] N *Fam (school)* boîte f à bac

cramming ['kræmɪŋ] N *Fam (for an exam)* bachotage m, bourrage m de crâne

cramp¹ [kræmp] N *Med* crampe f; **to have (an attack of) c.** être pris d'une crampe, avoir une crampe; **to get c.** *(frequently)* avoir des crampes; *Am* **to have cramps** *(period pains)* avoir des maux de ventre

VT *(hinder) (movements)* gêner; **to be cramped up in a small space** être à l'étroit; *Fam* **to c. sb's style** priver qn de ses moyens

cramp² N **1** *Carp* serre-joint m, pl serre-joints **2** *Constr (cramp iron)* crampon m, clameau m

VT **1** *Constr (stones etc)* cramponner, agrafer **2** *Carp* serrer *(au serre-joint)*
▸▸ *Constr* **c. iron** crampon, clameau

cramped [kræmpt] ADJ *(room)* exigu, f exiguë; *(writing)* serré; **it's very c. in this office** on est très à l'étroit dans ce bureau; **to live/work in c. conditions** vivre/travailler dans un espace restreint; **to be c. for space** être ou se sentir à l'étroit

crampon ['kræmpɒn] N crampon m à glace

cranberry ['krænbərɪ] N canneberge f
▸▸ **c. juice** jus m de canneberge; **c. sauce** sauce f à la canneberge

crane [kreɪn] N **1** *Tech etc* grue f, *Cin* grue (de prise de vue) **2** *(bird)* grue f
VT *(one's neck)* tendre, allonger
VI **to c. forward** tendre ou allonger le cou
▸▸ *Tech etc* **c. driver** conducteur, -trice de grue, grutier, -ière; *Entom* **c. fly** tipule f; *Tech etc* **c. operator** conducteur, -trice de grue, grutier, -ière; *Cin* **c. shot** prise f de vue sur grue

crane's-bill, cranesbill ['kreɪnzbɪl] N bec-de-grue m, pl becs-de-grue, géranium m

cranial ['kreɪnɪəl] ADJ *Anat (nerve etc)* crânien; *(fracture)* du crâne

craniology [kreɪnɪ'ɒlədʒɪ] N craniologie f

cranium, pl **crania** ['kreɪnɪəm, -ɪə] N *Anat* crâne m

crank¹ [kræŋk] N *Tech, Aut* manivelle f; *(crankpin)* maneton m
VT *(engine)* démarrer, lancer; *(with cranking handle)* faire démarrer à la manivelle
▸ **crank out** VT SEP *Fam* produire laborieusement

▸ **crank up** VT SEP *(engine)* lancer ou faire partir à la manivelle; *Fig Fam (person in morning)* mettre en route

crank² N *Fam* **1** *(eccentric)* excentrique mf; **a health food/religious c.** un dingue des aliments naturels/de religion **2** *Am (bad-tempered person)* grincheux, -euse

crankcase ['kræŋkkeɪs] N *Aut* carter m

crankiness ['kræŋkɪnɪs] N *Fam* **1** *(eccentricity)* excentricité f, *(whimsicality)* humeur f capricieuse **2** *Am (bad temper)* humeur f difficile

cranking ['kræŋkɪŋ] ADJ *Aut*
▸▸ **c. handle** manivelle f; **c. speed** vitesse f du démarreur, régime m de démarrage; **c. torque** couple m de démarrage

crankpin ['kræŋkpɪn] N *Aut* maneton m

crankshaft ['kræŋkʃɑːft] N *Aut* vilebrequin m
▸▸ **c. sensor** capteur m sur vilebrequin

cranky ['kræŋkɪ] ADJ *Fam* **1** *(eccentric)* excentrique; *(whimsical)* capricieux **2** *Am (bad-tempered)* grincheux

cranny ['krænɪ] N *(crack)* fente f, lézarde f

crap¹ [kræp] N *Sl* **1** *(excrement)* merde f, *Vulg* **to have** or **take a c.** chier
2 *Fig (worthless thing(s))* camelote f, saloperie f; *(nonsense)* foutaise(s) f(pl), connerie(s) f(pl); *(dirty, disgusting substance)* saloperie; **he's listening to that classical c. again** il est encore en train d'écouter ces conneries classiques; **he eats nothing but c.** il ne bouffe que des saloperies; **get all this c. off the table** enlève tout ce bordel ou toute cette merde de la table; **you don't believe all that c. about witches, do you?** tu ne crois quand même pas à toutes ces conneries sur les sorcières, hein?; **that's c.!, she never said that!** c'est de la connerie!, elle n'a jamais dit ça!; **what a load of c.!** quelles conneries!

ADJ *Sl (bad)* merdique; *(stupid)* con; **these books are c.** ces bouquins, c'est de la connerie ou de la merde

VT *Vulg* **to c. oneself** *(defecate, be scared)* faire dans son froc
VI *Vulg* chier

▸ **crap out** VT INSEP *Sl (lose one's nerve about)* **to c. out of sth** se défiler devant qch; **he crapped out of telling her she was fired** il aurait dû lui dire qu'on voulait la virer, mais il s'est défilé; **you can't c. out of it this time** tu ne peux pas te défiler cette fois-ci

crap² N *Am* = **craps**
▸▸ **c. game** jeu m de dés, craps m

crape [kreɪp] N **1** *(fabric)* crêpe m **2** *(for people in mourning)* crêpe m noir (de deuil)
▸▸ *Med* **c. bandage** bande f Velpeau®

crapper ['kræpər] N *Sl* **1** *(lavatory)* chiottes fpl **2** *(coward)* trouillard, -arde

crappy ['kræpɪ] ADJ *Sl* **1** *(dirty)* cradingue, crade **2** *(bad, stupid)* = **crap¹** ADJ

craps [kræps] NPL *(often with sing verb) Am* jeu m de dés, craps m; **to shoot c.** jouer aux dés

crapshooter ['kræpʃuːtər] N *Am* joueur, -euse de dés

crapulous ['kræpjʊləs], **crapulent** ['kræpjʊlənt] ADJ *Lit* intempérant

> Note that the French word **crapuleux** is a false friend. It means **villainous** or **dissolute**.

CRASH [kræʃ]

N	fracas **1**	▪ accident **2**	▪ krach **3**
▪ panne **4**			
INT	patatras		
VI	retentir **1**	▪ s'écraser **2, 3**	
▪ s'effondrer **4**	▪ tomber en panne **5**		
VT	avoir un accident avec **1**	▪ faire tomber en panne **2**	

N **1** *(noise)* fracas m; **there was a c. as the vase hit the ground** il y a eu un fracas quand le vase est tombé par terre; **the c. of thunder** le fracas du tonnerre; **there was a c. of thunder** il y eut un violent coup de tonnerre; **to fall with a c.** tomber avec fracas

2 *(accident)* accident m; **car/train/plane c.** accident de voiture/ferroviaire/d'avion; **we were in a c.** *(car accident)* nous avons eu un accident de voiture; **this car has been in a c.** cette voiture a eu un accident; **the force of the c.** la force de l'impact

3 *Fig (disaster)* catastrophe f, débâcle f; **(financial) c.** débâcle financière, krach m; *Fin* **the Wall Street C.** le krach de Wall Street

4 *(of computer)* panne f

INT patatras!; **c. went the vase** le vase tomba avec un grand fracas; **he drove c. into the wall** il est allé s'écraser contre le mur

VI **1** *(make sound)* retentir; *(of waves)* s'écra-

ser; **the thunder crashed** *(once)* il y eut un violent coup de tonnerre; *(repeatedly)* le tonnerre retentit

2 *(move)* **to c. (down)** tomber avec fracas; **the bottle crashed against the wall** la bouteille s'est écrasée contre le mur; **the bookcase came crashing down** la bibliothèque s'est écroulée avec fracas; **the vase crashed to the ground** le vase s'est écrasé par terre avec fracas; **the mast came crashing down** le mât s'abattit; **to c. through sth** passer à travers ou traverser qch avec fracas

3 *Aut, Rail* entrer en collision; *Aviat* s'écraser au sol; **the two cars crashed head on** les deux voitures se sont tamponnées de front; **to c. into a tree** s'écraser contre un arbre, rentrer dans un arbre; **to c. into sb** rentrer dans qn; **I crashed into him** je lui suis rentré dedans

4 *(of business)* faire faillite; *St Exch* s'effondrer

5 *(of network, system etc)* sauter; *(of computer)* tomber en panne

6 *Sl (sleep)* roupiller, pioncer; *(go to sleep)* se mettre à roupiller; **can I c. at your place tonight?** je peux pioncer chez toi ce soir?; **he crashed on the floor** il a roupillé par terre

VT **1** *(plane)* écraser au sol; **to c. one's car** *(accidentally)* avoir un accident avec sa voiture; *(deliberately)* démolir sa voiture

2 *Comput* faire tomber en panne

3 *(make noise with)* **to c. the gears** faire grincer la boîte de vitesses; **he crashed the books down on the table** il a posé les livres sur la table avec fracas

4 *Fam* **to c. a party** aller à une réception sans être invité

▸▸ **c. barrier** glissière f de sécurité; **c. course** cours m intensif; **c. diet** régime m choc; **c. dive** *(of submarine)* plongée f raide; *(of plane)* plongeon m; **c. helmet** casque m (de protection); **c. landing** atterrissage m forcé ou en catastrophe; *Fam* **c. pad** piaule f de dépannage; *Admin* **c. programme** programme m choc ou d'urgence; *Aut* **c. sensor** détecteur m de collision ou de choc; **c. test dummy** mannequin-test m, pl mannequins-test

▸ **crash out** VI *Sl* **1** *(go to sleep)* s'endormir; *(suddenly, when drunk etc)* s'écrouler; **he was crashed out on the sofa** il roupillait sur le divan

2 *(spend night, sleep)* pioncer

crash-dive *Naut* VT *(submarine)* faire plonger raide
VI plonger raide

crashing ['kræʃɪŋ] ADJ *Fam* **a c. bore** *(person)* une personne assommante; *(task)* une besogne assommante; *(party)* une soirée assommante; **to be a c. bore** être assommant

crashingly ['kræʃɪŋlɪ] ADV *Fam (boring)* incroyablement, terriblement

crash-land *Aviat* VI atterrir brutalement
VT *(plane, helicopter)* faire atterrir brutalement

crash-test VT **to c. a car** tester une voiture en situation d'accident

crashworthiness ['kræʃwɜːðɪnɪs] N *(of vehicle, helicopter)* résistance f aux chocs

crass [kræs] ADJ *(comment, person)* lourd; *(stupidity, behaviour)* grossier; *(ignorance)* grossier, crasse

crassly ['kræslɪ] ADV *(to behave, say)* avec grossièreté; **he's so c. stupid** il est d'une stupidité effarante

crassness ['kræsnɪs] N grossièreté f

crate [kreɪt] N **1** *(for wine, whisky etc)* caisse f, *(for apples, oranges etc)* cageot m; *(for glass, china)* harasse f, *(for bottles)* casier m

2 *Fam (car)* caisse *f*, *Old-fashioned (aircraft)* coucou *m*

VT *(goods)* mettre dans une caisse/des caisses

crater ['kreɪtər] **N** *Geol (of volcano, moon)* cratère *m*; *(shell hole)* entonnoir *m*, cratère; **the explosion had left a c. 20 feet wide** l'explosion avait laissé un cratère de 6 mètres de large

VT creuser; **a street cratered by shellfire** une rue défoncée par des éclats d'obus; **cratered face** visage *m* crevassé

▸▸ **c. lake** lac *m* de cratère

cravat [krə'væt] **N** foulard *m*

crave [kreɪv] **VT 1** *(long for, need)* désirer ardemment, réclamer; **child that craves affection** enfant qui a un grand besoin d'affection; **she craves tobacco** elle a une envie furieuse de fumer **2** *Lit (beg)* **to c. sb's pardon** demander pardon à qn; **to c. indulgence** solliciter l'indulgence

VI to c. for sth désirer ardemment qch, réclamer qch

craven ['kreɪv(ə)n] **ADJ** *Lit* lâche

cravenly ['kreɪv(ə)nlɪ] **ADV** *Lit* avec lâcheté, lâchement

craving ['kreɪvɪŋ] **N** désir *m* ardent, appétit *m* insatiable (**for** de); **c. for alcohol** passion *f* de l'alcool; *(need)* besoin *m* d'alcool; **I have a c. for chocolate** *(at this moment)* j'ai une envie furieuse de chocolat; *(in general)* j'ai une passion du chocolat; **pregnant women get strange cravings** les femmes enceintes ont souvent d'étranges envies

craw [krɔː] **N** *(of bird)* jabot *m*; *Fig* **it sticks in my c.** ça me reste en travers de la gorge

crawfish ['krɔːfɪʃ] **N** *esp Am* = **crayfish**

crawl [krɔːl] **N 1** *(action)* **the baby went for a c. along the floor** le bébé a rampé sur le sol **2** *(slow pace)* **to go along at a c.** *(on foot, in vehicle)* avancer très lentement; **the traffic had slowed to a c.** la circulation avait ralenti et on roulait au pas **3** *Swimming* crawl *m*; **to do the c.** nager le crawl, crawler **4** *TV (roller captions)* générique *m* sur déroulant

VI 1 *(of person)* *(on belly)* ramper, se traîner; *(on hands and knees)* marcher à quatre pattes; *(of snake, worm)* ramper; **to c. on one's hands and knees** aller à quatre pattes; **she was crawling about on the carpet** elle était à quatre pattes sur la moquette; **to c. into a hole** *(of reptile etc)* se glisser dans un trou; *(of person)* se traîner jusque dans un trou; **to c. to the door** aller jusqu'à la porte en rampant/à quatre pattes **2** *(move slowly)* avancer lentement; *Aut Fam* faire du surplace **3** *(be infested)* **to be crawling with vermin** grouiller de vermine; *Fam* **the streets were crawling with troops** les rues fourmillaient *ou* grouillaient de militaires; **to make sb's skin c.** donner un frisson de dégoût à qn **4** *Fam (be obsequious)* **to c. to sb** s'aplatir devant qn, lécher les bottes à qn; **I refuse to c.** je refuse de m'aplatir **5** *Swimming* crawler, nager le crawl

crawler ['krɔːlər] **N 1** *Fam (obsequious person)* lèche-botte *m*, *pl* lèche-bottes **2** *Comput* araignée *f*

▸▸ *Br Aut* **c. lane** file *f ou* voie *f* pour véhicules lents

crawlers **NPL** *(baby's overalls)* grenouillère *f*

crawling ['krɔːlɪŋ] **ADJ 1** *(baby)* qui marche à quatre pattes; **he's just got to the c. stage** il commence à marcher à quatre pattes; *Fig* **compared with the Japanese, we're still at the c. stage** comparés aux Japonais, nous en sommes encore aux balbutiements **2** *(infested)* grouillant (**with** de) **3** *Fam (obsequious)* lèche-bottes *inv*

N *Fam (obsequiousness)* **that's just c.** c'est du lèche-botte

crayfish ['kreɪfɪʃ] **N (freshwater) c.** écrevisse *f*, **(sea) c.** langouste *f*

crayon ['kreɪɒn, -ən] *Art* **N** *(pencil)* crayon *m* de couleur; *(pastel)* crayon *m* pastel; *(wax)* crayon *m* de cire

VT 1 *(draw)* dessiner au crayon/au pastel/au crayon de cire **2** *(colour in)* *(sketch)* colorier

craze [kreɪz] **N** manie *f* (**for sth** de qch); *(fad)* engouement *m*; **this is the latest dance c.** c'est la dernière danse à la mode

VT 1 *Lit (drive insane)* rendre fou **2** *Cer (porcelain)* craqueler

VI *Cer* se craqueler

crazed [kreɪzd] **ADJ 1** *(with grief)* fou, *f* folle (**with** de); *(with fear)* affolé (**with** par) **2** *Cer* craquelé

-crazed [kreɪzd] **SUFF** rendu fou par; **drug/power-c.** rendu fou par la drogue/le pouvoir; **he was half-c. with grief** la douleur l'avait rendu à moitié fou

crazily ['kreɪzɪlɪ] **ADV 1** follement; *(to behave)* bizarrement; **c., they …** ce qui est complètement fou, ils … **2** *(to lean)* bizarrement

craziness ['kreɪzɪnɪs] **N** *(of person)* folie *f*, démence *f*

crazy ['kreɪzɪ] **ADJ 1** *(person)* fou, *f* folle, *Fam* dingue; **c. with fear** fou de terreur; **to go c.** *(with anger)* devenir fou (**with** de colère); **to drive** *or* **send sb c.** rendre qn fou; **you're c.!** vous êtes fou!; **but that's c., we've only just arrived!** mais c'est dingue, nous venons juste d'arriver!; **to be c. about** *or* **over sb/sth** être fou de qn/qch; **like c.** comme un enragé **2** *(odd)* *(dress, building, angle etc)* bizarre **3** *esp Am Sl (very good)* fou, *f* folle, dément

N *esp Am Sl (person)* original, -ale

▸▸ *Am* **c. bone** petit juif *m*; **c. golf** minigolf *m*; *Am Sl* **c. house** asile *m ou* maison *f* de fous; *Br* **c. paving** = dallage *m* irrégulier en pierres plates

CRB [siːɑːˈbiː] **N** *(abbr* **Criminal Records Bureau***)* identité *f* judiciaire

CRC [siːɑːˈsiː] **N** *Typ (abbr* **camera-ready copy***)* épreuves *fpl* bonnes à filmer

CRE [siːɑːˈriː] **N** *Br Admin (abbr* **Commission for Racial Equality***)* commission *f* pour l'égalité raciale

creak [kriːk] **N** *(of hinge)* grincement *m*; *(of floor, chair, new shoes etc)* craquement *m*; **to give a c.** grincer/craquer

VI *(of hinge)* grincer; *(of floor, chair, shoes)* craquer; *Fig (of plot etc)* être boiteux; **the chair creaked under his weight** la chaise a craqué sous son poids

creaking ['kriːkɪŋ] **ADJ** *(hinge)* qui grince; *(timber, shoes)* qui craque

N *(of hinge)* grincement *m*; *(of timber, shoes)* craquement *m*

creaky ['kriːkɪ] **ADJ** *(hinge)* qui grince; *(timber, shoe)* qui craque; *Fig (dialogue, plot etc)* boiteux

cream [kriːm] **N 1** *(of milk)* crème *f*, *(used in cakes etc)* crème (fraîche); **single/double c.** crème fluide *ou* fleurette/épaisse; **strawberries and c.** fraises *fpl* à la crème; **c. of tomato/asparagus soup** crème de tomates/d'asperges

2 *Fig* **the c.** *(best part etc)* la crème, le dessus du panier; **they're the c. of the crop** *(of students, job applicants etc)* c'est le dessus du panier, c'est la crème; **the c. of society** la crème de la société

3 *(filling for chocolates, biscuits)* fondant *m*; *(individual chocolate)* chocolat *m* fourré à la crème

4 *(sauce)* **c. of horseradish** épaisse sauce *f* au raifort

5 *(for face, shoes)* crème *f*

6 *(colour)* crème *f*

ADJ *(colour)* crème *inv*; *Br Sl* **c. crackered** *(exhausted)* crevé, lessivé, naze

VT 1 *(remove cream from)* *(milk)* écrémer

2 *(add cream to)* *(coffee etc)* ajouter de la crème à

3 *(beat)* *(butter)* battre en crème; **to c. potatoes** réduire les pommes de terre en purée; **c. the butter and sugar** *(in recipe)* battre le beurre et le sucre jusqu'à ce qu'ils forment un mélange mousseux *ou* crémeux

4 *Am Fam (person) (beat up)* casser la figure à; *(defeat)* battre à plate couture, mettre la pâtée à

5 *Vulg* **to c. one's jeans** *(ejaculate in)* juter dans son froc; *(of woman)* mouiller

VI *Vulg (ejaculate)* décharger

▸▸ **c. bun** = petit pain *m* au lait servi avec de la crème chantilly; **c. cake** gâteau *m* à la crème; **c. cheese** ≃ fromage *m* frais; *Br* **c. cracker** biscuit *m* sec; **c. jug** pot *m* à crème; **c. puff** chou *m* à la crème; **c. sherry** sherry *m ou* xérès *m* doux; *Culin* **c. of tartar** crème de tartre; *Br* **c. tea** = goûter *m* composé de thé et de scones servis avec de la confiture et de la crème

▸ **cream off VT SEP** *(remove)* écrémer; **to c. off the best part of sth** écrémer *ou* prélever la meilleure partie de qch; **the universities c. off the best students** les universités écrèment toujours les meilleurs étudiants

cream-coloured, *Am* **cream-colored** **ADJ** crème *inv*

creamed [kriːmd] **ADJ** *Culin (chicken etc)* à la crème

▸▸ **c. potatoes** purée *f* de pommes de terre

creamer ['kriːmər] **N 1** *Am (jug)* pot *m* à crème **2** *(for coffee)* succédané *m* (de lait) **3** *(machine)* écrémeuse *f*

creamery ['kriːmərɪ] **N** *(dairy)* laiterie *f*, *(shop)* crémerie *f*

▸▸ **c. butter** beurre *m* laitier

creamy ['kriːmɪ] **ADJ** *(containing cream, resembling cream)* crémeux; **rich c. sauce** sauce *f* onctueuse

crease [kriːs] **N 1** *(made on purpose)* pli *m*; *(accidental)* faux pli *m*; **to remove the creases from sth** enlever les faux plis de qch; **to put a c. in a pair of trousers** faire le pli d'un pantalon **2** *Cr (batting)* **c.** ligne *f* du batteur

VT 1 *(on purpose)* plisser, faire des plis à; *(accidentally)* froisser, chiffonner; *(accidentally with iron)* faire un/des faux pli(s) à; **well-creased trousers** pantalon avec un pli impeccable; **to c. one's brow** froncer les sourcils **2** *(of bullet) (scalp etc)* érafler

VI 1 *(become creased)* se froisser **2** *Br Fam* = **crease up VI**

▸ **crease up** *Br Fam* **VI** *(laugh uncontrollably)* se tordre (de rire)

VT SEP *(make laugh uncontrollably)* faire rire à se tordre

crease-resistant **ADJ** infroissable

create [krɪˈeɪt] **VT** *(world, peer, jobs, role, difficulties etc)* créer; *(impression)* faire, produire; **she created a studio out of a shed** elle a créé un studio à partir d'une cabane; **if opportunities do not exist you must c. them** si les occasions n'existent pas, il faut les créer; **to c. a scene** *(fuss)* faire une scène; *Law* **to c. a disturbance** troubler l'ordre public

VI 1 *(be creative)* créer **2** *Br Fam (make a scene)* faire du tapage, faire une scène (**about** à propos de)

creation [krɪˈeɪʃən] **N 1** *(action) (of the world, a title etc)* création *f*; **job c.** création d'emplois **2** *(product)* création *f*; **the latest creations** *(fashions)* les dernières créations **3** *(universe)* création *f*; *Rel* **the C.** la Création

creative [krɪˈeɪtɪv] **ADJ** *(professional artist,*

designer etc) créateur, -trice; (activity, child, amateur artist etc) créatif; **I don't do anything c.** je ne fais rien de créatif

▸▸ Euph **c. accounting** (manipulation of accounts) comptabilité f fantaisiste; **c. brief** (in advertising) plan m de travail créatif, PTC m; **c. copy strategy** (in advertising) copie f stratégie créative; **c. department** service m de création; **c. director** directeur, -trice de la création; **c. instinct** instinct m créatif; **c. team** équipe f de création; **c. writing** techniques f pl de l'écriture; **c. writing workshop** atelier m d'écriture

creatively [krɪ'eɪtɪvlɪ] ADV avec créativité; **more c.** avec plus de créativité, de façon plus créative

creativeness [krɪ'eɪtɪvnɪs], **creativity** [krɪə'tɪvɪtɪ] N créativité f

creator [krɪ'eɪtər] N (of a fashion, role etc) créateur, -trice; Rel **the C.** le Créateur

creature ['kriːtʃər] N **1** (living being) créature f, être m (vivant); **creatures from outer space** extra-terrestres mpl **2** (animal) animal m, bête f **3** (person) **poor c.!** le/la pauvre!; Pej **c. of the government** créature f du gouvernement; **man is the c. of circumstances** l'homme dépend des circonstances; **I am a c. of habit** je suis un homme/une femme d'habitude

▸▸ **c. comforts** confort m matériel; **to like one's c. comforts** aimer ses aises

crèche [kreɪʃ, kreʃ] N **1** Br (nursery) crèche f, (in shopping centre, leisure complex) garderie f **2** Rel crèche f

▸▸ **c. facilities** garderie f

cred [kred] N Fam see **street cred**

credence ['kriːdəns] N croyance f, foi f; **to give or attach c. to sth** ajouter foi à qch; **letters of c.** lettres f pl de créance

credentials [krɪ'denʃəlz] NPL **1** (proof of identity) pièces f pl justificatives d'identité; (of a diplomat etc) lettres f pl de créance **2** (proof of ability) références f pl; **what are your c.?** quelles sont vos références?; Fig **a film director with excellent c.** un metteur en scène aux excellents antécédents

credibility [kredɪ'bɪlɪtɪ] N (of person, policy) crédibilité f; **the government has lost c. in the eyes of or with the public** le gouvernement a perdu sa crédibilité aux yeux du public; **the president's actions gave him some c.** les actions du président lui ont conféré une certaine crédibilité

▸▸ **c. gap** manque m de crédibilité

credible ['kredɪb(ə)l] ADJ crédible; **it is hardly c. that …** il est difficile à croire que … + sub

credibly ['kredɪblɪ] ADV de façon crédible

CREDIT ['kredɪt]

| N | crédit **1** ▪ croyance **2** ▪ mérite **3** ▪ générique **4** ▪ unité de valeur **5** |
| VT | créditer **1** ▪ attribuer **2** ▪ croire **3** |

N **1** Com, Fin crédit m; (in an account) avoir m; **to be in c.** avoir de l'argent sur son compte; (of account) être créditeur; **my account is still in c.** j'ai toujours de l'argent sur mon compte, esp Spec mon compte est toujours créditeur; **to get back into c.** rembourser un découvert; (of account) redevenir créditeur; **to give sb c.** faire crédit à qn; **we do not give c.** (of shop) la maison ne fait pas crédit; **to sell on c.** vendre à crédit; **to live on c.** vivre à crédit; **to enter a sum to sb's c.** porter une somme au crédit ou à l'actif de qn, créditer qn d'une somme; **his c. is good** Fin il a une bonne réputation de solvabilité; Fig (he is trusted) on lui fait toute confiance; Fig **he still has c. with the trade unions** les syndicats lui font encore confiance; Am **line of c.** ligne f de crédit

2 (belief) croyance f, **to give c. to or place c. in a rumour** ajouter ou accorder foi à un bruit; **facts that lend c. to a rumour** faits qui accréditent une rumeur; **to gain c.** (of theory etc) être accepté

3 (merit) mérite m, honneur m; **to give sb c. for sth** reconnaître le mérite de qn dans qch; **you'll have to give c. for that** il faudra bien que tu reconnaisses son mérite là-dedans; **I gave him c. for more sense** je lui supposais plus de jugement; **she's shrewder than most people give her c. for** elle est plus perspicace que la plupart des gens ne le pensent; **give me c. for some common sense!** fais-moi l'honneur de croire que j'ai un peu de bon sens!; **to take the c. for an action** s'attribuer le mérite d'une action; **they took the c., but she did all the work** ils se sont attribué le mérite, mais c'est elle qui a fait tout le travail; **I can't claim much of the c. for the project's success** je ne peux pas m'attribuer grand mérite pour la réussite du projet; **most of the c. should go to the actors** c'est aux acteurs que devrait revenir le plus grand mérite; **c. where c.'s due** il faut rendre à César ce qui lui appartient; **OK, but c. where c.'s due, it was he who …** d'accord mais il faut bien reconnaître que c'est lui qui …; **with c.** honorablement; Sch (in an examination) avec mention assez bien; **it must be said to her c. that …** il faut porter à son crédit que …; **the team have three wins to their c.** l'équipe compte trois victoires à son actif; **it does him c.** cela lui fait (grand) honneur; **your children do you c. or are a c. to you** vos enfants vous font honneur; **she is a c. to the school** elle fait honneur à l'école

4 Cin, TV **credits** générique m; **to give sb a c.** (in a book) mentionner le nom de qn dans la liste des collaborateurs

5 Univ unité f de valeur

VT **1** Com, Fin **to c. sb/an account with a sum** créditer qn/un compte d'une somme; **to c. a sum to an account** porter une somme au crédit d'un compte

2 (attribute) attribuer, prêter (**sb with a quality** une qualité à qn); **to c. sb with superior intelligence** prêter à qn d'une intelligence supérieure; **I credited you with more sense** je vous croyais ou supposais plus de jugement; **to be credited with having done sth** passer pour avoir fait qch

3 (believe) croire; **I wouldn't have credited it** je ne l'aurais pas cru possible; **you wouldn't c. it!, would you c. it!** tu te rends compte?

▸▸ **c. account** Banking compte m créditeur; Br Com (with shop) compte client; **c. advice** avis m de crédit; **c. agency** institution f de crédit; **c. agreement** accord m ou convention f de crédit; **c. balance** solde m créditeur; **c. bank** banque f de crédit; **c. broker** courtier, -ière en crédits ou en prêts; **c. card** carte f de crédit; **c. card reader** lecteur m de cartes; **c. ceiling** plafond m de crédit; Acct **c. column** colonne f créditrice; **c. control** (government restrictions) resserrement m ou encadrement m du crédit; (monitoring) surveillance f des crédits; **c. controller** contrôleur, -euse du crédit; **c. freeze** blocage m du crédit; **c. history** profil m crédit; **to obtain information on sb's c. history** établir des renseignements de solvabilité sur qn; **c. insurance** assurance-crédit f; Am **c. line** ligne f de crédit; Br **c. note** (in business) facture f ou note f d'avoir; (in shop) avoir; **c. period** délai m de crédit; **c. rating** (of person, company) degré m de solvabilité; (awarded by credit reference agency) notation f; **c. rating agency** agence f de notation; **c. risk** risque m de crédit; Acct **c. side** crédit; Fig **on the c. side, it must be said he was honest enough to own up** il faut dire en sa faveur

qu'il a eu l'honnêteté d'avouer; **c. squeeze** restriction f ou encadrement du crédit; **c. union** société f ou caisse f de crédit; **c. voucher** chèque m de caisse

creditable ['kredɪtəb(ə)l] ADJ (action) estimable, digne d'éloges

creditably ['kredɪtəblɪ] ADV honorablement, avec honneur

creditor ['kredɪtər] N créancier, -ière; **creditors' meeting** réunion f des créanciers

▸▸ **c. account** compte m créditeur; Econ **c. nation** nation f créditrice

creditworthiness ['kredɪtwɜːðɪnɪs] N solvabilité f

creditworthy ['kredɪtwɜːðɪ] ADJ solvable

credo, pl **credos** ['kriːdəʊ, 'kreɪ-, -əʊz] N credo m inv

credulity [krɪ'djuːlɪtɪ] N crédulité f; **his story stretched c.** son histoire était vraiment difficile à croire

credulous ['kredjʊləs] ADJ crédule

creed [kriːd] N **1** Rel credo m inv; **the (Apostles') C.** le Credo **2** (beliefs) croyance f, foi f; **political c.** credo m ou profession f de foi politique

creek [kriːk] N esp Br (small bay) crique f, anse f; Am, Austr, New Zealand (stream) ruisseau m, petit cours m d'eau; Fam **to be up the c. (without a paddle)** être dans le pétrin

creel [kriːl] N panier m de pêche

creep [kriːp] N **1** Sl (person) (disgusting) personnage m répugnant, salopard m, saligaud m; (obsequious) lèche-bottes m inv, lèche-cul m inv; **that c. she's married to** son salopard de mari

2 Fam **the creeps** la chair de poule; **to get the creeps** avoir la chair de poule; **to give sb the creeps** (scare) donner la chair de poule à qn; (annoy) horripiler qn

3 Aut rampage m

VI (pt, pp **crept** [krept]) **1** (of insect, animal) ramper; (of person) se glisser; **to c. into bed** se glisser dans son lit; **he crept into the room** il entra furtivement ou à pas de loup dans la chambre; Fig **a moralizing tone has crept into her writing** un ton moralisateur s'est insidieusement glissé dans ses écrits; **a feeling of uneasiness crept over me** un sentiment de gêne commençait à me gagner; **to make sb's flesh c.** donner la chair de poule à qn

2 Fam (be obsequious) ramper (devant les grands); **she's always creeping to the teacher** elle est toujours en train de ramper devant le professeur

3 (of plant) ramper; (upwards) grimper

▸ **creep along** VI (stealthily) s'avancer furtivement, marcher à pas de loup; (move slowly, in car etc) se traîner

▸ **creep away** VI s'éloigner à pas de loup

▸ **creep by** VI passer furtivement; **time or the hours crept slowly by** les heures passaient lentement

▸ **creep up** VI **1** (approach stealthily) approcher furtivement (**to** de); **she crept up behind me** elle est arrivée derrière moi tout doucement **2** (of inflation, prices etc) monter petit à petit; **the speedometer crept up to 120** l'aiguille de l'indicateur de vitesse est montée tout doucement jusqu'à 120

▸ **creep up on** VT INSEP surprendre, prendre par surprise; **don't c. up on me like that!** ne m'arrive pas comme ça dessus sans prévenir!; **old age has crept up on me** j'ai vieilli sans m'en rendre compte

creeper ['kriːpər] N **1** (plant) plante f rampante; (climbing) plante grimpante **2** **creepers** (shoes) chaussures f pl à semelles de crêpe; Am (crampons) crampons mpl à verglas **3** Am **creepers** (child's garment) barboteuse f

creeping ['kriːpɪŋ] ADJ **1** (animal) rampant **2** Fam (obsequious) servile, rampant **3** (plant) (along the ground) rampant; (upwards) grimpant
▸ N Fam (obsequiousness) servilité f
▸▸ Med **c. paralysis** paralysie f progressive

creepy ['kriːpɪ] ADJ Fam **1** (film, story, person) qui donne la chair de poule; **it was c.** c'était à vous donner la chair de poule; **a c. old house** une vieille maison sinistre **2** **I could feel something c. on my leg** je sentais quelque chose qui rampait sur ma jambe

creepy-crawly [-'krɔːlɪ] Fam N insecte m rampant, bestiole f rampante
▸ ADJ **a c. feeling** une sensation de fourmillement

cremate [krɪ'meɪt] VT (dead person) incinérer

cremation [krɪ'meɪʃən] N incinération f, crémation f

crematorium, pl **crematoria** [-'tɔːrɪəm, -ɪə] N crématorium m

crematory ['kriːmətɔːrɪ] N Am crématorium m

crenellated, Am **crenelated** ['krenəleɪtɪd] ADJ (wall etc) crénelé

Creole ['kriːəʊl] N **1** (person) Créole mf; Am (in Louisiana) = descendant, -ante des colons français ou espagnols de la Louisiane **2** Ling créole m
▸ ADJ créole; Am (in Louisiana) = qui descend des colons français ou espagnols de la Louisiane

creosote ['krɪəsəʊt] N créosote f
▸ VT (wood) créosoter

crêpe [kreɪp, krep] N **1** Tex crêpe m; **c. skirt** jupe f en crêpe **2** (crêpe rubber) crêpe m **3** (crêpe paper) papier m crépon **4** Culin (pancake) crêpe f
▸▸ **c. bandage** bande f Velpeau®; **c. de Chine** crêpe m de Chine; **c. paper** papier crépon; **c. rubber** crêpe m; **c. soles** semelles fpl de crêpe

crêpe-soled [-səʊld] ADJ à semelle(s) de crêpe

crept PP, PT see **creep** VI

Cres (abbr **Crescent**) rue (en croissant)

crescendo, pl **crescendos** [krɪ'ʃendəʊ, -əʊz] N Mus, Fig crescendo m inv; **to build up to a c.** aller crescendo; Fig **to reach a c.** atteindre son paroxysme
▸ ADV Mus crescendo

crescent ['kresənt] N (shape) croissant m; (street) rue f en croissant
▸ ADJ (shaped) en forme de croissant ou de demi-lune
▸▸ **c. moon** croissant m de la lune

cress [kres] N cresson m

crest [krest] N (of chicken, reptile) crête f; (of bird) huppe f, (of peacock) aigrette f, Anat (of bone) crête, arête f, (of helmet) cimier m, crête; (of hill, wave) crête, sommet m; (of roof) faîte m; (coat of arms) armoiries fpl; (insignia) écusson m; Fig **to be on the c. of a wave** être à son meilleur niveau; **she rode to power on the c. of a wave of popular enthusiasm** elle a été portée au pouvoir par l'enthousiasme populaire
▸ VT (wave, hill) arriver au sommet de

crested ['krestɪd] ADJ **1** (animal) à crête; (with feathered crest) à huppe, huppé; **white-c. waves** moutons mpl, vagues fpl aux crêtes blanches **2** (helmet) orné d'un cimier; (plumed) panaché **3** Her (coat of arms) armorié; (insignia) orné d'un écusson

crestfallen ['krestfɔːl(ə)n] ADJ (person) abattu, découragé; (look) déconfit, abattu, découragé

cretaceous [krɪ'teɪʃəs] ADJ crétacé
▸ N **the C.** le crétacé

Cretan ['kriːt(ə)n] ADJ crétois
▸ N Crétois, -oise

Crete [kriːt] N Crète f

cretin ['kretɪn] N Med Old-fashioned, Fam crétin, -ine

cretinism ['kretɪnɪz(ə)m] N Med Old-fashioned, Fam crétinisme m

cretinous ['kretɪnəs] ADJ Med Old-fashioned, Fam crétin

cretonne [kre'tɒn, 'kretɒn] N Tex cretonne f

Creutzfeldt-Jakob disease ['krɔɪtsfelt-'jækɒb] N Med maladie f de Creutzfeldt-Jakob

crevasse [krɪ'væs] N crevasse f (glaciaire)

crevice ['krevɪs] N fente f, (in wall) lézarde f, (in rock) crevasse f, fissure f

crew [kruː] VOIR GRAMMAIRE A11 **1** (of ship, plane) équipage m; (in rowing) équipe f; (gang, team) équipe; **ambulance/camera c.** équipe d'ambulanciers/de cameramen; Aviat **ground c.** personnel m au sol; Ind **maintenance c.** équipe d'entretien **2** Fam (group of people) bande f, troupe f, **sorry c.** triste engeance f; **they're a good c. to work with** c'est une bonne équipe avec qui travailler
▸ VT (ship) armer d'un équipage; (plane) fournir un équipage à; **crewed by less than six** yacht qui exige un équipage de six au moins; Naut **crewed charter** location f de bateau avec équipage
▸ VI **to c. for sb** servir d'équipier à qn
▸▸ **c. cut** coupe f de cheveux en brosse; **c. member** membre mf d'équipage; **c. neck** col m ras le ou du cou, ras-le-cou m inv

crib [krɪb] N **1** (cradle) berceau m; Am (cot) lit m d'enfant; Rel (in Nativity) crèche f **2** Agr (for feeding animals) mangeoire f, râtelier m **3** Br Fam (plagiarism) plagiat m; Sch antisèche f, (translation) traduction f (employée subrepticement)
▸ VT (-bb-) (passage from a book) reproduire, copier; Sch **to c. an exercise from sb** pomper un exercice sur qn
▸ VI (-bb-) Sch pomper; **to c. from an author** plagier un auteur
▸▸ Am **c. death** mort f subite (du nourrisson)

cribbage ['krɪbɪdʒ] N Cards = jeu m de cartes où l'on compte les points en enfonçant des chevilles dans une planche de bois

crick [krɪk] N **c. in the back** tour m de reins; **c. in the neck** torticolis m
▸ VT **to c. one's neck** attraper un torticolis; **c. one's back** se faire un tour de reins

cricket¹ ['krɪkɪt] N (insect) grillon m

cricket² N Sport cricket m; **to play c.** jouer au cricket; Old-fashioned Br Fig **that's not c.** cela n'est pas de jeu, cela ne se fait pas
▸▸ **c. ball** balle f de cricket; **c. bat** batte f de cricket; **c. field, c. pitch** terrain m de cricket

cricketer ['krɪkɪtər] N joueur, -euse de cricket

crier ['kraɪər] N **town c.** crieur m public ou municipal

crikey ['kraɪkɪ] INT Br Sl mince alors!

crim [krɪm] N Br, Austr Fam (criminal) criminel, -elle

Crimbo ['krɪmbəʊ] N Br Fam (Christmas) Noël m

crime [kraɪm] N (act) crime m; Law (minor offence) délit m; (phenomenon) criminalité f, **to commit a c.** commettre un crime/un délit; **a c. against nature/humanity** un crime contre nature/l'humanité; Law **a c. of passion** un crime passionnel; Fig **it's a c. to cut down this tree** c'est un crime d'abattre cet arbre; Fig **it's not a c. to …** ce n'est pas un crime de …
▸▸ **c. figures** chiffres mpl de la criminalité;

c. rate taux m de (la) criminalité; Journ **c. reporter** journaliste mf qui couvre les affaires criminelles; **c. scene** lieu m du crime; **c. series** série f policière; **c. story** (novel) roman m noir; (detective novel) roman policier; **c. wave** vague f de criminalité; **c. writer** auteur m de romans policiers

Crimea (the) [ðəkraɪ'mɪə] N la Crimée

Crimean [kraɪ'mɪən] ADJ de Crimée; Hist **the C. War** la guerre de Crimée

criminal ['krɪmɪn(ə)l] N criminel, -elle
▸ ADJ Law criminel; Fig **it would be c. to cut down these trees** ce serait un crime d'abattre ces arbres; **to take c. proceedings against sb** poursuivre qn en justice; **to bring a c. action against sb** intenter une action en justice contre qn
▸▸ **c. act** action f criminelle; Law **c. case** affaire f criminelle; Law **c. conversation** adultère m; Law **c. court** ≃ cour f d'assises; Br **C. Investigation Department** = police f judiciaire britannique, ≃ PJ f, **c. law** droit m pénal ou criminel; **c. lawyer** avocat, -ate au criminel, pénaliste mf; Law **c. liability** responsabilité f pénale, majorité f pénale; Law **c. negligence** négligence f coupable ou criminelle; Law **c. offence** délit m; Law **c. record** casier m judiciaire; **c. suit** action criminelle, procès m criminel

criminalization [krɪmɪnəlaɪ'zeɪʃən] N criminalisation f

criminalize ['krɪmɪnəlaɪz] VT criminaliser

criminally ['krɪmɪn(ə)lɪ] ADV criminellement; **to be c. insane** être dément; (of man) être un fou dangereux; **the c. insane** les fous dangereux; **this is c. negligent** c'est une négligence criminelle; **it's c. wasteful** c'est un crime de gaspiller comme ça

criminologist [krɪmɪ'nɒlədʒɪst] N criminologue mf

criminology [krɪmɪ'nɒlədʒɪ] N criminologie f

crimp [krɪmp] N (in hair) frisure f, (in sheet) pli m
▸ VT (hair) crêper; (pastry) gaufrer; (material) plisser, crêper

Crimplene® ['krɪmpliːn] N = synthétique m infroissable semblable au crêpe de Chine

crimson ['krɪmz(ə)n] ADJ, N cramoisi m; **to blush c.** devenir cramoisi; **c. with rage** rouge de colère

cringe [krɪndʒ] VI **1** (flinch) avoir un mouvement de recul; **the dog cringed in the corner** le chien se blottit dans le coin; **he stayed cringing in the background** il se fit tout petit **2** (be servile) s'humilier, ramper, s'aplatir (**before sb** devant qn) **3** Fam (be embarrassed) avoir envie de rentrer sous terre; **her singing makes me c.** quand elle chante, ça me donne envie de rentrer sous terre; **it makes you c.** c'est très pénible **4** (be disgusted) avoir un sentiment de dégoût

cringe-making ADJ Br Fam qui donne envie de rentrer sous terre

cringing ['krɪndʒɪŋ] ADJ **1** (afraid) craintif **2** (servile) servile, obséquieux

crinkle ['krɪŋk(ə)l] N pli m, ride f
▸ VT (paper) froisser, chiffonner; **to c. one's nose** froncer le nez
▸ VI se froisser; (of apples) se rider; **his nose crinkled at the smell** l'odeur lui fit froncer le nez

crinkle-cut ADJ (crisps, chips) dentelé

crinkly ['krɪŋklɪ] ADJ (skin) ridé; (paper) froissé, chiffonné; **my fingers have gone all c.** la peau de mes doigts est toute fripée

crinoline ['krɪn(ə)lɪn] N crinoline f

cripes ['kraɪps] INT Old-fashioned Br Sl mince alors!

cripple ['krɪp(ə)l] N estropié, -ée, infirme mf,

invalide *mf*, *Fig* **emotional c.** handicapé, -ée sur le plan affectif

vt 1 *(person)* estropier; **those who were crippled in the war** les mutilés *mpl* de guerre **2** *Fig (machine)* empêcher de fonctionner; *(ship)* désemparer; *(tank)* mettre hors de combat; *(industry, system)* paralyser

crippled [ˈkrɪp(ə)ld] **ADJ 1** *(person)* estropié, infirme; **c. with rheumatism** perclus de rhumatismes; **a c. arm** un bras malade **2** *Fig (ship)* désemparé; *(tank)* hors de combat; **the country is c. with debt** le pays est paralysé par les dettes

crippling [ˈkrɪplɪŋ] **ADJ 1** *(illness)* qui rend infirme **2** *Fig (taxation, strike etc)* paralysant; **the c. effect of the blockade** l'effet paralysant du blocus

crisis, *pl* **crises** [ˈkraɪsɪs, -iːz] **N** *(in business, one's personal life etc)* crise *f*; **in c.** en pleine crise; **things are coming to a c.** la situation devient critique; **to go through a c.** traverser une crise; **a minor family c.** un petit problème familial

▸▸ **c. management** gestion *f* des crises; **c. point** point *m* critique; **to reach c. point** atteindre un point critique

crisp [krɪsp] **ADJ** *(biscuit, pastry etc)* croquant, croustillant; *(apple, lettuce)* croquant, craquant; *(bacon)* croustillant; *(air)* vif; *(style)* vif et précis; *(tone)* tranchant; **the snow was c. underfoot** la neige craquait sous mes/nos/*etc* pas; **a c. five-pound note** un billet de cinq livres tout neuf; **a c. white shirt** *(appearance)* une chemise blanche impeccable; *(texture)* une chemise blanche fraîchement lavée

N 1 **cooked to a c.** rôti à point pour croquer sous la dent; **burnt to a c.** carbonisé **2** *Br* **(potato) crisps** (pommes *fpl*) chips *fpl*; **one c.** une chips

vt *(meat etc)* donner du croustillant *ou* du croquant à

crispbread [ˈkrɪspbred] **N** pain *m* suédois

crisper [ˈkrɪspər] **N** *(in refrigerator)* bac *m* à légumes

crisply [ˈkrɪsplɪ] **ADV** *(to speak)* d'un ton tranchant; *(to write)* d'un style vif et précis

crispness [ˈkrɪspnɪs] **N** *(of biscuit, pastry etc)* croustillant *m*, croquant *m*; *(of apple, lettuce)* craquant *m*; *(of bacon)* croustillant; *(of snow)* dureté *f*; *(of air)* fraîcheur *f*; *(of style)* vivacité *f* et précision *f*; **to lose its c.** *(of fabric etc)* perdre sa raideur

crispy [ˈkrɪspɪ] **ADJ** croustillant

criss-cross [ˈkrɪs-] **ADJ** *(pattern etc)* entrecroisé

N entrecroisement *m*

vt *(threads etc)* entrecroiser; **a brow crisscrossed with wrinkles** un front craquelé de rides; **a network of streets criss-crosses the town** un réseau de rues parcourt la ville dans tous les sens

vi s'entrecroiser

crit [krɪt] **N** *Fam (criticism)* critique *f*; *lit* c. critique littéraire

criterion, *pl* **criteria** [kraɪˈtɪərɪən, -ɪə] **N** critère *m*; **what criteria do you apply** *or* **what are your criteria when selecting candidates?** sur quels critères vous fondez-vous *ou* quels sont vos critères lorsque vous sélectionnez des candidats?

critic [ˈkrɪtɪk] **N** *(in general)* critiqueur, -euse; *(of other people's behaviour)* censeur *m*; *Cin, Liter etc* critique *mf*; **she has her critics** il y en a qui la critiquent; **there are few critics of the policy** peu de gens critiquent la politique; **music/drama/literary c.** critique musical/dramatique/littéraire; **film c.** critique de cinéma

critical [ˈkrɪtɪk(ə)l] **ADJ 1** *(criticizing)* critique; **a c. audience** un public exigeant; **to**

be c. of sb/sth *(of person)* se montrer *ou* être critique à l'égard de qn/qch; *(of report, article etc)* être critique à l'égard de qn/qch; **stop being so c.** arrête de critiquer

2 *Cin, Liter etc (essay, study)* critique; **the film received c. acclaim** le film a été salué unanimement par les critiques, le film a fait l'unanimité de la critique

3 *(decisive) (situation, moment, age etc)* critique; *Med* **she is in a c. condition** elle est dans un état critique; **she is going through a c. time** elle subit *ou* traverse une crise en ce moment; **the next few days will be c.** les prochains jours seront décisifs

▸▸ *Phys* **c. angle** angle *m* critique; *Phys* **c. mass** masse *f* critique; *Com, Tech* **c. path** chemin *m* critique; *Com, Tech* **c. path analysis** analyse *f* du chemin critique; *Com, Tech* **c. path method** méthode *f* du chemin critique; *Com, Tech* **c. path model** modèle *m* du chemin critique

critically [ˈkrɪtɪklɪ] **ADV 1** *(to consider sth)* en critique; *(to look at sth)* d'un œil critique **2** *(acclaimed etc)* par les critiques **3** *(seriously)* gravement; *Med* **she is c. ill** elle est gravement malade, elle est dans un état critique; **the c. ill** les grands malades *mpl*

criticism [ˈkrɪtɪsɪz(ə)m] **N 1** *(action, act of criticizing)* critique *f*; **it wasn't meant as a c.** ce n'était pas une critique; **to lay oneself open to c.** s'exposer à la critique; **the report contained strong c. of this department** le rapport contenait de graves critiques de ce service **2** *Cin, Liter etc* critique *f*; **to write a c. of a book** écrire la critique d'un livre

criticize [ˈkrɪtɪsaɪz] **vt 1** *(express disapproval of) (person, behaviour etc)* critiquer; **to c. sb for sth** critiquer qn pour qch; **to c. sb for doing sth** critiquer qn d'avoir fait qch; **they have been criticized for not trying** on leur a reproché de ne pas avoir essayé; **his report has been criticized for being too …** on a reproché à son rapport d'être trop …; **to c. sth severely** se répandre en critiques sur qch **2** *(film, book etc)* critiquer, faire la critique de

vi critiquer; **stop criticizing** arrête de critiquer *ou* de faire des critiques

critique [krɪˈtiːk] **N** critique *f*, *(of book etc)* article *m* critique

critter [ˈkrɪtər] **N** *Am Dial* = **creature**

CRN [siːɑːˈren] **N** *Com (abbr customs registered number)* numéro *m* d'enregistrement douanier

croak [krəʊk] **N** *(of frog)* coassement *m*; *(of raven)* croassement *m*; **…, he said in a c. …**, dit-il d'une voix rauque

vi 1 *(of frog)* coasser; *(of raven)* croasser; *(of person)* parler d'une voix rauque **2** *Sl (die)* crever, claquer

vt *(words, warning etc)* proférer d'une voix rauque; **I'm not well, she croaked** ça ne va pas, dit-elle d'une voix rauque

croaking [ˈkrəʊkɪŋ] **N** *(of frog)* coassement *m*; *(of raven)* croassement *m*

croaky [ˈkrəʊkɪ] **ADJ** *(voice)* rauque, enroué

Croat [ˈkrəʊæt] **ADJ** croate

N 1 Croate *mf* **2** *Ling* croate *m*

Croatia [krəʊˈeɪʃə] **N** Croatie *f*

Croatian [krəʊˈeɪʃən] **ADJ** croate

N 1 Croate *mf* **2** *Ling* croate *m*

croc [krɒk] **N** *Fam* crocodile *m*

crochet [ˈkrəʊʃeɪ, -ʃɪ] **N** *(travail m au)* crochet *m*

vt *(shawl, tablecloth etc)* faire au crochet; **crocheted sweater** pull au crochet

vi faire du crochet

▸▸ **c. hook** crochet *m*; **c. work** travail au crochet

crocheting [ˈkrəʊʃeɪɪŋ, -ʃɪ-] **N** *(travail m au)* crochet *m*

crock [krɒk] **N 1** *(pot)* pot *m* de terre; *(jug)* cruche *f*, *Vulg* **it's a c. of shit** *(nonsense)* c'est un tas de conneries **2** *(in gardening)* tesson *m* *(pour couvrir le trou d'un pot de fleurs)* **3** *Fam* **old c.** *(person)* vieux bonhomme *m* fini, croulant *m*; *(car)* vieux clou *m*, vieille bagnole *f*

crockery [ˈkrɒkərɪ] **N** *(no pl) (tableware)* vaisselle *f* de table *ou* de cuisine

crocodile [ˈkrɒkədaɪl] **N 1** *(animal)* crocodile *m* **2** *(skin)* peau *f* de crocodile, *Fam* croco *m* **c. handbag** sac *m* à main en crocodile *ou Fam* en croco **3** *Br Fam (line of pupils)* élèves *mpl* marchant en colonne par deux

▸▸ **c. clip** pince *f* crocodile; **c. skin** peau de crocodile, *Fam* croco; **c. tears** larmes *fpl* de crocodile

crocus, *pl* **crocuses** [ˈkrəʊkəs, -əsɪz] **N** crocus *m*

croft [krɒft] **N** *esp Scot* petite ferme *f*

crofter [ˈkrɒftər] **N** *esp Scot* petit fermier *m*

Crohn's disease [krəʊnz] **N** *Med* maladie *f* de Crohn

crone [krəʊn] **N** *Pej* **old c.** vieille bique *f*

crony [ˈkrəʊnɪ] **N** copain *m*, copine *f*; **a Labour c. is believed to have got the top advisory job** le principal poste de conseiller aurait été attribué à un membre du parti travailliste proche du pouvoir

▸▸ **c. capitalism** capitalisme *m* de copinage

cronyism [ˈkrəʊnɪɪzəm] **N** *Pej* copinage *m*

crook [krʊk] **N 1** *Fam (criminal, rogue)* escroc *m* **2** *(of shepherd)* houlette *f*; *(of bishop)* crosse *f* **3** *(curve)* **in the c. of her arm** dans le creux de son bras

vt courber, recourber; *(arm)* plier; **to c. one's finger** recourber son doigt

ADJ *Austr Fam* **1** *(ill)* malade; *(furious)* furieux; **to go c.** piquer une rage (**at sb** contre qn); **to feel a bit c.** ne pas se sentir dans son assiette **2** *(broken down) (machinery etc)* en panne **3** *(poor) (thing, place etc)* moche

crooked [ˈkrʊkɪd] **ADJ 1** *Fam (lawyer, salesman etc)* véreux; **c. means** moyens *mpl* douteux **2** *(not straight)* courbe; *(limb, tree)* déjeté; *(nose)* crochu; *(leg)* tors; **the painting was c.** le tableau était de travers; **his hat was on c.** son chapeau était de travers; **a c. smile** un sourire forcé **3** [krʊkt] *(with a hooked end)* **c. stick** bâton *m* recourbé

crookedly [ˈkrʊkɪdlɪ] **ADV 1** *Fam (to deal)* malhonnêtement **2** *(to hang)* de travers

crookedness [ˈkrʊkɪdnɪs] **N 1** *Fam (dishonesty)* malhonnêteté *f* **2** *(of outlines etc)* irrégularité *f*; *(of smile)* fausseté *f*

croon [kruːn] **vt 1** *(song)* chantonner, fredonner **2** *(say)* dire d'une voix charmeuse

vi chantonner

crooner [ˈkruːnər] **N** *(singer)* chanteur, -euse de charme, crooner *m*

crop [krɒp] **N 1** *Agr (of cereals)* récolte *f*, moisson *f*; *(of fruit, potatoes etc)* récolte; **a poor/good c.** une mauvaise/bonne récolte; **to harvest the crops** faire la récolte *ou* la moisson; *Fig* **a fine c. of hair** une belle chevelure; **this year's c. of films** les films de cette année

2 *(haircut)* coupe *f* (de cheveux); **to give sb a close c.** couper ras les cheveux de qn

3 *(handle of whip)* manche *m*; **(riding) c.** cravache *f*, **hunting c.** stick *m* de chasse

4 *(of bird etc)* jabot *m*

vt **(-pp-) 1** *(cut) (animal's ears, tail)* écourter, couper; *(hair)* couper ras; *Comput (graphic)* rogner; *(photograph)* couper

2 *(of cattle) (grass)* brouter

3 *Agr (potatoes etc)* cultiver; **to c. land with corn** mettre une terre en blé

vi **(-pp-) 1** *(of land)* donner une récolte; **to c. well** donner une bonne récolte

▸▸ **c. circle** = motif *m* circulaire tracé dans un champ, attribué par certains à l'intervention d'extraterrestres; *Agr* **c. rotation** assolement *m*, rotation *f* des cultures

▸ **crop up** VI *(arise)* se présenter, surgir; **her name cropped up in the conversation** son nom a surgi dans la conversation; **did anything c. up while I was away?** est-ce qu'il s'est passé quelque chose pendant mon absence?; **something has cropped up** *(I'll be late etc)* j'ai un empêchement

cropper ['krɒpər] N **1** *Fam* **to come a c.** *(fall)* faire une chute, *Fam* se prendre *ou* se ramasser une pelle; *Fig (fail)* se planter; **to come a c. over sth** se casser les dents sur qch **2** *Agr (person)* cultivateur, -trice **3** *(plant)* **good/bad c.** plante *f* qui donne de bonnes/de mauvaises récoltes *ou* qui donne bien/mal

cropping ['krɒpɪŋ] N *Comput (of graphics)* rognage *m*, recadrage *m*

croquet ['krəʊkeɪ, -kɪ] N *Sport* croquet *m*; **to play c.** jouer au croquet
▸▸ **c. mallet** maillet *m*; **c. player** joueur, -euse de croquet

croquette [krɒ'ket] N *Culin* croquette *f*; **potato c.** croquette de pomme de terre

crosier ['krəʊzɪər] N *Rel* crosse *f (d'évêque)*

CROSS [krɒs]

N croix **1** ▪ hybride **2**	
VT croiser **1, 5** ▪ traverser **2**	
▪ contrarier **3**	
VI se croiser **1** ▪ traverser **2**	
ADJ fâché **1** ▪ transversal **2**	

N **1** *(sign, shape)* croix *f*; *Fig* **everyone has their c. to bear** chacun a sa croix à porter; *Rel* **to make the sign of the c.** faire le signe de (la) croix; **market c.** croix de la place du marché; **St Andrew's c.** croix de Saint-André; **Military C.** Croix de Guerre; **to sign with a c.** signer d'une croix **2** *(hybrid)* hybride *m*, croisement *m*; **a c. between a horse and a donkey** un croisement *ou* hybride du cheval et de l'ânesse; *Fig* **to be a c. between sth and sth** être un mélange de qch et de qch; **it's a c. between a car and a van** c'est un compromis entre une voiture et une camionnette **3** *Boxing* cross *m*, coup *m* croisé

VT **1** *(form into the shape of a cross) (two sticks etc)* croiser; **to c. one's legs/arms** (se) croiser les jambes/les bras; **to c. one's eyes** loucher, faire exprès de loucher; *Fig* **to c. swords** croiser le fer (with avec); **let's keep our fingers crossed** croisons les doigts; **I've got my fingers crossed for you** je croise les doigts pour toi; *Rel* **to c. oneself** faire le signe de croix, se signer; *Fam* **c. my heart and hope to die)** croix de bois croix de fer (si je mens, je vais en enfer); *Fig* **we must have got our wires crossed** nous avons dû mal nous comprendre; *Prov* **c. my palm with silver** *(said by fortune-teller)* une petite pièce, s'il vous plaît

2 *(go across) (sea, river)* traverser, passer; *(street etc)* traverser; *(frontier)* traverser, franchir; *(threshold)* franchir; *(bridge)* passer (sur), traverser; **the bridge that crosses the river** le pont qui traverse *ou* enjambe la rivière; **to c. sb's path** se trouver sur le chemin de qn; *Br Pol* **to c. the floor (of the House)** changer de parti (politique); *Naut* **to c. the line** passer l'équateur; **to c. sb's mind** *(of thought)* traverser l'esprit de qn, venir à l'esprit *ou* à l'idée de qn; **didn't it c. your mind that she might have been lying?** est-ce qu'il ne t'est pas venu à l'idée qu'elle ait pu mentir?

3 *(oppose) (person, person's plans)* contrarier, contrecarrer; *(go against) (person)* s'opposer à; **to be crossed in love** avoir une déception amoureuse

4 *(in writing) (cheque)* barrer; **to c. one's t's** mettre les barres à ses t

5 *(in breeding etc)* croiser; *Fig (two styles)* mélanger, marier

VI **1** *(of roads, letters etc)* se croiser; *(of lines)* se croiser, s'entrecroiser

2 *(go across)* traverser; **to c. from Dover to Calais** faire la traversée de Douvres à Calais; **look before you c.** regarde avant de traverser

ADJ **1** *(angry)* fâché; **he looks c.** il a l'air fâché; **to get c.** se fâcher (**with** contre; **about** de); **Mummy's very c. with you!** Maman est très fâchée!; **don't be c. with me** il ne faut pas m'en vouloir; **to be c. with oneself** s'en vouloir; **you never hear a c. word from her** avec elle, on n'entend jamais un mot plus haut que l'autre; **we've never had a c. word** nous ne nous sommes jamais disputés

2 *(transverse)* transversal
▸▸ *Opt* **c. hairs** = fils *mpl* croisés d'une lunette qui déterminent la ligne de visée; *St Exch* **c. hedge** couverture *f* croisée; **c. section** coupe *f ou* section *f* transversale; **in c. section** en coupe transversale; *Fig* **a c. section of life** une tranche de vie; *Fig* **a c. section of the population** un groupe représentatif de la population; *Am* **c. street** rue *f* transversale

▸ **cross off** VT SEP *(remove) (name)* rayer, barrer; **to c. a name off a list** rayer un nom d'une liste
▸ **cross out** VT SEP *(word, phrase etc)* biffer, barrer, rayer
▸ **cross over** VT INSEP *(street)* traverser
VI *(go across street, sea, frontier etc)* traverser; **they crossed over to Cherbourg in their yacht** ils ont fait la traversée jusqu'à Cherbourg dans leur yacht

crossbar ['krɒsbɑːr] N (barre *f* de) traverse *f*, entretoise *f*; *(on man's bike)* barre; *Ftbl, Rugby etc* barre transversale

crossbeam ['krɒsbiːm] N *Constr* sommier *m*, traverse *f*; *(on piles)* chapeau *m*; *Gym* portique *m*

cross-bencher [-bentʃər] N *Br Parl (député m)* non-inscrit, -ite, *pl* non-inscrit(e)s

crossbill ['krɒsbɪl] N *(bird)* bec-croisé *m*, *pl* becs-croisés

crossbones ['krɒsbəʊnz] NPL **skull and c.** tête *f* de mort *(du pavillon des pirates)*

cross-border ADJ transfrontières *inv*, transfrontalier
▸▸ **c. talks** négociations *fpl* transfrontalières; **c. trade** commerce *m* transfrontalier

crossbow ['krɒsbəʊ] N arbalète *f*

crossbred ['krɒsbred] ADJ *(animal)* croisé; *(plant)* hybride

crossbreed ['krɒsbriːd] N croisement *m*; *(person)* métis, -isse
VT *(pt, pp* **crossbred**) croiser; *(humans)* métisser; *(plants)* hybrider

cross-Channel ADJ *(ferry)* trans-Manche *inv*

crosscheck ['krɒs'tʃek] N vérification *f* par recoupement
VT vérifier par recoupement; **I crosschecked my list against yours** j'ai vérifié que ma liste et la vôtre sont identiques, j'ai vérifié qu'il n'y a pas de disparités entre ma liste et la vôtre

cross-compiler N *Comput* compilateur *m* croisé

cross-country ADJ *(walk)* à travers champs; *(vehicle)* tout-terrain *inv*
N *Sport* **1** *(race, racing)* cross *m*, cross-country *m*, *pl* cross-countrys *ou* cross-countries **2** *(skiing)* ski *m* de fond
▸▸ **c. runner** coureur, -euse de cross, crossman *m*, *pl* crossmen, crosswoman *f*, *pl* crosswomen; **c. running** cross; **c. skier** fondeur, -euse; **c. skiing** ski de fond

cross-cultural ADJ interculturel

cross-currency swap N *St Exch* crédit *m* croisé

cross-current N *(in air, water)* contre-courant *m*, *pl* contre-courants

crosscut ['krɒskʌt] N **1** coupe *f* en travers **2** *Cin, TV* montage *m* alterné
▸▸ **c. file** lime *f* à taille croisée; **c. saw** scie *f* passe-partout

crosscutting ['krɒskʌtɪŋ] N *Cin, TV* montage *m* alterné

cross-dressing N travestisme *m*

crossed [krɒst] ADJ croisé; *Tel* **we seem to have a c. line** il y a des interférences sur la ligne; **the regimental badge is two c. rifles** le badge du régiment représente deux fusils croisés
▸▸ **c. cheque** chèque *m* barré

cross-examination N *Law* contre-interrogatoire *m*, *pl* contre-interrogatoires; *Fig* interrogatoire *m* serré

cross-examine VT *Law* soumettre à un contre-interrogatoire; *Fig* soumettre à un interrogatoire serré

cross-eyed ADJ qui louche; **to be c.** loucher

cross-fade N *Radio* fondu *m* enchaîné (sonore); *Cin, TV* fondu enchaîné

cross-fertilization N hybridation *f*, pollinisation *f* croisée; *Fig* échanges *mpl*

cross-fertilize VT *Bot* hybrider; *Fig (ideas)* échanger
VI *Bot* s'hybrider; *Fig (of teams, people at conference etc)* échanger des idées

crossfire ['krɒsfaɪər] N *Mil* feu *m* croisé; **to be caught in the c.** *Mil* être pris dans le feu croisé; *Fig (in argument)* être pris entre deux feux

cross-flow radiator N *Aut* radiateur *m* à flux transversal

cross-grained [-greɪnd] ADJ **1** *(wood)* aux fibres irrégulières, à fibres torses **2** *Fig (person)* difficile, acariâtre

crosshair pointer ['krɒsheər] N *Comput* pointeur *m* en croix

crosshatch ['krɒshætʃ] VT *(in drawing)* hachurer en croisillons

crosshatching ['krɒshætʃɪŋ] N (système *m* de) hachures *fpl* croisées *ou* en croisillons

cross-headed ADJ *Tech (screw, screwdriver)* cruciforme

cross-holding N *Fin* participation *f* croisée

cross-impact analysis N *Mktg* analyse *f* d'interférence

crossing ['krɒsɪŋ] N **1** *(of sea)* traversée *f*; *(of river, the Alps)* traversée, passage *m*; *Mil (of river)* franchissement *m*; **we had a fine or good c.** nous avons eu *ou* fait une belle traversée; **a sea c.** une traversée maritime **2** *(for pedestrians)* passage *m* pour piétons, passage clouté **3** *(of roads)* croisement *m*, intersection *f*, carrefour *m*; *Rail* **level** *or Am* **grade c.** passage *m* à niveau

cross-legged ADJ **in a c. position** les jambes croisées
ADV les jambes croisées; **to sit c.** être assis en tailleur

crossly ['krɒslɪ] ADV *(with annoyance)* avec mauvaise humeur; *(angrily)* d'un air/d'un ton fâché

cross-member N *Aut* traverse *f*

crossover ['krɒsəʊvər] N **1** croisement *m*; *(of roads)* (croisement par) pont *m* routier; *(for pedestrians)* passage *m* clouté; *Rail* voie *f* de croisement **2** *(singer)* = chanteur, -euse qui est passé(e) d'un style de musique à un autre
ADJ *Mus (music)* qui associe deux styles; *(singer)* = qui est passé d'un style de musique à un autre
▸▸ *Mus* **c. album** album *m* hybride

cross-party ADJ *Pol*

▸▸ **c. agreement** accord *m* entre partis; **c. support** = soutien *m* au-delà des clivages politiques; **c. talks** négociations *fpl* entre partis

crosspatch ['krɒspætʃ] N *Fam* ronchon, -onne

crosspiece ['krɒspi:s] N (barre *f* de) traverse *f*

cross-ply tyre N *Aut* pneu *m* à structure diagonale

cross-post VT *Comput* faire un envoi multiple de

cross-posting N *Comput* envoi *m* multiple

cross-pricing N fixation *f* de prix croisés

cross-purposes ['krɒs'pɜ:pəsɪz] N **to be (talking) at c.** ne pas parler de la même chose

cross-question VT = **cross-examine**

cross-refer VT (**-rr-**) renvoyer; **the reader is cross-referred to page 332** il y a un renvoi à la page 332

cross-reference N renvoi *m*
VT (*book*) établir les renvois de; **to c. X to Y** renvoyer de X à Y; **it's cross-referenced** (*to another article*) il y a un renvoi à un autre article
▸▸ *Comput* **c. table** table *f* de références

crossroad ['krɒsrəʊd] N *Am* (*across a road*) = route *f* qui en coupe une autre; (*between main roads*) route secondaire, route départementale

crossroads ['krɒsrəʊdz] N (*with sing verb*) carrefour *m*, croisement *m*; *Fig* **the city is at the c. of Europe** la ville est au carrefour de l'Europe; *Fig* **we are now at the c.** (*decisive moment*) c'est l'heure des décisions irrévocables

cross-stitch N *Sewing* point *m* de croix

crosstalk ['krɒstɔ:k] N **1** *Br* série *f* de répliques du tac au tac **2** *Tel* diaphonie *f*

cross-town ADJ *Am* (*bus, trolley*) qui traverse la ville

cross-trainer N (*gym equipment*) cross-trainer *m*, *pl* cross-trainers

cross-training N *Sport* = entraînement *m* dans d'autres disciplines afin d'améliorer ses performances dans sa discipline principale

crosswalk ['krɒswɔ:k] N *Am* passage *m* clouté, passage pour piétons

crossway ['krɒsweɪ] N *Am* = **crossroad**

crosswind ['krɒswɪnd] N vent *m* de travers

crosswise ['krɒswaɪz] ADV (*at right angles*) à angle droit; (*diagonally*) en travers

crossword ['krɒswɜ:d] N (*puzzle*) mots *mpl* croisés
▸▸ **c. puzzle** mots croisés

crotch [krɒtʃ] N (*of person*) entrejambe *m*; (*of trousers*) entrejambe, *Spec* fourche *f*

crotchet ['krɒtʃɪt] N *Mus* noire *f*

crotchety ['krɒtʃətɪ] ADJ (*person*) grognon; (*mood*) difficile, acariâtre

croton ['krəʊt(ə)n] N (*plant*) croton *m*

crouch [kraʊtʃ] N accroupissement *m*
VI (*of animal*) se tapir; (*of person*) s'accroupir; **the tiger was crouching for a spring** le tigre, tapi, était sur le point de sauter
▸ **crouch down** VI = **crouch** VI

croup¹ [kru:p] N (*of horse*) croupe *f*

croup² N *Med* croup *m*; **to have c.** avoir le croup

croupier ['kru:pɪər] N croupier *m*

crow¹ [krəʊ] N (*bird*) corneille *f*; *Am Fig* **to eat c.** s'humilier (*en reconnaissant qu'on s'est trompé*); **as the c. flies** à vol d'oiseau
▸▸ **c.'s nest** nid *m* de corneille; *Naut* nid-de-pie *m*, *pl* nids-de-pie

crow² N (*of cock*) chant *m* du coq, *Fam* cocorico *m*; *Fig* **he let out a c. of triumph** il a

crié victoire, *Fam* il a poussé un cocorico, il a fait cocorico
VI **1** (*of cock*) chanter; *Fig* chanter victoire, *Fam* faire cocorico (**about** à propos de) **2** (*of baby*) gazouiller

crowbar ['krəʊbɑ:r] N pince *f* (à levier)

crowd [kraʊd] N **1** (*large number of people*) foule *f*; (*in building*) foule, affluence *f*; **to come in a c.** *or* **in crowds** venir en foule; **to draw a c.** attirer la foule; **that's what happens when you get a c. of boys together** c'est ce qui se produit quand tout un groupe de garçons se trouve rassemblé; **there wasn't much of a c. at the game** il n'y avait pas grand monde au match; **there was quite a c. in the square** il y avait pas mal de monde dans le square; *Fig* **the c.** la foule; **to stand out from the c.** se distinguer (de la foule); *Fig* **to follow the c.** suivre le mouvement; *Theat, Cin* **the c.** les figurants *mpl*; *Theat, Cin* **to be a c. puller** attirer les foules
2 *Fam* (*group*) bande *f*, clique *f*; **they're a good c.** ce sont de braves types; **they stick to their own c.** ils font bande à part
VT **1** (*force in, on*) (*people, objects*) entasser; (*fill*) remplir, bourrer (**with** de); **they crowded 10,000 people into the square** ils ont entassé 10 000 personnes sur la place; **too many books had been crowded onto the shelf** on avait entassé trop de livres sur l'étagère; **the tourists crowding the streets** les touristes qui se pressaient dans les rues
2 (*come too close to*) *Sport* (*competitor*) tasser; (*another car*) serrer; *Am* (*debtor*) importuner; **don't c. me!** (*don't pressure me*) ne me pousse pas!; **to be crowded off the pavement** être forcé de quitter le trottoir
VI **to c. (together)** se serrer; **they all crowded into the room** ils se sont tous entassés dans la pièce; **to c. round sb** se presser autour de qn; **they all crowded round** ils se sont tous amassés
▸▸ *Cin, TV* **c. scene** scène *f* de foule; **c. surfing** = pratique *f* courante dans les concerts pop ou rock, qui consiste à se laisser transporter, allongé, au-dessus de la foule
▸ **crowd in on** VT INSEP assaillir; **memories c. in on me here** ici, des souvenirs m'assaillent en foule
▸ **crowd out** VT SEP (*force out*) (*person, object*) ne pas laisser de place à; **to c. sb out of a deal/a market** exclure qn d'une affaire/ d'un marché

crowded ['kraʊdɪd] ADJ (*train, cinema, restaurant etc*) bondé; (*street*) (*with people*) bondé; (*with cars*) encombré; (*day*) chargé; **they lived in a room c. with furniture** ils vivaient dans une pièce encombrée de meubles; **it's a bit c. in here** il y a un peu trop de monde ici; **crowded together** pressés *ou* serrés l'un contre l'autre; **we are too crowded here** on est trop serrés ici; **the hall was crowded with people** la salle était bondée; **the c. events of that day** les nombreux événements de cette journée

crowfoot ['krəʊfʊt] N (*pl usu* **crowfoots**) (*plant*) renoncule *f* (âcre)

crowing ['krəʊɪŋ] N (*of cock*) chant *m*; *Fig* fanfaronnades *fpl*

crown [kraʊn] N **1** (*of monarch, martyr, made of flowers etc*) couronne *f*; **c. of thorns** couronne d'épines; **to wear the c.** porter la couronne
2 *Pol* **the C. or c.** la Couronne (*symbole de l'État monarchique*)
3 (*of tooth, natural or artificial*) couronne *f*
4 (*coin*) couronne *f*
5 (*highest part*) (*of vault*) clef *f*; (*of bridge, road*) bombement *m*; (*of hill*) crête *f*; (*of roof*) faîte *m*; **the c. (of the head)** le sommet de la tête
6 (*of hat*) fond *m*

VT **1** (*person, person's head*) couronner (**with** de); **to c. sb king** couronner qn roi; **they crowned her head with a garland of flowers** ils lui ont couronné la tête d'une guirlande de fleurs; **the crowned heads of Europe** les têtes *fpl* couronnées d'Europe; *Br Fam* **I'll c. you!** (*hit you*) je vais te flanquer un de ces coups sur la tête!
2 *Fig* (*person's happiness*) combler, couronner; (*person's efforts*) récompenser; *Br Fam* **to c. it all** pour comble de malheur
3 (*be at summit of*) couronner; **the woods that c. the hill** les bois qui couronnent la colline
4 (*in dentistry*) (*tooth*) couronner
5 (*at draughts*) **to be crowned** aller à dame
▸▸ *Br* **c. cap** capsule *f* (de bouteille); *Br* **c. colony** colonie *f* de la Couronne; *Can* **C. corporation** société *f* d'État; *Br* **C. Court** ≃ Cour *f* d'assises; **c. estates** terres *fpl* domaniales *ou* appartenant à la Couronne; **c. gear** *Tech* roue *f* plate; *Aut* grande couronne; **c. jewels** (*crown, sceptre etc*) joyaux *mpl* de la Couronne; *Sl Hum* (*man's genitals*) bijoux *mpl* de famille; **c. lands** terres domaniales *ou* appartenant à la Couronne; **c. prince** prince *m* héritier; **C. rating system** (*for hotels*) système *m* de classement (des hôtels britanniques); **c. wheel** *Tech* roue plate; *Aut* grande couronne; *Law* **c. witness** témoin *m* à charge

crowning ['kraʊnɪŋ] ADJ (*ambition, achievement*) suprême; **the c. moment** l'apothéose *f*
N (*of monarch etc*) couronnement *m*
▸▸ *Hum* **c. glory** (*hair*) chevelure *f*; **the red hair that was her c. glory** la belle crinière rousse qui faisait l'admiration de tout le monde

crow's-foot, *pl* **crow's-feet** N (*wrinkle*) patte *f* d'oie

crozier ['krəʊzɪər] N *Rel* (*of bishop*) crosse *f*

CRT [si:ɑ:'ti:] N **1** (*abbr* **cathode ray tube**) tube *m* cathodique **2** *Comput* (*abbr* **carriage return**) retour *m* chariot

crucial ['kru:ʃ(ə)l] ADJ **1** (*point etc*) crucial, -aux, décisif, critique; **the c. test** l'épreuve *f* décisive; **to be c. to sth** être crucial pour qch **2** *Sl* (*excellent*) d'enfer, supergénial

crucible ['kru:sɪb(ə)l] N *Metal, Chem, Ind, Fig* creuset *m*; *Fig* **their friendship was forged in the c. of war** leur amitié fut forgée pendant les temps difficiles de la guerre

crucifix ['kru:sɪfɪks] N crucifix *m*, christ *m*; (*at roadside*) calvaire *m*

crucifixion [kru:sɪ'fɪkʃən] N crucifixion *f*, crucifiement *m*

cruciform ['kru:sɪfɔ:m] ADJ cruciforme

crucify ['kru:sɪfaɪ] VT **1** (*execute*) crucifier; **Christ Crucified** le Crucifié **2** *Sl* (*person*) (*defeat*) flanquer *ou* mettre la pâtée à; (*criticize*) descendre en flammes; **we were crucified** (*in match*) ils nous ont mis la pâtée; **my mum will c. us if she finds out!** ma mère va nous étriper si elle découvre ça!

crud [krʌd] N *Sl* (*dirt*) saletés *fpl*; (*nonsense*) bêtises *fpl*; (*person*) ordure *f*, saloperie *f*

cruddy ['krʌdɪ] ADJ *Sl* (*dirty*) cradingue; (*very bad*) merdique

crude [kru:d] ADJ **1** (*unsophisticated, unrefined*) (*method, idea, style etc*) grossier; (*tool etc*) grossier, primitif; **a c. statement of the facts** un exposé brutal des faits **2** (*vulgar*) (*language, joke*) grossier, cru; (*manners*) grossier
N *Petr* (*crude oil*) pétrole *m* brut *m*
▸▸ *Petr* **c. oil** (*pétrole*) brut

crudely ['kru:dlɪ] ADV **1** (*in an unrefined, unsophisticated manner*) d'une manière grossière, grossièrement; **a c. constructed canoe** un canoë construit sommairement;

to put it c. *(bluntly)* pour être tout à fait franc **2** *(vulgarly)* crûment, grossièrement

crudeness ['kruːdnɪs], **crudity** ['kruːdɪtɪ] N **1** *(lack of refinement)* *(of style)* nature *f* grossière; *(of tool etc)* caractère *m* grossier *ou* primitif **2** *(vulgarity)* *(of expression etc)* crudité *f*; *(of manners etc)* grossièreté *f*

cruel ['kruəl] ADJ *(person, joke, treatment, winter)* cruel; **to be c. to sb** être cruel envers qn; **a c. blow** un coup dur; *Prov* **you have to be c. to be kind** qui aime bien châtie bien

cruelly ['kruəlɪ] ADV cruellement

cruelty ['kruəltɪ] N cruauté *f* (**to** envers); *Law* sévices *mpl* (**to sb** envers qn); **an act of c.** une cruauté

cruet ['kruɪt] N **1** *(for oil, vinegar)* petit flacon *m* **2** *Culin* *(set of condiments)* service *m* à condiments **3** *Rel* burette *f*
  ▸▸ *Culin* **c. stand** service *m* à condiments

Cruft's [krʌfts] N = très importante exposition *f* canine qui se tient à Londres

cruise [kruːz] N **1** *Naut* croisière *f*; **(pleasure) c.** croisière *f*; **to go on a c.** partir en croisière **2** *Mil* *(missile)* missile *m* de croisière
  VI **1** *Naut* *(of yacht, liner)* croiser, être en croisière; *(of passenger)* être en croisière
  2 *(of taxi, car)* marauder, être en maraude; **he was cruising up and down the high street** il montait et redescendait la rue principale; **we went cruising around the streets in search of …** nous avons roulé dans les rues à la recherche de …; *Fam* **you're cruising for a bruising** tu vas droit vers les ennuis **3** *Aviat, Aut etc (maintain constant speed)* aller à une vitesse de croisière; **we were cruising at 60** nous allions à une vitesse de croisière de 60
  4 *Sl (look for sexual partner)* draguer
  VT **1** *(of ship)* croiser dans; *(of ship's passenger)* être en croisière dans
  2 *Sl* **he was out cruising the streets** il se baladait en voiture
  3 *Sl* **to c. the bars** draguer dans les bars
  ▸▸ *Aut* **c. control** régulateur *m* d'allure; **c. missile** missile de croisière; **c. ship** bateau *m* de croisière

cruiser ['kruːzər] N **1** *Naut* **(battle) c.** croiseur *m*; **(cabin) c.** yacht *m* de croisière *(à moteur)* **2** = **cruiserweight**

cruiserweight ['kruːzəweɪt] N *Br Boxing* poids *m* mi-lourd

cruising ['kruːzɪŋ] N *Naut* croisière(s) *f(pl)*
  ▸▸ *Aviat* **c. altitude** altitude *f* de croisière; **c. holiday** croisière *f*; *Aviat* **c. range** autonomie *f* à vitesse de croisière; *Aviat* **c. speed** vitesse *f* de croisière

crumb [krʌm] N **1** *(small piece) (of bread)* miette *f*, *(opposed to crust)* mie *f* (de pain); *Fig* **they make the profit and we get the crumbs from their table** ils réalisent les bénéfices et nous récupérons les miettes; **c. of comfort** brin *m* de consolation; **crumbs of news** fragments *mpl* d'information **2** *Fam (contemptible person)* minable *mf*
  VT *Culin (cutlet, fish)* paner, couvrir de chapelure

crumble ['krʌmb(ə)l] VI *(of stone, earth etc)* s'effriter; *(of bread, pastry)* s'émietter; *Fig (of empire, opposition, resistance, prices)* s'effondrer; **everything is crumbling to dust** tout tombe en poussière; **her world was crumbling (to pieces) around her** tout son univers s'effondrait autour d'elle
  VT *(bread)* émietter; *(stone)* désagréger
  N *Br Culin* **apple/rhubarb c.** = dessert *m* aux pommes/à la rhubarbe recouvert de pâte sablée

crumbling ['krʌmblɪŋ] ADJ *(stone, earth)* qui s'effrite; *(wall etc)* qui s'écroule, croulant; *Fig (empire, opposition, resistance)* qui s'effondre

N *(of stone, earth)* effritement *m*; *Fig (of empire, opposition, resistance, prices etc)* effondrement *m*

crumbly ['krʌmblɪ] ADJ *(cake, bread)* friable, qui s'émiette (trop); *(cheese)* qui s'émiette; *(stone, brick)* friable, qui se désagrège
  N *Br Fam (old person)* croulant, -ante

crumbs [krʌmz] INT *Br Fam* ça alors!, zut!

crummy ['krʌmɪ] ADJ *Fam (film, job, idea etc)* minable; **what a c. joint!** quel endroit minable!; **to feel c.** *(ill)* ne pas se sentir dans son assiette; *(unhappy, upset)* ne pas se sentir fier *(about doing* d'avoir fait)

crump [krʌmp] N *(of shells)* détonation *f* assourdie

crumpet ['krʌmpɪt] N **1** *Culin* = petite galette fronde et spongieuse que l'on sert avec du beurre, de la confiture etc **2** *(no pl) Br Sl (women)* nanas *fpl*; **a nice bit of c.** une belle nana; *Hum (man)* un beau gars *ou* garçon *ou* type; *Hum* **he's the thinking woman's bit of c.** il est le chéri des femmes intelligentes

crumple ['krʌmp(ə)l] VT *(material, dress etc)* froisser, friper, chiffonner; **to c. paper** chiffonner *ou* froisser du papier; *(make into a ball)* faire une boule avec du papier; **to get crumpled** se froisser *ou* friper
  VI *(of fabric)* se friper, se froisser, se chiffonner; *(of leaves, parchment)* se ratatiner; *(of mudguard, car)* se plier; *(of face)* se décomposer; *Fig (of opposition)* s'effondrer; **he crumpled as the bullet hit him** il s'est écroulé au moment où la balle l'a atteint
  ▸▸ *Aut* **c. zone** zone *f* d'absorption
  ▸ **crumple up** VT SEP *(screw up into a ball) (paper)* faire une boule avec
  VI *(of person)* s'écrouler; *(of car)* se plier

crumpled ['krʌmp(ə)ld] ADJ *(paper)* froissé, chiffonné; *(skirt etc)* froissé, fripé, chiffonné; *(car)* à la tôle froissée; *(car wing)* froissé

crunch [krʌntʃ] N **1** *(sound)* craquement *m*; *(of snow, gravel etc)* crissement *m* **2** *Fig (critical moment)* **when it comes to the c.** au moment critique *ou* crucial; **when it came to the c. he let them down** il les a laissés tomber au moment critique *ou* crucial; **if it comes to the c. we can sell the car** au pire nous pourrons vendre la voiture **3** *(exercise)* exercice *m* pour les abdominaux; **to do crunches** faire des abdominaux
  VT *(with teeth)* croquer; *Comput (numbers, data)* traiter à grande vitesse
  VI craquer, crisser; **the hard snow crunched underfoot** la neige durcie crissait sous les pieds; **they crunched through the snow** ils avançaient dans la neige qui crissait sous leurs pas; **he was crunching on an apple** il croquait dans une pomme
  ▸ **crunch up** VT SEP *(crush)* broyer; **the car had been crunched up** la voiture avait été broyée

crunching ['krʌntʃɪŋ] N = **crunch** N **1**

crunchy ['krʌntʃɪ] ADJ *(food)* croquant, croustillant; *(snow)* qui craque (sous les pas)

crupper ['krʌpər] N **1** *(part of harness)* croupière *f*, culière *f* **2** *(of horse)* croupe *f*

crusade [kruːˈseɪd] N *Hist, Fig* croisade *f*; **to go on a c.** partir en croisade; **a one-man c. against drug-dealing** une croisade contre la drogue menée par un seul homme; **to start a c.** lancer une croisade *(against* contre)
  VI **1** *Hist* partir en croisade **2** *Fig* mener une campagne (**against** contre; **for** pour); **she spent her life crusading against injustice/for women's rights** elle a passé sa vie à se battre contre l'injustice/pour les droits de la femme

crusader [kruːˈseɪdər] N **1** *Hist* croisé *m* **2** *Fig*

champion, -ionne (**for sth** de qch); **a c. against injustice** un champion de la lutte contre l'injustice
  ▸▸ *Hist* **c. castle** château *m* de croisé

crush [krʌʃ] N **1** *(crowd)* foule *f*; **there was a terrible c.** il y a eu une terrible bousculade; **two people were injured in the c.** deux personnes ont été blessées dans la bousculade **2** *Br (drink)* orange **c.** orangeade *f*; **lemon c.** citronnade *f* **3** *Fam (infatuation)* béguin *m*; **to have a c. on sb** avoir le *ou* un béguin pour qn, en pincer pour qn
  VT **1** *(person, object)* écraser; *(grapes etc)* exprimer le jus de; *(of boa constrictor) (victim)* comprimer; *(dress)* froisser; *(ice)* piler; *Min etc (ore)* broyer, concasser; **crushed together** *(people)* entassés, serrés; **we were nearly crushed to death** on a failli être écrasés; **he crushed the clothes into the suitcase** il a tassé les vêtements dans la valise
  2 *(destroy) (enemy)* écraser; *(revolt)* étouffer, écraser; **to c. sb's hopes** réduire les espoirs de qn à néant; **this remark crushed her** *(humiliated her)* cette remarque l'a profondément humiliée
  VI *(in order to get into a place)* se presser en foule, se bousculer
  ▸▸ *Theat* **c. bar** bar *m* des spectateurs; **c. barrier** barrière *f* de sécurité

crushing ['krʌʃɪŋ] ADJ *(news, defeat etc)* écrasant; *(reply, remark etc)* cinglant, humiliant; **to be dealt a c. blow** *(of army, hopes etc)* en prendre un sacré coup; **to treat sb with c. contempt** écraser qn de son mépris
  N *(of grapes)* pressage *m*; *(of ore)* broyage *m*, concassage *m*; *(of rebellion, uprising)* écrasement *m*; *(of hopes)* anéantissement *m*

crust [krʌst] N **1** *(of bread, pie)* croûte *f*; **there was not a c. to eat in the house** il ne restait absolument rien à manger dans la maison; *Fam* **we manage to earn a c.** nous arrivons à gagner notre croûte **2** *(of the earth, of ice etc)* croûte *f* **3** *(of wine)* dépôt *m* **4** *(on wound)* croûte *f*
  ▸ **crust over** VI *(become covered with a crust)* se couvrir d'une croûte; *(of wound etc)* former une croûte

crustacean [krʌsˈteɪʃən] ADJ crustacéen
  N crustacé *m*

crusted ['krʌstɪd] ADJ **to be c. with ice** être couvert d'une croûte de glace

crusty ['krʌstɪ] ADJ **1** *Culin (bread, roll)* croustillant **2** *(person)* bourru
  N *Br Fam* jeune hippie *mf* crado

crutch [krʌtʃ] N **1** *(support)* béquille *f*; *Fig* soutien *m*; *Fig* **a c. to lean on** un soutien; **to go about** *or* **walk on crutches** marcher avec des béquilles **2** = **crotch**

crux, *pl* **cruxes** [krʌks, 'krʌksɪz] N *(of discussion etc)* cœur *m*; **the c. of the matter** le nœud de la question

cry [kraɪ] N **1** *(call) (of person, animal)* cri *m*; **to give** *or* **utter a c.** pousser un cri; **a c. of pain** un cri de douleur; *also Fig* **a c. for help** un appel au secours; **there were cries of 'down with the king!'** on criait 'à bas le roi!'; **their c. was 'one man, one vote'** leur slogan était 'un homme, une voix'; **to be in full c.** *(of hounds etc)*, *Fig* être lancé dans une poursuite acharnée *(after* de); **it's a far c. from what they promised us** cela n'a rien à voir avec ce qu'ils nous avaient promis; **it's still a far c. from what I asked for** cela reste loin de ce que j'avais demandé
  2 *(weeping)* **to have a c.** pleurer; **to have a good c.** pleurer un bon coup
  VI *(pt, pp* **cried** [kraɪd]) **1** *(weep)* pleurer; **big girls don't c.** les grandes filles ne pleurent pas, on ne pleure pas quand on est une grande fille; **to c. over sth** pleurer *ou* verser des larmes sur qch; **to c. for joy** pleurer de

joie; **I laughed until I cried** j'ai ri aux larmes **2** *(shout, call)* crier, pousser un cri/des cris; **to c. aloud** pousser de grands cris; **to c. for help** appeler au secours *ou* à l'aide; **to c. for mercy** demander grâce

VT 1 *(exclaim) (name etc)* crier; **that's not true!, he cried** ce n'est pas vrai!, s'écria-t-il; *Old-fashioned* **to c. one's wares** vendre sa marchandise à la criée **2 to c. one's eyes** *or* **one's heart out** pleurer toutes les larmes de son corps; **she cried herself to sleep** elle s'est endormie en pleurant

▸ **cry down** VT SEP *(person, thing)* décrier, dénigrer

▸ **cry off** VI *(cancel acceptance of invitation)* se décommander

▸ **cry out** VI *(shout)* pousser un cri; *Fam* **for crying out loud!** nom de nom!, mais bon sang!

VT SEP *(name etc)* crier; **stop!, she cried out** arrêtez!, s'écria-t-elle

▸ **cry out for** VT INSEP **1** *(shout out for)* réclamer à grands cris **2** *Fig (need desperately)* avoir désespérément besoin de; **that wall is crying out for a coat of paint** ce mur a besoin d'un bon coup de peinture

▸ **cry up** VT INSEP **1** *(publicize, praise) (book, film)* vanter **2** *(exaggerate)* **to c. up one's opponent's chances** exagérer la force de son adversaire

crybaby ['kraɪbeɪbɪ] N *Fam* pleurnicheur, -euse

crying ['kraɪɪŋ] ADJ *(need etc)* urgent; **it's a c. shame that …** il est scandaleux que … + *sub* N **1** *(weeping)* pleurs *mpl* **2** *(shouting, calling)* cris *mpl*

cryogenics [kraɪə'dʒenɪks] N *(with sing verb)* cryogénie *f*

cryonics [kraɪ'ɒnɪks] N *(with sing verb)* cryoconservation *f*

cryosurgery [kraɪəʊ'sɜːdʒərɪ] N cryochirurgie *f*

crypt [krɪpt] N *(in church)* crypte *f*

cryptic ['krɪptɪk] ADJ *(message, silence, smile, look)* mystérieux, énigmatique; *(remark)* sibyllin; **he was very c. about his future plans** il a été très mystérieux sur ses projets d'avenir

▸▸ **c. crossword** = mots *mpl* croisés dont les définitions sont des énigmes qu'il faut résoudre

cryptically ['krɪptɪklɪ] ADV mystérieusement; *(to speak)* à mots couverts; **the book ends c.** le livre se termine de façon énigmatique *ou* sur une énigme

crypto- ['krɪptəʊ] PREF crypto-; **c.-communist** cryptocommuniste

cryptogram ['krɪptəɡræm] N cryptogramme *m*

cryptographer [krɪp'tɒɡrəfər] N cryptographe *mf*

cryptographic [krɪptə'ɡræfɪk] ADJ cryptographique

cryptography [krɪp'tɒɡrəfɪ] N cryptographie *f*

crystal ['krɪst(ə)l] N **1** *Chem, Miner* cristal *m*; **as clear as c.** clair comme le jour *ou* cristallin **2** *(chip)* cristal *m*; **salt crystals** cristaux *mpl* de sel; **in c. form** sous forme cristalline **3** *(on watch)* verre *m* de montre **4** *Electron etc* cristal *m*

ADJ *(clear)* limpide, cristallin; *(vase, glass)* de cristal

▸▸ **c. ball** boule *f* de cristal; **c. factory** cristallerie *f*, **c. gazing** divination *f* par la boule de cristal; *Radio* **c. set** poste *m* à galène

crystal-clear ADJ limpide, cristallin; *Fig (argument)* clair comme le jour *ou* de l'eau de roche; **it's all c. to me now** ça me paraît clair comme de l'eau de roche maintenant; **to make sth c.** rendre qch bien clair

crystalline ['krɪstəlaɪn] ADJ cristallin

▸▸ *Opt* **c. lens** cristallin *m*

crystallization [krɪstəlaɪ'zeɪʃən] N cristallisation *f*

crystallize ['krɪstəlaɪz] *Chem, Fig* VT cristalliser; **crystallized fruits** fruits *mpl* confits

VI se cristalliser

crystallography [krɪstə'lɒɡrəfɪ] N cristallographie *f*

CS ['siː'es] N

▸▸ **CS gas** gaz *m* lacrymogène

CSD [siːes'diː] N *Banking, St Exch (abbr* **Central Securities Depository***)* depositaire *m* national de titres

CSE [siːes'iː] N *Br Sch Formerly (abbr* **Certificate of Secondary Education***)* = diplôme *m* sanctionnant la fin des études du premier cycle dans l'enseignement secondaire

C-section N *Obst* césarienne *f*

CST [siːes'tiː] N *Am (abbr* **Central Standard Time***)* = heure *f* du centre de l'Amérique du Nord

CSV [siːes'viː] NPL *Comput (abbr* **comma-separated values***)* valeurs *fpl* séparées par des virgules

cub [kʌb] N **1** *(of fox)* renardeau *m*; *(of bear)* ourson *m*; *(of lion)* lionceau *m*; *(of wolf)* louveteau *m*; *Fig* **that impertinent young c.!** cette espèce de blanc-bec! **2** *(scout)* louveteau *m*; **he goes to Cubs on Fridays** il va à la réunion des louveteaux le vendredi

▸▸ **c. reporter** jeune journaliste *mf*, **C. scout** louveteau

Cuba ['kjuːbə] N Cuba *m*; **in C.** à Cuba

Cuban ['kjuːbən] ADJ cubain

N Cubain, -aine

▸▸ **C. heel** talon *m* cubain

cubbyhole ['kʌbɪhəʊl] N *(room)* cagibi *m*; *(cupboard)* placard *m*

cube [kjuːb] N **1** *Math, Geom* cube *m*; **27 is the c. of three** 27 est le cube de trois **2** *(piece) (of bread, meat etc)* dé *m*; *(of sugar)* morceau *m*; **cut the meat into cubes** coupez la viande en dés

VT **1** *Math* élever au cube; **27 cubed** 27 au cube **2** *(meat etc)* couper en dés

▸▸ *Math* **c. root** racine *f* cubique

cubic ['kjuːbɪk] ADJ **1** *(measurement)* cube **2** *(cube-shaped)* cubique

▸▸ **c. capacity** volume *m*, cube *m*; *(of engine)* cylindrée *f*, **c. centimetre** centimètre *m* cube; **c. measure** mesure *f* de volume; **c. metre** mètre *m* cube

cubicle ['kjuːbɪk(ə)l] N *(in swimming pool)* cabine *f*, *(for trying on clothes)* cabine d'essayage; *(in dormitory)* box *m*; *(of public toilet)* W.-C. *mpl*; **his office was little more than a c.** son bureau n'était pas plus grand qu'un box

cubism ['kjuːbɪz(ə)m] N *Art* cubisme *m*

cubist ['kjuːbɪst] ADJ, N *Art* cubiste *mf*

cuckold ['kʌkəld] *esp Lit* N cocu *m*

VT cocufier, faire cocu

cuckoo ['kʊkuː] N *(bird)* coucou *m*

ADJ *Fam (mad)* dingue; **to go c.** devenir dingue, perdre la boule

INT coucou!

▸▸ **c. clock** coucou *m (pendule)*; *Bot* **c. spit** crachat *m* de coucou

cucumber ['kjuːkʌmbər] N concombre *m*; *Fig* **to be (as) cool as a c.** *(in a crisis etc)* être d'un calme imperturbable; **…, she said, cool as a c.** … dit-elle avec un calme imperturbable; *(without showing any remorse)* … dit-elle comme si de rien n'était; *Zool* **sea c.** concombre de mer

▸▸ **c. sandwich** = petit sandwich *m* au pain de mie et au concombre *(l'expression est parfois utilisée pour évoquer certains milieux bourgeois)*

cud [kʌd] N *(of ruminant)* bol *m* alimentaire; **to chew the c.** *(of cow etc)* ruminer; *Fig (of person)* ruminer une idée, méditer

cuddle ['kʌd(ə)l] N câlin *m*; **to give sb a c.** faire un câlin à qn

VT *(person)* serrer dans ses bras, câliner; **to c. one another** se faire des câlins; **children need lots of cuddling** les enfants ont besoin d'être beaucoup câlinés

VI *(of two people)* se faire des câlins, se câliner; **two young people kissing and cuddling** deux jeunes gens en train de s'embrasser et de se faire des câlins

▸ **cuddle up** VI *(lie, sit etc closely)* se pelotonner; **to c. up to sb** se blottir *ou* se pelotonner contre qn; **they cuddled up to each other for warmth** ils se sont pelotonnés *ou* blottis l'un contre l'autre pour se tenir chaud; **c. up if you're cold** *(to me)* pelotonne-toi si tu as froid; *(to each other)* serrez-vous *ou* pelotonnez-vous l'un contre l'autre si vous avez froid

cuddly ['kʌdlɪ] ADJ *(teddy bear etc)* tout doux, *f* toute douce; *(child, animal etc)* mignon à croquer; *Hum (plump)* dodu

▸▸ **c. toy** peluche *f*

cudgel ['kʌdʒ(ə)l] N gourdin *m*, trique *f*, *Fig* **to take up the cudgels on sb's behalf** prendre fait et cause pour qn

VT *(-ll-, Am -l-) (person)* donner des coups de bâton à; *Fig Fam* **to c. one's brains** se creuser les méninges *ou* la cervelle

cue¹ [kjuː] N *(signal)* signal *m*, top *m*; *Theat (verbal)* réplique *f*; *Mus (for instrument)* indication *f* de rentrée; **to miss one's c.** *Theat* manquer la réplique; *TV, Cin* rater le signal; *Theat, Fig* **to give sb his/her c.** donner la réplique à qn; *Fig* **he nodded, and that was my c. to make the coffee** il a hoché la tête pour me faire signe de faire le café; **I suppose that's my c. to leave?** je dois comprendre que c'est le moment que je parte?; *Fig* **to take one's c. from sb** prendre exemple sur qn; *Fig (right)* **on c.** au bon moment

VT donner le signal à; *Theat (verbally)* donner la réplique à; **c. and cut!** moteur! et coupez!

▸▸ **c. card** carton *m* aide-mémoire; *Radio, TV* **c. sheet** feuille *f* de conducteur, feuille de mixage

▸ **cue in** VT SEP **1** donner le signal à; *Theat (verbally)* donner la réplique à **2** *esp Am (inform) (person)* mettre à la page

cue² N *(in billiards, snooker, pool)* queue *f*

▸▸ **c. ball** *(ball)* bille *f* de joueur; *Am Fam (bald person)* chauve *mf*, **c. rack** porte-queues *m inv*

cuff [kʌf] N **1** *(of shirt)* poignet *m*; *(that takes cuff links)* manchette *f*, *(of coat sleeve)* parement *m*; **double c.** poignet mousquetaire; *Fam* **off the c.** *(discours etc)* impromptu; *Fam* **to do sth off the c.** faire qch au pied levé; *Fam* **I can't tell you off the c.** je ne peux pas te le dire comme ça *ou* tout de suite **2** *Am (of trousers)* revers *m* de pantalon **3** *Fam* **cuffs = handcuffs 4** *(blow)* taloche *f*, calotte *f*; **he gave me a c. on the head** il m'a mis une taloche sur la tête

VT **1** *(hit) (person)* talocher, calotter **2** *Fam (put handcuffs on)* mettre les menottes à

▸▸ **c. link** bouton *m* de manchette

cuisine [kwɪ'ziːn] N cuisine *f*

cul-de-sac ['kʌldəsæk] N *(pl* **culs-de-sac, cul-de-sacs***)* cul-de-sac *m*, *pl* culs-de-sac, impasse *f*, *Fig* impasse

culinary ['kʌlɪnərɪ] ADJ *(skill, delight, purpose)* culinaire; *(implement)* de cuisine; *(herb)* pour la cuisine; **the c. art** l'art *m* culinaire

cull [kʌl] N **1** *(killing) (of deer, wild boar)* battue *f*, *(of seals)* abattage *m* **2** *(animal) (before killing)* bête *f* à abattre; *(after killing)* bête abattue

vt1 *(reduce by killing) (herd of deer, seal colony)* réduire la taille de; *(kill) (deer, seals)* abattre **2** *(choose)* choisir (**from** dans); **the poems have been culled from her early work** les poèmes ont été choisis parmi ses premières œuvres; **information culled from various sources** des renseignements pris à differentes sources

culminate [ˈkʌlmɪneɪt] **vi** **to c. in sth** *(undesirable)* se terminer en *ou* par qch; *(desirable)* aboutir à qch; **the protests culminated in a battle with the police** ces manifestations se sont terminées par un affrontement avec la police; **the excavations culminated in the discovery of a temple** les fouilles ont abouti à la découverte d'un temple

culminating [ˈkʌlmɪneɪtɪŋ] **adj** *(point, moment)* culminant

culmination [kʌlmɪˈneɪʃən] **n** *(of events etc)* point *m* culminant, sommet *m*

culottes [kuːˈlɒts] **npl** *(garment)* jupe-culotte *f*, *pl* jupes-culottes

culpability [kʌlpəˈbɪlɪtɪ] **n** *Fml* culpabilité *f*

culpable [ˈkʌlpəb(ə)l] **adj** *Law, Fml (negligence etc)* coupable

culprit [ˈkʌlprɪt] **n** *(guilty person), Fig* coupable *mf*, responsable *mf*, *(event)* cause *f*; **I'm the c.** c'est moi le coupable; **poor housing is the main c.** ce sont les mauvaises conditions de logement qui sont principalement responsables

cult [kʌlt] **n 1** *Rel, Fig (worship)* culte *m* (**of** de); **to make a c. of sth** avoir un culte pour qch; **a personality c., a c. of personality** un culte de la personnalité; **the film/band has a c. following** c'est un film-/groupe-culte; **c. book** livre *m* culte; **c. film** film *m* culte **2** *(sect)* secte *f*
► ► **c. figure** idole *f*

cultivate [ˈkʌltɪveɪt] **vt1** *(earth, field, vegetables etc)* cultiver **2** *Biol (bacillus)* faire une culture de **3** *(develop) (an art)* cultiver; *(friends, person's friendship, reputation, accent)* cultiver; *(approach, manner)* adopter

cultivated [ˈkʌltɪveɪtɪd] **adj 1** *Agr (land, plant)* cultivé **2** *(educated) (voice, manner)* qui témoigne d'une bonne éducation; *(mind)* cultivé

cultivation [kʌltɪˈveɪʃən] **n** culture *f*, **a field under c.** un champ cultivé

cultivator [ˈkʌltɪveɪtər] **n** *Agr* **1** *(machine) (for farm)* cultivateur *m*; *(for garden)* motoculteur *m* **2** *(person)* cultivateur, -trice

cultural [ˈkʌltʃər(ə)l] **adj** *(institute, development, attaché etc)* culturel
► ► **c. anthropology** culturologie *f*, **c. event** manifestation *f* culturelle; **c. exchange** échange *m* culturel; **c. heritage** patrimoine *m* culturel

culture [ˈkʌltʃər] **n1** *(artistic activity)* culture *f* **2** *(society)* culture *f*, **in Polynesian cultures** dans les cultures polynésiennes **3** *(refinement)* culture *f*, **he lacks c.** il n'a aucune culture **4** *Biol* culture *f*
vt *Biol (bacillus)* faire une culture de
► ► *Biol* **c. medium** milieu *m* de culture; **c. shock** choc *m* culturel; *Fam* **c. vulture** fana *mf* de culture, culturophage *mf*

cultured [ˈkʌltʃəd] **adj 1** *(educated)* cultivé **2** *(pearl)* de culture

culvert [ˈkʌlvət] **n** *Constr* canal *m* souterrain; *(for cable)* conduit *m* souterrain

cum[1] [kʌm] **prep** avec; **spare room c. study** chambre-bureau *f*, *pl* chambres-bureaux; **a translation c. rewrite** tout autant une réécriture qu'une traduction
► ► *St Exch* **c. dividend** coupon *m* attaché

cum[2] **n** *Sl* = **come n**

cumbersome [ˈkʌmbəsəm] **adj** *(clothing, luggage)* encombrant, gênant; *(system)* lourd, pesant; *(sentence)* lourd

cumin [ˈkʌmɪn, ˈkjuː-] **n** *Bot, Culin* cumin *m*

cummerbund [ˈkʌməbʌnd] **n** ceinture *f* de smoking

cumulative [ˈkjuːmjʊlətɪv] **adj** cumulatif; *Com (error)* cumulé
► ► *Fin* **c. balance** solde *m* cumulé; *Law* **c. evidence** preuve *f* par accumulation de témoignages; *Fin* **c. interest** intérêts *mpl* cumulatifs; *St Exch* **c. preference share** action *f* privilégiée; *Fin* **c. profit** bénéfice *m* cumulé; **c. total** cumul *m*; *Pol* **c. voting** vote *m* plural

cumulatively [ˈkjuːmjʊlətɪvlɪ] **adv** de façon cumulée

cumulonimbus [ˈkjuːmjʊləʊˈnɪmbəs] **n** *Met* cumulo-nimbus *m inv*

cumulus, *pl* **cumuli** [ˈkjuːmjʊləs, -laɪ] **n** *Met* cumulus *m*

cuneiform [ˈkjuːneɪɪfɔːm] **n** écriture *f* cunéiforme
adj cunéiforme

cunnilingus [kʌnɪˈlɪŋgəs] **n** cunnilingus *m*

cunning [ˈkʌnɪŋ] **n 1** *(deviousness)* ruse *f*, roublardise *f* **2** *(ingenuity)* astuce *f*, ingéniosité *f*
adj 1 *(devious)* rusé, roublard; *(look)* sournois; **c. as a fox** rusé comme un renard **2** *(ingenious) (device etc)* ingénieux, astucieux

cunningly [ˈkʌnɪŋlɪ] **adv 1** *(deviously)* avec ruse **2** *(ingeniously)* ingénieusement, astucieusement

cunt [kʌnt] **n** *Vulg* **1** *(vagina)* con *m*, chatte *f* **2** *(woman, women)* **he was out looking for c.** il cherchait une femme à baiser **3** *(unpleasant person)* salaud *m*, salope *f*

cup [kʌp] **n1** tasse *f*, *(metal)* gobelet *m*, timbale *f*, *(paper, plastic)* gobelet; **coffee/tea c.** tasse à café/à thé; **c. of coffee/of tea** tasse de café/de thé; *Fig Fam* **that's just my c. of tea** c'est tout à fait le genre de choses que j'aime; **science-fiction is not my c. of tea** la science-fiction n'est pas ma tasse de thé; **that's not everyone's c. of tea** tout le monde n'aime pas; **they're not my c. of tea** *(of people)* ils ne sont pas mon genre; *Culin* **cider/fruit c.** boisson *f* glacée au cidre/avec des fruits

2 *(measurement)* tasse *f*, **two cups of flour** deux tasses de farine

3 *Sport* coupe *f*, **to win a c.** remporter *ou* gagner une coupe; **the Davis C.** la coupe Davis; **c. winners** vainqueurs *mpl* de coupe

4 *Lit (goblet)* coupe *f*, *Rel* calice *m (du saint Sacrement)*; *Fig* **my c. runneth over** je déborde de joie; *Old-fashioned* **to be in one's cups** être gris

5 *(of flower)* calice *f*, *(of bra, swimming costume)* bonnet *m*; **what size c. do you take?** *(in bra etc)* quelle profondeur de bonnet est-ce que vous mettez?

vt (-pp-) **with one's chin cupped in one's hand** le menton dans le creux de la main; **to c. one's hand behind one's ear** mettre sa main en cornet; **to c. one's hands round one's mouth** mettre les mains en porte-voix; **she scooped up the water with her cupped hands** elle a recueilli l'eau dans ses mains jointes
► ► *Sport* **c. final** finale *f* de la coupe; **c. holder** *(in car)* support *m* de tasse; *Sport* **c. tie** match *m* de coupe

cup-and-ball joint **n** *Tech* joint *m* à rotule

cupbearer [ˈkʌpbeərər] **n** *Hist* échanson *m*

cupboard [ˈkʌbəd] **n** placard *m*; **store c.** placard *ou* armoire *f* à provisions;
► ► *Br* **c. love** amour *m* intéressé

cupcake [ˈkʌpkeɪk] **n** *Culin* petit gâteau *m (dans une caissette en papier)*

cupful [ˈkʌpfʊl] **n** tasse *f* (**of** de); **add two cupfuls of milk** ajouter deux tasses de lait

Cupid [ˈkjuːpɪd] **n** Cupidon *m*; *Art etc* Cupidon, Amour *m*

cupidity [kjuːˈpɪdɪtɪ] **n** *Fml* cupidité *f*

cupola [ˈkjuːpələ] **n 1** *Archit (ceiling, roof)* coupole *f*, dôme *m*; *(tower)* belvédère *m* **2** *Naut (gun turret)* coupole *f* **3** *(furnace)* cubilot *m*
► ► **c. furnace** cubilot

cuppa [ˈkʌpə] **n** *Br Fam* tasse *f* de thé

cupping glass [ˈkʌpɪŋ] **n** *Med* ventouse *f*

cupric [ˈkjuːprɪk] **adj** *Chem (acid)* cuprique

cup-shaped **adj** *Bot* cupulaire

cur [kɜːr] **n** *Lit* **1** *(dog)* sale cabot *m* **2** *(despicable man)* homme *m* méprisable, mufle *m*

curable [ˈkjʊərəb(ə)l] **adj** *Med, Fig* guérissable

curacy [ˈkjʊərəsɪ] **n** *Rel* vicariat *m*

curare [kjʊəˈrɑːrɪ] **n** curare *m*

curate[1] [ˈkjʊərət] **n** *Rel* vicaire *m*; **c. in charge** desservant *m*; *Fig* **his latest book/film is a bit of a c.'s egg** il y a du bon et du mauvais dans son dernier livre/film

curate[2] [kjʊˈreɪt] **vt** *(exhibition)* organiser

curative [ˈkjʊərətɪv] **adj** *(powers, effect, medicine)* curatif

curator [kjʊəˈreɪtər] **n** *(of museum, gallery)* conservateur, -trice

curb [kɜːb] **n1** *(check)* frein *m*; **to put a c. on sb's enthusiasm** mettre un frein à l'enthousiasme de qn; **to put a c. on one's passions** refréner ses passions, mettre un frein à ses passions **2** *Horseriding (chain)* gourmette *f* **3** *Am (of pavement etc)* bordure *f*, rebord *m*
vt1 *(one's passions)* réprimer, refréner; *(one's passions)* maîtriser, brider; *(impatience, enthusiasm, tendency)* modérer; *(inflation etc)* freiner; **you must learn to c. your tongue!** tu dois apprendre à tenir ta langue! **2** *(horse)* mettre la gourmette à
► ► *Horseriding* **c. bit** *(on harness)* mors *m*; *Horseriding* **c. chain** gourmette

curbstone [ˈkɜːbstəʊn] **n** *Am (of pavement)* pierre *f* de rebord

curd [kɜːd] **n** *(lait m)* caillé *m*; **curds and whey** lait caillé sucré

curdle [ˈkɜːd(ə)l] **vi** *(of milk)* se cailler; *Fig* **my blood curdled** mon sang s'est glacé *ou* figé
vt *(milk)* cailler; *Fig (blood)* glacer, figer; *Fam* **he had a face that would c. milk** il avait l'air aimable comme une porte de prison

cure [kjʊər] **n1** *(remedy), Fig* remède *m* (**for** contre); **there is no known c. for the condition** on ne connaît pas encore de remède pour cette maladie; **rest c.** cure *f* de repos; **to take a c.** faire une cure; **beyond** *or* **past c.** *(person)* incurable; *(situation)* irrémédiable; **the c. is worse than the disease** le remède est pire que le mal **2** *Rel* **c. of souls** cure *f ou* charge *f* d'âmes
vt1 *(person)* *(of illness)* guérir (**of** de); *(bad habit)* guérir, corriger; **this experience cured him of his infatuation** cette expérience l'a guéri de son engouement; *Prov* **what can't be cured must be endured** il faut savoir prendre son mal en patience **2** *(prepare) (food) (by salting)* saler; *(by smoking)* fumer; *(by drying)* faire sécher; *(hides)* traiter

cure-all **n** panacée *f*

curettage [kjʊəˈretɪdʒ] **n** *Med* curet(t)age *m*

curfew [ˈkɜːfjuː] **n** couvre-feu *m*, *pl* couvre-feux; **to ring the c. (bell)** sonner le couvre-feu; *esp Am Fig* **to be under c.** *(of teenager)* devoir rentrer à une heure précise

curing [ˈkjʊərɪŋ] **n** *(preparation) (by salting)* salaison *f*, *(by smoking) (of meat)* fumage *m*;

(of herring) saurissage *m*; *(by drying)* séchage *m*

curio ['kjʊərɪəʊ] N curiosité *f*, bibelot *m*

curiosity [kjʊərɪ'ɒsɪtɪ] N **1** curiosité *f*; **out of** *or* **from c.** par curiosité; **I was dying of c.** je mourais de curiosité; *Prov* **c. killed the cat** = la curiosité est un vilain défaut **2** *(object)* curiosité *f*, bibelot *m*

curious ['kjʊərɪəs] ADJ **1** *(inquisitive)* curieux, *Pej* indiscret, -ète; **to be c. to see/know** être curieux de voir/savoir; **they didn't seem at all c. as to** *or* **about how it had happened** ils n'avaient pas du tout l'air curieux de savoir comment cela s'était produit **2** *(strange)* *(way, circumstances)* curieux, singulier; **the two of them made a c. sight** ils formaient un étrange tableau tous les deux; **a c.-looking object** un objet bizarre

curiously ['kjʊərɪəslɪ] ADV **1** *(inquisitively)* avec curiosité, *Pej* indiscrètement **2** *(strangely)* curieusement, singulièrement; **c. enough ...** chose curieuse *ou* singulière ...

curl [kɜːl] N **1** *(of hair)* boucle *f*; *(of smoke)* spirale *f*; **in curls** *(hair)* bouclé, frisé; **to fall in curls** *(of hair)* tomber en boucles **2** *(action)* action *f* de se recourber; **with a c. of the lip** avec une moue dédaigneuse

▪ VT *(hair)* *(loosely)* boucler; *(tightly)* friser; **to c. one's lip** faire une moue dédaigneuse; **to c. sth round sth** enrouler qch autour de qch; **to c. oneself into a ball** *(of animal, person)* se rouler en boule

▪ VI *(of hair)* boucler; *(of paper)* rebiquer; *(of smoke)* s'élever en spirales; *(of waves)* onduler, déferler; *(of lip)* se relever avec dédain; *Fig* **stories that make your hair c.** histoires qui font dresser les cheveux sur la tête; **his language would make your hair c.** il jure comme un charretier; *Fig* **it made my toes c.** *(with embarrassment)* c'était vraiment pénible; *(with pleasure)* ça m'a donné des frissons de plaisir; **to c. round sth** *(of plant etc)* s'enrouler autour de qch

2 *Sport* jouer au curling

▸ **curl up** VI **1** *(lie, sit comfortably)* se blottir, se pelotonner; **I like to c. up in bed with a good book** j'aime me blottir au lit avec un bon livre; **to sleep curled up** dormir en chien de fusil; **curled up in bed** pelotonné dans son lit

2 *(form a curl)* se rouler en boule, se recroqueviller; **hedgehogs c. up into a ball for protection** les hérissons se roulent en boule pour se protéger

3 *(of leaves, paper)* se recroqueviller

4 *Fig Fam* *(be embarrassed)* être extrêmement gêné; **I wanted to c. up and die** je ne savais plus où me mettre

▪ VT SEP *(form into a curl)* **to c. oneself up** se rouler en boule, se recroqueviller; **to c. itself up** *(of cat etc)* se rouler en boule

curler ['kɜːlər] N **1** *(for hair)* bigoudi *m*; **in her curlers** avec ses bigoudis sur la tête, en bigoudis **2** *Sport* joueur, -euse de curling

curlew ['kɜːljuː] N *(bird)* courlis *m*

curlicue ['kɜːlɪkjuː] N trait *m* de plume en parafe

curliness ['kɜːlɪnɪs] N *(of hair)* *(loose)* boucles *fpl*; *(tight)* frisure *f*

curling ['kɜːlɪŋ] N *Sport* curling *m*

▸▸ **c. irons** fer *m* à friser; *Sport* **c. stone** pierre *f* de curling; **c. tongs** fer à friser

curly ['kɜːlɪ] ADJ *(hair)* *(loosely)* bouclé; *(tightly)* frisé; *(long piece of paper etc)* en spirale; **the dried leaves had gone c.** les feuilles séchées s'étaient recroquevillées

▪ N *Fam* **1** **to have sb by the short and curlies** pouvoir faire ce qu'on veut de qn; **they've got us by the short and curlies** ils nous tiennent **2** *(person with curly hair)* **hi there, c.** salut, le/la frisé(e)

▸▸ *Typ* **c. bracket** accolade *f*; **c. endive** frisée

f, **c. lettuce** *(laitue f)* frisée; *Br Typ* **c. quotes** guillemets *mpl* anglais

curly-headed, curly-haired ADJ *(with loose curls)* à la tête bouclée, aux cheveux bouclés; *(with tight curls)* aux cheveux frisés

currant ['kʌrənt] N **1** *(dried grape)* raisin *m* de Corinthe, raisin sec **2** *(soft fruit)* groseille *f*

▸▸ **c. bun** petit pain *m* aux raisins; **c. bush** groseiller *m*

currency ['kʌrənsɪ] N **1** *Fin (unit)* *(of a country)* unité *f* monétaire, monnaie *f*, devise *f*; *(specie)* numéraire *m*; **foreign c.** devise étrangère; **to buy foreign c.** acheter des devises étrangères; **hard/soft c.** devise forte/faible; **the world's major currencies** les principales monnaies du monde; **to buy c.** acheter des devises

2 *(circulation)* *(of ideas)* circulation *f*, cours *m*; **to give c. to a rumour** *(of person, newspaper etc)* faire courir un bruit; **to gain c.** *(of news)* s'accréditer; *(of expression, habit)* devenir de plus en plus courant; *(of ideas)* se répandre; **the expression is common c.** l'expression est monnaie courante; **this view had some c. at one time** cette opinion était accréditée à un moment donné

▸▸ *Fin* **c. adjustment factor** correctif *m* d'ajustement monétaire; **c. appreciation** appréciation *f* d'une monnaie; *Fin* **c. conversion** conversion *f* de monnaies; *Fin* **c. dealer** cambiste *mf*; **c. depreciation** dépréciation *f* monétaire; *Fin* **c. fluctuation** mouvement *m* des devises; *Econ, Fin* **c. market** marché *m* monétaire; *Fin* **c. risk** risque *m* de change; *Fin, St Exch* **c. speculation** spéculation *f* sur les devises; *Fin, St Exch* **c. speculator** spéculateur, -trice sur devises; *Fin, St Exch* **c. swap** échange *m* de devises; *Fin* **c. transfer** transfert *m* de devises; **c. unit** unité *f* monétaire

current ['kʌrənt] ADJ **1** *(existing, present)* *(feeling, tendency, situation)* actuel; **the c. theory is that ...** la théorie actuelle est que ...; **which is still c.** qui est toujours d'actualité; **the c. treasurer** le trésorier actuel (de l'association)

2 *(accepted, used)* courant, admis, reçu; **to be c.** avoir cours; **in c. use** d'usage courant; **the word is in c. use** le mot s'emploie couramment; **c. issue** *(of magazine)* dernier numéro *m*; **the c. month** le mois en cours

▪ N **1** *(of river, tide etc)* courant *m*; *Met* **air c.** courant d'air; *Fig* **the c. of opinion is against him** il y a un courant d'opinion contre lui; **to drift on the c.** se laisser aller au fil de l'eau, se laisser porter par le courant; *Fig* **to go with the c.** suivre le courant; **to swim against the c.** nager contre le courant *ou* à contre-courant; *Fig* **to go** *or* **swim against the c.** aller à contre-courant

2 *Elec* courant *m*

▸▸ *Br* **c. account** *Banking* compte *m* courant; *St Exch* liquidation *f* courante; **c. affairs** actualités *fpl*; *TV, Radio* **c. affairs programme** émission *f* d'actualités; *Acct* **c. assets** actif *m* de roulement; *Com, Fin* **c. cost** prix *m* courant *ou* du marché; *Acct* **c. cost accounting** comptabilité *f* en coûts actuels; *Acct* **c. earnings** bénéfices *mpl* de l'exercice, revenus *mpl* actuels; **c. expenditure** dépenses *fpl* courantes; *Br Acct* **c. financial year** exercice *m* en cours; *Am Acct* **c. fiscal year** exercice en cours; **c. income** *(in accounts)* produits *mpl* courants; *(actual earnings)* revenu *m* actuel; *Acct* **c. liabilities** passif *m* exigible à court terme; **c. net value** valeur *f* actuelle nette, VAN *f*; *St Exch* cours *m* instantané; **c. price** prix courant; *Acct* **c. ratio** coefficient *m* de liquidité; *Comput* **c. smoother** régulateur *m* de tension; *Acct* **c. value** valeur actuelle

---

Note that the most common meaning of the French adjective **courant** is **common**.

---

currently ['kʌrəntlɪ] ADV *(at present)* actuellement, en ce moment; **she is c. appearing in Othello** elle apparaît en ce moment dans Othello; **c. showing** *(at cinema)* à l'affiche

curriculum, pl curricula [kə'rɪkjʊləm, -ə] N *Sch* programme *m* (d'enseignement); **on the c.** au programme

▸▸ *Br* **c. vitae** curriculum *m* (vitae) *inv*

curry[1] ['kʌrɪ] *Culin* N *(spices, dish)* curry *m*, cari *m*; **beef/chicken/vegetable c.** bœuf *m*/ poulet *m*/légumes *mpl* au curry, cari de bœuf/poulet/légumes

▪ VT *(chicken etc)* apprêter au cari *ou* au curry; **curried chicken** poulet *m* au curry, cari *m* de poulet

▸▸ **c. powder** curry, cari

curry[2] VT **1** *Pej* **to c. favour with sb** s'insinuer dans les bonnes grâces de qn **2** *(groom)* *(horse)* étriller

currycomb ['kʌrɪkəʊm] N étrille *f*

curse [kɜːs] N **1** *(evil spell)* malédiction *f*, mauvais sort *m*; **to put a c. on sb** jeter un sort à qn; **a c. on ...!** maudit soit ...!; *Fig* **I feel as if I'm under a c.** j'ai l'impression qu'on m'a jeté un sort **2** *Old-fashioned (swearword)* imprécation *f*, juron *m*; **to let out a c.** lâcher un juron; *Hum* **curses!** diantre! **3** *(scourge)* fléau *m*; **rabbits are a c. here** ici les lapins sont un fléau; *Old-fashioned Fam* **to have the c.** *(be menstruating)* avoir ses règles

▪ VT *(person, object)* maudire; **he is cursed with a violent temper** il est affligé d'un mauvais caractère; **c. it!** le diable l'emporte!; **he cursed his luck** il a maudit son sort; **you'll c. the day you came here** tu maudiras le jour où tu es venu ici

▪ VI *(swear)* jurer; **to c. and swear** jurer comme un charretier; **to c. at sb** injurier qn

▸▸ *Am* **c. word** juron *m*

cursed ADJ **1** [kɜːst] *(under a curse)* maudit **2** ['kɜːsɪd] *Fam (annoying)* sacré, satané; **it's a c. nuisance** c'est bigrement embêtant

cursing ['kɜːsɪŋ] N jurons *mpl*

cursive ['kɜːsɪv] ADJ cursif; **c. handwriting** écriture cursive

▪ N écriture *f* cursive

cursor ['kɜːsər] N *(on slide rule)*, *Comput* curseur *m*; *Comput* **move the c. to the right/left** déplacez le curseur vers la droite/gauche; *Comput* **the word at the c.** le mot pointé

▸▸ *Comput* **c. blink rate** vitesse *f* de clignotement du curseur; **c. control** contrôle *m* du curseur; **c. key** touche *f* de curseur; **c. movement** déplacement *m* du curseur; **c. position** position *f* du curseur

cursorily ['kɜːsərɪlɪ] ADV *(to examine, look at)* superficiellement

cursoriness ['kɜːsərɪnɪs] N caractère *m* sommaire

cursory ['kɜːsərɪ] ADJ *(glance, examination, remarks)* superficiel

curt [kɜːt] ADJ *(manner)* brusque; *(tone, person)* cassant; *(reply, command)* sec, *f* sèche

curtail [kɜː'teɪl] VT **1** *(shorten)* *(visit)* abréger, écourter **2** *(limit)* *(person's freedom, privileges, spending)* réduire, restreindre; *(person's authority, powers)* diminuer

curtailment [kɜː'teɪlmənt] N *(of freedom, privileges, spending etc)* réduction *f*, restriction *f*; *(of authority, powers)* diminution *f*

curtain ['kɜːt(ə)n] N **1** *Br (on window etc)* rideau *m*; **to draw the curtains** *(open)* ouvrir les rideaux; *(close)* tirer *ou* fermer les rideaux **2** *Theat* rideau *m*; **safety c.** rideau de fer; *Fig Fam* **it's curtains for him** il est fichu

▪ VT *(alcove etc)* garnir de rideaux

▸▸ *Theat* **c. call** rappel *m*; **c. hook** crochet *m* de rideau; **c. material** tissu *m* à rideaux; **c. rail** tringle *f* à rideau; **c. ring** anneau *m* de rideau; **c. rod** tringle à rideau; **c. wall** *Archit* mur-rideau *m*, *pl* murs-rideaux; *Constr* enceinte *f*

▸**curtain off** VT SEP *(conceal) (part of room)* séparer par un rideau

curtain-raiser N *Theat (play)* lever *m* de rideau; *Fig* préambule *m*

curtainsider ['kɜːt(ə)nsaɪdər] N *Aut* camion *m* bâché

curtly ['kɜːtlɪ] ADV *(to say)* brusquement, d'un ton cassant; **a c. worded letter** une lettre au ton sec

curtness ['kɜːtnɪs] N *(of manner, words)* brusquerie *f*; *(of person)* ton *m* cassant; *(of letter)* ton sec

curts(e)y ['kɜːtsɪ] N révérence *f*; **to make a c. to sb** faire une révérence à qn
VI *(of woman, girl)* faire une révérence (**to** à)

curvaceous [kɜːˈveɪʃəs] ADJ *(woman)* qui a de jolies formes, *Fam* bien roulée; **c. figure** silhouette *f* de vamp

curvature ['kɜːvətʃər] N *(of the earth etc)* sphéricité *f*, *Phys, Opt (of space)* courbure *f*; *Med* **c. of the spine** courbure (de la colonne) vertébrale

curve [kɜːv] N courbe *f*, *(in road)* tournant *m*, virage *m*; **the c. of the bay** la courbe de la baie; **curves** *(of woman)* rondeurs *fpl*, formes *fpl*; *Am Fig* **to throw sb a c. (ball)** *(give unpleasant surprise to)* prendre qn par surprise; *(mislead)* induire qn en erreur
VI se courber; **the road curves round the castle** la route fait le tour du château; **to c. down(wards)/up(wards)** monter/descendre en courbe
VT courber, recourber; *(pipe, surface etc)* cintrer
▸▸*Comput* **c. smoothing** lissage *m* de courbes

curved [kɜːvd] ADJ *(intentionally bent)* courbe; *(bent out of shape)* courbé, cintré; *(nose)* busqué

curvilinear [kɜːvɪˈlɪnɪər] ADJ curviligne

curvy ['kɜːvɪ] ADJ **1** *(curved)* courbé, cintré **2** *Fam (woman)* qui a des formes

cushion ['kʊʃən] N **1** coussin *m*; **the mattresses acted as a c. when he fell** les matelas ont amorti sa chute; *Fig* **the annual increase in salary acts as a c. against inflation** l'augmentation annuelle des salaires amortit les effets de l'inflation **2** *Billiards* bande *f*, **off the c.** par la bande **3** *Tech (of air etc)* coussin *m*
VT *(reduce effect of) (blow, impact, fall etc)* amortir; **they have been cushioned against unemployment** ils ont été protégés contre le chômage

cushioning ['kʊʃənɪŋ] N *Tech* matelassage *m*; **as a c. against inflation** pour amortir les effets de l'inflation

cushy ['kʊʃɪ] ADJ *Fam (life etc)* pépère, peinard; **c. job** *or* **number** boulot *m* peinard

cusp [kʌsp] N **1** *Astron (of moon)* corne *f* **2** *Math (of curve)* sommet *m* **3** *(of tooth)* cuspide *f*

cuspidor ['kʌspɪdɔːr] N *Am* crachoir *m*

cuss [kʌs] N *Fam* **1** *(swear word)* juron *m*; **it isn't worth a (tinker's) c.** ça ne vaut pas un clou **2** *(person)* individu *m*, type *m*; **an awkward c.** un mauvais coucheur; **a stubborn c.** une tête de lard

cussed ['kʌsɪd] ADJ *Fam (annoying)* sacré, satané; *(stubborn)* entêté; **it's a c. nuisance** c'est bigrement embêtant

cussedness ['kʌsɪdnɪs] N *Fam* entêtement *m*; **out of sheer c.** par esprit de contradiction

custard ['kʌstəd] N *Culin* crème *f* anglaise; **baked c.** crème cuite au four
▸▸**c. apple** anone *f*; **c. cream** biscuit *m* fourré à la crème; **c. pie** tarte *f* à la crème; **c.**

powder ≃ crème *f* anglaise instantanée; **c. tart** tarte à la crème

custodial [kʌˈstəʊdɪəl] ADJ *Law* de prison
▸▸**c. sentence** peine *f* de prison *ou* de détention

custodian [kʌsˈtəʊdɪən] N **1** gardien, -ienne; *(of museum etc)* conservateur, -trice; **the police are the custodians of law and order** la police est la garante de l'ordre public **2** *Am St Exch* dépositaire *mf*, conservateur, -trice de titres

custody ['kʌstədɪ] N **1** *(guardianship) (of children etc)* garde *f*; **the court awarded c. (of the children) to the father** le tribunal a confié la garde des enfants au père; **to have c. of sb/sth** avoir la garde de qn/qch; **in safe c.** sous bonne garde **2** *Law* détention *f*, **to take sb into c.** arrêter qn; **to be in c.** être en détention préventive

custom ['kʌstəm] N **1** *(practice)* coutume *f*, usage *m*; *(of individual)* habitude *f*, **according to c.** selon l'usage; **it is the c. of the country** c'est la coutume du pays; **it is their c. to fast on that day** leur coutume veut qu'ils respectent ce jour-là; **it was a c. with him to ...**, **it was his c. to ...** il avait l'habitude de ...; **the manners and customs** *(of a country)* les us *mpl* et coutumes
2 *Law (of a country)* droit *m* coutumier, coutume *f*
3 *Com (of a company, shop)* clientèle *f*; **to lose sb's c.** perdre la clientèle de qn; **I'll take my c. elsewhere** je vais aller voir ailleurs, *Fam* je vais changer de crémerie
▸▸**c. car** voiture *f* customisée, custom *m*

customarily ['kʌstəmərɪlɪ] ADV habituellement, d'habitude; *(normally)* ordinairement

customary ['kʌstəm(ə)rɪ] ADJ **1** habituel, d'usage; **at the c. hour** à l'heure habituelle; **it is c. to ...** il est d'usage de ..., c'est la coutume de ...; **as is c.** comme il est d'usage; **her c. politeness** sa politesse habituelle *ou* coutumière **2** *Law* coutumier
▸▸*Law* **c. law** droit *m* coutumier; *Law* **c. right** droit d'usage

custom-built ADJ fait *ou* fabriqué sur commande; *Aut* **c. body** carrosserie *f* customisée

customer ['kʌstəmər] N **1** *(of shop etc)* client, -ente; **regular c.** *(of restaurant etc)* habitué, -ée; *Prov* **the c. is always right** le client a toujours raison, le client est roi **2** *Fam (person)* individu *m*, type *m*; **an awkward c.** un type pas commode; **a queer c.** un drôle de type; **an ugly c.** un sale type
▸▸*Com, Mktg* **c. acceptance test** test *m* d'acceptabilité auprès des consommateurs; *Com, Mktg* **c. base** base *f* de clientèle; **c. credit** crédit *m* client; *Com, Mktg* **c. satisfaction** satisfaction *f* de la clientèle; *Com, Mktg* **c. service** service *m* clientèle; *Com, Mktg* **c. service department** service clientèle; *Com, Mktg* **c. support** service service à la clientèle

customization [kʌstəmaɪˈzeɪʃən] N personnalisation *f*

customize ['kʌstəmaɪz] VT *(vehicle)* customiser; *(kitchen, computer etc)* personnaliser; **customized marketing** marketing *m* 'à la carte'
▸▸*Comput* **c. option** option *f* 'personnaliser'

custom-made ADJ *(car etc)* fait *ou* fabriqué sur commande; *(clothes etc)* fait sur mesure

customs ['kʌstəmz] N *Admin* douane *f*, **to go through (the) c.** passer la douane; **at c.** à la douane; *Br* **C. and Excise** ≃ la Régie
▸▸**c. agent** commissionnaire *mf* en douane; **c. allowance** tolérance *f ou* franchise *f* douanière; **c. barriers** barrières *fpl* douanières; **c. broker** agréé *m* en douane; **c. clearance** dédouanement *m*; **c. clearance**

area aire *f* de dédouanement; **c. clearance authorization** autorisation *f* de dédouanement; **c. control** contrôle *m* douanier; **c. declaration** déclaration *f* de *ou* en douane; **c. drawback** ristourne *f* de droits de douane; **c. duties** droits *mpl* de douane; **c. examination** contrôle douanier; **c. formalities** formalités *fpl* douanières; **c. house** (poste *m ou* bureau *m* de) douane; **c. inspector** inspecteur, -trice des douanes; **c. invoice** facture *f* douanière; **c. manifest** manifeste *m* de douane; **c. nomenclature** nomenclature *f* douanière, nomenclature générale des produits; **c. office** bureau de douane; **c. officer** douanier, -ière; **c. papers** dossier *m* de douane; **c. permit** permis *m* de douane; **c. procedure** procédure *f* douanière; **c. receipt** acquit *m* de douane; **c. regulations** réglementation *f* douanière; **c. system** régime *m ou* système *m* douanier; **c. tariff** tarif *m* douanier; **c. union** union *f* douanière; **c. value** valeur *f* en douane

---

CUT [kʌt]

N coupure **1, 4** ▪ réduction **1** ▪ coup **2** ▪ coupe **5, 9** ▪ morceau **6**	
VT couper **1–3, 6, 7, 9–11** ▪ tondre **5** ▪ trancher **1** ▪ réduire **3** ▪ monter **5** ▪ graver **7** ▪ percer **8**	
VI couper **1–3**	
ADJ coupé **1** ▪ réduit **2**	

N 1 *(in an object)* entaille *f*, *Com etc (in price, spending)* réduction *f*, *Cin, TV (in film etc)* coupure *f*, **to make a clean c.** trancher net; **power** *or* **electricity c.** coupure de courant; *Cin* **the sudden c. from the battlefield to the dinner scene** la coupure brutale entre le champ de bataille et la scène du dîner; **to make a c. in a text** faire une coupure dans un texte; **a two-hundred word c.** une réduction de deux cents mots; **wage cuts** réductions de salaires; **to take a c. in one's wages** accepter une réduction de salaire; **everyone has agreed to take a c. in their wages** tout le monde a accepté de voir son salaire réduit
2 *(blow) (with knife, sword)* coup *m*; *Cr, Tennis* coup tranchant; **c. with a whip** coup de fouet; *Fig* **the unkindest c. of all** le coup le plus dur; **she revels in the c. and thrust of debate** elle prend plaisir aux joutes oratoires
3 *(of machine tool)* passe *f*, **(saw) c.** trait *m* de scie
4 *(wound)* coupure *f*, *(gash)* balafre *f*, *Surg* incision *f*; **c. across the cheek** balafre à la joue
5 *(style) (of garment, hair)* coupe *f*, *(of jewel)* taille *f*
6 *(meat)* **c. off the joint** tranche *f* de rôti; **prime c.** morceau *m* de (premier) choix; **cheap cuts** bas morceaux
7 *Fig Fam (portion)* commission *f*, *Fam* gratte *f*, **he gets his c.** il a sa part
8 short c. raccourci *m*; *Fig* solution *f* de facilité; **to take a short c.** couper au plus court, prendre (par) un raccourci; *Fig* utiliser la solution de facilité
9 *Cards* coupe *f*
10 *Fam* **to be a c. above sb/sth** être un cran au-dessus de qn/qch
11 *(of tobacco)* **I prefer a finer/coarser c. of tobacco** je préfère le tabac plus fin/grossier
VT *(pt, pp* **cut**, *prp* **cutting) 1** couper; *(in slices)* trancher; *(rope)* sectionner; *(hay)* faucher; **to c. the grass (with mower)** tondre le gazon; *(with shears)* couper le gazon; **to c. one's finger** se couper le doigt; **to c. one's nails** se couper les ongles; **to c. one's throat** se trancher la gorge; **to c. sb's throat** trancher la gorge de qn; **to have one's hair c.** se faire couper les cheveux; *Fig* **this remark**

c. him to the quick cette parole l'a piqué au vif

2 *(separate)* **to c. sth in two** *or* **in half** couper qch en deux; **to c. a slice of cake** couper une tranche de gâteau; **to c. to pieces** *(object)* couper en morceaux; *(army)* tailler en pièces; **to c. one's way through the wood** se frayer un chemin à travers le bois; **to c. a dog loose** libérer un chien en coupant sa laisse; **to c. a horse loose** libérer un cheval en coupant sa longe; *Fig* **to c. oneself loose from sth** se libérer de qch

3 *(shorten, reduce)* *(film, scene, text etc)* couper; *(speech)* abréger, raccourcir; *(numbers, spending)* réduire; *(production)* diminuer; **the film was c. to 100 minutes** le film a été ramené à 100 minutes; **prices/wages have been c. by 10%** les prix/salaires ont été réduits de 10%; **this cuts their journey time by 20 minutes** cela réduit la durée de leur trajet de 20 minutes; **it helps to c. costs** cela permet de réduire les frais; **to c. a speech/a visit short** écourter un discours/une visite; **to c. sb short** couper la parole à qn; **to c. a long story short ...** bref ...; *Fig* **it's cutting it** *or* **things fine** cela va faire juste

4 *(omit, remove)* supprimer; **this scene was later c.** cette scène a été supprimée par la suite; *Sl* **c. the crap!** arrête tes conneries!

5 *(edit)* *(film)* monter

6 *Comput* couper; **to c. and paste sth** faire un couper-coller sur qch

7 *Tech etc (stone, glass etc)* couper, tailler; *(canal)* percer, creuser; *(characters on metal or stone)* tailler, ciseler; *(garment)* tailler, couper; *Mus (record)* graver; *Fig* **to c. one's coat according to one's cloth** faire avec ce que l'on a

8 **to c. a tooth** *(of child)* percer une dent; *Fig* **to c. one's teeth on sth** *(of lawyer etc)* se faire les dents sur qch

9 *Cards* **to c. the cards** *(in general)* couper les cartes; *(to decide who deals etc)* tirer une carte pour savoir qui fera la donne/*etc*

10 *Cr, Tennis (ball)* couper

11 *Elec etc (turn off)* couper

12 **to c. sb (dead)** *(ignore)* faire semblant de ne pas voir qn, ignorer qn complètement

13 *Sch Fam (class)* sécher

14 **to c. an elegant/a noble/a romantic figure** être très élégant/noble/romantique

VI 1 *(of knife, person)* couper; **those scissors don't c. very well** ces ciseaux ne coupent pas très bien; **cloth that cuts easily** tissu qui se coupe facilement; **that wind cuts like a knife** le vent te transperce; **to c. into a cake** entamer un gâteau; **to c. into the bark** inciser l'écorce; *Lit* **to c. through the waves** fendre les eaux; **that's an argument that cuts both ways** c'est un argument à double tranchant; *Am* **to c. loose** *(free oneself)* s'émanciper; *(escape)* s'évader; *Fam* **to c. and run** filer (en vitesse), décamper, se sauver

2 *Cin, TV, Theat (change scene)* **the action cuts to the street** l'action passe à la rue; *Cin* **c.!** coupez!

3 *Cards* couper

ADJ 1 *(crystal, diamond)* taillé; **well/elegantly c. suit** complet bien coupé/de coupe élégante; **c. and dried** *(opinions)* tout fait; **everything was c. and dried** *(decided)* tout était déjà décidé; **it's not as c. and dried as that** ce n'est pas aussi simple que ça

2 *(reduced, shortened)* réduit; **the c. version of the film** la version raccourcie du film

▸▸ **c. glass** cristal *m* taillé; **a c. glass jug** une cruche en cristal taillé; *Br Fig* **a c. glass accent** un accent bourgeois; *Comput* **c. sheet feed** dispositif *m* d'alimentation feuille à feuille; *(act)* alimentation *f* feuille à feuille; *Comput* **c. sheet feeder** dispositif d'alimentation feuille à feuille

▸ **cut across** VT INSEP *(playing field, forest etc)* couper à travers; *Fig* **concern for the envi-**

ronment **cuts across party lines** les préoccupations écologiques transcendent les clivages politiques

▸ **cut along** VI *Old-fashioned Br Fam* filer

▸ **cut away** VT SEP *(remove)* couper, ôter; **they had to c. away the wreckage to reach the victim** ils ont dû découper l'épave pour atteindre la victime; **c. away the fat** ôtez le gras

▸ **cut back** VT SEP **1** *(prune)* *(rosebush, undergrowth etc)* tailler; *(tree)* élaguer

2 *(reduce)* *(prices)* baisser; *(production etc)* diminuer; **arms spending has been c. right back** les dépenses d'armement ont été nettement réduites

VI **1** *(financially)* économiser, réduire les dépenses

2 *(go back)* s'en retourner, rebrousser chemin

3 *Cin (of action)* revenir en arrière; **we c. back to the scene in the kitchen** nous revenons à la scène de la cuisine

▸ **cut back on** VT INSEP *(financially)* économiser sur; *(time)* réduire; **we've already c. back on production** nous avons déjà diminué la production; **you'll have to c. back on the cakes** il faudra que vous mangiez moins de gâteaux; **to c. back on one's smoking** fumer moins

▸ **cut down** VT SEP **1** *(fell)* *(tree)* couper, abattre; *(wheat)* couper

2 *(kill)* abattre; *Lit* **to be c. down in one's prime** être fauché à la fleur de l'âge

3 *(shorten, reduce)* *(speech etc)* abréger; *(book for publication)* couper, réduire; *(spending)* couper, réduire; **to c. sth down to about 150,000 words** réduire qch à environ 150 000 mots; **we've been asked to c. down the amount of time we devote to sports** on nous a demandé de consacrer moins de temps au sport; **to c. trousers down** *(to make shorts)* transformer un pantalon en short

4 *(cut through ropes)* **to c. down a hanged man** couper la corde d'un pendu; **the parachutist had to be c. down from the tree** pour décrocher le parachutiste de l'arbre il a fallu couper les cordes de son parachute

VI *(make reductions)* réduire; **I drink too much coffee so I'm trying to c. down** je bois trop de café, alors j'essaie de réduire

▸ **cut down on** VT INSEP **we had to c. down on expenditure** nous avons dû réduire nos dépenses; **to c. down on the amount of time spent doing sth** passer moins de temps à faire qch; **try to c. down on the swearing** essayez de jurer un peu moins

▸ **cut in** VI **1** *(interrupt conversation)* intervenir dans la conversation; *Tel* interrompre la conversation; **she c. in (on me)** elle m'a coupé la parole; **you're wrong, she c. in** tu as tort, interrompit-elle

2 *Aut* faire une queue de poisson; **he c. in in front of me** il m'a fait une queue de poisson

3 *(at a dance)* **mind if I c. in?** vous permettez que je vous emprunte votre partenaire?

4 *Tech (of mechanism, safety device)* entrer en action

VT SEP *Fam (include in a deal)* **to c. sb in (on the deal)** donner à qn sa part du gâteau; **we could c. him in for £5,000** nous pourrions lui filer 5 000 livres

▸ **cut into** VT INSEP **1** *(interrupt)* **to c. into a conversation** intervenir dans *ou* interrompre brusquement la conversation

2 *(use)* **to c. into one's savings** entamer ses économies; **this work cuts into my free time** ce travail empiète sur mes heures de loisir

3 *(hurt)* blesser; **the rope was cutting into his arm/skin** la corde lui blessait le bras/lui entaillait la peau; **the string is cutting into me** le cordon me coupe la chair

▸ **cut off** VT SEP **1** *(remove by cutting)* *(piece)* couper, découper; **pages with the corners**

c. off pages dont les coins ont été coupés; **he's had all his hair c. off** il s'est fait couper les cheveux tout court; **to c. off sb's head** trancher la tête à qn; *Lit* **to be c. off in one's prime** être emporté *ou* fauché à la fleur de l'âge

2 *(isolate)* *(personne)* couper (du monde); **to c. off the enemy** couper la ligne de retraite de l'ennemi; **to c. off sb's retreat** couper la retraite à qn; **to be c. off** *(by snow, floods)* *(of person, village etc)* se trouver isolé; **the village is c. off from the outside world by snow** le village est coupé du monde par la neige; **I feel c. off** je me sens coupé du monde; **to c. oneself off from the world** se retirer du monde; **she c. herself off from her family** elle s'est coupée de sa famille

3 *Tel (person)* couper; **he's been c. off** *(during conversation)* il a été coupé; *(disconnected)* on lui a coupé le téléphone

4 *(electricity, steam, ignition)* couper; **to c. off sb's water/supplies** couper *ou* supprimer l'eau/les vivres à qn; **it c. off the supply of blood to the brain** cela a stoppé l'irrigation du cerveau

5 *(disinherit)* *(person)* déshériter; **the old man c. his son off without a penny** le vieillard n'a pas laissé un sou à son fils

▸ **cut out** VT SEP **1** *(remove by cutting)* couper, enlever; *Surg (tumour etc)* enlever; **to c. a picture out of a magazine** découper une photo dans un magazine

2 *(shape by cutting)* *(pictures)* découper; *(garment)* couper, tailler; *(neckline)* échancrer; **to c. a statue out of wood** tailler une statue dans le bois; *Fig* **to be c. out for sth** être fait pour qch, avoir des dispositions pour qch; **he's not c. out to be a leader** il n'a pas l'étoffe d'un dirigeant; **he's not c. out for it** il n'est pas fait pour cela; *Fig* **I've really got my work c. out** j'ai du pain sur la planche; **she's got her work c. out (for her) with those four kids** elle a de quoi faire avec ces quatre gamins

3 *(eliminate)* supprimer, éliminer; **to c. out luxuries** se passer du luxe; **to c. out smoking** arrêter de fumer; **I wish he'd c. out the jokes** j'aimerais bien qu'il arrête ses plaisanteries; *Fam* **c. it out!** ça suffit maintenant!, ça va comme ça!; **the new building cuts out a lot of the light** le nouveau bâtiment coupe une bonne partie de la lumière

4 *(oust)* **to c. sb out of a deal** évincer qn dans une affaire; **his father c. them out of his will** son père les a déshérités

VI *(stop)* *(of engine)* caler; *(of machine)* s'arrêter; *(of pilot light)* s'éteindre

▸ **cut through** VT INSEP **1** *(rope)* couper; *Fig* **to c. through red tape** éviter la paperasserie

2 *(take as a short cut)* **to c. through the park** couper par le parc

▸ **cut up** VT SEP **1** *(chop up)* *(wood, meat)* couper, débiter; *(chicken etc)* découper, dépecer; *(vegetables etc)* hacher, émincer; *(body)* couper en morceaux; **to c. sth up into small pieces** couper qch en petits morceaux

2 *Fam (usu passive) (upset)* **to be very c. up** être profondément affecté *ou* affligé (**about sth** par qch)

VI *Br Fam* **to c. up rough** *(physically)* devenir violent; *(verbally)* monter sur ses ergots

---

cut-and-paste *Comput* N couper-coller *m* VT & VI couper-coller

cutaneous [kjuː'teɪnɪəs] ADJ cutané

cutaway ['kʌtəweɪ] N **1** *(coat)* jaquette *f* **2** *Tech (drawing)* vue *f* en coupe **3** *Cin, TV* changement *m* de plan

▸▸ **c. coat** jaquette *f*; *Tech* **c. model** maquette *f* en coupe; *Cin, TV* **c. shot** changement de plan

cutback ['kʌtbæk] N *(in production, budget)* réduction *f*, dégonflement *m*

cute [kjuːt] ADJ *Fam* **1** *(attractive)* mignon; **what a c. little kitten** quel mignon petit chaton **2** *(clever)* malin, *f* maligne; *(idea)* original, -aux; **don't get c. with me!** ne fais pas le malin avec moi!

cuteness ['kjuːtnɪs] N *Fam* **1** *(attractiveness)* charme *m* **2** *(cleverness)* finesse *f*

cuticle ['kjuːtɪk(ə)l] N *Anat, Bot* cuticule *f*
▸▸**c. pen** repousse-peaux *m inv*

cutie(-pie) ['kjuːtɪ(paɪ)] N *Fam* **1** *(baby, child)* mignon, -onne; *(girl, woman)* beauté *f* **2** *(shrewd person)* malin *m*, maligne *f*

cutlass ['kʌtləs] N *Naut* sabre *m* d'abordage

cutler ['kʌtlər] N coutelier, -ière

cutlery ['kʌtlərɪ] N *(eating utensils)* couverts *mpl*, *Com, Ind* coutellerie *f*
▸▸**c. drawer** tiroir *m* à couverts

cutlet ['kʌtlɪt] N *Culin* **1** *(of lamb, veal)* côtelette *f* **2** *(croquette) (of chicken etc)* croquette *f*

cutoff ['kʌtɒf] N **1** *Am (short cut)* raccourci *m* **2** *Electron* déconnexion *f*, mise *f* hors de contact, mise hors circuit **3** *(stopping point)* limite *f* **4 cutoffs** *(shorts)* = jean *m* transformé en short
▸▸**c. date** date *f* limite; **c. point** limite; **we've taken a score of 370 as the c. point in deciding who to interview** *(no less than)* les candidats doivent avoir au minimum 370 points pour pouvoir passer l'entretien; **the c. point for remedial lessons is 150** *(no more than)* seuls les élèves qui obtiennent 150 points ou en deçà pourront bénéficier de cours de rattrapage

cutout ['kʌtaʊt] N **1 a cardboard c. of Humphrey Bogart** une silhouette en carton de Humphrey Bogart **2** *Elec* coupe-circuit *m inv*, disjoncteur *m*
▸▸*Aut* **c. device** dispositif *m* de coupure; *Aut* **c. valve** conjoncteur-disjoncteur *m*, *pl* conjoncteurs-disjoncteurs, disjoncteur

cut-price, *Am* **cut-rate** ADJ *Com (goods)* à prix réduit; *(as special offer)* bradé; **at cut-price rates** à un tarif réduit
▸▸**c. shop** solderie *f*

cutter ['kʌtər] N **1** *(person) (of garments)* coupeur, -euse; *(of stone, diamonds)* tailleur *m*; *Cin* monteur, -euse, découpeur, -euse **2** *(tool, device)* lame *f*, couteau *m*; **rotary c.** roue *f* à couteaux; **coal c.** haveuse *f* **3** *Naut* canot *m* *(d'un bâtiment de guerre)*

cutthroat ['kʌtθrəʊt] N *(murderer)* assassin *m*; *(razor)* rasoir *m* à main
ADJ féroce; *(competition)* acharné; *(prices)* très compétitif; **it's a c. business** la concurrence est acharnée
▸▸*Cards* **c. bridge** bridge *m* à trois; **c. razor** coupe-choux *m inv*, rasoir à main

cutting ['kʌtɪŋ] ADJ **1** *(wind)* cinglant, glacial, -aux; *(rain)* cinglant **2** *(remark etc)* mordant, blessant; *(criticism)* incisif; **she was rather c. about them** elle a dit des choses un peu dures sur eux
N **1** *(act)* coupe *f*; *(of jewel, stone)* taille *f*; *(film editing)* montage *m*; *(of trees)* coupe, abattage *m*
2 *(piece cut off) (from newspaper)* coupure *f*, *(of plant)* bouture *f*, *(of vine)* sarment *m*; **to grow a plant from a c.** faire pousser une plante à partir d'une bouture; **to take a c.** faire une bouture; **cuttings** *(of wood, metal etc)* rognures *fpl*, recoupes *fpl*; *(of carpet)* chutes *fpl*
3 *(railway)* **c.** (voie *f* en) déblai *m*
▸▸*Tech* **c. action** cisaillement *m*; *Tech* **c. an-**

gle angle *m* de coupe; **c. back** *(of tree)* élagage *m*; *(of production, budget)* réduction *f*; *Cin* **c. copy** copie *f* de montage *ou* de travail; **c. edge** tranchant *m*; *Fig* **to be at the c. edge (of technology)** être à la pointe; *Journ* **cuttings file** fichier *m* de coupures; *Journ* **cuttings library** archives *fpl* de coupures de presse; *Cin* **c. point** point *m* de coupe; *Cin* **c. room** salle *f* de montage; *Cin* **c. table** table *f* de montage; **c. tool** outil *m* tranchant

cuttingly ['kʌtɪŋlɪ] ADV *(to say)* d'un ton caustique; **c. brief** bref et caustique

cuttlebone ['kʌt(ə)lbəʊn] N os *m* de seiche

cuttlefish ['kʌt(ə)lfɪʃ] N seiche *f*

CV [siːˈviː] N *(abbr* **curriculum vitae***)* CV *m*

CV joint N *Aut (abbr* **constant velocity joint***)* joint *m* de cardan

CVP [siːviːˈpiː] N *Fin (abbr* **cost-volume-profit***)* étude *f* de coût-efficacité

cwo *Com (abbr* **cash with order***)* envoi contre paiement

cwt *abbr* **hundredweight**

CWU [siːdʌb(ə)ljuːˈjuː] N *(abbr* **Communication Workers Union***)* = syndicat *m* des travailleurs des postes et des télécommunications

cyan ['saɪən] N cyan *m*

cyanide ['saɪənaɪd] N *Chem* cyanure *m*; **potassium c.** cyanure de potassium

cyanosis [saɪəˈnəʊsɪs] N *Med* cyanose *f*

cyber ['saɪbər] N *Comput* cyber *m*

cyberbanking ['saɪbəbæŋkɪŋ] N transactions *fpl* bancaires en ligne

cybercafé ['saɪbəkæfeɪ] N cybercafé *m*

cybercrime ['saɪbəkraɪm] N cybercrime *m*

cyberculture ['saɪbəkʌltʃər] N cyberculture *f*

cybermall ['saɪbəmɔːl] N centre *m* commercial électronique, galerie *f* marchande électronique

cybernaut ['saɪbənɔːt] N cybernaute *m*

cybernetic [saɪbəˈnetɪk] ADJ cybernétique

cybernetics [saɪbəˈnetɪks] N [VOIR GRAMMAIRE A10] *(with sing verb)* cybernétique *f*

cyberpunk ['saɪbəpʌŋk] N cyberpunk *m*

cybersex ['saɪbəseks] N amour *m* virtuel

cyberspace ['saɪbəspeɪs] N cyber(e)space *m*

cybersquatter ['saɪbəskwɒtər] N *Comput* cybersquatteur *m*

cybersquatting ['saɪbəskwɒtɪŋ] N *Comput* cybersquatting *m*, cybersquattage *m*

cyberstalking ['saɪbəstɔːkɪŋ] N *Comput* cybertraque *f*, cyberharcèlement *m*

cyclamen ['sɪkləmən] N *Bot* cyclamen *m*

cycle ['saɪk(ə)l] N **1** *(pattern) (of movements etc)* cycle *m*; *Aut* **four-stroke c.** cycle à quatre temps; *Astron* **lunar c.** cycle lunaire; **trade c.** cycle économique **2** *(bicycle)* bicyclette *f*, vélo *m* **3** *Am* = **motorcycle**
VI faire de la bicyclette *ou* du vélo; **to c. to/from school** aller à/revenir de l'école à bicyclette *ou* à vélo
▸▸**c. lane** piste *f* cyclable; **c. path** piste *ou* bande *f* cyclable; **c. racing** courses *fpl* cyclistes; **c. racing track** vélodrome *m*; **c. shop** magasin *m* de cycles; **c. track** piste cyclable

cycler ['saɪklər] N *Am* cycliste *mf*

cyclic(al) ['sɪklɪk, -ɪk(ə)l] ADJ *(movement etc)* cyclique
▸▸**c. unemployment** chômage *m* conjoncturel

cycling ['saɪklɪŋ] N cyclisme *m*
▸▸**c. club** club *m* de cyclisme; **c. holidays** cyclotourisme *m*; **c. shorts** cuissard *m*; **c. track** piste *f* cyclable

cyclist ['saɪklɪst] N cycliste *mf*

cyclone ['saɪkləʊn] N *Met* cyclone *m*

cyclonic [saɪˈklɒnɪk] ADJ cyclonique, cyclonal

cyclorama [saɪkləʊˈrɑːmə] N cyclorama *m*
▸▸**c. light** éclairage *m* de cyclorama

cyclostyle ['saɪkləʊstaɪl] VT *Old-fashioned* polycopier

cyclotron ['saɪklətrɒn] N *Nucl* cyclotron *m*

cygnet ['sɪgnɪt] N *(bird)* jeune cygne *m*

cylinder ['sɪlɪndər] N **1** *Geom* cylindre *m* **2** *Tech, Comput etc* cylindre *m*; *(of pump, revolver)* barillet *m*; **to be firing on all cylinders** *(of engine)* tourner rond; *Fig (company)* fonctionner à plein régime; *(of person)* être en pleine forme; **four/eight-c. engine** moteur *m* à quatre/huit cylindres; **the engine isn't firing on all cylinders** le moteur boite; *Fig* **he's only firing on three cylinders, he's not firing on all cylinders** il n'est pas tout à fait dans son assiette
▸▸*Aut* **c. bank** rangée *f* de cylindres; *Tech* **c. block** bloc-cylindres *m*, *pl* blocs-cylindres; **c. bore** alésage *m* de cylindre; *Tech* **c. head** culasse *f* *(d'un moteur)*; **c. head gasket** joint *m* de culasse; **c. wall** paroi *f* des cylindres

cylindrical [sɪˈlɪndrɪk(ə)l] ADJ cylindrique

cymbal ['sɪmb(ə)l] N *Mus* cymbale *f*

Cymru ['kʊmrɪ] N = nom gallois du pays de Galles

cynic ['sɪnɪk] N cynique *mf*, *Antiq, Phil* cynique *m*

cynical ['sɪnɪk(ə)l] ADJ cynique

cynically ['sɪnɪklɪ] ADV cyniquement

cynicism ['sɪnɪsɪz(ə)m] N cynisme *m*

cypher ['saɪfər] N, VT = **cipher**

cypress ['saɪprəs] N *(tree)* cyprès *m*

Cypriot ['sɪprɪət] ADJ chypriote
N Chypriote *mf*

Cyprus ['saɪprəs] N Chypre *f*

Cyrillic [sɪˈrɪlɪk] ADJ cyrillique
N **in C.** en caractères cyrilliques

cyst [sɪst] N **1** *Biol, Anat* sac *m* **2** *Med* kyste *m*

cystic fibrosis ['sɪstɪk] N *Med* mucoviscidose *f*

cystitis [sɪsˈtaɪtɪs] N *Med* cystite *f*; **to have c.** avoir une cystite

cytological [saɪtəˈlɒdʒɪk(ə)l] ADJ *Med* cytologique

cytology [saɪˈtɒlədʒɪ] N *Biol* cytologie *f*

cytomegalovirus [saɪtəʊˈmegələʊvaɪrəs] N *Med* cytomégalovirus *m*

czar [zɑːr] N = **tsar**

czarevitch ['zɑːrəvɪtʃ] N = **tsarevitch**

czarina [zɑːˈriːnə] N = **tsarina**

czarist ['zɑːrɪst] ADJ, N = **tsarist**

Czech [tʃek] ADJ tchèque
N **1** Tchèque *mf* **2** *Ling* tchèque *m*
▸▸**C. Republic** République *f* tchèque

Czechoslovak [tʃekəʊˈsləʊvæk], **Czechoslovakian** [tʃekəʊsləʊˈvækɪən] *Formerly* ADJ tchécoslovaque
N Tchécoslovaque *mf*

Czechoslovakia [tʃekəʊsləˈvækɪə] N *Formerly* Tchécoslovaquie *f*

D¹, **d**¹ [diː] N **1** *(letter)* D, d *m*; **two d's** deux d **2** *Mus* ré *m* **3** *Sch* **to get a D** avoir une mauvaise note, ≃ avoir entre 7 et 9 sur 20

D² *Am Pol abbr* **Democrat**

d² **1** *(abbr* **deceased**) m. **2** *Br Hist (abbr* **denarius**) pence

DA [diːˈeɪ] N *Am Law abbr* **district attorney**

dab¹ [dæb] N **1** *(touch)* petit coup *m*; **a d. with a cloth** un petit coup de chiffon **2** *(portion) (of ink, paint)* tache *f*, *(of butter)* petit morceau *m*; *(of colour)* touche *f*; *(of perfume)* goutte *f*, *(of glue)* point *m*; **a few dabs of mustard** un peu de moutarde; **just give it a d. of paint** mets-y un coup de peinture **3** *Br Old-fashioned Fam* **dabs** *(fingerprints)* empreintes *fpl* digitales

VT (**-bb-**) *(touch)* donner un petit coup à; *(with pad etc)* tamponner; *(daub)* tapoter; **she dabbed the lump on her forehead with a wet facecloth** elle a tamponné la bosse qu'elle avait sur le front avec un linge humide; **to d. one's eyes (with a handkerchief)** se tamponner les yeux; **to d. paint on sth** donner un coup de peinture à qch

▸ **dab off** VT SEP ôter en tamponnant
▸ **dab on** VT SEP *(paint, antiseptic etc)* appliquer

dab² N *(fish)* limande *f*

dab³ ADJ *Fam* **to be a d. hand at (doing) sth** être doué pour (faire) qch

dabble [ˈdæb(ə)l] VT *(one's hands etc in water)* tremper; **she dabbled her feet in the brook** elle se trempa les pieds dans le ruisseau

VI *Fam* **to d. on the Stock Exchange** boursicoter; **to d. in politics** faire un peu de politique; **to d. in art/music** être un peu artiste/musicien; **to d. in black magic** toucher à la magie noire

dabbler [ˈdæblər] N *often Pej (amateur)* amateur *m*; **d. on the Stock Exchange** boursicoteur, -euse

dace [deɪs] N *(fish)* vandoise *f*, dard *m*

dacha [ˈdætʃə] N dacha *f*

dachshund [ˈdækshʊnd] N *(dog)* teckel *m*

dactyl [ˈdæktɪl] N *Liter* dactyle *m*

dad [dæd] N *Fam* papa *m*

Dada [ˈdɑːdɑː] N *Art, Liter* dada *m*, dadaïsme *m*

Dadaism [ˈdɑːdɑːɪz(ə)m] N *Art, Liter* dadaïsme *m*

daddy [ˈdædɪ] N *Fam* papa *m*

daddy-longlegs [-ˈlɒŋlegz] N *Fam (insect)* cousin *m*

dado [ˈdeɪdəʊ] N *Archit* **1** *(of pedestal)* dé *m* **2** *(of wall)* lambris *m* (d'appui)

daemon [ˈdiːmən] N *Arch, Lit* démon *m*

daff [dæf] N *Br Fam* = **daffodil** N

daffodil [ˈdæfədɪl] N *(flower)* jonquille *f*
ADJ *(colour)* jonquille *inv*
▸▸ **d. yellow** jonquille *inv*

daffy [ˈdæfɪ] ADJ *Fam (person)* timbré, toqué; *(idea, notion)* débile

daft [dɑːft] ADJ *Br Fam (person)* timbré, toqué; *(remark, idea, plan etc)* débile; **to act d.** faire l'idiot; **to go d.** devenir cinglé; *(become angry)* devenir fou de rage; **don't be d.!** ne sois pas bête!; **don't talk d.!** ne dis pas de bêtises!; **to be d. about sb/sth** être fou de qn/qch

daftie [ˈdɑːftɪ] N *Br Fam, Dial* toqué, -ée

daftness [ˈdɑːftnɪs] N *Br Fam* stupidité *f*

dag [dæg] N *Austr Fam* **1** *(unfashionable person)* ringard, -arde **2** *(untidy man)* type *m* négligé; *(untidy woman)* bonne femme *f* négligée

dagger [ˈdægər] N **1** poignard *m*, *Lit* dague *f*; *Fig* **to be at daggers drawn** être à couteaux tirés (**with** avec); **to look daggers at sb** foudroyer qn du regard **2** *Typ* croix *f*

dago [ˈdeɪgəʊ] N *Offensive Sl* métèque *m*

dahlia [ˈdeɪlɪə] N *(flower)* dahlia *m*

Dáil [dɔɪl] N = Chambre *f* des députés de la République d'Irlande

daily [ˈdeɪlɪ] ADJ ATTRIB quotidien; *(report, wage, output)* journalier; **on a d. basis** *(paid, employed, calculated)* à la journée; *(used)* tous les jours, de façon quotidienne; **d. takings** recette *f* journalière; **d. visitors** visiteurs *mpl* journaliers; **to earn one's d. bread** gagner son pain quotidien; *Rel* **give us this day our d. bread** donne-nous aujourd'hui notre pain de ce jour

ADV *(to phone, visit, happen)* tous les jours; **twice d.** deux fois par jour; **news of their defeat is awaited d.** on s'attend à apprendre leur défaite d'un jour à l'autre

N **1** *Journ* quotidien *m* **2** *Br Fam (for housework)* femme *f* de ménage **3** *TV, Cin* dailies rushes *mpl*

▸▸ *Admin* **d. allowance** indemnité *f* journalière; *Acct* **d. balance interest calculation** méthode *f* à échelles *ou* par échelles; *Br Old-fashioned Fam* **d. dozen** gym *f* quotidienne; *Fam* **the d. grind** métro *m* boulot dodo; **I've had enough of the d. grind** j'en ai assez du métro boulot dodo; *Br* **d. help** femme *f* de ménage; *St Exch* **D. Official List** cours *mpl* de clôture quotidiens; **d. paper** quotidien *m*; **d. press** presse *f* quotidienne; *Fin* **d. trading report** rapport *m* de situation journalière; *Br* **d. woman** femme de ménage

daintily [ˈdeɪntɪlɪ] ADV délicatement

daintiness [ˈdeɪntɪnɪs] N *(of movement, way of working etc)* délicatesse *f*, *(of taste)* raffinement *m*

dainty [ˈdeɪntɪ] ADJ **1** *(dish, food)* fin; *(morsel)* de choix **2** *(person) (in manners)* délicat; *(in build)* menu; **short d. steps** petits pas délicats **3** *(choosy)* délicat, difficile; **these animals are d. feeders** ces animaux sont délicats sur la nourriture **4** *(delicate) (porcelain, ornament)* fin, délicat

dairy [ˈdeərɪ] N **1** *(on farm)* laiterie *f* **2** *(shop)* crémerie *f*

▸▸ **d. butter** beurre *m* laitier; **d. cow** vache *f* laitière; **d. farm** ferme *f* laitière; **d. farming** industrie *f* laitière; **d. herd** troupeau *m* de vaches laitières; **d. ice cream** glace *f* à la crème; **d. produce** produits *mpl* laitiers

dairymaid [ˈdeərɪmeɪd] N fille *f* de laiterie

dairyman, *pl* **dairymen** [ˈdeərɪmən] N **1** *(on farm)* employé *m* de laiterie **2** *(who sells dairy products)* laitier *m*

dais [ˈdeɪɪs] N estrade *f*

daisy [ˈdeɪzɪ] N *(flower)* pâquerette *f*, *(bigger)* marguerite *f*; **as fresh as a d.** frais/fraîche comme une rose; *Sl* **he's pushing up the daisies** il mange les pissenlits par les racines

▸▸ **d. chain** guirlande *f* de pâquerettes; *Comput* **d. chaining** connexion *f* en boucle; *Comput, Typ* **d. wheel** marguerite *f*, **d. wheel printer** imprimante *f* à marguerite

daisy-chain VT *Comput* connecter en boucle

Dak *abbr* **Dakota**

Dalai Lama [ˈdælaɪˈlɑːmə] N dalaï-lama *m*, *pl* dalaï-lamas

dale [deɪl] N vallée *f*, *(smaller)* vallon *m*

dalliance [ˈdælɪəns] N *Lit* badinage *m*

dally [ˈdælɪ] VI **1** *Old-fashioned (trifle)* folâtrer (**with** avec qn); **to d. with an idea** caresser une idée **2** *(dawdle)* lambiner, traînasser; **to d. over sth** s'attarder à qch

Dalmatian [dælˈmeɪʃən] N *(dog)* dalmatien, -ienne

dam¹ [dæm] N *Tech (of reservoir)* barrage *m*; *(of canal)* digue *f*; *Tech* **d.** barrage-réservoir *m*, *pl* barrages-réservoirs

VT (**-mm-**) **to d. (up)** *(valley)* construire un barrage en aval de; *(river, lake)* endiguer; *(gutter)* obstruer; *Fig (one's feelings etc)* contenir

dam² N *Agr, Lit* mère *f*

damage [ˈdæmɪdʒ] N **1** *(physical)* dégâts *mpl*, *(to engine, ship etc)* avarie(s) *f(pl)*; **to pay for the d.** payer les dégâts; **smoking can cause serious d. to your health** le tabac nuit gravement à la santé; *Br Fam* **what's the d.?** *(how much do I owe?)* ça fait combien?; **there's no great d. done** il n'y a pas trop de mal; **d. to property** dommage *m* matériel **2** *(harm)* préjudice *m*; **to cause sb d.** porter préjudice à qn; **the d. is done** le mal est fait; **to do d. to a cause** faire du tort à une cause; **d. suffered** préjudice subi **3** *Law* **damages** dommages-intérêts *mpl*, intérêts *mpl* compensatoires; **to be liable for damages** être tenu au versement de dommages-intérêts; **to sue sb for damages** poursuivre qn en dommages et intérêts; **to be awarded damages of £5,000** *or* **£5,000 in damages** obtenir 5000 livres de dommages-intérêts

VT **1** *(physically) (engine, machine)* endommager; *(goods)* avarier; *(furniture)* endommager, abîmer; **the storm damaged a lot of trees** de nombreux arbres ont été endommagés par la tempête; *Com* **damaged in transit** abîmé en cours de route; **damaged goods** marchandises *fpl* avariées

2 *(harm) (chances)* compromettre; *(person)* faire du tort à; *(sb's interests)* léser; *(sb's reputation)* porter atteinte à, ternir

▸▸ **d. control, d. limitation** fait *m* de limiter les dégâts; **we have to do some d. limitation** il faut limiter les dégâts; **d. report** déclaration *f* de sinistre, constat *m* de dommages

damaging ['dæmɪdʒɪŋ] ADJ *(revelation, scandal, remark etc)* préjudiciable; **it's a d. blow to his re-election prospects/career** cela compromet sérieusement ses chances d'être réélu/sa carrière

Damascus [də'mɑːskəs] N Damas *m*; *Fig* **a conversion on the road to D.** une conversion subite

damask ['dæməsk] N **1** *Tex* damas *m* **2** *(colour)* rose foncé *m inv*
▸▸ **d. rose** rose *f* de Damas; **d. silk** soie *f* damassée; *Metal* **d. steel** acier *m* damassé

dame [deɪm] N **1** *Am Fam (woman)* femme *f*; *Br (in pantomime)* vieille femme comique *(dont le rôle est joué par un homme)* **2** *Br (title)* = titre *m* honorifique donné à certaines femmes en signe de distinction

dammit ['dæmɪt] INT *Fam* nom de Dieu; **it was as near as d.** il était moins une

damn [dæm] N *Fam* **I don't give** *or* **care a d.** je m'en fiche éperdument, je n'en ai rien à fiche; **I don't give a d. about the money** je me fiche pas mal de l'argent; **he doesn't give a d. about anything** il se fiche de tout; **it's not worth a d.** ça ne vaut rien
▸ VT **1** *(book, play etc) (criticize severely)* éreinter; *(condemn)* condamner; **to d. sb/sth with faint praise** faire de tièdes éloges de qn/qch, louer qn/qch avec si peu d'ardeur que cela revient à condamner; **you're damned if you do and damned if you don't** quoique tu fasses tu es perdant **2** *Rel* damner **3** *Fam* **well I'll be damned!** ça alors!; **I'm** *or* **I'll be damned if I'll do it** si tu crois que je vais le faire!; **d. the expense** au diable l'avarice; **d. the consequences** tant pis pour les conséquences
▸ INT **d. (it)!** zut!; **d. you!** va te faire fiche!; **d. and blast (it)!** sacré nom d'un chien!
▸ ADJ *Fam* = **damned** ADJ **2**
▸ ADV *Fam* **1 he's doing d. all** il n'en fout pas une (rame); **she knows d. all about it** elle y connaît que dal(l)e; **there's d. all in the fridge** il y a que dal(l)e dans le frigo; **it's got d. all to do with you** ça n'a absolument rien à voir avec toi; **what can you see? – d. all!** tu vois quelque chose? – que dalle! **2** = **damned** ADV

damnable ['dæmnəb(ə)l] ADJ **1** *Rel* damnable **2** *Fam (detestable)* maudit

damnably ['dæmnəblɪ] ADV *Old-fashioned Fam (difficult, expensive, rude etc)* diablement, rudement

damnation [dæm'neɪʃən] N *Rel* damnation *f*, **eternal d.** la peine du dam
▸ INT *Fam* **d.!** enfer et damnation!

damned [dæmd] ADJ **1** *Rel* damné **2** *Fam (intensifier)* **you d. fool!** espèce d'idiot!; **you have to be a d. fool to do that!** il faut être un sacré abruti pour faire ça!; **he's a d. nuisance!** ce qu'il peut être casse-pieds!; **well I'm d.!** elle est bien bonne celle-là!; **it's one d. thing after another** tout va de travers
▸ NPL *Rel* **the d.** les damnés *mpl*; **to suffer the tortures of the d.** souffrir comme un damné
▸ ADV *Fam* rudement, vachement; **it's d. hot** il fait rudement chaud; **I should d. well hope so** ah, ben j'espère bien!; **you can do what you d. well like!** fais ce que tu veux, je m'en

fiche!; **you know d. well what I mean** tu sais très bien ce que je veux dire; **they're d. good players** ils jouent vachement bien

damnedest ['dæmdest] *Fam* N **to do one's d.** faire tout son possible; **he did his d. to ruin the party** il a vraiment fait tout ce qu'il pouvait pour gâcher la soirée
▸ ADJ **if that isn't the d. thing!** c'est vraiment bizarre!, c'est incroyable!

damnfool ['dæm'fuːl] ADJ ATTRIB *Fam* idiot

damning ['dæmɪŋ] ADJ *(fact, evidence etc)* accablant; *(admission)* préjudiciable; **he was pretty d. about the film** il a été très critique vis-à-vis du film

Damocles ['dæməkliːz] N **the sword of D.** l'épée *f* de Damoclès

damp [dæmp] N *(of air)* humidité *f*; *(of skin)* moiteur *f*
▸ ADJ *(cloth, house, heat etc)* humide; *(skin)* moite; **d. patch** tache *f* d'humidité; **his hands are always d.** il a toujours les mains moites; *Fig* **to be a d. squib** faire l'effet d'un pétard mouillé
▸ VT *(diminish) (fire, sound)* étouffer; *(shocks)* amortir; **to d. down a furnace** boucher un haut fourneau

dampcourse ['dæmpkɔːs] N revêtement *m* d'étanchéité

dampen ['dæmp(ə)n] VT **1** *(wet) (cloth)* humecter **2** *(diminish) (enthusiasm)* refroidir; **to d. sb's spirits** décourager qn; **that dampened his ardour** cela a freiné son ardeur

damper ['dæmpər] N **1** *(on enthusiasm etc)* douche *f* froide; **to act as a d. on sb's spirits** saper le moral de qn; **the news put rather a d. on the celebrations/the company** la nouvelle a jeté un froid sur les réjouissances/la compagnie **2** *Mus (of piano, sound)* étouffoir *m* **3** *Tech (of hearth, chimney, furnace)* registre *m*; *(of stove pipe)* soupape *f* de réglage *ou* à papillon; *Aut* amortisseur *m*, damper *m*; *Elec* amortisseur; *Radio* sourdine *f*
▸▸ *Mus* **d. pedal** *(of piano)* pédale *f* forte

damping ['dæmpɪŋ] N *Aut* amortissement *m*

dampish ['dæmpɪʃ] ADJ un peu humide

dampness ['dæmpnɪs] N humidité *f*, *(of skin)* moiteur *f*

damp-proof ADJ hydrofuge
▸▸ **d. course** revêtement *m* d'étanchéité

damp-proofing N isolation *f* contre l'humidité

damsel ['dæmz(ə)l] N *Arch, Lit* demoiselle *f*, *Hum* **d. in distress** une belle éplorée; **to do the d. in distress act** jouer les belles éplorées
▸▸ **d. fly** *(insect)* demoiselle *f*

damson ['dæmz(ə)n] N prune *f* de Damas
▸▸ **d. tree** prunier *m* de Damas

dance [dɑːns] N **1** *(art form, steps)* danse *f*, *Mus (air m de)* danse; **will you have a d. with me?** voulez-vous danser?; *Fig Fam* **to lead sb a (merry) d.** donner du fil à retordre à qn **2** *(ball) (for teenagers)* soirée *f*, *(for older people)* soirée dansante; *(formal)* bal *m*, *pl* bals; **her parents are giving a d. for her birthday** ses parents organisent un bal pour son anniversaire
▸ VI danser; **are you dancing?** vous dansez?; **to d. with sb** danser avec qn; **to d. for joy** danser de joie; **to d. about** gambader; **they danced down the road with glee** ils descendaient la rue en dansant de joie
▸ VT *(waltz etc)* danser; **he danced the last dance with Claudia** il a fait la dernière danse avec Claudia; *esp Lit* **to d. attendance on sb** faire l'empressé auprès de qn
▸▸ **d. band** orchestre *m* de bal; **d. floor** piste *f* de danse; **d. hall** salle *f* de bal; **d. music** musique *f* dansante; *(modern)* dance *f*

dancer ['dɑːnsər] N danseur, -euse

dancing ['dɑːnsɪŋ] ADJ ATTRIB *(bear)* dansant; *Fig* **her d. eyes** son regard vif
▸ N danse *f*, **to go d.** aller danser
▸▸ **d. dervish** derviche *m* tourneur; **d. girl** danseuse *f*, **d. partner** cavalier, ière; **d. school** école *f* de danse; **d. shoes** chaussures *fpl* de danse

dandelion ['dændɪlaɪən] N pissenlit *m*
▸▸ **d. clock** aigrettes *fpl* de pissenlits

dander ['dændər] N *Fam* **to get sb's/one's d. up** mettre qn/se mettre en colère

dandified ['dændɪfaɪd] ADJ *Pej (dress, manner etc)* de dandy; **he had become rather d. in his dress** il s'habillait de plus en plus comme un dandy

dandle ['dænd(ə)l] VT *(child) (on knees)* faire sauter; *(in arms)* bercer

dandruff ['dændrəf] N pellicules *fpl*; **he has very bad d.** il a beaucoup de pellicules
▸▸ **d. shampoo** shampooing *m* antipelliculaire

dandy ['dændɪ] N *Old-fashioned usu Pej* dandy *m*, élégant *m*
▸ ADJ *Am Fam* épatant, chouette; **everything's just (fine and) d.** tout marche à merveille; **that's all fine and d., but …** c'est très joli tout ça, mais …

Dane [deɪn] N Danois, -oise VOIR GRAMMAIRE A19

dang [dæŋ] INT, ADJ, ADV *Old-fashioned Euph* = **damn**

danger ['deɪndʒər] N danger *m*; **out of d.** hors de danger; **to keep out of d.** rester à l'abri du danger; **d. keep out** *(on sign)* danger; **to be in d. of doing sth** risquer de faire qch, courir le risque *ou* être en danger de faire qch; **in d. of (losing) his life** en danger de mort; **to put sb/sth in d.** mettre qn/qch en danger; **there is some d. that …** il y a un risque que … + *subj*, **there is some d. that the engine will explode** *or* **of the engine exploding** le moteur risque d'exploser; **there is no d. that …** il n'y a pas de danger que … + *subj*, **there's no d. that he'll forget** *or* **of his forgetting** il ne risque pas d'oublier, il n'y a pas de danger qu'il oublie; **he's a d. to society** c'est un danger public; *Med* **to be on the d. list** être dans un état critique; *Med* **to be off the d. list** être hors de danger
▸▸ *Br* **d. money** prime *f* de risque; *Fig* **d. sign** signal *m* d'alarme; **d. signal** *Rail* signal d'arrêt; *Fig* signal d'alerte *ou* d'alarme

dangerous ['deɪndʒərəs] ADJ **1** dangereux; *(illness)* grave; **you are (treading) on d. ground** vous vous engagez sur un terrain dangereux **2** *(example, maxim)* pernicieux
▸▸ *Law* **d. driving** conduite *f* dangereuse; **d. goods** marchandises *fpl* dangereuses

dangerously ['deɪndʒərəslɪ] ADV dangereusement; **he came d. close to accusing me of lying** il m'a presque traité de menteur; **he came d. close to falling** il a failli tomber; **d. ill** gravement malade; **his energy was at a d. low ebb** ses forces avaient dangereusement diminué

dangle ['dæŋg(ə)l] VI pendiller; **with one's legs dangling** les jambes ballantes; **you can't keep him dangling like that** *(in state of uncertainty)* il ne faut pas le laisser dans l'incertitude
▸ VT *(object)* balancer; **to d. one's fingers/feet in the water** tremper les doigts/pieds dans l'eau; *Fig* **to d. sth in front of sb** faire miroiter qch à qn

Danish ['deɪnɪʃ] ADJ danois; *(ambassador, embassy, history)* du Danemark VOIR GRAMMAIRE A19
▸ N **1** *Ling* danois *m* **2** *Culin (pastry)* = sorte de chausson fourré
▸▸ **D. blue (cheese)** bleu *m* du Danemark; **D. pastry** = sorte de chausson fourré

dank [dæŋk] ADJ *(weather, dungeon)* humide (et froid)

Dantean [ˈdæntɪən, dænˈtiːən], **Dantesque** [dænˈtesk] ADJ dantesque

Danube (the) [ðəˈdænjuːb] N le Danube

dapper [ˈdæpər] ADJ *(man, suit)* coquet; *(beard)* soigné

dapple [ˈdæp(ə)l] N 1 *(on horse's coat)* tache f de couleur 2 *(horse)* pommelé m
VT tacheter; **a wall dappled with sunlight** un mur tacheté de lumière

dapple-grey N *(horse)* gris m pommelé

Darby and Joan [ˈdɑːbɪ] N = couple m uni de personnes âgés
▸▸ **D. club** club m du troisième âge *(en Grande-Bretagne)*

dare [deər] VOIR GRAMMAIRE A61; A41; B35 MO-DAL AUX V *(third sg pr* **dare;** *pt, pp* **dared;** **d. not** *often contracted to* **daren't)** oser; **I d. not** *or* **daren't speak to him** je n'ose pas lui parler; **don't you d. touch him!** ne touche pas un cheveu de sa tête!; **don't you d. (do that)!** ne t'avise pas de faire ça!; **how d. you!** comment oses-tu!, quelle audace!; **I d. say that …** je suppose que …; **I d. say** sans doute, c'est bien possible; **your opponent, d. I say it, has never been beaten** votre adversaire, si je puis me permettre de vous le faire remarquer, n'a jamais été battu
VT *(third sg pr* **dares;** *pt, pp* **dared)** 1 oser; **to d. to do sth** oser faire qch; **to d. to be different** avoir le courage d'être différent, oser être différent; **let him do it if he dare(s)!** qu'il le fasse s'il l'ose! 2 *(challenge)* **to d. sb to do sth** défier qn de faire qch; **I d. you!** fais-le si tu oses!, chiche! 3 *Fml (danger, death etc)* braver
N défi m; **to do sth for** *or* **as a d.** faire qch pour relever un défi

daredevil [ˈdeədev(ə)l] N casse-cou m inv
ADJ *(pilot, driver)* casse-cou inv; *(escape, exploits)* audacieux

daring [ˈdeərɪŋ] ADJ *(person)* audacieux, hardi; *(attempt, attack, escape etc)* audacieux; *(dress, film, writer)* provocant
N audace f

daringly [ˈdeərɪŋlɪ] ADV de manière audacieuse; **a d. low dress** une robe au décolleté audacieux; **to be d. different** *(of person)* avoir le courage d'être différent, oser être différent; **this is a d. different film** avec ce film, le metteur en scène ose être différent

dark [dɑːk] ADJ 1 *(without light)* sombre, obscur; **it's d.** *(outside)* il fait nuit, il fait noir; *(inside)* il fait sombre; **it's getting** *or* **growing d.** il commence à faire sombre *ou* à faire nuit; **everything suddenly went d.** soudain ce fut le noir complet; **the d. side of the moon** la face cachée de la lune

2 *(colour)* foncé, sombre; **d. blue dresses** robes fpl bleu foncé

3 *(eyes)* foncé; **to be d.** *(of white person)* être mat (de peau); *(of black person)* être très noir, avoir la peau très foncée; **she has d. hair** elle est brune

4 *(unhappy)* *(thought etc)* triste; *(future, days)* sombre; *(angry)* *(look)* sombre, noir; **to look on the d. side of things** voir tout en noir; **to mutter d. threats** marmonner des menaces; **to harbour d. designs** nourrir de noirs desseins; **d. powers** puissances fpl occultes

5 *(secret)* mystérieux, secret, -ète; **to keep sth d.** tenir qch secret; *Fig* **a d. horse** *(unknown competitor)* un concurrent inconnu; *(unexpected competitor)* un concurrent que l'on ne croyait pas dangereux; **he's a d. horse** *(a stranger)* on ne sait rien de lui; *(gave nothing away)* il a bien caché son jeu

6 *Hum* **they live in darkest Somerset** ils habitent au fin fond du Somerset
N ténèbres fpl, obscurité f; **the child is afraid of the d.** l'enfant a peur du noir; **after d.** à la tombée de la nuit; **until d.** jusqu'à ce qu'il fasse nuit; **in the d.** dans le noir; *Fig* **to be (kept) in the d.** être (laissé) dans l'ignorance; **we kept her in the d. about it** on ne lui en a rien dit
▸▸ *Hist* **the D. Ages** le haut Moyen Âge; *Fig* **we're still in the D. Ages** nous en sommes encore au Moyen Âge; *Hist* **the D. Continent** le Continent noir, l'Afrique f; **d. glasses** lunettes fpl noires

darken [ˈdɑːk(ə)n] VT *(room, sky)*, *Fig (future etc)* assombrir; *(colour)* foncer; *Fig Lit* **her life had been darkened by her son's death** la mort de son fils l'avait plongée dans la nuit; *Old-fashioned, Hum* **never d. my door again!** ne remettez plus les pieds chez moi!
VI *(of sky, thoughts)* s'assombrir; *(of colour)* se foncer, s'assombrir; *(of skin)* brunir; **his face** *or* **brow darkened** il *ou* son visage s'assombrit

darkening [ˈdɑːk(ə)nɪŋ] ADJ *(sky)*, *Fig (face)* qui s'assombrit; **he looked up at the d. sky** il regarda le ciel qui s'assombrissait
N *(of sky, painting)* assombrissement m

dark-eyed ADJ aux yeux foncés

dark-haired ADJ aux cheveux foncés

darkie [ˈdɑːkɪ] N *Old-fashioned Offensive Sl* moricaud, -aude

darkish [ˈdɑːkɪʃ] ADJ un peu sombre

darkly [ˈdɑːklɪ] ADV 1 *(dimly, not clearly)* obscurément; **the house loomed d. in the fog** la maison se dessinait, sombre dans le brouillard 2 *(to look at sb, to say)* d'un air sombre; **she contemplated the future d.** elle avait une sombre vision de l'avenir

darkness [ˈdɑːknɪs] N 1 obscurité f; **d. had fallen** il faisait sombre; **the room was in complete d.** il faisait tout à fait noir dans la pièce; **the house/village was in d.** *(no lights were on)* la maison/le village était dans l'obscurité 2 *(of colour)* teinte f foncée; *(of skin) (caused by weather)* hâle m; *(of white person)* teint m mat; *(of black person)* peau f très noire 3 *Arch (ignorance)* ignorance f

darkroom [ˈdɑːkruːm] N *Phot* chambre f noire

dark-skinned ADJ à la peau mate

darky [ˈdɑːkɪ] N = **darkie**

darling [ˈdɑːlɪŋ] N chéri, -ie; **(my) d.!** *(to male)* mon chéri!, mon chou!; *(to female)* ma chérie!, mon chou!; **she's a little d.** c'est un petit amour; **be a d. and get it for me** tu serais un amour si tu allais me le chercher; **a d. little place** un petit endroit charmant; **he's his mother's d.** c'est le chouchou de sa maman; **the d. of the people** l'idole f du peuple; **to be the d. of the court/media/public** être la coqueluche de la cour/des média/du public

darn¹ [dɑːn] N *(in stocking etc)* reprise f
VT *(stocking etc)* repriser

darn² *Fam* VT & VI **d. (it)!** zut!; **d. this car!** satanée voiture!; **d. him!** qu'il aille au diable!; **d. your father and his ideas!** ah ton père et ses satanées idées!
ADJ sacré; **it's a d. nuisance** c'est vachement embêtant; **the d. car won't start** cette sacrée bagnole ne veut pas démarrer
ADV vachement; **it's d. late** il est vachement tard; **we've been d. lucky** on a eu une sacrée veine; **don't be so d. stupid!** ce que tu peux être bête!

darned [dɑːnd] ADJ, ADV = **darn²**

darning [ˈdɑːnɪŋ] N reprise f
▸▸ **d. egg** œuf m à repriser; **d. needle** aiguille f à repriser; **d. wool** laine f à repriser

dart [dɑːt] N 1 *(weapon)* flèche f courte; **paper d.** avion m en papier 2 *(in games)* fléchette f, **darts** *(game)* fléchettes; **do you want a game of darts?** tu veux faire une partie de fléchettes? VOIR GRAMMAIRE A10 3 *Sewing* pince f 4 *(movement)* mouvement m soudain; **to make a sudden d.** foncer, se précipiter **(for, towards** sur, vers)
VT *(look)* lancer; *(tongue)* darder
VI se précipiter, foncer **(at sb/sth** sur qn/qch); **to d. in/out** entrer/sortir comme une flèche; **he darted across the road** il a traversé la rue comme une flèche; **her eyes darted from one face in the crowd to another** son regard passait rapidement d'un visage à l'autre dans la foule

dartboard [ˈdɑːtbɔːd] N cible f *(de jeu de fléchettes)*

dash [dæʃ] N 1 *(drop)* goutte f, *(of cognac etc)* larme f, *(of lemon juice, vinegar)* filet m, goutte; **add a d. of lemon** ajoutez-y un filet de citron; **d. of colour** *(in painting)* touche f de couleur; *Fig* **a d. of humour/cynicism** un rien d'humour/de cynisme

2 *(of pen, in Morse alphabet)* trait m; *Typ* tiret m

3 *(run)* course f à toute vitesse; *Am Sport* sprint m; **to make a d. forward** s'élancer en avant; **a quick d. across to Paris** un petit saut à Paris; **to make a d. at sth** se précipiter sur qch; **to make a d. at sb** foncer sur qn; **to make a d. for it** saisir l'occasion de s'enfuir

4 *(style)* élan m, entrain m; *Old-fashioned* **to cut a d.** faire de l'épate

5 *Aut Fam (dashboard)* tableau m de bord
VT 1 *(throw)* heurter violemment; **to d. sth to the ground** jeter qch à terre; **the ship was dashed against a rock** le navire a été jeté sur un écueil; **to d. sth to pieces** fracasser qch

2 *Fig (destroy) (sb's hopes)* détruire; *(enthusiasm)* refroidir; **to d. sb's spirits** abattre le courage de qn; **he saw his hopes dashed** il a vu tomber à l'eau ses espérances

3 *(rush)* **to d. sb to hospital** emmener qn à l'hôpital en urgence

4 *Fam* **d. (it)!** zut!
VI **to come dashing in** entrer comme un bolide, entrer en trombe; **to d. up to sb** se précipiter vers qn; **to d. up/down the stairs** monter/descendre l'escalier quatre à quatre; **to d. into the room** entrer précipitamment *ou* en coup de vent dans la salle; **I'm just going to d. home and …** je vais faire un saut chez moi et …; **to d. across the road** traverser la route en courant; **I've been dashing around like a mad thing all day** j'ai couru toute la journée; *Fam* **I must d.** il faut que je file

▸ **dash away** VI partir comme une flèche, filer à toute vitesse

▸ **dash off** VI *(leave quickly)* partir comme une flèche, filer à toute vitesse
VT SEP *(make or do quickly)* faire en vitesse; *(letter)* écrire en vitesse

▸ **dash out** VI sortir à toute vitesse; **she dashed out into the road** elle s'est précipitée sur la route; **I forgot my briefcase when I dashed out of the house** je suis sorti de chez moi à toute vitesse et j'ai oublié ma mallette; **I'll d. out to the garden/the shop for some parsley** je vais faire un saut au jardin/au magasin chercher du persil

dashboard [ˈdæʃbɔːd] N *Aut* tableau m de bord

dashed [dæʃt] *Old-fashioned Br Fam* ADJ sacré; **what a d. nuisance!** quel empoisonnement!
ADV vachement; **it's d. hot** il fait vachement chaud

dashing [ˈdæʃɪŋ] ADJ *(person)* fringant, *(coat, jacket etc)* élégant; **to cut a d. figure** avoir fière allure; **a d. young man** un beau jeune homme

dashingly [ˈdæʃɪŋlɪ] ADV avec élégance; **d. handsome** d'une beauté sublime

dashpot ['dæʃpɒt] N *Aut* dash-pot *m*, *pl* dash-pots

dastardly ['dæstədlɪ] ADJ *Old-fashioned, Lit* **1** *(person)* lâche **2** *(crime, plan, intentions)* infâme, ignoble

DAT [diːeɪˈtiː] N *(abbr* **digital audio tape)** DAT *m*
▸▸ **D. cartridge** cartouche *f* DAT; **D. drive** lecteur *m* DAT, lecteur de bande audionumérique; **D. recorder** magnétophone *m* numérique

data ['deɪtə, 'dɑːtə] N informations *fpl*; *Comput* données *fpl*; **an item of d.** une information; **what little d. we do have suggests that …** le peu d'informations que nous avons semble montrer que …; **to collect d. on sb/sth** recueillir des informations sur qn/qch
VOIR GRAMMAIRE A11
▸▸ **d. acquisition** collecte *f* de données, saisie *f* de données; **d. analysis** analyse *f* de données; **d. bank** banque *f* de données; **d. block** bloc *m* de données; **d. buffer** mémoire *f* tampon; **d. bus** bus *m* de données; **d. capture** saisie *f* de données; **d. carrier** support *m* de données; **d. collection** recueil *m* de données, collecte *f* de données; **d. communications** communication *f* ou transmission *f* de données, télématique *f*; **d. compression** compression *f* de données; **d. conversion** conversion *f* de données; **d. decryption** déchiffrement *m* de données; **d. encryption** cryptage *m* ou codage *m* de données; **d. entry** entrée *f* de données; **d. entry form** fiche *f* d'imputation; **d. exchange** échange *m* de données; **d. flow** flux *m* de données; **d. format** format *m* des données; **d. gathering** collecte de données; **d. input** entrée *f* de données; **d. integrity** intégrité *f* des données; **d. loss** perte *f* de données; **d. management** gestion *f* de données; **d. manipulation** manipulation *f* de données; **d. memory** mémoire *f* (pour les données); **d. mining** data mining *m*; **d. path** chemin *m* d'accès aux données; **d. pattern** modèle *m* de données; **d. pen** crayon *m* électronique; **d. privacy** secret *m* ou protection *f* des données; **d. processing** *(science)* informatique *f*; *(machine)* ordinateur *m*; *(person)* informaticien, -ienne; **d. protection** protection *f* de l'information; **d. protection act** ≃ loi *f* informatique et libertés; **d. reader** lecteur *m* de données; **d. reading system** système *m* de lecture de données; **d. recovery** récupération *f* de données; **d. security** sécurité *f* des données; **d. set** ensemble *m* de données; **d. storage** stockage *m* de données; **d. stream** flot *m* de données; **d. switch** commutateur *m* de données; **d. systems technology** technologie *f* informatique; **d. terminal** terminal *m* de traitement de données; **d. transfer** transfert *m* ou transmission *f* de données; **d. transfer protocol** protocole *m* de transfert de données; **d. transfer rate** taux *m* de transfert de données; **d. transmission** transmission *f* de données; **d. type** type *m* de données

database ['deɪtəbeɪs] N base *f* de données; **to have/put sth in a d.** avoir/mettre qch dans une base de données
VT intégrer dans une base de données
▸▸ **d. file** fichier *m* de base de données; **d. integration** intégration *f* de bases de données; **d. management** gestion *f* de base de données

datacomms ['deɪtəkɒms, 'dɑːtəkɒms] N *Comput* communication *f* ou transmission *f* de données, télématique *f*
▸▸ **d. linkup** liaison *f* télématique; **d. network** réseau *m* de communication de données; **d. software** logiciel *m* de communication

dataglove ['deɪtəglʌv] N *Comput* gant *m* de données

dataset ['deɪtəset, 'dɑːtəset] N *Comput* ensemble *m* de données

DATE¹ [deɪt]

N date **1** ▪ terme **2** ▪ rendez-vous **3** ▪ ami **3**		
VT dater **1** ▪ sortir avec **2**		
VI dater **1** ▪ se démoder **2**		

N **1** date *f*; *(on coins, books etc)* millésime *m*; **d. of birth** date de naissance; **d. of departure** date de départ; **d. of dispatch** date d'envoi ou d'expédition; **d. of issue** date d'émission; **what's the d. (today)?** le combien sommes-nous aujourd'hui?; **to fix a d. for sth** prendre date ou fixer une date pour qch; **shall we fix a d. now?** est-ce que nous prenons date ou fixons une date maintenant?; **have you set a d. yet?** *(for wedding)* est-ce que vous avez déjà décidé de la date du mariage?; **I'm not free on that d.** je ne suis pas libre à cette date; **(on) what dates are you free?** à quelles dates êtes-vous libre?; **to be up to d.** *(with work, reading)* être à jour (**with** dans); *(with what's happening)* être au courant (**with** de); *(in fashion)* être à la page; **to bring one's diary up to d.** mettre à jour son journal; **my assistant will bring you up to d.** mon assistant vous mettra au courant; **to d.** à ce jour VOIR GRAMMAIRE A81; B61 **2** *Com, Fin* terme *m*, échéance *f*; **d. of maturity, due d.** *(date f d')*échéance; **three months after d., at three months' d.** à trois mois de date ou d'échéance

3 *Fam (appointment)* rendez-vous *m inv*; *(boyfriend, girlfriend)* ami, -ie; **to make a d.** fixer un rendez-vous; **I have a d. tonight** j'ai un rendez-vous ce soir; *(with boyfriend etc)* je sors avec quelqu'un ce soir; *Am* **I don't have a d. for the prom** je n'ai pas de cavalier/de cavalière pour le bal de fin d'année; **where's your d.?** où est la personne qui t'accompagne?; **my d. didn't show up** on m'a posé un lapin

VT **1** *(letter, work of art etc)* dater; *(bottle of wine etc)* millésimer; *(with machine) (ticket)* composter; **the letter is dated the 12th** la lettre est datée du 12; **your letter dated …** votre lettre en date du …; **to d. back** antidater; **his clothes d. him** ses vêtements démodés montrent qu'il n'est pas jeune; **that dates you** *(shows how old you are)* ça montre ton âge

2 *esp Am Fam (person)* sortir avec, fréquenter; **they're dating each other** ils sortent ensemble

VI **1** *(originate)* dater (**from** de), remonter (**from** à); **church dating from** ou **back to the 13th century** église qui remonte au ou qui date du XIIIe siècle; **friendship dating back to the days of their youth** amitié qui remonte à leur jeunesse

2 *(go out of fashion)* se démoder; **his style is beginning to d.** son style commence à dater **3** *Fam (of couple)* sortir ensemble, se fréquenter
▸▸ **d. rape** = viol *m* commis par une connaissance, un ami etc; **d. stamp** timbre *m* à date, tampon *m* ou timbre dateur

Date
Pour donner une date en anglais, on n'emploie pas l'article à l'écrit. En anglais britannique, on écrira donc "Monday 25th December 2000" ou, de plus en plus souvent, "Monday 25 December 2000", et, en abrégé, "25.12.00". Notez cependant qu'à l'oral, on prononce "Monday the twenty-fifth of December". En anglais américain, le mois est indiqué avant le jour. On écrira ainsi "Monday December 25 2000" et, en abrégé, "12.25.00", et on prononcera "December twenty-five".

date² N *(fruit)* datte *f*
▸▸ *Bot* **d. palm** palmier *m* dattier

datebook ['deɪtbʊk] N *Am* agenda *m*

dated ['deɪtɪd] ADJ **1** démodé; **his style is rather d.** son style commence à dater **2** *Fin* **long-/short-d.** à longue/courte échéance

dateless ['deɪtlɪs] ADJ **1** *(timeless) (dress, style etc)* intemporel **2** *(not dated) (document, letter)* non daté

dateline ['deɪtlaɪn] N *Journ (of report etc)* date *f* de rédaction, dateline *f*

date-stamp VT composter

date-stamping N compostage *m*

dating ['deɪtɪŋ] N **1** *(of document etc)* datation *f*, datage *m*; *(of ticket) (with machine)* compostage *m* **2** *Archeol etc* datation *f*
▸▸ **d. agency** agence *f* matrimoniale

dative ['deɪtɪv] ADJ, N *Gram* datif *m*; **in the d.** au datif
▸▸ **d. case** datif

datum ['deɪtəm] N *(pl* **data)** *Fml* donnée *f*
VOIR GRAMMAIRE A11
▸▸ **d. point** *(in robotics)* point *m* de référence

daub [dɔːb] N **1** *Pej (picture)* croûte *f*, barbouillage *m* **2** *Constr* torchis *m*
VT **1** *Art Pej (painting, canvas)* barbouiller **2** *(smear)* barbouiller (**with** de)

daughter ['dɔːtər] N fille *f*

daughterboard ['dɔːtəbɔːd] N *Comput* carte *f* fille

daughter-in-law N belle-fille *f*, *pl* belles-filles, bru *f*

daunt [dɔːnt] VT *(somebody)* intimider; *Fml, Hum* **nothing daunted** intrépide(ment)

daunting ['dɔːntɪŋ] ADJ *(task etc)* impressionnant, intimidant

dauntless ['dɔːntlɪs] ADJ intrépide

dauntlessly ['dɔːntlɪslɪ] ADV intrépidement

davenport ['dævənpɔːt] N *Am* canapé(-lit) *m*, *pl* canapés(-lits)

davit ['dævɪt] N *Naut* bossoir *m* d'embarcation

Davy ['deɪvɪ] N *Naut Fam* **to go to D. Jones's locker** *(drown)* boire à la grande tasse; **he's in D. Jones's locker** il a bu à la grande tasse

dawdle ['dɔːd(ə)l] VI traînasser, lambiner
▸ **dawdle away** VT SEP **to d. the time away** passer le temps; *(waste)* perdre son temps

dawdler ['dɔːdlər] N traînard, -arde, lambin, -ine

dawdling ['dɔːdlɪŋ] N lambineries *fpl*, traînasseries *fpl*
ADJ traînard

dawn [dɔːn] N aube *f*, aurore *f*; *Fig (of life, civilization, new age)* aube *f*; **at d.** à l'aube; **at the crack of d.** à la pointe du jour; **from d. to dusk** du lever au coucher du soleil; **until d.** jusqu'à l'aube, jusqu'au petit jour
VI *(of day, morning)* se lever; *Fig (commencer à)* paraître; **day is dawning** le jour point ou se lève; *Fig* **when the truth dawned on him** quand il a compris la vérité; *Fig* **it dawned on me that …** j'ai commencé à me rendre compte que …; **another thought dawned on him** une autre pensée lui est venue à l'esprit
▸▸ **the d. chorus** le chant des oiseaux à l'aube; **d. raid** descente *f* à l'aube; *(by police)* descente ou rafle *f* à l'aube; *St Exch* raid *m* *(mené dès l'ouverture de la Bourse)*; *St Exch* **d. raider** raider *m* *(qui opère dès l'ouverture de la Bourse)*

dawning ['dɔːnɪŋ] ADJ *(day)* naissant
N aube *f*

DAY [deɪ]

▪ jour **1–5, 7** ▪ journée **2** ▪ temps **8**		

N 1 *(calendar unit)* jour *m*; **d. of the month** quantième *m* du mois; **what d. (of the week) is it (today)?** quel jour (de la semaine) sommes-nous?; **on this (d.) of all days!** justement aujourd'hui!; **of all (the) days to choose for a conference!** quelle idée d'avoir choisi de faire une conférence justement aujourd'hui!; **to take/get a d. off** prendre/obtenir un jour de congé; *Law etc* **ten clear days' notice** préavis *m* de dix jours francs; *Com* **d. of grace** jour de grâce; *Com* **days of grace** délai *m* de grâce VOIR GRAMMAIRE A81; B61

2 *(referring to duration)* journée *f*; **it's been a sunny/rainy d.** il a fait une journée de soleil/pluie; **on wet days we stay in** les jours où il pleut nous restons à la maison; **all d. (long)** toute la journée; **what sort of d. have you had?** tu as passé une bonne journée?; **to work/be paid by the d.** travailler/être payé à la journée; **it's all in a d.'s work** ça fait partie de la routine; **eight-hour d.** journée de huit heures; **in the course of the d.** dans la journée; **at the end of the d.** à la fin de la journée; *Fig* en fin de compte, au bout du compte; **to carry** *or* **win the d.** gagner la journée *ou* la bataille; *Lit* **d. is done** le jour s'achève VOIR GRAMMAIRE B61

3 *(time, frequency)* **the d. before/after he came** la veille/le lendemain de son arrivée; **two days previously** *or* **before** deux jours avant; **two days before/after his wedding** l'avant-veille/le surlendemain de son mariage; **the d. before yesterday** avant-hier; **the d. after tomorrow** après-demain; **the d. before yesterday was Sunday** il y a deux jours c'était dimanche; **two days later** deux jours après *ou* plus tard, le surlendemain; **I met him one d.** je l'ai rencontré un jour; **one d., some d., one of these days** *(future)* un jour (ou l'autre), un de ces jours; **the baby's due any d. now** le bébé va naître d'un jour à l'autre; **the other d.** l'autre jour; **a year ago to the d.** il y a un an jour pour jour; **I remember it to this (very) d.** je m'en souviens encore aujourd'hui; **until the d. I die, until my dying d.** jusqu'à ma mort; *Fam* **from d. one** dès le début; **from that d. on(wards)** depuis ce jour; **from this d. forth** dorénavant, à compter de ce jour; **once/twice a d.** une/deux fois par jour; **every other d.** tous les deux jours, un jour sur deux; **d. after d., d. in d. out** jour après jour; **by d.** jour après jour; **from d. to d.** de jour en jour, d'un jour à l'autre; **to live from d. to d.** vivre au jour le jour; **d.-old** *(chicks, baby)* d'un jour; *(bread)* de la veille

4 *(as distinguished from night)* **to work d. and night** travailler nuit et jour; **to travel by d.** voyager de jour; *Theat, Fam Hum* **don't give up the d. job** je ne crois pas que tu es prêt pour une carrière professionnelle; *Ind* **to be on days** *(of worker)* être de jour

5 *(dawn)* jour *m*; **before d.** avant le jour; **at break of d.** au point du jour; **they were waiting for d. to break** ils attendaient que le jour pointe

6 *(idioms) Fam* **he's sixty if he's a d.** il a soixante ans bien sonnés; **he doesn't look a d. older than 40/you** il n'a pas l'air d'avoir plus de 40 ans/d'être plus vieux que toi; **he doesn't look a d. older than when I last saw him** il n'a pas vieilli d'un poil depuis la dernière fois que je l'ai vu; **you've made my d.!** c'est la meilleure nouvelle de la journée; **it's not my d.!** c'est pas mon jour; *Fig* **let's call it a d.** *(finish work)* ça suffit pour aujourd'hui; *(end relationship)* finissons-en; *Fam* **let's make a d. of it!** allons faire la fête!; *Fam* **that'll be the d.!** j'aimerais voir ça!; **to pass the time of d. with sb** échanger quelques paroles de politesse avec qn

7 *(anniversary, celebration)* fête *f*; **Mother's/Father's D.** la fête des Mères/des Pères; **Saint David's D.** la Saint-David; **All Saints' D.** la

Toussaint; **All Souls' D.** le Jour des Morts; **Christmas D.** le jour de Noël; **to name the d.** *(of wedding)* fixer le jour du mariage; *Rel* **the D. of Judgement** le jour du jugement

8 *(time)* **the good old days** le bon vieux temps; **in the days of …** au *ou* du temps de …; **in my young days** au *ou* du temps de ma jeunesse; **in those days** en ce temps-là, à cette époque, alors; **these days** de notre temps; **in this d. and age** de nos jours; **those were the days** c'était la belle vie (alors); **in his d.** *(when he was young)* en son temps; *(when he was alive)* de son vivant; **she was a great actress in her d.** c'était une grande actrice en son époque; **he ended his days in poverty** il a fini ses jours pauvre; **in days to come** à l'avenir; **to have had its d.** *(of theory, fashion etc)* être démodé; *(of car, TV)* avoir fait son temps; **to have seen better days** *(of person)* avoir connu des jours meilleurs; *(of car, shoes)* avoir fait son temps; *Fam (of food)* avoir perdu de sa fraîcheur

▸▸ *Mktg* **d.-after recall** mémorisation *f* un jour après; *Mktg* **d.-after recall test** test *m* du lendemain; *Fin* **d. bed** lit *m* de repos; *Fin* **d. bill** effet *m* à date fixe; **d. cream** crème *f* de jour; **d. labourer** journalier, -ière; **d. nurse** infirmière, -ière qui est de service de jour; **d. nursery** garderie *f*; *St Exch* **d. order** ordre *m* valable pour la journée; *Sch* **d. pupil** (élève *mf*) externe *mf*; **d. rate** tarif *m* journalier; *Br Ind* **d. release** formation *f* continue en alternance; *Br Rail* **d. return** aller-retour *m* valable pour la journée *pl* allers-retours; **d. school** externat *m*; **d. shift** *(period worked)* service *m* de jour; *(workers)* équipe *f* de jour; *Met* **d. temperature** température *f* diurne; **d. tour** excursion *f* d'une journée; *St Exch* **d. trade** opération *f* de journée; **d. trip** excursion (d'une journée); **d. tripper** excursionniste *mf*; **d. visitor** excursionniste

> When translating **day**, note that **jour** and **journée** are not interchangeable. **Jour** is used to refer to a day as a distinct unit of time, while **journée** emphasizes duration.

daybook ['deɪbʊk] **N** *Com* journal *m*, -aux; *Acct* livre de main-courante, main *f* courante, brouillard *m*

dayboy ['deɪbɔɪ] **N** *Sch* externe *m*

daybreak ['deɪbreɪk] **N** point *m* du jour, lever *m* du jour; **at d.** au lever du jour, au point du jour

daycare ['deɪkeər] **N** *(for elderly, disabled)* service *m* d'accueil de jour; *(for children)* service *m* de garderie; **the children go to d.** les enfants vont à la garderie

▸▸ **d. centre** *(for elderly, disabled)* = centre *m* d'animation et d'aide sociale; *(for children)* garderie *f*; **d. facilities** *(for elderly, disabled)* service d'accueil de jour; *(for children)* service de garderie

daydream ['deɪdriːm] **N** rêverie *f*

VI rêvasser; **to d. about the future** rêver à l'avenir

daydreaming ['deɪdriːmɪŋ] **N** rêverie *f*, rêvasserie *f*; **d. will get you nowhere** les rêveries ne te mèneront nulle part

daygirl ['deɪgɜːl] **N** *Sch* externe *f*

daylight ['deɪlaɪt] **N 1** *(light)* jour *m*, lumière *f* du jour; **it was still d.** il faisait encore jour; **there were still two hours of d. left** il ferait jour pendant deux heures encore; *Fig* **to put d. between oneself and sb** distancer qn; *Fig* **to (begin to) see d.** *(come to the end of a task)* entrevoir la fin; *(understand)* (commencer à) voir clair **2** *(dawn)* aube *f*, point *m* du jour; **before d.** avant l'aube **2** *Fam* **to beat the living daylights out of sb** rosser qn, tabasser qn; **to scare** *or* **frighten the living daylights out of sb** flanquer la

trouille *ou* une peur bleue à qn

▸▸ **d. hours** heures *fpl* durant lesquelles il fait jour

daylight-saving N

▸▸ **d. time** heure *f* avancée d'été

daylong ['deɪlɒŋ] **ADJ** d'une journée

daytime ['deɪtaɪm] **N** jour *m*, journée *f*; **in the d.** pendant la journée, de jour; **d. classes** cours *mpl* pendant la journée

▸▸ **d. TV** émissions *fpl* télévisées pendant la journée

day-to-day ADJ *(task)* courant, quotidien; *(worry, concern)* quotidien; **d. management of a company** administration courante d'une entreprise; **on a d. basis** au jour le jour

daze [deɪz] **N 1** *(caused by drug, blow)* étourdissement *m*; **to be in a d.** être étourdi; *(stronger)* être hébété **2** *(caused by news)* ahurissement *m*; **to be in a d.** être hébété *ou* ahuri; **he was left in a d. by the news** la nouvelle l'a hébété *ou* ahuri

VT 1 *(of drug, blow)* étourdir; *(stronger)* hébéter **2** *(bewilder)* abasourdir, ahurir

dazed [deɪzd] **ADJ 1** *(by blow, lack of sleep)* tout étourdi, hébété **2** *(bewildered)* abasourdi, sidéré, hébété; **she had a d. look on her face, she looked d.** elle avait l'air abasourdi, elle paraissait abasourdie

dazzle ['dæz(ə)l] **N** *(of headlights)* lueur *f* éblouissante *ou* aveuglante; *Fig* éclat *m*

VT éblouir, aveugler; *Fig* éblouir; **dazzled with** *or* **by the light** aveuglé par la lumière; *Fig* **she was quite dazzled by him** il l'a complètement éblouie

dazzling ['dæzlɪŋ] **ADJ** *(light)* aveuglant, éblouissant; *(beauty, performance)* éblouissant; *(success)* éclatant

dazzlingly ['dæzlɪŋlɪ] **ADV d. beautiful** d'une beauté éblouissante; **d. bright** éblouissant, aveuglant

dB *(abbr* **decibel)** dB

DBMS [diːbiːem'es] **N** *Comput (abbr* **database management system)** SGBD *m*

DBS [diːbiː'es] **N** *Tel abbr* **direct broadcasting satellite**

DC [diː'siː] **N 1** *Elec abbr* **direct current 2** *Am Fam (abbr* **District of Columbia)** DC

D & C [diːən'siː] **N** *Med (abbr* **dilatation and curettage)** dilatation *f* et curetage *m*

DD [diː'diː] **N 1** *Univ abbr* **Doctor of Divinity 2** *Comput (abbr* **double density)** double densité *f*

D-day N le jour J

DDE [diːdiː'iː] **N** *Comput (abbr* **dynamic data exchange)** DDE *m*

DDT [diːdiː'tiː] **N** *Chem* DDT *m*

DEA [diːiː'eɪ] **N** *Am abbr* **Drug Enforcement Agency**

deacon ['diːkən] **N** *Rel* diacre *m*

deaconess ['diːkənɪs] **N** *Rel* diaconesse *f*

deactivate [diː'æktɪveɪt] **VT** désactiver

deactivation [diːæktɪ'veɪʃən] **N** désactivation *f*

DEAD [ded]

| ADJ | mort **1–3** ▪ engourdi **2** ▪ éteint **3** |
| ADV | vachement **1** ▪ absolument **2** |

ADJ 1 *(person, tree, flower)* mort; **he is d.** il est mort *ou* décédé; **the d. man** le mort; **the d. woman** la morte; **Fam over my d. body!** moi vivant, jamais!; **it'll be over my d. body!** il faudra me tuer d'abord!; **to step into a d. man's shoes** être promu à la suite du décès de son supérieur; *Prov* **d. men tell no tales** les morts ne parlent pas; **to shoot sb d.** tuer qn net (d'un coup de revolver); *Fam* **d. as a doornail, d. as mutton** mort et bien mort; **d. and gone, d. and buried** mort et enterré; **half**

d. with fright à moitié mort de peur; **d. or alive** mort ou vif; **more d. than alive** plus mort que vif; **to leave sb for d.** laisser qn pour mort; *Fig* **I wouldn't be seen d. wearing it** je ne porterais ça pour rien au monde; *Fig* **I wouldn't be seen d. there** je n'irais pour rien au monde; *Fam* **to be d. from the neck up** être idiot; *Fam* **you're a d. man** tu es un homme mort; *Fam* **if Dad finds out, you're d.** *or* **a d. duck** si Papa l'apprend, gare à toi!; **the plan's a d. duck** c'est un plan foireux

2 *(lacking sensitivity) (finger)* mort, engourdi; **to go d.** *(of limb)* s'engourdir; **to be d. to the world** *(asleep)* être profondément endormi; *(in drunken stupor)* être complètement hébété; **d. to all sense of honour** insensible à tout sentiment d'honneur

3 *(lacking power, energy, activity, validity etc) (fire)* mort; *(voice, eyes)* éteint; *(colour)* terne; *(sound)* mat; *Elec (wire)* hors *ou* sans tension; *(battery)* épuisé; *(town)* mort; **this place is d. in winter** cet endroit est mort l'hiver; *Tel* **the phone is** *or* **has gone d.** il n'y a pas de tonalité; **the line is** *or* **has gone d.** la ligne a été coupée; **the d. hand of tradition** le poids de la tradition

4 *(absolute, total)* **to fall into a d. faint** tomber en pâmoison, s'évanouir; *Naut* **by d. reckoning** à l'estime; *Fam* **to make a d. set at sb** chercher à tout prix à mettre le grappin sur qn; *Fam* **to make a d. set at sth** vouloir obtenir qch à tout prix

NPL *(deceased)* **the d.** les morts *mpl*; **to rise from the d.** ressusciter des morts

N *(depths)* **at d. of night** au plus profond de la nuit; **in the d. of winter** au plus fort de l'hiver

ADV 1 *Fam (very)* **d. easy/simple** facile/simple comme tout; **d. clever/interesting** super *ou* vachement intelligent/intéressant; **d. boring** vraiment rasoir

2 *(completely)* absolument; **d. beat** crevé; *Fam* **d. broke** fauché; **d. certain** sûr et certain, absolument certain; **d. drunk** ivre mort; **to be d. (set) against sth** être absolument opposé à qch; **with the tide running d. against us** avec le courant en plein contre nous; **d. ahead (of sb)** droit devant (qn); *Naut* **wind d. ahead** vent droit debout; **d. on the hour/half-past six** à l'heure/six heures et demi tapante(s); **he was d. right** il avait absolument raison; **d. slow** aussi lentement que possible; *(road sign)* au pas; *Hum* **he has two speeds – d. slow and stop** il a deux vitesses – la première et le point mort; **d. smooth surface** surface parfaitement plane; **d. sure** absolument certain, sûr et certain; **d. tired** mort de fatigue; **to be d. wrong** avoir complètement tort, se tromper du tout au tout; **to stop d.** s'arrêter net

▸▸ *Radio* **d. air** temps *m* mort; *Mil* **d. angle** angle *m* mort; *Ftbl* **d. ball** ballon *m* mort; *Naut* **d. calm** calme *m* plat; *Tech* **d. centre** point *m* mort; *(of lathe)* centre *m* fixe; **d. end** *(road)* cul-de-sac *m*, *pl* culs-de-sac, impasse *f*, voie *f* sans issue; *(of pipe)* bout *m* aveugle; *Fig* **to reach** *or* **come to a d. end** arriver à une impasse; **d.-end job** emploi *m* sans avenir; **d. heat** = course *f* dont les vainqueurs sont déclarés ex aequo; *Horseracing* dead-heat *m*, *pl* dead-heats; **it was a d. heat** il y a eu une arrivée exæquo; **d. language** langue *f* morte; **d. letter** lettre *f* de rebut; **to become a d. letter** *(of regulation)* tomber en désuétude; **d.-letter office** bureau *m* des rebuts; **d. level** niveau *m* parfait; **d. load** *Constr* poids *m* mort; *Aut* poids utile; *Br* **d. loss** *Com* perte *f* sèche; *Fam (person)* propre *mf* à rien; **this is a bit of a d. loss** *(party, meeting)* on perd notre temps ici; *Fig* **d. man** *(empty bottle)* cadavre *m*; **d. man's fingers** *(coral)* alcyon *m*; **d. man's handle** *(on train controls)* manette *f*, homme *m* mort; **d. march** marche *f* funèbre; *Fam* **d. ringer** sosie *m* (**for** de);

they're d. ringers ils se ressemblent comme deux gouttes d'eau; **the D. Sea** la mer Morte; **d. silence** silence *m* complet *ou* de mort; **d. stop** arrêt *m* brutal; **d. water** eau *f* stagnante; *Naut* remous *m* de sillage **d. weight** *Constr* poids mort; *Aut* poids utile; *Fig* **he's a d. weight** c'est un poids mort

dead-and-alive ADJ mort, triste; **a d. hole** un trou perdu, *Sl* un bled

deadbeat ['dedbiːt] **N** *esp Am Fam Pej (good-for-nothing)* bon *m* à rien, bonne *f* à rien; *(tramp)* épave *f*, loque *f*; *(parasite)* pique-assiette *mf*, *pl* pique-assiettes

deaden ['ded(ə)n] **VT** *(blow)* amortir; *(pain)* endormir; *(sound)* assourdir, étouffer; *(senses)* émousser; *(feeling)* étouffer; **they had become deadened to …** ils étaient devenus insensibles à …

deadening ['ded(ə)nɪŋ] **N** *(of blow)* amortissement *m*; *(of noise, sound)* assourdissement *m*
ADJ *(conformity, task)* engourdissant

deadhead ['dedhed] **N** *Fam* **1** *esp Am (dullard)* nullité *f* **2** *Am (person with free ticket) (in theatre)* personne *f* en possession d'un billet de faveur; *(on train)* personne en possession d'un titre de transport gratuit
VT to d. flowers *(in garden)* enlever les fleurs fanées
▸▸ **d. flight** parcours *m* à vide

deadline ['dedlaɪn] **N** *(day)* date *f* limite; *(time)* heure *f* limite; *(of journalist)* délai *m* de remise; **to work to a d.** travailler en fonction d'une date/heure limite; **the d. for returning your essays** la date limite *ou* la dernière limite pour rendre vos dissertations; **Monday is the absolute d.** c'est pour lundi dernier délai *ou* dernière limite; **to meet a d.** respecter un délai

deadliness ['dedlɪnɪs] **N 1** *(of poison etc)* nature *f* mortelle; *Fig (of wit, repartee)* mordant *m*, causticité *f* **2** *Fam (boredom)* ennui *m* mortel; **the utter d. of her style is difficult to describe** son style est tellement ennuyeux qu'on a peine à le décrire

deadlock ['dedlɒk] **N 1** impasse *f*; *Comput* interblocage *m*, impasse; **to reach d.** arriver à une impasse; **to break the d.** sortir de l'impasse **2** *Tech* serrure *f* à pêne dormant; *Aut* serrure passive
VT talks are deadlocked les discussions n'atteint une impasse, les discussions en sont au point mort

deadly ['dedlɪ] **ADJ 1** *(mortal) (poison, blow, enemy etc)* mortel; *(weapon)* meurtrier; *(hatred)* implacable, mortel; *(combat)* à mort; *Fig (pallor, silence etc)* de mort; *(wit, satire)* mordant, caustique; *also Fig* **to d. effect** de façon dévastatrice; **the seven d. sins** les sept péchés *mpl* capitaux **2** *Fam (boring)* mortel, rasant
ADV 1 *(pale)* comme un linge **2** *(completely)* **d. accurate** extrêmement précis; **d. boring** mortellement ennuyeux; *Fam* **d. dull** rasant; **to be d. serious** être tout à fait sérieux; **to speak in d. earnest** être absolument sincère
▸▸ *Bot* **d. nightshade** belladone *f*

deadpan ['dedpæn] **ADJ** *(face)* impassible, figé; *(humour)* de pince-sans-rire

deadweight ['dedweɪt] **N** *Com* port *m* en lourd
▸▸ **d. tonnage** *(of ship)* tonnage *m* port en lourd

deadwood ['dedwʊd] **N** *Fig (person)* personne *f* improductive; *(thing)* chose *f* inutile; **there is too much d. in this office** il y a trop de gens payés à ne rien faire dans ce bureau

deaf [def] **ADJ** sourd; **to go d.** devenir sourd; **d. in one ear** sourd d'une oreille; **d. and dumb** sourd-muet, *f* sourde-muette, *pl* sourds-muets, sourdes-muettes; **d. as a**

(door)post sourd comme un pot; *Prov* **there are none so d. as those that will not hear** il n'y a pire sourd que celui qui ne veut (pas) entendre; *Fig* **d. to entreaties** sourd aux supplications; **to turn a d. ear to** *(person)* refuser d'écouter; *(pleas)* rester sourd à; **to fall on d. ears** ne pas être entendu
NPL the d. les sourds *mpl*

deaf-aid **N** appareil *m* acoustique

deafen ['def(ə)n] **VT** *(somebody)* assourdir, rendre sourd; **you're deafening me** vous me cassez les oreilles

deafening ['def(ə)nɪŋ] **ADJ** *(noise)* assourdissant

deaf-mute **N** sourd-muet, *f* sourde-muette, *pl* sourds-muets, sourdes-muettes

deafness ['defnɪs] **N** surdité *f*, *Fig* **their d. to any appeal** le fait qu'ils sont restés sourds à tout appel

DEAL [diːl]

N	affaire **1** ▪ donne **2**
VT	donner **1**
VI	négocier **1** ▪ donner **2** ▪ dealer **3**

N 1 *Com etc* affaire *f*, marché *m*; **d. on the Stock Exchange** coup *m* de Bourse; **big d.** grosse affaire; *Fam Iron* la belle affaire!; **it's no big d.** *(no problem)* c'est pas un problème; **don't make such a big d. out of it!** c'est pas la peine d'en faire tout un plat; **cash d.** transaction *f* au comptant; *Hist* **the New D.** le New Deal; **package d.** contrat *m* global; **to do a d.** conclure une affaire *ou* un marché (**with sb** avec qn); **it's a d.!** d'accord!, entendu!; *Pol* **d. between parties** accord *m* entre partis; **to give sb a fair d.** offrir un bon prix à qn; *Fig* offrir un traitement équitable à qn

2 *Cards* donne *f*, **whose d. is it?** à qui de donner?; **your d.!** à vous la donne!

3 a good d. *(a lot)* beaucoup; **I have a great/good d. to do** j'ai beaucoup de/bien des choses à faire; **there's a great d. of truth in that** il y a beaucoup de vrai là-dedans; **a good d. of my time** une bonne partie de mon temps; **I think a great d. of him** je l'estime beaucoup; **not a great d.** pas énormément

VT *(pt, pp* **dealt** [delt]*)* **1** *(cards)* donner, distribuer

2 to d. sb a blow porter un coup à qn; **the news dealt a serious blow to her hopes of winning** la nouvelle a sérieusement entamé ses chances de gagner

3 *Fam (drugs)* dealer

VI 1 *(trade)* négocier, traiter; **the firm has been dealing for over 50 years** cette société est en activité depuis plus de 50 ans; **to d. in leather/in options** faire le commerce des cuirs/des primes

2 *Cards* faire la donne, donner, *Fam* faire

3 *(in drugs)* dealer

▸ **deal in** VT SEP **to d. sb in** *Cards* donner *ou* distribuer des cartes à qn, servir qn; *Fig (in criminal activity)* inclure qn dans l'affaire; *Fig* **d. me in!** je suis partant!

▸ **deal out** VT SEP *(supplies)* distribuer (**to**, **among** entre); *(cards)* donner, distribuer; **to d. out justice** rendre la justice; **to d. out criticism** critiquer à tour de bras

▸ **deal with** VT INSEP **1** *(do business with)* avoir affaire à *ou* avec; *Com* traiter *ou* négocier avec; *(get supplies from) (grocer etc)* se fournir chez; **man easy/difficult to d. with** homme commode/peu commode

2 *(be about) (subject)* traiter de

3 *(handle) (person, problem, situation)* s'occuper de; *Com (order)* donner suite à; **I know how to d. with him** je sais m'y prendre avec lui; **I'll d. with this** je m'en occupe

dealbreaker ['diːlbreɪkər] N = événement m ou décision f qui rend impossible toute poursuite des négociations

dealer ['diːlər] N **1** *Cards* donneur, -euse **2** *Com* négociant m (**in** en); *(supplier)* fournisseur m (**in** de); *St Exch* marchand, -ande de titres; *Aut etc* concessionnaire m, distributeur m; *(in drugs)* dealer m, trafiquant, -ante ▸▸ *Com* **d. brand** marque f de revendeur; *Mktg* **d. test** test m auprès des distributeurs

dealership ['diːləʃɪp] N *Aut* concession f

dealing ['diːlɪŋ] N *St Exch* transactions fpl; *(in drugs)* vente f ▸▸ **d. out** *(of supplies)* distribution f, *St Exch* **d. room** salle f de marchés

dealings ['diːlɪŋz] NPL relations fpl, rapports mpl; *Pej* tractations fpl (**with** avec); *Com* transactions fpl; **to have d. with sb** avoir des rapports avec qn; *Com* faire ou traiter des affaires avec qn

dean [diːn] N *Rel, Univ* doyen m

deanery ['diːnərɪ] N *Rel* résidence f du doyen

dear [dɪər] ADJ **1** *(loved)* cher, f chère (**to** à); **he is d. to me** il m'est cher; **a d. friend of mine** un de mes chers amis; **my dearest wish is that …** mon vœu le plus cher est que …; **a place d. to the hearts of …** un endroit qui est cher à …; *Old-fashioned* **my d. chap** *or* **fellow, …** mon cher ami, …; **all that I hold d.** tout ce qui m'est cher; **what a d. little child!** quel amour d'enfant!; **a d. little house** une petite maison coquette; *Fam* **to run for d. life** courir aussi vite que possible **2** *(in letter)* **D. Sir** Monsieur; **D. Madam** Madame; **D. Sir or Madam** Monsieur, Madame; **D. Mr Thomas** Cher Monsieur; **D. John Smith** Cher Monsieur Smith; **D. Alice** (Ma) chère Alice; **D. Alan and Avril** Chers Alan et Avril; *esp Am Fam* **a D. John letter** une lettre de rupture **3** *(costly)* cher, f chère, coûteux; **to get** *or* **become dearer** augmenter; **don't get the d./dearest ones!** ne prends pas les chers/plus chers!

N *(friend)* cher m, chère f, *(darling)* chéri, -ie; **you poor d.** mon/ma pauvre; **my d.** *(adult friend)* cher ami, f chère amie; *(darling)* mon chéri, f ma chérie; *(child)* mon petit chou; *Fam* **old d.** grand-mère f, pl grand(s)-mères; **you're a d.!** tu es un amour!; **be a d. and …** sois gentil/gentille et …

ADV *(to buy, sell, pay)* cher; *Fig* **he sold his life d.** il vendit chèrement sa vie

INT **d. d.!, d. me!** mon Dieu, mon Dieu!; **(dear) oh d.!** *(what have I done)* oh là là!; *(that's a pity)* hélas!; **oh d. no!** (oh) que non! ▸▸ *Fin* **d. money** argent m cher

dearie ['dɪərɪ] *Fam* N mon (petit) chéri, f ma (petite) chérie INT **d. me!** mon Dieu!

dearly ['dɪəlɪ] ADV **1** *(very much)* **I love him d.** je l'aime tendrement ou de tout mon cœur; **he d. loves to play jokes on people** il trouve tout son plaisir à jouer des tours aux gens; **I would d. like to meet her** je souhaite de tout mon cœur la rencontrer **2** *Fml (at great cost)* cher; **their success was d. won** leur victoire leur a coûté cher; **you shall pay d. for this** cela vous coûtera cher

dearness ['dɪənɪs] N **1** *(expensiveness) (of foodstuffs etc)* cherté f; **the d. of the prices** les prix élevés **2** *(lovableness)* **her d. to me** l'affection ou l'attachement que j'ai pour elle

dearth [dɜːθ] N *Fml (of supplies, books etc)* disette f, pénurie f, *(of ideas, information)* pénurie, pauvreté f

DEATH [deθ] N **1** *(end of life)* mort f, *Law, Admin* décès m; *Journ* **deaths** nécrologie f, **six food-poisoning deaths have been reported** on a signalé six décès par intoxication alimentaire; **there has been a d. in the family** il y a eu un décès dans la famille; **to die a violent d.** mourir de mort violente; **he died an easy d.** il n'a pas souffert; **at (the time of) his d.** à sa mort; **until d.** pour la vie; **till d. us do part** *(in marriage ceremony)* jusqu'à ce que la mort nous sépare; **a fight to the d.** une lutte à mort; **he fell to his d.** il a fait une chute mortelle; **to send sb to his/her d.** envoyer qn à la mort; **to be at d.'s door** *or* **on the verge of d.** être sur le point de mourir; **to drink/smoke oneself to d.** se tuer à force de boire/fumer; **to stab sb to d.** tuer qn à coups de couteau; **to work sb to d.** tuer qn à force de surmenage; **to be burnt to d.** *(accidentally)* périr dans les flammes; *(as form of martyrdom)* périr sur le bûcher; **to starve sb to d.** faire mourir qn de faim; **to beat sb to d.** battre qn à mort; **one false move could mean d.** *(for trapeze artist etc)* un faux mouvement pourrait entraîner la mort; **d. to traitors!** à mort les traîtres!

2 *(execution)* **to put sb to d.** mettre qn à mort, exécuter qn; **condemned to d., under sentence of d.** condamné à mort

3 *Fam (indicating exaggeration)* **to be sick to d. of sth** en avoir marre de qch; **you'll catch your d. (of cold)** vous allez attraper la crève; **that play has been done to d.** cette pièce a été beaucoup trop jouée; **he'll be the d. of me (yet)** il me fera mourir; **that car will be the d. of her** elle va se tuer avec cette voiture; **it would be the d. of him** ce serait sa mort; **to look like d. (warmed up)** avoir une mine de déterré

4 *Fig (end)* **the d. of one's hopes/plans** la fin de ses espoirs/projets; **to be in at the d.** assister au dénouement

▸▸ *Zool* **d. adder** acanthopis m, serpent m de la mort; *Fin* **d. benefit** capital m décès; **d. camp** camp m de la mort; *Bot* **d. cap** amanite f phalloïde; **d. cell** cellule f de condamné à mort; **d. certificate** acte m ou certificat m de décès; **deaths column** rubrique f nécrologique; *Formerly* **d. duties** droits mpl de succession; **d. knell** glas m; *Fig* **to sound the d. knell (for)** sonner le glas (de); **d. mask** masque m mortuaire; **d. penalty** peine f de mort, peine capitale; **d. rate** taux m de mortalité; **d. rattle** râle m d'agonie; **d. row** quartier m des condamnés à mort; *Am, Austr Fam* **d. seat** *(in a vehicle)* place f du mort; **d. squad** escadron m de la mort; **d. taxes** droits mpl de succession; **d. throes** agonie f, *(painful)* affres fpl de la mort; *Fig* **it was agonizing to watch her d. throes** c'était atroce de la voir à l'agonie; *Fig* **the project was in its d. throes** le projet était à ses dernières heures; **d. toll** nombre m de morts; **D. Valley** la Vallée de la Mort; **d. warrant** ordre m d'exécution; *Fig* **you've just signed your own d. warrant** tu viens de signer ton arrêt de mort; *Psy* **d. wish** désir m de mort

deathbed ['deθbed] N lit m de mort; **d. confession** confession f faite sur le lit de mort

deathblow ['deθbləʊ] N coup m mortel ou fatal; *Fig* **marriage was** *or* **dealt a d. to her career** le mariage a porté un coup mortel à sa carrière

deathless ['deθlɪs] ADJ *Lit* impérissable, immortel; *Hum Iron* **d. prose** prose f immortelle

deathlike ['deθlaɪk] ADJ *(pallor etc)* de mort

deathly ['deθlɪ] ADJ *(pallor)* de mort, cadavérique; *(calm)* sépulcral, -aux; **d. silence** silence m de mort

ADV comme la mort; **d. pale** d'une pâleur mortelle, mortellement pâle

death's-head ['deθshed] N tête f de mort ▸▸ **d. moth** (sphinx m) atropos m

deathtrap ['deθtræp] N *(place)* endroit m dangereux; *(vehicle)* véhicule m dangereux; **the house is a d.** cette maison est dangereuse

deathwatch beetle ['deθwɒtʃ] N *Entom* grande ou grosse vrillette f, horloger m de la mort

deb [deb] N *Br Fam* débutante f; **d.'s delight** beau parti m

debacle [deɪ'bɑːk(ə)l] N débâcle f

debag [diː'bæg] VT **(-gg-)** *Old-fashioned Br Fam* déculotter

debar [diː'bɑːr] VT **(-rr-)** **to d. sb from sth** exclure qn de qch, interdire qch à qn; **to d. sb from doing sth** interdire à qn de faire qch; **to be debarred from membership of sth** se voir refuser l'adhésion à qch

debase [dɪ'beɪs] VT **1** *(degrade) (person)* avilir, dégrader; *(one's style)* rabaisser **2** *(make less valuable) (metal)* altérer; *(currency)* déprécier

debasement [dɪ'beɪsmənt] N **1** *(of person)* avilissement m **2** *(of currency)* dépréciation f

debatable [dɪ'beɪtəb(ə)l] ADJ contestable, discutable; **it's d. whether he is to blame or she is** il est difficile de dire si c'est lui ou elle qui est à blâmer

debate [dɪ'beɪt] N discussion f, *(esp formal, parliamentary)* débat m; **after much d.** après bien des discussions; **there has been some d. over the effectiveness of the treatment** l'efficacité du traitement a été mise en doute; **he was a tough opponent in d.** c'était un rude adversaire dans les débats; **the issue has been in** *or* **under d. for some time** cette question est débattue depuis un certain temps

VT *(question etc)* débattre, discuter, agiter; *(subject)* mettre en discussion; **a much/fiercely debated question** une question fort controversée/vivement débattue; **we don't have time to d. the issue now** on n'a plus le temps de discuter le problème; **I was debating (with myself** *or* **in my mind) whether to go or not** je délibérais si j'irais ou non

VI discuter (**with sb on sth** avec qn sur qch); *(take part in a debate)* prendre part à un débat; **she frequently debated for her university** elle prenait souvent part à des débats pour son université

debater [dɪ'beɪtər] N spécialiste mf des débats

debating [dɪ'beɪtɪŋ] N **she took up d. at university** elle a pris part à des débats formels à l'université ▸▸ **d. society** société f de débats contradictoires

debauch [dɪ'bɔːtʃ] N débauche f, **it degenerated into a drunken d.** ça a tourné à l'ivrognerie

VT *Old-fashioned (person)* débaucher; *(taste)* corrompre

debauched [dɪ'bɔːtʃt] ADJ *(person)* débauché; *(morals, tastes)* corrompu; *(life)* de débauche

debauchee [dɪbɔː'tʃiː] N *Arch* débauché, -ée

debauchery [dɪ'bɔːtʃərɪ] N débauche f, **drunken d.** ivrognerie f, **his numberless debaucheries** ses innombrables descentes dans la débauche

debenture [dɪ'bentʃər] N *Fin* obligation f ADJ obligataire ▸▸ **d. bond** titre m d'obligation, *Can* débenture f, **d. holder** obligataire mf, détenteur, -trice d'obligations; **d. issue** émission f d'obligations; **d. loan** emprunt m obligataire; **d. stock** obligation f sans garantie

debilitate [dɪ'bɪlɪteɪt] VT débiliter

debilitating [dɪ'bɪlɪteɪtɪŋ] ADJ *(climate, heat)* débilitant; *(illness)* affaiblissant; **it**

had a d. effect on her concentration cela a provoqué une baisse de sa concentration

debility [dɪ'bɪlɪtɪ] N Med débilité f, asthénie f

debit ['debɪt] Fin N débit m; **to the d. of** au débit de; **d. and credit** doit m et avoir m ▸ VT (account) débiter; **to d. sb with a sum** porter une somme au débit de qn, débiter qn d'une somme; **to d. an amount to an account** porter un montant au débit d'un compte, débiter un compte d'un montant; **has this cheque been debited to my account?** est-ce que ce chèque a été débité de mon compte?
▸ ▸ **d. account** compte m débiteur; Fin **d. advice** avis m de débit; **d. balance** solde m débiteur ou déficitaire; Banking (of account) position f débitrice; Banking **d. card** = carte f de paiement à débit immédiat; Acct **d. column** colonne f débitrice ou des débits; **d. entry** Acct écriture f passée au débit; Banking article m porté au débit d'un compte; Fin **d. interest** intérêts mpl débiteurs; Acct **d. item** poste m débiteur; Fin **d. note** note f de débit; Acct **d. side** débit m; **to enter sth on the d. side of an account** porter qch au débit d'un compte; Fig **on the d. side** sur le plan négatif

debonair [debə'neər] ADJ (person) d'une élégance nonchalante; (smile, charm) nonchalant; **you look very d.** tu es vraiment élégant

debouch [dɪ'baʊtʃ] VI Geog, Mil déboucher (into dans)

debrief [diː'briːf] VT Mil, Aviat etc (pilot etc) faire faire un compte-rendu (de fin de mission) à; **to be debriefed** faire un rapport

debriefing [diː'briːfɪŋ] N rapport m (de fin de mission), debriefing m

debris ['debriː] N débris mpl, Fig (after party) détritus mpl, Fig **to salvage something from the d. of one's marriage** sauver quelque chose des restes de son mariage

debt [det] N dette f, (to be recovered) créance f, **bad d.** mauvaise créance; **to be in d.** être endetté, avoir des dettes; **to be £12,000 in d.** avoir 12 000 livres de dettes; **to be in d. to sb** être en dette envers qn; **to repay a d.** régler une dette; **to be out of d.** n'avoir plus de dettes, être quitte; **to get** or **run into d.** s'endetter, faire des dettes; Fam **to be up to the** or **one's ears in d.** être criblé de dettes; Fig **I shall always be in your d.** je vous serai toujours redevable; **to owe sb a d. of gratitude** avoir une dette de reconnaissance envers qn; **d. of honour** dette d'honneur
▸ ▸ **d. capacity** capacité f d'endettement; **d. chasing letter** lettre f de poursuite, lettre de relance des impayés; Fin **d. collection** recouvrement m ou récupération f des créances; **d. collection agency** bureau m de recouvrement ou récupération des créances; **d. collector** agent m de recouvrement; **d. due** créance f exigible; St Exch **d. equity swap** échange m de créances contre actifs; **d. financing** financement m par endettement; **d. instrument** titre m de créance; **d. rating** rating m de la dette; **d. ratio** ratio m d'endettement; **d. rescheduling** rééchelonnement m des dettes; **d. servicing** service m de la dette; **d. swap** échange m de créances

debtor ['detər] N débiteur, -trice
▸ ▸ Acct **d. account** compte m débiteur; **d. nation** pay m débiteur; Acct **d. side** débit m, doit m

debug [diː'bʌg] VT 1 (remove faults in) Comput (program) déboguer; (prototype etc) éliminer les erreurs de; (machine) dépanner 2 (remove microphones from) (room) débarrasser des microphones clandestins
▸ ▸ Comput **d. facility** option f de débogage, programme m débogueur

debugger [diː'bʌgər] N Comput (programme m) débogueur m

debugging [diː'bʌgɪŋ] N Comput débogage m

debunk [diː'bʌŋk] VT Fam (somebody) déboulonner, ridiculiser; (theory) discréditer; **to d. a myth** détruire un mythe

debut ['deɪbjuː] N début m; (in society) entrée f dans le monde; **to make one's d.** (of actor etc) débuter, faire ses débuts (**as** dans le rôle de)
▸ VI esp Am débuter; **she debut'd** ['deɪbjuːd] **in the role of …** elle a fait ses débuts ou a débuté dans le rôle de …

debutante ['debjʊtɑːnt, -tænt] N Br débutante f

Dec abbr December

decade ['dekeɪd] N 1 (ten years) décennie f, (of French republican calendar) décade; **a few decades ago** il y a quelques dizaines d'années 2 Rel (of rosary) dizaine f 3 Comput décade f

> Note that the French word **décade** is a false friend. It usually refers to a period of ten days.

decadence ['dekədəns] N 1 (of society etc) décadence f 2 Liter, Art décadentisme m

decadent ['dekədənt] ADJ décadent; **to become d.** tomber dans la décadence; Hum **how d.!** quelle décadence!
▸ N Liter, Art décadent m

decaf ['diːkæf] N Fam déca m

decaffeinate [diː'kæfineɪt] VT décaféiner

decaffeinated [diː'kæfineɪtɪd] ADJ décaféiné

decagram(me) ['dekəgræm] N décagramme m

decal [dɪ'kæl, 'diːkæl] N Am Fam décalcomanie f

decalcification [diːkælsɪfɪ'keɪʃən] N décalcification f

decalcify [diː'kælsɪfaɪ] VT (bones etc) décalcifier

Decalogue ['dekəlɒg] N Bible Décalogue m

decamp [diː'kæmp] VI Mil lever le camp; Fam (leave) aller s'installer ailleurs; (leave suddenly, secretively etc) décamper, filer, lever le camp; **to d. to another room** aller s'installer dans une autre pièce

decant [dɪ'kænt] VT (liquid) transvaser; (bottle of wine) décanter dans une carafe etc, Fam (move, transfer) (people to a different district etc) transférer

decanter [dɪ'kæntər] N (for wine etc) carafe f

decapitate [dɪ'kæpɪteɪt] VT décapiter

decapitation [dɪkæpɪ'teɪʃən] N décapitation f

decapod ['dekəpɒd] N (crustacean) décapode m

decarbonize [diː'kɑːbənaɪz] VT 1 Metal (steel etc) décarburer, décarboniser 2 Aut (cylinder head) décalaminer

decathlete [dɪ'kæθliːt] N Sport décathlonien, -ienne

decathlon [dɪ'kæθlɒn] N Sport décathlon m

decay [dɪ'keɪ] N 1 (rot) (of wood etc) pourriture f, corruption f, décomposition f, (of teeth) carie f 2 (decline) (of family, country etc) décadence f, déchéance f, (of beauty etc) déclin m; (of faculties) dégradation f, (of building) délabrement m; **moral d.** déchéance morale; **to fall into d.** (of house) tomber en ruine, se délabrer; (of state) tomber en décadence; **in a state of d.** (tooth) carié; (body) en état de décomposition; (building) délabré
▸ VT (teeth) carier

▸ VI 1 (rot) (of meat, fruit) se gâter, pourrir; (of timber) pourrir; (of teeth) se carier 2 (decline) (of nation, family) tomber en décadence; (of building) tomber en ruine, se délabrer; (of empire) décliner; (of beauty) (se) passer, se flétrir
▸ ▸ Phys **d. time** période f d'extinction

decayed [dɪ'keɪd] ADJ (civilization) en ruines; (building, part of town) délabré 2 (wood, fruit, flesh) pourri; (tooth) carié

decaying [dɪ'keɪɪŋ] ADJ 1 (in decline) (empire, civilization) sur le déclin; (building, part of town) qui se délabre; **his d. fortunes** ses richesses qui s'amenuisent 2 (rotting) pourrissant; (teeth) en train de former des caries

decease [dɪ'siːs] Law, Admin N décès m
▸ VI décéder

> Attention: ne pas confondre avec le nom **disease**.

deceased [dɪ'siːst] ADJ décédé; **son of Robert Martin, d.** fils de feu M. Robert Martin
▸ N **the d.** le défunt/la défunte/les défunt(e)s

decedent [dɪ'siːdənt] N Am Law défunt, -unte

deceit [dɪ'siːt] N 1 (action) supercherie f, tromperie f, Law fraude f, **to practice d. on sb** user de tromperie ou de fourberie envers qn 2 = **deceitfulness**

deceitful [dɪ'siːtfʊl] ADJ trompeur, -euse, fourbe; **to be d.** (of person) être faux; **it was very d. of her** c'était très malhonnête de sa part

deceitfully [dɪ'siːtfʊlɪ] ADV avec duplicité; **to obtain sth d.** obtenir qch en usant de duplicité; **the message was d. worded** le message avait été rédigé de manière à tromper; **d., she omitted to mention the fact** par duplicité, elle s'est gardée de mentionner ce fait

deceitfulness [dɪ'siːtfʊlnɪs] N fausseté f, duplicité f

deceive [dɪ'siːv] VT (person) tromper, abuser; (one's wife, husband) tromper; (sb's hopes) tromper, décevoir; **don't be deceived** ne vous y fiez pas; **to be deceived by appearances** se laisser tromper par les apparences; **to d. oneself** s'abuser, se méprendre; **don't d. yourself that it will be easy** ne croyez pas que ce sera facile; **to d. sb into thinking sth** faire croire qch à qn; **they deceived the electorate into voting for them by promising tax cuts** ils ont persuadé les électeurs de voter pour eux en promettant de diminuer les impôts; **I thought my eyes were deceiving me** je ne pouvais pas en croire mes yeux
▸ VI tromper; **it was not done with intent to d.** cela n'a pas été fait dans l'intention de tromper

> Note that the French verb **décevoir** is a false friend and is never a translation for the English verb **to deceive**. It means **to disappoint**.

deceiver [dɪ'siːvər] N trompeur, -euse

decelerate [diː'seləreɪt] VI ralentir

deceleration [diːselə'reɪʃən] N ralentissement m, décélération f
▸ ▸ **d. lane** voie f de décélération

December [dɪ'sembər] N VOIR GRAMMAIRE A81–2; B60–2 décembre m; **in D.** en décembre, au mois de décembre; **(on) the first/the seventh of D.** le premier/le sept décembre

decency ['diːsənsɪ] N 1 (of dress etc) décence f 2 (convention) bienséance f, convenances fpl, **common d.** les convenances (sociales); **he didn't even have the (common) d. to let us know** il n'a pas eu la bienséance élémentaire de nous informer; **the decencies** les convenances; **to observe the decencies** observer les convenances

decent ['diːsənt] ADJ **1** *(suitable)* bienséant, convenable; *(respectable)* décent, honnête; *Fam* **are you d.?** est-ce que tu es visible?; *Old-fashioned* **to do the d. thing** *(do what is required)* faire le nécessaire; *(marry sb)* faire son devoir *(et épouser la femme qu'on a mise enceinte)*; *Mil (commit suicide)* faire la seule chose possible dans les circonstances **2** *(acceptable)* passable; **this wine is quite d.** ce vin est très buvable *ou* se laisse boire; **the flat is quite a d. size** l'appartement est d'une taille raisonnable; **I earn a d. wage** je gagne un salaire décent; **wait until you have a d. amount of money** attends d'avoir suffisamment d'argent **3** *Fam (kind)* **a d. (sort of) chap** un bon type; **it's very d. of you** c'est très gentil de votre part

decently ['diːsəntlɪ] ADV **1** *(respectably)* décemment, convenablement; **I can't d. ...** décemment je ne peux pas ... **2** *Fam (acceptably well)* pas trop mal; **he pays quite d.** il ne paie pas mal **3** *(honourably)* de façon correcte, correctement; **he's treated me really d.** il m'a traité de façon vraiment correcte

decentralization [diːsentrəlaɪˈzeɪʃən] N décentralisation *f*

decentralize [diːˈsentrəlaɪz] VT décentraliser; *Comput* **decentralized processing** traitement *m* décentralisé

decent-sized ADJ *(house etc)* de bonnes dimensions

deception [dɪˈsepʃən] N tromperie *f*, supercherie *f*; **to obtain sth by d.** obtenir qch en usant de tromperie *ou* de supercherie; **thanks to their d. of the enemy** parce qu'ils étaient parvenus à tromper l'ennemi

Note that the French word **déception** is a false friend and is never a translation for the English word **deception**. It means **disappointment**.

deceptive [dɪˈseptɪv] ADJ *(thing, appearance)* trompeur, -euse; **he** *or* **his manner is very d.** on ne peut jamais deviner ce qu'il va faire/dire

deceptively [dɪˈseptɪvlɪ] ADV **he has a d. quiet manner** il a un air tranquille (bien) trompeur; **d. worded/written** trompeur; **it looks d. simple** *or* **easy** ce n'est pas aussi simple *ou* facile que ça en a l'air; **the mountains seem d. close** les montagnes paraissent plus proches qu'elles ne le sont en réalité; **the chair is d. light** en dépit de sa légèreté, la chaise est très robuste

deceptiveness [dɪˈseptɪvnɪs] N *(of sth)* caractère *m* trompeur

decibel ['desɪbel] N *Phys* décibel *m*
▸▸ **d. level** niveau *m* en décibels

decide [dɪˈsaɪd] VT *(question)* trancher; *(result of match, sb's fate, career etc)* décider de; **nothing has been** *or* **is decided yet** il n'y a encore rien de décidé; **that decided me** cela me décida (**to do** à faire); **to d. to do sth** se décider *ou* se résoudre à faire qch, décider *ou* résoudre de faire qch; **it was decided to wait for his reply** on a décidé d'attendre sa réponse

VI **have you decided?** êtes-vous décidé?; **you d.** décide, toi; **to d. on** *(plan of action)* arrêter; *(work procedure)* déterminer; *(day)* fixer; **have you decided on a date/a name?** vous êtes-vous décidés sur une date/un nom?; **I've decided on Greece for my holiday** j'ai décidé d'aller passer mes vacances en Grèce; **to d. on doing sth** décider de faire qch; **to d. against sth** *(give verdict)* se prononcer contre qch; **we've decided against a holiday this year** nous avons décidé de ne pas prendre de vacances cette année

decided [dɪˈsaɪd] ADJ **1** *(tone)* résolu; *(re-*

fusal) catégorique, net; *(opinion)* ferme; **they are quite d. about it** ils sont tout à fait décidés **2** *(distinct) (difference)* marqué, prononcé; *(change)* sensible; *(success)* incontestable; *(preference)* net, *f* nette; **it's a d. improvement** c'est nettement mieux

decidedly [dɪˈsaɪdɪdlɪ] ADV **1** *(to answer, say)* d'un ton résolu **2** *(distinctly)* franchement

Note that the French word **décidément** is a false friend and is never a translation for the English word **decidedly**.

decider [dɪˈsaɪdər] N *(factor)* facteur *m* décisif; *Sport (goal)* but *m* décisif; *(point)* point *m* décisif; **the d.** *(game, match)* la belle

deciding [dɪˈsaɪdɪŋ] ADJ *(factor, vote)* décisif; *Sport* **the d. game/set/match** la belle; **the chairman has the d. vote** la voix du président est décisive *ou* prépondérante

deciduous [dɪˈsɪdjʊəs] ADJ *Bot* à feuilles caduques; *Zool (antlers etc)* caduc

decilitre, *Am* **deciliter** ['desɪliːtər] N décilitre *m*

decimal ['desɪm(ə)l] [VOIR GRAMMAIRE A76; B59] ADJ *(fraction, system, coinage etc)* décimal, -aux; *Comput* **position** décimale; **correct to five d. places** exact jusqu'à la cinquième décimale; *Fam* **to go d.** adopter le système décimal
N fraction *f* décimale
▸▸ **d. coding** codification *f* décimale; *Math* **d. place** décimale *f*; *Math* **d. point** virgule *f*

decimalization [desɪməlaɪˈzeɪʃən] N décimalisation *f*

decimate ['desɪmeɪt] VT *(of disease etc) (population etc)* décimer

decimation [desɪˈmeɪʃən] N décimation *f*

decimetre, *Am* **decimeter** ['desɪmiːtər] N *(unit of measurement)* décimètre *m*

decipher [dɪˈsaɪfər] VT *(hieroglyphs, difficult handwriting)* déchiffrer; *(coded message)* déchiffrer, décoder

decipherable [dɪˈsaɪf(ə)rəb(ə)l] ADJ déchiffrable; **easily d.** facile à déchiffrer

decision [dɪˈsɪʒən] N **1** *(of question, to do sth)* décision *f*; *(on question)* vote *m*; **to give a d.** se prononcer; **to make a d.** prendre une décision; **the judge's d. is final** *(in competition etc)* la décision du juge est irrévocable; **to come to** *or* **arrive at** *or* **reach a d.** arriver à une décision (**about** quant à, touchant); **d. by arbitration** décision *f* arbitrale **2** *(decisiveness)* résolution *f*, fermeté *f*; **..., he said with d.** ..., dit-il fermement
▸▸ **d. model** modèle *m* décisionnel *ou* déterministe *ou* de décision; **d. theory** théorie *f* de la décision; **d. tree** modèle *m* de décision en arborescence

decision-maker N décideur, -euse; **to be a good/bad d.** savoir/ne pas savoir prendre des décisions

decision-making N prise *f* de décisions
▸▸ **d. tool** outil *m* d'aide à la décision; **d. unit** unité *f* de prise de décision(s)

decision-tree analysis N analyse *f* d'un modèle de décision en arborescence

decisive [dɪˈsaɪsɪv] ADJ **1** *(question, battle, proof etc)* décisif; *(experiment etc)* concluant **2** *(manner, tone, person etc)* décidé; *(approach)* tranché

decisively [dɪˈsaɪsɪvlɪ] ADV **1** *(conclusively)* d'une façon décisive **2** *(resolutely) (to act)* de façon décidée; *(to say)* d'un ton décidé

decisiveness [dɪˈsaɪsɪvnɪs] N **1** *(of battle, question)* caractère *m* décisif; *(of experiment)* caractère concluant **2** = **decision 2**

deck [dek] N **1** *Naut* pont *m*; **on d.** sur le pont; **below deck(s)** dans l'entrepont; **after d.** pont arrière; **lower/upper d.** pont inférieur/

supérieur; **to come/go on d.** monter sur le pont; **to clear the decks (for action)** faire le branle-bas de combat; *Fig* se préparer à agir; *Fam* **to hit the d.** *(to avoid injury)* tomber à plat ventre; *(get out of bed)* se lever; **hit the d.!** *(fall to the ground)* tout le monde à plat ventre!; *(get out of bed)* debout!; *also Fig* **all hands on d.!** tous sur le pont!

2 *(of vehicle)* plate-forme *f*, *pl* plates-formes; **top d.** *(of bus)* impériale *f*

3 *Constr* tablier *m*; *(of bridge)* plancher *m*; *Am (terrace)* terrasse *f*

4 *esp Am* **d. of cards** jeu *m* de cartes; *Fam* **he's not playing with a full d.** *(isn't very bright)* il a quelques cases de vides

5 *(for records etc)* platine *f*; **cassette d.** platine à cassette; **tape d.** platine à bande magnétique

6 *Am Aut (space behind back seat)* coffre *m*; *(cover of space)* plage *f* arrière

VT **1** *(decorate)* parer, orner (**sth with sth** qch de qch); **to d. oneself out** s'endimancher; **I decked myself out in my Sunday best** j'ai mis mes habits du dimanche; **they were decked out in their best clothes** ils étaient sur leur trente et un

2 *Naut (ship)* ponter

3 *esp Am Fam (knock to ground) (person)* flanquer par terre
▸▸ *Naut* **d. cargo** pontée *f*; **d. hand** matelot *m* de pont; **d. load** pontée *f*; **d. officer** officier *m* de pont

deckchair ['dektʃeər] N transat *m*

deckhouse ['dekhaʊs] N *Naut* rouf *m*

deckle ['dek(ə)l] N *(frame) (in papermaking)* cadre *m* volant, rebord *m*
▸▸ **d. edge** *(on paper)* bord *m* frangeux, barbes *fpl*

deckle-edged ADJ *(paper)* à barbes

declaim [dɪˈkleɪm] *Fml* VI déclamer (**against** contre)
VT *(verse etc)* déclamer

declamation [dekləˈmeɪʃən] N déclamation *f*

declamatory [dɪˈklæmətərɪ, -trɪ] ADJ *(style etc)* déclamatoire

declaration [dekləˈreɪʃən] N **1** *(of love, faith, war etc)* déclaration *f* **2** *Cards* annonce *f*
▸▸ **d. of bankruptcy** jugement *m* déclaratif de faillite, déclaration de faillite; *St Exch* **d. of dividend** déclaration de dividende; *Fin* **d. of income** déclaration de revenu; *Hist* **the D. of Independence** la Déclaration d'indépendance (américaine); **d. of intent** déclaration d'intention; **d. of solvency** déclaration de solvabilité; **d. of value** déclaration de valeur

declare [dɪˈkleər] VT **1** *(formally announce)* déclarer (**sth to sb** qch à qn); **to d. a change of policy** annoncer un changement de politique; **to d. war** déclarer la guerre (**on, against** à); **the two countries have declared war** *(on each other)* les deux pays se sont déclaré la guerre; **to d. a moratorium** décréter un moratoire; **to d. a strike** proclamer la grève; **she was declared the winner** elle a été déclarée vainqueur; *Fin* **to d. a dividend of ten per cent** déclarer un dividende de dix pour cent; **to d. sb guilty/innocent** déclarer qn coupable/innocent; **to d. sb bankrupt** prononcer la faillite de qn; **to d. a business bankrupt** déclarer une entreprise en faillite **2** *Cards (make public) (trumps, suit)* appeler; *Fig* **to d. one's hand** avouer ses intentions; **to d. oneself** prendre parti; *(of lover)* se déclarer, faire sa déclaration; **have you anything to d.?** *(at customs)* avez-vous quelque chose à déclarer?; **to d. an interest** déclarer un intérêt; **to d. itself** *(of disease)* se déclarer

VI *Cr* fermer son jeu (avant la chute des dix guichets); *Cards* annoncer son jeu; *Old-*

fashioned **well I d.!** ciel!, ça alors!; **to d. for/ against sth** se déclarer pour/contre qch

declared [dɪˈkleəd] **ADJ** avoué, déclaré

declassification [diːklæsɪfɪˈkeɪʃən] **N** *(of information, document)* levée *f* du sceau du secret (**of** portant sur)

declassify [diːˈklæsɪfaɪ] **VT** *(secret document etc)* lever le sceau du secret qui porte sur, déclassifier

declension [dɪˈklenʃən] **N** *Gram* déclinaison *f*

declinable [dɪˈklaɪnəb(ə)l] **ADJ** *Gram* déclinable

declination [deklɪˈneɪʃən] **N 1** *Astron* déclinaison *f* **2** *Am (refusal)* refus *m* courtois et formel

decline [dɪˈklaɪn] **N** *(of day, empire)* déclin *m*; *(in price, number, enthusiasm)* baisse *f*, *(of business)* ralentissement *m*; **sales have shown a rapid d. over the last six months** on a observé une forte chute des ventes au cours des six derniers mois; **to go into a d.** *(of health, patient)* décliner; *(of company shares, economy)* chuter; **to be on the d.** *(of crime, birth rate)* être sur le déclin, décliner, être en baisse; *(of prices)* être en baisse, être en diminution; *(of patient)* décliner

VT 1 *(refuse) (honour, invitation)* décliner; *(sb's help)* repousser; **to d. to do sth** refuser de faire qch **2** *Gram (noun etc)* décliner

VI 1 *(refuse)* refuser **2** *(go down, come to end) (of sun)* décliner; *(of day)* décliner, tirer à sa fin; *(of health, influence etc)* décliner, baisser; *Com (of prices, business)* être en baisse; **to d. in importance** perdre de l'importance

▸▸ *Mktg* **d. stage** *(of product)* phase *f* de déclin

declining [dɪˈklaɪnɪŋ] **ADJ 1** *(sun)* couchant; *Lit* **in one's d. years** au déclin de la vie; **she spent her d. years in a nursing home** elle a passé la fin de ses jours dans une maison de retraite **2** *Econ (industry)* déclinant, sur le déclin; *(market)* en baisse; **d. demand** demande *f* déclinante; **d. sales** ventes *fpl* en baisse

declivity [dɪˈklɪvɪtɪ] **N** *Fml* déclivité *f*, pente *f*

declutch [diːˈklʌtʃ] **VI** *Aut* débrayer

decoction [dɪˈkɒkʃən] **N** *Tech Fml* décoction *f*

decode [diːˈkəʊd] **VT** *(message)* déchiffrer, décoder, transcrire en clair; *Comput, TV* décoder; *Fig* déchiffrer; **decoded message** message transcrit en clair; **the file is automatically decoded when it is received** le fichier est décodé automatiquement à la réception

decoder [diːˈkəʊdər] **N** *(person, machine)* décodeur *m*, déchiffreur *m*; *Comput, TV* décodeur

decoding [diːˈkəʊdɪŋ] **N** *(of message)* déchiffrement *m*, décodage *m*, transcription *f* en clair; *Comput, TV* décodage

decoke [diːˈkəʊk] *Aut Fam* **N the car needs a d.** la voiture a besoin d'un décalaminage *ou* d'être décalaminée

VT décalaminer

▸▸ **d. machine** machine *f* de décalaminage

décolletage [deɪkɒlˈtɑːʒ] **N** décolleté *m*

décolleté [deɪˈkɒlteɪ] **ADJ** *(dress, woman)* décolleté

N décolleté *m*

decolonization [diːkɒlənaɪˈzeɪʃən] **N** décolonisation *f*

decolonize [diːˈkɒlənaɪz] **VT** décoloniser

decommission [diːkəˈmɪʃən] **VT** *(nuclear reactor, plant)* mettre hors service

decommissioning [diːkəˈmɪʃənɪŋ] **N** *(of nuclear reactor, plant)* mise *f* hors service

decompose [diːkəmˈpəʊz] **VI** *(of organic matter)* se décomposer, entrer en décomposition

VT *(matter, compound, light etc)* décomposer

decomposition [diːkɒmpəˈzɪʃən] **N** décomposition *f*

decompress [diːkəmˈpres] **VT** *Tech (gas etc)* décomprimer; *Med (diver)* faire séjourner dans une chambre de décompression; *Comput* décompresser

decompression [diːkəmˈpreʃən] **N** *Comput, Tech* décompression *f*

▸▸ **d. chamber** chambre *f* de décompression; *Med* **d. illness, d. sickness** *(suffered by divers)* maladie *f* des caissons; *Comput* **d. software** logiciel *m* de décompression

decompressor [diːkəmˈpresər] **N** *Comput* logiciel *m* de décompression

decongestant [diːkənˈdʒestənt] **ADJ, N** *Med* décongestionnant *m*

decongestion [diːkənˈdʒestʃən] *Med* décongestion *f*

deconsecrate [diːˈkɒnsəkreɪt] **VT** *Rel (church)* désaffecter

deconsignment [diːkənˈsaɪnmənt] **N** *Com* déconsignation *f*

decontaminate [diːkənˈtæmɪneɪt] **VT** décontaminer

decontamination [diːkəntæmɪˈneɪʃən] **N** décontamination *f*, **d. measures** mesures *fpl* de décontamination

decontrol [diːkənˈtrəʊl] **N** *(of prices, trade)* libération *f*

VT libérer des contraintes du gouvernement; *(prices, trade)* libérer; *(wages)* débloquer

décor, decor [ˈdeɪkɔːr] **N** *Theat etc* décor *m*; *Fam* **he's part of the d.** *(has been here for a long time)* il fait partie des meubles

decorate [ˈdekəreɪt] **VT 1** *(room, streets)* décorer, orner (**with sth** de qch); *(cake, Christmas tree)* décorer **2** *(paint and wallpaper etc) (room)* peindre et tapisser, décorer **3** *(person) (with medal)* décorer, remettre une décoration à; **she was decorated for bravery** elle a été décorée pour son courage

decorating [ˈdekəreɪtɪŋ] **N** décoration *f*, **to do the d.** *(in flat, house)* faire les travaux (de décoration)

decoration [dekəˈreɪʃən] **N 1** *(of room, cake, Christmas tree etc)* décoration *f*; **decorations** *(in town for festival etc)* décorations **2** *(with paint and wallpaper etc) (of room)* peinture *f* et pose *f* de la tapisserie, décoration *f*; **we did all the d. ourselves** nous avons fait tous les travaux nous-mêmes **3** *(with medal)* remise *f* d'une décoration (**of sb** à qn); *(medal)* décoration *f*, médaille *f*

decorative [ˈdek(ə)rətɪv] **ADJ** *(art, ornament)*, *Fam (woman)* décoratif; **the house is in excellent d. order** la décoration de la maison est en excellent état

decoratively [ˈdek(ə)rətɪvlɪ] **ADV** décorativement

decorator [ˈdekəreɪtər] **N** décorateur, -trice; *Br* **(painter and) d.** peintre *m* décorateur; *Br* **we're having the decorators in next week** les peintres viennent la semaine prochaine

decorous [ˈdekərəs] **ADJ** bienséant, convenable

decorously [ˈdekərəslɪ] **ADV** avec bienséance, convenablement

decorticate [diːˈkɔːtɪkeɪt] **VT** *Fml* décortiquer

decorum [dɪˈkɔːrəm] **N** décorum *m*, bienséance *f*, **a breach of d.** une inconvenance; **to have no sense of d.** ne pas avoir le sens du décorum; **her sense of d.** son sens des convenances *ou* du décorum; **to behave with d.** se comporter comme il faut

decouple [diːˈkʌp(ə)l] **VT** *Elec* découpler

decoupling [diːˈkʌplɪŋ] **N** *Elec* découplage *m*

decoy¹ [ˈdiːkɔɪ] **N 1** *(in hunting)* appât *m*, leurre *m*; *(bird)* moquette *f*, (oiseau *m*) appelant *m* **2** *Fig (person)* appât *m*; *(phone call)* piège *m*; **police d.** *(to trick criminal)* policier *m* en civil

▸▸ **d. bird** moquette, (oiseau) appelant

decoy² [dɪˈkɔɪ] **VT** *(birds, person)* leurrer; **to d. sb into a trap** attirer qn dans un piège; **to d. sb into doing sth** leurrer qn pour qu'il fasse qch; **the phone call decoyed her away from the office** le coup de téléphone était un piège pour la faire sortir du bureau

decrease¹ [ˈdiːkriːs] **N** *(in unemployment, crime, population)* diminution *f*, *(in prices, strength, value, number)* diminution, baisse *f*, *(in political power)* affaiblissement *m*; **to be on the d.** *(of crime etc)* baisser; **d. in speed** ralentissement *m*; **d. in stocks** *(profit and loss item)* déstockage *m* de production

decrease² [dɪˈkriːs] **VI** *(of population, unemployment, crime, inflation)* diminuer, baisser, décroître; *(of value, strength, prices, output)* diminuer, baisser; *(of power)* s'affaiblir; *Knitting* diminuer, faire une/des diminution(s)

VT diminuer, réduire; *(prices) (of government)* baisser; *(of economic forces)* faire baisser; *Knitting* **d. three stitches** diminuer de trois mailles, faire trois diminutions; **to d. the pain** faire diminuer la douleur

decreasing [dɪˈkriːsɪŋ] **ADJ** *(number, population, value, strength)* décroissant; *(prices, unemployment, crime, output)* en baisse; *(influence, importance)* déclinant, en déclin; **in d. order of importance** par ordre d'importance décroissante

▸▸ *Fin* **d. costs** frais *mpl* dégressifs; *Acct* **d. rate** taux *m* dégressif

decreasingly [dɪˈkriːsɪŋlɪ] **ADV** de moins en moins

decree [dɪˈkriː] **N 1** *Admin* décret *m*, arrêté *m*; **to issue a d.** promulguer un décret; **to rule by d.** régner par décret **2** *Rel* décret *m* **3** *Law* décision *f*, arrêt *m*, jugement *m*

VT *(order)* décréter, ordonner; *Law* arrêter (**that** que); **fate decreed that …** le sort avait voulu que …; **the film was decreed a threat to public morals** on a décrété que le film était une menace pour la morale publique

▸▸ *Law* **d. absolute** jugement définitif (de divorce); *Law* **d. nisi** jugement provisoire (de divorce)

decrepit [dɪˈkrepɪt] **ADJ 1** *(person)* décrépit **2** *(car, house, furniture etc)* délabré

decrepitude [dɪˈkrepɪtjuːd] **N** *Fml* **1** *(of person)* décrépitude *f* **2** *(of car, house etc)* délabrement *m*

decriminalization [diːkrɪmɪnəlaɪˈzeɪʃən] **N** *Law (of drug possession)* dépénalisation *f*

decriminalize [diːˈkrɪmɪnəlaɪz] **VT** *Law (possession of drugs)* dépénaliser

decry [dɪˈkraɪ] **VT** *Fml* décrier, dénigrer; **the union has decried the suggested increase as an insult** le syndicat a qualifié l'augmentation proposée d'insulte; **his intervention has been decried as worsening the problem** on l'a accusé, en intervenant, d'avoir aggravé le problème

decrypt [diːˈkrɪpt] **VT** *Comput* déchiffrer

decryption [diːˈkrɪpʃən] **N** *Comput* déchiffrement *m*

dedicate [ˈdedɪkeɪt] **VT 1** *(assign) (church)* dédier, consacrer; **to d. oneself** *or* **one's life to sb** se consacrer à qn, consacrer sa vie à qn; **to d. oneself** *or* **one's life to sth** se vouer à qch, se consacrer à qch **2** *(book, record)* dédicacer (**to** à)

dedicated [ˈdedɪkeɪtɪd] **ADJ 1** *(to one's pro-*

fession) consciencieux; *(doctor, nurse, teacher)* dévoué; *(socialist, supporter)* convaincu; **to be d. to one's job** être dévoué à son travail; **she was d. to the cause** elle se consacrait à cette cause; **d. to the cause of freedom** engagé dans la lutte pour la liberté **2** *(assigned for special purpose)* dédié, spécialisé

▸▸ **d. circuit** circuit *m* dédié; *Tel* **d. line** ligne *f* spécialisée; *Comput* **d. word processor** machine *f* exclusivement destinée au traitement de texte

dedication [dedɪˈkeɪʃən] **N 1** *(of church)* consécration *f*, *Am* *(of building)* inauguration *f* **2** *(of book)* dédicace *f*; **to write a d. in a book** dédicacer un livre; **to read out the dedications** *(of disc jockey)* lire les dédicaces **3** *(devotion) (to a cause)* attachement *m*, dévouement *m* (**to** à); *(to country, company)* dévouement; **a life of d.** une vie de dévouement; **to work with d.** travailler avec dévouement; **I admire your d. (to your work)** j'admire ton dévouement (à ton travail); **to work with great d. for the cause of freedom** travailler avec dévouement pour la liberté

deduce [dɪˈdjuːs] **VT** déduire (**from** de); **I d. therefore that you will not be there** j'en conclus donc que vous ne serez pas là

deduct [dɪˈdʌkt] **VT** déduire (**from** de); *(from a bill, price)* décompter; **to d. £50/10% from the price** rabattre 50 livres/10% sur le prix; **to d. a commission** prélever une commission; **to be deducted** à déduire; **tax is deducted at source** l'impôt est retenu *ou* prélevé à la source

deductibility [dɪdʌktɪˈbɪlɪtɪ] **N** déductibilité *f*

deductible [dɪˈdʌktɪb(ə)l] **ADJ** déductible

deduction [dɪˈdʌkʃən] **N 1** *(subtraction)* déduction *f* (**from a quantity** sur une quantité); *(from pay)* retenue *f*, prélèvement *m*; **d. of a sum** décompte *m* d'une somme; *Fin* **d. at source** retenue *f* à la source; **d. of tax at source** retenue *f* salariale à la source; **after deductions, I'm left with a salary of …** une fois les prélèvements *ou* les retenues décompté(e)s, il me reste un salaire de … **2** *(conclusion)* déduction *f* (**from** de); **by a process of d.** par déduction; **there is only one d. that can be made** on ne peut déduire qu'une seule chose

deductive [dɪˈdʌktɪv] **ADJ** *(reasoning)* déductif, par déduction

deed [diːd] **N 1** *(action)* action *f*, acte *m*; **to do one's good d. for the day** faire sa bonne action *ou* sa B. A. quotidienne; *Lit* **d. of valour** haut fait *m* **2** *Law (document)* acte *m* notarié; **mortgage d.** acte hypothécaire; **to change one's name by d. poll** changer légalement son nom; **the deeds to the house** les titres de propriété de la maison

VT *esp Am Law (transfer by deed)* transférer par un acte

▸▸ *Law* **d. of arrangement, d. of assignment** acte de transfert; **d. box** classeur *m* à documents; **d. of acknowledgment** acte récognitif; **d. of covenant** = déclaration *f* par laquelle on s'engage à verser régulièrement une certaine somme à un particulier, une association caritative, etc; **d. of partnership** acte constitutif *ou* de société; **d. of sale** acte de vente; **d. of transfer** acte de cession

deejay [ˈdiːdʒeɪ] **N** *Mus Fam* disc-jockey *m*, *pl* disc-jockeys

deem [diːm] **VT** *Arch, Lit* **I do not d. it necessary/proper to …** je ne juge pas *ou* ne crois pas *ou* ne considère pas nécessaire/convenable de …; **it is deemed necessary/proper to …** on juge *ou* croit nécessaire/convenable de …; **if it is deemed necessary** si c'est jugé nécessaire; **I d. it a great honour** je

considère cela comme un grand honneur; **he was deemed (to be) the winner** il a été considéré comme étant le vainqueur

▸▸▸ **DEEP** [diːp]

ADJ	profond **1**
ADV	profondément
N	océan

ADJ 1 *(water, wound, sleep, despair)*, *Tennis (serve)*, *Fig (thinker)* profond; *(shelf)* large, profond; **to be ten metres d.** avoir dix mètres de profondeur, avoir une profondeur de dix mètres; **to take a d. breath** respirer profondément; *Fig* respirer un grand coup; **to be in d. water** *(in serious difficulties)* être dans de sales draps, être en mauvaise posture; **I think we're getting into d. water here** je crois que nous sommes en train de nous engager sur un terrain dangereux; *Fam* **you're in d. trouble, my lad** tu as de sérieux problèmes, mon gars; **d. in debt** criblé de dettes; **he got deeper and deeper in debt** il s'est endetté de plus en plus; **d. in thought** plongé dans ses pensées; **to inflict a d. wound** *(of weapon)* pénétrer très profondément; **two/four d.** sur deux/quatre rangs; **his d. learning** ses connaissances profondes; **in deepest sympathy** *(on card)* avec toute ma sympathie; **d. concern** sincère *ou* vive préoccupation; *Hum* **in deepest Yorkshire** au fin fond du Yorkshire

2 *(colour)* foncé, sombre; *(sound)* grave; **d. blue** bleu foncé; **in a d. voice** d'une voix profonde

3 *Fam (not readily understandable)* **he's a d. one** il est plutôt mystérieux

ADV profondément; **the harpoon sank d. into the flesh** le harpon a pénétré très profondément dans la chair; **to walk d. into the forest** pénétrer profondément dans la forêt; **to look d. into sb's eyes** pénétrer qn du regard; **to work d. into the night** travailler tard dans la nuit; *Fam* **we're in too d. to pull out now** nous sommes trop impliqués pour faire marche arrière maintenant; *Fml* **to drink d.** boire à longs traits; **d.-lying causes** causes profondes; **d. down he's very kind** au fond, il est très gentil; **to run d.** être profond

N *Lit* **the d.** l'océan *m*; **to commit a body to the d.** immerger un mort

▸▸ *Com* **d. discount** forte remise *f*; **d. end** *(of swimming pool)* côté *m* le plus profond, grand bain *m*; *Cin, TV* **d. focus** grande profondeur *f* de champ; **the D. South** *(of the United States)* le sud profond; *Fam* **d. throat** *(informer)* informateur *m*, indicateur *m*

deep-dish ADJ
▸▸ *Am Culin* **d. pie** tourte *f*

deepen [ˈdiːp(ə)n] **VT 1** *(well etc)* approfondir, creuser; *(love, hatred, resentment etc)* rendre plus intense, accroître; **that only deepened his conviction** cela n'a fait que le conforter dans sa conviction **2** *(colour)* foncer; *(sound)* rendre plus grave

VI 1 *(of river, silence etc)* devenir plus profond; *(of conviction, belief)* augmenter; *(of mystery)* s'épaissir **2** *(of colour)* devenir plus foncé; *(of sound, voice)* devenir plus grave; *(of shadows)* s'épaissir

deep-fat frying N cuisson *f* en bain de friture

deep-freeze N congélateur *m*; *Fig* **to put sth in the d.** mettre qch au frigidaire
VT *(food)* congeler, surgeler

deep-frozen ADJ surgelé

deep-fry VT *(fish etc)* faire cuire dans la friture

deep-fryer N friteuse *f*

deep-laid ADJ *(plan, scheme)* habilement comploté

deeply [ˈdiːplɪ] **ADV** profondément; **to sigh**

d. pousser un profond soupir; **they gazed d. into each other's eyes leurs regards étaient plongés dans les yeux l'un de l'autre; *Fig* **to go d. into sth** pénétrer *ou* entrer profondément dans qch, approfondir qch; **she can't have looked into it very d.** elle n'a pas dû s'en occuper très sérieusement; **to fall d. in love with sb** tomber profondément amoureux de qn; **to care d. about sb** être profondément attaché à qn; **I care d. about your happiness/this country's future** ton bonheur/l'avenir de ce pays est très important pour moi; **d. interesting** fort intéressant; **d. offended** gravement offensé; **to be d. insulting** être très insultant

deepness [ˈdiːpnɪs] **N** *(of voice etc)* profondeur *f*, *Mus (of sound)* gravité *f*

deep-pan ADJ
▸▸ *Culin* **d. pizza** pizza *f* à pâte épaisse

deep-rooted ADJ *(tree)* profondément enraciné, aux racines profondes; *(affection, prejudice, dislike, antagonism etc)* profond; *(habit)* ancré

deep-sea ADJ *(plant, animal)* pélagique
▸▸ **d. diver** plongeur, -euse sous-marin(e); **d. fisherman** pêcheur *m* hauturier *ou* en haute mer; **d. fishery, d. fishing** pêche *f* hauturière

deep-seated [-ˈsiːtɪd] **ADJ** *(aversion)* profond, bien enraciné; *(affection, prejudice, conviction etc)* profond

deep-set ADJ *(eyes)* enfoncé

deep-six VT *Am Fam (throw away)* balancer; **we deep-sixed the project** on a balancé cette idée de projet

deep-vein thrombosis N *Med* thrombose *f* veineuse profonde

deer [dɪər] **N INV** cerf *m*
▸▸ **d. park** chasse *f* gardée pour le cerf

deerhound [ˈdɪəhaʊnd] **N** *(dog)* lévrier *m* d'Écosse

deerskin [ˈdɪəskɪn] **N** peau *f* de daim; *Com* daim *m*; **d. gloves** gants *mpl* en daim

deerstalker [ˈdɪəstɔːkər] **N 1** *(hunter)* chasseur *m* (de cerf) à l'approche **2** *(hat)* chapeau *m* de chasse (à la Sherlock Holmes)

deerstalking [ˈdɪəstɔːkɪŋ] **N** chasse *f* (au cerf) à l'approche

de-escalate [diːˈeskəleɪt] **VT** *(tension, bombing)* diminuer; *(crisis)* désamorcer
VI *(of tension)* diminuer; **the crisis shows no sign of de-escalating** la situation de crise ne semble pas se détendre

de-escalation [diːeskəˈleɪʃən] **N** *(of arms sales)* diminution *f*; *(of crisis, tension)* détente *f*

def [def] **ADJ** *Sl (excellent)* super, génial

deface [dɪˈfeɪs] **VT** *(statue)* dégrader; *(poster, walls)* barbouiller; *(book) (of child)* gribouiller; *(to express dissatisfaction with contents)* noircir

de facto [deɪˈfæktəʊ] **ADJ, ADV** *Law, Lit* de facto; *Law* **d. and de jure** de droit et de fait; *Law* **d. possession** possession *f* de fait

defamation [defəˈmeɪʃən] **N** diffamation *f*; **that's d. of character** c'est de la diffamation; **to sue for d. of character** engager des poursuites en diffamation, faire un procès en diffamation; **to sue sb for d. of character** poursuivre qn en diffamation

defamatory [dɪˈfæmət(ə)rɪ] **ADJ** *(remark etc)* diffamatoire, diffamant

defame [dɪˈfeɪm] **VT** *(person)* diffamer

default [dɪˈfɔːlt] **N 1** *Law (failure to appear in court)* défaut *m*, non-comparution *f*; *(in criminal law)* contumace *f*, **judgment by d.** jugement *m* par contumace; **by d.** *(if not otherwise specified)* implicitement; *Tech* par défaut; *Comput* **which is the d.?** quelle est la configuration/police/etc par défaut?; *Sport*

match won by d. match gagné par forfait; **the machine sets itself to 1 by d.** la machine se réglera sur 1 par défaut **2** *Com* défaut *m*, défaillance *f*; **d. in paying** défaut de paiement; *Fig* **in d. of ...** à défaut de ..., faute de ... **3** *Tennis* disqualification *f* **VT** *Tennis (player)* disqualifier **VI 1** *Law (fail to appear in court)* ne pas comparaître; *(in criminal law)* être en état de contumace **2** *(fail to pay)* *St Exch* manquer à ses engagements; **to d. on alimony payments** manquer aux versements de pension alimentaire **3** *Comput* **to d. to sth** sélectionner qch par défaut
► ►*Comput* **d. drive** lecteur *m* par défaut; *Comput* **d. font** police *f* par défaut; *Fin* **d. interest** intérêts *mpl* moratoires; *Comput* **d. setting** configuration *f* par défaut; *Comput* **d. value** valeur *f* par défaut

defaulter [dɪˈfɔːltər] **N 1** *Law* défaillant, -ante; *(in criminal law)* contumace *mf* **2** *(debtor)* débiteur *m* défaillant; **d. on a fine** = personne *f* qui ne paie pas une amende **3** *Mil, Naut* retardataire *m*, réfractaire *m*; *(undergoing punishment)* consigné *m*

defaulting [dɪˈfɔːltɪŋ] **ADJ** *Law* défaillant

defeasance [dɪˈfiːzəns] **N** *Banking, Law* defeasance *m*

defeat [dɪˈfiːt] **N 1** *(of army, team, government)* défaite *f*; **to suffer a d.** essuyer une défaite; **..., he said with an air of d.** ..., dit-il d'un air de vaincu; **to admit d.** s'avouer vaincu **2** *(of plan)* échec *m*, renversement *m*; *Parl (of measure)* rejet *m*
VT 1 *(army, opponent)* battre, vaincre; *(government)* mettre en minorité; **they were defeated by their own lack of preparation** ils ont été battus *ou* vaincus à cause de leur manque de préparation; **it defeats me** *(I don't understand)* cela me dépasse **2** *(plan, attempt to do sth)* déjouer, faire échouer; *(hope)* frustrer; *(of meeting) (proposal)* rejeter; *Parl (measure)* faire échouer, rejeter; **to d. the ends of justice** contrarier la justice; **to d. one's own ends** aller à l'encontre de ses propres intentions; **that does rather d. the object of the exercise** cela va plutôt à l'encontre du but de l'opération

defeatism [dɪˈfiːtɪz(ə)m] **N** défaitisme *m*; **an air/mood of d.** un air/une atmosphère défaitiste *ou* de défaite

defeatist [dɪˈfiːtɪst] **ADJ, N** défaitiste *mf*

defecate [ˈdefəkeɪt] **VI** *Fml* déféquer

defecation [defəˈkeɪʃən] **N** *Fml* défécation *f*

defect¹ [ˈdiːfekt] **N** *(in construction, physical)* défaut *m*; *Com* vice *m*; *(mental)* déficience *f*

defect² [dɪˈfekt] **VI** *Mil, Pol* passer à l'ennemi; *Pol Fig (of MP)* passer dans le camp adverse; *Pol Hist* **to d. to the West** passer à l'ouest; **she defected from the USSR in 1973** elle a quitté l'URSS en 1973; *Pol Fig* **to d. from the party** abandonner le parti; *Pol Fig* **to d. to the government** passer dans le camp du gouvernement; *Com Fig* **she's defected to our main competitor** elle est passée chez notre concurrent principal

defection [dɪˈfekʃən] **N** *Mil, Pol* défection *f*; **there have been a number of defections to the West** un certain nombre de gens sont passés à l'ouest

defective [dɪˈfektɪv] **ADJ 1** *(machine)* défectueux; *(theory)* imparfait; *(memory)* infidèle; *(brakes)* en mauvais état; *(reasoning)* défectueux, mauvais; *(hearing, method)* mauvais; **to be d. in sth** manquer de qch; *Ind* **d. part** pièce *f* défectueuse **2** *Gram (verb etc)* défectif

Attention: ne pas confondre avec l'adjectif anglais **deficient**.

defector [dɪˈfektər] **N** *Mil, Pol etc* transfuge *mf*

defence, *Am* **defense** [dɪˈfens] **N 1** *(action)* défense *f*; **to put up a stubborn d.** se défendre avec obstination; **I carry a knife for d.** je porte un couteau pour me défendre; **he killed the man in d. of his wife** il a tué l'homme pour défendre sa femme; **to come to sb's d.** venir à la défense de qn **2** *(means)* **defences** *(of country)* moyens *mpl* de défense; **Holland's defences against the flood waters** les défenses dont dispose la Hollande contre les inondations; **the body's natural defences** les défenses naturelles du corps; *Sport* **the d.** les défenseurs; **seaward defences** *(of port)* ouvrages *mpl* de défense face à la mer **3** *(argument)* défense *f*, justification *f*, *Law* défense; **to speak in d. of sb** défendre qn; **I must say, in my own d., that ...** je dois dire pour ma propre défense que ...; **to appear for the d.** *(of barrister)* représenter la défense; **to conduct one's own d.** défendre soi-même sa cause
► ►*Law* **d. counsel** défenseur *m*; *(in civil law)* avocat, -ate de la défense; **d. electronics** électronique *f* de défense; *Med* **d. mechanism** défenses *fpl* immunitaires; *Psy* mécanisme *m* de défense; *Pol* **d. spending** dépenses *fpl* pour la défense; *Law* **d. witness** témoin *m* à décharge

defenceless, *Am* **defenseless** [dɪˈfenslɪs] **ADJ** sans défense

defend [dɪˈfend] **VT 1** *(person, border, country etc)*, *Sport (title)* défendre (**from, against** contre) **2** *(opinion)* défendre, justifier; **to d. one's actions** justifier ses actions **3** *Law (defendant)* défendre
VI 1 *Law* assumer *ou* soutenir la défense **2** *Sport* défendre

defendant [dɪˈfendənt] **N** *Law* défendeur, -eresse; *(on appeal)* intimé, -ée; *(in criminal case)* accusé, -ée

defender [dɪˈfendər] **N** défenseur *m*
► ► **D. of the Faith** Défenseur *m* de la foi

defending [dɪˈfendɪŋ] **ADJ 1** *Sport* **d. champion** champion, -ionne en titre **2** *Law* de la défense
► ►*Law* **d. counsel** défenseur *m*

defense *Am* = **defence**

defensible [dɪˈfensəb(ə)l] **ADJ** *(cause)*, *Mil* défendable; *(position, point of view)* tenable; *(opinion, behaviour)* défendable, justifiable; **the town was easily d.** la ville était facile à défendre

defensive [dɪˈfensɪv] **ADJ** défensif, de défense; **don't be so d.!** ne te mets pas sur la défensive comme ça!; **to get d.** se montrer défensif (**about** au sujet de), se mettre sur la défensive
N défensive *f*; **to be/go on the d.** se tenir/se mettre sur la défensive
► ►*Mil* **d. action** action *f* défensive; **d. position** position *f* de défense; *St Exch* **d. stocks** titres *mpl* de placement, valeurs *fpl* d'investissement

defensively [dɪˈfensɪvlɪ] **ADV** *(to say)* d'un ton défensif; *(to react)* d'une manière défensive

defensiveness [dɪˈfensɪvnɪs] **N when she reacted/spoke with such d.** quand elle a réagi/parlé d'une manière aussi défensive; **her d. in the face of criticism** la façon qu'elle a de se mettre sur la défensive quand on la critique

defer [dɪˈfɜːr] **(-rr-) VT 1** *(delay, postpone)* *(question, case)* différer, ajourner, remettre; *(meeting, decision)* remettre, reporter; *(pay-*

ment) reculer, renvoyer; *(verdict)* suspendre; **to d. sth to a later date** remettre *ou* reporter qch à plus tard; **to d. doing sth** différer de faire qch **2** *Mil etc (person)* mettre en sursis (d'appel); **to d. sb on medical grounds** réformer qn
VI *(yield) (to sb's opinion)* se ranger (**to** à); *(to sb's wishes)* se soumettre (**to** à); *(to sb's knowledge)* s'en remettre (**to** à)

deference [ˈdefərəns] **N** déférence *f*, **to pay** *or* **show d. to sb, to treat sb with d.** témoigner de la déférence à *ou* envers qn; **out of** *or* **in d. to ...** par déférence pour ..., par égard pour ...

deferential [defəˈrenʃəl] **ADJ** *(air, tone)* de déférence, respectueux; *(behaviour)* respectueux; *(person)* déférent, respectueux; **to be d. to sb** se montrer plein de déférence *ou* de respect pour *ou* envers qn, se montrer respectueux envers qn

deferentially [defəˈrenʃəlɪ] **ADV** *(to speak, look at)* avec déférence, avec respect; *(to behave)* avec déférence, respectueusement

deferment [dɪˈfɜːmənt] **N 1** *(of case)* ajournement *m*, remise *f*; *(of payment)* renvoi *m* **2** *Mil etc (for health reasons)* réforme *f*, **to apply for d.** *(of call-up)* faire une demande de report d'appel

deferral [dɪˈfɜːrəl] **N** = **deferment**

deferred [dɪˈfɜːd] **ADJ** ajourné, retardé; *(shares)* différé
► ►*Fin* **d. depreciation** amortissements *mpl* différés; *Fin* **d. income** produit *m* constaté d'avance; *Fin* **d. payment** paiement *m* différé; *(in instalments)* paiement par versements échelonnés; *Law* **d. sentence** = jugement *m* dont le prononcé est suspendu, jugement ajourné

deffo [ˈdefəʊ] **ADV** *Br Fam* absolument; **are you coming tonight? – d.!** tu viens ce soir? – je veux!

defiance [dɪˈfaɪəns] **N** défi *m*; **a gesture of d.** un geste de défi; **in d. of** *(the law, an order)* au mépris de

defiant [dɪˈfaɪənt] **ADJ** *(gesture, look, remark)* de défi, provocant; *(person)* audacieux, *Pej* irrévérencieux

defiantly [dɪˈfaɪəntlɪ] **ADV** *(to say)* d'un ton provocant; *(to look at)* d'un air provocant *ou* de défi

defibrillation [dɪfɪbrɪˈleɪʃən] **N** *Med* défibrillation *f*

defibrillator [dɪˈfɪbrɪleɪtər] **N** *Med* défibrillateur *m*

deficiency [dɪˈfɪʃənsɪ] **N 1** *(lack)* manque *m*, insuffisance *f* (**of** de); *Med (of minerals, vitamins)* carence *f* (**in, of** de); *(of function, organ)* déficience *f* **2** *(flaw, defect)* défaut *m*, imperfection *f* **3** *(deficit)* manquant *m*, déficit *m*; *Com* découvert *m*; *Pol* déficit budgétaire
► ►*Med* **d. disease** maladie *f* de carence

deficient [dɪˈfɪʃənt] **ADJ** *(faulty)* défectueux; *(lacking)* insuffisant, incomplet; **to be d. in sth** manquer de qch

Attention: ne pas confondre avec l'adjectif **defective**.

deficit [ˈdefɪsɪt] **N** *Fin, Com* déficit *m*; **to be in d.** être en déficit; **budget d.** budget déficitaire; **to make up the d.** combler le déficit

defile¹ [ˈdiːfaɪl] **N** *(pass)* défilé *m*

defile² [dɪˈfaɪl] **VI** *Mil etc (of troops etc)* défiler

defile³ **VT** *(memory of sb, sth)* salir; *(sacred place, tomb)* profaner; *(painting, poster) (with racist etc remarks)* vandaliser; **they've defiled my home** *(entered uninvited)* ils ont violé l'intimité de ma maison; **I feel defiled** *(after rape)* je me sens souillé

defilement [dɪˈfaɪlmənt] N *(of sacred place, tomb)* profanation f; *(of sb's memory) (action)* fait m de salir; *(result)* souillure f

> Note that the French word **défilement** is a false friend and is never a translation for the English word **defilement**.

definable [dɪˈfaɪnəb(ə)l] ADJ définissable; **the border is not easily d.** la frontière n'est pas facile à déterminer

define [dɪˈfaɪn] VT **1** *(word, object)* définir **2** *(specify) (difference)* définir; *(one's attitude, position etc)* préciser; *(objectives etc)* formuler; *(scope, extent of sth)* déterminer; *(powers)* délimiter; **to d. what it means to be French** définir ce qu'être français signifie; **well-defined limits** limites bien déterminées **3 well-defined outlines** contours nettement dessinés *ou* dégagés **4** *Comput (value)* déclarer

defining [dɪˈfaɪnɪŋ] ADJ **1** *(decisive)* décisif; **a d. moment in history** un tournant de l'histoire **2** *(distinctive)* déterminant

definite [ˈdefɪnɪt] ADJ **1** *(distinct) (views, opinions)* bien arrêté; *(shape)* défini, bien déterminé; *(taste)* bien déterminé; **I can't put my finger on anything d.** je n'arrive pas à mettre le doigt sur quoi que ce soit de précis; **it shows a d. lack of ...** cela montre un manque évident de ...; **it's a d. advantage being a woman** c'est un véritable avantage d'être une femme; **there has been a d. improvement in her condition/work** il y a eu une amélioration certaine de son état/travail
2 *(sure, certain) (date)* définitif, certain; *(response)* précis, catégorique; *Com (order)* ferme; **it's not d. yet** ce n'est pas encore définitif *ou* sûr; **at a d. time** à une heure déterminée; **and that's d.!** et c'est sûr!; **she is very d. about it** elle est tout à fait sûre de cela; **I'm d. it was him** je suis certain *ou* sûr que c'était lui; **he's d. about getting married** il est décidé à se marier
3 *Gram (article)* défini; **past d.** passé m défini VOIR GRAMMAIRE A6–8; B3–4

> Attention: ne pas confondre avec l'adjectif **definitive**.

definitely [ˈdefɪnɪtlɪ] ADV **1** *(distinctly) (improved, superior)* nettement; *(to need, lack sth)* décidément
2 *(without doubt, certainly)* à coup sûr, sans aucun doute; **the meeting will d. be held next Monday** la réunion aura bien lieu lundi prochain; **he is d. mad/the man I saw** il n'y a pas de doute qu'il est fou/que c'est l'homme que j'ai vu, il est fou/c'est l'homme que j'ai vu, c'est sûr *ou* certain; **she's d. innocent** elle est innocente, c'est sûr *ou* certain; **are you going? – d.!** est-ce que vous y allez? – absolument!; **I'll d. be there** j'y serai à coup sûr; **I'll almost d. be there** j'y serai presque certainement, il est presque certain que j'y serai; **d. not!** certainement pas!; **I'll d. call you** je te téléphonerai sans faute; **that's d. my last offer** cette fois-ci, c'est ma dernière offre
3 *(clearly, without ambiguity)* **he told me very d. that he didn't want to come** il m'a dit très clairement qu'il ne voulait pas venir

> Attention: ne pas confondre avec l'adverbe **definitively**.

definition [defɪˈnɪʃən] N **1** *(meaning) (of word)* définition f; **by d.** par définition; **to give a d. of sth** donner une définition de qch, définir qch **2** *(specifying) (of powers, border etc)* délimitation f; *(of objectives)* formulation f **3** *(of image) Opt* netteté f; *TV* définition f

definitive [dɪˈfɪnɪtɪv] ADJ *(verdict, result)* définitif; *(authoritative) (biography, edition)* qui fait autorité; *(production of play)* inégalable; **she was, for me, the d. Juliet** pour moi, c'est une Juliette inégalable

> Attention: ne pas confondre avec l'adjectif **definite**.

definitively [dɪˈfɪnɪtɪvlɪ] ADV définitivement

> Attention: ne pas confondre avec l'adverbe **definitely**.

deflate [diːˈfleɪt] VT **1** *(ball, tyre)* dégonfler; *Fig (person)* remettre à sa place; **to d. sb's ego** porter un coup à l'orgueil de qn; **he looked quite deflated** *(had lost his self-esteem)* il était penaud; **I felt rather deflated** *(disappointed)* j'étais assez déçu **2** *Fin, Econ* **to d. the currency** provoquer la déflation de la monnaie; **to d. the economy** pratiquer une politique déflationniste; **to d. prices** faire baisser les prix
VI **1** *(of tyre etc)* se dégonfler **2** *Fin, Econ* provoquer la déflation de la monnaie; **since the government started deflating** depuis que le gouvernement pratique une politique déflationniste

deflation [diːˈfleɪʃən] N **1** *(of ball, tyre)* dégonflement m; *Fig (of person)* fait m de se dégonfler; **... which resulted in the d. of his ego** ... ce qui l'a complètement abattu **2** *Fin, Econ* déflation f

deflationary [diːˈfleɪʃən(ə)rɪ] ADJ *Econ* déflationniste

deflect [dɪˈflekt] VT *(ball, bullet)* (faire) dévier; *(light)* défléchir; *(sound)* renvoyer; *Fig (person)* détourner (**from** de); **to d. criticism** détourner la critique; **the government will not be deflected from its aims** le gouvernement ne se laissera pas détourner de ses objectifs; **to be deflected** *(of projectile)* dériver; **the ball was deflected into the net** le ballon a rebondi dans le filet
VI *(of projectile)* dévier; *(of light)* être défléchi; **the ball deflected off the post** le ballon a rebondi contre le poteau

deflection [dɪˈflekʃən] N *(of light)* déflexion f; *(of compass needle)* déviation f; *(of projectile)* déviation, détournement m; *(of criticism)* détournement; *Elec, Electron (of voltmeter etc)* déviation, déflexion; **it was a lucky d. off the post** heureusement la balle a été déviée par le montant du but; **he scored from a d. off the post** il a marqué un but après que le ballon ait rebondi contre le poteau

deflector [dɪˈflektər] N *Tech* déflecteur m; **sound d.** abat-son m inv

deflexion [dɪˈflekʃən] N = **deflection**

defloration [defləˈreɪʃən] N *Arch, Lit (of virgin)* défloration f

deflower [diːˈflauər] VT *Arch, Lit (virgin)* déflorer

deflowering [diːˈflauərɪŋ] N *Arch, Lit (of virgin)* défloration f

defocus [diːˈfəukəs] VI passer au flou

defoliant [diːˈfəulɪənt] N défoliant m

defoliate [diːˈfəulɪeɪt] VT *(trees etc)* défeuiller

defoliation [diːfəulɪˈeɪʃən] N défoliation f

deforest [diːˈfɒrɪst] VT *(region)* déboiser

deforestation [diːfɒrɪˈsteɪʃən] N *(of region)* déboisement m

deform [dɪˈfɔːm] VT déformer

deformation [diːfɔːˈmeɪʃən] N *(of bone etc)* déformation f

deformed [dɪˈfɔːmd] ADJ *(person)* malformé; *(limb)* difforme, malformé; **the baby was born d.** le bébé est né avec une malformation

deformity [dɪˈfɔːmɪtɪ] N *(of body)* difformité f

DEFRA [ˈdefrə] N *Br Admin (abbr* **Department of the Environment, Food and Rural Affairs**) = ministère m de l'Agriculture et de l'Environnement

defragment [diːˈfrægment] VT *Comput* défragmenter

defragmentation [diːfrægmenˈteɪʃən] N *Comput* défragmentation f

defragmenter [diːˈfrægmentər] N *Comput* défragmenteur m

defraud [dɪˈfrɔːd] VT *(taxman)* frauder; *(bank, employer)* escroquer; **to d. sb of sth** escroquer qch à qn, frustrer qn de qch
VI *Law* **conspiracy to d.** entente f délictueuse dans le but de frauder

defrauder [dɪˈfrɔːdər] N fraudeur, -euse

defray [dɪˈfreɪ] VT **to d. sb's expenses** rembourser les frais de qn, défrayer qn; **to d. the cost of sth** couvrir les frais de qch

defrayal [dɪˈfreɪəl] N **d. of expenses** remboursement m des frais

defrock [diːˈfrɒk] VT *Rel (priest)* défroquer

defrost [diːˈfrɒst] VT **1** *(refrigerator)* dégivrer **2** *(meat etc)* décongeler
VI **1** *(of refrigerator)* dégivrer **2** *(of meat)* se décongeler

defroster [diːˈfrɒstər] N *Aut* dégivreur m

deft [deft] ADJ adroit, habile

deftly [ˈdeftlɪ] ADV adroitement, habilement

deftness [ˈdeftnɪs] N adresse f, habileté f, dextérité f

defunct [dɪˈfʌŋkt] ADJ *(person)* défunt, décédé; *Fig (industry)* défunt; *(project, practice, law)* révolu; *(company)* dissous, f dissoute

defuse [diːˈfjuːz] VT *(bomb), Fig (crisis)* désamorcer

> Attention: ne pas confondre avec le verbe **to diffuse**.

defy [dɪˈfaɪ] VT *(somebody, the elements)* défier, braver; *(order, law)* braver; **to d. description** échapper à toute description, défier toute description; **I d. him to prove it** je le défie de le prouver

degearing [diːˈgɪərɪŋ] N *Fin* désendettement m

degeneracy [dɪˈdʒenərəsɪ] N dégénérescence f

degenerate¹ [dɪˈdʒen(ə)rət] ADJ, N dégénéré, -ée

degenerate² [dɪˈdʒenəreɪt] VI dégénérer (**from** de; **into** en); **the discussion degenerated into a fight** la discussion a dégénéré en bagarre

degeneration [dɪdʒenəˈreɪʃən] N dégénérescence f; *Med* **fatty d.** dégénérescence graisseuse

degenerative [dɪˈdʒenərətɪv] ADJ *Med (disease)* dégénératif; **she has a d. heart condition** elle a des troubles cardiaques qui s'aggravent

degradation [degrəˈdeɪʃən] N **1** avilissement m, dégradation f; **to live a life of d.** vivre dans la dégradation **2** *Phys* dégradation f, *Geol* désagrégation f **3** *Mil* dégradation f

degrade [dɪˈgreɪd] VT **1** *(person)* avilir, dégrader; **I won't d. myself by answering that** je ne m'abaisserai pas à répondre à ça **2** *Phys (energy)* dégrader; *Geol (rocks)* désagréger **3** *Mil (officer)* dégrader, casser

degrading [dɪˈgreɪdɪŋ] ADJ *(experience)* avilissant, dégradant

degree [dɪˈgriː] N **1** *(extent)* degré m; **to**

some *or* **a (certain) d.** à un certain degré, (jusqu')à un certain point; **she's right to a d.** elle a raison jusqu'à un certain point *ou* dans une certaine mesure; **to** *or* **in a high d.** éminemment; **in the highest d.** au plus haut *ou* au dernier degré; **to such a d. that ...** à tel point que ...; **by degrees** petit à petit, graduellement; **to feel a d. of optimism** ressentir un certain optimisme; *Law* **marriage within the prohibited** *or* **forbidden degrees** mariage entre parents ou alliés au degré prohibé

2 *Phys, Geog, Met etc* degré *m*; *Met* **it's 25 degrees** il fait 25 degrés; **we can expect temperatures of 15 to 20 degrees** nous pouvons nous attendre à des températures de 15 à 20 degrés; **degrees Fahrenheit/Celsius** degrés Fahrenheit/Celsius; **ten degrees of frost/below zero** dix degrés au-dessous de zéro; *Geom* **angle of 30 degrees, 30-d. angle** angle *m* de 30 degrés; *Math* **equation of the second/third d.** équation *f* du second/troisième degré; *Phys* **d. of humidity** titre *m* d'eau *ou* d'humidité

3 *Univ* diplôme *m* (universitaire); **to take** *or* **do a d.** passer un diplôme (in en); **when did you do** *or* **take your d.?** quand as-tu eu ton diplôme?

▸▸*Gram* **d. of comparison** degré *m* de comparaison

-degree [dəˈgriː] SUFF **first/second/etc-d. burn** brûlure *f* du premier/deuxième/etc degré; *Am* **first/second-d. murder** meurtre *m* avec/sans préméditation

dehire [diːˈhaɪər] VT *Am Euph (employee)* remercier

dehumanize [diːˈhjuːmənaɪz] VT déshumaniser; **it was a dehumanizing experience** c'était une expérience déshumanisante

dehumidification [diːhjuːmɪdɪfɪˈkeɪʃən] N déshumidification *f*

dehumidifier [diːhjuːˈmɪdɪfaɪər] N déshumidificateur *m*

dehumidify [diːhjuːˈmɪdɪfaɪ] VT déshumidifier

dehydrate [diːhaɪˈdreɪt] VT déshydrater; **to become dehydrated** se déshydrater

VI *(of person)* se déshydrater

dehydrated [diːhaɪˈdreɪtɪd] ADJ *(person, foodstuffs)* déshydraté; *(milk, eggs)* en poudre

dehydration [diːhaɪˈdreɪʃən] N déshydratation *f*

dehydrator [diːhaɪˈdreɪtər] N déshydrateur *m*

de-ice [diːˈaɪs] VT *Aut, Aviat* dégivrer

de-icer [diːˈaɪsər] N *Aut, Aviat* dégivreur *m*

de-icing [diːˈaɪsɪŋ] N *Aut, Aviat* dégivrage *m*

deification [diːɪfɪˈkeɪʃən, deɪ-] N déification *f*

deify [ˈdiːɪfaɪ, ˈdeɪ-] VT déifier

deign [deɪn] VT **to d. to do sth** condescendre à faire qch, daigner faire qch

deindex [diːˈɪndeks] VT *Fin (salaries)* désindexer par rapport au coût de la vie

deindustrialization [diːɪndʌstrɪəlaɪˈzeɪʃən] N désindustrialisation *f*

deinstall [diːɪnˈstɔːl] VT *Comput* désinstaller

deinstallation [diːɪnstəˈleɪʃən] N *Comput* désinstallation *f*

deinstaller [diːɪnˈstɔːlər] N *Comput* désinstallateur *m*

deionized water [diːˈaɪənaɪzd] N eau *f* déminéralisée

deism [ˈdiːɪz(ə)m, ˈdeɪ-] N déisme *m*

deity [ˈdiːɪti, ˈdeɪ-] N **1** *(god)* dieu *m*, déesse *f*, déité *f*, divinité *f*; *Rel* **the D.** la Divinité, Dieu *m* **2** *(divinity) (of Christ etc)* divinité *f*

déjà vu [ˈdeɪʒæˈvuː] N **I had a feeling of d.** j'ai eu une impression de déjà vu

deject [dɪˈdʒekt] VT *(person)* abattre, décourager

dejected [dɪˈdʒektɪd] ADJ abattu, découragé; **to become d.** se décourager

dejectedly [dɪˈdʒektɪdlɪ] ADV d'un air abattu *ou* découragé

dejection [dɪˈdʒekʃən] N découragement *m*

de jure [ˈdiːˈdʒʊərɪ] ADV *Law, Lit* de jure

dekko [ˈdekəʊ] N *Br Sl* coup *m* d'œil; **let's have a d.** fais/faites voir; **to take a d.** jeter un (coup d')œil (**at** sur)

Del *abbr* Delaware

delay [dɪˈleɪ] N retard *m*; **d. in delivery** retard à la livraison; **without d.** sans retard *ou* délai *m*; **without (any) further d.** sans plus tarder; **after much d.** après un long moment; **an hour's d.** une heure de retard; **all flights are subject to d.** tous les vols ont du retard; **delays of four hours can be expected** on peut s'attendre à des retards de quatre heures; **the road works caused traffic delays** les travaux ont retardé la circulation

VT **1** *(postpone) (one's departure)* retarder, remettre; *(payment)* différer, arriérer; **she delayed leaving until the last possible moment** elle a repoussé *ou* retardé son départ jusqu'au dernier moment; **I delayed writing to you until I knew the exact date** j'ai attendu de savoir la date exacte pour t'écrire

2 *(hold up) (somebody)* retenir, retarder; *(progress, traffic)* entraver, retarder; **they've been delayed by fog** ils ont été retardés par le brouillard; **she's suffering from delayed shock** elle souffre d'un choc après coup *ou* a posteriori

VI tarder (**in doing sth** à faire qch); *Mil* **delaying action** action *f* retardatrice; **don't d., book your holiday now** ne tardez pas, réservez vos vacances maintenant; **stop delaying and come to a decision!** arrête de remettre à plus tard ta décision!

> Note that the French word **délai** is a false friend and is never a translation for the English word **delay**. Its most common meaning is **deadline**.

delayed-action [dɪˈleɪd-] ADJ *(fuse, shutter)* à retardement

delayed cut-off N *(of courtesy light etc)* extinction *f* retardée

delayering [diːˈleɪərɪŋ] N *Com* suppression *f* d'échelons

del credere [delˈkreɪdərɪ] N *Com* ducroire *m*

▸▸**d. agent** commissionnaire *m* ducroire; **d. clause** clause *f* ducroire

delectable [dɪˈlektəb(ə)l] ADJ délectable, délicieux

delectation [diːlekˈteɪʃən] N *Fml* délectation *f*

delegate¹ [ˈdelɪgət] N délégué, -ée; **a d. to a conference** un membre d'une conférence; **a d. conference** une conférence de délégués syndicaux

delegate² [ˈdelɪgeɪt] VT **1** *(appoint) (person)* déléguer (**to do sth** pour faire qch) **2** *(powers)* déléguer

VI déléguer; **she's not very good at delegating** elle ne sait pas déléguer

delegation [delɪˈgeɪʃən] N *(act, representatives)* délégation *f*; **d. of power** délégation de pouvoir; **to send a d.** envoyer une délégation

delete [dɪˈliːt] VT *(erase)* effacer (**from** de); *(cross out)* rayer; *Comput* effacer, supprimer; **d. where applicable, d. as appropriate** *(on form)* rayer les mentions inutiles

VI *Comput* effacer

N **1** *Comput* touche *f* d'effacement **2** *Typ (symbol)* déléatur *m*

▸▸*Comput* **d. character** caractère *m* d'effacement; *Comput* **d. command** commande *f* d'effacement; *Comput* **d. key** touche d'effacement

deleterious [delɪˈtɪərɪəs] ADJ *Fml (to health)* nuisible, délétère

deleting [dɪˈliːtɪŋ] N effacement *m*

deletion [dɪˈliːʃən] N **1** *(action) (of word, paragraph etc)* suppression *f*, effacement *m* **2** *(passage/word deleted)* passage *m*/mot *m* effacé *ou* supprimé; **without deletions or additions** sans ratures ni surcharges

delft [delft] N *Cer* faïence *f* de Delft

▸▸**d. blue** bleu *m* de faïence

Delhi belly [ˈdelɪ] N *Br Fam Hum* **to have D.** avoir la courante

deli [ˈdelɪ] N *Fam* = delicatessen

deliberate¹ [dɪˈlɪb(ə)rət] ADJ **1** *(intentional) (mistake, lie, rudeness)* délibéré, intentionnel, voulu; *(insolence)* calculé; *(insult)* prémédité; **it was quite d.!** c'était voulu, c'était fait exprès!; **it wasn't d.** ce n'était pas voulu **2** *(unhurried) (person)* circonspect, avisé; *(movement etc)* mesuré; *(voice)* posé; **she has a very d. way of working** elle travaille de manière très réglée

deliberate² [dɪˈlɪbəreɪt] VI *(of individual)* délibérer, réfléchir (**on** sur); *(of people, committee etc)* débattre, délibérer, réfléchir (**on** sur); **to d. over** *or* **on a question** délibérer d'une question; **they deliberated whether or not to let him go** ils délibéraient de le laisser partir ou non

VT *(question)* délibérer de

deliberately [dɪˈlɪb(ə)rətlɪ] ADV **1** *(intentionally)* intentionnellement, exprès, à dessein; **I d. didn't invite her** c'est intentionnellement que je ne l'ai pas invitée **2** *(unhurriedly)* avec mesure; **he paused d.** il fit une pause calculée

deliberation [dɪlɪbəˈreɪʃən] N **1** *(thought, discussion)* délibération *f*; **after due d.** après mûre délibération; **the deliberations of an assembly** les débats *mpl* d'une assemblée **2** *(lack of haste)* mesure *f*; **with d.** *(to say sth)* posément; *(to do sth)* de façon réfléchie; *(to walk)* d'un pas mesuré; *(to act)* avec circonspection

deliberative [dɪˈlɪbərətɪv] ADJ *(function)* délibératif; *(assembly)* délibérant

delicacy [ˈdelɪkəsɪ] N **1** *(fineness) (of embroidery, carving, fingers, features)* délicatesse *f*

2 *(sensitivity) (of instrument, mechanism)* sensibilité *f*; *(tactfulness)* délicatesse *f*, tact *m*; **she showed great d. of feeling** elle a fait preuve d'une grande délicatesse *ou* sensibilité; **negotiations of the utmost d.** négociations très délicates

3 *(gentleness, lightness) (of touch)* légèreté *f* **4** *(fragility) (of health, fabric)* fragilité *f* **5** *(subtlety) (of colour, flavours)* délicatesse *f* **6** *(food)* mets *m* délicat

delicate [ˈdelɪkət] ADJ **1** *(fine) (embroidery, carving, fingers)* délicat; *(feature)* fin, délicat **2** *(sensitive) (mechanism, matter, situation etc)* délicat; *(question)* épineux; *(feelings)* sensible; *(person) (over-refined, easily shocked)* précieux; *(tactful)* délicat, sensible; **it's a matter that needs d. handling** c'est une affaire qui doit être traitée avec délicatesse; **we're at a very d. stage in our negotiations** nous en sommes à une étape très délicate de nos négociations; **to tread on d. ground** toucher à des questions délicates

3 *(gentle, light) (touch)* délicat **4** *(fragile) (person, glass)* délicat; *(health, fabric)* fragile, délicat **5** *(subtle) (colour, flavour)* délicat

NPL **delicates** linge *m* délicat

delicately [ˈdelɪkətlɪ] ADV **1** *(finely) (carved,*

embroidered etc) délicatement, finement **2** (sensitively) (to handle question, approach a subject etc) avec délicatesse; **the mechanism is very d. balanced** le réglage du mécanisme est très sensible **3** (gently, lightly) (to put sth down, pick sth up etc) délicatement **4** (with subtlety) (coloured) délicatement; **d. flavoured** aux saveurs délicates

delicateness ['delɪkətnɪs] N = **delicacy 1, 2, 3, 4, 5**

delicatessen [delɪkə'tesən] N **1** (shop) épicerie f fine, traiteur m **2** (food) plats mpl cuisinés

delicious [dɪ'lɪʃəs] ADJ délicieux, exquis

deliciously [dɪ'lɪʃəslɪ] ADV délicieusement

delight [dɪ'laɪt] N **1** (source of pleasure) délice m; **the film is a d.** le film est un délice; **he is a d. to work with** c'est un plaisir de travailler avec lui; **it is such a d. to …** c'est si bon de …; **a d. to the eye** un bonheur pour les yeux; **to be sb's d.** faire le bonheur de qn; **the delights of the countryside** les délices fpl de la campagne **2** (pleasure) plaisir m; **much to the d. of …, to the great d. of …** au grand plaisir de …, à la grande joie de …; **to take d. in (doing) sth** prendre grand plaisir à faire qch; **I take no d. in telling you this, but …** ce n'est pas de gaieté de cœur que je dois vous annoncer que … ▪ VT (somebody) enchanter, ravir; **to d. the ear/the eye** charmer les oreilles/enchanter la vue
▸ **delight in** VT INSEP se délecter de, aimer beaucoup; **to d. in doing sth** se délecter à ou aimer beaucoup faire qch; **he delights in the new baby** il est aux anges devant le bébé; **he delights in being a father** il est ravi d'être père

delighted [dɪ'laɪtɪd] ADJ ravi, enchanté (**with** de); **I'm d. to make your acquaintance** je suis ravi ou enchanté de faire votre connaissance; **I am d. for you** je suis ravi pour vous; **I'd be d. to!** j'en serais ravi!

delightedly [dɪ'laɪtɪdlɪ] ADV avec ravissement

delightful [dɪ'laɪtfʊl] ADJ (person, smile) délicieux, ravissant, charmant; (meal) délicieux, exquis; (place) ravissant, charmant; (weekend, evening, sense of humour) délicieux; **a d. child** un enfant charmant; **they have a d. home** ils ont une maison ravissante

delightfully [dɪ'laɪtfʊlɪ] ADV délicieusement; **he sings d.** il chante à ravir

delimit [diː'lɪmɪt] VT délimiter

delimitation [dɪlɪmɪ'teɪʃən] N délimitation f

delimiter [diː'lɪmɪtər] N Comput délimiteur m

delineate [dɪ'lɪnɪeɪt] VT **1** (draw) (triangle etc) tracer; Fml (sb's features) dessiner; (profile) délinéer **2** (describe) (plan, proposal) présenter en détails; (character in novel) faire le portrait de

delineation [dɪlɪnɪ'eɪʃən] N **1** (drawing) (of triangle etc) dessin m, tracé m **2** (description) (of plan, proposal etc) présentation f en détails; (of character in novel) portrait m

delinquency [dɪ'lɪŋkwənsɪ] N **1** Law délinquance f **2** Fin défaillance f, défaut m de paiement

delinquent [dɪ'lɪŋkwənt] N **1** Law délinquant, -ante **2** Fin défaillant, -ante ▪ ADJ **1** Law (behaviour etc) délinquant **2** Fin (person) défaillant; (taxes) impayé
▸▸ Banking **d. account** compte m en souffrance

delirious [dɪ'lɪrɪəs] ADJ Med en délire, délirant; Fig en délire; Med **to be d.** délirer; Fig **to be d. with joy** délirer de joie, être délirant de

joie; Fig **I'm d.** je suis ravi; Fig **I'm d. at** or **about the prospect** cette perspective me rend fou de joie; Fig **she's d. about being pregnant** elle est ravie d'être enceinte; Fig **I'm not exactly d. about the prospect** la perspective ne m'enchante guère

deliriously [dɪ'lɪrɪəslɪ] ADV **to talk d.** délirer; Fig **to cheer d.** applaudir frénétiquement ou avec frénésie; **d. happy** délirant de joie

delirium [dɪ'lɪrɪəm] N Med délire m; **to be in a d.** être en plein délire; Fig Lit **to be in a d. of joy** être transporté de joie;
▸▸ Med **d. tremens** delirium tremens m

delist [diː'lɪst] VT Com, Mktg (product) déréférencer; St Exch (company) radier de la cote

delisting [diː'lɪstɪŋ] N Com, Mktg (of product) déréférencement m; St Exch (of company) radiation f de la cote

deliver [dɪ'lɪvər] VT **1** (parcel, telegram etc) remettre (**to** à); (letters) distribuer (**to** à); (goods) livrer (**to** à); **do you want your newspaper (to be) delivered?** est-ce que vous voulez qu'on vous livre votre journal?, est-ce que vous voulez que votre journal vous soit livré?; **do you have your milk delivered?** est-ce que vous vous faites livrer votre lait?, est-ce qu'on vous livre votre lait?; **to d. a message** faire une commission; **to d. sth to sb's house** Com livrer qch au domicile de qn; (non-commercial) porter qch chez qn; Com **d. to domicile** livrer à domicile; **to d. the goods** livrer les marchandises; Fig remplir ses engagements; (of new product etc) tenir ses promesses
2 Obst **to d. a child** mettre un enfant au monde; Old-fashioned **to d. a woman (of a child)** accoucher une femme; Old-fashioned **to be delivered of a child** accoucher d'un enfant
3 (blow) porter, donner; (ball etc) lancer; Ftbl **to d. a pass** faire une passe
4 (speech) faire, prononcer; (lecture) faire; Law (verdict) prononcer, rendre
5 (provide) (service) assurer; (of machine, dynamo etc) (power) débiter, fournir; Aut (hp) développer; Fin **to d. a profit** rapporter ou faire un profit; Fin **to d. shares** délivrer des valeurs
6 (fulfil) **can the party d. its election promises?** est-ce que le parti arrivera à tenir ses promesses électorales?
7 (rescue) (person) délivrer (**from his enemies** de ses ennemis); **to d. sb from death** sauver qn de la mort; Rel **d. us from evil** délivre-nous du mal
▪ VI (of supplier) livrer; Fig (of new product supplier, political party etc) tenir ses promesses; **it/he just doesn't d.** il n'est pas à la hauteur; **can Brown d. on reform?** est-ce que Brown pourra tenir ses promesses en ce qui concerne les réformes?
▸ **deliver up** VT SEP (surrender) (town) restituer, rendre (**to** à); (hostage, prisoner) remettre, livrer (**to** à)

deliverance [dɪ'lɪv(ə)rəns] N Fml (rescue) délivrance f (**from** de)

delivered [dɪ'lɪvəd] ADJ Com **d. at domicile** rendu à domicile; **d. free** livraison franco; **d. free at domicile** livré franco domicile; **d. free on board** rendu franco bord; **d. at frontier** rendu à la frontière

deliverer [dɪ'lɪvərər] N **1** Fml (saviour) libérateur, -trice, sauveur m **2** (of goods) livreur m

delivery [dɪ'lɪv(ə)rɪ] N **1** (of parcel, goods etc) livraison f; (of letter) remise f; (of mail) distribution f; **to take d. of sth** prendre livraison de qch; **charge for d.** (frais mpl de) port m; **parcels awaiting d.** colis mpl en souffrance; **free d.** livraison franco; **to pay on d.** payer à ou sur livraison; Com **d. duty**

paid/unpaid droits mpl acquittés/non acquittés
2 Obst accouchement m; **it was an easy d.** l'accouchement a été facile
3 (of speech) prononciation f; (of speaker) diction f; **to have a good d.** avoir un bon débit
4 Sport (of ball) lancement m, envoi m; (of player) manière f de lancer (la balle); Mil (of rocket etc) lancement m
5 (of water, power etc) débit m; (of pump) refoulement m
6 (of prisoner) reddition f, Law (of property) tradition f, (of bequest etc) délivrance f (**to** à); **for d.** (of stocks) au comptant
▸▸ **d. address** adresse f de livraison; **d. boy** livreur m; **d. charges** frais mpl de livraison; **d. conditions** conditions fpl de livraison; **d. date** date f de livraison; **d. deadline** terme m de livraison; **d. girl** livreuse f, **d. man** livreur m ou bordereau m ou bulletin m de livraison; **d. note** bon m ou bordereau m ou bulletin m de livraison; **d. point** lieu m de livraison; **d. schedule** planning m de livraison; **d. time** délai m de livraison; **d. van** camion m de livraison; (smaller) camionnette f de livraison

dell [del] N vallon m

delouse [diː'laʊs] VT (something) ôter les poux de; (somebody) épouiller, ôter les poux de

delphinium [del'fɪnɪəm] N (flower) pied-d'alouette m, pl pieds-d'alouette

delta ['deltə] N **1** (in Greek alphabet) delta m inv **2** (of river) delta m
▸▸ Aviat **d. wing** aile f (en) delta

delude [dɪ'luːd] VT (somebody) tromper, induire en erreur; **to d. oneself** se faire des illusions; **he deluded himself/me into thinking she would agree** il s'est/m'a persuadé qu'elle accepterait

deluded [dɪ'luːdɪd] ADJ qui se fait des illusions

deluge ['deljuːdʒ] N **1** (flood) déluge m; **a d. of rain** une pluie diluvienne **2** Fig (of words) déluge m; (of letters, questions etc) avalanche f
▪ VT (flood), Fig inonder (**with** de)

delusion [dɪ'luːʒən] N illusion f, Psy fantasme m; (bordering on insanity) délire m; **to be under a d.** se faire des illusions, s'abuser; **to suffer from delusions** être sujet à des hallucinations; Psy **delusions of grandeur** folie f des grandeurs; Hum **you're suffering from delusions of grandeur!** tu te fais des illusions!

de luxe [dɪ'lʌks] ADJ de luxe; (apartment) (de) grand standing; **d. room** chambre f catégorie 'luxe'

delve [delv] VI fouiller; **to d. in(to) one's pocket** fouiller dans sa poche; **to d. into** (the past) remonter dans, fouiller dans; (person's past) fouiller dans; (records, archives) explorer

Dem [dem] Am Pol abbr Democrat

demagnetize [diː'mægnɪtaɪz] VT démagnétiser

demagogic [deməˈgɒgɪk] ADJ démagogique

demagogue ['deməgɒg] N démagogue m

demand [dɪ'mɑːnd] N **1** (request) demande f, réclamation f, **d. for payment** demande de paiement; **final d. (notice)** dernier rappel m; **payable on d.** payable sur demande
2 Econ demande f, **to be in (great) d.** être (très) demandé ou recherché; **to be much in d. as …** (of person) être très demandé en tant que …; **there's not much d. for it** ce n'est pas très demandé, ce n'est pas très recherché
3 demands (of workers, kidnappers) exigences fpl, (of a situation, job etc) nécessités fpl,

exigences *fpl*; **to give in to sb's demands** céder aux exigences de qn; **you make too many demands on her** tu exiges trop d'elle; **to make great demands on sb's patience** exiger de qn beaucoup de patience; **I have many demands on my time** je suis très pris; **with all of these demands on your time, how do you manage to …** tu es tellement pris, comment fais-tu pour …

VT1 *(something)* réclamer (**of, from** à); **to d. payment from sb** sommer qn de payer; **they're demanding payment** ils réclament le paiement; **to d. an apology/explanation** exiger des excuses/une explication; **I d. to speak to the manager** j'exige de parler au directeur; **to d. to know whether …** insister pour savoir si …; **to d. that …** exiger que … + *sub*

2 *(of situation, job etc)* demander, exiger; **the matter demands great care** l'affaire exige *ou* réclame beaucoup de soin

▸▸ *Com, Mktg* **d. analysis** analyse *f* de la demande; **d. curve** courbe *f* (d'évolution) de la demande; *Am Banking* **d. deposit** dépôt *m* à vue; *Am Banking* **d. deposit account** compte *m* à vue; *Com, Mktg* **d. driver** dynamisant *m* de la demande; *Com, Mktg* **d. forecasting** prévision *f* de la demande; **d. function** fonction *f* de demande; *Com* **d. management** contrôle *m* de la demande; *Fin* **d. note** bon *m* à vue

> Note that the most common meaning of the French word **demande** is *request* and that the most common meaning of the French verb **demander** is **to ask** or **to request**.

demanding [dɪ'mɑːndɪŋ] **ADJ** *(person)* exigeant; *(job)* exigeant, astreignant; *(task)* astreignant; **being a physiotherapist is physically d.** être kinésithérapeute est physiquement astreignant; **children are at their most d. between the ages of two and four** les enfants demandent le plus d'attention entre deux et quatre ans

demand-led **ADJ** *Econ* tiré par la demande

demand-pull inflation **N** *Econ* inflation *f* par la demande

demarcation [diːmɑː'keɪʃən] **N** démarcation *f*, délimitation *f*

▸▸ **d. dispute** conflit *m* d'attributions; **d. line** ligne *f* de démarcation

demarket [diː'mɑːkɪt] **VT** retirer du marché

demarketing [diː'mɑːkɪtɪŋ] **N** démarketing *m*

demean [dɪ'miːn] **VT to d. oneself** s'abaisser, s'avilir; **it was very demeaning having to …** c'était très avilissant de devoir …; **to d. one's office** rabaisser sa charge

demeanour, *Am* **demeanor** [dɪ'miːnər] **N** *(behaviour)* comportement *m*, attitude *f*, conduite *f*; *(bearing, mien)* air *m*

demented [dɪ'mentɪd] **ADJ** fou, *f* folle; *Med* dément; **to become d.** tomber en démence; **to be d. with grief/anger/worry** être fou de douleur/de colère/d'inquiétude; *Fig* **like one d.** *(to scream etc)* comme un fou

dementia [dɪ'menʃɪə] **N** *Med* démence *f*

demerara [demə'reərə] **N** cassonade *f*

▸▸ **d. sugar** cassonade *f*

demerger [diː'mɜːdʒər] **N** scission *f*; **several new companies were formed after the d. of the holding group** plusieurs entreprises nouvelles ont été créées à la suite de la scission du holding

demerit [diː'merɪt] **N 1** *Fml (fault)* démérite *m*, tort *m* **2** *Am Sch* blâme *m*

demesne [də'meɪn] **N 1** *Law (possession)* possession *f* **2** *Hist Fml (land)* domaine *m*

demigod ['demɪgɒd] **N** demi-dieu *m*, *pl* demi-dieux

demijohn ['demɪdʒɒn] **N** *Ind etc* dame-jeanne *f*, *pl* dames-jeannes, bonbonne *f*

demilitarization [diːmɪlɪt(ə)raɪ'zeɪʃən] **N** démilitarisation *f*

demilitarize [diː'mɪlɪtəraɪz] **VT** démilitariser

demi-pension [dəmɪ'pɑ̃sjɔ̃] **N** demi-pension *f*, *pl* demi-pensions

demise [dɪ'maɪz] **N** *Admin (of sb)* décès *m*, mort *f*, *Fig (of newspaper, empire etc)* disparition *f*; **this meant the d. of our hopes** cela a mis fin à nos espoirs

demisemiquaver ['demɪsemɪkweɪvər] **N** *Mus* triple croche *f*

demist [diː'mɪst] **VT** désembuer

demister [diː'mɪstər] **N** *Aut (dispositif m)* antibuée *m*, désembueur *m*

demisting [diː'mɪstɪŋ] **N** *Aut* désembuage *m*

demo ['deməʊ] **N** *Fam* **1** *(protest)* manif *f* **2** *(of singer, musician)* disque *m*/cassette *f*/vidéo *f* de démonstration

▸▸ *Comput* **d. disk** disquette *f* de démonstration *ou* d'évaluation; **d. tape** bande *f* démo; *Comput* **d. version** version *f* de démonstration *ou* d'évaluation

demob [diː'mɒb] *Old-fashioned Br Mil Fam* **VT (-bb-)** démobiliser

N démobilisation *f*

demobilization [diːməʊbɪlaɪ'zeɪʃən] **N** *Mil* démobilisation *f*

demobilize [diː'məʊbɪlaɪz] **VT & VI** *Mil* démobiliser

democracy [dɪ'mɒkrəsɪ] **N** démocratie *f*; **people's d.** démocratie populaire

democrat ['deməkræt] **N** démocrate *mf*; *Am Pol* **the Democrats** le parti démocrate

democratic [demə'krætɪk] **ADJ** démocratique

▸▸ **d. deficit** déficit *m* démocratique; **d. government** la démocratie *f*; **the D. Party** le parti *m* démocrate (américain); **d. socialism** socialisme *m* démocratique

democratically [demə'krætɪklɪ] **ADV** *(elected etc)* démocratiquement

democratize [dɪ'mɒkrətaɪz] **VT** démocratiser

VI se démocratiser

demodulation [diːmɒdjʊ'leɪʃən] **N** *Electron (of signal etc)* démodulation *f*

demodulator [diː'mɒdjʊleɪtər] **N** *Comput* démodulateur *m*

demographer [dɪ'mɒgrəfər] **N** démographe *mf*

demographic [deməʊ'græfɪk] **ADJ** démographique

▸▸ **d. analysis** analyse *f* démographique; **d. profile** profil *m* démographique; **d. segment** segment *m* démographique; **d. segmentation** segmentation *f* démographique; **d. trends** tendances *fpl* démographiques

demographics [deməʊ'græfɪks] **N** statistiques *fpl* démographiques; **the d. show that …** selon les statistiques démographiques … VOIR GRAMMAIRE A10

demography [dɪ'mɒgrəfɪ] **N** démographie *f*

demolish [dɪ'mɒlɪʃ] **VT** *(building, wall, argument)* démolir; *Fam (cake, meal etc)* dévorer; *Fig* **to d. sb** *(in argument)* démolir qn; *(in competition, fight)* mettre la pâtée à qn

demolition [demə'lɪʃən] **N** démolition *f*

▸▸ **d. contractor** démolisseur *m*; *Sport* **d. derby** = course *f* de voitures dans laquelle celles-ci sont délibérément détruites; **d. squad** équipe *f* de démolition; **d. work** travail *m* de démolition

demon ['diːmən] **N** démon *m*, diable *m*; **the d. drink** le démon de l'alcool; *Fig* **that child's**

a little d. cet enfant est un petit démon; *Fig* **he's a d. for work** c'est un monstre de travail; *Fig* **she's a d. for punctuality** elle insiste énormément sur la ponctualité

demonetize [diː'mʌnɪtaɪz] **VT** *Fin (currency)* démonétiser

demoniac [dɪ'məʊnɪæk] **ADJ, N** démoniaque *mf*

demoniacal [diːmə'naɪək(ə)l] **ADJ** démoniaque

demonic [dɪ'mɒnɪk] **ADJ** *(cruelty, rage)* démoniaque

▸▸ **d. possession** possession *f* diabolique

demonology [diːmə'nɒlədʒɪ] **N** démonologie *f*

demonstrable [dɪ'mɒnstrəb(ə)l, 'demən-] **ADJ** *(fact)* démontrable; **that is d. nonsense** c'est clairement absurde

demonstrably [dɪ'mɒnstrəblɪ, 'demən-] **ADV** **d. true/false statement** affirmation *f* visiblement *ou* manifestement vraie/fausse; **that's d. false** c'est faux de toute évidence; **that is d. not the case** de toute évidence *ou* manifestement ce n'est pas le cas

demonstrate ['demənstreɪt] **VT 1** *(prove)* *(truth)* démontrer; **that just demonstrates how stupid he is** ça ne fait que démontrer à quel point il est stupide **2** *(show, explain)* *(machine, alarm system etc)* donner une démonstration pratique du fonctionnement de; *(one's skills, use of sth)* faire une démonstration de; **to d. how sth works** montrer comment qch fonctionne

VI *Pol etc* manifester, faire une manifestation (**against** contre; **for, in favour of** pour, en faveur de)

demonstration [demən'streɪʃən] **N 1** *(of truth)* démonstration *f* **2** *(of machine, alarm system)* démonstration *f* pratique; *Sch* (séance *f* de) démonstration; **to give sb a d. of one's skills** faire une démonstration de ses talents à qn; **would you like a d.?** est-ce que vous voulez que je vous fasse une démonstration?; **a d. of affection** une manifestation *ou* un témoignage d'affection; **a d. of power** une démonstration de force **3** *(political etc)* manifestation *f*; **to hold** *or* **stage a d.** manifester

▸▸ **d. car** voiture *f* de démonstration; *Sch* **d. class** (séance de) démonstration

> Note that the French word **démonstration** is never used to describe a protest.

demonstrative [dɪ'mɒnstrətɪv] **ADJ 1** *(person)* démonstratif **2** *(argument etc)* démonstratif **3** *Gram (adjectif etc)* démonstratif VOIR GRAMMAIRE A30-1; B14-15

demonstrator ['demənstreɪtər] **N 1** *(of machine etc)* démonstrateur, -trice; *Sch* **science d.** préparateur, -trice en science **2** *Am (car)* voiture *f* de démonstration **3** *(political etc)* manifestant, -ante

demoralization [dɪmɒrəlaɪ'zeɪʃən] **N** démoralisation *f*

demoralize [dɪ'mɒrəlaɪz] **VT** démoraliser

demoralizing [dɪ'mɒrəlaɪzɪŋ] **ADJ** démoralisant

demote [dɪ'məʊt] **VT** *(person)* rétrograder; *Mil* **he's been demoted to private** il a été rétrogradé au grade de simple soldat; **she's been demoted to assistant manager** elle a été rétrogradée au poste de directeur-adjoint

demotic [dɪ'mɒtɪk] **ADJ** *Fml* populaire, du peuple; *Ling (Greek)* démotique

demotion [dɪ'məʊʃən] **N** rétrogradation *f*

demotivate [diː'məʊtɪveɪt] **VT** démotiver

demotivation [diːməʊtɪ'veɪʃən] **N** démotivation *f*

demur [dɪ'mɜːr] **N** *Fml* objection *f*; **without d.** sans faire d'objection

vi (**-rr-**) **1** *Fml* soulever des objections (**at, to** contre) **2** *Law* opposer une exception

demure [dɪˈmjʊər] **ADJ** modeste, réservé; *Pej* d'une modestie affectée

demurely [dɪˈmjʊəlɪ] **ADV** d'un air modeste *ou* réservé; *Pej* avec une modestie affectée

demureness [dɪˈmjʊənɪs] **N** modestie *f*, réserve *f*; *Pej* modestie affectée

demurrage [dɪˈmʌrɪdʒ] **N** *Com* surestarie *f*

demystify [diːˈmɪstɪfaɪ] **vt** démystifier

demythologize [diːmɪˈθɒlədʒaɪz] **VT** démythifier

den [den] **N 1** (*of wild animal*) tanière *f*, antre *m*; *Fig* (*of criminals, brigands*) nid *m*, repaire *m*; *Fig* **d. of thieves** repaire de voleurs; **gambling d.** maison *f* de jeu; **d. of iniquity** lieu *m* de débauche *ou* de perdition **2** *esp Am* (*in home*) petit salon *m* familial
▸▸*Am* **d. mother** (*in scout group*) cheftaine *f*

denationalization [diːnæʃənəlaɪˈzeɪʃən] **N** dénationalisation *f*

denationalize [diːˈnæʃənəlaɪz] **VT** dénationaliser

denature [diːˈneɪtʃər] **VT** (*product*) dénaturer

dengue [ˈdeŋgɪ] **N** *Med* dengue *f*
▸▸**d. fever** dengue

denial [dɪˈnaɪəl] **N 1** (*of right, request*) refus *m*; (*of justice*) déni *m* de justice **2** (*of truth of sth, guilt*) démenti *m*; **absolute** *or* **flat d.** dénégation *f* absolue *ou* catégorique; **to issue a d.** publier un démenti **3** *Psy* dénégation *f*; **to be in d.** refuser de se rendre à l'évidence **4** *Bible* **Peter's d. of Christ** le reniement de Pierre

denier [ˈdenɪər] **N** *Tex* (*of hosiery*) denier *m*; **a 30-d. stocking** un bas 30 deniers

denigrate [ˈdenɪgreɪt] **VT** *Lit* dénigrer

denim [ˈdenɪm] **N 1** (*fabric*) (toile *f* de) jean *m*; **d. skirt** jupe *f* en jean **2 denims** (*overalls*) bleus *mpl* (de travail); (*jeans*) jean *m*

denizen [ˈdenɪzən] **N** *Lit, Hum* habitant, -ante, hôte *mf*; **denizens of the deep** hôtes *ou* habitants des profondeurs

Denmark [ˈdenmɑːk] **N** Danemark *m*

denominate [dɪˈnɒmɪneɪt] **VT 1** *Fml* (*name*) dénommer **2** *Fin* libeller; **denominated in dollars** libellé en dollars

denomination [dɪnɒmɪˈneɪʃən] **N 1** *Rel* culte *m*, confession *f* **2** *Fin* valeur *f*; (*of share, of banknote*) coupure *f*; **in denominations of** en coupures de; **coins of all denominations** pièces *fpl* de toutes valeurs; **(notes of) small denominations** petites coupures **3** *Fml* (*name*) dénomination *f*

denominational [dɪnɒmɪˈneɪʃən(ə)l] **ADJ** confessionnel

denominator [dɪˈnɒmɪneɪtər] **N** *Math* dénominateur *m*; *also Fig* **lowest common d.** plus petit dénominateur commun; *also Fig* **to have a common d.** avoir un dénominateur commun

denotation [diːnəʊˈteɪʃən] **N** (*indication*) indication *f*; (*meaning*) signification *f*

denote [dɪˈnəʊt] **VT 1** (*indicate*) dénoter, montrer, indiquer (**sth** qch; **that** que) **2** (*mean*) signifier; *Ling* dénoter

denouement [deɪˈnuːmɒn] **N** (*of play, situation*) dénouement *m*

denounce [dɪˈnaʊns] **VT 1** (*inform against*) (*criminal, crime*) dénoncer; **to d. sb to the authorities** signaler qn à la justice; **to d. sb as an impostor** taxer qn d'imposture **2** (*protest about*) (*abuse, government action, drug-taking etc*) dénoncer, s'élever contre; (*modern art etc*) condamner; **they have been denounced as nothing more than murderers** ils ont été accusés de n'être rien de moins

que des assassins **3** (*declare termination of*) (*treaty*) dénoncer

dense [dens] **ADJ 1** *Phys* (*body, metal etc*) dense **2** (*smoke, fog etc*) épais, *f* -aisse; (*crowd*) compact; (*population*) nombreux; (*text, argument*) dense **3** *Fam* (*stupid*) stupide, bête

densely [ˈdenslɪ] **ADV d. wooded country** pays couvert de forêts épaisses; **d. populated region** région très peuplée; **to be d. packed together** être serrés les uns contre les autres; **d. written** écrit dans un style dense

denseness [ˈdensnɪs] **N 1** (*of fog*) épaisseur *f*, (*of text, writing*) densité *f*; **in spite of the d. of the crowd** bien que la foule fût si compacte **2** *Fam* (*of person*) stupidité *f*

density [ˈdensɪtɪ] **N 1** *Phys, Chem, Elec, Phot etc* densité *f*; *Tech* masse *f* volumique; *Nucl* **ion/neutron d.** densité ionique/neutronique **2** (*of population, traffic*) densité *f*
▸▸**d. chart** (*in hotel*) feuille *f* d'occupation journalière

dent [dent] **N** (*in saucepan etc*) bosse *f*, (*in ground*) trou *m*; (*in pillow, cushion*) creux *m*; **there's a d. in the car** la voiture a une bosse; *Fig* **to make a d. in one's fortune** faire une brèche à sa fortune; *Fig* **to make** *or* **put a d. in sb's self-confidence** entamer la confiance en soi *ou* l'assurance de qn; *Fig* **to make** *or* **put a d. in one's savings/budget** faire un trou dans ses économies/son budget
VT bosseler, cabosser; *Fig* **to d. sb's self-confidence** entamer la confiance en soi *ou* l'assurance de qn; **my self-confidence has been dented** mon assurance en a pris un coup

dental [ˈdent(ə)l] **ADJ 1** *Med* dentaire **2** *Ling* dental, -aux
▸▸**d. appointment** rendez-vous *m inv* chez le dentiste; **d. care** soins *mpl* dentaires; *Ling* **d. consonant** (consonne *f*) dentale *f*; **d. floss** fil *m* dentaire; **d. hygiene** hygiène *f* dentaire; **your d. hygiene is poor** vous avez une mauvaise hygiène dentaire; **d. hygienist** ≃ assistant, -ante de dentiste (*qui s'occupe du détartrage etc*); **d. nurse** assistant, -ante dentaire; *Am* **d. office** cabinet *m* dentaire; *Am* **d. practice** cabinet dentaire; **d. spa** = cabinet *m* dentaire proposant des soins tels que manucures ou soins de la peau afin de permettre aux patients de se détendre; *Br* **d. surgeon** chirurgien-dentiste *m*, *pl* chirurgiens-dentistes; **d. surgery** cabinet dentaire

dented [ˈdentɪd] **ADJ** bosselé, cabossé

dentifrice [ˈdentɪfrɪs] **N** *Old-fashioned* dentifrice *m*

dentine [ˈdentiːn] **N** dentine *f*

dentist [ˈdentɪst] **N** dentiste *mf*; **to go to the d.'s** aller chez le dentiste; *Fam* **the d.'s chair** le fauteuil du dentiste

dentistry [ˈdentɪstrɪ] **N** dentisterie *f*

dentition [denˈtɪʃən] **N** dentition *f*

dentures [ˈdentʃəz] **NPL** dentier *m*, prothèse *f* dentaire; **to wear d.** porter un dentier

Note that the French word **denture** is a false friend and is never a translation for the English word **dentures**. It means **set of teeth**.

denude [dɪˈnjuːd] **VT** dénuder, dépouiller; **a landscape denuded of trees** un paysage sans arbres

denunciation [dɪnʌnsɪˈeɪʃən] **N 1** (*of accomplice etc*) dénonciation *f* **2** (*condemnation*) (*of person, abuse, modern art etc*) condamnation *f* **3** (*of treaty*) dénonciation *f*

Denver [ˈdenvər]
▸▸*Fam* **D. boot** sabot *m* de Denver

deny [dɪˈnaɪ] **VT 1** (*fact, truth*) nier, refuser d'admettre; (*report*) démentir; (*accusation*)

repousser; (*statement*) opposer un démenti à; **the accused denies the charge** l'accusé nie; **to d. having done sth** nier avoir fait qch; **there is no denying the fact** c'est un fait indéniable; **there's no denying that ...** on ne saurait nier que ...; **to d. all knowledge of sth** nier avoir connaissance de qch **2** (*person, one's faith*) renier **3** (*request etc*) refuser; **to d. sb sth** *or* **sth to sb** refuser qch à qn; **to have one's request denied** se voir refuser sa demande; **to be denied access to sth/sb** se voir refuser l'accès à qch/qn; **to d. oneself sth** se priver de qch; **to d. oneself for one's children** se priver pour ses enfants

deodorant [diːˈəʊdərənt] **N** (*for body*) déodorant *m*; (*for room*) désodorisant *m*; **d. spray** déodorant/désodorisant en bombe

deodorize [diːˈəʊdəraɪz] **VT** désodoriser

deodorizer [diːˈəʊdəraɪzə(r)] **N** (*for home*) désodorisant *m*

deontology [diːɒnˈtɒlədʒɪ] **N** *Phil* déontologie *f*

deoxidize [diːˈɒksɪdaɪz] **VT** *Chem, Ind* désoxyder

deoxyribonucleic [diːˈɒksɪraɪbəʊnjuːˈkleɪk] **ADJ** désoxyribonucléique
▸▸**d. acid** acide *m* désoxyribonucléique

dep (*abbr* **departure/departs**) dép

depart [dɪˈpɑːt] **VI 1** *Fml* (*leave*) partir; **they departed for Canada from Portsmouth** ils sont partis pour le Canada depuis Portsmouth; **departing from** en partance de; **the train departing from platform four** le train au départ quai numéro quatre **2** (*differ, deviate*) **to d. from** (*version of events*) différer de, s'écarter de; (*custom*) abandonner; (*subject*) sortir de, s'écarter de; (*truth*) manquer à; **to d. from sb's wishes** ne pas respecter la volonté de qn
VT *Lit* **to d. this life** *or* **earth** quitter cette vie *ou* ce monde

departed [dɪˈpɑːtɪd] **ADJ 1** (*glory etc*) passé, évanoui **2** (*dead*) mort, défunt, décédé
N the d. le mort/la morte/les mort(e)s

department [dɪˈpɑːtmənt] **N 1** (*in company, organization*) département *m*, service *m*; (*in shop*) rayon *m*; *Univ* département *m*; **the French d.** (*at school*) la section de français; **personnel/accounts d.** service du personnel/de la comptabilité; *Fig* **that's not (really) my d.** ce n'est pas mon rayon **2** (*of government*) ministère *m* **3** *Geog* (*in France*) département *m*
▸▸*Am* **D. of Agriculture** ministère de l'Agriculture; *Br* **D. of Culture, Media and Sport** ministère de la Culture, de la Communication et des Sports; *Am* **D. of Defense** ministère de la Défense; *Am* **D. of Education**, *Br* **D. for Education and Skills** ≃ ministère de l'Éducation nationale; *Am* **D. of Energy** = ministère américain de l'Énergie; *Br* **D. of the Environment, Food and Rural Affairs** ≃ ministère de l'Agriculture et de l'Environnement; *Br* **D. of Health** ministère de la Santé; *Am* **D. of Health and Human Services** ministère de la Santé; *Am Formerly* **D. of Housing and Urban Development** ministère du logement et de la ville; *Am* **D. of the Interior** ≃ ministère de l'Intérieur; *Br* **D. for International Development** ≃ secrétariat *m* d'État à la Coopération; *Am* **D. of Justice** ministère de la Justice; *Am* **D. of Labor** ≃ ministère de l'Emploi et de la Solidarité; *Br* **D. of Public Works** ≃ ministère de l'Équipement; *Br* **D. of Social Security** ≃ ministère des Affaires sociales; *Am* **D. of State** Département d'État, ≃ ministère des Affaires étrangères; **d. store** grand magasin *m*; *Am* **D. of Trade** ministère du Commerce; *Br* **D. of Trade and Industry** ministère du Commerce et de l'Industrie; *Br* **D. of Transport**, *Am* **D. of Transportation** ministère des Transports; *Am* **D.**

of Veterans Affairs ministère des Anciens combattants; *Br* **D. of Work and Pensions** ≃ ministère de l'Emploi et de la Solidarité

departmental [dɪːpɑːtˈment(ə)l] ADJ départemental

▸▸ **d. head** chef *m* de service; *Univ* chef du département; **d. manager** chef de service; **d. meeting** réunion *f* de service

departure [dɪˈpɑːtʃər] N 1 *(from place) (of person, train etc)* départ *m*; *Aviat* **there's only one d. a day for Montreal** il n'y a qu'un départ par jour pour Montréal; *Fml* **to take one's d.** prendre congé; **her unexpected d. from politics** son départ inattendu de la scène politique 2 *Fig* déviation *f* (**from** de); *(from general rule)* exception *f*, *(from truth)* manquement *m* (**from** à); **d. from normal procedure** dérogation *f* à la procédure habituelle; **this type of holiday is something of a d. for him** ce type de vacances représente un grand changement pour lui; **a d. from his usual habits** une action contraire à ses habitudes; **politics is a new d. for her** la politique constitue un nouveau départ pour elle

▸▸ **departures book** *(in hotel)* registre *m* des départs; **d. date** date *f* de départ; **d. gate** *(in airport)* porte *f* (d'embarquement); **d. list** liste *f* des départs; **d. lounge** salle *f* d'embarquement; **d. quay** quai *m* de départ; **d. tax** taxe *f* de départ; **d. time** heure *f* de départ

depend [dɪˈpend] VI dépendre (**on** de); **that depends, it all depends** ça dépend; **that depends entirely on you** cela ne tient qu'à vous; **it depends on the weather** ça dépend du temps; **it depends on how much money I have** ça dépend de combien d'argent j'ai; **depending on whether ...** suivant que ...; **it depends on whether she accepts** ça dépend si elle accepte

▸**depend on** VT INSEP *(rely on) (person)* compter sur, faire confiance à; *(car, alarm system, weather etc)* compter sur; **we need somebody who can be depended on to be discreet** il nous faut quelqu'un dont on sait qu'il sera discret; **he can be depended on not to become discouraged** on peut être sûr qu'il ne se découragera pas; *Iron* **you can d. on him to be late** on peut être sûr qu'il arrive en retard; **you can never d. on what he says** on ne peut pas se fier à ce qu'il dit; **you can d. on it** tu peux compter dessus; **to d. on imports from abroad** être tributaire de l'étranger; **to d. financially/emotionally on sb** dépendre de qn financièrement/sur le plan affectif

dependability [dɪpendəˈbɪlɪtɪ] N *(of person)* sérieux *m*; *(of information)* véracité *f*, *(of machine)* fiabilité *f*; **I'm still not convinced of his d.** je ne suis pas encore convaincu de son sérieux *ou* qu'on peut compter sur lui

dependable [dɪˈpendəb(ə)l] ADJ *(person)* digne de confiance, sur qui l'on peut compter; *(information)* sûr; *(machine)* d'un fonctionnement sûr, fiable; **he is not d.** on ne peut pas compter sur lui; **to be a d. source of income** fournir un revenu régulier

dependance [dɪˈpendəns] N *Am* = **dependence**

dependant [dɪˈpendənt] N personne *f* à charge

Attention: ne pas confondre avec l'adjectif **dependent**.

dependence, *Am* **dependance** [dɪˈpendəns] N 1 *(reliance)* dépendance *f* (**on** de) 2 *(trust)* confiance *f* (**on** en) 3 *Med* (état *m* de) dépendance *f* (**on heroin** (à l'égard) de l'héroïne)

dependency [dɪˈpendənsɪ] N 1 *esp Am* = **dependence** 2 *(territory) (of country)* dépendance *f*

▸▸ **d. culture** = situation *f* d'une société dont les membres ont une mentalité d'assistés

dependent [dɪˈpendənt] ADJ 1 dépendant (**on** de); *Law* relevant (**on** de); **to be d. on** *(somebody, something)* dépendre de; *(financially) (somebody)* dépendre (financièrement) de; **institution d. on voluntary contributions** institution soutenue par des contributions bénévoles; **two d. children** deux enfants à charge 2 *Med* **to be d. on heroin/drugs** être héroïnomane/toxicomane; **to be d. on insulin** être insulinodépendant 3 *Gram (clause)* subordonné

Attention: ne pas confondre avec le nom **dependant**.

depict [dɪˈpɪkt] VT dépeindre, représenter

depiction [dɪˈpɪkʃən] N peinture *f*, description *f*

depilatory [dɪˈpɪlət(ə)rɪ] ADJ, N dépilatoire *m*

deplane [diːˈpleɪn] VI *Am* descendre d'avion, débarquer

deplete [dɪˈpliːt] VT réduire; **stocks are very depleted** les stocks sont très bas

depleted uranium [dɪˈpliːtɪd] N *Chem* uranium *m* appauvri

depletion [dɪˈpliːʃən] N réduction *f*

deplorable [dɪˈplɔːrəb(ə)l] ADJ déplorable, lamentable

deplorably [dɪˈplɔːrəblɪ] ADV déplorablement, lamentablement

deplore [dɪˈplɔːr] VT déplorer, regretter vivement; **to d. the fact that** déplorer le fait que

deploy [dɪˈplɔɪ] VT *(troops, resources)*, *Fig (argument)* déployer; **I think your talents would be better deployed elsewhere** je pense que vos talents seraient mieux utilisés ailleurs
VI se déployer

deployment [dɪˈplɔɪmənt] N *Mil, Fig* déploiement *m*

depolarization [diːpəʊləraɪˈzeɪʃən] N *Opt, Elec* dépolarisation *f*

depolarize [diːˈpəʊləraɪz] VT *Opt, Elec* dépolariser

deponent [dɪˈpəʊnənt] N 1 *Gram* verbe *m* déponent 2 *Law* témoin *m* déposant
ADJ *Gram (verb)* déponent

depopulate [diːˈpɒpjʊleɪt] VT *(country)* dépeupler; **to become depopulated** se dépeupler

depopulation [diːpɒpjʊˈleɪʃən] N *(of country)* dépopulation *f*, dépeuplement *m*; **rural d.** dépeuplement des campagnes

deport [dɪˈpɔːt] VT *(foreigner)* expulser; *(political prisoner etc)* déporter

deportation [diːpɒˈteɪʃən] N *(of foreigner)* expulsion *f*, *(of political prisoner etc)* déportation *f*

▸▸ **d. order** arrêt *m* d'expulsion

deportee [diːpɔːˈtiː] N *(foreigner)* expulsé, -ée; *(political prisoner etc)* déporté, -ée

deportment [dɪˈpɔːtmənt] N tenue *f*, maintien *m*

depose [dɪˈpəʊz] VT 1 *(monarch)* déposer, détrôner; *Fig (champion, head of party)* détrôner, destituer 2 *Law (testify)* déposer, attester (**that** que)
VI *Law* faire une déposition

deposit [dɪˈpɒzɪt] N 1 *Banking* dépôt *m*; **to make a d.** déposer de l'argent; **to make a d. of £500** déposer 500 livres en banque; **bank d.** dépôt bancaire *ou* en banque; **on d.** en dépôt
2 *Com (first payment)* acompte *m*; *(not returnable)* arrhes *fpl*; *(returnable)* caution *f*,

(on bottle) consigne *f*; **to pay** *or* **put down a d. on sth** verser un acompte/des arrhes sur qch; *Br Pol* **to lose one's d.** *(of candidate)* perdre sa caution
3 *(of minerals)* gisement *m*, couche *f*
4 *(material)* dépôt(s) *m(pl)*, précipité *m*; **alluvial deposits** alluvions *fpl*
5 *(coating)* dépôt *m*; *Tech* apport *m*; **d. of silver** précipité *m* d'argent
VT 1 *(money in bank)* déposer; *(document) (with a bank)* mettre en dépôt (**with** dans); *(with a solicitor etc)* confier (**with** à); *Fin* **to d. as security** nantir, gager; *Fin* **to d. security** déposer une caution
2 *(put down)* déposer, poser (**sth on sth** qch sur qch)
3 *(of liquid) (sediment)* déposer; **the flood waters deposited a layer of mud** les inondations ont laissé un dépôt de boue

▸▸ *Br Banking* **d. account** compte *m* livret, compte de dépôt; *(when notice has to be given before withdrawal)* compte à terme; *Banking* **d. bank** banque *f* de dépôt; *Banking* **d. book** livret *m* *ou* carnet *m* de dépôt; *Banking* **d. money** monnaie *f* de banque, monnaie scripturale; *Banking* **d. receipt** récépissé *m* de dépôt

deposition[1] [diːpəˈzɪʃən] N 1 *(of monarch)* déposition *f* 2 *Law* déposition *f*, témoignage *m*

deposition[2] VT *Mktg (product)* dépositionner

depositor [dɪˈpɒzɪtər] N *Banking* déposant, -ante

depository [dɪˈpɒzɪt(ə)rɪ] N dépôt *m*, magasin *m*, entrepôt *m*; **furniture d.** garde-meubles *m inv*

depot [ˈdepəʊ] N 1 *Mil* dépôt *m*; *Com etc* dépôt *m*, entrepôt *m*; **goods d.** dépôt de marchandises; **supply/ammunition d.** dépôt de ravitaillement/munitions 2 *Am (station)* **(railroad) d.** gare *f* (de chemin de fer); **bus d.** gare routière; **freight d.** gare des marchandises

depravation [deprəˈveɪʃən] N dépravation *f*

deprave [dɪˈpreɪv] VT dépraver, corrompre

depraved [dɪˈpreɪvd] ADJ *(person, taste)* dépravé, corrompu

depravity [dɪˈprævɪtɪ] N dépravation *f*, perversion *f*

deprecate [ˈdeprɪkeɪt] VT *(action)* désapprouver; **stop deprecating yourself** arrêtez de vous dévaloriser

deprecating [ˈdeprɪkeɪtɪŋ] ADJ 1 *(disapproving)* désapprobateur, -trice 2 *(apologetic)* modeste

deprecatingly [ˈdeprɪkeɪtɪŋlɪ] ADV 1 *(disapprovingly)* avec désapprobation 2 *(apologetically)* avec modestie, modestement

deprecatory [ˈdeprɪkeɪtərɪ] ADJ 1 *(modest) (smile etc)* de modestie; *(remark)* modeste 2 *(disapproving)* désapprobateur, -trice; **to be d. about sth/sb** désapprouver qch/qn

depreciate [dɪˈpriːʃɪeɪt] VT 1 *Com (value of sth)* déprécier, rabaisser; *Fin (currency)* dévaloriser, déprécier; *Com, Ind (property, equipment etc)* amortir 2 *(denigrate)* dénigrer, déprécier
VI *(of property etc)* se déprécier, diminuer de valeur; *(of prices, shares etc)* baisser; *(of equipment)* se dévaluer, s'avilir; **the pound has depreciated against the dollar** la livre a reculé par rapport au dollar; **the tractor depreciated by £200** la valeur du tracteur a baissé de 200 livres

depreciated [dɪˈpriːʃɪeɪtɪd] ADJ *Acct* amorti; *(currency)* déprécié

depreciation [dɪpriːʃɪˈeɪʃən] N 1 *(of money)*, *Ind (equipment etc)* dépréciation *f*, *Acct (of property, equipment)* amortissement *m*; *Fin (of currency)* dépréciation, dévalorisation *f*; *(amount)* moins-value *f* **2** *(denigration)* dénigrement *m*, dépréciation *f*

▸▸ **d. charges** frais *mpl* d'amortissement; **d. period** période *f* d'amortissement; *Acct* **d. rate** taux *m* d'amortissement; *Acct* **d. schedule** tableau *m ou* plan *m* d'amortissement

depreciatory [dɪˈpriːʃɪət(ə)rɪ] **ADJ** *(remark etc)* de dénigrement, critique

depredation [deprɪˈdeɪʃən] **N** *(usu pl) (of war)* déprédation(s) *f(pl)*; *(by soldiers, looters etc)* pillage *m*

depress [dɪˈpres] **VT 1** *(sadden, dishearten) (person)* déprimer, décourager **2** *Tech (press down)* (a)baisser; *Aut etc (pedal)* appuyer sur **3** *(cause to fall) (trade)* faire languir; *(price of sth)* faire baisser

depressant [dɪˈpresənt] **N** *Med (drug)* calmant *m*

depressed [dɪˈprest] **ADJ 1** *(person)* déprimé; **to feel d.** être déprimé, *Fam* avoir le cafard; **the winter makes me feel d.** l'hiver me déprime **2** *Com (market)* languissant, déprimé; **one of the most d. sectors of the economy** un des secteurs économiques les plus touchés par la crise; **the economy has been in a d. state for nearly three years** l'économie est dans un état de marasme depuis bientôt trois ans; **d. area** région touchée par la crise

depressing [dɪˈpresɪŋ] **ADJ 1** *(gloomy)* déprimant; *(countryside)* triste; **the unemployment figures make for d. reading** les chiffres du chômage sont plutôt déprimants **2** *Com* **to have a d. effect on the economy** déprimer l'économie

depressingly [dɪˈpresɪŋlɪ] **ADV** d'une manière déprimante

depression [dɪˈpreʃən] **N 1** *(of person)* dépression *f*; *Med* **state of d.** état *m* dépressif; *Med* **to suffer (from) acute d.** être en pleine dépression

  2 *Com (in business, region of country)* crise *f*; *(in industry)* crise, marasme *m*; **economic d.** dépression *f* économique; *Hist* **the (Great) D.** la crise de 29

  3 *Tech (pressing down) (of sth)* abaissement *m*; *Aut (of pedal)* enfoncement *m*; *Mil* **angle of d.** angle *m* de dépression

  4 *Met* dépression *f*

  5 *(sunken area) (in ground)* dépression *f*, enfoncement *m*, creux *m*

depressive [dɪˈpresɪv] **ADJ 1** *Psy (tendencies, person)* dépressif **2** *Com* **to have a d. effect on the economy** déprimer l'économie
N *Psy* dépressif, -ive

depressor [dɪˈpresər] **N** *Med (for tongue)* abaisse-langue *m inv*

depressurize [diːˈpreʃəraɪz] *Aviat* **VT** dépressuriser
VI se dépressuriser

deprivation [deprɪˈveɪʃən] **N 1** *(hardship)* privation *f*; **to suffer deprivations** souffrir de privations; **emotional d.** carence *f* affective **2** *(removal) (of rights, freedom etc)* privation *f*; *(of job, duties)* destitution *f*

deprive [dɪˈpraɪv] **VT** **to d. sb of sth** priver qn de qch, enlever qch à qn; **to d. oneself** se priver; **I won't d. you of the pleasure of telling him about it** je ne te priverai pas du plaisir de le lui dire; **to d. sb of office** déposséder qn de sa charge

deprived [dɪˈpraɪvd] **ADJ** *(child)* déshérité; **she had a d. childhood** elle a eu une enfance défavorisée

deprogram [dɪˈprəʊɡræm] **VT** déprogrammer

dept **N** *abbr* **department**

depth [depθ] **N 1** *(of river, thought etc)* profondeur *f*; *(of love, feelings, passion)* profondeur, intensité *f*; **in d.** en profondeur; *(to study sth)* à fond; **a study in d. of …** une

étude approfondie *ou* très poussée de …; **at a d. of 50 feet** par 50 pieds de fond; **to dive to a d. of 50 feet** descendre *ou* plonger à 50 pieds de fond; **I hadn't realised the d. of her feelings** je ne m'étais pas rendu compte de la profondeur de ses sentiments; *also Fig* **to go** *or* **get out of one's d.** perdre pied; **to be out of one's d.** *(of swimmer)* ne plus avoir pied; *Fig* avoir perdu pied, ne plus être sur son terrain; **I think she's a bit out of her d. in the new job** je crois qu'elle est un peu dépassée dans son nouveau travail; *Tech* **d. of cut** *(of machine tool)* profondeur de passe *ou* de coupe; *Opt* **d. of field/focus** profondeur de champ/de foyer

  2 *(of sound)* gravité *f*; *(of colour)* vigueur *f*, intensité *f*

  3 *(of forest etc)* fond *m*; *(of night)* milieu *m*; **in the depths of winter** en plein hiver; **the depths** *(of ocean etc)* les profondeurs *fpl*; *(of ignorance etc)* les ténèbres *fpl*; **in the depths of despair** dans le plus profond désespoir; **the lowest depths** *(of shame etc)* le dernier degré

  4 *Tech (of piston etc)* hauteur *f*; *(of layer)* épaisseur *f*

  5 *Mktg (of product, range)* profondeur *f*

  6 *Typ (of text)* encombrement *m*

  ▸▸ *Naut* **d. charge** grenade *f* sous-marine; *Tech* **d. finder** sondeur *m*; *Aut* **d. indicator** *(for tyres)* témoin *m* indicateur d'usure; *Mktg* **d. interview** *(in market research)* entretien *m* en profondeur

deputation [depjʊˈteɪʃən] **N 1** *(representatives)* députation *f* **2** *(action) (of sb)* députation *f*, délégation *f*

depute[1] [dɪˈpjuːt] **VT 1** *(person)* députer, déléguer (**to do sth** pour faire qch) **2** *(powers)* déléguer (**to** à)

depute[2] [ˈdepjuːt] **N** *Scot* = **deputy**

deputize [ˈdepjʊtaɪz] **VI to d. for sb** remplacer qn, faire l'intérim de qn, suppléer qn

deputy [ˈdepjʊtɪ] **N** *(second in command)* adjoint, -ointe; *(temporary replacement)* remplaçant, -ante; *(political representative)* député *m*; **to act as d. for sb** suppléer *ou* remplacer qn

  ▸▸ **d. director** directeur *m* adjoint; *Journ* **d. editor** rédacteur *m* en chef adjoint; **d. governor** sous-gouverneur *m*; *Sch* **d. head** directeur adjoint; **d. judge** juge *m* suppléant; *Pol* **D. Leader** *(of political party)* adjoint, -ointe du chef; **d. manager** directeur adjoint; **d. managing director** directeur général adjoint; **d. mayor** adjoint, -ointe au maire; *Can Admin* **D. Minister** Sous-Ministre *m*; *Pol* **D. Prime Minister** vice-Premier-Ministre *m*; *Parl* **D. Speaker** = adjoint *m* du président de l'Assemblée

DEQ [diːiːˈkjuː] *Com (abbr* **delivered ex quay***)* DEQ

derail [dɪˈreɪl] **VT** *(train)* faire dérailler; *Fig (project, negotiations)* faire avorter; **to be derailed** *(train)* dérailler; *Fig* avorter; **the discussions were derailed by their insistence on …** les pourparlers ont avorté parce qu'ils ont insisté sur …
VI dérailler

derailment [dɪˈreɪlmənt] **N** *(of train)* déraillement *m*; *Fig (of plans, negotiations etc)* échec *m*; **in spite of the d. of talks by their insistence on …** bien que les pourparlers aient avorté suite à leur insistance sur …

derange [dɪˈreɪndʒ] **VT** *(person)* déranger; **she has been quite deranged by the experience** cette expérience l'a profondément dérangée

deranged [dɪˈreɪndʒd] **ADJ** dérangé; **he** *or* **his mind is d.** il est dérangé, c'est un esprit dérangé

derangement [dɪˈreɪndʒmənt] **N** *Med* aliénation *f* mentale

Derby **N 1** [ˈdɑːbɪ] *Br Horseracing* **the D.** le derby d'Epsom; **donkey D.** course *f* d'ânes; *Ftbl* **local d.** derby **2** [ˈdɑːbɪ] *Am* **d.** *(hat)* chapeau *m* melon

deregulate [diːˈreɡjʊleɪt] **VT** *Com (industry, air transport, bus services)* déréglementer; *(prices)* libérer

deregulation [diːreɡjʊˈleɪʃən] **N** *Com (of industry, air transport, bus services)* déréglementation *f*; *(of prices)* libération *f*; **d. of trade** libération *f* des échanges commerciaux

derelict [ˈderəlɪkt] **ADJ 1** *(car)* abandonné; *(house)* abandonné, (tombé) en ruines **2** *Fml* **to be d. (in one's duty)** être négligent de son devoir
N *(person)* épave *f* humaine

dereliction [derɪˈlɪkʃən] **N 1** **d. of duty** manquement *m* au devoir **2** *(abandonment)* abandon *m*

derestricted [diːrɪˈstrɪktɪd] **ADJ** *(road)* sans limitation de vitesse

derestriction sign [diːrɪˈstrɪkʃən] **N** *Aut* fin *f* de limitation de vitesse

deride [dɪˈraɪd] **VT** *(person)* se moquer de, railler; *(something)* tourner en dérision

> Note that the French verb **dérider** is a false friend and is never a translation for the English verb **to deride**.

derision [dɪˈrɪʒən] **N** dérision *f*; **object of d.** objet *m* de dérision

derisive [dɪˈraɪsɪv] **ADJ** moqueur, -euse

derisively [dɪˈraɪsɪvlɪ] **ADV** *(to look at)* d'un air moqueur *ou* de dérision; *(to say)* d'un ton de dérision

derisory [dɪˈraɪsərɪ] **ADJ 1** *(offer)* dérisoire **2** = **derisive**

derivation [derɪˈveɪʃən] **N 1** dérivation *f*; **d. of a word from Latin** dérivation d'un mot du latin; **what is the d. of …?** quelle est l'origine de …? **2** *Math (of function)* dérivation *f*

derivative [dɪˈrɪvətɪv] **ADJ** *Gram (word)* dérivé; *Pej* **his work is very d.** *(of author)* il n'a pas encore trouvé son style propre, il emprunte beaucoup aux autres; **I find his paintings rather d.** je trouve que ses peintures ne sont pas très originales
N *Gram, Chem, Ind* dérivé *m*; *Math* dérivée *f*; *St Exch* produit *m* dérivé; **petroleum d.** dérivé du pétrole; **to be a d. of sth** être un dérivé de qch
  ▸▸ *St Exch* **d. market** marché *m* à terme des instruments financiers

derive [dɪˈraɪv] **VT** *(origin, income, profit)* tirer (**from** de); *(pleasure)* prendre (**from** à); *(satisfaction)* trouver, tirer; *(ideas)* trouver, puiser; **to be derived from** dériver de, (pro)venir de; **income derived from an investment** revenu provenant d'un placement; *Chem* **to d. one compound from another** dériver un composé d'un autre; **word derived from Latin** mot qui vient du latin; *Mktg* **derived demand** demande *f* dérivée
▸ **derive from** **VT INSEP** dériver de, (pro)venir de

dermatitis [dɜːməˈtaɪtɪs] **N** dermite *f*, dermatite *f*

dermatologist [dɜːməˈtɒlədʒɪst] **N** dermatologue *mf*, dermatologiste *mf*

dermatology [dɜːməˈtɒlədʒɪ] **N** dermatologie *f*

derogate [ˈderəɡeɪt] **VI** *Fml* déroger (**from** à)

derogation [derəˈɡeɪʃən] **N** *Fml* **1** dérogation *f* (**of** à une loi) **2** **d. from a right** atteinte *f* portée à un droit

derogatory [dɪˈrɒɡət(ə)rɪ] **ADJ** *(disrespectful) (meaning of word)* péjoratif; **d. remark** remarque *f* désobligeante; **to be d. to sb** se montrer désobligeant envers qn

derrick ['derɪk] N 1 *Petr* derrick *m*, tour *f* de forage 2 *Naut (crane)* mât *m* de charge

derring-do ['derɪŋ'duː] N *Arch* bravoure *f*; **deeds of d.** hauts faits *mpl*

derv [dɜːv] N *Br Aut* gazole *m*

dervish ['dɜːvɪʃ] N derviche *m*; **whirling** or **dancing d.** derviche tourneur

DES [diːiː'es] *Com (abbr* **delivered ex ship)** DES

desalinate [diː'sælɪneɪt] VT dessaler

desalination [diːsælɪ'neɪʃən] N *(of sea-water)* dessalement *m*, dessalaison *f*
▸▸ **d. plant** usine *f* de dessalement

descale [diː'skeɪl] VT *(kettle etc)* détartrer

descant ['deskænt] N *Mus* déchant *m*

descend [dɪ'send] VI descendre; *(of rain)* tomber; **as darkness descended** pendant que l'obscurité descendait; **a feeling of sadness descended upon him** un sentiment de tristesse s'empara de lui; **an air of gloom descended on the whole house** un sentiment de tristesse envahit la maison; **to d. on** *(attack) (group of people)* s'abattre *ou* tomber *ou* faire une descente sur; *(village, town)* faire une descente sur; *Fig* **to d. on sb** *(intrude on) (without warning)* arriver chez qn à l'improviste; *(be unwelcome)* s'imposer chez qn; **to d. to sb's level/to doing sth** s'abaisser au niveau de qn/(jusqu')à faire qch; **to d.** *or* **be descended from sb** descendre de qn; **to d. from sb to sb** *(of property)* passer de qn à qn
VT *(hill, stairs)* descendre

descendant [dɪ'sendənt] N descendant, -ante

descender [dɪ'sendər] N *Typ (of character)* descendante *f*, jambage *m*

descending [dɪ'sendɪŋ] N 1 *(scale etc)* descendant; *Math (progression)* décroissant; **in d. order** en ordre décroissant 2 *(movement)* de descente
▸▸ *Comput* **d. sort** tri *m* en ordre décroissant

descent [dɪ'sent] N 1 *(of mountaineer, plane etc)* descente *f* 2 *(path, road etc)* descente *f*, pente *f* 3 *(origins)* descendance *f*; **to trace one's d. back to …** faire remonter sa famille à …; **to be of Norman d.** descendre des Normands *Fig (attack, intrusion)* irruption *f* (on dans, sur) 5 *Law (of property)* transmission *f* par droit de succession *ou* par héritage

descramble [diː'skræmb(ə)l] VT *Comput (message)* déchiffrer

descrambler [diː'skræmblər] N *(for telephone)* déchiffreur *m*; *TV* désembrouilleur *m*

describe [dɪs'kraɪb] VT 1 *(somebody, something)* décrire; *(person wanted by police)* donner le signalement de; *Com (goods etc)* désigner; **can you d. the man?** pouvez-vous décrire cet homme?; **she described him as being tall and …** d'après sa description, il était grand et …; **the book describes how they escaped** le livre décrit la façon dont ils se sont évadés; **to d. sb/sth as stupid/as intelligent** qualifier qn/qch de stupide/d'intelligent; *Pej* **to d. oneself as an actor** se présenter comme acteur, se dire acteur 2 *(draw) (circle, line)* décrire; *(triangle)* tracer

description [dɪs'krɪpʃən] N 1 description *f*; *(for police purposes, on passport)* signalement *m*; *Com (of goods)* désignation *f*; **to be beyond d.** être indescriptible; **to give a d. of sb/sth** décrire qn/qch; **to answer (to)** *or* **fit the d.** répondre au signalement 2 *(sort, kind)* sorte *f*, espèce *f*; **people of this d.** les gens *mpl* de cette espèce; **people of all descriptions** les gens de toutes sortes

descriptive [dɪs'krɪptɪv] ADJ descriptif

descriptor [dɪ'skrɪptər] N *Comput* descripteur *m*

descry [dɪs'kraɪ] VT *Lit* discerner

desecrate ['desɪkreɪt] VT profaner, souiller

desecration [desɪ'kreɪʃən] N profanation *f*

desegregate [diː'segrɪgeɪt] VT *(country, school etc)* = mettre fin à la ségrégation raciale dans; **desegregated school** = école où la ségrégation raciale n'est plus pratiquée

desegregation [diːsegrɪ'geɪʃən] N déségrégation *f*

deselect [diːsɪ'lekt] VT 1 *Br Pol* ne pas resélectionner *(comme candidat à une élection)* 2 *Comput* désactiver

deselection [diːsɪ'lekʃən] N *Br Pol* = fait *m* de ne pas sélectionner *(comme candidat à une élection)*

desensitize [diː'sensɪtaɪz] VT *Phot, Med etc* désensibiliser

desert[1] ['dezət] N désert *m*; **the Sahara D.** le désert du Sahara
ADJ *(region, flora etc)* désertique
▸▸ **d. boots** = chaussures *fpl* en daim à lacets; **d. island** île *f* déserte; **d. rat** *Zool* gerboise *f*; *Br Mil Fam* = soldat *m* britannique combattant en Afrique du Nord (pendant la Seconde Guerre mondiale)

desert[2] [dɪ'zɜːt] VT *(place)* déserter, quitter; *(person)* abandonner; *Mil* **to d. one's post** déserter *ou* abandonner son poste; *Pol* **to d. one's party** tourner casaque; **to d. sb** *(of courage)* abandonner qn; **her sense of humour has deserted her** elle a perdu son sens de l'humour
VI *Mil* déserter; **to d. from the army** déserter l'armée; **to d. to the enemy** passer à l'ennemi

deserted [dɪ'zɜːtɪd] ADJ *(person)* abandonné; *(place)* désert; **the streets were d.** les rues étaient désertes

deserter [dɪ'zɜːtər] N *Mil* déserteur *m*; **to be shot as a d.** être fusillé pour désertion

desertification [dɪzɜːtɪfɪ'keɪʃən] N *(of land)* désertification *f*

desertion [dɪ'zɜːʃən] N 1 *(of sb)* abandon *m*, délaissement *m*; *Law* abandon du domicile conjugal; **he divorced her for d.** il a demandé le divorce parce qu'elle avait abandonné le domicile conjugal 2 *Mil* désertion *f*

deserts [dɪ'zɜːts] NPL mérites *mpl*, dû *m*; **he has got his (just) d.** il n'a que ce qu'il mérite

deserve [dɪ'zɜːv] VT *(something)* mériter; *(praise)* être digne de; **the idea deserves serious consideration** cette idée mérite qu'on y réfléchisse sérieusement; **she thoroughly deserves it!** elle ne l'a pas volé!; **she deserves better** elle mérite mieux que ça; **he deserves to be punished** il mérite qu'on le punisse; **he deserved to win** *(and did)* il méritait de gagner; *(but did not)* il aurait mérité de gagner

deserved [dɪ'zɜːvd] ADJ *(bien)* mérité

deservedly [dɪ'zɜːvɪdlɪ] ADV justement, à juste titre

deserving [dɪ'zɜːvɪŋ] ADJ *(person)* méritant, de mérite; *(action, cause)* méritoire; *Old-fashioned, Br Hum* **the d. poor** les pauvres méritants; **to be d. of** *(sympathy, recognition)* mériter; *(praise, respect)* être digne de

desiccate ['desɪkeɪt] VT dessécher; **desiccated coconut** noix *f* de coco déshydratée

desiderata [dɪzɪdə'rɑːtə] NPL *Lit* desiderata *mpl*

design [dɪ'zaɪn] N 1 *(intention)* dessein *m*, intention *f*; **by d.** à dessein, volontairement; **to have designs on sb/sth** avoir des desseins *ou* visées sur qn/qch
2 *(pattern) (on sweater, carpet etc)* motif *m*, dessin *m*

3 *(plan) (of novel etc)* plan *m*; *(for painting etc)* grandes lignes *fpl*, ébauche *f*; *Ind (for machine)* étude *f*, avant-projet *m*, *pl* avant-projets; *(of car, flat, house etc)* design *m*; **to study d.** étudier le design; **the sofa was made to** *or* **is of her own d.** le canapé a été fabriqué sur mesure pour elle; **industrial d.** esthétique *f* industrielle
4 *(arrangement of parts) (in machine etc)* dessin *m*; **machine of faulty d.** machine de construction défectueuse; *Com* **our latest d.** notre dernier modèle
VT 1 *(intend)* destiner (**for** à); **machine designed for a special purpose** machine conçue pour un but spécial; **a speech designed to inspire confidence** un discours fait pour inspirer la confiance
2 *(project)* préparer
3 *(by drawing etc) (building, plane, kitchen etc)* concevoir; *(dress, hat etc)* créer; *(syllabus etc)* mettre au point
▸▸ **d. centre** centre *m* d'exposition (de modèles); **d. department** service *m* d'études; **d. engineer** ingénieur *m* d'études; **d. office** bureau *m* d'études; **d. stage** phase *f* de conception; **d. team** équipe *f* des concepteurs

designate[1] ['dezɪgnət] ADJ désigné

designate[2] ['dezɪgneɪt] VT *(person)* désigner, nommer (**to an office** à une fonction); *(funds)* destiner; **to d. sb as one's successor** désigner qn comme son successeur; **the town is a designated special development area** la ville a été désignée *ou* classée zone de développement; **this area has been designated a no-smoking zone** cette zone est destinée aux non-fumeurs; *Aviat* **designated carrier** = compagnie *f* aérienne désignée dans un accord bilatéral pour assurer les liaisons entre deux pays

designation [dezɪg'neɪʃən] N 1 *(of successor)* désignation *f*, nomination *f*; *(of funds)* désignation *f*; **d. to a post** nomination à un emploi; **because of the d. of this building as a no-smoking zone** parce que le bâtiment est décrété zone non-fumeur 2 *(title, name)* désignation *f*, nom *m*

designedly [dɪ'zaɪnɪdlɪ] ADV à dessein, exprès

designer [dɪ'zaɪnər] N 1 *(of project)* auteur *m*, inventeur, -trice 2 *Art, Ind* dessinateur, -trice; *(of clothes)* styliste *mf*, créateur, -trice; *(of books, magazines)* maquettiste *mf*; *Theat, Cin* décorateur, -trice; **d. jeans/bed-linen/jewellery** jean *m*/literie *f*/bijoux *mpl* de marque;
▸▸ **d. drugs** drogues *fpl* de synthèse; **d. goods** produits *mpl* de marque; **d. label** griffe *f* de grande marque; *Hum* **d. stubble** barbe *f* de deux jours *(faisant partie d'un look étudié, faussement négligé)*

designing [dɪ'zaɪnɪŋ] ADJ *Pej (scheming)* intrigant

desirability [dɪzaɪərə'bɪlɪtɪ] N 1 caractère *m* désirable *ou* souhaitable; **she referred to the d. of change/improvement** elle a fait référence au fait que des changements/améliorations étaient désirables *ou* souhaitables 2 *(sexual)* attrait *m*

desirable [dɪ'zaɪərəb(ə)l] ADJ 1 *(worth having)* souhaitable; *(change, improvement)* désirable; **a knowledge of French is d.** *(in job advert)* connaissance du français souhaitée 2 *(sexually)* attrayant, désirable
▸▸ *Com* **d. property** *(house)* belle maison *f*; *(flat)* bel appartement *m*

desire [dɪ'zaɪər] N 1 désir *m*, souhait *m* (**for** de); **to have a d. for sth** désirer qch; **to have one's heart's d.** obtenir ce que l'on désire le plus (au monde); **to have a d. to do sth** avoir le désir *ou* avoir envie de faire qch; **to express the** *or* **a d.** exprimer le désir (**that** que; **to do** de faire); **I feel no d. to …** je n'ai aucune envie de … **2** *(sexual)* désir *m*

VT 1 *(something)* désirer, avoir envie de; **to d. to do sth** désirer faire qch; **what he desired most was to …** ce qu'il désirait le plus au monde, c'était de …; **it is to be desired that …** il est souhaitable que … + *subj*; **it leaves much** *or* **a lot to be desired** cela laisse beaucoup à désirer; **it leaves nothing to be desired** cela ne laisse rien à redire; *Lit* **to d. sth of sb** *(request)* demander qch à qn; *(want)* désirer qch de qn; **to d. sb to do sth** *(make request)* prier qn de faire qch; **it was clear that she desired him to leave** il était clair qu'elle voulait qu'il parte; **I d. nothing of you but your friendship** je ne désire rien d'autre de vous que votre amitié **2** *(sexually)* désirer

desirous [dɪˈzaɪərəs] **ADJ** *Fml* désireux (**of** de)

desist [dɪˈzɪst] **VI** *Lit* cesser (**from doing** de faire)

desk [desk] **N 1** *(in office, of teacher)* bureau *m*; *(for writing at)* secrétaire *m*; *(pupil's)* pupitre *m*; **to have a d. job** avoir un travail de bureau; **I couldn't stand being stuck behind a d. all day** je ne pourrais pas supporter de rester assis à un bureau toute la journée; **reading d.** pupitre; *Rel* lutrin *m*; *Comput etc* **control d.** pupitre de commande **2** *(in shop)* caisse *f*, *(in hotel)* réception *f*; **please leave your keys at the d.** *(in hotel)* prière de laisser les clefs à la réception; **pay at the d.** *(in shop)* payez à la caisse **3** *Journ (office)* **the news/sports d.** le service des informations/des sports; *Br* **Latin America d.** direction *f* des affaires latino-américaines
▸▸ *Am* **d. clerk** réceptionniste *mf*; **d. copy** *(of book)* livre *m* spécimen; **d. diary** agenda *m* de bureau; *Journ* **d. editor** rédacteur, -trice; **d. lamp, d. light** lampe *f* de bureau; **d. microphone** micro *m* de table; **d. pad** bloc *m* de bureau; **d. research** recherche *f* documentaire

deskill [diːˈskɪl] **VT** *(process, job)* automatiser; *(workforce)* déqualifier

deskman [ˈdeskmæn] **N** *Journ* deskman *m*

desktop [ˈdesktɒp] **N** *Comput (screen area)* bureau *m*
▸▸ **d. calculator** calculatrice *f*; **d. computer** ordinateur *m* de bureau *ou* de table; *Comput* **d. model** modèle *m* de table; *Comput* **d. publishing** publication *f* assistée par ordinateur, microédition *f*, *Can* éditique *f*; *Comput* **d. publishing package** logiciel *m* de mise en page

desolate¹ [ˈdesələt] **ADJ 1** *(house)* abandonné; *(place)* désert, vide; *(future, prospect)* sombre **2** *(person, look)* affligé; *(cry)* de désolation

desolate² [ˈdesəleɪt] **VT 1** *(region etc)* *(of invaders, natural catastrophe)* ravager; *(of epidemic)* ravager, dépeupler; *(of recession, unemployment)* dévaster **2** *(person)* accabler, affliger

desolately [ˈdesələtlɪ] **ADV** *(to say)* d'un ton désolé; *(to look at)* d'un air désolé

desolation [desəˈleɪʃən] **N 1** *(of defeated country etc)* désolation *f*, dévastation *f* **2** *(of landscape etc)* désolation *f* **3** *(of person)* désolation *f*, chagrin *m*

despair [dɪˈspeər] **N** désespoir *m*; **… she said in d.** …, dit-elle, désespérée; **to be in d.** être au désespoir; **to be in d. over** *or* **about sth** être désespéré par qch; **in d., she took the children and left** désespérée *ou* par désespoir, elle prit les enfants et partit; **to do sth out of d.** faire qch par désespoir; **to drive sb to d.** réduire qn au désespoir, désespérer qn; **child who is the d. of his parents** enfant qui fait le désespoir de ses parents
VI (se) désespérer, perdre espoir; **I d. of you** tu me désespères; **don't d.** ne désespère

pas; **to d. of doing sth** désespérer de faire qch; **I d. of her ever speaking French well** je désespère de la voir enfin parler français correctement; *Fml* **they d. of his life** ils craignent pour sa vie

despairing [dɪˈspeərɪŋ] **ADJ** désespéré

despairingly [dɪˈspeərɪŋlɪ] **ADV** désespérément, avec désespoir

despatch [dɪˈspætʃ] **N, VT** = **dispatch**

desperado [despəˈrɑːdəʊ] **N** desperado *m*, hors-la-loi *m*

desperate [ˈdesp(ə)rət] **ADJ 1** *(very serious)* *(condition)* désespéré; **they are in d. need of food** ils ont désespérément besoin de nourriture **2** *(characterized by despair)* *(struggle, remedy, attempt)* désespéré; *(resistance, fight, defence)* acharné; **refugees d. to save their children besieged the consulate** tenant désespérément à sauver leurs enfants, les réfugiés assiégèrent le consulat; **a d. man** un désespéré; **to do something d.** faire un malheur; **she made a d. attempt to save him** elle a tenté désespérément de lui sauver la vie; **to be d. for money/a job** avoir un besoin désespéré d'argent/de travail; **I'm d., it's d.** c'est urgent; *Fam* **I'm d. for a cup of tea** je meurs d'envie de boire une tasse de thé

desperately [ˈdesp(ə)rətlɪ] **ADV 1** *(with despair)* *(to fight, plead etc)* désespérément **2** *(extremely)* extrêmement; *(in love)* éperdument; **to be d. in love with sb** aimer qn à la folie; **d. ill** gravement malade; **to be d. sorry** être navré

desperation [despəˈreɪʃən] **N** désespoir *m*; **to drive sb to d.** pousser qn à bout, réduire qn au désespoir; **in d.** en désespoir de cause; **out of d.** par désespoir; **an act of d.** un acte de désespoir

despicable [dɪˈspɪkəb(ə)l] **ADJ** méprisable

despicably [dɪˈspɪkəblɪ] **ADV** bassement

despise [dɪˈspaɪz] **VT** *(person, attitude, cowardice etc)* mépriser; *(offer, proposal)* dédaigner; **these things are not to be despised** cela n'est pas à dédaigner

despite [dɪˈspaɪt] **PREP** en dépit de, malgré; **d. what she says** quoi qu'elle dise; **I did it d. myself** je l'ai fait malgré moi

despoil [dɪˈspɔɪl] **VT** *Fml* dépouiller, piller, spolier

despondency [dɪˈspɒndənsɪ] **N** découragement *m*, abattement *m*

despondent [dɪˈspɒndənt] **ADJ** découragé, abattu; **to become d.** se laisser abattre; **try not to be too d. about losing** ne te laisse pas trop abattre *ou* décourager par cette défaite

despondently [dɪˈspɒndəntlɪ] **ADV** d'un air découragé *ou* abattu; *(to say)* d'un ton découragé *ou* abattu

despot [ˈdespɒt] **N** *also Fig* despote *m*

despotic [dɪˈspɒtɪk] **ADJ** *also Fig* despotique

despotically [dɪˈspɒtɪklɪ] **ADV** *also Fig* despotiquement

despotism [ˈdespɒtɪz(ə)m] **N** despotisme *m*

des res [ˈdezˈrez] **N** *Fam (house)* jolie petite maison *f*, *(flat)* joli petit appartement *m*

dessert [dɪˈzɜːt] **N** dessert *m*; **what did you have for d.?** qu'est-ce que tu as eu comme dessert?
▸▸ **d. apple** pomme *f* à couteau; **d. knife** couteau *m* à dessert; **d. plate** assiette *f* à dessert; **d. spoon** cuillère *f* à dessert; **d. trolley** chariot *m* de desserts; **d. wine** vin *m* doux

dessertspoon [dɪˈzɜːtspuːn] **N** cuillère *f* à dessert

destabilization [diːsteɪbəlaɪˈzeɪʃən] **N** *(of government, economy)* déstabilisation *f*

destabilize [diːˈsteɪbəlaɪz] **VT** *(government, economy)* déstabiliser

destination [destɪˈneɪʃən] **N** destination *f*; **to reach one's d.** arriver à sa destination
▸▸ *Comput* **d. disk** *(hard disk)* disque *m*; *(floppy disk)* disquette *f* cible; *Comput* **d. drive** lecteur *m* de destination; **d. file** fichier *m* de destination; *Mktg* **d. purchase** achat *m* prévu

destine [ˈdestɪn] **VT** destiner (**for** à; **to a calling** à une carrière)

destined [ˈdestɪnd] **ADJ 1** *(meant)* destiné; **he was d. for the Church** il était destiné à l'église; **to do sth** destiné à faire qch; **she is d. to be successful** elle est destinée au succès; **he was d. never to see her again** il ne devait plus la revoir; **the marriage wasn't d. to last** leur mariage ne devait pas durer **2** *(of plane etc)* **d. for** à destination de

destiny [ˈdestɪnɪ] **N** destin *m*, sort *m*; **such was his d.** tel fut son destin

destitute [ˈdestɪtjuːt] **ADJ 1** *(needy)* indigent, sans ressources; **to be utterly d.** être dans la misère **2** *Fml (lacking)* dépourvu, dénué (**of** de)
NPL the d. les indigents *mpl*

destitution [destɪˈtjuːʃən] **N** *(extreme poverty)* indigence *f*, misère *f*

destock [ˈdiːˈstɒk] **VT** *(goods)* déstocker

destocking [ˈdiːˈstɒkɪŋ] **N** déstockage *m*

destroy [dɪˈstrɔɪ] **VT 1** *(demolish, wreck)* *(building, marriage, character of a place, letter etc)* détruire; *(sb's hopes, happiness, chances of doing sth)* anéantir; *(faith in sb)* détruire, anéantir; *(life, career)* gâcher; *(theory)* démentir; *(of failure, guilt etc)* *(person)* détruire, ravager; **to d. one's health** se détruire la santé; **to d. oneself with guilt** être ravagé par un sentiment de culpabilité **2** *(kill)* *(animal)* tuer, abattre; *(dog)* piquer

destroyer [dɪˈstrɔɪər] **N 1** *Naut* contre-torpilleur *m*, destroyer *m* **2** *(person or event causing destruction)* destructeur, -trice

destruct [dɪˈstrʌkt] **VI** s'autodétruire; **d. button/mechanism** bouton *m*/mécanisme *m* de destruction

destructible [dɪˈstrʌktɪb(ə)l] **ADJ** destructible

destruction [dɪˈstrʌkʃən] **N 1** *(of building)* destruction *f*, anéantissement *m*; *(of hopes, happiness, chances)* anéantissement **2** *(damage)* ravages *mpl*; **the d. caused by the fire/storm** les ravages du feu/de la tempête; **the army left a trail of d. in its wake** l'armée a tout détruit sur son passage; **the trail of d. left by soldiers on exercise** les dommages laissés par les soldats en exercice

destructive [dɪˈstrʌktɪv] **ADJ** destructeur, -trice; **d. child** enfant qui détruit tout
▸▸ **d. criticism** critique *f* négative *ou* non constructive; *Comput* **d. read** lecture *f* destructive

destructively [dɪˈstrʌktɪvlɪ] **ADV** d'une manière destructrice

destructiveness [dɪˈstrʌktɪvnɪs] **N** *(of explosive etc)* effet *m* destructeur *ou* destructif, pouvoir *m* destructeur *ou* destructif; *(of child etc)* penchant *m* à détruire, tendance *f* destructrice

desuetude [dɪˈsjuːɪtjuːd] **N** *Lit* désuétude *f*; **to fall into d.** tomber en désuétude

desultorily [ˈdesəltrɪlɪ] **ADV** *(to converse)* d'une manière décousue

desultory [ˈdesəlt(ə)rɪ] **ADJ** *(conversation)* décousu, sans suite; *(attempt)* peu convaincant; *(manner)* désinvolte

detach [dɪˈtætʃ] **VT 1** détacher; *(carriages)* dételer; *(trailer)* décrocher; *(stamp etc)* décoller; **to d. sth from sth** détacher *ou* séparer qch de qch; **she managed to d. herself**

from the rest of the group elle a réussi à s'éloigner du reste du groupe; **it took me a quarter of an hour to d. myself from him** ça m'a pris un quart d'heure pour me débarrasser de lui; **if you can bear to d. yourself from her** si tu pouvais t'arracher à elle **2** *Mil, Naut (troops, ship etc)* détacher **VI** *(of handle etc)* se détacher

detachable [dɪ'tætʃəb(ə)l] **ADJ** amovible

detached [dɪ'tætʃt] **ADJ 1** *(separate)* détaché, séparé (**from** de); **to become d.** *(of stamp), Med (retina)* se décoller; *(of price tag, carriage)* se détacher; *(of trailer)* se décrocher; **to become d. from the rest of the group** se détacher du reste du groupe **2** *Mil (officer)* en affectation spéciale **3** *(objective) (view, person)* objectif; *(disinterested) (person)* désintéressé; *(manner)* désinvolte; *(air)* détaché, indifférent; **you have to be d. in this job** il faut savoir garder ses distances dans ce travail
▸▸ *Br* **d. house** maison *f* individuelle, pavillon *m*; *Med* **d. retina** rétine *f* décollée

detachment [dɪ'tætʃmənt] **N 1** *(separation)* action *f* de détacher, séparation *f* (**from** de); *(of carriages)* dételage *m*; *(of stamp), Med (of retina)* décollement *m* **2** *Mil* détachement *m*; **on d.** détaché **3** *(objectivity, lack of involvement)* distance *f*, détachement *m* (**from** envers); *(lack of interest)* désintérêt *m*; *(of priest) (from worldly matters)* détachement (**from** envers); **I admire your d.** j'admire ton détachement; **with an air of d.** avec un air distancié *ou* détaché

detail ['diːteɪl] **N 1** détail *m*; **down to the last d.** jusqu'au moindre détail; **I'll remember every single d. of this day** je me souviendrai de cette journée dans les moindres détails; **the d. of the carving** le détail *ou* les détails de la sculpture; **to pay attention to d.** faire attention aux détails; **to go** *or* **enter into d.** *or* **(the) details** entrer dans *ou* donner tous les détails; **in d.** en détail; **in greater d.** plus en détail; **in every d.** dans le moindre détail; **in the fullest d.** dans le plus grand détail; **points** *or* **questions of d.** questions de détail; **minor details** petits détails (sans importance); **that's just a minor d.** ça n'a pas d'importance; **I can't give you any details** je ne peux vous donner aucune précision; **I'll send you the details of the property** je vous enverrai les informations concernant la propriété; **for further details please contact ...** pour plus de renseignements, veuillez contacter ...; **let me take down your details** laissez-moi vos coordonnées
2 *Mil (duty)* extrait *m* de l'ordre du jour; **details** l'ordre *m* du jour
3 *Mil (group of soldiers)* détachement *m*
VT 1 *(describe)* exposer en détail
2 *Mil etc* **to d. sb for a duty** désigner qn pour un service, affecter qn à un service
▸▸ *Cin, TV* **d. shot** très gros plan *m*

detailed ['diːteɪld] **ADJ** *(description)* détaillé; *(account)* détaillé, circonstancié; *(work)* minutieux; **to give a d. account of sth** raconter qch en détail

detailing ['diːteɪlɪŋ] **N** *Art etc (details)* détail *m*

detain [dɪ'teɪn] **VT** *(person) (in prison)* détenir; *(in hospital)* garder; *(hold back)* retenir, arrêter; *(prevent from leaving)* empêcher de partir; *Sch (pupil)* consigner; **this question need not d. us** cette question ne nous retiendra pas; **police have detained a man for questioning** la police a mis un homme en garde à vue; **I won't d. you for long** je ne vous garderai *ou* retiendrai pas longtemps; **I'm afraid I've been detained** *(when cancelling appointment)* je suis désolé, je suis retenu; **I'm sorry I'm late, I got detained** je suis désolé d'être en retard, j'ai été retenu

detainee [diːteɪ'niː] **N** détenu, -ue

detect [dɪ'tekt] **VT 1** *(notice) (of person) (sound, change)* percevoir; *(movement)* apercevoir; *(of alarm system etc)* détecter; **to d. a note of irony in sb's voice** déceler une nuance d'ironie dans la voix de qn **2** *(find) (pulse)* sentir; *(source of a problem, missile)* détecter; *(weakness)* déceler

detectable [dɪ'tektəb(ə)l] **ADJ** perceptible, discernable

detection [dɪ'tekʃən] **N 1** *(discovery)* découverte *f*, **to escape d.** *(of mistake, burglar etc)* passer inaperçu **2** *(location, finding) (of mines, planes etc)* détection *f* **3** *(by detective)* travail *m* de détective

detective [dɪ'tektɪv] **N** *(police officer)* agent *m* de la police judiciaire; *(private investigator)* détective *m* (privé)
▸▸ *Br* **d. chief inspector** ≃ inspecteur, -trice divisionnaire; *Br* **d. constable** ≃ inspecteur, -trice de police; **d. film** film *m* policier; *Br* **d. inspector** ≃ inspecteur, -trice de police principal(e); **d. series** série *f* policière; **d. story** roman *m* policier, polar *m*

detector [dɪ'tektər] **N** *(device)* détecteur *m*; **sound d.** détecteur par le son
▸▸ *Br* **d. van** = voiture-radar *f* utilisée pour la détection des postes de télévision non déclarés

détente [deɪ'tɒnt] **N** *Pol* détente *f*

detention [dɪ'tenʃən] **N 1** *Law (in prison)* détention *f*, **d. without trial** détention arbitraire; *Mil* **six weeks' d.** six semaines de prison **2** *Sch* retenue *f*, **to give a pupil d.** consigner un élève; **to be in d.** être consigné *ou* en retenue **3** *Naut (of ship)* arrêt *m*
▸▸ *Mil* **d. barracks** locaux *mpl* disciplinaires; *Br Law* **d. centre** = jusqu'en 1988, centre de détention pour jeunes délinquants (aujourd'hui appelé "young offenders' institution"); *Law* **d. order** ordre *m* de détention

deter [dɪ'tɜːr] **VT** (**-rr-**) dissuader (**from doing sth** de faire qch); **why should that d. you from going?** pourquoi est-ce que ça t'empêche d'y aller?

detergent [dɪ'tɜːdʒənt] **N** détergent *m*, lessive *f*
ADJ détersif
▸▸ **d. additive** additif *m* détergent; **d. oil** huile *f* détergente

deteriorate [dɪ'tɪərɪəreɪt] **VI** *(of relations, weather, economy, building)* se détériorer; *(of health, product)* se détériorer, s'altérer; *(of work, situation)* se dégrader; **her condition has deteriorated** *(of patient)* son état s'est aggravé; **the house has been allowed to d.** on a laissé la maison se détériorer; **to d. even further** *(of situation, work, condition, weather etc)* encore empirer; *(of building)* se détériorer encore davantage

deterioration [dɪtɪərɪə'reɪʃən] **N** *(of relations, weather, economy, building)* détérioration *f*, *(of health, product)* détérioration, altération *f*, **despite the continuing d. of the situation** bien que la situation continue à empirer; **d. in quality** baisse *f* de qualité

determinant [dɪ'tɜːmɪnənt] **N** facteur *m* déterminant

determination [dɪtɜːmɪ'neɪʃən] **N 1** *(resoluteness)* détermination *f*, résolution *f*, **air of d.** air résolu *ou* décidé *ou* déterminé **2** *(establishment) (of date, position of planet)* détermination *f* **3** *Law (decision, finding)* décision *f* **4** *Law (termination) (of contract etc)* résolution *f*, résiliation *f*

determine [dɪ'tɜːmɪn] **VT 1** *(resolve)* se décider, se déterminer, se résoudre (**to do** à faire)
2 *(establish) (nature, size of sth)* déterminer; *(date, price)* déterminer, fixer; *(border)* délimiter; **once I've determined the cost** *(found*

out) une fois que je saurai le prix **3** *(question etc)* décider, résoudre; *(point of dispute)* régler; **the magistrate determined that they were guilty** le magistrat les a déclarés coupables; **to d. sb's fate** décider du sort de qn; **this set will d. the outcome of the match** cette manche va déterminer le résultat du match
4 *Law (terminate) (contract, lease)* résoudre, résilier
VI 1 *(of person)* se décider, se déterminer, se résoudre (**on doing** à faire)
2 *Law (of contract)* être nul

determined [dɪ'tɜːmɪnd] **ADJ** *(person, attempt)* déterminé; *(effort)* résolu; **I'm d. that this year I'll learn how to ride a horse** je suis décidé *ou* résolu à apprendre à monter à cheval cette année; **I'm d. that he'll go to university** je suis déterminé *ou* décidé à ce qu'il aille à l'université; **with a d. air** d'un air déterminé *ou* résolu

determiner [dɪ'tɜːmɪnər] **N** *Gram* déterminant *m* **VOIR GRAMMAIRE A32**

determining [dɪ'tɜːmɪnɪŋ] **ADJ** *(factor)* déterminant

deterrence [dɪ'terəns] **N** dissuasion *f*; **nuclear d. is indispensable to national security** une force de dissuasion nucléaire est indispensable pour la sécurité nationale

deterrent [dɪ'terənt] **N 1 to act as** *or* **be a d.** *(of penalty etc)* exercer un effet dissuasif (**to crime** contre le crime) **2** *(weapon)* arme *f* de dissuasion
ADJ *(effect) (of nuclear bomb, policy)* dissuasif

detest [dɪ'test] **VT** détester, *Fml* abhorrer; **I d. having to wait** je déteste attendre

detestable [dɪ'testəb(ə)l] **ADJ** détestable

detestably [dɪ'testəblɪ] **ADV** détestablement

detestation [diːtes'teɪʃən] **N** *Fml* **1** *(hatred)* haine *f* **2** *(object of hatred)* chose *f* détestable, abomination *f*, **that's my particular d.** c'est ma bête noire

dethrone [dɪ'θrəʊn] **VT** détrôner

dethronement [dɪ'θrəʊnmənt] **N** détrônement *m*

detonate ['detəneɪt] **VT** *(explosive)* faire détoner; *(bomb)* faire exploser; *(mine)* faire sauter
VI détoner

detonation [detə'neɪʃən] **N** détonation *f*, explosion *f*

detonator ['detəneɪtər] **N 1** *(for explosive)* détonateur *m*, amorce *f*, **percussion d.** détonateur à percussion **2** *Rail (fog signal)* détonateur *m*

detour ['diːtʊər] **N** détour *m*; *(on sign)* déviation *f*, **to make a d.** faire un détour; **he took us on an elaborate d.** il nous a fait faire un détour très compliqué
VI faire un détour
VT *(traffic)* dévier

detox ['diːtɒks] **N** *Fam* désintoxication *f*
▸▸ **d. centre** centre *m* de désintoxication; **d. programme** cure *f* de désintoxication

detoxification [diːtɒksɪfɪ'keɪʃən] **N** désintoxication *f*, sevrage *m*
▸▸ **d. centre** centre *m* de désintoxication; **d. programme** cure *f* de désintoxication

▸ **detract from** **VT INSEP** *(sb's pleasure, beauty of sth)* diminuer, porter atteinte à; *(sb's worth, achievements)* déprécier; **it rather detracted from my enjoyment of the film** cela m'a quelque peu empêché d'apprécier le film

detractor [dɪ'træktər] **N** détracteur, -trice

detrain [diː'treɪn] **VT** *(troops)* débarquer (du train)
VI *Mil (of troops)* débarquer *ou* descendre

(du train); *Am* (*of passengers*) descendre du train

detriment ['detrɪmənt] N détriment *m*, préjudice *m*; **to the d. of ...** au détriment de ...; **without d. to ...** sans porter préjudice à ...

detrimental [detrɪ'ment(ə)l] ADJ nuisible, préjudiciable (**to** à); **to have a d. effect on** (*health, chances etc*) nuire à; (*paintwork, tyres, skin*) être mauvais pour; **to have a d. effect on sb** (*of treatment, stress etc*) être mauvais pour qn; **it would be d. to my interests** cela desservirait mes intérêts; **smoking is d. to your health** fumer est mauvais pour la santé

detritus [dɪ'traɪtəs] N *Geol* débris *mpl* de roches

de trop [də'trəʊ] ADJ PRED de trop

Dettol® ['detɒl] N = solution *f* antiseptique

deuce¹ [dju:s] N **1** (*of dice, dominoes, cards*) deux *m* **2** *Tennis* égalité *f*, quarante *f*, quarante partout; **to be at d.** être à égalité; **there were 16 deuces** il y a eu 16 égalités

deuce² N *Old-fashioned Fam* **what the d. does he mean?** que diable veut-il dire?; **what the d.!** bon sang!; **there's the d. of a difference** il y a une sacrée différence

deuced ['dju:sɪd, -u:st] *Old-fashioned Br Fam* ADJ sacré
ADV sacrément

devaluation [di:væljʊ'eɪʃən] N *Econ* dévaluation *f*

devalue [di:'vælju:] VT *Econ* dévaluer; *Fig* (*person, achievements, efforts*) dévaloriser

devastate ['devəsteɪt] VT (*crops, village*) dévaster, ravager; *Fig* (*of news*) (*person*) terrasser; (*hopes*) anéantir, briser; **I was devastated when I found out he'd been lying to me** ça m'a anéanti d'apprendre qu'il m'avait menti

devastating ['devəsteɪtɪŋ] ADJ (*storm, effect, accuracy etc*) dévastateur, -trice, ravageur, -euse; (*argument, news, admission etc*) accablant, dévastateur, écrasant; (*criticism, attack*) cinglant; (*discovery*) dévastateur; (*charm, beauty etc*) irrésistible; (*shock etc*) foudroyant

devastatingly ['devəsteɪtɪŋlɪ] ADV (*handsome, funny*) terriblement, irrésistiblement; **d. beautiful** d'une beauté irrésistible; **d. accurate fire** tir(s) *m(pl)* d'une précision dévastatrice

devastation [devəs'teɪʃən] N dévastation *f*, ravages *mpl*; **a scene of utter d.** un spectacle de dévastation complète

develop [dɪ'veləp] (**-p-** [dɪ'veləpt]) VT **1** (*expand*) (*skills, theme etc*) développer; (*theory, argument*) développer, exposer; (*thought*) développer, élargir; **to d. one's muscles** développer ses muscles, se muscler **2** *Econ* (*region*) mettre en valeur, développer; *Tech* (*new design, model etc*) mettre au point, réaliser; *Constr* (*site*) aménager; **to d. sth into sth** transformer qch en qch; **less developed countries** pays *mpl* moins développés; **developed countries** pays développés **3** (*acquire*) (*infection, bad habit, mannerism*) contracter; (*cold, flu*) attraper; (*symptoms*) manifester; **to d. a temperature or a fever** (se mettre à) avoir *ou* faire de la température; **he has developed cancer/Parkinson's disease** il est atteint de cancer/de la maladie de Parkinson; **to d. a dislike/taste or liking for sth** se mettre à détester/aimer *ou* apprécier qch; **to d. a tendency to do sth** prendre l'habitude de faire qch; **the machine has developed a fault** la machine s'est mise à mal fonctionner; **to d. a stoop** se voûter; **when did she d. the rash?** quand l'éruption s'est-elle déclenchée?; **I've developed a rash on my chest** j'ai fait une éruption sur la poitrine

4 *Phot* (*film*) développer
5 *Math* (*surface, function*) développer
6 *Phys etc* (*heat*) engendrer
VI **1** (*of body, the faculties etc*) se développer; **she has developed into a fine-looking young woman/a gifted pianist** elle est devenue une ravissante jeune femme/une pianiste douée
2 *Econ* (*of country, region*) se développer; **to d. into** devenir
3 (*become apparent*) se manifester, se révéler; (*of argument, crisis*) se produire; (*of fever*) se déclarer; **to d. into sth** devenir qch; (*bronchitis, riot*) se transformer en
4 *Phot* se développer

developer [dɪ'veləpər] N **1** *Econ* promoteur *m* **2** *Sch* **late d.** enfant *mf* qui se développe tard **3** *Phot* (*chemical*) (agent *m*) révélateur *m*; (*for laser printer*) développeuse *f*
▸▸ *Phot* **d. kit** (*for laser printer*) kit *m* développeur

developing [dɪ'veləpɪŋ] ADJ (*business*) en expansion; (*region*) qui se développe, en expansion; (*country*) en voie de développement; (*crisis*) en cours; **a d. interest in ...** un intérêt grandissant pour ...; **the d. situation in Iraq** la situation jour après jour en Irak
N **1** = **development 2** *Phot* développement *m*
▸▸ *Phot* **d. bath** (bain *m*) révélateur *m*; *Phot* **d. tank** cuve *f* à développement; *Phot* **d. tray** cuvette *f*

development [dɪ'veləpmənt] N **1** (*growth, expansion*) (*of body, faculties, concept*), *Mus* (*of theme*) développement *m*; (*of subject*) développement, amplification *f*, (*of idea*) élargissement *m*
2 *Econ* (*of region etc*) développement *m*, mise *f* en valeur; (*of area, land*) aménagement *m*, construction *f*; (*of Third World country*) développement; *Tech* (*of new design etc*) réalisation *f*, mise au point
3 (*progress, change*) développement *m*; (*of events etc*) déroulement *m*; (*of events, thought*) évolution *f*; **to await further developments** attendre la suite des événements; **a surprising d. in the situation** un développement étonnant de la situation; **the latest developments in the former Soviet Union** les derniers événements survenus dans l'ex-Union Soviétique; **the latest developments in medical research** les dernières découvertes médicales
4 *Phot* développement *m*
5 *Math* (*of surface, function*) développement *m*; (*of spiral*) développée *f*
▸▸ **d. aid** aide *f* aux pays en voie de développement; *Br* **d. area** = zone *f* économiquement sinistrée bénéficiant d'aides publiques en vue de sa reconversion; **d. assistance** crédits *mpl* de développement; *Fin* **d. capital** capital-développement *m*; **d. costs** coûts *mpl* de développement; **d. grant** subvention *f* pour le développement; **d. loan** crédits de développement; *Mktg* **d. stage** (*of product*) phase *f* de développement

deviant [di:vɪənt] ADJ, N *Psy* déviant, -ante

deviate ['di:vɪeɪt] VI (*from instructions, plans, intentions etc*) s'écarter (**from** de); (*from a path, course of action, line*) dévier (**from** de)

deviation [di:vɪ'eɪʃən] N (*from norm, principles, standard procedure*) écart *m* (**from** par rapport à); (*of magnetic needle, from path, course of action, line*) déviation *f* (**from** de)

deviationism [di:vɪ'eɪʃənɪz(ə)m] N *Pol* déviationnisme *m*

deviationist [di:vɪ'eɪʃənɪst] ADJ, N *Pol* déviationniste *mf*

device [dɪ'vaɪs] N **1** (*fitting, part of a machine etc*) dispositif *m*; (*machine, gadget*) appareil *m*, dispositif; *Comput* (*peripheral*) unité *f* périphérique, périphérique *m*; **locking d.** système *m* de verrouillage; **safety d.** dispositif de sécurité; **explosive/nuclear d.** engin *m* explosif/nucléaire **2** (*plan*) stratagème *m*, procédé *m*; **to leave sb to their own devices** (*alone*) laisser qn s'occuper comme bon lui semble; (*without help*) laisser qn se débrouiller **3** *Lit* (*on shield, flag etc*) emblème *m*, devise *f*
▸▸ *Comput* **d. driver** pilote *m* de périphérique; *Comput* **d. manager** gestionnaire *m* de périphériques

DEVIL ['dev(ə)l] N **1** (*evil being*) diable *m*, démon *m*; **the D.** le Diable
2 (*person*) diable *m*; **he's a bit of a d.** (*awkward to deal with*) il est un peu enquiquineur; (*not always honest*) il est un peu malhonnête; (*not always reliable*) on ne peut pas compter sur lui; **poor d.!** pauvre diable!; **the silly d.!** quelle espèce d'idiot!; **you little d.!** petit diable!; (*annoyed*) petit garnement!; (*to little girl*) petite diablesse!; (*annoyed*) petite peste!; *Br Fam* **go on, be a d.!** allez, laisse-toi tenter!
3 (*in phrases*) **to be (caught) between the d. and the deep (blue) sea** être pris entre deux feux; **talk of the d.!** quand on parle du loup (on en voit la queue); **to have the d.'s own luck, to have the luck of the d.** avoir une veine de cocu; *Old-fashioned* **d. take it!** que le diable l'emporte!; *Fam* **go to the d.!** allez au diable!; **to play the d. with sth** mettre la confusion dans qch; **to give the d. his due ...** pour être honnête, il faut admettre que ...; *Fam* **there'll be the d. to pay** ça va barder; **(and) d. take the hindmost** sauve qui peut; *Prov* **the d. looks after his own** il y en a qui ont de la chance; *Prov* **better the d. you know than the d. you don't** mieux vaut se contenter de ce qu'on a plutôt que risquer de trouver pire; *Prov* **the d. finds work for idle hands to do** l'oisiveté est la mère de tous les vices
4 *Fam* (*as intensifier*) **what the d. are you doing?** que diable faites-vous là?; **how the d. ...?** comment diable ...?; **like the d.** (*to work*) avec acharnement; **to have the d. of a job** *or* **the d.'s own job (to do sth)** avoir un mal de chien *ou* un mal de tous les diables (à *ou* pour faire qch); **he's got the d. of a temper** il a un fichu caractère
VI (**-ll-,** *Am* **-l-**) *Br Fam* **to d. for sb** (*lawyer etc*) servir de nègre à qn
VT *Culin* (*meat*) faire griller et poivrer fortement; **devilled eggs** œufs durs à la diable
▸▸ **d.'s advocate** avocat *m* du diable; **to play d.'s advocate** se faire l'avocat du diable

devilfish ['dev(ə)lfɪʃ] N **1** (*fish*) raie *f* manta **2** (*octopus*) pieuvre *f*

devilish ['dev(ə)lɪʃ] ADJ *also Fig* diabolique
ADV *Old-fashioned Fam* rudement

devilishly ['dev(ə)lɪʃlɪ] ADV diaboliquement; **d. clever/cruel** d'une habileté/cruauté diabolique

devil-may-care ADJ insouciant, *Fam* je-m'en-foutiste; **d. spirit** (*reckless*) esprit *m* téméraire; (*carefree*) esprit insouciant

devilment ['dev(ə)lmənt], **devilry** ['dev(ə)lrɪ] N **1** (*mischief*) malice *f*, diablerie *f*, espièglerie *f*; **to do sth out of** *or* **for sheer d.** faire qch par pure malice *ou* espièglerie; **a piece of d.** une diablerie, une espièglerie; **what d. is he up to now?** qu'est-ce qu'il nous prépare comme sottise? **2** (*wickedness*) méchanceté *f*

devil's food cake N *Am Culin* = gâteau *m* au chocolat

devious ['di:vɪəs] ADJ (*person*) retors; (*mind*) retors, tortueux; (*way, means, route*) détourné, tortueux; *(scheme)* tortueux; **that was a bit d. of you** c'était un peu sournois de ta part

deviously [d'iːvɪəslɪ] **ADV** *(to achieve sth)* d'une façon détournée *ou* tortueuse, par des voies détournées *ou* tortueuses; *(to act, behave)* d'une façon tortueuse; **d. worded** rédigé d'une façon tortueuse

deviousness ['diːvɪəsnɪs] **N** *(devious behaviour)* détours *mpl*; *(of person)* caractère *m* retors; *(of scheme, mind)* caractère tortueux; **the increasing d. of their attempts** leurs efforts de plus en plus tortueux

devise [dɪ'vaɪz] **N** *Law* legs *m* (immobilier) **VT 1** *(plan)* combiner, imaginer; *(solution, excuse, gadget)* inventer, imaginer; *(explanation, punishment, means of escape)* imaginer; *(plot)* tramer **2** *Law (real estate)* léguer

devising [dɪ'vaɪzɪŋ] **N a scheme of his own d.** un plan qu'il aurait imaginé lui-même

devitalize [diː'vaɪtəlaɪz] **VT** *(economy, country)* affaiblir

devoid [dɪ'vɔɪd] **ADJ PRED** dénué, dépourvu (**of** de)

devolution [diːvə'luːʃən] **N 1** *(of power, authority to individual)* délégation *f*, transmission *f*; *Pol* décentralisation *f* (administrative) **2** *Law* dévolution *f*, transmission *f* par succession

> **Devolution**
> Ce terme désigne la décentralisation parlementaire au sein du Royaume Uni, processus engagé depuis l'élection du gouvernement travailliste de Tony Blair en 1997. Après cette victoire, le nouveau gouvernement organisa des référendums en Écosse et au Pays de Galles, à la suite de quoi un parlement écossais fut instauré à Édimbourg et une assemblée nationale galloise à Cardiff, répondant ainsi aux attentes des nombreux Écossais et Gallois qui revendiquaient depuis longtemps un plus grand degré d'autonomie. (*Voir aussi encadrés sous* "**Scottish Parliament**" et "**Welsh Assembly**".)

devolve [dɪ'vɒlv] **VT** *(functions, powers)* déléguer, transmettre (**to sb** à qn)
► **devolve on, devolve to VT INSEP** *Fml* **1** *(of responsibility, duty etc) (somebody)* revenir à, incomber à **2** *Law (of property) (somebody)* être dévolu à

devote [dɪ'vəʊt] **VT** *(money, efforts)* consacrer (**to** à); *(time)* consacrer, accorder (**to** à); *(attention)* accorder (**to** à); **review specially devoted to history** revue entièrement consacrée à l'histoire; **to d. oneself to** *(occupation)* se vouer à, se consacrer à; *(study)* s'adonner à, se livrer à; **to d. oneself to sb/a cause** se dévouer à qn/une cause

devoted [dɪ'vəʊtɪd] **ADJ** *(father, daughter, service, care etc)* dévoué (**to** à); *(follower, fan)* fervent; *(couple)* uni; **they are d. to each other** ils sont dévoués l'un à l'autre

devotedly [dɪ'vəʊtɪdlɪ] **ADV** avec dévouement

devotee [devəʊ'tiː] **N** *(of person)* partisan, -ane; *(of sport)* passionné, -ée; *(of method)* adepte *mf*; *(of theory)* défenseur *m*; *(of god)* adorateur, -trice; **a d. of Haydn** un fervent *ou* un grand amateur de Haydn; **a d. of classical music** un passionné de musique classique

devotion [dɪ'vəʊʃən] **N 1** *(to a god)* dévotion *f* (**to** à) **2** *(prayers)* **devotions** dévotions *fpl*, prières *fpl* **3** *(to friend, family)* dévotion *f*, attachement *m* (**to** à); *(to leader of party, boss, cause)* dévouement *m* (**to sb** à *ou* pour

qn; **to sth** à qch); **d. to duty** dévouement; **d. to work** assiduité *f ou* ardeur *f* au travail

> When translating **devotion**, note that the French words **dévotion** and **dévouement** are not interchangeable. **Dévotion** usually refers to religious fervour and **dévouement** expresses the idea of dedication.

devotional [dɪ'vəʊʃən(ə)l] **ADJ** *Rel (book, articles etc)* de dévotion, de piété; *(writings, literature)* religieux

devour [dɪ'vaʊər] **VT** dévorer; *Fig* **to d. sb with one's eyes** dévorer qn des yeux; *Fig* **to d. a book** dévorer un livre; *Fig* **to be devoured by jealousy/hatred** être dévoré par la jalousie/la haine

devouring [dɪ'vaʊərɪŋ] **ADJ ATTRIB** *Fig (passion)* dévorant; *(enthusiasm)* débordant

devout [dɪ'vaʊt] **ADJ 1** *(person)* dévot, pieux; **a d. Catholic/Muslim** un catholique/ musulman fervent **2** *(wish etc)* fervent, sincère; **it is my d. wish that …** c'est mon vœu le plus sincère que …

devoutly [dɪ'vaʊtlɪ] **ADV 1** *(to pray)* avec dévotion; *(to live)* dans la dévotion **2** *(to wish, hope)* sincèrement; **it is d. to be wished that …** il faut sincèrement espérer que …

devoutness [dɪ'vaʊtnɪs] **N** dévotion *f*, piété *f*

dew [djuː] **N (morning) d.** rosée *f*; **evening d.** serein *m*
► ► *Met* **d. point** point *m* de rosée

dewclaw ['djuːklɔː] **N** *Zool (of dog etc)* ergot *m*

dewdrop ['djuːdrɒp] **N** goutte *f* de rosée

dewlap ['djuːlæp] **N** *(of cow)* fanon *m*; *(of person) (under chin)* plis *mpl* sous le menton, chairs *fpl* flasques sous le menton

dewy ['djuːɪ] **ADJ** couvert *ou* humide de rosée; *Fig* **complexion** teint *m* frais

dewy-eyed **ADJ 1** *(look)* humide; **she gets all d. about her husband/France** elle est tout émue quand elle parle de son mari/de la France **2** *(naive) (person)* naïf, -ïve, ingénu; *(optimism, enthusiasm)* naïf; **don't act the d. innocent with me** ne fais pas l'ingénu avec moi

dexterity [deks'terɪtɪ] **N** *(mental)* dextérité *f*, doigté *m*; *(physical)* habileté *f*, adresse *f*; **manual d.** habileté manuelle

dext(e)rous ['dekstrəs] **ADJ** adroit, habile (**in doing sth** à faire qch)

dext(e)rously ['dekstrəslɪ] **ADV** adroitement, avec dextérité

dextrin ['dekstrɪn] **N** *Chem, Ind* dextrine *f*

dextrose ['dekstrəʊs] **N** *Chem* dextrose *m*

DFC [diːef'siː] **N** *Br abbr* Distinguished Flying Cross

DFM [diːe'fem] **N** *Br abbr* Distinguished Flying Medal

DG [diː'dʒiː] **N** *Admin abbr* Director General

dhoti ['dəʊtɪ] **N** dhoti *m*

dhow [daʊ] **N** = petit bateau *m* arabe à une voile

DHSS [diːeɪtʃe'ses] **N** *Br Admin Formerly (abbr* Department of Health and Social Security) = ministère *m* de la Santé

diabetes [daɪə'biːtiːz] **N** *Med* diabète *m*; **to have d.** avoir du diabète
► ► **d. mellitus** diabète pancréatique

diabetic [daɪə'betɪk] *Med* **N** diabétique *mf*
ADJ diabétique; **to be in a d. coma** faire un *ou* être en coma diabétique; **d. biscuits/jam** biscuits/confiture pour diabétiques

diabolic [daɪə'bɒlɪk] **ADJ** *(cruelty etc)* diabolique, atroce; *(plot)* infernal, -aux; *(laugh)* satanique

diabolical [daɪə'bɒlɪk(ə)l] **ADJ** *Br Fam* **1**

(very bad) épouvantable, atroce; **it's d.!** *(of price)* c'est scandaleux!; **this wine tastes d.** ce vin est infect **2** *(intensifier)* **what a d. liberty** quel culot!

diabolically [daɪə'bɒlɪklɪ] **ADV 1** diaboliquement, de façon diabolique **2** *Br Fam (very badly)* de façon épouvantable; **it's d. expensive** c'est vachement cher

diacritic [daɪə'krɪtɪk] *Gram* **N** (signe *m*) diacritique *m*
ADJ *(sign)* diacritique

diacritical [daɪə'krɪtɪk(ə)l] **ADJ** *(sign)* diacritique

diadem ['daɪədem] **N** diadème *m*

diaeresis, *Am* **dieresis,** *pl* **diaereses** [daɪ'erəsɪs, -əsiːz] **N** *Gram* tréma *m*

diagnose ['daɪəgnəʊz] **VT** *(illness)* diagnostiquer, faire le diagnostic de; *(engine problem etc)* diagnostiquer; **the doctor has diagnosed pneumonia** le médecin a diagnostiqué une pneumonie; **she has been diagnosed as a schizophrenic** d'après le diagnostic, elle est schizophrène; **the book attempts to d. the causes of the crisis** le livre tente de faire le diagnostic de la crise

diagnosis, *pl* **diagnoses** [daɪəg'nəʊsɪs, -siːz] **N** *Med, Fig* diagnostic *m*; **to make** *or* **give a d.** faire un diagnostic; **d. is not her strong point** le diagnostic n'est pas son point fort

diagnostic [daɪəg'nɒstɪk] **ADJ** diagnostique; **d. skill/ability** talent *m*/capacité *f* à diagnostiquer
N diagnostic *m*
► ► *Com* **d. audit** audit *m* de diagnostic; *Aut* **d. bay** station *f* diagnostic; *Comput* **d. disk** disquette *f* de diagnostic; *Med* **d. kit** trousse *f* diagnostique; *Comput* **d. program** programme *m* de diagnostic; *Med, Comput, Sch* **d. test** test *m* de diagnostic

diagnostician [daɪəgnɒ'stɪʃən] **N** diagnostiqueur *m*; **she's an excellent d.** elle fait de très bons diagnostics

diagnostics [daɪəg'nɒstɪks] **N** *Med* diagnostique *f* VOIR GRAMMAIRE A10

diagonal [daɪ'ægən(ə)l] **ADJ** diagonal, -aux; *Constr (beam etc)* en écharpe
N diagonale *f*
► ► **d. ply** *(of tyre)* pli *m* diagonal

diagonally [daɪ'ægən(ə)lɪ] **ADV** diagonalement, en diagonale; **d. opposite sth** diamétralement opposé à qch

diagonal-ply tyre **N** pneu *m* à carcasse diagonale

diagram ['daɪəgræm] **N** diagramme *m*, schéma *m*; *Geom* figure *f*; *Phys etc (of temperature etc)* graphique *m*, courbe *f*; *Tech (of engine etc)* diagramme *m*, caractéristique *f*; **to make a d. of sth** faire un schéma de qch, schématiser qch; *Fig* **do I need to draw you a d.?** est-ce que je dois te faire un dessin?

diagrammatic [daɪəgrə'mætɪk] **ADJ** schématique

dial ['daɪəl] **N** *(of clock, scientific instrument)* cadran *m*; *Tel* cadran (d'appel); *Radio Old-fashioned Fam* **don't touch that d.** *(announcement)* restez avec nous
VT (-ll-, *Am* -l-) *Tel (number)* composer, faire; **to d.** *Br* **999** *or Am* **911** ≃ appeler Police Secours; **d.-a-recipe/-horoscope** recette/horoscope par téléphone
VI composer *ou* faire le numéro
► ► *Tel* **d. gauge, d. indicator** comparateur *m*; *Tel* **d. phone** téléphone *m* à cadran; *Am* **d. tone** tonalité *f*

dialect ['daɪəlekt] **N** dialecte *m*; **provincial d.** patois *m*

dialectic(al) [daɪə'lektɪk, -ɪk(ə)l] **ADJ** *Phil* dialectique;
► ► **d. materialism** matérialisme *m* dialectique

dialectic(s) [daɪə'lektɪk, -s] N *(pl) Phil* dialectique f

dialler ['daɪələr] N composeur m de numéros

dialling, *Am* **dialing** ['daɪəlɪŋ] N *Tel* composition f du numéro, numérotation f
▸▸ **d. code** indicatif m; **d. tone** tonalité f; **I can't get a d. tone** je n'arrive pas à avoir la tonalité

dialogue, *Am* **dialog** ['daɪəlɒg] N dialogue m; *Pol* **to enter into a d.** entamer le dialogue (**with sb** avec qn)
▸▸ *Comput* **d. box** zone f ou boîte f de dialogue; **d. coach** répétiteur, -trice de dialogues; *TV, Cin* **d. looping** doublage m du dialogue (en boucle); *Comput* **d. mode** mode m dialogue; *Comput* **d. screen** écran m de dialogue; *TV, Cin* **d. writer** dialoguiste mf

dial-up access N *Comput* accès m commuté

dial-up account N *Comput* compte m d'accès par ligne commutée

dial-up connection N *Comput* accès m commuté

dial-up line N *Tel* ligne f commutée

dial-up modem N modem m réseau commuté

dial-up service N service m de télétraitement

dialyse ['daɪəlaɪz] VT *Chem* dialyser

dialysis, *pl* **dialyses** [daɪ'ælɪsɪs, -iːz] N *Chem, Med* dialyse f; **she's in d.** elle est sous dialyse; **to have d. (treatment)** être sous dialyse
▸▸ **d. machine** dialyseur m

diamanté [daɪə'mænteɪ, dɪə-] N broderie f diamantée

diameter [daɪ'æmɪtər] N diamètre m; **the wheel is 60 cm in d.** la roue a 60 cm de diamètre; **internal d.** *(of tube)* calibre m; *(of cylinder etc)* alésage m

diametric(al) [daɪə'metrɪk, -ɪk(ə)l] ADJ **in d. opposition** *(opinion etc)* diamétralement opposé (**to** à)

diametrically [daɪə'metrɪklɪ] ADV **d. opposed** *(opinion etc)* diamétralement opposé (**to sth** à qch)

diamond ['daɪəmənd] N **1** *(gem)* diamant m; *Tech* **(cutting) d.** diamant de vitrier; **industrial d.** diamant industriel; **rough/cut d.** diamant brut/taillé; *Fig* **he's a rough d.** ses manières frustes cachent beaucoup de qualités; **d. necklace/ring** collier m/bague f de diamants **2** *(shape)* losange m; **d. pattern** dessin m en losanges **3** *Cards* carreau m; **the six of diamonds** le six de carreau **4** *Sport* terrain m de base-ball
ADJ *Br Fam* *(excellent)* super, génial, -aux; **he's a d. geezer** c'est un type super
▸▸ **d. cutter** *(person)* tailleur m de diamants; **d. cutting** taille f du diamant; **d. drill** foreuse f à pointe de diamant; **d. jubilee** (célébration f du) soixantième anniversaire m; **d. merchant** diamantaire m; **d. mine** mine f de diamants; **d. wedding (anniversary)** noces fpl de diamant

diamond-shaped ADJ en losange

diapason [daɪə'peɪsən] N *Mus* **1** *(of organ)* principaux jeux mpl de fond **2** *(tuning fork)* diapason m

diaper ['daɪəpər] N *Am (for baby)* couche f, lange m

diaphanous [daɪ'æfənəs] ADJ diaphane

diaphragm ['daɪəfræm] N **1** *Anat* diaphragme m **2** *(membrane)* diaphragme m, membrane f; *Phot* diaphragme m **3** *(contraceptive)* diaphragme m (contraceptif)

diarist ['daɪərɪst] N auteur m d'un journal (intime), diariste mf

diarrhoea, *Am* **diarrhea** [daɪə'rɪə] N *Med* diarrhée f; **to have d.** avoir la diarrhée

diary ['daɪərɪ] N **1** *(recording events)* journal m (intime); **to keep a d.** tenir un journal (intime) **2** *(for appointments)* agenda m; *(showing a week at a time)* semainier m; **desk d.** *(loose leaf)* bloc m calendrier; *(bound)* agenda
▸▸ *Journ* **d. column** billet m, rubrique f d'échos; *Journ* **d. job** reportage m prévu

Diaspora (the) [ðaɪ'æspərə] N *Rel* la Diaspora

diastole [daɪ'æstəlɪ] N *Med* diastole f

diatom ['daɪətəm] N *Biol* diatomée f

diatonic scale [daɪə'tɒnɪk] N *Mus* gamme f diatonique

diatribe ['daɪətraɪb] N diatribe f (**against** contre)

dibber ['dɪbər] N = **dibble**

dibble ['dɪb(ə)l] N *(for bulbs etc)* plantoir m
VT *(seeds)* semer au plantoir; *(plants)* repiquer au plantoir
VI semer/repiquer au plantoir

dibs [dɪbz] NPL *(game)* osselets mpl

dice [daɪs] N INV *(pl of* **die***)* **1** *(in game)* dé m; **to throw the d.** lancer le(s) dé(s); *Am Fig Fam* **no d.** pas question VOIR GRAMMAIRE A13 **2** *Culin* cube m
VI jouer aux dés; **to d. with death** risquer sa vie
VT *Culin (vegetables etc)* couper en cubes

dicey ['daɪsɪ] ADJ *esp Br Fam (uncertain)* hasardeux; *(dangerous)* risqué

dichotomous question [daɪ'kɒtəməs] N question f fermée à choix unique

dichotomy [daɪ'kɒtəmɪ] N dichotomie f

dick [dɪk] N **1** *esp Am Fam (detective)* détective m, flic m **2** *Vulg (penis)* bite f, queue f **3** *Vulg (contemptible man)* trou m du cul

dickens ['dɪkɪnz] N *Fam* **what the d. are you doing?** que diable fais-tu?; **the** *or* **a d. of a row** un bruit de tous les diables; **we had the** *or* **a d. of a time getting here** on a eu un mal fou pour arriver ici

Dickensian [dɪ'kenzɪən] ADJ *(scene, Christmas etc)* à la Dickens; *(conditions)* qui sort d'un roman de Dickens

dicker ['dɪkər] VI *Am Fam* marchander; **to d. for sth** marchander qch

dickface ['dɪkfeɪs] N *Vulg (idiot)* trou m du cul

dickhead ['dɪkhed] N *Br Vulg (idiot)* trou m du cul

dicky ['dɪkɪ] *Fam* N **1** *(of shirt)* faux plastron m **2** *Br Aut Old-fashioned (seat)* spider m
ADJ *Br (defective)* défectueux; *(heart)* malade, qui flanche; **to feel d.** se sentir tout chose
▸▸ *Br* **d. bird** *(in children's language)* (petit) oiseau m, zoziau m; **did you hear anything? – not a d. bird** est-ce que tu as entendu? – non, rien du tout; *Br* **they haven't heard a d. bird from her** elle n'a pas fait signe de vie; *Br* **not a d. bird to anyone about this** pas un mot de tout ça à quiconque; *Br* **d. bow** nœud m papillon

dicotyledon [daɪkɒtɪ'liːdn] N dicotylédone f

Dictaphone® ['dɪktəfəʊn] N Dictaphone® m

dictate ['dɪkteɪt] N ordre m; **to follow the dictates of one's conscience** écouter sa conscience; **the dictates of fashion** les exigences de la mode
VT **1** *(letter, passage)* dicter **2** *(conditions of peace etc)* dicter **3** *(determine)* déterminer; *(of circumstances)* imposer, demander; **the size of the harvest will be dictated by the weather** l'importance de la moisson dépendra du temps

VI **1** *(lay down law)* faire la loi; **I won't be dictated to** on ne me donne pas d'ordres **2** *(to secretary etc)* dicter

dictating [dɪk'teɪtɪŋ] N
▸▸ **d. machine** machine f à dicter

dictation [dɪk'teɪʃən] N dictée f; **to take d. from sb** écrire sous la dictée de qn; **to give d.** dicter; *Sch* **to do d.** faire la dictée
▸▸ **d. speed** vitesse f de dictée

dictator [dɪk'teɪtər] N *Pol, Fig* dictateur m

dictatorial [dɪktə'tɔːrɪəl] ADJ **1** *(power)* dictatorial **2** *(tone)* impérieux, autoritaire; *(person)* autoritaire

dictatorially [dɪktə'tɔːrɪəlɪ] ADV **1** *(to govern)* de façon dictatoriale **2** *(to say)* impérieusement, autoritairement; **to be d. inclined** avoir des tendances dictatoriales

dictatorship [dɪk'teɪtəʃɪp] N dictature f

diction ['dɪkʃən] N **1** *(pronunciation)* diction f **2** *(choice of words)* style m

dictionary ['dɪkʃən(ə)rɪ] N dictionnaire m (**of** de); **English-French d.** dictionnaire anglais-français; **d. of quotations** dictionnaire de citations

dictum, *pl* **dictums, dicta** ['dɪktəm, -əmz, -ə] N **1** *(statement)* affirmation f, dire m **2** *(saying)* maxime f, dicton m

did [dɪd] PT *see* **do¹**

didactic [dɪ'dæktɪk] ADJ didactique

didactically [dɪ'dæktɪklɪ] ADV didactiquement

diddle ['dɪd(ə)l] VT *Fam* **1** *(con)* duper, refaire, rouler; **he diddled me out of £500** il m'a refait *ou* roulé de 500 livres; **you've been diddled** tu t'es fait avoir *ou* rouler; **they diddled me into selling the house** ils ont réussi à m'embobiner et à me faire vendre la maison **2** *Am Vulg (have sex with)* baiser

diddler ['dɪdlər] N *Fam* escroqueur, -euse

diddly(-squat) ['dɪdlɪ-] N *Am Fam* que dalle; **I don't know d. about computers** l'informatique, j'y connais rien

didn't ['dɪd(ə)nt] CONTR = **did not,** *see* **do¹**

DIE¹ [daɪ] *(pt, pp* **died** [daɪd], *prp* **dying** ['daɪɪŋ])*

| VI | mourir 1, 2 ▪ caler 2 ▪ s'éteindre 2 |
| VT | mourir |

VI **1** mourir; **to be dying** être en train de mourir; **to d. of cancer** mourir d'un cancer; **to d. of grief/starvation** mourir de chagrin/faim; **he died yesterday** il est mort hier; **to d. in one's sleep** mourir pendant son sommeil; **to d. rich/a millionaire** mourir riche/millionnaire; **they died like heroes** ils sont morts en héros; **to d. from** *or* **of a wound** mourir des suites d'une blessure; **to d. in bed** mourir dans son lit; **to d. by one's own hand** se suicider, se donner la mort; **Dame Never say d.!** *(don't give up)* il ne faut jamais désespérer; *(stay cheerful)* courage!, tenez bon!; *Fam* **I thought I would d. of boredom/of curiosity** j'ai cru mourir d'ennui/de curiosité; *Fam* **I nearly died laughing/of shame** j'étais mort de rire/de honte; *Fam* **we were dying of cold** nous mourions de froid; *Fam* **to be dying to do sth** mourir *ou* mourir d'envie de faire qch; *Fam* **I'm dying for a drink/cigarette** je meurs de soif/d'envie de fumer une cigarette
2 *(of engine)* caler; *(of TV picture)* disparaître; *(of lights)* s'éteindre; *(of battery)* se mettre à plat; *(of love, passion, hopes, enthusiasm)* mourir; **old superstitions d. hard** les vieilles superstitions ont la vie dure; **the engine died (on me/us/etc)** le moteur a calé; *Lit* **day is dying** le jour s'en va; **their love died** leur amour s'est éteint; **his secret died with him** il a emporté son secret dans le tombeau

VT **to d. a natural death** *(not be murdered)*

mourir de mort naturelle; *(of old age)* mourir de sa belle mort; *(of fashion etc)* passer de mode; **to d. a violent death** mourir de mort violente; **to d. a hero's death** mourir héroïquement *ou* en héros; *Fig* **to d. the death** *(of play)* faire un four; *(be embarrassed)* être mortellement embarrassé; **to d. a thousand deaths** souffrir mille morts

▸ **die away** *vi (of sound)* s'affaiblir; *(of voice)* s'éteindre; *(of wind)* tomber; *Mus* **to let the sound d. away** éteindre le son

▸ **die back** *vi (of plant)* (se) faner

▸ **die down** *vi (of fire etc)* baisser; *(of wind)* tomber; *(of sound)* s'éteindre; *(of excitement, storm, scandal)* se calmer; *(of applause)* mourir

▸ **die off** *vi* mourir; **they're dying off like flies** ils meurent les uns après les autres *ou* comme des mouches

▸ **die out** *vi (of family etc)* s'éteindre; *(of species)* disparaître

die² N **1** *(pl* **dice***) (for playing, gambling)* dé *m; Fig* **the d. is cast** le sort est jeté, les dés sont jetés VOIR GRAMMAIRE A13 **2** *(pl* **dies** [daɪz]*) Metal (mould)* matrice *f;* **stamping** *or* **embossing d.** matrice *ou* machine *f* à estamper; **screw-cutting d.** mère *f* (de filet de vis) **3** *Metal (tool)* poinçonneuse *f* (à main)

▸▸ **d. casting** moulage *m* en coquille; **d. plate** *(for tickets)* plaque *f* d'imprimante de billets; **d. sinker** graveur *m* d'estampes *ou* de matrices; **d. stamping** matriçage *m*

die-hard N réactionnaire *mf; Pol* ultra-conservateur *m*

ADJ ATTRIB pur et dur; **d. policy** politique *f* réactionnaire; **his d. resistance to change** sa résistance obstinée au changement

dieresis [daɪˈerəsɪs] N *Am* = diaeresis

diesel [ˈdiːz(ə)l] ADJ *(engine, train)* diesel

N *(vehicle)* diesel *m; (oil, fuel)* gazole *m,* diesel, gasoil *m*

▸▸ *Aut* **d. emissions test** contrôle *m* des émissions de moteurs diesel; *Aut* **d. fuel** gazole, gasoil; *Aut* **d. injection** injection *f* diesel; *Aut* **d. knock** cognement *m* (du moteur) diesel; **d. oil** gazole, gasoil

diesel-electric ADJ diesel-électrique, *pl* diesel-électriques

dieselling [ˈdiːz(ə)lɪŋ] N *Aut* auto-allumage *m*

diet¹ [ˈdaɪət] N **1** *(what is eaten)* alimentation *f;* **their d. consists mainly of fish** leur nourriture se compose essentiellement de poisson; **to survive on a d. of fresh fruit and vegetables** survivre en se nourrissant de fruits et de légumes frais **2** *(for medical reasons)* régime *m,* diète *f; (to lose weight)* régime; **to be/go on a d.** être/se mettre au régime; **to put sb on a d.** mettre qn au régime; **d. drink** boisson *f* à basses calories **d. foods** *(for people with special requirements)* aliments *mpl* diététiques

vi être au régime; **he needs to d.** il faut qu'il se mette au régime

▸▸ **d. pill** pastille *f* amaigrissante

diet² *Pol* diète *f*

dietary [ˈdaɪət(ə)rɪ] ADJ alimentaire

N *Fml (of patient, prison etc)* régime *m* (alimentaire)

▸▸ **d. fibre** cellulose *f* végétale

dietetic [daɪəˈtetɪk] ADJ diététique

dietetics [daɪəˈtetɪks] N diététique *f* VOIR GRAMMAIRE A10

dietician, dietitian [daɪəˈtɪʃən] N diététicien, -ienne

differ [ˈdɪfər] *vi* **1** *(be different)* différer (**from** de), être différent (**from** de); **to d. in size/shape/colour** être de tailles/de formes/de couleurs différentes; **to d. in price** différer de prix; **how do the two species d.?** en quoi est-ce que les deux espèces diffè-

rent?, qu'est-ce qui différencie les deux espèces? **2** *(disagree)* être d'opinion différente *ou* d'avis différent; **I beg to d.** permettez-moi d'être d'un autre avis; **to agree to d.** garder chacun son opinion; **let's agree to d.** acceptons de dépasser nos différences; **that's where we d.** c'est sur ce point que nous sommes en désaccord; **I d. with her about** *or* **on** *or* **over the diagnosis** je ne suis pas d'accord avec elle sur le diagnostic

difference [ˈdɪf(ə)rəns] N **1** différence *f,* écart *m* (**between** entre); *(between two numbers etc)* différence; **d. in age/in altitude** différence d'âge/d'altitude; **d. in temperature** écart de température; **differences in price** écarts de prix; **there's a d. of two years between me and my brother** il y a une différence d'âge de deux ans entre mon frère et moi; **a world of d.** une différence énorme; **the d. in you is amazing** c'est incroyable à quel point tu as changé; **to notice a (big) d. in sb** remarquer que qn a (énormément) changé; **I don't quite see the d.** je ne saisis pas la nuance; **she doesn't make any d. between the children** *(of parent, teacher etc)* elle ne fait pas de distinction entre les enfants; **it doesn't make any d.** cela ne fait aucune différence; **it makes no d. (to me)** cela ne (me) fait rien, cela m'est parfaitement égal; **to make a d.** *(improve society)* faire avancer les choses; **the new colour scheme makes a big** *or* **all the d.** les nouvelles couleurs font toute la différence; **that makes all the d.** voilà qui change complètement les choses; **he's a businessman, but with a d.** c'est bien un homme d'affaires, mais pas comme les autres; **to split the d.** *(price, fee etc)* couper la poire en deux; **to pay** *or* **settle the d.** *(price, fee etc)* payer *ou* régler la différence; *Hum* **it's the same d.!** cela revient au même

2 *(disagreement)* désaccord *m,* différend *m* (**about sth** au sujet de qch); **d. of opinion** différence *f* d'opinion, désaccord; **to have a d. of opinion with sb** se disputer avec qn; **to settle a d.** *(of two people)* régler un différend, se mettre d'accord; **we have our differences** nous ne sommes pas toujours d'accord

different [ˈdɪf(ə)rənt] ADJ **1** différent (**from,** *Am also* **to** de); **she feels a d. person** elle ne se sent plus la même; **that dress makes you look d.** cette robe vous change; **I do it in a d. way** je m'y prends tout autrement; **that's quite a d. matter** ça c'est une autre affaire **2** *(various)* divers; **d. colours** couleurs diverses *ou* variées; **d. kinds of ...** diverses *ou* différentes espèces de ...; **at d. times** à différentes *ou* diverses reprises; **I talked to d. people about it** j'en ai parlé à plusieurs personnes; **d. people say d. things** les avis diffèrent **3** *(unusual)* hors de l'ordinaire; **he just wants to be d.** tout ce qu'il veut c'est être différent, *Pej* il cherche à se faire remarquer; **it's certainly d.** c'est original

differential [dɪfəˈrenʃəl] ADJ différentiel

N *Math* différentielle *f; Aut* différentiel *m; (in prices, salaries)* écart *m;* **weight d.** différence *f* de poids; **wage** *or* **pay differentials** hiérarchie *f* salariale

▸▸ *Math* **d. calculus** calcul *m* différentiel; *Aut* **d. gear** différentiel *m,* engrenage *m* différentiel; **d. pricing** établissement *m* des prix différentiels, tarification *f* différentielle; **d. tariff** tarif *m* différentiel

differentially [dɪfəˈrenʃəlɪ] ADV *(to pay)* à des taux différentiels

differentiate [dɪfəˈrenʃɪeɪt] *vt also Math* différencier (**sth from sth** qch de qch)

vi **1** *(distinguish)* faire la différence (**between two things** entre deux choses) **2** *(discriminate)* **to d. between male and female employees** traiter les employés hommes différemment des employées femmes

differentiation [dɪfərenʃɪˈeɪʃən] N différenciation *f*

differently [ˈdɪf(ə)rəntlɪ] ADV différemment

differently-abled ADJ *(in politically correct usage)* handicapé

difficult [ˈdɪfɪkəlt] ADJ **1** *(task, problem etc)* difficile; **she's at a d. age** elle est à l'âge ingrat; **this question is d. to answer** il est difficile de répondre à cette question; **I find it d.** *or* **it is d. for me to ...** j'ai de la peine à ..., j'ai du mal à ...; **it is d. to believe that ...** on a peine à croire que ... + *subj;* **why do you have to make life d. for people?** quel besoin as-tu de compliquer la vie aux gens?; **it makes life d. not knowing how long they'll be staying for** cela n'arrange pas les choses de ne pas savoir combien de temps ils vont rester; **he seems to have a habit of making things d. for himself** il semble avoir le chic pour se compliquer les choses

2 *(person)* difficile; **he's d. to get on with** il n'est pas commode; **don't be so d.!** ne fais pas le/la difficile!; **you're just being d.** tu fais le/la difficile; **why do you have to be d. about everything?** pourquoi faut-il que tout soit aussi compliqué avec toi?; **she's very d. to talk to** il est très difficile de lui parler

difficulty [ˈdɪfɪkəltɪ] N **1** difficulté *f,* **to have d. in doing sth** avoir du mal *ou* des difficultés à faire qch; **to have d. (in) breathing** avoir du mal à respirer; **with d.** avec difficulté, avec du mal; **without much d.** sans grande difficulté

2 *(obstacle, problem)* difficulté *f;* **the d. is to ...** ce qui est difficile, c'est de ...; **I see no d. about it** je n'y vois pas d'inconvénient; **the real d. is how to keep both sides happy** le plus difficile c'est de satisfaire les deux parties; **there will be no d. about that** cela ne fera pas de difficultés; **to raise** *or* **make difficulties** soulever des objections; **there's the d.!** voilà la difficulté; **to run into a d.** rencontrer une difficulté; **to be in d.** *or* **difficulties** *(of swimmer)* être en difficulté; *Fig (of company, marriage)* connaître des difficultés; **ship in difficulties** navire *m* en difficulté; **financial difficulties** embarras *m* pécuniaire; **to get into difficulties** se mettre dans un mauvais pas; **to get out of one's difficulties** se tirer d'affaire

diffidence [ˈdɪfɪdəns] N manque *m* de confiance en soi, manque d'assurance

diffident [ˈdɪfɪdənt] ADJ *(person)* qui manque d'assurance *ou* de confiance en soi; *(smile)* timide; *(manner, air)* peu assuré; **to be d. about doing sth** hésiter à faire qch; **to be d. about one's abilities** se montrer modeste en ce qui concerne ses propres capacités

diffidently [ˈdɪfɪdəntlɪ] ADV *(to smile)* timidement, d'un air peu assuré; *(to express oneself, say sth)* sur un ton peu assuré

diffract [dɪˈfrækt] VT *Opt (light)* diffracter

diffraction [dɪˈfrækʃən] N *Opt (of light)* diffraction *f*

diffuse¹ [dɪˈfjuːs] ADJ *(light, style etc)* diffus; *(sense of unease)* indéfini

diffuse² [dɪˈfjuːz] VT *(light)* diffuser, répandre; *Fml (news etc)* répandre

VI *(of light, gas etc)* se diffuser; *Fml (of knowledge)* se répandre

Attention: ne pas confondre avec le verbe **to defuse**.

diffused [dɪˈfjuːzd] ADJ

▸▸ **d. lighting** éclairage *m* diffus *ou* indirect

diffuseness [dɪˈfjuːsnɪs] N *(of style)* prolixité *f,* caractère *m* diffus

diffuser [dɪˈfjuːzər] N *(for hairdryer, light)*

diffuseur *m*; *TV, Cin (on a light)* (écran *m*) diffuseur *m*

diffusion [dɪˈfjuːʒən] N *(of liquid, style, news etc)* diffusion *f*; *(of ideas)* rayonnement *m*; *Phys (of rays)* dispersion *f*

diffusive [dɪˈfjuːsɪv] ADJ **1** *(property, characteristic)* diffusif **2** *(style)* diffus, prolixe

dig [dɪɡ] N **1** *(in garden etc)* coup *m* de bêche; *Archeol* fouille *f*; **give the ground a good d.** retournez bien le sol; *Archeol* **to go on a d.** faire des fouilles; **a d. in the ribs** un coup de coude dans les côtes

2 *(remark)* remarque *f* désobligeante (**at sb** à qn); **to get a d. in at sb, to have a d. at sb** lancer une remarque désobligeante à qn; **that's a d. at you** cette remarque t'est destinée

VT *(pt, pp* **dug** [dʌɡ], *prp* **digging** [ˈdɪɡɪŋ]) **1** *(hole, grave, well etc)* creuser; *(soil, garden)* bêcher; *Fig* **to d. one's own grave** creuser sa propre tombe

2 *(thrust)* enfoncer (**in** dans); **to d. sb in the ribs** donner un coup de coude à qn

3 *Old-fashioned Sl (understand)* comprendre, piger; *(like)* bien aimer; **she really digs you** *(likes you)* elle en pince vraiment pour toi; **I d. that** *(like it)* ça me plaît *ou* me botte, j'aime bien ça

VI *(of workmen, dog etc)* creuser; *(of gardener)* bêcher; *Archeol* faire des fouilles; **to d. for gold** faire des fouilles pour trouver de l'or; **the dog was digging for its bone** le chien creusait pour trouver son os

▸ **dig in** VT SEP *(compost etc)* enterrer; *Fig* **to d. one's heels** *or* **toes in** s'entêter; **she dug her heels in over the question** elle s'est montrée très intransigeante sur la question; **to d. oneself in** *Fam* s'incruster; *Mil* s'établir dans des tranchées

VI **1** *Mil (by digging trenches)* s'établir **2** *Fam (eat)* manger; *(start eating)* attaquer

▸ **dig into** VT INSEP **1** *Fam (eat)* manger **2** *(search)* *(sb's past, files)* fouiller dans **3** *(press into)* **my rucksack's digging into my back** mon sac à dos me blesse dans le dos

VT SEP enterrer dans; **to d. compost into the garden** enterrer du compost dans le jardin

▸ **dig out** VT SEP **1** *(remove)* *(bullet, splinter etc)* extraire; *(person from ruins, snow drift etc)* dégager **2** *Fam (find)* *(address, person etc)* dénicher

▸ **dig over** VT SEP retourner

▸ **dig up** VT SEP *(plant etc)* déraciner; *(treasure)* mettre à jour; *(road)* piocher; *(body)* déterrer, exhumer; *Fam (find)* dénicher

digest¹ [ˈdaɪdʒest] N **1** *(short account)* condensé *m*, *Fam* digest *m* **2** *Comput* synthèse *f*

digest² [dɪˈdʒest, daɪ-] VT *Physiol (food)* digérer; *Fig (insult)* digérer; *(reading matter)* digérer, assimiler

digestible [dɪˈdʒestəb(ə)l, daɪ-] ADJ digestible; **easily d.** digeste

digestion [dɪˈdʒestʃən, daɪ-] N *Physiol* digestion *f*, *Fig (of what one has read)* digestion, assimilation *f*; **to have a good d.** ne pas avoir de problèmes de digestion; **a glass of wine helps the d.** un verre de vin facilite la digestion *ou* aide à digérer

digestive [dɪˈdʒestɪv, daɪ-] ADJ digestif; **d. troubles** troubles *mpl* digestifs *ou* de digestion

N **1** *Pharm etc* digestif *m* **2** *Br (biscuit)* = sorte de sablé

▸▸ *Br* **d. biscuit** = sorte de sablé; **d. system** système *m* digestif; **d. tract** tube *m* digestif

Digger [ˈdɪɡər] N *Fam (Australian)* Australien, -ienne; *(New Zealander)* Néo-Zélandais, -aise

digger [ˈdɪɡər] N **1** *Constr* **(mechanical) d.** excavateur *m* **2** *(person)* *(with spade)* per-

sonne *f* qui bêche; *(for gold etc)* chercheur *m* **3** *(wasp)* guêpe *f* fouisseuse

▸▸ **d. wasp** guêpe fouisseuse

digging [ˈdɪɡɪŋ] N *(of soil)* bêchage *m*, labour *m* à la bêche; *(of well, ditches etc)* creusement *m*; *Archeol* fouilles *fpl*

digibox [ˈdɪdʒɪbɒks] N décodeur *m* numérique

digicam [ˈdɪdʒɪkæm] N *(abbr* **digital camera)** caméra *f* numérique

digit [ˈdɪdʒɪt] N **1** *Math* chiffre *m* (arabe); **double d. inflation** taux *m* d'inflation à deux chiffres **2** *(on hand)* doigt *m*; *(on foot)* orteil *m*; *Br Hum* **extract the d.!** grouille-toi!

▸▸ *Comput* **d. selector** sélecteur *m* d'indice

digital [ˈdɪdʒɪt(ə)l] ADJ **1** *Comput, Tel* numérique **2** *Anat* digital, -aux

▸▸ **d. analog(ue) converter** convertisseur *m* analogique numérique; **d. audio broadcasting** diffusion *f* audio numérique; **d. audio tape** cassette *f* numérique; **d. camera** appareil *m* photo numérique; *TV* **d. channel** chaîne *f* numérique; **d. clock** horloge *f* à affichage numérique; **d. computer** calculateur *m* numérique; **d. display** affichage *m* numérique; **d. economy** netéconomie *f*, **d. frequency display** affichage digital des fréquences; **d. graphics card** carte *f* graphique numérique; **d. imaging** photographie *f* numérique; **d. music** musique *f* en enregistrement numérique; **d. radio** radio *f* numérique; **d. readout** affichage digital; **d. recording** enregistrement *m* numérique; **d. signal** signal *m* numérique; *Comput* **d. signature** signature *f* électronique; **d. sound** son *m* numérique; **d. tape** bande *f* numérique; **d. television, d. TV** télévision *f* numérique; *Comput* **d. versatile disk** disque *m* vidéo numérique; **d. video** vidéo *f* numérique; **d. video disk** disque vidéo numérique; *Comput* **d. wallet** porte-monnaie *m inv* électronique; **d. watch** montre *f* à affichage numérique

digitalis [dɪdʒɪˈteɪlɪs] N **1** *Bot* digitale *f* **2** *Pharm* digitaline *f*

digitalization [dɪdʒɪtəlaɪˈzeɪʃən] N numérisation *f*

digitalize [ˈdɪdʒɪtəlaɪz] VT numériser

digitally [ˈdɪdʒɪtəlɪ] ADV numériquement; **d. recorded/remastered** enregistré/remixé en numérique

digitization [dɪdʒɪtaɪˈzeɪʃən] N numérisation *f*

digitize [ˈdɪdʒɪtaɪz] VT convertir en numérique, numériser

digitizer [ˈdɪdʒɪtaɪzər] N *Comput* numériseur *m*

diglossia [daɪˈɡlɒsɪə] N *Ling* diglossie *f*

dignified [ˈdɪɡnɪfaɪd] ADJ *(person)* digne, plein de dignité; *(air, silence)* digne; **to have a d. manner** avoir de la dignité dans ses manières

dignify [ˈdɪɡnɪfaɪ] VT *(something)* donner de la dignité à; **to d. sb with the name of …** honorer qn du nom de …; **I won't d. that remark with a response** je ne m'abaisserai pas à répondre à cette remarque

dignitary [ˈdɪɡnɪt(ə)rɪ] N dignitaire *m*

dignity [ˈdɪɡnɪtɪ] N dignité *f*, **a woman of great d.** une femme d'une grande dignité; **to be** *or* **stand on one's d.** se retrancher derrière sa dignité; **to consider sth beneath one's d.** considérer que qch est en-dessous de soi; **it was beneath my d. even to respond** je me serais abaissé à seulement répondre; **the d. of labour** la dignité du travail

digress [daɪˈɡres] VI faire une digression/des digressions; **to d. from a subject** s'écarter d'un sujet; **I'd like to d. for a moment** j'aimerais faire une parenthèse

digression [daɪˈɡreʃən] N digression *f*, **by way of a d.** par parenthèse

digs [dɪɡz] NPL *Br Fam (lodgings)* logement *m*; **to live in d.** loger en meublé; **where are your d.?** où est-ce que tu crèches?

dihedral [daɪˈhiːdrəl] N dièdre *m*

ADJ *(angle)* dièdre

dike [daɪk] N, VT = **dyke¹**

dilapidated [dɪˈlæpɪdeɪtɪd] ADJ *(building, car etc)* délabré, dans un état de délabrement; *Hum (hat, suit)* dépenaillé

dilapidation [dɪlæpɪˈdeɪʃən] N *(of building, car etc)* délabrement *m*, dégradation *f*, **in a state of d.** dans un état de délabrement

dilate [daɪˈleɪt] VT dilater

VI *(of eyes etc)* se dilater

▸ **dilate on** VT INSEP *Fml (subject)* s'étendre sur

dilation [daɪˈleɪʃən] N dilatation *f*, **d. and curettage** (dilatation *f* et) curetage *m*

dilatoriness [ˈdɪlət(ə)rɪnɪs] N lenteur *f* (à agir)

dilatory [ˈdɪlət(ə)rɪ] ADJ *Fml (person)* lent (à agir); *(action)* tardif; *(answer)* dilatoire; **to be d. in doing sth** tarder à faire qch

dildo [ˈdɪldəʊ] N **1** *(device)* godemiché *m* **2** *Sl (stupid person)* abruti, -ie

dilemma [daɪˈlemə] N embarras *m*; *(in logic)* dilemme *m*; **to be in a d.** être bien embarrassé; **you place** *or* **put me in a d.** tu me mets dans l'embarras; **to be in a d. over a decision** être pris dans un dilemme au sujet d'une décision; **she's in a bit of a d. over whether to tell him or not** elle ne sait pas trop si elle doit le lui dire ou non; **to be on the horns of a d.** être pris dans un dilemme

dilettante, *pl* **dilettanti** [dɪlɪˈtɑːntɪ] N dilettante *mf*

ADJ **in a d. manner** *(to do sth)* en dilettante

dilettantism [dɪlɪˈtɑːntɪz(ə)m] N dilettantisme *m*

diligence [ˈdɪlɪdʒ(ə)ns] N assiduité *f*, application *f*, zèle *m*

diligent [ˈdɪlɪdʒ(ə)nt] ADJ *(student, work)* assidu, appliqué; *(employee)* consciencieux, zélé; *(inquiries, search)* consciencieux, minutieux

diligently [ˈdɪlɪdʒ(ə)ntlɪ] ADV *(to study)* avec assiduité, assidûment; *(to work)* consciencieusement, avec zèle

dill [dɪl] N **1** *(herb)* aneth *m* **2** *Austr Fam* andouille *f*

dilly-dally [ˈdɪlɪˈdælɪ] VI **(dilly-dallied)** *Fam* **1** *(loiter)* traîner, traînasser, lambiner **2** *(vacillate)* hésiter, tergiverser; **to d. about whether to do sth** se tâter pour savoir si on fait qch

dilute [daɪˈluːt, dɪ-] VT **1** *(orange juice, acid)* diluer (**with** avec); *(sauce)* allonger (**with** de); **to d. wine with water** couper du vin avec de l'eau; **d. to taste** *(written on bottle)* diluer à votre convenance; **to become diluted** se diluer **2** *Fig (theory etc)* édulcorer; **diluted radicalism** radicalisme *m* à l'eau de rose

ADJ *(orange juice, acid)* dilué, étendu

dilution [daɪˈluːʃən, dɪ-] N dilution *f*, *Fig (of theory)* édulcoration *f*, *Fin* **d. of equity** dilution du bénéfice par action

dim [dɪm] ADJ **(dimmer, dimmest)** *(light)* faible, pâle; *(eyesight)* faible, trouble; *(forest, room, lighting)* sombre; *(outline, memory)* vague, faible, estompé; *Fam (chances, prospects)* faible, mince; *(person)* bête; **to grow d.** *(of light, faculties)* baisser; *(of recollection)* s'effacer; *(of eyesight)* se troubler; *(of outline)* s'effacer, s'estomper; *Fam* **to take a d. view of sth** avoir une piètre opinion de qch, désapprouver qch

VT **(-mm-)** *(light)* atténuer, réduire; *(sight)*

obscurcir; *(memory, intelligence)* troubler; *(beauty, surface of a mirror)* ternir; *Fig (sb's glory)* éclipser; **to d. the lights** baisser les lumières; *Am Aut* **to d. one's headlights** se mettre en code; **dimmed headlights** phares *mpl* code

vi *(of light)* baisser; *(of eyes)* s'obscurcir; *(of outline)* s'effacer, s'estomper

dimbo ['dɪmbəʊ] **N** *Fam* ballot *m*, nigaud, -e

dim-dip N *Aut* veilleuses-codes *fpl*

dime [daɪm] **N** *Am* dime *f (un dixième de dollar)*; **it's not worth a d.** ça ne vaut pas un clou; *Fig* **they're a d. a dozen** il y en a à la pelle; **arts graduates are a d. a dozen** des licenciés ès lettres, il y en a à la pelle, les licenciés ès lettres courent les rues

▸▸ *Am* **d. store** supérette *f* de quartier

dimension [daɪ'menʃən, dɪ-] **N** dimension *f*, **what are the dimensions of the room?** quelles sont les dimensions de la pièce?; **of large dimensions** de grandes dimensions; **the fourth d.** la quatrième dimension; *Fig* **there's another d. to the problem** le problème a une autre dimension **SEE GRAMMAR 859**

dimensional [daɪ'menʃən(ə)l, dɪ-] **ADJ** dimensionnel

-dimensional SUFF two/three-d. à deux/trois dimensions

diminish [dɪ'mɪnɪʃ] **VT** *(power, enthusiasm)* diminuer, réduire; *(sound, light)* diminuer, baisser; *(reputation)* diminuer, affaiblir; **to d. the importance of sth** diminuer l'importance de qch

vi *(of power, enthusiasm, reputation)* diminuer, s'affaiblir; *(of sound, light)* diminuer, s'atténuer, baisser

diminished [dɪ'mɪnɪʃt] **ADJ** *(power, reputation)* diminué, affaibli; *(light)* atténué; *Mus (interval)* diminué; **he's greatly d.** *(physically)* il est très diminué

▸▸ *Law* **d. responsibility** responsabilité *f* atténuée

diminishing [dɪ'mɪnɪʃɪŋ] **ADJ** *(light, power etc)* décroissant, qui diminue; *(value)* à la baisse; *(popularity)* en baisse

▸▸ *Econ* **d. marginal utility** utilité *f* marginale décroissante; **d. returns** rendements *mpl* décroissants; *Econ, Fig* **law of d. returns** loi *f* des rendements décroissants

diminuendo [dɪmɪnjʊ'endəʊ] **N** *Mus* diminuendo *m*

diminution [dɪmɪ'njuːʃən] **N** diminution *f*, réduction *f* (**in** de)

diminutive [dɪ'mɪnjʊtɪv] **N** *Gram* diminutif *m*

ADJ 1 *(tiny)* tout petit, minuscule **2** *Gram* diminutif

dimly ['dɪmlɪ] **ADV** *(to see)* indistinctement; *(to sense, remember)* vaguement; **d. lit room** pièce mal éclairée

dimmed [dɪmd] **ADJ** *Comput (command)* en grisé, estompé

▸▸ *Comput* **d. icon** icône *f* estompée

dimmer ['dɪmər] **N** *Elec* variateur *m*; *Cin* obscurateur *m* de salle; *Am Aut* **dimmers** *(headlights)* (phares *mpl*) codes *mpl*; *(parking lights)* feux *mpl* de position

▸▸ **d. bulb** ampoule *f* veilleuse; **d. switch** *Elec* variateur; *Cin* obscurateur de salle

dimness ['dɪmnɪs] **N** *(of lighting, sight)* faiblesse *f*, *(of room)* obscurité *f*, *(of memory)* imprécision *f*, vague *m*; *Fam (of person)* stupidité *f*, bêtise *f*

dimple ['dɪmp(ə)l] **N 1** *(on cheek, chin)* fossette *f* **2** *(on surface of water)* ride *f*

vt 1 *(of smile) (sb's cheeks)* creuser de fossettes dans **2** *(of wind) (surface of water)* rider

vi 1 *(of cheeks)* se creuser de fossettes **2** *(of water)* onduler

dimpled ['dɪmp(ə)ld] **ADJ** *(cheeks)* à fossettes

dimwit ['dɪmwɪt] **N** *Fam* idiot, -ote; **you d.!** imbécile!

dimwitted [dɪm'wɪtɪd] **ADJ** *Fam* idiot, bête

din [dɪn] **N** tapage *m*, vacarme *m*, boucan *m*; **the d. of the traffic** le vacarme *ou* le boucan que fait/faisait/*etc* la circulation; **to make** *or* **kick up a d.** faire du tapage *ou* du boucan *ou* du vacarme

▸ **din into VT SEP to d. sth into sb** enfoncer qch dans le crâne à qn; **to d. manners/the rules of the road into sb** inculquer les bonnes manières/le code de la route à qn

dinar ['diːnɑːr] **N** *(monetary unit)* dinar *m*

dine [daɪn] **vi** dîner

▸ **dine in vi** *(of hotel guest)* dîner à l'hôtel

▸ **dine off VT INSEP 1** *(use) (porcelain, silver)* manger dans **2** *(eat)* manger au dîner

▸ **dine on VT INSEP** *(eat)* manger au dîner

▸ **dine out vi** *(in restaurant)* dîner en ville *ou* dans un restaurant; *(of hotel guest)* dîner dehors; *(at friends' home)* dîner chez des amis; *Fig* **you'll be dining out on that for years** ça te fera une bonne histoire à raconter pendant des années

diner ['daɪnər] **N 1** *(person)* dîneur, -euse; **the restaurant serves two hundred diners every evening** ce restaurant sert deux cents repas chaque soir; **there were only a few late diners left in the restaurant** il n'y avait plus que quelques clients attardés dans le restaurant **2** *Am (restaurant)* petit restaurant *m*; *Rail* wagon-restaurant *m*, *pl* wagons-restaurants

dinette [daɪ'net] **N** coin-repas *m*, *pl* coins-repas

ding-a-ling ['dɪŋə'lɪŋ] **N** *Fam* **1** *(of bell, phone)* sonnerie *f*, **to go d.** sonner, faire ding-ding-ding **2** *Am (penis)* quéquette *f*, zizi *m*; *(idiot)* andouille *f*

dingbat ['dɪŋbæt] **N 1** *Am, Austr Fam* crétin *m*; **don't be such a d.!** quel crétin tu fais! **2** *Comput* symbole *m* Dingbat

ding-dong ['dɪŋdɒŋ] **N 1** *(of bells)* tintement *m*, sonnerie *f*, *(of doorbell)* sonnerie; **to go d.** faire ding-ding-dong **2** *Fam (fight)* bagarre *f*

ADJ *Fam* **to have a d. argument** *(of two people)* se disputer violemment; **d. match** partie *f* vivement disputée

dinghy ['dɪŋ(g)ɪ] **N** dinghy *m*, *pl* dinghies; **(ship's) d.** youyou *m*; **sailing d.** dinghy à voile; **rubber** *or* **inflatable d.** canot *m* pneumatique

> Attention: ne pas confondre avec le terme **dingy**.

dinginess ['dɪndʒɪnɪs] **N** *(dirtiness)* aspect *m* miteux; *(darkness)* aspect sombre

dingo ['dɪŋgəʊ] **N** *(animal)* dingo *m*

dingy ['dɪndʒɪ] **ADJ** *(room, furniture etc)* défraîchi; *(colour)* terne; *(hotel)* miteux

> Attention: ne pas confondre avec le terme **dinghy**.

dining ['daɪnɪŋ] **N**

▸▸ *Rail* **d. car** wagon-restaurant *m*, *pl* wagons-restaurants; **d. hall** réfectoire *m*, salle *f* à manger; **d. room** salle à manger; **d.(-room) table** table *f* de salle à manger

dink [dɪŋk] **N** *Hum (abbr* **double income, no kids)** = couple *m* sans enfants, qui touche deux salaires

dinkum ['dɪŋkəm] **ADJ** *Austr Fam (person)* sincère; *(object)* authentique; **fair d.** vrai de vrai

dinky ['dɪŋkɪ] **ADJ** *Br Fam (dainty)* mignon

N *Hum (abbr* **double income, no kids yet)** = membre *m* d'un couple à deux revenus qui n'a pas encore d'enfant

dinner ['dɪnər] **N** **VOIR GRAMMAIRE A7** **1** *(evening meal)* dîner *m*, *Can, Belg, Suisse* souper *m*; **what's for d.?** qu'y a-t-il au dîner?; **to go out to d.** *(in restaurant)* dîner en ville *ou* dans un restaurant; *(at friend's home)* dîner chez des amis; **to invite sb to d.** *(in restaurant)* inviter qn à dîner au restaurant; *(in one's home)* inviter qn à dîner; **at** *or* **during d.** au *ou* pendant le dîner; **to give the dog his d.** donner à manger au chien; **public d.** banquet *m*; *Mil* **regimental d.** repas *m* de corps; **to discuss sth at the d. table** parler de qch autour d'un repas; **when was the last time we all sat down at the d. table together?** à quand remonte la dernière fois où nous nous sommes assis ensemble autour de la table de la salle à manger? **2** *Fam (midday meal)* déjeuner *m*, *Can* dîner *m*

▸▸ **d. hour** *(at work)* heure *f* du déjeuner; *(at school)* pause *f* de midi; **d. jacket** smoking *m*; *Br* **d. lady** = employée *f* d'une cantine scolaire; **d. party** dîner *(sur invitation)*; **d. service, d. set** service *m* de table; **d. time** heure *f* du dîner; **(it's) d. time!** à table!; **d. trolley** chariot *m* à repas

dinner-dance **N** dîner-dansant *m*, *pl* dîners-dansants

dinnerware ['dɪnərweər] **N** vaisselle *f*

dinosaur ['daɪnəsɔːr] **N** dinosaure *m*

dint [dɪnt] **N** *Fml* **by d. of (doing) sth** à force de (faire) qch; **it was by d. of her efforts that ...** c'est grâce à ses efforts que ...

diocese ['daɪəsɪs] **N** *Rel* diocèse *m*

diode ['daɪəʊd] **N** *Electron* (lampe *f*) diode *f*

dioptre, Am diopter [daɪ'ɒptər] **N** *Opt* dioptrie *f*

dioxide [daɪ'ɒksaɪd] **N** *Chem* dioxyde *m*, bioxyde *m*

dioxin [daɪ'ɒksɪn] **N** *Chem* dioxine *f*

Dip *abbr* **diploma**

dip [dɪp] **N 1** *(in ground)* inclinaison *f*, dépression *f*, *(in road)* descente *f*, *(in prices etc)* baisse *f*

2 *(swim)* baignade *f*, **I'm going for a d.** je vais faire un petit tour dans l'eau

3 *Culin* = sauce *f* dans laquelle on trempe les crudités etc

4 *Agr* **(sheep) d.** bain *m* parasiticide (pour moutons)

5 *Naut (with flag)* salut *m*

6 *Sl (pickpocket)* pickpocket *m*

vt (-pp-) 1 *(insert, put) (hands etc)* plonger (**into** dans); *Ind (metal)* immerger, décaper; *Agr* **to d. sheep** baigner les moutons

2 *(lower)* baisser subitement; *Br Aut* **to d. one's headlights** se mettre en code; *Naut* **to d. a flag** (faire) marquer un pavillon

vi 1 *(in water etc)* plonger; **her head dipped below the surface** sa tête disparut sous l'eau

2 *(of ground)* descendre, être incliné; *(of prices, temperature etc)* baisser; *(of scale)* pencher; **the road dips sharply** la route descend brusquement; **the sun dipped below the horizon** le soleil est descendu derrière l'horizon; **shares dipped on the London Stock Market yesterday** les actions ont baissé à la Bourse des valeurs de Londres hier

▸▸ *Br Aut* **d. switch** basculeur *m* de phares

▸ **dip into VT INSEP 1** *(use part of) (one's capital)* prendre dans; **I'm always dipping into my pocket** je suis toujours à débourser **2** *(read or study parts of) (book)* feuilleter; *(subject)* effleurer

D. Ed ['dɪp'ed] **N** ≃ CAPES *m*

diphtheria [dɪf'θɪərɪə] **N** *Med* diphtérie *f*, **to have d.** être atteint de la diphtérie

diphthong ['dɪfθɒŋ] **N** *Ling* diphtongue *f*

diploid ['dɪplɔɪd] **ADJ** *Biol* diploïde *f*

diploma [dɪ'pləʊmə] **N** diplôme *m* (**in** de, **en** en); **to sit a d.** passer l'examen d'obtention d'un diplôme; **d. course** cours *m* conduisant à un diplôme

diplomacy [dɪˈpləʊməsɪ] **N** **1** *Pol* diplomatie *f* **2** *(tactfulness)* diplomatie *f*, tact *m*; **to attain one's ends by d.** user d'adresse pour atteindre son but

diplomat [ˈdɪpləmæt] **N** diplomate *mf*

diplomatic [dɪpləˈmætɪk] **ADJ** **1** *Pol* diplomatique **2** *(tactful) (person)* diplomate; *(answer)* diplomatique; **you should have been more d.** tu aurais dû être plus diplomate; **he knows how to be d.** il sait être diplomate *ou* agir avec diplomatie
▸▸ *Pol* **d. bag** valise *f* diplomatique; *Pol* **d. corps** corps *m* diplomatique; *Pol* **d. immunity** immunité *f* diplomatique; *Am* **d. pouch** valise diplomatique; **d. service** service *m* diplomatique, diplomatie *f*

diplomatically [dɪpləˈmætɪklɪ] **ADV** diplomatiquement

diplomatist [dɪˈpləʊmətɪst] **N** diplomate *mf*

dipole [ˈdaɪpəʊl] **N** *Elec* dipôle *m*

dipped [dɪpt] **ADJ** *(sloping)* incliné
▸▸ *Br Aut* **d. headlights** codes *mpl*, feux *mpl* de croisement

dipper [ˈdɪpər] **N** **1** *(bird)* cincle *m* plongeur **2** *Am Astron* **the Great** *or* **Big D.** la Grande Ourse; **the big d.** *(at fairground)* les montagnes *fpl* russes **3** *Br Aut* basculeur *m* de phares **4** *(ladle)* cuillère *f* à pot, louche *f*
▸▸ *Br Aut* **d. switch** basculeur *m* de phares

dipping [ˈdɪpɪŋ] **N** **1** *(plunging)* plongée *f*, immersion *f*; *Metal* décapage *m*; *Agr* *(of sheep)* baignage *m* **2** *Br Aut* *(of headlights)* mise *f* en code

dippy [ˈdɪpɪ] **ADJ** *Old-fashioned Fam* toqué

dipso [ˈdɪpsəʊ] **N** *Sl (drinker)* poivrot, -ote

dipsomania [dɪpsəˈmeɪnɪə] **N** dipsomanie *f*

dipsomaniac [dɪpsəˈmeɪnɪæk] **N** dipsomane *mf*

dipstick [ˈdɪpstɪk] **N** **1** *Aut* jauge *f* (de niveau) d'huile; *Med (for urine test etc)* bandelette *f* réactive **2** *Fam (idiot)* abruti, -ie

DIP switch [ˈdɪpswɪtʃ] **N** *Comput* interrupteur *m* DIP

dir *abbr* **1** *Admin* **director** **2** *Comput* **directory**

dire [ˈdaɪər] **ADJ** **1** *(foreboding)* lugubre; **d. necessity** dure nécessité; **to be in d. need of sth** avoir un besoin urgent de qch; **to be in d. straits** être dans une très mauvaise passe **2** *Fam (bad) (meal, book etc)* épouvantable

DIRECT [dɪˈrekt, daɪ-]

| **VT** adresser **1** ▪ diriger **1–3** ▪ réaliser **3** ▪ ordonner **4** ▪ instruire **4** |
| **VI** faire de la réalisation |
| **ADJ** direct **1, 2** |
| **ADV** directement |

VT **1** *(send, aim) (letter, remarks etc)* adresser (**to sb** à qn); *(light)* diriger (**at sth** sur qch); *(funds)* consacrer (**at sth** à qch); **to d. sb's attention to sth** appeler *ou* attirer l'attention de qn sur qch; **accusation directed against sb** accusation visant *ou* qui vise qn; **to d. one's steps towards …** diriger ses pas *ou* se diriger vers …; **can you d. me to the station?** pouvez-vous m'indiquer le chemin de la gare?; **to d. one's efforts at doing sth** consacrer ses efforts à faire qch
2 *(manage) (company, the economy)* diriger, mener, gérer; *(army, one's affairs)* conduire; **to d. traffic** régler la circulation
3 *Theat (play)* mettre en scène; *TV, Cin, Radio* réaliser; *(actors etc)* diriger; **directed by: …** *Theat* mise *f* en scène: …; *TV, Cin, Radio* réalisation *f*: …; **who directed it?** *(the play)* qui en fut le metteur en scène?; *(the*

film) de qui est la mise en scène?, de qui est ce film?
4 *(instruct) (somebody)* ordonner à, dire à (**to do** de faire); **as directed** *(as ordered)* conformément aux ordres; *(as instructed)* selon les instructions; *Law* **to d. the jury** *(of judge)* instruire le jury (sur un point de droit)
VI *Cin, Radio, TV* faire de la réalisation; *Theat* faire de la mise en scène
ADJ **1** *(straight, immediate) (route, control, influence, flight etc)* direct; *(cause)* immédiat; **to be a d. descendant of sb** descendre de qn en ligne directe
2 *(blunt)* direct; *(refusal)* catégorique; **in d. contradiction** en contradiction directe
ADV *(to go)* directement, tout droit; **to travel d. from London to Edinburgh** prendre un train/un vol/*etc* direct de Londres à Édimbourg; **to dispatch goods d. to sb** expédier des marchandises directement à qn; *Radio, TV* **the concert will be broadcast d. from Paris** ce concert sera transmis en direct de Paris
▸▸ **d. advertising** publicité *f* directe; **d. air link** liaison *f* aérienne directe; **d. banking** banque *f* à distance; *Tel* **d. broadcast satellite** satellite *m* de télédiffusion directe; **d.-comparison advertising** publicité comparative directe; **d. competition** concurrence *f* directe; **d. costing** méthode *f* des coûts variables *ou* proportionnels; **d. costs** charges *fpl* directes, frais *mpl* directs; *Elec* **d. current** courant *m* continu; *Br Banking, Fin* **d. debit** prélèvement *m* automatique; **to pay by d. debit** payer par prélèvement automatique; **d. debit advice** avis *m* de prélèvement; **d. democracy** démocratie *f* directe; *Tel* **d. dialling** automatique *m*; *Aut* **d. gear** prise *f* directe; **d. hit** coup *m* au but; **d. investment** investissement *m* direct; **d. labour** main-d'œuvre *f* directe; *Tel* **d. line** ligne *f* directe; *Com, Mktg* **d. mail** publipostage *m*; **d. mail advertising** publicité directe, publicité par publipostage; **d. mail campaign** campagne *f* de publicité directe; **d. marketing** marketing *m* direct; *Comput* **d. memory access** accès *m* direct à la mémoire; *Gram* **d. object** complément *m* (d'objet) direct; **d. purchasing** achats *mpl* directs; *Pol* **d. rule** = contrôle *m* direct du maintien de l'ordre par le gouvernement britannique en Irlande du Nord imposé en 1972; **d. response advert** publicité à réponse directe; **d. response television** télévision *f* à réponse directe; **d. sale** vente *f* directe; **d. selling** vente directe; *Br Gram* **d. speech** discours *m ou* style *m* direct; *Fin* **d. tax** impôt *m* direct; *Fin* **d. taxation** imposition *f* directe

direct-dial number **N** *Tel* numéro *m* direct

direct-dial telephone **N** ligne *f* téléphonique directe, téléphone *m* direct

direction [dɪˈrekʃən, daɪ-] **N** **1** *(management) (of company etc)* direction *f*, administration *f*; *(of traffic)* réglementation *f*; *Theat* mise *f* en scène; *TV, Cin, Radio* réalisation *f*; **under the d. of …** *(of orchestra)* sous la direction de …; *(of company)* dirigé par …
2 *(way)* direction *f*, sens *m*; **in the d. of …** dans la direction de …, en direction de …; *Aut* **d. of travel** sens *m* de la marche; **I'm going in your d.** je vais dans la même direction que toi; **we were going in the d. of Paris** nous nous dirigions vers Paris; **in every d.** dans tous les sens; **in all directions** dans tous sens, dans tous les sens; **you are not looking in the right d.** vous ne regardez pas dans la bonne direction *ou* du bon côté; *Fig* **a step in the right d.** un pas dans la bonne direction; **in the opposite d.** en sens inverse; **in which d.?** de quel côté?; **to have a good/bad sense of d.** avoir un bon/mauvais sens de l'orientation; **to lose one's sense of d.** perdre le sens de l'orientation; **to lack d.** *(in*

life) ne pas avoir de but; *(of novel, play)* ne mener nulle part; **change of d.** changement *m* de direction; *Aviat, Naut* changement de cap; *Fig* **improvements in many directions** améliorations sous bien des rapports
3 **directions** *(instructions)* instructions *fpl*; **directions (for use)** notice *f* (explicative), mode *m* d'emploi; **you have been given the wrong directions** on vous a mal renseigné; **to give sb directions to a place** indiquer à qn comment aller à un endroit; **to ask for directions** *(to a place)* demander son chemin; *Theat* **stage directions** indications *fpl* scéniques; *Law* **d. to the jury** = exposé *m* de la loi fait par le juge au jury
▸▸ **d. finder** radiogoniomètre *m*; *Aut* **d. sign** panneau *m* de signalisation

directional [dɪˈrekʃən(ə)l, daɪ-] **ADJ** directionnel
▸▸ *Electron* **d. aerial, d. antenna** antenne *f* directionnelle *ou* directive; *TV, Cin* **d. cut** montage *m* directionnel; *Aut* **d. indicator** indicateur *m* (de changement) de direction

directive [dɪˈrektɪv, daɪ-] **N** *Mil etc* directive *f*; **to issue a d.** donner une directive

directly [dɪˈrektlɪ, daɪ-] **ADV** **1** *(to go)* directement; *(to be descended from sb)* en ligne directe; **I'm flying d. from Glasgow** j'ai un vol direct au départ de Glasgow; **I am not d. concerned** je ne suis pas directement concerné; **d. opposite the church** juste en face de l'église; **to come d. to the point** aller droit au fait; **her views are d. opposite to my own** ses vues sont diamétralement opposées à les miennes **2** *(bluntly) (to answer, speak)* franchement; *(to attack, criticize)* directement **3** *(soon)* tout de suite, immédiatement; **I'm coming d.** je viens tout de suite **CONJ** aussitôt que, dès que; **I'll come d. I've finished** je viendrai dès que j'aurai fini

directness [dɪˈrektnɪs, daɪ-] **N** *(of answer etc)* franchise *f*; *(of criticism, questions)* caractère *m* direct; **his d. of speech** son franc-parler

director [dɪˈrektər, daɪ-] **N** **1** *(of company etc)* directeur, -trice; *(board member)* administrateur, -trice; **d. of music** *Rel* maître *m* de chapelle; *Mil etc* chef *m* de musique; *Sch* personne *f* chargée de l'organisation du programme d'études **2** *Theat* metteur *m* en scène; *TV, Cin, Radio* réalisateur, -trice
▸▸ **d.'s chair** régisseur *m*; *Cin* **d.'s cut** version *f* du réalisateur, director's cut *f*; *Fin* **d.'s fees** *(for attending meetings)* jetons *mpl* de présence; *Acct* **d.'s loan account** compte *m* courant d'administrateur; *Cin* **d. of photography** directeur, -trice de la photographie; *Radio, TV* **d. of programmes** directeur, -trice des programmes; *Br Law* **D. of Public Prosecutions** ≃ procureur *m* général; **directors' report** rapport *m* annuel; *Br Univ* **d. of studies** = enseignant *m* qui suit la scolarité d'un étudiant tout au long de son cursus universitaire

directorate [dɪˈrektər(e)ɪt, daɪ-] **N** conseil *m* d'administration

directorial [daɪrekˈtɔːrɪəl] **ADJ** de mise en scène; *Cin* **his d. début** son premier film derrière la caméra

directorship [dɪˈrektəʃɪp, daɪ-] **N** **1** *(position)* poste *m ou* fonctions *fpl* de directeur; **she holds directorships in several companies** elle fait partie du conseil d'administration de plusieurs entreprises **2** *(term of office)* **during my d.** *(in past)* pendant que j'étais directeur; *(in present)* depuis que je suis directeur

directory [dɪˈrektərɪ, daɪ-] **N** *Tel* annuaire *m*; *(of addresses)* répertoire *m* d'adresses; *Comput* répertoire *m*; **street d.** guide *m* des rues; **commercial d.** annuaire du commerce
▸▸ *Tel Am* **d. assistance,** *Br* **d. enquiries** ren-

seignements *mpl*; *Comput* **d. path** arborescence *f*; *Comput* **d. structure** structure *f* arborescente, structure du répertoire; *Comput* **d. tree** arborescence *f* des répertoires

dirge [dɜːdʒ] **N** hymne *m ou* chant *m* funèbre

dirigible ['dɪrɪdʒɪb(ə)l] **N, ADJ** *Fml (balloon)* dirigeable *m*

dirk [dɜːk] **N** *Scot* poignard *m*

dirt [dɜːt] **N 1** saleté *f*; *(earth)* terre *f*, *(mud)* boue *f*; *(on unwashed object, hands etc)* crasse *f*; *(excrement)* crotte *f*; *(in machine, solution etc)* corps *mpl* étrangers, saletés; **hands ingrained with d.** mains encrassées; **covered in d.** crasseux, couvert de crasse; **to show the d.** *(of material)* être salissant; *Fig* **to treat sb like d.** traiter qn comme le dernier des derniers; *Am Fam* **to be d. poor** être vachement pauvre; *Am Sl* **to do sb d.** *(treat meanly)* faire un sale coup à qn **2** *Fam (obscenities)* cochonneries *fpl*; **to talk d.** dire des obscénités, raconter des cochonneries **3** *(gossip)* ragot *m*; **to dig the d. on sb** chercher à salir qn

▸▸*Am* **d. farmer** exploitant *m* agricole; *Am* **d. farming** exploitation *f* agricole; **d. road** chemin *m* de terre *ou* non goudronné; **d. track** chemin *m* de terre; *Sport* (piste *f*) cendrée *f*, *Aut* **d.-track racing** courses *fpl* (motocyclistes) sur cendrée

dirtbag ['dɜːtbæg] **N** *Am Fam* nullard, -arde

dirt-cheap *Fam* **ADJ** vraiment pas cher; **that's d.** c'est donné

 ADV pour trois fois rien; **I got it d.** je l'ai eu pour trois fois rien

dirtily ['dɜːtɪlɪ] **ADV 1** *(to eat)* salement **2** *(crudely)* grossièrement **3** *(to play, fight)* déloyalement

dirtiness ['dɜːtɪnɪs] **N** saleté *f*

dirty ['dɜːtɪ] **ADJ 1** sale; *(with mud)* crotté; *(valve, piston etc)* encrassé; **d. dishes** vaisselle *f* sale; **to get d.** *(of child, clothes etc)* se salir; **to get one's hands d.** se salir les mains; **2** *(sexually)* cochon; *(story etc)* cochon, sale; *(book, film)* pornographique; **you've got a d. mind** tu as l'esprit mal tourné, tu as l'esprit entre le nombril et les genoux; **d. joke** blague *f* cochonne *ou* obscène; **to tell d. stories** raconter des cochonneries *ou* des obscénités; **d. word** gros mot *m*; *Fig* **competitiveness is a d. word nowadays** le mot 'compétitivité' est tabou de nos jours **3** *(nasty)* **it's a d. business** c'est une sale affaire; **d. job** sale boulot *m* **4** *Com (bill of lading)* clausé

 N *Br Fam* **to do the d. on sb** jouer un sale tour *ou* coup à qn

 ADV 1 *Fam (intensive)* **a d. great lorry** un énorme camion **2** **to talk d.** *(swearing)* dire des gros mots; *(sexually)* dire des trucs cochons

 VT *(one's clothes etc)* salir; **to d. one's hands** se salir les mains; *Fig* **to d. one's reputation** entacher *ou* salir sa réputation

 VI se salir, se souiller; **to d. easily** *(of material, car etc)* se salir facilement, être salissant

▸▸*Typ* **d. copy** manuscrit *m* brouillé *ou* peu clair; *St Exch* **d. float** taux *mpl* de change concertés; **d. look** *(angry)* sale coup *m* d'œil; **to give sb a d. look** regarder qn d'un sale œil *Fin* **d. money** argent *m* sale mal acquis; *Fam* **d. old man** vieux cochon *m*; *Br Fam Hum* **d. stop-out** débauché, -ée *(qui découche)*; **d. trick** *(malicious act)* sale tour *m*; **d. weather** sale temps *m*; *Naut* gros temps; *Fam* **d. weekend** week-end *m* coquin; **d. work** *(unpleasant)* travail *m* salissant; *Fam (dishonest)* sale boulot *m*

dis [dɪs] **VT** *(-ss-)* *Am Sl (disparage)* débiner

disability [dɪsə'bɪlɪtɪ] **N 1** *(infirmity)* infirmité *f*; *Admin* invalidité *f*; *(work-related)* incapacité *f* de travail; *Fig (handicap)* handicap *m* **2** *Law* incapacité *f* légale, inhabilité *f* (**to do** à faire)

▸▸**d. allowance, d. pension** pension *f* d'invalidité

disable [dɪ'seɪb(ə)l] **VT** *Mil (person)* mettre hors de combat; *(maim)* estropier; *(ship)* désemparer; *(machine)* mettre hors de service; *(function, feature)* désactiver

disabled [dɪ'seɪb(ə)ld] **ADJ** *(infirm)* infirme, handicapé; *(as result of accident etc)* handicapé, estropié; *(ship)* désemparé; **d. ex-serviceman** mutilé *m* de guerre

 NPL the d. *(people)* les handicapés; **facilities for the d.** aménagements *mpl* pour les handicapés;

▸▸**d. access** facilité *f* d'accès pour personnes handicapées

disablement [dɪ'seɪb(ə)lmənt] **N 1** *(physical handicap)* invalidité *f*; *Admin* **degree of d.** coefficient *m* d'invalidité **2** *(action)* *Mil* mise *f* hors de combat; *(of machine)* mise hors service

disabuse [dɪsə'bjuːz] **VT** détromper; **to d. sb of sth** *(of idea)* détromper qn de qch; *(of illusion)* faire perdre qch à qn

disadvantage [dɪsəd'vɑːntɪdʒ] **N** désavantage *m*, inconvénient *m*; **the d. of the plan is that ...** l'inconvénient de ce projet est que ...; **to be at a d.** être désavantagé (**owing to sth** par qch); **to put sb at a d.** désavantager qn

 VT désavantager

disadvantaged [dɪsəd'vɑːntɪdʒd] **ADJ** défavorisé

 NPL the d. les défavorisés *mpl*; **the educationally d.** les personnes *fpl* défavorisées en matière d'éducation

disadvantageous [dɪsædvən'teɪdʒəs] **ADJ** désavantageux (**to** pour), défavorable (**to** à)

disaffected [dɪsə'fektɪd] **ADJ** *(supporters, troops etc)* mécontent (**with** de)

disaffection [dɪsə'fekʃən] **N** mécontentement *m*, insatisfaction *f*; **d. among the troops is growing** le mécontentement grandit au sein des troupes

disagree [dɪsə'griː] **VI 1** *(of person)* ne pas être d'accord (**with** avec); *(quarrel)* se disputer, se brouiller (**with** avec); **to d. with sb** ne pas être du même avis que qn, ne pas être d'accord avec qn; **I d.** je ne suis pas de cet avis; **I can't say I d. with her** *(in opinion etc)* je ne peux pas dire que je ne suis pas de son avis; *(as regards an action)* je ne peux pas dire que je la désapprouve **2** *(not correspond)* *(of accounts, figures)* ne pas concorder **3** *(be unsuitable)* ne pas convenir (**with** à); **red wine disagrees with me** je ne supporte pas le vin rouge; **the climate disagrees with him** le climat ne lui convient pas *ou* ne lui va pas; **hard work disagrees with me** je ne suis pas fait pour les gros labeurs; **children d. with me** les enfants et moi, ça fait deux

disagreeable [dɪsə'griːəb(ə)l] **ADJ** *(person, job, smell)* désagréable; *(remark)* désobligeant; **he was very d. to her** il s'est montré très désagréable envers elle; **to make a d. impression on sb** faire une impression défavorable sur qn

disagreeableness [dɪsə'griːəb(ə)lnɪs] **N** *(of situation)* caractère *m* désagréable; *(of person)* mauvaise humeur *f*, *(of remark)* désobligeance *f* (**to** envers)

disagreeably [dɪsə'griːəblɪ] **ADV** désagréablement; **to behave d. to(wards) sb** se montrer désagréable envers qn

disagreement [dɪsə'griːmənt] **N 1** *(of figures)* différence *f* (**between** entre) **2** *(failure to agree)* désaccord *m* (**with sb about sth** avec qn sur qch), conflit *m* d'opinions; **we are in d.** nous sommes en désaccord; **to be in d. with sb** ne pas partager l'avis de qn,

être en désaccord avec qn **3** *(quarrel)* brouille *f*, différend *m*; **to have a d. with sb** se disputer avec qn

disallow [dɪsə'laʊ] **VT 1** *(reject)* *(hypothesis etc)* ne pas admettre, ne pas reconnaître; *Law (testimony)* rejeter **2** *Ftbl etc (goal, try)* annuler

disambiguate [dɪsæm'bɪgjʊeɪt] **VT** désambiguïser

disappear [dɪsə'pɪər] **VI** disparaître (**from a place** d'un endroit); **to d. in** *or* **into the crowd** se perdre dans la foule; **since she disappeared** depuis sa disparition

disappearance [dɪsə'pɪərəns] **N** disparition *f*

disappearing [dɪsə'pɪərɪŋ] **ADJ** *(race, species)* en voie de disparition; **where's that d. programme changer?** où est-ce que la télécommande a encore été se cacher?; **to do a d. act** *(of conjurer)* *(make sb/sth disappear)* faire disparaître quelqu'un/quelque chose; *(make self disappear)* disparaître; *Fig Fam (sneak away)* s'esquiver, s'éclipser; *Fam* **the scissors have done a d. act** les ciseaux ont disparu; **he's done his famous d. act again** il s'est encore éclipsé

disappoint [dɪsə'pɔɪnt] **VT** *(person)* décevoir; *(after promising)* manquer de parole à; *(person's hopes)* tromper

disappointed [dɪsə'pɔɪntɪd] **ADJ** *(person)* déçu; *(candidate)* refusé; **we were all d. that you couldn't come** nous avons tous été très déçus que tu ne puisses pas venir; **he was d. at** *or* **about not being invited** il a été déçu de ne pas être invité; **I am d. in** *or* **with you** tu m'as déçu; **I was d. with it** cela m'a déçu; **he was bitterly d.** il a eu une grande déception; **d. customers** clients insatisfaits; **to be d. in love** avoir des chagrins d'amour

disappointing [dɪsə'pɔɪntɪŋ] **ADJ** décevant; **how d.!** quelle déception!

disappointingly [dɪsə'pɔɪntɪŋlɪ] **ADV the unemployment figures are still d. high** il est décevant de constater que les chiffres du chômage restent élevés

disappointment [dɪsə'pɔɪntmənt] **N** déception *f*; **it was a bit of a d.** *(of film, holiday etc)* c'était un peu décevant; **bitter d.** vive contrariété *f*; **to suffer many disappointments** essuyer bien des déceptions; **you've been a great d. to your parents** tu as beaucoup déçu tes parents; **to their great d., she did not come** à leur grande déception, elle n'est pas venue; **book early to avoid d.** réservez bien à l'avance pour ne pas être déçu

disapprobation [dɪsæprəʊ'beɪʃən] **N** *Fml* désapprobation *f* (**of** à l'égard de)

disapproval [dɪsə'pruːv(ə)l] **N** désapprobation *f* (**of** de); **look of d.** regard désapprobateur; **to look at sb with d.** regarder qn avec désapprobation; **much to our d.** bien que nous n'approuvions pas

disapprove [dɪsə'pruːv] **VI I d.** je ne suis pas d'accord; *(stronger, in principle)* je désapprouve; **to d. of sth** désapprouver qch; **to d. of sth being done** désapprouver que l'on fasse qch; **she disapproves of her son-in-law** son gendre n'est pas à son goût; **your mother disapproves of me** ta mère ne m'aime pas

disapproving [dɪsə'pruːvɪŋ] **ADJ** *(look, tone etc)* désapprobateur, -trice; **he was a stern, rather d. man** c'était un homme sévère, qui portait sur toutes choses un œil désapprobateur

disapprovingly [dɪsə'pruːvɪŋlɪ] **ADV** *(to look)* d'un air désapprobateur; *(to say)* d'un ton désapprobateur

disarm [dɪs'ɑːm] **VT** *(prisoner, country etc)* désarmer; *(bomb etc)* désamorcer; *Fig* **her**

frankness quite disarmed us sa franchise nous a complètement désarmés vi désarmer

disarmament [dɪsˈɑːməmənt] N désarmement m

disarming [dɪsˈɑːmɪŋ] ADJ (smile, honesty etc) désarmant

disarmingly [dɪsˈɑːmɪŋlɪ] ADV he was d. frank il montrait une franchise désarmante; **to smile d.** sourire de façon désarmante

disarrange [dɪsəˈreɪndʒ] VT Fml déranger, mettre en désordre; **to d. sb's plans** déranger ou bouleverser les projets de qn

disarrangement [dɪsəˈreɪndʒmənt] N dérangement m

disarray [dɪsəˈreɪ] N désordre m; **in complete d.** (of person) en plein désarroi; (of objects, room, life) en désordre; (of troops) en déroute; **the news threw the company into complete d.** cette nouvelle a semé la panique dans l'entreprise

disassemble [dɪsəˈsemb(ə)l] VT démonter

disassembler [dɪsəˈsemblər] N Comput désassembleur m

disassociate [dɪsəˈsəʊʃɪeɪt] VT = **dissociate**

disassociation [dɪsəsəʊsɪˈeɪʃən] N = **dissociation**

disaster [dɪˈzɑːstər] N also Fig Fam désastre m; (by shipwreck, fire, earthquake etc) sinistre m; Fam (person) catastrophe f; **our journey was a series of disasters** notre voyage n'a été qu'une suite de malheurs; **they were near the summit when d. struck** ils avaient presque atteint le sommet quand la catastrophe a eu lieu; **he is heading for d.** il court à sa perte; **it would be a d.!** ce serait le désastre!; **to finish** or **end in d.** tourner à la tragédie; Fig **the party was an absolute d.** la soirée a été un vrai désastre; **air/railway d.** catastrophe aérienne/ferroviaire; **financial d.** désastre financier
▸▸ **d. area** région f sinistrée; Fig champ m de bataille; **d. fund** fonds m de secours; **d. movie** film m catastrophe

disastrous [dɪˈzɑːstrəs] ADJ désastreux; **just how d. would that be?** est-ce que ce serait vraiment une catastrophe?

disastrously [dɪˈzɑːstrəslɪ] ADV désastreusement; **the performance went d. wrong** la représentation a tourné au désastre; **the estimates were d. inaccurate** l'inexactitude des prévisions s'est révélée désastreuse; **his attitude was d. complacent** son attitude complaisante a eu des effets désastreux; **d. bad** désastreux; **d. optimistic** terriblement optimiste

disavow [dɪsəˈvaʊ] VT Fml désavouer, renier

disavowal [dɪsəˈvaʊəl] N Fml désaveu m

disband [dɪsˈbænd] VT (troops etc) licencier; (committee etc) dissoudre
vi (of troops) se débander; (on instructions) être licencié; (of committee etc) être dissout

disbar [dɪsˈbɑːr] VT (-rr-) Law (lawyer) rayer du barreau ou du tableau de l'ordre

disbarment [dɪsˈbɑːmənt] N Law (of lawyer) radiation f du tableau de l'ordre ou de la liste du barreau

disbelief [dɪsbɪˈliːf] N incrédulité f (in sth à l'égard de qch); **she looked at him in d.** elle l'a regardé, incrédule

disbelieve [dɪsbɪˈliːv] VT (somebody, something) ne pas croire
vi Fml **to d. in sb/sth** ne pas croire à qn/qch

disbeliever [dɪsbɪˈliːvər] N esp Rel incrédule mf

disbelieving [dɪsbɪˈliːvɪŋ] ADJ (look) incrédule

disbud [dɪsˈbʌd] VT Bot (fruit tree) ébourgeonner

disburse [dɪsˈbɜːs] VT Fml (money) débourser

disbursement [dɪsˈbɜːsmənt] N **1** (paying out) déboursement m **2** (money) débours m
▸▸ Fin **d. voucher** bon m de décaissement

disc, Am disk [dɪsk] N **1** (record) disque m **2** Comput = **disk 3** (of moon etc) disque m; Tech disque, plateau m; (made of cardboard etc) rondelle f; Mil etc **identity** or **identification d.** plaque f d'identité; Aut **parking d.** disque de stationnement; Aut **(tax) d.** vignette f **4** Anat disque m; **intervertebral d.** disque intervertébral; Med **slipped d.** hernie f discale; **to slip a d.** se faire une hernie discale
▸▸ Aut **d. brakes** freins mpl à disque; Phot **d. camera** appareil m photo à disque; Aut **d. clutch** embrayage m monodisque; Phot **d. film** disque m; Agr **d. harrow** pulvériseur m; **d. jockey** animateur, -trice; (on radio, in club) disc-jockey m, pl disc-jockeys; Agr **d. plough** charrue f à disques; Tech **d. valve** clapet m disque; **d. wheel** roue f pleine ou à voile plein

discard ['dɪskɑːd] N **1** Cards (action, card) (at cribbage) écart m; (at bridge) défausse f **2** Ind (rejected part) pièce f de rebut
VT **1** (object) se débarrasser de; (person, project) abandonner; (item of clothing, old car etc) mettre au rebut; **one of her discarded lovers** un de ses amants abandonnés; **his discarded coat still lay on the sofa** son manteau était toujours sur le canapé, tel qu'il l'y avait jeté **2** Cards (at cribbage) (card) écarter; (at bridge etc) (suit) se défausser de
vi Cards (at bridge) se défausser

discern [dɪˈsɜːn] VT distinguer, discerner, percevoir; **to d. a distant object** discerner ou reconnaître un objet dans le lointain

discernible [dɪˈsɜːnɪb(ə)l] ADJ perceptible

discernibly [dɪˈsɜːnɪblɪ] ADV perceptiblement

discerning [dɪˈsɜːnɪŋ] ADJ (person) éclairé, plein de discernement; (intelligence) pénétrant; (taste) délicat; **with a d. eye** d'un œil averti; **a house/car for the d. buyer** une maison/voiture pour l'acheteur avisé; **for the d. reader** pour le lecteur averti

discernment [dɪˈsɜːnmənt] N (judgement) discernement m, jugement m

discharge¹ ['dɪstʃɑːdʒ] N **1** (release), Med (of patient) renvoi m; Law (of prisoner) mise f en liberté, libération f; (of the accused) acquittement m; Fin (of bankrupt) réhabilitation f, **to apply for one's d.** (of bankrupt) demander sa réhabilitation
2 (dismissal) (of employee) renvoi m; (of servant) congé m; Mil (after active service) démobilisation f; Mil, Naut (for unfitness) réforme f; Mil, Naut **to take one's d.** prendre son congé
3 (firing) (of firearm, artillery) décharge f
4 (emission) (of water etc) décharge f, évacuation f; (of gas) décharge, dégagement m; (of steam) échappement m; (from pump) débit m; Elec (of electricity, battery) décharge; Med (of blood) perte f; (of pus) écoulement m; (vaginal) pertes fpl; Ind (water from factory etc) eaux fpl usées
5 (performance, fulfilment) (of duty) accomplissement m; (of debt) paiement m; **in the d. of his duties** dans l'exercice de ses fonctions
6 (unloading) (of ship, cargo) déchargement m
▸▸ Tech **d. nozzle** buse f de sortie; **d. pipe** tuyau m de décharge ou de débit; **d. pump** pompe f d'extraction ou d'épuisement

discharge² [dɪsˈtʃɑːdʒ] VT **1** (release) (patient) renvoyer; (prisoner) libérer, mettre en

liberté; (the accused) acquitter; Law (bankrupt) réhabiliter, décharger; (debtor) libérer; **he was discharged from hospital yesterday** il est sorti de l'hôpital hier; **to d. oneself from hospital** signer sa propre décharge; Law **to d. the jury** congédier les jurés; Fin **discharged bankrupt** failli m réhabilité; **to d. sb from an obligation** décharger ou acquitter qn d'une obligation
2 (dismiss) (employee) congédier, renvoyer; (workman) débaucher; (civil servant) destituer; (troops) licencier; (soldier) congédier, donner son congé à, désenrôler; Mil, Naut (for unfitness) (enlisted man) réformer; **to be discharged from the force** être congédié
3 (firearm) décharger, faire partir; (missile) lancer; Elec (battery etc) décharger
4 (emit) (steam) dégager; (of chemical reaction) (gas) dégager; (of gland) (hormones) sécréter; (of reservoir etc) (water) déverser; (of pump) débiter; **to d. pus** (of abscess) suppurer; **river that discharges its water into a lake** rivière qui déverse ses eaux dans un lac
5 (perform, fulfil) (one's duties) accomplir, s'acquitter de; Fin (debt) liquider, solder; (fine) payer; (account, obligation) apurer
6 (unload) (ship, tank etc) décharger; (cargo) décharger, débarquer; (of vehicle) (passengers) déposer
vi **1** (of gun) partir, se décharger
2 Med (of abscess, wound) suppurer
3 (of river) se jeter, déboucher (**into a lake** dans un lac)
4 Elec (of battery) se décharger

disciple [dɪˈsaɪp(ə)l] N Rel, Fig disciple m

disciplinarian [dɪsɪplɪˈneərɪən] N partisan, -ane d'une forte discipline; **he is a strict d.** il est strict en matière de discipline

disciplinary ['dɪsɪplɪnərɪ] ADJ (measures, committee) disciplinaire; (problems) de discipline; **to take d. action** (of employer) prendre des mesures disciplinaires
▸▸ **d. board** conseil m de discipline; **d. hearing** séance f du conseil de discipline; **d. procedure** procédure f disciplinaire

discipline ['dɪsɪplɪn] N **1** discipline f, **iron d.** discipline de fer; **to keep d.** (of teacher) maintenir la discipline **2** (branch of learning) discipline f
VT **1** (pupils, troops) discipliner; (punish) punir; **to d. oneself** se discipliner **2** (character) former

disciplined ['dɪsɪplɪnd] ADJ discipliné; (showing self-control) contrôlé

disclaim [dɪsˈkleɪm] VT **1** (deny) (knowledge, responsibility) nier **2** (reject) (person's authority) démentir, renier **3** Law (right etc) se désister de, renoncer à

disclaimer [dɪsˈkleɪmər] N **1** (denial) démenti m; (of responsibility) dénégation f, **to issue a d.** publier un démenti; **d. of authorship** désaveu m **2** Law désistement m, renonciation f (**of a right** à un droit)

disclose [dɪsˈkləʊz] VT **1** (make known) (secret, information etc) divulguer, révéler; **to d. that ...** révéler que ... **2** (show) révéler

disclosure [dɪsˈkləʊʒər] N **1** (of one's thoughts etc) révélation f, (of secret) divulgation f, révélation **2** (fact disclosed) révélation f **3** (of truth, fact) mise f à jour
▸▸ St Exch **d. threshold** seuil m d'annonce obligatoire

disco ['dɪskəʊ] N Fam (place) discothèque f, (event) soirée f disco; **we're having a d. at the party** il y aura une animation disco à la soirée
▸▸ **d. dancer** danseur, -euse de disco; **d. dancing** disco m; **d. music** musique f disco, disco

discography [dɪsˈkɒɡrəfɪ] N discographie f

discolour, Am discolor [dɪsˈkʌlər] VT (fabric

etc) ternir, délaver; **to become discoloured** se décolorer; *(of fabric)* se ternir; **discoloured by tobacco** jauni par le tabac
VI *(of fabric)* se ternir

discolo(u)ration, *Am* **discoloration** [dɪskʌlə'reɪʃən] **N** *(of fabric)* ternissure *f*, *(of teeth)* jaunissement *m*

discombobulate [dɪskəm'bɒbjʊleɪt] **VT** *Am Fam* déconcerter, confondre

discomfit [dɪs'kʌmfɪt] **VT** *Fml (confuse)* déconcerter

discomfiture [dɪs'kʌmfɪtʃər] **N** *Fml (confusion)* embarras *m*, trouble *m*; **he showed signs of d.** il avait l'air embarrassé; **much to his d.** à son grand embarras

discomfort [dɪs'kʌmfət] **N 1** *(lack of comfort)* inconfort *m* **2** *(pain)* malaise *m*, gêne *f*, **to be in some d.** *(of patient)* éprouver une sensation de gêne; **to cause (sb) d.** *(of stitches, wound etc)* gêner (qn)

discomposure [dɪskəm'pəʊʒər] **N** *Fml* trouble *m*, agitation *f*, *(of mind)* perturbation *f*

disconcert [dɪskən'sɜːt] **VT** déconcerter, troubler; **I don't want to d. you, but …** je ne veux pas vous alarmer, mais …

disconcerting [dɪskən'sɜːtɪŋ] **ADJ** *(news, attitude, habit etc)* déconcertant, troublant

disconcertingly [dɪskən'sɜːtɪŋlɪ] **ADV** d'une manière déconcertante; **they were d. eager to see him go** la hâte qu'ils avaient de le voir partir était déconcertante

disconnect [dɪskə'nekt] **VT 1** *(gas, water supply, electricity, phone)* couper; *Tel* **I've been disconnected** *(I cannot continue the call)* on a coupé la communication; *(because I haven't paid the bill)* ils m'ont coupé le téléphone *ou* la ligne; **to get the telephone disconnected** faire débrancher le téléphone **2** *(separate)* disjoindre, séparer, détacher **(sth from sth** qch de qch); *(carriages)* décrocher; *(machine etc)* débrayer, désembrayer; *Elec (battery, kettle etc)* déconnecter, débrancher; **to d. a waterpipe from the main supply** isoler un tuyau d'eau de l'arrivée

disconnected [dɪskə'nektɪd] **ADJ 1** *Elec* débranché; *Tech* débrayé **2** *(style etc) (lacking flow)* décousu; *(deliberately staccato)* entrecoupé **3** *(separate)* détaché, isolé

disconnection, **disconnexion** [dɪskə'nekʃən] **N 1** *(action) (of phone, gas, water, in phone call)* coupure *f*, *(of battery, kettle)* débranchement *m* **2** *(of carriage)* décrochage *m*; *(of part of machine)* démontage *m* **3** *(state)* séparation *f* **(between** entre)

disconsolate [dɪs'kɒnsələt] **ADJ** *(person)* tout triste, inconsolable; *(sigh, look, face)* accablé

disconsolately [dɪs'kɒnsələtlɪ] **ADV** tristement, désespérément

discontent [dɪskən'tent] **N** mécontentement *m*

discontented [dɪskən'tentɪd] **ADJ** mécontent **(with** de)

discontinue [dɪskən'tɪnjuː] **VT 1** *(service)* interrompre; *(practice)* abandonner; *(one's subscription)* résilier; *Com* **that item has been discontinued** cet article n'est plus suivi; *Com* **discontinued** *(on label)* fin de série; *Com* **discontinued line** fin de série **2** *Law (trial)* abandonner

discontinuity [dɪskɒntɪ'njuːɪtɪ] **N** *also Math* discontinuité *f*

discontinuous [dɪskən'tɪnjʊəs] **ADJ** *(with interruptions)*, *Ling* discontinu; *(intermittent)* intermittent

discord ['dɪskɔːd] **N 1** *(disagreement)* discorde *f*, **there was some d. over it** cela a été la source d'un certain désaccord, cela été

un sujet de discorde; **industrial/civil d.** dissensions *fpl* ouvrières/sociales **2** *Mus* dissonance *f*

discordance [dɪs'kɔːdəns] **N 1** *(of opinions etc)* discordance *f* **2** *(of sounds)* discordance *f*

discordant [dɪs'kɔːdənt] **ADJ 1 d. opinions** opinions opposées *ou* discordantes; **a d. atmosphere** une atmosphère de discorde **2** *(sound)* discordant; *(voice)* discordant, criard **3** *Mus* dissonant

discotheque ['dɪskətek] **N** discothèque *f*

discount[1] ['dɪskaʊnt] **N 1** *Com* remise *f*, rabais *m*; **to sell sth at a d.** vendre qch au rabais; **cash d.** escompte *m* de caisse; **trade d.** remise d'usage; **to allow a d. of 10%** consentir un rabais de 10%; **d. for early payment** escompte *m* de règlement **2** *Fin* escompte *m*; **discounts and allowances** remise, ristourne *f*, RRR; **to be at a d.** *(of shares)* être en perte, se trouver en moins-value; *Fig (of politeness etc)* être en défaveur
▸▸ **d. bank** banque *f* d'escompte; *St Exch* **d. bond** obligation *f* émise au dessous du pair; *Com* **d. card** carte *f* de réduction; **d. coach card** carte de réduction sur les lignes d'autocars; **d. house** comptoir *m* d'escompte; *Fin* **d. loan** prêt *m* escompté; **d. price** prix *m* réduit; *Fin* **d. rate** taux *m* d'escompte; *Com* **d. store** solderie *f*, magasin *m* de vente au rabais; **d. tariff** tarif *m* réduit; **d. ticket agency** agence *f* spécialisée dans la vente de billets bradés; **d. travel card** carte de réduction pour les transports; *Com* **d. voucher** bon *m* de réduction

discount[2] [dɪs'kaʊnt, 'dɪskaʊnt] **VT 1** *Fin* escompter; *(bill)* prendre à l'escompte **2** *(not consider) (somebody, something)* ne pas tenir compte de; *(ignore) (sb's advice, warning)* faire peu de cas de; *(fact, importance of sth)* négliger; **you must d. half of what he says** il ne faut croire que la moitié de ce qu'il dit; **police have discounted the possibility of suicide** la police a écarté la thèse du suicide
▸▸ *Fin* **discounted bill** effet *m* escompté; *Acct* **discounted cashflow** valeur *f* actualisée nette

discountable [dɪs'kaʊntəb(ə)l] **ADJ** *Fin* escomptable

discounted rate **N** *Fin* taux *m* d'escompte

discounted value **N** *Acct* valeur *f* actualisée

discounting [dɪs'kaʊntɪŋ] **N** remise *f*, *Fin* **d. of a bill** escompte *m* commercial

discourage [dɪs'kʌrɪdʒ] **VT 1** *(cause to lose heart)* décourager, abattre; **to become discouraged** se décourager; **don't get discouraged** ne te décourage pas **2** *(put difficulties in the way of) (project, suitor etc)* décourager; **to d. sb from (doing) sth** décourager qn de (faire) qch; **they were discouraged from going by the weather/the price** le temps/prix les a dissuadés d'y aller; **we (actively) d. smoking** nous essayons de dissuader les gens de fumer; **you should d. it** tu devrais l'en/les en dissuader

discouragement [dɪs'kʌrɪdʒmənt] **N 1** *(state)* découragement *m* **2** *(act of discouraging)* dissuasion *f*, **their d. of the use of this drug** le fait qu'ils déconseillent l'utilisation de ce médicament **3** *(something that discourages)* source *f* de découragement; **I hope this won't be a d. to you** j'espère que ceci ne te découragera pas; **to act as a d.** avoir un effet dissuasif

discouraging [dɪs'kʌrɪdʒɪŋ] **ADJ** décourageant; **he was very d. about my chances** il n'était pas du tout encourageant quant à mes chances

discourse ['dɪskɔːs] **N 1** *Lit (conversation)*

conversation *f*, entretien *m*; *Ling* discours *m*; **2** *Lit (dissertation)* dissertation *f* **(on** sur)
▸▸ *Ling* **d. analysis** analyse *f* du discours
▸ **discourse on, discourse upon** **VT INSEP** *Lit* **1** *(speak of)* discourir sur **2** *(discuss)* parler de, s'entretenir de

discourteous [dɪs'kɜːtɪəs] **ADJ** discourtois, impoli

discourteously [dɪs'kɜːtɪəslɪ] **ADV** impoliment, d'une façon impolie

discourtesy [dɪs'kɜːtəsɪ] **N** incivilité *f*, impolitesse *f*

discover [dɪ'skʌvər] **VT** *(the truth, a planet, the cause of a disease, actor etc)* découvrir; **we have discovered a good gardener** nous avons déniché un bon jardinier; **I discovered too late that …** je me suis rendu compte trop tard que …

discoverer [dɪ'skʌvərər] **N** découvreur *m*; **the d. of America** celui qui a découvert l'Amérique

discovery [dɪ'skʌvərɪ] **N** découverte *f*, *(thing found by chance)* trouvaille *f*, **he's quite a d.** *(of new actor, soccer player etc)* c'est une vraie révélation; **voyage of d.** voyage *m* d'exploration; **to make a d.** faire une découverte

discredit [dɪs'kredɪt] **N 1** *(doubt)* **to throw d. on a statement** mettre une affirmation en doute **2** *(dishonour)* **to be a d. to one's family** être une honte pour sa famille; **it does you no d. to admit you were mistaken** il n'y a aucune honte à admettre que tu t'es trompé; **much to their d.** ce qui ne leur faisait pas du tout honneur; **to bring d. on sb/sth** jeter le discrédit sur qn/qch, discréditer qn/qch; **to bring sth into d.** discréditer qch; **to bring d. on oneself** se discréditer
VT 1 *(rumour) (not believe)* ne pas croire; *(not trust)* mettre en doute; **such theories/methods have long been discredited** ces théories/méthodes sont discréditées depuis longtemps **2** *(lower in esteem) (person, opinion)* discréditer; **his conduct has discredited him with the public** sa conduite lui a fait perdre la considération du public

discreditable [dɪs'kredɪtəb(ə)l] **ADJ** peu digne, peu honorable; **conduct d. to a barrister** conduite *f* indigne d'un avocat; **there's nothing d. about being poor** il n'y a pas de honte à être pauvre

discreet [dɪ'skriːt] **ADJ** discret, -ète **(about** sur); **can you trust him to be d.?** peut-on compter sur sa discrétion? ; **to maintain a d. silence** observer un silence discret; **a d. smile** un petit sourire contenu

> Attention: ne pas confondre avec l'adjectif **discrete**.

discreetly [dɪ'skriːtlɪ] **ADV** discrètement, avec discrétion; *(to dress, be situated)* discrètement

discrepancy [dɪ'skrepənsɪ] **N** désaccord *m* **(between** entre); *(between accounts)* différence *f*, *(between statements)* divergence *f*, *(between styles, source text and target text)* décalage *m*; **there is a d. between the two stories** les deux récits ne cadrent pas; *Fin* **there is a d. in the accounts** les comptes ne concordent pas

discrete [dɪs'kriːt] **ADJ** *Math etc* discret, -ète

> Attention: ne pas confondre avec l'adjectif **discreet**.

discretion [dɪ'skreʃən] **N 1** *(liberty of action)* discrétion *f*, **I shall use my own d.** je ferai comme je jugerai à propos; **to leave sth to sb's d.** laisser qch à la discrétion de qn; **at the manager's d.** comme le directeur le décidera; **at your d.** comme vous jugerez bon, comme vous voudrez; *Law* **fine at** *or* **left to**

the d. of the judge amende laissée à l'appréciation du juge **2** *(good sense)* jugement *m*, prudence *f*; **the age of d.** l'âge *m* de raison; *Prov* **d. is the better part of valour** prudence est mère de sûreté **3** *(tact)* discrétion *f*, réserve *f*; **he is the soul of d.** il est la discrétion même

discretionary [dɪ'skreʃən(ə)rɪ] **ADJ** *Law* discrétionnaire
▸▸ *Banking* **d. account** compte *m* sous mandat de gestion; *St Exch* **d. order** ordre *m* à appréciation

discriminate [dɪ'skrɪmɪneɪt] **VI to d. between one thing and another** distinguer une chose d'une autre, établir une distinction entre une chose et une autre; **to d. in favour of sb** favoriser qn
VT distinguer (**from** de, d'avec)
▸ **discriminate against VT INSEP** faire de la discrimination envers; **to be (sexually/racially) discriminated against** être victime de discrimination (sexuelle/raciale)

discriminating [dɪ'skrɪmɪneɪtɪŋ] **ADJ 1** *(person)* plein de discernement, capable de juger; *(buyer)* avisé, averti; *(audience, eye)* averti; *(ear, judgement)* fin **2** *Admin (duty, tariff)* différentiel

discrimination [dɪskrɪmɪ'neɪʃən] **N 1** *(unfair treatment)* discrimination *f*; **without d.** sans distinction; **race** *or* **racial/sexual/religious d.** discrimination raciale/sexuelle/religieuse **2** *(in matters of taste)* jugement *m*, discernement *m* **3** *(of differences etc)* discrimination *f*, discernement *m* (**between ... and ...** entre ... et ...)

discriminatory [dɪ'skrɪmɪnət(ə)rɪ] **ADJ** *Pej (law etc)* discriminatoire
▸▸ **d. pricing** tarification *f* discriminatoire

discursive [dɪ'skɜːsɪv] **ADJ** *(style etc)* discursif

discus ['dɪskəs] **N** *Sport* disque *m*; **the d.** *(event)* le lancer du disque
▸▸ *Sport* **d. thrower** lanceur, -euse de disque

discuss [dɪ'skʌs] **VT** *(problem etc)* discuter, débattre; *(matter, question)* délibérer de; *(of book) (subject)* traiter de; **to d. a price** discuter *ou* débattre un prix; **I know they were discussing me** je sais qu'on parlait de moi; **I refuse to d. it** je refuse d'en parler; **have you discussed it with your parents?** est-ce que tu en as discuté avec tes parents?; **we were discussing what to do about the problem** nous discutions de ce qui devrait être fait pour résoudre le problème; **d.** *(in exam questions)* discutez

discussion [dɪ'skʌʃən] **N** discussion *f*; **a subject for d.** un sujet de discussion; **question under d.** question en discussion; **after much d. of sth** après avoir longtemps discuté qch; **the matter is not up for d.** le sujet n'est pas ouvert à la discussion
▸▸ *Comput* **d. list** *(on Internet)* liste *f* de diffusion; *Radio, TV* **d. programme** table *f* ronde; **d. table** table ronde

disdain [dɪs'deɪn] **N** dédain *m* (**of** de)
VT *(somebody, something)* dédaigner; **to d. to do sth** dédaigner de faire qch

disdainful [dɪs'deɪnfʊl] **ADJ** dédaigneux (**of** de)

disdainfully [dɪs'deɪnfʊlɪ] **ADV** dédaigneusement

disease [dɪ'ziːz] **N** maladie *f*; **to die of a d.** mourir d'une maladie; **skin d.** maladie de la peau

Attention: ne pas confondre avec le nom **decease**.

diseased [dɪ'ziːzd] **ADJ** *also Fig* malade

disembark [dɪsem'bɑːk] **VT & VI** débarquer (**from** de)

disembarkation [dɪsembɑː'keɪʃən] **N** débarquement *m*

disembodied [dɪsɪm'bɒdɪd] **ADJ** *(spirit)* désincarné

disembowel [dɪsɪm'baʊəl] **VT** éventrer, éviscérer

disenchant [dɪsɪn'tʃɑːnt] **VT** désillusionner; **a disenchanting experience/encounter** une expérience/rencontre décevante

disenchanted [dɪsɪn'tʃɑːntɪd] **ADJ** désillusionné; **she's d. with her job** son travail la déçoit beaucoup, elle n'a plus d'illusions quant à son travail

disenchantment [dɪsɪn'tʃɑːntmənt] **N** désillusion *f*

disencumber [dɪsɪn'kʌmbər] **VT** *Fml* **to d. oneself of sth** *(of coat etc)* se débarrasser de qch; *(of one's responsibilities, burdens)* s'affranchir de qch

disenfranchise [dɪsɪn'fræntʃaɪz] **VT** *(person)* priver du droit électoral *ou* de ses droits civiques; *(borough)* priver de ses droits de représentation

disenfranchisement [dɪsɪn'fræntʃɪzmənt] **N** *(of person)* déchéance *f* de ses droits civiques; *(of borough)* déchéance de ses droits de représentation

disengage [dɪsɪn'geɪdʒ] **VT** dégager, débarrasser (**sb/sth from sth** qn/qch de qch); *Tech (cogwheel)* désengrener; *(part, component)* débrayer, désembrayer; **to d. oneself from sb's embrace** se dégager de l'étreinte de qn; **to d. oneself from the struggle** se retirer de la lutte
VI *(of person)* se dégager; *Tech (of catch etc)* se déclencher, se défaire; *Mil (of troops)* se retirer

disengaged [dɪsɪn'geɪdʒd] **ADJ** *Tech* débrayé

disengagement [dɪsɪn'geɪdʒmənt] **N 1** *(of person)* détachement *m* (**from** de); *Tech (of part, component)* débrayage *m* **2** *Pol, Mil* désengagement *m*

disentangle [dɪsɪn'tæŋg(ə)l] **VT** débarrasser (**sb/sth from sth** qn/qch de qch); *(piece of string)* débrouiller, démêler; *(plot, mystery)* dénouer; **to d. itself** *(of rope etc)* se démêler; **to d. oneself from sth** se libérer *ou* se dégager de qch; *Fig (from scandal etc)* se sortir de qch

disequilibrium [dɪsiːkwɪ'lɪbrɪəm] **N** déséquilibre *m*
▸▸ *Econ* **d. price** prix *m* de déséquilibre

disestablish [dɪsɪ'stæblɪʃ] **VT** *(the Church)* séparer de l'État

disestablishment [dɪsɪ'stæblɪʃmənt] **N** **d. of the Church** séparation *f* de l'Église et de l'État

disfavour, *Am* **disfavor** [dɪs'feɪvər] **N** défaveur *f*; **to regard** *or* **view** *or* **look on sth with d.** être défavorable à qch; **to fall into d.** tomber en disgrâce; **to fall into d. with sb** perdre le soutien *ou* les faveurs de qn; **to be in d. with sb** être en disgrâce auprès de qn; **at the risk of incurring sb's d.** au risque de déplaire à qn

disfigure [dɪs'fɪgər] **VT** *(person, statue etc)* défigurer; *(of buildings etc) (landscape)* gâter, enlaidir; **a disfiguring disease** une maladie qui défigure

disfigured [dɪs'fɪgəd] **ADJ** *(person, statue etc)* défiguré; *(landscape)* enlaidi

disfigurement [dɪs'fɪgəmənt] **N** *(of person, statue)* défiguration *f*; *(of landscape)* enlaidissement *m*

disfranchise [dɪs'fræntʃaɪz] **VT** = **disenfranchise**

disgorge [dɪs'gɔːdʒ] **VT** *(smoke, information)* dégorger; *(food)* rendre
VI **river that disgorges into ...** rivière qui se déverse dans ...

disgrace [dɪs'greɪs] **N 1** *(disfavour)* disgrâce *f*, défaveur *f*; **to be in d.** *(out of favour)* être en disgrâce; *(of child)* être en pénitence; **she is in d. with the party** elle n'est pas en faveur auprès du parti **2** *(shame)* honte *f*, déshonneur *m*; **there is no d. in doing that** il n'y a pas de honte à faire cela; **to bring d. on one's family** déshonorer sa famille; **to be a d. to one's family** être la honte de sa famille, faire honte à sa famille; **it's a d.!** c'est une honte *ou* un scandale!; **you're a d.** tu me fais honte!; **house prices are a d.** c'est une honte de vendre les maisons si cher; **the state of their house is a d.!** leur maison est dans un état honteux!
VT 1 *(esp in passive)* **to be disgraced** *(out of favour)* être disgracié (**for** pour) **2** *(shame) (person)* déshonorer, faire déshonneur à; **to d. oneself** se couvrir de honte; **you disgraced me in front of all those people** tu m'as couvert de honte devant tous ces gens

disgraceful [dɪs'greɪsfʊl] **ADJ** honteux, infâme; **it's d.** c'est scandaleux *ou* honteux

Note that the French word **disgracieux** is a false friend and is never a translation for the English word **disgraceful**. It means **ungainly**.

disgracefully [dɪs'greɪsfʊlɪ] **ADV** honteusement; *(late, rude, expensive)* scandaleusement

disgruntled [dɪs'grʌnt(ə)ld] **ADJ** *(discontented)* mécontent (**at** de); *(sulky)* maussade; **what are you looking so d. about?** pourquoi cet air mécontent?, pourquoi est-ce que tu fais la tête?

disguise [dɪs'gaɪz] **N** *(costume)* déguisement *m*; **put this on as a d.** déguise-toi avec ça; **in d.** déguisé; **in the d. of a policeman** déguisé en agent de police
VT 1 *(change appearance of) (person)* déguiser, travestir; *(the truth, one's thoughts, feelings)* déguiser; *(one's voice, writing)* déguiser, contrefaire; **to d. oneself as a clown** se déguiser en clown; **there is no disguising the fact that ...** il faut avouer que ... **2** *(hide) (one's feelings, motives)* cacher, dissimuler; *(smell)* masquer; **to d. one's disappointment** cacher sa déception

disgust [dɪs'gʌst] **N 1** *(physical)* dégoût *m* (**at, for, towards** pour) **2** *(moral)* écœurement *m*, dégoût *m*; **that kind of attitude fills me with d.** ce genre d'attitude me dégoûte *ou* m'écœure; **she turned away from him in d.** dégoûtée *ou* écœurée, elle s'est détournée de lui; **much to my d.** à mon grand dégoût
VT 1 *(physically)* dégoûter, donner la nausée à **2** *(morally)* écœurer, dégoûter; **to be disgusted at** *or* **with** *or* **by sb/sth** être écœuré par qn/de qch; **he is disgusted that ...** cela l'écœure *ou* le dégoûte que ... + *subj*; **I feel disgusted with myself for not having protested** je me dégoûte de ne pas avoir protesté

disgusting [dɪs'gʌstɪŋ] **ADJ** *(sight, smell, prospect, behaviour, carpet)* dégoûtant, écœurant, répugnant, *Fam* dégueulasse; *(bad quality) (music, souvenirs)* épouvantable; *(salary) (very low)* ridicule; *(very high)* écœurant; **it's d.!** c'est dégoûtant *ou Fam* dégueulasse!

disgustingly [dɪs'gʌstɪŋlɪ] **ADV 1 d. dirty** d'une saleté répugnante; **d. sweet/bad** épouvantablement sucré/mauvais; **d. rich/underpaid** scandaleusement riche/sous-payé; **a joke in d. bad taste** une blague d'un mauvais goût détestable **2** *Fam* **d. good-looking/well-read** beau/instruit comme c'est pas permis; **you look d. fit** vous avez l'air vachement en forme; **he makes it look d. easy** on dirait que c'est facile comme tout quand il le fait

dish [dɪʃ] N **1** *(for food)* plat *m*; *(earthenware casserole)* terrine *f*; **vegetable d.** légumier *m*; **butter d.** beurrier *m*; **to wash** *or* **do the dishes** faire la vaisselle; **a d. of strawberries** un plat de fraises **2** *(food)* plat *m*, mets *m*; **it's not a d. I often make** ce n'est pas une recette *ou* un plat que je prépare souvent **3** *TV* antenne *f* parabolique **4** *Old-fashioned Fam (female)* belle fille *f*; *(male)* beau mec *m*; **she's/he's a real d.** ce qu'elle est belle/ce qu'il est beau **5** *(container)* récipient *m*; *Phot* cuvette *f* ▪ VT *Fam* **1 to d. sb's chances** gâcher les chances de qn **2 to d. the dirt on sb** faire des révélations sur qn
▸▸ *Br* **d. aerial**, *Am* **d. antenna** antenne *f* parabolique
▸ **dish out** VT SEP *Fam (meat etc)* servir; *(give) (sweets, money)* distribuer; **to d. out punishment to** *(of boxer)* assener des coups à; *(of schoolmaster)* punir; **to d. out advice** prodiguer des conseils; **he is really dishing it out** *(of boxer)* il en assène; **she can really d. it out** *(be very critical)* quand elle s'y met, c'est une vraie langue de vipère
▸ **dish up** VT SEP *(course, meal)* servir; *Fig Fam (of programme planners etc)* proposer, sortir
▪ VI *Culin* servir; **shall I d. up?** je peux servir?, je sers?

disharmonious [dɪshɑːˈməʊnɪəs] ADJ *(sound)* dissonant; *(relationship)* qui manque d'harmonie, peu harmonieux

disharmony [dɪsˈhɑːmənɪ] N **1** *(disagreement)* désaccord *m*, discorde *f*, manque *m* d'harmonie **2** *(of sound)* dissonance *f*

dishcloth [ˈdɪʃklɒθ] N *(for washing)* lavette *f*; *(for drying)* torchon *m* à (essuyer la) vaisselle

dishearten [dɪsˈhɑːt(ə)n] VT *(person)* décourager, abattre; **to become disheartened** perdre courage, se décourager

disheartening [dɪsˈhɑːt(ə)nɪŋ] ADJ décourageant

dishearteningly [dɪsˈhɑːt(ə)nɪŋlɪ] ADV de façon décourageante; **d. brief** d'une brièveté décourageante; **d. few people turned up** peu de monde est venu, ce qui était décourageant

dished [dɪʃt] ADJ *Tech* concave

dishevelled [dɪˈʃev(ə)ld] ADJ *(person)* échevelé, dépeigné; **his d. appearance** son air échevelé; **d. hair** cheveux ébouriffés

dishmop [ˈdɪʃmɒp] N lavette *f* (à vaisselle)

dishonest [dɪsˈɒnɪst] ADJ malhonnête

dishonestly [dɪsˈɒnɪstlɪ] ADV malhonnêtement

dishonesty [dɪsˈɒnɪstɪ] N malhonnêteté *f*; **an act of d.** un acte malhonnête, une malhonnêteté

dishonour, *Am* **dishonor** [dɪsˈɒnər] N **1** *(shame, source of shame)* déshonneur *m*; **to bring d. on one's family** déshonorer sa famille; **to his eternal d.** à son grand déshonneur **2** *Fin (of cheque)* non-paiement *m*, refus *m* de paiement; *(of bill)* non-acceptation *f*
▪ VT **1** *(shame) (one's family)* déshonorer **2** *(promise, agreement)* ne pas respecter; *Fin (bill)* ne pas accepter, refuser de payer; **dishonoured cheque** chèque impayé

dishonourable, *Am* **dishonorable** [dɪsˈɒnərəb(ə)l] ADJ *(person)* sans honneur; *(action, conduct)* honteux, indigne; **there's nothing d. about losing** perdre n'a rien de honteux; *Mil* **to receive a d. discharge** être renvoyé de l'armée pour manquement à l'honneur

dishonourably, *Am* **dishonorably** [dɪsˈɒnərəblɪ] ADV de façon déshonorante; *Mil*

to be d. discharged être renvoyé de l'armée pour manquement à l'honneur

dishpan [ˈdɪʃpæn] N *esp Am* cuvette *f*, bassine *f*; **to have d. hands** avoir les mains abîmées à force de faire la vaisselle

dishrag [ˈdɪʃræg] N lavette *f*

dishtowel [ˈdɪʃtaʊ(ə)l] N torchon *m* à (essuyer la) vaisselle

dishwasher [ˈdɪʃwɒʃər] N **1** *(person)* plongeur, -euse **2** *(machine)* lave-vaisselle *m inv*; *Can* laveuse *f* à vaisselle; **d. safe** *(glass, plate etc)* garanti lave-vaisselle

dishwashing liquid [ˈdɪʃwɒʃɪŋ] N *Am* produit *m* à vaisselle

dishwater [ˈdɪʃwɔːtər] N **1** eau *f* de vaisselle **2** *Fig Fam (tasteless soup, coffee etc)* lavasse *f*

dishy [ˈdɪʃɪ] ADJ *Br Fam* séduisant, sexy; **he's/she's very d.** ce qu'il est beau/ce qu'elle est belle

disillusion [dɪsɪˈluːʒən] VT désillusionner
▪ N = **disillusionment**

disillusioned [dɪsɪˈluːʒənd] ADJ désillusionné, désenchanté; **I'm very d. with her** elle me déçoit beaucoup; **to become d.** perdre ses illusions

disillusionment [dɪsɪˈluːʒənmənt] N désillusionnement *m*, désenchantement *m*

disincentive [dɪsɪnˈsentɪv] N *Econ etc* facteur *m* décourageant; **heavy taxation is a d. to expansion** les taxes élevées découragent toute expansion; **to act as a d. to sth** avoir un effet dissuasif sur qch

disinclination [dɪsɪŋklɪˈneɪʃən] N **because of his d. to ...** parce qu'il est/était peu enclin à ...; **to have** *or* **show a d. to do sth** montrer peu d'empressement *ou* être peu enclin à faire qch

disinclined [dɪsɪnˈklaɪnd] ADJ peu disposé, peu enclin (**to do sth** à faire qch)

disinfect [dɪsɪnˈfekt] VT désinfecter

disinfectant [dɪsɪnˈfektənt] N désinfectant *m*

disinfection [dɪsɪnˈfekʃən] N désinfection *f*; **d. of the wound is vital** il est vital de désinfecter la plaie

disinflation [dɪsɪnˈfleɪʃən] N *Econ* désinflation *f*, déflation *f*

disinflationary [dɪsɪnˈfleɪʃənərɪ] ADJ *Econ* désinflationniste

disinformation [dɪsɪnfəˈmeɪʃən] N désinformation *f*
▸▸ **d. campaign** campagne *f* de désinformation

disingenuous [dɪsɪnˈdʒenjʊəs] ADJ *(person)* qui manque de franchise, peu sincère; **it was utterly d. of her to pretend that ...** ce n'était pas du tout honnête de sa part de prétendre que ...

disingenuously [dɪsɪnˈdʒenjʊəslɪ] ADV peu franchement; **d. worded** formulé en termes peu sincères

disingenuousness [dɪsɪnˈdʒenjʊəsnɪs] N manque *m* de franchise

disinherit [dɪsɪnˈherɪt] VT *(one's son)* déshériter

disintegrate [dɪsˈɪntɪgreɪt] VI *(of stone etc)* se désagréger, se désintégrer, s'effriter; *(of exploding plane, crashing train etc)* se désintégrer; *(of calm, confidence)* s'effriter; *(of health)* se dégrader, s'effriter; *Nucl* se désintégrer; **her family was disintegrating around her** sa famille se désagrégeait autour d'elle
▪ VT désagréger

disintegration [dɪsɪntɪˈgreɪʃən] N *(of stone etc)* désagrégation *f*, désintégration *f*, effritement *m*; *(of health)* dégradation *f*; *(of organization, family)* désagrégation; *Nucl* désintégration

disinter [dɪsɪnˈtɜːr] VT **(-rr-)** *(corpse, antiques)* déterrer, exhumer; *Fig (scandal)* déterrer; **to d. sth from the archives** aller repêcher qch dans les archives

disinterest [dɪsˈɪnt(ə)rɪst] N = **disinterestedness**

disinterested [dɪsˈɪnt(ə)rɪstɪd] ADJ *(unbiased)* désintéressé, impartial

> Attention: ne pas confondre avec l'adjectif **uninterested**.

disinterestedness [dɪsˈɪnt(ə)rɪstɪdnɪs] N **1** *(lack of bias)* désintéressement *m* **2** *(indifference)* indifférence *f* (**in** à)

disintermediation [dɪsɪntəmiːdɪˈeɪʃən] N désintermédiation *f*

disinterment [dɪsɪnˈtɜːmənt] N déterrement *m*, exhumation *f*

disinvest [dɪsɪnˈvest] VT & VI désinvestir (**from, in** de)

disinvestment [dɪsɪnˈvestmənt] N *(from a country)* désinvestissement *m*

disjointed [dɪsˈdʒɔɪntɪd] ADJ *(speech)* sans suite, incohérent; *(style)* haché, décousu; *(movements, delivery of speech)* entrecoupé

disk [dɪsk] N **1** *Comput* disque *m*; *(floppy)* disquette *f*; **to put sth on d.** enregistrer qch sur disque/disquette **2** *Am* = **disc**
▸▸ **d. access time** temps *m* d'accès disque; **d. box** boîte *f* à disquettes; **d. capacity** capacité *f* de disque/disquette; **d. controller** contrôleur *m* de disque; **d. controller card** carte *f* contrôleur de disque; **d. drive** lecteur *m* de disquettes; **d. file** fichier *m* disque; **d. mailer** pochette *f* d'expédition de disquette; **d. memory** mémoire *f* à disque; **d. operating system** système *m* d'exploitation de disques; **d. space** espace *m* disque

disk-based [-beɪst] ADJ *Comput* conçu pour disque; *(for floppy)* conçu pour disquettes

diskcopy [ˈdɪskkɒpɪ] N *Comput* copie *f* de disquette

diskette [dɪsˈket] N *Comput* disquette *f*
▸▸ **d. box** boîte *f* à disquettes; *Am* **d. drive** lecteur *m* de disquettes

diskless [ˈdɪsklɪs] ADJ *Comput* sans disque, sans unité de disque
▸▸ **d. workstation** station *f* de travail sans unité de disque

dislike [dɪsˈlaɪk] N aversion *f* (**of, for** pour); **they have the same likes and dislikes** ils ont les mêmes goûts et dégoûts; **to have a d. of sth** ne pas aimer qch; **to take a d. to** *or* **conceive a d. for sb** prendre qn en grippe; **to take a d. to** *or* **conceive a d. for sth** prendre qch en horreur
▪ VT ne pas aimer; **I don't d. him** il ne me déplaît pas; **to d. doing sth** détester *ou* ne pas aimer faire qch; **to get oneself disliked** se rendre antipathique

dislocate [ˈdɪsləkeɪt] VT **1** *Med (shoulder, knee)* luxer, démettre, disloquer; **to d. one's jaw** se décrocher la mâchoire **2** *(business)* désorganiser; *(plan)* bouleverser

dislocation [dɪsləˈkeɪʃən] N **1** *Med (of shoulder, knee)* luxation *f*, déboîtement *m*, dislocation *f*; *(of jaw)* déboîtement **2** *(of business)* désorganisation *f*; *(of plan etc)* bouleversement *m*

dislodge [dɪsˈlɒdʒ] VT *(enemy troops)* déloger, débusquer (**from** de); *(brick etc)* détacher; *(sth stuck)* dégager; **several bricks had become dislodged** plusieurs briques s'étaient détachées; **now he's been made manager nobody is ever going to d. him** maintenant qu'il a été nommé au poste de directeur, personne ne l'en fera jamais sortir; *Fig* **nothing would d. him from his position on arms control** rien ne pouvait ébranler sa conviction sur le contrôle des armements

disloyal [dɪsˈlɔɪəl] **ADJ** *(to one's king, friendship)* infidèle (**to** à); *(behaviour)* déloyal (**to** envers)

disloyalty [dɪsˈlɔɪəltɪ] **N** déloyauté *f*

dismal [ˈdɪzməl] **ADJ** *(face, person)* lugubre, sombre, triste; *(countryside, future)* morne; *(failure, performance)* lamentable; *(weather)* maussade; **my prospects look d.** mes chances sont maigres; *Hum* **the d. science** = l'économie *f*

dismally [ˈdɪzməlɪ] **ADV** *(to say)* tristement; *(to fail, perform)* lamentablement

dismantle [dɪsˈmænt(ə)l] **VT** *(machine, rifle etc)* démonter; *(fortress, network)* démanteler

dismast [dɪsˈmaːst] **VT** *Naut (ship)* démâter

dismay [dɪsˈmeɪ] **N** consternation *f*, **in d.** consterné, atterré; **to my d.** à ma grande consternation; **to be filled with d.** être consterné *ou* atterré

VT consterner; **we were dismayed at** *or* **by the news** cette nouvelle nous jeta dans la consternation; **the dismaying news** la nouvelle accablante *ou* consternante

dismember [dɪsˈmembər] **VT** *also Fig* démembrer

dismemberment [dɪsˈmembəmənt] **N** démembrement *m*

dismiss [dɪsˈmɪs] **VT 1** *(cease employing)* *(employee, servant)* congédier, renvoyer, licencier; *(civil servant)* révoquer; *Mil* **to d. sb from the service** *(career member)* rayer qn des cadres de l'armée; *(on military service)* réformer qn
2 *(send away)* *(person)* congédier, donner la permission de se retirer à; *(door-to-door salesman etc)* congédier, éconduire; *(meeting)* dissoudre; *Mil* **to d. a parade** faire rompre les rangs (aux troupes); *Mil* **d.!** rompez (les rangs)!; *Cr* **dismissed for ten** *(of batsman)* mis hors jeu quand il n'a marqué que dix points; **you are dismissed** vous pouvez vous retirer
3 *(cease or refuse to consider)* *(topic of conversation etc)* quitter, abandonner; *(threat, rumours)* ne pas tenir compte de; *(danger)* mépriser; *(theory, explanation)* **to d. sth from one's mind** chasser *ou* éloigner qch de ses pensées; **the incident was dismissed as a mere schoolboy prank** on n'a vu dans cet incident qu'une simple farce d'écolier; **she is dismissed as an intellectual lightweight** on la considère comme une non-valeur sur le plan intellectuel
4 *(reject)* *(proposal)* écarter; *Law (request, appeal)* rejeter; **to d. a case** *(of judge)* rendre une fin de non-recevoir; **to d. a charge** rendre une ordonnance de non-lieu

dismissal [dɪsˈmɪs(ə)l] **N 1** *(of employee)* congédiement *m*, renvoi *m*, licenciement *m*; *(of civil servant)* révocation *f*, **unfair d.** licenciement non justifié; **d. with/without notice** licenciement avec/sans préavis **2** *(of danger)* mépris *m*; *(of theory, explanation)* rejet *m* **3** *Law (of case)* fin *f* de non-recevoir; *(of request, appeal)* rejet *m*

dismissive [dɪsˈmɪsɪv] **ADJ** *(laugh, person)* méprisant, dédaigneux; *(gesture)* de rejet; **to be d. about** *or* **of sth** *(of danger)* mépriser qch; *(of proposal)* ne pas accorder la moindre valeur à qch; **he was d. about** *or* **of my chances of winning** il pensait que je n'avais pas la moindre chance de gagner; **you shouldn't be so d. about the proposal** tu ne devrais pas condamner la proposition aussi vite

dismissively [dɪsˈmɪsɪvlɪ] **ADV** *(to reply, comment etc)* dédaigneusement

dismount [dɪsˈmaʊnt] **VI** *(from horse, bicycle)* descendre

VT 1 *(rider)* démonter, désarçonner **2** *(cannon, machine)* démonter

disobedience [dɪsəˈbiːdɪəns] **N** désobéissance *f* (**to sb** à qn); **civil d.** résistance *f* passive

disobedient [dɪsəˈbiːdɪənt] **ADJ** *(dog, child)* désobéissant; **to be d. to sb** désobéir à qn; **that was very d. of you** c'était très désobéissant de ta part

disobey [dɪsəˈbeɪ] **VT** *(person, order)* désobéir à; *(order, the law)* enfreindre

disobliging [dɪsəˈblaɪdʒɪŋ] **ADJ** désobligeant (**to** envers)

disobligingly [dɪsəˈblaɪdʒɪŋlɪ] **ADV** avec désobligeance; **someone had very d. left the doors locked** quelqu'un avait eu l'extrême désobligeance de laisser les portes verrouillées

disorder [dɪsˈɔːdər] **N 1** *(confusion)* désordre *m*; **in d.** en désordre; **in a terrible state of d.** terriblement en désordre; **to throw sth into d.** *(room once)* mettre du désordre dans qch; *(plans)* bouleverser qch; **they fled in d.** ils se sont enfuis en débandade **2** *(unrest)* désordre *m*, trouble *m*; **serious disorders have broken out** de graves désordres ont éclaté **3** *Med* trouble(s) *m(pl)*; **heart d.** troubles cardiaques; **nervous d.** troubles nerveux, affection *f* nerveuse; **personality d.** trouble caractériel *ou* de la personnalité

VT déranger, mettre en désordre; **the crisis had disordered his thoughts** la crise avait mis de la confusion dans ses idées

disordered [dɪsˈɔːdəd] **ADJ** *(room, existence)* désordonné; *(mind)* malade; *(stomach)* dérangé

disorderliness [dɪsˈɔːdəlɪnɪs] **N 1** *(untidiness)* désordre *m*; **the d. of the room** le désordre dans lequel se trouvait la pièce; **the d. of their life** leur vie désordonnée **2** *(of mob)* turbulence *f*

disorderly [dɪsˈɔːdəlɪ] **ADJ 1** *(untidy)* *(person, work etc)* désordonné; *(room etc)* en désordre **2** *(unruly)* *(mob etc)* turbulent, tumultueux; *(person, behaviour)* désordonné, déréglé; **to lead a d. life** mener une vie désordonnée *ou* déréglée; *Law* **to charge sb with being drunk and d.** inculper qn pour ivresse et atteinte à l'ordre public
▶▶ *Law* **d. conduct** conduite *f* portant atteinte à l'ordre public; *Law* **d. house** *(brothel)* maison *f* de débauche; *(gaming house)* maison de jeu

disorganization [dɪsɔːgənaɪˈzeɪʃən] **N** désorganisation *f*

disorganize [dɪsˈɔːgənaɪz] **VT** désorganiser

disorganized [dɪsˈɔːgənaɪzd] **ADJ** *(person)* désorganisé; *(room)* désordonné; *(memories, ideas)* confus, désordonné

disorientate [dɪsˈɔːrɪənteɪt], **disorient** [dɪsˈɔːrɪənt] **VT** désorienter; **to be disorient(at)ed** être désorienté; **with disorient(at)ing speed** à une vitesse hallucinante

disorientation [dɪsɔːrɪənˈteɪʃən] **N** désorientation *f*

disorienting [dɪsˈɔːrɪəntɪŋ] **ADJ** déroutant

disown [dɪsˈəʊn] **VT** *(novel, painting)* désavouer; *(person)* renier; **to d. a child** *(deny paternity)* désavouer (la paternité d')un enfant; **if you go out looking like that I'll d. you!** si tu sors habillé comme ça, je ne te connais plus!

disparage [dɪsˈpærɪdʒ] **VT** *(somebody, something)* déprécier, décrier, dénigrer

disparagement [dɪsˈpærɪdʒmənt] **N** dénigrement *m*, dépréciation *f*

disparaging [dɪsˈpærɪdʒɪŋ] **ADJ** *(term)* de dénigrement; **d. remark** remarque désobligeante; **he was extremely d. about the**

whole idea il s'est montré extrêmement méprisant à l'égard de cette idée

disparagingly [dɪsˈpærɪdʒɪŋlɪ] **ADV** *(to say)* d'un ton méprisant; *(to look at)* d'un air méprisant; **to speak d. of sb** parler de qn en termes de mépris, faire des remarques désobligeantes à l'égard de qn

disparate [ˈdɪspərɪt] **ADJ** *Fml* disparate

disparity [dɪsˈpærɪtɪ] **N** *(of wealth, status etc)* disparité *f*, écart *m* (**of** entre); *(between ideas, opinions)* différence *f* (**between** entre); *(between accounts, stories)* contradiction *f* (**between** entre); **d. of age** différence d'âge; **the d. in their ages** la différence d'âge entre eux

dispassionate [dɪsˈpæʃənət] **ADJ 1** *(calm)* sans passion, dépassionné, calme **2** *(impartial)* impartial, -aux; **to take a d. view of things** juger impartialement les choses

dispassionately [dɪsˈpæʃənətlɪ] **ADV 1** *(calmly)* sans passion **2** *(impartially)* sans parti pris, impartialement

dispatch [dɪsˈpætʃ] **N 1** *(sending)* *(of object)* expédition *f*, envoi *m*
2 *Old-fashioned (speed)* promptitude *f*, **with (all due) d.** promptement
3 *(message, report)* *(diplomatic, by journalist)* dépêche *f*, *Com, Mil etc* **to be mentioned in dispatches** être cité à l'ordre (du jour)
4 *(finishing off)* *(of a piece of business)* expédition *f*
5 *(execution)* *(of condemned man)* exécution *f*

VT 1 *(send)* *(messenger, squadron)* dépêcher; *(letter)* expédier; **to d. an order** envoyer une commande
2 to d. a piece of business/a job expédier une affaire/un travail
3 *Fam (eat up)* *(meal)* expédier
4 *(kill)* *(animal)* achever; *(person)* expédier dans l'autre monde
▶▶ **d. box** *(for documents)* boîte *f* à documents; *Br Parl* tribune *f*, **d. case** serviette *f*, porte-documents *m inv*; **d. department** expéditions *fpl*, **d. note** bordereau *m* d'expédition; **d. rider** estafette *f*

dispatcher [dɪsˈpætʃər] **N 1** *Com etc* expéditeur, -trice **2** *Rail, Aviat etc* régulateur *m*, contrôleur *m*

dispel [dɪsˈpel] **VT** (-ll-) *(doubt, clouds, fear)* chasser, dissiper; **to d. sb's illusions** faire perdre ses illusions à qn

dispensable [dɪsˈpensəb(ə)l] **ADJ** dont on peut se passer; **nobody here is d.** il n'y a personne ici dont on peut se passer, il n'y a personne en trop ici; **I felt I had become d.** j'avais l'impression qu'on pouvait se passer de moi

dispensary [dɪsˈpensərɪ] **N 1** *(of pharmacy)* officine *f* **2** *(in hospital)* pharmacie *f*

dispensation [dɪspenˈseɪʃən] **N 1** *Law, Rel (exemption)* **d. from sth** dispense *f* de qch; **d. from fasting** dispense du jeûne **2** *Fml (distributing)* *(of prizes, alms)* distribution *f*, *(of justice)* administration *f*, exercice *m* **3** *(of Providence)* décret *m*, arrêt *m* **4** *(organization, way of running things)* système *m*; **under the present d.** dans le système actuel

dispense [dɪsˈpens] **VT 1** *(administer)* *(justice)* administrer, rendre; **to d. charity** faire la charité; **to d. advice** donner des conseils **2** *(of vending machine etc)* *(chocolate, condoms)* distribuer; *(change)* donner **3** *Pharm (medication, prescription)* préparer **4** *(exempt)* *(person)* dispenser, exempter (**from doing** de faire); *Rel* **to d. sb from fasting** dispenser qn du jeûne
▶ **dispense with** **VT INSEP** se passer de; **let's d. with the formalities** passons-nous des formalités; *Euph* **we've dispensed with her services** *(dismissed her)* nous nous sommes

passés de ses services; **to d. with the need for sth** rendre qch superflu

dispenser [dɪ'spensər] N **1** *Pharm* pharmacien, -ienne **2** *(machine) (for cigarettes, sweets etc)* distributeur m **3** *Rel (of alms)* dispensateur, -trice, distributeur, -trice

dispensing [dɪ'spensɪŋ] ADJ
▸▸*Br* **d. chemist** pharmacien m diplômé; **d. machine** distributeur m; **d. optician** = opticien, -ienne ne pouvant fournir que des montures de lunettes (et non pas des verres)

dispersal [dɪ'spɜːs(ə)l] N dispersion f

dispersant [dɪ'spɜːsənt] N dispersant m

disperse [dɪ'spɜːs] VT **1** *(scatter) (crowd, seeds etc)* disperser, éparpiller; *(clouds)* dissiper, chasser; *Med (tumour)* résoudre, dissoudre; *(of prism etc) (light)* disperser; *(knowledge, information)* faire circuler **2** *(arrange) (troops etc)* disperser
VI *(of crowd, troops etc)* se disperser, s'éparpiller; *(of light)* se disperser; *(of darkness, clouds)* se dissiper

dispersing agent [dɪ'spɜːsɪŋ] N agent m dispersant

dispersion [dɪ'spɜːʃən] N **1** *(of light)* dispersion f **2** *Rel* **the D.** la Diaspora

dispirit [dɪ'spɪrɪt] VT *(person)* décourager, abattre

dispirited [dɪ'spɪrɪtɪd] ADJ découragé, abattu, démoralisé

dispiritedly [dɪ'spɪrɪtɪdlɪ] ADV *(to say)* d'un ton découragé *ou* abattu; *(to look)* d'un air découragé *ou* abattu; *(to play, do sth)* sans enthousiasme

dispiriting [dɪ'spɪrɪtɪŋ] ADJ décourageant, démoralisant

dispiritingly [dɪ'spɪrɪtɪŋlɪ] ADV de façon décourageante *ou* démoralisante; **their reply was d. unenthusiastic** le manque d'enthousiasme de leur réponse était décourageant *ou* démoralisant; **d., no-one had come to meet them** personne n'était venu à leur rencontre, ce qui les démoralisait

displace [dɪs'pleɪs] VT **1** *(shift)* déplacer; **weight of water displaced by a body** poids de l'eau déplacée par un corps; *Pol* **displaced persons** personnes déplacées; *Med* **to d. a bone** se déplacer un os **2** *(supplant)* remplacer (**by** par); *(person)* évincer; *(in sb's affections)* supplanter

displacement [dɪs'pleɪsmənt] N **1** *(of water, people)* déplacement m; *Naut (of ship)* déplacement m; **ship of 5,000 tons d.** navire d'un déplacement de 5 000 tonnes **2** *(substitution)* **d. of A by B** remplacement m de A par B **3** *Psy* déplacement m
▸▸*Psy* **d. activity** activité f de déplacement; *Aut* **d. volume** cylindrée f

displacer unit [dɪs'pleɪsər] N *Aut* amortisseur m à déplacement de fluide

display [dɪ'spleɪ] N **1** *Com (of merchandise)* étalage m, exposition f; **for d. only** *(on product)* en démonstration uniquement; **on d. is merchandise from all over the world** des produits du monde entier sont exposés
2 *(show)* **the treasures are on d. in the museum** les trésors sont exposés dans le musée; **you'll have a fine d. of flowers** vous aurez un beau déploiement de fleurs
3 *Fig (of feelings, opinions etc)* affichage m, étalage m; *(of affection)* étalage m; *(of strength, skill, incompetence)* démonstration f; *(of luxury)* étalage m; **to be fond of d.** aimer l'ostentation
4 *(event) (of paintings etc)* exposition f; *(of regional dances, handicraft)* démonstration f
5 *Typ* lignes fpl en vedette
6 *Comput etc (screen)* écran m; *(screen, display unit)* afficheur m *(text appearing)* affichage m
7 *(of bird)* parade f

VT **1** *(put on show) (merchandise)* étaler, exposer; *(notice)* afficher; **to d. prices** afficher les prix
2 *(exhibit) (ignorance, bad manners)* afficher, étaler; *(talent, irritation, interest)* manifester; *(courage, tact)* faire preuve de
3 *Typ (line)* mettre en vedette
4 *Comput etc* afficher, visualiser
VI *(of bird)* parader
▸▸ **d. ad(vertisement)** pavé m *ou* placard m publicitaire; **d. area** *Comput* surface f d'affichage, zone f d'affichage; *Mktg (in store)* espace m d'exposition; **d. cabinet** *(in shop)* étalage, vitrine f; *(in home)* vitrine; **d. case** *(in shop)* étalage, vitrine; *(in home)* vitrine; **d. copy** *(of book)* exemplaire m de démonstration; *Comput* **d. driver** pilote m d'affichage; **d. furniture** mobilier m de présentation; **d. material** matériel m de présentation; *Com, Mktg* **d. pack** emballage m de présentation, emballage présentoir; *Aut* **d. panel** tableau m *ou* panneau m d'affichage; **d. rack** présentoir m; **d. screen** écran m de visualisation; **d. shelf** présentoir m; **d. space** surface f d'exposition; **d. staff** étalagistes mpl; **d. stand** présentoir m; *Comput* unité f de visualisation *ou* d'affichage; *(for goods)* présentoir m; **d. window** *(of shop)* vitrine, étalage; *(of calculator)* viseur m

displease [dɪs'pliːz] VT *(person)* fâcher, contrarier; **to be displeased at** *or* **with sb/sth** être mécontent de qn/de qch; *(stronger)* être fâché contre qn/de qch

displeasing [dɪs'pliːzɪŋ] ADJ déplaisant, désagréable (**to** à)

displeasure [dɪs'pleʒər] N mécontentement m, déplaisir m; **much to my/his/etc d.** à mon/son/*etc* grand déplaisir; **to incur sb's d.** s'attirer le mécontentement de qn

disport [dɪs'pɔːt] VT & VI *Lit* **to d. (oneself)** s'amuser, s'ébattre

disposable [dɪ'spəʊzəb(ə)l] ADJ **1** *(towel, lighter, nappy etc)* jetable, à jeter; *(bottle)* non consigné; *(wrapping, packaging)* perdu **2** *Fin (funds, assets)* disponible
N *Fam (nappy)* couche f jetable
▸▸ **d. camera** appareil m photo jetable; *Fin* **d. income** revenus mpl disponibles (après impôts)

disposal [dɪ'spəʊz(ə)l] N **1** *(getting rid of)* mise f au rebut; *(of rubbish etc)* enlèvement m; **(refuse) d. plant** dépotoir m; **waste d.** traitement m des ordures; **waste d. unit** broyeur m d'ordures; **for the d. of the body, they …** pour se débarrasser du corps, ils …
2 *(availability)* **to be at sb's d.** être à la disposition de qn; **I am entirely at your d.** je suis à votre entière disposition; **to put sth at sb's d.** mettre qch à la disposition de qn; **to have a sum of money at one's d.** disposer d'une somme; **to have a boat at one's d.** avoir un bateau à sa disposition; **with the limited means at our d.** avec les moyens limités qui sont à notre disposition
3 *(of goods, property)* aliénation f; **for d.** à vendre; **d. of assets** cession f d'actifs; **d. of stocks** écoulement m de stocks; **I will decide on the d. of my property** *(who my heirs will be)* c'est moi qui prendrai les dispositions testamentaires relatives à ma propriété
4 *Fml (arrangement)* disposition f

dispose [dɪ'spəʊz] VT **1** *(make willing)* disposer, porter (**sb to (do) sth** qn à (faire) qch); **I am not disposed to help him** je ne suis pas disposé à l'aider **2** *Fml (arrange) (objects)* disposer, arranger; *(troops)* disposer, placer; **they had disposed themselves around the room** ils s'étaient répartis dans la pièce
VI *Prov* **man proposes, God disposes** l'homme propose et Dieu dispose

▸ **dispose of** VT INSEP **1** *(get rid of)* se débarrasser de, mettre au rebut
2 *Com (merchandise)* écouler; *(item)* vendre; *(a business, lease)* céder
3 *(settle) (matter)* régler
4 *Fam (eat) (food)* liquider; *(kill) (person)* liquider; *(beat) (opponent)* mettre la pâtée à
5 *Fml (use) (one's time)* employer
6 *Fml (have at one's disposal)* disposer de

> Note that the French **disposer de** only means **to have at one's disposal**.

disposed [dɪ'spəʊzd] ADJ **d. to sth** enclin *ou* porté à qch; **d. to do sth** porté à faire qch

-disposed SUFF **well/ill-disposed** bien/mal intentionné (**to, towards** envers, pour)

disposition [dɪspə'zɪʃən] N **1** *(temperament)* nature f, humeur f; **child of a pleasant d.** enfant d'un bon naturel; **she is of** *or* **has a kindly d.** c'est une bonne nature **2** *Fml (arrangement) (of furniture)* disposition f, arrangement m; *(of troops)* disposition **3** *Law* disposition f testamentaire **4** *(inclination)* désir m, intention f (**to do sth** de faire qch); *(tendency)* tendance f, inclination f (**to sth** à qch; **to do sth** à faire qch)

dispossess [dɪspə'zes] VT *(person)* déposséder; *(of house, land)* exproprier; **to d. sb of sth** déposséder *ou* *Law* dessaisir qn de qch

dispossession [dɪspə'zeʃən] N dépossession f; *Law* dessaisissement m; *(of house, land)* expropriation f

disproportion [dɪsprə'pɔːʃən] N disproportion f

disproportionate [dɪsprə'pɔːʃənət] ADJ disproportionné (**to** à)

disproportionately [dɪsprə'pɔːʃənətlɪ] ADV d'une façon disproportionnée; **d. long/ expensive** d'une longueur/d'un prix disproportionné(e)

disprove [dɪs'pruːv] VT *(pp* **disproved,** *Law* **disproven** [dɪs'prəʊv(ə)n]) *(statement, hypothesis etc)* réfuter

disputable [dɪ'spjuːtəb(ə)l] ADJ contestable, discutable

disputant [dɪ'spjuːtənt, 'dɪspjʊtənt] N **1** *Fml* personne f participant à un débat **2** *Am Law* partie f en litige

disputation [dɪspjʊ'teɪʃən] N *Fml* **1** *(debate)* discussion f **2** *(argument)* controverse f, débat m

dispute[1] ['dɪspjʊt, dɪ'spjuːt] N **1** *(debate)* contestation f, controverse f; **the matter in d.** l'affaire contestée *ou* en contestation; **the fact is beyond d.** le fait est incontestable; **there's some d. about their true intentions** il y a un doute quant à leurs véritables intentions; **it's open to d.** c'est contestable **2** *(argument)* querelle f, dispute f (**as to** relative à); **to settle a d.** régler une querelle; **industrial d.** conflit m du travail; **wages** *or* **pay d.** conflit salarial; **to be in d.** être en conflit (**with** avec)

dispute[2] [dɪ'spjuːt] VI se disputer, se quereller
VT *(subject)* discuter; *(statement etc)* contester; **to d. (the possession of) sth with sb** disputer qch à qn; **I'm not disputing that** je ne conteste pas cela, je ne dis pas le contraire

disqualification [dɪskwɒlɪfɪ'keɪʃən] N **1** *(from competition)* disqualification f **2** *(disqualifying factor)* cause f d'incapacité (**for** à) **3** *Law* inhabilité f (**to act** à agir); **a year's d. (from driving)** un retrait de permis d'un an

disqualify [dɪs'kwɒlɪfaɪ] VT *Sport (player)* disqualifier; *(from military service)* rendre inapte à; **he was disqualified (from the competition) for failing to turn up on time**

il a été éliminé *ou* exclu (de la compétition) pour ne s'être pas présenté à l'heure; **her youth disqualifies her from participating** son jeune âge ne l'autorise pas à participer; **it automatically disqualifies you from standing for election/for the job** ceci vous met automatiquement dans l'incapacité de vous présenter aux élections/d'accéder à ce poste; **being a woman doesn't d. me from expressing an opinion** le fait que je suis une femme ne m'interdit pas de donner mon avis; **to d. sb from driving** retirer son permis de conduire à qn; **she was fined for driving while disqualified** on lui a mis une amende pour avoir conduit alors qu'on lui avait retiré son permis; *Law* **disqualified from making a will** inhabile à tester

disquiet [dɪs'kwaɪət] *Lit* **N** inquiétude *f*
VT inquiéter, troubler

disquieting [dɪs'kwaɪətɪŋ] **ADJ** *(news, development etc)* inquiétant, troublant

disregard [dɪsrɪ'ɡɑːd] **N** *(for facts, one's own safety)* mépris *m* (**of, for** de); *(of the law, convention)* inobservation *f*; **to show complete d. for the feelings of others** ne pas du tout prendre les sentiments des autres en considération; **with a complete d. for his own safety he …** au mépris total du danger qu'il courait, il …
VT *(somebody, warning, fact)* ne tenir aucun compte de; *(regulations)* mépriser; *(an order)* enfreindre; *Mil (orders)* manquer à; **I'll d. what you've just said** je ne tiendrai pas compte de ce que vous venez de dire

disremember [dɪsrɪ'membər] **VT** *Am* ne pas se souvenir de

disrepair [dɪsrɪ'peər] **N** *(no pl)* délabrement *m*; **to fall into d.** *(of building)* tomber en ruine, se délabrer; **the building is in d.** le bâtiment est délabré

disreputable [dɪs'repjʊtəb(ə)l] **ADJ 1** *(action, methods)* déshonorant, peu honorable; *(life)* peu honorable **2** *(person)* de mauvaise réputation; *(neighbourhood, pub)* mal famé; **to look d.** avoir l'air louche; *(untidy)* être peu soigné; **she has some d. friends** elle a des amis pas très fréquentables

disreputably [dɪs'repjʊtəblɪ] **ADV** honteusement, d'une façon peu honorable

disrepute [dɪsrɪ'pjuːt] **N** **to bring sb into d.** ruiner la réputation de qn; **to bring the law/game into d.** discréditer la loi/le sport; **to fall into d.** tomber en discrédit; **to be in d.** être en défaveur (**with, among** auprès de)

disrespect [dɪsrɪ'spekt] **N** irrévérence *f*, irrespect *m*, manque *m* de respect (**for** envers); **to treat sb/sth with d.** manquer de respect à qn/pour qch; **I mean no d.** je ne veux pas paraître irrespectueux; **no d., but isn't that a bit daft?** sans vouloir vous manquer de respect *ou* sauf votre respect, n'est-ce pas un peu idiot?

disrespectful [dɪsrɪ'spektfʊl] **ADJ** irrespectueux, irrévérencieux; **to be d. to sb** manquer de respect à qn

disrespectfully [dɪsrɪ'spektfʊlɪ] **ADV** *(to speak of sb, behave)* d'une manière irrespectueuse *ou* irrévérencieuse

disrobe [dɪs'rəʊb] **VT** *(judge, priest)* aider à se dévêtir de sa robe
VI *(take off robe)* se dévêtir de sa robe; *Fml, Hum (undress)* se déshabiller

disrupt [dɪs'rʌpt] **VT** *(administration, plan etc)* désorganiser; *(railway, bus service, traffic)* perturber; *(meeting) (of power failure etc)* interrompre; *(of hecklers etc)* perturber; *(life, routine) (seriously)* bouleverser; *(less seriously)* déranger

disruption [dɪs'rʌpʃən] **N** *(of railway, bus service, traffic)* perturbation *f*, *(of meeting) (by power failure etc)* interruption *f*, *(by*

hecklers etc) perturbation; *(of life, routine) (major)* bouleversement *m*; *(minor)* dérangement *m*; **there were several disruptions to the meeting** la réunion a été perturbée/interrompue à plusieurs reprises; **all the disruptions to everyday life caused by the earthquake** tous les bouleversements de la vie quotidienne provoqués par le tremblement de terre; **we apologize to viewers for the d. to this evening's programmes** nous prions les téléspectateurs de bien vouloir nous excuser pour les changements intervenus dans les programmes de la soirée

disruptive [dɪs'rʌptɪv] **ADJ** *(element)* perturbateur; *(pupil)* turbulent; **she has** *or* **is a d. influence on the class** c'est un élément perturbateur dans la classe
▸ ▸ **d. strike** grève *f* paralysante

dissatisfaction [dɪssætɪs'fækʃən] **N** insatisfaction *f*, mécontentement *m* (**with** de)

dissatisfied [dɪs'sætɪsfaɪd] **ADJ** mécontent, insatisfait (**with** de); **I am very d. with the service I received** je suis très mécontent *ou* je ne suis pas du tout satisfait du service que j'ai reçu; **the meal/explanation left me d.** le repas/l'explication m'a laissé sur ma faim

dissaving [dɪs'seɪvɪŋ] **N** *Econ* désépargne *f*

dissect [dɪ'sekt, daɪ-] **VT** *also Fig* disséquer

dissecting [dɪ'sektɪŋ, daɪ-] **ADJ ATTRIB** *(table, room)* de dissection
▸ ▸ **d. knife** scalpel *m*

dissection [dɪ'sekʃən, daɪ-] **N** *also Fig* dissection *f*

dissemble [dɪ'semb(ə)l] *Fml* **VT** *(one's feelings, intentions etc)* dissimuler, cacher
VI dissimuler

disseminate [dɪ'semɪneɪt] **VT** *(opinions etc)* disséminer, propager, répandre; *(information)* diffuser

disseminated [dɪ'semɪneɪtɪd] **ADJ**
▸ ▸ *Med* **d. sclerosis** sclérose *f* en plaques

dissemination [dɪsemɪ'neɪʃən] **N** *(of opinions, beliefs)* dissémination *f*, propagation *f*, *(of information)* diffusion *f*

dissension [dɪ'senʃən] **N** dissension *f*; **to sow d.** semer la dissension *ou* le désaccord

dissent [dɪ'sent] **N 1** *(opposition)* dissensions *fpl*; **d. within the party** dissensions au sein du parti; **d. from the party line** désaccord *m* par rapport à la politique du parti; **to express one's d. from sth** exprimer son désaccord par rapport à qch; **voices of d.** voix discordantes **2** *Rel, Hist* dissidence *f*
VI 1 différer (**from sb about sth** de qn sur qch); **to d. from a report** avoir une opinion contraire à celle exprimée dans un rapport; **I'd like to d. from the idea** j'aimerais exprimer mon désaccord par rapport à cette idée **2** *Rel, Hist* être dissident

dissenter [dɪ'sentər] **N 1** dissident, -ente **2** *Rel, Hist* personne *f* qui n'appartient pas à l'Église anglicane

dissenting [dɪ'sentɪŋ] **ADJ ATTRIB** *(opinion, voice)* dissident

dissertation [dɪsə'teɪʃən] **N** *Univ* mémoire *m*, *Am* thèse *f*, *Fig (long explanation etc)* exposé *m*

disservice [dɪs'sɜːvɪs] **N** mauvais service *m*; **to do sb a d.** rendre un mauvais service à qn; **to do oneself a d.** se faire du tort

dissidence ['dɪsɪdəns] **N** *Pol* dissidence *f*, *(disagreement)* désaccord *m*, divergence *f*

dissident ['dɪsɪdənt] **ADJ, N** *Pol* dissident, -ente

dissimilar [dɪ'sɪmɪlər] **ADJ** dissemblable (**to** à, de); **they are not d.** ils se ressemblent; **a proposal not at all d. to your own** une proposition qui ne diffère pas énormément de la vôtre

dissimilarity [dɪsɪmɪ'lærɪtɪ] **N** dissemblance *f*, dissimilarité *f* (**to** de; **between** entre)

dissimulate [dɪ'sɪmjʊleɪt] *Fml* **VT** dissimuler
VI dissimuler, feindre

dissimulation [dɪsɪmjʊ'leɪʃən] **N** *Fml* dissimulation *f*

dissipate ['dɪsɪpeɪt] **VT** *(clouds, heat, fears, suspicions etc)* dissiper; *(fortune, one's energy)* gaspiller, dissiper
VI *(of cloud, heat, fears suspicions etc)* se dissiper; *Phys (of energy)* se dégrader

dissipated ['dɪsɪpeɪtɪd] **ADJ** *(life)* dissipé; *(person)* débauché; **to be d.** *(of person)* vivre dans la dissipation *ou* la débauche

dissipation [dɪsɪ'peɪʃən] **N 1** *(of person)* vie *f* dissipée *ou* désordonnée **2** *Fml (of fog, one's assets)* dissipation *f*, *(of fortune)* gaspillage *m*, dissipation

dissociate [dɪ'səʊsɪeɪt] **VT 1** dissocier (**from** de); **the two functions have become dissociated** ces deux fonctions se sont dissociées; **to d. oneself from sb/a policy** se désolidariser de qn/d'une politique **2** *Chem (compound etc)* dissocier
VI *Chem* se dissocier

dissociation [dɪsəʊsɪ'eɪʃən] **N** dissociation *f*

dissolute ['dɪsəluːt] **ADJ** *(person)* dissolu, débauché; *(conduct)* licencieux; *(life)* dissolu, déréglé; **to lead a d. life** vivre dans la débauche, mener une vie dissolue

dissoluteness ['dɪsəluːtnɪs] **N** débauche *f*, dissolution *f*

dissolution [dɪsə'luːʃən] **N** *(of parliament, marriage etc)* dissolution *f*

dissolve [dɪ'zɒlv] **N** *Cin, TV* fondu *m* enchaîné
VT *(sugar)* (faire) dissoudre, faire fondre; *(cloud, illusion)* dissiper; *(marriage, partnership, Parliament)* dissoudre
VI 1 *(of sugar, metal in acid)* se dissoudre, fondre; *(of cloud, illusion)* se dissiper; *(of crowd)* se disperser; *Pol (of Parliament, opposition)* se dissoudre; *Fig* **to d. into tears** fondre en larmes; *Fig* **to d. into thin air** partir *ou* s'en aller en fumée **2** *Cin, TV* faire un fondu enchaîné

dissonance ['dɪsənəns] **N** *Mus* dissonance *f*, *Fig (of views)* discordance *f*

dissonant ['dɪsənənt] **ADJ** *Mus* dissonant; *Fig (voice, opinion)* discordant

dissuade [dɪ'sweɪd] **VT** **to d. sb from doing sth** dissuader qn de faire qch; **to d. sb from a particular course of action** dissuader qn de suivre une certaine ligne de conduite

dissuasion [dɪ'sweɪʒən] **N** dissuasion *f* (**from** de); **no amount of d. would have convinced him to stay** rien n'aurait pu le persuader de rester

distaff ['dɪstɑːf] **N** quenouille *f*, *Fig* **on the d. side** *(of family)* du côté maternel

DISTANCE ['dɪstəns] **N 1** distance *f*; **at a d. of …** à une distance de …; **within five minutes' walking d.** à cinq minutes de marche; **a short d. away** tout près, à deux pas; **some d. away** assez loin; **it is quite a d. (away)** *(of house etc)* ce n'est pas tout près; **to see sth from a d.** voir qch de loin; **to see sth in the d.** voir qch au loin; **in the middle d.** au second plan; *Mil* **within striking d.** *(of target)* à portée de fusil/de canon/*etc*; *(of own forces)* à portée de l'ennemi SEE GRAMMAR B59
2 *(between two places)* distance *f*, *(between two things)* distance, intervalle *m*; *(in time)* intervalle; **to go part of the d. on foot** faire une partie du trajet à pied; **to keep sb at a d.** tenir qn à distance; **at this d. in time** à cet intervalle de temps

3 *Sport* parcours *m*; *(of boxing match)* durée *f*; **long-/medium-d. race/runner** course *f*/coureur *m* de fond/de demi-fond; *Sport, Boxing, Fig* **to go** *or* **last** *or* **stay the d.** tenir la distance; **the fight went the d.** le combat est allé jusqu'à la limite

4 *(reserve)* réserve *f*, air *m* distant; **to keep one's d., to keep sb at a d.** *(from other people)* se tenir sur la réserve, garder ses distances; *(from sth dangerous, infectious)* garder ses distances, ne pas s'approcher; **to keep sb at a d.** se tenir sur la réserve avec qn, garder la distance avec qn

VT *(competitor)* distancer; *Fig* **to d. oneself from sb/sth** prendre ses distances à l'égard de qn/par rapport à qch

▸ ▸ **d. banking** banque *f* à distance; **d. education, d. learning** enseignement *m* à distance *ou* par correspondance; *Aut* **d. table** tableau *m* des distances entre les villes

distant ['dɪstənt] **ADJ 1** *(place, object, relation)* éloigné; *(country, memory, resemblance)* lointain; *(in time)* éloigné, lointain; **in the d. future** dans un avenir lointain; **in the not too d. future** dans un futur relativement proche; **in the (dim and) d. past** dans le temps, il y a bien longtemps **2** *(reserved) (person, manner)* réservé, distant; **to be d. with sb** se montrer réservé *ou* distant avec qn; **d. look** regard perdu dans le vague

ADV three miles d. à trois mil(l)es de distance; **not far d. from …** à peu de distance de …

▸ ▸ *Rail* **d. signal** signal *m* à distance

distantly ['dɪstəntlɪ] **ADV 1** *(in the distance)* au loin; **he could d. hear …** il entendait … au loin; **d. related** d'une parenté éloignée; **to be d. related to sb** avoir un lien de parenté éloigné avec qn **2** *(to treat sb)* d'un air réservé, avec réserve

distaste [dɪs'teɪst] **N** dégoût *m* **(for** de), répugnance *f* **(for** pour**)**; **she was unable to hide her d. for his attitude** il lui était impossible de cacher le dégoût que lui inspirait son attitude; **if you could only overcome your initial d. for opera** si seulement tu parvenais à surmonter ta répugnance pour l'opéra

distasteful [dɪs'teɪstfʊl] **ADJ** *(task, thought etc)* désagréable, déplaisant; *(joke)* de mauvais goût

distastefulness [dɪs'teɪstfʊlnɪs] **N** *(of task, thought etc)* caractère *m* désagréable *ou* répugnant; *(of joke)* mauvais *m* goût

distemper¹ [dɪ'stempər] **N** *Vet* maladie *f* des jeunes chiens, maladie de Carré

distemper² **N** *Art* détrempe *f*

VT *(wall)* badigeonner en couleur; *Art (painting, wall)* peindre à la *ou* en détrempe

distend [dɪ'stend] **VT** *(cheeks)* gonfler; *(nostrils)* dilater; *(stomach)* distendre, ballonner **VI** *(of cheeks)* se gonfler; *(of nostrils)* se dilater; *(of stomach)* se ballonner, se distendre

distension [dɪ'stenʃən] **N** dilatation *f*, distension *f*

distich ['dɪstɪk] **N** *Liter (couplet)* distique *m*

distil, *Am* **distill** [dɪ'stɪl] **(-ll-)** *Chem, Ind* **VT** *(water etc)* distiller **VI** *(of liquid, secretion etc)* distiller **(from** de**)** ▸ **distil off, distil out** **VT SEP** *Chem, Ind* chasser par la distillation

distillate ['dɪstɪleɪt] **N** *Chem, Ind* distillat *m*

distillation [dɪstɪ'leɪʃən] **N 1** *Chem, Ind (process)* distillation *f* **2** *(result) Chem, Ind* produit *m* de la distillation; *Fig (of ideas, theories)* condensé *m*

distilled water [dɪ'stɪld] **N** eau *f* distillée

distiller [dɪ'stɪlər] **N** *Ind* distillateur *m*

distillery [dɪ'stɪlərɪ] **N** *Ind* distillerie *f*

distinct [dɪ'stɪŋkt] **ADJ 1** *(different)* distinct,

différent **(from** de**)**; **to keep two things d.** faire la distinction entre deux choses; **women, as d. from men** les femmes, par opposition aux hommes **2** *(clear)* distinct; *(difference)* net, *f* nette, clair; *(memory)* clair, net, précis; *(order)* formel, précis; *(promise)* formel; *(preference)* marqué; *(impression)* net; **to have a d. memory of sth** se souvenir clairement de qch; **the coast becomes more d.** la côte se précise

> Attention: ne pas confondre avec l'adjectif **distinctive**.

distinction [dɪ'stɪŋkʃən] **N 1** *(difference)* distinction *f* **(between** entre**)**; **to make** *or* **draw a d. between two things** faire une distinction entre deux choses; **without d. of age** sans distinction d'âge; **class d.** distinction de classes **2** *(honour)* distinction *f*, **academic distinctions** distinctions académiques **3** *(excellence)* distinction *f*; *Univ* mention *f*; **to gain d.** se distinguer; **man of d.** homme distingué; *Univ* **with d.** *(thesis etc)* avec mention

distinctive [dɪ'stɪŋktɪv] **ADJ** *(feature, style)* distinctif, -ive; **to be d. of sth** être caractéristique de qch

> Attention: ne pas confondre avec l'adjectif anglais **distinct**.

distinctively [dɪ'stɪŋktɪvlɪ] **ADV** de manière distinctive *ou* caractéristique

> Attention: ne pas confondre avec l'adverbe **distinctly**.

distinctly [dɪ'stɪŋktlɪ] **ADV 1** *(clearly) (to speak, hear, see)* distinctement, clairement; **I d. remember telling you** je me rappelle clairement te l'avoir dit; **I told him d.** je le lui ai dit expressément **2** *(definitely)* décidément; **she is d. better** elle va sensiblement mieux; **by now the weather was d. cold** à présent il faisait vraiment froid

> Attention: ne pas confondre avec l'adverbe **distinctively**.

distinctness [dɪ'stɪŋktnɪs] **N 1** *(clearness)* clarté *f*, netteté *f* **2** *(separate nature)* spécificité *f*, **not to lose sight of the d. of these two issues** ne pas perdre de vue le fait que ces deux questions sont distinctes

distinguish [dɪ'stɪŋgwɪʃ] **VT 1** *(recognize) (object, sound)* distinguer, discerner; **I could not d. him among the crowd** je n'ai pu le distinguer dans la foule **2** *(characterize, differentiate)* distinguer, différencier **(from** de**)**; **reason distinguishes man from the other animals** la raison sépare l'homme des autres animaux; **to d. oneself by …** se distinguer par … **VI to d. between two things** faire la distinction entre deux choses

distinguishable [dɪ'stɪŋgwɪʃəb(ə)l] **ADJ 1** *(recognizable)* reconnaissable; *(sound, difference)* perceptible; *(improvement)* sensible; **the coast was hardly d.** c'est à peine si l'on distinguait la côte **2** *(that can be differentiated)* que l'on peut distinguer, qui se distingue **(from** de**)**; **the two ideas are barely d.** les deux idées diffèrent à peine

distinguished [dɪ'stɪŋgwɪʃt] **ADJ** *(air, appearance)* distingué; *(author etc)* de distinction; *(performance)* brillant; **to look d.** avoir l'air distingué

distinguishing mark [dɪ'stɪŋgwɪʃɪŋ] **N** signe *m* distinctif

distort [dɪ'stɔːt] **VT 1** *(physically) (metal)* déformer; *(features, face)* décomposer, déformer; *(limbs)* distordre; *(surface)* fausser, déjeter **2** *Fig (the truth)* déformer; *(facts, words)* fausser, dénaturer; **to d. the mean-**

ing of a text dénaturer un texte **3** *Electron, Radio (reception etc)* déformer **VI 1** *(of metal, wood)* se déformer, se fausser **2** *Electron, Radio* se déformer

distorted [dɪ'stɔːtɪd] **ADJ 1** *(physically)* tordu, déformé; *(features, face)* déformé; **face d. by rage** visage convulsé de fureur **2** *Fig (version, account of event)* déformé, faussé **3** *Radio, TV* déformé

distorting [dɪ'stɔːtɪŋ] **ADJ** déformant; *Fig* **those changes had a d. effect on the inflation index** ces changements ont faussé l'indice de l'inflation

▸ ▸ **d. mirror** glace *f* déformante

distortion [dɪ'stɔːʃən] **N 1** *(physical)* distorsion *f*; *(of features)* altération *f*; *(of body)* contorsion *f* **2** *Fig (of text)* altération *f*; *(of facts, truth)* déformation *f* **3** *Electron, Radio, Opt (of transmission)* distorsion *f*, déformation *f*; *(of sound)* distorsion sonore; *(of magnetic field)* déviation *f*; *Tech (of part)* distorsion

distract [dɪ'strækt] **VT 1** *(mind, attention)* distraire, détourner **(from** de**)**; **stop distracting me!** arrête de me distraire!; **I don't want to d. you if you're working** je ne veux pas te déranger si tu travailles; **see if you can d. him from his problems** essaie de le distraire de ses problèmes **2** *(trouble)* préoccuper

distracted [dɪ'stræktɪd] **ADJ** préoccupé; *(look)* absent

> Note that the French word **distrait** is a false friend and is never a translation for the word **distracted**. Its most common meaning is **absent-minded**.

distractedly [dɪ'stræktɪdlɪ] **ADV** *(to pace about, look about)* d'un air préoccupé; *(to answer)* distraitement

distracting [dɪ'stræktɪŋ] **ADJ** qui distrait l'attention; **I find noise d. when I'm working** le bruit me dérange quand je travaille; **she has a d. influence on him** elle le distrait

distraction [dɪ'strækʃən] **N 1** *(interruption) (when working etc)* distraction *f*, **I could do without the d. of you asking me that every five minutes** ça m'aiderait si tu ne me dérangeais pas pour me demander ça toutes les cinq minutes **2** *(amusement)* distraction *f*, divertissement *m*; **he's seeking d.** il cherche à se distraire **3** **to drive sb to d.** rendre qn fou/*f* folle, faire perdre la tête à qn; **to love sb to d.** aimer qn éperdument *ou* à la folie

distrain [dɪ'streɪn] **VI** *Law* **to d. upon sb** contraindre qn par saisie de biens; **to d. upon a debtor** exécuter une saisie sur un débiteur

distraint [dɪ'streɪnt] **N** *Law* saisie *f*, (saisie-) exécution *f*, *pl* (saisies-) exécutions

distraught [dɪ'strɔːt] **ADJ** bouleversé; **he is d. over his wife's illness** la maladie de sa femme le bouleverse; **d. with grief/anger** fou/*f* folle de douleur/colère

distress [dɪ'stres] **N 1** *(mental suffering)* angoisse *f*, *(physical suffering)* douleur *f*; **to be in a state of great d.** *(unhappy)* être désespéré; *(anxious)* être fou/*f* folle d'angoisse; **to cause sb d.** *(unhappiness)* faire de la peine à qn; *(anxiety)* alarmer qn **2** *(difficulty)* détresse *f*, embarras *m*; *Naut* **ship in d.** navire en détresse **3** *Law (action)* saisie *f*, *(goods)* biens *mpl* saisis

VT 1 *(somebody)* affliger, angoisser, faire de la peine à **2** *(piece of furniture)* vieillir

▸ ▸ *Com* **d. merchandise** = marchandises *fpl* écoulées à bas prix parce qu'elles sont endommagées ou pour permettre de régler des dettes importantes; *Com* **d. sale** = vente *f* d'articles à bas prix parce qu'ils sont endommagés ou pour permettre de régler des dettes importantes; **d. signal** signal *m* de détresse; *Law* **d. warrant** mandat *m* de saisie

distressed [dɪ'strest] **ADJ 1** *(suffering)* affligé, désespéré; **to be d. about sth** *(unhappy)* être affligé par qch; *(anxious)* être angoissé par qch **2** *(in difficulty)* dans la détresse **3** *(piece of furniture)* vieilli **4** *Law* saisi

distressing [dɪ'stresɪŋ] **ADJ** affligeant, pénible

distribute [dɪ'strɪbju:t] **VT 1** *(give out)* *(alms, prizes, leaflets)* distribuer; *(property)* répartir, partager; *Com, Cin (be distributor of)* distribuer; *(books, newspapers)* distribuer, diffuser; *Fin (dividend)* répartir **2** *(spread out) (over a surface etc)* disperser, répartir; **evenly distributed load** charge uniformément répartie

distributed database [dɪ'strɪbju:tɪd] **N** *Comput* base *f* de données répartie

distribution [dɪstrɪ'bju:ʃən] **N 1** *Com, Cin* distribution *f*, *(of books, newspapers)* distribution, diffusion *f*, **d. of profits** distribution *ou* répartition *f* des bénéfices **2** *(of population, manpower etc)* répartition *f*, *(of property)* répartition, partage *m*; **d. of wealth** distribution *f* des richesses
▸ ▸ *Elec* **d. board** tableau *m* de distribution; *Elec* **d. box** boîte *f* de dérivation *ou* de jonction; *Com* **d. centre** centre *m* de distribution; *Com* **d. chain** chaîne *f* de distribution; *Com* **d. channel** canal *m* de distribution; *Com* **d. contract** contrat *m* de distribution; *Com* **d. costs** frais *mpl* de distribution, coût *m* de la distribution; **d. depot** dépôt *m* de distributeur; *Com* **d. market** marché *m* de la distribution; **d. method** mode *m* de distribution; *Com* **d. network** réseau *m* de distribution, circuit *m* de distribution; *Com* **d. outlet** point *m* de distribution; *Cin* **d. rights** droits *mpl* de distribution; *Elec* **d. switchboard** tableau de distribution; **d. system** système *m* de distribution

distributive [dɪ'strɪbjʊtɪv] **ADJ, N** *Gram* distributif *m*

distributor [dɪ'strɪbjʊtər] **N 1** *(person)* distributeur, -trice; *(of particular make of car etc)* concessionnaire *m*; *Cin* distributeur *m* **2** *Elec, Aut etc (device)* distributeur *m*
▸ ▸ *Elec* **d. box** boîte *f* de dérivation *ou* de jonction; *Com* **d. brand** marque *f* de distributeur; *Aut* **d. cap** tête *f* de Delco® *ou* d'allumeur; *Com* **d. discount** remise *f* au distributeur; *Com* **d.'s margin** marge *f* du distributeur; *Com* **d. panel** panel *m* de distributeurs

distributorship [dɪ'strɪbjʊtəʃɪp] **N** *Com* **to have the d. for ...** distribuer ...

district ['dɪstrɪkt] **N 1** *(of country)* région *f*, territoire *m*; *Admin* district *m*, secteur *m*; **electoral d.**, *Am* **congressional d.** circonscription *f* électorale; **mining d.** région minière; **postal d.** secteur postal; **urban d.** district urbain **2** *(of town)* quartier *m*; *Admin (of city)* ≃ arrondissement *m*
▸ ▸ *Am Law* **d. attorney** ≃ procureur *m* de la République; *Br Admin* **d. council** conseil *m* municipal; *Am Law* **d. court** ≃ tribunal *m* d'instance (fédéral); *Com* **d. manager** directeur, -trice régional(e); *Br* **d. nurse** infirmière *f* visiteuse

distrust [dɪs'trʌst] **N** méfiance *f*, défiance *f* (**of** de); **to have a d. of sth** se méfier *ou* se défier de qch
VT se méfier de, se défier de; **to d. one's own eyes** ne pas en croire ses propres yeux

distrustful [dɪs'trʌstfʊl] **ADJ** méfiant, défiant (**of** de); **he was d. of his own capabilities** il ne croyait pas à *ou* manquait de foi en ses propres capacités; **to be d. of a policy/sb's intentions** ne pas se fier à une politique/à qn

disturb [dɪ'stɜːb] **VT 1** *(interrupt) (person)* déranger; *(criminal)* surprendre; *(sb's rest etc)* troubler; *Phys (magnetic field)* perturber; **to d. the peace** troubler l'ordre public; **do not d.** ne pas déranger **2** *(disarrange) (papers, room)* déranger; *(surface, ground)* agiter, remuer **3** *(worry) (somebody)* inquiéter, troubler; *Law (interfere with the rights of)* inquiéter *ou* troubler dans la jouissance d'un droit; **I am disturbed by his apparent indifference** l'indifférence qu'il montre m'inquiète *ou* me trouble

disturbance [dɪ'stɜːbəns] **N 1** *(interruption)* dérangement *m* **2** *(disarrangement)* trouble *m*; **atmospheric d.** perturbation *f* atmosphérique; **emotional disturbances** troubles *mpl* émotifs **3** *(noise)* bruit *m*, tumulte *m*; *(fight)* bagarre *f*, *(riot)* émeute *f*, **political disturbances** troubles *mpl* politiques; **to cause** *or* **create a d.** troubler l'ordre public; *(at meeting etc)* semer la confusion; **it will cause major disturbances to traffic** cela perturbera énormément la circulation **4** *Law (interference with rights)* trouble *m* de jouissance

disturbed [dɪ'stɜːbd] **ADJ 1** *(night, sleep etc)* agité **2** *(mentally, emotionally) (at a particular time)* perturbé; *(as a characteristic)* qui souffre de troubles du comportement; *Psy* **d. behaviour** troubles *mpl* du comportement

disturbing [dɪ'stɜːbɪŋ] **ADJ** *(news, development etc)* inquiétant, troublant; *(stronger)* perturbant, dérangeant

disunite [dɪsju'naɪt] **VT** *(family etc)* désunir, jeter la désunion dans; *(party)* diviser

disunited [dɪsju'naɪtɪd] **ADJ** *(family)* désuni; *(party)* divisé

disunity [dɪs'ju:nɪtɪ] **N** désunion *f*

disuse [dɪs'ju:s] **N** *(of term etc)* désuétude *f*, *(of machine etc)* abandon *m*, mise *f* au rancart; **to fall into d.** *(of word, custom)* tomber en désuétude

disused [dɪs'ju:zd] **ADJ** *(machine)* mis au rancart; *(public building)* désaffecté; *(mine, well, railway line)* abandonné

disyllabic [dɪsɪ'læbɪk] **ADJ** dissyllabe, dissyllabique

ditch [dɪtʃ] **N** fossé *m*; *(between fields)* douve *f*, *Aviat Sl (sea)* baille *f*, **drainage d.** rigole *f* d'écoulement
VT *Fam (get rid of) (object)* jeter, se débarrasser de; *(car, project etc)* abandonner; *(inconvenient person)* se débarrasser de; *(boyfriend, girlfriend)* plaquer; *(friend)* laisser tomber
VI 1 *Aviat* faire un amerrissage forcé **2** *Agr* creuser un fossé

ditcher ['dɪtʃər] **N** personne *f* qui creuse des fossés

ditching ['dɪtʃɪŋ] **N** *Aviat* amerrissage *m* forcé

ditchwater ['dɪtʃwɔːtər] **N** *(of ditch)* eaux *fpl* stagnantes; *Fam* **as dull as d.** ennuyeux comme la pluie *ou* un jour de pluie

dither ['dɪðər] *Fam* **N** **to be all of a** *or* **in a d.** ne plus savoir où donner de la tête, paniquer
VI hésiter; **stop dithering!** décide-toi!; **she was dithering over whether to come or not** elle n'arrivait pas à se décider si elle viendrait ou pas

ditherer ['dɪðərər] **N** *Fam* indécis, -ise; **don't be such a d.!** allez, décide-toi!

dithery ['dɪðərɪ] **ADJ** *Fam* indécis

ditto ['dɪtəʊ] **ADV** idem, de même; *Fam* **I'm hungry – d.** j'ai faim – moi aussi *ou* moi pareil *ou* moi de même

ditty ['dɪtɪ] **N** *Fam* chanson *f*, chansonnette *f*

ditz [dɪts] **N** *Am Fam* courge *f*, andouille *f*

ditzy ['dɪtsɪ] **ADJ** *Am Fam* étourdi

diuretic [daɪjʊ'retɪk] **ADJ, N** *Med* diurétique *m*

diurnal [daɪ'ɜːn(ə)l] **ADJ** *Astron, Biol* diurne **N** *Rel* diurnal *m*, -aux

div [dɪv] **N** *Br Fam (idiot)* abruti, -ie

diva ['diːvə] **N** *Mus* diva *f*

divan [dɪ'væn] **N** divan *m*
▸ ▸ **d. base** sommier *m*; **d. bed** divan-lit *m*, *pl* divans-lits

dive [daɪv] **N 1** *Swimming* plongeon *m*; *(of submarine, deep-sea diver)* plongée *f*, *Aut (on braking)* plongée (au freinage); *Swimming* **high d.** plongeon de haut vol; *Aviat* **vertical d., nose d.** piqué *m*; *Aviat* **to go into a d.** faire un piqué; *Aviat* **to pull out of a d.** effectuer un rétablissement; **he made a d. for the shelter** il s'est précipité vers l'abri; **the goalie made a d. for the ball** le goal a plongé pour attraper le ballon; **to take a d.** *(of boxer)* se coucher; *(of salary, exchange rate)* plonger, chuter
2 *Fam Pej (place)* bouge *m*
VI *(pt* **dived**, *Am Fam* **dove** [dəʊv], *pp* **dived)** plonger (**into** dans); *(of submarine)* plonger, effectuer une plongée; *(of aircraft)* piquer, descendre en piqué; **to d. (for the ball)** *(of goalkeeper)* plonger pour attraper le ballon; **to d. for pearls** pêcher des perles; *Aviat* **to d. down on an enemy** piquer de haut sur un ennemi; **to d. into one's pocket** plonger la main dans sa poche; **to d. into a doorway for shelter** se précipiter dans une entrée pour s'abriter; *Fam* **they all dived into the pub** ils se sont précipités dans le pub
▸ ▸ *Aviat* **d. bomber** chasseur *m* bombardier; *Aviat* **d. bombing** bombardement *m* en piqué
▸ **dive in VI 1** *(into water)* plonger **2** *Fam (start eating)* attaquer **3** *Fam (start doing sth)* s'y mettre; *(do sth without preparation)* se jeter à l'eau

dive-bomb **VT** *Aviat* attaquer en piqué

diver ['daɪvər] **N 1** plongeur, -euse; *(in deep sea)* scaphandrier *m* **2** *Orn (bird)* plongeon *m*, plongeur *m*

diverge [daɪ'vɜːdʒ] **VI** *(of rays, lines etc)* diverger, s'écarter; *(of roads)* s'écarter; *(of opinions, persons)* diverger; *Fig* **our paths diverged** nos chemins se sont séparés
VT *(rays etc)* faire diverger

divergence [daɪ'vɜːdʒəns] **N** divergence *f*

divergent [daɪ'vɜːdʒənt], **diverging** [daɪ'vɜːdʒɪŋ] **ADJ** divergent; **we take d. views on certain points** nos opinions divergent *ou* diffèrent sur certains points

diverging beam [daɪ'vɜːdʒɪŋ] **N** *Aut* faisceau *m* divergent

divers ['daɪvəz] **ADJ** *Arch (several)* divers, plusieurs

diverse [daɪ'vɜːs] **ADJ 1** *(different)* divers, différent; **they are very d. in their approach** ils ont une approche très différente **2** *(varied)* divers, varié

diversely [daɪ'vɜːslɪ] **ADV** diversement

diversification [daɪvɜːsɪfɪ'keɪʃən] **N 1** *(of company etc)* diversification *f* **2** *(of tastes etc)* diversification *f*

diversify [daɪ'vɜːsɪfaɪ] **VI** *(of company etc)* se diversifier; **to d. into furniture** se diversifier et commencer à fabriquer *ou* produire/vendre/etc des meubles; **to d. into software/banking** se diversifier en pénétrant le secteur du logiciel/le secteur bancaire
VT diversifier; **we must aim to d. our product portfolio** il nous faut essayer de diversifier notre portefeuille de produits

diversion [daɪ'vɜːʃən] **N 1** *(of traffic etc)* déviation *f*, *(of plane, funds)* détournement *m*; *Elec* dérivation *f*, **to create** *or* **make a d.** *(to distract attention)* faire diversion **2** *(amusement)* distraction *f*, divertissement *m*; **to**

seek **d. from sth** chercher à se distraire de qch **3** *Mil* diversion *f*

diversionary [daɪˈvɜːʃən(ə)rɪ] ADJ **1** *(activity)* destiné à faire diversion **2** *Mil (manœuvre)* de diversion

diversity [daɪˈvɜːsɪtɪ] N diversité *f*, variété *f*

divert [daɪˈvɜːt] VT **1** *(river, traffic)* détourner, dériver; *(blow)* parer, écarter; *(criticism)* parer; *(attention, conversation, sb from course of action, funds)* détourner **(from** de); *Elec (current)* dévier; *Naut* dérouter; *Aviat (plane, flight)* détourner; **I managed to d. his attention from the problem** j'ai réussi à détourner son attention de ce problème **2** *(amuse)* divertir, amuser; **to d. oneself by doing sth** faire qch pour se distraire

diverting [daɪˈvɜːtɪŋ] ADJ divertissant, amusant

divest [daɪˈvest] VT **1** *Fml (person)* priver, dénuer **(of** de); **to d. oneself of** *(one's coat)* enlever; *(one's authority)* se dévêtir de; *(a duty)* se désinvestir de; *(right)* renoncer à **2** *Law (somebody)* déposséder **(of** de)

divestment [daɪˈvestmənt] N *Fin* **d. of assets** scission *f* d'actifs

divide [daɪˈvaɪd] VT **1** *(split) (inheritance etc)* diviser; *(kingdom)* démembrer; *(land)* morceler; *(meat etc)* détailler; *(family)* mettre le désaccord dans, désunir; *(party)* diviser, scinder; **to d. sth in two** couper *ou* diviser qch en deux; **to d. sth into parts** diviser qch en parties

2 *(distribute)* partager, répartir **(among** entre); *(spending, one's time, resources)* répartir; **to d. proportionally** répartir au prorata; **to d. profits among shareholders** répartir les bénéfices entre les actionnaires; **we d. the work among us** nous nous partageons le travail

3 *Math* diviser

4 *(separate)* séparer **(from** de); **the mountains that d. France from Spain** les montagnes qui séparent la France de l'Espagne

VI **1** se diviser, se partager **(into** en); *(of political party)* se scinder, se diviser; *(of road)* bifurquer

2 *Pol (of House)* aller aux voix

3 *Math* **twelve divides by three** douze est divisible par trois; **they're learning to d.** ils apprennent à faire des divisions

N *Geog* ligne *f* de partage des eaux; *Fig (racial, political, emotional etc)* fossé *m*; **the North-South d.** le fossé entre le nord et le sud

▸ **divide off** VT SEP séparer

▸ **divide out** VT SEP *(distribute)* partager, répartir **(among** entre)

▸ **divide up** VT SEP partager; **they divided the area/work up between them** ils se sont partagé le secteur/travail

divided [daɪˈvaɪdɪd] ADJ **1** *(territory etc)* divisé; *(attention)* distrait; **we are d. on this issue** nous sommes partagés sur ce sujet; **opinions are d.** les avis sont partagés; **house/family d. against itself** maison/famille désunie; **a (political) party d. against itself** un parti divisé **2** *(work)* partagé **3** *(scale, thermometer etc)* gradué

▸▸ *Am* **d. highway** route *f* à quatre voies; **d. skirt** jupe-culotte *f*, *pl* jupes-culottes

dividend [ˈdɪvɪdend] N *Math, Fin* dividende *m*; *Fin* **d. on shares** dividende d'actions; **the company has declared a d. of 10%** la société a déclaré un dividende de 10%; *Fig* **to pay dividends** porter des fruits

▸▸ **d. cover** taux *m* de couverture du dividende; **d. share** action *f* de jouissance; **d. tax** impôt *m* sur les dividendes; **d. warrant** chèque-dividende *m*, *pl* chèques-dividendes, coupon *m* d'arrérages; **d. yield** taux *m* de rendement des actions

divider [dɪˈvaɪdər] N *(in room)* cloison *f* de séparation; *(for files)* intercalaire *m*

dividers [dɪˈvaɪdəz] NPL *(instrument)* compas *m* à pointes sèches

dividing [dɪˈvaɪdɪŋ] ADJ

▸▸ *Elec* **d. box** boîte *f* de dérivation; **d. line** ligne *f* de démarcation; *Fig* séparation *f*, distinction *f*; **she has crossed the d. line between confidence and arrogance** elle a franchi la limite entre confiance en soi et arrogance; **d. wall** mur *m* de séparation, cloison *f*

divination [dɪvɪˈneɪʃən] N divination *f*

divine [dɪˈvaɪn] ADJ *(judgement, worship etc)*, *Fig* divin; **to attend d. service** aller à l'église; *Fig Fam* **you look d. in that dress** vous êtes divine *ou* adorable dans cette robe

N théologien *m*

VT **1** *(the future, sb's intentions)* deviner **2** *(water)* découvrir, détecter

▸▸ *Fig* **d. inspiration** inspiration *f* divine; *Hist* **the d. right of kings** la monarchie de droit divin

divinely [dɪˈvaɪnlɪ] ADV *also Fig* divinement; **she was looking d. beautiful** elle était divine

diviner [dɪˈvaɪnər] N devin *m*, devineresse *f*; **(water) d.** radiesthésiste *mf*, sourcier *m*

diving [ˈdaɪvɪŋ] N *(underwater)* plongée *f* (sous-marine); *(from diving board)* plongeon *m*

▸▸ **d. bell** cloche *f* à plongeur *ou* de plongée; **d. board** plongeoir *m*; *Naut* **d. rudder** *(of submarine)* gouvernail *m* de profondeur; **d. suit** scaphandre *m*

divining [dɪˈvaɪnɪŋ] N divination *f*, **(water) d.** radiesthésie *f*

▸▸ **d. rod** baguette *f* de sourcier

divinity [dɪˈvɪnɪtɪ] N **1** *(divine nature, god)* divinité *f*, **the D.** la Divinité **2** *(subject)* théologie *f*, *Univ* **Doctor of D.** docteur *m* en théologie **3** *Sch* instruction *f* religieuse

divisible [dɪˈvɪzɪb(ə)l] ADJ divisible **(by** par)

division [dɪˈvɪʒən] N **1** *(splitting)* division *f*, partage *m* **(into** en); *(of party)* scission *f*, *(of land)* morcellement *m*; *(of scale etc)* graduation *f*, *(distribution) (of profit etc)* répartition *f*, partage; **d. of labour** division du travail; **d. of votes** partage de voix

2 *(discord)* division *f*, désunion *f*, **to sow d.** semer la zizanie *ou* la discorde

3 *Math* division *f*; **long d.** = division décomposée en ses différentes étapes VOIR GRAMMAIRE A77; B59

4 *Parl* vote *m*; **to come to a d.** voter; **without a d.** sans avoir à voter

5 *(section)*, *Ftbl, Mil* division *f*; *Biol* groupe *m*, classe *f*; *Law (of court)* section *f*, *esp Am Rail* section de ligne; *(of scale, thermometer etc)* degré *m*; *Pol* **parliamentary d.** *(area)* circonscription *f* électorale

6 *Constr etc* cloison *f*, séparation *f*

▸▸ *Br Pol* **d. bell** = sonnerie *f* à la Chambre des communes prévenant les députés qu'il faut venir voter; *Br Pol* **d. list** = liste *f* des députés qui ont voté pour ou contre une motion; *Br Pol* **d. lobby** = nom *m* des deux salles dans lesquelles les députés britanniques se répartissent pour voter; *Math* **d. sign** symbole *m* de division

divisional [dɪˈvɪʒən(ə)l] ADJ de la division

▸▸ **d. account** compte *m* divisionnaire; **d. director** directeur, -trice de division

divisive [dɪˈvaɪsɪv] ADJ qui divise, qui crée des divisions

divisor [dɪˈvaɪzər] N *Math* diviseur *m*

divorce [dɪˈvɔːs] N **1** *Law* divorce *m*; **I want a d.** je veux divorcer; **to get a d.** divorcer; **to ask for a d.** demander le divorce; **d. case** cas *m* de divorce; **to specialize in d. (cases)** *(of lawyer)* se spécialiser dans les cas de di-

vorce; **to sue for (a) d.**, *Am* to file a petition for d. demander le divorce; **their marriage ended in d.** ils ont divorcé; **one in three marriages ends in d.** un couple sur trois divorce **2** *Fig* divorce *m*, séparation *f* **(between sth and sth** de qch et de qch)

VT **1** *Law (of judge) (two people)* prononcer le divorce de; **to get divorced from sb, to d. sb** divorcer d'avec qn **2** *Fig* **you cannot d. form from content** on ne peut pas séparer le fond et la forme

VI *(of husband and wife)* divorcer

▸▸ **d. proceedings** action *f* en divorce

divorced [dɪˈvɔːst] ADJ divorcé; **she is divorced from him** elle est divorcée d'avec lui; *Fig* **d. from reality** *(life, idea)* chimérique; **passage d. from the context** passage isolé du contexte; **d. from commonsense** dénué de bon sens

divorcee [dɪvɔːˈsiː] N divorcé, -ée

divot [ˈdɪvət] N motte *f* de terre

divulge [daɪˈvʌldʒ] VT divulguer; **to d. sb's whereabouts** divulguer l'endroit où se trouve qn

divvy [ˈdɪvɪ] N *Br Fam* **1** *Fin* dividende *m* **2** *(idiot)* abruti, -ie; **stop being such a d.** arrête tes bêtises

▸ **divvy up** VT SEP *Fam* partager

dixie, dixy [ˈdɪksɪ] N *esp Mil Fam* gamelle *f*

dixieland [ˈdɪksɪlænd] N *Mus* dixieland *m*

▸▸ **d. jazz** dixieland

DIY [diːaɪˈwaɪ] *Br (abbr* **do-it-yourself)** N bricolage *m*

ADJ ATTRIB de bricolage; **a D. expert** un spécialiste du bricolage

dizzily [ˈdɪzɪlɪ] ADV **1** *(to stagger etc)* pris de vertige **2** *(to rise) (of cliffs, share prices etc)* vertigineusement **3** *Fig (to behave, laugh)* étourdiment

dizziness [ˈdɪzɪnɪs] N étourdissement *m*, vertige(s) *m(pl)*, malaise *m*; **fit of d.** éblouissement *m*

dizzy [ˈdɪzɪ] ADJ **1** *Med* pris de vertige; **to feel d.** avoir le vertige; **to make sb d.** donner le vertige à qn; **d. with desire/fear** fou/folle de désir/peur **2** *Fig (height, speed etc)* vertigineux **3** *Fig (scatterbrained)* écervelé

▸▸ **d. blonde** blonde *f* évaporée; **d. spell** éblouissement *m*, malaise *m*

DJ [diːˈdʒeɪ] N **1** *abbr* disc jockey **2** *Fam abbr* dinner jacket

Djibouti [dʒɪˈbuːtɪ] N Djibouti

D Lit(t) [diːˈlɪt] N *abbr* Doctor of Letters

DNA [diːeˈneɪ] N *Chem (abbr* deoxyribonucleic acid) ADN *m*

D-notice N *Journ* = consigne *f* donnée par le gouvernement britannique à la presse pour empêcher la diffusion d'informations touchant à la sécurité du pays

DNS [diːeˈnes] N *Comput (abbr* **Domain Name System)** système *m* de nom de domaine, DNS *m*

DO¹ [duː] (**he does** [dʌz], *pt* **did** [dɪd], *pr sub sg, pl* **do;** *pp* **done** [dʌn], *pr sub sg* **don't** [dəʊnt], **didn't** [ˈdɪd(ə)nt] *are common for* **do not, did not; doesn't** [ˈdʌz(ə)nt] *for* **does not)**

V AUX	in questions **1** ▪ in negative statements **1** ▪ for emphasis **2** ▪ in tag questions **6** ▪ elliptically **6**
VT	faire **1–6** ▪ étudier **1**
VI	aller **2, 3**

V AUX **1** *(usual form in questions and negative statements except with* **have**, *but see* **have²**, **be**, *and modal verbs; also in negative commands)* **did you see him?** l'avez-vous vu?; **we do not know** nous ne le savons pas; **do not speak!** ne parlez pas!; **don't do it!** n'en faites rien!; **don't be afraid** n'ayez pas peur; **do you mind?** ça ne vous fait rien?; *Iron* vous permettez? VOIR GRAMMAIRE A46–8

2 *(used for emphasis)* **he did go** il y est bien allé; **I do believe he is a thief** je crois vraiment que c'est un voleur; **it doesn't matter – it does (matter)!** ça ne fait rien – si, ça fait quelque chose!; **why don't you work? – I do (work)!** pourquoi ne travaillez-vous pas? – mais si, je travaille!; **do you remember him? – do I remember him** *or* **do I!** vous souvenez-vous de lui? – si je m'en souviens!; **do sit down** asseyez-vous donc!; **yes, people did live there** oui, des gens ont vécu là; **I don't like coffee, but I do like tea** je n'aime pas le café, mais j'aime bien le thé; **rarely does it happen that …** il arrive rarement que … VOIR GRAMMAIRE A57

3 *(replacing vi)* **they work in the fields as their fathers did** ils travaillent aux champs comme le faisaient leurs pères; **he writes better than I do** il écrit mieux que moi; **they have always existed and still do** ils ont toujours existé et existent encore; **if you want to speak to him, do it now** si vous désirez lui parler, faites-le maintenant VOIR GRAMMAIRE A57

4 *(replacing vt and taking its construction)* **he envies me as much as I do him** il m'envie autant que je l'envie

5 *(replacing vt and object)* **if you understood the question as well as I do** si vous compreniez la question aussi bien que moi

6 *(in replies, tag questions etc)* **may I open these letters? – (please) do** puis-je ouvrir ces lettres? – je vous en prie!; **did you see him? – I did** l'avez-vous vu? – oui(, je l'ai vu); **do you like her? – no I don't** tu l'aimes bien? – non(, je ne l'aime pas); **you don't like it – yes I do** vous ne l'aimez pas – mais si; **you like him, don't you?** vous l'aimez bien, n'est-ce pas?; **she lives here, doesn't she?** elle habite ici, n'est-ce pas?; **that does you good, doesn't it?** ça fait du bien, hein?; **he doesn't believe that, does he?** il ne croit pas ça, hein?; **you like Paris? so do I** vous aimez Paris? moi aussi VOIR GRAMMAIRE A47

7 *Law* **charged that he did on the 15th of August utter threats** accusé d'avoir proféré des menaces le 15 août

VT 1 *(carry out, complete)* *(good deed, one's duty, housework, calculation etc)* faire; *Math (problem)* résoudre; **she's doing medicine** *(studying it)* elle étudie la médecine; **to do the interpreting** faire l'interprète; **to do ten years (in prison)** faire dix ans de prison; **the car was doing sixty** la voiture faisait du soixante

2 *(with reference to general activity)* **what do you do (for a living)?** qu'est-ce que vous faites (dans la vie)?; **what are you doing?** qu'est-ce que vous faites?; **it gives me something to do** cela me donne de l'occupation; **don't do it again!** ne recommencez pas!; **don't!** ne faites pas ça!; **do as you're told** fais ce qu'on te dit; **what is to be done?** que faire?; **it can't be done** cela n'est pas possible, c'est impossible; **there's nothing to be done** il n'y a rien à faire; **it's as good as done** c'est une affaire faite; **she did nothing but cry** elle n'a fait que pleurer; **I don't know what to do** je ne sais que faire, je ne sais pas quoi faire; **what can I do for you?** que puis-je faire pour vous?; **what are you going to do about it?** que proposez-vous de faire?; **what would he do without you?** que deviendrait-il sans vous?; **it was all I could do to lift it** c'est à peine si j'ai pu le soulever; **it was all I could do not to laugh** j'ai eu du mal à ne pas rire; *Fam* **that's done it!** ça y est! VOIR GRAMMAIRE A46–8

3 *(with reference to behaviour, conduct)* **to do right/wrong** bien/mal faire; **to do right/wrong by sb** bien/mal agir envers qn; **you would do well to …** vous feriez bien de

…; **well done!** très bien!, bravo!; **it isn't done** *(is not the practice)* cela ne se fait pas; **it is quite commonly done** c'est de pratique courante

4 *(arrange, fix)* **to do sb's/one's hair** coiffer qn/se coiffer; **to do one's teeth** se brosser les dents; **he does repairs** il fait des réparations; **she's doing the flowers for the wedding** c'est elle qui s'occupe des fleurs pour le mariage

5 *Fam (look around)* *(town, museum)* visiter, faire

6 *Theat (Hamlet etc)* faire

7 *Fam (with reference to crime, dishonest conduct)* **to do sb** *(cheat)* refaire qn, faire qn; *(beat up)* casser la figure à qn, mettre une raclée à qn; **he got done last night** *(arrested)* il s'est fait ramasser la nuit dernière; **I've been done!** *(cheated)* j'ai été roulé!, on m'a eu!; **they did three other houses in the neighbourhood** *(burgled them)* ils sont passés dans trois autres maisons dans le quartier

8 *Fam (use)* **to do drugs** se droguer; **I don't do drugs** je ne me drogue pas, je ne prends pas de drogues

9 **let's do lunch** il faudra qu'on déjeune ensemble un de ces jours

10 *Fam (provide, serve, help)* Old-fashioned **they do you very well at this hotel** on est très bien servi dans cet hôtel; *Com* **we can do you this article at …** nous pouvons vous faire cet article à …; **that dress/hairstyle does something/nothing for you** cette robe/coiffure t'arrange *ou* te met en valeur/ne t'arrange pas *ou* ne te met pas du tout en valeur; **this music doesn't do anything for me** cette musique ne me dit rien, je n'aime pas cette musique

11 *(in perfect tenses and past participle)* **to have done** *(finished)* avoir fini; *Lit* **day is done** la journée tire à sa fin; **have you done shouting?** as-tu fini de crier?; **done!** *(after a bargain made)* entendu!, marché conclu!; **to be done** *(of meat, vegetable)* être prêt *ou* cuit; **meat well done** viande bien cuite; **done to a turn** cuit à point

VI 1 **how do you do?** *(on first introduction)* enchanté (de faire votre connaissance); **to be doing well** *(of patient)* être sur la voie de la guérison; *(in business)* être en bonne voie, faire de bonnes affaires; *(of business)* bien aller, réussir; *(of plant)* bien pousser; **that young man will do well** c'est un garçon qui réussira; **he did brilliantly** il a réussi brillamment; **to do very well** *or* **nicely for oneself** *(prosper)* s'en tirer pas mal du tout

2 *(serve, suffice)* **that will do** *(is satisfactory)* c'est bien (comme cela), c'est bon; *(stop it)* ça suffit, c'est assez; **tea will do** *(if you haven't got coffee)* du thé fera l'affaire; **this room will do for the office** cette pièce ira bien pour le bureau; **will this one do?** ceci fera l'affaire?; **that will never do** cela n'ira jamais, ça n'ira pas du tout; **to make do with what one has** s'arranger avec ce qu'on a; **we'll just have to make do** il faudra faire avec; **that will do me** cela fera mon affaire; **it would never do for them to see me** il ne faudrait pas qu'ils me voient

3 *(happen)* **let's see what's doing next door** allons voir ce qui se passe à côté; **there's never anything doing at this time of year** il ne se passe jamais rien à cette période de l'année; **nothing doing!** *(I, she etc won't)* rien à faire!, ça ne prend pas!

N 1 **the do's and don'ts** ce qu'il faut faire et ce qu'il ne faut pas faire; **the do's and don'ts of society** ce qui se fait et ce qui ne se fait pas dans le monde; *Fam* **come on, fair do's!** *(I want my share)* dis donc, donne-moi ma part!; *(be fair)* dis donc, sois juste!

2 *Fam (party etc)* réception f

3 *Old-fashioned Fam (state of affairs)* **it's a poor do!** c'est triste!

▸ **do away with** VT INSEP **1** *(abolish)* *(custom)* abolir, abandonner; *(death penalty, monarchy)* abolir; *(practice, paperwork, homework)* supprimer; **we've done away with the typists** *(got rid of them)* nous nous sommes défaits des dactylos; *Fam* **they should do away with school** ils devraient supprimer l'école

2 *Fam (kill)* supprimer; **she has threatened to do away with herself** elle a menacé de se supprimer

▸ **do by** VT INSEP *Fam (treat)* **to do well** *or* **right/badly** *or* **wrong by sb** bien/mal agir *ou* se conduire envers qn; **she did very well by her granddaughter at Christmas** *(gave her lots of gifts)* elle a gâté sa petite-fille à Noël; **he has been hard done by** il a été traité durement; **he'll feel very hard done by if you don't at least send him a birthday card** il se sentira vraiment blessé si tu ne lui envoies même pas de carte d'anniversaire; *Prov* **do as you would be done by** ne fais pas aux autres ce que tu ne voudrais pas qu'ils te fassent

▸ **do down** VT SEP **1** *(swindle)* estamper

2 *(say bad things about)* dire du mal de; **to do oneself down** se rabaisser; **there's always someone ready to do you down** il y a toujours des gens prêts à dire du mal des autres

▸ **do for** VT INSEP *Fam* **1** *(murder)* tuer, faire son affaire à; **he's done for** *(will be killed)* c'est un homme mort; *(is ruined)* il est fini *ou Fam* fichu; **if he keeps on treating her this way, she'll do for him** s'il continue à la traiter de cette façon, elle va le descendre

2 *(exhaust)* épuiser; **it was that last hill that did for me** c'est la dernière colline qui m'a épuisé

3 *(clean house for)* faire *ou* tenir le ménage de; **who does for you?** qui fait votre ménage?

VT SEP *(charge with, convict of)* **to do sb for sth** *(murder, shoplifting)* condamner qn pour qch; **they'll do you for double-parking** ils vont te mettre une amende si tu restes garé en double file; *Hum* **she'll get done for child-molesting if she goes out with him** on va l'accuser de les prendre au berceau si elle sort avec lui

▸ **do in** VT SEP *Fam* **1** *(murder)* descendre, faire son affaire à; **somebody on our street was done in last night** quelqu'un de notre rue a été descendu cette nuit

2 *(exhaust)* crever; **I'm absolutely done in** je suis crevé *ou* vanné

3 *(injure, damage)* *(of shoes etc)* *(toes etc)* faire mal à; **to do one's back/knee** se niquer le dos/genou; *Sl* **that girl really does my head in** *(annoys me)* cette fille, elle me prend la tête

▸ **do out** VT SEP **1** *(clean)* *(the kitchen, a room)* faire, nettoyer; *(drawer, cupboard)* ranger

2 *(decorate)* *(room)* faire (**in** en); *(woodwork)* peindre (**in** en)

▸ **do out of** VT SEP *Fam (cheat)* **to do sb out of sth** soutirer *ou* carotter qch à qn; *(money)* refaire *ou* escroquer qn de qch; **to do sb out of a job** *(of person)* prendre le travail de qn; **all this automation is doing people out of jobs** toute cette automatisation supprime des emplois; **the new structure did him out of his job** la nouvelle structure lui a fait perdre son travail; **you've done me out of a possible job** tu m'as fait perdre un emploi; **she's been done out of her share of the money** elle s'est fait escroquer de sa part de l'argent

▸ **do over** VT SEP **1** *Am (redecorate)* *(house)* refaire la décoration de

2 *Br Fam (beat up)* *(person)* casser la figure à, mettre une raclée à

3 *Fam (search)* *(flat etc)* retourner; **their place really got done over while they were**

away *(burgled)* on a tout retourné chez eux pendant qu'ils étaient partis

4 *Am (repeat) (homework)* refaire

▶ **do up** VT SEP **1** *(fasten) (jacket, skirt, button, zip)* fermer; *(laces)* faire; *(hair)* relever

2 *(wrap) (parcel)* faire; *(objects)* emballer, empaqueter

3 *(improve appearance of)* remettre à neuf; *(room, inside of house etc)* décorer; *Fam* **to do oneself up** se faire beau/belle; **to be done up to the nines** être sur son trente et un

VI *(of clothes)* s'agrafer

▶ **do with** VT SEP **1 what did you do with my umbrella?** qu'avez-vous fait de mon parapluie?; **she didn't know what to do with herself** *(to keep busy)* elle ne savait que faire *ou* à quoi s'occuper; *(for joy)* elle ne se tenait pas de joie; *(for awkwardness)* elle était gênée, elle ne savait plus où se mettre; **I can't do a thing with my hair** je n'arrive pas à me coiffer; **I'll see if Bob can do anything with the car** je vais voir si Bob peut faire quelque chose à la voiture; **I can't do a thing with him** *(child)* je ne sais plus quoi faire

2 *(need) (usually formed with* could*)* **I could do with a cup of tea** je prendrais bien une tasse de thé; **we can do with your help** vous n'êtes pas de trop; **you could do with a haircut** une coupe de cheveux ne te ferait pas de mal; **the house could do with a lick of paint** la maison aurait bien besoin d'un coup de pinceau; **we could do with something like that for the spare room** ce serait bien si on avait quelque chose comme ça pour la chambre d'ami

3 *(be connected with)* **she's something to do with insurance** elle est dans les assurances; **it has to do with your mother, I'm afraid** j'ai bien peur que ça concerne ta mère; **I want nothing to do with him** je ne veux pas avoir affaire à lui; **to have nothing to do with sth** *(not be involved in or responsible for)* n'être pour rien dans qch, n'avoir rien à voir avec qch; *(not be connected with)* n'avoir rien à faire avec qch; **you should have nothing to do with it** *(don't get involved)* tu ne devrais pas t'en mêler; **I had nothing to do with it** je n'y suis pour rien; **it's nothing to do with the colour of your skin** cela n'a rien à voir avec la couleur de la peau; **it's nothing to do with you** vous n'avez rien à voir là-dedans

4 *(finish)* **to have done with sth** en avoir fini avec qch; **I've done with trying to help people** j'en ai fini d'aider les gens; **let's have done with it!** finissons-en!; **to have done with sb** *(terminated relationship with lover, girlfriend etc)* avoir rompu avec qn; *(with friend)* en avoir fini avec qn; **I haven't done with him yet!** *(haven't finished scolding him)* je n'en ai pas encore fini avec lui!; **that's all over and done with!** c'est fini, tout ça!

5 *Fam (finish using) (newspaper, scissors etc)* finir avec; **once you've done with it** quand tu auras fini

6 *Fam (with negative) (not like)* **I can't be doing with getting up early** je n'aime pas me lever tôt; **I can't be doing with television** je n'aime pas la télévision; **I can't be doing with her** je ne l'aime pas

▶ **do without** VT INSEP *(manage without) (something)* se passer de; **to do without food** se passer de nourriture; *Fam* **I could do without him** je me passerais de lui; **we can do without the sarcasm** on n'a pas besoin de ces sarcasmes; **you could do without the heavy eye make-up** tu serais mieux avec moins de maquillage sur les yeux; **you'll just have to do without** il faudra s'en passer

do ² [dəʊ] N *Mus (fixed)* do m, ut m; *Scot Fam* **to be up to high do** être dans tous ses états

DOA [diːəʊ'eɪ] ADJ *Med (abbr* **dead on arri-**

val**) to be D.** être mort avant son arrivée à l'hôpital

doc [dɒk] N *(abbr* **doctor***) Fam* toubib m; **thanks d.** merci docteur

▶▶ **D. Martens®** *(shoes)* Doc Martens® fpl

docile ['dəʊsaɪl] ADJ docile

docility [dəʊ'sɪlɪtɪ] N docilité f

dock ¹ [dɒk] N **1** *Naut (of port)* bassin m; **to go into d.** entrer au bassin; **the docks** les docks mpl, *Fam* **in d.** *(of car, plane)* en réparation; **floating d.** dock flottant, chantier m à flot **2** *Theat* **scene d.** remise f à décors

VT **1** *Naut (ship)* faire entrer au bassin *ou* à quai; *(for repairs)* faire entrer en cale sèche; *(on canal, river) (barge etc)* garer **2** *(two spacecraft)* arrimer

VI **1** *(of ship)* entrer *ou* arriver au port *ou* aux docks *ou* à quai; *(for repair)* entrer en cale sèche; **when do we d.?** quand arrivons-nous à quai?; **we'll be docking at New York** nous entrerons à quai à New York **2** *(of two spacecraft)* s'arrimer

▶▶ **d. strike** grève f des dockers; **d.-warehouse** dock m entrepôt

dock ² N *Law* banc m des accusés *ou* des prévenus; **prisoner in the d. Murphy** accusé Murphy

dock ³ VT **1** *(sb's pay)* diminuer; **to d. two pounds from sb's wages** supprimer deux livres du salaire de qn **2 to d. a horse('s tail)/a dog('s tail)** couper la queue à un cheval/un chien

dock ⁴ N *(weed)* patience f

docker ['dɒkər] N docker m, débardeur m; **dockers' strike** grève f des dockers

docket ['dɒkɪt] N **1** *(piece of paper) (accompanying parcel, file)* bordereau m **2** *Law (summary)* registre m des jugements rendus; *Am (list of cases)* rôle m des causes **3** *Br (customs document)* récépissé m de douane

VT **1** *Law (decision)* enregistrer; *Am (case)* porter sur le rôle des causes **2** *(file, merchandise)* étiqueter

docking ['dɒkɪŋ] N **1** *Naut* mise f au bassin; *(for repairs)* radoub m **2** *(of two spacecrafts)* arrimage m

▶▶ **d. manoeuvre** accostage m; *Comput* **d. station** *(for notebook)* station f d'accueil

dockland ['dɒklænd] N quartiers mpl des docks

dockyard ['dɒkjɑːd] N chantier m naval *ou* de constructions navales; **naval d.** arsenal m maritime

doctor ['dɒktər] N **1** *Med* médecin m, docteur m; **to go to the doctor('s)** aller chez le docteur; **the d. will see you now** le docteur va vous recevoir maintenant; **good morning d.** bonjour docteur; *Br Fam* **to be under the d. for sth** être suivi par le docteur pour qch; **I would like to see D. Brown** j'aimerais voir le docteur Brown; **I am a d.** je suis médecin; **woman d.** femme f médecin; **family d.** médecin de famille; **ship's d.** médecin de bord; **army d.** médecin militaire; *Br* **National Health (Service) d.** ≃ médecin conventionné; *Fig Fam* **that's just what the d. ordered** c'est exactement ce qu'il me fallait

2 *Univ* docteur m; **D. of Divinity/Law/Medicine** docteur en théologie/droit/médecine; **D. of Literature/Science** docteur ès lettres/sciences; *Rel* **Doctors of the Church** docteurs *ou* pères m de l'Église; **d.'s degree** doctorat m

VT **1** *Pej Fam (falsify, adulterate) (text)* falsifier; *(accounts, evidence)* falsifier, fausser; *(dice, cards)* piper; *(wine etc)* frelater

2 *(drug) Horseracing (horse)* doper; **to d. sb's drink** mettre de la drogue dans le verre de qn *(à son insu)*

3 *Old-fashioned (patient)* soigner

4 *Vet Fam (cat etc)* châtrer

doctoral ['dɒktər(ə)l] ADJ *(thesis, research etc)* de doctorat; *(robes)* de docteur

doctorate ['dɒktərət] N *Univ* doctorat m; **to have a d. in history** avoir un doctorat en histoire

doctoring ['dɒktərɪŋ] N **1** *Pej Fam (of text etc)* falsification f **2** *(of horse)* doping m **3** *Med Fam* profession f de médecin **4** *(care)* soins mpl *(of sb* donnés à qn) **5** *Vet (of cat etc)* castration f

doctrinaire [dɒktrɪ'neər] ADJ *Pej* doctrinaire

doctrinal [dɒk'traɪn(ə)l] ADJ doctrinal

doctrine ['dɒktrɪn] N doctrine f

docudrama ['dɒkjʊdrɑːmə] N *TV* docudrame m

document ['dɒkjʊmənt] N document m; **legal d.** acte m authentique; *Com* **documents against acceptance/payment** documents mpl contre acceptation/paiement; *Law* **documents relating to a case** dossier m d'une affaire; *Law* **to draw up a d.** rédiger un acte

VT documenter; *(of photographer)* faire un reportage sur; **the film documents the lives of the long-term unemployed** le film montre en détail la vie des chômeurs de longue durée; **well-documented book** livre bien documenté; **his involvement in the affair is well documented** on dispose de nombreux témoignages montrant qu'il a été impliqué à cette affaire; **the first documented case of …** le premier cas établi de …

▶▶ **d. case** porte-documents m inv; **d. collator** unité f de classement de documents; **d. cover** pochette f, *Comput* **d. file** fichier m document; **d. handling** manipulation f de documents; **d. holder** *(for keyboarder)* bras m porte-copies; *Comput* **d. reader** lecteur m de documents; *Law* **d. of title** acte m de propriété

documentary [dɒkjʊ'ment(ə)rɪ] ADJ *(film)* documentaire; *(proof)* littéral, -aux

N *Cin, TV* documentaire m

▶▶ *Com, Fin* **d. bill** traite f documentaire; **d. charges** frais mpl de crédit documentaire; **d. credit** crédit m documentaire; **d. credit application** demande f d'ouverture de crédit documentaire; **d. credit department** service m des crédits documentaires; **d. evidence** preuve f littérale; **d. interview** interview-document f, pl interviews-documents; **d. letter of credit** lettre f de crédit documentaire; **d. maker** documentariste mf; **d. remittance** remise f documentaire

documentation [dɒkjʊmen'teɪʃən] N documentation f

docusoap ['dɒkjʊsəʊp] N docu-soap m

dodder ['dɒdər] VI *(walk)* marcher d'un pas branlant; *Hum* **I'm doddering along** je vais mon petit bonhomme de chemin; **he's beginning to d. a bit** *(mentally)* il commence à devenir un peu gâteux

dodderer ['dɒdərər] N *Pej* croulant, -ante

doddering ['dɒdərɪŋ] ADJ **1** *(walk)* branlant **2** *Pej (person)* gaga inv; gâteux; **a d. old fool** un vieux gâteux

doddery ['dɒdərɪ] ADJ *Fam (shaky)* branlant, tremblotant; **I still feel a bit d. (on my feet)** *(after illness)* je ne me sens pas encore d'aplomb; *Pej* **a d. old fool** un vieux croulant

doddle ['dɒd(ə)l] N *Br Fam* **it's a d.** *(easy)* c'est simple comme bonjour

dodge [dɒdʒ] N **1** *(to avoid sth)* saut m de côté; **she made a d. to the left** elle a fait un saut vers la gauche **2** *Fam usu Pej (trick)* truc m, combine f; **he's up to all the dodges** il connaît toutes les combines; **tax d.** combine pour payer moins d'impôts

VI se jeter de côté; *Boxing, Ftbl* esquiver; **to d. behind a tree** se glisser prestement derrière un arbre

VT 1 *(blow)* esquiver; *(person)* éviter; *(police, search party)* échapper à, se dérober à **2** *Fam Pej (difficulty)* esquiver, éluder; *(question)* éluder, escamoter; **to d. doing one's duty** se dérober à son devoir; **to d. doing the housework/buying one's round** se défiler pour ne pas faire le ménage/payer sa tournée; **to d. military service** couper au service militaire; **stop dodging the issue** arrête d'éluder le problème

dodgem® ['dɒdʒəm] **ADJ, N** *Br* **d. cars, dodgems**® autos *fpl* tamponneuses; **to have a ride** *or* **a go on the dodgems**® faire un tour d'autos tamponneuses

dodger ['dɒdʒər] **N** *Fam (shirker)* tire-au-flanc *m inv*; *Old-fashioned* **an artful d.** un fin matois; **fare d.** voyageur, -euse sans billet; **they're after tax dodgers** ils cherchent à coincer ceux qui fraudent le fisc

dodgy ['dɒdʒɪ] **ADJ** *Br Fam* **1** *(risky, dangerous) (plan, idea)* risqué; **the house is nice, but it's in a really d. area** la maison est bien mais elle est dans un quartier vraiment craignos; **investing money in a scheme like that is just too d.** c'est vraiment trop risqué d'investir dans ce genre de truc; **the weather looks pretty d.** *(unreliable)* le temps a l'air plutôt douteux *ou* menaçant

2 *(untrustworthy) (person)* louche; *(scheme)* douteux, suspect; **he's OK, but all his friends are well d.** lui, ça va, mais ses amis craignent vraiment; **they were involved in a couple of d. business deals** ils ont été impliqués dans des transactions plutôt louches

3 *(not working properly, unstable)* merdique; **the brakes are really d.** les freins sont très douteux; **the engine sounds a bit d.** le moteur fait un bruit suspect; **don't sit on that chair, it's a bit d.** ne t'assieds pas sur cette chaise, elle est un peu branlante; **the ceiling looks a bit d.** le plafond n'a pas l'air en très bon état; **my stomach's been a bit d. for the last couple of days** ça fait deux jours que j'ai l'estomac un peu dérangé

dodo, *pl* **dodoes, dodos** ['dəʊdəʊ, -z] **N 1** *(bird)* dronte *m*, dodo *m*; *Fig* **(as) dead as a d.** mort et enterré **2** *Fam (fool)* andouille *f* **3** *Mktg* poids *m* mort, produit *m* dodo

DOE [di:əʊ'i:] **N** *Br Admin Formerly (abbr* **Department of the Environment)** ≃ ministère *m* de l'Environnement

doe [dəʊ] **N 1** *(deer)* biche *f*; *(of fallow deer)* daine *f*; **d.-eyed** aux yeux de biche **2** *(of rabbit)* lapine *f*; *(of wild rabbit, hare)* hase *f*

doer ['du:ər] **N** *(dynamic person)* personne *f* dynamique; **she's a d.** c'est une femme très active; **we need a d. rather than a talker** c'est un homme d'action qu'il nous faut plutôt qu'un orateur

doeskin ['dəʊskɪn] **N** peau *f* de daim; **d. glove** gant *m* peau de daim

doesn't ['dʌz(ə)nt] **CONTR = does not,** *see* **do**[1]

doff [dɒf] **VT** *Lit, Hum (one's hat)* enlever, ôter; **to d. one's cap/hat to sb** se découvrir devant qn

DOG [dɒg] **N 1** *(animal)* chien *m*; **beware of the d.** *(sign)* (attention) chien méchant; **to set the dogs on sb** lancer les chiens sur qn; **sporting d.** chien de chasse; *Br Sport Fam* **the dogs** les courses *fpl* de lévriers

2 *Zool (of certain animals)* mâle *m*

3 *Old-fashioned (person)* **you lucky d.!** veinard! *m*; **sly d.** fin renard *m*; **gay d.** coureur *m* (de jupons); **dirty d.** salaud *m*, sale type *m*

4 *Am Sl (failed film, party etc)* fiasco *m*; *Pej (ugly woman)* cageot *m*; **dogs** *(feet)* panards *mpl*

5 *Mktg (product)* poids *m* mort, gouffre *m* financier

6 *Tech (pawl)* cliquet *m*

7 *(idioms)* **to die like a d.** mourir comme un chien; **to treat sb like a d.** traiter qn comme un chien; **to follow sb like a d.** suivre qn comme un petit chien; *Fig* **he's a d. in the manger** il fait l'empêcheur de tourner en rond; **to lead a d.'s life** mener une vie de chien; **to lead sb a d.'s life** faire mener une vie de chien à qn; **it's a d.'s life being a teacher** c'est une vie de chien que d'être professeur; *Prov* **you can't teach an old d. new tricks** = on ne peut pas apprendre un nouveau métier *etc* à quelqu'un qui a dépassé un certain âge; *Prov* **every d. has his day** à chacun vient sa chance; *Prov* **give a d. a bad name (and hang him)** = il est très difficile de se débarrasser de sa mauvaise réputation, qu'elle soit méritée ou non; *Br Fam* **to give sb d.'s abuse** traiter qn de tous les noms; *Fam* **what a d.'s breakfast** *or* **dinner!** quel gâchis!; *(of text)* quel torchon!; *Fam* **to make a d.'s breakfast** *or* **dinner of sth** gâcher qch; *Br Fam* **to be dressed up like a d.'s dinner** être habillé comme un clown; *esp Am Fam* **to put on the d.** *(put on airs and graces)* prendre des grands airs; *(spend a lot of money)* faire des frais; *Fam* **he doesn't stand a d.'s chance** il n'a pas la moindre chance; *Fam* **I'm going to see a man about a d.** *(going to the toilet)* je vais aux toilettes; *(going somewhere unspecified)* j'ai un truc à faire; **it's a case of d. eat d.** les loups se mangent entre eux; **it's a d.-eat-d. world** c'est un monde où les loups se mangent entre eux, c'est la loi de la jungle; **to go to the dogs** *(of business, country)* aller à la ruine; **he's really gone to the dogs** c'est la déchéance totale pour lui; **this restaurant has gone to the dogs since he took over** ce restaurant ne vaut plus rien du tout depuis qu'il l'a racheté

VT (**-gg-** [dɒgd]) *(person)* suivre à la trace; **to d. sb's footsteps** marcher sur les talons de qn; **he is dogged by misfortune** il est poursuivi par la malchance; **she has been dogged by injury for the last year** elle a eu blessure sur blessure au cours de l'année passée

▸ ▸ **d. biscuit** biscuit *m* pour chien; **d. breeder** éleveur, -euse de chiens; **d. breeding** élevage *m* de chiens; *Tech* **d. clutch** embrayage *m* à crabot, crabot *m*; **d. collar** *(for dog)* collier *m* pour *ou* de chien; *Fam (of clergyman)* col *m* d'ecclésiastique; **d. days** canicule *f*; **d. fox** renard *m* mâle; **d. handler** maître-chien *m*, *pl* maîtres-chiens; **d.** *Latin* latin *m* de cuisine; *Br* **d. licence** = permis *m* de posséder un chien; **d. paddle** nage *f* du petit chien; **d. racing** courses *fpl* de lévriers; **d. rose** *(flower)* églantine *f*, *(bush)* églantier *m*, rosier *m* sauvage; **d. show** exposition *f* canine; **D. Star** Sirius *f*; **d. tag** *(for dog, soldier)* plaque *f* d'identification

---

dogcart ['dɒgkɑ:t] **N** *(vehicle)* dog-cart *m*, *pl* dog-carts

dog-catcher N = employé *m* municipal qui est chargé d'attraper les chiens errants

doge [dəʊdʒ] **N** *Hist* doge *m*

dog-eared ADJ *(book)* aux pages cornées; *(page)* corné; **I'm afraid your book got a bit d.** je crois bien que les pages de ton livre se sont un peu cornées

dog-end N *Fam* mégot *m*

dogfight ['dɒgfaɪt] **N** combat *m* de chiens; *Mil, Aviat* combat aérien; *Fig (brawl)* bagarre *f*

dogfish ['dɒgfɪʃ] **N** chien *m* de mer, roussette *f*

dogfood ['dɒgfu:d] **N** pâtée *f* (pour chiens)

dogged ['dɒgɪd] **ADJ** *(person)* résolu, tenace; *(research, refusal, pursuit)* tenace; *(attachment)* fidèle

doggedly ['dɒgɪdlɪ] **ADV** avec ténacité, ré-

solument; **to work d.** travailler sans relâche; **to be d. intent on doing sth** avoir la ferme intention de faire qch

doggedness ['dɒgɪdnɪs] **N** ténacité *f*

doggerel ['dɒgərəl] **N** *(silly and comical)* poésie *f* burlesque; *(worthless, mediocre)* vers *mpl* de mirliton

▸ ▸ **d. verse** *(silly and comical)* poésie burlesque; *(worthless, mediocre)* vers de mirliton

doggie ['dɒgɪ] **N** *Fam* toutou *m*, chienchien *m*; **to do it d. fashion** *(sex)* faire l'amour en levrette

▸ ▸ **d. bag** = petit sac *m* fourni par certains restaurants pour emporter les restes; **d. paddle** nage *f* à la chien

doggo ['dɒgəʊ] **ADV** *Br Fam* **to lie d.** se tenir coi

doggone ['dɒgɒn] *Am Fam* **INT d. (it)!** zut!, nom d'un chien!

ADJ fichu; **I've lost the d. car keys** j'ai perdu ces saletés de clés de bagnole

ADV vachement; **it's so d. hot!** il fait une chaleur à crever!

doggy ['dɒgɪ] **ADJ 1** *(smell etc)* de chien **2** *Fam (person)* qui adore les chiens

N *Fam* = **doggie**

doghouse ['dɒghaʊs] **N** *esp Am* chenil *m*; *Fig* **to be in the d.** être en défaveur *ou* en disgrâce; **you're in the d. with Mum** tu n'es pas en odeur de sainteté avec Maman

dogleg ['dɒgleg] **N** *(in pipe, road, golf course)* coude *m*

VI *(of pipe, road, on golf course)* faire un coude

doglike ['dɒglaɪk] **ADJ** *(devotion)* de chien

dogma, *pl* **dogmas** ['dɒgmə, -əz] **N** dogme *m*

dogmatic [dɒg'mætɪk] **ADJ** dogmatique

dogmatically [dɒg'mætɪklɪ] **ADV** dogmatiquement; *(to say)* d'un ton dogmatique

dogmatism ['dɒgmətɪz(ə)m] **N** *(of opinion, person etc)* dogmatisme *m*

dogmatist ['dɒgmətɪst] **N** dogmatique *mf*

dogmeat ['dɒgmi:t] **N** viande *f* pour chiens

do-gooder ['du:'gʊdər] **N** *Fam Pej* âme *f* charitable, faiseur, -euse de bonnes œuvres

dog-paddle VI nager comme un chien

dogsbody ['dɒgzbɒdɪ] **N** *Fam* factotum *m*; **she's the general d.** c'est la bonne à tout faire

dogsled ['dɒgsled] **N** luge *f* tirée par des chiens

dog's-tooth ['dɒgztu:θ] **N = dogtooth**

dog-tired ADJ *Fam* claqué, crevé, mort de fatigue

dogtooth ['dɒgtu:θ] **N** *(tooth)* canine *f*

▸ ▸ *Tex* **d. check** pied *m* de poule; *Bot* **d. violet** érythrone *m*, dent-de-chien *f*, *pl* dents-de-chien

dogtrot ['dɒgtrɒt] **N** petit trot *m*; **to go somewhere at a d.** aller quelque part au petit trot

dogwatch ['dɒgwɒtʃ] **N** *Naut* petit quart *m*

dogwood ['dɒgwʊd] **N** *Bot* cornouiller *m*

DOH ['di:əʊ'eɪtʃ] **N** *Br Admin (abbr* **Department of Health)** ≃ ministère *m* de la Santé

doh[1] [dəʊ] **N** *Mus* = **do**[2]

doh[2] **INTERJ** d! que je suis bête!

doily ['dɔɪlɪ] **N 1** *(underneath plate etc)* petit napperon *m* **2** *(on plate)* dessus *m* d'assiette

doing ['du:ɪŋ] **N** talking is one thing, **d. is another** c'est bien beau de parler, encore faudrait-il agir; **that takes some d.** ça ne se fait pas en un tour de main; **this is his d.** c'est son ouvrage; **all this is your d.** c'est vous qui êtes la cause de tout cela; **it was none of my d.** ce n'est pas moi qui suis responsable; *Br Fam* **to give sb a d. (over)** casser la figure à qn, mettre une raclée à qn; **d. up** *(renovation)* remise fà neuf

doings ['duːɪŋz] NPL **1** *(of person)* ce qu'on fait, *Pej* agissements *mpl*; **to be informed of sb's d.** être au courant des faits et gestes de qn **2** *Fam (events)* événements *mpl*; **there have been great d. at their house** il y a eu bien du mouvement chez eux **3** *Br Fam (gadget etc)* machin *m*, truc *m*

do-it-yourself N bricolage *m*; **d. enthusiast** passionné, -ée de bricolage
▸▸**d. shop, d. store** magasin *m* de bricolage

do-it-yourselfer [-jə'selfər] N bricoleur, -euse

dol *(abbr dollar)* dol(l)

Dolby® ['dɒlbɪ] N Dolby® *m*;
▸▸**D. system** système *m* Dolby® stéréo

doldrums (the) [ðə'dɒldrəmz] NPL *Naut* la zone calme; *Fig* le cafard, les idées *fpl* noires; **to be in the d.** *(of person)* avoir le moral à zéro, être au trente-sixième dessous; *(of business, market)* être dans le marasme

dole [dəʊl] N *Br Fam (money)* indemnité fde chômage; **to be on the d.** être au chômage; **to go on the d.** s'inscrire au chômage; **d. queues are lengthening** le nombre des chômeurs s'accroît
▸▸**d. money** indemnité de chômage
▸**dole out** VT SEP *Fam (money, food, clothing)* distribuer; **I'm tired of doling out sympathy to everyone** j'en ai assez de réconforter tout le monde

doleful ['dəʊlfʊl] ADJ *(expression, look, song)* lugubre; *(cry)* plaintif; *(person)* triste, affligé

dolefully ['dəʊlfʊlɪ] ADV tristement

doll [dɒl] N **1** *(for child)* poupée f, *(of ventriloquist)* marionnette f, **baby d.** baigneur *m*; **to play with a d.** jouer à la poupée **2** *Fam (woman)* poupée f, *(pretty woman)* belle poupée **3** *Am Fam (kind person)* amour *m*
▸▸**d.'s house** maison fde poupée; *Fig* jolie petite maisonnette f
▸**doll up** VT SEP *Fam (person)* bichonner; **to d. oneself up** *(of woman)* se pomponner; *(of man)* se faire beau; **to be all dolled up** être sur son trente et un; **they've dolled their house up** ils ont retapé leur maison

dollar ['dɒlər] N dollar *m*; **dollars in real terms** dollars *mpl* constants
▸▸*Econ, Fin* **d. area** zone fdollar; **d. sign** (signe *m* du) dollar

dollop ['dɒləp] N *Fam (of butter)* gros morceau *m*; *(of cream, mashed potato)* bonne cuillerée f, *(of mud)* tas *m*; **a good d. of cream** une bonne cuillerée de crème

dolly ['dɒlɪ] N **1** *Fam (for child)* poupée f **2** *Old-fashioned Br Fam (young woman)* **d. (-bird)** poupée f **3** *TV, Cin* travelling *m*, chariot *m* **4** *(for clothes)* agitateur *m*
▸ VI *TV, Cin* faire un travelling; **to d. in/out** faire un travelling avant/arrière
▸▸*TV, Cin* **d. operator** machiniste *m* caméra; **d. tub** *(for laundry)* baquet *m* à lessive

dolman ['dɒlmən] N
▸▸**d. sleeve** manche fchauve-souris

dolmen ['dɒlmen] N *Archeol* dolmen *m*

dolomite ['dɒləmaɪt] N *Miner* dolomite f, *Geol (rock)* dolomie f

Dolomites (the) [ðə'dɒləmaɪts] NPL les Dolomites *fpl*

dolphin ['dɒlfɪn] N *(mammal)* dauphin *m*

dolphinarium [dɒlfɪ'neərɪəm] N aquarium *m* pour dauphins

dolt [dəʊlt] N sot *m*, nigaud *m*, gourde f

doltish ['dəʊltɪʃ] ADJ sot, fsotte, bête

domain [də'meɪn] N **1** *(property)*, *Fig* domaine *m*; *Fig* **that is outside my d.** ce n'est pas mon domaine **2** *Math, Phys (of function)* domaine *m* **3** *Comput* domaine *m*

▸▸*Comput* **d. name** nom *m* de domaine; **D. Name System** système *m* de nom de domaine

dome [dəʊm] N **1** *Archit* dôme *m*, coupole f **2** *Fig (of sky)* dôme *m*, voûte f, *(of hill)* dôme; *(of skull)* calotte f, *Fam (head)* tête f **3** *Metal (of furnace)* dôme *m*, voûte f
▸▸*Am* **d. fastener** bouton-pression *m*, *pl* boutons-pression, pression f

domed [dəʊmd] ADJ **1** *(building)* à dôme, à coupole **2** *(shaped like a dome)* en forme de dôme; *(skull)* ovoïde

Domesday ['duːmzdeɪ] N
▸▸*Hist* **D. Book** = (livre *m* du) cadastre *m* de l'Angleterre *(établi en 1086 par Guillaume le Conquérant)*

domestic [də'mestɪk] ADJ **1** *(misfortune, problem)* domestique; *(fuel)* de ménage; **she does d. work** *(to earn a living)* elle fait des ménages; **to be in d. service** être employé(e) de maison; **newlyweds living in d. bliss** des jeunes mariés au comble du bonheur **2** *(trade, dissent, flight etc)* intérieur; *(production, currency)* national, -aux **3** *(person)* casanier
▸ N domestique *mf*
▸▸*Aviat* **d. airline** ligne f intérieure; **d. animal** animal *m* domestique; **d. appliances** appareils *mpl* ménagers; **d. duties** travaux *mpl* ménagers; *Old-fashioned* **d. economy** économie f domestique; **d. excursionist** excursionniste *mf* (dans son propre pays); **d. life** vie fde famille; *Am* **d. mail** correspondance f à destination de l'intérieur; *Com, Econ* **d. market** marché *m* intérieur; *Com, Econ* **d. products** denrées *fpl* du pays; *Aviat* **d. route** ligne intérieure; **d. sales** ventes *fpl* domestiques; *Br Sch Formerly* **d. science** enseignement *m* ménager; **d. servant** domestique; **d. tasks** travaux ménagers; **d. tourism** tourisme *m* national; **d. tourist** touriste *m* national; **d. travel** voyages *mpl* domestiques; **d. virtues** talents *mpl* de femme/d'homme d'intérieur; **d. visitor** touriste *m* du pays

domestically [də'mestɪk(ə)lɪ] ADV à l'intérieur du pays

domesticate [də'mestɪkeɪt] VT **1** *(tame) (animal)* domestiquer, apprivoiser **2** *(naturalize) (animal, plant)* acclimater **3** **to be domesticated** *(of person)* être casanier, aimer la vie d'intérieur; **to become domesticated** prendre goût à la vie d'intérieur; **her husband is quite domesticated** son mari fait sa part des travaux ménagers

domesticity [dəʊme'stɪsɪtɪ] N **1** *(liking for home)* attachement *m* au foyer **2** *(home life)* vie fde famille; **the cosy d. of their life** leur petite vie tranquille

domicile ['dɒmɪsaɪl] N *Com, Law, Fin* domicile *m*
▸ VT **1** *Fml (usu passive) (person)* **domiciled at Leeds** domicilié *ou* demeurant à Leeds **2** *Com* domicilier; *Fin* **domiciled bill** effet *m* domicilié; **bills domiciled in France** traites *fpl* payables en France; *Fin* **to d. acceptances** domicilier des acceptations

domiciliary [dɒmɪ'sɪlɪərɪ] ADJ *Fml (visit etc)* domiciliaire; *(assistance)* à domicile

domiciliation [dɒmɪsɪlɪ'eɪʃən] N *Fin* domiciliation f
▸▸**d. papers** dossier *m* de domiciliation

dominance ['dɒmɪnəns] N *(of disease, gene etc)* dominance f, *(of race, political party)* prédominance f, **Manchester's d. of English football** la suprématie exercée par Manchester sur le football anglais

dominant ['dɒmɪnənt] ADJ *(character, gene, force etc)* dominant; *(person)* dominateur, -trice
▸ N *Mus* dominante f

▸▸*Mus* **d. chord** accord *m* de dominante; *Mus* **d. seventh** septième fde dominante

dominantly ['dɒmɪnəntlɪ] ADV d'une manière dominante

dominate ['dɒmɪneɪt] VT **1** *(person, a people)* dominer (sur); **to d. a match/game** *(of player, team)* dominer un match/un jeu; **to be dominated by sb** subir la loi de qn; **man dominated by ambition** homme en proie à l'ambition; **the wedding dominated his thoughts to the exclusion of everything else** le mariage prédominait sur toute autre chose dans ses pensées **2** *(of mountain etc) (landscape)* dominer; **the fortress dominates the town** la forteresse domine *ou* commande la ville

dominating ['dɒmɪneɪtɪŋ] ADJ *(feature, colour etc)* dominant; *(personality)* dominateur, -trice

domination [dɒmɪ'neɪʃən] N domination f *(over sur)*; **to be under sb's d.** être dominé par qn; **Manchester's d. of English football** la suprématie exercée par Manchester sur le football anglais

domineer [dɒmɪ'nɪər] VI se montrer autoritaire
▸**domineer over** VT INSEP tyranniser

domineering [dɒmɪ'nɪərɪŋ] ADJ *(person, character etc)* dominateur, -trice, autoritaire

Dominica [də'mɪnɪkə] N la Dominique

dominical [də'mɪnɪk(ə)l] ADJ *Rel* dominical, -aux

Dominican¹ [də'mɪnɪkən] ADJ, N *Rel* dominicain, -aine

Dominican² *Geog* ADJ dominicain
▸▸**the D. Republic** la République Dominicaine
▸ N Dominicain, -aine

dominion [də'mɪnjən] N **1** *(rule)* autorité f, empire *m*; **to have** *or* **hold d. over …** exercer son empire *ou* dominer sur … **2** *(land)* dominion *m*

domino, *pl* **dominoes** ['dɒmɪnəʊ, -əʊz] N **1** *(in game)* domino *m*; **dominoes** *(game)* (jeu *m* de) dominos; **to play dominoes** jouer aux dominos VOIR GRAMMAIRE A10 **2** *(mask)* domino *m*
▸▸**d. effect** effet *m* d'entraînement; *Pol, Fig* **the d. theory** la théorie des dominos

don¹ [dɒn] N **1** *Br Univ* professeur *m* (d'université) *(surtout à Oxford et Cambridge)* **2** *(Spanish title)* Don *m*

don² VT *(-nn-)* *Fml (uniform, clothes)* revêtir, endosser; *(hat)* mettre, coiffer

donate [dəʊ'neɪt] VT faire un don de; *Med* **d. blood** donner du *ou* son sang; **how much did you d.?** combien est-ce que tu as donné?; **to d. one 's time** faire don de son temps
▸ VI faire un don

donation [dəʊ'neɪʃən] N donation f, don *m*; **all donations are tax-deductible** tous les dons sont déductibles des impôts; **to make a d. to a charity** faire un don *ou* une donation à une œuvre de bienfaisance

donator [dəʊ'neɪtər] N donateur, -trice

done PP *see* do¹

doner kebab ['dɒnə, 'dəʊnə] N chiche-kebab *m*

dong [dɒŋ] N *Vulg (penis)* bite f, queue f

dongle ['dɒŋg(ə)l] N *Comput* fiche fgigogne, clé fgigogne

donkey ['dɒŋkɪ] N **1** *(animal)* âne *m*, *Fam* baudet *m*; *(female)* ânesse f, *Fam* **he would talk the hind legs off a d.** il est bavard comme une pie; *Fam* **it happened d.'s years ago** ça s'est passé il y a des années; *Fam* **I haven't seen him for d.'s years** je ne l'ai pas vu depuis une éternité **2** *Fig (idiot)* âne *m*, imbécile *mf*

▸▸*Naut* **d. boiler** chaudière *f* auxiliaire; *Tech* **d. engine** moteur *m* auxiliaire; *Br* **d. jacket** = veste *f* longue en tissu épais, généralement bleu foncé; **d. race** course *f* d'ânes

donkey-work N (*drudgery*) travail *m* pénible

donnish ['dɒnɪʃ] ADJ (*person, air, tone*) intellectuel, -elle, *Pej* pédant; **he's a bit d.** il a un petit air professoral

donor ['dəʊnər] N 1 *Med* (*of blood, organ etc*) donneur, -euse 2 (*to charity etc*) donateur, -trice
▸▸ **d. card** carte *f* de don d'organe

don't [dəʊnt] CONTR = **do not**, *see* **do**[1]
▸▸ *Fam* **d. know** (*voter*) indécis, -ise

donut ['dəʊnʌt] N *esp Am Culin* beignet *m*, *Can* beigne *m*

doobie ['du:bɪ] N *Fam* (*cannabis cigarette*) joint *m*

doodah ['du:dɑ:] N *Fam* truc *m*, machin *m*

doodle ['du:d(ə)l] N *Fam* gribouillis *m*, griffonnage *m*
VT griffonner *ou* gribouiller (distraitement)
VI griffonner *ou* gribouiller (distraitement); *Fig* (*on piano*) pianoter

doodlebug ['du:d(ə)lbʌg] N *Hist Fam* bombe *f* volante

doo-doo ['du:du:] N *Fam* 1 (*excrement*) crotte *f*, caca *m*; **the dog's done a d. on the doormat** le chien a fait sa crotte sur le paillasson 2 (*trouble*) pétrin *m*; **we're in deep d.!** on est vraiment dans le pétrin!

doofus ['du:fəs] N *Am Fam* (*idiot*) andouille *f*

doolally [du:'lælɪ] ADJ *Sl* (*crazy, confused*) timbré

doom [du:m] N destin *m* (funeste), sort *m* (malheureux); **an air/a feeling of d.** un air/ sentiment funeste; *Lit* **he met his d.** il trouva la mort; *Fig* **to be full of** *or* **all d. and gloom** (*of person, forecast etc*) être pessimiste; **the situation's not all d. and gloom** la situation n'est pas aussi sombre qu'il y paraît
VT condamner (**to** à); **doomed** (*town*) condamné; (*person*) perdu; (*ship, aircraft*) marqué par le destin; **an attempt doomed to failure** une tentative condamnée à l'insuccès *ou* vouée à l'échec

doom-laden ADJ (*forecast, words etc*) funeste, lugubre

Doomsday ['du:mzdeɪ] N **D. Book** *see* **Domesday**

doomsday ['du:mzdeɪ] N le (jour du) jugement dernier; *Fam* **till d.** indéfiniment; **to put off sth till d.** renvoyer qch aux calendes grecques

door [dɔ:r] N (*of house, refrigerator etc*) porte *f*; (*of train, car etc*) portière *f*, porte; (*of wardrobe*) porte, battant *m*; **two doors away** deux portes plus loin; **the house next d.** la maison à côté; **I live next d.** j'habite à côté; **the journey takes twenty-five minutes d. to d.** le voyage prend vingt-cinq minutes de porte à porte; **will you answer the d.?** tu peux aller ouvrir (la porte)?; **it was Bob who answered the d.** (to me) c'est Bob qui m'a ouvert (la porte); **to show sb the d.** éconduire *ou* congédier qn; **to show sb to the d.** conduire qn à la porte, reconduire qn; **out of doors** dehors, en plein air; **to shut the d. in sb's face** fermer la porte au nez de qn; *Fig* **doors kept being closed in our faces** tout le monde nous a fermé la porte au nez; **to leave the d. open to** *or* **for negotiations** laisser la porte ouverte à des négociations; **to close** *or* **shut the d. on any discussion** rendre impossible toute discussion; **behind closed doors** (*discussions etc*) entre quatre murs, à huis-clos; **to meet behind closed doors** se rencontrer à huis-clos; **to lay a charge at sb's d.** imputer qch à qn; **to put one's foot in the d.** mettre le pied dans l'em-

brasure de la porte; **the foot in the d. technique** (*of salesman*) = la vente (en porte-à-porte) forcée
▸▸ **d. attendant** portier *m*; *Aut* **d. bin** vide-poche *m*, *pl* vide-poches; **d. chain** chaînette *f* de sûreté; **d. curtain** portière *f*; *Mktg* **d. drop** distribution *f* à domicile; **d. handle** poignée *f* de porte; *Aut* poignée de portière; **d. knocker** marteau *m* de porte, heurtoir *m*; *Aut* **d. mirror** rétroviseur *m* extérieur; *Aut* **d. pocket** vide-poche

doorbell ['dɔ:bel] N sonnette *f*; **to ring the d.** sonner à la porte

do-or-die ADJ (*effort, attempt etc*) acharné; **this d. attitude** cette attitude de détermination inébranlable

doorframe ['dɔ:freɪm] N chambranle *m ou* châssis *m* de porte

doorjamb ['dɔ:dʒæm] N montant *m* de porte

doorkeeper ['dɔ:ki:pər] N portier *m*, concierge *mf*

doorknob ['dɔ:nɒb] N poignée *f* (ronde) de porte

doorman, *pl* **doormen** ['dɔ:mən] N portier *m*

doormat ['dɔ:mæt] N 1 (*for door*) paillasson *m* 2 *Fig* (*person*) lavette *f*, chiffe *f* molle; **don't be such a d.** ne te laisse pas marcher sur les pieds comme ça; **to treat sb like a d.** traiter qn comme une chose insignifiante

doornail ['dɔ:neɪl] N *Fam* **(as) dead as a d.** mort et bien mort

doorpost ['dɔ:pəʊst] N montant *m* de porte

doorstep ['dɔ:step] N 1 seuil *m*, pas *m* (de la porte); **don't leave him standing on the d.** ne le laisse pas sur le pas de la porte; *Fig* **there are shops and a library on your d.** tu as des boutiques et une bibliothèque à ta porte 2 *Br Fam* (*slice of bread*) grosse tranche *f* de pain
VI (*of canvasser*) faire du porte-à-porte

doorstepping ['dɔ:stepɪŋ] N *Journ Fam* = technique *f* des journalistes qui importunent les gens à leur domicile

doorstop ['dɔ:stɒp] N (*fixed*) butoir *m*; (*wedge*) cale-porte *m*, *pl* cale-portes

door-to-door ADJ
▸▸ **d. canvassing** porte-à-porte *m*; **to do d. canvassing** faire du porte-à-porte; **d. salesman** vendeur *m* à domicile; **d. selling** porte-à-porte; **to do d. selling** faire du porte-à-porte

doorway ['dɔ:weɪ] N (baie *f* de) porte *f*; (*frame*) encadrement *m* de la porte; **in the d.** dans l'embrasure de la porte

dopamine ['dəʊpəmɪn] N dopamine *f*

dope [dəʊp] N 1 (*drugs*) drogue *f*, *Sport* doping *m*, stimulant *m*
2 *Sl* (*cannabis*) shit *m*
3 *Fam* (*idiot*) crétin, -ine; **what a d.!** quelle nouille!, quel andouille!
4 *Old-fashioned Sl* (*information*) rencard *m*, tuyau *m*; **to give sb the d. on sth** rencarder qn sur qch
5 *Aviat, Aut* (*varnish*) enduit *m*
6 (*in petrol*) additif *m*, dopant *m*; (*for explosives*) absorbant *m*
ADJ *Am Fam* (*excellent*) génial, -aux, super
VT 1 (*drug*) (*person, horse*) (*to prevent from winning*) droguer; (*to increase chances*) doper; (*drink*) verser une drogue dans
2 *Aviat, Aut* (*varnish*) enduire
3 *Aut* **doped fuel** carburant dopé *ou* additionné d'anti-détonant
▸▸ **d. test** *n* antidopage *ou* antidoping; **to fail/take a d. test** être déclaré positif à/ subir un test antidopage *ou* antidoping

dopehead ['dəʊphed], **doper** ['dəʊpər] N *Sl* (*drug user*) camé, -ée; (*heavy cannabis user*)

= personne *f* qui fume beaucoup de cannabis

dopey ['dəʊpɪ] ADJ *Fam* 1 (*drugged*) drogué; (*from sleep*) endormi 2 (*stupid*) stupide; **what a d. thing to say** que c'était stupide de dire une chose pareille

doping ['dəʊpɪŋ] N 1 (*to incapacitate*) administration *f* d'un narcotique (**of** à); (*to increase chances of winning*) dopage *m*, doping *m* 2 *Aviat, Aut* (*varnishing*) enduisage *m* 3 *Petr* (*of fuel*) dopage *m*

Doppler effect ['dɒplər] N *Phys* effet *m* Doppler

do-re-mi [dəʊre'mi:] N *Am Fam* (*money*) fric *m*, blé *m*

Doric ['dɒrɪk] ADJ, N *Archit* dorique *m*; *Ling* = dialecte *m* de l'anglais parlé dans le nord-est de l'Écosse

dork [dɔ:k] N *Fam* (*idiot*) abruti, -ie

dorky ['dɔ:kɪ] ADJ *Fam* ringard, nul, *f* nulle

dorm [dɔ:m] N *Sch Fam* dortoir *m*

dormant ['dɔ:mənt] ADJ 1 (*passion etc*) assoupi, endormi; (*conflict*) latent; **to lie d.** être en sommeil 2 (*plant, bud*) dormant 3 (*volcano*) en repos
▸▸ *Banking* **d. account** compte *m* sans mouvement

dormer (window) ['dɔ:mər] N fenêtre *f* en mansarde

dormitory ['dɔ:mɪt(ə)rɪ] N 1 dortoir *m* 2 *Am Univ* (*residence*) maison *f ou* foyer *m* d'étudiants
▸▸ **d. town** cité-dortoir *f*, *pl* cités-dortoirs

dormouse, *pl* **dormice** ['dɔ:maʊs, -maɪs] N *Zool* loir *m*

dorsal ['dɔ:s(ə)l] ADJ dorsal, -aux; *Anat* (*towards back of body*) postérieur
▸▸ **d. fin** nageoire *f* dorsale

dory ['dɔ:rɪ] N 1 (*fish*) (**John) D.** dorée *f*, saint-pierre *m inv* 2 *Am* (*boat*) doris *m*

DOS [dɒs] N *Comput* (*abbr* **disk operating system**) DOS *m*
▸▸ **D. command** commande *f* du DOS; **D. prompt** indicatif *m* (du) DOS, invite *f* du DOS; **D. switch** clé *f ou* paramètre *m* du DOS

dosage ['dəʊsɪdʒ] N (*of medicine*) dosage *m*, posologie *f*

dose [dəʊs] N 1 *Med, Nucl* dose *f*, *Fig* **she's bearable in small doses** elle est supportable à petites doses; *Fam* **to get through sth like a d. of salts** faire qch en deux temps trois mouvements *ou* en deux coups de cuillère à pot; **that curry went through me like a d. of salts** ce curry est passé tout droit 2 *Fam* (*bout*) (*of flu etc*) attaque *f* 3 *Sl* (*venereal disease*) vérole *f*
VT 1 (*person*) administrer un médicament à; **to d. oneself with quinine** se bourrer de quinine 2 (*medicine*) doser
▸ **dose up** VT *Fam* bourrer (**with** de)

dosh [dɒʃ] N *Br Sl* (*money*) fric *m*

doss [dɒs] N *Br Sl* 1 (*bed*) lit *m*, pieu *m*; **I'm looking for a d. for tonight** je cherche un endroit où dormir ce soir 2 (*sleep*) somme *m*, roupillon *m*; **to have a d.** faire un somme 3 **it was a real d.** (*easy*) c'était de la tarte *ou* du gâteau
VI (*sleep*) pieuter; (*in doss house*) coucher à l'asile de nuit
▸ **doss around** VI *Br Sl* (*hang around*) se la couler douce
▸ **doss down** VI *Br Sl* (*sleep*) se coucher, se pieuter; **do you mind dossing down on the floor?** est-ce que ça t'embête de coucher par terre?; **I need somewhere to d. down for the night** j'ai besoin d'un endroit où coucher cette nuit

dosser ['dɒsər] N *Br Sl* 1 (*person*) clochard, -arde 2 (*place*) asile *m* de nuit

doss-house N *Br Sl* asile *m* de nuit

dossier ['dɒsɪeɪ, -ɪər] N dossier *m*; **to keep a d. on sb** avoir un dossier sur qn

dot [dɒt] N *(in dotted line, over the letter i etc)*, Comput point *m*; Mus point d'augmentation; **'i' with two dots** 'i' surmonté de deux points; **dots and dashes** *(Morse code)* points et traits; Comput "**gwilson at transex, dot, co, dot, uk**" gwilson at *ou* arobase transex, point, co, point, uk; Fam **on the d.** *(to arrive)* à l'heure tapante; **on the d. of three o'clock, at three o'clock on the d.** à trois heures pile; Fam **since the year d.** depuis des siècles; Fam **that was in the year d.** c'était il y a une éternité; Fam **but she left early, d. d. d.** mais elle est partie de bonne heure, si vous voyez ce que je veux dire

  VT (-tt-) **1** *(an i)* mettre un point sur; Fig **to d. one's i's (and cross one's t's)** mettre les points sur les i

  2 *(surface)* marquer de points; *(drawing)* pointiller; **dotted with flowers/etc** *(of surface etc)* parsemé de fleurs/etc; **his shirt was dotted with flecks of tomato sauce** sa chemise était tachetée de sauce tomate; **the islands are dotted all round the coast** les îles sont éparpillées tout autour de la côte

  3 Mus *(note)* pointer

  4 Old-fashioned Fam **to d. and carry one** *(when walking)* boiter

  5 Sl **to d. sb one** *(hit)* flanquer un gnon à qn

  ▸▸ Comput **d. com** *(company)* start-up *f inv*; Comput **d. command** commande *f* avec point; Comput **d. matrix** imprimante *f* matricielle, matricielle *f*; Comput **d. prompt** repère *m* de saisie de commandes

dotage ['dəʊtɪdʒ] N gâtisme *m*; **to be in one's d.** être gâteux

dote [dəʊt] VI être gâteux

  ▸ **dote on, dote upon** VT INSEP *(somebody)* adorer

doting ['dəʊtɪŋ] ADJ ATTRIB *(parents, grandparents)* qui montre une tendresse *ou* une indulgence exagérée; **a d. husband** un mari qui gâte sa femme

dotted ['dɒtɪd] ADJ **1** *(contour)* pointillé; **2** Mus *(note)* pointé

  ▸▸ **d. line** *(on form)* ligne *f* en pointillés; Aut ligne discontinue; **to sign on the d. line** *(on form)* signer à l'endroit indiqué; Fig donner son consentement; **tear along the d. line** déchirer en suivant les pointillés

dottle ['dɒt(ə)l] N *(in pipe)* culot *m*

dotty ['dɒtɪ] ADJ Fam toqué, piqué; **he's d. about her** il est toqué *ou* fou d'elle; **I'm not d. about him** je ne raffole pas de lui; **she wasn't d. about moving house** l'idée de déménager ne l'enchantait pas

DOUBLE ['dʌb(ə)l]

ADJ	double **1, 2**
ADV	en deux ▪ deux fois
N	double **1, 3–6**
VT	doubler **1, 2, 4** ▪ plier en deux **2** ▪ contrer **3**
VI	doubler **1**

ADJ **1** *(having two, two together)* double; **'all' is spelt 'a, d. l'** 'all' s'écrit 'a, deux l'; **d. two d. three** *(when giving telephone number, address)* vingt-deux trente-trois; **to reach d. figures** *(of inflation etc)* atteindre les deux chiffres; Br Univ **she took a d. first in English and History** elle a deux licences avec mention très bien, une en anglais et l'autre en histoire; Am **to go on a d. date** sortir à deux couples; Comput **d.-sided** *(disk etc)* à deux faces, à double face; **to have a d. yolk** *(of egg)* avoir deux jaunes; **a d. whisky** un double whisky

  2 *(misleading, ambiguous)* double; **with a d. meaning** à deux *ou* double sens; *(ambiguous)* ambigu, -uë; **to play a d. game** jouer

double jeu; **to lead a d. life** mener une double vie; **to apply a d. standard** utiliser deux poids, deux mesures

  ADV **to see d.** voir double; **to fold a sheet (of paper) d.** plier une feuille (de papier) en deux; **bent d.** *(of person)* courbé en deux; **bent d. with pain/laughter** plié en deux de douleur/rire; **the number** le double, deux fois autant; **it took me d. the time I expected** ça m'a pris le double du temps que je pensais; **to pay d. (the price)** payer le double (du prix); **I am d. your age** je suis deux fois plus âgé que vous, j'ai deux fois votre âge

  N **1** *(of person)* double *m*, Fam sosie *m*; Theat, Cin doublure *f*

  2 Fam *(hotel room)* chambre *f* à deux personnes

  3 *(measure of drink)* double *m*; **make mine a d.** un double pour moi

  4 Tennis **men's/women's/mixed doubles** double *m* messieurs/dames/mixte; **a doubles match** un double; **to play doubles** jouer des doubles

  5 Horseracing pari *m* couplé; **to bring off a d.** réussir un double

  6 Cards *(at bridge)* contre *m*; *(at dominoes)* double *m*; Billiards doublé *m*; **d. or quits** quitte ou double

  7 **on** *or* **at the d.** Mil au pas de gymnastique, au pas de course; Fig *(quickly)* en moins de deux; *(immediately, right away)* tout de suite, sur-le-champ

  VT **1** *(increase)* *(amount, salary etc)* doubler; *(figure)* porter au double, multiplier par deux; **to d. the stakes** doubler la mise

  2 *(fold)* *(paper, blanket etc)* plier en deux; *(thread)* doubler

  3 Cards *(at bridge)* contrer; Billiards **to d. the red** doubler la rouge

  4 Naut *(headland)* doubler

  VI **1** *(of population, salary etc)* doubler; **to d. in value** doubler de valeur

  2 to d. as servir de; **the smallest bedroom doubles as my study** la chambre la plus petite me sert également de bureau; Theat **to d. as sb** jouer qn en plus d'un rôle principal

  ▸▸ **d. ace** *(in dice game, dominoes)* double-as *m*, *pl* doubles-as; **d. agent** agent *m* double; Mus **d. bass** contrebasse *f*; Mus **d. bassoon** contrebasson *m*; **d. bed** grand lit *m*, lit à deux places; **d. bedroom** chambre *f* pour deux personnes; **d. bill** Cin = séance *f* avec deux longs métrages à la suite; TV = programmation *f* de deux longs métrages à la suite; Psy **d. bind** double contrainte *f*; Br **d. bluff** = technique *f* consistant à faire croire qu'on bluffe alors qu'on dit la vérité; **d. boiler** casserole *f* à double fond; **d. chin** menton *m*; Comput **d. click** double-clic *m*, *pl* doubles-clics; Br **d. cream** crème *f* épaisse, Can crème à fouetter, Suisse double crème; Typ **d. dagger** diésis *m*; **d. Dutch** Br Fam charabia *m*, baragouin *m*; Am *(game)* double dutch *m*; **d. entendre** mot *m* *ou* expression *f* à double sens; Acct **d. entry book-keeping** comptabilité *f* en partie double; Phot **d. exposure** surimpression *f*; Sport **d. fault** double faute *f*; Cin **d. feature** = séance avec deux longs métrages à la suite; **d. helix** double hélice *f*; Med **d. incontinence** incontinence *f* double; Am Ins **d. indemnity** = clause *f* d'une assurance-vie qui stipule qu'en cas de mort accidentelle de l'assuré la prime est doublée; **d. knitting** grosse laine *f*; Gram **d. negative** double négation *f*; **d. occupancy** *(of hotel room)* occupation *f* double; St Exch **d. option** stellage *m*; Journ **d. page spread** page *f* centrale, double page; *(advert)* pub *f* double page; **d. parking** stationnement *m* en double file; Med **d. pneumonia** pneumonie *f* double; **to have d. pneumonia** faire une pneumonie double; Typ **d. quotes** guillemets *mpl*; Br **d. saucepan** casserole *f* à double fond; **d. sink** évier *m* à

deux bacs; Typ **d. spacing** double interligne *m*; Comput **d. strike** double passage *m* (de la tête d'impression); **d. strike printing** impression *f* à double frappe; TV, Cin **d. take** double prise *f*, Fam **to do a d. take** marquer un temps d'arrêt *(par surprise)*; **he did a d. take when I told him** lorsque je le lui ai dit il a marqué un temps d'arrêt; **d. talk** propos *mpl* ambigus *ou* équivoques; Fin **d. taxation** double imposition *f*; **d. time** *(pay)* salaire *m* double; Mil pas *m* redoublé; Mus mesure *f*; **in d. time** Mil au pas de gymnastique, au pas de course; Fam *(very quickly)* en moins de rien; *(immediately, right away)* tout de suite, sur-le-champ; Typ **d. underlining** double soulignement *m*; Med **d. vision** double vision *f*, Fam **d. whammy** double coup *m* de malchance; Br **d. white line** *(on road)* double ligne *f* blanche *(d'interdiction de doubler)*; **d. yellow line** *(on road)* double ligne jaune *(qui indique une zone de stationnement interdit)*

  ▸ **double back** VT SEP *(blanket etc)* replier, rabattre

  VI **to d. back (on one's tracks)** *(of person, hunted animal etc)* revenir sur ses pas; **to d. back on itself** *(of road)* tourner en épingle à cheveux

  ▸ **double for** VT INSEP remplacer; Theat doubler; Cin *(of stuntman)* être la doublure de

  ▸ **double over** VI se plier; **to d. over with pain** se plier en deux de douleur, se tordre de douleur

  VT SEP replier, rabattre

  ▸ **double up** VI **1** *(bend over)* se plier (en deux), se courber (en deux); **to d. up with laughter/pain** se tordre de rire/douleur

  2 *(share room)* partager une chambre

  VT SEP **1** *(paper, material etc)* plier en deux

  2 *(of blow, pain etc)* *(person)* faire plier en deux

double-acting ADJ Tech à double effet

double-barrelled [-'bærəld] ADJ *(shotgun)* à deux coups

  ▸▸ Br **d. name** = nom *m* de famille composé (p.ex. Burnes-Jones) indiquant souvent une origine aristocratique

double-blind ADJ Med *(test)* test *m* à double insu

double-book VT *(seat, room)* réserver pour deux personnes différentes, sur-réserver; **we've been double-booked again** nous sommes encore en double réservation; **I've double-booked myself for next Friday** *(doing two things)* je me suis engagé à faire deux choses différentes vendredi prochain

  VI *(of hotel, airline)* faire une/des double(s) réservation(s)

double-booking N double réservation *f*

double-bottomed [-'bɒtəmd] ADJ *(saucepan, suitcase etc)* à double fond; *(dinghy etc)* à double coque

double-breasted [-'brestɪd] ADJ *(jacket)* croisé

double-check VT & VI revérifier

double-click VT cliquer deux fois sur, double-cliquer

  VI Comput cliquer deux fois, faire un double-clic

double-clutch VI Am Aut faire un double débrayage

double-cross Fam VT doubler, trahir

  N trahison *f*, tromperie *f*

double-crosser ['dʌb(ə)l'krɒsər] N traître, -esse

double-dealer N fourbe *m*

double-dealing N duplicité *f*

  ADJ déloyal, -aux

double-decker ['dʌbəl'dekər] N **1** Br *(bus)* autobus *m* à impériale **2** *esp Am (sandwich)* sandwich *m* double

double-declutch vi *Br Aut* faire un double débrayage

double-declutching [ˈdʌb(ə)ldiːˈklʌtʃɪŋ] N *Br Aut* double débrayage *m*

double-density ADJ *Comput (disk)* à double densité

double-edged ADJ *(sword, compliment, argument)* à deux tranchants

double-faced [-ˈfeɪst] ADJ **1** *Tex* réversible **2** *Pej (person)* à double face, hypocrite

double-glaze vt **to have the windows double-glazed** poser du double vitrage; **they've just had their house double-glazed** ils viennent de faire poser du double vitrage chez eux

double-glazed ADJ à double vitrage

double-glazing N double vitrage *m*; **to put in d.** installer *ou* poser du double vitrage

double-headed ADJ à deux têtes, *Spec* bicéphale; *TV (programme)* animé par deux présentateurs
► ► **d. coin** pièce *f* de monnaie à deux faces; *Her* **d. eagle** aigle *f* à deux têtes

double-header N *Am Sl* = deux matchs *mpl* disputés l'un après l'autre

double-jointed ADJ *(person, limb)* désarticulé

double-lock vt *(door etc)* fermer à double tour

double-park vt & vi *Aut* stationner en double file

double-pointed ADJ *Knitting (needle)* à double pointe

double-quick ADJ, ADV **in d. time, d.** *Mil* au pas de gymnastique, au pas de course; *Fam (very quickly)* en moins de rien; *(immediately, right away)* tout de suite, sur-le-champ

double-space vt *(write/type) (text)* écrire/ taper en double interligne, mettre en double interligne; **double-spaced** en double interligne

double-speak N propos *mpl* ambigus *ou* équivoques; **rationalization is just d. for more unemployment** rationalisation n'est qu'un euphémisme pour plus de chômage

double-speed ADJ *Comput (CD-ROM)* double vitesse

double-stop vi (-pp-) *Mus (on violin)* faire des doubles-cordes

double-stopping N *Mus* double-corde *f*

doublet [ˈdʌblɪt] N **1** *Ling* doublet *m* **2** *Hist (jacket)* pourpoint *m*, justaucorps *m*

double-think N raisonnement *m* contradictoire

doubling [ˈdʌblɪŋ] N *(of number etc)* doublement *m*

doubly [ˈdʌb(ə)lɪ] ADV doublement; **to be d. careful/interested** redoubler de prudence/ d'intérêt

doubt [daʊt] N doute *m*; **to be in d.** *(of person)* être en *ou* dans le doute; *(of future, event)* être douteux *ou* incertain; **I'm in no d. as to …** je ne doute absolument pas de …; **to raise doubts in sb's mind** soulever des doutes dans l'esprit de qn; **the whole thing raised doubts about his abilities** toute cette affaire a mis ses capacités en question; **when in d.** dans le doute; **to cast doubt(s) on sth** mettre qch en doute; **to have one's doubts about sth** avoir des doutes sur *ou* au sujet de qch; **I have my doubts whether this is true** je doute que cela soit vrai; **beyond (a shadow of a) d.** sans aucun doute; **the facts have been established beyond (all) d.** ces faits ont été avérés sans le moindre doute; **no d. he will come** il viendra sans doute; **there is** *or* **seems to be no d. that …** il ne semble faire aucun doute que …; **there is no d. about her guilt** il n'y a au-

cun doute sur sa culpabilité; **there is some d. about her guilt** il y a des doutes quant à sa culpabilité; **is there any d. in your mind?** est-ce qu'il y a un doute dans votre esprit?; **do you have any doubts?** est-ce que vous avez des doutes?; *(about getting married etc)* est-ce que vous hésitez?; **I have no doubts** je n'ai aucun doute; **to leave no (room for) d.** ne laisser aucun doute (**that** sur le fait que); **without (a** *or* **any** *or* **the slightest) d.** sans aucun doute
► vt *(person)* douter de; *(person's word)* douter de, mettre en doute; **I d. we'll be hearing** *or* **I d. if we'll hear from him again** je doute que nous entendions à nouveau parler de lui; **I d. it** j'en doute; **he made me d. the evidence of my own eyes** il m'a fait douter de ce que je voyais de mes propres yeux; **I d. whether** *or* **if he will come** je doute qu'il vienne
► vi *(have doubts)* douter

doubter [ˈdaʊtər] N sceptique *mf*

doubtful [ˈdaʊtfʊl] ADJ **1** *(undecided) (person)* indécis, incertain; *(future, outcome, weather)* incertain; **to be d. of** *or* **about sth** avoir des doutes sur qch; **I'm d. about going** j'hésite à y aller; **I'm d. about the wisdom/ advisability of it** je doute que ce soit bien sage/conseillé; **John's a bit d. for Saturday** il n'est pas sûr qu'on puisse compter sur John samedi; **she's a d. starter (for the race)** il n'est pas certain qu'elle prenne le départ (de la course); **it is d. whether …** il est douteux *ou* à douter que … **2** *(questionable) (character, appearance)* équivoque, suspect; *(origin, decision, food)* douteux; **in d. taste** d'un goût douteux
► ► *Fin* **d. debt** créance *f* douteuse; **d. loan** prêt *m* douteux

doubtfully [ˈdaʊtfʊlɪ] ADV *(to say)* d'un ton dubitatif, dubitativement; *(to watch)* d'un air dubitatif; *(to stand etc)* en hésitant, d'une façon indécise

doubting [ˈdaʊtɪŋ] ADJ incrédule, sceptique
► ► **d. Thomas** incrédule *mf*; **you're always such a d. Thomas** tu es toujours tellement sceptique

doubtless(ly) [ˈdaʊtlɪs(lɪ)] ADV **1** *(certainly)* sans aucun doute **2** *(probably)* sans doute, sûrement

douche [duːʃ] N **1** *(cleansing)* douche *f*, *Med* lavage *m* interne; *(as contraceptive)* douche vaginale; **to be like a d. of cold water** faire l'effet d'une douche froide **2** *Med (instrument)* poire *f* à injection
► vt doucher

dough [dəʊ] N **1** *(for bread etc)* pâte *f* **2** *Old-fashioned Sl (money)* fric *m*, pognon *m*

doughboy [ˈdəʊbɔɪ] N *Hist* = soldat *m* américain de la première guerre mondiale

doughnut [ˈdəʊnʌt] N *Culin* beignet *m*, *Can* beigne *m*; **jam d.** beignet à la confiture

doughty [ˈdaʊtɪ] ADJ *Arch, Lit* vaillant

doughy [ˈdəʊɪ] ADJ **1** *(bread)* pâteux **2** *Fig (face)* terreux

dour [dʊər] ADJ austère, sévère

douse [daʊs] vt **1** *(splash) (person, object)* arroser, asperger (**with** de); *(plunge)* plonger, tremper; **he doused himself with** *or* **in aftershave** il s'est aspergé d'après-rasage **2** *(extinguish) (light, fire)* éteindre

dove [dʌv] N *(bird)* colombe *f*; **ring d.** (pigeon *m*) ramier *m*, palombe *f*; **d. of peace** colombe de la paix; *Pol* **the doves and the hawks** les colombes et les faucons
ADJ **d.(-coloured** *or* **-grey)** colombin, gorge-de-pigeon *inv*

dovecote [ˈdʌvkɒt] N colombier *m*, pigeonnier *m*

Dover [ˈdəʊvər] N Douvres; **the Straits of D.** le Pas de Calais

dovetail [ˈdʌvteɪl] N *Carp* queue-d'aronde *f*, *pl* queues-d'aronde
► vt *Carp* assembler à queue-d'aronde; *Fig* **to d. two schemes (together** *or* **into each other)** harmoniser deux projets
► vi *(of schemes etc)* se rejoindre, se raccorder (**with** à)
► ► **d. joint** assemblage *m* à queue-d'aronde

dovish [ˈdʌvɪʃ] ADJ *esp Am Pol (person)* partisan de la manière douce; *(speech)* conciliateur

dowager [ˈdaʊədʒər] N douairière *f*
► ► **d. duchess** duchesse *f* douairière; *Fam* **d.'s hump** = bosse *f* qui se développe chez les femmes d'un certain âge suite à une carence de calcium, bosse de sorcière

dowdiness [ˈdaʊdɪnɪs] N manque *m* d'élégance *ou* de chic

dowdy [ˈdaʊdɪ] ADJ peu élégant; *(dress, image)* démodé

dowel [ˈdaʊəl] N *Carp, Tech (location device)* téton *m* (de positionnement)
► ► **d. pin** *(wooden)* cheville *f*, goujon *m*, tourillon *m*

dowelling [ˈdaʊəlɪŋ] N *(material)* bois *m* à goujons *ou* tourillons

dower [ˈdaʊər] N
► ► *Br* **d. house** petit manoir *m* (de douairière)

Dow-Jones [ˈdaʊˈdʒəʊnz] N *St Exch* index *m* Dow Jones
► ► **D. average, D. index** index Dow Jones

Down [daʊn] N
► ► *Med* **D.'s syndrome** mongolisme *m*, *Spec* trisomie *f* 21; **D.'s syndrome baby** bébé *m* mongolien *ou* *Spéc* trisomique

DOWN¹ [daʊn]

ADV	vers le bas **1** ▪ en bas **3**
PREP	le long de ▪ en bas de
ADJ	déprimé
VT	abattre **1** ▪ descendre **2**

ADV **1** *(motion)* vers le bas; **I'll be d. in a minute** je descends dans une minute; **to lay d. one's arms** mettre bas les armes; **to shoot** *or* **bring d. an aircraft** abattre *ou Fam* descendre un avion; **to fall d.** tomber à terre *ou* par terre; **d. to the ground** jusqu'à terre; *Fam* **it suits me d. to the ground** ça me va parfaitement; **d. with traitors!** à bas les traîtres!; **d. with it!** *(of medicine etc)* avalez!; **d.!** *(to dog)* couché!; **d. you go!** allez, descends!
2 *(in crossword)* verticalement; **I can't get five d.** je ne trouve pas le cinq vertical
3 *(position, level)* **d. below** en bas, en contre-bas; **d. here** ici; *Am* **d. South** dans les États du sud; *Br Fam* **d. under** aux antipodes *(toujours en référence à l'Australie et à la Nouvelle-Zélande)*; **d. there** là-bas; **further d.** plus bas; **the blinds were d.** les stores étaient baissés; **to lay sth face d.** placer qch face en dessous *ou* à l'envers; **head d.** la tête en bas; *Fig* **to hit a man when he's d.** frapper un homme à terre; **she's d. with flu** elle est grippée; *Fam* **that gets me d.** ça me déprime; *Tel* **the lines are d.** les lignes sont coupées; **the wind is d.** le vent est tombé *ou* s'est apaisé; **the river is d.** la rivière est basse; **the price of gold is d.** le prix de l'or a baissé; **he's £20 d. on the deal** il en est pour 20 livres de sa poche; **bookings are d. on last week's** les réservations sont en baisse par rapport à la semaine dernière; **takings are several hundred pounds d. on last year** les recettes ont baissé de plusieurs centaines de livres par rapport à l'année dernière; *Fin* **to be d. 12% on last year** être en baisse de 12% par rapport à l'année précédente; **your team is five-two d.** ton équipe est en train de perdre par cinq à deux
4 *(order, time)* **everyone from the boss d.**

tout le monde, y compris le patron; **from prince d. to beggar** du prince jusqu'au mendiant; **I'm d. to my last cigarette/cheque** j'en suis à ma dernière cigarette/mon dernier chèque; **d. to recent times** jusqu'au temps présent; **d. to here** (en descendant) jusqu'ici; **one d., nine to go!** un de moins, plus que neuf!

5 (*in writing*) **to put** *or* **get sth d. (in writing)** coucher *ou* mettre qch par écrit; **if I was you, I'd get that d. in writing** *or* **on paper** (*as opposed to taking sb's word for it*) à ta place, j'essaierais d'obtenir ça noir sur blanc; **there's nothing d. on paper yet** il n'y a encore rien d'officiel; **but there's nothing d. on paper to that effect** mais il n'y a aucun écrit à cet effet; **she's d. for 20 boxes** (*has reserved*) elle a réservé 20 boîtes; **she's d. for £20** (*has agreed to donate*) elle est inscrite pour une cotisation de 20 livres; **he's d. for the 100 metres** il est inscrit pour le 100 mètres; **I've got you d. to present the bouquet** tu as été désigné pour offrir le bouquet

6 (*phrases*) **to be d. on sb** en vouloir à qn; *Comput* **to be d.** être en panne; **it's d. to you whether or not we go** (*it's your decision*) c'est à toi de décider si nous y allons ou pas; **this is all d. to you!** (*your fault*) tout cela est de ta faute!; **our lack of cash is all d. to the repairs to the roof** (*is attributable to*) notre manque d'argent est entièrement dû aux réparations du toit; **it was d. to his hard work that we managed to finish** c'est grâce à son travail acharné que nous avons réussi à terminer; **money d., cash d.** argent (au) comptant *ou* sur table; **you can have it for £50 d.** c'est à vous pour 50 livres au comptant; **to go d. by the bows** (*of ship*) piquer de l'avant

PREP to slide d. sth glisser le long de qch; **the tears ran d. his face** les larmes lui coulaient le long des joues; **d. the side of his trousers/the box** le long de son pantalon/de la boîte; **to go d. the street/a hill** descendre la rue/une colline; **to fall d. the stairs** tomber en bas de l'escalier; *Fam* **get that d. you** (*food, drink*) avale ça!; *Fam* **he's gone d. the pub** il est allé au pub; *Fam* **to go d. the shops** aller faire des courses; **they live further d. the street** ils habitent plus bas dans cette rue; *Lit* **d. the centuries/years** au long des siècles/années; *Rail* **d. the line** en aval

ADJ (*depressed*) découragé, déprimé; **to be d. (in the mouth)** être découragé *ou* déprimé; **you look very d.** tu as l'air très déprimé

N *Fam* **to have a d. on sb** en vouloir à qn
VT 1 (*person*) terrasser; *Boxing* (*opponent*) abattre; (*aircraft*) descendre, abattre
2 *Ind* **d. tools** cesser le travail
3 *Fam* **to d. a drink** s'envoyer un verre; **he downed his beer and left** il a descendu sa bière et est parti; **to d. sth in one (go)** *or* **in a oner** avaler qch d'un coup

▸▸ *Comput* **d. arrow** flèche *f* vers le bas; *Comput* **d. arrow key** touche *f* de déplacement vers le bas; *Fin* **d. payment** acompte *m*; **d. time** (*of machine*) temps *m* de non-disponibilité *ou* d'immobilisation; *Rail Old-fashioned* **d. train** train *m* descendant

down² N (*on bird, person, fruit*) duvet *m*; (*on plant*) poil *m*, coton *m*, duvet

down³ N *Geog* (*usu pl*) **downs** chaîne *f* de collines crétacées; *Br* **the (North/South) Downs** les Downs *mpl*

down-and-out ADJ **to be d.** être sans le sou
N clochard, -arde

down-at-heel ADJ **1** (*shoe*) éculé **2** (*person*) miteux

downbeat ['daʊnbiːt] N *Mus* (temps *m*) frappé *m*
ADJ *Fam* **1** (*gloomy*) (*ending, story*) triste;

(*speech, person*) pessimiste **2** (*relaxed*) relaxe

downcast ['daʊnkɑːst] ADJ **1** (*person*) abattu, déprimé; **there's no need to be so d.** il ne faut pas se laisser abattre *ou* se décourager comme ça; **to look d.** avoir l'air découragé **2** (*look, eyes etc*) baissé

downdraught, *Am* **downdraft** ['daʊndrɑːft] N *Met* courant *m* d'air descendant
▸▸ *Aut* **d. carburettor** carburateur *m* inversé

downer ['daʊnər] N *Sl* **1** (*drug*) tranquillisant *m* **2** (*depressing situation, experience*) **to be on a d.** avoir le moral à zéro, être au trente-sixième dessous; **she's a real d.** elle vous met le moral à zéro; **it was a real d. to find out I hadn't even got an interview** ça m'a mis le moral complètement à zéro de savoir que je n'avais même pas obtenu d'entretien

downfall ['daʊnfɔːl] N (*of person*) ruine *f*, (*of government etc*) écroulement *m*, effondrement *m*; **drink brought about** *or* **was his d.** la boisson l'a perdu

downgrade ['daʊngreɪd] VT (*move to lower position*) (*employee*) rétrograder, déclasser à une échelle de salaire inférieure; (*goods*) classer dans une catégorie inférieure; **he was downgraded to area manager** il a été rétrogradé au rang de responsable régional; **the hurricane has been downgraded to a storm** l'ouragan n'est maintenant plus qu'une tempête
N *esp Am* descente *f*, déclivité *f*, *Fig* **to be on the d.** baisser, être sur le déclin *ou Fam* sur le retour

downgrading ['daʊngreɪdɪŋ] N (*of employee*) = déclassement *m* à une échelle de salaire inférieure, rétrogradation *f*, (*of goods*) classement *m* dans une catégorie inférieure

downhearted [daʊn'hɑːtɪd] ADJ découragé, déprimé; **don't be d.!** ne te décourage pas!, ne te laisse pas abattre!; **to become d.** se décourager

downhill ['daʊn'hɪl] N **1** descente *f*, pente *f* **2** *Ski* descente *f*
ADJ (*slope*) descendante; **the d. journey** la descente
ADV **to go d.** (*of road, car*) descendre; *Fig Fam* (*of person*) être sur le déclin; (*of business etc*) péricliter; (*of sb's work*) devenir moins bon; **it's d. all the way** ça descend tout le long du chemin; *Hum* **it's d. all the way after you're 40** après 40 ans, on ne fait que décliner; **after January it'll be d. all the way** (*easier*) après janvier le pire sera passé
▸▸ **d. skier** descendeur, -euse; **d. skiing** ski *m* alpin

Downing Street ['daʊnɪŋstriːt] N *Br Pol* = résidence *f* officielle du Premier ministre (n° 10) et du ministre des Finances (n° 11); **there has been no confirmation from D.** le Premier ministre n'a pas apporté de confirmation

---

Downing Street

C'est à Downing Street à Londres que se trouvent les résidences officielles du Premier ministre, au n° 10, et du ministre des Finances, au n° 11. Le terme "Downing Street" est souvent employé pour désigner le gouvernement.

---

download ['daʊnləʊd] *Comput* N téléchargement *m*
VT télécharger
VI effectuer un téléchargement; **graphic files take a long time to d.** le téléchargement de fichiers graphiques est très lent
▸▸ **d. font** police *f* téléchargeable

downloadable [daʊn'ləʊdəb(ə)l] ADJ *Comput* téléchargeable

downloading [daʊn'ləʊdɪŋ] N *Comput* téléchargement *m*

down-low N *Am Fam* **on the d.** (*confidential*) confidentiel; **I'm telling you this on the d.** je te dis ça, mais c'est entre nous

down-market ADJ (*car, house etc*) bas de gamme; (*person*) ordinaire; (*district, accent*) populaire
ADV **to move d.** passer au bas de gamme; (*go to a cheap restaurant etc*) donner dans le populaire

downpipe ['daʊnpaɪp] N *Constr* tuyau *m* de descente

downplay [daʊn'pleɪ] VT minimiser

downpour ['daʊnpɔːr] N averse *f*

downright ['daʊnraɪt] ADV (*idiotic etc*) tout à fait, complètement; (*rude, disgusting, nosy*) carrément
ADJ **1** (*complete, absolute*) (*stupidity, carelessness, dishonesty*) absolu; (*lie*) éclatant; **d. fool** parfait *ou* franc imbécile **2** (*blunt, frank*) (*person, language*) direct, franc, *f* franche

downshift ['daʊnʃɪft] VI **1** *Am Aut* rétrograder **2** (*change one's lifestyle*) = passer à un emploi moins stressant

downshifting ['daʊnʃɪftɪŋ] N = passage *m* à un emploi moins stressant

downside ['daʊnsaɪd] N désavantage *m* (**to sth** de qch); **there's a d. to everything** toute médaille a son revers; **on the d., however, the situation has worsened in the South** mais par contre la situation a empiré dans le sud; **on the d., we'll have to sleep in the train** le désavantage, c'est que nous devrons dormir dans le train
▸▸ *St Exch* **d. potential** potentiel *m* de baisse; *St Exch* **d. risk** risque *m* de baisse

downsize [daʊn'saɪz] VT *Electron* microniser; (*project*) réduire l'envergure de; (*of designers*) (*car*) réduire les dimensions de; **downsized car** voiture aux dimensions réduites
VI (*of company*) réduire ses effectifs

downsizing [daʊn'saɪzɪŋ] N **1** *Electron* micronisation *f* **2** (*of company*) réduction *f* des effectifs

downspout ['daʊnspaʊt] N tuyau *m* de descente

downstage ['daʊnsteɪdʒ] *Théâtre* ADV, sur le devant (de la scène), à l'avant-scène; **to stand d. of sb** se tenir plus en avant que qn sur la scène; **take two paces d.** fais deux pas vers le devant de la scène
N avant-scène *f*

downstairs ADV [daʊn'steəz] **1** (*down the stairs*) en bas; **to come/go d.** descendre (l'escalier); **to run d.** descendre (l'escalier) en courant **2** (*on a lower floor*) en bas; **our neighbours d.** nos voisins d'en-dessous
ADJ ['daʊnsteəz] **the d. rooms** les pièces d'en bas *ou* du bas
N ['daʊnsteəz] l'étage *m* du bas

downstate ['daʊnsteɪt] *Am* ADJ **in d. New York** dans le sud de l'État de New York
ADV au sud de l'État

downstream ADV [daʊn'striːm] en aval, à l'aval (**from** de); **a few miles d. from here** quelques miles en aval d'ici
ADJ ['daʊnstriːm] d'aval
▸▸ *TV* **d. keyer** incrustateur *m* après mélange; *Petr* **d. operations** opérations *fpl* en aval

downstroke ['daʊnstrəʊk] N **1** (*in writing*) plein *m* **2** *Tech* course *f* descendante; (*of piston*) mouvement *m* de descente **3** *Orn* (*of wing*) abaissée *f*

downswept ['daʊnswept] ADJ *Aviat* (*wings*) surbaissé

downswing ['daʊnswɪŋ] N *(in economy etc)* tendance *f* à la baisse

down-to-earth ADJ *(person, approach, attitude)* terre(-)à(-)terre *inv*, réaliste

downtown ['daʊn'taʊn] *Am* ADV dans/vers (le centre de) la ville; **he gave me a lift d.** il m'a descendu en ville; **to live d.** habiter en ville

ADJ **d. New York** le centre de New York; **d. theatres** théâtres *mpl* du centre

N *(of town)* centre *m*

downtrodden ['daʊntrɒd(ə)n] ADJ **1** *Fig (people, wife etc)* opprimé **2** *(grass etc)* piétiné

downturn ['daʊntɜːn] N *(in inflation, unemployment figures)* baisse *f*, *(in economy)* ralentissement *m*; **to take a d.** *(of economy)* ralentir; *(of inflation, unemployment)* baisser; **their fortunes took a sudden d. when ...** leur fortune a connu un soudain revers quand ...

downward ['daʊnwəd] ADJ *(movement, path)* descendant; **to take a d. glance** *or* **look at sth** jeter un coup d'œil par en dessous à qch; *Fig* **to be on the d. path** aller à sa perte; *Fin* **d. movement** mouvement *m* de baisse; **d. trend** *(in prices etc)* tendance *f* à la baisse

ADV = **downwards**

downward-compatible ADJ *Comput* compatible vers le bas

downwards ['daʊnwədz] ADV vers le bas, en descendant; *(on river)* en aval; *(to look)* en bas; **to slope d.** descendre; **to lay sth face d.** placer qch face en dessous; **from the twelfth century d.** à partir du *ou* depuis le douzième siècle; **children of five and d.** enfants de cinq ans et au-dessous; **every member of the cabinet, from the Prime Minister d.** tout le monde, du Premier ministre au dernier membre du gouvernement

downwind ADV ['daʊn'wɪnd] *Aviat (to land)* vent arrière; **to move d. of an animal** se déplacer sous le vent d'un animal; *Hum* **it's best to stand d. of old Mr Wilson** il vaut mieux ne pas trop s'approcher du vieux M. Wilson

ADJ ['daʊnwɪnd] *Aviat (landing)* vent arrière

downy ['daʊnɪ] ADJ duveteux, duveté; *(fruit)* velouté, duveté

dowry ['daʊrɪ] N dot *f*

dowse[1] ['daʊz] VI faire de la radiesthésie; **to d. for water** chercher de l'eau à l'aide d'une baguette de sourcier

dowse[2] ['daʊs] VT = **douse**

dowser ['daʊzər] N sourcier *m*, radiesthésiste *mf*

dowsing ['daʊzɪŋ] N radiesthésie *f*
▸▸ **d. rod** baguette *f* (de sourcier)

doyen ['dɔɪjən] N doyen *m* (d'âge)

doyenne ['dɔɪjen] N doyenne *f* (d'âge)

doz *(abbr* **dozen)** d(ou)z

doze [daʊz] N petit somme *m*; **to have a d.** faire un petit somme; **to fall into a d.** s'assoupir

VI somnoler
▸ **doze off** VI s'assoupir

dozen ['dʌz(ə)n] N VOIR GRAMMAIRE A12–13; B60
1 *(inv)* douzaine *f*; **a d. eggs** une douzaine d'œufs; **half a d., a half d.** une demi-douzaine; **£5 a d./half d.** cinq livres la douzaine/demi-douzaine; **six d. bottles of wine** six douzaines de bouteilles de vin; **by the d.** à la douzaine **2** *(pl* **dozens) they arrived in their dozens** ils arrivèrent par douzaines; **dozens of people have asked me about it** des dizaines de personnes me l'ont demandé; **to have dozens of things to do** avoir des tas de choses à faire; **dozens and dozens of times** maintes et maintes fois; **a baker's d., thirteen to the d.** treize à la douzaine;

Fam **to talk nineteen to the d.** bavarder comme une pie

dozenth ['dʌz(ə)nθ] ADJ douzième

dozily ['dəʊzɪlɪ] ADV *(to watch)* d'un œil somnolent; *(to answer)* d'une voix endormie

doziness ['dəʊzɪnɪs] N **1** somnolence *f* **2** *Br Fam (stupidity)* bêtise *f*

dozy ['dəʊzɪ] ADJ **1** somnolent, assoupi; **to feel d.** avoir envie de dormir **2** *Br Fam (stupid)* nunuche

DP [di:'pi:] N *Comput (abbr* **data processing)** traitement *m* des données, informatique *f*; **DP manager** chef *m* des traitements

D Phil [di:'fɪl] N *Univ abbr* **Doctor of Philosophy**

dpi [di:pi:'aɪ] *Comput (abbr* **dots per inch)** dpi, ppp

DPP [di:pi:'pi:] N *Br Law abbr* **Director of Public Prosecutions**

dpt *abbr* **department**

Dr 1 *(abbr* **doctor)** Dr. **2** *(abbr* **Drive)** av.

drab [dræb] ADJ **1** *(colour)* terne; *(clothing)* de couleur terne **2** *Fig (surroundings, routine)* morne, monotone; *(existence)* terne, monotone; *(person)* insignifiant

N **1** *(colour)* olivâtre *m* **2** *(material) (grey)* tissu *m* gris; *(brown)* tissu brun

drably ['dræblɪ] ADV de façon terne; **d. coloured** aux couleurs ternes *ou* mornes

drabness ['dræbnɪs] N *(of surroundings, existence)* monotonie *f*; **the d. of her clothes** ses vêtements ternes

drachm [dræm] N *(measurement)* drachme *f*

drachma, *pl* **drachmas** ['drækmə, -məz] N *Formerly* drachme *f*

draconian [drə'kəʊnɪən] ADJ draconien, -ienne

draft[1] [drɑːft] N **1** *(of letter)* brouillon *m*; *(of law)* projet *m*; *(of treaty)* avant-projet *m*, *pl* avant-projets; *Archit, Tech etc* dessin *m* schématique, tracé *m*; **rough d.** *(of map etc)* ébauche *f*, *(of novel)* premier jet *m* d'un roman; **do you want it in d.?** tu le veux au brouillon?; **first d. of a novel** premier jet *m* d'un roman

2 *Com* traite *f*, **banker's d.** chèque *m* bancaire

3 *Am Mil (conscription)* conscription *f*, **to be d. age** être en âge de faire son service

4 *Mil (group) (of troops)* détachement *m*; *(of recruits)* contingent *m*

VT **1** *(letter)* faire le brouillon de; *(deed, project)* rédiger; *Pol* **to d. a bill** établir un projet de loi

2 *Am Mil (conscript)* appeler sous les drapeaux

3 *Mil (detach) (troops)* détacher, envoyer en détachement; *(soldier)* affecter (**to** à); **to d. troops into ...** faire passer des troupes dans ...; *Fig* **could we d. in some outside help?** est-ce que nous pourrions obtenir de l'aide à l'extérieur?; **she had been drafted in from the Foreign Office** on l'avait fait venir du ministère des affaires étrangères

▸▸ **d. agreement** projet *m* de contrat; *Am Mil* **d. board** conseil *m* de révision; **d. budget** projet de budget; *Am Mil* **d. card** ordre *m* d'incorporation; **d. contract** projet de contrat; *Am Mil* **d. dodger** réfractaire *m*; *Am Mil* **d. dodging** insoumission *f*, **d. legislation** projet d'acte législatif; *Br Comput* **d. mode** mode *m* rapide *ou* brouillon; *Comput* **d. printout** brouillon *m*; *Br Comput* **d. quality** qualité *f* brouillon; *Comput* **d. quality printing** impression *f* en qualité brouillon; *Comput* **d. version** version *f* brouillon

draft[2] N *Am* = **draught**[1]

draftsman, draftsmanship *etc Am* = **draughtsman, draughtsmanship** *etc*

drafty ['drɑːftɪ] ADJ *Am* = **draughty**

drag [dræg] N **1** *(in aerodynamics)* résistance

f de l'air; *Aviat* traînée *f*, *Billiards* effet *m* rétrograde

2 *Fam (bore) (person)* raseur, -euse; **it's an awful d.** c'est la barbe, c'est barbant; **the party was a d.** la soirée était rasante; **I don't want to be a d. but ...** je ne voudrais pas être rasoir, mais ...; **what a d. for you!** quelle barbe!

3 *Sl* **to have a d.** *(on cigarette)* tirer une taffe; **she took a quick d. on her cigarette** elle tira vivement sur sa cigarette

4 *Sl (women's clothes worn by man)* costume *m* féminin (porté par un homme); **he was in d.** il portait des vêtements de femme

5 *esp Am Fam* **the (main) d.** la rue principale

6 *Am Fam* **to have d.** *(influence)* avoir du piston

7 *(in hunting)* voie *f* artificielle

8 *(brake)* **to put a d. on a wheel** enrayer une roue; *Fig* **she was a d. on his career** elle entravait sa carrière, elle le freinait dans sa carrière; **I don't want to be a d. on you** *(in career, on walk, climb etc)* je ne veux pas te freiner

9 *(trek)* **it's a long d. to the top of the hill** c'est une sacrée tirée jusqu'en haut de la colline

10 *(for dredging)* drague *f*, *(for retrieving lost object)* araignée *f*, *Naut* grappin *m* à main; *(for helping drowning person)* gaffe *f* de sauvetage

VT **(-gg-) 1** *(pull)* traîner, tirer; *(by force) (person)* entraîner de force *ou* contre sa volonté; **to d. sb's feet** traîner les pieds; *Fig* **to d. one's feet** *or* **heels** tarder (**over doing** à faire); **she dragged her feet over the decision** elle a tardé à se décider; *Fig* **I wish you'd stop dragging your feet** je voudrais bien que tu arrêtes d'atermoyer; **he dragged himself to the door** il se traîna jusqu'à la porte; **to d. its anchor** *(of ship)* déraper; *Fig* **I don't want to d. you through it** je ne veux pas te faire subir ça; *Fig* **he dragged me to the football match** il m'a traîné au match de football; *Fig* **to d. sb through the courts** traîner qn devant les tribunaux

2 *(search) (pond, river)* draguer

3 *Comput (with mouse)* faire glisser; **d. and drop** glisser-lâcher

VI **1** *(of skirt etc)* traîner (à terre)

2 *(progress slowly) (of lawsuit)*, *Theat (of scene etc)* traîner en longueur; *(of conversation)* languir; *(of work)* se traîner; **time is dragging** les heures se traînent; **the meeting finally dragged to a close at 10 pm** la réunion s'est enfin terminée à 10 heures

3 *Tech* offrir de la résistance; *(of brakes)* frotter (sur les roues)

4 *Fam* **to d. on** *or* **at a cigarette** tirer des bouffées d'une cigarette

5 *(search)* draguer (**for sth** pour retrouver qch)

6 *Fishing* pêcher à la drague; **to d. for oysters** pêcher les huîtres à la drague

7 *Comput* **to d. and drop** faire un glisser-lâcher

▸▸ **d. act** numéro *m* de travesti(s); **d. artist** travesti *m*; **d. coefficient** coefficient *m* aérodynamique, coefficient de pénétration dans l'air, Cx *m*; **d. factor** coefficient de traînée; **d. hunt** chasse *f* à courre où la meute suit une piste artificielle, drag *m*; *Aut* **d. link** biellette *f* de direction; *Aut* **d. link bar** bielle *f* pendante; *Fam* **d. queen** travelo *m*; *Am Aut* **d. race** concours *m* d'accélération; **d. show** spectacle *m* de travesti

▸ **drag along** VT SEP *(somebody, something)* traîner

VI *(of dress)* traîner; *(of person)* être à la traîne

▸ **drag apart** VT SEP séparer

▸ **drag away** VT SEP *(person)* entraîner, emmener de force; *(somebody, something)* arracher (**from** de); **I couldn't d. myself away** j'étais cloué sur place; **if you could d. yourself away from the television** si tu pouvais t'arracher de devant la télévision

▸ **drag behind** VT SEP traîner derrière (soi) VI être à la traîne; **stop dragging behind** arrête de traîner comme ça

▸ **drag down** VT SEP **1** (person, object) entraîner en bas; (by force) (person) faire descendre de force; also Fig **he dragged me down with him** il m'a entraîné dans sa chute; **to d. sb down to one's level** faire descendre qn à son niveau **2** (of illness etc) (person) déprimer

▸ **drag in** VT SEP **1** (pull in) traîner; (by force) faire entrer de force **2** Fam (refer to) faire allusion à; **why do you always have to d. in my one mistake?** pourquoi est-ce que tu te crois obligé de faire sans arrêt allusion à ma seule erreur?

▸ **drag into** VT SEP **1** (involve) **don't d. me into this!** ne me mêle pas à ça!; **he keeps dragging her name into the conversation** il n'arrête pas de glisser son nom dans la conversation

▸ **drag off** VT SEP = **drag away**

▸ **drag on** VI (of meeting, business etc) s'éterniser, traîner en longueur; **to let a matter d. on** laisser traîner une affaire; **the play dragged on and on** la pièce n'en finissait pas; **the exams seemed to d. on for ages** les examens semblaient n'en plus finir

▸ **drag out** VT SEP **1** (heavy object, person) traîner à l'extérieur; (by force) (person) faire sortir de force; **to d. sb out of bed** tirer qn de son lit; **to d. the truth/a confession out of sb** arracher la vérité/des aveux à qn; **I finally managed to d. out of him the reason why he was so upset** j'ai finalement réussi à lui faire dire pourquoi il était si retourné **2** (speech, presentation, matter) faire traîner; Lit **to d. out a wretched existence** traîner une existence misérable

▸ **drag up** VT **1** (object, person) entraîner ou tirer jusqu'en haut; Fam **you dragged me up to London for this?** et c'est pour ça que tu m'as fait venir à Londres? **2** Fam (refer to) (old story) déterrer **3** Fam (raise badly) **those children are being dragged up** ces enfants sont élevés n'importe comment; **where were you dragged up?** où as-tu été élevé?

drag-and-drop N Comput glisser-lâcher m inv

dragging ['drægɪŋ] ADJ **d. step** pas m traînant

N **1** (of something heavy behind one etc) traînement m; Naut **d. of the anchor** dérapage m **2** (of pond, river) dragage m

draggy ['drægɪ] ADJ Fam **1** (boring) (evening, party) ennuyeux, barbant **2** (listless) pas dans son assiette; **to feel a bit d.** ne pas être dans son assiette

draglift ['dræglɪft] N tire-fesses m inv

dragnet ['drægnet] N **1** (organized by police) cordon m de police; **twenty suspects were picked up in the d.** vingt personnes suspectes furent arrêtées dans la rafle **2** Fishing seine f, drège f

dragon ['drægən] N **1** Myth, Fig Fam dragon m; Sl **to chase the d.** (smoke heroin) chasser le dragon **2** (lizard) dragon m
▸▸ Mil **d.'s teeth** (anti-tank defence) rangées fpl de tétraèdres de béton

dragonfly ['drægənflaɪ] N libellule f

dragoon [drə'guːn] N Mil dragon m
VT Fam **to d. sb into doing sth** forcer qn à faire qch

dragrope ['drægrəʊp] N **1** Mil bricole f, combleau m **2** Aviat (of hot-air balloon) guide-rope m, pl guide-ropes

dragster ['drægstər] N Aut dragster m

drain [dreɪn] N **1** (in street) égout m; (of

house) canalisation f sanitaire; **a smell of drains** une odeur d'égout; **the drains are overflowing** les égouts débordent; **to pour sth down the d.** (dé)verser qch dans les égouts; Fig **to throw money down the d.** jeter son argent par la fenêtre; Fam **that's five years' work down the d.** voilà cinq années de travail perdues; Fam **that's my holiday down the d.** mes vacances sont à l'eau; Fam **to laugh like a d.** rire à gorge déployée **2** (loss) (of energy etc) perte f, fuite f; (of capital etc) drainage m; **this constant d. on our resources** cette hémorragie continuelle de nos ressources; **the car is a continual d. on our resources** la voiture nous cause constamment des dépenses; **the brain d.** l'exode m ou la fuite des cerveaux **3** Tech etc tuyau m d'écoulement; Med **drain** m; **overflow d.** (tube m de) trop-plein m, pl trop-pleins

VT **1** (liquid) (from field, pond) évacuer; **d. the water from the vegetables** égoutter les légumes; Med **to d. pus from a wound** faire sortir le pus d'une blessure; Fig **to d. wealth from a country** drainer les richesses d'un pays **2** (glass, pond, radiator etc) vider; (land, swamp), Med (wound, abscess) drainer; (sump) vidanger; Culin (vegetables etc) égoutter; Agr **well/poorly-drained soil** sol m perméable/peu perméable; Fig **to d. a country of its wealth** épuiser les richesses d'un pays; **the company is being drained of its top executives** la société perd ses cadres supérieurs **3** Fig (person) épuiser; **to d. sb's energy** épuiser qn; **to feel drained** (of energy) être épuisé; (of emotions) être vidé; **to be drained of emotion** ne plus ressentir aucune émotion; **to d. sb of their strength** épuiser les forces de qn

VI (of dishes) égoutter; (of sink, washing machine) se vider; **the river drains into the sea** la rivière se jette dans la mer; **the colour drained from her face** elle est devenue blême
▸▸ **d. hole** vis m de purge, trou m d'évacuation; Aut etc **d. plug** bouchon m de vidange

▸ **drain away** VT SEP (remove) (oil, water etc) faire couler
VI (of water) s'écouler; (of strength, enthusiasm, energy etc) s'épuiser; (of fear, tension) s'envoler, s'en aller

▸ **drain off** VT SEP (water, oil) évacuer
VI (of water) s'écouler

drainage ['dreɪnɪdʒ] N **1** = **draining 2** Constr (for draining land etc) système m d'écoulement des eaux; (drains) système d'égouts; **main d.** tout-à-l'égout m inv; Agr **soil with good d.** sol m perméable; **to improve the d. of the soil** rendre le sol plus perméable **3** (water) eaux fpl de surface; (sewage) eaux d'égout
▸▸ Geog **d. area, d. basin** bassin m hydrographique; Agr **d. ditch** fossé m d'écoulement; Med **d. tube** drain m

drainer ['dreɪnər] N égouttoir m

draining ['dreɪnɪŋ] N (of water) écoulement m; (of swamp) drainage m, assèchement m; Agr (of land) drainage, assainissement m; (of bottles etc) égouttement m; (of sump etc) vidange f, Med (of wound) drainage
▸▸ **d. board** égouttoir m (d'évier)

drainpipe ['dreɪnpaɪp] N tuyau m d'écoulement ou de drainage; Fam **drainpipes** pantalon m étroit ou en tuyau de poêle
▸▸ **d. trousers** pantalon étroit ou en tuyau de poêle

drake [dreɪk] N (bird) canard m mâle; **wild d.** malard m

DRAM ['diːræm] N Comput (abbr **dynamic random access memory**) DRAM f

dram [dræm] N **1** Pharm drachme f (= un seizième d'once, = 1,77 grammes) **2** esp Scot Fam (of whisky) goutte f; **to take a d.** prendre un petit verre (de whisky)

drama ['drɑːmə] N **1** Theat (play), Fig drame m; Fig **to make a d. out of sth** faire un drame de qch; **there's no need to make such a d. out of it** ce n'est pas la peine d'en faire tout un drame; **she always has to make a d. out of everything** elle est toujours à dramatiser **2** (art form) l'art m dramatique, le théâtre; **the masterpieces of French d.** les chefs-d'œuvre du théâtre français; **to teach d.** donner des cours d'art dramatique ou de théâtre **3** Fig (excitement) action f, **packed with d., full of d.** (film etc) plein d'action ou de rebondissements; **the d. of the situation is heightened by the fact that …** le caractère dramatique de la situation est renforcé par le fait que …
▸▸ TV **d. documentary** docudrame m; Fam Pej **d. queen** comédien, -ienne; **don't be such a d. queen!** arrête ton cinéma!; **d. school** école f d'art dramatique, école de théâtre; TV **d. series** série f dramatique; **d. student** étudiant, -ante en art dramatique; **d. studio** studio m d'enregistrement

> Note that the French word **drame** also means **tragedy, disaster**.

dramadoc ['drɑːmədɒk] N TV Fam docudrame m

dramatic [drə'mætɪk] ADJ **1** (book, ending, actor etc) dramatique; **the d. works of Corneille** le théâtre de Corneille **2** Fig (substantial) (developments, rise, decline, change etc) considérable, très important **3** Fig (theatrical) (gesture, effect) théâtral **4** (spectacular) (landscape, scenery, skyline) spectaculaire

> Note that the most common meaning of the French word **dramatique** is **tragic**.

dramatically [drə'mætɪklɪ] ADV **1** Theat (to end) sur un coup de théâtre; **d., the play doesn't work** du point de vue dramatique, la pièce ne tient pas debout **2** Fig (substantially) considérablement **3** Fig (theatrically) théâtralement; **the room is decorated rather d. in red and black** la pièce est décorée avec beaucoup d'effet en rouge et noir

> Note that the French word **dramatiquement** is a false friend and is never a translation for the English word **dramatically**.

dramatics [drə'mætɪks] N amateur d. théâtre m amateur; Pej **this is no time for d.** ce n'est pas le moment de faire un drame ou de dramatiser VOIR GRAMMAIRE A10

dramatis personae ['dræmətɪs pɜː'səʊnaɪ] NPL Theat personnages mpl

dramatist ['dræmətɪst] N Theat auteur m dramatique, dramaturge mf

dramatization [dræmətaɪ'zeɪʃən] N Radio, TV, Theat (of novel etc) adaptation f, Fig (of event) dramatisation f

dramatize ['dræmətaɪz] VT Radio, TV, Theat (novel) adapter; Fig (event) dramatiser; **there's no need to d. it** il ne faut pas en faire un drame
VI **novel that would d. well** (for stage/screen/radio) roman qui s'adapterait bien à la scène/à l'écran/à la radio; Fig **there's no need to d. it** il ne faut pas en faire un drame; **he tends to d.** il a tendance à dramatiser

drape [dreɪp] VT (table, window, neckline, material) draper (**with, in** de); **to d. sth over sth** draper qch sur qch; **the hall was draped in black** la salle était tendue de noir; **she was draped over the sofa** elle s'était étalée sur le canapé; **she draped herself round him** elle l'a enlacé; **he had a coat draped over his**

arm il avait un manteau sur le bras
vi *(of material)* se draper
n 1 *(of dress etc)* drapé *m* **2 drapes** tentures *fpl*; *Am (curtains)* rideaux *mpl*

draper ['dreɪpər] **n** *Old-fashioned Br* marchand, -ande de tissus; **d.'s shop** magasin *m* de tissus

drapery ['dreɪpərɪ] **n 1** *Old-fashioned Br (trade)* commerce *m* des tissus; *(shop)* magasin *m* de tissus **2** *(hangings)* tentures *fpl*

drastic ['dræstɪk] **adj** *(action)* énergique; *(measures, solution, change)* radical, drastique; *(cuts)* draconien, -ienne, sombre; *(remedy)* drastique; *(decline, rise, improvement, change)* dramatique; *(shortage)* dramatique, critique; *(need)* urgent; **things are getting d.** la situation devient critique; **that's quite a d. haircut you've got** tu as la boule à zéro; **d. reductions** *(sign)* soldes monstres; **that's a bit d.** *(of proposal etc)* c'est un peu exagéré

drastically ['dræstɪklɪ] **adv** *(to act)* énergiquement; *(shortened, improved etc)* radicalement; **to be d. short of sth** manquer dramatiquement de qch; **they're not d. different** ils ne sont pas fondamentalement différents; **d. reduced prices** prix *mpl* cassés

drat [dræt] **int** *Old-fashioned Fam* **d. (it)!** sacristi!, nom de nom!; **d. the child!** au diable cet enfant!

dratted ['drætɪd] **adj** *Old-fashioned Fam (boy etc)* maudit

draught[1], *Am* **draft** [drɑːft] **n 1** *(wind)* courant *m* d'air; **I'm in a d., I feel a d.** je suis dans un courant d'air; **d.-proof** à l'épreuve des courants d'air; *Fig Fam* **we're (all) feeling the d.** les choses vont mal (pour tout le monde) **2** *(of chimney)* tirage *m* **3** *Lit (drink)* trait *m*, gorgée *f*; **he took a long d. of beer** il a bu une grande gorgée de bière **4** *Med Arch* potion *f*, **poisoned d.** potion empoisonnée **5** *Naut (of ship)* tirant *m* d'eau **6 beer on d., d. beer** bière *f* à la pression **7** *(for playing draughts)* pion *m*
▸▸ **d. animal** bête *f* de trait; *Br* **d. excluder** bourrelet *m* (de porte)

draught[2] **n, vt** = **draft**[1]

draughtboard ['drɑːftbɔːd] **n** damier *m*

draughts ['drɑːfts] **n** *Br* (jeu *m* de) dames *fpl*; **to play d.** jouer aux dames; **a game of d.** une partie de dames VOIR GRAMMAIRE A10

draughtsman, *Am* **draftsman**, *pl* **draughtsmen** ['drɑːftsmən] **n 1** *Ind (of plans, drawings etc)* dessinateur *m* industriel **2** *Art* dessinateur *m*

draughtsmanship, *Am* **draftsmanship** ['drɑːftsmənʃɪp] **n 1** *Ind* l'art *m* du dessin industriel **2** *(ability to draw well)* talent *m* de dessinateur; **a fine piece of d.** un très bon dessin; **the d. is excellent** c'est très bien dessiné; **d. was never his strong point** le dessin n'a jamais été son fort

draughtswoman, *Am* **draftswoman**, *pl* **draughtswomen** ['drɑːftswʊmən, -wɪmɪn] **n 1** *Ind (of plans, drawings etc)* dessinatrice *f* industrielle **2** *Art* dessinatrice *f*

draughty, *Am* **drafty** ['drɑːftɪ] **adj** *(room, corridor etc)* plein de courants d'air; *(street corner)* exposé à tous les vents; **it's d. here** il y a des courants d'air ici

---

▮N▮	partie nulle **1**	▪ loterie **2**
▪ attraction **3**		
▮VT▮	dessiner **1**	▪ tirer **2, 3, 7**	▪ attirer **2,**
6	▪ retirer **3**	▪ toucher **5**
▮VI▮	dessiner **1**	▪ faire partie nulle **2**
▪ faire ex æquo **2**	▪ tirer **4**	

DRAW [drɔː]

n 1 *(game)* partie *f* nulle; *Ftbl, Boxing* match *m* nul; **it ended in a d.** ils ont fait partie/

---

match nul(le); *(of competition)* ils ont fini à égalité; *Ftbl* **a one-all/nil-nil d.** un match nul un à un/zéro à zéro; **it's a d. so far** pour l'instant, ils sont à égalité
2 *(lottery)* loterie *f*, tombola *f*, *(selection of winners, competitors)* tirage *m* (au sort); *Sport (list)* = tableau *m* des concurrents à chaque tour d'une série d'épreuves de championnat etc; **an easy/difficult d.** un tirage favorable/défavorable; *Ftbl* **the d. for the World Cup** le tirage de la Coupe du Monde; *Fam* **that's just the luck of the d.** c'est la vie!
3 *(attraction)* attraction *f*, *Theat* pièce *f* qui fait recette; **the match/film was a big d.** le match/film a remporté un grand succès; **she was a big d.** elle a attiré beaucoup de monde
4 **to take a d. at one's pipe** tirer une bouffée de sa pipe; **she had a quick d. on her cigarette** elle tira vivement sur sa cigarette; *Fam* **to be quick on the d.** *(with gun)* avoir la gâchette facile; *(with answers)* avoir la repartie facile; **to be a fast d.** avoir la gâchette facile; **the fastest d. in the West** le tireur le plus rapide de l'Ouest
5 *Br Sl (cannabis)* shit *m*
vt *(pt* **drew** [druː], *pp* **drawn** [drɔːn]*)* **1** *Art (landscape, figure etc)* dessiner; *Geom (circle, plan)* tracer; *(triangle, hexagon)* tracer, construire; *(line)* tirer, tracer; **to d. a map** dessiner une carte; *(of surveyor)* dresser une carte; **to d. sb's picture** faire le portrait de qn; *Fig* **the author has drawn the characters skilfully** l'auteur a tracé les personnages avec adresse
2 *(pull) (person)* attirer **(towards** vers); *(cart)* tirer; *(bow)* tendre; *(blind)* baisser; **to d. the curtains** tirer les rideaux; **drawn by a locomotive** remorqué par une locomotive; **to d. breath** souffler; *Fig* **I haven't drawn breath all day** *(I've been very busy)* je n'ai pas arrêté de la journée; **she drew his head down towards her** elle attira sa tête vers elle; **to d. a comb/brush through one's hair** se donner un coup de peigne/brosse
3 *(extract)* retirer, ôter **(sth from** or **out of sth** qch de qch); *(screw)* ôter, enlever; *(cork)* retirer, tirer, faire sauter; *(tooth, nail etc)* arracher; **to d. one's sword** tirer l'épée, dégainer; **to d. one's revolver** *(from holster/pocket)* sortir son revolver de l'étui/de sa poche, dégainer; **to d. a gun on sb** sortir un revolver et le pointer sur qn; **to d. a knife on sb** sortir un couteau (et en menacer qn); *Cards* **to d. a card (from the pack)** tirer une carte; *Cards* **to d. trumps** faire tomber les atouts; **to d. money from the bank** retirer de l'argent à la banque; **to d. blood** *(of weapon)* faire couler le sang; *(of dog)* mordre jusqu'au sang; *(of cat)* griffer jusqu'au sang; *Fig (of remark, criticism)* avoir un effet dévastateur; **to d. water from the river/the well** puiser *ou* tirer de l'eau à la rivière/au puits; **to d. wine (from a barrel)** tirer du vin (d'un tonneau); **to d. lots for sth** tirer qch au sort; **to d. straws** tirer à la courte paille; **to be drawn** *(of winning number, bonds)* sortir au tirage; **to d. a team/player against another** tirer une équipe/un joueur au sort contre un(e) autre; **it was the second time Czechoslovakia had been drawn against Scotland** c'était la deuxième fois que la Tchécoslovaquie tombait contre l'Écosse; **to d. a confession from sb** arracher un aveu à qn; **to d. a conclusion from sth** tirer *ou* déduire une conclusion de qch
4 *Sport* **to d. a game with sb** faire match nul avec qn; *(in chess etc)* faire partie nulle avec qn; **the match was drawn** ils ont fait match nul
5 *(receive) (salary)*, *Mil (rations)* toucher; **to d. supplies from sb** s'approvisionner chez qn

---

6 *(attract) (criticism, praise, person's gaze)* attirer; **to d. a crowd** *(of incident)* créer un attroupement; *(of play)* attirer le public; **to feel drawn to sb** se sentir attiré par qn; *Mil* **to d. the enemy's fire** attirer sur soi le feu de l'ennemi; **to d. sb's fire** *(of policeman)*, *Fig (deliberately)* faire diversion; *Fig (accidentally)* s'attirer les foudres de qn; **his accusation drew an instant denial** son accusation provoqua un démenti immédiat; **the government refused to be drawn** le gouvernement refusa de se commettre; **she would not be drawn on what she intended to do** elle a refusé de faire connaître ses intentions
7 *(take, derive) (strength, comfort, consolation etc)* tirer **(from** de); **our members are drawn from all walks of life** nos membres appartiennent à tous les milieux
8 *Fin (cheque)* libeller, rédiger; **to d. a cheque on** tirer *ou* disposer d'un chèque sur; **to d. a bill on** tirer une traite sur
9 *Culin (chicken etc)* vider
10 *Naut* **to d. twenty feet of water** *(of ship)* tirer *ou* jauger vingt pieds d'eau, avoir vingt pieds de tirant d'eau
11 *Med (abscess)* faire aboutir
12 *Metal (wire, tubes etc)* étirer, tirer
13 **to d. tea** faire infuser du thé
vi 1 *Art* dessiner
2 *Sport* faire match nul; *(in chess etc)* faire partie nulle; **they drew two all** ils ont fait deux partout; **they drew for third place** ils ont fait troisième ex æquo
3 *(move)* **to d. ahead of sb** devancer qn; **to d. level with a competitor** arriver à (la) hauteur d'un concurrent; **to d. to an end** tirer *ou* toucher à sa fin; **to d. near** *(of elections, Christmas)* se rapprocher; *(of person)* se rapprocher, s'approcher **(to sb** de qn); **the bird flew away as they drew near** à leur approche l'oiseau s'est envolé; **as they drew nearer, they could see ...** en s'approchant, ils ont vu ...; **to d. to a halt** *(stop)* s'arrêter
4 *(of chimney, pipe etc)* tirer; *(of pump)* la aspirer
5 *(in dominoes)* **to d. (from the pool)** piocher
6 *(infuse) (of tea)* infuser
7 *Fin* **to d. at sight** tirer à vue

▸ **draw alongside vt insep** *(and stop)* se ranger à côté de; *(keep moving)* rouler à la hauteur de; **the train drew alongside the platform** le train s'est rangé le long du quai
vi *(of vehicle)* **to d. alongside of a car/the platform** *(and stop)* se ranger à côté d'une voiture/le long du quai; **the police car drew alongside and signalled him to stop** la voiture de police a roulé à sa hauteur et lui a fait signe d'arrêter

▸ **draw apart vt sep** séparer, écarter
vi *(of people)* se séparer, s'écarter; *(in relationship)* s'éloigner l'un de l'autre; **they drew apart from the rest of the crowd** ils se sont écartés du reste de la foule

▸ **draw aside vt sep** *(person)* tirer *ou* prendre à l'écart; *(chair, suitcase)* tirer en arrière; *(curtain, sheet)* tirer, écarter
vi s'écarter

▸ **draw away vt sep** *(person)* entraîner, détourner **(from sth** de qch); **she drew us away from the other guests** elle nous a entraîné à l'écart des autres invités; **to d. one's hand away** retirer sa main
vi 1 *(of car etc)* s'éloigner; *Sport* **the first half-dozen runners are now beginning to d. away** les six premiers coureurs commencent à devancer les autres; *Sport* **to d. away from a competitor** prendre de l'avance sur un concurrent **2** *(recoil)* reculer, avoir un mouvement de recul

▸ **draw back vt sep 1** *(pull) (table, chair etc)* tirer en arrière; *(sheet, veil etc)* tirer, écarter; *Mil (troops)* retirer; **she drew her hand back** from the fire elle a retiré sa main du feu; **to d. back the curtains** ouvrir les rideaux **2** *(attract back)* **what drew you back to your home town?** qu'est-ce qui t'a poussé à revenir dans ta ville natale?; **I'm increasingly being drawn back to folk music** je reviens de plus en plus à la musique folk

vi 1 *(recoil)* reculer; **to d. back from making a decision** ne pas vouloir prendre une décision; **caution made him d. back from telling anyone about his new job** par prudence il résista à l'envie de parler à quiconque de son nouveau travail **2** *(from commitment etc)* faire marche arrière

▶ **draw in vt sep 1** *(net)* haler à bord; *(of cat etc)* *(claws)* rentrer, rétracter; *(of horseman)* *(reins, bridle)* serrer; *Fig Fam* **to d. in one's horns** faire des économies **2** *(air)* aspirer **3** *(involve)* *(person)* impliquer; **they're arguing and I don't want to be drawn in** ils se disputent et je ne veux pas y être mêlé

vi 1 *(of days, nights)* diminuer, raccourcir **2** *(of train, bus)* arriver

▶ **draw into vt insep** *(arrive at)* **the train drew into the station** le train entra en gare; **a car drew into the kerb** une voiture s'est rangée le long du trottoir

vt sep *(involve)* **to get drawn into an argument** être mêlé à une dispute; **to d. sb into conversation** entamer une conversation avec qn; **to d. sb into the conversation** faire entrer qn dans la conversation

▶ **draw off vt sep** *(liquid)* soutirer

▶ **draw on vt insep 1** *(use)* se servir de; **to d. on one's savings** prendre sur ses économies; **to d. on the reserves** puiser dans les réserves; **to d. on sb's experiences for a novel** s'inspirer des expériences de qn pour un roman **2** *(pipe, cigarette)* tirer sur **3** *Fam* **to d. on sb** sortir un revolver et le pointer sur qn

vt sep *(put on)* mettre; **she drew on a pair of gloves** elle a enfilé une paire de gants

vi 1 *(approach)* approcher; **evening was drawing on** la nuit approchait **2** *(go past slowly)* s'avancer; **as the day gradually drew on** au fur et à mesure que la journée avançait; **as time drew on his health improved** avec le temps sa santé s'améliora

▶ **draw out vt sep 1** *(sth from sth)* sortir, retirer; *(nail)* arracher; **to d. money out (of the bank)** retirer de l'argent (de la banque) **2** *(person)* faire sortir de sa réserve; **I managed to d. her out (of herself)** j'ai réussi à la faire sortir de sa réserve **3** *(prolong)* *(meal, speech)* prolonger; *(situation)* tirer en longueur, (faire) traîner; *Mus (note)* tenir; **they drew the meeting out on purpose** ils ont fait exprès de faire traîner la réunion **4** *Metal (stretch)* *(iron)* étirer; *(gold)* étendre

vi 1 *(of bus, train etc)* partir; **the train drew out of the station** le train a quitté la gare; *Aut* **to d. out in order to overtake** déboîter pour doubler **2** *(of days)* se prolonger

▶ **draw to vt sep** *(curtains)* tirer, fermer

▶ **draw together vt sep** *(people, objects)* rassembler, réunir; **the child's illness had drawn them together** la maladie de l'enfant les avait rapprochés

vi se rassembler

▶ **draw up vt sep 1** *(pull)* tirer vers le haut; *(heavy object)* hisser; *(water from well)* tirer; **he drew the blankets up to his chin** il ramena les couvertures jusqu'à son menton; **to d. oneself up** se redresser; **she drew herself up to her full height** elle s'est dressée de toute sa hauteur; *Naut* **to d. up a boat (on the beach)** tirer un bateau à sec; **to d. up a chair** approcher une chaise (**to** de)

2 *(prepare)* *(document)* dresser, rédiger; *(account, budget, itinerary)* établir; *(programme, procedure)* dresser, établir; *(plan)* élaborer; **document drawn up before a lawyer** acte passé devant (un) notaire; *Law* **to d. up a will** dresser un testament; **to d. up**

a **commercial bill** créer un effet de commerce; **to d. up an invoice** rédiger une facture

3 *(arrange in formation)* *(troops, chairs)* ranger, aligner

vi 1 *(of car etc)* s'arrêter, stopper; **to d. up at the kerb** se ranger le long du trottoir

2 *(of troops)* se mettre en rang, s'aligner; **to d. up in line** se mettre en ligne

3 to d. up to the table s'approcher de la table

drawback ['drɔːbæk] **N 1** *(disadvantage)* inconvénient *m*, désavantage *m* (**to** de) **2** *Admin* remboursement *m* (à la sortie) des droits d'importation

drawbar ['drɔːbɑː] **N** *Aut* crochet *m* (d'attelage)

drawbridge ['drɔːbrɪdʒ] **N 1** *(over moat)* pont-levis *m*, *pl* ponts-levis **2** *Constr* pont *m* basculant *ou* à bascule

drawcord ['drɔːkɔːd] **N** *(of curtains etc)* cordon *m*

drawdown ['drɔːdaʊn] **N** *Fin* tirage *m*

drawee [drɔːˈiː] **N** *Com (of bill of exchange)* tiré *m*, payeur *m*

drawer ['drɔːər] **N 1** *Art* dessinateur, -trice; **she's a good d.** *(of child, amateur)* elle dessine bien **2** *Fin* tireur *m*; *(of bill)* souscripteur *m* **3** *(of water)* puiseur, -euse **4** [drɔːr] tiroir *m*; **chest of drawers** commode *f*; *Old-fashioned* **bottom d.** *(trousseau)* trousseau *m* (de mariage); *Old-fashioned Fam* **they're not really (out of the) top d.** ils n'appartiennent pas vraiment à l'élite; *Com* **cash d.** tiroir-caisse *m*, *pl* tiroirs-caisses

drawers ['drɔː(ə)z] **NPL** *Old-fashioned* **(pair of) d.** *(for women)* culotte *f*, *(for men)* caleçon *m*

drawing ['drɔːɪŋ] **N 1** *Art (picture, art)* dessin *m*; **to make a d. of sth** dessiner qch; **her talent for d.** son talent pour le dessin; **line d.** dessin au trait; **rough d.** ébauche *f*, croquis *m*; **pencil d.** dessin au crayon; *Ind, Tech* **engineering d.** dessin industriel; **sectional d.** (vue *f* en) coupe *f* **2** *(pulling)* *(of cart)* tirage *m* **3** *(extraction)* *(of water)* puisage *m*; *(of teeth)* extraction *f*, *(of lots)* tirage *m* **4** *(attraction)* attraction *f* (**towards** vers) **5** *Com, Fin* **drawings** prélèvements *mpl*, levées *fpl* **6** *Culin (of poultry)* vidage *m* **7** *Metal (of metal)* étirage *m*

▶▶ **d. board** planche *f* à dessin; **d. book** cahier *m* de dessin; **d. card** *Com* valeur *f* sûre; *Am Fig (of festival etc)* attraction *f*, clou *m*; **she's always a big d. card** elle attire toujours beaucoup de monde; **d. off** *(of liquid)* soutirage *m*; **d. office** atelier *m* *ou* bureau *m* d'études; **d. paper** papier *m* à dessin; *Br* **d. pin** punaise *f* (à papier); **d. power** pouvoir *m* d'attraction; *Comput* **d. program** programme *m* de dessin, logiciel *m* de dessin; *Fin* **d. rights** droits *mpl* de tirage; **d. room** *(living room)* salon *m*; *(reception room)* salle *f* *ou* salon de réception; *Am Rail* compartiment *m* privé; **d. up** *(of deed, document, will)* rédaction *f*; *(of constitution, plan)* élaboration *f*, *(of bill, list, budget, itinerary)* établissement *m*

drawl [drɔːl] **N** voix *f* traînante; **to speak with a d./a Texan d.** parler d'une voix traînante/avec un accent Texan; **to speak with an affected d.** traîner la voix avec affectation

vi traîner la voix en parlant, parler d'une voix traînante

vt ..., **he drawled** ..., dit-il d'une voix traînante; **to d. one's vowels** traîner sur les voyelles

▶ **drawl out vt sep** = **drawl vt**

drawling ['drɔːlɪŋ] **ADJ** *(voice, tone)* traînant

N affectation *f* de langueur dans le débit

drawn [drɔːn] **ADJ 1** *(face)* hagard; *(features)* tiré; **to look d.** avoir les traits tirés **2 with d. sword(s)** sabre *m* au clair **3** *(battle)* indécis

▶▶ *Sport* **d. match** match *m* nul; *Sewing* **d.(-thread) work** ouvrage *m* *ou* travail *m* à jour(s)

drawsheet ['drɔːʃiːt] **N** *Med* alaise *f*, alèse *f*

drawstring ['drɔːstrɪŋ] **N** cordon *m*; **d. trousers, trousers with a d. waist** = pantalon *m* qui se ferme par un cordon autour de la taille

dray [dreɪ] **N** *(cart)* haquet *m*, camion *m*

drayhorse ['dreɪhɔːs] **N** cheval *m* de roulage

drayman, *pl* **draymen** ['dreɪmən] **N** conducteur *m* de haquet

dread [dred] **N** terreur *f*, épouvante *f*; **I have a d. of dentists** j'ai la hantise des dentistes; **she has a terrible d. of heights** elle a effroyablement peur du vide; **I have this d. that he'll find out where I am** j'ai la hantise qu'il apprenne où je suis; **she waited in d. for the phone to ring** angoissée, elle attendait que le téléphone sonne; **to be** *or* **stand in d. of sb/sth** craindre *ou* redouter qn/qch

ADJ ATTRIB *Old-fashioned* redouté

vt redouter, appréhender, craindre; **I'm dreading Monday** je redoute la journée de lundi; **I'm dreading my driving test** j'appréhende de passer le permis de conduire; **to d. that ...** redouter que (ne) ... + *subj*; **I d. to think!** je n'ose même pas y penser!; **I d. having them both here** j'appréhende de les avoir tous les deux en même temps; **the dreaded Monday finally arrived** le lundi si redouté est finalement arrivé; **she said the dreaded words** elle prononça les mots tant redoutés

dreadful ['dredfʊl] **ADJ 1** *(pain, noise etc)* atroce, épouvantable; **it is d. that nothing can be done** c'est affreux qu'on ne puisse rien faire; **to feel/look d.** ne pas se sentir/avoir l'air bien du tout; **I really feel d. about it!** ça m'ennuie terriblement!; **the shops were d.** *(very busy)* c'était l'horreur dans les magasins; **I'm a d. dancer** je danse atrocement mal; **to be d. at maths** être nul en maths **2** *Fam (intensive)* terrible; **it's a d. bore!** c'est assommant!; **it's a d. pity** *or* **shame** c'est vraiment dommage **3** *Fml (causing dread)* terrible, redoutable

dreadfully ['dredfʊlɪ] **ADV 1** terriblement, horriblement; **I was d. frightened** j'avais horriblement peur; **the children behaved d.** les enfants se sont terriblement *ou* horriblement mal conduits; **she suffers d. from backache** son dos la fait atrocement souffrir **2** *Fam (intensive)* terriblement; **d. ugly** affreusement laid; **our neighbours are d. noisy** nos voisins sont terriblement bruyants; **I am d. sorry** je regrette infiniment

dreadlocks ['dredlɒks], **dreads** [dredz] **NPL** dreadlocks *fpl*

dream [driːm] **N** rêve *m*, songe *m*; **to have a d.** faire un rêve; **to have a d. about sb/sth** rêver de qn/qch; **to have beautiful/bad dreams** faire de beaux/mauvais rêves; **sweet dreams!** faites de beaux rêves!; **to see sth in a d.** voir qch en rêve *ou* en songe; **to go about in a d.** être comme dans un rêve; **my d. house, the house of my dreams** la maison de mes rêves; **a d. holiday** des vacances de rêve; **it's my d. to go to Australia** je rêve d'aller en Australie; **I've always had this d. that one day I would have ...** j'ai toujours rêvé d'avoir ...; **it's everybody's d. to win the lottery** tout le monde rêve de gagner à la loterie; **I've long cherished a d. to be my own boss** je caresse depuis longtemps le rêve de me mettre à mon compte; *Fam* **a d. of a car** la voiture rêvée; **it's a d.** c'est le rêve; **it's a d. come true** c'est un rêve devenu réalité, mon rêve s'est réalisé; **it worked like a d.** cela a réussi à merveille; *Fam* **in your dreams!** tu peux toujours rêver!; *Austr* **in the d. time** *(of native people)* au temps où l'homme n'était pas encore arrivé sur la terre; *Fig Fam* **il y a des siècles**

VI *(pt, pp* **dreamt** [dremt], **dreamed** [dri:md]) **1** *(in sleep, daydream)* rêver; **to d. of** *or* **about sb/sth** rêver de qn/qch; **you must have been dreaming!** vous l'avez rêvé!; **to d. of one's youth** rêver à sa jeunesse; *Fam* **d. on!** tu peux toujours rêver! **2** *(think)* **I wouldn't d. of doing it** jamais je ne m'aviserais de faire cela; **I wouldn't d. of it!** je n'y songerais même pas!; **no one would have dreamt of suspecting him** personne n'aurait songé à le soupçonner

VT **I dreamt (that) you were ill** j'ai rêvé que vous étiez malade; **little did I d. that …** je ne songeais guère que …; **I never dreamt you would take me seriously** je n'aurais jamais pensé que tu me prendrais au sérieux; **you must have dreamt it!** vous l'avez rêvé!

▸▸ *Cin* **d. sequence** séquence *f* onirique; *Sport* **d. team** équipe *f* rêvée; *Pol* **d. ticket** combinaison *f* rêvée; **d. world** monde *m* imaginaire

▸ **dream away** VT SEP *(one's time)* passer à rêver; **he'll d. his whole life away** il passera sa vie à rêver

▸ **dream up** VT SEP *Fam (idea etc)* inventer, imaginer; **what have you dreamed up now?** qu'est-ce que tu as encore inventé?

dreamboat ['dri:mbəʊt] N *Old-fashioned Fam (attractive man, woman)* canon *m*

dreamer ['dri:mər] N rêveur, -euse

dreamily ['dri:mɪlɪ] ADV *(to look at, smile)* d'un air rêveur; *(to say)* d'un ton rêveur; *(to wander)* comme dans un rêve; **to think d. of the future** rêvasser à l'avenir

dreaming ['dri:mɪŋ] N rêves *mpl*; **this d. will get you nowhere** ça ne te mènera à rien de rêver comme ça

dreamland ['dri:mlænd] N le pays *ou* le monde des rêves, le pays des songes

dreamless ['dri:mlɪs] ADJ *(sleep)* sans rêves

dreamlessly ['dri:mlɪslɪ] ADV *(to sleep)* d'un sommeil sans rêves

dreamlike ['dri:mlaɪk] ADJ *(unreal)* onirique

dreamy ['dri:mɪ] ADJ **1** *(person, mood)* rêveur, -euse, songeur, -euse; **d. look/smile** air/sourire rêveur; **the d. look in her eye** son regard rêveur **2** *Fam (wonderful)* magnifique, superbe

drearily ['drɪərɪlɪ] ADV tristement; *(to look at)* d'un air morne; *(to say)* d'un ton morne

dreariness ['drɪərɪnɪs] N *(of life, countryside etc)* caractère *m* morne; *(of book, speech etc)* platitude *f*, monotonie *f*; **the d. of the weather** la grisaille

dreary ['drɪərɪ] ADJ *(weather, countryside)* triste, morne; *(speech, routine, person etc)* morne, ennuyeux; *(diet)* monotone; **we had a d. time (of it)** ce n'était pas très gai

dredge¹ [dredʒ] N **1** *(boat)* (bateau *m*) dragueur *m* **2** *(machine)* drague *f* **3** *Fishing (net)* (filet *m* de) drague *f*

VT *(canal)* draguer, dévaser; **to d. away mud** enlever la vase avec une drague; **to d. one's memory for sth** chercher qch dans ses souvenirs *ou* sa mémoire

VI **to d. for sth** draguer à la recherche de qch

▸▸ **d. bucket** godet *m* de drague; *Fishing* **d. net** (filet de) drague

▸ **dredge up** VT SEP *(silt)* enlever avec une drague; *(submerged object)* pêcher *ou* recueillir avec une drague; *Fig (scandal)* déterrer; **to d. sth up out of one's memory** ressortir qch de sa mémoire; **where did you**

d. these old photographs up from? où as-tu été repêcher ces vieilles photos?

dredge² VT *Culin* saupoudrer (**with** de); **to d. flour over meat** saupoudrer la viande de farine

dredger¹ ['dredʒər] N **1** *(boat)* (bateau *m*) dragueur *m* **2** *(machine)* drague *f*; **bucket d.** drague à godets; **grab d.** drague à benne piocheuse **3** *(person)* (ouvrier *m*) dragueur *m*; **oyster d.** dragueur d'huîtres

dredger² N *Culin (for sugar etc)* saupoudroir *m*

dredging ['dredʒɪŋ] N *(of canal etc)* dragage *m*

dregs [dregz] NPL **1** *(solid particles) (in glass)* lie *f*, fond *m*; *(of coffee)* marc *m*; **to drink sth to the d.** boire qch jusqu'à la lie; *Fig* **the d. of society** les bas-fonds *mpl* de la société **2** *(remainder, residue)* fond *m*

drench [drentʃ] VT *(soak)* tremper, mouiller (**with** de); *(earth) (of gardener)* arroser abondamment; *(of rain)* détremper; **to d. sb with water/a hosepipe** arroser qn d'eau/avec un tuyau; **to get drenched (with rain)** se faire tremper, *Fam* se faire saucer; **drenched to the skin** trempé jusqu'aux os; **to be drenched with sweat** être en nage

drenching ['drentʃɪŋ] ADJ *(rain)* battant, diluvien, -ienne

N **we got a d.** nous avons été trempés, *Fam* nous nous sommes fait saucer

Dresden ['drezdən] N Dresde; *(china)* porcelaine *f* de Saxe

▸▸ **D. china** porcelaine de Saxe

dress [dres] N **1** *(for woman)* robe *f*; **ball d.** robe de bal

2 *(attire)* costume *m*; **to wear Western d.** s'habiller à l'occidentale; **evening d.** tenue *f* de soirée; **to be casual in one's d.** s'habiller de façon décontractée; **to have good d. sense** savoir s'habiller; **to have no d. sense** ne pas savoir s'habiller; *Mil* **mess d.,** formal **d.** uniforme *m* de cérémonie *ou* de soirée; **in full d.** *(of men)* en grande tenue; *(of women)* en grande toilette; *Mil* en grande tenue, en uniforme de parade; *Mil* **full d. parade** parade *f* en grande tenue

VT *(* **dressed** [drest] *)* **1** *(put clothes on) (person)* habiller, vêtir; *Theat (play)* costumer; **to d. oneself, to get dressed** s'habiller; **to be dressed in black/silk** être vêtu de noir/soie; **dressed in rags** vêtu *ou* couvert de haillons; **dressed for the country/for climbing** en tenue de campagne/d'escalade; **I'm not dressed for it** je ne suis pas habillé pour; **well/badly dressed** bien/mal habillé; **to be plainly** *or* **simply dressed** avoir une mise simple, être simplement vêtu; *esp Mil* **to be improperly dressed** ne pas porter la tenue réglementaire; **dressed as a clown/a witch** *(for a party)* déguisé en clown/en sorcière; *Fam* **dressed to kill** sur son trente et un

2 *(decorate)* orner, parer (**sth with sth** qch de qch); *Naut (ship)* pavoiser; **dressed over all** *(of ship)* sous le grand pavois; *Com* **to d. the window** faire la vitrine; *TV etc* **to d. set** habiller le décor; *Old-fashioned* **to d. sb's hair** coiffer qn

3 *Mil (troops, tents etc)* aligner

4 *Med (wound)* panser

5 *Tech (prepare, finish) (surface, hide)* apprêter; *(land, fields)* engraisser; *(leather)* corroyer; *(stone)* dresser, tailler; *(wood)* dresser, corroyer; *(ore)* trier; *Culin (poultry, meat)* habiller; *(dish)* accommoder; *(salad)* assaisonner, garnir; **dressed poultry** volaille prête à cuire *ou* parée; **dressed crab** crabe tout préparé pour la table; **dressed timber** bois dégrossi

VI s'habiller; **she dresses like a man** elle s'habille comme un homme; **to d. in black** s'habiller de noir; **to d. (for dinner)** *(of man)*

se mettre en habit; *(of woman)* se mettre en robe du soir; **they always d. for dinner** ils s'habillent toujours pour le dîner

▸▸ *Theat* **d. circle** premier balcon *m*, corbeille *f*; **d. designer** modéliste *mf*, dessinateur, -trice de mode; *(famous)* couturier, -ière; **d. material** tissu *m* pour robes; *Theat* **d. rehearsal** (répétition *f*) générale *f*; *Fig (practice)* répétition générale; **d. shield** dessous-de-bras *m inv*; **d. shirt** chemise *f* de soirée; **d. suit** habit *m*, tenue *f* de soirée; **d. uniform** uniforme de cérémonie *ou* de soirée

▸ **dress down** VT SEP *Fam (reprimand)* passer un savon à

VI s'habiller plus simplement qu'à l'accoutumée

▸ **dress up** VT SEP **1** *(put elegant clothes on)* **to d. oneself up** se faire beau/belle, s'habiller; **to be all dressed up, to be dressed up to the nines** être sur son trente et un **2** *(put fancy dress on)* **you could d. yourself up as Batman** tu pourrais te déguiser en Batman; **to d. sb up** costumer qn, déguiser qn (**as sth en** qch); *Fig* **we'll have to d. it up a bit** il faudra améliorer un peu la présentation; *Fig* **however you d. it up** de quelque façon qu'on le présente

VI **1** *(wear elegant clothes)* se faire beau/belle, s'habiller **2** *(wear fancy dress)* se déguiser

dressage ['dresɑ:ʒ] N *Horseriding* dressage *m* (supérieur)

dress-down Friday N = journée *f* du vendredi où, contrairement au reste de la semaine, les employés sont libres de s'habiller comme ils le souhaitent

dresser ['dresər] N **1** *(for plates etc)* buffet *m*; **(Welsh) d.** vaisselier *m* **2** *Am (dressing table)* table *f* de toilette, coiffeuse *f* **3** **to be a smart d.** s'habiller avec chic **4** *Theat, Cin, TV* habilleur, -euse **5** *(tool) (for wood)* raboteuse *f*; *(for stone)* rabotin *m*

dressing ['dresɪŋ] N **1** *(putting clothes on)* habillement *m*

2 *Naut (of ship)* pavoisement *m*

3 *Mil (of troops)* alignement *m*

4 *Med (of wound)* pansement *m*; **to apply a d.** mettre *ou* faire un pansement; **surgical d. case** trousse *f* de pansement

5 *Agr* engrais *m*; **a heavy d. of manure** un gros apport de fumier; **surface d., top d.** engrais en couverture, couche *f* d'engrais

6 *Culin* **(salad) d.** assaisonnement *m*, sauce *f*, **French d.** vinaigrette *f*

7 *Tech (of hide)* apprêt *m*; *(of stone)* dressage *m*, taille *f*; *(of wood)* dressage, corroyage *m*; *(of ore)* préparation *f* mécanique; *Tex* apprêt, empois *m*; *Culin (of poultry)* habillage *m*; *(of dish)* assaisonnement *m*

8 *Am Culin (stuffing)* farce *f*

▸▸ *Old-fashioned* **d. case** trousse *f* de toilette, nécessaire *m* de toilette; **d. gown** robe *f* de chambre, peignoir *m*; **d. room** *(at home)* dressing-room *m*, *pl* dressing-rooms, dressing *m*, vestiaire *m*; *(at gym, sports ground)* vestiaire; *Theat* loge *f* (d'acteur); *Am (in shop)* cabine *f* d'essayage; *Mil* **d. station** poste *m* de secours; **d. table** coiffeuse *f*, (table *f* de) toilette *f*; **d.-table set** garniture *f* de toilette; **d. up** *(children's activity)* déguisement *m*

dressing-down N *Fam* verte semonce *f*, savon *m*; **to give sb a d.** passer un savon à qn; **to get a d.** se faire passer un savon

dressmaker ['dresmeɪkər] N couturier, -ière

dressmaking ['dresmeɪkɪŋ] N *(by tailor, dress designer)* couture *f*, *Ind* confection *f* de robes

dress-run N *TV, Theat etc* répétition *f* générale

dressy ['dresɪ] ADJ **1** *(clothes)* chic, élégant;

(party) habillé; **it's a bit d. for a barbecue** c'est un peu trop habillé pour un barbecue; **I wanted something a bit more d.** je cherchais quelque chose d'un peu plus habillé **2** *Pej (person)* trop (élégamment) habillé

drib [drɪb] N *only used in* **in dribs and drabs** petit à petit, peu à peu

dribble ['drɪb(ə)l] N **1** *(of water etc)* petite(s) goutte(s) *f(pl)*; *Fig* **supplies are coming through in dribbles** les approvisionnements sont livrés au compte-gouttes; **there's only a d. left** il n'en reste que quelques gouttes

  2 *(of person, dog)* bave *f*

  3 *Ftbl etc* dribble *m*

VI 1 *(of water etc) (drop by drop)* dégoutter, tomber goutte à goutte; *(in a trickle)* dégouliner; **the wine dribbled down his chin** le vin lui dégoulina le long du menton; **half the flour/water had dribbled out** la moitié de la farine/l'eau s'était échappée; *Fig* **to d. in/ out** *(of people)* entrer/sortir au compte-gouttes; **news has started to d. back** des nouvelles commencent à filtrer

  2 *(of baby etc)* baver

  3 *Ftbl etc* dribbler

  4 *Billiards* **to d. into the pocket** *(of ball)* rouler doucement dans la blouse

VT 1 **to d. (out)** *(liquid)* laisser couler goutte à goutte; **I had dribbled juice all down my tie** je m'étais mis plein de jus de fruit sur la cravate; **d. some oil over it** versez quelques gouttes d'huile dessus

  2 *Ftbl etc (ball)* dribbler

  3 *Billiards* **to d. the ball into the pocket** faire rouler tout doucement la bille dans la blouse

dribbler ['drɪblər] N *Ftbl etc* dribbleur *m*

dribbling ['drɪblɪŋ] N **1** *(of baby etc)* écoulement *m* de bave; **people were disgusted by his d.** les gens étaient dégoûtés de le voir baver comme ça **2** *Ftbl etc* dribbling *m*

driblet ['drɪblɪt] N *(of water etc)* gouttelette *f*, petite goutte *f*; *Fig* petite somme *f* d'argent; **in driblets** goutte à goutte, au compte-gouttes; *Fig* au compte-gouttes

dried [draɪd] ADJ séché

dried-up ADJ *(river bed, lake etc)* asséché; *(grass, bread)* sec; *Fig Pej* **a d. old maid** une vieille bique au cœur asséché

drier ['draɪər] N = **dryer**

drift [drɪft] N **1** *(movement)* mouvement *m*; *(of current)* direction *f*, sens *m*; *(of business, events)* cours *m*; *(of plane, ship)* dérive *f*; *(of missile etc)* dérivation *f*, *Constr (of borehole)* déviation *f*, *Electron* glissement *m*; **carried along by the d. of the current** emporté par le courant; *Fig* **policy of d.** politique *f* de laisser-faire; **the d. towards war** la descente vers la guerre; **the d. from the land** la lente désertification des campagnes; **the d. towards the cities** l'exode *m* rural; *Sch* **the d. away from science** le désintéressement envers la science

  2 *(meaning) (of person's words)* sens *m* général, portée *f*; **I catch** *or* **follow his d.** je vois où il veut en venir; *Fam* **I get the/your d.** je pige

  3 *(of sand, leaves etc)* amoncellement *m*; *Geog* apport(s) *mpl*; *(of snow)* congère *f*

  4 *Min (of gallery)* direction *f*; *(passage)* (galerie *f* de) chassage *m*; *(exploratory)* galerie d'exploration

VI 1 *(of boat)* dériver, aller à la dérive; *Aviat* déporter; *(of questions, events)* tendre (**towards sth** vers qch); *Fig* **she's been drifting** elle ne s'est pas fixée; **you can't go on drifting like this** tu ne peux pas continuer à te laisser porter par les événements comme ça; **to d. from job to job** aller d'un travail à un autre; **to let things d.** laisser aller les choses; **to d. apart** *(of friends)* se perdre de

vue; *(of married couple)* devenir peu à peu des étrangers l'un pour l'autre; **wisps of smoke were drifting across the sky** la fumée formait des traînées dans le ciel; **conversation drifted from one subject to another** la conversation passait d'un sujet à un autre; **a few tramps had drifted in in search of warmth** attirés par la chaleur, quelques vagabonds étaient entrés; **the cigarette smoke was drifting into his eyes** la fumée de cigarette lui venait dans les yeux; **to d. into war/ crime** être entraîné dans la guerre/vers le crime; **the yacht drifted onto a sandbank** le yacht a dérivé et s'est échoué sur un banc de sable; **the audience started to d. towards the exit** les spectateurs se dirigeaient lentement vers la sortie; **to d. with the current** se laisser aller au fil de l'eau; *Fig* se laisser porter par les événements

  2 *(of sand etc)* s'amonceler, s'amasser; *(of snow)* se former en congères, s'amasser; **some snow had drifted in through the open door** de la neige s'était infiltrée par la porte ouverte

VT 1 *(logs)* flotter; *(of current) (something)* entraîner **2** *(of wind) (snow, sand)* amonceler, entasser; **the wind was drifting snow in through the window** de la neige entrait par la fenêtre, portée par le vent

  ▸▸**d. ice** glaces *fpl* flottantes *ou* en dérive; *Fishing* **d. net** filet *m* traînant

▸ **drift off** VI **to d. off (to sleep)** s'assoupir

VT INSEP *Naut, Aviat* **to d. off course** dévier de son cap

drifter ['drɪftər] N **1** *Fishing* bateau *m* de pêche à filets traînants **2** *Fig* personne *f* qui se laisse aller; **he's been a d. all his life** il ne s'est jamais fixé; **she's a bit of a d.** elle n'a pas vraiment de but dans la vie

drifting ['drɪftɪŋ] ADJ *(ship etc)* à la dérive; *(cloud)* traînant; **d. snow** neige *f* soulevée par le vent; **d. banks of fog/cloud** des traînées de brouillard/de nuages

  N *(caused by current)* entraînement *m* par le courant; *(caused by wind)* entraînement par le vent; *(formation of drifts) (of snow)* amoncellement *m*; **caused by the d. of the snow across the road** causé par la neige soulevée par le vent en travers de la route

driftwood ['drɪftwʊd] N *(in the sea)* bois *m* flottant *ou* flotté; *(on the shore)* bois rejeté *ou* ruléé par la mer

drill¹ [drɪl] N **1** *Carp, Metal (for wood, metal)* foret *m*, mèche *f*; *(for metal)* foreuse *f*, drille *f*, *(power-driven)* perceuse *f*; *(of dentist)* fraise *f*, **electric d.** perceuse électrique; **hand d.** perceuse à main; **percussion d.** perceuse à percussion; **spoon d.** cuiller *f*, cuillère *f* **2** *Min, Constr* perforateur *m*, perforatrice *f*, *(for taking borings)* sondeuse *f*, sonde *f*, *(for oil)* trépan *m* **3** *(training)* exercice(s) *mpl*; *Fig* **to know the d.** savoir ce qu'il faut faire *ou* comment s'y prendre; *Fam* **what's the d.?** *(what do you want me to do?)* qu'est-ce qu'il y a à faire?; *(for working the photocopier etc)* comment on fait?; *Sch* **verb d.** exercices *mpl* oraux sur les verbes; *Mil*

firing d. instruction *f* du tir; **recruit d.** école *f* du soldat; **rifle d.** maniement *m* du fusil

VT 1 *(well etc)* forer; *(wood, metal)* faire un trou dans; *(hole)* percer; *(tooth)* fraiser **2** *Min (rock etc)* (per)forer **3** *Gym etc (people)* faire faire l'exercice à; *Mil (soldiers)* instruire, exercer; *Naut* **well-drilled crew** équipage bien exercé; *Fam* **to d. sb (in what to do/say)** faire la leçon à qn (sur ce qu'il faut faire/dire); **I can't d. (it) into him that …** je ne peux pas lui faire comprendre que …; **it had always been drilled into her that …** on lui avait enfoncé dans la tête que …; **to d. good manners into sb** enseigner les bonnes manières à qn; *Sch* **to d. pupils in French**

verbs faire faire aux élèves des exercices oraux sur les verbes français

VI 1 *Petr* forer; **to d. for oil** forer pour trouver du pétrole **2** *(do exercises)* s'exercer, s'entraîner; *(of troops)* faire l'exercice

  ▸▸**d. bit** foret, mèche; **d. chuck** mandrin *m* *(de tour)* porte-mèche; **d. ground** terrain *m* d'exercice *ou* de manœuvres; **d. hole** trou *m* à la foreuse; *Petr* trou de forage; *Mil* **d. sergeant** sergent *m* instructeur

drill² *Agr* N **1** *(row)* rayon *m*, sillon *m*; **to sow the grain in drills** semer la graine en rayons **2** *(machine)* semoir *m* (à cuillers)

VT semer en rayons

  ▸▸**d. harrow** herse *f* à semer

drill³ N *Tex* coutil *m*; *(for denims etc)* treillis *m*

drilling ['drɪlɪŋ] N **1** *Metal* forage *m*, perçage *m*; *Min (of rock etc)* perforation *f*, *Min (of well)* forage, sondage *m* **2** *Petr* forage *m* **3** *(of tooth)* fraisage *m* **4** *Mil* exercices *mpl*, manœuvres *fpl*

  ▸▸**d. machine** foreuse *f*, **d. mud** boue *f* (de forage); **d. operations** opérations *fpl* de forage; *Petr* **d. platform** plate-forme *f* (de forage), *pl* plates-formes; *Petr* **d. rig** *(on land)* derrick *m*, tour *f* de forage; *(at sea)* plate-forme (de forage)

drily ['draɪlɪ] ADV = **dryly**

DRINK [drɪŋk]

N	boisson **1** ▪ verre **1** ▪ alcool **1**
VT	boire
VI	boire **1, 2**

N 1 boisson *f*, *(said by waiter, barkeeper etc)* consommation *f*, *(alcoholic)* verre *m*, *Fam* pot *m*; **to give sb food and d.** donner à boire et à manger à qn; **to give sb a d.** donner à boire à qn; **to have a d.** boire *ou* prendre quelque chose; **I'd love a d. of water** je voudrais bien un verre d'eau; **will you join me in a d.?** tu prends un verre avec moi?; **pour yourself a d.** sers-toi un verre *ou* à boire; **we're going for a d.** nous allons prendre un verre *ou Fam* un pot; **how about a d. after work?** on prend un verre *ou Fam* un pot après le travail?; **to pay for the drinks** payer les consommations; **I haven't had a d. in six months** je n'ai pas bu d'alcool depuis six mois; **long d.** = gin/vodka/*etc* allongé de jus d'orange/de limonade/*etc*; **short d.** = gin/whisky/*etc* non dilué; **strong d.** *(spirits)* boissons fortes; **soft drinks** boissons sans alcool; **to take to d.** s'adonner à la boisson, se mettre à boire; **to have a d. problem** *(trop)* boire; **to smell of d.** sentir l'alcool; **to be the worse for d.** être plein *ou* ivre; **he can't hold his d.** *(gets drunk quickly)* il ne tient pas l'alcool; *(vomits)* il vomit le moindre verre d'alcool; *Fam* **I didn't mean it, it was the d. talking** je n'étais pas sérieux, j'avais juste un peu trop bu; **to be under the influence of d.** avoir trop bu; *Law* **to drive a car while under the influence of d.** conduire en état d'ébriété; **to drive sb to d.** pousser qn à l'ivrognerie; **drinks dispenser** *ou* **machine** distributeur *m* automatique de boissons

  2 *Fam* **the d.** *(sea)* la baille; **to fall into the d.** tomber à la baille

VT *(pt* **drank** [dræŋk], *pp* **drunk** [drʌŋk], *Arch* **drunken** ['drʌŋkən]) *(water etc)* boire; **will you have something to d.?** voulez-vous boire *ou* prendre quelque chose?; **what are you drinking?** qu'est-ce que tu prends *ou* bois?; **to d. sb's health** boire à la santé de qn; **to d. sb under the table** faire rouler qn sous la table; **the wine is best drunk at room temperature** ce vin se boit chambré; **fit to d.** bon à boire, potable

VI 1 *(take in liquid)* boire; **to d. straight from the bottle** boire à la bouteille

  2 *(take alcohol)* boire, être adonné à la

boisson; **I don't d.** je ne bois pas; **to d. heavily** s'alcooliser; **you're drinking yourself to death** l'alcool est en train de te détruire; **to d. oneself into debt** s'endetter à cause de la boisson; **don't d. and drive** ≃ boire ou conduire, il faut choisir; **to d. like a fish** boire comme un trou; **to d. to sb** boire à la santé de qn; **to d. to sth** arroser qch; **I'll d. to that!** et comment!

3 *(of wine)* **the wine is now drinking superbly** ce vin a atteint toute sa saveur; **it won't d. quite as well in two years' time** dans deux ans il aura perdu de sa saveur

► **drink away** VT SEP *(one's pay)* boire
► **drink down** VT SEP *(water etc)* boire, avaler
► **drink in** VT SEP *(person's words)* boire; *(scenery, fresh air)* se délecter de, se repaître de
► **drink off** VT SEP *(glass)* boire d'un coup; *(bottle)* avaler
► **drink up** VT SEP finir (de boire); **I want you to d. that all up!** *(not leave any)* bois tout! VI **d. up!** videz votre verre/vos verres!

drinkable ['drɪŋkəb(ə)l] ADJ buvable; *(water)* potable; **the wine's very d.** ce vin se laisse boire

drink-driver N *Br Fam* conducteur, -trice ivre; **he's a notorious d.** tout le monde sait qu'il conduit souvent en état d'ébriété

drink-driving N *Br Fam* **he was arrested for d.** il a été arrêté pour conduite en état d'ivresse

drinker ['drɪŋkər] N buveur, -euse; **I'm not much of a d.** je ne bois pas beaucoup; **wine/beer/tea drinkers** buveurs de vin/de bière/de thé; **he's a heavy** or **hard d.** il boit beaucoup; **she's a social d.** elle ne boit que pour les grandes occasions

drinking ['drɪŋkɪŋ] ADJ **I'm not a d. man** je n'ai pas l'habitude de boire

N **1** boire *m* **2** *(to excess)* ivrognerie *f*, alcoolisme *m*; **d. bout** beuverie *f*; **they'd been doing some heavy d.** ils avaient beaucoup bu; **it was her d. that destroyed the marriage** c'est son alcoolisme qui a détruit leur mariage; **d. companions** compagnons *mpl* de boisson;

►► **d. chocolate** chocolat *m* à boire; *(powder)* chocolat *m* en poudre; *(hot drink)* chocolat *m* chaud; **d. fountain** *(in street)* fontaine *f* publique; *(in corridor, public conveniences)* jet *m* d'eau potable; **d. laws** = lois *fpl* sur les débits de boissons; **d. song** chanson *f* à boire; **d. straw** paille *f*; **d. trough** abreuvoir *m*; **d. water** eau *f* potable

drinking-up time N *Br* = dans les pubs, temps *m* accordé aux clients pour finir leur verre après l'heure de fermeture officielle

drip [drɪp] N **1** *(sound)* **the d. of water** le bruit de l'eau qui tombe *ou* qui s'écoule; **the d. of a tap** le bruit d'un robinet qui goutte **2** *(drop)* goutte *f*; **there's a d. coming from the ceiling** le plafond goutte, il tombe des gouttes du plafond; **you're getting drips all over the floor** tu fais tomber des gouttes partout sur le sol; **the drips from the trees** les gouttes qui tombent/tombaient des arbres; **the d. method of making coffee** la méthode filtre de faire le café **3** *Med* goutte-à-goutte *m inv*; **he's on a d.** il est sous perfusion **4** *Sl (feeble person)* **he's/she's a d.** c'est un mou/une molle, c'est un ramolli/une ramollie

VI *(-pp-)* *(of rain, water)* tomber goutte à goutte, (dé)goutter; **the perspiration was dripping from his forehead** la sueur lui dégouttait du front, son front était ruisselant de sueur; **just leave it to d.** *(of shirt etc)* laisse-le s'égoutter; **the tap has been dripping all night** le robinet a fui *ou* goutté toute la nuit

VT *(liquid)* faire dégoutter, laisser tomber goutte à goutte; **you're dripping water/**

paint everywhere! tu mets des gouttes d'eau/de peinture partout!; **the ceiling was dripping water** le plafond gouttait, des gouttes d'eau tombaient du plafond

►► *Mktg* **d. advertising** publicité *f* continue, publicité goutte à goutte; *Tech* **d. feed** *(for oil)* distributeur *m* compte-gouttes; *Tech* **d.-feed lubricator** *(graisseur m)* compte-gouttes *m inv*; **d. mat** dessous-de-verre *m inv*

drip-dry ADJ *Tex (shirt etc)* ne nécessitant aucun repassage

drip-feed VT *(pt, pp drip-fed)* *Med (patient)* nourrir *ou* alimenter par perfusion

drip-feeding N alimentation *f* par perfusion

dripping ['drɪpɪŋ] ADJ ruisselant; *(tap)* qui goutte; **to be d. wet** être trempé; **d. with perspiration/blood** ruisselant de sueur/sang; *Fig* **to be d. with jewels** être couvert de bijoux

N **1** égouttement *m* **2** *Br Culin* graisse *f* de rôti; **bread and d.** tartine *f* à la graisse;
►► *Br Culin* **d. pan** lèchefrite *f*

drippy ['drɪpɪ] ADJ *Fam (person)* mou, *f* molle; *(film, novel)* *(inane)* plat, fade; *(sentimental)* mélo

━━━━━━━━━━━━━━━━━━━━━━━━
DRIVE [draɪv]
━━━━━━━━━━━━━━━━━━━━━━━━
| **N** promenade en voiture **1** ▪ conduite **2–4** ▪ dynamisme **6** ▪ campagne **7** ▪ allée **9** |
| **VT** conduire **1, 2** ▪ pousser **3** ▪ surmener **4** ▪ faire marcher **7** |
| **VI** conduire **1** ▪ aller en voiture **1** ▪ rouler **1** |
━━━━━━━━━━━━━━━━━━━━━━━━

N **1** *Aut (trip)* promenade *f* en voiture; *(in taxi)* course *f*; **a 50-km d.** un parcours *ou* un trajet de 50 km; **it's an hour's d. away** c'est à une heure en voiture; **to go for** *or* **take a d.** aller faire une promenade *ou* un (petit) tour en voiture, faire une promenade en voiture; **it's a very pleasant d. to the coast** la route est très belle jusqu'à la côte; *Aut* **test d.** conduite *f* d'essai

2 *(of cattle)* conduite *f*; *(of deer)* battue *f*; *Am (guiding of logs)* *(transport m du bois par le)* flottage *m*, *Can* drave *f*, *(logs)* train *m* (de bois flotté)

3 *Tech (mouvement m de)* propulsion *f*; *(by component)* commande *f*, transmission *f*, actionnement *m*; *Aut (for any shaft)* entraînement *m*; *(on automatic gearbox)* conduite *f* normale; **belt/chain d.** entraînement *ou* transmission par courroie/chaîne; **gear d.** commande par engrenages; *Aut* **direct d.** prise *f* directe; *(for interdependent parts)* courroie de commande

4 *Aut (location of steering wheel)* conduite *f*, **left-hand d.** conduite à gauche; **car with left-hand d.** voiture *f* avec conduite à gauche

5 *(shot)* *Golf, Tennis* drive *m*; *Cr* coup *m* droit long et appuyé

6 *Fig (initiative)* énergie *f*, dynamisme *m*; **to have plenty of d.** être énergique *ou* entreprenant

7 *(campaign)* *(to increase sales etc)* campagne *f*, *(against stronghold, abuse)* offensive *f*, **membership d.** campagne *f* pour attirer des membres

8 *Psy (urge)* *(sexual etc)* pulsions *fpl*

9 *(of house)* allée *f*, **the car's sitting in the d.** la voiture est garée dans l'allée

10 *Cards (for bridge, whist)* tournoi *m*

11 *Comput (for disk)* lecteur *m*, unité *f*, **d. a:/b:** unité de disque a:/b:

VT *(pt* **drove** [drəʊv]*, pp* **driven** ['drɪv(ə)n]*)* **1** *(car, train)* conduire; *(racing car)* conduire, piloter; *Horseracing (trotting horse)* driver; **can you d. a car?** savez-vous conduire?; **to d. sb to a place** conduire qn en voiture

quelque part; **I haven't driven all this way just to …** je n'ai pas fait tout ce chemin juste pour …

2 *(cattle)* conduire, mener; *(deer etc)* rabattre; *(prisoners)* faire aller (devant soi); *(log train)* diriger; **thousands of people have been driven from their homes** des milliers de personnes ont été obligées de quitter leur maison; **to d. the enemy from his position** déloger l'ennemi; **the wind is driving the rain against the window panes** le vent rabat la pluie contre les vitres; **the waves drove the ship onto the rocks** les vagues ont poussé le navire contre les rochers

3 *(force)* *(sb to do sth)* pousser; **I was driven to resign** j'ai été forcé de démissionner; **he won't be driven** on ne le mène pas comme on veut; **to d. sb mad** *or* **out of his/her mind** rendre qn fou/folle; **she drove me to it** c'est elle qui m'y a poussé; **to d. sb to despair** réduire qn au désespoir; **to be driven by ambition** être mû par l'ambition

4 *(one's employees)* surmener; **to d. oneself too hard** se surmener; **she drives herself as hard as she drives us** elle se surmène autant qu'elle nous surmène

5 **to d. a bargain** conclure un marché; **to d. a hard bargain** chercher à gagner le dernier centime, négocier serré

6 **to d. the ball** *Cr* chasser la balle; *Tennis* jouer un drive, driver; *Golf* driver

7 *Tech (machine)* actionner, faire marcher; *(of part) (component)* actionner; *Comput (of program)* commander, piloter; **to be driven by electricity** fonctionner à l'électricité

VI **1** *Aut* conduire; **can you d.?** savez-vous conduire?; **I don't d.** *(I never learned)* je n'ai pas mon permis; **who was driving?** qui était au volant?; **to d. to work** aller *ou* se rendre au travail en voiture; **to d. slowly/fast** rouler lentement/vite; **to d. on the right (of the road)** circuler à droite, tenir la droite; **car that drives well** voiture facile à conduire

2 **the rain driving against the window panes** la pluie qui fouette les vitres; *Lit* **to d. before the wind** *(of clouds etc)* chasser devant le vent

►► *Aut* **d. belt** courroie *f* d'entraînement; *Comput* **d. door** porte *f* de l'unité de disquette; *Aut* **d. shaft** arbre *m* d'entraînement *ou* de commande

► **drive along** VI rouler (en voiture); **I was driving along slowly** je roulais lentement; **to d. along the road** rouler sur la route
► **drive at** VT INSEP **what are you driving at?** où voulez-vous en venir?; **what do you think she was driving at?** où croyez-vous qu'elle voulait en venir?
► **drive away** VT SEP **1** *(dog, intruder)* chasser, éloigner, écarter; *(lover, spouse)* faire partir; *(friend)* éloigner; *(doubt, suspicion)* écarter; *(fear)* chasser

2 *Aut (person)* emmener en voiture; **the men came in a car and drove her away** des hommes sont arrivés et l'ont emmenée en voiture; **they were driven away in a taxi** ils ont été conduits en taxi

VI partir *ou* s'en aller en voiture; *(of car, bus)* s'éloigner; **he jumped into his car and drove away** il a sauté dans sa voiture et s'en est allé
► **drive back** VT SEP **1** *(repel)* *(attack, demonstrators)* repousser; *(of flames)* faire reculer

2 *Aut (person)* reconduire *ou* ramener en voiture

VI *Aut* rentrer en voiture
► **drive down** VT SEP **1** *Econ (prices, inflation etc)* faire baisser

2 *Aut* **to d. sb down to London** conduire qn à Londres

VI *Aut (from north to south)* se rendre en voiture; **how did you get here?** – **we drove down** comment êtes-vous venus? – nous sommes venus *ou* descendus en voiture; **to d. down to Marseilles** descendre à Marseille en voiture; **she had driven down from Inverness the day before** elle était descendue d'Inverness en voiture la veille

▸ **drive home** VT SEP **1** *(nail)* enfoncer, renfoncer

2 *(make understood)* **to d. sth home to sb** faire comprendre qch à qn, *Fam* faire rentrer qch dans la tête de qn; **d. it home to them that they mustn't speak to strangers** faisleur comprendre qu'ils ne doivent pas parler à des inconnus

3 *Aut* **to d. sb home** reconduire qn chez lui

▸ **drive in** VT SEP *(nail)* enfoncer

VI *Aut (into garage)* entrer (en voiture); **he had driven in from the countryside** il était venu de la campagne en voiture

▸ **drive into** VT SEP **to d. a nail into the wall** enfoncer un clou dans le mur; **he drove his fist into the other man's face** il a mis un coup de poing à l'autre

VT INSEP *Aut (garage)* entrer dans (en voiture); **I'm driving into town** je vais en ville en voiture

▸ **drive off** VT SEP **1** *(repel) (attack, attackers)* repousser; *(mosquitoes)* chasser

2 *Aut (person)* emmener en voiture; **they were driven off in a taxi** ils ont été conduits en taxi

VI **1** *Aut* partir *ou* s'en aller en voiture; *(of car, bus)* s'éloigner; **he jumped into his car and drove off** il a sauté dans sa voiture et s'en est allé

2 *Golf* commencer la partie

▸ **drive on** VT SEP *(somebody)* pousser (**to do sth** à faire qch)

VI *Aut* continuer (sa route); **the policeman told us to d. on** le gendarme nous a dit de circuler

▸ **drive out** VT SEP *(somebody, something)* chasser; **I will not be driven out of my home** on ne me chassera pas de ma maison; **we're being driven out of business by the supermarkets** les supermarchés nous font faire faillite

VI *Aut* **he had driven out from Glasgow** il était venu de Glasgow en voiture; **he drove out of the petrol station** il est sorti de la station d'essence

▸ **drive through** VT SEP *Constr* **to d. a tunnel through rock** percer *ou* forer un tunnel dans le rocher; *Constr* **to d. a railway through the desert** tracer *ou* construire une ligne de chemin de fer à travers le désert; **to d. one's sword through sb's body** passer son sabre à travers le corps à qn

VT INSEP *Aut (town)* traverser en voiture

VI *Aut* passer en voiture; **we'll just d. through** *(not stop)* nous ne ferons que passer en voiture

▸ **drive up** VT SEP *Econ (prices, inflation etc)* faire monter

VI *Aut* s'approcher; **they've just driven up** ils viennent de s'approcher; **a car drove up to the door** une voiture vint s'arrêter devant la porte

driveability [draɪvə'bɪlɪtɪ] N *(of vehicle)* facilité *f ou* agrément *m* de conduite

drive-in N *(cinema)* = cinéma *m* en plein air auquel on assiste en voiture, drive-in *m inv*, *Can* ciné-parc *m*, *pl* ciné-parcs; *(restaurant)* = restaurant *m* où les clients sont servis dans leurs voitures; *(bank)* = banque *f* dont les guichets sont accessibles aux clients depuis leur voiture

drivel ['drɪv(ə)l] *Fam* N bêtises *fpl*, balivernes *fpl*; **to talk d.** radoter; **the film was absolute d.** le film n'était qu'un tas de balivernes

VI **(-ll-,** *Am* **-l-)** radoter; **what are you drivelling (on) about?** qu'est-ce que tu radotes?

driveline ['draɪvlaɪn] N *Aut* chaîne *f* cinématique

drivelling, *Am* **driveling** ['drɪv(ə)lɪŋ] ADJ *Fam* radoteur, -euse; **you d. idiot!** espèce d'idiot!

driven ['drɪv(ə)n] ADJ **1** *(person)* mû comme par une obsession **2** *Tech* **electrically d.** actionné par l'électricité

▸▸ **d. snow** neige *f* vierge

driver ['draɪvər] N **1** *(of car, bus)* conducteur, -trice, chauffeur, -euse; *(of taxi, truck)* chauffeur, -euse; *(of train)* mécanicien, -ienne; *(of tram)* mécanicien, -ienne, wattman *m*; *(of horse-drawn vehicle)* conducteur, -trice; *(of horse-drawn carriage)* cocher *m*; *Horseracing (of trotting horse)* driver *m*; **he's a very good/bad d.** il conduit très bien/mal **2** *Comput (software)* programme *m* de gestion, pilote *m*, gestionnnaire *m* (de périphérique) **3** *(of cattle)* conducteur *m* **4** **log d.** flotteur *m*, driver *m*, *Can* draveur *m* **5** *Golf* driver *m*

▸▸ *Am* **d.'s license** permis *m* de conduire; **d.'s seat** siège *m* du conducteur; *Fig* **to be in the d.'s seat** mener l'affaire; **that win really puts them in the d.'s seat** cette victoire les met dans une position dominante

drive-time programme N *Radio* = émission *f* aux heures de grande écoute en voiture

drivetrain ['draɪvtreɪn] N *Aut* chaîne *f* cinématique

driveway ['draɪvweɪ] N *(of house)* allée *f*

driving ['draɪvɪŋ] ADJ **1** *Tech (wheel etc)* moteur, -trice **2** *(rain)* battant; **d. snow** neige *f* fouettée par le vent

N **1** *(of car etc)* conduite *f*; **d. is fun** c'est amusant de conduire; **his d. is awful** il conduit affreusement mal **2** **log d.** flottage *m* du bois, *Can* drave *f*

▸▸ *Aut* **d. axle** essieu *m* moteur; *Tech* **d. belt** courroie *f* de commande; **d. conditions** conditions *fpl* de conduite; *Tech* **d. force** force *f* motrice; *Fig* **the d. force behind the scheme** le moteur du projet; **d. gear** (engrenage *m* de) transmission *f*, pignon *m* d'entraînement; *Br* **d. instructor** moniteur, -trice de conduite *ou* d'auto-école; *Golf* **d. iron** grand fer *m*, driver *m*; **d. lamp** feu *m* de route; **d. lessons** leçons *fpl* de conduite; *Br* **d. licence** permis *m* de conduire; **d. mirror** rétroviseur *m*; **d. school** auto-école *f*, *pl* auto-écoles; **d. seat** place *f* du conducteur; *Tech* **d. shaft** arbre *m* moteur; **d. test** examen *m* du permis de conduire; *Tech* **d. wheel** roue *f* motrice; *(of locomotive etc)* roue de transmission

drizzle ['drɪz(ə)l] N bruine *f*, crachin *m*; **the rain came down in a steady d.** il tombait un crachin persistant

VI bruiner; **it was drizzling** il bruinait

drizzly ['drɪz(ə)lɪ] ADJ *(day)* bruineux

drogue [drəʊg] N **1** *Naut* cône-ancre *m*, *pl* cônes-ancres **2** *Aviat (for slowing descent)* parachute *m* de queue

droll [drəʊl] ADJ drôle, comique; *Iron* **oh, very d.!** très drôle!

dromedary ['drɒmɪd(ə)rɪ] N dromadaire *m*

drone [drəʊn] N **1** *(bee)* abeille *f* mâle, fauxbourdon *m*, *pl* faux-bourdons; *Fig Pej (parasite)* fainéant *m*, parasite *m* **2** *(noise) (of bee, conversation, traffic)* bourdonnement *m*; *(of engine)* ronronnement *m*; *Mus (of bagpipe)* bourdon *m*; *Fig (of speaker etc)* débit *m* monotone **3** *Mil, Aviat* avion *m* téléguidé, drone *m*

VI *(of bee etc)* bourdonner; *(of engine)* ronronner; *Fig (of person)* parler d'un ton monotone; **a droning sound** un bourdonnement; **a droning voice** une voix monotone

VT dire d'un ton monotone

▸ **drone away, drone on** VI **he droned on for hours** il n'a pas cessé de parler de sa voix

monotone; **to d. on** *or* **away about sth** parler de qch ad nauseam

drongo ['drɒŋgəʊ] N *Austr Fam (idiot)* abruti, -ie

drool [druːl] VI *(dribble)* baver; *Fig (gloat)* baver d'admiration; *Fig* **the sight of her in her bikini made him d.** ça le faisait baver de la voir dans son bikini®

▸ **drool over** VT INSEP *(something)* baver d'admiration à la vue de

droop [druːp] **he could tell from the d. of her shoulders/head** il savait à ses épaules tombantes/à la façon dont elle penchait la tête

VI *(of head)* (se) pencher; *(of shoulders, moustache)* tomber; *(of eyelids)* s'abaisser; *(of feathers)* pendre; *(of flower)* commencer à se faner; *Fig (of person)* languir; **his spirits drooped at the thought** cette pensée le démoralisa

VT *(head)* baisser, pencher

drooping ['druːpɪŋ] ADJ *(shoulders, moustache)* tombant; *(head)* baissé, penché; *(eyelids)* abaissé; *(flower)* qui commence à faner; *Fig (person)* languissant; **to revive sb's d. spirits** remonter le moral à qn

droopy ['druːpɪ] ADJ *(moustache)* tombant; *Fig (weak, not very well)* patraque, mal fichu

---

DROP [drɒp]

N	goutte **1** · baisse **2** · chute **2**
VI	tomber **1–3** · se laisser tomber **1** · baisser **3**
VT	laisser tomber **1, 4** · baisser **2** · déposer **3** · abandonner **4** · omettre **5** · perdre **6**

N **1** *(of water, blood)* goutte *f*; *(of wine)* doigt *m*, larme *f*; *(of vinegar)* filet *m*; *(of necklace, chandelier etc)* pendant *m*, pendeloque *f*; **d. by d.** goutte à goutte; *Fig* **it's only a d. in the ocean** *or* **bucket** ce n'est qu'une goutte d'eau dans la mer; *Pharm* **drops** gouttes *fpl*; *Fam* **to take a d.** boire un verre; **you've had a d. too much (to drink)** tu as un peu trop bu; **he likes a wee d.** il aime bien prendre la goutte; **I haven't touched a d. since** je n'y ai pas touché depuis; **acid d.** bonbon *m* acidulé; **chocolate d.** pastille *f* de chocolat

2 *(fall) (in price, enrolments etc)* chute *f*, baisse *f*; *(in pressure)* perte *f*, chute *f*; **a d. of a couple of inches** un différence de niveau de quelques centimètres; **a d. of a hundred metres** *(sharp)* un à-pic de cent mètres; *careful,* **it's a long d.** attention, c'est haut; **d. in the ground** dénivellation *f* du terrain; *Fig* **at the d. of a hat** sans hésiter, sans la moindre hésitation; *(without any warning)* sur-le-champ, immédiatement; **he gets angry at the d. of a hat** il se met en colère pour un oui pour un non

3 *Aviat* parachutage *m*, droppage *m*

4 *Old-fashioned Fam* **the d.** *(hanging)* la potence; **he's for the d.** il est bon pour la potence; *Fig Hum* son compte est bon

5 *(for spies to leave letters etc)* boîte aux lettres *f*, planque *f*

6 *Fam* **to have/get the d. on sb** *(have advantage)* avoir/prendre l'avantage sur qn

7 *(length) (of curtain, blind, earring)* hauteur *f*

VI **(-pp-** [drɒpt]**) 1** *(of object)* tomber; *(of person)* se laisser tomber; *(of ground)* s'abaisser, s'affaisser; *Med (of womb etc)* descendre; **the book dropped from** *or* **out of his hands** le livre lui tomba des mains; **his jaw dropped** il en est resté bouche bée; **to d. into a chair** s'affaler dans un fauteuil; **I'm ready to d.** *(with fatigue)* je tombe de fatigue, je ne tiens plus sur mes jambes; *(with sleep)* je tombe de sommeil; **people are dropping like flies** *(succumbing quickly to flu etc)* les gens tombent comme des mouches; **to d. (down)**

dead tomber (raide) mort; *Sl* **d. dead!** va te faire voir!; **he can d. dead for all I care** il peut aller se faire voir; **he's dropped to sixth place** il est descendu à la sixième place; **to d. to the rear** passer à l'arrière; *Fam* **let it d.!** n'en parlons plus!; **I'm not going to let it d.** *(grievance etc)* je ne vais pas laisser passer cela

2 *(of liquid)* tomber doucement (**from** de); *(of rain)* tomber

3 *(of prices, temperature, voice etc)* baisser; *(of share prices)* reculer; *(of wind)* tomber; *(of speed)* diminuer; **the pound dropped three points against the dollar** la livre a reculé de *ou* a perdu trois points par rapport au dollar; **interest rates have dropped by 1%** les taux d'intérêt ont baissé de 1%

vt 1 *(object)* laisser tomber, lâcher; *(bomb, parachutist)* lâcher; *Naut (anchor)* jeter, mouiller; *Comput (icon)* lâcher; **d. it!** *(to dog)* lâche ça!; **he dropped it from the balcony to his accomplice** il l'a lancé à son complice depuis le balcon; **to d. a word in sb's ear** glisser *ou* couler un mot à l'oreille de qn; **to d. a letter into the pillar box** mettre une lettre à la poste; **to d. sb a line/a card** envoyer *ou* écrire un mot/une carte à qn

2 *(lower)* *(one's eyes, veil, curtain)* baisser; *(one's arms)* laisser tomber; **to d. a curtsey** faire une révérence; **to d. the hem of a dress** allonger une robe; *Aviat* **to d. a wing** piquer de l'aile

3 *(set down)* *Aut (person)* déposer, descendre (de voiture); *Naut (pilot)* débarquer

4 *(give up, stop)* *(work)* abandonner, délaisser; *(pursuit)* cesser, lâcher; **to d. the idea of doing sth** renoncer à (l'idée de) faire qch; **I've dropped the idea** j'y ai renoncé; **let's d. the subject** ne parlons plus de cela!; *Fam* **d. it!** en voilà assez!; **just d. it, okay?** laisse tomber, hein?; **to d. everything** laisser tout tomber; *Sch* **to d. maths** arrêter les maths; **to d. sb** laisser tomber qn; *Fam* **to d. sb like a hot brick** *or* **potato** laisser tomber qn du jour au lendemain; *Sport* **to d. a player** laisser tomber un équipier; **she's been dropped from the team** elle a été écartée de l'équipe; *Law* **to d. the charges** abandonner l'accusation (**against** contre)

5 *(omit)* *(letter, syllable)* omettre, supprimer; *(when speaking)* *(the r etc)* ne pas prononcer; **cases in which the article is dropped** cas où l'on supprime l'article; **you can d. the 'sir' when we're on our own** inutile de m'appeler 'monsieur' quand nous sommes seuls

6 *(lose)* *(money, Sport points, serve, stitch)* perdre

7 *Zool (of sheep etc) (young)* mettre bas

▸▸ *Aut* **d. arm** bielle *f* pendante; *Theat* **d. curtain** rideau *m* d'entr'acte; *Metal* **d. forge** marteau-pilon *m, pl* marteaux-pilons; *Sport* **d. goal** *(in rugby)* drop-goal *m, pl* drop-goals, drop *m*; *Metal* **d. hammer** marteau-pilon, *pl* marteaux-pilons; **d. handlebars** guidon *m* renversé; *Sport* **d. kick** *(in rugby)* coup *m* de pied tombé; **d.-leaf table** table *f* à battants; *Comput, Typ* **d. letter** lettrine *f*; *Tennis* **d. shot** amorti *m*; *Aut* **d. test** essai *m* de chute

▸ **drop away** vi *(of support, attendance etc)* diminuer

▸ **drop back** vi = drop behind vi

▸ **drop behind** vi *(in race)* se laisser distancer; *(with work)* prendre du retard (**with** dans); **she dropped behind to talk to John** elle est passée vers l'arrière pour parler à John

vt INSEP *(somebody)* se laisser distancer par

▸ **drop by** vi passer (chez qn); **I thought I'd d. by for a chat** je me suis dit que je passerais pour bavarder deux minutes

▸ **drop down** vi **1** *(of person) (accidentally)* tomber par terre; *(deliberately)* se mettre par *ou* à terre; **to d. down dead** tomber

(raide) mort; **they dropped down into the Second Division** ils sont descendus en deuxième division

2 *(of flap etc)* s'abaisser

▸ **drop in** vt SEP *(something)* laisser tomber dedans, mettre dedans; **d. this letter in the box for me** mets cette lettre à la boîte; *Fam* **you dropped me right in it** tu m'as mis dans la merde

vi **to d. in at the butcher's** passer chez le boucher; **to d. in on sb** *(for a few minutes)* faire une petite visite à qn; *(arrive unexpectedly)* venir en visite chez qn à l'improviste; **I'll d. in on my way home** *(to see you)* je passerai (chez toi) en rentrant; **they're always dropping in on us** ils nous tombent toujours dessus à l'improviste

▸ **drop off** vt SEP **1** *(deposit) (letter, parcel etc)* déposer

2 *(let out of car) (person)* déposer; **where do you want to be dropped off?** où veux-tu que je te dépose?

vi **1** *(fall, become detached) (of leaves etc)* tomber, se détacher; **I feel as if my arm is going to d. off** *(because this case is so heavy etc)* j'ai l'impression que mon bras va lâcher

2 *Fam* **to d. off (to sleep)** s'assoupir, s'endormir; **it was two o'clock before I finally dropped off** je ne me suis pas endormi avant deux heures du matin; **she dropped off for a few hours** elle a dormi quelques heures

3 *(decline) (of membership, attendance etc)* diminuer

▸ **drop out** vt SEP laisser tomber dehors; **he dropped it out of the window** il l'a laissé tomber par la fenêtre

vi **1** *(from pocket, briefcase etc)* tomber

2 *Fam (from school)* abandonner ses études; *(from class)* abandonner *ou* laisser tomber (un cours); *(from contest)* se retirer; *(from society)* rejeter la société; **he dropped out at the age of 14** il a abandonné ses études à 14 ans; **to d. out of university** laisser tomber l'université

▸ **drop round** vi = drop in vi

drop-dead gorgeous ADJ *Fam* hyper canon

drop-deadline N *Fam* délai *m* de rigueur

drop-down menu N *Comput* menu *m* déroulant

drop-forge vt *Metal* étamper, estamper

drop-forging N *Metal* **1** *(process)* estampage *m* **2** *(result)* pièce *f* emboutie *ou* étampée

drophead ['drɒphed] N *Aut* capote *f* rabattable

▸▸ **d. coupé** coupé *m* décapotable *ou* cabriolet

drop-in centre N *Br* centre *m* de permanence *(où l'on est reçu sans rendez-vous)*

droplet ['drɒplɪt] N gouttelette *f*

dropout ['drɒpaʊt] N **1** *Sch, Univ Fam* étudiant, -ante qui abandonne ses études; *(from society)* marginal, -ale **2** *(on a tape)* blanc *m*, perte *f* de signal

dropped ['drɒpt] ADJ *Aut etc (axle etc)* surbaissé

▸▸ *Sport* **d. goal** *(in rugby)* drop-goal *m, pl* drop-goals

dropper ['drɒpər] N compte-gouttes *m inv*

dropping ['drɒpɪŋ] N **1** *(of object)* descente *f*, chute *f*, *Aviat (of parachutist, package)* largage *m*, droppage *m*

2 *(reduction) (of prices)* baisse *f*, chute *f*

3 *(omission) (of word)* suppression *f*

4 *(abandonment) (of project, course)* abandon *m*

5 *Aut (of chassis)* surbaissement *m*

6 *Vet* **d. (of young)** mise *f* bas

▸▸ **d. off** *(of membership, attendance etc)* di-

minution *f*; *Fam* **d. out** *(of school, university)* abandon *m*; *(from society)* désinsertion *f* sociale; *Aviat* **d. zone** zone *f* de largage *ou* de droppage

droppings ['drɒpɪŋz] NPL *(of animals, birds)* fiente *f*; *(of sheep)* crottes *fpl*

dropsical ['drɒpsɪk(ə)l] ADJ *Med* hydropique

dropsy ['drɒpsɪ] N *Med* hydropisie *f*

dross [drɒs] N **1** *Metal* scories *fpl*, crasse *f* **2** *(waste)* impuretés *fpl*, déchets *mpl*; *Fam (rubbish)* rebut *m*

drought [draʊt] N sécheresse *f*

drove [drəʊv] N **1** *(of cattle etc)* troupeau *m* en marche **2 droves** *(of people)* foules *fpl* (de personnes en marche); **to arrive** *or* **come in droves** *(of sightseers, tourists etc)* arriver en foule

drover ['drəʊvər] N conducteur *m ou* toucheur *m* de bestiaux

drown [draʊn] vt **1** *(kill)* noyer; **to d. oneself** se noyer; **to be drowned** *(by accident)* se noyer; *(on purpose)* être noyé; **drowned at sea** noyé en mer; *Fig* **to d. one's sorrows (in drink)** noyer son chagrin dans la boisson **2** *(flood) (meadow, city)* inonder, submerger; **eyes drowned in tears** yeux noyés de larmes; **don't d. it!** *(when adding water etc to alcoholic drink)* ne le noie pas! **3** *(make inaudible) (sound)* étouffer; **the noise of the waterfall drowned her voice** le bruit de la cascade a couvert sa voix

vi se noyer; *Fig (be unable to cope)* être dépassé; **I'm drowning in a sea of paper** je suis dans la paperasse jusqu'au cou

▸ **drown out** vt SEP *(sound)* couvrir; *(person)* couvrir la voix de

drowned [draʊnd] ADJ **1** *(person, animal)* noyé; **a d. man/woman** un noyé/une noyée; *Fig* **he came home like a d. rat** il est rentré trempé comme une soupe **2** *(land)* inondé

drowning ['draʊnɪŋ] ADJ **a d. man** un homme qui se noie

N **1** *(case of)* **d.** noyade *f*; **to save sb from d.** sauver qn qui se noie, sauver qn de la noyade **2** *(of fields)* inondation *f*

drowse [draʊz] vi somnoler

drowsily ['draʊzɪlɪ] ADV *(to look at)* d'un air somnolent, à demi endormi; *(to say)* d'une voix endormie *ou* ensommeillée, à demi endormi; *(to think, reflect)* à moitié endormi

drowsiness ['draʊzɪnɪs] N somnolence *f*; **may cause d.** *(notice on bottle of cough mixture etc)* peut entraîner une somnolence

drowsy ['draʊzɪ] ADJ *(person)* somnolent; *(atmosphere)* engourdi; *(voice)* endormi, ensommeillé; **to be** *or* **feel d.** avoir envie de dormir, avoir sommeil

drub [drʌb] vt (-bb-) *(somebody, the enemy)* battre, rosser

▸ **drub into** vt SEP **to d. sth into sb** faire entrer qch de force dans la tête de qn

drubbing ['drʌbɪŋ] N *(with stick, fists)* volée *f* de coups; *Fig* défaite *f*; **to give an opponent a d.** battre un adversaire à plates coutures

drudge [drʌdʒ] N bête *f* de somme; **the household d.** la bonne à tout faire

vi trimer, peiner

drudgery ['drʌdʒərɪ] N travail *m* pénible *ou* ingrat, corvée(s) *f(pl)*; **just two more weeks of d.** plus que deux semaines à trimer; **the d. of housework** le caractère pénible *ou* ingrat des tâches ménagères

drug [drʌg] N **1** *(medication)* médicament *m*, drogue *f* **2** *(narcotic)* drogue *f*, stupéfiant *m*; **hard/soft drugs** drogues dures/douces; **to take** *or* **be on** *or* *Fam* **do drugs** se droguer; **to be arrested on d. charges** *(for using/possessing/dealing)* être arrêté pour utilisation/possession/trafic de stupéfiants; **athletes who take drugs** les athlètes qui se dopent;

the whole question of drugs in sport tout le problème du dopage dans le sport; *Fig* **computer games are a d.** les jeux électroniques sont une véritable drogue; *Mktg Fig* **d. on the market** produit *m* invendable; **to be a d. on the market** être invendable; **truth d.** sérum *m* de vérité

vt (**-gg-**) (*person, guard dog, wild animal, horse*) droguer; (*horse*) (*to increase performance*) doper; **they had drugged his wine/ food** on avait mis un narcotique dans son vin/sa nourriture; *Fam* **he's drugged up to the eyeballs** (*after operation*) il est bourré de médicaments; **to be in a drugged sleep** dormir profondément sous l'effet d'un narcotique

▸▸ **d. abuse** usage *m* de stupéfiants; **d. addict** drogué, -ée, toxicomane *mf*; **d. addiction** toxicomanie *f*; **d. baron** gros bonnet *m* de la drogue; **d. company** compagnie *f* de produits pharmaceutiques; **d. dealer** dealer *m*; **d. dependency** dépendance *f* à l'égard des drogues, toxicomanie, *Spec* pharmacodépendance *f*; **d. money** argent *m* de la drogue; **d. peddler** revendeur, -euse de drogue; **d. peddling** trafic *m* de drogue; **d. pusher** revendeur, -euse de drogue; **d. pushing** trafic de drogue; **d. smuggler** trafiquant, -ante de drogue; **d. smuggling** trafic de drogue; **d. squad** (*of police force*) brigade *f* des stupéfiants; **d. taking** dopage *m*; **d. trafficker** narco-trafiquant, -ante *mf*; **d. trafficking** trafic de drogue

druggist ['drʌgɪst] **N** *Am* pharmacien, -ienne; **wholesale d.** pharmacien, -ienne en gros

druggy ['drʌgɪ] **N** *Fam* camé, -ée

drugstore ['drʌgstɔːr] **N** *Am* drugstore *m*

druid ['druːɪd] **N** druide *m*

drum [drʌm] **N 1** *Mus* tambour *m*; **the drums** la batterie; **to beat the d.** battre du tambour; **to play the drums** jouer de la batterie; **big** *or* **bass d.** grosse caisse *f*, *Fig* **to bang** *or* **beat the d. for sb/sth** battre le tambour pour qn/ qch **2** (*container*) tonneau *m* en fer, fût *m*; (*for oil*) bidon *m*, tambour *m* **3** *Tech etc* tambour *m*; (*of winch*) cylindre *m*; **concrete mixing d.** mélangeur *m* à béton, bétonnière *f*, **cable d.** tambour, dévidoir *m* (*de câble électrique*) **4** (*for laser printer*) tambour *m*

vi (**-mm-**) *Mus* jouer de la batterie; *Mil* battre du tambour; **he drummed with** *or* **for the Beatles** il était batteur *ou* il jouait de la batterie pour les Beatles; **to d. on the window panes** (*of person, rain*) tambouriner sur les vitres; **her fingers were drumming on the table** elle tapotait sur la table

vt to d. a tune on sth tambouriner un air sur qch; **she was drumming her fingers on the table** elle tapotait sur la table

▸▸ **d. kit** batterie *f*, *Mil* **d. major** tambour-major *m*, *pl* tambours-majors; *Am* **d. majorette** majorette *f*; **d. plotter** traceur *m* à tambour; **d. roll** roulement *m* de tambour

▸ **drum into vt sep to d. sth into sb** enfoncer qch dans la tête de qn; **d. it into them that they mustn't take sweets from strangers** mets-leur bien dans la tête qu'ils ne doivent pas accepter de bonbons offerts par des inconnus

▸ **drum out vt sep 1** *Mil, Hist* (*soldier*) renvoyer (**of** de) **2** *Fig* (*from a club etc*) (*person*) expulser avec ignominie

▸ **drum up vt sep** (*supporters*) racoler; (*friends*) battre le rappel de; **to d. up customers** rechercher de la clientèle; **to d. up support for sth** rechercher du soutien pour qch

drumbeat ['drʌmbiːt] **N** coup *m* de tambour

drumhead ['drʌmhed] **N** *Mus* dessus *m* de tambour

▸▸ *Mil* **d. court-martial** conseil *m* de guerre

(*tenu sur le champ de bataille*); *Mil, Rel* **d. service** office *m* divin en plein air

drumlin ['drʌmlɪn] **N** drumlin *m*

drummer ['drʌmər] **N** (*of drum*) tambour *m*; (*of kettle-drum*) timbalier *m*; (*playing jazz, rock*) batteur *m*; *Fig* **to march to a different d.** suivre son propre chemin

▸▸ **d. boy** tambour

drumming ['drʌmɪŋ] **N 1** (*sound*) (*of rain, fists*), *Mus* tambourinage *m*; **the d. of her fingers on the table was driving me crazy** la façon qu'elle avait de tapoter sur la table me rendait fou **2** (*action*) (*of woodpecker*) tambourinage *m*; *Mus* **his d. has improved** il s'est amélioré à la batterie

drumstick ['drʌmstɪk] **N 1** *Mus* baguette *f* de tambour *ou* de timbale **2** *Culin* (*of chicken*) pilon *m*

drunk [drʌŋk] **pp** *see* **drink**

ADJ ivre, soûl, gris; *Fig* enivré (**with success** par le succès); **to get d.** se soûler (**on sth** à qch); **to make** *or* **get sb d.** soûler qn; **d. as a lord** soûl comme un Polonais; *Law* **d. and disorderly** = en état d'ivresse manifeste dans un lieu public; *Fig* **d. with joy/power** ivre de joie/puissance; **he is d. with power** le pouvoir lui a monté à la tête

N homme *m* soûl/femme *f* soûle; (*habitual*) ivrogne *mf*; **the city centre was full of drunks** le centre-ville était plein de gens soûls *ou* ivres; **some old d. came up to me** un vieil ivrogne s'est approché de moi

▸▸ **d. driver** = personne *f* qui conduit en état d'ivresse

drunkard ['drʌŋkəd] **N** ivrogne *mf*

drunken ['drʌŋk(ə)n] **ADJ** (*person*) ivre; (*fury, stupor*) alcoolique; (*party, celebration*) bien arrosé; (*laughter, voice*) d'ivrogne; **d. brawl** querelle *f* d'ivrognes; **d. state** état *m* d'ivresse

drunkenly ['drʌŋk(ə)nlɪ] **ADV** (*to sing, speak*) d'une voix d'ivrogne; **to stagger d.** tituber; **to quarrel d.** avoir une querelle d'ivrognes; **he slumped d. onto his chair** complètement soûl, il s'est affalé sur sa chaise

drunkenness ['drʌŋk(ə)nnɪs] **N** ivresse *f*, (*habitual*) ivrognerie *f*

drunkometer [drʌŋ'kɒmɪtər] **N** *Am* alcootest® *m*

drupe [druːp] **N** *Bot* drupe *f*

dry [draɪ] **ADJ** (**drier, driest**) **1** (*weather, cold, bread, clothing etc*) sec, *f* sèche; (*well, spring*) tari, à sec; (*river*) asséché; *Ind, Chem etc* (*process, analysis*) par voie sèche; **tomorrow will be d. and bright** demain sera une journée sans pluie et ensoleillée; **to be** *or* **feel d.** (*of thirsty person*) avoir la gorge sèche; **to pump a well d.** épuiser l'eau d'un puits; **to run** *or* **go d.** (*of river*) s'assécher; (*of spring, well*) s'épuiser, (*se*) tarir; (*of pump*) se désamorcer; **to run d.** (*of speaker*) être à sec; **I've run d.** (*of author*) mon inspiration s'est tarie; **to be kept d.** (*notice on container*) garder au sec; *Fam* **d. as a bone, bone d.** sec comme une allumette; **d. country** pays *m* aride; *Fig* pays sec (*où les boissons alcoolisées sont prohibées*); *Fig* **to go d.** (*prohibit alcohol*) prohiber la consommation des boissons alcoolisées; **there wasn't a d. eye in the house** tout le monde pleurait; **to have d. skin** avoir la peau sèche; *Met* **d. spell** éclaircie *f*, **d. work** (*causing thirst*) travail *m* qui donne soif

2 (*wine*) sec; **medium-d.** demi-sec; **extra d.** champagne champagne *m* brut

3 (*dull, boring*) (*subject*) aride; (*book, lecture*) ennuyeux; **to be as d. as dust** être ennuyeux comme la pluie

4 (*ironic*) (*person*) pince-sans-rire *inv*; (*wit, humour*) teinté d'ironie; **he has a d. manner** il est plutôt pince-sans-rire

5 *Br Pol Fam* dur

▸▸ **1** *Br Pol Fam* dur, *f* dure

2 *Austr* *Fam* **the d.** la saison sèche

3 to stay in the d. rester au sec *ou* à couvert

vt (**dried** [draɪd]) sécher; (*clothes*) faire sécher; (*skin*) dessécher; **to d. the dishes** essuyer la vaisselle; **to d. one's eyes** s'essuyer les yeux; **to d. one's hair** se sécher les cheveux; **to d. one's tears** sécher ses larmes

vi 1 (*of clothes, paint, cement*) sécher; (*of skin*) se dessécher; **to put sth out to d.** mettre qch à sécher dehors; **it's my turn to d.** (*when doing the dishes*) c'est à moi d'essuyer la vaisselle; **ink that dries black** encre qui vire au noir en séchant

2 *Fam* (*of actor*) oublier son texte

▸▸ **d. battery, d. cell** pile *f* sèche; *Naut* **d. dock** cale *f* sèche; *Fishing* **d. fly** mouche *f* sèche; *Com* **d. goods** *Br* marchandises *fpl* sèches; *Am* tissus *mpl* et articles *mpl* de bonneterie; **d. ice** neige *f* carbonique; **d. land** terre *f* ferme; *Aviat, Naut* **d. lease** location *f* d'avion/de bateau sans carburant ni équipage; **d. martini** martini *m* dry; **d. measure** = unité *f* de mesure des matières sèches; **d. rot** (*in wood, potatoes*) pourriture *f* sèche; **d. run** (*trial, practice*) coup *m* d'essai, test *m*; *Mil* entraînement *m* avec tir à blanc; **d. stone walling** murs *mpl* en pierres sèches; (*process*) construction *f* en pierres sèches; **d. weather tyre** pneu *m* temps sec

▸ **dry off vt sep** (*person*) sécher; **come and d. yourself off in front of the fire** viens te sécher devant le feu

vi (*of varnish, paint etc*) sécher; (*of person*) se sécher

▸ **dry out vt sep 1** *Fam* (*alcoholic*) désintoxiquer **2** (*water*) faire évaporer; (*skin*) dessécher; (*ground, football pitch, wood*) sécher

vi 1 *Fam* (*of alcoholic*) se faire désintoxiquer **2** (*of moisture*) s'évaporer, sécher; (*of skin, wooden furniture*) se dessécher; (*of soil, wood*) sécher; **leave your wet things in the bathroom to d. out** laisse tes affaires à sécher dans la salle de bain

▸ **dry up vt sep** (*dishes*) essuyer; (*roads, ground*) sécher; (*skin*) dessécher

vi (*of well, pool etc*) se dessécher, tarir; *Fig* (*of funds, conversation*) tarir; (*of inspiration*) se tarir; (*of author etc*) épuiser son inspiration; (*of speaker, actor etc*) oublier son texte; **the well has dried up** le puits est à sec; *Sl* **d. up!** (*be quiet!*) la ferme!, ta gueule!

dryad ['draɪæd] **N** *Myth* dryade *f*

dry-clean **vt** nettoyer à sec

dry-cleaner **N** nettoyeur *m* à sec, teinturier *m*; **take it to the d.'s** portez-le à la teinturerie *ou* au pressing

dry-cleaning **N 1** (*process*) nettoyage *m* à sec; **d. is not recommended** (*on label*) le nettoyage à sec n'est pas recommandé **2** (*clothes*) vêtements *mpl* laissés chez le teinturier; **pick up the d. for me** va me chercher les vêtements chez le teinturier

dry-dock **vt** (*ship*) mettre en cale sèche

vi (*of ship*) entrer en cale sèche

dryer ['draɪər] **N 1** (*device*) *Ind* sécheur *m*, séchoir *m*; **hair d.** (*hand-held*) séchoir (à cheveux), sèche-cheveux *m inv*; (*on stand*) casque *m* sèche-cheveux; **clothes-d.** (*hanging from ceiling, folding etc*) séchoir; **spin d.** essoreuse *f* (centrifuge); **tumble d.** séchoir rotatif (à air chaud); *Phot* **plate d.** sèche-cliché *m*, *pl* sèche-clichés **2** (*in paint etc*) siccatif *m*

dry-eyed **ADJ** les yeux secs, l'œil sec

drying ['draɪɪŋ] **ADJ 1** (*wind*) desséchant; **a good d. wind** (*for drying clothes*) un bon vent pour sécher le linge **2 quick-d.** (*oil, varnish*) siccatif

N séchage *m*; (*of skin*) dessèchement *m*; (*with a cloth*) essuyage *m*

▸▸*Fam* **d. out** *(of alcoholic)* désintoxication *f*; **d. rack** séchoir *m*; **d. up** *(of stream, river etc)* tarissement *m*

dryly ['draɪlɪ] **ADV** *(with irony)* avec une pointe d'ironie, d'un air de pince-sans-rire

dryness ['draɪnɪs] **N 1** *(of region, weather, ground)* sécheresse *f* **2** *(of speech)* aridité *f* **3** *(of tone)* ironie *f*; **the d. of her wit** son humour pince-sans-rire

dry-roasted [draɪ'rəʊstɪd] **ADJ** *(peanuts)* grillé à sec

DSC [diːes'siː] **N** *Br Mil abbr* **Distinguished Service Cross**

D. Sc. [diːes'siː] **N** *Univ abbr* **Doctor of Science**

DSL [diːe'sel] **N** *Comput (abbr* **Digital Subscriber Line)** ligne *f* d'abonné numérique, DSL *m*

DSM [diːe'sem] **N** *Br Mil abbr* **Distinguished Service Medal**

DSO [diːe'səʊ] **N** *Br Mil abbr* **Distinguished Service Order**

DSS [diːe'ses] **N** *Br Admin Formerly abbr* **Department of Social Security**

DST [diːes'tiː] **N** *Am (abbr* **daylight saving time)** HAE *f*

DTI [diːtiː'aɪ] **N** *Br Admin abbr* **Department of Trade and Industry**

DTP [diːtiː'piː] **N** *Comput (abbr* **desktop publishing)** PAO *f*
▸▸ **D. operator** opérateur, -trice de PAO; **D. software** logiciel *m* de PAO

DTs [diː'tiːz] **NPL** *Fam (abbr* **delirium tremens) to have the D.** *(of alcoholic)* faire une crise de delirium tremens

DTT [diːtiː'tiː] **N** *(abbr* **digital terrestrial television)** TNT *f*

dual ['djuːəl] **ADJ 1** double; **to have d. nationality** avoir la double nationalité; **to have a d. function** *or* **purpose** avoir une double fonction **2** *Math* dual
▸▸ *Br Aut* **d. carriageway** route *f* à quatre voies; *Aut* **d.-control car** voiture *f* à double commande; **d. currency** deux monnaies *fpl*; **d. economy** économie *f* duale; *St Exch* **d. listing** cotation *f* sur deux Bourses; *Br* **d. ownership** copropriété *f*; *Psy* **d. personality** dédoublement *m* de la personnalité; **d. pricing** régime *m* du double prix; *(display)* double affichage *m* (des prix); *Aut* **d. wheels** roues *fpl* jumelées

Attention: ne pas confondre avec le nom anglais **duel**.

dual-band **ADJ** *Tel* bi-bande

dualism ['djuːəlɪz(ə)m] **N** dualité *f*; *Phil* dualisme *m*

duality [djuː'ælɪtɪ] **N** dualité *f*; *Psy (of personality)* dédoublement *m*

dual-mode **ADJ** *Tel* Dual Mode

dual-purpose **ADJ** à double emploi

dual-venturi ['djuːəlven'tjʊərɪ] **ADJ** *Aut* à double venturi

dub¹ [dʌb] *Cin, TV* **N** *(sound)* repiquage *m*; *(video)* copie *f*; *(action)* doublage *m*
VT (-bb-) *(film)* *(into foreign language)* doubler (**into** en); *(original voice soundtrack)* sonoriser; *(sound)* post-synchroniser; *(video)* faire une copie dans un autre format

dub² **VT (-bb-) 1 to d. sb (a) knight** armer *ou* adouber qn chevalier; *Fig* **he was dubbed the king of tennis** on l'a surnommé le roi du tennis **2** *(leather)* préparer au dégras

dubbin ['dʌbɪn] **N** *(for leather)* dégras *m*
VT *(shoes)* enduire de dégras

dubbing ['dʌbɪŋ] **N** *Cin, TV (into foreign language)* doublage *m*; *(of original voice soundtrack)* sonorisation *f*; *(of sound)* post-synchronisation *f*, repiquage *m* du son, mixage *m*

▸▸ **d. mixer** mélangeur *m* de son, ingénieur *m* du son; **d. suite** studio *m* de doublage

dubiety [djuː'baɪətɪ] **N** *Fml* = **dubiousness**

dubious ['djuːbɪəs] **ADJ 1** *(uncertain)* *(person)* qui doute; *(outcome)* incertain; **she looked d.** elle avait l'air d'avoir des doutes; **d. as to what he should do** ne sachant trop ce qu'il devait faire; **I'm still a bit d.** j'ai encore quelques doutes; **we were d. about the scheme** nous avions des doutes sur le projet; **d. expression** air *m* de doute; **it is d. whether they will succeed in persuading him** il n'est pas certain qu'ils réussissent à le persuader **2** *Pej (suspect, questionable)* *(origin)* douteux; *(advantage)* contestable; *(distinction, honour)* triste; *(compliment)* équivoque; *(company)* douteux, louche

dubiously ['djuːbɪəslɪ] **ADV** *(to say)* d'un ton de doute; *(to look at)* d'un air de doute

dubiousness ['djuːbɪəsnɪs] **N 1** *(uncertainty)* *(of outcome)* incertitude *f*; *(in voice, of expression)* doute *m*; **their increasing d. about the whole enterprise** leurs doutes croissants à propos de toute cette affaire **2** *(suspect nature)* *(of origin, proposal, person's background)* caractère *m* douteux; *(of advantage)* caractère contestable; *(of compliment etc)* caractère équivoque; **the d. of this distinction** ce triste honneur

Dubliner ['dʌblɪnə(r)] **N** = **personne** *f* née ou habitant à Dublin

ducal ['djuːk(ə)l] **ADJ** *USU ATTRIB* ducal, -aux

ducat ['dʌkət] **N** *Hist (coin)* ducat *m*; *Am Fam (money)* fric *m*, blé *m*

duchess ['dʌtʃɪs] **N** duchesse *f*

duchesse ['duːʃes] **N**
▸▸ *Culin* **d. potatoes** pommes *fpl* (de terre) duchesse

duchy ['dʌtʃɪ] **N** duché *m*

duck¹ [dʌk] **N 1** *(bird)* canard *m*; *(female)* cane *f*; *Culin* canard; **wild d.** canard sauvage; *Culin* **Peking d.** canard à la Pékinoise; *Culin* **Bombay d.** poisson *m* sec assaisonné de cari; **d.-egg blue** bleu-vert *m* pâle; *Fig* **to take to sth like a d. to water** mordre à qch; **criticism runs off him like water off a d.'s back** les critiques glissent sur lui comme de l'eau sur les plumes d'un canard; **to play at ducks and drakes** faire des ricochets (sur l'eau); *Fig* **to play ducks and drakes with one's money** jeter l'argent par les fenêtres;
2 *Eng Dial (form of address)* **what do you want, ducks?** *(to woman)* et pour vous, ma petite dame?; *(to man)* et pour le monsieur, qu'est-ce que ce sera?
3 *Cr* zéro *m*; **to be out for a d., to make a d.** faire chou blanc; **to break one's d.** marquer son premier point
▸▸ *Sl* **d.'s arse** *(hairstyle)* = coiffure *f* masculine populaire dans les années cinquante *(cheveux courts plaqués vers l'arrière)*; **d. pond** mare *f* aux canards

duck² **VI 1** *(to avoid being hit)* baisser la tête, se baisser; **to d. behind a tree/car** se cacher derrière un arbre/une voiture; **to d. out of sight** se cacher **2** *(under water)* plonger sous l'eau; **he ducked under the surface** il a plongé sous la surface de l'eau
VT 1 *(one's head)* baisser subitement; **to d. a blow** esquiver un coup **2** *Fig (obligations, embarrassing question etc)* se dérober à; *(problem)* contourner; **to d. the issue** s'esquiver *(in reply)* user de faux-fuyants; **to d. a challenge** ne pas relever un défi **3** *(under water)* *(person)* plonger dans l'eau, faire faire le plongeon à
N *(movement)* *(to avoid being hit etc)* mouvement *m* instinctif de la tête; *Boxing* esquive *f*

▸ **duck out** **VI** se défiler; **to d. out of doing sth** éviter de faire qch; **I managed to d. out**

of it j'ai réussi à me défiler, j'ai réussi à y couper

duck³ **N** *Tex* coutil *m*; *Old-fashioned* **ducks** *(trousers)* pantalon *m* de coutil *ou* de toile

duck-billed [-bɪld] **ADJ**
▸▸ **d. platypus** ornithorynque *m*

duckboards ['dʌkbɔːdz] **NPL** caillebotis *m*

duckie ['dʌkɪ] **N, ADJ** = **ducky**

ducking ['dʌkɪŋ] **N** *(under water)* plongeon *m* (involontaire); **to give sb a d.** faire boire la tasse à qn; **to get** *or* **take a d.** boire la tasse

duckling ['dʌklɪŋ] **N** canardeau *m*; *(male)* caneton *m*; *(female)* canette *f*; *Culin* caneton; **the Ugly D.** le vilain petit Canard

duckweed ['dʌkwiːd] **N** *(plant)* lentille *f* d'eau

ducky ['dʌkɪ] **N** *Eng Dial (to man)* mon petit chou; *(to woman)* ma cocotte
ADJ *Am Fam* tout mignon

duct [dʌkt] **N 1** *(tube)* conduit *m*; *Constr etc (for cables etc)* caniveau *m*; **air d.** manche *f* à air, gaine *f* de ventilation **2** *Anat* canal *m*, vaisseau *m*; **tear d.** conduit *m* lacrymal
▸▸ **d. tape** ruban *m* adhésif en toile

ductile ['dʌktaɪl] **ADJ** *(metal)* ductile; *Fig Lit (character)* malléable

ductility [dʌk'tɪlɪtɪ] **N** *(of metal)* ductilité *f*; *Fig Lit (of character)* malléabilité *f*

dud [dʌd] **N** *Fam (person)* incapable *mf*; *Mil (shell)* obus *m* non éclaté; **several fireworks were duds** plusieurs pièces d'artifice ont foiré; **I'm a d. at history** je suis nul en histoire; **the note was a d.** le billet était faux
ADJ **it was a d. idea** c'était nul comme idée
▸▸ **d. cheque** chèque *m* en bois; **d. note** faux billet *m*; *Mil* **d. shell** obus *m* non éclaté

dude [djuːd, duːd] **N** *Am Fam* **1** *(dandy)* gommeux *m* **2** *(man)* type *m*; **a real cool d.** un type formidable **3** *(vacationer on ranch)* hôte *m* d'un ranch qui propose des activités touristiques
▸▸ *Am* **d. ranch** = ranch *m* qui propose des activités touristiques

dudgeon ['dʌdʒən] **N** *only used in* **in high d.** sur ses grands chevaux

duds [dʌdz] **NPL** *Fam (clothes)* fringues *fpl*

DUE [djuː] **ADJ 1** *(owed)* *Com, Fin (debt)* exigible; *(bill)* échu; **bill d. on 1st May** effet payable le premier mai; **balance d.** solde *m* dû; **debts d. to us** dettes *fpl* actives; **debts d. by us** dettes passives; **bond d. for repayment** obligation *f* amortie; **to fall** *or* **become d.** *(of bill etc)* échoir, devenir payable; **falling d.** échéance *f*; **are you d. any money from him?** est-ce qu'il te doit de l'argent?; **the money d. to you** l'argent qui vous est dû; **on the d. date** à l'échéance, à terme échu; **redemption before d. date** remboursement *m* anticipé; **you're d. an apology** je vous dois/il vous doit/etc une excuse; **they are d. our thanks** ils méritent nos remerciements; **I'm (still) d. three days' holiday** j'ai encore trois jours de congé à prendre; **I'm d. (for) a rise** j'attends une augmentation de salaire
2 *(merited, proper)* dû, juste, mérité; **to give sb d. warning** avertir qn dans les formes; **with d. care** avec tout le soin requis; **he was received with d. ceremony** il fut reçu avec tout le cérémonial qui lui était dû; **in d. form** en bonne et due forme, en due forme; **after d. consideration** après mûre réflexion; **with all d. respect** avec tout le respect que je vous dois; **to treat sb with d. respect** *or* **the respect d. to him/her** traiter qn avec le respect qui lui est dû; **all in d. time** chaque chose en son temps; **in d. course** *(be told about something, learn of decision etc)* en temps voulu; *(come into inheritance, sit an exam)* en temps venu; **the impostor was unmasked in d. course** l'imposteur a finalement été démasqué

3 d. to *(caused by)* causé par, attribuable à, à cause de; *(as a result of)* par suite de, en raison de; **it is d. to his negligence** c'est sa négligence qui en est (la) cause, c'est dû à sa négligence; **what is it d. to?** à quoi cela tient-il?, à quoi est-ce que c'est dû?; **d. to fog the boat arrived late** par suite du brouillard, le bateau est arrivé en retard; **d. to circumstances beyond our control** en raison de circonstances indépendantes de notre volonté

4 *(expected)* **the train/he is d. (to arrive) at two o'clock** le train/il doit arriver à deux heures; **there's a bus d. now** un bus doit arriver d'un moment à l'autre; **when is the baby d.?** pour quand la naissance est-elle prévue?, quand le bébé doit-il naître?

ADV d. north droit vers le nord, plein nord

N *(what is owed)* dû *m*; **to give sb their d.** donner à qn ce qui lui est dû *ou* ce qui lui revient; *Fig* **to give him his d., he did apologize** pour lui rendre justice, il faut reconnaître qu'il s'est excusé

NPL dues *(for membership)* droits *mpl*, frais *mpl*; *(club subscription)* cotisation *f* annuelle; *(in publishing)* *(books on order)* livres *mpl* en commande; *esp Am Fig* **she's paid her dues** *(merits respect)* elle mérite le respect; *(has worked hard)* elle a peiné pour en arriver où elle en est; *Naut* **harbour dues** droits de port

▶▶ **d. date** *(of bill, payment)* échéance *f*, *(of baby)* date *f* prévue pour la naissance

duel ['djʊəl] **N** duel *m*; *Fig* lutte *f*, **a d. to the death** un duel à mort; **to fight a d.** se battre en duel

VI (**-ll-**, *Am* **-l-**) se battre en duel

> Attention: ne pas confondre avec l'adjectif **dual**.

duelling, *Am* **dueling** ['djʊəlɪŋ] **N** le duel
▶▶ **d. pistols** pistolets *mpl* de duel

duellist, *Am* **duelist** ['djʊəlɪst] **N** duelliste *m*

duet [dju:'et] **N** duo *m*; *(for piano)* morceau *m* à quatre mains

duettist [dju:'etɪst] **N** *Mus* duettiste *mf*

duff [dʌf] **N 1** *Culin* **(plum) d.** pudding *m* aux raisins **2** *Br Fam* **up the d.** *(pregnant)* en cloque; **to get sb up the d.** mettre qn en cloque **3** *Am Fam* *(buttocks)* cul *m*, derche *m* **ADJ** *Br Fam* nul; **it was a d. idea** c'était nul comme idée

▶ **duff up VT SEP** *Br Sl* *(beat up)* rosser; **to get duffed up** se faire rosser

duffel ['dʌf(ə)l] **N**
▶▶ **d. bag** sac *m* marin; **d. coat** duffle-coat *m*, *pl* duffle-coats, *Can* corvette *f*

duffer ['dʌfər] **N** *Fam* **1** *(incompetent person)* bousilleur, -euse; *Sch* cancre *m*; **to be a d. at** *(history etc)* être nul en **2** **an old d.** *(old man)* un vieux croulant

duffle ['dʌf(ə)l] **N** = **duffel**

dug[1] [dʌg] **PT, PP** *see* **dig**

dug[2] **N** *(of cow)* pis *m*; *Pej (of woman)* mamelle *f*, tétine *f*

dugout ['dʌgaʊt] **N 1** *(canoe)* canot *m* creusé dans un tronc d'arbre, pirogue *f* **2** *(shelter)* *Mil* tranchée-abri *f*, *pl* tranchées-abris; *Ftbl* banc *m* abri de touche

DUI *abbr* **driving under the influence**

duke [dju:k] **N 1** duc *m* **2** *Old-fashioned Sl* **dukes** *(fists)* poings *mpl*, **put up your dukes** en garde!

▶ **duke out VT SEP** *Am Old-fashioned* **to d. it out** se bagarrer (**with** avec)

dukedom ['dju:kdəm] **N 1** *(territory)* duché *m* **2** *(title)* titre *m* de duc; *(rank)* dignité *f* de duc

dulcet ['dʌlsɪt] **ADJ ATTRIB** *Lit, Iron (sound)*

doux, *f* douce, suave, agréable; **to say sth in d. tones** dire qch d'un ton suave; *Hum* **I recognize those d. tones** je reconnais le son harmonieux de cette voix

dulcimer ['dʌlsɪmər] **N** *Mus* tympanon *m*

dull [dʌl] **ADJ 1** *(not intelligent) (person)* lent, lourd; **to be d.-witted** être lent d'esprit; *Prov* **all work and no play makes Jack a d. boy** on s'abrutit à ne penser qu'au travail

2 *(boring) (book, film, person)* ennuyeux; *(life)* monotone; *(party)* assommant; *(style)* terne; **things have been pretty d. since she left** c'est plutôt monotone depuis qu'elle est partie; **as d. as ditchwater** ennuyeux comme la pluie; **deadly d.** abrutissant, assommant; **it's deadly d. here** on s'ennuie à mourir ici; **never a d. moment!** pas le temps de s'ennuyer!

3 *(not sharp) (pain)* sourd; *(sound)* sourd, étouffé; *(blunt) (edge)* émoussé; **to become d.** *(of tool, senses etc)* s'émousser

4 *(not bright) (colour, surface)* terne, mat; *(glow)* faible, terne; *(eyes)* sans éclat; *(voice)* terne; *(weather, sky, cloud)* sombre; **paper with a d. finish** papier mat *ou* non satiné

5 *Com, Fin (market)* calme, inactif; **business is d.** les affaires ne marchent pas fort

VT 1 *(the mind)* engourdir, alourdir

2 *(make less sharp) (pain)* endormir, calmer; *(pleasure)* rendre moins vif; *(sound)* amortir, assourdir; *(tool, the senses)* émousser; **sorrow is dulled by the passage of time** le temps émousse la douleur

3 *(make less bright) (colours)* ternir; *(surface)* dépolir; *(metal)* mater; *(eyes)* faire perdre son éclat à; *(voice)* ternir

VI 1 *(become less sharp) (of senses, eyesight)* s'émousser

2 *(become less bright) (of colour)* se ternir; *(of metal etc)* se dépolir; *(of eyes)* perdre son éclat

dullard ['dʌləd] **N** *Fml* lourdaud, -aude; *Sch* cancre *m*

dullness ['dʌlnɪs] **N 1** *(of mind)* lourdeur *f* d'esprit **2** *(tedium)* ennui *m*, tristesse *f*, *(of life, speech)* monotonie *f*, **a film of such d.** un film aussi ennuyeux **3** *(lack of sharpness) (of blade etc)* manque *m* de tranchant; *(of point, senses)* émoussement *m*; *(of pain)* caractère *m* sourd **4** *(lack of brightness) (of colour, eyes)* manque *m* d'éclat; *(of sound, light)* faiblesse *f*, *(of voice)* caractère *m* terne; **the d. of the weather** la grisaille **5** *Com, Fin (of business)* stagnation *f*, *(of market)* inactivité *f*

dully ['dʌlɪ] **ADV 1** *(stupidly)* lourdement, lentement **2** *(boringly)* d'une manière ennuyeuse **3** *(not sharply) (to echo)* sourdement, faiblement; *(to throb)* sourdement **4** *(not brightly) (lit, to gleam)* faiblement; **..., she said d.** ..., dit-elle d'une voix terne

Dulux dog ['dju:lʌks] **N** *Br Fam* bobtail *m*

duly ['dju:lɪ] **ADV 1** *(properly)* dûment; **d. appointed** *(member)* régulièrement désigné **2** *(as expected)* comme prévu; **rent d. paid** loyer payé exactement; **and all the shops were d. shut** et tous les magasins étaient bien entendu fermés

dumb [dʌm] **ADJ 1** *(unable or unwilling to speak)* muet, *f* muette; **I was struck d. with astonishment** la stupeur m'a rendu muet **2** *esp Am Fam (stupid) (person, mistake)* bête; *(worthless)* nul, *f* nulle; **to play** *or* **act d.** faire le niais; **I don't want to go to some d. theatre!** je ne veux pas aller au théâtre, c'est nul!
▶▶ **d. animal** bête *f*, *Pej* **d. blonde** blonde *f* évaporée; *Fam* **d. cluck** imbécile *mf*; **d. insolence** silence *m* insolent; **d. show** = pantomime *m* faisant partie d'une pièce de théâtre; *Comput* **d. terminal** terminal *m* passif

▶ **dumb down VT SEP** *(education, news programme)* faire baisser le niveau de

dumbass ['dʌmæs] *Am Sl* **N** taré, -ée, débile *mf*, abruti, -ie
ADJ débile

dumbbell ['dʌmbel] **N 1** *(weight)* haltère *f* **2** *esp Am Sl (idiot)* lourdaud, -aude

dumbfound [dʌm'faʊnd] **VT** abasourdir, ahurir, ébahir

dumbfounded [dʌm'faʊndɪd] **ADJ** abasourdi, ahuri, ébahi (**at** de); **I'm d.** je n'en reviens pas; **we were d. at the news** la nouvelle nous frappa de stupeur

dumbing down ['dʌmɪŋ] **N** *(of education, news programme)* baisse *f* de niveau

dumbly ['dʌmlɪ] **ADV** *(to follow, stare)* sans rien dire; **to be d. obedient** obéir silencieusement

dumbness ['dʌmnɪs] **N 1** mutisme *m*; **deaf and d.** surdi-mutité *f* **2** *Fam (stupidity)* sottise *f*, bêtise *f*

dumbo ['dʌmbəʊ] **N** *Fam* andouille *f*, imbécile *mf*

dumbstruck ['dʌmstrʌk] **ADJ** = **dumbfounded**

dumbwaiter [dʌm'weɪtər] **N** *(food stand)* guéridon *m*; *(revolving)* plateau *m* tournant; *(lift)* monte-plats *m inv*

dumdum ['dʌmdʌm] **N 1** *Mil (bullet)* (balle *f*) dum-dum *f*, *pl* dum-dums **2** *Fam (idiot)* idiot, -ote
▶▶ *Mil* **d. bullet** (balle *f*) dum-dum *f*, *pl* dum-dums

dummy ['dʌmɪ] **N 1** *(in clothes shop window)*, *Sewing* mannequin *m*; *(of ventriloquist)* marionnette *f*, *Fam* **standing there like a stuffed d.** planté comme un piquet **2** *(imitation object)* objet *m*/paquet *m*/bouteille *f*/etc factice; *(book)* maquette *f*, **it's just a d.** ce n'en est pas un vrai **3** *Offensive (person who cannot speak)* muet, *f* muette; *Fig Pej (idiot)* abruti, -ie, lourdaud, -aude **4** *Br (for baby)* tétine *f* **5** *Cards (player or hand at bridge, whist)* mort *m*; **to be** *or* **play d.** faire le mort **6** *Ftbl etc* feinte *f*

ADJ *(fake)* factice
▶▶ **d. bridge** bridge *m* à trois personnes; **d. run** *(trial)* essai *m*; *Fig Fam* coup *m* d'essai; *Aviat, Mil* attaque *f* simulée *ou* d'entraînement; **d. whist** whist *m* avec un mort

dump [dʌmp] **N 1** *(for refuse)* (lieu *m* de) décharge *f*, refuse *or* rubbish *or Am* garbage d. décharge

2 *Fam (house etc)* taudis *m*; **what a d.!** *(of place)* quel trou!, quel bled!; *(of office etc)* quelle saloperie de boîte!

3 *(store)* dépôt *m*; *Mil* **ammunition d.** dépôt de munitions, parc *m* à munitions;

4 *Comput* cliché *m* mémoire; **(memory) d.** vidage *m* (de) mémoire; **(screen) d.** impression *f* écran

5 *Sl* **to take** *or* **have a d.** *(defecate)* chier

VT 1 *(put down) (lorryload of sand etc)* décharger, déverser; *(package etc)* laisser tomber lourdement; *(somebody, something) (on chair etc)* déposer rudement; *Aviat (cargo)* se délester de; **I'm just going home to d. my suitcase** je vais déposer ma valise chez moi; **d. your bags in the corner** déposez *ou* laissez vos sacs dans le coin; **can we d. the kids here for the weekend?** est-ce que nous pouvons laisser les enfants ici ce week-end?

2 *(throw away, dispose of) (refuse)* jeter à la voirie; *(waste in the sea)* déverser; *Fam (car, unwanted object etc)* se débarrasser de; *(lover, boyfriend etc)* plaquer

3 *Com* **to d. goods on a foreign market** faire du dumping, écouler des marchandises à perte à l'étranger

4 *Comput (memory)* vider

VI *Com* faire du dumping
▶▶ *Mktg* **d. bin** panier *m* de présentation en vrac, panier présentoir; *Am Rail* **d. car** wa-

gon *m* à bascule; **d. truck** dumper *m*, tombe-reau *m*

▸**dump on** VT INSEP *Am Fam* **1** *(criticize)* *(somebody, something)* s'en prendre à **2** *(tell one's problems to)* *(somebody)* se décharger de ses problèmes sur

dumper ['dʌmpər] N *Br* tombereau *m*, dumper *m*
▸▸**d. truck** tombereau, dumper

dumping ['dʌmpɪŋ] N **1** 'no d.' *(sign)* 'décharge interdite' **2** *Com (of goods)* dumping *m* **3** *Comput (of memory)* vidage *m*
▸▸**d. ground** *(for rubbish)* décharge *f*, dépôt *m* d'ordures; *Fig (for inferior goods)* dépotoir *m*; *Fig* **people use the home as a d. ground for their elderly parents** les gens utilisent la maison de retraite pour se débarrasser de leurs parents âgés; **they just use this house as a d. ground** ici ce n'est qu'un dépôt pour eux

dumpling ['dʌmplɪŋ] N **1** *Culin (in stew)* boulette *f* de pâte; **apple d.** pomme *f* enrobée dans de la pâte et cuite au four **2** *Fig Fam (plump person)* boulot, -otte, petit gros, *f* petite grosse; **he's become a bit of a d.** il est devenu un peu boulot

dumps [dʌmps] NPL *Fam (depression)* cafard *m*, idées *fpl* noires; **to be down in the d.** broyer du noir, avoir le cafard

dumpster ['dʌmpstər] N *Am* benne *f* à ordures

dumpy ['dʌmpɪ] ADJ *(person etc)* boulot, -otte

dun[1] [dʌn] ADJ brun grisâtre; *(horse)* gris louvet
N *(horse)* cheval *m* gris louvet

dun[2] VT (-nn-) *Old-fashioned (debtor)* importuner, harceler; **dunned by his creditors** pressé par ses créanciers; **a dunning letter** une lettre de relance *ou* de poursuite

dunce [dʌns] N *Sch* cancre *m*; **the d. of the class, the class d.** le dernier de la classe; **to be a d. at physics** être nul en physique; **d.'s cap** bonnet *m* d'âne

dunderhead ['dʌndəhed] N *Fam* imbécile *mf*

dune [dju:n] N **(sand) d.** dune *f*
▸▸**d. buggy** buggy *m*

dung [dʌŋ] N **1** *(excrement)* crotte *f*, *(of wild animal)* fumées *fpl*; *(of cow)* bouse *f*, *(of horse)* crottin *m* **2** *Agr (manure)* fumier *m*, engrais *m*
▸▸**d. beetle** bousier *m*

dungaree [dʌŋgə'ri:] N **1** dungarees *(with bib)* salopette *f*, *(workman's)* bleu(s) *m(pl)* (de travail); **to be wearing (a pair of) dungarees** porter une salopette, être en salopette; *(workman's)* porter un *ou* des bleu(s) (de travail), être en bleu(s) (de travail) **2** *Tex* treillis *m*

dungeon ['dʌndʒ(ə)n] N **1** *(prison)* cachot *m* **2** *Hist (tower)* donjon *m*

dunghill ['dʌŋhɪl] N tas *m* de fumier, fumier *m*

dunk [dʌŋk] VT *(bread, croissant) (in coffee etc)* tremper
VI faire trempette

Dunkirk [dʌn'kɜːk] N Dunkerque

dunlin ['dʌnlɪn] N *(bird)* bécasseau *m* variable

dunno [dʌ'nəʊ] CONTR *Sl* = **don't know** j'sais pas!

dunnock ['dʌnək] N *(bird)* accenteur *m* mouchet

dunny ['dʌnɪ] N *Austr Fam (toilet)* chiottes *fpl*

duo ['dju:əʊ] N **1** *Mus* duo *m* **2** *(two people)* couple *m*

duodecimal [dju:əʊ'desɪm(ə)l] ADJ duodécimal

NPL **duodecimals** *(system)* système *m* de numérotation duodécimal

duodenal [dju:əʊ'di:n(ə)l] ADJ *Anat, Med (ulcer etc)* duodénal

duodenum pl **duodena, duodenums** [dju:əʊ'di:nəm, -nə, -nəmz] N *Anat* duodénum *m*

dupe [dju:p] N dupe *f*
VT duper, tromper; **to be duped** se laisser duper; **to d. sb into doing sth** duper qn pour qu'il fasse qch; **she duped him into believing that …** elle lui a fait gober que …

duple ['dju:p(ə)l] ADJ
▸▸*Mus* **d. time** rythme *m* binaire *ou* à deux temps

duplex ['dju:pleks] ADJ **1** *Elec, Tel (line)* duplex *inv*; *(operation etc)* en duplex **2** *Am (apartment)* duplex
N *Am (apartment)* (appartement *m*) duplex *m*; *(house)* maison *f* jumelée
▸▸*Am* **d. house** maison jumelée

duplicate[1] ['dju:plɪkət] ADJ (en) double; **I have a d. key** j'ai un double de la clé; **d. set of tools** outils *mpl* de rechange; **d. receipt** quittance *f* double
N *(of work of art etc)* double *m*; *(of cheque etc)* duplicata *m*; *(of written document)* double, contrepartie *f*, **in d.** en double (exemplaire), en deux exemplaires, *Fml* en duplicata

duplicate[2] ['dju:plɪkeɪt] VT **1** *(make a copy of) (key)* faire un double de; *(document)* copier, reproduire en double exemplaire **2** *(on duplicator)* reprographier, polycopier; **to d. sth** tirer plusieurs exemplaires de qch au duplicateur, polycopier qch **3** *(do again)* refaire; **that's just duplicating what they've already done** cela revient à refaire ce qu'ils ont déjà fait

duplicating ['dju:plɪkeɪtɪŋ] N *(of document)* reproduction *f*
▸▸**d. machine** duplicateur *m*, machine *f* à polycopier

duplication [dju:plɪ'keɪʃən] N reproduction *f*; **unnecessary d. of work** répétition *f* inutile du travail

duplicator ['dju:plɪkeɪtər] N duplicateur *m*, machine *f* à polycopier

duplicity [dju:'plɪsɪtɪ] N duplicité *f*

durability [djʊərə'bɪlɪtɪ] N durabilité *f*, *Ind* résistance *f*

durable ['djʊərəb(ə)l] ADJ *(peace)* durable; *(fabric)* résistant
NPL *Com* **(consumer) durables** biens *mpl* durables
▸▸*Com* **d. goods** biens durables *ou* non périssables

duration [djʊ'reɪʃən] N durée *f*, *(of life)* étendue *f*; **the peace was of short d.** la paix fut de courte durée; **for the d.** *Mil (to enlist)* pour la durée de la guerre; *Fig* jusqu'à la Saint-Glinglin

duress [djʊ'res] N *Law* contrainte *f*, coercition *f*; **to act under d.** agir sous la contrainte

Durex® ['djʊəreks] N préservatif *m*

during ['djʊərɪŋ] PREP pendant, durant; **d. the whole week** toute la semaine; **d. the winter** au cours de *ou* pendant l'hiver; **d. the journey** en cours de route; **d. the last year** dans le courant de l'année dernière; **killed d. a brawl** tué au cours d'une rixe; **d. that time** pendant ce temps

durum ['djʊərəm] N
▸▸**d. wheat** blé *m* dur

dusk [dʌsk] N crépuscule *m*; **at d.** à la nuit tombante, à la tombée de la nuit

duskiness ['dʌskɪnɪs] N **1** *(darkness of skin)* teint *m* mat **2** *Lit (dimness)* demi-jour *m*, pénombre *f*

dusky ['dʌskɪ] ADJ **1** *(dark) (complexion)*

mat; *(dark-skinned)* au teint mat **2** *Lit (dim)* crépusculaire

dust [dʌst] N **1** *(dirt, powder)* poussière *f*, *(of marble)* sciure *f*; **these ornaments just collect the d.** ces bibelots ne sont que des nids à poussière; **to raise a cloud of d.** soulever un nuage de poussière; *Fig* **to bite the d.** *(die, fail)* mordre la poussière; *(of hopes)* s'envoler; *Fig* **to throw d. in sb's eyes** jeter de la poudre aux yeux à qn; *Fig* **to blow the d. off sth** dépoussiérer qch; *Old-fashioned Fam* **to kick up** *or* **raise a d.** *(a fuss)* faire du foin; *Fig* **once the d. has settled** une fois que les choses seront revenues à la normale, une fois que la situation se sera apaisée; **all their hopes had turned to d. and ashes** tous leurs espoirs s'étaient anéantis; *Fam* **when there's work to be done you can't see him for d.!** dès qu'il y a du travail, il n'y a plus personne!; **… or you won't see me for d.!** … ou tu ne me reverras pas de sitôt!; **brick d.** poussière de brique; *Phys* **cosmic d.** poussière cosmique; **to take a d. bath** *(of bird)* s'ébrouer dans la poussière
2 *(action)* **to give the table a d.** passer un coup de chiffon sur la table (pour enlever la poussière)
VT **1** *(remove dust from) (room, furniture)* épousseter
2 *(sprinkle)* **to d. a cake with sugar, to d. sugar over a cake** saupoudrer un gâteau de sucre; **sugar-dusted doughnuts** beignets saupoudrés de sucre; *Fam* **to d. a gun for fingerprints** examiner un revolver pour y relever des empreintes digitales
▸▸**d. bag** *(for vacuum cleaner) (disposable)* sac *m* à poussière; *(fixed)* sac tissu; *Am* **d. ball** mouton *m*; *Geog* **d. bowl** zone *f* semi-désertique; **the D. Bowl** *(in US)* le Dust Bowl; *Am* **d. bunny** mouton *m*; **d. cap** capuchon *m* anti-poussière; *Am* **d. cloth** chiffon *m* à poussière; **d. coat** cache-poussière *m inv*; *Tech* **d. collector** capteur *m* de poussières; **d. cover** *(for book)* jaquette *f*, *(for machine)* housse *f* de rangement; *(for furniture)* housse de protection; **d. devil** tourbillon *m* de poussière; **d. jacket** *(for book)* jaquette; *Am* **d. kitten** mouton *m*; **d. storm** tempête *f* de poussière; **d. trap** nid *m* à poussière; *Ind* attrape-poussières *m inv*

▸**dust down, dust off** VT SEP *(furniture)* épousseter; *Fig (legislation, lecture)* dépoussiérer; *(one's French etc)* rafraîchir, dérouiller; **to d. oneself off** *or* **down** se brosser (pour enlever la poussière); **she dusted the crumbs off the chair** elle brossa la chaise pour en enlever les miettes

dustbin ['dʌstbɪn] N *Br* poubelle *f*

dustcart ['dʌstkɑːt] N *Br* camion *m* d'enlèvement des ordures ménagères, camion des éboueurs

dustcloud ['dʌstklaʊd] N nuage *m* de poussière

duster ['dʌstər] N **1** *Br (cloth)* chiffon *m* (à poussière); *Sch (for blackboard) (cloth)* chiffon *m* (à effacer); *(pad)* tampon *m* (à effacer); **feather d.** plumeau *m* **2** *Naut Sl (flag)* pavillon *m*; **red d.** = pavillon de la marine marchande britannique **3** *(coat)* manteau *m* léger
▸▸**d. coat** manteau léger

dustiness ['dʌstɪnɪs] N état *m* poudreux *ou* poussiéreux

dusting ['dʌstɪŋ] N **1** *(of room, furniture etc)* époussetage *m*; **to give a room a d.** épousseter une pièce; **have you done the d.?** tu as fait les poussières? **2** *(of cake etc)* saupoudrage *m*; **the cake had a d. of chocolate powder** le gâteau était saupoudré de chocolat; **there was a d. of snow on the pavement** le trottoir était saupoudré de neige
▸▸**d. powder** talc *m*

dustman, *pl* **dustmen** [ˈdʌstmən] **N** *Br* éboueur *m*, *Fam* boueur *m*, boueux *m*

dustpan [ˈdʌstpæn] **N** pelle *f* (à poussière)

dustproof [ˈdʌstpruːf] **ADJ** imperméable à la poussière

dustsheet [ˈdʌstʃiːt] **N** *(for furniture)* housse *f*

dust-up N *Fam (quarrel)* coup *m* de torchon, querelle *f*; *(brawl)* bagarre *f*; **to have a d. with sb** se quereller/se bagarrer avec qn; **they've had a bit of a d.** le torchon a brûlé entre eux

dusty [ˈdʌstɪ] **ADJ** poussiéreux, couvert de poussière; **to get d.** se couvrir de poussière; *Old-fashioned Sl* **it's not so d.** *(not bad)* c'est pas mal du tout; *Old-fashioned Fam* **a d. answer** une réponse un peu sèche

Dutch [dʌtʃ] **ADJ 1** hollandais; *(cheese etc)* de Hollande; *(government)* néerlandais; *Fig Fam* **to talk to sb like a D. uncle** faire la morale à qn **2** *Am* **(Pennsylvania) D.** allemand de Pennsylvanie
 N 1 the D. (people) les Hollandais *mpl* **2** *Ling* hollandais *m*; **Cape D.** afrikaans *m*
 ADV *Fam* **to go D.** payer son écot; **let's go D.** payons chacun notre part
 ▸▸ **D. auction** vente *f* à la baisse; *Br* **D. barn** hangar *m* à récoltes; *Br* **D. cap** diaphragme *m (contraceptif)*; *Fam* **D. courage** = courage *m* trouvé dans la boisson; **I'll need a little D. courage** il faut que je boive un peu pour me donner du courage; *Am* **D. door** porte *f* à deux vantaux; **D. elm disease** maladie *f* de l'orme, graphiose *f*; **D. oven** *(casserole)* marmite *f*, fait-tout *m inv*; *Fam* **D. treat** = sortie *f* où chacun paye son écot; **as long as it's a D. treat** tant que chacun paie sa part *ou* son écot

dutch [dʌtʃ] **N** *Br Sl (wife)* **my old d.** ma femme, ma vieille

Dutchman, *pl* **Dutchmen** [ˈdʌtʃmən] **N** Hollandais *m*, Néerlandais *m*; *Fam* **if that's a real diamond (then) I'm a D.** si c'est un vrai diamant je mange mon chapeau

Dutchwoman, *pl* **Dutchwomen** [ˈdʌtʃwʊmən, -wɪmɪn] **N** Hollandaise *f*, Néerlandaise *f*

dutiable [ˈdjuːtɪəb(ə)l] **ADJ** *(goods purchased abroad)* soumis aux droits de douane, imposable, taxable

dutiful [ˈdjuːtɪfʊl] **ADJ** *(son, daughter)* obéissant; **a d. husband** un mari plein d'égards pour sa femme

dutifully [ˈdjuːtɪfʊlɪ] **ADV** avec soumission

duty [ˈdjuːtɪ] **N 1** *(obligation)* devoir *m* (**to** envers); **to do one's d.** faire son devoir; **to fail in one's d.** manquer à son devoir (**as** a de); **to do one's d. by sb** remplir son devoir envers qn; **I shall make it my d. to …** je considérerai de mon devoir de …; **it is your d. to …** il est de ton devoir de …; **from** *or* **out of a sense of d.** par devoir; **to have no sense of d.** n'avoir aucun sens du devoir; *Hum* **I must go, d. calls** je dois y aller, le devoir m'appelle; **to pay a d. call** faire une visite de politesse
 2 *(task) (usu pl)* **duties** fonctions *fpl*, attributions *fpl*; *Mil* mission *f*; **public duties** fonctions publiques; **to take up** *or* **assume one's duties** entrer en fonctions *ou* en charge; **to hand over one's duties** *(resign)* résigner ses fonctions; *(transfer them)* remettre ses fonctions (**to** à); **to carry out** *or* **perform one's duties** exercer ses fonctions
 3 to be on d. être de service; *(in factory, playground etc)* être de surveillance; *Naut* être de service *ou* de corvée; *Mil, Naut etc* **while on d.** pendant le service; **to be off d.** ne pas être de service; **to do d. for sb** remplacer qn (dans son service); **to do d. for sth** servir de qch; *Mil* **tour of d.** tour *m* de ser-vice; *Am* **active d.** service actif; **fatigue d.** corvée *f*
 4 *Fin (tax)* droit *m*; **customs d.** droit(s) *m(pl)* de douane; **liable to d.** passible de droits; **d. paid** franc de douane, droits acquittés; **to pay d. on sth** payer une taxe sur qch
 ▸▸ **d. chart** tableau *m* de service; *Journ* **d. editor** rédacteur, -trice en chef de service; **d. manager** directeur, -trice de service; **d. officer** officier *m* de service; **d. roster** tableau de service

duty-bound **ADJ PRED** tenu; **you are d. to do it** votre devoir vous y oblige, vous y êtes tenu; **I feel d. to …** je me sens tenu par mon devoir de …

duty-free **ADJ** exempt de droits (de douane); *(wine, cigarettes etc for personal use)* hors taxe
 N *(purchase)* achat *m* hors taxe
 ADV **how much wine can I bring back d.?** quelle quantité de vin est-ce que j'ai le droit de ramener hors taxe?
 ▸▸ **d. allowance** quantité *f* de marchandises hors taxe autorisée; **d. entry** admission *f* en franchise; **d. goods** marchandises *fpl* franches de douane, marchandises hors taxe; **d. sales** ventes *fpl* hors taxe; **d. shop** magasin *m* hors taxe; **d. zone** zone *f* en franchise

duty-paid goods **NPL** marchandises *fpl* libérées *ou* acquittées

duvet [ˈduːveɪ] **N** couette *f*, *Suisse* duvet *m*
 ▸▸ **d. cover** housse *f* de couette; *Fam* **d. day** = journée *f* de congé supplémentaire pouvant être prise de façon impromptue

dux [dʌks] **N** *Scot Sch* premier, -ière de la classe/l'école

DV [diːˈviː] **ADV** *(abbr* **deo volente***)* si Dieu le veut

DVD [diːviːˈdiː] **N** *Comput (abbr* **Digital Versatile Disk, Digital Video Disk***) (format)* DVD *m*; *(player)* lecteur *m* de DVD; *(disk)* DVD *m*; **on DVD** sur DVD; **D. recordable** DVD enregistrable; **D. rewritable** DVD réinscriptible
 ▸▸ **D. drive** lecteur (de) DVD; **D. player** lecteur (de) DVD

DVD-R [-ɑːr] **N** *Comput (abbr* **digital video disk-recordable***)* DVD-R *m*

DVD-ROM **N** *Comput (abbr* **digital video disk-read only memory***)* DVD-ROM *m*
 ▸▸ **D. drive** lecteur (de) DVD-ROM

DVD-RW [-ɑːdʌbˈljuː] **N** *Comput (abbr* **digital video disk-rewritable***)* DVD-RW *m*

DVT [diːviːˈtiː] **N** *(abbr* **deep-vein thrombosis***)* TVP *f*

dwarf, *pl* **dwarfs, dwarves** [dwɔːf, dwɔːvz] **N** *(person)*, *Myth* nain, *f* naine
 ADJ *(plant, tree)* nain
 VT 1 écraser; *Fig (sb's achievements, success)* éclipser; **tower that dwarfs the main building** tour dont la hauteur écrase le corps de bâtiment; **the church is dwarfed by the skyscraper** l'église est écrasée par le gratte-ciel; **at nearly six feet, Jack dwarfed his classmates** avec son mètre 80, Jack semblait un géant par rapport à ses camarades de classe **2** *(stunt growth of) (plant)* rabougrir

dwarfish [ˈdwɔːfɪʃ] **ADJ** *(legs)* de nain; *(man, stature)* très petit

dweeb [dwiːb] **N** *Am Fam* crétin, -ine, abruti, -ie

dwell [dwel] **VI** *(pt, pp* **dwelt** [dwelt]*)* **1** *Lit* habiter, demeurer; **he dwells in Edinburgh/in Spain** il habite à Édimbourg/en Espagne **2** *Fig (remain)* rester; **to let one's eye d. on sb** arrêter son regard sur qn; *Lit* **this hope dwells within our hearts** cet espoir repose dans notre cœur
 N *Tech* dwell *m*
 ▸▸ **d. angle** angle *m* de dwell *ou* de fermeture

▸ **dwell on, dwell upon** **VT INSEP** *(brood about)* remâcher, ressasser; *(memories)* s'attarder sur; *(discuss) (in speech, book)* s'appesantir sur; *(syllable etc)* appuyer sur; **don't d. or don't let your mind d. on it** essaie de ne pas y penser

dweller [ˈdwelər] **N** habitant, -ante (**in, on** de); **city-d.** citadin, -ine; **flat-d.** personne *f* qui habite dans un appartement

dwelling[1] [ˈdwelɪŋ] **N** *Lit* lieu *m* de séjour; *Admin* domicile *m*, demeure *f*
 ▸▸ *Law* **d. house** maison *f* d'habitation; **d. place** domicile, demeure

-dwelling[2] **SUFF** **tree-d.** arboricole, qui vit sur les arbres; **ocean-/cave-d.** qui vit dans l'océan/dans les caves

DWEM [dwem] **N** *(abbr* **dead white European male***)* = écrivain/musicien/*etc* européen blanc mort depuis longtemps

DWI **N** *Am (abbr* **driving while intoxicated***)* conduite *f* en état d'ivresse

dwindle [ˈdwɪnd(ə)l] **VI** **to d. (away)** diminuer; **to d. to nothing** se réduire à rien

dwindling [ˈdwɪnd(ə)lɪŋ] **ADJ** *(audience, funds, membership)* en baisse; *(enthusiasm)* faiblissant; **a d. number of people** de moins en moins de gens
 N *(of supplies, enthusiasm, support)* baisse *f*, diminution *f*, *Fin (of capital)* déperdition *f*

dye [daɪ] **N** *(for clothes, hair)* teinture *f*; **fast d.** *(on label)* bon teint; *Lit* **villain of the deepest d.** fieffé coquin *m*
 VT teindre; **to d. sth black/red** teindre qch en noir/rouge; **to have a dress dyed** faire teindre une robe; **to d. one's hair** se teindre les cheveux
 VI (se) teindre; **material that dyes well** tissu qui prend bien la teinture
 ▸▸ *Phot* **d. solution** bain *m* colorant

dyed-in-the-wool [ˈdaɪd-] **ADJ** *Fig* invétéré, inébranlable; **a d. Englishman/conservative** un Anglais/conservateur bon teint

dyeing [ˈdaɪɪŋ] **N 1** *(of material, hair)* teinture *f* **2** *(trade)* teinturerie *f*

dyer [ˈdaɪər] **N** teinturier *m*; **d. and cleaner** teinturier dégraisseur

dyestuff [ˈdaɪstʌf] **N** matière *f* colorante, colorant *m*

dyeworks [ˈdaɪwɜːks] **NPL** *(usu with sing verb)* teinturerie *f*

dying [ˈdaɪɪŋ] **ADJ** *(person)* mourant, agonisant; *Fig (industry, ideology)* agonisant; *(traditions)* en voie de disparition; **d. words** dernières paroles; **in a d. voice** d'une voix éteinte; **with his d. breath** de sa voix agonisante; **it was my mother's d. wish that …** les dernières volontés de ma mère étaient que …; **I shall remember it to my d. day** je m'en souviendrai jusqu'à la mort; *Fig Fam* **to look like a d. duck (in a thunderstorm)** avoir l'air pitoyable
 N *(death throes)* agonie *f*, *(death)* mort *f*
 NPL **the dead and the d.** les morts *mpl* et les moribonds *mpl*; **prayers for the d.** prières *fpl* des agonisants

dyke[1] [daɪk] **N 1** *Tech* digue *f*, levée *f*; *(embankment)* chaussée *f* surélevée *ou* en remblai **2** *(ditch)* fossé *m*, chenal *m*, -aux
 VT *Tech (river)* endiguer; *(land)* protéger par des digues

dyke[2] **N** *Fam (lesbian)* gouine *f*

dynamic [daɪˈnæmɪk] **ADJ** *Phys*, *Fig* dynamique; *Fig* **to have a d. personality** être plein de dynamisme
 N dynamique *f*
 ▸▸ *Comput* **d. data exchange** échange *m* dynamique de données; *Comput* **d. RAM** mémoire *f* RAM dynamique

dynamically [daɪˈnæmɪklɪ] **ADV** dynamiquement

dynamics [daɪˈnæmɪks] **NPL** *(usu with sing verb)* *Phys, Fig* dynamique *f*; **the d. of change/progress** la dynamique du changement/progrès VOIR GRAMMAIRE A10

dynamism [ˈdaɪnəmɪz(ə)m] **N** *Phys, Fig* dynamisme *m*

dynamite [ˈdaɪnəmaɪt] **N** dynamite *f*; *Fam* **subject that is political d.** sujet explosif sur le plan politique; **it/she could be political d. for the Government** ça/elle pourrait faire des dégâts au niveau du gouvernement; *Fam* **this information is d.** cette information c'est de la dynamite; *Fam* **it's d.!** *(marvellous)* c'est du tonnerre!; *Fam* **this new band is d.** ce nouveau groupe déménage
 VT *(rocks etc)* faire sauter à la dynamite; *(building etc)* dynamiter

dynamiting [ˈdaɪnəmaɪtɪŋ] **N** dynamitage *m*

dynamo, *pl* **dynamos** [ˈdaɪnəməʊ, -əʊz] **N** *Elec* dynamo *f*; *Fig* **she's a human d.** elle a une énergie extraordinaire

dynastic [dɪˈnæstɪk] **ADJ** dynastique

dynasty [ˈdɪnəstɪ, *Am* ˈdaɪnəstɪ] **N** dynastie *f*

dyne [daɪn] **N** *Phys (unit of force)* dyne *f*

dysentery [ˈdɪsəntrɪ] **N** *Med* dysenterie *f*; **to have d.** avoir la dysenterie

dysfunction [dɪsˈfʌŋkʃən] **N** *Med (of organ)* insuffisance *f*

dysfunctional [dɪsˈfʌŋkʃənəl] **ADJ a d. family** une famille à problèmes

dyslectic [dɪsˈlektɪk] = **dyslexic**

dyslexia [dɪsˈleksɪə] **N** *Med* dyslexie *f*; **to have d.** être dyslexique

dyslexic [dɪsˈleksɪk] **ADJ, N** *Med* dyslexique *mf*

dysmenorrhoea, *Am* **dysmenorrhea** [dɪsmenəˈrɪə] **N** *Med* dysménorrhée *f*

dyspepsia [dɪsˈpepsɪə] **N** *Med* dyspepsie *f*; **acid d.** aigreurs *fpl*

dyspeptic [dɪsˈpeptɪk] **N** *Med* dyspepsique *mf*, dyspeptique *mf*
 ADJ 1 *Med* dyspepsique, dyspeptique **2** *Fig (bad-tempered)* ronchon, -onne, grognon, -onne

dysphasia [dɪsˈfeɪzɪə] **N** *Med* dysphasie *f*

dystrophy [ˈdɪstrəfɪ] **N** *Med* dystrophie *f*

E, e¹ [iː] N **1** *(letter)* E, e *m*; **two e's** deux e **2** *Mus* mi *m*; **in E flat** en mi bémol **3** *Sch* **to get an E** avoir une très mauvaise note, ≃ avoir une note inférieure à 7 sur 20 **4** *Sl (ecstasy)* ecsta *f*, X *f* **5** *Fam* **to give sb the big E** *(reject)* plaquer qn

e² *(abbr* **east)** E.

EACH [iːtʃ] VOIR GRAMMAIRE A35–6; 815–16

> ADJ chaque
> PRON chacun **1**

ADJ chaque; **e. day** chaque jour, tous les jours; **e. one of us** chacun/chacune de nous *ou* d'entre nous

PRON **1** *(both or all)* chacun, -une; **e. of us** chacun/chacune de nous *ou* d'entre nous; **we e. earn £10, we earn £10 e.** nous gagnons 10 livres chacun; **peaches at 25p e.** pêches à 25 pence chacune *ou* 25 pence pièce; **a little of e.** un peu de chaque

2 *(reciprocal)* **e. other** l'un l'autre, l'une l'autre, *pl* les uns les autres, les unes les autres; **separated from e. other** séparés l'un de l'autre/les uns des autres; **to fight e. other** se battre; **we can help e. other** nous pouvons nous aider l'un l'autre, nous pouvons nous aider mutuellement, *(to study, work)* avec passion; *(to study, work)* avec passion; nous pouvons nous entraider; **they flatter e. other** ils se flattent réciproquement *ou* mutuellement

eager ['iːgər] ADJ *(desire, hope)* vif; *(look)* avide; *(voice, face)* exalté; *(supporter)* fervent; **to be e. for sth** désirer qch vivement; **the crowd were e. for blood** la foule était assoiffée de sang; **the audience were still e. for more when the show ended** le public en voulait encore quand le spectacle s'est terminé; **to be e. to do sth** être impatient de faire qch; **to be e. to please** être très désireux de plaire; **they were e. to learn** ils étaient avides d'apprendre; **I didn't want to seem too e.** *(in relationship etc)* je ne voulais pas sembler trop empressé; *Fam* **to be an e. beaver** être zélé; **I've never seen such an e. beaver** je n'ai jamais vu quelqu'un d'aussi zélé

eagerly ['iːgəlɪ] ADV *(to listen)* avidement; *(to ask, smile)* avec empressement; *(to wait)* impatiemment; *(to study, work)* avec passion; **to desire sth e.** désirer qch passionnément; **her e. awaited second album** son deuxième album très attendu

eagerness ['iːgənɪs] N *(to see sb)* impatience *f*, *(to make oneself useful etc)* empressement *m*; *(to learn sth etc)* vif désir *m*; **to show e. in doing sth** montrer un intérêt très vif à faire qch; **to show** *or* **have no e. for sth** n'avoir aucune envie de qch; **he thought he detected a certain lack of e. in her voice** il lui sembla déceler un certain manque d'ardeur dans sa voix; **e. to succeed** ardent désir de réussir

eagle ['iːg(ə)l] N **1** *(bird)* aigle *m* **2** *Her* aigle *f*,

double-headed e. aigle à deux têtes **3** *Am Mil* aigle *f* (= insigne de grade de colonel) **4** *Golf* eagle *m*, *Can* aiglon *m*
▸▸*Rel* **e. lectern** aigle *m*

eagle-eyed ADJ aux yeux d'aigle

eaglet ['iːglɪt] N *(bird)* aiglon *m*

ear [ɪər] N **1** oreille *f*, *Anat* **the external** *or* **outer/middle/internal** *or* **inner e.** l'oreille externe/moyenne/interne; **deaf in one e.** sourd d'une oreille; **she was smiling** *or* **grinning from e. to e.** elle avait un sourire épanoui jusqu'aux oreilles; **to go in one e. and out the other** *(of words)* entrer par une oreille et sortir par l'autre; **your ears must have been burning** les oreilles ont dû vous siffler; **up to one's ears in work** accablé de travail; **up to one's ears in debt** endetté jusqu'au cou; *Fam* **to be (thrown) out on one's e.** se faire jeter dehors *ou* sur le pavé; **after only two months in the job he found himself out on his e. again** après seulement deux mois de travail il s'est retrouvé de nouveau sur le pavé

2 *(hearing)* **to have sharp ears** avoir l'ouïe fine; *Mus* **to have a good/poor e.** avoir de l'oreille/ne pas avoir d'oreille; **to have an e. for music** avoir l'oreille musicale; *Mus* **to play by e.** jouer sans notes; *Fig* **to play it by e.** aller au pifomètre, improviser; **to have an e. for poetry** avoir le sens de la poésie; **to have an e.** *or* **a good e. for languages** avoir une bonne oreille pour les langues; **to have sb's e.** être dans les faveurs *ou* les petits papiers de qn; **to keep one's ears open** *or* **one's e. to the ground** se tenir aux écoutes; **I'm all ears** je suis tout ouïe; **to close one's ears to the truth** fermer l'oreille à la vérité; **word reached their ears of the enemy's plan** les projets de l'ennemi leur sont venus à l'oreille **3** *Tech (of vase)* anse *f*, oreille *f*, *(of bell)* anse *f* **4** *(of seashell)* oreillette *f* **5** *(of wheat etc)* épi *m*; **wheat in the e.** blé *m* en épi
▸▸*Anat* **e. lobe** lobe *m* de l'oreille; *Med* **e., nose and throat specialist** oto-rhino-(laryngologiste) *mf*, *pl* oto-rhinos-(laryngologistes); **e., nose and throat department** service *m* d'oto-rhino-laryngologie; **e. protector** *(against cold)* protège-tympan *m inv*; *(against noise)* casque *m* anti-bruit; **e. trumpet** cornet *m* acoustique

earache ['ɪəreɪk] N mal *m* d'oreille(s); *Med* otalgie *f*; **to have e.** avoir mal à l'oreille/aux oreilles

earbashing ['ɪəbæʃɪŋ] N *Br* **to give sb an e.** passer un savon à qn, souffler dans les bronches à qn; **to get an e.** se faire passer un savon, se faire souffler dans les bronches

eardrops ['ɪədrɒps] NPL *Med* gouttes *fpl* pour les oreilles

eardrum ['ɪədrʌm] N *Anat* tympan *m*

-eared ['ɪəd] SUFF **long/short-e.** aux oreilles longues/courtes

earflap ['ɪəflæp] N *(of cap)* oreillette *f*

earful ['ɪəfʊl] N **I got an e. of water** j'ai pris de l'eau plein l'oreille; *Fam* **to give sb an e.** *(reprimand)* donner une verte semonce à qn, passer un savon à qn; *Fam* **a right** *or* **real e.** un bon savon; *Fam* **get an e. of this!** écoute un peu ça!

earhole ['ɪəhəʊl] N *Br Fam* trou *m* de l'oreille

earl [ɜːl] N comte *m*

earldom ['ɜːldəm] N **1** *(land)* comté *m* **2** *(title)* titre *m* de comte

EARLY ['ɜːlɪ] (**earlier, earliest**)

> ADJ matinal **1** ▪ premier **2, 3** ▪ en avance **4** ▪ précoce **5**
> ADV de bonne heure **1** ▪ en avance **3**

ADJ **1** *(in the day)* matinal, -aux; **in the e. morning** de bon matin; **e. morning walk** promenade matinale; **I'm not a great believer in e. rising** se lever de bonne heure, ce n'est pas pour moi; **to be an e. riser** être matinal, se lever de bon matin; **an e. bird** un lève-tôt, un matinal; *Prov* **the e. bird catches the worm** l'avenir appartient à ceux qui se lèvent tôt; **e. morning call** appel *m* matinal; **e. morning tea** thé du matin

2 *(at beginning of period of time)* **in (the) e. summer, in the e. part of summer** dans les *ou* aux premiers jours de l'été, au début de l'été; **in the e. afternoon** au début de l'après-midi; **to have an e. dinner** dîner de bonne heure; **I'm going to have an e. night** je vais me coucher de bonne heure; **in the e. nineteenth century** au début du XIXe siècle; **in the e. sixties** au début des années soixante; **e. youth** première jeunesse *f*, **e. medieval music** musique *f* du début du Moyen Âge; **e. Debussy/Racine** première(s) œuvre(s) *f(pl)* de Debussy/Racine; **at an e. age** tout jeune; **from the earliest age** dès la plus tendre enfance; **from (the) earliest times** depuis les temps les plus reculés; **it's e. days yet** il est encore tôt

3 *(first)* **the e. Church** l'Église *f* primitive; **e. Christians** les premiers chrétiens *mpl*; **the earliest legends** les premières légendes *fpl*; **a very e. example of ...** un des premiers exemples de ...; **this e. pottery** ces exemples des premières formes de poterie; *Art* **the e. masters** les primitifs *mpl*; **e. radios didn't have loudspeakers** les premières radios n'avaient pas de haut-parleurs; **my earliest recollections** mes souvenirs les plus lointains; **he received his e. education at ...** il reçut sa première éducation à ...

4 *(ahead of time)* **you're e.** tu es en avance; **I am half an hour e.** je suis en avance d'une demi-heure

5 *(premature)* précoce, hâtif; *(death)* prématuré; **e. beans** haricots de primeur; **e. vegetables/fruit/produce** primeurs *fpl*; **we're having an e. winter** l'hiver est précoce; **Easter is e. this year** Pâques est tôt cette année

6 *(future)* **at an e. date** prochainement, à une date prochaine; **at an earlier date** à une date plus rapprochée; **to take an e. opportunity to do sth** faire qch à la première occasion; **at the earliest possible moment** le plus tôt possible; **at your earliest convenience** dès que possible

7 *(previous)* **at an earlier date** à une date antérieure

ADV **1** *(in the day)* de bonne heure, tôt; **e. in the morning** le matin de bonne heure, de grand matin; **e. in the evening** tôt dans la soirée; **to get up e.** se lever de bonne heure; **as e. as possible** le plus tôt possible

2 *(at beginning of period of time etc)* **e. in the winter** au début *ou* à l'entrée de l'hiver; **e. in the year** au début de l'année; **e. on, it was apparent that ...** dès l'abord, il est apparu que ...; **e. in (his) life** dans ses jeunes années, dans sa jeunesse; **e. in his career** au début de sa carrière; **as e. as the tenth century** dès le dixième siècle; **e. in the list** tout au commencement de la liste

3 *(ahead of time)* en avance; **too e.** trop tôt; **to arrive five minutes (too) e.** arriver avec cinq minutes d'avance; **they left the party e.** ils ont quitté la soirée tôt

4 *(prematurely)* **to die e.** *(young)* mourir jeune; *(sooner than expected)* mourir prématurément; **this flower blooms very e.** cette fleur s'épanouit très précocement

5 *(soon)* **next week at the earliest** la semaine prochaine au plus tôt

6 *(previously)* **earlier** plus tôt; **as I mentioned earlier** *(in time)* comme je l'ai mentionné plus tôt; *(in writing)* comme je l'ai mentionné ci-dessus *ou* plus haut

▸▸ *Mktg* **e. adopter** réceptif *m* précoce, adopteur *m* précoce; *Br Com* **e. closing** = jour *m* où les magasins ferment tôt; **e. edition** *(of newspaper)* première édition *f*, premier tirage *m*; *Mktg* **e. follower** suiveur *m* immédiat; *Mktg* **e. majority** majorité *f* innovatrice; **e. music** *(baroque)* musique *f* ancienne; *(earlier)* première forme *f* de musique; *Fin* **e. redemption** amortissement *m* anticipé; **e. retirement** retraite *f* anticipée; **to take e. retirement** prendre la retraite anticipée; *Mil* **e. warning system** réseau *m* de radars de guet *ou* de pré-alerte

early-closing ADJ
▸▸ *Br Com* **e. day** = jour *m* où les magasins ferment tôt

early-purchase discount N *Mktg* discompte *m* sur achat dans un bref délai

earmark ['ɪəmɑːk] N *Agr (of sheep etc)* marque *f* à l'oreille; *Fig* **to have all the earmarks of embezzlement/another of her silly ideas** porter tous les signes d'un détournement de fonds/d'une de ses idées stupides

VT **1** *(assign) (funds)* donner à une affectation spéciale; **to e. funds for a project** assigner des fonds à un projet; **the land has been earmarked for a new school** le terrain a été affecté à la construction d'une nouvelle école; **the building is earmarked for closure** il est prévu que ce bâtiment soit fermé; *Fam* **to e. sth for oneself** se réserver qch **2** *(mark the corner of) (document, cheque)* faire une marque au coin de **3** *Agr (sheep etc)* marquer à l'oreille

earmuff ['ɪəmʌf] N protège-oreilles *m inv*, cache-oreilles *m inv*

earn [ɜːn] VT **1** *(money)* gagner; **how much do you e.?** combien gagnez-vous?; **to e. one's living by writing** gagner sa vie de sa plume; *Fin* **to e. interest** *(of money)* produire des intérêts **2** *(deserve) (rest, respite)* mériter; *(sb's affection, respect)* gagner; **to e. sb's love** gagner le cœur de qn; **you've earned it** *(this break, rise etc)* tu l'as bien mérité; **his**

conduct earned him universal praise/many votes sa conduite lui valut les éloges de tous/de nombreuses voix; **it earned her nothing but criticism** cela ne lui a valu que des critiques; **this action earned her many enemies** cette action lui a valu de nombreux ennemis, par cette action elle s'est attiré de nombreux ennemis; **her attitude has earned her a lot of friends/supporters** son attitude lui a gagné de nombreux amis/partisans

earned [ɜːnd] ADJ
▸▸ *Com* **e. income** revenus *mpl* salariaux; *Fin* **e. interest** revenu *m* des intérêts; *Acct* **e. surplus** bénéfices *mpl* non distribués

earner ['ɜːnər] N **1** *(person)* **(wage) e.** salarié, -ée; **she's not a big e.** elle ne gagne pas beaucoup; **the high/low earners** les gros/petits salaires *mpl* **2** *Br Fam (activity, business)* **a nice little e.** une bonne petite affaire, un bon plan

earnest ['ɜːnɪst] ADJ *(person, effort, discussion)* sérieux; *(expression)* pénétré, grave; *(demand, voice)* pressant; *(request)* fervent; *(desire, wish)* profond

N **1** **in e.** sérieusement; **to be in e.** être sérieux; **are you in e.?** *(in what you're saying)* parlez-vous sérieusement?; **to speak in e.** parler sérieusement; **she's leaving him in e. this time** cette fois elle le quitte pour de bon; **to set to work in e.** se mettre sérieusement à l'ouvrage **2** *Com etc Old-fashioned* arrhes *fpl*

earnestly ['ɜːnɪstlɪ] ADV *(to speak, discuss, consider)* sérieusement; *(to hope, believe)* sincèrement; *(to desire)* profondément; *(to pray)* avec ferveur

earnestness ['ɜːnɪstnɪs] N *(of discussion)* caractère *m* sérieux; *(of tone, person)* gravité *f*, sérieux *m*; *(of hope, desire)* sincérité *f*; *(of request)* ferveur *f*

earning ['ɜːnɪŋ] N *(act)* gain *m*
▸▸ **e. capacity, e. power** *(of business)* rapport *m*; *(of person)* revenu *m* potentiel

earnings ['ɜːnɪŋz] NPL **1** *(salary)* salaire *m*; **my e.** ce que je gagne; **e. related** *(pensions, benefits etc)* proportionnel au salaire **2** *(profits)* profits *mpl*, bénéfices *mpl*
▸▸ *Fin* **e. forecast** résultats *mpl* prévisionnels; *Fin* **e. growth** accroissement *m ou* augmentation *f* des bénéfices; *Fin* **e. before interest and tax** bénéfices avant impôts et charges; *Fin* **e. retained** bénéfices non distribués

earphone ['ɪəfəʊn] N *Radio, Tel* écouteur *m*

earpiece ['ɪəpiːs] N *Tel (of handset)* écouteur *m*; *(in TV studio)* écouteur auriculaire

ear-piercing ADJ *(scream)* à vous percer les tympans

N *(for earrings)* **do you know anywhere in town that does e.?** connais-tu un endroit en ville où l'on peut se faire percer les oreilles?

earplug ['ɪəplʌg] N *(for sleeping)* boule *f* Quiès®; *(for protection from noise)* protège-tympan *m inv*

earring ['ɪərɪŋ] N boucle *f* d'oreille

earshot ['ɪəʃɒt] N **within/out of e.** à portée/hors de portée de voix

ear-splitting ADJ à vous déchirer *ou* crever les tympans

earth [ɜːθ] N **1** *(planet)* terre *f*, *(world)* monde *m*; **the e.** *ou* **E.** *(planet)* la Terre; **the e.'s crust/atmosphere** l'écorce *f*/l'atmosphère *f* terrestre; **on e.** sur terre; *Bible* **on e. as it is in heaven** sur la terre comme au ciel; *Fam* **where/why on e. ...?** où/pourquoi diable ...?; **what on e. have you done to your hair?** que diable as-tu fait à tes cheveux?; *Fam* **how on e. should I know?** comment veux-tu que je le sache?; *Fam* **to look like nothing on e.** ne

ressembler à rien; *Fam* **to feel like nothing on e.** ne vraiment pas être dans son assiette; **there's no reason on e.** il n'y a absolument aucune raison; **it wouldn't cost the e.** ça ne coûterait pas les yeux de la tête; **to pay the e. for sth** payer qch les yeux de la tête; **he promised people the e.** il a promis la lune aux gens

2 *(ground)* sol *m*; *Fig* **to come back to e. (with a bump)** revenir (brutalement) sur terre; **it brought her down to e. with a bit of a bump** ça l'a ramenée sur terre un peu brutalement; **the e. moved** la terre a tremblé; *Hum* **did the e. move for you?** *(while making love)* est-ce que tu as eu le grand frisson?

3 *(of soil)* terre *f*, **e. floor** *(of hut etc)* sol *m* en terre battue; **loose/heavy e.** terre(s) meuble(s)/lourde(s)

4 *Br Elec* terre *f*, masse *f*, *(terminal)* mise *f* à terre; **dead e.** contact *m* parfait avec le sol; **e. to frame** *(of car etc)* contact à la masse; *Aut* câble *m* de masse

5 *(of fox)* terrier *m*, tanière *f*, **to go to e.** *(of fox, fugitive)* se terrer; **I've been trying to get in touch with him but he seems to have gone to e.** j'ai essayé de le joindre mais on dirait qu'il s'est volatilisé; **to run to e.** *(fox)* chasser jusqu'à son terrier; *(fugitive)* dépister; *(person)* dénicher; *(mistake in the figures)* découvrir la source de

VT **1** *Br Elec* mettre à la terre **2** *(in hunting)* poursuivre jusqu'à son terrier **3** = **earth up**

VI *(of fox)* se terrer
▸▸ *Br Elec* **e. cable** câble *m* de terre; *Br Elec* **e. connection** prise *f* de terre; **e. creature** *(in science fiction)* créature *f* terrestre; *Astron* **e. orbit** *(of satellite)* orbite *f* terrestre; *Astron* **e. satellite** satellite *m* terrestre; **e. sciences** sciences *fpl* de la terre; *TV* **e. station** station *f* terrestre; *Br Elec* **e. wire** fil *m* de terre
▸ **earth up** VT SEP *(in gardening) (plant)* butter, chausser

earthbound ['ɜːθbaʊnd] ADJ **1** *(mundane)* terre à terre *inv* **2** **e. spirit** esprit *m* qui ne peut pas quitter le monde des vivants **3** *(heading towards earth)* qui se dirige vers la terre

earthen ['ɜːθ(ə)n] ADJ **1** *(crockery etc)* en *ou* de terre (cuite) **2** *(floor)* en terre battue

earthenware ['ɜːθ(ə)nweər] N poterie *f* (de terre); **e. jug** cruche *f* en *ou* de terre (cuite); **glazed e.** faïence *f*, *(stoneware)* grès *m* flambé

earthfall ['ɜːθfɔːl] N éboulement *m* de terres

earthiness ['ɜːθɪnɪs] N truculence *f*, *Pej* grossièreté *f*

earthlight ['ɜːθlaɪt] N *Astron (of moon)* lumière *f* cendrée

earthling ['ɜːθlɪŋ] N *(in science fiction)* habitant, -ante de la terre, terrien, -enne

earthly ['ɜːθlɪ] ADJ terrestre; **the E. Paradise** le Paradis terrestre; *Fam* **there's no e. reason for ...** il n'y a absolument aucune raison pour que ...; *Fam* **it's of no e. use to me** ça ne me sert *ou* ne me servirait absolument à rien; *Fam* **he hasn't got an e. chance** *or* **hope** il n'a pas la moindre chance

N *Br Fam* **he hasn't got an e.** il n'a pas la moindre chance

earthman, *pl* **earthmen** ['ɜːθmæn, -mɛn] N *(in science fiction)* terrien *m*

earthmover ['ɜːθmuːvər] N bulldozer *m*

earthmoving ['ɜːθmuːvɪŋ] N
▸▸ **e. equipment** engins *mpl* de terrassement

earthquake ['ɜːθkweɪk] N *also Fig* tremblement *m* de terre, séisme *m*; **e. survivor** survivant *m ou* rescapé *m* d'un tremblement de terre

earth-shaking [ˈɜːθʃeɪkɪŋ] ADJ = **earth-shattering**

earth-shattering ADJ **1** *(discovery, news)* stupéfiant; *(defeat)* accablant **2** *(explosion, crash etc)* assourdissant

earthwoman, *pl* **earthwomen** [ˈɜːθwʊmən, -wɪmɪn] N *(in science fiction)* terrienne *f*

earthwork [ˈɜːθwɜːk] N **e. embankment** terrassement *m* en remblai; **earthworks** *(banked earth)* travaux *mpl* en terre *ou* de terrassement; *(prehistoric)*, *Mil* fortifications *fpl* en terre

earthworm [ˈɜːθwɜːm] N lombric *m*, ver *m* de terre

earthy [ˈɜːθɪ] ADJ **1** terreux; **to have an e. smell** sentir la terre **2** *(coarse)* *(person)* truculent; *(humour, language)* truculent, vert; **an e. laugh** un gros rire **3** **e. common sense** sens *m* pratique

earwax [ˈɪəwæks] N cire *f (sécrétée par les oreilles)*, *Fml* cérumen *m*

earwig [ˈɪəwɪɡ] N *(insect)* perce-oreille *m*, *pl* perce-oreilles
▸ VT *Fam* écouter de façon indiscrète
▸ VI *Fam* écouter aux portes

ease [iːz] N **1** *(facility)* *(when speaking, moving etc)* facilité *f*, *(of manners, movements etc)* aisance *f*; **the e. with which they adapted** la facilité avec laquelle ils se sont adaptés; **with e.** *(to defeat, adapt)* facilement; *(to answer)* aisément; *(to speak)* avec facilité; **with the utmost *or* the greatest of e.** avec la plus grande facilité, le plus facilement du monde; **the e. with which we entered the building** la facilité avec laquelle nous sommes entrés dans le bâtiment; **e. of use** confort *m ou* facilité d'emploi
2 *(peace)* *(mental)* tranquillité *f*, *(physical)* repos *m*, bien-être *m*; **to be at e.** *(mentally)* avoir l'esprit tranquille; **to be at e. with sb/in a place** être à l'aise avec qn/dans un endroit; **to be *or* feel ill at e.** *(awkward)* être mal à l'aise; *(worried)* être inquiet *(about* au sujet de); **a nation at e. with itself** une nation qui s'accepte; **to be at one's e.** *(relaxed)* être à son aise; *(calm)* être tranquille; **to put sb at e.** mettre qn à l'aise; **set your mind at e.** rassurez-vous, soyez tranquille; **to take one's e.** se mettre à l'aise; **Mil etc to stand at e.** se mettre *ou* se tenir au repos; **at e.!** repos!
3 *(leisure)* loisir *m*; *(idleness)* oisiveté *f*; **a life of e.** une vie d'oisiveté
▸ VT **1** *(alleviate)* *(suffering, pain)* adoucir, calmer, soulager; *(the mind)* tranquilliser; **to e. sb's anxiety/fears** calmer les inquiétudes/craintes de qn
2 *(free)* débarrasser, délivrer **(sb of *or* from sth** qn de qch); **to e. oneself of a burden** se soulager d'un fardeau
3 *(relax)* *(rope, spring)* détendre, relâcher; *(screw)* desserrer; *(pressure)* soulager; *(tension)* réduire; **to e. the congestion in a street** décongestionner la circulation d'une rue
4 *(move carefully, slowly)* déplacer doucement; **to e. a box open** ouvrir doucement une boîte; **to e. one's way through the crowd** se faufiler à travers la foule
5 *Sewing (dress, item of clothing)* donner plus d'ampleur à; *Tech (part)* donner du jeu à
▸ VI *(of pain, pressure etc)* s'atténuer; *(of tension)*, *St Exch (market etc)* se détendre; **the wind/rain has eased** le vent/la pluie s'est calmé(e); **the situation has eased** la situation s'est détendue
▸ **ease off** VT SEP **1** *(release)* enlever doucement; **she eased the lid off the jar** elle a doucement enlevé le couvercle de sur le pot
2 *Naut (let out)* *(rigging)* filer, choquer
▸ VI **1** *(work less)* moins travailler, *Pej* se relâcher

2 *(diminish)* *(of pain)* s'atténuer; *(of rain)* se calmer; *St Exch (of rates)* se détendre
3 *Naut* s'éloigner un peu du rivage
▸ **ease up** VI **1** = **ease off** VI **1, 2**
2 *(slow down)* ralentir

easel [ˈiːz(ə)l] N *(of painter)* chevalet *m*

easily [ˈiːzɪlɪ] ADV **1** *(without difficulty)* facilement, sans difficulté; **you can e. imagine my disappointment** vous concevez sans peine ma déception; **he is not e. satisfied** il n'est pas facile à satisfaire; *Sport etc* **he came in first e.** il est arrivé bon premier; **the car holds six people e.** six personnes tiennent à l'aise dans cette voiture; **that's e. said** c'est vite dit **2** *(in relaxed manner)* à son aise; **to take things *or* life e.** prendre les choses comme elles viennent, prendre la vie comme elle vient, *Pej* se laisser vivre, se la couler douce **3** *(undoubtedly)* **e.** largement plus grand; **e. the best/worst/biggest** de loin le meilleur/le pire/le plus gros; **he is e. forty** il a bien quarante ans; **it's e. 20 kilometres to the next village** il y a bien 20 kilomètres jusqu'au prochain village **4** *(possibly)* **the information could e. be wrong** les informations pourraient très bien être fausses

easiness [ˈiːzɪnɪs] N **1** *(of task)* facilité *f*, **I was surprised at the e. with which the door opened** j'ai été surpris de la facilité avec laquelle la porte s'est ouverte **2** *(easy-going nature)* *(of person)* décontraction *f*, *(of approach)* caractère *m* décontracté; **his e. with children** la facilité de ses rapports avec les enfants

easing [ˈiːzɪŋ] N **1** *(of suffering, pressure)* atténuation *f*, *(caused by medication)* soulagement *m*; *(of beam etc)* allègement *m* **2** *(relaxation)* *(of conflict, pressure)* atténuation *f*, *(of restrictions)* allègement *m*; **e. of tension** *(political etc)* détente *f*, *Com* **e. of the market** détente du marché
▸ ▸ **e. off** *(of pain)* atténuation *f*, *(from work)* relâchement *m*

east [iːst] N est *m*; **the house faces the e.** la maison est orientée à l'est; **on the e., to the e.** à l'est *(of* de); **the E.** *(the Orient)* l'Orient *m*; **the Middle E.** le Moyen-Orient; **the Far E.** l'Extrême-Orient; **the e. of England** l'est de l'Angleterre; **to pray to the e.** prier en direction de l'est
▸ ADV à l'est; **to travel e.** voyager vers l'est; **e. of the Rhine** à l'est du Rhin
▸ ADJ est *inv*; *(wind)* d'est; *(wall, window)* qui fait face à l'est; **the e. coast** la côte est
▸ ▸ **E. Africa** Afrique *f* orientale; **E. End** *(of city)* = quartiers *mpl* est; **the East End** = quartier industriel de Londres, connu pour ses docks et, autrefois, pour sa pauvreté; *esp Am* **E. Europe** Europe *f* de l'Est; *Formerly* **E. Germany** Allemagne *f* de l'Est; *Hist* **E. India Company** compagnie des Indes Orientales; *Hist* **the E. Indies** les Indes *fpl* orientales; **the E. Side** l'East Side *m (quartier situé à l'est de Manhattan)*

eastbound [ˈiːstbaʊnd] ADJ *(traffic)* en direction de l'est; *(lane, carriageway)* de l'est; *(road)* vers l'est; **e. traffic is subject to delays** la circulation est ralentie dans le sens est; **there's a jam on the e. carriageway** il y a un bouchon en direction de l'est

Easter [ˈiːstər] N Pâques *m*; **at E.** à Pâques; **to celebrate E.** fêter Pâques
▸ ▸ **E. Day** le jour de Pâques; **E. egg** œuf *m* de Pâques; **E. Island** l'île *f* de Pâques; **E. Monday** le lundi de Pâques; **E. Sunday** le dimanche de Pâques; **E. week** *(following Easter)* la semaine de Pâques; *(Holy Week)* la semaine sainte

easterly [ˈiːstəlɪ] ADJ *(wind)* d'est, qui vient de l'est; *(current)* qui se dirige vers l'est; **e.**

point point situé à *ou* vers l'est; **in an e. direction** vers l'est
▸ ADV vers l'est
▸ N vent *m* d'est

eastern [ˈiːstən] ADJ est *inu*; de l'est; *(of Far East)* oriental, -aux; **the e. side of the country** la partie de l'est
▸ ▸ *Rel* **the E. Church** l'Église *f* d'Orient; **E. Europe** Europe *f* de l'Est; **E. Standard Time** heure *f* d'hiver de New York; **the E. Townships** *(of Canada)* les Cantons *mpl* de l'Est

Easterner [ˈiːstənər] N *(from Far East)* oriental, -ale; *(in US)* = personne *f* qui vient de l'est des États-Unis

Eastertide [ˈiːstətaɪd] N Pâques *m*

east-facing [ˈiːstfeɪsɪŋ] ADJ orienté à l'est

eastward [ˈiːstwəd] ADJ vers l'est, en direction de l'est
▸ ADV = **eastwards**

eastwards [ˈiːstwədz] ADV vers l'est, en direction de l'est

EASY [ˈiːzɪ] **(easier, easiest)** ADJ **1** *(not difficult)* *(work)* facile, aisé; *(question, test)* facile; *(method, solution)* simple; **e. to please** pas difficile; **to be e. to annoy/upset** s'énerver/se vexer facilement; **he's e. to keep entertained** un rien l'amuse; **e. to get on with** d'un commerce facile; **e. to live with** facile à vivre; **don't worry, it's e. to do on your first day** ne t'inquiète pas, ça arrive à tout le monde le premier jour; **that is e. to see** cela se voit; **it is e. for him to …** il lui est facile de …; **it's e. to say …** on a vite fait de dire …; **this will make your job easier** ceci vous facilitera la tâche; **it makes life much easier not having to fill in these forms** ça facilite bien les choses de ne pas avoir à remplir ces formulaires; **within e. reach of …** à distance commode de …; **it's within e. walking distance** on peut facilement y aller à pied; *Fam* **as e. as ABC *or* as falling off a log *or* as pie** simple comme bonjour; **it isn't e. being a mother** ce n'est pas facile d'être mère; **the e. way out *or* option** la solution de facilité; **there are no e. answers** c'est un problème qui est loin d'être facile à résoudre; **to have an e. time (of it)** se la couler douce; **by e. stages** *(travel)* à petites étapes; **learn how to drive/French in five e. steps *or* stages** apprendre à conduire/le français sans peine en cinq leçons; **the film is very e. on the eye** le film est reposant à regarder; **he's/she's e. on the eye** il/elle n'est pas mal du tout; *Com* **by e. payments, on e. terms** avec facilités de paiement; *Sport etc* **to come in an e. first** arriver bon premier
2 *(easy-going, relaxed)* *(person)* d'un caractère facile; *(manners etc)* libre, dégagé; *(style)* facile, naturel; *(grace)* naturel; **they're usually fairly e. about deadlines** ils sont assez accommodants sur les délais; **the e. familiarity of her welcome instantly reassured them** la familiarité dégagée de son accueil les a immédiatement rassurés; *Fam* **I'm e.!** *(I don't mind)* ça m'est égal!; *Old-fashioned* **woman of e. virtue** femme *f* de mœurs faciles *ou* légères; *Sl* **an e. lay** une femme/fille facile
3 *(movement)* aisé, souple; *(of jeans, clothes)* lâche, de coupe confortable; *Tech* **e. fit** ajustage *m* lâche; **my coat is an e. fit** mon manteau est de coupe confortable
4 *(comfortable)* *(pace)* tranquille; *(life)* sans souci; **to be e. in one's mind** avoir l'esprit tranquille; **at an e. pace** tranquillement; **with an e. conscience** la conscience tranquille; *Fam* **to be on e. street** ne pas avoir de problèmes financiers
5 *Com (market)* tranquille; **prices are (getting) easier** on accuse une détente dans les prix; **cotton was easier** le coton a accusé une détente

ADV 1 to take things *or* **it e.** *(in relaxed manner)* prendre les choses en douceur; **to take things** *or* **life e.** *(lead a life of ease)* mener une vie tranquille; *(not overdo things)* ralentir; **take it e.!** doucement!; *(don't get upset)* ne vous en faites pas!; **you'll have to go e. for a bit** il va falloir ralentir *ou* freiner un peu; **to go e. with sb/sth** ménager qn/qch; **e. does it!** (allez-y) doucement!; **go e. on the electricity/the curry powder** allez-y doucement avec l'électricité/le curry; **e. (ahead)!** *(in rowing)* (en avant) doucement!; *Mil* **stand e.!** repos!

2 *Fam (without difficulty)* **I can do it e.** cela me sera facile; **(it's) easier said than done** c'est plus facile à dire qu'à faire; *Prov* **e. come e. go** ce qui vient de la flûte s'en va par le tambour

▸▸ **e. chair** fauteuil *m*; *Mus* **e. listening** variété *f*, *Fam* **e. money** argent *m* gagné sans peine

easy-going ADJ **1** *(not given to anger)* qui prend les choses tranquillement; *(not worrying)* qui ne se fait pas de bile, décontracté; *(undemanding)* accommodant, coulant, peu exigeant; *(permissive)* qui a la conscience élastique; **the police take an e. attitude to such cases** dans de tels cas, la police se montre assez conciliante **2** *(horse)* à l'allure douce

eat [iːt] *(pt* **ate** [et, *esp Am* eɪt], *pp* **eaten** [ˈiːt(ə)n]) VT **1** *(bread, soup etc)* manger; **to e. one's breakfast** déjeuner, prendre son petit déjeuner; **to e. one's dinner/supper** dîner/souper; **to e. a good dinner** faire un bon dîner; **to e. a card** *(credit card)* avaler une carte; **fit to e.** bon à manger, mangeable; **I don't e. meat** je ne mange pas de viande; **to e. one's fill** manger à sa faim; **he won't e. you** il ne vous mangera pas; *Fam* **(I'm so hungry) I could e. a horse!** j'ai une faim de loup!; *Fam* **we e. teams like you for breakfast** nous ne faisons qu'une seule bouchée d'équipes comme la vôtre; *Am Fam Fig* **to e. sb's lunch** *(defeat)* battre qn à plates coutures; **to e. one's words** se rétracter; **if it comes off, I'll e. my hat** si ça réussit, je mange mon chapeau!; **to e. sb out of house and home** ruiner qn en nourriture; **she ate her way through six packets of biscuits** elle a réussi à engloutir six paquets de biscuits; *Am Vulg* **e. shit!** va te faire voir!

2 *Fam (trouble)* **what's eating you?** qu'est-ce qui vous inquiète *ou* tracasse?

VI **1** manger; **to e. like a horse** manger comme un ogre; **to e. like a bird** avoir un appétit d'oiseau, manger trois fois rien; **he eats out of my hand** *(of bird)* il vient manger dans ma main; *Fig (of person)* il fait tout ce que je veux; **treat them right and you'll have them eating out of your hand** traite-les bien et ils te mangeront dans la main

2 *(have meal)* dîner; **we e. at seven** nous dînons à sept heures; **to e. well** bien manger; **let's e.!** on mange?; **have you eaten?** est-ce que tu as mangé?

▸ **eat away** VT SEP *(erode)* *(rocks, cliff, self-confidence)* éroder, miner; *(foundations)* saper; *(part of body)* ronger; *(of acid)* dissoudre

▸ **eat away at** VT INSEP = eat away, eat into

▸ **eat in** VI *(of hotel guest)* consommer sur place

▸ **eat into** VT INSEP **1** *(attack)* ronger; **rust had eaten into the metal** la rouille avait rongé le métal; **to e. into wood** *(of insect, worm)* ronger le bois **2** *(diminish)* entamer; **these expenses had eaten into their savings** ces dépenses avaient entamé leurs économies

▸ **eat off** VT SEP *Fam* **to e. one's head off** s'empiffrer

▸ **eat out** VI **1** *(eat in restaurant)* manger au restaurant **2** *(of hotel guest)* déjeuner/dîner à l'extérieur

VT SEP *Fam* **to e. one's heart out** se ronger le cœur; **e. your heart out, USA!** = dommage pour les États-Unis!

▸ **eat up** VT SEP **1** *(eat completely)* *(cake etc)* manger jusqu'à la dernière miette; **e. up your bread!** finis ton pain! **2** *(consume)* consumer sans profit; *Fam* **stove that eats up the coal** poêle qui mange beaucoup de charbon; **to e. up the miles** *(of car etc)* dévorer la route; **jealousy is eating him up** la jalousie le dévore; **to be eaten up with** *(pride)* être dévoré de; *(ambition)* être consumé par **3** *(exhaust)* *(provisions)* épuiser

VI *(eat everything)* finir son assiette; **e. up!** *(there's lots more)* vas-y, mange!

eatable [ˈiːtəb(ə)l] ADJ comestible; *(fit to eat)* mangeable, bon à manger; **fruit that is quite e.** fruit qui se laisse manger

NPL *esp Hum* **eatables** provisions *fpl* de bouche, comestibles *mpl*

eater [ˈiːtər] N **1** *(person)* mangeur, -euse; **he isn't as good an e. as his sister** il ne mange pas aussi bien que sa sœur; **to be a fussy e.** être difficile (sur la nourriture); **to be a messy e.** manger salement; **small/big e.** petit/gros mangeur **2** *(apple)* pomme *f* à couteau *ou* de dessert

eatery [ˈiːtərɪ] N *Fam* (café-)restaurant *m*, *pl* (cafés-)restaurants

eating [ˈiːtɪŋ] N manger *m*; **healthy e.** alimentation *f* saine; **these birds make good e.** ces oiseaux sont bons à manger

▸▸ **e. apple** pomme *f* à couteau; **e. habits** habitudes *fpl* alimentaires; **e. house, e. place** restaurant *m*

eats [iːts] NPL *Fam* bouffe *f*, **plenty of e.** plein à bouffer; **let's get some e.** allons chercher de la bouffe

eau-de-Cologne [ˈəʊdəkəˈləʊn] N eau *f* de Cologne

eaves [iːvz] NPL *Constr* avant-toit *m*

eavesdrop [ˈiːvzdrɒp] VI **(-pp-)** écouter aux portes; **to e. on a conversation** tendre l'oreille pour écouter une conversation privée; **I found myself eavesdropping on their conversation** j'ai entendu leur conversation sans le vouloir; **stop eavesdropping!** arrête d'espionner le monde!

eavesdropper [ˈiːvzdrɒpər] N oreille *f* indiscrète

ebb [eb] N **1** *(of tide)* reflux *m*; **the e. and flow** le flux et le reflux; **the e. and flow of marital life** les hauts et les bas de la vie conjugale; **the e. and flow of political change** les fluctuations de la vie politique; **the tide is on the e.** la marée baisse **2** *(of fortune, life)* déclin *m*; **to be at a low e.** *(of patient)* être très bas; *(be depressed)* être déprimé; *(of business)* être au ralenti; **her spirits were at a low e./their lowest e.** elle était abattue/très abattue; **their funds were at a low/their lowest e.** ils étaient à bout de ressources

VI *(of tide)* baisser; **to e. and flow** monter et baisser **2** = ebb away

▸▸ **e. tide** marée *f* descendante

▸ **ebb away** VI *(of enthusiasm, courage, strength)* faiblir, baisser; *(of rage, indignation)* se calmer; *(of support)* s'amenuiser; *(of time, water)* s'écouler; **his life was ebbing away** il baissait d'heure en heure

ebbing [ˈebɪŋ] ADJ **1** *(water)* qui reflue **2** *(fortunes etc)* sur le déclin; *(popularity)* en baisse; *(strength, enthusiasm)* faiblissant

EBIT [ˈiːbiːaɪˈtiː, ˈebɪt] N *Fin (abbr* **earnings before interest and tax)** bénéfices *mpl* avant impôts et charges

EBITDA [ebɪtˈdaː] N *Fin (abbr* **earnings before interest, tax, depreciation and amortization)** EBITDA *m*

ebonics [əˈbɒnɪks] N *Ling* = anglais *m* parlé par une partie de la communauté Noire américaine

ebony [ˈebənɪ] N **1** *(wood)* (bois *m* d')ébène *f*, **e. box** boîte *f* en bois d'ébène **2** *(tree)* ébénier *m* **3** *(colour)* ébène *f*, **e. skin** peau *f* noire d'ébène

▸▸ **e. tree** ébénier *m*

e-book N livre *m* numérique, livre électronique, e-book *m*

EBRD [iːbiːɑːˈdiː] N *(abbr* **European Bank for Reconstruction and Development)** BERD *f*

e-broker N *St Exch* courtier, -ière électronique

e-broking N *St Exch* courtage *m* électronique

ebullience [ɪˈbʌlɪəns] N bouillonnement *m*, effervescence *f*, **the e. of youth** l'exubérance *f* de la jeunesse

ebullient [ɪˈbʌlɪənt] ADJ enthousiaste, exubérant; **they were in (an) e. mood** *or* **in e. spirits** ils étaient d'une humeur exubérante

e-business N *Comput* commerce *m* électronique

EC [iːˈsiː] N *(abbr* **European Community)** CE *f*, **EC directive** directive *f* européenne

ADJ ATTRIB de la CE

e-cash N *Comput* argent *m* électronique, argent virtuel, e-cash *m*

ECB [iːsiːˈbiː] N *(abbr* **European Central Bank)** BCE *f*

eccentric [ekˈsentrɪk] ADJ **1** *(person, behaviour)* excentrique **2** *Math, Astron (circle, orbit etc)* excentrique; *Tech (camshaft)* excentré

N **1** *(person)* excentrique *mf*, original, -ale **2** *Tech* excentrique *m*

▸▸ *Tech* **e. shaft** arbre *m* à excentrique

eccentrically [ekˈsentrɪklɪ] ADV *Tech* excentriquement; *(to dress, behave)* de manière excentrique, excentriquement

eccentricity [eksenˈtrɪsɪtɪ] N **1** *(of character, behaviour etc)* excentricité *f*, **eccentricities** *(of person)* excentricités **2** *Math (of ellipse)* excentricité *f*, *Tech* excentricité, désaxage *m*

ecclesiastic [ɪkliːzɪˈæstɪk] N *Fml* ecclésiastique *m*

ecclesiastical [ɪkliːzɪˈæstɪk(ə)l] ADJ ecclésiastique

ECE [iːsiːˈiː] N *abbr* **Economic Commission for Europe**

ECG [iːsiːˈdʒiː] N *Med* **1** *(abbr* **electrocardiogram)** ECG *m* **2** *(abbr* **electrocardiograph)** électrocardiographe *m*

ECGD [iːsiːdʒiːˈdiː] N *(abbr* **Export Credit Guarantee Department)** COFACE *f*

echelon [ˈeʃəlɒn] N **1** *(level)* **the higher** *or* **upper echelons of industry/the Civil Service** les niveaux supérieurs de l'industrie/de l'administration **2** *Mil* échelon *m*; **in e.** en échelon

echinacea [ekɪˈneɪʃə] N *Bot, Med* échinacée *f*

echo, *pl* **echoes** [ˈekəʊ, -əʊz] N écho *m*; **this room has a bit of an e./a good e.** il y a un peu d'écho/un bon écho dans cette pièce; **to cheer sb to the e.** applaudir qn à tout rompre; *Fig* **there are echoes of the 18th century in this novel** il y a des accents du XVIIIᵉ siècle dans ce roman; **echoes of Churchill/Godard** du Churchill/du Godard; **her words found an e. in many hearts** ses mots ont fait vibrer la corde sensible dans beaucoup de cœurs

VT répéter (en écho); **to e. sb's words** répéter ce que qn a dit; **to e. sb's opinions** se faire l'écho des opinions de qn; **'we're going to the beach', she said – 'the beach?' he echoed** 'nous allons à la plage', dit-elle – 'à la plage?', répéta-t-il; *Fig* **the yellow of the** walls is **echoed in the curtains** le jaune des murs se trouve rappelé dans les rideaux

VI faire écho; **the woods echoed with the songs of birds** les bois retentissaient des chants des oiseaux; **his voice echoes through the room** sa voix résonne dans la salle

▸▸**e. chamber** chambre *f* de réverbération; **e. sounder** échosondeur *m*; **e. sounding** sondage *m* par ultrasons

ECHR [iːsiːeɪtʃ'ɑːr] **N** (abbr **European Court of Human Rights**) CEDH *f*

éclair [eɪ'kleər] **N** Culin éclair *m*; **chocolate e.** éclair au chocolat

eclectic [ɪ'klektɪk] **ADJ, N** éclectique *mf*; **an e. blend** un mélange varié

eclecticism [ɪ'klektɪsɪz(ə)m] **N** éclectisme *m*

eclipse [ɪ'klɪps] **N 1** Astron éclipse *f*; **solar/lunar e.** éclipse de soleil/de lune; **total/partial e.** éclipse totale/partielle **2** Naut (of lighthouse) éclipse *f* **3** Fig (overshadowing) éclipse *f*; **the e. of this team by a younger one** l'éclipse de cette équipe par une équipe plus jeune; **to suffer** or **go into an e.** être éclipsé

VT 1 Astron, Naut etc éclipser **2** Fig (overshadow, supersede) éclipser

Ecofin ['iːkəʊfɪn] **N** (abbr **Economic and Financial Council of Ministers**) (Conseil *m*) Ecofin *m*

ecofreak ['iːkəʊfriːk] **N** Fam écologiste *mf* enragé(e)

eco-friendly ['iːkəʊ-] **ADJ** (product) qui ne nuit pas à l'environnement; (lifestyle, person) qui respecte l'environnement

ecological [iːkə'lɒdʒɪk(ə)l] **ADJ** écologique

ecologically [iːkə'lɒdʒɪklɪ] **ADV** écologiquement; **to be e. harmful/sound** nuire/ne pas nuire à l'environnement

ecologist [ɪ'kɒlədʒɪst] **N** écologiste *mf*

ecology [ɪ'kɒlədʒɪ] **N** écologie *f*

e-commerce **N** Comput commerce *m* électronique

▸▸**e. site** site *m* marchand

econometric [ɪkɒnə'metrɪk] **ADJ** économétrique

▸▸**e. model** modèle *m* économétrique; **e. modelling** modélisation *f* économétrique

econometrics [ɪkɒnə'metrɪks] **N** économétrie *f* VOIR GRAMMAIRE A10

economic [iːkə'nɒmɪk] **ADJ 1** Econ économique **2** Br (profitable) rentable; **to make sth e.** rentabiliser qch **3** Fam (inexpensive) économique

▸▸**e. adviser** conseiller, -ère économique; **e. aid** aide *f* économique; **e. analysis** analyse *f* économique; **e. analyst** analyste *mf* économique; **e. appraisal** évaluation *f* économique; **e. circumstances** conjoncture *f*, EU **E. Commission for Europe** Commission *f* économique pour l'Europe; **e. cost** coût *m* économique; **e. crisis** crise *f* économique; **e. development** croissance *f* par habitant ou per capita; **e. forecast** prévisions *fpl* économiques; **e. forecasting firm** = organisme *m* spécialisé dans les prévisions économiques; **e. geography** géographie *f* économique; **e. goods** biens *mpl* économiques; **e. indicator** indicateur *m* économique; EU **E. and Monetary Union** union *f* économique et monétaire; **e. pressure** pression *f* économique; **e. rate of return** taux *f* de rentabilité économique; **e. recovery** reprise *f* ou redressement *m* économique; **e. sanctions** sanctions *fpl* économiques; **e. situation** conjoncture *f* économique; EU **E. and Social Committee** Comité *m* Économique et Social; **e. trend** tendance *f* ou conjoncture *f* économique; **e. zone** zone *f* économique

Il faut noter que les adjectifs **economic** et **economical** ne sont pas interchangeables. **Economic** signifie qui se rapporte à l'économie, alors que **economical** signifie qui permet d'économiser.

economical [iːkə'nɒmɪk(ə)l] **ADJ** (person) économe; (machine, method, approach) économique; (style) concis, sobre; **to be e. with sth** économiser qch; **to be e. with the truth** dire la vérité avec parcimonie; **it's more e. to buy larger packets** c'est plus économique d'acheter des paquets plus grands

▸▸**e. speed** (of ship etc) vitesse *f* économique

Voir note ci-dessus.

economically [iːkə'nɒmɪklɪ] **ADV** économiquement; **to use sth e.** (electricity, fuel) économiser qch; **e. viable** économiquement viable, rentable; **e. written** écrit avec concision

economics [iːkə'nɒmɪks] **N** VOIR GRAMMAIRE A10 **1** Econ les sciences *fpl* économiques; **socialist/supply-side e.** économie *f* socialiste/de l'offre **2** (financial aspects) aspects *mpl* économiques ou financiers; (profitability) rentabilité *f*, **we must consider the e. of the project before making any decisions** nous devons considérer l'aspect financier du projet avant de prendre une décision

economist [ɪ'kɒnəmɪst] **N** Econ économiste *mf*

economize [ɪ'kɒnəmaɪz] **VI** économiser, faire des économies; **to e. on sth** économiser sur qch

VT (time, money etc) économiser, ménager

economizer [ɪ'kɒnəmaɪzər] **N** Aut économiseur *m*

economy [ɪ'kɒnəmɪ] **N 1** (careful use, saving) (of money, resources etc) économie *f*, **to practise e.** économiser; **to make economies** faire des économies; **it's a false e.** ça revient aussi cher; **with e. of effort** sans effort *m* inutile; **e. of style** concision *f* de style; **economies of scale** économies *fpl* d'échelle **2** Econ (of country) économie *f*, régime *m* économique; Old-fashioned **political e.** économie politique; **(centrally) planned e.** économie planifiée

▸▸Com **e. brand** marque *f* économique; **e. class** classe *f* touriste; **e. drive** (of company, government) politique *f* de réduction des dépenses; **e. fare** tarif *m* économique; **e. measure** mesure *f* de réduction des dépenses; Aut **e. mode** (with automatic gears) mode *m* économique; Com **e. pack** paquet *m* économique; Com **e. size** format *m* économique

ECOSOC ['iːkəʊsɒk] **N** EU (abbr **Economic and Social Committee**) CES *m*

ecosphere ['iːkəʊsfɪər] **N** écosphère *f*

ecosystem ['iːkəʊsɪstəm] **N** écosystème *m*

ecotax ['iːkəʊtæks] **N** taxe *f* écologique, écotaxe *f*

ecoterrorist ['iːkəʊ'terərɪst] **N** = militant, -ante écologiste ayant recours à des actions violentes

ecotourism [iːkəʊ'tʊərɪz(ə)m] **N** tourisme *m* écologique

ecowarrior ['iːkəʊwɒrɪər] **N** écoguerrier, -ière

ecru ['ekruː] **N, ADJ** Tex écru *m*

ECSC [iːsiːes'siː] **N** Admin (abbr **European Coal and Steel Community**) CECA *f*

ecstasy ['ekstəsɪ] **N 1** (joyful feeling) joie *f* délirante, ravissement *m*; **to be in an e. of joy** se pâmer de joie; **to go into/be in ecstasies over sth** s'extasier/être en extase devant qch; **to send sb into ecstasies** faire tomber

qn en extase **2** Rel, Psy etc extase *f* **3** Sl (drug) ecstasy *f*

ecstatic [ek'stætɪk] **ADJ** extatique; **he was e. about** or **over the news/their arrival** la nouvelle/leur arrivée le rendait fou de joie

ecstatically [ek'stætɪklɪ] **ADV** avec extase; (to look at) d'un air extasié; **e. happy** heureux jusqu'au ravissement

ECT [iːsiː'tiː] **N** (abbr **electroconvulsive therapy**) = traitement *m* par électrochocs

ectopic [ek'tɒpɪk] **ADJ**

▸▸Obst **e. pregnancy** grossesse *f* extra-utérine, grossesse ectopique

ectoplasm ['ektəʊplæz(ə)m] **N** (in spiritualism) ectoplasme *m*

ECU, **ecu** ['eɪkjuː, occ iːsiː'juː] Formerly (abbr **European Currency Unit**) écu *m* **2** [iːsiː'juː] abbr **European Customs Union 3** [iːsiː'juː] abbr **electronic control unit**

Ecuador ['ekwədɔːr] **N** (la République de) l'Équateur *m*

Ecuadoran [ekwə'dɔːrən], **Ecuadorian** [ekwə'dɔːrɪən] **ADJ** écuadorien, équatorien **N** Écuadorien, -ienne, Équatorien, -ienne

ecumenical [iːkjʊ'menɪk(ə)l] **ADJ** Rel (council) œcuménique

ecumenism [iː'kjuːmənɪz(ə)m], **ecumenicism** [iːkjuː'menɪsɪz(ə)m] **N** Rel œcuménisme *m*

eczema ['eksɪmə] **N** Med eczéma *m*; **to have** or **suffer from e.** avoir ou faire de l'eczéma

ed 1 (abbr **edition**) éd(it) **2** abbr **editor 3** abbr **edited**

EDC [iːdiː'siː] **N** (abbr **European Defence Community**) CED *f*

eddy ['edɪ] **N** (of water, wind) remous *m*, tourbillon *m*; (of leaves, dust) tourbillon **VI** (of water) faire des remous; (of wind, smoke, snow) tourbillonner, tournoyer; (of crowds) tournoyer

▸▸Elec **e. currents** courants *mpl* de Foucault

edelweiss ['eɪd(ə)lvaɪs] **N** (plant) edelweiss *m*

edema [ɪ'diːmə] **N** Am œdème *m*

Eden ['iːd(ə)n] **N** Bible (the Garden of) **E.** l'Éden *m*, le Paradis terrestre

EDF [iːdiː'ef] **N** (abbr **European Development Fund**) FED *m*

EDGE [edʒ] **N 1** (of blade) fil *m*, tranchant *m*; (of tool) angle *m*; (of skate) carre *f*; (of stone etc) arête *f*, angle; **sharp/rounded e.** arête vive/mousse; **inside/outside e.** dedans *m*/dehors *m*; **knife with a keen e.** couteau à tranchant aigu; **to put an e. on a tool** aiguiser ou affiler un outil; **to take the e. off** (blade, appetite etc) émousser; (pleasure) gâter; (argument) couper tout l'effet de

2 (rim, border, limit) (of table) bord *m*, rebord *m*; (of plank, medal, book) tranche *f*; (of wood) lisière *f*, bordure *f*, orée *f*; (of river) bord, rive *f*; (of plain) limite *f*, (of road, path) bordure, bord; (sewn onto material) liséré *m*; **it fell off the e. of the table** il est tombé de la table; **it fell off the e.** il est tombé; **gilt edges** tranches dorées; **with gilt edges** doré sur tranches; **to be on the e. of …** (new age) être à l'orée de …; (final conflict, great discoveries) être au bord de …; **at the e. of the road** au bord ou en bordure de la route; **the flag had a golden fringe round the e.** le drapeau était bordé d'une frange dorée; Phot etc **white e.** (of print) liséré blanc; **at the water's e.** au bord de l'eau; **at the e. of a precipice** au bord d'un précipice; **on e.** (of brick) de chant, de can; **to set sth on e.** (tilt) mettre qch de chant ou de can

3 (idioms) Fam **to have an** or **the e. on sb** être avantagé par rapport à qn; **to have an e. to one's voice** avoir une voix coupante; **to**

speak with a sarcastic/nervous/contemptuous e. to one's voice parler avec une pointe de sarcasme/de nervosité/de mépris dans la voix; on e. *(of person)* énervé, nerveux; to set sb on e. crisper qn, énerver qn; to set *or* put sb's teeth on e. faire grincer des dents à qn; to set sb's nerves on e. taper sur les nerfs de qn; to send sb over the e. porter le coup de grâce à qn; a movie that will have you on the e. of your seat un film au suspense insoutenable; to give sb the rough e. of one's tongue dire son fait à qn

VT 1 *Tech (sharpen) (knife, tool)* affiler, aiguiser; *(millstone)* repiquer

2 *(border) (material)* border (with de); *(skirt etc)* lisérer

3 *(move slowly)* to e. one's way into a room/through the crowd se faufiler dans une pièce/à travers la foule; to e. one's chair nearer rapprocher *ou* avancer sa chaise peu à peu

VI *(move slowly)* to e. towards sb/sth s'approcher tout doucement de qn/qch; to e. through the crowd/past the guards se faufiler à travers la foule/devant les gardes; could you possibly e. a little closer? pourriez-vous vous rapprocher un petit peu?; the drivers were edging forwards in the traffic jam les conducteurs avançaient lentement dans l'embouteillage

▶▶ e. cutter, e. trimmer *(for grass)* coupebordure(s) *m, pl* coupe-bordures

▶ **edge away VI** *(move away slowly)* s'éloigner *ou* s'écarter tout doucement (from sb de qn)

▶ **edge out VI** *(move cautiously)* I opened the window and edged out j'ai ouvert la fenêtre et me suis doucement glissé dehors; the driver/car edged out le conducteur/la voiture se dégagea lentement

VT SEP 1 to e. one's way out se frayer un chemin; she edged her way out onto the ledge elle gagna le rebord de la fenêtre avec précaution

2 *(supplant)* évincer; to e. sb out of the chairmanship évincer qn de la présidence

▶ **edge past VI** *(move past cautiously)* passer prudemment

VT INSEP I edged past her je suis passé discrètement à côté d'elle

▶ **edge up VI** *(climb slowly) (of prices)* grimper petit à petit

VT SEP they edged their way up the cliff ils ont escaladé la falaise à grand peine

edged [edʒd] **ADJ** *(tool, weapon etc)* tranchant, acéré

-edged [edʒd] **SUFF** double-e. à double tranchant; *Fig* a double-e. weapon une arme à double tranchant; sharp-e. au tranchant affilé *ou* bien aiguisé; a razor-e. knife/tongue un couteau/une langue bien affilé(e)

edgeways ['edʒweɪz], **edgewise** ['edʒwaɪz] **ADV 1** *(on its edge)* de chant; to lay *or* set a plank e. placer une planche de chant; *Fam* I can't get a word in e. je n'arrive pas à placer un mot (dans la conversation) **2** *(from side)* latéralement, de côté; seen e. (on) vu de côté

edginess ['edʒɪnɪs] **N** nervosité *f*

edging ['edʒɪŋ] **N 1** *(action) (of dress)* pose *f* d'un liséré *ou* d'une ganse; *(of lawn)* entretien *m* de la bordure **2** *(border) Sewing* liséré *m*, passement *m*, ganse *f*; *(of flower bed)* bordure *f*

▶▶ e. shears cisaille *f* à gazon; e. tool coupe-gazon *m inv*, molette *f*

edgy ['edʒɪ] **ADJ** *(person)* énervé; to get e. s'énerver

EDI [iːdiːˈaɪ] **N 1** *Comput (abbr* **Electronic Interchange)** EDI *m* **2** *Fin (abbr* **European Data Interchange)** EED *m*

edible ['edɪb(ə)l] **ADJ** comestible; *(fit to eat)*

bon à manger, mangeable; it was so hot it was barely e. c'était si chaud que c'était à peine mangeable; it's very e. c'est très bon

▶▶ e. oil huile *f* comestible

edict ['iːdɪkt] **N** *Law, Pol* édit *m*

▶▶ *Hist* the E. of Nantes l'Édit de Nantes

edification [edɪfɪˈkeɪʃən] **N** *Fml* édification *f*, instruction *f*; *esp Iron* for your e. pour votre édification

edifice ['edɪfɪs] **N** édifice *m*

edify ['edɪfaɪ] **VT** *Fml* édifier

edifying ['edɪfaɪɪŋ] **ADJ** *Fml (spectacle, book etc)* édifiant

Edinburgh ['edɪnbrə] **N** Édimbourg

edit ['edɪt] **VT 1** *(in publishing), Journ (prepare)* préparer pour la publication; *(work)* donner une édition annotée de; *(series of texts etc)* diriger; *(be in charge of) (newspaper, magazine)* rédiger, diriger; edited by ... *(series, newspaper etc)* sous la direction de ... **2** *(film, TV programme, tape)* monter; edited master master *m* monté, montage *m* original **3** *Comput (text on screen)* éditer

N *(in publishing)* révision *f*; *TV* point *m* de montage; *(in newspaper, text)* correction *f*, révision; *Comput (menu heading)* Edition *f*

▶▶ *Comput* e. key touche *f* de modification; *Comput* e. mode mode *m* Edition; *TV* e. suite régie *f ou* salle *f* de montage

> Note that the French verb **éditer** is a false friend. It means **to publish**.

▶ **edit in VT SEP** insérer

▶ **edit out VT SEP** *(scene)* couper; *(from text)* supprimer; *(write out of TV series)* faire disparaître; he was edited out of the film when he broke his contract on a coupé toutes les scènes du film où il apparaissait quand il a rompu son contrat

editable ['edɪtəb(ə)l] **ADJ** pouvant être édité

editing ['edɪtɪŋ] **N 1** *(in publishing) (of text)* préparation *f*, édition *f*; *(of newspaper, magazine)* rédaction *f*; a book on e. un manuel d'édition **2** *(of film, TV programme, tape)* montage *m*; *(removal) (of scene, passage etc)* suppression *f* **3** *Comput* édition *f*

▶▶ *TV* e. desk table *f ou* banc *m* de montage; *Comput* e. function fonction *f* d'édition; *TV* e. table table *f* de montage; *TV* e. terminal terminal *m* de montage; *Comput* e. window fenêtre *f* d'édition

edition [ɪˈdɪʃən] **N** *(in publishing), Journ* édition *f*; the earlier editions of the newspapers les premières éditions des journaux; this error was corrected in later editions cette erreur a été corrigée dans les éditions ultérieures; the hardback/paperback e. l'édition reliée/de poche; in Tuesday's e. of the programme dans l'émission de mardi; school e. édition scolaire; cheap e. édition populaire; book in its fourth e. livre à sa quatrième édition

▶▶ e. time *(for newspaper)* bouclage *m*, heure *f* de l'édition, tombée *f*

> Note that the French word **édition** also means **publishing**.

editor ['edɪtər] **N 1** *(in publishing), Journ (of text)* éditeur, -trice; *(of critical edition)* auteur *m*; *(in charge of publication)* surveillant *m* de la publication; *(of series)* directeur, -trice; *(of magazine, newspaper)* rédacteur, -trice en chef, directeur, -trice; *(of dictionary)* rédacteur *m*; news e. rédacteur au service des informations; series e. directeur de la publication; sports/political/fashion e. rédacteur sportif/politique/de mode; **2** *Cin (of film)* monteur *m*; *TV, Radio* programme e. réalisateur *m* **3** *Comput (software)* éditeur *m*

▶▶ editors' conference conférence *f* de ré-

daction; e.'s note note *f* de la rédaction; *Comput* e. program programme *m* éditeur

editorial [edɪˈtɔːrɪəl] **ADJ** *(in publishing), Journ* de rédaction; that's an e. decision c'est une décision qui appartient à la rédaction

N *Journ* éditorial *m*; *Fam* édito *m*;

▶▶ e. advertisement reportage *m* publicitaire; e. advertising publicité *f* rédactionnelle; e. changes corrections *fpl*; e. column colonne *f* rédactionnelle; e. conference conférence *f* de rédaction; e. content contenu *m* rédactionnel; e. department service *m* de la rédaction, rédaction *f*, direction *f* de la rédaction; e. director *(of newspaper)* rédacteur, -trice en chef, directeur, -trice de la rédaction; *(of publishing company)* directeur, -trice de la rédaction; e. freedom liberté *f* des rédacteurs; e. interference ingérence *f* rédactionnelle; e. office (salle *f* de) rédaction; e. opinion *(in press)* avis *m* éditorial; e. policy politique *f* éditoriale; *(in press)* politique de la rédaction; the e. staff la rédaction; e. writer éditorialiste *mf*

editorialist [edɪˈtɔːrɪəlɪst] **N** *Am* éditorialiste *mf*

editorialize [edɪˈtɔːrɪəlaɪz] **VI** émettre des opinions personnelles, être subjectif; as the Times editorialized, ... comme l'affirmait l'éditorial du Times, ...

editorially [edɪˈtɔːrɪəlɪ] **ADV** du point de vue de la rédaction

editor-in-chief, *pl* **editors-in-chief N** rédacteur, -trice en chef

editorship ['edɪtəʃɪp] **N** rédaction *f*, direction *f*; during her e. quand elle dirigeait la rédaction; the series was produced under the general e. of ... la série a été produite sous la direction générale de ...

EDP [iːdiːˈpiː] **N** *(abbr* **electronic data processing)** informatique *f*

▶▶ E. department service *m* informatique

educable ['edjʊkəb(ə)l] **ADJ** éducable

educate ['edjʊkeɪt] **VT 1** *Sch (person)* donner de l'instruction à, instruire; he was educated in France/at Oxford il a fait ses études en France/à Oxford; to have one's child educated faire faire des études à son enfant; to be impossible to e. être inéducable **2** *(train, develop) (person, sb's taste/mind)* former; the series aims to e. the viewers in the ways of this strange people cette série a pour objectif d'instruire les téléspectateurs sur les coutumes de ce peuple étrange; she was educated always to think of others before herself on lui a enseigné à toujours penser aux autres avant elle-même

educated ['edjʊkeɪtɪd] **ADJ** *(person)* instruit, lettré; half-e. peu instruit; an e. guess une supposition éclairée; self-e. autodidacte; he was well e. in the ways of the locals il était bien renseigné sur le mode de vie des gens de la région

education [edjʊˈkeɪʃən] **N 1** *(instruction)* enseignement *m*, instruction *f*; to study E. étudier les Sciences de l'Éducation; the e. of young people in the use of birth control methods l'éducation des jeunes pour l'utilisation des méthodes contraceptives; he has had a good e. il a reçu une bonne instruction; to receive a classical/literary e. recevoir une éducation *ou* un enseignement classique/littéraire; to get oneself an e. faire des études; he never completed his e. il n'a jamais fini *ou* terminé ses études; *Iron* it was an e. working over there c'était instructif de travailler là-bas; adult e. enseignement des adultes; compulsory e. enseignement obligatoire; full-time e. enseignement à temps complet; further e. enseignement post-scolaire; higher *or* university e. *(system)* enseignement supérieur; *(of person)* études *fpl* supérieures; pri-

mary/secondary e. enseignement primaire/secondaire; *Br* **Department for Education** = Ministère *m* de l'Éducation nationale; *Br* **(local) e. authority** = Direction *f* de l'enseignement

2 *(learning)* éducation *f*; **a man without e.** un homme sans éducation; **gaps in one's e.** des lacunes dans son éducation

▸▸ **E. Act** ≃ réforme *f* (de l'Éducation); *Journ* **e. correspondent** correspondant, -ante chargé(e) des problèmes d'enseignement; **e. page** page *f* éducation; **e. supplement** supplément *m* éducation

> Note that the French noun **éducation** refers both to education and to upbringing.

educational [edjʊ'keɪʃən(ə)l] ADJ *(institution, work)* d'éducation, d'enseignement; *(role, function)* éducatif, éducateur, -trice; *(film)* éducatif; *(programme, publisher)* scolaire; *(method)* éducatif, pédagogique; **working over there was very e.** c'était très instructif de travailler là-bas; **it was an e. experience/visit** c'était une expérience/visite instructive; **for e. purposes** dans un but pédagogique

▸▸ **e. adviser** conseiller, -ère d'orientation; **e. holiday** vacances *fpl* studieuses; **e. psychologist** *(practical)* psychologue *mf* scolaire; *(academic)* psychopédagogue *mf*; **e. qualification** diplôme *m*; *Comput* **e. software** logiciel *m* didactique; **e. tour** ≃ Éductour *m*, voyage *m* d'études

education(al)ist [edjʊ'keɪʃənɪst, -əlɪst] N éducateur, -trice, pédagogue *mf*

educationally [edjʊ'keɪʃən(ə)lɪ] ADV du point de vue de l'éducation *ou* de l'enseignement; **e. subnormal** *(child)* arriéré

educative ['edjʊkətɪv] ADJ *(function, purpose)* éducatif; *(experience, remark)* instructif

educator ['edjʊkeɪtər] N *esp Am* éducateur, -trice

edutainment [edju:'teɪnmənt] N apprentissage *m* par le jeu, édutainment *m* ◊ ADJ ludo-éducatif

Edwardian [ed'wɔːdɪən] ADJ qui a rapport à l'époque du roi Édouard VII; **the E. era** ≃ la Belle Époque

Edward the Confessor ['edwəd] N Édouard *m* le Confesseur

EEA [iːiː'eɪ] *(abbr* **European Economic Area)** N EEE *m*

EEC [iːiː'siː] N *Formerly (abbr* **European Economic Community)** CEE *f*

e-economy N économie *f* en ligne

EEG [iːiː'dʒiː] N *Med* **1** *(abbr* **electroencephalogram)** EEG *m* **2** *(abbr* **electroencephalograph)** appareil *m* à EEG

eejit ['iːdʒɪt] N *Ir, Scot* andouille *f*, couillon *m*

eel [iːl] N anguille *f*; **e. basket** *or* **pot** nasse *f* à anguilles; *Br Culin* **jellied eels** anguilles en gelée

eelworm ['iːlwɜːm] N anguillule *f*

EEPROM ['iːprɒm] N *Comput (abbr* **electrically erasable programmable ROM)** EEPROM *f*

eerie ['ɪərɪ] ADJ *(calm, sound)* inquiétant, sinistre; *(atmosphere)* qui donne des frissons; **an e. silence** *(after explosion, in empty house etc)* un silence de mort; **I had the e. feeling that I was being watched** j'avais l'étrange impression qu'on m'observait; **it was e. to think that …** cela donnait des frissons *ou* la chair de poule de penser que …

eerily ['ɪərɪlɪ] ADV étrangement, à donner des frissons; **the cat's eyes glowed e. in the dark** les yeux du chat brillaient d'une lueur surnaturelle dans le noir; **e. quiet** *(house etc)* d'un calme inquiétant; **the whole town was e. silent** dans toute la ville régnait un silence inquiétant *ou* sinistre

eeriness ['ɪərɪnɪs] N *(of place, sound etc)* étrangeté *f* surnaturelle

eery ['ɪərɪ] ADJ = **eerie**

eff [ef] VI *Br Sl Euph* **he's always effing and blinding** il n'arrête pas de jurer

▸ **eff off** VI *Br Sl Euph* **e. off!** va te faire foutre!; **she told him to e. off** elle lui a dit d'aller se faire foutre

efface [ɪ'feɪs] VT effacer; *(memory of sth)* oblitérer, effacer; *(remnants of past)* faire disparaître; **to e. oneself** s'effacer

effacement [ɪ'feɪsmənt] N effacement *m*

effect [ɪ'fekt] N **1** *(result)*, *Phys* effet *m*; *(of deed)* résultat *m*, conséquence *f*; **the e. of heat on metals** l'action de la chaleur sur les métaux; **the e. of this action was to bring prices down** cette action a eu pour effet de faire baisser les prix; **to have an e. on sb/sth** faire *ou* produire de l'effet sur qn/qch, affecter qn/qch; **to have no e.** ne faire *ou* ne produire aucun effet; **let's see what e. the addition of hydrogen has** voyons l'effet que produit l'addition d'hydrogène; **to take e.** *(of regulation, law etc)* agir, opérer; *(of drug)* agir, opérer; *(of vaccination)* prendre; **law that comes into e. today** loi qui entre en vigueur à partir d'aujourd'hui; **to no e.** en vain, sans résultat; **to put sth into e.** *(plan)* mettre qch à exécution; *(decision)* donner suite à qch

2 *(purpose, meaning) (of document)* sens *m*, teneur *f*; **to the e. that …** *(clause)* portant que …; **we have made provisions to this e.** nous avons pris des dispositions dans ce sens; **that is what he said, or words to that e.** voilà ce qu'il a dit, ou quelque chose d'approchant

3 *(simulation)* **moonlight e.** effet *m* de lune; **clever use of lighting created the e. of a thunderstorm** une utilisation adroite de la lumière donnait l'impression qu'il y avait un orage; **stage effects** jeux *mpl* scéniques; *Cin, TV etc* **(special) effects** trucage *m*, effets spéciaux; **sound effects** bruitage *m*

4 *(impression)* effet *m*, impression *f*; **the combination of colours creates** *or* **has a pleasing e.** le mélange des couleurs laisse une impression agréable; **for e.** *(to impress)* pour faire de l'effet; **words meant for e.** phrases à effet

5 in e. en fait, en réalité; **that is in e. a refusal** c'est de fait un refus

6 *(always pl) (belongings) Fml* **personal effects** effets *mpl ou* biens *mpl* personnels; **household effects**, *Law* **movable effects** biens mobiliers

◊ VT *(repair, change)* effectuer; *(plan, wish, saving)* réaliser; *(plan, law)* exécuter; *(reconciliation)* parvenir à; **to e. an entry** entrer de force; **to e. a cure for sth** apporter un remède à qch; **to e. a solution to sth** apporter une solution à qch; *Mil* **to e. a retreat** battre en retraite; **to e. a payment** effectuer un paiement

effective [ɪ'fektɪv] ADJ **1** *(efficient, having desired effect)* efficace; *(speech)* qui fait de l'effet; *(response)* plein d'à-propos; **the medicine was e.** le médicament a produit son effet; **an e. argument** un argument de poids; **she is an e. speaker** ses paroles font de l'effet *ou* portent **2** *(actual) Econ etc (yield, return)* effectif; *(value)* réel; *Elec (charge)* efficace; *(frequency)* utile; **this resulted in the e. silencing of all opposition** *(was tantamount to)* cela a eu en effet pour résultat de faire taire les opposants **3** *(striking) (contrast)* frappant, saisissant **4 to become e.** *(of law etc)* entrer en vigueur; **e. as from 10 October** applicable à partir du 10 octobre

NPL *Mil* **effectives** effectifs *mpl*

▸▸ *Fin* **e. annual rate** taux *m* annuel effectif; *Admin* **e. date** date *f* d'entrée en vigueur; *Econ* **e. demand** demande *f* effective; *Tech*

e. power rendement *m*; **e. range** *(of firearm, missile)* portée futile; *Aviat* rayon *m* d'action; *Electron* étendue *f* de mesure; *Fin* **e. tax rate** taux *m* d'imposition effectif

effectively [ɪ'fektɪvlɪ] ADV **1** *(really, in effect)* en fait, en réalité; **the country was e. ruled by the military** en fait *ou* en réalité, le pays était dirigé par les militaires; **the match was e. over** c'était comme si le match était déjà terminé **2** *(efficiently)* efficacement; **the building has been designed very e.** le bâtiment a été conçu avec un grand souci d'efficacité; **he spoke e. in favour of the government's motion** il a fait un éloge percutant *ou* persuasif de la motion du gouvernement **3** *(strikingly)* d'une façon frappante

> Note that the French word **effectivement** is a false friend and is never a translation for the English word **effectively**. It means **actually**.

effectiveness [ɪ'fektɪvnɪs] N **1** *(efficiency)* efficacité *f* **2** *(of colour scheme, design)* effet *m* percutant; **the e. of the white houses outlined against a darkening sky** l'effet de contraste percutant *ou (stronger)* saisissant des maisons blanches qui se découpaient sur un ciel de plus en plus sombre

effectual [ɪ'fektjʊəl] ADJ **1** *Fml* efficace **2** *Law (contract)* valide; *(ruling)* en vigueur

effectually [ɪ'fektjʊəlɪ] ADV efficacement

effeminacy [ɪ'femɪnəsɪ] N caractère *m* efféminé

effeminate [ɪ'femɪnət] ADJ efféminé

effervesce [efə'ves] VI **1** être en effervescence; *(start to effervesce)* entrer en effervescence; *(of drinks)* pétiller **2** *Fig (of person)* pétiller de joie *ou* d'animation

effervescence [efə'vesəns] N **1** *(of liquid)* effervescence *f* **2** *Fig (of youth etc)* pétillement *m*

effervescent [efə'vesənt] ADJ **1** effervescent; *(drink)* gazeux, pétillant **2** *Fig (person, mood)* effervescent; **to be e. with enthusiasm/joy** pétiller d'enthousiasme/de joie

effete [ɪ'fiːt] ADJ *(person)* mou, *f* molle veule; *(nation, civilization etc)* amorphe

efficacious [efɪ'keɪʃəs] ADJ *Fml* efficace

efficacy ['efɪkəsɪ], **efficaciousness** [efɪ'keɪʃəsnɪs] N efficacité *f*

efficiency [ɪ'fɪʃənsɪ] N *(of method, organization)* efficacité *f*; *(of machine, business etc) (output)* rendement *m*; *(functioning)* bon fonctionnement *m*; *(of person)* capacité *f*, compétence *f*

▸▸ **e. expert** expert *m* en organisation

efficient [ɪ'fɪʃənt] ADJ *(method, work, organization)* efficace; *(machine) (productive)* à bon rendement, performant; *(functioning well)* d'un fonctionnement sûr; *(person)* performant, capable, compétent; *(software)* performant; **to be e. at sth** faire qch avec compétence; **to be e. in one's work** se montrer capable dans son travail; **e. use of one's time** utilisation rationnelle de son temps; **energy e.** *(machine)* qui ne consomme pas beaucoup d'énergie

efficiently [ɪ'fɪʃəntlɪ] ADV *(effectively)* efficacement; *(competently)* avec compétence; **to organize one's time e.** utiliser son temps de manière rationnelle; **this car runs more e. than any of its competitors** cette voiture a un meilleur rendement que toutes ses concurrentes

effigy ['efɪdʒɪ] N effigie *f*; **to burn/hang sb in e.** brûler/pendre qn en effigie

effing ['efɪŋ] *Br Sl Euph* ADJ foutu; **this e. weather** ce temps de merde ◊ ADV **how e. stupid!** quelle connerie!

N *(swearing)* there's too much e. and blinding on entend trop de grossièretés

efflorescence [eflə'resəns] N **1** *Bot* floraison *f* **2** *Chem, Med etc* efflorescence *f*

efflorescent [eflə'resənt] ADJ *Bot, Chem* efflorescent

effluence ['efluəns] N *Lit* émanation *f*, effluence *f*

effluent ['efluənt] ADJ effluent
N effluent *m*

effluvium, *pl* **effluvia** [e'flu:vɪəm, -ɪə] N effluve *m*, émanation *f, Pej* émanation désagréable *ou* fétide

effort ['efət] N **1** effort *m*; **physical e.** effort physique; **without e.** sans effort; **to make an e. to do sth** faire (un) effort pour faire qch; **he made no e. to contact us** il n'a fait aucun effort pour nous joindre; **put some e. into it!** fais un effort!; **she put all her e. into her work** elle s'est jetée corps et âme dans son travail; **their efforts were rewarded** leurs efforts ont été récompensés; *Fml* **we make every e. to ensure our products reach you in perfect condition** nous faisons tout ce qui est en notre pouvoir pour que nos produits vous parviennent en bon état; *Fam* **it's an e. to get up so early** il faut vraiment faire un effort pour se lever si tôt; **wasted e.** peine *f* perdue
2 *Fam (attempt)* tentative *f*, **that's not a bad e.** ce n'est pas mal réussi; **some of my first efforts at making pots were pretty awful** certains de mes premiers essais en poterie étaient plutôt ratés; **literary/artistic e.** œuvre *f* littéraire/artistique; *Fam* **what do you think of his latest e.?** qu'est-ce que vous pensez de sa dernière performance?
3 *Phys (of traction etc)* effort *m*, poussée *f*, travail *m*
4 *Sl (thing, gadget)* truc *m*; **there's this sort of lever e.** il y a une espèce de levier

effortless ['efətlɪs] ADJ *(victory, success etc)* facile; *(skill, grace)* aisé; **she won with an almost e. ease** elle a gagné avec une facilité presque absolue

effortlessly ['efətlɪslɪ] ADV sans effort; **to be e. graceful/skilful** être naturellement gracieux/talentueux; **her voice soars e. to the high notes** elle peut chanter très haut sans aucun effort

effrontery [ɪ'frʌntərɪ] N effronterie *f*, **she had the e. to correct me!** elle a eu l'audace de me corriger!

effusion [ɪ'fju:ʒən] N effusion *f*

effusive [ɪ'fju:sɪv] ADJ *(person)* démonstratif, expansif; *(style)* exubérant; *(compliments)* sans fin; *(welcome, speech)* enthousiaste; **to be e. in one's thanks** se confondre en remerciements; **to be e. in one's praise/congratulations** louer/féliciter qn avec grand enthousiasme

effusively [ɪ'fju:sɪvlɪ] ADV avec effusion; **to thank sb e.** se confondre en remerciements; **to praise/congratulate/welcome sb e.** louer/féliciter/accueillir qn avec enthousiasme

effusiveness [ɪ'fju:sɪvnɪs] N effusion *f*, **the e. of his praise** l'enthousiasme *m* de ses louanges

E-fit® N portrait-robot *m* électronique

EFL [i:e'fel] N *Sch (abbr* **English as a Foreign Language)** anglais *m* langue étrangère; **to have an E. qualification** avoir une qualification en anglais langue étrangère

EFT [i:ef'ti:] N *Comput (abbr* **electronic funds transfer)** transfert *m* de fonds électronique

EFTA ['eftə] N *(abbr* **European Free Trade Association)** AELE *f*

EFTPOS ['eftpɒs] N *Comput (abbr* **electronic funds transfer at point of sale)** transfert *m*

de fonds électronique sur point de vente

eg [i:'dʒi:] *(abbr* **exempli gratia)** ex

EGA [i:dʒi:'ei] N *Comput (abbr* **enhanced graphics adaptor)** EGA *m*

egalitarian [ɪgælɪ'teərɪən] ADJ égalitaire
N égalitariste *mf*

egalitarianism [ɪgælɪ'teərɪənɪz(ə)m] N égalitarisme *m*

e-generation N génération *f* électronique, E-génération *f*

egg [eg] N *(of hen, animal, insect etc)* œuf *m*; *(of louse)* lente *f*; **bacon and eggs** œufs au bacon; **e. sandwich** sandwich *m* à l'œuf; *Fam* **as sure as eggs is eggs** aussi sûr que deux et deux font quatre; *Fam* **you've got e. on your chin** *(fly is undone)* ta braguette est ouverte; *Fig Fam* **to have e. on one's face** s'être couvert de ridicule; *Old-fashioned Fam* **a bad e.** *(person)* un vaurien; *Old-fashioned Fam* **a good e.** *(man)* un gars épatant; *(woman)* une fille épatante; *Prov* **don't put all your eggs in one basket** il ne faut pas mettre tous ses œufs dans le même panier
▸▸ **e. cup** coquetier *m*; *Br Culin* **e. custard** ≃ crème *f* anglaise; **e. flip** *(with milk)* lait *m* de poule; *(with alcohol)* lait de poule alcoolisé; **e. mayonnaise** œufs *mpl* mayonnaise; **e. nog** lait de poule alcoolisé; **e. spoon** cuillère *f* à œufs (à la coque); **e. timer** sablier *m*; **e. tooth** dent *f* d'éclosion; **e. white** blanc *m* d'œuf; **e. yolk** jaune *m* d'œuf
▸ **egg on** VT SEP **to e. sb on (to do sth)** pousser *ou* inciter qn (à faire qch); **don't e. him on** ne l'encourage pas

egg-and-spoon ADJ
▸▸ **e. race** = course *f* dans laquelle les coureurs doivent porter un œuf dans une cuillère

eggbeater ['egbi:tər] N **1** *Culin* batteur *m ou* fouet *m* à œufs **2** *Am Fam (helicopter)* hélico *m*

eggbox ['egbɒks] N boîte *f* à œufs

egghead ['eghed] N *Hum, Pej* intello *mf*, cerveau *m*

egg-laying ADJ ovipare
N ponte *f*

eggplant ['egplɑ:nt] N *esp Am* aubergine *f*

egg-shaped ADJ ovoïde, ovoïdal, -aux

eggshell ['egʃel] N **1** coquille *f* (d'œuf); **e. finish** *(on paint)* fini *m* coquille d'œuf **2** *(colour)* (couleur *f)* coquille *f* d'œuf, blanc *m* cassé
▸▸ **e. blue** bleu *m* pâle; *Cer* **e. china** coquille d'œuf

eggwhisk ['egwɪsk] N = **eggbeater**

eggy ['egɪ] ADJ *Fam (stained)* taché *ou* souillé de jaune d'œuf; **an e. taste/smell** un goût/une odeur d'œuf

egis ['i:dʒɪs] N *Am* = **aegis**

eglantine ['eglantaɪn] N *(plant)* églantier *m*

EGM [i:dʒi:'em] N *(abbr* **extraordinary general meeting)** AGE *f*

ego ['i:gəʊ, 'egəʊ] N **the e.** l'ego *m inv*; *Psy* le moi, l'ego; **you've got an enormous e.** tu as un ego démesuré; **it gave my e. a boost** mon ego en est ressorti gonflé; **his bruised e.** son ego blessé; **to feed/deflate sb's e.** entretenir/rabaisser l'ego de qn; *Fam* **it was a real e. trip for her** c'était une occasion pour elle de donner libre cours à sa vanité

egocentric [i:gəʊ'sentrɪk] ADJ égocentrique

egocentricity [i:gəʊsen'trɪsɪtɪ] N égocentrisme *m*

egoism ['i:gəʊɪz(ə)m] N égoïsme *m*

egoist ['i:gəʊɪst] N égoïste *mf*

egoistic(al) [i:gəʊ'ɪstɪk, -ɪk(ə)l] ADJ égoïste

egoistically [i:gəʊ'ɪstɪklɪ] ADV égoïstement

egomania [i:gəʊ'meɪnɪə] N manie *f* égocentrique

egotism ['i:gəʊtɪz(ə)m] N égotisme *m*

egotist ['i:gəʊtɪst] N égotiste *mf*

egotistic(al) [i:gəʊ'tɪstɪk, -ɪk(ə)l] ADJ égotiste

egregious [ɪ'gri:dʒəs] ADJ *Fml Pej (error, mistake)* monumental, -aux, énorme; *(lie)* énorme; *(cowardice, incompetence)* extrême

egress ['i:gres] N **1** *Fml (exit)* sortie *f*, issue *f* **2** *Astron* émersion *f*

egret ['i:grɪt] N *(bird)* aigrette *f*

Egypt ['i:dʒɪpt] N Égypte *f*

Egyptian [ɪ'dʒɪpʃən] ADJ égyptien, d'Égypte
N Égyptien, -ienne

eh [eɪ, e] INT eh!, hé!, hein?

EIB [i:aɪ'bi:] N *(abbr* **European Investment Bank)** BEI *f*

eider ['aɪdər] N eider *m* à duvet
▸▸ **e. duck** eider *m* à duvet

eiderdown ['aɪdədaʊn] N **1** *(quilt)* édredon *m* **2** *(feathers)* duvet *m* d'eider

eight [eɪt] N **1** *(number, numeral)* huit *m inv*; **e. and e. are sixteen** huit et huit font seize; **to be e.** *(in age)* avoir huit ans; **it's e. o'clock** il est huit heures; **it's five past e.** il est huit heures cinq; **to reach the last e.** *(in knockout competition)* être en huitième de finale; *Br* **to have had one over the e.** avoir bu plus que son compte **2** *Sport (in rowing)* huit *m* (de pointe)
PRON huit; **there are e. (of them)** *(people)* ils sont huit; *(objects)* il y en a huit
NUM ADJ huit; **to work an e.-hour day** travailler huit heures par jour, faire des journées de huit heures
▸▸ *Am* **e. ball** *(ball)* bille *f* numéro huit; *(game)* = variante du billard; *Fig Fam* **to be behind the e. ball** être dans une situation délicate; *Am* **e. hundred number** ≃ numéro *m* vert

eight-bit byte N *Comput* octet *m*

eight-bit character N *Comput* caractère *m* à huit bits

eighteen [eɪ'ti:n] NUM ADJ, N dix-huit *m*; **she is e. (years old)** elle a dix-huit ans; **at e. thirty (hours)** à dix-huit heures trente

eighteenth [eɪ'ti:nθ] ADJ dix-huitième; **Louis the E.** Louis Dix-huit
N **1** *(on)* **the e. of May** le dix-huit mai; **on the e.** le dix-huit **2** *(fraction)* dix-huitième *m*

eightfold ['eɪtfəʊld] ADJ octuple; **an e. increase** une augmentation à l'octuple
ADV huit fois autant; **to increase e.** octupler

eighth [eɪtθ] ADJ huitième; **in the e. place** huitièmement; **Henry the E.** Henri Huit
N **1** *(on)* **the e. of April** le huit avril; **on the e.** le huit **2** *(fraction)* huitième *m*; **three eighths** trois huitièmes
▸▸ *Am Mus* **e. note** croche *f*

eightieth ['eɪtɪɪθ] ADJ, N quatre-vingtième *m*, *Suisse, Belg* huitantième *m*, *Suisse, Can* octantième *m*

eighty ['eɪtɪ] NUM ADJ, N quatre-vingts *m*, *Suisse, Belg* huitante *m*, *Suisse, Can* octante *m*; **e.-one** quatre-vingt-un; **page e.** page quatre-vingt; **in the eighties** *(decade)* dans les années quatre-vingt; **she is in her eighties** elle a quatre-vingts ans passés SEE
GRAMMAR 858–9

eighty-six *Am Sl* ADJ **to be e. on sth** *(in restaurant, bar)* être à court de qch; **tell the customer we're e. on the chicken** dis au client qu'il n'y a plus de poulet
VT **1** *(eject)* vider **2** *(kill)* buter, refroidir

Eire ['eərə] N Eire *f*

eisteddfod [aɪ'stedfəd] N = festival *m* gallois de poésie et de musique

either ['aɪðər, *esp Am* 'i:ðər] ADJ, PRON VOIR

GRAMMAIRE A37 **1** *(each of the two)* l'un(e) et l'autre; **on e. side** de chaque côté, des deux côtés

2 *(one or other)* l'un(e) ou l'autre; **e. of them** soit l'un(e), soit l'autre; **I don't believe e. of you** je ne vous crois ni l'un ni l'autre; **I do not want e. of them** je ne veux ni l'un(e) ni l'autre; **e. candidate may win** l'un ou l'autre candidat pourra l'emporter; **there is no evidence e. way** les preuves manquent de part et d'autre

▸ CONJ, ADV **1 e. … or …** (ou) … ou …, soit …, soit …; **e. you or your brother** (ou) vous ou votre frère, soit vous, soit votre frère; **it's e. that motorbike or me!** c'est cette moto ou moi!; **e. come in or go out!** entrez ou sortez! VOIR GRAMMAIRE A73-4

2 not … e. ne … non plus; **if you don't go, I won't go e.** si vous n'y allez pas, je n'irai pas non plus; **she's caught a cold, and she isn't very strong e.** elle s'est enrhumée, elle qui n'est déjà pas si forte

either-or ADJ **an e. situation** = une situation dans laquelle il faut choisir entre deux maux le moindre

ejaculate [ɪ'dʒækjʊleɪt] VI **1** *Physiol* éjaculer **2** *Old-fashioned, Lit (exclaim)* s'écrier
▸ VT *(cry)* pousser; **'help!', he ejaculated** 'à l'aide!', s'écria-t-il

ejaculation [ɪdʒækjʊ'leɪʃən] N **1** *Physiol* éjaculation *f* **2** *Old-fashioned, Lit (exclamation)* cri *m*, exclamation *f*; **an e. of surprise/joy/horror** un cri de surprise/de joie/d'horreur

eject [ɪ'dʒekt] VT **1** *(troublemaker etc)* expulser (**from** de) **2** *(of volcano etc) (lava)* projeter; *(flames etc)* jeter, émettre; *(of tape recorder, rifle)* éjecter
▸ VI *Aviat (of pilot)* s'éjecter

ejection [ɪ'dʒekʃən] N **1** *(of person)* expulsion *f*, *(of tape, cartridge, pilot)* éjection *f* **2** *(by volcano) (of flames, lava)* projection *f*
▸▸ *Am* **e. seat** siège *m* éjectable; **to use the e. seat** s'éjecter

ejector [ɪ'dʒektər] N *(on firearm)* éjecteur *m*
▸▸ *Br* **e. seat** siège *m* éjectable; **to use the e. seat** s'éjecter

▸ **eke out** [iːk] VT SEP **1 to e. out a living** gagner péniblement sa vie; **they eked out a miserable existence on the barren land** ils tiraient leur maigre subsistance du sol aride **2** *(supplement) (one's income etc)* suppléer à l'insuffisance de **3** *(make last) (rations)* économiser, faire durer

El [el] N *Am Rail (abbr* **elevated railroad)** chemin *m* de fer *ou* métro *m* aérien

elaborate¹ [ɪ'læbərət] ADJ *(style)* travaillé; *(plan, arrangements, inspection etc)* minutieux; *(description, explanation)* détaillé; *(dress etc)* recherché; *(hairstyle, pattern, design)* compliqué; *(work)* soigné; *(excuse)* alambiqué; *(apparatus, network etc)* complexe; *(meal, dish)* élaboré; **I haven't cooked anything e.** je n'ai pas préparé quelque chose de compliqué; **the cake was a very e. affair** c'était un gâteau très élaboré

elaborate² [ɪ'læbəreɪt] VI donner plus de détails (**on sth** sur qch); **could you e.?** est-ce que vous pouvez être plus précis?
▸ VT *(formulate) (plan)* élaborer; *(flesh out)* développer

elaborately [ɪ'læbərətlɪ] ADV *(planned, drawn)* minutieusement, de façon détaillée; *(designed)* avec recherche

elaboration [ɪlæbə'reɪʃən] N *(working out from scratch)* élaboration *f*, *(fleshing out)* développement *m*

élan [eɪ'lɑːn] N *Lit* élan *m*, impétuosité *f*

eland [ˈiːlənd] N *(animal)* éland *m*; **common e.** éland du Cap

elapse [ɪ'læps] VI *(of time)* s'écouler, passer;

years have elapsed since then des années ont passé depuis

elapsed time N *Comput* temps *m* écoulé

elastic [ɪ'læstɪk] ADJ *Phys (body)* élastique; *(movement)* souple; *Econ (supply, demand)* élastique; *Pej* **e. conscience** conscience *f* élastique
▸ N **1** élastique *m* **2** *esp Am (rubber band)* élastique *m*
▸▸ *Br* **e. band** élastique, caoutchouc

elasticated [ɪ'læstɪkeɪtɪd] ADJ *(clothing)* extensible

elasticity [iːlæs'tɪsɪtɪ] N *Phys (of body)* élasticité *f*, *(of wood, metal)* flexibilité *f*, *Med (of muscles)* tonicité *f*, **e. of interpretation** *(of law)* élasticité; *Econ* **e. of supply and demand** l'élasticité de l'offre et de la demande

elastomer [ɪ'læstəmər] N *Chem* élastomère *m*

Elastoplast® [ɪ'læstəplɑːst] N sparadrap *m*

elate [ɪ'leɪt] VT exalter

elated [ɪ'leɪtɪd] ADJ transporté, exalté; **to feel e.** se sentir plein de joie; **to be e. with success** être enivré de succès

elation [ɪ'leɪʃən] N exaltation *f*

Elba [ˈelbə] N **(the island of) E.** l'île *f* d'Elbe

elbow ['elbəʊ] N *(of arm, sleeve, pipe)* coude *m*; **to lean one's e. on sth** s'accouder sur qch; *Fig* **to stand e. to e.** être coude à coude; **to be at sb's e.** être *ou* se tenir aux côtés de qn; **to be out at the elbows** *(of person)* être déguenillé; *(of jacket etc)* être troué aux coudes; **I'm up to my elbows in work** je suis submergé de travail; **to rub elbows with all sorts of people** fréquenter *ou* coudoyer toutes sortes de gens; *Fam* **to give sb the e.** *(of employer)* virer qn; *(of boyfriend etc)* plaquer qn; *Fam* **to get the e.** *(of employee)* se faire jeter; *(of boyfriend etc)* se faire plaquer; *Fam* **to bend** *or* **lift the e.** *(drink)* lever le coude
▸ VT pousser du coude; **to e. sb aside** écarter qn d'un coup de coude; **to e. one's way through the crowd** se frayer un passage à travers la foule en jouant des coudes; *Fig* **she elbowed aside anyone in the office who might have opposed her** elle a joué des coudes pour écarter quiconque au bureau se serait opposé à elle
▸▸ *Fam* **e. grease** huile *f* de coude; **use a bit of e. grease!** mets un peu d'huile de coude!; **e. joint** *Anat* articulation *f* de coude; *Tech* raccord *m* coudé; **e. patch** coude *m*

▸ **elbow out** VT SEP *(remove) (person)* évincer; **there have been attempts to e. him out as chairman** on a essayé de l'évincer de la présidence

elbow-length ADJ **e. gloves** gants *mpl* longs (montant jusqu'au coude)

elbow-rest N accoudoir *m*

elbowroom ['elbəʊrʊm] N *Fig* **to have (enough) e.** avoir ses coudées franches; **give me some more e.** laisse-moi les coudées franches

El Cheapo [el'tʃiːpəʊ] *Hum Fam* N article *m* bas de gamme
▸ ADJ bas de gamme

elder¹ ['eldər] VOIR GRAMMAIRE A26-7 ADJ *(of two people)* aîné, plus âgé; **my e. brother** mon frère aîné; **Pliny the E.** Pline l'Ancien
▸ N **1** aîné, -ée; **he is my e. by two years** il est de deux ans mon aîné; **children should obey their elders** les enfants devraient obéir à leurs aînés **2** *Hist, Rel (of tribe, church, village)* ancien *m*
▸▸ **e. statesman** vétéran *m*; *(politician)* vétéran de la politique

elder² N sureau *m*
▸▸ **e. tree** sureau

elderberry ['eldəberɪ] N *(fruit)* baie *f* de sureau
▸▸ **e. wine** vin *m* de sureau

elderflower ['eldəflaʊər] N fleur *f* de sureau

elderly ['eldəlɪ] ADJ âgé; *Fig* **an e. typewriter** une machine à écrire qui a fait son temps
▸ NPL **the e.** les personnes *fpl* âgées

eldest ['eldɪst] ADJ aîné; **my e. daughter** ma fille aînée, mon aînée; **their e. son** leur fils aîné VOIR GRAMMAIRE A26-7
▸ N aîné, -ée

elect [ɪ'lekt] VT **1** *Pol* élire; **to e. sb to the presidency** élire qn à la présidence; **to get elected** être élu; **she was elected president** elle a été élue présidente **2** *Fml (choose)* choisir (**to do** de faire)
▸ ADJ élu; **the president e.** le président élu
▸ NPL *Rel* **the e.** les élus *mpl*

elected [ɪ'lektɪd] ADJ *Pol* élu
▸▸ **e. dictatorship** = gouvernement *m* élu qui se comporte comme une dictature

election [ɪ'lekʃən] N *(of candidate etc)* élection *f*; **to hold an e.** procéder à une élection; **to stand for e.** se présenter aux élections; **on the e. trail** en tournée électorale
▸▸ **e. agent** directeur, -trice de campagne électorale; **e. campaign** campagne *f* électorale; **e. committee** comité *m* électoral; **e. day** jour *m* des élections; **e. programme** programme *m* électoral; **e. promise** promesse *f* électorale; **e. results** résultat *m* des élections; **e. speech** discours *m* électoral

electioneer [ɪlekʃə'nɪər] VI faire de la propagande électorale

electioneering [ɪlekʃə'nɪərɪŋ] N propagande *f* électorale

elective [ɪ'lektɪv] ADJ **1** *Pol (office etc)* électif; *(body etc)* électoral **2** *esp Am Sch, Univ (subject)* facultatif
▸ N *esp Am Sch, Univ (course)* cours *m* facultatif; **I'm taking two electives in psychology** je suis deux cours facultatifs en psychologie
▸▸ **e. surgery** chirurgie *f* de confort

elector [ɪ'lektər] N électeur, -trice, votant, -ante; *Hist (of Holy Roman Empire)* électeur

electoral [ɪ'lektər(ə)l] ADJ électoral, -aux
▸▸ **e. body** corps *m* électoral; **e. college** collège *m* électoral *(qui élit le président des États-Unis)*; *Br* **E. Commission** commission *f* électorale; **e. district** circonscription *f* électorale; **e. pact** pacte *m* électoral; **e. process** processus *m* électoral; *Br* **e. reform** réforme *f* électorale; **e. roll** liste *f* électorale; **e. system** système *m* électoral, régime *m* électoral

electorate [ɪ'lektərət] N *Pol* corps *m* électoral, électeurs *mpl*

electret microphone [ɪ'lektrət] N microphone *m* à électret

electric [ɪ'lektrɪk] ADJ *(light, cooker, car etc)* électrique; *Fig* **the atmosphere of the meeting was e.** l'atmosphère de la réunion était électrique; **the effect of her words was e.** ses mots ont eu un effet électrisant
▸▸ *Br* **e. blanket** couverture *f* chauffante; **e. blue** bleu *m* électrique; **e. chair** chaise *f* électrique; **e. charge** charge *f* électrique; **e. eel** anguille *f* électrique; **e. eye** œil *m* électrique; **e. fence** clôture *f* électrique; **e. field** champ *m* électrique; **e. generator** générateur *m*, génératrice *f*; **e. guitar** guitare *f* électrique; **e. heater** appareil *m* de chauffage électrique; **e. motor** moteur *m* électrique; **e. power station** centrale *f* électrique; **e. ray** torpille *f*; **e. shock** décharge *f* électrique; **e. wave** onde *f* électrique; *Aut* **e. window** glace *f* ou vitre *f* électrique

electrical [ɪ'lektrɪk(ə)l] ADJ électrique
▸▸ **e. appliance** appareil *m* électrique; **e. engineer** ingénieur *m* électricien; **e. engineering** électrotechnique *f*; **e. failure** panne *f* d'électricité; **e. fault** défaut *m* dans le système électrique

electrically [ɪˈlektrɪklɪ] ADV électriquement; *Fig* an e. charged atmosphere une atmosphère électrique; e. controlled window vitre *f* à commande électrique; *Comput* e. erasable ROM mémoire *f* morte effaçable électriquement

electrician [ɪlekˈtrɪʃən] N électricien, -ienne

▸▸ e.'s screwdriver tournevis *m* d'électricien

electricity [ɪlekˈtrɪsɪtɪ] N électricité *f*; lit by e. éclairé à l'électricité; many homes are without e. (*temporarily*) de nombreux foyers sont privés d'électricité; (*not installed*) de nombreux foyers n'ont pas l'électricité; *Fig* you could feel the e. in the air il y avait de l'électricité dans l'air

▸▸ *Br Formerly* E. Board ≃ EDF *f* (Électricité de France); e. meter compteur *m* d'électricité

electrics [ɪˈlektrɪks] NPL *Br Fam* (*of car etc*) circuits *mpl* électriques

electrification [ɪlektrɪfɪˈkeɪʃən] N (*of railways etc*) électrification *f*

electrify [ɪˈlektrɪfaɪ] VT 1 (*convert to electricity*) (*railway line etc*) électrifier 2 (*charge with electricity*) (*fence*), *Fig* (*auditorium*) électriser

electrifying [ɪˈlektrɪfaɪɪŋ] ADJ (*effect etc*) électrisant

electroacoustic [ɪˈlektrəʊəˈkuːstɪk] ADJ électroacoustique

electrocardiogram [ɪlektrəʊˈkɑːdɪəʊgræm] N *Med* électrocardiogramme *m*

electrocardiograph [ɪlektrəʊˈkɑːdɪəʊgræf] N *Med* électrocardiographe *m*

electrocardiography [ɪlektrəʊkɑːdɪˈɒgrəfɪ] N *Med* électrocardiographie *f*

electrochemical [ɪˈlektrəʊˈkemɪkl] ADJ électrochimique

electrochemistry [ɪlektrəʊˈkemɪstrɪ] N électrochimie *f*

electroconvulsive [ɪlektrəʊkənˈvʌlsɪv] ADJ

▸▸ *Med* e. therapy traitement *m* par électrochocs

electrocute [ɪˈlektrəkjuːt] VT électrocuter; to e. oneself s'électrocuter

electrocution [ɪlektrəˈkjuːʃən] N électrocution *f*

electrode [ɪˈlektrəʊd] N électrode *f*

▸▸ e. gap écartement *m* des électrodes; e. holder porte-électrodes *m inv*

electrodynamics [ɪlektrəʊdaɪˈnæmɪks] N électrodynamique *f* VOIR GRAMMAIRE A10

electroencephalogram [ɪlektrəʊenˈsefələʊgræm] N *Med* électroencéphalogramme *m*

electroencephalograph [ɪlektrəʊenˈsefələʊgræf] N *Med* appareil *m* à EEG

electrolysis [ɪlekˈtrɒlɪsɪs] N électrolyse *f*

electrolyte [ɪˈlektrəʊlaɪt] N *Elec* électrolyte *m*

electrolytic [ɪlektrəʊˈlɪtɪk] ADJ électrolytique

electromagnet [ɪlektrəʊˈmægnɪt] N électro-aimant *m*, *pl* électro-aimants

electromagnetic [ɪlektrəʊmægˈnetɪk] ADJ (*field, wave etc*) électromagnétique

electromagnetism [ɪlektrəʊˈmægnɪtɪz(ə)m] N électromagnétisme *m*

electromotive [ɪlektrəʊˈməʊtɪv] ADJ électromoteur, -trice

▸▸ e. force force *f* électromotrice

electron [ɪˈlektrɒn] N *Phys* électron *m*; positive/negative e. électron positif/négatif

▸▸ e. beam faisceau *m* d'électrons; e. gun canon *m* électronique *ou* à électrons; *Biol* e. microscope microscope *m* électronique

electronic [ɪlekˈtrɒnɪk] ADJ électronique

▸▸ *Comput* e. banking banque *f* électronique; e. book livre *m* numérique, livre électronique, e-book *m*; e. brain cerveau *m* électronique; e. business commerce *m* électronique; e. card lock serrure *f* à carte perforée; *Comput* e. cash argent *m* électronique, argent virtuel; *Comput* e. catalogue catalogue *m* en ligne; *Comput* e. commerce commerce électronique; *Comput* e. computer calculateur *m* électronique; *Comput* e. control unit centrale *f* électronique; *Comput* e. data interchange échange *m* de données informatisé; *Comput* e. data processing traitement *m* électronique de l'information; *Phot* e. flash flash *m* électronique; *Aut* e. fuel injection injection *f* à commande numérique, injection électronique; *Fin, Comput* e. funds transfer transfert *m* de fonds électronique; *Fin, Comput* e. funds transfer at point of sale transfert de fonds électronique au point de vente; *Comput* e. journal journal *m* en ligne; e. keycard carte-clé *f*, *pl* cartes-clés; e. lock serrure *f* électronique; *Comput* e. mail courrier *m* électronique; *Comput* e. mailbox boîte *f* à *ou* aux lettres électronique; e. media médias *mpl* électroniques; *Comput* e. money argent électronique, argent virtuel; (*concept*) monétique *f*; e. music musique *f* électronique; *TV* e. news gathering journalisme *m* électronique de télévision; e. newssheet bulletin *m* électronique; *Mus* e. organ orgue *m* électronique; *Com* e. payment paiement *m* électronique; *Comput* e. point of sale point *m* de vente électronique; *Comput* e. publishing édition *f* électronique, éditique *f*; *Comput* e. purse porte-monnaie *m inv* électronique; *Aut* e. ride control contrôle *m* électronique de confort; *Aut* e. route finder guide *m* électronique d'itinéraire; *Comput* e. shopping téléachat *m*, achats *mpl* en ligne; e. tagging étiquetage *m* électronique; *St Exch* e. trading transactions *fpl* boursières électroniques; e. wallet porte-monnaie *m* électronique

electronically [ɪlekˈtrɒnɪklɪ] ADV électroniquement

electronics [ɪlekˈtrɒnɪks] N 1 électronique *f* 2 (*of machine*) système *m* électronique VOIR GRAMMAIRE A10

▸▸ e. company société *f* d'électronique; e. engineer ingénieur *m* électronicien, électronicien, -ienne; e. industry industrie *f* électronique

electroplate [ɪˈlektrəʊpleɪt] *Metal* N 1 (*material*) (métal *m*) plaqué *m* 2 (*no pl*) (*articles*) articles *mpl* plaqués; (*plated with silver*) articles argentés

VT plaquer; (*with silver*) argenter

electroplated [ɪˈlektrəʊpleɪtɪd] ADJ plaqué (*par électrodéposition*)

electro-sensitive [ɪˈlektrəʊ'-] ADJ électrosensible

electroshock [ɪˈlektrəʊʃɒk] ADJ *Med* e. therapy *or* treatment traitement *m* par électrochocs

electrostatic [ɪlektrəʊˈstætɪk] ADJ *Phys* (*generator etc*) électrostatique

electrostatics [ɪlektrəʊˈstætɪks] N *Phys* électrostatique *f* VOIR GRAMMAIRE A10

electrotechnic(al) [ɪlektrəʊˈteknɪk, -ɪk-(ə)l] ADJ *Elec* électrotechnique

electrotherapy [ɪlektrəʊˈθerəpɪ] N *Med* électrothérapie *f*

electrotype [ɪˈlektrəʊtaɪp] *Typ* N galvanotype *m*

VT galvanotyper

elegance [ˈelɪgəns] N élégance *f*

elegant [ˈelɪgənt] ADJ 1 (*appearance, person etc*) élégant; e. furniture meubles *mpl* d'un goût raffiné 2 *Am Fam* (*excellent*) excellent, de premier ordre

elegiac [elɪˈdʒaɪək] *Lit* ADJ élégiaque

NPL elegiacs vers *mpl* élégiaques

elegy [ˈelɪdʒɪ] N élégie *f*

element [ˈelɪmənt] N 1 (*aspect*) e. of uncertainty/danger/chance part *f* d'incertitude/de danger/de chance; there is an e. of risk involved cela comporte un risque; disturbing e. élément *m* d'instabilité; the personal/time e. le facteur humain/temps; the film has all the elements of a hit movie le film a tous les ingrédients d'un film à succès; a key e. in selling is … un des facteurs clés dans la vente est …

2 (*part of whole*) élément *m*, partie *f*, *Elec* (*of kettle, fire etc*) résistance *f*, elements (*basics*) (*of science*) rudiments *mpl*, *Comput* data e. élément d'information; the hooligan e. (in our society/in a football crowd) les hooligans (dans notre société/parmi les spectateurs d'un match de football); undesirable elements (in society) éléments indésirables (de la société)

3 *Chem* corps *m* simple

4 *Met* the four elements les quatre éléments *mpl*; to brave the elements braver les éléments; exposed to the elements exposé aux intempéries; *Fig* to be in one's e. être dans son élément; *Fig* to be out of one's e. ne pas être dans son élément

5 *Rel* the elements (of bread and wine) les espèces *fpl*

elemental [elɪˈment(ə)l] ADJ 1 (*belonging to the elements*) qui appartient aux éléments *ou* aux forces de la nature; (*spirit*) élémentaire; (*rage, fury*) déchaîné 2 (*primitive*) élémentaire, primitif 3 *Chem* élémentaire 4 (*basic*) fondamental, -aux, essentiel; to be e. to sth être essentiel à qch

▸▸ e. forces éléments *mpl*

elementary [elɪˈment(ə)rɪ] ADJ élémentaire; *Sch* e. algebra rudiments *mpl* d'algèbre

▸▸ *Am* e. school école *f* primaire

elephant [ˈelɪfənt] N éléphant *m*; *Fam* baby e. éléphanteau *m*

▸▸ e. calf éléphanteau; e. seal éléphant *m* de mer

elephantiasis [elɪfænˈtaɪəsɪs] N *Med* éléphantiasis *m*

elephantine [elɪˈfæntaɪn] ADJ (*proportions etc*) éléphantesque; (*movement etc*) lourd et gauche; *Fig* (*humour*) lourd

elevate [ˈelɪveɪt] VT 1 (*raise*) élever, hausser; *Mil* (*gun*) pointer en hauteur; *Rel* (*host, mind*) élever; to e. sb to a high rank élever qn à un haut rang 2 (*exalt*) (*person*) exalter; (*sb's soul*) élever; they had elevated their legends into a religion ils avaient élevé leurs légendes au rang de religion

elevated [ˈelɪveɪtɪd] ADJ 1 (*raised, exalted*) élevé; e. thoughts hautes pensées *fpl*; he has an e. opinion of himself il a une haute opinion de lui-même 2 (*overhead*) surélevé

▸▸ e. motorway autoroute *f* surélevée; e. position position *f* élevée; *Br* e. railway, *Am* e. railroad chemin *m* de fer *ou* métro *m* aérien; *Cin, TV* e. shot plongée *f*

elevating [ˈelɪveɪtɪŋ] ADJ (*discourse etc*) édifiant; the experience was far from e. l'expérience n'a rien eu de bien inspirant

N élévation *f*, levage *m*

elevation [elɪˈveɪʃən] N 1 (*of sth to certain height, of sb to superior position*) élévation *f*, *Rel* the E. (of the Host) l'Élévation *f* 2 *Geog* (*height*) altitude *f*, hauteur *f*; e. above sea level altitude *f ou* hauteur *f* au-dessus du niveau de la mer 3 (*hill*) élévation *f*, éminence *f* 4 *Astron* (*of star*) élévation *f* 5 *Mil* (*of gun*) hausse *f*, pointage *m* en hauteur; angle of e. angle *m* de hausse 6 *Archit etc* élévation *f*; front e. façade *f*; side e. façade latérale; rear e. derrière *m* 7 (*nobility, refine-*

ment) (of style) élévation *f*, dignité *f*, *(of character)* noblesse *f*, grandeur *f*
▸▸ **e. mechanism** dispositif *m* de pointage en hauteur

elevator ['elɪveɪtər] N **1** *(lifting device)* élévateur *m*; *Am (for goods)* monte-charge *m inv*; **bucket e.** élévateur à godets; **grain e.** élévateur *m* à grains; *(silo)* silo *m* **2** *Am (lift)* ascenseur *m*; *Fam Hum* **the e. doesn't go up to the top floor** c'est pas une lumière **3** *Aviat* gouvernail *m* de profondeur *ou* d'altitude
▸▸ **e. angle** angle *m* de braquage; *Am* **e. attendant** liftier *m*; **e. shoe** chaussure *f* à semelle compensée

eleven [ɪ'lev(ə)n] NUM ADJ, N **1** *(numeral)* onze *m*; **the e. o'clock train** le train de onze heures **2** *Sport (team)* onze *m*; **the French e.** le onze de France

elevenses [ɪ'lev(ə)nzɪz] NPL *Br Fam* collation *f ou* casse-croûte *m inv (de onze heures du matin)*

eleventh [ɪ'lev(ə)nθ] ADJ onzième; *Fig* **at the e. hour** au dernier moment, à la dernière minute
N **1 on the e. of May** le onze mai; **on the e.** le onze **2** *(fraction)* onzième *m*

eleventh-hour ADJ de la dernière heure *ou* chance, de dernière minute; **an e. rescue attempt** une tentative de sauvetage de dernière heure

elf, *pl* **elves** [elf, elvz] N *Myth* elfe *m*, lutin *m*, lutine *f*

elfin ['elfɪn] ADJ *(grace, features)* d'elfe, de lutin; *(music)* féerique

elfish ['elfɪʃ] ADJ **1** = **elfin 2** *(mischievous)* espiègle

elicit [ɪ'lɪsɪt] VT **1** *(extract) (truth)* découvrir; *(facts)* tirer au clair; *(answer from sb)* obtenir; **to e. sth from sb** tirer qch de qn **2** *(give rise to) (response)* provoquer

elide [ɪ'laɪd] VT *Ling* élider

eligibility [elɪdʒɪ'bɪlɪtɪ] N **1** *(as a candidate)* éligibilité *f*, *(for grant, benefit)* droit *m* (**for** à) **2** *(of suitor etc)* acceptabilité *f*

eligible ['elɪdʒɪb(ə)l] ADJ **1** *(entitled)* éligible; **to be e.** avoir droit (**for** à); **she wasn't e. for a tax rebate/early retirement** elle n'avait pas droit à une réduction d'impôts/ la retraite anticipée; **e. for promotion** qualifié pour une promotion **2** *(worthy of being chosen)* digne d'être élu *ou* choisi, acceptable; **e. bachelor/young man** bon parti *m*

eliminate [ɪ'lɪmɪneɪt] VT *(toxic substances, names from list, poverty etc)* éliminer; *(hypothesis, possible explanation)* écarter; *(possibility of error, risk etc)* supprimer; *Euph (kill)* supprimer; *Math* **to e. x** éliminer x; **the police have eliminated him from their enquiries** la police l'a écarté de son enquête; *Sport* **they were eliminated in the first round** ils ont été éliminés au premier tour

eliminating [ɪ'lɪmɪneɪtɪŋ] ADJ ATTRIB éliminateur, -trice
▸▸ *Sport* **e. heats, e. rounds** épreuves *fpl* éliminatoires

elimination [ɪlɪmɪ'neɪʃən] N élimination *f*, **in spite of her e. from the list** bien qu'elle ait été éliminée de la liste; **by (a) process of e.** en procédant par élimination

eliminator [ɪ'lɪmɪneɪtər] N éliminateur *m*; **the next match will be the e.** le prochain match décidera de qui sera éliminé

elision [ɪ'lɪʒən] N *Ling (of vowel etc)* élision *f*

élite, elite [eɪ'liːt] N élite *f*; **the é. of society** l'élite de la société; *Mil* **é. regiment** corps *m* d'élite

elitism [eɪ'liːtɪz(ə)m] N élitisme *m*; **the e. of his attitude** son attitude élitiste

elitist [eɪ'liːtɪst] ADJ, N élitiste *mf*

elixir [ɪ'lɪksər] N élixir *m*; **the e. of life** l'élixir de longue vie

Elizabethan [ɪlɪzə'biːθ(ə)n] ADJ *(house, literature etc)* élisabéthain
N = Anglais, -aise vivant sous le règne de la reine Élisabeth 1re

Elizabeth I [ɪ'lɪzəbəθθə'fɜːst] N Élisabeth *f* Ire

elk [elk] N *(Scandinavian)* e. élan *m*; *(American)* e. wapiti *m*, orignal *m*

ell [el] N *Arch (measurement)* aune *f*

ellipse [ɪ'lɪps] N *Math* ellipse *f*

ellipsis [ɪ'lɪpsɪs, -siːz] N **1** *Gram* ellipse *f* **2** *Typ* points *mpl* de suspension

ellipsoid [ɪ'lɪpsɔɪd] N *Math* ellipsoïde *m*

elliptic(al) [ɪ'lɪptɪk, -ɪk(ə)l] ADJ *Gram, Math, Fig* elliptique

elliptically [ɪ'lɪptɪklɪ] ADV elliptiquement

elm [elm] N *(tree, wood)* orme *m*
▸▸ **e. grove** ormaie *f*

elocution [elə'kjuːʃən] N élocution *f*, diction *f*, **e. lessons** cours *mpl* de diction

elocutionist [elə'kjuːʃənɪst] N *(teacher)* professeur *m* de diction

elongate ['iːlɒŋgeɪt] VT allonger, étendre; *(line, platform)* prolonger
VI s'allonger, s'étendre

elongated ['iːlɒŋgeɪtɪd] ADJ allongé

elongation [iːlɒŋ'geɪʃən] N **1** allongement *m*; *(of line)* prolongement *m* **2** *Astron* élongation *f*

elope [ɪ'ləʊp] VI s'enfuir (pour se marier); **they eloped together** ils se sont enfuis pour se marier

elopement [ɪ'ləʊpmənt] N fuite *f*

eloquence ['eləkwəns] N éloquence *f*

eloquent ['eləkwənt] ADJ éloquent; **to be an e. speaker** être éloquent, avoir de l'éloquence; *Fig* **an e. gesture** un geste éloquent; **the state of the economy is an e. indictment of this policy** la situation économique en dit long sur cette politique

eloquently ['eləkwəntlɪ] ADV éloquemment; **to pause e.** faire une pause éloquente

ELSE [els] ADV **or e.** *(otherwise)* autrement; *(if not, then)* ou bien; **come tomorrow or e. it will be too late** venez demain, autrement il sera trop tard; **he must be joking, or e. he's mad** il plaisante, ou bien alors il est fou; **do what I tell you, or e.!** fais ce que je te dis, sinon!
ADJ, ADV **1** *(with -one/-body)* anyone *or* anybody e. toute autre personne, n'importe qui d'autre; **he is no more stupid than anyone e.** il n'est pas plus bête qu'un autre; **can I speak to anyone e.?** y a-t-il quelqu'un d'autre à qui je puisse parler?; **it couldn't be anyone e.'s** ça ne pouvait être celui de personne d'autre; **I couldn't find anyone e. to help me** je n'ai pu trouver personne d'autre pour m'aider; **someone** *or* **somebody e.** quelqu'un d'autre; **you are taking me for someone e.** vous me prenez pour quelqu'un d'autre; **everyone** *or* **everybody e. knows it** tous les autres le savent; **you're kind to everyone e., why are you so horrible to me?** tu es gentil avec tout le monde, pourquoi es-tu si horrible avec moi?; **no one e., nobody e.** personne d'autre, aucun autre; **I knew nobody e. would do it for me** je savais que personne d'autre ne le ferait pour moi; **no one e. could do it** il n'y a que lui/elle *etc* qui puisse le faire
2 *(with -thing)* anything e. n'importe quoi d'autre; **have you anything e. to do?** avez-vous autre chose à faire?; **he wouldn't accept anything e.** il n'a rien voulu accepter d'autre; **anything e. I produce is impossible to sell** tout ce que je fais d'autre est invendable; **anything e., madam?** *(in shop)* et avec cela, madame?; **something e.** quelque chose d'autre, autre chose; **is there something**

e. you want me to do? y a-t-il quelque chose d'autre *ou* autre chose que tu voudrais que je fasse?; **I was thinking of something e.** je pensais à autre chose; *Fam* **she's/it's something e.!** elle est/c'est génial!; **everything e.** tout le reste; **nothing e.** rien d'autre; **nothing e., thank you** c'est tout, merci
3 *(with -where)* somewhere e. autre part, ailleurs; **I'm sure somewhere e. will give them a room** je suis sûr qu'ailleurs on leur donnera une chambre; **anywhere e.** n'importe où (ailleurs); **anywhere e. would have turned them away** n'importe où ailleurs on les aurait renvoyés; **can I find some anywhere e.?** puis-je en trouver ailleurs?; **everywhere e.** partout ailleurs; **everywhere e. was shut** *(other shops)* tous les autres magasins étaient fermés; **nowhere e.** nulle part ailleurs; **nowhere e. was willing to accept them** nulle part ailleurs on ne voulait les accepter
4 *(with interr pronouns)* who e.? qui d'autre?, qui encore?; **do you think they'll give the prize to Whippleton? – who e.?** tu crois qu'ils attribueront le prix à Whippleton? – à qui d'autre veux-tu qu'ils le donnent?; **what e.?** quoi encore?, quoi de plus?; **do you use fresh pasta for this dish? – what e.?** utilises-tu des pâtes fraîches pour ce plat? – que veux-tu que j'utilise d'autre?; **what e. can I say?** qu'est-ce que je peux dire de plus?; **where e.?** *(did you go, look etc)* où encore?; *(did you think you would find it, her etc)* où est-ce que tu pensais le/la/*etc* trouver sinon là?; **when e.?** à quel autre moment/date?; **when e. has this happened?** quand cela est-il déjà arrivé?; **how e.?** de quelle autre manière?; **did you come by taxi? – how e.?** tu es venu en taxi? – comment serais-tu venu sinon?; **why e.?** pour quelle autre raison?
5 *(with little/(not) much)* little e. pas grandchose d'autre; **he eats bread but little e.** il ne mange guère que du pain; **there isn't much e. to be done** il ne reste pas beaucoup à faire; *(we've no choice)* il n'y a pas grand chose d'autre à faire; *Fml* **much e. could be said on this topic** on pourrait encore en dire long sur ce sujet; *Fml* **much e. remained to be done** restait encore beaucoup à faire

elsewhere ['elsweər] ADV ailleurs, autre part; **e. the weather will be fine** ailleurs, il fera beau; **his ambitions lie e.** ses ambitions se situent à un autre niveau

ELT [iːel'tiː] N *Sch (abbr English Language Teaching)* = enseignement *m* de l'anglais à des étudiants étrangers

elucidate [ɪ'luːsɪdeɪt] VT élucider, éclaircir; *(reference)* clarifier, éclaircir
VI s'expliquer, être plus clair; **can you e.?** peux-tu être plus clair?

elucidation [ɪluːsɪ'deɪʃən] N élucidation *f*, éclaircissement *m* (**of** de)

elude [ɪ'luːd] VT *(question)* éluder; *(blow)* esquiver, éviter; *(death, police, capture)* échapper à; *(justice)* se soustraire à; **to e. sb's grasp** échapper aux mains de qn; *Fig* **to e. sb** *(mentally)* échapper à qn

elusive [ɪ'luːsɪv] ADJ *(enemy, happiness)* insaisissable; *(answer)* évasif; *(concept)* flottant; *(memories)* fugitif; *(scent, perfume)* indéfinissable; **but, for him, success remained e.** mais le succès lui a échappé

elusiveness [ɪ'luːsɪvnɪs] N *(of enemy, happiness)* nature *f* insaisissable; *(of answer)* caractère *m* évasif; *(of scent, perfume)* caractère indéfinissable; **a concept of great e.** un concept extrêmement flottant

elver ['elvər] N *(young eel)* civelle *f*

elvish ['elvɪʃ] ADJ = **elfish**

Elysian [ɪ'lɪzɪən] ADJ *Myth* Élyséen
▸▸ **E. fields** champs *mpl* Elysées

em [em] N Typ cadratin m
▸▸ **em dash** tiret m cadratin

'em [əm] PRON Fam = **them**

emaciate [ɪ'meɪsɪeɪt] VT (body) émacier, dessécher

emaciated [ɪ'meɪsɪeɪtɪd] ADJ émacié, décharné

emaciation [ɪmeɪsɪ'eɪʃən] N (of body) émaciation f, dessèchement m

e-mail, email ['iːmeɪl] N e-mail m, Can courriel m; **to send an e. to sb** envoyer un e-mail à qn; **to send sth by e.** envoyer qch par courrier électronique; **to check one's e.** consulter sa boîte à lettres électronique
VT **to e. sth to sb** envoyer qch à qn par courrier électronique; **can I e. you?** est-ce que je peux vous contacter par courrier électronique?; **e. us at...** envoyez-nous vos messages à l'adresse suivante...
▸▸ **e. account** compte m de courrier électronique; **e. address** adresse f électronique; **e. bomb** bombe f e-mail; **e. box** boîte f à ou aux lettres électronique; **e. program** programme m de courrier électronique; **e. software** logiciel m de courrier électronique

emanate ['eməneɪt] VI émaner (**from** de); (of light) provenir (**from** de)
VT dégager

emanation [emə'neɪʃən] N émanation f; (of light) émission f

emancipate [ɪ'mænsɪpeɪt] VT (minor, women etc) émanciper; (slave) affranchir; **an emancipating realization** une réflexion émancipatrice

emancipated [ɪ'mænsɪpeɪtɪd] ADJ émancipé; (slave) affranchi

emancipation [ɪmænsɪ'peɪʃən] N émancipation f; (of slave) affranchissement m

e-marketing N marketing m électronique

emasculate [ɪ'mæskjʊleɪt] VT émasculer, châtrer; Fig émasculer

emasculation [ɪmæskjʊ'leɪʃən] N émasculation f, castration f

embalm [ɪm'bɑːm] VT embaumer

embalmer [ɪm'bɑːmər] N embaumeur m

embalming [ɪm'bɑːmɪŋ] N embaumement m
▸▸ **e. fluid** fluide m de thanatopraxie

embankment [ɪm'bæŋkmənt] N Rail etc talus m, remblai m; (to contain river) digue f; (alongside river etc) berge f, quai m

embargo, pl **embargoes** [em'bɑːgəʊ, -əʊz] N embargo m; **to be under (an) e.** être sous embargo; (of ship) être séquestré; **to put an e. on** (goods etc) mettre un embargo sur; **to lift the e.** lever l'embargo; **trade/oil/arms e.** embargo commercial/pétrolier/sur les armes
VT mettre l'embargo sur

embark [em'bɑːk] VT Naut embarquer, prendre à bord
VI Naut, Aviat s'embarquer; Fig **to e. (up)on** (adventure etc) s'embarquer dans

embarkation [embɑː'keɪʃən] N Naut, Aviat embarquement m
▸▸ **e. card** carte f d'accès à bord ou d'embarquement

embarrass [ɪm'bærəs] VT embarrasser

embarrassed [ɪm'bærəst] ADJ embarrassé, gêné; **an e. silence** un silence embarrassé

embarrassing [ɪm'bærəsɪŋ] ADJ embarrassant, gênant; **a financially e. situation** un embarras financier; **how e.!** comme ça a dû être/c'est/ce serait embarrassant!

embarrassingly [ɪm'bærəsɪŋlɪ] ADV d'une manière embarrassante ou gênante; **there were e. few in the audience** le public était si réduit que c'en était embarrassant; **e., we seem to have omitted the principal's name** il

semble que nous ayons oublié le nom du directeur, ce qui est plutôt embarrassant

embarrassment [ɪm'bærəsmənt] N 1 (feeling) embarras m, gêne f; **much to my e.** à mon grand embarras; **blushing with e.** rouge de confusion; **to be in a state of financial e.** avoir des embarras d'argent 2 (person, thing) source f d'embarras

embassy ['embəsɪ] N (building) ambassade f; **the French E.** l'ambassade de France
▸▸ **e. official** fonctionnaire mf d'ambassade; **e. staff** personnel m d'ambassade

embattled [ɪm'bæt(ə)ld] ADJ (engaged in battle) pris d'assaut; Fig (under attack) assiégé

embed [ɪm'bed] VT (-dd-) 1 (nail in wall) enfoncer; (frame in wall) encastrer; (diamond in gold etc) incruster; **to be embedded in sth** (of hook, tooth etc) être enfoncé dans qch; **embedded in concrete** noyé dans le béton; **to be embedded in sb's memory** être gravé dans la mémoire de qn; **to be embedded in sb's mind** être ancré dans l'esprit de qn; **to be embedded in sb's personality** être enraciné dans la personnalité de qn 2 Comput intégrer, imbriquer

embedded [ɪm'bedɪd] ADJ **a deeply e. feeling of inferiority** un sentiment d'infériorité profondément ancré
▸▸ Gram **e. clause** proposition f enchâssée; Comput **e. command** commande f intégrée; Journ **e. journalist** = journaliste mf incorporé(e) à une unité combattante

embellish [ɪm'belɪʃ] VT orner, embellir; (prose) embellir; Fig (account, story) enjoliver

embellishment [ɪm'belɪʃmənt] N embellissement m, ornement m; (of story) enjolivure f

ember ['embər] N (usu pl) **embers** braise f, charbons mpl ardents

embezzle [ɪm'bez(ə)l] VT (funds) détourner, distraire, s'approprier
VI commettre des détournements de fonds

embezzlement [ɪm'bezəlm(ə)nt] N détournement m de fonds, appropriation f de fonds

embezzler [ɪm'bezlər] N escroc m

embitter [ɪm'bɪtər] VT (person) aigrir, remplir d'amertume; (character) aigrir; (quarrel etc) envenimer

embittered [ɪm'bɪtəd] ADJ (person) aigri (**by** par); (laugh) amer

embittering [ɪm'bɪtərɪŋ] ADJ (experience) qui aigrit

emblazon [ɪm'bleɪz(ə)n] VT Her blasonner, décorer d'armoiries; **emblazoned with the arms of the town** peint aux armes de la ville; **she didn't want to see her name emblazoned across the front page of the Sun** elle ne voulait pas voir son nom étalé en première page du Sun

emblem ['embləm] N (symbol) emblème m; Her emblème, devise f; Aut (on radiator) écusson m; **sporting e.** insigne m sportif

emblematic [emblə'mætɪk] ADJ emblématique

embodiment [ɪm'bɒdɪmənt] N incarnation f, personnification f; **he is the e. of kindness** il est la bonté même

embody [ɪm'bɒdɪ] VT (embodied; embodying) 1 (give form to) incarner 2 (personify) (quality) personnifier 3 (incorporate) (clause in law) incorporer; (principles in treatise) renfermer, rédiger

embolden [ɪm'bəʊldən] VT 1 enhardir (**sb to do sth** qn à faire qch) 2 Typ (characters) renforcer, graisser

embolism ['embəlɪz(ə)m] N Med embolie f

embolus ['embələs] N Med embole m

embonpoint [ɒmbɒn'pwæn] N Hum embonpoint m, rondeurs fpl

emboss [ɪm'bɒs] VT (leather, metal) estamper, repousser; (cloth, paper) gaufrer

embossed [ɪm'bɒst] ADJ (leather, metal) estampé, repoussé; (cloth, paper) gaufré

embossing [ɪm'bɒsɪŋ] N 1 (technique, activity) (of leather, metal) estampage m, repoussage m; (of paper) gaufrage m 2 (result) (on leather, metal) estampage m, repoussé m; (on cloth, paper) gaufrure f
▸▸ **e. press** (in paper making) presse f à imprimer en relief; **e. punch** repoussoir m

embrace [ɪm'breɪs] N étreinte f, (of lovers) étreinte amoureuse; **to hold sb in a warm e.** étreindre qn chaleureusement; Lit **winter's iron e.** l'étreinte glacée de l'hiver
VT 1 (person) étreindre; (in official ceremony) donner une accolade à; **to e. one another tenderly** s'étreindre tendrement 2 (adopt) (religion) embrasser; (cause) adopter 3 (include) embrasser, contenir (**in** dans); (subjects) comprendre; **the view from the terrace embraces the whole valley** de la terrasse la vue s'étend sur toute la vallée ou embrasse toute la vallée
VI (of two people) s'étreindre

> Note that the most common meaning of the French verb **embrasser** is **to kiss**.

embrasure [ɪm'breɪʒər] N 1 Archit embrasure f, ébrasement m 2 Mil embrasure f, sabord m

embrocation [embrə'keɪʃən] N Med embrocation f

embroider [ɪm'brɔɪdər] VT 1 Sewing broder 2 (exaggerate) (account, report) enjoliver
VI 1 Sewing broder 2 (exaggerate) broder, enjoliver, Fam en rajouter
▸ **embroider on** VT INSEP (truth, facts) enjoliver

embroidering [ɪm'brɔɪdərɪŋ] N = **embroidery**

embroidery [ɪm'brɔɪdərɪ] N 1 Sewing broderie f 2 (added details) (of account, report) enjolivement m, fioriture f; **their e. of the facts** les enjolivements qu'ils avaient apportés aux faits
▸▸ Sewing **e. frame** métier m à broder; Sewing **e. thread** fil m à broder

embroil [ɪm'brɔɪl] VT (usu passive) (involve) **embroiled in a quarrel** entraîné dans une querelle; **to become** or **get embroiled in sth** se trouver impliqué dans qch; **I wouldn't get embroiled with her if I was you** à ta place je ne me compliquerais pas la vie avec elle, Fam à ta place je ne me laisserais pas embringuer avec elle

embroilment [ɪm'brɔɪlmənt] N (involvement) implication f

embryo, pl **embryos** ['embrɪəʊ, -əʊz] N Biol, Fig embryon m; **in e.** (foetus, plan) à l'état embryonnaire;
▸▸ **e. research** recherche f portant sur les embryons

embryogenesis [embrɪəʊ'dʒenɪsɪs] N Med embryogenèse f

embryology [embrɪ'ɒlədʒɪ] N embryologie f

embryonic [embrɪ'ɒnɪk] ADJ Biol embryonnaire; Fig (plan, idea etc) à l'état embryonnaire

embus [ɪm'bʌs] Mil VT (troops) embarquer dans un autocar
VI monter dans un autocar

emcee ['em'siː] Fam N maître m de cérémonies; Radio, TV animateur, -trice
VT (show) animer

emend [ɪ'mend] VT corriger

emendation [iːmen'deɪʃən] N 1 (action) (of

text) correction *f* **2** *(proposed alteration)* variante *f* proposée

emerald ['em(ə)rəld] **N 1** *Miner* émeraude *f* **2** *(colour)* (vert *m* d')émeraude *m*
▸▸ **e. green** (vert d')émeraude; *Lit* **the E. Isle** la verte Irlande

emerge [ɪ'mɜːdʒ] **VI** *(appear)* *(from liquid, the shadow, fog)* émerger (**from** de); *(from hole, from behind sth etc)* déboucher (**from** de); *(from house, hole, darkness)* sortir; *(arise)* *(of difficulty etc)* se dresser, surgir; *(of truth, facts)* émerger, se faire jour; **the moon is emerging from behind the clouds** la lune sort de derrière les nuages; **she emerged as an important politician** elle est devenue une personnalité politique importante; **from these facts it emerges that …** de ces faits il ressort que …; **it later emerged that …** il est apparu par la suite que …; **he was soon to e. from his father's shadow** il allait bientôt sortir de l'ombre de son père

emergence [ɪ'mɜːdʒəns] **N** *(of theory etc)* émergence *f*, *(of new state, new leader)* apparition *f*; **they still awaited the e. of a convincing account of the events** ils attendaient encore qu'un récit convainquant des événements se fasse jour

emergency [ɪ'mɜːdʒənsɪ] **N** circonstance *f* critique, cas *m* urgent; *Med* urgence *f*, **to provide for emergencies** parer aux éventualités *ou* à l'imprévu; **this is an e.** c'est une urgence; **to meet an e.** faire face à une situation critique; **in an e.,** in case of **e.** en cas d'urgence; **state of e.** état *m* d'urgence; **to declare a state of e.** déclarer l'état d'urgence; **national e.** catastrophe *f* nationale
▸▸ **e. aid** secours *mpl* d'urgence; *Aut* **e. brake** frein *m* de secours; *Am (handbrake)* frein *m* à main; *Br Parl* **e. debate** débat *m* d'urgence; **e. exit** sortie *f ou* issue *f* de secours; **e. fund** fonds *m* de secours; **e. goods** produits *mpl* de dépannage; *Aviat* **e. landing** atterrissage *m* forcé; *Cin etc* **e. lighting** éclairage *m* de sécurité; *Med* **e. operation** opération *f* à chaud; **e. rations** vivres *mpl* de secours *ou* de réserve; **e. regulations** mesures *fpl* d'exception; **e. repairs** réparations *fpl* d'urgence; **e. services** services *mpl* d'urgence; **e. supply** réserve *f*, *Aviat* **e. tank** réservoir *m* auxiliaire; *Fin* **e. tax** impôt *m* extraordinaire; **e. telephone** téléphone *m* d'urgence, poste *m* d'appel d'urgence; *Br Med* **e. ward** salle *f* des urgences

emergent [ɪ'mɜːdʒənt] **ADJ** *(talent, ability)* naissant;
▸▸ **e. nation** nation *f* en voie de développement

emerging market [ɪ'mɜːdʒɪŋ] **N** *Econ* marché *m* émergeant

emeritus [ɪ'merɪtəs] **ADJ**
▸▸ *Univ* **e. professor** professeur *m* honoraire

emery ['emərɪ] **N** émeri *m*
▸▸ **e. board** lime *f* à ongles; **e. cloth** toile *f* (d')émeri; **e. paper** papier *m* (d')émeri; **e. powder** poudre *f* d'émeri; **e. wheel** meule *f* (en) émeri

emetic [ɪ'metɪk] **ADJ, N** *Med* émétique *m*

EMF [iːe'mef] **N 1** *Elec (abbr* **electromotive force)** force *f* électromotrice **2** *Econ, Pol (abbr* **European Monetary Fund)** FME *m*

EMI [iːe'maɪ] **N** *Econ, Pol (abbr* **European Monetary Institute)** IME *m*

emigrant ['emɪɡrənt] **ADJ** émigré
N émigrant, -ante

emigrate ['emɪɡreɪt] **VI** émigrer

emigrating ['emɪɡreɪtɪŋ] **ADJ** émigrant

emigration [emɪ'ɡreɪʃən] **N** émigration *f*

émigré ['emɪɡreɪ] **N** émigré, -ée; **e. writer** écrivain *m* émigré

eminence ['emɪnəns] **N 1** *(position of impor-*

tance) position *f* éminente; *(of office)* grandeur *f*, distinction *f*; **to rise to e.** parvenir à une haute position **2** *(raised ground)* éminence *f*, élévation *f* **3** *Rel* **E.** *(title of cardinal)* Éminence *f*; **Your E.** Votre Éminence

eminent ['emɪnənt] **ADJ** éminent; **in view of his e. suitability for the job** du fait qu'il convient tout à fait pour le poste

eminently ['emɪnəntlɪ] **ADV** éminemment; **an e. respectable family** une famille éminemment honorable *or* des plus honorables; **an e. suitable place** un endroit *ou* une place parfaitement adapté(e) (**for** à); **what an e. sensible idea!** quelle sage idée!; **an e. believable story** une affaire tout à fait crédible

emir [e'mɪər] **N** émir *m*

emirate ['emɪreɪt] **N** émirat *m*

emissary ['emɪsərɪ] **N** émissaire *m*

emission [ɪ'mɪʃən] **N 1** *(action) (of gas, heat, light etc)* émission *f*, dégagement *m*; *(of pollutant)* émission; *Banking etc (of bank notes)* émission **2** *(substance)* émanation *f*, **nocturnal emissions** pollutions *fpl* nocturnes
▸▸ *Aut* **e. limit** seuil *m* d'émission

emit [ɪ'mɪt] **VT** *(heat, light etc)* émettre, dégager; *(signal, sigh, cry)*, *Banking (paper money)* émettre; *(smell)* exhaler, dégager; *(sparks)* lancer, jeter; *(sound)* rendre

emitter [ɪ'mɪtər] **N** *Nucl* émetteur *m*

Emmy ['emɪ] **N** *Am TV* ≃ Sept *m* d'Or

emollient [ɪ'mɒlɪənt] **ADJ, N** *Med* émollient *m*

emolument [ɪ'mɒljʊmənt] **N** *(usu pl)* **emoluments** émoluments *mpl*, appointements *mpl*, honoraires *mpl*

e-money **N** monnaie *f* électronique

emote [ɪ'məʊt] **VI** donner dans l'emphase

emoticon [ɪ'məʊtɪkɒn] **N** *Comput* emoticon *m*, *Can* binette *f*

emotion [ɪ'məʊʃən] **N** émotion *f*, **to show one's emotions** laisser paraître ses émotions; **to appeal to the emotions** faire appel aux sentiments; **to be in control of one's emotions** maîtriser ses émotions; **full of e.** plein d'émotion, ému; **she felt a mixture of emotions** ses sentiments étaient partagés

emotional [ɪ'məʊʃən(ə)l] **ADJ 1** *(reaction)* émotif; *(problems)* émotionnel; *(motive)* affectif; **she's an e. wreck** elle a de gros problèmes émotionnels; **e. shock** choc *m* émotif *ou* émotionnel; **he was something of an e. cripple** il était quelque peu handicapé sur le plan affectif; **to have** *or* **carry a lot of e. baggage** avoir accumulé les échecs sentimentaux; **why is my life such an e. mess?** pourquoi ma vie affective est-elle si compliquée?; **for e. reasons** pour des raisons émotives

2 *(liable to emotion)* émotif; **to be e.** *(of person)* s'attendrir facilement; **he got very e.** *(tearful)* il a pris ça très à cœur; *(tearfully angry)* il a pris ça très mal

3 *(full of emotion)* *(plea, ceremony etc)* émouvant
▸▸ **e. blackmail** chantage *m* affectif

emotionalism [ɪ'məʊʃənəlɪz(ə)m] **N** sentimentalisme *m*; **it's a piece of e.** c'est du sentimentalisme; **the e. of his writing** son style sentimentaliste

emotionally [ɪ'məʊʃən(ə)lɪ] **ADV 1** **to be e. involved with sb** être attaché à qn; **I'm too e. involved with the whole situation** cette situation me touche de trop près; **I don't want to get e. involved** je ne veux pas m'attacher; **e. deprived** en manque d'affection; **e. disturbed/exhausted** troublé/vidé sur le plan émotionnel **2** *(with strong emotion)* avec beaucoup d'émotion

emotionless [ɪ'məʊʃənlɪs] **ADJ** *(person)* in-

différent; *(face, look)* impassible; *(style)* sobre

emotive [ɪ'məʊtɪv] **ADJ** qui déchaîne les passions; **e. speech/language** discours *m*/ langage *m* sensationnaliste; **racism is a very e. issue** le racisme est un sujet qui déchaîne les passions; **an e. word** un mot chargé

empanel [ɪm'pæn(ə)l] **VT** (**-ll-,** *Am* **-l-**) *Law* **e. a juror** inscrire un juré sur la liste du jury

empathetic [empə'θetɪk] **ADJ** compatissant; **to feel e. towards sb** éprouver de la compassion pour qn

empathetically [empə'θetɪklɪ] **ADV** avec compassion

empathize ['empəθaɪz] **VI** compatir; **to e. with sb** avoir de la compassion pour qn; **to e. with sb's suffering/problems** compatir à la souffrance/aux problèmes de qn

empathy ['empəθɪ] **N** empathie *f*; **to feel e. for sb** éprouver de l'empathie pour qn

emperor ['empərər] **N** empereur *m*
▸▸ **e. moth** saturnie *f*, paon *m* de nuit; **e. penguin** manchot *m* empereur

emphasis ['emfəsɪs] **N 1** *(insistence)* insistance *f*, **to lay** *or* **place e. on** *(fact)* appuyer *ou* insister sur; *(word)* souligner; **too much e. is placed on individualism** l'individualisme l'emporte trop souvent; **the e. is on written work** l'accent est mis sur le travail écrit **2** *(stress) (in words)* force *f*, accentuation *f*, *Gram* mise *f* en relief; *Ling* accent *m*

emphasize ['emfəsaɪz] **VT** *(stress) (word, fact)* accentuer, appuyer sur; *(draw attention to) (fact)* attirer l'attention sur; *(quality etc)* faire ressortir, mettre en relief; **she emphasized the need for caution** elle a bien insisté sur la nécessité d'être prudent; **you should e. the first syllable** il faut accentuer la première syllabe

emphatic [ɪm'fætɪk] **ADJ 1** *(manner, gesture)* énergique; *(speaker)* vigoureux; *(refusal, response)* positif, net, *f* nette; *(victory)* net; **he was quite e. on that point** il s'est montré très catégorique sur ce point **2** *Ling (syllable)* accentué

emphatically [ɪm'fætɪk(e)lɪ] **ADV 1** *(to say)* énergiquement; *(to refuse)* carrément, catégoriquement; *(to deny)* catégoriquement; **they had been e. defeated** ils avaient été largement battus **2** *(intensive)* **he is most e. a leader** c'est un chef s'il en fut jamais; **e. yes!** tout à fait, oui!

emphysema [emfɪ'siːmə] **N** *Med* emphysème *m*; *(pulmonary)* emphysème pulmonaire

empire ['empaɪər] **N** empire *m*; *Hist* **the (British) E.** l'Empire britannique; *Fig* **a shipbuilding e.** un empire dans le monde de la construction navale; *Br Hist* **E. troops** *(of British Empire)* armée *f* coloniale; **E. furniture** meubles *mpl* Empire; *Archit etc* **E. style** style *m* Empire

empire-builder **N** *also Fig* constructeur *m* d'empires

empire-building **N** *also Fig* construction *f* d'empires

empiric [em'pɪrɪk] **ADJ** = **empirical**
N empiriste *mf*

empirical [em'pɪrɪk(ə)l] **ADJ** empirique; **e. evidence** preuve *f* empirique

empiricism [em'pɪrɪsɪz(ə)m] **N** empirisme *m*

emplacement [ɪm'pleɪsmənt] **N** *Mil (of gun)* emplacement *m*

emplane [ɪm'pleɪn] *Mil* **VI** monter en avion
VT *(person, troops)* faire monter en avion

employ [ɪm'plɔɪ] **VT 1** *(give work to)* employer; **to e. sb as secretary** employer qn comme secrétaire **2** *(occupy)* **to e. oneself, to be employed** s'occuper, être occupé (**in**

doing sth à faire qch); **she employed herself by tidying up the room** elle s'est occupée en rangeant la pièce **3** *(use) (means, time, technique)* employer; *(force, argument)* se servir de; *(one's skills, tact)* user de

N *Fml* emploi *m*; **to be in sb's e.** être au service de qn, être employé par qn

employable [ɪmˈplɔɪəb(ə)l] **ADJ** employable, susceptible d'être employé; **qualifications make you more e.** il est plus facile de se faire embaucher quand on a des qualifications

employed [ɪmˈplɔɪd] **ADJ** employé

NPL employers and e. le patronat et le salariat

employee [ɪmplɔɪˈiː, emˈplɔɪiː] **N** employé, -ée; **employees** effectif *m*, salariés *mpl*; **relations between management and employees** relations entre la direction et le personnel

▸▸ **e. association** comité *m* d'entreprise; *Fin* **e. buyout** reprise *f* de l'entreprise par les salariés, RES *f*; *Fin* **e. contributions** cotisations *fpl* salariales, charges *fpl* sociales salariales; **e. file** fichier *m* salarié; *Fin* **e. profit-sharing scheme** intéressement *m* aux résultats; **e. representative** délégué, -ée du personnel; **e. share ownership plan** plan *m* d'actionnariat des salariés

employer [ɪmˈplɔɪər] **N** patron, -onne, *Fml* employeur, -euse; **she's a good e. (to work for)** c'est une bonne patronne; **this company is the town's largest e.** c'est cette entreprise qui emploie le plus de gens dans la ville; **(body of) employers** patronat *m*

▸▸ **employers' association** organisation *f* patronale, syndicat *m* patronal; **e.'s contributions** cotisations *fpl* ou retenues *fpl* patronales; **e.'s liability** responsabilité *f* patronale; **e.'s organization** organisation patronale, syndicat patronal

employment [ɪmˈplɔɪmənt] **N 1** *(work)* emploi *m*, travail *m*; **to be looking for e.** chercher un emploi ou du travail; **to be without e.** être sans emploi ou sans travail; **to be in e.** avoir un emploi; **the firm gives e. to 2,000 (people)** l'entreprise emploie 2 000 personnes **2** *(act of giving work)* embauche *f*; **the e. of 200 more staff** l'embauche de 200 employés supplémentaires **3** *(use) (of money, force etc)* usage *m*

▸▸ **e. agency, e. bureau** bureau *m* ou agence *f* de placement; *(for manual workers)* service *m* d'embauche; **e. law** code *m* ou législation *f* du travail; **e. protection** protection *f* de l'emploi; **e. tax** taxe *f* sur les salaires

emporium [ɪmˈpɔːrɪəm] **N** *Old-fashioned, Lit (shop)* grand magasin *m*

empower [ɪmˈpaʊər] **VT 1** *(person)* donner du pouvoir à; *Law* donner pouvoir ou procuration à **2** *(authorize)* **to e. sb to do sth** autoriser qn à faire qch, donner ou conférer plein(s) pouvoir(s) à qn pour faire qch

empress [ˈemprɪs] **N** impératrice *f*

emptiness [ˈemptɪnɪs] **N** *(of room, existence etc)* vide *m*; *(of feelings, way of life, words)* vacuité *f*; **to feel an e.** *(after bereavement, divorce etc)* sentir un vide

empty [ˈemptɪ] **ADJ 1** vide *(of* de); *(street)* désert; *(building)* inoccupé; *(stomach)* vide; *(wagon)* sans chargement; **to come back e.** *(of lorry etc)* revenir à vide; **you shouldn't run on an e. stomach** tu ne devrais pas courir à jeun **2** *Fig (existence)* vide; *(words, threats, pleasure)* vain; **word e. of meaning** mot vide de sens; **to feel e.** *(after bereavement etc)* sentir un vide

N *Com (crate)* caisse *f* vide; *(bottle)* bouteille *f* vide; **returnable empties** *(bottles)* bouteilles consignées

VT *(glass etc)* vider *(into* dans); *(truck)* décharger; *Min* verser; *(streets)* dépeupler;

(cesspool, tank etc) vidanger; **he emptied (the contents of) the bucket over her head** il a vidé le seau sur sa tête; **she emptied the cigarette butts into a plant pot** elle a versé les mégots dans un pot de fleurs; **she emptied the water out of her boots** elle a vidé l'eau qui était dans ses bottes

VI *(of river etc)* se déverser *(into* dans); *(of theatre etc)* se vider; **the crowd emptied onto the streets** la foule s'est répandue dans les rues

▸▸ **e. weight** poids *m* à vide

▸ **empty out VT SEP** *(pockets)* vider; **he emptied (the contents of) his pockets out onto the table** il a vidé le contenu de ses poches sur la table

empty-handed **ADV** les mains vides; **to leave e.** repartir les mains vides; **to return e.** rentrer les mains vides, rentrer bredouille

empty-headed **ADJ** sans cervelle

emptying [ˈemptɪɪŋ] **N** *(of glass etc)* vidage *m*; *(of barrel etc)* vidange *f*; *(of wagon)* déchargement *m*; *(of streets)* dépeuplement *m*

EMS [iːeˈmes] **N 1** *Formerly (abbr* **European Monetary System)** SME *m* **2** *(abbr* **engine management system)** EMS *f* **3** *Comput (abbr* **expanded memory specification)** = mémoire *f* paginée, spécifications *fpl* de la mémoire paginée **4** *Comput (abbr* **enhanced messaging service)** EMS *m*

EMU [iːemˈjuː] **N** *Econ, Pol (abbr* **Economic and Monetary Union)** UME *f*

emu [ˈiːmjuː] **N** *(bird)* émeu *m*

emulate [ˈemjʊleɪt] **VT** *(imitate)* imiter; *(try to equal or surpass) (person)* être l'émule de; *Comput* émuler; **to e. sb's success** égaler le succès de qn

emulation [emjʊˈleɪʃən] **N** *also Comput* émulation *f*

emulator [ˈemjʊleɪtər] **N** *also Comput* émulateur *m*

emulsifier [ɪˈmʌlsɪfaɪər] **N** émulsifiant *m*

emulsify [ɪˈmʌlsɪfaɪ] **VT** émulsionner

emulsion [ɪˈmʌlʃən] **N 1** émulsion *f*, *Phot* **plate e.** émulsion pour plaques **2** *(paint)* peinture *f* mate

▸▸ **e. paint** peinture mate

en [en] **N** *Typ* demi-cadratin *m*, *pl* demi-cadratins

▸▸ **en dash** tiret *m* demi-cadratin

enable [ɪˈneɪb(ə)l] **VT 1 to e. sb to do sth** mettre qn à même ou en état de faire qch; *Law* habiliter qn à faire qch; **this legacy enabled him to retire** cet héritage lui permit de prendre sa retraite **2** *(option)* activer

enabled [ɪˈneɪb(ə)ld] **ADJ** *Comput (option)* activé

enabling [ɪˈneɪb(ə)lɪŋ] **ADJ** *Law* habilitant

▸▸ **e. act** loi *f* d'habilitation; **e. legislation** décret *m* d'application

enact [ɪˈnækt] **VT 1** *(act out) (tragedy, play)* jouer, représenter; **the political drama currently being enacted** le drame politique qui se joue ou se déroule actuellement **2** *Law (law)* décréter; *(measure)* ordonner, décréter

enactment [ɪˈnæktmənt] **N 1** *(of play)* représentation *f* **2** *Law (of law)* établissement *m*, promulgation *f*; *(decree)* ordonnance *f*, décret *m*; **by legislative e.** par un texte législatif

enamel [ɪˈnæm(ə)l] **N 1** *Art etc* émail *m*, *pl* émaux; **e. saucepan** casserole *f* émaillée **2** *Anat (of teeth)* émail *m* **3** *(varnish)* vernis *m*, émail *m*, *pl* émails

VT *(-ll-, Am -l-)* émailler

▸▸ **e. paint** peinture *f* laquée ou vernie; **e. ware** ustensiles *mpl* en fer émaillé; **e. work** émaillure *f*, *(painting on enamel)* peinture sur émail

enamelled [ɪˈnæm(ə)ld] **ADJ 1** *(covered with enamel) (brick etc)* émaillé; *(tile)* vernissé; **e. saucepan** casserole *f* émaillée **2** *(painted)* peint en émail

enamelling [ɪˈnæm(ə)lɪŋ] **N** *(art)* émaillure *f*, *(painting)* peinture *f* en émail

enamour [ɪˈnæmər] **VT his behaviour did little to e. me of him** son comportement ne me l'a guère rendu plus sympathique

enamoured [ɪˈnæməd] **ADJ** passionné *(of sth* pour qch), amoureux *(of sb* de qn); **to become e. of sb** s'éprendre de qn; **I am scarcely e. of the suggestion** cette suggestion ne m'enchante guère

encage [ɪnˈkeɪdʒ] **VT** *Fml (animal)* encager

encamp [ɪnˈkæmp] **VT** *(army)* (faire) camper; **the army had been encamped outside the city for nearly three months** l'armée campait aux portes de la ville depuis près de trois mois

VI camper

encampment [ɪnˈkæmpmənt] **N** campement *m*, camp *m*; **an army e.** un campement militaire

encapsulate [ɪnˈkæpsjʊleɪt] **VT 1** *(summarize)* résumer; **this film encapsulates the atmosphere of the times** ce film contient ou renferme l'atmosphère de l'époque **2** *Pharm* capsuler

encase [ɪnˈkeɪs] **VT 1** *(provide with covering)* envelopper; **encased in concrete** noyé dans le béton **2** *(put in case)* encaisser, enfermer *(in* dans)

encash [ɪnˈkæʃ] **VT** *Br Banking (cheque)* encaisser

encashment [ɪnˈkæʃmənt] **N** *Br Banking (of cheque)* encaissement *m*

encaustic [enˈkɔːstɪk] **ADJ** *Art (painting etc)* à l'encaustique; *(paint)* encaustique

N *Art* encaustique *f*

▸▸ **Cer e. tile** carreau *m* céramique

encephalitis [ensefəˈlaɪtɪs] **N** *Med* encéphalite *f*

encephalopathy [ensefəˈlɒpəθɪ] **N** encéphalopathie *f*

enchant [ɪnˈtʃɑːnt] **VT 1** *(delight)* enchanter, ravir; **he was less than enchanted by the prospect** l'idée ne l'enchantait guère **2** *(put under a spell)* ensorceler

enchanted [ɪnˈtʃɑːntɪd] **ADJ 1** *(delighted)* enchanté *(with* de) **2** *(under a spell, magic)* enchanté, ensorcelé; **an e. wood** une forêt enchantée

enchanter [ɪnˈtʃɑːntər] **N** enchanteur *m*

enchanting [ɪnˈtʃɑːntɪŋ] **ADJ** *(smile, scenery)* enchanteur, -eresse; *(voice, person)* ravissant, charmant; *(idea, thought)* délicieux; **an e. little cottage** une charmante petite maison de campagne

enchantingly [ɪnˈtʃɑːntɪŋlɪ] **ADV** à ravir; *(to sing, to smile etc)* de façon enchanteresse; **she looked quite e. beautiful** elle était belle à ravir

enchantment [ɪnˈtʃɑːntmənt] **N 1** *(delight)* ravissement *m*, enchantement *m*; **he professed his e.** il a déclaré qu'il était enchanté; *Lit* **distance lends e. (to the view)** tout paraît beau (vu) de loin; **it filled us with a sense of e.** cela nous a remplis de ravissement ou jetés dans le ravissement **2** *(placing under spell)* enchantement *m*, ensorcellement *m*

enchantress [ɪnˈtʃɑːntrɪs] **N** enchanteresse *f*

enchilada [entʃɪˈlɑːdə] **N 1** *(food)* enchilada *f*; *Fam* **big e.** *(person)* huile *f*; **the whole e.** *(everything)* tout le tremblement

encircle [ɪnˈsɜːk(ə)l] **VT** *(of roads, walls)* entourer, ceindre; *(of army, police)* encercler, cerner; **she encircled him with her arms** elle a mis ses bras autour de lui

encirclement [ɪn'sɜːkəlmənt] N encerclement m
▶▶*Mktg* **e. attack** attaque f par encerclement; *Mktg* **e. strategy** stratégie f d'encerclement

encircling [ɪn'sɜːk(ə)lɪŋ] N encerclement m
ADJ *Mil* **e. movement** manœuvre f d'encerclement

encl (*abbr* **enclosure**) p. j.

enclave ['enkleɪv] N enclave f

enclose [ɪn'kləʊz] VT 1 (*include*) inclure, (r)enfermer (**in** dans); **to e. sth in a letter** joindre qch à une lettre; **letter enclosing a cheque** lettre contenant un chèque; **enclosed herewith** sous ce pli; **enclosed please find ...** veuillez trouver ci-inclus *ou* ci-joint ... 2 (*surround*) (*field*) clôturer (**with** de); (*the enemy, town*) entourer, investir; **garden enclosed with** *or* **in** *or* **by high walls** jardin entouré *ou* ceint de hauts murs 3 (*cover*) (*electric motor etc*) blinder; (*mechanism*) enfermer (*dans un carter*)

enclosed [ɪn'kləʊzd] ADJ 1 (*in letter*) joint, ci-joint, ci-inclus; **the e. documents** les pièces jointes 2 (*field etc*) clos, enclos; (*army*) entouré, cerné; (*city*) investi; (*order, monk etc*) cloîtré; (*existence, way of life*) reclus; **e. space** espace m clos 3 *Tech etc* (*covered*) recouvert, enfermé; (*mechanism*) en carter

enclosure [ɪn'kləʊʒər] N 1 (*area*) enclos m, clos m, enceinte f, *Br Hist* enclosure f, *Horse-racing* **the e.** le pesage; **the public enclosures** la pelouse 2 (*fence, wall etc*) enceinte f, clôture f 3 *Com* (*in letter*) pièce f annexée *ou* incluse, annexe f, **enclosures** pièces jointes

encode [en'kəʊd] VT (*text etc*) chiffrer; *Comput* encoder

encoder [en'kəʊdər] N *Comput* encodeur m

encoding [en'kəʊdɪŋ] N *Comput* codage m, encodage m

encomium, *pl* **encomia** [ɪn'kəʊmɪəm, -ɪə] N *Lit* apologie f, panégyrique m

encompass [ɪn'kʌmpəs] VT 1 (*include*) englober, envelopper, renfermer (**with, within** dans); **their repertoire encompasses most musical styles** leur répertoire englobe la plupart des genres musicaux; **the state education system encompasses children of all ability levels** le système d'éducation nationale regroupe des enfants de tous les niveaux d'aptitude 2 *Fml* (*surround*) entourer (**with** de); (*of army, enemy*) encercler, cerner

encore ['ɒŋkɔːr] *Théâtre* N 1 (*song etc*) = chanson f *ou* morceau m exécuté(e) à la fin d'un spectacle ou d'un concert etc par un artiste que l'on a bissé; **to call for an e.** (*of audience*) bisser; **to give an e.** (*of pianist, singer etc*) bisser; **to play/sing an e.** jouer/chanter un morceau supplémentaire; (*repeating sth*) bisser un morceau 2 (*shout*) bis m
INT **e.!** bis!
VT (*passage, actor etc*) bisser

encounter [ɪn'kaʊntər] N 1 (*meeting*) (*of friends etc*) rencontre f 2 (*confrontation*) rencontre f (hostile); (*fight*) combat m; *Sport, Journ* confrontation f; **the e. between colonised and colonizer** la confrontation entre colonisés et colonisateurs
VT (*person, obstacle*) rencontrer; (*difficulties*) éprouver; (*the enemy*) affronter; (*resistance*) rencontrer, trouver; (*storm, objection*) essuyer
▶▶*Psy* **e. group** = séance f de psychothérapie de groupe

encourage [ɪn'kʌrɪdʒ] VT 1 (*person*) encourager; **to e. sb to do sth** encourager *ou* inciter qn à faire qch; **don't e. him!** ne l'encourage pas! 2 (*support*) (*good works*) appuyer; (*the arts, commerce*) favoriser;

(*belief*) encourager; **they encouraged their daughter's ambition** ils ont encouragé leur fille à réaliser ses ambitions

encouragement [ɪn'kʌrɪdʒmənt] N encouragement m; **to give** *or* **offer sb e.** encourager qn; **to get** *or* **receive e. from sb** être encouragé par qn; **her success was a great e. to us** sa réussite nous a beaucoup encouragés; *Iron* **he doesn't need any e.** il n'a pas besoin qu'on l'encourage; **to draw e. from sth** trouver des motifs d'encouragement dans qch

encouraging [ɪn'kʌrɪdʒɪŋ] ADJ (*news, person*) encourageant; **he wasn't very e. to me** il ne s'est pas montré très encourageant à mon égard; **it is e. to see the progress that has been made** c'est encourageant de constater les progrès qui ont été faits

encouragingly [ɪn'kʌrɪdʒɪŋlɪ] ADV (*to say sth*) d'une manière encourageante; (*to smile*) d'un air encourageant; **he looked e. healthy** sa bonne mine était encourageante

▶**encroach on, encroach upon** [ɪn'krəʊtʃ] VT INSEP (*land etc*) empiéter sur; (*sb's rights*) usurper; *Law* léser; **the sea is encroaching on the land** la mer gagne du terrain

encroachment [ɪn'krəʊtʃmənt] N 1 **e. upon sb's rights** usurpation f des droits de qn, empiètement m sur les droits de qn 2 (*of sea*) ingression f

encrust [ɪn'krʌst] VT 1 (*decorate*) **encrusted with diamonds** incrusté de diamants 2 (*cover with hard outer layer*) couvrir (d'une croûte), incruster (**with** de); **encrusted with mud/blood** couvert de boue/sang

encrypt [en'krɪpt] N *Comput* crypter, chiffrer

encryption [en'krɪpʃən] N *Comput* chiffrement m
▶▶**e. key** clé f de chiffrement; **e. software** logiciel m de chiffrement

encumber [ɪn'kʌmbər] VT 1 encombrer (**with** de); (*person, movement*) gêner; **the party remains encumbered by the legacy of its Stalinist past** le parti pâtit encore du legs encombrant de son passé stalinien 2 *Law* **encumbered estate** (*with debts*) propriété f grevée de dettes; (*with mortgage*) propriété grevée d'hypothèques

encumbrance [ɪn'kʌmbrəns] N 1 embarras m; **to be an e. to sb** (*physically*) encombrer qn; (*financially*) être à la charge de qn; **to be an e. to sb's plans** gêner les projets de qn; **the suitcase was something of an e.** la valise était plutôt encombrante 2 *Law* (*of inheritance*) charges fpl; **to free an estate from encumbrances** dégrever une propriété

encyclic [ɪn'sɪklɪk] ADJ *Cathol* encyclique

encyclical [ɪn'sɪklɪk(ə)l] *Cathol* N encyclique f
ADJ (*letter*) encyclique

encyclop(a)edia [ɪnsaɪklə'piːdɪə] N encyclopédie f, **an e. entry** un article d'encyclopédie

encyclop(a)edic [ɪnsaɪklə'piːdɪk] ADJ encyclopédique

encyclop(a)edist [ɪnsaɪklə'piːdɪst] N encyclopédiste mf

END [end]

N bout 1 ▪ fin 2, 3 ▪ but 3		
VT terminer		
VI se terminer 1, 2		

N 1 (*extremity, limit etc in space*) (*of stick, road etc*) bout m, extrémité f; (*of football pitch*) camp m; (*limit*) limite f, borne f; (*of book*) fin f; (*of procession etc*) queue f; (*of beam*) about m; (*of mast*) tronçon m; (*of cable*) tronche f, (*remnant*) (*of candle*) bout; (*of cigarette*) bout, mégot m; **the e. of the**

table le bout de la table; **to the ends of the earth** jusqu'au bout du monde; **from one e. of the country to the other** d'un bout à l'autre du pays; **to come to the e. of the road** arriver au bout de la route; (*in one's career*) arriver au bout de sa carrière; (*in one's life*) arriver au bout de sa vie; (*be unable to make progress*) être dans une impasse; *Ftbl etc* **to change ends** changer de camp; **the third from the e.** le troisième avant la fin; *Tel* **at the other e. of the line** à l'autre bout de la ligne, au bout du fil; **what's the weather like at your e.?** quel temps fait-il chez vous?; **the problem's at the supplier's e.** le problème est chez le fournisseur; **it's at the other e. of town** c'est à l'autre bout de la ville; **at the northern e. of the park/town/lake** à l'extrémité nord du parc/de la ville/du lac; **e. to e.** bout à bout; **from e. to e.** d'un bout à l'autre; **e. on** bout à bout; **on e.** (*of barrel etc*) debout, sur bout; **to stand a box (up) on e.** dresser une boîte debout; **the deep/shallow e.** (*of swimming pool*) le grand/le petit bain 2 (*limit in time, quantity etc*) fin f; (*of process etc*) terme m; **five hours on e.** cinq heures de suite *ou* d'affilée; **for hours on e.** pendant des heures et des heures; *Fig* **we shall never hear the e. of it** on n'a pas fini d'en entendre parler; **and that's the e. of it!** et voilà tout!; **let that be an e. to the matter!** qu'on en finisse là!, qu'on n'en parle plus!; **there's no e. to it** cela n'en finit pas; *Fam* **no e. of ...** infiniment de ...; *Fam* **it'll do you no e. of good** ça te fera énormément de bien; *Fam* **it helped me no e.** ça m'a énormément aidé; **to make an e. of, to put an e. to** (*something*) en finir avec; (*evil etc*) mettre fin à; (*competition*) supprimer; **to draw to an e.** tirer *ou* toucher à sa fin; **to come to an e.** prendre fin; **to come to an abrupt e.** terminer abruptement; **to come to the e. of the supplies/ what one wants to say** arriver au bout des réserves/de ce qu'on a à dire; **to come to a bad** *or* *Fam* **sticky e.** mal finir; **to bring sth to an e.** mettre fin à qch; **the war was at an e.** la guerre était terminée; **to be at the e. of one's resources** être au bout de ses ressources; **I am at the e. of my patience** je suis à bout de patience; **at the e. of** (*month, winter, century, contract, class*) à la fin de; (*six months etc*) au bout de; **at the e. of the day** à la fin de la journée; *Fig* en fin de compte, au bout du compte; **in the e.** à la longue, à la fin; **you'll get used to it in the e.** tu t'y habitueras à la longue; **she gave me the money back in the e.** elle m'a rendu l'argent à la fin, elle a fini par me rendre l'argent; **he always pays me back in the e.** il finit toujours par me rendre ce qu'il me doit; **e. of the world** fin du monde; **it's not the e. of the world** ce n'est pas la fin du monde; *Rel* **world without e.** pour les siècles des siècles; **until the e. of time** jusqu'à la fin des temps; **the e. of one's life** la fin *ou* le terme de la vie; **to meet one's e.** trouver la mort; **e. of the financial year** clôture f de l'exercice 3 (*aim, purpose*) fin f, but m, dessein m; **e. in itself** une fin en soi; **to attain** *or* **achieve one's end(s)** en arriver *ou* parvenir à ses fins, atteindre son but; **to this e.** à ces fins; **to no good e.** avec de mauvaises intentions; **with this e. in view** avec cet objectif en vue; *Fml* **to what e.?** dans quel but?; *Prov* **the e. justifies the means** la fin justifie les moyens 4 (*technical uses*) east e. (*in church architecture*) chevet m; *Aut* **big e.** tête f de bielle; *Aut* **small e.** pied m de bielle; *Rail* **e. carriage** le wagon de queue; *Rail* **e. of line** tête f de ligne 5 (*idioms*) **his hair was standing on e.** ses cheveux se dressaient sur sa tête *ou* se hérissaient; *Fam* **to keep one's e. up** (*stay cheerful*) ne pas se laisser démonter; (*contribute*) y mettre du sien; *Fig* **to make (both)** ends meet joindre les deux bouts; *Fig* to get hold of the wrong e. of the stick mal comprendre; *Fig* to begin at the wrong e. ne pas commencer par le commencement; *Fig* I don't know one e. of a tennis racket/a computer from the other je ne sais même pas à quoi ressemble une raquette de tennis/un ordinateur; *Fam* you're the e.! tu es impossible!; *Br Vulg* to get one's e. away tremper son biscuit

VT (work, task etc) finir, terminer, achever; (speech) conclure; (meeting) clore; to e. one's days peacefully terminer ses jours en paix; to e. a speech with a quotation terminer un discours avec une citation; *Fam* to e. it all en finir; the war to e. all wars la dernière des dernières (guerres), la der des ders; it's the horror film to e. all horror films c'est le nec plus ultra des films d'horreur; a headache to e. all headaches une migraine de première

VI 1 finir, se terminer (in dans, en); (of subscription) expirer; to e. happily (of story) avoir une fin heureuse, bien se terminer; the path ends at the lakeside le chemin aboutit au bord du lac; to e. in a point (of stick) se terminer en pointe; it ended in a fight ça a fini en bagarre, ça s'est terminé par une bagarre; this will e. in tears! ça va se finir par des larmes!; to e. in bitterness/acrimony se terminer dans l'amertume/l'acrimonie; his extravagance will e. by ruining him son extravagance aboutira à sa ruine; I must e. by thanking Mr Brown pour conclure, je dois remercier M. Brown; the film ends with her saying ... le film se termine sur elle disant ...; let us e. with a song finissons par une chanson; the story ends on a happy note l'histoire se termine sur une note gaie; how will it all e.? (what is the world coming to?) comment tout cela va-t-il se terminer?; will this torment/the bad weather never e.? ce tourment/ce mauvais temps n'en finira donc jamais?; *Prov* all's well that ends well tout est bien qui finit bien

2 (of word) se terminer (in -er*etc* en -er*etc*); a word ending in s un mot qui se termine par s

▸▸ *Comput* **e. key** touche *f* fin; *Publishing, Typ* **e. matter** parties *fpl* annexes; *Tech* **e. piece** embout *m*; **e. product** *Com, Ind* produit *m* final; *Fig* résultat *m*; **e. result** résultat final; *Cin, TV* **e. titles** générique *m* de fin

▸ **end up VI** (finish) finir; no one thought she'd e. up in prison personne ne pensait qu'elle finirait en prison; we ended up going to see a movie en fin de compte, nous sommes allés voir un film; he ended up dead il a fini par se faire tuer; our luggage ended up in Hong Kong nos bagages se sont retrouvés à Hongkong; she'll e. up killing someone if she carries on driving like that elle finira par tuer quelqu'un si elle continue à conduire comme ça

end-all N *see* be-all and end-all

endanger [ɪn'deɪndʒər] **VT** (somebody, something) mettre en danger; (one's life) exposer, risquer; (interests, health, chances) compromettre

endangered [ɪn'deɪndʒəd] **ADJ ATTRIB** menacé; an e. way of life un mode de vie qui menace de disparaître

▸▸ **e. species** espèce *f* en voie de disparition

end-consumer N utilisateur *m* final; (of foodstuffs) consommateur *m* final, utilisateur final

endear [ɪn'dɪər] **VT** (somebody, something) rendre cher (to à); he has endeared himself to all il s'est fait aimer de tous; her outspokenness did not e. her to the régime sa franchise ne l'a pas rendue populaire auprès du régime; the melancholy of his songs endears him to many a listener la mélancolie de ses chansons le fait apprécier de nombreux auditeurs

endearing [ɪn'dɪərɪŋ] **ADJ** (person, smile, look) attachant; (quality) sympathique; (word) tendre; he has a less than e. habit of ... il a l'habitude peu plaisante de ...

endearingly [ɪn'dɪərɪŋlɪ] **ADV** d'une manière attachante; he's e. coy/modest il est d'une pudeur/modestie attachante

endearment [ɪn'dɪəmənt] **N** term of e. terme *m* affectif; endearments mots *mpl* tendres

endeavour, *Am* **endeavor** [ɪn'devər] **N** effort *m*; to wish sb good luck in their endeavours souhaiter bonne chance à qn dans ses entreprises; to use *or* make every e. to ... faire tout son possible *ou* tous les efforts possibles pour ...; in an e. to persuade them dans une tentative pour les persuader; in the field of human e. dans l'histoire des réussites humaines

VT to e. to do sth s'efforcer *ou* tenter de faire qch, chercher à faire qch

endemic [en'demɪk] **ADJ** *Bot, Med, Fig* endémique

N *Med* endémie *f*

endgame ['endgeɪm] **N** *Chess* fin *f* de partie; *Mktg* objectif *m* (mercatique)

ending ['endɪŋ] **N 1** (of nuclear tests etc) cessation *f*, (of restrictions) levée *f* **2** (of story etc) fin *f*, conclusion *f*, happy e. dénouement *m* heureux; a surprise e. une fin surprenante **3** *Gram* (of word) terminaison *f*, désinence *f*, feminine/masculine/neuter e. terminaison féminine/masculine/neutre; accusative/genitive/*etc* e. désinence de l'accusatif/du génitif/*etc*; verb/noun/*etc* e. désinence *ou* flexion *f* verbale/nominale/*etc*; case e. flexion casuelle

endive ['endaɪv] **N** *Culin* **1** (curly) e. chicorée *f* frisée **2** *Am* (chicory) endive *f*

endless ['endlɪs] **ADJ 1** (in space) infini, sans bornes; (journey, list etc) interminable, sans fin; *Tech* (cable, screw) sans fin; **e. space** l'infini *m* **2** (in time) interminable, sans fin; (discussion, meeting) à n'en plus finir, interminable; (pain) continuel, incessant; (chatter) intarissable; it's an e. task, it's an e. job cela n'en finit pas; after what seemed like an e. wait après une attente qui m'a/lui a/ *etc* semblé une éternité **3** (in number) innombrable; a seemingly e. number of ... un nombre apparemment infini de ...; to take e. pains to do sth se donner une peine infinie à faire qch; the possibilities are e., there are e. possibilities les possibilités sont innombrables

endlessly ['endlɪslɪ] **ADV** (to speak, discuss) interminablement; (to repeat, revise sth) sans cesse; (to stretch out) à l'infini, à perte de vue

endnote ['endnəʊt] **N** *Comput* note *f* de fin de document, NfD *f*

endocardium [endəʊ'kɑːdɪəm] **N** *Anat* endocarde *m*

endocarp ['endəʊkɑːp] **N** *Bot* endocarpe *m*

endocranium, *pl* **endocrania** [endəʊ'kreɪnɪəm, -ɪə] **N** endocrâne *m*

endocrine ['endəʊkraɪn] *Physiol* **ADJ** (gland) endocrine

N (glande *f*) endocrine *f*

endocrinology [endəʊkraɪ'nɒlədʒɪ] **N** *Med* endocrinologie *f*

end-of-month ADJ de fin de mois

▸▸ *Fin* **e. balance** solde *m* de fin de mois; *Fin* **e. payments** échéances *fpl* de fin de mois; *Fin* **e. statement** relevé *m* de fin de mois

end-of-year ADJ de fin d'année

▸▸ *Com* **e. bonus** gratification *f* de fin d'année

endogamy [en'dɒgəmɪ] **N** endogamie *f*

endogenous [en'dɒdʒɪnəs] **ADJ** endogène

endometrium [endəʊ'miːtrɪəm] **N** *Anat* endomètre *m*

endomorph ['endəʊmɔːf] **N** endomorphe *mf*

endorphin [en'dɔːfɪn] **N** *Physiol* endorphine *f*

endorse [ɪn'dɔːs] **VT 1** *Admin, Fin etc* (document, cheque) endosser; (passport) viser; (bill) avaliser **2** *Br Admin* to e. a driving licence = décompter des points sur un permis de conduire **3** (approve) (action) appuyer, sanctionner; (decision) souscrire à; (opinion) souscrire à, sanctionner; *Law* (appeal) approuver; *Pol* to e. sb as a candidate, to e. sb's candidature appuyer la candidature de qn; (by party) investir qn; I e. all you have done j'approuve tout ce que vous avez fait; *Com* our products are endorsed by leading athletes nos produits sont signés par les plus grands athlètes

endorsee [endɔː'siː] **N** *Fin* endossataire *mf*

endorsement [ɪn'dɔːsmənt] **N 1** *Admin, Fin etc* (of cheque) endossement *m*, endos *m*; (of bill) aval *m*; (on passport) mention *f* spéciale; (in insurance) avenant *m* **2** *Br Admin* (on driving licence) contravention *f* inscrite sur le permis de conduire **3** (approval) (of action) approbation *f*, (of opinion) adhésion *f* (of à)

▸▸ *Fin* **e. fee** commission *f* d'endos

endorser [ɪn'dɔːsər] **N** *Fin* (of document, cheque) endosseur *m*; (of bill) avaliste *mf*, avaliseur *m*

endoscope ['endəskəʊp] **N** *Med* endoscope *m*

endoscopic [endəʊ'skɒpɪk] **ADJ** *Med* endoscopique

endoscopy [en'dɒskəpɪ] **N** *Med* endoscopie *f*

endoskeleton ['endəʊskelətən] **N** *Zool* endosquelette *m*

endosperm ['endəʊspɜːm] **N** *Bot* endosperme *m*

endow [ɪn'daʊ] **VT 1** doter; endowed with great talents doué de grands talents; woman endowed with great beauty femme dotée d'une grande beauté; *Fam Hum* to be well endowed (of man, woman) avoir tout ce qu'il faut **2** *Fin* (person, company) doter (with de); (hospital bed, university chair etc) fonder

endowment [ɪn'daʊmənt] **N 1** *Fin* (action, fund) dotation *f*, (bequeathed to home) fondation *f*, (ordinary) e. assurance assurance *f* mixte; (pure) e. assurance *or* policy assurance en cas de vie, assurance à capital différé **2** (talent) don *m* (naturel), talent *m*

▸▸ *Fin* **e. fund** fonds *m* de dotation; *Fin* **e. mortgage** = prêt-logement *m* lié à une assurance-vie

endpaper ['endpeɪpər] **N** (of book) page *f* de garde

endue [ɪn'djuː] **VT** *Lit* revêtir (with de)

endurable [ɪn'djʊərəb(ə)l] **ADJ** supportable

endurance [ɪn'djʊərəns] **N** résistance *f*, physical e. endurance *f* (physique); to have great powers of e. avoir une grande endurance; beyond e. insupportable, intolérable; it was boring/irritating him beyond e. cela l'ennuyait/l'irritait atrocement *ou* insupportablement;

▸▸ **e. test** épreuve *f* d'endurance; *Fig* this is a real e. test c'est une véritable épreuve d'endurance

endure [ɪn'djʊər] **VT** endurer; (insults etc) supporter; it was more than she could e.

c'était plus qu'elle ne pouvait supporter; **it is something I (just) can't e.** c'est une chose que je ne supporte pas; **these days she just endures him** à présent elle le souffre avec patience

VI rester; *(of relationship)* durer; *(of work of art)* (bien) supporter le passage du temps; **monuments which e. to this day** des monuments qui subsistent jusqu'à ce jour; **their names will e. forever in our hearts** leurs noms resteront pour toujours dans nos cœurs

enduring [ɪnˈdjʊərɪŋ] **ADJ** *(influence, memory, friendship)* durable, qui dure, permanent; *(peace)* stable; *(evil)* persistant, qui persiste

enduro [ɪnˈdjʊərəʊ] **N** *(motor race)* enduro *m*

end-user N utilisateur *m* final; *(of foodstuffs)* consommateur *m* final, utilisateur final
▸▸ *Mktg* **e. specialist** spécialiste *mf* du marché utilisateur final

endways [ˈendweɪz], **endwise** [ˈendwaɪz] **ADV 1** *(end up)* de chant, debout; **e. on** le bout en avant; **I could only see the object e. on** je ne voyais que la face latérale de l'objet; **the house stands e. on to the road** la maison est perpendiculaire à la route **2** *(end to end)* bout à bout; **to put things together e.** mettre des choses bout à bout **3** *(lengthways)* longitudinalement; **we'll have to take it through e.** il faudra que nous le passions dans le sens de la longueur

enema [ˈenəmə] **N** *Med* lavement *m*; **they gave him an e.** ils lui ont administré un lavement

enemy [ˈenəmɪ] **N** ennemi, -ie; **to be one's own (worst) e.** se desservir soi-même; **to make enemies** se faire des ennemis; *Mil etc* **the e.** *(no pl)* l'ennemi; *Fig* **the e. at the gates** l'ennemi qui menace VOIR GRAMMAIRE A11 **ADJ** *(country, ship etc)* ennemi
▸▸ **e. alien** ressortissant, -ante d'un pays ennemi

enemy-occupied ADJ
▸▸ *Mil* **e. territory** territoire *m* occupé par l'ennemi

energetic [enəˈdʒetɪk] **ADJ** *(person, action)* énergique; **I'll join you later if I'm feeling e.** je vous rejoindrai plus tard si je m'en sens l'énergie; **I'm not feeling very e.** je ne me sens pas beaucoup d'énergie

energetically [enəˈdʒetɪklɪ] **ADV** énergiquement, avec énergie; *(to deny, reply etc)* énergiquement

energetics [enəˈdʒetɪks] **N** *Phys* énergétique *f* VOIR GRAMMAIRE A10

energize [ˈenədʒaɪz] **VT 1** *(person)* donner de l'énergie à, stimuler; **an energizing effect** un effet énergisant *ou* stimulant **2** *Elec* alimenter; *(dynamo)* amorcer; *(core of coil)* aimanter

energy [ˈenədʒɪ] **N 1** *(vitality)* énergie *f*, vigueur *f*; **to have no e.** ne pas avoir d'énergie; **I don't have the e.** *(to do it, go out etc)* je n'en ai pas l'énergie; **to run out of e.** ne plus avoir d'énergie; **I am running out of e.** je n'ai plus beaucoup d'énergie; **man of considerable e.** homme très énergique; **to devote** *or* **apply all one's e.** *or* **energies to a task** consacrer *ou* apporter *ou* appliquer tous ses efforts *ou* toute son énergie à une tâche; **to shout/work/etc with all one's e.** crier/travailler/*etc* de toutes ses forces; **to conserve one's energies** économiser ses forces **2** *Phys* énergie *f*; **e. consumed** puissance *f* absorbée; **kinetic e.** énergie cinétique; **atomic e.** énergie atomique; **to save e.** faire des économies d'énergie; **the e. crisis** la crise de l'énergie
▸▸ **e.-absorbing bumper** pare-chocs *m inv*

à absorption d'énergie; *Pol* **E. Minister** ministre *m* de l'Énergie; *Pol* **E. Secretary** ministre de l'Énergie

energy-saving ADJ *(device)* d'économie d'énergie, pour économiser l'énergie, qui économise l'énergie

enervate [ˈenəveɪt] **VT** *(body, the will)* affaiblir

enervating [ˈenəveɪtɪŋ] **ADJ** *(climate)* débilitant

enervation [enəˈveɪʃən] **N** *(state)* mollesse *f*

enfeeble [ɪnˈfiːb(ə)l] **VT** *(of pain, age)* affaiblir

enfilade [ˈenfɪleɪd] *Mil* **N** tir *m* d'enfilade **VT** enfiler, prendre en enfilade

enfold [ɪnˈfəʊld] **VT** envelopper (**sth in sth** qch dans qch); **to e. sb in one's arms** étreindre qn, serrer qn dans ses bras

enforce [ɪnˈfɔːs] **VT 1** *(put into effect)* *(a law etc)* mettre en vigueur, appliquer; *(rights)* faire valoir; *(the law)* faire respecter, faire obéir; *(ruling)* imposer, faire observer; **such a law would be impossible to e.** une telle loi serait impossible à appliquer; **to e. compliance with the law/regulations** faire respecter la loi/les réglementations; **to e. obedience** se faire obéir **2** *Fml (reinforce)* *(argument)* donner de la force à, faire valoir

enforceable [ɪnˈfɔːsəb(ə)l] **ADJ** *(ruling, policy)* applicable; *(contract)* exécutoire

enforced [ɪnˈfɔːst] **ADJ** *(silence, inactivity etc)* forcé

enforcement [ɪnˈfɔːsmənt] **N** *Law (of law)* exécution *f*, mise *f* en vigueur, application *f*; **law e. officers** fonctionnaires *mpl* chargés de l'application de la loi

enfranchise [ɪnˈfræntʃaɪz] **VT 1** *(give vote to)* admettre au suffrage, accorder le droit de vote à **2** *(free) (slave)* affranchir

enfranchisement [ɪnˈfræntʃaɪzmənt] **N 1** *Pol (of citizen)* admission *f* au suffrage **2** *(freeing) (of slave)* affranchissement *m*

ENG [iːenˈdʒiː] **N** *(abbr* **electronic news gathering)** journalisme *m* électronique de télévision

engage [ɪnˈɡeɪdʒ] **VT 1** *Fml (employ, hire)* *(domestic employee etc)* engager; *(workers)* embaucher; *Naut (men)* recruter; **to e. sb's services** employer les services de qn **2** *(occupy) (person)* occuper; *(attention)* fixer; *(sb's affection)* attirer, gagner; **to e. sb in conversation** entrer en conversation avec qn, engager la conversation avec qn; **to be engaged in doing sth** être occupé à faire qch **3** *Mil* **to e. the enemy** attaquer l'ennemi; **to e. an enemy aircraft** ouvrir le feu sur un appareil ennemi **4** *Tech (cog, gear)* mettre en prise; **to e. first (gear)** mettre en première *(vitesse)*; **to e. the clutch** embrayer **5** *Fml (pledge)* **to e. oneself to do sth** s'engager à faire qch

VI 1 *(take part)* **to e. in** *(sport etc)* s'adonner à; **to e. in conversation** commencer une conversation **2** *Mil* attaquer; **to e. in an action** se lancer dans une action **3** *Tech (of cog wheel)* (s')engrener, (s')engager (**with** avec); *(of clutch)* s'embrayer **4** *Fml (pledge)* s'engager (**to do** à faire)

engaged [ɪnˈɡeɪdʒd] **ADJ 1** **to be e. (to be married)** être fiancé(e); **to get e.** se fiancer; **the e. couple** les fiancés *mpl* **2** *(busy)* heavily e. très occupé; **to be deeply e. in conversation** être en pleine conversation; **I am (otherwise) e.** je suis pris **3** *Br Tel* **the number is e.** la ligne est occupée; **to get the e. tone** *or* **signal** entendre le signal de ligne occupée **4** *(on lavatory door)* occupé **5** *Tech (gear wheels)* en prise

engagement [ɪnˈɡeɪdʒmənt] **N 1** *(to be married)* fiançailles *fpl* **2** *(meeting etc)* rendez-vous *m*; **owing to a previous** *or* **prior e.**

---

en raison d'un engagement antérieur; **public e.** engagement *m* à paraître en public; **she has many social engagements** elle est très demandée; **to have an e.** être pris, être occupé **3** *(obligation)* engagement *m*, promesse *f*, obligation *f*; **to make an e./a formal e. to do sth** s'engager/s'engager formellement à faire qch; *Com* **to carry out** *or* **meet one's engagements** faire face à ses engagements, remplir ses engagements **4** *Mil (action)* combat *m*, engagement *m*; *(of unit)* intervention *f* **5** *Tech* mise *f* en prise; *(of clutch)* embrayage *m*; *(of pinion with wheel etc)* prise *f* **6** *(employment) (of domestic staff, actor)* engagement *m*; *Naut (of men)* recrutement *m*
▸▸ **e. book** agenda *m*; **e. ring** bague *f* de fiançailles

engaging [ɪnˈɡeɪdʒɪŋ] **ADJ** *(smile)* engageant, attrayant, attirant; *(tone)* liant, engageant; **to have an e. manner** être liant

engagingly [ɪnˈɡeɪdʒɪŋlɪ] **ADV** d'une manière engageante; *(to smile)* gentiment; **e. honest/modest** d'une honnêteté/modestie engageante

engender [ɪnˈdʒendər] **VT** *(effect)* faire naître, produire; *(illness, feeling)* engendrer; **it engendered some respect for her among her colleagues** cela fit naître chez ses collègues un certain respect à son égard

engine [ˈendʒɪn] **N 1** *Tech etc* moteur *m*; *(for ship)* machine *f*, *Comput (in laser)* mécanique *f*, base *f*, cœur *m*; *Fig* **the e. of progress/reform/etc** le moteur du progrès/de la réforme/etc; **car e.** moteur de voiture; *Br* **petrol** *or Am* **gas e.** moteur à essence; *Aut* **e. trouble** panne *f* de moteur **2** *(Br* **railway** *or Am* **railroad) e.** locomotive *f*; **circular e. shed** rotonde *f* **3** *Arch (machine, device)* machine *f*, appareil *m*
▸▸ *Aut* **e. block** bloc-moteur *m*, *pl* blocs-moteurs; *Aut* **e. braking** frein *m* moteur; *Aut* **e. bulkhead** pare-feu *m inv* de moteur; *Aut* **e. compartment** compartiment *m* moteur; *Br* **Rail e. driver** mécanicien, -ienne, conducteur, -trice; **e. house** bâtiment *m* des machines *ou* des moteurs; *(for fire engines)* dépôt *m*; *Aut* **e. immobilizer** (dispositif *m)* antidémarrage *m*; **e. management system** commande *f* électronique du moteur; *Tech* **e. mounting** support *m* moteur; **e. oil** huile *f* à *ou* de moteur; *Naut* **e. room** salle *f* des machines; *Rail* **e. shed** dépôt (des locomotives); *(circular)* rotonde *f*

Note that the French word **engin** is a false friend and is rarely a translation for the English word **engine**. Its most common meaning is **machine**.

engineer [endʒɪˈnɪər] **N 1** *(technical specialist)* ingénieur *m*; *(mechanic, repairman)* dépanneur *m*; **civil e.** ingénieur civil; **marine e.** ingénieur du génie maritime; **mechanical e.** ingénieur mécanicien; **mining e.** ingénieur des mines; **consulting e.** ingénieur conseil; **production e.** ingénieur (chargé) de la production; *Tel* **telephone e.** technicien *m* des télécommunications *ou* du téléphone **2** *Naut* ingénieur *m*, mécanicien *m*; **chief e.** chef *m* mécanicien; **second e.** officier *m* mécanicien en second **3** *Aviat* **flight e.** *(on military aircraft)* mécanicien *m* navigant; *(on civil aircraft)* mécanicien de bord; **aircraft e.** mécanicien de piste **4** *Mil* soldat *m* du génie, sapeur *m*; **the engineers** le génie, l'arme *f* du génie; *Br* **the Royal Engineers,** *Am* **the Corps of Engineers** = le Génie **5** *Am Rail (driver) (of locomotive)* conducteur *m*, mécanicien *m* **6** *Fig (instigator) (of plan, plot)* âme *f*, instigateur *m*; **her ex-husband was the e. of her downfall** son ex-mari a été l'instigateur de sa ruine

VT 1 *usu Pej (cause, bring about) (coup, sb's downfall, defeat)* machiner; *(situation)* manigancer; *Sport (goal)* amener; **she engineered his escape** elle a organisé son évasion; **he had carefully engineered the seating arrangements** il avait disposé les convives avec soin **2** *(build) (bridges, roads)* construire (en qualité d'ingénieur); **the bridge has been superbly engineered** le pont est un superbe travail d'ingénierie
▸▸ **e. officer** ingénieur mécanicien

Note that the French word **ingénieur** is never used to mean **repairman**.

---

engineering [endʒɪ'nɪərɪŋ] **N 1** *Tech* ingénierie *f*, technique *f ou* science *f* de l'ingénieur; **a degree in e.** une licence en ingénierie; **a tremendous feat of e.** une remarquable prouesse technique; **agricultural e.** génie *m* agricole *ou* rural; **civil e.** génie civil; **industrial e.** organisation *f* industrielle; **light e.** petite mécanique *f*; **marine e.** génie maritime; **mechanical e.** mécanique *f*; **precision e.** mécanique de précision; **production e.** technique de la production **2** *usu Pej (planning)* machinations *fpl*, manœuvres *fpl*; **he had participated in the e. of her downfall** il avait participé aux machinations *ou* manœuvres qui ont conduit à sa ruine
▸▸ *Mktg* **e. attributes** qualités *fpl* techniques; **e. consultant** ingénieur-conseil *m, pl* ingénieurs-conseils; **e. department** service *m* technique; **e. and design department** bureau *m* d'études; **e. test** test *m* technique; **e. works** atelier *m* de constructions mécaniques

engineman, *pl* **enginemen** [ˈendʒɪnmən, -men] **N** *Am Rail* mécanicien *m*

England [ˈɪŋɡlənd] **N** l'Angleterre *f*; **in E.** en Angleterre; **to go to E.** aller en Angleterre; *Sport* **the E. team** l'équipe d'Angleterre; **an E. player** un joueur de l'équipe d'Angleterre

English [ˈɪŋɡlɪʃ] **ADJ** anglais; **E. born** *or* **by birth** de naissance anglaise; *Archit* **early E. (style)** premier style *m* gothique; **E. history** histoire *f* d'Angleterre
NPL the E. les Anglais *mpl*
N *Ling* anglais *m*; **she speaks excellent E.** elle parle un anglais excellent, son anglais est excellent; **E. E., British E.** l'anglais d'Angleterre; **American/Australian/Indian/Nigerian E.** l'anglais américain/australien/indien/nigérian; **the King's/Queen's E.** l'anglais correct; **to study E.** étudier l'anglais; **to speak E.** parler anglais; **E. speaking** anglophone, de langue anglaise; **in E.** en anglais; **E. teacher** professeur *m* d'anglais
▸▸ **E. breakfast** petit déjeuner *m* anglais *ou* à l'anglaise, breakfast *m*; **the E. Channel** la Manche; *Am* **E. muffin** muffin *m*; *Fig* **E. rose** = le type idéal de la femme anglaise; **E. service** *(in restaurant)* service *m* à l'anglaise

---

English Breakfast
Le petit déjeuner traditionnel anglais se compose d'un plat chaud (des œufs au bacon, par exemple), de céréales ou de porridge, et de toasts à la marmelade d'oranges, le tout accompagné de café ou de thé; aujourd'hui il est généralement remplacé par une collation plus légère.

Englishman, *pl* **Englishmen** [ˈɪŋɡlɪʃmən] **N** Anglais *m*; *Prov* **an E.'s home is his castle** tout homme est maître chez lui

Englishwoman, *pl* **Englishwomen** [ˈɪŋɡlɪʃwʊmən, -wɪmɪn] **N** Anglaise *f*

engrave [ɪnˈɡreɪv] **VT** graver; **to e. on wood** graver sur bois; **engraved on the memory** gravé dans la mémoire; *Fig* **to be engraved on tablets of stone** être parole d'évangile

engraved [ɪnˈɡreɪvd] **ADJ ATTRIB** gravé
engraver [ɪnˈɡreɪvər] **N** *(person)* graveur *m*
engraving [ɪnˈɡreɪvɪŋ] **N** *(process, print)* gravure *f*; *(print)* estampe *f*; **line e.** gravure au burin

engross [ɪnˈɡrəʊs] **VT 1** *(person)* absorber, occuper; **engrossed in her reading** plongée dans sa lecture, toute à sa lecture; **to become engrossed in sth** s'absorber *ou* s'abstraire dans qch **2** *Law (document) (draw up)* rédiger; *(copy)* grossoyer

engrossing [ɪnˈɡrəʊsɪŋ] **ADJ** *(study, article, work)* absorbant; *(film, account, book)* captivant

engrossment [ɪnˈɡrəʊsmənt] **N 1** *(absorption) (of attention)* absorption *f* (**in** dans); **her total e. in the project meant she ...** ce projet l'absorbait tellement qu'elle ... **2** *Law* rédaction *f* de la grosse

engulf [ɪnˈɡʌlf] **VT** engloutir, engouffrer; **to be engulfed by the waves** sombrer dans les flots; **engulfed by the flames** englouti par les flammes; **the house was suddenly engulfed in darkness** la maison a été soudain plongée dans l'obscurité; **a feeling of despair engulfed him** le désespoir l'a terrassé

enhance [ɪnˈhɑːns, -ˈhæns] **VT** *(quality of life, performance, chances)* améliorer; *(sth's worth)* rehausser; *(ability, effect)* renforcer; *(pleasure)* accroître; *(sb's beauty)* mettre en valeur; *(reputation)* agrandir; *Fin (pension)* augmenter; *Comput* améliorer

enhancement [ɪnˈhɑːnsmənt, -ˈhæns-] **N** *(of value)* rehaussement *m*; *(of pleasure)* augmentation *f*; *Comput* **computer e.** amélioration *f* par ordinateur

enharmonic [enhɑːˈmɒnɪk] **ADJ** *Mus* enharmonique

enigma [ɪˈnɪɡmə] **N** énigme *f*; *(person)* personne *f* énigmatique *ou* mystérieuse

enigmatic [enɪɡˈmætɪk] **ADJ** énigmatique, mystérieux

enigmatically [enɪɡˈmætɪklɪ] **ADV** énigmatiquement, mystérieusement

enjoin [ɪnˈdʒɔɪn] **VT** *Fml* enjoindre (**sth on sb** qch à qn); **to e. sb to do sth** enjoindre à qn de faire qch

enjoy [ɪnˈdʒɔɪ] **VT 1** *(take pleasure from)* aimer, prendre plaisir à; *(pipe, meal)* savourer; *(music, film, play etc)* aimer; **I don't think you would e. the concert** je ne pense pas que tu aimerais le concert *ou* que le concert te plairait; **I couldn't e. the film knowing what was really happening there** je n'ai pas pu apprécier le film en sachant ce qui se passait réellement là-bas; **you won't e. the party** tu ne t'amuseras pas à la soirée; **he's someone who really enjoys his food** c'est quelqu'un qui aime la bonne chère; **to e. the fine weather** jouir du beau temps; **to e. life** profiter de la vie; **to e. oneself** s'amuser, se divertir; **they enjoyed themselves hiding in the bushes** ils se sont amusés à se cacher dans les buissons; **e. yourself!** amusez-vous bien!; **to e. doing sth** aimer faire *ou* trouver du plaisir à faire qch; **I e. cooking** j'aime (bien) faire la cuisine; **I enjoyed seeing them make fools of themselves** j'ai pris plaisir à les voir se ridiculiser; **I don't e. being woken up in the middle of the night** je n'aime pas qu'on me réveille en plein milieu de la nuit
2 *esp Fml (benefit from) (wealth, sb's confidence)* jouir de, posséder; **to e. good health/a high standard of living** jouir d'une bonne santé/d'un haut niveau de vie; *Hum* **to e. bad health** se complaire dans ses maux
VI *Am* **e.!** *(before meal)* bon appétit!

enjoyable [ɪnˈdʒɔɪəb(ə)l] **ADJ** *(stay, trip, wine)* agréable; **that was a very e. meal**

c'était très bon; **we had a most e. evening** nous avons passé une soirée des plus agréables

enjoyably [ɪnˈdʒɔɪəblɪ] **ADV** agréablement; **we spent the week most e.** nous avons passé une semaine des plus agréables

enjoyment [ɪnˈdʒɔɪmənt] **N 1** *(pleasure)* plaisir *m*; **to get e. out of sth/doing sth** retirer du plaisir de qch/à faire qch; **to take great e. in doing sth** prendre un grand plaisir à faire qch; **the noise spoiled our e. of the music** le bruit nous a empêchés de profiter pleinement de la musique **2** *Fml (benefit) (of right etc)* jouissance *f*

enlarge [ɪnˈlɑːdʒ] **VT 1** *(increase in size)* agrandir; *(property)* étendre; *(wealth)* accroître, augmenter; *(hole)* élargir; *Med (heart, liver)* hypertrophier; *Phot (photograph)* agrandir; **to have** *or* **get a photograph enlarged** faire agrandir une photo **2** *(develop) (idea)* développer
VI 1 *(increase in size)* s'agrandir; *(of property)* s'étendre; *(of wealth)* augmenter; *(of hole)* s'élargir, s'agrandir; *Med (of heart, liver)* s'hypertrophier **2** *(speak or write at greater length)* **to e. on** *(subject, importance of sth)* s'étendre sur

enlarged [ɪnˈlɑːdʒd] **ADJ** *(majority)* accru; *(photograph)* agrandi; *Med (tonsil, liver)* hypertrophié
▸▸ **e. edition** *(of reference book)* édition *f* augmentée

enlargement [ɪnˈlɑːdʒmənt] **N 1** *(increase)* agrandissement *m*; *(of property)* extension *f*; *(of wealth)* accroissement *m*; *(of EU)* élargissement *m*; *(of hole)* élargissement *m* **2** *Phot (print, action)* agrandissement *m* **3** *Med (of heart, spleen)* hypertrophie *f*

enlarger [ɪnˈlɑːdʒər] **N** *Phot* agrandisseur *m*

enlighten [ɪnˈlaɪt(ə)n] **VT** *(person)* éclairer (**on, as to** sur); **can somebody e. me as to what is going on?** est-ce que quelqu'un peut m'expliquer ce qui se passe?; **the programme didn't really e. me as to why ...** l'émission ne m'a pas vraiment éclairé sur la raison pour laquelle ...

enlightened [ɪnˈlaɪt(ə)nd] **ADJ** *(person, criticism)* éclairé; **to be sexually e.** *(liberal)* avoir les idées larges sur le plan de la sexualité; *(knowledgeable)* avoir de bonnes connaissances en matière de sexualité
▸▸ *Hist* **e. despot** despote *m* éclairé

enlightenment [ɪnˈlaɪt(ə)nmənt] **N 1** éclaircissement *m* (**on** sur); **for your e.** pour votre édification **2** *Hist* **the (Age of) E.** le Siècle des lumières

enlist [ɪnˈlɪst] **VT** *(supporters)* recruter; *Mil (soldier)* enrôler, engager; *(sb's support, help, sympathy)* s'assurer; **to e. sb's support for a cause** rallier qn à une cause; **she enlisted the help of two bystanders** elle a obtenu de l'aide de la part de deux spectateurs
VI *Mil (of soldier)* s'engager

enlisted [ɪnˈlɪstɪd] **ADJ** *Mil* enrôlé, engagé, appelé (sous les drapeaux);
▸▸ *Am Mil* **e. man** *(simple)* soldat *m*

enlistment [ɪnˈlɪstmənt] **N** *Mil* engagement *m*

enliven [ɪnˈlaɪv(ə)n] **VT** *(person, conversation)* animer; *(party)* égayer, animer; **she had been enlivened by the visit of her grandson** la visite de son petit-fils l'avait égayée

en masse [ˈɒnˈmæs] **ADV** en masse, tous ensemble

enmesh [ɪnˈmeʃ] **VT** *(person)* prendre dans un piège; *(in net)* prendre au filet; *Fig* **to be enmeshed in a situation** être empêtré dans une situation

enmity [ˈenmɪtɪ] **N** inimitié *f*, hostilité *f*; **she felt no e. for** *or* **towards him** elle ne ressentait aucune inimitié *ou* hostilité à son égard; **religious and ethnic enmities** hostilités religieuses et ethniques

ennoble [ɪˈnəʊb(ə)l] **vt 1** *(raise to the nobility)* *(commoner)* anoblir **2** *(make nobler)* *(person, character)* ennoblir

ennoblement [ɪˈnəʊb(ə)lmənt] **n 1** *(of commoner)* anoblissement *m* **2** *(of character etc)* ennoblissement *m*

ennobling [ɪˈnəʊblɪŋ] **adj** *(effect, experience)* ennoblissant

ennui [ɒnˈwiː] **n** ennui *m*; **this feeling of e.** cet ennui

enormity [ɪˈnɔːmɪtɪ] **n** *(of crime)* énormité *f*, **enormities** atrocités *fpl*

enormous [ɪˈnɔːməs] **adj** *(building, hands, sum, difference, improvement)* énorme; *(gratitude, patience)* immense; *(power, intelligence)* colossal, -aux; *(loss)* gigantesque; *(idiot, stupidity)* monumental, -aux

enormously [ɪˈnɔːməslɪ] **adv** énormément; **I was e. grateful** j'étais infiniment reconnaissant

enormousness [ɪˈnɔːməsnɪs] **n** immensité *f*, *(of problems)* énormité *f*

ENOUGH [ɪˈnʌf]

| **adj, n** | assez ▪ assez de |
| **adv** | assez **1** |

adj, n assez (de); **(not) e. money** (pas) assez d'argent; **will this be e.?** est-ce que ça suffira?; **I've had e. of it/them** *(fed up with)* j'en ai assez; **I've had e. to drink** j'ai assez bu; **that's e. for me** cela me suffit; **that's e.** *(to eat, drink)* c'est assez, ça suffit; *(of your behaviour)* en voilà assez!, ça suffit!; **e. is e.** il ne faut pas exagérer; **he started to help her but then decided that e. was e.** il a d'abord essayé de l'aider mais il a ensuite décidé qu'il en avait déjà assez fait; **more than e.** plus qu'il n'en faut, plus que suffisant; **there was more than e.** il y en avait de reste; **you've said more than e. already** tu en as déjà largement assez dit; **have you e. to pay?** avez-vous de quoi payer?; **wages that are not e. to live on** salaire qui ne suffit pas pour vivre; **he has e. to live on** il a de quoi vivre; **e. said!** assez parlé!; **e. of this nonsense!** assez de ces bêtises!; **one word was e. to prove that …** il a suffi d'un mot pour prouver que …; **it was e. to drive you crazy** c'était à vous rendre fou; *Prov* **e. is as good as a feast** assez vaut (un) festin

adv VOIR GRAMMAIRE A23 **1** *(sufficiently)* assez; **good e.** assez bon; **fair e.!** ça va!, d'accord!; **it's a good e. reason** c'est une raison comme une autre; **she is not strong e.** elle n'est pas assez forte; **to be near e. to see** être assez près pour voir; **I haven't been here long e. to say** cela ne fait pas assez longtemps que je suis ici pour le savoir; **he didn't try (hard) e.** il n'a pas assez essayé
2 *(intensive)* **you know well e. what I mean** vous savez très bien ce que je veux dire; **curiously** *or* **oddly e., nobody knew anything about it** chose curieuse, personne n'en savait rien

en passant [ɒnpæˈsɒn] **adv** *Chess, Fig* en passant

enplane [enˈpleɪn] **vt** embarquer

enprint [ˈenprɪnt] **n** *Phot* format *m* normal

enquire [ɪŋˈkwaɪər] **vt & vi** = **inquire**

enquiry [ɪnˈkwaɪ(ə)rɪ] **n** = **inquiry**

enrage [ɪnˈreɪdʒ] **vt** *(person)* rendre furieux; **she was enraged by the government's complacency** la complaisance du gouvernement la rendait furieuse

enrapture [ɪnˈræptʃər] **vt** éblouir, émerveiller

enraptured [ɪnˈræptʃəd] **adj** ébloui, émerveillé

enrich [ɪnˈrɪtʃ] **vt** *(person, language, text etc)* enrichir; *(soil)* fertiliser, amender; *Aut* **to e. the mixture** enrichir le mélange

enriched [ɪnˈrɪtʃd] **adj** enrichi; **e. with gold** rehaussé d'or; **e. with vitamin C** enrichi à la vitamine C
▸▸ *Phys* **e. uranium** uranium *m* enrichi

enriching [ɪnˈrɪtʃɪŋ] **adj** *(experience)* enrichissant

enrichment [ɪnˈrɪtʃmənt] **n** enrichissement *m*; *(of soil)* fertilisation *f*, amendement *m*

enrol, *Am* **enroll** [ɪnˈrəʊl] (**enrolled; enrolling**) **vt** *(recruits)* enrôler, encadrer; *(workers)* embaucher; *(students)* immatriculer; **to e. oneself** *(in army)* s'enrôler, s'engager (**in** dans); *(in a society)* s'inscrire
▸ **vi** s'enrôler, s'engager; *(in a society)* s'inscrire (**in** dans); *(for course)* s'inscrire (**for** à); **to e. for a course of lectures** s'inscrire pour une série de conférences

enrolment, *Am* **enrollment** [ɪnˈrəʊlmənt] **n** *(of soldiers etc)* enrôlement *m*; *(of workers)* embauche *f*, *(of students)* immatriculation *f*

Ens *abbr* **Ensign**

ensconce [ɪnˈskɒns] **vt** **to e. oneself** *(in armchair)* s'installer confortablement; *(in corner)* se nicher; **she was ensconced in her favourite chair** elle était confortablement installée dans son fauteuil préféré

ensemble [ɒnˈsɒmb(ə)l] **n** *(clothing etc), Mus* ensemble *m*

enshrine [ɪnˈʃraɪn] **vt** *Rel* enchâsser (**in** dans); *Fig* **this right is enshrined in the constitution** ce droit fait partie intégrante de la constitution

ensign [ˈensaɪn] **n 1** *(flag)* drapeau *m*; *Naut* pavillon *m* national; *Br Naut* **white e.** = pavillon de la Marine anglaise et du Royal Yacht Squadron; *Br Naut* **red e.** = pavillon marchand **2** *Am (officer)* enseigne *m* (*de vaisseau de deuxième classe*)

ensilage [enˈsaɪlɪdʒ] **n** *Agr* ensilage *m*, silotage *m*

enslave [ɪnˈsleɪv] **vt** réduire à l'esclavage, asservir

enslavement [ɪnˈsleɪvmənt] **n** *(of nation etc)* réduction *f* à l'esclavage, asservissement *m*

ensnare [ɪnˈsneər] **vt** *(animal)* prendre au piège; *Pej (of woman) (lover)* attirer dans ses filets; **she used her beauty to e. him into marrying her** elle s'est servi de sa beauté comme d'un appât pour qu'il l'épouse; **he was ensnared by her charms** il a été enjôlé par ses charmes

ensue [ɪnˈsjuː] **vi** s'ensuivre; **a long silence ensued** il se fit un long silence

ensuing [ɪnˈsjuːɪŋ] **adj** *(in the past)* qui a/ont suivi, suivant; *(in the future)* qui suivra/suivront; *(negotiations)* ultérieur, postérieur

en suite [ˈɒnswiːt] **n** *(bathroom)* salle *f* de bain particulière
▸ **adv** **with a bathroom e.** avec salle de bain particulière
▸ **adj** *(bathroom)* particulier

ensure [ɪnˈʃʊər] **vt** assurer; **I have taken steps to e. that …** j'ai pris des mesures pour que … + *sub*; **it is the police's job to e. that the public are protected** c'est à la police de faire en sorte que le public soit protégé

ENT [iːenˈtiː] **n** *Med (abbr ear nose and throat)* O.R.L. *f*

entail[1] [ˈenteɪl] **n 1** *Law (act)* substitution *f* **2** *(property)* bien *m* substitué **3** *(inheritance)* héritage *m* inéluctable

entail[2] [enˈteɪl] **vt 1** *(involve) (expenditure)* entraîner, occasionner; *(a lot of work)* impo-

ser; *(difficulties)* comporter; *(in logic)* entraîner; **it entailed my going to London** cela exigeait que je me rende à Londres; **the job entails working unsociable hours** ce travail nécessite que l'on travaille en dehors des heures régulières **2** *Law* **to e. an estate** substituer un bien (**on sb** au profit de qn); **entailed estate** bien *m* substitué

entangle [ɪnˈtæŋg(ə)l] **vt 1** *(catch)* empêtrer; **to get** *or* **become entangled in sth** *(of person, animal)* s'empêtrer dans qch; *(of string, raincoat belt, hair)* s'enchevêtrer dans qch **2** *(mix up) (hair, thread)* enchevêtrer; **to get** *or* **become entangled** s'emmêler, s'embrouiller **3** *Fig* embarrasser, empêtrer; **to become entangled in lies/sb's problems** s'empêtrer dans des mensonges/les problèmes de qn; **to get entangled with sb** *(emotionally)* avoir une liaison avec qn; **he got himself entangled with criminals** il s'est retrouvé mêlé à *ou Fam* embringué avec des criminels

entanglement [ɪnˈtæŋg(ə)lmənt] **n 1** embrouillement *m*, enchevêtrement *m*; *Mil* **barbed wire e.** réseau(x) *m(pl)* de fil de fer barbelé **2** *Fig* **e. with the law/the police** accrochage *m* avec la loi/la police; **emotional entanglements** complications *fpl* sentimentales; **an e. with a woman** une liaison avec une femme

entente [ɒnˈtɒnt] **n** entente *f*
▸▸ **e. cordiale** entente *f* cordiale

ENTER [ˈentər]

vt	entrer dans **1, 2** ▪ s'inscrire à **2**
	▪ inscrire **4** ▪ entrer **6**
vi	entrer **1** ▪ s'inscrire **2**

vt (-r-) 1 *(go or come into) (house, country etc)* entrer dans; **to e. the war** entrer en guerre; **the bullet had entered his heart** la balle lui avait pénétré dans le cœur; **it never entered my head that …** il ne m'est pas venu à l'esprit que …
2 *(join) (university)* s'inscrire à, se faire inscrire à; *(profession)* entrer dans; **to e. the Army/Navy** entrer dans l'armée/dans la marine; **to e. the Church** entrer dans les ordres; **to e. a university/convent** entrer à une université/dans un couvent; **to e. politics** se lancer dans la politique; **to e. sb's service** entrer au service de qn
3 *(begin)* **to e. one's sixtieth year** entrer dans sa soixantième année
4 *(include, register)* **to e. a name on a list** inscrire *ou* porter un nom sur une liste; **to e. sb for an exam** inscrire qn à un examen; **to e. sb for a race** inscrire qn au nombre des participants d'une course; **to e. a horse for a race** engager un cheval dans une course; *Com* **to e. goods** *(in customs)* déclarer des marchandises en douane; *Acct* **to e. an item in the ledger** inscrire *ou* porter un article au grand livre; *Acct* **to e. sth to** *or* **against sb** porter *ou* inscrire qch au compte de qn; *Acct* **to e. sth in the accounts** comptabiliser qch;
to e. a protest protester formellement
5 *(take part in) (race, competition)* participer à
6 *Comput (data)* entrer, introduire
▸ **vi 1** entrer (**through** par); *Theat* **e. Hamlet** entre Hamlet
2 *(register)* s'inscrire; **she entered for the race/for the exam** elle s'est inscrite pour la course/à l'examen; **are you going to e.?** *(for competition, exam)* est-ce que tu vas te présenter?
▸ **n** *Comput* touche *f* (d')entrée; **press e.** appuyer sur la touche entrée
▸▸ *Comput* **e. key** touche *f* (d')entrée

▸ **enter into vt insep 1** *(begin) (service, relationship)* entrer en; *(business, dispute)* entrer dans; *(negotiations)* engager; *(agreement)* conclure, passer; *(contract)* passer; **to e. into partnership with sb** s'associer avec qn; *Lit* **to e. into holy matrimony** se marier; **to e. into (a) conversation with sb** engager une conversation avec qn

2 *(have part in) (decision)* peser sur, influencer; **money doesn't e. into it** l'argent n'entre pas en jeu *ou* en ligne de compte

3 to e. into the spirit of the game entrer dans le jeu

▸ **enter on** VT INSEP **1** *(commence)* débuter (dans), commencer, entamer; **she has entered on a new career** elle a commencé une nouvelle carrière

2 *Law (property)* entrer en possession de, prendre possession de

▸ **enter up** VT SEP **to e. up an item in the ledger** inscrire *ou* porter un article au grand livre

▸ **enter upon** VT INSEP = **enter on**

enteric [en'terɪk] ADJ *Med* entérique
▸▸ **e. fever** *(fièvre f)* typhoïde *f*

entering ['entərɪŋ] N *Comput (of command, character)* entrée *f*; *(of data)* entrée *f*, introduction *f*; **e. of an order** enregistrement *m* d'une commande

enteritis [entə'raɪtɪs] N *Med* entérite *f*

enterprise ['entəpraɪz] N **1** *(undertaking)* entreprise *f* (difficile) **2** *Com (business)* entreprise *f*; **free e.** la libre entreprise; **private e.** l'entreprise privée **3** *(initiative)* **to show e.** faire preuve d'un esprit entreprenant; **man of great e.** homme entreprenant; **to lack e.** manquer d'initiative; **to be full of e., to have a lot of e.** être très entreprenant
▸▸ *Br* **e. area** = zone *f* d'encouragement à l'implantation d'entreprises dans les régions économiquement défavorisées; *Com* **e. culture** = attitude *f* favorable à l'essor de l'esprit d'entreprise; *Econ* **e. economy** = type d'économie qui facilite la création d'entreprises; *Br* **e. zone** = zone d'encouragement à l'implantation d'entreprises dans les régions économiquement défavorisées

enterprising ['entəpraɪzɪŋ] ADJ entreprenant; *(imaginative)* plein d'imagination; *(solution)* imaginatif, ingénieux

enterprisingly ['entəpraɪzɪŋlɪ] ADV d'une façon entreprenante; *(to repair sth)* ingénieusement

entertain [entə'teɪn] VT **1** *(amuse)* divertir, amuser; **she entertained us with stories of her travels** elle nous a divertis en nous racontant ses histoires de voyages; **to keep sb entertained** divertir *ou* amuser qn **2** *esp Fml* **to e. guests** recevoir (des invités); **we are entertaining them to dinner next Tuesday** nous les avons invités à dîner mardi prochain **3** *(consider, accept) (proposition, opinion)* admettre, accueillir; *(request)* faire un accueil favorable à; **he wasn't prepared to e. the idea** il se refusait à considérer cette idée **3** *(harbour) (fears, suspicions)* éprouver; *(hope, idea, doubts)* nourrir; *(illusion)* chérir, caresser
VI offrir une réception; **they e. a great deal** ils reçoivent beaucoup (de monde)

> Note that the French verb **entretenir** is a false friend and is never a translation for the English verb **to entertain**. Its most common meaning is **to maintain**.

entertainer [entə'teɪnər] N **1** *Theat etc* artiste *mf* de cabaret, fantaisiste *mf*; *(comedian)* comique *mf*; **TV e.** animateur, -trice de la télé **2** *(of guests)* **they never were big entertainers** ils n'ont jamais beaucoup reçu

entertaining [entə'teɪnɪŋ] ADJ divertissant; *(funny, amusing)* amusant
N *(of guests)* réception *f*; **they do a lot of e.** ils reçoivent beaucoup; **he never liked e.** il n'a jamais aimé recevoir

entertainingly [entə'teɪnɪŋlɪ] ADV d'une manière divertissante; *(in funny or amusing way)* d'une manière amusante

entertainment [entə'teɪnmənt] N **1** *(amusement)* divertissement *m*, amusement *m*; **much to the e. of the crowd** au grand amusement de la foule; **to be good e. value** être amusant *ou* divertissant **2** *Theat etc* spectacle *m*, divertissement *m*; **the e. business** l'industrie *f* du spectacle **3** *(hospitality)* hospitalité *f*; *(reception)* réception *f*, fête *f*
▸▸ *Com* **e. allowance** frais *mpl* de représentation; **e. centre** système *m* audio-vidéo; **entertainments director** *(at holiday centre etc)* directeur *m* de l'animation; *Com* **e. expenses** frais de représentation; **entertainments guide** guide *m* des spectacles; **entertainments officer** *(on ship)* = officier *m* chargé des spectacles, animateur *m*; **entertainments team** équipe *f* d'animation; **e. system** système audio-vidéo; **e. tax** taxe *f* sur les spectacles

enthral, *Am* **enthrall** [ɪn'θrɔːl] VT (**enthralled; enthralling**) *(of spectacle, speaker)* captiver, passionner; *(of object, beauty)* fasciner; *(of prospect, idea)* enthousiasmer, exalter; **we were enthralled by his stories** nous étions captivés par ses histoires

enthralling [ɪn'θrɔːlɪŋ] ADJ *(spectacle, speaker etc)* captivant, passionnant; *(object, beauty)* fascinant; *(prospect, idea)* exaltant, enthousiasmant

enthrallingly [ɪn'θrɔːlɪŋlɪ] ADV d'une manière captivante; **e. beautiful** d'une beauté fascinante

enthrone [ɪn'θrəʊn] VT *(king)* mettre sur le trône; *(bishop)* introniser

enthronement [ɪn'θrəʊnmənt] N intronisation *f*

enthuse [ɪn'θjuːz] VI s'enthousiasmer (**over, about** pour)
VT enthousiasmer

enthusiasm [ɪn'θjuːzɪæz(ə)m] N enthousiasme *m* (**for, about** pour); **to show/feel little e. for sth** faire preuve de/se sentir peu d'enthousiasme pour qch

enthusiast [ɪn'θjuːzɪæst] N enthousiaste *mf*; *(of golf etc)* fanatique *mf*; *(of music)* passionné, -ée; **Harold, long an e. of privatization** Harold, partisan *ou* adepte de longue date de la privatisation; **a great Shakespeare e.** un grand amateur de Shakespeare

enthusiastic [ɪnθjuːzɪ'æstɪk] ADJ enthousiaste; *(angler etc)* passionné; **to be very e. about sth** être très enthousiaste à l'égard de qch; **to become e. about sth** s'enthousiasmer pour qch; *Iron* **don't sound so e.!** tu pourrais te montrer un peu plus enthousiaste!

enthusiastically [ɪnθjuːzɪ'æstɪklɪ] ADV avec enthousiasme; **to accept e.** accepter d'enthousiasme

entice [ɪn'taɪs] VT attirer, séduire; **to e. sb to do sth** convaincre *ou* persuader qn de faire qch; **she'll never be able to e. him away from his wife** elle n'arrivera jamais à le séduire au point de lui faire quitter sa femme; **to e. sb away from a company** appâter qn pour qu'il quitte une entreprise; **they used a prostitute to e. him into the bar** ils se sont servi d'une prostituée pour le séduire et l'attirer dans le bar; **she used it to e. the mouse out from under the cooker** elle s'en est servi pour faire sortir la souris de sous la cuisinière

enticement [ɪn'taɪsmənt] N **1** *Law (act)* séduction *f* **2** *(charm)* attrait *m*, charme *m* **3** *(lure)* appât *m*; **to offer an e.** offrir une gratification

enticing [ɪn'taɪsɪŋ] ADJ *(offer, idea etc)* séduisant, tentant, attrayant; *(publicity pos-*

ter) tentant; *(dish)* alléchant; *(smile)* charmeur, séduisant; **the water doesn't look very e.** l'eau n'est pas très tentante

enticingly [ɪn'taɪsɪŋlɪ] ADV d'une manière séduisante *ou* attrayante; **the sky was e. blue** le ciel était d'un bleu tentant; **she smiled at him e.** elle lui adressa un sourire charmeur *ou* séduisant; **the food smelt e. good** la nourriture dégageait une odeur alléchante; **the holiday was e. cheap** le prix de ces vacances était tentant *ou* attrayant

entire [ɪn'taɪər] ADJ **1** *(whole)* entier, tout; **the e. population** la population (tout) entière; **the e. day** toute la journée; **she read the e. book in an afternoon** elle a lu le livre en entier *ou* tout le livre en l'espace d'un après-midi; **she didn't say one new thing in the e. speech** elle n'a pas dit une seule chose nouvelle dans tout le discours; **the e. business had proved to be a complete waste of time** toute l'affaire s'est résumée à une pure perte de temps; **to enjoy sb's e. confidence** jouir de l'entière confiance de qn **2** *(intact)* entier, intact

entirely [ɪn'taɪəlɪ] ADV entièrement, tout à fait, complètement; **to agree e. with sb** être entièrement *ou* tout à fait d'accord avec qn; **almost e.** presque entièrement *ou* complètement; **you are e. mistaken** vous vous trompez du tout au tout

entirety [ɪn'taɪərətɪ] N intégralité *f*, intégrité *f*; *(of domain etc)* totalité *f*; **in its e.** en entier, intégralement, dans son entier; **to consider sth in its e.** considérer qch dans son entier; **the skeleton had been preserved in its e.** le squelette avait été intégralement conservé

entitle [ɪn'taɪt(ə)l] VT **1** *(give right to)* donner le droit à (**to** à); **to e. sb to do sth** donner (le) droit à qn de faire qch; **to be entitled to sth** avoir droit à qch; **to be entitled to do sth** avoir le droit de faire qch; **the very least I am entitled to is an explanation!** je pourrais quand même avoir une explication, c'est la moindre des choses!; *Law* **to be entitled to inherit** être apte *ou* habilité à hériter **2** *(give title to) (book, chapter, song etc)* intituler **3** *(give aristocratic title to)* **to e. sb duke/prince/etc** donner à qn le titre de duc/prince/etc

entitlement [ɪn'taɪt(ə)lmənt] N = ce qui revient de droit à qn; *(money)* allocation *f* (**à laquelle on a droit**); **(annual) holiday e.** congé *m* annuel *(auquel on a droit)*

entity ['entɪtɪ] N entité *f*

entomb [ɪn'tuːm] VT *(bury)* mettre dans la tombe, mettre au tombeau; *(of ruins etc) (person)* ensevelir

entombment [ɪn'tuːmmənt] N mise *f* au tombeau; *(by ruins)* ensevelissement *m*

entomological [entəmə'lɒdʒɪk(ə)l] ADJ entomologique

entomologist [entə'mɒlədʒɪst] N entomologiste *mf*

entomology [entə'mɒlədʒɪ] N entomologie *f*

entourage [ɒntʊ'rɑːʒ] N entourage *m*

entr'acte ['ɒntrækt] N *Theat* entracte *m*

entrails ['entreɪlz] NPL entrailles *fpl*; *Fig* **to study the e.** prendre les augures

entrain [ɪn'treɪn] *Mil* VT *(troops etc)* embarquer, faire embarquer en train
VI s'embarquer (en train)

entrance[1] ['entrəns] N **1** *(way in)* entrée *f*; **main e.** entrée principale; **the e. is at the rear** *(of bus etc)* l'entrée s'effectue par l'arrière **2** *(act of entering)* entrée *f*; *Theat, Fig* **to make one's e.** faire son entrée; **to force an e. into a house** forcer l'entrée d'une maison; **to gain e. to a building** s'introduire *ou* pénétrer dans un immeuble **3** *(admission)* (to association, club etc) admission f, (to cinema) entrée f, **to refuse sb e.** (to association, restaurant) refuser l'accès à qn

▸▸**e. examination** (for school) examen m d'entrée; (for job) concours m de recrutement; **e. fee** (to exhibition, fair etc) droit m d'entrée; Br (to club, organization etc) droit ou frais mpl d'inscription; **e. gate** grille f d'entrée; **e. hall** (in house) vestibule m; (in hotel) hall m; Univ **e. qualifications, e. requirements** conditions fpl d'admission

entrance 2 [ɪn'trɑːns] VT (person) extasier, ravir, transporter; **to be entranced by ...** s'extasier sur ..., être en extase devant ...; **I was entranced by the music** j'étais transporté par la musique; **they all sat entranced** ils étaient tous fascinés

entrancing [ɪn'trɑːnsɪŋ] ADJ (beauty, sight) enchanteur, -eresse; (story) passionnant; (melody) ravissant

entrancingly [ɪn'trɑːnsɪŋlɪ] ADV à ravir; (to sing, to smile etc) de façon enchanteresse; **to be e. beautiful** être beau à ravir

entrant ['entrənt] N (in race, competition) inscrit, -ite; (in examination) candidat, -ate; (in profession) débutant, -ante; Com (on market) acteur m

entrap [ɪn'træp] VT (-pp-) also Am Law prendre au piège, piéger; **to e. sb into doing sth** prendre qn au piège ou piéger qn pour qu'il fasse qch; **he claimed that his client had been entrapped into committing a crime** il prétendait que son client avait été piégé et forcé à commettre un crime

entrapment [ɪn'træpmənt] N Am Law = coup m monté par la police pour piéger un criminel; Journ = fait, pour un journaliste, d'inciter quelqu'un à commettre un délit dans le cadre d'un reportage

entreat [ɪn'triːt] VT **to e. sb to do sth** prier ou implorer ou supplier qn de faire qch; **they entreated him to stay** ils l'implorèrent ou le supplièrent de rester; Lit **be merciful, I e. you** ayez pitié, je vous en implore ou supplie

entreating [ɪn'triːtɪŋ] ADJ (tone, look) suppliant, implorant

entreatingly [ɪn'triːtɪŋlɪ] ADV d'un air suppliant ou implorant

entreaty [ɪn'triːtɪ] N Fml prière f, supplication f; **at sb's urgent e.** sur les vives instances de qn; **look of e.** regard suppliant

entrée ['ɒntreɪ] N **1** Culin (dish before the main course) entrée f, Am (as main course) plat m de résistance **2** (right of entry) entrée f (**to, into** dans)

entrench [ɪn'trentʃ] VT Mil, (camp, town) retrancher; Fig **e. oneself behind** or **in sth** se retrancher ou se terrer derrière qch

entrenched [ɪn'trentʃt] ADJ Mil, Fig retranché; (views, ideas) arrêté; (customs) enraciné; **an e. position** une position de retranchement

entrenchment [ɪn'trentʃmənt] N Mil, Fig retranchement m

entrepôt ['ɒntrəpəʊ] N entrepôt m

entrepreneur [ɒntrəprə'nɜːr] N entrepreneur, -euse

entrepreneurial [ɒntrəprə'nɜːrɪəl] ADJ (skills, talents) d'entrepreneur; (person, class) qui a l'esprit d'entreprise; **his e. success** son succès en tant qu'entrepreneur

entrepreneurship [ɒntrəprə'nɜːʃɪp] N esprit m d'entreprise

entropy ['entrəpɪ] N entropie f

entrust [ɪn'trʌst] VT **to e. sth to sb** confier qch à qn; **to e. a secret/a child to sb** confier un secret/un enfant à qn; **to e. sb with** (task etc) charger qn de; (mission) investir qn de; **to e. sb with the task** or **job of doing sth** charger qn de faire qch; **to e. sb with the**

care of sth commettre qch à la garde de qn; **to be entrusted with the sale of sth** être chargé de la vente de qch

entry ['entrɪ] N **1** (act of entering) entrée f ((**in)to** dans); (to world of politics etc) début m ((**in)to** dans); **to gain e. to a house** pénétrer dans une maison; Law **illegal e. (of a dwelling)** violation f de domicile; **to make one's e.** faire son entrée; (of actor) entrer en scène; (of new politician, artist) faire ses débuts; **right of free e.** droit m de passer librement les frontières; **no e.** entrée interdite; (in one way street) sens interdit

2 (way in) entrée f (**to** de)

3 (writing down) (of a record) enregistrement m; (of name in a list, in bookkeeping) inscription f; (item) article m, poste m, écriture f; (in dictionary, encyclopedia) article; Acct **single/double e.** comptabilité f en partie simple/double; **to make an e.** (in bookkeeping) porter un article à compte; (in journal etc) inscrire quelque chose; **author/subject entries** (in cataloguing) fiches fpl auteur/sujet; Naut **e. in the log** élément m du journal de bord

4 Sport etc (of competitor) inscription f; (list of competitors) liste f de concurrents; **there are twenty entries** il y a vingt participants; **a big/small e.** une forte/faible participation

▸▸**e. card** (for entry to a country) fiche f de police (au débarquement); **e. form** feuille f d'inscription; **e. tax** taxe f d'entrée; **e. visa** visa m d'entrée

entryism ['entrɪɪz(ə)m] N Pol entrisme m, noyautage m

entryist ['entrɪɪst] N, ADJ Pol entriste mf

entry-level ADJ (car, computer) d'entrée de gamme

Entryphone® ['entrɪfəʊn] N Interphone® m

entwine [ɪn'twaɪn] VT **to e. sth round sth** enlacer qch autour de qch; **to become entwined** (of one thing, ribbon etc) s'enlacer; (of two or more things, ribbons etc) s'entrelacer; **with arms entwined** les bras entrelacés; **her hair was entwined with ribbons** ses cheveux étaient entrelacés de rubans VI s'enlacer (**round** autour de); (of two or more things) s'entrelacer

E-number N additif m (dont le code commence par E)

enumerate [ɪ'njuːməreɪt] VT (reasons, one's services etc) énumérer, détailler, dénombrer

enumeration [ɪnjuːmə'reɪʃən] N énumération f, dénombrement m, recensement m

enunciate [ɪ'nʌnsɪeɪt] VT **1** (pronounce clearly) (sounds, words) prononcer, articuler **2** Fml (state clearly) (opinion etc) énoncer, déclarer
VI **to e. clearly** articuler distinctement

enunciation [ɪnʌnsɪ'eɪʃən] N **1** (pronunciation) articulation f; (of word) prononciation f **2** Fml (of opinion etc) énonciation f; Math (of problem) énoncé m

enuresis [enjʊ'riːsɪs] N Med énurésie f

envelop [ɪn'veləp] VT (-p-) envelopper (**in** dans, de); **enveloped in mist/cloud** (countryside) enveloppé ou voilé de brume/par les nuages

envelope ['envələʊp, occ 'ɒnvələʊp] N **1** (for letter) enveloppe f; **window e.** enveloppe à fenêtre; **to put a letter in an e.** mettre une lettre sous enveloppe; **in a sealed e.** sous pli cacheté; **in the same e.** sous le même pli **2** (covering) enveloppe f; Biol (of organ) enveloppe, tunique f

▸▸**e. file** chemise f (de carton)

envelopment [ɪn'veləpmənt] N enveloppement m

envenom [ɪn'venəm] VT envenimer

enviable ['envɪəb(ə)l] ADJ enviable, digne

d'envie; **in the e. position of being offered two jobs** dans la position enviable de se voir proposer deux emplois

enviably ['envɪəblɪ] ADV d'une manière enviable; **e. rich/well-read** d'une richesse/culture enviable

envious ['envɪəs] ADJ envieux; **I'm so e.!** comme je t'/l'/etc envie!; **my sister's got a big house, but I'm not e.** ma sœur a une grande maison, mais je ne l'envie pas; **to be e. of sb/sth** envier qn/qch; **e. glances** regards mpl d'envie; **to look at sb with e. eyes** regarder qn d'un œil jaloux; **to make sb e.** rendre qn jaloux

enviously ['envɪəslɪ] ADV (to speak) avec envie; (to look at sth) d'un œil jaloux

environment [ɪn'vaɪrənmənt] N **1** (surroundings) milieu m; **in an office/a hospital e.** dans un bureau/milieu hospitalier; **natural e.** milieu naturel **2** Ecol **the e.** l'environnement m; **Department** or **Ministry of the Environment** ≃ ministère m de (la Protection de la Nature et de) l'Environnement **3** Comput environnement m

environmental [ɪnvaɪrən'ment(ə)l] ADJ (conditions) qui ont rapport à l'environnement; (change) de l'environnement; (brought about by the environment) produit par l'environnement; **chemicals that cause e. damage** produits chimiques nuisibles à l'environnement; **the company must improve its e. performance** la société doit améliorer ses performances en matière d'environnement

▸▸**e. audit** = rapport m sur l'impact des activités d'une entreprise sur l'environnement; **e. economics** économie f de l'environnement; **e. impact** impact m sur l'environnement; **e. (protection) group** groupe m écologiste, groupe de protection de l'environnement

environmentalist [ɪnvaɪrən'mentəlɪst] N écologiste mf
ADJ (issues, politics) écologique

environmentally [ɪnvaɪrən'mentəlɪ] ADV du point de vue de l'environnement; **e. friendly** qui ne nuit pas à l'environnement, non polluant, non nuisible à l'environnement

▸▸**E. Sensitive Area** = zone f de protection de la nature désignée par l'Union européenne où les agriculteurs doivent utiliser des méthodes traditionnelles

environment-friendly ADJ (product) qui ne nuit pas à l'environnement; **to be e.** ne pas nuire à l'environnement

environs [ɪn'vaɪrənz] NPL (of town) environs mpl, alentours mpl; **New York and its e.** New York et ses environs

envisage [ɪn'vɪzɪdʒ] VT (difficulty etc) envisager; **I can easily e. something of the kind happening** j'envisage sans peine qu'arrive une chose de ce genre

envision [en'vɪʒən] VT Am envisager

envoy ['envɔɪ] N (person) envoyé, -ée

envy ['envɪ] N **1** envie f, jalousie f; **to be green with e.** être dévoré d'envie; **to do sth out of e.** faire qch par envie ou jalousie; **to excite sb's e.** exciter ou s'attirer l'envie de qn **2** (object of envy) **to be the e. of sb** être un objet d'envie pour qn
VT (person) envier, porter envie à; **I don't e. you** je ne t'envie pas; **to e. sb sth** envier qch à qn; **I don't e. him having to catch such an early train** je ne l'envie pas d'avoir à prendre le train de si bonne heure; **a job to e.** un travail que beaucoup aimeraient avoir

enzyme ['enzaɪm] N Biol, Chem enzyme f, diastase f

EOC [iːəʊ'siː] N Br Admin (abbr **Equal Opportunities Commission**) = organisme m désigné par le gouvernement pour veiller à l'application des dispositions relatives aux droits des femmes au travail

Eocene [ˈiːəʊsiːn] ADJ, N Geol éocène m

E & OE [iːəndˈəʊiː] Com (abbr **errors and omissions excepted**) s. e. & o.

eon [ˈiːən] N Am = **aeon**

EONIA [iːˈəʊnɪə] N Fin (abbr **Euro Overnight Index Average**) EONIA m, TEMPÉ m

EP [iːˈpiː] N (abbr **extended-play (record)**) disque m double durée

EPA [iːpiːˈeɪ] N Am (abbr **Environmental Protection Agency**) ≃ Agence f pour la Protection de l'Environnement

epaulette, Am **epaulet** [epəˈlet] N Mil épaulette f

ephedrine [ˈefɪdrɪn] N Pharm éphédrine f

ephemera, pl **ephemerae, ephemeras** [ɪˈfemərə, -iː, -əz] N **1** chose f éphémère **2** (insect) éphémère m

ephemeral [ɪˈfemərəl] ADJ éphémère; (passion) fugitif; (beauty) passager, -ère

ephemerid [ɪˈfemərɪd] N (insect) éphémère m

epic [ˈepɪk] ADJ épique
◾ N (poem) poème m épique, épopée f; (film) film m à grand spectacle

epicarp [ˈepɪkɑːp] N Bot épicarpe m

epicene [ˈepɪsiːn] ADJ Fml androgyne

epicentre, Am **epicenter** [ˈepɪsentər] N (of earthquake) épicentre m

epicure [ˈepɪkjʊər] N (gourmet) gourmet m, gastronome mf

epicurean [epɪkjʊˈriːən] ADJ, N Phil, Fig épicurien, -ienne

epicyclic [epɪˈsaɪklɪk] ADJ
▸▸ Tech **e. gear** engrenage m épicycloïdal

epidemic [epɪˈdemɪk] ADJ (disease) épidémique; Fig **corruption has reached e. proportions** la corruption prend des allures d'épidémie
◾ N Med, Fig épidémie f

epidemiological [epɪdiːmɪəˈlɒdʒɪk(ə)l] ADJ Med (evidence, research, study) épidémiologique

epidemiologist [epɪdiːmɪˈɒlədʒɪst] N Med épidémiologiste mf

epidemiology [epɪdiːmɪˈɒlədʒɪ] N Med épidémiologie f

epidermis [epɪˈdɜːmɪs] N Anat épiderme m

epidural [epɪˈdjʊər(ə)l] ADJ Anat épidural
◾ N Med péridurale f; **she had an e.** on lui a fait une péridurale

epiglottis [epɪˈglɒtɪs] N Anat épiglotte f

epigram [ˈepɪɡræm] N Liter épigramme f

epigrammatic [epɪɡrəˈmætɪk] ADJ épigrammatique

epigraph [ˈepɪɡrɑːf] N épigraphe f

epilepsy [ˈepɪlepsɪ] N épilepsie f

epileptic [epɪˈleptɪk] N épileptique mf
◾ ADJ épileptique
▸▸ **e. fit** crise f d'épilepsie

epilogue [ˈepɪlɒɡ] N Liter, Fig épilogue m

Epiphany [ɪˈpɪfənɪ] N Rel Épiphanie f

epiphyte [ˈepɪfaɪt] N Bot (plante f) épiphyte m

episcopacy [ɪˈpɪskəpəsɪ] N Rel épiscopat m

Episcopal [ɪˈpɪskəp(ə)l] ADJ Rel
▸▸ Am, Scot **the E. Church** l'Église f épiscopale

episcopal [ɪˈpɪskəp(ə)l] ADJ Rel épiscopal, -aux
▸▸ **e. palace** évêché m; **e. ring** anneau m pastoral

Episcopalian [ɪpɪskəˈpeɪlɪən] N Rel Am Scot membre m de l'Église épiscopale
◾ ADJ de l'Église épiscopale

episcopalian [ɪpɪskəˈpeɪlɪən] Rel ADJ, N épiscopalien, -ienne

episcopate [ɪˈpɪskəpeɪt] N Rel épiscopat m

episiotomy [əpiːzɪˈɒtəmɪ] N Obst épisiotomie f

episode [ˈepɪsəʊd] N (of story etc) épisode m; (incident) incident m

episodic [epɪˈsɒdɪk] ADJ épisodique

epistemic [epɪˈstiːmɪk] ADJ Phil, Ling épistémique

epistemology [ɪpɪstɪˈmɒlədʒɪ] N Phil épistémologie f

epistle [ɪˈpɪs(ə)l] N **1** Rel épître f **2** Arch, Hum (letter) épître f, lettre f
▸▸ **e. side** (of altar) côté m de l'épître

epistolary [ɪˈpɪstələrɪ] ADJ (style, novel) épistolaire

epitaph [ˈepɪtɑːf] N épitaphe f

epithelium [epɪˈθiːlɪəm] N Anat épithélium m

epithet [ˈepɪθet] N épithète f VOIR GRAMMAIRE A17

epitome [ɪˈpɪtəmɪ] N **1** (perfect example) **to be the e. of sth** incarner qch; **he is the e. of elegance** il est l'élégance même **2** Arch (summary) épitomé m, abrégé m

epitomize [ɪˈpɪtəmaɪz] VT (embody) incarner; **this situation epitomizes what we're up against** cette situation est le parfait exemple de ce contre quoi nous luttons

epizootic [epɪzəʊˈɒtɪk] Vet ADJ (disease) épizootique
◾ N épizootie f

EPO [iːpiːˈəʊ] N (abbr **European Patent Office**) OEB m

epoch [ˈiːpɒk] N époque f, âge m; **to mark an e.** faire époque, faire date

epoch-making ADJ (discovery, event) qui fait époque, qui fait date

eponymous [ɪˈpɒnɪməs] ADJ Lit éponyme

EPOS [ˈiːpɒs] N Com (abbr **electronic point of sale**) point m de vente électronique

epoxy [ɪˈpɒksɪ] Chem N époxyde m
▸▸ Chem **e. resin** résine f époxyde ou époxy

EPROM [ˈiːprɒm] N Comput (abbr **erasable programmable ROM**) EPROM f, mémoire f morte programmable et effaçable

eppy [ˈepɪ] N Br Fam **to have an e.** (lose one's temper) péter une durite, péter les plombs

EPS [iːpiːˈes] N **1** Fin (abbr **earnings per share**) BPA m **2** Comput (abbr **encapsulated PostScript**) EPS

Epsom [ˈepsəm] N
▸▸ **E. salts** sel m d'Epsom, epsomite f

e-publishing N édition f électronique

equability [ekwəˈbɪlɪtɪ, iːk-] N (of climate, temperature) uniformité f; (of moods) égalité f

equable [ˈekwəb(ə)l] ADJ (climate, temperature) uniforme, régulier, -ière; **e. temperament** humeur égale; **an e. companion** un compagnon/une compagne à l'humeur égale

equably [ˈekwəblɪ] ADV d'humeur égale; (to reply, say) calmement

equal [ˈiːkwəl] ADJ **1** (same) égal (**to, with** à); **e. numbers of boys and girls** un nombre égal de garçons et de filles; **to finish e. first/second** finir premier/deuxième ex æquo; **on e. terms** à conditions égales; **to be on e. terms** or **on an e. footing with sb** être sur un pied d'égalité avec qn; **in e. measure** en quantité égale; **e. distribution of taxes** péréquation f de l'impôt; **all things** or **other things being e.** si tout se déroule normalement, si tout va bien; **to be an e. opportunity employer** offrir des chances égales d'emploi à tous; **e. pay for e. work** à travail égal, salaire égal;

2 (of sufficient calibre etc) **to be e. to (doing) sth** être à la hauteur de (faire) qch; **I don't feel e. to (doing) it** (I'm too tired etc) je ne m'en sens pas le courage ou la force; (I'm not good enough) je ne m'en sens pas à la hauteur; **a cinema e. to any in London** un cinéma à l'instar des cinémas de Londres
◾ N égal, -ale; **the service is the e. of a five star hotel** le service est du niveau d'un hôtel cinq étoiles; **your equals** vos pareils, vos égaux; **you won't find her e.** vous ne trouverez pas son semblable; **she's easily his e. at tennis/chemistry** elle l'égale facilement au tennis/en chimie; **to treat sb as an e.** traiter qn d'égal à égal
◾ VT (-ll-, Am -l-) **1** (be equal to) égaler, être égal à (in en); **nothing can e. this splendour** rien ne saurait égaler cette splendeur; **no one has equalled her record** personne n'a égalé son record; **not to be equalled** sans égal, qui n'a pas son égal; **her clumsiness is only equalled by her lack of manners** sa maladresse n'a d'égal que ses mauvaises manières; **I've never seen anything to e. it** je n'ai jamais rien vu qui l'égale
2 Math (total) faire; **four fives e.** or **four times five equals twenty** quatre fois cinq font vingt; **let x e. 20** soit x égal à 20
▸▸ **e. rights** égalité f des droits; Math **e. sign** signe m égal ou d'égalité; Radio, TV **e. time** droit m de réponse

equality [ɪˈkwɒlɪtɪ] N égalité f (**with sb** avec qn); **e. of opportunity** égalité des chances

equalization [iːkwəlaɪˈzeɪʃən] N **1** égalisation f; Fin (of taxes, wealth) péréquation f; (of dividends) régularisation f **2** Tech équilibrage m
▸▸ Fin **e. fund** fonds m de parité; Fin **e. payment** soulte f

equalize [ˈiːkwəlaɪz] VT égaliser (**sth with sth** qch avec qch); (taxes, wealth) faire la péréquation de; (dividends) régulariser; (chances) équilibrer; (forces etc) compenser, équilibrer
◾ VI Sport égaliser

equalizer [ˈiːkwəlaɪzər] N **1** Elec égaliseur m de potentiel; (for sound) égaliseur; Tech compensateur m **2** Sport (point) point m égalisateur; (goal) but m égalisateur **3** Am Fam (handgun) flingue m

equalizing [ˈiːkwəlaɪzɪŋ] ADJ (current etc) compensateur, -trice; (pressure) de compensation; Sport **the e. goal** le but égalisateur

equally [ˈiːkwəlɪ] ADV **1** (to an equal degree) tout aussi; **it would be e. wrong/mistaken/rash** etc **to ...** ce serait tout aussi faux/erroné/imprudent etc de ...; **I'm e. interested in the Baroque period** la période baroque m'intéresse tout autant; **she worked e. hard** elle a travaillé tout aussi dur **2** (in equal amounts) **to contribute e. to the expenses** contribuer pour une part égale à la dépense; **the money was divided e. between the children** l'argent a été partagé de façon égale entre les enfants **3** (likewise) **e., they may be telling the truth** il se pourrait tout aussi bien qu'ils disent la vérité

equals sign N signe m égal

equanimity [iːkwəˈnɪmɪtɪ, ek-] N Fml égalité f d'âme, équanimité f; **to disturb sb's e.** troubler la sérénité de qn; **to recover one's e.** se ressaisir; **with e.** d'une âme égale, avec équanimité

equate [ɪˈkweɪt] VT **1** (make equal) rendre égal (**to, with** à); Math (two expressions etc) mettre en équation **2** (think of as equal) **I e. communism with the Soviet Union** j'assimile le communisme à l'Union Soviétique; **to e. Jupiter with Zeus** donner Jupiter comme l'équivalent de Zeus; **to e. Picasso**

with **Michelangelo** voir en Picasso l'égal de Michel-Ange

equating [ɪˈkweɪtɪŋ] **N 1** *(making equal)* égalisation *f*; *Math* mise *f* en équation **2** *(thinking of as equal)* assimilation *f*

equation [ɪˈkweɪʒən] **N 1** *Math, Chem, Astron* équation *f*; *Math* **simple/quadratic e.** équation du premier/deuxième degré **2** *(making equal) (of expenditure to income etc)* égalisation *f* **3** *(thinking of as equal)* assimilation *f*; **the e. of fame with success** l'assimilation de la célébrité au succès

equator [ɪˈkweɪtər] **N** équateur *m* (de la terre); **at the e.** sous l'équateur

equatorial [ekwəˈtɔːrɪəl] **ADJ** équatorial

equerry [ˈekwərɪ] **N** écuyer *m*

equestrian [ɪˈkwestrɪən] **ADJ** USU ATTRIB *(statue etc)* équestre; **e. performances** exercices *mpl* d'équitation
▪ **N** cavalier, -ière; *(in circus)* écuyer, -ère
▸▸ *Sport* **e. event** tournoi *m* équestre

equidistant [iːkwɪˈdɪstənt] **ADJ** *Fml* équidistant (**from** de)

equilateral [iːkwɪˈlæt(ə)rəl] **ADJ** *Geom* équilatéral, -aux

equilibrium [iːkwɪˈlɪbrɪəm] **N 1** équilibre *m*, aplomb *m*; **stable/unstable e.** équilibre stable/instable; **to lose one's e.** perdre l'équilibre; **to maintain one's (inner) e.** garder son équilibre; **to keep sth in e.** maintenir qch en équilibre; **in a state of e.** en équilibre **2** *Econ* équilibre *m*
▸▸ *Econ* **e. price** prix *m* d'équilibre

equine [ˈiːkwaɪn, ˈekwaɪn] **ADJ** équin; *(race, face)* chevalin
▪ **N** équidé *m*

equinoctial [iːkwɪˈnɒkʃəl, ek-] **ADJ** *Met (line, year etc)* équinoxial, -aux; *(storm etc)* d'équinoxe; **e. tides** marées *fpl* d'équinoxe, grandes marées

equinox [ˈiːkwɪnɒks, ˈek-] **N** *Met* équinoxe *m*; **spring** *or* **vernal e.** équinoxe du printemps, point *m* vernal; **autumn(al) e.** équinoxe d'automne

equip [ɪˈkwɪp] **VT** (-pp-) **1** *(provide with equipment) (soldier, expedition, kitchen etc)* équiper; *(house)* meubler, monter; *(factory)* outiller, monter; **to e. sb with sth** munir *ou* équiper qn de qch; **to e. oneself with sth** s'équiper *ou* se munir de qch **2** *(prepare)* préparer (**to do sth** pour faire qch); **her training had not equipped her for such an eventuality** sa formation ne l'avait pas parée à une telle éventualité

equipage [ˈekwɪpɪdʒ] **N** *Horseriding (vehicle)* équipage *m*

equipment [ɪˈkwɪpmənt] **N 1** *(items)* équipement *m*; *(in house)* appareils *mpl*, *(in factory)* installations *fpl*, matériel *m*; **camping e.** matériel de camping; **electrical e.** équipement électrique; **emergency e.** matériel *ou* installations de secours; **heavy e.** matériel lourd; **kitchen e.** ustensiles *mpl* de cuisine; **laboratory/office e.** matériel de laboratoire/bureau; *Mil* **regulation** *or* **standard e.** matériel réglementaire; **sports e.** équipement sportif; **surplus e.** matériel en excédent; **2** *Fig* **intellectual e.** capacité *f* intellectuelle **3** *(act) (of expedition)* équipement *m*; *(of house)* aménagement *m*; *(of factory)* outillage *m*; *(of laboratory etc)* installation *f*
▸▸ **e. allowance** subvention *f* pour l'achat de matériel

equipped [ɪˈkwɪpt] **ADJ 1** *(soldier, expedition etc)* équipé (**with** de); **the aircraft is e. to take aerial photographs** *or* **for aerial photography** l'avion est équipé pour prendre des photos aériennes **2** *(prepared)* préparé; **she is well e. to succeed/for the job** elle est préparée pour réussir/pour ce travail; *(pos-*

sessing adequate skills) elle a les qualités requises pour réussir/pour ce travail

equitable [ˈekwɪtəb(ə)l] **ADJ** équitable

equitably [ˈekwɪt(ə)blɪ] **ADV** équitablement

equitation [ekwɪˈteɪʃən] **N** *Fml* équitation *f*

Equity [ˈekwɪtɪ] **N** = principal syndicat *m* britannique des gens du spectacle

equity [ˈekwɪtɪ] **N 1** *(fairness)* équité *f* **2** *Law* équité *f* **3** *Fin (of shareholders)* capitaux *mpl ou* fonds *mpl* propres, avoir *m* des actionnaires; *(of company)* capital *m* actions; **equities** actions *fpl* ordinaires
▸▸ *Fin* **e. dilution** dilution *f* du capital; *Fin* **e. financing** financement *m* par actions, financement par capitaux propres; *Fin* **e. investment** placement *m* en actions; *Fin* **e. issue** augmentation *f* du capital par émission d'actions; *Fin* **e. loan** prêt *m ou* titre *m* participatif; *Fin* **e. market** marché *m* des actions ordinaires; *Fin* **e. risk premium** prime *f* de risque de variation du prix des actions; *Fin* **e. share capital** capital en actions ordinaires; *Fin* **e. trading** marché des actions, courtage *m* sur actions; *Fin* **e. unit trust** SICAV *f* actions

equity-linked **ADJ** *Fin (policy)* libellé, investi en actions

equivalence [ɪˈkwɪvələns] **N** équivalence *f*

equivalent [ɪˈkwɪvələnt] **ADJ** équivalent; **to be e. to sth** être équivalent à qch, équivaloir à qch; **to be e. in meaning/weight to sth** avoir un sens/un poids équivalent à celui de qch; **that would be e. to saying that …** cela reviendrait à dire que …
▪ **N** équivalent *m*; **to drink the e. of one glass of wine** boire la valeur d'un verre de vin; **the Soviet e. of the FBI** l'équivalent soviétique du FBI; **to be an acceptable e.** être un substitut acceptable

equivocal [ɪˈkwɪvək(ə)l] **ADJ 1** *(ambiguous) (reply, attitude)* équivoque, ambigu, -uë; *(word)* à double sens, équivoque; **he was rather e.** il s'est montré plutôt ambigu **2** *(uncertain)* incertain, douteux

equivocally [ɪˈkwɪvəklɪ] **ADV** d'une manière équivoque

equivocate [ɪˈkwɪvəkeɪt] **VI** user d'équivoque, tergiverser

equivocation [ɪkwɪvəˈkeɪʃən] **N** tergiversation *f*; **to resort to equivocation(s)** user d'équivoque, tergiverser

ER [iːˈɑːr] **1** *Br (abbr* **Elizabeth Regina)** la Reine Élisabeth **2** *Am (abbr* **Emergency Room)** urgences *fpl*

er [ər, ɜːr] **INT** euh

ERA [iːɑːˈreɪ] **N** *Am (abbr* **Equal Rights Amendment)** = modification *f* proposée à la constitution relative aux droits de la femme et aux droits des citoyens, indépendamment de leur race ou de leur religion

era [ˈɪərə] **N** *Hist, Geol etc* ère *f*; **the end of an e.** la fin d'une époque; **to mark an e.** faire date; **the post-war e.** l'après-guerre *m*

eradicate [ɪˈrædɪkeɪt] **VT** *(prejudice, evil)* extirper, déraciner; *(disease)* éradiquer, faire disparaître; *(resistance, poverty)* éliminer

eradication [ɪrædɪˈkeɪʃən] **N** *(of prejudice, evil etc)* extirpation *f*, *(of disease)* éradication *f*, *(of resistance, poverty)* élimination *f*

erasable [ɪˈreɪzəbl] **ADJ** effaçable

erase [ɪˈreɪz] **VT** *(written material, sth on tape, disk, file)* effacer; *(with eraser)* gommer; *(memory)* oblitérer
▸▸ **e. button** bouton *m* d'effacement; **e. head** tête *f* d'effacement

eraser [ɪˈreɪzər] **N** *(rubber)* gomme *f* (à effacer); **ink e.** gomme à encre

erasing [ɪˈreɪzɪŋ] **N** effacement *m*

erasure [ɪˈreɪʒər] **N 1** *(act)* effacement *m* **2** *(what is erased)* mot *m*/chiffre *m*/etc effacé; **there were a number of mysterious erasures** un certain nombre de choses avaient été mystérieusement effacées

ERDF [iːɑːdiːˈef] **N** *(abbr* **European Regional Development Fund)** FEDER *m*

ere [eər] **Arch, Lit** **PREP** avant; *(by this time)* déjà; **e. long** bientôt; **e. now** *(in the past)* auparavant
▪ **CONJ** avant que + *subj*; **e. you forget** avant que tu (n')oublies

erect [ɪˈrekt] **ADJ** *(person)* droit, debout; *(carriage)* droit; *(penis, nipples etc)* en érection; *(dog's ears)* dressé; **with head e.** la tête haute *ou* relevée; **to stand e.** se tenir droit
▪ **VT** *(building, theory)* ériger; *(statue)* élever (**to** à); *(scaffolding, altar, mast)* dresser; *(machine)* installer; *(tent)* monter

erectile [ɪˈrektaɪl] **ADJ** *Physiol (tissue)* érectile
▸▸ *Med* **e. dysfunction** troubles *mpl* érectiles

erection [ɪˈrekʃən] **N 1** *(act)* *(of building)* construction *f*, érection *f*; *(of statue)* érection; *(of mast)* dressage *m*; *(of machine)* installation *f* **2** *Physiol (of organ)* érection *f*; **to have/get an e.** avoir une érection **3** *often Pej (building, structure)* bâtisse *f*, construction *f*, édifice *m*

erectness [ɪˈrektnɪs] **N** attitude *f* droite; **the e. of his bearing** sa posture droite

erector [ɪˈrektər] **N 1** *(person)* *(of buildings)* constructeur *m* **2** *Anat (muscle)* (muscle *m*) érecteur *m*
▸▸ *Anat* **e. muscle** (muscle *m*) érecteur

erg [ɜːg] **N** *Phys* erg *m*

ergo [ˈɜːgəʊ, ˈeəgəʊ] **ADV** *Fml, Hum* ergo, donc

ergonomic [ɜːgəˈnɒmɪk] **ADJ** ergonomique

ergonomically [ɜːgəˈnɒmɪklɪ] **ADV** **e. designed** *(chair etc)* d'une conception ergonomique

ergonomics [ɜːgəˈnɒmɪks] **N** ergonomie *f*
VOIR GRAMMAIRE A10

ergot [ˈɜːgɒt] **N** *Agr, Pharm* ergot *m*

ergotism [ˈɜːgətɪz(ə)m] **N** *Med* ergotisme *m*

Erie [ˈɪərɪ] **N** *Geog* **Lake E.** le lac Érié

erigeron [ɪˈrɪdʒərən] **N** *Bot (plant)* érigéron *m*

Erin [ˈerɪn] **N** *Arch, Lit* la verte Érin

Eritrea [erɪˈtreɪə] **N** Érythrée *f*

Eritrean [erɪˈtreɪən] **N** Érythréen, -enne

ERM [iːɑːˈrem] **N** *Fin Formerly (abbr* **Exchange Rate Mechanism)** mécanisme *m* de change

erm [ɜːm] **INT** euh

ermine [ˈɜːmɪn] **N** hermine *f*

erode [ɪˈrəʊd] **VT** *(of elements)* éroder; *(of acid, corrosive substance)* ronger, corroder; *(confidence)* miner, entamer; *Fig* **the power of the church has been eroded** le pouvoir de l'église a été miné; **our savings have been eroded by inflation** nos économies se sont trouvées grignotées par l'inflation
▪ **VI** *(of metal)* s'éroder, se corroder; *(of confidence, popularity)* baisser, se détériorer; *(of prices)* s'effriter

erogenous [ɪˈrɒdʒɪnəs] **ADJ** érogène
▸▸ **e. zone** zone *f* érogène

Eros [ˈɪərɒs] **N** Éros *m*

erosion [ɪˈrəʊʒən] **N** *(marine etc)* érosion *f*; *Fig (of confidence, popularity)* détérioration *f*; **wind e.** érosion éolienne; **soil e.** érosion du sol; *Fig* **the e. of real earnings by inflation** la diminution du salaire réel causée par l'inflation; **e. of prices** effritement *m* des prix

erosive [ɪˈrəʊzɪv] **ADJ** érosif

erotic [ɪˈrɒtɪk] **ADJ** *(art, book, film etc)* érotique

erotica [ɪ'rɒtɪkə] NPL écrits mpl/dessins mpl/etc érotiques

erotically [ɪ'rɒtɪklɪ] ADV érotiquement; **to be e. charged** avoir un contenu érotique

eroticism [ɪ'rɒtɪsɪz(ə)m] N érotisme m

err [ɜːr] VI 1 (make mistake) faire erreur, esp Lit errer; **to e. in one's judgement** faire une erreur de jugement; Prov **to e. is human** l'erreur est humaine 2 (sin) pécher; **he does not e. on the side of modesty** il ne pèche pas par excès de modestie; **let's e. on the side of caution and do ...** par mesure de prudence, faisons ...; **it's better to e. on the side of generosity** il vaut mieux pécher par générosité, il vaut mieux être trop généreux que pas assez 3 (stray) s'égarer, s'écarter (from de); Hum **to e. from the straight and narrow** s'égarer du droit chemin

errand ['erənd] N commission f, course f; **to send sb on an e.** envoyer qn faire une commission ou une course; **to go on** or **run errands** (aller) faire des commissions ou des courses; Lit **e. of mercy** mission f humanitaire
▶▶ **e. boy** garçon m de courses

errant ['erənt] ADJ (erring) dévoyé; **e. husband** mari m infidèle **e. ways** vie f dévoyée

errata [ɪ'rɑːtə] NPL Typ errata mpl

erratic [ɪ'rætɪk] ADJ 1 (irregular) irrégulier, -ière; (light) intermittent, discontinu; Aut **e. driving** conduite mal assurée 2 (person) capricieux, bizarre, velléitaire; (life) désordonné; (changes of mood) imprévisible; **her playing is e.** (of sportswoman, musician) son jeu est inégal; **the road/river follows an e. course** la route/rivière suit un cours irrégulier 3 Med (pain) erratique

erratically [ɪ'rætɪklɪ] ADV sans méthode, sans règle; **to work e.** (of person) travailler irrégulièrement; (of machine) fonctionner irrégulièrement ou par à-coups; **to play e.** (of sportsman, musician) avoir un jeu inégal; Aut **to drive e.** conduire d'une façon mal assurée

erratum, pl **errata** [ɪ'rɑːtəm, -tə] N erratum m, pl errata

erring ['ɜːrɪŋ] ADJ (sinning) dévoyé, égaré; (mistaken) tombé dans l'erreur; (husband, wife) infidèle; **e. ways** vie f dévoyée

erroneous [ɪ'rəʊnɪəs] ADJ esp Fml (calculation, premise, conclusion) erroné, faux, f fausse; (supposition) faux

erroneously [ɪ'rəʊnɪəslɪ] ADV esp Fml à tort; **e. accused of ...** accusé à tort de ...

erroneousness [ɪ'rəʊnɪəsnɪs] N esp Fml erreur f, fausseté f

error ['erər] N 1 (mistake) erreur f, faute f; **to make an e.** faire ou commettre une erreur; **to make an e. in one's calculations** faire une erreur de calcul; **e. of judgement** erreur de jugement; **printing** or **printer's e.** faute d'impression; Com **errors and omissions excepted** sauf erreur ou omission 2 Tech erreur f, aberration f, déviation f; Comput error; **allowable e.** erreur permise, tolérance f 3 (being wrong) **to do sth in e.** faire qch par erreur; **to be in e.** être dans l'erreur, avoir tort; **to fall into e.** tomber dans l'erreur 4 (wrongdoing) écart m (de conduite); **errors of youth** erreurs fpl ou écarts de jeunesse; **he has seen the e. of his ways** il est revenu de ses égarements; **to show sb the e. of his ways** montrer à qn qu'il est dans le mauvais chemin
▶▶ Comput **e. checking** vérification f d'erreurs; Comput **e. code** code m d'erreur; Comput **e. correction** correction f d'erreur; Comput **e. message** message m d'erreur; Comput **e. routine** sous-programme m de correction d'erreurs, pl sous-programmes de correction d'erreurs

ersatz [eə'zæts, 'ɜːzæts] N ersatz m, succédané m
ADJ Pej **e. coffee** succédané m de café; Fig **e. religion** ersatz m de religion

Erse [ɜːs] Ling N 1 (Gaelic) erse m, gaélique m 2 (Irish Gaelic) irlandais m
ADJ (see n) 1 gaélique 2 irlandais

erstwhile ['ɜːstwaɪl] ADJ ATTRIB Arch, Lit (pupil, friend, belief etc) ancien

eructate ['iːrʌkteɪt] VI Fml éructer

eructation [iːrʌk'teɪʃən] N Fml éructation f

erudite ['eruːdaɪt] ADJ érudit, savant

erudition [eruː'dɪʃən] N érudition f; **work of monumental e.** vrai monument d'érudition

erupt [ɪ'rʌpt] VI 1 (of volcano) entrer en éruption 2 (of violence, anger, sound) éclater; (of person) exploser; **the stadium erupted in a huge roar** le stade a éclaté d'un énorme rugissement 3 (of teeth) percer; (of spot) sortir; **his face erupted in spots** son visage s'est couvert de boutons

eruption [ɪ'rʌpʃən] N 1 (of volcano) éruption f, **volcano in e.** volcan m en éruption 2 (of anger, joy etc) éruption f, éclat m 3 (of teeth) éruption f, (of spots) éruption, poussée f

erysipelas [erɪ'sɪpɪləs] N Med érysipèle m

erythema [erɪ'θiːmə] N Med érythème m

erythrocyte [e'rɪθrəʊsaɪt] N Physiol érythrocyte m

ESA [iːe'seɪ] N (abbr European Space Agency) ASE f

escalate ['eskəleɪt] VI 1 (of prices etc) monter (en flèche) 2 (of conflict etc) s'aggraver; **small incidents can easily e. into a world war** de simples incidents (militaires) peuvent facilement mener à une guerre mondiale
VT intensifier; **to e. the situation** aggraver la situation

escalation [eskə'leɪʃən] N 1 (of prices etc) augmentation f (rapide), montée f en flèche; (of interest rates) escalade f 2 (of war, situation) escalade f

escalator ['eskəleɪtər] N 1 (moving stairway) escalier m mécanique, escalator m 2 Econ clause f d'échelle mobile
▶▶ Econ **e. clause** clause d'échelle mobile

escalope ['eskəlɒp] N Culin escalope f

escapade ['eskəpeɪd] N escapade f, frasque f, fredaine f

escape [ɪs'keɪp] N 1 (flight) fuite f, évasion f, **to make one's e.** s'échapper, se sauver; **to make good one's e.** réussir à s'échapper; **to have a narrow e.** l'échapper belle; **to have a miraculous e.** échapper comme par miracle; Fig **the cinema provided an e. from their daily routine** le cinéma leur offrait un moyen de s'évader de leur routine quotidienne 2 (of gas, water etc) échappement m, fuite f, dégagement m 3 Tech déversoir m 4 Comput échappement m
VI 1 (of person) échapper, s'échapper, prendre la fuite; **to e. from prison** s'évader de prison; **escaped prisoner** évadé, -ée; **the lion escaped from the zoo** le lion s'est échappé du zoo; **to e. by the skin of one's teeth** échapper tout juste; **to e. uninjured** s'en tirer indemne; **he escaped with a fright** il en a été quitte pour la peur; **he was lucky to e. with his life** il a eu de la chance de s'en sortir vivant; Fig **to e. from reality** s'évader ou s'échapper de la réalité 2 (of gases, fluids) s'échapper, fuir
VT 1 (of person, animal) (danger) échapper à; **he narrowly escaped death** il a échappé tout juste à la mort; **he just escaped being killed** il a bien failli être tué, il a manqué (de) se faire tuer; **they escaped punishment/justice** ils ont échappé à la punition/justice 2 (go unnoticed by) échapper à; **noth-**

ing escapes her eagle eye rien n'échappe à son regard perçant; **to e. notice** échapper à l'attention, passer inaperçu 3 (of name, date etc) échapper à; **his name escapes me** son nom m'échappe 4 (of sound) **a cry escaped him** un cri lui a échappé
▶▶ Law **e. clause** clause f échappatoire; **e. hatch** trappe f de secours; Comput **e. key** touche f d'échappement, touche Echap; **e. road** talus m de protection; **e. route** (from fire) itinéraire m de sortie de secours; (of criminal) itinéraire ménagé pour s'échapper; Tech **e. valve** soupape f d'échappement; Astron **e. velocity** vitesse f de libération; Tech **e. wheel** roue f d'échappement

escapee [eskeɪ'piː] N évadé, -ée

escapement [ɪs'keɪpmənt] N (of clock, piano etc) échappement m

escaper [ɪs'keɪpər] N fugitif, -ive

escapism [ɪs'keɪpɪz(ə)m] N évasion f (de la réalité); **the movie is pure e.** ce film permet de s'évader totalement de la réalité

escapist [ɪs'keɪpɪst] N **she had always been a bit of an e.** elle avait toujours un peu cherché à s'évader de la réalité
ADJ (film, story) qui permet de s'évader de la réalité; **e. literature** littérature f d'évasion

escapologist [eskə'pɒlədʒɪst] N prestidigitateur m spécialiste de l'évasion

escapology [eskə'pɒlədʒɪ] N art m de l'évasion

escarpment [ɪs'kɑːpmənt] N escarpement m

ESCB [iːessiː'biː] N (abbr European System of Central Banks) SEBC m

eschatology [eskə'tɒlədʒɪ] N Rel eschatologie f

eschew [ɪs'tʃuː] VT Lit (notions, ideas) éviter; **to e. violence** s'abstenir de recourir à la violence; **to e. sb's company** fuir ou éviter qn

e-science N e-science f

esc key N Comput touche f d'échappement, touche Echap

escort¹ ['eskɔːt] N 1 (for convoy etc) escorte f; (for tourists etc) guide m; (woman from agency) hôtesse f, Old-fashioned (to woman) cavalier m; (to man) cavalière f, (ship) escorteur m, bâtiment m d'escorte; **a police e.** une escorte de police 2 (act of escorting) escorte f; **under the e. of ...** sous l'escorte de ...; **to conduct a prisoner under e.** conduire un prisonnier sous escorte

escort² [ɪs'kɔːt] VT (convoy) escorter, faire escorte à, servir d'escorte à; (lady) servir de cavalier à; (prisoner) conduire sous escorte; **to be escorted to safety** être escorté jusqu'à un lieu sûr
▶▶ **e. agency** service m ou bureau m d'hôtesses; Mil **e. duty** service d'escorte; Aviat, Mil **e. fighter** chasseur m d'escorte; **e. girl** hôtesse

escrow ['eskrəʊ] N Banking dépôt m fiduciaire; **to put money in e.** placer de l'argent en dépôt fiduciaire
▶▶ Law **e. account** compte m bloqué; **e. agent** dépositaire mf légal(e)

escutcheon [ɪs'kʌtʃ(ə)n] N Her écu m, écusson m

ESF [iːe'sef] N (abbr European Social Fund) FSE m

e-signature N Comput signature f électronique, e-signature f

Eskimo, pl **Eskimos, Eskimo** ['eskɪməʊ, -əʊz] ADJ esquimau (occ -aude in feminine), -aux, eskimo inv
N Esquimau, -aude

ESL [iːe'sel] N Sch (abbr English as a Second Language) anglais m deuxième langue

ESOP [iːesəʊ'piː] N (abbr employee Br share or Am stock ownership plan) plan m d'actionnariat des salariés

esophagus [ɪˈsɒfəgəs] N *Am Anat* œsophage *m*

esoteric [esəʊˈterɪk] ADJ ésotérique

ESP [iːesˈpiː] N **1** (*abbr* **extrasensory perception**) perception *f* extra-sensorielle **2** *Sch* (*abbr* **English for Specific or Special Purposes**) anglais *m* appliqué

esp (*abbr* **especially**) spécialt

espadrille [ˈespədrɪl] N espadrille *f*

espalier [ɪsˈpælɪər, -ɪeɪ] N *Bot* espalier *m*

esparto [esˈpɑːtəʊ] N *Bot* sparte *m*, alfa *m*
▸▸*Bot* **e. grass** sparte, alfa

especial [ɪsˈpeʃəl] ADJ spécial, -aux, particulier; **of e. importance** d'une importance toute particulière

especially [ɪsˈpeʃəlɪ] ADV surtout; **we were e. lucky with the weather** le temps nous a été particulièrement favorable; **he likes birds, e. parrots** il aime les oiseaux, spécialement les perroquets; **I did it e. for you** je l'ai fait spécialement *ou* exprès pour vous; **I was e. pleased to hear about your success** cela m'a fait tout particulièrement plaisir d'apprendre la nouvelle de votre succès; **these figures are surprisingly good, e. given recent developments** ces chiffres sont étonnamment bons, surtout si l'on considère les derniers développements

> Attention: ne pas confondre avec **specially**.

Esperanto [espəˈræntəʊ] N *Ling* espéranto *m*

espionage [ˈespɪɑːnɑːʒ] N espionnage *m*

esplanade [espləˈneɪd] N esplanade *f*, (*in seaside town*) digue *f*

espousal [ɪsˈpaʊz(ə)l] N **the e. of a cause** l'adhésion *f* à une cause

espouse [ɪsˈpaʊz] VT (*cause, belief etc*) épouser, embrasser

espresso [esˈpresəʊ] N (café *m*) expresso *m*
ADJ expresso
▸▸**e. machine** machine *f* à express

espy [ɪsˈpaɪ] VT *Arch, Lit* apercevoir, aviser

Esq *Old-fashioned abbr* **Esquire**

Esquire [ɪsˈkwaɪər] N *Old-fashioned (respectful title)* **David Thomas, E.** = Monsieur David Thomas

essay[1] [ˈeseɪ] N **1** (*piece of writing*) *Liter* essai *m*; *Sch* composition *f*, (*for younger students*) rédaction *f* **2** *Fml* (*attempt*) essai *m*, tentative *f* (**at** de)

essay[2] [eˈseɪ] VT *Fml* tenter; **to e. a smile** tenter de sourire

essayist [ˈeseɪɪst] N *Liter* essayiste *mf*, auteur *m* d'essais

essence [ˈesəns] N **1** *Phil, Rel etc* essence *f*, (*of question*) fond *m*; (*of speech*) essentiel *m*; **the very e. of authority/bravery/stupidity** l'autorité/le courage/la stupidité même; **in e.** essentiellement; **speed/time is of the e.** la vitesse/le temps est le facteur prioritaire; **diplomacy is of the e.** la diplomatie s'impose *ou* est de rigueur; **the e. of the matter is that ...** le fond de l'affaire, c'est que ... **2** *Chem, Culin* essence *f*, extrait *m*; **meat e.** extrait de viande; **vanilla e.** extrait de vanille

essential [ɪˈsenʃəl] ADJ **1** (*basic*) (*difference etc*) essentiel **2** (*indispensable*) essentiel, indispensable; **an e. part** *or* **feature** un élément essentiel; **it is e. to do that** il est essentiel *ou* absolument nécessaire de faire cela; **the e. thing** l'essentiel *m*; **prudence is e.** la prudence s'impose
N (*usu pl*) **reduced to its essentials** dépouillé; **to concentrate on the essentials** s'attacher à l'essentiel; **one of the essentials of a business man** une des qualités indispensables à un homme d'affaires
▸▸**e. foodstuffs** denrées *fpl* de première nécessité; **e. information** (*on package label*) mentions *fpl* obligatoires; **e. oil** huile *f* essentielle

essentially [ɪˈsenʃ(ə)lɪ] ADV essentiellement; **her analysis is e. correct** pour l'essentiel son analyse est correcte

Essex man [ˈesɪks-] N *Br Fam* = stéréotype du réactionnaire bête et vulgaire

> ### Essex
> Il s'agit de stéréotypes sociaux apparus au cours des années 80. L'"Essex Girl" (originaire de l'Essex, comté situé à l'est de Londres) est censée être une jeune femme d'origine modeste aux mœurs légères, vulgaire, bruyante, et peu intelligente. L'"Essex Man" est lui aussi vulgaire et bruyant; de plus, il est réactionnaire et inculte.

EST [iːesˈtiː] N *Am* (*abbr* **Eastern Standard Time**) HNE *f*

est 1 *Com* (*abbr* **established**) établi, fondé; **A. Jones, e. 1885** A. Jones, établi en 1885 **2** (*abbr* **estimated**) estimatif

establish [ɪsˈtæblɪʃ] VT **1** (*set up*) (*government*) établir; (*system*) établir, édifier; (*business*) fonder; (*agency*) créer; (*company*) constituer; (*peace*) mettre sur pied; **to e. close relations with sb** nouer des relations avec qn; **to e. oneself in business** s'établir dans les affaires; *Pej* **to e. oneself in sb's house** s'installer *ou* s'incruster chez qn; *Com* **established 1885** établi en 1885 **2** (*make firm*) (*one's faith*) affermir; (*power*) asseoir; (*rule of law*) instaurer; *Law* (*will*) confirmer, ratifier; **to e. one's right** faire apparaître son bon droit; **to e. a reputation** se faire une réputation; **to e. sb's reputation as an author** faire la réputation de qn comme auteur; **the film established her as an important director** avec ce film, elle s'est affirmée comme un metteur en scène important **3** (*prove, become clear about*) (*fact, sb's innocence etc*) établir; **research has established links between the two diseases** la recherche a permis d'établir des liens entre les deux maladies **4** *Rel, Pol* (*Church*) ériger en Église d'État

established [ɪsˈtæblɪʃt] ADJ établi; (*friendship*) solide; (*fact*) avéré; (*reputation*) solide, bien établi; **once the company becomes e.** quand la société sera bien établie; **when you become e. as an opera singer** quand ta réputation de chanteur d'opéra sera faite; **e. scientific fact** fait acquis à la science; *Rel, Pol* **the e. Church** l'Église *f* établie; **the e. religion** la religion d'État; **the e. order** l'ordre *m* établi

establishing shot [ɪsˈtæblɪʃɪŋ] N *TV, Cin* plan *m* de situation *ou* de mise en place *ou* d'ensemble

establishment [ɪsˈtæblɪʃmənt] N **1** (*established order*) **the E.** (*national institutions*) les institutions *fpl*; (*dominant group*) l'establishment *m*; (*prevailing values*) l'ordre *m* établi; **the liberal/academic/etc E.** les sommités *fpl* libérales/académiques/*etc*; **E. figure** membre *m* de la classe dirigeante; **to be against the E., to be anti-E.** être anticonformiste; **to revolt against the E.** se révolter contre l'ordre établi; *Rel* **the (Church) E.** l'Église *f* établie **2** *Com* (*company etc*) établissement *m*; **business e.** maison *f* de commerce; **a family e.** (*hotel, restaurant*) un établissement familial **3** (*staff*) personnel *m*; *Mil etc* (*of unit etc*) effectif *m*; *Fml* **to be on the e.** faire partie du personnel; *Mil* **peacetime e.** effectifs *mpl* de paix **4** *Pol* (*of government, Church*) établissement *m*; (*of system*) création *f*, *Com* (*of business*) fondation *f*, (*of company*) constitution *f* **5** (*of fact etc*) constatation *f*, (*of one's faith*) affermissement *m*; *Law* (*of will*) homologation *f*

estate [ɪsˈteɪt] N **1** *Law* (*possessions*) bien *m*; (*of deceased person*) succession *f*, biens *mpl*, (*of bankrupt*) actif *m* **2** (*land*) terre *f*, propriété *f*; **country house and e. for sale** à vendre château et domaine; *Br* (*housing*) **e.** lotissement *m*; (*council houses*) cité *f* HLM; *Br* (*industrial*) **e.** zone *f* industrielle **3** *Br* (*car*) break *m* **4** *Lit, Arch* (*state*) état *m*, condition *f*; **man's e.** l'âge *m* d'homme; **of high/ low e.** (*social condition*) de haut rang/ d'humble condition **5** *Pol* **the third e.** le tiers (état); **the fourth e.** le quatrième pouvoir; *Hist* **the Estates (of the Realm)** les états *mpl*, les ordres *mpl* (de l'ancien régime)
▸▸*Br* **e. agency** agence *f* immobilière; *Br* **e. agent** (*salesperson*) agent *m* immobilier; (*manager*) intendant *m*, régisseur *m*; *Br* **e. car** break *m*; *Br* **e. duty,** *Am* **e. tax** droits *mpl* de succession

esteem [ɪsˈtiːm] N estime *f*, considération *f*, **to hold sb in high e.** avoir qn en haute estime; **to hold sb in low e.** avoir peu d'estime *ou* de considération pour qn; **to go up/ down in sb's e.** monter/baisser dans l'estime *ou* la considération de qn
VT **1** (*regard highly*) (*person*) estimer; (*something*) priser; **to e. sth lightly** faire peu de cas de qch; **highly esteemed** (*person*) fort estimé **2** *Fml* (*consider*) estimer, regarder (**sth as sth** qch comme qch); **to e. it an honour that ...** se sentir honoré que ...; **I would e. it a favour if you did this** je vous serais reconnaissant de le faire
▸▸*Mktg* **e. needs** besoin *m* d'estime

ester [ˈestər] N *Biol, Chem* ester *m*

esthete, **esthetic** *etc Am* = **aesthete, aesthetic** *etc*

estimable [ˈestɪməb(ə)l] ADJ estimable, digne d'estime

estimate[1] [ˈestɪmət] N **1** (*rough calculation*) (*of contents of sth, of force of sth*) appréciation *f*, évaluation *f*, calcul *m*; **it's only an e.** ce n'est qu'une estimation; **rough e.** approximation *f* grossière; **at a rough e.** à vue de nez; **at the lowest e.** au bas mot **2** *Com* devis *m* (estimatif); **to ask for an e.** demander un devis; **to give** *or* **put in an e. for decorating work** donner un devis pour des travaux de décoration, soumissionner des travaux de décoration; *Pol* **the Estimates** les prévisions *fpl* budgétaires; **building e.** devis de construction; **free e.** devis gratuit; **preliminary e.** devis de prévision

estimate[2] [ˈestɪmeɪt] VT (*costs etc*) estimer, évaluer; **to e. sth at £10,000** estimer *ou* calculer qch à 10 000 livres; **his fortune is estimated at ...** on évalue sa fortune à ...; **I e. that it will take three years** j'estime que cela prendra trois ans

estimated [ˈestɪmeɪtɪd] ADJ (*cost*) estimatif; (*value*) estimé; **it will cost an e. £500,000** estime que cela coûtera 500 000 livres; **it is only an e. figure** ce n'est qu'une estimation; **e. time of arrival** heure *f* d'arrivée prévue

estimation [estɪˈmeɪʃən] N **1** (*rough calculation*) estimation *f*, appréciation *f*, évaluation *f*, (*of costs etc*) calcul *m* **2** (*judgement*) jugement *m*; **in my e.** d'après moi, à mon avis **3** (*regard*) estime *f*, considération *f*, **she is rising in the e. of the public** elle monte dans l'estime du public; **he's gone down in my e.** il est descendu dans mon estime *ou* ma considération

estimator [ˈestɪmeɪtər] N *Fin* expert *m*

Estonia [esˈtəʊnɪə] N Estonie *f*

Estonian [esˈtəʊnɪən] ADJ estonien
N Estonien, -ienne

estrange [ɪsˈtreɪndʒ] **VT** s'aliéner l'affection de; **to become estranged from sb** se détacher de qn; **the quarrel estranged her from her family** cette dispute l'a brouillée avec sa famille

estranged [ɪsˈtreɪndʒd] **ADJ an e. couple** des époux séparés; **her e. husband** son mari dont elle est séparée; **their e. son** leur fils avec qui ils sont brouillés

estrangement [ɪsˈtreɪndʒmənt] **N** (of person) aliénation f; (of two people) brouille f (**between** entre); (of married couple) séparation f

estrogen [ˈiːstrədʒən] **N** Am Biol, Chem œstrogène m

estrous [ˈiːstrəs] **ADJ** Am Biol (cycle) œstral

estrus [ˈiːstrəs] **N** Am Biol œstrus m

estuary [ˈestjʊ(ə)rɪ] **N** estuaire m; **the Thames e.** l'estuaire de la Tamise
▸▸ **e. English** = accent m standard teinté d'accent Cockney, prédominant à Londres et dans le sud-est de l'Angleterre, ne permettant pas d'identifier l'appartenance sociale du locuteur

ETA [iːtiːˈeɪ] **N** Aviat (abbr **estimated time of arrival**) heure f d'arrivée prévue

e-tail N vente f en ligne

et al [etˈæl] (abbr **et alii**) et autres

etc [etˈsetrə] **ADV** (abbr **et cetera**) etc; Fam **you have to fill in the form in duplicate e. e.** il faut remplir le formulaire en deux exemplaires etc, etc

et cetera [etˈsetrə] **ADV** et cætera

etceteras [etˈsetrəs] **NPL** extras mpl

etch [etʃ] **VT** Art, Typ (drawing etc) graver à l'eau-forte; (plate) graver; **to e. away the metal** enlever le métal à l'eau-forte; Fig **the scene was etched in his memory** la scène était gravée dans sa mémoire
VI faire de la gravure à l'eau-forte

etcher [ˈetʃər] **N** Art graveur m à l'eau-forte

etching [ˈetʃɪŋ] **N** Art (art) art m de graver à l'eau-forte; (individual work) gravure f à l'eau-forte, eau-forte, pl eaux-fortes; Hum **come up and see my etchings** monte, je vais te montrer ma collection d'estampes japonaises

ETD [iːtiːˈdiː] **N** (abbr **estimated time of departure**) = heure f de départ prévue

eternal [ɪˈtɜːn(ə)l] **ADJ** éternel; (continual) continuel, sans fin; **e. life** la vie éternelle; **e. quarrelling/complaints/gossip** querelles/plaintes/commérages incessant(e)s
N the E. l'Éternel m
▸▸ Fig **the e. triangle** l'éternel triangle m

eternally [ɪˈtɜːn(ə)lɪ] **ADV** éternellement; **I shall be e. grateful to you** je vous serai éternellement reconnaissant

eternity [ɪˈtɜːnɪtɪ] **N** éternité f; Fam **I waited an e.** j'ai attendu pendant une éternité
▸▸ **e. ring** = bague f entièrement sertie de pierres symbolisant l'éternité du mariage

ethane [ˈiːθeɪn] **N** Chem éthane m

ether [ˈiːθər] **N 1** Phys, Chem éther m **2** Arch, Lit **the e.** (heavens) la voûte éthérée, l'éther m

ethereal [ɪˈθɪərɪəl] **ADJ** éthéré; (form) léger, impalpable

ethereally [ɪˈθɪərɪəlɪ] **ADV** **e. beautiful** d'une beauté éthérée

etherize [ˈiːθəraɪz] **VT** Med éthériser

Ethernet® [ˈiːθənet] **N** Comput Ethernet® m

ethic [ˈeθɪk] **ADJ**
N (set of values) éthique f, work **e.** conception f du travail
▸▸ Gram **e. dative** datif m éthique

ethical [ˈeθɪk(ə)l] **ADJ** éthique, moral, -aux; **it's not e.** (morally wrong) ce n'est pas moral;

the doctor's behaviour was not e. (against professional ethics) le comportement du médecin n'était pas conforme au code déontologique
▸▸ Pharm **e. drug** = remède m vendu uniquement sur l'ordonnance d'un médecin; Fin **e. investment** investissement m éthique; Liter **e. writer** moraliste m

ethically [ˈeθɪklɪ] **ADV** d'après (les doctrines de) l'éthique; **she has behaved quite e.** son comportement a été tout à fait éthique ou moral; **e. questionable** d'une éthique douteuse

ethics [ˈeθɪks] **N** Phil éthique f, morale f; (of profession) déontologie f; **e. code, code of e.** code m déontologique VOIR GRAMMAIRE A10

Ethiopia [iːθɪˈəʊpɪə] **N** Éthiopie f

Ethiopian [iːθɪˈəʊpɪən] **ADJ** éthiopien
N Éthiopien, -ienne

ethnic [ˈeθnɪk] **ADJ** ethnique
N Am membre m d'une minorité ethnique
▸▸ **e. cleansing** purification f ethnique, nettoyage m ethnique; **e. community** communauté f ethnique; **e. minority** minorité f ethnique; **e. tourism** (travel to ancestral country) tourisme m ethnique

ethnically [ˈeθnɪklɪ] **ADV** du point de vue ethnique

ethnicity [eθˈnɪsɪtɪ] **N** appartenance f ethnique

ethnocentric [eθnəʊˈsentrɪk] **ADJ** ethnocentrique

ethnographer [eθˈnɒgrəfər] **N** ethnographe mf

ethnography [eθˈnɒgrəfɪ] **N** ethnographie f

ethnological [eθnəˈlɒdʒɪk(ə)l] **ADJ** ethnologique

ethnologically [eθnəˈlɒdʒɪklɪ] **ADV** ethnologiquement

ethnologist [eθˈnɒlədʒɪst] **N** ethnologue mf

ethnology [eθˈnɒlədʒɪ] **N** ethnologie f

ethological [iːθəˈlɒdʒɪk(ə)l] **ADJ** éthologique

ethology [ɪˈθɒlədʒɪ] **N** éthologie f

ethos [ˈiːθɒs] **N** (of people) génie m; (of company, class) culture f

Ethyl® [ˈeθɪl] **N** Chem éthyle m
▸▸ **e. alcohol** alcool m éthylique, éthanol m

ethylene [ˈeθɪliːn] **N** Chem éthylène m

etiolate [ˈiːtɪəʊleɪt] **VT** (plant) étioler

etiological [iːtɪəˈlɒdʒɪk(ə)l] **ADJ** Am étiologique

etiology [iːtɪˈɒlədʒɪ] **N** Am étiologie f

etiquette [ˈetɪket] **N** étiquette f, court **e.** cérémonial m de cour; **e. demands that ...** l'étiquette veut ou exige que ...; **professional e.** usages mpl professionnels

Etonian [iːˈtəʊnɪən] **N** Sch élève m (du collège) d'Eton; Old **E.** ancien élève d'Eton

Etruscan [ɪˈtrʌskən] Antiq **ADJ** étrusque
N Étrusque mf

etymological [etɪməˈlɒdʒɪk(ə)l] **ADJ** étymologique

etymologically [etɪməˈlɒdʒɪklɪ] **ADV** étymologiquement

etymologist [etɪˈmɒlədʒɪst] **N** étymologiste mf

etymology [etɪˈmɒlədʒɪ] **N** étymologie f

EU [iːˈjuː] **N** (abbr **European Union**) UE f; **EU legislation** législation f européenne

eucalyptus, pl **eucalypti, eucalyptuses** [juːkəˈlɪptəs, -taɪ, -təsɪz] **N** (tree) eucalyptus m
▸▸ **e. oil** essence f d'eucalyptus

Eucharist (the) [ðəˈjuːkərɪst] **N** Rel l'eucharistie f; **to receive the E.** recevoir l'eucharistie

Euclidean [juːˈklɪdɪən] **ADJ** (geometry) euclidien

eugenics [juːˈdʒenɪks] **N** eugénique f, eugénisme m VOIR GRAMMAIRE A10

eulogist [ˈjuːlədʒɪst] **N** panégyriste mf

eulogize [ˈjuːlədʒaɪz] **VT** (person, thing) faire l'éloge ou le panégyrique de

eulogy [ˈjuːlədʒɪ] **N** panégyrique m; **to pronounce a e. on sb** faire l'éloge ou le panégyrique de qn

eunuch [ˈjuːnək] **N** eunuque m

euphemism [ˈjuːfɪmɪz(ə)m] **N** euphémisme m

euphemistic [juːfɪˈmɪstɪk] **ADJ** euphémique

euphemistically [juːfɪˈmɪstɪklɪ] **ADV** par euphémisme; **e. known as ...** auquel on se réfère par euphémisme sous le terme de ...

euphonious [juːˈfəʊnɪəs] **ADJ** euphonique

euphonium [juːˈfəʊnɪəm] **N** Mus saxhorn m basse, basse f (des cuivres)

euphony [ˈjuːfənɪ] **N** euphonie f

euphorbia [juːˈfɔːbɪə] **N** Bot (plant) euphorbe f

euphoria [juːˈfɔːrɪə] **N** euphorie f

euphoric [juːˈfɒrɪk] **ADJ** euphorique

Eurasia [jʊəˈreɪʃə, -ʒə] **N** Eurasie f

Eurasian [jʊəˈreɪʃən, -ʒən] **ADJ** eurasien; (fauna etc) eurasiatique
N Eurasien, -ienne

eureka [juːˈriːkə] **INT** eurêka

eurhythmics [juːˈrɪðmɪks] **N** gymnastique f rythmique VOIR GRAMMAIRE A10

EURIBOR [ˈjʊərɪbɔːr] **N** Fin (abbr **Euro Interbank Offered Rate**) EURIBOR m, TIBEUR m

euro [ˈjʊərəʊ] **N** euro m
▸▸ **E. area** zone f euro; **E. MP** membre m du Parlement européen; **E. zone** zone euro

Euro- PREF euro-

Eurobank [ˈjʊərəʊbæŋk] **N** eurobanque f

Eurobarometer [jʊərəʊbəˈrɒmɪtər] **N** Eurobaromètre m

Eurobond [ˈjʊərəʊbɒnd] **N** euro-obligation f

eurocard [ˈjʊərəʊkɑːd] **N** Banking eurocarte f

Eurocheque [ˈjʊərəʊtʃek] **N** Banking eurochèque m

Eurocommunism [jʊərəʊˈkɒmjʊnɪz(ə)m] **N** Pol eurocommunisme m

Eurocrat [ˈjʊərəʊkræt] **N** eurocrate mf

eurocredit [ˈjʊərəʊkredɪt] **N** Com eurocrédit m

eurocurrency [ˈjʊərəʊkʌrənsɪ] **N** eurodevise f
▸▸ **e. market** marché m des eurodevises

Eurodollar [ˈjʊərəʊdɒlər] **N** eurodollar m

Euro-election N the Euro-elections les élections fpl européennes

Eurofranc [ˈjʊərəʊfræŋk] **N** eurofranc m

Euroland [ˈjʊərəʊlənd] **N** Euroland(e) f

Euroloan [ˈjʊərəʊləʊn] **N** eurocrédit m

Euromarket [ˈjʊərəʊmɑːkɪt] **N** marché m des eurodevises

Europe [ˈjʊərəp] **N** Europe f; **in E.** en Europe

European [jʊərəˈpiːən] **ADJ** européen
N Européen, -éenne
▸▸ Fin **E. Central Bank** Banque f centrale européenne; Pol **E. Coal and Steel Community** Communauté européenne de charbon et de l'acier; **E. Commission** Commission f européenne; Pol **E. Community** Communauté européenne; **E. Convention for the Protection of Human Rights and Fundamental Freedoms** Convention f européenne de sauvegarde des droits de l'homme et des libertés fondamentales; **E. Court of Human Rights** Cour européenne des droits de

l'homme; **E. Court of Justice** Cour européenne de justice; *Fin Formerly* **E. Currency Unit** Unité *f* monétaire européenne; **E. Customs Union** Union *f* douanière européenne; *Fin* **E. Development Fund** Fonds *m* européen de développement; *Pol* **E. Economic Area** Espace *m* économique européen; *Formerly* **E. Economic Community** Communauté économique européenne; *Fin Formerly* **E. Exchange Rate Mechanism** mécanisme *m* de change européen; **E. Free Trade Association** Association *f* européenne de libre-échange; *Fin* **E. Investment Bank** Banque européenne d'investissement; *Fin* **E. Monetary Institute** Institut *m* monétaire européen; *Fin Formerly* **E. Monetary System** Système *m* monétaire européen; **E. Parliament** Parlement *m* européen; **E. Patent Office** Office *m* européen des brevets; *Am* **E. plan** *(in hotel)* chambre *f* sans pension; **E. Political Cooperation** coopération *f* en matière de politique étrangère; **E. Regional Development Fund** Fonds européen de développement régional; *Fin* **E. Social Fund** Fonds social européen; **E. Standards Commission** Comité *m* européen de normalisation; **E. Union** Union européenne

Europeanize [jʊərə'piːənaɪz] **VT** européaniser

European-style option **N** *St Exch* option *f* européenne

Eurosceptic ['jʊərəʊskeptɪk] **N** eurosceptique *mf*

Eurotourism ['jʊərəʊtʊərɪz(ə)m] **N** eurotourisme *m*

Eurotunnel ['jʊərəʊtʌnəl] **N** Eurotunnel *m*

Eurovision ['jʊərəʊvɪʒən] **N** Eurovision *f*; **the E. song contest** le concours Eurovision de la chanson

euroyen ['jʊərəʊjen] **N** *Fin* euroyen *m*

Eustachian [juːˈsteɪʃən] **ADJ**
▸▸ *Anat* **E. tube** trompe *f* d'Eustache

euthanasia [juːθəˈneɪzɪə] **N** euthanasie *f*

EVA [iːviːˈeɪ] **N** *(abbr* **economic value added)** VAE *f*

evacuate [ɪˈvækjʊeɪt] **VT** *(place, population)* évacuer; *Tech (exhaust gases)* refouler; *Phys (create vacuum in)* faire le vide dans; **children were evacuated to the countryside** les enfants ont été évacués vers la campagne; *Physiol* **to e. the bowels** vider les intestins

evacuation [ɪvækjʊˈeɪʃən] **N** *(of place, people, bowels)* évacuation *f*; *Tech (of exhaust gases)* refoulement *m*; *Phys (creation of vacuum)* production *f* du vide

evacuee [ɪvækjʊˈiː] **N** évacué, -ée; **e. children** enfants évacués

evade [ɪˈveɪd] **VT** *(blow)* éviter, esquiver; *(danger)* éviter; *(creditors)* esquiver; *(justice, responsibility)* se soustraire à; *(obstacle, the law)* éluder, tourner; *(question, problem)* éluder; *(sb's vigilance)* déjouer; *(one's pursuers, detection)* échapper à, se dérober à; **to e. customs duty on sth** passer qch en fraude; **to e. tax** frauder le fisc; **success evades him** le succès lui échappe

> Note that the French verb **s'évader** is a false friend and is never a translation for the English verb **to evade**. It means **to escape**.

evader [ɪˈveɪdər] **N** **tax e.** fraudeur, -euse du fisc

evaluate [ɪˈvæljʊeɪt] **VT** *(danger, strength)* évaluer; *(damages)* évaluer, estimer le montant de

evaluation [ɪvæljʊˈeɪʃən] **N** évaluation *f*

evanescent [evəˈnesənt] **ADJ** évanescent, éphémère

evangelical [iːvænˈdʒelɪk(ə)l] *Rel* **ADJ** *(rela-*

ting to Gospels) évangélique; **an e. Christian/ church/sect** un chrétien/une église/une secte évangélique; **he's one of these e. Christians** c'est un de ces évangélistes; **e. preacher** évangéliste *mf*; **e. zeal** zèle *m* religieux; *Fig* **an e. vegetarian/communist** un végétarien/communiste à tout crin
N protestant, -ante évangélique

evangelicalism [iːvænˈdʒelɪkəlɪz(ə)m] **N** *Rel* évangélisme *m*

evangelism [ɪˈvændʒɪlɪz(ə)m] **N** *Rel* évangélisme *m*, prédication *f* de l'Évangile

evangelist [ɪˈvændʒɪlɪst] **N** *Rel* évangéliste *mf*

evangelize [ɪˈvændʒɪlaɪz] *Rel* **VT** évangéliser; *(person)* prêcher l'Évangile à
VI prêcher l'Évangile; *Fig* **to e. for a cause** prêcher une cause; **he has been evangelizing about jazz for years** il prêche les mérites du jazz depuis des années

evaporate [ɪˈvæpəreɪt] **VT** *(liquid)* (faire) évaporer; **evaporated milk** lait *m* condensé (non sucré)
VI *(of liquid etc)* s'évaporer; *(of acid)* se volatiliser; *Fig (of money)* disparaître comme par enchantement; *(of enthusiasm, hope etc)* s'envoler

evaporation [ɪvæpəˈreɪʃən] **N** *(of liquid)* évaporation *f*, *(of acid)* volatilisation *f*, *(of fears)* disparition *f*

evaporator [ɪˈvæpəreɪtər] **N** *Ind* évaporateur *m*

evasion [ɪˈveɪʒən] **N 1** *(act of dodging a commitment)* dérobade *f*; **by skilful e. of the more difficult questions** en se dérobant adroitement aux questions plus difficiles; **tax e.** évasion *f* fiscale **2** *(subterfuge)* subterfuge *m*, échappatoire *f*, faux-fuyant *m*, *pl* faux-fuyants; **without e.** sans détours

> Note that the French word **évasion** is a false friend and is rarely a translation for the English word **evasion**. Its most common meaning is **escape**.

evasive [ɪˈveɪsɪv] **ADJ** *(person)* évasif; *(personality)* fuyant; **to give an e. answer** faire une réponse évasive, répondre évasivement; *Mil etc* **to take e. action** faire une manœuvre d'évitement

evasively [ɪˈveɪsɪvlɪ] **ADV** *(to answer)* évasivement

evasiveness [ɪˈveɪsɪvnɪs] **N** caractère *m* évasif; **her e. increased our suspicions** ses propos évasifs ont renforcé nos soupçons

EVC [iːviːˈsiː] **N** *Mktg (abbr* **economic value to the customer)** valeur *f* économique apporté au consommateur

Eve [iːv] **N** Ève; *Br Culin* **E.'s pudding** = compote *f* de pommes recouverte de génoise

eve [iːv] **N 1** *(day before)* veille *f*, **Christmas E.** la veille de Noël; **New Year's E.** la Saint-Sylvestre; **on the e. of …** à la veille de …; *Fig* **to be on the e. of success** être à la veille du succès **2** *Arch, Lit (evening)* soir *m*

EVEN ['iːv(ə)n]

ADJ	plat **1** ▪ égal **1–3** ▪ pair **5**
ADV	même **1, 3** ▪ encore **2**
VT	égaliser

ADJ 1 *(surface, ground etc) (level)* plat, plan; *(smooth)* uni, égal, -aux; **to be e. with sth** être au niveau de *ou* à ras de qch; **to make e.** *(foundations of building)* araser; *(surface)* aplanir; *(edges of two planks etc)* affleurer **2** *(regular) (pulse)* égal, régulier; **to make e.** *(spacing)* égaliser; **e. temperature** température égale; **e. disposition** caractère *m* calme **3** *(equal)* égal, -aux; **he has an e. chance of succeeding** il a une chance sur deux de réus-

sir; **the chances** *or* **odds are about e. that …** il y a à peu près une chance sur deux que …; *Sport* **to be e.** être à égalité; **they are an e. match** ils sont à partie égale; *Fig* **to get e. with sb** prendre sa revanche sur qn; **to be e. with sb** être quitte avec qn; **I'll get e. with him yet** je la lui rendrai; *Sl* **to be e. Stevens** être quitte; *Sl* **to go e. Stevens with sb** partager fifty-fifty avec qn
4 *(fair)* **with an e. hand** impartialement; **e. bargain** marché *m* équitable *ou* juste
5 *(number)* pair; **odd or e.** pair ou impair
ADV 1 même; **it isn't e. amusing any more** ce n'est même plus amusant; **or e. …** ou même …; **e. the cleverest** même les plus habiles; **e. the children knew** même les enfants savaient; **I never e. saw it** je ne l'ai même pas vu; **without e. speaking** sans même dire un mot; **e. then she wouldn't believe me** même alors elle ne voulait pas me croire; **this would be sad, tragic e.** ça serait triste, tragique même
2 *(with comparatives)* encore; **e. more/less** encore plus/moins; **that would be e. worse/better** ce serait encore pis/mieux; **bring a friend – e. better, bring two** amène un ami – mieux encore, amène-en deux; **e. sadder than usual** encore plus triste que d'habitude
3 *(giving conditions)* même; **e. supposing that …** même en supposant que …; **e. if** même si; **e. if she came** même si elle venait; **e. though** même si; **e. though he has a car** bien que qu'il ait une voiture; **e. with a computer, the work would take months** même avec un ordinateur, le travail prendrait des mois; **e. so** cependant, quand même
4 *(with time)* **e. as I speak** au moment même où je parle; **e. now** à l'instant même; **e. now, four years later, I still haven't got over it** aujourd'hui encore, quatre ans plus tard, je ne m'en suis pas encore remis; **e. then** *(already)* déjà (à cette époque)
VT 1 *(make smooth) (surface etc)* aplanir, niveler, égaliser; *(two planks etc)* affleurer; *(foundations of a wall)* araser
2 *(make equal)* rendre égal; *Typ (spacing)* égaliser; **to e. the odds** égaliser les chances
▸▸ *Horseracing* **e. money** pari *m* avec enjeu égal; **horse quoted at e. money** cheval coté à égalité; *Fig* **I'll give you e. money that …** je te parie que …, je suis prêt à te parier que …; *Comput* **e. parity** parité *f*

▸ **even out** **VI** *(become smooth, flat)* s'aplanir, s'égaliser, se niveler; *(of curve on graph)* s'aplanir; **the road goes uphill and then evens out** la route monte, puis s'aplanit; **prices finally evened out** les prix ont fini par s'égaliser; **that should e. out over the lifetime of the entire project** cela devrait s'équilibrer sur la durée totale du projet
VT SEP *(make more equal, fairer) (taxation etc)* répartir également; **that evens things out** on est quitte(s)

▸ **even up** **VT SEP 1** *(make equal) (score etc)* égaliser; **that will e. things up** *(financially)* on sera quitte(s); *(in competition)* cela équilibrera les choses
2 *(sum)* arrondir au chiffre supérieur; **let's e. it up to a pound** arrondissons la somme à une livre

even-handed [-'hændɪd] **ADJ** équitable, juste, impartial, -aux

evening ['iːvnɪŋ] **N 1** soir *m*; *(duration)* soirée *f*; **tomorrow e.** demain soir; **yesterday e.** hier soir; **in the e.** le soir; **what do you do in the evenings?** qu'est-ce que vous faites le soir?; **at nine o'clock in the e.** à neuf heures du soir; **I'm going out this e.** je sors ce soir; **to have an e. out** sortir; **(on) that e.** ce soir-là; **(on) the e. before, (on) the previous e.** la veille au soir; **the next e.** le lendemain soir; **one** *or* **on a fine summer e.** (par) un beau soir d'été; **long winter evenings** longues soirées d'hiver; **every e.** tous les soirs; **every Monday e.** tous les lundis soir; **on the e. of Monday, 29th March** dans la soirée du lundi 29 mars; **all (the) e.** toute la soirée; **during the e.** pendant la soirée; *Fig Lit* **in the e. of life** au déclin de la vie SEE GRAMMAR B61 **2** *(evening party)* soirée *f*; **musical/cultural e.** soirée musicale/culturelle

▸▸ **e. class** cours *m* du soir; **e. dress** *(for men)* tenue *f* de soirée; *(for women)* robe *f* du soir; **in e. dress** en tenue de soirée; *Sport* **e. fixture** nocturne *f*, **e. gown** robe *f* de soirée *ou* du soir; *Sport* **e. match** nocturne; **e. paper** journal *m* du soir; *Theat* **e. performance** représentation *f* de soirée; *Rel* **e. prayers** office *m ou* service *m* du soir; **e. primrose oil** huile *f* d'onagre; *Rel* **e. service** office *ou* service du soir; *Astron* **e. star** étoile *f* du berger; **e. wear** *(for men)* tenue de soirée; *(for women)* robe du soir; **in e. wear** en tenue de soirée

> When translating **evening**, note that **soir** and **soirée** are not interchangeable. **Soir** is used to refer to the evening as part of the day as opposed to the morning or the afternoon. For **soirée**, the emphasis is on duration.

evenly [ˈiːv(ə)nlɪ] ADV **1** *(to stretch, knit)* uniment; **spread the glue e.** étaler la colle régulièrement **2** *(to breathe)* régulièrement; *(to say sth)* calmement **3** *(fairly)* *(to divide)* également; **e. matched** *(of equal size)* de grandeur égale; *(of equal strength)* de force égale

evenness [ˈiːvənnɪs] N **1** *(smoothness)* caractère *m* plat *ou* égal *ou* nivelé **2** *(regularity)* égalité *f*; *(of movement)* régularité *f* **3** *(calm)* *(of character)* calme *m*; *(of mood)* égalité *f*

even-numbered [ˈiːvənˈnʌmbəd] ADJ (portant un nombre) pair

evens [ˈiːv(ə)nz] NPL *(in betting)* **to lay e.** parier à l'égalité; **horses quoted at e.** chevaux cotés à égalité; **the bookmakers are offering e.** les bookmakers offrent un enjeu égal

evensong [ˈiːv(ə)nsɒŋ] N *Church of Eng* office *m* du soir

event [ɪˈvent] N **1** *(occurrence)* événement *m*; **it is going to be quite an e.** ça va être un véritable événement; **in the course of events** par la suite; **to be swept along by the tide** *or* **course of events** être emporté par le cours des événements; **as recent events have shown** comme l'ont montré de récents événements; *Fam* **a happy e.** *(birth)* un heureux événement; **when's the happy e.?** quand l'heureux événement doit-il avoir lieu? **2** *(outcome)* issue *f*, résultat *m*; **in either e.** dans l'un ou l'autre cas; **wise after the e.** sage après coup; **at all events, in any e.** en tout cas; **in the e. of his refusing** au cas *ou* dans le cas où il refuserait, pour le cas où il refuserait; **in the e. of (his) death** en cas de décès; **in the e. of rain** au cas où il pleuvrait, en cas de pluie **3** *Sport (meeting)* réunion *f* sportive; *(individual category, contest)* épreuve *f*, *Boxing, Fencing etc* rencontre *f*, **sporting e.** manifestation *f* sportive; **what was your best e.?** quelle a été ta meilleure discipline?

▸▸ *Mktg* **e. advertising** publicité *f* par l'événement; **e. management, events management** gestion *f* d'événements; **e. manager, events manager** organisateur, -trice d'événements; *Mktg* **e. promotion** communication *f* événementielle

even-tempered ADJ *(person)* d'humeur égale; **of an e. disposition** d'humeur égale

eventer [ɪˈventər] N *Horseriding* participant, -ante au concours complet

eventful [ɪˈventfʊl] ADJ *(life, journey, day)* mouvementé, plein d'incidents

eventide [ˈiːv(ə)ntaɪd] N *Lit* soir *m*
▸▸ *Br* **e. home** maison *f* de retraite

eventing [ɪˈventɪŋ] N *Horseriding* concours *m* complet d'obstacles

eventual [ɪˈventjʊəl] ADJ **1** *(final)* final, -als *ou* -aux, définitif; **his prodigality and his e. ruin** sa prodigalité et sa ruine finale **2** *Com (possible)* éventuel; **the e. profits from his new deal** les profits éventuels de sa nouvelle affaire

> Note that the French word **éventuel** is a false friend and is never a translation for the English word **eventual**. It means **possible**.

eventuality [ɪventjʊˈælɪtɪ] N éventualité *f*; **in that e.** dans cette éventualité

eventually [ɪˈventjʊəlɪ] ADV *(in the end)* finalement, en fin de compte; *(at future date)* par la suite; **he e. became a judge** il finit par être nommé juge; **they e. reached the castle** ils ont fini par arriver au château; **I'll get round to mending that door e.** je finirai par réparer cette porte un de ces jours; **don't worry, I will do it e.** ne t'en fais pas, tôt ou tard je le ferai

> Note that the French word **éventuellement** is a false friend and is never a translation for the English word **eventually**. It means **possibly**.

▸ **eventuate in** [ɪˈventjʊeɪt] VT INSEP *Fml* conduire à

EVER [ˈevər]

■ jamais **1**	■ toujours **2**

ADV **1** jamais; **I don't know if I'll e. see him again** je ne sais pas si je le reverrai un jour; **have you e. eaten caviar?** as-tu déjà mangé du caviar?; **I seldom, if e., read French** je lis rarement le français, pour ne pas dire jamais; **if I e. catch him** si jamais je l'attrape; **nothing e. happens** il n'arrive jamais rien; **hardly e., scarcely e.** presque jamais; **he's a liar if e. there was one** c'est un menteur s'il en fût jamais; **it started to rain faster than e.** il s'est mis à pleuvoir de plus belle; **without e. having thought of it** sans jamais y avoir pensé; **the best mother that e. was** la meilleure mère qui fût jamais; **it was the best/worst e.** c'était le meilleur/pire de tous; *Sl* **did you e.!** par exemple! **2** *(always)* toujours; **all she e. does is criticize** elle ne fait que critiquer; **e.-increasing influence** influence toujours plus grande; **e. the gentleman, he opened the door for her** en gentleman, comme toujours, il lui a ouvert la porte; **she was as cheerful as e.** elle était aussi gaie qu'à l'habitude; **for e.** pour toujours, à jamais; **to go away for e.** partir sans retour *ou* pour toujours; *Rel* **for e. and e.** à tout jamais, pour l'éternité; **Scotland for e.!** vive l'Écosse!; **to live for e.** vivre éternellement; **they lived happily e. after** ils vécurent heureux à tout jamais; *Old-fashioned* **yours e., e. yours** *(letter ending)* bien cordialement à vous, tout(e) à vous **3** *(intensive)* **it was the funniest sight e.** c'était à se tordre; *Fam* **e. so pretty** joli comme tout; *Fam* **it was e. so long ago** ça fait tellement longtemps; *Fam* **e. so many times** je ne sais combien de fois; *Fam* **thank you e. so much, thanks e. so** merci mille fois; *Fam* **I'm e. so pleased** j'en suis tellement content; *Fam* **e. so slightly ...** légèrement ...; *Fml* **be he e. so clever/handsome** si intelligent/beau qu'il soit; *Fam* **e. such a lot of money** une somme d'argent tellement importante; *Fam* **as if I e. would!** comme si

j'étais capable d'une chose pareille!; *Old-fashioned* **as quickly as e. you can** aussi vite que possible **4** *(in what/where/etc questions)* **what e. shall we do?** qu'est-ce que nous allons bien faire?; **what e.'s the matter with you?** mais qu'est-ce que vous avez donc?; **what e. can it be?** qu'est-ce que ça peut bien être?; **when e. will he come?** quand donc viendra-t-il?; **where e. have you been?** d'où venez-vous donc?; **who e. told you that?** qui est-ce qui a bien pu vous dire cela?; **why e. not?** mais pourquoi pas?; **how e. are we going to get back?** comment allons-nous bien pouvoir rentrer?; **how e. you manage I don't know** je me demande comment vous faites **5** **e. since (then)** dès lors, depuis; **I have been here e. since lunch** je suis là depuis le déjeuner; **he came to Scotland in 1990 and he's been here e. since** il est arrivé en Écosse en 1990 et il y est toujours resté **6** *esp Am Sl* **is he/she/it/etc e.!** *(generous, stupid, a beautiful day etc)* et comment!; **was I e. grateful for your help!** je te suis vraiment reconnaissant de m'avoir donné un coup de main!

evergreen [ˈevəgriːn] ADJ *Bot* à feuilles persistantes; *Fig* **e. topic** question *f* toujours d'actualité
N *(tree)* arbre *m* à feuilles persistantes; *(song)* classique *m*
▸▸ *Fin* **e. facility** possibilité *f* de crédit permanent; *Fin* **e. fund** fonds *m* de crédit permanent non confirmé; **e. oak** chêne *m* vert

everlasting [evəˈlɑːstɪŋ] ADJ **1** *(eternal)* éternel; *Bible* **the e. Father** le Père éternel; **Henry, to his e. credit, said nothing** Henry n'a rien dit, ce qui est tout à son honneur **2** *(material)* inusable, solide **3** *(continual)* perpétuel, continuel, sans fin
N **the E.** l'Éternel *m*
▸▸ *Bot* **e. flower** immortelle *f*, *Bot* **e. pea** pois *m* vivace

everlastingly [evəˈlɑːstɪŋlɪ] ADV *(eternally)* éternellement; *(continually)* perpétuellement

evermore [evəˈmɔːr] ADV *Lit* toujours; **for e.** à jamais

EVERY [ˈevrɪ]

■ chaque **1, 2**	■ tout **1**	■ tous les ... **1**
■ chacun **2, 4**		

ADJ VOIR GRAMMAIRE A35-6; B15-16 **1** *(indicating regular occurrence)* chaque, tout, tous les ...; **e. week** toutes les semaines, chaque semaine; **e. day** chaque jour, tous les jours; **it's not e. day you get married** ce n'est pas tous les jours qu'on se marie; **confidence is increasing e. day** la confiance s'accroît de jour en jour; **e. other** *or* **second day** tous les deux jours, un jour sur deux; **e. other Sunday** un dimanche sur deux; **e. other line/page** une ligne/page sur deux, toutes les deux lignes/pages; **e. second or third day** tous les deux ou trois jours; **e. third man was chosen** on choisissait un homme sur trois; **at e. quarter past the hour** toutes les heures, au quart; **e. few minutes** toutes les cinq minutes; **e. so often, e. now and again** *or* **then** de temps en temps, de temps à autre; **e. mile/few miles or so** tous les miles/deux ou trois miles **2** *(each)* chaque; **e. one** chacun, *f* chacune; **e. one of us was there** nous étions tous là; **they are my friends, e. one of them** ils sont tous mes amis; **I've checked e. single one** j'ai vérifié chacun d'entre eux; **at e. opportunity** chaque fois que c'est/c'était possible; **from e. side of** tous (les) côtés; **of e. kind** *or* **sort** de toute sorte; **of e. variety/age** de toutes les variétés/tous les âges; **e. word he says is a lie** tout ce qu'il dit est mensonge; **I have co-**

pied e. word of it je l'ai copié mot pour mot; **e. time (that) she comes** chaque fois qu'elle vient; **perseverance wins e. time** la persévérance l'emporte toujours; **e. man for himself** chacun pour soi; *(in danger)* sauve qui peut!; **e. person has this right** chacun a ce droit; **e. man Jack of them** tous sans exception

3 *(intensive)* he was e. inch a republican il était républicain jusqu'au bout des ongles; **I have e. reason to believe that ...** j'ai tout lieu de croire que ...; **you have e. right to be angry** tu as tout à fait le droit d'être en colère; **e. bit as good/intelligent as ...** tout aussi bon/ intelligent que ...; **she's e. bit as much to be pitied as he is** elle est tout autant à plaindre que lui; **I shall give you e. assistance** je vous aiderai de tout mon pouvoir; **I look forward with e. confidence to the future** j'envisage l'avenir avec une pleine confiance; **there's e. chance that he'll pull through** il a toutes les chances de s'en sortir; **we have e. hope that ...** nous avons grand espoir que ...; *Am* **e. which way I look** où que je regarde; *Am* **to look e. which way for sb** chercher qn partout; *Am* **(from) e. which way** de tous les côtés

4 *esp Fml* her e. action chacune de ses actions; **they hung on his e. word** ils ne perdaient pas un seul mot de ce qu'il disait; **his desire to meet your e. wish** son désir d'aller au-devant de chacun de vos désirs

everybody ['evrɪbɒdɪ] INDEF PRON tout le monde; **e. has his/her** *or* **their own way of doing things** chacun/chacune a sa manière de faire les choses; **I don't know about e. else, you guys, but I'm going home** je ne sais pas ce que vous comptez faire, les mecs, mais moi je rentre chez moi; **I don't know about e. else, but I'll be there** je ne sais pas ce que les autres comptent faire, mais moi je serai là; **e. knows that** tout le monde *ou* n'importe qui sait cela; **not e. can do it** ce n'est pas tout le monde qui pourrait le faire; **e. who is anybody** toutes les personnes importantes; **e. else** tous les autres; **e. seems to know e. else** tout le monde semble se connaître VOIR GRAMMAIRE A36

everyday ['evrɪdeɪ] ADJ ATTRIB **1** *(daily)* journalier, quotidien; *(ordinary)* fait banal; **e. occurrence** *(happening every day)* fait *m* journalier; **it's an e. occurrence** cela arrive tous les jours; **e. life** la vie quotidienne; **e. routine** train-train *m* quotidien **2** *(used every day)* de tous les jours; **for e. wear** pour porter tous les jours **3** *(ordinary)* usuel, ordinaire; **e. English** l'anglais de tous les jours; **e. expression** expression *f* courante; **words in e. use** mots d'usage courant

everyone ['evrɪwʌn] INDEF PRON = **everybody**

everyplace ['evrɪpleɪs] ADV *Am Fam* = **everywhere**

everything ['evrɪθɪŋ] INDEF PRON tout; **he has eaten e.** il a tout mangé; **e. good** tout ce qu'il y a de bon; **e. I did seemed to go wrong** tout ce que je faisais semblait mal tourner; **(a place for e. and) e. in its place** chaque chose à sa place; **they sell e.** on y vend de tout; *Com* **e. for cyclists** tout ce qui concerne le cyclisme; **money is not e.** l'argent n'est pas tout; **beauty isn't e.** il n'y a pas que la beauté (qui compte); **she's e. to me** elle est tout pour moi; *Fam* **to call sb e.** traiter qn de tous les noms; *Fam* **we're in a bad way with strikes and e.** ça marche mal à cause des grèves et de tout ça VOIR GRAMMAIRE A36; B15–16

everywhere ['evrɪweər] ADV partout, en tous lieux; **to look e. for sb/sth** chercher qn/qch partout; **e. you go** partout où vous allez, où que vous alliez; **e. you look there is poverty** de quelque côté que l'on se

tourne, on voit la pauvreté; **e. in France** partout en France

evict [ɪ'vɪkt] VT *(tenant)* évincer, expulser (**from** de); *(from meeting, court-room)* expulser; **evicted tenant** locataire *m* évincé

eviction [ɪ'vɪkʃən] N *Law (of tenant)* éviction *f*, expulsion *f*; **e. notice, e. order** avis *m* d'expulsion

evidence ['evɪdəns] N **1** *(reason for belief)* preuve *f*; **there was clear e. that ...** il était clair *ou* manifeste que ...; **there is no e. to suggest a link between the two diseases** il n'y a aucune preuve suggérant qu'il y ait un lien entre les deux maladies; **they gave no e. of this** ils n'en laissaient paraître aucun signe; **on the e. of their past performances** si l'on en juge par leurs performances passées; **on this e., the answer would seem to be 'yes'** autant qu'on puisse en juger ici, la réponse semblerait être 'oui'

2 *(indication)* signe *m*, marque *f*; **to bear e. of sth** porter la marque de qch; **there was no e. of his stay in the house** rien ne marquait qu'il eût séjourné dans la maison; **the books were e. of her interest in the subject** les livres étaient le signe *ou* l'indication de son intérêt pour le sujet; **to be in e.** *(of person, thing)* être en évidence; **the army was much in e. on the streets** l'armée était très fortement présente dans les rues

3 *Law* preuves *fpl*; *(testimony)* témoignage *m*; **there wasn't enough e. to convict them** il n'y avait pas suffisamment de preuves pour qu'on les condamne; **internal e.** preuves intrinsèques; **external e.** preuves extrinsèques; **oral e.** preuve orale; **written/ documentary e.** preuve littérale/documentaire; **to give e.** témoigner, déposer (en justice); **to give e. in sb's favour** témoigner en faveur de qn; **to call sb in e.** appeler qn à la barre des témoins; **the e. was strongly against him** les témoignages pesaient contre lui; **whatever you say may be given in e.** tout ce que vous direz pourra être retenu contre vous; **to turn** *Br* **King's/Queen's** *or Am* **State's e.** témoigner contre ses complices *(sous promesse de pardon)*

VT *Fml* témoigner de; **as evidenced by ...** comme en témoigne ...

Note that the French noun **évidence** is a false friend and is never a translation for the English word **evidence**. It means **obviousness**.

evident ['evɪdənt] ADJ évident, manifeste; *(fact, truth)* patent; **it was e. that ...** il était évident *ou* clair que ...; **that was far from e.** c'était loin d'être évident

evidently ['evɪdəntlɪ] ADV **1** *(clearly)* à l'évidence, manifestement; **he was e. afraid** il était évident *ou* clair qu'il avait peur; **e. worried** manifestement inquiet; **e., such a dangerous criminal must be caught** il est évident qu'un criminel aussi dangereux doit être arrêté; **I got held up – e.** j'ai été retardé – c'est ce qu'il semblerait **2** *(apparently)* apparemment; **he's been away** apparemment il a été absent, il semblerait qu'il ait été absent; **e. not** il semble bien que non, apparemment non

Note that the French word **évidemment** is a false friend and is never a translation for the English word **evidently**. It means **of course**.

evil ['iːv(ə)l] ADJ **1** *(person, look)* mauvais, malveillant; *(spirit)* malfaisant, malin; *(moment)* funeste; **the E. One** le Malin; **to silence e. tongues** faire taire la médisance; **house of e. repute** lieu *m* mal famé; *Lit* **to fall on e. days** tomber dans l'infortune *ou* dans le malheur; *Fam* **to put off the e. hour** *(of visit to*

dentist etc) repousser le moment fatal; **e. influence** influence *f* néfaste; **e. intentions** mauvaises intentions *fpl*; **e. omen** présage *m* de malheur; **e. tongue** mauvaise langue *f* **2** *(smell)* mauvais, nauséabond

N mal *m*, *pl* maux; **to choose the lesser of two evils** choisir entre deux maux le moindre; **a social e.** une plaie sociale; **to speak e. of sb** dire du mal de qn; **the evils of drink** les effets néfastes de la boisson

▸▸ **the e. eye** le mauvais œil

evildoer ['iːv(ə)lduːər] N *Lit* malfaiteur *m*

evil-looking ADJ *(man)* louche; *(knife)* vilain

evilly ['iːvɪlɪ] ADV *(to laugh, leer etc)* avec malveillance; *(to look at sb)* d'un mauvais œil, d'un air méchant

evil-minded ADJ malintentionné, malveillant

evil-smelling ADJ nauséabond

evince [ɪ'vɪns] VT *Fml (quality, talent etc)* faire montre de, témoigner; *(curiosity, enthusiasm etc)* manifester

Note that the French verb **évincer** is a false friend and is never a translation for the English verb **to evince**. It means **to oust**.

eviscerate [ɪ'vɪsəreɪt] VT **1** éviscérer, éventrer **2** *Fig (literary work etc)* émasculer

evisceration [ɪvɪsə'reɪʃən] N éviscération *f*

evocation [evə'keɪʃən] N évocation *f*

evocative [ɪ'vɒkətɪv] ADJ évocateur, -trice (**of** de)

evoke [ɪ'vəʊk] VT **1** *(conjure up) (memory)* évoquer **2** *(provoke)* **this remark evoked a smile** cette observation a provoqué *ou* suscité un sourire

evoked set [ɪ'vəʊkt] N *Mktg* ensemble *m* évoqué

evolution [iːvə'luːʃən] N **1** *Biol, Fig (of species, project etc)* évolution *f*, développement *m*; **the theory of e.** la théorie de l'évolution des espèces; *Fig* **the e. of events** le déroulement des événements; **her e. from journalist to revolutionary leader** son passage de la carrière de journaliste à celle de dirigeante d'un groupe révolutionnaire **2** *(manoeuvre) (of acrobat, troops etc)* évolution *f*

evolutionary [iːvə'luːʃən(ə)rɪ] ADJ *Biol (character, symptom, disease)* évolutif

evolutionism [iːvə'luːʃənɪz(ə)m] N *Biol* évolutionnisme *m*

evolutionist [iːvə'luːʃənɪst] ADJ, N *Biol* évolutionniste *mf*

evolve [ɪ'vɒlv] VT *(plan)* dérouler, développer; *(theory, truth)* développer, déduire (**from** de); **some species evolved wings** des ailes se sont développées chez certaines espèces

VI *(of events)* se dérouler; *(of situation, race etc)* se développer, évoluer; **the scheme evolved from a pilot project** ce programme a été développé à partir d'un projet-pilote; **medicine has evolved into a sophisticated science** la médecine est devenue une science sophistiquée

ewe [juː] N brebis *f*

ewer ['juːər] N *Old-fashioned* pot *m* à eau; *(on washstand)* broc *m* de toilette

ex [eks] PREP **1** *Com (out of)* **ex quay** à quai; **ex ship** à bord; **ex warehouse** à (prendre à) l'entrepôt, en entrepôt; **ex works** départ usine, sortie d'usine; **price ex works** prix *m* départ usine, prix sortie d'usine **2** *Fin (without)* **ex all, ex allotment** ex-répartition *f*; **ex bonus** ex-capitalisation *f*; **ex cap, ex capitalisation** ex-capitalisation; **ex coupon** ex-coupon *m*, coupon *m* détaché; **ex dividend** ex-dividende *m*, dividende *m* détaché; **ex in-**

terest sans *ou* exonéré d'intérêts; **ex rights** ex-droit *m*

N *Fam (former husband, girlfriend etc)* ex *mf inv*

ex- [eks] **PREF** *(former)* ancien, ex-; **ex-minister** ex-ministre *m*; **an ex-teacher** un ancien professeur; **ex-wife** ex-femme *f*; **ex-husband** ex-mari *m*; **all her ex-boyfriends** tous ses ex

exacerbate [eg'zæsəbeɪt] **VT 1** *(pain, situation, sb's difficulties etc)* exacerber, aggraver **2** *(person)* irriter, exaspérer

exact [ɪg'zækt] **ADJ** exact, précis; **at the e. moment when ...** au moment précis *ou* au moment même où ...; **she was very e. in her reporting of events** elle a été très précise dans son compte-rendu des événements; **in the south of France, the Dordogne, to be more e.** dans le sud de la France, en Dordogne, pour être plus précis; **to give e. details** donner des détails précis *ou* des précisions, préciser; **an e. replica** une réplique exacte; **those were her e. words** c'est ce qu'elle a dit mot pour mot; **the e. word to describe Joanna** le mot juste pour décrire Joanna; **that wasn't the e. word he used** ce n'est pas exactement le mot qu'il a employé; **to tender the e. amount** *(on bus)* faire l'appoint; **the e. opposite** exactement le contraire; *Fml* **to be e.** *(in payments)* être exact; *(in business)* être strict **VT** *(take) (tax)* exiger (**from** de); *(ransom, promise)* extorquer (**from** à); *(insist on) (obedience)* exiger, réclamer (**from** de)
▸▸ **e. sciences** sciences *fpl* exactes

exacting [ɪg'zæktɪŋ] **ADJ** *(person)* exigeant; *(work)* astreignant

exaction [ɪg'zækʃən] **N** *Fml (of taxes, money)* exaction *f*; *(of promise)* extorsion *f*

exactitude [ɪg'zæktɪtjuːd] **N** *Fml (of report)* exactitude *f*, précision *f*; *(of reasoning, calculation)* exactitude, justesse *f*; **to say sth with e.** dire qch précisément *ou* exactement

exactly [ɪg'zæktlɪ] **ADV 1** exactement, précisément; *(of time)* juste; **I don't know e. what happened** je ne sais pas au juste ce qui est arrivé; **I don't e. know where he is** je ne sais pas exactement où il se trouve; **I'm not e. sure what you mean** je ne suis pas tout à fait sûr de ce que tu veux dire; **where e. in France did you go?** où exactement êtes-vous allés en France?; **that's e. right!** c'est exactement cela!; **but that's e. what I mean!** mais c'est précisément ce que je veux dire!; **it's e. the same thing** c'est exactement la même chose; **at e. the right/wrong moment** exactement *ou* juste au bon/mauvais moment; **e.!** précisément!, parfaitement!; **e. so!** exactement!; **it is e. five** il est cinq heures juste; **not e.** pas précisément; **she didn't e. agree, but ...** elle n'était pas vraiment d'accord, mais ...; **he is not e. a scholar** ce n'est pas précisément un savant **2** *(with precision)* précisément, exactement; **e. calibrated** précisément étalonné

exactness [ɪg'zæktnɪs] **N** exactitude *f*

exaggerate [ɪg'zædʒəreɪt] **VT** exagérer **VI** exagérer; **let's not e.!** n'exagérons rien!

exaggerated [ɪg'zædʒəreɪtɪd] **ADJ** exagéré; *(praise)* outré; **e. behaviour** comportement *m* excessif; **to have an e. opinion of oneself** avoir une trop haute opinion de soi-même; **to attach e. importance to sth** prêter une importance excessive à qch

exaggeratedly [ɪg'zædʒəreɪtɪdlɪ] **ADV** exagérément

exaggeration [ɪgzædʒə'reɪʃən] **N** exagération *f*; **it would be no e. to say that ...** on pourrait dire sans exagérer *ou* sans exagération que ...; **without e.** sans exagération; **that's an e.!** vous exagérez!/ils exagèrent!/*etc*

exalt [ɪg'zɔːlt] **VT 1** *(praise) (sb's virtues)* exalter, vanter; **to e. sb to the skies** porter qn jusqu'aux nues **2** *(raise in rank)* élever

exalted [ɪg'zɔːltɪd] **ADJ 1** *(sentiment)* exalté; *(tone)* élevé **2** *(rank)* élevé; *(person)* haut placé

exam [ɪg'zæm] **N** = examination 1

examination [ɪgzæmɪ'neɪʃən] **N 1** *Sch etc* examen *m*; **competitive e.** concours *m*; **to take** *or* **sit an e.** passer *ou* subir un examen; **to pass/fail an e.** être reçu/refusé à un examen

2 *(inspection)* examen *m*; *Med (of vagina, rectum)* toucher *m*; *(of machines etc)* inspection *f*, visite *f*; *(of accounts)* vérification *f*; *(of report)* dépouillement *m*; *Law (of files etc)* compulsation *f*; **on e.** après examen, examen fait; **on further e.** après un examen plus approfondi; **the matter is under e.** l'affaire est à l'étude; **to undergo a medical e.** passer une visite médicale

3 *Law (of accused)* interrogatoire *m*; *(of witness)* audition *f*, *(of case)* instruction *f*; **to be put under e.** *(accused)* subir un interrogatoire; *(witness)* être entendu; **he admitted, under e., ...** il a admis, lors de l'interrogatoire/l'audition, ...
▸▸ **e. paper** *(set of questions)* sujet *m* d'examen; *(written answer)* copie *f* (d'examen)

examine [ɪg'zæmɪn] **VT 1** *(inspect) (machine)* examiner, inspecter; *(in Customs) (baggage)* fouiller, examiner; *(accounts)* vérifier; *(passport)* contrôler; *(files etc)* compulser, étudier, examiner; *(inventory, account)* dépouiller; *Med (patient)* examiner; **to e. one's conscience** faire son examen de conscience; **to e. a question thoroughly** examiner une question à fond

2 *Sch etc (pupil)* examiner, faire passer un examen à; **to e. a candidate in Latin** examiner un candidat en latin

3 *Law etc (accused)* interroger, faire subir un interrogatoire à; *(witness)* interroger, entendre; *(case)* instruire

examinee [ɪgzæmɪ'niː] **N** *Sch etc* candidat, -ate

examiner [ɪg'zæmɪnər] **N 1** *(of baggage etc)* inspecteur, -trice; *(of files etc)* compulseur *m* **2** *Sch etc* examinateur, -trice; **the examiners** le jury (d'examen)

examining [ɪg'zæmɪnɪŋ] **ADJ**
▸▸ **e. body** jury *m* d'examen; *Br Law* **e. magistrate** juge *m* d'instruction

example [ɪg'zɑːmp(ə)l] **N 1** exemple *m*; **to give an e.** donner un exemple; **to give just one e., ...** pour ne donner *ou* citer qu'un exemple, ...; **to quote sth as an e.** citer qch à titre d'exemple; **she showed me some examples of her work** elle m'a montré des spécimens de son travail; **a perfect e. of what not to do in a crisis** un exemple parfait de ce qu'il ne faut pas faire dans une crise; **for e.** par exemple; **large towns, (as) for e. London** les grandes villes, telles que Londres (par exemple); **by way of e.** en guise d'exemple

2 *(model)* exemple *m*; **to set an e.** donner l'exemple; **to set a good/bad e. for sb** donner le bon/mauvais exemple à qn; **I wish you would set a better e. for your sister** j'aimerais bien que tu donnes un peu mieux l'exemple à ta sœur; **to be an e.** *or* **a good e. to sb** être un exemple *ou* un bon exemple pour qn; **their father wasn't a very good e.** leur père n'a pas été un très bon exemple; **let that be an e. to you!** que ça te serve d'exemple!; **to make an e. of sb** faire un exemple de qn, punir qn pour l'exemple; **to take sb as an e.** prendre exemple sur qn; **to follow sb's e.** suivre l'exemple de qn

exasperate [ɪg'zɑːspəreɪt] **VT** exaspérer, irriter; **exasperated at** *or* **by his insolence** exaspéré par son insolence; **an exasperated look/voice** un regard/une voix exaspéré(e); **an exasperated gesture** un geste d'exaspération

exasperating [ɪg'zɑːspəreɪtɪŋ] **ADJ** exaspérant, irritant

exasperatingly [ɪg'zɑːspəreɪtɪŋlɪ] **ADV** d'une manière exaspérante *ou* irritante; **to be e. slow/obstinate** être d'une lenteur/obstination exaspérante; **they had come e. close to winning** ils avaient frôlé la victoire de si près que c'en était exaspérant

exasperation [ɪgzæspə'reɪʃən] **N** exaspération *f*; **to drive sb to e.** pousser qn à bout; **'shut up!', she screamed in e.** 'tais-toi!', cria-t-elle, exaspérée

excavate ['ekskəveɪt] **VT** *(tunnel)* excaver, creuser; *(soil)* fouiller; *(canal)* approfondir; *(ruins etc)* déterrer; *Archeol* **to e. a site** faire des fouilles
VI *Archeol* faire des fouilles; *Constr* procéder à une/des excavation(s)

excavation [ekskə'veɪʃən] **N 1** *(action)* excavation *f*, *(of ground, soil)* approfondissement *m*; **the e. of a site** les fouilles *fpl* conduites dans un site **2** *(site)* terrain *m* excavé; *Archeol* fouille *f*; **the excavations at Pompeii** les fouilles de Pompéi

excavator ['ekskəveɪtər] **N 1** *Constr (machine)* excavateur *m*, excavatrice *f*, pelleteuse *f* **2** *Archeol (person)* personne *f* qui fait des fouilles

exceed [ɪk'siːd] **VT** *(limits etc)* excéder, dépasser; *(hopes, fears, ambitions)* dépasser; *(other products)* surpasser (**in** en); **not exceeding ten pounds** ne dépassant pas dix livres; **not exceeding 250 g** *(parcels etc)* jusqu'à 250 g; **do not expose to temperatures exceeding 50°C** ne pas exposer à des températures excédant 50°C; **to e. one's instructions** aller au-delà des instructions reçues; **to e. one's rights/one's powers** outrepasser ses droits/sa compétence; *Aut* **to e. the speed limit** dépasser *ou* excéder la limitation de vitesse; **he was fined for exceeding the speed limit** il a eu une contravention pour excès de vitesse; **the outcome exceeded all our hopes** le résultat a dépassé toutes nos espérances; **demand exceeded supply** la demande a excédé l'offre

exceedingly [ɪk'siːdɪŋlɪ] **ADV** extrêmement

excel [ɪk'sel] (**-ll-**) **VI** exceller (**at doing sth** à faire qch); **to e. at a game** exceller à un jeu; **at school, she excelled in chemistry** à l'école, elle excellait en chimie
VT *(person)* surpasser; **to e. oneself** se surpasser; *Iron* **he's excelled himself this time** il s'est surpassé cette fois-ci

excellence ['eksələns] **N** qualité *f*, supériorité *f*, excellence *f*; **students are expected to strive for e.** on demande aux étudiants de s'efforcer à atteindre l'excellence; **centre of e.** centre *m* d'excellence

excellency ['eksələnsɪ] **N** *(title)* **Your E.** Votre Excellence *f*; **his E. the French Ambassador** Son Excellence l'ambassadeur de France

excellent ['eksələnt] **ADJ** excellent, parfait

excellently ['eksələntlɪ] **ADV** admirablement; **she had done e. in her exams** elle avait excellé à ses examens, elle avait obtenu d'excellents résultats à ses examens

except¹ [ɪk'sept] **PREP** sauf, excepté, à l'exception de; **nobody e. him** personne excepté *ou* sauf lui; **all e. the doctor** tous, à l'exception du docteur, tous, sauf le docteur; **nobody heard me. (for) me** personne ne l'a entendu sauf moi; **e. by agreement between the parties** sauf accord entre les parties; **they could do nothing e. pray** ils ne pouvaient rien faire d'autre que prier; **e.**

when sauf quand; **e. for** à part, si ce n'est; **e. for getting a few scratches, she came out of it uninjured** à part quelques égratignures, elle s'en est tirée indemne; **we would have lost e. for you** sans toi nous aurions perdu; **the dress is ready e. for the buttons** la robe est prête, à l'exception des boutons; **you cannot obtain such permission e. by paying a bribe to local officials** on ne peut obtenir une telle permission qu'en soudoyant les autorités locales

CONJ e. (that) excepté que, si ce n'est que; **he came out of it unscathed, e. that he lost his hat** il en est sorti indemne, si ce n'est qu'il a perdu son chapeau; **I would go, e. I'm busy** j'irais bien, mais je suis occupé

except² VT excepter, exclure (**from** de); **present company excepted** les présents exceptés

excepting [ɪk'septɪŋ] PREP à l'exception de, sauf; **not e. my wife** sans excepter ma femme

exception [ɪk'sepʃən] N **1** exception f; **to make an e. (of sth/for sb)** faire une exception (pour qch/qn); *Prov* **the e. proves the rule** l'exception confirme la règle; **without e.** sans (aucune) exception; **with the e. of ...** à l'exception de ..., exception faite de ...; **with a few exceptions** sauf de rares exceptions, à quelques exceptions près; **with certain exceptions** sauf exceptions **2 to take e. to sth** *(object)* trouver à redire à qch; *(take offence)* se formaliser ou s'offenser de qch; **to take e. to sb's doing sth** trouver mauvais que qn fasse qch; **I take great e. to that remark** je trouve cette remarque très offensante

exceptionable [ɪk'sepʃənəb(ə)l] ADJ *Fml (usu with negative)* critiquable; *(offensive)* offensant; **nothing e.** rien de critiquable/d'offensant; **to find nothing e. in sth** ne rien trouver à redire à qch; *(offensive)* ne rien trouver d'offensant à qch

exceptional [ɪk'sepʃən(ə)l] ADJ *(unusual, outstanding)* exceptionnel
▸▸*Acct* **e. item** poste *m* extraordinaire

exceptionally [ɪk'sepʃən(ə)lɪ] ADV *(unusually)* exceptionnellement, extraordinairement; **e. cheap** d'un prix exceptionnellement bas; **an e. fine day** un jour exceptionnellement beau; **e., no bail was granted** à titre exceptionnel, il n'a pas été accordé de remise en liberté sous caution; **e. gifted child** enfant remarquablement doué; **an e. well-made film** un film d'une qualité exceptionnelle

excerpt ['eksɜːpt] N *Liter, Mus* extrait *m* (**from** de)

excess [ɪk'ses] N **1** *(of light, enthusiasm etc)* excès *m*; **to eat/drink to e.** manger/boire à l'excès; **indulgence carried to e.** indulgence poussée trop loin; **to commit excesses** commettre des excès; *(cruel acts)* commettre des cruautés; **to be given to e.** avoir le goût des excès; **to indulge in e.** tomber dans l'excès **2** *(quantity, sum etc)* excédent *m*; **to pay the e. (on one's ticket)** prendre un supplément; **sum in e.** somme f en surplus; **sum in e. of 50** somme au-dessus de 50; **there has been an e. of expenditure over revenue** les dépenses ont excédé les recettes **3** *Br Fin (in insurance)* franchise f
▸▸**e. baggage** *(on plane)* excédent de bagages; *Br* **e. fare** supplément *m* de prix; **e. luggage** *(on plane)* excédent de bagages; **e. profit** surprofit *m*; **e. supply** suroffre f; **e. weight** excédent de poids

excessive [ɪk'sesɪv] ADJ *(heat, fine, expenses, amount)* excessif; *(zeal, desire)* immodéré; *(virtue)* outré, exagéré; *(ambition)* démesuré; **to be an e. drinker/smoker** boire/fumer à l'excès

excessively [ɪk'sesɪvlɪ] ADV *(expensive, hot)* excessivement; *(clever, stupid, polite)* extrêmement, particulièrement; *(to eat, drink)* à l'excès; **it was hot/damaged, but not e. so** il faisait chaud/il était endommagé, mais pas trop; **to be e. generous** être (par) trop généreux; **he's not e. intelligent** il n'est pas particulièrement intelligent

exchange¹ [ɪks'tʃeɪndʒ] N **1** *(of prisoners, blows etc)* échange *m*; **e. of views** échange de vues; **we had an angry** *or* **heated e.** nous avons eu des mots; **in e. (for sth)** en reprise f, *Admin* **e. of posts** *(of two officials, civil servants)* permutation f, **2** *Fin (of currency)* change *m*; **foreign e.** change; **dollar e.** change du dollar ou en dollars; *Am* **exchanges** *(bills)* lettres fpl de change, traites fpl; **(foreign) e. broker** cambiste mf, **(foreign) e. office** bureau *m* de change; **(foreign) e. reserves** réserves fpl en devises (étrangères); **at the current rate of e.** au cours du jour, au taux du change du jour **3** *Fin* **(Stock) E.** Bourse f (des valeurs); **commodities e.** bourse de commerce; **corn e.** bourse des céréales; *Am Mil* **post e.** économat *m* de l'armée **4** *(telephone)* **e.** central *m* téléphonique; **local e. area** = réseau *m* urbain
▸▸**e. bank** = banque f s'occupant d'opérations de change; *Br Fin* **e. control** contrôle *m* des changes; *Fin* **e. dealer** cambiste mf, agent *m* de change, courtier, -ière de change; *Fin* **e. gain** gain *m* de change; *Fin* **e. index** indice *m* boursier; *Fin* **e. loss** perte f de change; *Fin* **e. market** marché *m* des changes; **e. office** bureau *m* central (téléphonique); *Fin* **e. premium** prime f de change; *Fin* **e. rate** taux *m* de change, cours *m* de change; *Fin Formerly* **E. Rate Mechanism** mécanisme *m* (des taux) de change (du SME); **e. rate parity** parité f du change; **e. rate stability** stabilité f des changes; *Nucl* **e. reaction** réaction f d'échange; *Fin* **e. restrictions** contrôle des changes; *Sch, Univ* **e. student** = étudiant qui participe à un échange; *Fin* **e. transaction** opération f de change; *Med* **e. transfusion** transfusion f d'échange; *Fin* **e. value** contre-valeur f, pl contre-valeurs, valeur f d'échange; *Sch* **e. visit** échange *m*

exchange² VT *(blows, words, prisoners)* échanger; *(foodstuffs etc)* troquer; **to e. sth for sth** échanger/troquer qch pour ou contre qch, faire un échange de qch pour ou contre qch; **records exchanged for money** *(sign)* rachat de disques; **to e. glances** échanger un regard/des regards; **to e. views** échanger ses vues; *Admin* **to e. posts with sb** permuter avec qn

exchangeable [ɪks'tʃeɪndʒəb(ə)l] ADJ échangeable (**for** pour, contre); **a voucher which is e. for goods** un bon qui peut être échangé contre des marchandises

exchequer [eks'tʃekər] N *Br Admin* **the E.** *(money)* le Trésor public; *(government department)* ≃ le Ministère des Finances; **the Chancellor of the E.** le Chancelier de l'Exchiquier, ≃ le Ministre des Finances
▸▸*Fin* **e. bill** bon *m* du Trésor

excise¹ ['eksaɪz] N *Admin (tax)* contributions fpl indirectes, *Belg* accise f, *(department)* service *m* des contributions indirectes, régie f, *Br* **Customs and E.** la Régie
▸▸**e. documents** documents mpl administratifs de régie; **e. duties** droits mpl de régie; **e. officer** receveur *m* des douanes

excise² [ɪk'saɪz] VT *Surg (tumour etc)* exciser; *Fig (passage)* couper (**from a book** d'un livre)

exciseman, pl **excisemen** ['eksaɪzmən] N *Br Hist* employé *m* de l'excise ou de la régie

excision [ɪk'sɪʒən] N excision f, coupure f; *Surg* excision f, abscission f, ablation f

excitable [ɪk'saɪtəb(ə)l] ADJ **1** *(person, temperament)* émotif; **young children tend to be easily e.** les jeunes enfants ont tendance à être facilement surexcités; **they are an easily e. people** c'est un peuple exubérant; **be careful with him, he's rather easily e.** fais attention avec lui, il est assez excitable **2** *Elec, Physiol* excitable

excite [ɪk'saɪt] VT **1** *(get worked up)* agiter, énerver, surexciter; **don't e. him** ne l'énerve pas; **easily excited** surexcitable **2** *(arouse enthusiasm in)* enthousiasmer, *Fam* emballer; **the idea/prospect clearly excited them** il était évident que l'idée/la perspective les animait ou enthousiasmait; **it really excites me** ça m'emballe vraiment; **what excites you in life?** qu'est-ce qui vous passionne dans la vie? **3** *(stimulate)* exciter, animer; *(feeling, passion)* stimuler; *(sexually)* exciter; *Physiol (nerve)* exciter, stimuler **4** *(give rise to)* provoquer, exciter, soulever; *(feeling, admiration, fear)* inspirer, provoquer; *(interest)* susciter; *(sb's curiosity)* piquer **5** *Elec (dynamo, relay etc)* exciter, amorcer

excited [ɪk'saɪtɪd] ADJ **1** *(worked up)* énervé, surexcité, agité; *(impatient)* impatient; *(upset)* troublé; **e. children** enfants surexcités; **e. crowd** foule surexcitée ou en émoi; *(impatient)* foule impatiente; **to get e.** s'exciter; *(to get angry)* s'énerver; **don't get e.!** ne vous énervez pas!, du calme!; **he gets e. over nothing** il s'emballe pour un rien; **it's nothing to get e. about** il n'y a pas de quoi en faire toute une histoire
2 *(enthusiastic)* animé, enthousiaste; **she was very e. about her trip to Canada** elle était très excitée ou animée à l'idée de son voyage au Canada; **the medical world is very e.** *(by discovery etc)* le monde médical est très enthousiaste; **doctors are e. by this discovery** les médecins sont enthousiasmés par cette découverte; **she was not in the least bit e. at the thought of his visit/about going to university** elle n'était pas du tout enthousiaste ou *Fam* emballée à l'idée de sa visite/à l'idée d'aller à l'université; **I can't get e. about it** ça ne me dit vraiment rien; **I don't understand what everyone's getting so e. about** je ne comprends pas ce qu'ils ont tous à s'exciter ou *Fam* s'emballer comme ça; **he was e. at the prospect of earning all this money** la perspective de gagner tout cet argent l'enthousiasmait ou *Fam* l'emballait
3 *Elec, Physiol* excité; **e. state** *Nucl Phys* état *m* excité ou d'excitation; *Elec* état d'amorçage

excitedly [ɪk'saɪtɪdlɪ] ADV *(to speak, laugh)* avec animation; *(to wait)* avec une impatience fébrile; **she was jumping up and down e.** elle sautait dans tous les sens, très animée; **she was watching the road e., waiting for the car to appear** elle regardait la route anxieusement, guettant la voiture; **he was waving his arms e.** il agitait les bras frénétiquement

excitement [ɪk'saɪtmənt] N **1** *(agitation)* agitation f; **he mustn't have too much e.** il ne faut pas qu'il s'agite; **to avoid e.** éviter les sensations fortes; **to be in a state of e.** *(person)* être surexcité
2 *(enthusiasm, excited state)* animation f, enthousiasme *m*; **the thirst for e.** la soif des sensations fortes; **the e. of departure** l'émoi *m* du départ; **to cause great e.** faire (grande) sensation; **there is some e. in the city** il y a un certain émoi dans la ville; **a sense** *or* **feeling of e.** un sentiment d'exaltation; **there was an air of e. surrounding the event** l'événement baignait dans une atmosphère exaltée; **in the e. of the moment** dans l'exci-

tation du moment; **we had a bit of e. at the office this morning** il y a eu de l'animation au bureau ce matin; **I wouldn't want to miss the e.** je ne veux pas rater ça; **it put the e. back into life for him** ça a remis du sel dans sa vie; **all the e. has gone out of my life** ma vie a perdu tout son piquant

3 *Physiol (of organ)* surexcitation *f*

exciting [ɪk'saɪtɪŋ] ADJ *(film, story, person etc)* passionnant; *(idea, prospect, proposal)* enthousiasmant; *(situation, scene)* sensationnel; *(full of suspense)* plein de suspense; **e. developments in medical research** développements passionnants dans la recherche médicale; **it was e. for him to be involved in such a project** c'était exaltant *ou* excitant pour lui de faire partie d'un tel projet; *Sport* **an e. finish** une arrivée palpitante; **an e. game** une partie mouvementée

▸▸ *Elec* **e. coil** bobine *f* inductrice; *Elec* **e. dynamo** dynamo *f* d'excitation

excitingly [ɪk'saɪtɪŋlɪ] ADV d'une manière sensationnelle; *(to dress)* avec originalité; **e. different** d'une originalité enthousiasmante *ou* électrisante; **the most e. dangerous thing she has ever done** la chose la plus dangereuse et la plus excitante qu'elle ait jamais faite; **the match finished as e. as it had started** le match s'est terminé de façon aussi palpitante qu'il avait commencé; **e., nobody knew exactly what might happen** ce qui était excitant *ou* exaltant, c'est que personne ne savait ce qui allait se passer

exclaim [ɪks'kleɪm] VI s'écrier, s'exclamer; **to e. in anger/surprise/delight** pousser une exclamation de colère/surprise/ravissement

VT **'leave me alone!', he exclaimed** 'laissez-moi!', s'est-il écrié

exclamation [eksklə'meɪʃən] N exclamation *f*

▸▸ *Br* **e. mark,** *Am* **e. point** point *m* d'exclamation

exclamatory [eks'klæmət(ə)rɪ] ADJ exclamatif

exclude [ɪks'kluːd] VT exclure (**from** de); *(draught)* empêcher d'entrer; *(doubt, suspicion)* écarter; **to e. sb from a society** *(expel)* exclure qn d'une société; *(not allow to join)* refuser à qn l'entrée d'une société; **the figures e. deaths from other causes** ces chiffres ne tiennent pas compte des morts provoquées par d'autres causes; **to e. sb from voting/working** dénier le droit de vote/de travailler à qn; **excluding ...** à l'exclusion de ...; **this excludes all possibility of doubt** le doute n'est plus permis

exclusion [ɪks'kluːʒən] N **1** exclusion *f* (**from** de); **to the e. of ...** à l'exclusion de ... **2** *(refusal to allow to join)* refus *m* d'admission (**from** à); **the e. of blacks from certain jobs** l'exclusion des noirs de certains postes; **the e. of women from voting** la dénégation du droit de vote aux femmes

▸▸ **e. order** ordre *m* d'exclusion

exclusive [ɪks'kluːsɪv] ADJ **1** *(right etc)* exclusif; **to have e. rights in a production** avoir l'exclusivité d'une production; **you don't have an e. right to use this park!** vous n'avez pas l'exclusivité de ce parc! **2** *(only)* seul, unique; **it has been his e. occupation for ten years** cela a été son occupation unique pendant dix ans **3** *(expensive, upper-class)* huppé; *(club, social circle etc)* très fermé; *(boutique)* de luxe; *(clothing, jewellery)* de grande marque **4** *(in logic)* exclusif; **two qualities that are mutually e.** deux qualités qui s'excluent **5** *(with numbers, dates etc)* exclusivement; **chapters one to twenty e.** chapitres un à vingt exclusivement **6** *(not including extras)* sans compter les extras; **rent £10,000 a year e.** loyer 10 000 livres

par an, contributions et charges non comprises **7** *(not including)* **e. of** non compris; **e. of wrappings** sans compter l'emballage, emballage non compris; **price of dinner e. of wine** prix du dîner, vin non compris; **all prices are e. of postage and packing** les prix indiqués ne tiennent pas compte des frais d'envoi et d'emballage; **e. of tax** hors taxe, HT

N *Journ* article *m* en exclusivité; *(interview)* interview *f* exclusive; **aTimes e.** une exclusivité duTimes

▸▸ *Com* **e. distribution** distribution *f* exclusive; *Journ* **e. interview** interview exclusive

exclusively [ɪks'kluːsɪvlɪ] ADV exclusivement; **to be published e. in the Sunday Express** paraître en exclusivité dans le Sunday Express; **brought to you e. on ITV** diffusé en exclusivité sur ITV

exclusivity [ekskluː'sɪvɪtɪ] N **1** *(of restaurant, area)* caractère *m* huppé; *(of club, social circle)* caractère fermé **2** *Com (of dealership etc)* exclusivité *f*

▸▸ *Com* **e. arrangement** accord *m* d'exclusivité; *Com* **e. clause** clause *f* d'exclusivité

excommunicate¹ [ekskə'mjuːnɪkeɪt] VT excommunier

excommunicate² [ekskə'mjuːnɪkət] ADJ, N excommunié, -ée

excommunication [ekskəmjuːnɪ'keɪʃən] N excommunication *f*

ex-con N *Sl* ancien taulard *m*

excrement ['ekskrɪmənt] N excrément *m*

excrescence [eks'kresəns] N excroissance *f*

excrescent [eks'kresənt] ADJ *Fml* **1** *(outward-growing)* qui forme une excroissance **2** *(superfluous)* superflu, redondant

excreta [ɪks'kriːtə] NPL excrétions *fpl*

excrete [ɪks'kriːt] VT excréter; *(of plant)* sécréter

excretion [ɪks'kriːʃən] N excrétion *f*, *(of plant)* sécrétion *f*

excruciating [ɪks'kruːʃɪeɪtɪŋ] ADJ *(pain)* atroce, horrible; *Fam (music, TV programme)* atroce; **she was in e. pain** elle souffrait atrocement *ou* horriblement

excruciatingly [ɪks'kruːʃɪeɪtɪŋlɪ] ADV atrocement; *Fam* **e. boring** à en mourir d'ennui; **e. embarrassing/shy** horriblement embarrassant/timide; *Fam* **e. funny** *(story)* tordant; **e. painful** atrocement douloureux

exculpate ['ekskʌlpeɪt] VT *Fml* disculper, exonérer (**from** de)

exculpation [ekskʌl'peɪʃən] N *Fml* disculpation *f*, exonération *f* (**from** de)

excursion [ɪks'kɜːʃən] N **1** *(journey)* excursion *f*, *Aut, Cycling etc* randonnée *f*, **to make** *or* **go on an e.** faire une excursion; **a shopping e.** un tour dans les magasins **2** *(digression)* *(in speech)* digression *f*, **after a brief e. into sculpture, she returned to painting** après une brève incursion dans la sculpture, elle est retournée à la peinture

▸▸ *Br Rail Formerly* **e. ticket** billet *m* circulaire *(bénéficiant de tarifs réduits)*

excursionist [ɪks'kɜːʃənɪst] N excursionniste *mf*

excusable [ɪks'kjuːzəb(ə)l] ADJ *(error etc)* excusable, pardonnable

excusably [ɪks'kjuːzəblɪ] ADV de manière excusable; **she was e. reluctant to help** on pouvait l'excuser de ne pas vouloir aider

excuse¹ [ɪks'kjuːs] N **1** *(justification)* excuse *f*; **there is no e. for his behaviour** sa conduite est inexcusable; **there was no e. for doing that** il n'y avait aucun prétexte à faire cela; **ignorance of the law is no e.** nul n'est censé ignorer la loi; **that's no e.!** ce n'est pas une excuse!

2 *(pretext)* excuse *f*, prétexte *m*; **poor** *or*

feeble **e.** faible excuse; **I'm not interested in excuses** tes excuses ne m'intéressent pas; **their e. was that they'd forgotten** leur prétexte était qu'ils avaient oublié; **to make excuses** s'excuser; **I make no excuses for these views** je ne ressens pas le besoin de justifier ces opinions; **stop making excuses for him** arrête de lui trouver des excuses; **to look for an e.** chercher des excuses; *(in order not to do sth)* chercher des faux-fuyants *ou* une échappatoire; **to look for an e. to celebrate** chercher un prétexte pour faire la fête; **to find an e. for sth** trouver une excuse à qch; **any e. to get out of the house!** tout prétexte est bon pour sortir de la maison!; **he's just using his broken leg as an e. to ...** il se sert du fait qu'il a une jambe cassée comme excuse pour ...

3 *(example)* **a poor e. for a letter** un semblant de lettre; **a poor e. for a car** un vieux tacot délabré

excuse² [ɪks'kjuːz] VT **1** *(forgive)* excuser, pardonner; **to e. sb's laziness, to e. sb's being lazy** excuser la paresse de qn; **e. my being late** excusez-moi d'être en retard; **e. me yawning** je vous demande pardon si je bâille; **to e. sb's absence** excuser l'absence de qn; **he may be excused for laughing** il est excusable d'avoir ri; **you could be excused for thinking it was spring** on aurait pu facilement penser que c'était le printemps; **if you will e. the expression** si vous voulez me pardonner l'expression; **if you will e. me, I have to finish my work** si vous voulez bien m'excuser, il faut que je finisse mon travail; **e. me!** *(let me past, sorry)* pardon!, excusez-moi!; **e. me?** *(what did you say?)* pardon?; **e. me, it was yesterday that ...** *(expressing contradiction)* pardon, c'était hier que ...

2 *(exempt)* exempter, dispenser (**from doing sth** de faire qch); **to e. sb from attendance** excuser qn; **may I be excused?** *(leave the table)* puis-je sortir de table?; *Sch* est-ce que je peux sortir?; *Mil, Naut* **to be excused a fatigue** être exempté d'une corvée

3 *(justify)* excuser; **his youth excuses him** sa jeunesse l'excuse *ou* peut lui servir d'excuse

4 to e. oneself *(give excuse)* s'excuser; **I excused myself** *(apologized for leaving)* je me suis excusé de devoir partir

excuse-me N = danse *f* où on change de partenaire lorsque quelqu'un s'approche en disant 'excusez-moi'

ex-directory ADJ *Br Tel* **they** *or* **their number must be e.** ils doivent être sur la liste rouge; **to go e.** *(of subscriber)* se faire inscrire sur la liste rouge

▸▸ **e.** numéro *m* ne figurant pas dans l'annuaire, numéro se trouvant sur la liste rouge

ex dividend ADV coupon échu

execrable ['eksɪkrəb(ə)l] ADJ exécrable, abominable

execrably ['eksɪkrəblɪ] ADV exécrablement, abominablement

execrate ['eksɪkreɪt] VT *Fml* **1** *(abhor)* exécrer **2** *(curse)* maudire

execration [eksɪ'kreɪʃən] N *Fml* **1** *(abhorrence)* exécration *f* (**of** de); **to hold sb/sth in e.** avoir qn/qch en exécration **2** *(curse)* malédiction *f*

executable file ['eksɪkjuːtəb(ə)l] N *Comput* fichier *m* exécutable

execute ['eksɪkjuːt] VT **1** *(carry out)* (task, order) exécuter; *(plan)* mettre à exécution; *(operation)* accomplir; *Fin (transfer)* effectuer; *Law (will)* exécuter; *(deed)* souscrire, signer; *Mus (piece)* exécuter, jouer; *Admin* **executed on ...** fait le ... **2** *(put to death)* exécuter **3** *Comput* exécuter

▸▸*Comput* e. **cycle** cycle *m* d'exécution; *Comput* e. **file** fichier *m* exécutable

execution [eksɪ'kjuːʃən] **N 1** *(of project, order)* exécution *f*; *(of purpose, goal etc)* accomplissement *m*; *Law (of deed)* souscription *f*; *(of will)* exécution; *Mus (of piece of music)* exécution; *(of musician)* jeu *m*; **to put** *or* **carry a plan into e.** mettre un projet à exécution; **in the e. of one's duty** dans l'exercice de ses fonctions; *St Exch* e. **at market** exécution *f* au prix du marché **2** *Law (seizure of property)* saisie-exécution *f*, *pl* saisies-exécutions **3** *(killing) (of criminal)* exécution *f*; e. **by firing squad** exécution par un peloton d'exécution **4** *Comput* exécution *f*

executioner [eksɪ'kjuːʃənər] **N** bourreau *m*

executive [ɪg'zekjʊtɪv] **ADJ 1** *(in business) (post etc)* de cadre; *(in politics) (power)* exécutif; *Pol* **chief e. officer** président-directeur *m* général **2** *(luxury)* de luxe

N 1 *(in business)* cadre *m*; **executives** encadrement *m*, cadres *mpl*; ; **sales e.** directeur *m* commercial **2** *(of government)* (pouvoir *m*) exécutif *m* **3** *(of political party, union)* bureau *m*, comité *m* central; **the union's national e.** le bureau national du syndicat

▸▸*Am Pol* e. **agreement** accord *m* en forme simplifiée *(qui ne nécessite pas l'approbation du Sénat)*; *Com* e. **board** directoire *m*; e. **briefcase** attaché-case *m*, *pl* attachés-cases; e. **chef** cuisinier *m* en chef, maître-coq *m*, *pl* maîtres-coqs; *Aviat* e. **class** classe *f* affaires; e. **committee** comité *m* de direction; e. **decision** décision *f* prise par un cadre; *Fig* décision capitale; *Com* e. **director** directeur *m* exécutif; *Mil* e. **duties** service *m* de détail; e. **housekeeper** *(in hotel)* gouvernante *f* générale; e. **jet** jet *m* privé; e. **model** *(of car etc)* modèle *m* de (grand) luxe; *Com* e. **officer** cadre *m* supérieur; *Cin* e. **producer** producteur *m* délégué; e. **recruitment agency** association *f* pour l'emploi des cadres, APEC *f*; *Com* e. **secretary** secrétaire *mf* de direction; *Am Pol* e. **session** *(of Senate)* séance *f* à huis clos; e. **suite** *(in hotel)* suite *f* de luxe; *(in company)* bureaux *mpl* de la direction; e. **travel** voyages *mpl* d'affaires

executor [ɪg'zekjʊtər] **N** *Law* exécuteur *m* testamentaire; **literary e.** exécuteur littéraire

executrix, *pl* **executrices** [ɪg'zekjʊtrɪks, -trɪsiːz] **N** *Law* exécutrice *f* testamentaire

exegesis [eksɪ'dʒiːsɪs] **N** exégèse *f*

exegetical [eksɪ'dʒetɪk(ə)l] **ADJ** exégétique

exemplary [ɪg'zemplərɪ] **ADJ 1** *(outstanding) (conduct)* exemplaire; *(husband)* modèle **2** *(serving as example) (punishment)* exemplaire

▸▸*Law* e. **damages** dommages-intérêts *mpl* exemplaires *ou* à titre exemplaire

exemplification [ɪgzemplɪfɪ'keɪʃ(ə)n] **N** exemplification *f*; **in e. of his remarks** pour exemplifier ses remarques

exemplify [ɪg'zemplɪfaɪ] **VT 1** *(show by example)* exemplifier, illustrer **2** *(serve as example of) (rule)* servir d'exemple à; *(problem)* être un exemple de

exempt [ɪg'zempt] **ADJ** exempt, dispensé, exempté (**from** de); *(from tax)* exempt, franc, *f* franche; **he was declared e. from any blame** il a été délivré de toute responsabilité; *Mil* **to be e. from fatigues** être dispensé *ou* exempté des corvées

VT exempter, dispenser (**from** de); **to e. sb from doing sth** exempter *ou* dispenser qn de faire qch; *Mil* **exempted from military service** exempté *ou* dispensé du service militaire; **to e. sb from VAT** exempter les livres de TVA; **to e. sb from responsibility for sth** délivrer qn de la responsabilité de qch

exemption [ɪg'zem(p)ʃən] **N** *(from tax, military service)* exemption *f*, dispense *f*; e. **from customs duty** franchise *f* douanière; e. **from liability** exonération *f* de responsabilité; e. **from VAT** exonération *f* de TVA

▸▸*Law* e. **clause** clause *f* de non-responsabilité

exercise ['eksəsaɪz] **N 1** *(physical)* exercice *m*; **outdoor e.** exercice au grand air; **to take e.** prendre de l'exercice; **I don't get much e.** je ne fais pas beaucoup d'exercice; *Gym* **physical exercises** exercices physiques; **breathing exercises** gymnastique *f* respiratoire, exercices respiratoires **2** *(mental, educational)* exercice *m*; **school/grammar e.** exercice scolaire/de grammaire; **piano exercises** exercices pour piano **3** *Mil, Naut* exercice *m*; **tactical exercises** évolutions *fpl* tactiques; **to be on e.** être à l'exercice **4** *(activity)* **religious exercises** pratiques *fpl* religieuses; **it was an interesting e.** c'était une expérience intéressante; **sending an ambassador would be a pointless e.** envoyer un ambassadeur ne servirait à rien; **it was just an e. in public relations** ce n'était que pour les apparences *ou* pour l'effet d'annonce **5** *(use, practice) (of faculty, duty)* exercice *m*; *(of profession, religion)* pratique *f*; **in the e. of one's duties/rights** dans l'exercice de ses fonctions/droits; *St Exch* e. **of an option** levée *f* d'une prime

VT 1 *(train etc) (body, mind)* exercer; *(troops)* faire faire l'exercice à; **to e. a horse** exercer un cheval; *(take for a walk)* promener un cheval **2** *(practise) (right)* exercer, user de; *(profession)* exercer, pratiquer; **to e. one's influence in sb's favour** user de son influence en faveur de qn; **to e. one's will/authority** faire acte de volonté/d'autorité; **we must e. caution/restraint** nous devons user de prudence/de retenue; *Fin* **to e. an option** lever une prime, exercer une option **3** *Fml (bother) (person)* tracasser; *Old-fashioned (sb's patience)* mettre à l'épreuve

VI prendre de l'exercice; *(train)* s'entraîner

▸▸e. **bike** vélo *m* d'appartement; e. **book** *(for writing in)* cahier *m* d'exercices; *(containing exercises)* livre *m* d'exercices; e. **class** cours *m* de gymnastique; *St Exch* e. **date** date *f* d'échéance; *St Exch* e. **notice** avis *m* de levée; *St Exch* e. **price** *(of share)* prix *m* d'exercice, cours *m* de base; e. **yard** *(in prison)* cour *f*, préau *m*

exerciseable ['eksəsaɪzɪb(ə)l] **ADJ** *St Exch* exerçable

exert [ɪg'zɜːt] **VT 1** *(use) (force)* employer, faire usage de; *(influence, pressure, authority)* exercer **2 to e. oneself** se remuer, se donner du mal; **to e. oneself to do sth** faire des efforts pour faire qch; *Iron* **don't e. yourself!** ne te donne pas trop de mal, surtout!

exertion [ɪg'zɜːʃən] **N 1** *(of force)* usage *m*, emploi *m*; **he was accused of undue e. of influence** il a été accusé d'exercer une influence abusive **2** *(effort)* effort *m*

exeunt ['eksɪənt] **VI** *Theat* e. **Romeo and Juliet** Roméo et Juliette sortent

exfoliant [eks'fəʊlɪənt] **N** exfoliant *m*

exfoliate [eks'fəʊlɪeɪt] **VI** *Biol, Geol* s'exfolier

exfoliating [eks'fəʊlɪeɪtɪŋ] **ADJ** *Biol, Geol* exfoliant

▸▸e. **cream** crème *f* exfoliante

exfoliation [eksfəʊlɪ'eɪʃən] **N** *Biol, Geol* exfoliation *f*

ex gratia [eks'greɪʃɪə] **ADJ, ADV** *Law, Fml* à titre de faveur, à titre gracieux; **ex gratia payment** paiement *m* à titre gracieux

ex-growth **N** *Com (decline)* baisse *f*; **to go e.** être en déclin

exhalation [eksə'leɪʃən] **N 1** *(of breath)* ex-

piration *f*; **on e.** lors de l'expiration **2** *(thing exhaled)* effluve *m*, exhalaison *f*

exhale [eks'heɪl] **VT** *(air from lungs)* expirer; *(one's last breath, smoke, gas etc)* exhaler

VI expirer

exhaust [ɪg'zɔːst] **N 1** *Aut, Tech* échappement *m*; *(what is ejected)* gaz *m* d'échappement; **2** *(pipe)* (tuyau *m* d')échappement *m*

VT 1 *(tire) (person)* épuiser, éreinter, exténuer; **to e. oneself in useless efforts** se consumer en efforts inutiles; **this/he is exhausting me** cela/il m'épuise **2** *(use up) (reserves, topic of conversation)* épuiser; **to e. sb's patience** venir à bout de la patience de qn

▸▸*Aut* e. **emission** émission *f* de gaz d'échappement; *Aut* e. **fumes** gaz *mpl* d'échappement; *Aut* e. **manifold** collecteur *m* d'échappement; *Br Aut* e. **pipe** pot *m ou* tuyau d'échappement; *Aut* e. **stroke** *(in internal combustion engine)* temps *m* d'échappement

exhausted [ɪg'zɔːstɪd] **ADJ 1** *(person)* épuisé, exténué, éreinté; **I'm e.** je n'en peux plus, je suis épuisé *ou* exténué; **this baby's got me e.** ce bébé m'épuise **2** *(land, resources)* épuisé; **my patience is e.** je suis à bout de patience

exhaustible [ɪg'zɔːstɪb(ə)l] **ADJ** limité; **her patience is easily e.** elle est vite à bout de patience

exhausting [ɪg'zɔːstɪŋ] **ADJ** *(effort, climate)* épuisant; *(work, person)* épuisant, éreintant

exhaustion [ɪg'zɔːstʃən] **N 1** *(of person, animal) (state of)* e. épuisement *m*; **mental e.** extrême fatigue *f* mentale; **to be in a state of complete e.** être complètement à bout de forces; **I was ready to drop with e.** je tombais de fatigue **2** *(of resources, land)* épuisement *m* **3** *Phys (of gas)* aspiration *f*

exhaustive [ɪg'zɔːstɪv] **ADJ** *(list)* exhaustif; *(analysis, description)* détaillé, minutieux; *(investigation, enquiry, search)* approfondi; **in e. detail** très en détail; **to make an e. study of a subject** traiter un sujet à fond

exhaustively [ɪg'zɔːstɪvlɪ] **ADV** *(detailed, to list)* exhaustivement; *(to describe)* minutieusement; *(to study)* à fond; **this is an e. researched book** ce livre est le résultat de recherches approfondies *ou* très poussées

exhibit [ɪg'zɪbɪt] **N 1** *Art etc* objet *m* exposé; **how many exhibits will there be?** combien d'objets seront exposés?; **we'll need more exhibits** nous aurons besoin d'autres objets à exposer **2** *Law (in criminal proceedings)* pièce *f* à conviction

VT 1 *Art etc (of artist) (paintings etc)* exposer **2** *Law (items of supporting evidence)* exhiber, produire **3** *(show) (object)* exhiber, montrer, faire voir; *(in shop window)* exposer; *(courage, bad grace etc)* faire preuve de; **to e. signs of stress/anxiety** donner des signes de tension/d'anxiété; **parking permits must be clearly exhibited on the windscreen** les permis de stationnement doivent être disposés bien en vue derrière le pare-brise; **he exhibited no remorse** il n'a manifesté aucun remords

VI *(of artist)* exposer

exhibition [eksɪ'bɪʃən] **N 1** *(event)* exposition *f*; **Ideal Home Exhibition** ≃ Salon *m* des Arts ménagers; **2** *(display) (of merchandise etc)* exposition *f*, étalage *m*; *(of talent)* manifestation *f*; *(of procedure etc)* démonstration *f*; *Law (of items in evidence)* production *f*; *Fam* **to make an e. of oneself** se donner en spectacle; **it was a disgraceful e.** ce fut un spectacle de mauvais goût; **to give an e. of bad manners/bad temper** faire montre d'impolitesse/de mauvaise humeur; **I've never seen such an e. of bad manners** je n'ai jamais vu une telle impolitesse **3**

Am Sch = séance *f* musicale etc donnée par les élèves et à laquelle sont invités les parents **4** *Br Univ (award)* bourse *f*
▶▶ **e. centre** centre *m* d'expositions; **e. hall** salle *f ou* hall *m* d'exposition; **e. insurance** assurance *f* foire; **e. stand** stand *m* (d'exposition)

> Note that the French word **exhibition** is a false friend and is never a translation for the English word **exhibition**.

exhibitionism [eksɪ'bɪʃənɪz(ə)m] **N 1** *(showing off)* désir *m* de se faire remarquer **2** *Psy (exposing oneself)* exhibitionnisme *m*

exhibitionist [eksɪ'bɪʃənɪst] **N 1** he's an e. *(shows off)* il aime se faire remarquer **2** *Psy* exhibitionniste *mf*

exhibitor [ɪg'zɪbɪtər] **N 1** *Art (at exhibition)* exposant, -ante **2** *Br Cin* exploitant, -ante

exhilarate [ɪg'zɪləreɪt] **VT** *(of mountain air)* vivifier; *(of experience, news etc)* faire exulter; **they had been exhilarated by the thought that …** ils exultaient à la pensée que …

exhilarated [ɪg'zɪləreɪtɪd] **ADJ** exultant, fou, *f* folle de joie; *(laugh, cry)* d'exultation; **they felt e. by the news** la nouvelle les faisait exulter; **to feel e.** *(physically, after sauna etc)* se sentir grisé

exhilarating [ɪg'zɪləreɪtɪŋ] **ADJ** *(air, wind, walk etc)* vivifiant; *(experience, ride)* grisant; *(news)* réjouissant

exhilaration [ɪgzɪlə'reɪʃən] **N** gaieté *f* de cœur, joie *f* de vivre; **a mood/an atmosphere of e.** une humeur/une atmosphère joyeuse; **the thought filled him with e.** cette pensée le faisait exulter; **this feeling of e.** cette exultation

exhort [ɪg'zɔːt] **VT** *(person)* exhorter, encourager (**to do** à faire); **to e. sb to greater efforts** exhorter qn à plus d'efforts

exhortation [ɪgzɔː'teɪʃən] **N** exhortation *f* (**to do** à faire)

exhumation [ekshjuː'meɪʃən] **N** exhumation *f*
▶▶ **e. order** permis *m* d'exhumer

exhume [eks'hjuːm] **VT** exhumer, déterrer

exigency ['eksɪdʒənsɪ], **exigence** ['eksɪdʒəns] **N** *Fml* **1** *(necessity)* exigence *f*, nécessité *f* **2** *(situation)* cas *m* pressant, situation *f* urgente **3** **exigencies** *(requirements)* exigences *fpl*, impératifs *mpl*

exigent ['eksɪdʒənt] **ADJ** *Fml* **1** *(urgent)* urgent, pressant **2** *(demanding)* exigeant

exiguity [eksɪ'gjuːɪtɪ] **N** *Fml (of accommodation etc)* exiguïté *f*; *(of income etc)* modicité *f*

exiguous [ɪg'zɪgjʊəs] **ADJ** *Fml* exigu, -uë, fort petit; *(diet)* maigre; *(income)* modique

exile ['eksaɪl] **N 1** *(banishment)* exil *m*, bannissement *m*; **to send sb into e.** envoyer qn en exil, bannir qn; **to go into e.** partir en exil *ou* pour l'exil; *(voluntarily)* s'exiler; **he lives in e. in Madrid** il vit en exil à Madrid; **government in e.** gouvernement en exil **2** *also Fig (person)* exilé, -ée
VT exiler (**from** de)

exist [ɪg'zɪst] **VI 1** *(be in existence)* exister; *(of conditions etc)* régner; **fairies don't e.** les fées n'existent pas; **a legend/tradition exists that …** il y a une légende/tradition selon laquelle …; **to cease to e.** cesser d'exister; **to continue to e.** subsister; **the Institute exists to carry out research** la raison d'être de l'Institut est d'effectuer des recherches; **these old shops still e. in a few places** ces vieilles boutiques existent encore dans quelques endroits; *Fam* **as far as you're concerned, I don't e., do I?** en ce qui te concerne, c'est comme si je n'existais pas, hein? **2** *(live)* se

maintenir en vie; **I can't e. on that** cela ne me suffit pas pour vivre; **they managed to e. on a handful of rice a day** ils parvenaient à se maintenir en vie avec une poignée de riz par jour

existence [ɪg'zɪstəns] **N 1** *(state of existing)* existence *f*; **the e. of these laws is not enough** l'existence de ces lois ne suffit pas; **to be in e.** exister; **the oldest manuscript in e.** le plus ancien manuscript existant; **it's the only one still in e.** c'est le seul qui existe encore; **to come into e.** naître; *Lit* **to call sth into e.** créer qch; **to spring into e.** naître soudainement; **to go out of e.** disparaître, cesser d'exister **2** *(life)* existence *f*, vie *f*; **to lead a pleasant e.** mener une existence agréable

existent [ɪg'zɪstənt] **ADJ 1** *(that exists)* existant; **these conditions have been e. since …** ces conditions existent depuis … **2** *(current)* actuel

existential [egzɪs'tenʃəl] **ADJ** *Phil* existentiel

existentialism [egzɪs'tenʃəlɪz(ə)m] **N** *Phil* existentialisme *m*

existentialist [egzɪs'tenʃəlɪst] **ADJ, N** *Phil* existentialiste *mf*

existing [ɪg'zɪstɪŋ] **ADJ** existant, actuel, -elle; *(equipment)* existant; **in e. circumstances** dans les circonstances actuelles *ou* présentes
▶▶ *Mktg* **e. customer** client *m* actuel; *Mktg* **e. market** marché *m* existant, marché actuel

exit ['eksɪt] **N 1** *(way out) (from theatre etc)* sortie *f*, issue *f*; *(from highway)* sortie; *(roadway)* bretelle *f* de sortie; **e. only** *(passage etc)* réservé à la sortie **2** *(act of going out)* sortie *f*; **to make a hurried e.** sortir en vitesse; *Theat* **to make one's e.** sortir, quitter la scène; **the audience must have free e. at all times** le public doit pouvoir sortir librement à tout moment; **3** *Comput* sortie *f*
VI (**-t-**) **1** *Theat* faire sa sortie; **e. Macbeth** Macbeth sort **2** *(leave)* sortir **3** *Comput* sortir
VT *Comput (program, session etc)* sortir de
▶▶ **e. barrier** *(in store)* barrière *f* à la sortie; *Fin* **e. charges** frais *mpl* de sortie; **e. door** porte *f* de sortie; *Com* **e. interview** = entretien *m* entre un employeur et son employé lors du départ de ce dernier; *Br* **e. permit** permis *m* de sortie; *Pol* **e. poll** = sondage *m* effectué lorsque les électeurs viennent de voter; *Comput* **e. routine** routine *f* de sortie; **e. sign** panneau *m* indiquant une/la sortie; **e. staircase** escalier *m* de sortie; **e. visa** visa *m* de sortie

exocrine ['eksəʊkraɪn] **ADJ** *Physiol* exocrine
▶▶ **e. gland** glande *f* exocrine

exodus ['eksədəs] **N 1** *Bible (of the Jews etc)* exode *m*; **(the Book of) E.** l'Exode **2** *Fml, Hum (departure) (of group of people etc)* départ *m*, sortie *f*; **a mass e. towards the beaches** un exode en direction des plages; **there was a general e.** il y eut une sortie générale; *Fin* **e. of capital** évasion *f ou* fuite *f* des capitaux

ex officio ['eksə'fɪʃɪəʊ] *Admin* **ADJ** *(member)* de droit, à titre d'office
ADV *(to act)* d'office

exonerate [ɪg'zɒnəreɪt] **VT 1** *(absolve)* **to e. sb (from blame)** disculper *ou* justifier qn **2** *(exempt)* exonérer, décharger (**sb from an obligation** qn d'une obligation)

exoneration [ɪgzɒnə'reɪʃən] **N 1** **e. (from blame)** disculpation *f*, justification *f* **2** *(exemption)* exonération *f*, décharge *f* (**from** de)

exorbitance [ɪg'zɔːbɪt(ə)ns] **N** *(of prices, demands)* énormité *f*

exorbitant [ɪg'zɔːbɪt(ə)nt] **ADJ** exorbitant,

exagéré, excessif; *(interest)* usuraire; **e. price** prix exorbitant

exorbitantly [ɪg'zɔːbɪt(ə)ntlɪ] **ADV** *(priced)* d'une manière exorbitante; **e. expensive** excessivement cher, d'un prix exorbitant

exorcism ['eksɔːsɪz(ə)m] **N** *Rel* exorcisme *m*

exorcist ['eksɔːsɪst] **N** *Rel* exorciste *m*

exorcize ['eksɔːsaɪz] **VT** *Rel* exorciser; *(demon, possessed etc)* conjurer; *(spirit, fears)* faire disparaître

exoskeleton ['eksəʊskelətən] **N** *Zool* exosquelette *m*, cuticule *f*

exotic [ɪg'zɒtɪk] **ADJ** exotique; **a taste for the e.** le goût de l'exotique; **she is e.-looking** elle a un charme exotique; **an e.-sounding name** un nom aux consonances exotiques
N *Bot* plante *f* exotique

exotica [ɪg'zɒtɪkə] **NPL** objets *mpl* exotiques

exotically [ɪg'zɒtɪklɪ] **ADV** exotiquement; **e. flavoured/coloured** aux saveurs/couleurs exotiques

exoticism [ɪg'zɒtɪsɪz(ə)m] **N** exotisme *m*

expand [ɪks'pænd] **VT** *(production, output)* augmenter; *(gas)* dilater; *(boundaries of empire)* étendre; *(idea, algebraic formula, chest)* développer; *(mind, circle of friends, range of products)* élargir; *(wings)* déployer; **it's an idea that could easily be expanded into a novel** c'est une idée qu'on pourrait facilement développer pour en faire un roman; **the police force is to be expanded** les effectifs de la police doivent être augmentés
VI 1 *(of solid, air, gas)* se dilater; *(of balloon)* se gonfler; *(of steam)* se détendre; *(of chest)* se développer; *(of sail etc)* s'étendre, se déployer; *(of company)* s'agrandir; *Tech (of belt)* s'allonger; **they want to e. into plastics** ils veulent se développer en s'introduisant sur le marché des plastiques; **as the Empire expanded** à mesure que l'Empire grandissait *ou* s'étendait **2** *(talk, write at greater length)* préciser sa pensée; **could you e.?** est-ce que vous pourriez préciser ce que vous voulez dire par là?
▶ **expand on, expand upon VT INSEP** *(talk, write at greater length about)* développer; **I'd like to e. on that** j'aimerais développer ce point

expandable [ɪks'pændɪb(ə)l] **ADJ** *Comput* extensible; **4MB e. to 64MB** 4 Mo extensible à 64 Mo

expanded [ɪks'pændɪd] **ADJ** étendu; *(wings)* déployé;
▶▶ *Comput* **e. keyboard** clavier *m* étendu; *Comput* **e. memory** mémoire *f* paginée *ou* expansée; *Comput* **e. memory specification** spécifications *fpl* de la mémoire paginée; **e. polystyrene** polystyrène *m* expansé

expander [ɪks'pændər] **N 1** *Gym* **(chest) e.** extenseur *m* **2** *Aut (in brake drum)* came *f* de frein

expanding [ɪks'pændɪŋ] **ADJ 1** *(market, sector, field)* en expansion; *(gas)* qui se dilate; *(balloon etc)* qui se gonfle, qui enfle; *(commerce)* qui se développe, qui prend de l'extension; *(demand, production)* croissant; *(interests, circle of friends)* qui s'élargit; **the e. universe** l'univers *m* en expansion **2** *(watch strap, headband)* extensible; *(suitcase)* à soufflets

expanse [eks'pæns] **N** *(of country, water etc)* étendue *f*; **a vast e.** *(of water, snow etc)* une vaste étendue; *(of sand)* une mer; **a wide e. of cloudless sky** une immensité de ciel sans nuages

expansion [ɪks'pænʃən] **N 1** *(making larger) (of gas)* dilatation *f*; *(of subject, chest etc)* développement *m* **2** *(becoming larger) (of solid, liquid, commerce etc)* expansion *f*; *(of gas, metal etc)* dilatation *f*; *(of flower, heart)* épanouissement *m*; *Econ* relance *f*, colo-

nial/territorial e. expansion coloniale/territoriale
▸▸**e. bit** foret *m ou* mèche *f* extensible; *Comput* **e. board, e. card** carte *f* d'extension; *Tech* **e. joint** joint *m* de dilatation; *Comput* **e. slot** emplacement *m ou* logement *m* pour carte d'extension; *Constr* **e. tank** réservoir *m* d'expansion

expansionism [ɪks'pænʃənɪz(ə)m] N *Pol* expansionnisme *m*

expansionist [ɪks'pænʃənɪst] *Pol* ADJ, N expansionniste *mf*

expansive [ɪks'pænsɪv] ADJ **1** *(force)* expansif; *(gas)* expansible, dilatable **2** *(person)* expansif; **in an e. mood** en veine d'épanchement; **to welcome sb with an e. gesture** accueillir qn à bras ouverts

> Attention: ne pas confondre avec l'adjectif **expensive**.

expansively [ɪks'pænsɪvlɪ] ADV *(to welcome)* chaleureusement; **to gesture e. towards the skyline/paintings** désigner l'horizon/les tableaux d'un grand geste

expansiveness [ɪks'pænsɪvnɪs] N **1** *(of gas)* expansibilité *f* **2** *(of person)* expansivité *f*, nature *f* expansive

expat [eks'pæt] ADJ, N *Br Fam* expatrié, -ée

expatiate [eks'peɪʃɪeɪt] VI *Fml* discourir (longuement) (**on** sur)

expatriate[1] [eks'pætrɪət] N expatrié, -ée; **an e. Scot** un Écossais expatrié

expatriate[2] [eks'pætrɪeɪt] VT *(person)* expatrier

expatriation [ekspætrɪ'eɪʃən] N expatriation *f*

expect [ɪks'pekt] VT **1** *(anticipate) (person, letter, phone call etc)* attendre; *(event)* s'attendre à; *(sb's arrival etc)* compter sur; **to e. sb for dinner** attendre qn à dîner; **the delivery isn't expected until Thursday** on n'attend pas la livraison avant jeudi; **I expected as much** je m'y attendais; **I expected more from you** je m'attendais à mieux de ta part; **I knew what to e.** je savais à quoi m'attendre; **to e. the worst** s'attendre au pire; **as one might e., as might be expected** comme on doit s'y attendre, comme de raison; **she played with the brilliance (which) we have come to e. (from her)** elle a joué avec le brio auquel elle nous a maintenant habitués; **to e. that sb will do sth/that sth will happen** s'attendre à ce que qn fasse qch/à ce que qch arrive; **I half expected him to say no** je m'attendais plus ou moins à ce qu'il dise non; **I fully expected him to agree** je comptais bien qu'il soit d'accord; **to e. to do sth** compter *ou* espérer faire qch; **I don't e. them to be pleased** je ne m'attends pas à ce qu'ils soient contents; **the movie was better than I expected (it to be)** le film était meilleur que je ne m'y attendais; **she was angry – well, what did you e.?** elle était en colère – et alors, ça t'étonne?; **some slight initial difficulty is to be expected** il faut s'attendre à rencontrer quelques légères difficultés initiales; **that's only to be e.** ce n'est pas du tout surprenant; **he is not expected to recover** on ne s'attend pas à ce qu'il se rétablisse; **they arrived later than expected** ils sont arrivés plus tard que prévu; **she's expecting a baby** elle attend un bébé

2 *(require)* **to e. sth from sb** exiger qch de qn; **I e. you to be punctual** je vous demande d'arriver à l'heure; **I don't e. you to be perfect** je ne te demande pas d'être parfait; **it is expected that the candidate will be willing to undertake some travel** on attend du candidat qu'il soit disposé à voyager; **how do you e. me to do it?** comment voulez-vous que je le fasse?; **where do they e. them to**

go if there's nowhere else? où veulent-ils qu'ils aillent si c'est le seul endroit?; **is it too much to e. a little courtesy?** est-ce qu'un peu de courtoisie est trop demander?; **it's too much to e. of a child** c'est trop attendre d'un enfant; **I know what is expected of me** je sais ce qu'on attend de moi; **people e. too much from marriage** les gens attendent trop du mariage

3 *(suppose)* **to e. (that)** penser que; **I e. he'll pay** je pense qu'il payera; **I e. so/not** je crois bien que oui/que non
VI *Fam* **she's expecting** elle attend un bébé

expectancy [ɪks'pektənsɪ] N **1** *(expectation)* attente *f*; **an air/atmosphere of e.** un air/une atmosphère d'expectative *f*; **a look of e.** un regard plein d'espoir; **eager e.** vive impatience *f*; **life e.** espérance *f* de vie; *Mktg* **e.-value model** modèle *m* de valeur attendue **2** *Law (of inheritance etc)* expectative *f*

expectant [ɪks'pekt(ə)nt] ADJ **1** *(expecting)* (qui est) dans l'attente (**of sth** de qch); *(crowd, face)* impatient; *(air, hush)* d'expectative; **the e. look on the children's faces** l'expectative qui se lisait sur le visage des enfants **2** *Law (property, heir etc)* en expectative
▸▸**e. mother** future maman *f*

expectantly [ɪks'pekt(ə)ntlɪ] ADV dans l'expectative, dans l'attente; **fans waiting e. at the stage door** des fans qui attendent à la sortie des artistes, pleins d'espoir; **he looked at me e.** il m'a regardé avec l'air d'attendre quelque chose

expectation [ekspek'teɪʃən] N **1** *(thing expected)* attente *f*, espérance *f*; **to come up to/fall short of sb's expectations** remplir *ou* répondre à/tromper l'attente de qn; **it didn't come up to e.** il n'a pas été à la hauteur de ce qu'on attendait; **to succeed beyond one's expectations** réussir au delà de ses espérances; **contrary to all expectations** contrairement à *ou* contre toute attente; **to have high expectations of sb/sth** attendre beaucoup de qn/qch; **in (the) e. of** dans l'attente de **2** *(anticipation)* **with eager e.** avec une vive impatience; **to live in e.** vivre dans l'expectative **3** *Law* expectative *f* d'héritage; **expectations** espérances *fpl*; **uncle from whom one has expectations** oncle *m* à héritage **4** *(probability) (of event)* probabilité *f*; **there is every/no e. that we shall be seeing them again soon** il y a de grandes chances/peu de chance pour que nous les revoyions bientôt; **e. of life** espérance *f* de vie

expected [ɪks'pektɪd] ADJ attendu; *(hoped for)* espéré
▸▸*Mktg* **e. product** produit *m* attendu; *Mktg* **e. service** service *m* attendu

expectorant [ɪks'pektərənt] ADJ, N *Med* expectorant *m*

expectorate [eks'pektəreɪt] *Med, Fml* VT *(mucus)* expectorer
VI cracher

expectoration [ekspektə'reɪʃən] N *Med, Fml* expectoration *f*

expedience [ɪks'piːdɪəns], **expediency** [ɪks'piːdɪənsɪ] N **1** *(convenience) (of measure etc)* convenance *f*, opportunité *f*; **I questioned the e. of doing ...** j'ai douté qu'il soit opportun de faire ...; **on grounds of e.** pour des raisons de convenance **2** *Pej (opportunism)* opportunisme *m*

expedient [ɪks'piːdɪənt] ADJ **1** *(convenient)* expédient, convenable; **do what you think e.** faites ce que vous jugerez à propos **2** *Pej (opportunist)* opportun
N expédient *m*, moyen *m*

expedite ['ekspɪdaɪt] VT **1** *Fml (hasten) (measure)* activer, pousser, hâter; *(procedure)* accélérer; **I'll do what I can to e. matters** je ferai ce que je pourrai pour accélérer

les choses **2** *Old-fashioned (deal with speedily) (matter)* expédier, dépêcher

expedition [ekspə'dɪʃən] N **1** *(trip)* expédition *f*; **an e. to the North Pole** une expédition au pôle Nord; *Fam* **a shopping e.** une expédition dans les magasins; *Fam* **getting here was quite an e.** ça a été toute une expédition pour arriver jusqu'ici **2** *Old-fashioned, Fml (promptness)* promptitude *f*

expeditionary [ekspə'dɪʃ(ə)nərɪ] ADJ *Mil (unit etc)* expéditionnaire

expeditious [ekspə'dɪʃəs] ADJ *Fml (procedure)* expéditif; *(reply)* prompt

expeditiously [ekspə'dɪʃəslɪ] ADV *Fml* promptement

expel [ɪks'pel] VT (**-ll-**) *(person)* expulser; *(foreign body, enemy etc)* chasser, expulser; *(liquid, gas)* chasser, refouler; *(breath)* exhaler; *Admin (foreigner)* expulser, refouler; **to e. a pupil (from school)** renvoyer un élève (de l'école)

expend [ɪks'pend] VT *(time, resources)* consacrer, employer; *(money)* dépenser, employer; *(ammunition)* utiliser; **to e. one's energies on sth** consacrer ses énergies à qch; **all our stocks have been expended** toutes nos réserves sont épuisées

expendable [ɪks'pendəb(ə)l] ADJ **he/it is e.** il n'est pas irremplaçable *ou* indispensable; **the general considered these troops to be e.** le général considérait qu'on pouvait sacrifier ces troupes

expenditure [ɪks'pendɪtʃər] N **1** *(of money, energy etc)* dépense *f*, *(of ammunitions)* consommation *f* **2** *(amount)* dépense(s) *f(pl)*; **heavy e.** une forte dépense, de fortes dépenses; **e. on arms** les dépenses pour l'armement

expense [ɪks'pens] N **1** *(cost)* dépense *f*, frais *mpl*; *(of energy)* dépense; *(of funds)* utilisation *f*, *(of fuel, ammunition)* consommation *f*; **regardless of e.** sans regarder à la dépense; **at great/little e.** à grands/peu de frais; **at no extra e.** sans supplément de frais; **at my own e.** à mes propres frais; **book published at the author's e.** livre édité à compte d'auteur; **to go to great e.** faire beaucoup de dépenses; **they didn't want to go to the e. of hiring a car** ils ne voulaient pas faire les frais de louer une voiture; **it's not worth the e.** c'est trop cher pour ce que c'est; **don't go to any e. over ...** ne faites pas de frais pour ...; **they went to considerable e.** ils ont dépensé des sommes considérables; **to put sb to e.** faire faire des dépenses à qn; **no e. was spared to ...** on n'a pas regardé à la dépense pour ...; *Fig* **a joke at my e.** une plaisanterie à mes dépens; **at the e. of the poor/his social life** aux dépens des pauvres/de sa vie sociale

2 *Com* **expenses** frais *mpl*, dépenses *fpl*; **to meet/cover sb's expenses** rembourser/couvrir les frais de qn; **it's on expenses** c'est la société qui paie, ça va sur la note de frais; **to offer sb £100 and expenses** offrir à qn 100 livres, plus les frais; **travelling expenses** frais de déplacement, indemnité *f* de voyage; **living expenses** frais de séjour; **general expenses** frais généraux; **incidental expenses** faux frais; **to incur expenses** faire des dépenses; **to cut down on e.** réduire les frais; **to have all expenses paid** être défrayé de tout; **an all-expenses-paid trip to Paris** un voyage à Paris tous frais payés

3 *(financial burden)* **to be a great e. to sb** être une grande charge pour qn
▸▸**e. account** note *f* de frais; **expenses claim form** note *f* de frais

expensive [ɪks'pensɪv] ADJ *(object)* cher, *f* chère, coûteux; *(shop, restaurant)* cher; *(procedure, habit)* dispendieux; *(pastime, treatment)* onéreux; *(mistake)* qui coûte cher; **he has e. tastes** il a des goûts dispendieux *ou* de luxe; **that butcher's very e.** ce boucher est très cher; **to be** *or* **come e.** revenir cher; **that can be e.** ça peut être cher; **travelling is e.** les voyages coûtent cher

---

Attention: ne pas confondre avec l'adjectif **expansive**.

---

expensively [ɪks'pensɪvlɪ] **ADV** *(to dress)* coûteusement; *(to eat, decorate)* à grands frais; **to live e.** mener la vie large, vivre dispendieusement; **e. priced** coûteux, cher

expensiveness [ɪks'pensɪvnɪs] **N** *(of commodity, life etc)* cherté *f*; **the e. of his tastes** ses goûts dispendieux

experience [ɪks'pɪərɪəns] **N 1** expérience *f*; **to gain e. of life** faire l'apprentissage de la vie; **practical e.** pratique *f*; **driving e.** expérience de la route; **he still lacks e.** il manque encore de pratique; **she has several years' e.** elle a plusieurs années d'expérience; **have you had any previous e.?** avez-vous déjà travaillé dans ce métier?; **I have enough business e. to** ... j'ai assez de pratique des affaires pour ...; **a man of e.** un homme d'expérience; **he shows that** ... l'expérience démontre que ...; **to know sth from e.** savoir qch par expérience; **to learn from e.** tirer les leçons de l'expérience; **I know from bitter e. that** ... je sais, pour l'avoir éprouvé cruellement, que ...; **he was clearly speaking from e.** de toute évidence, il parlait en connaissance de cause *ou* il parlait d'expérience; **in my e.** d'après mon expérience; **my e. has been that** *or* **in my e. people appreciate politeness** j'en ai fait l'expérience, les gens apprécient la politesse; **I had no e. of looking after disabled people** je ne m'étais jamais occupé de personnes handicapées; **the black e. in this country** la condition des noirs dans ce pays; **I lost a lot of money, but I'll just have to put it down to e.** j'ai perdu beaucoup d'argent, mais au moins ça me servira de leçon; **well, it's all e.** voilà qui est à mettre au compte de l'expérience
2 *(individual event)* expérience *f*; **to have a nasty e.** faire une mauvaise expérience; **the journey was an e.** le voyage a été enrichissant; *Iron* le voyage a été une drôle d'expérience; **it was his first e. of love** c'était la première fois qu'il tombait amoureux
VT *(emotions, feeling, pain)* ressentir; *(real hunger, poverty, success)* connaître, faire l'expérience de; *(difficulties, problems)* avoir
▸▸*Mktg* **e. curve** courbe *f* d'expérience; *Mktg* **e.-curve pricing** tarification *f* en fonction de la courbe d'expérience; *Mktg* **e. quality** qualité *f* reconnue après achat

experienced [ɪks'pɪərɪənst] **ADJ** qui a de l'expérience, expérimenté, chevronné; *(observer)* averti; *(eye)* exercé; **to be e. in sth** avoir l'expérience de qch, s'y connaître en qch; **to be politically e.** avoir de l'expérience en matière de politique; **e. in business** rompu aux affaires; **a more e. doctor** un médecin plus expérimenté; **sexually e.** qui a de l'expérience en matière de sexualité

experiment [ɪks'perɪmənt] **N** expérience *f*; **to carry out** *or* **do an e.** faire ou procéder à une expérience; **as an e., by way of e.** à titre d'essai *ou* d'expérience
VI expérimenter, faire une expérience/des expériences (**on** sur); **an artist should be prepared to e.** un artiste devrait être prêt à toutes les expériences; **to e. with** *(new technique, style)* s'essayer à; *(philosophy, religion)* goûter à; **to e. with drugs** faire l'expérience de la drogue; **to e. with smoking** goûter à la cigarette

experimental [ɪksperɪ'ment(ə)l] **ADJ 1** *(subject)* d'expérience; *(physics, evidence, method)* expérimental, -aux; **e. rocket** fusée

expérimentale; **this new reactor is at the e. stage** ce nouveau réacteur est à l'essai *ou* en cours d'expérimentation **2** *(based on experiment)* *(knowledge)* expérimental, -aux, fondé sur l'expérience
▸▸**e. research** recherche *f* (expérimentale)

experimentally [ɪksperɪ'ment(ə)lɪ] **ADV 1** *(as experiment)* à titre d'essai **2** *(to discover sth)* expérimentalement

experimentation [ɪksperɪmen'teɪʃən] **N** expérimentation *f*

expert ['ekspɜːt] **ADJ** expert, habile; **to be e. in** *or* **at sth** être expert en qch; **to be e. in** *or* **at doing sth** être habile à faire qch; **an e. opinion** une opinion avisée
N spécialiste *mf*, *(professional, with qualifications)* expert *m*; **I'm no e.** je ne suis pas un expert; *Law* **medical e.** médecin *m* légiste; **according to the experts** selon les experts; **to be an e. at doing sth** être habile à faire qch; **she is an e. in this field** elle est expert en la matière; **the eye of an e.** un œil expert
▸▸**e. advice** avis *m* autorisé; **e. panel** commission *f* d'experts; **e.'s report** expertise *f*, *Comput* **e. system** système *m* expert; *Law* **e. witness** expert *m inv* (appelé comme témoin)

expertise [ekspɜː'tiːz] **N** *(technical, financial etc)* connaissances *fpl*; *(as a cook, carpenter etc)* savoir-faire *m inv*; adresse *f*, habileté *f* (**in** à)

expertly ['ekspɜːtlɪ] **ADV** habilement, de manière experte

expiate ['ekspɪeɪt] **VT** *(sin)* expier

expiation [ekspɪ'eɪʃən] **N** expiation *f*, **in e. of his crime** pour expier *ou* en expiation de son crime

expiration [ekspɪ'reɪʃən] **N 1** *(expiry)* *(of lease)* cessation *f*, expiration *f*, *(of option)* échéance *f*, *(of term)* fin *f*, *(of insurance policy)* expiration, déchéance *f*, **date of e.** *(of guarantee etc)* date *f* d'expiration **2** *Physiol* *(of air from lungs)* expiration *f*

expire [ɪks'paɪər] **VI 1** *(of law, treaty, deadline etc)* expirer, venir à expiration; **expired policy** *(in insurance)* police déchue; **this passport expires on** ... ce passeport expire le ...; **expired passport** passeport périmé **2** *Lit (die)* expirer, mourir; *(of hope)* s'évanouir
VT *Physiol* *(air from lungs)* expirer, exhaler

expiring [ɪks'paɪərɪŋ] **ADJ 1** *Law (lease, contract)* qui expire, qui est à son terme **2** *Lit (dying)* expirant, qui se meurt; **with an e. voice** d'une voix mourante

expiry [ɪks'paɪərɪ] **N** *(of term, contract, deadline)* expiration *f*, fin *f*, *(of period)* terme *m*
▸▸**e. date** *(of contract, lease, insurance policy)* date *f* d'expiration *ou* d'échéance; *(of visa, passport)* date d'expiration; *(on food labels)* date limite de consommation; *(on ticket, on voucher)* date à utiliser avant le, valable jusqu'au; *(on bank card)* valable jusqu'au

explain [ɪks'pleɪn] **VT 1** *(make clear)* expliquer; **that explains everything** voilà qui explique tout; **that is easily explained** cela s'explique facilement; **that explains his embarrassment** cela explique son embarras; **she explained to us how the system works** elle nous a expliqué comment le système fonctionne; **I explained that we were tourists** j'ai expliqué que nous étions des touristes **2** *(justify)* *(one's behaviour etc)* justifier **3 to e. oneself** *(make oneself understood)* s'expliquer; *(justify oneself)* se justifier; **I don't understand, please e. yourself** je ne comprends pas, veuillez vous expliquer
VI donner des explications; **you'd better e.** allons, expliquez-vous
▸ **explain away VT SEP** donner une explica-

tion satisfaisante de; **how did he manage to e. away the broken vase?** quelle raison a-t-il trouvée pour expliquer que le vase soit cassé?; **he tried to e. away the women's underwear in the car** il a essayé de fournir une raison expliquant la présence de dessous féminins dans la voiture; **e. that away, if you can!** explique donc ça!; **he tried to e. away his absence from the meeting** il a essayé de justifier son absence à la réunion

explainable [ɪks'pleɪnəb(ə)l] **ADJ** *(behaviour etc)* explicable; **it's easily e.** cela s'explique facilement; **to become e.** s'expliquer

explanation [eksplə'neɪʃən] **N** explication *f*, éclaircissement *m*; **to give explanations** fournir des explications; **to give an e. of one's behaviour** justifier sa conduite; **one e. is that** ... l'une des explications est que ...; **the e. is that** ... cela s'explique par le fait que ...; **I hope you've got a good e. for this!** j'espère que vous avez une explication satisfaisante à me donner à propos de ceci!; **she wasn't able to offer any e. of why it had happened** elle a été incapable d'expliquer pourquoi c'était arrivé

explanatory [ɪks'plænət(ə)rɪ] **ADJ** explicatif; **e. notes** commentaires *mpl*

expletive [ɪks'pliːtɪv] **N 1** *(swearword)* juron *m* **2** *Gram etc* particule *f* explétive, explétif *m*
ADJ *Gram etc* explétif

explicable [eks'plɪkəb(ə)l] **ADJ** explicable; **to become e.** s'expliquer; **this phenomenon is not e. by sociological factors alone** ce phénomène ne peut s'expliquer par les seuls facteurs sociologiques

explicit [eks'plɪsɪt] **ADJ** explicite; **to be more e. (in one's statements)** préciser (ses affirmations); **to make sth e.** rendre qch explicite; **e. language** *(vulgar)* langage susceptible d'offenser la pudeur; **e. sex and violence** *(on television etc)* de la violence et du sexe montrés de façon explicite; **sexually e. scenes** scènes au contenu sexuel non voilé

explicitly [eks'plɪsɪtlɪ] **ADV** explicitement, de manière explicite

explode [ɪks'pləʊd] **VT 1** *(detonate etc)* *(shell)* faire éclater; *(mine)* faire sauter; *(gas)* faire exploser **2** *(show to be false)* démontrer la fausseté de; *(theory)* discréditer; *(myth)* détruire **3** *(in diagram)* éclater
VI *(of boiler, shell etc)* éclater; *(of mine)* sauter; *(of gas, dynamite etc)* exploser, détoner; *(of car, plane etc)* exploser; *Fig* **to e. with laughter** éclater de rire; *Fig* **he'll e.** *(with anger)* il va exploser (de colère), il va sortir de ses gonds; *(with repressed feeling)* il va craquer; *(with overeating)* il va exploser; *Fig* **the population exploded after the war** il y a eu une explosion démographique après la guerre

exploded [ɪks'pləʊdɪd] **ADJ 1** *(shell)* éclaté; *(mine)* qui a sauté **2** *(theory)* abandonné, reconnu pour faux
▸▸*Phot, Tech* **e. view** vue *f* éclatée

exploit¹ ['eksplɔɪt] **N** exploit *m*, haut fait *m*

exploit² [eks'plɔɪt] **VT 1** *(take unfair advantage of)* exploiter; **immigrant workers are being exploited** les travailleurs immigrés se font exploiter **2** *(use)* *(mine, forest etc)* exploiter; *(talents)* mettre à profit; *(scandal)* exploiter

exploitation [eksplɔɪ'teɪʃən] **N** exploitation *f*

exploration [eksplə'reɪʃən] **N 1** *(trip)* exploration *f*, **voyage of e.** voyage *m* de découverte; **Magellan called here on his explorations** au cours de ses explorations, Magellan est passé par ici **2** *(act)* *(of terrain)* exploration *f*, reconnaissance *f*, **e. work** travaux *mpl* de recherches; **the e. of a possibi-lity** l'étude d'une possibilité **3** *Med (of wound)* exploration *f*

explorative [ɪks'plɒrətɪv] **ADJ** explorateur, -trice

exploratory [ɪks'plɒrət(ə)rɪ] **ADJ** *(well, poll)* d'exploration; *(voyage)* de découverte; *(dia-logue)* préliminaire
▸ ▸ *Med* **e. surgery** opération *f* exploratoire; *Med* **e. test** exploration *f*

explore [ɪks'plɔːr] **VT 1** *(region, town)* explorer; *(continent)* aller à la découverte de; *(country)* faire l'exploration de; *(terrain)* tâter; *(possibility, idea)* étudier; *(theory)* étudier en détail; **to e. sth with one's hands/tongue** explorer qch de ses mains/de la langue; *Com* **to e. the market** prospecter le marché **2** *Med (wound)* explorer, sonder

explorer [ɪks'plɔːrər] **N** *(person)* explora-teur, -trice

explosion [ɪks'pləʊʒən] **N** *(of gases, shell etc)* explosion *f*; *(of gas)* déflagration *f*; *(noise)* détonation *f*; *Fig (of anger, joy)* débordement *m*; *(of laughter, artistic creativity, new writing)* explosion; **to cause an e.** provoquer une explosion; *Fig* **population e.** explosion démographique

explosive [ɪks'pləʊsɪv] **ADJ 1** explosif, déto-nant; **e. mixture** mélange *m* détonant; *Fig* **an e. situation/combination** une situation/ combinaison explosive **2** *Ling (consonant)* explosif
▸ **N 1** *(material)* explosif *m* **2** *Ling* (consonne *f*) explosive *f*
▸ ▸ **e. device** dispositif *m* explosif; *Nucl* **e. fission** fission *f* explosive

exponent [ɪks'pəʊnənt] **N 1** *(of system etc)* interprète *mf*; *(of theory, idea, opinion)* avocat, -ate, défenseur *m*; *Mus (of work)* interprète, exécutant, -ante; *(of sport)* protagoniste *mf*; **the leading exponents of this genre** les principaux représentants de ce genre **2** *Math (of quantity)* exposant *m*

exponential [ekspəʊ'nenʃəl] **ADJ** exponen-tiel
▸ ▸ *Math* **e. curve** courbe *f* exponentielle

exponentially [ekspəʊ'nenʃəlɪ] **ADV** de ma-nière exponentielle

export¹ ['ekspɔːt] **N 1** *(product)* article *m* d'exportation; **coffee is an important e.** le café est une des exportations principales; **exports** *(of country)* exportations *fpl*; **vi-sible/invisible exports** exportations visi-bles/invisibles **2** *(trade)* exportation *f*; **the e. of coal** l'exportation de charbon; **for e. on-ly** réservé à l'exportation
▸ ▸ **e. agent** commissionnaire *m* exporta-teur; **e. ban** interdiction *f* d'exporter; **e. bid** offre *f* export; **e. company** entreprise *f* ex-portatrice; **e. credit** crédit *m* à l'exportation; **e. credit guarantee** garantie *f* de crédit à l'exportation; **E. Credit Guarantee Depart-ment** COFACE *f*; **e. department** service *m* des exportations, service export; **e. director** directeur *m* export; **e. drive** = campagne *f* visant à stimuler l'exportation; **e. duty** droit *m* de sortie *ou* d'exportation; **e. earnings** re-venus *mpl ou* recettes *fpl* de l'exportation; **e. financing** financement *m* des exportations; **e. guarantee** garantie *f* à l'exportation; **e. li-cence** permis *m* d'exportation; **e. manage-ment company** société *f* de portage; **e. manager** directeur export; **e. market** mar-ché *m* à l'export, marché à l'exportation; **e. order** commande *f* export; **e. quota** contin-gent *m* d'exportation; **e. reject** produit *m* im-propre à l'exportation; **e. restrictions** restrictions *fpl* aux exportations; **e. sales** ventes *fpl* export *ou* à l'exportation; **e. sales director** directeur des ventes export; **e. ta-riff** tarif *m* export; **e. tax** taxe *f* à l'exporta-tion; **e. tourism** tourisme *m* d'exportation;

e. trade commerce *m* d'exportation **a flou-rishing e. trade** une exportation florissante

export² [eks'pɔːt] **VT 1** *(goods)*, *Fig (way of life)* exporter **2** *Comput* exporter
▸ **VI** exporter; **exporting country** pays *m* exportateur

exportable [eks'pɔːtəb(ə)l] **ADJ** exportable

exportation [ekspɔː'teɪʃən] **N** exportation *f*

exporter [eks'pɔːtər] **N** exportateur, -trice (**of** de)

expose [ɪks'pəʊz] **VT 1** *(put in unprotected position)* exposer; *(new-born child)* aban-donner; *Phot (film)* exposer; **to be exposed to the weather** être exposé aux intempé-ries; **to e. sb/oneself to danger** exposer qn/s'exposer au danger; **to e. one's flank to the enemy** prêter le flanc à l'ennemi; **to e. oneself to ridicule/sb's anger** s'exposer à la risée publique/à la colère de qn **2** *(lay bare) (wire etc)* mettre à découvert *ou* à nu *ou* à jour **3** *(display) (one's ignorance, feelings)* af-ficher; *(goods for sale)* étaler; *Rel (the Blessed Sacrament)* exposer; **to e. oneself** faire de l'exhibitionnisme; **a man exposed himself to her** un exhibitionniste l'a appro-chée **4** *(reveal) (secret)* éventer; *(crime)* dé-voiler; *(criminal activity, network)* mettre à jour; *(traitor)* démasquer; **they're trying to e. him as …** ils essaient de démontrer que c'est …; **he feared being exposed as a ho-mosexual** il craignait que son homosexua-lité ne soit découverte *ou* mise à jour

exposé [eks'pəʊzeɪ] **N** *(article, documentary, book etc)* exposé *m*; *(of scandal etc)* révéla-tion *f*; **the newspaper's e. of the MP's activi-ties** l'enquête du journal sur les activités du parlementaire

exposed [ɪks'pəʊzd] **ADJ 1** *(to sight, ele-ments)* exposé; *(gears)* à découvert; *Phot (film)* exposé, impressionné; *Mil* **e. position** endroit exposé; *Fig* **this leaves the Prime Mi-nister in an e. position** cela laisse le Premier ministre dans une position fragile; *Mil* **to be e.** *(of troops)* être en l'air **2** *(laid bare)* à nu

exposition [ekspə'zɪʃən] **N 1** *(explanation)* exposé *m*, exposition *f*, présentation *f*; *(in novel)*, *Mus* exposition **2** *(exhibition)* exposi-tion *f* **3** *Rel* exposition *f*

expostulate [ɪks'pɒstjʊleɪt] **VI** vitupérer (**about** contre); **to e. with sb about sth** faire des remontrances à qn sur *ou* à propos de qch

expostulation [ɪkspɒstjʊ'leɪʃən] **N** *(to per-son)* vitupérations *fpl*, remontrance(s) *f(pl)*

exposure [ɪks'pəʊʒər] **N 1** *(to air, cold, dan-ger)* exposition *f*; *(of new-born child)* aban-don *m*; *Fin* exposition *f* aux risques; **to die of e.** mourir de froid; *Nucl* **e. (to radiation)** irradiation *f* **2** *(display) (of goods for sale)* ex-position *f*, étalage *m*; *(on market)* exposi-tion; *Law* **indecent e.** outrage *m* public à la pudeur **3** *Journ etc* **press e.** couverture *f* mé-diatique; **to get a lot of e.** recevoir une im-portante couverture médiatique; **politicians eager for e.** les hommes politiques anxieux de paraître dans les médias **4** *(of crime etc)* dévoilement *m*; *(of crook)* dénonciation *f*; **to threaten sb with e.** menacer de mettre à jour les activités de qn **5** *Phot (shot)* prise *f* de vue; **time e.** pose *f*; **a 36-e. film** une pelli-cule 36 poses **6** *(outlook of building, place)* exposition *f*, orientation *f*
▸ ▸ *Phot* **e. counter** compteur *m* de prises de vue; *Phot* **e. meter** exposimètre *m*, posemè-tre *m*; *Phot* **e. time** temps *m* de pose

expound [ɪks'paʊnd] **VT** *(doctrine, princi-ples)* exposer; *Rel (Holy Scriptures)* interpréter

express [ɪks'pres] **ADJ 1** *(clear) (law, stipula-tion etc)* exprès, *f* expresse; *(order)* formel, explicite; **for this e. purpose** dans ce but

même; **it was her e. instruction that we …** elle nous a formellement *ou* explicitement demandé de … **2** *(image)* exact, fidèle (**of** de)
▸ **ADV** sans arrêt; **to send a letter e.** envoyer une lettre par *ou* en exprès; **lift that goes e. to the twentieth floor** ascenseur qui monte directement au vingtième étage
▸ **N 1** *(train)* express *m*, rapide *m* **2** *Am Fam (freight company)* compagnie *f* de message-ries
▸ **VT 1** *(one's feelings, intention)* exprimer; *(one's will, desire)* manifester; *(opinion)* émettre; *(wish)* formuler; *(gratitude)* témoi-gner; **a millionaire has expressed an inter-est in (buying) the castle** un millionnaire s'est déclaré intéressé par le château; **well/badly expressed** bien/mal rendu; **to e. one-self** s'exprimer; *Math* **to e. sth as an equation** exprimer qch sous forme d'équation **2** *(re-move) (oil etc)* extraire (**out of, from** de); *(milk)* exprimer **3** *(letter)* envoyer par *ou* en exprès; *Am (package) (by freight company)* envoyer *ou* expédier par les messageries
▸ ▸ *Am* **e. company** entreprise *f* de livraison exprès; **e. delivery** envoi *m* par exprès; **e. freight** fret *m* express; **e. letter** lettre *f* ex-près; **e. messenger** messager *m* exprès; *Rail* **e. train** train *m* express, express *m*

expression [ɪks'preʃən] **N 1** *(of face, eyes)* expression *f*; **he had a strange e. (on his face)** il avait une drôle d'expression **2** *(phrase)* expression *f*, locution *f*, **it's just an e.** ce n'est qu'une expression; *Math* **algebra-ical e.** expression *ou* formule *f* algébrique **3** *(act of expressing) (of thought, joy etc)* ex-pression *f*, manifestation *f*, **beyond e.** au de-là de toute expression, inexprimable; **freedom of e.** liberté *f* d'expression; **these feelings found e. in her poetry** sa poésie a su exprimer ses sentiments; **he raised his fist in an e. of defiance** il brandit le poing en signe de défi **4** *(feeling)* **with e.** *(to sing, act)* avec expression

expressionism [ɪks'preʃənɪz(ə)m] **N** *Art* ex-pressionnisme *m*

expressionist [ɪks'preʃənɪst] **ADJ**, **N** *Art* ex-pressionniste *mf*

expressionless [ɪks'preʃənlɪs] **ADJ** *(voice)* sans expression; *(face)* impassible, sans ex-pression; **there was something rather e. about her performance** quelque chose dans sa performance manquait d'expression

expressive [ɪks'presɪv] **ADJ** *(face, eyes)* ex-pressif, plein d'expression; *(gesture, silence)* éloquent; *(person)* démonstratif; *(language)* expressif; **attitude e. of disdain** attitude qui exprime le dédain

expressively [ɪks'presɪvlɪ] **ADV** avec expression

expressiveness [ɪks'presɪvnɪs] **N** *(of face etc)* caractère *m* expressif, force *f* d'expression

expressly [ɪks'preslɪ] **ADV 1** *(clearly)* ex-pressément, formellement; **e. forbidden** ex-pressément *ou* formellement défendu; **I e. told you to buy a lettuce** je t'ai bien dit d'acheter une salade **2** *(with a clear purpose)* **to do sth e. to …** faire qch dans le seul but de …

expressway [ɪks'presweɪ] **N** *Am* autoroute *f*, voie *f* rapide

expropriate [eks'prəʊprɪeɪt] **VT** *(owner, property)* exproprier

expropriation [eksprəʊprɪ'eɪʃən] **N** expro-priation *f*

expulsion [ɪks'pʌlʃən] **N** *(from country, po-litical party etc)* expulsion *f*; *(from school)* renvoi *m*

expunge [ɪks'pʌndʒ] **VT** *Fml (name from list)* effacer, rayer; *(passage from book)* suppri-mer; *(memory, thought)* effacer

expurgate ['ekspɜːgeɪt] **VT** (book) expurger; (text) épurer; (passage etc) supprimer; **expurgated edition** édition expurgée

expurgation [ekspɜː'geɪʃən] **N** (of book) expurgation f, (of text) épuration f, (of passage) suppression f

exquisite ['ekskwɪzɪt] **ADJ 1** (food, wine, afternoon) exquis; (pleasure etc) vif, f vive; **the relief was e.** ce fut un merveilleux soulagement **2** (delicate) très sensible, délicat, subtil **3** (torture) raffiné; (pain) exquis

exquisitely [eks'kwɪzɪtlɪ] **ADV 1** (delightfully) d'une manière exquise; **e. done** (of needlework etc) perlé; **an e. warm afternoon** un après-midi délicieusement chaud **2** (intensely) extrêmement

exquisiteness [eks'kwɪzɪtnɪs] **N 1** (delicacy, subtlety) (of work of art) perfection f délicate; (of hearing) finesse f **2** (extreme degree) (of pleasure etc) caractère m vif; (of pain) acuité f

ex-serviceman, pl **ex-servicemen N** militaire m en retraite

ex-servicewoman, pl **ex-servicewomen N** femme f militaire en retraite

ex ship ADV ex navire

ext Tel abbr **extension**

extant [eks'tænt] **ADJ** existant encore, qui existe encore

extemporaneous [ɪkstempə'reɪnɪəs] **ADJ** Fml improvisé, impromptu

extemporaneously [ɪkstempə'reɪnɪəslɪ] **ADV** Fml (to speak etc) impromptu

extempore [ɪks'tempərɪ] Fml **ADV** (to speak) impromptu, sans préparation
  ADJ (speech) improvisé, impromptu; (speaker) qui parle sans préparation

extemporization [ɪkstempəraɪ'zeɪʃən] **N** improvisation f

extemporize [ɪks'tempəraɪz] **VT** (speech) improviser
  VI (speak) improviser, parler à l'impromptu; Mus improviser (**on the organ**/etc à l'orgue/etc)

extend [ɪks'tend] **VT 1** (stretch) (body, arm) étendre, allonger; **the giraffe extended its neck** la girafe a allongé ou tendu le cou; **to e. an aerial/telescope** développer une antenne/un télescope
  2 (prolong) (period of time, rail ticket, contract) prolonger; (Com (expiry of bill) proroger; (research) continuer; **the deadline has been extended until 25 May** la date limite a été repoussée au 25 mai
  3 (broaden, lengthen, increase) (line) prolonger; (boundaries) étendre, porter plus loin; (sense of word) étendre; (knowledge) accroître; (power, lands) agrandir, augmenter; (agreement, scope) élargir; (house, room) agrandir; (frontiers of state) reculer; **we are going to e. our premises** nous allons nous agrandir
  4 (offer) (hand) tendre; (thanks, sympathy) présenter; (support) offrir; **to e. a welcome to sb** souhaiter la bienvenue à qn; Banking **to e. credit to sb** accorder un crédit à qn
  5 Sport etc (push to limit) (horse, runner etc) faire rendre son maximum à, pousser; **to e. oneself** donner son maximum; **they haven't really been extended by any of their opponents** aucun de leurs adversaires ne les a vraiment poussés au bout de leurs limites
  VI 1 (in space) s'étendre, s'allonger; **to e. beyond the wall** s'avancer au-delà du mur; **the government's concern with austerity does not e. to its own departments** la volonté du gouvernement de mener une politique d'austérité ne s'étend pas jusqu'à ses propres départements
  2 (of period of time) se prolonger, continuer; **enquiries extending over a number**

of years investigations prolongées pendant un grand nombre d'années

extendable [ɪks'tendɪb(ə)l] **ADJ** (aerial, pole) télescopique; (ladder) à coulisse; (contract of employment) renouvelable

extended [ɪks'tendɪd] **ADJ 1** (body, arm) étendu, allongé; Mil **in e. order** en ordre dispersé **2** (in time) (long) long, prolongé; (prolonged) prolongé **3** (increased) augmenté, agrandi
  ▸▸ Comput **e. ASCII** ASCII m étendu; **e. coverage** (in insurance) couverture f multirisque; Radio, TV = informations fpl détaillées sur un événement; **e. family** famille f élargie; **e. maintenance insurance** assurance f maintenance étendue; Comput **e. memory** mémoire f étendue; Horseriding **e. trot** trot m allongé; **e. warranty** garantie f prolongée

extended-play record N disque m double durée

extender lens [ɪks'tendər] **N** bague f rallonge

extending [ɪks'tendɪŋ] **ADJ** (table) à rallonges; (ladder) à coulisse

extension [ɪks'tenʃən] **N 1** (act of stretching out) (of arm) extension f, (of canal, railway etc) prolongement m; (of factory etc) agrandissement m, extension; Surg (of broken leg) extension; Aviat (of landing gear) sortie f, (of table, jack etc) (r)allonge f
  2 (development) extension f, accroissement m; **there has been a considerable e. of his business** son commerce a pris une extension considérable
  3 (extra part) (of table etc) (r)allonge f, (of cable) allonge f, (on building) annexe f; **we're having an e. built (onto the house)** nous faisons agrandir la maison; **an e. is being added to the museum** on construit une annexe au musée
  4 Tel poste m supplémentaire; Tel **e. 35** poste 35
  5 Gram (of subject, attribute) complément m
  6 (in time) (of leave, railway ticket etc) prolongation f; **to get/give an e.** (of deadline) obtenir/accorder un délai
  7 Comput (of file) extension f
  ▸▸ **e. cable** câble m de raccordement; Sch etc **e. courses** formation f continue; **e. ladder** échelle f à coulisse; **e. loudspeaker** haut-parleur m séparé, pl haut-parleurs séparés; Tel **e. number** numéro m de poste; Tech **e. piece** pièce f formant un prolongement

extensive [ɪks'tensɪv] **ADJ 1** étendu, vaste; (repairs, alterations, reworking) considérable, important; **there was e. damage to both wings** les deux ailes ont été très endommagées; **e. knowledge** vastes connaissances fpl; **e. research** travaux mpl approfondis; **to make e. use of sth** faire un usage considérable de qch **2** (agriculture) extensif

extensively [ɪks'tensɪvlɪ] **ADV** (to travel, read etc) énormément; (rewritten, revised etc) largement; **to use sth e.** se servir beaucoup de qch, faire un usage considérable de qch; **it was e. damaged/repaired** il a subi des dommages/réparations considérables

extensor [ɪks'tensər] **N** Anat (muscle) extenseur m

extent [ɪks'tent] **N** (of lands, knowledge etc) étendue f, (of damage etc) importance f; Typ (of book) nombre m de pages; **credit to the e. of £500** crédit jusqu'à concurrence de 500 livres; **to an e., to a certain e., to some e.** jusqu'à un certain point, dans une certaine mesure; **to a great e., to a large e.** en grande partie, dans une large mesure; **to such an e. that …** à tel point que …; **to what e. is this true?** jusqu'à quel point est-ce vrai?; **to the e. that he can play a few tunes, he is a musician** dans la mesure où il peut jouer quel-

ques airs, c'est un musicien; **the e. to which the strike affected production is unclear** les conséquences de la grève sur la production sont mal définies

extenuate [ɪks'tenjʊeɪt] **VT** (crime) atténuer, amoindrir

> Note that the French verb **exténuer** is a false friend and is never a translation for the English verb **to extenuate**. It means **to exhaust**.

extenuating [ɪks'tenjʊeɪtɪŋ] **ADJ**
  ▸▸ **e. circumstances** circonstances fpl atténuantes

extenuation [ɪkstenjʊ'eɪʃən] **N to say sth in e. of an offence/an act** dire qch pour atténuer la gravité d'un délit/d'un acte

exterior [ɪks'tɪərɪər] **ADJ** extérieur (**to** à), en dehors (**to** de)
  N 1 extérieur m, dehors mpl; **on the e.** à l'extérieur; **house with an imposing e.** maison aux dehors imposants; **despite her stern e., she is very likeable** malgré un extérieur ou une apparence sévère, elle est très sympathique **2** Theat, Cin extérieur m
  ▸▸ Math **e. angle** angle m externe; **e. wall** mur m extérieur

exteriorize [ɪks'tɪərɪəraɪz] **VT** extérioriser

exterminate [ɪks'tɜːmɪneɪt] **VT** (insects, population etc) exterminer; (belief, disease) supprimer

extermination [ɪkstɜːmɪ'neɪʃən] **N** extermination f, (of belief) suppression f, (of disease) éradication f

exterminator [ɪks'tɜːmɪneɪtər] **N** (person) exterminateur, -trice; **a rodent e.** un employé de la dératisation

extern [eks'tɜːn] **N** Am Med externe mf

external [ɪks'tɜːn(ə)l] **ADJ** (wall, reality, world, trade, debt) extérieur; (angle, damage) externe; (interference, pressure) du dehors, de l'extérieur; (affairs) étranger, -ère, extérieur; (student) libre; **in e. appearance** en apparence; **to judge sth by (its) e. appearance** juger qch d'après ses apparences; Med **for e. use only** à usage externe
  N (usu pl) **1** (appearance) **externals** extérieur m, formes fpl extérieures, dehors mpl; **to judge by externals** juger les choses selon les apparences **2** (inessential things) **externals** choses fpl secondaires
  ▸▸ Banking **e. account** compte m d'étranger, Can compte de non-résident; Fin **e. audit** audit m externe; Fin **e. auditing** vérification f externe, audit externe; Fin **e. auditor** audit ou auditeur, -trice externe; Comput **e. command** commande f externe; Fin **e. deficit** déficit m extérieur; Comput **e. device** dispositif m externe, périphérique m; Comput **e. drive** unité f (de disque) externe; (printer) imprimante f, Univ **e. examiner** examinateur, -trice venant de l'extérieur; Fin **e. financing** financement m externe, fonds mpl extérieurs; Comput **e. hard disk** disque m dur externe; Comput **e. modem** modem m externe

externality [ekstɜː'nælɪtɪ] **N** Econ externalité f

externalize [ɪks'tɜːnəlaɪz] **VT** (feelings) exprimer

externally [ɪks'tɜːn(ə)lɪ] **ADV** (damaged, calm) extérieurement; **to apply e.** appliquer en usage externe

extinct [ɪks'tɪŋkt] **ADJ** (animal, plant) disparu, qui n'existe plus; (office, title) aboli, tombé en désuétude; (volcano, passion) éteint; **to become e.** (of race) s'éteindre, disparaître; (of way of life) disparaître, se perdre

extinction [ɪks'tɪŋkʃən] **N** (of fire, race) extinction f, (of hope) anéantissement m; **to**

hunt an animal to e. chasser un animal jusqu'à extinction de la race; **race threatened with e.** race *f* en passe de disparaître

extinguish [ɪksˈtɪŋgwɪʃ] **VT** *(fire, cigarette, candle)* éteindre; *(hope, race)* anéantir

extinguisher [ɪksˈtɪŋgwɪʃər] **N 1** *(for fire)* (appareil *m*) extincteur *m* (d'incendie), appareil d'extinction; **foam e.** extincteur à mousse **2** *(for candle)* éteignoir *m*

extirpate [ˈekstɜːpeɪt] **VT** *Fml (evil)* extirper, déraciner

extirpation [ekstɜːˈpeɪʃən] **N** *Fml (of evil)* extirpation *f*, éradication *f*

extn *Tel (abbr* **extension)** poste *m*

extol, *Am* **extoll** [ɪksˈtəʊl] **VT** *(Br &Am* **extolled, extolling)** *esp Lit* exalter, vanter, prôner; *(sb's beauty)* célébrer, chanter; **she was extolling the virtues of central heating** elle vantait les vertus du chauffage central; **to e. sb to the skies** porter qn aux nues

extort [ɪksˈtɔːt] **VT** *(money etc)* extorquer (**from sb** à qn); *(promise, confession)* arracher (**from sb** à qn)

extortion [ɪksˈtɔːʃən] **N** *(of money etc)* extorsion *f*; *(of promise, confession)* arrachement *m*; **£15 for this? that's sheer e.!** 15 livres pour ça? c'est du vol!

extortionate [ɪksˈtɔːʃənɪt] **ADJ 1** *(price)* exorbitant **2** *(person)* rapace

extortioner [ɪksˈtɔːʃənər], **extortionist** [ɪksˈtɔːʃənɪst] **N** extorqueur, -euse

extra [ˈekstrə] **ADJ 1** *(additional)* de plus, supplémentaire; **an e. pint of milk** une pinte de lait supplémentaire *ou* de plus; **it costs 15p e.** ça coûte 15 pence de plus; **I took an e. £5, just in case** j'ai pris 5 livres de plus, au cas où; **500 e. police officers** 500 officiers de police supplémentaires; **no e. charge** sans supplément de prix; **at no e. cost** sans supplément; **e. pay** prime *f*, supplément *m* de salaire; *Mil, Naut* supplément de solde; **e. work** *(hours)* heures *fpl* supplémentaires; *(work)* surcroît *m* de travail; *Br Sport* prolongation *f*; *Br Sport* **to go into e. time** jouer les prolongations; **as an e. precaution** pour plus de précaution; **to make an e. effort** faire un surcroît d'effort **2** *(spare)* de réserve, de rechange; **bring some e. batteries** prends des piles de rechange; **these ones are e., take them!** ceux-là sont en trop, prends-les!

ADV 1 *(more than usual)* plus que d'ordinaire, extra-; **to be e. kind/polite** être particulièrement gentil/poli; **an e. special wine for those e. special occasions** un grand vin pour les grandes occasions; **this is an e. special cake for your birthday** voici un gâteau exceptionnel pour ton anniversaire; **e. strong binding/rope** reliure *f*/corde *f* extra-solide; **e. smart** ultra-chic; **e. white/fast** extra-blanc/-rapide; **e. large** *(clothing)* grand patron **2** *(in addition)* en plus; **meals taken in the bedroom are charged (for)** il y a un supplément pour les repas servis dans la chambre; **I had to pay e. for the sunroof** il a fallu que je paye un supplément pour le toit ouvrant; **packing e.** emballage en sus; **a few e.** quelques-uns en plus

N 1 *(on restaurant bill)* supplément *m*; *(of newspaper)* édition *f* spéciale; *(on car)* option *f* **2** *Cin, Theat (actor)* figurant, -ante; **to be** *or* **work as an e.** faire de la figuration **3** **extras** *(expenses)* frais *mpl ou* dépenses *fpl* supplémentaires; *(on invoice)* suppléments *mpl*; **extras bill** facture *f* des extras **4** *(luxuries)* **little extras** petits à-côtés *mpl*, extras *mpl*

▸▸**e. charge** supplément (de prix); *Sch* **e. subject** matière *f* facultative; **e. time** *(to pay, finish)* délai *m*; *Sport* prolongations *fpl*

extra- [ˈekstrə] **PREF** *(outside)* extra-; **extragalactic** extragalactique; **extravascular** extravasculaire

extract¹ [ˈekstrækt] **N 1** *(of substance)* extrait *m*, concentré *m*; **malt/beef e.** extrait de malt/de bœuf; **meat e.** concentré de viande **2** *Liter etc* extrait *m*; **selected extracts** *(from author, works)* morceaux *mpl* choisis

extract² [ɪksˈtrækt] **VT** *(tooth)* extraire, arracher; *(oil, metal, data, passage from book etc)* extraire (**from** de); *(letter from pocket etc)* tirer (**from** de); *(passage from book)* extraire (**from** de); **to e. money/a confession from sb** arracher de l'argent/un aveu à qn, tirer de l'argent/un aveu de qn; *Math* **to e. the square root of a number** extraire la racine carrée d'un nombre

extraction [ɪksˈtrækʃən] **N 1** *(removal) (of juice from lemon etc)* extraction *f*, *(of nail, tooth)* arrachage *m*; **she needs two extractions and three fillings** il faut lui arracher deux dents et en plomber trois; **e. of stone from a quarry** extraction de la pierre d'une carrière **2** *(origin)* extraction *f*, origine *f*; **of humble e.** de basse extraction; **of Italian e.** d'origine italienne

extractor [ɪksˈtræktər] **N 1** *(tool)* pince *f*, *(in dentistry)* davier *m*; *Surg (of stones etc)* extracteur *m* **2** *(person) (of teeth etc)* extracteur *m*

▸▸**e. fan** ventilateur *m*, aérateur *m*; **e. hood** *(on stove)* hotte *f* aspirante

extracurricular [ˈekstrəkəˈrɪkjʊlər] **ADJ** *Sch* hors-programme *inv*

▸▸**e. activities** activités *fpl* extrascolaires; *Fig Hum* frasques *fpl*

extraditable [ˈekstrədaɪtəb(ə)l] **ADJ** *(person)* passible d'extradition; *(crime, offence)* qui justifie l'extradition

extradite [ˈekstrədaɪt] **VT** *Law (criminal) (hand over)* extrader; *(obtain extradition of)* obtenir l'extradition de; **the authorities were unable to e. him from the USA** les autorités n'ont pas réussi à obtenir son extradition des États-Unis

extradition [ekstrəˈdɪʃən] **N** extradition *f*; **the Spanish government is seeking/has obtained his e.** le gouvernement espagnol a demandé/obtenu son extradition

▸▸**e. treaty** accord *m* d'extradition

extra-dry **ADJ** *(wine)* très sec

extra-fine **ADJ** extra-fin

extrajudicial [ˈekstrədʒuːˈdɪʃəl] **ADJ** extrajudiciaire

extramarital [ˈekstrəˈmærɪt(ə)l] **ADJ** extraconjugal

extramural [ˈekstrəˈmjʊər(ə)l] **ADJ** **e. course** cours *m* de formation continue; *Br Univ* **e. lecturer** = conférencier *m* en dehors de la Faculté accrédité pour certains cours; *Br Univ* **Department of E. Studies** Département *m* de la formation continue

extraneous [ɪksˈtreɪnɪəs] **ADJ** *(considerations)* en dehors de la question; *(details)* sans rapport; **to be e. to sth** n'avoir aucun rapport avec qch

extraordinarily [ɪksˈtrɔːd(ə)nərɪlɪ] **ADV** extraordinairement; **it was an e. brave/foolish action** c'était un acte particulièrement courageux/inconscient

extraordinary [ɪksˈtrɔːd(ə)nrɪ] **ADJ 1** *(remarkable) (extent, success, coincidence, story)* extraordinaire; *(behaviour, suggestion, idea)* surprenant, singulier, étrange; *(appearance)* surprenant, bizarre; **the e. thing is that …** ce qu'il y a d'étrange *ou* de singulier, c'est que …; **that's e., he was here only an hour ago!** c'est incroyable, il était là il y a une heure à peine!; **I find it e. that you did not inform the police** je trouve incroyable *ou* extraordinaire que vous n'ayez pas prévenu la police; **they went to e. lengths to conceal the truth** ils se sont

donné un mal fou pour cacher la vérité **2** *(special)* extraordinaire; **ambassador e.** ambassadeur *m* extraordinaire

▸▸*Com* **e. general meeting** assemblée *f* générale extraordinaire; *Acct* **e. income** produits *mpl* exceptionnels; *Acct* **e. item** poste *m* extraordinaire; *Acct* **e. loss** résultats *mpl* exceptionnels *(pertes)*; **e. powers** pouvoirs *mpl* extraordinaires; **e. profit** résultats *mpl* exceptionnels *(profits)*

extrapolate [ekˈstræpəleɪt] **VT & VI** extrapoler; **to e. from sth** extrapoler à partir de qch; **we can e. a prediction** nous pouvons extrapoler et établir une prévision

extrapolation [ɪkstræpəˈleɪʃən] **N** extrapolation *f*

extrasensory [ˈekstrəˈsensərɪ] **ADJ** extrasensoriel

▸▸**e. perception** perception *f* extrasensorielle; **to have e. perception** avoir des dons de perception extra-sensorielle

extraterrestrial [ˈekstrətɪˈrestrɪəl] **ADJ, N** extraterrestre *mf*

extraterritorial [ˈekstrəterɪˈtɔːrɪəl] **ADJ** *(privilege)* d'exterritorialité

extravagance [ɪksˈtrævəgəns] **N 1** *(excessive, wasteful expenditure)* folles dépenses *fpl*, prodigalités *fpl*; **the e. of your tastes** tes goûts dispendieux *ou* de luxe; **it was real e.** c'était de la folie; **she accused the government of e.** elle a accusé le gouvernement de dilapider le trésor public; **a piece of e., an e.** une dépense inutile, une folie **2** *(exaggeration)* extravagance *f*

> Note that the most common meaning of the French word **extravagance** is eccentricity.

extravagant [ɪksˈtrævəgənt] **ADJ 1** *(wasteful) (person)* dépensier, gaspilleur; *(tastes)* dispendieux; **it was very e. of them to come by taxi** ils ont fait une folie en venant en taxi; **don't be so e. with the butter** ne gaspillez pas le beurre; **he considered two baths a week (to be) e.** il trouvait que deux bains par semaine, c'était du gaspillage **2** *(exaggerated)* extravagant; *(claim)* exagéré, déraisonnable; *(praise)* outré; *(style)* exagéré; *(price)* exorbitant, prohibitif; **e. claims have been made for the drug** certaines propriétés ont été attribuées abusivement à ce médicament

> Note that the most common meaning of the French word **extravagant** is eccentric.

extravagantly [ɪksˈtrævəgəntlɪ] **ADV 1** *(excessively)* **e. priced items** des articles à des prix exorbitants; **he spent money e.** il jetait l'argent par la fenêtre; **to live e.** vivre sur un grand pied, dépenser sans compter; **e. furnished house** maison meublée avec un luxe exagéré **2** *(exaggeratedly)* d'une façon extravagante; **to talk/act e.** dire/faire des folies *ou* des extravagances

extravaganza [ekstrævəˈgænzə] **N** *(lavish show)* grand spectacle *m*

extravasation [ɪkstrævəˈseɪʃən] **N** *Med* épanchement *m*

extravert [ˈekstrəvɜːt] **ADJ, N** = **extrovert**

extreme [ɪksˈtriːm] **ADJ 1** *(heat, difficulty, pleasure etc)* extrême; *(nationalism)* outrancier; *(opinions, views)* extrême, extrémiste; **to be in e. danger** *or* **peril** être en (très) grand danger; **to be in e. pain** souffrir à l'extrême; **to behave with e. awkwardness** se conduire avec la dernière gaucherie; **an e. case** un cas exceptionnel; **the question is one of e. delicacy** le problème est délicat entre tous **2** *(far)* extrême; **the e. opposite** l'extrême opposé; **at the e. end of the quay** tout au bout du quai; *Pol* **the e. left** l'extrême gauche; **on the e. left of the photograph** à l'extrême gauche de la photo

N extrême *m*; **they were rude in the e.** ils étaient mal polis à l'extrême; **to go from one e. to the other** passer d'un extrême à l'autre; **to go to the e. of calling the police** aller jusqu'à appeler la police; **now he's going to the other e. and …** il est passé d'un extrême à l'autre et maintenant …; **to go to extremes** pousser les choses à l'extrême; **extremes of temperature** extrêmes de température

▸▸*Cin, TV* **e. close-up** plan *m* très rapproché; *Cin, TV* **e. long shot** plan très éloigné; *Fml* **the e. penalty** le dernier supplice; **e. sports** sports *mpl* extrêmes; *Rel* **e. unction** extrême-onction *f*

extremely [ɪks'tri:mlɪ] **ADV** extrêmement; **to be e. witty** avoir énormément d'esprit

extremism [ɪks'tri:mɪz(ə)m] **N** *Pol* extrémisme *m*

extremist [ɪks'tri:mɪst] **ADJ, N** *Pol* extrémiste *mf*

extremity [ɪks'tremɪtɪ] **N 1** *(end)* extrémité *f*, point *m* extrême; **the southernmost e. of Europe** l'extrême sud de l'Europe **2 the extremities** *(of the body)* les extrémités *fpl* **3** *(need)* gêne *f*; **how had they arrived at such an e.?** comment étaient-ils parvenus à de telles extrémités?; **to be reduced to the last e.** en être réduit à la dernière extrémité

extricate ['ekstrɪkeɪt] **VT** dégager, tirer (**sb from a critical position** qn d'un mauvais pas); **to e. oneself from a danger** se tirer d'un danger; **to e. oneself from a conversation** se dégager d'une conversation; **to e. oneself from difficulties** se débrouiller, se tirer d'affaire

extrinsic [eks'trɪnsɪk] **ADJ** extrinsèque

▸▸*Fin* **e. value** valeur *f* extrinsèque

extrovert, extravert ['ekstrəvɜːt] **N** extraverti, -ie, extroverti, -ie; **a bit (too much) of an e.** un peu (trop) extraverti; **she's much more of an e. than her sister** elle est bien plus extravertie que sa sœur, c'est une extravertie bien plus que sa sœur

ADJ extraverti, extroverti; **to have e. tendencies** être d'un naturel extraverti

extrude [eks'tru:d] **VT** expulser, faire jaillir (**from** de); *Metal* filer, profiler; *Ind (plastics)* boudiner (à chaud); **extruded section** *or* **shape** profilé *m*

VI *Geol (of rock etc)* s'épancher

extrusion [eks'tru:ʒən] **N** expulsion *f*, *(of secretion)* émission *f*, *Geol* épanchement *m*; *Metal* extrusion *f*, filage *m* (à chaud); *Ind (of plastics)* boudinage *m*, extrusion

exuberance [ɪg'zju:b(ə)rəns] **N** exubérance *f*, *(of person)* exubérance, gaieté *f* débordante; *(of vegetation)* luxuriance *f*, richesse *f*

exuberant [ɪg'zju:b(ə)rənt] **ADJ** *(person)* exubérant, débordant de vie; *(imagination)* exubérant; *(vegetation)* luxuriant, riche; *(health, vitality)* débordant; **she felt e. at the news** la nouvelle la remplit d'une joie exubérante

exuberantly [ɪg'zju:b(ə)rəntlɪ] **ADV** avec exubérance; **e. cheerful** d'une gaieté exubérante; **e. healthy** débordant de santé

exude [ɪg'zju:d] **VT** exsuder; *Fig* **she exudes health** elle respire la santé; **he exudes (an air of) confidence/well-being/charm** un halo de confiance en soi/de bien-être/de charme se dégage de tout son être

VI exsuder, suinter; *(of sap)* couler, s'écouler

exult [ɪg'zʌlt] **VI 1** *(rejoice)* exulter, se réjouir (**at, in** de); **they exulted at their enemies' confusion** ils exultaient de voir la confusion dans laquelle se trouvaient leurs ennemis; **to e. in the name of 'Mad Mitch'** porter le nom singulier de 'Mad Mitch' **2** *(triumph)* **to e. over sb** triompher de qn

exultant [ɪg'zʌltənt] **ADJ** *esp Lit (feeling)* joyeux; *(cry)* de triomphe; **to be e. at sth** *(of person)* exulter de qch

exultantly [ɪg'zʌltəntlɪ] **ADV** *(to speak etc)* d'un air triomphant

exultation [egzʌl'teɪʃən] **N** exultation *f*; **to sing in e.** chanter le cœur plein de joie

ex voto [eks'vəʊtəʊ] **N** *Rel* **e. (offering)** ex-voto *m inv*

ex warehouse **ADV** départ entrepôt

ex works **ADV** départ usine

EYE [aɪ] **N 1** *(of human, animal)* œil *m*, *pl* yeux; **to have blue eyes** avoir les yeux bleus; **a man with green eyes** un homme aux yeux verts; **to have good eyes** avoir de bons yeux; **to open/close one's eyes** ouvrir/fermer les yeux; **to open one's eyes wide** ouvrir les yeux tout grands; **to have the sun/the light in one's eyes** avoir le soleil/la lumière dans les yeux; **I've got something in my e.** j'ai quelque chose dans l'œil; **with tears in one's eyes** les larmes aux yeux; **dry your eyes** essuyez vos larmes; **he could not keep his eyes open** il dormait debout; **at e. level** à la hauteur des yeux; **to maintain e. contact with sb** soutenir le regard de qn; **to make e. contact with sb** regarder qn (droit) dans les yeux; **to try to make e. contact with sb** chercher le regard de qn; **she always avoids e. contact (with me)** elle évite tout le temps mon regard; **to look sb straight in the e.** regarder qn droit dans les yeux; *Zool* **simple e.** œil simple, ocelle *m*; *Zool* **compound e.** œil composé *ou* à facettes

2 *(idioms of observation, awareness etc)* **as far as the e. can see** à perte de vue; **to keep one's eyes and ears open** avoir l'œil et l'oreille aux aguets; **to keep one's eyes open** *or Fam* **peeled** *or Fam* **skinned** avoir *ou* ouvrir l'œil; *Fig* **to open sb's eyes** ouvrir les yeux à qn, dessiller les yeux à qn (**to** sur); *Fig* **to do sth with one's eyes open** faire qch en connaissance de cause; **I could do it with my eyes shut** je pourrais le faire les yeux fermés; **to shut** *or* **close one's eyes to sb's faults** fermer les yeux sur les défauts de qn; **to be all eyes** être tout yeux; **all eyes were upon her** elle était au centre de tous les regards, tous les regards étaient posés sur elle; **to strike/catch the e.** frapper/attirer l'œil *ou* les regards; **to catch sb's e.** *(of person, thing)* attirer l'attention de qn; *Parl* **to catch the Speaker's e.** obtenir la parole; **it pleases/delights the e.** cela charme/réjouit les yeux *ou* les regards; **he has eyes in** *or* **at the back of his head** il a des yeux d'Argus; **he has eyes for nobody but her** il n'a d'yeux que pour elle; **to set** *or* **lay eyes on sth** poser les yeux sur qch, apercevoir qch, voir qch; **it was the biggest fish I'd ever laid eyes on** c'était le plus gros poisson que j'aie jamais vu; **to see sth with one's own eyes** voir qch de ses propres yeux; **it took place before my (very) eyes** cela s'est passé sous mes yeux; **to see sth in one's mind's e.** voir qch en imagination *ou* en idée; *Fig* **where are your eyes?** êtes-vous aveugle?; **use your eyes!** ouvre les yeux!; **to run** *or* **cast one's e. over sth** jeter un coup d'œil sur qch; **to look at sth with a critical/experienced e.** regarder qch d'un œil critique/exercé; **with jealous eyes** d'un œil jaloux; **you can see that with half an e.** cela saute aux yeux; **anyone with half an e. can see it's a fake** du premier coup d'œil, n'importe qui verrait que c'est un faux; **with half an e. on the weather** sans quitter le ciel des yeux; **to keep an e. on sb/sth** surveiller qn/qch; **keep your e. on him!** ne le quittez pas des yeux!; **I couldn't keep my eyes off him/it** je ne pouvais pas en détacher mes yeux; **to keep an e. out for sth** être à l'affût de qch; **keep an e. out for anyone trying to sell it** soyez à l'affût au cas où quelqu'un essaierait de le vendre; **keep an e. on the children/potatoes** surveille les enfants/les pommes de terre; **a neighbour is keeping an e. on the house while we're away** un de nos voisins a l'œil sur la maison quand nous sommes absents; **to keep one's e. on the ball** suivre *ou* Fam fixer la balle; **keep your eyes on the road** regarde la route; **to have one's e. on sb/sth** *(be watching)* avoir qn/qch à l'œil; *(have in mind, be thinking of acquiring)* avoir l'œil sur qn/qch; **the police have had their e. on him for some time** cela fait un certain temps que la police l'a à l'œil; **under the (watchful) e. of …** sous la surveillance de …

3 *(point of view, perception)* **everyone is equal in the eye(s) of the law** tout le monde est égal devant la loi; **in the eyes of all, he is guilty** aux yeux de tous, il est coupable; **through sb else's eyes** du point de vue de qn d'autre; **to be very much in the public e.** occuper une position très en vue; **to have an e. for a horse** s'y connaître en chevaux, être bon juge des chevaux; **to have an e. for a bargain** savoir reconnaître une bonne affaire; **with the e. of a painter** d'un œil de peintre; **an e. for detail/colour** l'œil pour le détail/la couleur

4 *(idiomatic expressions)* **to be up to the** *or* **one's eyes in work/debt** avoir du travail/des dettes par-dessus la tête; **to see e. to e. with sb** voir les choses du même œil que qn; **for your eyes only** confidentiel; *Fam* **that's one in the e. for him!** ça lui fait les pieds!; *Old-fashioned Fam* **my e.!** mon œil!; *Bible* **an e. for an e., a tooth for a tooth** œil pour œil, dent pour dent; **to pass through the e. of a needle** passer par le trou d'une aiguille; *Fig* **at the e. of the hurricane** dans un havre de paix, dans un îlot préservé; **to make eyes at sb,** *Fam* **to give sb the (glad) e.** lancer des œillades *ou* faire de l'œil à qn; *Fam* **to make sheep's eyes at sb** lancer des œillades amoureuses à qn; **with an e. to …** en vue de …; **he does everything with an e. for** *or on* *or* **to the main chance** il fait tout avec son propre intérêt en vue

5 *(specialist uses) (bud)* œil *m*, *pl* yeux, bourgeon *m*; *(on potato)* germe *m*; *(in grafting)* œilleton *m*; *(hole) (of needle, rigging)* œil, *pl* œils; *(of support, prop)* collet *m*, œillet *m*; *(with screw thread)* piton *m*; *Met (of storm)* œil; *Mil* **eyes right/left!** tête (à) droite/(à) gauche!; *Mil* **eyes front!** fixe!; *Sport* **to get one's e. in** se faire la main; **eyes** *(on peacock's tail)* yeux *mpl*, miroirs *mpl*; **bird's eyes** *(in mahogany etc)* tourbillons *mpl*; *Electron* **electric** *or* **magic e.** cellule *f* photoélectrique

6 *Fam (private detective)* détective *m ou* enquêteur *m* privé

VT (**eyed; eyeing**) *(look at)* regarder, observer (**with suspicion** d'un air soupçonneux); *(weigh up) (person, obstacle etc)* mesurer des yeux; **to e. sb up and down** regarder qn de la tête aux pieds

▸▸**e. bank** banque *f* des yeux; **e. camera** caméra *f* oculaire; *Fam* **e. candy** beaux mecs/belles nanas; **his latest piece of e. candy** sa dernière nana; **e. contact** croisement *m* des regards; **e. drops** gouttes *fpl* pour les yeux; **e. end** *(of cable)* œil, piton; **e. hospital** centre *m* hospitalier d'ophtalmologie; **e. make-up** maquillage *m* pour les yeux; **e. movement camera** caméra oculaire; **e. shadow** ombre *f* à paupières; **e. socket** orbite *f*; **e. test** examen *m* de la vue

▸ **eye up** **VT SEP** *Fam* **1** *(with sexual interest)* **to e. up the girls/boys** reluquer les filles/les garçons; **he eyed her up** il l'a reluquée

2 *(estimate strength etc of) (opponent etc)* jauger (d'un coup d'œil)

eyeball ['aɪbɔːl] N globe *m* oculaire; *Fig* **to come e. to e.** *(of two people)* s'affronter; **to come e. to e. with sb** affronter qn; **an e. to e. confrontation** un affrontement direct **VT** *Fam* regarder en face

eyebath ['aɪbɑːθ] N *Br Med* **1** œillère *f* **2** *(liquid)* bain *m* d'œil

eyebrow ['aɪbraʊ] N sourcil *m*; *Fig* **he never raised an e.** *(in disapproval, astonishment)* il n'a pas sourcillé; *Fig* **(some) eyebrows were raised at this suggestion** *(in disapproval)* cette proposition a suscité des grimaces de désapprobation; *(in astonishment)* cette proposition a suscité de l'étonnement
▸ ▸ **e. pencil** crayon *m* à sourcils; **e. tweezers** pince *f* à épiler

eye-catching ADJ *(design, dress, title)* accrocheur, -euse; *(advertisement)* tapageur, -euse

eyecup ['aɪkʌp] N *Am* = **eyebath 1**

-eyed [aɪd] SUFF **blue-e.** aux yeux bleus; **wide-e.** aux grands yeux

eyeful ['aɪfʊl] N **to get an e. of mud/sand/water** recevoir de la boue/du sable/de l'eau plein les yeux; *Fam* **to get an e.** *(look)* se rincer l'œil; *Fam* **she's quite an e.** elle vaut le coup d'œil

eyeglass ['aɪɡlɑːs] N *(monocle)* monocle *m*; **watchmaker's e.** loupe *f* d'horloger

eyeglasses ['aɪɡlɑːsɪz] NPL *Am (spectacles)* lunettes *fpl*

eyehole ['aɪhəʊl] N **1** *(in mask)* **eyeholes** ouvertures *fpl* pour les yeux **2** *(small opening)* petite ouverture *f*, judas *m*; *Tech* trou *m* de regard *ou* de visite

eyelash ['aɪlæʃ] N cil *m*
▸ ▸ **e. curlers** recourbe-cils *m inv*

eyelet ['aɪlɪt] N œillet *m*

eyelevel ['aɪlev(ə)l] ADJ qui est à la hauteur des yeux
▸ ▸ **e. grill** gril *m* surélevé

eyelid ['aɪlɪd] N paupière *f*; *Fig* **he didn't bat an e.** il n'a pas sourcillé

eye-line N *TV etc* direction *f* du regard

eyeliner ['aɪlaɪnər] N eye-liner *m*, *pl* eye-liners

eye-opener N **1** **that was an e. for him** cela lui a ouvert les yeux, ça a été une révélation pour lui **2** *Am (drink)* petit verre *m* du matin

eye-opening ADJ qui ouvre les yeux, révélateur, -trice; **it was very e.** ça a été très révélateur

eyepatch ['aɪpætʃ] N cache *m* (sur l'œil); **eyepatches** caches (pour les yeux)

eyepiece ['aɪpiːs] N *Opt (of microscope etc)* oculaire *m*, viseur *m*; *(on camera)* œilleton *m*, oculaire *m* de visée; *Metal (of furnace)* lunette *f* de regard; *(of gas mask)* lunette *f*

eyepopping ['aɪpɒpɪŋ] ADJ *Am Fam* sensationnel

eyeshade ['aɪʃeɪd] N visière *f*

eyesight ['aɪsaɪt] N vue *f*; **to lose one's e.** perdre la vue; **to have good e.** avoir une bonne vue *ou* de bons yeux; **my e. is failing** ma vue baisse

eyesore ['aɪsɔːr] N **the building is an e.** le bâtiment est une horreur *ou* blesse la vue

eyespot ['aɪspɒt] N *(of butterfly etc)* ocelle *m*

eyestrain ['aɪstreɪn] N **to suffer from e.** avoir les yeux fatigués; **you'll give yourself e.** tu vas te fatiguer les yeux

eyetooth, *pl* **eyeteeth** ['aɪtuːθ, -tiːθ] N (dent *f*) canine *f*; **to cut one's eyeteeth** faire ses canines; *Fam (come to end of childhood)* sortir de sa première enfance; **I'd give my eyeteeth to go with them** je donnerais n'importe quoi pour aller avec eux

eyewash ['aɪwɒʃ] N *Pharm* collyre *m*; *Fig* **that's a lot** *or* **load of e.** *(nonsense)* tout ça, c'est du boniment

eyewitness ['aɪwɪtnɪs] N témoin *m* oculaire (**of** de); **an e. account** le récit d'un témoin oculaire

eyrie ['ɪərɪ] N *(of eagle)* aire *f*

ezine, e-zine ['iːziːn] N ezine *m*, e-zine *m*

F, f [ɛf] N **1** *(letter)* F, f *m*; **two f's** deux f **2** *Mus* fa *m*; **in F** en fa **3** *Sch* **to get an F** être recalé ▸▸ *Br Euph* **the F word** ≃ le mot de Cambronne

FA [ɛ'feɪ] N **1** *Br Ftbl (abbr Football Association)* = fédération *f* anglaise de football; **FA Cup** coupe *f* de la fédération anglaise de football **2** *Sl* **sweet FA** rien du tout, nib de nib

fa [fɑː] N *Mus* fa *m*

fab [fæb] ADJ *Br Fam* super, génial, -aux ▸▸ **the f. Four** = surnom des Beatles

Fabian ['feɪbɪən] ADJ *Pol* fabien, -ienne

fable ['feɪb(ə)l] N fable *f*, conte *m*

fabled ['feɪb(ə)ld] ADJ de la fable; *Fig* légendaire

fabric ['fæbrɪk] N **1** *Tex etc* tissu *m*, étoffe *f*; **dress fabrics** tissus pour robes; **silk, woollen and cotton fabrics** soieries *fpl*, lainages *mpl* et cotonnades *fpl* **2** *(of building, system)* structure *f*; **the f. of society** l'édifice *m* social; **the urban f.** le tissu urbain

> Note that the French word **fabrique** is a false friend and is never a translation for the English word **fabric**. Its most common meaning is **factory**.

fabricate ['fæbrɪkeɪt] VT *(news, story, alibi)* forger, fabriquer; *(document)* contrefaire

fabrication [fæbrɪ'keɪʃən] N *(of news, story, alibi)* fabrication *f*; *(of document)* contrefaçon *f*; **it's pure f.** c'est de la pure fabrication; **a pure f.** *(lie)* une histoire inventée de toutes pièces

fabulous ['fæbjʊləs] ADJ **1** *(marvellous)* prodigieux, fabuleux; *(price)* fou, *f* folle; **we had a f. evening** on a passé une soirée merveilleuse *ou* fabuleuse **2** *(fairy story)* fabuleux; *(character, city)* légendaire

fabulously ['fæbjʊləslɪ] ADV *(rich etc)* fabuleusement, prodigieusement

façade [fæ'sɑːd] N *Archit, Fig* façade *f*; **they put on a f. of family happiness** ils adoptent une façade de bonheur familial

FACE [feɪs]

> N visage **1** ▪ figure **1** ▪ mine **2**
> ▪ apparence **3** ▪ surface **5** ▪ face **6**
> ▪ façade **6**
> VT faire face à **1, 2** ▪ être confronté à **1**
> ▪ revêtir **3**
> VI être orienté

N 1 *(of person)* figure *f*, visage *m*; *Fam* **shut your f.!** ferme-la!, la ferme!; **you should have told him to shut his f.** tu aurais dû lui dire de la fermer *ou* boucler; **to hide one's f. in shame** se cacher le visage de honte; **to set one's f. against sth** s'opposer résolument à qch; **he won't show his f. here again!** il ne remettra pas les pieds ici!; **I told him so to his f.** je le lui ai dit en face; **I shall never be able to look her in the f. again** je ne pourrai jamais plus la regarder en face; *Fam* **I'm just going to put my f. on** je vais me maquiller; **her f. doesn't fit** *(in job, company etc)* sa tête ne nous/leur/*etc* revient pas; *Br Sl* **to be off one's f.** *(drunk)* être pété *ou* bourré; *(on drugs)* être défoncé; **the f. of Britain is changing** le visage de la Grande-Bretagne est en train de changer; **the unacceptable f. of capitalism** le visage inacceptable du capitalisme; **Communism with a human f.** le communisme à visage humain; **in the f. of danger** devant le danger; **in the f. of an enemy** en face d'un ennemi; **in the f. of this threat, he …** confronté à cette menace, il …; **full-f.** portrait portrait *m* de face

2 *(expression)* mine *f*, physionomie *f*; **to pull a long f.** tirer une tête longue comme ça, *Fam* tirer une tête de six pieds de long; **to make** *or* **pull faces** faire des grimaces (**at** à); **to keep a straight f.** garder son sérieux; **to put a good f. on it** faire contre mauvaise fortune bon cœur

3 *(appearance)* *(of sth)* apparence *f*, aspect *m*; **on the f. of it** au premier aspect, à première vue; **to save/lose f.** sauver/perdre la face; **loss of f.** humiliation *f*

4 *Fam (cheek)* culot *m*, front *m*, toupet *m*

5 *(surface)* *(of the earth)* surface *f*; **they disappeared from** *or* **off the f. of the earth** ils ont disparu de la surface du globe; **my keys can't just have disappeared off the f. of the earth!** mes clés n'ont pas pu se volatiliser tout de même!

6 *(side)* *(of coin, cliff, polyhedron, golf club etc)* face *f*; *(of material)* endroit *m*; *(of document)* recto *m*; *(of building)* devant *m*, façade *f*; *(of crystal)* facette *f*, plan *m*; *(of hammer)* plat *m*; *(on valve seat)* portée *f*; **bearing f.** (sur)face portante; **the north f. of the Eiger** la face nord de l'Eiger; **f. up/down** face en dessus/en dessous; **the toast landed f. up/down** le toast est tombé du bon/mauvais côté; *Min* **(coal) f.** front *m* de taille (du charbon)

7 *(of clock, watch)* cadran *m*

8 *Typ (of character)* œil *m*; **bold/light f.** (caractère *m*) gras *m*/maigre *m*

VT 1 *(confront)* *(difficulties, enemy)* affronter, faire face à; *(danger)* braver, affronter; **to f. facts** regarder les choses en face; **f. it** sois réaliste; **let's f. it** voyons les choses comme elles sont; **f. it – you've lost/she's not coming back** accepte-le – tu as perdu/elle ne reviendra pas; **the problem that faces us** le problème qui se pose à nous, le problème auquel nous sommes confrontés; **to be faced with a difficulty** se heurter à une difficulté; **to be faced with a decision** être confronté à une décision; **to f.** *or* **be faced with a crisis/a grim future** être confronté à une crise/un avenir lugubre; **he dared not f. me** il n'a pas osé me rencontrer face à face; *Fig* **to f. the music** faire front

2 *(look towards)* faire face à; **to f. the front**

regarder devant soi; **sunflowers always f. the sun** le tournesol est toujours tourné vers le soleil; **hotel facing the square** hôtel en façade sur la place; **the picture facing page 10** la gravure en regard de la page 10; **facing each other** l'un en face de l'autre; *Rail* **seat facing the direction of travel** place *f* dans le sens de la marche

3 *Metal etc (dress)* dresser, planer, surfacer; *Constr (cover) (wall etc)* revêtir (**with** de)

VI être orienté; **the house faces north** la maison est exposée au nord *ou* regarde le nord; **terrace facing south** terrasse orientée au sud; **to f. both ways** faire face des deux côtés; *Fig* ménager la chèvre et le chou; *Mil* **right/left f.!** face à droite/à gauche!

▸▸ **f. card** figure *(de jeu de cartes)*; **f. cloth** ≃ gant *m* de toilette; **f. cream** crème *f* pour le visage; *Br* **f. flannel** ≃ gant *m* de toilette; *Sport* **f. guard** masque *m* protecteur; **f. mask** *(cosmetic)* masque *(de beauté)*; *Sport* masque; **f. pack** masque *(de beauté)*; **f. powder** poudre *f*, *TV, Cin* **f. shot** plan de visage; *Am* **f. time** *(meeting)* = rencontre *f* en face à face entre deux personnes *(par opposition aux contacts par téléphone ou courrier électronique)*; *(on TV)* temps *m* de présence à l'écran; **we need some f. time to solve this** il faut qu'on se voie pour régler ça; **f. value** *(of bank note, traveller's cheque)* valeur *f* nominale; *(of stamp)* valeur faciale; **I took him at (his) f. value** je l'ai jugé sur les apparences; **to take what sb says at f. value** prendre ce que qn dit pour argent comptant

▸ **face about** VI *Mil* faire demi-tour

▸ **face down** VT SEP *(confront)* *(enemy, critic)* faire face à

▸ **face on to** VT INSEP *(garden, street)* donner sur

▸ **face out** VT SEP *(deal with, confront)* *(problems, difficult situation)* faire face à; *(threat)* défier; *(oppose, resist)* *(person)* résister à; **to f. it out** ne pas broncher; **to f. out opposition** résister à l'opposition

▸ **face up to** VT INSEP **1** *(confront)* *(person, danger)* affronter; **to f. up to one's fears** faire face à ses craintes; **you have to f. up to him over his treatment of you** il faut que tu lui dises en face que tu n'aimes pas la façon dont il te traite

2 *(accept)* regarder en face, faire face à; **to f. up to one's responsibilities** faire face à ses responsabilités

▸ **face with** VT SEP **to f. sb with sth** *(confront with)* confronter qn à qch; **why don't you f. them with it?** *(what they said or did)* pourquoi est-ce que tu ne le leur dis pas en face?; **he confessed when faced with the evidence/the dead man's wife** il a avoué lorsqu'il a été confronté aux preuves/à la femme du défunt

faceless ['feɪslɪs] ADJ *Fig* anonyme

face-lift N **1** lifting *m*; **to have a f.** se faire faire un lifting **2** *Fig (of facade of building)* restauration f, (of flat, house) rénovation f, retapage m; **Glasgow's had a f.** Glasgow a été remis à neuf

facer ['feɪsər] N Br Fam **that's a f.!** quelle tuile!

face-saving ADJ (agreement, compromise etc) qui sauve la face

facet ['fæsɪt] N **1** (of diamond, insect's eye) facette f **2** Fig (of situation) aspect m; **there are several facets to this problem/question** ce problème/cette question a plusieurs facettes
▶ VT (-tt-, Am -t-) (precious stone) facetter

facetious [fə'siːʃəs] ADJ (person, remark) facétieux, plaisant, bouffon; **I was being f.** je plaisantais; **there's no need to be so f.** il n'y a pas de quoi se moquer

facetiously [fə'siːʃəslɪ] ADV facétieusement; (to say sth) d'un ton facétieux; **do you have to behave so f.?** faut-il absolument que tu fasses le bouffon?

facetiousness [fə'siːʃəsnɪs] N caractère m facétieux, bouffonnerie f, (mood) humeur f facétieuse; **I find his f. a bit tiresome** je trouve ses bouffonneries un peu lassantes; **there's no need for f.** il n'y a pas de quoi se moquer

face-to-face ADJ (meeting) face-à-face; **a f. encounter** un face-à-face; **to bring sb f. with sb/the consequences of one's actions** confronter qn avec qn/aux conséquences de ses actions; **to come f. with sb** se trouver face à face avec qn; **to meet sb f.** rencontrer qn face à face

facetted ['fæsɪtɪd] ADJ à facettes

facia ['feɪʃə] N Br Aut tableau m de bord

facial ['feɪʃ(ə)l] ADJ (nerve, tic) facial, -aux; (expression, hair) du visage
▶ N soins mpl du visage; **to have a f.** se faire faire des soins du visage
▶▶ **f. scrub** exfoliant m

facialist ['feɪʃəlɪst] N = esthéticienne f spécialisée dans les soins du visage

facile ['fæsaɪl, -ɪl] ADJ **1** (simplistic) simpliste **2** Old-fashioned Pej facile; **to be a f. liar** être un menteur habile

facilitate [fə'sɪlɪteɪt] VT (action) faciliter

facilitator [fə'sɪlɪteɪtər] N Mktg auxiliaire mf

facility [fə'sɪlɪtɪ] N **1** (ease) facilité f, **f. in speaking/writing** facilité à parler/écrire; **to do sth with great f.** faire qch avec une grande facilité; **to have a f. at or for doing sth** avoir de la facilité à ou pour faire qch
2 (means) (usu pl) **facilities** aménagements mpl; **the building has limited facilities for the handicapped** le bâtiment est doté d'aménagements limités pour les handicapés; **storage/cooking facilities** installations fpl de stockage/cuisine; **transport facilities** moyens mpl de transport; **play/educational facilities** équipements mpl récréatifs/scolaires; **the village has few shopping facilities** le village ne compte pas beaucoup de magasins; **we have no facilities for it** nous ne sommes pas équipés pour cela; **facilities for payment** facilités fpl de paiement; **they are given every f. for improving their French** on leur accorde toutes facilités de se perfectionner en français; Aviat **ground facilities** installations au sol; Euph **can I use the facilities?** (toilet) est-ce que je peux utiliser les toilettes?; TV etc **facilities man** technicien m, prestataire m
3 esp Am (establishment) établissement m; (hotel) hôtel m; **training/research f.** établissement de formation/recherche

facing ['feɪsɪŋ] N **1** Sewing (material) revers m; (on outside) parement m; (on inside) parementure f, Constr (of wall etc) revêtement m; Mil **regimental facings** = parements mpl (de

la manche ou du col) servant à distinguer les différents corps **2** (in shop) frontal m, frontale f
▶ ADJ (page) ci-contre
▶▶ Constr **f. brick** brique f de parement; **f. pages** pages fpl en regard

facsimile [fæk'sɪmɪlɪ] N **1** (copy) fac-similé m, pl fac-similés; Law (of will etc) copie f figurée; **to reproduce sth in f., to make a f. of sth** faire un fac-similé de qch; **f. signature** signature f autographiée **2** Tel télécopie f
▶▶ **f. machine** télécopieur m

fact [fækt] N **1** fait m; **f. and fiction** le réel et l'imaginaire; **scientific facts** les vérités fpl scientifiques; **to stick to the facts** s'en tenir aux faits; **just give me the facts** donnez-moi simplement les faits; **the f. that you're a woman** le fait que vous soyez une femme; **the f. (of the matter) is that …** le fait est que …; **owing to the f. that …** du fait que …; **it's a f. that …** il est de fait que …; **to know for a f. that …** savoir pertinemment que …; **apart from the f. that …** hormis que …; **in f.** de fait; **in point of f.** en fait; Law **the jury only decides issues of f.** les jurés ne sont juges que du fait; **the facts of life** les choses de la vie; **it's a f. of life** c'est une réalité
▶▶ **f. sheet** fiche f d'informations

fact-finding ADJ (mission etc) d'information, d'enquête

faction¹ ['fækʃən] N (group) faction f

faction² N Cin, TV docudrame m

factious ['fækʃəs] ADJ factieux

factitious [fæk'tɪʃəs] ADJ factice, artificiel, -elle

factor ['fæktər] N **1** facteur m; Math diviseur m, facteur; Tech (of drag, amplification etc) coefficient m; Math **the highest common f.** le plus grand commun diviseur; Econ **f. of production** facteur de production; **demand f.** facteur de consommation; **f. of safety, safety f.** facteur de sécurité; Tech **load f.** coefficient m de charge; **the human f.** le facteur humain **2** Com (agent) agent m, dépositaire m; Scot (of estate) intendant m **3** Fin (factoring company) société f d'affacturage
▶▶ Math **f. analysis** analyse f factorielle; Econ **f. market** marché m des facteurs de production

factorage ['fæktərɪdʒ] N Fin courtage m, commission f (d'affacturage)

factoring ['fæktərɪŋ] N Com affacturage m
▶▶ **f. company** société f d'affacturage

factory ['fækt(ə)rɪ] N usine f, **munitions f.** fabrique f de munitions; **biscuit f.** biscuiterie f
▶▶ **f. farm** ferme f industrielle; **f. farming** élevage m industriel; **f. inspection** inspection f du travail; **f. inspector** inspecteur, -trice d'usine; **f. manager** directeur, -trice d'usine; **f. overheads** frais mpl généraux de fabrication; **f. price** prix m usine, prix sortie usine; **f. (retail) outlet** magasin m d'usine; **f. ship** navire-usine m, pl navires-usine; **f. shop** magasin d'usine; **f. work** travail m en usine ou d'usine; **f. worker** ouvrier, -ère en usine

factotum [fæk'təʊtəm] N factotum m, homme m/femme f à tout faire

factual ['fæktʃʊəl] ADJ (account, information, description) factuel, -elle, reposant sur les faits; (knowledge) des faits

factually ['fæktʃʊəlɪ] ADV en ce qui concerne les faits; (to report, describe etc) objectivement

facultative ['fækəltətɪv] ADJ facultatif, -ive

faculty ['fækəltɪ] N **1** (of mind, body) faculté f, pouvoir m; **the f. of speech** le don de la parole; **to be in possession of all one's faculties** jouir de toutes ses facultés **2** (ability) facilité f, talent m; **to have a f. for doing sth** avoir

des facilités pour faire qch; **to have the f. of observation** être observateur **3** Univ (departments) faculté f, Am (teaching staff) professorat m, corps m enseignant

fad [fæd] N lubie f, **it's only a passing f.** ce n'est qu'une toquade, ce n'est qu'un engouement passager; **the f. for macrobiotic food** la lubie pour les aliments macrobiotiques; **to have a f. about sth** se toquer de qch

faddiness ['fædɪnɪs] N his f. ses goûts mpl difficiles

faddy ['fædɪ] ADJ capricieux, maniaque; **he's f. about his food, he's a f. eater** il est difficile sur la nourriture

fade [feɪd] VI **1** (of flowers) se faner, se flétrir; (of colours) passer; (of material) se décolorer, déteindre; (of hope) s'éteindre; (of light, sound) s'affaiblir; **the light is fading** (daylight) le jour baisse; TV, Cin **to f. to black** faire un fondu au noir; **colours that f. into each other** couleurs qui se fondent; **summer fades into autumn** peu à peu l'automne succède à l'été; **to f. from memory** s'effacer de la mémoire **2** TV, Cin faire un fondu; **to f. to black** faire un fondu au noir **3** Am Fam (leave) s'esbigner, calter
▶ VT **1** faner, décolorer; **curtains faded by the sun** rideaux décolorés par le soleil **2** TV, Cin fondre
▶ N **1** TV, Cin fondu m **2** (of drum brakes) fading m, évanouissement m

▶ **fade away** VI (of light, sound) s'affaiblir; Fig (of person) dépérir

▶ **fade in** VI (of scene in film) ouvrir en fondu; (of music) commencer en fondu sonore
▶ VT SEP TV, Cin ouvrir en fondu; Radio (sound) monter; **to f. the music in** introduire la musique en fondu sonore

▶ **fade out** VI (of scene in film) se terminer en fondu; (of music) se terminer en fondu sonore
▶ VT SEP TV, Cin fermer en fondu; (music) terminer par un fondu sonore

faded ['feɪdɪd] ADJ (flower, memory) fané, flétri; (material) décoloré; (beauty, colour) défraîchi, passé; (photograph) jauni

fade-in N (of scene, music) ouverture f en fondu

fade-in-fade-out Cin, Radio, TV N fondu m enchaîné
▶ VI faire un fondu enchaîné

fade-out N (of scene, music) fermeture f en fondu

fader ['feɪdər] N TV, Cin potentiomètre m

fading ['feɪdɪŋ] ADJ (flower) qui se fane; (light) pâlissant
▶ N **1** (of plant) flétrissure f, (of material) décoloration f **2** Radio fading m **3** Cin fondu m

faecal, Am **fecal** ['fiːk(ə)l] ADJ fécal, -aux
▶▶ **f. matter** matières fpl fécales, déjections fpl

faeces, Am **feces** ['fiːsiːz] NPL Physiol fèces fpl, matières fpl fécales

faff [fæf] Br Fam N (panic) panique f, (effort) **it's too much of a faff** c'est trop compliqué
▶ VI **1** (waste time) glander; **stop faffing!** arrêtez de tourner en rond! **2** (potter) s'occuper, bricoler

▶ **faff about, faff around** VI **1** (waste time) glander; **stop faffing about!** arrêtez de tourner en rond! **2** (potter) s'occuper, bricoler; **stop faffing about with the radio** arrête de tripoter la radio

fag [fæg] N **1** Br Fam (unpleasant job) corvée f **2** Am Pej Sl (homosexual) pédé m, pédale f **3** Br Fam (cigarette) clope m, sèche f **4** Br Sch (pupil) = jeune élève m attaché au service d'un grand
▶ VI (-gg-) **1** Br Sch **to f. for a senior** (of pupil) faire les corvées d'un grand **2** Old-fashioned Fam (work hard) travailler dur, s'échiner

▸▸ *Br Fam* **f. end** *(of cigarette)* mégot *m*; *Fig (remainder)* reste *m*; *(of material, winter)* bout *m*; *(of conversation)* dernières bribes *fpl*; *Sl* **f. hag** fille *f* à pédés

▸ **fag out vt sep** *Fam (of work etc)* éreinter; **fagged out** épuisé, éreinté

fagged [fægd] **ADJ** *Br Fam* **I can't be f.** ça ne me dit pas; **I could never really be f. about things like that** ces trucs-là ne m'ont jamais trop rien dit; **I don't know how he can be f. doing that** je ne sais pas comment il peut s'embêter à faire ça

faggot ['fægət] **N** **1** *Am Pej Sl (homosexual)* pédé *m*, pédale *f* **2** *Br Culin* boulette *f* (de viande) **3** *(bundle of wood)* fagot *m*

faggy ['fægɪ] **ADJ** *Am Pej Sl* qui fait tapette

fah [fɑ:] **N** *Mus* = **fa**

Fahrenheit ['færənhaɪt] **ADJ** *Phys (scale, thermometer)* Fahrenheit; **ten degrees F.** dix degrés Fahrenheit

faience [faɪ'jɑ:ns] **N** *Cer* faïence *f*

FAIL [feɪl]

N	échec **1**
VI	recaler ▪ rater
VT	échouer **1** ▪ baisser **2** ▪ tomber en panne **2** ▪ manquer **2**

N 1 *(in exam)* échec *m*; **she got three passes and two fails** elle a réussi trois examens et en a raté deux; **he had never had a single f. in his life** il n'avait jamais raté un examen de sa vie

2 *Comput (when logging in)* erreur *f*

3 without f. sans faute

VI 1 *(not succeed) (of person)* ne pas réussir, échouer, manquer son coup; *(in exam)* échouer; *(of negotiations etc)* ne pas aboutir; *(of play)* faire fiasco; *(of business)* faire faillite; *(of project)* échouer; **he failed in his attempt to ...** il a échoué dans sa tentative de ...; **I f. to see why/how ...** je ne vois pas pourquoi/comment ...; **the discussions have failed to bring any progress** les discussions n'ont pas réussi à produire le moindre progrès; **the high proportions of pupils who are failing** la forte proportion d'élèves qui échouent à leurs examens

2 *(be inadequate)* manquer, faire défaut; *(of health, patient)* décliner; *(of health, light, memory, strength)* baisser; *(of eyesight)* faiblir, baisser; *(of brakes, heart, support)* lâcher; *(of engine)* tomber en panne; **his parachute failed** son parachute ne s'est pas ouvert; **if all else fails** en désespoir de cause; **to f. in one's duty** manquer à son devoir; **to f. to do sth** négliger de faire qch; **she was charged with failing to report an accident** elle a été inculpée pour avoir manqué de signaler un accident; **he failed to mention that ...** il a omis de faire remarquer que ...; **the cheque failed to arrive** le chèque n'est pas arrivé; **the engine failed to start** le moteur a refusé de démarrer; **she never fails to visit me on Sundays** elle ne manque jamais de me rendre visite le dimanche; **it never fails** *(it always happens)* ça ne manque jamais; *(of remedy)* ça ne rate jamais

VT *Sch (candidate)* refuser, recaler; *(exam)* être refusé *ou* recalé à; *(essay)* rater; **to f. a drugs test** être positif au contrôle antidopage; **words f. me** les mots me manquent; **his nerve failed him** le courage lui a fait défaut, il a manqué de courage; **I won't f. you** vous pouvez compter sur moi; **he had failed her before** il lui avait déjà fait faux bond; **his memory/eyesight was beginning to f. him** sa mémoire/vue commençait à lui faire défaut

failed [feɪld] **ADJ** *(candidate)* refusé, recalé; *Com (company)* en faillite; *(project, scheme)*

qui n'a pas abouti; *(artist, politician)* raté

▸▸ *Comput* **f. login** ouverture *f* de session avortée

failing ['feɪlɪŋ] **ADJ** *(sight, strength etc)* défaillant, baissant; **to be in f. health** avoir une santé défaillante

N *(fault)* faiblesse *f*, défaut *m*; **with all her failings** malgré tous ses défauts

PREP = *ou* au défaut de; **f. a satisfactory reply** faute de réponse satisfaisante; **f. which** faute de quoi; **f. all else** en désespoir de cause; **call me at home or, f. that, at the office** appelle-moi à la maison ou, à défaut, au bureau

failsafe ['feɪlseɪf] **ADJ** *(system)* protégé contre les incidents; **f. device** dispositif *m* de sécurité positive

failure ['feɪljər] **N 1** *(lack of success)* insuccès *m*, non-réussite *f*; *(in exam, of play)* échec *m*; *Com* faillite *f*; **the experiment was or proved or turned out a f.** l'expérience n'a pas réussi *ou* a raté; **the expedition ended in f.** l'expédition s'est soldée par un échec; **the team's f. to win the championship was a great surprise** cela a été une grande surprise que l'équipe n'ait pas remporté le championnat; **the f. of his new film** l'échec qu'a rencontré son nouveau film

2 *(person)* raté, -ée; *(play etc)* four *m*, fiasco *m*; **I'm a complete f. as a teacher** comme professeur, je suis complètement nul; *Sch* **there are too many failures** trop de candidats ont été recalés

3 *(neglect)* manque *m*; **f. to keep a promise** manquement *m* à une promesse; **f. to pay a bill** défaut *m* de paiement d'un effet; **your f. to apologise is inexcusable** tu es inexcusable de ne pas avoir demandé pardon; **he was angry at her f. even to write** il était en colère qu'elle n'écrive même pas

4 *(of machine)* panne *f*; *(of software, hardware)* panne, défaillance *f*; *(of organ)* insuffisance *f*; *Elec* **power f.** panne de courant;

▸▸ *Am Com* **f. investment** investissement *m* en valeurs de redressement *ou* de retournement; **f. rate** taux *m* de panne

fain [feɪn] **ADV** *Arch, Lit* volontiers

faint [feɪnt] **ADJ 1** *(weak) (hope, light, sound, possibility etc)* faible; *(praise)* tiède; *(colour)* pâle, délavé; *(sound, touch, bruise etc)* léger, -ère; *(idea)* vague, peu précis; *(mark etc)* à peine visible; *(inscription)* indistinct; **to give a f. smile** *(not be amused or pleased)* sourire du bout des lèvres; **I could detect a f. smile on her lips** j'ai décelé un petit sourire sur ses lèvres; **a f. tinge of blue** une légère nuance bleuâtre; **I haven't the faintest (idea)** je n'en ai pas la moindre idée; **the sound of the footsteps grew fainter** le bruit des pas s'affaiblit

2 to feel *or* **be f.** se sentir mal; **I was feeling f. with hunger** j'avais tellement faim que la tête me tournait; **to be f. with tiredness** tomber de fatigue

3 *Arch, Lit (timid)* timide; *Prov* **f. heart never won fair lady** jamais honteux n'eut belle amie

N *Med* évanouissement *m*, défaillance *f*; **to fall down in a f.** tomber évanoui

VI s'évanouir, défaillir; **she fainted with pain** elle s'évanouit de douleur

faint-hearted [-'hɑ:tɪd] **ADJ** pusillanime

faint-heartedly [-'hɑ:tɪdlɪ] **ADV** avec pusillanimité

faint-heartedness [-'hɑ:tɪdnɪs] **N** pusillanimité *f*

fainting ['feɪntɪŋ] **N** évanouissement *m*

▸▸ **f. fit** évanouissement

faintly ['feɪntlɪ] **ADV** *(to hear, shine)* faiblement; *(uneasy, amused, ridiculous)* légèrement; *(to remember, see)* vaguement; **f. visible** à peine visible; **to smile f.** esquisser

un sourire; **it is f. possible that ...** il y a une faible possibilité pour que ...

faintness ['feɪntnɪs] **N** *(of voice, sound etc)* faiblesse *f*; *(of breeze etc)* légèreté *f*; *Med* malaise *f*, **have you been suffering from f.?** avez-vous souffert d'évanouissements?; **it's the f. of the writing that's the problem** le problème c'est que l'écriture est pâle

fair¹ [feər] **N** foire *f*, world **f.** exposition *f* universelle; *Br* **(fun)** fête *f* foraine; **village f.** kermesse *f*

FAIR²

| **ADJ** | juste **1** ▪ équitable **1** ▪ assez bon **2** ▪ favorable **3** ▪ beau **4** ▪ blond **6** |
| **ADV** | loyalement **1** |

ADJ 1 *(just)* juste, équitable; *(price)* raisonnable; *(wage)* équitable; *(fight)* loyal, -aux; **to get a f. trial** être jugé de façon équitable; **f.'s f.** il faut être juste; **that's only f.** ce n'est que juste; **it's not f.** ce n'est pas juste; **it isn't f. to expect children to ...** ce n'est pas raisonnable de demander à des enfants de ...; **f. enough!** ça va!, d'accord!; **it's all f. and above board** *or* **all f. and square** c'est de bonne guerre; **he is strict but f.** il est sévère mais juste *ou* sans parti pris; **it is only f. to say that ...** il faut dire que ...; **but, to be f.** mais, pour être honnête; **as is only f.** comme il se doit; *Sl* **f. do's** ce n'est que justice; **a f. example** un bon exemple; **a f. exchange** un échange équitable; *Prov* **f. exchange is no robbery** tout le monde est content; **everyone deserves their f. share** chacun mérite d'avoir ce qui lui est dû; **he got more than his f. share!** il a eu plus que ce qui lui revenait!; **he's had more than his f. share of criticism/problems** il a eu largement sa part de critiques/problèmes; **by f. means or foul** d'une manière ou d'une autre; *Prov* **all's f. in love and war** à la guerre comme à la guerre

2 *(quite good)* assez bon; **a f. amount of** pas mal de; **he has a f. chance of success** il a des chances de réussir; **in f. condition** acceptable; **a f. idea** une bonne idée; **a f. number of ...** un nombre respectable de ...; **a f. pace** un bon pas *ou* rythme; **f. to middling** comme ci comme ça; **in a f. way to recovering** en bonne voie de rétablissement

3 *(wind etc)* propice, favorable; **f. weather** beau temps

4 *esp Lit, Arch (attractive)* beau, *f* belle; **the fair(er) sex** le beau sexe; *Hum* **to make sth with one's own f. hands** faire qch de ses propres mains; *Hum* **faire qch tout seul comme un grand**

5 *(specious)* spécieux; **f. promises/words** de belles promesses/paroles

6 *(light-coloured) (person, hair)* blond; *(skin)* blanc, *f* blanche

7 *Sl (intensive)* **we had a f. old time of it at the party** nous nous sommes drôlement bien amusés à la fête

ADV 1 *(to act)* loyalement; **to play f.** jouer franc jeu; **to fight f.** se battre loyalement; **you can't say fairer than that** il n'y a pas plus équitable

2 *(completely)* complètement; **struck f. (and square) on the chin** frappé en plein menton

▸▸ *Br* **f. copy** copie *f* au propre *ou* au net; **f. game** proie *f* légitime; **f. play** fair-play *m inv*, franc-jeu *m inv*; *Com* **f. trade** commerce *m*

fairground ['feəgraʊnd] **N** champ *m* de foire

fair-haired **ADJ** blond, aux cheveux blonds; *Am Fig* **f. boy** chouchou *m*

fairing ['feərɪŋ] **N** *Aviat, Aut* carénage *m*

fairish ['feərɪʃ] **ADJ 1** *(hair)* plutôt blond **2** *(quite good)* assez bon

fairly ['feəlɪ] **ADV 1** *(to judge etc)* équitablement, avec justice; **to treat sb f.** traiter qn équitablement *ou* avec impartialité **2** *(to act, play etc)* honnêtement; *(to fight)* loyalement; **to come by sth f. (and squarely)** obtenir qch par des moyens honnêtes; **to win f. and squarely** *(clearly, easily)* remporter une nette victoire; *(without dishonest means)* vaincre honnêtement

3 *(quite) (rich, skilful etc)* assez; **f. good wine** vin passablement *ou* assez bon; **it is f. certain that ...** il est à peu près certain que ...; **to do sth f. well** faire qch d'une façon acceptable *ou* passable

4 *(well)* bien; **once the ship was f. under way** une fois le navire en bonne route; **we f. raced through the work** nous avons fait notre travail à bonne allure

5 *Fam (completely)* complètement, absolument

fair-minded ADJ équitable, juste

fairness ['feənɪs] N **1** *(of decision)* impartialité *f*; *(of person)* équité *f*, impartialité; *(of law, share)* équité; **in all f.** en toute justice; **in f. to him, he did help us a lot** pour lui rendre justice, il faut dire qu'il nous a beaucoup aidés **2** *Arch, Lit (beauty)* beauté *f* **3** *(of hair)* blondeur *f*; *(of skin)* blancheur *f*

fair-sized ADJ assez grand

fairway ['feəweɪ] N **1** *Golf* fairway *m* **2** *Naut* chenal *m*, passe *f*, passage *m*

fair-weather ADJ *(boat)* qui convient seulement pour le beau temps; **a f. friend** un ami des beaux *ou* bons jours

fairy ['feərɪ] N **1** fée *f*; **the wicked f.** la fée Carabosse **2** *Sl, Pej (homosexual man)* pédé *m*, tapette *f*, tante *f*
▸ ADJ féerique; **f. footsteps** des pas *mpl* légers; **f. voices** des voix *fpl* de fées
▸▸ **f. godmother** bonne fée *f*, *Fig* marraine *f* gâteau; **f. lights** guirlande *f* électrique; **f. queen** reine *f* des fées; **f. story** conte *m* de fées; *Fig (lie)* histoire *f* à dormir debout; **f. tale** conte *m* de fées; *Fig (lie)* histoire à dormir debout

fairyland ['feərɪlænd] N pays *m* ou royaume *m* des fées; *Fig (imaginary world)* féerie *f*

faith [feɪθ] N **1** *(trust)* foi *f*; **to have (every) f. in sb/sth** avoir (entièrement) confiance en qn/qch; **I don't have much f. in doctors** je ne fais pas beaucoup confiance aux médecins; **to have f. in God** avoir foi en Dieu; **to put one's f. in sb** accorder toute sa confiance à qn; **an act of f.** un acte de foi **2** *(religion)* religion *f*, foi *f*, croyance *f*; **what f. are you?** de quelle religion êtes-vous?; **to be of the Catholic/Jewish f.** être de religion catholique/juive; **the Christian f.** la foi chrétienne; **to lose one's f.** perdre la foi **3** *(loyalty)* **to keep f. with sb** tenir ses engagements envers qn; **to break f. with sb** manquer de foi *ou* de parole à qn; **good f.** bonne foi; **to say sth in good f.** dire qch en toute bonne foi; **to do sth in all good f.** faire qch en tout honneur; **bad f.** perfidie *f*
▸▸ **f. healer** guérisseur, -euse spirituel(elle); **f. healing** guérison *f* par la foi; **f. school** école *f* religieuse

faithful ['feɪθfʊl] ADJ **1** *(friend etc)* fidèle, loyal, -aux; *(copy)* exact, juste; *(translation, description, account)* fidèle; **to remain f. to sb/one's promises** rester fidèle à qn/ses promesses; **f. in every detail** exact jusqu'au moindre détail **2** *Rel* **the f.** les fidèles *mpl*; *(Islam)* **the party f.** les croyants *mpl*; *Pol* **the party f.** les fidèles du parti

faithfully ['feɪθfʊlɪ] ADV **1** *(loyally)* fidèlement, loyalement; **yours f.** *(in formal letter)* recevez l'expression de mes/nos sentiments distingués; **he promised f. to come tomorrow** il a promis formellement de venir demain **2** *(to copy)* exactement; *(to translate, follow instructions)* fidèlement

faithfulness ['feɪθfʊlnɪs] N **1** *(loyalty)* fidé-

lité *f*, loyauté *f* (**to** envers) **2** *(accuracy) (of report etc)* fidélité *f*, exactitude *f*

faithless ['feɪθlɪs] ADJ **1** *Rel (lacking faith)* infidèle, sans foi **2** *(to husband, wife etc)* infidèle (**to** à); *(to party, friend)* déloyal, -aux

faithlessness ['feɪθlɪsnɪs] N **1** *(lack of trust)* manque *m* de confiance **2** *(to husband, wife etc)* infidélité *f* (**to** à); *(to party, friend)* déloyauté *f*

fake [feɪk] N *(object)* article *m* faux *ou* truqué; **it's a f.** c'est un faux; **he's a f.** c'est un bluffeur
▸ ADJ faux, *f* fausse
▸ VT *(calculations etc)* truquer; *(signature)* contrefaire; *(illness)* simuler; **faked balance sheet** bilan truqué; **to f. a story** inventer une histoire; **she faked her own death** elle a fait croire à sa propre mort; **it's all faked** *(in cinema etc)* c'est du trucage
▸ VI *(pretend)* faire semblant, jouer la comédie

faker ['feɪkər] N *Fam (who pretends)* comédien, -ienne

faking ['feɪkɪŋ] N **it's just f.** c'est de la comédie

fakir ['feɪkɪr, fə'kɪər] N fakir *m*

falcon ['fɔːlkən] N *(bird)* faucon *m*

falconer ['fɔːlkənər] N fauconnier *m*

falconry ['fɔːlkənrɪ] N fauconnerie *f*

Falkland ['fɔːlklənd] N **the F. Islands, the Falklands** les (îles *fpl*) Malouines *fpl*, les îles Falkland

---

FALL [fɔːl]

N	chute **1, 3, 5, 8, 9** ▪ automne **2**
	▪ chutes **3** ▪ baisse **4, 5**
VI	tomber **1–3, 6–8** ▪ s'écouler **3**
	▪ baisser **4, 5**

N 1 *(of body etc)* chute *f*; *(in wrestling)* tomber *m*; *Theat (of curtain)* baisser *m*; *(of snow, rain)* précipitations *fpl*; **a f. of earth/rock** *(actual earth, rocks)* un éboulis de terre/pierres; **there's been another f.** il y a encore eu un éboulement; **to have a f.** faire une chute; **a bad f.** une mauvaise chute; **there has been a heavy f. of snow** il est tombé beaucoup de neige; *Fig* **to be heading** *or* **riding for a f.** courir à sa perte

2 *Am (autumn)* automne *m*

3 *(waterfall) (usu pl)* **falls** chute *f* (d'eau); **Victoria Falls** les chutes Victoria; **Niagara Falls** les chutes du Niagara

4 *(lowering) (of water)* décrue *f*, baisse *f*; *(of tide)* reflux *m*, jusant *m*; *(of voice)* cadence *f*

5 *(decrease) (in weight, number etc)* diminution *f*; *(of barometer, in pressure etc)* chute *f*; *(in temperature, interest, income, frequency)* baisse *f*; *Com, Fin (of prices, shares)* baisse; *(of currency)* dépréciation *f*; **f. in prices** baisse de prix

6 *(slope) (of road etc)* pente *f*

7 *(ruin) (of person)* perte *f*, ruine *f*; **after this f. from grace** après être tombé en disgrâce

8 *(capture) (of city)* chute *f*; *(of empire etc)* chute, déchéance *f*; **the F. of the Roman Empire** la chute de l'Empire romain; **the F. of the Bastille** la prise de la Bastille

9 *Rel* **the F. (of Man)** la chute

▸ VI *(pt* **fell** [fel]*, pp* **fallen** ['fɔːlən]*)* **1** *(from a height)* tomber; *Astron (of star)* filer; **to f. to the ground** tomber à terre; **she fell to her death** elle a fait une chute mortelle; **to f. off a ladder** tomber d'une échelle; **to f. 20 feet** faire une chute de six mètres; **the water falls over 800 m to the valley below** l'eau tombe dans une cascade de plus de 800 m de haut jusque dans la vallée; **the cliff falls sheer to the ocean below** la falaise descend à pic vers l'océan; **to f. out of the window** tomber par la fenêtre; **to f. on one's feet** retomber sur ses pieds; *Fig* avoir de la chance;

to f. short of a target manquer la cible; **to f. short of a past performance** être loin d'une performance passée; **to f. into a trap** tomber *ou* donner dans un piège; **to f. into sb's hands** tomber entre les mains de qn; **night is falling** la nuit tombe; **rain/snow had fallen overnight** il avait plu/neigé pendant la nuit; **his hair fell to his shoulders** *(hung down)* ses cheveux lui descendaient *ou* tombaient jusqu'aux épaules; **his hair keeps falling into his eyes** ses cheveux n'arrêtent pas de lui tomber dans les yeux

2 *(from standing or perpendicular position)* **to f. to the ground** tomber par terre; **to f. on one's knees** tomber à genoux; **to f. (in battle)** tomber au champ d'honneur; *Fig* **the scheme fell flat** le projet est tombé à l'eau

3 *(collapse) (of building)* s'écrouler, s'effondrer; **to f. to pieces** *or* **bits** tomber en morceaux; **when Liège fell** lorsque Liège capitula; **the government has fallen** le gouvernement a été renversé *ou* est tombé

4 *(diminish) (of price etc)* diminuer, baisser, chuter; *(of exchange etc)* baisser, se déprécier; *(of wind)* tomber; *Fig* **his stock is falling** son crédit est en baisse; **the thermometer/temperature has fallen ten degrees** le thermomètre/la température a baissé *ou* chuté de dix degrés

5 *(become lower) (of ground)* aller en pente, s'incliner; *(of tide etc)* baisser; **her eyes fell** elle a baissé les yeux; **his face fell** sa figure s'allonge; **my spirits fell** j'ai perdu tout courage; **to f. from one's position** déchoir de sa position; **to f. to the bottom of the league/list** tomber en bas du classement/de la liste; **to f. in sb's estimation** baisser dans l'estime de qn

6 *Rel (sin)* tomber, pécher; **to f. from grace** perdre la grâce; *Fig* **to f. from grace with sb** tomber en disgrâce auprès de qn

7 *(alight)* **a shadow fell on the wall** une ombre se projeta sur le mur; **his eye fell on a box/a curious headline** son regard est tombé sur une boîte/un titre curieux

8 *(occur)* tomber; **Christmas falls on a Thursday** Noël tombe un jeudi; **the accent falls on the last syllable** l'accent tombe sur la dernière syllabe; **it fell to me to break the bad news** c'est à moi qu'il est revenu d'annoncer la mauvaise nouvelle; **these facts f. under another category** ces faits entrent dans une autre catégorie; **that falls outside the scope of our investigation** ceci dépasse les limites de notre enquête

9 *(enter into given state)* **to f. under suspicion** *(of person)* devenir l'objet des soupçons, devenir suspect; **the country has fallen on hard times** le pays connaît des jours difficiles; **I soon fell in with their ways** *(became used to their way of doing things)* je me suis vite accoutumé à leur manière de faire; *(learnt routine)* j'ai bientôt appris la routine; **to f. in love with sb/sth** tomber amoureux de qn/qch; **to f. into a habit** contracter une habitude; **to f. into error** être induit en erreur; **to f. into despair** sombrer dans le désespoir; **to f. into line with** s'aligner sur

10 *(become)* **to f. asleep** s'endormir; **to f. ill** *or* **sick** tomber malade; **to f. silent** *(of person, guns)* se taire; **the room fell silent** le silence se fit dans la salle; **to f. vacant** *(of post)* se trouver vacant; **to f. (a) victim to ...** être victime de ...

11 *(begin)* **they fell to work/discussing (again)** ils se (re)mirent au travail/à discuter
▸▸ *Fam* **f. guy** *(dupe)* pigeon *m*; *(scapegoat)* bouc *m* émissaire

▸ **fall about** VI *(fall in different directions)* tomber de côté et d'autre; **to f. about (laughing)** se tordre de rire

▸ **fall apart** VI *(fall to pieces)* se désintégrer,

tomber en morceaux; *(of marriage)* se désintégrer, sombrer

▸ **fall away** VI 1 *(of ground)* s'affaisser

2 *(crumble)* se désintégrer; *(of plaster, paint)* s'écailler

3 *(of attendance)* diminuer; *(of followers etc)* déserter

4 *(of prejudice etc)* disparaître

▸ **fall back** VI 1 *(fall)* tomber à la renverse *ou* en arrière; **to f. back on the cushions** *(after trying to get up)* retomber sur les coussins; *(sink back)* se basculer en arrière sur les coussins; *(from standing position)* tomber à la renverse sur les coussins

2 *(of troops)* se replier, reculer; **to f. back a pace** reculer d'un pas

3 *StExch, Fin* **to f. back two points** se replier de deux points

▸ **fall back on** VT INSEP *(resort to)* avoir recours à; **she fell back on the usual clichés** elle a eu recours aux clichés habituels; **to have some money to f. back on** avoir de l'argent en réserve au cas où; **he knew he could always f. back on his parents** il savait qu'il pouvait compter sur ses parents

▸ **fall behind** VI *(of runner, political party etc)* être à la traîne, se faire distancer, rester en arrière; **to f. behind with the rent** être en retard pour payer son loyer; **to f. behind with one's work** prendre du retard dans son travail

▸ **fall down** VI 1 *(fall to ground)* tomber à terre *ou* par terre

2 *(of building etc)* s'écrouler, s'effondrer

3 *(fail)* échouer; **that's where their argument falls down** c'est sur ce point que leurs arguments ne tiennent plus debout; **where the whole thing falls down is …** là où plus rien ne tient debout *ou* où tout s'écroule, c'est …; **I fell down badly on the first question** j'ai complètement raté la première question; **to f. down on the job** ne pas être à la hauteur

▸ **fall for** VT INSEP *Fam* 1 *(fall in love with)* *(person)* tomber amoureux de; **I've fallen for that antique chair** j'ai eu le coup de foudre pour cette vieille chaise

2 *(be deceived by)* *(story etc)* se laisser prendre à; **to f. for it** s'y laisser prendre; **I'm not falling for that one!** ça ne prend pas!, à d'autres!

▸ **fall in** VI 1 *(of building, roof etc)* s'écrouler, s'effondrer; *(of trench etc)* s'ébouler; **I was running along the edge of the pool when I fell in** je courais le long de la piscine quand je suis tombé dedans

2 *Mil (of troops)* former les rangs; **f. in!** rassemblement!

▸ **fall in with** VT INSEP 1 *(person)* *(meet up with)* rencontrer par hasard; *(associate with)* fréquenter; **my son fell in with a bad crowd** mon fils s'est mis à avoir de mauvaises fréquentations

2 *(agree with)* *(suggestion)* accepter; *(request)* accéder à; **I fell in with the plans for a picnic** j'ai accepté le projet d'un pique-nique

▸ **fall off** VI 1 *(fall from something)* tomber; **I picked the violin up and the neck fell off** j'ai pris le violon et le manche est tombé

2 *(of followers etc)* faire défection; *(of profits)* diminuer; *(of speed)* ralentir; *(of wind)* tomber; *(of zeal)* se relâcher; *(of popularity)* baisser

3 *(of skills, standards, quality)* baisser

4 *Naut* abattre sous le vent

▸ **fall on** VT INSEP 1 *(of blame, responsibility, suspicion)* retomber sur

2 *(attack)* *(enemy)* attaquer; *(food)* se jeter sur; **they fell on each other in delighted relief** vivement soulagés, ils tombèrent dans les bras l'un de l'autre

▸ **fall out** VI 1 *(fall from inside sth)* tomber dehors; *(of hair)* tomber

2 *Mil (of troops)* rompre les rangs; **f. out! rompez!**

3 *(quarrel)* se brouiller, se fâcher *(with* avec*)*; **they have fallen out** ils sont fâchés *ou* brouillés

4 *(occur)* se passer, se dérouler; **as things fell out** en fin de compte

▸ **fall over** VI *(of person)* tomber (par terre); *(of thing)* se renverser, être renversé

VT INSEP *(stumble on)* trébucher sur; **move that suitcase before someone falls over it** déplace cette valise avant que quelqu'un ne se prenne les pieds dedans; *Fam* **publishers were falling over each other for her new book** les éditeurs se disputaient avec acharnement son nouveau livre; **he was falling over himself to please her** il se mettait en quatre pour lui plaire

▸ **fall through** VI *(of scheme etc)* ne pas aboutir, échouer, *Fam* tomber à l'eau

▸ **fall to** VI *Old-fashioned Fam (begin eating)* s'attaquer au repas

▸ **fall upon** VT INSEP = **fall on**

fallacious [fə'leɪʃəs] ADJ erroné

fallacy ['fæləsɪ] N erreur *f*, *(in logic)* sophisme *m*; **it is a f. that …** ce serait une erreur de croire que …; **the f. of this argument is that …** ce qui est faux dans ce raisonnement, c'est que …

fallback ['fɔːlbæk] N solution *f* de remplacement

ADJ de remplacement, alternatif

fallen ['fɔːlən] ADJ 1 *(leaf, tree etc)* tombé; *(angel)* déchu; *(idol)* tombé en disgrâce **2** *(immoral)* perdu

NPL *Mil, Lit* **in memory of the f.** en mémoire des soldats tombés au combat

▸▸ *Med* **f. arches** affaissement *m* de la voûte plantaire; *Old-fashioned* **f. woman** femme *f* déchue, fille *f* perdue

fallibility [fælɪ'bɪlɪtɪ] N faillibilité *f*

fallible ['fælɪb(ə)l] ADJ faillible

falling ['fɔːlɪŋ] ADJ *(piece of masonry, tile)* qui tombe; *(darkness etc)* tombant; *(temperature, membership, standards)* en baisse; *Com (prices)* qui baisse; *(market)* avec tendance à la baisse

N chute *f*, *(of prices, barometer etc)* baisse *f*

▸▸ **f. away** *(of support)* affaiblissement *m*; *(of supporters)* défection *f*, désertion *f*; **f. rocks** chute *f* de pierres; *Arch* **f. sickness** épilepsie *f*, **f. star** étoile *f* filante

fall(ing)-off N *(of support)* affaiblissement *m*; *(of supporters)* désertion *f*, défection *f*, *(of figures, rate etc)* diminution *f*, baisse *f*, *(of power, popularity)* déclin *m*; *(of zeal)* relâchement *m*; *(of orders, business)* ralentissement *m*

Fallopian [fə'ləʊpɪən] ADJ

▸▸ *Anat* **F. tube** trompe *f* de Fallope

fallout ['fɔːlaʊt] N retombées *fpl* (radioactives); *Fig* **the political f. from the scandal** les retombées politiques du scandale

fallow¹ ['fæləʊ] *Agr* N jachère *f*

ADJ *(land)* en jachère; **to lie f.** être en jachère; *Fig* **a f. period** une période de régénération

fallow² ADJ

▸▸ *Zool* **f. deer** daim *m*

false [fɔːls] ADJ 1 *(incorrect)* faux, *f* fausse; *(idea)* erroné; **to give sb a f. impression of sth** donner à qn une fausse impression sur qch; **to put a f. interpretation on sb's actions/words** mal interpréter les actions/paroles de qn; **one f. move and he would have killed me** si j'avais fait un faux mouvement, il m'aurait tué; **to put sb in a f. position** donner de qn l'image qu'il est en tort

2 *(dishonest)* hypocrite; *(unfaithful)* infidèle; *(promise etc)* mensonger; **he turns on the charm for them – it's all so f.!** il veut leur

faire du charme – quelle hypocrisie!; **to be in a f. position** être dans une situation délicate; **under f. pretences** par des moyens frauduleux; *(by lying)* sous des prétextes fallacieux

3 *(not real)* *(beard, nose etc)* faux, *f* fausse, artificiel, -elle, postiche; *(action etc)* feint, prétendu; *(coin, seal, document)* faux, contrefait; **it's a f. economy** ça ne revient pas moins cher

ADV *Lit, Old-fashioned* **to play sb f.** trahir qn; **his memory played him f.** sa mémoire l'a trahi *ou* lui a joué des tours

▸▸ **f. alarm** fausse alerte *f*, *Fam* canard *m*; **f. bottom** *(of box etc)* double fond *m*; **f. claim** *(made for product)* promesse *f* mensongère; **f. dawn** lueurs *fpl* annonciatrices de l'aube; *Acct* **f. entry** fausse écriture *f*, *Ling* **f. friend** faux ami *m*; **f. invoice** fausse facture *f*, *Psy* **f. memory syndrome** syndrome *m* des faux souvenirs; **f. modesty** fausse modestie *f*, **f. name** faux nom *m*; *Mus* **f. note** fausse note *f*, *Fig* **to strike a f. note** créer une fausse note; **f. positive** *(pregnancy etc test)* résultat *m* faussement positif; **f. report** fausse nouvelle *f*, *Sport* **f. start** faux départ *m*; **to get off to a f. start** faire un faux départ; **f. teeth** fausses dents *fpl*, dentier *m*; **f. trade description** description *f* commerciale erronée *ou* mensongère; **f. witness** faux témoin *m*; **to bear f. witness** faire un faux témoignage

false-hearted [-'hɑːtɪd] ADJ *Lit* fourbe

falsehood ['fɔːlshʊd] N 1 **to distinguish truth from f.** distinguer le vrai du faux **2** *Fml (lie)* mensonge *m*; **to tell a f.** dire un mensonge

falsely ['fɔːlslɪ] ADV faussement; **to smile f.** affecter un sourire; *esp Lit* **to act f.** agir déloyalement

falseness ['fɔːlsnɪs] N 1 *(of report, manner etc)* fausseté *f* **2** *Old-fashioned (of lover etc)* infidélité *f*

falsers ['fɔːlsəz] NPL *Br Fam Hum (teeth)* râtelier *m*, dentier *m*

falsetto [fɔːl'setəʊ] *Mus* N 1 *(voice)* voix *f* de fausset; **to sing (in) f.** chanter en fausset **2** *(singer)* fausset *m*

ADJ *(voice)* de fausset

falsies ['fɔːlsɪz] NPL *Fam* 1 *(padding for breasts)* soutien-gorge *m* rembourré **2** *(false breasts)* faux seins *mpl*

falsifiable [fɔːlsɪ'faɪb(ə)l] ADJ *Phil* falsifiable

falsification [fɔːlsɪfɪ'keɪʃən] N falsification *f*

falsify ['fɔːlsɪfaɪ] VT **(falsified; falsifying)** 1 *(make false)* *(document)* falsifier; *(balance sheet)* fausser; *(facts etc)* dénaturer **2** *(disprove)* prouver la fausseté de

falsity ['fɔːlsɪtɪ] N = **falseness**

falter ['fɔːltər] VI *(of voice)* hésiter, trembler; *(of person)* chanceler; *(in one's belief, conviction)* vaciller; *(of courage, determination)* défaillir; **his steps faltered as he neared the room** ses pas se firent hésitants tandis qu'il s'approchait de la pièce; **he faltered in his speech** il eut un moment d'hésitation

VT dire d'une voix hésitante; **he faltered his way through his speech** *(nervously)* il a prononcé son discours d'une voix hésitante; *(losing thread)* il n'a pas arrêté de perdre le fil de son discours

▸ **falter out** VT SEP *(excuse etc)* balbutier

faltering ['fɔːltərɪŋ] ADJ *(voice etc)* hésitant; *(courage, memory etc)* défaillant; *(legs)* chancelant; **to speak in a f. voice** parler d'une voix mal assurée; **to reply in f. Spanish** répondre dans un espagnol mal assuré; **with f. steps** d'un pas mal assuré *ou* chancelant; **a child's first f. steps** les premiers pas hésitants d'un enfant

fame [feɪm] N renom m, renommée f; **to win f.** devenir célèbre; **to rise** or **come to f. as an explorer** atteindre la renommée en tant qu'explorateur; **to seek f. and fortune** rechercher la gloire et la fortune; **house of ill f.** maison mal famée; **not Chandler of Philip Marlowe f.?** le Chandler célèbre pour son Philip Marlowe?

famed [feɪmd] ADJ célèbre, bien connu (**for** pour); **she was f. for her rudeness** elle était bien connue pour son impolitesse

familiar [fəˈmɪlɪər] ADJ **1** (well-known) familier, -ière, bien connu; **a f. face** un visage familier; **she looks f.** je l'ai déjà vue quelque part; **an experience that will be f. to everyone** une expérience bien connue de tous; **it strikes one as f.** (seen before) cela laisse une impression de déjà vu; (heard before) cela laisse une impression de déjà entendu; **to be on f. ground** être sur son terrain; **an all too f. story of drug addiction and homelessness** c'est une histoire malheureusement banale de gens qui se droguent et sont à la rue; **his voice sounded f. to me** il me sembla reconnaître sa voix; **there was something f. about him/it** il/cela me disait quelque chose

2 (acquainted) **to be f. with sb/sth** bien connaître qn/qch; **to be f. with the customs** être au courant des usages; **to become more f. with sb/sth** se familiariser avec qn/qch **3** (intimate) familier, intime; Ling familier; **to adopt a f. tone** prendre un ton familier ou d'intimité; **to be on f. terms with sb** bien connaître qn; Old-fashioned **you are rather too f.** vous prenez trop de privautés; **don't let the pupils get too f. (with you)** ne laissez pas les élèves prendre trop de familiarités (avec vous)

▪ N **1** (in witchcraft) (spirit) démon m familier **2** Old-fashioned (friend) familier m, intime m ▸ ▸ **f. spirit** (in witchcraft) démon m familier

familiarity [fəmɪlɪˈærɪtɪ] N **1** (intimacy) familiarité f; Prov **f. breeds contempt** la familiarité engendre ou fait naître le mépris **2** (acquaintance) connaissance f (**with** de); **her f. with French** sa connaissance du français

familiarization [fəmɪlɪəraɪˈzeɪʃən] N **after a period of f. with ...** après une période de familiarisation avec ...; **greater f. with the details of the proposal** une connaissance plus poussée des détails de la proposition ▸ ▸ Com **f. trip** voyage m d'études ou de familiarisation

familiarize [fəˈmɪlɪəraɪz] VT **1** (acquaint) **to f. sb with sth** faire connaître qch à qn, familiariser qn avec qch; **to f. oneself with a language/the rules** se familiariser avec une langue/le règlement **2** (make known) rendre familier; **science-fiction had long familiarized us with the idea** la science-fiction nous avait depuis longtemps rendu cette idée familière ou habitués à cette idée

familiarly [fəˈmɪlɪəlɪ] ADV familièrement; **f. known as ...** communément connu comme ...

family [ˈfæmlɪ, -ɪlɪ] N **1** VOIR GRAMMAIRE A11 famille f; **large f.** famille nombreuse; **a friend of the f., a f. friend** un ami de la famille; **they don't want (to have** or **start) a f. yet** ils ne veulent pas encore avoir un enfant ou fonder de famille; **to be one of the f.** être de la maison; Fam **we've got f. coming to stay** nous allons avoir de la famille en visite; Fam **she's like f.** c'est comme si elle était de la famille; **it runs in the f.** cela tient de famille; **disease that runs in the f.** maladie f héréditaire; **the painting has been in the f. for generations** ce tableau est dans la famille depuis des générations; **we will keep it in the f.** (of heirloom, land etc) ça restera dans la famille; (of scandal) ça ne sortira pas de la famille; **you can see the f. resemblance** or **likeness** on ne peut pas ne pas remarquer un air de famille; Fam **she's in the f. way** elle est enceinte; **to get** or **put sb in the f. way** mettre qn enceinte; **f. business** entreprise f familiale; **f. butcher** boucher m du coin; **f. doctor** médecin m de famille; **f. hotel** hôtel m de famille; **a f. dinner** un dîner en famille; **a f. celebration** une fête de famille; Fam **f. get-together** réunion f familiale; **f. life** vie f familiale; **f. likeness** air m de famille; **f. portraits** portraits mpl d'ancêtres; **sorry, it's a f. joke** désolé, c'est une plaisanterie qu'on ne peut comprendre que si l'on fait partie de la famille; Com **f.-size(d) jar/packet** pot m/paquet m familial; **f. programme** émission f tout public; **unsuitable for f. viewing** non approprié aux enfants; **I wouldn't call it f. viewing** ce n'est pas exactement un spectacle à conseiller aux enfants; **this film is not f. viewing** ce n'est pas un film tout public **2** Biol, Ling (of plants, words etc) famille f ▸ ▸ Br Admin Formerly **f. allowance** ≃ allocations fpl familiales; **f. car** familiale f; Br Admin Formerly **f. income supplement** ≃ complément m familial; Fam Hum **f. jewels** (man's genitals) bijoux mpl de famille; **f. man** père m de famille; **f. name** nom m de famille; **f. planning** planning m familial; **f. planning clinic** centre m de planning familial; **f. rate** tarif m famille; **f. room** (in hotel) chambre f familiale; Am (in house) salle f de séjour; Br (in pub) salle réservée aux familles; **f. saloon** berline f familiale; **f. tree** arbre m généalogique

family-run ADJ (hotel, restaurant) géré en famille, familial, -aux

famine [ˈfæmɪn] N (food shortage) famine f; **to die of f.** mourir de faim; **f. prices** prix mpl exorbitants ou faramineux

famished [ˈfæmɪʃt] ADJ affamé; Fam **to be** or **feel f.** (hungry) mourir de faim, être affamé

famous [ˈfeɪməs] ADJ **1** célèbre, renommé (**for** pour, par); **many f. names have stayed here** beaucoup de personnes célèbres ont séjourné ici; **f. in history** célèbre dans l'histoire; **town f. for its monuments** ville célèbre ou renommée pour ou par ses monuments; Iron **f. last words!** c'est cela, oui! **2** Old-fashioned Fam (excellent) parfait, fameux

▪ NPL **the f.** les célébrités fpl

famously [ˈfeɪməslɪ] ADV **1 the castle has often been the scene of important events, most f. when ...** le château a souvent été la scène d'événements importants, le plus célèbre d'entre eux ayant eu lieu quand ... **2** Old-fashioned Fam (very well) fameusement, à merveille; **I get on f. with him** je m'entends à merveille

fan[1] [fæn] N **1** (hand-held) éventail m **2** (mechanical) ventilateur m; Ind soufflet m; Sl **when the shit** or **it hits the fan** quand la merde me/nous/lui/etc tombera dessus; Aut **radiator f.** ventilateur m **3** Agr (winnowing machine) tarare m

▪ VT (-nn-) **1** (blow air on) (person) éventer; (fire, embers) souffler sur; Fig (stir up) (passions) attiser, exciter; (quarrel) attiser, envenimer; **these remarks had fanned the flames of nationalist feeling** ces remarques avaient exacerbé le sentiment nationaliste; **to f. the embers of sb's passion** raviver les flammes de la passion de qn; **terraces fanned by cool sea breezes** terrasses rafraîchies par les brises de mer **2** Agr (winnow) (grain) vanner

▸ ▸ Aut **f. belt** courroie f de ventilateur; **f. heater** radiateur m soufflant; **f. palm** palmier-éventail m, pl palmiers-éventails; Archit **f. vaulting** voûte(s) f(pl) en éventail

▸ ▸ **fan out** VI (spread out) se déployer en éventail

▪ VT SEP (spread out) étaler (en éventail)

fan[2] N Fam (enthusiast) (of television, sport etc) fanatique mf, fana mf; (of singer, actor) fan mf; **a f. of sb/sth** un fana de qn/qch; **I'm a big f. (of hers)** je suis un de ses fans les plus fervents; **I'm not a great f. of his** il est loin d'être mon idole; **football f.** fana de football

▸ ▸ **f. base** public m; **f. club** cercle m ou club m de fans; **f. mail** courrier m des admirateurs

fan(-assisted) oven [(əsɪstɪd)] N four m à chaleur pulsée

fanatic [fəˈnætɪk] ADJ, N fanatique mf

fanatical [fəˈnætɪk(ə)l] ADJ fanatique

fanatically [fəˈnætɪklɪ] ADV fanatiquement

fanaticism [fəˈnætɪsɪz(ə)m] N fanatisme m

fanciable [ˈfænsɪəb(ə)l] ADJ Fam attirant

fancied [ˈfænsɪd] ADJ (imaginary) imaginaire

fancier [ˈfænsɪər] N (of dogs etc) connaisseur, -euse

fanciful [ˈfænsɪfʊl] ADJ **1** (unrealistic) (project, idea etc) chimérique; **he was being rather f.** (being unrealistic) il se faisait des idées, il rêvait; (indulging his imagination) il se laissait porter par son imagination **2** (imaginative) (person) capricieux, fantasque; (work etc) fantaisiste; (portrait) plein de fantaisie

fancifully [ˈfænsɪfʊlɪ] ADV d'une manière fantasque; (decorated) de manière fantaisiste; **somewhat f. described as ...** désigné sous le terme plutôt fantaisiste de ...

fan-cooled [-kuːld] ADJ refroidi par ventilateur

fancy [ˈfænsɪ] N **1** (imagination) imagination f, fantaisie f; (imagined thing) chose f imaginaire; **the realm of f.** le domaine de l'imaginaire ou de l'imagination; **it's only f.!** c'est pure imagination!; **idle fancies** vaines imaginations

2 (whim) fantaisie f, caprice m; **just as the f. takes me** comme l'idée me prend, Fam comme ça me chante

3 (liking) **he took a f. to the house** la maison lui a plu; **to take an immediate f. to sth** s'enticher de qch; **to take a f. to sb** (become fond of) prendre qn en affection; (become sexually attracted to) s'éprendre ou s'enticher de qn; **it took** or **caught my f. at once** cela m'a séduit du premier coup

▪ ADJ (jewels, gadget, hat) de fantaisie; (writing style) recherché; **just a bottle of ordinary wine, nothing f.** juste une bouteille de vin ordinaire, rien de spécial; **f. biscuits** biscuits assortis; **f. footwork** beau jeu de jambes; Fig **I had to do a bit of f. footwork** j'ai dû faire des pieds et des mains; Fam **to cut out the f. stuff** élaguer, faire moins de fantaisies; **f. price** prix excessif ou exorbitant

▪ VT **1** (imagine) s'imaginer, se figurer; Fam **f. now!, just f.!, f. (that)!** figurez-vous ça!; **f. meeting you!** tiens, toi ici!; **f. him not knowing that!** il ne sait pas ça! incroyable!

2 (have impression) **f. (that)** croire ou penser que; **I f. I have seen her before** j'ai l'impression de l'avoir déjà vue; **he fancied he heard footsteps** il a cru entendre des pas **3** Br Fam (feel desire for) **to f. sb** être attiré par qn; **he fancies you** tu lui plais; **I like him as a person but I don't f. him** je l'aime bien en tant que personne mais il ne m'attire pas; **he fancies her rotten** elle lui plaît vachement

4 Fam (have good opinion of) **to f. oneself** être infatué de sa petite personne, se gober; **he fancies himself as a speaker** il se croit orateur; **I don't f. their chances of winning** je ne crois pas qu'ils aient des chances de gagner; **they were not fancied to win** personne ne pensait qu'ils gagneraient; *Horseracing* **strongly fancied horse** cheval très coté

5 *Br Fam* **to f. sth** *(like)* bien aimer qch; *(feel like)* avoir envie de qch; **I don't f. his offer** son offre ne me dit rien; **I f. a bit of chicken** je mangerais volontiers un morceau de poulet, j'ai envie d'un morceau de poulet; **I wouldn't f. being in her shoes** je ne voudrais pas être à sa place; **I don't f. going** ça ne me dit rien d'y aller, je n'ai pas envie d'y aller; **she wasn't sure if she fancied the idea** elle n'était pas sûre que l'idée la tentait; **I didn't really f. the sound of her second novel** son deuxième roman ne m'a trop rien dit

▸▸ *Fam* **F. Dan** *(dandy)* dandy *m*; *(show-off)* frimeur *m*; *Br* **f. dress** déguisement *m*, costume *m*; **f. dress party** fête *f* déguisée; *Br* **f. goods** articles *mpl* de fantaisie; *Fam Pej* **f. man** jules *m*; *Fam Pej* **f. woman** maîtresse *f*, poule *f*

fancy-free ADJ **to be f.** avoir le cœur libre

fancywork ['fænsɪwɜːk] N *Sewing* broderie *f*, *(crochet work)* crochet *m*

fanfare ['fænfeər] N fanfare *f*

fanfold ['fænfəʊld] ADJ

▸▸ *Comput* **f. paper** papier *m* continu plié en accordéon

fang [fæŋ] N *(of dog etc)* croc *m*; *(of viper)* crochet *m*; *(of vampire)* canine *f*

fanlight ['fænlaɪt] N imposte *f*

fanny ['fænɪ] N **1** *Br Vulg (vagina)* chatte *f* **2** *Am Fam (buttocks)* derrière *m*, fesses *fpl* **3** *Br Sl Euph* **sweet f. adams** rien du tout, nib de nib

▸▸ *Am* **f. pack** banane *f* *(pochette)*
▸ **fanny about, fanny around** VI *Br Sl* perdre son temps à des bricoles, glander

fan-shaped ADJ en éventail

fantabulous [fæn'tæbjʊləs] ADJ *Fam* sensass

fantail ['fænteɪl] N *(bird)* pigeon *m* paon

fantailed ['fænteɪld] ADJ

▸▸ **f. pigeon** pigeon *m* paon

fantasia [fæn'teɪzɪə] N *Mus* fantaisie *f*

fantasize ['fæntəsaɪz] VI fantasmer *(about* sur); **he fantasized about being able to read people's minds** son fantasme était de pouvoir lire les pensées; **she was still fantasizing about making love to Robert Redford when ...** elle fantasmait encore qu'elle faisait l'amour avec Robert Redford quand ...
VT **to f. that ...** imaginer que ...

fantastic [fæn'tæstɪk] ADJ **1** *Fam (excellent)* formidable, fantastique; **we had a f. time** nous nous sommes vraiment bien amusés **2** *(enormous) (price, size etc)* énorme; **a f. sum** une somme faramineuse; *Com* **f. reductions** soldes *mpl* monstres **3** *(unbelievable) (person, thing)* bizarre; *(thing)* fantastique, grotesque; *(animals)* fantastique; *(claim)* grotesque, absurde; **that's the most f. thing I've ever heard** c'est la chose la plus grotesque *ou* absurde que j'aie jamais entendue; **what is absolutely f. about all this is that ...** ce qu'il y a de vraiment fantastique dans toute cette histoire, c'est que ...; **it sounds f., but it's true** *(unbelievable)* ça paraît inouï, mais c'est vrai; **it's f. to suppose/claim that ...** *(absurd)* c'est absurde de penser/de prétendre que ...

fantastically [fæn'tæstɪklɪ] ADV **1** *Fam* **f. beautiful/old/mean** incroyablement beau/vieux/méchant **2** somewhat **f., the story ends with ...** l'histoire se termine d'une manière un peu invraisemblable ...

fantasy ['fæntəsɪ, -zɪ] N **1** *(imagined event)* vision *f* bizarre; *(idea)* idée *f* fantasque; *(proposal)* extravagance *f*, **sexual f.** fantasme *m* sexuel; **his f. was to own a house**

in the country son rêve était d'avoir une maison à la campagne **2** *(imagination)* fantaisie *f*, **you live in a f. world!** tu vis dans un monde imaginaire!; **he has a strong sense of f.** il a énormément de fantaisie; **the realm of f.** le domaine de l'imaginaire **3** *(work)* Art œuvre *f* fantastique; *Mus* fantaisie *f*

> Note that the French word **fantaisie** is a false friend.

fanzine ['fænziːn] N fanzine *m*

FAO [efeɪ'əʊ] N *(abbr* **Food and Agriculture Organization)** FAO *f*
PREP *(abbr* **for the attention of)** à l'attention de

FAQ [efeɪ'kjuː] N *Comput (abbr* **frequently asked questions)** FAQ *f*
▸▸ *Comput* **F. file** fichier *m* FAQ

FAR [fɑːr]

ADV	loin **1** ▪ beaucoup **3**
ADJ	lointain **1** ▪ éloigné **1** ▪ autre **2** ▪ extrême **2**

VOIR GRAMMAIRE A26 ADV *(*farther, farthest ['fɑːðər, -ɪst], further, furthest ['fɜːðər, -ɪst]*)* **1** *(distance)* loin; **to go f.** aller loin; **how f. did you go?** jusqu'où êtes-vous allé?; **I got as f. as Birmingham** je suis allé jusqu'à Birmingham; *Fig* **this young man will go f.** ce jeune homme ira loin; **a pound does not go very f. nowadays** on ne va pas loin avec une livre de nos jours; **to go so f. as to do sth** aller jusqu'à faire qch; **I'll go so f. as to say that ...** j'irai jusqu'à dire que ...; **things went so f. that ...** les choses sont allées si loin que ...; *Fig* **to go too f.** aller trop loin; **that is going too f.** cela passe la mesure; **to live f. away** *(from here)* habiter loin d'ici; *(from there)* habiter loin; **her thoughts were f. away** sa pensée était ailleurs; **it isn't f. off** ce n'est pas loin; **f. from ...** loin de ...; **not f. from ... à peu de distance de ...; *Fig* **f. from it** loin de là; *Fig* **not f. from it** pas son faut; **f. be it from me to ...** loin de moi l'idée de ...; **f. from admiring him, I loathe him** bien loin de l'admirer, je le déteste; **f. out at sea** au (grand) large; **f. beneath/above us** loin audessous/au-dessus de nous; **f. and wide** *or* **near** de tous côtés; **they searched f. and wide for a suitable site** ils ont cherché partout un emplacement convenable; **the story so f.** = résumé *m* des chapitres précédents; **how f. have you got?** *(with your reading etc)* où en êtes-vous?; **as f. as the eye can see** à perte de vue; **as f. as I can judge ...** pour autant que je puisse en juger ...; **as f. as I know** autant que je sache; **I will help you as f. as I can** *or* **as f. as possible** je vous aiderai de mon mieux; **as f. as I can see** pour autant que je puisse en juger; **as f. as ...** dans la mesure où ...; **by f.** de loin; **by f. the best** de beaucoup *ou* de loin le meilleur

2 *(time)* **so f.** jusqu'ici; **so f. so good** jusqu'ici tout va bien; **have you seen him? – not so f.** l'avez-vous vu? – pas encore; **as f. back as I can remember** aussi loin que je puisse me rappeler; **as f. back as 1990** déjà en 1990; **she is not f. off sixty** elle n'est pas loin de la soixantaine; **to work f. into the night** travailler fort avant dans la nuit

3 *(much)* beaucoup; **it is f. better** c'est beaucoup mieux; **she's f. too intelligent to do that** elle est bien trop intelligente pour faire ça; **to be f. too many/little/etc** être beaucoup trop nombreux/petit/etc, **f. and away the best** de beaucoup *ou* de loin le meilleur; **the night was f. advanced** la nuit était fort avancée

ADV *(*farther, farthest ['fɑːðər, -ɪst], further, furthest ['fɜːðər, -ɪst]*)* **1** *(distant)* lointain, éloigné; **a f. country** un pays lointain; **in the f. distance** tout au loin

2 *(other)* **the f. end** *(of plank etc)* l'autre bout, le bout le plus éloigné; **the f. bank of the river** la rive opposée de la rivière; *Pol* **the f. left/right** l'extrême-gauche/-droite *f*
▸▸ **the F. East** l'Extrême-Orient *m*

farad ['færæd] N *Elec* farad *m*

faraway ['fɑːrəweɪ] ADJ lointain, éloigné; *(country)* lointain; **his eyes had a f. look** il avait le regard perdu dans le vague

farce [fɑːs] N *Theat* farce *f*, **knockabout f.** grosse farce; *Fig* **the trial was a f.** le procès relevait de la farce *ou* était grotesque; **this is an absolute f.!** c'est grotesque!; **the whole thing was a f.** tout a tourné à la farce; **their marriage had been little more than a loveless f.** leur mariage n'avait été qu'une comédie sans amour

farcical ['fɑːsɪk(ə)l] ADJ *Theat* bouffon, burlesque; *Fig (incident, idea, accusation)* absurde, grotesque; **the whole thing is becoming f.** c'est en train de tourner à la farce

farcically ['fɑːsɪklɪ] ADV d'une manière absurde *ou* grotesque

fare[1] [feər] N **1** *Rail, Aviat* prix *m* du voyage; *(in bus)* prix du trajet; *(in taxi)* prix de la course; **half f.** demi-place *f*, *pl* demi-places; **single f.** aller *m* (simple); **return f.** aller et retour *m*; **to pay one's f.** payer son billet; *(in taxi)* payer sa course; **fares, please!** *(in bus)* tickets, s'il vous plaît!; **rail/bus fares are going up** les billets de train/les tickets de bus augmentent **2** *(taxi passenger)* client, -ente **3** *esp Fml (food)* chère *f*, **traditional f.** cuisine *f* traditionnelle; **good f.** bonne chère; **prison f.** régime *m* de prison
▸▸ **f. structure** structure *f* tarifaire

fare[2] VI **how is he faring?** comment ça marche pour lui?, comment se débrouille-t-il?; *(after operation etc)* comment va-t-il?; **she fared badly** elle ne s'en est pas bien tirée; **she fared well** elle s'en est bien tirée, elle s'est bien débrouillée; **he went out to see how the lambs were faring** il est sorti pour voir ce que devenaient les agneaux

farewell [feə'wel] INT, N adieu *m*; **to bid sb f.** dire adieu à qn; **to say** *or* **make one's farewells** faire ses adieux; **a f. dinner** un dîner d'adieu

far-fetched [-fetʃt] ADJ *(idea, example, story)* tiré par les cheveux

far-flung ADJ **1** *(large)* *(empire etc)* très étendu **2** *(distant) (countries)* lointain; *(villages, places)* éloigné

farinaceous [færɪ'neɪʃəs] ADJ farineux, farinacé; **f. foods** farineux *mpl*, féculents *mpl*

farm [fɑːm] N **1** *Agr* ferme *f*, exploitation *f* agricole; **I work on a f.** je travaille dans une ferme; **dairy f.** ferme laitière; **fish f.** établissement *m* piscicole; **poultry f.** exploitation avicole; **sheep/trout f.** élevage *m* de moutons/truites; **stud f.** haras *m*; *Am Sl* **to buy the f.** *(die)* clamser, calancher **2** *(installation)* **sewage f.** champs *mpl* d'épandage **3** *(centre)* **health f.** établissement *m* de cure
VT *(land)* cultiver, exploiter; **to f. 400 acres** = exploiter 160 hectares; *(animals)* élever
VI être cultivateur
▸▸ *(of)* **f. animals** animaux *mpl* de ferme; **f. buildings** bâtiments *mpl* de la ferme; *(outhouses)* dépendances *fpl*; **f. hand** ouvrier, -ière agricole; **f. holiday** vacances *fpl* à la ferme; **f. horse** cheval *m* de ferme; **f. labourer** ouvrier, -ière agricole; **f. machinery** machines *fpl* agricoles; **f. tourism** tourisme *m* agricole, agritourisme *m*; **f. worker** ouvrier, -ière agricole
▸ **farm out** VT SEP *Fam (send to other people) (children)* confier à l'extérieur; **she farmed out the children to their aunty** elle a confié les enfants à leur tante; **to f. out work** don-

ner du travail à des collaborateurs extérieurs; *(subcontract)* sous-traiter du travail

farmable ['fɑːməbl] **ADJ** *(land)* cultivable

farmer ['fɑːmər] **N** agriculteur, -trice, cultivateur, -trice; **(tenant)** f. fermier, -ière; **sheep f.** éleveur, -euse de moutons; **poultry f.** aviculteur, -trice
▸▸ **farmers' market** marché *m* fermier

farmhouse ['fɑːmhaʊs] **N** (corps *m* de) ferme *f*

farming ['fɑːmɪŋ] **ADJ**
N agriculture *f*; **the f. of the land** la culture de la terre; **mixed f.** polyculture *f*; **sheep f.** élevage *m* de moutons; **poultry f.** aviculture *f*
▸▸ **f. communities** communautés *fpl* rurales

farmland ['fɑːmlænd] **N** terre(s) *f(pl)* arable(s)

farmstead ['fɑːmsted] **N** ferme *f*

farmyard ['fɑːmjɑːd] **N** cour *f* de ferme

Faroe ['feərəʊ] **N** the F. Islands, the Faroes les îles *fpl* Féroé

far-off **ADJ** *(place)* lointain, éloigné; *(country)* lointain; *(time)* reculé; **the day was not f. when** … le jour était proche où …

far-out **ADJ** *Fam (avant-garde)* avant-gardiste; *(fantastic)* super

far-reaching ['fɑːˈriːtʃɪŋ] **ADJ** de grande envergure, d'une grande portée; **to have a f. influence** avoir une grande portée

farrier ['færɪər] **N** *Br* maréchal-ferrant *m, pl* maréchaux-ferrants

farrow ['færəʊ] **N** *(piglets)* portée *f* de cochons
VT *(of sow) (piglets)* mettre bas
VI *(of sow)* **to f. (down)** faire des petits, cochonner

far-seeing **ADJ** clairvoyant; *(providing for the future)* prévoyant; **to be f.** voir loin

far-sighted **ADJ 1** *(providing for the future) (person)* prévoyant; *(decision etc)* avisé, sage **2** *(long-sighted)* hypermétrope; *(because of old age)* presbyte

far-sightedness [-ˈsaɪtɪdnɪs] **N 1** *(of government, leader)* prévoyance *f*, perspicacité *f*, *(of decision)* sagesse *f* **2** *(long-sightedness)* hypermétropie *f*, *(because of old age)* presbytie *f*

fart [fɑːt] *Fam* **N** pet *m*; *Fig* **a boring old f.** un vieux rasoir; **you stupid f.!** espèce de con!
VI péter, lâcher un pet
▸ **fart about, fart around** **VI** *Fam* **1** *(play the fool)* déconner **2** *(waste time)* glander; **he's been farting about with the car for days** il a passé des journées entières à trifouiller la voiture; **if you hadn't spent so much time farting about with your make-up** si tu n'avais pas autant traîné en te maquillant

farther ['fɑːðər] *(comp of far)* <u>VOIR GRAMMAIRE A26</u> **ADV 1** *(place)* plus loin (**than** que); **f. off** plus éloigné, plus loin; **they stopped a little f. on** ils se sont arrêtés un peu plus loin; **f. on in the book** plus loin dans le livre; **I can go no f.** je ne saurais aller plus loin; *(exhausted)* je n'en peux plus; **f. down/west** plus bas/à l'ouest; **before she could get any f. with her story …** avant qu'elle ne puisse continuer son histoire … **2** *(time)* **f. (back)** plus en arrière; **f. back than 1500** avant 1500
ADJ plus lointain; **at the f. end of the room** à l'autre bout de la salle

farthest ['fɑːðɪst] *(superl of far)* <u>VOIR GRAMMAIRE A26</u> **ADV** le plus loin; **this is the f. east they reached** voici le point le plus à l'est qu'ils ont atteint
ADJ 1 *(distant)* **f. (off)** le plus éloigné, le plus reculé **2** *(distance etc)* le plus long

farthing ['fɑːðɪŋ] **N** *Br Hist (coin)* quart *m* d'un penny; *Fig Fam* **not to have a f.** n'avoir pas le sou; *Old-fashioned Fam* **I don't care a brass f.** je m'en moque éperdument

farthingale ['fɑːðɪŋgeɪl] **N** *Hist* vertugadin *m*

FAS *Com (abbr* **free alongside ship**) FLQ, FAS, franco quai

fascia, *pl* **fascias** ['feɪʃə, -z] **N 1** *Archit* bandelette *f*, bande *f*; *(on shop front)* enseigne *f* en forme d'entablement **2** *(dashboard)* tableau *m* de bord; *(for mobile phone)* coque *f*
▸▸ **f. panel** planche *f* de bord

fascicle ['fæsɪk(ə)l], **fascicule** ['fæsɪkjuːl] **N** *Typ* fascicule *m*

fascinate ['fæsɪneɪt] **VT** *(person)* fasciner; **insects f. him** les insectes le fascinent; **to be fascinated by sth** être fasciné par qch

fascinating ['fæsɪneɪtɪŋ] **ADJ** fascinant

fascination [fæsɪˈneɪʃən] **N** fascination *f*, attrait *m*; **I don't understand the f. of tennis** je ne comprends pas l'attrait que peut avoir le tennis; **the sport has** *or* **holds a f. for millions** ce sport fascine des millions de gens; **he has always had a f. for dinosaurs** les dinosaures ont toujours exercé une fascination sur lui, il a toujours été fasciné par les dinosaures; **she watched/listened in f.** elle regardait/écoutait, fascinée

fascism ['fæʃɪz(ə)m] **N** *Pol* fascisme *m*

fascist ['fæʃɪst] **ADJ, N** *Pol* fasciste *mf*

fash [fæʃ] **VT** *Scot (person)* agacer, ennuyer; **dinna f. yersel** ne te fais pas de bile

fashion ['fæʃən] **N 1** *(in clothes etc)* mode *f*, vogue *f*; **in f.** à la mode, en vogue; **out of f.** passé de mode, démodé; **in the latest f.** à la dernière mode; **to set the f.** lancer la mode; **to follow f.** suivre la mode; **to become the f., to come into f.** devenir à la mode; **to go out of f.** se démoder; **the Costa del Sol was going out of f. with British holidaymakers** la Costa del Sol n'était plus aussi à la mode pour les vacanciers britanniques; **it's all the f.** c'est la grande vogue; **it's the latest f.** c'est la dernière mode **2** *(manner)* manière *f*; **crabs walk in a peculiar f.** les crabes marchent d'une façon étrange; **we rubbed noses, Eskimo f.** nous nous sommes frotté le nez à la manière des Esquimaux; **after a f.** tant bien que mal; **he loved her, after a f.** il l'aimait à sa façon
VT façonner, former; *(dress etc)* confectionner; **to f. a log into a canoe** façonner un tronc d'arbre en canot
▸▸ **f. designer** modéliste *mf*; **f. editor** rédacteur, -trice de mode; **f. house** maison *f* de (haute) couture; **f. magazine** journal *m* de mode; **f. model** mannequin *m*; *Old-fashioned* **f. parade** défilé *m* de mode; **f. photographer** photographe *mf* de mode; **f. photography** photo *f* de mode; **f. show** présentation *f* des modèles *ou* des collections, défilé *m* de mode; *Hum* **f. victim** esclave *mf* de la mode **f. writer** chroniqueur, -euse de mode, critique *m* de mode

fashionable ['fæʃənəb(ə)l] **ADJ** à la mode, en vogue; **a f. film director** un metteur en scène en vogue; **a f. part of town** un quartier très en vogue *ou* à la mode *ou* branché

fashionably ['fæʃənəblɪ] **ADV** *(dressed)* à la mode; *Hum* **they arrived f. late** ils sont arrivés en retard, comme il se doit

<u>**FAST¹**</u> [fɑːst]

| **ADJ** rapide **1** ▪ en avance **2** ▪ solide **3** |
| **ADV** vite **1** ▪ solidement **2** |

ADJ 1 *(rapid)* rapide; *Phot (film)* rapide; **you're a f. walker** vous marchez vite; **he likes f. cars** il aime les voitures qui vont vite; *Sport* **a f. time** *(in race etc)* un bon temps, un

bon chrono; *Fam* **he pulled a f. one on me** il m'a joué un mauvais tour; **he's a f. worker** il travaille vite
2 *(clock, watch)* en avance; **my watch is** *or Fam* **I'm five minutes f.** ma montre avance *ou* j'avance de cinq minutes
3 *(secure) (stake etc)* ferme, fixe, solide; *(grip etc)* ferme; *(door, lid etc)* bien fermé; *(colour)* solide, résistant; **these colours are not f.** ces couleurs ne résistent pas au lavage; *Naut* **to make f. (to a buoy)** prendre le corps-mort; **to make f. (alongside)** s'amarrer
4 *(immoral)* **f. living** débauche *f*, **f. woman** femme légère
ADV 1 *(rapidly)* vite, rapidement; **she was walking faster than me** elle marchait plus vite *ou* rapidement que moi; **not so f.!** pas si vite!, doucement!; **bad news travels f.** les mauvaises nouvelles courent vite
2 *(securely)* ferme, solidement; **to hold f.** tenir ferme, tenir bon; **to stick f.** bien tenir; *(be stuck)* rester pris, rester collé; **the door was shut f.** la porte était bien fermée; *Tex* **f. dyed** grand teint *inv*; **to be f. asleep** dormir d'un sommeil profond; *Fam* **to play f. and loose** prendre des risques; **to play f. and loose with sb's emotions** se jouer des émotions de qn; **to play f. and loose with the statistics** truquer *ou* falsifier les statistiques
▸▸ **f. food** fast-food *m*, prêt-à-manger *m inv*; **f. forward (button)** *(on tape recorder)* avance *f* rapide; *Aut* **f. idle** ralenti *m* accéléré; **the f. lane** *(on motorway)* la voie rapide; *Fig* **life in the f. lane** la vie à cent à l'heure; *Cin, TV* **f. motion** accéléré *m*; *Mktg* **f. mover** *(product)* article *m* à forte rotation; *Br* **f. train** rapide *m*

fast² **N** jeûne *m*; **to break one's f.** rompre le jeûne; *Rel* **a f. day** un jour de jeûne
VI jeûner; *Med* être à la diète

fastback ['fɑːstbæk] **N** *Aut* arrière *m* profilé *(car)* voiture *f* à l'arrière profilé

fasten ['fɑːs(ə)n] **VT 1** *(attach)* attacher (**to** à); **to f. papers together with a clip** attacher des papiers (ensemble) avec une agrafe; **to f. one's eyes/attention on sth** fixer le regard/son attention sur qch **2** *(hold)* fixer; **to f. a door with a bolt** fermer une porte au verrou, verrouiller une porte; **to f. one's seatbelt** accrocher *ou* attacher sa ceinture; **to f. one's buttons** se boutonner; **to f. one's coat** boutonner son manteau
VI s'attacher, se fixer; *(of garment)* s'agrafer, se boutonner (**at the back** par derrière); *(of door etc)* se verrouiller; *(of attention, eyes)* se fixer; **door that fastens with a bolt** porte qui se ferme au verrou
▸ **fasten down** **VT SEP** fixer (en place); *(tent, furniture)* fixer au sol; *(patient)* accrocher
▸ **fasten on, fasten onto** **VT INSEP 1** *(seize)* s'accrocher à; *(of eyes)* se fixer sur **2** *(evidence, statement, idea etc)* s'accrocher à; **she fastened on(to) this kiss as evidence of his affection** elle se raccrochait à ce baiser comme à une preuve de son affection; **she quickly fastened on(to) this excuse** elle saisit l'excuse à la volée; **the assessor fastened on(to) the irregularities in the accounts** le contrôleur des impôts s'obstinait sur les irrégularités que contenaient les comptes
▸ **fasten up** **VT SEP** *(one's dress etc)* agrafer, boutonner
VI this dress fastens up at the back cette robe se boutonne *ou* s'agrafe dans le dos
▸ **fasten upon** **VT INSEP** = **fasten on, fasten onto**

fastener ['fɑːs(ə)nər] **N** attache *f*, *(of garment) (hook)* agrafe *f*, *(of purse)* fermoir *m*; *(of window etc)* fermeture *f*, *(of French window)* espagnolette *f*, **(snap) f.** (bouton *m* à) pression *f*, **(zip) f.** fermeture à glissière, fermeture Éclair®

fastening ['fɑːs(ə)nɪŋ] N (device) = **fastener; fastenings** attaches fpl

fast-forward VT (cassette) mettre en avance rapide

VI (of tape) se dérouler en avance rapide; (of person) (faire) avancer; **I'm just waiting for the tape to f.** j'attends que la cassette ait fini de se dérouler

fastidious [fæ'stɪdɪəs] ADJ difficile (**about sth** sur qch); (about manners, hygiene, details) pointilleux; (about appearance) méticuleux; (about choice of friends) exigeant, difficile; **she's always been a very f. eater** elle a toujours été très difficile sur la nourriture

Note that the French word **fastidieux** is a false friend and is never a translation for the English word **fastidious**. It means **tedious**.

fastidiously [fæ'stɪdɪəslɪ] ADV méticuleusement

fastidiousness [fæ'stɪdɪəsnɪs] N (about appearance, details) méticulosité f; **I was unused to such f. about hygiene** je n'étais pas accoutumé à ce qu'on soit aussi pointilleux sur l'hygiène; **because of his f. about what he eats** parce qu'il est difficile sur la nourriture

fasting ['fɑːstɪŋ] N jeûne m; Med diète f (absolue)

fast-moving ADJ rapide; **f. events** des événements mpl rapides
▸▸ Mktg **f. consumer goods** biens mpl de consommation à forte rotation

fastness ['fɑːstnɪs] N **1** (of colour, dye) solidité f **2** (of moorings etc) sûreté f, fiabilité f **3** Lit (stronghold) mountain f. forteresse f

FAT Comput (abbr file allocation table) Fat f

fat [fæt] ADJ (fatter; fattest) **1** (person) gros, f grosse, gras, f grasse, corpulent; (meat) gras; (tissue) adipeux; Fam (cheque, salary) gros; **to get f.** engraisser; Fig **to grow f. on sth/at the expense of others** s'engraisser de qch/aux dépens d'autrui; Fam **a f. lot of good that'll do you!** cela vous fera une belle jambe!; Fam **that was a f. lot of good** or **use!** on est bien aidé avec ça!; Fam **a f. lot of difference that has made!** ça a bien avancé les choses!; Fam **a f. lot you know about it!** comme si vous en saviez quelque chose!; Fam **f. chance he's got!** il est mal barré!; **a f. volume** un gros tome; **a f. wallet** un portefeuille bien garni

2 (land) riche, fertile, gras; (clay, lime etc) gras

N graisse f; (of meat) gras m; **fats** matières fpl grasses; **animal/vegetable f.** graisse animale/végétale; Fig, Fam **the f.'s in the fire!** ça va chauffer!; **to live off the f. of the land** vivre comme un coq en pâte
▸▸ Fam Fig **f. cat** (rich, prosperous) richard m; (in industry) = personne f touchant un salaire extrêmement élevé de façon injustifiée; **f. content** (teneur f en) matières grasses; **f. intake** ration f de corps gras

fatal ['feɪt(ə)l] ADJ **1** (blow, accident, disease) mortel, -elle; **this condition can prove f.** cela peut être mortel **2** (action, consequences) désastreux, catastrophique; (mistake) fatal, -als, grave **3** Lit (ordained by fate) fatal, -als; **the f. hour** l'heure f fatale
▸▸ **f. accident enquiry** enquête f à la suite d'un accident mortel; Comput **f. error** erreur f fatale

fatalism ['feɪtəlɪz(ə)m] N fatalisme m

fatalist ['feɪtəlɪst] N fataliste mf

fatalistic [feɪtə'lɪstɪk] ADJ fataliste

fatality [fə'tælɪtɪ] N **1** (person killed) mort m, victime f **2** (fatal nature) fatalité f

Note that the most common meaning of the French word **fatalité** is **fate**.

fatally ['feɪt(ə)lɪ] ADV (wounded) mortellement; **f. ill** condamné; **to be f. damaging to sth, to f. damage sth** causer un tort irréparable à qch; **f. damaged** qui a subi un tort irréparable

Note that the French word **fatalement** is a false friend and is never a translation for the English word **fatally**. It means **inevitably**.

fate [feɪt] N destin m, sort m; **stroke of f.** coup m du destin ou du sort; **f. decreed that …** le sort a voulu que …; Myth **the Fates** les Parques fpl; **to leave sb to their f.** abandonner qn à son sort; **to meet one's f.** trouver la mort; **to escape one's f.** échapper à son destin; **to suffer** or **share a similar f.** avoir le même sort; **a f. worse than death** un destin pire que la mort

fated ['feɪtɪd] ADJ **1** (destined) destiné, condamné (**to do sth** à faire qch); **this was f. to be the last time they would ever meet** le sort a voulu que ce soit la dernière fois qu'ils se voyaient **2** (doomed) voué à la destruction

fateful ['feɪtfʊl] ADJ **1** (words) fatidique **2** (day) fatidique; (event) fatal, -als

fathead ['fæthed] N Fam imbécile mf

fatheaded [fæt'hedɪd] ADJ Fam abruti, bête

father ['fɑːðər] N **1** père m; **from f. to son** de père en fils; **he's his f.'s son** c'est bien le fils de son père; **on the f.'s side** du côté paternel; **like a f.** paternellement; **he was like a f. to me** il était comme un père pour moi; **like f. like son** tel père tel fils

2 Lit (ancestor) **our fathers** nos ancêtres mpl, nos aïeux mpl

3 (founder) (of science, art etc) père m, fondateur m; **the Fathers of the Church** les Pères de l'Église

4 Rel (God) Père m; **God the F.** Dieu le Père; **Our F. which** or **who art in Heaven** notre Père qui êtes aux cieux

5 Rel (priest) père m; **the Holy F.** (Pope) le Saint-Père; **F. O'Riley** (in monastic order) l'abbé O'Riley; (priest) le Père O'Riley; **yes, F.** oui, mon Père

6 (leader) Pol **the F. of the House** = titre m traditionnel donné au doyen (par l'ancienneté) des parlementaires britanniques; **f. of chapel** (in printing or publishing union) représentant m du personnel

VT (child) engendrer; (steam engine etc) inventer; (project, idea) concevoir
▸▸ Br **F. Christmas** le Père Noël; **f. confessor** directeur m de conscience, père spirituel; **F.'s Day** la fête des pères; **f. figure** = personne f qui joue le rôle du père; **F. Time** le Temps

fatherhood ['fɑːðəhʊd] N paternité f

father-in-law, pl **fathers-in-law** N beau-père, pl beaux-pères

fatherland ['fɑːðəlænd] N patrie f

fatherless ['fɑːðəlɪs] ADJ sans père, orphelin, -ine de père

fatherly ['fɑːðəlɪ] ADJ (person, tone, manner etc) paternel, -elle; **to behave in a f. way towards sb** se montrer paternel envers qn

fathom ['fæðəm] N Naut (measurement) brasse f

VT Naut sonder; Fig (mystery) pénétrer, sonder; **I can't f. him** (out) je ne le comprends pas; **I can't f. out why he did it at all** je n'arrive pas à me figurer pourquoi il a fait cela

fatigue [fə'tiːg] N **1** (tiredness) fatigue f; **to be suffering from f.** être épuisé; **mental f.** fatigue cérébrale; **to be dropping with f.**

tomber de fatigue **2** Tech (in material) fatigue f; **metal f.** fatigue des métaux **3** Mil (chore) corvée f; **to put sb on f.** mettre qn de corvée; **cookhouse f.** corvée de cuisine(s); **fatigues** treillis m

VT **1** (person) fatiguer; (stronger) épuiser; **to f. oneself doing sth** se fatiguer/s'épuiser à faire qch **2** Tech (metal etc) fatiguer
▸▸ Mil **f. dress** treillis m; Mil **f. duty** corvée f; Mil **f. party** (détachement m de) corvée

fatiguing [fə'tiːgɪŋ] ADJ fatigant; (stronger) épuisant

fatness ['fætnɪs] N (of person) embonpoint m, corpulence f; (of stomach, buttocks) grosseur f; (of flesh etc) adiposité f

fatso ['fætsəʊ] N Fam gros m; (woman) grosse (bonne femme) f; (more insulting) gros lard m; (woman) grosse vache f

fatted ['fætɪd] ADJ Prov **to kill the f. calf** tuer le veau gras

fatten ['fæt(ə)n] VT (sheep, calves etc) engraisser
VI engraisser
▸ **fatten up** VT SEP = **fatten** VT; Fam (person) faire grossir, engraisser; **we'll have to f. you up a bit** il va falloir qu'on t'engraisse un peu

fattening ['fæt(ə)nɪŋ] ADJ (food) qui fait grossir
N (of animals) engraissement m, engraissage m

fatty ['fætɪ] ADJ graisseux; (tissue etc) adipeux; (meat) gras, f grasse; **avoid f. foods** évitez les matières grasses ou les aliments gras
N Fam gros (bonne femme) f; **hey, f.!** ohé, mon gros!/ma grosse!; **they always called him f.** ils l'appelaient toujours le gros
▸▸ Chem **f. acid** acide m gras

fatuity [fæ'tjuːɪtɪ] N sottise f, imbécillité f; **the utter f. of his efforts/the enterprise** l'absurdité de ses efforts/de l'entreprise

fatuous ['fætjʊəs] ADJ imbécile, idiot; (attempt) ridicule; (smile) béat

fatuously ['fætjʊəslɪ] ADV sottement, d'un air imbécile

fatuousness ['fætjʊəsnɪs] N = **fatuity**

faucet ['fɔːsɪt] N Am robinet m

fault [fɔːlt] N **1** (flaw) défaut m; **in spite of all his faults** malgré tous ses défauts ou travers; **scrupulous to a f.** scrupuleux à l'excès; **to find f. with sb/sth** trouver à redire contre qn/qch; **she's always finding f.** elle trouve toujours quelque chose à redire

2 Tech (inherent) problème m, défaut m; **a f. has developed on the line** il y a un problème sur la ligne

3 (guilt) faute f; **to be at f.** être en faute, être coupable; **you were at f. in not warning us** vous avez eu tort de ne pas nous prévenir; **his memory was at f.** sa mémoire lui a fait défaut; **whose f. is it?** à qui la faute?; **I am afraid it was (all) my f.** je crains bien que ce ne soit de ma faute; **it's his own silly f.** c'est de sa faute, à cet imbécile; **through no f. of mine** sans que je sois en cause

4 Tennis faute f; **double f.** double faute; **foot f.** faute de pied

5 Geol faille f

VT (person) prendre en défaut; (something) trouver un défaut dans; **I can't f. her research** je ne trouve aucune erreur dans ses recherches
▸▸ **f. line** ligne f de faille; **f. plane** plan m de faille; Com **f. tree** arbre m de défaillances

Note that the most common meaning of the French word **faute** is **error**.

fault-finder N (person) critiqueur, -euse; (device) détecteur m de fuites

fault-finding ADJ (critical) ergoteur, -euse, pinailleur, -euse

N 1 *(criticism)* disposition *f* à critiquer; **I'd had enough of her petty f.** j'en avais assez de ses pinailleries **2** *Tech* localisation *f* des défauts

faultiness ['fɔːltɪnɪs] **N** défectuosité *f*, imperfection *f*

faultless ['fɔːltlɪs] **ADJ** *(work, performance, craftmanship etc)* sans faute, impeccable; *(dress, behaviour)* impeccable, irréprochable

faultlessly ['fɔːltlɪslɪ] **ADV** impeccablement

fault-tolerant **ADJ** *Comput* quasi insensible aux défaillances, tolérant les pannes

faulty ['fɔːltɪ] **ADJ** *(work, device etc)* défectueux; *(style etc)* incorrect; *(reasoning etc)* erroné; *(logic)* défaillant; *Gram (construction etc)* vicieux; **f. workmanship** mauvaise construction *f*

faun [fɔːn] **N** *Myth* faune *m*

fauna ['fɔːnə] **N** *(of region, country)* faune *f*

faux pas ['fəʊ'pɑː] **N** faux pas *m*, gaffe *f*

favour, *Am* **favor** ['feɪvər] **N 1** *(approval)* faveur *f*, approbation *f*; **to be in/out of f.** *(of person)* être bien/mal vu; *Fam* avoir/ne pas avoir la cote; *(of style)* être à la mode/démodé; **to look on sb/sth with f.** être favorable à qn/qch, être bien disposé envers qn/qch; **to find f. with sb** trouver grâce aux yeux de qn; *(of theory, explanation)* être favorablement reçu auprès de qn; **to gain sb's f.** gagner la faveur de qn; **to be restored** *or* **to return to f.** rentrer en grâce; **to fall out of f. with sb** perdre les bonnes grâces de qn, tomber en défaveur aux yeux de qn; **this method has rather fallen out of f. in recent years** cette méthode a été plus ou moins abandonnée au cours de ces dernières années **2** *(service)* service *m*; **to ask sb a f., to ask a f. of sb** solliciter un service *ou* une faveur de qn; **as a f.** à titre gracieux; **as a personal f.** à titre personnel; **to do sb a f.** faire une faveur à qn, obliger qn; **you could at least do me the f. of listening** tu pourrais au moins me faire la faveur d'écouter; **will you do me a great f.?** voulez-vous me rendre un grand service?; *Br Sl* **do me a f.!** *(you must be joking!)* tu rigoles?; *Fam* **why don't you do everyone a f. and shut up?** tu vas faire plaisir à tout le monde et la fermer, d'accord?; **she's not doing herself any favours by being so arrogant** son arrogance la dessert **3** *(preference)* partialité *f*, préférence *f*; **to show f. towards sb** favoriser qn; **to speak in sb's f.** parler en faveur de qn; **he has everything in his f.** tout lui sourit; **design C has everything in its f.** le projet C a tous les avantages; **in f. of ...** en faveur de ...; **all those in f. raise your hand** *(in meeting, debate etc)* que tous ceux qui sont pour lèvent la main; **this route was abandoned in f. of a more direct one** cette route a été abandonnée pour une autre qui était plus directe; **to be in f. of sth** être partisan de qch, préconiser qch; **he's in f. of introducing subsidies** il est favorable à *ou* partisan de la mise en place de subventions; **a point in sb's/sth's f.** un élément en faveur de qn/qch; *Fin* **balance in your f.** solde en votre faveur **4** *Arch (ribbon etc)* faveur *f*, cocarde *f* **5** *Lit, Hum* **favours** *(of woman)* faveurs *fpl*; **she was rather too free with her favours** elle était un peu trop prodigue de ses faveurs

VT 1 *(approve of)* *(something)* approuver, préférer; *(project)* être pour; *(person)* accorder une préférence à; **I f. allowing more time for the planning stage** je suis partisan d'accorder plus de temps au stade préparatoire **2** *(bestow favour on)* *(person)* favoriser; **to f.**

sb **with a smile** gratifier qn d'un sourire; *Iron* **we have not, as yet, been favoured with a reply** on ne nous a pas encore fait la faveur de nous répondre **3** *(give advantage to)* *(person)* avantager, montrer de la partialité pour; *(something)* faciliter; **to be favoured by circumstances** avoir les circonstances en sa faveur; **the town is uniquely favoured as a holiday destination** cette ville est exceptionnellement avantagée en tant que destination de vacances **4** *(of fact etc)* *(theory etc)* soutenir

favourable, *Am* **favorable** ['feɪv(ə)rəb(ə)l] **ADJ** favorable; *(weather, wind etc)* propice; *(reception etc)* bienveillant; *(terms etc)* bon, *f*bonne, avantageux; *(report etc)* bon, rassurant; **in a f. light** sous un jour favorable; *Com* **on f. terms** à des conditions avantageuses

favourably, *Am* **favorably** ['feɪv(ə)rəblɪ] **ADV** favorablement; **to be f. disposed to(-wards) sb/sth, to look f. on sb/sth** être favorable à qn/qch, être bien disposé à l'égard de qn/qch; **I hope everything goes f. for you** j'espère que tout ira bien pour toi; **to compare f. with sth** n'avoir rien à envier à qch; **I was f. impressed** j'ai été favorablement impressionné

favoured, *Am* **favored** ['feɪvəd] **ADJ 1** *(person)* favorisé, avantagé; **he is one of our most f. clients** c'est un de nos clients privilégiés; **most-f. nation status** statut *m* de nation la plus favorisée; **the f. few** les élus *mpl* **2** *Old-fashioned* **ill-f.** laid, de mauvaise mine

favourite, *Am* **favorite** ['feɪv(ə)rɪt] **N** favori, *f*favorite, préféré, -ée; *(song)* succès *m*, tube *m*; *Comput* **favorites** *(websites)* favoris *mpl*; *Sport* **to back the f.** jouer le favori; **chocolate cake is a firm f. with children** c'est vraiment le gâteau au chocolat que les enfants préfèrent; **it's a great f. of mine** c'est l'un/l'une de mes préféré(e)s; **he's a great f. with the old ladies** les vieilles dames l'affectionnent particulièrement; **roast duck? (that's) my f.!** du canard rôti? c'est mon plat préféré!

ADJ favori, préféré

▸▸ **f. son** *(family member)* enfant *m* chéri; *Am Pol* = candidat *m* favorisé par les électeurs du même état que lui

favouritism, *Am* **favoritism** ['feɪv(ə)rɪtɪz(ə)m] **N** favoritisme *m*

fawn [fɔːn] **N 1** *(deer)* faon *m* **2** *(colour)* fauve *m*

ADJ fauve

VI to f. on sb ramper devant qn

fawning ['fɔːnɪŋ] **ADJ** *(flattering)* adulateur, -trice; *(servile)* servile

N adulation *f*

fax [fæks] **N 1** *(machine)* télécopieur *m*, fax *m*; **to send sth by f.** envoyer qch par fax *ou* par télécopie **2** *(copy, message)* fax *m*; **to send sb a f.** envoyer un fax à qn

VT *(document)* faxer, envoyer par fax *ou* télécopie; *(person)* envoyer un fax *ou* une télécopie à; **I'll f. the figures to you** je vous faxe les chiffres, je vous envoie les chiffres par fax *ou* télécopie

▸▸ **f. board** carte *f* fax, carte de télécopie; *Comput* **f. card** carte fax; **f. machine** télécopieur, fax; **f. message** fax, télécopie; *Comput* **f. modem** modem-fax *m*, *pl* modems-fax; **f. number** numéro *m* de fax *ou* de télécopie; **f. shot** publicité *f*directe par télécopie; **f. software** logiciel *m* de télécopie

▸ **fax back VT SEP** *(return by fax)* renvoyer par fax *ou* par télécopie (**to** à); **I'll f. you back** je vous réponds par fax

faxable ['fæksəb(ə)l] **ADJ** *(document)* faxable, télécopiable

faze [feɪz] **VT** *Fam (person)* déconcerter

FBI [efbiː'aɪ] **N** *Am (abbr* **Federal Bureau of Investigation)** FBI *m*, ≃ Police *f*Judiciaire

▸▸ **F. agent** agent *m* du FBI

FC [ef'siː] **N** *(abbr* **Football Club)** Club *m* de Football

FCL-FCL *Com (abbr* **full container load-full container load)** FCL-FCL

FCL-LCL *Com (abbr* **full container load-less than container load)** FCL-LCL

FD *(abbr* **floppy disk)** disquette *f*

FDA [efdiː'eɪ] **N** *Am (abbr* **Food and Drug Administration)** = office *f* du contrôle pharmaceutique et alimentaire

FDD *(abbr* **floppy disk drive)** unité *f* de disquette

FDI [efdiː'aɪ] **N** *Econ (abbr* **foreign direct investment)** IED *m*

fealty ['fiːltɪ] **N** *Hist* fidélité *f*

fear [fɪər] **N 1** crainte *f*, peur *f*; **my greatest f. was that they would forget** ce que je craignais le plus, c'est qu'ils oublient; **f. seized her** la peur l'envahit; **deadly f.** effroi *m*; **in f. and trembling** tremblant de peur; **to be overcome by** *or* **with f.** être en proie à la frayeur; **to be** *or* **stand** *or* **go in f. of sb/sth** avoir peur de *ou* redouter *ou* craindre qn/qch; **to go in f. of one's life** craindre pour sa vie; **there are fears for her life** sa vie est en danger; **for f. of waking the baby** de crainte de réveiller le bébé; **for f. of making a mistake** de crainte d'erreur; **there is no f. that he will come back** il n'y a pas de danger qu'il revienne; **without f. or favour** sans distinction de personnes; *Fam* **no f.!** pas de danger!, jamais de la vie! **2** *(respect)* *(of God, the law etc)* respect *m*, crainte *f*, *Fam* **to put the f. of God into sb** *(reprimand)* faire à qn une semonce dont il se souviendra longtemps; *(frighten)* inspirer une peur bleue à qn

VT 1 *(somebody, something)* craindre, redouter; *(event)* appréhender, craindre; **what they most feared** ce qu'ils craignaient le plus; **he fears failure above all else** l'échec est ce qu'il craint *ou* redoute par-dessus tout; **she is an adversary to be feared** c'est une adversaire redoutable; **it is to be feared that ...** il est à craindre que ...; *Fml* **I f. it is too late** j'ai peur *ou* je crains qu'il ne soit trop tard; *Fml* **I f. he will not come** je crains qu'il ne vienne pas; *Fml* **I f. so/not** je crains que oui/que non; *Fml* **I f. he may be out** je crains qu'il ne soit pas là; *Fml* **I f. I'm late** je crois bien être en retard; **I f. the worst!** je crains *ou* redoute le pire! **2** *(respect)* *(God etc)* craindre

VI avoir peur; **we'll be here tomorrow, never f.** nous serons là demain, ne crains rien; *Old-fashioned* **f. not** *or* **never f.,** help is at hand n'ayez crainte, l'assistance ne saurait tarder; **to f. for sb/sth** s'inquiéter au sujet de qn/qch; **I was beginning to f. for her sanity** je commençais à m'inquiéter pour son état mental; **we feared for our lives** nous craignions pour nos vies

feared [fɪəd] **ADJ** *(person etc)* redouté

fearful ['fɪəfʊl] **ADJ 1** *(consequences, doubt)* affreux, effrayant; *(pain, accident)* atroce, affreux; *esp Old-fashioned Fam (terrible)* affreux; **he's a f. bore** il est affreusement rasoir; **a f. mess** un désordre effrayant *ou* formidable **2** *(person)* peureux, craintif; **don't look so f.!** n'aie pas l'air aussi apeuré!; **f. of ...** qui craint *ou* a peur de ...; **f. of what would happen ...** par crainte de ce qui arriverait ...

fearfully ['fɪəfʊlɪ] **ADV 1** *(frighteningly)* affreusement, terriblement **2** *esp Old-fashioned Fam (very)* affreusement; **f. clever/interesting** terriblement intelligent/intéressant **3** *(out of fear)* peureusement

fearfulness ['fɪəfʊlnɪs] N **1** (of noise etc) caractère m terrifiant; **the f. of his appearance** son aspect terrifiant **2** (of person) (fear) crainte f, (concern) appréhension f

fearless ['fɪəlɪs] ADJ intrépide, courageux; **f. of …** sans peur de …; **he was f. of danger** il ne reculait devant aucun danger

fearlessly ['fɪəlɪslɪ] ADV intrépidement

fearlessness ['fɪəlɪsnɪs] N intrépidité f, courage m

fearsome ['fɪəsəm] ADJ (weapon, opponent) effrayant, redoutable; (bark, growl) effrayant

feasibility [fiːzə'bɪlɪtɪ] N (of plan etc) faisabilité f; **to doubt the f. of a suggestion** douter qu'une suggestion puisse être mise en pratique; **the f. of finding backers** la possibilité de trouver des garants
▸▸ **f. report** rapport m de faisabilité; **f. stage** f de faisabilité; **f. study** étude f de faisabilité; **f. test** essai m probatoire

feasible ['fiːzəb(ə)l] ADJ **1** (plan etc) faisable, réalisable, praticable **2** (story etc) vraisemblable

feast [fiːst] N **1** (large meal) festin m, banquet m; **f. for the eyes/the senses** un plaisir pour les yeux/les sens **2** Rel fête f
VI faire festin, festoyer; **to f. (up)on sth** se régaler de qch
VT Old-fashioned (person) régaler, fêter; **to f. one's eyes on sth** repaître ses yeux de qch
▸▸ **f. day** (jour m de) fête; Rel **F. of Tabernacles** fête des Tabernacles

feasting ['fiːstɪŋ] N Lit festoiement m

feat [fiːt] N **1** (exploit) exploit m; **f. of arms** fait m d'armes **2** (achievement) tour m de force; **a remarkable f. of modern technology** une remarquable prouesse technologique; **feats of engineering** triomphes mpl de l'ingénieur; **f. of skill** tour m d'adresse

feather ['feðər] N **1** plume f, (of tail, wing) penne f, (on arrow) (em)penne f; **as light as a f.** léger comme une plume; **in fine f.** dans une forme éblouissante; Fig **to show the white f.** manquer de courage; **you could have knocked me down with a f.** je n'en revenais pas; Fig **that's a f. in her cap** elle peut en être fière; Fig **to smoothe sb's ruffled feathers** rasséréner qn; Fig **to make the feathers fly** déclencher les hostilités **2** (in rowing) plate f
VT **1** (arrow) empenner; Fig **to f. one's nest** faire sa pelote ou son beurre **2** (in rowing) (oar) ramener à plat; **f. your oars!** avirons à plat! **3** Aviat (propeller) mettre en drapeau
VI (in rowing) nager plat
▸▸ **f. bed** lit m de plumes; Fig sinécure f, **f. boa** boa m de plumes; **f. cut** (hairstyle) coupe f en dégradé; **f. duster** plumeau m

featherbed ['feðəbed] VT Econ protéger par des subventionnements excessifs; Fig (children) élever dans du coton

featherbedding ['feðəbedɪŋ] N Econ subventionnement m excessif

featherbrain ['feðəbreɪn] N Fam tête f de linotte; **he's a real f.** c'est une vraie tête de linotte

featherbrained ['feðəbreɪnd] ADJ Fam étourdi; (scheme, idea) insensé

feather-edge N Carp etc biseau m

feather-edged ADJ taillé en biseau, biseauté

feathering ['feðərɪŋ] N **1** (of birds) plumage m **2** (of arrow) empennage m **3** (in rowing) nage f plate **4** Aviat (of propeller) mise f en drapeau

featherstitch ['feðəstɪtʃ] N Sewing point m d'épines

featherweight ['feðəweɪt] N Boxing poids m plume; Fig **he's a bit of a f.** il ne fait pas vraiment le poids

feathery ['feðərɪ] ADJ (snow, wheat etc) plumeux; **it has a light, f. feel to it** c'est doux et léger comme la plume

feature ['fiːtʃər] N **1** (of face) trait m; **prominent features** traits accusés
2 (of landscape, person, car) caractéristique f, (of software) fonction f, **a f. of the course is …** un des aspects de la formation est …; **paper that makes a f. of sports** journal qui fait une large place aux sports; **to make a f. of the fact that …** attirer l'attention sur le fait que …; **they decided to make a f. of the huge pillar in the dining area** ils ont décidé de mettre en valeur l'énorme pilier qui se trouve dans la salle à manger; **physical features of a country** topographie f d'un pays; **distinguishing f.** trait distinctif; **distinguishing features** (in passport) signes mpl particuliers; **main features** grands traits; **prominent** or **salient f.** trait saillant; **the redeeming f.** (of sth) le bon côté; **special f.** particularité f
3 (film) long métrage m; **double-f. programme** programme m à deux longs métrages
4 Journ (item) article m vedette; (news report etc) grand reportage m
VT **1** Cin (person) représenter; **a film featuring John Wayne** un film avec John Wayne en vedette; **also featuring Mark Williams** avec Mark Williams
2 Journ (news item) mettre en manchette; **the story was featured in all the main newspapers** cette affaire a fait la manchette de tous les grands quotidiens
3 (have as special feature) présenter, comporter; **the new model features four-wheel drive** le nouveau modèle comporte quatre roues motrices
VI **1** Cin (of actor) faire une apparition
2 (appear) figurer
▸▸ Journ **f. article** article de fond; Journ **features department** service m des rubriques; Journ **features editor** rédacteur, -trice de rubrique; journaliste mf responsable d'une rubrique; Cin **f. film** long métrage; Journ **f. story** article de fond; Journ **features writer** grand reporter mf, éditorialiste mf

feature-length Cin ADJ
▸▸ **f. cartoon** film m d'animation; **f. film, f. movie** long métrage m

featureless ['fiːtʃəlɪs] ADJ sans caractéristiques bien marquées

Feb abbr February

febrile ['fiːbraɪl] ADJ Med, Fig fébrile

February ['februərɪ] N **VOIR GRAMMAIRE A81; B60** février m; in **F.** au mois de février, en février; **(on) the first/the seventh of F.** le premier/le sept février

fecal, feces Am = faecal, faeces

feckless ['feklɪs] ADJ **1** (irresponsible) (person) étourdi, irréfléchi; (lifestyle) inconscient, irresponsable **2** (ineffectual) (person) propre à rien, incapable; (attempt) inepte

fecklessness ['feklɪsnɪs] N **1** (irresponsibility) étourderie f **2** (of plan) ineptie f

fecund ['fiːkənd] ADJ esp Fml fécond

fecundity [fɪ'kʌndɪtɪ] N fécondité f

Fed [fed] N Am **1** Fin (abbr **Federal Reserve Board**) banque f centrale (des États-Unis) **2** Fin (abbr **Federal Reserve (System)**) (système m de) Réserve f fédérale **3** Fam (abbr **Federal Agent**) agent m du FBI

fed [fed] PT, PP see feed

federal ['fedərəl] ADJ (government etc) fédéral, -aux
N Am Hist fédéral m, nordiste m
▸▸ Am **the F. Reserve** la Réserve fédérale

federalism ['fedərəlɪz(ə)m] N fédéralisme m

federalist ['fedərəlɪst] ADJ, N fédéraliste mf

federalize ['fedərəlaɪz] VT **1** fédéraliser **2** Am (put under federal control) charger le gouvernement fédéral du contrôle de

federate[1] ['fedərət] ADJ (state etc) fédéré

federate[2] ['fedəreɪt] VT fédérer
VI se fédérer

federation [fedə'reɪʃən] N fédération f, **employers' f.** association f patronale

fedora [fɪ'dɔːrə] N feutre m

fed up ADJ Fam **to be f.** en avoir marre, en avoir ras le bol; **she's f. with him** elle en a marre de lui; **she's f. with it** elle en a marre; **to be f. (to the back teeth) with sb/sth** en avoir (vraiment) marre ou ras le bol de qn/qch; **what are you looking so f. about?** pourquoi as-tu l'air aussi écœuré?; **you sound f.** tu as l'air d'en avoir marre ou ras le bol

fee [fiː] N **1** (of physician, lawyer etc) honoraires mpl; (of actor) cachet m; (of company director) jeton m de présence; **for a small f.** moyennant une légère redevance; **is there a f. for joining?** est-ce que l'inscription est payante?; **school fees** frais mpl de scolarité; **boarding-school fees** pension f, **entrance f.** droit m d'entrée; **membership fee(s)** droit d'inscription; **registration f.** (for conference etc) droit d'inscription; (for letter) taxe f de recommandation **2** Law **property held in f. simple** propriété sans conditions ou libre **3** Hist (fief) fief m
▸▸ **f. note** note f d'honoraires

feeb [fiːb] N Am Fam crétin, -ine

feeble ['fiːb(ə)l] ADJ **1** (weak) faible; Fam **that's pretty f.** (as an excuse, attempt) c'est un peu léger; (as a joke) ce n'est pas très drôle **2** Fam (ineffectual) mou, f molle, peu capable; (film) faible, médiocre

feeble-minded ADJ d'esprit faible, arriéré
NPL **the f.** les débiles mpl mentaux

feeble-mindedness [-'maɪndɪdnɪs] N faiblesse f d'esprit, arriération f

feebleness ['fiːb(ə)lnɪs] N (of person) faiblesse f, (of excuse) pauvreté f, faiblesse; (of film, book, play) médiocrité f, faiblesse

feebly ['fiːblɪ] ADV **1** (weakly) faiblement **2** (ineffectually) mollement; **to say sth f.** dire qch d'un ton peu convaincu

feed [fiːd] N **1** (animal food) nourriture f, pâture f, (for horses etc) fourrage m; Fam (meal) repas m; **to have a good f.** bien manger; **the horse is off his f.** le cheval boude sur son avoine; Fam **to be off one's f.** (of baby) bouder sur la nourriture; **it's time for baby's f.** il faut donner à manger au bébé **2** (portion) (of food for animals) mesure f, ration f, **f. of oats** picotin m d'avoine **3** Theat etc (actor) acteur, -trice qui donne la réplique; (of comedian) faire-valoir m inv **4** Tech (of machine etc) (process) alimentation f, (device) appareil m ou système m d'alimentation; (pipe) conduit m d'alimentation
VT (pt, pp fed [fed]) **1** (give food to) (person) nourrir, donner à manger à; (family etc) nourrir; (country etc) approvisionner; (army) ravitailler; (dog etc) faire manger; (livestock) affourager; (breastfeed) allaiter; (of mother bird) (chicks) donner la becquée à; **to f. the birds** donner à manger aux oiseaux, nourrir les oiseaux; **he can f. himself already** il arrive déjà à manger tout seul; **we were well fed** nous étions bien nourris; Fam **to f. one's face** s'en mettre plein la lampe, se goinfrer; **the animals are fed a diet of fruit** les animaux sont nourris de fruits; **we were fed bread and water** on nous donnait de l'eau et du pain; **they were fed to the lions** ils ont été jetés en pâture aux lions; **field that feeds three cows** champ qui nourrit trois vaches; **manure feeds the ground** le fumier nourrit la terre; **to f. the mind/sb's anger/**

sb's obsession nourrir l'esprit/la colère de qn/l'obsession de qn

2 *(supply with)* Tech *(machine, fire etc)* alimenter; *(furnace etc)* charger; *Comput (paper)* faire avancer, alimenter; *Comput* **to f. data into a computer** entrer des données dans un ordinateur; **to f. coins into a parking meter** mettre des pièces dans un parcmètre; **to f. sb with false information** fournir de fausses informations à qn; *Ftbl etc* **to f. the forwards** alimenter les avants

3 *Theat (actor)* donner la réplique à VI manger; *(of cattle, sheep)* paître, brouter; **to f. on sth** se nourrir *ou* vivre de qch

▸▸ **f. belt** *(of machine gun)* bande-chargeur *f* (souple), *pl* bandes-chargeurs; **f. line** *(of comedian)* réplique *f*, *Tech* **f. pipe** tuyau *m* d'alimentation; *Tech* **f. pump** pompe *f* d'alimentation

▸ **feed back** VT SEP *(information)* envoyer; *(send back again)* retransmettre
VI **to f. back into a system** être incorporé à un système

▸ **feed in** VT SEP *Comput* introduire en machine *ou* en mémoire; **to f. sth into the computer** entrer qch dans l'ordinateur, mettre qch en mémoire

▸ **feed up** VT SEP *(animals)* engraisser; **he needs feeding up** *(person)* il a besoin d'engraisser un peu

feedback ['fiːdbæk] N **1** *Electron etc* réaction *f*, rétroaction *f*, *Fam* feed-back *m inv*; *(in microphone)* effet *m* Larsen **2** *(of information)* retour *m*, remontée *f*, *(reaction)* réactions *fpl*; **we haven't had much f.** nous n'avons pas eu beaucoup d'écho; **positive/negative f.** réactions positives/négatives

feedbag ['fiːdbæg] N **1** *(container)* sac *m* à nourriture; *(containing food)* sac de nourriture **2** *Am (for horse)* musette *f*, mangeoire *f* portative

feeder ['fiːdər] N **1** *(person) (of machine etc)* alimenteur, -euse; *(of furnace etc)* chargeur, -euse; *(eater)* mangeur, -euse; **heavy f.** gros mangeur **2** *(feeding bottle)* biberon *m*; *Br (bib) (for baby)* bavette *f*, bavoir *m* **3** *Geog (of river)* affluent *m*, *Tech* canal *m* d'alimentation *ou* d'amenée; *(road)* route *f* de raccordement; *(air route)* ligne *f* régionale *(regroupant les passagers vers un aéroport principal)*; *Rail* embranchement *m*; *(for gas etc)* canalisation *f*, *Elec* câble *m ou* ligne *f* d'alimentation **4** *(device)* dispositif *m* d'alimentation **5** *(for printer, scanner, photocopier)* chargeur *m*

▸▸ **f. airline** compagnie *f* aérienne d'apport; **f. flight** vol *m* d'apport; **f. network** *(for airport)* réseau *m* d'apport; *Br Sch* **f. (primary) school** = école *f* primaire d'où arrivent les élèves d'un collège donné

feeding ['fiːdɪŋ] N **1** *(of person, machine etc)* alimentation *f*, *(of livestock)* affourragement *m* **2** *Tech* avance *f*, avancement *m*

▸▸ **f. bottle** biberon *m*; *Med* **f. cup** canard *m*; **f. frenzy** *(of sharks)* = frénésie *f* causée par la présence de nourriture; *Fig* **speculators were in a f. frenzy** les spéculateurs se sont déchaînés; *Zool* **f. grounds** = endroit *m* où les animaux viennent trouver leur nourriture; *Ind* **f. mechanism** mécanisme *m* d'avance *ou* d'avancement; *(for liquid)* mécanisme d'alimentation; **f. time** *(for child, animal)* heure *f* des repas

FEEL [fiːl]

N	toucher **1, 2**
VT	toucher **1** ▪ sentir **2** ▪ ressentir **2** ▪ penser **2**
VI	avoir **1** ▪ se sentir **1–3** ▪ avoir envie de **1, 2** ▪ être **3** ▪ chercher **4**

N **1** *(act of touching)* toucher *m*; **rough to the f.** rude au toucher; **to have a f. of sth** tou-

cher qch, tâter qch; **to have a f. in a drawer for sth** chercher qch à tâtons dans un tiroir; *Fig* **I don't like the f. of this** ça ne me dit rien qui vaille; *Sl* **to give sb a (quick) f.** tripoter qn

2 *(texture) (of paper etc)* toucher *m*; **it has a nice f. to it** *(fabric)* c'est agréable au toucher; *(place)* il y a une bonne atmosphère; *(name)* ça sonne bien; **there's a funny f. to this gearstick** le levier de vitesses fait un peu drôle; **to recognize sth by the f. of it** reconnaître qch au toucher

3 *(sensation)* sensation *f*; **the f. of silk against your skin** le contact de la soie contre la peau

4 *(knack)* **he has the f. of his car** il a sa voiture bien en main; **you'll soon get the f. of the work** vous allez bientôt vous habituer au travail; **to have a f. for translation** avoir le sens de la traduction; **you need to have a f. for it** il faut l'avoir en soi

VT *(pt, pp* felt *[felt])* **1** *(touch) (sth with one's hand)* toucher; *(pulse, pocket etc)* tâter; *(organ)* palper; **to f. one's way** *(in darkness)* avancer à tâtons; *Fig* explorer le terrain, y aller doucement; *Fig* **to f. one's way towards sth** avancer vers qch à tâtons; **to f. one's way into sth** se faire à qch; **to f. one's way around** essayer de s'y retrouver; **he felt her scalp to see if there was a lump** il tâta son crâne pour voir s'il y avait une bosse

2 VOIR GRAMMAIRE A41; B35 *(be conscious of, experience)* sentir; *(bitterness, pain, joy etc)* éprouver, ressentir; **I felt the floor tremble** *or* **trembling** j'ai senti trembler le sol; **she felt his arms around her** elle sentait ses bras l'entourant; **f. the weight of that!** pèse un peu ça!; **to f. the heat** être sensible à la chaleur; **to f. the cold** être sensible au froid, être frileux; **to make one's authority felt** affirmer son autorité, faire sentir son autorité; **she felt nothing, only emptiness** elle ne ressentait rien, seulement un vide; **do you f. anything for her?** est-ce que tu éprouves *ou* ressens quelque chose à son égard?; **I f. it in my bones that I shall succeed** quelque chose en moi me dit que je réussirai; **I felt it necessary to intervene** j'ai jugé nécessaire d'intervenir; **what do you f. about ...?** qu'est-ce que vous pensez de ...?; **what I f. about it is ...** mon sentiment là-dessus, c'est que ...; **I felt that he could have tried harder** j'avais le sentiment qu'il aurait pu faire plus d'efforts; **to f. a fool** se sentir bête *ou* stupide; **to f. a new woman/man** se sentir comme neuve/neuf

VI **1** *(of person)* **to f. hot/cold** avoir chaud/froid; **to f. tired** se sentir fatigué; **to f. ill** ne pas se sentir bien; **I f. really stupid** je me sens vraiment stupide; **to f. sick** *Br (about to vomit)* avoir envie de vomir; *Am (ill)* ne pas se sentir bien, se sentir malade; **she felt sick when she thought of ...** ça la rendait malade de penser à ...; **he felt really bad about leaving her** ça l'ennuyait vraiment de la laisser; **they felt betrayed** ils se sont sentis trahis; **my foot feels better** mon pied va mieux; **how do you f.?, how are you feeling?** comment te sens-tu?; **to f. all the better for it** s'en trouver mieux; **I f. ten years younger** je me sens dix ans de moins; **not to f. oneself** ne pas être dans son assiette; **I f. quite myself again** je me sens tout à fait rétabli; **to f. up to doing sth** *(well enough)* se sentir assez bien pour faire qch; *(competent enough)* se sentir de taille à faire qch; **to f. certain/convinced that ...** être certain/convaincu que ...; **how would you f. if I were to offer you a job?** qu'est-ce que vous diriez si je vous offrais un emploi?; **how would you f. if she left you?** qu'est-ce que tu ressentirais si elle te quittait?; **how do you think I f.?** *(that's a stupid question)* qu'est-ce que tu crois?; **how would you f.?** *(if sb did that to you)* qu'est-ce que tu ressen-

tirais, toi?; **she feels strongly about it** elle a des idées très arrêtées là-dessus; **I f. as if ...** j'ai l'impression que ...; **I felt as if I'd seen him before** j'avais l'impression de l'avoir déjà vu; **I felt as if** *or Fam* **like I was wasting my time** j'avais l'impression de perdre mon temps; **to f. like a fool** se sentir bête *ou* stupide; **to f. like a new man/woman** se sentir comme neuf/neuve

2 *(want sth/to do sth)* **to f. like doing sth** se sentir d'humeur à faire qch; **I felt like crying** j'avais envie de pleurer; **if you f. like it** si ça vous dit, si le cœur vous en dit; **I don't f. like it** ça ne me dit rien; **I f. like a cup of tea** j'ai envie d'une tasse de thé

3 *(of things)* **to f. hard/soft** être dur/doux au toucher; **the wall/her forehead felt hot** le mur/son front était chaud au toucher; **his legs/head felt heavy** il se sentait les jambes/la tête lourde(s); **the atmosphere felt tense** on sentait une certaine tension dans l'air; **my hands f. cold** j'ai froid aux mains; **my arm feels as if it's broken** j'ai l'impression que je me suis cassé le bras; **the room feels damp** la pièce (me) paraît humide; **it feels like ...** cela donne la sensation de ...; **it feels like (it's going to) rain** on dirait qu'il va pleuvoir; **it felt good to be alive** c'était bon d'être en vie; **it feels different/dead now she's gone** c'est différent/mort depuis qu'elle est partie; **what did it f. like when you won?** qu'est-ce que vous avez ressenti en gagnant?

4 *(explore, touch with fingers)* **to f. in one's pockets for sth** chercher qch dans ses poches; **he felt on the ground for his keys** il cherchait ses clefs à tâtons sur le sol

▸ **feel about, feel around** VI *(search by touching)* chercher à tâtons; **to f. about** *or* **around for sth** chercher qch à tâtons

▸ **feel for** VT INSEP *(feel sympathy for)* éprouver de la compassion à l'égard de; **I f. for her** elle a toute ma sympathie; **to f. for sb in their sorrow** partager la douleur de qn; **I really felt for you then** je t'ai sincèrement plaint à ce moment

▸ **feel up** VT SEP *Sl (touch sexually)* peloter

feeler ['fiːlər] N **1** *Biol (of insect etc)* antenne *f*, *(of snail)* corne *f*, *(of mollusc etc)* tentacule *m* **2** *Fig (tentative enquiry etc)* ballon *m* d'essai; **to put out feelers** lancer un ballon d'essai, tâter le terrain **3** *Tech (gauge)* calibre *m* d'épaisseur (à lames)

▸▸ *Tech* **f. gauge** calibre d'épaisseur (à lames)

feel-good factor N sentiment *m* de bien-être

feeling ['fiːlɪŋ] ADJ *(person)* sensible
N **1** *(sense of)* **f.** toucher *m*; **to have no f. in one's arm** avoir le bras mort; **to lose the f. in one's arm/leg** ne plus avoir aucune sensation dans le bras/la jambe

2 *(sensation)* sensation *f*

3 *(emotion)* sentiment *m*; **there is a f. of grief/joy throughout the country** le chagrin/la joie règne dans tout le pays; **a f. of emptiness** une impression de vide; **to hurt sb's feelings** blesser qn; **I don't want anybody to have hurt feelings about it** je ne veux pas que cela blesse qui que ce soit; **her feelings are hurt** elle est blessée; **she had a f. of elation** elle éprouvait un sentiment d'allégresse; **his feelings towards me** ses sentiments envers moi; **to have no feelings** n'avoir aucun cœur; **I know the f.!** je sais ce que c'est!; **I had a f. I might find you here** je pensais bien vous trouver ici; **I've got a nasty** *or* **unpleasant f. that ...** j'ai la désagréable impression que ...; **no hard feelings!** sans rancune!; **with f.** *(to speak etc) (emotionally)* avec émotion; *(warmly)* chaleureusement; *(angrily)* avec emportement; *(to sing etc)* avec expression *ou* âme

4 *(opinion)* **what are your feelings about fox-hunting?** qu'est-ce que vous pensez de la chasse au renard?; **I don't have any strong feelings about it** ça m'est plus ou moins égal; **feelings are running very high** les esprits sont très échauffés; **public f. ran high against the proposal** le sentiment populaire s'élevait contre cette proposition; **there is a general f. that …** l'impression règne (dans le public) que …, le sentiment général est que …

5 *(sensitivity)* sensibilité *f;* **to have a f. for music/nature** être sensible à la musique/la nature; **to have a f. for sth** *(do well)* être doué pour qch

feelingly ['fiːlɪŋlɪ] **ADV** *(to speak)* avec émotion; *(warmly)* chaleureusement; *(to sing, play)* avec expression

feet NPL *see* **foot N**

feign [feɪn] **VT** *(anger etc)* feindre, simuler; *(surprise)* affecter; **to f. illness** feindre *ou* simuler la maladie; **to f. sleep** faire semblant de dormir

feigned [feɪnd] **ADJ** *(illness)* simulé; *(surprise)* feint

feint [feɪnt] **N** *Mil* fausse attaque *f, Boxing, Fencing etc* feinte *f;* **his anger is only a f.** sa colère n'est qu'une simulation
▸ **VI** *Mil* faire une fausse attaque; *Boxing etc* feinter; *Boxing* **to f. with the right** feinter du droit

feint-ruled [-ruːld] **ADJ** *(paper)* à réglure légère

feistiness ['faɪstɪnɪs] **N** *esp Am* **1** *(spirit, energy)* fougue *f,* impétuosité *f* **2** *(pugnacity)* attitude *f* contestataire

feisty ['faɪstɪ] **ADJ** *esp Am* **1** *(full of energy)* impétueux, fougueux **2** *(pugnacious)* contestataire

feldspar ['feldspɑːr] **N** *Miner* feldspath *m*

felicitous [fɪ'lɪsɪtəs] **ADJ** *Lit (choice, decision)* heureux; *(word, expression etc)* bien trouvé, à propos

felicity [fɪ'lɪsɪtɪ] **N** *Lit* **1** *(happiness)* félicité *f,* bonheur *m* **2** *(aptness) (of remark, expression etc)* à-propos *m,* bien-trouvé *m;* *(of choice, decision)* caractère *m* heureux

feline ['fiːlaɪn] **ADJ** félin; **f. grace** grâce *f* féline, grâce de chat
▸ **N** félin *m*

fell[1] [fel] **VT** *(opponent etc)* abattre, terrasser; *(tree)* abattre, couper; **felled wood** *or* **timber** abattis *m,* bois *m* gisant, vente *f*

fell[2] **PT** *see* **fall VI**

fell[3] **ADJ at one f. swoop** d'un seul coup

fell[4] **N** *Br (hill, mountain)* colline *f;* **the fells** *(high moorland)* les landes *fpl* des plateaux
▸▸ **f. running** course *f* en basse montagne; **f. walking** randonnée *f* en basse montagne

fell[5] **N** *(animal skin)* peau *f*

fella, feller ['felə, -ər] **N** *Br Fam* mec *m,* type *m;* *(boyfriend)* copain *m,* mec, *Can* chum *m*

fellatio [fə'leɪʃɪəʊ] **N** fellation *f*

felling ['felɪŋ] **N** *(of cow, forest)* abattage *m;* *(of timber)* abattage, coupe *f*

fellow ['feləʊ] **N** **1** *(comrade)* camarade *mf,* compagnon *m*

2 *(colleague)* semblable *mf,* pareil *m;* *(one of a pair)* pendant *m;* **a vase and its f.** un vase et son pendant

3 *(at university) (professor)* = professeur *m* titulaire; *(postgraduate student)* chargé, -ée de cours; *(of learned society)* membre *m;* **F. of the Royal Society** = membre de la Société royale (de Londres)

4 *Br Fam (boyfriend)* copain *m,* mec *m, Can* chum *m*

5 *Old-fashioned, Fam (man)* homme *m,* gars *m;* **a good f.** un brave garçon; **a decent f.** un bon gars; **he's a queer f.** c'est un drôle de

type; **the poor little f.** le pauvre petit
▸ **ADJ f. being** *or* **creature** semblable *mf;* **f. citizen** concitoyen, -enne; **f. countryman/countrywoman** compatriote *mf;* **f. passenger/sufferer** compagnon de voyage/misère; **f. soldier** compagnon d'armes, camarade de régiment; **f. student** camarade d'études
▸▸ **f. feeling** sympathie *f;* **f. traveller** *(companion on journey)* compagnon, *f* compagne de voyage *ou* de route; *Fig* compagnon *m* de route; *Pol* communisant, -ante

fellowship ['feləʊʃɪp] **N** **1** *(friendship)* **(good) f.** amitié *f,* camaraderie *f* **2** *(association)* association *f,* corporation *f* **3** *(at university)* bourse *f* universitaire *(avec obligation de faire un cours, des recherches);* *(of learned society)* titre *m* de membre

felon ['felən] **N** *Law Arch* criminel, -elle

felonious [fe'ləʊnɪəs] **ADJ** *Law Arch* criminel, -elle; **f. act** action *f* qui constitue un crime

felony ['felənɪ] **N** *Law Arch* crime *m;* **to compound a f.** pactiser avec un crime

felspar ['felspɑːr] **N** = **feldspar**

felt[1] [felt] **N** *Tex etc* feutre *m;* **tarred f.** feutre bitumé
▸ **VT** *Tex (wool, hairs)* feutrer; *Constr (roof etc)* couvrir de feutre bitumé

felt[2] **PT, PP** *see* **feel VT, VI**

felt-tip **N** *(stylo m)* feutre *m*
▸▸ **f. pen** *(stylo)* feutre

female ['fiːmeɪl] **ADJ** *(person)* féminin; *(voice etc)* de femme; *(animal, plant etc)* femelle; *Tech* femelle; **the young f. giraffe** la jeune girafe femelle; **f. company** la compagnie féminine *ou* des femmes; **f. executive** femme *f* cadre; *Tech* **f. screw** écrou *m; Tech* **male-f. coupling/connection/adapter** accouplement *m*/accordement *m*/adaptateur *m* mâle-femelle
▸ **N** **1** *(animal, plant)* femelle *f;* *(person)* femme *f* **2** *Pej (woman)* bonne femme *f;* **some f. called for you** il y a une bonne femme qui t'a demandé au téléphone
▸▸ **f. impersonator** travesti *m (dans un spectacle)*

> Note that the French word **femelle** is never used to refer to human beings.

feminine ['femɪnɪn] VOIR GRAMMAIRE A16–17; B7–8; B9–10 **ADJ** féminin; *Gram* **this word is f.** ce mot est féminin
▸ **N** *Gram* féminin *m;* **in the f.** au féminin

femininity [femɪ'nɪnɪtɪ] **N** féminité *f*

feminism ['femɪnɪz(ə)m] **N** féminisme *m*

feminist ['femɪnɪst] **ADJ, N** féministe *mf*

femoral ['femərəl] **ADJ** *Anat* fémoral, -aux

femur, *pl* **femurs, femora** ['fiːmər, -əz, 'femərə] **N** *Anat* fémur *m*

fen [fen] **N** marais *m,* marécage *m;* **the Fens** = les plaines *fpl* marécageuses de l'est de l'Angleterre

fence [fens] **N** **1** *(for delimiting an area)* clôture *f,* *(more solid, for preventing entry)* barrière *f,* **sunk f.** saut *m* de loup; *Fig* **to sit on the f.** ménager la chèvre et le chou; **to get** *or* **come off the f.** arrêter de ménager la chèvre et le chou; *Fig* **to be on the other side of the f.** être de l'autre côté de la barricade, avoir une opinion contraire; **I don't often find myself on the same side of the f. as you** je n'ai pas souvent les mêmes opinions que toi; *esp Am Fig* **to mend one's fences** *(of politician)* regagner la confiance des électeurs; *Am Fig* **to mend one's fences with sb** se remettre en bons termes avec qn

2 *Horseriding (in steeplechasing)* obstacle *m,* haie *f,* *(in showjumping)* obstacle, barrière *f*

3 *Tech (of circular saw etc)* guide *m;* *(of machine tool etc)* garde *f*

4 *Sl (receiver of stolen property)* receleur, -euse (d'objets volés)
▸ **VT** *(field)* clôturer
▸ **VI** **1** *Sport* faire de l'escrime; *Fig* **to f. with a counsel** répondre en éludant les questions d'un avocat; *Fig* **stop fencing!** arrête d'éluder la question! **2** *Sl (receive stolen property)* faire du recel
▸▸ **f. post** piquet *m* de clôture
▸ **fence in VT SEP** *(land etc)* clôturer
▸ **fence off VT SEP** séparer par une clôture

fence-mending **N** *esp Am Fig* reprise *f* des relations

fencer ['fensər] **N** *Sport* escrimeur, -euse

fencing ['fensɪŋ] **N** **1** *(barrier etc)* clôture *f,* barrière *f;* *(material)* matériaux *mpl* pour clôture; **wire f.** treillage *m* en fil de fer **2** *(action) (of land etc)* action *f* de clôturer **3** *Sport* escrime *f,* **f. master** maître *m* d'armes; **f. match** assaut *m* d'armes; **f. school** salle *f* d'escrime *ou* d'armes **4** *Sl (receiving)* recel *m*

fend [fend] **VI** **to f. for oneself** se débrouiller
▸ **fend off VT SEP** *(blow, questions etc)* parer, détourner; *(attack)* parer

fender ['fendər] **N** *Am Aut* aile *f,* *(protecting wall, door, post etc)* bouteroue *f,* *(for fireplace)* garde-feu *m inv; Am Rail (on train engine, tram)* pare-chocs *m inv;* *(for clearing track)* chasse-pierres *m inv; Naut* bourrelet *m* de défense

fender-bender **N** *Am Fam* (petit) accrochage *m*

feng shui [fəŋ'ʃweɪ] **N** Feng Shui *m*

fenland ['fenlænd] **N** pays *m* marécageux

fennel ['fen(ə)l] **N** *Bot, Culin* fenouil *m*

feral ['ferəl] **ADJ** *Fml (cat, dog etc)* féral, -als, *ou* -aux

ferment ['fɜːment] **N 1** *(yeast etc)* ferment *m* **2** *(fermentation) (of liquid)* fermentation *f,* *Fig (commotion)* effervescence *f,* agitation *f;* **the whole town was in a (state of) f.** toute la ville était en effervescence *ou* dans un état d'agitation
▸ **VI** *(of liquids etc), Fig (of sedition)* fermenter; *(of wine)* travailler
▸ **VT** *(liquid)* laisser fermenter

fermentation [fɜːmen'teɪʃən] **N** *(of liquid etc)* fermentation *f,* *(of wine)* travail *m; Fig* agitation *f*

fern [fɜːn] **N** *(plant)* fougère *f,* **hillside covered with f.** coteau couvert de fougères

ferocious [fə'rəʊʃəs] **ADJ** *(animal, person, look etc)* féroce

ferociously [fə'rəʊʃəslɪ] **ADV** férocement, avec férocité

ferocity, ferociousness [fə'rɒsɪtɪ, fə'rəʊʃəsnɪs] **N** férocité *f*

ferret ['ferɪt] **N** *(animal)* furet *m*
▸ **VI** **(-t-) 1** *(hunt)* chasser au furet **2** *Fam* **to f. (about) in one's pockets** fouiller dans ses poches **(for sth** pour trouver qch); **what are you ferreting for?** qu'est-ce que tu cherches?
▸ **VT** *(rabbits etc)* chasser au furet
▸ **ferret out VT SEP** *(dislodge) (somebody, something)* dénicher; *(secret, the truth)* déterrer

ferreting ['ferɪtɪŋ] **N** *(hunting)* chasse *f* au furet

ferrety ['ferɪtɪ] **ADJ** de furet; *Pej* **f. eyes/face** yeux *mpl*/visage *m* de fouine

ferric ['ferɪk] **ADJ** *Chem* ferrique

Ferris wheel ['ferɪs] **N** *(at fairground)* grande roue *f*

ferrite ['feraɪt] **N** ferrite *f*

ferroconcrete ['ferəʊ'kɒŋkriːt] **N** béton *m* armé

ferromagnetic ['ferəʊmæg'netɪk] ADJ ferromagnétique

ferrous ['ferəs] ADJ Chem (oxide etc) ferreux
▸▸ **f. sulphide** pyrite f de fer

ferrule ['ferəl, -uːl] N (of walking stick) bout m ferré, embout m

ferry ['ferɪ] N (boat) bac m, ferry m; **to take the f.** prendre le bac ou le ferry; **passenger/car f.** bac ou ferry à piétons/à voitures; **train f.** bac transbordeur; **air f.** avion m transbordeur
VT **to f. sb/a car across a river** passer qn/une voiture en bac ou en ferry de l'autre côté de la rivière; **to f. voters to the polls** transporter des électeurs aux urnes; **she ferries her children backwards and forwards to school by car** elle fait la navette pour conduire ses enfants à l'école et les en ramener
▸▸ **f. port** port m de ferry; **f. service** ligne f de ferry

ferryboat ['ferɪbəʊt] N bac m, ferry m

ferrying ['ferɪɪŋ] N transport m en ou par bac ou ferry

ferryman, pl **ferrymen** ['ferɪmən] N passeur m

fertile ['fɜːtaɪl] ADJ (soil, woman, imagination etc) fertile, fécond (**in** en); (man) fécond; (egg) fécondé

fertility [fɜː'tɪlɪtɪ] N (of soil, person's imagination, woman etc) fertilité f, fécondité f
▸▸ Med **f. clinic** centre m de traitement de la stérilité; Med **f. drug** médicament m pour le traitement de la stérilité; **f. symbol** symbole m de fertilité; Med **f. treatment** traitement m de la stérilité

fertilization [fɜːtɪlaɪ'zeɪʃən] N (of egg etc) fertilisation f, fécondation f, Biol **self f.** autofécondation f

fertilize ['fɜːtɪlaɪz] VT **1** (egg, plant etc) fertiliser, féconder **2** Agr (soil) fertiliser, engraisser

fertilizer ['fɜːtɪlaɪzər] N Agr engrais m; **artificial fertilizers** engrais chimiques

fervent ['fɜːvənt] ADJ (prayer, supporter, belief) ardent, fervent; (wish, desire) ardent

fervently ['fɜːvəntlɪ] ADV (to plead, believe, pray etc) avec ferveur; (to wish, support etc) avec ardeur

fervid ['fɜːvɪd] ADJ = fervent

fervour, Am **fervor** ['fɜːvər] N (of prayer, speech, belief) ferveur f, (of wish, supporter) ardeur f

▸ **fess up** [fes] VI Am Fam (confess) se mettre à table

fester ['festər] VI (of wound etc) suppurer, s'envenimer; (of conflict, resentment) s'envenimer; (of dislike, sense of injustice) s'aviver

festering ['festərɪŋ] ADJ (wound etc) ulcéreux, suppurant; (conflict, resentment) qui s'envenime; (dislike, sense of injustice) aggravé, de plus en plus vif

festival ['festɪv(ə)l] N (of music, drama etc) festival m, pl -als; (religious) fête f, esp Rel **harvest f.** = office m d'action de grâces (célébré après la rentrée des récoltes); **film f.** festival du film; **street f.** fête de quartier

festive ['festɪv] ADJ (day etc) de fête; **the f. season** l'époque f des fêtes; **to be in (a) f. mood** (of person) avoir le cœur en fête

festivity [fes'tɪvɪtɪ] N (merriness) gaieté f, **an air/atmosphere of f.** un air/une atmosphère de fête; **festivities** (celebrations) festivités, réjouissances

festoon [fes'tuːn] N feston m, guirlande f
VT festonner (**with** de); (flowers etc) disposer en festons

feta ['fetə] N feta f
▸▸ **f. cheese** feta

fetal ['fiːt(ə)l] ADJ = foetal

fetch [fetʃ] VT **1** (go to get) aller chercher; **to f. water from the river** aller puiser de l'eau dans la rivière; **to f. sb from the airport** aller chercher qn à l'aéroport; **I'll f. you** je viendrai te chercher; **f.!** (to dog) va chercher!
2 Com rapporter; (specific price) atteindre; **it fetched a high price** cela s'est vendu cher; **it fetched £100,000** cela a atteint les 100 000 livres; **I'd be surprised if it fetched that much** cela m'étonnerait que cela rapporte autant ou que cela se vende aussi cher
3 (hit) **to f. sb a blow** flanquer un coup à qn **4** Lit (utter) (sigh, moan) pousser
VI **I'm not going to f. and carry for you!** je ne vais pas être ta bonne à tout faire!
▸ **fetch back** VT SEP (bring back) (somebody) ramener; (something) rapporter
▸ **fetch up** VI (reach) **to f. up at a port** parvenir ou arriver à un port; **the kite fetched up in the branches of a tree** le cerf-volant est resté accroché dans les branches d'un arbre; Fam **they finally fetched up at our house** ils ont finalement atterri chez nous; Fam **the car fetched up against a wall** la voiture s'est (finalement) arrêtée en heurtant un mur
VT SEP **1** (bring from lower place) (somebody) faire monter; (something) remonter **2** Fam (vomit) dégueuler

fetching ['fetʃɪŋ] ADJ (woman, air) séduisant, attrayant; (hat, smile) ravissant

fête [feɪt] N fête f, **village f.** fête communale
VT (person, event) fêter; (person) faire fête à

Fête
En Grande-Bretagne, les "village fêtes" sont des manifestations en plein air où l'on vend des produits faits maison et où l'on organise des manifestations sportives et des jeux pour enfants; elles sont généralement destinées à réunir des fonds pour une œuvre de charité.

fetid ['fetɪd, 'fiːtɪd] ADJ fétide, puant

fetish ['fetɪʃ] N (magic object), Psy fétiche m; **he has a f. for black silk** il est obsédé par la soie noire; **to make a f. of sth** être obsédé par qch

fetishism ['fetɪʃɪz(ə)m] N Psy fétichisme m

fetishist ['fetɪʃɪst] N Psy fétichiste mf

fetishistic [fetɪ'ʃɪstɪk] ADJ Psy fétichiste

fetlock ['fetlɒk] N (of horse) (part of leg) partie f postérieure du pied; (joint) boulet m; (hair) fanon m

fetter ['fetər] N (usu pl) **fetters** (of prisoner etc) chaînes fpl, fers mpl; **in fetters** enchaîné, dans les fers; **to put sb in fetters** mettre qn aux fers; Fig **to place fetters on sb/on sb's freedom** entraver qn/la liberté de qn; **the fetters of marriage** les chaînes du mariage
VT (person) enchaîner; (horse) entraver; Fig (unions etc) garrotter

fettle ['fet(ə)l] N **to be in fine** or **good f.** être en condition ou en forme

fetus ['fiːtəs] N = foetus

feud [fjuːd] N (between families, clans etc) inimitié f, **blood f.** vendetta f, **family f.** querelle f familiale
VI se quereller (**over** au sujet de); **the feuding parties** les opposants mpl, les parties fpl en conflit

feudal ['fjuːd(ə)l] ADJ Hist (system, service etc) féodal, -aux; Pej (attitude, approach to sth) moyenâgeux

feudalism ['fjuːdəlɪz(ə)m] N le système féodal; **under late f.** pendant les dernières années du système féodal

feudally ['fjuːd(ə)lɪ] ADV féodalement

fever ['fiːvər] N Med (high temperature, disease) fièvre f, **high f.** forte fièvre; **she's got** or **she is running a f.** elle a de la fièvre; Fig **to be in a f. of excitement** être animé d'une excitation fébrile ou fiévreuse; **expectation had reached f. pitch** l'attente était fiévreuse; **things are at f. pitch** l'atmosphère est enfiévrée; **gold f.** fièvre de l'or

fevered ['fiːvəd] ADJ (brow) fiévreux; Fig (imagination) enfiévré

feverish ['fiːvərɪʃ] ADJ Med fiévreux, fébrile; **to be f.** avoir de la fièvre, être fiévreux ou fébrile; **to feel f.** se sentir fiévreux; Fig **f. activity** activité fébrile ou fiévreuse

feverishly ['fiːvərɪʃlɪ] ADV fiévreusement, fébrilement

feverishness ['fiːvərɪʃnɪs] N Med état m fébrile; (of activity) fébrilité f

FEW [fjuː] VOIR GRAMMAIRE A6

ADJ peu de **1** ▪ quelques **2**	
PRON peu **1** ▪ quelques-uns **2**	

ADJ **1** (not many) (people, things) peu de; **to have f. friends** avoir peu d'amis; **very f. opportunities** très peu d'occasions; **with f. exceptions** à de rares exceptions près; **on the f. occasions I've spoken to her** les rares fois où je lui ai parlé; **his visits/tourists are f. and far between** ses visites/les touristes sont rarissimes; **trains every f. minutes** trains toutes les deux ou trois minutes; **every f. days** tous les deux ou trois jours; **too f. points** pas suffisamment de points; **f. in number** peu nombreux; **f. novelists have equalled her** peu de romanciers l'ont égalée
2 (some) **a f.** quelques; **I have only a f. pounds** je n'ai que quelques livres; **he had a good f. enemies** il avait pas mal d'ennemis; **in a f. minutes** dans quelques minutes; **quite a f. minutes passed** un bon moment s'est écoulé; **in the next f. days** dans les jours qui suivent/suivaient
PRON **1** (not many) (people etc) peu; **there are very/too f. of us** nous sommes très peu/trop peu nombreux; **f. (of them) could speak French** peu parmi eux parlaient français; **there are so f. of them** ils sont tellement peu nombreux
2 (some) **a f. of these cakes/oranges** quelques-uns de ces gâteaux/quelques-unes de ces oranges; **a f. of the survivors** quelques-uns des survivants; **I know a f. of them** j'en connais quelques-uns; **a f. of us** quelques-uns d'entre nous; **I've seen/read a f.** j'en ai vu/lu quelques-uns; Fam **you've had a f. too many** (drunk too much) tu as un peu trop bu; **she only knew a f. (of them)** elle ne connaissait que quelques-uns d'entre eux
NPL **the f.** la minorité; **the fortunate f.** les heureux élus mpl; **the f. who came** les rares personnes qui sont venues

fewer ['fjuːər] ADJ (comp of few) moins de; **there are f. trees here** il y a moins d'arbres ici; **no f. than thirty** pas moins de trente; **the houses became f.** les maisons devenaient plus rares ou moins nombreuses; **f. and f. people** de moins en moins de gens
PRON moins; **there are f. (of them) than I thought** il y en a moins que je n'avais pensé

fewest ['fjuːɪst] ADJ (superl of few) le moins de; **the f. people possible** le moins de gens possible; **the area where there are the f. houses** la région où il y a le moins de maisons
PRON **the region where the f. live** la région où vit le moins grand nombre de gens

fey [feɪ] ADJ **1** (charming) qui possède un charme éthéré **2** (silly) un peu idiot **3** Scot (foreseeing death) qui a des pressentiments de mort ou des visions de l'au-delà; *(having second sight)* doué de seconde vue

fez [fez] **N** *(hat)* fez *m*

fiancé, *f* **fiancée** [fɪ'ɒnseɪ] **N** fiancé, -ée

fiasco [fɪ'æskəʊ] **N** fiasco *m*; **to be a f.** faire un four, être un fiasco

fiat ['faɪæt] **N** *(decree)* décret *m*
▸▸ *Am Fin* **f. money** monnaie *f* fiduciaire

fib [fɪb] *Fam* **N** petit mensonge *m*; **that's a f.!** ce n'est pas vrai!, c'est des histoires!; **you're telling me fibs** tu me racontes des histoires; **I told them a f. about having to do some work** je leur ai raconté qu'il fallait que je travaille
VI (**-bb-**) *(lie)* raconter des histoires; **you're fibbing to me again** tu es encore en train de me raconter des histoires; **I'm sure he was fibbing about how much he earns** je suis sûr qu'il a menti *ou* raconté des histoires à propos de l'argent qu'il gagne; **I fibbed to them about having to do some work** je leur ai raconté qu'il fallait que je travaille

fibber ['fɪbər] **N** *Fam* menteur, -euse; **she's a terrible f.** elle raconte tout le temps des histoires; **what a f. you are!** quel menteur tu fais!

fibre, *Am* **fiber** ['faɪbər] **N 1** fibre *f*; *(of cloth, wood)* fibre; **artificial/natural fibres** fibres artificielles/naturelles; *Fig* **moral f.** force *f* morale; *Fig* **to love sb/sth with every f. of one's being** aimer qn/qch de tout son être **2** *(in diet)* fibres *fpl*; **to be high in f.** *(foodstuff)* être riche en fibres; **high-f. diet** régime *m ou* alimentation *f* riche en fibres
▸▸ *Comput* **f. optics** fibre(s) *f(pl)* optique(s)

fibreboard, *Am* **fiberboard** ['faɪbəbɔːd] **N** panneau *m* de fibres agglomérées

fibreglass, *Am* **fiberglass** ['faɪbəɡlɑːs] **N** fibre *f* de verre; **it's (made of) f.** c'est en *ou* la fibre de verre

fibre-optic, *Am* **fiber-optic** **ADJ** *(technology)* de la fibre optique; *(system)* qui utilise la fibre optique; *(components)* en fibre optique
▸▸ **f. cable** câble *m* optique, câble en fibres optiques

fibrescope, *Am* **fiberscope** ['faɪbəskəʊp] **N** *Med, Opt* fibroscope *m*

fibrillation [faɪbrɪ'leɪʃən] **N** fibrillation *f*

fibroid ['faɪbrɔɪd] **ADJ** *(tumour etc)* fibroïde **N** *Med* fibrome *m*

fibroma, *pl* **fibromata** [faɪ'brəʊmə, -mətə] **N** *Med* fibrome *m*

fibrosis [faɪ'brəʊsɪs] **N** *Med* fibrose *f*

fibrositis [faɪbrəʊ'saɪtɪs] **N** *Med* fibrosite *f*

fibrous ['faɪbrəs] **ADJ** *(tissue etc)* fibreux

fibula ['fɪbjʊlə] **N** *Anat* péroné *m*

fickle ['fɪk(ə)l] **ADJ** inconstant, capricieux; *(character)* changeant, versatile; *(esp romantically)* volage; *(weather)* capricieux

fickleness ['fɪk(ə)lnɪs] **N** inconstance *f*, humeur *f* volage; **the f. of luck** les caprices *mpl* de la chance

fiction ['fɪkʃən] **N 1** *(creation of imagination)* fiction *f*, création *f* de l'imagination; *Law* **legal f.** fiction légale; **these tales are pure f.** tous ces contes sont totalement imaginaires; *Fig* **his entire statement is a piece of f.** sa déposition est fabriquée de toutes pièces **2** *(in library, bookshop)* romans *mpl*; **light f.** romans de lecture facile; **a piece of f.** une œuvre de fiction; **f. writer** auteur *m* d'ouvrages de fiction

fictional ['fɪkʃən(ə)l] **ADJ** fictif; **a f. autobiography** une autobiographie romancée

fictionalize ['fɪkʃənəlaɪz] **VT** romancer

fictitious [fɪk'tɪʃəs] **ADJ** *(character, events)* fictif; *(account)* inventé; **her statement is entirely f.** sa déposition est fabriquée de toutes pièces

▸▸ *Fin* **f. assets** actif *m* fictif; *Fin* **f. person** personne *f* fictive

fictitiously [fɪk'tɪʃəslɪ] **ADV** fictivement

fiddle ['fɪd(ə)l] **N** *Fam* **1** *(violin)* violon *m*; *(musician)* (joueur, -euse de) violon; **bass f.** contrebasse *f*; *Fig* **to play second f.** jouer un rôle secondaire (**to sb** auprès de qn) **2** *Br (swindle)* combine *f*, magouille *f*; **to be on the f.** faire du fricotage
VI 1 *(play violin)* jouer du violon; *Pej* racler du violon; *Fig* **to f. while Rome burns** = s'occuper de choses futiles au lieu de lutter contre une calamité **2** *(play, fidget)* **to f. (about** *or* **around) with** jouer avec, tripoter, trifouiller; *(details etc)* chipoter sur, ergoter sur; **to f. with one's watch** jouer avec sa montre; **don't f. with the switch** laisse l'interrupteur tranquille, ne tripote pas l'interrupteur; **she fiddled with a few knobs** elle a manipulé quelques boutons; **stop fiddling about** *or* **around and get down to some work!** arrête de tourner en rond et mets-toi au travail! **3** *Br Fam (swindle)* combiner, fricoter
VT *Br Fam (tamper with) (meter etc)* bricoler; *(obtain dishonestly)* carotter; **to f. the accounts** truquer les comptes; **he fiddled a week's leave** il a carotté huit jours de permission; **he fiddled it** *or* **things so that ...** il s'est arrangé pour que ... + *sub*

fiddlededee [fɪd(ə)ldɪ'diː] **INT** *Old-fashioned Fam* bah!, turlututu!

fiddle-faddle [-fæd(ə)l] *Old-fashioned Fam* **N** bagatelles *fpl*, balivernes *fpl*, fadaises *fpl* **INT** = **fiddlededee**

fiddler ['fɪdlər] **N** *Fam* **1** *Mus* joueur, -euse de violon; *Pej* violoneux *m* **2** *Br (swindler)* combinard, -arde

fiddlesticks ['fɪd(ə)lstɪks] **INT** *Old-fashioned Fam (nonsense)* balivernes!, quelle blague!; *(annoyance)* zut de zut!

fiddling ['fɪdlɪŋ] **ADJ** *(insignificant)* futile, insignifiant
N 1 *Fam Pej (on violin)* raclage *m* **2** *(fidgeting)* trifouillage *m*, tripotage *m*; **his f. with the details of my reports** la manière qu'il avait de chipoter *ou* d'ergoter sur les détails de mes rapports **3** *Br Fam (dishonest dealing)* combines *fpl*, fricotage *m*; **a lot of f. goes on around here** ça magouille *ou* ça fricote pas mal par ici

fiddly ['fɪdlɪ] **ADJ** *(work)* délicat, minutieux; *(details)* minutieux; **it was f. getting this nut off** ça a été délicat d'enlever cet écrou

fidelity [fɪ'delɪtɪ] **N 1** *(of person, to person)* fidélité *f* **2** *(of translation, sound reproduction)* fidélité *f*; **f. to the original** fidélité à l'original; *Radio etc* **high f.** haute fidélité

fidget ['fɪdʒɪt] **N 1** *(usu pl)* **the fidgets** l'agitation *f* nerveuse; **to have the fidgets** ne pas tenir en place **2** *(person)* **he's a f.** il ne tient pas en place; **what a f. you are!** mais tu ne tiens donc pas en place!; **don't be such a f.!** mais tiens-toi donc tranquille!
VI (**-t-**) être agité, ne pas tenir en place; *(become excited)* s'énerver; **to f. around with sth** tripoter qch; **don't f.!** *(to child)* tiens-toi tranquille!

fidgetiness ['fɪdʒɪtɪnɪs] **N** agitation *f* nerveuse

fidgety ['fɪdʒɪtɪ] **ADJ** agité, qui ne tient pas en place; *(excited)* nerveux, impatient

fiduciary [fɪ'djuːʃərɪ] *Law, Fin* **ADJ** fiduciaire
N fiduciaire *m*; *(trustee)* dépositaire *m*
▸▸ **f. account** compte *m* fiduciaire; **f. issue** émission *f* fiduciaire

fief [fiːf] **N** *Hist Fig* fief *m*

field [fiːld] **N 1** *(land)* champ *m*; *(under pasture)* pré *m*; *(of oil, gas, coal, diamonds etc)* gisement *m*; **to work in the fields** travailler

dans les champs; **to cut across the fields** couper à travers champs; **f. of wheat** champ de blé; **strawberry f.** plantation *f* de fraisiers; **in the open f.** en plein champ; *Aviat* **landing f.** terrain *m* d'atterrissage **2** *Mil* **f. (of battle)** champ *m* de bataille; **in the f.** en campagne; **to hold the f.** se maintenir sur ses positions; *(of theory etc)* faire autorité; **to take the f.** entrer en campagne; **f. of honour** champ d'honneur **3** *Sport (ground)* *Ftbl, Cr etc* terrain *m*; *(for baseball)* champ *m*; *Cr (bowlers)* chasseurs *mpl* **4** *(in race), Horseracing* **the f.** les partants *mpl*; **big f.** champ *m* fourni; **a strong f.** un bel éventail de concurrents; *Fig* **there are three candidates in the f.** trois candidatures ont été déposées; **well ahead of the rest of the f.** loin devant les autres; **to lead the f.** *Sport* mener le peloton; *Fig (of theory, ideas etc)* faire autorité; **our company leads the f. when it comes to fitted kitchens** notre entreprise est en tête du marché pour ce qui est des cuisines encastrées; *Fam* **to play the f.** *(keep options open)* ne pas s'engager; *(in relationships)* papillonner, avoir de nombreuses aventures amoureuses **5** *(domain) (of operation etc)* théâtre *m*, champ *m*; *(of science)* domaine *m*; **in the political f.** sur le plan politique; **she is the leading artist in her f.** elle est la plus grande artiste dans son domaine; **they were first in the f. with miniaturized TVs** ils ont été les premiers à commercialiser les télévisions miniaturisées; **that's not my f.** ce n'est pas mon domaine; **to work in the f.** *(not in office etc)* travailler sur le terrain; **to test a product in the f.** essayer un produit sur le terrain **6** *Opt, Phot etc* champ *m*; **f. of view** *or* **of vision** champ visuel; *Phys* **f. of force** champ de force; **magnetic f.** champ magnétique **7** *Her* champ *m*, sol *m*; *Art (of painting etc)* champ, fond *m*; *(of medal)* champ **8** *Comput (in database)* champ *m*
VT 1 *Sport (team)* réunir; *Mil etc* **to be able to f. 50,000 men** pouvoir mettre 50 000 hommes en ligne; *Pol* **to f. 500 candidates** présenter 500 candidats **2** *Cr* **to f. a ball** arrêter (et relancer) une balle; **to f. a question (well)** bien répondre à une question
VI *Cr* tenir le champ
▸▸ **f. agent** agent *m* sur le terrain; *Mil* **f. artillery** artillerie *f* de campagne; *Mil* **f. battery** batterie *f* de campagne; *Opt, Phot* **f. coil** bobine *f* d'excitation *ou* d'inducteur, bobine inductrice; **f. day** *Sch* journée *f* en plein air; *Mil* jour *m* des grandes manœuvres; *Fig* **to have a f. day** s'en donner à cœur joie; *Comput* **f. delimiter** délimiteur *m* de champ; **f. engineer** ingénieur *m* de chantier *ou* sur le terrain; *Sport* **f. events** concours *mpl* de saut et de lancer; *Mil* **f. exercise** exercice *m* en campagne, manœuvre *f*; **f. experiment** expérience *f* sur le terrain; **f. glasses** jumelles *fpl*; *Mil* **f. gun** canon *m*; *Am* **f. hockey** hockey *m* (sur gazon); *Mil* **f. hospital** antenne *f* chirurgicale, hôpital *m* de campagne; *Mktg* **f. interviewing** sondage *m* sur le terrain; **f. label** *(in dictionary)* rubrique *f*, indicateur *m* de domaine; *Mil* **f. marshal** maréchal *m*; *Mil* **f. officer** officier *m* supérieur; *Mil* **f. rations** ration *f* de guerre; **f. research** études *fpl* sur le terrain; **f. research executive** responsable *mf* des études sur le terrain; **f. sales manager** directeur, -trice des ventes sur le terrain; **f. sales personnel** personnel *m* de vente sur le terrain; *Comput* **f. separator** séparateur *m* de champs; *Mil* **f. service** service *m* en campagne; *Comput* **f. size** taille *f* de champ; **f. study** étude *f* sur le terrain; *Mil* **f. telegraph** télégraphe *m* militaire; **f. trials** *(for machine)* essais *mpl* sur le terrain; *Sch, Univ* **f. trip** voyage *m* d'études; *(of one afternoon, one*

day) sortie *f* d'études; **f. work** *(research etc)* travaux *mpl ou* recherches *fpl* sur le terrain *ou* sur les lieux; **f. worker** *(social worker)* travailleur, -euse social(e); *(researcher)* chercheur, -euse de terrain

fielder ['fiːldər] **N** *Cr etc* chasseur *m*

fieldmouse, *pl* **fieldmice** ['fiːldmaʊs, -maɪs] **N** mulot *m*

fiend [fiːnd] **N 1** *(demon)* démon *m*, diable *m* **2** *(evil person)* monstre *m* (de cruauté) **3** *Fam (fanatic)* **fresh-air f.** maniaque *mf ou* fanatique *mf* du plein air; *Old-fashioned* **dope f.** toxicomane *mf*

fiendish ['fiːndɪʃ] **ADJ** diabolique, satanique; *Fig* diabolique; *(weather)* atroce, abominable; **to take a f. pleasure in sth** prendre un plaisir diabolique à qch

fiendishly ['fiːndɪʃlɪ] **ADV** diaboliquement; **to laugh f.** avoir un rire diabolique; **a f. clever plan/piece of software/virus** un plan/logiciel/virus drôlement malin; **f. complicated/expensive** affreusement compliqué/cher; *Fam* **f. difficult** d'une difficulté infernale; *Fam* **it was f. cold** il faisait un froid de tous les diables

fierce [fɪəs] **ADJ** *(person)* redoutable; *(animal)* féroce; *(fire etc)* ardent; *(heat)* torride; *(battle, competition, opposition)* acharné; *(critic, opponent)* ardent; *(wind etc)* furieux, violent; **to give sb a f. look** jeter un regard féroce à qn; **f. encounter** rencontre violente; **there was f. criticism of the policy** la politique a suscité des critiques violentes; **she was f. in her defence of him** elle le défendait avec acharnement; **f. fighting** lutte *f* acharnée; *Aut etc* **f. brake** frein *m* brutal

fiercely ['fɪəslɪ] **ADV** *(to lash out, criticize)* violemment; *(to glare)* d'un œil féroce; *(to defend, fight)* avec acharnement; **to be f. opposed to sth** être ardemment opposé à qch; **the sun beat down f.** le soleil frappait très fort

fierceness ['fɪəsnɪs] **N** *(of person, opposition, criticism)* violence *f*, véhémence *f*; *(of animal)* férocité *f*; *(of fire etc)* ardeur *f*; *(of battle)* acharnement *m*; *(of wind etc)* fureur *f*, *Aut etc (of brakes)* brutalité *f*; **the f. of her tone** son ton véhément

fieriness ['faɪərɪnɪs] **N 1** *(of sun)* ardeur *f*; **the f. of the seasoning** l'assaisonnement très relevé ou épicé **2** *(of character)* ardeur *f*, fougue *f*, impétuosité *f*, emportement *m*

fiery ['faɪərɪ] **ADJ 1** brûlant, enflammé; *(alcoholic drink)* extrêmement fort, brûlant; **f. coal(s)** charbons *mpl* ardents; **f. furnace** fournaise *f* ardente; **f. red** rouge *m* ardent, rouge feu; **f. sky** ciel *m* embrasé; **f. taste** saveur *f* très épicée, goût *m* piquant **2** *(person, character)* fougueux, emporté, impétueux; **to make f. speeches against sb** vomir feu et flamme contre qn; **f. temper** tempérament *m* fougueux *ou* emporté
  ▸▸ *Am* **the f. cross** la croix en flammes *(symbole du Ku Klux Klan)*

FIFA ['fiːfə] **N** *(abbr* **Fédération Internationale de Football Association)** FIFA *f*

fife [faɪf] **N** *Mus* fifre *m*

FIFO [fiːfəʊ] *Com (abbr* **first in, first out)** PEPS

fifteen [fɪf'tiːn, 'fɪftiːn] **N 1** quinze *m*; **she is f. (years old)** elle a quinze ans; **the plane will land at f. thirty (hours)** l'avion va atterrir à quinze heures trente **2** *Rugby* **the French f.** le quinze de France

fifteenth [fɪf'tiːnθ, 'fɪftiːnθ] **ADJ** quinzième; **Louis the F.** Louis Quinze; **(on) the f. (of the month)** le quinze du mois
  N 1 *(person, thing)* quinzième *mf* **2** *(fraction)* quinzième *m*

fifth [fɪfθ] **ADJ** cinquième; **Henry the F.** Henri Cinq

N 1 *(of month)* cinq *m*; **on the f.** le cinq **2** *(person, thing)* cinquième *mf* **3** *(fraction)* cinquième *m* **4** *Mus* quinte *f*
  ▸▸ *Am* **F. Amendment** Cinquième Amendement *m (de la Constitution des États-Unis, permettant à un accusé de ne pas répondre à une question risquant de jouer en sa défaveur); Law, Hum* **to plead the F. Amendment, to take the F. Amendment** = refuser de répondre pour ne pas dire quelque chose pouvant être utilisé contre soi; *Pol* **f. column** cinquième colonne *f*; *Pol* **f. columnist** membre *m* de la cinquième colonne; *Br Sch* **f. form** ≃ classe *f* de seconde; *Aut* **f. gear** cinquième vitesse *f*, *Aut* **f. wheel** *(trailer coupling)* sellette *f*; *(on test car)* cinquième roue *f*, *Am* **to feel like a f. wheel** avoir l'impression d'être la cinquième roue du carrosse

fifth-generation **ADJ** *Comput* de la cinquième génération

fifthly ['fɪfθlɪ] **ADV** cinquièmement

fifth-rate **ADJ** *Fam* médiocre

fiftieth ['fɪftɪəθ] **ADJ** cinquantième
  N 1 *(person, thing)* cinquantième *mf* **2** *(fraction)* cinquantième *m*

fifty ['fɪftɪ] **NUM ADJ, N** cinquante *m*; **f.-one** cinquante et un; **f.-two** cinquante-deux; **about f. books** une cinquantaine de livres; **the fifties** les années cinquante; **to be f.** avoir cinquante ans; **to be in one's fifties** avoir entre cinquante et soixante ans; **to be over f.** avoir cinquante ans passés, avoir plus de cinquante ans

fifty-fifty **ADJ, ADV** *(partnership)* à parts égales; **to split the profits f.** partager les bénéfices à parts égales; **to go f. on sth** partager le coût de quelque chose à parts égales; **her chances are f.** *(of surviving)* elle a cinquante pour cent de chances de s'en tirer; *(of winning)* elle a cinquante pour cent de chances de gagner

fig[1] [fɪg] **N 1** *(fruit)* figue *f*; **fresh** *or* **green figs** figues fraîches; **dried figs** figues sèches; *Old-fashioned Fam* **he doesn't give** *or* **care a f. what you think** il se fiche éperdument de ce que tu penses **2** *(tree)* figuier *m*
  ▸▸ **f. leaf** *Bot* feuille *f* de figuier; *(on statue, in painting)* feuille *f* de vigne; *Fig* camouflage *m*; *Fig* **it's just a f. leaf** ce n'est qu'une couverture; *Fig* **f. tree** figuier

fig[2] *(abbr* **figure)** *(in book etc)* fig; **see f. 21b** voir fig 21b

fight [faɪt] **N** *Boxing, Mil etc* combat *m*; *(brawl)* bagarre *f*, *(argument)* dispute *f*, **f. to the death** lutte *f* à mort; **they had a f.** *(in which they hit each other)* ils se sont battus; *(they argued)* ils se sont disputés; **to get into a f. with sb** se battre avec qn; *(argue)* se disputer avec qn; **I don't want us to get into a f. over this, but ...** je ne veux pas que nous nous disputions pour ça, mais ...; **do you want a f.?** tu veux te battre?; **a fair f.** un combat loyal; **the f. for life** la lutte pour la vie; **her f. against cancer** sa lutte contre le cancer; **to carry on a stubborn f. against sb** soutenir une lutte opiniâtre contre qn; **to show some f.** résister, offrir de la résistance; **I won't give in without a f.** je ne vais pas me laisser faire sans me battre; *Sport* **to put up a good f.** bien se défendre; **there was no f. left in him** il n'avait plus le cœur à se battre; **he still has a lot of f. left in him** il n'a pas dit son dernier mot; **you'll have a f. on your hands** *(it will be difficult)* tu vas avoir du mal; **the f. for the leadership of the party** la lutte pour la tête du parti

  VI *(pt, pp* **fought** [fɔːt]) *(physically)* se battre; *(struggle)* lutter; *(argue)* se disputer; *Mil* **he fought in Russia** il s'est battu en Russie; **to f. against the enemy** combattre l'ennemi; **to f. against adversity/disease** lutter contre l'adversité/la maladie; **to f. against sleep**

lutter contre le sommeil; **to f. for sb** se battre pour qn; **to f. for sth** *(on behalf of)* se battre pour qch; *(to get sth)* se battre pour obtenir qch; **to f. for breath** avoir beaucoup de mal à respirer; **to f. for one's rights/freedom** se battre *ou* lutter pour ses droits/sa liberté; **she fought to clear her name** elle s'est battue pour prouver son innocence; **to f. on two fronts** se battre sur deux fronts; **two dogs fighting over a bone** deux chiens qui se disputent un os; **to f. fair** se battre loyalement; **they were fighting over some islands/who would sleep where** ils se battaient pour des îles/pour décider qui allait dormir où; **to f. for one's life** *(of someone seriously ill, competitor)* lutter pour sa vie; **to f. to the finish** se battre jusqu'au dernier moment; **to go down fighting** se battre jusqu'au bout

  VT *(person)* se battre avec *ou* contre; *(enemy, fire, new measure, decision)* combattre; *(illness, temptation)* lutter contre; *(match)* disputer; *Boxing* **to f. the champion** affronter le champion; **I'll f. you in the courts** je vous traînerai en justice; **I'll f. you for custody** je me battrai contre toi pour obtenir la garde des enfants; **to f. a battle** livrer (une) bataille; **to f. a duel** se battre en duel; *Fig* **to f. a losing battle** livrer *ou* mener une bataille perdue d'avance; **to f. a losing battle to do sth** tenter vainement de faire qch; *Rel etc* **to f. the good f.** combattre pour la bonne cause; *Fig* **to f. sb's battles** prendre le parti de qn; **I'm not going to f. your battles for you** c'est à vous de vous débrouiller; **he fought his way through the crowd** il se fraya un chemin à travers la foule; **to f. one's way out** se frayer un passage pour sortir; **to f. one's way to the top** *(of one's profession)* se battre pour atteindre le sommet; **to f. an action (at law)** se défendre dans un procès; **to f. an election** se présenter à une élection; **she will be fighting a popular businessman** *(in election)* elle sera opposée à un homme d'affaires populaire; **to f. an emotion** lutter contre une émotion; **f. it!** résiste!
  ▸▸ **the f. game** la boxe

▸ **fight back** **VT SEP 1** *(suppress) (emotion etc)* lutter contre; *(tears)* refouler **2 to f. one's way back again** remonter le courant
  VI *(retaliate)* riposter, résister; **to f. back against an illness** lutter contre une maladie

▸ **fight down** **VT SEP** *(suppress) (passion, resistance etc)* vaincre; *(impulse, urge)* réprimer

▸ **fight off** **VT SEP** *(repel) (enemy, attack, sb's advances etc)* repousser; *(illness etc)* combattre; *(inflation)* juguler; **to f. off one's fear** lutter contre *ou* combattre sa peur

▸ **fight out** **VT SEP to f. it out** se mesurer l'un à l'autre; **you'll have to f. that out with him** tu régleras ça avec lui

fighter ['faɪtər] **N 1** *(person who fights)* combattant *m*; *(boxer)* boxeur *m*; *Fig* **she's a f.** c'est une battante **2** *Mil, Aviat (plane)* chasseur *m*, avion *m* de chasse
  ▸▸ *Mil, Aviat* **f. aircraft** chasseur, avion de chasse; *Mktg* **f. model** modèle *m* d'attaque; *Mil, Aviat* **f. pilot** pilote *m* de chasse; *Mil, Aviat* **f. plane** chasseur, avion de chasse; *Mil, Aviat* **f. squadron** escadron *m* de chasse

fighter-bomber **N** chasseur-bombardier *m*, *pl* chasseurs-bombardiers

fighting ['faɪtɪŋ] **ADJ that's f. talk!** tu cherches la bagarre?/il cherche la bagarre!/*etc*; *Fam* **I still have a f. chance** j'ai encore de bonnes chances; **to be f. fit** être dans une forme éblouissante; **to get f. drunk** se saouler et chercher la bagarre
  N *Mil* combat *m*; *Boxing* boxe *f*; **there was a lot of f. at my school** il y avait beaucoup de bagarre dans mon école; **the f. on the eastern front** les combats sur le front est

▸▸**f. cock** coq *m* de combat; *Mil* **f. forces** effectifs *mpl* sous les armes; *Mil* **f. men** combattants *mpl*; *Mil* **f. unit** unité *f* de combat

figment ['fɪgmənt] **N a f. of the imagination** un phénomène imaginaire; **it's a f. of your imagination** tu te fais des idées, c'est le fruit de ton imagination; **is this a f. of my imagination, or …?** est-ce que je me fais des idées, ou bien …?

figurative ['fɪgərətɪv] **ADJ 1** *(language, meaning)* figuré, métaphorique; **in the f. sense** au (sens) figuré **2** *(art)* figuratif

figuratively ['fɪgərətɪvlɪ] **ADV 1** *(to speak, write)* au figuré, métaphoriquement; **f. speaking, …** métaphoriquement parlant, … **2** *Art* figurativement

FIGURE ['fɪgər, *Am* 'fɪgjər]

| **N** chiffre **1** ▪ figure **2, 6, 7** ▪ silhouette **2** ▪ ligne **2, 3** ▪ personnage **4** |
| **VI** figurer **1** ▪ sembler logique **3** |
| **VT** penser **1** ▪ supposer que **2** |

N 1 *(number)* chiffre *m*; **it's difficult to give an exact f.** il est difficile de donner un chiffre exact; **figures** *(for project etc)* détails *mpl* chiffrés; *(involving calculation)* calculs *mpl*; *(statistics)* statistiques *fpl*; **the figures for 2001** les statistiques de 2001; **to find a mistake in the figures** trouver une erreur de calcul; **there must be a mistake in the figures** il doit y avoir une erreur dans les calculs; *Com* **sales figures** chiffres *mpl* de vente; **unemployment figures** le taux de chômage; **in round figures** en chiffres ronds; **to put a f. on sth** *(assess price, cost)* évaluer le prix/coût de qch; *(assess quantity)* évaluer le nombre de qch; **to be good at figures** être bon en calcul; **to fetch a high f.** se vendre cher; **his score barely managed to get into double figures** son score s'élevait tout juste à un nombre à deux chiffres; **our takings have reached four figures** nous avons décroché les quatre chiffres; **to get inflation down to single figures** réduire l'inflation à un taux inférieur à dix pour cent

2 *(shape)* figure *f*; *(of person)* silhouette *f*; **to have a good f.** être bien fait de sa personne; *(of woman)* avoir une jolie silhouette; **to look after/keep one's f.** soigner/garder sa ligne; **to be f.-conscious** faire attention à sa ligne

3 *(human form)* ligne *f*; **a fine f. of a man** un bel homme; **a fine f. of a woman** une belle femme; *Art* **reclining f.** corps *m* au repos

4 *(person, character)* personnage *m*; **a distinguished f.** une personnalité; **a f. of fun** un objet de ridicule; **a hate f.**, a f. that un objet de haine; **the central f. of a painting** le personnage principal d'un tableau

5 *(appearance)* apparence *f*, air *m*; **to cut a sorry f.** faire piètre figure; **to cut an elegant f.** être élégant de sa personne; **to cut a pathetic f.** avoir l'air lamentable

6 *(illustration)* illustration *f*, **see f. 21b** *(in book)* voir figure 21b; **geometrical f.** figure *f* géométrique

7 *(pattern)* figure *f*; *(on material)* dessin *m*; **the figures of a dance** les figures d'une danse

8 *(rhetorical)* **f. of speech** façon *f* de parler; **it was just a f. of speech** ce n'était qu'une façon de parler

VI 1 *(appear)* figurer; **his name figures on the list** son nom figure sur la liste

2 *(calculate)* calculer

3 *esp Am Fam (make sense)* sembler logique *ou* normal; **that doesn't f.** ce n'est pas logique, ça n'a pas de sens; **that figures** ça colle

4 *esp Am* **go f.!** allez *ou* va comprendre!

VT 1 *esp Am (think)* penser; **I figured that**

she might be feeling lonely je me suis dit qu'elle se sentait peut-être seule

2 *esp Am (estimate)* **I f. that it will take three years** j'estime que cela prendra trois ans

3 *(put pattern on) (silk etc)* brocher, gaufrer; *(cotton etc)* imprimer

4 *(bass)* chiffrer

5 *esp Lit (imagine) (person, landscape etc)* figurer, représenter; **f. to yourself a happy family** imaginez une famille heureuse

▸▸ **f. of eight** *(shape)* (figure en forme de) huit *m*; *Sport* **to cut figures of eight** *(in skating etc)* faire des huits; **to draw figures of eight** décrire des huits; **f. skater** patineur, -euse artistique; **f. skating** patinage *m* artistique

▸ **figure on** **VT INSEP** *esp Am Fam* s'attendre à; *(plan on)* compter sur; **to f. on doing sth** avoir l'intention de *ou* compter faire qch; **I didn't f. on this happening** je ne m'attendais pas à ce que cela se produise; **he didn't f. on a woman for the position** *(did not consider hiring one)* il ne pensait pas à une femme pour le poste; *(did not think one would get it)* il ne s'attendait pas à ce qu'une femme obtienne le poste

▸ **figure out** *Fam* **VT SEP** *(work out) (amount)* calculer; *(problem)* résoudre; **he couldn't f. out what she meant** il n'arrivait pas à comprendre ce qu'elle voulait dire; **we couldn't f. out what to do next** nous n'arrivions pas à décider ce que nous devions faire; **we couldn't f. out where we were** nous n'arrivions pas à découvrir où nous étions; **we figured out that they must have paid more than we did** nous avons réalisé qu'ils avaient dû payer plus que nous; **she can't f. you out at all** elle n'arrive pas du tout à te comprendre

VI *Am* **it will f. out at about $100** cela coûtera une centaine de dollars

▸ **figure up** **VI** *Am (amount)* **to f. up to sth** s'élever à qch

---

Note that when referring to the human body, the French noun **figure** means **face**.

-figure **SUFF** **three/four/etc-f.** à trois/quatre/*etc* chiffres; **four-f. number** nombre *m* à quatre chiffres

figured ['fɪgəd] **ADJ 1** *(material, velvet etc)* façonné; *(silk etc)* broché **2** *Mus (counterpoint)* figuré; *(bass)* chiffré

figurehead ['fɪgəhed] **N** *(on ship)* figure *f* de proue; *Fig, Pej (man)* homme *m* de paille; **she's just a f.** elle n'agit qu'en prête-nom

figure-hugging **ADJ** moulant

figurine ['fɪgəriːn] **N** *Art etc* figurine *f*

Fiji ['fiːdʒiː] **N F., the F. Islands** les îles *fpl* Fidji

Fijian [fiː'dʒiːən] **ADJ** fidjien **N** Fidjien, -ienne

filament ['fɪləmənt] **N 1** *Elec* filament *m* **2** *Biol* filament *m*, filet *m*

▸▸ **f. lamp** lampe *f* à incandescence

filbert ['fɪlbət] **N** aveline *f*, *(hazelnut)* grosse noisette *f*

filch [fɪltʃ] **VT** *Fam* faucher, piquer (**sth from sb** qch à qn)

file¹ [faɪl] **N** *(tool)* lime *f*, **nail f.** lime à ongles **VT** *(metal etc)* limer; **to f. one's nails** se limer les ongles

file² **N 1** *(folder)* classeur *m*; *(documents)* dossier *m*; **the f. on James Brown, the James Brown f.** le dossier James Brown; **to keep a f. on sb/sth** constituer un dossier sur qn/qch; **have we got anything on f. about it?** y a-t-il quelque chose là-dessus dans les dossiers?; **files** archives *fpl*, **we have placed your report on our files** nous avons classé votre rapport dans nos dossiers; **card-index f.** fichier *m*; **card f.** fichier sur cartes

2 *Comput* fichier *m*

VT 1 *(classify) (documents, letters etc)* classer; **it was filed under 'jazz'** c'était classé dans la catégorie 'jazz'; **the books are filed according to author** les livres sont classés par auteur

2 **to f. a petition** *(of court official)* déposer une requête; *(of plaintiff)* enregistrer une requête; **to f. one's petition (in bankruptcy)** déposer son bilan; **to f. a claim for damages** intenter une action en dommages-intérêts; **to f. an insurance claim** faire une déclaration de sinistre; *Am* **to f. one's tax return** remplir sa déclaration d'impôts; **to f. a story** *(of journalist)* boucler un sujet; **to f. copy** *(of journalist)* rapporter une copie

3 *esp Am Admin (document, complaint)* déposer (**with sb** auprès de qn)

VI to f. for divorce faire une demande de divorce

▸▸ *Comput* **f. allocation table** table *f* des fichiers; *Am* **f. cabinet** classeur *m*; **f. card** fiche *f* (de classeur); *Am* **f. clerk** documentaliste *mf*; *Comput* **f. compression** compression *f* de fichiers; *Comput* **f. conversion** conversion *f* de fichiers; **f. copy** copie *f* à classer; **f. divider** carte-guide *f*, *pl* cartes-guides, guide-classement *m*, *pl* guide-classements; *Comput* **f. extension** extension *f* du nom de fichier; *Comput* **f. format** format *m* de fichier; *Comput* **f. management** gestion *f ou* tenue *f* des fichiers; *Comput* **f. management system** système *m* de gestion de fichiers; *Comput* **f. manager** gestionnaire *m* des fichiers; **f. number** *(of document in file)* cote *f*; *Comput* **f. protection** protection *f* de fichiers; **f. separator** carte-guide, guide-classement; *Comput* **f. server** serveur *m* de fichiers; *Comput* **f. sharing** partage *m* de fichiers; *Comput* **f. structure** structure *f* de fichiers; *Comput* **f. transfer** transfert *m* de fichiers; *Comput* **f. transfer protocol** protocole *m* de transfert de fichiers; **f. trolley** bac *m* roulant; *Comput* **f. viewer** visualiseur *m*

▸ **file away** **VT SEP 1** *(documents etc)* classer, archiver; *Fig (mentally)* enregistrer

2 = **file down 1**

file³ **N** *(line)* file *f*, **in single** *or* **Indian f.** en file indienne; **to walk in single f.** marcher à la file *ou* en file indienne; *Mil* **in f.** (en rang) par deux

VI *Mil etc (walk in line)* marcher à la file *ou* en ligne de file; **to f. off** défiler; **to f. past** défiler; **to f. past sb/sth** défiler devant qn/qch; **to f. in/out** entrer/sortir un à un

▸ **file down** **VT SEP 1** *(remove by filing) (rough edge etc)* enlever à la lime, limer

2 *(smooth by filing) (surface)* polir à la lime, limer; *(of blacksmith etc) (horseshoe)* raboter

▸ **file off** **VT SEP** = **file down 1**

file-compatible **ADJ** *Comput* compatible du point de vue des fichiers

filename ['faɪlneɪm] **N** *Comput* nom *m* de fichier

▸▸ **f. extension** extension *f* du nom de fichier

filer ['faɪlər] **N** *Comput* classeur *m*, gestionnaire *m* de fichiers et de répertoires

filial ['fɪlɪəl] **ADJ** *Fml* filial, -aux

filibuster ['fɪlɪbʌstər] **N 1** *Pol* obstruction *f*, **a six-hour f.** un discours obstructionniste de six heures **2** *Hist (pirate)* flibustier *m*

VI *Pol* faire de l'obstruction; **filibustering tactics** manœuvres *fpl ou* tactiques *fpl* obstructionnistes

filigree ['fɪlɪgriː] **N** filigrane *m*; **f. work** (travail *m* en) filigrane

filing¹ ['faɪlɪŋ] **N 1** *(of metal etc)* limage *m* **2** *(small pieces of metal etc) (usu pl)* **filings** limaille *f*

filing² **N 1** *(of documents, letters etc)* classement *m*; *(for long-term storage)* archivage *m*; **f. by subject** classement *m* par sujet **2** *Law* *(of petition) (by court official)* enregistrement *m; (of claim) (by plaintiff)* dépôt *m*

▸▸**f. cabinet** classeur *m*; **f. clerk** documentaliste *mf*; **f. system** méthode *f* de classement; **f. tray** corbeille *f* pour correspondance à classer

Filipino [ˌfɪlɪˈpiːnəʊ] **ADJ** philippin **N** Philippin, -ine

FILL [fɪl]

| **VT** remplir **1** ■ boucher **2** ■ occuper **3** ■ répondre à **4** |
| **VI** se remplir **1** |

N 1 to have had one's f. of sth en avoir assez de qch; **to eat one's f.** manger à sa faim; **the horse ate its f. of straw** le cheval s'est rassasié de paille

2 *Tech* matériau *m* de remplissage; *Constr* remblai *m*; **a f. of tobacco** une pipée de tabac

VT 1 *(jug etc)* remplir, emplir (**with** de); *(pipe)* bourrer; *(cart etc)* charger; **to f. sb's glass** servir à boire à qn; *(to the brim)* verser une rasade à qn; **to f. the air with one's cries** remplir l'air de ses cris; **a smell of cooking filled the house** une odeur de cuisine envahissait la maison; **to f. one's head with useless things** se farcir la tête de choses inutiles; **to be filled with admiration** être rempli d'admiration; **the thought filled him with jealousy** cette pensée le remplissait de jalousie; **to be filled with hope** être plein d'espoir; **to be filled with fear/envy** être dévoré de peur/d'envie

2 *(plug) (opening, gap etc)* combler, boucher; *(tooth)* plomber; *(of employer) (vacancy)* pourvoir à; **to f. the woodwork** *(before painting)* mastiquer les boiseries; **I'm having two teeth filled tomorrow** on va me faire deux plombages demain; **two places remain to be filled** deux postes restent à pourvoir; **the position has already been filled** le poste a déjà été pourvu

3 *(occupy) (time)* occuper; **a position she has filled for some time** un poste qu'elle occupe depuis quelque temps; **to f. sb's shoes** *(take on sb's responsibilities)* prendre les fonctions de qn; **it's going to be difficult to f. his shoes** ça va être difficile de trouver quelqu'un pour le remplacer; **the thoughts that filled his mind** les pensées qui occupaient son esprit; **reading fills my evenings** la lecture remplit mes soirées

4 *(fulfil) (order, prescription)* exécuter; *esp Am* **to f. every requirement** répondre à tous les besoins

5 *(pour)* verser

VI 1 *(of tank, bath, container, hall etc)* se remplir; *(of hole)* se combler; **her eyes filled with tears** ses yeux se sont remplis de larmes

2 *(of sails)* se gonfler

▸ **fill in VT SEP 1** *(make level) (hole)* combler, boucher; *(ditch)* remblayer; *(block off) (door)* condamner

2 *(complete) (form)* remplir; **to f. in a gap in one's knowledge** combler un vide *ou* une lacune dans ses connaissances; **to f. in the blanks** remplir les blancs

3 *(insert) (date etc)* insérer

4 *Fam* **to f. sb in on the details** mettre qn au courant des détails; **she quickly filled us in on what had been happening** elle nous a rapidement mis au courant de ce qui s'était passé

5 *(use up)* **to f. in time** occuper son temps

VI **to f. in for sb** remplacer qn; **I'm filling in while she's on holiday** je la remplace pendant ses vacances

▸ **fill out VT SEP 1** *(pad out) (speech etc)* étoffer

2 *(complete) (form)* remplir

VI *(of sails)* se gonfler; *(of person)* s'étoffer; *(of adolescent female)* prendre des formes; **her cheeks are filling out** ses joues se remplissent, elle prend des joues

▸ **fill up VT SEP 1** *(with liquid) (glass)* remplir jusqu'au bord; *Aut Fam* **f. her up** (faites) le plein

2 *(plug) (hole with putty etc)* boucher

3 *(complete) (form)* remplir

VI 1 *(become full) (of tank, container etc)* se remplir (**with** de); *(of hole)* se combler, se remplir

2 *(fill tank etc)* **to f. up with petrol/water** faire le plein d'essence/d'eau

filler ['fɪlər] **N 1** *(person)* remplisseur, -euse; *(machine)* remplisseuse *f*; **oil f.** entonnoir *m*; **2** *(substance)* (matière *f* de) remplissage *m*; *(of cigar)* tripe *f*, *(for wood etc)* bouche-pores *m inv*; *(before painting)* mastic *m*; *Fig (between main acts etc)* bouche-trou *m, pl* bouche-trous; *(in media)* bouche-trou, passe-partout *m inv* **3** *(word)* mot *m* de remplissage

▸▸*Aut* **f. cap** bouchon *m* du réservoir d'essence; *TV* **f. light** éclairage *m* d'appoint; *TV* **f. mike** micro *m* d'appoint; **f. paste** mastic *m* de bouchage; **f. word** mot de remplissage

fillet ['fɪlɪt] **N 1** *Culin (of beef, sole)* filet *m*; *(of veal)* rouelle *f* **2** *(for hair)* ruban *m* **3** *Typ* filet *m*

VT (-t-) *Culin (fish)* détacher les filets de; **filleted sole** filets *mpl* de sole

▸▸*Culin* **f. steak** filet de bœuf

filling ['fɪlɪŋ] **ADJ** *(food)* bourratif

N 1 *(of hole)* comblement *m*; *(of tooth)* plombage *m* **2** *(substance)* (matière *f* de) remplissage *m*; *(in dentistry)* plombage *m*; *Carp* mastic *m*; *Constr* remplissage; *(rubble)* blocage *m*; *Culin (for pie, sandwich)* garniture *f*; **cake with a chocolate f.** gâteau fourré au chocolat

▸▸**f. station** station-service *f, pl* stations-service, station *f* d'essence

fillip ['fɪlɪp] **N** *(stimulus)* stimulant *m*, encouragement *m*; **to give a f. to business** stimuler *ou* doper les affaires

fill-up **N** *Aut* plein *m*; **do you want a f.?** *(more to drink)* je te remplis ton verre?

filly ['fɪlɪ] **N 1** *(horse)* pouliche *f* **2** *Old-fashioned Fam (girl)* jeune fille *f*

film [fɪlm] **N 1** *Cin* film *m*; *(celluloid strip)* bande *f*; **the f. of the book** le film tiré du livre; **full-length/short f.** long/court métrage *m*; **news f.** actualités *fpl*; **to shoot** *or* **make a f.** tourner un film; **to be in films** faire du cinéma **2** *Phot* pellicule *f*, film *m*; **I've run out of f.** ma pellicule est finie; **a roll of f.** un rouleau de pellicule, une pellicule; **colour f.** pellicule *ou* film couleur(s) **3** *(layer) (of ice, oil)* pellicule *f*, couche *f*, *(of plastic)* film *m*; *(of mist, smoke etc)* voile *m*; *Med (over eye)* taie *f*, **wrapped in plastic f.** emballé dans un film en plastique

VT *Cin (scene)* filmer, tourner; *(novel)* porter à l'écran; *(person, interview etc)* filmer

VI 1 *Cin, TV* filmer; **we start filming next week** on commence à tourner la semaine prochaine **2** = **film over**

▸▸**f. actor** acteur *m* de cinéma; **f. actress** actrice *f* de cinéma; **f. archives** cinémathèque *f*, **f. buff** cinéphile *mf*; **f. camera** caméra *f*; **f. cassette** cartouche *f* de pellicule *ou* de film; **f. clip** séquence *f ou* extrait *m* de film; **f. club** ciné-club *m, pl* ciné-clubs; **f. crew** équipe *f* de tournage; **f. critic** critique *m* de cinéma; **f. director** réalisateur, -trice, metteur *m* en scène; **f. editor** monteur, -euse; **f. festival** festival *m* cinématographique *ou* du cinéma; **the f. industry** l'industrie *f* cinématographique *ou* du cinéma; **f. laboratory** laboratoire *m* de film, labo *m*; **f. library** cinémathèque *f*; **f. maker** cinéaste

mf; **f. producer** producteur, -trice de cinéma; **f. projector** appareil *m* de projection; **f. reel** bobine *f* de film; **f. review** critique *f* cinématographique; **f. reviewer** critique *m* de cinéma; **f. rights** droits *mpl* film; **f. scanner** lecteur *m* de télé-cinéma, analyseur *m* de film; **f. script** scénario *m*; **f. set** plateau *m* de tournage; **f. star** vedette *f* de cinéma; **f. stock** pellicule vierge; **f. strip** bande (de film) fixe; **f. studies** filmologie *f*; **f. studio** studio *m* (de cinéma); **f. test** bout *m* d'essai

▸ **film over VI** se couvrir d'une pellicule; *Med (of eyes)* se couvrir d'une taie

filmgoer ['fɪlmɡəʊər] **N** amateur *m* de cinéma, cinéphile *mf*; **she is a regular f.** elle va régulièrement au cinéma

filmic ['fɪlmɪk] **ADJ** filmique

filming ['fɪlmɪŋ] **N** *Cin* tournage *m*; **to get permission for f.** obtenir l'autorisation de tourner

filmless camera ['fɪlmlɪs] **N** caméra *f* sans film

film-making **N** production *f* cinématographique

filmography [fɪlˈmɒɡrəfɪ] **N** filmographie *f*

filmset ['fɪlmset] **VT** *Br Typ* photocomposer

filmsetter ['fɪlmsetər] **N** *Br Typ (machine)* photocomposeuse *f*, *(person)* photocompositeur *m*

filmsetting ['fɪlmsetɪŋ] **N** *Br Typ* photocomposition *f*

filmy ['fɪlmɪ] **ADJ** *(eye)* couvert d'une taie; *(lace, cloud etc)* léger, -ère, diaphane

Filofax® ['faɪləʊfæks] **N** organiseur *m*

filter ['fɪltər] **N 1** filtre *m*; *(for oil etc)* épurateur *m*; *(cigarette)* cigarette *f* à filtre; *Br* **a packet of Regal®** f. un paquet de Regal® filtres; **coffee f.** filtre à café **2** *Opt, Phot, Cin* filtre *m*; **colour f.** filtre *m* de couleur, écran *m* filtre **3** *Elec, Electron etc* **frequency f.** filtre *m* de fréquences **4** *Br Aut (signal) (on traffic light)* flèche *f* de dégagement

VT *(water etc)* filtrer; *(air etc)* épurer

VI 1 *(of water etc)* filtrer (**through** à travers); *(seep)* suinter **2** *Br Aut etc* changer de file; **to f. to the right/left** prendre la voie de dégagement vers la droite/la gauche **3** *Fam* **to f. into a building** entrer par petits groupes dans un immeuble

▸▸*Constr* **f. bed** couche *f* de filtration; **f. circuit** circuit *m* de filtrage; **f. coffee** café *m* filtre, *pl* cafés-filtre; *Aut* **f. element** cartouche *f* filtrante; *Br Aut* **f. lane** voie *f* de dégagement; **f. paper** papier *m* filtre; **f. tip** *(tip)* (bout *m*) filtre; *(cigarette)* cigarette (bout) filtre; *Br Aut* **f. signal** *(on traffic light)* flèche de dégagement

▸ **filter down VI** filtrer; **the information finally filtered down to them** les informations ont fini par filtrer jusqu'à eux

▸ **filter out VT SEP** *(remove with filter) (impurities)* séparer par filtrage; *Fig (in selection procedure etc)* éliminer; **f. out the solids** retenir les solides par filtrage

VI *(leave slowly)* quitter lentement; **information is beginning to f. out that …** des informations commencent à filtrer selon lesquelles …; **to f. out of a building** sortir par petits groupes d'un édifice

▸ **filter through VI** *(pass slowly)* passer lentement; **the news soon filtered through** les nouvelles n'ont pas tardé à filtrer

VT INSEP **the light filtered through the branches** la lumière filtrait à travers les branches

filterable ['fɪltərəb(ə)l] **ADJ** *Med (virus)* filtrant

filtering ['fɪltərɪŋ] **N** filtrage *m*, filtration *f*

▸▸*Comput* **f. software** logiciel *m* de filtrage

filth [fɪlθ] **N 1** *(dirt)* immondices *fpl*, *(excreta)* ordure *f*; **to live in f.** vivre dans la saleté **2** *(obscenity)* **to talk f.** dire des obscénités;

what are you reading that **f. for?** pourquoi est-ce que tu lis ces cochonneries?; **this isn't art, it's f.!** ce n'est pas de l'art, c'est de la pornographie! **3** *Br Sl, Pej* **the f.** *(the police)* les flics *mpl*, les poulets *mpl*

filthy ['fɪlθɪ] **ADJ 1** *(very dirty)* (très) sale; **your hands are f.!** tes mains sont dégoûtantes!; **to get f.** *(of person)* se salir; *(of part of machine)* s'encrasser; **my hands got f.** je me suis sali les mains; **my jacket got f.** j'ai sali ma veste **2** *Fam* **he gave me a f. look** il m'a jeté un sale regard, il m'a regardé d'un sale œil; *Fam* **in a f. temper** d'une humeur massacrante; *esp Br Fam* **f. weather** temps *m* de chien **3** *(obscene) (language, talk etc)* ordurier, obscène; *(suggestion)* obscène, dégoûtant; *(person)* dégoûtant; **you've got a f. mind!** tu as l'esprit mal tourné!; **you f. beast!** espèce de gros dégoûtant!

ADV *Fam* **f. dirty** dégoûtant; **f. rich** pourri de fric; **the f. rich** les gros richards *mpl*

filtration [fɪl'treɪʃən] **N** filtration *f*, filtrage *m*

fin [fɪn] **N 1** *(of fish, whale etc)* nageoire *f*; *(of shark)* aileron *m*; **fins** *(for swimmer, diver)* palmes *fpl* **2** *(of boat)* dérive *f*; *(of plane)* empennage *m*; *(of bomb etc)* ailette *f*; *Aut etc (of radiator etc)* ailette; **cooling fins** ailettes de refroidissement; **stabilizer f.** aileron stabilisateur **3** *Am Fam (five-dollar bill)* billet *m* de cinq dollars

finagle [fɪ'neɪg(ə)l] **VT** *Fam* **= wangle VT**

final ['faɪn(ə)l] **ADJ 1** *(last)* final, -als *ou* -aux, dernier, -ière; **f. details/preparations** derniers détails/préparatifs; **to make a f. effort** faire un dernier effort; **to put the f. touches to sth** mettre la dernière main à qch **2** *(definitive)* définitif; **f. text** texte *m* définitif; **the umpire's decision is f.** la décision de l'arbitre est sans appel; **take this as f.** tenez-le-vous pour dit **3** *Gram, Phil (clause, cause)* final, -als *ou* -aux

N 1 *Sport* **the f.** *or* **finals** la finale; **to be through to the final(s)** être en finale; *Ftbl* **cup f.** finale de coupe **2** *Univ* **to sit** *or* **take one's finals** = passer son dernier examen de licence **3** *Journ* dernière édition *f*; **late f.** dernière édition du soir

▸ ▸ *Com* **f. acceptance** réception *f* définitive; *Cin* **f. cut** final cut *m*; **f. date** date *f* limite; *Com* **f. demand** dernier rappel *m*; *St Exch* **f. dividend** dividende *m* définitif *ou* final; **f. edition** *(of newspaper)* dernière édition *f*; *Com* **f. handover** réception *f* définitive; **f. instalment** dernier versement *m*, versement de libération; *Law* **f. judgment** jugement *m* définitif *ou* sans appel; **f. offer** dernière proposition *f*; *Fin* **f. settlement** solde *m* de tout compte; **f. warning** dernier avertissement *m*

finale [fɪ'nɑːlɪ] **N** *Mus* finale *m*; *Theat etc* conclusion *f*; **grand f.** apothéose *f*; **there was a grand f. to the match** le match s'est terminé en apothéose

finalist ['faɪnəlɪst] **N** finaliste *mf*

finality [faɪ'nælɪtɪ] **N 1** *(of decision)* caractère *m* définitif, irrévocabilité *f*; **to say sth with f.** dire qch d'un ton irrévocable *ou* sans appel **2** *Phil* finalité *f*

finalization [faɪnəlaɪ'zeɪʃən] **N** *(of details, plans etc)* mise *f* au point

finalize ['faɪnəlaɪz] **VT** *(details, plans etc)* mettre au point; *(deal, arrangement)* conclure; **details of the visit have yet to be finalized** les détails de la visite restent à préciser

finally ['faɪn(ə)lɪ] **ADV 1** *(lastly)* à la fin, en dernier; **and f., I would like to thank Mr Smith** et enfin *ou* et pour finir, j'aimerais remercier M. Smith **2** *(at last)* finalement, enfin **3** *(irrevocably)* définitivement

finance [faɪ'næns, fɪ-] **N 1** finance *f*; *(funding)* finances *fpl*; **high f.** la haute finance **2** *(funds)* fonds *mpl*; **his finances are low** ses fonds sont bas; **what state are your finances in?** comment vont tes finances?; **it's a problem of f.** c'est un problème financier; **where are they going to get the f. from?** où vont-ils trouver les fonds nécessaires?

VT *(project)* financer; *(person, company etc)* financer, commanditer; *Acct* **financed from cashflow** autofinancé

▸ ▸ **f. charges** frais *mpl* financiers; **f. company** société *f* financière; **f. costs** frais financiers *ou* de trésorerie; **f. department** service *m* financier; **f. director** directeur, -trice financier(ère); *Br* **f. house** société financière; = société britannique de financement pour les achats à crédit

financial [faɪ'nænʃəl, fɪ-] **ADJ** *(difficulty, planning, scandal etc)* financier, -ière

▸ ▸ **f. accountant** comptable *mf* financier(ère); **f. accounting** comptabilité *f* générale *ou* financière; **f. adviser** conseiller, -ère financier(ère); **f. aid** aide *f* financière; **f. analyst** analyste *mf* financier(ère); **f. appraisal** évaluation *f* financière; **f. assistance** appui *m* financier, aide financière; **f. backing** financement *m*, aide financière; **f. centre** place *f* financière; **f. circles** sphères *fpl* de la finance; **f. consultant** conseiller, -ère financier(ère), conseil *m* financier; **f. control** contrôle *m* financier; **f. controller** contrôleur, -euse financier(ère); **f. correspondent** correspondant, -ante sur les questions financières; *Acct* **f. costs** frais *mpl* financiers; **f. deal** opération *f* financière; **f. department** service *m* financier; **f. director** directeur, -trice financier(ère); **f. engineering** ingénierie *f* financière; *St Exch* **f. future** instrument *m* financier à terme; **f. gearing** effet *m* de levier financier; **f. healthcheck** diagnostic *m* financier; **f. institution** établissement *m* financier; **f. instrument** instrument financier; **f. intermediary** intermédiaire *mf* financier(ère); **f. management** direction *f ou* gestion *f* financière; **f. management accounting** comptabilité-gestion *f* financière; **f. manager** directeur, -trice financier(ère); **f. market** marché *m* financier; **f. marketplace** marché financier; *(centre)* place *f* financière; *Radio, TV* **f. news** chronique *f* financière; **f. ombudsman** arbitre *m* financier; **f. pages** pages *fpl* financières; **f. period** période *f* comptable; **f. position** position *f ou* situation *f* financière; **f. press** presse *f* financière; **f. services** services *mpl* financiers; **f. statement** état *m* financier, déclaration *f* de résultats; **f. statements** document *m* de synthèse; **The F. Times** = quotidien *m* britannique d'information financière; **F. Times-Stock Exchange 100 Share Index** = principal indice *m* boursier du Financial Times basé sur 100 actions cotées à la Bourse de Londres; **f. transaction** opération financière; **f. transactions** flux *m* financier; *Br* **the f. year** *(in business)* l'exercice *m* financier; *(in politics)* l'année *f* budgétaire

---

Financial Year

Pour les impôts sur le revenu en Grande-Bretagne, l'année fiscale commence le 5 avril.

---

financially [faɪ'nænʃəlɪ, fɪ-] **ADV** financièrement; **f. sound** solvable; **f. successful** aux finances prospères

financier [faɪ'nænsɪər, fɪ-] **N** financier *m*

financing [faɪ'nænsɪŋ, fɪ-] **N** *(of project etc)* financement *m*

▸ ▸ **f. gap** déficit *m* de financement; **f. plan** plan *m* de financement; **f. terms** modalités *fpl* de financement

finch [fɪntʃ] **N** *(bird)* fringillidé *m*

FIND [faɪnd]

N	découverte ▪ trouvaille
VT	trouver **1, 2, 4** ▪ retrouver **1**
	▪ chercher **2** ▪ constater **3** ▪ se
	trouver **4** ▪ déclarer **5**
VI	prononcer

N découverte *f*, trouvaille *f*; *(artist, actor etc)* découverte; **he's quite a f.** c'est une perle rare; **it's quite a f.** c'est une fameuse trouvaille

VT *(pt, pp* **found** [faʊnd]) **1** *(discover by chance)* trouver, découvrir; **to f. happiness with sb** trouver *ou* rencontrer le bonheur auprès de qn; **to f. sb at home** *or* **in** trouver qn chez lui; **they found him dead** on l'a trouvé mort; **I found her waiting in the hall** je l'ai trouvée qui attendait dans le vestibule; **we must leave everything as we f. it** il faut tout laisser dans l'état où nous l'avons trouvé; **I often f. myself smiling** je me surprends souvent à sourire; **I found myself in London** je me suis retrouvé à Londres; **they found an unexpected supporter in Mr Smith** ils ont trouvé en M. Smith un partisan inattendu

2 *(discover by searching)* **to try to f. sth** chercher qch; **to f. an answer/a solution** trouver une réponse/une solution; **f. some paper** allez chercher du papier; *Comput* **to f. and replace** trouver et remplacer; **I ran to f. a doctor** j'ai couru chercher un médecin; **the (lost) key has been found** la clef a été retrouvée; **she was nowhere to be found** elle était introuvable; **you won't f. a better motorbike at this price** vous ne trouverez pas une meilleure moto à ce prix; **to f. a job for sb** trouver un emploi à qn; **to f. sth for sb to do** trouver qch à faire à qn; **to f. a leak in a main** localiser une fuite dans une conduite; **the bullet found its mark** la balle a atteint son but; **I can f. no reason for ...** je ne vois pas de raison pour ...; **he keeps finding excuses** il arrive toujours à trouver des excuses; **to f. it in one's heart to do sth** avoir le cœur de faire qch; **he couldn't f. it in his heart to tell her** il n'avait pas le cœur de le lui dire; **to f. favour with sb** gagner la faveur de qn; **to f. one's balance** trouver son équilibre; **to f. one's way** trouver son chemin; *Fig* trouver sa voie; **such ideas can easily f. their way into the minds of the young** de telles idées peuvent facilement entrer dans les jeunes esprits; **to f. a way to do sth** trouver moyen de faire qch; **to f. oneself** *(one's true self)* se trouver

3 *(learn, be told)* apprendre; *(come to realize, discover)* constater; **you will f. that I am right** vous verrez que j'ai raison; **I was surprised to f. that ...** j'ai été surpris de constater que ...; **after his death, his family found that ...** après sa mort, sa famille a appris que ...

4 *(experience)* **to f. some difficulty in doing sth** éprouver quelque difficulté à faire qch; **they will f. it easy/difficult** cela leur sera facile/difficile; **to f. it impossible/necessary to do sth** se trouver dans l'impossibilité/la nécessité de faire qch; **I found it almost impossible to understand him** j'ai eu un mal fou à le comprendre; **how do you f. this wine?** comment trouvez-vous ce vin?; **how did you f. the meal?** le repas vous a-t-il plu?; **I f. her rather offhand/friendly** je la trouve plutôt désinvolte/aimable

5 *Law* **to f. sb guilty/innocent** déclarer qn coupable/innocent

6 *(provide)* **to f. the money for an undertaking** procurer les capitaux *ou* fournir l'argent pour une entreprise; **to f. half the costs for a project** financer la moitié des coûts d'un projet; **cost £20, all found** prix 20 livres, tout compris

VI *Law* **to f. for/against sb** prononcer *ou* rendre un verdict en faveur de/contre qn
▸▸ *Comput* **f. command** commande *f* de recherche
▸ **find out** **VT SEP 1** *(discover) (facts)* se rendre compte de; *(truth)* découvrir; **we found out that she was French** nous avons découvert qu'elle était française; **did you f. anything out?** est-ce que vous avez découvert quoi que ce soit?
2 to f. sb out *(learn truth about)* découvrir le vrai caractère de qn; *(catch doing wrong)* prendre qn en défaut; **we've been found out** nous nous sommes fait prendre; **they had found her out for the liar she was** ils avaient découvert quelle menteuse elle était; **she had been found out transferring money into her own account** on avait découvert qu'elle transférait de l'argent sur son propre compte
VI *(discover)* **I'll f. out** je le saurai; **your mother had better not f. out!** j'espère pour toi que ta mère ne l'apprendra pas!; **to f. out about sth** se renseigner sur qch; **I have found out all about it** j'ai tout appris à ce sujet

finder ['faɪndər] **N 1** *(of lost item)* **there's a reward for the f.** la personne qui le trouvera recevra une récompense; **well, it's yours then, finders keepers** eh bien, c'est à toi maintenant, puisque tu l'as trouvé **2** *(of telescope)* chercheur *m*

finding ['faɪndɪŋ] **N** *(usu pl)* **findings** *(of scientist, enquiry, investigation etc)* résultat *m*; *(of tribunal, jury, committee, report)* conclusion *f*; **he published his findings in a scientific journal** il a fait publier les résultats de ses recherches dans un journal scientifique; **his f. is that …** il est arrivé à la conclusion que …

fine¹ [faɪn] *Law* **N** amende *f*; **to impose a f. on sb** infliger une amende à qn; **to pay a f.** payer une amende; **parking f.** amende pour stationnement illégal
VT condamner à une amende; **to f. sb £20** frapper qn d'une amende de 20 livres

FINE²

ADJ	excellent **1** ▪ bien **1** ▪ beau **3, 4**
	▪ fin **7, 8, 10** ▪ subtil **9**
ADV	bien **1**

ADJ 1 *(excellent)* excellent, magnifique; **meat/wine of the finest quality** viande/vin de premier choix; **a f. athlete** un excellent athlète; **that's f.!** c'est parfait!; **that's f. by** *or* **with me** ça me va; **she's/everything is f.** elle/tout va bien; **we had a f. time** nous nous sommes bien amusés; *Iron* **he had a f. time explaining what he was doing there** il a passé un mauvais quart d'heure quand il a fallu qu'il explique ce qu'il faisait là-bas; *Iron* **you're a f. one, you are!** vous êtes joli, vous!; *Iron* **you're a f. one to talk!** vous pouvez bien parler!
2 *Fam (intensive)* **he was in a f. (old) temper!** ce qu'il rageait!; **this is another f. mess you've got us into!** tu nous a encore mis dans un beau pétrin!
3 *(beautiful)* beau, bel, *f* belle; **a f. piece of writing** un bon texte
4 *(weather)* beau, bel, *f* belle; **when the weather is f.** quand il fait beau; **a f. day** une belle journée; **it's turned out f. again** aujourd'hui encore il fait beau
5 *(noble, admirable)* **to appeal to sb's finer feelings** faire appel aux sentiments élevés de qn; **she's a f. woman** c'est une femme admirable
6 *Old-fashioned* **a f. lady** *(elegant)* une dame élégante; *(of high rank)* une grande dame
7 *(texture, hair, rain etc)* fin; *(gravel etc)* menu, fin

8 *(pointed)* effilé; *(writing)* délié, mince; *(needle)* fin; *(blade)* affilé, aigu; *(pen)* pointu; **f. print** petits caractères *mpl*; **to read the f. print** lire ce qui est écrit en petits caractères
9 *(subtle)* subtil; **a f. distinction** une distinction subtile; **she's got washing the car down to a f. art** elle est passée maître dans l'art de laver la voiture; **there's a f. line between eccentricity and madness** il n'y a qu'un pas de l'excentricité à la folie; **not to put too f. a point on it** pour parler franchement
10 *(pure) (metals, oil etc)* fin; **gold twenty-two carats f.** or à vingt-deux carats de fin
INT *(agreed)* bon!, entendu!, d'accord!
ADV 1 **to get on** *or* **do f.** *(in new job etc)* se débrouiller très bien; *(be well)* aller bien; **to get on f.** *(of two people)* bien s'entendre
2 **to chop meat f.** hacher menu la viande; *Fig* **to cut it (a bit) f.** calculer un peu juste; **that's cutting it a bit f.** là tu calcules/il calcule/*etc* un peu juste; *Billiards* **to cut the ball too f.** prendre la bille trop fine *ou* trop fine
▸▸ **f. arts** beaux-arts *mpl*
▸ **fine down** **VT SEP 1** *(refine) (beer)* clarifier
2 *(make thinner) (metal, wood)* amincir, désépaissir; *(plans, proposals)* dégrossir

fine-cut **ADJ 1** *(features)* finement *ou* délicatement ciselé **2** *(tobacco)* haché fin

fine-drawn **ADJ 1** *(features etc)* fin **2** *(distinction)* subtil **3** *(wire)* finement étiré; *(thread)* délié

fine-grained [-greɪnd] **ADJ** *(wood, leather)* à grain fin

fine-looking **ADJ** beau, bel, *f* belle

finely ['faɪnlɪ] **ADV 1** *(excellently)* magnifiquement **2** *(skilfully)* habilement **3** *(delicately)* délicatement; **f. drawn features** traits *mpl* fins **4** *(in small size)* **f. powdered** finement pulvérisé; **f. chopped** haché fin; **f. ground** moulu très fin

fineness ['faɪnnɪs] **N 1** *(excellence)* qualité *f* supérieure, excellence *f* **2** *(splendour) (of dress etc)* splendeur *f*, magnificence *f* **3** *(in texture) (of hair, material etc)* finesse *f* **4** *(purity) (of gold)* titre *m*, aloi *m*

finery ['faɪnərɪ] **N** parure *f*; **decked out in all his f.** paré de ses plus beaux atours

fine-spun **ADJ 1** *Tex* au fil ténu *ou* délié **2** *(reasoning etc)* subtil

finesse [fɪ'nes] **N 1** *(skill) (of style etc)* finesse *f*, délicatesse *f* **2** *(ruse)* finesse *f*, ruse *f* **3** *Cards* impasse *f*

fine-tooth **ADJ** *(comb)* fin; *Fig* **to go through sth with a f. comb** passer qch au peigne fin

fine-tune **VT** *(radio, engine etc)* régler avec précision; *Fig (plan, proposals)* peaufiner

finger ['fɪŋɡər] **N 1** *(of hand, glove etc)* doigt *m*; **first** *or* **index f.** index *m*; **middle f.** médius *m*, doigt du milieu; **ring f.** annulaire *m*; **little f.** auriculaire *m*; **to eat sth with one's fingers** manger qch avec les doigts; **to keep one's fingers crossed** croiser les doigts; **they could be counted on the fingers of one hand** on pourrait les compter sur les doigts de la main; *Fig* **he's got them (wrapped) round his little f.** il fait d'eux ce qu'il veut; **the f. (of suspicion) is pointed at him** on le soupçonne; **he has a f. in every pie** il est mêlé à tout; **I've been working my fingers to the bone** je me suis tué à la tâche; **don't you dare lay a f. on him** je vous défends de le toucher; *Fig* **I can't quite put my f. on it** je n'arrive pas à mettre le doigt dessus; **to lay** *or* **put one's f. on the source of the trouble** mettre le doigt sur la source du mal; **she wouldn't lift a f. to help you** elle ne remuerait pas le petit doigt pour vous aider; **he's so lazy, I've never seen him lift a f.** il est si paresseux, je ne l'ai jamais vu faire le moindre effort; *Br Fam* **get** *or* **pull your f. out!** remue-

toi!, *Sl* bouge ton cul!; *Fam* **to put the f. on sb** *(inform on)* balancer qn; **to give sb the f.** *(rude gesture)* faire un doigt d'honneur à qn
2 *(measure etc)* **f. of brandy** doigt *m* de cognac; **f. of cake** petit morceau *m* (rectangulaire) de gâteau
VT 1 *(feel)* toucher, tâter; **stop fingering that food!** arrête de tripoter la nourriture!
2 *Mus (piece of music)* doigter; **to f. the piano** tapoter sur le piano
3 *Sl (inform on)* balancer
▸▸ *Culin* **f. biscuit** biscuit *m* à la cuiller; **f. board** *(of violin etc)* touche *f*; **f. bowl** rince-doigts *m inv*; **f. buffet** = buffet *m* où sont servis des petits sandwiches, des petits fours, des légumes crus, etc; *Mus* **f. exercises** exercices *mpl* de doigté; **f. food** = petits fours, petits sandwiches et légumes crus, etc, servis à un buffet et que l'on mange avec les doigts; *Mus* **f. hole** trou *m*; **f. painting** peinture *f* avec les doigts; **she's being doing f. paintings all afternoon** elle a peint avec ses doigts tout l'après-midi; **f. plate** *(on door etc)* plaque *f* de propreté

fingering ['fɪŋɡərɪŋ] **N** *Mus* doigté *m*

fingermark ['fɪŋɡəmɑːk] **N** trace *f* de doigt

fingernail ['fɪŋɡəneɪl] **N** ongle *m* (de la main)

fingerprint ['fɪŋɡəprɪnt] **N** empreinte *f* digitale; **to take sb's fingerprints** prendre les empreintes digitales de qn
VT *(person)* prendre les empreintes digitales de; **the police fingerprinted him** la police a pris ses empreintes digitales
▸▸ **f. expert** spécialiste *mf* en empreintes digitales *ou* en dactyloscopie; **f. identification** dactyloscopie *f*

fingerstall ['fɪŋɡəstɔːl] **N** *Med* doigtier *m*

fingertip ['fɪŋɡətɪp] **N** bout *m* du doigt; **he is a Frenchman to his fingertips** il est français jusqu'au bout des ongles; **to have sth at one's fingertips** savoir qch sur le bout des doigts
▸▸ **f. controls** commandes *fpl* à touches

finial ['fɪnɪəl] **N** *Archit* fleuron *m*

finicky ['fɪnɪkɪ] **ADJ** *(person)* méticuleux, *Pej* tatillon, vétilleux; *(style, layout)* alambiqué; *(job, task)* minutieux; *(device, recipe)* compliqué; **to be a very f. eater** être très difficile sur la nourriture; **this is a f. dish to make** c'est un plat très délicat à préparer; **there are all these f. little bits and pieces** il y a toutes ces petites pièces embêtantes à manier

FINISH ['fɪnɪʃ]

N	fin **1** ▪ finition **2**
VT	finir **1, 3** ▪ terminer **1** ▪ achever **2**
VI	se terminer ▪ finir

N 1 *(end)* fin *f*; *Sport (of race)* arrivée *f*; **she was exhausted by the f.** sur la fin elle était épuisée; *Sport* **he has a fast f.** il a un bon finish; *Sport* **it's going to be a close f.** l'arrivée va être serrée; *Fam* **that was the f. (of him)** ce fut le coup de grâce; **to be in at the f.** être là pour voir la fin; *St Exch* **price at the f.** prix *m* de clôture
2 *(workmanship) (of work etc)* fini *m*; *Tech (operation)* finition *f*; *(surface)* apprêt *m*; **paint with a gloss/matt f.** peinture vernie/mate; **paper with a gloss/matt f.** papier glacé/mat; **all the woodwork has been given a pine f.** toute les boiseries ont été teintées imitation pin; **car with a metallic/silver f.** voiture métallisée/argentée
VT 1 *(end)* finir, terminer, achever; *(cake, food)* finir; *(meal)* finir, terminer; **to f. doing sth** terminer *ou* finir de faire qch; **you can f. telling me tomorrow** tu peux me raconter la fin demain; **to f. what one was saying** finir ce qu'on avait à dire; **when do you f. work?**

à quelle heure est-ce que tu finis?; **f. your soup!** finis ta soupe!

2 *(ruin, kill) (person)* achever; **he's finished!** il est fini *ou* achevé!; **this defeat has finished the team's chances** cette défaite a mis un terme aux chances de l'équipe; **she was finished as a singer** sa carrière de chanteuse était finie; **you're finished here** *(I'm sacking you)* tu es viré

3 *(put finishing touches) (to piece of work etc)* finir, donner du fini à; *Tex (fabric)* apprêter; *Metal (part)* usiner; *Sewing* **to f. a buttonhole** brider une boutonnière; **the wood/paintwork hasn't been very well finished** le bois/la peinture n'a pas un très bon fini

VI se terminer, s'achever; **they finished long before the others** ils ont fini *ou* terminé bien avant les autres; **the meeting finished in a brawl** le meeting se termina par des coups; **when do you f.?** *(leave work)* quand est-ce que tu finis?; **have you finished?** *(eating, shouting etc)* tu as terminé?; **to f. in a point** *(of blade, shape etc)* se terminer en pointe; **the book finishes with him returning to the family house** à la fin du livre, il retourne à la maison familiale; **I'd like to f. on an optimistic note** je voudrais terminer *ou* finir sur une note optimiste; **he finished by calling me a liar** il a fini par me traiter de menteur; *Sport* **to f. fourth** finir *ou* arriver quatrième; *Sport* **where did she f.?** à quelle place est-ce qu'elle a fini?

▸ **finish off** **VT SEP 1** *(complete) (task)* terminer; *Sewing* **to f. off a buttonhole** brider une boutonnière

2 *(have the last of) (cake, milk etc)* finir

3 *Fam (kill)* achever; *(exhaust)* achever, épuiser; *(ruin) (company, industry)* causer la ruine de; *(hopes)* ruiner, anéantir; **to f. off a wounded animal** donner le coup de grâce à une bête; **this fly killer will soon f. them off!** ce tue-mouches aura bientôt raison d'elles!; **cirrhosis of the liver finally finished him off** une cirrhose du foie a fini par avoir raison de lui

VI *(end)* finir, terminer; **we should be finishing off soon** nous devrions bientôt avoir fini *ou* terminé; **they finished off with some fruit/a song** ils ont fini avec des fruits/une chanson

▸ **finish up** **VT SEP 1** *(complete)* finir, terminer; **f. up your soup!** finis ta soupe!

2 *(have the last of)* finir; **don't f. up the pie** ne mange pas toute la tourte

VI *(end up)* finir; **we finished up in a ditch** nous avons fini dans un fossé; **I'm going to f. up a nervous wreck!** je vais finir par m'user les nerfs!; **I'm going to f. up hating him** je vais finir par le détester

▸ **finish with** **VT INSEP 1** *(stop using)* ne plus avoir besoin de; **have you finished with the dictionary/mustard?** est-ce que tu as fini avec le dictionnaire/la moutarde?; **I've finished with it** je n'en ai plus besoin

2 *(stop doing)* en avoir fini avec; **I've finished with acting** j'en ai fini avec le théâtre; **I've finished with trying to help people** plus jamais je n'essaierai d'aider les gens

3 *(finish dealing with)* **I haven't finished with you!** je n'en ai pas fini avec toi!; **wait until I've finished with him!** *(threat)* attendez que je lui aie réglé son compte!

4 *(end relationship with)* rompre avec; **I've finished with you** tout est fini entre nous; **I've finished with men forever!** les hommes et moi, c'est fini!

finished ['fɪnɪʃt] **ADJ 1** *(item etc)* fini, apprêté; *(product)* ouvré; **machine f.** apprêté à la machine; **badly f. goods** marchandises mal finies; **beautifully/professionally f.** d'un fini magnifique/professionnel **2** *(appearance etc)* soigné, fini; *(performance)* au

---

point, parfait **3** *(ruined)* he's f. as a boxer sa carrière de boxeur est finie; **if I can't raise the money, I'm f.!** si je n'arrive pas à trouver l'argent, je suis fichu!

finisher ['fɪnɪʃər] **N** *Ind, Sport (person)* finisseur, -euse; *Sport* **he's a fast f.** c'est un bon finisseur, il a un bon finish

finishing ['fɪnɪʃɪŋ] **ADJ** dernier, -ière; **f. coat** *(of paint etc)* dernière couche *f*, **the f. stroke** le coup de grâce

N 1 *(completion) (of task etc)* achèvement *m*; **2** *Tech* finition *f*, *(of leather, paper)* apprêtage *m*

▸▸ *Br Sport* **f. line** ligne *f* d'arrivée; **f. school** = école *f* privée de jeunes filles surtout axée sur l'enseignement des bonnes manières; *Ind* **f. shop** atelier *m* de finitions; **f. touches** finitions *fpl*; **to put the f. touches to sth** mettre la dernière main à qch

finite ['faɪnaɪt] **ADJ** *(universe)* fini, limité; *(resources, means)* limité; *Gram (verb)* à un mode fini; **a f. number of possibilities** un nombre limité de possibilités

N the f. and the infinite le fini et l'infini

fink [fɪŋk] *Am Fam, Pej* **N 1** *(unpleasant person)* salaud *m* **2** *(strikebreaker)* jaune *m* **3** *(informer)* balance *f*, indic *m*

VI moucharder; **to f. on sb** balancer qn

Finland ['fɪnlənd] **N** Finlande *f*

Finn [fɪn] VOIR GRAMMAIRE A19 Finlandais, -aise, Finnois, -oise

finnan ['fɪnən] **N**

▸▸ *Scot Culin* **f. haddie** haddock *m*

Finnish ['fɪnɪʃ] VOIR GRAMMAIRE A19 **ADJ** finlandais, finnois

N *Ling* finlandais *m*, finnois *m*

fiord [fjɔːd] **N** *Geog* fjord *m*, fiord *m*

fir [fɜːr] **N** *(tree, wood)* sapin *m*

▸▸ *Br* **f. cone** pomme *f* de pin; **f. tree** sapin *m*

FIRE ['faɪər]

N feu **1–3** ▪ radiateur **1** ▪ incendie **2** ▪ enthousiasme **5**
VT enthousiasmer **2** ▪ tirer **6** ▪ décharger **6** ▪ virer **7**
VI tourner **1** ▪ tirer **2**

N 1 *(in hearth etc)* feu *m*; **to make** *or* **light a f.** faire du feu; **to set** *or* **lay a f.** préparer un feu; **wolves are afraid of f.** les loups ont peur du feu; *Fig* **to go through f. and water for sb** subir des épreuves pour qn; *Fig* **to play with f.** jouer avec le feu; *Fig* **to fight f. with f.** combattre le mal par le mal; **gas/electric f.** radiateur *m* à gaz/électrique; **to throw sth into the f.** jeter qch au feu; **open f.** feu de cheminée; **a roaring f.** une belle flambée; **blacksmith's f.** feu de forge

2 *(large, destructive)* incendie *m*; **bush f.** feu *m* de brousse; **to cause** *or* **start a f.** provoquer un incendie; *Br* **to catch f.,** *Am* **to catch on f.** prendre feu; **f.!** au feu!; **on f.** en feu; **to set f. to sth, to set sth on f.** mettre le feu à qch; *Fam* **my singing isn't going to set the world** *or* *Br* **the Thames on f.** la façon dont je chante n'a rien de fantastique; *Fam* **to get on like a house on f.** *(of work etc)* marcher rondement; *(of two people)* s'entendre à merveille

3 *Mil etc (act)* feu *m*, tir *m*; *(shots)* coups *mpl* de feu; **individual f., f. at will** tir *ou* feu à volonté; **to open f.** ouvrir le feu; **to hold one's f.** *(stop firing)* arrêter de tirer, cesser le feu; *(postpone firing)* ne pas tirer; **to cease f.** cesser le feu; **to return (sb's) f.** riposter (au tir de qn); **under enemy f.** sous le feu de l'ennemi; **we are under f.** on nous tire dessus; **to come under f.** être exposé aux tirs (**from sb** de qn); *Fig* **to be/come under f.** être exposé à de sévères critiques (**from** de la part de); **to draw sb's f.** attirer sur soi les tirs de qn; *Mil, Fig* **between two fires** entre deux feux; *Fig*

---

to hang f. *(of project etc)* être en attente

4 *(of diamond)* lumière *f*, éclat *m*

5 *(enthusiasm)* enthousiasme *m*; *(ardour)* fougue *f*; **the f. of youth** l'enthousiasme de la jeunesse; **the speech lacked f.** le discours manquait de mordant; **he lacks the f. of his predecessor** il n'a pas l'ardeur de son prédécesseur

VT 1 *Fml, Lit (set on fire)* mettre le feu à

2 *(fill with enthusiasm)* animer, enthousiasmer; *(the imagination)* exciter; **she was fired with an intense desire to help others** elle était animée d'un désir intense d'aider autrui; **to be fired with enthusiasm for sth** brûler d'enthousiasme pour qch; **the speech had fired them with enthusiasm** le discours les avait remplis d'un enthousiasme ardent

3 *Cer (pottery etc)* cuire

4 *(heat) (locomotive etc)* chauffer; *(boiler)* allumer; **oil-fired/gas-fired central heating** chauffage *m* central au mazout/au gaz

5 *(fuel mix in engine)* enflammer

6 *Mil etc (shot, salvo)* tirer; *(rifle, pistol)* décharger; *(rocket, torpedo)* lancer; *(cannon)* tirer un coup de feu; **to f. a gun at sb** tirer un coup de fusil sur qn; **without firing a shot** sans tirer un seul coup de feu; *Fig* **to f. a question at sb** poser une question à qn à brûle-pourpoint

7 *Fam (dismiss) (employee etc)* virer, saquer; **you're fired!** vous êtes viré!

VI 1 *(of spark plug)* s'allumer; *(of engine)* tourner; **to f. on all (four) cylinders** tourner rond; *Fig* **I'm not firing on all (four) cylinders this morning** je ne tourne pas tout à fait rond ce matin

2 *Mil etc (of person)* tirer; *(of shot)* partir; **we could hear the guns firing** on entendait le bruit des canons; **the revolver failed to f.** le revolver a fait long feu; **to f. at** *or* **on sb/sth** tirer sur qn/qch; **to f. at sb with a revolver** tirer un coup de revolver sur qn; **f.!** feu!; **to f. at will** tirer à volonté; **we were fired on** nous avons reçu des coups de feu, on nous a tiré dessus

▸▸ **f. alarm** alarme *f* d'incendie; **f. blanket** couverture *f* pare-flamme; *Br* **f. brigade** brigade *f* des pompiers *ou* sapeurs-pompiers, *Suisse* service *m* du feu; *Naut, Aviat* **f. bulkhead** cloison *f* pare-feu; *Comput* **f. button** *(on joystick)* bouton *m* feu; **f. chief** capitaine *m* des pompiers *ou* sapeurs-pompiers; **f. clay** argile *f* réfractaire; **f. damage** dégâts *mpl* causés par le feu; *Am* **f. department** brigade des pompiers *ou* sapeurs-pompiers, *Suisse* service du feu; **f. door** porte *f* coupe-feu; **f. drill** exercice *m* de sécurité *(en cas d'incendie)*; **f. engine** voiture *f* de pompiers; **f. escape** escalier *m* de secours *ou* d'incendie; **f. fighter** pompier *m*, sapeur-pompier *m* (volontaire), *Suisse* homme *m* du feu; **f. fighting** lutte *f* contre l'incendie; **f. hazard** risque *m* d'incendie; **that old gas cooker must be a f. hazard** cette vieille cuisinière à gaz doit présenter un risque d'incendie; **f. hose** tuyau *m* de pompe à incendie; *Br* **f. hydrant** bouche *f* d'incendie, *Suisse* hydrant *m*; **f. insurance** assurance-incendie *f*, **f. irons** accessoires *mpl* de cheminée; *Am* **f. marshal** capitaine des pompiers *ou* sapeurs-pompiers; **f. master** capitaine des pompiers; **f. notice** *(in hotel etc)* consignes *fpl* en cas d'incendie; **f. power** puissance *f* de tir; **f. raiser** incendiaire *mf*; **f. regulations** consignes en cas d'incendie; *(posted in hotel room)* consignes d'incendie; **f. safety** sécurité *f* incendie; **f. sale** = vente *f* au rabais de marchandises ayant subi de légers dégâts à la suite d'un incendie; **f. screen** écran *m* de cheminée; **f. station** caserne *f* de pompiers; **f. tender** voiture *f* de pompiers; *Am* **f. truck** voiture *f* de pompiers; **f. worship** culte *m* du feu

▸ **fire away** **VI** *Mil etc* tirer à feu continu (**at**

sur); *Fig* **f. away!** allez-y!, commencez!
► **fire off** VT SEP *Mil etc (round etc)* tirer; *Fig (questions)* poser à brûle-pourpoint; **she fired off a letter of complaint** elle a envoyé une lettre de réclamation sur-le-champ

fire-and-brimstone ADJ *(sermon, preacher)* annonçant les feux de l'enfer

firearm ['faɪərɑːm] N arme f à feu; **firearms training** formation f à l'utilisation des armes à feu

fireball ['faɪəbɔːl] N **1** *Met* éclair m en boule **2** *Astron* bolide m **3** *(ball of fire)* boule f de feu; **he heard a loud noise and saw a f. in the sky** il a entendu un grand bruit et il a vu une boule de feu dans le ciel **4** *Fig* **she's a real f.** elle déborde d'énergie

fireboat ['faɪəbəʊt] N bateau-pompe m, pl bateaux-pompes

firebox ['faɪəbɒks] N foyer m, boîte f à feu

firebrand ['faɪəbrænd] N **1** *(burning wood)* tison m, brandon m **2** *(agitator)* brandon m de discorde

firebreak ['faɪəbreɪk] N *(in forest etc)* coupe-feu m inv

firebrick ['faɪəbrɪk] N brique f réfractaire

firebug ['faɪəbʌg] N *Fam* incendiaire mf, pyromane mf

firecracker ['faɪəkrækər] N *Am* pétard m

firedamp ['faɪədæmp] N *Min* grisou m
► ► **f. explosion** coup m de grisou

firedog ['faɪədɒg] N *(in fireplace)* chenet m

fire-eater N **1** *(at fair etc)* avaleur m de feu **2** *Fam (aggressive person)* batailleur, -euse

fire-extinguisher N extincteur m (d'incendie)

fire-fighting N lutte f contre les incendies
► ► **f. equipment** matériel m de lutte contre l'incendie

firefly ['faɪəflaɪ] N *(insect)* luciole f

fireguard ['faɪəgɑːd] N **1** *(in front of open fire)* écran m pare-étincelles, garde-feu m inv; devant m de cheminée **2** = **firebreak**

firehouse ['faɪəhaʊs] N *Am* poste m d'incendie; *(with living quarters)* caserne f de (sapeurs-)pompiers

firelight ['faɪəlaɪt] N **to read by f.** lire à la lumière du feu; **in the f.** à la lumière du feu

firelighter ['faɪəlaɪtər] N allume-feu m, pl allume-feux

fireman, pl **firemen** ['faɪəmən] N **1** *(firefighter)* (sapeur-)pompier m **2** *Rail (of steam engine)* chauffeur m

fireman's lift N **to give sb a f.** transporter qn sur l'épaule

fireplace ['faɪəpleɪs] N cheminée f

fireplug ['faɪəplʌg] N *esp Am* bouche f d'incendie

fireproof ['faɪəpruːf] ADJ *(door, safe)* à l'épreuve du feu; *(clothing, toys)* ininflammable; *(dish)* allant au feu
VT rendre ininflammable, ignifuger

fire-retardant ADJ ignifuge

fireside ['faɪəsaɪd] N coin m du feu; **sitting by the f.** assis au coin du feu
► ► **f. chair** fauteuil m; **f. chat** *(by politician)* causerie f au coin du feu

firestorm ['faɪəstɔːm] N tempête f de feu

firetrap ['faɪətræp] N **this building's a real f.** ce bâtiment est un véritable piège (en cas d'incendie)

firewall ['faɪəwɔːl] N **1** *Am Aut* pare-feu m inv de moteur **2** *Comput* mur m coupe-feu, garde-barrière f

firewarden ['faɪəwɔːdən] N *Am* guetteur, -euse d'incendies

firewatcher ['faɪəwɒtʃər] N *Br* guetteur, -euse d'incendies

firewatching ['faɪəwɒtʃɪŋ] N *Br* surveillance f contre les incendies

firewater ['faɪəwɔːtər] N *Fam* gnole f, gnôle f, gniole f

firewood ['faɪəwʊd] N bois m de chauffage; **bundle of f.** fagot m; **to go out in search of f.** aller chercher du bois; **to chop sth up for f.** couper qch en morceaux pour en faire du bois de chauffage

firework ['faɪəwɜːk] N **1** *(device)* pièce f d'artifice **2** *(display) (usu pl)* **fireworks** feu m d'artifice; *Fig Fam* **there'll be fireworks** il va y avoir du grabuge
► ► **f. display** feu d'artifice

firing ['faɪərɪŋ] N **1** *Mil etc (of rocket)* tir m; *(shooting)* tir, feu m; **heavy f. could be heard** on entendait une vive fusillade; **they could hear the f. of the guns** ils entendaient les coups de feu **2** *(heating) (of oven, locomotive etc)* chauffage m, chauffe f; **coal/oil f.** chauffe au charbon/mazout **3** *Cer (of bricks, pottery etc)* cuisson f; **they'll be given a second f.** elles seront cuites une deuxième fois **4** *(of engine)* allumage m
► ► *Mil* **f. line** ligne f de tir; *Aut* **f. order** *(of cylinders)* ordre m d'allumage; **f. party** *(for execution)* peloton m d'exécution; *(for ceremonial duties)* = peloton chargé de tirer la salve d'honneur; **f. pin** percuteur m; **f. position** *(of weapon)* position f de tir; *(of person)* position du tireur; **f. practice** exercice m de tir; **f. range** champ m de tir; **within f. range** à portée de fusil; **f. sequence** *(of cylinders)* ordre d'allumage; **f. squad** *(for execution)* peloton d'exécution; *(for ceremonial duties)* = peloton chargé de tirer la salve d'honneur

firm¹ [fɜːm] N VOIR GRAMMAIRE A11 *Com* maison f (de commerce), entreprise f, firme f; **the f.'s giving us a rise** la firme nous accorde une augmentation; **a large f.** une grosse entreprise; **f. of auditors** cabinet m comptable; **f. of solicitors** étude f de notaires

firm² ADJ **1** *(flesh, mattress, handshake etc)* ferme; *(post, nail, foundations etc)* solide; **as f. as a rock** inébranlable; **to rule with a f. hand** gouverner d'une main ferme; **to walk with a f. step** *or* **tread** marcher d'un pas assuré; **I'm on firmer ground when it comes to the marketing side** je suis plus à mon affaire pour ce qui touche au marketing

2 *(intention, person etc)* ferme; *(voice)* ferme, assuré; *(friendship)* solide; *(date)* fixe; *(evidence)* convaincant; **a f. favourite for the Derby/with the crowd** un grand favori dans le Derby/auprès de la foule; **there has been no f. news** il n'y a aucune nouvelle certaine; **to be f. about sth** tenir bon sur qch; **she was polite but f.** elle a été polie mais ferme; **to have a f. belief that ...** avoir la ferme conviction que ...; **I'm a f. believer in corporal punishment** je suis résolument partisan du châtiment corporel; **I'm a f. believer in the value of a high fibre diet** je crois fermement à la valeur d'un régime riche en fibres

3 *(offer, sale, order)* ferme; **these shares remain f. at ...** ces actions se maintiennent à ...; **the dollar remained f. against the yen** le dollar est resté fort contre le yen
ADV **to stand f.** tenir bon *ou* ferme; **to stand f. about sth** tenir bon sur qch; **to hold f.** tenir bon, résister; **to hold f. to one's principles/beliefs** être fidèle à ses principes/croyances
VT **to f. the soil** affermir *ou* tasser le sol
VI = **firm up** VI
► **firm up** VT SEP *(make firm)* raffermir; *(details)* préciser
VI *(become firm) (of price, muscles etc)* se raffermir

firmament ['fɜːməmənt] N *Lit* firmament m; *Fig* **one of the brightest stars in the Holly-**wood f. l'une des plus grandes stars de l'univers hollywoodien

firmly ['fɜːmlɪ] ADV *(tied, to deny)* fermement; *(to nail down, screw on)* solidement; *(to walk)* d'un pas assuré; *(to say)* d'un ton ferme, fermement; *(to act)* avec fermeté; **I f. believe that ...** j'ai la ferme conviction que ...; **to deal f. with sb** traiter qn fermement *ou* avec fermeté; **she remains f. entrenched in her views** elle demeure fermement retranchée derrière ses opinions

firmness ['fɜːmnɪs] N **1** *(solidity)* fermeté f; *(of character etc)* force f; *(of tread)* assurance f **2** *(of intention, person, voice etc)* fermeté f; *(of friendship)* solidité f; **the f. of her voice** l'assurance qu'il y avait dans sa voix **3** *Com, Fin etc (of shares etc)* stabilité f

firmware ['fɜːmweər] N *Comput* microprogrammation f, microprogrammes mpl constructeurs

FIRST [fɜːst]

ADJ	premier
N	le premier **1** ▪ première **3**
ADV	d'abord **1** ▪ pour la première fois **2** ▪ plutôt **3** ▪ le premier **4**

ADJ SEE GRAMMAR B59 *(in time, order)* premier, -ière; **the f. (day) of the month** le premier (jour) du mois; **twenty-f.** vingt et unième; **eighty-f.** quatre-vingt-unième; **ninety-f.** quatre-vingt-onzième; **one hundred and f.** cent unième; **the f. of April** le premier avril; **the f. three years** les trois premières années; **Charles the F.** Charles Premier m; **to use** *or* **wear sth for the f. time** étrenner qch; **it was my f. flight** c'était mon baptême de l'air; **to be the f. person to do sth** être le premier/la première à faire qch; **English is my f. language** l'anglais est ma langue maternelle; **English is my f. foreign language** l'anglais est ma première langue; **to have news at f. hand** tenir une nouvelle de première main; **to put f. things f.** commencer par le commencement; **f. things f.!** commençons par le commencement!; **f. things f., let's talk about financing** avant tout, parlons du financement; **I don't know the f. thing** *or* **have the f. idea about motorbikes** je ne connais absolument rien aux motos; **f. thing in the morning** *(as soon as I get up)* dès que je me lève; *(as soon as I arrive at the office etc)* dès que j'arrive; *(immediately the shop etc opens)* à l'ouverture; **at the f. attempt** au premier *ou* de prime abord; **at f. light** aux premières lueurs du jour; **at f. sight** à première vue; *Gram* **in the f. person** à la première personne; **in the f. place, I didn't ask for your help** d'abord *ou* pour commencer, je ne t'ai rien demandé; **why didn't you tell me that in the f. place?** pourquoi ne me l'as-tu pas dit dès le début?; **of the f. water** de la plus belle eau; **on the f. floor** *Br* au premier étage; *Am* au rez-de-chaussée; **f. draft** premier jet m; *Br* **f. year** *Univ* première année f; *Sch* = sixième f

N **1** *(person, thing)* premier, f première; **we were the very f. to arrive** nous sommes arrivés les tout premiers; **we were the f. to tell him** nous avons été les premiers à le lui dire; **she was the f. to finish** elle a terminé la première; **you'll be the f. to know** vous serez le premier à le savoir; *Sport etc* **to come in an easy f.** arriver bon premier; **to be the f. to do sth** être le premier/la première à faire qch; *Univ* **to get a f.** avoir une licence avec mention très bien; **the inflatable life jacket was a Scottish f.** *(it was invented there)* le gilet de sauvetage gonflable est une invention écossaise; **this is a f. for France** *(the first time it has won the competition)* c'est une première pour la France; **it's the f. I've heard of it!** première nouvelle!

2 *(beginning)* commencement *m*; **from f. to last** depuis le début jusqu'à la fin; **from the f.** dès le commencement *ou* début; **at f.** d'abord

3 *Aut (gear)* première *f* (vitesse); **in f.** en première (vitesse); **to put the car into f.** se mettre en première, passer la première

ADV 1 *(firstly)* d'abord; **I shall f. have to give it careful consideration** il faudra d'abord que j'examine cela soigneusement; **f., make sure the parts are clean** premièrement, assurez-vous que les différentes pièces sont propres; **do this f.** *(before anything else)* commence par ça; **what should I do f.?** par quoi est-ce que je dois commencer?; **f. and foremost** avant toute chose; **f. of all** pour commencer, en premier lieu; *Fam* **f. off, why did you do it?** pour commencer *ou* et d'abord, pourquoi est-ce que tu as fait cela?; **f., forget that …** commencez par oublier que …

2 *(for the first time)* pour la première fois; **when did you f. see him?** quand l'avez-vous vu pour la première fois?

3 *(rather)* plutôt; **I'll see him damned f.** qu'il aille plutôt au diable

4 *(before others)* le premier, la première; **he arrived/left/died f.** il est arrivé/parti/mort le premier; **you go f.!** *(in queue)* passez devant!; **to claim the right to speak f.** réclamer la priorité de parole; **to come f.** passer en premier; **to come f. in an examination** être reçu premier à un examen; **f. come f. served** premier arrivé, premier servi; **it's a case of f. come f. served** les premiers arrivés sont les premiers servis; **tickets were handed out on a f. come f. served basis** les billets ont été distribués par ordre d'arrivée; **ladies f.!** place aux dames!; **women and children f.!** les femmes et les enfants d'abord!; **to fall head f.** tomber la tête la première; **he was carried out feet f.** on l'a emporté les pieds devant

▸▸ **f. aid** secourisme *m*, premiers secours *mpl*; **I've had f. aid training** j'ai une formation de secouriste; **f. aid certificate** brevet *m* de secourisme; **f. aid class** cours *m* de secourisme; **f. aid kit** trousse *f* de secours; **f. aid post** poste *m* de (premiers) secours; **f. aider** secouriste *mf*; **f. cousin** cousin, -ine germain(e); **f. edition** édition *f* originale; *Mktg* **f. entry** premier lancement *m*; *Mktg* **f. gear** première (vitesse); **F. Lady** *(in US)* = femme *f* du président des États-Unis; *Fig* **the f. lady of rock/of the detective novel** la grande dame du rock/du roman policier; **f. lieutenant** *Naut* lieutenant *m* de vaisseau; *Am Mil, Aviat* lieutenant *m*; **f. love** premier amour *m*; *Naut* **f. mate** second *m*; *Pol* **F. Minister** *(of Scottish Parliament, Welsh Assembly, Northern Ireland Assembly)* Premier ministre *m*; *Mktg* **f. mover** premier entré *m*; *Mktg* **f. mover advantage** avantage *m* du premier entré; **f. name** prénom *m*; *Theat etc* **f. night** première *f*; *Law* **f. offence** premier délit *m*; *Law* **f. offender** délinquant, -ante primaire; *Naut* **f. officer** second *m*; *Theat etc* **f. performance** première *f*; *Fin* **f. quarter** *(of financial year)* premier trimestre *m*; *Parl* **f. reading** *(of bill)* première lecture *f*; *Pol* **F. Secretary** premier secrétaire *m*; *Cin* **f. showing** première exclusivité *f*; *Mus* **f. violin** *(person, instrument)* premier violon *m*; **the F. World War** la Première Guerre mondiale

first-born ADJ, N *esp Lit (boy)* premier-né *m*, *pl* premiers-nés; *(girl)* première-née *f*, *pl* premières-nées

first(-)class ADJ **1** *(compartment, ticket)* de première (classe); *(item)* de première qualité; *(hotel, player, performance etc)* de premier ordre; **the food was f.** la nourriture était excellente **2** *(letter, stamp)* au tarif normal; **to send a letter by f. mail** envoyer une

lettre au tarif normal **3** *Br Univ* **she got a f. honours degree (in French)** elle a eu mention très bien (en français); **to graduate with f. honours** obtenir son diplôme avec mention très bien

ADV **to travel f.** voyager en première; **to send a letter f.** envoyer une lettre au tarif normal

first-day ADJ
▸▸ *Philat* **f. cover** (enveloppe *f*) premier jour *m* (d'émission)

first-degree ADJ
▸▸ *Med* **f. burn** brûlure *f* au premier degré; *Am Law* **f. murder** meurtre *m* avec préméditation

first-foot *Scot* N = première personne *f* à se rendre chez quelqu'un pour souhaiter la bonne année
VI **to f. sb** = être le premier à se rendre chez qn pour souhaiter la bonne année

first-hand ADJ, ADV *(news)* de première main; **she had the news f.** elle a appris la nouvelle de première main; **to experience sth f.** faire personnellement l'expérience de qch

first-in first-out ADJ *Comput, Ind* premier entré, premier sorti

firstly ['fɜːstlɪ] ADV premièrement, en premier lieu; **f. she rang the office** elle téléphona d'abord au bureau

first-nighter [fɜːst'naɪtər] N *Theat* habitué, -ée des premières

first-notice day N *St Exch* premier jour *m* de notification

first-off N *Mktg* produit *m* vedette

first-past-the-post ADJ *Br Pol (system)* majoritaire à un tour; **the f. electoral system** le scrutin majoritaire à un tour

first-rate ADJ excellent, de première classe; **f. idea** fameuse idée *f*; **of f. quality** de toute première qualité; **I feel f.!** je suis en pleine forme!

first-strike ADJ *(missile, capability etc)* de première frappe

first-time ADJ **f. visitors to the country** les personnes visitant le pays pour la première fois
▸▸ **f. buyer** *(of property)* = personne *f* devenant propriétaire pour la première fois; **f. user** nouvel utilisateur *m*

firth [fɜːθ] N *Scot Geog* estuaire *m*; **the F. of Forth** le golfe du Forth

fiscal ['fɪsk(ə)l] ADJ *Fin (resources, control)* fiscal, -aux; *(policy)* budgétaire
N *Scot* **(procurator)** f. procureur *m* général
▸▸ *Fin* **f. austerity** austérité *f* fiscale; *Fin* **f. balance** équilibre *m* fiscal; *Am Acct* **f. period** période *f* comptable; *Am* **f. year** *Fin* exercice *m* (financier), année fiscale *ou* d'exercice; *Admin* année *f* budgétaire

---

Fiscal Year

En Grande-Bretagne, l'année fiscale commence le 1er avril pour les entreprises et le 6 avril pour les particuliers. Aux États-Unis, l'année fiscale correspond à l'année civile pour les particuliers.

---

fish, *pl* **fishes** *or* **fish** [fɪʃ, 'fɪʃɪz] N **1** VOIR GRAMMAIRE A12 poisson *m*; **I don't like f.** *(as food)* je n'aime pas le poisson; *Br* **f. and chips** poisson frit avec des frites; *Fig Fam* **I've other f. to fry** j'ai d'autres chats à fouetter; *Fig* **there are plenty more f. in the sea** un(e) de perdu(e), dix de retrouvé(e)s; **to feel like a f. out of water** ne pas se sentir dans son élément; **a big f. in a small pond** une gloire locale; **at university, she was a small f. in a big pond** à l'université, elle se sentait complètement perdue dans la masse; *Fig* **neither f.**

nor fowl ni chair ni poisson **2** *Astron* **the Fish** les Poissons *mpl*
VI pêcher; **to f. for trout/pearls** pêcher la truite/des perles; **to go fishing** aller à la pêche; *Fam* **to f. for compliments** chercher des compliments
VT **1** *(salmon etc)* pêcher **2** *(river)* pêcher dans **3** *(remove)* **to f. sb/sth from somewhere** tirer qn/qch de quelque part; **they fished the body from the pond** ils ont repêché le corps de l'étang
▸▸ **f. bone** arête *f* (de poisson); **f. cake** croquette *f* de poisson; **f. course** plat *m* de poisson; **f. dish** plat de poisson; **f. farm** établissement *m* piscicole; **f. farmer** pisciculteur, -trice; **f. farming** pisciculture *f*; *Br* **f. fingers** bâtonnets *mpl* de poisson; **f. fork** fourchette *f* à poisson; **f. kettle** poissonnière *f*; **f. knife** couteau *m* à poisson; **f. market** marché *m* au poisson; **f. meal** farine *f* de poisson; **f. pond** étang *m*; **f. shop** poissonnerie *f*; **f. slice** pelle *f* à poisson; *Am* **f. sticks** bâtonnets de poisson; **f. tank** *(in house)* aquarium *m*; *(on fish farm)* vivier *m*
▸ **fish out** VT SEP *(remove from water)* repêcher; **to f. out a dead body** (re)pêcher un cadavre; **she put her hand in the drawer and fished out a twenty-dollar bill** elle a mis la main dans le tiroir et en a sorti un billet de vingt dollars; **he fished a pencil out of his pocket** il a fouillé dans sa poche et en a tiré un crayon
▸ **fish up** VT SEP *(bring up from water)* repêcher; *(dead body)* (re)pêcher; *(mine)* relever; *(information)* dénicher

fish-and-chip ADJ
▸▸ *Br* **f. shop** = boutique *f* qui vend du poisson frit et des frites

fisherman, *pl* **fishermen** ['fɪʃəmən] N pêcheur *m*
▸▸ **f.'s bend** *(knot)* nœud *m* de grappin

fishery ['fɪʃərɪ] N *(fishing ground)* pêcherie *f*, *(fishing industry)* pêche *f*
▸▸ **f. protection vessel** garde-pêche *m inv*

fisheye *Phot* N *Fam* grand-angle *m*
▸▸ **f. lens** objectif *m* ultra grand angle, objectif fish-eye

fish-hook N hameçon *m*

fishing ['fɪʃɪŋ] N pêche *f*; **there's good f. to be had here** il y a du poisson par ici; **trout f.** pêche à la truite; **pearl f.** pêche des perles; **fly f.** pêche à la mouche
▸▸ **f. boat** bateau *m* de pêche; **f. ground** zone *f* de pêche; **f. line** ligne *f* de pêche; **f. net** filet *m* de pêche; **f. port** port *m* de pêche; **f. rights** droits *mpl* de pêche; **f. rod** canne *f* à pêche, gaule *f*; **f. smack** bateau *m* de pêche; **f. tackle** articles *mpl* de pêche; **f. trip** partie *f* de pêche; **f. vessel** navire *m* de pêche, pêcheur *m*; **f. village** village *m* de pêcheurs

fishmonger ['fɪʃmʌŋɡər] N *esp Br (person)* poissonnier, -ière; **f.'s (shop)** poissonnerie *f*

fishnet ['fɪʃnet] N *esp Am Fishing* filet *m* de pêche
▸▸ **f. stockings** bas *mpl* résille; **f. tights** collant *m* résille

fishplate ['fɪʃpleɪt] N *Rail* éclisse *f*

fishpole mike ['fɪʃpəʊl] N micro *m* sur perche

fishwife, *pl* **fishwives** ['fɪʃwaɪf, -waɪvz] N marchande *f* de poisson, poissonnière *f*; **she swears like a f.** elle jure comme un charretier

fishy ['fɪʃɪ] ADJ **1** *(smell, taste)* de poisson **2** *Fam (suspicious) (business etc)* louche; **f. story** histoire *f* qui ne tient pas debout; **there's something f. going on here** il y a quelque chose de louche

fissile ['fɪsaɪl] ADJ fissile

fission ['fɪʃən] N **1** *Phys* fission *f*; **nuclear/**

thermal f. fission nucléaire/thermique **2** *Biol* scissiparité *f*

fissure ['fɪʃər] **N** (*in wall, rock etc*) fissure *f*, fente *f*
VT (*rock etc*) fissurer, fendre
VI (*of rock etc*) se fissurer, se fendre

fist [fɪst] **N** poing *m*; **to clench one's f., to make a f.** serrer le poing; **to shake one's f.** *or* **fists at sb** menacer qn du poing; **he went for them with his fists** il tomba sur eux à coups de poing

fistful ['fɪstfʊl] **N** (*of money etc*) poignée *f*

fisticuffs ['fɪstɪkʌfs] **NPL** *Br Old-fashioned, Hum* coups *mpl* de poing; **if he finds out, there'll be f.!** s'il s'en rend compte il va y avoir de la bagarre *ou* du grabuge

fistula ['fɪstjʊlə] **N** *Med* fistule *f*

fit¹ [fɪt] **N** (*of madness etc*) accès *m*; (*of coughing*) quinte *f*, (*apoplexy*) crise *f* d'apoplexie; **(epileptic) f.** crise d'épilepsie; **to have** *or Fam* **throw a f.** piquer une crise; *Fam* **he'll have a f. when he finds out** il va avoir une attaque quand il apprendra ça; **in a f. of temper** dans un mouvement de colère; **f. of crying** crise de larmes; **f. of laughter** accès de rire; **to be in fits** (*of laughter*) avoir le fou rire; **to have sb in fits** donner le fou rire à qn; **in a f. of carelessness** dans un moment d'inattention; **to work by fits and starts** travailler par à-coups

---

FIT²

ADJ bon **1** ▪ en forme **4**
VT s'accorder **1** ▪ aller à **2** ▪ adapter, ajuster **3** ▪ assembler **4** ▪ munir, pourvoir **5**
VI aller

ADJ (**fitter; fittest**) **1** (*appropriate*) bon, propre (**for sth** à qch); **f. to eat** bon à manger, mangeable; **f. to drink** buvable, potable; **I've nothing f. to wear** je n'ai rien à me mettre; **story that is not f. to be repeated** histoire qu'il ne serait pas convenable de répéter; **a meal f. for a king** un repas digne d'un roi; **I'm not f. to be seen** je ne suis pas présentable; **to think f.** *or* **see f. to do sth** trouver bon de faire qch; **do as you see** *or* **think f.** faites comme bon vous semble; **this is no f. way to behave** ce comportement est inacceptable; **this is no f. way to run a company** ce n'est pas comme ça qu'on dirige une entreprise; **he's not f. to polish my boots** il n'est même pas bon à cirer mes chaussures

2 (*capable*) capable; **f. to do sth** capable de faire qch; **that's all he's f. for** il n'est bon qu'à cela; **she's not a f. mother** c'est une mère indigne

3 (*ready*) **I felt f. to drop** je me sentais prêt à tomber (de fatigue); **she worked until she was f. to drop** elle a travaillé jusqu'à tomber de fatigue

4 (*healthy*) en forme; **to get f.** retrouver la forme; **I'm a lot fitter** je suis bien plus en forme; **to be (fighting) f.** être en forme; **to keep f.** se maintenir en forme; **he is not yet f. to go back to work** il n'est pas encore en état de reprendre son travail; **f. for duty** bon pour le service; *Mil* valide; *Fam* **to be as f. as a fiddle** être en parfaite santé, se porter comme un charme

5 *Br Fam* (*attractive*) bien foutu(e)

N **your coat is a perfect/poor f.** votre manteau vous va parfaitement/ne vous va pas très bien; **easy/tight f.** coupe *f* confortable/ajustée; **it was a tight f. but everyone squeezed in** il n'y avait pas beaucoup de place mais tout le monde a tenu

VT (**-tt-**) **1** (*be suitable for*) s'accorder avec; **to make the punishment f. the crime** proportionner la peine au délit

2 (*of clothes*) **to f. sb** aller à qn; **it fits/they f. me** elle me va/elles me vont; **it fitted her perfectly** il était exactement à sa taille; **key that fits the lock** clef qui va à la serrure

3 (*install*) adapter, ajuster (**sth to sth** qch à qch); **to f. a nozzle on the end of a pipe** adapter un ajutage à l'extrémité d'un tuyau; **to f. a handle to a broom** emmancher un balai; **to f. one part into another** emboîter une pièce dans une autre; **to f. a carpet** poser une moquette; **I'm going to be fitted for my new dress** je vais faire l'essayage de ma nouvelle robe

4 (*assemble*) **to f. parts together** monter *ou* assembler des pièces; **to f. a machine together** assembler une machine

5 (*equip*) munir, pourvoir (**sth with sth** qch de qch); **fitted with two propellers** pourvu de deux hélices

6 (*insert*) **to f. sb/sth into/onto sth** mettre *ou Fam* caser qn/qch dans/sur qch; **we can f. another two (people) inside** il y a de la place pour deux personnes de plus

VI aller; **the lid doesn't f.** ce n'est pas le bon couvercle; **your dress fits well/badly** votre robe vous va/ne vous va pas bien; **she no longer fits into her dress** elle n'entre plus dans sa robe; **I can't f. into these jeans any more** je n'arrive plus à rentrer dans ce jean; **to f. (together)** s'ajuster, s'adapter; **to f. into sth** (*of piece etc*) s'emboîter dans qch; **all her tools easily fitted into the bag** tous ses outils tenaient largement dans le sac; **we won't all f. into the car** nous ne tiendrons pas tous dans la voiture; **the photos just f. onto the page** les photos tiennent juste sur la page; **the phrase/colour has to f.** l'expression/la couleur doit bien aller avec le reste; *Fam* **his face didn't f.** on n'aimait pas sa gueule

▸ **fit in VT SEP** (*find room, time for*) **I can't f. any more clothes in** je ne peux plus mettre aucun vêtement; **the hairdresser says she can f. me in tomorrow** la coiffeuse dit qu'elle peut s'arranger pour me prendre demain; **I'll check my diary and see if I can f. you in** je vais regarder mon agenda et voir si je trouve un moment pour toi

VI 1 (*go into place*) tenir; **there's no way they'll all f. in** ils ne tiendront jamais tous; **to f. in between two things** s'emboîter entre deux choses

2 (*harmonize*) **to f. in with sth** (*of piece of furniture, building, colour*) être en accord avec qch; **your plans don't f. in with mine** vos projets ne cadrent pas avec les miens; **to f. in with sb's plans** (*of person*) s'adapter aux projets de qn; **he doesn't f. in there** il n'y est pas dans son élément; **you'll have to make more of an effort to f. in** il va falloir que tu fasses plus d'efforts pour t'adapter *ou* t'intégrer

3 (*agree*) correspondre (**with** à); *Fam* coller (**with** avec); **that doesn't f. in with what I was told** ça ne correspond pas à ce qu'on m'a dit; *Fam* ça ne colle pas avec ce qu'on m'a dit

▸ **fit out VT SEP** équiper (**sth with sth** qch de qch); (*ship*) armer; (*new ship*) équiper; **to f. sb out** équiper qn (**with clothes/etc** de vêtements/*etc*)

▸ **fit up VT SEP 1** (*provide*) doter, pourvoir, munir (**with** de); **they fitted me up with an artificial leg** ils m'ont mis une jambe artificielle

2 *Fam* **to f. sb up (for a crime)** monter un coup contre qn; **they claim to have been fitted up by the Serious Crimes Squad** ils se prétendent tous victimes d'un coup monté organisé par la Brigade criminelle

fitful ['fɪtfʊl] **ADJ** (*sleep, night*) agité; **to make f. progress** progresser par à-coups

fitfully ['fɪtfəlɪ] **ADV** (*to sleep*) d'un sommeil agité; (*to work*) par à-coups

fitment ['fɪtmənt] **N 1** *Br* (*piece of furniture*) élément *m* **2** (*of machine*) accessoire *m*

fitness ['fɪtnɪs] **N 1** (*health*) forme *f* (physique) **2** (*suitability*) (*of person*) aptitude *f* (**for a job/etc** à un emploi/*etc*); (*of remark*) justesse *f*, à-propos *m*; **her f. for government** *or* **power** son aptitude à gouverner
▸▸ *Br* **f. centre** club *m* de gym; *Fam* **f. freak** fana *mf* d'exercice physique; **f. room** salle *f* de musculation

fitted ['fɪtɪd] **ADJ 1** (*garment*) ajusté **2** (*suitable*) (*of person, thing*) **to be f. for sth** convenir à qch
▸▸ **f. carpet** moquette *f*; **f. cooker** four *m* encastré; **f. kitchen** cuisine *f* intégrée; **f. sheet** drap-housse *m*, *pl* draps-housses; **f. wardrobe** garde-robe *f* encastrée, *pl* garde-robes encastrées

fitter ['fɪtər] **N 1** *Tech, Aut etc* ajusteur *m*, assembleur, -euse; **electrical f.** installateur *m* d'appareils électriques **2** *Sewing* essayeur, -euse

fitting ['fɪtɪŋ] **ADJ** convenable, approprié (**to** à); (*remark*) à propos; **it was a f. tribute to a great athlete** c'était un hommage mérité rendu à un grand athlète; **it was only f. he should score the winning goal** ce n'était que justice qu'il marque le but gagnant; **a f. end for a murderer** une fin appropriée pour un meurtrier

N 1 (*of clothes*) essayage *m*; *Com* **made in three fittings** fabriqué en trois tailles; (*of shoes*) fabriqué en trois largeurs **2** (*usu pl*) **fittings** (*of office etc*) installations *fpl*; (*of bathroom etc*) accessoires *mpl*; **door fittings** ferrures *fpl* de porte; **brass fittings** garnitures *fpl* en cuivre; *Elec* **light f.** appareil *m* d'éclairage; **ceiling f.** plafonnier *m*; **wall f.** applique *f*
▸▸ **f. out** (*of expedition etc*) équipement *m*; (*of ship*) armement *m*; **f. room** salon *m ou* salle *f* d'essayage; (*cubicle*) cabine *f* d'essayage; *Ind* **f. shop** atelier *m* d'ajustage

fittingly ['fɪtɪŋlɪ] **ADV** convenablement, à propos; **f., he was buried in his home town** comme il convenait, il a été enterré dans sa ville natale; **f., he died the sort of violent death he had inflicted on so many others** ce n'est que justice qu'il soit mort de la même mort violente qu'il avait infligée à tant d'autres

five [faɪv] **N 1** (*number, numeral*) cinq *m inv*; **f. times table** table *f* des cinq; **f. and f. are ten** cinq et cinq font dix; *Cards* **the f. of hearts** le cinq de cœur; **to be f.** (*in age*) avoir cinq ans; **it's f. o'clock** il est cinq heures; **it's f. to/past f.** il est cinq heures moins cinq/cinq heures cinq; **come at f.** venez à cinq heures; **to get f. out of ten** avoir cinq sur dix; **a table for f.** une table pour cinq (personnes); *Fam* **to take f.** faire un break de cinq minutes; *Fam* **give me f.!** tope là! (*pour conclure un marché, dire bonjour ou manifester son approbation*) **2** *Sport* **fives** (*game*) balle *f* au mur

PRON cinq; **f. is not enough** cinq, ce n'est pas assez; **I need f. (of them)** il m'en faut cinq, j'en ai besoin de cinq

NUM ADJ cinq; **f. people** cinq personnes; **on page f.** (à la) page cinq; **they live at number f.** ils habitent au numéro cinq

five-day week **N** semaine *f* de cinq jours

five-door model **N** *Aut* (version *f*) cinq portes *f*

five-finger **ADJ**
▸▸ *Mus* **f. exercises** exercices *mpl* de doigté

fivefold ['faɪvfəʊld] **ADJ** quintuple; **a f. increase/rise** une augmentation au quintuple
ADV au quintuple; **to increase f.** quintupler, augmenter au quintuple

fiver ['faɪvər] **N** *Fam Br* billet *m* de cinq livres, *Am* billet de cinq dollars; *Br* **it'll cost you a f.** ça te coûtera cinq livres

five-seater N *Aut* cinq places *f*

five-speed gearbox N *Aut* boîte *f* cinq-vitesses, boîte de vitesses cinq rapports

fivespot ['faɪvspɒt] N *Am Fam* billet *m* de cinq dollars

five-star ADJ *(hotel)* cinq étoiles, quatre étoiles-luxe; **f. accommodation** hébergement *m* en hôtel cinq étoiles

five-year ADJ quinquennal, -aux

Five-Year Plan N *Econ* Plan *m* quinquennal

FIX [fɪks]

N	pétrin **1** ■ dose **2**
VT	fixer **1, 2, 6** ■ arranger **2, 3**
	■ réparer **3** ■ préparer **3**

N **1** *Fam (difficulty)* embarras *m*, difficulté *f*; **to be in a f.** être dans le pétrin; **to get into a f.** se mettre dans l'embarras *ou* dans le pétrin; **I'm in a bit of a f. financially** j'ai quelques difficultés financières
2 *Sl (of drug)* dose *f*, *(injection)* piqûre *f* (de drogue); **to give oneself a f.** se piquer, se shooter; *Fam Fig* **my daily f. of television news** ma dose quotidienne de journaux télévisés
3 *Aviat, Naut* position *f*; **to get a f. on a ship/** *etc* déterminer la position d'un navire/*etc*
4 *Fam (set-up)* **the match/quiz was a f.** le match/jeu était truqué; **it's a f.!** c'est de l'arnaque!
VT **1** *(attach securely)* fixer; *(bait to a line etc)* accrocher; **to f. sth in one's memory** graver qch dans sa mémoire; **to f. one's attention on sth** fixer son attention sur qch; **to f. one's eye(s) on sb** fixer qn (du regard)
2 *(decide) (limits, interest rates etc)* fixer, établir; *(meeting place)* choisir; *(itinerary, date, price etc)* fixer; *(meeting etc)* arranger; **there's nothing fixed yet, nothing is fixed yet** il n'y a encore rien de décidé *ou* de fixé
3 *(repair)* réparer, retaper; *(prepare) (meal etc)* préparer; **to f. sth with sb** arranger qch avec qn; **I've fixed it with her** je me suis arrangé avec elle; *Fam* **I'll f. him!** je lui ferai son affaire!; **just wait while I f. my hair** attends que je me coiffe
4 *(set up) (camp)* établir
5 *(bribe)* graisser la patte à; *(rig) (match, jury etc)* truquer
6 *Chem, Phot etc (mercury, dye etc)* fixer
7 *Am Dial* **to be fixing to do sth** envisager de faire qch
▸ **fix on** VT SEP *(attach)* fixer
VT INSEP *(choose, decide) (holiday destination, dress, house etc)* se décider pour; *(date, itinerary, price, time)* fixer
▸ **fix up** VT SEP *Fam* **1** *(assemble, put up) (tent)* monter; **they fixed up a temporary telephone** ils ont installé une ligne de téléphone provisoire; **to f. up a room as a study** transformer une pièce en bureau
2 *(arrange) (business, meeting)* arranger; **it's all fixed up** c'est une affaire réglée, tout est arrangé; **I've already fixed up to go out tonight** j'ai déjà prévu de sortir ce soir
3 *(improve) (car, bike)* réparer, retaper; *(house, apartment)* retaper; **you should f. yourself up a bit** tu devrais t'arranger un peu
4 *(provide)* **to f. sb up with a job/room** trouver un travail/une chambre pour *ou* à qn; **I've fixed you up with a date** je t'ai arrangé un rendez-vous; **they've been trying to f. me up with her for weeks** ça fait des semaines qu'ils essaient de me monter un plan avec elle

---

fixated [fɪk'seɪtɪd] ADJ **to be f. on** *or* **with sth** être obsédé par qch; **he was still f. by the idea** cette idée l'obsédait encore

fixation [fɪk'seɪʃən] N *Psy* fixation *f*; **to have a mother f.** faire une fixation sur sa mère

fixative ['fɪksətɪv] ADJ, N *Art* fixatif *m*

fixed [fɪkst] ADJ **1** fixe; *(rule)* établi, absolu; *(smile)* figé; **of f. length** de longueur constante; **to have f. ideas** avoir des idées (bien) arrêtées; **to have no f. plans** ne pas avoir de projets bien déterminés **2** *Fam* **how are you f. for money/for condoms?** tu as assez d'argent/de capotes?; **how are you f. for time?** tu as du temps libre?; **how are you f. for accommodation/transport?** est-ce que tu as un endroit où loger/un moyen de transport?; **how are we f. for disks?** on a des disquettes? **3** *Chem (oil, salt)* fixe **4** *Fam Pej (rigged)* truqué
▸▸ *Acct, Fin* **f. asset** actif *m* immobilisé; *Acct, Fin* **f. assets** immobilisations *fpl*, actif immobilisé; *Cin, TV* **f. camera** caméra *f* fixe; *Fin* **f. charge** frais *mpl* fixes; *Fin* **f. cost** charge *f* fixe, coût *m* fixe *ou* constant; *Com* **f. deposit** dépôt *m* à terme (fixe) *ou* à échéance fixe; *Comput* **f. disk** disque *m* fixe; *Fin* **f. exchange rate** taux *m* de change fixe; *Fin* **f. income** revenu *m* fixe; *Fin* **f. interest** intérêt *m* fixe; *Fin* **f. investment** immobilisations *f*; *Fin* **f. point** point *m* fixe, point de repère; *Math* **f. point arithmetic** arithmétique *f* en virgule fixe; **f. price** prix *m* fixe *ou* forfaitaire; *Fin* **f. rate** taux *m* fixe; *Com* **f. salary** salaire *m* fixe

fixed-income ADJ *Fin* à revenu fixe
▸▸ **f. investment** placement *m* à revenus fixes; **f. securities** valeurs *fpl* à revenu fixe

fixed-interest ADJ *Fin* à intérêt fixe
▸▸ **f. market** marché *m* des obligations; **f. securities** valeurs *fpl* à intérêt fixe

fixedly ['fɪksɪdlɪ] ADV fixement

fixed-price menu N menu *m* à prix fixe

fixed-rate ADJ *Fin (loan, mortgage)* à taux fixe; *(investment)* à revenu fixe
▸▸ **f. bond** obligation *f* à revenu fixe; **f. borrowing** emprunts *mpl* à taux fixe

fixed-term ADJ *Com* à terme fixe
▸▸ *Fin* **f. bill** effet *m* à date fixe; *Com* **f. contract** contrat *m* à durée déterminée, CDD *m*; *Fin* **f. credit** crédit *m* à durée déterminée; *Fin* **f. deposit** dépôt *m* à terme fixe *ou* à échéance fixe

fixer ['fɪksər] N **1** *Fam (person)* combinard *m* **2** *Art* fixatif *m*; *Phot* fixateur *m*

fixing ['fɪksɪŋ] N **1** *(repairing)* réparation *f* **2** *Com (of prices etc)* établissement *m*; *St Exch* fixage *m* **3** *(usu pl) Am* **fixings** *(trimmings)* accessoires *mpl*; *(food)* accompagnements *mpl*, garnitures *fpl*; **roast turkey with all the fixings** dinde rôtie avec tout ce qui s'ensuit
▸▸ *Phot* **f. bath** *(container)* cuvette *f* de fixage; *(solution)* bain *m* de fixage; *Phot* **f. solution** solution *f* de fixage

fixity ['fɪksɪtɪ] N fixité *f*; *Fml* **f. of purpose** détermination *f*

fixture ['fɪkstʃər] N **1** *(installation)* appareil *m* fixe; **fixtures** *(of house etc)* aménagements *mpl*; *(electrical etc)* appareils; **fixtures and fittings** agencements *mpl*, installations *fpl* fixes; **£3,000 for fixtures and fittings** 3 000 livres de reprise; **bathroom fixtures and fittings** installations et accessoires de salles de bain; *Fam* **he's become a f. here** il fait partie des meubles à présent; **she was something of a f. at his parties** elle apparaissait inévitablement à chacune de ses soirées; **she was becoming a f.** elle commençait à faire partie des meubles **2** *Br Sport* rencontre *f* (prévue), match *m* (prévu)
▸▸ *Sport* **f. list** calendrier *m*

fizz [fɪz] N **1** *(sound) (of champagne etc)* pétillement *m*; *(of steam)* sifflement *m*; *(fizziness)* gaz *m* **2** *Fam (soft drink)* boisson *f* gazeuse; *(champagne)* champagne *m*

VI *(of champagne)* pétiller; *(of steam, firework)* siffler; **the champagne fizzed out of the bottle** le champagne est sorti de la bouteille en pétillant; **the Coke® fizzed up and spilled onto the table** le Coca® a moussé et s'est répandu sur la table

fizzle ['fɪz(ə)l] VI *(of wine)* pétiller; *(of gas burner etc)* siffler
▸ **fizzle out** VI *Fam (of plan)* tomber à l'eau; *(of enthusiasm, interest, desire)* tomber; *(of hope)* s'envoler; *(of story, film)* finir en queue de poisson; **the evening fizzled out** la soirée se traîna lamentablement

fizzy ['fɪzɪ] ADJ *(mineral water, drink)* gazeux; *(wine)* mousseux

fjord [fjɔːd] N *Geog* fjord *m*, fiord *m*

Fla *abbr* Florida

flab [flæb] N *Fam (fat)* graisse *f*; **he was trying to get rid of his f.** il essayait de perdre sa graisse

flabbergast ['flæbəgɑːst] VT *Fam* abasourdir, ahurir; **I was flabbergasted** j'en étais sidéré

flabbiness ['flæbɪnɪs] N *(of flesh, skin)* flaccidité *f*, manque *m* de fermeté; *(of person)* flaccidité *f*; *(of person's grip)* mollesse *f*; *(of prose, writing, novel)* prolixité *f*; *(of argument, idea)* manque de rigueur

flabby ['flæbɪ] ADJ *(muscles etc)* flasque, mou, *f* molle; *(cheeks)* pendant; *(person)* grassouillet; *(grip)* mou; *Fig (prose)* prolixe; *(reasoning, ideas, morals)* qui manque de rigueur

flaccid ['flæsɪd] ADJ mou, *f* molle; *(flesh)* flasque

flag¹ [flæg] N **1** *(cloth, emblem)* drapeau *m*; *Naut* pavillon *m*; *Fig* **to fly the f. for one's country** défendre les couleurs de son pays; *also Fig* **to show the f.** faire acte de présence; **black f.** *(of pirate)* pavillon noir; **yellow f.** pavillon de quarantaine **2** *(of taxi)* drapeau *m*; **taxi with the f. up** taxi *m* libre **3** *Comput (marker)* drapeau *m*, marqueur *m* **4** *(for file, folder)* papillon *m*
VT *(-gg-)* **1** = **flag down 2** *(mark)* marquer; *(error in text etc)* marquer, signaler
VI *(of sail)* battre; *(of plant)* s'étioler, languir; *(of person)* s'alanguir; *(of conversation)* traîner, languir; *(of attention, courage, determination)* faiblir; **our spirits were flagging** notre moral faiblissait; **his strength was flagging** ses forces baissaient
▸▸ **f. airline** compagnie *f* aérienne nationale; *Naut* **f. captain** commandant *m* du navire amiral; **f. carrier** *(airline)* compagnie aérienne nationale; *(shipping company)* compagnie maritime nationale; *Naut* **f. of convenience** pavillon de complaisance; *Am* **F. Day** le 14 juin *(fête nationale des États-Unis)*; *Br* **f. day** *m* jour de quête d'une œuvre de charité; *Naut* **f. officer** contre-amiral *m*, *pl* contre-amiraux; **f. signals** signalisation *f* par fanions
▸ **flag down** VT SEP *(stop)* arrêter, stopper
▸ **flag out** VT SEP *Sport (racetrack)* jalonner
▸ **flag up** VT SEP *(mark, indicate)* marquer; *(mistake)* signaler, marquer

flag² N = **flagstone**
VT *Constr (pave)* daller; *(pavement etc)* paver de carreaux

flag³ N *(plant)* iris *m*

flagellate ['flædʒəleɪt] ADJ, N *Zool* flagellé *m*
VT flageller, fouetter

flagellation [flædʒə'leɪʃən] N flagellation *f*

flageolet ['flædʒəlet, flædʒə'let] N *Mus, Culin* flageolet *m*

flagged [flægd] ADJ *(floor)* dallé

flagging¹ ['flægɪŋ] ADJ *(conversation etc)* languissant; *(courage, determination, attention)* faiblissant; *(strength, health)* baissant; **to revive sb's f. spirits** remonter le moral à qn

flagging² N *(paving)* dallage *m*

flagon ['flægən] N **1** *(large bottle)* grosse bouteille *f* (ventrue), bonbonne *f* **2** *(jug)* pot *m* (à anse)

flagpole ['flægpəʊl] N mât *m* de drapeau; *Fig, Fam* **to run sth up the f.** proposer qch pour voir les réactions

flagrant ['fleɪgrənt] ADJ *(offence, miscarriage of justice, lie)* flagrant; **a f. injustice** une injustice criante; **this f. disobedience** cet acte de désobéissance effronté; **what a f. cheek!** ça alors, quel culot!

flagrante delicto, in flagrante delicto [ɪnfləˈgræntɪdɪˈlɪktəʊ] ADV *Law* en flagrant délit

flagrantly ['fleɪgrəntlɪ] ADV d'une manière flagrante; **f. dishonest** d'une malhonnêteté flagrante; **f. unfair** d'une injustice criante

flagship ['flægʃɪp] N *Naut* (navire *m*) amiral *m*; *Fig* **the London store is the f. of the chain** le magasin de Londres est le plus important de la chaîne; **this latest model is the f. of their new range** ce dernier modèle est le produit vedette de leur nouvelle gamme; **the Conservatives' f. council** le conseil municipal qui est le fleuron du parti Conservateur

flagstaff ['flægstɑːf] N mât *m* de drapeau; *Naut* mât de pavillon

flagstone ['flægstəʊn] N dalle *f*
▸▸ **f. pavement** dallage *m* en pierre

flag-waving N *Pej, Fam (patriotic remarks)* déclarations *fpl* cocardières; **f. speech** discours *m* cocardier

flail [fleɪl] N *Agr* fléau *m*
VT **1** *Agr* battre au fléau **2** **he flailed his fists at me** il balançait les poings dans ma direction; **the animal was flailing its legs in the air** l'animal battait l'air de ses pattes
VI *(of rope, cable)* se balancer violemment; **I dodged my assailant's flailing arms** j'ai esquivé les coups de mon assaillant
▸ **flail about, flail around** VI *(wave wildly) (of arms, legs)* s'agiter dans tous les sens; **she was flailing about in the water** elle se débattait des mains et des pieds dans l'eau

flair ['fleər] N *(skill)* aptitude *f* (**for** à); *(skill in detecting things etc)* flair *m*; *(energy etc)* dynamisme *m*; **to have a f. for languages/cooking** avoir le don des langues/pour cuisiner; **to dress/write with f.** *(stylishness)* s'habiller/écrire avec style; **he had no f. for business** il n'avait pas le sens des affaires; **they have a real f. for making the right choices** ils ont vraiment le don de faire les bons choix

flak [flæk] N **1** *(artillery)* artillerie *f* anti-aérienne; *(fire)* tir *m* contre-avions **2** *Fam (criticism)* critique *f*; **she got a lot of f. for this decision** on l'a beaucoup critiquée pour cette décision
▸▸ **f. jacket** gilet *m* pare-balles

flake [fleɪk] N **1** *(of snow, oat, corn)* flocon *m*; *(of metal etc)* écaille *f*, éclat *m*, paillette *f*, *(of paint, plaster)* écaille *f*; **soap flakes** savon *m* en paillettes; **a f. of skin** un petit morceau de peau morte **2** *Am Fam (crazy person)* barjo *mf*
VI *(of metal, paint etc)* s'écailler; *(of arms, nose)* peler; **my skin was flaking** je pelais
▸ **flake away, flake off** VI *(of metal, paint etc)* s'écailler; **the skin on my nose is flaking off** mon nez pèle, j'ai le nez qui pèle
▸ **flake out** VI *Fam (fall asleep)* s'endormir; **I just want to f. out on the sofa** j'ai envie de m'effondrer sur le canapé et roupiller; **she's gone upstairs to f. out** elle est montée roupiller; **to be flaked out** *(exhausted)* être vidé *ou* crevé; *(asleep)* roupiller

flaking ['fleɪkɪŋ] ADJ *(paint)* qui s'écaille; *(skin)* qui se détache

flaky ['fleɪkɪ] ADJ **1** *(mineral etc)* écailleux; *(paint)* écaillé; **her skin was all dry and f.** elle avait la peau toute sèche qui pelait **2** *Fam (crazy)* barjo
▸▸ *Br Culin* **f. pastry** pâte *f* feuilletée

flamboyance [flæmˈbɔɪəns] N *(of personality, manner, clothes, car)* extravagance *f*, *(of physical gesture)* caractère *m* magistral

flamboyant [flæmˈbɔɪənt] ADJ *(personality, generosity, manner, clothes, car)* extravagant; *(physical gesture)* magistral

flamboyantly [flæmˈbɔɪəntlɪ] ADV *(to behave, dress)* avec extravagance; *(designed)* aux lignes extravagantes

flame [fleɪm] N **1** flamme *f*, **in flames** en flammes, en feu; **to go up in flames** être détruit par le feu; *Fig (of hopes, chances)* s'envoler, partir en fumée; **to burst into flame(s)** s'enflammer, se mettre à flamber **2** *(light)* éclat *m* **3** *Lit (passion)* passion *f*, ardeur *f*, *Fam (lover)* béguin *m*; **he is an old f. of mine** c'est un de mes anciens amoureux; **the f. of passion** les feux de la passion; **the f. of enthusiasm** la flamme de l'enthousiasme; **to keep the f. of freedom burning** ne pas laisser s'éteindre la flamme de la liberté **4** *Comput* message *m* injurieux
VI **1** *(of fire etc)* flamber, flamboyer; *Lit (of passions etc)* brûler; **her cheeks flamed** ses joues s'empourprèrent **2** *(of diamond etc)* briller **3** *Comput* rédiger un message injurieux
VT **1** *Culin* flamber **2** *Comput* incendier
▸▸ *Tech* **f. cutter** chalumeau *m* à découper; *Agr* **f. gun** agriflamme *m*; **f. red** rouge *m* feu; **f. red hair** chevelure *f* rouge flamboyante; *Bot* **f. tree** flamboyant *m*; *Comput* **f. war** guerre *f* d'insultes
▸ **flame up** VI *(blaze)* s'enflammer

flame-coloured ADJ ponceau *inv*, couleur de feu *inv*

flamenco [fləˈmeŋkəʊ] N *Mus* flamenco *m*

flameproof ['fleɪmpruːf] ADJ ininflammable; *(material)* ignifugé; *Elec* anti-déflagrant

flamer ['fleɪmər] N *Comput* auteur *m* d'un message injurieux

flamethrower ['fleɪmθrəʊər] N *Mil etc* lance-flammes *m inv*

flaming ['fleɪmɪŋ] N *Comput* = échange *m* d'insultes sur l'Internet
ADJ **1** *(fire)* flambant, flamboyant **2** *(sun)* ardent; *(sunset)* embrasé; *(sky)* embrasé; **f. red** rouge feu *inv*; *Fam* **in a f. temper** d'une humeur massacrante **3** *Br Fam (intensifier)* sacré; **you f. idiot!** sacré imbécile!; **a f. cheek** un culot monstre
ADV *Br Fam* complètement, carrément; **he's so f. stupid** il est complètement stupide; **he's so f. brilliant** il est carrément génial; **it was f. expensive** c'était super cher

flamingo, *pl* **flamingos, flamingoes** [fləˈmɪŋgəʊ, -əʊz] N *(bird)* flamant *m*

flammable ['flæməb(ə)l] ADJ inflammable

flan [flæn] N *Culin* tarte *f*, *(savoury)* quiche *f*
▸▸ **f. case** fond *m* de tarte

Flanders ['flɑːndəz] N Flandre *f*

flange [flændʒ] N *(of tube, pipe)* bourrelet *m*, collerette *f*, *(of piece of sheet metal)* collet *m*, rebord *m*; *(of wheel)* boudin *m*, rebord; *(of beam)* aile *f*, *Rail (of rail)* patin *m*; **cooling f.** ailette *f* de refroidissement
▸▸ **f. coupling** raccordement *m* à bride

flanged [flændʒd] ADJ *(tube)* à bride(s); *(wheel)* à boudin; *(rail)* à patin; *(beam)* à aile; *(piece of sheet metal)* à bord tombé; *Aut (radiator)* à ailettes

flank [flæŋk] N **1** *(of person, animal)* flanc *m*; *Culin (of beef)* flanchet *m* **2** *(of mountain etc)* côté *m*, flanc *m* **3** *Mil (of army etc)* flanc *m*;

left/right f. aile *f* gauche/droite; **to protect one's flanks** se couvrir sur les flancs
VT **1** flanquer; **to f. sth with** *or* **by sth** flanquer qch de qch; **flanked by two policemen** encadré de deux gendarmes **2** *Mil (the enemy)* prendre de flanc; *(trench)* enfiler; **flanking movement** attaque *f* par le/les flanc(s)
▸▸ *Mktg* **f. attack** attaque *f* latérale; **to launch a f. attack** lancer une attaque latérale

flanker ['flæŋkər] N **1** *Rugby* avant-aile *m*, *pl* avant-ailes **2** *Mktg* produit *m* de protection latérale
▸▸ *Mktg* **f. brand** marque *f* de protection latérale, marque dérivée

flannel ['flæn(ə)l] N **1** *Tex (material)* flanelle *f*, **flannels** *(trousers)* pantalon *m* de flanelle **2** *Br* **(face) f.** = gant *m* de toilette **3** *Br Fam (wordy language)* blabla(bla) *m*; *(flattery)* flatteries *fpl*
ADJ *(trousers etc)* de flanelle
VI *Br Fam* faire du baratin; **stop flannelling** arrête ton baratin

flannelette [flænəˈlet] N pilou *m*, veloutine *f*

flap [flæp] N **1** *(movement, sound) (of wing)* battement *m*, coup *m*; *(of sail)* claquement *m* **2** *(piece of material etc) (of envelope, dustcover for book, tent)* rabat *m*; *(of pocket)* patte *f*, *(of table)* abattant *m*; *(of cellar door)* trappe *f*, *(on studio light)* volet *m*; *Aviat* volet; *Tech* clapet *m* (à charnière); **desk with a writing f.** secrétaire *m*; **a f. of skin** un lambeau de peau **3** *Fam (panic)* affolement *m*; **to get into a f.** s'affoler, se mettre dans tous ses états; **to be in a f.** ne plus savoir où donner de la tête; **there's a big f. on** c'est la panique, c'est l'affolement total
VT **(-pp-)** *(wings)* battre de; *(hands, piece of paper)* agiter; **the bird flaps its wings** l'oiseau bat des ailes; **to f. one's arms about** agiter les bras
VI **1** *(of sail)* battre, claquer; *(of wings)* battre; **the eagle flapped off/away** l'aigle s'envola/s'éloigna en battant des ailes; **when she started talking to me it really set his ears flapping** quand elle a commencé à me parler il a tendu l'oreille **2** *Fam (panic)* s'affoler, se mettre dans tous ses états; **once he stopped flapping (about)** une fois son affolement passé
▸▸ *Aut* **f. valve** *(in throttle)* valve *f* papillon, papillon *m*

flapjack ['flæpdʒæk] N *Culin* **1** *Am (pancake)* crêpe *f* **2** *Br (biscuit)* biscuit *m* à l'avoine

flapper ['flæpər] N = jeune femme *f* (des années 20)

flapping ['flæpɪŋ] N *(of wings)* battement *m*; *(of sail)* claquement *m*

flare [fleər] N **1** *(bright flame)* flamboiement *m*; *(of jet engine etc)* flammes *fpl* **2** *(signal)* feu *m* de signal; *(rocket)* fusée *f* éclairante, **3** *(of pipe etc)* évasement *m*; *(of skirt)* godet *m*; **(pair of) flares** *(trousers)* pantalon *m* (à pattes d'éléphant)
VI **1** *(of lamp, light etc)* flamboyer **2** *(of skirt etc)* s'évaser; *(of nostrils)* se dilater (**with** de) **3** *(of temper)* s'échauffer; **tempers flared at the council meeting** le ton est monté pendant la réunion du conseil
VT *(pipe, skirt etc)* évaser; *(nostrils)* dilater
▸▸ **f. gun** pistolet *m* de signalisation; *Br* **f. path** piste *f* à balises lumineuses; **f. pistol** pistolet de signalisation
▸ **flare up** VI **1** *(of candle etc)* s'enflammer brusquement **2** *(of anger, fighting etc)* éclater; *(of person)* s'emporter; *(of medical condition, skin condition)* se déclencher; **he flares up at the slightest thing** il monte comme une soupe au lait

flared [fleəd] ADJ *(skirt, pipe etc)* évasé; **f. trousers** pantalon *m* à pattes d'éléphant

flare-up N **1** *(with flames)* flambée f soudaine **2** *(outbreak)* *(of war)* déclenchement m; *(of anger)* éruption f; *(renewal of anger, war)* recrudescence f; *(argument)* altercation f; *(of person)* flambée f ou éclat m de colère; *(of violence)* explosion f; **there has been a new f. in the Balkans** il y a eu une nouvelle recrudescence des combats dans les Balkans

---

FLASH [flæʃ]

N	éclat **1** ▪ flash **2, 4** ▪ torche **3**
VI	briller **1** ▪ clignoter **1** ▪ passer comme un éclair **2**
VT	lancer **1** ▪ diriger **1** ▪ montrer rapidement **2** ▪ projeter **2**
ADJ	tape-à-l'œil

N **1** *(light)* éclair m; *(of diamond etc)* éclat m; *(of firearm)* lueur f; éclair; **a f. of lightning** un éclair; **f. of wit** saillie f; **f. of inspiration** éclair de génie; **(as) quick as a f.** vif comme l'éclair; **in a f.** en un rien de temps, en un clin d'œil; **it came to her in a f.** ça lui est venu subitement; *Fig* **a f. in the pan** un feu de paille
2 *Phot* flash m, pl flashes; **I took this one with a f.** celle-ci je l'ai prise au flash ou avec le flash
3 *Am Fam (torch)* torche f (électrique)
4 *Journ* flash m; **news f.** flash d'information
5 *Br Mil (badge)* écusson m
VI **1** *(of light, diamonds)* briller; *(of light on police car etc)* clignoter; *(of eyes)* jeter des éclairs; *(with enthusiasm)* briller; **the light flashed once then went out** la lumière s'est allumée puis s'est éteinte; **his eyes flashed with anger** ses yeux lançaient des éclairs de colère
2 *(move fast)* **to f. past** passer comme un éclair; **she flashed past me on a skateboard** elle m'a doublé en skateboard à la vitesse de l'éclair; **he flashed through the exercises** il a fait les exercices à toute vitesse; **the days seemed to f. by** les journées ont passé à toute vitesse; **it flashed across my mind that …** l'idée m'est venue tout d'un coup que …; **my life flashed before me** ma vie a défilé devant mes yeux; **a look of panic flashed across his face** une expression de panique passa rapidement sur son visage; **a smile flashed across her lips** un sourire se dessina soudain sur ses lèvres
3 *Br Fam (expose oneself)* s'exhiber (**at** devant)
VT **1** *(smile, look)* lancer (**at sb** à qn); **to f. a light in sb's eyes** diriger une lumière dans les yeux de qn; **she flashed her headlights at us** elle nous a fait un appel de phares; **she flashed a mirror to signal for help** elle a fait des signaux avec un miroir pour appeler à l'aide; **he was flashing a fat wad of money** il exhibait un gros paquet de billets; **she flashed a report to head office** elle a envoyé un rapport-éclair au siège social
2 *(show quickly)* montrer rapidement; *(picture etc on screen)* projeter; **he flashed a photo in front of me** il m'a passé une photo sous les yeux; **he flashed a £50 note at them** il leur passa un billet de cinquante livres sous le nez
3 *Am Fam (expose oneself to)* s'exhiber devant
ADJ *Br Fam (showy)* tape-à-l'œil inv; voyant, extravagant; inv; *(spiv)* filou m
▸▸ **f. burn** brûlure f *(causée par un éclat très violent et brûlant, comme celui d'une bombe)*; **f. flood** crue f subite; *Phot* **f. gun** flash; *Br Fam* **f. Harry** frimeur m; *Com* **f. pack** *(discounted)* = emballage m portant une réduction de prix; **f. photography** photographie f au flash; **f. point** *Tech (of oil etc)* point m d'inflammabilité; *Fig* situation f critique ou explosive; **f. welding** soudure f par étincelage

▸ **flash around** VT SEP *Fam (show off)* montrer, exhiber; **he likes flashing his money around** il aime étaler sa richesse; **don't f. your money around here!** ne montre ou n'exhibe pas ton argent ici!
▸ **flash back** VI *Cin (of film)* revenir en arrière, faire un retour en arrière ou un flashback; *(of mind)* remonter (dans le passé); **my thoughts flashed back to the last time we had all been together** j'ai soudain repensé à la dernière fois où nous étions tous ensemble
▸ **flash forward** VI *(of film)* faire un saut en avant

flashback ['flæʃbæk] N *Cin* retour m en arrière, flash-back m; **their story is told in f.** leur histoire est racontée par flash-back ou par retours en arrière; *Fig* **he had a f. to that fateful day** cette journée fatidique lui revint soudain à l'esprit

flashbulb ['flæʃbʌlb] N *Phot* ampoule f (de) flash

flashcard ['flæʃkɑːd] N étiquette f

flashcube ['flæʃkjuːb] N *Phot* flash m cube

flasher ['flæʃər] N **1** *Br Fam (man exposing himself)* exhibitionniste m **2** *Aut Fam (lamp)* clignotant m
▸▸ *Aut* **f. unit** centrale f clignotante

flash-forward N *Cin, TV* projection f en avant

flashily ['flæʃɪlɪ] ADV *Fam Pej* d'une manière tapageuse ou tape-à-l'œil, tapageusement; **f. dressed** habillé tapageusement

flashing[1] ['flæʃɪŋ] ADJ *(signal, light, torch)* clignotant; *(eyes, gems)* étincelant
N *(of diamond)* éclat m; *(of mirror)* miroitement m; *(of signal)* clignotement m

flashing[2] N *(on roof)* revêtement m

flashlamp ['flæʃlæmp] N torche f (électrique)

flashlight ['flæʃlaɪt] N **1** *Phot* flash m **2** *esp Am (torch)* torche f (électrique)
▸▸ *Phot* **f. photography** photographie f au flash

flashover ['flæʃəʊvər] N *Elec* étincelle f de rupture

flashy ['flæʃɪ] ADJ *Pej (clothes, car, jewellery)* voyant, tapageur, -euse; *(taste)* tapageur; **f. young man** jeune homme habillé tapageusement; **you and your f. friends** toi et tes copains aux goûts tapageurs

flask [flɑːsk] N flacon m; *Chem* fiole f, *(spherical)* ballon m; **brandy f.** flacon à cognac; **(vacuum) f.** Thermos® m ou f; **a f. of tea** un(e) Thermos® de thé

FLAT [flæt]

ADJ	plat **1** ▪ net **2** ▪ catégorique **2** ▪ terne **3** ▪ éventé **3** ▪ à plat **3** ▪ fixe **4** ▪ en dessous du ton **5**
ADV	à plat **1** ▪ nettement **2** ▪ en dessous du ton **4**
N	plat **1** ▪ appartement **5** ▪ bémol **7** ▪ crevaison **8**

ADJ **1** *(countryside, chest, stomach, shoes)* plat; *(roof)* plat, en terrasse; *(curve etc)* aplati; *(surface)* plat, uni; *(nose)* camus; *Med (feet)* plat; *(picture)* sans relief; *(in painting) (colour)* mat; *Archit (vault)* plat; *(arch)* déprimé; **to beat sth f.** aplatir qch; **the city had been bombed f.** les bombardements avaient rasé la ville; **as f. as a pancake** plat comme une galette; *Fam* **to go into a f. spin** *(of person)* s'affoler
2 *(absolute)* net, f nette; *(denial)* formel, absolu; *(refusal)* net, catégorique; **to give a f. refusal** refuser net; *Fam* **and that's f.!** voilà qui est net!; **I'm not going, and that's f.** je n'y vais pas, un point c'est tout
3 *(existence etc)* monotone, ennuyeux;

(style etc) terne; *(voice)* terne, blanc; *(drink)* éventé, plat; *(battery)* à plat; **to go f.** *(of drink)* s'éventer; **business has been a bit f. lately** les affaires sont calmes ces derniers temps
4 *Com (rate, fee)* fixe
5 *(sound)* sourd; *Mus* bémol; **symphony in D f.** symphonie f en ré bémol; **you're f.** *(singing)* vous chantez en dessous du ton; *(playing)* vous jouez en dessous du ton; **her voice went a bit f. at the end** elle a fini un peu en dessous du ton
ADV **1** *(in level position)* à plat; *also Fig* **to knock sb f.** faire tomber qn à la renverse; **to fall f. on one's face** tomber à plat ventre; *Fam (be humiliated)* essuyer une humiliation; **to fall f.** *(of joke etc)* manquer son effet, tomber à plat; *(of play etc)* faire un four; **stretched out f. on the ground** étendu à plat sur le sol; **to fold f.** se plier; **he pressed himself f. against the wall** il s'est collé au mur
2 *(absolutely)* nettement, positivement; *Fam* **he told me f. that …** il m'a dit carrément que …; **to turn sb down f.** envoyer qn balader, envoyer qn sur les roses; *Fam* **to be f. broke** être à sec; **to work f. out** travailler d'arrache-pied; **to go f. out** *(run)* filer à toute allure; *Fig* **she was going f. out for the championship** elle mettait tout en jeu pour le championnat; **to lie f. out** être allongé à plat; **to be f. out** *(exhausted)* être à plat
3 *(exactly)* **in twenty seconds f.** en vingt secondes pile; **in less than ten seconds f.** en moins de dix secondes
4 *Mus (to sing, play etc)* en dessous du ton
N **1** *(of sword etc)* plat m; **the f. of the hand** le plat de la main
2 *(land)* plaine f, *(left exposed at low tide)* sèche f
3 **on the f.** *(horizontally)* horizontalement; *Rail (track)* en palier; *Sport* sur le plat
4 *Horseracing* **the f.** *(season)* la saison du plat; *(racing)* les courses de plat, le plat
5 *esp Br (rooms)* appartement m; **furnished/unfurnished f.** appartement meublé/non meublé; **service f.** appartement avec service
6 *Theat (scenery)* panneau m de décor
7 *Mus* bémol m
8 *Fam (puncture)* crevaison f, *(flat tyre)* pneu m à plat; *(punctured)* pneu crevé
▸▸ **f. bed** *(of lorry)* plateau m; **f. blade screwdriver** tournevis m (à lame) plate; *Naut* **f. calm** calme m plat; *Br* **f. cap** casquette f, **f. fare** *(on bus etc)* tarif m unique; *Comput* **f. file** fichier m de données non structurées; *Comput, TV* **f. monitor** écran m plat; *Comput* **f. panel display** moniteur m à écran plat; *Horseracing* **f. race** course f de plat; *Horseracing* **f. racing** *(races)* plat m; *(season)* saison f des courses de plat; *Comput, TV* **f. screen** écran plat; **f. screen television** téléviseur m à écran plat; **f. screen tube** tube m cathodique plat; **f. sheets** *(in bookbinding)* feuilles fpl à plat; *Aut* **f. spot** point m mort; **f. swapping** échange m d'appartement; *Fam* **f. top** *(haircut)* brosse f, *Am Fam (aircraft carrier)* porte-avions m inv; **f. tyre** pneu m à plat; *(punctured)* pneu crevé

flatbed ['flætbed] ADJ
▸▸ *Br* **f. lorry** semi-remorque m à plateau, pl semi-remorques à plateau; *Comput* **f. plotter** traceur m à plat; *Comput* **f. scanner** scanneur m à plat; **f. truck** semi-remorque à plateau

flat-bottomed ['-'bɒtəmd] ADJ à fond plat

flatcar ['flætkɑːr] N *Am Rail* wagon m en plateforme

flat-chested [-'tʃestɪd] ADJ plat

flatfish, pl **flatfishes** or **flatfish** ['flætfɪʃ, -fɪʃɪz] N poisson m plat

flatfoot ['flætfʊt] N **1** *Med* pied m plat **2** *Old-*

fashioned Br Fam (policeman) agent *m* de police, *Fam* poulet *m*

flat-footed ADJ **1** *Med* à pied plat, aux pieds plats **2** *Br Fig, Fam (clumsy, inelegant)* maladroit

flatiron ['flætaɪən] N fer *m* à repasser

flat-leaf parsley N *Bot, Culin* persil *m* plat

flatlet ['flætlɪt] N *esp Br* petit appartement *m*, studio *m*

flatline ['flætlaɪn] *Med* N électrocardiogramme *m* plat
VI avoir un électrocardiogramme plat

flatly ['flætlɪ] ADV **1** *(absolutely)* nettement, carrément; *(to refuse)* net; *(to deny)* absolument; *(to say)* sèchement **2** *(monotonously)* d'une façon monotone; **the speaker's voice droned f. on** l'orateur continuait de sa voix lassante et monotone

flatmate ['flætmeɪt] N *Br* colocataire *mf (d'un appartement)*; **we used to be flatmates** avant, nous partagions un appartement

flatness ['flætnɪs] N **1** *(of surface etc)* nature *f* plate; *(of countryside)* absence *f* de relief; *(of curve etc)* aplatissement *m* **2** *(of refusal)* netteté *f* **3** *(of existence etc)* monotonie *f*; *(of style etc)* insipidité *f*, platitude *f*; *(of beer etc)* évent *m*; *(of colour)* caractère *m* terne; *(of sound)* caractère sourd; **there was a f. in his voice which suggested that …** le détachement que l'on décelait dans sa voix suggérait que …

flat-rate ADJ
▸▸ *Comput* **f. connection** *(to Internet)* connexion *f* à tarif forfaitaire; *Comput* **f. monthly charge** *(to Internet)* forfait *m* mensuel

flatten ['flæt(ə)n] **(-n-)** VT **1** aplatir; *(road)* aplanir; *(of wind, rain) (corn etc)* coucher; **to f. oneself against a wall** se plaquer *ou* se coller contre un mur; *Fam* **to f. sb** *(in fight)* mettre la pâtée à qn; *(humiliate)* écraser qn **2** *(make dull)* rendre fade *ou* insipide; *(make less striking)* atténuer **3** *Mus (note)* bémoliser
VI **1** s'aplatir **2** *(become dull)* devenir fade *ou* insipide; *(of colour)* se ternir
▸ **flatten out** VI **1** *Aviat* reprendre le vol horizontal; *(after dive)* se redresser; *(of inflation, unemployment etc)* se stabiliser (**at** à) **2** *(of terrain, slope)* s'aplanir

flattened ['flæt(ə)nd] ADJ **1** aplati; *(nose)* épaté **2** *Mus (note)* bémolisé

flatter ['flætər] VT flatter; **the portrait/dress flatters her** ce portrait/cette robe la flatte *ou* l'avantage; **he flatters himself that he will succeed** il est persuadé de sa réussite; **I f. myself on my goulash/my ability to judge people** je me flatte de faire un bon goulasch/de savoir juger les gens; *Fam* **don't f. yourself!** tu rêves!
VI être flatteur

flatterer ['flætərər] N flatteur, -euse; *(who exaggerates)* flagorneur, -euse

flattering ['flætərɪŋ] ADJ *(words, photo etc)* flatteur, -euse; *(exaggerated)* adulatoire; **it is f. to be asked to give this speech** c'est flatteur d'être sollicité pour faire ce discours; **to speak in f. terms of sb, to make f. remarks about sb** parler de qn en termes flatteurs; **I didn't get a very f. impression of the city/ your boss** la ville/ton patron ne m'a pas fait une impression très favorable

flatteringly ['flætərɪŋlɪ] ADV *(to speak)* en termes flatteurs; **the photograph had been f. lit** la photo avait été prise dans une lumière flatteuse

flattery ['flætərɪ] N flatterie *f*, *(exaggerated)* flagornerie *f*; **f. will get you nowhere!** ça ne vous apportera rien de flatter les gens!

flatulence ['flætjʊləns] N *Med* flatulence *f*,

to suffer from f. avoir des vents; **to cause f.** provoquer des flatulences

flatulent ['flætjʊlənt] ADJ **1** *Med (person)* qui souffre de flatulences **2** *Fig (style)* boursouflé

flatware ['flætweər] N *Am* vaisselle *f* plate

flaunt [flɔːnt] VT *(wealth, knowledge)* étaler, afficher, faire parade de; *(jewels)* étaler, arborer; *(bad manners, ignorance)* afficher

Attention: ne pas confondre avec le verbe **to flout.**

flautist ['flɔːtɪst] N *Mus* flûtiste *mf*

flavour, *Am* **flavor** ['fleɪvər] N saveur *f*, goût *m*; *(of tea etc)* arôme *m*; *(of ice cream etc)* parfum *m*; **what f. (of) ice cream did you want?** quel parfum tu voulais?; *Fam* à quoi tu voulais ta glace?; **it comes in six different flavours** il existe en six parfums différents; **her stories have a Mediterranean f.** ses histoires sentent bon la Méditerranée; **there was a f. of regret about his remarks** ses remarques contenaient une pointe de regret; **her book gives the true f. of the Mexican hinterland** son livre fleure bon l'arrière-pays mexicain; *Fam* **I'm not f. of the month** je ne suis pas en odeur de sainteté; **she's definitely f. of the month** décidément, elle a la cote ce mois-ci
VT *(dish etc)* assaisonner, parfumer; **to f. a sauce with garlic** relever une sauce avec de l'ail; **vanilla flavoured** (parfumé) à la vanille
▸▸ **f. enhancer** agent *m* de sapidité

flavouring, *Am* **flavoring** ['fleɪvərɪŋ] N *(savoury)* assaisonnement *m*; *(sweet)* parfum *m*; **artificial f.** arôme *m* artificiel

flavourless, *Am* **flavorless** ['fleɪvəlɪs] ADJ *(food etc)* sans saveur, fade, insipide; *(wine)* plat

flaw [flɔː] N **1** défaut *m*, imperfection *f*, *(in plan)* point *m* faible; **there is one f. in their argument** il y a une faille dans leur argument; **to have a f. in one's character** avoir un défaut **2** *Law (in document etc, making it null and void)* vice *m* de forme
VT *(spoil)* endommager, défigurer; **the plan is flawed by the lack of …** le point faible de ce plan est le manque de …

flawed [flɔːd] ADJ *(reasoning)* défectueux; *(novel, film)* qui a des défauts; *(sweater, scarf, fabric)* qui a un/des défaut(s); *(wood)* gercé; *(diamond)* qui a un crapaud *ou* un défaut

flawless ['flɔːlɪs] ADJ sans défaut, parfait; *(technique)* impeccable

flawlessly ['flɔːlɪslɪ] ADV parfaitement

flawlessness ['flɔːlɪsnɪs] N perfection *f*

flax [flæks] N *(plant)* lin *m*
▸▸ **f. field** linière *f*

flaxen ['flæksən] ADJ *(hair)* blond de lin *inv*, blond filasse *inv*

flay [fleɪ] VT **1** *(skin) (animal)* écorcher; **to be flayed alive** être écorché vif **2** *(whip)* fouetter; *Fig* **the critics flayed him** les critiques l'ont éreinté

flea [fliː] N *(insect)* puce *f*, **to have fleas** avoir des puces; *Fig Fam* **she sent him away with a f. in his ear** elle l'a envoyé promener
▸▸ **f. collar** collier *m* antipuces; **f. market** marché *m* aux puces

fleabag ['fliːbæg] N *Sl* **1** *Br (person)* pouilleux, -euse; *(animal)* sac *m* à puces **2** *Am (hotel)* hôtel *m* pouilleux

fleabite ['fliːbaɪt] N **1** morsure *f* de puce **2** *Fig (trifle)* vétille *f*, bagatelle *f*

flea-bitten ADJ *(dog, cat, person)* plein de puces; *(hotel)* pouilleux; *(old jacket)* miteux

fleapit ['fliːpɪt] N *Old-fashioned Br Sl (cinema)* cinéma *m* pouilleux

fleck [flek] N **1** *(mark) (of light etc)* petite tache *f*, *(of colour, paint)* moucheture *f* **2** *(particle) (of dust)* particule *f*

VT tacheter; **flecked with clouds** moucheté de nuages; **hair flecked with grey** cheveux qui grisonnent; **flecked material** tissu moucheté

fled PT, PP *see* **flee**

fledged [fledʒd] ADJ *(bird)* qui a toutes ses plumes; *see* **fully-fledged**

fledgling ['fledʒlɪŋ] N **1** *(young bird)* oisillon *m* **2** *(beginner)* novice *mf*, débutant, -e; **a f. lawyer** un avocat novice; **a f. industry/ state** une industrie/un État jeune

flee [fliː] *(pt, pp* **fled)** VI *(of person)* s'enfuir, prendre la fuite; *(of time etc)* voler; *(of hope)* s'envoler; **to f. from a place** s'enfuir d'un endroit; **to f. from temptation/persecution** fuir la tentation/les persécutions; **to f. to America** s'enfuir en Amérique
VT *(country etc)* s'enfuir de; *(person, temptation etc)* fuir

fleece N **1** *(of sheep)* toison *f*, *Liter* **the Golden F.** la Toison d'or **2** *Tex (material)* laine *f* polaire; *(garment)* polaire *f*
VT *Fam (cheat, overcharge)* écorcher; **I've been fleeced** je me suis fait estamper

fleece-lined ADJ doublé de laine polaire

fleecing ['fliːsɪŋ] N *Fam (overcharging)* estampage *m*

fleecy ['fliːsɪ] ADJ *(wool)* floconneux; *(material etc)* laineux; *(cloud)* moutonné

fleeing ['fliːɪŋ] ADJ *(army etc)* en fuite

fleet [fliːt] N **1** *Naut* flotte *f*, *(naval unit)* escadre *f*; **the F.** ≃ la Marine nationale; **the Atlantic F.** l'escadre de l'Atlantique; **merchant f.** flotte de commerce; **fishing f.** flottille *f* de pêche **2** *(of cars, taxis)* parc *m*; **air f.** flotte aérienne; **a f. of coaches took the tourists to their hotel** une caravane de cars a amené les touristes à leur hôtel
ADJ *Lit* vite, leste; **f. of foot** au pied léger
▸▸ *Naut* **f. admiral** ≃ amiral *m* de France; *Naut* **the F. Air Arm** = l'aéronavale *f* britannique; **F. Street** = rue *f* de Londres, dont le nom sert à désigner les grands journaux britanniques; **F. Street journalist** journaliste *mf* de la presse nationale

Fleet Street
Traditionnellement, cette rue de la City était celle des journaux. Aujourd'hui, beaucoup de journaux ont établi leur siège dans d'autres quartiers, notamment les Docklands. Cependant, le terme "Fleet Street" est encore employé pour désigner la presse et le monde du journalisme.

fleet-footed ADJ *Lit* au pied léger

fleeting ['fliːtɪŋ] ADJ *(time, moment)* fugitif, fugace; *(beauty)* passager; *(happiness)* éphémère; *(relationship)* de courte durée; **for a f. moment** l'espace d'un instant; **to pay sb a f. visit** faire une courte visite à qn; **to catch a f. glimpse of sth** entrevoir qch, apercevoir qch; **to give sb a f. glance** lancer un regard fugace à qn

fleetingly ['fliːtɪŋlɪ] ADV *(to glimpse, appear)* un court instant; **she has been f. involved with a number of men** elle a eu un certain nombre d'aventures de courte durée

Fleming ['flemɪŋ] N Flamand, -ande

Flemish ['flemɪʃ] ADJ flamand
N *Ling* flamand *m*

flesh [fleʃ] N **1** *(of person, fruit)* chair *f*, **to put on f.** *(of animal)* prendre chair; *(of person)* grossir, prendre de l'embonpoint; **to put some f. on an idea** étoffer *ou* développer une idée; **there he was in the f.** c'était lui en chair et en os; **to make sb's f. creep** *or* **crawl** donner la chair de poule à qn; **his own f. and blood** la chair de sa chair; **it is more than f. and blood can stand** *or* **bear** c'est plus que la nature humaine ne saurait endurer; **I'm only f. and blood!** je ne suis pas un surhomme!; *Fam* **to press the f.** serrer des mains

2 *(as opposed to spirit) Rel* **to mortify the f.** mortifier sa chair; *Rel, Lit* **to go the way of all f.** payer sa dette à la nature; *Rel, Lit* **the sins of the f.** le péché de la chair; *Rel, Prov* **the spirit is willing but the f. is weak** l'esprit est prompt, mais la chair est faible

3 *Arch (meat)* viande *f*; **f.-eating animals** les animaux *mpl* carnivores; *Rel* **to eat f.** faire gras

► ► **f. colour** couleur *f* chair; *Theat* **f. tights** collant *m* chair; *Art* **f. tints** carnations *fpl*; **f. wound** blessure *f* superficielle *ou* légère

► **flesh out** VT SEP *(plan, character, remarks)* étoffer

VI *(become fatter)* s'étoffer

flesh-coloured ADJ *(tights etc)* (couleur) chair

fleshpots ['fleʃpɒts] NPL *Lit, Hum* **the f.** les lieux *mpl* de perdition

fleshy ['fleʃɪ] ADJ *(limb, fruit etc)* charnu; *(leaf)* succulent

fleur-de-lis, *pl* **fleurs-de-lis** ['flɜːdə'liː] N *Her* fleur *f* de lis

flew PT *see* **fly**³

flex [fleks] VT *(one's arm, knees etc)* fléchir; *(one's muscles)* faire jouer; *Fig* **he's just flexing his muscles** ce n'est qu'une démonstration d'autorité de sa part

VI *(of spring)* fléchir

N *Br Elec* cordon *m*, câble *m*

flexibility [fleksɪ'bɪlɪtɪ] N *(of material, plan, person)* flexibilité *f*; *(of character)* souplesse *f*

flexible ['fleksɪb(ə)l] ADJ *(material, plans)* flexible, souple; *(character, principles)* souple; **when would you like the appointment? – I'm f.** quand désirez-vous prendre rendez-vous? – je suis disponible à peu près tout le temps; **f. ticket** billet *m* sans condition; **f. working hours** horaire *m* à la carte *ou* flexibles, *Can* horaire flexible

flexion ['flekʃən] N **1** *(of spring etc)* flexion *f*, courbure *f* **2** *(bend)* courbe *f*

flexitime ['fleksɪtaɪm], **flextime** ['flekstaɪm] N *Ind etc* horaire *m* à la carte, *Can* horaire flexible; **we're on f.** nous avons des horaires à la carte

flexor ['fleksər] N *Anat (muscle)* fléchisseur *m*

flibbertigibbet [flɪbətɪ'dʒɪbɪt] N *Fam* écervelé, -ée, évaporé, -ée, hurluberlu *m*

flick [flɪk] N **1** *(of whip, tail etc)* petit coup *m*; *(with finger)* chiquenaude *f*, **a f. of the wrist** un tour de main; **at the f. of a switch** juste en appuyant sur un bouton **2** *Old-fashioned Br Fam (film)* film *m*; **the flicks** *(cinema)* le ciné, le cinoche; **to go to the flicks** aller au ciné *ou* au cinoche

VT *(with whip etc) (horse etc)* effleurer; *(with finger)* donner une chiquenaude à; **he had to keep flicking the hair out of his eyes** il n'arrêtait pas de chasser du doigt les cheveux qui lui tombaient dans les yeux; **she was flicking cigarette ash all over the floor** elle faisait tomber de la cendre de cigarette partout; **she flicked the dust from her shoulders** du doigt elle fit envoler la poussière qui se trouvait sur ses épaules; **to f. a duster over sth** donner un coup de torchon à qch

► ► *Br* **f. knife** (couteau *m* à) cran *m* d'arrêt; *Aut* **f. wipe** balayage *m* unique

► **flick away** VT SEP chasser; *(with fingers)* repousser d'une chiquenaude

► **flick off** VT SEP *(with fingers)* enlever d'une chiquenaude; **to f. sth off with a duster** faire envoler qch d'un coup de torchon; **he flicked the dandruff off his collar** il secoua les pellicules qui se trouvaient sur son col

► **flick on** VT SEP **to f. on the lights** allumer; *Aut* allumer les phares

► **flick out** VI sortir; **the snake's tongue was flicking in and out** la langue du serpent sortait et rentrait à petits coups rapides

► **flick through** VT INSEP *(book)* feuilleter; *(photographs)* jeter un œil parmi

flicker ['flɪkər] N petit mouvement *m* vacillant; *(of eyelids)* battement *m*; *Cin* scintillement *m*; *(of TV, computer screen)* papillotement *m*; *Fig* **without a f.** sans un battement de cil; **a f. of light** une petite lueur tremblotante; **a f. of recognition** une lueur de reconnaissance; **a f. of hope/a smile** l'ombre d'un espoir/d'un sourire; **a f. of interest/annoyance** une pointe d'intérêt/d'énervement

VI *(of flame etc)* trembloter, vaciller; *(of eyelids)* cligner; *(of light)* clignoter; *(of snake's tongue)* onduler; *(of instrument needle etc)* osciller; *Cin* scintiller; *(of TV, computer screen)* papilloter; **the candle flickered out** la bougie vacilla et s'éteignit; **a smile flickered on his lips** il eut un petit sourire

flicker-free ADJ *(screen)* anti-scintillements

flickering ['flɪkərɪŋ] ADJ *(light)* clignotant; *(shapes, images, candle)* vacillant

N *Cin* scintillement *m*; *(of TV, computer screen)* papillotement *m*

flier ['flaɪər] N **1** *(pilot etc)* aviateur, -trice; **I'm not a good f.** *(passenger)* je n'aime pas prendre l'avion

2 *Fam (fall)* **to take a f. over the handlebars** faire un vol plané par-dessus le guidon

3 *(leaflet)* feuille *f* volante, prospectus *m*

4 *(in race) (of sprinter)* départ *m* en flèche

5 **to take a f.** *(financial risk)* prendre un risque financier

flight¹ [flaɪt] N **1** *(act of flying) (of bird, plane etc)* vol *m*; *(of projectile, star etc)* course *f*; **these birds are not capable of f.** ces oiseaux ne peuvent pas voler; **very graceful in f.** très gracieux en vol; **once we're in f.** quand nous serons à notre altitude de croisière; *Aviat* **level f.** vol horizontal *ou* en palier; *Fig* **f. of fancy** essor *m* de l'imagination

2 *(distance) (of bird etc)* volée *f*, distance *f* parcourue; *(of birds etc)* migration *f*; *(of projectile)* trajectoire *f*; *Aviat* **it's an hour's f. from London** c'est à une heure de vol de Londres

3 *(specific trip)* vol *m*; **f. A200 to Brussels** vol A200 pour Bruxelles; **I don't want to miss my f.** je ne veux pas rater mon avion; **my f. is at 2.15** mon avion est à 2h15; **how was your f.?** comment s'est passé le vol?; **f. only** vol sec

4 *(group) (of birds etc)* vol *m*, volée *f*; *(of planes)* escadrille *f*; *Fig* **in the top f.** parmi les tout premiers; *Aviat* **the Queen's/King's F.** = avions *mpl* au service de la famille royale

5 **f. (of stairs)** escalier *m*; **you go up two flights** tu montes deux étages *ou* de deux volées d'escalier; **they live six flights up from me** ils habitent six étages au-dessus de chez moi; **he lives up four flights (of stairs)** il habite au quatrième; *Sport* **f. of hurdles** *(in obstacle race)* série *f* de haies

6 *(on arrow, dart)* plume *f*

► ► **f. attendant** *(male)* steward *m*; *(female)* hôtesse *f* de l'air; **f. clearance** autorisation *f* de vol; **f. control** *(action of individual aircraft)* conduite *f*; *(from ground)* contrôle *m* de la navigation aérienne; *Mil* contrôle des missions aériennes; *(place)* contrôle aérien; *(people)* contrôleurs *mpl* aériens; **f. crew** équipage *m* *(d'un avion)*; **f. deck** *(of aircraft carrier)* pont *m* d'envol; **f. engineer** mécanicien, -ienne navigant(e) *(d'avion)*, ingénieur *m* de vol; *Orn* **f. feather**

(of bird) penne *f*, **f. formation** formation *f* de vol; **f. lieutenant** = capitaine *m* de l'armée de l'air britannique; **f. log** journal *m* de vol; **f. mechanic** mécanicien, -ienne navigant(e); **f. number** numéro *m* de vol; **f. path** trajectoire *f* de vol; **f. pattern** formation de vol; **f. personnel** personnel *m* navigant; **f. plan** plan *m* de vol; **f. recorder** enregistreur *m* de vol; **f. simulator** simulateur *m* de vol; **f. time** *(duration)* durée *f* de vol; *(take-off time)* heure *f* du vol

flight² N *(escape)* fuite *f*; **his sudden f. from the room** sa sortie précipitée de la pièce; **in the course of her f. from justice** alors qu'elle fuyait la justice; **to take (to) f.** prendre la fuite; **to put the enemy to f.** mettre l'ennemi en fuite; **in full f.** en pleine déroute; *Fin* **f. of capital** exode *m ou* fuite *f* des capitaux

► ► *Fin* **f. capital** capitaux *mpl* flottants *ou* fébriles

flightiness ['flaɪtɪnɪs] N inconstance *f*

flightless ['flaɪtlɪs] ADJ *(bird)* coureur

flighty ['flaɪtɪ] ADJ inconstant; *(emotionally)* volage

flimsily ['flɪmzɪlɪ] ADV *(built, constructed)* d'une manière peu solide

flimsiness ['flɪmzɪnɪs] N **1** *(of dress, cloth)* légèreté *f*; *(of building, plane)* manque *m* de solidité; *(of walls, wooden beams)* minceur *f* **2** *(of excuse etc)* faiblesse *f*, pauvreté *f*

flimsy ['flɪmzɪ] ADJ **1** fragile, peu solide; *(paper etc)* fin, fragile; *(dress, cloth)* léger **2** *(excuse)* faible, pauvre; *(evidence, alibi)* peu convaincant; *(novel, plot)* faible; **to condemn sb on the flimsiest evidence** condamner qn en s'appuyant sur des preuves très peu convaincantes

N **1** *(paper)* papier *m* pelure **2** *Journ (copy)* copie *f* (de reporter)

flinch [flɪntʃ] VI **1** *(shy away)* **not to f. from doing sth** ne pas hésiter à faire qch; **she didn't f. from carrying out her duty** elle ne s'est pas dérobée à son devoir **2** *(with pain)* tressaillir (**with** de); **to bear pain without flinching** supporter la douleur sans broncher; **I flinched at the thought of it** ça m'a fait tressaillir d'y penser; **the very thought of telling her about it made him f.** la simple pensée de lui en parler le faisait frémir

fling [flɪŋ] N **1** *(throw)* jet *m*, coup *m*

2 *Fam (attempt)* **I'll have a f. at it** je vais essayer; **to give sth a f., to have a f. at sth** essayer qch; **to have a f. at doing sth** essayer de faire qch; **he had given French a f. a few years before** il avait essayé de se mettre au français quelques années auparavant

3 *(dance)* **(highland) f.** = pas *m* seul écossais

4 *Fam (impulsive behaviour)* **to have one's f.** faire la fête; **the summer seemed to be having one last f.** l'été semblait avoir un dernier sursaut

5 *Fam (affair)* **to have a f.** avoir une aventure (**with** avec qn)

VT *(pt, pp* **flung** [flʌŋ]*)* jeter; *(ball etc)* lancer; **to f. sb into prison** jeter qn en prison; **to f. oneself into sb's arms/an armchair** se jeter dans les bras de qn/un fauteuil; **to f. oneself into a task** se lancer dans une tâche; **to f. one's arms around sb** jeter ses bras autour de qn

► **fling about** VT SEP *(objects)* jeter de côté et d'autre; **to f. one's arms about** gesticuler violemment; **to f. one's money about** mener grand train

► **fling away** VT SEP *(throw)* jeter de côté; *(get rid of)* se débarrasser de; **to f. one's money away** gaspiller son argent

► **fling back** VT SEP *(sheets, blanket)* rejeter; **to f. back one's head** rejeter la tête en arrière

► **fling down** VT SEP *(to the ground, floor)* jeter par terre; *(blinds, hatch)* refermer brusquement; *Fig (ultimatum)* imposer; **he flung the books down on the table** il a jeté les livres sur la table; **f. down my keys, will you?** lance-moi mes clés, s'il te plaît

▸ **fling off** VT SEP **1** *(rid oneself of) (impositions, restrictions)* se débarrasser de; *Lit* **to f. off the yoke of tyranny** secouer le joug de la tyrannie **2** *(take off) (one's coat etc)* retirer brusquement

▸ **fling open** VT SEP *(window, door etc)* ouvrir toute grande

▸ **fling out** VT SEP **1** *(throw out)* jeter dehors; *(get rid of) (unwanted object)* jeter, balancer; *(bill, legislation, case)* rejeter; *Fam* **to f. sb out** flanquer qn à la porte; **she flung him out of the house** elle l'a flanqué à la porte, elle l'a viré de chez elle **2** *(extend)* **to f. out one's arm** étendre le bras d'un grand geste; **he flung out a fist and knocked his assailant out** il mit son assaillant K-O d'un coup de poing; **he flung out a foot and turned the ball into the net** il tendit le pied et dévia la balle vers le filet

▸ **fling up** VT SEP **1** *(throw in air)* jeter en l'air; **he flung the bag up to her** il lui a envoyé le sac **2** *Fam (possibility)* entraîner; **what did your investigations f. up?** qu'ont produit vos recherches?

flint [flɪnt] N *Miner* silex *m*; *(for making fire)* pierre *f* à feu; *(for cigarette lighter)* pierre à briquet; *Hist* **f. tools** outils *mpl* en silex taillés

▸▸ **f. glass** flint(-glass) *m*

flinty ['flɪntɪ] ADJ **1** *(of or resembling flint)* de silex **2** *Fig (heart)* de pierre, dur; *(person)* au cœur de pierre; *(expression, manner)* dur; **cold f. eyes** un regard froid et dur

flip[1] [flɪp] N *(flick)* chiquenaude *f*, pichenette *f*

VT (-pp-) **1** *(flick) (pancake, card etc)* retourner vivement; **to f. a coin** *(to decide)* jouer à pile ou face; **she flipped the coin into the air** elle lança la pièce en l'air; **he flipped the leaflet into the bin** il balança le prospectus dans la poubelle; *Fam* **to f. one's lid** *(get very angry)* sortir de ses gonds, piquer une crise; *(go crazy)* perdre la boule; **he absolutely flipped his lid at us** il a piqué une drôle de crise contre nous **2** *Elec (switch)* basculer **3** *Fam (turn over) (record)* retourner

VI *Sl* **1** *(get very angry)* sortir de ses gonds, piquer une crise; *(go crazy)* perdre la boule **2** *(become ecstatic)* flasher, flipper (**over** sur)

▸▸ **f. card** *(as prompt)* aide-mémoire *m inv*; **f. chart** tableau *m* à feuilles; *Fam* **f. side** *(of record)* face *f* B; *Fig (of policy, situation)* face *f* cachée; **there is, of course, a f. side to the expansion of industry** l'expansion de l'industrie a, comme toute médaille, son revers

▸ **flip open** VT SEP ouvrir

▸ **flip out** VI **1** *esp Am Fam (get very angry)* sortir de ses gonds, piquer une crise **2** *(of end of lorry)* déraper

▸ **flip over** VT SEP *(turn over) (record)* retourner; **to f. over the pages of a magazine** feuilleter les pages d'un magazine

VI *(turn over)* se retourner

▸ **flip through** VT INSEP *(book)* feuilleter; *(photos, posters, wallpaper samples etc)* jeter un coup d'œil à

flip[2] ADJ *Fam (flippant)* léger, désinvolte, cavalier

flip-flop N **1** *(sandal) (usu pl)* **flip-flops** tongs *fpl* **2** *(jump)* saut *m* périlleux; *(change of opinion)* volte-face *f inv* **3** *(circuit)* (circuit *m*) basculeur *m* monostable

▸▸ *Electron* **f. circuit** (circuit) basculeur monostable

flippancy ['flɪpənsɪ] N légèreté *f*, désinvolture *f*

flippant ['flɪpənt] ADJ désinvolte, cavalier

flippantly ['flɪpəntlɪ] ADV *(to say)* d'un ton ou d'une manière désinvolte

flipper ['flɪpər] N *(of whale, seal)* nageoire *f*; *(of scuba diver etc)* palme *f*

flipping ['flɪpɪŋ] *Br Fam* ADJ fichu; **don't be such a f. idiot!** arrête donc de faire l'imbécile!

ADV sacrément; **it's f. hot** il fait sacrément chaud; **he's so f. stupid** il est bête comme ses pieds; **not f. likely!** il n'y a pas de risque!

flip-top ADJ *(carton, pack)* à rabat

flirt [flɜːt] N flirteur, -euse

VI faire du charme (**with sb** à qn); **to f. with danger/Marxism** flirter avec le danger/le Marxisme; **to f. with an idea/death** jouer avec une idée/la mort

flirtation [flɜː'teɪʃən] N flirt *m*; **to have a f. with sb** flirter avec qn; **to have a f. with danger/an idea** jouer avec le danger/une idée

flirtatious [flɜː'teɪʃəs] ADJ *Fam* charmeur; *(look, smile)* enjôleur; **to be f. with sb** faire du charme à qn

flirtatiously [flɜː'teɪʃəslɪ] ADV *(to say sth)* d'un ton charmeur; **she smiled f. at him** elle lui fit un sourire enjôleur

flit [flɪt] N *Br Fam* **to do a (moonlight) f.** déménager à la cloche de bois

VI (-tt-) **1** *(of bird etc)* **to f. by** passer légèrement; **to f. about** aller et venir d'un pas léger; *Fig* **to f. from one thing to another** passer d'une chose à l'autre **2** *Scot, North Eng (move house)* déménager **3** *Br Fam (leave stealthily)* déménager à la cloche de bois

flitch [flɪtʃ] N *(of bacon)* flèche *f*

float [fləʊt] N **1** *(of boiler, carburettor etc)* flotteur *m*

2 *Fishing (on fishing line, net)* flotteur *m*, bouchon *m*

3 *Biol (of aquatic plant)* flotteur *m*; *(of fish)* vessie *f* natatoire

4 *(raft)* radeau *m*; *(floating logs)* train *m* (de bois); *(swimming aid)* flotteur *m*

5 *Theat* **the floats** *(footlights)* la rampe

6 *(vehicle, in carnival etc)* char *m* de carnaval; *Br* **milk f.** voiture *f* de livraison du lait

7 *Com esp Am (petty cash)* petite caisse *f*; *esp Br (in cash till etc)* fond *m* de caisse; *(advance)* avance *f*; **they gave me a f. of £200 for the trip** *(advance)* ils m'ont donné une viatique de 200 livres, ils m'ont donné 200 livres pour le voyage

8 *esp Am Culin (drink)* = soda *m*, jus *m* de fruit ou milk-shake *m* dans lequel on ajoute une boule de glace

9 *St Exch* flottant *m*; **clean f.** taux *mpl* de change libres ou flottants; **dirty f.** taux *mpl* de change concertés

VI **1** *(in water)* flotter; *(of boat)* être à flot; *Swimming* faire la planche; **to f. down the stream** descendre le courant

2 *(move as if in water)* **to f. to the surface** revenir à la surface; **to f. in the air** planer dans l'air; **she floated out of the room** elle est sortie de la pièce d'un pas léger; **he seems to just f. through life** *(has no worries)* il semble ne jamais avoir de soucis; *(has no goals)* il semble se laisser porter par les événements

3 *Tech (of part of machine)* avoir du jeu

VT **1** *(timber etc)* flotter; *(launch) (ship)* mettre à flot ou à l'eau; *(refloat) (ship)* renflouer **2** *Com (company etc)* lancer; *Fin (loan)* émettre, lancer; *(idea, rumour)* lancer; *(proposal)* introduire; **to f. sth on the Stock Exchange** introduire qch en Bourse

▸▸ *Am* **f. bowl** *(in engine)* cuve *f*; **f. chamber** *(in engine)* cuve; **f. glass** verre *m* flotté

▸ **float about, float around** VI *(of news etc)* circuler, courir; *(in a daze etc)* flotter; **there were rumours floating about that …** le bruit courait que …; *Fam* **he's floating**

around somewhere il traîne dans les parages; *Fam* **he just floats around all day** il traîne sans rien faire toute la journée

▸ **float off** VI *(of ship etc)* se déséchouer

VT INSEP *(of ship etc)* **the boat floated off the sandbank at high tide** à marée haute, le bateau s'est dégagé du banc de sable

VT SEP *(wrecked ship etc)* renflouer, déséchouer; **they floated off the sandbank** ils ont remis à flot ou renfloué le bateau échoué sur un banc de sable

floating ['fləʊtɪŋ] ADJ **1** flottant, à flot; **this ship is, in effect, a f. hotel** en fait, ce bateau est un hôtel flottant **2** *(population)* flottant, fluctuant; *Fin (currency, exchange rate)* flottant; *(capital)* circulant, mobile; *Tech (bearing)* flottant

N *(of ship)* mise *f* à flot; *(of wrecked ship etc)* renflouage *m*; *(of timber)* flottage *m*; *Com (of company etc)* lancement *m*; *(onto stock market)* introduction *f* en Bourse; *Fin (of loan, bonds)* émission *f*

▸▸ *Acct* **f. assets** actif *m* circulant; **f. bridge** pont *m* de bateaux ou de radeaux; *Banking* **f. charge** nantissement *m* général; **f. crane** ponton-grue *m*, *pl* pontons-grues; *Fin* **f. debt** dette *f* flottante ou non consolidée; *Culin* **f. islands** île *f* flottante; *Med* **f. kidney** rein *m* flottant; **f. off** *(of wrecked ship etc)* renflouage; *Comput* **f. point** virgule *f* flottante; *Fin* **f. rate** taux *m* flottant; *Anat* **f. ribs** côtes *fpl* flottantes; *Pol* **f. vote** *(voters)* indécis *mpl*, électorat *m* flottant; *Pol* **f. voter** électeur, -trice indécis(e); *Comput* **f. window** fenêtre *f* flottante

floating-point ADJ *Comput* à ou en virgule flottante

▸▸ **f. arithmetic** arithmétique *f* en virgule flottante; **f. notation** notation *f* en virgule flottante; **f. processor** coprocesseur *m* arithmétique

floating-rate ADJ *Fin* à taux flottant

▸▸ **f. bond** obligation *f* à taux flottant ou variable; **f. interest** intérêt *m* à taux flottant; **f. investment** investissement *m* à taux flottant ou variable; **f. note** effet *m* à taux flottant; **f. securities** titres *mpl* à taux flottant ou variable

flock[1] [flɒk] N *(of sheep, geese)* troupeau *m*; *(of animals)* bande *f*, *(of birds)* volée *f*; **a pastor and his f.** un pasteur et ses ouailles *fpl*; **a f. of visitors** une foule de visiteurs

VI *(gather)* s'attrouper, s'assembler; **everybody is flocking to see the exhibition** tout le monde vient en masse pour voir l'exposition; **in summer people f. to the sea** en été les gens vont en foule au bord de la mer; **people flocked towards the park** les gens se sont dirigés en foule vers le parc; **crowds flocked to the stadium** des foules de gens sont allés au stade

flock[2] N *(material)* bourre *f* (de laine)

▸▸ **f. mattress** matelas *m* en bourre de laine; **f. wallpaper** papier *m* tontisse

▸ **flock together** VI s'assembler

floe [fləʊ] N *(ice)* **f.** masse *f* de glaces flottantes, banquise *f*

flog [flɒg] VT (-gg-) **1** *(person)* flageller, fouetter; *(with stick)* frapper à coups de bâton; **to f. a horse** cravacher un cheval; *Fam Fig* **to f. a dead horse** se dépenser en pure perte; *Fam Fig* **to f. a subject to death** s'étendre indéfiniment sur une question; **we've flogged the subject to death** nous avons épuisé le sujet **2** *Br Fam (sell)* vendre; *(sell off quickly)* bazarder; *(stolen goods etc)* fourguer

▸ **flog off** VT SEP *Br Fam (sell off)* bazarder

flood [flʌd] N inondation *f*; **the river was in f.** la rivière débordait; **the victims of the f.** les inondés *mpl*; *Bible* **the F.** le Déluge; **the floods of the Nile** les crues *fpl* du Nil; **a f. of**

light des flots *mpl* de lumière; **floods of tears/abuse** un torrent de larmes/d'injures; **VT** *(land, the bathroom etc)* inonder; *Naut (hold)* noyer; *Agr (for irrigation)* irriguer; *Aut (carburettor)* noyer; *(engine)* étouffer, noyer; **the river flooded its banks** la rivière est sortie de son lit, la rivière a débordé; **to be flooded** *(of ship)* être envahi par l'eau; *(of house)* être inondé; **to f. the market with …** inonder le marché de …; **to be flooded with letters/telephone calls** être submergé de lettres/de coups de téléphone; **flooded with light** *(room)* inondé de lumière **VI** *(of river etc) (overflow)* déborder; *(be in flood)* être en crue; *Fig* **the sun's rays came flooding through the window** les rayons du soleil entraient à flots par la fenêtre; **spectators were flooding into the stadium** les spectateurs affluaient dans le stade ▸▸ **f. plain** plaine *f* d'inondation, lit *m* majeur; **f. tide** flux *m*, marée *f* montante; **f. water** inondation; **the f. waters receded** les inondations ont diminué ▸ **flood back** **VI** *(return to memory)* revenir (à l'esprit); **it all came flooding back** tout m'est/leur est/*etc* soudain revenu; **all the feelings came flooding back** un flot d'émotions familières m'envahit/l'envahit/*etc*; **it all comes flooding back** tout me/te/*etc* revient, tout à coup ▸ **flood in** **VI** *(of light, water)* arriver à flots; *(of correspondence, people, thanks)* affluer ▸ **flood out** **VT SEP** *(force to leave)* forcer à partir; **many families have been flooded out** les inondations ont forcé beaucoup de familles à évacuer leur maison **VI** *(of people)* sortir à flots; **light flooded out of the open casement** des flots de lumière s'échappaient de la fenêtre ouverte; **money flooded out of the country** il y eut d'énormes fuites de capitaux

flooded ['flʌdɪd] **ADJ** *(land)* inondé; *(carburettor)* noyé

floodgate ['flʌdgeɪt] **N** vanne *f* (de décharge), porte *f* d'écluse; **to open/close the floodgates** lever/mettre les vannes; *Fig* **to open the floodgates to immigration/immorality/**etc ouvrir les vannes de l'immigration/l'immoralité/*etc*

flooding ['flʌdɪŋ] **N** *(of land etc)* inondation *f*, *(of river etc)* débordement *m*; *Agr (for irrigation)* irrigation *f*, *Naut (of hold)* noyage *m*; **road liable to f.** *(road sign)* route inondable; **there has been f. in many parts of the country** il y a eu des inondations dans de nombreuses régions

floodlight ['flʌdlaɪt] **N** projecteur *m*; *Phot* (lampe *f*) flood *f*; **under** *or* **by f.** à la lumière des projecteurs **VT** *(pt, pp* **floodlighted** *or* **floodlit**) illuminer aux projecteurs

floodlighting ['flʌdlaɪtɪŋ] **N** illumination *f* aux projecteurs; *(lights)* projecteurs *mpl*

floodlit ['flʌdlɪt] **ADJ** illuminé (aux projecteurs)

floor [flɔːr] **N 1** sol *m*; *(wooden)* plancher *m*; *(of Stock Exchange, the House)* parquet *m*; *(of studio)* plateau *m*; **parquet f.** parquet *m*; **tiled f.** carrelage *m*; *Fam* **to wipe the f. with sb** battre qn à plate(s) couture(s); **to take the f.** *(at meeting)* prendre la parole; *(at dance)* se joindre aux danseurs; **Mr Taylor has the f.** la parole est à M. Taylor; **questions from the f.** *(at meeting)* questions du public; **to give sb the f.** donner la parole à qn; **dance f.** piste *f* de danse; *Ind* **the factory** *or* **shop f.** l'atelier *m* **2** *(storey)* étage *m*; **house on two floors** maison avec étage; *Br* **ground f.** rez-de-chaussée *m inv*; **first f.** *Br* premier étage, *Am* rez-de-chaussée; **to live on the fifth f.** *Br* habiter au cinquième, *Am* habiter au qua-

trième; **we live on the same f.** nous habitons sur le même palier, nous sommes voisins de palier; **on the f. above/below** à l'étage du dessus/dessous; **we're ten floors up** nous sommes au dixième étage; **their offices are two floors down** leurs bureaux sont deux étages plus bas **3** *(of ocean)* fond *m*; *Min (of gallery)* sole *f*; **on the ocean f.** au fond de l'océan; **the forest f.** le sol de la forêt **VT 1** *(room) (with floorboards)* planchéier; *(with wooden blocks)* parqueter; *(with tiles)* carreler **2** *(knock down) (opponent)* terrasser, envoyer au tapis **3** *Fam (of problem, question)* **to f. sb** réduire qn à quia, clouer le bec à qn ▸▸ *TV* **f. assistant** assistant, -ante de plateau; **f. cleaner** (produit *m*) nettoyant *m* pour sols; **f. clerk** *(in hotel)* responsable *m* d'étage; *TV* **f. crew** personnel *m* de plateau; **f. housekeeper** *(in hotel)* gouvernante *f* d'étage; **f. manager** *(in department store)* chef *m* de rayon; *TV* régisseur, -euse de plateau; **f. plan** plan *m*; **f. polish** encaustique *f*, cire *f*, *Com* **f. price** prix *m* seuil; *Aut* **f. shift** levier *m* (de vitesses) au plancher; **f. show** spectacle *m* de cabaret; **f. tile** carreau *m*; *St Exch* **f. trader** commis *m*; *St Exch* **f. trading** cotation *f* à la criée; **f. waiter** *(in hotel)* garçon *m* d'étage

floorboard ['flɔːbɔːd] **N** planche *f*

floorcloth ['flɔːklɒθ] **N** serpillière *f*

flooring ['flɔːrɪŋ] **N 1** *(action) (with floorboards)* planchéiage *m*; *(with wooden blocks)* parquetage *m*; *(with tiles)* carrelage *m*; *(with large slabs)* dallage *m* **2** *(floor)* plancher *m*; *(tiles)* carrelage *m*

floorspace ['flɔːspeɪs] **N** *(of room etc)* surface *f* (couverte), superficie *f*; *(of vehicle)* surface au plancher; **there was barely enough f. for all of them** il y avait tout juste assez d'espace pour eux tous

floorwalker ['flɔːwɔːkər] **N** *Am* inspecteur, -trice, surveillant, -ante (de magasin)

floozie, floozy ['fluːzɪ] **N** *Fam* pouffiasse *f*

flop [flɒp] **N** *Fam* **1** *(failure)* four *m*, fiasco *m*, bide *m*; *(novel, product)* bide; *(person) (in life)* raté, -ée; *(in film, play)* nul, *f* nulle; **it was a f.** ça a fait un four ou bide, c'était un fiasco **2** *Am (hotel)* hôtel *m* borgne; *(hostel)* asile *m* de nuit **VI** (-pp-) **1** *(fall)* faire plouf, faire floc; *(of person)* se laisser tomber, s'affaler; *(into water)* tomber; **to f. down on(to) a seat** tomber lourdement sur un siège, se laisser tomber comme un sac sur un siège **2** *Fam (fail)* échouer; *(of play, novel, product etc)* faire un bide; *(of jokes, sketch)* tomber à plat

flophouse ['flɒphaʊs] **N** *Am Sl* asile *m* de nuit

floppy ['flɒpɪ] **ADJ** *(hat)* mou; *(garment)* lâche, trop large; **with f. ears** à oreilles pendantes **N** *Comput* disquette *f*, disque *m* souple; **on f.** sur disquette ▸▸ *Comput* **f. disk** disquette *f*; **f. (disk) controller** contrôleur *m* d'unité de disquette; **f. (disk) drive** unité *f* de disquettes

floptical ['flɒptɪk(ə)l] **ADJ** *Comput* ▸▸ **f. disk** *(hard)* disque *m* optique; *(floppy)* disquette *f* optique; **f. drive** *(hard)* unité *f* de disque optique; *(floppy)* unité de disquette optique

flora ['flɔːrə] **N** *(of country, region)* flore *f*; **the f. and fauna of a region** la flore et la faune d'une région

floral ['flɔːrəl] **ADJ** floral, -aux; **dress with a bold f. design** robe *f* à grands ramages ▸▸ **f. tribute** bouquet *m* ou gerbe *f* de fleurs; *(funeral wreath)* couronne *f* de fleurs

floret ['flɒrɪt] **N** *Bot* fleuron *m*

florid ['flɒrɪd] **ADJ** *(style etc)* fleuri, orné à l'excès; *(complexion)* coloré

Florida ['flɒrɪdə] **N** Floride *f*

florin ['flɒrɪn] **N** *Br Hist (coin)* pièce *f* de deux shillings

florist ['flɒrɪst] **N** fleuriste *mf*; **f.'s (shop)** magasin *m* de fleurs; **to go to the f.'s** aller chez le fleuriste

floss [flɒs] **N** *(dental)* **f.** fil *m* (de soie) dentaire **VT** **to f. one's teeth** se nettoyer les dents avec du fil dentaire ▸▸ *Tex* **f. silk** bourre *f* de soie

flotation [fləʊ'teɪʃən] **N 1** *Com (of company)* lancement *m*; *(onto Stock Market)* introduction *f* en Bourse **2** *Fin (of loan)* émission *f*; *(of currency)* flottement *m*

flotilla [flə'tɪlə] **N** *Naut* flottille *f*, *(of small boats)* escadrille *f*

flotsam ['flɒtsəm] **N** épave(s) *f(pl)* flottante(s); **f. and jetsam** choses *fpl* refoulées par la mer; **sometimes the f. and jetsam of a wrecked ship would be washed up on the shore** parfois les restes d'une épave, refoulés par la mer, venaient s'échouer sur la rive; *Fig* **the f. of the war/of society** *(people)* les laissés-pour-compte *mpl* de la guerre/de la société

flounce [flaʊns] **N 1** *(of indignation, impatience)* mouvement *m* vif; **with a f. of her long skirt, she marched out of the room** elle sortit de la pièce d'un pas ferme, en faisant voltiger sa longue jupe **2** *Sewing* volant *m* **VI** **to f. in/out/off** entrer/sortir/partir brusquement; **don't you go flouncing off!** ne te sauve pas si vite! **VT** *Sewing* garnir de volants; **flounced skirt** jupe *f* à volants

flouncy ['flaʊnsɪ] **ADJ** *(dress, skirt)* froufroutant

flounder¹ ['flaʊndər] **N** *(fish)* flet *m*, carrelet *m*

flounder² **VI** *(in water, mud etc)* patauger; **to f. about in the water** se débattre dans l'eau; **to f. along** avancer en trébuchant; **to f. in a speech/course** patauger dans un discours/cours

flour ['flaʊər] **N** farine *f*; **to dust sth with f.** (en)fariner qch; **potato f.** fécule *f* de pommes de terre **VT** (en)fariner, saupoudrer de farine ▸▸ **f. dredger** saupoudreuse *f* à farine; **f. mill** minoterie *f*

flourbin ['flaʊəbɪn] **N** farinière *f*, huche *f*, maie *f*

flourish ['flʌrɪʃ] **N 1** *(in writing, style)* fioriture *f*, *(after signature)* parafe *m* **2** *(gesture)* grand geste *m*; *(of sword)* brandissement *m*; **with a f. of his sword/umbrella** en brandissant son épée/parapluie; **to raise one's hat with a f.** saluer d'un grand coup de chapeau; **to carry things off with a f.** faire les choses avec panache **3** *Mus* fioriture(s) *f(pl)*, ornement *m*; *(of trumpets)* fanfare *f* **VI** *(of plant)* croître, se développer; *(of person, business etc)* être florissant, prospérer; *(of arts)* fleurir; **to f. in sandy soil** se plaire dans un terrain sablonneux; **trade is flourishing** le commerce est prospère **VT** *(sword, stick, newspaper etc)* brandir

flourishing ['flʌrɪʃɪŋ] **ADJ** *(plant, industry etc)* florissant; *(business)* prospère

floury ['flaʊərɪ] **ADJ 1** *(hands etc)* enfariné, couvert de farine **2** *(potatoes, texture etc)* farineux; *(rolls)* saupoudré de farine

flout [flaʊt] **VT** *(person's authority, convention etc)* faire fi de; *(person)* passer outre à la volonté de

> Attention: ne pas confondre avec le verbe **to flaunt**.

FLOW [fləʊ] **N 1** *(movement) (of liquid)* coulée *f*; *(of river, blood)* écoulement *m*; *Elec (of current)* passage *m*; *(of air, fuel etc)* passage, arrivée *f*; *(of tide)* flot *m*, flux *m*; *Fin (of capital)* mouvement *m*; *(of information)* circulation *f*; **a steady f. of immigrants** un flot ininterrompu d'immigrés; **a f. of ideas/proposals** un flot d'idées/de propositions; **f. of funds** mouvement de fonds; **f. of money** flux monétaire; **the speaker was interrupted in full f.** l'orateur a été interrompu en plein discours; **to follow the f. of sb's argument** suivre le fil de l'argumentation de qn; **to go with the f.** suivre le mouvement
2 *(volume) (of liquid)* volume *m*; *(of river, pump, electric current)* débit *m*; **the f. of traffic** le flux de la circulation; **there was a heavy f. of traffic** il y avait beaucoup de circulation
3 *(stream)* courant *m*, cours *m* (d'eau); *(of lava)* coulée *f*; *(of blood etc)* flot *m*; *Physiol* **menstrual f.** règles *fpl*
4 *Sewing (of garment)* drapé *m*
VI 1 *(of water, river)* couler, s'écouler; *(of electric current, blood in veins)* circuler; *(of traffic, crowd)* s'écouler; *(of hair etc)* flotter; *(of tide)* monter, remonter; *Fin (of capital, money)* circuler; **to f. into the sea** se verser dans la mer; **lava that flows down the mountain** lave qui s'écoule le long de la montagne; **the tears flowed down her cheeks** les larmes coulaient sur ses joues; **blood flowed from the wound** le sang s'écoulait de la blessure; **blood flowing to the head** sang qui afflue à la tête; *Prov* **land flowing with milk and honey** pays *m* de cocagne, terre *f* d'abondance; **you can feel the energy f.** on sent circuler l'énergie; **the work is flowing nicely** le travail suit bien son cours; **the ideas are really flowing today** les idées affluent aujourd'hui
2 *(of literary style, prose)* couler; **to keep the conversation flowing** entretenir la conversation; **these two paragraphs don't f.** ces deux paragraphes ne s'enchaînent pas bien; **the film flows very nicely** tout s'enchaîne vraiment bien dans le film
3 *(result)* dériver, découler (**from** de); **God from whom all blessings f.** Dieu, de qui découlent toutes les grâces
▸▸**f. chart** organigramme *m*; **f. diagram** organigramme, graphique *m* d'évolution; *Comput* ordinogramme *m*; *Comput* **f. path** branche *f* de traitement
▸ **flow away VI** *(of liquid)* s'écouler; **the small craft flowed away on the tide** le petit bateau s'éloigna dans le flot de la marée
▸ **flow back VI** *(of water)* refluer; *(in pipe etc)* regorger
▸ **flow in VI** *(of liquid)* entrer; *(of people, money)* affluer; **the stream flowed in to the river** le ruisseau se jetait dans la rivière
▸ **flow out VI** *(of liquid)* sortir, s'écouler; *(of people)* partir; *(of money)* disparaître; **people flew out of the country in their thousands** les gens quittèrent le pays par milliers

flower ['flaʊər] **N 1** fleur *f*; **in f.** *(of plant)* en fleur; **in full f.** en plein épanouissement; **to burst into f.** fleurir; *Fig* **in the (first) f. of youth** dans la première fleur de la jeunesse; **to put flowers on a grave** fleurir une tombe; **no flowers by request** ni fleurs ni couronnes
2 *Chem* **flowers of sulphur** fleurs *fpl* de soufre **3** *Fig (best part) (of an army etc)* fine fleur *f*, crème *f*
VI *(of plant) (action)* fleurir; *(state)* être en fleur; *(of art etc)* fleurir, s'épanouir
▸▸**f. arrangement** *(art)* art *m* floral; *(example)* composition *f* florale; **f. arranging** art floral; **f. child** hippie *mf* *(surtout des années soixante)*; **f. garden** jardin *m* d'agrément; **f. girl** *(selling flowers)* marchande *f* de fleurs; *(at wedding)* = petite fille *f* qui porte des fleurs dans un mariage; ≃ demoiselle *f* d'honneur; **f. head** capitule *m*; **f. market** marché *m* aux fleurs; **f. people** hippies *mpl* *(surtout des années soixante)*; **f. power** = pacifisme *m* prôné par les hippies, surtout dans les années soixante; **f. seller** *(in street)* marchand, -ande de fleurs; **f. show** exposition *f* de fleurs; *(outdoors, on a large scale)* floralies *fpl*; **f. vase** vase *m* à fleurs

flowerbed ['flaʊəbed] **N** plate-bande *f*, *pl* plates-bandes; *(round)* corbeille *f*

-flowered ['flaʊəd] **SUFF** white/yellow/etc**f.** à fleurs blanches/jaunes/etc; **many-f.** multiflore

flowering ['flaʊərɪŋ] **ADJ 1** *(in flower) (garden, plant)* fleuri, en fleur **2** *(that flowers) (shrub)* à fleurs
N *(of plant)* fleuraison *f*; *Fig* **her late f. as an artist** son épanouissement tardif en tant qu'artiste

flowerpot ['flaʊəpɒt] **N** pot *m* de fleurs; *(ornamental)* cache-pot *m inv*

flowery ['flaʊərɪ] **ADJ 1** *(meadow)* fleuri; *(dress, carpet)* à fleurs **2** *(language, speech)* fleuri

flowing ['fləʊɪŋ] **ADJ** *(style etc)* coulant, fluide; *(movement)* fluide; *(hair)* tombant (dans le cou); *(beard)* long; **a fast f. stream** un ruisseau au cours rapide

flowline ['fləʊlaɪn] **N** *(on organization chart)* ligne *f* de jonction de symboles

flowmeter ['fləʊmiːtər] **N** *(for liquid etc)* débitmètre *m*, indicateur *m* d'écoulement *ou* de débit

flown PP *see* **fly**[3]

flu [fluː] **N** *Med* grippe *f*; **I've got (the) f.** j'ai la grippe, je suis grippé; **a bad dose** *or* **case of (the) f.** une mauvaise grippe
▸▸**f. epidemic** épidémie *f* de grippe; **f. jab** vaccin *m* contre la grippe; **f. virus** virus *m* de la grippe

flub [flʌb] *Am Fam* **N** gaffe *f*, bourde *f*
VI (-bb-) faire une gaffe, gaffer
VT to f. a question répondre de travers à une question

fluctuate ['flʌktjʊeɪt] **VI 1** fluctuer; *(of pulse, heartbeat)* être irrégulier; *(of conditions etc)* varier; *Fin (of exchange rate, share prices)* fluctuer; **to f. between sth and sth** osciller entre qch et qch **2** *(of person) (in one's opinions etc)* vaciller, balancer

fluctuating ['flʌktjʊeɪtɪŋ] **ADJ** *(temperature etc)* variable; *(rate, prices)* oscillant, fluctuant; *(heartbeat)* irrégulier; *(interest)* variable, fluctuant

fluctuation [flʌktjʊ'eɪʃən] **N** *(of temperature etc)* variations *fpl*; *(of support, interest)* fluctuation(s) *f(pl)*; *Fin* **exchange f.** fluctuation(s) *f(pl)* du change

flue [fluː] **N 1** *Constr* tuyau *m* de cheminée, conduit *m* de fumée **2** *Mus (of organ)* bouche *f* (de tuyau d'orgue)
▸▸**f. boiler** chaudière *f* à tubes-foyers; **f. brush** hérisson *m inv*; *Mus* **f. pipe** *(of organ)* tuyau à bouche; **f. stop** jeu *m* de flûte

fluency ['fluːənsɪ] **N** *(of speech, style)* facilité *f*; **her f. in French** son aisance à s'exprimer en français

fluent ['fluːənt] **ADJ** *(speech etc)* coulant, facile; **to be a f. speaker** s'exprimer avec aisance; **he is a f. speaker of French, he speaks f. French, he is f. in French** il parle le français couramment

fluently ['fluːəntlɪ] **ADV** *(to speak a language, read a language)* couramment; *(to express oneself)* avec facilité, avec aisance

fluff [flʌf] **N 1** *(of fabric)* duvet *m*; *(of wool)* coton *m*; **a bit of f.** une peluche; *Old-fash-*ioned *Br Fam (girl)* une poule; **(pieces of) f.** *(under bed etc)* moutons *mpl* **2** *(of rabbit etc)* fourrure *f* douce; *(of chicks)* duvet *m* **3** *Theat Fam (mistake)* raté *m* **4** *(trifle)* frivolités *fpl*
VT 1 = fluff out, fluff up 2 *Fam (entrance, line, exam, interview)* rater, louper; *Sport* **to f. a shot** rater un coup
▸ **fluff out, fluff up VT SEP** *(one's hair, cushions)* faire bouffer; **to f. up its feathers** *(of bird)* hérisser ses plumes; **f. up the potatoes with a fork** fouetter la purée avec une fourchette

fluffy ['flʌfɪ] **ADJ** *(sheet)* pelucheux; *(woollen material) (naturally)* duveteux; *(after wear)* pelucheux; *(chick, beard, hair etc)* duveteux; *(clouds)* cotonneux; *(mashed potatoes, cake mixture)* léger et mousseux
▸▸**f. toy** (jouet *m* en) peluche *f*

fluid ['fluːɪd] **ADJ** *(substance)* fluide, liquide; *Tech (transmission)* fluide; *(style etc)* coulant, facile; *(movement, grace)* fluide, coulant; *(opinions etc)* changeant, inconstant; **industry in a f. state** industrie en voie de transformation rapide
N fluide *m*, liquide *m*; **body fluids** sécrétions *fpl*; *Med* **fluids only** liquides uniquement
▸▸*Tech* **f. clutch** embrayage *m* hydrodynamique; **f. ounce** *(in UK)* = 0,028 litre; *(in US)* = 0,03 litre

fluidity [fluː'ɪdɪtɪ] **N** *(of style etc)* fluidité *f*, aisance *f*; *(of opinions etc)* caractère *m* changeant *ou* fluctuant

fluke[1] [fluːk] **N 1** *(fish)* flet *m* **2** *(worm) (in liver)* douve *f*
▸▸**f. worm** *(in liver)* douve

fluke[2] **N 1** *Naut (of anchor)* patte *f*, aile *f* **2** *(of whale)* **flukes** nageoires *fpl*

fluke[3] *Fam* **N** *(coincidence)* hasard *m*; *(stroke of luck)* coup *m* de veine, coup de pot; **it was a pure f.** c'était un véritable coup de veine *ou* de pot; *(just coincidence)* c'était un pur hasard; **his success was due to a f.** c'est un hasard qu'il ait réussi; **by a pure f.** purement par hasard
ADJ that was a f. goal il a marqué ce but complètement par hasard; **it was a f. guess** c'est par hasard qu'il a deviné juste

fluky ['fluːkɪ] **ADJ** *Fam (person)* chanceux; **that was a f. goal** il a marqué ce but complètement par hasard; **it was a f. guess** c'est par hasard qu'il a deviné juste

flume [fluːm] **N 1** *(of watermill)* buse *f* **2** *(for logs etc)* canal *m* d'amenée; *(water chute in amusement park)* toboggan *m* **3** *Am (ravine)* ravin *m*

flummox ['flʌməks] **VT** *Fam* réduire à quia

flung PT, PP *see* **fling**

flunk [flʌŋk] *esp Am Fam* **VI** *(in exam)* se faire recaler, se faire coller
VT 1 *(of teacher) (person in exam)* recaler, coller **2** *(of student) (exam)* rater, se faire coller *ou* recaler à

flunkey ['flʌŋkɪ] **N** *Pej* laquais *m*

fluorescence [fluə'resəns] **N** fluorescence *f*

fluorescent [fluə'resənt] **ADJ** fluorescent
▸▸**f. lighting** éclairage *m* au néon

fluoridation [fluərɪ'deɪʃən] **N** *Chem* fluoration *f*

fluoride ['fluəraɪd] **N** *Chem* fluorure *m*
▸▸**f. toothpaste** dentifrice *m* au fluor

fluorine ['fluəriːn] **N** *Chem* fluor *m*

fluoroscope ['fluərəskəʊp] **N** *Med* fluoroscope *m*

flurry ['flʌrɪ] **N 1** *(of snow)* rafale *f* **2** *(agitation)* agitation *f*, bouleversement *m*, émoi *m*; **f. of excitement/protest** vague *f* d'excitation/de protestations
VT to get flurried perdre la tête

flush[1] **N 1** *(of lavatory)* chasse *f* (d'eau); *(of* *drain)* curage *m;* **to pull the f.** tirer la chasse (d'eau) **2** *(of light, beauty etc)* éclat *m; (of emotion etc)* accès *m; (of enthusiasm)* élan *m;* **in the first f. of victory** dans l'ivresse de la victoire; **in the first f. of youth** dans le premier éclat de la jeunesse **3** *(redness of face)* rougeur *f; Med* suffusion *f;* **the words brought a f. to her cheeks** ces mots l'ont fait rougir

vt 1 *(water)* faire jaillir; **to f. a drain** donner une chasse à un égout; **to f. the lavatory** tirer la chasse d'eau; **to f. sth down the lavatory** jeter qch dans les toilettes (et tirer la chasse d'eau) **2** *(redden)* faire rougir; **the exercise had flushed their cheeks** l'exercice leur avait fait monter le sang au visage

vi 1 *(of person)* rougir (**with** de); **he** *or* **his face flushed** il a rougi; **she flushed crimson** elle est devenue écarlate **2** *(in lavatory) (of person)* tirer la chasse d'eau; **the lavatory isn't flushing properly** la chasse d'eau ne fonctionne pas bien

▸ **flush away vt sep** *(dispose of in lavatory)* jeter dans les toilettes (et tirer la chasse d'eau)

vi it wouldn't f. away ça ne voulait pas partir

flush² n *Cards (in poker)* flush *m,* longue couleur *f;* **straight f.** quinte *f* flush

flush³ adj **1** *(surface etc)* de niveau; *(door, lock etc)* encastré; *(screw, nail)* noyé; *(rivet)* à tête noyée *ou* perdue; **to be f. with sth** être à fleur de qch, être de niveau avec qch; **f. mounted** monté à fleur; **f. with the ground** à ras de sol **2** *Fam* **to be f. (with money)** *(of person)* être en fonds

adv 1 *Typ* **f. left/right** justifié à gauche/droite **2** *(fit, be positioned)* **this piece has to fit f. into the frame** ce morceau doit être de niveau avec la charpente

flush⁴ vt *(in hunting)* *(partridge etc)* (faire) lever, faire partir

▸ **flush out vt sep 1** *(force to emerge)* forcer à sortir, faire sortir de force; *(force to reveal oneself)* faire se trahir; **they used tear gas to f. the students out** ils ont utilisé des gaz lacrymogènes pour faire sortir les étudiants **2** *(clean)* rincer par circulation d'eau; **to f. out a drain** donner une chasse à un égout

flushed [flʌʃt] adj *(face)* empourpré, congestionné; **f. with anger/joy** rouge de colère/plaisir; **f. with success** exalté par le succès

fluster ['flʌstər] n agitation *f,* trouble *m;* **in a f.** paniqué

vt *(person)* décontenancer; *(cause to panic)* faire perdre la tête à; *(make nervous)* rendre nerveux; **to get flustered** se troubler, perdre contenance

vi he doesn't f. easily il ne se trouble pas facilement, il ne perd pas facilement contenance

flustered ['flʌstəd] adj *(look)* paniqué; *(reaction)* de panique; **it was a rather f. Jim that came out of the meeting** Jim était plutôt décontenancé quand il est sorti de la réunion

flute [fluːt] n **1** *Mus* flûte *f* traversière; **transverse f.** flûte traversière; *Theat* **the Magic F.** la Flûte Enchantée **2** *(groove)* *(of column)* cannelure *f* **3** *(glass)* flûte *f*
▸▸ **f. glass** flûte; **f. player** joueur, -euse de flûte, flûtiste *mf;* **f. stop** *(on organ)* jeu *m* de flûte

fluted ['fluːtɪd] adj *(wood etc)* à cannelures; *(column)* cannelé

fluting ['fluːtɪŋ] n *(no pl)* *(grooves)* cannelures *fpl*

flutist ['fluːtɪst] n *esp Am Mus* flûtiste *mf*

flutter ['flʌtər] n **1** *(of bird)* volettement *m; (of wings, eyelids)* battement *m; (of heart)* palpitation *f, (of flag etc)* flottement *m; (of*

sound) pulsation *f, (on tape)* pompage *m;* **she thinks she can get whatever she wants with a f. of her eyelashes** elle croit pouvoir obtenir tout ce qu'elle veut d'un simple battement de cils

2 *Fig (agitation)* agitation *f,* trouble *m;* **to be in a f. of excitement** *or Fam* **all in a f.** être tout en émoi

3 *Br Fam (bet)* **to have a little f.** faire un ou deux petits paris; *(in gambling house etc)* risquer de petites sommes au jeu; **to have a f. on the horses** risquer de petites sommes au tiercé

vi *(of birds, insects) (fly)* voleter; *(flap wings)* battre des ailes; *(of flag etc)* flotter, s'agiter (au vent); *(of heart)* palpiter; *(of pulse)* battre irrégulièrement; **to make sb's heart f.** faire tressaillir le cœur de qn; **the letter fluttered to the ground** la lettre a volé par terre; **the pigeons fluttered off** *or* **away** les pigeons s'éloignèrent en voletant; **he was fluttering about nervously** il s'agitait nerveusement; **she fluttered happily round the house** elle virevoletait gaiement dans toute la maison

vt to f. its wings *(of bird)* battre des ailes; **she fluttered her eyelashes at him** elle l'a regardé en battant des cils

fluvial ['fluːvɪəl] adj fluvial, -aux

flux [flʌks] n **1** *Med (of blood etc)* flux *m* **2** *(constant change)* changement *m* continuel; **to be in a (constant) state of f.** être sujet à des changements continuels **3** *Phys* flux *m* **4** *Metal* fondant *m,* flux *m;* **gold f.** *(in glassmaking)* aventurine *f*

fluxion ['flʌkʃən] n *Med (of blood etc)* fluxion *f*

fluxmeter ['flʌksmiːtər] n *Phys* fluxmètre *m*

fly¹, *pl* **flies** [flaɪ, -z] n **1** *(insect)* mouche *f;* **they were dying** *or* **dropping like flies** ils tombaient comme des mouches; **he wouldn't hurt a f.** il ne ferait pas de mal à une mouche; *Fam* **a f. in the ointment** un os; *Fig* **to catch flies** bayer aux corneilles; *Fam* **there are no flies on her** elle n'est pas bête; **I wish I could be a f. on the wall** *(at that interview, meeting etc)* si je pouvais être une petite souris; *TV* **f.-on-the-wall documentary** documentaire *m* intimiste, documentaire avec caméra cachée

2 *Fishing* mouche *f,* **wet-f.** mouche mouillée *ou* noyée; **wet-/dry-f. fishing** pêche *f* à la mouche noyée/sèche
▸▸ **f. agaric** amanite *f* tue-mouches; **f. orchid** *(plant)* ophrys *m* mouche; **f. spray** bombe *f* insecticide; **f. swat(ter)** tapette *f* tue-mouches; **f. whisk** chasse-mouches *m inv*

fly² n **1** *(often in pl)* **flies, f.** *(of trousers)* braguette *f;* **your flies are** *or* **f. is undone** *or* **open** ta braguette est ouverte **2** *(roof)* double toit *m* **3** *Theat* **the flies** les cintres *mpl*

FLY³ *(pt* **flew** [fluː], *pp* **flown** [fləʊn]) **vi 1** *(of bird etc)* voler; **a flock of geese flew across the sky** un troupeau d'oies traversa le ciel à tire d'aile; *Fig, Fam* **the bird has flown** l'oiseau s'est envolé; **to f. high** voler haut; *Fig (of person)* avoir de l'ambition

2 *Aviat (of aircraft, pilot, missile)* voler; *(passenger)* prendre l'avion, voyager en avion; **I've never flown before** c'est la première fois que je prends l'avion; **it's cheaper to f.** il est moins cher de prendre l'avion; **I've never flown in a 747** je n'ai jamais voyagé en 747; **to f. blind** voler sans visibilité; **to f. over London** survoler Londres; **to f. across the Channel** traverser la Manche en avion; **we flew 400 miles** nous avons parcouru 640 kilomètres en avion; **who did you f. with?** *(which airline)* avec quelle compagnie est-ce que tu as voyagé?; **to f. direct** effectuer un vol direct; **to f. via London** faire escale à

Londres; **we f. to over a dozen destinations** *(of airline)* nous desservons plus d'une douzaine de destinations; **we f. to Berlin four days a week** nous avons des vols pour Berlin quatre jours par semaine; **the airline only flies to Hong Kong via Karachi** tous les vols de la compagnie à destination de Hongkong s'effectuent via Karachi; **they don't f. from Heathrow any more** ils n'ont plus de vols au départ de Heathrow

3 *(of hair etc)* flotter; *(of flag)* flotter, battre; **the American flag flew above the building** le drapeau américain flottait au-dessus du bâtiment

4 *(move quickly etc) (of person etc)* courir *ou* aller à toute vitesse; *(flee)* s'enfuir; *(of time)* filer; *(of cork etc)* voler, sauter en l'air; **the insults were really flying** les insultes fusaient de toutes parts; **to f. to sb's aid** voler au secours de qn; *Fam* **it's late, I must f.** il se fait tard, il faut que je me sauve; *Fam* **I flew home to change** j'ai filé à la maison pour me changer; **time is flying** le temps passe à toute vitesse; **the door flew open** la porte s'ouvrit brusquement; **to f. into a rage** *or Fam* **off the handle** s'emporter, sortir de ses gonds; **to f. into a temper** se mettre en colère; **to f. at sb** *(attack them)* se jeter sur qn; **to let f.** *(lose one's temper)* s'emporter; *(arrow)* décocher; *(string of insults)* lâcher; **to let f. at sb** *(abuse, reprimand)* passer un savon à qn, sonner les cloches à qn; *(hit)* flanquer un coup à qn; *Fam* **to send sb/sth flying** envoyer rouler qn/qch; **to f. (in)to pieces** *or* **to bits** éclater, voler en éclats; *Fig* **to f. in the face of the evidence/current thinking** aller à l'encontre de l'évidence/des idées actuelles; **to f. in the face of reason/logic** défier la raison/toute logique

vt 1 *Aviat (plane)* piloter; *(person, object)* emmener en avion, transporter par avion; **we'll f. it to you tomorrow** nous vous l'enverrons par avion demain; **we were flown to Norway** on nous a emmenés en Norvège en avion; **to f. ABC airlines** voyager avec la compagnie aérienne ABC; **several airlines f. this route** plusieurs compagnies aériennes empruntent cette route; **he had flown three missions** il avait effectué trois missions en vol; **I'd never flown the Atlantic before** je n'avais jamais traversé l'Atlantique en avion auparavant; **her employers flew her to the States** ses employeurs l'ont envoyée aux États-Unis en avion; **we're flying them home on the first flight** nous les rapatrions par le premier vol

2 *Naut (flag)* déployer; **the ship was flying the Italian flag** le bateau arborait le pavillon italien

3 to f. a kite faire voler un cerf-volant; *Fig* lancer un ballon d'essai; *esp Am* **go f. a kite!** *(go away)* fiche-moi le camp!; *(I'm not going to do it)* va te faire voir!

4 *(flee)* **to f. the country** s'enfuir du pays; *esp Am* **to f. the coop** disparaître; **to f. the nest** *(of fledgling, child)* quitter le nid

▸ **fly about, fly around vi** *(of bird)* voler çà et là; *(of butterfly etc)* voltiger; *Fig (of rumours)* courir; **there are lots of figures flying about** *or* **around** on entend tellement de chiffres différents

▸ **fly away vi** *(of bird etc)* s'envoler

▸ **fly by vi 1** *(of time)* passer à toute vitesse; **the time has flown by!** comme le temps a passé!; **as the days flew by** à mesure que les jours s'enfuyaient

2 *Aviat (of aircraft)* passer

▸ **fly in vi 1** *(arrive by aircraft)* arriver en avion

2 *(approach) (of pilot, aircraft)* arriver; **the planes flew in over the coast** les avions sont arrivés en survolant la côte

vt sep *(transport by aircraft)* amener en avion; **the air force flew in supplies/rein-**

forcements les forces aériennes ont amené des ravitaillements/du renfort

▶**fly off** VI *(of bird, aircraft etc)* s'envoler; *(leave in aircraft)* partir en avion; *(of button, lid etc)* sauter

VT SEP *(transport by aircraft)* envoyer par avion; **they were flown off by helicopter** ils ont été évacués par hélicoptère

▶**fly out** VI **1** *(of bird)* sortir en volant

2 *(leave in aircraft)* partir en avion; **a medical team flew out to the disaster area** une équipe médicale s'est rendue en avion dans la région sinistrée

3 *(be ejected)* être éjecté; **the knife flew out of his hand** le couteau lui a échappé de la main

VT SEP *(transport by aircraft)* emmener en avion; **her husband's employer flew her out to be with him** l'employeur de son mari lui a payé le billet d'avion pur qu'elle aille retrouver celui-ci

▶**fly past** VI **1** *(of bird, aircraft)* passer (en volant); *Mil, Aviat (in formation)* exécuter un défilé aérien; *Fig* **he flew past on a bicycle** il est passé à toute vitesse en bicyclette

2 *(of time)* passer vite

▶**fly up** VI **1** *(of bird etc)* s'envoler; **I flew up from London on Saturday** j'ai pris l'avion depuis Londres samedi

2 *(become vertical) (of arm etc)* s'élever; **the other end of the broom flew up** l'autre extrémité du balai s'est relevée

fly ⁴ ADJ **1** *Br Sl* malin, *f* -igne; *(scheme)* rusé, astucieux; **he's very f.** c'est un malin; **on the f.** en douce **2** *Am Sl (excellent)* génial, -aux, géant; *(stylish, attractive)* chouette

flyaway ['flaɪəweɪ] ADJ **1** *(hair)* indiscipliné **2** *(person)* léger, étourdi

flyblown ['flaɪbləʊn] ADJ *(meat)* plein *ou* couvert d'œufs de mouches

flyby ['flaɪbaɪ] N *Mil, Aviat* défilé *m* aérien

fly-by-night *Fam Pej* ADJ *(company etc)* douteux, véreux

N *(dishonest person)* personne *f* qui file à l'anglaise pour éviter de payer; *(who doesn't pay rent)* déménageur *m* à la cloche de bois; *(firm)* entreprise *f* douteuse *ou* véreuse

flycatcher ['flaɪkætʃər] N *(bird)* gobemouches *m inv*; *Am* moucherolle *f*; **spotted f.** gobe-mouches gris

fly-drive N formule *f* avion plus voiture
▸▸ **f. holiday** formule avion plus voiture

flyer ['flaɪər] N = **flier**

fly-half N *Rugby* demi *m* d'ouverture

flying ['flaɪɪŋ] ADJ **1** *(bird, fish etc)* volant; *(ribbon, hair etc)* volant, léger; **they were hurt by f. glass** ils ont été blessés par des bris de verre; **unidentified f. object** objet *m* volant non identifié

2 *(rapid)* rapide; **to take a f. leap** *or* **jump over sth** franchir qch d'un saut

3 to pass an exam with f. colours réussir un examen haut la main

4 *(school)* d'aviation; *(staff)* navigant

5 *(fleeing)* en fuite

N **1** *(flight)* vol *m*; *(of plane)* pilotage *m*; *Aviat (activity)* aviation *f*; **he loves f.** *(as pilot)* il adore piloter; *(as passenger)* il adore prendre l'avion; **I don't like f.** *(as passenger)* je n'aime pas prendre l'avion; **I haven't done much f.** *(as pilot)* je n'ai pas beaucoup piloté; *(as passenger)* je n'ai pas pris l'avion très souvent; **night f.** vol *m* de nuit

2 *(of flag)* déploiement *m*

▸▸ **f. ambulance** avion-ambulance *m, pl* avions-ambulances; **f. boat** hydravion *m*; **f. bomb** bombe *f* volante; *Constr* **f. buttress** arc-boutant *m, pl* arcs-boutants; **f. circus** *(exhibition)* voltige *f* aérienne; *(group)* groupe *m* de voltige aérienne; **f. club** aéro-club *m, pl* aéro-clubs; *Mil* **f. column** colonne *f* mobile, groupement *m* mobile; *Am Aviat* **f.**

---

corps corps *m* d'armée aérien; **f. doctor** médecin *m* volant; **the F. Dutchman** *(legend)* le Hollandais volant; *Zool* **f. fox** roussette *f*; **f. machine** machine *f* volante; *Ind* **f. picket** piquet *m* de grève volant; **f. saucer** soucoupe *f* volante; **the F. Squad** = brigade *f* de détectives britanniques spécialisés dans la grande criminalité; *Sport* **f. start** départ *m* lancé; **the runner got off to a f. start** le coureur est parti comme une flèche; *Fig* **the campaign got off to a f. start** la campagne a démarré sur les chapeaux de roues; **f. time** heures *fpl ou* temps *m* de vol; **200 hours f. time** 200 heures de vol; **f. visit** visite *f* éclair; **to pay a f. visit to London** faire une visite éclair à Londres

fly-kick N *Rugby* coup *m* de pied à suivre

flyleaf ['flaɪliːf] N *(of book)* page *f* de garde

Flymo® ['flaɪməʊ] N = tondeuse *f* à gazon sur coussin d'air

flyover ['flaɪəʊvər] N **1** *Br (elevated road)* pont *m* routier **2** *Am Aviat* survol *m*; *(ceremonial)* défilé *m* aérien

▸▸ *Br* **f. crossing** croisement *m* à niveaux différents

flypaper ['flaɪpeɪpər] N papier *m* tue-mouches

fly-past N *Mil, Aviat* défilé *m* aérien

flypost ['flaɪpəʊst] VI coller illicitement des affiches

flyposting ['flaɪpəʊstɪŋ] N affichage *m* illégal

flysheet ['flaɪʃiːt] N **1** *(on tent)* auvent *m* **2** *(leaflet)* feuille *f* volante

fly-tipping N *Br* dépôt *m* d'ordures illégal

flyweight ['flaɪweɪt] N *Boxing (boxer, category)* poids *m* mouche; **f. champion** champion *m* poids mouche

flywheel ['flaɪwiːl] N *Tech etc* volant *m* (de commande)

FM [e'fem] N *Radio (abbr frequency modulation)* FM *f*; **FM radio** *(radio f)* FM; **a station on FM, an FM station** une station FM

f-number N *Phot* échelle *f* d'ouverture

FO [e'fəʊ] N *Br Admin (abbr Foreign Office)* ministère *m* des Affaires étrangères

foal [fəʊl] N poulain *m*, pouliche *f*; *(of donkey)* ânon *m*, bourriquet *m*; **mare in** *or* **with f.** jument *f* pleine

VI pouliner

VT *(colt, filly)* mettre bas

foam [fəʊm] N **1** *(on sea)* écume *f*; *(on beer)* mousse *f*; **waves white with f.** vagues moutonneuses; **to break into f.** *(of wave)* déferler; **f.-flecked** moucheté d'écume **2** *(from mouth)* bave *f*, écume *f* **3** *(artificial substance)* mousse *f*; **polystyrene f.** mousse *f* de polystyrène; **f.-backed** doublé de mousse

VI *(of sea etc)* écumer; *(of beer etc)* mousser; **to f. at the mouth** avoir l'écume aux lèvres; *(of dog etc)* baver; *Fam Fig (be furious)* écumer (de rage); **he was foaming at the mouth about the latest price rises** il écumait de rage en évoquant les dernières hausses de prix

▸▸ **f. bath** bain *m* moussant; **f. fire extinguisher** extincteur *m* à mousse carbonique; **f. rubber** caoutchouc *m* Mousse®

▶**foam up** VI mousser, faire de la mousse

foaming ['fəʊmɪŋ] ADJ *(sea, horse etc)* écumant; *(sea)* moutonnant; *(blood, saliva)* spumeux; *(beer etc)* moussant

▸▸ *Hum* **f. ale** bière *f*

foamy ['fəʊmɪ] ADJ *(sea)* écumant; *(drink)* mousseux

fob [fɒb] N *(chain)* chaîne *f* (de gousset); *(pocket)* gousset *m*; *(watch)* montre *f* de gousset

▸▸ **f. pocket** gousset *m*; **f. watch** montre *f* de gousset

---

▶**fob off** VT SEP **1 to f. sb off** se débarrasser de qn; **they fobbed him off with some excuse** ils lui ont donné la première excuse venue; **she'll try to f. it off on(to) some unsuspecting buyer** elle essaiera de le vendre *ou Fam* fourguer à un acheteur peu soupçonneux **2 to f. sth off as sth** faire passer qch pour qch

f.o.b., FOB [efəʊ'biː] ADJ *Com (abbr free on board)* f. à b., FAB, FOB; **F. port of embarkation** FAB port d'embarquement

focal ['fəʊk(ə)l] ADJ **1** *Phys, Opt, Math* focal, -aux **2** *Med (infection)* focal, -aux

▸▸ *Opt* **f. distance** distance *f* focale, focale *f*; *Opt* **f. length** distance focale, focale *f*; *Phot* **f. plane shutter** obturateur *m* focal *ou* à rideau; **f. point** *Opt* foyer *m*; *Fig (of room)* point *m* de convergence; *(of discussion etc)* point central

focalization ['fəʊkəlaɪ'zeɪʃn] N focalisation *f*

fo'c'sle ['fəʊks(ə)l] N = **forecastle**

focus N *(pl* **foci, focuses** ['fəʊkəs, 'fəʊsaɪ, 'fəʊkəsɪz]) **1** *Opt, Math etc (of lens etc)* foyer *m*; **in f.** *(of image)* net, au point; *(of instrument)* réglé; **out of f.** *(of image)* flou, pas au point; *(of instrument)* non réglé, déréglé; **to bring sth into f.** *(image)* mettre qch au point; **to bring a problem into f.** mieux définir un problème, clarifier la nature d'un problème; **these unemployment figures bring the economic crisis into an even sharper f.** ces chiffres du chômage mettent la crise économique encore plus en relief; *Phot* **fixed-f. camera** appareil *m* à mise au point fixe

2 *(of discontent, unrest)* foyer *m*; *(of interest, attention)* centre *m*; *Med (of illness)* siège *m*; **she was the f. of attention** elle était le centre d'attention; *Med* **f. of infection** foyer d'infection; **these proposals have been the f. of much concern** ces propositions ont fait l'objet de profondes inquiétudes; **the organization will provide some kind of a f. for opposition to the project** l'organisation fournira un point de ralliement à l'opposition au projet; **this became a f. of people's discontent** le mécontentement s'est concentré là-dessus

VT (-s-) **1** *(rays of light etc)* concentrer (**in** dans; **on** sur); *(rays)* faire converger; *(one's interest, concern)* centrer; *(one's energies)* concentrer; **all eyes were focused on him** il était le point de mire de tous les regards; **to f. one's attention on sth** concentrer son attention sur qch; **to f. attention on sth** attirer l'attention des gens sur qch

2 *(microscope, camera etc)* mettre au point; **to f. a camera on sth** faire la mise au point d'un appareil photo sur qch

VI **1 to f. on sth** *(with eyes)* fixer qch; *(of debate, speaker etc)* se concentrer sur qch; *Phot* **to f. on an object** mettre au point sur un objet

2 *(of light, sound etc)* converger (**on** sur)

▸▸ *Phot* **f. control** *(on camera)* mise *f* au point; *Mktg, Pol* **f. group** groupe *m* témoin; *Phot* **f. knob** bouton *m* de mise au point; *Phot* **f. puller** responsable *m* point, assistant cameraman *m*

focusing ['fəʊkəsɪŋ] N *(of camera, microscope etc)* mise *f* au point

▸▸ **f. screen** loupe *f* de mise au point

fodder ['fɒdər] N fourrage *m*; **green/dry f.** fourrage (en) vert/(en) sec

VT *(animal)* donner le fourrage à

foe [fəʊ] N *Lit* ennemi *m*, adversaire *m*

foetal ['fiːt(ə)l] ADJ *Biol* fœtal, -aux

▸▸ **f. heartbeat** rythme *m* cardiaque du fœtus; **f. position** position *f* fœtale; **in a f. position** en position fœtale

foetid ['fiːtɪd] ADJ = **fetid**

foetus, *pl* **foetuses** ['fi:təs, -əsɪz] N *Biol* fœtus *m*

fog [fɒg] N **1** *Met* brouillard *m*; **in the f.** dans le brouillard; *Fig* **I'm in a f.** je ne sais plus où j'en suis; **she was in a complete f. about what she was supposed to be doing** elle ignorait complètement ce qu'elle était censée faire; **he is in a f. on anything related to economics** il est complètement perdu pour tout ce qui touche à l'économie **2** *Phot (on negative)* voile *m*
▶ VT (**-gg-**) **1** *Fig (ideas)* brouiller; *(person, issue)* embrouiller; **I am a bit fogged** je ne sais plus très bien où j'en suis; **don't be fogged by all the long words he uses** ne vous laissez pas embrouiller par ses grands mots **2** *Phot (negative)* voiler **3** *(mirror etc)* embuer, couvrir de buée
▶ VI **1** = **fog up 2** *Phot (of negative)* se voiler
▷ ▶ **f. bank** banc *m* de brume; *Aviat etc* **f. dispersal** dénébulation *f*; **f. lamp** feu *m* de brouillard; **f. light** feu *m* de brouillard; **f. signal** *Naut* signal *m* de brume; *Rail* pétard *m*
▶ **fog up** VI *(of spectacles, windows)* se couvrir de buée, s'embuer

fogbound ['fɒgbaʊnd] ADJ *(airport)* bloqué par le brouillard

fogey ['fəʊgɪ] N *Fam* **old f.** vieille baderne *f*; **I'm afraid I'm turning into a bit of an old f.** je crois que je suis en train de m'encroûter; **he dresses like such an old f.** il s'habille tellement vieux jeu; **young f.** pépère *m*

fogginess ['fɒgɪnɪs] N **1** *(of weather)* temps *m* brumeux **2** *(of person's ideas)* confusion *f*; *Phot* voile *m*

foggy ['fɒgɪ] ADJ **1** *(weather, climate etc)* brumeux; **on a f. day** par un jour de brouillard; **it's f.** il y a du brouillard; **due to f. conditions** pour cause de brouillard; **the roads are rather f.** il y a du brouillard sur les routes **2** *(photograph etc)* voilé; **to have only a f. idea of sth** n'avoir qu'une vague idée de qch; *Fam* **I haven't the foggiest (idea)!** je n'en ai pas la moindre idée!

foghorn ['fɒghɔ:n] N *Naut* corne *f* de brume, sirène *f*; *Fam* **voice like a f.** voix *f* de stentor

foible ['fɔɪb(ə)l] N *(idiosyncrasy)* particularité *f*, *(weakness)* point *m* faible

foil[1] [fɔɪl] N **1** *(metal sheet, gold etc)* feuille *f*, **silver f.** feuille d'argent; *Culin* **cooking** *or* **kitchen f.** papier *m* aluminium; **sandwiches wrapped in f.** sandwiches enveloppés dans du papier aluminium **2** *(person, thing)* repoussoir *m*; **to serve as a f. to sb's beauty** servir de repoussoir à la beauté de qn **3** *Aviat, Naut (of hydrofoil)* patin *m*, aile *f* **4** *Archit (of arch etc)* lobe *m*

foil[2] N *Fencing* fleuret *m*; **foils** *(event)* escrime *f* au fleuret

foil[3] VT *(thwart)* *(attempt etc)* faire échouer; *(plan, plot)* contrecarrer; **to be foiled at all points** *(of person)* échouer sur toute la ligne; **foiled again!** encore raté!; **once again they have been foiled by their own incompetence** une fois encore ils ont échoué à cause de leur propre incompétence

foist [fɔɪst] VT refiler *(sth on sb* qch à qn); **to f. oneself on sb** s'imposer à qn *ou* chez qn; **I try not to f. my opinions/ideas on people** j'essaie de ne pas imposer mes opinions/idées à autrui

fold[1] [fəʊld] N **1** *(crease) (in paper, skirt etc)* pli *m*; **folds of fat** bourrelets *mpl* de graisse **2** *Geol* pli *m*, plissement *m*
▶ VT **1** *(sheet of paper etc)* plier; **to f. sth in two** *or* **in half** plier qch en deux; **to f. sth in paper** envelopper qch dans du papier; **to f. sb in one's arms** enlacer qn, serrer qn dans ses bras; **to f. one's arms** (se) croiser les bras; **with folded arms** les bras croisés; **to f. one's hands** joindre les mains **2** *Culin* **f. the whites**

into the mixture incorporer les blancs dans le mélange
▶ VI **1** *(of screen etc)* se (re)plier **2** *Fam (of business)* cesser ses activités; *Theat* **the play folded after a week** la pièce a été retirée de l'affiche au bout d'une semaine
▶ **fold away** VI *(of table etc)* se replier, être escamotable
▷ VT SEP *(store)* plier et ranger; **f. your clothes away neatly** plie tes affaires et range-les; **I slept on a campbed which I folded away every morning** je dormais sur un lit de camp que je repliais tous les matins
▶ **fold back** VT SEP *(collar etc)* rabattre; *(bedcovers, page)* replier
▷ VI *(of door etc)* se rabattre
▶ **fold down** VT SEP *(bedcovers)* replier
▷ VI *(of seat etc)* se rabattre; *(of sofa)* se déplier
▶ **fold in** VT SEP *Culin* **to f. in the whites of the eggs** incorporer les blancs d'œuf
▶ **fold over** VT SEP plier; **she had folded the top of the paper over** elle avait replié le haut de la feuille par-dessus
▶ **fold under** VT SEP *(edges)* replier en dessous
▶ **fold up** VT SEP *(seat, table)* (re)plier; *(screen)* replier, fermer
▷ VI se (re)plier

fold[2] N **1** *Agr (sheep)* **f.** parc *m* à moutons **2** *Fig (of Church, family)* sein *m*; **to return to the f.** *(of member of family)* rentrer au bercail; *(of politician etc)* rentrer dans les rangs; **to welcome sb back to the f.** accueillir l'enfant prodigue; **they welcomed Paul back to the f.** ils ont accueilli Paul comme l'enfant prodigue
▷ VT *Agr (sheep)* (em)parquer

-fold [fəʊld] SUFF **three/eleven/twenty/etc-f.** *(in three/eleven etc parts)* en trois/onze/vingt/etc parties; *(to increase)* (par) trois/onze/vingt/etc fois

foldaway ['fəʊldəweɪ] ADJ *(bed, table)* pliant, escamotable; *(seat)* pliant, rabattable

foldback ['fəʊldbæk] N *TV etc* ré-injection *f*, retour *m*, play-back *m inv*

folder ['fəʊldər] N **1** *(for papers etc)* chemise *f* **2** *Com (leaflet)* prospectus *m* (plié) **3** *(device)* plioir *m* **4** *Comput (directory)* dossier *m*

folding ['fəʊldɪŋ] ADJ pliant; *(joint, shutter)* brisé; **car with a f. top** voiture *f* décapotable
▷ N **1** *(of material etc)* pliage *m*; *(in bookbinding) (of pages)* pliure *f*, *Geol (of land)* plissement *m* **2** *Br Sl (paper money)* biffetons *mpl*, fafiots *mpl*
▷ ▶ **f. camera** appareil *m* à soufflet; **f. door** porte *f* (en) accordéon; **f. machine** *(for documents)* machine *f* à plier les documents; *Fam* **f. money** billets *mpl* de banque; **f. screen** paravent *m*; **f. seat** pliant *m*; **f. stool** pliant; **f. table** table *f* pliante *ou* escamotable; *(with extending sections)* table à battants; **f. tray** *(in plane, train)* tablette *f* (qui se relève)

foldout ['fəʊldaʊt] N dépliant *m*

foliage ['fəʊlɪɪdʒ] N feuillage *m*, frondaison *f*
▷ ▶ **f. plant** plante *f* cultivée pour son feuillage

foliate ['fəʊlɪeɪt] ADJ *Bot* feuillu

foliation [fəʊlɪ'eɪʃən] N **1** *(of plant)* foliation *f*, feuillaison *f* **2** *Archit (ornementation fen)* rinceaux *mpl* **3** *Geol (of rock)* foliation *f* **4** *(of book)* foliotage *m*

folic acid ['fəʊlɪk] N acide *m* folique

folio, *pl* **folios** ['fəʊlɪəʊ, -əʊz] N *(in bookbinding) (sheet)* folio *m*, feuille *f*, *Typ (page number)* numéro *m*; **(book in) f.** (livre *m*) in-folio *m inv*
▷ ▶ **f. book** livre *m* in-folio, in-folio *m inv*

folk [fəʊk] N *(pl* **folk,** *esp Am* **folks)** VOIR GRAMMAIRE A11 *(people)* gens *mpl*; *(music)*

folk *m*; **I don't care what f. think** je me moque de ce que les gens pensent; **country f.** campagnards *mpl*; **my f./your f.** les miens, ma famille/les vôtres, votre famille; *esp Am Fam* **hi, folks!** salut, tout le monde!
▷ ▶ **f. concert** concert *m* de folk; **f. dance** danse *f* folklorique; **f. festival** festival *m* de folk; **f. medicine** remèdes *mpl* de bonne femme; **f. museum** musée *m* folklorique, musée des arts et traditions populaires, musée du folklore; **f. music** *(traditional)* musique *f* folklorique; *(contemporary)* musique folk, folk; **f. singer** *(traditional)* chanteur, -euse de chansons folkloriques; *(contemporary)* chanteur, -euse folk; **f. song** *(traditional)* chanson *f ou* chant *m* folklorique; *(contemporary)* chanson folk; **f. tale** conte *m* folklorique

folklore ['fəʊklɔ:r] N folklore *m*

folksy ['fəʊksɪ] ADJ *Fam (friendly)* sociable; *(smile, greeting, cheerfulness)* bon enfant; *(dress)* traditionnel

foll *(abbr* **following)** suiv

follicle ['fɒlɪk(ə)l] N *Anat, Bot etc* follicule *m*

FOLLOW ['fɒləʊ] VT **1** *(person, car, suspect etc)* suivre; **to f. sb about** suivre qn partout; **to f. sb up the stairs/into a room** monter l'escalier/entrer dans une pièce à la suite de qn; *Fam* **to f. one's nose** y aller à l'instinct
2 *(go along) (path, road, itinerary)* suivre; **the road follows the coast** la route longe la côte
3 *(succeed)* succéder à; **the years followed one another and nothing changed** les années passèrent et rien ne changea; **as sure as day follows night** aussi sûr que deux et deux font quatre; **in the months that followed his resignation** dans les mois qui ont suivi sa démission; **George IV was followed by William IV** Guillaume IV a succédé à George IV; **dinner followed by a dance** dîner suivi d'un bal; **how do you expect me to f. that?** comment veux-tu passer après un truc comme ça?; **following our correspondence** (comme) suite à notre échange de lettres
4 *(imitate, adhere to) (person)* être le disciple de; *(the old masters)* imiter; *(person's example, teaching, pattern, fashion)* suivre; *(diet)* s'assujettir à, suivre; **to f. instructions** suivre les consignes
5 *(practise, carry out) (profession)* exercer, suivre; *(career)* poursuivre; **to f. suit** *(do the same)* faire de même; **you're not following the music** vous ne suivez pas la musique
6 *(understand) (explanation etc)* suivre, comprendre; **I don't quite f. you** je ne vous comprends *ou* suis pas très bien; **I didn't f. why they killed him** je n'ai pas compris pourquoi ils l'ont tué
7 *(pay attention to) (speech etc)* prêter attention à; *(events, news, programme)* suivre; **I don't f. the tennis any more** je ne suis plus le tennis
8 *(support)* **to f. a football team** être supporter d'une équipe de foot
▷ VI **1** *(come after) (of person, event)* suivre, venir après; **my husband is following later** mon mari viendra plus tard; **in the days that followed** dans les jours qui ont suivi; **a long silence followed** un long silence s'ensuivit; **roast beef, with strawberries to f.** du rosbif, suivi par des fraises; **proceed as follows** procéder comme suit; **our method is as follows** notre méthode est la suivante; **what follows is a brief account** ce qui suit est un bref compte-rendu
2 *(result)* s'ensuivre, résulter (**from** de); **it follows that ...** il s'ensuit que ...; **it does not f. that ...** ça ne veut pas nécessairement dire que ... + *ind*; **it follows from this that ...** il en résulte que ...; **I don't see how that conclusion follows** je ne vois pas comment

tu arrives/il arrive/*etc* à cette conclusion; *(in logic etc)* je ne vois pas comment cette conclusion s'ensuit; **that doesn't f.** pas nécessairement, pas forcément

3 *(understand)* suivre; **I don't f.** je ne suis pas ► ► *Cin, TV* **f. shot** plan *m* d'accompagnement

► **follow on** VI **1** *(come after)* suivre; **you go ahead, we'll f. on** partez en avant, nous vous suivons; **she said she would f. on later** elle a dit qu'elle nous rejoindrait plus tard

2 *(result)* **it follows on from this that …** il en résulte que …; **I don't see how that follows on at all** je ne vois pas du tout comment on en arrive là

3 *Cr* = reprendre la garde du guichet au commencement de la seconde partie du match (au lieu d'alterner avec l'autre équipe)

► **follow out** VT SEP *(orders)* exécuter; *(instructions)* suivre; *(investigation)* procéder à

► **follow through** VT SEP *(execute)* **to f. a project through (to the end)** poursuivre un projet jusqu'à sa conclusion; **she seems incapable of following anything through** on dirait qu'elle est incapable de mener quoi que ce soit à bien
VI *Sport* suivre le coup

► **follow up** VT SEP *(take further)* poursuivre; *Com (letter)* faire suivre d'une seconde lettre; *(person)* relancer; *(advantage)* poursuivre; *(enquiry, order etc)* donner suite à; *(opportunity)* saisir; *(success)* exploiter; *(victory etc)* donner suite immédiate à; *(tip-off)* suivre; **to f. up a clue** suivre une piste
VI *(add to previous action)* continuer; *(in selling)* faire de la relance; **he followed up with a right to the jaw** il a continué avec un droit à la mâchoire; **it's up to you now to f. up** c'est à toi d'agir maintenant

follower ['fɒləʊər] N **1** *(supporter)* partisan, -ane, disciple *mf*; *(of football club)* supporter *m*; **as followers of this programme will be aware, …** comme les personnes qui suivent cette émission le savent, …; **she had never really been much of a f. of the arts** elle ne s'était jamais beaucoup intéressée à l'art **2** *(servant) (of prince etc)* serviteur *m*; **the King and his followers** le roi et sa suite **3** *Mktg* suiveur *m*

following ['fɒləʊɪŋ] ADJ suivant; **on the f. day** le jour suivant, le jour d'après, le lendemain; **the f. Monday** le lundi suivant; **the f. resolution** la résolution que voici *ou* suivante; **the f. persons** les personnes dont les noms suivent, les personnes suivantes; **two days f.** deux jours de suite
N **1** *Pol etc (of leader)* partisans *mpl*; *(of prince)* suite *f*; **to have a big f.** avoir un grand nombre de partisans *ou* de disciples; **a television programme that commands a wide f.** une émission télévisée très suivie; **a team with a large f.** une équipe qui a beaucoup de supporters **2 the f.** *(things, points)* ce qui suit; *(people)* les personnes suivantes *ou* dont les noms suivent; **the f. is the full list** voici la liste complète
PREP après, à la suite de
► ► *TV, Cin* **f. pan** pano *m* de poursuite; *Naut* **f. wind** vent *m* arrière

follow-me product N *Mktg* produit *m* tactique

follow-my-leader N *Br* = sorte *f* de jeu dans lequel les participants se déplacent en file indienne et doivent répéter les gestes de celui qui ouvre la marche

follow-on N *Cr* **to try to avoid** *or* **save the f.** = s'efforcer de marquer le nombre de points requis pour ne pas avoir à reprendre la garde du guichet

follow-the-leader N *Am* = **follow-myleader**

follow-through N *Sport* fin *f* du coup

follow-up N suite *f*; *Com etc (of advertising etc)* relance *f*; *(of order)* suivi *m*; *Med (appointment)* examen *m* de contrôle
► ► **f. action** suite; **to take f. action on sth** donner suite à qch; *Med* **f. care** soins *mpl* post-hospitaliers; **f. interview** *(for job, research)* deuxième entretien *m*; **f. letter** lettre *f* de rappel *ou* de relance; *Mktg* **f. publicity** publicité *f* de rappel; **f. story** suite *f*; **f. system** système *m* de relance; **f. visit** *(medical)* visite *f* de contrôle; *(in selling)* visite de relance

folly ['fɒlɪ] N **1** folie *f*, sottise *f*; **an act of f., a f.** une folie; **it would be the height of f. to …** ce serait la plus grande folie de …; **this decision is sheer f. on the part of the government** c'est de la folie furieuse pour le gouvernement d'avoir pris cette décision **2** *Archit* folie *f*

foment [fə'ment] VT **1** *(discord, discontent)* fomenter **2** *Med (wound)* fomenter

fomentation [fəʊmen'teɪʃən] N **1** *(of discord, discontent)* fomentation *f* **2** *Med (of wound)* fomentation *f*

fond [fɒnd] ADJ **1 to be f. of sb/sth** *(to like)* bien aimer qn/qch; **they are f. of each other** ils s'aiment bien; **I'm f. of you but I don't love you** je t'aime bien mais c'est tout; **he was very f. of me** il me portait beaucoup d'affection; **to become f. of sb** s'attacher à qn; **to be f. of music** être amateur de musique; **f. of sweets** friand de sucreries; **to be passionately f. of reading** adorer la lecture; **he is rather too f. of the sound of his own voice** il aime un peu trop s'écouter parler; **he was f. of the odd whisky** il aimait bien prendre un petit whisky de temps à autre

2 *(loving) (person, embrace)* affectueux, tendre; *(smile)* attendri; *(parent)* indulgent, bon; **with f. regards** *(in letter)* bien amicalement

3 *(memory)* agréable

4 *(foolish)* **in the f. hope of catching a glimpse of my idol** dans le fol espoir d'apercevoir mon idole; **she still retained the f. belief that he would return** elle persistait à croire qu'il reviendrait

fondant ['fɒndənt] N fondant *m*

fondle ['fɒnd(ə)l] VT *(person)* caresser, câliner; *(of lover, mother)* faire des câlins à; *(dog, cat etc)* caresser; **he was fondling her leg under the table** il lui caressait la jambe sous la table

fondly ['fɒndlɪ] ADV **1** *(lovingly) (to smile, stroke etc)* tendrement, affectueusement **2** *(naively) (to hope, believe etc)* naïvement; **I f. believed that …** j'ai naïvement cru que …

fondness ['fɒndnɪs] N **1** *(affection)* affection *f*, tendresse *f* (**for** pour, envers) **2** *(liking)* penchant *m*, prédilection *f*, goût *m* (**for sth** pour qch); *(strong liking)* goût profond (**for sth** de qch)

fondue ['fɒndu:] N *Culin* fondue *f*; **beef/cheese f.** fondue bourguignonne/savoyarde

font¹ [fɒnt] N *Rel* fonts *mpl* baptismaux

font² N *Typ, Comput* police *f*, fonte *f*
► ► **f. cartridge** cartouche *f* de polices; **f. cassette** cassette *f* de polices de caractères, cassette de fontes; **f. size** taille *f* de police

fontanel(le) [fɒntə'nel] N *Anat* fontanelle *f*

food [fu:d] N **1** *(no pl)* nourriture *f*; *(as opposed to drink)* manger *m*; *(for expedition)* vivres *mpl*; *Agr (for animals)* pâture *f*; *(for poultry)* mangeaille *f*; **f. and drink** le boire et le manger; *Com* **f. and non-f.** alimentaire et non-alimentaire; **there's some f. in the fridge** il y a à manger dans le Frigidaire®; **f. is expensive here** la nourriture est chère ici; **take some f. for the journey** prenez de quoi manger pendant le voyage; **a hotel where**

the f. is good un hôtel où la cuisine *ou* la table est bonne; **to be off one's f.** ne pas avoir d'appétit; **to hunt** *or* **search for f.** *(of animal)* chercher sa nourriture; **f. for the mind** nourriture de l'esprit; **to give sb f. for thought** donner à penser à qn

2 *(type of food)* aliment *m*; **canned** *or Br* **tinned foods** aliments de conserve (en boîte); **health foods** *(for special diet)* produits *mpl* diététiques; *(natural foods)* produits alimentaires naturels
► ► **f. allergy** allergie *f* alimentaire; *Ecol* **f. chain** chaîne *f* alimentaire; **f. combining** combinaisons *fpl* alimentaires; **f. counter** *(in large store)* buffet *m*; **f. critic** critique *mf* gastronomique; **f. hall** rayon *m* d'alimentation; **f. hygiene** hygiène *f* alimentaire; **f. hygiene regulations** réglementation *f* sur l'hygiène alimentaire; **f. industry** industrie *f* alimentaire; **f. manufacturer** fabricant *m* de produits comestibles; **f. mixer** mixeur *m*; **f. packaging** emballage *m* des produits alimentaires; **f. poisoning** intoxication *f* alimentaire; **f. processor** robot *m* ménager *ou* de cuisine; **f. products** produits *mpl* alimentaires; *Am* **f. stamp** bon *m* alimentaire *(accordé aux personnes sans ressources)*; **the F. Standards Agency** = organisme *m* britannique de contrôle de la sécurité alimentaire; **f. value** valeur *f* nutritive

foodie ['fu:dɪ] N *Fam* fin gourmet *m*

foodstore ['fu:dstɔ:r] N magasin *m* d'alimentation

foodstuff ['fu:dstʌf] N *(usu pl)* **foodstuffs** produits *mpl* alimentaires *ou* d'alimentation

fool¹ [fu:l] N imbécile *mf*, idiot, -ote; *Hist (jester)* fou *m*; **to play** *or* **act the f.** faire l'idiot; **to make a f. of oneself** se couvrir de ridicule; **no one likes being made a f. of** personne n'aime être ridiculisé; **I felt such a f.** je me sentais vraiment idiot; **you'd be a f. to buy it** tu serais bête de l'acheter; **only a f. would pay that much for it** il faudrait être bête pour le payer aussi cher; **what f. was responsible for this decision?** quel est l'idiot *ou* l'imbécile qui a pris cette décision?; *Fam* **silly f.!** espèce d'idiot!; **what a f.!** quel idiot!; **he's no f.** il n'est pas bête; **he's a bigger f. than I thought** il est plus bête que je ne le pensais; **more f. you!** *(for believing them, buying it etc)* ce que tu es bête!; **if you agreed to that, then more f. you** si tu as accepté, c'est que tu es vraiment bête; **like a f., I agreed** comme un idiot, j'ai accepté; **any f. knows that** le premier imbécile venu sait cela; **some f. doctor** un imbécile de docteur; *Prov* **there's no f. like an old f.** il n'y a pire imbécile qu'un vieil imbécile; **to make a f. of sb** *(make look ridiculous)* exposer qn au ridicule, ridiculiser qn; *(tease)* se moquer de qn; **she's nobody's** *or* **no one's f.** c'est une maline *ou* une rusée; **to go on a f.'s errand** y aller pour des prunes *ou* pour le roi de Prusse; **I went on a f.'s errand trying to buy a turkey on Christmas Eve** j'ai essayé de trouver une dinde la veille de Noël mais il n'y a pas eu moyen; **the sales trip promised to be nothing but a f.'s errand** ce voyage d'affaires s'annonçait comme une perte de temps; **to send sb on a f.'s errand** envoyer qn décrocher la lune; **All Fools' Day, April Fools' Day** le premier avril; **they're living in a f.'s paradise** ils rêvent tout éveillés *ou* debout
ADJ *esp Am* stupide; **what a damn f. idea!** quelle idée stupide!
VI **1** *(act foolishly)* faire l'idiot; **stop fooling!** assez de bêtises!; **I'm becoming tired of your fooling** je commence à en avoir assez de tes bêtises **2** *(not be serious)* dire des blagues; **I was only fooling** je plaisantais
VT *(deceive)* duper; *(tease)* faire marcher; **you can't f. me** on ne m'a pas comme ça; **to**

(allow oneself to) **be fooled** se laisser duper; **to be fooled into doing sth** être amené à faire qch par duperie; **he fooled me into believing it** il me l'a fait croire; **he had tried to f. her into providing him with an alibi** il avait essayé de l'embobiner pour qu'elle lui fournisse un alibi; **they had me completely fooled** ils m'ont bien eu; **you didn't have me fooled for a moment** je n'ai pas été dupe un seul instant; **at that point I knew I had them fooled** à ce moment-là j'ai su qu'ils avaient mordu; *Iron* **her?** *a socialist?* **you could've fooled me!** elle? une socialiste? je ne l'aurais pas cru!

▸▸ *Miner* **f.'s gold** pyrite *f* de fer; **f.'s parsley** petite ciguë *f*

▸**fool about, fool around** *vi* **1** *(act foolishly)* faire l'imbécile; **to f. about** *or* **around with sth** *(with electrical appliance etc)* tripoter qch; *(with gun)* jouer avec qch; **I still enjoy fooling around with my old train set** j'aime encore bien m'amuser avec mon vieux train électrique; **she fooled around with drugs** elle a touché à la drogue **2** *(waste time)* traîner; **this is no time to f. around, young man** ce n'est pas le moment de traîner, jeune homme **3** *(have affair)* avoir *ou* se payer des aventures; **if I thought my husband/wife was fooling around …** si je pensais que mon mari/ma femme me trompait …; **to f. around with sb** coucher avec qn; **if I found that he'd been fooling around while I was away** si j'apprenais qu'il m'avait fait des infidélités pendant que j'étais en voyage

▸**fool with** *vt insep Am (handle or play with carelessly) (electrical appliance etc)* tripoter; *(gun)* jouer avec; **to f. with drugs** toucher à la drogue; **don't f. with me!** ne me cherche pas!; **nobody fools with Mental Mickey** on ne plaisante pas avec Mental Mickey

fool² *n Br Culin* = dessert *m* à base de crème et de fruits; **gooseberry f.** crème *f* de groseilles (à maquereau)

foolery ['fu:lərɪ] *n* **1** *(stupidity)* **(piece of) f.** sottise *f*, folie *f* **2** *(playing the fool)* bouffonnerie *f*, pitreries *fpl*

foolhardiness ['fu:lhɑ:dɪnɪs] *n* témérité *f*, imprudence *f*

foolhardy ['fu:lhɑ:dɪ] *adj* téméraire, imprudent; **he was brave to the point of being f.** son courage frôlait la témérité

foolish ['fu:lɪʃ] *adj (stupid)* bête; *(imprudent)* insensé; **don't be so f.!** ne sois pas bête!; **it is f. of him to …** c'est stupide de sa part de …; **a f. hope** un fol espoir; **to do something f.** faire une bêtise; **to look f.** avoir l'air penaud; **to make sb look f.** tourner qn en ridicule, ridiculiser qn; **to feel f.** se sentir idiot

foolishly ['fu:lɪʃlɪ] *adv* bêtement; **she looked at him rather f.** elle le regardait d'un air plutôt bête; **f., he decided to invade the country** il prit la folle décision d'envahir le pays

foolishness ['fu:lɪʃnɪs] *n (of person)* bêtise *f*, *(of plan, decision, idea etc)* stupidité *f*; **it is sheer f. to believe that …** il est absolument stupide de croire que …; **they've described the project as nothing but f.** ils ont qualifié le projet d'absurdité; *Old-fashioned* **what f. is this?** qu'est-ce que c'est que ces bêtises?

foolproof ['fu:lpru:f] *adj (mechanism)* indéréglable, indétraquable, de sûreté, à toute épreuve; *(scheme)* à toute épreuve, sûr; *(method, system)* infaillible; **it's f.** *(electrical appliance etc)* il n'y a aucun risque, ça marche à tous les coups; **if this plan of yours is so f.** si ton plan est aussi sûr que tu le dis

foolscap ['fu:lskæp] *n esp Br (paper)* papier *m* ministre

FOOT [fʊt] *n (pl* **feet** [fi:t]) **1** *(of human, animal with cloven hoof)* pied *m*; *(of dog, cat, bird etc)* patte *f*, **the fore/hind feet** *(of horse)* le bipède antérieur/postérieur; **to put one's feet up** *(have a rest)* se reposer; **she put her feet up on the table** elle a mis les pieds sur la table; **to put one's f. in the door** *(of salesperson etc)* coincer son pied dans la porte; **to set f. on an island** mettre pied sur une île; **I shall never set f. in his house again** jamais je ne remettrai les pieds chez lui; **to rise to one's feet** *(stand)* se lever; *(in debate)* prendre la parole; **he jumped to his feet** d'un bond il fut debout; **to be on one's feet** se tenir debout; **she is on her feet all day** elle est sur ses jambes du matin au soir; **to be on one's feet again** être de nouveau sur pied; **he's constantly getting under my feet** je l'ai toujours dans les pattes; **on f.** à pied; **to go on f.** aller à pied; **under f.** sous les pieds; **to trample** *or* **tread sth under f.** fouler qch aux pieds; **feet first** les pieds devant

2 *(idioms) Fam* **to have/get cold feet** avoir la frousse; **to have one's feet firmly on the ground** avoir les pieds sur terre; **to have one f. in the grave** avoir un pied dans la tombe; **not to put a f. wrong** ne faire aucune erreur; **to catch sb on the wrong f.** prendre qn au dépourvu; *Tennis etc* prendre qn à contrepied; **to start** *or* **get off on the wrong f.** *(of two people)* faire un mauvais départ; **to put one's best f. forward** *(get on with task)* abattre la besogne; *(make rapid progress)* avancer vite *ou* à toute allure; **to put one's f. down** *(be firm)* faire preuve de fermeté; *(stop sth)* mettre le holà; *Aut Fam* mettre le pied au plancher; *Fam* **to put one's f. in it, to put one's f. in one's mouth** faire une gaffe; **to sit at sb's feet** être le disciple de qn; **to set sb on their feet** (re)mettre qn sur pied, (r)établir qn; **to begin to find one's feet** *(in new job, situation etc)* commencer à s'adapter; **to get a f. in the door** établir un premier contact; **it's not much of a job, but it's a f. in the door** ce n'est pas terrible comme travail, mais ça fait un contact; **to have feet of clay** être un colosse aux pieds d'argile; *Fam* **my f.!** mon œil!

3 *(no pl) Mil, Arch (infantry)* fantassins *mpl*, soldats *mpl* d'infanterie; **a regiment of f.** un régiment d'infanterie; **the 42nd F.** le 42ème d'infanterie

4 *(lower part) (of stocking)* pied *m*; *(of table)* bout *m*, pied; *(of bed, tombstone, glass)* pied; *(of lake)* extrémité *f* inférieure; *(of column etc)* base *f*, *(of mountain, ladder)* pied, bas *m*; *Typ (of letter)* pied; **at the f. of the stairs** au bas *ou* en bas de l'escalier; **at the f. of the page/list** au bas de la page/liste

5 *Liter (in poetry)* pied *m*

6 *(measurement)* pied *m* anglais (= *30,48 cm)*; **square f.** pied carré; **cubic f.** pied cube; **to be five f.** *or* **feet high/thick** avoir cinq pieds de haut(eur)/d'épaisseur; **three f.** *or* **feet six (inches)** trois pieds six pouces; **a f. of water** un pied d'eau; **at 2,000 feet (above sea level)** à 2 000 pieds (au-dessus du niveau de la mer)

vt Fam **1** **to f. it** *(walk)* marcher

2 *(pay)* **to f. the bill** payer la note *ou* les dépenses

3 *Am* = **foot up**

▸▸ **f. control** commande *f* au pied; *Tennis* **f. fault** faute *f* de pied; **f. passenger** passager, -ère sans véhicule; *Br Mil* **f. patrol** patrouille *f* à pied; **f. pump** pompe *f* à pied; *Bot, Vet* **f. rot** piétin *m*; **f. scraper** gratte-pieds *m inv*; **f. soldier** *Mil* fantassin *m*; *(of political party)* militant, -ante de base; **f. spa** bain *m* de pieds à remous

▸ **foot up** *vt sep Am Fam (add up) (bill)* additionner

footage ['fʊtɪdʒ] *n* **1** *(length)* longueur *f* (en

pieds) **2** *Cin (length of film)* métrage *m* **3** *Cin (sequence, film)* séquences *fpl*

foot-and-mouth disease *n Vet* fièvre *f* aphteuse

football ['fʊtbɔ:l] *n* **1** *(soccer)* football *m*; *Fam* foot *m*; *Am* football américain **2** *(ball)* ballon *m* (de football); *Fig* **it has become a political f.** c'est devenu une question que tous les politiciens espèrent utiliser à leur avantage

▸▸ **f. boot** chaussure *f* de football; *Br* **f. club** club *m* de football; **f. fan** supporteur, -trice d'une équipe de football; *Am* **f. field** terrain *m* de football; *Br* **f. ground** terrain de football; **f. hooligan** hooligan *m*; **f. hooliganism** vandalisme *m*, hooliganisme *m*; **the F. League** = association *f* réunissant la majorité des clubs de football professionnels en Angleterre; *Br* **f. pitch** terrain de football; **f. player** *Br* joueur, -euse de football, footballeur, -euse; *Am* joueur, -euse de football américain; *Br* **f. pools** ≃ Loto *m* sportif; **f. season** saison *f* de football; *Br Rail* **f. special** = train *m* mis en service spécialement pour un match de foot; **f. supporter** supporteur, -trice d'une équipe de football

footballer ['fʊtbɔ:lər] *n Br* footballeur, -euse; *Am* joueur, -euse de football américain

footbath ['fʊtbɑ:θ] *n* bain *m* de pieds

footbrake ['fʊtbreɪk] *n Aut* frein *m* à pédale *ou* à pied

footbridge ['fʊtbrɪdʒ] *n* pont *m* pour piétons; *(narrow)* passerelle *f*

footer ['fʊtər] *n* **1** *Comput* bas *m* de page **2** *Old-fashioned Br Fam (soccer)* foot *m*

footfall ['fʊtfɔ:l] *n* **1** *(sound)* (bruit *m* de) pas *m*; **I heard a light f.** j'ai entendu un pas léger **2** *Mktg (people entering shop, airport etc)* taux *m* de fréquentation

foot-fault *Tennis vi* faire une faute de pied

vt (of umpire) **to f. a player** pénaliser un joueur pour faute de pied

footgear ['fʊtgɪər] *n* (grosses) chaussures *fpl*

foothills ['fʊthɪlz] *npl* collines *fpl* basses *ou* avancées; *(of mountain range)* avant-monts *mpl*

foothold ['fʊthəʊld] *n* prise *f* pour le pied; **to get a f.** prendre pied; *Fig* **enemy troops gained a f. on the island** les troupes ennemies ont pris pied sur l'île

footie ['fʊtɪ] *n Br Fam (soccer)* foot *m*

footing ['fʊtɪŋ] *n* **1** **to lose one's f.** *(in bathing etc)* perdre pied; **to miss one's f.** poser le pied à faux **2** *(situation) (of person)* position *f*, condition *f*; *(of institution etc)* condition, état *m*; **on a war f.** *(of troops)* sur le pied de guerre; *(of country, economy)* en état de guerre; **to be on a sound f.** *(of company, economy)* être sain *ou* ferme *ou* bien établi; **to place two people on the same f.** mettre deux personnes au même niveau; **to be on an equal f.** être de pair *ou* sur un pied d'égalité (**with** avec); **to be on a friendly f. with sb** avoir des rapports amicaux avec qn

▸**footle about, footle around** ['fu:t(ə)l] *vi Fam (waste time)* traînailler; **to f. about** *or* **around with sth** jouer avec qch, tripoter qch

footlights ['fʊtlaɪts] *npl Theat* rampe *f*

footling ['fu:tlɪŋ] *adj Fam* insignifiant

footloose ['fʊtlu:s] *adj (person)* libre; *(existence)* sans attaches; **to be f. and fancy-free** être libre comme l'air

footman, *pl* **footmen** ['fʊtmən] *n* valet *m* de pied

footnote ['fʊtnəʊt] *n* note *f* de bas de page; *Fig* détail *m*; **he is now little more than a f. to the history of the period** il n'a guère plus qu'un rôle d'arrière-plan dans l'histoire de l'époque

footpath ['fʊtpɑːθ] N sentier m (pour piétons); (alongside canal, railway) banquette f, accotement m; (in street) trottoir m

footplate ['fʊtpleɪt] N Rail (of railway engine) plate-forme f, pl plates-formes, tablier m

footplateman, pl **footplatemen** ['fʊtpleɪtmən] N Rail mécanicien m de locomotive

foot-pound N (pl **foot-pounds**) Phys (measurement) pied-livre m, pl pieds-livres

footprint ['fʊtprɪnt] N 1 empreinte f de pas; **footprints in the sand** (empreintes de) pas mpl sur le sable 2 (of object, appliance), Comput encombrement m 3 (of satellite) empreinte f

footrest ['fʊtrest] N (on chair, motorcycle) repose-pied(s) m, pl repose-pieds; Med porte-pieds m inv, repose-pied(s); (on bicycle) cale-pied m, pl cale-pieds

foot-second N (pl **foot-seconds**) Phys (measurement) pied m par seconde

Footsie ['fʊtsi] N (abbr **Financial Times-Stock Exchange 100 Index**) = principal indice boursier du Financial Times basé sur la valeur de 100 actions cotées à la Bourse de Londres

footsie N Fam **to play f. with sb** faire du pied à qn

footslog ['fʊtslɒg] VI (-gg-) marcher, faire la route à pied

footsore ['fʊtsɔːr] ADJ qui a mal aux pieds; **they arrived f. and weary** ils sont arrivés les pieds en compote et épuisés

footstall ['fʊtstɔːl] N Archit socle m

footstep ['fʊtstep] N 1 (sound) pas m; **I hear footsteps** j'entends des pas ou un bruit de pas 2 (footprint) (empreinte f de) pied m ou pas m; Fig **to follow** or **tread** or **walk in sb's footsteps** marcher sur les traces ou pas de qn; Fig **to follow in one's father's footsteps** suivre les traces de son père

footstool ['fʊtstuːl] N tabouret m (pour les pieds)

footwarmer ['fʊtwɔːmər] N chancelière f

footway ['fʊtweɪ] N chemin m (pour piétons)

footwear ['fʊtweər] N chaussures fpl

footwell ['fʊtwel] N Aut place f aux pieds

footwork ['fʊtwɜːk] N (in dancing, sports etc) jeu m de pieds ou de jambes; Fig **it required some rather fancy f. on his part** il a dû faire des pieds et des mains

footy ['fʊti] = footie

fop [fɒp] N Pej bellâtre m, dandy m

foppish ['fɒpɪʃ] ADJ (man) qui met trop de recherche à sa toilette; (clothes, manners) d'une élégance affectée; (taste, elegance) de bellâtre, de dandy

FOR [efəʊˈɑːr] Com (abbr **free on rail**) franco wagon

FOR [fɔːr, unstressed fər]

PREP pour **2–5, 7–13, 16** ■ en raison de **7** ■ de **7** ■ à **9** ■ pendant **10**
CONJ car

PREP 1 (representing) **A f. Andrew** A comme André; **what's the Russian f. 'book'?** comment dit-on 'livre' en russe?

2 (as) **to have sb f. a teacher** avoir qn comme professeur; **f. the first time** pour la première fois

3 (in return for) **you can hire a car f. five pounds a day** on peut louer une voiture pour cinq livres par jour; **to sell sth f. ten euros** vendre qch dix euros; **three f. £5** trois

pour 5 livres; **to be paid f. one's services** recevoir un paiement pour ses services; **oh, f. some peace and quiet!** que ne donnerais-je pas pour un peu de tranquillité!

4 (in favour of) **he is f. free trade** il est partisan du libre-échange, il est pour le libre-échange; **I'm all f. it** je suis tout à fait pour; Law **judgment f. the plaintiff** arrêt m en faveur du demandeur

5 (purpose) **garments f. men** vêtements pour hommes; **can you give me something f. the pain?** est-ce que vous pouvez me donner quelque chose pour ou contre la douleur?; **f. books on gardening, try Jackson's bookshop** pour trouver des livres sur le jardinage, essayez la librairie Jackson

6 (in trouble) Fam **he's f. it!** ['fɔːrɪt], **he's in f. it!** ['ɪnfərɪt] qu'est-ce qu'il va prendre!; **I really thought I was in f. it** j'ai bien crû que mon compte était bon

7 (because of) **to choose sb f. his/her ability** choisir qn en raison de sa compétence; **he's well known f. his views on taxation** il est célèbre pour ses opinions sur l'impôt; **she couldn't sleep f. the pain** elle ne pouvait pas dormir à cause de la douleur; **I feel all the better f. it** je me sens vraiment mieux, ça m'a fait du bien; **I'm a few million poorer and I'm all the better f. it** j'y ai laissé quelques millions et je ne m'en porte que mieux

8 (considering) **f. all the use he is, he might as well go and play** pour ce qu'il fait d'utile, il pourrait aussi bien aller jouer; **f. all the sense it made** pour ce que c'était clair

9 (direction) **ship (bound) f. America** navire à destination de l'Amérique; **the train f. London** le train pour ou à destination de ou en direction de Londres; **I'm leaving f. France** je pars pour la France; **his feelings f. you** ses sentiments envers vous ou à votre égard; **to swim f. sth** nager vers qch

10 (extent) **the road is lined with trees f. two miles** la route est bordée d'arbres pendant deux mil(l)es; **bends f. one mile** (on sign) virages sur un mil(l)e; **I'm going away f. a fortnight** je pars pour quinze jours; **he will be away f. a year** il sera absent pendant un an; **she won't be back f. a month** elle ne sera pas de retour avant un mois; **we have food f. three days** nous avons des vivres pour trois jours; **I lived there f. five years** j'y ai vécu (pendant) cinq ans; **I have not seen him f. three years** il y a trois ans que je ne l'ai pas vu; **I have been here f. three days** il y a trois jours que je suis ici, je suis ici depuis trois jours; **I had known him f. years** je le connaissais depuis des années, il y avait des années que je le connaissais; **f. now, f. the time being** pour l'instant, pour le moment SEE GRAMMAR B31

11 (intention, destination) **this box is f. you** cette boîte est pour vous; **it's f. you** (letter, phone call) c'est pour toi; **your job f. tomorrow** votre travail pour demain; **you are the man f. me/the job** vous êtes l'homme qu'il me faut/qui convient pour ce poste; **that is just the thing f. you** c'est juste ce qu'il vous faut; **there's no time f. that** il n'y a pas le temps pour ça; **it'll do f. temporary accommodation** ça ira comme logement provisoire

12 (to the amount of) **a cheque f. £50** un chèque de 50 livres; **put me down f. £5** inscrivez-moi pour 5 livres

13 (with regard to) **he is big f. his age** il est grand pour son âge; **not bad f. a beginner!** pour un débutant ce n'est pas si mal!; **f. sheer impudence, his remarks are hard to beat** pour ce qui est de l'effronterie, ses commentaires sont imbattables; **as f. him** quant à lui; **as f. that** pour ce qui est de cela; **f. myself, f. my part** pour moi, quant à moi, pour ma part; **this shop is better f. books** ce magasin est mieux pour les livres

14 (in spite of) **f. all that** malgré tout, malgré cela, tout de même; esp Lit **f. all that he wanted to believe them** pour autant qu'il veuille les croire; **she loved him, f. all his faults** elle l'aimait malgré tous ses défauts

15 (owing to) **were it not f. her** or **but f. her, I should have died** sans elle, je serais mort

16 (corresponding to, in opposition to) **they sell twenty red bikes f. every black one** pour chaque vélo noir vendu, il y en a vingt rouges

17 (introducing an infinitive clause) **it is easy/difficult/impossible f. him to come** il lui est facile/difficile/impossible de venir; **it is too late f. us to set off** il est trop tard pour que nous partions; **they made way f. him to pass** on se rangea pour le laisser passer; **I have brought it f. you to see** je l'ai apporté pour que vous le voyiez; **it is not f. me to decide/to criticize him** ce n'est pas à moi de décider/de le critiquer; **it is usual f. the mother to accompany her daughter** il est d'usage que la mère accompagne sa fille; **it's no good f. him to talk** il a beau dire; (because he is similarly guilty etc) il peut parler; **f. that to be done** pour que ça soit fait; **it took an hour f. the taxi to get to the station** le taxi a mis une heure pour aller jusqu'à la gare; **the best plan will be f. you to go away** le mieux sera que vous vous absentiez pour quelque temps; **it would be a disgrace f. you to back out now** vous retirer maintenant serait honteux

CONJ Lit car; **f. it was too late** car il était trop tard

forage ['fɒrɪdʒ] N (animal food) fourrage(s) m(pl); **to go on the f.** (search for provisions) chercher de la nourriture; **to have a f. for sth** (search for sth) fouiller ou fourrager pour trouver qch
▶ VI fourrager; **to f. for sth** fourrager ou fouiller pour trouver qch; **never mind me, I'll f. for myself** ne t'occupe pas de moi, je me débrouillerai
▶ ▶ Mil **f. cap** calot m
▶ **forage about, forage around** VI (rummage) fourrager, fouiller (**in** dans)

foray ['fɒreɪ] N razzia f, incursion f, raid m; **she was on one of her forays round the bookshops** elle procédait à l'une de ses expéditions dans les librairies; Fig **to make a brief f. into the business world** faire une courte incursion dans le monde des affaires
▶ VI faire des incursions ou des raids

forbear¹ ['fɔːbeər] N = forebear

forbear² [fɔːˈbeər] (pt **forbore** [fɔːˈbɔːr], pp **forborne** [fɔːˈbɔːn]) Lit VT s'abstenir de
▶ VI **to f. from doing sth** s'abstenir de ou se garder de faire qch

forbearance [fɔːˈbeərəns] N 1 patience f, Lit longanimité f; **to show f. towards sb** montrer de l'indulgence envers qn 2 Fml **your f. from doing this** le fait que vous vous soyez abstenu de faire ceci

forbearing [fɔːˈbeərɪŋ] ADJ patient, indulgent

forbid [fəˈbɪd] VT (pt **forbade** [fəˈbæd, -ˈbeɪd], pp **forbidden** [fəˈbɪd(ə)n]) 1 (prohibit) défendre, interdire; (custom etc) proscrire; Law prohiber; **I f. it!** je l'interdis!; **to f. sb sth** défendre qch à qn; **to f. sb to do sth** défendre ou interdire à qn de faire qch; **I am forbidden (to drink) tea** le thé m'est défendu; **smoking is strictly forbidden** il est formellement interdit de fumer; **to be forbidden from doing sth** ne pas avoir le droit de faire qch; **he was forbidden from seeing her again** on lui a interdit de la revoir

2 (prevent) empêcher; **my condition forbids strenuous exercise** mon état ne me permet pas de me livrer à des exercices violents; **Heaven f. that I should do such a**

thing! Dieu me préserve de faire une telle chose!; **God f.!** à Dieu ne plaise! (*that que + sub*)

forbidden [fə'bɪd(ə)n] ADJ défendu, interdit; **to tread on f. ground** empiéter sur un terrain défendu; *Fig* toucher à un sujet tabou
▸▸ *Bible, Fig* **f. fruit** fruit *m* défendu

forbidding [fə'bɪdɪŋ] ADJ *(face, aspect)* sinistre; *(character)* peu avenant; *(sky, weather)* sombre; *(rock, building)* menaçant; *(look, stare)* sombre, menaçant; **a text of f. density/complexity** un texte d'une densité/complexité rébarbative

forbiddingly [fə'bɪdɪŋlɪ] ADV **the castle towered f. over the town** le château, menaçant, dominait la ville; **f. difficult/complex** d'une difficulté/complexité rébarbative

---

FORCE [fɔːs]

> N force **1, 3–5** ▪ autorité **2** ▪ poids **6**
> ▪ en vigueur *(in force)* **7**
> VT forcer **1, 2** ▪ arracher **1**
> ▪ imposer **1**

N 1 *(strength, violence)* force *f*; **by sheer or brute f.** de vive force; **by sheer f. of will** à force de volonté; **by f. of circumstance(s)** par la force des choses; **f. of habit** force de l'habitude; **f. of personality** force de personnalité; **to use f. against the strikers** avoir recours à la force contre les grévistes; **armed f.** force armée
2 *(authority)* influence *f*, autorité *f*; **f. of example** influence de l'exemple; **moral f.** force morale
3 *(effort)* énergie *f*; *(power) (of blow, wind etc)* intensité *f*; *(of imagination etc)* vigueur *f*; **a blow with plenty of f. behind it** un coup bien appuyé *ou* bien assené; **considerable f. would be needed to break the door down** il faudrait une force considérable pour défoncer la porte; **the full f. of the explosion** toute la force de l'explosion; **the forces of Nature** les forces de la Nature; **a f. for good** une influence positive; **to be a f. for change** être le moteur du changement; **the forces at work here** les forces en jeu ici; **several forces conspired to bring about his downfall** plusieurs facteurs ont conspiré à provoquer sa chute
4 *Phys* force *f*, effort *m*; **f. exerted by an engine** effort d'un moteur; **f. of gravity** (force de la) pesanteur *f*; *Met* **f. ten on the Beaufort scale** force dix sur l'échelle de Beaufort
5 *Mil etc (group)* force *f*, troupe *f*, élément(s) *m(pl)*; **a f. of 20,000 men** une troupe de 20 000 hommes; **an armed f.** une force (armée); **the (armed) forces** les forces armées; **he was in the forces** il était dans l'armée; **forces large argot** *m* militaire; **the police f.**, *Fam* **the F.** la Police; **a strong f. of police** un gros détachement de police; **two different police forces** deux forces de police différentes; **we turned out in (full) f.** nous sommes venus en masse
6 *(value) (of argument)* poids *m*; *(sense) (of word, document)* signification *f*; *(of word, expression)* valeur *f*; **I mean it with the full f. of the word** je le dis et je pèse mes mots
7 *(of law, rule etc)* **to be in f.** être en vigueur; **to put the law into f.** appliquer la loi; **to come into f.** entrer en vigueur

VT 1 *(compel)* **to f. sb to do sth** *or* **into doing sth** forcer *ou* obliger qn à faire qch; **no one's forcing you!** *(to go etc)* personne ne t'y force *ou* oblige!; **I am forced to conclude that …** je suis forcé de conclure que …; **to be forced to give way** céder à la force; **that forced me to think** cela m'a obligé à réfléchir; **to f. sb into/out of the room** faire entrer/sortir qn de force; **to f. sth on sb** imposer qch à qn; **to f. drink on sb** contraindre qn à boire; **to**

f. a promise/confession from sb arracher une promesse/confession à qn
2 *(obtain, produce etc by effort) (break open) (door, window)* forcer, enfoncer; *(lock)* forcer; **to f. sb's hand** forcer la main à qn; **to f. the issue** précipiter les choses; **to f. the pace** forcer l'allure *ou* le pas; **she forced a smile** elle s'est forcée à sourire; **to f. (the meaning of) a word** forcer le sens d'un mot; **to f. legislation through Parliament** forcer le Parlement à voter une législation; **to f. a plant** forcer une plante; *Aut* **to f. the engine** trop pousser le moteur; **to f. a car/sb off the road** faire sortir une voiture/qn de la route; **to f. one's way into a house** pénétrer de force dans une maison; **to f. one's way through the crowd** se frayer un passage à travers la foule; **to f. sth into sth** faire entrer qch de force dans qch; **to f. oneself on sb** s'imposer à qn; **compressed air forces the liquid up the pipe** l'air comprimé fait monter le liquide dans le tuyau
▸ **force back** VT SEP *(enemy forces etc)* repousser, faire reculer; *(air, water, tears etc)* refouler; *(impulse, laugh)* réprimer
▸ **force down** VT SEP faire descendre de force; *(suitcase lid)* fermer de force; **to f. prices down** faire baisser les prix; *Aviat* **the plane was forced down** on a forcé l'avion à atterrir; **to f. down food/medicine/etc** avaler un aliment/un médicament/etc à contrecœur; **to f. food/medicine/etc down sb** faire avaler un aliment/un médicament/etc de force à qn
▸ **force open** VT SEP *(door, window)* ouvrir de force, forcer; *(lock)* forcer; **it took all his strength to f. open the dog's jaws** il a dû y aller de toutes ses forces pour réussir à ouvrir la mâchoire du chien
▸ **force out** VT SEP faire sortir de force; *(in engine) (exhaust gas)* refouler au dehors; **shopkeepers were forced out of the town centre by the rising rents** la hausse des loyers a chassé les petits commerçants du centre-ville; **to be forced out of business** être forcé à fermer boutique; **to f. out a few words of congratulation** féliciter qn du bout des lèvres
▸ **force up** VT SEP faire monter de force; *(prices)* faire monter

forced [fɔːst] ADJ **1** forcé **2** *(smile)* forcé, artificiel; **to give a f. laugh** rire du bout des lèvres, avoir un rire forcé **3** *(plant, fruit, vegetables)* forcé
▸▸ **f. feeding** *(of person)* alimentation *f* de force; *(of livestock)* gavage *m*; **f. labour** travail *m* forcé; *Aviat* **f. landing** atterrissage *m* forcé; *Mil* **f. march** marche *f* forcée; **f. sale** vente *f* forcée; *Fin* **f. saving** épargne *f* forcée

force-feed VT *(pt, pp* **force-fed** [-fed]*) (goose)* gaver; *(person)* nourrir de force

forceful ['fɔːsfʊl] ADJ *(personality)* énergique; *(argument, case)* puissant; *(language)* musclé; *(reason)* bon

forcefully ['fɔːsfʊlɪ] ADV *(to speak, act)* énergiquement; *(to express oneself, reason, write)* avec vigueur; *(to argue)* énergiquement, avec force; **I was f. struck by it** ça m'a fortement marqué

forcefulness ['fɔːsfʊlnɪs] N vigueur *f*

force-land VI *Aviat* faire un atterrissage forcé

forcemeat ['fɔːsmiːt] N *Culin* farce *f*

forceps ['fɔːseps] NPL **(pair of) f.** pince *f*; *Surg* forceps *m*; *(in dentistry)* davier *m*;
▸▸ *Obst* **f. delivery** accouchement *m* au forceps

forcible ['fɔːsɪb(ə)l] ADJ **1** *(by force)* de force **2** *(argument)* vigoureux, plein de force; *(reminder)* brutal, -aux
▸▸ *Law* **f. entry** effraction *f*

forcibly ['fɔːsɪblɪ] ADV **1** *(by force)* de force; **to detain sb f.** retenir qn de force **2** *(convincingly)* vigoureusement; **she argued f. for their release** elle a argumenté énergiquement *ou* avec force en faveur de leur libération; **they put their case very f.** ils se sont défendus avec force *ou* vigueur; **we were all f. reminded of our own mortality** nous avons été brutalement rappelés à notre condition de mortels

forcing ['fɔːsɪŋ] N **1** *(of lock)* forcement *m*; *(of door)* enfoncement *m* **2** *(in gardening)* forçage *m*, culture *f* forcée
▸▸ *Culin* **f. bag** poche *f* à douille; **f. frame** châssis *m*; **f. house** *(for plants)* forcerie *f*; *Fig Fam* **it's just an academic f. house** dans cette boîte, tout ce qui compte ce sont les résultats aux examens

ford [fɔːd] N *(in river)* gué *m*
VT *(river)* guéer, traverser à gué

fordable ['fɔːdəb(ə)l] ADJ *(river)* guéable

fore [fɔːr] ADJ **1** *(front)* à l'avant, antérieur; **the f. and hind legs** les pattes de devant et de derrière **2** *Naut* (de l')avant
N *Naut* avant *m*; **at the f.** au mât de misaine; *Fig* **to the f.** *(prominent)* en vue, en évidence, en vedette; **this question has been very much to the f. in the talks** cette question a été au tout premier plan au cours des discussions; **to come to the f.** *(of person)* commencer à être connu; **this issue came to the f. during last year's negotiations** ce problème a été mis en évidence lors des négociations de l'an dernier; **to bring to the f.** *(aspect, problem, importance of sth)* mettre en évidence, souligner; *(theory, philosophy)* mettre au premier plan
ADV *Naut* de l'avant; **f. and aft** de l'avant à l'arrière
INT *Golf* gare devant!
▸▸ *Typ* **f. edge** petit fond *m*, goutière *f*; *Naut* **f. hatch** panneau *m* avant

fore-and-aft ADJ *Naut* aurique
▸▸ *Naut* **f. bulkhead** cloison *f* médiane; *Mil* **f. cap** calot *m*; *Naut* **f. movement** *(of engine)* déplacement *m* longitudinal; *Naut* **f. sail** voile *f* aurique

forearm¹ ['fɔːrɑːm] N avant-bras *m inv*

forearm² [fɔːr'ɑːm] VT *(person)* prémunir; **he came forearmed** il est venu prémuni *ou* préparé; **she would always ensure that she was forearmed before going** elle prenait toujours soin de se prémunir avant d'y aller

forebear ['fɔːbeər] N aïeul *m*, *pl* aïeux, aïeule *f*, ancêtre *mf*; *Fig* ancêtre *mf*

forebode [fɔː'bəʊd] VT **to f. disaster** présager *ou* laisser prévoir le désastre

foreboding [fɔː'bəʊdɪŋ] N *(intuition)* (mauvais) pressentiment *m*; **she was filled with (a sense of) f.** elle était envahie par un mauvais pressentiment; **to have a f. that …** avoir le pressentiment que …; **she thought with f. of what the future would hold** elle songea avec appréhension à ce que l'avenir lui réservait

forecast ['fɔːkɑːst] N prévision *f*; **his f. was wrong/right** ses prévisions étaient fausses/exactes; **forecasts of higher interest rates** des prévisions d'augmentation des taux d'intérêts; **racing f.** pronostic *m* des courses; **(weather) f.** prévisions météorologiques, *Fam* météo *f*; **long-/short-range f.** prévision à longue échéance/sur période courte
VT *(pt, pp* **forecast(ed)***) (events, storm etc)* prévoir; *Sport (result)* pronostiquer; **I wouldn't like to f. a winner** je ne voudrais pas avoir à prédire qui va gagner
▸▸ *Acct* **f. balance sheet** bilan *m* prévisionnel

forecaster ['fɔːkɑːstər] N pronostiqueur,

-euse; *Econ* expert *m*; **weather f.** météorologiste *mf*

forecasting ['fɔːkɑːstɪŋ] N *(of result etc)* pronostication *f*, *(of weather, economic matters, sports)* prévision *f*
▸▸ **f. firm** société *f* de prévisions; **f. model** modèle *m* de prévisions

forecastle ['fəʊks(ə)l] N *Naut* gaillard *m*; *(in merchant vessel)* poste *m* de l'équipage

foreclose [fɔːˈkləʊz] *Law* VT **to f. the mortgage** saisir l'immeuble hypothéqué
VI *(on a mortgage)* saisir l'immeuble hypothéqué; *(on a loan)* récupérer le prêt; **to f. on a loan** interrompre un crédit, rompre un crédit avant son terme; **the bank has foreclosed on us** la banque nous a saisi l'immeuble hypothéqué/a décidé de récupérer le prêt

foreclosure [fɔːˈkləʊʒər] N *Law (on a mortgage)* saisie *f* (d'une hypothèque), forclusion *f*

forecourt ['fɔːkɔːt] N avant-cour *f*, *pl* avant-cours; *(of garage, station)* devant *m*; *(of car dealer)* parc *m* d'exposition

foredoomed [fɔːˈduːmd] ADJ condamné d'avance (**to** à)

forefather ['fɔːfɑːðər] N *Lit* aïeul *m*, *pl* aïeux; *Fig* ancêtre *m*

forefinger ['fɔːfɪŋɡər] N index *m*

forefoot, *pl* **forefeet** ['fɔːfʊt, -fiːt] N *(of dog, cat, bird)* patte *f* de devant; *(animal with cloven hoof)* pied *m* antérieur

forefront ['fɔːfrʌnt] N **to bring sth to the f.** mettre qch au premier plan; **this question is still in the f.** cette question occupe toujours le premier plan

foregather [fɔːˈɡæðər] VI = **forgather**

forego [fɔːˈɡəʊ] VT = **forgo**

foregoing ['fɔːɡəʊɪŋ] ADJ *esp Fml* précédent, antérieur; *(previously cited)* cité ci-avant; **the f.** ce qui précède

foregone ['fɔːɡɒn] ADJ **it was a f. conclusion** c'était couru d'avance

foreground ['fɔːɡraʊnd] N *Art, Phot etc* premier plan *m*; **in the f.** au premier plan; **they must be hoping that this issue will fade from the f.** ils doivent espérer que ce problème ne restera pas longtemps au premier plan
VT *Art etc* mettre au premier plan; *Fig* privilégier
▸▸ *TV, Cin* **f. matte** cache *m* d'avant-plan; *Comput* **f. processing** traitement *m* en avant-plan; *Comput* **f. program** programme *m* prioritaire

forehand ['fɔːhænd] N *Tennis* coup *m* droit; **to have a strong/weak f.** avoir un coup droit puissant/faible; **to play a f.** jouer un coup droit; **to serve to one's opponent's f.** servir sur le coup droit adverse
▸▸ **f. drive** drive *m* de coup droit; **f. stroke** coup droit

forehead ['fɒrɪd, 'fɔːhed] N *Anat* front *m*

foreign ['fɒrɪn] ADJ 1 *(from different country, countries)* étranger; **she looked f.** elle paraissait étrangère; **a f.-sounding name** un nom aux consonances étrangères; **f. countries, f. parts** pays *mpl* étrangers, l'étranger *m*; **our relations with f. countries** nos rapports avec l'extérieur; **I don't like f. food** je n'aime pas la cuisine étrangère; **f. investment** investissement *m* à l'étranger; **f. travel** voyages *mpl* à l'étranger 2 *(not belonging)* étranger (**to** à); **such feelings are f. to his nature** de tels sentiments lui sont étrangers; **lying is f. to her nature** ce n'est pas dans sa nature de mentir
▸▸ *Fin* **f. account** compte *m* étranger; **f. affairs** affaires *fpl* étrangères; **f. aid** *(to foreign country)* aide *f* aux pays étrangers; *(from for-*

eign country) aide de l'étranger; *Med* **f. body** corps *m* étranger; *Journ* **f. correspondent** correspondant, -ante à l'étranger; *Fin* **f. currency** devises *fpl* étrangères; *Fin* **f. currency account** compte en devises étrangères; *Fin* **f. currency earnings** apport *m* de devises étrangères; *Fin* **f. currency holding** avoir *m* en devises étrangères; *Fin* **f. currency loan** prêt *m* en devises étrangères; *Fin* **f. currency option** option *f* de change; *Fin* **f. currency reserves** réserves *fpl* de change, réserves en devises; *Fin* **f. debt** dette *f* extérieure; *Econ* **f. direct investment** investissement *m* étranger direct; *Fin* **f. exchange** devises étrangères; *Fin* **f. exchange gain** gain *m* de change; *Fin* **f. exchange loss** perte *f* de change; *Fin* **f. exchange market** marché *m* des changes; *Fin* **f. exchange option** option sur devises; *Fin* **f. exchange rate** cours *m* des devises; *Fin* **f. exchange reserves** réserves de change, réserves en devises; *Fin* **f. exchange risk** risque *m* de change; **f. legion** légion *f* étrangère; **f. market** marché extérieur; *Pol* **f. minister** ministre *m* des affaires étrangères; **the F. Office** le Foreign Office, le ministère britannique des Affaires étrangères; **the F. Secretary** = le ministre britannique des Affaires étrangères; *Am* **f. service** service *m* diplomatique; **f. trade** commerce *m* extérieur

foreign-built ADJ *(car)* de marque étrangère; *(ship)* construit à l'étranger

foreigner ['fɒrɪnər] N étranger, -ère; **I feel like a f. here** je me sens étranger ici

Attention: ne pas confondre avec **stranger.**

foreignness ['fɒrɪnnɪs] N air *m* étranger; *(of place)* caractère *m* étranger; *(exotic nature)* exotisme *m*; **the f. of the food/their way of life** la nourriture/leur mode de vie bien à part; **given the f. of this concept to our culture** étant donné que ce concept est étranger à notre culture

foreknowledge [fɔːˈnɒlɪdʒ] N *esp Fml* connaissance *f* anticipée; **to have f. of sth** avoir connaissance à l'avance de qch

foreland ['fɔːlənd] N cap *m*, promontoire *m*

foreleg ['fɔːleɡ] N patte *f* de devant; *(of horse)* jambe *f* de devant

forelock ['fɔːlɒk] N *(of person)* mèche *f* (de cheveux) sur le front; **to touch** *or* **tug one's f.** = porter la main à son front (pour saluer qn); *Fig* faire une révérence

foreman, *pl* **foremen** ['fɔːmən] N 1 *Ind etc* contremaître *m*; *Typ* prote *m*; *(of gang of workmen)* chef *m* d'équipe *ou* de brigade; **works f.** conducteur *m* de travaux 2 *(of jury)* président *m*

foremast ['fɔːmɑːst] N *Naut* mât *m* de misaine

forementioned [fɔːˈmenʃənd] ADJ *Law, Admin* précité

foremost ['fɔːməʊst] ADJ *(in importance)* le plus important; *(in place)* le plus en avant; **of the f. importance** de la plus haute importance
ADV **to rank f.** se classer parmi les premiers; **I shall only leave this room feet f.** je ne quitterai cette pièce que les pieds devant

forename ['fɔːneɪm] N prénom *m*

forenoon ['fɔːnuːn] N *esp Scot, Irish* matinée *f*, **in the f.** dans *ou* pendant la matinée

forensic [fəˈrensɪk, fɒ-] ADJ légal, -aux
N *Fam* **forensics** *(department)* service *m* médico-légal; **did forensics come up with anything?** est-ce que le service médico-légal a trouvé quelque chose?
▸▸ **f. evidence** = preuves *fpl* relevées lors d'une expertise criminalistique; **f. laboratory** laboratoire *m* de criminalistique; **f. medi-**

cine médecine *f* légale; **f. science** criminalistique *f*, **f. scientist** expert *m* légiste *ou* en criminalistique

foreordain ['fɔːrɔːˈdeɪn] VT *Fml* prédestiner (**sb to sth** qn à qch; **sb to do sth** qn à faire qch)

foreplay ['fɔːpleɪ] N *(sexual)* préliminaires *mpl*; **he doesn't go in much for f.** il n'est pas très porté sur les préliminaires

forequarter ['fɔːkwɔːtər] N *(of cow etc)* quartier *m* de devant; **forequarters of a horse** avant-main *m ou* avant-train *m* d'un cheval

forerunner ['fɔːrʌnər] N ancêtre *m*; *(person)* précurseur *m*

foresail ['fɔːseɪl, 'fɔːs(ə)l] N *Naut* (voile *f* de) misaine *f*

foresee [fɔːˈsiː] VT *(pt* **foresaw** [fɔːˈsɔː], *pp* **foreseen** [fɔːˈsiːn]) *(misfortune, event, development)* prévoir; **I f. difficult times/a problem** j'entrevois des moments difficiles/un problème; **it was an accident which should have been foreseen** c'était un accident qu'on aurait dû prévoir

foreseeable [fɔːˈsiːəb(ə)l] ADJ *(future, consequence, result etc)* prévisible; **not in the f. future** pas dans un avenir prévisible

foreshadow [fɔːˈʃædəʊ] VT *(event etc)* annoncer, présager

foreshore ['fɔːʃɔːr] N laisse *f* de mer; *(beach)* plage *f*

foreshorten [fɔːˈʃɔːt(ə)n] VT *Art (object)* dessiner en raccourci *ou* en perspective; **foreshortened figure** figure vue en raccourci; **the distances are foreshortened** les distances sont réduites (par la perspective)

foreshortening ['fɔːʃɔːt(ə)nɪŋ] N *Art* raccourci *m*

foresight ['fɔːsaɪt] N 1 prévoyance *f*, **lack of f.** manque *m* de prévoyance, imprévoyance *f*, **with f. this could all have been avoided** avec un peu de prévoyance tout ceci aurait pu être évité 2 *(on gun)* guidon *m*, bouton *m* de mire

foreskin ['fɔːskɪn] N *Anat* prépuce *m*

forest ['fɒrɪst] N forêt *f*, **deciduous/coniferous f.** forêt à feuilles caduques/de conifères; **f.-covered hills** collines *fpl* boisées; *Fig* **a f. of masts/telegraph poles** une forêt de mâts/poteaux télégraphiques
VT *(region)* boiser (**with** de)
▸▸ **f. fire** incendie *m* de forêt; *Am* **f. ranger** garde *m* forestier

forestall [fɔːˈstɔːl] VT *(attempt, criticism)* anticiper, devancer; *(rivals)* devancer

forestay ['fɔːsteɪ] N *Naut* étai *m* de misaine

forested ['fɒrɪstɪd] ADJ boisé (**with** de)

forester ['fɒrɪstər] N (garde *m*) forestier *m*

forestry ['fɒrɪstrɪ] N sylviculture *f*
▸▸ **the F. Commission** = organisme *m* britannique de gestion des forêts domaniales, ≃ les eaux et forêts *fpl*

foretaste ['fɔːteɪst] N avant-goût *m*, *pl* avant-goûts; **to give** *or* **offer sb a f. of sth** donner un avant-goût de qch à qn

foretell [fɔːˈtel] VT *(pt, pp* **foretold** [fɔːˈtəʊld]) *(of person)* prédire

forethought ['fɔːθɔːt] N prévoyance *f*, **to do sth with a lack of f.** manquer de prévoyance en faisant qch; **if you had given it some f.** si tu y avais un peu réfléchi à l'avance

forever [fəˈrevər] ADV 1 *(until end of time)* pour toujours, à jamais; **a good bike should last f.** un vélo de bonne qualité devrait durer pour toujours; **to live f.** vivre éternellement *ou* pour toujours; **nobody lives f.** personne n'est éternel; **nothing lasts f.** tout a une fin; *(object, possession)* rien n'est éternel; **the**

journey seemed to last **f.** le voyage a semblé durer une éternité **2** *(ceaselessly)* sans cesse, sans arrêt; **he was f. changing his mind** il changeait sans cesse *ou* sans arrêt d'avis
N *Fam* **to take f. to do sth** prendre *ou* mettre une éternité à faire qch; **it took me f. to persuade him to come** ça m'a pris une éternité pour le persuader de venir

forewarn [fɔː'wɔːn] VT prévenir, avertir; **to f. sb of sth** prévenir *ou* avertir qn de qch; *Prov* **forewarned is forearmed** un homme averti en vaut deux

forewoman, *pl* **forewomen** ['fɔːwʊmən, -wɪmɪn] N **1** *Ind etc* contremaîtresse *f* **2** *Law (of jury)* présidente *f*

foreword ['fɔːwɜːd] N *(to book)* avant-propos *m inv*, préface *f*

forex ['fɒreks] N, ADJ *Fin (abbr* **foreign exchange)** devises *fpl* étrangères
▸▸ **f. trading** transactions *fpl* en devises étrangères

forfaiting ['fɔːfeɪtɪŋ] N *Banking* forfaitage *m*, forfaitisation *f*

forfeit ['fɔːfɪt] ADJ *Hist, Law* confisqué; **his lands were f.** on lui a confisqué ses terres
N **1** *Law (fine)* amende *f*; *(for non-performance of contract)* dédit *m*; **to have to pay a f.** être mis à l'amende **2** *(in game)* gage *m*; **to play forfeits** jouer aux gages
VT **1** *(have confiscated) (object)* perdre par confiscation; *(right)* être déchu de **2** *(lose)* perdre; *(give up)* renoncer à, abandonner; **to f. one's life** payer de sa vie; **to f. one's honour** forfaire à l'honneur; **he had forfeited his independence in return for financial security** il avait sacrifié son indépendance au profit de la sécurité financière; *Fin* **to f. a deposit** perdre les arrhes

forfeiture ['fɔːfɪtʃər] N **1** *Law (act of having confiscated) (of property)* perte *f* par confiscation; *Law, Fin (of shares, right)* déchéance *f*, forfaiture *f* **2** *esp Fml (loss) (of sb's respect, one's life, honour etc)* perte *f*

forgather, foregather [fɔː'gæðər] VI *Fml* se réunir

forge [fɔːdʒ] N atelier *m* de forgeron, forge *f*
VT **1** *(of blacksmith etc) (horseshoe etc)* forger; *Metal (iron)* forger, cingler; *Fig* **to f. an alliance/a friendship** forger une alliance/une amitié **2** *(counterfeit) (signature, banknotes, cheque)* contrefaire; *(document, passport)* faire un faux de
▸▸ **f. hammer** marteau-pilon *m*, *pl* marteaux-pilons

Note that the French verb **forger** never means **to counterfeit**.

▸ **forge ahead** VI **1** *(press forward)* faire des progrès; *(in race, election campaign)* prendre de l'avance; *(in business, undertaking)* aller de l'avant; **to f. ahead with one's plans** aller de l'avant dans ses projets, mener ses projets de l'avant **2** *(outstrip competitors)* dépasser ses concurrents; **to f. ahead of one's rivals** prendre de l'avance sur ses rivaux

forged [fɔːdʒd] ADJ **1** *Metal (iron)* forgé **2** *(document, banknote, signature)* faux, *f* fausse, contrefait; **f. document** faux *m*; *(identity paper)* faux papier

forger ['fɔːdʒər] N *(of banknotes)* contrefacteur *m*, faussaire *mf*; *(of signature etc)* faussaire *mf*

forgery ['fɔːdʒərɪ] N **1** *(activity)* contrefaçon *f*, *(of documents)* falsification *f*; *Law* **to be guilty of f.** être coupable de faux **2** *(thing forged)* faux *m*; **it's a f.** *(of signature)* c'est une fausse signature; **it's a clever/obvious f.** c'est une contrefaçon bien/mal réussie; **it's a f. of my signature** c'est une contrefaçon de ma signature

forget [fə'get] *(pt* **forgot** [fə'gɒt], *pp* **forgotten** [fə'gɒt(ə)n], *prp* **forgetting)** VT **1** VOIR GRAMMAIRE A44 *(fact, person, knowledge)* oublier; *(one's French)* désapprendre; **to f. to do sth** oublier *ou* omettre de faire qch; **don't f. to …** n'oubliez *ou* ne manquez pas de …; **to f. how to do sth** oublier comment on fait qch, ne plus savoir faire qch; **to f. oneself** s'oublier; **have I forgotten anyone?** est-ce que j'ai oublié quelqu'un?; **to f. sb's birthday** oublier *(de souhaiter)* l'anniversaire de qn; **to f. one's manners** oublier ses bonnes manières; **have you forgotten your manners?** où sont tes bonnes manières?; *(to child)* veux-tu être poli!; **f. it!** *(in reply to apology, thanks)* il n'y a pas de quoi!; **f. it, it wasn't important** *(what I said)* non, non, ça n'a pas d'importance; **look, f. it, will you?** *(stop talking about it)* écoute, laisse tomber, d'accord?; **you can f. it!** *(they're being unreasonable)* ils peuvent faire une croix dessus *ou* *Fam* aller se faire voir!; *(they've no chance)* ils peuvent faire une croix dessus!, *Fam* ils sont foutus!; **you can f. the holiday** *(we can't afford it)* tu peux laisser tomber l'idée d'aller en vacances; **he's only ten years old, don't f.** n'oubliez pas qu'il n'a que dix ans; **to be forgotten** tomber dans l'oubli; **he felt that he had been forgotten by his friends** il avait l'impression que ses amis l'avaient oublié; **it's best forgotten** il vaut mieux ne plus en parler; **it's all been forgotten now** tout ça c'est du passé; **things best forgotten** des choses qu'il vaut mieux oublier
2 *(leave by mistake) (handkerchief, gloves etc)* oublier; **I forgot my hat on the train** j'ai oublié mon chapeau dans le train
VI oublier; **before I f.** *(can you do sth?)* avant que j'oublie *ou* que je n'oublie; **to f. about sb/sth** oublier qn/qch; **he warned me of the danger but I forgot (all) about it** il m'a averti du danger mais je n'y ai plus pensé; **and you can f. about going to London!** et ce n'est pas la peine de songer à aller à Londres!

forgetful [fə'getfʊl] ADJ **1** **to be very f.** avoir très mauvaise mémoire **2** *(negligent)* oublieux *(* **of** de); **to be f. of one's duty** être oublieux de *ou* négliger son devoir

forgetfulness [fə'getfʊlnɪs] N manque *m* *(habituel)* de mémoire; **a moment of f.** un moment de distraction

forget-me-not N *(plant)* myosotis *m*

forging ['fɔːdʒɪŋ] N *Metal (activity)* travail *m* de forge; *(forged item)* pièce *f* forgée;
▸▸ **f. mill** forge *f*; **f. press** marteau-pilon *m*, *pl* marteaux-pilons

forgivable [fə'gɪvəb(ə)l] ADJ excusable, pardonnable

forgivably [fə'gɪvəblɪ] ADV de façon excusable *ou* pardonnable; **he was f. angry/surprised** il est compréhensible *ou* naturel qu'il ait été en colère/surpris; **f. so, in my opinion** ce qui est tout à fait compréhensible *ou* naturel, à mon avis

forgive [fə'gɪv] *(pt* **forgave** [fə'geɪv], *pp* **forgiven** [fə'gɪv(ə)n]*)* VT **1** *(something)* pardonner; *Rel, Arch (mistake, insult)* pardonner; **to f. sb sth** pardonner qch à qn; **to f. sb a debt** faire grâce d'une dette à qn; **if you'll f. the pun** pardonnez-moi ce jeu de mots; **she was not prepared to f. his rudeness** elle n'était pas prête à lui pardonner sa grossièreté
2 **to f. sb** pardonner à qn; **he asked me to f. him** il m'a demandé pardon, il m'a demandé de le pardonner; **am I forgiven?** est-ce que tu me pardonnes?; **I'll never f. him for what he did** je ne lui pardonnerai jamais ce qu'il a fait; **one might perhaps be forgiven for thinking that …** il n'est pas interdit de pen-

ser que …; **f. me for intruding/interrupting** excusez-moi de vous déranger/interrompre
VI pardonner; **f. and forget** il faut oublier et pardonner

forgiveness [fə'gɪvnɪs] N **1** *(act) (of sins)* rémission *f*; **to ask sb's f.** demander pardon à qn; **she pleaded for his f.** elle l'a imploré pour qu'il la pardonne **2** *(quality)* indulgence *f*; **to show f.** faire preuve d'indulgence, se montrer indulgent

forgiving [fə'gɪvɪŋ] ADJ indulgent *(* **of** envers)

forgo, forego [fɔː'gəʊ] VT *(pt* **forwent** [fɔː'went], *pp* **forgone** [fɔː'gɒn]*)* renoncer à; **to f. doing sth** s'abstenir de faire qch

forgotten [fə'gɒt(ə)n] ADJ oublié; **the f. man of Scottish football** le laissé-pour-compte du football écossais

fork [fɔːk] N **1** *(for food)* fourchette *f*; *Agr* fourche *f*; **garden f.** fourche à bêcher; *Mus* **tuning f.** diapason *m* **2** *(sth with shape of fork) (of water diviner)* baguette *f* divinatoire; *(to support branch etc)* poteau *m* fourchu; **f. of lightning** zigzag *m* (d'éclair); *Cycling* **front f.** fourche *f* avant *ou* de direction **3** *(division) (in road)* bifurcation *f*, jonction *f*; *(of branches)* fourche *f*; **take the left f.** prenez la route/le sentier de gauche
VI *(of tree etc)* fourcher; *(of road)* faire une fourche, bifurquer; **follow the road until it forks** suivez la route jusqu'à la bifurcation *ou* fourche; **f. right for York** *(on sign)* prenez à droite pour York
VT *Agr (earth, hay)* fourcher; **they were forking hay onto the truck** ils chargeaient du foin à la fourche dans le camion
▸▸ **f. lunch** buffet *m*

When translating **fork**, note that **fourchette** and **fourche** are not interchangeable. **Fourchette** is an item of cutlery, whereas **fourche** is an agricultural implement.

▸ **fork in** VT SEP *(compost)* enfouir en fourchant
▸ **fork off** VI *(of road, driver)* bifurquer
▸ **fork out** *Fam* VT SEP *(provide, often unwillingly)* **to f. out money** raquer, casquer
VI *(pay out money)* **to f. out for sth** casquer pour qch; **he had to f. out (for it)** il a dû allonger la monnaie, il a dû casquer; **come on, f. out** *(what you owe me)* allez, aboule
▸ **fork over** VT SEP *(flowerbed)* retourner légèrement à la fourche

forked [fɔːkt] ADJ *(branch, pipe)* fourchu, bifurqué, en fourche; *(road)* qui bifurque, à bifurcation; *(tongue)* fourchu; *(lightning)* ramifié

forkful ['fɔːkfʊl] N **1** *(of food etc)* fourchetée *f* **2** *(of hay etc)* fourchée *f*

fork-lift N chariot *m* élévateur à fourche
▸▸ **f. truck** chariot élévateur à fourche

forlorn [fə'lɔːn] ADJ *Lit* **1** *(place)* désert, abandonné; *(look)* triste; *Am* **f. of hope** privé de tout espoir; **to look f.** avoir l'air triste; **a f. expression** une expression de tristesse **2** *(desperate) (attempt)* désespéré; **it's a f. hope** c'est un vain espoir; **to do sth in the f. hope that …** faire qch dans le fol espoir que …

FORM [fɔːm]

N	forme **1-4, 6, 10** ▪ silhouette **1**
	▪ formulaire **5** ▪ classe **8**
VT	former **1-3** ▪ façonner **1** ▪ se
	former **1** ▪ contracter **2**
	▪ constituer **3**
VI	se former **1**

N **1** *(shape) (of object)* forme *f*, configuration *f*, *(of person, animal)* silhouette *f*; **to take f.** prendre forme

2 *(manifestation)*, Biol, Gram, Liter, Mus forme f; **f. and content** *(of book etc)* la forme et le fond; **work that lacks f.** œuvre qui manque de forme; **tonic taken in the f. of pills** remontant pris sous (la) forme de pilules; **what f. did the lesson take?** quelle forme la leçon a-t-elle prise?; **poverty in every f.** la misère sous toutes ses formes; **it's a f. of disease** c'est une forme spéciale de maladie; **the different forms of worship** les différentes pratiques religieuses

3 *(formality)* formalité f; Law etc **in due or proper f.** en bonne (et due) forme; **a receipt in due f.** une quittance régulière; **to go through the f. of refusing** faire semblant de refuser; **for f.'s sake** pour la forme; **as a matter of f.** par manière d'acquit; **it is a mere matter of f.** c'est une pure formalité; Fam **to know the f.** *(what to do)* savoir ce qu'il faut faire; **it is good f.** c'est de bon ton; **good f. demands that ...** la politesse exige que ...; **it is not good f., it's bad f.** c'est de mauvais ton, ça fait mauvais genre; **it is bad f. to ask a lady her age** ce n'est pas poli de demander son âge à une dame; **it would have been good f. to at least tell me** la moindre des politesses aurait été de me le dire

4 *(formula)* *(of legal document etc)* formule f, forme f; **correct f. of words** tournure f de phrase correcte; **forms of address** *(when writing)* formules de politesse; *(when speaking)* titres mpl de politesse

5 *(printed document with spaces)*, Comput formulaire m; **order f.** bulletin m de commande

6 esp Sp *(condition)* forme f, condition f; Horseracing *(of horse)* performances fpl; *(in newspaper etc)* *(of horses)* tableau m des performances; **to be in/out of f.** être/ne pas être en forme; **to be in good f.** *(at a party etc)* être en train ou en forme; **in excellent f.** dans une forme excellente; **he felt in good f.** il se sentait en forme; **on present f.** *(the company will make a profit etc)* si l'on en juge par la situation actuelle; Horseracing **to study (the) f.** étudier les performances des chevaux

7 Br Sl **he's got f.** *(a criminal record)* son casier judiciaire n'est pas vierge; **has he got f.?** est-ce qu'il a un casier judiciaire?

8 Br Sch *(class)* classe f; **first f.** (classe f de) sixième f; **sixth f.** (classe de) première f

9 Br Old-fashioned *(bench)* banc m, banquette f

10 *(mould)* Metal forme f, moule m; Constr etc *(for reinforced concrete)* coffrage m, coffre m; Am Typ *(frame)* forme

11 *(of hare)* gîte m, forme f

VT 1 *(shape)* former, faire, façonner; *(the mind)* développer; *(character)* former; *(idea etc)* se former, se faire; *(doubts)* concevoir; **to f. the impression that ...** avoir l'impression que ...

2 *(habit etc)* contracter; *(relationship)* établir; *(plan)* arrêter; **to f. a friendship** *(of two people)* devenir amis; **to f. a friendship with sb** devenir ami avec qn; **to f. a successful partnership** former une association réussie; **he had formed a plan to ...** il avait projeté de ...

3 *(constitute)* former, faire; *(government, organisation)* constituer; *(company etc)* former, organiser; *(republic etc)* instituer, établir; *(new word etc)* former, faire; **to f. an obstacle to sth** faire obstacle à qch; **Portugal formed the last remaining obstacle** le Portugal constituait le dernier obstacle; **the walls f. a square** les murs forment un carré; **to f. part of sth** faire partie de qch; **they formed themselves into a committee** ils se constituèrent en comité; **the past tense is formed by the addition of -ed** le passé se forme en ajoutant -ed

VI 1 *(of ideas, opinions)* prendre forme, se former; *(of character, personality)* se former; *(of company)* se constituer; *(of friendship, relationship)* naître

2 Mil **to f. into a line** se mettre en ligne

▶▶ Comput **f. document** document m canevas; Comput **f. feed** avancement m du papier; Comput **f. field** champ m de saisie; **f. letter** lettre f circulaire; Br Sch **f. master** ≃ professeur m principal; Br Sch **f. mistress** ≃ professeur principal; Br Sch **f. room** salle f de classe, f; Br Sch **f. teacher** = ≃ professeur principal; Br Sch **f. tutor** = ≃ professeur principal

▶ **form up** VI Mil former des rangs

formal ['fɔːm(ə)l] **ADJ 1** *(welcome, reception, occasion etc)* cérémonieux, solennel; *(invitation)* officiel; **a f. dinner** un grand dîner; **is it f.?** *(the party, dance etc)* est-ce que c'est habillé?

2 esp Pej *(person)* compassé, formaliste; *(tone, manner)* guindé; *(language)* soutenu; **f. style** style m empesé ou compassé

3 *(procedure, notification)* formel, en règle; *(order, denial, agreement)* formel; *(contract)* en due forme; *(logic, grammar)* formel; *(garden)* à la française; **f. request for payment** mise f en demeure de payer; **to give sb a f. warning** avertir qn dans les formes; **a purely f. arrangement** un arrangement purement formel; **a f. similarity** une similarité de forme; **she had no f. schooling** elle n'a pas fait d'études conventionnelles

N Am *(dress)* robe f de soirée; *(occasion)* soirée f de cérémonie; *(with dancing)* bal m de cérémonie

▶▶ **f. demand** mise f en demeure; **f. dress** *(for ceremony)* tenue f de cérémonie; *(for evening)* tenue de soirée; **f. notice** mise f en demeure; **f. religion** religion f officielle

formaldehyde [fɔː'mældɪhaɪd] **N** Chem formaldéhyde m, aldéhyde m formique

formalin ['fɔːməlɪn] **N** Chem formol m

formalism ['fɔːməlɪz(ə)m] **N** formalisme m

formality [fɔː'mælɪtɪ] **N 1** *(procedure)* formalité f; **legal formalities** formes fpl ou formalités juridiques; **a mere f.** une pure formalité; **to dispense with the formalities** se dispenser des formalités **2** *(stiffness) (of speech)* compassement m; **the f. of the dance** le caractère cérémonieux du bal

formalize ['fɔːməlaɪz] **VT** *(contract, relations etc)* donner une forme officielle à; Ling, Phil *(grammar, proposition)* formaliser

formally ['fɔːməlɪ] **ADV 1** *(with formality)* cérémonieusement; **they greeted her f.** ils l'ont accueillie cérémonieusement; **to dress f.** s'habiller de façon stricte; *(in evening dress)* porter une tenue de soirée

2 *(openly, officially)* officiellement; **the organization f. renounced violence** l'organisation a officiellement renoncé à la violence

3 *(procedurally)* **f. correct** correct quant à la forme, dans les formes; **the institute is f. subordinate to the Department** sur le papier l'institut est subordonné au Département

Note that the French word **formellement** is a false friend. Its most common meaning is **strictly** or **categorically**.

format ['fɔːmæt] **N** *(of book, disk, TV programme etc)* format m; *(of meeting, evening etc)* organisation f

VT *(-tt-)* Comput *(disk)* formater; *(page, text)* mettre en forme, formater

formation [fɔː'meɪʃən] **N 1** *(act of creating)* *(of plural, coal, new policy, character etc)* formation f, *(of opinions, child's mind)* développement m; *(of company etc)* constitution f, formation; *(of republic etc)* établissement m

2 Mil etc *(arrangement)* *(of troops)* formation f, dispositif m; **battle f.,** Am **combat f.** formation de combat; **close f.** ordre m serré; **to break f.** décrocher

3 Mil *(unit)* unité f; **armoured f.** formation blindée

4 Geol **granite f.** formation f granitique

▶▶ **f. dancing** danse f en formation; **f. flying** vol m en formation

formative ['fɔːmətɪv] **ADJ** *(experience, influence etc)* formateur, -trice; **the f. years** les années de formation

N Ling élément m formateur

formatted ['fɔːmætɪd] **ADJ** *(disk)* formaté; *(text, page)* mis en forme, formaté

formatting ['fɔːmætɪŋ] **N** Comput *(of disk)* formatage m; *(of page, text)* mise f en forme, formatage

▶▶ **f. command** commande f de formatage; **f. instructions** instructions fpl pour le formatage

forme [fɔːm] **N** Br Typ forme f

former ['fɔːmər] **ADJ 1** *(previous)* antérieur, -eure, précédent; *(pupil, servant, colleague etc)* ancien; **my f. pupils** mes anciens élèves; **a f. convict** un repris de justice; **in f. times** autrefois; **in a f. life** dans une vie antérieure; **he is a mere shadow of his f. self** il n'est plus que l'ombre de lui-même

2 VOIR GRAMMAIRE A77 *(as opposed to the latter)* premier; **I prefer the f. alternative to the latter** je préfère la première alternative à la deuxième

PRON VOIR GRAMMAIRE A77 **the f.** celui-là, f celle-là, pl ceux-là, celles-là; **the f. ..., the latter ...** le premier ..., le second ...; **of the two methods I prefer the f.** des deux méthodes je préfère celle-là

-former ['fɔːmər] **SUFF** Br Sch **first/second/etc-f.** élève mf de sixième/cinquième/etc

formerly ['fɔːməlɪ] **ADV** autrefois, jadis; **Mr Martin, f. a liberal** M. Martin, autrefois libéral; **Mrs Boyle, f. Miss Reid** Madame Boyle, auparavant Mademoiselle Reid; **f. of London** résidant auparavant à Londres; **Burkina Faso, f. Upper Volta** le Burkina Faso, ancienne Haute-Volta

formic ['fɔːmɪk] **ADJ** Chem *(acid)* formique

Formica® [fɔː'maɪkə] **N** Formica® m; **F. worktop** plan m de travail en Formica®

formidable ['fɔːmɪdəb(ə)l] **ADJ** *(opponent, difficulty, appearance, weapon)* redoutable; *(performance, talent, defence)* formidable

Note that the most common meaning of the French word **formidable** is **fantastic, excellent.**

formidably [fɔː'mɪdəblɪ] **ADV** *(armed, difficult)* redoutablement; *(talented, thorough, equipped)* formidablement, remarquablement

forming ['fɔːmɪŋ] **N 1** *(of company etc)* constitution f, formation f **2** Metal formage m, façonnage m

▶▶ Mil **f. up** rassemblement m

formless ['fɔːmlɪs] **ADJ** informe, sans forme; *(desire, idea)* indéfini, flou

Formosa [fɔː'məʊsə] **N** Formerly Formose f

formula, pl **formulas, formulae** ['fɔːmjʊlə, -əz, -iː] **N 1** *(scheme, plan)* formule f; **an infallible f. for success/happiness** une recette infaillible pour réussir/trouver le bonheur; **a f. acceptable to all parties** une formule qui soit acceptable à tous les partis; **these romantic novels are all done to the same f.** ces romans à l'eau de rose sont tous écrits selon la même formule **2** *(recipe)*, Chem, Math etc pl usu **formulae** formule f; **gentle f.** *(shampoo, make-up remover etc)* formule douce **3** *(for feeding baby)* lait m en poudre

▶▶ Aut **F. 1** la formule 1; Aut **F. 1 car** voiture f formule 1

formulaic [fɔːmjʊˈleɪɪk] **ADJ** *Fml* stéréotypé

formulate [ˈfɔːmjʊleɪt] **VT 1** *(law, doctrine, theory etc)* formuler; *(plan, strategy, policy)* élaborer **2** *(one's opinion, objections)* formuler, exprimer; *(one's response)* formuler; **difficult to f. in words** difficile à exprimer en paroles

formulation [fɔːmjʊˈleɪʃən] **N 1** *(development)* (of plan, policy) formulation f, élaboration f **2** *(putting into words, expressing)* expression f **3** *(wording)* formulation f

formwork [ˈfɔːmwɜːk] **N** *(for reinforced concrete)* coffrage m

fornicate [ˈfɔːnɪkeɪt] **VI** forniquer

fornication [fɔːnɪˈkeɪʃən] **N** fornication f

fornicator [ˈfɔːnɪkeɪtər] **N** *(man)* fornicateur m; *Fam* coureur m de jupons; *(woman)* coureuse f

forsake [fəˈseɪk] **VT** (*pt* **forsook** [fəˈsʊk], *pp* **forsaken** [fəˈseɪk(ə)n]) *esp Lit* **1** *(abandon)* *(person)* abandonner, délaisser; *(shelter)* abandonner; **his habitual assurance had forsaken him** son assurance habituelle l'avait abandonné **2** *(renounce)* *(belief, career etc)* renoncer à, abandonner; *(conduct, life of ease)* renoncer à

forsooth [fəˈsuːθ] *Arch, Lit* **ADV** *(in truth)* en vérité

INT par exemple!, ma foi!

forswear [fɔːˈsweər] **VT** (*pt* **forswore** [fɔːˈswɔːr], *pp* **forsworn** [fɔːˈswɔːn]) *Fml* **1** renoncer à; *Rel* abjurer, renier **2** *Law* **to f. oneself** se parjurer

forsythia [fɔːˈsaɪθɪə] **N** *(shrub)* forsythia m

fort [fɔːt] **N** *Mil* fort m, forteresse f; *Fam* **to hold the f.** *(look after house etc)* garder la maison; *(look after office, shop etc)* tenir la boutique

forte[1] [fɔːt, ˈfɔːtɪ] **N** *(strong point)* fort m

forte[2] [ˈfɔːtɪ] *Mus* **ADJ, ADV** forte *inv*

N forte m

forth [fɔːθ] **ADV 1** *(forwards)* en avant; **to walk back and f.** marcher de long en large, faire les cent pas; **the ferry goes back and f. between ...** le ferry fait la navette entre ...; *Arch* **from this time f.** désormais, dorénavant; **from that/this day f.** à partir de ce jour/d'aujourd'hui **2 and so f.** *(etcetera)* et ainsi de suite, et cetera

forthcoming [fɔːθˈkʌmɪŋ] **ADJ 1** *(imminent)* prochain, à venir; *(book, film)* qui va sortir; **the f. session** la prochaine session **2** *(available)* **to be f.** ne pas se faire attendre; **the money will be f.** on trouvera l'argent nécessaire; **no answer was f.** aucune réponse n'est venue (**from** de); **the promised help was not f.** les secours promis ont fait défaut **3** *(person)* *(sociable)* sociable, expansif; *(frank)* ouvert, franc, f franche; **not (very) f.** réservé, renfermé (**about** au sujet de)

forthright [ˈfɔːθraɪt] **ADJ** *(person, reply)* franc, f franche

forthrightness [ˈfɔːθraɪtnɪs] **N** franchise f (**about** au sujet de)

forthwith [fɔːθˈwɪθ] **ADV** *Fml* tout de suite, immédiatement, aussitôt; **the council must be summoned f.** il faut convoquer le conseil d'urgence; **to dispense with sb's services f.** se dispenser sur-le-champ *ou* immédiatement des services de qn

fortieth [ˈfɔːtɪɪθ] **ADJ** quarantième

N 1 *(person, thing)* quarantième mf **2** *(fraction)* quarantième m

fortification [fɔːtɪfɪˈkeɪʃən] **N** fortification f

fortified [ˈfɔːtɪfaɪd] **ADJ** *Mil* fortifié

▸▸ **f. town** ville f fortifiée, place f forte; *Br* **f. wine** vin m de liqueur, vin doux naturel

fortify [ˈfɔːtɪfaɪ] **VT 1** *(ship etc)* renforcer,

fortifier; *(person)* fortifier; *Fig (person, person's resolve)* affermir, fortifier; **to f. oneself for the coming struggle** rassembler ses forces pour la lutte à venir; **fortified with the rites of the Church** muni des sacrements de l'Église; **to f. oneself against the cold** se prémunir contre le froid **2** *(wine)* viner; *(food)* augmenter la valeur nutritive de **3** *Mil (place)* fortifier

fortifying [ˈfɔːtɪfaɪɪŋ] **ADJ** fortifiant; *(drink etc)* remontant

fortissimo [fɔːˈtɪsɪməʊ] *Mus* **ADV** fortissimo

N fortissimo m *inv*

fortitude [ˈfɔːtɪtjuːd] **N** force f morale

fortnight [ˈfɔːtnaɪt] **N** *esp Br* quinzaine f, quinze jours mpl; **today f.** (d')aujourd'hui en quinze; **a f. tomorrow** demain en quinze; **in a f.'s time** dans une quinzaine (de jours); **a f. ago** il y a quinze jours; **to adjourn a case for a f.** remettre une cause à quinzaine; **to take a f.'s holiday** prendre quinze jours de vacances

fortnightly [ˈfɔːtnaɪtlɪ] *esp Br* **ADJ** bimensuel, semi-mensuel

ADV *(to appear)* bimensuellement, tous les quinze jours; *(to meet)* tous les quinze jours

FORTRAN [ˈfɔːtræn] **N** *Comput* FORTRAN m

fortress [ˈfɔːtrɪs] **N** forteresse f, *(town)* place f forte; **the place was built like a f.** l'endroit était construit comme une forteresse

▸▸ **f. city** cité f fortifiée

fortuitous [fɔːˈtjuːɪtəs] **ADJ** *esp Fml* fortuit, imprévu

fortuitously [fɔːˈtjuːɪtəslɪ] **ADV** *esp Fml* fortuitement, par hasard

fortunate [ˈfɔːtʃənət, -tʃ-] **ADJ 1** *(person etc)* **to be f.** avoir de la chance; **to be f. enough to ...** avoir la chance de ...; **I consider myself f. to know her** j'ai la chance de la connaître; **we've been quite f. in the weather** nous avons eu de la chance pour ce qui est du temps; **we've been quite f. in our choice** nous avons fait un choix très heureux; **the less f. among them** les plus infortunés d'entre eux

2 *(occasion etc)* propice, favorable, heureux; **a f. choice of words** une tournure heureuse; **it was f. that you remembered** encore heureux que tu t'en sois souvenu; **how f.!** quel bonheur!, quelle chance!

> Note that the French adjective **fortuné** is a false friend. It means **wealthy**.

fortunately [ˈfɔːtʃənətlɪ, -tʃ-] **ADV** heureusement, par bonheur; **we're quite f. situated as far as the shops are concerned** nous sommes plutôt bien lotis en ce qui concerne les magasins

fortune [ˈfɔːtʃən] **N 1** *(prosperity)* prospérité f, richesse f, *(riches)* richesses fpl, biens mpl; **a man of f.** un homme riche; **to make a** *or* **one's f.** faire fortune; **you must be making a f.** tu dois gagner un argent fou; **she has made and lost several fortunes** elle a fait fortune plusieurs fois dans sa vie; **to come into a f.** hériter une fortune; **her jewels are worth a f.** ses bijoux valent une fortune; *Fam* **it cost me a (small) f.** cela m'a coûté un argent fou *ou* une fortune *ou* les yeux de la tête *ou Fam* la peau des fesses; **to spend a (small) f. on books/decorating the house** dépenser une fortune en livres/pour décorer la maison; **her face is her f.** son visage est son grand atout

2 *(luck)* fortune f, *(chance)* hasard m, chance f, *(destiny)* destinée f, sort m; *Myth* le Sort, le Destin; **ill f.** malchance f, mauvais sort; **piece of good f.** coup m de chance, bonheur m; **by (sheer) good f.** par bonheur; **f. favours** *or* **is kind to him** la fortune lui sourit; **the fortunes of war** le sort des armes; **he**

followed the team's changing fortunes il a suivi l'équipe bon an mal an; **despite its changing fortunes over the years, the company ...** en dépit des adversités qu'elle a rencontré au fil des ans, la compagnie ...; **to tell fortunes** dire la bonne aventure; **to tell sb's f.** dire la bonne aventure à qn; **to tell sb's f. by the cards** tirer les cartes à qn

▸▸ **f. cookie** = biscuit m chinois dans lequel est caché un horoscope; *Fin* **F. 500** = les cinq cents plus grosses entreprises fpl américaines (dont la liste est établie, chaque année, par le magazine Fortune)

fortune-hunter **N** *(man)* coureur m de dot; *(woman)* croqueuse f de diamants

fortune-teller **N** diseur, -euse de bonne aventure; *(with cards)* tireur, -euse de cartes

fortune-telling **N** la bonne aventure; *(with cards)* cartomancie f

forty [ˈfɔːtɪ] **ADJ, N** quarante m; **f.-one** quarante et un; **f.-two** quarante-deux; **about f. guests** une quarantaine d'invités; **to be f. (years old)** avoir quarante ans; *Prov* **life begins at f.** la vie commence à quarante ans; **the forties** les années quarante; **to be in one's forties** avoir passé la quarantaine; *Fam* **to have f. winks** piquer *ou* faire un petit somme

forty-five **N** *Old-fashioned (record)* (disque m) quarante-cinq tours m

fortyish [ˈfɔːtɪɪʃ] **ADJ** d'une quarantaine d'années; **I'd say she was f.** je lui donne la quarantaine *ou* une quarantaine d'années; **he was balding, f. and plump** il perdait ses cheveux et avait la quarantaine rondouillarde

forum [ˈfɔːrəm] **N 1** tribune f libre, forum m; *Antiq (square)* forum m; **a f. in which workers can put forward their views** un forum permettant aux ouvriers d'exprimer leurs opinions **2** *Comput (on Internet)* forum m (de discussion)

forward [ˈfɔːwəd, *Naut* ˈfɒrəd] **ADJ 1** *(of place)* de devant, situé en avant; *Naut* (de l')avant, sur l'avant; *(movement etc)* en avant; **f. and backward movement** mouvement m d'avant en arrière

2 *(of time)* *(plants)* avancé, précoce; *(child)* précoce, en avance; **a f. thinking company** une entreprise tournée vers l'avenir

3 *(impudent, bold)* effronté, hardi; **it would have been thought f. of a woman to ...** cela aurait été considéré comme effronté de la part d'une femme de ...

4 *Fin (price etc)* à terme

ADV *(occ* **forwards** [ˈfɔːwədz]*)* **1** *(of time)* **from this/that day f.** à partir d'aujourd'hui/de ce jour-là

2 *(of direction)* en avant; **to go** *or* **move f.** (s')avancer; **to step f.** faire un pas en avant; **f.!** en avant!; *Mil* **f. march!** en avant, marche!

3 *(of position)* à l'avant; **the seat is too far f.** la banquette est trop avancée *ou* trop en avant; **we're sitting too far f.** nous sommes assis trop à avant; *Naut* **f. of the beam** sur l'avant du travers; **the crew's quarters are f.** le logement de l'équipage est à l'avant

4 *Com* **(carried) f.** report m; *Com* **charges f.** frais mpl à percevoir à la livraison; *Com, Fin* **to sell f.** vendre à terme

N *Sport (player)* avant m

VT 1 *(send)* *(letter, e-mail)* faire suivre; *(goods etc)* expédier, envoyer, *Spec* transiter; **please f.** *(on letter)* prière de faire suivre, à faire suivre; **to f. sth to sb** faire parvenir qch à qn; **we'll f. your complaint/report to the relevant department** nous transmettrons votre plainte/rapport au service correspondant

2 *(promote)* *(person's interests etc)* favoriser

▸▸ *Fin* **f. account** compte m à terme; *Fin* **f. buying** achat m à terme; *Fin* **f. contract** contrat *m* à terme; *Fin, Com* **f. dealing** opérations *fpl* à terme; *Com* **f. delivery** livraison *f* à terme; *Fin* **f. exchange** change *m* à terme; *Fin* **f. exchange market** marché *m* des changes à terme; *Aut* **f. gears** marches *fpl* avant; *Econ* **f. integration** intégration *f* en aval, intégration descendante; *Mktg* **f. invention** invention *f* de produits totalement nouveaux; *Fin, Com* **f. market** marché à terme; **f. motion** marche *f* (en) avant; *Sport* **f. pass** *(in rugby)* passe *f* en avant; *Mil* **f. positions** premières positions *fpl*; **f. post** avant-poste *m, pl* avant-postes; *Fin, Com* **f. purchase** achat à terme; *Fin* **f. rate** cours *m* à terme, taux *m* pour les opérations à terme; *Fin* **F. Rate Agreement** accord *m* de taux à terme; *Com* **f. requirement** commande *f* prévisionnelle; *Com* **f. sale** vente *f* à terme; *Comput* **f. search** recherche *f* avant; *Br Comput* **f. slash** barre *f* oblique; *Fin, Com* **f. trading** opérations *fpl* à terme; *Naut* **f. turret** tourelle *f* avant

forwardation [fɔːwəˈdeɪʃən] N *Fin* report *m*

forwarder [ˈfɔːwədər] N *Com* transitaire *m*; **f. and consolidator** transitaire-groupeur *m*

forwarding [ˈfɔːwədɪŋ] N *(sending)* expédition *f*, envoi *m*;
▸▸ **f. address** adresse *f* pour faire suivre le courrier; *Com* adresse pour l'expédition; *Com* **f. agent** transitaire *m*; *Com* **f. charges** frais *mpl* d'expédition; *Com* **f. instructions** indications *fpl* concernant l'expédition

forward-looking ADJ progressiste

forwardness [ˈfɔːwədnɪs] N **1** *(eagerness)* empressement *m*, ardeur *f* **2** *(boldness)* hardiesse *f*, présomption *f*

forwards [ˈfɔːwədz] ADV *see* **forward** ADV

forwent PT *see* **forgo**

Fosbury flop [ˈfɒzbərɪ] N *Sport* Fosbury *m*

fossil [ˈfɒs(ə)l] N fossile *m*; *Fam Pej* **an old f.** *(person)* un vieux croûton, un vieux fossile
ADJ *(plant, bones etc)* fossile
▸▸ **f. fuel** combustible *m* fossile

fossilization [fɒsɪlaɪˈzeɪʃən] N fossilisation *f*

fossilize [ˈfɒsɪlaɪz] VT fossiliser
VI se fossiliser; *Fig (of person)* s'encroûter

fossilized [ˈfɒsɪlaɪzd] ADJ fossilisé; *(ideas, attitudes etc)* fossile

foster [ˈfɒstər] VT **1** *(child)* prendre en famille d'accueil; **to f. a child (out)** mettre un enfant en famille d'accueil **2** *(promote)* *(idea, hope, belief etc)* entretenir, nourrir; *(person's plans, sense of responsibility)* encourager, favoriser; *(the arts etc)* protéger; **to f. friendship between peoples** stimuler l'amitié entre les peuples
▸▸ **f. child** enfant *m* placé dans une famille d'accueil; **f. father** père *m* de la famille d'accueil; **f. home** famille *f* d'accueil; **f. mother** mère *f* de la famille d'accueil; **f. parents** famille d'accueil

fostering [ˈfɒstərɪŋ] N **1** *(of child)* prise *f* en famille d'accueil; *(fostering out)* mise *f* en famille d'accueil **2** *(of the arts etc)* patronage *m*, encouragement *m*

fought PP, PT *see* **fight**

foul [faʊl] ADJ **1** *(disgusting)* *(smell)* infect, nauséabond; *(thoughts)* immonde, impur, corrompu; *(language)* grossier, ordurier; *(water)* croupi; *Fam* **that soup was f.!** cette soupe était infecte!; *Fam* **what f. weather!** quel sale temps!, quel temps infect!; *Naut* **f. weather** gros temps *m*; **to be f. to sb/about sth** être infect *ou* abject avec qn/au sujet de qch; **f. air** air *m* vicié; **f. breath** mauvaise haleine *f*, *esp Lit* **f. deed** infamie *f*, **f.-smelling/-tasting** qui a une odeur/un goût infect(e); *Fam* **I'm in a f. temper today** je suis d'une humeur massacrante aujourd'hui; **she has a f.**

temper elle a un sale caractère; **she's got a f. tongue** elle a une langue de vipère
2 *(gun, spark plug)* encrassé; **f. bottom** *(of anchorage)* mauvais fond *m*; *(of ship)* carène *f* sale
3 *Sport etc (unfair)* déloyal, -aux, illicite; *(criminal behaviour)* action criminelle; *(underhand dealings)* intrigue *f*
N *Sport* coup *m* illicite *ou* déloyal; *Ftbl, Rugby* faute *f*
ADV **1 it smells f.!** ça pue!; **it tastes perfectly f.** c'est infect; **it looks f.** c'est horrible *ou* atroce; *Fam* **to feel f.** ne pas se sentir bien
2 *(unfairly)* irrégulièrement, déloyalement; *Old-fashioned* **to fight f.** se battre déloyalement; *Naut* **to run f. of another ship** *(collide with)* entrer en collision avec *ou* aborder *ou* heurter un autre navire; **to fall** *or* **run f. of the law/sb** avoir des démêlés avec la justice/qn
VT **1** *(dirty)* *(place, reputation etc)* salir, souiller; *(of dog)* *(pavement)* souiller; *(gun barrel, spark plugs)* encrasser
2 *(obstruct, jam)* *(ropes etc)* s'emmêler dans; *(collide with)* *(ship)* entrer en collision avec, (se) heurter contre; **weeds fouled the anchor** l'ancre était prise *ou* coincée dans des algues; **the ropes fouled the propeller** les cordes avaient bloqué l'hélice
3 *Sport (another player)* commettre une faute contre
VI **1** *(of gun barrel etc)* s'encrasser; *(of pump)* s'engorger **2** *Naut (of anchor, rope etc)* se coincer; *(of anchor)* surjaler; *Tech (of moving part)* toucher
▸▸ *Sport* **f. play** jeu *m* irrégulier *ou* déloyal; *(in cards, games)* tricherie *f*, **f. play is not suspected** on ne croit pas à un crime

▸ **foul up** VT SEP **1** *(put out of order)* *(machine)* dérégler **2** *Fam (ruin)* *(plan)* gâcher; **it will f. things up if he finds out** ça va tout gâcher s'il l'apprend
VI **1** *Sl (of person)* merder; **don't f. up again/this time!** tâche de ne plus merder/ne pas merder cette fois! **2** *(of gun barrel etc)* s'encrasser; *(of pump)* s'engorger

fouler [ˈfaʊlər] N *Sport* **he's a persistent f.** il commet des fautes sans arrêt

fouling [ˈfaʊlɪŋ] N **1** *(of pipes)* engorgement *m*; *(of spark plugs)* encrassement *m* **2** *Sport* **a lot of f.** beaucoup de jeu déloyal

foully [ˈfaʊlɪ] ADV **1** *(to speak etc)* grossièrement **2** *(to behave)* bassement, ignoblement; *Lit* **he was f. murdered** il fut ignoblement assassiné

foul-mouthed [ˈfaʊlˈmaʊðd] ADJ *(person)* au langage ordurier, grossier, -ière; *(reply, tirade)* ordurier, grossier

foulness [ˈfaʊlnɪs] N **1** *(dirtiness)* saleté *f*, *(of air etc)* fétidité *f*, **the f. of the smell** l'odeur infecte, la puanteur **2** *(of language etc)* grossièreté *f*, obscénité *f* **3** *(of a deed, behaviour)* infamie *f*, ignominie *f*

foul-tempered ADJ **to be f.** avoir un sale caractère

foul-up N *Fam (mistake)* cafouillage *m*; **there's been a f.** quelque chose a cloché *ou* cafouillé, il y a eu un cafouillage

found [faʊnd] VT **1** *(city, hospital, dynasty)* fonder; *(college, club, organization etc)* fonder, créer; *(company, business etc)* établir, créer; **to f. a fortune** *(lay foundations of fortune)* établir les bases d'une fortune; *(make fortune)* bâtir une fortune **(on** sur**) 2** *(suspicions, hope, social order etc)* baser, fonder **(on** sur**); founded on fact** *(of novel etc)* reposant sur des faits véridiques

found [2] PT, PP *see* **find**
ADJ *(with adv prefixed)* *(ship etc)* **well-f.** bien équipé **(in** de**)**

found [3] VT *Metal (metals)* fondre; *(casting)* mouler

foundation [faʊnˈdeɪʃən] N **1** *(action)* *(of city etc)* fondation *f*, *(of empire)* établissement *m*, institution *f*, *(of company)* établissement *m*, création *f*, *(of hospital)* fondation et dotation *f*
2 *Constr (base)* *(of building)* fondement *m*, fondation *f*, *(of road)* assiette *f*, *(of machine etc)* assise *f*, *Fig* **to lay the foundation(s) of an alliance** jeter les bases d'une alliance; **the foundations of modern society** les assises *ou* fondations de la société moderne; *Constr* **to lay the f. stone** poser la première pierre
3 *(basis)* *(of theory etc)* fondement *m*, base *f*, *(of doubt)* motif *m*, cause *f*, **rumour without f.** bruit dénué de fondement
4 *(institution)* institution *f* dotée, fondation *f*, *(legacy)* capital *m* légué pour œuvres de bienfaisance, fondation; **a charitable f.** une institution charitable; **the Ford f.** la fondation Ford
5 *(in clothing)* **embroidery on a silk f.** broderie *f* sur fond de soie
6 *(make-up)* fond *m* de teint
▸▸ *Br* **f. course** cours *m* introductif; **f. cream** fond de teint; *Old-fashioned* **f. garment** *(girdle)* gaine *f*, *(full-length)* combiné *m*; *Br* **f. hospital** = hôpital *m* dépendant du NHS mais possédant une autonomie importante en ce qui concerne le budget, les salaires et les conditions de travail; **f. scholar** élève *mf* boursier; *Br* **f. school** = école *f* privée qui reçoit une subvention de l'État

founder [1] [ˈfaʊndər] N *(of hospital etc)* fondateur *m*
▸▸ *Br* **f. member** membre *m* fondateur

founder [2] N *Metal* fondeur *m*

founder [3] VI *(of hopes, horse)* s'effondrer; *(of talks, negotiations)* avorter; *(of project, scheme)* péricliter; *(of ship)* sombrer, couler; **to f. on the rocks** s'échouer sur les rochers
VT *(horse)* courbaturer

foundering [ˈfaʊndərɪŋ] N *(of hopes)* effondrement *m*

founding [1] [ˈfaʊndɪŋ] ADJ *(member)* fondateur, -trice
N = **foundation 1**
▸▸ **f. father** père *m* fondateur; *Hist* **the F. Fathers** les pères *mpl* fondateurs *(aux États-Unis)*

founding [2] N *Metal* fonderie *f*, moulage *m*

foundling [ˈfaʊndlɪŋ] N *Old-fashioned* enfant *mf* trouvé(e)
▸▸ *Hist* **f. hospital** hospice *m* des enfants trouvés

foundry [ˈfaʊndrɪ] N *Metal (iron etc)* fonderie *f*
▸▸ **f. iron** fonte *f* de moulage

fount [1] [faʊnt] N *Lit (spring)* source *f* (d'eau); *Fig (of happiness etc)* source *f*

fount [2] [faʊnt, fɒnt] N *Typ* fonte *f*

fountain [ˈfaʊntɪn] N *(natural)* fontaine *f*, source *f* (d'eau); *(man-made)* fontaine; *(in park etc)* jet *m* d'eau; **a f. of water shot from the broken pipe** un jet d'eau jaillit du tuyau cassé
▸▸ **f. pen** stylo *m* à encre

fountainhead [ˈfaʊntɪnhed] N *esp Fig* source *f*

four [fɔːr] N **1** *(number, numeral)* quatre *m inv*; **twenty-f.** vingt-quatre; **f. fives are twenty** quatre fois cinq font vingt; **it's f. o'clock** il est quatre heures; **at f. thirty** à quatre heures et demie; **to be f.** *(in age)* avoir quatre ans; **on all fours** à quatre pattes; **to get down on all fours** se mettre à quatre pattes
2 *Sport (in rowing)* quatre *m*; **would you like to make up a f.?** *(for a game of bridge)* voudriez-vous vous joindre à nous pour faire une partie à quatre?; *Cr* **to hit a f.** marquer

quatre points; *Golf* a **f.-ball (match)** une partie à quatre joueurs et quatre balles
PRON quatre
ADJ quatre; **the f. corners of the earth** les quatre coins du monde; **open to the f. winds** ouvert à tous les vents *ou* aux quatre vents; **the F. Horsemen of the Apocalypse** les quatre cavaliers de l'Apocalypse

four-colour, *Am* **four-color** **ADJ** *Typ etc* à quatre couleurs
▸▸**f. printing** impression *f* en quadrichromie; **f. work** (*process*) quadrichromie *f*

four-cornered **ADJ** à quatre coins; (*quadrangular*) quadrangulaire

four-cycle **ADJ** *Am* (*engine, cylinder etc*) à quatre temps

four-door **ADJ** *Aut* à quatre portes; **f. model** quatre portes *f*; **f. saloon** berline *f* à quatre portes

four-engined [-'endʒɪnd] **ADJ** (*plane*) quadrimoteur

four-eyes [-aɪz] **N** *Fam* binoclard, -arde

four-figure **ADJ** *Math* (*number, sum*) à quatre chiffres; (*logarithm*) à quatre décimales

fourfold ['fɔːfəʊld] **ADJ a f. increase** une augmentation au quadruple
ADV quatre fois autant, au quadruple; **to increase f.** quadrupler

four-footed [-'fʊtɪd] **ADJ** (*animal*) quadrupède, à quatre pattes; *Fam* **a f. friend** un animal à quatre pattes

four-handed [-'hændɪd] **ADJ 1** *Cards* (*game*) à quatre (personnes) **2** *Mus* (*piece*) à quatre mains

four-in-hand **N** (*carriage*) véhicule *m* à quatre chevaux

four-leaf clover **N** trèfle *m* à quatre feuilles

four-leaved **ADJ** (*plant*) quadrifolié
▸▸**f. clover** trèfle *m* à quatre feuilles

four-legged **ADJ** (*animal*) quadrupède; (*table*) à quatre pieds; **our f. friends** nos amis les bêtes

four-letter word **N** *Fam* gros mot *m*, obscénité *f*; **for some people, 'socialism' seems to be a f. w.** pour certains, il semble que le mot 'socialisme' soit tabou

four-part **ADJ** *Mus* à quatre parties; (*singing*) à quatre voix

four-phase **ADJ** *Elec* (*system*) tétraphasé

four-poster **N** lit *m* à colonnes *ou* à baldaquin
ADJ (*bed*) à colonnes

fourscore [fɔː'skɔːr] **ADJ** *Arch, Lit* quatre-vingts

four-seater **N** *Aut* voiture *f* à quatre places

foursome ['fɔːsəm] **N** (*four people*) groupe *m* de quatre personnes; (*two couples*) deux couples; *Golf* (*game*) partie *f* (de) double *ou* à deux contre deux; **to go out in a f.** (*of four people*) sortir à quatre; (*of two couples*) sortir à deux couples; **to make up a f.** (*of four people*) former un groupe de quatre personnes; (*of two couples*) former deux couples; (*be the fourth person*) faire le quatrième

four-speed **ADJ** *Aut* à quatre vitesses

foursquare ['fɔː'skweər] **ADJ 1** (*refusal*) carré **2** (*building*) solide
ADV (*to refuse*) carrément; (*to build*) solidement; **to stand f. behind sb** soutenir qn fermement *ou* résolument

four-star **N** *Br* (*petrol*) super *m*
▸▸**f. hotel** hôtel *m* quatre étoiles *ou* de première catégorie; **f. petrol** super, super-carburant *m*; **f. unleaded** super sans plomb

four-stroke **ADJ** (*engine*) à quatre temps

fourteen ['fɔː'tiːn] **ADJ, N** quatorze *m*; **she is f.** elle a quatorze ans; **the plane will arrive at**

f. thirty (hours) l'avion arrivera à quatorze heures trente

fourteenth [fɔː'tiːnθ] **ADJ** quatorzième; **Louis the F.** Louis Quatorze
N 1 (*of month*) quatorze *m*; (on) **the f. of May** le quatorze mai **2** (*fraction*) quatorzième *m* **3** (*person, thing*) quatorzième *mf*

fourth [fɔːθ] **ADJ** quatrième; **Henry the F.** Henri Quatre
N 1 (*of month*) quatre *m*; **on the f.** le quatre; **the f. of January, January the f.** le quatre janvier
2 (*fraction*) quart *m*; **three-fourths of the globe** les trois quarts du globe
3 (*in series*) quatrième *mf*
4 *Mus* quarte *f*
5 *Aut* quatrième *f*
6 *Cards* **to make a f.** faire le quatrième
▸▸**the f. estate** (*press*) la presse; *Aut* **f. gear** quatrième vitesse *f*; *Am* **F. of July** = anniversaire *m* du jour de l'indépendance (*fête nationale américaine*); *Pol* **the F. World** le quart-monde; *Br Sch* **f. year** ≃ classe *f* de troisième

fourthly ['fɔːθlɪ] **ADV** quatrièmement, en quatrième lieu

four-wheel **ADJ** (*vehicle*) à quatre roues
▸▸*Aut* **f. drive** propulsion *f* à quatre roues; **does it have f. drive?** est-ce qu'il a quatre roues motrices?; **it's a f. drive** c'est un quatre-quatre; *Aut* **f. steering** quatre roues *fpl* directrices

four-wheeled **ADJ** à quatre roues

four-wheeler **N** voiture *f* à quatre roues

fowl [faʊl] **N 1** (*domesticated bird*) volaille *f*, **to keep fowl(s)** élever de la volaille *ou* des volailles; *Culin* **boiling f.** poule *f* (au pot) **2** (*wild bird*) (*pl* **fowl**) gibier *m* ailé **3** *Lit* (*bird*) oiseau *m*
▸▸**f. pest** peste *f* aviaire; **f. pox** diphtérie *f* aviaire

fowling ['faʊlɪŋ] **N to go f.** aller à la chasse au gibier ailé
▸▸**f. piece** carabine *f*, fusil *m* de chasse léger

fox [fɒks] **N** renard *m*; **red f.** renard commun; **Arctic f.** renard bleu; **silver f.** renard argenté; *Fam* **an old f.** (*cunning man*) un vieux renard, un vieux madré; *Fam* **a sly f.** un fin renard, un roublard
VT 1 (*mystify*) (*person*) mystifier, tromper; **you've got me foxed** je suis perplexe; **it foxes me why he did it** je n'arrive pas à saisir pourquoi il a fait ça; **she was absolutely foxed by the problem** le problème la laissait complètement perplexe **2** (*trick, deceive*) tromper, duper **3** (*discolour*) (*pages of book*) tacher de roux; (*engraving*) maculer
▸▸**f. brush** queue *f* de renard; **f. cub** renardeau *m*; **f. fur** (*peau f de*) renard *m*; **a f. fur coat** un manteau *m* en renard

foxglove ['fɒksglʌv] **N** (*plant*) digitale *f* (pourprée)

foxhole ['fɒkshəʊl] **N 1** renardière *f*, terrier *m* de renard **2** *Mil* abri *m* individuel; (*for sniper*) trou *m* de tirailleur

foxhound ['fɒkshaʊnd] **N** fox-hound *m*, *pl* fox-hounds

foxhunt ['fɒkshʌnt] **N** chasse *f* au renard

foxhunting ['fɒkshʌntɪŋ] **N** chasse *f* au renard

foxiness ['fɒksɪnɪs] **N 1** (*craftiness*) roublardise *f* **2** *Am Fam* (*of woman*) air *m* sexy

foxtail ['fɒksteɪl] **N 1** (*flower*) queue *f* de renard **2** (*plant*) vulpin *m*
▸▸**f. grass** vulpin

fox-terrier **N** fox-terrier *m*, *pl* fox-terriers, *Fam* fox *m*

foxtrot ['fɒkstrɒt] **N** (*dance*) fox-trot *m inv*
VI (-**tt-**) danser le fox-trot

foxy ['fɒksɪ] **ADJ 1** (*crafty*) rusé, astucieux, *esp Pej* roublard **2** *Am Fam* (*woman*) sexy; **a f. lady** une nana sexy

foyer ['fɔɪeɪ, 'fwæjeɪ] **N** *Theat* foyer *m* du public; *Cin* (*hall m d'*)entrée *f*, (*of hotel*) hall (de réception)

FPA [efpiː'eɪ] **N** (*abbr* **Family Planning Association**) = association *f* pour le planning familial

FPU [efpiː'juː] **N** *Comput* (*abbr* **floating-point unit**) FPU *f*, coprocesseur *m* arithmétique

Fr 1 *Rel* (*abbr* **Father**) Père **2** *abbr* **France 3** *Fin abbr* **franc**

FRA [efɑː'reɪ] **N** *Fin* (*abbr* **Future Rate Agreement, Forward Rate Agreement**) ATF *m*

fracas ['fræka:] **N** remue-ménage *m inv*; **to cause a f.** faire du remue-ménage

fractal ['frækt(ə)l] **N** fractal *m*

fraction ['frækʃən] **N 1** VOIR GRAMMAIRE A76; B59 *Math* fraction *f*, **vulgar** *or* **common f.** fraction ordinaire; **compound f.** fraction de fraction; **decimal f.** fraction décimale **2** (*small part*) petite portion *f*, petite partie *f*; **the new method takes only a f. of the time** la nouvelle méthode prend bien moins de temps; **he escaped death by a f. of a second** il a été à deux doigts de la mort; **a f. too small/large** un tout petit peu trop petit/grand; **a f. earlier/too late** un tout petit peu plus tôt/trop tard; **she won by a f.** elle a gagné d'un rien **3** *Fin* (*of share*) fraction *f*, rompu *m* **4** *Chem* (*of distillation*) fraction *f* **5** *Pol* (*of party*) fraction *f*, groupe *m* fractionnaire

fractional ['frækʃən(ə)l] **ADJ 1** *Math* fractionnaire; *Fig* **the difference is only f.** la différence est minime **2** *Chem* fractionné
▸▸*Chem* **f. distillation** distillation *f* fractionnée

fractionally ['frækʃən(ə)lɪ] **ADV** légèrement, un tout petit peu

fractionate ['frækʃəneɪt] **VT** *Chem, Ind* (*petroleum etc*) fractionner

fractionize ['frækʃənaɪz] **VT** *Math* fractionner

fractious ['frækʃəs] **ADJ** de mauvaise humeur; (*tone of voice, expression*) irrité; (*baby*) pleurnicheur; **to be f.** *or* **in a f. mood** être de mauvaise humeur; (*baby*) pleurnicher

fractiousness ['frækʃəsnɪs] **N** mauvaise humeur *f*, (*of baby*) pleurnicherie *f*, pleurnichage *m*; **the f. of her voice** l'irritation qu'il y avait dans sa voix

fracture ['fræktʃər] **N 1** *Med* fracture *f*, **to set a f.** réduire une fracture **2** (*of axle etc*) fracture *f*, rupture *f*, *Geol* cassure *f*, fracture
VT 1 *Med* (*bone*) fracturer; **fractured skull** crâne fracturé; **fractured ribs** côtes cassées **2** (*break*) casser, briser
VI 1 *Med* (*of bone, limb*) se fracturer **2** (*break*) se casser, se briser

fragile ['frædʒaɪl] **ADJ 1** (*cup, peace*) fragile **2** (*person*) (*weak*) fragile, faible; (*delicate*) délicat; **she was a f. child** c'était une enfant fragile; **he's become very f. recently** il s'est beaucoup affaibli ces derniers temps; **emotionally f.** fragile sur le plan émotionnel; **he sounded rather f. over the phone** il avait l'air plutôt abattu au téléphone; *Fam* **I'm feeling a bit f. this morning** (*hung over*) j'ai mal aux cheveux ce matin

fragilely ['frædʒaɪlɪ] **ADV** fragilement

fragility [frə'dʒɪlɪtɪ] **N 1** (*of ornament, peace*) fragilité *f* **2** (*of person*) (*weakness*) fragilité *f*, faiblesse *f*, (*delicateness*) délicatesse *f*, **emotional f.** fragilité émotionnelle

fragment[1] ['frægmənt] **N 1** (*of porcelain etc*) fragment *m*, morceau *m*; (*of paper*) morceau; (*of mortar shell*) éclat *m*; (*of story, account*) fragment; **to fly into fragments** voler en morceaux *ou* en éclats **2** *Liter* fragment *m*; *(of book)* extrait *m*; *(of author)* œuvre *f* inachevée

fragment[2] [ˈfræɡˈment] vɪ se fragmenter

vт réduire en fragments, briser en morceaux; **the family structure/the party has been fragmented** la structure familiale/le parti a été fragmenté(e)

fragmentary [ˈfræɡmənt(ə)rɪ] ADJ fragmentaire

fragmentation [fræɡmənˈteɪʃən] N fragmentation *f*

▸▸ **f. bomb** bombe *f* à fragmentation

fragrance [ˈfreɪɡrəns] N parfum *m*; **bubble bath with the f. of bilberries** bain moussant (parfumé) à la myrtille

fragrant [ˈfreɪɡrənt] ADJ parfumé, odorant, fragrant; *(scent)* embaumé; **to be** *or* **smell f.** sentir bon; **woods f. with wild strawberries** bois qui embaument les fraises sauvages

fraidy cat [ˈfreɪdɪ] N *Am Fam* poule *f* mouillée

frail [freɪl] ADJ **1** *(person)* faible, frêle; **a f. old man** un vieil homme frêle *ou* fragile; **to be in f. health** avoir une santé délicate **2** *(object)* peu solide, fragile; *(beauty)* éphémère; *(happiness)* précaire; *(hope)* fragile

frailness [ˈfreɪlnɪs] N **1** *(of person)* faiblesse *f*, *(of character)* faiblesse morale; **the f. of his health** sa santé délicate **2** *(of glass etc)* fragilité *f*, *(of beauty)* caractère *m* éphémère; *(of happiness)* précarité *f*

frailty [ˈfreɪltɪ] N **1** = **frailness 1 2** *(moral flaw)* faible *m*, défaut *m*; **human f.** faiblesse *f* des hommes

frame [freɪm] N **1** *(of picture, mirror, web page)* cadre *m*, encadrement *m*; *(of window, door)* chambranle *m*, châssis *m* dormant; *(picture) TV* trame *f* (double); *Cin (of reel of film)* image *f*, *(of comic strip)* case *f* **2** *(framework)* *(of person, animal, wing of plane)* ossature *f*, *(of building, bridge etc)* charpente *f*, *(of bicycle etc)* cadre *m*; *(of railway engine, car)* châssis *m*; *(of machine)* bâti *m*; *(of umbrella)* monture *f*, *(of racket)* armature *f*, *(of bed)* châlit *m*; *(of ship)* membrure *f*, carcasse *f*, *(in gardening)* châssis *m*; **his huge f. filled the doorway** sa large carrure s'encadrait dans la porte; **man of gigantic f.** homme bâti comme un colosse; *(spectacle)* **frames** monture (de lunettes); **glasses with metal frames** lunettes à monture de métal **3 f. of mind** état *m ou* disposition *f* d'esprit; **he is in a bad f. of mind** il est mal disposé; **f. of reference, reference f.** *Math* système *m* de coordonnées, référentiel *m*; *Fig* système *m* de référence **4** *(in embroidery)* *(floor-standing)* métier *m* (à broder); *(hand-held)* tambour *m* (à broder) **5** *Sport (in snooker)* *(wooden device)* triangle *m*; *(game)* partie *f*

vт 1 *(surround)* *(picture etc)* encadrer; *TV (the picture)* cadrer, centrer; *Phot, TV (subject)* cadrer; **black hair framed her face** des cheveux noirs encadraient son visage **2** *(compose)* *(poem etc)* composer; *(law)* rédiger; *(one's thoughts)* mettre de l'ordre dans; *(opinion)* formuler; *(answer, reply)* composer, formuler **3** *Fam (falsely incriminate)* *(person)* monter une accusation *ou* un coup contre; **I've been framed** c'est un coup monté (contre moi); **she was framed by the police for a bank robbery** la police a monté un coup contre elle et l'a accusée d'avoir dévalisé une banque

▸▸ *Comput* **f. format** *(of network)* protocole *m*; *Am* **f. house** maison *f* en bois

framer [ˈfreɪmər] N *(of pictures)* encadreur *m*

frame-up N *Sl (false incrimination)* coup *m* monté

framework [ˈfreɪmwɜːk] N *(of building, ship)* charpente *f*, carcasse *f*, *(of novel, play)* charpente; *(of negotiations)* structure *f*; **a political/legal/constitutional f.** un cadre politique/légal/constitutionnel; **it comes within the f. of the UN** cela entre dans le cadre de l'ONU

framing [ˈfreɪmɪŋ] N **1** *(of picture etc)* encadrement *m*; *Cin, Phot* cadrage *m* **2** *(structuring) (of poem etc)* composition *f* **3** *Fam (false incrimination)* accusation *f* inventée de toutes pièces **4 metal f.** *(for window)* vitrière *f*

franc [fræŋk] N **1** *(Swiss currency)* franc *m* **2** *Formerly (French and Belgian currency)* franc *m*

France [frɑːns] N France *f*, **in F.** en France

franchise [ˈfræntʃaɪz] N **1** *Com (granted by public body)* concession *f*, *(granted by manufacturer)* franchise *f*, *(shop, outlet)* établissement *m* en franchise **2** *Pol* droit *m* de vote

▸▸ *Com* **f. agreement** accord *m* de franchise; *Com* **f. holder** franchisé, -ée

franchisee [fræntʃaɪˈziː] N *Com* franchisé, -ée

franchising [ˈfræntʃaɪzɪŋ] N *Com* franchisage *m*

franchisor [ˈfræntʃaɪzər] N *Com* franchiseur, -euse

Franciscan [frænˈsɪskən] N, ADJ franciscain *m*

Francis of Assisi [ˈfrɑːnsɪs] N saint François d'Assise

franco [ˈfræŋkəʊ] *Com* ADJ franco

ADV franco

francophile [ˈfræŋkəʊfaɪl] ADJ, N francophile *mf*

francophobe [ˈfræŋkəʊfəʊb] ADJ, N **2** francophobe *mf*

francophone [ˈfræŋkəʊfəʊn] ADJ, N francophone *mf*

frangible [ˈfrændʒɪb(ə)l] ADJ cassant, fragile

frangipane [ˈfrændʒɪpeɪn] N frangipane *f*

Franglais [ˈfrɒŋɡleɪ] N franglais *m*

Frank [fræŋk] N *Hist* Franc *m*, Franque *f*

frank[1] [fræŋk] ADJ *(person, answer)* franc, *f* franche, sincère; *(speech)* direct, ouvert; *(discussion, exchange of views)* à cœur ouvert; **to be quite f. with you** pour être franc avec vous; **I don't think you're being f. with me** je ne crois pas que tu me dises la vérité

frank[2] vт *(letter)* affranchir *(à la machine)*; *(by post office)* oblitérer

Frankenstein food [ˈfræŋkənstaɪn] N *Fam* = surnom donné aux aliments génétiquement modifiés par leurs détracteurs

Frankfurt [ˈfræŋkfɜːt] N Francfort

frankfurter [ˈfræŋkfɜːtər] N saucisse *f* de Francfort

frankincense [ˈfræŋkɪnsens] N encens *m*

franking [ˈfræŋkɪŋ] N *(of letter)* affranchissement *m (à la machine)*

▸▸ **f. machine** machine *f* à affranchir

Frankish [ˈfræŋkɪʃ] ADJ *Hist* franc, *f* franque

Franklin stove [ˈfræŋklɪn] N *Am* poêle *m* à bois

frankly [ˈfræŋklɪ] ADV franchement; **I tell you f. that …** je vous dis carrément que …; **(quite) f., no!** franchement, non!; **I'll speak f. to you** je vais vous parler franchement *ou* à cœur ouvert

frankness [ˈfræŋknɪs] N franchise *f*, sincérité *f*; **I admire her f. in telling him** j'admire la franchise *ou* la sincérité avec laquelle elle le lui a dit

frantic [ˈfræntɪk] ADJ *(rush, pace)* fréné-

tique, forcené; **in a f. attempt to …** dans une folle tentative pour …; **everyone was quite f. in their efforts to meet the deadline** tout le monde se déchaînait *ou* travaillait comme des fous pour essayer de respecter la date limite; **the last month had been absolutely f.** le mois précédent avait été complètement fou; **f. with pain/worry** fou, *f* folle de douleur/d'inquiétude; **it drives him f.** cela le met hors de lui; **I'm f.** je suis hors de moi; **I was f. when I heard she'd had an accident** j'ai paniqué en apprenant qu'elle avait eu un accident

frantically, *esp Am* **franticly** [ˈfræntɪklɪ] ADV **1** *(to work, try)* frénétiquement, avec frénésie; **to rush f. around** courir frénétiquement dans tous les sens; **she was f. trying to help** elle essayait désespérément d'apporter son aide; **f. worried** fou, *f* folle d'inquiétude **2** *Fam* affreusement, terriblement; **I'm f. busy** je ne sais plus où donner de la tête

frat [fræt] ADJ *Am Univ Fam* = confrérie *f* d'étudiants

▸▸ **f. house** maison *f* communautaire (où résident des étudiants appartenant à une même organisation); **f. rat** = membre *m* d'une confrérie d'étudiants

fraternal [frəˈtɜːn(ə)l] ADJ fraternel

fraternally [frəˈtɜːn(ə)lɪ] ADV fraternellement

fraternity [frəˈtɜːnɪtɪ] N **1** *(brotherliness)* fraternité *f* **2** *(group engaged in same activity)* confrérie *f*; **the banking/medical f.** la confrérie des banquiers/des médecins; **the sporting f.** la grande famille du sport **3** *Am Univ* = confrérie *f* d'étudiants

▸▸ *Am Univ* **f. house** maison *f* communautaire (où résident des étudiants appartenant à une même confrérie)

fraternization [frætənaɪˈzeɪʃən] N fraternisation *f* (**with** avec); **f. with the enemy is forbidden** il est interdit de fraterniser avec l'ennemi

fraternize [ˈfrætənaɪz] vɪ fraterniser (**with** avec); **they tend not to f. with each other** ils ont tendance à ne pas fraterniser

fraud [frɔːd] N **1** *(deception)* supercherie *f*, tromperie *f*, *Law* fraude *f*, dol *m*; **to obtain sth by f.** obtenir qch frauduleusement *ou* par fraude; **guilty of f.** coupable de manœuvres frauduleuses; **he had carried out a wages f.** il avait fraudé sur les salaires **2** *(person)* imposteur *m*; *(thing, place)* farce *f*, attrape *f*; **this place is a f.** cet endroit ne répond pas à la réputation qu'on lui a faite

▸▸ *Br* **the F. Squad** brigade *f* de répression des fraudes

fraudulence [ˈfrɔːdjʊləns] N *(of transaction)* caractère *m* frauduleux; *(of concerns, sentiments)* fausseté *f*

fraudulent [ˈfrɔːdjʊlənt] ADJ *(false) (sympathy, feelings)* faux, *f* fausse, affecté; *(charge, accusation)* faux; *Law (bankrupt, transaction)* frauduleux

▸▸ **f. bankruptcy** faillite *f* frauduleuse

fraudulently [ˈfrɔːdjʊləntlɪ] ADV frauduleusement

fraught [frɔːt] ADJ **1** plein (**with problems** de problèmes); **the voyage was f. with danger** la traversée a été remplie *ou* pleine d'embûches; **an atmosphere f. with emotion/tension** une atmosphère chargée d'émotion/de tension; **things have been rather f.** l'atmosphère est assez tendue; **a f. day** une journée stressante **2** *(distressing)* pénible; **it's a f. subject** c'est un thème ardu **3** *(person) (distressed)* désespéré; *(anxious)* inquiet

fray[1] [freɪ] N *(brawl)* bagarre *f*, échauffourée *f*, mêlée *f*; **in the thick of the f.** au plus épais de la mêlée; **to enter the f.** descendre dans l'arène; **to return to the f.** rentrer en lice; **ready for the f.** prêt à entrer dans la mêlée

fray² VT *(material etc)* érailler, effiler ▮ VI **1** *(of material) (at edges)* s'effilocher, s'effiler; *(at collar, seams)* s'élimer **2** *(of nerves)* être à vif; *(of tempers)* s'échauffer

frayed [freɪd] ADJ **1** *(cloth, garment etc) (at edges)* effiloché, effrangé; *(at collar, seams)* élimé; *(rope)* usé **2** *(nerves)* à vif; **my nerves are f.** je suis à bout de nerfs; **tempers were getting a little f.** tout le monde commençait à être à bout de nerfs

frazzle ['fræz(ə)l] N *Fam* **to be worn to a f.** *(of person)* être complètement éreinté; **a joint cooked** *or* **burnt to a f.** un rôti calciné; **you look burnt to a f.** *(by sun)* tu as l'air d'avoir pris un de ces coups de soleil

frazzled ['fræzəld] ADJ *Fam* **1** *(mentally)* à bout de nerfs; **his nerves were still f.** il était encore à bout de nerfs **2** *(burnt)* calciné; **I got f. on the beach** je me suis pris un gros coup de soleil sur la plage

freak [friːk] N **1 f. (of nature)** monstre *m*, phénomène *m*; **a circus f.** un phénomène de cirque; **what kind of a f. would do something like that?** il faut être taré pour faire un truc pareil!; **people treat me as some kind of f.** *(because of what I think, do etc)* les gens me trouvent anormal; **by some f. (of fortune) he won** par un coup de chance il a gagné **2** *(enthusiast)* fana *mf*; **jazz/film f.** fana de jazz/cinéma

ADJ *(storm)* anormal, -aux; *(accident)* insolite, bizarre; **f. weather conditions** des conditions atmosphériques anormales

VI **= freak out 1**

▸ **freak out** *Fam* VI **1** *(become angry)* piquer une crise (**at** contre; **about** à propos de); *(be shocked, scared)* flipper, avoir les boules; *(become mentally unbalanced)* être déboussolé; *(of drug taker)* se défoncer; **mum'll f. out when she sees that mess** Maman va piquer une crise quand elle verra tout ce désordre; **f. show** exhibition *f* de monstres **2** *(abandon restraint)* s'éclater; **look at him freaking out on the dancefloor!** regarde-le s'éclater sur la piste de danse!

VT SEP *(person) (shock, scare)* mettre les boules à, faire flipper; *(mentally unbalance)* rendre dingue

freaking ['friːkɪŋ] *Am Sl* ADJ *(for emphasis)* sacré, foutu; **where are those f. kids?** mais où sont passés ces foutus gamins?

ADV *(for emphasis)* vachement; **it's f. cold out there** ça pince vachement dehors; **I don't f. know!** j'en sais foutre rien!

freakish ['friːkɪʃ] ADJ **1** *(weather etc)* insolite, anormal, -aux **2** *(imagination, idea, appearance, hairdo)* bizarre; *(stronger)* délirant

freaky ['friːkɪ] ADJ *Fam (person, appearance etc)* bizarre; *(stronger)* délirant

freckle ['frek(ə)l] N tache *f* de rousseur; **she's got freckles** elle a des taches de rousseur

freckled ['frek(ə)ld], **freckly** ['freklɪ] ADJ **1** *(person, face, arm etc)* couvert de taches de rousseur **2** *(animal's coat)* tacheté

Frederick the Great ['fred(ə)rɪk] N *Hist* Frédéric le Grand

FREE [friː]

ADJ	libre **1, 2** ▪ gratuit **3** ▪ franco **3** ▪ généreux **4**
ADV	gratuitement **1**
VT	libérer **1** ▪ dégager **2**

ADJ **1** *(unrestricted) (person, animal, movement, translation)* libre; *Chem (gas)* (à l'état) libre, non combiné; **to set f.** *(prisoner, hostage)* relâcher, remettre en liberté; *(slave)* affranchir; *(person) (from relationship, contract)* libérer; *(bird)* laisser s'envoler; **to break f. (of bonds)** se dégager (**of** de); *(escape)* s'échapper; **to be allowed to go f.** être mis en liberté, être relâché; **to be (entirely) f. to do sth** être (entièrement) libre de faire qch; **I am f. to do what I please** je suis libre de mes mouvements; **f. from** *or* **of sth** débarrassé de qch; **the area is now f. of** *or* **from contamination** cette zone a été complètement décontaminée; **to remain f. of** *or* **from sth** être préservé de qch; **to be f. of sb** être débarrassé de qn; **to be f. from care** *or* **worry** *or* **anxiety** être sans souci; **she's f. and graceful in all her actions** elle fait tout avec aisance et grâce; **as f. as the air** *or* **a bird** libre comme l'air; *Fig* **it's a f. country** on est en démocratie; **f. end** *(of rope)* extrémité *f* libre; *Fig* **with his f. hand** avec sa main libre; *Fig* **to have a f. hand** avoir pleine liberté d'action, avoir ses coudées franches (**to do** pour faire); **to give** *or* **allow sb a f. hand** donner carte blanche à qn; **to make a f. choice** décider librement *ou* en toute liberté; **right of f. entry** droit *m* de passer librement les frontières

2 *(unoccupied)* libre; *Tel (line)* libre; **is this table f.?** est-ce que cette table est libre?; **I am f. tomorrow** je suis libre demain; **to have some time f.** avoir du temps libre; **f. time** temps *m* libre, loisir *m*

3 *(without charge) (concert, sample etc)* gratuit; *Theat (ticket)* de faveur; **it came f. with the magazine** c'était en prime pour l'achat du magazine; *Fig* **there's no such thing as a f. lunch** tout se paie; **admission f.** entrée gratuite; *Com* **delivery f.** livré franco *inv*; **post f.** franco de port; **f. in and out** bord à bord; *Com* **f. alongside ship** franco long du quai; **f. overside** franco allège; *Com* **f. at franco** rendu; *Com* **f. at frontier** franco frontière; *Com* **f. carrier** franco transporteur; *Com* **f. destination** franco rendu point de destination; *Com* **f. of average** franc de toute avarie; **f. of customs duty** franco de douane; *Fin* **f. of duty** *(in customs)* exempt de droits d'entrée; **to import sth f. of duty** faire entrer qch en franchise; **f. of packing charges** franco d'emballage; **f. of tax** franc d'impôts; *Fin* **interest f. of tax** intérêts nets *ou* exempts d'impôt; **f. of VAT** en franchise de TVA; **f. on board** franco à bord; *Com* **f. on rail** franco wagon; **f. on truck** franco camion

4 *(generous) (person)* libéral, -aux, généreux; **to be f. with one's time** être généreux de son temps; **to be f. with one's money** être prodigue de son argent; **he was very f. with his advice** il a été très prodigue en conseils

5 *esp Pej (uninhibited)* **you'll like it here, things are f. and easy** tu te plairas ici, on ne fait pas de façons; **things are a bit too f. and easy here** ici on est un peu trop sans gêne *ou* désinvolte; **he's pretty f. and easy as a boss** il est plutôt décontracté comme patron; **to make f. with sth** se servir de qch sans se gêner; **he made very f. with my whisky** il ne se gênait pas pour boire mon whisky; **to be rather f. in one's conversation** tenir des propos peu convenables; *Fam* **feel f.** faites comme chez vous; *Fam* **may I take another? – feel f. puis-j'en reprendre? – je vous en prie; **feel f. to speak your mind** n'hésitez pas à dire ce que vous pensez

ADV **1** *(without charge)* franco, gratuitement; **catalogue sent f. on request** catalogue gratuit sur demande; **the museum is open f. on Saturdays** l'entrée du musée est gratuite le samedi; **for f.,** *Fam* **f. gratis and for nothing** gratis; **to get sth for f.** obtenir qch gratis; **you are allowed to bring in half a litre f.** *(exempt from duty)* il y a une tolérance d'un demi-litre

2 *(followed by a present participle)* **f. flow-**

ing qui coule abondamment; **f. flowering** qui fleurit abondamment

VT **(freed; freeing) 1** *(prisoner, caged animal etc)* libérer, relâcher; *(of rescuer) (hostage, prisoner)* délivrer; *(slave, colony)* affranchir; *(sth stuck, one's foot etc)* dégager; *(funds)* dégager; *(time, space)* libérer; **to f. sb's hands** *(untie)* détacher les mains de qn; **to f. oneself from sb's grasp** se dégager des mains de qn; **to f. sb from an obligation** libérer qn d'une obligation; **to f. oneself from one's commitments** se libérer *ou* se délier de ses engagements; **to f. sb to do sth** libérer qn pour qu'il puisse faire qch; **to f. the pound/franc** libéraliser le cours de la livre/du franc

2 *(clear obstructions from)* débarrasser (**from, of** de); *(path etc)* dégager; *Tech etc (part)* dégager; *(blocked filter)* désobstruer; *(pump)* dégorger; **to f. a property (from mortgage)** déshypothéquer une propriété

▸▸ **f. agent** personne *f* libre *ou* indépendante; *(sports player)* joueur, -euse indépendant(e); *Fig* **to be a f. agent** être libre de ses mouvements; *Psy* **f. association** association *f* libre; *Sport* **f. climbing** escalade *f* libre; *Sch* **f. composition** composition *f* libre; **f. copy** *(in publishing)* spécimen *m*; **f. demonstration** démonstration *f* gracieuse; **f. diving** plongée *f* sous-marine autonome; *Econ* **F. enterprise** libre entreprise *f*; **f. fall** chute *f* libre; *Hist* **F. France** la France libre; *Hist* **the F. French** les Français *mpl* libres; *Com* **f. gift** cadeau *m*; *Br* **f. house** = pub *m* libre de ses approvisionnements (et non lié à une brasserie particulière); *St Exch* **f. issue** attribution *f* d'actions gratuites; *Sport* **f. kick** coup *m* franc; **f. love** union *f* libre; *Econ* **f. market** économie *f* de marché; *Law* **f. pardon** grâce *f*; *Customs* **f. port** port *m* franc; **f. press** liberté *f* de la presse; *Med* **f. radical** radical *m* libre; **f. speech** liberté de parole *ou* d'expression; **f. spirit** non-conformiste *mf*, *pl* non-conformistes; *Econ* **f. trade** libre-échange *m*; *Econ* **f. trade area** zone *f* de libre-échange; *Econ* **f. trade policy** politique *f* antiprotectionniste, politique de libre-échange; *Com* **f. trial** essai *m* gratuit; *Com* **f. trial period** période *f* d'essai gratuit; **f. verse** vers *m* libre; **f. vote** vote *m* libre; **f. will** libre arbitre *m*; **of one's own f. will** de (son) plein gré; *Pol* **the F. World** le monde libre; *Com* **f. zone** zone franche

▸ **free up** VT SEP *(funds)* dégager; *(time, space)* libérer; **this will f. up sales people to do more actual selling** cela donnera plus de temps au personnel de vente pour se consacrer à la vente même

-free [friː] SUFF sans; **sugar/gluten/etc-f.** sans sucre/gluten/etc

freebie, freebee ['friːbiː] N *Fam (for customer etc)* cadeau *m*; **it was a f. with the magazine** c'était un cadeau offert avec le magazine

freeboard ['friːbɔːd] N *Naut* (franc-)bord *m*

freeborn ['friːbɔːn] ADJ libre de naissance, né libre

freedom ['friːdəm] N **1** liberté *f*; **in f.** en liberté; **we have less f. now** nous sommes moins libres maintenant; **f. to do sth** liberté de faire qch; **f. to overfly a country without landing** droit *m* de survol d'un État; **f. of action** liberté d'action; **f. of entry** liberté d'entrée; **f. of the press** liberté de la presse

2 *(frankness) (of a conversation etc)* franchise *f*, *Pej (uninhibitedness)* sans-gêne *m*, familiarité *f*; **to speak with complete f.** parler en toute liberté

3 *(exemption)* exemption *f*, franchise *f*; **f. from tax** exemption d'impôts; **with my new f. from worry** désormais libéré de mes inquiétudes

4 *(free use)* the f. of sth le libre usage de qch; **the f. of the seas** la liberté de la haute mer; **f. of the air** liberté *f* de l'air; **f. of the city** droit *m* de cité; *(honorary citizenship)* citoyenneté *f* d'honneur d'une ville; **to receive the f. of a city** être nommé citoyen/citoyenne d'honneur d'une ville; **to give sb the f. of one's library** mettre sa bibliothèque à la disposition de qn

▸▸ **f. of expression** liberté d'expression; **f. fighter** guérillero *m*, révolutionnaire *mf*; **f. of information** liberté d'information; **f. of movement** liberté de mouvement; **f. of religion** liberté de culte; **f. of speech** liberté d'expression; **f. of worship** liberté de culte

free-flowing ADJ **1** *(river, stream)* qui coule librement; *(traffic, substance)* fluide **2** *(information)* librement accessible; *Fin (capital)* flottant

Freefone® ['fri:fəʊn] N *Br Tel* appel *m* gratuit, numéro *m* vert; **call F. 123** composez le numéro vert 123

free-for-all N mêlée *f* générale; **when the food arrived, the queue quickly turned into a f.** quand la nourriture est arrivée, la file d'attente s'est transformée en pagaille générale

free-form ADJ *Art* à forme libre
▸▸ *Mus* f. jazz free-jazz *m inv*

freehand ['fri:hænd] ADJ, ADV *Art* à main levée

free-handed [-'hændɪd] ADJ généreux

freehold ['fri:həʊld] *Law* ADJ tenu en propriété perpétuelle et libre
N *(property)* propriété *f* foncière perpétuelle et libre; **to buy the f.** acheter en pleine propriété

freeholder ['fri:həʊldər] N propriétaire *m* foncier (à perpétuité)

freeing ['fri:ɪŋ] N *(of prisoner)* libération *f*, *(of slave)* affranchissement *m*; *(of funds, resources)* dégagement *m*

freelance ['fri:lɑ:ns] N indépendant, -ante, free-lance *mf inv*, *(esp journalist etc)* indépendant, -ante, pigiste *mf*; **to work as a f.** travailler en indépendant *ou* free-lance; *(esp journalist)* travailler comme pigiste *ou* en indépendant, travailler à la pige
ADJ *(contributor, worker)* free-lance, indépendant; *(esp journalist etc)* qui travaille à la pige, free-lance; *(rates)* du travail free-lance
ADV **to work f.** travailler en indépendant *ou* en free-lance; *(esp journalist)* travailler comme pigiste *ou* en indépendant, travailler à la pige
VI travailler en indépendant *ou* en free-lance; *(esp journalist)* faire de la pige, travailler comme pigiste *ou* en indépendant
▸▸ **f. work** travail *m* indépendant *ou* à la pige *ou* (en) free-lance

freelancer ['fri:lɑ:nsər] N free-lance *mf*, *(esp journalist)* pigiste *mf*

freeload ['fri:ləʊd] VI *esp Am Fam* parasiter

freeloader ['fri:ləʊdər] N *esp Am Fam* pique-assiette *mf inv*, parasite *m*

freely ['fri:lɪ] ADV **1** *(copiously, abundantly)* librement; **to give f. to sb** faire des libéralités à qn; **to give out advice f.** se répandre en conseils; **the wine was flowing f.** le vin coulait à flots **2** *(without hindrance)* librement; *(to speak, act etc)* en toute liberté; **to speak f. to sb** parler à qn à cœur ouvert; **f. available** *(for sale)* en vente libre; *(easy to get hold of)* qu'on peut se procurer facilement; **I f. admit that …** j'avoue sans peine que …

freeman, *pl* **freemen** ['fri:mən] N **1** *Hist* homme *m* libre **2** *(of city)* citoyen *m* d'honneur; **to be made a f. of the city** être nommé citoyen d'honneur

free-marketeer N libéral, -ale

freemason ['fri:meɪs(ə)n] N franc-maçon *m*, *pl* francs-maçons

freemasonry ['fri:meɪs(ə)nrɪ] N franc-maçonnerie *f*

freenet ['fri:net] N *Comput* libertel *m*

Freepost® ['fri:pəʊst] N *Br* correspondance-réponse *f*

free-range ADJ *(eggs, chicken)* de ferme

freesia ['fri:ʒə] N *(plant)* freesia *m*

free-spoken ADJ *(person)* franc, *f* franche, qui parle ouvertement

freestanding ['fri:'stændɪŋ] ADJ *(wall etc)* auto-portant; *Archit (column)* isolé; *(clinic, restaurant, machine)* autonome

freestyle ['fri:staɪl] N *Swimming* nage *f* libre; *(wrestling)* lutte *f* libre

freethinker [fri:'θɪŋkər] N *Old-fashioned* libre penseur, -euse

free-trader N *Econ* libre-échangiste *mf*, *pl* libre-échangistes

freeware ['fri:weər] N *Comput* freeware *m*, logiciel *m* public
▸▸ **f. programs** freewares *mpl*, logiciels *mpl* publics

freeway ['fri:weɪ] N *Am* autoroute *f* (gratuite)

freewheel ['fri:wi:l] VI **1** *Cycling* être en roue libre; *Aut* rouler au point mort; **to f. down a hill** descendre une côte en roue libre/au point mort **2** *esp Am (travel in carefree fashion)* se laisser aller, aller sans but précis
N roue *f* libre

freewheeling ['fri:wi:lɪŋ] ADJ *Fam (discussion)* libre; **her f. approach to such serious matters** sa façon un peu légère *ou* désinvolte de traiter des questions aussi sérieuses; **to lead a f. existence** mener une existence insouciante

freeze [fri:z] N **1** *Met* gel *m*, gelée *f*, **the big f.** la grande gelée; **we had a big f. last winter** il a gelé très fort l'hiver dernier **2** *(act of fixing) price and wage* f. blocage *m ou* gel *m* des prix et des salaires; **to put a f. on further changes/expenditure** bloquer le processus de changement/les dépenses
V IMPERS *(pt* froze [frəʊz], *pp* frozen ['frəʊz(ə)n]) **it's freezing** il gèle
VI **1** *(of liquid, washing on line)* geler; *(of food)* se congeler; **the river has frozen** la rivière est prise *ou* a gelé; **the earth had frozen** la terre avait gelé; **the sausages had frozen together** les saucisses s'étaient congelées et ne formaient plus qu'un bloc; **his hand had frozen to the ice axe** le gel avait collé sa main au piolet; **it has frozen solid** *(mud)* elle a gelé; *(food)* ça s'est congelé; *(milk)* il est gelé; **to f. to death** mourir de froid; *Fam* **I'm freezing** je meurs de froid, je gèle; *Fam* **we froze in our thin clothes** on n'était pas assez couvert, on s'est caillé; **the smile froze on his lips** le sourire se figea sur ses lèvres
2 *(of person) (not move)* rester cloué sur place, se figer; *(stiffen)* se raidir, se guinder; *(become speechless)* rester sans voix; **f.!** on ne bouge plus!; **I froze at the sound of his voice** je me suis immobilisé au son de sa voix
3 *Comput (of screen, computer)* se bloquer
VT **1** *(turn to ice)* geler, congeler; *(food)* congeler; **to f. the blood (in one's veins)** glacer le sang *ou* le cœur; **she froze them with a look** d'un regard, elle les glaça sur place; **to be frozen to death** mourir de froid
2 *Fin (credit, currency, prices)* geler; *(wages)* bloquer; **to f. assets** immobiliser des actifs
3 *Med* insensibiliser par anesthésie locale
4 **to f. a film** *or* **a frame** faire un arrêt sur image; **f. it!** arrêtez l'image!
▸ **freeze out** VT SEP *Fam (exclude) (person)* évincer; *(rival)* supplanter; **to f. sb out of**

the conversation exclure qn de la conversation
▸ **freeze over** VI the pond has/is frozen over l'étang a/est complètement gelé
▸ **freeze up** VI *(become frozen)* geler; *Fig (of person)* rester sans voix; **the river has frozen up** la rivière est prise *ou* gelée; **the radiator froze up** le radiateur a gelé

freeze-dried ADJ lyophilisé(e)

freeze-dry VT lyophiliser

freeze-frame N *Cin* arrêt *m* sur image

freezer ['fri:zər] N congélateur *m*; *(in refrigerator)* freezer *m*; **chest f.** congélateur bahut
▸▸ **f. compartment** compartiment *m* à glace *(d'un réfrigérateur)*, freezer *m*

freeze-up N *Met* gelée *f*

freezing ['fri:zɪŋ] ADJ *(weather, room, temperature etc)* glacial, -als *ou* -aux; **it's f. in here!** ça caille ici!; **I'm f.** je gèle
ADV **the weather's f. cold** il fait un temps glacial; **I'm f. cold** je suis gelé; **a f. cold shower** une douche glacée
N **1** *(becoming frozen)* congélation *f*, gel *m*; **the temperature was below f.** la température était inférieure à zéro **2** *(making frozen) (of liquid etc)* réfrigération *f*, *(of meat)* congélation *f* **3** *Fin (of wages etc)* blocage *m*; *(of credit, prices)* gel *m*
▸▸ **f. compartment** *(in refrigerator)* freezer *m*, compartiment *m* à glace *(d'un réfrigérateur)*; **f. instructions** *(for food)* consignes *fpl* pour la congélation; **f. mixture** mélange *m* réfrigérant; **f. point** point *m* de congélation

freight [freɪt] N **1** *(transport)* fret *m*, transport *m* *(de marchandises)*; **air f.** transport par air **2** *(cargo)* fret *m*, cargaison *f*, chargement *m*; *Rail, Aviat* marchandises *fpl* (transportées) **3** *(price of transport)* fret *m*
VT **1** *(load) (vessel)* charger **2** *(hire) (ship)* (af)fréter; *(of owner)* donner à fret **3** *esp Am (transport)* transporter
▸▸ **f. bill** connaissement *m*; *Am* **f. car** wagon *m* de marchandises, fourgon *m*; **f. charges** fret, frais *mpl* de transport; **f. collect** port *m* avancé; **f. consolidator** groupeur *m*; **f. depot** gare *f* de marchandises; **f. forward** port avancé; **f. forwarder** agent *m* de fret, transitaire *m*; **f. forwarding** transit *m*; **f. insurance** assurance *f* sur fret; **f. plane** avion-cargo *m*, *pl* avions-cargos; avion *m* de fret; **f. price** prix *m* de transport; **f. release** bon *m* à délivrer; **f. shipping** messageries *fpl* maritimes; **f. terminal** terminal *m* de fret; **f. ton** tonne *f* d'affrètement; *Am* **f. train** train *m* de marchandises; **f. vehicle** véhicule *m* de transport de marchandises

freightage ['freɪtɪdʒ] N fret *m*; *(transport)* transport *m*

freighter ['freɪtər] N **1** *(ship)* cargo *m*, navire *m* de charge; *Am Rail* wagon *m* de marchandises; *Aviat* avion-cargo *m*, *pl* avions-cargos, avion *m* de fret **2** *(hirer) (of ship)* affréteur *m* **3** *Am (of goods carried overland)* consignateur, -trice **4** *(operator of transport company)* entrepreneur *m* de transports, exportateur *m*

Freightliner® ['freɪtlaɪnər] N *Rail* train *m* de marchandises en conteneurs, train *m* conteneur

French [frentʃ] ADJ français; *(dish, fashion etc)* à la française; *(class, teacher)* de français; **the F. ambassador** l'ambassadeur, -drice de France; *Fam* **to take F. leave** filer à l'anglaise
N **1** *Ling* français *m*; **to speak F.** parler français; **to learn/know F.** apprendre/savoir parler le français; **say it in F.** dites-le en français; **her F. is excellent** elle parle très bien (le) français; **Canadian F.** français canadien *ou* du Canada; *Hum* **excuse my F.** passez-moi l'expression **2** **the F.** *(people)* les Français *mpl* **3** *Sl Old-fashioned (fellatio)* pipe *f*

▶▶ **F. bean** haricot *m* vert; **F. bread** baguette *f*; **F. Canada** le Canada français; **F. Canadian** *(person)* Canadien, -ienne français(e); *(language)* français *m* canadien; **F. chalk** craie *f* de tailleur; *Am* **F. doors** porte-fenêtre *f*, *pl* portes-fenêtres; *Culin* **F. dressing** *(in UK)* vinaigrette *f*, *(in US)* = sauce *f* de salade à base de mayonnaise et de ketchup; **F. Foreign Legion** Légion *f* étrangère; **F. fried potatoes** pommes *fpl* frites; **F. fries** frites *fpl*; **F. Guiana** Guyane *f* française; **F. horn** cor *m* d'harmonie; **F. kiss** baiser *m* avec la langue, *Fam* patin *m*; *Br Fam* **F. letter** *(condom)* capote *f* anglaise; **F. loaf** baguette *f*; **F. plait** *(hairstyle)* natte *f* africaine; *Br* **F. polish** vernis *m* (à l'alcool); **F. roll** *(hairstyle)* chignon *m* banane; **F. service** *(in restaurant)* service *m* à la française *ou* au guéridon; **F. stick** baguette *f*; **F. Switzerland** la Suisse Romande; **F. toast** pain *m* perdu; **F. West Indies** Antilles *fpl* Françaises; *Br* **F. window** porte-fenêtre

Frenchify ['frentʃɪfaɪ] **VT** *Pej (one's style etc)* franciser

French-kiss *Fam* **VT** rouler une pelle *ou* un patin à
VI se rouler une pelle *ou* un patin

Frenchman, *pl* **Frenchmen** ['frentʃmən] **N** Français *m*

French-polish **VT** *Br (table etc)* vernir au tampon

French-speaking **ADJ** *(native speaker)* francophone; *(who can speak French)* qui parle français; **the F. world** la francophonie

Frenchwoman, *pl* **Frenchwomen** ['frentʃwʊmən, -wɪmɪn] **N** Française *f*

Frenchy ['frentʃɪ] **N** *Old-fashioned Fam* Français, -aise

frenetic [frə'netɪk] **ADJ** *(person, action etc)* frénétique

frenetically [frə'netɪklɪ] **ADV** frénétiquement

frenzied ['frenzɪd] **ADJ** *(person)* affolé, forcené; *(rage)* fou, *f* folle; *(applause, activity)* frénétique; *(attack, mob)* déchaîné; **f. with worry/rage** fou d'inquiétude/de rage; **there was a f. look in her eye** elle avait un regard halluciné

frenzy ['frenzɪ] **N** *(of despair etc)* frénésie *f*, folie *f*; **in a f. of excitement/hatred** dans un accès d'excitation/de haine; **to work oneself into a f.** *(get angry, upset)* se mettre dans tous ses états; **the children worked themselves into a f. (of excitement)** les enfants se sont mis dans un état de surexcitation folle

frequency ['fri:kwənsɪ] **N 1** fréquence *f*; **to recur with increasing f.** se faire de plus en plus fréquent; **the increasing f. of his absences** ses absences de plus en plus fréquentes; *Math* **f. of errors** répartition *f* des erreurs **2** *Phys* fréquence *f*; *Elec* **high/low f.** haute/basse fréquence; *Radio* **very high f.** très haute fréquence
▶▶ *Radio* **f. band** bande *f* de fréquences; **f. modulation** modulation *f* de fréquence; **f. range** gamme *f* de fréquences

frequent[1] ['fri:kwənt] **ADJ** *(visits etc)* fréquent; *(visitor)* assidu; *(customer)* habituel; *(widespread)* très répandu; *(explanation, state of affairs etc)* commun, habituel; **he became a f. visitor to our house** c'est devenu un habitué de la maison; **it is a f. occurrence** cela se produit souvent; **it is a f. sight in the summer months** on en voit souvent pendant les mois d'été; **this bird is a f. visitor to our shores** cet oiseau visite régulièrement nos rivages; **f. theatregoers** des gens qui vont souvent au théâtre; **the doctor recommended f. changes of the dressing** le docteur a recommandé que le pansement soit changé souvent; **it's quite a f. practice** c'est une coutume assez répandue

▶▶ **f. flyer club** club *m* de fidélité de compagnie aérienne; **f. flyer programme** programme *m* de fidélisation des passagers de compagnies aériennes; *Mktg* **f. user card** carte *f* de fidélité; *Mktg* **f. user programme** programme de fidélisation

frequent[2] [frɪ'kwent] **VT** fréquenter; *(theatres, pubs etc)* hanter

frequenter [frɪ'kwentər] **N** *(of a house etc)* habitué, -ée, familier *m*; **a great f. of public houses** un pilier de bar

frequently ['fri:kwəntlɪ] **ADV** fréquemment; **I f. can't remember my address** il m'arrive fréquemment de ne pas pouvoir me souvenir de mon adresse; **how f.?** avec quelle fréquence?, *Fam* tous les combien?; **I can't say how f. it happened** je ne saurais pas dire avec quelle fréquence cela se produisait

fresco, *pl* **frescos, frescoes** ['freskəʊ, -əʊz] **N** *Art* fresque *f*; **to paint in f.** peindre à fresque; **f. painter** fresquiste *mf*

fresh [freʃ] **ADJ 1** *(fruit, eggs, fish, colour etc)* frais, *f* fraîche; *(person) (full of vigour)* vigoureux, alerte; *(refreshed) (after sleep, rest)* dispos; *(horse)* fougueux, animé; *(complexion)* frais, fleuri; **as f. as a daisy** frais et dispos; **a f.-faced youth** un jeune homme au teint frais; **I felt fresher after a shower** une douche m'a ragaillardi
2 *(new)* nouveau, -el, *f* -elle; *(news, blood, footprints)* frais, *f* fraîche; **a f. change of clothes/socks** des habits/chaussettes de rechange; **f. dangers to face** de nouveaux dangers à affronter; **to make a f. start on a problem** reprendre un problème à zéro; **to put f. courage into sb** ranimer le courage de qn; **to put f. water in the fish tank** changer l'eau de l'aquarium; **f. outbreak of fire/disease** reprise *f* du feu/de la maladie; **it is still f. in my mind** je l'ai encore frais à la mémoire; **the wound was f.** la plaie était récente; **f. from London** nouvellement arrivé de Londres; **and now, f. from his tour of the States, we present ...** et maintenant, tout juste rentré de sa tournée aux États-Unis, nous vous présentons ...; **the bread was f. from the oven** le pain sortait du four; **f. paragraph** nouveau paragraphe; **f. troops** troupes fraîches
3 *(air)* frais, *f* fraîche, pur; *(cool)* frais; **it's f. this morning** il fait frais ce matin; **in the f. air** au grand air, en plein air; **to let f. air into a room** aérer une pièce; *Fam* **f.-air fiend** fanatique *mf* d'air frais; *(outdoor person)* fanatique du grand air; *Naut* **f. breeze** bonne brise; **f. water** eau douce
4 *esp Am Fam (impudent)* effronté; **to get f. with a girl** prendre des libertés avec une jeune fille; **don't (you) get f. with me!** ne te fiche pas de moi!
ADV *(arrived, painted etc)* fraîchement, nouvellement, récemment; **f.-cut flowers** fleurs nouvellement cueillies; *esp Am* **to be f. out of sth** ne plus avoir de qch; **f.-frozen** *(food)* congelé à la fabrication; *(fish)* congelé sur le bateau

freshen ['freʃən] **VI** *(of temperature)* (se) rafraîchir; *(of wind, weather)* fraîchir
VT *(air, one's memory etc)* rafraîchir; *esp Am* **can I f. your drink?** est-ce que je vous sers un autre verre?
▶ **freshen up** **VI** *(wash)* faire un brin de toilette
VT SEP 1 *(renew) (make-up)* retoucher; **to f. up the paint** (r)aviver la couleur; **to f. up one's lipstick** se remettre du rouge à lèvres; **to f. oneself up** faire un brin de toilette **2** *(change air in) (room)* aérer

fresher ['freʃər] **N** *Br Fam* = **freshman**

freshly ['freʃlɪ] **ADV** *(with pp only)* fraîchement; **f. baked** sortant du four; **f. picked pea-**

ches des pêches fraîchement cueillies; **f. squeezed orange juice** orange *f* pressée

freshman, *pl* **freshmen** ['freʃmən] **N** *Univ Fam* étudiant, -ante de première année

freshness ['freʃnɪs] **N 1** *(of fruit, fish etc)* fraîcheur *f* **2** *(of event)* caractère *m* récent; *(of impression, approach etc)* fraîcheur *f* **3** *(of wind etc)* fraîcheur *f* **4** *(liveliness)* vigueur *f*, vivacité *f* **5** *esp Am Fam (impudence)* effronterie *f*

freshwater ['freʃwɔːtər] **ADJ**
▶▶ **f. fish** poisson *m* d'eau douce; **f. fishing** pêche *f* en eau douce

fret[1] [fret] **N** *Fam* **to be in a f.** être dans tous ses états; *(extremely worried)* se faire du mauvais sang *ou* de la bile
VI (-tt-) *(worry)* s'inquiéter, se tourmenter; **don't f.!** *(don't worry)* ne vous inquiétez pas!; *(don't upset yourself)* ne vous faites pas de bile!, ne vous faites pas de mauvais sang!; **child fretting for his mother** enfant qui réclame sa mère en pleurnichant; **she's fretting because her pony is missing** elle est dans tous ses états parce que son poney a disparu; **children always tend to f. in hospital** les enfants ont toujours tendance à se tourmenter quand ils sont à l'hôpital
VT 1 *(worry)* **don't f. yourself!** ne te tracasse pas!; **to f. one's life away** passer sa vie à se tracasser *ou* se tourmenter **2** *(wear away)* ronger; **to f. a rope** érailler un cordage

fret[2] **N** *Mus (on guitar etc)* touchette *f*, touche *f*

fret[3] **VT** *Carp (wood)* découper
▶▶ **f. saw** scie *f* à découper

fretful ['fretfʊl] **ADJ** *(anxious) (person)* inquiet, qui se fait du mauvais sang; *(voice)* inquiet; *(peevish)* grincheux; **a f. baby** un bébé agité

fretfully ['fretfʊlɪ] **ADV** *(to speak, complain)* d'un ton grincheux; *(to look at sb)* d'un air chagrin

fretfulness ['fretfʊlnɪs] **N** irritabilité *f*

fretting ['fretɪŋ] **N 1** *(worrying)* inquiétude *f* *(over* à propos de*)*; *(being upset)* agitation *f*; **I wish he'd stop his f.!** si seulement il pouvait arrêter de se faire du mauvais sang! **2** *(of rope etc)* usure *f*

fretwork ['fretwɜːk] **N** *Carp (technique)* découpage *m*; *(finished work)* travail *m* ajouré, bois *m* découpé *ou* chantourné

Freudian ['frɔɪdɪən] **ADJ** *Psy* freudien
▶▶ **F. slip** lapsus *m*

Freudianism ['frɔɪdɪənɪzm] **N** freudisme *m*

FRG [efɑː'dʒiː] **N** *Formerly (abbr* **Federal Republic of Germany***)* RFA *f*

Fri *abbr* **Friday**

friable ['fraɪəb(ə)l] **ADJ** *(soil etc)* friable

friar ['fraɪər] **N** *Cathol* moine *m*, frère *m*, religieux *m*; **Grey Friars** Franciscains *mpl*; **Black Friars** Dominicains *mpl*; **White Friars** Carmes *mpl*
▶▶ *Pharm* **f.'s balsam** baume *m* de benjoin

friary ['fraɪərɪ] **N** monastère *m*

fricassee [frɪkə'siː] *Culin* **N** fricassée *f*, *(of rabbit or hare)* gibelotte *f*
VT fricasser

fricative ['frɪkətɪv] *Ling* **ADJ** *(consonant)* fricatif
N fricative *f*

friction ['frɪkʃən] **N 1** *Phys* friction *f*, frottement *m*; *(of two bodies)* frottement *m*; *(of scalp etc)* friction *f* **2** *(disagreement)* friction *f*, désaccord *m*; **there's f. between them** il y a du tirage entre eux
▶▶ *Aut* **f. clutch** embrayage *m* à friction; *Aut* **f. cylinder** cylindre *m* de friction; *Aut* **f. drive** entraînement *m* par friction; *Comput* **f. feed** avancement *m* par friction; **f. glove** *(for massage)* gant *m* de crin; *Aut* **f. lining** garni-

ture *f* de friction; *Aut* **f. plate** plateau *m* de friction; *Am* **f. tape** chatterton *m*

Friday ['fraɪdɪ] N VOIR GRAMMAIRE A81; B61 vendredi *m*; **F. 26 February** vendredi 26 février; **F. morning/evening** vendredi matin/soir; **it's F. today** nous sommes vendredi aujourd'hui; **she comes on Fridays** elle vient le vendredi; **he's coming on F.** il vient vendredi; **every F.** tous les vendredis; **(Man) F.** *Liter* Vendredi; *Fig* factotum *m*, homme *m* à tout faire; *Fam* **girl F.** aide *f* de bureau

fridge [frɪdʒ] N *Fam* frigo *m*

fridge-freezer N *Fam* frigo *m* avec congélateur

fried [fraɪd] ADJ **1** *(food)* frit; **they eat a lot of f. food** ils mangent beaucoup de friture **2** *Am Fam (drunk)* bourré, pété; *(on drugs)* raide, parti
  PT, PP *see* fry[1]
  ▸▸ **f. egg** œuf *m* sur le plat; **f. potatoes** pommes *fpl* de terre sautées

friend [frend] N **1** ami, *f* amie; *(acquaintance)* connaissance *f*; **we're the best of friends** nous sommes les meilleurs amis du monde; **let's be friends again** faisons la paix; **I'm offering you a bargain, my f.** *(to stranger)* cher ami, c'est une affaire que je vous propose; **I am speaking to you as a f.** je vous parle en ami(e); **that's what friends are for** c'est à ça que servent les amis; **she's been a good f. to us** elle a beaucoup fait pour nous; **we're just good friends** nous sommes bons amis, c'est tout; **school f.** ami(e) *ou* camarade *mf* d'école; **man f.** *(pl* **men friends)** ami homme, *pl* amis hommes; **woman f.** *(pl* **women friends)** amie femme, *pl* amies femmes; *Old-fashioned* **lady f.** petite amie *f*; **to be friends with sb** être ami avec qn; **they've been friends for years** ils sont amis depuis des années; **to be more than friends** être plus qu'amis; **to make friends** *(with others)* se faire des amis; **they made friends** *(with each other)* ils sont devenus amis; **I made friends with them** nous sommes devenus amis, je suis devenu ami avec eux; *Prov* **a f. in need is a f. indeed** c'est dans le besoin que l'on connaît ses amis; **he has been a real f. in need** il ne m'a/t'a/*etc* pas abandonné dans le besoin; **you'd better be** *or* **stay friends with them** vous feriez bien de ne pas vous brouiller avec eux; **let us part friends** séparons-nous (en) bons amis; **he's no f. of mine** *(he's an enemy)* je ne le compte pas parmi mes amis; *(he means me no good)* il ne me veut pas de bien; **Britain is no f. of those who seek to ...** la Grande-Bretagne n'est pas favorable à ceux qui cherchent à ...; *Fig* **to have friends in high places** *or* **at court** avoir des amis influents; *Fig* **a f. at court** un ami en haut lieu *ou* bien placé; **f. or foe?** *(said by sentry)* qui va là?
  2 *(supporter) (of law and order etc)* ami, *f* amie, partisan *m*; *(of the arts etc)* patron, -onne; **f. of the poor** bienfaiteur, -trice des pauvres; **she's no f. of trade unionism** elle n'est pas favorable au syndicalisme; **the Friends of Canterbury Cathedral** la Société des Amis *ou* les Amis de la Cathédrale de Cantorbéry
  3 *Rel* **F.** *(Quaker)* Quaker, -eresse, Ami, -ie; **the Society of Friends** la Société des Amis

friendless ['frendlɪs] ADJ sans amis; **I am totally f. now** je n'ai plus aucun ami

friendliness ['frendlɪnɪs] N amabilité *f* **(to, towards** envers); **to show great f. towards sb** se montrer très aimable envers qn

friendly ['frendlɪ] ADJ **1** *(people, smile, slap on the back, welcome)* amical, -aux; *(city, neighbours, face)* sympathique; *(well disposed)* favorable, favorablement disposé; *(dog)* gentil; *(quarrel, argument)* entre amis; **you should try to be a bit more f. to people**

tu devrais essayer d'être un peu plus aimable; **why is he so f. all of a sudden?** pourquoi est-il aussi aimable tout à coup?; **to be f. with sb** être ami avec qn; **she's very f. with the boss all of a sudden** elle est très copine avec le patron tout d'un coup; **they became very f.** *(to each other)* ils se sont pris d'amitié l'un pour l'autre; **to get too f. with sb** se montrer trop familier avec qn; **piece of f. advice** avis amical; **someone ought to have a f. word with him and explain that ...** quelqu'un devrait lui expliquer gentiment que ...; **f. gathering** réunion *f* d'amis; **in a f. manner** *or* **way** *(to talk, argue, smile)* amicalement; **to be on f. terms with sb** être en bons termes avec qn; **he gave me a f. wave** il m'a fait un signe amical de la main
  2 *(software, layout etc)* convivial, -aux
  3 *Mil* **is this aircraft f.?** est-ce que cet avion est des nôtres?; **a f. nation** un pays ami
  N *Sport* match *m* amical
  ▸▸ *Mil* **f. fire** tirs *mpl* amis; **to come under f. fire** tomber sous les tirs des siens; **f. forces** troupes *fpl* amies *ou* alliées; **the F. Islands** Tonga *m*, les îles *fpl* des Amis; *Br Fin* **f. society** société *f* de mutualité; *Fin* **f. takeover bid** OPA *f* amicale

-friendly ['frendlɪ] SUFF **ozone-f.** qui préserve la couche d'ozone; **environment-f.** qui respecte l'environnement

friendship ['frendʃɪp] N amitié *f*; **to form a f. with sb** se lier (d'amitié) avec qn; **to lose sb's f.** perdre l'amitié de qn; **her f. means more to me than anything** notre amitié est ce qu'il y a de plus important pour moi; *esp Fml* **to enjoy the f. of sb** côtoyer qn

fries [fraɪz] NPL *esp Am Fam* **(French) f.** frites *fpl*

Friesian ['friːʒən] ADJ frison
  N **1** *(person)* Frison, -onne; *(cow)* frisonne *f*
  2 *Ling* frison *m*

frieze [friːz] N **1** *Archit* frise *f* **2** *(of wallpaper)* frise *f*

frig [frɪg] VT *Vulg (have sex with)* baiser avec
  VI *Vulg (of woman)* se masturber, se toucher
  ▸ **frig about, frig around** VI *Sl (waste time)* traînailler, glandouiller; *(play the fool)* déconner
  ▸ **frig off** VI *Sl* **f. off!** va te faire foutre!

frigate ['frɪgət] N **1** *Naut* frégate *f*, escorteur *m* **2** *(bird)* frégate *f*
  ▸▸ **f. bird** frégate *f*

frigging ['frɪgɪŋ] *Sl* ADJ foutu; **this f. car** cette foutue bagnole, cette putain de bagnole; **what a f. waste of time!** putain, quelle perte de temps!; **he's a f. nuisance** il est chiant comme pas deux
  ADV foutrement; **don't f. lie to me!** ne me mens pas, bordel!

fright [fraɪt] N **1** peur *f*, effroi *m*; **to take f.** s'effrayer (**at** de); **to give sb a f.** faire peur à qn; **to get** *or* **be given the f. of one's life** avoir une peur bleue; *Fam* **I got an awful f.** j'ai eu une sacrée peur **2** *Fam* **what a f. you look!** tu es à faire peur!; **that dress makes you look a real f.!** tu es moche à faire peur dans cette robe!

frighten ['fraɪt(ə)n] VT effrayer, faire peur à; **it frightens him/her** cela lui fait peur; **it frightens me that so many people believe him** ça m'effraie que tant de personnes le croient; **he is easily frightened** il s'effraie pour un rien; **these animals are easily frightened** ces animaux s'effarouchent d'un rien; **to f. sb into doing sth** faire peur à qn pour qu'il fasse qch; **to f. sb out of doing sth** faire peur à qn et le dissuader de faire qch; *Fam* **to f. the life** *or* **the living daylights out of sb** faire mourir qn de peur; *Fam* **to f. sb out of their wits, to f. the wits out of sb** rendre qn fou de peur; **you frightened me to death** vous m'avez fait une peur bleue

VI **I don't f. easily** c'est difficile de me faire peur; **he frightens easily** il s'effraie pour un rien
  ▸ **frighten away, frighten off** VT SEP *(scare) (animal)* effaroucher; *(person)* faire peur à, faire fuir

frightened ['fraɪt(ə)nd] ADJ *(look, voice etc)* apeuré; **to be** *or* **feel f.** avoir peur (**of** de); **I wasn't as f. as you were** je n'avais pas aussi peur que vous; **he's a very f. man** il a très peur; **I was f. of waking her** j'avais peur de la réveiller; **he's out of one's wits** terrifié; **f. to death** mort de peur

frighteners ['fraɪtnəz] NPL *Br Sl* **to put the f. on sb** menacer qn

frightening ['fraɪt(ə)nɪŋ] ADJ effrayant

frighteningly ['fraɪt(ə)nɪŋlɪ] ADV à faire peur; **they were f. close** ils se rapprochaient dangereusement; **they look f. similar** ils se ressemblent tellement que c'en est effrayant; **f. expensive** terriblement cher, hors de prix

frightful ['fraɪtfʊl] ADJ effroyable, épouvantable, affreux

frightfully ['fraɪtfʊlɪ] ADV affreusement; **he is f. ugly** il est laid à faire peur; **I am f. sorry** je regrette énormément; **f. rich/stupid** incroyablement riche/stupide; **f. expensive** affreusement cher; *Fam Hum* **f. f.** = maniérisme *m* utilisé pour décrire les manières et l'accent de la haute bourgeoisie britannique

frightfulness ['fraɪtfʊlnɪs] N atrocité *f*

frigid ['frɪdʒɪd] ADJ **1** *(sexually)* frigide **2** *Geog etc* glacial, -als *ou* -aux, (très) froid **3** *(style, smile, atmosphere)* glacial, -als *ou* -aux; *(response, silence)* glacé

frigidity [frɪ'dʒɪdɪtɪ] N **1** *(sexual)* frigidité *f* **2** *(of style, response, atmosphere)* froideur *f*

frigidly ['frɪdʒɪdlɪ] ADV *(to answer, reply etc)* d'un ton glacial; **f. polite** d'une politesse glaciale

frill [frɪl] N *(on clothing etc)* volant *m*, ruche *f*; *Culin (on ham etc)* papillote *f*; **shirt f.** jabot *m*; *Fig* **a plain meal without frills** un repas simple sans présentation compliquée

frilled [frɪld] ADJ *(ribbon etc)* froncé, ruché; *(shirt)* à jabots
  ▸▸ *Zool* **f. lizard** iguane *m* australien

frilly ['frɪlɪ] ADJ *(shirt, sleeves)* froncé, ruché; *(style, language)* fleuri

fringe [frɪndʒ] N **1** *(of tablecloth, scarf etc)* frange *f* **2** *esp Br (of hair)* frange *f* **3** *(edge)* bordure *f*, bord *m*; **the outer fringe(s) of London** la grande banlieue de Londres; **to live on the f. of society** vivre en marge de la société; **to be on the radical f. of a party** appartenir à la frange radicale d'un parti
  VT *(carpet etc)* franger; **eyes fringed with black lashes** yeux bordés de cils noirs
  ▸▸ **f. benefits** avantages *mpl* annexes *ou* en nature; **f. group** frange *f*; **f. market** marché *m* marginal; *Pol* **f. meeting** réunion *f* parallèle; *Br* **f. theatre** théâtre *m* d'avant-garde *ou* expérimental

frippery ['frɪpərɪ] N *(usu pl)* fripperies *(ornaments)* colifichets *mpl*

Frisbee® ['frɪzbɪ] N Frisbee® *m*; **to play F.** jouer au Frisbee®

Frisco ['frɪskəʊ] N *Am Fam* San Francisco

frisk [frɪsk] N **1** *(search)* fouille *f*; **to give sb a f.** fouiller qn **2** *(movement)* **with a f. of its tail** en donnant un coup de queue
  VT **1** *(search) (suspect etc)* fouiller; **to be frisked for weapons/alcohol** être fouillé pour vérifier qu'on ne cache pas d'armes/d'alcool **2** *(of dog etc)* **to f. its tail** remuer la queue
  VI *(of lambs etc)* s'ébattre, gambader, folâtrer
  ▸ **frisk about** VI = **frisk** VI

friskiness ['frɪskɪnɪs] **N** vivacité f

frisking ['frɪskɪŋ] **N** (of suspect, traveller) fouille f; **to get a f. from a policeman, to be given a f. by a policeman** se faire fouiller par un policier

frisky ['frɪskɪ] **ADJ** vif; (horse) qui fait des cabrioles; **to feel f.** (of person) se sentir plein d'entrain; Fam (sexually) avoir le feu au derrière; Fam **to get f.** s'échauffer; **for an old man, he was still remarkably f.** il avait un tempérament encore très ardent pour son âge

fritillary [frɪ'tɪlərɪ] **N 1** (plant) fritillaire f **2** (butterfly) damier m

fritter ['frɪtər] **N** Culin beignet m; **apple/banana f.** beignet aux pommes/à la banane
▸ **fritter away VT SEP** Fam (fortune) dissiper; (money, time) gaspiller; **to f. away one's money on clothes/jewellery** gaspiller son argent dans des vêtements/des bijoux; **I feel as if I've just frittered away the day** j'ai l'impression d'avoir perdu ma journée

frivolity [frɪ'vɒlɪtɪ] **N** frivolité f

frivolous ['frɪvələs] **ADJ** (person etc) frivole; (remark) frivole, futile; (objection, criticism) futile

frivolously ['frɪvələslɪ] **ADV** (to behave, say sth) frivolement

frivolousness ['frɪvələsnɪs] **N** (of person) frivolité f; (of objection etc) futilité f

frizz [frɪz] **VT** (hair) crêper, frisotter
VI (of hair) frisotter

frizziness ['frɪzɪnɪs] **N** the f. of my hair mes cheveux crépus

frizzle ['frɪz(ə)l] **VI** (of meat etc in frying pan) grésiller
VT Culin (burn) laisser brûler

frizzy ['frɪzɪ] **ADJ** (hair) crêpelé, crépu

FRN [efɑː'ren] **N** Banking (abbr floating-rate note) effet m à taux flottant

fro [frəʊ] **ADV** **to go to and f.** aller et venir

frock [frɒk] **N** (for child, woman) robe f; (of monk) froc m, bure f
▸▸ **f. coat** redingote f

frog[1] [frɒg] **N 1** (animal) grenouille f; Fam **to have a f. in one's throat** avoir un chat dans la gorge **2** Br Offensive Sl **F.** (French person) Français, -aise

frog[2] **N** Mil etc **1** (for sword) porte-épée m inv; (for bayonet) porte-baïonnette m inv **2** (braid) brandebourg m

frogged [frɒgd] **ADJ** (uniform, tunic etc) orné de brandebourgs

frogging ['frɒgɪŋ] **N** (on uniform etc) brandebourgs mpl

Froggy ['frɒgɪ] **N** Br Offensive Sl (French person) Français, -aise

frogman, pl **frogmen** ['frɒgmən] **N** homme-grenouille m, pl hommes-grenouilles

frogmarch ['frɒgmɑːtʃ] **VT** (person) emmener de force; **they frogmarched her out of the room** ils l'ont fait sortir de la pièce de force

frogspawn ['frɒgspɔːn] **N** (no pl) œufs mpl de grenouille

frolic ['frɒlɪk] **N** (of young animal, child etc) ébats mpl; **to have a f. in the fields** s'ébattre ou gambader dans les champs
VI (frolicked) s'ébattre

FROM [frɒm, unstressed frəm]

- de **1, 2, 5, 8, 9** ▪ à partir de **3, 4**
- depuis **4** ▪ d'après **7**

PREP 1 (place) de; **he returned f. London** il est revenu de Londres; **f. Paris to London** de Paris à Londres; **f. town to town** de ville en ville; **f. here** d'ici

2 (origin) **to take/remove/steal/etc sth f. sb**

prendre/ôter/voler/etc qch à qn; **to take sth f. somewhere** prendre qch quelque part; **to remove sth f. somewhere** enlever qch de quelque part; **where do you come f.?, where are you f.?** d'où viens-tu?; **a train/plane f. Manchester** un train/avion en provenance de Manchester; **wheat f. Russia** blé (venant) de Russie; **a quotation f. Shakespeare** une citation tirée de Shakespeare; **he grabbed a revolver f. the table** il saisit un revolver sur la table; **I have brought it to you f. a friend** je vous l'apporte de la part d'un ami; **tell her that f. me** dites-lui cela de ma part; **f. ...** (on parcel) expéditeur/expéditrice ...

3 (range) à partir de; **potatoes f. 50 pence a kilo** des pommes de terre à partir de 50 pence le kilo; **the bird lays f. four to six eggs** l'oiseau pond de quatre à six œufs; **wine f. four euros a bottle** vins à partir de quatre euros la bouteille; **the price has been increased f. fifty pence to sixty pence** on a augmenté le prix de cinquante pence à soixante pence; **every flavour of ice cream f. vanilla to pistachio** tous les parfums de glace de la vanille à la pistache

4 (time) depuis, dès, à partir de; **f. that day** depuis ce jour, à partir de ce jour; **f. tomorrow on** à partir de demain; **house let f. 1 June** maison louée à compter du 1er juin; **f. his childhood** depuis ou dès son enfance; **she remembered him f. her childhood** elle se souvenait de lui dans son enfance; **he remembered the name f. his time with the BBC** il se souvenait du nom de l'époque où il était à la BBC; **f. morning till night** du matin au soir

5 (distance) **not far f. ...** pas loin de ...; **ten kilometres f. Paris** à dix kilomètres de Paris

6 (change) **f. bad to worse** de mal en pis

7 (because of) **to act f. conviction** agir par conviction; **I know him f. seeing him at the club** je le reconnais pour l'avoir vu au cercle; **f. his looks you might suppose that ...** à le voir on dirait que ...; **f. what I heard ...** d'après ce que j'ai entendu dire ...; **f. what I can see ...** à ce que je vois ...

8 (with adv, prep) **f. above** d'en haut; **I saw him f. a long way off** je l'ai vu de loin; **f. among the trees ...** de parmi les arbres ...; **take one f. among ...** prenez-en un parmi ...

9 (after adv) **to come down f. one's room** descendre de sa chambre; **to move away f. sb** s'éloigner de qn

frond [frɒnd] **N** (of fern) fronde f; (of palm tree) feuille f

FRONT [frʌnt]

N	devant **1, 5** ▪ avant **1** ▪ façade **1, 3** ▪ front **4** ▪ en avant (in front) **5**
ADJ	de devant
VT	diriger **2**

N 1 devant m; (of building) façade f; (of shop) devanture f; (of car) avant m; (of shirt) devant; **carriage at the f. of the train** voiture en tête du train; **at the f. of the book** au début du livre; **I spilled soup all down my f.** je me suis renversé de la soupe dessus; Theat **out f.** dans la salle; Br **the f.** (promenade at seaside) la promenade; Br **house on the f.** maison faisant face à la mer

2 (first row) premier rang m; **to push one's way to the f.** se frayer un chemin jusqu'au premier rang; Fig **se pousser (en avant)**

3 (outward appearance) **to put on a bold f.** faire bonne contenance; **it's only a f. on his part** (way of behaving etc) ce n'est qu'une façade; **the company was just a f. for their arms dealing operation** la société n'était qu'une couverture pour leur trafic d'armes; Br Fam **to have the f. to do sth** (nerve) avoir l'effronterie ou le front de faire qch

4 Mil, Pol, Met front m; Pol **common f.** front

commun; **popular f.** front populaire; Fig **to make progress on all fronts** faire des progrès sur tous les fronts; Met **warm/cold f.** front chaud/froid

5 in f. devant, en avant; (in race, contest) en tête; **Manchester United are now five points in f.** Manchester United mène par cinq points; **to send sb on in f.** envoyer qn devant; **in f. of**, Am **f. of** devant; (opposite) en face de; **he was standing right in f. of me** (facing me) il se trouvait juste en face de moi; (in queue, crowd etc) il se trouvait juste devant moi; **it's right in f. of you** (what you are looking for) c'est juste devant vous; **he opened it/talked about it in f. of her** il l'a ouvert/en a parlé devant elle

6 Fam **I want the money up f.** je veux mon argent avant; **to pay up f.** payer d'avance; Fam **he was very up f. about it** il a été franc sur ce point

ADJ (garden, teeth) de devant; **the f. part of the brain** la partie antérieure du cerveau; **f. carriage** (of train) voiture f de tête; Theat **f.-row seat** siège m de premier rang; **to have a f.-row seat** Theat être assis au premier rang; Fig être aux premières loges; Aut **f. wheel** (of car, bicycle) roue f avant

VI 1 (of building) **the house fronts north** la maison est exposée ou orientée au nord
2 Mil faire front; **left f.!** à gauche front!, à gauche, gauche!
VT 1 (building) donner une (nouvelle) façade à
2 (government) diriger; TV (programme) présenter; Mus **to f. a band** (lead it) diriger un orchestre
3 Am Fam (pay in advance) avancer; **the cashier can f. you the money** le caissier peut vous faire une avance ou vous avancer l'argent
4 Am Fam (give, lend money to) filer; **can you f. me five bucks?** tu pourrais pas me filer cinq dollars?
▸▸ Journ **f. cover** (of magazine) couverture f, première f de couverture, Fam première f de couve; **to appear on the f. cover** faire la une; **f. desk** réception f, **f. door** (of house) porte f d'entrée; (of vehicle) portière f avant; Theat **f. of house** = partie f d'un théâtre où peuvent circuler les spectateurs; **f.-of-house manager** (in hotel) directeur m administratif, directeur de l'hébergement; Theat directeur m administratif; Mil **the f. line** la première ligne; **f. man** prête-nom m, pl prête-noms, homme m de paille; (presenter) présentateur m; **to act as a f. man for sb** servir de prête-nom ou d'homme de paille à qn; Banking **f. office** front-office m, pl front-offices; **f. organization** couverture f, façade f; **f. page** (of newspaper) première page f, Fam **to be f. page news** faire la une; **f. panel** face f avant; Cin **f. projection** projection f frontale; **f. room** (at front of house) = pièce f qui donne sur le devant de la maison; (sitting room) salon m; **f. row** premier rang m; Rugby première ligne f; **in the f. row** au premier rang; Rugby **f.-row forward** avant m de première ligne; Aut **f. seat** siège m avant; **f. view** vue f de face; Archit **élévation** f du devant
▸ **front on, front onto VT INSEP** (of building) (be opposite) faire face à; (point towards) être tourné vers; **the river and the houses fronting on it** (overlooking) le fleuve et les maisons qui donnent dessus

frontage ['frʌntɪdʒ] **N 1** (of building) longueur f de façade; (of shop) devanture f; **premises with frontages on two streets** local avec façades sur deux rues **2** (of river etc) terrain m en bordure **3** (land at front of building etc) espace m sur le devant d'un immeuble

frontal ['frʌnt(ə)l] **N 1** Rel devant m d'autel, fronteau m **2** (of building) façade f

ADJ *Anat* frontal, -aux; *Archit (view etc)* de face
▸▸ f. **attack** *Com* attaque f frontale; *Mil* attaque de front; *Aut* f. **impact** choc m frontal; *Aut* f. **impact test** test m de choc frontal; *Met* f. **system** système m de fronts

frontbench [frʌnt'bentʃ] N *Br Pol (members of the government)* ministres mpl; *(members of the opposition)* ministres du cabinet fantôme; **he's never been on the f.** *(government)* il n'a jamais été ministre; *(opposition)* il n'a jamais été membre du cabinet fantôme; **the frontbenches** *(in Parliament)* = à la Chambre des communes, bancs mpl situés à droite et à gauche du Président et occupés respectivement par les ministres du gouvernement en exercice et ceux du gouvernement fantôme
▸▸ f. **MP** *(member of the government)* ministre m; *(member of the opposition)* membre m du cabinet fantôme; f. **spokesperson** *(of cabinet)* porte-parole m inv; *(of shadow cabinet)* porte-parole du cabinet fantôme; f. **team** *(cabinet)* équipe f ministérielle; *(shadow cabinet)* cabinet m fantôme

frontbencher [frʌnt'bentʃər] N *Br Pol (member of the government)* ministre m; *(member of the opposition)* membre m du cabinet fantôme

front-end N *Comput* interface f
▸▸ *Comput* f. **computer** ordinateur m frontal; *Fin* f. **fee** frais mpl d'entrée; *Fin* f. **loading** = système m de prélèvement des frais sur les premiers versements; *Comput* f. **processor** processeur m frontal

frontier [frʌn'tɪər] N frontière f, **natural frontiers** frontières naturelles; **the frontiers of human knowledge** les bornes fpl des connaissances humaines
▸▸ f. **guard** garde-frontière m, pl gardes-frontière; f. **town** = ville f de l'Ouest américain, à l'époque des pionniers

frontispiece ['frʌntɪspiːs] N *Typ* frontispice m

front-line ADJ *Mil (soldiers, troops)* en première ligne
▸▸ *Am Sport* f. **player** avant m

front-loader N *(washing machine)* machine f à laver avec chargement frontal

front-loading ADJ *(washing machine)* avec chargement frontal

frontrunner ['frʌntrʌnər] N *(leader)* coureur/cheval/concurrent m de tête; *(in election etc)* favori, -ite

front-wheel drive N traction f avant

frosh [frɒʃ] N *Am Univ Fam* étudiant, -ante de première année

frost [frɒst] N *Met* gelée f, gel m; **there was a f. last night** il a gelé la nuit dernière; **there was f. on the ground** le sol était gelé; **ground f.** gelée blanche; **heavy/light f.** grosse/petite gelée; **ten degrees of f.** dix degrés au-dessous de zéro
VT 1 *(windows etc)* givrer 2 *esp Am Culin (cake etc)* glacer 3 *(damage by frost) (fruit tree etc)* geler 4 *(in glassmaking) (glass)* dépolir
VI = **frost over, frost up**
▸ **frost over, frost up** VI *(of windscreen etc)* se givrer, se couvrir de givre

frostbite ['frɒstbaɪt] N *Med (of feet etc)* gelure f; **to have f.** avoir des gelures

frostbitten ['frɒstbɪt(ə)n] ADJ 1 *(nose etc)* gelé 2 *(plant)* brûlé par le froid, grillé (par la gelée)

frostbound ['frɒstbaʊnd] ADJ *(earth)* gelé

frosted ['frɒstɪd] ADJ 1 *(windscreen)* givré 2 *esp Am Culin (cake)* glacé 3 *(glass)* dépoli

frost-free ADJ *(refrigerator, freezer)* à dégivrage automatique

frostily ['frɒstɪlɪ] ADV *(to say)* sur un ton glacial; **to greet sb f.** faire un accueil glacé à qn; **she smiled f.** elle fit un sourire glacial

frostiness ['frɒstɪnɪs] N 1 *(of the morning etc)* froid m glacial 2 *(of person)* manière f glaciale; **the f. of her smile/behaviour** son sourire/comportement glacial

frosting ['frɒstɪŋ] N *esp Am Culin (on cake)* glaçage m; *Fig* **the f. on the cake** la cerise sur le gâteau

frostproof ['frɒstpruːf] ADJ résistant à la gelée

frosty ['frɒstɪ] ADJ 1 *(night, air etc)* glacial, -als ou -aux 2 *(answer, smile, greeting)* glacial, -als ou -aux 3 *(window)* couvert de givre; *(ground)* gelé

froth [frɒθ] N 1 *(foam)* écume f, *(on beer, fizzy drink etc)* mousse f 2 *Pej (empty words)* paroles fpl creuses
VI écumer, mousser; *(of beer, fizzy drink etc)* mousser; *(of waves)* moutonner; **he was frothing at the mouth** il avait l'écume aux lèvres; **the frothing water** *(of sea)* les eaux écumantes
▸ **froth up** VI mousser

frothy ['frɒθɪ] ADJ 1 écumeux, mousseux; *(waves)* moutonneux; *(beer, fizzy drink etc)* mousseux 2 *(speech, play, style)* léger; *Pej* vide, creux

frown [fraʊn] N froncement m de sourcils; *(disapproving look)* air m désapprobateur; *(stern look)* regard m sévère; **to say sth with a f.** dire qch en fronçant les sourcils
VI *(of person)* froncer les sourcils, se renfrogner; **she frowned disapprovingly/in annoyance** elle fronça les sourcils d'un air désapprobateur/irrité; **to f. at sb** regarder qn en fronçant les sourcils
▸ **frown on, frown upon** VT INSEP *(disapprove of) (suggestion etc)* désapprouver; **such behaviour was frowned upon** un tel comportement était mal vu

frowning ['fraʊnɪŋ] ADJ *(expression)* renfrogné

frowsty ['fraʊstɪ] ADJ *Br Fam (room)* qui sent le renfermé; *(smell, atmosphere)* de renfermé

frowzy ['fraʊzɪ] ADJ *Fam* 1 *(musty) (room)* qui sent le renfermé 2 *(person, clothes etc)* peu soigné

froze PT see **freeze**

frozen ['frəʊz(ə)n] ADJ 1 gelé, glacé; *(meat, peas etc)* congelé, surgelé; *Fam* **my hands are f.** j'ai les mains gelées ou glacées 2 *Fin (credit, wages)* gelé, bloqué; *(assets, currency, prices)* gelé; *(account)* bloqué 3 *Comput (screen)* bloqué
PP see **freeze**
▸▸ f. **food** *(in refrigerator)* aliments mpl congelés; *(industrially frozen)* surgelés mpl; f. **food compartment** congélateur m; f. **yoghurt** yaourt m glacé

fructify ['frʌktɪfaɪ] VI fructifier
VT faire fructifier

fructose ['frʌktəʊs] N *Chem* fructose m

frugal ['fruːg(ə)l] ADJ *(person, life)* frugal, -aux; *(meal etc)* frugal, -aux, sobre; *(thrifty)* économe; **to be f. with sth** ménager qch

frugality [fruː'gælɪtɪ] N *(of person, life)* frugalité f, *(of meal)* frugalité, sobriété f, *(thriftiness)* économie f

frugally ['fruːg(ə)lɪ] ADV frugalement

fruit [fruːt] N 1 fruit m; **would you like some f.?** prendrez-vous un fruit?; **apples and other fruit(s)** les pommes et autres fruits; **a piece of f.** un fruit; **eat more f.** mangez plus de fruits; *Br* **soft f.**, *Am* **small f.** petits fruits; **to bear f.** *(of tree)* donner des fruits, porter fruit; *Fig (of labour)* porter ses fruits; **my enquiries bore f.** mes recherches furent cou-

ronnées de succès 2 *Fig* fruit m; *Lit* **the fruits of the earth** les fruits de la terre; *Lit* **the f. of her womb** le fruit de ses entrailles 3 *Old-fashioned Br Fam* **yes, old f.** oui, mon vieux 4 *Am Offensive Sl (homosexual)* pédé m
VI *(of tree)* porter des fruits
▸▸ f. **basket** *(for display)* corbeille f à fruits; *Zool* f. **bat** chauve-souris f frugivore, pl chauves-souris frugivores; f. **bowl** coupe f à fruits, compotier m; f. **bud** bourgeon m à fruit; f. **cocktail** macédoine f ou salade f de fruits; f. **cup** *(dessert)* coupe de fruits; *(drink)* boisson f aux fruits *(parfois alcoolisée)*; f. **dish** *(individual)* coupe, coupelle f, *(large)* coupe à fruits, compotier; f. **drop** bonbon m aux fruits; f. **farmer** producteur, -trice de fruits; f. **farming** arboriculture f (fruitière); f. **fly** mouche f du vinaigre, drosophile f, f. **grower** fruiticulteur, -trice; f. **juice** jus m de fruits; f. **knife** couteau m à fruit(s); *Br* f. **machine** machine f à sous; f. **salad** macédoine ou salade de fruits; f. **shop** fruiterie f ou étalage m de fruit; f. **tree** arbre m fruitier

fruit-bearing ADJ *(tree etc)* frugifère, fructifère

fruitcake ['fruːtkeɪk] N 1 *Culin* cake m 2 *esp Br Fam (eccentric, mad person)* cinglé, -ée, fou, f folle; **he's as nutty as a f.** il est complètement cinglé

fruit-eating ADJ *(animal)* frugivore

fruiterer ['fruːtərər] N *esp Br Old-fashioned* fruitier, -ière; **f.'s (shop)** fruiterie f

fruitful ['fruːtfʊl] ADJ 1 *(work, discussion etc)* fructueux 2 *(tree etc)* fructueux, productif; *(soil etc)* fertile, fécond

fruitfully ['fruːtfʊlɪ] ADV fructueusement; **they had spent the day f.** la journée avait été fructueuse pour eux

fruitfulness ['fruːtfʊlnɪs] N 1 *Fig (of work, discussion etc)* caractère m fructueux 2 *(of tree etc)* productivité f, *(of earth etc)* fertilité f

fruiting ['fruːtɪŋ] ADJ *(tree etc)* frugifère, fructifère

fruition [fruː'ɪʃən] N *(of plan, hope)* réalisation f, **to come to f.** porter ses fruits; **to bring sth to f.** mener qch à bien

fruitless ['fruːtlɪs] ADJ *(discussions, negotiations)* stérile, infructueux; *(efforts, attempt)* infructueux, vain; **at least the trip won't have been entirely f.** au moins le voyage n'aura pas tout à fait servi à rien

fruity ['fruːtɪ] ADJ 1 *(taste etc)* de fruit; *(wine)* fruité, fruiteux 2 *Fam* **a f. voice** une voix *(trop)* étoffée; **a f. laugh** un rire généreux 3 *esp Br Old-fashioned (novel, scandal etc)* corsé 4 *Am Offensive Sl (homosexual)* de pédé 5 *Am (crazy)* toqué, cinglé

frump [frʌmp] N femme f mal attifée; **she's a f.** elle est ficelée comme l'as de pique

frumpish ['frʌmpɪʃ], **frumpy** ['frʌmpɪ] ADJ *(clothes)* tarte, moche; *Fam* f. **woman** femme f mal attifée ou mal fagotée

frustrate [frʌs'treɪt] VT 1 *(upset, annoy) (person)* décevoir, frustrer 2 *(thwart) (person)* contrecarrer; *(plan)* faire échouer; **to f. sb's hopes** frustrer qn dans son espoir, frustrer l'espoir de qn

frustrated [frʌs'treɪtɪd] ADJ *(writer etc)* frustré; **(sexually) f.** frustré

frustrating [frʌs'treɪtɪŋ] ADJ *(experience etc)* frustrant

frustration [frʌs'treɪʃən] N 1 *(emotion)* frustration f 2 *(of person's plans)* anéantissement m; *(of hopes, ambitions)* frustration f

fry[1] [fraɪ] *(fried)* VT 1 *Culin (fish etc)* (faire) frire; **to f. an egg** faire cuire un œuf sur le plat 2 *esp Am Sl (convict)* faire passer à la chaise électrique
VI 1 *(of food)* frire 2 *esp Am Sl (of convict)* passer à la chaise électrique

fry² N (no pl) (of fish) frai m, fretin m, alevin m; **small f.** menu fretin; Fig (insignificant people) menu fretin, gens mpl insignifiants; (children) gosses mpl; **salmon f.** saumoneaux mpl dans la deuxième année

fry³ N (offal) issues fpl; (of lamb, pig) fressure f

fryer ['fraɪər] N Culin **1** (person) = personne f qui fait de la friture **2** (frying pan) poêle f à frire; **(deep) f.** friteuse f **3** (chicken) poulet m à frire

frying ['fraɪɪŋ] N friture f
▸ ▸ **f. pan** poêle f (à frire); Prov **to jump out of the f. pan into the fire** tomber de Charybde en Scylla

fry-pan N Am poêle f à frire

fry-up N Br Culin Fam = bacon, saucisses, tomates etc frits ensemble, généralement consommés au petit déjeuner

FSA [efes'eɪ] N **1** Fin (abbr **Financial Services Authority**) = organisme m gouvernemental britannique chargé de contrôler les activités du secteur financier **2** (abbr **Food Standards Agency**) = organisme m britannique de contrôle de la sécurité alimentaire

f-stop N Phot ouverture f du diaphragme

ft (abbr **foot/feet**) p., pd.

FT 100 index [ef'ti:] N St Exch (abbr **Financial Times-Stock Exchange 100 Index**) = principal indice m boursier du Financial Times basé sur la valeur de 100 actions cotées à la Bourse de Londres

FTP [efti:'pi:] Comput N (abbr **File Transfer Protocol**) FTP
vT télécharger par FTP
▸ ▸ **F. server** serveur m FTP; **F. site** site m FTP

FTSE ['fʊtsɪ] N St Exch (abbr **Financial Times Stock Exchange**) = principal indice m boursier du Financial Times basé sur la valeur de 100 actions cotées à la Bourse de Londres, ≃ indice m CAC 40

fuchsia ['fju:ʃə] N (plant) fuchsia m

fuck [fʌk] Vulg N **1** (intercourse) baise f; **they had a quick f.** ils ont baisé ou tiré un coup en vitesse; **to be a good f.** bien baiser; **to be an easy f.** coucher avec tout le monde
2 (as intensifier) **what the f. is that?** qu'est-ce que c'est que ça, bordel de merde?; **I can't really afford it, but what the f.!** c'est un peu cher pour moi, mais je m'en fous!; **who the f. told you about it/did this?** quel est le connard qui t'en a parlé/qui a fait ça?; **as stupid/rich as f.** foutrement con/riche; **he ran like f.** il a couru comme un dératé; **shut the f. up!** ferme ta gueule putain ou bordel!; **get the f. out of here!** casse-toi connard!; **for f.'s sake!** bordel!, putain!; **f. knows why I agreed to come!** putain ou bordel, pourquoi est-ce que j'ai accepté de venir?; **not to care or give a f.** n'en avoir rien à foutre (about sth de qch); **why should I give a f. about what you think?** qu'est-ce que ça peut me foutre, ce que tu penses?; **she'd like you to apologize – like f. I will!** elle voudrait que tu t'excuses – qu'elle aille se faire foutre!; **did you invite them? – like f. I did!** tu les as invités? – tu déconnes ou quoi?; **like f. I'm going to help that bastard!** qu'il aille se faire foutre, ce connard, je ne l'aiderai pas!; **get to f.!** va te faire foutre!
INT merde!, bordel!
vT 1 (person) baiser **2 f. it!** merde!; **f. this!** et puis merde!; **f. you!, go f. yourself!** va te faire foutre!, je t'emmerde!; **f. him!** qu'il aille se faire foutre!; **f. what he thinks/says!** je m'en fous de ce qu'il pense/dit!; **f. me!** putain!; **f. the President!** aux chiottes le Président!; **f. all** que dalle; **she does f. all work** elle en fout pas une rame
vI baiser
▸ **fuck about, fuck around** Vulg vI (play the fool) déconner; (waste time) glander; **to f. about or around with sth** (car, radio) trifouiller qch; **if you spent less time fucking about or around with your computer program …!** si tu passais moins de temps sur ton putain de logiciel …!
vT SEP (person) (treat badly) emmerder; (waste time of) faire tourner en bourrique
▸ **fuck off** Vulg vI (go away) se casser; **to tell sb to f. off** dire à qn d'aller se faire foutre, envoyer qn se faire foutre; **f. off!** va te faire foutre!
vT SEP (annoy) (person) emmerder, faire chier; **she's been feeling really fucked off about work recently** le boulot la fait vraiment chier ces temps-ci
▸ **fuck over** vT SEP Am Vulg **to f. sb over** (cheat) baiser qn, arnaquer qn; **I really got fucked over on that one** là je me suis vraiment fait baiser ou arnaquer; **he had been fucked over for a thousand dollars** il s'était fait baiser de mille dollars
▸ **fuck up** Vulg vT SEP (ruin) foutre en l'air, niquer; (person) foutre en l'air; **I think I've fucked up the exam/the meringue** je crois que j'ai loupé ce putain d'examen/cette putain de meringue; **she was badly fucked up by her parents** ses parents l'ont complètement foutue en l'air; **to be fucked up** (of person) être à côté de ses pompes
vI (bungle sth) déconner, merder

fucked [fʌkt] ADJ Vulg (car, stereo etc) foutu, naze; **I'm f.!** (exhausted) je suis mort ou crevé!; **his knee/heart/eye is f.** son genou/cœur/œil est naze ou niqué; **his chances of winning the race were completely f.!** il n'avait plus une chance de gagner cette putain de course!

fucker ['fʌkər] N Vulg **1** (person) stupid f. connard m; **old f.** vieux con m **2** (thing, object) saloperie f; **I can't get the f. out** je n'arrive pas à retirer cette saloperie

fuckface ['fʌkfeɪs] N Vulg tête f de con

fucking ['fʌkɪŋ] Vulg ADJ foutu; **this f. car** cette voiture de mes deux, cette putain de voiture; **I've cut my f. finger** bordel ou putain, je me suis coupé le doigt!; **he's a f. idiot!** c'est un connard!; **you're a f. liar!** tu n'es qu'un connard de menteur!; **that's a f. lie!** c'est des conneries!; **you haven't got a f. clue, have you?** tu n'y connais foutrement rien, hein?; **f. hell!** bordel de merde!; **who the f. hell does she think she is?** mais merde, pour qui elle se prend?; **why/when the f. hell did you do that?** pourquoi/quand est-ce que tu as fait ça putain ou bordel?
ADV (cold, expensive, good) vachement; (stupid) foutument; **it's f. cold** putain, il fait vachement froid; **you're f. well out of your mind!** bordel, ça va vraiment pas dans ta tête!; **what did you f. expect?** mais qu'est-ce que tu croyais putain ou bordel?
N baise f

fuck-up N Vulg gâchis m; **the whole thing was a complete f.** tout a merdé; **to make a f. of sth** (task, job) saloper qch; (marriage) foutre qch en l'air; **I made a real f. of the exam/interview** j'ai complètement merdé à l'examen/l'entretien

fuckwit ['fʌkwɪt] N Vulg connard m, connasse f

fuddle ['fʌd(ə)l] vT (person) embrouiller; **he had fuddled his brain with drink and drugs** l'alcool et la drogue lui avaient embrouillé le cerveau

fuddled ['fʌd(ə)ld] ADJ Fam **1** (drunk) soûl; **to get f.** se soûler, s'enivrer; **slightly f.** un peu gris **2** (confused) embrouillé

fuddy-duddy ['fʌdɪdʌdɪ] Fam N vieil encroûté m; **don't be such an old f.!** arrête de t'encroûter comme ça!
ADJ vieux jeu inv

fudge [fʌdʒ] N **1** Culin fondant m **2** Journ (late news) dernières nouvelles fpl **3** (evasion) **his answer was a f.** sa réponse n'était qu'une dérobade
vT Fam (botch) (piece of work etc) bousiller; (falsify) (accounts etc) truquer; **to f. an issue** (avoid) éluder une question
vI Fam se dérober; **I've had enough of their fudging** j'en ai assez de leurs dérobades

fuel [fjʊəl] N combustible m; (for engine) carburant m; **domestic or household f.** combustible de ménage; Fig **to add f. to the flames** jeter de l'huile sur le feu; Fig **to add fresh f. to a quarrel** alimenter une querelle
vT (-ll-, Am -l-) (furnace etc) alimenter, charger; (vehicle, machine etc) ravitailler ou alimenter en carburant; Fig (speculations) nourrir; (doubts, hatred, argument) alimenter
vI se ravitailler en carburant
▸ ▸ **f. bill** (of household) facture f de chauffage; (of region) dépenses fpl énergétiques; **f. consumption** consommation f d'énergie; (of car) consommation de carburant; **f. costs** (of household) coûts mpl de chauffage; (of region) coûts de l'énergie; **f. element** élément m combustible; **f. gauge** jauge f d'essence; Tech **f. injection** alimentation f par injection, injection f (de carburant); Tech **f. injection system** système m d'injection (de combustible); Tech **f. injector** injecteur m de carburant; **f. level** niveau m de carburant; **f. oil** mazout m, fuel m, fioul m; **f. pipe** tuyau m d'alimentation en carburant; **f. pressure** pression f de carburant; **f. pump** pompe f d'alimentation; Nucl **f. rod** assemblage m d'éléments combustibles; **f. tank** (in home) cuve f à mazout; (in car) réservoir m de carburant ou d'essence; (in ship) soute f à mazout ou à fuel; **f. tank shield** bouclier m de réservoir de carburant; **f. tax** taxe f sur les carburants; **f. temperature gauge** jauge f de température du carburant

fuel/air mixture N mélange m air/carburant

fuel-injected ['fjʊəlɪndʒektɪd] ADJ Aut etc à injection

fuelling, Am fueling ['fjʊəlɪŋ] N ravitaillement m en carburant
▸ ▸ **f. stop** escale f de ravitaillement (en carburant)

fug [fʌg] N esp Br Fam forte odeur f de renfermé; (in smoke-filled room) air m saturé de fumée de cigarette; **there's a terrible f. in here!** ce que ça pue le renfermé/le tabac là-dedans!

fuggy ['fʌgɪ] ADJ esp Br Fam (room etc) qui sent le renfermé; (atmosphere) confiné

fugitive ['fju:dʒɪtɪv] N fugitif, -ive, fuyard, -arde; (refugee) réfugié, -ée; **f. from justice** fugitif recherché par la justice
ADJ 1 (prisoner) fugitif, fuyard **2** esp Lit (happiness) fugitif, fugace; (smile, impression, thought) fugitif

fugue [fju:g] N Mus, Psy fugue f

fulcrum, pl fulcra, fulcrums ['fʌlkrəm, -krə, -krəmz] N (of lever) pivot m

fulfil, Am fulfill [fʊl'fɪl] vT (Br fulfils, Am fulfills; Br, Am fulfilled, fulfilling) (task, prophecy) accomplir; (expectations) répondre à, remplir; (wish) satisfaire; (prayer, plea) exaucer; (obligation, duties) remplir, s'acquitter de; (conditions, instructions, purpose, contract) remplir; (requirements, need, purpose) répondre à, satisfaire à; (promise) exécuter; (commandment) obéir à; (ambition, plan, potential) réaliser; **to f. oneself** se réaliser, s'épanouir; **administrative work doesn't f. me** le travail de bureau ne me permet pas de me réaliser; **to feel fulfilled** (of person) se sentir épanoui

fulfilling [fʊlˈfɪlɪŋ] **ADJ** *(work etc)* épanouissant

fulfilment, *Am* **fulfillment** [fʊlˈfɪlmənt] **N** *(of prophecy, duty, wish etc)* accomplissement *m; (of prayer, plea)* exaucement *m; (of plan, contract)* exécution *f; Law (of condition)* accomplissement; *(of ambition)* réalisation *f, (of promise)* exécution; **to find** *or* **achieve f.** se réaliser; **to have a feeling** *or* **sense of f.** avoir un sentiment de plénitude

FULL [fʊl]

ADJ plein **1, 2, 4, 5** ▪ rempli **1** ▪ ample **3** ▪ complet **4** ▪ large **5** **N** intégralement **ADV** complètement **1** ▪ carrément **2**

ADJ 1 *(receptacle, cupboard)* plein, rempli; *(room)* comble; *(bus etc)* plein; *(day)* chargé; *(sail)* plein, gonflé; *(disk)* saturé; **f. to the brim** rempli jusqu'au bord *ou* à ras bord; **f. to overflowing** plein à ras bord; **don't speak with your mouth f.** ne parle pas la bouche pleine; **to be f. (up)** *(of person)* être repu *ou* rassasié; **on a f. stomach** le ventre plein; **the bus is f. up** l'autobus est au complet; **the sails are f.** les voiles portent bien; **to be f. of sth** être plein de qch; **the (news)papers were f. of it** les journaux ne parlaient que de ça; **to become f.** *(of disk)* arriver à saturation; **to have one's pockets f. of money** avoir les poches pleines d'argent; **her eyes were f. of tears** ses yeux étaient remplis de larmes; **f. of holes** plein de trous

2 look f. of hatred regard chargé de haine; **to be f. of hope** être rempli d'espoir; **to be f. of ideas** être plein d'idées; **to be f. of life/ energy/vitality** être plein de vie/d'énergie/ de vitalité; **to be f. of praise for sb** ne pas tarir d'éloges sur qn; **to be f. of one's own importance** être pénétré de sa propre importance; *Pej* **f. of oneself** plein de soi-même

3 *(written notes, details etc)* ample, copieux; **she received her f. share of the money** elle a reçu tout l'argent qui lui revenait; **in the fullest detail** dans le plus grand détail; **to ask for fuller information about sth** demander des précisions sur qch

4 *(complete)* complet, entier; **the f. horror of the situation** toute l'horreur de la situation; **roses in f. bloom** roses épanouies; **to be in f. cry** *(of hounds)* donner de la voix; *Fig* **the press was in f. cry after the minister** la presse se déchaînait contre le ministre; **in f. flow** en plein discours; **on f. beam** en feux de route, en pleins phares; *Mil, Fig* **in f. flight/retreat** en pleine déroute/retraite; *Mil, Fig* **at f. strength** au grand complet; **below f. strength** pas au complet; **in f. uniform** en grande tenue; **to be in f. swing** *(of party, sales etc)* battre son plein; **in f. view of the police/the enemy** sous les yeux de la police/de l'ennemi; **to lead a f. life** mener une vie bien remplie; **I waited two f. hours** *or* **a f. two hours** j'ai attendu deux bonnes heures; **we were under f. sail** nous avions toutes voiles dehors; **to give f. scope to sb** donner libre carrière à qn; **to give f. scope to sb's talents** donner libre champ aux talents de qn; **f. amount** somme totale; **at f. blast** à fond; **f. cargo** plein chargement; *Phot* **in f. colour** tout en couleur; *Sch* **f. marks** dix sur dix/ vingt sur vingt/*etc, Fig* **f. marks for all those who spotted the mistake** bravo à tous ceux qui ont trouvé l'erreur; **f. meal** repas complet; *Com* **f. set of bills of lading** jeu *m* complet de connaissances; **(at) f. speed** à toute vitesse, à fond; *Naut* **f. speed ahead!** en avant toute!; *Fig* **it's f. speed ahead** maintenant on peut y aller

5 *(face)* plein, rond; *(sleeve etc)* large, bouffant; **f. face portrait** portrait de face; **a f. fi-**gure *(of woman)* une silhouette généreuse; **f. lips** grosses lèvres, lèvres charnues; **f. skirt** jupe *f* bouffante; **f. voice** voix pleine *ou* ronde

N to publish a letter in f. publier une lettre intégralement; **money refunded in f.** *(on notice etc)* on rembourse intégralement l'argent *ou* l'argent en totalité; **to pay in f.** payer intégralement; **name in f.** nom et prénoms; **to write out a word in f.** écrire un mot en toutes lettres; **to the f.** tout à fait; **to live life to the f.** vivre sa vie pleinement; **to indulge one's tastes to the f.** donner libre cours à ses goûts

ADV 1 *(completely)* complètement, entièrement; **to turn a tap f. on** *or* **on f.** ouvrir un robinet en grand; **to turn the radio f. on** *or* **on f.** mettre la radio à fond; **to drive (one's car) f. out** *(at top speed)* conduire à toute vitesse; **to work f. out** travailler à toute vitesse; **I know it f. well** je le sais bien *ou* parfaitement

2 *(right)* carrément; **lying f. in the sun** couché en plein (au) soleil; **hit f. in the face** atteint en pleine figure

▸▸**f. board** pension *f* complète; *Fin* **f. consolidation** intégration *f* globale; *Com* **f. container load** conteneur *m* chargé complètement; *Acct* **f. cost accounting (method)** méthode *f* de capitalisation du coût entier; *Fin* **f. costing** méthode du coût complet; *Fin* **f. discharge** quitus *m; Tel* **f. duplex** bidirectionnel *m* simultané, full duplex *m; Econ* **f. employment** plein emploi *m,* **f. employment policy** politique *f* de plein emploi; **f. house** *Cards* full *m; Theat* salle *f* comble; *Aut* **f. licence** permis *m* tous véhicules; **f. member** membre *m* à part entière; *Fam* **the f. Monty** *(everything)* la totale; **to do a f. Monty** *(strip)* faire un strip-tease intégral; **f. moon** pleine lune *f,* **f. name** *(on form)* nom *m* en toutes lettres; **what is your f. name?** quels sont vos nom et prénoms?; **f. pay** paie *f* entière; **leave on f. pay** congé *m* à solde entière; *Fin* **f. payment** paiement *m* intégral; **to make f. payment for a share** libérer entièrement une action; *Typ* **f. point** *(in punctuation)* point *m;* **f. price** prix *m* fort; **to pay f. price** payer place entière; **to pay the f. price for sth** payer le prix fort pour qch; *Am* **f. professor** professeur *m* d'université *(titulaire d'une chaire); Comput* **f. screen** plein écran *m;* **f. session** *(of a committee etc)* réunion *f* plénière; *TV, Cin* **f. shot** plan *m* d'ensemble, plan général; *Br* **f. stop** *(pause)* arrêt *m* complet; *Gram* point; *Comput* point final; **f. text** texte *m* intégral; **f. time** *(of working week)* temps *m* complet; *Sport* fin *f* de match; **f. warranty** garantie *f* totale; *Com* **f. weight** poids *m* juste

fullback [ˈfʊlbæk] **N** *Sport* arrière *m;* **at f.** à l'arrière

full-blooded **ADJ 1** *(racially)* de race pure; *(horse)* de sang, pur-sang *inv* **2** *(vigorous)* vigoureux

full-blown **ADJ 1** *(rose etc)* épanoui, en pleine fleur **2** *(crisis)* de la plus grande envergure; **a f. argument** une vraie dispute **3** *Fig (doctor etc)* qualifié; **she is a f. lawyer** elle a (obtenu) tous ses diplômes; **to have f. AIDS** avoir le sida avéré

full-bodied [ˈfʊlˈbɒdɪd] **ADJ** *(wine)* corsé, qui a du corps

full-cost pricing **N** *Mktg* fixation *f* du prix en fonction du coût

full-cream **ADJ**
▸▸**f. milk** lait *m* entier

full-dress **ADJ** *(attire)* en habit de cérémonie
▸▸**f. debate** débat *m* de fond; **f. uniform** tenue *f* de cérémonie, grande tenue

fuller [ˈfʊlər] **N f.'s earth** terre *f* à foulon

full-faced [ˈfʊlˈfeɪst] **ADJ** *(person)* à la figure ronde, au visage plein

full-fledged **ADJ** *Am* = **fully-fledged**

full-frontal **ADJ** *(attack, assault)* de front **N** nudité *f* vue de face, nu *m* de face **ADV** nu de face
▸▸**f. nudity** *(in show)* nu *m* intégral

full-grown **ADJ** *(tree)* qui a atteint son développement complet; *(person, cow)* adulte

full-length **ADJ** *(portrait)* en pied; *(mirror)* qui permet de se voir en pied; *(evening dress)* long; **a f. novel** un vrai roman **ADV he was stretched out f. on the floor** il était étendu de tout son long par terre
▸▸*TV, Cin* **f. film** long métrage *m; TV, Cin* **f. shot** plan *m* général

ful(l)ness [ˈfʊlnɪs] **N 1** *(of receptacle)* état *m* plein; **out of the f. of his heart** comme son cœur débordait; **to speak out of the f. of one's grief** parler le cœur débordant de chagrin **2** *(of strength)* plénitude *f,* perfection *f,* totalité *f,* **in the f. of time** avec le temps **3** *(of skirt, report etc)* ampleur *f, (of detail)* abondance *f, (of figure)* rondeur *f, (of style etc)* richesse *f*

full-out **ADJ** *Typ* au fer, sans alinéa

full-page **ADJ** pleine page
▸▸**f. advertisement** annonce *f* pleine page; *Comput* **f. display** écran *m* pleine page

full-scale **ADJ 1** = **full-size(d) 2** *(reform)* complet, intégral, -aux; *(panic, drought, retreat)* total, -aux; *(attack, war)* de grande envergure; *(emergency)* absolu

full-screen **ADJ** *Comput* plein écran
▸▸*Comput* **f. menu** menu *m* plein écran

full-size(d) **ADJ** *(drawing, model etc)* grandeur nature; *(tree)* adulte; *(keyboard, wheel)* aux dimensions standard; *(violin, bicycle)* d'adulte

full-strength **ADJ** de force normale

full-time **ADV** *(work)* à plein temps, à temps complet **ADJ** *(work, employee, job)* à temps complet, à plein temps; *Fig* **looking after the baby is a f. job** s'occuper du bébé ne laisse pas une minute de libre
▸▸*Sport* **f. score** score *m* final

fully [ˈfʊlɪ] **ADV 1** *(completely) (involved, occupied in sth, taken up)* entièrement; *(satisfied, justified, convinced)* pleinement, entièrement; *(to understand)* parfaitement; *(to treat subject etc)* à fond; **to be f. aware** *or* **conscious of the fact that ...** être parfaitement conscient du fait que ...; **I f. expect to be back here on Monday** je pense vraiment être de retour lundi; **f. licensed** *(hotel, restaurant etc)* qui a obtenu une licence pour la vente d'alcool; **f. loaded** *(van, plane etc)* en pleine charge; **f. paid** payé intégralement; **f. paid up** *(capital)* intégralement libéré; **this topic is dealt with more f. below** ce thème est traité plus en détail ci-après **2** *(at least)* it takes f. two hours cela prend bien *ou* au moins deux heures

fully-fashioned [ˈfʊlɪˈfæʃənd] **ADJ** *(stockings, sweater)* bien ajusté

fully-fledged **ADJ** *(bird)* qui a toutes ses plumes; *Fam (doctor etc)* qualifié; **now you're a f. actor!** maintenant tu es un vrai acteur!

fulmar [ˈfʊlmər] **N** *(bird)* pétrel *m* glacial

fulminate [ˈfʌlmɪneɪt] **VI** fulminer (**against** contre)

fulmination [fʌlmɪˈneɪʃən] **N** malédiction *f,* imprécation *f*

fulsome [ˈfʊlsəm] **ADJ** *(praise)* enthousiaste; *(excessive)* excessif, exagéré; *(welcome, greeting)* plein d'effusion; **to be f. in one's praise of sb/sth** porter qn/qch aux nues

fulsomely ['fʊlsəmlɪ] ADV to praise sb/sth f. porter qn/qch aux nues; **'it's gorgeous!'**, **she said f.** 'c'est magnifique!', dit-elle pleine d'enthousiasme

fumarole ['fju:mərəʊl] N *Geol* fumerolle f

fumble ['fʌmb(ə)l] VI *(in enclosed space)* fouiller (au hasard); *(on floor, in dark etc)* tâtonner; **to f. (about or around) in a drawer for sth** fouiller dans un tiroir pour trouver qch; **to f. (about or around) in a dark room for sth** chercher qch à tâtons dans une pièce obscure; **to f. for words** chercher ses mots; **to f. with sth** manier qch maladroitement
  VT manier maladroitement; *(opportunity)* gâcher; **to f. a question** répondre à une question en bafouillant; *Sport* **to f. the ball** mal attraper la balle

fumbling ['fʌmblɪŋ] ADJ maladroit, gauche

fume [fju:m] N *(vapour)* vapeur f; *(gas)* gaz m; **petrol fumes** vapeurs d'essence; *Aut* **exhaust fumes** gaz d'échappement
  VI *Fam (be angry)* rager; **I was fuming** je rageais (**at** contre), j'étais exaspéré (**at** par)

> Note that the French verb **fumer** is a false friend and is never a translation for the English verb **to fume**. It means **to smoke**.

fumigate ['fju:mɪgeɪt] VT *(flat etc)* désinfecter par fumigation

fumigation [fju:mɪ'geɪʃən] N fumigation f

fumigator ['fju:mɪgeɪtər] N *(device)* appareil m fumigatoire

fumitory ['fju:mɪtərɪ] N *(plant)* fumeterre f

fun [fʌn] N amusement m, gaieté f; *(joking)* plaisanterie f; **to have f.** s'amuser, se divertir; **to get a lot of f. out of doing sth** bien s'amuser en faisant qch; **we had lots of or great or good f.** on s'est bien amusé; **to have f. at sb's expense** s'amuser aux dépens de qn; **there'll be f. and games** ça va chauffer, il va y avoir du grabuge; **it was great f.** c'était très amusant; **he is great f. or full of f.** il est très drôle; **she's f. to be with** on s'amuse avec elle; **to make f. of or poke f. at sb/sth** se moquer de qn/qch, rire de qn/qch; **to say sth in f.** dire qch en plaisantant; **in f.** *(as a joke)* par plaisanterie; **for f.** *(for enjoyment)* pour se distraire; **I did it for the f. of the thing or of it** je l'ai fait pour le plaisir; **where's the f. in that?** je ne vois pas ce que ça a d'agréable; **it wasn't much f. walking home in the rain** rentrer à pied sous la pluie n'avait rien d'une partie de plaisir; **it won't be half as much f. without you** ce ne sera pas si drôle sans toi; **all the f.'s gone out of it** ce n'est plus drôle du tout; *esp Am Fam* **a f. party** une soirée où l'on s'amuse bien; **she's a f. person to be with** on s'amuse bien avec elle; **I don't want to spoil your f.** je ne veux pas vous empêcher de vous amuser; **to take the f. out of sth** rendre qch plus drôle du tout; **to put the f. back into sth** redonner tout son charme à qch; **that's half the f. as far as I'm concerned** c'est là tout le charme de la chose pour moi; **to join in the f.** s'amuser avec tout le monde; *Iron* **that's when the f. began** *(trouble)* c'est là que ça a commencé à barder; **all the f. of the fair** toutes les attractions de la foire; **what f.!** comme c'est amusant!; *Iron* très amusant!; **f.-loving** qui aime s'amuser; **a f.-packed or -filled holiday** des vacances pendant lesquelles on n'a pas le temps de s'ennuyer
  ▸▸ **f. fur** fourrure f synthétique; **f. run** course f à pied pour amateurs *(pour collecter des fonds pour des organisations caritatives)*

funboard ['fʌnbɔ:d] N funboard m

function ['fʌŋkʃən] N 1 *(of body, machine, institution)* fonction f; *(of person)* fonction, charge f; **in his f. as a magistrate** en sa qualité de magistrat; **he combines the functions of servant and gardener** il tient le double emploi de domestique et de jardinier; **to discharge one's functions** s'acquitter de ses fonctions; **my f. in life** ma raison d'être; **the spring performs the f. of a shock absorber** le ressort joue le rôle d'(un) *ou* fait fonction d'amortisseur
  2 *(occasion) (reception)* réception f, réunion f; *(public ceremony)* cérémonie f publique; **society f.** réception mondaine
  3 *Math etc* fonction f; *also Fig* **to be a f. of sth** être fonction de qch
  VI *(operate, work)* fonctionner; **to f. as sth** *(fill a role)* faire fonction de qch
  ▸▸ *Comput* **f. key** touche f de fonction; **functions manager** *(at hotel)* responsable m des réceptions; **f. room** salle f de réception

functional ['fʌŋkʃən(ə)l] ADJ 1 *(furniture etc)* fonctionnel, utilitaire 2 *(operational)* **to be f.** fonctionner; **I'm barely f. before ten o'clock** je ne suis guère opérationnel avant dix heures 3 *Math, Med* fonctionnel
  ▸▸ *Med* **f. disorder** trouble m fonctionnel; **f. illiterate** illettré, -ée

functionality [fʌŋkʃə'nælɪtɪ] N fonctionnalité f

functionally ['fʌŋkʃən(ə)lɪ] ADV **to be f. illiterate** = être illettré au point de ne pas pouvoir faire face aux situations courantes; **to be f. equivalent to sth** avoir la même fonction que qch; **the human appendix is f. unnecessary** l'appendice humain est inutile du point de vue fonctionnel

functionary ['fʌŋkʃənərɪ] N *often Pej* fonctionnaire mf

functioning ['fʌŋkʃənɪŋ] N *(of machine etc)* fonctionnement m

fund [fʌnd] VOIR GRAMMAIRE A10 1 *Fin etc* fonds m, caisse f; **to start a f.** lancer une souscription 2 **funds** *(money)* fonds mpl, ressources fpl pécuniaires; *(of government)* fonds publics; **to be in funds** être en fonds; **funds are low** les fonds sont bas; **to be short of or low on funds** être à court d'argent; *Banking* **'no funds'** 'défaut de provision', 'manque de fonds'; **f.-holder** rentier, -ière 3 *(supply) (of wit)* fonds m; *(of information)* source f, **unfailing f. of humour** des ressources d'humour intarissables; **a f. of anecdotes** un stock d'anecdotes
  VT *Fin (project)* financer; *(company etc)* pourvoir de fonds; *(public debt)* consolider; **to f. money** placer de l'argent dans les fonds publics; *Acct* **funded from cashflow** autofinancé
  ▸▸ *Fin* **funds flow statement** tableau m des emplois et ressources; **f. of funds** fonds de fonds; **f. management** gestion f de fonds; **f. manager** gestionnaire mf de fonds

fundamental [fʌndə'ment(ə)l] ADJ 1 fondamental, -aux, essentiel; *(question)* principal, -aux, de fond; **of f. importance** d'une importance capitale; **to be f. to one's understanding/the success of sth** être fondamental pour *ou* essentiel à la compréhension/essentiel au succès de qch 2 *Mus* fondamental
  N 1 **fundamentals** principe(s) m(pl); *(of science)* notions fpl fondamentales, fondements mpl; *(of system)* partie f essentielle; **to reach agreement on fundamentals** réaliser un accord sur les points essentiels; **let's get down to fundamentals** allons à l'essentiel 2 *Mus* fondamentale
  ▸▸ *Mus* **f. note** note f fondamentale

fundamentalism [fʌndə'mentəlɪz(ə)m] N *Rel* fondamentalisme m

fundamentalist [fʌndə'mentəlɪst] ADJ, N *Rel* fondamentaliste mf

fundamentally [fʌndə'mentəlɪ] ADV *(honest, incorrect, important)* fondamentale-

ment; **f., there's nothing wrong with the idea** l'idée en soi n'est pas mauvaise; **f., it's a question of who's got more money** au fond, ce qui importe c'est qui a le plus d'argent

funded ['fʌndɪd] ADJ *Fin (assets)* en rentes
  ▸▸ **f. capital** capitaux mpl investis; **f. debt** dette f consolidée; **f. pension scheme** régime m de retraite par capitalisation

fundholder ['fʌndhəʊldər] N *(person)* rentier, -ière

funding ['fʌndɪŋ] N 1 *(for project)* financement m 2 *(of debt)* consolidation f, *(of annuity)* assiette f
  ▸▸ **f. operation** opération f de financement; **f. plan** plan m de financement

fund-raiser N 1 *(professional)* = personne f employée par une œuvre de bienfaisance pour rassembler des fonds 2 *(event)* = match m/concert m/etc au profit d'une œuvre de bienfaisance

fund-raising N collecte f de fonds pour une œuvre de bienfaisance; **Nadia is in charge of f.** Nadia est chargée de rassembler les fonds
  ADJ *(dinner, project, sale)* organisé pour collecter des fonds

funeral ['fju:nərəl] N funérailles fpl, obsèques fpl; *(including burial)* enterrement m; **to attend sb's f.** assister à l'enterrement de qn; *Fam* **that's your f.!** ça, c'est votre problème!
  ▸▸ **f. ceremony** cérémonie f funèbre; **f. director** entrepreneur, -euse de pompes funèbres; *Am* **f. home** établissement m de pompes funèbres; **f. march** marche f funèbre; **f. parlour** établissement de pompes funèbres; **f. procession** cortège m funèbre; **f. pyre** bûcher m *(funéraire)*; **f. service** service m ou office m funèbre

funereal [fju:'nɪərɪəl] ADJ lugubre, funèbre, triste; *(voice)* lugubre, sépulcral, -aux; *(pace)* lent; **to proceed at a f. pace** avancer à un pas d'enterrement

funfair ['fʌnfeər] N *(travelling)* fête f foraine, foire f, *(fixed)* parc m d'attractions

fungal ['fʌŋgəl] ADJ fongique
  ▸▸ *Med* **f. infection** mycose f

fungible ['fʌndʒɪb(ə)l] ADJ *St Exch* fongible

fungicide ['fʌndʒɪsaɪd] N fongicide m

fungicidal ['fʌndʒɪ'saɪdl] ADJ antifongique, fongicide

fungoid ['fʌŋgɔɪd] ADJ 1 *Bot* fongoïde 2 *Med* fongueux

fungous ['fʌŋgəs] ADJ *Med* fongueux

fungus, *pl* **funguses, fungi** ['fʌŋgəs, -əsɪz, -gaɪ, -dʒaɪ] N 1 *Bot* champignon m; *(on walls)* moisissure f, *Hum* **face f.** *(moustache)* moustache f, bacchantes fpl, *(beard)* barbe f 2 *Med* fongus m

funicular [fju:'nɪkjʊlər] N, ADJ *(railway)* funiculaire m

funk¹ [fʌŋk] *Old-fashioned esp Br Sl* N *(fright)* frousse f, **to be in a (blue) f.** avoir une peur bleue, avoir une frousse de tous les diables; **to get into a f.** caner
  VT **to f. sth/doing sth** avoir peur de qch/de faire qch; **to f. it** caner, se dégonfler
  VI caner, se dégonfler
  ▸▸ *Mil Fam* **f. hole** abri m, planque f

funk² N *Mus* funk m; **f. band** groupe m funk

funky ['fʌŋkɪ] ADJ 1 *Mus* funky, funk 2 *Am Fam (smelly)* puant 3 *esp Am Old-fashioned Fam (fashionable)* cool, branché 4 *esp Br Old-fashioned Sl (cowardly)* froussard

funnel ['fʌn(ə)l] N 1 *(of locomotive, steamship)* cheminée f 2 *(for filling)* entonnoir m; *Ind* **(loading) f.** trémie f, hotte f 3 *(for ventilation)* tuyau m ou cheminée f d'aération
  VI (-ll-, *Am* -l-) **the crowd funnelled into a**

narrow passage/through the gates la foule s'est engouffrée dans un passage étroit/entre les grilles

VT *(direct)* canaliser; **to f. a liquid into a bottle** verser un liquide dans une bouteille à l'aide d'un entonnoir; **complaints are funnelled to the head office** les réclamations sont canalisées vers le bureau central

funnelling, *Am* **funneling** ['fʌn(ə)lɪŋ] **N** *Mktg (in questionnaire construction)* entonnoir *m*

funnily ['fʌnɪlɪ] **ADV 1** *(amusingly)* comiquement **2** *(curiously)* curieusement, bizarrement; **f. enough** … chose curieuse …

funniness ['fʌnɪnɪs] **N 1** *(amusing nature) (of person)* caractère *m* amusant *ou* drôle **2** *(strangeness)* bizarrerie *f*

funny ['fʌnɪ] **ADJ 1** *(amusing)* drôle, amusant; **it was really too f.!, it was too f. for words!** c'était vraiment trop drôle!, c'était tordant!; **she's a very f. woman** *(comic, actress)* elle est très drôle; **none of your f. tricks!, don't try to be f.!** pas de blagues!; **the f. thing about it is …** le comique de la chose, c'est que …

2 *(strange)* curieux, bizarre; **he is a f. person** c'est un drôle d'homme; **he was f. that way** il était comme ça; **a f. idea** une drôle d'idée; **well, that's f.!** voilà qui est curieux *ou* étrange; **f., I thought I'd locked the door** tiens, c'est drôle, je pensais avoir fermé la porte à clé; **(it's) f. you should say that** c'est drôle que vous disiez cela; **it's a f. thing, but … c'est drôle, mais …; there's something f. about the entire business** il y a quelque chose de louche dans cette affaire; *Fam* **no f. business!** pas de blagues!, pas de bêtises!; **this butter tastes/smells f.** ce beurre a un drôle de goût/une drôle d'odeur; **it feels f.** ça fait drôle; **the engine sounds f.** le moteur fait un drôle de bruit; **his voice sounded f.** il avait une drôle de voix; *Fam* **I came over all f.** je me suis senti(e) tout(e) drôle; **I've got a f. feeling in my stomach** j'ai un peu mal au cœur; **I had a f. feeling we were going to meet again** j'avais comme l'impression que nous nous reverrions; **he went a bit f. in his old age** il devint un peu bizarre en vieillissant; *Fam* **f. peculiar or f. ha-ha?** comment ça, drôle? bizarre ou rigolo?

NPL *esp Am Fam* **the funnies** *(in magazine)* bandes *fpl* dessinées, pages *fpl* comiques

▸▸ *Br Fam* **f. bone** petit juif *m*; *Fam* **f. farm** maison *f* de fous; *Fam* **f. money** des sommes *mpl* mirobolantes *ou* astronomiques

fur [fɜːr] **N 1** *Com* fourrure *f, Zool* poil *m; Fam* **to make the f. fly, to set the f. flying** *(make a scene)* faire une scène violente; *(fight)* se battre avec acharnement; **furs** *(of animals)* peaux *fpl*, **f.-lined boot** bottillon *m* fourré; **f.-lined coat** manteau doublé de fourrure **2** *(deposit) (in kettle, boiler)* tartre *m; Med (on tongue)* enduit *m*

▸▸ **f. coat** (manteau *m* de) fourrure *f*; **f. farm** élevage *m* d'animaux à fourrure; **f. seal** phoque *m*; **f. skins** peaux *fpl*; **f. trade** commerce *m* de fourrures, pelleterie *f*

▸ **fur up** **VI** *(of boiler etc)* s'incruster, s'entartrer; *Med (of tongue)* se charger, s'empâter

furbish ['fɜːbɪʃ] **VT 1** *(polish) (piece of metal)* fourbir, polir, astiquer **2** *(renovate) (furniture)* remettre à neuf

furious ['fjʊərɪəs] **ADJ** furieux; *(look)* furibond; *(battle, activity, efforts etc)* acharné, forcené; *(storm, sea, wind)* déchaîné; **to drive at a f. speed** conduire à une allure folle; **to get f.** entrer en fureur; **to be f. with sb/oneself** être furieux contre qn/soi-même

furiously ['fjʊərɪəslɪ] **ADV** furieusement; *(to work)* avec acharnement; *(to fight)* avec acharnement, avec furie; *(to drive)* à une al-

lure folle; **the fire was blazing f.** l'incendie faisait rage

furl [fɜːl] **VT** *(umbrella, flag etc)* rouler; *Naut (sail)* serrer, ferler

furlong ['fɜːlɒŋ] **N** *(measurement)* furlong *m* *(= 201 mètres)*; **a race over seven furlongs** une course de 1400 mètres

furlough ['fɜːləʊ] **N** *Mil etc* congé *m*, permission *f*; **to be/go on f.** être/aller en permission

furnace ['fɜːnɪs] **N 1** fourneau *m*, four *m; Fig* fournaise *f*; **this room is like a f.** cette pièce est une (vraie) fournaise **2** *(central-heating)* **f.** calorifère *m*

furnish ['fɜːnɪʃ] **VT 1** *(house, flat etc)* meubler; **to f. one's room/home/flat** se meubler **2** *esp Fml (provide) (information)* fournir, donner; *(funds)* pourvoir; *(reasons)* produire, alléguer; *(opportunity)* offrir, présenter, fournir; *(needs)* pourvoir à; **to f. sb with sth** fournir qch à qn, pourvoir *ou* munir qn de qch; **to f. an army (with provisions)** fournir une armée en provisions

furnished ['fɜːnɪʃt] **ADJ 1** *(flat, room)* meublé; **to live in f. rooms** loger en meublé **2** *(provided)* pourvu, fourni, équipé (**with** de); **well f. shop** magasin bien achalandé

furnishing ['fɜːnɪʃɪŋ] **N f. fabrics** tissus *mpl* d'ameublement

furnishings ['fɜːnɪʃɪŋz] **NPL** *(furniture) (of house)* ameublement *m*; **soft f.** *(fabrics)* tissus *mpl* d'ameublement; *(carpets and curtains)* tapis *mpl* et rideaux *mpl*

furniture ['fɜːnɪtʃər] **N 1** *(in house etc)* meubles *mpl*, mobilier *m*; **a piece of f.** un meuble; *Fam* **I feel as if I'm part of the f.** j'ai l'impression de faire partie des meubles; **dining-room f.** mobilier *ou* meubles de salle à manger **2** *(of door, coffin etc)* ferrures *fpl*

▸▸ **f. polish** encaustique *f*, cire *f*, **f. remover** déménageur *m*; **f. showroom** magasin *m* de meubles; **f. van** camion *m* de déménagement

Note that the French noun **fourniture** is a false friend. Its most common meaning is **supplies**.

furore [fjʊˈrɔːreɪ], *Am* **furor** ['fjʊərɔːr] **N** *(uproar)* tumulte *m* (**over** au sujet de); *(enthusiasm)* enthousiasme *m* démesuré; **to cause** *or* **create a f.** *(cause uproar)* provoquer un tumulte; *(be very popular)* faire fureur; **there's been a great f. over those scenes** ces scènes ont provoqué un énorme tumulte

furred [fɜːd] **ADJ** *(boiler etc)* entartré, encrusté; *(kettle, pipe)* entartré; *(tongue)* pâteux, chargé

furrier ['fʌrɪər] **N** pelletier, -ière, fourreur *m*

furring ['fɜːrɪŋ] **N** *(in boiler etc)* tartre *m*

furrow ['fʌrəʊ] **N** *(in field), Fig (in stone)* sillon *m; Fig (on face)* ride *f* profonde, sillon; *Fig* **to plough a lonely f.** *(of inventor, reformer etc)* poursuivre seul une idée; *(keep oneself to oneself)* faire bande à part

VT 1 *(earth)* creuser des sillons dans; *Lit* **the boats furrowed the seas** les bateaux sillonnaient les mers **2** *(forehead etc)* rider profondément; **his brow is furrowed with wrinkles** des rides profondes lui sillonnent le front

furrowed ['fʌrəʊd] **ADJ** *(forehead, brow)* coupé de rides profondes; **f. with concentration** plissé de concentration

furry ['fɜːrɪ] **ADJ 1** *(animal)* à poil; *(tail, ears)* poilu; *(insect)* velu; *(moss etc)* qui ressemble à (de) la fourrure; **the husky has a f. coat** le husky a de longs poils; **a f. little kitten** un chaton tout doux **2** *(boiler, kettle)* entartré; *(tongue)* chargé, pâteux

ADV plus loin **1** ▪ plus **1** ▪ de plus **2** ▪ suite à *(further to)* **3**
ADJ plus éloigné **1** ▪ additionnel **2**

ADV 1 *(distance)* plus loin (**than** que); *(extent)* davantage, plus; **to penetrate f. into the country** pénétrer plus avant dans le pays; **I can go no f.** je ne peux pas aller plus loin; *(I'm exhausted)* je n'en peux plus; *Fam* **this mustn't go any f.** ceci ne doit pas se propager; **to move f. away** s'éloigner; **I didn't question him any f.** je ne l'ai pas interrogé davantage; **until you hear f.** jusqu'à nouvel avis; **I've nothing f. to say** je n'ai rien d'autre à dire; **to go no f. into the matter** en rester là; **to add water to the wine to make it go f.** allonger le vin d'eau; **that doesn't get us much f.** cela ne nous avance pas beaucoup; **f. back** *(in time)* à une période plus reculée; **f. back than the last century** antérieurement au siècle dernier

2 *(moreover)* d'ailleurs, de plus; **we would f. add that …** nous nous permettons d'ajouter en outre que …

3 *Fml* **f. to** *(following)* suite à

ADJ 1 *(of two)* plus éloigné, plus lointain; **at the f. end of the room** à l'autre bout *ou* au fond de la salle; **the f. bank of the river** la rive opposée de la rivière; **the f. of the two villages** le plus éloigné des deux villages

2 *(additional)* additionnel, supplémentaire; **upon f. consideration** après plus ample(s) réflexion(s); **do you have any f. instructions?** est-ce que vous avez d'autres consignes?; **one or two f. details** encore un ou deux détails; **without f. loss of time** sans perdre plus de temps; **to await f. news** attendre de plus amples nouvelles; **until f. notice** jusqu'à nouvel ordre; **without f. warning** sans plus d'avertissement; *(about)* au sujet de); **f. information** renseignements *mpl* complémentaires; *Com* **I would like to place a f. order** je voudrais passer une nouvelle commande; *esp Mil* **to await f. orders** attendre les ordres

VT *(cause, person's interests)* servir; *(one's attempts, efforts, career)* favoriser

▸▸ *Br* **f. education** enseignement *m* postscolaire

furtherance ['fɜːðərəns] **N** *(of work etc)* avancement *m*; **for the f. or in f. of sth** pour servir qch

furthermore [fɜːðəˈmɔːr] **ADV** en outre, de plus, par ailleurs

furthermost ['fɜːðəməʊst] **ADJ** *(place etc)* le plus lointain, le plus reculé, le plus éloigné; *Lit* **to the f. ends of the earth** jusqu'au bout du monde

furthest ['fɜːðɪst] *(superl of* **far**) VOIR GRAMMAIRE A26 **ADV** he went f. il est allé le plus loin; **when it's f. from the sun** lorsqu'il se trouve le plus éloigné du soleil; **this is the f. north I've ever been** c'est le plus au nord que j'aie jamais été

ADV **the f. part of the cave** la partie la plus reculée de la caverne

furtive ['fɜːtɪv] **ADJ** *(manner, person)* sournois, cachottier; *(smile, look etc)* furtif, dérobé

furtively ['fɜːtɪvlɪ] **ADV** *(behave)* sournoisement; *(smile, look)* furtivement

fury ['fjʊərɪ] **N 1** *(of person)* furie *f*, fureur *f*, *(of wind etc)* déchaînement *m*, violence *f*; **to be in a f.** *(of person)* être furieux, être en furie *ou* fureur; **to get into a f.** entrer en furie *ou* fureur, s'emporter; *Fam* **to work like f.** travailler avec acharnement; **to run like f.** courir comme un dératé **2** *Myth* **the Furies** les Furies *fpl*

furze [fɜːz] N (plant) ajonc m

fuse, Am **fuze** [fjuːz] N **1** Mil etc (for shell etc) fusée f, (for bomb) amorce f, Min étoupille f, mèche f, **safety f.** cordeau m (Bickford); **time f.** fusée à retard(ement); **to set a f.** régler une fusée; Fig **the incident which lit the f. of the revolution** l'incident qui a déclenché la révolution; Fig Fam **to have a short f.** démarrer au quart de tour **2** Elec **(safety) f.** fusible m (de sécurité), Fam plomb m; **to blow a f.** faire sauter un plomb; Fig Fam (of person) sortir de ses gonds; **the f. has blown** or Fam **gone** le plomb a sauté

vт **1** (melt) (metal etc) fondre, mettre en fusion; **to f. two pieces together** réunir deux pièces par fusion **2** (join) fusionner, amalgamer **3** Br Elec (circuit) faire sauter les plombs de; **to f. the lights** faire sauter les plombs **4** Mil etc (bomb) amorcer

vι **1** (of metals etc) fondre; **the parts had fused together** les pièces avaient fondu et s'étaient collées les unes aux autres **2** (of parties etc) fusionner **3** Br Elec **the lights have fused** les plombs ont sauté

▸▸ **f. box** boîte f à fusibles, coupe-circuit m inv; Aut porte-fusible m, pl porte-fusibles; **f. wire** fusible m

fused [fjuːzd] ADJ Elec muni d'un fusible

fuselage [ˈfjuːzəlɑːʒ] N Aviat fuselage m

fusilier [fjuːzɪˈlɪər] N Mil fusilier m

fusillade [fjuːzɪˈleɪd] N Mil **a f. (of shots)** une fusillade; **a f. of criticism/questions** une avalanche de critiques/questions

fusion [ˈfjuːʒən] N **1** Phys fusion f, (of metal) fonte f, Phys **cold f.** fusion à froid; Nucl, Phys **controlled f.** fusion contrôlée **2** (amalgamation) (of banks etc) fusionnement m; Pol (of parties etc) fusion f

▸▸ Nucl **f. bomb** bombe f thermonucléaire ou à hydrogène; Culin **f. food** = cuisine f qui mêle saveurs d'orient et d'occident

fuss [fʌs] N (exaggeration) histoires fpl; **what's all the f. about?** qu'est-ce que c'est que toutes ces histoires?; (what's wrong) qu'est-ce qui cloche?; **without any f.** (to get married) sans cérémonies; (to get through customs) sans aucun problème; **can you have him ejected from the studio without too much f.?** est-ce que vous pouvez le faire évacuer du studio discrètement?; **I don't want any f. made when I retire** je ne veux pas qu'on fasse tout un cinéma quand je prendrai ma retraite; **a lot of f. about** or **over nothing** beaucoup de bruit pour rien; **if you knew the f. your letter caused** si tu savais le remue-ménage que ta lettre a provoqué; **a great f.** bien des cérémonies; Fam **to kick up a f.** (complain loudly) faire un tas d'histoires, faire tout un cinéma; **don't make such a f. about it** ne faites pas tant d'histoires; **I don't see what all the f. is about** (I think it's a harmless, poor-quality film/product etc) je ne vois pas pourquoi on fait un tel cinéma; **to make a f. of** or **over sb** être aux petits soins pour qn; (talk about with excessive admiration) faire grand cas de qn; **he likes to be made a f. of** or **over** (of person) il aime qu'on fasse grand cas de lui; (of dog) il aime qu'on le caresse

vι faire des embarras ou des histoires; **stop fussing!** arrête de faire des histoires!; **she never stops fussing with her hair** elle ne cesse pas d'arranger nerveusement ses cheveux

vт (person) tracasser, agiter; Fam **I'm not fussed** ça ne me fait rien

▸ **fuss about, fuss around** vι (be busy) s'affairer

▸ **fuss over** vт INSEP (person) être aux petits soins pour

fussily [ˈfʌsɪlɪ] ADV **1** (to arrange things) d'une manière tatillonne; (to say sth) d'un air important **2** (over-ornately) de façon tarabiscotée; **f. dressed** vêtu avec trop de recherche; **the room was rather f. decorated** la décoration de la pièce était surchargée

fussiness [ˈfʌsɪnɪs] N **1** (of person) (behaviour) tendance f à faire beaucoup d'embarras; (character) esprit m tracassier; **his f. about food is ridiculous** il est si difficile sur la nourriture que c'en est ridicule; **her f. about details** l'attention exagérée qu'elle porte aux détails **2** (of dress, decor etc) manque m de simplicité

fusspot [ˈfʌspɒt] N Br Fam Pej (finicky person) (about preparing food, cleaning house) tatillon, -onne; (about getting wet, dirty etc) chichiteux, -euse; **don't be such a f. about a little bit of rain** ne sois pas aussi chichiteux, ce n'est qu'une petite pluie; **don't be such a f., leave the housework for one day** ne sois pas aussi tatillon, laisse tomber le ménage pour aujourd'hui; **don't be such a f., I'm sure he is safe** ne te tracasse pas comme ça, je suis sûr qu'il est en sécurité

fussy [ˈfʌsɪ] ADJ **1** (person) (who worries) tracassier, qui fait des histoires; (who is finicky, particular) tatillon, -onne; **I'm not the f. kind** je ne suis pas difficile; **I'm not f.** cela m'est égal; **we can't afford to be too f.** nous ne pouvons pas nous permettre d'être trop difficiles; **to be f. about one's food** être difficile sur la nourriture **2** (dress, decor) surchargé; (style) qui manque de simplicité, surchargé

fustian [ˈfʌstɪən] N Tex futaine f, Fig Lit (pompousness) grandiloquence f, emphase f

fustiness [ˈfʌstɪnɪs] N **1** (smell) odeur f de moisi **2** Fig (of theory etc) caractère m démodé

fusty [ˈfʌstɪ] ADJ **1** (house, clothes) qui sent le renfermé; (smell) de renfermé **2** Fig (ideas etc) suranné, démodé

futile [ˈfjuːtaɪl] ADJ **1** (vain) inutile; (attempt, protest) vain **2** (trifling) (remark etc) futile

futility [fjuːˈtɪlɪtɪ] N futilité f, (of efforts etc) inutilité f, **an exercise in f.** une vaine entreprise

futon [ˈfuːtɒn] N futon m

future [ˈfjuːtʃər] ADJ futur; (events) à venir; **my f. wife** ma future épouse; **at some f. date** dans l'avenir; **for f. reference** à titre d'information; Com **goods for f. delivery** marchandises livrables ultérieurement; Fin **to sell for f. delivery** vendre livrable à terme

N **1** avenir m; **in (the) f., for the f.** à l'avenir; **in the near f.** dans un proche avenir, sous peu; **in the distant f.** dans un avenir lointain; **at some point** or **stage in the f.** un jour; **what does the f. hold for us?** qu'est-ce que l'avenir nous réserve?; **the public transport of the f.** les transports en commun de l'avenir

2 (of person) avenir m; **job with a (good) f.** situation d'avenir; **to ruin one's f.** briser son avenir; **she has a brilliant f. (before her)** elle a un bel avenir devant elle

3 Fin contrat m à terme; **futures** opérations fpl à terme; **futures and options** contrats mpl à terme et options

4 VOIR GRAMMAIRE A50–2; B31 Gram (temps m) futur m; **verb in the f.** verbe au futur

▸▸ Fin **futures contract** contrat à terme; Fin **futures exchange** marché m à terme; Fin **futures market** marché à terme; Fin **futures option** option f sur contrats à terme; Gram **f. perfect** futur antérieur; Gram **f. tense** futur, temps futur VOIR GRAMMAIRE A50–2; B31 ; Fin **futures trading** négociations fpl à terme; Fin **f. value** valeur f capitalisée

future-proof esp Comput ADJ évolutif vт rendre évolutif

futurism [ˈfjuːtʃərɪz(ə)m] N Art futurisme m

futurist [ˈfjuːtʃərɪst] ADJ, N Art futuriste mf

futuristic [ˈfjuːtʃəˈrɪstɪk] ADJ futuriste

futurologist [fjuːtʃəˈrɒlədʒɪst] N futurologue mf

futurology [fjuːtʃəˈrɒlədʒɪ] N futurologie f

fuze [fjuːz] N, VT Am = **fuse**

fuzz [fʌz] N **1** (on blankets etc) peluches fpl, bourre f **2** (on peach, skin) duvet m NPL Sl **the f.** (the police) les flics mpl

fuzziness [ˈfʌzɪnɪs] N **1** (of outline, recording etc) manque m de netteté; (of photo etc) flou m **2** **the f. of my hair** mes cheveux crépus

fuzzy [ˈfʌzɪ] ADJ **1** (outline etc) sans netteté; (recording) qui manque de netteté; (idea, look) flou, vague; Art, Phot flou; **everything looks f. to me** j'ai une vue confuse de tout; **I feel a bit f.-headed** je n'ai pas les idées très claires **2** (hair) crépu; (cloth etc) floconneux ▸▸ Comput **f. logic** logique f floue

fwd abbr **forward**

FX [efˈeks] NPL Cin effets mpl spéciaux N Fin (abbr **foreign exchange**) devises fpl étrangères

▸▸ Fin **FX broker** cambiste mf, courtier, -ière en devises; Fin **FX market** marché m des changes; Fin **FX option** option f sur devises

FYI (abbr **for your information**) à titre indicatif

G, g¹ [dʒiː] N **1** (*letter*) G, g *m*; **two g's** deux g **2** *Mus* sol *m*; **in G minor** en sol mineur **3** *Fam Br* (*thousand pounds*) mille livres *fpl*; *Am* (*thousand dollars*) mille dollars *mpl* **4** *Phys* conductance *f* **5** *Am, Austr* Cin visible par tous **6** **G7** G7 *m*, groupe *m* des 7; **G7 summit** sommet *m* du G7; **G8** G8 *m*, groupe des 8

g² (*abbr* **gramme**) gr.

Ga *abbr* **Georgia**

GAAP [dʒiːeɪeɪˈpiː] NPL *Acct* (*abbr* **generally-accepted accounting principles**) PCGR *mpl*

gab [gæb] *Fam* N (*chat, talk*) **we had a good g. on the phone** on a taillé une bonne bavette au téléphone; **to have the gift of the g.** avoir la langue bien pendue; (*be convincing talker*) avoir du bagou(t)
▸ VI (**-bb-**) (*chat*) bavarder, *Pej* papoter; (*gossip*) caqueter, jaser

gabardine [gæbəˈdiːn, ˈgæbədiːn] N gabardine *f*

gabble [ˈgæb(ə)l] N bredouillement *m* (*de paroles prononcées trop vite*); **to speak in a g.** bredouiller; **to listen to the g. of voices** écouter le bruit des conversations; **there was an incomprehensible g. coming from the garden** on entendait une conversation inintelligible dans le jardin
VI bredouiller, manger ses mots
VT (*speech*) débiter à toute vitesse
▸ **gabble away** VI baragouiner; **two foreigners were gabbling away to each other** deux étrangers baragouinaient dans leur langue
▸ **gabble out** VT SEP = **gabble** VT

gaberdine [gæbəˈdiːn, ˈgæbədiːn] N gabardine *f*

gable [ˈgeɪb(ə)l] N pignon *m*
▸▸ **g. end** pignon *m*; **g. roof** comble *m* sur pignon(s); **g. window** fenêtre *f* sur pignon

gabled [ˈgeɪb(ə)ld] ADJ *Archit* (*house*) à pignon(s); (*wall*) en pignon; (*roof*) sur pignon(s)

Gabon [gæˈbɒn] N Gabon *m*

Gabonese [gæbəˈniːz] ADJ gabonais
N Gabonais, -aise

▸ **gad about** [gæd] VI courir le monde; **he spent a year gadding about Europe** il a passé un an à parcourir l'Europe; **she's been out gadding about (town) all night** elle a passé toute la nuit à faire la fête (en ville)

gadfly [ˈgædflaɪ] N (*insect*) taon *m*; *Fig* casse-pieds *mf inv*

gadget [ˈgædʒɪt] N gadget *m*; **it's just another g.** c'est un gadget de plus; **what's that g. for?** à quoi sert ce truc-là?

gadgetry [ˈgædʒɪtrɪ] N gadgets *mpl*

Gaelic [ˈgeɪlɪk] ADJ gaélique
N *Ling* gaélique *m*

gaff¹ [gæf] N **1** *Fishing* gaffe *f* **2** *Naut* corne *f*
VT *Fishing* gaffer
▸▸ *Naut* **g. topsail** voile *f* de flèche

gaff² N *Fam* **to blow the g.** vendre la mèche; **to blow the g. on** (*sb's plans*) dévoiler; (*corruption*) dénoncer; **to blow the g. on sb** dénoncer qn, vendre qn

gaff³ N *Br Fam* (*home*) baraque *f*; **he's staying at my g. for the weekend** il crèche chez moi ce week-end

gaffe [gæf] N (*blunder*) gaffe *f*, bourde *f*

gaffer [ˈgæfər] N **1** *Br Fam* (*foreman*) contremaître *m*, chef *m* d'équipe; (*boss, owner*) patron *m*, singe *m*; *Cin, TV* chef électricien, gaffer *m* **2** *Fam* (*old man*) vieux *m*
▸▸ *Cin, TV* **g. grip** pince *f* pour projecteur; **g. tape** ruban *m* adhésif en toile

gag [gæg] N **1** (*on mouth*) bâillon *m*; *Surg* ouvre-bouche *m inv*; *Fig* **the law was used as a g. on the freedom of the press** la loi servait à bâillonner la presse **2** *Fam* (*joke*) blague *f*, (*visual*) gag *m*; **to do sth for a g.** faire qch pour rire *ou* pour s'amuser
VT (**-gg-**) (*put a gag on*) (*person, the press*) bâillonner
VI *Fam* (*retch*) avoir des haut-le-cœur; **to make sb g.** donner envie de vomir à qn

gaga [ˈgɑːgɑː] ADJ *Fam* gaga *inv*, gâteux; **to go g.** devenir gaga *ou* gâteux

gage¹ [geɪdʒ] N *Old-fashioned* (*pledge*) gage *m*, garantie *f*

gage² N, VT *Am* = **gauge**

gage³ N = **greengage**

gagging [ˈgæɡɪŋ] N (*of person, press*) bâillonnement *m*
▸▸ *Law* **g. order** = décision *f* de justice visant à interdire à la presse de publier tout article à propos d'une affaire, *Can* ordonnance *f* imposant le secret

gaggle [ˈɡæɡ(ə)l] N (*of geese*) troupeau *m*; *Fig* **a g. of young schoolgirls** un troupeau de jeunes élèves
VI (*of goose*) cacarder

gagman, *pl* **gagmen** [ˈɡæɡmən] N *Am Cin, Theat* auteur *m* de gags, gagman *m*, *pl* gagmen

gaiety [ˈɡeɪətɪ] N **1** (*cheerfulness*) gaieté *f* **2** *Old-fashioned* (*festivities*) (*usu pl*) **gaieties** réjouissances *fpl*

gaily [ˈɡeɪlɪ] ADV **1** (*happily*) gaiement, allègrement **2** (*with bright colours*) de couleurs gaies; **g. coloured** aux couleurs gaies *ou* vives

gain [ɡeɪn] N **1** (*profit*) gain *m*, profit *m*, avantage *m*; **to do sth for g.** faire qch par intérêt; **my g. is your loss** le profit de l'un est le dommage de l'autre
2 (*increase*) augmentation *f*, (*in value*) hausse *f*, *Fin* **g. in value** plus-value *f*, **g. in weight** prise *f* de poids; **there has been a net g. in their income** leurs revenus ont nettement augmenté; *St Exch* **there has been a g. of 100 points on the Dow Jones** l'indice Dow Jones a gagné 100 points; *Pol* **Labour made important gains in London** le parti travailliste a beaucoup progressé à Londres
3 *Electron* gain *m*
VT **1** (*acquire*) (*reputation*) acquérir; (*sympathy*) gagner; **you will g. nothing by it** vous n'y gagnerez rien; **to g. permission** obtenir une permission; **to g. sb's affection** gagner l'affection de qn; **to g. experience** acquérir de l'expérience; **to g. entrance** *or* **admission** s'introduire; **to g. the impression that …** avoir l'impression que …; **to g. an advantage** obtenir un avantage; **we have not so much lost a daughter as gained a son, we're not losing a daughter, we're gaining a son** nous n'avons pas perdu une fille mais gagné un fils
2 (*acquire more of*) gagner, prendre; (*time*) gagner; (*strength*) (re)prendre; **to g. weight** prendre du poids; **to g. popularity** devenir plus populaire; **he has gained prestige through this action** cette action a rehaussé son prestige; **the party has gained support** le parti a gagné des voix; **to g. ground** (*of racer, pursuer*) gagner du terrain (**on** sur); (*of a custom*) se répandre, se développer; **to g. share** (*of market*) gagner des parts de marché
3 (*win*) **to g. a victory** remporter une victoire; **they gained two points** ils ont gagné deux points; **to g. the upper hand** prendre le dessus
4 (*of clock*) **to g. five minutes a day** avancer de cinq minutes par jour
VI **1** (*benefit*) **to g. by** bénéficier de, être aidé par; **we have all gained by his hard work** nous avons tous bénéficié de son labeur; **we have gained by having her in the team** cela nous a aidés de l'avoir dans l'équipe; **I had a good teacher and I think I gained by that** j'ai eu un bon professeur et je crois que ça m'a servi
2 (*increase*) **to g. in popularity/experience** gagner en popularité/acquérir de l'expérience; **to g. in self-confidence** gagner *ou* prendre de l'assurance; **to g. in number** devenir plus nombreux
3 (*of clock*) avancer
4 (*of racer, pursuer*) gagner du terrain
▸ **gain on** VT INSEP (*adversary, competitor*) gagner du terrain sur

gainer [ˈɡeɪnər] N gagnant, -ante

gainful [ˈɡeɪnfʊl] ADJ profitable, rémunérateur, -trice; **to be in g. employment** avoir un emploi rémunéré

gainfully [ˈɡeɪnfʊlɪ] ADV **to be g. employed** (*doing sth useful*) faire quelque chose d'utile; (*earning money*) avoir un emploi rémunéré

gainsay [ɡeɪnˈseɪ] VT (*pt, pp* **gainsaid** [ɡeɪnˈsed]) *usu Lit* contredire; **there's no gainsaying his honesty/skill** son honnêteté/son adresse est indéniable

gait [ɡeɪt] N démarche *f*, (*of horse*) train *m*; **unsteady g.** pas *m* mal assuré

gaiter ['geɪtər] N **1** *(clothing)* guêtre *f* **2** *Aut* soufflet *m*

gal¹ *abbr* **gallon(s)**

gal² [gæl] N *Old-fashioned Fam (girl)* fille *f*

gala ['gɑːlə] N gala *m*; **swimming g.** grand concours *m* de natation; **in g. dress** en habit de gala
▸▸ **g. evening** soirée *f* de gala; **g. performance** représentation *f* de gala

galactic [gə'læktɪk] ADJ *Astron (pole etc)* galactique

Galahad ['gæləhæd] N *Myth* **Sir G.** Galaad *m*; *Fig* personne *f* noble et généreuse, seigneur *m*

Galapagos [gə'læpəgəs] N **the G. (Islands)** les (îles *fpl*) Galapagos *fpl*

galaxy ['gæləksɪ] N **1** *Astron* galaxie *f*; **the G.** *(Milky Way)* la Voie Lactée **2** *Fig (of famous people, film stars etc)* pléiade *f*

gale [geɪl] N grand (coup *m* de) vent *m*, vent fort; **the roof was blown off in a g.** un grand coup de vent a emporté le toit; **it's blowing a g.** le vent souffle en tempête; *Fig* **a g. of laughter** un éclat de rire
▸▸ *Met* **g.-force winds** vents forts; *Met* **g. warning** avis *m* de coup de vent, avis de tempête

galena [gə'liːnə] N *Miner* galène *f*

Galilean [gælɪ'liːən] *Bible* ADJ galiléen N Galiléen, -éenne

Galilee ['gælɪliː] N Galilée *f*; **the Sea of G.** la mer *ou* le lac de Galilée

Galileo [gælɪ'leɪəʊ] N Galilée *m*

gall¹ *abbr* **gallon(s)**

gall² [gɔːl] N **1** *Physiol* bile *f* **2** *(impudence)* effronterie *f*, culot *m*, toupet *m*; **she had the g. to …** elle a eu le culot *ou* le toupet de …
▸▸ *Anat* **g. bladder** vésicule *f* biliaire

gall³ N *(sore) (on horse etc)* écorchure *f*, *Fig* **the criticism was a g. to his pride** la critique l'a piqué au vif
VT **1** *(make sore)* écorcher *(par frottement)* **2** *(annoy)* irriter, exaspérer

gall⁴ N *Bot* galle *f*, cécidie *f*

gallant ADJ **1** ['gælənt] *(brave)* brave, vaillant; **the ship and her g. crew** le navire et son vaillant équipage; **g. deed** acte de bravoure **2** [gə'lænt] *(with women)* galant

gallantly ADV **1** ['gæləntlɪ] *(bravely)* bravement, vaillamment **2** [gə'læntlɪ, 'gæləntlɪ] *(with women)* galamment, en homme galant

gallantry ['gæləntrɪ] N **1** *(bravery)* vaillance *f*, bravoure *f*; **a medal for g.** une médaille de bravoure **2** *(with women)* galanterie *f*

galleon ['gælɪən] N *Naut, Hist* galion *m*

gallery ['gælərɪ] N **1** *(in hall etc)* galerie *f*, *TV* régie *f*; **strangers' or public g.** *(in Houses of Parliament)* tribune *f* du public; **press g.** tribune de la presse; *Theat* **the g.** *(seats)* la (troisième) galerie, *Fam* le paradis; *Fig* **to play to the g.** jouer pour la galerie **2** *(private)*, *Com* **(art) g.** galerie *f*, *(museum)* musée *m* (d'art) **3** *Min* galerie *f* **4** **shooting g.** stand *m* de tir **5** *Am (balcony)* balcon *m*; *(veranda)* véranda *f*

galley ['gælɪ] N **1** *(ancient ship)* galère *f*, *(rowing boat)* yole *f* **2** *Naut, Aviat (kitchen)* cuisine *f* **3** *Typ* galée *f*, *(proof)* (épreuve *f* en) placard *m*
▸▸ *Typ* **g. proof** (épreuve en) placard *f*; **g. slave** galérien *m*

Gallic ['gælɪk] ADJ **1** *(French) (flair, charm, sophistication)* français; **a G. shrug** un haussement d'épaules (typiquement français) **2** *Hist (of Gaul)* gaulois; **the G. Wars** la guerre des Gaules

gallicism ['gælɪsɪz(ə)m] N *Ling* gallicisme *m*

gallicize ['gælɪsaɪz] VT franciser VI se franciser

galling ['gɔːlɪŋ] ADJ irritant, exaspérant; **it was g. to reflect that …** ça me/la/*etc* rendait malade de penser que …

gallium ['gælɪəm] N *Chem* gallium *m*

▸ **gallivant about, gallivant around** ['gælɪvænt] *Fam* VI partir en vadrouille; **he goes out gallivanting around every night** il part en vadrouille tous les soirs
VT INSEP *(travel around)* **I'm fed up with gallivanting about the country** j'en ai marre de toujours être par monts et par vaux; **he's gallivanting around the South of France** il est parti en vadrouille dans le Midi

gallon ['gælən] N gallon *m* (= 4,54 l, *Am* = 3,78 l); *Aut* **miles per g.** = consommation *f* d'essence aux cent kilomètres; *Fam* **they drink gallons of beer** ils boivent de la bière à tire-larigot

gallop ['gæləp] N **1** *(pace)* galop *m*; **at a g.** au galop (allongé); **(at) full g.** au grand galop **2** *(ride)* galopade *f*, **to have** *or* **go for a g.** faire une galopade
VI **(-p-)** *(of horse)* galoper; *(of horse, rider)* aller au galop; **to g. away** *or* **off** partir au galop; **he came galloping down the steps** *(of person)* il a descendu les escaliers quatre à quatre *ou* au grand galop; *Fig* **to g. through one's work/a task** expédier un travail/une tâche; *Fig* **to g. through prayers** réciter les prières à toute vitesse
VT *(horse)* faire galoper

galloping ['gæləpɪŋ] ADJ *(horse)* au galop; *Fig* **at a g. pace** à la vitesse grand V
▸▸ **g. inflation** inflation *f* galopante

Gallo-Roman ['gæləʊ'rəʊmən] ADJ gallo-romain, *pl* gallo-romains

gallows ['gæləʊz] NPL *(often with sing verb)* potence *f*, gibet *m*
▸▸ *Old-fashioned* **g. bird** gibier *m* de potence; *Br* **g. humour** humour *m* noir; **g. tree** potence, gibet

gallstone ['gɔːlstəʊn] N *Med* calcul *m* biliaire; **to have gallstones** avoir des calculs

Gallup ['gæləp] N
▸▸ **G. poll** sondage *m* Gallup

galore [gə'lɔːr] ADV *Fam* à gogo; **children g.** une flopée d'enfants; **books/money g.** des livres/de l'argent à gogo

galoshes [gə'lɒʃɪz] NPL caoutchoucs *mpl*

galumph [gə'lʌmf] VI *Fam* galoper lourdement (et bruyamment)

galvanic [gæl'vænɪk] ADJ galvanique

galvanism ['gælvənɪz(ə)m] N galvanisme *m*

galvanization [gælvənaɪ'zeɪʃən] N galvanisation *f*

galvanize ['gælvənaɪz] VT galvaniser; *Fig* **to g. sb/sth into life** galvaniser qn/qch

galvanized ['gælvənaɪzd] ADJ galvanisé
▸▸ **g. iron** fer *m* galvanisé

galvanizing ['gælvənaɪzɪŋ] ADJ
▸▸ **g. effect** effet *m* de galvanisation; *Fig* **the imminent danger had a g. effect on us** la proximité du danger nous a galvanisés

galvanometer [gælvə'nɒmɪtər] N galvanomètre *m*

Gambia ['gæmbɪə] N **the G.** la Gambie; **the G. (River)** la Gambie

Gambian ['gæmbɪən] N Gambien, -ienne ADJ gambien

gambit ['gæmbɪt] N *Chess* gambit *m*; *Fig* tactique *f*, stratagème *m*; *Fig* **opening g.** manœuvre *f* d'approche; **a g. to get their sympathy** un stratagème pour gagner leur sympathie

gamble ['gæmb(ə)l] N *(risk)* risque *m*; **I know it's a g. but …** je sais que c'est risqué mais …; **to take a g.** prendre un risque; **it's a g. but it may pay off** c'est un risque *ou* c'est risqué mais ça peut être payant

VI jouer de l'argent; **I don't g.** je ne joue pas pour de l'argent; **to g. on a throw of the dice** miser sur un coup de dé(s); **to g. on the Stock Exchange** jouer en Bourse, spéculer; **to g. on a rise in prices** jouer à la hausse; *Fig* **they're gambling on there not being an inspector on the train** ils misent sur le fait qu'il n'y aura pas de contrôleur dans le train; *Fig* **she's gambling on getting home by 8 o'clock** elle compte rentrer avant 8 heures; *Fig* **Napoleon gambled and lost** Napoléon a joué et perdu
VT **to g. one's money on horses** jouer son argent aux courses; *Fig* **the government has gambled its political future on the plan's success** le gouvernement a joué son avenir sur le succès du projet
▸ **gamble away** VT SEP *(fortune)* perdre au jeu

gambler ['gæmblər] N joueur, -euse (pour de l'argent)

gambling ['gæmblɪŋ] N jeu *m*, jeux *mpl* d'argent; **g. on the Stock Exchange** la spéculation en Bourse; **my father was a g. man** mon père jouait
▸▸ **g. debts** dettes *fpl* de jeu; *Pej* **g. den**, **g. house**, *Am* **g. joint** tripot *m*

gambol ['gæmb(ə)l] N cabriole *f*, gambade *f* VI **(-ll-, *Am* -l-)** gambader, cabrioler

gambrel ['gæmbrəl] N *Archit* toit *m* en croupe

game¹ [geɪm] N **1** *(activity, sport)* jeu *m*; **g. of skill/chance** jeu d'adresse/de hasard; **outdoor games** jeux de plein air; *Br Sch* **games** sports *mpl*; **games teacher** professeur *m* d'éducation physique; *Br Sch* **he's good at games** il est bon en sport, c'est un sportif; **the children were playing a g. of cowboys and Indians** les enfants jouaient aux cowboys et aux Indiens
2 *(contest)* *Sport* match *m*; *(friendly) (of cards, chess, golf, snooker etc)* partie *f*, *(part of a game of cards)* manche *f*, *(in tennis match)* jeu *m*; **how's the g. going?** comment marche la partie?; **we're having a g. of football after work** on va jouer au football après le travail; **anyone for darts/tennis? – I'll give you a g.** quelqu'un veut faire une partie de fléchettes/de tennis? – oui, moi; **you might get a g.** *(if someone is absent)* tu pourras peut-être jouer; **he played 65 games for England** il a joué 65 fois pour l'Angleterre; **we had a good g.** *(played well)* nous avons bien joué; **he plays a good g. of cards/billiards** il joue bien aux cartes/au billard; *Tennis* **g., set and match** jeu, set et match; *Chess* **opening/middle/end g.** début *m*/milieu *m*/fin *f* de partie
3 *Fig* **to play the g.** jouer le jeu, jouer selon les règles; **that's not playing the g.** ce n'est pas loyal; **to beat sb at his own g.** battre qn à son propre jeu; **two can play at that g.** on peut jouer à deux à ce petit jeu-là; *Fam* **what's his g.?** où veut-il en venir?, à quoi joue-t-il?; **I know your (little) g.!** je sais bien où vous voulez en venir!; **so that's your g.!** voilà donc ce que vous manigancez!; **politics is just a g. to him** la politique n'est qu'un jeu pour lui; **it isn't a g.!** *(it's serious)* ce n'est pas un jeu!; **to play games with sb** jouer avec qn; **let's stop playing games and come to the point** trêve de plaisanteries, passons aux choses sérieuses; **to play a dangerous g.** jouer un jeu dangereux; **he's up to his old games again** voilà qu'il refait des siennes; **the g.'s up** l'affaire est à l'eau; **the g. is not worth the candle** le jeu n'en vaut pas la chandelle; **I've been in this g. a long time** ça fait longtemps que je suis de la partie; *Fam* **how long have you been in the newspaper g.?** ça fait combien de temps que tu es dans les journaux?; *Br Sl* **to be on the g.** *(be a prostitute)* faire le trottoir; **to spoil sb's little**

g. déjouer les plans de qn; **what a g.!** (a lot of trouble) quel cinéma!; **they were just playing a g., pretending to be angry** ils faisaient semblant d'être en colère

4 Culin, (in hunting) gibier m; **small g.** menu gibier; **big g.** les grands fauves mpl; **big-g. hunting** la chasse aux grands fauves

vi jouer (de l'argent)

ADJ Fam (brave) courageux; **to be g. (to do sth)** (willing) être partant (pour faire qch); **I'm g.!** d'accord (j'en suis)!, je suis partant!; **he's g. for anything** il est toujours partant, Pej il est prêt à tout ou capable de tout

▸▸ **g. birds** gibier m à plumes; **g. licence** permis m de chasse; Culin **g. pie** tourte f au gibier, ≃ pâté m en croûte; Tennis **g. point** balle f de jeu; Comput **games port** port m (de connexion pour) jeux, sortie f jeux; **g. reserve** réserve f (pour animaux sauvages); **games room** salle f de jeux; Math **g. theory** théorie f des jeux

game² ADJ = gammy

gamebag ['geɪmbæg] N gibecière f

gamecock ['geɪmkɒk] N coq m de combat

gamekeeper ['geɪmkiːpər] N garde-chasse m, pl gardes-chasse(s)

gamely ['geɪmlɪ] ADV courageusement

gameplan ['geɪmplæn] N Chess, Fig stratégie f, Mktg stratégie (de mercatique)

gamer ['geɪmər] N **1** (who plays computer games) = amateur m de jeux vidéo **2** Am (athlete, sportsperson) = sportif m très compétitif

gameshow ['geɪmʃəʊ] N TV jeu m télévisé; Radio jeu radiophonique

gamesmanship ['geɪmzmənʃɪp] N astuce f, **this is just a g.** ce n'est qu'une astuce pour déstabiliser son adversaire

gamete ['gæmiːt, gæˈmiːt] N Biol gamète m

gameware ['geɪmweər] N Comput ludiciel m

gamey ['geɪmɪ] ADJ = gamy

gaming ['geɪmɪŋ] N **1** (gambling) jeu m **2** (playing of computer games) (pratique f des) jeux mpl électroniques

▸▸ **g. house** maison f de jeu; **g. table** table f de jeu

gamma ['gæmə] N (in Greek alphabet) gamma m

▸▸ **g. ray** rayon m gamma

gamma-ray therapy N Med gammathérapie f

gammon ['gæmən] N (bacon) quartier m; (ham) jambon m fumé

▸▸ Br **g. steak** = épaisse tranche f de jambon fumé

gammy ['gæmɪ] ADJ Fam **a g. leg** une patte folle

gamp [gæmp] N Br Old-fashioned Fam parapluie m, pépin m

gamut ['gæmət] N (of colours), Mus, Fig gamme f, **this character runs the whole g. of emotions** ce personnage passe par toute la gamme des émotions

gamy ['geɪmɪ] ADJ faisandé

gander ['gændər] N **1** (male goose) jars m **2** Br Sl (look) coup m d'œil; **just take a g.!** mate-moi ça!

gang [gæŋ] N (of criminals) bande f, gang m; (of children) bande; (of workmen) équipe f, (of prisoners) convoi m; **can I join your g.?** (of children) je peux faire partie de votre bande?; Fam **the whole g.** (of friends, colleagues) toute la bande; Pol, Hist **the G. of Four** la Bande des Quatre VOIR GRAMMAIRE A11

▸▸ **g. rape** viol m collectif; **g. war(fare)** guerre f des gangs

▸ **gang up** vi Fam former un gang; **to g. up with sb** s'allier avec qn; **to g. up on sb** se liguer contre qn

ganga ['gændʒə] N = ganja

gangbang ['gæŋbæŋ] N Sl **1** (group rape) viol m collectif **2** (group sex) partouse f

ganger ['gæŋər] N Br Rail chef m d'équipe

Ganges (the) [ðǽndʒiːz] N le Gange

gangland ['gæŋlænd] N (area) (in big city) territoire m contrôlé par des gangsters; (underworld) le milieu

▸▸ **g. boss** chef m de gang; **g. killing** règlement m de compte (entre gangsters); **g. warfare** guerre f des gangs

gangling ['gæŋglɪŋ] ADJ dégingandé; **a g. youth** un jeune dégingandé

ganglion, pl **ganglia** ['gæŋglɪən, -ɪə] N Anat ganglion m

gangplank ['gæŋplæŋk] N Naut passerelle f, **to make sb walk the g.** forcer qn à marcher sur la planche (de telle sorte qu'il tombe dans la mer)

gang-rape VT commettre un viol collectif sur; **women who have been gang-raped** les femmes qui ont été victimes de viols collectifs; **they gang-raped her** ils l'ont violée

gangrene ['gæŋgriːn] N Med gangrène f, nécrose f, **to have g.** avoir la gangrène

gangrenous ['gæŋgrɪnəs] ADJ gangreneux, gangrené; **to go g.** (of wound) se gangrener

gangster ['gæŋstər] N gangster m; **g. film** film m de gangsters

▸▸ **g. capitalism** = système m économique débridé exclusivement basé sur la recherche du profit

gangsterism ['gæŋstərɪz(ə)m] N gangstérisme m

gangway ['gæŋweɪ] N **1** (passage) passage m; (of bus etc) couloir m central; **when you set the chairs out, leave a g.** laissez un passage entre les chaises quand vous les installerez; **g.!** dégagez, s'il vous plaît! **2** Naut (gangplank) passerelle f de service; Aviat (for plane) passerelle

ganja ['gændʒə] N Sl (marijuana) herbe f

gannet ['gænɪt] N (bird) fou m (de Bassan); Hum Fig (glutton) goinfre mf

gantry ['gæntrɪ] N **1** (for travelling crane) pont m roulant; (for rocket) portique m de lancement; Rail **signal g.** portique de signalisation; **travelling g.** portique roulant **2** (for barrel) chantier m

▸▸ **g. crane** grue f (à) portique

gaol [dʒeɪl] N, VT Br = jail

gaolbird ['dʒeɪlbɜːd] N Br = jailbird

gaolbreak ['dʒeɪlbreɪk] N Br évasion f de prison

gaolbreaker ['dʒeɪlbreɪkər] N Br évadé, -ée de prison

gaoler ['dʒeɪlər] N Br = jailer

gap [gæp] N **1** (hole, opening) (which needs mending) trou m; (in floorboards) interstice m; (created deliberately) trouée f, ouverture f, (in a wall) brèche f, (in clouds) trou; (in trees) trouée; (of spark plug, points) écartement m; (in piston ring) jeu m à la coupe (des segments); **that fills a g.** (of snack) ça cale bien; **a g. in the bookshelf** un vide sur l'étagère; **the demolition of the house left a g. in the street** la démolition de la maison a laissé un espace vide dans la rue; **a g. of 2 cm** un intervalle de 2 cm; **leave a g. of six centimetres between the chairs** laissez un espace de six centimètres entre les chaises; **there's a g. in the curtains** les rideaux bâillent; **the g. in his teeth** l'écart entre ses dents; **there were gaps in his teeth** il avait les dents écartées; **the shelling had opened great gaps in the ranks** le bombardement avait éclairci les rangs; Aut **(spark) g.** intervalle m d'allumage; Com **g. in the market** créneau m

2 (difference) différence f, **age g.** différence

d'âge; **the g. between us and our competitors** l'écart entre nos concurrents et nous; **to close the g.** réduire l'écart; **there is a vast g. in ability between the two teams** il y a une grande différence de niveau entre les deux équipes; **the g. between rich and poor has widened** le fossé entre les riches et les pauvres s'est élargi

3 (in time) écart m; **there is a g. of two years in the records** il y a un trou de deux ans dans les archives; **after a g. of over twenty years** après un intervalle de plus de vingt ans

4 Fig (in memory etc) trou m, lacune f, vide m; **his death leaves a g. in all of our lives** sa mort laisse un vide dans nos vies; **to fill the gaps in one's education** combler les lacunes de son éducation; **there are a lot of gaps in her account of the event** il y a beaucoup d'omissions dans sa version des événements

5 Geog (opening in hills, mountains) trouée f, esp Am (pass) col m

6 (in recording) blanc m sonore; (in recorded tape) plage f de silence

▸▸ Mktg **g. analysis** étude f des créneaux; Mktg **g. level** écart m de performance; Br **g. year** = année f, souvent passée à voyager, que s'accorde un étudiant avant son entrée à l'université ou à la fin de ses études

gape [geɪp] vi **1** (stare) être ou rester bouche bée; **to g. in admiration/astonishment** être bouche bée d'admiration/d'étonnement; **to g. at sb/sth** regarder qn/qch bouche bée; **what are you gaping at?** qu'est-ce que tu regardes bouche bée?; **stop gaping!** remets-toi! **2** **to g. (open)** (of thing) s'ouvrir (tout grand); (of seam etc) bâiller; (of hole) être béant

N I could tell from his astonished g. that ... je savais à son air éberlué que ...; **with a g. of disbelief** la bouche ouverte ou bée en signe d'incrédulité

gaping ['geɪpɪŋ] ADJ ATTRIB (hole etc) béant

gappy ['gæpɪ] ADJ (list etc) incomplet; **g. smile** sourire m édenté; Fam **g. teeth** dents fpl écartées

gap-toothed [-tuːθt] ADJ aux dents écartées

garage ['gærɑːʒ, -rɪdʒ] N Aut garage m; (multistorey) parking m; **there is g. space for two cars** il y a de la place pour garer deux voitures

vt (car) rentrer; (for longer period) remiser

▸▸ **g. attendant** gardien m de parking; **g. mechanic** garagiste mf, mécanicien, -ienne; **g. owner, g. proprietor** garagiste mf; **g. sale** vente f d'occasion, ≃ vide-greniers m inv

garb [gɑːb] N Lit costume m, habit m; **in clerical g.** en habit ecclésiastique

vt (usu passive) habiller, vêtir (in de); **garbed all in black** tout de noir vêtu

garbage ['gɑːbɪdʒ] N **1** esp Am (waste) ordures fpl (ménagères); Comput **g. in, g. out** mauvaises données à l'entrée égale mauvais résultats à la sortie **2** Fig Fam (nonsense) bêtises fpl; **he's talking g.** il dit n'importe quoi **3** Fig Fam (worthless things) **their new album is a load of g.** leur dernier album est vraiment nul; **I've been eating too much g. lately** je mange trop de cochonneries en ce moment

▸▸ Am **g. can** poubelle f, **g. collector** éboueur m; Am **g. disposal unit** broyeur m d'ordures; Am **g. heap** tas m d'ordures; **g. man** éboueur m

garbanzo [gɑːˈbænzəʊ] N Am pois m chiche

garble ['gɑːb(ə)l] VT (news, quotation) fausser; (facts) dénaturer; (text) altérer; **garbled account** compte rendu m trompeur ou mensonger; **garbled message** message m confus

Garda, pl **Gardai** ['gɑːdə, 'gɑːdiː] N **1** (police force) police f (de la République d'Irlande) **2**

(policeman) policier *m (de la République d'Irlande)*

garden ['gɑːd(ə)n] **N** jardin *m*; **back/front g.** jardin de derrière/de devant; **g. of remembrance** = jardin en souvenir des défunts; **public garden(s)** jardin public, parc *m*; *Fig Fam* **to lead sb up the g. path** duper qn, faire marcher qn
VI *(usu continuous)* jardiner, faire du jardinage
▸▸ **g. centre** jardinerie *f*; **g. chair** chaise *f* de jardin; **g. city** cité-jardin *f*, *pl* cités-jardins; *Br* **g. flat** rez-de-jardin *m inv*; **g. furniture** meubles *mpl* de jardin; **g. hose** tuyau *m* d'arrosage; *Br* **g. party** garden-party *f*, *pl* garden-parties *ou* garden-partys; **g. plant** plante *f* de jardin; **g. produce** produits *mpl* maraîchers; **g. suburb** banlieue *f* verte; **g. tools** outils *mpl* de jardinage

gardener ['gɑːdnər] **N** jardinier, -ière *m*; **he's a keen g.** c'est un adepte du jardinage

gardenia [gɑːˈdiːnɪə] **N** *(flower)* gardénia *m*

gardening ['gɑːdnɪŋ] **N** jardinage *m*
▸▸ **g. book** livre *m* de jardinage; **g. expert** spécialiste *mf* du jardinage; **g. programme** émission *f* sur le jardinage; **g. tools** outils *mpl* de jardinage

gargantuan [gɑːˈgæntjʊən] **ADJ** gargantuesque

gargle ['gɑːg(ə)l] *Med* **N** gargarisme *m*
VI se gargariser

gargoyle ['gɑːgɔɪl] **N** *Archit etc* gargouille *f*

garish ['geərɪʃ] **ADJ 1** *(clothes)* voyant; *(wallpaper)* criard; *(taste)* vulgaire **2** *(light, colour)* cru

garishly ['geərɪʃlɪ] **ADV** de façon criarde

garishness ['geərɪʃnɪs] **N 1** *(of clothes)* aspect *m* voyant *ou* tapageur; *(of wallpaper)* aspect criard; *(of taste)* vulgarité *f* **2** *(of light, colour)* crudité *f*

garland ['gɑːlənd] **N** guirlande *f*
VT parer de guirlandes, enguirlander; **garlanded with flowers** paré de guirlandes de fleurs

garlic ['gɑːlɪk] **N** ail *m*, *pl* ails *ou* aulx; **clove of g.** gousse *f* d'ail; **head of g.** bulbe *m* d'ail
▸▸ **g. bread** = pain *m* chaud au beurre d'ail; **g. butter** beurre *m* d'ail; **g. press** presse-ail *m inv*; **g. sausage** saucisson *m* à l'ail

garlicky ['gɑːlɪkɪ] **ADJ** qui sent l'ail; *(taste)* d'ail

garment ['gɑːmənt] **N** *Fml* vêtement *m*; **the g. industry** l'industrie *f* du vêtement

garner ['gɑːnər] **VT** *(collect) (information)* recueillir

garnet ['gɑːnɪt] **N** *Miner* grenat *m*; **g. necklace** collier *m* de grenat

garnish ['gɑːnɪʃ] **N** garniture *f*
VT garnir, orner (**with** de); *Culin (dish)* garnir

garnishee [gɑːnɪˈʃiː] **N**
▸▸ *Law* **g. order** ordonnance *f* de saisie-arrêt

garnishing ['gɑːnɪʃɪŋ] **N** garnissage *m*; *Culin* garniture *f*

garret ['gærət] **N** mansarde *f*; **to live in a g.** habiter sous les combles

garrison ['gærɪs(ə)n] *Mil* **N** garnison *f*
VT *(station)* mettre en garnison; **troops garrisoned at Lille** troupes en garnison à Lille; **to g. a town** *(provide with a garrison)* mettre une garnison dans une ville
▸▸ **g. duty** service *m* de place *ou* de garnison; **g. town** ville *f* de garnison

garrotte, *Am* **garrote** [gəˈrɒt] **N 1** *(device)* garrot *m* **2** *(execution)* supplice *m* du garrot
VT 1 *(strangle)* étrangler *(avec un fil, une corde etc)* **2** *(execute)* faire subir le supplice du garrot à

garrotting, *Am* **garroting** [gəˈrɒtɪŋ] **N 1**

(strangling) strangulation *f (avec un fil, une corde)* **2** *(execution)* supplice *m* du garrot

garrulity [gæˈruːlɪtɪ], **garrulousness** ['gærʊləsnɪs] **N** loquacité *f*

garrulous ['gærʊləs] **ADJ** loquace, bavard

garrulously ['gærʊləslɪ] **ADV** avec volubilité, de façon loquace

garter ['gɑːtər] **N** jarretière *f*; *Am (suspender) (for stockings)* jarretelle *f*; *Am (for socks)* fixe-chaussette *m*, *pl* fixe-chaussettes; *Br* **Knight of the (Order of the) G.** chevalier *m* de l'Ordre de la Jarretière
▸▸ *Am* **g. belt** porte-jarretelles *m inv*; **g. snake** couleuvre *f*; *Knitting* **g. stitch** point *m* mousse

gas, *pl* **gases** [gæs, ˈgæsɪz] **N 1** gaz *m inv*; **to pay the g. bill** payer le gaz; **the g. has been cut off** le gaz a été coupé; **to cook with** *or* **by g.** faire la cuisine au gaz; **to have g.** *(as anaesthetic)* se faire anesthésier au gaz; **town g.** gaz de ville
2 *Mil* gaz *m* de combat
3 *Min* grisou *m*
4 *Am (gasoline)* essence *f*; **to fill up with g.** faire le plein d'essence; **to step on the g.** *Aut* appuyer sur le champignon; *Fig (hurry)* se presser, *Fam* se grouiller
5 *Fam (worthless talk)* bavardage *m*, verbiage *m*
6 *esp Am* **what a g.!** *(situation, activity)* quelle rigolade!; **we did it for a g.** on l'a fait pour rigoler
VT (**-ss-**) *(person)* asphyxier *(avec un gaz)*; *(deliberately)* gazer; **to g. oneself** *(deliberately)* se suicider au gaz; *(accidentally)* être asphyxié
VI *Fam (chat)* bavarder, jaser
▸▸ **g. attack** attaque *f* aux gaz; *Admin* **G. Board** compagnie *f* du gaz; **g. burner** brûleur *m* à gaz; **g. chamber** chambre *f* à gaz; **g. cooker** cuisinière *f* à gaz; **g. cylinder** bouteille *f* de gaz; **g. explosion** *(in home or street)* explosion *f* due à une fuite de gaz; *(in mine)* coup *m* de grisou; **g. field** gisement *m* de gaz; *Br* **g. fire** *(appareil m de)* chauffage *m* au gaz; **g. fitter** installateur, -trice d'appareils à gaz; **g. furnace** fourneau *m* à gaz; **g. gangrene** gangrène *f* gazeuse; *Am Fam* **g. guzzler** = voiture *f* qui consomme beaucoup; **g. holder** gazomètre *m*, réservoir *m* à gaz; **g. industry** industrie *f* du gaz; *Br* **g. lamp** *(in street)* bec *m* de gaz; **g. leak** fuite *f* de gaz; **g. lighter** *(for cooker)* allume-gaz *m inv*; *(for cigarettes)* briquet *m* à gaz; **g. main** conduite *f* de gaz; *(large)* gazoduc *m*; **g. mantle** manchon *m* à incandescence; **g. mask** masque *m* à gaz; **g. meter** compteur *m* à gaz; **g. oven** *(domestic)* four *m* à gaz; *(cremation chamber)* four crématoire; **she threatened to put her head in a g. oven** elle a menacé de se suicider; **g. pipe** tuyau *m* à gaz; *Comput* **g. plasma screen** écran *m* à plasma; *Br* **g. poker** allume-gaz *m inv*; *Br* **g. ring** *(part of cooker)* brûleur *m*; *(small cooker)* réchaud *m* à gaz; *Am* **g. station** poste *m* d'essence, station-service *f*, *pl* stations-service; **g. stove** cuisinière *f* à gaz; **g. tank** *(domestic)* cuve *f* à gaz; *Am Aut (petrol tank)* réservoir *m* à essence; **g. tap** *(on cooker)* bouton *m* de gaz; *(at mains)* robinet *m* de gaz; **g. turbine** turbine *f* à gaz; **g. turbine engine** moteur *m* à turbine à gaz; **g. warfare** guerre *f* chimique

gasbag ['gæsbæg] **N** *Fam* bavard, -arde; *(boaster)* vantard, -arde

Gascony ['gæskənɪ] **N** la Gascogne

gas-cooled reactor [-'kuːld] **N** réacteur *m* à refroidissement par gaz

gaseous ['gæsɪəs, 'geɪsɪəs, geɪʃ ɪəs] **ADJ** gazeux

gas-fired [-'faɪəd] **ADJ** au gaz

gash [gæʃ] **N** *(on body)* coupure *f*, entaille *f*;

(on face) balafre *f*; *(in earth's surface etc)* fente *f*; **the iceberg had ripped a great g. in the ship's side** l'iceberg avait fait une grande déchirure sur le côté du bateau
VT *(wound)* entailler, couper; *(face)* balafrer; **to g. one's chin** se faire une entaille au menton

gasholder ['gæshəʊldər] **N** réservoir *m* à gaz

gasify ['gæsɪfaɪ] **VT** gazéifier
VI se gazéifier

gasket ['gæskɪt] **N** *Tech (of joint)* joint *m* d'étanchéité, garniture *f*; *Aut (of cylinder head)* joint de culasse; **to blow a g.** *Aut* faire sauter un joint de culasse; *Fig Fam* se mettre en rage, piquer une colère; *Fam* **he just about blew a g.** il a pété les plombs

gaslight ['gæslaɪt] **N** lumière *f* du gaz; **by g.** à la lumière du gaz

gasman, *pl* **gasmen** ['gæsmæn, -men] **N** *Fam* contrôleur *m* *ou* employé *m* du gaz, gazier *m*

gasoline ['gæsəliːn] **N** *Am* essence *f*

gasometer [gæˈsɒmɪtər] **N** gazomètre *m*, réservoir *m* à gaz

gasp [gɑːsp] **N** *(of surprise)* hoquet *m*, sursaut *m*; **there were gasps of admiration from the audience** il y a eu des sursauts d'admiration dans le public; **..., she said with a g.** ..., dit-elle, le souffle coupé; **to be at one's last g.** agoniser, être à l'agonie; *Fig Fam* être sur le point de rendre son dernier soupir; **to give one's last g.** rendre le dernier soupir; **to defend sth to the last g.** défendre qch jusqu'à son dernier souffle
VI *(with surprise, fright, horror)* avoir le souffle coupé (**with** de); **to make sb g.** couper le souffle à qn; **to g. for breath** *or* **for air** haleter, suffoquer; *Fam* **I'm gasping (for a drink)** je meurs de soif; *Fam* **I'm gasping (for a cigarette)** je meurs d'envie de fumer une cigarette
VT dire d'une voix entrecoupée; **she managed to g. her name** elle a réussi à dire son nom d'une voix entrecoupée
▸ **gasp out VT SEP** = **gasp VT**

gasper ['gɑːspər] **N** *Fam (cigarette)* tige *f*

gas-permeable **ADJ** *(contact lens)* semi-rigide

gassed [gæst] **ADJ** *Fam (drunk)* bourré

gassing ['gæsɪŋ] **N 1** *(of person) (deliberate)* gazage *m* **2** *Fam (talk)* bavardage *m*

gassy ['gæsɪ] **ADJ** *(beer etc)* trop gazeux

gastrectomy [gæs'trektəmɪ] **N** *Med* gastrectomie *f*

gastric ['gæstrɪk] **ADJ** gastrique
▸▸ **g. flu** grippe *f* intestinale *ou* gastro-intestinale; **g. juices** sucs *mpl* gastriques; **g. ulcer** ulcère *m* de l'estomac, gastrite *f* ulcéreuse

gastritis [gæs'traɪtɪs] **N** *Med* gastrite *f*; **to have g.** avoir *ou* faire une gastrite

gastro-enteritis [gæstrəʊentə'raɪtɪs] **N** *Med* gastro-entérite *f*, *pl* gastro-entérites

gastroenterology [gæstrəʊentə'rɒlədʒɪ] **N** *Med* gastro-entérologie *f*

gastro-intestinal ['gæstrəʊ-] **ADJ** *Anat* gastrointestinal, -aux; **the g. tract** les voies *f* digestives

gastronome ['gæstrənəʊm] **N** gastronome *mf*

gastronomic(al) [gæstrə'nɒmɪk, -ɪk(ə)l] **ADJ** gastronomique

gastronomy [gæs'trɒnəmɪ] **N** gastronomie *f*

gastropod ['gæstrəpɒd] **N** *(mollusc)* gastéropode *m*

gastropub ['gæstrəʊpʌb] **N** *Br* pub *m* gastronomique

gasworks ['gæswɜːks] **NPL** *(usu with sing verb)* usine *f* à gaz

gate [geɪt] N **1** *(of castle, city, factory)* porte *f*; *(of manor house)* portail *m*; **the gate(s) of hell** les portes de l'enfer

2 *(of garden)* portail *m*; *(metal)* grille *f*; *(of field)* barrière *f*, *Ski* porte *f*, *Aviat* g. **15** *(at airport)* porte 15; *Sport* **(starting)** g. starting-gate *m*, *pl* starting-gates

3 *(at stadium)* entrée *f*; **to pay at the g.** payer à l'entrée; *Sport* **the g.** *(spectators)* le public; *(takings)* la recette, les entrées

4 *Tech* **(lock)** g. vanne *f* (d'écluse)

5 *Aut* **(for gearstick)** grille *f* (de changement de vitesse)

6 *Electron* porte *f*, **(logic)** g. porte logique

▸ VT *Br Sch, Univ* **to be gated** se faire consigner

▸▸ *Aviat* g. **lounge** salle *f* d'embarquement; *Sport* g. **money** la recette, les entrées; g. **pattern** *(of gearbox)* disposition *f* de grille, type *m* de grille

gâteau ['gætəʊ] N gros gâteau *m* à la crème

gate-crash VI resquiller

▸ VT **to g. a party** aller à une soirée sans y être invité

gate-crasher [-kræʃər] N resquilleur, -euse

gatefold ['geɪtfəʊld] N page *f* qui se déplie, dépliant *m* (dans un magazine)

gatehouse ['geɪthaʊs] N **1** *(of an estate)* loge *f* **2** *(of a castle)* corps-de-garde *m inv*

gatekeeper ['geɪtkiːpər] N **1** gardien, -ienne **2** *Mktg* contrôleur *m*, relais *m*, filtre *m* **3** *Rail* garde-barrière *mf. pl* gardes-barrière(s)

gate-leg(ged) [-leg(d)] ADJ *(table)* à abattants

gatepost ['geɪtpəʊst] N montant *m* (de barrière); *Fam* **between you, me and the g.** entre nous soit dit

gateway ['geɪtweɪ] N **1** porte *f*, entrée *f*, *Fig* **the g. to the Continent** la porte du Continent; **a g. to a successful career** un passeport pour une carrière réussie **2** *Comput* passerelle *f* de connexion

gather ['gæðər] VT **1** *(collect) (people)* assembler, rassembler; *(things)* rassembler; *(flowers)* cueillir; *(information)* recueillir; *(wood, papers)* ramasser; *(strawberries etc)* cueillir, faire la cueillette de; *(one's skirts)* serrer autour de ses jambes; *(in bookbinding) (pages of a book)* rassembler; **to g. the harvest** rentrer la moisson; **to g. honey from the flowers** *(of bees)* butiner les fleurs; **we are gathered here today …** nous sommes rassemblés ici aujourd'hui …; **to g. one's thoughts** rassembler ses idées; **to g. all one's strength (in order) to do sth** rassembler toutes ses forces pour faire qch; **to g. one's hair into a bun/a ponytail/bunches** se faire un chignon/une queue de cheval/des couettes; *Lit Euph* **to be gathered to one's fathers** expirer

2 *(accumulate)* **to g. dirt** s'encrasser; **to g. dust** ramasser la poussière; **to g. force** *(of argument)* gagner du terrain; **to g. momentum, to g. speed** prendre de la vitesse; **to g. strength** *(of person)* reprendre des forces

3 *(pull together) Sewing (skirt etc)* froncer; **to g. the blankets round one** se serrer dans les couvertures; **he gathered her in his arms** il l'a serrée dans ses bras

4 *(conclude, understand)* conclure; **so far as I can g.** à ce que je sache; **I g. from the papers that …** à en croire les journaux …; **I g. he has been ill** j'ai appris qu'il a été malade; **I g. from the evidence given that …** je déduis *ou* j'infère de ces témoignages que …; **as you may/must already have gathered** comme vous l'avez peut-être/sûrement déjà compris; **I had (already) gathered as much** *(it was not news to me)* j'avais déjà compris; **prices have gone up – so I g.** les prix ont augmenté – c'est bien ce qu'il me semble

VI **1** *(of people)* se réunir, s'assembler, se rassembler; **a crowd gathered** une foule se forma **2** *(of objects, dust)* s'accumuler, s'amonceler; **tears were gathering in her eyes** ses yeux se remplissaient de larmes; **the clouds are gathering** les nuages s'amoncellent; **a storm is gathering** un orage se prépare **3** *Med (of abscess)* mûrir, aboutir; **the pus gathers** le pus s'accumule

▸ **gather in** VT SEP **1** *(collect) (crops, harvest)* rentrer; *(sheep)* faire rentrer; *(exam papers, questionnaires)* ramasser **2** *Sewing* froncer

▸ **gather round** VT INSEP se rassembler autour de

VI s'approcher; **g. round!** approchez-vous!

▸ **gather together** VT SEP *(collect) (belongings, children etc)* rassembler

VI *(assemble)* se rassembler

▸ **gather up** VT SEP *(collect) (belongings, things)* ramasser; **she gathered up her skirts** elle a serré sa jupe autour de ses jambes; **to g. up one's hair** attacher *ou* relever ses cheveux; **he gathered her up in his arms** il l'a serrée dans ses bras

gathered ['gæðəd] ADJ *Sewing (flounce etc)* froncé, à fronces

▸▸ g. **pages** *(in bookbinding)* feuilles *fpl* assemblées

gathering ['gæðərɪŋ] N **1** *(people) (in a hall etc)* assemblée *f*, réunion *f*; *(in a street)* rassemblement *m*, attroupement *m*; **the g. of the clans** le rassemblement des clans; **a small g. was listening to him** quelques personnes attroupées l'écoutaient **2** *(of information, data)* collecte *f*; *(of fruit etc)* cueillette *f*, *Sewing (pleats)* fronces *fpl*

ADJ ATTRIB **in the g. darkness** dans la nuit grandissante; **with g. force** avec une force croissante

gathers ['gæðəz] NPL *Sewing* fronces *fpl*

gator ['geɪtər] N *Am Fam (alligator)* alligator *m*

GATS [gæts] N *(abbr General Agreement on Trade in Services)* AGCS *m*

GATT [gæt] N *(abbr General Agreement on Tariffs and Trade)* GATT *m*, AGETAC *m*

gauche [gəʊʃ] ADJ gauche, maladroit

gaucheness ['gəʊʃnɪs] N gaucherie *f*, maladresse *f*

gaudily ['gɔːdɪlɪ] ADV d'une manière voyante; *(painted)* avec des couleurs criardes

gaudiness ['gɔːdɪnɪs] N *(of colour etc)* éclat *m* criard

gaudy ['gɔːdɪ] ADJ *(colour)* voyant, criard; *(display)* de mauvais goût

gauge [geɪdʒ] N **1** *(size) (of screw etc)* calibre *m*; *Rail (of track)* écartement *m* **2** *(standardization device)* étalon *m*; *(for liquid)* jauge *f*; **wire g.** calibre *m* pour fils métalliques **3** *(control instrument)* indicateur *m*; *Tech* **water-/oil g.** indicateur *ou* jauge *f* de niveau d'eau/d'huile; **pressure g.** manomètre *m*; *Aut* **(petrol or fuel) g.** jauge d'essence; *Fig* **an opinion poll is a useful g. of public opinion** un sondage constitue un indicateur utile de l'opinion

VT *(screw etc)* calibrer; *(oil)* jauger, mesurer; **in order to g. the amount of petrol/water necessary to …** pour évaluer la quantité d'essence/d'eau nécessaire à …; *Fig* **to g. a situation** évaluer une situation; **it was difficult to g. how interested they were/their enthusiasm** il était difficile de juger dans quelle mesure ils étaient intéressés/de juger de leur enthousiasme

gauging ['geɪdʒɪŋ] N

▸▸ g. **rod**, g. **stick** jauge *f*

Gaul [gɔːl] N *Antiq* **1** *(region)* Gaule *f* **2** *(inhabitant)* Gaulois, -oise

Gaullist ['gəʊlɪst] ADJ, N *Pol* gaulliste *mf*

gaunt [gɔːnt] ADJ **1** *(person, face)* maigre, décharné **2** *(place)* désolé

gauntlet[1] ['gɔːntlɪt] N **1** *(part of armour)* gantelet *m*, gant *m*; *Fig* **to throw** *or* **fling down the g.** jeter le gant; *Fig* **to take up the g.** relever le gant **2** *(glove)* gant *m* à crispins *ou* à manchette

▸▸ g. **glove** gant à crispins *ou* à manchette

gauntlet[2] N *(glove)* to run the g. *Mil* passer par les baguettes; *Naut* courir la bouline; *Fig* soutenir un feu roulant (de critiques adverses); **they had to run the g. of enemy fire** ils ont dû soutenir le feu roulant de l'ennemi; **he had to run the g. of their abuse** il a dû soutenir le feu roulant de leurs injures

gauntness ['gɔːntnɪs] N *(of person, face)* maigreur *f*; *(of place)* désolation *f*; **the g. of his face** son visage hâve

gauze [gɔːz] N gaze *f*, *Med* **(antiseptic) g.** gaze aseptique; **(wire) g.** toile *f* métallique

▸▸ *Med* g. **bandage** bande *f* de gaze

gave PT *see* give

gavel ['gæv(ə)l] N *(of auctioneer, of judge)* marteau *m*

gavotte [gə'vɒt] N *Mus* gavotte *f*

Gawd [gɔːd] N *Sl* = God

gawk [gɔːk] *Fam* N lourdaud, -aude

VI = gawp

gawker ['gɔːkər] N *Am* badaud *m*, curieux, -ieuse

gawkiness ['gɔːkɪnɪs] N gaucherie *f*, *Fam* air *m* empoté

gawky ['gɔːkɪ] ADJ gauche, *Fam* empoté

gawp [gɔːp] VI *Fam* rester bouche bée, gober les mouches; **to g. at sth** regarder qch d'un air bête; **stop gawping!** ne reste pas planté là à regarder!

gay [geɪ] ADJ **1** *(homosexual)* homosexuel, gay *inv*; **the g. community** la communauté homosexuelle *ou* gay; **g. club/magazine** boîte de nuit/magazine pour homosexuels **2** *Sl (stupid)* nul **3** *Old-fashioned (happy)* gai, allègre; *(laugh)* enjoué; *(colour)* vif, *f* vive, gai; **to have a g. old time** bien s'amuser

N homosexuel, -elle

gayness ['geɪnɪs] N *(homosexuality)* homosexualité *f*

Gaza ['gɑːzə] N Gaza; **the G. Strip** la Bande de Gaza

gaze [geɪz] N regard *m* fixe; **she turned her g. on the dog** elle a tourné son regard vers le chien; **to meet sb's g.** regarder qn dans les yeux; **exposed to the public g.** exposé aux regards inquisiteurs de tous

VI regarder fixement; **they gazed around them** ils ont regardé autour d'eux; **to g. at** *or* **on sb/sth** fixer *ou* contempler *ou* considérer qn/qch

gazebo [gə'ziːbəʊ] N *(with a view)* belvédère *m*; *(without a view)* kiosque *m*

gazelle [gə'zel] N *(animal)* gazelle *f*

gazette [gə'zet] N *(official journal)* journal *m* officiel; **the Police G.** ≃ la Gazette des tribunaux

VT *(bankruptcy, appointment etc)* annoncer *ou* publier dans un journal officiel

gazetteer [gæzɪ'tɪər] N répertoire *m* géographique

gazump [gə'zʌmp] VT *Br Fam* **to g. sb** = revenir sur une promesse de vente faite à qn pour accepter une offre plus élevée; **we were gazumped** le propriétaire est revenu sur la promesse de vente qu'il nous avait faite

gazumping [gə'zʌmpɪŋ] N *Br Fam* = fait de revenir sur une promesse de vente pour accepter une offre plus élevée

GB ['dʒiː'biː] N **1** *Aut (abbr* Great Britain*)* GB plate plaque *f* GB; **GB sticker** autocollant *m* GB **2** *Comput (abbr* gigabyte*)* Go *m*

GBH [dʒiːbiːˈeɪtʃ] N Law (abbr **grievous bodily harm**) coups mpl et blessures fpl

GCE [dʒiːsiːˈiː] Br Sch Formerly (abbr **General Certificate of Education**) N = certificat m britannique de fin d'études secondaire en deux étapes (O level et A level) dont la première est aujourd'hui remplacée par le GCSE

GCHQ [dʒiːsiːeɪtʃˈkjuː] N Br (abbr **Government Communications Headquarters**) = centre m de renseignement du gouvernement britannique

GCSE [dʒiːsiːesˈiː] N Br Sch (abbr **General Certificate of Secondary Education**) = première partie f de l'examen de fin d'études secondaires

---

GCSE

Cet examen a remplacé les "O levels", ou le "GCE O level", et le "CSE". On le passe après cinq ans de scolarité dans l'enseignement secondaire. Chaque élève choisit les matières dans lesquelles il veut se présenter (généralement entre cinq et dix) selon un système d'unités de valeur. Le nombre d'unités et les notes obtenues déterminent le passage dans la classe supérieure. Les élèves qui sont admis au GCSE peuvent ensuite préparer les "**A levels**" (l'équivalent du baccalauréat français). En Écosse, l'examen équivalent au GCSE s'appelle le "Standard Grade".

GDP [dʒiːdiːˈpiː] N Econ (abbr **gross domestic product**) PIB m; **G. per capita** PIB par habitant

GDR [dʒiːdiːˈɑːr] N Formerly (abbr **German Democratic Republic**) RDA f

Gds abbr **Gardens**

gear [ɡɪər] N 1 (speed) vitesse f; (mechanism) appareil m, mécanisme m; Tech etc (gearwheel) engrenage m; **in g.** (car) embrayé, en prise; Sl **get your arse in g.!** remue-toi!; **out of g.** (car) au point mort; **to throw** or **put out of g.** (car) débrayer; Fig (plan, process) perturber; **a ten-g. racing bike** un vélo de course à dix vitesses; Aut **neutral g.** point m mort; Aut **first** or **bottom g.** première vitesse; Aut **top g.** cinquième/sixième vitesse; Fig **we're not operating in top g.** nous ne sommes pas à notre maximum ou au top de notre forme; **to change** or Am **shift g.** Aut, Fig changer de vitesse; Cycling changer de vitesse ou de braquet

2 (equipment) équipement m; Naut apparaux mpl; (for camping, fishing, photography) équipement, matériel m; Fig Fam **he arrived with all his g.** (belongings) il est arrivé avec tout son attirail **3** Fam (clothes) fringues fpl **4** Br Sl (drugs) dope f **5** (harness) (of draught horse) harnais m, harnachement m

VT **1** Tech engrener, embrayer **2** Fin (link) indexer (**to** à); **salaries are geared to the cost of living** les salaires sont indexés au coût de la vie

▸▸**g. change** changement m de vitesse; **g. lever** levier m (de changement) de vitesse; **g. ratio** rapport m du changement de vitesse

▸ **gear down** VI (of factory etc) ralentir la production

VT SEP **1 to g. down production** ralentir la production **2** Tech démultiplier

▸ **gear to** VT SEP (intend for) **to g. sth to sth** adapter qch en fonction de qch; **wages geared to the cost of living** salaires indexés sur le coût de la vie; **this book is geared to the needs of students** ce livre est spécialement adapté aux besoins des étudiants

▸ **gear up** VI (prepare) se préparer; **the shops are gearing up for Christmas** les magasins se préparent pour Noël

VT SEP **1** (prepare) préparer; **businesses were getting geared up for the single European market** les entreprises se préparaient en vue du marché unique européen **2** (increase) augmenter; **we must g. up production to meet the demand** il nous faut augmenter la production pour faire face à la demande **3** Tech multiplier

gearbox [ˈɡɪəbɒks] N Aut boîte f de vitesses
▸▸**g. ratio** rapport m de boîte

gearing [ˈɡɪərɪŋ] N **1** Tech etc (gears) engrenage m, embrayage m, système m ou jeu m d'engrenages; (drive) transmission f **2** Fin (leverage) effet m de levier; (as percentage) ratio m d'endettement

▸▸Fin **g. adjustment** redressement m financier; Tech **g. down** démultiplication f; Tech **g. up** multiplication f

gearshift [ˈɡɪəʃɪft] N Am Aut (lever) levier m de vitesses; (action) changement m de vitesse; **automatic g.** changement de vitesse automatique

gearstick [ˈɡɪəstɪk] N levier m de vitesses

gearwheel [ˈɡɪəwiːl] N Tech engrenage m; Cycling pignon m

gecko, pl **geckos**, **geckoes** [ˈɡekəʊ, -əʊz] N gecko m

gee [dʒiː] INT **1** (to horse) **g. up!** hue! **2** Am **g. (whiz(z))!** ça alors!, mince alors!

gee-gee [ˈdʒiːdʒiː] N Fam (horse) dada m

geek [ɡiːk] N Fam crétin, -ine, débile mf

geeky [ˈɡiːkɪ] ADJ Fam ringard, débile

geese [ɡiːs] NPL see **goose**

geezer [ˈɡiːzər] N Fam **1** Br (man) type m; **old g.** vieux type; **funny old g.** drôle m de bonhomme **2** Am (old person) vioque mf

Geiger counter [ˈɡaɪɡər] N compteur m Geiger

geisha [ˈɡeɪʃə] N geisha f

gel [dʒel] N Chem colloïde m (coagulé); (for hair, eyes) gel m

VI (-ll-) se coaguler; Fig (of ideas, plans) prendre corps ou forme; Fig **the musicians didn't g.** la cohésion ne s'est pas faite entre les musiciens

gelatine [ˈdʒeləˌtiːn] N gélatine f
▸▸**g. paper** papier m gélatine

gelatinize [dʒɪˈlætɪnaɪz] VT gélatiniser
VI se gélatiniser

gelatinous [dʒɪˈlætɪnəs] ADJ gélatineux

geld [ɡeld] VT (animal) châtrer; (horse) hongrer

gelding [ˈɡeldɪŋ] N (animal) animal m châtré; (horse) (cheval m) hongre m

gelignite [ˈdʒelɪɡnaɪt] N gélignite f

gem [dʒem] N **1** (precious stone) pierre f précieuse **2** Fig (marvellous thing or person) perle f; **he's a g. of a husband** c'est la perle des maris; **the g. of the collection** le joyau de la collection **3** Typ diamant m

Gemini [ˈdʒemɪnaɪ] NPL Astrol Gémeaux mpl; **to be (a) G.** être (des) Gémeaux

gemstone [ˈdʒemstəʊn] N pierre f gemme

Gen Mil (abbr **General**) gal

gen [dʒen] N Br Fam renseignements mpl, tuyaux mpl (**on sth** sur qch)

▸ **gen up** VT SEP Br Fam (provide with information) (person) rencarder (**on** sur)

▸ **gen up on** VT INSEP Br Fam se rencarder sur

gender [ˈdʒendər] N **1** Gram genre m; **to agree in g.** s'accorder en genre (**with** avec) SEE GRAMMAR B5–7 **2** (sex) sexe m; **the male/female g.** le sexe masculin/féminin; **it is not a question of g.** ce n'est pas une question de sexe

▸▸**g. bias** discrimination f sexuelle; **g. reassignment** réassignation f sexuelle

gender-bender N Fam **1** (person) travesti, -ie **2** Comput commutateur m, changeur m de genre

gender-changer N Comput commutateur m, changeur m de genre

gene [dʒiːn] N Biol gène m; Fig **music's in his genes** chez lui la musique, c'est héréditaire; **it's in his genes** c'est inné, il est né comme ça
▸▸**g. pool** patrimoine m génétique; **g. therapy** thérapie f génique

genealogical [dʒiːnɪəˈlɒdʒɪk(ə)l] ADJ généalogique
▸▸**g. chart, g. tree** arbre m généalogique

genealogist [dʒiːnɪˈælədʒɪst] N généalogiste mf

genealogy [dʒiːnɪˈælədʒɪ] N généalogie f

genera [ˈdʒenərə] NPL see **genus**

general [ˈdʒen(ə)r(ə)l] ADJ **1** (paralysis, improvement etc) général, -aux; **the rain has been pretty g.** il a plu un peu partout; **the g. tone of her remarks was that …** ce qui ressortait de ses remarques, c'est que …; **he made himself a g. nuisance** il a été embêtant à tout point de vue; **I had a g. tidy-up** j'ai fait du rangement un peu partout; **g. effect** effet m d'ensemble; **a word in g. use** un mot couramment employé; **to come into g. use** se généraliser; **as a g. rule** en règle générale; **in g. terms** en termes généraux; **speaking in a g. way** d'une manière générale

2 (in titles) **inspector g.** inspecteur m général ou en chef; Hist **Estates G.** États mpl généraux

N **1 in g.** en général; **what effect will this have in g.?** quel effet général est-ce que cela va avoir?; **to argue from the g. to the particular** aller du général au particulier **2** Mil général m; (rank) général d'armée; Rel (of religious order) général

▸▸Banking **g. account manager** chargé, -ée de clientèle grand public; **g. accounts** comptabilité f générale; **G. Agreement on Tariffs and Trade** accord m général sur les tarifs douaniers et le commerce; Med **g. anaesthetic** anesthésie f générale; **G. Assembly** assemblée f générale; Com **g. business** (on agenda) questions fpl diverses; Rel **g. confession** confession f en commun; Am **g. delivery** poste f restante; **g. election** élections fpl législatives; Acct, Fin **g. expenses** frais mpl généraux; **g. hospital** centre m hospitalier; **g. knowledge** culture f générale; Law **g. lien** privilège m général; **g. manager** directeur, -trice général(e); **G. Manager, European Operations** Directeur des Opérations européennes; **g. meeting** assemblée f générale; Fin **g. obligation bond** emprunt m de collectivité locale; **g. officer** général m en chef; **g. overheads** frais d'administration générale; Com **g. partnership** société f commerciale en nom collectif; **g. practice** médecine f générale; **g. practitioner** médecin m généraliste, omnipraticien, -ienne; **the g. public** le grand public; **g. staff** état-major m, pl états-majors; **g. strike** grève f générale; **g. wholesaler** grossiste m généraliste

general-interest ADJ TV généraliste
▸▸**g. channel** chaîne f généraliste; **g. station** station f généraliste

generalissimo [dʒenərəˈlɪsɪməʊ] N Mil généralissime m

generality [dʒenəˈrælɪtɪ] N **1** (statement) **to confine oneself to generalities** s'en tenir aux généralités **2** (quality) (of remarks, opinions) caractère m général **3** Fml (majority) **the g. of mankind** la plupart des hommes

generalization [dʒen(ə)rəlaɪˈzeɪʃən] N généralisation f; **to make generalizations** généraliser

generalize [ˈdʒen(ə)rəlaɪz] VI **1** généraliser,

faire des généralisations; **I don't like generalizing, but ...** je n'aime pas faire de généralisations, mais ... **2** Med (of disease) généraliser

VT 1 (conclusion, facts etc) généraliser à partir de **2** (make widespread) (custom etc) généraliser; **to become generalized** (of practice) se généraliser

generalized ['dʒen(ə)rəlaɪzd] ADJ généralisé

generally ['dʒenrəlɪ] ADV **1** (widely) généralement; **the word is g. understood to mean ...** le mot veut généralement dire ...; **this information is not g. available** le public n'a pas accès à ces informations; **it is not g. known that ...** beaucoup de gens ignorent que ...
2 (taken overall) dans l'ensemble; **to make oneself g. useful** se rendre généralement utile; **she behaved in a g. antisocial manner** d'une manière générale, elle s'est comportée de façon antisociale
3 (as a general rule) en règle générale, généralement, en général; **g. speaking** d'une manière générale; **the roads are g. crowded at this time** en général, les routes sont très encombrées à cette heure-ci

general-purpose ADJ universel, à usages multiples

generalship ['dʒen(ə)rəlʃɪp] N Mil (skill) l'art m d'être général; **his g.** la compétence de général dont il a fait preuve

generate ['dʒenəreɪt] VT (result, electric current, heat etc) produire; (income) créer; (feeling, reaction, response) provoquer, engendrer; (interest, ideas) créer, générer; Comput créer, générer; Math engendrer; Ling générer; **tourism generated three million pounds for the region** le tourisme a rapporté trois millions de livres à la région; **environment that generates crime** environnement qui engendre la délinquance

generating ['dʒenəreɪtɪŋ] ADJ générateur, -trice
N génération f
▶▶ **g. station** centrale f électrique

generation [dʒenə'reɪʃən] N **1** (period, people, computers etc) génération f; **from g. to g.** de génération en génération, de père en fils; **for generations there had always been a doctor in the family** ils étaient médecins de père en fils; **people of my g. will remember ...** les gens de ma génération se souviendront ...; **he's my g.** il est de ma génération; **we're a different g.** nous appartenons à des générations différentes; **the younger/older g.** la jeune/l'ancienne génération; **the g. gap** l'écart m ou le fossé entre les générations VOIR GRAMMAIRE A11
2 (production) (of ideas etc) génération f, formation f, Elec, Phys etc (of heat etc) génération, production f, Math génération; Ling production, génération; Comput création f, génération

-generation SUFF second-g. immigrant immigrant de la deuxième génération; **third-g. fax machines** télécopieurs de la troisième génération

generative ['dʒenərətɪv] ADJ Ling génératif

generator ['dʒenəreɪtər] N Elec génératrice f, dynamo f; (backup device) groupe m électrogène; Comput (programme m) générateur m; Tech (of heat etc) générateur m; **tourism is a major g. of income** le tourisme est une source importante de revenus

generatrix, pl **generatrices** ['dʒenəreɪtrɪks, -ɪsiːz] N Math génératrice f

generic [dʒɪ'nerɪk] ADJ (term, noun) générique
N Mktg produit m générique
▶▶ Mktg **g. advertising** publicité f générique; Com, Mktg **g. brand** marque f géné-

rique; **g. drug** médicament m générique, générique m; **g. market** marché m générique; **g. name** Biol nom m du genre; Com, Mktg (of product, drug) nom générique; Mktg **g. product** produit générique

generically [dʒɪ'nerɪklɪ] ADV génériquement; **they are g. distinct** ils se distinguent en genre

generosity [dʒenə'rɒsɪtɪ] N (with money, gifts) générosité f, libéralité f, (of spirit) grandeur f, magnanimité f, **in a spirit of g.** (to act) par générosité; **thanks to the g. of Mr Jones** grâce à la générosité de M. Jones

generous ['dʒenərəs] ADJ (person) (with money, gifts) généreux; (remarks, comments) bienveillant; **he has a g. nature** c'est une âme généreuse; **he's a bit too g. with his advice** il n'est pas avare de conseils; **that's a g. interpretation of his motives** c'est faire preuve de bienveillance que d'interpréter ainsi ses raisons; **to be g. in victory** se montrer magnanime; **to be g. in defeat** être bon perdant; **g. mark** (for homework etc) note généreuse; **she's g. with her money** elle n'est pas avare de son argent; **a g. helping of food/measure of whisky** une portion généreuse de nourriture/un bon verre de whisky; **he took a g. helping of the stew** il s'est servi amplement de ragoût; Fam **she's built on g. lines** elle a des formes généreuses

generously ['dʒen(ə)rəslɪ] ADV (to give, donate etc) généreusement; **he g. congratulated her on her victory** bon joueur, il l'a félicité pour sa victoire; **he helped himself g. to the stew** il s'est servi amplement de ragoût; **she g. offered to help** elle a généreusement proposé son aide; **her g. proportioned figure** ses formes généreuses

genesis ['dʒenɪsɪs] N genèse f, origine f, Bible (the Book of) G. la Genèse

genetic [dʒɪ'netɪk] ADJ Biol génétique
▶▶ **g. code** code m génétique; **g. engineering** génie m génétique; **g. fingerprint** empreinte f génétique; **g. fingerprinting** analyse f de l'empreinte génétique; **g. modification** modification f génétique

genetically [dʒɪ'netɪklɪ] ADV Biol génétiquement; **g. modified** (plant, food) génétiquement modifié; **to g. alter a mouse** faire des manipulations génétiques sur une souris

geneticist [dʒɪ'netɪsɪst] N Biol généticien, -ienne

genetics [dʒɪ'netɪks] N Biol génétique f VOIR GRAMMAIRE A10

Geneva [dʒɪ'niːvə] N Genève f, **Lake G.** le lac Léman; Hist **the G. Convention** la Convention de Genève

Genghis Khan ['geŋgɪs'kɑːn] N Gengis Khan

genial ['dʒiːnɪəl] ADJ (person, tone, manner) plein de bienveillance, affable, plein de bonne humeur

Note that the French word **génial** is a false friend and is never a translation for the English word **genial**. It means **brilliant**.

geniality [dʒiːnɪ'ælɪtɪ] N bienveillance f, bonne humeur f

genially [dʒiːnɪəlɪ] ADV affablement, avec affabilité

genie, pl **genii** ['dʒiːnɪ, 'dʒiːnɪaɪ] N djinn m, génie m

genital ['dʒenɪt(ə)l] ADJ génital, -aux
NPL **genitals** organes mpl génitaux externes
▶▶ Med **g. herpes** herpès m génital

genitalia [dʒenɪ'teɪlɪə] NPL organes mpl génitaux externes

genitive ['dʒenɪtɪv] VOIR GRAMMAIRE A15–16

Gram N génitif m; **in the g.** au génitif
ADJ génitif
▶▶ **g. case** génitif m

genito-urinary [-'jʊərɪnərɪ] ADJ Med génito-urinaire

genius ['dʒiːnɪəs] N **1** (pl geniuses ['dʒiːnɪəsɪz]) (person) génie m; **she's a mathematical g.** c'est un génie en mathématiques
2 (no pl) (great talent) génie m; **man/work of g.** homme m/œuvre f de génie; **to show g.** faire preuve de génie; **that goal was pure g.** ce goal, c'était du génie pur et simple
3 (no pl) (aptitude) aptitudes fpl naturelles; **to have a g. for business** avoir le génie des affaires; **to have a g. for doing sth** avoir le don de faire qch
4 Lit (no pl) (of a nation, era) génie m
5 Lit (pl genii ['dʒiːnɪaɪ]) (spirit) (of place etc) génie m ou esprit m tutélaire; **she is his good/evil g.** c'est son bon/mauvais génie

Genoa ['dʒenəʊə] N Gênes f

genocidal [dʒenə'saɪd(ə)l] ADJ génocide

genocide ['dʒenəsaɪd] N génocide m

Genoese [dʒenəʊ'iːz] ADJ génois
N Génois, -oise

genome ['dʒiːnəʊm] N Biol génome m

genotype ['dʒenəʊtaɪp] N Biol génotype m

genre ['ʒɑːnrə] N genre m
▶▶ Cin **g. film** film m de genre; **g. painting** peinture f de genre

gent [dʒent] N Br Fam **1** monsieur m; **he's a real g.** c'est un gentleman; **gents' footwear** chaussures pour hommes **2** gents (toilets) toilettes fpl pour hommes; **where's the gents?** où sont les toilettes?

genteel [dʒen'tiːl] ADJ **1** Pej (affected) maniéré, affecté **2** (respectable) comme il faut; **g. poverty** pauvreté f digne; **g. society** la bonne société

Note that the French word **gentil** is a false friend and is never a translation for the English word **genteel**. It means **kind**.

gentian ['dʒenʃən] N (plant) gentiane f
▶▶ **g. bitter** (amer m de) gentiane; **g. blue** bleu m gentiane

Gentile ['dʒentaɪl] N Gentil
ADJ des Gentils

gentility [dʒen'tɪlɪtɪ] N **1** Pej (affectation) prétention f au bon ton **2** Old-fashioned (respectability) respectabilité f, **the g.** (people) la haute bourgeoisie; **shabby g.** la misère en habit noir

gentle ['dʒent(ə)l] ADJ (gentler, gentlest) **1** (delicate, kind) doux, f douce; (reprimand) peu sévère; (tap on shoulder etc) léger; (exercise) modéré; (slope) doux, faible; **to be g. with sb** être doux avec qn; **g. as a lamb** doux comme un agneau; **the gentle(r) sex** le sexe faible; **a g. breeze** une petite brise; **a g. giant** un bon géant **2** Old-fashioned (noble) of g. **birth** bien né

Note that the French word **gentil** is a false friend and is never a translation for the English word **gentle**. It means **kind**.

gentlefolk ['dʒent(ə)lfəʊk] NPL Old-fashioned personnes fpl de bonne famille

gentleman, pl **gentlemen** ['dʒent(ə)lmən] N **1** (well-bred man) homme m bien élevé, gentleman m; **to act or behave like a g.** se conduire en gentleman; **he's no g.** il est mal élevé; **thank you, you're a g.** merci, vous êtes un gentleman
2 (man) monsieur m, homme m; **Ladies and Gentlemen!** (to audience) mesdames et messieurs! **there's a g. to see you** il y a un monsieur qui voudrait vous parler; **this young g.'s lost** ce petit jeune homme est perdu; Old-fashioned **g. friend** (of woman)

ami *m*; **gentlemen** *(on toilet)* messieurs; **g.'s g.** valet *m* de chambre; *Hum* **g. of the road** *(tramp)* clochard *m*

  3 *(nobleman etc)* gentilhomme *m, pl* gentilshommes; **g. (of independent means)** rentier *m*; **g. in waiting** gentilhomme de service *(près du roi)*

  4 *Sport Old-fashioned* amateur *m*

  ▸▸ **g.'s agreement** gentleman's agreement *m*; **gentlemen's club** club *m* dont l'accès est réservé aux hommes

gentleman-farmer N gentleman-farmer *m, pl* gentlemen-farmers

gentlemanly ['dʒent(ə)lmənlɪ] ADJ bien élevé; **it would have been more g. to say nothing** un homme bien élevé *ou* un gentleman n'aurait rien dit

gentleness ['dʒent(ə)lnɪs] N douceur *f*

gently ['dʒentlɪ] ADV *(to handle etc)* doucement; *(to remind, imply, dissuade)* gentiment; **to speak g.** parler d'un ton doux *ou* avec douceur; **to deal g. with sb** traiter qn avec douceur; **g. (does it)!** allez-y doucement!; **the road slopes g. down to the beach** la route descend en pente douce jusqu'à la plage

gentrification [dʒentrɪfɪ'keɪʃən] N *Br* embourgeoisement *m*

gentrified ['dʒentrɪfaɪd] ADJ *Br (area, street)* qui s'est embourgeoisé

gentry ['dʒentrɪ] N *(no pl)* petite noblesse *f*; **landed g.** aristocratie *f* terrienne

genuflect ['dʒenjʊflekt] VI faire une génuflexion

genuflection, genuflexion ['dʒenjʊ-'flekʃən] N génuflexion *f*

genuine ['dʒenjʊɪn] ADJ **1** *(manuscript etc)* authentique, véritable; *Com (article)* garanti d'origine; *(champagne)* authentique; *(diamond)* véritable **2** *(sincere)* sincère, franc, *f* franche; *(belief)* sincère; *(friend)* loyal, -aux; **I think he's being g.** je crois qu'il est sincère; **she comes across as a g. person** elle donne l'impression d'être une personne sincère; **it was a g. mistake on her part** elle ne l'a pas fait exprès; *Com* **g. buyer** acheteur *m* sérieux; **a g. surprise** une véritable surprise

genuinely ['dʒenjʊɪnlɪ] ADV **1** authentiquement **2** *(to believe, be sorry etc)* sincèrement; **g. surprised** vraiment surpris

genuineness ['dʒenjʊɪnnɪs] N **1** *(of manuscript etc)* authenticité *f* **2** *(sincerity)* sincérité *f*

genus, *pl* **genera** ['dʒiːnəs, 'dʒenərə] N *Biol* genre *m*

geo- ['dʒiːəʊ] PREF géo(-)

geode ['dʒiːəʊd] N *Geol* géode *f*

geodemographic [dʒiːəʊdeməˈɡræfɪk] ADJ *Mktg* géodémographique

  ▸▸ **g. profile** profil *m* géodémographique; **g. segment** segment *m* géodémographique; **g. segmentation** segmentation *f* géodémographique

geodesic [dʒiːəʊ'diːzɪk] ADJ géodésique

  ▸▸ **g. dome** dôme *m* géodésique

geodesy [dʒɪ'ɒdɪsɪ] N géodésie *f*

geodynamics [dʒiːəʊdaɪ'næmɪks] N géodynamique *f*

geographer [dʒɪ'ɒɡrəfər] N géographe *mf*

geographic(al) [dʒɪə'ɡræfɪk, -ɪk(ə)l] ADJ géographique; **a g. survey** un relevé topographique

  ▸▸ *Mktg* **g. pricing** tarification *f* géographique

geographically [dʒɪə'ɡræfɪklɪ] ADV géographiquement

geography [dʒɪ'ɒɡrəfɪ] N géographie *f*; **I haven't quite got a grasp of the g. of the building** je ne m'oriente pas encore très bien

dans le bâtiment; **g. book** livre *m* de géographie

geologic(al) [dʒɪə'lɒdʒɪk, -ɪk(ə)l] ADJ géologique

  ▸▸ **g. survey** relevé *m* géologique

geologically [dʒɪə'lɒdʒɪklɪ] ADV géologiquement

geologist [dʒɪ'ɒlədʒɪst] N géologue *mf*

geology [dʒɪ'ɒlədʒɪ] N géologie *f*

geometer [dʒɪ'ɒmɪtər] N géomètre *mf*

geometric(al) [dʒɪə'metrɪk, -ɪk(ə)l] ADJ géométrique; **g. design** dessin *m* géométrique

  ▸▸ **g. progression** progression *f* géométrique

geometrically [dʒɪə'metrɪklɪ] ADV géométriquement

geometrician [dʒɪɒmɪ'trɪʃən] N géomètre *mf*

geometry [dʒɪ'ɒmɪtrɪ] N géométrie *f*

geomorphologic(al) [dʒiːəʊmɔː'fɒlɒdʒɪk, -ɪk(ə)l] ADJ géomorphologique

geomorphology [dʒiːəʊmɔː'fɒlədʒɪ] N géomorphologie *f*

geophysical [dʒiːəʊ'fɪzɪk(ə)l] ADJ géophysique

geophysicist [dʒiːəʊ'fɪzɪsɪst] N géophysicien, -ienne

geophysics [dʒiːəʊ'fɪzɪks] N géophysique *f* VOIR GRAMMAIRE A10

geopolitics [dʒiːəʊ'pɒlɪtɪks] N géopolitique *f* VOIR GRAMMAIRE A10

Geordie ['dʒɔːdɪ] *Br Fam* N *(resident)* habitant, -ante de Newcastle-upon-Tyne ou de sa région; *(by birth)* originaire *mf* de Newcastle-upon-Tyne ou de sa région; *(dialect)* dialecte *m* parlé dans la région de Newcastle-upon-Tyne

  ADJ *(dialect etc)* de Newcastle-upon-Tyne

George [dʒɔːdʒ] N **1** *Old-fashioned Fam* **by G.!** sapristi! **2** *Aviat Fam (automatic pilot)* George *m*

  ▸▸ **G. Cross** = décoration *f* britannique décernée aux civils pour des actes de bravoure; **G. Medal** = décoration britannique décernée aux civils ou aux militaires pour des actes de bravoure

georgette [dʒɔː'dʒet] N *Tex* crêpe *m* georgette

Georgia ['dʒɔːdʒɪə] N Géorgie *f*

Georgian[1] ['dʒɔːdʒɪən] ADJ *Br Hist* **1** du règne des quatre rois George; **a G. house** une maison datant de l'époque 1720-1830 **2** *(of George V)* du règne de George V

Georgian[2] *Geog* ADJ géorgien

  N Géorgien, -ienne

geoscience [dʒiːə'saɪəns] N sciences *fpl* de la terre

geosphere ['dʒiːəʊsfɪər] N géosphère *f*

geostationary [dʒiːəʊ'steɪʃənərɪ] ADJ géostationnaire

  ▸▸ **g. orbit** orbite *f* géostationnaire; **g. satellite** satellite *m* géostationnaire

geothermal [dʒiːəʊ'θɜːməl] ADJ géothermique

geotropism [dʒɪ'ɒtrəpɪz(ə)m] N géotropisme *m*

geranium [dʒə'reɪnɪəm] N **1** *(plant)* géranium *m* **2** *(colour)* vermeil *m*

  ▸▸ **g. red** vermeil

gerbil ['dʒɜːbɪl] N gerbille *f*

geriatric [dʒerɪ'ætrɪk] *Med* N malade *mf* gériatrique; *Pej (old person)* vieux croulant *m*, vieille croulante *f*

  ADJ gériatrique

  ▸▸ **g. medicine** gériatrie *f*; **g. ward** service *m* de gériatrie

geriatrician [dʒerɪə'trɪʃən] N gériatre *mf*

geriatrics [dʒerɪ'ætrɪks] N SING *Med* gériatrie *f* VOIR GRAMMAIRE A10

germ [dʒɜːm] N **1** *Med (of disease)* germe *m*, microbe *m*; **I don't want your germs!** je ne veux pas de tes microbes! **2** *Biol (of organism)* germe *m*; *Fig* **the g. of an idea** le germe d'une idée

  ▸▸ **g. cell** cellule *f* germinale *ou* reproductrice; **g. warfare** guerre *f* bactériologique

German ['dʒɜːmən] ADJ allemand; *Formerly* **West/East G.** ouest-/est-allemand

  N **1** Allemand, -ande; *Formerly* **West/East G.** Allemand de l'Ouest/de l'Est **2** *Ling* allemand *m*; **High/Low G.** haut/bas allemand

  ▸▸ *Formerly* **G. Democratic Republic** République *f* démocratique Allemande; *Med* **G. measles** rubéole *f*; *esp Am* **G. shepherd** *(dog)* berger *m* allemand

germander [dʒɜː'mændər] N *(plant)* germandrée *f*

germane [dʒɜː'meɪn] ADJ *Fml* se rapportant (**to** à)

germanic [dʒɜː'mænɪk] ADJ germanique

Germanist ['dʒɜːmənɪst] N *Ling* germaniste *mf*

Germanize ['dʒɜːmənaɪz] VT germaniser

Germany ['dʒɜːmənɪ] N Allemagne *f*; *Hist* **West/East G.** l'Allemagne de l'Ouest/de l'Est; **the two Germanies** les deux Allemagnes

germ-free ADJ *(environment)* stérile

germicidal [dʒɜːmɪ'saɪd(ə)l] ADJ germicide

germicide ['dʒɜːmɪsaɪd] N germicide *m*

germinate ['dʒɜːmɪneɪt] VI *(of seed)*, *Fig (of idea)* germer

  VT *(seeds)* faire germer

germination [dʒɜːmɪ'neɪʃən] N germination *f*

gerontocracy [dʒerɒn'tɒkrəsɪ] N gérontocratie *f*

gerontologist [dʒerɒn'tɒlədʒɪst] N gérontologue *mf*

gerontology [dʒerɒn'tɒlədʒɪ] N gérontologie *f*

gerrymander ['dʒerɪmændər] *Pol* VT & VI **to g. (constituencies)** faire du tripatouillage électoral

  N tripatouillage *m* électoral

gerrymandering [dʒerɪ'mændərɪŋ] N *Pol* tripatouillage *m* électoral

gerund ['dʒerənd] N *Gram* gérondif *m*, nom *m* verbal; **in the g.** au gérondif VOIR GRAMMAIRE A43–4

gerundive [dʒɪ'rʌndɪv] *Gram* ADJ du gérondif

  N adjectif *m* verbal

gesso ['dʒesəʊ] N *Art (coating) (for frescos)* enduit *m* de plâtre; *(substance)* plâtre *m* de Paris, gypse *m*

gestalt [gə'ʃtælt] N *Psy* gestalt *f*

  ▸▸ **g. therapist** gestalt thérapeute *mf*; **g. therapy** gestalt-thérapie *f*

Gestapo [gəs'tɑːpəʊ] N Gestapo *f*

gestate [dʒes'teɪt] VI être en gestation

gestation [dʒes'teɪʃən] N *Physiol, Fig* gestation *f*

  ▸▸ **g. period** période *f* de gestation

gesticulate [dʒes'tɪkjʊleɪt] VI gesticuler

gesticulation [dʒestɪkjʊ'leɪʃən] N gesticulation *f*

gesture ['dʒestʃər] N geste *m*; **to make a g.** faire un geste; **with a sweeping g.** d'un geste large; **g. of defiance** geste de défi; *Fig* **as a g. of friendship** en témoignage d'amitié; **a g. towards peace** un geste indiquant une volonté de paix

  VI faire des gestes; **she gestured to them to be silent** elle leur a fait signe de se taire

  VT exprimer par gestes; **he gestured us over** il nous a fait signe d'approcher

GET [get] (*pt* **got** [gɒt], *pp* **got**, *Arch, Am also* **gotten** ['gɒt(ə)n], *prp* **getting**['getɪŋ])

| **VT** obtenir **1** ▪ acheter **1** ▪ prendre **1**, **4** ▪ recevoir **2** ▪ gagner **2** ▪ avoir **2, 3**, **17** ▪ attraper **4** ▪ atteindre **5** ▪ comprendre **8** ▪ aller chercher **10** ▪ préparer **11** ▪ faire faire **12, 14–16** |
| **VI** aller **1** ▪ devenir **4** |

vt 1 (*obtain*) obtenir; **to g. sth for sb** procurer qch à qn; (*buy*) acheter qch pour qn; **where did you g. that?** où avez-vous trouvé/acheté cela?; **where can we g. some information?** où est-ce que nous pouvons obtenir des informations?; **to g. something to eat** (*find*) trouver de quoi manger; (*eat in restaurant etc*) manger quelque chose; **we g. our eggs from the farm next door** nous achetons nos œufs à la ferme d'à-côté; **I got this car cheap** j'ai eu *ou* j'ai acheté cette voiture à un bon prix; **if you're going to buy shoes, g. good ones** si tu achètes des chaussures, prends-en de bonnes; **to g. a job** trouver un travail; **I haven't got the right answer** je n'ai pas trouvé la solution; **to g. sb's permission to do sth** obtenir la permission de qn de faire qch; **to g. one's own way** faire valoir sa volonté; **I'll do it if I g. the time/a moment** je le ferai si j'ai le temps/si je trouve un moment; **I've got six more to g.** (*in collection*) il m'en manque six; **you g. a fine view from here** il y a une vue magnifique d'ici; **you g. a lot of people marrying young here** il y a beaucoup de gens qui se marient jeunes par ici; **we don't g. many accidents here** nous n'avons pas beaucoup d'accidents par ici; **I finally got her on her own** *or* **alone** j'ai fini par réussir à la voir en tête à tête; **you need to g. (yourself) a good lawyer** il te faut un bon avocat

2 (*receive*) (*present, medal etc*) recevoir; (*prize*) gagner, remporter; **what did you g. for your birthday?** qu'est-ce que tu as eu pour ton anniversaire?; **I got your letter last week** j'ai eu *ou* reçu ta lettre la semaine dernière; **I didn't g. a reply** je n'ai pas eu de réponse; **room that gets no sun** pièce où le soleil ne donne pas; **we g. quite a lot of rain in summer** il pleut beaucoup en été; **he gets his shyness from his mother** il tient sa timidité de sa mère; **I got the idea from a book** j'ai trouvé l'idée dans un livre; **I need all the advice I can g.** j'ai besoin de tous les conseils qu'on peut me donner; **to g. ten years** prendre dix ans de prison; **to g. £15,000 a year** gagner 15 000 livres par an; **to g. 10% interest** recevoir 10% d'intérêt; **to g. a good price for sth** obtenir un bon prix pour qch; **what did you g. for your car?** combien est-ce que tu as vendu ta voiture?; **she got very little from her lessons** elle a tiré peu appris de ses leçons

3 *Radio, TV* **we can't g. Moscow/Channel 4** nous ne pouvons pas avoir Moscou/Channel 4; **we can only g. three channels here** nous ne pouvons recevoir que trois chaînes ici; **we g. the Guardian** (*newspaper*) nous achetons le Guardian; *Tel* **I had a job getting you** j'ai eu du mal à vous joindre; *Tel* **I couldn't g. her at the office** je n'ai pas pu l'avoir au bureau; *Tel* **g. me Washington 330 330** (*to operator*) appelez-moi Washington 330 330; **could you g. the phone/the door?** (*answer*) est-ce que tu peux décrocher?/ouvrir la porte?

4 (*catch*) prendre, attraper; (*train, bus*) prendre; (*cold, illness*) attraper; (*note down, record*) noter; *Fam* **we'll g. them yet!** on les aura!; **I'll g. you for that** je te revaudrai ça; **you've got me this time** (*caught me*) cette fois-ci vous m'avez eu; (*I don't know the answer*) je donne ma langue au chat; **the piranhas got him in the end** les piranhas ont fini par l'avoir

5 (*hit*) (*with fist, foot*) atteindre; (*with bullet, arrow, stone etc*) toucher; **he got a bullet in his shoulder** il a reçu une balle dans l'épaule

6 *Fam* (*move emotionally*) émouvoir; **the play didn't really g. me** la pièce ne m'a pas fait grand-chose

7 *Fam* (*annoy*) mettre en boule; **that gets me** *or* **gets my goat** ça me met en boule; **what gets me is that …** ce qui me met en boule, c'est que …

8 *Fam* (*understand*) comprendre; **I don't g. your meaning** je ne vous comprends pas; **if you g. my meaning** si tu vois ce que je veux dire; **g. me?** tu y es?, tu piges?; **oh, I g. you!** ah! j'ai pigé!; **I don't g. it** je ne comprends pas; **to g. a joke** comprendre une blague; **g. it?** (*do you understand the joke?*) tu piges?

9 *Sl* (*consider*) **g. a load of this!** (*listen*) écoute un peu ça!; **g. him!** (*he looks outrageous*) regarde-le, celui-là!; (*he made an outrageous remark*) écoute-le, celui-là!; **g. him, riding around in a Rolls when he's on the dole!** tu te rends compte, il roule en Rolls alors qu'il touche le chômage!

10 (*fetch*) aller chercher; **he went and got a book from the library** il est allé chercher un livre à la bibliothèque; **go and g. a doctor** allez chercher un médecin; **g. me the big screwdriver** allez me chercher le gros tournevis; **can I g. you anything?** (*to sb ill etc*) est-ce vous avez besoin de quelque chose?; **g. him a chair, someone** est-ce quelqu'un peut lui apporter une chaise?

11 (*prepare*) faire, préparer; **can I g. you an omelette?** est-ce que je peux vous faire une omelette?; **she got herself some breakfast** elle s'est préparé un petit déjeuner; **to g. lunch (ready)** préparer le déjeuner

12 (*move, send*) faire parvenir, faire transporter; **you'll never g. that box through the door** tu n'arriveras jamais à faire passer cette boîte par la porte; **they got her to the airport on time** ils l'ont amenée à l'aéroport à l'heure; **I got a message to them** je leur ai fait parvenir un message; **how can I g. it to you?** comment puis-je vous le faire parvenir?; **how am I to g. this parcel home?** (*by myself*) comment vais-je faire pour transporter ce paquet jusqu'à chez moi?; **to g. the children to bed** coucher les enfants, mettre les enfants au lit; *Fig* **where has all this got us?** (*our hard work, arguing*) où est-ce que tout ça nous a menés?; **this is getting us nowhere** (*of method, argument*) ça ne nous mène nulle part, ça ne nous mène à rien; **to g. sb on(to) a subject** amener qn à parler sur un sujet

13 (*cause to be*) **to g. sth dry/wet** sécher/mouiller qch; **to g. sth clean/dirty** nettoyer/salir qch; **to g. sb angry** mettre qn en colère; **to g. sb nervous** rendre qn nerveux; **I got myself terribly agitated** je me suis rendu malade; **they've got me so I don't know whether I'm coming or going** c'en est à un tel point que je ne sais plus où j'en suis; **I couldn't g. the drawer open** je n'arrivais pas à ouvrir le tiroir; **to g. the answer right** trouver la bonne réponse; **I got his name wrong** j'ai fait erreur sur son nom; **you've got him worried** tu l'as fait s'inquiéter; **to g. people interested (in sth)** intéresser les gens (à qch)

14 (*with pp or inf or prp*) (*cause*) **to g. sth done by sb, to g. sb to do sth** faire faire qch à *ou* par qn; **to g. sth mended** faire réparer qch; **to g. oneself noticed** se faire remarquer; **g. him to read it** faites-le-lui lire; **to g. sb to agree** décider qn à consentir; **you'll never g. him to admit to it** tu ne le lui feras jamais admettre; **we must g. him to come and see us** il faut le persuader de venir nous voir; **I can't g. the door to shut** je n'arrive pas à fermer la porte; **to g. one's work finished** venir à bout de son travail; **to g. one's dress**

torn déchirer sa robe; **to g. sb doing sth** faire faire qch à qn; **if you want to g. him going …** (*angry*) si tu veux le mettre en colère …; (*cause him to talk a lot*) si tu veux le faire parler …; **once he gets going, there's no stopping him** quand il commence, il n'y a plus moyen de l'arrêter; *Aut* **to g. the engine running** mettre le moteur en marche; **that got him guessing** ça l'a intrigué **VOIR GRAMMAIRE A56–7**

15 (*do eventually*) **to g. to do sth** finir par faire qch; **you'll g. to like him** vous finirez par l'aimer; **to g. to know sth** apprendre qch; **when you g. to know him** quand on le connaît mieux; **they got to be friends** ils sont devenus amis; **she got to be very rich** elle est devenue très riche

16 (*have opportunity to do*) **to g. to do sth** avoir l'occasion de faire qch; **as a diplomat she got to visit many countries** en tant que diplomate elle a pu visiter *ou* a eu l'occasion de visiter de nombreux pays; **I didn't g. to speak to him in person** je n'ai pas pu lui parler en personne; **I finally got to see the Taj Mahal** j'ai finalement réussi à voir le Taj Mahal

17 (*have*) **to have got** avoir; **have you got any children?** avez-vous des enfants?; **I haven't got any** je n'en ai pas; **have you got a light?** avez-vous du feu?; **what have you got there?** qu'avez-vous là?; **she's (really) got something** elle a (vraiment) quelque chose; **it's got something** (*of play, poem, song etc*) il y a quelque chose là-dedans; **he's got measles** il a la rougeole; **what's that got to do with it?** qu'est-ce que cela a à voir?; *Fam* **you've got it!** vous y êtes!, c'est ça! **VOIR GRAMMAIRE A56**

18 (*must*) **to have got to do sth** être obligé de *ou* devoir faire qch; **it has got to be done** il faut que cela soit fait; **have you really got to work on Sundays?** est-ce que vous êtes vraiment obligé de travailler le dimanche?; **but that's got to be the right answer!** c'est forcément la bonne réponse! **VOIR GRAMMAIRE A60**

vi 1 (*reach, make one's way*) arriver, se rendre (**to** à); **how does one g. there?** comment fait-on pour y aller?; **when I got home** quand je suis arrivé à la maison; **how do I g. to the station?** (*asking one's way*) où se trouve la gare?; **to g. there** (*reach a place*) arriver; (*reach a goal*) y arriver, réussir; **we're not getting anywhere, we're getting nowhere** nous n'aboutissons à rien, nous n'arrivons à rien, nous n'allons nulle part; **to g. to the top of a tree/ladder** monter jusqu'en haut d'un arbre/d'une échelle; **where has he got to?** où est-ce qu'il est passé?; **where have you got to?** (*in your work etc*) où en êtes-vous?; **she got to the door and turned round** elle est allée jusqu'à la porte et s'est retournée; **to g. to one's feet** se lever; **to g. to university** aller à l'université; **they only got as far as Marseilles** ils ne sont pas allés plus loin que Marseille; **he got as far as saying …** il a été jusqu'à dire …; **we got onto (the subject of) divorce** nous en sommes venus à parler de divorce; **it got to the point where they weren't speaking to one another** c'en est venu au point qu'ils ne se parlaient plus; **eventually we got to talking about politics** nous avons fini par en venir à parler de politique; *Sl* **it really gets to me** (*annoys me*) ça me met hors de moi; (*thrills me*) ça me fait quelque chose

2 (*move*) **to g. behind a tree** se mettre derrière un arbre; **she got inside the barrel** elle est rentrée dans le tonneau

3 **to g. to work** (*start working*) se mettre au travail; (*reach workplace*) arriver à son (lieu de) travail

4 (*with adj complement*) (*become*) devenir; **to g. old** devenir vieux, vieillir; **I'm getting**

used to it je commence à m'y habituer; **to g. angry** se mettre en colère; **to g. better** *(improve)* s'améliorer; *(after illness)* se remettre

5 *(with pp)* **to g. dressed** s'habiller; **to g. married** se marier; **to g. shaved** *(by self)* se raser; *(by barber)* se faire raser; **to g. killed** se faire tuer; **to g. drowned** se noyer; **to g. caught** *(by police etc)* se faire prendre; *(by rain etc)* être surpris; **he got sacked** il s'est fait renvoyer; **to g. started** commencer **VOIR** **GRAMMAIRE A54-5**

6 *(with prp)* *(start)* **to g. going** *(leave)* partir, se mettre en route; *(start work)* se mettre au travail; *(hurry)* se dépêcher; **let's g. going** allons-y!; **to g. talking with sb** entrer en conversation avec qn

▶ **get about VI 1** *(move around)* circuler; **he gets about a great deal** il se déplace beaucoup; **she can't g. about very easily** *(of invalid)* elle se déplace difficilement; **I don't g. about so much these days** *(of old person)* je ne sors plus tellement ces temps-ci

2 *(of news etc)* se répandre, circuler; **it got about that she was planning to resign** le bruit s'est répandu qu'elle projetait de démissionner

▶ **get across VI 1** *(succeed in crossing)* traverser

2 *(communicate)* communiquer; **she can't g. across to her audience** elle ne peut pas communiquer avec son public; **our message is not getting across** notre message ne passe pas; *Theat* **the play didn't g. across to the audience** la pièce n'a pas passé la rampe

VT SEP 1 *(over water, over street)* *(person)* faire traverser; **we couldn't g. the supplies across** *(across the river)* nous ne pouvions pas faire passer les vivres de l'autre côté; **it was easy to g. the people across** *(across the border)* il était facile de faire passer les gens

2 *Fam (communicate)* **I couldn't g. it across to him** je n'ai pas réussi à le lui faire comprendre; **we're not getting our message across** notre message ne passe pas

▶ **get ahead VI 1** *(make progress)* avancer; **you'll never g. ahead unless you work hard** tu n'arriveras à rien si tu ne travailles pas dur

2 *(move in front)* prendre la tête

▶ **get along VI 1** *(leave)* s'en aller, partir; **it's time for me to be getting along, it's time I was getting along** il est temps que je parte; *Fam* **g. along with you!** *(go away)* allez-vous-en!; *(that's silly, not true)* allons donc!, vous plaisantez!

2 *(progress)* **how are you getting along in your new job?** comment ça va, ton nouveau travail?; **how are you getting along in the new house?** comment ça va, dans la nouvelle maison?; **we've got along all right without their help/them** nous nous sommes bien débrouillés sans leur aide/eux

3 *(be on good terms)* *(bien)* s'entendre *(with* avec*)*; **I wish I got along better with my neighbours** j'aimerais bien m'entendre mieux avec mes voisins

▶ **get around VI 1** *(be active)* bouger; *(gain experience)* rouler sa bosse; **old people find it hard to g. around** les personnes âgées ont du mal à se déplacer; **she gets around a great deal** *(travels)* elle voyage beaucoup; **you g. around, don't you!** tu sors beaucoup, hein!

2 *(spread)* se répandre; **the word got around that he had some information** on a raconté qu'il avait des informations

VT INSEP *(avoid, circumvent)* *(difficulties)* couper à, échapper à; **there's no getting around it, we'll have to tell her** il n'y a pas d'autre moyen, il va falloir que nous le lui disions; **there's no getting around the fact that he lied to us** il reste qu'il nous a menti

▶ **get around to VT INSEP to g. around to doing sth** trouver le temps de faire qch; **I'll g.**

around to it one day je trouverai le temps de le faire un de ces jours; **could you g. around to telling me why you're here?** est-ce que tu pourrais enfin me dire pourquoi tu es ici?

▶ **get at VT INSEP 1** *(reach, have access to)* *(place, person)* atteindre; **the study is locked and I can't g. at my books** le bureau est fermé à clef et je ne peux pas accéder à mes livres; **it's on the top shelf where the children can't g. at it** c'est sur l'étagère du haut où les enfants ne peuvent pas l'atteindre; **to g. at the truth** découvrir la vérité; *Fam* **just let me g. at him!** si jamais il me tombe sous la main!

2 *(imply)* **what are you getting at?** où voulez-vous en venir?

3 *Fam (suborn)* *(witness)* suborner

4 *Fam (criticize unfairly)* *(person)* attaquer; **she's always getting at her husband** elle est toujours à dénigrer son mari; **you're not being got at, no one's getting at you** on ne s'en prend pas à toi, personne ne s'en prend à toi

▶ **get away VI** *(leave)* partir; *(escape)* s'échapper, se sauver; **to g. away for a few days** s'absenter pendant quelques jours; **g. away!** allez-vous-en!; *Fam* **g. away (with you)!** *(stop joking)* tu plaisantes!, ça ne prend pas!; **car that gets away quickly** voiture qui a une bonne reprise

VT SEP *(remove)* *(person)* emmener; *(object)* s'emparer de

▶ **get away from VT INSEP** *(leave, escape from)* *(place)* quitter; **to g. away early from the office** quitter le bureau de bonne heure; **I couldn't g. away from him** *(he wouldn't stop talking)* je ne pouvais pas m'en défaire; **how wonderful to g. away from it all!** quel plaisir de tout quitter!; *Fig* **there's no getting away from it** il faut bien l'admettre

VT SEP *(remove from)* **g. that child away from the road!** éloignez cet enfant de la route!; **g. me away from here!** fais-moi sortir d'ici!; **g. your dog away from my garden!** faites sortir votre chien de mon jardin!; **they managed to g. him away from the TV** ils ont fini par l'arracher de devant la télévision; **to g. sth away from sb** prendre qch à qn

▶ **get away with VT INSEP 1** *(escape with)* **the burglars got away with £10,000** les cambrioleurs sont repartis avec *ou* ont raflé 10,000 livres

2 *(be let off with)* s'en tirer avec; **he got away with a small fine** il s'en est tiré avec une petite amende

3 *(not be punished for)* **that child gets away with murder** on laisse tout faire à ce gamin; **children who play truant mustn't be allowed to g. away with it** les enfants qui font l'école buissonnière doivent être punis; **she pretended she was a doctor and she got away with it** elle a fait semblant d'être médecin et ça a marché; **her skirt is really short but she gets away with it** sa jupe est vraiment très courte mais elle peut se le permettre

▶ **get back VI 1** *(return)* revenir, retourner; **when did you g. back?** quand est-ce que tu es rentré?; **I got back from Italy yesterday** je suis rentré d'Italie hier; **to g. back home** rentrer chez soi; **to g. back into bed** se recoucher

2 *(move away, step back)* reculer *(from* de*)*; **g. back or I'll shoot!** reculez ou je tire!

VT SEP 1 *(recover)* *(something)* récupérer; *(one's strength)* reprendre; **I'll g. the book back from her tomorrow** je lui demanderai de rendre le livre demain; **to g. one's money back** *(loan returned)* récupérer son argent; *(reimbursed)* se faire rembourser

2 *(return)* *(something)* rendre; **g. the file back to me as soon as possible** *(in person)* rendez-moi le dossier dès que possible; *(by*

post etc) faites en sorte que je récupère le dossier dès que possible

3 *(put back)* *(something)* remettre; **to g. sth back into its box** faire rentrer qch dans sa boîte

▶ **get back at VT INSEP** *(have revenge on)* se venger de

▶ **get back to VT INSEP 1** *(return to)* retourner à; **to g. back to London** rentrer à Londres; **to g. back to work** *(after illness)* reprendre le travail; *(after short break)* se remettre au travail; **to g. back to nature** retourner à la nature

2 *(contact again)* recontacter; **can we g. back to you on that later?** est-ce que nous pouvons vous donner une réponse à ce sujet plus tard?

▶ **get behind VI** *(become delayed)* prendre du retard; **to g. behind with** *or* **in one's work** prendre du retard dans son travail; **to g. behind with the rent** être en retard pour payer son loyer

VT INSEP 1 *(move to the back of)* se mettre derrière; **g. behind that tree** mets-toi derrière cet arbre

2 *esp Am Fam (support, sympathize with)* appuyer

▶ **get by VI 1** *(pass)* passer

2 *Fam (manage)* se débrouiller; **we just g. by** on s'en tire, sans plus; **he thinks he'll g. by without studying** il croit qu'il va s'en tirer sans étudier; **you can g. by on a few dollars a day** vous pouvez vous en tirer avec quelques dollars par jour

VT INSEP 1 *(move past)* **can you g. by the washing machine?** est-ce que vous avez assez de place pour passer à côté de la machine à laver?

2 *(escape attention of)* *(censor, editor)* échapper à

▶ **get down VI 1** *(from wall, tree etc)* descendre *(from, off* de*)*

2 *(lower one's body)* **g. down or she'll see us!** baisse-toi sinon elle va nous voir!; **to g. down on one's knees** se mettre à genoux; **g. down!** *(to dog)* couché!

3 *(leave table)* quitter la table, sortir de table; **may I g. down?** est-ce que je peux quitter la table?

VT SEP 1 *(bring, fetch down)* *(book from shelf etc)* descendre

2 *(reduce)* *(temperature, inflation etc)* faire baisser; **to g. one's weight down** perdre du poids

3 *(make a note of)* noter *(in writing, on paper* par écrit*)*

4 *(depress)* déprimer; **this rain is getting me down** cette pluie me déprime

5 *(swallow)* avaler; **try and g. this down (you)** essaye d'avaler ça

▶ **get down to VT INSEP** *(tackle)* se mettre à; **to g. down to work** se mettre au travail; **to g. down to doing sth** se mettre à faire qch; **we'd better g. down to the facts** il faut en venir aux faits; **we eventually got down to details** nous avons fini par arriver aux détails; **when you g. down to it, there's very little difference between them** en fin de compte, il y a très peu de différence entre eux

▶ **get in VI 1** *(gain entrance)* entrer; **how did the thieves g. in?** comment est-ce que les voleurs sont entrés?; **water had got in everywhere** l'eau avait pénétré partout

2 *(arrive)* *(of train etc)* arriver; **when does the London train g. in?** à quelle heure est-ce que le train de Londres arrive?; **we got in at about eleven** *(home)* nous sommes rentrés (chez nous) vers onze heures

3 *Pol (be elected)* être élu; **the Conservatives didn't g. in** les conservateurs n'ont pas été élus

VT INSEP *(enter)* **g. in the car!** monte dans la voiture!; **the smoke got in our eyes** la fumée nous est venue dans les yeux

VT SEP 1 (summon) (doctor, police etc) faire venir

2 (bring in, bring inside) (washing, harvest etc) rentrer; (dog) faire rentrer; **shouldn't Jack be in on this meeting? – of course, could you g. him in?** on n'a pas besoin de Jack pour cette réunion? – si, bien sûr, tu peux lui demander de venir?

3 (plant in the ground) planter, mettre en terre

4 (manage to do) réussir à faire; **she got in some last-minute revision before the exam** elle a réussi à faire des révisions de dernière minute avant l'examen; **I'd like to g. in some golf over the weekend** j'aimerais trouver le temps de faire un peu de golf ce week-end

5 (insert) faire pénétrer; **I couldn't g. a word in** je n'ai pas pu placer un mot, je n'ai pas pu en placer une

6 (stock up with) (food, coal etc) faire provision de; **to g. coal in for the winter** faire une provision de ou faire rentrer du charbon pour l'hiver; **to g. in a round of drinks** (in pub) payer une tournée; **I'll g. the pints in** je m'occupe des bières

7 (assure of admission) permettre d'entrer; **a press card should g. you in** une carte de presse devrait vous permettre d'entrer; **these exam results will g. you in** (to university) les notes que vous avez obtenues à l'examen vous permettront d'être admis

8 (ensure election of) (person, party) assurer l'élection de; **her reputation for integrity got her in** sa réputation d'intégrité a assuré son élection

▸ **get into VT INSEP 1** (gain entrance to) (house etc) entrer dans; (car, train etc) monter dans; **to g. into Parliament** être élu député; **to g. into university** entrer à la faculté

2 (put on) (clothes) mettre, enfiler; (overcoat etc) mettre, enfiler, endosser; **I can't g. into this dress any more** je n'entre plus dans cette robe

3 (affect) **I don't know what's got into her** je ne sais pas ce qu'elle a ou ce qui lui prend

4 (become involved in) **to g. into (a) conversation** entamer une conversation; **to g. into a fight** se bagarrer; **to g. into trouble** s'attirer des ennuis; **I got into trouble at school today** je me suis fait disputer à l'école aujourd'hui; **to g. into debt** s'endetter

5 to g. into the way of doing sth prendre l'habitude de faire qch; **the system may seem difficult but you'll soon g. into it** le système peut sembler difficile mais tu t'y feras vite

6 Fam (become interested in) (music etc) commencer à s'intéresser à; **it's a hard book to g. into** c'est un livre dans lequel il est difficile de rentrer

7 (phrases) **to g. into a panic** être pris de panique; **to g. into a rage** se mettre en rage; **to g. into a bad habit** acquérir ou prendre une mauvaise habitude

VT SEP 1 (insert into) **to g. sth into sth** (faire) (r)entrer qch dans qch; **to g. the key into the lock** mettre ou introduire la clef dans la serrure; **to g. an article into a paper** faire accepter un article par un journal; **to g. an idea into one's head** se mettre une idée en tête; **when are you going to g. it into your thick head that that isn't how things work?** quand est-ce que tu te mettras dans la tête que les choses ne se passent pas comme ça?

2 you got me into this mess tu m'as mis dans ce pétrin; **to g. sb into a rage** mettre quelqu'un en rage; **to g. sb into a good mood** mettre qn de bonne humeur; Fam **he got me into jazz** c'est lui qui m'a fait connaître le jazz

▸ **get in with VT INSEP 1** (ingratiate oneself with) s'insinuer dans les bonnes grâces de, se mettre bien avec; **if you want to g. in**

with him … si tu veux te mettre bien avec lui …

2 (associate with) (person, group etc) fréquenter; **he has got in with …** il fréquente …; **she got in with the wrong crowd at school** elle avait de mauvaises fréquentations à l'école

▸ **get off VI 1** (descend from vehicle) descendre; Fig **I told him where to g. off** (rebuked him) je lui ai dit ses quatre vérités

2 (let go of sth) lâcher; **hey! g. off! that's my book!** hé! laisse ça! c'est mon livre!

3 (go unpunished) s'en tirer; **to g. off lightly** s'en tirer à bon compte

4 (leave, especially referring to work) quitter, sortir; **I'd like to g. off early tomorrow** j'aimerais bien quitter (le travail) tôt ou sortir tôt (du travail) demain

5 to g. off (to sleep) s'endormir

6 to g. off to a late start commencer avec du retard; **to g. off to a good/bad start** bien/mal commencer

VT INSEP 1 (descend from) descendre de; **to g. off a bike** descendre d'une bicyclette; **g. off that wall!** descends de ce mur!; **g. off the grass!** ne marche pas sur la pelouse!

2 (let go of) **g. off me!** laisse-moi tranquille!, lâche-moi!

3 (be exempted from) couper à, échapper à; **he managed to g. off military service** il s'est débrouillé pour couper au service militaire

VT SEP 1 (remove) (lid etc) enlever; (stain) faire partir; **g. your feet off the table!** enlève tes pieds de sur la table!; **g. your hands off me/that cake** ne me touche pas/ne touche pas ce gâteau; **we got his clothes off** nous lui avons enlevé ses vêtements; Fig **to g. sth off one's chest** vider son sac

2 (send) (letter) expédier, envoyer; **to g. the children off to bed** envoyer les enfants au lit; **to g. a baby off (to sleep)** endormir un bébé; Naut **to g. a ship off** (from sandbank etc) renflouer un bateau, remettre un bateau à flot

3 (save from punishment) **to g. sb off** tirer qn d'affaire; Law (person standing trial) faire acquitter qn

4 (have as holiday) **to g. a day/week off** prendre un jour/une semaine de congé; **can you g. tomorrow afternoon/next week off?** est-ce que tu peux prendre un congé demain après-midi/la semaine prochaine?

5 Fam (obtain) **to g. sth off sb** obtenir qch de qn; **I got this story off the woman next door** je tiens cette histoire de la voisine; **I got this cold off the woman next door** la voisine m'a passé son rhume

6 (free from) **to g. sb off doing sth** dispenser qn de faire qch; **those burns got him off work** ces brûlures l'ont dispensé d'aller travailler

7 that got the meeting off to a late start la réunion a commencé en retard à cause de ça

▸ **get off on VT INSEP** Fam prendre son pied avec

▸ **get off with VT INSEP 1** (a fine etc) s'en tirer avec; **he got off with it for years before the police caught him** on l'a laissé tranquille pendant des années avant que la police ne l'arrête

2 Br Fam **to g. off with sb** (have sex with) coucher avec qn; **did you g. off with anybody at the party?** (meet anybody) tu as rencontré quelqu'un d'intéressant à la soirée?; **to g. off with each other** (kiss etc) se peloter

▸ **get on VI 1** (board) monter

2 (succeed, progress) réussir, progresser; **to g. on in life** or **in the world** arriver dans la vie

3 (continue with work, journey) continuer; **right, let's g. on, shall we?** bien, si on continuait?

4 (cope, manage) **how are you getting on?** (how are you) comment ça va?; (at work)

comment va votre travail?; **how did you g. on?** (in exam, at dentist's) comment ça s'est passé?; **I was getting on perfectly well without you** je me débrouillais très bien sans vous; **I'll let you know how he's getting on** je vous donnerai de ses nouvelles

5 (have good relationship) s'entendre; **to g. on well/badly with sb** bien/mal s'entendre avec qn

6 (become late) se faire tard; **time's getting on** l'heure tourne

7 (age) **to be getting on (in years)** se faire vieux

VT SEP (put on) (clothing) mettre, enfiler; **I can't g. these trousers on any more** je n'entre plus dans ce pantalon; **she's just getting her coat on** elle est en train de mettre ou d'enfiler son manteau; **I can't g. the lid on** je n'arrive pas à mettre le couvercle

VT INSEP 1 (board, enter) (bus, train, plane etc) monter dans

2 (climb onto) (chair, ladder) monter sur; (with some effort) grimper sur

3 how did these papers g. on my desk? comment est-ce que ces papiers se sont retrouvés ou se sont arrivés sur mon bureau?

▸ **get on at VT INSEP** harceler; **he keeps getting on at me to have my hair cut** il est toujours après moi pour que je me fasse couper les cheveux; **you'll have to really g. on at her if you want her to do something** il va falloir que tu sois toujours derrière elle si tu veux qu'elle fasse quelque chose

▸ **get on for VT INSEP** (approach) **he must be getting on for forty** il doit approcher de ou friser la quarantaine; **it's getting on for midnight** il est presque minuit; **there were getting on for 200 people at the wedding** il y avait près de 200 personnes au mariage

▸ **get onto VT INSEP 1** (contact) contacter, se mettre en contact avec, se mettre en rapport avec; **I'll g. onto the bank about it** je vais contacter la banque à ce sujet; **I'll g. onto him to finish the work** je vais le contacter pour lui dire de finir le travail

2 (locate, find name of) (person) trouver le nom ou les coordonnées de; **how did you g. onto me?** comment est-ce que vous avez trouvé mon nom?

3 (move forward to) en arriver à; **they eventually got onto (the subject of) money** ils ont fini par en arriver à parler d'argent

4 = get on with VT INSEP

▸ **get on with VT INSEP 1** (have good relationship with) s'entendre bien avec; **I don't g. on with my parents** je ne m'entends pas avec mes parents

2 (continue with) **how are you getting on with the painting?** alors, ça avance la peinture?; **just g. on with what you are supposed to be doing** (said by teacher etc) continuez ce que vous avez à faire; **let Dad g. on with his work** laissez Papa travailler en paix; **I wish the press would let me g. on with my life** si la presse pouvait me laisser vivre en paix; **I've got enough work to be getting on with** j'ai assez de travail à faire, j'ai assez de pain sur la planche

▸ **get out VI 1** (leave) sortir; (from car) descendre; Fam **g. out, you bastard!** fiche(-moi) le camp, espèce de salaud!

2 (be released from prison, hospital) sortir; **when does she g. out?** quand est-ce qu'elle sort?; **how did the news g. out?** comment la nouvelle s'est-elle répandue?; **the secret got out** le secret a transpiré

3 (leave one's house, flat) sortir (de chez soi); **he ought to g. out more** il devrait sortir plus

VT SEP 1 (bring out) (tools, books etc) sortir; **to g. one's car out** (from garage) sortir sa voiture; **to g. a book out from the library** emprunter un livre à la bibliothèque; **he could hardly g. a word out** c'est à peine s'il a pu sortir un mot; **we have to g. this report out by Monday** nous devons sortir ce rapport pour lundi

2 *(free) (hostages etc)* libérer

3 *(remove)* enlever; *(nail etc)* arracher; *(cork)* retirer; *(stain)* faire disparaître

4 *Cr (batsman)* renverser le guichet à

▸ **get out of** VT INSEP **1** *(leave)* sortir de; *(car)* descendre de; **let's g. out of here** partons d'ici; **he managed to g. out of the country** *(of criminal, refugee)* il a réussi à quitter le pays; **to g. out of bed** se lever; **to g. out of prison/the army** sortir de prison/quitter l'armée; **to g. out of sb's way** s'écarter du chemin de qn, faire place à qn; *Sl* **g. the hell out of here!** fiche(-moi) le camp!

2 *(extricate oneself from)* se faire exempter de; **to g. out of doing sth** se faire exempter de faire qch; **he always gets out of doing the washing-up** il arrive toujours à couper à la corvée de vaisselle; **to g. out of a difficulty** se tirer d'une position difficile; **I'd like to see her g. out of this one** j'aimerais bien voir comment elle va s'en tirer cette fois

3 *(become unaccustomed to)* **to g. out of (the habit of) doing sth** perdre l'habitude de faire qch

VT SEP **1** *(bring out of)* sortir de; **g. the phone book out of the drawer** sors l'annuaire du tiroir; **she got the nail out of her shoe** elle a retiré le clou de sa chaussure; **to g. a secret out of sb** arracher un secret à qn; **I can't g. anything out of him** je ne peux rien en tirer; **we finally got the truth out of her** nous avons fini par lui arracher la vérité; **I can't g. the idea out of my mind** je ne peux pas chasser cette idée de mon esprit; **to g. money out of sb** soutirer de l'argent à qn; **I got ten pounds out of it** j'y ai gagné dix livres; **to g. sb out of a difficulty** tirer qn d'affaire; **the firemen got us out of the building** les pompiers nous ont fait sortir du bâtiment; **to g. a stain out of a carpet** enlever une tache d'un tapis

2 *(derive from)* **I didn't g. much out of my lessons** je n'ai pas tiré grand-chose de mes leçons; **he could have got more out of the experience** il aurait pu tirer davantage de l'expérience

▸ **get over** VI **1** *(over road etc)* traverser; **to g. over to France/America** aller en France/Amérique; **to g. over to visit sb** *(in another city, country etc)* aller rendre visite à qn; **we'll try to g. over next weekend** *(to visit)* nous essayerons de venir vous voir le week-end prochain; **the wall was low, it was easy to g. over** le mur était bas, il a été facile de le franchir

2 *(communicate)* **to g. over to sb** se faire comprendre de qn

VT INSEP **1** *(cross) (wall etc)* escalader, passer par-dessus; *(road, river etc)* franchir

2 *(recover from) (illness)* se remettre de; *(difficulties)* venir à bout de; *(surprise)* revenir de; **she can't g. over it** *(illness, emotional shock, trauma)* elle ne s'en remet pas; *(surprise, shock etc)* elle n'en revient pas; *(loss)* elle est inconsolable; **it will take her a long time to g. over it** elle s'en ressentira longtemps, ça lui prendra longtemps pour s'en remettre

3 *(overcome) (fear etc)* surmonter

VT SEP **1** *(communicate)* faire passer; **she got her point over very well** elle a très bien fait passer ce qu'elle voulait dire

2 *(to other side of something)* faire passer; **we got the children over the road** nous avons fait traverser la route aux enfants

▸ **get over with** VT SEP *(complete)* terminer, finir; **she got her work over with as quickly as possible** elle a fini son travail aussi vite que possible; **when I g. my exams over with, I'll be able to relax** quand j'aurai terminé mes examens, je pourrai me détendre; **let's**

---

g. it over with as quickly as possible finissons-en au plus vite

▸ **get round** VI **1** **it would take a day to g. round** *(round the exhibition, museum)* ça prendrait une journée pour en faire le tour

2 **the doctor said she'd g. round as soon as she could** le docteur a dit qu'elle viendrait ou passerait dès qu'elle pourrait; **I didn't manage to g. round to each pupil in the class** je n'ai pas réussi à m'occuper de chaque élève de la classe

3 *(of news, rumour)* se répandre; **news gets round pretty quickly in small towns** les nouvelles circulent vite dans les petites villes

VT INSEP **1** *(exhibition, museum)* faire le tour de; *(corner)* passer

2 *(circumvent) (difficulty, regulations etc)* contourner; *(persuade) (person)* embobiner; **there's no getting round it** *(you'll have to own up)* il n'y a pas moyen d'y couper; **will you be able to g. round your dad?** est-ce que tu réussiras à persuader ton père?; **how did they g. round the regulations?** comment est-ce qu'ils ont réussi à contourner les réglementations?

VT SEP **1** *(bring, take)* **I'll g. the books round (to you) as soon as I can** je t'apporterai les livres dès que je le pourrai

2 *(persuade)* **we eventually got him round to our way of thinking** nous avons finalement réussi à le convaincre

▸ **get round to** VT INSEP = **get around to**

▸ **get through** VI **1** *(arrive)* **the road was blocked and no one could g. through** la route était bloquée et personne ne pouvait passer; **the message didn't g. through** le message n'est pas passé; **only a few trains got through to the besieged city** seuls quelques trains sont arrivés jusqu'à la ville assiégée; **the news got through to them** la nouvelle leur est parvenue

2 *Tel* obtenir la communication (**to sb** avec qn); *Fig (communicate)* se faire comprendre (**to sb** de qn); *Fig* **I'm not getting through (to you), am I?** je ne me fais pas bien comprendre, hein?

3 *Am (finish)* finir, terminer; **the class doesn't usually g. through until six o'clock** la leçon ne se termine généralement pas avant six heures

4 *(pass exam)* être reçu

VT INSEP **1** *(pass through) (hole etc)* passer à travers; **I thought I'd never g. through the day** j'ai cru que la journée n'en finirait jamais; **they got through the day without a single argument** ils ne se sont pas disputés une seule fois de toute la journée; **the Government may have difficulty getting through another six months** le gouvernement aura peut-être du mal à tenir encore six mois; **I couldn't g. through another winter in Moscow** je ne pourrais pas passer un hiver de plus à Moscou; **you won't g. through the roadblock** tu n'arriveras pas à franchir le barrage routier

2 *(succeed in) (exam)* être reçu à, réussir

3 *(finish) (work etc)* achever, arriver au bout de; *(food, drink etc)* consommer; **to g. through a lot of work** abattre beaucoup de travail

4 *(use up)* **he gets through eight shirts a week** il salit huit chemises par semaine; **we'll never g. through all this food** nous ne viendrons jamais à bout de toute cette nourriture; **she gets through her wages very quickly** elle dépense son salaire très rapidement

VT SEP **1** *(transport, send successfully)* faire parvenir; **they got the food supplies through** ils ont réussi à faire parvenir les provisions alimentaires (à destination); **to g. sth through customs** (faire) passer qch à la douane; **they got a message through** ils ont fait passer un message; **you'll never g.**

---

that desk through tu n'arriveras jamais à faire passer ce bureau; *Parl* **to g. a bill through** faire adopter un projet de loi

2 **I finally got it through to him that I wasn't interested** j'ai fini par lui faire comprendre que je n'étais pas intéressé

3 *(cause to succeed)* **it was your essay that got you through (the exam)** c'est grâce à ta dissertation que tu as réussi l'examen

4 *(enable to endure)* **I need four cups of coffee to g. me through the day** il me faut mes quatre tasses de café par jour

▸ **get together** VI *(of people)* se réunir, se rassembler (**to do** pour faire); **the two countries got together to deal with coastal pollution** les deux pays ont collaboré pour s'attaquer au problème de la pollution côtière

VT SEP *(collect) (objects)* rassembler; *(friends etc)* réunir; **g. your things together, we're going** rassemble tes affaires, nous partons; **to g. some money together** réunir une somme d'argent; **let me g. my thoughts together** laisse-moi rassembler mes idées

▸ **get under** VT INSEP *(get into position beneath) (table etc)* se mettre sous; **they got under the fence and escaped** ils sont passés sous la clôture et se sont enfuis

VT SEP *(place beneath)* mettre ou placer sous; **I can't g. the carpet under the table** je n'arrive pas à placer le tapis sous la table

▸ **get up** VI **1** *(get out of bed)* se lever; *(stand up)* se lever, se mettre debout; **g. up!** levez-vous!; **to g. up from a chair/the table** se lever de sa chaise/de table

2 *Met* **the wind/a storm was getting up** le vent/une tempête se levait

VT INSEP *(climb) (stairs)* monter; *(ladder)* monter à; *(mountain)* faire l'ascension de

VT SEP **1** **to g. up speed** prendre de la vitesse

2 *(organize) (party etc)* organiser; *Pol* **to g. up a petition** organiser ou faire une pétition

3 *(move up)* monter; **how are we going to g. this desk up to the fifth floor?** comment allons-nous monter ce bureau jusqu'au cinquième étage?; **to g. sb up the stairs** *(help climb)* aider qn à monter l'escalier

4 *(rouse)* faire (se) lever; **have you got the children up?** est-ce que tu as fait lever les enfants?

5 **to g. oneself up as sb/sth** *(dress up)* se déguiser en qn/qch

6 *Vulg* **to g. it up** *(achieve an erection)* bander; **he couldn't g. it up** il n'a pas réussi à bander

▸ **get up to** VT INSEP **1** *(reach)* arriver à; **it took ages to g. up to the top of the hill** ça a pris une éternité pour arriver en haut de la colline; **I've got up to chapter 5** j'en suis au chapitre 5; **where have you got up to?** *(in your reading etc)* où en êtes-vous?

2 *(do)* **those children are always getting up to something** or **to some mischief** ces enfants sont toujours en train de faire des bêtises; **what have you been getting up to?** qu'est-ce que tu as fabriqué?; **the dog's been getting up to his usual tricks** le chien a encore fait des siennes

getatable, get-at-able [get'ætəb(ə)l] ADJ *Fam* accessible, d'accès facile

getaway ['getəweɪ] N *(of criminal)* fuite *f*; **to make one's g.** s'enfuir

▸▸ **g. car** = voiture *f* utilisée pour s'enfuir

get-go N *Am Fam* **from the g.** *(from the beginning)* dès le début; **he's a crook from the g.** *(completely)* c'est un escroc total, c'est un véritable escroc

Gethsemane [geθ'semənɪ] N Gethsémani *m*

get-rich-quick ADJ *Fam* **a g. scheme** un stratagème pour s'enrichir rapidement

get-together N *Fam* réunion *f*; **I'm having a**

g. with some friends nous faisons une petite soirée entre amis; **you and I must have a little g. one day** il faut qu'on se voie un de ces jours tous les deux

get-up N *Fam* **1** *(clothes)* accoutrement *m*, tenue *f*; *(fancy dress)* déguisement *m*; **what a g.!** quel accoutrement! **2** *Com (of merchandise)* présentation *f*

get-up-and-go N *Fam* allant *m*, entrain *m*; **where's your g.?** allez, remue-toi!

get-well(-soon) card N = carte *f* que l'on envoie à un malade pour lui souhaiter un prompt rétablissement

gewgaw ['gjuːgɔː] N babiole *f*

geyser ['giːzər] N **1** *Geol* geyser *m* **2** *Old-fashioned Br (water heater)* chauffe-eau *m inv* à gaz

G-force N pesanteur *f*

Ghana ['gɑːnə] N Ghana *m*

Ghanaian, Ghanian [gɑː'neɪən, 'gɑːnɪən] N Ghanéen, -éenne
ADJ ghanéen

ghastliness ['gɑːstlɪnɪs] N *(of crime)* horreur *f*

ghastly ['gɑːstlɪ] ADJ **1** *(experience)* horrible, affreux, épouvantable; *Fam* **what g. weather!** quel temps épouvantable *ou* abominable!; **a g. mistake** une erreur monstrueuse **2** *(pale)* blême; *(pallor)* mortel; *(light)* blafard; **he looked g.** il avait l'air d'un déterré

ghee [giː] N *Culin* beurre *m* clarifié

Ghent [gent] N Gand *m*

gherkin ['gɜːkɪn] N cornichon *m*; **pickled gherkins** cornichons au vinaigre

ghetto ['getəʊ] N ghetto *m*
▸▸ *Fam* **g. blaster** = grand radiocassette *m* portatif

ghillie ['gɪlɪ] N = gillie

ghost [gəʊst] N **1** fantôme *m*, spectre *m*; **to believe in ghosts** croire aux revenants *ou* fantômes; **you look as if you've seen a g.** comme tu es pâle, tu as l'air d'avoir reçu un sacré choc; **to be the mere g. of one's former self** n'être plus que l'ombre de soi-même; **not the g. of a chance** pas la moindre chance; **g. of a smile** esquisse *f* de sourire **2** *Rel* **the Holy G.** l'Esprit *m* Saint, le Saint-Esprit **3** *Arch (soul)* âme *f*; *Fig* **to give up the g.** *(die)* rendre l'âme, expirer; *Fig Fam* **the car finally gave up the g. yesterday** la voiture a finalement rendu l'âme hier **4** *Opt* spectre *m* secondaire, image *f* blanche; *TV* écho *m* **5** *Liter (ghostwriter)* nègre *m*
VI *Liter* servir de nègre (**for an author** à un écrivain)
VT *Liter (sb's speeches)* écrire; **to g. a book** servir de nègre pour l'écriture d'un livre; **ghosted work** ouvrage écrit par un nègre
▸▸ **g. ship** vaisseau *m* fantôme; *Mktg* **g. shopping** achats *mpl* simulés pour audit; **g. story** histoire *f* de revenants; **g. town** ville *f* fantôme

ghosting ['gəʊstɪŋ] N *TV* images *fpl* fantôme

ghostly ['gəʊstlɪ] ADJ spectral, -aux

ghostwrite ['gəʊstraɪt] VT = ghost VT

ghostwriter ['gəʊstraɪtər] N nègre *m*

ghoul [guːl] N **1** *(evil spirit)* goule *f*; *Fig (person)* personne *f* qui a des goûts macabres *ou* morbides; **a crowd of ghouls had gathered at the scene of the accident** une foule d'amateurs de spectacles macabres s'était assemblée sur la scène de l'accident **2** *Old-fashioned (grave robber)* déterreur *m* de cadavre

ghoulish ['guːlɪʃ] ADJ **1** *(humour etc)* macabre **2** *Myth* de goule

GHQ [dʒiːeɪtʃ'kjuː] N *Mil (abbr* General Headquarters*)* QG *m inv*

GHz *(abbr* gigahertz*)* GHz *m*

GI [dʒiː'aɪ] N *Fam* GI (Joe) soldat *m* américain, GI *m inv*; **GI bride** = femme *f* étrangère ayant épousé un GI

giant ['dʒaɪənt] N *Myth, Fig* géant *m*
ADJ *(oak, package)* géant; **with g. strides** à pas de géant
▸▸ *Br Sport* **g. killer** vainqueur *m* surprise

giantess [dʒaɪən'tes] N géante *f*

Gib [dʒɪb] N *Fam* Gibraltar *m*

gibber ['dʒɪbər] VI *(like a monkey, an idiot)* produire des sons inarticulés; *(of foreigners speaking amongst themselves)* baragouiner; **he was gibbering with rage/fear** il bégayait de rage/frayeur; **it reduced him to a gibbering wreck** il en est devenu bègue; *Fam* **gibbering idiot** espèce de crétin

gibberish ['dʒɪbərɪʃ] N baragouin *m*, charabia *m*; **to talk g.** raconter n'importe quoi

gibbet ['dʒɪbɪt] N gibet *m*, potence *f*

gibbon ['gɪbən] N *(monkey)* gibbon *m*

gibbous ['gɪbəs] ADJ *Astron (moon)* gibbeux

gibe [dʒaɪb] N raillerie *f*, quolibet *m*; **to make a g.** lancer une raillerie *ou* un quolibet (**at** à)
VI **to g. at sb** railler qn, se moquer de qn

giblets ['dʒɪblɪts] NPL *(of poultry)* abats *mpl*, abattis *mpl*

Gibraltar [dʒɪ'brɔːltər] N Gibraltar *m*

giddily ['gɪdɪlɪ] ADV **1** *(to rise)* de manière vertigineuse **2** *(frivolously)* étourdiment

giddiness ['gɪdɪnɪs] N **1** *(vertigo)* étourdissement *m*, vertige *m*; **fits of g.** des étourdissements, des vertiges **2** *(frivolousness)* frivolité *f*

giddy ['gɪdɪ] ADJ **1** *(dizzy) (person)* étourdi; **to be** *or* **feel g.** avoir le vertige; **I feel g.** la tête me tourne; **it makes me (feel) g.** cela me donne le vertige **2** *(height)* vertigineux, qui donne le vertige **3** *(frivolous)* frivole; **g. round of pleasures** tourbillon *m* de plaisirs; *Br Old-fashioned* **oh my g. aunt!** ciel!

GIF [gɪf] N *Comput (abbr* Graphic Information Format*)* GIF *m*

gift [gɪft] N **1** *(to individual)* cadeau *m*; **it was a g.** c'était un cadeau; *(of bargain)* c'était donné; *Fam (easy victory)* c'était un jeu d'enfants; **I wouldn't have it as a g.** je n'en voudrais pas même si on m'en faisait cadeau; *Prov* **never look a g. horse in the mouth** à cheval donné on ne regarde pas la bouche **2** *(donation)* don *m*; **a g. of £2,000** un don de 2 000 livres; **to make a g. of sth to sb** faire don de qch à qn; *Law* **as a g.** en cadeau; **in the g. of sb** à la discrétion de qn **3** *Com (on presentation of coupons)* prime *f*; **free g.** cadeau *m* **4** *(talent)* don *m*; **to have a g. for mathematics** avoir le don *ou Fam* la bosse des mathématiques
▸▸ **g. shop** boutique *f* de cadeaux; *Fin* **g. tax** impôt *m* sur les donations; **g. token,** *Br* **g. voucher** bon *m* d'achat

gifted ['gɪftɪd] ADJ doué; *(artist)* de talent

giftwrap ['gɪftræp] VT emballer *(et faire un paquet-cadeau)*; **shall I g. it?** je vous fais un paquet-cadeau?

giftwrapped ['gɪftræpt] ADJ *Com (article)* sous paquet-cadeau; **would you like it g.?** c'est pour offrir?, je vous fais un paquet-cadeau?

giftwrapping ['gɪftræpɪŋ] N *(paper, ribbons etc)* emballage-cadeau *m*

gig[1] [gɪg] N **1** *(carriage)* cabriolet *m* **2** *Naut* yole *f*

gig[2] N *Mus Fam* concert *m*

giga- ['gɪgə] PREF giga-

gigabyte ['gɪgəbaɪt] N *Comput* gigaoctet *m*

gigahertz ['gɪgəhɜːts] N gigahertz *m*

gigantic [dʒaɪ'gæntɪk] ADJ géant, gigantesque; *(building, bridge)* colossal

gigantically [dʒaɪ'gæntɪklɪ] ADV de façon démesurée

giggle ['gɪg(ə)l] N petit rire *m*; *(of young girl)* gloussement *m*, rire *m* bébête; **to have (a fit of) the giggles** avoir le fou rire; **to give a nervous g.** avoir un petit rire nerveux; *Fam* **to do sth for a g.** pour se marrer *ou* pour rigoler; **the evening was a g. from start to finish** on s'est marré toute la soirée; **she was a real g. as usual** elle était tordante comme d'habitude
VI avoir un petit rire; *(nervously)* rire nerveusement; *(of young girls)* glousser, rire bêtement; **what are you giggling about?** qu'est-ce qui vous fait rire?

giggling ['gɪg(ə)lɪŋ] ADJ qui pousse de petits rires; *(nervously)* qui rit avec nervosité; *(young girl)* qui glousse, qui rit bêtement
N petits rires *mpl*; *(nervous)* petits rires nerveux; *(of young girl)* rires bébêtes, gloussements *mpl*

giggly ['gɪg(ə)lɪ] ADJ qui se met à rire bêtement pour un rien; **to get** *or* **go all g.** se mettre à rire bêtement; **to be in a g. mood** être d'humeur joyeuse

GIGO [dʒiːaɪdʒiː'əʊ] *Comput Sl abbr* **garbage in, garbage out**

gigolo ['dʒɪgələʊ] N gigolo *m*

gigot ['dʒɪgət] N gigot *m*

gild [gɪld] VT *(pt* gilded; *pp* gilded, *occ* gilt [gɪlt]) dorer; *Fig* **to g. the lily** surcharger; *Lit* **gilded youth** la jeunesse dorée; **to be like a bird in a gilded cage** vivre dans une prison dorée

gilding ['gɪldɪŋ] N dorure *f*

gill[1] [gɪl] N *(usu pl)* **1** *(of fish)* gills ouïes *fpl*, branchies *fpl* **2** *gills (of mushroom)* lamelles *fpl* **3** *Fam* **to be** *or* **look green about the gills** *(look ill)* avoir le teint verdâtre *ou* jaune; *(through disgust, shock etc)* être vert; **he went green about the gills** *(looked ill)* son teint est devenu verdâtre *ou* jaune; *(through disgust, shock etc)* il est devenu vert

gill[2] [dʒɪl] N *(measure)* quart *m* de pinte (= 0,142 l)

gillie ['gɪlɪ] N *Scot* serviteur *m* *(de chasseur, pêcheur etc)*

gillyflower ['dʒɪlɪflaʊər] N **1** *(wallflower)* giroflée *f* jaune *ou* des murailles **2** *(clove)* g. œillet *m* giroflée

gilt [gɪlt] PP see gild
ADJ *(frame etc)* doré
N *(gold)* dorure *f*, doré *m*; *St Exch* **gilts** fonds *mpl* d'État, *Fam* valeurs *fpl* de tout repos *ou* de père de famille; *Fam* **that takes the g. off the gingerbread** voilà qui enlève le charme *ou* l'attrait

gilt-edged ADJ *(book)* doré sur tranche
▸▸ *St Exch* **g. market** marché *m* des valeurs de premier ordre; *St Exch* **g. market maker** teneur *m* de marché de valeurs de premier ordre; *St Exch* **g. stock(s)** fonds *mpl* d'État

gimbals ['dʒɪmb(ə)lz] NPL *Aviat, Naut etc* suspension *f* à cardan *m*

gimcrack ['dʒɪmkræk] ADJ *Old-fashioned (furniture)* de pacotille; *(house)* en carton; *(jewellery)* en toc; *(scheme, theory etc)* à la noix

gimlet ['gɪmlɪt] N **1** *Carp (tool)* vrille *f*, foret *m* à bois; *Fig* **g. eyes** yeux *mpl* perçants **2** *(cocktail)* = cocktail *m* à base de gin ou de vodka et de jus de citron vert

gimme ['gɪmɪ] CONTR *Sl* = give me

gimmick ['gɪmɪk] N truc *m*, astuce *f*; **advertising g.** astuce *ou* truc publicitaire

gimmickry ['gɪmɪkrɪ] N astuces *fpl*

gimmicky ['gɪmɪkɪ] ADJ plein d'astuces; **a bit too g.** trop artificiel

gin¹ [dʒɪn] N *(drink)* gin *m*; *(made in Holland)* genièvre *m*
▶▶*Fam Hum* **g. palace** troquet *m*; *Cards* **g. rummy** gin-rummy *m*, gin-rami *m*

gin² N **1** *(trap)* piège *m* **2** *Tex* *(cotton)* **g.** égreneuse *f* de coton

ginger ['dʒɪndʒər] N **1** *Bot, Culin* gingembre *m*; **preserved** or **crystallized g.** gingembre confit; **g. biscuit** biscuit *m* au gingembre **2** *Fam (liveliness)* énergie *f* **3** *(redhead)* **hi, g.!** ohé, poil de carotte! **4** *Scot Fam (fizzy drink)* boisson *f* gazeuse
ADJ *Fam (hair)* roux, *f* rousse
▶▶**g. ale** = boisson *f* gazeuse aux extraits de gingembre pouvant servir à couper un alcool; **g. beer** = limonade *f* au gingembre; **g. group** = dans une organisation politique ou autre, faction dynamique cherchant à faire bouger les choses en incitant à l'action; **g. snap,** *Br* **g. nut** biscuit au gingembre; **g. wine** = boisson alcoolisée à base de gingembre
▶**ginger up** VT SEP *Fam (apathetic person)* secouer les puces à; *(film, text, storyline etc)* donner du punch à; **we need something to g. up the party** il nous faut quelque chose pour mettre un peu d'animation dans la soirée

gingerbread ['dʒɪndʒəbred] N *Culin* pain *m* d'épice
▶▶**g. man** bonhomme *m* en biscuit parfumé au gingembre

gingerly ['dʒɪndʒəlɪ] ADV avec précaution; *(trying not to make a noise)* doucement; **he stepped g. between the cowpats** il a avancé précautionneusement entre les bouses de vache

gingery ['dʒɪndʒərɪ] ADJ **1** *(taste)* de gingembre **2** *(hair, colour)* qui tire sur le roux

gingham ['gɪŋəm] N *Tex* vichy *m*; **g. curtains/dress** rideaux/robe en vichy

gingivitis [dʒɪndʒɪˈvaɪtɪs] N *Med* gingivite *f*

ginormous [dʒaɪˈnɔːməs] ADJ *Fam* gigantesque, énorme

ginseng ['dʒɪnseŋ] N ginseng *m*

gippo ['dʒɪpəʊ] N *Br Offensive Sl* romanichel, -elle

gippy ['dʒɪpɪ] ADJ *Fam* **to have a g. tummy** avoir la courante

gipsy ['dʒɪpsɪ] N bohémien, -ienne, *Pej* romanichel, -elle; *(Spanish)* gitan, -ane
▶▶**g. caravan** roulotte *f*, **g. moth** zigzag *m*, bombyx *m* disparate

gipsyish ['dʒɪpsɪɪʃ] ADJ comme un bohémien ou *Pej* un romanichel; *(dark-skinned)* brun de peau

giraffe [dʒɪˈræf, -ˈrɑːf] N girafe *f*

gird [gɜːd] VT *(pt, pp* **girded, girt** [gɜːt]) *Arch, Lit* **1** *(wrap around with a belt)* ceindre; **to g. up one's loins** se ceindre les reins; **to g. (on) one's sword** ceindre son épée **2** *(surround)* ceindre *(with* de)

girder ['gɜːdər] N *Constr* poutre *f* (métallique)

girdle¹ ['gɜːd(ə)l] N *(corset)* gaine *f*, *(belt)* ceinture *f*
VT *Lit* ceindre, entourer

girdle² N = **griddle**

girl [gɜːl] N fille *f*; *(young woman)* jeune fille, jeune femme *f*; **little g.** petite fille, fillette *f*; **when I was a g.** quand j'étais petite; **g.'s name** prénom *m* féminin ou de fille; **girls' school** école *f* de filles; *Br Sch* old **g.** ancienne élève *f*; **a French/an Indian g.** une jeune Française/Indienne; **his g.** *(daughter)* sa fille; *Old-fashioned (girlfriend)* sa petite amie; **the Smith(s') g.** la fille (des) Smith;

that's my g.! *(well done)* bravo!, très bien!; *Old-fashioned* **my dear g.!** ma chère!; *Old-fashioned Fam* **the old g.** la vieille femme, *Pej* la vieille; *(wife)* ma femme, la bourgeoise; *(mother)* ma mère; *(boss)* la patronne; *(car)* ma vieille voiture ou bagnole; *Old-fashioned* **hello, old g.!** salut, ma vieille!
▶▶**g. band** girls band *m*; **G. Guide** éclaireuse *f*, **g. power** = slogan *m* associé au groupe féminin britannique The Spice Girls, revendiquant l'égalité des sexes; **G. Scout** éclaireuse

girlfriend ['gɜːlfrend] N *(of boy, man)* petite amie *f*, *(of girl, woman)* amie, *Fam* copine *f*

girlhood ['gɜːlhʊd] N *(childhood)* enfance *f*, *(young womanhood)* jeunesse *f*, **in my g.** dans ma jeunesse, quand j'étais jeune fille

girlie ['gɜːlɪ] N *Fam* **1** *(effeminate boy)* fillette *f* **2** *Br (young woman)* (jeune) fille *f*, **to have a g. chat** bavarder entre filles
▶▶**g. magazine** magazine *m* de femmes à poil

girlish ['gɜːlɪʃ] ADJ **1** *(behaviour)* de fille; *(figure)* de jeune fille; **g. laughter** un rire de (petite) jeune fille **2** *(boy)* efféminé; **g. good looks** air enfantin ou de très jeune fille

girlishly ['gɜːlɪʃlɪ] ADV *(to behave, dress)* comme une petite fille

giro ['dʒaɪrəʊ] N *Br* **1** *(system)* = système *m* de virement interbancaire introduit par la Poste britannique; *Banking* **National G.** = service *m* de chèques postaux; **bank g.** virement *m* bancaire **2** *Fam (for unemployed)* chèque *m* d'allocation de chômage; **I haven't had my g. (cheque) yet** *(unemployment benefit)* mon allocation de chômage ne m'a pas encore été payée
▶▶**g. account** compte *m* chèque postal, CCP *m*; **g. cheque** chèque *m* postal, chèque de virement; **g. transfer** transfert *m* par CCP

Girobank ['dʒaɪrəʊbæŋk] N = service *m* bancaire de la Poste britannique

girt PT, PP *see* **gird**

-girt [gɜːt] SUFF *Lit* **sea-g. isle** île *f* encerclée par les mers

girth [gɜːθ] N **1** *(circumference)* *(of tree etc)* circonférence *f*, *(of chest, waist)* tour *m*; **of considerable g.** *(of person)* d'une belle corpulence **2** *(on harness)* sangle *f*, **saddle g.** sangle de selle

gismo ['gɪzməʊ] N = **gizmo**

gist [dʒɪst] N *(of conversation)* essentiel *m*; *(of question)* point *m* essentiel; **to get the g. (of the matter)** saisir l'essentiel; **could you just give me the g. (of it) now?** pourrais-tu m'en donner l'essentiel?; **I got the g. of what she was saying** j'ai compris l'essentiel de ce qu'elle disait; **the g. of what she was saying was …** elle a dit en substance …

git [gɪt] N *Br Sl* con, *f* conne; **stupid g.!** espèce de con/conne!

GIVE *(pt* **gave** [geɪv], *pp* **given** ['gɪv(ə)n])

VT	donner **1–3, 5, 7, 8** ▪ accorder **6** ▪ faire **9** ▪ rendre **10**
VI	donner **1** ▪ céder **2**
N	élasticité

VT **1** *(present, bestow, pledge, provide)* **to g. sth to sb, to g. sb sth** donner qch à qn; **to g. sb a present** faire ou donner un cadeau à qn; **to g. an example** donner un exemple; **to g. a discount** accorder un escompte; *Fml* **to g. a dinner** *(in honour of sb)* donner un dîner; **to g. sb one's hand** *(to hold)* donner ou tendre la main à qn; **to g. sb a note from sb** remettre à qn un petit mot de qn; **to g. no sign of life** ne donner aucun signe de vie; **to g. sth to eat/drink** donner à manger/à boire à qn; **to g. sb six months' imprisonment** condamner qn à six mois de prison; **he was**

given life il a été condamné à perpétuité; **to g. a child a name** donner un nom à un enfant; **to g. sb a job to do** assigner une tâche à qn; **g. her my love** embrasse-la pour moi; **to g. sb one's support** prêter son appui à qn; *Euph* **she gave herself to him** elle s'est donnée à lui; **g. me the good old days!** parlez-moi du bon vieux temps!; **g. me British weather any day!** rien ne vaut le climat de la Grande-Bretagne!

2 *(in exchange)* donner; **to g. a good price for sth** donner ou payer un bon prix pour qch; **I'll g. you £10 for it** je vous en donnerai 10 livres; **to g. sth in exchange for sth** donner qch en échange de ou contre qch; **to g. one's life for one's beliefs** donner sa vie pour ses convictions; **I would g. a lot** or **a great deal to know …** je donnerais beaucoup pour savoir …

3 *(devote)* donner, consacrer; **to g. oneself to one's studies** se consacrer entièrement ou s'adonner à ses études; **to g. one's attention to sth** porter son attention sur qch; **he gave it considerable thought** il y a beaucoup réfléchi; **I've given you six years of my life** je t'ai donné six ans de ma vie; **he gave this job the best years of her life** elle a consacré à ce travail les plus belles années de sa vie

4 *(do)* **to g. a laugh** rire, laisser échapper un rire; **to g. a sigh** soupirer, pousser un soupir; **to g. sb's hand a squeeze** serrer la main à qn; **to g. sb a smile** faire un sourire à qn; **he gave me an odd look** il m'a lancé un regard singulier; **she gave her hair a comb** elle s'est donné un coup de peigne; **he gave his face a wash** il s'est lavé le visage; **he gave the table a wipe** il a essuyé la table

5 *(reason, explanation, opinion, answer, reference number)* donner; **the answer (that) he gave me** la réponse qu'il m'a faite ou donnée; **he gave his age as twenty** il a déclaré avoir vingt ans; **to g. a decision** faire connaître sa décision; *Law* rendre un arrêt; **don't g. me that!** *(don't try to fool me)* ne me raconte pas d'histoires!, à d'autres!; **don't g. me that stuff about how hard your life is** épargne-moi le récit de tous tes malheurs

6 *(grant)* **she gave him her hand (in marriage)** elle lui a accordé sa main; **to g. sb an interview** accorder une interview à qn; **we were given a choice** on nous a fait choisir; **g. me a break!** fais-moi des vacances!, lâche-moi les baskets!; **g. me a chance!** donne-moi une chance!; **g. me five minutes** accorde-moi cinq minutes; **I can g. you 10 minutes** je peux te consacrer ou t'accorder 10 minutes; **we'll get there in two hours, g. or take a few minutes** on fera le trajet en deux heures, à quelques minutes près; **g. us a song!** chante-nous quelque chose!; **aren't you going to g. me a kiss?** tu ne m'embrasses pas?; **married? those two? I'll g. it a year at the outside** mariés? ces deux-là? je leur donne un an au grand maximum; **he's keen, I'll g. you that** il est très enthousiaste, je te l'accorde

7 *(perform, execute) (concert etc)* donner; **she gave an outstanding performance** *(of actress)* son interprétation était remarquable; **I g. you our host** *(in proposing toast)* je bois à la santé de notre hôte

8 *(pass on)* **he gave me his cold** il m'a donné ou passé son rhume; **that gave me the idea of travelling** cela m'a donné l'idée de voyager; **don't go giving him ideas!** ne va pas lui mettre des idées dans la tête!

9 *(cause) (embarrassment, pleasure)* faire, causer; **to g. oneself trouble** se donner du mal; **to g. sb to believe** or **understand that …** faire croire ou donner à entendre à qn que …

10 *(yield)* rendre; **investment that gives 10%** placement qui rend ou rapporte 10%; **this lamp gives a poor light** cette lampe éclaire mal; **to g. an average of ...** donner une moyenne de ...

11 *Fam (hit etc)* **to g. it (to) sb** *(beat up)* rosser qn; *(reprimand)* laver la tête à qn; **g. it to them!** allez-y!; **I gave him what for!** *(reprimanded him)* je lui ai passé un savon!; **caviare on toast? I'll g. him caviare on toast!** *(in annoyance at request)* du caviar et des toasts! je vais lui en donner, moi, du caviar et des toasts!

VI 1 *(give gift etc)* donner, offrir; *Prov* **it is better** *or* **more blessed to g. than to receive** donner vaut mieux que recevoir; **please g. generously** *(to charity collection)* soyez généreux; **to g. generously of one's time** donner beaucoup de son temps; **to g. and take** faire des concessions; **to g. as good as one gets** rendre coup pour coup

2 *(of cloth, elastic)* se détendre; *Fig (of person)* céder; **something's got to g.** ça va exploser; **the springs don't g. enough** les ressorts manquent de souplesse; **the door will g. if you push hard enough** la porte cédera si vous la poussez assez fort

3 *esp Am Fam* **what gives?** *(hi!)* salut!; *(what's going on?)* qu'est-ce qui se passe?; *(what's the news?)* quoi de neuf?

4 *Sl* **g.!** *(tell me etc)* vide ton sac!

N élasticité *f*, *(in mechanism etc)* jeu *m*

▸▸ **g. way sign** signal *m* de priorité

▸ **give away VT SEP 1** *(give for nothing)* donner, faire cadeau de; **I'm practically giving them away!** *(said by salesman)* c'est pratiquement donné!; **you couldn't g. them away** tu n'arriveras pas à t'en débarrasser (même si tu en faisais cadeau)

2 *(at ceremony)* **to g. away the prizes** distribuer les prix; **to g. the bride away** conduire la mariée à l'autel

3 *(betray, reveal)* *(of person)* trahir, vendre; *(of accent, clothes etc)* trahir; **to g. oneself away** se trahir; **to g. the game** *or* **show away** vendre la mèche; **I'm not going to g. anything away** *(that might help you)* je ne veux rien vous révéler

▸ **give back VT SEP** *(something)* rendre, restituer (**to sb** à qn); *(echo)* renvoyer; *(image)* refléter; **to g. sb back his liberty** rendre la liberté à qn

▸ **give in VT SEP** *(hand over)* donner, remettre; **I gave the wallet in to the police** j'ai remis le portefeuille à la police; **to g. in one's name** donner son nom; **to g. in one's examination paper** remettre sa copie d'examen

VI *(under pressure)* céder; *(in fight, battle)* se rendre; *(of rebel)* se soumettre; *(not know the answer)* renoncer, abandonner; **to g. in to intimidation** se laisser intimider; **to g. in too easily** tu abandonnes trop facilement; **to g. in to sb** céder à qn

▸ **give off VT SEP** *(emit) (smell)* dégager, émettre; *(heat)* émettre, répandre; *Chem (gas)* dégager

▸ **give onto VT INSEP** *(of window, door etc)* *(garden, street)* donner sur

▸ **give out VT SEP 1** *(distribute)* *(supplies, books etc)* distribuer

2 *(emit) (smell)* dégager; *(heat)* répandre; *(sound)* émettre

3 *(make known)* **it was given out that ...** on a annoncé *ou* dit que ...

VI 1 *(become used up)* manquer, faire défaut; *(of supplies)* s'épuiser; **my strength/patience was giving out** j'étais à bout de forces/patience; **my luck has finally given out** finalement, la chance a tourné

2 *(of radio, car etc)* tomber en panne

▸ **give over VT SEP 1** *(transfer)* remettre (**to sb** entre les mains de qn)

2 *(devote)* *(afternoon, rest of the evening etc)* consacrer (**to** à)

3 *(usu passive) (abandon)* **given over to despair** abandonné *ou* en proie au désespoir

VI *Fam (stop)* **g. over, will you?** vraiment, ça

suffit!; **g. over kicking your sister** arrête de donner des coups de pieds à ta sœur

▸ **give up VT SEP 1** *(abandon)* *(possessions, pretensions)* abandonner; *(plan etc)* renoncer à; **to g. up the idea of doing sth** renoncer à (l'idée de) faire qch; **he gave up all hope of being promoted** il a abandonné tout espoir d'être promu; **to g. up smoking** cesser de fumer; **to g. up one's job** quitter son emploi; **to g. up the game/struggle** abandonner la partie/renoncer à la lutte; **to g. sth up as a bad job** renoncer à qch (en raison du manque de résultats); **to g. sb up (for lost)** considérer qn comme perdu; **the doctors have given him up** les médecins disent qu'il est perdu; **I'd given you up!** *(giving up waiting)* je ne vous attendais plus!; **he gave himself up to grief** il s'est laissé aller au désespoir

2 *(surrender) (prisoner)* livrer; **to g. up one's seat to sb** céder sa place à qn; **to g. oneself up** se constituer prisonnier, se rendre; **I want to g. myself up** je veux me rendre; **she gave herself up to her studies** elle s'est consacrée entièrement à ses études; **his mornings were given up to business** ses matinées étaient consacrées aux affaires

VI 1 *(surrender)* se rendre; **I g. up** *(I don't know the answer)* j'abandonne, je donne ma langue au chat

2 *(abandon a course of action, struggle etc)* abandonner, laisser tomber; **you mustn't g. up now** tu ne peux pas abandonner maintenant; **I g. up!** *(you're or it's etc hopeless)* j'abandonne!

▸ **give up on VT INSEP** *(stop having faith in)* even his mother had given up on him même sa mère avait perdu tout espoir à son sujet; **don't g. up on me** ne me laisse pas tomber

▸ **give way VI 1** *(collapse)* s'effondrer; *(of ladder)* se casser, se rompre; *(of cable)* céder, partir; **the ground gave way under our feet** le sol s'est affaissé *ou* s'est dérobé sous nos pieds; **my legs are giving way (under me)** mes jambes fléchissent *ou* mollissent *ou* se dérobent sous moi; **his health is giving way** sa santé s'affaiblit

2 *(yield)* **to g. way to sb** *(in argument)* céder à qn; **to g. way to despair/grief** s'abandonner au désespoir/à la douleur; **g. way** *(on sign)* cédez le passage; **to g. way (to a car)** céder le passage (à une voiture)

3 *(be superseded by)* **her tears gave way to laughter** le rire l'a emporté sur ses larmes; **natural fibres have given way to synthetics** les fibres naturelles ont été remplacées par les synthétiques

give-and-take N *(mutual concession)* concessions *fpl* (mutuelles); **there has to be some g.** il faut que chacun fasse des concessions, il faut que chacun y mette du sien

giveaway ['gɪvəweɪ] N *Fam* **1** *(revelation)* révélation *f* involontaire; *(clue)* indice *m*; **her remark about inflation was the g.** sa remarque sur l'inflation l'a trahie; **it was a dead g.** c'était un geste/un mot/*etc* qui en disait long **2** *Com (free gift)* prime *f*, cadeau *m* **3** *Am Radio* jeu *m* radiophonique; *TV* jeu télévisé

▸▸ **g. paper** journal *m* gratuit; **g. price** prix *m* défiant toute concurrence; *Am* **g. program** *Radio* jeu radiophonique; *TV* jeu télévisé

given ['gɪv(ə)n] ADJ **1** *(specific)* donné, déterminé; **at a g. time** dans une période donnée; **at any g. time** à tout moment; **at a g. point** à un point donné **2** *(apt, likely)* **to be g. to forgetfulness** avoir tendance à être distrait; **I'm g. to losing my temper** c'est dans ma nature de me mettre en colère

PREP **g. these facts, explain why ...** à partir de ces données, expliquez pourquoi ...; **g.**

her age *(considering it)* étant donné son âge; **g. a triangle ABC** soit un triangle ABC

▸▸ *Am* **g. name** prénom *m*

giver ['gɪvər] N *(of blood, organ)* donneur, -euse; *(of money)* donateur, -trice

giving ['gɪvɪŋ] ADJ *(person)* généreux, -euse; **of a g. nature** d'une nature généreuse

gizmo ['gɪzməʊ] N *esp Am Fam* machin *m*, truc *m*, bidule *m*

gizzard ['gɪzəd] N gésier *m*; *Fig Fam* **that sticks in my g.** j'ai du mal à le digérer

glacé ['glæseɪ] ADJ

▸▸ *Culin* **g. cherries** cerises *fpl* confites

glacial ['gleɪsɪəl, -ʃəl] ADJ **1** *Geol (erosion, valley etc)* glaciaire **2** *(wind, Fig manner etc)* glacial, -als

glaciation [gleɪsɪ'eɪʃən, -ʃɪ'eɪ-] N glaciation *f*

glacier ['glæsɪər, 'gleɪs-, *Am* 'gleɪʃər] N *Geol* glacier *m*

glad [glæd] ADJ (**gladder, gladdest**) **1** *(person)* heureux, content; **to be g. to hear sth** apprendre qch avec plaisir, être heureux *ou* content d'apprendre qch; **I'm g. you like him** je suis content que vous l'aimiez; **I'm (so) g.** *(to know that you're better etc)* ça me fait plaisir (de l'apprendre); **he is only too g. to help you** il ne demande pas mieux que de vous aider; **they would be g. of your help** ils seraient bien heureux d'avoir votre aide; **to be g. of an opportunity to do sth** se réjouir de l'occasion de faire qch; **it makes my heart g. to hear him** cela me réjouit le cœur de l'entendre

2 *(smile)* de contentement; *(shout)* de plaisir; **g. news,** *Lit* **g. tidings** bonne nouvelle *f*; *Old-fashioned Fam* **to give sb the g. eye** faire de l'œil à qn; *Am* **to give sb the g. hand** faire un accueil chaleureux à qn *(souvent dans un but intéressé)*; *Fam Hum* **to put on one's g. rags** se mettre sur trente et un

gladden ['glæd(ə)n] VT *(person)* rendre heureux; **it gladdens my heart to see them** cela me réjouit le cœur de les voir

glade [gleɪd] N *esp Lit (in forest)* clairière *f*

glad-hand VT *Am (welcome warmly)* faire un accueil chaleureux à; *(of politician etc)* serrer la main à *(souvent dans un but intéressé)*

gladiator ['glædɪeɪtər] N gladiateur *m*

gladiatorial [glædɪə'tɔːrɪəl] ADJ *(combats)* de gladiateurs

▸▸ *Fig* **g. politics** = politique *f* qui fait de la confrontation son moyen d'action

gladiolus, *pl* **gladioli** [glædɪ'əʊləs, -laɪ] N glaïeul *m*

gladly ['glædlɪ] ADV *(willingly)* avec plaisir, volontiers; **I accept g.** j'accepte avec grand plaisir

gladness ['glædnɪs] N joie *f*, allégresse *f*

Gladstone bag ['glædstən] N = petit sac *m* de voyage

Glam *abbr* Glamorganshire

glam [glæm] ADJ *Fam* = **glamorous**

glamorize ['glæməraɪz] VT rendre séduisant *ou* attrayant; **to g. war** présenter la guerre de telle sorte qu'elle apparaisse attrayante; **a TV programme that glamorizes violence** une émission de télé qui rend la violence attrayante; **an advertising campaign that seeks to g. smoking** une campagne publicitaire qui cherche à redorer l'image des fumeurs

glamorous ['glæmərəs] ADJ *(person)* chic et élégant; *(dress)* habillé; *(job, football club etc)* prestigieux, -ieuse; *(job as model etc)* qui fait rêver; **a g. grandmother** une grand-mère sophistiquée; **working in the film industry is not always g.** il n'y a pas que des métiers de prestige dans le cinéma

glamour, *Am* **glamor** ['glæmər] N *(of person)* glamour *m*, chic *m* fascinant; *(of name, lifestyle)* prestige *m*; *(of ceremony etc)* éclat *m*; **the false g. of war** la fascination trompeuse qu'exerce la guerre; **g. is back in fashion** le chic revient à la mode
▸▸*Fam* **g. boy** beau gosse *m*; *Fam* **g. girl** pin-up *f inv*, *(model)* mannequin *m*

glam-rock N *Mus* glam-rock *m*

glance [glɑːns] N *(quick look)* regard *m*, coup *m* d'œil; **at a g.** d'un coup d'œil; **at first g.** à première vue, au premier coup d'œil; **to give sth a g., to have a g. at sth** jeter un coup d'œil sur qch
VI *(look quickly)* **to g. at sb/sth** jeter un regard sur qn/qch, lancer un coup d'œil à qn/sur qch; **to g. around** jeter un coup d'œil autour de soi; **to g. through** *or* **over sth** *(examine)* parcourir rapidement qch; **to g. through a book** parcourir *ou* feuilleter un livre; **he glanced up briefly when I came in** il a brièvement levé la tête quand je suis entré
▸ **glance off** VI *(of bullet etc)* ricocher
VT INSEP ricocher sur; *(of light)* se refléter sur; **the blow glanced off his helmet** le coup a ricoché sur son casque

glancing ['glɑːnsɪŋ] ADJ *(blow)* oblique; **she caught him with a g. blow** elle lui a donné un coup sur le côté

gland¹ [glænd] N glande *f*

gland² N *Tech* **packing g.** bague *f* de presse-étoupe

glanders ['glændəz] NPL *(with sing verb)* *Vet* morve *f*

glandular ['glændjʊlər] ADJ *Physiol, Med* glandulaire
▸▸**g. fever** mononucléose *f* (infectieuse)

glans [glænz], *pl* **glandes** ['glændiːz] N *Anat* gland *m*

glare [gleər] N **1** *(angry stare)* regard *m* fixe et furieux **2** *(of sun, headlight etc)* éclat *m*, lumière *f* éblouissante; *Fig* **in the full g. of publicity** sous le feu croisé des médias
VI **1** *(stare angrily)* fixer un regard furieux *ou* furibond (**at sb** sur qn) **2** *(of sun etc)* être aveuglant
▸▸*Comput* **g. filter** filtre *m* antireflet; *Comput* **g. screen** écran *m* antireflet

glaring ['gleərɪŋ] ADJ **1** *(eyes)* furieux **2** *(light)* éblouissant, éclatant; *(sun)* aveuglant; *(colour etc)* voyant **3** *Fig (fact etc)* manifeste, patent, qui saute aux yeux; *(error, injustice, omission)* flagrant; *(abuse)* scandaleux, choquant

glaringly ['gleərɪŋlɪ] ADV **it's g. obvious** ça saute aux yeux

glasnost ['glæznɒst] N *Pol* glasnost *f*

glass [glɑːs] N **1** *(material)* verre *m*; **g. bottle** bouteille de *ou* en verre; **g. door** porte vitrée, porte de *ou* en verre; **g. partition** cloison *f* de *ou* en verre; **the g. industry** l'industrie *f* du verre; *Prov* **people who live in g. houses shouldn't throw stones** il faut être sans défauts pour critiquer autrui; **to keep/display sth under g.** garder/exposer qch sous verre
2 *(single piece) (of window)* vitre *f*, carreau *m*; *(of car)* glace *f*, vitre; *(of watch, lamp)* verre *m*
3 *(cup)* verre *m*; **wine g.** verre à vin; **g. of wine** verre de vin; **to sell wine by the g.** vendre le vin au verre
4 *(no pl) (glassware)* verrerie *f*
5 *(lens) (of optical instrument)* lentille *f*
6 *(telescope)* **(field) g.** lunette *f* d'approche, longue-vue *f*, *pl* longues-vues
7 *(mirror) (looking) g.* glace *f*, miroir *m*
8 *Old-fashioned (barometer)* baromètre *m* (à cadran); **the g. is falling** le baromètre baisse
9 *(in gardening)* **grown under g.** *(in cold*

frame) cultivé sous verre *ou* sous châssis; *(in glasshouse)* cultivé en serre
▸▸**g. case** *(for display)* vitrine *f*; **to keep/display sth in a g. case** garder/exposer qch sous verre; **g. ceiling** = plafond *m* de verre qui désigne métaphoriquement l'ensemble des facteurs qui empêchent les femmes de parvenir aux postes les plus élevés dans le monde professionnel; **g. cutter** *(person)* vitrier *m*; **g. cutting** taille *f* du verre; **g. eye** œil *m* de verre; **g. fibre** fibre(s) *f(pl)* de verre; *Boxing etc Fam* **g. jaw** mâchoire *f* fragile; **g. manufacturer** verrier *m*; **g. roof** verrière *f*; **g. wool** laine *f* de verre
▸ **glass in** VT SEP *(balcony etc)* entourer d'une cloison vitrée

glass-blower N souffleur *m* de verre

glass-blowing N soufflage *m* de verre

glasscloth ['glɑːsklɒθ] N torchon *m* (pour essuyer les verres)

glasses ['glɑːsɪz] NPL *(spectacles)* lunettes *fpl* VOIR GRAMMAIRE A10

glassful ['glɑːsfʊl] N *(of water etc)* (plein) verre *m*

glasshouse ['glɑːshaʊs] N **1** *Br (in garden)* serre *f* **2** *Br Mil Fam* prison *f* militaire, *Fam* trou *m* **3** *Am (factory)* verrerie *f*

glasspaper ['glɑːspeɪpər] N papier *m* de verre

glassware ['glɑːsweər] N verres *mpl*, *(stylish)* verrerie *f*

glassworks ['glɑːswɜːks] NPL *(usu with sing verb)* verrerie *f*, *(for crystal)* cristallerie *f*

glassy ['glɑːsɪ] ADJ *(smooth)* vitreux; **g. look/eye** regard/œil terne

Glaswegian [glæz'wiːdʒən] N *(resident)* habitant, -ante de Glasgow; *(by birth)* originaire *mf* de Glasgow
ADJ de Glasgow

glaucoma [glɔː'kəʊmə] N *Med* glaucome *m*; **to have g.** avoir un glaucome

glaucous ['glɔːkəs] ADJ glauque

glaze [gleɪz] N **1** *Cer* vernis *m* (luisant) **2** *Culin* glaçage *m* **3** *Art* vernis *m* **4** *Am (ice)* verglas *m*
VT **1** *(window, house)* vitrer **2** *Cer (pottery)* vernisser; *(tiles etc)* vitrifier **3** *Culin* glacer **4** *Art (painting)* glacer; *Phot (print)* émailler
▸ **glaze over** VI *(of eyes)* devenir vitreux

glazed [gleɪzd] ADJ **1** *(door)* vitré **2** *Cer* verni; *(brick)* vitrifié **3** *Culin* glacé **4** *(eye, look)* vitreux

glazier ['gleɪzɪər] N vitrier *m*

glazing ['gleɪzɪŋ] N **1** *(fitting of windows etc)* pose *f* des vitres **2** *(no pl) (windows)* vitrerie *f*; *Cer* vernissage *m*

GLC [dʒiːel'siː] N *Formerly (abbr* Greater London Council) = anciennement, conseil *m* municipal du grand Londres

gleam [gliːm] N *(of light)* rayon *m*, trait *m*; *(of knife etc)* reflet *m*; **there's a strange g. in his eye** il y a une drôle de lueur dans son regard; *Hum* **when you were just a g. in your father's eye** bien avant ta naissance
VI luire, reluire; *(of water)* miroiter; *(of eyes)* briller; **she polished the silverware until it gleamed** elle a astiqué l'argenterie jusqu'à ce qu'elle reluise

gleaming ['gliːmɪŋ] ADJ luisant; *(surface of water)* miroitant; *(silverware etc)* reluisant; **g. eyes** yeux brillants

glean [gliːn] VT *(corn, information etc)* glaner; **I couldn't g. much from the brochure** je n'ai pas pu tirer grand-chose de la brochure
VI *Agr* faire la glane

gleaner ['gliːnər] N *Agr* glaneur, -euse

gleaning ['gliːnɪŋ] N **gleanings** *(of crops)* glanes *fpl*; *Fig* **gleanings from the newspapers** informations *fpl* glanées dans les journaux

glebe [gliːb] N *Rel* terre *f* assignée à un bénéfice

glee [gliː] N **1** *(delight)* joie *f*, allégresse *f*; *(malicious pleasure)* jubilation *f*; **the children gave shouts of g.** les enfants ont poussé des cris de joie; **she announced it with some g.** elle l'a annoncé avec un malin plaisir **2** *Mus* petit chant *m* à trois ou quatre parties *(pour voix d'hommes)*
▸▸*Am Mus* **g. club** chorale *f*

gleeful ['gliːfʊl] ADJ joyeux, allègre; *(maliciously)* plein d'une joie malicieuse

gleefully ['gliːfʊlɪ] ADV allègrement, plein de joie; *(maliciously)* avec une joie malicieuse

glen [glen] N vallée *f*, *(narrower)* gorge *f*

glengarry (bonnet) [glen'gærɪ] N *Scot* béret *m* écossais

glib [glɪb] ADJ *(answer)* spécieux; *(speaker)* qui a du bagou(t); **his explanation was a bit too g.** son explication était un peu trop facile

glibly ['glɪblɪ] ADV *(to reply)* spécieusement; *(to speak)* avec aisance

glibness ['glɪbnɪs] N *(of excuse, reply)* spéciosité *f*, *(of person)* bagou(t) *m*

glide [glaɪd] N **1** *(movement)* glissement *m*; *(in dancing)* glissade *f*, glissé *m* **2** *(of glider)* vol *m* plané; *(of aircraft)* descente *f* en (vol) plané **3** *Mus* port *m* de voix **4** *Ling* son *m* transitoire
VI **1** *(slide)* glisser; **to g. (along) over the water** glisser sur l'eau **2** *(of birds)* planer; *(of aircraft)* planer, faire un vol plané; *(in glider)* faire du vol à voile
▸▸**g. path** *(of aircraft)* trajectoire *f* d'atterrissage

glider ['glaɪdər] N *Aviat* planeur *m*
▸▸**g. pilot** pilote *m* de planeur

gliding ['glaɪdɪŋ] N *Aviat* vol *m* plané; *(sport)* vol à voile

glimmer ['glɪmər] N *(of candle etc)* faible lueur *f*, *(of water etc)* reflet *m*; **g. of hope/intelligence** lueur d'espoir/d'intelligence; **not a g. of interest** pas le moindre intérêt
VI jeter une faible lueur; *(of water)* miroiter

glimmering ['glɪmərɪŋ] ADJ *(water)* miroitant; **a g. light** une faible lueur

glimpse [glɪmps] N vision *f* momentanée; **to catch a g. of sb/sth** entrevoir qn/qch; **she had only caught a g. of her assailant** elle n'avait fait qu'entrevoir son assaillant; **a g. of the future** un aperçu de ce que sera le futur
VT entrevoir

glint [glɪnt] N *(of light) (flash)* éclair *m*; *(continuous)* scintillement *m*; *(of knife etc)* reflet *m*; **hair with glints of gold** chevelure à *ou* aux reflets d'or
VI étinceler; *(on water)* miroiter; **the blade glinted in the sunlight** la lame miroita/miroitait au soleil; **his eyes were glinting with fury** ses yeux étincelaient de fureur

glissando [glɪ'sændəʊ] N *Mus* glissando *m*

glisten ['glɪs(ə)n] VI *(re)luire, scintiller; *(of sea)* miroiter; **his forehead glistened with sweat** la sueur perlait sur son front

glistening ['glɪs(ə)nɪŋ] ADJ luisant, scintillant; *(sea)* miroitant

glitch [glɪtʃ] N *Fam (problem etc)* pépin *m*; *Comput* défaillance *f* subite

glitter ['glɪtər] N scintillement *m*; *Fig (of occasion etc)* éclat *m*
VI briller, scintiller, (re)luire; **her eyes glittered with excitement** ses yeux brillaient *ou* scintillaient de joie; *Prov* **all that glitters is not gold** tout ce qui brille n'est pas or

glitterati [glɪtə'rɑːtiː] NPL *Fam* **the g.** le beau monde

glittering ['glɪtərɪŋ] ADJ scintillant; *(occa-*

sion) brillant; *Fig* **the g. world of showbusiness** le monde de lumière du show-business

glitz [glɪts] N *Fam (of showbusiness etc)* tape-à-l'œil *m*

glitzy ['glɪtsɪ] ADJ *Fam (party etc)* tape-à-l'œil *inv*

gloaming ['gləʊmɪŋ] N *Lit* crépuscule *m;* **in the g.** au crépuscule

gloat [gləʊt] VI jubiler; **don't g.** ne te réjouis pas; **to g. about sth** se réjouir à l'idée de qch
N **to have a g. about sth** se réjouir à l'idée de qch
▸ **gloat over** VT INSEP **to sit gloating over one's possessions** jubiler à la vue de ses possessions; **to g. over sb's misfortune** se réjouir du malheur de qn; **he was gloating over his victory/success** il jubilait en pensant à sa victoire/son succès

gloating ['gləʊtɪŋ] ADJ *(eye)* avide; *(smile, look)* jubilant

glob [glɒb] N *Fam (of cream etc)* petite boule *f*

global ['gləʊb(ə)l] ADJ **1** *(worldwide)* mondial, -aux, international, -aux; **on a g. scale** à l'échelle mondiale **2** *(comprehensive)* global, -aux
▸▸ *Mktg* **g. audience** audience *f* globale; *Fin* **g. banking** banque *f* universelle; *Comput* **g. change** changement *m* global; **g. corporation** multinationale *f,* **g. custody** conservation *f* globale; **g. economy** économie *f* mondiale; *Fin* **g. equities market** marché *m* mondial des actions; **g. finance** la finance internationale; *Com* **g. market** marché global; *Mktg* **g. marketing** marketing *m* global *ou* international; *Com* **g. marketplace** marché global; *Com* **g. player** acteur *m* international; *Comput* **g. search and replace** recherche *f* et remplacement *m* global; **g. village** village *m* planétaire; **g. war(fare)** guerre *f* mondiale; **g. warming** réchauffement *m* de la planète

globalism ['gləʊbəlɪzm] N mondialisme *m*

globalization [gləʊb(ə)laɪ'zeɪʃən] N **1** *(making worldwide)* mondialisation *f* **2** *(generalization)* globalisation *f*

globalize ['gləʊb(ə)laɪz] VT **1** *(make worldwide)* mondialiser **2** *(generalize)* globaliser

globally ['gləʊbəlɪ] ADV **1** *(generally)* globalement **2** *(worldwide)* mondialement; **the problem of over-population must be dealt with g.** on doit résoudre le problème de la surpopulation à l'échelle planétaire

globe [gləʊb] N *(sphere)* sphère *f; (with map)* globe *m* terrestre; *(lampshade)* globe (de lampe); *Anat (of eye)* globe; **to go round the g.** faire le tour du globe; *Sl* **globes** *(breasts)* nichons *mpl,* nénés *mpl*
▸▸ **g. artichoke** artichaut *m;* **g. lightning** éclair *m* en boule

globe-fish N poisson-globe *m, pl* poissons-globes

globetrotter ['gləʊbtrɒtər] N *Fam* globe-trotter *m, pl* globe-trotters

globetrotting ['gləʊbtrɒtɪŋ] N *Fam* voyages *mpl* dans le monde entier

globular ['glɒbjʊlər] ADJ *(globe-shaped)* globulaire; *(composed of globules)* globuleux

globule ['glɒbjuːl] N *(of fat etc)* globule *m; (of wax, molten metal)* gouttelette *f*

globulin ['glɒbjʊlɪn] N *Biol, Chem* globuline *f*

glockenspiel ['glɒkənʃpiːl] N *Mus* glockenspiel *m*

glomerulus [glɒ'merʊləs] N *Anat* glomérule *m*

gloom [gluːm] N **1** *(darkness)* obscurité *f,* ténèbres *fpl* **2** *(melancholy)* mélancolie *f,* tristesse *f* empreinte de pessimisme; **to cast** *or*

throw a **g.** over *or* on the company jeter une ombre *ou* un voile de tristesse sur l'assemblée; **there is g. in the City** la Bourse de Londres est pessimiste

gloomily ['gluːmɪlɪ] ADV avec mélancolie, mélancoliquement

gloominess ['gluːmɪnɪs] N **1 the g. of the sky** le ciel gris; **the g. of the weather** ce temps maussade **2** *(melancholy)* tristesse *f,* mélancolie *f*

gloomy ['gluːmɪ] ADJ **1** *(dark)* sombre, *Lit* ténébreux; **the weather is g.** il fait sombre; **to turn g.** s'assombrir **2** *(melancholy)* morne, sombre; *(stronger)* lugubre; *(prediction etc)* sombre; **to become g.** *(of person)* devenir sombre, se rembrunir; **g. thoughts** de noires pensées; *Fig* **to paint a g. picture** faire un tableau plutôt sombre

glorification [glɔːrɪfɪ'keɪʃən] N glorification *f*

glorified ['glɔːrɪfaɪd] ADJ **1** *Rel* glorifié; *(body)* glorieux **2 it's just a g. motor scooter** ce n'est qu'un scooter amélioré; **in fact he's just a g. janitor** en fait ce n'est qu'un simple concierge

glorify ['glɔːrɪfaɪ] VT glorifier, célébrer; *(God)* rendre gloire à; **the book glorifies war** ce livre glorifie la guerre

glorious ['glɔːrɪəs] ADJ **1** *(reign, martyr)* glorieux; *(victory)* éclatant; *(action)* remarquable; *Br Hist* **the G. Revolution** la *(seconde)* Révolution d'Angleterre; **the G. Twelfth** = le 12 août, début de la chasse à la grouse **2** *(splendid, beautiful)* resplendissant, radieux; **g. in her youth and beauty** resplendissante de jeunesse et de beauté **3** *(excellent)* magnifique, splendide; **what g. weather!** quel temps superbe!

gloriously ['glɔːrɪəslɪ] ADV glorieusement; *Fam* **g. drunk** ivre bien comme il faut

glory ['glɔːrɪ] N **1** *(honour)* gloire *f,* **the athletes get all the g.** ce sont les athlètes qui remportent toute la gloire; **to give g. to God** rendre gloire à Dieu; **g. be to God!** gloire à Dieu!; *Old-fashioned Fam* **g. be!** oh mon Dieu!; *(thank heaven)* Dieu soit loué! **2** *(thing)* sujet *m* de gloire; **to be the g. of the age** faire la gloire du siècle **3** *(splendour) (of spectacle etc)* splendeur *f,* éclat *m;* **in all her g.** parée de ses plus beaux atours; **Spain, in the days of her g.** l'Espagne, au temps de sa splendeur; **the glories of the Irish countryside** les splendeurs de la campagne irlandaise **4** *Rel* gloire *f,* **the saints in g.** les glorieux *mpl* **5** *(halo) (of saint)* gloire *f*
▸▸ **g. hole** *Naut (locker)* petit placard *m; (storeroom)* soute *f, Br Fam (cupboard)* débarras *m; (untidy place)* capharnaüm *m*
▸ **glory in** VT INSEP *(rejoice in)* se glorifier de; **to g. in one's freedom** profiter pleinement de sa liberté; **the dog gloried in the name of Marmaduke** le chien portait le nom ronflant de Marmaduke

Glos *abbr* Gloucestershire

gloss[1] [glɒs] N *(shine)* lustre *m,* vernis *m,* brillant *m; Tex* cati *m; (paint)* peinture *f* brillante; *Fig (veneer) (of legality etc)* vernis *m; Fig* **to take the g. off sth** gâcher qch
VT *(make shine)* lustrer
▸▸ **g. paint** peinture *f* brillante
▸ **gloss over** VT INSEP **1** *(deal hurriedly with)* ne pas s'étendre sur; *(sb's shortcomings)* glisser *ou* passer sur **2** *(conceal, cover up)* dissimuler

gloss[2] *Liter* N glose *f*
VT *(text)* annoter

glossary ['glɒsərɪ] N glossaire *m,* lexique *m*

glossiness ['glɒsɪnɪs] N lustre *m,* vernis *m*

glossy ['glɒsɪ] ADJ lustré, brillant; *(paper)*

glacé; *(coat) (of dog)* lustré; *Phot (paper)* brillant
N *(pl* **glossies)** *Journ* magazine *m (sur papier glacé); (women's magazine)* magazine féminin de luxe; **the glossies** la presse féminine de luxe
▸▸ **g. magazine** magazine *m (sur papier glacé); Phot* **g. print** épreuve *f* sur papier brillant

glottal ['glɒt(ə)l] ADJ *Ling* glottal, -aux; *Anat* glottique
▸▸ *Ling* **g. stop** coup *m* de glotte

glottis ['glɒtɪs] N *Anat* glotte *f*

glove [glʌv] N gant *m;* **to put on one's gloves** mettre ses gants, se ganter; **to take off one's gloves** enlever ses gants, se déganter; **it fits like a g.!** ça me/te/lui/*etc* va comme un gant!; *Fig* **the gloves were off** on n'a pas mis de gants, on y est allé carrément
VT ganter
▸▸ *Aut* **g. compartment** boîte *f* à gants; **g. counter, g. department** *(in large store)* rayon *m* des gants, ganterie *f,* **g. maker, g. manufacturer** gantier, -ière; *Br* **g. puppet** marionnette *f (à gaine)*

glovebox ['glʌvbɒks] N *Aut* boîte *f* à gants

glover ['glʌvər] N gantier, -ière

glow [gləʊ] N **1** *(light)* lueur *f, (of hot metal)* rougeoiement *m,* incandescence *f,* **the g. of the setting sun** l'embrasement *m* du ciel au couchant **2** *(of complexion)* to have a healthy g. in one's cheeks avoir les joues bien rouges; **g. of health** bonne mine *f,* **a g. of pleasure** une rougeur de plaisir **3** *Fig (warm feeling)* it gave him a g. of pride cela le faisait rayonner d'orgueil; **he felt a warm g.** spread over him as the whisky went down il sentit une sensation de chaleur dans tout le corps après avoir bu le whisky; **it gives you a warm g.** *(of news, scene etc)* ça vous fait chaud au cœur
VI *(of light, fire, hot metal)* rougeoyer; *(of person, face)* rayonner; **her face was glowing with pleasure** son visage rayonnait de plaisir; **to g. with enthusiasm** brûler d'enthousiasme; **to be glowing with health** être rayonnant de santé; **his cheeks were glowing** il avait les joues en feu

glower ['glaʊər] VI avoir un air renfrogné; **to g. at sb** *(with disapproval or anger)* lancer un/des regard(s) noir(s) à qn

glowering ['glaʊərɪŋ] ADJ *(expression)* renfrogné; **to give sb a g. look** lancer à qn un regard noir

glowing ['gləʊɪŋ] ADJ **1** *(metal)* (chauffé au) rouge, incandescent, rougeoyant **2** *(coal, embers, cigarette)* rougeoyant; *(eyes)* de braise **3** *(complexion)* rayonnant; *(cheeks)* rouge **4** *(colours, words)* chaleureux; *(description)* en termes chaleureux; *Fig* **to paint sth in g. colours** présenter qch sous un jour des plus favorables; **the reviews were g.** les critiques étaient très élogieuses; **to speak in g. terms of sb** faire les louanges de qn

glow-worm N ver *m* luisant

gloxinia [glɒk'sɪnɪə] N *(plant)* gloxinia *m*

glucose ['gluːkəʊs] N glucose *m*

glue [gluː] N colle *f* (forte), glu *f, Fam* **he sticks to me like g.** il me suit partout comme un petit chien
VT *(* **glued; gluing)** coller (à la colle forte); **to g. sth on** *or* **to sth** coller qch sur qch; **I glued it on** je l'ai collé dessus; **to g. two things together** coller deux choses (ensemble); *Fig* **with her face glued to the window** le visage collé à la fenêtre; *Fig* **they were glued to the television** ils étaient rivés à la télévision; *Fig* **keep your eyes glued to the road** gardez les yeux rivés *ou* fixés sur la route
▸▸ *Med* **g. ear** otite *f* séreuse
▸ **glue down** VT SEP coller

gluepot ['glu:pɒt] N pot *m* de colle

glue-sniffer N sniffeur, -euse (de colle)

glue-sniffing ['glu:snɪfɪŋ] N inhalation *f* de colle; **to be into g.** sniffer de la colle

gluey ['glu:ɪ] ADJ gluant, poisseux

glug [glʌg] *Fam* N g. (g.) glouglou *m*
VI (-gg-) faire glouglou

glum [glʌm] ADJ (face, expression) renfrogné, maussade; (appearance) morne, maussade

glumly ['glʌmlɪ] ADV d'un air maussade

glumness ['glʌmnɪs] N air *m* maussade

glut [glʌt] N *Com* (on market) encombrement *m*; (of commodity) surabondance *f*; **g. of money** pléthore *f* de capitaux
VT (-tt-) **1** *Com* (market) encombrer, inonder; **the market is glutted with ...** le marché regorge de ... **2 to g. oneself** se rassasier, se gorger (**on** de)

glutamine ['glu:təmɪn] N glutamine *f*

gluten ['glu:tən] N gluten *m*

glutinous ['glu:tɪnəs] ADJ glutineux

glutted ['glʌtɪd] ADJ (market) encombré

glutton ['glʌt(ə)n] N (person) glouton, -onne, goinfre *m*; **she's a g. for work** c'est un bourreau de travail; **you're a g. for punishment** tu cherches les complications

gluttonous ['glʌtənəs] ADJ glouton

gluttonously ['glʌtənəslɪ] ADV gloutonnement

gluttony ['glʌtənɪ] N gloutonnerie *f*, goinfrerie *f*

glycaemia [glaɪ'si:mɪə] N *Med* glycémie *f*

glycerin(e) ['glɪsərɪn, -i:n] N *Chem etc* glycérine *f*

glycerol ['glɪsərɒl] N *Chem etc* glycérol *m*

glyceryl trinitrate ['glɪsərɪltraɪ'naɪtreɪt] N *Pharm* trinitrine *f*

glycol ['glaɪkɒl] N *Chem* glycol *m*

GM [dʒi:'em] ADJ **1** abbr **genetically modified 2** abbr **grant maintained**

G-man, pl **G-men** ['dʒi:mæn, -men] N *Am Fam* agent *m* du FBI

GMC [dʒi:em'si:] N (abbr **general management committee**) comité *m* de direction

GMO [dʒi:em'əʊ] N (abbr **genetically modified organism**) OMG *m*

GMT [dʒi:em'ti:] N (abbr **Greenwich Mean Time**) G. M. T. *m*

gnarled [nɑ:ld] ADJ **1** (tree) (knotty) noueux; (twisted) tordu **2** (hands, fingers) noueux; (old man, woman) fripé

gnarly ['nɑ:lɪ] ADJ *Am Fam* (excellent, awful) mortel

gnash [næʃ] VT **to g. one's teeth** grincer des dents

gnashing ['næʃɪŋ] N grincement *m*; *Lit, Hum* **there was much weeping and g. of teeth** il y eut moult pleurs et grincements de dents

gnat [næt] N (insect) moucheron *m*

gnaw [nɔ:] VT (pt gnawed; pp gnawed, gnawn) (of rodent) ronger; **to g. a bone** (of dog) ronger un os; *Fig* **gnawed by hunger** tenaillé par la faim; **gnawed by remorse** rongé par le remords

▸ **gnaw at, gnaw into, gnaw through** VT INSEP ronger

gnawing ['nɔ:ɪŋ] ADJ (hunger, anxiety) dévorant; **the g. pains of hunger** les tiraillements *mpl* de la faim

GNE [dʒi:en'i:] N *Econ* (abbr **gross national expenditure**) DNP *f*, dépense *f* nationale brute

gneiss [naɪs] N *Geol* gneiss *m*

gnome [nəʊm] N *Myth* gnome *m*; (garden) g. = statue *f* de nain qui décore un jardin; *Fam*

Pej **the gnomes of Zurich** les banquiers *mpl* internationaux de Zurich

gnomic ['nəʊmɪk] ADJ *Lit* gnomique

gnosis ['nəʊsɪs] N gnose *f*

gnostic ['nɒstɪk] ADJ, N *Rel* gnostique *mf*

gnosticism ['nɒstɪsɪz(ə)m] N *Rel, Hist* gnosticisme *m*

GNP [dʒi:en'pi:] N *Econ* (abbr **Gross National Product**) PNB *m*; **G. per capita** PNB par habitant

gnu [nu:] N (animal) gnou *m*

GO [gəʊ]

VT		
aller **1, 3, 15, 16**	▪	marcher **2, 3**
▪ passer **4**	▪	faire **6**	▪ aller ensemble **7**
▪ s'en aller **8**	▪	partir **8**
▪ disparaître **9**	▪	s'user **10**	▪ sauter **10**
▪ se casser **10**	▪	se vendre **11**
▪ aller (+ infinitive) **12, 13**	▪	future tense **13**	▪ entrer **14**	▪ contribuer **17**
▪ s'étendre **18**	▪	devenir **19**
VI	dire **2**	
N	allant **2**	▪ coup **3**	▪ essai **3**
▪ tour **3**		

VI (he goes; pt went [went], pp gone [gɒn]) **1** aller; **to go to a place** aller *ou* se rendre à un endroit; **to go to Paris/to the country** aller à Paris/à la campagne; **to go to France/Japan** aller en France/au Japon; **to go home** aller *ou* rentrer chez soi; **to go to church/Mass** aller à l'église/à la messe; **to go to the doctor's** aller chez le médecin; **to go to prison** aller en prison; **to go to the lavatory** aller aux toilettes; **do you need to go?** (to toilet) tu as besoin de faire pipi?; **I went before I came** (to toilet) j'ai fait (pipi) avant de venir; **to go to sb's house** aller chez qn; **to go on foot/by train/by car** aller à pied/par le train/en voiture; **there he goes!** le voilà (qui passe)!; *Mil* **who goes there?** qui va là?; **the car was going very slowly/fast** la voiture allait très lentement/vite; **to go at 100 km an hour** faire 100 km *ou* du cent à l'heure; **you go first** (after you) à vous l'honneur, vous d'abord; (you leave first) partez le premier *ou* devant; **to go up/down/across a street** remonter/descendre/traverser une rue; **which road goes to London?** quelle est la route de Londres?; *Fig* **where do we go from here?** et maintenant?; **to go one's own way** faire à sa guise; **there you go!** (handing sth to sb) voilà!; **it's expensive, but there you go** (that's how it is) c'est cher, mais c'est comme ça; **there you go again!** vous voilà reparti!; **to go riding** (aller) se promener à cheval; **to go hunting/fishing** aller à la chasse/à la pêche; **to go looking for sth** partir à la recherche de qch

2 (be active, function) marcher; **to set** *or* **get a piece of machinery going** mettre une machine en marche *ou* en mouvement; *Fam* **get going!** file!, vas-y!; **my watch has stopped going** ma montre ne marche plus; **the bell went ten minutes ago** la cloche a sonné il y a dix minutes; **enough timber to keep three sawmills going** assez de bois pour alimenter trois scieries; **to keep the conversation going** entretenir la conversation; **when he gets going, he never stops** quand il est lancé *ou* une fois lancé, il ne sait pas s'arrêter

3 (progress) **everything's going well** tout marche bien; **things are going badly** cela va mal; **how are things going?, how is it going?** comment ça va?; **if all goes well** si tout va bien; **the rehearsal went well/badly** la répétition a bien/mal marché; **the way things are going** au train où vont les choses; **I forget how the tune goes** l'air m'échappe; **how does the chorus go?** quelles sont les paroles du refrain?; **how does it go?** (of

tune, music) c'est comment?; **as things go today** par les temps qui courent; **that's not dear as things go today** ce n'est pas cher au prix où sont les choses; **which way will the decision go?** que décidera-t-on?; **I don't know how things will go** je ne sais pas comment cela tournera

4 (of time) passer; **there were only five minutes to go before ...** il ne restait que cinq minutes avant ...; **how's the time going?** combien de temps nous reste-t-il?; **it has just gone eight** il est un peu plus de huit heures

5 (be the rule) **what she says goes** c'est elle qui commande; **anything goes** (do, wear etc whatever you like) on fait ce qu'on veut

6 *Fam* (make sound, perform action) **to go crack/bang** faire crac/pan; **go like this with your left foot** fais comme ça du pied gauche

7 (match) **these colours don't go** ces couleurs jurent; **these colours go perfectly** ces couleurs vont parfaitement ensemble

8 (leave) partir, s'en aller; **after** *or* **when I had gone** après mon départ, après que je sois parti; **we must go** *or* **must be going** il est temps de partir; **let me go** laissez-moi partir; **go!** (go away) allez-vous-en!; *Sport* (in race etc) partez!; **from the word go** dès le début; **that old chair will have to go** il va falloir se débarrasser de cette vieille chaise; **a hundred employees will have to go** il va falloir mettre cent employés à la porte; *Euph* **his wife went first** (died) sa femme est partie avant lui; *Euph* **when I am gone, after I have gone** (died) quand je ne serai plus là

9 (disappear) disparaître; **my hat has gone** mon chapeau a disparu; **it's all gone** il n'y en a plus; **that's the way the money goes** voilà comme l'argent file; **most of my money goes on food** la plus grande partie de mon argent passe dans la nourriture; **her sight is going** elle est en train de perdre la vue

10 (break) (se) casser; **the spring went** le ressort s'est cassé; **the batteries are going** les piles sont presque mortes; *Elec* **a fuse went** un plomb a sauté; **my dress is going at the seams** ma robe s'use aux coutures

11 (be on sale, available) **they are going for ten euros each** on les vend dix euros pièce; **the lot went for £20** (at auction) le lot fut adjugé à 20 livres; **going! going! gone!** (at auction) une fois! deux fois! adjugé!; **let's see if there's any lunch going** allons voir si le déjeuner est prêt; **there are drinks going in the drawing room** on sert l'apéritif dans le salon; **there's a job going at the factory** il y a une place à l'usine

12 (introducing an action) **to go and do sth** aller faire qch; **to go to dinner with sb** aller dîner avec qn; (at their place) aller dîner chez qn; **to go to** *or* **and see sb** aller voir qn; **go and see** *or* **esp** *Am* **go see what's happening** va voir ce qui se passe; **to go and look for sth** aller chercher qch; *Fam* **and then he went and got married!** et puis, il a eu l'idée de se marier!; *Fam* **what did you have to go and tell him for?** qu'est-ce qui t'a pris d'aller le lui dire?; *Fam* **you've gone and done it now!** vraiment, tu as tout gâché!; **he went (forward) to help her, but ...** il a fait un mouvement pour l'aider, mais ...

13 (aux forming future) **I'm going to tell you a story** je vais vous raconter une histoire; **the shortage is not going to last** la disette ne durera pas; **I'm going to have my own way** je vais faire comme je l'entends; **I'm not going to be cheated** je ne me laisserai pas abuser; **I was going to walk** (intention) j'avais l'intention d'y aller à pied; **I'm going to go to France for my holiday** je compte passer mes vacances en France; **he knew it was going to be difficult** il savait que ce serait difficile; **she was going to telephone the police when she was shot** elle s'apprêtait à téléphoner à la police quand la balle l'a frappée VOIR GRAMMAIRE A51

14 *(fit)* too big to go into the basket trop grand pour entrer dans le panier; **the key won't go in(to) the lock** la clef n'entre pas dans la serrure; **the piano won't go through the door** le piano ne passe pas par la porte; *Math* **six into twelve goes twice** douze divisé par six fait deux; **four into three won't go** trois n'est pas divisible par quatre

15 *(belong)* **where does this book go?** où va ce livre?; **the scissors go in the drawer** les ciseaux vont *ou* se rangent dans le tiroir

16 *(be given)* **the proceeds will go to charity** les bénéfices iront à des œuvres de charité; **the estate will go to his eldest son** la propriété va revenir à son fils aîné

17 *(contribute)* **the qualities that go to make a great man** les qualités qui font un grand homme; **ingredients that go to make a good dish** ingrédients qui contribuent à faire un bon plat; **these reforms go some way to(wards) improving the situation** ces réformes contribuent à améliorer la situation; **this money will go to(wards) building a new school** cet argent servira à construire une nouvelle école; **to go to prove sth** servir à prouver qch; **it only goes to show that …** cela montre bien que …

18 *(extend)* s'étendre; **the garden goes down to the river** le jardin s'étend jusqu'à la rivière; **that's true, as far as it goes** c'est vrai jusqu'à un certain point; **her essay's quite good, as far as it goes** malgré ses faiblesses, sa dissertation n'est pas mauvaise

19 *(become)* devenir; **to go Communist** devenir communiste; **you'll just have to go hungry** il va falloir que tu supportes la faim; **while half the world go hungry** tandis que la moitié du monde n'a rien à manger *ou* connaît la faim; **he went cold all over** son sang s'est glacé; **the tea's gone cold** le thé a refroidi; **to go red** rougir; **to go white** blanchir; **my hair is going grey** mes cheveux grisonnent *ou* deviennent gris; **to go to the bad** mal tourner

VT 1 *Fam* **that's really going it!** *(that's fast)* ça, c'est de la vitesse!; **to go it alone** agir tout seul; *(in business)* se lancer tout seul; *Fam* **I could really go a beer** je me paierais bien une bière; **to go 10** *(in gambling)* risquer 10; *Cards* **to go no/two/three trumps** annoncer sans/deux/trois atout(s); **to go one better** surenchérir *(* than sb sur qn)

2 *Fam (say)* dire; **so she goes, 'you're lying!', and I go, 'no, I'm not!'** alors elle me fait 'tu mens!', et je lui fais 'non, je mens pas!'

N *(pl* goes**) 1** *(activity)* **to be always on the go** être toujours à trotter *ou* à courir, *Fam* avoir la bougeotte; **to keep sb on the go** faire trimer qn; **it's all go** on n'a pas une minute à soi, ça n'arrête pas

2 *(energy)* **to be full of** *or* **have plenty of go** avoir de l'allant

3 *(try)* coup *m*, essai *m*; **to make a go of it** *(succeed)* y réussir; **(it's) your go!** *(in game)* à vous de jouer!; **to have a go (at doing sth)** essayer (de faire qch); **can I have a go?** je peux essayer?; **let's have a go!** tentons le coup!, allons-y!; *(let me try)* laisse-moi essayer!; **she had a go at me** *(abused me verbally)* elle s'en est prise à moi; *Fam* **to have a go** *(stop or arrest criminal)* tenter quelque chose *(alors qu'on n'est pas de la police)*; **(it's) no go!** rien à faire!; **at one go** d'un (seul) coup; **£1 a go** *(at fair etc)* une livre la partie *ou* le tour; **to have a go on the Dodgems®** faire un tour d'autos tamponneuses; **he wouldn't let me have** *or* **give me a go** *(on his bicycle etc)* il ne voulait pas me laisser l'essayer; **you've had three goes already** *(attempts)* tu as déjà essayé trois fois; *(on bicycle etc)* tu as déjà fait trois tours

4 *Old-fashioned* **it's all the go** *(fashionable)* ça fait fureur *ou* rage

ADJ *Astronaut* **all systems are go** tout est paré et en ordre de marche (pour le départ)

▸ **go about** **VI** *(move)* circuler; *(of rumour)* courir; *Naut (turn)* virer de bord; **policemen usually go about in pairs** en général, les policiers circulent par deux; **you can't go about saying things like that!** il ne faut pas raconter des choses pareilles!; **someone has been going about saying that …** quelqu'un a été raconter que …; **she's been going about with that Smith boy** on l'a vue traîner avec le fils Smith

VT INSEP 1 *(country)* parcourir; **to go about the streets** circuler dans les rues

2 *(tackle)* **how to go about it** comment s'y prendre; **how do I go about getting a licence?** que dois-je faire pour obtenir un permis?

3 *(one's work, business)* vaquer à

▸ **go across** **VI** traverser; **she's gone across to Mrs McGinty's** elle est en face, chez Mme McGinty

VT INSEP *(bridge etc)* traverser

▸ **go after** **VT INSEP** *(pursue)* essayer d'obtenir; *(person)* courir après; **she really goes after what she wants** elle fait tout pour obtenir ce qu'elle veut

▸ **go against** **VT INSEP** *(conflict with, act contrary to)* aller contre; **to go against sb's wishes** contrarier les désirs de qn; **this goes against everything I believe in** ceci est contraire à tout ce en quoi je crois; **the judgement/decision went against them** le jugement/la décision leur a été défavorable

▸ **go ahead** **VI 1** *(proceed)* continuer, poursuivre; **may I say something? – go ahead** puis-je dire quelque chose? – allez-y; **to go ahead with sth** commencer qch; **he went ahead and did it** *(without hesitating)* il l'a fait sans l'ombre d'une hésitation; *(despite warnings)* rien ne l'a arrêté; **the building work was finally able to go ahead** la construction a pu commencer; **they went straight a.** ils sont allés droit devant eux; **the project is going a.** *(has been approved)* le projet a été accepté; **they're going ahead with the project after all** ils ont finalement décidé de mener le projet à bien

2 *(go in front)* avancer; **you go (on) ahead** *(I'll follow later)* partez devant; **to go ahead of sb** devancer qn

▸ **go along** **VI 1** *(walk, ride, drive etc)* avancer; **as we go along** en chemin; **we were going along quite slowly when …** nous avancions plutôt lentement quand …

2 *(proceed)* **I check the figures as I go along** je vérifie les chiffres au fur et à mesure; **you'll have to make it up as you go along** il faudra que tu improvises au fur et à mesure

3 *(go to meeting, party etc)* aller

▸ **go along with** **VT INSEP** *(agree with)* *(person)* coopérer avec; *(something)* approuver, accepter; **she wouldn't go along with it** elle n'était pas d'accord

▸ **go around** **VI** = **go about VI**

▸ **go at** **VT INSEP** *(somebody, something)* s'attaquer à; **to go at it hard** ne pas y aller de main morte; **he was still going at it when I left** *(working hard)* il était encore à la tâche quand je suis parti; **they went at the task with a will** ils se sont mis à la tâche avec beaucoup de détermination

▸ **go away** **VI** *(leave)* s'en aller, partir; **go away!** va-t-en!; **to go away on business/for the weekend** s'absenter pour affaires/pour le week-end; **to go away with sth** emporter qch

▸ **go back** **VI 1** *(return)* revenir, s'en retourner; *(turn back)* retourner (en arrière); *(move back)* reculer; **go back! it's dangerous!** recule! c'est dangereux!; **to go back home** retourner *ou* rentrer chez soi; **to go back to Paris** retourner à Paris; **he's never gone back** *(to that place)* il n'y est jamais retourné; **let's go back the way we came** reprenons le même chemin qu'à l'aller; **to go back two paces** faire deux pas en arrière; **to go back to the beginning** reprendre depuis le début; **he went back to his reading** il s'est replongé dans sa lecture; **to go back to sleep** se rendormir; **to go back to one's old ways** retomber dans ses anciennes habitudes; **to go back to doing sth** *(resume task, habit)* se remettre à faire qch; **he went back to teaching** il est revenu à l'enseignement

2 *(date back)* remonter (to à); **there are records going back to 1700** il y a des récits qui remontent à 1700; **we go back a long way** *(our acquaintance)* ça fait longtemps qu'on se connaît

3 *(extend)* **the garden goes back 40 metres behind the house** le jardin s'étend sur 40 mètres derrière la maison

4 **the clocks go back tonight** on retarde les pendules d'une heure cette nuit

▸ **go back on** **VT INSEP** *(abandon, alter)* *(decision, promise)* revenir sur

▸ **go before** **VI** précéder; *Euph* **those who have gone before** *(the dead)* ceux qui nous ont précédés

VT INSEP *(tribunal, committee etc)* se présenter devant; *Law* comparaître devant; **the case goes before the court/the judge tomorrow** l'affaire passe au tribunal/devant le juge demain; **it goes before the committee tomorrow** elle passe en commission demain

▸ **go below** **VI** *Naut* descendre

▸ **go by** **VI 1** *(pass)* passer; **to watch people going by** regarder passer les gens; *Fig* **to let an opportunity go by** laisser passer une occasion

2 *(elapse)* s'écouler; **half an hour went by** une demi-heure s'est écoulée; **as the years go by** à mesure que les années passent

VT INSEP 1 *(judge on the basis of)* juger d'après; **don't go by what he says/his opinion** ne juge pas d'après ce qu'il dit/ne tiens pas compte de ses opinions; **to go by appearances** juger d'après les apparences

2 *(follow)* **to go by the rules** suivre *ou* respecter les règles; **promotion goes by seniority** l'avancement se fait à l'ancienneté; **go by your sister's example** suis l'exemple de ta sœur

3 *(be known by)* **to go by a different/false name** être connu sous un nom différent/un faux nom; **the product goes by the name of 'Bango' in France** ce produit est vendu sous le nom de 'Bango' en France

▸ **go down** **VI 1** *(descend)* descendre; *(of sun)* se coucher; *(of ship)* sombrer; **going down!** *(in lift)* on descend!, pour descendre!; **go down and answer the door** descends ouvrir; **to go down on one's knees** se mettre à genoux; *Sl* **to go down on sb** *(perform oral sex on)* sucer qn; *Fam* **to go down with flu** attraper la grippe; **to have gone down in the world** avoir connu des jours meilleurs; **the captain went down with his ship** le capitaine a sombré avec son navire; **I'm not going to go down without a fight** *(be defeated)* je me battrai jusqu'à la fin

2 *(decrease)* *(of floods, temperature)* baisser, s'abaisser; *(of wind)* baisser, tomber; *(of prices, value)* baisser; **to go d. in sb's estimation** baisser dans l'estime de qn

3 *(be received)* **to go down well** *(of drink)* se laisser boire; *(of food)* se laisser manger; *(of entertainment, speech, suggestion)* plaire, être bien reçu; **he went down in history as a tyrant** l'histoire a retenu de lui l'image d'un tyran

4 *(shrink)* *(of swelling)* désenfler, se dégonfler; *(of tyre, balloon)* se dégonfler

5 *(extend)* continuer; *(to end of page etc)* aller jusqu'à; **the mineshaft goes down three hundred metres** le puits de mine a trois cents mètres de profondeur

6 *Br Univ (esp Oxford and Cambridge)* **to go down (from university)** *(at end of studies)* quitter l'université; *(at end of term)* partir en vacances

7 *Cards (bridge)* chuter

8 *Am Fam* **what's going down?** *(happening)* qu'est-ce qui se passe?

9 *Comput* tomber en panne; *(of computer network)* planter

VT INSEP *(descend)* *(hill, ladder, street)* descendre; *Sch* **to go down a class/a grade** descendre d'une classe; **some of his food went down the wrong way** il a avalé de travers; **my weight has gone down a few pounds** j'ai perdu quelques kilos; *Fig* **I don't want to go down that road** je ne veux pas m'engager là-dedans

▸ **go for** **VT INSEP 1** *(attack)* *(person)* attaquer, tomber sur; **go for him!** *(to dog)* attaque!; **they went for each other in court** *(physically)* ils se sont empoignés devant le tribunal; *(verbally)* ils se sont disputés *ou Fam* engueulés devant le tribunal

2 *(strive to attain)* essayer d'obtenir; **if you really want the job, go for it!** si tu veux vraiment le poste, mets-y le paquet!; **with his next jump, he's going for the gold** avec son prochain saut, il vise la médaille d'or

3 *(like)* **I don't go for him much** *(don't like him)* je ne l'aime pas tellement; *(don't think him attractive)* il ne m'attire pas spécialement; **tabloid newspapers go for stories like those** la presse à scandales adore ce genre d'histoires

4 *(choose)* prendre; **I'll go for the blue one** je prendrai le bleu

5 **she's got a lot going for her** elle a tout pour elle; **the third proposal has a lot going for it** la troisième proposition a bien des avantages

6 **the same goes for you** ça s'applique à vous aussi

▸ **go forth** **VI** *Rel* **go forth and multiply** croissez et multipliez; *Lit* **the word went forth that ...** on a fait savoir que ...; *Hum* **the word has gone forth that the boss would like ...** le patron a fait savoir qu'il voudrait ...

▸ **go forward** **VI** (s')avancer; **the clocks go forward tomorrow** on avance les pendules demain; **if this scheme goes forward ...** si ce projet est accepté ...

▸ **go in** **VI 1** *(enter)* entrer, rentrer; **let's go in!** entrons!; **it's too big, it won't go in** c'est trop grand, ça ne rentrera pas

2 *(of sun)* se cacher

3 *Cr* prendre son tour au guichet

4 *Mil etc Fam (attack)* attaquer

VT INSEP *(enter)* *(house, room etc)* entrer dans, rentrer dans

▸ **go in for** **VT INSEP 1** *(use, produce, show interest in)* **they don't go in for injections so much nowadays** ils ne sont pas tellement pour les piqûres de nos jours; **why do scientists go in for all that jargon?** pourquoi est-ce que les scientifiques utilisent tout ce jargon?; **this publisher doesn't really go in for fiction** cet éditeur ne fait pas tellement dans le roman; **we don't go in for pop music** nous ne sommes pas très musique pop

2 *(engage in)* s'adonner à, se consacrer à; **he doesn't go in for team sports** il n'est pas très porté sur les sports d'équipe; **to go in for painting** *(as hobby)* faire de la peinture; **to go in for teaching** *(as career)* entrer dans l'enseignement

3 *(enter)* **to go in for an examination** se présenter à un examen; **to go in for a competition** prendre part à un concours

▸ **go into** **VT INSEP 1** *(enter)* entrer dans, rentrer dans; **she's gone into hospital** elle est

(r)entrée à l'hôpital; **to go into fits of laughter** avoir des crises de fou rire; **to go into the army** s'engager (dans l'armée); *(be called up)* partir au régiment; **to go into teaching** *(as career)* entrer dans l'enseignement; **to go into a convent** entrer au couvent

2 *(examine)* *(question)* examiner, étudier; **I shall go into the matter** je vais m'occuper de l'affaire; **to go into the reasons (given) for sth** rechercher les raisons de qch

3 *(explain, provide the reasons for)* expliquer; **to go into details** entrer dans les détails

4 *(embark on)* *(description)* s'embarquer dans, se lancer dans

5 *(collide with)* entrer dans

▸ **go in with** **VT INSEP** *(person in a business etc)* se joindre à

▸ **go off** **VI 1** *(leave)* partir, s'en aller; *Theat* quitter la scène; *Fam* **she's gone off and left him** elle l'a quitté; **he went off with the woman next door** il est parti avec la voisine; **to go off with sth** emporter qch, enlever qch

2 *(deteriorate)* *(of milk)* tourner; *(of butter)* rancir; *(of fish, meat)* se gâter; *(of tennis player etc)* perdre sa forme

3 *(proceed)* **everything went off well** tout a bien marché, tout s'est bien passé; **how did the concert go off?** comment le concert s'est-il passé?

4 *(cease working, be disconnected)* **the power/light went off** l'électricité a été coupée/la lumière s'est éteinte

5 *(of gun)* partir, se décharger; *(of bomb)* éclater; **the pistol didn't go off** le coup n'est pas parti; **the firework went off in my face** la fusée m'a explosé dans la figure; *Fam* **to go off at the deep end** piquer une crise, péter les plombs

6 *(of alarm)* se déclencher; *(of alarm clock)* sonner

7 *(go to sleep)* s'endormir

VT INSEP *(lose liking for)* *(something)* perdre le goût de; **I've gone off cheese** je ne mange plus de fromage; **I've completely gone off him** *(husband, boyfriend)* je ne suis complètement détachée de lui; *(actor, singer, writer)* je ne l'aime plus du tout; **funny how you can go off people** c'est drôle comme on se lasse des gens parfois; **I've gone off the idea** cette idée ne me dit plus rien

▸ **go on** **VI 1** *(continue)* continuer (**doing sth** à faire qch); **'and that's not all'**, he went on 'et ce n'est pas tout', a-t-il poursuivi; **go on with what we were doing** continuez ce que vous étiez en train de faire; **I must go on with my work** il me faut continuer mon travail; **as time went on, her intentions became clear** à mesure que le temps passait, ses intentions devenaient plus claires; **the lecture went on rather a long time** le cours a duré assez longtemps; **I have enough to be going on with** j'en ai assez pour le moment; **to go on to another question** passer à une autre question; **go on, take one** allez, prends-en un; **go on, try it** allez, essaie-le; **can I? – yes, go on** est-ce que je peux? – oui, vas-y; *Old-fashioned Fam* **go on (with you)!** allons donc!

2 *(talk excessively, unreasonably)* parler à n'en plus finir (**about** de); **how he goes on!** impossible de l'arrêter!; **once he starts, he goes on and on** une fois qu'il est parti, il n'y a plus moyen de l'arrêter; **what are you going on about now?** qu'est-ce que vous racontez?; **she went on a bit** elle s'est un peu étendue sur la question; **he's always going on at me** il est toujours à me faire des remontrances

3 *(happen)* **this has been going on for years** cela fait des années que ça dure; **what's going on here?** qu'est-ce qui se passe ici?

4 *(begin to operate, be connected)* se mettre

en marche; *(of streetlight)* s'allumer

5 *Theat (walk on stage)* entrer en scène; **the band went on at 10 o'clock** le groupe est entré en scène à 10 heures

6 *(fit)* **I can't get the lid to go on** je n'arrive pas à mettre le couvercle; **these shoes won't go on** ces chaussures ne vont pas; **these jeans won't go on any more** je ne rentre plus dans ce jean

VT INSEP 1 *(enter)* *(boat, train)* monter dans

2 *(embark on)* **to go on a journey/a holiday** partir en voyage/en vacances; **to go on a diet** se mettre au régime; **to go on social security** s'inscrire au chômage

3 *(approach)* aller sur; **she's two going on three** elle va sur ses trois ans

4 *(be guided by)* se fonder sur; **the police have nothing to go on** la police n'a rien sur quoi se fonder

▸ **go on for** **VT INSEP** *(approach)* approcher de, aller sur; **he's going on for forty** il va sur ses quarante ans

▸ **go out** **VI 1** *(leave house etc)* sortir; **to go out for a meal** aller au restaurant; **she's gone out to get a paper** elle est sortie (pour) acheter un journal; **to go out for a walk** sortir se promener; **we don't go out much in the evenings** nous ne sortons pas beaucoup le soir; **she was dressed to go out** elle était en tenue de ville; **she's decided to go out to work** elle a décidé de travailler à l'extérieur; **what time did he go out to work?** à quelle heure est-il parti travailler?; *Ind* **to go out (on strike)** se mettre en grève; **the magic seemed to have gone out of their marriage** leur mariage semblait avoir perdu de son charme; **her heart went out to them** elle a ressenti de la compassion pour eux; **my heart goes out to you** je partage votre douleur; *Iron* j'en ai les larmes aux yeux

2 *(date)* **they've been going out (together) for a month** ils sortent ensemble depuis un mois; **to go out with sb** sortir avec qn, fréquenter qn; **he went out with her for two years before they got married** il l'a fréquentée pendant deux ans avant de l'épouser

3 *(of fire, light)* s'éteindre; **the lights go out at midnight** on éteint les lumières à minuit; *Fam* **I went out like a light** *(fell asleep)* je me suis endormi tout de suite

4 *(of tide)* baisser, se retirer

5 *(become unfashionable)* passer de mode, se démoder

6 *Sport (be eliminated)* être éliminé, *Fam* se faire sortir; **I bet they go out in the next round** je parie qu'ils vont être éliminés à la prochaine manche; **Henman went out to Agassi** Henman s'est fait sortir par Agassi

7 *(of letter)* être envoyé

8 *TV, Radio (of programme)* être diffusé

▸ **go over** **VI 1** *(cross)* **I went over and tapped him on the shoulder** je suis allé vers lui et je lui ai tapé sur l'épaule

2 *(transfer allegiance)* **to go over to the enemy** passer à l'ennemi; **to go over to the other side** changer de parti; **he's thinking of going over to cigars** il songe à passer aux cigares

3 *(be received)* **to go over well/badly** *(of suggestion, joke)* bien/mal passer; *(of play)* être bien/mal reçu; *Fam* **to go over big** avoir un grand succès

4 *(turn upside down)* se retourner

VT INSEP 1 *(pass across)* **to go over a bridge** passer un pont; **to go over a river** passer par-dessus une rivière; **the ball went over the wall** la balle est passée par-dessus le mur

2 *(examine)* *(accounts, report)* examiner, revoir; *(papers etc)* passer en revue; *(document)* relire; *(lesson)* repasser, revoir; **to go over sth in one's mind** repasser qch dans son esprit

3 *(discuss)* parler de; *Fig* **we are just going**

over the same old ground on ressasse les mêmes choses

4 *(rehearse)* refaire; *(bars of music)* rejouer; *(sing)* rechanter

▸ **go round** VI **1** *(make a detour)* faire un détour

2 *(spin)* tourner; **my head's going round** la tête me tourne

3 *(visit)* **I said I'd go round (and see her)** j'ai dit que j'irais la voir; **he's gone round to a friend's** il est allé chez un ami

4 *(circulate)* *(of rumour)* circuler, courir; *(of bottle, cold, flu)* circuler

5 *(suffice)* **the food only just went round** il y avait juste assez de nourriture pour tout le monde; **to make the food go round** ménager la nourriture; **there isn't enough to go round** il n'y en a pas assez pour tout le monde

VT INSEP **1** *(make a detour by)* **to go round the long way** faire un long détour

2 *(tour)* *(museum)* faire le tour de; **I hate going round the shops** j'ai horreur de faire les boutiques; **they went round the neighbourhood looking for their cat** ils ont fait le tour du quartier pour chercher leur chat

3 *(be sufficient for)* suffire pour; **will the soup go round twenty?** est-ce qu'il y aura assez de soupe pour vingt?

▸ **go through** VI **1** *(travel through, penetrate)* passer, traverser; **the gates were open and we went through** les barrières étaient ouvertes et nous sommes passés

2 *(be completed, accepted)* *(of deal)* être conclu; *(of divorce)* être prononcé; *Parl (of bill)* passer

VT INSEP **1** *(penetrate)* traverser

2 *(suffer)* *(trials and tribulations)* subir, essuyer; **he went through agony** *(wondering what had happened)* il était au supplice; **in spite of all she had gone through** malgré tout ce qu'elle avait enduré

3 *(complete)* *(formalities)* remplir

4 *(examine)* *(documents)* examiner; *(lesson, accounts)* revoir

5 *(search)* *(suitcases)* fouiller; **to go through sb's pockets** fouiller dans les poches de qn, *Fam* faire les poches à qn

6 *(use up)* *(money)* dépenser; *(supplies, paper, toner etc)* utiliser; *(food)* consommer; **to go through all one's money** dépenser tout son argent; **have we gone through the salmon already?** est-ce qu'on a déjà fini le saumon?

▸ **go through with** VT INSEP *(carry out)* réaliser, exécuter, aller jusqu'au bout de; **she decided that she couldn't go through with the wedding** elle a décidé qu'elle ne pouvait pas se marier; **I mean to go through with it** j'ai l'intention d'aller jusqu'au bout

▸ **go together** VI **1** *(harmonize)* aller ensemble

2 *(date)* sortir ensemble; **they've been going together for a long time** ils sortent ensemble depuis longtemps

▸ **go under** VI **1** *(of drowning man)* couler, s'enfoncer; *(of ship)* couler, sombrer

2 *(go bankrupt)* faire faillite

3 *(under anaesthetic)* s'endormir

VT INSEP **to go under a false/different name** utiliser *ou* prendre un faux nom/un nom différent; **since the divorce she's been going under her old name** depuis le divorce, elle utilise son nom de jeune fille; **a glue that goes under the name of Stikit** une colle qui s'appelle Stikit

▸ **go up** VI **1** *(climb, rise)* monter; **to go up to bed** monter se coucher; **to go up in a helicopter** monter en hélicoptère; **going up!** *(in lift)* on monte!, pour monter!; *Theat* **before the curtain goes up** avant le lever du rideau; **a shout went up from the crowd** un cri s'éleva de la foule; *Br Univ* **to go up (to Oxford/etc)** entrer à l'université (d'Oxford/etc); **to go**

up in the world faire son chemin

2 *(of prices, temperature etc)* monter; **bread is going up** *(in price)* le pain augmente; **to go up in sb's estimation** monter dans l'estime de qn

3 *(explode, be destroyed)* sauter; **to go up in flames** se mettre à flamber; *Fig* **their plans went up in smoke** leurs projets sont partis en fumée

▸ **go up to** VT INSEP **1** *(approach)* **to go up to sb/sth** se diriger vers qn/qch; **the path goes up to the front door** le chemin mène à la porte d'entrée

2 *(go as far as)* **the book only goes up to the end of the war** le livre ne va que jusqu'à la fin de la guerre; **I will go up to £100** je veux bien aller jusqu'à 100 livres

▸ **go with** VT INSEP **1** *(accompany)* aller de pair avec; **mathematical ability usually goes with skill at chess** des capacités en mathématiques vont souvent de pair avec un don pour les échecs; **a company car goes with the job** ce poste donne droit à une voiture de fonction

2 *(harmonize with)* s'accorder avec, aller avec; *(of colours)* se marier avec; **the carpet doesn't go with the furniture** le tapis n'est pas assorti aux meubles; **this behaviour doesn't go with what I know about her** un tel comportement ne cadre pas avec ce que je sais d'elle

3 *(date)* *(person)* sortir avec, fréquenter; **is she going with someone?** est-ce qu'elle sort avec quelqu'un?

4 *(have sex with)* coucher avec

▸ **go without** VI *(not have sth)* **I'd rather go without** je préfère m'en passer; **as children, they often went without** lorsqu'ils étaient enfants, ils on souvent été privés; **they went without so that the children got enough to eat** ils ont dû se priver pour que les enfants aient assez à manger

VT INSEP *(not have)* se passer de; **I went without breakfast so I wouldn't be late** je me suis passé de petit déjeuner pour ne pas être en retard

goad [gəʊd] N *also Fig* aiguillon *m*

VT *(cattle)* aiguillonner, piquer; *(sb's curiosity)* piquer, stimuler; **to g. sb into doing sth** talonner qn jusqu'à ce qu'il fasse qch

▸ **goad on** VT SEP aiguillonner; **don't g. him on!** arrête de l'exciter!

go-ahead *Fam* ADJ *(enterprising)* entreprenant

N **to give sb the g.** donner le feu vert à qn; **to give sth the g.** donner le feu vert pour qch

goal [gəʊl] N **1** *(aim)* but *m*, objectif *m*; **to achieve a g.** atteindre un but, réaliser un objectif; **my g. is in sight** j'approche de mon but *ou* du but **2** *Sport* but *m*; *(structure)* but, cages *fpl*; **Macleod was in g. for Rangers** Macleod était dans les buts des Rangers

▸▸ **g. kick** coup *m* de pied au but, dégagement *m* aux six mètres; **g. line** ligne *f* de but; **g. scorer** buteur *m*; **the leading** *or* **top g. scorer** le meilleur buteur

goalkeeper ['gəʊlkiːpər], *Fam* **goalie** ['gəʊli] N *Ftbl etc* gardien *m* de but, goal *m*

goalless ['gəʊlls] ADJ *Ftbl etc* sans but marqué

▸▸ **g. draw** match *m* nul 0-0

goalmouth ['gəʊlmaʊθ] N *Ftbl etc* entrée *f* de but; **there was no shortage of g. incident** il y avait beaucoup d'action devant les cages

goalpost ['gəʊlpəʊst] N *Ftbl etc* montant *m ou* poteau *m* (de but); *Fig* **to move** *or* **shift the goalposts** changer les règles du jeu

goat [gəʊt] N **1** chèvre *f*; **she g.** chèvre, *Fam* bique *f*; **he g.** bouc *m*; **g.'s milk** lait *m* de chèvre; **g.'s (milk) cheese** fromage *m* de chèvre; *Fig Fam* **it really gets my g.!** ça me met en boule!, ça me tape sur les nerfs!; *Fig* **to act**

or play the g. faire l'idiot **2** *Fam Pej* **old g.** *(lecherous man)* vieux *m* cochon; *Am (old woman)* vieille toupie *f*, *(old man)* vieux schnock *m*

goatee [gəʊ'tiː] N *(beard)* barbiche *f*, bouc *m*

goatherd ['gəʊthɜːd] N chevrier, -ière

goatskin ['gəʊtskɪn] N **1** peau *f* de chèvre *ou Fam* de bique **2** *(bottle)* outre *f* (en peau de bouc)

goatsucker ['gəʊtsʌkər] N *Am (bird)* engoulevent *m*

gob [gɒb] N **1** *Br Fam (spittle)* crachat *m*; **a g. of spit** un crachat **2** *esp Br Sl (mouth)* gueule *f*; **shut your g.!** ferme-la!, ta gueule!

VI *Br Sl (spit)* cracher (**at** sur)

gobble ['gɒb(ə)l] VT *Fam (eat)* avaler gloutonnement, dévorer, *Fam* bouffer; **don't g. (your food)!** *(to child)* n'avale pas si vite!

N *(of turkey)* glouglou *m*

VI *(of turkey)* glouglouter

▸ **gobble down** VT SEP *(eat quickly)* avaler gloutonnement, *Fam* bouffer

▸ **gobble up** VT SEP *(eat quickly)* engloutir, engouffrer, *Fam* bouffer; *Fig (money, pay rise)* engloutir; *Fig* **the empire gobbled up these territories** l'empire a absorbé ces territoires

gobbledegook, gobbledygook ['gɒb(ə)ldɪguːk] N *Fam* charabia *m*

go-between N intermédiaire *mf*; **to act** *or* **serve as a g.** servir d'intermédiaire (**to** à)

goblet ['gɒblɪt] N verre *m* à pied; *Lit (drinking cup)* coupe *f*

goblin ['gɒblɪn] N lutin *m*

gobo ['gəʊbəʊ] N *(camera matte)* drapeau *m*

gobshite ['gɒbʃaɪt] N *Sl (bastard)* trouduc *m*

gob-smacked [-smækt] ADJ *Br Sl* **I was g.** j'en étais tout estomaqué

gobstopper ['gɒbstɒpər] N *Br* gros bonbon *m* rond

go-by N *Fam* **to give sb the g.** snober qn

GOC [dʒiːəʊ'siː] N *Mil (abbr* **general officer commanding***)* général *m* commandant en chef

go-cart N **1** *(child's toy)* petit chariot *m*; *Sport* kart *m* **2** *Am (baby-walker)* trotteur *m*; *(pushchair)* poussette *f*

▸▸ **g. racing** karting *m*

God [gɒd] N Dieu *m*; *Rel* **G. the Father, G. the Son and G. the Holy Ghost** Dieu le père, le fils et le Saint-Esprit; **a man of G.** un homme de Dieu; **to play G.** se prendre pour Dieu; **I wish to G. ...** plût à Dieu ...; **in G.'s name, in the name of G.** au nom du Ciel; *Fam* **G. knows** Dieu seul le sait; **G. willing** si Dieu le veut; *Fam* **for G.'s sake!, for the love of G.!** pour l'amour de Dieu!; *Fam* **what in G.'s name are you doing?** que faites-vous là, grand Dieu!; *Fam* **she's G. knows where** elle est Dieu sait où; *Fam* **oh G.!, my G.!** mon Dieu!; **G. forbid!** à Dieu ne plaise!; *Fam* **he thinks he's G.'s gift to women** il croit que toutes les femmes vont tomber à ses pieds; **he's not exactly G.'s gift to women** ce n'est pas vraiment l'homme dont rêvent toutes les femmes; **an act of G.** un cas de force majeure

god [gɒd] N dieu *m*; **the g. of war** le dieu de la guerre; **a river g.** une divinité de la rivière; **to make a g. of money** diviniser l'argent; *Theat Fam* **the gods** *(gallery)* le poulailler

god-awful ADJ *Fam* dégueulasse

god-botherer [-bɒðərər] N *Fam* cul-bénit *m*, *pl* culs-bénits

godchild, *pl* **godchildren** ['gɒdtʃaɪld, -tʃɪldrən] N filleul, -eule

goddammit [gɒd'dæmɪt] INT *Am Sl* bordel!

goddamn [gɒd'dæm] *esp Am Sl* **INT** nom de Dieu!
ADJ (*also* **god-damned**) fichu, sacré; **don't be such a g. fool!** ne sois donc pas si bête!

goddaughter ['gɒddɔːtər] **N** filleule *f*

goddess ['gɒdɪs] **N** déesse *f*; *Fig* **a g. of the screen, a screen g.** une idole du grand écran

godfather ['gɒdfɑːðər] **N** parrain *m*

god-fearing ['gɒdfɪərɪŋ] **ADJ** (*person*) très religieux; **decent g. folk** les gens croyants bien comme il faut

godforsaken ['gɒdfəseɪk(ə)n] **ADJ** (*place, town*) perdu; **what a g. place!** quel bled!

godhead ['gɒdhed] **N** divinité *f*

godless ['gɒdlɪs] **ADJ** (*person, action etc*) impie

godlike ['gɒdlaɪk] **ADJ** divin, de dieu

godliness ['gɒdlɪnɪs] **N** piété *f*

godly ['gɒdlɪ] **ADJ** dévot, pieux; **to lead a g. life** vivre pieusement

godmother ['gɒdmʌðər] **N** marraine *f*

godparent ['gɒdpeərənt] **N** (*woman*) marraine *f*; (*man*) parrain *m*; **my godparents** mon parrain et ma marraine

godsend ['gɒdsend] **N** aubaine *f*; **this money is a g. to him** cet argent est un don du ciel; **the president's gaffe was a g. to the opposition** la gaffe du président a été une aubaine pour l'opposition

godson ['gɒdsʌn] **N** filleul *m*

godsquad ['gɒdskwɒd] **N** *Fam* bondieusards *mpl*

goer ['gəʊər] **N 1 to be a good/bad g.** (*of horse*) courir bien/mal; (*of car*) marcher bien/mal **2** *Fam* **she's a real g.!** (*promiscuous*) c'est une femme facile!; (*good in bed*) c'est un bon coup!

-goer ['gəʊər] **SUFF** **church/cinema/theatre-g.** personne qui va souvent à l'église/au cinéma/au théâtre

gofer, gopher ['gəʊfər] **N 1** *esp Am Fam* (*menial assistant*) (*male*) grouillot *m*, homme *m* à tout faire; (*female*) bonne *f* à tout faire **2** *Comput* (*serveur m*) gopher *m*

go-getter [-getər] **N** *Fam* battant, -ante

go-getting [-getɪŋ] **ADJ** *Fam* (*person, approach*) entreprenant, dynamique

goggle ['gɒg(ə)l] **VI** (*of person*) rouler de gros yeux; (*of eyes*) être saillant; **to g. at sb/sth** regarder qn/qch en roulant de gros yeux

gogglebox ['gɒg(ə)lbɒks] **N** *Br Fam* télé *f*

goggle-eyed **ADJ** *Fam* qui a les yeux en boules de loto; **they watched g.** ils regardaient, les yeux en boules de loto

goggles ['gɒg(ə)lz] **NPL** (*for motorcyclist*) lunettes *fpl* protectrices *ou* de moto; (*for skier*) lunettes (de ski); (*for diver, swimmer*) lunettes (de plongée); *Ind* lunettes de travail; (*for welder*) lunettes (protectrices); *Hum* (*spectacles*) carreaux *mpl*

go-go dancer **N** = homme *m* ou femme *f* légèrement vêtu(e) qui danse sur un podium de boîte de nuit

going ['gəʊɪŋ] **ADJ 1** (*functioning*) qui marche; **to start** *or* **set sth g.** mettre qch en marche; **the business is a g. concern** c'est une affaire qui marche; **to be sold as a g. concern** à vendre avec fonds **2** (*current*) **the g. price** *or* **rate** le prix courant *ou* actuel

N 1 (*progress*) **that's very good g.!** voilà qui n'est pas mal du tout!; **it was slow g.** (*walking, climbing*) on progressait lentement; (*working, learning*) ça avançait lentement; **it was hard g.** (*walking, climbing*) on progressait difficilement; (*learning, working*) c'était dur; *Typ* **g. to press** mise *f* sous presse **2** (*leaving*) départ *m*

3 g. back (*return*) retour *m*; **g. back on one's word** manque *m* de parole; **there's no g.**

back now il n'y a pas moyen de revenir en arrière
4 *Horseracing etc* (*condition of ground*) état *m* du sol; **the g. is rough** le chemin est rude; *Horseracing* **good/heavy g.** bon terrain/terrain lourd; *Fig* **heavy g.** (*of film, book etc*) indigeste; *Fig* **it's heavy g. getting him to talk** on a du mal à le faire parler; *Fig* **while the g. is good** tant que c'est favorable; **to get out while the g.'s good** partir tant que les choses vont bien

-going ['gəʊɪŋ] **SUFF 1** theatre/cinema-g. fréquentation *f* des théâtres/des cinémas **2** slow/fast-g. qui marche lentement/vite

going-away **ADJ** **a g. party/present** une soirée/un cadeau d'adieu
▸▸ **g. dress** robe *f* de voyage de noce

going-over **N** *Fam* **to give sb a g.** (*beating*) tabasser qn; (*criticism*) sonner les cloches à qn; **the burglars had given the flat a real g.** les cambrioleurs avaient laissé l'appartement sens dessus dessous; **the auditors gave the accounts a thorough g.** les experts ont soigneusement examiné les comptes

going-rate pricing **N** *Mktg* alignement *m* sur les prix du marché

goings-on ['gəʊɪŋzɒn] **NPL** *Fam* (*events*) événements *mpl*; (*behaviour*) conduite *f*, **the g. of the Royals** les activités *fpl* des membres de la famille royale; **there were strange g.** il se passait de drôles de choses; **what extraordinary g.!** quelles histoires extraordinaires!

goitre, *Am* **goiter** ['gɔɪtər] **N** *Med* goitre *m*

go-kart **N** *Sport* kart *m*
▸▸ **g. racing** karting *m*

gold [gəʊld] **N 1** or *m*; **to pay sb in g.** payer qn en or **2** (*medal*) médaille *f* d'or; **to win g.** gagner la médaille d'or **3** (*colour*) or *m*; **the reds and golds of autumn** les rouges et les ors de l'automne
ADJ (*made of gold*) en or; (*gold-coloured*) doré; **g. brooch/necklace** broche/collier en or; **g. dress** robe couleur d'or *ou* dorée; **lamé dress** robe lamée d'or; **g. paint** peinture dorée
▸▸ *Fin* **g. bond** obligation *f* or; **g. braid** galon *m* d'or; **g. bullion** or en barre *ou* en lingots, encaisse *f* or; **the G. Coast** (*in Australia*) = suite *f* de stations balnéaires sur la côte est de l'Australie; *Am* (*expensive area*) les beaux quartiers *mpl*; *Formerly* (*Ghana*) le Ghana; **g. coin** pièce *f* d'or; **g. content** teneur *f* en or; **g. currency** monnaie *f* d'or; *Fig* **tickets for the game are like g. dust** il est pratiquement impossible de se procurer des billets pour le match; **g. fever** fièvre *f* de l'or; **g. filling** (*in tooth*) obturation *f* à l'or *ou* en or; **g. foil** feuille *f* d'or, or en feuille; **g. ingot** lingot *m* d'or; **g. leaf** feuille d'or, or en feuille; **g. market** marché *m* de l'or; **g. medal** médaille *f* d'or; *also Fig* **g. mine** mine *f* d'or; **g. money** monnaie d'or; **g. plate** (*utensils*) orfèvrerie *f*, vaisselle *f* d'or; (*plating*) plaque *f* d'or; *Mus* **g. record** disque *m* d'or; *Fin* **g. reserve** réserve *f* d'or; **g. rush** ruée *f* vers l'or; **g. standard** étalon-or *m inv*

goldbrick ['gəʊldbrɪk] *Am Fam* **N 1 to sell sb a g.** rouler qn **2** (*malingerer*) tire-au-flanc *m*
VT (*swindle*) rouler
VI (*malinger*) tirer au flanc

goldcrest ['gəʊldkrest] **N** (*bird*) roitelet *m* huppé

gold-digger **N** chercheur *m* d'or; *Pej Fig* (*woman*) croqueuse *f* de diamants

golden ['gəʊld(ə)n] **ADJ 1** (*made of gold*) en or; *Bible, Fig* **to worship the g. calf** adorer le veau d'or **2** (*gold-coloured*) **g. hair** cheveux d'or **3** (*excellent, best*) **a g. opportunity** une occasion en or; **g. boy/girl** enfant *mf* chéri/chérie

▸▸ **the g. age** l'âge *m* d'or; **G. Delicious** (*apple*) golden *f*; **g. eagle** aigle *m* royal; *Myth* **the G. Fleece** la Toison d'or; **the G. Gate Bridge** le Golden Gate; *Cin, TV* **G. Globe** Golden Globe *m*; *Ftbl* **g. goal** but *m* en or; *Fig* **g. goose** poule *f* aux œufs d'or; *Fam* **g. handcuffs** primes *fpl* (*versées à un cadre à intervalles réguliers pour le dissuader de partir*); *Fam* **g. handshake** gratification *f* de fin de service; *Fam* **g. hello** prime *f* d'embauche; **g. jubilee** (fête *f* du) cinquantième anniversaire *m*; **the g. mean** le juste milieu; *Fam* **g. oldie** vieux tube *m*; *Fam* **g. parachute** prime *f* de licenciement (*versé à certains cadres supérieurs en cas de rachat de l'entreprise*); **g. pheasant** faisan *m* doré; **g. rule** règle *f* d'or; *Fin* **g. share** participation *f* majoritaire (*souvent détenue par le gouvernement britannique dans les entreprises privatisées*); **the G. State** = la Californie; *Br* **g. syrup** mélasse *f* raffinée; **g. wedding** noces *fpl* d'or

goldenrod ['gəʊld(ə)nrɒd] **N** *Bot* (*plant*) verge *f* d'or

goldfield ['gəʊldfiːld] **N** champ *m* ou région *f* aurifère

goldfinch ['gəʊldfɪntʃ] **N** chardonneret *m*

goldfish ['gəʊldfɪʃ] **N** poisson *m* rouge
▸▸ **g. bowl** bocal *m* (à poissons rouges); *Fig* **it's like living in a g. bowl** c'est comme être en vitrine

Goldilocks ['gəʊldɪlɒks] **N** Boucle d'Or *f*

gold-plated **ADJ** plaqué or

gold-rimmed **ADJ** (*glasses*) à monture dorée

goldsmith ['gəʊldsmɪθ] **N** orfèvre *m*

gold-tipped **ADJ** à bout doré

golf [gɒlf] *Sp* **N** golf *m*
VI jouer au golf; **I went golfing yesterday** hier, j'ai fait du golf *ou* j'ai joué au golf
▸▸ **g. ball** (*for golf*) balle *f* de golf; (*for typewriter*) boule *f*, **g. ball typewriter** machine *f* à écrire à boule; **g. club** (*stick*) club *m ou* crosse *f ou* canne *f* de golf; (*building, association*) club de golf; **g. course** terrain *m ou* parcours *m* de golf, golf; **g. links** links *mpl*; **g. umbrella** parapluie *m* de golf

golfer ['gɒlfər] **N** golfeur, -euse, joueur, -euse de golf

golfing ['gɒlfɪŋ] **N** golf *m*
▸▸ **g. holiday** = vacances *fpl* prises pour jouer au golf

Goliath [gə'laɪəθ] **N** *Bible, Fig* Goliath *m*

golliwog ['gɒlɪwɒg] **N** = poupée *f* en étoffe représentant un Noir

golly ['gɒlɪ] **INT** *Old-fashioned Fam* fichtre!, mince (alors)!
N *Br* = **golliwog**

goloshes [gə'lɒʃɪz] **NPL** = **galoshes**

gonad ['gɒnæd, 'gəʊ-] **N** *Biol* gonade *f*

gondola ['gɒndələ] **N 1** (*boat*) gondole *f* **2** *Aviat* (*of airship, balloon*) nacelle *f*, *Am* (*cable car*) nacelle *ou* cabine *f* de téléphérique **3** *Am Rail* wagon *m* plat **4** *Mktg* (*in supermarket etc*) gondole *f*
▸▸ *Am Rail* **g. car** wagon plat; *Mktg* **g. end** tête *f* de gondole

gondolier [gɒndə'lɪər] **N** gondolier *m*

gone [gɒn] **PP** *see* **go**
ADJ 1 to be g. (*dead*) être mort, être parti; **when I'm g.** quand je ne serai plus là; *Fam* **oh well, that's that g.!** (*of broken machine etc*) bon, ben c'est foutu!
2 to be pretty far g. (*drunk*) être complètement bourré; (*on drugs*) être complètement camé; (*of dying patient*) être très mal; *Fam* **to be six months g.** (*pregnant*) être enceinte de six mois; **how far g. is she?** (*pregnant*) elle est enceinte de combien?
3 *Fam* **g. on sb** amoureux *ou* *Fam* toqué de qn

4 *(past)* **it's g. ten o'clock** il est plus de dix heures, il est dix heures passées

goner ['gɒnər] N *Fam* mourant, -ante; **I thought she was a g.** je pensais qu'elle allait mourir; **if the engine fails now, we'll all be goners** si le moteur tombe en panne, on va tous crever *ou* on est tous foutus; *Fig* **I'm a g. if she finds out where I've been** je suis fichu *ou* foutu si elle apprend où je suis allé

gong [gɒŋ] N **1** *Mus etc* gong *m*; **to sound the g.** faire retentir le gong **2** *Br Fam (medal)* médaille *f*; **he was wearing all his gongs** il exhibait toute sa batterie de cuisine

gonna ['gɒnə] CONTR *Fam* = **going to**

gonorrhoea, *Am* **gonorrhea** [gɒnəˈriːə] N *Med* blennorragie *f*; **to have g.** avoir *ou* faire une blennorragie

goo [guː] N *Fam* **1** *(sticky substance)* substance *f* visqueuse **2** *(sentimentality)* mièvrerie *f*

goober ['guːbər] N *Am Fam* crétin, -ine

GOOD [gʊd]

ADJ bon **1–7, 10–12, 15, 17** ▪ beau **1** ▪ sage **8** ▪ aimable **9**	
ADV bien **1–3**	
N bien **1, 2** ▪ pour de bon *(for good)* **4**	
INT bien	

ADJ (**better, best**) **1** *(of fine quality)* bon, *f* bonne; **a g. wine** un bon vin; **g. handwriting** belle écriture; **to have a g. ear (for music)** avoir de l'oreille; **she was wearing her g. dress** elle portait sa belle robe; **we only use the g. cutlery when we have guests** nous n'utilisons nos beaux couverts que lorsque nous avons des invités; **he has a g. style, but ...** son style est agréable, mais ...; **g. weather** beau temps; **g. to eat** bon à manger; **the leaves are g. to eat as well as the root** les feuilles, de même que la racine, sont comestibles *ou* bonnes à manger; **this fruit is a bit bashed, but it's still g. to eat** ce fruit est un peu écrasé, mais il est encore bon; **is the meat still g.?** est-ce que la viande est encore bonne?; *Fam* **that's a g. one!** *(of story, joke)* elle est bien bonne, celle-là!; **he's too g. for that job** il mérite une meilleure situation; **I suppose he thinks he's too g. for us** j'imagine qu'il se trouve trop bien pour nous; **if it's g. enough for you, it's g. enough for me** si ça vous va, alors ça me va aussi; **this isn't g. enough!** *(you will have to do better)* c'est insuffisant!; **it's looking g.** ça a l'air de bien se passer; *(is going to succeed)* ça se présente bien; **he's looking g.** *(of boxer, athlete, candidate in election)* il a toutes ses chances; **g. living, the g. life** la belle vie

2 *(appropriate)* bon, *f* bonne; **a g. opportunity** une bonne occasion; **to be in a g. position to do sth** être bien placé pour faire qch; **it is not always g. to ...** il n'est pas toujours bon de ...

3 *(pleasant, enjoyable)* heureux; **g. news** bonnes *ou* heureuses nouvelles; **to have a g. time** (bien) s'amuser; **to show sb a g. time** faire passer un bon moment à qn; **a g. time was had by all** tout le monde s'est bien amusé; **too g. to be true** trop beau pour être vrai; **it's g. to be alive!** que la vie est belle!; **it's g. to know you've got friends** ça fait plaisir de savoir qu'on a des amis; **it's g. to see you** je suis/nous sommes content(s) de te voir; **it's been g. seeing you again** ça m'a/nous a fait plaisir de vous revoir

4 *(attractive)* bon, beau; **she looks g. in that hat** ce chapeau lui va bien; **that pizza looks g.** cette pizza a l'air bonne; **the vase looks g. there** le vase rend très bien là; **(that) sounds g.!** *(good idea)* bonne idée!; **to have a g. figure** être bien fait

5 *(beneficial)* **this medicine is very g. for coughs** ce remède est très bon pour la toux; **beer is not g. for me** la bière ne me vaut rien; **you'll accept, if you know what's g. for you** tu accepteras, si tu as deux sous de bon sens; **to drink more than is g. for one** boire plus que de raison; **it will be g. for them to have some company** ça leur fera du bien d'avoir de la compagnie; **it isn't g. for people to live alone** il n'est pas bon de vivre seul; **it's g. for your health** c'est bon pour la santé; **he's not g. for her** il a une mauvaise influence sur elle; **to be g. for business** être bon pour les affaires

6 *(skilful, effective etc)* bon, *f* bonne; **to be g. with one's hands** être adroit *ou* habile de ses mains; **to be g. with children** *(of person)* savoir y faire avec les enfants; **to be g. at maths** être bon *ou* fort en math; **to be g. at sport** être bon en sport; **to be g. for doing sth** *(of equipment, medicine, chemical etc)* être bien pour faire qch; **to be g. on French history/contract law** *(of author)* être bon en histoire de France/sur le droit des contrats; **to be g. on sth** *(of book)* être complet sur qch; **to be g. in bed** être un bon/une bonne partenaire sexuel(le); **g. for nothing** bon à rien

7 *(morally good)* bon, *f* bonne; **g. Christian** bon chrétien, bonne chrétienne; **to lead a g. life** vivre en homme de bien, pratiquer le bien; **he proved to be a g. friend** il s'est montré un véritable ami; **g. nature** bon naturel *m*; **they take advantage of his g. nature** ils profitent de son bon caractère

8 *(well-behaved)* sage; **answer would you, there's a g. boy** sois gentil, réponds; **be g.!** *(to child)* sois sage!; **g. dog!** *(encouraging)* oh, le beau chien!; *(congratulating)* c'est bien, le chien!; **he's g. with children** *(of dog, pony etc)* il est très doux avec les enfants; **g. conduct** *or* **behaviour** bonne conduite *f*, **as g. as gold** sage comme une image

9 *(kind)* aimable; **that's very g. of you** c'est bien aimable *ou* gentil de votre part; **he was very g. about it** il s'est montré très compréhensif; **would you be g. enough to ...?** auriez-vous l'amabilité *ou* la gentillesse de ...?; **she has always been g. to me** elle s'est toujours montrée bonne pour moi; **life has been g. to me** j'ai eu de la chance dans la vie; **he's a g. sort** *or* **chap** c'est un brave type; **to do sb a g. turn** rendre service à qn

10 *(valid)* **a g. reason** une bonne raison, une raison valable; **he** *or* **his credit is g. for £25,000** on peut lui faire jusqu'à 25 000 livres de crédit; **he should be g. for a couple of hundred pounds** on devrait pouvoir en tirer quelques centaines de livres; **how much is he g. for?** de combien dispose-t-il?; **this car ought to be g. for another five years** cette voiture devrait me faire encore cinq ans; **this pass is g. for another six months** cette carte d'abonnement est encore valable six mois; *Fam* **she's g. for another ten years yet** elle est bonne pour encore dix ans

11 *(substantial)* **it makes a g. meal for four** ça fait un bon repas pour quatre; **to earn g. money** bien gagner sa vie; **you've got a g. chance** tu as toutes tes chances; **of a g. size** de bonne taille; **a g. way into the first act** bien après le début du premier acte; **it's a g. distance** *or* **way (from here)** c'est assez loin d'ici; **I was a g. way into the book when I realized that ...** j'avais déjà bien avancé dans ma lecture quand je me suis rendu compte que ...

12 *(thorough)* bon; **a g. spanking/beating** une bonne fessée/correction; **to have a g. look at sb/sth** bien regarder qn/qch; **to have a g. cry** pleurer un bon coup (**about sth** à propos de qch); **I had a g. sleep last night** j'ai bien dormi la nuit dernière; **we had a g. laugh (about it)** on (en) a ri un bon coup

13 **to make g.** *(of person)* prospérer, faire son chemin; **an immigrant made g.** un immigrant qui a fait son chemin; **to make g. a loss** remplacer ce qu'on a perdu; **to make g. one's losses** compenser ses pertes; **to make g. a deficiency** pallier une insuffisance; **to make g. an injustice/damage** réparer une injustice/des dégâts; **to make g. one's promise** remplir *ou* tenir sa promesse; **he made g. his escape** il a réussi son évasion

14 *(expressions with 'as')* **it's as g. a way as any other** c'est une façon qui en vaut une autre; **it's as g. a place as any to stay** qu'on séjourne là ou ailleurs, ça ne fait pas de différence; **this is as g. as you can get** c'est ce qui se fait de mieux; **to give as g. as one gets** rendre coup pour coup; **this method is as g., if not better** cette méthode est aussi bonne, pour ne pas dire meilleure; **it's as g. as new** il/elle est comme neuf/neuve; **to make sth as g. as new** remettre qch à neuf; **it's as g. as settled** c'est comme si c'était fait; **are you married? – as g. as** *(I'm living with sb)* tu es marié? – non, mais c'est tout comme; **it is as g. as saying that ...** ça revient à dire que ...; **he as g. as told me it would be a disaster** il m'a quasiment dit que ce serait un désastre; **he as g. as called me a liar to my face** c'est comme s'il m'avait traité de menteur

15 *(used affectionately)* **g. old Anne, I knew she wouldn't let us down!** cette brave Anne, je savais bien qu'elle ne nous laisserait pas tomber!; **g. old London** le bon vieux Londres; **the g. old days** le bon vieux temps; *Old-fashioned* **his g. lady (wife)** son épouse; **your g. lady** votre dame; *Old-fashioned* **my g. man** mon brave

16 *(greetings, exclamations)* **g. morning/afternoon!** bonjour (monsieur/etc)!; *Fml* **g. day** *(hello)* bonjour; *(goodbye)* au revoir; **g. night!** *(when going to bed)* bonne nuit!; *(when leaving)* bonsoir!; **very g.!** *(well done, congratulations etc)* très bien!, parfait!; **very g., sir!** bien, monsieur!; *esp Fml* **(I'll do as you say)** très bien, je m'en charge!; **g. for you!**, *esp Austr* **g. on you!** tant mieux pour toi!; **g. Lord!** grand Dieu!; **g. heavens!, g. gracious!** bon sang!; **g. grief!** fichtre!

17 *(with quantity, number)* **a g. half** une bonne moitié; **a g. two hours** deux bonnes heures; **a g. while, a g. time** pas mal de temps; **a g. round sum** une somme rondelette; **a g. twenty years ago** il y a bien vingt ans; **a g. deal, a g. many** beaucoup; **a g. few people** pas mal de gens; **to come in a g. third** arriver bon troisième

ADV 1 bien; **a g. long break** une pause bien longue; **to have a g. long soak in the bath** rester des heures dans le bain

2 *Fam* **they beat us g. and proper** ils nous ont écrasés; **he was g. and mad** il était absolument furieux; **I'll do it when I'm g. and ready** je le ferai quand ça me chantera; **I like my coffee g. and strong** j'aime le café bien fort; **make sure it's stuck on g. and hard** vérifie que c'est vraiment bien collé; **put the paint on g. and thick** appliquer la peinture en couches bien épaisses

3 *esp Dial Fam (well)* bien; **she sure sings g.** elle chante bien, c'est sûr; **how are you? – g., thanks** comment allez-vous? – bien, merci

N 1 *(morally good behaviour)* bien *m*; **to return g. for evil** rendre le bien pour le mal; **to do g.** faire le bien; **he's up to no g.** il prépare un mauvais coup; **to come to no g.** finir mal; **there is g. and bad everywhere** il y a du bien et du mal partout; **there's g. and bad in everyone** il y a du bon et du mauvais en chacun de nous; **to see the g. in sb/sth** voir le bon côté de qn/qch

2 *(benefit, use)* **I did it for your own g.** je l'ai fait pour votre bien; **for the g. of one's health** pour sa santé; **to act for the common g.** agir dans l'intérêt général; **it will do you g.**

(to spend a week in the country) cela vous fera du bien (de passer une semaine à la campagne); **what g. will that do you?, what g. will it be to you?** à quoi cela vous avancera-t-il?; **that won't be much g.** ça ne servira pas à grand-chose; **for all the g. it will do** pour la différence que cela fera; **what's the g. of (doing) that?** à quoi bon?; **it's no g. talking about it** inutile d'en parler; **that's no g.** *(pointless)* cela ne sert à rien; *(worthless)* ça ne vaut rien; **he's no g.** il est nul; **it's no g. complaining** se plaindre ne sert à rien **3** *(profit)* **to be five pounds to the g.** avoir cinq livres de gagné *ou* de profit; **it is all to the g.** c'est autant de gagné **4 for g. (and all)** *(permanently)* pour de bon; **he is gone for g.** il est parti pour de bon; **to settle down for g.** se fixer définitivement **5 the g. and the bad** *(pl)* *(people)* les bons et les méchants

INT bien; **g., that's settled then** eh bien, c'est arrangé alors; **I feel better today – g.!** je me sens mieux aujourd'hui – tant mieux!

▸▸ **the G. Book** la sainte Bible; **G. Friday** le vendredi saint; **G. Housekeeping seal** label *m* britannique de bonne qualité; **g. looks** *(attractive appearance)* beauté *f*, *Bible* **the G. Samaritan** le bon Samaritain

---

Good Friday

En Grande-Bretagne, il est traditionnel, le jour du vendredi saint, de manger des "hot cross buns" (petits pains ronds aux fruits secs, marqués d'une croix).

---

goodbye ['gʊd'baɪ] **INT, N** au revoir *m*; **g. for now!** à bientôt!; **to say g. to sb** dire au revoir à qn; **she said her goodbyes** elle a dit au revoir; *(for good)* elle a fait ses adieux; **it was g. to Paris for the time being** il fallait dire au revoir à Paris pour le moment; **that was g. to £5,000** j'ai dû dire adieu à mes 5 000 livres; **he can say g. to any hope of an ambassadorship** il peut dire adieu à ses espoirs de devenir ambassadeur; **to give sb a g. kiss/hug** embrasser qn/serrer qn dans ses bras pour lui dire au revoir

▸▸ **g. present** cadeau *m* d'adieu

good-for-nothing **ADJ** *(person)* qui n'est bon à rien; **her g. husband** son bon à rien de mari

N bon *m* à rien, bonne *f* à rien, vaurien, -ienne

good-hearted [-'hɑːtɪd] **ADJ** qui a bon cœur; *(gesture)* généreux

good-humoured, *Am* **good-humored** [-'hjuːməd] **ADJ** *(person)* d'un caractère agréable, facile à vivre; *(on particular occasion)* de bonne humeur; *(smile, air)* bon enfant *inv*; *(answer)* plaisant; *(joke etc)* sans malice; **he is always g.** il a bon caractère; **in that g. way of hers** avec sa bonne humeur habituelle

good-humouredly, *Am* **good-humoredly** [-'hjuːmədlɪ] **ADV** avec bonhomie; *(to laugh)* avec bonne humeur

goodish ['gʊdɪʃ] **ADJ** *Fam* **1** *(quite good)* assez bon, passable **2** *(number etc)* assez grand; **it's a g. step from here** c'est à un bon bout de chemin d'ici; **it's a g. size** c'est assez grand; **add a g. pinch of salt** ajoutez une bonne pincée de sel

good-looker **N** *Fam* **he's/she's a g.** il/elle est beau/belle

good-looking **ADJ** (**better-looking, best-looking**) beau, *f* belle; **he's very g.** il est beau garçon; **she's quite g.** elle n'est pas mal; **hey, g.!** *(to woman)* eh, ma jolie!; *(to man)* eh, beau gosse!

goodly ['gʊdlɪ] **ADJ** *Old-fashioned, Lit* *(por-* *tion etc)* large, ample; *(number)* considérable; **a g. sum (of money)** une belle somme (d'argent)

good-natured [-'neɪtʃəd] **ADJ** *(person)* accommodant, d'un caractère agréable; *(laugh)* jovial

good-naturedly [-'neɪtʃədlɪ] **ADV** avec bonhomie

goodness ['gʊdnɪs] **N 1** *(of person)* bonté *f*, *Fml* **would you have the g. to inform me next time?** auriez-vous la bonté de m'informer la prochaine fois? **2** *(of thing)* bonne qualité *f*, **contains all the g. of full cream milk** *(in advert)* contient toutes les bonnes choses du lait entier; **to extract all the g. out of sth** extraire tout ce qu'il y a de bon de qch; **it's where the g. is** *(in fruit etc)* c'est ce qu'il y a de plus nutritif **3** *(as euphemism)* **g. gracious (me)!** bonté divine!, mon Dieu!; **g. (me)!** mon Dieu!, oh là là!; **thank g.!** Dieu merci!; **for g.' sake, be quiet!** taisez-vous, pour l'amour de Dieu!; **I wish to g. he'd shut up!** je prie le ciel qu'il se taise!; **g. (only) knows what I'm going to do** Dieu seul sait ce que je dois faire

goodnight [gʊd'naɪt] **N after they had said their goodnights** *(and gone to bed)* après qu'ils se furent dit bonne nuit; *(and left)* après qu'ils se furent dit bonsoir; **to give sb a g. kiss** donner un baiser à qn pour lui dire bonne nuit

goods [gʊdz] **NPL 1** *Law* biens *mpl*, effets *mpl*, **g. and chattels** possessions *fpl* **2** *Com, Econ* marchandises *fpl*, **manufactured g.** produits *mpl* manufacturés; **leather g.** articles *mpl* en cuir, maroquinerie *f*, **to deliver the g.** livrer la marchandise *ou* les marchandises; *Fig (keep one's promise)* remplir ses engagements, tenir parole; *Fig* **a computer that can deliver the g.** un ordinateur qui tient ses promesses; *Fig* **to come up with the g.** faire le nécessaire; *Am Fam* **to have the g. on sb** avoir la preuve de la culpabilité de qn

▸▸ *Rail* **g. depot** dépôt *m* de marchandises; *Rail* **g. station** gare *f* de marchandises; *Rail* **g. train** train *m* de marchandises; *Br* **g. vehicle** poids *m* lourd, véhicule *m* utilitaire

good-tempered **ADJ** d'un caractère facile, qui a bon caractère; *(reply, discussion)* aimable

good-till-cancelled order **N** *St Exch* ordre *m* à révocation

good-time **ADJ** *Fam* qui ne pense qu'à s'amuser

▸▸ **g. girl** fille *f* rigolote; *(sexually)* fille facile

goodwill [gʊd'wɪl] **N 1** *(benevolence)* bienveillance *f*, bon vouloir *m* (**towards** pour, envers); **a gesture of g.** un geste de bonne volonté; **a g. tour** un voyage d'amitié; **to retain sb's g.** conserver les bonnes grâces de qn **2** *(willingness)* bonne volonté *f* **3** *Com* fonds *m* de commerce, actif *m* incorporel

▸▸ **g. mission** mission *f* de conciliation

goody ['gʊdɪ] *Fam* **N 1** *(person)* brave type *m*; *(too good)* petit saint *m*; **the goodies and the baddies** les bons *mpl* et les méchants **2** **goodies** *(treats)* bonnes choses *fpl*

INT (g.) g.! chouette!

goody-goody *Fam Pej* **N** petit saint *m*, petite sainte *f*

ADJ de petit saint; **she's awfully g.** elle prend toujours des airs de petite sainte

goody-two-shoes **N** = **goody-goody**

gooey ['guːɪ] **ADJ** *Fam* **1** *(sticky)* gluant, collant **2** *(sentimental)* à l'eau de rose

goof [guːf] **N 1** *(blunder)* gaffe *f*, bourde *f* **2** *(idiot)* cave *m*

VI 1 *(blunder)* gaffer, faire une gaffe *ou* une bourde **2** *(joke)* rigoler; **to g. with sb** *(tease)*

faire enrager qn **3** *(stare)* **to g. at sb/sth** regarder qn/qch bêtement

▸▸ **g. sheet** pense-bête *m*, *pl* pense-bêtes

▸ **goof about, goof around** **VI** *Fam (act foolishly)* faire l'idiot; *(waste time)* glander, glandouiller

▸ **goof off** **VI** *Am Fam (evade work, waste time)* glander, glandouiller

▸ **goof up** *Am Fam* **VT SEP to g. sth up** foirer qch

VI merder

goofball ['guːfbɔːl] **N** *Am Sl* **1** *(fool)* cave *m* **2** *(drug)* somnifère *m*

goofy ['guːfɪ] **ADJ** *Fam* **1** *(stupid)* loufoque **2** *Br (teeth)* en avant

googly ['guːglɪ] **N** *Cr* = balle *f* lancée avec de l'effet qui prend le batteur à contre-pied alors qu'il pensait l'avoir bien anticipée; *Fig* **to bowl sb a g.** essayer de tromper qn

gook [guːk] **N** *Am* **1** *Offensive Sl (Oriental)* Chinetoque *mf* **2** *Fam (muck)* saleté *f*, crasse *f*

goolies ['guːlɪz] **NPL** *Br Sl* couilles *fpl*

goon [guːn] **N** *Fam* **1** *(stupid person)* imbécile *mf* **2** *Am (criminal)* gorille *m*

goosander [guː'sændər] **N** *(bird)* harle *m* bièvre

goose, *pl* **geese** [guːs, giːs] **N 1** *(bird)* oie *f*, *Fig* **you've cooked your g., your g. is cooked** tu es fichu; *Fig* **to cook sb's g.** couler qn; *Fig* **to kill the g. that lays the golden egg** tuer la poule aux œufs d'or; *Fig* **all his geese are swans** à l'entendre, tout ce qu'il touche est du prodige; **goose('s) egg** œuf *m* d'oie **2** *Old-fashioned Fam (silly person)* niais *m*, niaise *f*, **I'm not such a g.** je ne suis pas si bête que ça

VT *Sl* pincer les fesses à

▸▸ *esp Am* **g. bumps** chair *f* de poule; **to have g. bumps** avoir la chair de poule; **g. fat** graisse *f* d'oie; *Br* **g. flesh, g. pimples** chair de poule; **to get g. flesh** *or* **pimples** avoir la chair de poule; *Mil* **g. step** pas *m* de l'oie

gooseberry ['gʊzb(ə)rɪ] **N** *(fruit)* groseille *f* à maquereau, groseille verte; *(bush)* groseillier *m*; *Culin* **g. fool** crème *f* de groseilles (à maquereau); *Br Fam* **to play g.** tenir la chandelle

▸▸ **g. bush** groseillier *m*; **I told her children were found under a g. bush** je lui ai dit que les petites filles naissent dans les roses et les petits garçons dans les choux

goosegog ['gʊzgɒg] **N** *Br Fam* groseille *f* à maquereau

goose-step **VI** (**-pp-**) *Mil* marcher au pas de l'oie

GOP [dʒiːəʊ'piː] **N** *Am Pol* (*abbr* **Grand Old Party**) le Parti républicain

gopher ['gəʊfər] **N 1** *(rodent)* (**pocket**) **g.** géomys *m* **2** *(ground squirrel)* spermophile *m* **3** = **gofer**

gorblimey ['gɔːblaɪmɪ] **INT** *Eng Dial* nom d'un chien!

Gordian ['gɔːdɪən] **ADJ** *Fig* **to cut the G. knot** trancher le nœud gordien

gore [gɔːr] **N** *(blood)* sang *m*; **blood and g.** du sang et encore du sang; **there's plenty of g. in this movie** ce film est sanglant à souhait; *Lit* **he lay in his g.** il baignait dans son sang

VT *(of bull)* blesser avec les cornes, encorner; **gored to death** tué d'un coup/à coups de corne

gorge[1] [gɔːdʒ] **N 1** *Geog* gorge *f*, défilé *m* **2** *Lit (throat)* gorge *f*, **it makes my g. rise** cela me soulève le cœur

gorge[2] **VI** se gorger, se repaître, se rassasier, *Fam* s'empiffrer (**on** de)

VT *(person)* rassasier; **to g. oneself** se gaver, *Fam* s'empiffrer

gorgeous ['gɔːdʒəs] **ADJ** magnifique; *(weather)* superbe, magnifique; *(meal)* somptueux; *Lit (palaces)* fastueux; *Fam* **hello, g.!** *(usu to young woman)* bonjour, ma beauté!

gorgeously ['gɔːdʒəslɪ] **ADV** magnifiquement, somptueusement

gorgon ['gɔːgən] **N** *Myth* gorgone *f*

gorilla [gəˈrɪlə] **N** *(animal), Fam (bodyguard)* gorille *m*

gormless ['gɔːmlɪs] **ADJ** *Br Fam* idiot, imbécile

gorse [gɔːs] **N** *Bot (shrub)* ajoncs *mpl*
▸▸ **g. bush** ajonc *m*

gory ['gɔːrɪ] **ADJ** sanglant, ensanglanté; *(film)* sanglant; **in g. detail** avec les détails les plus sanglants; *Fig* **spare me the g. details** épargne-moi les détails

gosh [gɒʃ] **INT** *Fam* zut (alors)!, mince (alors)!

goshawk ['gɒshɔːk] **N** *(bird)* autour *m*

gosling ['gɒzlɪŋ] **N** oison *m*

go-slow N *Br Ind* grève *f* du zèle

gospel ['gɒsp(ə)l] **N** évangile *m*; *Mus* gospel *m*; **St Mark's G., the G. according to St Mark** l'Évangile selon saint Marc; *Fig* **to take sth as g.** accepter qch comme parole d'évangile; *Fig* **it's the g. truth** c'est parole d'évangile; *Rel* **the g. for the day** l'évangile du jour; **to preach the g.** prêcher l'évangile; *Fig* **to preach the g. of monetarism** prêcher le monétarisme
▸▸ **g. music** gospel *m*; **g. oath** serment *m* prêté sur l'Évangile; **g. singer** chanteur, -euse de gospels

gospeller ['gɒspələr] **N (hot) g.** évangélisateur, -trice

gossamer ['gɒsəmər] **N 1** *(spider's web)* fils *mpl* de la Vierge, filandres *fpl* **2** *Tex* gaze *f* légère
ADJ *(cloth)* très léger, arachnéen
▸▸ **g. thread** filandre *f*

gossip ['gɒsɪp] **N 1** *(person)* bavard, -arde; *(ill-natured)* commère *f*, cancanier, -ière **2** *(talk)* bavardage *m*; *(ill-natured)* commérage(s) *m(pl)*, *Fam* cancans *mpl*, potins *mpl*; **to have a good g.** se raconter les derniers potins
VI bavarder; *(ill-naturedly) Fam* cancaner, potiner; **to g. about sb** faire des commérages sur qn
▸▸ **g. column** échos *mpl*, **g. columnist, g. writer** échotier *m*, rédacteur, -trice mondain(e)

gossiping ['gɒsɪpɪŋ] **N** bavardage *m*; *(ill-natured)* commérage *m*
ADJ ATTRIB cancanier

gossipmonger ['gɒsɪpmʌŋgər] **N** commère *f*

gossipy ['gɒsɪpɪ] **ADJ** *(style)* anecdotique; *(person)* cancanier, -ière; **g. letter** lettre pleine de petits potins

got PT, PP *see* **get**

gotcha ['gɒtʃə] **INT** *Fam (I understand)* pigé!; *(cry of success)* ça y est (je l'ai)!; *(when catching someone doing something)* je t'y prends!; *(when one has an advantage over someone)* je te tiens!

Gothic ['gɒθɪk] **ADJ** *Archit, Art, Ling, Typ etc* gothique
N 1 *Art* gothique *m* **2** *Ling* gotique *m*, gothique *m*
▸▸ **G. novel** roman *m* gothique

gotta ['gɒtə] **CONTR** *Fam* = **got to**

gotten *Am, Arch* **PP** *see* **get**

gouache [gʊˈɑːʃ] **N** *Art* gouache *f*

gouge [gaʊdʒ] **N** *Carp, Surg* gouge *f*
VT *Carp (wood)* gouger
▸ **gouge out VT SEP** *(groove, channel etc)* creuser; **to g. sb's eye out** arracher un œil à qn

goulash ['guːlæʃ] **N** *Culin* goulasch *m*, goulache *m*

gourd ['gʊəd] **N 1** *(plant)* gourde *f* **2** *(container)* gourde *f*, calebasse *f* **3** *Fam* **out of one's g.** maboul

gourmand ['gʊəmənd] **N** *(glutton)* glouton, -onne; *(gourmet)* gourmet *m*

gourmet ['gʊəmeɪ] **N** gourmet *m*, gastronome *mf*; **g. cooking** cuisine *f* gastronomique; **g. restaurant** restaurant *m* gastronomique

gout [gaʊt] **N** *Med* goutte *f*; **to have g.** avoir la goutte

gouty ['gaʊtɪ] **ADJ** *(person, joint etc)* goutteux

Gov 1 *abbr* **government 2** *abbr* **governor**

.gov [dɒt'gʌv] *Comput* = abréviation *f* désignant les sites gouvernementaux dans les adresses électroniques

govern ['gʌvən] **VT 1** *(rule)* *(state etc)* gouverner, régir; *(province etc)* administrer **2** *(control)* *Gram (the accusative etc)* se construire avec; **laws that g. chemical reactions** lois qui régissent les réactions chimiques **3** *(restrain)* *(emotions)* maîtriser, contenir
VI *(rule)* gouverner

governance ['gʌvənəns] **N** *Lit* **1** *(act, manner)* *(of state etc)* gouvernement *m*; *(of province etc)* administration *f* **2** *(control)* emprise *f*

governess ['gʌvənɪs] **N** gouvernante *f*

governing ['gʌvənɪŋ] **ADJ 1** *Pol etc* gouvernant; **the g. party/coalition** le parti/la coalition au pouvoir **2** *Fig* dominant; **the g. concept of his philosophy** le principe qui sous-tend toute sa philosophie
N gouvernement *m*
▸▸ **g. body** conseil *m* d'administration

government ['gʌv(ə)nmənt] **N 1** *Pol* gouvernement *m*; *Mil* **it's g. issue** c'est fourni par le gouvernement VOIR GRAMMAIRE A11 **2** *(cabinet)* ministère *m*; **to form a g.** former un gouvernement *ou* un ministère
▸▸ **g. action** action *f* gouvernementale; **g. advertising** publicité *f* gouvernementale; **g. adviser** conseiller *m* du gouvernement; **g. aid** aide *f* gouvernementale *ou* de l'État; *Fin* **g. bond** obligation *f* du gouvernement; **g. borrowings** emprunts *mpl* de l'État; *Br* **g. broker** agent *m* du Trésor; **g. expenditure** dépenses *fpl* publiques; **g. finance** financement *m* par l'État; **g. grant** subvention *f* d'État; *Br* **G. House** palais *m* du gouverneur; **g. intervention** intervention *f* du gouvernement; **g. loan** emprunt *m* public *ou* d'État; **g. market** marché *m* de l'État; **g. monopoly** monopole *m* d'État; **g. offices** bureaux *mpl* du Gouvernement; **g. organization** collectivité *f* publique; **g. representative** représentant *m* du gouvernement; **g. restraints, g. restrictions** restrictions *fpl* gouvernementales; **g. revenue** recettes *fpl* publiques; **g. sector** secteur *m* public; **g. securities** effets *mpl* publics, fonds *mpl* publics *ou* d'État; **g. spending** dépenses *fpl* publiques; **g. spending review** examen *m* des dépenses publiques; **g. stocks** rentes *fpl* de l'État, bons *mpl* du Trésor

governmental [gʌvənˈment(ə)l] **ADJ** gouvernemental, aux

government-sponsored [-spɒnsəd] **ADJ** parrainé par le gouvernement

governor ['gʌv(ə)nər] **N 1** *(of colony, bank, US state)* gouverneur *m*; *(of prison, reform school etc)* directeur *m*; *(member of board of governors of a school etc)* membre *m* du conseil d'administration; *Br Fam* **the g.** *(boss)* le patron, le singe; *Fam* **where to, g.?** *(said by a taxi driver)* on va où, patron? **2** *Tech (device)* régulateur *m*; *(of speed)* modérateur *m*
▸▸ **g. general** gouverneur *m* général

governorship ['gʌvənəʃɪp] **N** *(post)* poste *m* de gouverneur; *(function)* fonctions *fpl* de gouverneur

Govt *abbr* **government**

gown [gaʊn] **N 1** *(woman's)* robe *f* **2** *(of magistrate, academic etc)* robe *f*, toge *f*; *(of surgeon)* blouse *f*; *Univ* **town and g.** = les gens *mpl* de la ville et les étudiants *mpl*

goy, *pl* **goys, goyim** [gɔɪ, -z, 'gɔɪɪm] **N** goy *m*, *pl* goyim

GP [dʒiːˈpiː] **N** *Br Med* *(abbr* **general practitioner)** (médecin *m*) généraliste *mf*

GPA [dʒiːpiːˈeɪ] **N** *Am (abbr* **grade point average)** moyenne *f*

GPO [dʒiːpiːˈəʊ] **N** *Br Formerly (abbr* **General Post Office)** Poste *f* principale

GPRS [dʒiːpiːɑːˈres] **N** *Tel (abbr* **General Packet Radio Service)** GPRS *m*

GPS [dʒiːpiːˈes] **N** *(abbr* **Global Positioning System**) GPS *m* *(système de navigation par satellite)*

gr *(abbr* **gramme(s))** g.

grab [græb] **N 1** *(movement)* **to make a g. at sth** faire un mouvement vif pour saisir qch; *Fam* **to be up for grabs** être à prendre; *(be on market, for sale)* être à vendre; **they're getting rid of all the furniture, so those chairs are up for grabs** ils se débarrassent de tous leurs meubles, alors ces chaises sont à qui veut les prendre; **is that last chocolate up for grabs?** est-ce que je peux prendre le chocolat qui reste?; **you can take it if you like, it's up for grabs** vous pouvez le prendre si vous voulez, il est là pour ça **2** *Constr* benne *f* preneuse *ou* piocheuse **3** *Aut (of brakes)* blocage *m*
VT(**-bb-) 2** *(hold of)* sb/sth saisir qn/qch (d'un geste brusque), empoigner qn/qch; **he grabbed a revolver from the table** il a saisi un revolver sur la table; **she grabbed the letter from my hands** elle m'a arraché la lettre des mains; **he grabbed me by the lapels** il m'a empoigné par le revers; **to g. a rope** *(to save oneself)* se raccrocher à un cordage; **to g. a chance/an opportunity** saisir une chance/une occasion; **to g. sb's attention** retenir *ou* (stronger) accaparer l'attention de qn; **I'll g. something to eat on the way** j'avalerai quelque chose en chemin; *Fam Fig* **how does that g. you?** *(my suggestion)* ça te dit?; **the idea doesn't g. me** ça ne me dit rien
VI **to g. at sb** s'agripper à qn; **to g. at sth** se saisir de qch, se jeter sur qch; **don't g.!** *(esp to children)* ne m'arrache/ne lui arrache/etc pas les choses/la nourriture/etc des mains!
▸▸ *Am* **g. bag** *(game)* = jeu *m* consistant à chercher des cadeaux enfouis dans un grand sac; *(assortment)* fourre-tout *m inv*; *Constr* **g. bucket** benne preneuse *ou* piocheuse

grabby ['græbɪ] **ADJ** *Fam* **don't be so g.** *(don't grab things)* ne te jette pas sur les choses; *(don't grab me)* ne t'agrippe pas à moi; **he's very g.** *(of child picking things up)* il touche à tout

grace [greɪs] **N 1** *(of movement, dancer etc)* grâce *f*; *(of language)* élégance *f*
2 *(of manners)* grâce *f*; **to do sth with (a) good/bad g.** faire qch de bonne/mauvaise grâce; **to have the (good) g. to apologize** avoir la bonne grâce de faire des excuses; **the social graces** le savoir-vivre
3 *(favour)* faveur *f*; **to be in/get into sb's good graces** être dans/entrer dans les bonnes grâces de qn; *Rel* **the g. of God** la grâce de Dieu; **there, but for the g. of God, go I** je

remercie le ciel de m'avoir épargné; **in a state of g.** en état de grâce; **to fall from g.** perdre la grâce; *Old-fashioned* **in the year of g. 1066** en l'an de grâce 1066
4 *Fin (for payment of a bill)* **days of g.** délai *m*; **to give a creditor seven days' g.** accorder à un créancier sept jours de grâce *ou* de faveur; *Com* **period of g.** jours *mpl* de grâce
5 *(prayer) (before meal)* bénédicité *m*; *(after meal)* grâces *fpl*; **to say g.** réciter le bénédicité
6 *(address)* **His G.** *(the duke)* Monsieur (le duc de …); *(the archbishop)* Monseigneur (l'archevêque de …); **Her G.** *(the duchess)* Madame (la duchesse de …)
7 *Myth* **the Graces** les Grâces *fpl*
8 *Arch (pardon)* grâce *f*, pardon *m*
vt 1 *(honour)* honorer (**with** de); **to g. a meeting with one's presence** honorer une réunion de sa présence **2** *(ornament)* embellir, orner
▸▸ *Comput* **g. log in** connexion *f* de grâce; *Mus* **g. note** note *f* d'agrément, ornement *m*

grace-and-favour ADJ *Br (residence etc)* = prêté gratuitement par le souverain à un sujet qui lui a rendu service

graceful ['greɪsʊl] ADJ **1** *(person, movement)* gracieux; **g. figure** silhouette élégante; **she is a g. dancer** elle danse avec grâce **2** *(speech)* gracieux, poli, bien tourné

gracefully ['greɪsfʊlɪ] ADV avec grâce, avec élégance

gracefulness ['greɪsfʊlnɪs] N grâce *f*, élégance *f*

graceless ['greɪslɪs] ADJ *(inelegant)* gauche, inélégant; *(rude)* effronté

gracious ['greɪʃəs] ADJ **1** *(kind, polite)* poli, affable; *(generous, noble-minded)* courtois; **to be g. to sb** être affable avec *ou* envers qn; **to be g. in accepting sth** accepter qch avec courtoisie; **our g. King/Queen** notre gracieux souverain **2** *(God)* plein de grâce *ou* de miséricorde (**to** envers) **3** *(living, house etc)* luxueux
INT **g. (me)!**, **good(ness) g.!** miséricorde!, mon Dieu!; **good g. no!** jamais de la vie!

graciously ['greɪʃəslɪ] ADV *(to accept, allow)* gracieusement, de bonne grâce; *(to reply, behave)* avec politesse; *Fml* **to be g. pleased to do sth** daigner faire qch

graciousness ['greɪʃəsnɪs] N **1** *(kindness)* gentillesse *f*, *(politeness)* courtoisie *f* **2** *(of God)* bonté *f*, miséricorde *f* **3** *(of life, house etc)* luxe *m*

gradate [grə'deɪt] VI se dégrader (**into** en)
vt *(colours)* dégrader

gradation [grə'deɪʃən] N **1** *Art (of colours)*, *Phot* gradation *f* **2** *(degree) (on thermometer etc)* degré *m*; **gradations of meaning** nuances *fpl* de sens

grade [greɪd] N **1** *(of hierarchy etc)* grade *m*, rang *m*; *(of administration)* échelon *m* **2** *(quality) (of paper, coffee, flour)* qualité *f*; *(of potato)* calibre *m*; *(of petrol)* grade *m*; *Fig* **to make the g.** se montrer à la hauteur **3** *esp Am (gradient)* pente *f* **4** *esp Am Sch (mark)* note *f*; **to get high grades** avoir de bonnes notes **5** *Am Sch (year at school)* classe *f*; *Am* **the grades** ≃ l'école *f* primaire **6** *Agr* **grades** bétail *m* amélioré par croisement
vt **1** *(classify) (produce, oil, jobs)* classer; *(potatoes)* calibrer; *Am Sch* **to g. essays** noter des dissertations **2** *Am Rail (track)* ménager *ou* régulariser la pente de; *Constr (land)* niveler **3** *Agr (breed etc)* améliorer
▸▸ *Agr* **g. cattle** bétail *m* amélioré par croisement; *Am Rail* **g. crossing** passage *m* à niveau; **g. crossing gate** barrière *f* de passage

à niveau; *Com* **g. label** étiquette *f* de calibrage; *Am* **g. point average** moyenne *f*, *Am* **g. school** école *f* primaire
▸ **grade down** VT SEP *(move to lower category)* classer dans une catégorie inférieure
▸ **grade up** VT SEP **1** *(move to higher category)* classer dans une catégorie supérieure **2** *Agr (breed etc)* améliorer

graded ['greɪdɪd] ADJ calibré; **g. exercises** exercices gradués
▸▸ **g. tax** *(upwards)* impôt *m* progressif; *(downwards)* impôt dégressif

gradient ['greɪdɪənt] N **1** *Constr etc* inclinaison *f*, *(of ground)* dénivellation *f*; **downward g.** pente *f*, déclivité *f*; **upward g.** rampe *f*, montée *f*; **a g. of 1 in 6, a 1 in 6 g.** une dénivellation d'un sixième; **steep/low g.** forte/ faible pente **2** *Math, Phys (of temperature etc)* gradient *m*

grading ['greɪdɪŋ] N **1** *(classification) (of oil, tasks, exercises)* classement *m*, gradation *f*, *(of potatoes)* calibrage *m*; *(of ore etc)* triage *m*; *Am Sch (marking)* correction *f* **2** *Am Constr, Rail (of slope)* (a)ménagement *m*

gradual ['grædjʊ(ə)l] ADJ progressif, graduel; **a g. process** un processus graduel; **a g. slope** une pente douce; **a g. transition** une transition progressive (**from … to …** de … à …)
N *Rel* graduel *m*

gradualism ['grædjʊəlɪzm] N gradualisme *m*

gradually ['grædjʊ(ə)lɪ] ADV petit à petit, progressivement; **it happened very g.** ça s'est produit très progressivement; **g. you'll be able to type without looking at the keyboard** graduellement *ou* petit à petit *ou* progressivement, tu seras capable de taper sans regarder le clavier

graduate¹ ['grædjʊət] N diplômé, -ée; *Univ* ≃ licencié, -ée; **biology g.** ≃ licencié, -ée en biologie; *Am Sch* **high school g.** ≃ titulaire *mf* du baccalauréat
▸▸ **g. entry** échelon *m* d'entrée pour les diplômés; *Am Univ* **g. school** = école *f* où l'on poursuit ses études après la licence; *Am Univ* **g. studies** études *fpl* de troisième cycle; **g. training scheme** programme *m* de formation professionnelle pour les diplômés

graduate² ['grædjʊeɪt] VI obtenir son diplôme; *Univ (complete one's degree)* obtenir sa licence; *(receive one's degree certificate)* recevoir son diplôme de licence; **he graduated from Oxford** il a fait ses études à Oxford; **I graduated in 2002** j'ai eu ma licence en 2002; *Am Sch* **to g. from high school** terminer ses études au lycée; *Fig* **to g. from sth to sth** passer de qch à qch; **she learnt on a cheap violin before graduating to a better instrument** elle a appris à jouer avec un violon bon marché avant de passer à un meilleur instrument
vt **1** *(scale, thermometer etc)* graduer; **graduated in centimetres** gradué en centimètres **2** *Am Sch, Univ* remettre un diplôme/un diplôme de licence à

graduated ['grædjʊeɪtɪd] ADJ *(thermometer etc)* gradué; **a g. pay rise/tax increase** une augmentation de salaire/des impôts progressive; **g. income tax** impôt *m* progressif; *Am Fin* **g. payment mortgage** hypothèque *f* à paiements échelonnés

graduation [grædjʊ'eɪʃən] N **1** *Univ* remise *f* des diplômes; *(by student)* réception *f* d'un diplôme; *Fig* **my g. to the post of supervisor** ma promotion au poste de surveillant **2** *(of thermometer etc)* graduation *f*, *(of tax)* progressivité *f*, **graduations** degrés *mpl*, grades *mpl*
▸▸ *Univ* **g. ceremony** cérémonie *f* de remise des diplômes

---

Graduation

Dans les pays anglo-saxons, la "graduation" est la cérémonie officielle au cours de laquelle les étudiants reçoivent leur diplôme des mains du président de l'université. La cérémonie de remise des diplômes est une occasion solennelle – dans certaines universités elle se fait en latin – et les étudiants doivent porter la toge traditionnelle avec capuchon et mortier. Le diplôme ainsi que la photo prise le jour de la cérémonie sont ensuite gardés précieusement par la famille. Aux États-Unis, le terme "graduation" désigne également la cérémonie organisée en l'honneur des élèves qui achèvent leurs études secondaires.

---

graffiti [græ'fiːtiː] NPL graffiti *mpl*; **a piece of g.** un graffiti; **there's some g. on the wall** il y a des graffiti sur le mur
▸▸ **g. artist** tagueur, -euse

graft¹ [grɑːft] N **1** *(from a plant)* greffon *m*; *(from a tree)* ente *f* **2** *Surg* greffe *f*, **bone/skin g.** greffe osseuse/de peau; **I had to have a skin g.** on a dû me faire une greffe de peau
vt *(onto a plant)* greffer; *(onto a tree)* enter; *Surg* greffer (**onto** sur); *Fig* **this piece was grafted onto the symphony later** ce morceau a été rajouté à la symphonie plus tard; **the tower was grafted onto the original edifice** la tour a été ajoutée à l'édifice d'origine

graft² *Fam* N **1** *Am (bribery etc)* pot-de-vin *m*, *pl* pots-de-vin **2** *Br (work)* **to achieve sth by hard g.** réussir qch en bossant dur
vi **1** *Am (engage in bribery etc) (give)* verser des pots-de-vin; *(take)* recevoir des pots-de-vin **2** *Br (work hard)* bosser dur

grafter ['grɑːftər] N *Br Fam (hard worker)* bosseur, -euse

grafting ['grɑːftɪŋ] N *(in horticulture, arboriculture)* greffe *f*, greffage *m*; *Surg* greffe; **skin g.** greffe de peau

Grail [greɪl] N **the G., the Holy G.** le Saint-Graal; *Fig* **the G. of full employment/world peace** la croisade pour parvenir au plein emploi/instaurer la paix mondiale

grain [greɪn] N **1** *(of wheat, pepper, salt, sand etc)* grain *m*; *Fig* **there's not a g. of truth in what he says** il n'y a pas un grain de vérité dans ce qu'il dit; *Fig* **not a g. of common sense** pas un grain *ou* pas deux sous de bon sens, pas une once de bon sens
2 *(no pl) (cereals)* céréales *fpl*; **a shipment of g.** une cargaison de céréales
3 *(measurement)* grain *m* (= 0,0648 g)
4 *(in wood, photo, stone)* grain *m*; *(in meat)* fil *m*; *(in leather)* grain, grenure *f*, **against** *or* **across the g.** contre le fil, à contre-fil; *Fig* **it goes against the g. for me to do it** ça m'est difficile de le faire, c'est contre ma nature de le faire
▸▸ **g. alcohol** alcool *m* de grains; **g. crop** récolte *f* de céréales, récolte céréalière; **g. elevator** silo *m* à céréales; **g. market** marché *m* céréalier

grainy ['greɪnɪ] ADJ *Phot* granuleux

gram [græm] N gramme *m*

grammage ['græmɪdʒ] N *(of paper)* grammage *m*

grammar ['græmər] N **1** grammaire *f*, **that's not good g.** ce n'est pas grammaticalement correct **2** *(book)* grammaire *f*, **a French g.** une grammaire française
▸▸ **g. book** grammaire *f*; *Comput* **g. checker** correcteur *m* grammatical; **g. school** *(in UK)* = type d'école secondaire; *(in US)* ≃ école *f* primaire

Grammar School

En Grande-Bretagne, ce terme désigne une école secondaire recevant une aide de l'État mais pouvant être privée, réputée dispenser un enseignement de qualité de type traditionnel et préparant aux études supérieures. L'admission se fait sur concours ("eleven-plus") ou sur dossier. Moins de cinq pour cent des élèves britanniques fréquentent ce type d'école, qui existe en Angleterre, au pays de Galles et en Irlande du Nord.

grammarian [grə'meərɪən] **N** grammairien, -ienne

grammatical [grə'mætɪk(ə)l] **ADJ 1** grammatical, -aux; **g. mistake** faute de grammaire **2** *(correct)* grammaticalement correct

grammatically [grə'mætɪklɪ] **ADV** grammaticalement

gramme [græm] **N** gramme *m*

Grammy ['græmɪ] **N** = distinction *f* récompensant les meilleures œuvres musicales américaines de l'année (classique exclu)

Gramophone® ['græməfəʊn] **N** *Old-fashioned Br* gramophone *m*
▶▶ **g. record** disque *m*

grampus ['græmpəs] **N** *(killer whale)* épaulard *m*, orque *f*

gran [græn] **N** *esp Br Fam (grandmother)* grand-mère, *pl* grands-mères *(in children's language)* mamie *f*, mémé *f*

granary ['grænərɪ] **N** *Agr* grenier *m*; *Com* entrepôt *m* de grain; **Egypt was the g. of the ancient world** l'Égypte était le grenier de l'antiquité
▶▶ *Br* **Granary®. bread, Granary®. loaf** = pain *m* complet avec des morceaux de blé non moulu

grand [grænd] **ADJ 1** *(imposing)* grand, imposant, magnifique; **to do things on a g. scale** faire les choses en grand; **to entertain on a g. scale** recevoir des gens en grande pompe; **to invest on a g. scale** faire de gros investissements; **to build on a g. scale** réaliser de grands projets de construction; **in g. style** en grande pompe; **it was all part of his g. design** tout cela faisait partie de son grand projet; **the g. manner of the aristocracy** le faste de l'aristocratie; **the mayor looked very g. in his robes** le maire avait un air très imposant avec ses vêtements de cérémonie; **the g. old man of trade unionism/Scottish folk music** le patriarche du syndicalisme/de la musique folklorique écossaise; **a g. lady** une grande dame; **'lexicographer' is just a g. name for someone who writes dictionaries** 'lexicographe' est simplement un mot pompeux pour désigner une personne qui écrit des dictionnaires **2** *Fam (excellent) (food, accommodation)* excellent; *(weather)* magnifique; **I'm not feeling too g.** je ne suis pas dans mon assiette; **she sounded absolutely g. when I spoke to her on the phone** elle avait l'air en pleine forme quand je l'ai eue au téléphone; **to have a g. time** bien s'amuser; *Iron* **we had a g. old time trying to find the house!** on s'est marré pour trouver la maison!

N 1 *Fam Am (thousand dollars)* mille dollars *mpl*, *Br (thousand pounds)* mille livres *fpl*; **two g.** *Am* deux mille dollars; *Br* deux mille livres **2** *Mus* piano *m* à queue

▶▶ **g. concert** grand concert; **g. duchess** grande-duchesse *f*, *pl* grandes-duchesses; **g. duke** grand-duc *m*, *pl* grands-ducs; **g. finale** apothéose *f*; *Am* **g. jury** jury *m* d'accusation; *Am* **g. larceny** vol *m* qualifié; **G. Master** *(in chess)* grand maître *m*; *(of maso-*

nic lodge) Grand Maître *m*; *Horseracing* **the G. National** = la plus importante course d'obstacles de Grande-Bretagne, qui se déroule à Aintree, dans la banlieue de Liverpool; **g. opera** grand opéra *m*; **g. piano** piano *m* à queue; *Sport, Cards* **g. slam** grand chelem *m*; **g. total** total *m*; **a g. total of £4575** une somme totale de 4575 livres; **the G. Tour** le tour d'Europe *(entrepris jadis par les jeunes aristocrates pour compléter leur éducation)*; *Hum* **would you like a g. tour of the house?** veux-tu que je te fasse visiter la maison?

grandad ['grændæd] **N** *Fam* papi *m*, pépé *m*

grandaddy ['grændædɪ] **N** = **grandad**; *Fig* **the g. of them all** *(of car, locomotive etc)* l'ancêtre *mf*

grandchild, *pl* **grandchildren** ['græntʃaɪld, -tʃɪldrən] **N** *(boy)* petit-fils *m*, *pl* petits-fils; *(girl)* petite-fille *f*, *pl* petites-filles; **that will be something to tell your grandchildren** voilà quelque chose que tu pourras raconter à tes petits-enfants

granddad ['grændæd] **N** *Fam* papi *m*, pépé *m*

granddaughter ['grændɔːtər] **N** petite-fille *f*, *pl* petites-filles

grandee [græn'diː] **N** *Hist* grand *m* *(d'Espagne)*; *Fig* **Tory grandees** = personnes *fpl* influentes du parti conservateur

grandeur ['grændʒər] **N 1** *(of person)* grandeur *f*, noblesse *f*, éminence *f* **2** *(of building, surroundings etc)* splendeur *f*, magnificence *f*; **the g. of the landscape** la majesté du paysage; **an air of g.** quelque chose de grandiose; **faded g.** *(of house, furnishings etc)* splendeur passée

grandfather ['grænfɑːðər, 'grænd-] **N** grand-père *m*, *pl* grands-pères
▶▶ **g. clock** horloge *f* (de parquet)

grandfatherly ['grænfɑːðəlɪ] **ADJ** de grand-père

grandiloquence [græn'dɪləkwəns] **N** grandiloquence *f*, emphase *f*

grandiloquent [græn'dɪləkwənt] **ADJ** grandiloquent

grandiose ['grændɪəʊs, -əʊz] **ADJ** *(building etc)* grandiose, magnifique; *(term, theory, title etc)* pompeux; *(idea, scheme)* grandiose

grandly ['grændlɪ] **ADV 1** *(impressively)* de façon grandiose *ou* impressionnante **2** *(pompously)* pompeusement

grandma ['grænmɑː, 'grænd-, 'græm-] **N** *Fam* mamie *f*, mémé *f*

grandmother ['grænmʌðər, 'grænd-] **N** grand-mère *f*, *pl* grands-mères

grandnephew ['grænnefjʊ, 'grænd-] **N** petit-neveu *m*, *pl* petits-neveux

grandness ['grændnɪs] **N** grandeur *f*, *Pej* caractère *m* pompeux

grandniece ['grænniːs, 'grænd-] **N** petite-nièce *f*, *pl* petites-nièces

grandpa ['grænpɑː] **N** *Fam* papi *m*, pépé *m*

grandparent ['grænpeərənt, 'grænd-] **N** *(male)* grand-père *m*; *(female)* grand-mère *f*; **grandparents** grands-parents; **children are often looked after by a g.** les enfants sont souvent gardés par un de leurs grands-parents

grandson ['grænsʌn, 'grænd-] **N** petit-fils *m*, *pl* petits-fils

grandstand ['grænstænd, 'grænd-] **N** *Sport* tribune *f* (d'honneur); **to have a g. view of sth** être bien placé pour voir qch
vi *Fig* faire le mariolle
▶▶ **g. finish** *(of race)* arrivée *f* palpitante; *(of match)* fin *f* palpitante

grange [greɪndʒ] **N 1** *Br (country house)* petit manoir *m* **2** *Arch (granary)* grange *f*

granite ['grænɪt] **N** granit(e) *m*; **g. building** édifice en granit(e)

granitic [grə'nɪtɪk] **ADJ** granitique, graniteux

grannie, granny ['grænɪ] **N** *Fam* mamie *f*, mémé *f*; **an old g.** une vieille mémé
▶▶ **g. flat** = partie *f* d'une maison aménagée indépendamment pour héberger un parent âgé; **g. knot** nœud *m* de ménagère *ou* de soldat

Granny Smith **N** *(apple)* granny-smith *f inv*

grant [grɑːnt] **N 1** *(financial aid)* subvention *f*; *Univ* bourse *f* d'études; **I can't live on my g.** je n'arrive pas à m'en sortir avec seulement ma bourse d'études; **to make a g. to sb** accorder une subvention/une bourse d'études à qn; **to receive a g.** être subventionné, recevoir une subvention; *Univ* recevoir *ou* se voir accorder une bourse d'études
2 *(action)*, *Com (of patent)* délivrance *f*, *Law (of property etc)* cession *f*
vt 1 *(permission)* donner; *(interview, audience, request etc)* accorder; *(authorization, patent)* délivrer; *Law (property etc)* faire cession de; **he was granted permission to …** il reçut la permission de …; **the countries that have been granted autonomy** les pays qui se sont vus accorder l'autonomie; **God g. that …** Dieu veuille que …; **to take sth for granted** considérer qch comme allant de soi *ou* comme normal; **you take too much for granted** vous présumez trop; **he takes it for granted that he can borrow my books** il se croit permis d'emprunter mes livres; **we take all this for granted** tout cela nous semble aller de soi; **she felt that she was being taken for granted** elle avait le sentiment qu'elle ne comptait pas; **I'm tired of the way everybody just takes me for granted** j'en ai assez que personne ne fasse attention à moi; **the party has been accused of taking its members for granted** on a accusé le parti de ne pas tenir compte de ses membres
2 *(subsidy)* accorder, allouer (**to** à)
3 *(admit)* admettre; **it must be granted that …** il faut reconnaître que …; **I g. you he is lazy** il est paresseux, je vous l'accorde; **I'll g. you that** je vous l'accorde

grant-aided **ADJ** subventionné par l'État

grant-in-aid **N** subvention *f*

grant-maintained school **N** *Br Sch* = école *f* privée qui reçoit une subvention de l'État

granular ['grænjʊlər] **ADJ** *(surface, texture)* granulaire, granuleux

granulate ['grænjʊleɪt] **vt** *(powder etc)* granuler, grener, grainer; *(sugar)* cristalliser

granulated sugar ['grænjʊleɪtɪd] **N** sucre *m* cristallisé

granulation [grænjʊ'leɪʃən] **N** granulation *f*

granule ['grænjʊl] **N** grain *m*, granule *m*; **coffee/tea granules** granules de café/thé

grape [greɪp] **N** grain *m* de raisin; **a (variety of) g.** un raisin; **to eat grapes** manger du raisin; **to pick grapes** faire les vendanges, cueillir le raisin
▶▶ **g. harvest** vendanges *fpl*; *Bot* **g. hyacinth** muscari *m*; **g. juice** jus *m* de raisin; **g. picker** vendangeur, -euse

> Note that the French word **grappe** is a false friend. It means **bunch** or **cluster**.

grapefruit ['greɪpfruːt] **N** pamplemousse *m*
▶▶ **g. juice** jus *m* de pamplemousse; **g. tree** pamplemoussier *m*

grapeshot ['greɪpʃɒt] **N** *(ammunition)* mitraille *f*

grapevine ['greɪpvaɪn] **N 1** vigne *f*, treille *f* **2** *Fig* téléphone *m* arabe; **I heard on the g.**

graph 409 **gravely**

that ... j'ai appris par le téléphone arabe que ...

graph [grɑːf] N graphique *m*, diagramme *m* VT faire la représentation graphique de
▸▸ g. **paper** papier *m* quadrillé; *(in milli-metres)* papier millimétré

graphic ['græfɪk] ADJ 1 *Math (also* **graphical)** *(representation etc)* graphique 2 *(vivid) (description etc)* très vivant; *(shocking)* cru 3 *Art* graphique
N graphique *m*
▸▸ g. **art** art *m* graphique; g. **artist** graphiste *mf*; g. **design** conception *f* graphique; g. **designer** graphiste, maquettiste *mf*; g. **equalizer** égaliseur *m* graphique; *Comput* g. **interface** interface *f* graphique

> Note that the French adjective **graphique** never means vivid or shocking.

graphically ['græfɪklɪ] ADV 1 *Math (to solve a problem)* graphiquement 2 *(vividly)* de façon très vivante; *(in a shocking way)* crûment

graphical user interface ['græfɪk(ə)l] N *Comput* interface *f* utilisateur graphique

graphics ['græfɪks] N VOIR GRAMMAIRE A10 1 *(art)* arts *mpl* graphiques 2 *Comput* graphismes *mpl*, graphiques *mpl*
▸▸ *Comput* g. **accelerator** accélérateur *m* graphique; *Comput* g. **accelerator card** carte *f* accélérateur graphique; *Comput* g. **capability** aptitude *f* graphique; *Comput* g. **card** carte graphique; g. **designer** concepteur *m* graphiste; g. **digitizer** convertisseur *m* numérique de graphiques; *Comput* g. **display** affichage *m* graphique; g. **generator** générateur *m* graphique; *Comput* g. **mode** mode *m* graphique; *Comput* g. **package** grapheur *m*; g. **resolution** résolution *f* graphique; *Comput* g. **software** logiciel *m* graphique

graphite ['græfaɪt] N graphite *m*, mine *f* de plomb

graphologist [græ'fɒlədʒɪst] N grapholo-gue *mf*

graphology [græ'fɒlədʒɪ] N graphologie *f*

grapnel ['græpnəl] N *Naut* grappin *m*, cro-chet *m*; *Aviat (of balloon)* ancre *f*

grapple ['græp(ə)l] N = **grapnel**
VI *(fight)* lutter corps à corps; *Fig* **to g. with** *(difficulty, problem, computer, machine etc)* se débattre avec; **to g. with inflation** être aux prises avec l'inflation
VT *Am (person)* empoigner; **to g. sb to the floor** mettre qn à terre

grappling ['græp(ə)lɪŋ] N *Naut* g. **iron** *or* **hook** grappin *m*, crochet *m*

grasp [grɑːsp] N 1 *(hold)* prise *f*; **to wrest sth from sb's g.** arracher qch des mains de qn; **to have a strong g.** *(handshake)* avoir de la poigne; *Fig* **to have sth within one's g.** avoir qch à sa portée; *Fig* **it is now within every-one's g.** *(financially etc)* c'est maintenant à la portée de tout le monde; *Fig* **to let an op-portunity slip from one's g.** rater une occa-sion 2 *Fig (understanding)* compréhension *f*; **to have a good g. of modern history** avoir une bonne connaissance de l'histoire mo-derne; **his g. of the problem was poor** il do-minait mal le problème
VT 1 *(hold firmly)* saisir, empoigner; **to g. sb's hand** serrer la main à qn; **I grasped his arm** je l'ai agrippé par le bras; *Fig* **to g. the opportunity** saisir l'occasion (**of doing sth** de faire qch) 2 *Fig (understand)* comprendre, saisir; **to g. the importance of sth** saisir l'im-portance de qch
▸ **grasp at** VT INSEP *(attempt to take hold of)* tenter de saisir *ou* d'atteindre; *Fig (seize) (op-portunity, offer)* saisir avidement; *Fig* **to g. at straws** se raccrocher à de faux espoirs

grasping ['grɑːspɪŋ] ADJ *(mean)* avide, cupide

grass [grɑːs] N 1 *(plant)* herbe *f*; *Fig* **she doesn't let the g. grow under her feet** elle ne perd pas son temps
2 *(lawn)* pelouse *f*, gazon *m*; *Tennis* gazon; **keep off the g.** défense de marcher sur le gazon *ou* sur la pelouse, pelouse interdite; *Prov* **the g. is always greener (on the other side of the fence)** c'est toujours mieux ail-leurs; *Tennis* **she plays well on g.** elle joue bien sur gazon
3 *(pasture)* herbage *m*; **to put** *or* **turn a horse out to g.** mettre un cheval en pâture; *Fig* **to put sb out to g.** mettre qn à la retraite; **to be (out) at g.** *(of animal)* être au vert; **to put land under g.** enherber une terre, met-tre une terre en herbe
4 *Fam (marijuana)* herbe *f*
5 *Br Sl (informer)* balance *f*, indicateur *m*
VT 1 *(cover with grass) (field)* mettre en herbe, enherber; *(garden)* gazonner 2 *Sl (in-form on)* **to g. sb** balancer, dénoncer
VI *Br Sl (inform)* parler; **to g. on sb** balancer *ou* dénoncer qn
▸▸ g. **box** *(on lawn mower)* panier *m* à her-bes; *Tex* g. **cloth** *(toile f de)* ramie *f*; *Tennis* g. **court** court *m* (en gazon); **the g. roots** *(of political party etc)* la base; **the feeling at the g. roots is that ...** le sentiment à la base est que ...; g. **seed** *(for lawn)* graine *f* pour gazon; *(as feed)* graine fourragère; g. **snake** couleuvre *f* à collier; g. **widow** = femme *f* dont le mari est toujours en déplacement; *(who is divorced or separated)* femme divor-cée/séparée (de son mari); **I'm a g. widow this weekend** je suis célibataire ce week-end
▸ **grass over** VT SEP *(garden)* gazonner; *(field)* mettre en herbe, enherber
▸ **grass up** VT SEP *Br Fam* **to g. sb up** balancer qn, moucharder qn

grass(-)green ADJ *(colour)* vert gazon *inv*

grasshopper ['grɑːshɒpər] N sauterelle *f*

grassland ['grɑːslænd] N prairies *fpl*, prés *mpl*

grass-root(s) ADJ de base, qui émane de la base; **there is no g. support for their policy** il n'y a pas de soutien de la base pour leur politique; **the g. feeling is that ...** le senti-ment à la base est que ...; **at g. level** à la base
▸▸ *Mktg* g. **forecasting** prévision *f* de la base

grassy ['grɑːsɪ] ADJ herbu, herbeux; *(lane)* vert; *(plain)* verdoyant

grate [greɪt] N *(of hearth)* grille *f*, *(fireplace)* foyer *m*, âtre *m*; **a fire in the g.** un feu dans la cheminée
VT 1 *(cheese, carrot, nutmeg etc)* râper 2 *(scrape)* **to g. sth on sth** frotter qch contre qch *(avec un grincement)*; **to g. one's teeth** grincer des dents
VI 1 *(of machinery)* grincer; *(of chalk on blackboard)* crisser 2 *(irritate)* taper sur les nerfs (**on sb** à qn); **it really grates (on me)** ça me tape vraiment sur les nerfs; **to g. on the ear** *(of music, particular accent)* écorcher l'oreille; *(of noise)* faire mal aux oreilles

G-rated ADJ *Am Cin (movie)* tous publics

grateful ['greɪtfʊl] ADJ reconnaissant (**to sb for sth** à *ou* envers qn de qch); **I'm g. for all you've done** je vous suis reconnaissant de tout ce que vous avez fait, *esp Fml* je vous sais gré de tout ce que vous avez fait; **he gave her a g. smile** il lui a adressé un sourire reconnaissant; **I would be g. if you could let me know as soon as possible** je vous serais reconnaissant de m'informer dès que pos-sible; **I was g. it wasn't me** j'étais bien content que ce ne soit pas moi; **I suppose we should be g. for that** on devrait s'en esti-mer heureux

gratefully ['greɪtfʊlɪ] ADV avec reconnais-

sance; **to smile g.** faire un sourire re-connaissant

grater ['greɪtər] N râpe *f*

gratification [grætɪfɪ'keɪʃən] N satisfac-tion *f*, plaisir *m*; **to do sth for one's own g.** faire qch pour sa propre satisfaction; **she had the g. of knowing that she'd been pro-ved right** elle avait la satisfaction de savoir qu'on lui avait donné raison

gratified ['grætɪfaɪd] ADJ satisfait, content (**with** de); *(smile)* de satisfaction

gratify ['grætɪfaɪ] VT 1 *(please) (person)* faire plaisir à 2 *(satisfy) (passion etc)* satis-faire, contenter; **to g. sb's whims** satisfaire les caprices de qn

gratifying ['grætɪfaɪɪŋ] ADJ satisfaisant

grating [1] ['greɪtɪŋ] ADJ *(noise)* discordant, grinçant; *(voice)* éraillé; g. **laugh** ricane-ment *m*; g. **sound** grincement *m*
N *Culin* râpage *m*

grating [2] N *(bars) (of window)* grille *f*

gratis ['grɑːtɪs] ADJ gratis, gratuit
ADV gratis, gratuitement

gratitude ['grætɪtjuːd] N gratitude *f*, recon-naissance *f* (**to** envers); **to show one's g.** té-moigner de sa reconnaissance

gratuitous [grə'tjuːɪtəs] ADJ *(unnecessary)* gratuit, sans raison; g. **violence** violence *f* gratuite

gratuitously [grə'tjuːɪtəslɪ] ADV gratuite-ment, sans raison

gratuity [grə'tjuːɪtɪ] N *Fml (tip)* pourboire *m*; **no gratuities** pourboires interdits

> Note that the French word **gratuité** is a false friend and is never a translation for the English word **gratuity**. It indicates that something is free of charge.

grave [1] [greɪv] N tombe *f*, tombeau *m*; **(mass) g.** fosse *f* commune; *(in wartime)* charnier *m*; **to be in one's g.** être dans la tombe; **she worked herself into an early g.** elle s'est tuée au travail; **he took his secret with him to the g.** il a emporté son secret dans la tombe; **he drank himself into an early g.** l'alcool l'a pré-maturément tué; **he's drinking himself into an early g.** il se détruit à force de boire; *Fig* **he must have turned in his g.** il a dû se re-tourner dans sa tombe; **it would make her turn in her g.** elle se retournerait dans sa tombe; **someone has just walked over my g.** j'ai eu un frisson; **to be digging one's own g.** creuser sa propre tombe; **to have one foot in the g.** avoir un pied dans la tombe; **from beyond the g.** d'outre-tombe
ADJ *(serious)* grave, sérieux; *(tone)* solennel; *(situation)* grave; *(error)* lourd; g. **news** de graves nouvelles; **to make a g. mistake** se tromper lourdement
▸▸ g. **robber** *(who robs valuables from graves)* = personne *f* qui vole les objets de valeur laissés dans les tombes, pilleur *m* de tombes; *(body snatcher)* déterreur, -euse de cadavres

grave [2] [grɑːv] ADJ grave
N accent *m* grave; **it's spelt with an "e" g.** ça s'écrit avec un "e" accent grave
▸▸ g. **accent** accent grave

gravedigger ['greɪvdɪgər] N fossoyeur *m*

gravel ['græv(ə)l] N gravier *m*
VT (-ll-, *Am* -l-) 1 *(cover with gravel)* couvrir de gravier; **gravelled path** chemin *m* de gra-vier 2 *esp Am Fam (perplex) (person)* embar-rasser
▸▸ g. **path** chemin de gravier; g. **pit** gra-vière *f*, carrière *f* de gravier

gravelly ['græv(ə)lɪ] ADJ *(containing gravel)* graveleux; *(river bed)* pierreux; g. **voice** voix râpeuse

gravely ['greɪvlɪ] ADV *(to say)* gravement,

solennellement; **to be g. mistaken** se tromper lourdement; **g. ill** gravement malade; **g. wounded** grièvement blessé

graven ['greɪvən] ADJ *Arch, Lit* **g. on his memory** gravé dans sa mémoire
▸▸ *Rel* **g. image** idole *f*, image *f*

graveness ['greɪvnɪs] N *(of manner, tone)* gravité *f*

Graves' disease ['greɪvz-] N *Med* maladie *f* de Basedow

graveside ['greɪvsaɪd] N **at the g.** près de la tombe; **his next of kin were there at the g.** ses proches étaient présents à l'enterrement

gravestone ['greɪvstəʊn] N pierre *f* tombale

graveyard ['greɪvjɑːd] N *(for people)*, *Fig (for cars)* cimetière *m*; *Fig* **this town is a g.** cette ville est mortelle; **this department has been the g. of more than one young hopeful's ambitions** ce service a mis fin aux ambitions de plus d'un jeune
▸▸ **g. shift** équipe *f* de nuit; *Radio, TV* **g. slot** tranche *f* nocturne

graving dock ['greɪvɪŋ] N *Naut* bassin *m* de radoub

gravitate ['grævɪteɪt] VI *Phys* graviter (**towards** vers; **round** autour de); *Fig* **most of the guests had gravitated towards the bar/kitchen** la plupart des invités s'étaient rapprochés du bar/de la cuisine; **at a party, she gravitates towards anybody who can help her career** dans les soirées, elle est tout de suite attirée par les personnes qui peuvent l'aider dans sa carrière; **he had gravitated towards a pro-European position** il s'était rallié à la cause européenne

gravitation [grævɪ'teɪʃən] N *Phys* gravitation *f*, *Fig* **there was a general g. towards the bar** tout le monde s'est dirigé vers le bar; *Phys* **law of g.** loi *f* de la gravitation

gravitational [grævɪ'teɪʃ(ə)l] ADJ *Phys* gravitationnel; *(field)* de gravitation
▸▸ **g. pull** gravitation *f*

gravity ['grævɪtɪ] N **1** *Phys* gravité *f*, pesanteur *f*, **law of g.** loi *f* de la pesanteur **2** *(of person)* gravité *f*, sérieux *m*; *(of situation, injury)* gravité *f*
▸▸ *Phys* **g. feed** alimentation *f* par gravité

gravure [grə'vjʊər] N *Typ (process, impression)* gravure *f*, *(plate)* plaque *f* gravée

gravy ['greɪvɪ] N **1** *Culin* jus *m*; *(thickened)* sauce *f* (au jus) **2** *Am Sl (money) (gained easily)* bénef *m*; *(gained illegally)* profit *m* illicite; **to get on the g. train** trouver le filon; **she's been on the g. train for years** elle a eu la vie facile pendant des années; **it's just a g. train for him and his friends** c'est une véritable mine d'or pour lui et ses amis
▸▸ **g. boat** saucière *f*

gray [greɪ] ADJ, N, VI *Am* = **grey**

grayling ['greɪlɪŋ] N **1** *(fish)* ombre *m* (de rivière) **2** *(butterfly)* (papillon *m*) agreste *m*

graze¹ [greɪz] *Agr* VI *(of cattle etc)* paître, brouter; **to g. on grass** brouter l'herbe; **to g. in a field** paître au champ
VT *(of farmer) (herd)* (faire) paître; *(field)* mettre en pâturage; *(of cattle etc) (field)* pâturer; *(grass)* brouter, paître

graze² N écorchure *f*, *(slighter)* éraflure *f*
VT **1** *(scrape) (knees etc)* écorcher; *(slighter)* érafler **2** *(brush past)* effleurer; **the bullet grazed his shoulder** la balle lui rasa l'épaule

grazing ['greɪzɪŋ] N *Agr* **1** *(of herd etc)* pâturage *m* **2** *(land)* pâture *f*, pacage *m*
▸▸ **g. ground, g. land** pâture, pacage; **g. rights** droit *m* de pâturage

grease [griːs] N *Culin, Tech etc* graisse *f*, *Tech (dirty)* cambouis *m*; **g. stain** *(on clothing etc)* tache *f* de gras *ou* de graisse
VT *Tech (machine)* graisser, lubrifier; *Culin*

(cake tin) beurrer; *Fig Fam* **to g. sb's palm** graisser la patte à qn
▸▸ **g. box** boîte *f* à graisse *ou* de graissage; **g. gun** *(pistolet m)* graisseur *m*, pompe *f* à graisse; *Am Fam (submachine gun)* mitraillette *f*, *Fam* **g. monkey** mécano *m*; **g. nipple** graisseur
▸ **grease back** VT SEP **to g. back one's hair** se gominer les cheveux

greased [griːst] ADJ *Fam* **like g. lightning** en quatrième vitesse; **he's like g. lightning** c'est un rapide

greasepaint ['griːspeɪnt] N maquillage *m* (de théâtre); **stick of g.** crayon *m* gras (de maquillage); *Fig* **the smell of g.** le mirage du théâtre

greaseproof ['griːspruːf] ADJ *(paper)* sulfurisé

greaser ['griːsər] N **1** *Br esp Aut Sl (mechanic)* mécano *m* **2** *Old-fashioned Br Sl (motorcyclist)* motard *m* **3** *Am Offensive Sl (Mexican)* Mexicain, -aine

greasiness ['griːsɪnɪs] N **1** état *m* graisseux *ou* gras **2** *Fam (of manner)* onctuosité *f*

greasy ['griːsɪ] ADJ **1** *(containing, covered in grease)* graisseux, huileux; *(sausage etc)* gras; *(grease-stained)* taché de graisse; **his hands felt g.** il avait les mains grasses; **you'll get your jacket all g.** tu vas mettre plein de graisse sur ta veste; **g. complexion** peau grasse; **g. hair** cheveux gras **2** *(slippery) (road etc)* glissant **3** *Fam (manner)* onctueux, mielleux
▸▸ *Sport, Fig* **the g. pole** le mât de cocagne; *Fam* **g. spoon** boui-boui *m*, *pl* bouis-bouis

GREAT [greɪt] ADJ **1** *(large, important)* grand; **a g. crowd** une foule nombreuse *ou* énorme; **a g. deal of time/money** beaucoup de temps/d'argent; **I expect a g. deal from my staff** j'attends beaucoup de mon personnel; **you're expecting a g. deal if you think that ...** tu espères trop si tu crois que ...; **a g. many people** beaucoup de gens *ou* de monde; **the g. majority, the greater part** la plupart, la majeure partie (**of** de); **to a g. extent, in g. part** en grande partie; **to reach a g. age** parvenir à un âge avancé; **his greatest fault** son plus grand défaut, son défaut capital; **to take g. care** prendre grand soin (**of** de); **g. difference** grande *ou* forte différence; **the g. divide between rich and poor/the two communities** le fossé immense qui sépare les riches et les pauvres/les deux communautés; **to take a g. interest in sb/sth** s'intéresser beaucoup à qn/qch; **with g. pleasure/with the greatest of pleasure** avec grand/avec le plus grand plaisir; **it gives me g. pleasure to inform you that ...** j'ai l'immense plaisir de vous informer que ...; **they are g. friends** ce sont de grands amis; **it is no g. matter** ce n'est pas une grosse affaire; **to have no g. opinion of sb** ne pas avoir une haute opinion de qn; **the g. thing is that ...** le grand avantage *ou* ce qui est bien, c'est que ...; **g. artist** grand artiste; **a g. man** un grand homme; *Old-fashioned Fam* **G. Scott!** grands dieux!

2 *(in proper names)* **Alexander the G.** Alexandre le Grand

3 *Fam (very good)* **to have a g. time** bien s'amuser; **(that's) g!** parfait!, (c'est) super!; *Iron* bravo!; **he's a g. guy** c'est un gars super; **a g. idea** une idée géniale; **isn't he g.!** qu'est-ce qu'il est bien!; **to be g. at tennis** être excellent au tennis; **she's g. at making the past come alive** elle arrive merveilleusement bien à faire revivre le passé; **I'm not g. on Roman history** je ne suis pas très fort *ou* calé en histoire romaine; *Iron* **she's a g. one for borrowing things without asking people** elle est spécialiste pour emprunter les choses sans demander l'autorisation

4 *(enthusiastic)* **she's a g. hillwalker** elle fait beaucoup de randonnée; **I'm a g. reader** je lis énormément; **to be a g. believer in sth** croire beaucoup en qch
ADV *Fam* **1** *(well)* très bien; **I feel g.!** je me sens super bien!; **I don't feel g. about what I did** je ne me sens pas très fier de ce que j'ai fait; **you look g. in that suit** il te va vraiment bien ce costume; **you look g.** *(very healthy)* tu as vraiment bonne mine; **he's doing g.** *(in health)* il se porte à merveille
2 *(intensifier)* **a g. big dog** un énorme chien; **be careful with your g. clumsy feet!** fais attention avec tes grands pieds maladroits!; **you g. fat slob!** espèce de gros lard!
N **1** *(person)* grand *m*, grande *f*, **one of the greats of world cinema** un des grands du cinéma mondial
2 the g. and the good les gens influents
▸▸ *Zool* **the g. apes** les grands singes *mpl*; *Astron* **the G. Bear** la Grande Ourse; **G. Britain** Grande-Bretagne *f*, **G. Dane** danois *m*; **the G. Lakes** les Grands Lacs *mpl*; **the G. Plains** les Grandes Plaines *fpl*, *Am* **g. room** séjour *m* cathédrale, *Can* salle *f* de séjour à toit cathédrale; **the G. Wall of China** la Grande Muraille (de Chine); **the G. War** la Grande Guerre, la guerre de 14 *ou* de 14–18

great-aunt N grand-tante *f*, *pl* grands-tantes

greatcoat ['greɪtkəʊt] N **1** pardessus *m* **2** *Mil (worn by cavalry)* manteau *m*; *(worn by infantry)* capote *f*

Greater London [greɪtə] N Londres *m* et son agglomération

Greater Manchester N Manchester *m* et son agglomération

greater-than sign N signe *m* plus grand que, signe supérieur à

greatest ['greɪtɪst] N *Fam* **to be the g.** *(best)* être le meilleur/la meilleure

great-grandchild, *pl* **great-grandchildren** N *(boy)* arrière-petit-fils *m*, *pl* arrière-petits-fils; *(girl)* arrière-petite-fille *f*, *pl* arrière-petites-filles; **great-grandchildren** arrière-petits-enfants *mpl*

great-granddaughter N arrière-petite-fille *f*, *pl* arrière-petites-filles

great-grandfather N arrière-grand-père *m*, *pl* arrière-grands-pères, bisaïeul *m*

great-grandmother N arrière-grand-mère *f*, *pl* arrière-grands-mères, bisaïeule *f*

great-grandparents NPL arrière-grands-parents *mpl*, bisaïeuls *mpl*

great-grandson N arrière-petit-fils *m*, *pl* arrière-petits-fils

great-great-grandfather N arrière-arrière-grand-père *m*, trisaïeul *m*

great-great-grandmother N arrière-arrière-grand-mère *f*, trisaïeule *f*

great-hearted [-'hɑːtɪd] ADJ généreux

greatly ['greɪtlɪ] ADV très; **to be g. influenced/surprised/amused** être très influencé/surpris/amusé; **g. irritated** très *ou* fortement irrité; **the difficulties have been g. exaggerated** on a beaucoup exagéré les difficultés; **he has g. improved since last year** il a fait beaucoup de progrès depuis l'année dernière; **I would g. prefer ...** je préférerais nettement ...; **to contribute g. to a result** largement contribuer à un résultat; **g. though I admired/respected him ...** j'avais beau l'admirer/le respecter beaucoup ...

great-nephew N petit-neveu *m*, *pl* petits-neveux

greatness ['greɪtnɪs] N **1** *(of person, action etc)* grandeur *f*, *(of thought)* élévation *f*, noblesse *f*, **g. of soul** grandeur d'âme *f* **2** *(extent, size)* grandeur *f*, importance *f*

great-niece N petite-nièce f, pl petites-nièces

great-uncle N grand-oncle m, pl grands-oncles

grebe [griːb] N (bird) grèbe m; **great crested g.** grèbe huppé

Grecian ['griːʃən] ADJ grec, f grecque; **in the G. style** à la grecque

Greece [griːs] N Grèce f

greed [griːd] N **1** (for material things) avidité f, cupidité f; **g. for fame/power** la recherche avide de célébrité/pouvoir; **it's sheer g.!** c'est de l'avidité pure et simple **2** (gluttony) gourmandise f

greedily ['griːdɪlɪ] ADV **1** (to hoard, keep for oneself etc) avidement, cupidement **2** (to eat) goulûment; (to look, say) avec gourmandise

greediness ['griːdɪnɪs] N = greed

greedy ['griːdɪ] ADJ **1** (for material things) avide, cupide **2** (gluttonous) gourmand
▸▸ Sl **g. guts** goinfre mf

Greek [griːk] ADJ grec, f grecque; **the G. Church** l'Église grecque
N **1** (person) Grec m, Grecque f; Prov **beware of Greeks bearing gifts** = méfiez-vous des étrangers qui vous veulent du bien **2** Ling grec m; **modern G.** le grec moderne; Fam **it's all G. to me** c'est de l'hébreu pour moi

green [griːn] ADJ **1** (colour) vert; **to paint sth g.** peindre qch en vert; Lit **to keep sb's memory g.** entretenir la mémoire de qn; **to give sb the g. light** donner le feu vert à qn (**to do sth** pour faire qch); **to go** or **turn g.** (of traffic lights) passer au vert; (of person) verdir, blêmir; (of lawn, fields) verdir; **she has** Br **g. fingers** or Am **a g. thumb** elle a la main verte; **to grow g.** verdir; (of grass) verdoyer; Agr **the g. revolution** la révolution verte; **g. with envy** vert de jalousie, pâle d'envie; **to make sb g. with envy** faire pâlir qn d'envie
2 Fam (young, inexperienced) jeune, inexpérimenté; (naive) naïf, f naïve; **he's not as g. as he looks** il n'est pas si niais qu'il en a l'air; **she's as g. as grass** (person) elle est extrêmement naïve
3 Pol (consumer, policy etc) vert, écologiste
N **1** (colour) vert m
2 (of trees, plants etc) verdure f
3 greens (vegetables) légumes mpl verts
4 (grassy area) pelouse f, gazon m; **village g.** pelouse communale, pré m communal; **the g.** la pelouse; Golf le green; **bowling g.** (terrain m pour) jeu m de boules
5 Pol (person) écologiste mf
▸▸ **g. audit** = rapport m sur l'impact des activités d'une entreprise sur l'environnement; **g. bean** haricot m vert; **g. belt** ceinture f verte; **the G. Berets** les Bérets mpl verts; **g. card** (for insurance) carte f verte (prouvant qu'un véhicule est assuré pour un voyage à l'étranger); (work permit) carte de séjour (temporaire, aux États-Unis); **g. channel** (at customs) file f "rien à déclarer"; **g. keeper** (of bowling green, golf course) préposé, -ée à l'entretien des pelouses; **g. marketing** marketing m vert ou écologique; Br Pol **G. Paper** livre m blanc; **G. Party** (in UK) parti m écologiste; **g. pea** petit pois m; **g. pepper** poivron m vert; Br Econ **g. pound** livre f verte; Mktg **g. product** produit m vert ou écologique; **g. rate** taux m vert; **g. salad** salade f (verte); Fin **g. taxation** fiscalité f écologique; **g. tourism** tourisme m vert; Br Fam **g. wellies** = bottes fpl de caoutchouc vertes (le terme évoque les classes bourgeoises ou aristocratiques habitant à la campagne)

greenback ['griːnbæk] N Am Fam billet m vert

greenery ['griːnərɪ] N verdure f

green-eyed ['griːnaɪd] ADJ aux yeux verts; Lit **the g. monster** (jealousy) la jalousie

greenfield site ['griːnfiːld] N (for factory etc) terrain m non-bâti

greenfinch ['griːnfɪntʃ] N (bird) verdier m

greenfly ['griːnflaɪ] N (insect) puceron m; **to have g.** (of plant) avoir des pucerons; **g. spray** produit m à vaporiser contre les pucerons

greengage ['griːngeɪdʒ] N reine-claude f, pl reines-claudes

greengrocer ['griːngrəʊsər] N esp Br marchand, -ande de fruits et légumes; **g.'s (shop)** magasin m de fruits et légumes

greenhorn ['griːnhɔːn] N Fam blanc-bec m, pl blancs-becs; Mil bleu m

greenhouse ['griːnhaʊs] N serre f
▸▸ **g. effect** effet m de serre; **g. gas** gaz m à effet de serre

greening ['griːnɪŋ] N **the recent g. of the Labour Party** la récente conversion du Parti travailliste à l'écologie

greenish ['griːnɪʃ] ADJ verdâtre

Greenland ['griːnlənd] N Groenland m; **in G.** au Groenland

Greenlander ['griːnləndər] N Groenlandais, -aise

greenmail ['griːnmeɪl] N Fin greenmail m

greenness ['griːnnɪs] N (of fruit etc) immaturité f, (inexperience) inexpérience f, (naivety) naïveté f, simplicité f, (of countryside etc) vert m, verdure f, **the g. of the wood made the fire difficult to light** le feu avait du mal à prendre parce que le bois était vert

greenroom ['griːnruːm] N TV salle f de détente; Theat foyer m des artistes

greenstick fracture ['griːnstɪk] N Med fracture f en bois vert

greenstuff ['griːnstʌf] N **1** Br (vegetables) légumes mpl verts **2** Am Sl (paper money) billets mpl

greensward ['griːnswɔːd] N Lit pelouse f, (tapis m de) gazon m

Greenwich [-'grenɪdʒ-] N Greenwich
▸▸ **G. Mean Time** heure f (du méridien) de Greenwich; **G. meridian** méridien m de Greenwich

greenwood ['griːnwʊd] N Lit bois m, forêt f (en été)

greet [griːt] VT (person) saluer; (welcome) accueillir avec quelques paroles aimables; **to g. a speech with cheers** acclamer un discours; **the announcement was greeted with cheers** l'annonce a été saluée par des acclamations; **his words were greeted with resentful silence** ses mots ont été accueillis par un silence désapprobateur; **the first thing to g. my ear was** … la première chose que j'ai entendue a été …; **to g. the eyes** s'offrir à l'œil
VI Scot (cry) pleurer
N Scot (cry) **to have a g.** pleurer (**about sth** à cause de qch)

greeting ['griːtɪŋ] N salutation f, salut m; **to send greetings to sb** envoyer ses salutations à qn; **New Year/Christmas greetings** vœux mpl de bonne année/Noël; **greetings card** carte f de vœux

gregarious [grɪ'geərɪəs] ADJ (person) sociable; Zool, Bot grégaire

> Note that the French adjective **grégaire** is a false friend. It never means **sociable**.

gregariously [grɪ'geərɪəslɪ] ADV Zool (to live) en groupe; **she was not g. inclined** elle n'avait pas le tempérament grégaire

gregariousness [grɪ'geərɪəsnɪs] N (of person) sociabilité f, Zool, Bot grégarisme m, instinct m grégaire

Gregorian [grɪ'gɔːrɪən] ADJ Rel (chant, calendar etc) grégorien

gremlin ['gremlɪn] N Fam lutin m; Fig **to get all the gremlins out of the system** se débarrasser de toutes les petites bêtises qui ralentissent le système

Grenada [grə'neɪdə] N la Grenade

grenade [grə'neɪd] N Mil grenade f
▸▸ **g. attack** attaque f à la grenade; **g. launcher** lance-grenade m, pl lance-grenades

grenadier [grenə'dɪər] N Mil grenadier m

grenadine ['grenədiːn] N (syrup) grenadine f

grew PT see **grow**

grey, Am **gray** [greɪ] ADJ **1** gris; **to turn** or **go g.** grisonner; Fig **it's a g. area** c'est une zone d'ombre **2** (complexion) blême; **to turn g.** blêmir **3** (outlook etc) sombre, morne; **a g. dismal morning** un matin gris et triste; **a g. existence** une existence morne
N **1** (colour) gris m; **hair touched with g.** cheveux grisonnants; Comput **shades of g.** niveaux de gris **2** (horse) cheval m gris
VI (of hair) grisonner; **to be greying at the temples** avoir les tempes grisonnantes, grisonner aux tempes
▸▸ **g. import** importation f grise; St Exch **g. knight** chevalier m gris; St Exch, Com **g. market** marché m gris; Anat **g. matter** matière f grise; Hum **to exercise the g. matter** faire marcher sa matière grise; **G. Panthers** = groupe m de pression composé de personnes âgées; **g. power** = pouvoir m économique, social etc des personnes âgées; **g. squirrel** écureuil m gris, petit-gris m, pl petits-gris; **g. wolf** loup m (gris); **g. zone** zone f grise

greybeard ['greɪbɪəd] N esp Lit (old man) vieillard m sage, Pej vieux barbon m

grey-eyed ADJ aux yeux gris

grey-haired, grey-headed ['greɪ'heəd, -'hedɪd] ADJ aux cheveux gris; (greying) grisonnant

greyhound ['greɪhaʊnd] N lévrier m
▸▸ **g. racing** course f de lévriers; **g.(-racing) track** cynodrome m

greying ['greɪɪŋ] ADJ grisonnant; **a g. population** une population vieillissante

greyish ['greɪɪʃ] ADJ grisâtre

greylag ['greɪlæg] N oie f cendrée
▸▸ **g. goose** oie cendrée

greyness ['greɪnɪs] N **1** (colour) teinte f grise; **the g. of London** la grisaille de Londres **2** (depressing quality) caractère m morne ou sombre, tristesse f

greyscale ['greɪskeɪl] N Comput niveau m de gris
▸▸ **g. monitor** moniteur m de niveau de gris

grid [grɪd] N **1** (of bars etc) grille f, grillage m **2** (electrode) grille f, Br **the national g.** le réseau électrique national **3** (on chart) grille f, (lines on map) quadrillage m **4** Sport (of motor racing circuit) (starting) **g.** grille f de départ **5** Comput **g.** f **6** = gridiron
▸▸ **g. layout** (of town) quadrillage, damier m; **g. lines** droites fpl du quadrillage; **g. reference** coordonnées fpl de la grille; **g. system** réseau m de quadrillage

griddle ['grɪd(ə)l] N Culin (iron plate) plaque f en fonte; (on top of stove) plaque chauffante
▸▸ **g. cake** = sorte de galette épaisse

gridiron ['grɪdaɪən] N Am Ftbl (field) terrain m de football; (game) football m américain

gridlock ['grɪdlɒk] N (on road) embouteillage m; Fig impasse f

grief [griːf] N **1** (pain) chagrin m, douleur f, **to die of g.** mourir de chagrin; **to come to g.** (of person) (in undertaking) échouer; (have an accident) avoir un accident; (of rider)

faire une chute; *(of plan etc)* échouer, mal tourner; **she came to g. in the written exam** elle a échoué à l'écrit; *Fam* **good g.!** mon Dieu! **2** *Fam (trouble, inconvenience)* embêtements *mpl*; **to give sb g.** embêter qn
► ► *Am* **g. counselor** = conseiller *m* qui propose une assistance psychologique aux personnes qui ont perdu un être cher

> Note that the French word **grief** is a false friend and is never a translation for the English word **grief**. It means **grievance**.

grief-stricken ADJ accablé de douleur *ou* de chagrin

grievance ['griːvəns] N **1** *(feeling of having been wronged)* grief *m*; **to have a g. against sb** avoir un grief contre qn; **to air** *or* **state one's grievances** conter *ou* exprimer ses doléances **2** *(wrong)* doléance *f*; **to redress a g.** réparer un tort
► ► **g. procedure** = procédure *f* permettant aux salariés de faire part de leurs revendications

grieve [griːv] VI se chagriner, s'affliger (**over** *or* **about** sth de qch); **the whole nation grieved at his death** la nation entière pleura sa mort; **he was grieving for his lost daughter** il pleurait sa fille perdue; **she is still grieving** elle a encore de la peine
VT *(person)* chagriner, affliger; **we are grieved to learn ...** nous apprenons avec peine ...; **it grieves me to ...** cela me peine de ...

grieved [griːvd] ADJ chagriné, affligé (**at** de); **deeply g.** navré (**at** de)

grieving ['griːvɪŋ] ADJ éploré

grievous ['griːvəs] ADJ *Fml* **1** *(causing grief)* douloureux, pénible; *(news)* affligeant, douloureux; *(loss)* cruel **2** *(wound etc)* grave
► ► *Law* **g. bodily harm** coups *mpl* et blessures *fpl*; **to cause g. bodily harm** causer de graves blessures

grievously ['griːvəslɪ] ADV *(seriously)* gravement; *(wounded)* grièvement

griffin ['grɪfɪn] N *Myth* griffon *m*

griffon ['grɪfən] N **1** *(dog)* griffon *m* **2** *Myth* griffon *m* **3** *(bird)* vautour *m* fauve
► ► **g. vulture** vautour fauve

grift [grɪft] VT *Am Sl* escroquer

grifter ['grɪftər] N *Am Sl* escroc *m*

grill [grɪl] N *Br Culin* **1** *(food)* grillade *f*; **a mixed g.** un assortiment de grillades **2** *(room in restaurant)* grill-room *m*, *pl* grill-rooms; *(restaurant)* rôtisserie *f* **3** *(device)* gril *m*; **to cook sth under the g.** cuire qch sur le *ou* au gril
VT **1** *Br (cook) (meat etc)* faire griller **2** *Fam (interrogate) (prisoner etc)* cuisiner
VI *Br Culin* griller

grill(e) [grɪl] N *(bars) (of gate)* grille *f*, **(counter) g.** *(in bank etc)* grille de comptoir; *Aut* **(radiator) g.** calandre *f*

grilled [grɪld] ADJ *Br Culin* grillé; **g. meat** viande *f* grillée, grillade *f*

grilling ['grɪlɪŋ] N **1** *Br (of food)* cuisson *f* sur le *ou* au gril **2** *Fam (interrogation)* **to give sb a g.** cuisiner qn

grillroom ['grɪlrʊm] N *(in restaurant)* grill-room *m*, *pl* grill-rooms; *(restaurant)* rôtisserie *f*

grim [grɪm] ADJ *(countryside, surroundings)* sinistre, lugubre; *(news, report)* sombre; *(face)* sévère; *(smile)* sardonique; *(humour)* macabre; **g. determination** volonté inflexible; **to hold on like g. death** se cramponner (**to sb/sth** à qn/qch); **to look g.** *(of person) (serious)* avoir une mine sévère; *(very ill)* avoir très mauvaise mine; **things are looking g.** ça s'annonce mal; **the g. prospect of another famine** la perspective sinistre d'une autre famine; *Fam* **how do you**

feel? – pretty g. comment ça va? – plutôt mal; *Fam* **I thought it was pretty g.** *(not well done, of poor quality)* j'ai trouvé ça plutôt minable
► ► **the G. Reaper** La Faucheuse

grimace [grɪ'meɪs] N grimace *f*; **to make a g.** faire la grimace
VI grimacer, faire la grimace

grime [graɪm] N saleté *f*; *(dust)* poussière *f* de charbon *ou* de suie

griminess ['graɪmɪnɪs] N saleté *f*, noirceur *f*

grimly ['grɪmlɪ] ADV sinistrement, de façon lugubre; *(to fight, hold on)* avec acharnement

grimness ['grɪmnɪs] N *(of surroundings, landscape)* caractère *m* sinistre *ou* lugubre; *(of face)* sévérité *f*; *(of struggle)* acharnement *m*; **the g. of the situation in the country** la situation désespérée du pays; **the g. of the news from the front** les sombres nouvelles du front

grimy ['graɪmɪ] ADJ sale, encrassé, noirci; *(with soot)* noir (de suie)

grin [grɪn] N **1** *(smile)* large sourire *m*; **to give a broad g.** avoir la bouche fendue jusqu'aux oreilles **2** *(grimace)* grimace *f* (qui découvre les dents)
VI *(-nn-)* **1** *(smile)* sourire; *(broadly)* faire un large sourire; **he grinned broadly** son visage s'est épanoui en un large sourire, il fit un large sourire; *Fig* **to g. and bear it** (tâcher de) garder le sourire, *Fam* encaisser (sans broncher) **2** *(grimace)* grimacer en montrant les dents

grind [graɪnd] N **1** *Fam (work)* labeur *m* monotone et continu; **the daily g.** le labeur quotidien; **what a g.!** quelle corvée! **2** *(erotic dance)* déhanchement *m* **3** *(sound)* grincement *m*, crissement *m*
VT *(pt, pp* ground [graʊnd]*)* **1** *(pulverize) (grain, coffee, pepper)* moudre; *Am (meat)* hacher; *also Fig* **to g. sth to dust** pulvériser qch; **to g. sth under one's heel** écraser qch avec le talon; *Fig* écraser qch; *Fig* **to g. the faces of the poor** opprimer les pauvres; **to g. one's teeth** grincer des dents **2** *(polish) (glass)* dépolir; *Opt* **to g. lenses** polir les lentilles **3** *(sharpen)* aiguiser, affûter; *(on grindstone)* passer à la meule **4** **to g. a barrel organ** jouer de l'orgue de Barbarie; **to g. a pepper mill** moudre du poivre
VI **1** *(of wheels)* grincer, crisser; *(of gears)* craquer; **to g. to a halt** *(of vehicle)* s'immobiliser; *(of machine)*, *Fig (production)* stopper; **the whole country ground to a halt** *or* **standstill during the General Strike** le pays a été complètement paralysé pendant la grève générale **2** *Old-fashioned Fam (work hard)* bûcher, turbiner; *Sch* bachoter
► **grind away** VI **1** *(working)* progresser laborieusement; **to g. away at sth** travailler laborieusement à qch **2** *Fam (sexually)* s'envoyer en l'air
► **grind down** VT SEP **1** *(opposition)* écraser; **a people ground down by poverty** un peuple accablé par une pauvreté extrême; *Fam* **don't let the bastards g. you down!** ne te laisse pas enfoncer par ces salauds! **2** *(pulverize) (grain, coffee)* moudre **3** *(sharpen)* aiguiser, affûter
VI *(of substance)* **it grinds down easily** c'est facile à moudre
► **grind on** VI *(proceed relentlessly)* ne pas en finir; *(of negotiations, speech)* traîner en longueur, s'éterniser; **the accordion music ground on in the background** en fond sonore on entendait l'accordéon, intermittable et monotone
► **grind out** VT SEP **1** *(produce without originality) (articles, poems)* pondre; **to g. out a tune** jouer un air avec monotonie; **he ground out the same jokes night after night**

il a débité les mêmes plaisanteries soir après soir **2** *(cigarette)* écraser
► **grind up** VT SEP *(pulverize)* pulvériser; **to g. sth up small** moudre qch fin

grinder ['graɪndər] N **1** *(device)* appareil *m* broyeur, broyeuse *f*; *(for coffee)* moulin *m* à café; *(for sharpening)* meule *f*; *Fig* **to put sb through the g.** faire passer un mauvais quart d'heure à qn **2** *(person)* broyeur, -euse; *(of knives etc)* rémouleur *m* **3** *(molar)* molaire *f* **4** *Am Fam (sandwich)* gros sandwich *m*

grinding ['graɪndɪŋ] ADJ *(boredom, monotony etc)* mortel; *(worry, insecurity)* accablant; *(of gears)* craquement *m*; **to come to a g. halt** *(of vehicle)* s'immobiliser en grinçant; *(of machine)*, *Fig (production)* stopper; **to bring sth to a g. halt** *(production)* stopper qch; *(country, rail network)* paralyser qch; **g. poverty** extrême pauvreté; **g. sound** *(of machine, car, lift)* grincement *m*
N *(of corn)* mouture *f*; *(sound) (of machine, factory)* grincement *m*; *(of gears)* craquement *m*

grindingly ['graɪndɪŋlɪ] ADV **g. boring/monotonous** ennuyeux/monotone à mourir

grindstone ['graɪndstəʊn] N meule *f*; *Fig Fam* **he keeps our noses to the g.** il ne nous laisse aucun répit; **it's going to be noses to the g.** il va y avoir du boulot

gringo ['grɪŋgəʊ] N *Fam usu Pej (English speaker in Latin America)* gringo *m*

grip [grɪp] N **1** *(hold, grasp)* prise *f*; *(of wheels on road)* adhérence *f*; **to have a strong g.** *(of person)* avoir une bonne poigne; **your g. is wrong** *(on tennis racket, golf club etc)* tu ne tiens pas ta raquette/ton club/*etc*/comme il faut; *Fig* **I can't get to grips with Shakespeare** je n'arrive pas à comprendre Shakespeare; **to come to grips with sb** *(physically)* s'en prendre à qn; **to get a g. on sth** avoir une prise sur qch; *Fig* **to get a g. on the situation** *(bring under control)* prendre la situation en mains; *Fig* **to get** *or* **take** *or* **keep a g. on oneself** se maîtriser; **to have a firm g. on sth** *(physically)* tenir qch bien en main; *Fig* **although he has officially retired, Sir Charles retains a firm g. on financial decisions** bien qu'il soit officiellement à la retraite, Sir Charles est toujours très impliqué dans les décisions financières; *Br Fig Fam* **get a g.!** *(control yourself)* reprends-toi!; *(behave normally, be realistic)* arrête de déconner!; **to lose one's g.** *(on rope etc)* lâcher prise; *Fig (mentally)* baisser; **I must be losing my g.** je vieillis, je baisse; **to lose one's g. on reality** perdre le sens des réalités; **he was beginning to lose his g. on the situation** il commençait à perdre le contrôle de la situation; **in the g. of a disease/despair/pessimism** en proie à une maladie/au désespoir/au pessimisme; *Fig* **the country was in the g. of the worst winter for years** le pays connaissait l'hiver le plus rigoureux qu'il ait avait connu depuis des années
2 *(handle) (of oar, handlebars)* poignée *f*; *(of pistol)* poignée, crosse *f*; *Tennis (of racket)* manche *m*
3 *Tech etc (device)* pince *f*
4 *(hair)* **g.** pince *f* (à cheveux)
5 *Old-fashioned Am (bag)* mallette *f*
6 *TV, Cin* **grip(s)** machiniste *m* (de plateau)
VT *(-pp-)* *(seize)* saisir, prendre; *(hold)* empoigner, agripper; **to g. sth in a vice** serrer qch dans un étau; **the tyres g. the road well** les pneus adhèrent bien (à la route); *Fig* **to be gripped by panic** être pris *ou* saisi de panique; **the region has been gripped by cold weather** la région a été saisie par une vague de froid; *Fig* **the play gripped the audience** la pièce a captivé les spectateurs
VI *(of tyre)* adhérer

gripe [graɪp] N **1** *Fam (complaint)* sujet *m* de mécontentement; **what's your g.?** de quoi est-ce que tu te plains?; **they've always got some g.** ils sont toujours en train de râler **2** *(pain)* **gripes** coliques *fpl*

VI *(complain)* ronchonner, râler (**about sth** à propos de qch)

▸▸ **g. water** calmant *m* (pour coliques)

griping ['graɪpɪŋ] ADJ **g. pains** coliques *fpl*

N *Fam (complaining)* plaintes *fpl*

gripping ['grɪpɪŋ] ADJ *(book, film)* passionnant

grisly ['grɪzlɪ] ADJ *(murder, discovery)* macabre, sinistre; *(story, sight)* effrayant, épouvantable

grist [grɪst] N blé *m* à moudre; *Fig* **it's all g. to their mill** cela apporte de l'eau à leur moulin

gristle ['grɪs(ə)l] N *(in meat)* nerfs *mpl*

gristly ['grɪslɪ] ADJ *(meat)* nerveux

grit [grɪt] N **1** *(particles)* grès *m*, sable *m*; *(for icy roads)* sable; *Tech etc* impuretés *fpl* **2** *Fig (courage, determination)* cran *m*, courage *m*; **to have a lot of g.** avoir beaucoup de cran **3** *(stone)* grès *m* (dur)

VT (**-tt-**) **1** *(put grit on) (slippery road surface etc)* sabler **2 to g. one's teeth** grincer des dents; *Fig* **you'll just have to g. your teeth** il va falloir que tu prennes ton mal en patience

VI *(put grit on roads)* sabler (les routes)

grits [grɪts] NPL *Am (dish)* gruau *m* d'avoine

gritstone ['grɪtstəʊn] N grès *m* (dur)

gritter ['grɪtər] N *Br (vehicle)* camion *m* de sablage

gritting ['grɪtɪŋ] N *Br (of roads)* sablage *m*

▸▸ **g. lorry** camion *m* de sablage

gritty ['grɪtɪ] ADJ **1** *(soil)* cendreux; *(texture)* graveleux **2** *Fam (brave)* qui a du cran, résolu; **g. determination** détermination farouche **3** *(realistic) (writing etc)* très réaliste; **g. realism** *(of book, film etc)* réalisme cru

grizzle ['grɪz(ə)l] VI *esp Br Fam (complain)* ronchonner, râler; *(whine)* pleurnicher, geindre

grizzled ['grɪz(ə)ld] ADJ *(hair, person)* grisonnant

grizzling ['grɪzlɪŋ] N *esp Br Fam (whining)* pleurnicherie *f*, pleurnichement *m*

grizzly ['grɪzlɪ] ADJ **1** *(hair, person)* grisonnant **2** *Fam (whining)* grognon

N *(bear)* grizzli *m*, grizzly *m*

▸▸ **g. bear** grizzli, grizzly

groan [grəʊn] N *(of pain)* gémissement *m*; *(at boring story, bad joke)* grognement *m* désapprobateur; *(of disappointment, dismay)* grognement; *(of tree, timber)* grincement *m*; **to give or utter a deep g.** pousser un profond gémissement

VI *(in pain)* gémir, pousser un gémissement; *(complain)* geindre; *(at bad joke, in dismay)* grogner; *(of tree, timber)* grincer; **to g. inwardly** étouffer une plainte *ou* un gémissement; **to g. under the weight of sth** grincer sous le poids de qch; **the cart is groaning under the load** la charrette grince sous le fardeau

VT *(say)* gémir

groats [grəʊts] NPL *(of oats, wheat)* gruau *m* d'avoine/de froment

grobag® ['grəʊbæg] N = sac *m* de terreau que l'on perfore et qui sert directement de pépinière

grocer ['grəʊsər] N épicier, -ière; **the g.'s will be closed** l'épicerie sera fermée; **to go to the g.'s** aller à l'épicerie *ou* chez l'épicier

groceries ['grəʊsərɪz] NPL (articles *mpl* d')épicerie *f*

grocery ['grəʊsərɪ] N *(shop)* épicerie *f*; **to be in the g. business** être dans l'épicerie

grog [grɒg] N *(drink)* grog *m*

groggy ['grɒgɪ] ADJ *Fam* chancelant, titubant; *(boxer)* groggy; **to feel g.** avoir les jambes en coton; **I'm feeling a bit g.** je ne suis pas dans mon assiette

grogshop ['grɒgʃɒp] N *Austr Fam* = magasin *m* où l'on vend des boissons alcoolisées

groin [grɔɪn] N **1** *Anat* aine *f*; *Euph* **she kicked him in the g.** elle lui a donné un coup de pied dans les parties; **g. injury** blessure *f* à l'aine **2** *Archit (of vault)* arête *f*

grommet ['grɒmɪt] N *Tech* bague *f* d'étoupe; *Naut* erse *f*, erseau *m*

groom [gruːm] N **1** *(of horse)* palefrenier *m* **2** *(at wedding)* marié *m* **3** *(of King's bedchamber etc)* gentilhomme *m*, valet *m*

VT **1** *(horse)* panser **2** *Fig (candidate)* préparer, former *(en vue d'un poste ou d'une fonction dans la politique etc)*; **the dictator groomed his successor for power** le dictateur a préparé son successeur au pouvoir

groomed [gruːmd] ADJ **well-g.** *(horse)* bien entretenu; *(person)* bien soigné, soigné de sa personne

grooming ['gruːmɪŋ] N **1** *(of horse)* pansage *m* **2** *(of person)* **good g. is very important** il est important d'avoir une bonne présentation **3** *Fig (of candidate)* préparation *f*

groove [gruːv] N **1** *(slot)* rainure *f*; *(of gun etc)* rayure *f*; *(of column etc)* cannelure *f*; *(on record)* sillon *m* sonore; *(for sliding shutter etc)* coulisse *f*, glissière *f* **2** *Fig (routine)* routine *f*; **to get into a g.** s'encroûter, devenir routinier

VT rainer; *(gun etc)* rayer; *(column)* canneler

VI *Fam (dance)* danser; **to g. to the beat** danser en rythme

groovy ['gruːvɪ] ADJ *Old-fashioned Fam* sensass

grope [grəʊp] N **1** *(in dark etc)* tâtonnement *m* **2** *Fam (sexual)* pelotage *m*; **they were having a g.** ils se pelotaient

VI tâtonner; **to g. for sth** chercher qch à tâtons *ou* à l'aveuglette; **to g. for a word** chercher un mot

VT **1 to g. one's way** avancer à tâtons, se diriger en tâtonnant (**towards sth** vers qch) **2** *Fam (sexually)* peloter

groper ['grəʊpər] N *(fish)* mérou *m*

groping ['grəʊpɪŋ] ADJ tâtonnant

N **1** *(in dark etc)* tâtonnement *m* **2** *(sexual)* pelotage *m*

grosbeak ['grəʊsbiːk] N *(bird)* gros-bec *m*, *pl* gros-becs

grosgrain ['grəʊgreɪn] N *Tex* gros-grain *m*

gross[1] [grəʊs] N INV *(twelve dozen)* douze douzaines *fpl*, grosse *f* VOIR GRAMMAIRE A12–13

gross[2] ADJ **1** *(fat)* gras, *f* grasse **2** *(blatant) (error)* grossier; *(ignorance)* crasse; *(injustice, carelessness, idiocy)* flagrant; *(abuse)* choquant **3** *(vulgar) (joke, person)* grossier; *esp Am Fam* **that's g.!** *(repulsive)* c'est dégoûtant! **4** *Com, Fin (profit, income)* brut **5** *Naut (displacement)* global, -aux, total, -aux

N *(whole amount)* montant *m* brut

VT *Com etc (of company)* gagner brut; *(of sale)* produire brut; *(of film)* rapporter une recette brute de

▸▸ **g. amount** montant *m* brut; **g. assets** actif *m* brut; *Fin* **g. dividend** dividende *m* brut; **g. domestic product** produit *m* intérieur brut; **g. income** *(in accounts)* produit brut; *(of individual)* revenu *m* brut; *Fin* **g. margin** marge *f* brute; **g. national expenditure** dépense *f* nationale brute; **g. national income** revenu national brut; **g. national product** produit national brut; *Law* **g. negligence** faute flourde; *Acct* **g. operating profit** bénéfice *m ou* résultat *m* brut d'exploitation; **g. profit** bénéfice brut; *Acct* **g. profit margin** marge commerciale brute; *Acct* **g. receipts** recettes *fpl* brutes; *Acct* **g. redemption yield** rendement *m* actuariel brut; *Naut* **g. register tonnage** (tonnage *m* de) jauge *f* brute, tonnage brut; *Fin* **g. return** rendement brut; *Naut* **g. ton** tonne *f* de jauge; *Naut* **g. tonnage** (tonnage de) jauge brute, tonnage brut; **g. weight** poids *m* brut, brut *m*; *Fin* **g. yield** rendement brut

▸ **gross out** VT SEP *Fam* **to g. sb out** répugner qn, dégoûter qn

grossed-up price [grəʊst-] N prix *m* fort, plein tarif *m*

grossly ['grəʊslɪ] ADV **1** *(vulgarly)* grossièrement **2** *(exaggerated, negligent)* énormément; **to be g. mistaken** se tromper grossièrement; **his skills have been g. overrated** ses capacités ont été vraiment surestimées

grossness ['grəʊsnɪs] N **1** *(obesity)* obésité *f* **2** *(of abuse, stupidity, error etc)* énormité *f* **3** *(vulgarity)* grossièreté *f*

grossout ['grəʊsaʊt] N *Am Fam* = chose *f* ou situation *f* répugnante; **what a g.!** c'est vraiment dégueulasse!

grot [grɒt] N *Fam (muck)* crasse *f*

grotesque [grəʊ'tesk] ADJ *(bizarre)* grotesque

N *Art* grotesque *m*

grotesquely [grəʊ'tesklɪ] ADV grotesquement

grotto, *pl* **grottoes, grottos** ['grɒtəʊ, -əʊz] N grotte *f*

grotty ['grɒtɪ] N *Br Fam* dégueulasse; *(ill)* vaseux

grouch [graʊtʃ] *Fam* N **1** *(person)* râleur, -euse **2** *(complaint)* plainte *f*; **to have a g. about sth** se plaindre de qch; **to have a g. against sb** en vouloir à qn

VI râler, ronchonner (**to sb** après qn; **about sth** à propos de qch)

grouchy ['graʊtʃɪ] ADJ *Fam* râleur, ronchonneur

ground[1] [graʊnd] ADJ **1** *(coffee, wheat)* moulu **2** *(steel)* meulé; *(glass)* dépoli

▸▸ *Am* **g. beef** bœuf *m* haché; *Am* **g. meat** viande *f* hachée; **g. rice** farine *f* de riz

GROUND[2]

N		
terre **1, 7**	sol **1**	terrain **2**
parc **3**	fond **4, 5**	raison **6**
motif **6**		
VT		
fonder **1**	former **2**	mettre à la terre **3**

N **1** *(earth etc)* sol *m*, terre *f*; **sitting on the g.** assis par terre; **to pick sth up off the g.** ramasser qch par terre; **to fall to the g.** tomber à *ou* par terre; **above/below g.** sur/sous terre; **curtains down to the g.** rideaux qui pendent jusqu'à terre; **burnt (down) to the g.** brûlé de fond en comble; *Fam* **that suits me** *Br* **down to the g.** *or Am* **from the g. up** *(of arrangement etc)* ça me convient parfaitement; *Fig* **to cut the g. from under sb's feet** couper l'herbe sous le pied à qn; **the plane didn't get off the g.** l'avion n'a pas décollé, l'avion n'a pas quitté le sol; *Fig* **the idea never got off the g.** l'idée n'a jamais abouti à rien; *Fig* **the idea may take a while to get off the g.** l'idée risque de mettre du temps à prendre forme; **when the project eventually did get off the g.** quand le projet a enfin démarré; *Fig* **to work oneself into the g.** se tuer au travail; *Fig* **he's driven this car into the g.** il a usé cette voiture jusqu'au bout; **to go to g.** *(of fox)*, *Fig* se terrer; **to run a fox to g.** traquer un renard jusqu'à son terrier; *Fig* **to run sb to g.** *(criminal, person sought by police)* traquer qn; **I finally ran him to g. in the library** j'ai fini par le trouver à la bibliothèque

2 *(land, for sport)* terrain *m*; *Fig* **to find common g. for negotiations** trouver un terrain d'entente en vue de négocier; *Fig* **to be on firm g.** être sûr de soi; *Fig* **to be on shaky g.** marcher sur des œufs; *Fig* **to change** *or* **shift one's g.** changer de tactique; *Fig* **to break new** *or* **fresh g.** faire œuvre de pionnier, innover; **to cover a lot of g.** *(travel a great distance)* faire beaucoup de chemin *ou* de kilomètres; *Fig (deal with many subjects)* couvrir de très nombreux domaines; **to cover a lot of g. looking for sb** rechercher qn dans un vaste rayon; **to gain g.** gagner du terrain, progresser; *(of idea)* faire son chemin; **to lose g.** *(of troops, company, government)* perdre du terrain; **we are losing g. to the competition** la concurrence gagne du terrain; **to give g.** *(of troops, company, government)* céder du terrain; **to stand** *or* **hold one's g.** tenir bon, tenir ferme; *Fig* **to confront/defeat sb on his own g.** affronter/battre qn sur son propre terrain

3 grounds *(of school, hospital, country house)* parc *m*; **the school has extensive grounds** l'école est entourée d'un immense parc; **country house with extensive grounds** château avec domaine

4 *(of sea)* fond *m*; *Naut* **to touch g.** *(of ship)* talonner, heurter le fond

5 *(background) (of painting)* fond *m*, champ *m*; **light colour on a dark g.** couleur claire sur un fond sombre

6 grounds *(reasons)* raison *f*, cause *f*, motif *m*; *(of suspicions etc)* base *f*; **g.** *or* **grounds for complaint** raisons de se plaindre; **she has no g. for complaint** elle n'a aucune raison de se plaindre; **to have (good) g.** *or* **grounds for doing sth** avoir de bonnes raisons de faire qch; **they had no grounds for treating her like that** ils n'avaient pas le droit de la traiter de cette manière; **... and with good g.** ... et avec raison; **what grounds have you for saying that?** qu'est-ce qui vous permet d'affirmer cela?; **it gives us grounds to suspect that ...** cela nous donne des raisons de suspecter que ...; **on what grounds?** à quel titre?; **on personal/medical/moral grounds** pour des raisons personnelles/médicales/morales; **on grounds of ill-health** pour raisons de santé; *Law* **grounds for divorce** motifs de divorce; *Law* **grounds for appeal** voies *fpl* de recours

7 *Am Elec* terre *f*, masse *f*; **to connect to g.** *(pole)* mettre à la masse, relier à la terre

8 grounds *(of coffee)* marc *m*

vt 1 *(base)* fonder, baser, appuyer (**on** *or* **in** sth *sur* qch); *(belief)* asseoir (**on** sur)

2 to g. sb in sth *(give a grounding in)* former qn en qch

3 *Am Elec (current)* mettre à la masse *ou* à la terre

4 *(ship)* échouer; *(airplane)* interdire de vol; *Fam* **to be grounded** *(of teenager)* ne pas avoir le droit de sortir; *Mil* **g. arms!** reposez armes!

vi *(of ship)* échouer, s'échouer (**on** sur); *(of balloon)* atterrir

▸▸ *Mil* **g. attack** offensive *f* terrestre; *Mus* **g. bass** basse *f* contrainte; *Am Aut* **g. cable** câble *m* de masse; *Aut* **g. clearance** hauteur *f* du châssis au-dessus du sol, garde *f* au sol; *Am Elec* **g. connection** prise *f* de terre; *Aviat* **g. control** contrôle *m* au sol; *Aviat* **g. crew** personnel *m* au sol, personnel non-navigant; *Br* **g. floor** rez-de-chaussée *m inv*; *Mil* **g. forces** armée *f* de terre; **g. frost** gelée *f* blanche; *TV, Cin* **g. lamp** lampe *f* de rampe; **g. level** *(ground floor)* rez-de-chaussée; *(lowest level in organization)* base *f*; *Fishing* **g. line** ligne *f* de fond; **g. note** son *m* fondamental; *Aviat* **g. operator** *(who organizes services, transfers etc)* voyagiste *m ou* agence *f* de réceptif, réceptif *m*; **g. personnel** personnel au sol, personnel non-navigant; **g. plan** *(plan of ground floor)* plan *m* au sol; *(plan of action)* plan préparatoire; **g.**

rent redevance *f* foncière *(as source of income)* rente *f* foncière; **g. rule** procédure *f*, règle *f*; **g. staff** *Sport* = personnel responsable de l'entretien d'un terrain de sport; *Br Aviat* personnel au sol, personnel non-navigant; *TV* **g. station** station *f* terrestre; *TV* **g. transmitter** émetteur *m* terrestre; *Mil* **g. zero** hypocentre *m*, point *m* zéro; **G. Zero** *(in New York)* Ground Zero

groundbait ['graʊndbeɪt] N *Fishing* amorce *f* de fond

ground-breaking ADJ révolutionnaire; **this is g. technology** c'est une véritable percée technologique

grounded ['graʊndɪd] ADJ **1** *(based) (argument, belief etc)* fondé; **well/ill g.** *(belief)* bien/mal fondé **2** *Am Elec* (mis) à la masse, relié à la terre

groundhog ['graʊndhɒg] N marmotte *f* d'Amérique
▸▸ *Am* **G. Day** = le 2 février, jour où les marmottes sont censées avoir fini leur hibernation et sortir de leur terrier, annonçant l'arrivée prochaine du printemps si elles restent dehors, et le prolongement de l'hiver si elles ne font qu'une brève apparition

grounding ['graʊndɪŋ] N **1** *(of argument on sth)* fondement *m* **2** *Am Elec (of current)* mise *f* à la terre *ou* à la masse **3** *(of ship)* échouage *m*; *(of airplane)* interdiction *f* de vol; *(of balloon)* atterrissage *m* **4 to have a good g. in Latin** avoir de bonnes bases en latin

groundless ['graʊndlɪs] ADJ *(suspicion etc)* mal fondé, sans fondement

groundnut ['graʊndnʌt] N *Br* arachide *f*
▸▸ **g. oil** huile *f* d'arachide

groundsel ['graʊndsəl] N *(weed)* séneçon *m*

groundsheet ['graʊndʃiːt] N *(of tent)* tapis *m* de sol

groundsman, *pl* **groundsmen** ['graʊndzmən] N *Sport* responsable *m* de l'entretien d'un terrain de sport

groundspeed ['graʊndspiːd] N *Aviat* vitesse *f* au sol

groundswell ['graʊndswel] N *Naut* lame *f* de fond; *Fig* **g. of public opinion** grand mouvement *m* d'opinion publique; **there has been a g. of support for the proposal** il y a eu un raz-de-marée en faveur de la proposition

ground-to-air ADJ *Mil (missile etc)* sol-air *inv*

ground-to-ground ADJ *Mil (missile etc)* sol-sol *inv*

groundwork ['graʊndwɜːk] N *(initial work)* travail *m* préparatoire; *Fig* **to do** *or* **lay the g. for a project/economic reform** jeter les fondations d'un projet/de réformes économiques; **I've laid the g., the rest is up to you** j'ai préparé le terrain, le reste dépend de toi

group [gruːp] N VOIR GRAMMAIRE A11 **1** *(of people, companies)*, *Mus* groupe *m*; *(of things)* groupe, ensemble *m*; **to form a g.** se grouper; **(arranged) in groups of three** répartis en groupes de trois; **g. of accounts** classe *f* de comptes; **political g.** groupe(ment) *m* politique **2** *Mil, Aviat (unit)* groupe *m*

vt grouper

vi se grouper (**round** autour de)
▸▸ **g. booking** réservation *f* de groupe; **g. captain** colonel *m* de l'armée de l'air; **g. decision** décision *f* collective; **g. discount** remise *f* pour les groupes; *Psy* **g. dynamics** dynamique *f* de groupe; **g. fare** tarif *m* de groupe; **g. insurance** assurance *f* collective; **g. interview** entretien *m* de groupe; **g. leader** *(on package tour)* accompagnateur, -trice; *(for group of children)* moniteur, -trice; **g. manager** chef *m* de groupe; **g. meeting** réunion *f*

de groupe; **g. photograph** photographie *f* de groupe; *Med* **g. practice** cabinet *m* médical; *(of dentists)* cabinet dentaire; **g. product manager** chef *m* de groupe de produits; **g. rate** tarif de groupe; **g. sex** relations *fpl* sexuelles à plusieurs; *Cin, TV* **g. shot** plan *m* de groupe *(de personnages)*; **g. subscription** abonnement *m* collectif; **g. therapy** thérapie *f* de groupe; **g. travel** voyages *mpl* en groupe; *Fin* **g. turnover** chiffre *m* d'affaires consolidé *ou* du groupe

groupage ['gruːpɪdʒ] N groupage *m*
▸▸ *Com* **g. bill** connaissement *m* de groupage

grouped consignment [gruːpt] N *Com* envoi *m* groupé

grouper ['gruːpər] N *(fish)* mérou *m*

groupie ['gruːpɪ] N *Fam* groupie *f*

grouping ['gruːpɪŋ] N **1** *(putting together) (of packages, consignments etc)* groupage *m*; *(of figures etc)* groupement *m* **2** *(group)* groupe *m*; **political g.** groupement *m* politique

groupware ['gruːpweər] N *Comput* logiciel *m* de groupe, synergiciel *m*

grouse¹ [graʊs] N INV *(bird)* tétras *m*, grouse *f*, **red g.** lagopède *m* (rouge) d'Écosse; **black g.** tétras *m*
▸▸ **g. shooting** chasse *f* à la grouse

grouse² N *(grumble)* grogne *f*, *(complaint)* plainte *f*; **he enjoys a good g.** il aime ronchonner

vi ronchonner, grogner (**at, about** contre)

grouser ['graʊsər] N râleur, -euse

grousing ['graʊsɪŋ] N ronchonneries *fpl*; **I've had enough of your g.!** j'en ai assez de t'entendre ronchonner!

grout [graʊt] *Constr* N coulis *m*, mortier *m* clair *ou* liquide; **cement g.** lait *m ou* laitance *f* de ciment

vt jointoyer

grove [grəʊv] N futaie *f*, bosquet *m*; **beech g.** hêtraie *f*, **olive g.** oliveraie *f*, *Lit* **the groves of Academe** les hautes sphères de l'université

grovel ['grɒv(ə)l] VI (**-ll-,** *Am* **-l-**) être à quatre pattes; **what are you doing grovelling around on the floor?** qu'est-ce que tu fais à quatre pattes?; *Fig* **to g. to** *or* **before sb** ramper devant qn

grovelling, *Am* **groveling** ['grɒv(ə)lɪŋ] ADJ *(humble)* servile; **a g. apology** une excuse obséquieuse

N servilité *f*, *(before sb)* obséquiosité *f*

grow [grəʊ] *(pt* **grew** [gruː], *pp* **grown** [grəʊn]) VI **1** *(of plants, hair)* pousser; *(of seeds)* germer; **to g. back** *(of plants, hair)* repousser; **she let her hair g. long** elle a laissé pousser ses cheveux, elle s'est laissé pousser les cheveux; **olives do not g. in England** les oliviers ne poussent pas en Angleterre

2 *(of person, animal)* grandir; *(of company)* s'agrandir; **you've grown** tu as grandi; **you've grown really tall** qu'est-ce que tu as grandi; **this variety of tree will g. fairly tall in five years** cette variété d'arbre atteint une taille assez importante en cinq ans; **she has grown 2 inches** elle a grandi de 5 cm

3 *(increase)* augmenter, s'accroître; **the crowd grew** la foule augmenta *ou* grossit; **the economy has grown by 5% in the last two years** la croissance de l'économie a été de 5% au cours des deux dernières années; **his influence grew** son influence a grandi; **support for the strike is growing** la grève est de plus en plus soutenue; **the rumour was growing** la rumeur grandissait; **to g. in wisdom/beauty** grandir en sagesse/beauté

4 *(become)* devenir; **to g. old** vieillir; **to g. younger** rajeunir; **to g. big/bigger** *(of person)* grandir; *(of animal, database, crowd, tumour)* grossir; *(of town, company)* s'agrandir;

(of plant, tree) pousser; (of problem) s'accroître; **to g. smaller** (of person) rapetisser; (of swelling, problem) diminuer; **the noise grew louder** le bruit a augmenté ou s'est amplifié; **to g. alarmed/excited** s'alarmer/s'exciter; **to g. angry** se fâcher; **to g. less** diminuer; **it is growing dark** il commence à faire sombre

5 (reach point) **I have grown to think that ...** j'en suis venu à penser que ...; **they grew to like the house** ils ont fini par aimer la maison

VT 1 (roses, vegetables) cultiver; **soil that will not g. asparagus** sol peu propice aux asperges

2 (beard) se laisser pousser; **to g. one's hair (long)** se laisser pousser les cheveux, laisser pousser ses cheveux; **the stag grows fresh antlers every year** de nouveaux andouillers poussent au cerf chaque année

3 Com **to g. the business** augmenter le chiffre d'affaires; **to g. a company** développer une entreprise

▸ **grow apart** VI (of people) s'éloigner; **we gradually grew apart as we got older** nous nous sommes progressivement éloignés l'un de l'autre en vieillissant

▸ **grow in** VI (of hair) repousser; (of nail) s'incarner

▸ **grow into** VT INSEP **1** (become) devenir; **she had grown into a woman** elle était devenue femme; **the company grew into a huge organization** l'entreprise est devenue une énorme société **2** (become big enough for) **he has grown into his brother's shirts** les chemises de son frère lui vont maintenant

▸ **grow on** VT INSEP Fam **that picture grows on me** plus je regarde ce tableau plus il me plaît; **this music grows on you** plus on écoute cette musique plus on l'aime; **it's grown on me** je me suis mis à l'aimer petit à petit; **it will g. on you** tu finiras par l'aimer; **the idea was beginning to g. on me** l'idée commençait à me séduire

▸ **grow out** VI **she let the dye g. out** elle a laissé pousser ses cheveux jusqu'à ce que les traces de teinture aient disparu

▸ **grow out of** VT INSEP **1** (become too large for) ne plus rentrer dans; **he's grown out of his shoes** ses chaussures sont maintenant trop petites pour lui **2** (become too old for) **to g. out of doing sth** passer l'âge de faire qch; **she grew out of her dolls** elle a passé l'âge de jouer à la poupée; **it's just a phase, he'll g. out of it** ce n'est qu'une tocade, ça lui passera; **to g. out of one's friends** ne plus avoir grand-chose en commun avec ses amis

▸ **grow up** VI **1** (become adult) grandir; **I want to be a doctor when I g. up** je veux être docteur quand je serai grand; **we didn't have television when I was growing up** nous n'avions pas la télévision quand j'étais petit

2 (behave like adult) **I wish you'd g. up!** j'aimerais bien que tu cesses tes gamineries!; **g. up!** (be realistic) reviens sur terre!

3 (develop) se développer, se faire jour; **a theory has grown up that ...** une théorie s'est fait jour selon laquelle ...; **a custom has grown up** la coutume s'est établie; **a legend grew up around these events** une légende s'est développée autour de ces événements; **the town grew up around the castle** la ville s'est développée autour du château; **a close friendship gradually grew up between them** une étroite amitié s'est développée entre eux petit à petit

grower ['grəʊər] N **1** (person) cultivateur, -trice **2** (plant) **fast/slow g.** plante f qui pousse vite/lentement

growing ['grəʊɪŋ] ADJ **1** (child) en pleine croissance; (town, population etc) en pleine

expansion **2** (increasing) (debt) qui augmente; (opinion, belief) de plus en plus répandu; (discontent, opposition, problem) grandissant; **there was a g. fear that ...** on craignait de plus en plus que ...; **there is g. support for this party** le parti a de plus en plus d'adhérents; **there are g. problems** il y a de plus en plus de problèmes

▸▸ **g. pains** (of children) douleurs fpl de croissance; (of business, project) difficultés fpl de croissance, problèmes mpl de départ

-growing ['grəʊɪŋ] SUFF **wheat/potato-g.** culture f du blé/de la pomme de terre; **a potato-g. region** une région à pommes de terre; **fast/slow-g.** (plant) qui pousse vite/lentement

growl [graʊl] N (of dog, bear, tiger etc) grondement m, grognement m

VT & VI **1** (of dog, lion etc) grogner, gronder (**at** contre) **2** (of person) grogner, grommeler (**at** sb contre qn)

growling ['graʊlɪŋ] N (of dog, bear etc) grognement m, grondement m

grown [grəʊn] ADJ grand; **a g. woman** une femme adulte; **when fully g., these animals can ...** lorsqu'ils ont atteint l'âge adulte, ces animaux peuvent ...

PP see **grow**

grown-up N ['grəʊnʌp] grand m, grande personne f; **the grown-ups** les grands, les grandes personnes

ADJ [grəʊn'ʌp] adulte; **he's very g. for his age** il est très mûr pour son âge

growth [grəʊθ] N **1** (of person, plant) croissance f, Med (**human**) **g. hormone** hormone f somatotrope ou de croissance, somatotrophine f

2 (increase) accroissement m; (of business) croissance f, (of business, company, population) expansion f, (**economic**) **g.** croissance économique; **to go for g.** favoriser la croissance; **rate of g.** taux m d'expansion ou de croissance; **the recent g. in the number of small businesses** l'augmentation récente du nombre de petites entreprises

3 (something that has grown) **the entrance was covered by a dense g. of weeds** l'entrée était envahie par les mauvaises herbes; **g. of hair** poussée f de cheveux; **with a week's g. (of beard) on his chin** le menton couvert d'une barbe de huit jours; **yearly g.** (of plant) pousse f annuelle

4 (tumour) grosseur f, excroissance f; **benign/malignant g.** tumeur f bénigne/maligne; **I have a g. on my neck** j'ai une grosseur au cou

▸▸ **g. area** secteur m en expansion; **alternative medicine has really been a g. area in recent years** les médecines parallèles ont connu un boom ces dernières années; Mktg **g. developer** stimulateur m de croissance; **g. industry** industrie f en plein essor ou de pointe; Mktg **g. inhibitor** inhibiteur m de croissance; **g. market** marché m porteur; St Exch **g. shares, g. stock** valeurs fpl d'avenir ou de croissance; **g. strategy** stratégie f de croissance

growth-share matrix N Mktg matrice f croissance-part de marché

groyne [grɔɪn] N brise-lames m inv

grub [grʌb] N **1** (larva) larve f; (maggot) asticot m, Fam ver m (blanc) **2** Sl (food) bouffe f, **g.'s up!** à la bouffe!

▸▸ **G. Street** le monde des plumitifs

▸ **grub about, grub around** VI (search) fouiller, farfouiller; **I was grubbing about in the dirt looking for my key** j'étais en train de farfouiller par terre dans les saletés pour trouver ma clef

▸ **grub out** VT SEP (roots etc) extirper

▸ **grub up** VT SEP (root) extirper; (plant) déraciner; (of bird, animal) déterrer

grubbiness ['grʌbɪnɪs] N (dirtiness) saleté f, malpropreté f, Fig (immorality) bassesse f

grubby ['grʌbɪ] ADJ (dirty) crasseux, malpropre; Fig (immoral) sordide, sale; Fig **I felt g. when I found out he was married** je me suis méprisée quand j'ai appris qu'il était marié; **I don't want him getting his g. hands on these documents** je ne veux pas que cet animal mette la main sur ces documents

grubstake ['grʌbsteɪk] N Am = provisions fpl données à un prospecteur contre un pourcentage de ses profits

grudge [grʌdʒ] N rancune f; **to bear sb a g., to have a g. against sb** tenir rancune à qn, en vouloir à qn; **she's not one to bear a g.** elle n'est pas du genre rancunier

VT **1** (give unwillingly) **to g. sb sth** donner qch à contrecœur à qn; **she grudged them every penny she gave them** elle leur donnait chaque penny à contrecœur; **to g. sb the food they eat** lésiner sur la nourriture de qn **2** (resent) **to g. sb their pleasures** mal supporter que qn passe du bon temps; **she grudges him his success** elle lui en veut à cause de son succès; **I don't g. spending money but ...** je ne répugne pas à dépenser mais ...; **I g. having to get up so early** je supporte très mal d'avoir à me lever si tôt

▸▸ **g. match** règlement m de compte

grudging ['grʌdʒɪŋ] ADJ (praise, gift) fait/donné à contrecœur

grudgingly ['grʌdʒɪŋlɪ] ADV (to do sth) à contrecœur, à regret

gruel ['gruːəl] N gruau m (d'avoine); (thin) brouet m

gruelling, Am **grueling** ['gruːəlɪŋ] ADJ (race, interview) éreintant, épuisant; (match) âprement disputé; **we had a g. time** ça a été très dur

gruesome ['gruːsəm] ADJ horrible, abominable; Hum **the g. twosome** les deux terreurs fpl

gruesomely ['gruːsəmlɪ] ADV horriblement, abominablement

gruff [grʌf] ADJ (tone) bourru, brusque; **a g. voice** une grosse voix

gruffly ['grʌflɪ] ADV d'un ton bourru

gruffness ['grʌfnɪs] N brusquerie f; **the g. of his tone** son ton bourru

grumble ['grʌmb(ə)l] N grommellement m, grognement m; **his letter contained the usual grumbles** sa lettre contenait les plaintes habituelles; **to obey without a g.** obéir sans murmurer; Fam **to have a good old g.** rouspéter un bon coup

VI grommeler, grogner, Fam rouspéter; Fig (of thunder) gronder; **(we) mustn't g.** il ne faut pas se plaindre; **to g. about the food** se plaindre de la nourriture; **to g. at sb** grommeler ou rouspéter contre qn; **my stomach's grumbling** j'ai l'estomac qui gargouille

VT **'I do all the work here', he grumbled,** 'c'est moi qui fait tout ici', a-t-il grommelé

grumbler ['grʌmblər] N grognon m, ronchonneur, -euse, Fam rouspéteur, -euse

grumbling ['grʌmblɪŋ] ADJ grognon; **the g. crowd waited impatiently** la foule attendait avec des ronchonnements d'impatience; **g. noises** des ronchonnements mpl

N Fam rouspétance f

▸▸ Med **g. appendix** appendicite f chronique

grummet ['grʌmɪt] N = **grommet**

grump [grʌmp] N Fam **1** (person) grincheux, -euse **2** Old-fashioned **to have the grumps** être grincheux

grumpily ['grʌmpɪlɪ] ADV (to agree, wonder, say) en ronchonnant; (to look at) d'un air ronchon

grumpiness ['grʌmpɪnɪs] N mauvaise humeur f

grumpy ['grʌmpɪ] ADJ (person) ronchon, grincheux; (attitude, tone) renfrogné; (answer) grincheux; **a g. old man** un vieux grincheux ▪ N **what's wrong, g.?** qu'est-ce qui ne va pas, grincheux?

grundyism ['grʌndɪɪzm] N pudibonderie f

grunge [grʌndʒ] N Fam **1** (dirt) crasse f **2** (fashion, music) grunge m

grungy ['grʌndʒɪ] ADJ Fam (town) nul; (flat, hotel) miteux; (sweater, trainers) crasseux; (mood) désagréable

grunt[1] [grʌnt] N (of pig, person) grognement m; **to give a g.** pousser ou faire entendre un grognement ▪ VI (of pig, person) grogner, pousser un grognement ▪ VT **to g. an answer** grogner une réponse

grunt[2] N Am Mil Sl (private) bidasse m

grunting ['grʌntɪŋ] N grognement(s) m(pl)

gryphon ['grɪfən] N = **griffin**

GSM [dʒiːes'em] N Tel (abbr **global system for mobile communication**) GSM m

G-spot N point m G

GST [dʒiːes'tiː] N Can Fin (abbr **goods and services tax**) TPS f (taxe sur les produits et services)

G-string N **1** Mus corde f de sol **2** (underwear) cache-sexe m inv; string m

G-suit N combinaison f spatiale

gt (abbr **great**) grand

Guadeloupe [gwɑːdə'luːp] N Geog Guadeloupe f

guano ['gwɑːnəʊ] N guano m

guarantee [gærən'tiː] N **1** Com (document, promise) garantie f; **a clock with a 12-month g.** une horloge garantie 12 mois; **this camera's still got two months' g. left** cet appareil photo est encore garanti deux mois; **it's still under g.** il est encore sous garantie **2** (security) garantie f, caution f; **to leave sth as a g.** laisser qch en garantie **3** (assurance) garantie f ▪ VT (stand surety for) se porter garant ou caution pour; (debt, product) garantir; **watch guaranteed for two years** montre garantie deux ans; **it's guaranteed not to rust** c'est garanti anti-rouille; **I can't g. that she'll come** je ne garantis pas qu'elle viendra; **to g. sb against loss** garantir qn contre les pertes ▪ ▸ **g. certificate** certificat m de garantie; **g. commission** commission f de garantie; **g. company** société f de sécurité; **g. fund** fonds m de garantie

guaranteed [gærən'tiːd] ADJ (success) garanti, assuré; Fin **g. by** (on document) pour aval, bon pour aval ▪ ▸ Fin **g. bond** obligation f garantie; Fin **g. loan** prêt m garanti

guarantor [gærən'tɔːr] N garant, -ante, caution f; (of bill) donneur d'aval m, avaliste mf; **to stand as g. for sb** se porter garant ou caution pour qn

guaranty ['gærəntɪ] N = **guarantee**

guard [gɑːd] N **1** (readiness) garde f; **to be on one's g.** être ou se tenir sur ses gardes; **to be on one's g. against sth** être sur ses gardes contre qch; **to put sb on his g.** mettre qn en garde; **to be caught off one's g.** être pris au dépourvu; Fencing, Boxing **on g.!** en garde! **2** (of sentry etc) **to be on g. (duty)** être en ou de faction, être de garde; **to go on g., to mount g.** monter la garde; **to come off g.** descendre de garde; **to keep g.** monter la garde, être de garde; **to keep a prisoner under g.** garder un prisonnier à vue; **he was marched off under g.** il fut emmené sous escorte

3 (no pl) Mil (men) garde f; **one of the old g.** un vieux de la vieille; **g. of honour** garde d'honneur; **to form a g. of honour** faire une haie d'honneur; **to set a g. on a bridge** faire surveiller un pont **4** (person) Mil soldat m de garde; Br Rail chef m de train; Am (prison) g. gardien m de prison; Br Mil **the Guards** les Gardes mpl du corps **5** (device) dispositif m protecteur, protection f; (on machine) protecteur m; Fencing (of foil) garde f, (fire) g. garde-feu m inv ▪ VT **1** (entrance etc) garder; **to g. sb from** or **against a danger** garder ou protéger qn d'un danger **2 to g. one's tongue** tenir sa langue **3** Tech (gears etc) protéger ▪ ▸ **g. dog** chien m de garde; Br Mil **Guards officer** un officier de la Garde; Br Rail **g.'s van** wagon m du chef de train; (for luggage etc) fourgon m

▸ **guard against** VT INSEP (be careful to avoid) se garder de; **to g. against colds** se protéger ou se prémunir contre les rhumes; **to g. against an error** prendre garde à ne pas commettre une erreur

guarded ['gɑːdɪd] ADJ **1** (speech, reply, comments etc) prudent; **he was very g.** il est resté très prudent **2** (mechanism) protégé **3** (prisoner) gardé à vue; (building) gardé, surveillé

guardedly ['gɑːdɪdlɪ] ADV avec circonspection, avec prudence

guardhouse ['gɑːdhaʊs] N Mil corps m de garde

guardian ['gɑːdɪən] N gardien, -ienne; Law (of minor) tuteur, -trice ▪ ▸ **g. angel** ange m gardien

guardianship ['gɑːdɪənʃɪp] N garde f, Law gestion f tutélaire, tutelle f

guardrail ['gɑːdreɪl] N garde-fou m, pl garde-fous, parapet m; (on ship) bastingage m

guardroom ['gɑːdruːm] N Mil **1** (for guards) corps m de garde **2** (for prisoners) salle f ou poste m de police

guardsman, pl **guardsmen** ['gɑːdzmən] N Mil **1** Br (soldier) soldat m de la Garde; (officer) officier m de la Garde **2** Am (National) G. soldat m de la Garde Nationale

Guatemala [gwætɪ'mɑːlə] N Geog Guatemala m

Guatemalan [gwætɪ'mɑːlən] Geog ADJ guatémaltèque ▪ N Guatémaltèque mf

guava ['gwɑːvə] N **1** (fruit) goyave f **2** (tree) goyavier m ▪ ▸ **g. tree** goyavier

gubernatorial [guːbənə'tɔːrɪəl] ADJ esp Am (residence) du gouverneur; (election) au poste de gouverneur

gudgeon[1] ['gʌdʒən] N (fish) goujon m

gudgeon[2] N Tech goujon m, tourillon m, axe m ▪ ▸ **g. pin** axe de piston; (in machine) tourillon de la crosse

guelder-rose ['geldə'rəʊz] N (shrub) boule-de-neige f, pl boules-de-neige

gueridon ['gerɪdən] N guéridon m

Guernsey ['gɜːnzɪ] N **1** Geog Guernesey f **2** (sweater) jersey m; (cow) vache f de Guernesey

guer(r)illa [gə'rɪlə] N Mil guérillero m; **band of guer(r)illas** groupe m de guérilleros ▪ ▸ **g. attack** attaque f de guérilleros; **g. leader** chef m de guérilla; **g. warfare** guérilla f

Note that the French word **guérilla** is a false friend and is never a translation for the English word **guerrilla**. It means **guerrilla warfare**.

guess [ges] N conjecture f, estimation f; **to have** or **make a g.** deviner; **that was a lucky g.!** je suis/tu es/etc tombé juste!; **it was just a lucky g.** c'était un coup de chance; **your g. is as good as mine** j'en sais autant que toi; **it's anybody's g.** qui sait?, Dieu seul le sait; **it's my g. ...** à mon avis, ...; **I give you three guesses** tu as droit à trois essais; **at a g., I'd say he's German** a priori, je dirais qu'il est allemand; **at a rough g., I'd say he's forty** je dirais qu'il a quarante ans; **at a g., there will be 40 people at the party** je pense qu'il y aura environ 40 personnes à la soirée; **40 at a rough g.** environ quarante ▪ VT **1** deviner; (estimate) (the length of sth etc) estimer; **g. who did it!** devine qui a fait ça!; **I guessed him to be twenty-five** je lui ai donné vingt-cinq ans; **to g. sth from sb's manner** deviner qch d'après l'attitude de qn; **g. what! I saw Ian yesterday** tu sais quoi? j'ai vu Ian hier; **g. who!** devine qui!; **you've guessed it!** vous l'avez deviné! **2** esp Am (think) croire, penser; **I g. you're right** tu as raison; **I g. so/not** je crois ou oui/non ▪ VI deviner; **to g. right** deviner juste; **to g. wrong** se tromper; **you'll never g.** tu ne devineras jamais; **to keep sb guessing** laisser qn dans l'ignorance; **to g. at sth** (essayer de) deviner qch; **we could only g. at their plans** nous ne pouvions qu'essayer de deviner leurs intentions; **I couldn't begin to g.** je n'en ai pas la moindre idée; Iron **I would never have guessed** je n'aurais jamais deviné

guessing ['gesɪŋ] N estimation f ▪ ▸ **g. game** devinette f

guesstimate ['gestɪmɪt] N Fam calcul m au pif

guesswork ['geswɜːk] N estimation f, conjecture f; **it's pure** or **sheer g.** c'est de la pure conjecture; **by g.** au jugé; **by sheer** or **pure g.** à vue de nez

guest [gest] N **1** invité, -ée; (at meal) convive mf; also Iron **be my g.!** faites comme chez vous!; **with a g. appearance from ...** avec comme invité, -ée d'honneur ...; **to make a g. appearance in a programme** être invité dans une émission; Cin, TV **g. star ...** (in credits) avec la participation de ...; **our thanks to this week's g. star, Billy Connolly** nous remercions Billy Connolly, qui nous a fait la gentillesse d'être avec nous cette semaine **2** (at hotel) client, -iente; **the landlord and his guests** l'hôtelier et ses hôtes; **g. comments** commentaires mpl clients ▪ VI TV, Radio **to g. on sb's show** faire une apparition dans l'émission de qn; Mus **another guitarist guested on one of the numbers** un autre guitariste a participé à l'un des morceaux ▪ ▸ **g. artist** invité-vedette m, invitée-vedette f, m pl invités-vedettes, f pl invitées-vedettes; **g. book** (in house, hotel), Comput (of Web page) livre m d'or; **g. list** liste f des invités; **g. night** (in club) = soirée f d'un club où les non-membres sont invités; **g. occupancy** taux m d'occupation des lits; **g. room** chambre f d'ami(s); **g. speaker** conférencier, -ière (invité à parler par une organisation, une association)

guesthouse ['gesthaʊs] N **1** (hotel) pension f de famille **2** (of monastery etc) hôtellerie f

guff [gʌf] N Fam bêtises fpl, âneries fpl; **don't talk g.!** ne dis pas d'âneries!; **the film was a load of g.** le film était vraiment débile

guffaw [gʌ'fɔː] N gros rire m ▪ VI s'esclaffer

GUI ['guːi] N Comput (abbr **graphical user interface**) interface f utilisateur graphique

Guiana [gaɪ'ɑːnə] N (region) Guyane f

guidance ['gaɪdəns] N **1** direction f,

conduite *f*; **under the g. of ...** sous la direction de ...; **sent for your g.** envoyé à titre d'indication **2** *(of missile)* guidage *m*

▸▸**g. counsellor** conseiller, -ère d'orientation; *Aviat* **g. system** système *m* de guidage

guide [gaɪd] **N 1** *(person)* guide *m*; *Br* **(Girl) G.** guide *f*, éclaireuse *f* **2** *(book)* guide *m*; *(of railways)* indicateur *m*; **g. to Switzerland** guide de la Suisse; **the book is a useful g. to the world of finance** le livre constitue un guide utile du monde de la finance **3** *(indication)* indication *f*, exemple *m*; **as a g.** à titre indicatif

VT guider, conduire; **to g. a child's first steps** guider les premiers pas d'un enfant; **I will be guided by your advice** je suivrai vos conseils

▸▸**g. dog** chien *m* d'aveugle; *Rail* **g. rail** contre-rail *m*, *pl* contre-rails; **g. rope** *(for hoist)* corde *f* de guidage; *(for hot-air balloon)* guiderope *m*

guidebook ['gaɪdbʊk] **N** guide *m*

guided ['gaɪdɪd] **ADJ** *(tour etc)* guidé

▸▸**g. missile** missile *m* guidé *ou* téléguidé

guideline ['gaɪdlaɪn] **N 1** *(indication)* directive *f* (**on** concernant); **as a general** *or* **rough g.** en règle générale **2** *(line)* ligne *f*

guidepost ['gaɪdpəʊst] **N** poteau *m* indicateur

guiding ['gaɪdɪŋ] **ADJ ATTRIB** *(principle)* directeur, -trice; **without his g. hand** sans ses conseils; *Fig* **g. star** *or* **light** guide *m*

guild [gɪld] **N 1** *Hist* corporation *f*, **merchant g.** guilde *f* de commerçants **2** *(organization)* association *f*, confrérie *f*, **church** *or* **parish g.** cercle *m* paroissial

guilder ['gɪldər] **N** *Formerly (Dutch currency)* florin *m*

guildhall ['gɪldhɔːl] **N 1** *(of a guild)* salle *f* de réunion d'une guilde **2** *(town hall)* hôtel *m* de ville

guile [gaɪl] **N** ruse *f*; **she is without g.** elle est candide

guileless ['gaɪllɪs] **ADJ** *(naive)* candide

guillemot ['gɪlɪmɒt] **N** *(bird)* guillemot *m*

guillotine ['gɪləti:n] **N 1** *(for execution)* guillotine *f*, **to be executed by g.** être guillotiné; **to go to the g.** aller à la guillotine, être mené à la guillotine **2** *(for cutting paper)* massicot *m* **3** *Parl* = imposition *f* d'une limite de temps pour les débats parlementaires

VT 1 *(execute)* guillotiner **2** *(cut) (paper etc)* massicoter **3** *Parl (bill)* imposer une limite de temps pour la discussion de

guilt [gɪlt] **N 1** culpabilité *f* (**for sth** pour qch); **the g. does not lie with him alone** il n'est pas le seul coupable **2** *(feeling)* culpabilité *f*, **to feel g.** ressentir de la culpabilité; **feelings of g.** sentiments *mpl* de culpabilité; **to be on a g. trip** culpabiliser

▸▸**g. complex** complexe *m* de culpabilité

guiltily ['gɪltɪlɪ] **ADV** coupablement, d'un air coupable; **she looked away g.** elle a détourné les yeux d'un air coupable

guiltless ['gɪltlɪs] **ADJ** innocent (**of sth** de qch)

guilty ['gɪltɪ] **ADJ 1** coupable (**of** de); **g. person** coupable *mf*; **he is not the only g. party** il n'est pas le seul coupable; *Law* **to plead g./not g.** plaider coupable/non coupable; *Law* **to find sb g./not g.** déclarer qn coupable/non coupable; *Law* **verdict of g./not g.** verdict *m* de culpabilité/d'acquittement

2 *(feeling guilt)* **I feel g. about not telling them** je me sens coupable *ou* je culpabilise de ne pas leur avoir dit; **you're making me feel g.** tu me culpabilises; **she looked very g.** elle avait un air très coupable; **g. conscience** mauvaise conscience *f*, *(more serious)* conscience chargée

3 *(act)* coupable

Guinea ['gɪnɪ] **N** *Geog* Guinée *f*

guinea ['gɪnɪ] **N 1** *Br (money)* guinée *f* *(ancienne monnaie britannique)* **2** *Am Sl Pej (Italian)* Rital, -ale, macaroni *mf*

▸▸**g. fowl** pintade *f*, **g. pig** cobaye *m*, cochon *m* d'Inde; *Fig* **to be a g. pig** servir de cobaye

Guinea-Bissau [-bɪˈsaʊ] **N** la Guinée-Bissau

Guinean [gɪˈneɪən] **N** Guinéen, -enne

ADJ guinéen

guise [gaɪz] **N** dehors *m*, apparence *f*, **under** *or* **in the g. of friendship** sous l'apparence *ou* sous le masque de l'amitié; **under the g. of religion** sous le manteau *ou* le couvert de la religion; **it's the same idea in a new g.** c'est la même idée présentée sous une autre forme

guitar [gɪˈtɑːr, *Am* also 'gɪtɑːr] **N** guitare *f*, **to play the g.** jouer de la guitare

▸▸**g. player** guitariste *mf*

guitarist [gɪˈtɑːrɪst] **N** guitariste *mf*

gulch [gʌltʃ] **N** *Am* ravin *m*

gulf [gʌlf] **N 1** *Geog* golfe *m*; **the (Persian) G.** le Golfe **2** *(abyss)* gouffre *m*, abîme *m*; *Fig* **there is a g. between the two ideologies** un abîme sépare les deux idéologies

▸▸**the G. Stream** le Gulf Stream; **the G. War** la guerre du Golfe; **G. War syndrome** syndrome *m* de la guerre du Golfe

gull[1] [gʌl] **N** *(bird)* mouette *f*, *(bigger)* goéland *m*; *Aut* **g.-wing doors** portes *fpl* papillon

gull[2] **VT** *Arch, Lit (person)* duper, rouler

gullet ['gʌlɪt] **N** *Anat* œsophage *m*; *Fam (throat)* gosier *m*; *Fam Fig* **it really sticks in my g.** ça me reste en travers du gosier

gulley ['gʌlɪ] **N** = **gully**

gullibility [gʌlɪˈbɪlɪtɪ] **N** crédulité *f*

gullible ['gʌlɪb(ə)l] **ADJ** crédule

gully ['gʌlɪ] **N** *Geol* petit ravin *m*

gulp [gʌlp] **N 1** *(act of gulping)* coup *m* de gosier; **to swallow sth at one g.** avaler qch d'un coup; **he confessed with a g. that ...** il admit, la gorge serrée, que ... **2** *(mouthful)* grosse bouchée *f*, *(of drink)* goulée *f*

VT 1 *(swallow)* = **gulp down 2** *(say nervously, with shock)* **'me?'**, **she gulped** 'moi', dit-elle, la voix étranglée

VI essayer d'avaler; **he gulped** sa gorge se serra; **g.!** *(as in comic strip)* gulp!, glup!

▸ **gulp back** **VT SEP** **to g. back one's tears** avaler *ou* refouler ses larmes

▸ **gulp down** **VT SEP** *(swallow)* avaler à grosses bouchées; *(oyster etc)* avaler; **he gulped it down** *(in one mouthful)* il n'en fit qu'une bouchée; *(drinking)* il n'en fit qu'une gorgée

gum[1] [gʌm] **N 1** *Bot* gomme *f*, *(adhesive)* colle *f*, gomme **2** (**chewing) g.** chewing-gum *m*; **two sticks of g.** deux chewing-gums; (**wine/fruit/***etc*) **g.** boule *f* de gomme

VT (**-mm-**) **1** *(coat with adhesive) (paper)* gommer, encoller **2** *(stick with adhesive) (page in book etc)* coller; **to g. two pages together** coller deux feuilles **3** = **gum up**

▸▸**g. arabic** gomme *f* arabique; **g. tree** gommier *m*; *Fig Fam* **to be up a g. tree** être dans le pétrin

gum[2] **N** *Anat* gencive *f*

▸▸**g. disease** gingivite *f*

gum[3] **INT** *Old-fashioned Br Fam* **by g.!** fichtre!, mazette!

▸ **gum up** **VT SEP** *Tech (piston)* gommer; *(file)* encrasser; *Fam* **to g. up the works** enrayer le mécanisme; *Fig* compliquer les choses

gumboil ['gʌmbɔɪl] **N** abcès *m* à la gencive, *Spec* parulie *f*

gumboot ['gʌmbuːt] **N** botte *f* en *ou* de caoutchouc

gumdrop ['gʌmdrɒp] **N** *(sweet)* boule *f* de gomme

gummed [gʌmd] **ADJ** *(label etc)* gommé

gummy ['gʌmɪ] **ADJ 1** gommeux; *(sticky)* gluant **2** **he gave her a g. smile** il lui sourit, découvrant ses gencives encore sans dents

gumption ['gʌmʃən, 'gʌmp-] **N** *Fam* jugeote *f*, sens *m* pratique; **she's got plenty of g.** c'est une débrouillarde

gumshield ['gʌmʃiːld] **N** *Boxing etc* protège-dents *m inv*

gumshoe ['gʌmʃuː] **N 1** *(rubber overshoe)* caoutchouc *m* **2** *Fam (detective)* privé *m*

gun [gʌn] **N 1** *Mil (artillery)* canon *m*, pièce *f* (d'artillerie); **the guns** l'artillerie *f*, le canon; **the big guns** la grosse artillerie, les grosses pièces; *Fam* **big g.** *(important person)* gros manitou *m*, grosse légume *f*, **do you hear the guns?** entendez-vous le canon?; **21-g. salute** salve de 21 coups de canon; *Fam* **it was blowing great guns** il faisait un vent à décorner les bœufs; *Fam* **to be going great guns** *(of work, sale)* marcher très fort; **to jump the g.** *(in race)* faire un faux départ; *Fig* s'emballer

2 *(rifle)* fusil *m*; *(handgun)* revolver *m*, pistolet *m*; **machine g.** mitrailleuse *f*, *Fig* **to stick to one's guns** rester sur ses positions, tenir bon; **a party of six guns** *(hunters)* une bande de six chasseurs

3 *Tech etc* **(grease) g.** seringue *f*, injecteur *m* (à graisse); **(spray) g.** pistolet *m* (à peinture); *Electron* **(electron) g.** canon *m* à électrons

VT (**-nn-**) *Aut (engine)* (faire) emballer

VI *Fam* **to go along** *(of car, driver)* foncer

▸▸**g. barrel** *(of rifle)* canon *m* de fusil; *(of revolver)* canon de revolver; **g. carriage** affût *m* de canon; *(at military funeral)* prolonge *f* d'artillerie; **g. dog** chien *m* d'arrêt; **g. licence** permis *m* de port d'armes; **g. mike** micro *m* canon; **g. room** *(in house)* armurerie *f*, *(on warship)* poste *m* des aspirants; **g. turret** tourelle *f*

▸ **gun down** **VT SEP** *(kill)* abattre

▸ **gun for** **VT INSEP** *(only in continuous tenses)* **1** *(want to reprimand, punish)* en avoir après; **he's gunning for us** il nous en veut, il en a après nous **2** *(try to get)* pourchasser; **he's gunning for the heavyweight title** il vise le titre poids lourd

gunboat ['gʌnbəʊt] **N** aviso-torpilleur *m*, *pl* avisos-torpilleurs

▸▸**g. diplomacy** diplomatie *f* imposée par la force, politique *f* de la canonnière

guncotton ['gʌnkɒt(ə)n] **N** fulmicoton *m*

gundeck ['gʌndek] **N** *Naut* batterie *f*

gunfight ['gʌnfaɪt] **N** fusillade *f*, échange *m* de coups de feu

gunfighter ['gʌnfaɪtər] **N** *(in Western film, novel)* bandit *m* armé

gunfire ['gʌnfaɪər] **N** *Mil (of artillery)* canonnade *f*, feu *m* (des pièces); *(of smaller guns)* coups *mpl* de feu; **we heard g.** nous avons entendu des coups de feu

gunge [gʌndʒ] **N** *(no pl)* *Fam* crasse *f* graisseuse

gung-ho [gʌŋˈhəʊ] **ADJ** *(enthusiastic)* tout feu tout flamme; *(ready to fight)* belliqueux

gunk [gʌŋk] **N** *Fam* = **gunge**

gunmaker ['gʌnmeɪkər] **N** armurier *m*

gunman, *pl* **gunmen** ['gʌnmən] **N 1** *(terrorist)* terroriste *m*; *(robber)* bandit *m* armé **2** *Am* = **gunmaker**

gunmetal ['gʌnmet(ə)l] **N 1** *(bronze)* bronze *m* à canon **2** *(colour)* gris métallisé *m inv*; **a car with a g. finish** une voiture gris métallisé

▸▸**g. grey** gris métallisé

gunnel ['gʌn(ə)l] **N** = **gunwale**

gunner ['gʌnər] **N** artilleur *m*; *Naut (warrant officer)* canonnier *m*; **(machine) g.** mitrailleur *m*

gunnery ['gʌnərɪ] N *Mil (guns)* artillerie *f*
▸▸**g. officer** officier *m* d'artillerie

gunny ['gʌnɪ] N *esp Am (material)* toile *f* de jute; *(bag)* sac *m* en jute
▸▸**g. sack** sac en jute

gunplay ['gʌnpleɪ] N *esp Am* coups *mpl* de revolver

gunpoint ['gʌnpɔɪnt] N **at g.** sous la menace d'un pistolet/d'un fusil; **to hold sb at g.** menacer qn d'un pistolet/d'un fusil

gunport ['gʌnpɔːt] N *Naut* sabord *m* de batterie

gunpowder ['gʌnpaʊdər] N poudre *f* (à canon); *Br Hist* **the G. Plot** la Conspiration des Poudres

gunrunner ['gʌnrʌnər] N trafiquant, -ante d'armes

gunrunning ['gʌnrʌnɪŋ] N trafic *m* d'armes

gunship ['gʌnʃɪp] N **(helicopter) g.** hélicoptère *m* de combat

gunshot ['gʌnʃɒt] N coup *m* de feu; *(of rifle)* coup de fusil; **within/out of g.** à/hors de portée de fusil
▸▸**g. wound** blessure *f* par balle; **to receive a g. wound** être blessé par balle

gun-shy ADJ *(dog)* qui a peur des coups de feu

gunslinger ['gʌnslɪŋər] N *Am Fam* bandit *m* armé

gunsmith ['gʌnsmɪθ] N armurier *m*; **g.'s (shop)** armurerie *f*

gunstock ['gʌnstɒk] N fût *m* (de fusil)

gunwale ['gʌn(ə)l] N *Naut* plat-bord *m*, *pl* plats-bords; **full to the gunwales** plein à ras bord

guppy ['gʌpɪ] N *(fish)* guppy *m*

gurgle ['gɜːg(ə)l] N *(of liquid)* glouglou *m*; *(of stream)* murmure *m*; *Fig (of pleasure, delight)* gloussement *m*, roucoulement *m*; **happy gurgles could be heard coming from the baby's cot** on entendait l'enfant gazouiller dans son berceau; *Fig* **gurgles of laughter** des gloussements
VI *(of liquid)* glouglouter, faire glouglou; *(of stream)* murmurer, gargouiller; *(of person)* glousser, roucouler; *(of baby)* gazouiller; **he gurgled with laughter** il eut un rire perlé
VT **she gurgled her delight** elle roucoula de plaisir

gurgling ['gɜːg(ə)lɪŋ] ADJ *(liquid in bottle)* glougloutant, qui fait glouglou; *(stream)* murmurant; **a g. laugh** un rire perlé

Gurkha ['gɜːkə] N Gurkha *m*

gurnard ['gɜːnəd], **gurnet** ['gɜːnɪt] N *(fish)* grondin *m*

gurney ['gɜːnɪ] N *Am* chariot *m* (d'hôpital)

guru ['gʊruː] N *Rel, Fig* gourou *m*

gush [gʌʃ] N *(of spring, fountain)* jaillissement *m*; *(of tears)* torrent *m*; *(of blood)* jet *m*, flot *m*; *Fig* **a g. of words** un flot de paroles; *Fig* **a g. of enthusiasm** un élan d'enthousiasme; **a g. of anger/emotion** une bouffée de colère/d'émotion
VI **1** *(spurt, pour)* jaillir, couler à flots; **tears gushed from her eyes** un torrent de larmes coulait de ses yeux **2** *Pej (talk effusively)* faire de longs discours sentimentaux, *Fam* la faire au sentiment; **she gushed over their baby** elle s'attendrissait sur leur bébé
VT **1 to g. water/oil** lancer des jets d'eau/un jet de pétrole **2 'how wonderful to see you!',** **she gushed** 'qu'est-ce que ça me fait plaisir de te voir!', s'exclama-t-elle
▸ **gush forth, gush out** VI = **gush** VI

gusher [gʌʃər] N **1** *Pej (person)* personne *f* trop exubérante **2** *Petr* source *f* (de pétrole) jaillissante, puits *m* jaillissant

gushing ['gʌʃɪŋ] ADJ **1** *(water)* jaillissant; **the car was swept away by a g. torrent of**

water la voiture a été emportée par un véritable torrent d'eau; **a g. stream fed by melting snow** les flots déchaînés d'un ruisseau grossi par la fonte des neiges **2** *Pej (person)* trop exubérant; *(compliments)* très élogieux

gushy ['gʌʃɪ] ADJ *Pej* = **gushing 2**

gusset ['gʌsɪt] N *Sewing* soufflet *m*; *(in sleeve)* gousset *m*

gust [gʌst] N **g. (of wind)** rafale *f*, bourrasque *f*; *Naut* grain *m*; **g. of rain** ondée *f*, giboulée *f*; **a g. of hot air** une bouffée d'air chaud; *Fig* **a g. of anger** une bouffée de colère
VI *(of wind)* souffler par rafales

gustatory [gʌs'teɪtərɪ] ADJ *Fml* gustatif

gusto ['gʌstəʊ] N délectation *f*, goût *m*; **to eat sth with g.** manger qch en savourant; **to do sth with g.** faire qch avec grand plaisir

gusty ['gʌstɪ] ADJ *(weather)* venteux; *(wind)* soufflant en rafales; *(day)* de grand vent

gut [gʌt] N **1** *(intestine)* *(of animal)* boyau *m*; *(of human)* intestin *m*; *Fig Fam* **to sweat** *ou* **work one's guts out** se casser les reins; *Fig Fam* **she hates my guts** elle ne peut pas me saquer *ou* m'encadrer; *Fig Fam* **I'll have his guts for garters** je vais le massacrer; *Fig* **it's just a g. feeling** c'est une intuition; **g. reaction** réaction *f* instinctive *ou* viscérale
2 *Fig Fam (courage)* **to have guts** avoir du cran, avoir du cœur au ventre; **I didn't have the guts to tell them** je n'ai pas eu le courage de le leur dire; **he hasn't any guts** il manque de cran
3 *Fam (stomach)* bide *m*; **pull in your g.** rentre ton bide; **to have sore guts** avoir mal au bide; **g. ache** mal *m* de bide
4 *(for violins etc)* corde *f* de boyau
VT (-tt-) **1** *(animal)* étriper; *(fish, poultry)* vider **2 the house had been gutted by the fire** la maison avait été ravagée par l'incendie; **she gutted the house and completely redecorated it** elle a cassé tout l'intérieur de la maison et a tout refait

gutless ['gʌtlɪs] ADJ *Fam (cowardly)* lâche

gutsy ['gʌtsɪ] ADJ *Fam* **1** *(brave)* qui a du cran, courageux **2** *(powerful) (prose etc)* vigoureux **3** *(greedy)* goinfre

gutted ['gʌtɪd] ADJ *Br Fam (disappointed)* dégoûté, hyper déçu

gutter ['gʌtər] N **1** *(in street)* caniveau *m*; *(on roof)* gouttière *f*, chéneau *m*; *Fig* **to end up in the g.** finir sous les ponts; *Fig* **to drag oneself out of the g.** se sortir de la misère; **the language of the g.** la langue de la rue **2** *Typ* gouttière *f*, petits fonds *mpl* (de deux pages en vis-à-vis)
VI *(of candle)* vaciller
▸▸**g. pipe** tuyau *m* de descente; *Pej* **g. press** presse *f* de bas étage, presse à scandale **g. tile** tuile *f* creuse

guttered ['gʌtəd] ADJ *Br Fam (drunk)* bourré, pété

guttering ['gʌtərɪŋ] N *Constr (on building)* gouttières *fpl*

guttersnipe ['gʌtəsnaɪp] N *Old-fashioned Pej* gamin, -ine des rues

guttural ['gʌtərəl] ADJ guttural, -aux
N *Ling* gutturale *f*

guv [gʌv], **guv'nor** ['gʌvnər] N *Br Sl* **the g.** *(boss)* le patron, le singe; *Old-fashioned (father)* le vieux, le paternel; **all right, g.** d'accord, chef

guy¹ [gaɪ] N **1** *Fam (man)* type *m*, mec *m*; **a great g.** un type *ou* mec super; **a tough g.** un dur; **I didn't like the look of those guys** ces types avaient une sale tête **2** *esp Am Fam (as second person plural)* **hurry up, you guys!** allez, dépêchez-vous!; **what are you guys doing tonight?** vous faites quoi, vous, ce soir?; **ok guys, let's go** OK, les amis, on y va; **do you guys want to go out?** vous voulez sortir?; **hi guys!** salut tout le monde! **3** *Br*

(effigy) = effigie *f* burlesque de Guy Fawkes, le chef de la Conspiration des Poudres (1605)

> ### Guy Fawkes Night
> Cette fête se déroule le 5 novembre en plein air autour d'un grand feu de joie sur lequel on est censé brûler une effigie ("the Guy") de Guy Fawkes, l'instigateur de la conspiration des poudres. Des feux d'artifice sont également organisés.

guy² VT *Old-fashioned* se moquer de, *Fam* charrier, mettre en boîte

guy³ N corde *f* de tente
▸▸**g. rope** corde de tente

Guyana [gaɪ'ænə] N *(country)* Guyana *f*

Guyanese [gaɪə'niːz] ADJ guyanais
N Guyanais, -aise

guzzle ['gʌz(ə)l] *Fam* VT *(food)* bâfrer, bouffer; *(drink)* descendre; *esp Am* **to g. gas** *(of car)* bouffer de l'essence
VI *(of eater)* s'empiffrer, goinfrer; *(of drinker)* boire avidement

guzzler ['gʌzlər] N *Fam (of food)* bâfreur, -euse, goinfre *m*; *(of drink)* soiffard, -arde

gym [dʒɪm] N **1** *(hall, building)* gymnase *m*; *(fitness club)* club *m* de gym **2** *(activity, school subject)* gym *f*; **we have g. today** on a gym aujourd'hui
▸▸**g. shoes** (chaussures *fpl* de) tennis *mpl*

gymkhana [dʒɪm'kɑːnə] N *Br (for horses)* concours *m* hippique; *esp Am Aut* gymkhana *m*

gymnasium, *pl* **gymnasiums, gymnasia** [dʒɪm'neɪzɪəm, -ɪəmz, -ɪə] N *Sport* gymnase *m*

gymnast ['dʒɪmnæst] N gymnaste *mf*

gymnastic [dʒɪm'næstɪk] ADJ gymnastique

gymnastics [dʒɪm'næstɪks] N gymnastique *f*, **to do g.** faire de la gymnastique; *Fig* **mental/verbal g.** gymnastique intellectuelle/verbale VOIR GRAMMAIRE A10

gymnosperm ['dʒɪmnəʊspɜːm] N gymnosperme *m*

gymslip ['dʒɪmslɪp] N *esp Br Sch* tunique *f*

gynaecologic(al), *Am* **gynecologic, gynecological** [gaɪnɪkə'lɒdʒɪk, -ɪk(ə)l] ADJ gynécologique

gynaecologist, *Am* **gynecologist** [gaɪnɪ-'kɒlədʒɪst] N gynécologue *mf*

gynaecology, *Am* **gynecology** [gaɪnɪ-'kɒlədʒɪ] N gynécologie *f*

gyp [dʒɪp] N *Br Fam* **to give sb g.** *(of aching tooth etc)* faire souffrir qn

gypsum ['dʒɪpsəm] N *Miner* gypse *m*

gypsy ['dʒɪpsɪ] N = **gipsy**

gyrate [dʒaɪ'reɪt] VI tourner; *(less regularly) (of dancers)* tournoyer

gyration [dʒaɪ'reɪʃən] N giration *f*

gyratory ['dʒaɪrətrɪ, -ərɪ, dʒaɪ'reɪtərɪ] ADJ giratoire; **g. (traffic) system** (système *m* de circulation en) sens *m* giratoire

gyrfalcon ['dʒɜːfɔːlkən] N *(bird)* gerfaut *m*

gyro ['dʒaɪrəʊ] ADJ gyroscopique
N **1** = **gyroscope 2** = **gyrocompass**
▸▸**g. control** commande *f* gyroscopique

gyrocompass ['dʒaɪrəʊkʌmpəs] N *Naut* gyrocompas *m*, compas *m* gyroscopique

gyromagnetic [dʒaɪrəʊmæg'netɪk] ADJ gyromagnétique

gyropilot ['dʒaɪrəʊpaɪlət] N *Aviat* pilote *m* automatique, gyropilote *m*; *Naut (compass)* gyropilote

gyroplane ['dʒaɪrəpleɪn] N *Aviat* autogyre *m*

gyroscope ['dʒaɪrəskəʊp] N gyroscope *m*, gyro *m*

gyroscopic [dʒaɪrə'skɒpɪk] ADJ gyroscopique

gyrostat ['dʒaɪrəstæt] N gyrostat *m*

H, h [eɪtʃ] **N 1** *(letter)* H, h *m*; **two h's** deux h; **to drop one's h's** [ˈeɪtʃɪz] avaler ses h *(et révéler par là ses origines populaires)* **2** *Sl (heroin)* héro *f*, blanche *f*
▸ ▸ **H bomb** bombe *f* H

ha [hɑː] **INT** ha!, ah!; *Fam* **ha bloody ha!** ha ha ha!, très drôle!

habeas corpus [ˈheɪbɪəsˈkɔːpəs] **N** *Law* (writ of) **h.** habeas corpus *m*

haberdasher [ˈhæbədæʃər] **N** *Com Old-fashioned* **1** *Br (for sewing articles)* mercier, -ière **2** *Am (for men's clothes)* chemisier *m*

haberdashery [ˈhæbədæʃərɪ] **N** *Com Old-fashioned* **1** *Br (sewing articles)* mercerie *f* **2** *Am (men's clothes)* chemiserie *f*

habit [ˈhæbɪt] **N 1** *(custom, practice)* habitude *f*, coutume *f*, *(picking nose, biting nails etc)* habitude; **bad habits** mauvaises habitudes; **to be in the** *or* **make a h. of doing sth** avoir l'habitude de faire qch; **I try not to make a h. of working late** j'essaye de ne pas prendre l'habitude de travailler tard; **don't make a h. of it** ne recommence pas; **it's a h. with him** c'est une habitude chez lui; **to get into the h. of doing sth** prendre l'habitude de faire qch; **to get sb into the h. of doing sth** habituer qn à faire qch; **to get into bad habits** prendre de mauvaises habitudes; **to get out of a h.** perdre une habitude; **from force of h.** poussé par l'habitude; **to do sth by sheer force of h.** faire qch (simplement) par habitude
2 *Fam (addiction)* **to have a (drug) h.** être accro; **to have a cocaine/heroin h.** être accro à la cocaïne/à l'héroïne
3 *(costume) (of monk, nun)* habit *m*; **riding h.** tenue *f* d'équitation

habitable [ˈhæbɪtəb(ə)l] **ADJ** habitable; **to make a room h.** rendre une pièce habitable

habitat [ˈhæbɪtæt] **N** habitat *m*

habitation [hæbɪˈteɪʃən] **N 1** *(occupation) (of house)* habitation *f*; **fit for h.** habitable; **unfit for h.** inhabitable; **there were no signs of h.** l'endroit ne semblait pas habité **2** *(dwelling place)* habitation *f*, demeure *f*

habit-forming **ADJ** *(drug)* qui crée une accoutumance

habitual [həˈbɪtjʊəl] **ADJ 1** *(customary)* habituel **2** *(liar, drunk)* invétéré; **h. criminal** *or* **offender** récidiviste *mf*
▸ ▸ *Mktg* **h. buying behaviour** comportement *m* d'achat habituel

habitually [həˈbɪtjʊəlɪ] **ADV** habituellement, d'habitude

habituate [həˈbɪtjʊeɪt] **VT to h. sb to sth/to doing sth** habituer *ou* accoutumer qn à qch/à faire qch; **to become habituated to sth/to doing sth** s'habituer à qch/à faire qch

Habsburg [ˈhæpsbɜːɡ] **N** *Hist* Habsbourg

hacienda [hæsɪˈendə] **N** ranch *m*, hacienda *f*

hack¹ [hæk] **N** *(cut)* taillade *f*, entaille *f*, *(blow) (with foot, arm)* coup *m*; *Ftbl etc (kick)* coup de pied
VT 1 *(cut)* hacher; **to h. sb/sth to pieces** mettre *ou* tailler qn/qch en pièces; *Fig* **my article has been hacked to pieces** mon article a été massacré; **to h. sb to death** lacérer qn à mort; **to h. one's way through the jungle** se frayer un chemin à coups de machette dans la jungle **2** *Ftbl etc* **to h. sb's shins** donner délibérément un coup de pied dans le tibia à qn; **to h. the ball** donner un petit coup de pied dans le ballon **3** *Fam* **he can't h. it** *(cope)* il ne s'en sort pas, il est complètement dépassé
VI 1 *(cut)* taillader, entailler; **to h. (away) at a tree** entailler un arbre à coups de hache; **to h. at one's meat** taillader son morceau de viande; **to h. away at a text** sabrer un texte *ou* des passages d'un texte **2** *(cough)* émettre une toux sèche **3** *(kick)* **to h. at sb's shins** essayer de donner un coup de pied/ des coups de pied dans le tibia à qn
▸ **hack about** **VT SEP** *(often passive) (body)* mutiler; **the piece of wood had been hacked about** on avait taillé ce morceau de bois; **the article had been hacked about a bit** on avait pas mal remanié l'article
▸ **hack down** **VT SEP** *(tree)* abattre
▸ **hack into** **VT INSEP** *Comput* **to h. into a database/system** s'introduire en fraude dans une base de données/un système, *Fam* pirater une base de données/un système
▸ **hack off** **VT SEP 1** *(chop off)* trancher **2** *Fam (annoy)* **to h. sb off** prendre la tête à qn; **to be hacked off (with)** en avoir marre (de)
▸ **hack up** **VT SEP** *(chop up)* mettre en pièces

hack² **N 1** *Fam Pej (journalist)* journaleux, -euse, tâcheron *m*; **there were all the usual Labour Party hacks** on y trouvait tous les habitués du parti travailliste; **literary h.** écrivaillon *m* **2** *(horse for hire)* cheval *m*, -aux de louage; *(for riding)* cheval de selle; *Fam (nag)* rosse *f* **3** *Am Fam (taxi)* taxi *m*; *(taxi driver)* chauffeur *m* de taxi
▸ ▸ *Fam* **h. writer** écrivaillon; *Fam* **h. writing** travail *m* d'écrivaillon

hack³ **VI** *Br (ride)* se promener à cheval

hacker [ˈhækər] *Comput Fam* **N 1** *(illegal user)* pirate *m* informatique **2** *(expert user)* bidouilleur, -euse

hacking¹ [ˈhækɪŋ] **N 1** *Ftbl etc* coups *mpl* de pied (sur le tibia) **2** *Comput Fam (illegal)* piratage *m* informatique
ADJ **h. cough** toux *f* sèche

hacking² **N** *Br (riding)* promenade(s) *f(pl)* à cheval
▸ ▸ **h. jacket** veste *f* de cheval

hackle [ˈhæk(ə)l] **N** *(of bird)* plume *f* du cou; **hackles** camail *m*; **his hackles rose** *(of dog)*, *Fig (of person)* il s'est hérissé; *Fig* **to get one's hackles up** se hérisser, monter sur ses ergots; *Fig* **his hackles are up** il se prépare pour

la bagarre; *Fig* **to make sb's hackles rise** hérisser qn

hackney [ˈhæknɪ] **N 1** *(taxi)* **h. cab** *or* **carriage** fiacre *m* **2** *(carriage for hire)* cabriolet *m* de louage **3** *(horse)* cheval *m*, -aux de selle; *(trotter)* trotteur *m*

hackneyed [ˈhæknɪd] **ADJ** *(language)* rebattu, usé, banal, -als; **a h. argument** un argument éculé; **h. phrase** formule *f* stéréotypée, cliché *m*

hacksaw [ˈhæksɔː] **N** scie *f* à métaux

hackwork [ˈhækwɜːk] **N** *Fam* **to do h.** *(of writer)* écrire au kilomètre; **it's just h.** *(routine work)* c'est du travail alimentaire; **the report was a piece of shoddy h.** ce rapport, c'était du travail d'écrivaillon

had **PT, PP** *see* **have**

haddock [ˈhædək] **N** *(fish)* aiglefin *m*, églefin *m*; *Culin* **smoked h.** haddock *m*

Hades [ˈheɪdiːz] **N** *Myth* les Enfers *mpl*

hadn't [ˈhæd(ə)nt] **CONTR** = **had not**, *see* **have**

Hadrian's Wall [ˈheɪdrɪənzwɔːl] **N** le Mur d'Hadrien

haema- [ˈhiːmə] **PREF** *Med etc* héma-

haematite, *Am* **hematite** [ˈhiːmətaɪt] **N** hématite *f*

haemato- [ˈhiːmətɒ, -təʊ] **PREF** *Med etc* hémato-

haematology, *Am* **hematology** [hiːməˈtɒlədʒɪ] **N** *Med* hématologie *f*

haematoma, *Am* **hematoma,** *pl* **haematomas, haematomata** [hiːməˈtəʊmə, -əʊməz, -əʊmətə] **N** *Med* hématome *m*

haemo- [ˈhiːməʊ, -mə] **PREF** *Med etc* hémo-

haemoglobin, *Am* **hemoglobin** [hiːməʊˈɡləʊbɪn] **N** *Med* hémoglobine *f*

haemophilia, *Am* **hemophilia** [hiːməʊˈfɪlɪə] **N** *Med* hémophilie *f*

haemophiliac, *Am* **hemophiliac** [hiːməʊˈfɪlɪæk] **N** *Med* hémophile *mf*

haemophilic, *Am* **hemophilic** [hiːməʊˈfɪlɪk] **ADJ** *Med* hémophile

haemorrhage, *Am* **hemorrhage** [ˈhemərɪdʒ] **N** *Med, Fig* hémorragie *f*
VI *Med* faire une hémorragie; *Fig (disappear, fade fast) (of support etc)* s'évanouir, se dissiper; **party membership was haemorrhaging badly** les effectifs du parti diminuaient de façon spectaculaire; **foreign capital would h. if …** il y aurait une hémorragie *ou* fuite de capitaux si …

haemorrhoids, *Am* **hemorrhoids** [ˈhemərɔɪdz] **NPL** *Med* hémorroïdes *fpl*; **to have h.** avoir des hémorroïdes

haemostat, *Am* **hemostat** [ˈhiːməʊstæt] **N** *Med (instrument)* pince(s) *f(pl)* hémostatique(s)

haft [hɑːft] **N** *(of tool etc)* manche *m*, poignée *f*

hag [hæɡ] **N** *(witch)* (vieille) sorcière *f*, *Fam*

(unpleasant old woman) vieille taupe *f*, vieux chameau *m*

haggard ['hægəd] **ADJ 1** *(gaunt)* hâve; *(face)* décharné **2** *(wild) (face)* égaré, hagard

haggis ['hægɪs] **N** *Scot Culin* = panse *f* de brebis farcie (d'un hachis d'abats et de farine d'avoine très épicé)

haggle ['hæg(ə)l] **VI** marchander, *Fam* chipoter; **I'm not going to h.** je ne vais pas chipoter; **to h. about** *or* **over the price of sth** chicaner sur le prix de qch

haggler ['hæglər] **N** *(over details etc)* chipoteur, -euse

haggling ['hæg(ə)lɪŋ] **N** marchandage *m*

hagiographer [hægɪ'ɒgrəfər] **N** hagiographe *mf*

hagiography [hægɪ'ɒgrəfɪ] **N** hagiographie *f*

hag-ridden **ADJ** *(by nightmares)* tourmenté par des cauchemars; *(by an idea etc)* obsédé, tourmenté

Hague (the) [ðeheɪg] **N** La Haye

hah [hɑː] **INT** ha!, ah!

ha-ha¹ [hɑː'hɑː] **INT** ha, ha!

ha-ha² ['hɑːhɑː] **N** *(ditch)* saut-de-loup *m*, *pl* sauts-de-loup

haiku ['haɪkuː] **N** haïku *m*

hail¹ [heɪl] **N** *Met* grêle *f*; **h. of blows/stones** grêle *ou* volée *f* de coups/pierres; **a h. of bullets** une pluie de balles; **a h. of fire** un déluge de feu; **a h. of abuse** une pluie d'injures; **to be met by a h. of insults** être reçu sous *ou* par une pluie d'insultes
V IMPERS *Met* grêler; **it's hailing** il grêle
VT to h. blows on sb donner une volée de coups à qn; **to h. insults/abuse/obscenities on sb** asséner des insultes/des injures/des obscénités à qn
► **hail down** **VI** **blows/missiles hailed down on our heads** nous avons reçu une volée de coups/une pluie de missiles; **criticism hailed down on him** il a subi une avalanche *ou* un déluge de critiques
VT SEP *(throw)* **they hailed stones down on us** ils nous ont bombardés de cailloux; **they hailed insults down on the President** ils ont déversé un flot d'insultes à l'intention du président

hail² **INT** *Arch, Lit* salut!; **h., Caesar!** Avé César!; **h., Mary, full of grace!** je te salue, Marie, pleine de grâce!
N *Old-fashioned* **within h.** à portée de (la) voix
VT 1 *Old-fashioned (greet) (person)* saluer **2** *(attract attention of) (person, ship, taxi)* héler; **within hailing distance** à portée de (la) voix **3** *(acclaim)* acclamer; **he has been hailed as the new ...** il a été acclamé comme le nouveau ...; **the bridge was hailed as an engineering marvel** le pont a été salué comme une merveille de technicité; **the plan was hailed as the solution to their problems** le projet a été salué comme la solution à tous leurs problèmes
VI where does he h. from? d'où vient-il?; **to h. from a port** *(of ship) (be based at)* venir *ou Spec* dépendre d'un port; *(come from)* venir *ou* arriver d'un port
► ► *Rel* **H. Mary** *(prayer)* Je vous salue Marie *m inv*, Ave (Maria) *m inv*; **to say two H. Marys** dire deux Ave Maria

hail-fellow-well-met **ADJ** **to be h. with everyone** être à tu et à toi avec tout le monde

hailstone ['heɪlstəʊn] **N** grêlon *m*

hailstorm ['heɪlstɔːm] **N** averse *f* de grêle

hair [heər] **N 1** *(of human head)* cheveux *mpl*; *(single)* cheveu *m*; **the h.** les cheveux, la chevelure; **to have fair h.** avoir les cheveux clairs; **woman with short h.** femme aux cheveux courts; **I like your h.** j'aime bien ta

coiffure; **to wash one's h.** se laver la tête; **to have** *or* **get one's h. cut** se faire couper les cheveux; **to do one's h.** se coiffer; **to have one's h. done** aller chez le coiffeur; **if you harm** *or* **touch a h. on that child's head ...** si tu touches un cheveu de cet enfant ...; **it was enough to make your h. stand on end** c'était à faire dresser les cheveux sur la tête; *Fam* **keep your h. on!** calmez-vous!; *Fam* **to get in sb's h.** taper sur les nerfs de qn, enquiquiner qn; **to comb one's h.** se peigner; **h. crack** *(in metal)* gerçure *f*

2 *(individual hair, of human face and body, animals, plants)* poil *m*; **(body) h.** *(of human)* poil; **(facial) h.** *(of human)* poils *mpl* du visage; *Fig* **h. of the dog** *(for hangover)* antidote *m*; *Fam Hum* **this'll put hairs on your chest!** tiens, bois/mange ça, c'est bon pour la santé!

3 *(coat) (of animal)* poil *m*, pelage *m*; *(of horse)* crin *m*; *(of pig)* soie *f*

4 *Opt (of gun sight etc)* cheveu *m*, fil *m*; **cross hairs** réticule *m*

► ► **h. conditioner** après-shampooing *m*; **h. cream** crème *f* pour les cheveux; **h. drier, h. dryer** *(hand-held)* sèche-cheveux *m inv*; *(over the head)* casque *m*; **h. gel** gel *m* pour les cheveux; **h. lacquer** laque *f* (pour les cheveux); **h. lotion** lotion *f* capillaire; **h. mattress** matelas *m* de crin; **h. mousse** mousse *f* coiffante; **h. oil** huile *f* capillaire; **h. remover** crème dépilatoire; *Br* **h. restorer** produit *m* pour la repousse des cheveux; **h. shirt** haire *f*, cilice *m*; **h. slide** barrette *f*, *Typ* **h. space** espace *f* fine; **h. spray** laque; **h. straighteners** *(appliance)* fer *m* à défriser, défriseur *m*; **h. tonic** lotion capillaire; **h. trigger** *(in firearm)* détente *f ou* gâchette *f* sensible

hairball ['heəbɔːl] **N** *(in cat's stomach)* boule *f* de poils

hairband ['heəbænd] **N** bandeau *m*

hairbrush ['heəbrʌʃ] **N** brosse *f* à cheveux

haircut ['heəkʌt] **N 1** *(act)* coupe *f* de cheveux; **to have a h.** se faire couper les cheveux **2** *(hairstyle)* coupe *f* de cheveux, coiffure *f*

hairdo ['heəduː] **N** *Fam* coiffure *f*

hairdresser ['heədresər] **N** coiffeur, -euse; **to go to the h.'s** aller chez le coiffeur

hairdressing ['heədresɪŋ] **N** coiffure *f*
► ► **h. salon** salon *m* de coiffure; **h. school** école *f* de coiffure

-haired [heəd] **SUFF** **short/grey/etc-h.** aux cheveux courts/gris/*etc*

hairgrip ['heəgrɪp] **N** *esp Br* pince *f* à cheveux

hairless ['heəlɪs] **ADJ** *(bald)* chauve; *(face)* glabre, imberbe; *(body, animal)* sans poils

hairline ['heəlaɪn] **N 1** *(of person)* racine *f* des cheveux; **his h. is receding** son front commence à se dégarnir, il commence à se dégarnir **2** *Typ* délié *m* **3** *Tech (in metal)* gerçure *f* **4** *Opt (of gun sight etc)* cheveu *m*, fil *m*; **hairlines** réticule *m*
► ► **h. crack** fêlure *f*, *Med* **h. fracture** fêlure; *Typ* **h. space** espace *f* fine

hairnet ['heənet] **N** filet *m*, résille *f*

hairpiece ['heəpiːs] **N** mèche *f* postiche

hairpin ['heəpɪn] **N** épingle *f* à cheveux
► ► **h. bend** virage *m* en épingle à cheveux

hair-raising ['heəreɪzɪŋ] **ADJ** effrayant; *(adventure)* effroyable; *(account)* à vous faire dresser les cheveux sur la tête

hair's-breadth **N** épaisseur *f* d'un cheveu; **he escaped death by a h.** il a été à deux doigts de la mort, il a frisé la mort; **to be within a h. of disaster** être à un cheveu de la ruine

hair-splitting **N** ergotage *m*; *(dispute)* chicane *f*
ADJ *(distinction etc)* (trop) subtil

hairspring ['heəsprɪŋ] **N** *(of watch, clock etc)* spiral *m*, *pl* spiraux

hairstyle ['heəstaɪl] **N** coiffure *f*

hairstylist ['heəstaɪlɪst] **N** coiffeur, -euse

hairy ['heərɪ] **ADJ 1** *(hands, chest etc)* velu, poilu; *(person)* hirsute **2** *Fam (dangerous)* périlleux; *(frightening)* effrayant; **things are getting rather h.** la situation devient assez désespérée

Haiti ['heɪtɪ, 'haɪ-] **N** Haïti *m ou f*

Haitian ['heɪʃən, 'heɪtɪən] **ADJ** haïtien
N Haïtien, -ienne

hake [heɪk] **N** *(fish)* merluche *f*, colin *m*

halal [hæ'læl] **ADJ** *Muslim Rel* hal(l)al *inv*

halation [hæ'leɪʃən] **N** *Phot* halo *m*, irradiation *f*

halberd ['hælbəd] **N** *Mil, Hist* hallebarde *f*

halcyon ['hælsɪən] **N** *(kingfisher)* halcyon *m*
► ► *Lit* **h. days** bon vieux temps *m*, jours *mpl* heureux

hale [heɪl] **ADJ** vigoureux, robuste, encore gaillard; **to be h. and hearty** être frais et gaillard

---

HALF, *pl* **halves** [hɑːf, hɑːvz]

N	demi **1-3**	▪ moitié **1**	▪ mi-temps **3**
	▪ camp **3**		
ADJ	demi		
ADV	à moitié		

N **VOIR GRAMMAIRE A5** **1** moitié *f*; *(of beer, hour)* demi *m*; **to fold/cut sth in h.** *or* **into halves** plier/couper qch en deux; **three and a h.** trois et demi; **what is h. of twelve?** quelle est la moitié de douze?; **h. a dozen** une demi-douzaine; **a h. of lager** un demi de blonde; *Fig* **h. the time he isn't there** les trois quarts du temps, il n'est pas là; **h. of them were students** la moitié d'entre eux étaient étudiants; **the first h. of the year** la première moitié de l'année; **she gave each of us h.** elle nous en a donné la moitié à chacun; **I'll be with you in h. a second** *or Br Fam* **(give me) h. a tick** je suis à vous dans une seconde; **I've got h. a mind to complain** j'ai bien envie de faire une réclamation; *Fam* **my better** *or* **other h.** ma (chère) moitié; *Fam* **how the other h. lives** comment vivent les autres; **bigger by h.** plus grand de moitié; *Fam* **she is too clever by h.** elle est beaucoup trop maligne; *Fam* **you haven't heard the h. of it!** tu n'en sais pas encore le quart!; **but that's h. the fun of it!** mais c'est le plus amusant!; **that was h. the point of going there** c'était tout l'intérêt d'y aller; **they don't do things by halves** ils ne font pas les choses à moitié; **to go halves with sb** partager avec qn; *Br* **one and two halves** *(on bus, train)* un tarif normal, deux tarifs enfant; *Rail* **outward/return h.** *(of ticket)* coupon *m* d'aller/de retour; **chicken halves** *(portions)* demi-poulets *mpl*

2 *(time)* **h. an hour** une demi-heure; **h. past twelve** midi/minuit et demi; **it's h. past two** *or Fam* **h. two** il est deux heures et demi; **I waited for two and a h. hours** j'ai attendu pendant deux heures et demi

3 *Sport (player)* demi *m*; **the first/second h. (of the game)** la première/seconde mi-temps; **in our h. (of the pitch)** dans notre camp

ADJ demi; **at h. price** à moitié prix; *Br Fam* **h. seas over** gris, soûl, ivre

ADV à moitié; **she only h. understands** elle ne comprend qu'à moitié; **he h. opened the door** il entrouvrit la porte; **the bottle was h. full/empty** la bouteille était à moitié *ou* à demi pleine/vide; **you're h. right** tu n'as pas tout à fait tort; **h. laughing, h. crying** moitié riant, moitié pleurant; **I was h. afraid that you wouldn't come** j'avais quelque crainte que vous ne veniez pas; **h. as big** moitié moins grand; **h. as big again** plus grand de moitié; **it was not h. as expensive as I thought it would be** c'était bien moins cher que je ne le pensais; **he gets h. as much money as you** il reçoit moitié moins d'argent que vous; *Br Fam* **it isn't h. bad** ce n'est pas mal du tout; *Br Fam* **it isn't h. cold!** il fait rudement froid!; *Br Fam* **he doesn't h. say some stupid things!** il dit vraiment n'importe quoi *ou* des âneries!; *Br Fam* **not h.!** et comment!

PREF **h. dressed** à demi vêtu; **h. naked/asleep/dead** à moitié nu/endormi/mort; **h. done** *(work)* fait à moitié; *(cooked meat etc)* à moitié cuit

▸▸ *Tech* **h. bearing** demi-palier *m, pl* demi-paliers; **h. board** demi-pension *f*; *Admin* **h. day** demi-journée *f, pl* demi-journées; *Comput* **h. duplex** semi-duplex *m inv*; *Ftbl etc* **h. time** (la) mi-temps; **the h. time score** le score à la mi-temps; *Tennis* **h. volley** demi-volée *f, pl* demi-volées; **h. year** semestre *m*

half-a-crown N *Br Arch* demi-couronne *f*

half-and-half ADJ, ADV moitié l'un moitié l'autre, fam moitié-moitié; **how shall I mix them? – h.** comment faut-il les mélanger? – à doses égales; **how do you like your coffee? – h.** comment prenez-vous le café? – moitié café, moitié lait
▪ N *Am (milk and cream)* = mélange *m* de lait et de crème liquide

half-arsed [hɑːfˈɑːst], *Am* **half-assed** [hɑːfˈæst] ADJ *Sl* foireux

halfback [ˈhɑːfbæk] N **1** *Ftbl Old-fashioned* demi-arrière *m, pl* demi-arrières **2** *(in rugby)* demi *m*

half-baked ADJ *Fam (poorly planned)* nul; *(idea)* qui ne tient pas debout, ridicule

half-binding N demi-reliure *f*

half-blood N = halfbreed

halfbreed [ˈhɑːfbriːd] N **1** *Old-fashioned Offensive Sl (person)* métis, -isse **2** *(horse)* cheval *m* demi-sang, *pl* chevaux demi-sang *ou* demi-sangs

half-brother N demi-frère *m, pl* demi-frères; *Law (through mother)* frère utérin; *(through father)* frère consanguin

half-caste ADJ, N *Old-fashioned usu Offensive* métis, -isse

half-circle N demi-cercle *m, pl* demi-cercles; *Naut* **to turn a h.** faire demi-tour

half(-)cock N **at h.** *(rifle etc)* à moitié armé, sur le cran de sûreté; *Fig Fam* **to go off at h.** mal partir, mal démarrer

half-crown N = half-a-crown

half-cut ADJ *Br Fam (drunk)* bourré, pété, fait

half-fare ticket N billet *m* demi-tarif

halfhearted [hɑːfˈhɑːtɪd] ADJ sans enthousiasme; *(effort)* timide, hésitant

halfheartedly [hɑːfˈhɑːtɪdlɪ] ADV sans enthousiasme

halfheartedness [hɑːfˈhɑːtɪdnɪs] N tiédeur *f*, manque *m* d'enthousiasme

half-hour N demi-heure *f*; **on the h.** à la demie

half-hourly ADV toutes les demi-heures
ADJ **there is a h. train service** il y a des trains toutes les trente minutes; **he needs his h. break** il lui faut faire une pause toutes les trente minutes; **at h. intervals** toutes les demi-heures, toutes les trente minutes

half-inch VT *Br Sl (pinch)* piquer, faucher; **he got his wallet half-inched** il s'est fait piquer son portefeuille

half-length N **1** *Horseracing* demi-longueur *f, pl* demi-longueurs **2** *(portrait)* en buste

half-life N *Nucl etc (of isotope etc)* demi-vie *f, pl* demi-vies

half-light N demi-jour *m, pl* demi-jours

half-mast N *Br* **at h.** à mi-mât; **flag at h.** pavillon *m* en berne; *Hum* **to be at h.** *(of trousers)* arriver à mi-mollet; *(of socks)* descendre

half-moon N **1** demi-lune *f, pl* demi-lunes **2** *(of fingernail)* lunule *f*

half-nelson N *(in wrestling)* simple prise *f* de tête à terre

half-note N *esp Am Mus* blanche *f*

half-pay N demi-salaire *m*; *(in civil service)* demi-traitement *m*; *Mil* demi-solde *f*; **on h.** à mi-salaire/à demi-traitement/en demi-solde

halfpenny [ˈheɪpnɪ, ˈhɑːfpenɪ] N *Br Arch* demi-penny *m*, sou *m*; *Fam* **it isn't worth a h.** ça ne vaut pas un sou!; **he's down to his last h.** il ne lui reste que quelques sous

half-price ADJ *(ticket)* demi-tarif
ADV *(à)* demi-tarif; **children get in h.** les enfants payent demi-tarif

half-shaft N demi-arbre *m, pl* demi-arbres

half-sister N demi-sœur *f, pl* demi-sœurs; *Law (through mother)* sœur utérine; *(through father)* sœur consanguine

half-size N *(in dress)* demi-taille *f, pl* demi-tailles; *(in shoes)* demi-pointure *f, pl* demi-pointures; **we don't stock half-sizes of that shoe** nous n'avons pas les demi-pointures de ce modèle en stock

half-staff N *Am* = half-mast

half-term N *Br Sch* congé *m* de mi-trimestre

half-timbered ADJ *Archit (house)* à colombages

half-title N *Typ (of book)* faux-titre *m, pl* faux-titres

halftone [hɑːfˈtəʊn] N **1** *Art* demi-teinte *f, pl* demi-teintes; *Phot* similigravure *f* (tramée) **2** *Am Mus* demi-ton *m, pl* demi-tons

half-track N *Aut (auto)* chenille *f*, half-track *m*

half-truth N demi-vérité *f, pl* demi-vérités

halfway [hɑːfˈweɪ] ADV **1** à mi-chemin; *(of piston)* à mi-course; **h. between the two towns** à mi-chemin entre les deux villes; **h. to Paris** à mi-chemin de Paris; **we're h. there** nous sommes à mi-chemin, nous avons fait la moitié du chemin; *(in project etc)* nous sommes à mi-chemin; **h. up (the hill)** à mi-côte, à mi-pente; **I was h. up/down the stairs** j'étais à mi-hauteur de l'escalier; **the lift got stuck h. up** l'ascenseur s'est bloqué à mi-hauteur; **h. through the project** j'ai à mi-projet; **we're h. through the year and …** six mois ont déjà passé et …; **we're h. through the summer holidays/week** nous sommes à la moitié des grandes vacances/de la semaine; **it happened h. through the holidays** ça s'est passé en plein milieu des vacances; **we're h. through the work** nous avons fait la moitié du travail; **to meet sb h.** *(in distance)* aller à la rencontre de qn à mi-chemin; **let's meet up h. in Bath** disons que chacun fait la moitié du chemin et qu'on se retrouve à Bath; **let's meet h.** *(in distance)* faisons chacun la moitié du chemin; **I'll meet you h.** *(in price)* faisons moitié-moitié, trouvons un compromis; *(in concessions asked for)* faisons un arrangement

2 *(partly)* à peu près; **haven't you got a h. acceptable shirt?** tu n'as pas une chemise à peu près convenable?

▸▸ **h. house** *(on journey)* (auberge *f*) relais *m*; *(for rehabilitation)* centre *m* de réadaptation *(pour anciens détenus, malades mentaux, drogués etc)*; *Fig (halfway stage)* (stade *m* de) transition *f*; *(compromise)* compromis *m*; *Sport* **h. line** ligne *f* médiane

halfwit [ˈhɑːfwɪt] N faible *mf* d'esprit, simple *mf* d'esprit

halfwitted [hɑːfˈwɪtɪd] ADJ faible d'esprit, simple

half-yearly ADJ semestriel; **h. result** demi-résultat *m*, résultat à six mois
ADV une fois par semestre, tous les six mois

halibut [ˈhælɪbət] N *(fish)* flétan *m*

halitosis [hælɪˈtəʊsɪs] N *Med* mauvaise haleine *f*; **to suffer from h.** avoir mauvaise haleine

hall [hɔːl] N **1** *(entrance)* **h.** *(of house)* entrée *f*; *(of hotel)* hall *m* **2** *Am (corridor)* couloir *m*, corridor *m* **3** *(room, building)* salle *f*; *(dining)* **h.** *(of stately home)* salle à manger; *Univ* réfectoire *m*; **the servants' h.** l'office *m*; *Br Univ* **h. (of residence)** résidence *f* universitaire, maison *f* d'étudiants; *Br Univ* **to eat in h.** manger au réfectoire *ou* RU; *Br Univ* **to live in h.** loger en résidence universitaire **4** *(manor house)* manoir *m*; **she works up at the h.** elle travaille au château; **Ludgely H.** le château de Ludgely

▸▸ *esp Am* **H. of Fame** ≃ Panthéon *m*; **he's in the baseball h. of fame** il fait partie du panthéon de l'histoire du baseball; **h. porter** *(in hotel)* portier *m*; **h. stand** portemanteau *m*

hallelujah [hælɪˈluːjə] INT, N alléluia *m*

hallmark [ˈhɔːlmɑːk] N *(on silver)* (cachet *m* de) contrôle *m*, poinçon *m*; *Fig* **the h. of genius** l'empreinte *f* du génie; **to bear all the hallmarks of …** porter l'empreinte de …, avoir tous les signes de …
VT *(silver)* contrôler, poinçonner

hallo [həˈləʊ] INT = hello

hallow [ˈhæləʊ] *Rel Old-fashioned* **All Hallows' (Day)** (le jour de) la Toussaint
VT sanctifier, consacrer; **hallowed be Thy name** que Ton nom soit sanctifié

hallowed [ˈhæləʊd] ADJ béni, sanctifié
▸▸ *Rel* **h. ground** terre *f* sainte *ou* bénie; *Fig* lieu *m* de culte

Hallowe'en [hæləʊˈiːn] N = veille *f* de la Toussaint, *Can* halloween *f*

> **Hallowe'en**
> Il s'agit d'une fête d'origine païenne célébrée dans les pays anglo-saxons la veille de la Toussaint, à l'époque de l'année où les morts étaient censés rendre visite aux vivants. Aujourd'hui la tradition demeure: on évide des citrouilles pour les transformer en lanternes en forme de crâne, et les enfants vont de maison en maison déguisés en sorcières ou en fantômes. De nos jours, la coutume britannique a adopté la tradition américaine de "trick or treat", consistant pour les enfants à demander un petit cadeau aux habitants des maisons visitées et à les menacer d'un mauvais tour s'ils refusent.

hallucinate [həˈluːsɪneɪt] VT he was hallucinating that his skin had turned green dans ses hallucinations, il se voyait avec la peau verte
VI avoir des hallucinations

hallucination [həluːsɪˈneɪʃən] N hallucination *f*

hallucinatory [həˈluːsɪnət(ə)rɪ] ADJ hallucinatoire

hallucinogen [həˈluːsɪnədʒen] N hallucinogène *m*

hallucinogenic [həluːsɪnəʊˈdʒenɪk] ADJ hallucinogène

hallway [ˈhɔːlweɪ] N **1** vestibule *m*, entrée *f* **2** *Am (corridor)* couloir *m*

halo, *pl* **halos, haloes** [ˈheɪləʊ, -əʊz] N **1** *(of saint)* auréole *f*, nimbe *m*; *Hum* **your h.'s slipping!** tu te dévergondes! **2** *Astron, Opt, Phot* halo *m*; *(of moon)* auréole *f*
▸▸ *Mktg* **h. effect** effet *m* de halo

halogen ['hælədʒən] ADJ, N Chem halogène *m*; **h. headlights** phares *mpl* halogènes

halt¹ [hɒlt] N 1 (act of stopping) arrêt *m*, interruption *f* (momentanée), halte *f*, pause *f*; **a brief h. at an inn** une brève halte dans une auberge; **to bring to a h.** (process etc) arrêter; (movement, action) provoquer l'interruption momentanée de; (vehicle, crowd etc) arrêter, faire stopper; **to come to a h.** marquer un temps d'arrêt, s'interrompre momentanément, s'arrêter, stopper; (on journey) faire halte; (in a speech) rester sans rien dire; **to call a h.** (demander à) faire une halte; **to call a h. to sth** arrêter qch **2** Br Rail (small station) halte *f*

VI faire halte, s'arrêter; **to h. at …** faire un arrêt à …, s'arrêter à …; Mil **company h.!** compagnie halte!; Mil **h.! who goes there** halte! qui va là?

VT (person) faire faire (une) halte à; (something) (for good) arrêter, mettre un terme ou un point final à; (temporarily) interrompre

▸▸ Aut **h. sign** stop *m*

halt² Bible, Arch ADJ boiteux

NPL **the h. and the lame** les estropiés *mpl*

halter ['hɔːltər] N 1 (for horse) licou *m* **2** (on women's clothing) bain *m* de soleil; **dress with a h. neck, h.-neck dress** robe *f* dos nu ou bain de soleil **3** (rope) (for hanging person) corde *f*

▸▸ **h. top** bain *m* de soleil

halting ['hɔːltɪŋ] ADJ (words, speech etc) hésitant; (style) heurté

haltingly ['hɔːltɪŋlɪ] ADV en hésitant

halve [hɑːv] VT 1 (cut) diviser en deux (moitiés), couper en deux (moitiés) **2** (share) partager en deux **3** (reduce) (expenses, costs etc) réduire de moitié

halves [hɑːvz] NPL see half

halyard ['hæljəd] N Naut drisse *f*

ham [hæm] N 1 Culin jambon *m*; **h. sandwich** sandwich *m* au jambon **h. and eggs** œufs *mpl* au jambon **2** Fam (buttocks) **the hams** les fesses *fpl*, le derrière **3** Fam (actor) cabotin *m* **4** Radio Fam (enthusiast) **(radio) h.** radioamateur *m*

VI (-mm-) Fam jouer comme un pied

VT Fam **he hams all his parts** il charge tous ses rôles, il en fait trop

▸▸ Fam **h. acting** cabotinage *m*; Fam **h. actor** cabotin *m*

▸ **ham up** VT SEP Fam **to h. it up** jouer comme un pied

Hamburg ['hæmbɜːg] N Hambourg

Hamburger ['hæmbɜːgər] N (person) Hambourgeois, -oise

hamburger ['hæmbɜːgər] N Culin hamburger *m*; Am (meat) viande *f* hachée

ham-fisted [hæm'fɪstɪd] ADJ Fam maladroit

Hamitic [hə'mɪtɪk] ADJ chamitique

hamlet ['hæmlɪt] N hameau *m*

hammer ['hæmər] N 1 (tool) marteau *m*; (heavy) masse *f*, Pol **the h. and sickle** la faucille et le marteau; **to go at it h. and tongs** (work etc energetically) y aller de bon cœur, ne pas y aller de main morte; (quarrel) se quereller; (fight) se bagarrer; Am Fam **to let the h. down** appuyer sur le champignon, mettre les gaz; Sport **throwing the h.** lancement *m* du marteau

2 (of auctioneer) marteau *m*; **to come under the h.** être mis aux enchères

3 (in clock, alarm, piano etc) marteau *m*

4 Anat (of inner ear) marteau *m*

5 (of firearm) chien *m*

VT marteler; Fam (beat) (person) tabasser; (of boxer etc) (opponent) cogner dur sur; (defeat) (opponent, other side) battre à plate(s) couture(s), écraser; (criticize) (person, book

etc) massacrer, descendre; **to h. a nail into sth** enfoncer un clou dans qch avec un marteau; **to h. into shape** (pot etc) façonner à coups de marteau; Fig Fam (plan etc) perfectionner; Fam **to h. sth into sb** faire entrer qch dans la tête de qn; **I'll h. it into her** je veux lui faire entrer ça dans la tête; **to h. prices** écraser les prix

VI 1 travailler avec un marteau, travailler au marteau; **to h. at** or **on the door** frapper à la porte à coups redoublés **2** Fam **to h. down the motorway** foncer sur l'autoroute

▸▸ **h. thrower** lanceur, -euse de marteau

▸ **hammer along** VI Fam (in car) foncer

▸ **hammer away** VI 1 (with hammer) **they've been hammering away all evening** ils ont donné des coups de marteau toute la soirée; **to h. away at sth** marteler qch **2** (of heart) battre très fort (dans la poitrine) **3** Fig **to h. away at sth** (at agreement) travailler d'arrache-pied à qch; **to h. away at the keyboard** frapper de toutes ses forces sur le clavier

▸ **hammer home** VT SEP 1 (something) enfoncer (à l'aide d'un marteau); **make sure you h. the nails home** assure-toi que tu as bien enfoncé les clous **2** Fig (insist on) **to h. sth home** insister sur qch, répéter cent fois qch

▸ **hammer in** VT SEP (nail) enfoncer à coups de marteau

▸ **hammer out** VT SEP 1 (in metalwork) (gold etc) étendre sous le marteau; (copper) panner; **to h. out a dent in sth** débosseler qch **2** **to h. out a tune** (on the piano) pianoter un air; **to h. out a message on the pipes** tapoter un message sur les conduits **3** Fig Fam (draw up) élaborer, mettre au point; **unions and management hammered out an agreement** les syndicats et le patronat sont parvenus à un accord

hammered ['hæməd] ADJ Fam (drunk) bourré, beurré, pété

hammerhead ['hæməhed] N 1 (shark) requin *m* marteau **2** (bird) ombrette *f* (du Sénégal)

▸▸ **h. shark** requin marteau

hammering ['hæmərɪŋ] N (with hammer) martelage *m*; (noise) martèlement *m*; (of iron) battage *m*; Fam (with fists) volée *f* de coups; **to give sb a h.** (hit) cogner dur sur qn, rouer qn de coups; (defeat) battre qn à plate(s) couture(s), écraser qn; (criticize) descendre qn; **to give sth a h.** (criticize) descendre qch; **our team got a h.** notre équipe a été battue à plate(s) couture(s)

hammertoe ['hæmətəʊ] N Med orteil *m* en marteau ou en cou de cygne

hammock ['hæmək] N hamac *m*

hammy ['hæmɪ] ADJ Fam (acting) outrancier; **h. actor** cabotin *m*, acteur *m* qui en fait trop

hamper¹ ['hæmpər] N panier *m*; (for oysters etc) bourriche *f*; **Christmas h.** panier rempli de gourmandises de Noël

hamper² VT (person) embarrasser, gêner, entraver; **to h. the progress of business** entraver la marche des affaires; **high winds hampered the rescue work** les sauveteurs ont été gênés dans leur travail par la force des vents; **they were hampered in their efforts (to do sth) by the terrible weather** ils furent gênés dans leurs efforts (pour faire qch) par le mauvais temps; **she was hampered by her long cloak** elle était empêtrée dans son grand manteau

hamster ['hæmstər] N hamster *m*

hamstring ['hæmstrɪŋ] N tendon *m* du jarret; **h. injury** lésion *f* du tendon du jarret

VT (pt, pp **hamstringed** or **-strung**) **1** (cut hamstrings of) (person, horse) couper le(s) jarret(s) à **2** Fig paralyser; (financially) (person) couper les moyens à; **we are ham-**

strung by a lack of funds nous sommes paralysés par l'absence de fonds suffisants

┌─────────────────────────────────┐
HAND [hænd]

| N | main **1–9, 12** ▪ ouvrier **10** ▪ écriture **11** ▪ paume **13** ▪ aiguille **14**
| VT | passer ▪ donner
└─────────────────────────────────┘

N 1 (part of body) main *f*, **on one's hands and knees** à quatre pattes; **give me your h.** donnez-moi la main; **to hold in one's h.** (sword, hat) tenir à la main; (grain) tenir dans la main; (success) tenir entre les mains; **to hold hands** se tenir (par) la main; **keep your hands to yourself** ne touche pas, enlève ou retire tes mains de là; **to lay hands on sth** mettre la main sur qch; **to lay hands on sb** faire violence à qn; **to pass sth from h. to h.** passer qch de main en main; **I can't put my h. on it** je n'arrive pas à mettre la main dessus; **to take sb by the h.** prendre qn par la main; **he writes with his left h.** il écrit de la main gauche; **I only have one pair of hands!** je n'ai que deux mains!; **made/done by h.** fait à la main; **to wash clothes by h.** laver du linge à la main; **by h.** (on letter etc) = remise par porteur (sans timbre); **to send/deliver a letter by h.** envoyer/distribuer une lettre par porteur; **sword in h.** sabre au poing; **hands off!** n'y touchez pas!; (off me) bas les pattes!; **hands up!** haut les mains!

2 (responsibility, control, ownership etc) **to have a h. in sth** être impliqué dans qch, être mêlé à qch; **I had no h. in this crime** je n'ai absolument rien à voir avec ce crime; **the h. of God** le doigt de Dieu; **I see Moriarty's h. in this** je reconnais la griffe de Moriarty dans cette affaire; **to have one's hands full** (literally) avoir les mains prises; Fig (be busy) avoir du pain sur la planche, être débordé; **I've got my hands full trying to cope as it is** j'ai déjà assez à faire comme ça; **to fall into enemy hands** tomber aux mains de l'ennemi; **in the wrong hands this knowledge could be very dangerous** si elles tombaient aux mains de personnes malintentionnées, ces connaissances pourraient être très dangereuses; **to be in good hands** être en (de) ou entre (de) bonnes mains; **to put oneself in sb's hands** se confier à qn; **it's in your own hands what happens next** la suite dépend de vous; **to put a matter in the hands of a lawyer** confier une affaire à un avocat; **the matter's in their hands now** désormais, l'affaire est entre leurs mains; **it's out of my hands** je ne peux (plus) rien y faire; **the case is off our hands** l'affaire ne dépend plus de nous; **to get sth off one's hands** se débarrasser de qch; **to change hands** (of goods etc) changer de mains; (of business etc) changer de propriétaire

3 (skill) **to try one's h. at sth** essayer de faire qch, s'essayer à qch; **to get one's h. in** se faire la main; **to keep one's h. in** garder la main; **she can turn her h. to anything** c'est une femme qui peut tout faire

4 (idioms) Fml **he asked for her h. (in marriage)** il lui a demandé sa main; Fam **he never does a h.'s turn** il ne fait jamais rien de ses dix doigts; Fam **to give sb a big h.** (applaud) applaudir vivement qn; **to give** or **lend sb a (helping) h.** aider qn, donner un coup de main à qn; **to lend a h.** mettre la main à la pâte; Fig **to have one's hands tied** avoir les mains liées; **I could beat you at tennis with one h. tied behind my back** je pourrais te battre au tennis même avec une main dans le dos; Fam **to put** or **dip one's h. in the till** puiser dans la caisse; **to be h. in glove with sb** être d'intelligence ou Péj de mèche avec qn; Fam **to make money h. over fist** s'enrichir rapidement; **to be living from h. to mouth** vivre au jour le jour; Sport etc **to win hands down** gagner haut la main; **to**

beat sb hands down battre qn à plate(s) couture(s)

5 (*phrases with* **at**) **to be (near) at h.** (*of object etc*) être à portée de la main *ou* sous la main; (*of event etc*) approcher, être proche; **the hour is at h.** l'heure est proche; **there is always a doctor at h.** il y a toujours un médecin de service; **to suffer at the hands of ...** souffrir aux mains de *ou* entre les mains de ...

6 (*phrases with* **in**) **to walk h. in h. with sb** marcher avec qn la main dans la main; **to work h. in h. with sb** agir de concert avec qn; **to have so much money in h.** avoir tant d'argent disponible; **stock in h.** marchandises en magasin; **I've five minutes in h.** j'ai encore cinq minutes; **the matter in h.** l'affaire en question; **work in h.** travail en cours *ou* en chantier; **the situation is well in h.** la situation est bien en main; **to take sb in h.** prendre qn en main

7 (*phrases with* **on**) **work on h.** travail en cours *ou* à faire; **to have sb/sth on one's hands** avoir qn/qch à sa charge *ou* *Fam* sur les bras; **to have an hour on one's hands** avoir une heure à tuer; **to have time on one's hands** avoir du temps libre; **she's got a lot on her hands at the moment** elle est très occupée en ce moment; **I'm on h. if you need me** je suis à votre disposition si vous avez besoin de moi; **on the one h.** d'une part; **on the other h.** d'autre part

8 (*phrases with* **out of**) **these birds will eat out of your h.** ces oiseaux te mangeront dans la main; *Fig* **I'll soon have him eating out of my h.** bientôt, il me mangera dans la main; **to do sth out of h.** faire qch sur-le-champ; **to shoot sb out of h.** abattre qn sans autre forme de procès; **to get out of h.** (*of situation, inflation etc*) échapper à notre/leur/*etc* contrôle; (*of children, class etc*) perdre toute discipline

9 (*phrases with* **to**) **to come to h.** tomber sous la main; **you can use anything that comes to h.** tu peux utiliser tout ce qui te tombe sous la main; **your parcel came to h. this morning** votre paquet m'est parvenu ce matin; **use whatever is to h.** utilisez ce que vous avez sous la main; **the first excuse to h.** le premier prétexte venu

10 (*worker*) ouvrier, -ière; *Naut* matelot *m*; *Ind etc* **to take on hands** embaucher de la main-d'œuvre; *Naut* **the (ship's) hands** l'équipage *m*; **all hands on deck!** tout le monde sur le pont!; **to be lost with all hands** (*of ship*) périr corps et biens; **an old h. (at sth)** un expert (en/dans qch), un spécialiste (en/de qch); **an old h. at doing sth** un expert *ou* spécialiste pour ce qui est de faire qch; **he was an old h. at spotting such tricks** c'était un expert dans l'art de reconnaître de telles ruses

11 (*handwriting*) écriture *f*; **in one's own h.** (*write a letter*) de sa propre main; *Law, Arch* **to set one's h. to a deed** apposer sa signature à un acte

12 *Cards* (*cards received*) main *f*, jeu *m*; (*player*) joueur, -euse; (*round*) partie *f*; **to have a good h.** avoir un beau jeu, avoir du jeu; **first/fourth h.** (*player*) premier *m*/dernier *m* en cartes; **to show one's h.** faire voir son jeu

13 (*measurement*) paume *f*; **horse fifteen hands high** cheval de quinze paumes

14 *Typ* index *m*; (*of signpost, barometer*) indicateur *m*; (*of clock, watch*) aiguille *f*; **the little h. is pointing to three** la petite aiguille est sur le trois

15 (*of bananas*) régime *m*

vt passer, remettre, donner (**sth to sb** qch à qn); **he handed her the letter to read** il lui a donné la lettre à lire; *Fig* **to h. sth to sb on a plate** apporter à qn qch sur un plateau; *Fig Fam* **to h. it to sb** reconnaître la supériorité

de qn; **you've got to h. it to him** devant lui, chapeau!; **you've got to h. it to these Russians, they know how to dance!** il faut reconnaître que ces Russes savent danser!

▸▸ **h. baggage** bagages *mpl* à main; *Ftbl* **h. ball** (*foul*) (faute *f* de) main *f*; **h. basin** lavabo *m*; **h. controls** commandes *fpl* manuelles; **h. cream** crème *f* pour les mains; *TV etc* **h. cue** signal *m* de départ de la main; *Old-fashioned* **h. glass** (*for reading*) loupe *f*; (*mirror*) miroir *m* de sac; *Mil* **h. grenade** grenade *f* à main; **h. lotion** lotion *f* pour les mains; **h. luggage** bagages à main; **h. microphone** micro *m* portatif; *Theat* **h. puppet** marionnette *f*; **h. signal** signal *m* de la main

▸ **hand around** VT SEP = **hand round**

▸ **hand back** VT SEP (*return*) repasser; **she handed me back the bottle** elle m'a repassé la bouteille; **should Britain h. Gibraltar back to Spain?** est-ce que la Grande-Bretagne devrait rétrocéder Gibraltar à l'Espagne?

▸ **hand down** VT SEP **1** (*give*) **h. me down that bottle** descends-moi cette bouteille

2 (*help down*) **to h. sb down** donner la main à qn pour l'aider à descendre

3 (*bequeath etc*) (*necklace, tradition*) transmettre (**from** de; **to** en); **all her clothes had been handed down from her older sisters** tous ses vêtements venaient de ses sœurs aînées

4 *Law* **to h. down a sentence** prononcer une sentence

▸ **hand in** VT SEP remettre, déposer; **to h. in one's resignation** démissionner; **to h. in a piece of homework** rendre un devoir; **to h. a piece of lost property in (to the police)** remettre un objet trouvé (à la police)

▸ **hand off** VT SEP *Rugby* (*player*) raffûter

▸ **hand on** VT SEP (*custom*) transmettre; (*news*) passer (**to** à)

▸ **hand out** VT SEP **1** (*distribute*) (*leaflets, biscuits*) distribuer **2** (*give*) donner; **he's always handing out advice** il se permet de donner des conseils, *Fam* il est sans cesse à donner des conseils; **he's fond of handing it out, but can't take it** (*criticism*) il se permet de critiquer les autres mais il déteste qu'on le critique

▸ **hand over** VT SEP **1** (*give*) donner, remettre

2 (*deliver*) remettre, livrer; **she handed over the documents to a lawyer** elle a remis les documents à un avocat

3 (*surrender*) (*property*) céder; **h. over your wallet!** donne ton portefeuille!; **to h. sb over to justice** livrer qn à la justice, remettre qn aux mains de la justice

4 (*transfer*) (*power*) transmettre; **we now h. you over to our foreign affairs correspondent** nous passons maintenant la parole au responsable des affaires étrangères; **to h. over the command to ...** remettre le commandement à ...

VI **1** (*transfer*) **I now h. over to the weatherman** je passe maintenant la parole au présentateur de la météo; **when will she h. over to the new president?** quand va-t-elle laisser la place au nouveau président?

2 *Fam* (*give*) **I know you have it, so h. over!** passe-le moi, je sais que tu l'as!

▸ **hand round** VT SEP (*circulate*) (*bottle etc*) faire passer, faire circuler; **to h. round a hat** faire passer (à la ronde) un chapeau

---

hand- [hænd] PREF à la main; **h.-sewn** cousu (à la) main; **h.-operated** à commande manuelle

handbag ['hændbæg] N sac *m* à main, *Can* sacoche *m*

handball ['hændbɔːl] N *Sport* (*game*) handball *m*

handbell ['hændbel] N sonnette *f*, clochette *f*

handbill ['hændbɪl] N prospectus *m*

handbook ['hændbʊk] N **1** (*for traveller, tourist*) guide *m*; (*for use in museum etc*) livret *m* **2** *Sch etc* (*of science etc*) manuel *m*

handbrake ['hændbreɪk] N frein *m* à main

handcart ['hændkɑːt] N charrette *f* à bras

handclap ['hændklæp] N **to give sb a slow h.** ≃ siffler qn

handcuff ['hændkʌf] VT (*person*) mettre *ou* passer les menottes à, menotter; **to h. sb to sb** attacher qn à qn d'autre avec des menottes; **to h. sb to sth** attacher qn à qch avec des menottes

handcuffs ['hændkʌfs] NPL menottes *fpl*

handful ['hændfʊl] N **1** (*of sand etc*) poignée *f* **2** (*small number*) petit nombre *m*; **there was** *or* **were only a h. of people there** il n'y avait là que quelques personnes **3** *Fam* (*difficult person*) **that child is a real h.** cet enfant-là me donne du fil à retordre

handgrip ['hændgrɪp] N *Cycling etc* poignée *f*

handgun ['hændgʌn] N revolver *m*, pistolet *m*

hand-held N *Comput* ordinateur *m* de poche ▸▸ *Cin, TV* **h. camera** caméra *f* portable; *Comput* **h. computer** ordinateur *m* de poche; *Comput* **h. scanner** scanner *m* *ou* scanneur *m* à main

handhold ['hændhəʊld] N prise *f*

handicap ['hændɪkæp] N **1** (*disadvantage*) handicap *m*, désavantage *m*; *Med* handicap; **to have a severe h.** avoir un lourd handicap **2** *Sport* handicap *m*; **(weight) h.** (*of racehorse*) surcharge *f*, handicap; **time/distance h.** handicap en temps/distance

VT (*-pp-*) **1** (*disadvantage*) handicaper, désavantager; **their lack of preparation handicapped them** ils ont été désavantagés par leur manque de préparation **2** *Sport* handicaper

handicapped ['hændɪkæpt] ADJ handicapé NPL **the (physically/mentally) h.** les handicapés *mpl* (physiques/mentaux)

handicraft ['hændɪkrɑːft] N (*usu pl*) **1** (*trade*) artisanat *m*, métier *m* manuel **2** (*result*) artisanat *m*, produit *m* artisanal

handily ['hændɪlɪ] ADV commodément; **h. shaped** d'une forme très pratique; **they h. left their fingerprints** ils ont laissé leurs empreintes, ce qui était bien pratique

handiness ['hændɪnɪs] N **1** (*of tool etc*) commodité *f*; **the h. of the house for the shops** l'emplacement très commode de la maison près des magasins **2** (*skill with hands*) adresse *f*, dextérité *f*, habileté *f* (manuelle)

handing down N (*of tradition*) transmission *f*

handing over N (*of hostages, keys*) remise *f* (**to** aux mains de); *Law* (*of property*) cession *f*; (*of power*) transmission *f*

handiwork ['hændɪwɜːk] N **1** (*action*) travail *m* manuel **2** (*result*) ouvrage *m*, travail *m*, œuvre *f*; **the repair/fruit bowl is Jenny's h.** c'est Jenny qui a fait la réparation/la corbeille à fruits; *Iron* **is this your h.?** c'est ton œuvre?; **this quarrel (of theirs) is your h.** c'est de ta faute s'ils se disputent

hand-job N *Sl* **to give sb a h.** branler qn

handkerchief ['hæŋkətʃɪf] N mouchoir *m*

hand-knit(ted) ADJ (*sweater etc*) tricoté (à la) main

handle ['hænd(ə)l] N **1** (*of broom, knife, tool etc*) manche *m*; (*of pump*) bras *m*, balancier *m*; (*of wheelbarrow*) bras; (*of stretcher*) brancard *m*; (*of frying pan*) queue *f*; (*of sword, lever, box, suitcase etc*) poignée *f*; (*of tap*) clef *f*; (*of basket, bucket etc*) anse *f*, **(door) h.** poignée *f*; *Fam* **to fly off the h.** s'emballer; **to get a h. on a problem** savoir comment s'y prendre pour résoudre un problème

2 *Fam (title)* titre *m*; *(CB radio user's call name)* indicatif *m*, code *m*; **to have a h. to one's name** avoir un nom à rallonge(s)

VT 1 *(touch, hold)* tâter, toucher; **to h. a material** tâter *ou* toucher un tissu; **h. with care** *(on package)* ≃ fragile; **to h. stolen goods** receler des objets volés; *Ftbl* **to h. the ball** toucher la balle, faire une main

2 *(operate) (object)* manier, manipuler; *(ship, sails etc)* manœuvrer; *(ship)* gouverner; *(car)* conduire; **how to h. a gun** comment se servir d'un fusil

3 *(treat)* traiter; **to h. sb roughly** malmener qn, rudoyer qn; **the author handles the subject well** l'auteur traite bien le sujet

4 *(manage, cope with)* **to h. a situation** prendre en main une situation; **you handled that very well** vous vous en êtes très bien sorti; **to h. a crisis** résoudre une crise; **don't worry, I'll h. this/him** ne vous inquiétez pas, je vais m'en occuper/je vais m'occuper de lui; **to h. oneself (well) in a crisis** bien se comporter *ou* se conduire en cas de crise; *Fam* **I can't h. interviews** je n'arrive pas à affronter les interviews; *Fam* **he can't h. it when people get aggressive** il n'arrive pas à faire face aux gens agressifs; **she can h. would-be Romeos** elle sait comment faire avec ce genre de dragueurs; *Fam* **could you h. another potato?** tu reprendras bien une autre pomme de terre?

5 *(deal with)* **we h. a lot of business for them** nous travaillons beaucoup pour eux; **who handles your business in …?** qui s'occupe de votre entreprise en …?; **we don't h. that sort of business** nous ne nous occcupons pas de ce genre d'affaires; **to h. large orders** s'occuper de grosses commandes; **to h. a lot of money** brasser beaucoup d'argent; **we h. 10,000 passengers a week** 10 000 passagers passent par nos services chaque semaine; **we don't h. that kind of material/product any more** nous ne faisons plus ce genre de matériel/produit; **who handles your products in France?** qui distribue vos produits en France?; **to h. figures/words** manier les chiffres/les mots

VI 1 *(of car, boat)* être agréable à conduire; **how does it h.?** elle/il est comment?

handlebar ['hænd(ə)lbɑːr] N *(usu pl)* **handlebars** guidon *m*
▸▸ **h. moustache** moustache *f* en guidon de vélo

handler ['hændlər] N *Com* manutentionnaire *mf*; *(of spy)* contact *m*; *(dog)* **h.** maître *m* (de) chien

handling ['hændlɪŋ] N **1** *(touching, holding)* manipulation *f*, action *f* de toucher; *(of stolen goods)* recel *m*
2 *(of tool)* maniement *m*; *(of explosives)* manipulation *f*; *(of a ship)* manœuvre *f*
3 *(of a car)* maniabilité *f*, comportement *m* routier
4 *(treatment) (of person, subject etc)* traitement *m*; **rough h.** traitement brutal
5 *(of crisis, situation)* prise *f* en main; *(of funds)* maniement *m*
6 *Com* manutention *f*, distribution *f*
7 *Ftbl* (faute *f* de) main *f*
▸▸ **h. capacity** capacité *f* de traitement; **h. charges** frais *mpl* de traitement; *(for physically shifting goods)* frais de manutention; **h. fee** frais d'administration

handmade ['hænd'meɪd] ADJ fait *ou* fabriqué à la main, fait main

handmaid ['hænd'meɪd], **handmaiden** ['hændmeɪd(ə)n] N *Old-fashioned* servante *f*

hand-me-down N *Fam* hand-me-downs, **h. clothes** vêtements usagés *ou* d'occasion, frusques *fpl*; **I used to wear my brother's hand-me-downs** je récupérais les vêtements usagés de mon frère

hand-out, handout ['hændaʊt] N **1** *Pej (alms)* aumône *f*; *(food)* = nourriture *f* distribuée aux pauvres; **I don't want to live off hand-outs** je ne veux pas vivre de la charité des autres; **state** or **government h.** aumône du gouvernement **2** *Journ* compte rendu *m* communiqué à la presse, communiqué *m*; *Sch, Univ* notes *fpl* (polycopiées), polycopié *m* (donné aux élèves etc) **3** *Com (brochure)* prospectus *m*, brochure *f*, tract *m*; *(sample)* cadeau *m* publicitaire

handover ['hændəʊvər] N *(of hostage, ransom)* remise *f*; **h. of power** passation *f* de pouvoirs

hand-pick VT *(fruit etc)* cueillir à la main; **the volunteers have been hand-picked** les volontaires ont été triés sur le volet

hand-picked ['hænd'pɪkt] ADJ *(fruit etc)* cueilli à la main; *(person, team)* trié sur le volet

handrail ['hændreɪl] N *(of staircase etc)* rampe *f*, main *f* courante; *(of bridge etc)* garde-fou *m*, *pl* garde-fous, garde-corps *m inv*, *Naut, Rail* rambarde *f*

handsaw ['hændsɔː] N scie *f* à main

handset ['hændset] N *Tel* **1** *(of telephone)* combiné *m* **2** *(mobile phone)* téléphone *m* portable

hands-free ADJ *Tel (phone, dialling)* mains libres; **phone with h. facility** téléphone *m* avec fonction mains-libres

handshake ['hændʃeɪk] N **1** poignée *f ou* serrement *m* de main **2** *Comput* dialogue *m* d'établissement de liaison
▸▸ *Comput* **h. message** message *m* d'établissement de liaison, message de prise de contact

handshaking ['hændʃeɪkɪŋ] N *Comput* établissement *m* d'une liaison

hands-off ADJ *Pol* non-interventionniste; **the director has a h. style of management** le directeur est partisan de laisser de l'autonomie à son personnel, *Pej* le directeur a un sens très large de la délégation de pouvoir

handsome ['hænsəm] ADJ **1** *(good-looking)* beau, *f* belle; **a h. man** un bel homme; **she was a h. woman** c'était une belle femme; **a h. building** une belle construction **2** *(conduct etc)* gracieux, généreux; *(praise, apology)* sincère, sans réserve; **he received very h. treatment** on l'a traité d'une façon très généreuse **3** *(considerable) (price)* bon; *(gift)* généreux; **to make a h. profit** faire *ou* réaliser de beaux bénéfices; **h. fortune** belle fortune; **a h. sum** une coquette somme

handsomely ['hænsəmlɪ] ADV **1** *(dressed, furnished etc)* bien **2** *(to act)* généreusement; *(to treat, praise, apologize)* avec sincérité, sans réserve; *(to pay)* libéralement

handsomeness ['hænsəmnɪs] N **1** *(of person, monument etc)* beauté *f* **2** *(of an action)* générosité *f*; *(of reward)* libéralité *f*; *(of an apology)* sincérité *f*

hands-on ADJ *(experience)* pratique; **h. exhibition** *(at museum)* = exposition *f* où les gens sont encouragés à toucher aux objets; **the director has a h. style of management** le directeur n'a pas peur de mettre la main à la pâte

handspring ['hændsprɪŋ] N *Gym* saut *m* de mains

handstand ['hændstænd] N *Gym* **to do a h.** faire un équilibre sur les mains, faire l'arbre droit

hand-to-hand ADJ *(fighting)* corps-à-corps
ADV **to fight h.** se battre au corps-à-corps

hand-to-mouth ADJ, ADV **to live h.**, **to lead a h. existence** tirer le diable par la queue

hand-tooling N **1** *Tech (on a lathe etc)* tra-

vail *m* à la main **2** *(in bookbinding)* dorure *f* à froid faite à la main

handwork ['hændwɜːk] N travail *m* fait à la main, travail manuel

handwriting ['hændraɪtɪŋ] N écriture *f*
▸▸ **h. expert** graphologue *mf*; *Comput* **h. recognition** reconnaissance *f* de l'écriture manuscrite

handwritten ['hændrɪt(ə)n] ADJ *(letter etc)* manuscrit

handy ['hændɪ] ADJ **1** *(useful) (tool etc)* pratique; *(ship)* maniable; **that would come in very h.** ça serait bien utile; **a h. tip** un bon conseil
2 *(convenient)* commode; **the flat's h. for the shops** l'appartement est tout près des commerces
3 *(within reach)* à portée (de la main); **I always keep my tools h.** j'ai toujours mes outils sous la main
4 *(skilful) (with one's hands)* adroit, habile *(de ses mains)*; **he's very h. about the house** *(good at making, repairing things)* c'est un bon bricoleur; **h. at sth/at doing sth** adroit à qch/à faire qch; **to be h. with one's fists** savoir se servir de ses poings

handyman, *pl* **handymen** ['hændɪmæn, -men] N *(employee)* homme *m* à tout faire *ou* à toutes mains; *(DIY expert etc)* bricoleur *m*; *Am* **h.'s special** = maison *f* qui a besoin de beaucoup de travaux

HANG [hæŋ] N **1** *(of clothing)* tombé *m*; *(material)* drapé *m*
2 *Fam* **to get the h. of sth** *(understand)* comprendre qch, piger qch; **when you've got the h. of it** *(acquired skill)* quand tu auras attrapé le coup; **I haven't got the h. of this new keyboard yet** je ne connais pas encore très bien ce nouveau clavier!; **when you've got the h. of things** *(in new office, job etc)* quand vous serez au courant
3 *Fam* **I don't give** or **care a h.** je m'en moque *ou* m'en fiche

VT *(pt, pp* hung [hʌŋ]) **1** *(suspend)* pendre, accrocher, suspendre **(on, from** à); *(door)* monter; **to h. a coat on a hook** pendre *ou* suspendre un manteau à une patère; **to h. sth on the wall** accrocher qch au mur; **they hung banners from their windows** ils ont accroché des bannières à leurs fenêtres; **to h. a picture** suspendre un tableau; *(exhibit)* exposer un tableau *(au Salon etc)*; **to h. wallpaper** poser du papier peint
2 *(droop)* **to h. one's head** baisser la tête
3 *(decorate)* **to h. a room with tapestries** tendre une salle de tapisseries; **hall hung with flags** salle ornée de drapeaux
4 *Culin (meat, game)* faire faisander
5 **to h. fire** *(of troops etc)* suspendre le feu; *Fig (of decision etc)* traîner (en longueur), faire traîner les choses
6 *(pt, pp* hanged [hæŋd]) *(criminal)* pendre; **he hanged himself** il s'est pendu; *Br Pol Fam Pej* **the h. 'em and flog 'em brigade** = les partisans *mpl* de la peine de mort et des châtiments corporels; *Fam* **I'm hanged if I know!** je n'en sais fichtre *ou* foutre rien!; **h. it!** zut!, mince alors!; *Prov* **as well be hanged for a sheep as for a lamb** quitte à avoir des ennuis, autant que ça en vaille la peine; *Hist* **to be hanged, drawn and quartered** être pendu, éventré et écartelé; *Fig* **he was hanged, drawn and quartered by the press** il s'est fait étriper par la presse

VI 1 *(be suspended)* pendre, être suspendu; *Culin (of game)* se faisander; **a picture hanging on the wall** un tableau pendu *ou* accroché au mur; **he was hanging by his arms from the tree** il était suspendu à l'arbre par les bras; **to h. out of the window** *(of person)* se pencher à la fenêtre; *(of object)* pendre à la fenêtre

2 *(of drapery, clothes etc)* tomber, se draper; **to h. loose** *or* **limply** pendiller, *Fam* pendouiller; **his clothes h. loosely on him** il flotte dans ses vêtements; *esp Am Sl* **h. loose!** relax, Max!; *Am Sl* **to h. tough** s'accrocher; *Sl* **how's it hanging?** *(how are you?)* comment ça va?; **this door hangs badly** cette porte est mal suspendue (sur ses gonds); **time hangs heavy (on my hands)** le temps me pèse *ou* me semble long

3 *Am Fam (spend time)* traîner; **he's hanging with his friends** il traîne avec ses copains

4 *(of criminal)* être pendu; **to h. for murder** être pendu pour meurtre; *Fig Fam* **if he doesn't like it he can go h.** si ça ne lui plaît pas, qu'il aille se faire pendre; *Old-fashioned* **you'll h. for this!** tu seras pendu pour ça!

▸ **hang about, hang around** vi *Fam* **1** *(wait)* poireauter; **to keep sb hanging about** faire poireauter qn; **h. about, that's not what I said!** eh, minute! ce n'est pas ce que j'ai dit!

2 *(waste time)* traîner, flâner; **to h. about the house doing nothing** traîner à la maison sans rien faire; **young men hanging about on street corners** jeunes qui traînent dans les rues; **don't h. about or we'll never finish!** ne perds pas de temps ou nous n'aurons jamais fini!; *Fam* **you don't h. about, do you!** vous êtes un/une rapide, vous!; *Fam* **this car doesn't h. about** cette voiture est un vrai bolide

3 *(associate)* **to h. about with sb** traîner avec qn

vt insep *(frequent) (place)* fréquenter, traîner dans

▸ **hang back** vi *(not go forward)* rester en arrière; *(hesitate)* hésiter; **to h. back from doing sth** hésiter à faire qch

▸ **hang down** vi pendre **(from sth** de qch)

▸ **hang in** vi *esp Am Fam (persevere, not lose heart)* tenir bon, persévérer; **just h. in there** courage, tenez bon

▸ **hang on** vi **1** *(hold)* se cramponner, s'accrocher; **h. on tight!** cramponne-toi bien!

2 *Fam (wait)* patienter, attendre; *Tel* **h. on!** ne quittez pas!; **h. on for a moment** attendez un moment, patientez un instant

3 *(survive)* supporter, *Fam* tenir le coup; **to h. on by the skin of one's teeth** s'en sortir de justesse

vt insep **1** *(hold)* **to h. on sb's arm** *(of thing)* pendre au bras de qn; *(of person)* se pendre au bras de qn

2 *(be attentive to)* **to h. on sb's lips** *or* **words** être pendu aux lèvres de qn; **the children hung on his every word** les enfants buvaient ses paroles *ou* étaient suspendus à chacune de ses paroles

3 *(depend on)* dépendre de, tenir à; **everything hangs on his answer** tout dépend de sa réponse

vt sep *Am Sl* **to h. one on** *(get drunk)* prendre une cuite

▸ **hang on to** vt insep **1** *(hold tightly)* se cramponner à, ne pas lâcher; **he hung on to the cliff face** il s'est agrippé à la paroi de la falaise

2 *(keep)* garder; **I'd h. on to those documents if I were you** je garderais précieusement ces documents; **he hung on to these outdated ideas** il se raccrochait à ces idées démodées; **to h. on to an opinion** persister dans son opinion; **he hung on to his version of events** il a maintenu sa version des faits

▸ **hang out** vt sep *(suspend) (object)* pendre *ou* mettre au dehors; **to h. out the washing** étendre le linge; **to h. out a flag** arborer un pavillon

vi **1** *(be suspended)* pendre (au dehors); **the rocks h. out over the gully** les rochers surplombent le ravin; **his shirt was hanging out** sa chemise dépassait; *Sl* **to let it all h. out** se défouler

2 *Fam (spend time)* traîner; **to h. out with one's friends** traîner avec ses amis; **he hangs out at the local bar** c'est un habitué du café du coin

▸ **hang over** vt insep *(hover over)* planer *ou* peser sur; **a thick fog hangs over the town** un épais brouillard plane sur la ville; **a heavy silence hung over the meeting** un lourd silence pesait sur l'assemblée; **to have a threat hanging over one** avoir une menace qui pèse sur soi; **a question mark is hanging over the outcome of the debate** il reste un point d'interrogation quant à l'issue du débat; **I have an appointment with the dentist hanging over me** il y a une visite chez le dentiste qui me pend au nez; **we've got the threat of eviction hanging over us** nous risquons d'être expulsés d'une minute à l'autre

▸ **hang together** vi **1** *(of people)* rester unis **2** *(of statements etc)* s'accorder, *Fam* tenir debout

▸ **hang up** vt sep *(hat, picture etc)* accrocher, pendre, suspendre; *Fig* **to h. up one's boots/ racket** *(retire)* raccrocher

vi *Tel* raccrocher (l'appareil); **to h. up on sb** raccrocher au nez de qn

hangar ['hæŋər] N *esp Aviat* hangar *m*

hangdog ['hæŋdɒg] ADJ **h. look** air *m* de chien battu

hanger ['hæŋər] N **(coat** *or* **clothes) h.** cintre *m*

hanger-on, *pl* **hangers-on** N parasite *m*, pique-assiette *m inv*

hang-glide vi faire du deltaplane

hang-glider N *(craft)* deltaplane® *m*; *(person)* libériste *mf*

hang-gliding N *(sport m* du) deltaplane® *m*; **to go h.** faire du deltaplane®

hanging ['hæŋɪŋ] ADJ *(hook etc)* pendant; *Geog (valley)* suspendu

N **1** *(execution)* pendaison *f*, *Fig* **it's not a h. offence** ce n'est pas un crime gravissime **2** *(of picture etc)* suspension *f*, *(of door)* montage *m*, accrochage *m*; *(of wallpaper)* pose *f* **3 (wall) h.** tenture *f*, tapisserie *f*

▸▸ *Art* **h. committee** = comité *m* de réception *ou* jury d'admission des tableaux; **h. cupboard** armoire *f* murale; **the H. Gardens of Babylon** les jardins *mpl* suspendus de Babylone; *Comput* **h. indent** présentation *f* en sommaire; *Law* **h. judge** juge *m* à la main lourde; **h. paragraph** paragraphe *m* en sommaire; **h. valley** vallée *f* suspendue; **h. wardrobe** penderie *f*

hangman, *pl* **hangmen** ['hæŋmən] N **1** bourreau *m* **2** *(game)* le pendu

hangnail ['hæŋneɪl] N envie *f*

hang-out N *Fam (haunt)* repaire *m*, nid *m*, endroit *m* favori; **this is one of his hang-outs** c'est l'un des endroits où on le trouve le plus souvent; **it's a real student h.** c'est un endroit très fréquenté par les étudiants

hangover ['hæŋəʊvər] N **1** *(from drinking)* **to have a h.** avoir la gueule de bois, *Hum* avoir mal aux cheveux **2** *(practice, belief etc)* reliquat *m*; **a h. from the past** un reliquat du passé

hang-up N **1** *Fam (complex)* complexe *m*; **he's got a h. about driving** il fait un blocage, il ne veut pas conduire; **you've got a lot of hang-ups** tu es très complexé **2** *Comput* arrêt *m* imprévu

hank [hæŋk] N *(of wool etc)* écheveau *m*; *(of thread)* peignée *f*

hanker ['hæŋkər] vi **to h. after** *or* **for sth** avoir bien envie de qch, soupirer après qch, convoiter qch

hankering ['hæŋkərɪŋ] N vif désir *m*, grande envie *f* (**after, for** de); **to have a h. for sth** avoir grande envie de qch

hankie, hanky ['hæŋkɪ] N *Fam* mouchoir *m*

hanky-panky ['hæŋkɪ'pæŋkɪ] N *Fam* **1** *(sexual activity)* batifolage *m*, galipettes *fpl* **2** *(underhand behaviour)* coup *m* fourré, entourloupette *f*

Hanoverian [hænə'vɪərɪən] ADJ hanovrien N Hanovrien, -ienne

Hansard ['hænsɑːd] N *Br Parl* = compte *m* rendu officiel des débats parlementaires

Hanseatic [hænsɪ'ætɪk] ADJ *Hist* **the H. League** la Ligue hanséatique

hansom ['hænsəm] N *Hist* cab *m* ▸▸ *Hist* **h. cab** cab *m*

Hants [hænts] *abbr* Hampshire

ha'penny, *pl* **ha'pence** ['heɪpənɪ, -pəns] N *Br Fam* = **halfpenny**

haphazard [hæp'hæzəd] ADJ *(attempt)* au petit bonheur (la chance); *(arrangement)* fortuit; **to choose in a h. way** choisir à l'aveuglette

haphazardly [hæp'hæzədlɪ] ADV au petit bonheur (la chance), à l'aveuglette

hapless ['hæplɪs] ADJ *Arch, Lit* infortuné, malheureux

HAPPEN ['hæp(ə)n] vi *(take place)* arriver, se passer, se produire; **it happened ten years ago** cela s'est passé il y a dix ans; **did anyone see what happened?** *(of accident, incident)* quelqu'un a-t-il vu ce qui s'est passé *ou* est arrivé?; **it happens over and over again** c'est toujours la même chose; **don't let it h. again!** que cela n'arrive plus!, que cela ne se reproduise pas!; **it couldn't h. here** ce n'est pas ici que ça arriverait; **I don't like what's happening in this country** je n'aime pas ce qui se passe dans ce pays; **just as if nothing had happened** comme si de rien n'était; **whatever happens** quoi qu'il arrive; **as it happens** justement, précisément; **as often happens** comme il est fréquent; **what has happened to him?** *(what has occurred?)* qu'est-ce qui lui est arrivé?; *(what has become of him?)* qu'est-ce qu'il est devenu?; **if anything happens to me** *(if I die)* s'il m'arrive quelque chose; **what's happened to my pen?** *(where is it?)* qu'est-ce qu'on a fait de mon stylo?; *(what's wrong with it?)* qu'est-il arrivé à mon stylo?

vt *(chance)* **I happened to pass that way** il se trouve que je passais par là; **a taxi happened to be passing** par hasard *ou* par bonheur, un taxi passait; **I h. to know that …** il se trouve que je sais que …; **do you h. to know whether …?** sauriez-vous par hasard si …?; **it just so happens that …** il se trouve justement que …; **if you h. to find it** s'il arrive que vous le trouviez; **she happens to be my sister** il se trouve qu'elle est ma sœur

▸ **happen along, happen by** vi *(arrive by chance)* arriver par hasard

▸ **happen on, happen upon** vt insep *(come across) (person, object)* tomber sur

happening ['hæp(ə)nɪŋ] N événement *m*; *Theat* happening *m*

ADJ *Fam (fashionable)* branché, dans le coup

happenstance ['hæp(ə)nstæns] N *esp Am* **it was h.** c'était le hasard, c'était le fait d'un heureux hasard

happily ['hæpɪlɪ] ADV **1** heureusement; **they laughed h.** ils rirent de bon cœur; **we were sitting there quite h. watching television** nous étions installés tout tranquillement devant la télévision; **to live h.** vivre heureux; **a h. married couple** un ménage heureux; **they lived h. ever after** *(at end of fairy story)* ≃ ils furent heureux et eurent beaucoup d'enfants; **he'll quite h. say one**

thing and do the opposite ça ne le gêne pas de dire une chose et de faire exactement le contraire **2** *(fortunately)* heureusement

happiness ['hæpɪnɪs] **N** bonheur *m*, félicité *f*

happy ['hæpɪ] **ADJ 1** *(content)* heureux; **to be h. to do sth** être heureux *ou* content de faire qch; **h. to oblige** ravi de rendre service; **to make sb h.** rendre qn heureux; **his money hasn't made him h.** l'argent n'a pas fait son bonheur; **a h. life** une vie heureuse; **a h. ending** une fin heureuse; **to have a h. ending** bien se terminer; **to be as h. as the day is long** être heureux comme un poisson dans l'eau; **as h. as a lark** *or* **a sandboy** gai comme un pinson; **those were h. days** c'était le bon temps; **in happier circumstances** dans des circonstances plus favorables; **in happier times** en des jours meilleurs; **I'm very h. with his work** je suis très satisfait *ou* content de son travail; **I'm not at all h. about it** cela ne me plaît pas du tout; **if you are h. with these conditions ...** si vous êtes satisfait de ces conditions ...; **give me a good book and I'm h.** un bon livre suffit à me satisfaire; **to keep sb h.** satisfaire qn; **this game keeps the children h. for hours** avec ce jeu, les enfants sont contents pendant des heures; *Fam* **he's not a h. camper** *or Br* **chappy** *or* **bunny** il est pas jouasse; *Old-fashioned Fam* **to be h.** *(drunk)* être un peu gris; **h. birthday!** joyeux *ou* bon anniversaire!; **h. Christmas!** joyeux Noël!; *Fam* **h. days!** *(as toast)* à votre santé!
2 *(wording etc)* bien choisi, à propos; *(coincidence)* heureux
▸▸ **h. families** *(card game)* jeu *m* des sept familles; **h. hour** *(in pub, bar)* happy hour *f (heure, généralement en début de soirée, pendant laquelle les boissons sont moins chères)*; **h. medium** équilibre *m*, juste milieu *m*

happy-clappy [hæpɪ'klæpɪ] *Br Fam Pej* **ADJ** *(service, meeting, Christian)* d'une joie exubérante et agaçante
N chrétien, -ienne évangélique

happy-go-lucky **ADJ** *(person)* sans souci, insouciant; **to do sth in a h. fashion** faire qch au petit bonheur

Hapsburg ['hæpsbɜːg] **N** *Hist* Habsbourg

harangue [hə'ræŋ] **N** harangue *f*
VT haranguer; **to h. sb into doing sth** sermonner qn pour qu'il fasse qch

harass ['hærəs, hə'ræs] **VT 1** *Mil (enemy forces)* harceler, tenir en alerte **2** *(pester) (person)* tracasser, tourmenter, harceler; *(sexually)* harceler; **to h. sb to do sth** harceler qn pour qu'il fasse qch; **to h. sb into doing sth** harceler qn jusqu'à ce qu'il fasse qch; **he was harassing me for money** il me harcelait pour que je lui donne de l'argent

Note that the French verb **harasser** is a false friend and is never a translation for the English verb **to harass**. It means **to exhaust**.

harassed [hə'ræst] **ADJ** stressé

harassment ['hærəsmənt, hə'ræs-] **N** *(pestering)*, *Mil* harcèlement *m*; **police h.** tracasseries *fpl* policières; **sexual h.** harcèlement sexuel

harbinger ['haːbɪndʒər] **N** *Lit* avant-coureur *m*, *pl* avant-coureurs; **the riot was a h. of things to come** la bagarre annonçait ce qui allait arriver

harbour, *Am* **harbor** ['haːbər] **N** *Naut* port *m*; *(of small port)* lieutenant de port
VT *(person)* héberger, donner asile à; *(criminal)* receler, cacher; *(dirt)* attirer, garder, retenir; *(suspicions)* entretenir, nourrir; **to h. a grudge against sb** garder rancune à qn

▸▸ **h. dues** droits *mpl* de port; **h. lights** lumières *fpl* du port; **h. master** capitaine *m* de port; **h. terminal** gare *f* maritime

HARD [haːd]

| **ADJ** | dur **1–3** ▪ concret **1** ▪ difficile **2** ▪ rude **4** |
| **ADV** | dur **1** ▪ fort **1** ▪ difficilement **2** |

ADJ 1 *(substance etc)* dur; *(snow)* durci; **to become** *or* **get h.** *(of cement etc)* durcir; **to become harder** durcir *ou* se durcir davantage; *Fig* **h. fact** fait *m* brut; **the h. facts** la dure réalité; **the h. fact is that there isn't enough money** la vérité, c'est qu'il n'y a pas assez d'argent; **the argument was not backed up by any h. fact** l'argument ne s'appuyait sur rien de concret; **there's no h. evidence** il n'y a pas de preuve tangible; *Br Fam* **h. luck!, h. lines!**; **h. cheese!** pas de chance!, quelle guigne!
2 *(difficult)* difficile; *(task)* pénible; **to learn the h. way** apprendre à ses dépens; **I learnt it the h. way** j'en ai bavé et maintenant, je le sais; **to do things the h. way** *(through choice)* se compliquer la vie; *(due to circumstances)* en baver; **h. work** *(working hard)* travail *m* assidu; *(hard task)* *(difficult)* tâche *f* difficile; *(strenuous)* travail ingrat; **he's not afraid of h. work** le travail ne lui fait pas peur; **it was h. work to convince him** j'ai eu fort à faire pour le convaincre; **it is h. work for me to ...**, **I find it h. work to ...** j'ai beaucoup de peine *ou* bien du mal à ...; **it was h. work!** (que) c'était dur!; **the hardest part of the job is done** le plus dur est fait; **to play h. to get** jouer les insaisissables; **to be h. to please** être exigeant *ou* difficile à contenter; **to be h. of hearing** être dur d'oreille; **the h. of hearing** les malentendants *mpl*; **the laws make it h. to leave the country** à cause des lois, il est difficile de quitter le pays; **I find it h. to believe that ...** j'ai peine à croire que ... **+ subj**; **it is h. to understand** c'est difficile à comprendre; **it's h. to say** c'est difficile à dire; **that book was h. to read** ce livre était difficile à lire; **to have a h. fight** *or* **struggle on one's hands** avoir une lourde tâche devant soi
3 *(severe, harsh)* *(person, manner etc)* dur, sévère (**to, towards** envers); *(master)* sévère, exigeant; *(heart)* dur; *Phot (print)* heurté, contrasté; **a h. man** *(tough)* un dur; **he's h.** *(a hard man)* c'est un dur; **to be h. on sb** être sévère envers qn; **it's hardest on the children** le plus dur, c'est pour les enfants; **it's h. to lose a child** c'est une épreuve de perdre un enfant; **to say h. things to sb** avoir des mots très durs pour qn, dire des choses très dures à qn; **it's a h. blow for him** c'est un coup terrible pour lui; **no h. feelings?** tu ne m'en veux pas?; **a h. life** une vie difficile *ou* dure; **times are h.** les temps sont durs *ou* difficiles; **he's been giving her a h. time** il lui en a fait voir de toutes les couleurs; **to have a h. time of it** en voir de rudes; **to be as h. as nails** ne pas avoir de cœur; *(physically)* être un vrai dur
4 *(intense)* **to try one's hardest** faire tout son possible; **to be a h. worker** travailler dur; **a h. winter** un hiver rude *ou* rigoureux; **a h. frost** une forte gelée; *Com* **to give sth the h. sell** promouvoir qch de façon très agressive
5 h. drinker gros *ou* grand buveur *m*; *Fam* **a drop of the h. stuff** une goutte d'alcool *ou* d'eau-de-vie
6 *Fin (stock, rates)* soutenu, ferme
ADV 1 *(vigorously)* fort; **as h. as one can** de toutes ses forces; **to hit** *or* **strike h.** cogner dur; **to push/pull h.** pousser/tirer fort; **to jam on the brakes h.** serrer les freins à bloc; **to look** *or* **gaze** *or* **stare h. at sb** regarder fixement qn; **we can't find it – well, look**

harder! nous ne le trouvons pas – et bien cherchez mieux!; **you didn't look very h.!** tu n'as pas bien cherché; **to try h.** faire de son mieux; **to try harder** faire plus d'efforts; **to think h.** réfléchir profondément; **to work h. at sth** travailler dur à qch; **she works too h.** elle se surmène; **to be h. at work** être en plein travail; **he works h. and plays h.** il se dépense beaucoup dans son travail et dans ses loisirs; **to play h.** *(roughly)* avoir un jeu *(très)* physique; **to drink h.** boire beaucoup; **it's raining h.** il pleut à verse; **to turn h. to the left** braquer à gauche, faire un virage très sec vers la gauche; **to swim h. for the shore** nager de toutes ses forces vers le rivage; *Naut* **h. over!** la barre toute!
2 *(with difficulty)* difficilement, avec peine; **you'd be h. pushed** *or* **pressed** *or* **put to find a shop open at this time** tu vas avoir du mal à trouver une boutique ouverte à cette heure-ci; **she took the news h.** elle a très mal pris la nouvelle; *Old-fashioned* **it will go h. with him if ...** cela sera sérieux (pour lui) si ...
3 *(near)* **to follow h. (up)on** *or* **after** *or* **behind sb** suivre qn de près; **his resignation followed h. (up)on this news** sa démission a suivi tout de suite cette nouvelle; *Old-fashioned* **h. by** tout près, tout contre
4 *Fam (harshly)* **to feel h. done by** se sentir traité de façon injuste
▸▸ *Typ, Comput* **h. carriage return** retour *m* chariot obligatoire; **h. cash** (argent *m*) liquide *m*; *Fin* **h. commodities** minerais *mpl*, *Ling* **h. consonant** consonne *f* dure; *Comput* **h. copy** copie *f* sur papier, sortie *f* papier; **h. core** *(nucleus)* noyau *m* dur; *Constr* empierrement *m*; *Mus* **hard rock** *m* inv; **hard** *m* inv; *(pornography)* porno *m* hard; *Br Tennis* **h. court** court *m* en ciment; **h. currency** monnaie *f ou* devise *f* forte; *Comput* **h. disk** disque *m* dur; *Comput* **h. drive** unité *f* de disque dur; **h. drug** drogue *f* dure; *Horseriding* **h. gallop** galop *m* soutenu; **h. hat** *(of construction worker)* casque *m*; *Am Fam (construction worker)* ouvrier *m* du bâtiment; *Typ, Comput* **h. hyphen** césure *f* imposée, trait *m* d'union imposé; **h. labour** travaux *mpl* forcés; *Metal* **h. lead** plomb *m* aigre; *Pol* **the h. left** l'extrême gauche *f*; *Tech* **h. light** lumière *f* crue; **h. line** ligne *f* de conduite dure; **the president takes a h. line on drugs** le président a pris une position très ferme concernant la drogue; **h. liquor** spiritueux *mpl*; *Fin* **h. loan** prêt *m* aux conditions du marché; *Journ* **h. news** nouvelles *fpl* sûres *ou* vérifiées; *Typ, Comput* **h. page break** fin *f* de page obligatoire; *Anat* **h. palate** voûte *f* du palais, palais *m* dur; **h. porn** porno *m* hard; *Comput* **h. reset** réinitialisation *f* totale de la machine; *Typ, Comput* **h. return** saut *m* de ligne manuel; *esp Am Culin* **h. sauce** = sauce *f* au beurre, au sucre et au brandy *ou* au rhum servie avec le pudding; **h. sell** vente *f* agressive; *Aut* **h. shoulder** bande *f* d'arrêt d'urgence; *Typ* **h. space** espace *m* insécable; *Econ* **h. terms** conditions *fpl* du marché; **h. water** eau *f* calcaire *ou* dure

hard-and-fast **ADJ** *(rule etc)* absolu

hardback ['haːdbæk] **N** livre *m* cartonné; **the book is only available in h.** ce livre n'est disponible qu'en version cartonnée
ADJ *(book)* cartonné

hard-bitten **ADJ** *Fam (person)* dur à cuire

hardboard ['haːdbɔːd] **N** *Constr* carton *m* dur, Isorel® *m*

hard-boiled **ADJ** *Fam (person)* dur à cuire
▸▸ *Culin* **h. egg** œuf *m* dur

hard-core **ADJ** *(reactionary, supporter)* de la tendance dure
▸▸ *Mktg* **h. loyal** fidèle *mf* absolu(e); *Mktg*

loyalty fidélité *f* absolue; **h. pornography** pornographie *f* hard

hardcover [ˈhɑːdkʌvər] **N** *esp Am* = **hardback**

hard-earned **ADJ** *(money etc)* péniblement gagné; *(prize)* bien mérité; **don't waste your h. wages** ne gaspille pas l'argent que tu as péniblement gagné

harden [ˈhɑːd(ə)n] **VT 1** *(something)* durcir, endurcir; *(steel etc)* tremper; *Med (muscles etc)* scléroser; **to h. oneself** *or* **to become hardened to the cold** s'endurcir *ou* s'aguerrir au froid; **to h. sb's heart** endurcir le cœur à qn (**to sb** à l'égard de qn) **2** *Metal* = **case-harden 3** = **harden off**

VI 1 *(of substance)* (se) durcir, s'endurcir; *(of person, constitution)* s'endurcir, s'aguerrir; **attitudes have hardened** les attitudes se sont durcies; **scientific opinion has hardened to the view that ...** de plus en plus, les scientifiques sont d'avis que ... **2** *Fin (of shares etc)* se raffermir; **prices are hardening** les prix sont en hausse

▶ **harden off** **VT SEP** **to h. off seedlings** fortifier de jeunes plantes

▶ **harden up** **VI** *Fin (of shares etc)* se raffermir

hardened [ˈhɑːd(ə)nd] **ADJ** *(substance)* durci, endurci; *(steel, glass)* trempé; *(criminal)* endurci

hardener [ˈhɑːd(ə)nər] **N** *(for paint, glue)* durcisseur *m*

hardening [ˈhɑːd(ə)nɪŋ] **N 1** durcissement *m*, endurcissement *m*, affermissement *m*; *Metal (of steel)* trempe *f*, *Med* **h. of the arteries** durcissement *m ou* sclérose *f* des artères; *Fig* **a h. of attitudes** un durcissement des attitudes; *Fin* **a h. of prices** un raffermissement des prix **2** *Metal* = **case-hardening**

hard-faced, **hard-featured** [ˈhɑːdˈfeɪst, -ˈfiːtʃəd] **ADJ** *(person)* aux traits durs *ou* sévères

hard-fought **ADJ** vivement contesté

hard-hat **ADJ** *esp Am* = caractéristique des attitudes conservatrices et des préjugés attribués aux ouvriers de la construction

hard-headed **ADJ 1** *(tough)* dur, réaliste; *(realism)* sans concession; *(attitude)* réaliste; **h. business man** homme d'affaires réaliste **2** *esp Am (stubborn)* obstiné, têtu

hard-hearted [ˈhɑːdˈhɑːtɪd] **ADJ** *(person)* impitoyable, au cœur dur; *(attitude)* impitoyable

hard-hit **ADJ** gravement atteint *ou* touché; **one particularly h. village** un village touché de façon particulièrement dure

hard-hitting [hɑːdˈhɪtɪŋ] **ADJ** *(boxer)* qui frappe dur; *(critic, speech)* très dur; **the speech was a h. attack on this policy** le discours était une attaque directe contre cette politique

hardiness [ˈhɑːdɪnɪs] **N** robustesse *f*, vigueur *f*

hardline [ˈhɑːdlaɪn] **ADJ** *Pol etc (Conservative etc)* convaincu; *(policy)* intransigeant

hardliner [ˈhɑːdˈlaɪnər] **N** *Pol etc* dur *m*, dure *f*

hardly [ˈhɑːdlɪ] **ADV** *(scarcely)* à peine, ne ... guère; **h. anyone/anything** presque personne/rien; **h. ever** presque jamais; **she can h. read** c'est à peine si elle sait lire; **I need h. say ...** il va sans dire ...; **she would h. set her own house on fire** elle n'aurait sûrement pas mis le feu à sa propre maison; **he could h. have said that** il n'aurait sûrement pas dit cela VOIR GRAMMAIRE A78

hardness [ˈhɑːdnɪs] **N 1** *(of substance, water)* dureté *f*; *(of steel)* trempe *f*; *(of print, painting)* tons *mpl* heurtés **2** *(of task, problem)* difficulté *f*; *Med* **h. of hearing** surdité *f* partielle **3** *(harshness) (of rule etc)* sévérité *f*, ri-

gueur *f*; *(of person)* caractère *m* insensible, dureté *f*; **h. of heart** sécheresse *f* de cœur **4** *Fin (of market, shares)* raffermissement *m*

hard-nosed [ˈhɑːdnəʊzd] **ADJ** *esp Am Fam* = **hard-headed**

hard-on **N** *Sl* **to have a h.** bander, avoir la trique

hard-packed **ADJ** **h. snow** congère *f*

hard-pressed, **hard-pushed** [hɑːdˈprest, -ˈpʊʃt] **ADJ** *(troops, personnel)* très sollicité; *(funds, finances)* qui s'épuisent; *(debtor)* aux abois, fort embarrassé; *(tolerance, patience)* presqu'à bout; **to be h. to do sth** avoir du mal à faire qch; **to be h. for time** manquer de temps; **to be h. for money** être à court d'argent

hard-sectored [ˈhɑːdsektəd] **ADJ** *(disk)* à secteurs pré-définis

hardship [ˈhɑːdʃɪp] **N 1** *(circumstance)* privation *f*, (dure) épreuve *f*; **he has suffered great hardship(s)** il en a vu de rudes **2** *(suffering)* souffrance *f*, *(deprivation)* privation *f*; **to live in h.** vivre dans la misère

▶▶ **h. allowance** = aide *f* accordée à un étudiant en cas de graves problèmes financiers

hardtack [ˈhɑːdtæk] **N** *Naut* biscuit *m* de mer

hardtop [ˈhɑːdtɒp] **N** *Aut* hard-top *m*

hard-up **ADJ** *Fam* **to be h. (for money)** être fauché *ou* à sec; *Fam* **to be h. for volunteers/suggestions** manquer de bénévoles/suggestions

hardware [ˈhɑːdweər] **N** *(no pl)* **1** *Com* quincaillerie *f* **2** *Comput* matériel *m*, hardware *m*; **h. problem** problème *m* de matériel **3** *(weapons)* armement *m*; *Sl (gun)* pétard *m*, soufflant *m*

▶▶ **h. dealer** quincaillier, -ière; **h. shop, h. store** quincaillerie *f*

hard-wearing **ADJ** *(garment etc)* de bon usage; *(material)* durable

hard-wired [ˈhɑːdwaɪəd] **ADJ** *Comput* câblé

hard-won **ADJ** *(trophy, victory)* âprement disputé, remporté de haute lutte

hardwood [ˈhɑːdwʊd] **N** bois *m* dur

hard-working **ADJ** laborieux, travailleur, -euse, assidu

hardy [ˈhɑːdɪ] **ADJ 1** *(robust)* robuste; *Bot* résistant; *(shrub)* vivace; *(plant)* de pleine terre **2** *(courageous)* hardi, courageux, audacieux

▶▶ *Bot* **h. annual** plante *f* annuelle

hare [heər] **N** lièvre *m*; **doe h.** hase *f*, *Fig* **to run with the h. and hunt with the hounds** ménager la chèvre et le chou; *(play double game)* jouer double jeu; **to start a h.** *(in hunting)* lever un lièvre; *(in conversation)* donner un nouveau tour à la conversation; *Sport* **h. and hounds** ≃ jeu *m* de piste, rallye *m*

VI *Fam (of person)* courir comme un lièvre *ou* à toutes jambes; **to h. off after sb** s'élancer à la poursuite de qn

▶▶ *Sport* **h. coursing** chasse *f* à courre au lièvre

harebell [ˈheəbel] **N** *(plant)* campanule *f*

harebrained [ˈheəbreɪnd] **ADJ** écervelé, étourdi; **h. scheme** projet *m* insensé

harelip [ˈheəlɪp] **N** *Med* bec-de-lièvre *m*, *pl* becs-de-lièvre

harem [hɑːˈriːm, ˈheərəm] **N** harem *m*

haricot [ˈhærɪkəʊ] **N** haricot *m* blanc

▶▶ **h. bean** haricot blanc

hark [hɑːk] **VI** *esp Arch, Lit* prêter l'oreille (**at, to** à); **h.!** écoutez!; *Fam* **h. at him!** comme il y va!

▶ **hark back** **VI** *(recall)* **to h. back (to the past)** ressasser le passé; **to h. back to sth** *(in conversation)* ramener la conversation sur qch

harlequin [ˈhɑːlɪkwɪn] **N** *Theat* arlequin *m*; **h. coat** habit *m* bigarré

harlot [ˈhɑːlət] **N** *Arch, Lit* prostituée *f*

harm [hɑːm] **N** mal *m*; *(to reputation etc)* tort *m*; **to do h. to sb** faire du mal/du tort à qn; **what h. has she done you?** quel mal vous a-t-elle fait?; **it will do more h. than good** cela fera plus de mal que de bien; **that won't do any h.** cela ne gâtera rien; **it won't do him any h.** cela ne lui fera pas de mal; **to see no h. in sth** ne pas voir de mal à qch; **you will come to no h.** il ne vous arrivera pas de mal; **out of h.'s way** *(of fragile object etc)* à l'abri du danger, en sûreté; *(of dangerous object etc)* mis dans l'impossibilité de nuire à personne; **they put the china in a cupboard, out of h.'s way** ils ont mis la porcelaine à l'abri dans un placard; **put these chemicals where they'll be out of h.'s way** mets ces produits chimiques en lieu sûr; **there's no h. in saying so** il n'y a pas de mal à le dire; **there's no h. in trying** on peut toujours essayer

VT *(person) (physically)* faire du mal à; *(non-physically)* faire du mal *ou* du tort à, causer du tort à, nuire à; *(reputation)* salir; *(person's interests)* léser; *(health)* nuire à

harmful [ˈhɑːmfʊl] **ADJ** *(substances)* nocif; *(remarks)* nuisible; *(ideas, influence)* malfaisant, pernicieux; **it's h. to your health** cela nuit à votre santé; **in small doses the drug is not h.** à petites doses, ce médicament n'est pas dangereux; **it had a h. effect on her education** cela a eu des conséquences fâcheuses sur son éducation; **h. side-effects** effets secondaires dangereux

harmfully [ˈhɑːmfʊlɪ] **ADV** de façon nuisible *ou* dangereuse, dangereusement

harmfulness [ˈhɑːmfʊlnɪs] **N** nocivité *f*, nature *f* nuisible

harmless [ˈhɑːmlɪs] **ADJ** *(animal, person)* inoffensif; *(pastime)* innocent; *(drug, sex scenes etc)* anodin; **to render h.** *(explosives)* désamorcer; *(chemical)* neutraliser; **it was just a bit of h. fun** c'était pour rire; **h. gossip** propos inoffensifs

harmlessly [ˈhɑːmlɪslɪ] **ADV** sans faire de mal; *(to enjoy oneself)* innocemment; *(to tease)* gentiment

harmonic [hɑːˈmɒnɪk] **ADJ** harmonique **N 1** *Mus (of root)* harmonique *m*; *(on stringed instrument)* harmonique, son *m* flûté; **harmonics** sons harmoniques; *(science)* harmonie *f* **2** *Math, Phys (of wave motion)* harmonique *m*

▶▶ *Phys* **h. motion** mouvement *m* sinusoïdal; **h. series** *Mus* échelle *f* harmonique; *Math, Phys* série *f* harmonique

harmonica [hɑːˈmɒnɪkə] **N** harmonica *m*

harmonious [hɑːˈməʊnɪəs] **ADJ 1** *(combination, relationship)* harmonieux **2** *(music)* mélodieux

harmoniously [hɑːˈməʊnɪəslɪ] **ADV** harmonieusement; *(to work, live)* en harmonie

harmonium [hɑːˈməʊnɪəm] **N** *Mus* harmonium *m*

harmonization [hɑːmənaɪˈzeɪʃən] **N** harmonisation *f*

harmonize [ˈhɑːmənaɪz] **VT 1** *Mus (melody)* harmoniser **2** *(ideas etc)* harmoniser; *(texts etc)* faire s'accorder; *(colours etc)* allier, harmoniser (**with** avec)

VI 1 *Mus (of singer)* chanter en harmonie; *(of musician)* jouer en harmonie **2** *(of sounds, colours etc)* s'harmoniser; *(of people, ideas etc)* se mettre en harmonie, s'accorder (**with** avec); **colours that h. well** *(with one another)* couleurs qui vont bien ensemble

harmony [ˈhɑːmənɪ] **N 1** *Mus* harmonie *f*, **to study h.** étudier l'harmonie; **songs full of h.** chants mélodieux **2** *(of people, ideas etc)* harmonie *f*, accord *m*; *(of voices, instruments)* concert *m*; *(of texts)* concordance *f*; **to live in perfect h. (with sb)** vivre en parfaite intelligence (avec qn); **in h. with …** en accord avec …; **to be in h. with sb/sth** être en harmonie avec qn/qch

harness ['hɑːnɪs] **N 1** *(of horse)* harnais *m*, harnachement *m*; **draught h.** harnais d'attelage; *Fig* **to get back into h.** *(of person)* reprendre le collier; *Fig* **to die in h.** mourir à la peine *ou* au travail *ou* à la tâche; **to work in h. (with sb)** travailler de concert (avec qn) **2** *Aviat* **(parachute) h.** ceinture *f ou* harnais *m* (de parachutiste); *Ind, Aut etc* **(safety) h.** harnais (de sécurité) **3** *Tex (of loom)* harnais *m*

VT 1 *(horse)* harnacher; **to h. a horse to a cart** atteler un cheval à une charrette; *Fig* **to be harnessed to sth** être étroitement lié à qch **2** *(waterfall etc)* aménager; **to h. atomic energy for industrial purposes** mettre l'énergie nucléaire au service de l'industrie
▸▸**h. horse** cheval *m* d'attelage; *Sport* **h. race** course *f* attelée; **h. room** sellerie *f*

harnessing ['hɑːnɪsɪŋ] **N 1** *(of a horse)* harnachement *m* **2** *(of waterfall etc)* aménagement *m*; *(of energy)* exploitation *f*

harp [hɑːp] **N** *Mus* harpe *f*
▸ **harp on** **VI** revenir sans arrêt sur la même chose; **he's always harping on about inflation** il est toujours en train de nous rebattre les oreilles avec l'inflation

harpist ['hɑːpɪst] **N** *Mus* harpiste *mf*

harpoon [hɑː'puːn] **N** harpon *m*, lance *f*
VT harponner
▸▸**h. gun** *(on deck of ship)* canon *m* lance-harpon; *(hand-held)* fusil *m* à harpon

harpsichord ['hɑːpsɪkɔːd] **N** *Mus* clavecin *m*

harpsichordist ['hɑːpsɪkɔːdɪst] **N** *Mus* claveciniste *mf*

harpy ['hɑːpɪ] **N** *Myth* harpie *f*; *Fam* **old h.** vieille mégère *f*
▸▸**h. eagle** harpie *f*

harridan ['hærɪd(ə)n] **N** *Lit* vieille sorcière *f*

harrier ['hærɪər] **N** *(bird)* busard *m*

harrow ['hærəʊ] *Agr* **N** herse *f*
VT *(soil)* herser; *Fig* **to h. sb's feelings, to h. sb** déchirer le cœur à qn

harrowed ['hærəʊd] **ADJ ATTRIB** *Fig (appearance)* meurtri

harrowing ['hærəʊɪŋ] **ADJ** *(story etc)* poignant, navrant; *(cry)* déchirant; *(experience)* très douloureux, cruel

Harry ['hærɪ] **N** *Old-fashioned Br Fam* **to play old H. with sb** en faire voir des vertes et des pas mûres à qn; **to play old H. with sb's health** ruiner la santé de qn

harry ['hærɪ] **VT** *(enemy forces)* attaquer, harceler; **he was being harried by his creditors** il était harcelé par ses créanciers

harsh [hɑːʃ] **ADJ 1** *(rough to the touch)* dur, rêche, rude; *(taste)* âpre; *(sound)* strident; *(voice)* rude, rauque **2** *(severe, brutal) (character)* bourru; *(treatment)* dur; *(master, answer, climate, winter)* rude; *(punishment)* sévère, rude; *(light)* cru; **to be h. things to sb** dire des choses (très) dures à qn; **she was very h. about them** elle a été très dure à leur égard; **to be h. on sb** être dur avec qn; **h. words** mots *mpl* durs

harshly ['hɑːʃlɪ] **ADV** *(to answer etc)* durement, rudement; *(to treat sb)* sévèrement

harshness ['hɑːʃnɪs] **N 1** *(roughness to the touch)* dureté *f*, rudesse *f*; *(of light)* dureté, crudité *f*; *(of style, voice)* aspérité *f*; *(of climate etc)* rudesse; **the h. of these sounds** ces sons stridents **2** *(severity) (of punishment, law)* sévérité *f*

hart [hɑːt] **N** cerf *m*; *(in hunting)* cerf âgé de plus de cinq ans

harum-scarum ['heərəm'skeərəm] *Fam* **ADJ** étourdi, écervelé
ADV étourdiment
N écervelé, -ée

harvest ['hɑːvɪst] **N 1** *(of corn)* moisson *f*; *(of fruit)* récolte *f*, cueillette *f*; *(of wine)* vendange *f*, *Fig* récolte *f*; **a good/poor h.** une bonne/mauvaise récolte; **to get in the h.** faire la moisson; **to help with the h.** aider à la moisson; *Fig* **it yielded a rich h. of information** on a récolté beaucoup d'informations **2** *(time of year)* (temps *m ou* époque *f* de la) moisson; **at h. (time)** à l'époque de la moisson
VT *(corn)* moissonner; *(fruit)* récolter, faire la cueillette de; *Fig* récolter; *(market)* exploiter
VI rentrer *ou* faire la moisson
▸▸*Br* **h. festival** = action *f* de grâce après la rentrée des récoltes; *Br* **h. home** *(festival)* fête *f* de la moisson; *(harvesting)* moisson *f*; **h. moon** pleine lune *f* (de l'équinoxe d'automne); *Zool* **h. mouse** rat *m* des moissons; *Am, Scot* **h. thanksgiving** = action de grâce après la rentrée des récoltes

harvester ['hɑːvɪstər] **N 1** *(person)* moissonneur, -euse **2** *(machine)* moissonneuse *f*

harvesting ['hɑːvɪstɪŋ] **N** (rentrée *f* de la) moisson *f*

has-been **N** *Fam Pej (person)* ringard, -arde, has been *mf inv*; **he's a h.** il est fini, c'est un ringard

hash [hæʃ] **N 1** *Culin* hachis *m* **2** *Fam (mess)* **to make a h.(-up) of sth** faire un beau gâchis de qch; **he made a h. of everything** il a tout bousillé *ou* saboté; **to settle sb's h.** régler son compte à qn **3** *Sl (hashish)* hasch *m* **4** *(symbol)* dièse *m*
VT 1 *Culin* **to h. meat** hacher de la viande (en petits morceaux) **2** *Fam* = **hash up**
▸▸*Culin* **h. browns** = pommes *fpl* de terre rapées et sautées (présentées parfois sous forme de galette); *Typ* **h. sign** dièse *m*
▸ **hash over** **VT SEP** *esp Am Fam (discuss sth)* discuter
▸ **hash up** **VT SEP** *Fam (mess up) (something)* bousiller

hashed index [hæʃt] **N** *Comput* index *m* de totalisation

hashish ['hæʃiːʃ] **N** hachisch *m*

hasn't ['hæz(ə)nt] **CONTR** = **has not**, *see* **have**

hasp [hɑːsp] **N** *(on door)* loquet *m*; *(on book etc)* fermoir *m*; **(staple) h.** *(for padlocking)* moraillon *m*

hassle ['hæs(ə)l] *Fam* **N 1** *(inconvenience)* problème *m*, embêtement *m*; **it's too much h. going by train** c'est trop d'embêtements d'aller par le train; **all the h. of filling out the form** tous les embêtements pour remplir le formulaire **2** *(argument)* dispute *f*, **I don't want any h., right?** pas d'histoires, d'accord?; **the police give us a lot of h.** la police nous fait des tas d'histoires
VT *(person)* ennuyer, embêter; **he keeps hassling me for money** il n'arrête pas de m'embêter pour que je lui donne de l'argent

hassock ['hæsək] **N** *Rel* agenouilloir *m*

haste [heɪst] **N** hâte *f*, célérité *f*, **to do sth in h.** faire qch à la hâte *ou* en hâte; **a note written in h.** un billet écrit à la hâte; *Fml* **to make h.** se hâter, se presser, se dépêcher (**to do sth** de faire qch); *Prov* **more h. less speed** plus on se hâte moins on avance

hasten ['heɪs(ə)n] *esp Lit, Fml* **VT** *(one's pace etc)* accélérer; *(person's departure)* hâter, presser, avancer; **to h. the hour when …** hâter l'heure où …
VI se hâter, se dépêcher, se presser (**to do sth** de faire qch); **I don't agree with him, I h. to add** je m'empresse d'ajouter que je ne suis pas d'accord avec lui

hastily ['heɪstɪlɪ] **ADV 1** *(quickly)* à la hâte, précipitamment **2** *(rashly)* de façon irréfléchie; *(to speak)* sans réfléchir; *(to judge sth)* à la légère, trop vite

hastiness ['heɪstɪnɪs] **N 1** *(speed)* précipitation *f*, hâte *f* **2** *(rashness)* irréflexion *f*

hasty ['heɪstɪ] **ADJ 1** *(departure, farewell)* précipité; *(sketch)* fait à la hâte; *(meal)* sommaire; **I sent him a h. note** je lui ai envoyé un billet écrit à la hâte; **to be too h. in doing sth** mettre trop de hâte à faire qch; **a h. decision** une décision hâtive; **to jump to a h. conclusion** conclure à la légère **2** *(short-tempered)* vif; **to have a h. temper** s'emporter facilement

hat [hæt] **N** chapeau *m*; **paper h.** chapeau en papier; *Fig* **I'm saying that with my lawyer's h. on** je dis ça en ma qualité de juriste; *Fig* **she wears several different hats in the company** elle remplit plusieurs rôles dans la société; **to put on/take off one's h.** mettre/enlever son chapeau; *Fig* **I take my h. off to him/you/etc!** chapeau!; **hats off!** chapeaux bas!; *Fig* **to hang up one's h.** raccrocher; *Fig* **to pass the h. round** faire passer le chapeau (à la ronde), faire la quête (**for sb/sth** pour qn/qch); *Fig* **to throw one's h. into the ring** se porter candidat; *Old-fashioned Fam* **my h.!** mon Dieu!; *Fam* **to talk through one's h.** parler à tort et à travers; *Fig Fam* **to keep sth under one's h.** garder qch pour soi; *Fam* **if that comes off I'll eat my h.** si ça réussit, je mange mon chapeau; *Fam* **that's old h.** c'est vieux jeu
▸▸*Br* **h. trick** *(three goals)* hat-trick *m*, *pl* hat-tricks; *(three wins)* trois victoires *fpl* consécutives; *Cr* = mise *f* hors jeu de trois batteurs avec trois balles de suite

hatband ['hætbænd] **N** ruban *m* de chapeau

hatbox ['hætbɒks] **N** carton *m* à chapeau

hatch[1] [hætʃ] **N 1** *Naut* descente *f*, écoutille *f*; *(cover)* panneau *m* de descente, panneau (d'écoutille); **cargo h.** panneau de chargement *ou* de déchargement; *Fam* **down the h.!** *(when drinking)* cul sec! **2** *(trap door)* trappe *f*, panneau *m* d'accès; **(service or serving) h.** passe-plats *m inv*; *Aviat etc* **(escape) h.** panneau d'évacuation **3** *Tech* vanne *f* d'écluse
▸▸**h. cover** panneau de descente, panneau (d'écoutille)

hatch[2] **N** *Agr* **1** *(of egg, clutch of birds)* éclosion *f* **2** *(clutch of birds)* couvée *f*
VT *(chickens)* faire éclore; *(eggs)* incuber, (faire) couver; *(in fish farming, of fish) (eggs)* incuber; *Fig* **to h. a plot** ourdir *ou* tramer un complot
VI *(of young birds, eggs)* éclore; **newly hatched chickens** poussins qui sortent de la coquille
▸ **hatch out** **VI** = **hatch**[2] **VI**

hatch[3] **VT** *(drawing)* hacher, hachurer

hatchback ['hætʃbæk] **N** *Aut* **1** *(car)* voiture *f* à hayon (arrière) **2** *(part, door)* hayon *m* (arrière)

hatchery ['hætʃərɪ] **N** *Agr* couvoir *m*, couveuse *f*; *(in fish farming)* appareil *m* à éclosion

hatchet ['hætʃɪt] **N** hachette *f*; *Fig* **to bury the h.** enterrer la hache de guerre
▸▸**h. face** visage *m* en lame de couteau; *Fam* **h. job** démolissage *m*; *Fam* **to do a h. job on sb/sth** démolir qn/qch; *Fam* **h. man** *(killer)* tueur *m* à gages; *Ind, Pol* = personne *f* dont le rôle est de restructurer une entreprise ou une organisation, le plus souvent à l'aide de mesures impopulaires

hatching ['hætʃɪŋ] **N** *(in drawing)* hachure(s) *f(pl)*

hatchway ['hætʃweɪ] **N** *Naut* descente *f*, écoutille *f*

hate [heɪt] **N 1** *(hatred)* haine *f* **2** *(object of dislike)* objet *m* d'aversion; **her pet h.** sa bête noire
VT *(somebody, something)* haïr, détester, exécrer; **I h. him** je le déteste, je le hais; **I h. classical music** je déteste la musique classique; **I h. myself for agreeing to it** je m'en veux d'y avoir consenti; **I h. it when he's in a bad mood** je déteste quand il est de mauvaise humeur; **to h. to do sth** détester (de) faire qch; **to h. doing sth** détester faire qch; **she hates having her hair washed** elle déteste qu'on lui lave les cheveux; **he hates to be contradicted** il ne peut pas souffrir qu'on le contredise; **she hates being kissed** elle a horreur qu'on l'embrasse; **I'd h. anyone to find out** je ne supporterais pas que quelqu'un l'apprenne; *Fam* **I h. to tell you, but I think you've missed your train** je regrette de devoir te le dire mais je pense que tu as raté ton train
▸ **h. mail** lettres *fpl* d'injures

hated [ˈheɪtɪd] **ADJ** détesté, haï
hateful [ˈheɪtfʊl] **ADJ** *(person, thing)* odieux, détestable
hatefully [ˈheɪtfʊlɪ] **ADV** odieusement, détestablement
hater [ˈheɪtər] **N** ennemi *m* **(of** de); **to be an animal-h.** détester les animaux
hatless [ˈhætlɪs] **ADJ** *(person)* sans chapeau, tête nue
hatpeg [ˈhætpeg] **N** patère *f*
hatpin [ˈhætpɪn] **N** épingle *f* à chapeau
hatrack [ˈhætræk] **N** porte-chapeaux *m inv*
hatred [ˈheɪtrɪd] **N** haine *f* **(of sb** de *ou* contre qn)
hatshop [ˈhætʃɒp] **N** *(for men)* chapellerie *f*, *(for women)* boutique *f* de modiste
hatstand [ˈhætstænd] **N** porte-chapeaux *m inv*
hatter [ˈhætər] **N** chapelier, -ière; *Prov* **he's as mad as a h.** il a un grain, il travaille du chapeau
haughtily [ˈhɔːtɪlɪ] **ADV** hautainement, d'une manière hautaine *ou* arrogante
haughtiness [ˈhɔːtɪnɪs] **N** hauteur *f*, arrogance *f*
haughty [ˈhɔːtɪ] **ADJ** hautain, arrogant
haul [hɔːl] **N 1** *(pull)* **to give a h. on sth** tirer sur qch
2 *(fish caught)* prise *f*, pêche *f*, *Fig (of thieves etc)* butin *m*; **drugs h.** saisie *f* de drogue; **to make** *or* **get a good h.** *(of fishermen)* faire (une) bonne pêche; *Fig (of thieves etc)* faire son butin; **you've got a good h.!** *(of presents)* c'est un joli tas de cadeaux que tu viens de recevoir!
3 *Fam (distance, journey)* parcours *m*, trajet *m*; *Aviat etc* **short/long h.** étape *f ou* distance *f* courte/longue; **there's still a long h. ahead** il reste un long chemin à parcourir; **it's a long h. from Glasgow to Naples** *(by road)* c'est un long trajet de Glasgow à Naples; **it's a real h.** c'est un sacré trajet
VT 1 *(pull)* tirer; *(load)* traîner; *(boat, train)* remorquer; *Fam* **to h. sb over the coals** réprimander qn, *Fam* passer un savon à qn **2** *Com (transport by road) (goods)* transporter par camions
VI 1 *(pull)* tirer, traîner; **they all hauled together** ils ont tous tiré ensemble; *Naut* **to h. on a rope** haler sur une manœuvre **2** *Naut (sail, move etc)* **to h. alongside** accoster
▸ **haul down VT SEP** *(bring down) (something)* descendre; *Naut (sails etc)* haler bas, affaler; *(flag)* rentrer
▸ **haul in VT SEP** *(bring in) (something)* tirer (à l'intérieur); *Naut (sail, nets)* amener; *Fam (suspects, people for questioning)* emmener; *Fam* **they hauled in some experts to back up**

their case ils ont amené des experts pour les soutenir
▸ **haul up VT SEP 1** *(hoist) (something)* monter; *Naut (flag)* hisser; **to h. up a boat** *(on ship)* rentrer une embarcation; *(on the beach)* haler un bateau à sec **2** *(call to account)* **to h. sb up** demander des comptes à qn **(for sth** de qch**); to be hauled up before the court** être traîné devant les tribunaux; **he was hauled up before the headmaster** il a dû se présenter devant le principal
haulage [ˈhɔːlɪdʒ] **N** *Com* **1** *(transportation)* *(transport m par)* roulage *m*, charriage *m*, camionnage *m*; **road h.** transports *mpl* routiers **2** *(costs)* frais *mpl* de roulage *ou* de transport
▸▸ **h. contractor** entrepreneur *m* de transports routiers
haulier [ˈhɔːlɪər], *Am* **hauler** [ˈhɔːlər] **N** *Com* camionneur *m*, entrepreneur *m* de transports, transporteur *m*; *(driver)* routier *m*
hauling [ˈhɔːlɪŋ] **N** *Naut* halage *m*
▸▸ **h. rope** câble *m* de halage
haunch [hɔːntʃ] **N 1** *Anat* hanche *f*; **haunches** arrière-train *m*; **sitting** *or* **squatting on his haunches** *(person)* accroupi; *(dog)* assis **2** *Culin (of venison)* cuissot *m*
haunt [hɔːnt] **N** retraite *f*, repaire *m*; *(of group of people)* rendez-vous *m inv*; **this pub was one of his haunts** ce pub était l'un de ses repaires; **the h. of existentialists** le lieu de rendez-vous des existentialistes
VT 1 *(of ghost) (house etc)* hanter **2** *(of person, animal) (place, person)* fréquenter **3** *(of thoughts etc) (person)* obséder, poursuivre; *(mind, sleep)* troubler, hanter; **to be haunted by memories** être obsédé par des souvenirs; **a lack of finance haunted the project** le problème du manque de moyens les a hantés tout le long du projet; **these problems have returned to h. us** ces problèmes nous minent une fois de plus
haunted [ˈhɔːntɪd] **ADJ** *(castle, room etc)* hanté; **he has a h. look** il a l'air égaré
haunting [ˈhɔːntɪŋ] **ADJ** *(melody, memory)* qui vous hante; *(memory etc)* obsédant
Havana [həˈvænə, -ˈvɑː-] **N 1** La Havane **2 a H. (cigar)** un havane

HAVE [hæv]

avoir **1–4, 6, 7, 10–12, 19** ▪ obtenir **3**
▪ prendre **5** ▪ faire faire **14**
▪ vouloir **15,16** ▪ mettre **17** ▪ devoir **18**
▪ être **19**

N *Fam* **the haves and the h.-nots** les riches *mpl* et les pauvres
VT VOIR GRAMMAIRE A55–7 *(pr* **have***; 3rd pers sing* **has** [hæz]*, 3rd pers pl* **have***; pr sub sing, pl* **have***; past, past* **had** [hæd]*, plural* **had**; *prp* **having***; pp* **had; have not, has not, had not** *are frequently shortened into* **haven't, hasn't, hadn't; I have, he has, we have** *etc into* **I've, he's, we've** *etc;* **I had** *etc into* **I'd** *etc)*
1 avoir; **a week has seven days** une semaine a sept jours; **he had no friends** il n'avait pas d'amis; **all I h.** tout ce que je possède *ou* que j'ai; **she has a shop** elle tient *ou* a une boutique; **he has big hands** il a de grosses mains; **my bag has no name on it** ma valise ne porte pas de nom; **she had the pen in her desk** le stylo était dans son bureau; **I h. nothing to do** je n'ai rien à faire; **I h. work to do** j'ai à travailler *ou* du travail; **to h. a right** avoir un droit, jouir d'un droit; **I h. it!** *(solution)* j'y suis!; *Br Fam* **come on!, let's be having you!** *(come forward)* allez, venez par ici!; *(hurry up!)* allez!, dépêche-toi; *Fam* **he had it coming to him** c'est bien fait pour lui, il a bien mérité; *Sl* **I'm not having any** *(I don't believe it)* ça ne prend pas avec moi; *(I'm not getting involved)* je ne vais pas m'en mêler

2 *(invite etc)* **we're having visitors tomorrow** nous attendons des invités demain; **to h. friends to dinner** avoir des amis à dîner
3 *(obtain)* **there was no work to be had** on ne pouvait pas obtenir de travail; **they were the cheapest seats to be had** ce sont les places les moins chères qu'on pouvait trouver; **to h. one's wish** obtenir ce que l'on désire
4 *(receive etc)* **to h. news from sb** recevoir des nouvelles de qn; **I h. it on good authority** je l'ai appris de bonne source; **I will let you h. it for £5** je vous le céderai pour cinq livres; **let me h. your keys** donnez-moi vos clefs; **you shall h. it back tomorrow** je vous le rendrai demain; *Fam* **I let him h. it** *(verbally)* je lui ai dit son fait; *(physically)* je lui ai flanqué un coup; *Fam* **I've had it!** *(if sb finds out)* je suis foutu!; *(I'm exhausted)* je suis crevé!; *Fam* **this coat has had it** *(is worn out)* ce manteau est foutu; *Fam* **the car has just about had it** la voiture va bientôt rendre l'âme; *Fam* **he's had it** *(dead, dying)* il a sa dose; *Fam* **I've had it up to here with him** j'en ai jusque-là de ce type-là; *Fam* **I've had it up to here with you** j'en ai marre de toi
5 *(take) (meal)* prendre; **to h. tea with sb** prendre le thé avec qn; **what will you h., sir? – I'll h. lasagne, please** que prendra monsieur? – donnez-moi *ou* je prendrai les lasagnes
6 *(in numerous verbal phrases)* **to h. measles** avoir la rougeole, *Fam* faire une rougeole; **to h. a cold** avoir un rhume, être enrhumé; **to h. the choice** avoir le choix; **to h. an idea** avoir une idée; **to h. a dream** faire un rêve; **to h. a game** faire une partie; **to h. a fall** faire une chute; **to h. a lesson** prendre une leçon; **to h. a bath** prendre un bain; **to h. a wash** se laver; **to h. a shave** se raser; **to h. a cigarette** fumer une cigarette
7 *(experience)* **I had a pleasant evening** j'ai passé une soirée agréable; **I didn't h. any trouble in finding it** je n'ai eu aucune peine à le trouver; **we had a rather strange adventure** il nous est arrivé une aventure assez étrange; **to h. fine/wet weather** avoir du beau temps/de la pluie
8 *(claim)* **public opinion has it that he is not telling the truth** on pense généralement qu'il ne dit pas la vérité; **she has it that John has been having an affair** elle prétend que John a une liaison; **rumour has it that …** le bruit court que …; **as Plato has it** comme dit Platon, comme l'a écrit Platon
9 *(hold)* **to h. sb in one's power** avoir qn en son pouvoir; **he had me by the throat** il me tenait à la gorge
10 *Fam (outwit)* **to be had** donner dans le panneau, *Fam* donner dedans; **you've been had!** on vous a eu!; *(for a purchase)* on vous a refilé un rossignol; **you h. me there!** là, je donne ma langue au chat!
11 *(give birth to)* avoir; **our cat has had kittens** notre chatte a fait des petits
12 **he had two children by her** il a eu d'elle deux enfants
13 *Sl (have sexual intercourse with)* prendre, coucher avec
14 *(causative)* **to h. sth done** faire faire qch; **to h. sb do sth** faire faire qch à qn; **to h. one's hair cut** se faire couper les cheveux; **three houses had their windows shattered** trois maisons ont eu leurs fenêtres brisées; **I had my watch stolen** je me suis fait voler ma montre; **to h. a tooth out** se faire arracher une dent; **I shall h. everything ready** je veillerai à ce que tout soit prêt VOIR GRAMMAIRE A56; B37
15 *(want)* **which one will you h.?** lequel voulez-vous?; **she won't h. him** elle ne veut pas de lui; **as luck would h. it he arrived too late** la malchance voulut qu'il arrivât trop tard; **what would you h. me do?** *(despairing)* que voulez-vous que j'y fasse?;

I'll h. you know that ... sachez que ...

16 *(allow)* **I will not h. such conduct** je ne supporterai pas une conduite pareille; **I won't h. you coming in here** je ne veux pas que vous entriez ici; *Fam* **he wouldn't h. it** *(that he was wrong)* il n'a pas voulu me/nous/etc écouter, il ne voulait pas en convenir; *Fam* **we tried to give the dog a bath but he wasn't having any of it!** nous avons essayé de donner un bain au chien, mais rien n'y a fait; **I'm not having any of your nonsense** pas de bêtises

17 *(place)* mettre; **I'll h. the television in that corner** *(when I get one)* je mettrai la télé dans ce coin; *(to person holding it)* mettez la télé dans ce coin; *Horseracing* **to h. money on a horse** *(a bet)* miser (de l'argent) sur un cheval

18 *(be compelled)* **to h. to do sth** devoir faire qch, être obligé *ou* forcé de faire qch; **I had to go away** j'ai dû m'en aller; **I don't h. to work** je n'ai pas besoin de travailler; *Iron* **of course you had to go and tell him!** bien sûr, il a fallu que tu ailles le lui dire!; **the clock will h. to be mended** la pendule a besoin d'une réparation; **I don't like housework but it has to be done** je n'aime pas faire le ménage mais il faut bien que quelqu'un le fasse; **first the potatoes h. to be washed** il faut d'abord laver les pommes de terre

19 *(as auxiliary)* **to h. been/given/done** avoir été/donné/fait; **to h.** être arrivé; **to h. hurt oneself** s'être blessé; **I h. lived in London for three years** j'habite Londres depuis trois ans; **well, you have grown!** ce que tu as grandi!; **you h. forgotten your gloves – so I h.!** vous avez oublié vos gants – en effet! *ou* tiens, c'est vrai!; **you h. been in prison before – I haven't!** vous avez déjà fait de la prison – c'est faux!; **you've forgotten, haven't you?** vous avez oublié, n'est-ce pas?; **you haven't forgotten, h. you?** vous n'avez pas oublié, n'est-ce pas? VOIR GRAMMAIRE A50; B26–8

20 *(with better, sooner)* **I had better say nothing** je ferais mieux de ne rien dire; **I'd sooner leave at once** j'aimerais bien mieux partir tout de suite VOIR GRAMMAIRE A41

▸ **have around** VT SEP **1** *(keep available)* garder *ou* avoir sous la main; **I h. the documents around somewhere** les documents sont là quelque part, j'ai les documents quelque part; **she's a useful person to h. around** il est bon de l'avoir sous la main; **I don't like having children around** je n'aime pas la compagnie des enfants

2 *(invite)* inviter; **we must h. them around for dinner** il faudra qu'on les invite à dîner

▸ **have away** VT SEP *Br Sl (have sexual intercourse)* **to h. it away (with sb)** s'envoyer en l'air (avec qn)

▸ **have back** VT SEP **1** *(invite)* **we're having them back on Saturday** *(in return)* nous leur rendons leur invitation samedi prochain; *(for second visit)* nous les réinvitons samedi prochain

2 *(invite after an event)* **after the movie we had them back for coffee** après le cinéma, nous les avons invités à venir prendre le café chez nous

▸ **have down** VT SEP *(invite from upstairs, the north)* inviter; **we're having the neighbours down for dinner tomorrow** nous avons invité nos voisins du dessus à venir dîner demain

▸ **have in** VT SEP **1** *(summon)* appeler, faire venir; **we had to h. the doctor in** nous avons dû faire venir le médecin; **we're having the painters in next week** les peintres viennent la semaine prochaine

2 *(invite)* inviter, recevoir; **let's h. him in to discuss it** *(ask to come in)* demandons-lui de venir nous en parler; **she had friends in for tea** elle a reçu quelques amis pour le thé

3 *Fam* **to h. it in for sb** *(have a grudge against)* en avoir après qn, garder à qn un chien de sa chienne; **they had it in for me from the day I arrived** ils en ont eu après moi dès mon arrivée

▸ **have off** VT SEP **1** *(remove)* retirer; **the barber nearly had my ear off** le coiffeur a failli me couper l'oreille

2 *(have removed)* faire retirer; **she's having the plaster off next week** on lui retire son plâtre la semaine prochaine

3 *Br Sl (have sexual intercourse)* **to h. it off (with sb)** s'envoyer en l'air (avec qn)

▸ **have on** VT SEP *(wear)* porter; **they had nothing on** ils étaient nus; **she had her black dress on** elle avait *ou* portait sa robe noire

VT SEP **1** *Fam (fool) (person)* faire marcher; **I was only having you on** c'était juste pour te faire marcher

2 *(have arranged)* **he has a lot on this week** il est très occupé cette semaine; **I h. something else on tonight** j'ai d'autres projets pour ce soir

3 *(install, put on)* installer, mettre; **they soon had the roof-rack on** très vite, ils ont installé *ou* mis la galerie; **she had her coat on in no time** en un clin d'œil, elle a mis son manteau

VT SEP **to h. sth on sb** avoir qch sur qn; **the police h. nothing on him** la police n'a rien sur lui

▸ **have out** VT SEP **1** *(remove) (object)* retirer; *(of dentist) (tooth)* extraire, arracher

2 *(have extracted) (tooth)* se faire arracher

3 *(resolve)* **to h. it out with sb** mettre les choses au point avec qn; **let's h. this out once and for all** mettons les choses au point une fois pour toutes

▸ **have over, have round** VT SEP = **have around 2**

▸ **have up** VT SEP **1** *(usu passive) (bring to court)* **to be had up (for vagrancy/etc)** passer devant le tribunal (pour vagabondage/etc)

2 *(erect, install)* installer, mettre en place; **they had the decorations up in a few hours** ils ont installé les décorations en quelques heures

3 *(invite from downstairs, the south)* inviter; **we'd better h. him up for a chat** *(ask to come up)* on devrait lui demander de venir; **he had them up (to his flat) for tea** il les a invités à venir prendre le thé

---

haven ['heɪv(ə)n] N *(shelter)* abri *m*, asile *m*, refuge *m*; *Lit (port)* havre *m*, port *m*; **safe h.** enclave *f* de protection; **to provide a safe h. for sb** offrir une terre d'asile à qn; *(within a war zone)* offrir un refuge à qn

have-not N démuni, -ie; **the have-nots of our society** les (plus) démunis de notre société

haven't ['hæv(ə)nt] CONTR = **have not**, *see* **have**

haversack ['hævəsæk] N havresac *m* *(de camping)*; *Mil* musette *f*

havoc ['hævək] N ravage *m*, dégâts *mpl*, dévastation *f*; **to cause** *or* **wreak h.** *(in a country etc)* faire de grands dégâts *ou* de grands ravages; **to play h. with** *(harvest etc)* ravager; *(person's health etc)* déranger, détraquer; *(person's plans etc)* désorganiser complètement

haw [hɔː] N *Bot* cenelle *f*

Hawaii [hə'waɪiː] N Hawaï *m*, Hawaii *m*

Hawaiian [hə'waɪən] ADJ hawaïen

N Hawaïen, -ïenne

▸▸ *Mus* **H. guitar** guitare *f* hawaiienne *ou* hawaïenne

hawk¹ [hɔːk] N **1** *(bird)* faucon *m*; **he has eyes like a h.** *(sharp eyesight)* il a des yeux d'aigle *ou* de lynx; *(misses nothing)* rien ne lui échappe; **to watch sb/sth like a h.** ne

pas lâcher qn/qch des yeux, ne pas quitter qn/qch du regard **2** *Pol* faucon *m*; **hawks and doves** faucons et colombes *fpl*

VI *(hunt)* chasser au faucon

▸▸ **h. moth** sphinx *m*, crépusculaire *m*, smérinthe *m*

hawk² VT *(sell) (goods)* colporter; *(rumour etc)* répandre; **to h. one's wares** *(in market etc)* vendre ses marchandises à la criée; *(from door to door)* faire du porte-à-porte; *Hum (of prostitute)* offrir ses services

hawk³ VI *(clear throat)* se racler la gorge; *(spit)* cracher

▸ **hawk up** VT SEP expectorer

hawker¹ ['hɔːkər] N *(hunter)* fauconnier *m*

hawker² N *(seller)* colporteur *m*, démarcheur, -euse

hawk-eyed ADJ *(sharp-sighted)* aux yeux d'aigle; *(who misses nothing)* à qui rien n'échappe

hawking¹ ['hɔːkɪŋ] N *(hunting)* chasse *f* au faucon, fauconnerie *f*

hawking² N *(selling)* colportage *m*

hawkish ['hɔːkɪʃ] ADJ *Pol etc* belliciste; **h. politician** faucon *m*

hawknosed ['hɔːknəʊzd] ADJ *(person)* au nez aquilin

hawser ['hɔːzər] N *Naut* haussière *f*, aussière *f*; *(for mooring only)* amarre *f*; **steel h.** aussière/amarre en fil d'acier

hawthorn ['hɔːθɔːn] N *(shrub)* aubépine *f*

hay [heɪ] N foin *m*; **to make h.** faire le(s) foin(s), faner; *Prov* **to make h. while the sun shines** ≃ battre le fer pendant qu'il est chaud; *Sl* **to hit the h.** se coucher

▸▸ **h. rake** râteau *m*, fauchet *m*

haycart ['heɪkɑːt] N fourragère *f* de foin

haycock ['heɪkɒk] N tas *m* *ou* meulette *f* de foin

hayfever ['heɪfiːvər] N *Med* rhume *m* des foins

hayfork ['heɪfɔːk] N fourche *f* à foin

haying ['heɪɪŋ] N fenaison *f*

hayloft ['heɪlɒft] N fenil *m*

haymaker ['heɪmeɪkər] N **1** *(person)* faneur, -euse; *(machine)* faneuse *f*, tourne-foin *m inv* **2** *Fam (punch)* uppercut *m*, swing *m*

haymaking ['heɪmeɪkɪŋ] N fenaison *f*

hayrack ['heɪræk] N râtelier *m* d'écurie

hayrick ['heɪrɪk] N meule *f* de foin; *(square)* barge *f*

hayride ['heɪraɪd] N *Am* = promenade *f* dans un chariot rempli de paille; *Fig* **it was no h.** ça n'a pas été une partie de plaisir

hayseed ['heɪsiːd] N *Am Fam (yokel)* péquenaud *m*

haystack ['heɪstæk] N = **hayrick**

haywire ['heɪwaɪər] ADJ *Fam* confus, embrouillé; **to go h.** *(of plan)* louper, finir en queue de poisson; *(of mechanism etc)* se détraquer; **he's gone h.** *(crazy)* il déménage, il perd la boule

hazard ['hæzəd] N **1** *(danger)* risque *m*, danger *m*, péril *m*; *Aut etc (place)* point *m* dangereux; **ice presents another h. for drivers** le verglas est un danger supplémentaire pour les automobilistes **2** *Golf* accident *m* de terrain

VT *(one's life, fortune)* risquer, hasarder; **to h. an opinion** risquer une opinion; **to h. a guess** tenter de deviner

▸▸ *Mktg* **h. forecasting** prévision *f* événementielle; *Aut* **h. lights** feux *mpl* de détresse

Note that the French word **hasard** is a false friend and is never a translation for the English word **hazard**. It means **chance**.

hazardous [ˈhæzədəs] **ADJ** *(risky)* hasardeux, chanceux; *(dangerous) (journey, job etc)* dangereux; *(uncertain) (project, undertaking)* incertain, hasardeux, aventureux

Hazchem *(abbr* **hazardous chemicals**) produits dangereux

haze [heɪz] **N** *(mist)* brume *f* légère; **a h. of uncertainty surrounded the affair** une atmosphère d'incertitude entourait l'affaire; **she** *or* **her mind was in a h.** son esprit était embrouillé; **to see everything through an alcohol-induced h.** voir tout sous l'emprise de l'alcool

haze[2] **VT** *Am Univ (new student etc)* brimer, bizuter

hazel [ˈheɪz(ə)l] **N 1** *(tree)* noisetier *m*, coudrier *m*, avelinier *m* **2** *(colour)* (couleur *f* de) noisette *f*
 ADJ *(couleur)* noisette *inv*; **h. eyes** yeux (couleur) noisette
 ▶▶ **h. tree** noisetier, coudrier, avelinier

hazelnut [ˈheɪz(ə)lnʌt] **N** *Bot* noisette *f*, aveline *f*

hazily [ˈheɪzɪlɪ] **ADV** vaguement

haziness [ˈheɪzɪnɪs] **N** *(of atmosphere, mind)* état *m* brumeux *ou* nébuleux; *(of memory)* imprécision *f*

hazing [ˈheɪzɪŋ] **N** *Am Univ* bizutage *m*

hazy [ˈheɪzɪ] **ADJ** *(air etc)* brumeux, embrumé; *(outline)* flou, estompé; *(idea etc)* nébuleux, flou; *(memory, knowledge)* vague; **to be h. about** *(knowledge)* n'avoir qu'une connaissance imprécise de; *(memory)* n'avoir qu'un souvenir vague de

h & c *(abbr* **hot and cold**) eau *f* courante chaude et froide

HD [eɪtʃˈdiː] *Comput* **1** *(abbr* **hard disk**) DD **2** *(abbr* **high density**) HD

HDD *Comput (abbr* **hard disk drive**) unité *f* de disque dur

HDTV [eɪtʃdiːtiːˈviː] **N** *TV (abbr* **high-definition television**) TVHD *f*

he [hiː] **PERS PRON 1** *(unstressed)* il; **he loves her** il l'aime; **what is he saying?** que dit-il?; **here he comes** le voici *ou* voilà qui vient *ou* arrive; **he's a strange man** c'est un homme étrange VOIR GRAMMAIRE A27–8 **2** *(stressed)* lui; **he and I** lui et moi; **I am as tall as he (is)** je suis aussi grand que lui; *esp Lit* **he who believes** celui qui croit
 N 1 *Fam (male)* mâle *m*; **it's a he** *(of newborn child)* c'est un garçon; *(of animal)* c'est un mâle **2** *(children's game)* (jeu *m* de) chat *m*; **you're he!** c'est toi le chat!

he- [hiː] **PREF** **he-bear** ours *m* mâle; **he-goat** bouc *m*

HEAD [hed] **VT 1** *(lead) (procession)* conduire, mener, venir en tête de; *(party)* être à la tête de, diriger; *(the poll)* venir en tête de; **she headed the attack on the Government's economic policy** elle menait l'attaque contre la politique économique du gouvernement; **to h. the list** être *ou* venir en tête de (la) liste **2** *(direct)* diriger; **they are heading the country into chaos** ils conduisent le pays au chaos; **just h. me towards the nearest bar** dirigez-moi vers le bar le plus proche; *Naut* **to h. the ship for Southampton** mettre le cap sur Southampton **3** *(put a title on)* **the article is headed …** l'article est intitulé … **4** *Old-fashioned (skirt around) (lake)* contourner par l'amont; *(river)* contourner par sa source **5** *Ftbl (ball)* jouer de la tête
 VI *(go)* **to h. east** *or* **to the East** *(of ship)* aller vers l'Est; **where are you heading** *or* **headed?** où allez-vous?; **you're heading in the right direction** vous allez dans la bonne direction; **he was headed** *or* **heading for an early death** il allait mourir jeune

N 1 tête *f*; **from h. to foot** *or* **toe** de la tête aux pieds, des pieds à la tête; *Fig* **he gave orders over my h.** il a donné des ordres sans me consulter; *Fig* **to be in over one's h.** *(in difficult situation)* être dépassé; **to stand on one's h.** faire le poirier; *Fam* **I could do it standing on my h.** c'est simple comme bonjour; **that's the kind of thing he could do standing on his h.** c'est le genre de choses qu'il peut faire les yeux fermés; **to stand** *or* **turn sth on its h.** poser qch la tête en bas; *Fig* **recent events have turned the situation on its h.** les événements récents ont retourné la situation; **to fall** *or* **go** *or* **turn h. over heels** faire la culbute; **to fall h. over heels in love with sb** tomber follement amoureux de qn; **to be a h. taller than sb** avoir une tête de plus que qn; **she stands h. and shoulders above me** elle fait une tête de plus que moi; *Fig* **she's h. and shoulders above the other athletes** elle est bien supérieure aux autres athlètes, elle surpasse les autres athlètes; *Horseracing* **to win by a h.** *(of horse)* gagner d'une tête; **to win by a short h.** gagner de justesse; **they'll have your h. (on a plate) for this** ils auront ta tête pour ça; **to let sb have their h.** lâcher les rênes à qn; *Lit* **his blood will be upon your h.** la responsabilité de sa mort pèsera sur vos épaules; **on your own h. be it** assumez-en la responsabilité; **to cut off sb's h.** décapiter qn, couper la tête à qn; *Fam* **to shout one's h. off** crier à tue-tête *ou* à pleins poumons; *Fam* **to talk one's h. off** bavarder comme une pie; *Fam* **to bite** *or* **snap sb's h. off** rembarrer qn; **a fine h. of hair** une belle chevelure; **to have a (good) h. for heights** ne pas avoir le vertige; **I haven't got a h. for heights** j'ai le vertige; **to have a good** *or* **strong h. for drink** bien supporter l'alcool; **the wine went (straight) to my h.** le vin m'a fait tourner la tête, le vin m'est monté à la tête; **all the praise went to his h.** toutes les louanges lui sont montées à la tête; **to have one's h. in the clouds** être dans les nuages *ou* dans la lune; *Fig* **to bang** *or* **bash** *or* **knock one's h. against a (brick) wall** se heurter à un mur; *Fig* **to bury** *or* **have one's h. in the sand** se cacher la tête dans le sable; *esp Am Sl* **to give sb h.** *(oral sex)* sucer qn **2** *(intellect, mind)* **to do sums in one's h.** calculer de tête; **to have a good h. for business** avoir le sens des affaires, s'entendre aux affaires; **to have a good h. for figures** être à l'aise avec les chiffres; **to let the h. be ruled by the heart** laisser son cœur gouverner sa raison; **to get sth into one's h.** se mettre qch dans la tête; **I can't get that into his h.** je n'arrive pas à le lui faire comprendre; **he has taken it into his h. that …** il s'est mis dans la tête *ou* en tête que …; **it never entered my h. that …** je n'aurais jamais pensé que …; **to put ideas into sb's h.** donner des idées à qn; **to put an idea into sb's h.** mettre une idée dans la tête à qn; **to get one's h. around sth** piger qch; **his name has gone right** *or* **clean out of my h.** j'ai complètement oublié son nom; **the girl's got a good h. on her shoulders** cette fille a la tête sur les épaules; *Prov* **he's an old h. on young shoulders** il est très mûr pour son âge; **we put our heads together** nous avons réfléchi ensemble; *Prov* **two heads are better than one** à deux, on réfléchit mieux; **I think he made it up out of his own h.** je crois que c'est lui qui a inventé ça; **not off the top of my h.** *(I'd have to check)* pas au pied levé; **she made some figures up off the top of her h.** elle a inventé des chiffres; **off the top of my h., I'd say somewhere like Paris** à tout hasard, je dirais un endroit comme Paris; **to be over the heads of the audience** *(of speech, lecture etc)* dépasser l'entendement de l'auditoire; **it's (way) over his h.** il n'y

comprend rien (du tout); *Fam* **to lose one's h.** perdre la tête *ou* la boule *ou* la boussole; *Fam* **to keep one's h.** *(in crisis)* garder la tête sur les épaules; *Fam* **to be off one's h.** être fou *ou* timbré *ou* toqué; *Fam* **to go off one's h.** devenir fou; *Fam* **he's not quite right in the h., he's a bit soft in the h.** il est faible d'esprit *ou* un peu timbré; *Fam* **to be out of one's h.** *(on drugs, alcohol)* se défoncer **3** *Fam (headache)* **I've got a bad h.** *or* **an awful h.** j'ai mal à la tête *ou* une de ces maux de tête; *(after drinking)* j'ai mal aux cheveux **4** *Culin* **sheep's h.** tête *f* de mouton; **calf's h.** tête de veau; **potted h.** fromage *m* de tête **5** *(antlers) (of stag)* bois *mpl*, tête *f*; **deer of the first/second h.** cerf *m* à la première/deuxième tête **6** *(top part, end) (of pin, hammer, violin, flower, volcano, piston, boil, tennis racket)* tête *f*; *(of cabbage, cane, stick)* pomme *f*; *(of asparagus)* pointe *f*; *(of celery)* pied *m*; *(of lance etc)* fer *m*; *(of page, stairs)* haut *m*; *(heading of page)* en-tête *m*, *pl* en-têtes; *(of column, rocket, still)* chapiteau *m*; *Typ (of chapter etc)* tête, intitulé *m*; *(of mineshaft)* bouche *f*; *(of cylinder)* tête, culasse *f*; *(of torpedo)* cône *m*; *(of cask etc)* fond *m*; *(of drum)* peau *f*; *(of bed)* chevet *m*, tête; *(of the table)* haut bout *m*; *(of river)* source *f*; *(in bookkeeping)* rubrique *f*; *(on beer)* mousse *f*, *Fam* faux col *m*; *(on fermenting liquid)* chapeau *m*; **at the h. of the lake** à l'extrémité du lac; **to come to a h.** atteindre un paroxysme; **things are coming to a h.** la crise est proche; **to bring matters to a h.** forcer une décision **7** *(heading, grouping)* rubrique *f*; **under this h.** sous cette rubrique **8** *Naut Fam (latrine)* latrines *fpl* **9** = **headland 10** *(front or chief place)* **at the h. of a procession** à la *ou* en tête d'un cortège; **to be at the h. of the list** venir en tête de liste; **at the h. of the queue** en tête de file; **to sit at the h. of the table** présider la table **11** *(person in charge) (of family, the Church, business)* chef *m*; **h. (of department)** *Sch* chef de département; *(in company)* chef de service; *(in store)* chef de rayon; **h. of section** chef de service; *Hum* **h. cook and bottlewasher** factotum *m* **12** *(no pl) (unit)* **six h. of cattle** six têtes de bétail; **thirty h. of oxen** trente bœufs **13** *(person)* **to pay £50 per h.** *or* **a h.** payer 50 livres par tête *ou* par personne **14** *(of coin)* face *f*; *Art etc* **coin bearing the h. of George III** pièce (frappée) à l'effigie de Georges III; **heads or tails?** pile ou face?; **heads I win, tails you lose** pile je gagne, face tu perds, je gagne de toutes les façons *ou* de toute façon; *Fam* **I can't make h. or tail of this** je n'y comprends rien de rien, ça n'a ni queue ni tête **15** *Phys etc (of a fluid, gas etc)* charge *f*, pression *f*; **h. of water** *(pressure)* charge *ou* pression d'eau; **full h. of steam** charge *ou* pression de vapeur; *Phys* **loss of h.** perte *f* de pression **16** *(on tape recorder, disk drive)* tête *f*
 ▶▶ **heads of agreement** *(draft)* protocole *m* d'accord; **h. barman** chef *m* barman; *Br Sch* **h. boy** = élève *m* chargé d'un certain nombre de responsabilités et qui représente son école aux cérémonies publiques; **h. cashier** chef caissier; *Com* **h. clerk** premier commis *m*, chef de bureau; **h. cold** rhume *m* de cerveau; **h. concierge** chef concierge; *Comput, Tech* **h. crash** crash *m ou* écrasement *m* de tête; **h. foreman** chef d'atelier; *Mining* **h. frame** chevalement *m*; **h. gardener** jardinier, -ière en chef; *Aut* **h. gasket** joint *m* de culasse; *Tech* **h. gate** *(of lock)* porte *f* d'amont; *Br Sch* **h. girl** = élève *f* chargée d'un certain nombre de responsabilités et qui représente son école aux cérémonies pu-

bliques; **h. housekeeper** (in hotel) gouvernante f générale; **h. louse** pou m; **h. office** siège m social, bureau m central; **it's h. office on the phone** c'est le siège au téléphone; **h. porter** (in hotel) chef m portier; (in university college) appariteur m principal; **h. receptionist** chef de réception; Mus **h. register** voix f de tête; Br Aut **h. restraint** appuie-tête m, pl appuie-tête ou appuie-têtes, repose-tête m, pl repose-tête ou repose-têtes; TV, Cin **h. shot** gros plan m de tête; **h. start** (lead) avance f; (advantage) avantage m; **h. of state** chef d'État; Sch **h. teacher** (man) proviseur m, directeur m, chef d'établissement; (woman) directrice f, chef d'établissement; Mus **h. voice** voix de tête; **h. waiter** maître m d'hôtel

▸ **head back** VI rentrer, retourner; **it's time we were heading back** il est temps que nous rentrions

▸ **head for** VT INSEP (go towards) **to h. for a place** s'avancer ou se diriger vers un endroit; Naut avoir le cap sur un endroit; **we were heading for ...** nous étions en route pour ...; **let's h. for home** rentrons; **where are you headed for?** vous allez ou dans quelle direction allez-vous?; **the country is heading for civil war** le pays va droit à la guerre civile; **you're heading for trouble** vous allez avoir des ennuis; **they're heading for disaster** ils vont ou courent à la catastrophe; **to be heading for a fall** aller tout droit vers un échec

▸ **head in** VT SEP Ftbl **to h. the ball in** marquer (un but) de la tête

▸ **head off** VT SEP (divert) (person, enemy troops) barrer la route à; (fugitives) intercepter; (question) parer; **I'll h. them off at the pass** je les intercepterai au col

▸ **head up** VT SEP (team etc) diriger

headache ['hedeɪk] N **1** mal m de tête, pl maux de tête; **to have a h.** avoir mal à la tête; Fig Fam **you give me a h.** vous me cassez la tête **2** Fam (worry, problem) embêtement m, casse-tête m, plaie f; **it can be a h. finding somewhere to park** certains jours, c'est une plaie de trouver à se garer; **this injury is another h. for the team's manager** cette blessure, c'est un nouveau casse-tête pour le manager de l'équipe

headband ['hedbænd] N bandeau m

headbanger ['hedbæŋə(r)] N Fam **1** (heavy metal fan) hardeux, -euse **2** Br (mad person) cinglé, -ée, toqué, -ée

headboard ['hedbɔːd] N dosseret m

headbutt ['hedbʌt] N coup m de tête; **to give sb a h.** donner un coup de tête à qn
VT donner un coup de tête à

headcase ['hedkeɪs] N Br Fam cinglé, -ée

headcheese ['hedtʃiːz] N Am Culin fromage m de tête

headcount ['hedkaʊnt] N dénombrement m des personnes présentes; **let's do a h.** on va les compter

headdress ['heddres] N coiffe f

headed ['hedɪd] ADJ **h. (note)paper** papier m à en-tête

-headed ['hedɪd] SUFF **big/two/etc-h.** qui a la grosse tête/qui a deux têtes/etc

header ['hedər] N **1** Typ, Comput en-tête m, pl en-têtes **2** Ftbl tête f, coup m de tête **3** Fam (fall) **to take a (flying) h.** (into water) tomber (à l'eau) la tête la première; (onto ground) tomber (par terre) la tête la première **4** Constr boutisse f
▸ ▸ Br Aut **h. tank** collecteur m de tête

headfirst ['hedˈfɜːst] ADV (to fall) la tête la première; **he was hanging h. from the window** il était suspendu à la fenêtre la tête en bas

headgear ['hedɡɪər] N (no pl) couvre-chef

m; **all kinds of h.** toutes sortes de couvre-chefs

head-hunt VT Com **to be head-hunted** être recruté par un chasseur de têtes; **we'll have to h. someone** il va falloir y aller à la manière d'un chasseur de têtes

head-hunter N (tribal warrior), Com chasseur m de têtes

head-hunting N (recruitment) recrutement m de cadres par approche directe; **a h. firm** un cabinet de chasseurs de têtes

headiness ['hedɪnɪs] N **1** (of wine etc) qualité f capiteuse **2** (rashness) impétuosité f; **the h. of the moment** la griserie ou l'ivresse f du moment

heading ['hedɪŋ] N **1** (in book etc) (of chapter) tête f; (of article) rubrique f; (of page etc) en-tête m, pl en-têtes; (in bookkeeping) poste m, rubrique; Comput titre m; **it falls under the h. of ...** c'est à mettre à la rubrique de ...; **this subject comes under the h. of rhetoric** cette discipline fait partie de la rhétorique **2** Ftbl jeu m de tête **3** Min (head of tunnel) avancée f, avancement m; (tunnel) galerie f d'avancement **4** Constr assise f de boutisses
▸ ▸ Constr **h. course** assise de boutisses

headlamp ['hedlæmp] N (of car) phare m; (of locomotive) feu m d'avant
▸ ▸ **h. washer** lave-phare m, pl lave-phares; **h. wiper** essuie-phare m, pl essuie-phares

headland ['hedlənd] N Geog cap m, promontoire m

headless ['hedlɪs] ADJ sans tête; (body) décapité; Fam **to run about like a h. chicken** courir dans tous les sens, paniquer **2** Biol (animal etc) acéphale

headlight ['hedlaɪt] N (of car) phare m; (of locomotive) feu m d'avant

headline ['hedlaɪn] N **1** Journ titre m, gros titre; **to get into** or **hit** or **make the headlines** faire la une, faire les gros titres; **pollution has been in the headlines a lot recently** la pollution a beaucoup fait la une récemment; Radio, TV **... and here are the headlines ...** et voici les grands titres (de l'actualité); **the disappearance of a dog isn't normally h. news** la disparition d'un chien ne fait pas normalement la une de l'actualité **2** Typ en-tête m, pl en-têtes, ligne f de tête
VT Journ mettre en vedette ou en première page; **the story was headlined 'Tragic accident'** l'article s'intitulait 'un accident tragique'
VI Mus etc (be chief attraction of a show) être en vedette
▸ ▸ **h. writer** titreur m

headlong ['hedlɒŋ] ADV **to fall h. (on the floor)** tomber de tout son long (par terre); **to rush h. to one's ruin** courir à sa ruine; **they rushed h. into the deal** ils se sont jetés à corps perdu dans l'affaire; **they rushed h. into marriage** ils se sont mariés trop vite et sans réfléchir
ADJ (fall) la tête la première; **to take a h. dive** piquer une tête; **there was a h. rush to buy the shares** tout le monde s'est précipité pour acheter les actions; **h. flight** sauve-qui-peut m inv

headman, pl **headsmen** ['hedmən] N (of tribe etc) chef m

headmaster [hed'mɑːstər] N (of school) directeur m; (of comprehensive) principal m; (of high school) proviseur m

headmistress [hed'mɪstrɪs] N (of school) directrice f; (of comprehensive) principale f; (of high school) proviseur m

head-on ADJ, ADV de front; **to meet sb h.** prendre qn de front; **they met h. over the issue of taxation** ils se sont affrontés sur la question des impôts; **h. confrontation** affrontement m direct

▸ ▸ Mktg **h. attack** attaque f frontale; **h. collision** collision f frontale ou de plein fouet

headphones ['hedfəʊnz] NPL casque m, écouteurs mpl

headquarter ['hedkwɔːtər] Am VI (of company) **to h. in Glasgow** établir son siège à Glasgow
VT **to be headquartered in Glasgow** avoir son siège à Glasgow

headquarters [hed'kwɔːtəz] NPL (often with sing verb) **1** (of private company, bank) siège m social; (of organization, government office) bureau m principal; (of UN etc) administration f centrale; **to have its h. in ...** siéger ou avoir son siège à ... **2** Mil (of lower units) poste m de commandement; (of higher units) quartier m général; (staff) état-major m, pl états-major; **company/platoon h.** (staff) groupe m de commandement de la compagnie/de la section

headrest ['hedrest] N appui-tête m ou appuie-tête, pl appuis-tête ou appuie-tête

headroom ['hedruːm] N hauteur f; (of arch) échappée f; (in car) hauteur au plafond; (under bridge) hauteur (de passage); **there wasn't enough h. for the bus** il n'y avait pas un dégagement suffisant au-dessus du bus

headscarf ['hedskɑːf] N foulard m

headset ['hedset] N Radio, TV casque m, écouteurs mpl

headship ['hedʃɪp] N Br Sch (of school) direction f

headshrinker ['hedʃrɪŋkər] N (savage) réducteur m de têtes; Fam Hum (psychiatrist) psychiatre mf, psy mf

headstall ['hedstɔːl] N (for horse) têtière f, licou m

headstand ['hedstænd] N Gym poirier m; **to do a h.** faire le poirier

headstone ['hedstəʊn] N **1** (on grave) pierre f tombale **2** Archit, Constr clef f de voûte

headstrong ['hedstrɒŋ] ADJ volontaire, têtu, entêté

head-up display N (in aeroplane, car) affichage m tête-haute

headway ['hedweɪ] N progrès m; **to make h.** avancer, faire des progrès; (of ship) faire route; **to make no h.** ne pas avancer; **the two sides have made some h. in their negotiations** les deux parties ont avancé dans leurs négociations

headwind ['hedwɪnd] N Naut vent m contraire, vent debout

headword ['hedwɜːd] N (in dictionary) entrée f

heady ['hedɪ] ADJ (vin) capiteux; (perfume) capiteux, troublant; (height etc) vertigineux; **the h. heights of international finance** les sommets de la finance internationale; **to be h. with success** être grisé par le succès; **the h. times during the revolution** les moments grisants de la révolution

heal [hiːl] VT guérir (**sb of a disease** qn d'une maladie); Med, Fig (wound) guérir, cicatriser; Fig **to h. the breach (between two people)** amener une réconciliation (entre deux personnes)
VI (of wound) se cicatriser, se refermer; **the wound hasn't healed properly** la blessure ne s'est pas bien cicatrisée ou n'a pas bien cicatrisé
▸ **heal over, heal up** VI = **heal** VI

healer ['hiːlər] N guérisseur, -euse; Prov **time is a great h.** le temps guérit toutes les blessures

healing ['hiːlɪŋ] ADJ (remedy etc) curatif; (ointment, plant, remedy) cicatrisant
N guérison f; (of wound) cicatrisation f, guérison

health [helθ] N santé f; **exercise is good for**

the *or* one's h. l'exercice est bon pour la santé; **good h.** bonne santé; **ill** *or* **poor h.** mauvaise santé; **to be in good h.** être en bonne santé *ou* bien portant; **to be in bad** *or* **poor h.** se porter mal, être mal portant; *Fig* **the economy is in good h.** l'économie se porte bien; **to restore sb to (full** *or* **good) h.** rendre la santé à qn; **to endanger one's h.** mettre en danger sa santé; **to regain one's h.** recouvrer la santé; **to suffer from ill h.** être de santé fragile; **to drink to sb's h.** boire à la santé de qn; **(your very) good h.!** (à votre) santé!; **public h.** santé *ou* hygiène *f* publique; **(public) h. officer** *or* **inspector** inspecteur *m* de la santé publique; *Br Admin* **(local) h. authority** = organisme *m* régional responsable de l'administration de la santé publique

▸▸ **h. care** soins *mpl ou* services *mpl* médicaux; **h. centre** centre *m* médico-social; **h. certificate** certificat *m* sanitaire; **h. check** contrôle *m* sanitaire; **h. club** club *m* de remise en forme; *Br* **h. cover** assurance *f* médicale; **h. farm** centre *m* de remise en forme; **h. food** aliments *mpl* diététiques *ou* biologiques; **h. food shop** magasin *m* de produits diététiques; **h. hazard** risque *m* pour la santé; **h. insurance** assurance maladie; **h. resort** station *f* climatique; *(by sea)* station balnéaire; **h. risk** risque pour la santé; **h. and safety committee** comité *m* d'hygiène et de sécurité; *Br* **h. and safety regulations** réglementation *f* sur l'hygiène et la sécurité; *Br* **H. Secretary** ≃ ministre *m* de la Santé; *Br* **h. service** = système *m* créé en 1946 en Grande-Bretagne et financé par l'État, assurant la gratuité des soins et des services médicaux, ≃ Sécurité *f* sociale; **the epidemic has put a terrible strain on the h. services** l'épidémie a mis les services médicaux à rude épreuve; **h. tourism** tourisme *m* de santé; *Br* **h. visitor** = infirmière *f* visiteuse qui s'occupe surtout des enfants en bas âge, des personnes âgées etc

health-giving ADJ *(effect etc)* bienfaisant, salutaire; *(air etc)* tonifiant, vivifiant

healthily ['helθɪlɪ] ADV sainement, salubrement

healthiness N *(of place, climate)* salubrité *f*; *(of person)* bonne santé; *(of relationship)* caractère *m* sain

healthy ['helθɪ] ADJ *(person, animal)* en bonne santé, bien portant; *(skin, lungs, relationship)* sain; *(plant)* robuste; *(climate, food etc)* salubre, sain; **a h. appetite** un solide appétit; **h. eating habits** bonne alimentation *f*; **to look healthier** avoir meilleure mine; **a h. interest in the opposite sex** un intérêt naturel à l'égard du sexe opposé; **to have a h. respect for sb/sth** avoir beaucoup de respect pour qn/qch; **to have a h. disregard for traditions** avoir un mépris louable des traditions; **it isn't h. for a child to spend so much time reading** il n'est pas sain pour un enfant de passer tant de temps à lire; **a h. democracy** une démocratie qui se porte bien; **a h. economy** une économie saine *ou* prospère; **h. living** une vie saine; **to make a h. profit** faire de bons bénéfices; **it is a h. sign that ...** il est encourageant que ... + *sub*

heap [hi:p] N **1** *(pile)* *(of wood, stones etc)* tas *m*, monceau *m*, amas *m*, amoncellement *m*; **the books were in a h. on the floor** les livres étaient en tas sur le sol; *Fig* **at the top/bottom of the h.** en haut/au bas de l'échelle (sociale); **h. of junk** tas de ferraille; **a h. of rubble** un tas de ruines; **to lie in a h.** être en tas; **to fall in a h.** *(of person)* s'affaisser (sur soi-même); *Fam* **to be struck all of a h.** en rester abasourdi *ou* stupéfait

2 *Fam (large number) (usu pl)* **she had heaps of children** elle avait une ribambelle d'enfants; **I've got heaps of things to do** j'ai un tas de choses à faire; **you've got heaps of time** vous avez largement le temps; **to have heaps of room/money** avoir plein de place/ d'argent

3 *Sl (car)* **this old h.** cette vieille bagnole, ce vieux tas de ferraille

VT **1** *(pile) (wood, stones etc)* entasser, amonceler, mettre en tas; **to h. riches/praise on sb** couvrir qn de richesses/d'éloges; **to h. scorn on sb/sb's proposal** ridiculiser qn/la proposition de qn; **to h. insults on sb('s head)** accabler qn d'injures

2 *(cover, fill)* **the table was heaped with food** la table était couverte de victuailles; **the lorry was heaped with food supplies** le camion regorgeait de provisions; **she heaped my plate with cherries** elle a rempli mon assiette de cerises

▸ **heap up** VT SEP *(make pile of)* empiler, entasser

heaped [hi:pt] ADJ *(container, bowl)* entassé, amoncelé; *Culin* **a h. teaspoonful/ tablespoonful** *(in recipe)* une bonne cuillère à café/à soupe

heaps [hi:ps] ADV *Fam (a lot)* vachement

HEAR [hɪər] *(pt, pp* **heard** [hɜːd]*)* VT **1** *(perceive)* entendre; **I heard a ring** j'ai entendu sonner; **let's h. it** *(tell us)* dites donc, racontez-nous ça; **let's h. it for ...** *(applaud)* applaudissons ...; **I heard my name (mentioned)** j'ai entendu dire mon nom; **to h. sb speak** entendre parler qn, entendre qn parler; **I could hardly make myself heard/h. myself speak** je pouvais à peine me faire entendre; *Iron* **he hears what he wants to h.** il n'entend que ce qu'il veut; *Fam* **I've heard that one before!** j'ai déjà entendu ça (quelque part)!; **you heard!** ne faites pas celui/ celle qui n'a pas entendu! VOIR GRAMMAIRE A40–1; B35–6

2 *(listen to)* écouter; *Law (witness, testimony)* entendre; **h. me out** écoutez-moi jusqu'au bout; **h.! h.!** *(at meeting)* très bien! très bien!; *esp Am Fam* **I h. you, I h. what you're saying** je comprends, j'ai compris; *Rel* **to h. Mass** assister à la messe; **to h. sb's confession** entendre qn en confession; **to h. a prayer** exaucer *ou* écouter *ou* entendre une prière; *Law* **to h. a case** juger une affaire; **the case was heard in camera** l'audience a eu lieu à huis clos; **when is your case going to be heard?** quand ton affaire va-t-elle être jugée *ou* passer au tribunal?

3 *(learn) (piece of news)* apprendre; *(the truth)* apprendre, savoir; **I heard it from a friend** je l'ai su par un ami, je l'ai appris par un ami; **I heard a rumour that she was in Spain** j'ai entendu une rumeur selon laquelle elle serait en Espagne; **I have heard that ...** j'ai appris *ou* on m'a appris que ...; **I h. you're getting married** j'apprends que tu vas te marier; **for six months we heard nothing** *(received no news)* pendant six mois nous n'avons pas eu de nouvelles; **she was very famous for a while then we heard no more about her** elle a été célèbre pendant un moment puis on n'a plus entendu parler d'elle; **let me h. how you get on** donnez-moi de vos nouvelles; **from what I h. à** ce qu'on dit; **I have heard a great deal about him** on m'a beaucoup parlé de lui; **I don't want to h. any more about it** je ne veux plus en entendre parler; **I've heard nothing but good about them** je n'ai entendu que du bien à leur propos; **to h. tell of ...** entendre parler de ...

VI **1** *(have hearing)* entendre (bien); **I can't h. properly** je n'entends pas bien

2 *(receive news, word)* **to h. from sb** recevoir des nouvelles de qn; **you'll h. from me!** *(as threat)* vous aurez de mes nouvelles!; **you'll be hearing from my lawyer!** mon avocat vous contactera!, on en reparlera

devant les tribunaux!; **to h. about sb/sth** avoir des nouvelles de qn/qch, entendre parler de qn/qch; **haven't you heard?** vous ne savez pas?

▸ **hear of** VT INSEP **1** *(learn about) (person, thing)* entendre parler de; **he has not been heard of since** depuis on n'a plus entendu parler; **this is the first I have heard of it** c'est la première fois que j'en entends parler; **I only heard of it yesterday** je n'en ai eu connaissance qu'hier; **I never heard of such a thing!** a-t-on jamais entendu une chose pareille!, je n'ai jamais vu une chose pareille!

2 *(in neg) (allow)* **I won't h. of you going to a hotel** il est hors de question que vous alliez à l'hôtel; **I won't h. of it** je ne veux pas en entendre parler

hearer ['hɪərər] N auditeur, -trice; **hearers** auditoire *m*

hearing ['hɪərɪŋ] N **1** *(ability to hear)* ouïe *f*; **my h. is very bad** mon ouïe est très faible; **loud noise can permanently damage your h.** trop de bruit peut endommager l'ouïe de façon irréversible; **he has very little h. left** son ouïe est défaillante, il n'entend presque plus; **the h. impaired** les malentendants *mpl*

2 *(range)* **within h.** à portée de voix; **out of h.** hors de portée de voix; **it was said in my h.** on l'a dit devant moi *ou* en ma présence

3 *(act of listening)* audition *f*, audience *f*; **he was refused a h.** on a refusé de l'entendre; **to condemn sb without a h.** condamner qn sans l'écouter; **we should give her a fair h. first** on devrait l'entendre d'abord

4 *Law* **h. of witnesses** audition *f* des témoins; **the h. of the case** l'audience *f*; *(by judge alone)* l'audition de la cause par le juge; **the case comes up for h. tomorrow** l'affaire passera en jugement demain

5 *(meeting)* séance *f*, *(investigation) (of Senate etc)* enquête *f*

▸▸ **h. aid** appareil *m* acoustique, audiophone *m*

hearken ['hɑːk(ə)n] VI *Arch, Lit* écouter

hearsay ['hɪəseɪ] N ouï-dire *m inv*; **that's only h.** ce ne sont que des on-dit; **I know it** *or* **have it only from h.** je ne le sais que par ouï-dire

▸▸ *Law* **h. evidence** déposition *f* sur la foi d'un tiers *or* d'autrui

hearse [hɜːs] N corbillard *m*, fourgon *m* mortuaire

HEART [hɑːt] N **1** *Anat* cœur *m*; *Med* **to have h. trouble, to have a weak** *or* **bad h.** être cardiaque; **to press** *or* **clasp sb to one's h.** serrer *ou* presser qn sur son cœur

2 *Fig (seat of the emotions)* **to have a big h.** avoir très bon cœur; **h. of gold** cœur d'or; **h. of stone** cœur de pierre; **you've got no h.** tu n'as pas de cœur; **have a h.!** ayez un peu de cœur!; **it did my h. good to see her again** ça m'a fait chaud au cœur de la revoir; **her h.'s in the right place** *(she is kind)* elle a bon cœur; **(has good intentions)** elle a de bonnes intentions; **his h. was full** *or* **heavy** il avait le cœur gros; **with a heavy h.** le cœur serré *ou* gros; **my h. sank at the news** cette nouvelle m'a désespéré; *Fam* **my h. was in my boots** *(disheartened)* j'étais complètement découragé; *(afraid)* je n'en menais pas large; **to have one's h. in one's mouth** avoir le cœur qui bat la chamade; **to break sb's h.** briser le cœur à qn; **it was enough to break your h.** c'était à fendre le cœur *ou* l'âme; **to cry one's h. out** pleurer toutes les larmes de son corps; **to be sick at h.** avoir le cœur gros *ou* serré; **to wear one's h. on one's sleeve** ne pas cacher ses préférences

3 *(representing romantic love)* **to win sb's h.** gagner le cœur de qn; **to lose one's h. to sb** tomber amoureux de qn; **affairs** *or* **matters of the h.** affaires *fpl* de cœur

4 *(representing sincerity, one's deepest preferences)* **in my h. of hearts** au plus profond de mon cœur; **from the bottom of one's h.** *(thank sb, congratulate sb)* de tout son cœur; **to love sb with all one's h.** aimer qn de tout son cœur; **to have sb's welfare at h.** avoir à cœur le bonheur de qn; **she's a socialist at h.** au fond, elle est socialiste; **a cause close to my h.** une cause qui me tient à cœur; **to take sth to h.** prendre qch à cœur; **to have set one's h. on sth/on doing sth** avoir qch à cœur/avoir *ou* prendre à cœur de faire qch; **I have set my h. on it** j'y tiens; **he's a man after my own h.** c'est un homme qui me ressemble, il est comme moi; **to one's h.'s content** à cœur joie, à souhait; **to eat/drink to one's h.'s content** manger/boire tout son soûl; **to be all h.** être plein de bonne volonté; *Iron* **you're all h.** tu es charmant!

5 *(enthusiasm, courage)* **to put (all) one's h. into it** y aller de tout son cœur; **his/my h. isn't in it** le cœur n'y est pas; **to put one's h. and soul** *or* **to throw oneself h. and soul into sth** se donner corps et âme à qch; **to put new h. into sb** donner du courage *ou* du cœur à qn; **to take h.** (re)prendre courage; **to lose h.** se décourager; **she didn't have the h. to tell him** elle n'a pas eu le cœur de le lui dire

6 to learn/know sth (off) by h. apprendre/savoir qch par cœur

7 *(centre)* *(of cabbage)* cœur *m*; *(of tree)* cœur, vif *m*; *(of cable)* âme *f*, mèche *f*; **h. of oak** homme *m* courageux; **the h. of the matter** le fond du problème; **in the h. of** *(town, country)* au cœur de; *(forest)* au (beau) milieu de

8 *Cards* **heart(s)** cœur *m*; **to play a h./hearts** jouer du cœur/cœur; **king/queen of hearts** roi *m* /dame *f* de cœur

▸▸ *Med* **h. attack** crise *f* cardiaque; *Med* **h. disease** maladie *f* de cœur, maladie cardiaque; *Med* **h. failure** *(condition)* défaillance *f* cardiaque; *(cessation of heartbeat)* arrêt *m* du cœur; *Med* **h. murmur** souffle *m* au cœur; *Mktg* **h. share** préférence *f*; *Med* **h. surgery** chirurgie *f* du cœur; **h. transplant** greffe *f* du cœur, greffe cardiaque

heartache ['hɑːteɪk] N chagrin *m* *ou* peine *f* de cœur

heartbeat ['hɑːtbiːt] N battement *m* *ou* pulsation *f* du cœur; *Fig* **a h. away from sth** à un cheveu de qch

heartbreak ['hɑːtbreɪk] N peine *f* immense, chagrin *m*; *(romantic)* chagrin d'amour; **I've had my share of heartbreak(s)** j'ai eu ma part de chagrins d'amour

heartbreaker ['hɑːtbreɪkər] N *(man)* bourreau *m* des cœurs; *(woman)* mangeuse *f* d'hommes

heartbreaking ['hɑːtbreɪkɪŋ] ADJ navrant, accablant, déchirant; *(sigh, news)* à fendre le cœur; *(sight)* navrant; **it was h.** c'était à fendre l'âme; **h. cries** cris déchirants

heartbroken ['hɑːtbrəʊk(ə)n] ADJ **to be h.** avoir le cœur brisé

heartburn ['hɑːtbɜːn] N *Med* brûlures *fpl* d'estomac

hearten ['hɑːt(ə)n] VT *(person)* encourager, donner du courage à

heartening ['hɑːt(ə)nɪŋ] ADJ *(advice, words)* encourageant

heartfelt ['hɑːtfelt] ADJ *(emotion, vow)* sincère, qui vient *ou* part du cœur; **to express one's h. thanks to sb** adresser de sincères remerciements à qn

hearth, *pl* **hearths** [hɑːθ, hɑːθs] N foyer *m*, âtre *m*; **without h. and home** sans feu ni lieu

▸▸ **h. rug** devant *m* de foyer

hearthstone ['hɑːθstəʊn] N pierre *f* de la cheminée, (marbre *m* du) foyer *m*

heartily ['hɑːtɪlɪ] ADV **1** *(cordially)* *(to greet)* cordialement; *(to welcome, applaud)* chaleureusement; *(to work, laugh)* de bon cœur; *(to rejoice)* sincèrement; *Fam* **to be h. sick of sth** être profondément dégoûté de qch **2** *(to eat)* de bon appétit, avec appétit

heartiness ['hɑːtɪnɪs] N **1** *(cordiality)* *(of welcome)* cordialité *f*, chaleur *f*; *(of consent)* sincérité *f* **2** *(vigour)* *(of appetite)* vigueur *f*

heartland ['hɑːtlænd] N *Pol, Econ, Geog* centre *m*, cœur *m*; **the country's industrial h.** le centre industriel du pays; **this is Tory h.** c'est une place forte du parti conservateur

heartless ['hɑːtlɪs] ADJ *(person)* sans cœur, insensible; *(action, remark)* dur, cruel; **it was h. of you to say that** c'était cruel de ta part de dire ça

heartlessly ['hɑːtlɪslɪ] ADV sans cœur, sans pitié; *(cruelly)* cruellement

heartlessness ['hɑːtlɪsnɪs] N manque *m* de cœur, insensibilité *f*; *(cruelty)* cruauté *f*

heart-lung ADJ

▸▸ *Med* **h. machine** cœur-poumon *m* artificiel, *pl* cœurs-poumons artificiels; *Med* **h. transplant** greffe *f* cœur-poumon

heart-rending ['hɑːtrendɪŋ] ADJ = heartbreaking

heart-searching N **after much h.** après avoir longuement réfléchi

heartsick ['hɑːtsɪk] ADJ *esp Lit* écœuré; **to be** *or* **feel h.** avoir le cœur serré *ou* gros

heartstrings ['hɑːtstrɪŋz] NPL *Fig* **to tug at sb's h.** serrer le cœur de qn

heart-throb N *Fam (person)* idole *f*, coqueluche *f*; **he thinks he's a real h.** il se prend pour Johnny

heart-to-heart ADJ *(conversation)* intime, à cœur ouvert; **to have a h. talk with sb** parler avec qn à cœur ouvert

N conversation *f* intime *ou* à cœur ouvert; **I think it's time we had a h.** il est temps que nous parlions franchement

heart-warming ADJ réconfortant, qui réchauffe le cœur; **it was h. to see father and child getting on so well** ça vous réchauffait le cœur de voir le père et l'enfant s'entendre si bien

hearty ['hɑːtɪ] ADJ **1** *(cordial)* cordial, -aux; *(sentiment)* sincère, qui part du cœur; *(laugh)* jovial, -als *ou* -aux; **my heartiest congratulations** mes félicitations les plus chaleureuses; **h. cheers** acclamations nourries; **she has a h. dislike of hypocrisy** elle a une sainte horreur de l'hypocrisie **2** *(vigorous)* vigoureux, robuste, bien portant; **he is still (hale and) h.** il est encore gaillard **3** *(substantial)* *(meal)* copieux, abondant; **h. appetite** gros appétit, *Fam* rude appétit; **he's a h. eater** c'est un gros mangeur

N joyeux luron *m*; *Naut, Arch* **my hearties** les gars

heat [hiːt] N **1** chaleur *f*; *(of sun, fire)* ardeur *f*, **in the h. of the day** au plus chaud de la journée; *Culin* **cook at a low h.** cuire à faible température *ou* à feu doux; **we've been without h. for over a week** *(heating)* nous n'avons plus de chauffage depuis plus d'une semaine; *Fam Fig* **if you can't stand the h., get out of the kitchen** si tu ne peux pas t'y faire, laisse tomber

2 *(passion)* **to reply with some h.** répondre avec (une certaine) vivacité; **to take the h. out of the situation** dédramatiser la situation; **in the h. of the moment** sur le moment; **in the h. of the argument** dans le feu de la discussion; **in the h. of battle** dans le feu de la bataille; **to do sth in the h. of passion** faire qch dans le feu de la passion

3 *Sl (pressure)* **to turn up the h.** *(in interrogation etc)* faire pression, mettre la pression;

until the h. is off jusqu'à ce que les choses se calment

4 *(of female animal)* chaleur *f*, rut *m*; **to be on** *or* **in h.** être en chaleur

5 *Sport* (épreuve *f*) éliminatoire *f*; **it was a dead h.** ils ont fini à égalité *ou* ex-æquo

6 *Am Sl* **the h.** *(police)* les flics *mpl*

VT *(water, house etc)* chauffer; **to h. sth to (a temperature of) 80°** porter qch à 80°; **to h. a house with gas** chauffer une maison au gaz

VI *(of water etc)* chauffer

▸▸ *Phys* **h. constant** constante *f* calorifique; *Tech* **h. engine** machine *f* *ou* moteur *m* thermique; *Phys* **h. exchange** échange *m* de chaleur; *Phys* **h. exchanger** échangeur *m* de chaleur; *Med* **h. exhaustion** épuisement *m* dû à la chaleur; **h. haze** brume *f* de chaleur; **h. loss** perte *f* *ou* déperdition *f* de chaleur; *Med* **h. prostration** épuisement *m* dû à la chaleur; *Tech* **h. pump** pompe *f* à chaleur; *Med* **h. rash** irritation *f* *ou* inflammation *f* due à la chaleur; *Aviat* **h. shield** bouclier *m* thermique; *Med* **h. treatment** traitement *m* par la chaleur, *Spec* thermothérapie *f*

▸ **heat up** VT SEP *(warm)* *(food etc)* (faire) réchauffer

VI *(of water)* chauffer; *(of room)* se réchauffer; *(of discussion etc)* s'échauffer

heat-conducting ADJ thermoconducteur, -trice

heated ['hiːtɪd] ADJ **1** *(swimming pool, apartment)* chauffé; *(towel rail)* chauffant **2** *(passionate, angry)* *(discussion)* chaud, animé; **to become h.** *(of discussion, person)* s'échauffer; **things got a bit h.** l'atmosphère a commencé à s'échauffer

▸▸ **h. rear window** lunette *f* (arrière) chauffante; **h. seat** siège *m* chauffant

heatedly ['hiːtɪdlɪ] ADV avec chaleur, avec emportement

heater ['hiːtər] N **1** *(for room etc)* radiateur *m*; *(for water)* chauffe-eau *m inv*; *Tech* réchauffeur *m*; *Electron* filament *m* incandescent; **(immersion) h.** thermoplongeur *m* **2** *Am Sl (pistol etc)* revolver *m*

heath [hiːθ] N **1** *(tract of land)* bruyère *f*, lande *f* **2** *(heather)* bruyère *f*

heathen ['hiːð(ə)n] ADJ *(pagan)* païen, -ïenne

NPL *Lit* **the h.** les païens *mpl*; *Old-fashioned (barbarians)* les barbares *mpl*

heathenish ['hiːðənɪʃ] ADJ *(pagan)* païen, -ïenne

heathenism ['hiːðənɪz(ə)m] N paganisme *m*

heather ['heðər] N *(shrub)* bruyère *f*, brande *f*

Heath Robinson [hiːθ'rɒbɪnsən] ADJ *Br* de bric et de broc

heating ['hiːtɪŋ] N *(system)* chauffage *m*; **there's no h. in the bathroom** il n'y a pas de chauffage dans la salle de bain; **to put the h. on** mettre le chauffage

▸▸ **h. apparatus** appareil *m* de chauffage; **h. bill** facture *f* de chauffage; *Tech etc* **h. coil** serpentin *m* de chauffage, réchauffeur *m*; **h. element** élément *m* chauffant; **h. engineer** chauffagiste *mf*; **h. power** puissance *f* *ou* pouvoir *m* calorifique; *Elec* puissance de chauffage; **h. system** (système *m* de) chauffage *m*; **h. unit** élément chauffant

heatproof ['hiːtpruːf] ADJ *(clothing, material)* résistant à la chaleur; *(varnish, dish etc)* allant au feu; *(asbestos)* incombustible; **is it h.?** *(dish)* est-ce que ça va au feu?

heat-resistant, heat-resisting ['hiːtrɪzɪstənt, -rɪzɪstɪŋ] ADJ résistant à la chaleur; *Tech* thermorésistant

heat-seeking ['hiːtsiːkɪŋ] ADJ *(missile)* guidé par la chaleur

heatsink ['hiːtsɪŋk] N dissipateur *m* thermique *ou* de chaleur

heatstroke ['hi:tstrəʊk] N *Med* coup *m* de chaleur

heatwave ['hi:tweɪv] N *Met* vague *f* de chaleur, canicule *f*

heave [hi:v] N 1 effort *m*; **with a mighty h.** avec un énorme effort; *Naut* **h. of the sea** houle *f* 2 *(retch)* haut-le-cœur *m inv*
  VT *(pt, pp* **heaved** *or esp Naut* **hove** [həʊv]*)* 1 *(lift) (load)* faire un effort pour lever *ou* soulever; *(pull)* faire un effort pour tirer; *(push)* faire un effort pour pousser; *(drag)* faire un effort pour traîner; *(throw)* faire un effort pour lancer; **he heaved the sacks of coal onto the truck** il a hissé les sacs de charbon dans le camion (à grand-peine); **she heaved herself out of her chair** elle s'est soulevée de la chaise avec effort; *Naut* **to h. the anchor** lever l'ancre; **to h. a sigh of relief** pousser un soupir de soulagement
  2 *Naut* **to h. the ship ahead/astern** virer le navire de l'avant/de l'arrière
  VI 1 **h.!** *(push)* poussez!; *(pull)* tirez!; *(lift)* soulevez!; **they heaved on the rope** ils ont tiré très fort sur la corde
  2 *(swell)* (se) gonfler, se soulever; *(of sea)* s'agiter, se soulever; *(of ship)* se soulever sur la lame; *(of bosom)* palpiter
  3 *(retch) (of person)* avoir des haut-le-cœur; *(of stomach)* se soulever
  4 *Naut (of land, ship)* **to h. into sight** paraître (à l'horizon)
  ▸ **heave to** *Naut* VI se mettre en panne *ou* à la cape; *(in gale)* caranguer
  VT SEP mettre en panne

heave-ho INT *Naut* oh hisse!
  N *Fam* **to give sb the h.** *(of employer)* sacquer qn, virer qn; *(of boyfriend etc)* plaquer qn; **to get** *or* **be given the h.** se faire jeter

heaven ['hev(ə)n] N ciel *m, pl* cieux; **in h.** au ciel, *Fig (overjoyed)* au paradis, aux anges; **to go to h.** aller au ciel *ou* en *ou* au paradis; **this is h.!** c'est merveilleux!; **h. on earth** c'est le paradis sur terre; **to move h. and earth to do sth** remuer ciel et terre pour faire qch; **the heavens opened** il s'est mis à pleuvoir à torrents; *Fam* **stinks to high h.** ça pue; **(good) heavens!, heavens above!** bon Dieu!; **thank h. (for that)!** Dieu merci!; **h. (alone) knows!** Dieu seul le sait!; **h. knows why/when**/*etc* ... Dieu seul sait pourquoi/quand/*etc* ...; **for h.'s sake!** pour l'amour de Dieu!, pour l'amour du ciel!; **where in the name of h.** *or* **in h.'s name is he?** où diable est-il?; **h. forbid!** que le ciel nous (en) préserve!

heavenly ['hev(ə)nlɪ] ADJ 1 *(from God) (gift, mercy etc)* du ciel; *(music etc)* céleste; **our H. Father** notre Père céleste 2 *Fam (wonderful)* divin; **what h. peaches!** quelles pêches délicieuses!; **to have a h. evening** passer une soirée merveilleuse
  ▸▸**h. body** corps *m* céleste

heaven-sent ADJ providentiel

heavily ['hevɪlɪ] ADV 1 *(to fall, lean)* lourdement; *(to walk)* lourdement, d'un pas pesant; **time hangs h. on his hands** le temps lui pèse
  2 *(to a considerable extent)* fortement, fort; **h. underlined** souligné d'un gros trait; **to drink/smoke h.** boire/fumer beaucoup; **it was raining h.** il pleuvait fort, il pleuvait beaucoup; **to rely** *or* **depend h. on sth** dépendre beaucoup de qch; **to lose h.** perdre gros; **to be h. defeated** subir une lourde défaite; **h. in debt** fortement endetté; **the secret service was h. involved in training guerillas** les services secrets étaient lourdement impliqués dans la formation des guérilleros; **to be h. hit** *(by financial misfortune etc)* être gravement atteint; **to be h. taxed** être fortement imposé

  3 *(deeply) (to sigh, sleep)* profondément
  4 *(with difficulty) (to breathe)* péniblement

heaviness ['hevɪnɪs] N 1 *(of body, gait)* lourdeur *f*, pesanteur *f*, *(of burden)* poids *m*; *(of food)* lourdeur *f* 2 *(of limbs)* engourdissement *m*; **h. of heart** serrement *m* de cœur

heaving ['hi:vɪŋ] ADJ *Br Fam (extremely busy)* hyper animé

HEAVY ['hevɪ]

> ADJ lourd 1–5, 7 ▪ grave 1 ▪ gros 2, 3, 7 ▪ pénible 5 ▪ chargé 5 ▪ sérieux 6
> ADV lourd
> N dur 1

ADJ 1 *(in weight)* lourd, pesant; *(step)* pesant, lourd, alourdi; *(style)* lourd; *Phys (body)* grave; *Nucl (atom)* lourd; **h. blow** coup violent; **fate had dealt her a h. blow** le destin lui avait porté un coup très rude; **h. meal** repas lourd à digérer; **h. with sleep** lourd de sommeil
  2 *(large, thick) (coat, shoes)* gros, *f* grosse; **h. beard** forte barbe; **h. features** gros traits *mpl*; **h. losses** lourdes *ou* fortes pertes; **h. wire** fil *m* (de) grosse épaisseur
  3 *(intense)* fort; **h. rain** forte pluie; **a h. shower** une grosse averse; *Med* **a h. cold** un gros rhume; **h. period(s)** règles *fpl* abondantes; **h. sleep** profond sommeil, sommeil de plomb
  4 *(oppressive) (smell)* fort; *(smell of perfume)* lourd; *(sky)* sombre, morne; **air h. with scent** air chargé de parfums; **h. responsibility** lourde responsabilité; **h. fine** lourde amende; **to rule with a h. hand** gouverner de façon très autoritaire
  5 *(hard) (work)* pénible, difficile, dur; *(breathing)* pénible; *(task)* lourd; *(day)* chargé; *(football pitch, race course)* lourd; *Fam* **to be h. on electricity/petrol** consommer beaucoup d'électricité/d'essence; **she did the h. work** c'est elle qui a fait le gros travail; **this book is h. reading** *or* **going** ce livre est indigeste; **to find it h. going** trouver cela difficile; **h. soil** sol *m* gras; **h. user** gros utilisateur *m*; **he made h. weather of it** il s'est noyé dans un verre d'eau; **to make h. weather of sth** faire une montagne de qch, se compliquer la vie (en ce qui concerne qch); **h. sea** forte mer, grosse mer
  6 *(serious) Theat* **h. part** rôle *m* sérieux; *Fam* **to come the h. father** prendre un ton de père autoritaire
  7 *(eater, drinker)* gros; **to be a h. sleeper** avoir le sommeil lourd; **to be a h. smoker** fumer beaucoup
  8 *Sl (tense, frightening) (situation etc)* difficile, menaçant; **to get h. with sb** devenir agressif avec qn; **things started to get a bit h.** ça a commencé à craindre
  ADV **to weigh h.** *(of time, duty etc)* peser lourd; **food that lies h. on the stomach** nourriture lourde *ou* indigeste *ou* qui pèse sur l'estomac
  N 1 *Fam (thug)* dur *m*
  2 *Theat (serious part)* rôle *m* sérieux; *(role of villain)* rôle de scélérat
  3 *Journ Fam* **heavies** journaux *mpl* sérieux
  ▸▸*Naut* **h. armament** artillerie *f* lourde; *Mil* **h. fire** feu *m* nourri, feu intense; *Br Transp* **h. goods vehicle** poids *m* lourd; *Am* **h. hitter** *(in baseball)* = joueur *m* qui frappe fort et marque beaucoup de points; *Fig* homme *m* influent, gros bonnet *m*; *Ind* **h. industry** industrie *f* lourde; *St Exch* **h. market** marché *m* lourd; **h. metal** *Phys* métal *m* lourd; *Mus* **heavy metal** *m inv*, *Typ* **h. type** caractères *mpl* gras; *Phys* **h. water** eau *f* lourde

heavy-duty ADJ *(machine)* à grand *ou* fort rendement, de grande puissance; *(clothing)* résistant; *(boots)* solide, robuste; *Aut (tyre)* tout-terrain; **h. oil** huile *f* HD

heavy-eyed ADJ aux yeux battus

heavy-handed [hevɪ'hændɪd] ADJ 1 *(clumsy)* maladroit, gauche 2 *(harsh)* oppressif, cruel

heavy-hearted [hevɪ'hɑ:tɪd] ADJ qui a le cœur lourd *ou* gros; **to feel h.** avoir le cœur gros

heavy-laden ADJ 1 lourdement chargé 2 *(with cares)* accablé de soucis

heavyweight ['hevɪweɪt] N 1 *Boxing* poids lourd *m* 2 *(serious, important person)* personne *f* de poids *ou* d'influence; **he is not a literary h.** ce n'est pas un grand de la littérature
  ADJ 1 *Boxing* (catégorie (des)) poids lourd(s) 2 *Tex* lourd
  ▸▸*Boxing* **h. champion** champion *m* poids lourd *ou* dans la catégorie poids lourd

hebe [hi:b] N *Am Offensive Sl* youpin, -ine

Hebrew ['hi:bru:] ADJ *Bible* hébreu, *f* hébraïque
  N 1 *Bible (person)* Hébreu *m* 2 *Ling* hébreu *m*

Hebridean [hebrɪ'di:ən] ADJ des Hébrides

Hebrides (the) [ðe'hebrɪdi:z] N les Hébrides *fpl*

heck [hek] *Fam* INT sapristi!, zut!
  N **what the h. are you doing here?** que diable fais-tu là?; **a h. of a lot** *(quantity)* tout un tas; **not a h. of a lot** *(not greatly)* pas tellement, pas beaucoup, pas des masses; **that's a h. of a lot of money!** c'est une sacrée somme d'argent!; **we saw a h. of a good film** on a vu un vachement bon film!; **oh, what the h.!** et puis flûte!

heckle ['hek(ə)l] VT *(at public meetings) (speaker)* interpeller; **he was heckled non-stop** il s'est fait chahuter tout le temps
  VI chahuter

heckler ['heklər] N *Pol etc* **there were two hecklers in the audience** il y avait deux membres du public qui faisaient du chahut

heckling ['hek(ə)lɪŋ] N chahut *m*

hectare ['hekteə] N *(measurement)* hectare *m*

hectic ['hektɪk] ADJ 1 *(busy)* agité, fiévreux; *(existence, morning)* mouvementé; **to lead a h. existence** mener une vie trépidante; **it gets very h. in the post office at Christmas** c'est la bousculade à la poste à Noël; **we had a h. time** nous ne savions où donner de la tête 2 *Med (fever)* hectique

hectically ['hektɪklɪ] ADV fiévreusement

hectolitre, *Am* **hectoliter** ['hektəlɪːtər] N hectolitre *m*, *Fam* hecto *m*

hector ['hektər] VT *(person)* rudoyer
  VI prendre des tons autoritaires

hectoring ['hektərɪŋ] ADJ *(tone etc)* autoritaire, impérieux

hectowatt ['hektəwɒt] N hectowatt *m*

he'd [hi:d] CONTR 1 = **he had,** *see* **have** = **he would,** *see* **will**

hedge [hedʒ] N 1 haie *f*, *Fig* **to buy sth as a h. against inflation** acheter qch pour se mettre à l'abri de l'inflation 2 *St Exch* couverture *f*
  VT *(field)* mettre une haie autour de; *St Exch (position)* protéger, couvrir; **to h. one's bets** *(in betting)* répartir les risques; *Fig (cover oneself)* se couvrir, éviter de se compromettre; **the laws are hedged about with exceptions** les lois sont remplies d'exceptions
  VI 1 *(in discussion)* se réserver, éviter de se compromettre 2 *Horseracing* parier pour et contre 3 *St Exch* se couvrir (**against** contre)
  ▸▸**h. clippers** taille-haies *m inv*; *St Exch* **h. fund** société *f* d'investissement; *St Exch* **h. ratio** ratio *m* de couverture; **h. shears** taille-haies
  ▸ **hedge in** VT SEP *(surround) (field)* entourer d'une haie; *(person)* entourer; **hedged in with difficulties** entouré de difficultés

▸ **hedge off** VT SEP (*separate with a hedge*) (*field*) séparer par une haie (**from** de)

hedgehog [ˈhedʒhɒg] N hérisson *m*; *Am* (*porcupine*) porc-épic *m*, *pl* porcs-épics; **to curl up like a h.** se pelotonner, se recroqueviller (sur soi-même)

hedgehop [ˈhedʒhɒp] VI (**-pp-**) *Aviat Fam* voler en rase-mottes, faire du rase-mottes

hedgerow [ˈhedʒrəʊ] N bordure *f* d'arbres *ou* d'arbustes formant une haie; **animals of the hedgerows** animaux qui vivent dans les haies

hedging [ˈhedʒɪŋ] N **1** (*care of hedges*) entretien *m* des haies; **h. and ditching** entretien des haies et des fossés **2** (*hedges*) bordure *f* **3** *Horseracing* répartition *f* des risques **4** *St Exch* couverture *f* **5** (*in discussion etc*) hésitation *f* à prendre des décisions

hedonism [ˈhiːdənɪz(ə)m, ˈhed-] N hédonisme *m*

hedonist [ˈhiːdənɪst, ˈhed-] N hédoniste *mf*

hedonistic [hiːdəˈnɪstɪk, hed-] ADJ hédoniste

heebie-jeebies [ˈhiːbɪˈdʒiːbɪz] NPL *Fam* **to have the h.** (*be nervous*) avoir la frousse; **he gives me the h.** (*revolts me*) il me hérisse; (*scares me*) il me donne la chair de poule

heed[1] [hiːd] *esp Lit* N **to give** *or* **pay h. to sth/sb** faire attention à qch/qn; **to take h.** prendre garde; **to take h. of a warning** tenir compte d'un avertissement

VT tenir compte de; **his advice was not heeded** on n'a tenu aucun compte de ses conseils

heedful [ˈhiːdfʊl] ADJ *Fml* **to be h. of ...** être attentif à ...

heedless [ˈhiːdlɪs] ADJ **to be h. of** (*what is happening*) être inattentif à; (*the future etc*) être peu soucieux de; **they continued, h. of her warning/the danger** ils ont continué sans se soucier de son avertissement/du danger

heedlessly [ˈhiːdlɪslɪ] ADV étourdiment, avec insouciance

hee-haw [ˈhiːhɔː] N hi-han *m*
VI braire, faire hi-han

heel[1] [hiːl] N **1** (*of foot*) talon *m*; **to have the police at one's heels** avoir la police à ses trousses; **to tread on sb's heels** marcher sur les talons de qn; **to follow close on sb's heels** suivre qn de près, emboîter le pas à qn; **to take to one's heels** prendre ses jambes à son cou; *Fam* **to cool** *or* **kick one's heels** poireauter; **to turn on one's h.** tourner les talons; **to be down at h.** (*of shoes*) être éculé; (*of person*) avoir l'air miteux; **to come to h.** (*of dog*) venir au pied; *Fam* (*of person, state*) se soumettre; **h.!** (*to dog*) au pied!; **to bring sb to h.** rappeler qn à l'ordre; *Aut* **h. and toe** talon-pointe *m*

2 (*of shoe, sock*) talon *m*; **high heels** talons hauts; **she was wearing heels** elle portait des talons

3 (*of bread*) croûton *m*

4 *Sl* (*contemptible person*) chameau *m*, salaud *m*

5 *Tech etc* (*of tool*) talon *m*; *Naut* (*of mast*) pied *m*, caisse *f*, (*of rudder*) talon

6 (*of hoof of horse etc*) derrière *m* du sabot

VT **1** (*shoe*) (*fit with a heel*) mettre un talon à; (*repair*) réparer le talon de; **to get one's shoes heeled** (faire) refaire le talon de ses chaussures **2** *Rugby* (*ball*) talonner

▸ ▸ **h. bar** talon-minute *m*, *pl* talons-minutes, réparations-minute *fpl*

heel[2] *Naut* N (*of ship*) bande *f*, gîte *f*, inclinaison *f*
VI (*of ship*) avoir *ou* donner de la bande, prendre de la gîte

▸ **heel over** VI = **heel**[2] VI

heelpiece [ˈhiːlpiːs] N (*of shoe*) contrefort *m* du talon

heeltap [ˈhiːltæp] N (*in shoe*) rondelle *f* en cuir (*pour talon*)

heft [heft] VT *Am Fam*, *Br Dial* **1** (*lift*) soulever **2** (*guess weight of*) soupeser

hefty [ˈheftɪ] ADJ *Fam* **1** (*person*) fort, solide, costaud **2** (*heavy*) lourd, pesant; **a h. blow** un coup violent **3** (*substantial*) gros, important; **a h. bill** une note de taille

Hegelian [heˈgeɪlɪən] ADJ, N hégélien, -ienne

hegemony [hɪˈgemənɪ] N hégémonie *f*

hegira [hɪˈdʒaɪrə] N *Muslim Rel* hégire *f*

heifer [ˈhefər] N *Agr* génisse *f*

heigh-ho [ˈheɪˈhəʊ] INT eh bien!

height [haɪt] N **1** hauteur *f*, (*of person*) taille *f*, stature *f*; **wall two metres in h.** mur qui a deux mètres de haut; **a h. of 20 metres** une hauteur de 20 mètres; **overall h.** (*of vehicle*) hauteur totale; **what's your h.?, what h. are you?** combien mesurez-vous?; **of average h.** de taille moyenne

2 (*of an arch*) flèche *f*, montée *f*

3 (*altitude*) altitude *f*; **h. above sea level** altitude au-dessus du niveau de la mer; *Aviat* **cruising h.** altitude de croisière; **the plane was gaining/losing h.** l'avion prenait/perdait de l'altitude; **to have a good head for heights** ne pas avoir le vertige; **I'm scared of heights** j'ai le vertige

4 *Fig* (*highest point*) (*of career, glory etc*) apogée *m*; (*of eloquence*) sommet *m*; **at the h. of his glory** au faîte de la gloire; **it's the h. of madness!** c'est de la folie pure!; **this is the h. of insolence!** c'est de la plus haute insolence!; **at the h. of the storm** au plus fort de l'orage; **an actress at the h. of her career** une actrice à l'apogée de sa carrière; **at the h. of summer** en plein été; **the season is at its h.** la saison bat son plein; **it's the h. of fashion** c'est la dernière mode *ou* le dernier cri

▸ ▸ *Aviat* **h. indicator** altimètre *m*

height-adjustable ADJ réglable en hauteur

heighten [ˈhaɪt(ə)n] VT **1** (*increase etc*) (*pleasure*) accroître, augmenter; (*contrast*) accentuer; (*colour etc*) relever, faire ressortir; (*impression, speculation*) renforcer; **to h. the interest in sth** augmenter l'intérêt pour qch; **to h. public awareness** sensibiliser le public; **the riots have heightened racial tensions in the city** les émeutes ont accentué *ou* aggravé les tensions raciales dans la ville **2** (*increase height of*) (*wall etc*) surélever, rehausser

VI (*of tension*) s'accroître

heightened [ˈhaɪt(ə)nd] ADJ accru; (*sensitivity*) exacerbé; **there is a h. awareness of the dangers of pollution** il y a une prise de conscience accrue des dangers de la pollution

heightening [ˈhaɪt(ə)nɪŋ] N **1** (*increase etc*) (*of response*) accroissement *m*; **there has been a h. of speculation** il y a eu un renforcement de la spéculation **2** (*raising of height*) (*of wall etc*) surélévation *f*, rehaussement *m*

heights [haɪts] NPL (*area of high ground*) éminence *f*, hauteurs *fpl*

heinous [ˈheɪnəs] ADJ *Fml* (*crime*) odieux, atroce, abominable

> Note that the French word **haineux** is a false friend and is never a translation for the English word **heinous**. It means **full of hatred**.

Heinz [haɪnz] N *Fam Hum* (*dog*) bâtard *m*

heir [eər] N héritier *m*; **to be h. to an estate** être l'héritier d'une propriété; **the h. to the throne** l'héritier du trône

▸ ▸ **h. apparent** *Law* héritier *m* présomptif; *Fig* (*of political party, company*) dauphin *m*; *Law* **h. presumptive** héritier présomptif (*sauf naissance d'un héritier en ligne directe*)

heir-at-law, *pl* **heirs-at-law** N *Law* héritier *m* légitime

heiress [ˈeərɪs] N héritière *f*

heirloom [ˈeəluːm] N héritage *m*; **a family h.** (*furniture*) un meuble de famille; (*jewellery*) un bijou de famille

heist [haɪst] N *esp Am Sl* fric-frac *m*, casse *m*; **to pull a h.** faire un casse

Helen of Troy [ˈhelɪnəvˈtrɔɪ] N Hélène de Troie

helianthus [hiːlɪˈænθəs] N (*flower*) hélianthe *m*, tournesol *m*

heliboarding [ˈhelɪbɔːdɪŋ] N héliboarding *m*, snowboard *m* avec dépose en hélicoptère

helical [ˈhelɪk(ə)l] ADJ *Tech* (*gear etc*) hélicoïdal, -aux; (*spring*) hélicoïde, en hélice; **h. shell** coquille *f* contournée

helicopter [ˈhelɪkɒptər] N *Aviat* hélicoptère *m*

▸ ▸ **h. gunship** hélicoptère *m* de combat; **h. pilot** pilote *mf* d'hélicoptère

▸ **helicopter in** VT SEP (*troops, supplies*) amener en hélicoptère, héliporter

▸ **helicopter out** VT SEP (*people*) emmener en hélicoptère, héliporter

heliograph [ˈhiːlɪəgræf] N (*for signalling*) héliographe *m*

heliotrope [ˈhiːlɪətrəʊp] N (*flower*) héliotrope *m*
ADJ (*colour*) héliotrope *inv*

helipad [ˈhelɪpæd] N *Aviat* zone *f* d'atterrissage pour hélicoptère

heliport [ˈhelɪpɔːt] N *Aviat* héliport *m*

heliskiing [ˈhelɪskiːɪŋ] N héliski *m*, ski *m* avec dépose en hélicoptère

helium [ˈhiːlɪəm] N *Chem* hélium *m*

▸ ▸ **h. balloon** ballon *m* gonflé à l'hélium

helix, *pl* **helices** [ˈhiːlɪks, ˈhiːlɪsiːz] N **1** *Math* hélice *f*, *Archit etc* spirale *f* **2** *Anat* (*of the ear*) hélix *m* **3** (*snail*) hélice *f*, colimaçon *m*

hell [hel] N *Myth* les enfers

2 *Fam* (*unpleasant state or experience*) **it was h. working in the mine** c'était l'enfer de travailler dans la mine; **it can be h. trying to park here** quelquefois, c'est l'enfer pour se garer ici; **to make sb's life h.** *or* **a h. on earth** faire un enfer de la vie de qn; **I feel like h.** je suis au trente-sixième dessous, je me sens horriblement mal; **to give sb h.** (*tell off*) passer un savon à qn, engueuler qn; (*give a hard time*) faire une vie d'enfer à qn; **these shoes are giving me h.** ces chaussures me font un mal de chien; **it was all h. let loose** c'était infernal; **all h. broke loose** c'était l'horreur; **there'll be h. to pay if your mother finds out** ça va barder si ta mère l'apprend

3 *Fam* (*idioms*) **go to h.!** va au diable!; (*stronger*) va te faire voir!; **to go to h. and back** connaître des moments très difficiles (mais s'en sortir); **to h. with him!** qu'il aille au diable!; **get the h. out of here!** fiche-moi le camp d'ici!; *Br* **it's as cold as h.** il fait un froid de canard; **to run like h.** courir comme un dératé; **to work like h.** travailler comme un malade; **like h. (I will)!, the h. I will!** jamais de la vie!; **(you can wait) till h. freezes over** tu peux attendre jusqu'à la saint-Glinglin; **I wish to h. I could remember** si seulement je pouvais me souvenir; **come h. or high water** quoi qu'il arrive; **to go h. for leather** (*running*) courir ventre à terre; (*driving*) conduire comme un fou; (*working, playing music*) travailler/jouer comme un malade; **to do sth for the h. of it** faire qch sans raison particulière; **I did it for the h. of it** je l'ai fait parce que cela me chantait;

why don't you just do it for the h. of it? et si tu le faisais juste comme ça?; **to play merry h. with sth** foutre qch en l'air; *esp Am* **the whole country's going to h. in a handcart** tout fout le camp dans ce pays

4 *Fam (intensifier)* **a h. of a price** un prix salé *ou* démentiel *ou* ahurissant; **you've got a h. of a nerve!** tu as un culot du diable!; **there was a** *or* **one h. of a fight** il y a eu une bagarre terrible; **he's a h. of a guy** c'est un type formidable *ou* un mec super; **it was a h. of a good film** c'était un sacrément bon film; **we had a h. of a time** *(bad)* on en a bavé; *(good)* on s'est super marrés; **you'll have a h. of a time** *(bad)* tu vas en baver; *(good)* tu vas te marrer; **I had a h. of a time getting here** *(bad)* j'en ai bavé pour arriver jusqu'ici, ça a été l'enfer pour arriver ici; **a h. of a lot of ...** énormément de ...; **not a h. of a lot** pas des masses; **what the h. do you think you're doing?** qu'est-ce que tu fous?; **what the h.'s going on?** qu'est-ce qui se passe, nom de Dieu?; **who the h. are you?** qui diable êtes-vous?; **what the h., you only live once** que diable, on ne vit qu'une fois

INT *Fam* **(oh) h.!** zut alors!; *(stronger)* merde alors!; *Fam* **h.'s bells!, h.'s teeth!, h. and damnation!** (sacré) nom de nom!

he'll [hi:l] = **he will,** *see* **will²**

hellacious [hel'eɪʃəs] ADJ *Am Fam* **1** *(bad, unpleasant)* infernal, -aux **2** *(excellent)* super, génial, -aux

hellbender ['helbendər] N *Am Fam (drinking bout)* (séance *f* de) beuverie *f*

hellbent ['helbent] ADJ *Fam* **to be h. on doing sth** vouloir à tout prix faire qch; **the human race seems h. on self-destruction** la race humaine semble vouloir s'autodétruire à tout prix

hellcat ['helkæt] N *Fam* sorcière *f*, mégère *f*

hellebore ['helɪbɔːr] N *(plant)* ellébore *m*

Hellene ['heliːn] N Hellène *mf*

Hellenic [he'lenɪk] ADJ *(people)* hellène; *(language, history)* hellénique

hellfire ['helfaɪər] N feu *m* de l'enfer
▸▸**h. preacher** prédicateur *m* fanatique *(qui est toujours en train de rappeler aux pécheurs qu'ils sont voués à la damnation éternelle)*

hellhole ['helhəʊl] N *Fam (bar, club etc)* bouge *m*, boui-boui *m*

hellish ['helɪʃ] *Fam* ADJ *(unpleasant)* infernal, -aux; **I feel h.** je ne me sens vraiment pas bien
ADV terriblement, vachement

hellishly ['helɪʃlɪ] ADV *Fam* diaboliquement, vachement

hello [he'ləʊ] INT bonjour!, *Fam* salut!; *(in evening)* bonsoir!, *Fam* salut!; *Tel* allô!; **h. there, wake up!** *(calling attention)* holà! réveille-toi!; **h., what's this?** *(indicating surprise)* tiens!, qu'est-ce que c'est que ça?; **to say h.** dire bonjour; **say h. to him for me** dis-lui bonjour de ma part; **she gave them a cheery 'h.'** elle leur a lancé un 'bonjour' joyeux

hell-raiser N *Fam* chahuteur *m*

hell-raising N *Fam* vie *f* de patachon, vie de bâton de chaise; **his h. days** sa vie de patachon

helluva ['heləvə] *Fam* = **hell of a,** *see* **hell** N4

helm [helm] N *Naut* gouvernail *m*, timon *m*; **the man at the h.** *Naut* l'homme de barre; *Fig* l'homme qui tient le gouvernail *ou* qui dirige l'entreprise; *Naut, Fig* **to be at the h.** être à la barre; *Fig* **to take (over) the h.** prendre la direction des affaires
VT *Naut* gouverner, barrer; *Fig* diriger; *(film)* mettre en scène

helmet ['helmɪt] N *(of soldier, fireman etc)* casque *m*; **(crash) h.** casque protecteur

helmsman, *pl* **helmsmen** ['helmzmən] N *Naut* homme *m* de barre, timonier *m*

▐**HELP**▐ [help]

┌─────────────────────────────────────┐
│ ▌N▐ aide **1–3** ▪ secours **1** ▪ personnel │
│ **4**   │
│ ▌VT▐ aider **1** ▪ faciliter **2** ▪ servir **3** │
│ ▌VI▐ aider **1**   │
└─────────────────────────────────────┘

N **1** aide *f*, assistance *f*; *(when in danger etc)* secours *m*, aide; **with God's h.** avec l'aide de Dieu, grâce à Dieu; **to shout for h.** crier au secours, appeler à l'aide; **he's past h.** *(is dying)* il est perdu; *(is crazy, stupid)* on ne peut rien pour lui; **can I be of (any) h.?** puis-je vous aider?; **to be of h. to sb** être d'un grand secours à qn; **some students need h. to decide which course to take** certains étudiants ont besoin qu'on les aide à choisir leur cursus; **she needs h.** *(from a psychiatrist etc)* il faut qu'elle voie un psychiatre, elle a des problèmes psychologiques; **if you think that's funny, you need h.** si tu trouves ça drôle, c'est que tu dois avoir un problème; **to give h. to sb** aider qn; *(at accident etc)* porter secours à qn; **to provide some financial h.** offrir une aide financière; **the map wasn't much h.** la carte n'a pas servi à grand-chose; **for all the h. you've been** pour ce que tu nous as aidés; **I had h.** *(I didn't do it on my own)* on m'a aidé; *Fam* **a (fat) lot of h. you are** tu parles d'une aide!; **to come to sb's h.** venir au secours de qn

2 **to be a h. to sb** rendre service à qn; **my daughter's been a great h.** ma fille m'a bien rendu service; **that was a big h. (to me)** ça m'a beaucoup aidé; *Iron* **you're a great h.!** merci pour ton aide!

3 *(helper)* aide *mf*, *esp Br* **daily h.** femme *f* de ménage; *esp Br* **home h.** aide *f* ménagère; **mother's h.** aide *f* familiale

4 *esp Am (pl* **help)** *(worker)* **a hired h.** un ouvrier *ou (white collar)* employé intérimaire; **we need more h.** on a besoin de plus de personnel

5 *(alternative)* **there was no h. for it** il n'y avait rien d'autre à faire

VT **1** *(person)* aider; **to h. one another** s'entraider; **can I** *or* **may I h. you?** puis-je vous aider?; *(in shop, restaurant)* que désirez-vous?; *(on telephone)* que puis-je faire pour vous?; *Law* **do you swear to tell the truth, so h. you God?** jurez-vous de dire la vérité, que Dieu vous vienne en aide?; **so h. me God!** *(it's the truth)* je le jure *ou* sur la vérité!; *Fam* **so h. me** je jure; **come and h. me** venez m'aider *ou* me donner un coup de main; **he helped me with my homework** il m'a aidé à faire mes devoirs; **to h. sb (to) do sth** aider qn à faire qch; **he helped the old lady up the stairs** il a aidé la vieille dame à monter l'escalier; **to h. sb on/off with their coat** aider qn à mettre/enlever son manteau; **to h. sb out of a difficulty** aider qn à se tirer d'une difficulté; **he helped the ball into the goal** il a donné un petit coup au ballon pour le faire entrer dans les buts; *Prov* **God helps those who h. themselves** aide-toi et le ciel t'aidera; **it helped me knowing that someone was waiting for me** ça m'a aidé de savoir que quelqu'un m'attendait; **a man is helping the police with their enquiries** un homme est interrogé par la police; **it helped to give the impression that ...** cela a contribué à donner l'impression que ..., à cause de cela, on avait l'impression que ...; **h.!** *(when in danger etc)* au secours!; **h.!, I'm late!** mon Dieu!, je suis en retard! VOIR GRAMMAIRE A41

2 *(improve)* *(digestion, progress)* faciliter; **that doesn't h. the situation, that doesn't h.**

much cela ne nous avance pas (beaucoup); *Iron* **to h. matters, we had a puncture** pour ne rien arranger, nous avons crevé

3 *(at table)* *(person)* servir; **to h. sb to soup/wine** servir du potage/verser du vin à qn; **to h. oneself to sth** *(serve)* se servir en *ou* de qch; *Fam, Iron (steal)* voler *ou* prendre *ou* chiper qch; **h. yourself!** servez-vous!

4 *(prevent)* *(with negation expressed or implied)* **it can't be helped!** tant pis!, il n'y a rien à faire, on n'y peut rien; **I can't h. laughing** je ne peux pas m'empêcher de rire; **I couldn't h. overhearing** je n'ai pu m'empêcher de surprendre la conversation; **I can't h. wondering** je ne peux pas m'empêcher de poser la question; **I can't h. it** c'est plus fort que moi, je ne peux pas m'en empêcher; *(it can't be helped)* je n'y peux rien; **they can't h. being born there** ils n'ont pas demandé à naître là; **I'm not going back if I can h. it** si j'ai le choix, je n'y retournerai pas

VI **1** aider; **can I h.?** est-ce que je peux faire quelque chose?; **I was only trying to h.!** je voulais seulement vous/les/*etc* aider!; **he offered to h. with the clearing up** il a proposé de nous/les/*etc* aider à ranger; **it helps if you can speak the language** c'est plus facile si on parle la langue; **forgetting the map didn't h. (much)** le fait d'avoir oublié la carte n'a pas arrangé les choses; **it's near the post office if that helps** *(of information)* c'est près du bureau de poste si ça peut vous aider; **every little helps** les petits ruisseaux font les grandes rivières

2 *(avoid)* **don't be away longer than you can h.** tâchez d'être absent le moins de temps possible

▸▸ *Comput* **h. button** case *f* d'aide; **h. desk** service *m* d'assistance téléphonique; *Comput (for computing queries)* service d'assistance; *Comput* **h. file** fichier *m* d'aide; **h. function** fonction *f* d'aide; *Comput* **h. key** touche *f* d'aide; *Comput* **h. menu** menu *m* d'aide; *Comput* **h. screen** écran *m* d'aide; *Comput* **h. window** fenêtre *f* d'aide

▸ **help out** VI *(help)* aider; **everyone helped out with the cleaning up** tout le monde a aidé à nettoyer; **I could h. out with the cooking** je pourrais vous/les/*etc* aider à faire les repas

VT SEP *(help)* aider; **I need £20, can you h. me out?** j'ai besoin de 20 livres, est-ce que tu peux me les avancer?; **they helped him out with food and money** ils l'ont aidé en lui donnant de la nourriture et de l'argent, ils lui ont donné de la nourriture et de l'argent pour l'aider

helper ['helpər] N aide *mf*, *(assistant)* assistant, -ante; **voluntary h.** bénévole *mf*

helpful ['helpfʊl] ADJ **1** *(person)* secourable, serviable; **he always tries to be h.** il essaie toujours de rendre service; **he was not being very h.** il n'a pas fait grand-chose pour nous aider; *(wasn't telling us much)* il ne disait pas grand-chose **2** *(book, advice)* utile; **this dictionary is not very h.** ce dictionnaire ne sert pas à grand-chose

helpfully ['helpfʊlɪ] ADV **she very h. offered/lent us ...** elle a eu la gentillesse *ou* l'amabilité de nous offrir/prêter ...; **it's very h. indexed** l'index est très utile; **it's h. explained in the brochure** c'est très bien expliqué dans la brochure; *Iron* **someone had very h. let the battery run down** quelqu'un a eu l'amabilité de décharger la pile

helpfulness ['helpfʊlnɪs] N **1** *(of person)* serviabilité *f* **2** *(of book etc)* utilité

helping ['helpɪŋ] ADJ **to lend a h. hand** aider; **to give sb a h. hand** donner un coup de main à qn
N *(of food)* portion *f*; **two helpings of soup** deux assiettes *fpl* de soupe; **I had two hel-**

pings *or* **a second h.** j'en ai repris, je me suis resservi

helpless ['helplɪs] ADJ *(powerless)* faible, impuissant; *(orphan etc)* sans appui, délaissé; *(handicapped person)* infirme; *(ship)* désemparé; **I am h. in the matter** je n'y puis *ou* peux rien; **a h. onlooker** un spectateur impuissant; **we were h. to prevent what was happening** nous ne pouvions rien faire contre ce qui se passait; **I was h. with laughter** je n'en pouvais plus de rire; *Fam* **he's one of the h. sort** il est incapable de se débrouiller; **carry it yourself, you're not h.** débrouille-toi, tu peux très bien le porter tout seul

helplessly ['helplɪslɪ] ADV *(to struggle)* en vain; **to gesture h.** lever les mains en signe d'impuissance; **to watch h.** regarder en spectateur impuissant; **they were h. convulsed with laughter** ils n'en pouvaient plus de rire

helplessness ['helplɪsnɪs] N impuissance *f*; **because of his h. around the house** parce qu'il est incapable de se débrouiller tout seul chez lui

helpline ['helplaɪn] N *Tel (for information)* ligne *f* d'assistance; *(for battered women)* ≃ SOS femmes battues; *(for victims of child abuse)* ≃ SOS enfants martyrs

Helsinki [hel'sɪŋkɪ] N Helsinki

helter-skelter ['heltə'skeltər] ADV *(to run, flee)* pêle-mêle, à la débandade
▪ N *Br (at fairground)* toboggan *m*

hem¹ [hem] *Sewing* N **1** *(of garment)* bord *m*; *(turned over part)* ourlet *m*; **let the h. down** j'ai rallongé ma jupe en en défaisant l'ourlet **2** = **hemline**
▪ VT ourler, faire l'ourlet de
▸ **hem in** VT SEP *(surround) (enemy troops)* entourer, cerner; *(place)* investir; **hemmed in by high mountains** enserré entre de hautes montagnes

hem² INT hem!, hum!

hem³ VI = **hum**¹ VI 2

hema- ['hiːmə] PREF *Am Med* = **haema-**

he-man, *pl* **he-men** ['hiːmæn, -men] N *Fam* homme *m* viril

hemato- [hiːmə'təʊ] PREF *Am Med* = **haemato-**

hemicycle ['hemɪsaɪk(ə)l] N *Archit* hémicycle *m*

hemiplegia [hemɪ'pliːdʒɪə] N *Med* hémiplégie *f*

hemisphere ['hemɪsfɪər] N hémisphère *m*; *Geog* **the northern/southern h.** l'hémisphère nord *ou* boréal/sud *ou* austral; **left/right h.** *(of brain)* hémisphère gauche/droit

hemispherical [hemɪ'sferɪk(ə)l] ADJ hémisphérique

hemline ['hemlaɪn] N *Sewing* bas *m* de l'ourlet; **hemlines are coming down** la mode rallonge; **daring hemlines** des jupes très courtes

hemlock ['hemlɒk] N ciguë *f*

hemo- ['hiːməʊ] pref *Am Med* = **haemo-**

hemp [hemp] N **1** *(plant)* chanvre *m*; *Tex* chanvre, filasse *f* **2** *Pharm etc* **Indian h.** chanvre *m* indien, hachisch *m*

hemstitch ['hemstɪtʃ] *Sewing* N ourlet *m* à jour
▪ VT *(handkerchief etc)* ourler à jour

hen [hen] N **1** *(chicken)* poule *f* **2** *(female bird)* femelle *f* **3** *Scot Fam (term of address)* ma poule, ma cocotte
▸▸ **h. bird** oiseau *m* femelle; **h. harrier** busard *m* Saint-Martin; *Fam* **h. night, h. party** = soirée *f* où une femme enterre sa vie de jeune fille; **h. pheasant** poule faisane

henbane ['henbeɪn] N *(plant)* jusquiame *f*, herbe *f* aux poules

hence [hens] ADV **1** *(referring to consequence)* de là, d'où, en conséquence; **h. his anger** de là *ou* d'où sa fureur **2** *(referring to time)* dorénavant, désormais, à partir d'aujourd'hui; **five years h.** dans cinq ans **3** *Arch, Lit (referring to place) (from)* h. d'ici; **five miles h.** à deux lieues d'ici

henceforth [hens'fɔːθ], **henceforward** [hens'fɔːwəd] ADV *Fml* désormais, dorénavant, à l'avenir

henchman, *pl* **henchmen** ['hentʃmən] N *Pol etc Pej* acolyte *m*

hencoop ['henkuːp] N cage *f* à poules

henhouse ['henhaʊs] N poulailler *m*

henna ['henə] N *(shrub, dye)* henné *m*
▪ VT **to h. one's hair** se faire un henné; **hennaed hair** cheveux teints au henné

henpecked ['henpekt] ADJ **h. husband** mari mené par le bout du nez; **he's h.** sa femme le mène par le bout du nez

henroost ['henruːst] N **1** *(perch)* juchoir *m*, perchoir *m* **2** = **henhouse**

Henry the Eighth, **Henry VIII** ['henrɪ ðiː'eɪtθ] N Henri VIII

hep [hep] ADJ *Old-fashioned Fam* à la page, dans le vent

heparin ['hepərɪn] N *Pharm* héparine *f*

hepatic [he'pætɪk] ADJ *Anat etc* hépatique

hepatitis [hepə'taɪtɪs] N *Med* hépatite *f*; **h. A/B/C** hépatite A/B/C

hepatology [hepə'tɒlədʒɪ] N *Med* hépatologie *f*

heptagon ['heptəgən] N *Math* heptagone *m*

her [VOIR GRAMMAIRE A27–8; B18–19] *(unstressed)* [hər], *stressed* [hɜːr]) PERS PRON **1** *(unstressed) (direct)* la; *(before a vowel sound)* l'; *(indirect)* lui; *(reflexive, after preposition)* elle; **I hate h.** je la déteste; **have you seen h.?** l'avez-vous vue?; **I shall tell h. so** je le lui dirai; **look at h.** regardez-la; **tell h.** dites-lui; **I am thinking of h.** je pense à elle; **I remember h.** je me souviens d'elle; **she closed the door behind h.** elle referma la porte derrière elle; *Fml* **Poland's friends deserted h.** *(country)* la Pologne a été abandonnée par ses amis; **the enemy sank h.** *(ship)* il a été coulé par l'ennemi; *Fam* **I'll get h. started** *(car etc)* je vais le faire démarrer
2 *(stressed)* elle; *Lit (with dem force)* celle; **I can forgive h. son but not her** je peux pardonner à son fils, mais pas à elle; *Lit* **to h. who should take offence at this I would say** ... à celle qui s'en offenserait je dirais ...; **who better than h. to break the news?** qui, mieux qu'elle, saurait annoncer la nouvelle?
3 *(complement of verb* **to be***)* **it's h.!** c'est elle!; **that's h.!** la voilà!
POSS ADJ son, *f* sa, *pl* ses; **h. dress/dresses** sa robe/ses robes; **h. hat** son chapeau; **h. father and mother** son père et sa mère; *Admin* ses père et mère; **h. eyes are blue** elle a les yeux bleus; **she has hurt h. hand** elle s'est fait mal à la main; **H. Majesty** sa Majesté; *Fml* **France reassured h. allies** la France rassura ses alliés; **the ship and h. crew** le navire et son équipage [VOIR GRAMMAIRE A30; A43; B21–2]
▪ N *Fam* **it's a h. not a him** *(of baby)* c'est une fille, pas un garçon; *(of animal)* c'est une femelle, pas un mâle

herald ['herəld] N **1** héraut *m* **2** *Fig (of spring etc)* présage *m*
▪ VT *Fml, Lit (arrival etc)* annoncer, proclamer; **these negotiations h. a new era for world peace** ces négociations marquent le début d'une ère nouvelle pour la paix mondiale; **to h. the dawn** annoncer l'aube

heraldic [hɪ'rældɪk] ADJ héraldique; **h. bearing** armoirie *f*, blason *m*

heraldry ['herəldrɪ] N héraldique *f*; *(coat of arms)* blason *m*; **book of h.** armorial *m*, -aux

herb [hɜːb, *Am* ɜːb] N *(plant)* herbe *f*; *Culin* **herbs** (fines) herbes; **herbs and spices** condiments *mpl*; **medicinal herbs** plantes *fpl* médicinales
▸▸ *Hort* **h. garden** jardin *m* d'herbes aromatiques; *Bot* **h. Robert** herbe à Robert, géranium *m* robertin; **h. tea** infusion *f*, tisane *f*

herbaceous [hɜː'beɪʃəs] ADJ *Bot* herbacé
▸▸ **h. border** bordure *f* de plantes herbacées

herbage ['hɜːbɪdʒ] N *(plants)* herbes *fpl*, herbage(s) *m(pl)*

herbal ['hɜːb(ə)l, *Am* 'ɜːb(ə)l] N *Old-fashioned (book)* herbier *m*
▪ ADJ *(drink)* fait avec des plantes; *(remedy)* à base d'herbes *ou* de plantes
▸▸ **h. cigarettes** cigarettes *fpl* aux plantes; **h. infusion** infusion *f*, tisane *f*; **h. medicine** *(practice)* phytothérapie *f*, *(medication)* médicament *m* à base de plantes; **h. tea** infusion, tisane

herbalist ['hɜːbəlɪst, *Am* 'ɜːbəlɪst] N herboriste *mf*

herbarium [hɜː'beərɪəm, *Am* ɜː'beərɪəm] N herbier *m*

herbicide ['hɜːbɪsaɪd, *Am* 'ɜːbɪsaɪd] N herbicide *m*

herbivore ['hɜːbɪvɔːr] N *(animal)* herbivore *m*

herbivorous [hɜː'bɪvərəs, *Am* ɜː'bɪvərəs] ADJ *(animal)* herbivore

Herculean [hɜːkjʊ'liːən] ADJ *(effort, strength)* herculéen

Hercules ['hɜːkjʊliːz] N *Myth, Astron* Hercule; *Fig (strong man)* hercule *m*
▸▸ *Comput* **H. monitor** moniteur *m* Hercules

herd [hɜːd] N *(of cattle, elephants etc)* troupeau *m*; *(of deer)* troupeau, *Spec* harde *f*, *(of horses etc)* troupe *f*, bande *f*, *(of people)* troupeau, foule *f*; **the h. instinct** *(in animals, people)* l'instinct grégaire; **the common h.** le peuple, *Pej* la canaille, la populace
▪ VT *(cattle)* garder, surveiller; *Fam (tourists etc)* diriger; **the cattle were herded into the barn** on a fait entrer le bétail dans la grange; **the candidates were then all herded into the waiting room** on a entassé les candidats dans la salle d'attente; **the prisoners were herded onto trucks** on a entassé les prisonniers dans des camions
▸ **herd together** VI *(of animals) (live in herds)* vivre en troupeaux; *(form a herd)* s'assembler en troupeau; *Fam (of people)* se regrouper
▪ VT SEP *(cattle etc)* rassembler en troupeau

herder ['hɜːdər] N *esp Am* = **herdsman**

herdsman, *pl* **herdsmen** ['hɜːdzmən] N *esp Br* gardien *m* de troupeau

HERE [hɪər] ADV [VOIR GRAMMAIRE A21] **1** *(this place)* ici; **come h.!** (venez) ici!; **in h., please** par ici, s'il vous plaît; **near h.** près d'ici; **over h.** par ici; **from h. to there** d'ici à là-bas; **Mr Green's not h. today** M. Green n'est pas là aujourd'hui; **over h. in Scotland** ici, en Écosse; **h. and now** immédiatement, tout de suite; **it's h. to stay** *(of fashion)* cela restera; **h. lies ...** *(on tombstone)* ci-gît ...; *Lit* **h. below** *(on this earth)* ici-bas
2 *(point in time, argument etc)* **I think we could break h. for lunch** je crois que nous pouvons nous arrêter là pour déjeuner; **h. I am referring to taxation** *(at this point)* c'est aux impôts que je fais allusion; **we disagree h.** c'est là que nous ne sommes pas d'accord; **h.'s what you have to do** voilà ce que tu as à faire

3 h.'s your hat! voici *ou* voilà votre chapeau!; **h. you are!** *(on seeing, finding sb)* vous voici!, vous voilà!; *(giving sth)* tenez!; **h. we are!** *(on finding sth)* voilà! j'ai trouvé!; *(on arriving somewhere)* nous y sommes!, nous voilà arrivés! *ou* rendus!; **h. she comes!** la voici (qui vient)!; **h. I am!** me voici!, me voilà!; **h. is** *or* **h. we have a woman who ...** voici une femme qui ...; **my friend h. will tell you** mon ami que voici vous le dira; *Fam* **this h. ...** ce..., *f* cette ...; **h. goes!** allons-y!; **h. we go (again)!** *(said with a sigh)* c'est reparti!; *(annoyed)* encore?

4 *(esp over drink etc)* h.'s **to you!** à votre santé!; **h.'s to the success of your venture!** à votre succès!

5 h. and there partout, çà et là, *Lit* par-ci, par-là; **h., there and everywhere** (un peu) partout; **neither h. nor there** ni ici ni ailleurs; *Fig* **that's neither h. nor there** cela n'a aucun rapport

INT 1 *(at roll call)* présent!

2 *(to attract sb's attention)* h.! come and look at this eh! viens voir ça!; **h., take this** tiens, prends ça

3 *(to express annoyance)* h., that's my chair! eh, c'est ma chaise!; **h., stop that!** écoute, tu arrêtes un peu!

N the h. and now le présent

hereabout(s) [ˈhɪərəbaʊt(s)] **ADV** près d'ici, par ici

hereafter [hɪərˈɑːftər] **ADV** *Fml* **1** *(of position)* *(in book, writings etc)* ci-après, ci-dessous **2** *esp Jur* *(of time)* dorénavant, désormais **3** *(after death)* dans l'autre monde

N *Lit* **the h.** l'au-delà *m*; **in the h.** dans l'autre monde, dans l'au-delà

hereby [hɪəˈbaɪ, ˈhɪəbaɪ] **ADV** *Fml* par ceci, par ce moyen, par là; *Law* par la présente *ou* les présentes; **the council h. declares that ...** le conseil déclare par le présent acte que ...

hereditary [hɪˈredɪt(ə)rɪ] **ADJ** *(disease etc)* héréditaire

heredity [hɪˈredɪtɪ] **N** hérédité *f*

herein [hɪərˈɪn] **ADV** *Law, Lit* **1** *(of place, position)* ici, en ce lieu; *(in document)* dans ce document; **the letter enclosed h.** la lettre ci-incluse **2** *(in this matter)* sur ce point

heresy [ˈherəsɪ] **N** *Rel, Fig* hérésie *f*; **it smacks of h.** *(of opinion)* c'est une hérésie

heretic [ˈheratɪk] **N** *Rel, Fig* hérétique *mf*

heretical [hɪˈretɪk(ə)l] **ADJ** *Rel, Fig* hérétique

hereto [hɪəˈtuː, ˈhɪətuː] **ADV** *Law* annexed h., **h. annexed** ci-joint

heretofore [ˈhɪətʊˈfɔːr] **ADV** *Arch, Lit* jusqu'ici; **as h.** comme par le passé

hereunder [hɪərˈʌndər] **ADV** *Law etc* ci-dessous

hereupon [ˈhɪərəpɒn] **ADV** *Law etc* là-dessus; **h. he left** sur ce *ou* là-dessus, il partit

herewith [hɪəˈwɪθ] **ADV 1** = **hereby 2** *Com* **price list h. enclosed** prix-courant ci-inclus *ou* sous ce pli

heritable [ˈherɪtəb(ə)l] **ADJ 1** *Biol (disease)* héréditaire **2** *Law (right)* héréditaire; *(property)* dont on peut hériter; *(person)* capable d'hériter

heritage [ˈherɪtɪdʒ] **N** héritage *m*, patrimoine *m*; *(of nation, humanity)* patrimoine

▸▸ **h. site** site *m* patrimoine; **h. tourism** tourisme *m* culturel; **h. trail** = parcours *m* touristique qui va d'un lieu historique à un autre

hermaphrodite [hɜːˈmæfrədaɪt] **ADJ, N** *Zool, Bot* hermaphrodite *m*

hermaphroditic [hɜːmæfrəˈdɪtɪk] **ADJ** hermaphrodite

hermetic [hɜːˈmetɪk] **ADJ** hermétique; *Fig*

the university was a h. world l'université était un monde très fermé *ou* hermétique

hermetically [hɜːˈmetɪklɪ] **ADV** *(sealed)* hermétiquement

hermit [ˈhɜːmɪt] **N** ermite *m*; **to live like a h.** vivre en solitaire *ou* en ermite

▸▸ **h. crab** bernard-l'ermite *m inv*, pagure *m*

hermitage [ˈhɜːmɪtɪdʒ] **N** ermitage *m*

hernia [ˈhɜːnɪə] **N** *Med* hernie *f*; **to have a h.** avoir une hernie

hero, *pl* **heroes** [ˈhɪərəʊ, -əʊz] **N** héros *m*; **a sporting h.** un champion sportif; *Fam* **my h.!** mon héros!

▸▸ **h. worship** *(admiration)* adulation *f*, culte *m* (du héros); *Antiq* culte *m* des héros

Herod [ˈherəd] **N** *Hist* Hérode

heroic [hɪˈrəʊɪk] **ADJ** héroïque; **h. deed** acte *m* d'héroïsme

▸▸ **h. couplet** distique *m* héroïque; *Liter* **h. poem** poème *m* épique; *Liter* **h. verse** vers *m* décasyllabe héroïque

heroically [hɪˈrəʊɪklɪ] **ADV** héroïquement

heroics [hɪˈrəʊɪks] **NPL 1** *Pej (behaviour)* coup *m* d'éclat; *(in opera)* emphase *f* **2** *(heroic efforts)* efforts *mpl* héroïques

heroin [ˈherəʊɪn] **N** *Chem, Pharm* héroïne *f*

▸▸ **h. addict** héroïnomane *mf*; **h. chic** = apparence *f* cultivée par certains mannequins, inspirée de celle des héroïnomanes (extrême maigreur, mauvaise mine etc)

> Attention: ne pas confondre avec **heroine**.

heroine [ˈherəʊɪn] **N** héroïne *f*

> Attention: ne pas confondre avec **heroin**.

heroism [ˈherəʊɪz(ə)m] **N** héroïsme *m*

heron [ˈherən] **N** *(bird)* héron *m*

hero-worship **VT** *(person)* idolâtrer

herpes [ˈhɜːpiːz] **N** *Med* herpès *m*; **to have h.** avoir de l'herpès

▸▸ *Med* **h. simplex** herpès *m*; **h. virus** virus *m* de l'herpès; *Med* **h. zoster** zona *m*

herring [ˈherɪŋ] **N** *(fish)* hareng *m*

▸▸ **h. boat** harenguier *m*; **h. fleet** flotille *f* de harenguiers

herringbone [ˈherɪŋbəʊn] **N 1** *(pattern)* dessin *m* à chevrons **2** *Sewing (stitch)* point *m* croisé, point d'épine **3** *Ski* montée *f* en ciseaux *ou* en pas de canard

▸▸ **h. pattern** dessin à chevrons; *Sewing* **h. stitch** point croisé, point d'épine

hers [hɜːz] **POSS PRON** le sien, la sienne, *pl* les siens, les siennes; **this book is h.** ce livre est à elle *ou* lui appartient; **a friend of h.** un(e) de ses ami(e)s, un(e) ami(e) à elle; **it's no business of h.** ce n'est pas son affaire **VOIR GRAMMAIRE A30; B21**

herself [hɜːˈself] **PERS PRON** **VOIR GRAMMAIRE A29–30 1** *(emphatic)* elle-même; **she did all the work h.** elle a fait tout le travail elle-même *ou* toute seule; **she's looking (quite) h. again** *(after illness)* elle paraît complètement remise; **she's not h. today** elle n'est pas elle-même aujourd'hui, elle n'est pas dans son état normal aujourd'hui

2 *(reflexive)* se; **she hurt h.** elle s'est fait mal **SEE GRAMMAR B28–9**

3 *(after preposition)* elle(-même); **'well, well!' she said to h.** 'eh bien!' se dit-elle; **she isn't being honest with h.** elle n'est pas honnête avec elle-même; **she kept one for h.** elle s'en est gardé un/une pour elle; **she painted a picture of h.** elle a fait son autoportrait; **she was living by h.** elle vivait seule

Herts [hɑːts] *abbr* **Hertfordshire**

hertz [hɜːts] **N** *Elec* hertz *m*

he's [hiːz] **CONTR 1** = **he is,** *see* **be 2** = **he has,** *see* **have**

hesitancy [ˈhezɪtənsɪ] **N** hésitation *f*

hesitant [ˈhezɪtənt] **ADJ** hésitant, irrésolu; **I would be h. to ...** j'hésiterais à ...; **he's a very h. speaker** il hésite beaucoup en parlant

hesitantly [ˈhezɪtəntlɪ] **ADV** avec hésitation

hesitate [ˈhezɪteɪt] **VI** *(in speaking, acting)* hésiter; **without hesitating** sans hésiter **VT to h. to do sth** hésiter à faire qch

hesitation [hezɪˈteɪʃən] **N** hésitation *f*; **without (the slightest) h.** sans (la moindre) hésitation; **he has no h. about it** il n'a pas le moindre doute à ce sujet

hessian [ˈhesɪən] **N** *Tex* toile *f* de jute

hetero [ˈhetərəʊ] **ADJ, N** *Fam* = **heterosexual**

heterodox [ˈhetərədɒks] **ADJ** hétérodoxe

heterogeneous [hetərəˈdʒiːnɪəs] **ADJ** hétérogène

heterosexism [hetərəˈseksɪzm] **N** discrimination *f* envers les homosexuels

heterosexual [hetərəʊˈseksjʊəl] **ADJ, N** hétérosexuel, -elle

het up [hetˈʌp] **ADJ** *Br Fam (annoyed)* fâché, en rogne; *(upset, tense)* énervé, à cran; **don't get h. up about it** ne t'en fais pas pour cela

heuristic [hjʊˈrɪstɪk] **ADJ** heuristique

N heuristics heuristique *f* **VOIR GRAMMAIRE A10**

▸▸ *Math, Phil* **h. model** modèle *m* heuristique

hew [hjuː] **VT** *(pt* **hewed** [hjuːd]*, pp* **hewed, hewn** [hjuːn]*)* *(with axe, chisel etc)* couper, tailler; *(stone)* tailler, équarrir, dresser; **to h. coal** abattre le charbon

▸ **hew down VT SEP** *(cut down) (tree)* abattre

▸ **hew off VT SEP** *(branch)* abattre

▸ **hew out VT SEP** creuser; **the cavern had been hewn out of the rock** la caverne a été creusée dans la pierre

hewer [ˈhjuːər] **N** *(of stones)* tailleur *m*

hex¹ [heks] *Am Fam* **N** *(spell)* sortilège *m*, *(mauvais)* sort *m*; **to put a h. on sb/sth** jeter un sort à qn/qch

VT jeter un sort à

hex² *Comput* **N** notation *f* hexadécimale; **in h.** en hexadécimal

▸▸ **h. code** code *m* hexadécimal, notation hexadécimale; **h. file** fichier *m* hexadécimal

hexadecimal [heksəˈdesəm(ə)l] **ADJ** *Comput* hexadécimal, -aux

hexagon [ˈheksəgən] **N** *Math* hexagone *m*

hexagonal [hekˈsægən(ə)l] **ADJ** hexagonal, -aux

hexameter [hekˈsæmɪtər] **N** *Liter* hexamètre *m*

hey [heɪ] **INT 1** *(to attract attention)* hé!, holà! **2 h. presto!** passez muscade!, le tour est joué!; **h., that's a good idea!** hé, c'est une bonne idée, ça!

heyday [ˈheɪdeɪ] **N** apogée *m*; **in its h. it was one of the busiest ports in the world** à son heure de gloire, c'était l'un des ports les plus importants du monde; **to be in the h. of youth** être dans *ou* à la fleur de l'âge

HFEA [eɪtʃefiːˈeɪ] **N** *Br (abbr* **Human Fertilization and Embryology Authority)** = organisme *m* chargé de réglementer les traitements de la stérilité et la recherche en embryologie

HGH [eɪtʃdʒiːˈeɪtʃ] **N** *Biol (abbr* **human growth hormone)** hormone *f* de croissance

HGV [eɪtʃdʒiːˈviː] **N** *Br Admin (abbr* **heavy goods vehicle)** poids lourd *m*

▸▸ **H. licence** permis *m* PL

hi [haɪ] **INT 1** *Fam (hello)* salut! **2** *(to attract attention)* hé!, là-bas!, ohé!

hiatus, *pl* **hiatuses** [haɪˈeɪtəs, -əsɪz] **N 1** *Fml (gap in series, text etc)* lacune *f* **2** *Fml (pause in conversation etc)* silence *m*; *(pause in negotiation etc)* interruption *f*, **apart from a h.**

between **1993** and **1995** mis à part une interruption entre 1993 et 1995 **3** *Gram* hiatus *m*
▸▸*Med* **h. hernia** hernie *f* hiatale

hibernate ['haɪbəneɪt] *vi* hiberner

hibernation [haɪbə'neɪʃən] *n also Comput* hibernation *f*; **to go into h.** hiberner

hibiscus [hɪ'bɪskəs] *n (plant)* ketmie *f*, hibiscus *m*

hiccup, hiccough ['hɪkʌp] *n* **1** hoquet *m*; **to have (the) hiccups** avoir le hoquet **2** *Fig (problem)* problème *m*, *Fam* hic *m*; **there's been some sort of h. with the delivery** il y a eu un hic à la livraison
vi hoqueter

hick [hɪk] *Am Fam n* paysan *m*, rustaud *m*
adj **a h. town** un bled

hickey ['hɪkɪ] *n Am Fam* **1** *(spot)* bouton *m*; *(love bite)* suçon *m* **2** *(gadget)* machin *m*, truc *m*

hickory ['hɪkərɪ] *n (tree or wood)* noyer *m* (blanc) d'Amérique, hickory *m*

hid *pt see* **hide**[1]

hidden ['hɪd(ə)n] *pp see* **hide**[1]
adj (difficulty, treasure etc) caché; **she has h. talents** elle a des talents cachés
▸▸**h. camera** caméra *f* cachée, caméra invisible; *Fin* **h. cost** coût *m* caché; *Com* **h. defects** défauts *mpl ou* vices *mpl* cachés; *Com* **h. extras** dépenses *fpl* supplémentaires inattendues; **no h. extras** garanti tout compris; *Comput* **h. file** fichier *m* caché; *Fig* **h. hand** influence *f* occulte; *Fin* **h. reserves** réserve *f* latente; **I have h. reserves** j'ai encore des réserves

hide[1] [haɪd] *n Br (place for hunter etc)* affût *m*, cachette *f*
vt (pt **hid** [hɪd], *pp* **hidden** ['hɪd(ə)n]*)* cacher; *(feelings, emotions)* dissimuler; **to h. sth from sb** cacher qch à qn; *(not divulge information)* taire qch à qn; **I've got nothing to h.** je n'ai rien à cacher; **to h. one's face** se cacher le visage; **where has she hidden herself?** où est-elle allée se cacher *ou Fam* se fourrer?; **they hid him from the police** ils l'ont caché pour que la police ne le trouve pas; **to h. sth from sight** soustraire qch aux regards; **trees h. the house from sight** les arbres cachent la maison; **clouds hid the sun** des nuages voilaient le soleil; *Fig* **to h. one's light under a bushel** cacher son talent; *Fig* **he doesn't exactly h. his light under a bushel** il ne se prend pas pour le quart de la moitié d'un citron, ce n'est pas la modestie qui l'étouffe
vi se cacher (**from sb** de qn); **have you been hiding from me?** tu te caches?; **she was hiding in a corner** *(of shy person)* elle restait dans son coin; **to h. behind an excuse/statistics** prétexter une excuse/les statistiques; *Fig* **to h. behind sb** se réfugier derrière qn
▸ **hide away** *vi* = **hide**[1] *vi*
vt sep = **hide**[1] *vt*
▸ **hide out** *vi (be in hiding)* se cacher, se terrer

hide[2] *n (skin) (of animal)* peau *f*, dépouille *f*; *Com (leather)* cuir *m*; *Fam* **to save one's h.** sauver sa peau; *Fam* **to tan sb's h.** tanner le cuir à qn; *Fam* **I haven't seen h. nor hair of her** je ne l'ai pas vue du tout

hide-and-seek, *Am* **hide-and-go-seek** *n* cache-cache *m*; **to play h.** jouer à cache-cache

hideaway ['haɪdəweɪ] *n* cachette *f*, *Fam* planque *f*

hidebound ['haɪdbaʊnd] *adj (person)* aux vues étroites, plein de préjugés; *(attitude)* rigide; **the country's h. legal profession** les hommes de loi conservateurs et bornés de ce pays

hideous ['hɪdɪəs] *adj (appearance etc)* hi-

deux, affreux, effroyable; *(crime)* horrible, odieux; **what a h. painting!** quelle peinture abominable!

hideously ['hɪdɪəslɪ] *adv* hideusement, affreusement

hideousness ['hɪdɪəsnɪs] *n* laideur *f*; **the h. of his wounds/the crime** ses blessures abominables/le crime abominable

hide-out *n* cachette *f*, *Fam* planque *f*; **so this is your h. !** alors, c'est ici que tu te caches!

hidey-hole ['haɪdɪhəʊl] *n Fam* cachette *f*

hiding[1] ['haɪdɪŋ] *n* **to go into h.** se cacher; **to be in h.** se tenir caché, se cacher; **to live in h.** vivre dans la clandestinité; **to come out of h.** sortir de sa cachette; *(stop living in hiding)* sortir de la clandestinité
▸▸**h. place** cachette *f*

hiding[2] *n Fam (beating)* raclée *f*, rossée *f*, volée *f*; **to give sb a good h.** donner une raclée à qn; **to be on a h. to nothing** n'avoir aucune chance (de réussir)

hierarchic(al) [haɪə'rɑːkɪk, -ɪk(ə)l] *adj* hiérarchique; **in h. order** par ordre hiérarchique

hierarchy ['haɪərɑːkɪ] *n* hiérarchie *f*

hieroglyph ['haɪərəglɪf] *n* hiéroglyphe *m*

hieroglyphic [haɪərə'glɪfɪk] *adj* hiéroglyphique

hieroglyphics [haɪərə'glɪfɪks] *n (system)* hiéroglyphes *mpl*; *(characters)* signes *mpl* hiéroglyphiques; *Fig Fam (bad handwriting)* hiéroglyphes VOIR GRAMMAIRE A10

hifalutin(g) [haɪfə'luːtɪn, -tɪŋ] *adj Fam* = **highfalutin**

hi-fi ['haɪfaɪ] *n* hi-fi *f inv*; *(stereo system)* chaîne *f* (hi-fi)
adj hi-fi *inv*
▸▸**h. system** chaîne (hi-fi)

higgledy-piggledy ['hɪg(ə)ldɪ'pɪg(ə)ldɪ] *adv Fam* en pagaïe, pêle-mêle

HIGH [haɪ]	
ADJ haut **1, 3, 7**	▪ élevé **1, 2, 4**
▪ grand **2** ▪ noble **4** ▪ aigu **7**	
ADV haut **1** ▪ en haut **1**	
N haut **1**	

ADJ 1 haut, élevé; **built on h. ground** construit sur un terrain élevé; **this house is much higher (up) than the village** cette maison est située à beaucoup plus haute altitude que le village; **the highest mountain in the country** la plus haute montagne du pays; **wall two metres h.** mur haut de deux mètres, mur d'une hauteur de deux mètres, mur de deux mètres de hauteur; **at h. water** *or* **tide** à marée haute; **h. neck** *(on garment)* col montant; **h. cheekbones** pommettes saillantes; **with one's head h.** la tête haute **2** *(in number, degree) (price)* élevé; *(percentage)* gros; *(speed)* grand; **to fetch a h. price** se vendre cher; **to pay a h. price** payer le prix fort; **to make a h. bid** faire une offre supérieure, surenchérir; **highest bidder** surenchérisseur *m*; *Cards, Fig* **to play for h. stakes** jouer gros (jeu); **ore with a h. mineral content** minerai à haute teneur; **cheese is h. in calcium** le fromage est riche en calcium; **h. latitudes** hautes latitudes; **to have a h. opinion of sb** avoir une haute opinion de qn, tenir qn en haute estime; **of the highest importance** de première importance; **to be h. farce** tourner à la farce; **h. quality** bonne qualité; *Com* **h. value added** à haute valeur ajoutée; **a h. fever** une forte *ou* grosse fièvre; **h. winds** vents forts **3** *(superior, advanced)* haut; **of h. rank** de haut rang; **she is h. up in the government** elle est haut placée dans le gouvernement; **to be in a h. position** être haut placé; **she's**

acting all **h. and mighty** elle agit avec beaucoup d'arrogance; **higher posts** postes *ou* emplois supérieurs; **higher mathematics** mathématiques *fpl* supérieures **4** *(noble) (principles, character etc)* élevé, noble; **h. ideals** idéaux élevés; **she has very h. moral standards** elle a des principes (de moralité) très élevés **5** *(strong)* **h. colour** couleur *f* vive **6** *(good)* **to be in h. spirits** être plein d'entrain; **our spirits were h.** nous avions le moral; **the h. life** la vie mondaine; **the h. point of the match** le point culminant du match; **one of the h. points of the evening** un des points forts de la soirée **7** *Mus etc* **h. voice** voix élevée *ou* haute; *(thin)* voix grêle; **h. note** note *f* aiguë; *Fig* **h. point** *m* culminant **8 h. summer** plein été; **it's h. time he went to school** il est grand temps qu'il aille à l'école; *Br Com* **h. season** la haute saison **9** *(meat etc)* avancé; *(bad)* avarié; *(game)* faisandé; **to get h.** *(of game)* se faisander; **to smell h.** avoir une forte odeur **10** *Fam (person)* **to be h.** *(on drugs)* planer; *Fig (euphoric)* être dans un état d'euphorie; **h. on cocaine** défoncé à la cocaïne; *Fig* **they were h. on success** ils ne se sentaient plus après ce succès **11** *Fam (lively)* **to have a h. old time** faire la noce **12 h. and dry** *(of ship)* échoué au plein; *(pulled up on beach etc)* à sec; *Fam* **to be left h. and dry** *(of person)* être laissé en plan
ADV 1 *(to aim, jump etc)* haut, en haut; **higher (up)** plus haut; **higher and higher** de plus en plus haut; **to rise h. in public esteem** monter très haut dans l'estime du public; **to hunt h. and low for sth** chercher qch partout; **higher up the river** en amont **2** *(in bidding etc)* **to go as h. as £2,000** aller jusqu'à 2 000 livres; *Cards etc* **to play** *or* **stake h.** jouer gros jeu **3** **to run h.** *(of sea)* être grosse *ou* houleuse; *(of prices)* être élevés; **feelings are running h.** les passions s'exacerbent; *(between countries)* la tension monte; **tempers were running h.** les esprits s'échauffaient **4** **to have memory loaded h.** avoir chargé en mémoire haute
N 1 *(high point)* **highs and lows** *(of share prices etc)* hausses *fpl* et baisses *fpl*; *(of career etc)* hauts *mpl* et bas *mpl*; **prices have reached a new h.** les prix ont atteint un nouveau maximum **2** *Met* aire *f* anticyclonique **3** *Fam* **to be on a h.** *(from drugs etc)* planer; *(from success etc)* être sur son petit nuage **4** *Rel* **the Most H.** le Très-Haut, le Tout-Puissant; **on h.** en haut, dans le ciel; *Rel, Fig* **from on h.** d'en haut
▸▸*Rel* **h. altar** maître-autel *m*, *pl* maîtres-autels; **h. beam** *Am Aut* feux *mpl* de route; *(in gym)* poutre *f*; *Med* **h. blood pressure** hypertension *f*; *Br Rel* **H. Church** Haute Église *f*; *Mil* **h. command** haut commandement *m*; **H. Commission** = représentation *f* officielle d'un pays, équivalente à une ambassade; **H. Commissioner** = représentant *m* officiel d'un pays, équivalent à un ambassadeur; *Law* **H. Court** Tribunal *m* de grande instance; *Com, Mktg* **h. end** *(of market)* haut *m*; *Mil* **h. explosive** explosif *m* puissant; **h. fashion** haute couture *f*; **h. fidelity** haute-fidélité *f*; *Electron* **h. frequency** haute fréquence *f*; **H. German** haut allemand *m*; **h. hat** *Mus* cymbales *fpl*; *Old-fashioned Fam (person)* arrogant *m*, snob *mf*; *Cin, TV* petit pied *m* de caméra, pied de sol; **h. heels** talons *mpl* hauts; *Sport* **h. jump** saut *m* en hauteur; *Sport* **h. jumper** sauteur, -euse *(qui fait du saut en hauteur)*; *Rel* **H. Mass** grand-messe *f*, *pl* grand(s)-messe, grande messe *f*; *Comput* **h. memory** mémoire *f* haute; *Comput* **h. me-**

mory area zone *f* de mémoire haute; **h. noon** plein midi *m*; *Rel* **h. priest** grand prêtre *m*; *Fig* **the h. priests of fashion** les grands noms de la mode; *Rel* **h. priestess** grande prêtresse *f*, **h. school** *(in UK)* = établissement *m* d'enseignement secondaire regroupant collège et lycée; *(in US)* lycée *m*; *Naut* **the h. seas** la haute mer; *Br Admin* **H. Sheriff** = dans les comtés anglais et gallois, représentant *m* officiel du monarque; **h. society** haute société *f*, grand monde *m*; *Br* **the h. street** *(street)* la grand-rue, la rue principale; *(shops)* les commerçants *mpl*, le commerce; **the h. table** la table d'honneur; *Sch, Univ* la table des professeurs *(au réfectoire)*; *Br* **h. tea** = repas *m* léger pris en début de soirée et accompagné de thé; **h. tech** haute technologie *f*, **h. treason** haute trahison *f*, *Elec* **h. voltage** haute tension *f*, **h. wire** corde *f* raide *ou* de funambule

high-ability ADJ **h. children** enfants *mpl* surdoués

high-angle shot N *Cin* plan *m* en plongée

highball ['haɪbɔːl] N = whisky-soda *m* avec de la glace servi dans un grand verre

highborn ['haɪbɔːn] ADJ de haute naissance

highboy ['haɪbɔɪ] N *Am (furniture)* commode *f* haute

highbrow ['haɪbraʊ] *Fam* N intello *mf* ADJ intello

highchair ['haɪtʃeər] N *(for baby)* chaise *f* haute

high-class ADJ *(merchandise etc)* de premier ordre, de première qualité; *(hotel)* de grande classe; *(prostitute)* de luxe

high-definition TV N télévision *f* haute définition

high-density ADJ **1** *Comput (disk, graphics, printing)* haute densité; *(in high-rise buildings)* grands ensembles *mpl* **2** *(housing)* à forte concentration de population

high-diving N plongeon *m* de haut vol, haut vol *m*

high-end ADJ *(top-of-the-range)* haut de gamme

Higher ['haɪər] N *Scot* = diplôme *m* de fin d'études secondaires sanctionnant une matière déterminée

higher court N *Law* instance *f* supérieure

higher education N enseignement *m* supérieur

higher-income group N groupe *m* de contribuables à revenus élevés

highfalutin(g) [haɪfə'luːtɪn, -ɪŋ] ADJ *Fam (style, language)* ampoulé, prétentieux, pompeux

high-fibre ADJ *Culin* riche en fibres

high-fidelity ADJ de haute fidélité

high-five N *Fam* = tape *f* amicale donnée dans la paume de quelqu'un, bras levé, en signe de victoire

high-flier, high-flyer N *(successful person)* ambitieux, -euse; *(company)* société *f* qui va de l'avant; **she's a real h.** elle ira loin

high-flown ADJ *(style, language)* ampoulé, pompeux

high-flying ADJ *(successful)* ambitieux, qui ira loin

high-frequency ADJ *Elec (current)* à haute fréquence; *(amplifier)* de haute fréquence

high-grade ADJ *(ore etc)* à haute teneur; *(merchandise)* de première qualité, de (premier) choix; *Aut* **h.** *Br* **petrol** *or Am* **gasoline** supercarburant *m*

high-handed ['haɪ'hændɪd] ADJ *(person, behaviour etc)* trop autoritaire, tyrannique; **was there any need to be so h. about it?** était-il nécessaire de te montrer si autoritaire?

high-heeled shoes [haɪ'hiːld] NPL chaussures *fpl* à hauts talons, talons *mpl* hauts

high-income ADJ à haut revenu
▸▸ **h. group** groupe *m* des gros salaires, groupe des salaires élevés

high-involvement ADJ *Mktg (purchasing)* à forte participation des consommateurs

highjack, highjacker *etc* = **hijack**, **hijacker** *etc*

highland ['haɪlənd] N pays *m* montagneux; **the Highlands** *(of Scotland)* les Highlands *mpl* ADJ des montagnes; *(from Scotland)* des Highlands
▸▸ **H. cattle** race *f* bovine des Highlands

Highland Games

En Écosse, il s'agit d'une sorte de kermesse locale en plein air où se déroulent simultanément toutes sortes de concours (danse, cornemuse) et d'épreuves sportives (courses, lancer du marteau, mais aussi "tossing the caber", "tug o' war" etc).

highlander ['haɪləndər] N montagnard, -arde; **H.** *(from Scotland)* Highlander *m*, habitant, -ante de la Haute Écosse; *Mil* = soldat *m* d'un régiment écossais

high-level ADJ *(discussion)* à haut niveau; *(official, officer)* de haut niveau
▸▸ *Comput* **h. language** langage *m* évolué *or* de haut niveau; *Comput* **h. programming language** langage *m* de programmation évolué

highlight ['haɪlaɪt] N **1** *(important moment)* grand moment *m*; *(of celebration etc)* clou *m*; *(of match etc)* point *m* culminant; *TV* **they didn't show the whole match, just the highlights** ils n'ont pas retransmis tout le match, seulement les meilleurs moments; **the news highlights** les grands titres de l'actualité **2** *Phot* rehaut *m*; **highlights** *(in a painting)* rehauts *mpl*, clairs *mpl* **3** **highlights** *(in hair)* reflets *mpl*, mèches *fpl* **4** *Comput* relief *m* VT **1** *(problem, need)* souligner **2** *(with coloured marker)* surligner **3** *Comput (text block)* sélectionner; **to be highlighted** *(of text)* apparaître en surimpression *ou* en surbrillance

highlighted ['haɪlaɪtɪd] ADJ *Comput* lumineux, contrasté

highlighter ['haɪlaɪtər] N *(pen)* surligneur *m*, stylo *m* surligneur, marqueur *m* surligneur

highly ['haɪlɪ] ADV **1** **h. placed official** haut fonctionnaire *m*; **to be h. placed** être haut placé; **his services are h. paid** on paie très cher ses services; **to think h. of sb** avoir une haute opinion de qn **2** *(extremely)* fort, très, fortement; **h. amusing** très amusant; **h. coloured** *(painting, style)* haut en couleur; *(account, report)* coloré, haut en couleur; **h. displeased** fort mécontent; **h. seasoned** fortement assaisonné; **to be h. sexed** avoir une forte libido; **h. strung** *(person)* très sensible, *Fam* hypersensible

high-margin product N produit *m* à forte marge

high-minded ADJ aux sentiments nobles, généreux; *(action, nature)* magnanime; **to be too h.** avoir trop de principes

high-mindedness ['haɪ'maɪndɪdnɪs] N noblesse *f* de sentiments, grandeur *f* d'âme; *(of action etc)* magnanimité *f*

Highness ['haɪnɪs] N *(title)* Altesse *f*, **His/Her Royal H.** son Altesse Royale

high-octane ADJ *(fuel)* à indice d'octane élevé

high-performance ADJ *(car, engine)*, *Comput (chip)* (à) haute performance

high-pitched ADJ **1** *(sound)* aigu, -uë; *(voice)* aigu, criard **2** *Constr (roof)* à forte inclinaison, à forte pente

high-powered ADJ *(engine, car, telescope)* très puissant; *(microscope)* à fort grossissement; *Fig (person)* dynamique et compétent; **a h. businessman** un homme d'affaires de poids; **she is something h. in the City** elle a un poste important à la Cité de Londres; **a h. job** un poste très important, *Fam* un super boulot

high-pressure ADJ **1** *Tech (cylinder, machine)* à haute pression, à haute tension; *Met (area)* anticyclonique, de hautes pressions **2** *Pej (salesman)* agressif

high-principled ADJ aux principes élevés

high-profile ADJ *(politician etc)* en vue; *(company)* connu; *(campaign etc)* de grande envergure

high-quality ADJ haut de gamme

high-resolution ADJ *Phot, TV etc (screen, graphics)* à haute résolution

high-rise N tour *f*
▸▸ **h. building** tour

high-risk ADJ *(occupation, category etc)* à haut(s) risque(s)

highroad ['haɪrəʊd] N **1** *Old-fashioned* grand-route *f* **2** *Fig* **on the h. to success** sur la route du succès

high-sounding ADJ *(title)* pompeux, ronflant

high-speed ADJ ultra-rapide; *(machine)* à marche rapide; *(engine)*, *Phot* grande vitesse; *Comput* à grande vitesse
▸▸ *Comput* **h. access** accès *m* rapide; *Comput* **h. bus** bus *m* rapide; **h. camera** caméra *f* grande vitesse; **h. printer** imprimante *f* rapide; *Rail* **h. train** train *m* à grande vitesse, TGV *m*

high-spirited ADJ plein d'ardeur *ou* de feu; *(horse)* fougueux

high-street ADJ **a h. bank** une banque populaire, une banque de dépôt; **h. shops** commerces *mpl*; **prices in the h. shops** prix dans le commerce

high-strung ADJ *(character, person)* très sensible

hightail ['haɪteɪl] VT *esp Am Fam* **to h. it** se tirer en vitesse; **he hightailed it out of town** il a fichu le camp de la ville; **he hightailed it back to the ranch** il est retourné au ranch en quatrième vitesse

high-tech ['haɪtek] ADJ, N = **hi-tech**

high-tensile steel N acier *m* à haute résistance élastique

high-tension ADJ *Elec (wire, tension, coil)* (à) haute tension

high-up *Fam* N gros bonnet *m*, grosse légume *f*
ADJ *(judge, politician etc)* haut placé

high-viscosity ADJ *(oil)* à haute viscosité

highway ['haɪweɪ] N **1** *esp Am (main road)* route *f* nationale, autoroute *f*, **highways and byways** chemins *mpl* et sentiers *mpl*; *Fam* **that's h. robbery!** c'est du vol! **2** *Br Admin (public road)* voie *f* publique
▸▸ *Br Aut* **the H. Code** le code de la route; *Br* **h. engineer** ≃ ingénieur *m* des Ponts et Chaussées; *Am* **h. patrol** police *f* de la route; *Am* **h. patrolman** membre *m* de la police de la route

highwayman, *pl* **highwaymen** ['haɪweɪmən] N *Hist* voleur *m* de grand(s) chemin(s)

high-yield ADJ *Fin (bond, security)* à rendement élevé

hijack ['haɪdʒæk] N détournement *m* VT *(plane in flight)* détourner; *(vehicle)* s'emparer de force de; *Fig* **the government hi-**

jacked the opposition's policy le gouvernement s'est approprié la politique de l'opposition

hijacker ['haɪdʒækər] N (of aircraft) pirate mf de l'air; (of vehicle) pirate de la route; **the hijackers of the Israeli Boeing** les pirates de l'air du Boeing israélien

hijacking ['haɪdʒækɪŋ] N (of aircraft) (general practice) piraterie f aérienne; (single incident) détournement m; (of vehicle) = vol m à main armée d'un véhicule et de son contenu

hike [haɪk] N **1** (walk) (longue) promenade f à pied, randonnée f; **to go on** ou **for a h.** faire une (longue) promenade à pied, faire une randonnée; Am Fam **he can take a h.!** il peut aller se faire voir! **2** (in interest rates etc) augmentation f, hausse f
▸ VI (walk) faire une (longue) promenade à pied, faire une randonnée
▸ **hike up** VT SEP (trousers, skirt) remonter; (interest rates) augmenter; **to h. oneself up on to sth** se hisser jusqu'à qch

hiker ['haɪkər] N randonneur, -euse (à pied)

hiking ['haɪkɪŋ] N randonnée f pédestre; **to go on a h. holiday** partir en vacances faire de la randonnée
▸ ▸ **h. boots** chaussures fpl de marche

hilarious [hɪ'leərɪəs] ADJ (very amusing) hilarant, Fam marrant; **it was h.!** c'était à se tordre (de rire)!

hilariously [hɪ'leərɪəslɪ] ADV (unlikely, old-fashioned looking) à vous faire tordre de rire; (to laugh) aux éclats; **it was h. funny** c'était à se tordre (de rire)

hilariousness [hɪ'leərɪəsnɪs] N (of scene, joke) caractère m hilarant

hilarity [hɪ'lærɪtɪ] N hilarité f

hill [hɪl] N **1** colline f, (sloping ground) coteau m; **up h. and down dale** par monts et par vaux; Mil **h.** 304 la cote 304; Fig Fam **to be over the h.** commencer à se faire vieux; Am Fam **it ain't worth a h. of beans, it doesn't amount to a h. of beans** (of opinion etc) ça ne vaut pas tripette; **to be as old as the hills** (of joke, person etc) dater de ou remonter à Mathusalem **2** (on road) côte f, (uphill) montée f, (downhill) descente f, **steep h.** (uphill) montée abrupte; (downhill) descente abrupte
▸ ▸ **h. country** pays m de collines; Aut **h. start** démarrage m en côte; **h. station** (in India) station f de montagne

hillbilly ['hɪlbɪlɪ] N Am Fam Pej villageois, -oise un peu rustaud(e)
▸ ▸ **h. music** folk m (des Appalaches) (du sud-est des États-Unis)

hill-climbing N randonnée f (en pays vallonné), (of vehicle) montée f

hillfarm ['hɪlfɑːm] N ferme f à flanc de coteau

hilliness ['hɪlɪnɪs] N vallonnement m

hillock ['hɪlək] N petite colline f, (smaller) butte f, tertre m

hillside ['hɪlsaɪd] N flanc m de coteau, coteau m

hilltop ['hɪltɒp] N sommet m de (la) colline

hill-walker N randonneur, -euse (en pays vallonné)

hill-walking N randonnée f (en pays vallonné)

hilly ['hɪlɪ] ADJ (country) montagneux; (terrain) accidenté; (road) montueux, à fortes pentes

hilt [hɪlt] N (of sword) poignée f, (of dagger, knife etc) manche m; Fig **right up to the h.** jusqu'au bout; **to back** ou **support sb to the h.** soutenir qn sans réserve ou à fond; **mortgaged up to the h.** (person) endetté jusqu'au cou, qui doit rembourser des emprunts énormes; (property) fortement hypothéqué

him [hɪm] PERS PRON **1** (direct) le; (before a vowel sound) l'; **I hate h.** je le déteste; **do you love h.?** l'aimez-vous?; **have you seen h.?** l'avez-vous vu?; **I remember h.** je me souviens de lui VOIR GRAMMAIRE A27–8; A43
2 (indirect and reflexive, after prepositions) lui; **I shall tell h. so** je le lui dirai; **tell h. I have come** dites-lui que je suis là; **we are thinking of h.** nous pensons à lui; **he took his luggage with h.** il a pris ses bagages avec lui; **he closed the door behind h.** il a fermé la porte derrière lui; **I object to h. borrowing the car** je m'oppose à ce qu'il emprunte la voiture
3 (as complement of verb **to be**) **it's h.!** c'est lui!
4 (stressed) lui; Lit (with dem force) celui; **we can forgive his parents but not him** nous pouvons pardonner à ses parents, mais pas à lui; **who better than h. to break the news?** qui, mieux que lui, pourrait annoncer la nouvelle?; Lit **to h. who should take offence at this I would say ...** à celui qui s'en offenserait, je dirais ...

Himalayan [hɪmə'leɪən] ADJ himalayen, -enne

Himalayas [hɪmə'leɪəz] NPL **the H.** (les) montagnes fpl de) l'Himalaya m

himbo ['hɪmbəʊ] N Fam beau mec m pas très futé

himself [hɪm'self] PERS PRON VOIR GRAMMAIRE A29–30 **1** (emphatic) lui-même; **he doesn't want to do it h.** il ne veut pas le faire lui-même; **he's not (quite) h. again yet** (after illness) il n'est pas encore complètement remis; **he's not h. today** il n'est pas lui-même aujourd'hui, il n'est pas dans son état normal aujourd'hui; **I spoke to the author h.** j'ai parlé à l'auteur lui-même ou en personne
2 (reflexive) se; **he hurt h.** il s'est fait mal; **he lives by h.** il vit seul; **'well, well!', he said to h.** 'eh bien!', se dit-il; **he kept one for h.** il s'en est gardé un/une VOIR GRAMMAIRE B28–9
3 (used impersonally) soi(-même); **everyone for h.** chacun pour soi

hind [haɪnd] N (female deer) biche f
▸ ▸ **h. calf** faon m femelle

hind [haɪnd] ADJ de derrière, postérieur; **h. legs/feet** pattes fpl de derrière; Fam **to get up on one's h. legs** (of person) se lever

hinder ['hɪndər] VT **1** (impede) gêner, embarrasser; (movement) entraver; (delay) retarder **2** (prevent) empêcher, retenir (**from doing** de faire)

hinder ['haɪndər] ADJ de derrière, postérieur

Hindi ['hɪndɪ] N Ling hindi m

hindmost ['haɪndməʊst] ADJ dernier; Prov **devil take the h.!** chacun pour soi; **it's a case of devil take the h.** vu les circonstances, c'est chacun pour soi

hindquarters ['haɪndkwɔːtəz] NPL arrière-train m

hindrance ['hɪndrəns] N empêchement m, obstacle m, entrave f, **he is a h.** il gêne; **they were more of a h. than a help** ils nous/les/etc gênaient plus qu'ils ne nous/les/etc aidaient

hindsight ['haɪndsaɪt] N recul m, sagesse f que donne le recul; **with (the benefit of) h.** après coup, avec le recul; **with all the advantages of h.** avec tous les avantages que donne le recul

Hindu [hɪn'duː] ADJ hindou N hindou, -oue

Hinduism ['hɪnduːɪz(ə)m] N hindouisme m

Hindustan [hɪndʊ'stɑːn] N Geog Hindoustan m

Hindustani [hɪndʊ'stɑːnɪ] Ling N hindoustani m
ADJ hindi

hinge [hɪndʒ] N charnière f, (of door) gond m; **the door came off its hinges** la porte est sortie de ses gonds; (stamp) **h.** charnière
▸ VT (mount on hinges) (door etc) monter sur ses gonds; (put hinges on) (box etc) mettre des charnières à
▸ VI Tech tourner, pivoter (**on** autour de); **to h. forward** (of seat etc) basculer vers l'avant
▸ **hinge on, hinge upon** VT INSEP (depend on) dépendre de; **everything hinges on his answer** tout dépend de sa réponse

hinged [hɪndʒd] ADJ (door, lid etc) à charnière(s); **h. flap** (of counter) abattant m; (of aircraft) volet m articulé

hinky ['hɪŋkɪ] ADJ Am Fam (suspect) louche

hint [hɪnt] N **1** (allusion) allusion f (indirecte); **broad h.** allusion évidente ou claire; **gentle h.** allusion discrète; **to give** or **drop sb a h.** toucher un mot à qn; **to know how to take a h.** comprendre à demi-mot; **we can take a h.** nous avons compris l'allusion; **he can't take a h.** il faut lui mettre les points sur les i
2 (sign) signe m, indication f, suggestion f, **not a h. of surprise** pas une ombre de surprise; **not the slightest h. of ...** pas le moindre soupçon de ...; **there was a h. of garlic in the stew** il y avait un soupçon d'ail dans le ragoût
3 (piece of advice) petit conseil m; **the book is full of useful hints on how to save money** le livre est plein de tuyaux pour faire des économies; **can you give me some hints?** (about how I should proceed) pouvez-vous me donner quelques conseils?; (about the right answer) pouvez-vous me mettre sur la voie?
▸ VT **to h. that ...** insinuer que ...; **to h. to sb that ...** laisser entendre à qn que ...
▸ **hint at** VT INSEP faire (une) allusion à

hinterland ['hɪntəlænd] N arrière-pays m

hip[1] [hɪp] N **1** Anat hanche f, **to have narrow/wide hips** avoir les hanches fines/larges; **he stood with his hands on his hips** il était debout, les mains sur les hanches; esp Am Fig **he shoots from the h.** réagir de façon impulsive; **2** Constr arêtier m, arête f
▸ ▸ Br **h. bath** bain m de siège; **h. flask** flasque f, Anat **h. joint** articulation f de la hanche; **h. measurement** tour m de hanches; Constr **h. piece** (of roof) arêtier, arête; Br **h. pocket** poche f revolver; Constr **h. rafter** (of roof) arêtier, arête; Med **h. replacement (operation)** mise f en place d'une prothèse de la hanche; **h. size** tour m de hanches

hip[2] N (fruit) cynor(r)hodon m, fruit m du rosier

hip[3] ADJ Fam (trendy) branché; **to be h. to sth** être branché sur qch

hip[4] INT **h.! h.!, hurray!** hip! hip! hourra!

hipbone ['hɪpbəʊn] N os m iliaque

hip-huggers ['hɪp'hʌɡəz] NPL Am = **hipster 2**

-hipped [hɪpt] SUFF **broad-h.** aux hanches fortes; **narrow-h.** aux hanches fines ou étroites

hippie ['hɪpɪ] ADJ, N hippie mf, Hum **ageing h.** vieillissant(e) hippie

hippo ['hɪpəʊ] N Fam hippopotame m

Hippocrates [hɪ'pɒkrətiːz] N Hippocrate

Hippocratic [hɪpə'krætɪk] ADJ Med hippocratique
▸ ▸ **H. oath** serment m d'Hippocrate

hippodrome ['hɪpədrəʊm] N hippodrome m; (not for racing) arène f

hippopotamus, pl **hippopotamuses, hippopotami** [hɪpə'pɒtəməs, -məsɪz, -maɪ] N hippopotame m

hippy[1] ['hɪpɪ] ADJ (with large hips) aux hanches larges

hippy[2] ADJ, N = **hippie**

hipster ['hɪpstər] N **1** *esp Am Old-fashioned* beatnik *mf (des années 40 et 50)* **2** *Br* **hipsters** *(trousers)* pantalon *m* (à) taille basse

hire ['haɪər] N **1** *Br (of car, room)* location *f*; **for h.** *(sign on taxi)* libre; **for** *or* **on h.** à louer **2** *Am (of labour)* embauche *f*; *(of servant)* louage *m* **3** *Lit (wages)* salaire *m*, gages *mpl* VT **1** *Br (car etc)* louer **2** *(take on) (lawyer, private detective etc)* s'assurer les services de, engager **3** *Am (worker)* embaucher, engager; *(domestic staff)* prendre à son service VI *esp Am (take on workers)* embaucher
▸▸ *Br* **h. car** voiture *f* de location; **h. charges** *(frais mpl ou prix m de)* location
▸ **hire out** VT SEP *Br* louer, donner en location (**to sb** à qn)

hired ['haɪəd] ADJ *Br (car etc)* de location
▸▸ **h. gun** tueur *m* à gages; **h. hand** ouvrier *m* agricole; **h. killer** tueur à gages; **h. man** *Am (servant)* domestique *m*; *(farmworker)* ouvrier agricole

hireling ['haɪəlɪŋ] N *Pej* laquais *m*

hire-purchase N *Br Com* location-vente *f*; **to buy sth on h.** acheter qch en location-vente
▸▸ **h. agreement** contrat *m* de location-vente

hi-res ['haɪrez] ADJ *Comput Fam (abbr high-resolution)* (à) haute résolution

hiring ['haɪ(ə)rɪŋ] N **1** *Br (of a car etc)* location *f* **2** *(of staff etc)* embauche *f*; *Fam* **he does the h. and firing** il est chargé des embauches et des licenciements

hirsute [hɜː'sjuːt] ADJ *Lit* hirsute, velu, poilu

his [hɪz] POSS ADJ son, *f* sa, *pl* ses; **one of h. friends** un de ses amis, un ami à lui; **h. father and mother** son père et sa mère; *Admin* ses père et mère; **h. own son** son propre fils; **he has hurt h. hand** il s'est fait mal à la main; **h. eyes are brown** il a les yeux bruns; **I object to h. borrowing the car** je m'oppose à ce qu'il emprunte la voiture VOIR GRAMMAIRE A30; A43; B21–2
POSS PRON le sien, la sienne, *pl* les siens, les siennes; **he took my pen as well as h.** il a pris mon stylo avec le sien; **this book is h.** ce livre est à lui, c'est son livre à lui; **a friend of h.** un de ses amis, un ami à lui; **it is no business of h.** cela ne le regarde pas; **it's no business of h. to tell me what to do** ce n'est pas à lui de me dire quoi faire VOIR GRAMMAIRE A30; B21–2

Hispanic [hɪ'spænɪk] ADJ hispanique
N *Am* Hispano-Américain, -aine

Hispano-American [hɪ'spænəʊə'merɪk(ə)n] ADJ hispano-américain
N Hispano-Américain, -aine

hiss [hɪs] N **1** *(sound)* sifflement *m*; *Theat etc* sifflets *mpl*; *(on tape)* bruit *m* parasite, bruit de piste **2** *Ling* sifflante *f*
VT & VI *(of person, steam, geese etc)* siffler; *(of steam, gas)* chuinter; **to h. (at) an actor** siffler un acteur; **to be hissed** être sifflé

hissing ['hɪsɪŋ] ADJ **h. noise** sifflement *m*; *(of gas)* chuintement *m*
N sifflement *m*; *(of gas)* chuintement *m*

hissy fit ['hɪsɪ] N *Fam* **to have a h.** faire une crise

histamine ['hɪstəmɪn, -miːn] N *Physiol* histamine *f*

histogram ['hɪstəgræm] N histogramme *m*

historian [hɪs'tɔːrɪən] N historien, -ienne

historic [hɪs'tɒrɪk] ADJ **1** historique; **h. event/moment** événement/moment historique **2** *Gram* **past h.** passé *m* simple VOIR GRAMMAIRE B30
▸▸ **h. building** monument *m* historique

Il faut noter que les adjectifs **historic** et **historical** ne sont pas interchangeables. *Historic* signifie **important d'un point de vue historique** alors que *historical* signifie **qui se rapporte à l'histoire**.

historical [hɪs'tɒrɪk(ə)l] ADJ *(character, event, novel)* historique; **h. background** contexte *m* historique; **of purely h. interest** d'intérêt purement historique; **h. record/account** historique *m*; **h. research** recherche *f* en histoire
▸▸ *Acct* **h. cost accounting** comptabilité *f* par coûts historiques; **h. linguistics** linguistique *f* diachronique

Voir note ci-dessus.

historically [hɪs'tɒrɪklɪ] ADV historiquement

historiographer [hɪstɔːrɪ'ɒgrəfər] N historiographe *mf*

historiography [hɪstɔːrɪ'ɒgrəfɪ] N historiographie *f*

history ['hɪst(ə)rɪ] N **1** *(of country, ship etc)* histoire *f*; **French h.** l'histoire de France; **ancient/modern h.** l'histoire ancienne/moderne; *Fig* **that's h.** c'est du passé; *Fam* **he's h.!** *(in trouble)* il est fini!; *(no longer in my/her/etc life)* avec lui, c'est terminé!; **that's ancient h.** c'est une vieille histoire, c'est de l'histoire ancienne; **we're making h.** nous faisons l'histoire, nous entrons dans l'histoire; *Sch* **h. book/teacher/etc** livre *m*/professeur *m*/etc d'histoire; **Shakespeare's h. plays** les pièces *fpl* historiques de Shakespeare
2 *(book)* histoire *f*; *(chronological account)* historique *m*
3 *(tradition)* tradition *f*; **there is a long h. of cultural links between these cities** il existe une longue tradition de liens culturels entre ces villes; **there is a h. of heart disease in her family** il y a des antécédents de maladie cardiaque dans sa famille
4 *Comput* historique *m*
▸▸ *Comput* **h. file** fichier *m* historique; *Comput* **h. list** historique *m*

histrionic [hɪstrɪ'ɒnɪk] ADJ **1** histrionique **2** *Theat, Liter* théâtral, -aux

histrionics [hɪstrɪ'ɒnɪks] NPL *Pej* démonstrations *fpl* affectées *(de colère etc)*; **I've had enough of his h.** j'en ai assez de ses simagrées *ou Fam* son cinéma; **it's just h. on her part** elle nous joue la comédie

HIT [hɪt]

N	coup **1, 2** ▪ succès **3** ▪ tube **3** ▪ hit **6**
VT	frapper **1** ▪ heurter **1** ▪ atteindre **1–3** ▪ toucher **2, 3** ▪ arriver à **5** ▪ buter sur **6**
VI	frapper

N **1** *(blow)* coup *m*; *Fig Fam* **that's a h. at you** c'est à vous que s'adresse l'allusion
2 *Fencing* touche *f*, coup *m*; *Billiards* touche; *Baseball* coup de batte; *Hockey* coup de crosse; *Hockey* **free h.** coup franc; **to score a h.** *Fencing* toucher; *(in shooting)* atteindre la cible; *Fig* **to score a h. against sb** marquer des points contre qn; **to score a direct h.** *(of bomber, tank etc)* taper dans le mille; **to score a direct h. on sth** *(of bomber etc)* toucher qch en plein dans le mille; *(of bomb)* tomber en plein dans qch; **built to withstand a direct h.** construit pour résister à une bombe; **the ship suffered two direct hits from missiles** le bateau a été touché par deux missiles
3 *Theat, TV etc (success)* succès *m*; *(song, record)* tube *m*; **she had a h. with her song 'Spinning Around'** sa chanson 'Spinning Around' a été un tube; **h. show** spectacle *m* à succès; **Frank Sinatra's greatest hits** les plus grands succès de Frank Sinatra; **to make** *or* **score a h. with sb** faire bonne impression à qn; *(romantically)* avoir une touche avec qn; **one-h. wonder** *(group, singer)*

= groupe *m* ou chanteur *m* qui n'a eu qu'un seul tube
4 *Sl (murder)* meurtre *m*
5 *Sl (of hard drugs)* fix *m*; *(of joint)* taffe *f*; *(effect of drugs)* effet *m (procuré par une drogue)*; **you get a good h. off that grass** cette herbe fait rapidement de l'effet
6 *Comput (visit to website)* hit *m*, accès *m*; **this website counted 20,000 hits last week** ce site Web a été consulté 20 000 fois la semaine dernière
VT *(pt, pp hit; prp hitting)* **1** *(of person)* frapper; *Comput (key)* appuyer sur; *(of bullet) (person)* atteindre; *(of car etc) (tree, bus)* percuter; **to h. sb in the face** frapper qn au visage; **to h. one's foot against a stone** se cogner le pied contre une pierre; *(and stumble)* buter contre une pierre; **to h. one's head on the ceiling** se cogner la tête contre le plafond; **to h. a reef** *(of ship, boat)* heurter un récif; **the bullet h. her in the arm** la balle l'a touchée au bras; **to h. the target** *(with gun, missile etc)* toucher la cible; *Am Fam* **that really h. the spot** *(is just what was needed)* c'est juste ce qu'il me fallait; *Journ* **to h. the headlines** défrayer la chronique; *Fig* **to h. the nail on the head** tomber juste; *Fig* **to h. the roof** être furieux; *Sl* **to h. the bottle** picoler; *Sl* **to h. the hay** *or Am* **the sack** se pieuter; **it suddenly h. me that ...** j'ai réalisé tout d'un coup que ...; **he didn't know what had h. him** il se demandait ce qui lui était arrivé
2 *(reach)* atteindre; *Fencing, Billiards* toucher; **to h. the wrong note** *(on the piano etc)*, *Fig* faire une fausse note; *(in singing)* chanter faux; **I can't h. those high notes any more** je n'arrive plus à chanter ces notes aiguës; **to h. ninety (miles an hour)** faire du 140 km/h; **to h. an all-time low** *(of investment, relationship etc)* être au plus bas; **to h. rock-bottom** atteindre son point le plus bas
3 *(affect)* **to be hard h.** *(by losses etc)* être sérieusement touché; **the strike has h. several factories** la grève a atteint plusieurs usines
4 *Am Fam (borrow from)* **he h. his friend for $100** il a tapé son ami de 100 dollars
5 *Fam (arrive at) (place, town)* arriver à; **the circus hits town tomorrow night** le cirque arrive en ville demain soir; **to h. the beach** *(of troops)* atteindre la plage; **let's h. the beach!** allons à la plage!; **when it hits the shops** quand il arrivera sur le marché; **to h. the trail** *or* **the road** *(start)* se mettre en route; *Fig* **to h. the ground running** être opérationnel immédiatement
6 *(encounter) (problem, difficulty)* buter sur; **the tunnellers h. rock** les ouvriers qui creusaient le tunnel sont tombés sur de la roche; **we h. a terrible snowstorm** nous nous sommes trouvés dans une tempête de neige terrible; **to h. a sticky** *or* **bad patch** rencontrer des difficultés
7 *esp Am Sl (murder)* buter
VI frapper; *(collide)* se heurter; **to h. hard** frapper fort, *Fam* cogner fort; *Fig* **the remark h. home** la remarque a eu l'effet escompté
▸▸ *Comput* **h. counter** compteur *m* d'accès; *Fam* **h. list** liste *f* noire; *Fam* **h. man** tueur *m* à gages; *Old-fashioned* **h. parade** hit-parade *m*, *pl* hit-parades; *Mus* **h. record** tube
▸ **hit back** VI **1** *(return blow)* rendre coup pour coup (**at sb** à qn)
2 *Fig (answer accusation, criticism etc)* riposter, répondre
VT SEP *(return blow to)* **to h. sb back** donner un coup en retour à qn
▸ **hit off** VT SEP **1** *(imitate) (in satirical drawing)* caricaturer; *(impersonate)* imiter
2 *Fam* **to h. it off** *(get on well)* bien s'entendre (**with** avec)
▸ **hit on** VT INSEP **1** *Am Fam* **to h. on sb** draguer qn, faire du plat à qn
2 = **hit upon**

▸ **hit out** VI **1** *(punch etc)* frapper; **she h. out at her attackers** elle a frappé ses agresseurs; **he h. out in all directions** il donnait des coups dans tous les sens **2** *(verbally)* attaquer (verbalement); **to h. out at sb** s'en prendre à qn

▸ **hit up** VT SEP *Sl* **to h. it up** *(inject drugs)* se piquer

▸ **hit upon** VT INSEP *(discover) (idea, method etc)* trouver

hit-and-run N *(accident)* accident *m* avec délit de fuite
  ▸▸ **h. accident** accident avec délit de fuite; **h. driver** conducteur, -trice coupable de délit de fuite; *Mil* **h. raid** raid *m* éclair

hitch [hɪtʃ] N **1** *(difficulty)* empêchement *m*, anicroche *f*, contretemps *m*; **there's a h. somewhere** il y a quelque chose qui cloche; **there's been a h.** il y a eu un problème; **without a h.** sans anicroches, sans accroc; *Radio, TV etc* **technical h.** incident *m* technique **2** *(knot)* nœud *m*; **half h.** demi-clef *f* **3** *Am Fam (length of time)* **a three-year h. in the army** (une période de) trois ans dans l'armée; **to do a three-year h. in prison** faire trois ans de prison **4** *(movement)* saccade *f*, secousse *f*; *(of horse)* léger boitement *m*
  VT **1** *(attach)* accrocher, attacher; *Naut* amarrer (**to** à); **she hitched her horse to a post** elle a attaché son cheval à un poteau; **they hitched the horses to the cart** ils ont attelé les chevaux à la charrette **2** *Fam (hitchhike)* **to h. a lift** *ou* **ride** faire du stop, *Can* faire du pouce; **we hitched a ride to Paris** on nous a pris en stop jusqu'à Paris **3** *Fam* **to get hitched** *(married)* se caser
  VI **1** *Fam* =**hitchhike 2** *(of person)* **to h. on to sth** s'accrocher à qch
  ▸ **hitch up** VT SEP **1** *(harness) (horse)* harnacher **2** *(lift) (trousers, skirt)* remonter

hitchhike [ˈhɪtʃhaɪk] VI faire de l'auto-stop *ou* du stop, *Can* faire du pouce; **to h. to Paris** aller à Paris en stop

hitchhiker [ˈhɪtʃhaɪkər] N auto-stoppeur, -euse

hitchhiking [ˈhɪtʃhaɪkɪŋ] N *(auto-)*stop *m*

hi-tech [ˈhaɪtek] ADJ de haute technologie, de pointe; *(furniture)* hi-tech; **they've adopted a h. approach** ils ont eu recours à la technologie de pointe; **we're very h. here** nous faisons un usage intensif de l'automatisation *ou* de l'informatique ici
  N technologie *f* de pointe, hi-tech *f*; *Archit* hi-tech

hither [ˈhɪðər] ADV *Arch, Lit* ici; **h. and thither** çà et là; *Hum* **to give sb a 'come h.' look** jeter un coup d'œil coquin à qn

hitherto [ˈhɪðəˈtuː] ADV jusqu'ici, jusqu'à présent

hit-or-miss ADJ *(method)* aléatoire, *Fam* au pif, au pifomètre; **it was all rather h.** c'était au pifomètre *ou* au pif; **in a h. sort of way** au pifomètre, au pif; **to reply in a h. sort of way** répondre au hasard *ou* au petit bonheur; **their method is rather h.** ils font les choses au pif
  ADV *(to answer)* au petit bonheur, *Fam* au pif

HIV [eɪtʃaɪˈviː] N *Med (abbr* **human immuno-deficiency virus)** HIV *m*, VIH *m*; **H. case** cas *m* de séropositivité; **H. deaths** morts liées à la séropositivité **H. patients** patients *mpl* séropositifs; **to be H. positive** être séropositif; **to be H. negative** être séronégatif

hive [haɪv] N *(for bees)* ruche *f*; *Fig* **a h. of industry** une véritable ruche *ou* fourmilière
  VT *(swarm)* mettre dans une ruche
  VI *(of swarm)* entrer dans la ruche
  ▸ **hive off** VT SEP *(separate)* détacher *ou* séparer (d'un tout); **to h. off work** sous-traiter, donner du travail en sous-traitance; *Br Com*

part of the industry was hived off to private ownership une partie de cette industrie a été privatisée
  VI *(split off)* se séparer (**from** de)

hives [haɪvz] NPL *Med* urticaire *f*; **to have h.** avoir de l'urticaire

hiya [ˈhaɪjə, haɪˈjaː] INT *Fam* salut!

HM [eɪtʃˈem] *Br abbr* **His/Her Majesty**

h'm [hm] INT *(expressing doubt)* heu!, hum!

HMG [eɪtʃemˈdʒiː] *Br Admin abbr* **His/Her Majesty's Government**

HMI [eɪtʃemˈaɪ] *Br (abbr* **His/Her Majesty's Inspector)** inspecteur *m* de l'éducation nationale (britannique)

HMS [eɪtʃeˈmes] *Br Naut abbr* **His/Her Majesty's Ship**

HMSO [eɪtʃemeˈsəʊ] N *Br (abbr* **Her/His Majesty's Stationery Office)** ≃ Imprimerie *f* nationale

HNC [eɪtʃenˈsiː] N *Br (abbr* **Higher National Certificate)** = diplôme *m* technique préparé en un an

HND [eɪtʃenˈdiː] N *Br (abbr* **Higher National Diploma)** = diplôme *m* technique préparé en deux ans

HO N *Br (abbr* **Home Office)** = le ministère britannique de l'Intérieur

ho [həʊ] INT **1** *Old-fashioned (to attract attention)* hé!, ohé!; *Naut* **land ho!** terre! **2 ho! ho!** *(laughter)* ha! ha!

hoar [hɔːr] N gelée *f* blanche

hoard [hɔːd] N amas *m*; *(of provisions, food etc)* réserve *f*; **h. of money** trésor *m*, *Fam* magot *m*; **he has a whole h. of stories** il a une réserve d'histoires assez extraordinaire
  VT *(corn, information)* amasser; *(provisions, food etc)* mettre *ou* tenir en réserve; *(causing shortage for others)* accaparer; *(money)* thésauriser
  ▸ **hoard up** VT SEP =**hoard** VT

> Attention: ne pas confondre avec le nom anglais **horde**.

hoarder [ˈhɔːdər] N *(animal)* animal *m* prévoyant; **petrol hoarders were arrested** ceux qui accaparaient l'essence ont été arrêtés; **she's a real h.** elle garde absolument tout, elle ne jette absolument rien

hoarding[1] [ˈhɔːdɪŋ] N *(of provisions)* mise *f* en réserve

hoarding[2] N **1** *Br (for advertising)* panneau *m* d'affichage **2** *(fencing)* clôture *f* en planches; *(around worksite etc)* palissade *f*
  ▸▸ *Com* **h. site** emplacement *m* d'affichage

hoarfrost [ˈhɔːfrɒst] N gelée *f* blanche

hoarse [hɔːs] ADJ *(voice etc)* enroué, rauque; **to be h.** être enroué; **to shout oneself h.** s'enrouer à force de crier

hoarsely [ˈhɔːslɪ] ADV d'une voix rauque *ou* enrouée

hoarseness [ˈhɔːsnɪs] N enrouement *m*

hoary [ˈhɔːrɪ] ADJ **1** *Lit (hair)* blanchi, chenu; *Bot, Entom (foliage, insect)* couvert d'un duvet blanc **2** *(old)* vieux, *f* vieille

hoax [həʊks] N canular *m*, farce *f*, *Journ Fam* canular, canard *m*; **(bomb) h.** fausse alerte *f* à la bombe; **it turned out to be a h.** finalement, c'était un canular; **to play a h. on sb** faire un canular à qn
  VT monter *ou* faire un canular à
  ▸▸ *Br* **h. call** canular *m* téléphonique; *Br* **h. caller** mauvais plaisant *m (qui donne de fausses informations par téléphone)*

hoaxer [ˈhəʊksər] N farceur, -euse; *(hoax caller)* mauvais plaisant *m (qui donne de fausses informations par téléphone)*

hob [hɒb] N *(on electric cooker)* plaque *f*, *(on hearth)* plaque de côté

hobble [ˈhɒb(ə)l] N **1** *(limp)* boitillement *m* **2** *(for horses etc)* entrave *f*
  VI boitiller, clopiner; **to h. along** marcher en boitillant
  VT *(horse etc)* entraver
  ▸▸ **h. skirt** jupe *f* entravée

hobby [ˈhɒbɪ] N passe-temps *m inv*, hobby *m*, violon *m* d'Ingres; **to take up a h.** se trouver un hobby; **to take up sth as a h.** se mettre à qch pendant son temps libre

hobbyhorse [ˈhɒbɪhɔːs] N *(toy) (of merry-go-round)* cheval *m* de bois; *(rocking-horse)* cheval à bascule; *Fig* dada *m*, cheval de bataille; *Fig* **to get on one's h.** enfourcher son dada *ou* son cheval de bataille

hobgoblin [hɒbˈgɒblɪn] N *Myth* lutin *m*

hobnail [ˈhɒbneɪl] N clou *m*, fer *m (pour les chaussures)*; **hobnail(ed) boot** chaussure *f* ferrée

hobnob [ˈhɒbnɒb] VI *(-bb-) Fam* **to h. with sb** frayer avec qn

hobo [ˈhəʊbəʊ] N *Am* **1** *(tramp)* clochard *m* **2** *(itinerant worker)* ouvrier *m* saisonnier

Hobson [ˈhɒbsən] N **it's H.'s choice** je n'ai pas/il n'a pas/*etc* vraiment le choix *(se dit d'une situation où le choix n'est qu'apparent)*

hock[1] [hɒk] N *(of horse)* jarret *m*

hock[2] N *(wine)* vin *m* du Rhin

hock[3] *Fam* N **in h.** *(of watch etc)* en gage, *Fam* au clou, *Fam* chez ma tante; *(of person) (in debt)* endetté; **to put sth in h.** *(pawn)* mettre qch en gage; **to be in h. to the bank** devoir de l'argent à la banque
  VT *(pawn)* mettre au clou

hockey [ˈhɒkɪ] N *Sport* **1** *Br* hockey *m* (sur gazon); **to play h.** jouer au hockey **2** *Am (ice hockey)* hockey *m* (sur glace), *Can* hockey
  ▸▸ **h. stick** *Br* crosse *f* de hockey; *Am* crosse de hockey sur glace

hockshop [ˈhɒkʃɒp] N *Am Fam* crédit *m* municipal, mont-de-piété *m*, *pl* monts-de-piété

hocus-pocus [ˈhəʊkəsˈpəʊkəs] N **1** *(formula used by conjurers)* abracadabra **2** *(trickery)* tromperie *f*, supercherie *f*

hod [hɒd] N **1** *(of bricklayer)* oiseau *m*, hotte *f* **2** *(for coal)* seau *m*, caisse *f*
  ▸▸ **h. carrier** apprenti *m ou* aide *m* maçon

hodgepodge [ˈhɒdʒpɒdʒ] N *esp Am* = **hotchpotch**

Hodgkin's disease [ˈhɒdʒkɪnz] N *Med* maladie *f* de Hodgkin

hoe [həʊ] N houe *f*, binette *f*, **(weeding) h.** sarcloir *m*; **(Dutch) h.** griffe-bineuse *f*, *pl* griffes-bineuses
  VT **(hoed; hoeing)** *(soil)* biner; *(weeds)* sarcler

hoedown [ˈhəʊdaʊn] N *esp Am* bal *m* populaire

hog [hɒg] N **1** *(castrated pig)* porc *m* châtré; *Am (pig)* porc, cochon *m*, pourceau *m*; *Fam* **to go the whole h.** aller jusqu'au bout; **they went the whole h. for the party** *(didn't stint)* ils n'ont pas fait les choses à moitié; *Am Fig Fam* **to live high on the h.** mener joyeuse vie **2** *Fig (glutton)* goinfre *m*, glouton *m* **3** *Am Fam (motorbike)* grosse bécane *f*
  VT *(-gg-) Fam (take, use etc more than one's fair share of)* prendre plus que sa part de; **to h. the television** monopoliser la télé; **to h. the limelight** accaparer la vedette; *Aut* **to h. the road** prendre toute la place; *Aut* **to h. the centre lane** monopoliser la voie centrale

Hogmanay [ˈhɒgməˈneɪ] N *Scot* la Saint-Sylvestre

hogshead ['hɒgzhed] N (barrel) tonneau m, barrique f

hogtie ['hɒgtaɪ] VTAm (animal) lier les quatre pattes de; Fig (the economy etc) entraver

hogwash ['hɒgwɒʃ] N (swill) eaux fpl grasses (que l'on donne aux porcs); Fam (nonsense) foutaise f

hogweed ['hɒgwi:d] N (plant) berce f commune

hoi polloi [hɔɪpə'lɒɪ] NPL Pej the h. la foule f, les masses fpl

hoist [hɔɪst] N 1 (act) levage m; Fam to give sb a h. (up) aider qn à monter; (from beneath also) faire la courte échelle à qn 2 (device) appareil m ou engin m de levage; (winch) treuil m, grue f, palan m; Min bourriquet m; (for goods) monte-charge m inv

▪ VT (load) lever, hisser; Naut (ship's boat, flag) hisser; to h. boats in/out embarquer/débarquer les canots; h. away! hissez!; she hoisted herself on to the wall elle s'est hissée sur le mur; Fig to be h. with one's own petard tomber dans son propre piège

hoity-toity ['hɔɪtɪ'tɔɪtɪ] INT ta, ta, ta!, tara-tata!

▪ ADJ qui se donne des airs, qui fait l'important; she can get quite h. elle fait l'importante quelquefois

hokey ['həʊkɪ] ADJ Am Fam (nonsensical) absurde; (sentimental) à l'eau de rose

hokey-cokey [həʊkɪ'kəʊkɪ] N Br = danse f et chanson traditionnelles londoniennes

hokum ['həʊkəm] N Am Fam (in film etc) niaiseries fpl; (nonsense) bêtises fpl, âneries fpl

HOLD [həʊld]

N prise 1 ▪ cale 4 ▪ soute 4	
VT tenir 1, 3, 4, 6, 10, 11 ▪ maintenir 1	
▪ retenir 2, 6, 8 ▪ contenir 5	
▪ stocker 5 ▪ réserver 8 ▪ avoir 9	
▪ détenir 9	
VI tenir bon 1 ▪ durer 2 ▪ attendre 4	

N 1 (grip) prise f; Boxing tenu m; (in wrestling) prise; to have h. of sb/sth tenir qn/qch; to catch or get or take h. of sb/sth saisir ou empoigner qn/qch; to get h. of sth (find) mettre la main sur qch; where did you get h. of that? où vous êtes-vous procuré cela?; they prevented us from getting h. of the code ils nous ont empêchés de nous emparer du code; to get h. of the wrong idea mal comprendre; it's difficult to get h. of this book (find a copy of it) ce livre est difficile à trouver; to relax one's h. relâcher son étreinte; to let go one's h. lâcher prise; to lose one's h. on reality perdre le sens des réalités; to have a h. on or over sb avoir prise ou de l'emprise sur qn; to gain a firm h. over sb acquérir un grand pouvoir sur qn; no holds barred tous les coups sont permis; a no-holds-barred argument/contest une dispute/compétition où tous les coups sont permis; a no-holds-barred

discussion une discussion très franche

2 (in rockclimbing etc) point m d'appui

3 on h. (of project) en suspens; to put sth on h. mettre qch en suspens; the road building programme is on h. la construction de la route est interrompue; Tel to put sb on h. mettre qn en attente ou en parcage; Tel to be on h. (of caller) attendre, être en attente

4 (of ship) cale f; (for luggage on plane) soute f

▪ VT (pt, pp held [held]) 1 (grip) (child etc) tenir; to h. sth in one's hand tenir qch à la main; (something very small) tenir qch dans la main; to h. sth/sb tight(ly) serrer qch/qn, tenir qch/qn serré; they held (each other's) hands ils se tenaient (par) la main; to h. one's sides with laughter se tenir les côtes de rire; to h. one's nose se boucher le nez; to h. sth in position tenir ou maintenir qch en place; four screws h. the shelf to the wall l'étagère est fixée au mur par quatre vis; the table is held in place by steel bolts la table est maintenue par des boulons d'acier

2 (detain etc) Law to be held on remand être incarcéré (en détention provisoire); to h. sb prisoner retenir qn prisonnier; to h. sb (as) hostage retenir qn en otage; she was held without trial for six weeks elle est restée en prison six semaines sans avoir été jugée

3 (command etc) to h. one's ground tenir bon, ne pas lâcher pied; to h. one's own se maintenir, se défendre; Mil to h. a fort défendre une forteresse; to h. a position tenir une position; to h. the stage (of actor) captiver son auditoire; Fig (in discussion etc) occuper le devant de la scène; Naut etc to h. course tenir la route; car that holds the road well voiture qui tient bien la route

4 (carry) tenir; to h. one's head high garder la tête haute; to h. oneself straight/well se tenir droit/bien

5 (contain) contenir, renfermer; Comput stocker; barrel that holds twenty litres tonneau d'une contenance de vingt litres; how much data will this disk hold? quelle quantité de données cette disquette peut-elle stocker?; car that holds six people voiture à six places; to h. water (of cask etc) être étanche; Fig (of theory, story etc) tenir debout; the theory doesn't h. water la théorie ne tient pas (debout); to be able to h. one's drink bien supporter l'alcool; what the future holds for us ce que l'avenir nous réserve; sport held no interest for them pour eux, le sport ne présentait aucun intérêt

6 (conduct etc) (meeting) tenir; (party etc) donner; the meeting will be held at 8pm la réunion aura lieu à 8 heures du soir; to h. a conversation with sb s'entretenir avec qn; the two sides held talks des discussions ont eu lieu entre les deux parties; to h. a surgery for one's patients recevoir ses patients

7 (restrain) to h. one's breath retenir sa respiration ou son souffle; there's no holding him (une fois lancé) il n'y a pas moyen de l'arrêter; h. your tongue! taisez-vous!; Fam h. it!, h. your horses! arrêtez!, attendez!, stop!; h. it! (at photographer's) ne bougez plus!, on ne bouge plus!; Mil to h. the enemy contenir l'ennemi; to h. the front page garder la une

8 (keep) (airline seat) réserver; to h. sb's interest retenir l'attention de qn; the film doesn't h. the attention for long le film ne retient pas l'attention très longtemps; to h. one's audience retenir l'attention de son auditoire; to h. sb to their promise obliger ou contraindre qn à tenir sa promesse; we can h. a room for you until tomorrow la chambre vous sera réservée jusqu'à demain, on vous gardera la chambre jusqu'à demain; Am h. the onions (in restaurant) sans oignons

9 (possess) (title) avoir, posséder; (opinion)

avoir; (position, post) occuper; (record, shares) détenir; (passport) être porteur ou détenteur de; to h. 5% of the shares in a company détenir 5% du capital d'une société; she had held (government) office before elle avait déjà assumé des fonctions au gouvernement; Com to h. sb's commercial bill détenir un effet sur qn

10 (consider) to h. sth lightly faire peu de cas de qch, attacher peu d'importance à qch; to h. sth sacred tenir qch pour sacré; to h. sb responsible tenir qn responsable; to be held in respect être respecté de tous; to h. that … soutenir que …

11 Mus to h. a note tenir ou prolonger une note

12 Tel h. the line! ne quittez pas!; h. all my calls ne me passez aucun appel

▪ VI 1 (of rope etc) tenir (bon); h. tight! tenez bon!; Aut tyres that h. in the wet pneus qui tiennent bien la route par temps de pluie

2 (last) (of agreement etc) durer, persister; (of weather) se maintenir; if your luck holds si votre chance dure

3 (be valid) to h. (good or true) être vrai ou valable; the same holds true in respect of … il en est de même pour …

4 Tel attendre

▶ **hold against** VT SEP (dislike for) to h. sth against sb tenir rigueur de qch à qn; I won't h. it against you je ne t'en voudrai pas

▶ **hold back** VI 1 (stay in the background) rester en arrière

2 (restrain oneself) se retenir; to h. back from doing sth attendre avant de faire qch; (stronger) se retenir de faire qch; buyers are holding back les acheteurs s'abstiennent

▪ VT SEP 1 (restrain) (person, anger, tears) retenir; (anger, tears, crowd) contenir

2 (impede) freiner, entraver; lack of investment is holding industry back l'absence d'investissements freine l'industrie

3 (withhold) (truth) cacher, dissimuler; he's holding something back il cache quelque chose

▶ **hold down** VT SEP 1 (restrain) (person) maintenir à terre; to h. down interest rates empêcher l'augmentation des taux d'intérêt

2 to h. down a job (occupy) avoir un emploi; (keep) garder un emploi; although she is a student, she holds down a full-time job bien qu'elle étudie, elle occupe un poste à plein temps; he never holds down a job for more than a week il ne peut jamais garder un emploi plus d'une semaine

3 Comput (key, mouse button) maintenir enfoncé

▶ **hold forth** VI (speak pompously) disserter (on sth sur qch); he's always got something to h. forth about il trouve toujours quelque chose sur quoi disserter

▶ **hold in** VT SEP (laughter) réprimer; (emotion) maîtriser; (anger) contenir; (horse) serrer la bride à, contenir; to h. one's stomach or oneself in rentrer son ventre; to h. oneself in (emotionally) se maîtriser

▶ **hold off** VT SEP 1 (keep away) (enemy) tenir à distance; he held off his assailants il a tenu ses assaillants en respect; she held the press off by promising to make a statement elle a fait attendre les journalistes en leur promettant un communiqué

2 (refrain from) (decision, choice etc) remettre à plus tard; to h. off doing sth attendre pour faire qch; they held off buying a new car ils ont repoussé l'achat d'une nouvelle voiture

▪ VI (keep away) se tenir à distance (from de); (refrain from doing sth, from deciding) différer, surseoir; the rain is holding off jusqu'ici il ne pleut pas

▶ **hold off from** VT INSEP (decision, choice etc) remettre à plus tard; to h. off from doing sth attendre avant de faire qch

▸**hold on** VI 1 (endure) tenir, résister

2 (wait) attendre, patienter; **h. on (a minute)!** (not so fast) pas si vite!; Tel **h. on a moment** ne quittez pas

3 (keep one's grip) se tenir; **h. on (tight)!** (on bus, motorbike etc) tiens-toi bien!

VT SEP (keep attached) (piece of wood etc) fixer; **the tiles are held on with glue** les carreaux sont maintenus en place par de la colle

▸**hold on to** VT INSEP 1 (grip) (thing) s'agripper à; Fig (idea, hope etc) se raccrocher à

2 (keep) garder; **h. on to that book** (it may be valuable) garde ce livre précieusement; **she held on to her money** elle se cramponnait à son argent

▸**hold out** VT SEP 1 (stretch out) (one's hand) tendre

2 (offer) (hope) offrir, laisser; **the doctor doesn't h. out much hope** le docteur ne laisse pas beaucoup d'espoir

VI 1 (resist) tenir (le coup); **to h. out against an attack** résister à une attaque; **to h. out for a higher price** espérer un prix plus élevé

2 (of supplies etc) durer

▸**hold out on** VT INSEP (not give information to) **you've been holding out on me** (I didn't know you played the piano etc) tu m'as caché des choses

▸**hold over** VT SEP 1 (postpone) remettre (à plus tard); (decision) ajourner; (payment) arriérer

2 **to h. sth over sb** (threaten with) menacer qn de qch

▸**hold to** VT INSEP (abide by) s'en tenir à; **to h. to a belief** rester attaché à une croyance; **to h. to one's decision** s'en tenir ou maintenir sa décision

▸**hold together** VT SEP (two objects) maintenir ensemble; (party, alliance) maintenir la cohésion de; **the two pieces of wood are held together by nails** les deux morceaux de bois sont cloués ensemble

VI (of objects) tenir (ensemble); (of ideas) être cohérent; **the story doesn't h. together** l'histoire ne tient pas debout

▸**hold up** VT SEP 1 (support) soutenir; **these ropes h. the tent up** ces cordes maintiennent la tente bien droite

2 (raise) lever (en l'air); **to h. one's head up (with pride)** lever la tête (avec fierté); **she held the book up** (so that everyone could see) elle brandit le livre; Fig **to h. sb up as an example** citer qn comme exemple; **to h. sb up to ridicule** tourner qn en ridicule

3 (delay) (person) retenir, retarder; (train, kick-off etc) retarder; (traffic, agreement, decision) bloquer; **the car was held up at the traffic lights** la voiture a dû s'arrêter au feu rouge; **our departure was held up by bad weather** notre départ a été retardé par le mauvais temps; **the goods were held up at customs** les marchandises ont été retenues à la douane; **financial difficulties are holding the project up** le projet est freiné par des difficultés financières

4 (in order to rob) (person, bank) attaquer; (train) attaquer à main armée

VI 1 (stay in place) (of shelf etc) tenir (en place); (of good weather) se maintenir; **the old building is still holding up** le vieux bâtiment est toujours debout; **I hope the good weather holds up** j'espère que le beau temps va durer; **she's holding up well under the pressure** elle supporte bien la pression; **my finances are holding up well** je tiens le coup financièrement

2 (of theory etc) tenir debout

▸**hold with** VT INSEP (usu neg) **I don't h. with such behaviour/his opinions** je n'approuve pas une telle conduite/ses opinions

holdall ['həʊldɔːl] N Br sac m de voyage, fourre-tout m inv

holder ['həʊldər] N 1 (person) (of passport, permit etc) possesseur m, détenteur, -trice; (of ticket) possesseur; (of degree, record, shares) détenteur, -trice; (of opinion, belief) tenant m; Fin (of bonds, bill) porteur, -euse; (of right, post, account, degree etc) titulaire mf; (of championship) tenant; Sport **the present h.** (of the title) l'actuel tenant du titre 2 (device) support m; (drill) **h.** porte-foret m, pl porte-forets; (soap) **h.** porte-savon m, pl porte-savons; **pot plant h.** cache-pot m, pl cache-pots; (cigarette) **h.** porte-cigarettes m inv

holding ['həʊldɪŋ] N 1 Agr (property) terre f affermée, ferme f; Fin effets mpl en portefeuille; (shares in company) participation f; **he has holdings in several companies** il est actionnaire de plusieurs sociétés 2 (action) (of congress etc) tenue f; Mus (of note) tenue; (lengthening) prolongation f 3 Aviat (delay) attente f; **h. letter/reply** réponse f d'attente

▸▸Fin **h. company** (société f en) holding m, société à portefeuille; **h. costs** coûts mpl de détention; **h. operation** opération f de maintien; Fig **we need a h. operation** il faut trouver un moyen de retarder les choses; Aviat **h. pattern** circuit m d'attente

hold-up N 1 (delay) arrêt m; (on road) embouteillage m; **there's been a h. on the line** il y a eu des perturbations sur la ligne; **there have been no hold-ups with the project** le projet n'a eu à souffrir d'aucun retard 2 (armed robbery) attaque f à main armée, hold-up m; **this is a h.** c'est un hold-up

hole [həʊl] N 1 (in the ground) trou m, creux m, cavité f; Golf trou; (of rabbit) terrier m; (of fox) tanière f; (of mouse etc) trou; **to dig a h.** creuser un trou; **what a h.!** (of room etc) quel gourbi!; (of house) quel taudis!; (of town) quel bled!; Golf **h. in one** trou réussi en un coup

2 (opening) trou m; (in metal plate etc) perforation f, (of drive belt etc) point m; (of flute) perce f, (in theory etc) point faible; Comput (punch) **h.** perforation f, Med **h. in the heart** trou dans le cœur; **h. in the wall** restaurant/café/endroit exigu; **to make a h. in** faire un trou dans ou à; (piece of clothing) trouer; Fig **to make a h. in one's savings** (of expenditure) faire un (gros) trou dans ses économies; **this jersey is full of holes** ce tricot est tout troué ou est plein de trous; **to pick holes in sth** relever des erreurs dans qch; **to pick holes in a theory** relever les points faibles d'une théorie

3 Fam (difficult situation) situation f difficile; **to be or find oneself in a h.** être ou se trouver dans une situation délicate

VT 1 (make a hole in) trouer, faire un trou dans; **the ship was holed below the water line** le navire avait des avaries au-dessous de la ligne de flottaison; **the building had been holed by shellfire** le bâtiment a été endommagé par les obus 2 (put into a hole) **to h. the ball** Golf envoyer ou mettre la balle dans le trou; Billiards bloquer; Fig **holed in one!** vous avez deviné juste!

VI (of stockings etc) se trouer, se percer

▸▸**h. punch** perforatrice f, Fam **h. in the wall** (cashpoint) guichet m automatique; (restaurant) petit restaurant m; (shop) petite boutique f, Am (apartment) appartement m minuscule

▸**hole out** VI Golf mettre la balle dans le trou

▸**hole up** VI Fam (hide) se terrer

hole-and-corner ADJ Fam clandestin; (affair) un peu louche

holey ['həʊlɪ] ADJ Fam (tout) troué, plein de trous

holiday ['hɒlɪdɪ, -deɪ] N 1 Br vacances fpl; **a month's h.** un mois de vacances; **how much h. do you get?** combien est-ce que tu as de vacances?; **the summer holidays** les gran-

des vacances; **to be on h.** être en vacances; **to take a h.** prendre des vacances; **when are you going on h.?** quand est-ce que vous allez prendre vos vacances?; **where are you going on h.** or **for your holidays?** où allez-vous pour vos vacances?; **camping h.** vacances passées à faire du camping; **ski** or **skiing h.** vacances de neige

2 Br (day off) (jour m de) congé m; Sch **half-day h.** demi-journée f de congé; **I'm going to take a h. today** je vais prendre un jour de congé aujourd'hui

3 (day of festival) (jour m de) fête f, jour férié; **public** or Br **bank h.** fête légale

VI Br passer les vacances

▸▸**h. brochure** catalogue m de vacances; Br **h. camp** = centre m de vacances familial (avec animations et activités diverses); **h. centre** centre m de vacances; **h. club** club m de vacances; Br **h. cottage** gîte m; **h. entitlement** nombre m de jours de vacances auquel un employé a droit, droit m aux vacances; Br **h. home** maison f de vacances, résidence f secondaire; **h. market** marché m du tourisme; **h. period** période f de fêtes; Br **h. resort** lieu m de vacances ou de séjour; Br **h. season** saison f des vacances; **h. village** village m des vacances; **h. worker** vacataire mf

holiday-maker N Br vacancier, -ière f, (in summer) estivant, -ante

holier-than-thou ['həʊlɪəðən'ðaʊ] ADJ (attitude etc) hypocritement pieux

holiness ['həʊlɪnɪs] N sainteté f, **His/Your H.** (of the Pope) Sa/Votre Sainteté

holism ['həʊlɪz(ə)m] N Phil, Med holisme m

holistic [həʊ'lɪstɪk] ADJ Phil, Med holistique

Holland ['hɒlənd] N Hollande f

holland ['hɒlənd] N Tex toile f de Hollande, toile bise

holler ['hɒlər] N braillement m

VI crier à tue-tête, brailler

hollow ['hɒləʊ] ADJ 1 creux; (cheek) creux, rentré; (eye) cave; Fig **to feel h.** (emotionally) se sentir vide ou vidé; (hungry) avoir le ventre ou l'estomac creux; Fig **he's got h. legs** (can eat a lot) il mange comme quatre, il a le ver solitaire 2 (sound) sourd; **in a h. voice** d'une voix caverneuse; **a h. laugh** un ricanement 3 (insincere) (promise, friendship etc) faux, f fausse, trompeur, -euse; (worthless) qui sonne creux; **a h. victory** une victoire sans signification

ADV 1 **to sound h.** sonner creux 2 Br Fam **to beat sb h.** battre qn à plate(s) couture(s)

N (of hand, tree, in field etc) creux m; (larger depression in ground) dépression f (du sol); Geog (basin) cuvette f

▸▸Mil, Hist **h. square** carré m

▸**hollow out** VT SEP (carve, scrape out etc) creuser, évider; **to h. out the ground** (of water) raviner le terrain

hollow-cheeked [-'tʃiːkt] ADJ aux joues creuses

hollow-eyed ADJ aux yeux caves

hollowness ['hɒləʊnɪs] N 1 (of tree etc) creux m, cavité f 2 (of voice) timbre m caverneux 3 (of promise etc) manque m de sincérité; (worthlessness) (of victory etc) absence f de signification

holly ['hɒlɪ] N houx m

▸▸**h. berry** baie f de houx, cenelle f, **h. tree** houx

hollyhock ['hɒlɪhɒk] N (plant) rose f trémière

Hollywood ['hɒlɪwʊd] N Hollywood

ADJ hollywoodien

holm[1] [həʊm] N Eng Dial (island) petite île f, îlot m (de rivière)

holm[2] N (tree) yeuse f, chêne m vert

▸▸**h. oak** yeuse, chêne vert

holocaust [ˈhɒləkɔːst] N holocauste *m*; *Hist* the H. l'Holocauste; a H. survivor/victim un survivant/une victime de l'Holocauste

hologram [ˈhɒləgræm] N *Phot* hologramme *m*

holograph [ˈhɒləgrɑːf] N document *m*/testament *m* (h)olographe

holographic [hɒləˈgræfɪk] ADJ *Phot* holographique

holography [hɒˈlɒgrəfɪ] N *Phot* holographie *f*

hols [hɒlz] NPL *Br Fam* vacances *fpl*, vacs *fpl*

holster [ˈhəʊlstər] N étui *m* (de revolver); *(for rifle)* fonte *f*

holy [ˈhəʊlɪ] ADJ (**holier, holiest**) saint, sacré; *(person)* saint, pieux; *Fig Fam* **to swear by all that is h.** jurer sur ce qu'on a de plus sacré; *Fig* **to have a h. fear of sth** avoir une peur bleue de qch; *Fam* **that child is a h. terror** cet enfant est une terreur; *Sl* **h. cow!, h. smoke!, h. mackerel!** sapristi!

▪ N **the H. of Holies** le Saint des Saints
▸▸ **the H. Bible** la sainte Bible; **h. bread** pain *m* bénit; **the H. City** la Ville sainte; *Rel* **H. Communion** la Sainte Communion; **the H. Father** le Saint-Père, le pape; **the H. Ghost** le Saint-Esprit; **h. ground** terre *f* sacrée; *Fam* **H. Joe** *Br (religious person)* bigot *m*; *Am (parson, chaplain)* curé *m*; **the H. Land** la Terre Sainte; **h. matrimony** les liens *mpl* sacrés du mariage; **h. orders** ordres *mpl*; **h. place** lieu *m* saint; **the H. Roman Empire** le Saint-Empire romain germanique; **the H. Spirit** le Saint-Esprit; **the H. Trinity** la Sainte Trinité; **h. war** guerre *f* sainte; **h. water** eau *f* bénite; *Rel* **H. Week** la Semaine sainte

homage [ˈhɒmɪdʒ] N hommage *m*; **to pay** or **do h. to sb** rendre hommage à qn

homburg [ˈhɒmbɜːg] N *(hat)* chapeau *m* mou, feutre *m* souple

---

HOME [həʊm]

N	maison **1** ▪ chez soi **1** ▪ habitat **1**
	▪ patrie **2** ▪ hospice **3** ▪ début **6**
ADV	à la maison **1** ▪ chez soi **1** ▪ au
	pays **2**

N **1** *(house)* maison *f*, *(flat)* appartement *m*; *Biol (of animal, plant)* habitat *m*; **this is my h.** ici, c'est chez moi; **a house without love is not a h.** sans l'amour, une maison n'est pas un foyer; **to come from a broken h.** avoir des parents divorcés; **a happy h.** une famille heureuse; **I've come straight from h.** je viens (directement) de chez moi; *Br* **the Ideal H. Exhibition,** *Am* **the H. Show** ≃ le Salon des Arts Ménagers; **to work from h.** travailler à domicile; **to have a h. of one's own** avoir un chez-soi ou un foyer; **to own one's own h.** être propriétaire (de sa maison); **television brings the world into your own h.** la télévision vous apporte le monde à domicile; *Iron* **don't you have a h. to go to?** vous avez l'intention de passer la nuit ici?; **to buy some things for the h.** acheter des choses pour sa maison/son appartement; **to make one's h. in France** s'établir en France; **Glasgow is her second h.** Glasgow est sa deuxième patrie; **it's a h. from h.** on y est comme chez soi; **there's no place like h.** on n'est nulle part si bien que chez soi; **to leave h.** quitter la maison; *(for good)* partir (définitivement); **to be away from h.** être parti ou absent ou en voyage; **at h.** à la maison, chez soi; *Sport (to play)* à domicile; **to stay at h.** rester à la maison; **to find no one at h.** trouver la maison vide; **how are things at h.?** comment ça va chez vous?; **these children have problems at h.** ces enfants ont des problèmes chez eux; **I don't feel at h. here** je me sens dépaysé ici, je ne me sens pas chez moi ici; **he is at h. on** or **with any topic** il est

à l'aise sur tous les sujets; **make yourself at h.** fais comme chez toi; **he insulted me in my own h.!** il m'a insulté sous mon propre toit!; **to come from a good h.** venir d'une bonne famille; **good h. wanted for three kittens** *(on notice)* on recherche de gentils maîtres pour trois chatons

2 *(country, region)* patrie *f*, pays *m* (natal), terre *f* natale; **at h. and abroad** dans notre pays et à l'étranger; **our policy at h. and abroad** notre politique intérieure et extérieure; **to take an example nearer h.** sans aller chercher si loin; **Greece, the h. of the arts** la Grèce, patrie des beaux-arts; **Valencia is the h. of paella** Valence est le pays de la paella

3 *(for old people etc)* asile *m*, hospice *m*; **old people's h.** maison *f* de retraite; **she didn't want her father to go into a h.** elle ne voulait pas que son père aille à l'hospice; **children's h.** home *m* d'enfants

4 *(in games)* le but

5 **first-time h. buyer** personne *f* qui achète une maison pour la première fois; **h. purchase loan** crédit *m* épargne logement; **h. ownership is increasing** le nombre des personnes propriétaires de leur logement augmente;

6 *Comput (key)* (touche *f*) début *m*

ADV **1** *(to/at one's house)* à la maison, chez soi; **to go/come h.** rentrer (à la maison); *(after period of absence)* retourner/revenir dans sa famille; **on her way h.** en rentrant ou en retournant/revenant chez elle; **to bring work h.** emporter du travail à la maison; **to be h.** être de retour; **he's h. again!** il est de retour!; **we'll be h. soon** nous serons bientôt arrivés chez nous

2 *(to/in one's country)* au pays; **to go/come h.** retourner au pays; **to send sb h.** renvoyer qn chez lui; *(repatriate)* rapatrier qn

3 **his speech went h.** son discours fit forte impression; **her remarks/criticisms hit h.** ses remarques/critiques ont fait mouche; **it will come h. to him some day** il s'en rendra compte un jour; **to drive sth h. to sb** faire entrer qch dans la tête à qn; **to push an attack h.** pousser à fond une attaque; **to push h. one's advantage** profiter au maximum d'un avantage

4 *(all the way)* à fond; **to screw a piece h.** visser ou serrer une pièce à bloc; **she drove the knife h. with all her strength** elle enfonça le couteau de toutes ses forces; **the bolt slid h.** le verrou glissa dans la serrure

VI *(of pigeon)* revenir au colombier; **to h. on** or **towards ...** *(of aircraft, missile etc)* mettre le cap sur ..., se diriger vers ou sur ...
▸▸ **h. address** *(on form)* domicile *m* (permanent); *(not business address)* adresse *f* personnelle; *Comput* **h. automation** domotique *f*; **h. banking** banque *f* à domicile; *Obst* **h. birth** accouchement *m* à la maison; **h. cinema** cinéma *m* à domicile, home cinéma *m*; *Comput* **h. computer** ordinateur *m* familial; *Comput* **h. computing** informatique *f* à domicile; **h. cooking** cuisine *f* familiale; **the H. Counties** = l'ensemble *m* des comtés limitrophes de Londres, à la population aisée et conservatrice; **h. delivery** livraison *f* à domicile; *Sch* **h. economics** économie *f* domestique; **h. economist** spécialiste *mf* d'économie domestique; *Am Fin* **h. equity loan** prêt *m* sur valeur nette de la propriété; *Sport* **h. ground** terrain *m* du club; *Hist* **the H. Guard** = section *f* de volontaires de l'armée britannique restée sur le territoire pour le défendre en cas d'invasion; *Br* **h. help** aide *f* ménagère; **h. improvements** travaux *mpl* de rénovation; **h. journey** voyage *m* de retour; *Comput* **h. key** touche *f* début; *Sport* **h. leg** match *m* à domicile; **h. life** vie *f* de famille; *Fin* **h. loan** prêt *m* immobilier, prêt d'épargne-logement; *Econ* **h. market** marché *m* in-

térieur; *Sport* **h. match** match à domicile; **h. news** nouvelles *fpl* nationales; *Pol* **the H. Office** = le ministère britannique de l'Intérieur; **h. owner** propriétaire *mf*, *Comput* **h. page** *(initial page)* page *f* d'accueil; *(start page in browser)* page d'accueil; *(personal page)* page personnelle; *Mktg* **h. party selling** vente *f* domiciliaire; *Econ* **h. products** produits *mpl* nationaux ou domestiques; **h. rule** *(devolution)* décentralisation *f*, **h. run** *Sport (in baseball)* coup *m* de circuit *(coup de batte qui permet au batteur de marquer un point en faisant un tour complet en une seule fois)*; *Fig (last leg of trip)* dernière étape *f* du circuit; **to hit a h. run** faire un coup de circuit; **h. sales** ventes *fpl* sur le marché intérieur; *Pol* **H. Secretary** = ministre *mf* de l'Intérieur en Grande-Bretagne; *Com* **h. shopping** téléachat *m*; *Sport* **the h. straight, the h. stretch** la dernière ligne droite; *Sport* **h. team** équipe *f* qui reçoit; **h. town** *(of birth)* ville *f* natale; **h. truth** vérité *f* bien sentie; **to tell sb a few h. truths** dire son fait ou ses quatre vérités à qn; *Comput* **h. user** utilisateur *m* domestique; **h. video** = film *m* vidéo réalisé par un particulier, généralement sur sa vie de famille; *Sport* **h. win** victoire *f* à domicile

▸ **home in** VI *(approach or reach target) (of airplane, missile etc)* arriver au but
▸ **home in on** VT INSEP *(aim for)* viser; **to h. in on a target** *(of missile)* se diriger en plein vers un objectif; *Fig* **she homed in on this error** elle a relevé ou repéré cette erreur, elle n'a pas manqué de relever cette erreur

---

home-baked ADJ *(bread, cake)* fait ou cuit à la maison; *(bread)* de ménage

homebird [ˈhəʊmbɜːd] N *Fam (person)* casanier, -ière

homebody [ˈhəʊmbɒdɪ] N *esp Am Fam* casanier, -ière

homeboy [ˈhəʊmbɔɪ] N *Am Fam (man from one's home town)* compatriote *m*; *(friend)* pote *m*; *(fellow gang member)* = membre *m* de la même bande

home(-)brew N *(beer)* bière *f* brassée à la maison

home-brewed [ˈhəʊmˈbruːd] ADJ *(beer)* brassé à la maison

homecoming [ˈhəʊmkʌmɪŋ] N retour *m* (au foyer ou à la maison); *(to one's country)* retour au pays

homegirl [ˈhəʊmgɜːl] N *Am Fam (woman from one's home town)* compatriote *f*, *(friend)* copine *f*; *(fellow gang member)* = membre *m* de la même bande

home-grown ADJ *(from garden)* du jardin; *(from one's own country)* du pays; *Fig* **many people prefer Japanese cars to the h. product** beaucoup de gens préfèrent les voitures japonaises à celles qu'on fabrique chez eux

homeland [ˈhəʊmlænd] N *esp Lit* patrie *f*, *(in South Africa)* bantoustan *m*, homeland *m*

homeless [ˈhəʊmlɪs] ADJ sans foyer, sans abri; **to be h.** être à la rue ou sur le pavé
▪ NPL **the h.** les sans-abri *mpl*, les sans-logis *mpl*

homelessness [ˈhəʊmlɪsnɪs] N = fait *m* de ne pas avoir de logis; **h. among the young is growing** de plus en plus de jeunes sont sans abri

homeloving [ˈhəʊmlʌvɪŋ] ADJ casanier, -ière

homely [ˈhəʊmlɪ] ADJ **1** *(food)* simple, ordinaire; *(tastes)* modeste; *(atmosphere)* accueillant; *Br (person)* simple **2** *Am (plain) (person)* au physique ingrat

home-made ADJ *(cake, wine)* fait à la maison; *(bread)* de ménage; **the bookshelves looked rather h.** les étagères semblaient plutôt artisanales

homemaker ['həʊmmeɪkər] N *Am* **1** femme *f*/homme *m* d'intérieur, ménagère *f* **2** *(social worker)* aide *f* ménagère

homeopath ['həʊmɪəʊpæθ] N homéopathe *mf*

homeopathic [həʊmɪəʊ'pæθɪk] ADJ homéopathique

homeopathy [həʊmɪ'ɒpəθɪ] N homéopathie *f*

homeostasis [həʊmɪəʊ'steɪsɪs] N homéostasie *f*

homeostatic [həʊmɪəʊ'stætɪk] ADJ homéostatique

Homer ['həʊmər] N Homère *m*; *Prov* **even H. nods, H. sometimes nods** même les meilleurs font des erreurs

homer ['həʊmər] N **1** *Am Baseball Fam* coup *m* de circuit **2** *Fam (homing pigeon)* pigeon *m* voyageur **3** *Br Fam (work)* = séance *f* de travail au noir effectuée chez un particulier par un artisan, généralement le soir ou le week-end

Homeric [həʊ'merɪk] ADJ *(poem, hero)* homérique

homesick ['həʊmsɪk] ADJ **1** *(for one's country)* nostalgique, qui a le mal du pays; **to feel h.** avoir le mal du pays **2** *(for one's home)* **a h. little boy** un petit garçon qui s'ennuie de ses parents; **are you h.?** tu t'ennuies de chez toi?

homesickness ['həʊmsɪknɪs] N mal *m* du pays, nostalgie *f*

homespun ['həʊmspʌn] ADJ **1** *(simple)* simple, sans apprêt **2** *Tex (cloth)* fait à la maison N *Tex* tissu *m* fait à la maison

homestead ['həʊmsted] N **1** *Agr* ferme *f (avec dépendances)* **2** *Am Law (land granted)* concession *f* statutaire de 160 acres

homeward ['həʊmwəd] ADJ qui se dirige vers sa maison; *(from abroad)* qui se dirige vers son pays; **h. journey** voyage *m* de retour; **h. leg** *(of a journey)* dernière étape *f*, *Naut* **h. voyage** voyage de retour ADV = **homewards**

homeward-bound ADJ *Naut (ship)* à destination de son port d'attache, retournant au port, sur le retour; *(container)* de retour; **to be h.** *(of person)* rentrer chez soi

homewards ['həʊmwədz] ADV *(to one's house)* vers sa maison, vers sa demeure; *(from abroad)* vers son pays

homework ['həʊmwɜːk] N **1** *Sch* devoirs *mpl*, *Fig Fam* **it was plain that the chairman had not done his h.** il était évident que le président ne maîtrisait pas son sujet **2** *(paid work)* travail *m* à domicile

Attention: ne pas confondre avec **homework**, qui signifie **travaux ménagers**.

homeworker ['həʊmwɜːkər] N travailleur, -euse à domicile

homeworking ['həʊmwɜːkɪŋ] N travail *m* à domicile

homey ['həʊmɪ] ADJ *esp Am* accueillant N *Am Fam* = **homeboy, homegirl**

homicidal [hɒmɪ'saɪd(ə)l] ADJ homicide, meurtrier

homicide ['hɒmɪsaɪd] N **1** *(crime)* homicide *m*; *Law* **wilful h.** homicide volontaire; *Scot* **culpable h.** homicide involontaire; *Law* **justifiable h., h. in self-defence** homicide en état de légitime défense **2** *esp Am (person)* homicide *mf*

homily ['hɒmɪlɪ] N homélie *f*, *Fig* sermon *m*

homing ['həʊmɪŋ] ADJ *Tech* directionnel, de radioguidage
▸▸ **h. device** mécanisme *m* d'autoguidage; **h. instinct** *(of animals)* instinct *m* d'orientation; **h. pigeon** pigeon *m* voyageur

hominy grits ['hɒmɪnɪ] N *Am Culin* maïs *m* concassé et bouilli

homo ['həʊməʊ] N *Fam Pej* homo *m*, pédé *m*

homoeopath, homoeopathic *etc* = **homeopath, homeopathic** *etc*

homoerotic [həʊməʊɪ'rɒtɪk] ADJ homoérotique

homogeneity [hɒməʊdʒɪ'niːɪtɪ] N homogénéité *f*

homogeneous [hɒməʊ'dʒiːnɪəs] ADJ homogène; *Mktg* **h. shopping goods** produits *mpl* d'achat réfléchi homogènes

homogenize [hə'mɒdʒənaɪz] VT *(milk)* homogénéiser

homograft ['hɒməgrɑːft] N *Med* allogreffe *f*, autogreffe *f*

homograph ['hɒməgrɑːf] N *Ling* homographe *m*

homologous [hə'mɒləgəs] ADJ *Biol, Math etc* homologue

homonym ['hɒmənɪm] N *Ling* homonyme *m*

homophobe ['hɒməʊfəʊb] N adversaire *mf* des homosexuels

homophobia [hɒməʊ'fəʊbɪə] N haine *f* des homosexuels

homophobic [hɒməʊ'fəʊbɪk] ADJ antihomosexuel

homophone ['hɒməfəʊn] N homophone *m*

homosexual [hɒməʊ'seksjʊəl] ADJ, N homosexuel, -elle

homosexuality [hɒməʊseksjʊ'ælɪtɪ] N homosexualité *f*

Hon *Br Parl* **the H.** ABBR **the Honourable**

hon [hʌn] N *Am Fam (abbr* **honey)** *(term of address)* chéri, chérie

honcho ['hɒntʃəʊ] N *Fam* **the head h.** le boss

Honduras [hɒn'djʊərəs] N Honduras *m*

hone [həʊn] VT aiguiser, affiler; *Fig (sense of humour)* aiguiser; *Fig* **finely honed musicianship** sens aigu de la musique

honest ['ɒnɪst] ADJ **1** *(trustworthy)* honnête, probe, droit; *(in business)* loyal, -aux; **he has an h. face** il a une figure d'honnête homme **2** *(sincere, truthful)* sincère, de bonne foi; **the h. truth** la vérité vraie; **I gave you an h. answer** je t'ai répondu avec sincérité; **is that your h. opinion?** est-ce que c'est ce que tu penses vraiment?; **to be h. (with you)** pour être franc; **if you're h. (with yourself)** si tu étais sincère avec toi-même; **an h. piece of work** un travail consciencieux; *Sl* **I couldn't help it, h.** c'était plus fort que moi, je t'assure **3** *(legitimate)* juste, légitime; *(means)* légitime; **to earn an h. living** gagner honnêtement sa vie; **an h. day's work** une bonne journée de travail; **he's never done an h. day's work in his life** *(real work)* il n'a jamais rien fait de ses dix doigts; *(honest work)* il n'a jamais rien fait d'honnête; **an h. day's pay for an h. day's work** toute peine mérite salaire **4** *Old-fashioned, Hum* **to make an h. woman of sb** faire de qn une honnête femme *(en l'épousant)* **5** *Old-fashioned (usu used condescendingly) (respectable)* brave; **they are h. folk** ce sont de braves gens

honestly ['ɒnɪstlɪ] ADV **1** *(in legitimate manner)* honnêtement **2** *(sincerely)* sincèrement; **quite h.** en toute sincérité; **I can h. say that …** je peux dire en toute sincérité que …; **do you h. believe that?** est-ce que tu le crois vraiment?; **I didn't do it, h.!** ce n'est pas moi qui l'ai fait, je t'assure! INT *(expressing indignation)* **h.! some people!** y'a des gens, je te jure!

honesty ['ɒnɪstɪ] N **1** *(trustworthiness)* honnêteté *f*, *Prov* **h. is the best policy** l'honnê-

teté est la meilleure des tactiques **2** *(sincerity)* sincérité *f*, bonne foi *f*, *(of a speech)* franchise *f*, **in all h.** en toute sincérité **3** *(plant)* lunaire *f*, *Fam* monnaie-du-pape *f*

honey ['hʌnɪ] N **1** miel *m*; **clear/thick h.** miel liquide/solide; **comb h.** miel en rayon; *Fig* **he was all h.** il a été tout sucre et tout miel **2** *esp Am (term of endearment)* chéri, *f* chérie **3** *esp Am (nice person)* amour *m*; *(excellent thing)* bijou *m*; **she's a real h., isn't she?** c'est un amour, tu ne trouves pas?; **it's a h. of an apartment** cet appartement est un bijou
▸▸ *Zool* **h. bear** *(in Europe, Asia)* ours *m* brun; *(in South America)* kinkajou *m*; **h. coloured** miellé, couleur de miel

honeybee ['hʌnɪbiː] N abeille *f*

honeybun(ch) ['hʌnɪbʌn, -tʃ] N *Am Fam (term of endearment)* mon chéri, ma chérie, mon amour

honeycomb ['hʌnɪkəʊm] N rayon *m* de miel; *(for eating)* gâteau *m* de miel; *Tex* nid *m* d'abeilles
VT **to be honeycombed with sth** être criblé de qch; **the city was honeycombed with narrow streets** la ville était un dédale de rues étroites
▸▸ *Geol* **h. structure** structure *f* alvéolée *ou* alvéolaire

honeydew ['hʌnɪdjuː] N miellée *f*, miellure *f*
▸▸ *Bot* **h. melon** melon *m* d'hiver *ou* d'Espagne

honeyed ['hʌnɪd] ADJ *(tones, words)* mielleux

honeymoon ['hʌnɪmuːn] N *(of couple)* lune *f* de miel; *Fig* état *m* de grâce; **they're on their h.** ils sont en voyage de noces; *Fig* **the h. is over** c'est la fin de l'état de grâce
VI être en voyage de noces; *(go on honeymoon)* aller en voyage de noces
▸▸ **h. couple** couple *m* en voyage de noces; **h. suite** *(in hotel)* suite *f* nuptiale; **h. trip** voyage *m* de noces

honeymooners ['hʌnɪmuːnəz] NPL couple *m* en voyage de noces

honeypot ['hʌnɪpɒt] N **1** pot *m* à miel **2** *Sl (vagina)* minette *f*

honeysuckle ['hʌnɪsʌk(ə)l] N *(shrub)* chèvrefeuille *m*

Hong Kong ['hɒŋ'kɒŋ] N Hongkong

honk[1] [hɒŋk] N **1** *(of goose)* cri *m* **2** *(of car horn)* coup *m* de klaxon
VI **1** *(of goose, seal etc)* pousser un cri **2** *(of car horn etc)* retentir; **she honked twice on the horn** elle a donné deux coups de klaxon
VT **to h. the horn** klaxonner

honk[2] VI *Br Sl* **1** *(vomit)* dégueuler **2** *(smell bad)* schlinguer

honker ['hɒŋkər] N *Am Sl* **1** *(nose)* blaire *m*, tarin *m* **2** *(breast)* nichon *m*

honky ['hɒŋkɪ] N *esp Am Offensive Sl (white person)* blanc *m*, blanche *f*

honky-tonk ['hɒŋkɪtɒŋk] N *Am Fam* **1** *(bar)* bouge *m*, boui-boui *m*, *pl* bouis-bouis **2** *Mus* musique *f* de bastringue
▸▸ **h. joint** bouge, boui-boui

honorarium, *pl* **honoraria, honorariums** [ɒnə'reərɪəm, -ɪə, -ɪəmz] N *(of doctor, lawyer)* honoraires *mpl*

honorary ['ɒnərərɪ] ADJ *(without pay)* bénévole; *(without duties)* honorifique; *(president)* d'honneur; *(member)* honoraire; **to have an h. doctorate** être docteur honoris causa
▸▸ *Univ* **h. degree** diplôme *m* honoris causa; **h. membership** honorariat *m*; *Mil* **h. rank** grade *m* honorifique

honor, honorable *etc Am* = **honour, honourable** *etc*

honorific [ɒnəˈrɪfɪk] **ADJ** *(title)* honorifique

honour, *Am* **honor** [ˈɒnər] **N 1** *(respect)* honneur *m*; **to put up a statue in h. of sb** ériger une statue à la gloire de qn; **dinner in your h.** dîner en votre honneur; **in h. of the occasion** pour l'occasion; **to do sb h.** honorer qn; **you would do yourself h.** ce serait tout à ton honneur; *Prov* **h. where h. is due** à tout seigneur tout honneur **2** *(privilege)* honneur *m*; **to consider it an h. to do sth** considérer comme un honneur de faire qch; **it is a great h. to be selected for the team** c'est un grand honneur que d'être sélectionné pour l'équipe; **it was an h. to have worked with her** cela a été un honneur que de travailler avec elle; *Fml* **whom have I the h. of addressing?** à qui ai-je l'honneur de parler?; *Fml* **I don't believe I've had the h.** je ne crois pas avoir eu l'honneur d'être présenté; **we had the h. of a visit from the president** nous avons eu l'honneur de recevoir la visite du président; **to have the h.** *Golf* avoir l'honneur; *(at bowls)* avoir la boule; *Fml* **may I have the h.?** *(at dance)* me ferez-vous l'honneur de cette danse? **3** *(good name)* honneur *m*; **to come out of an affair with h.** se tirer honorablement d'une affaire; **she acquitted herself with h.** *(of player)* elle s'en est tirée honorablement; **their courage does them h.** leur courage leur fait honneur; **to make it a point of h. to do sth** mettre son (point d')honneur à faire qch; **I'm h. bound to ...** l'honneur m'oblige à ...; **I felt h. bound to stay** je sentis que l'honneur me commandait de rester; **man of h.** homme d'honneur; **to swear on one's h.** jurer sur son honneur; **to put sb on their h.** faire promettre à qn sur son honneur; **you're on your h.** tu as promis sur ton honneur; **to give one's word of h.** engager sa parole (d'honneur); **on my (word of) h.!** je vous donne ma parole (d'honneur)!, sur l'honneur!; *Prov* **(there is) h. among thieves** les loups ne se mangent pas entre eux; **h. is satisfied** l'honneur est sauf **4** *Old-fashioned (chastity)* honneur *m*; *Old-fashioned, Hum* **to defend one's h.** défendre son honneur **5** *(award)* distinction *f* honorifique **6** *(civilities)* **to receive sb with full honours** recevoir qn avec tous les honneurs qui lui sont dus; *Fam Hum* **to do the honours** *(serve food, drinks)* servir; *(do introductions)* faire les présentations; *Hist* **the honours of war** les honneurs de la guerre; **he was buried with full military honours** il a été enterré avec tous les honneurs militaires **7** *Cards (at bridge etc)* **honours** honneurs *mpl* (as, roi, dame et valet) **8** *(person)* **to be an h. to one's country** faire honneur à sa patrie **9** *Law (in title)* **Your/His H.** Votre Honneur/ Monsieur le juge, Monsieur le président

VT 1 *(somebody, sb's memory)* honorer; *Iron* **the manager honoured us with his presence today** le directeur nous a fait l'honneur de sa présence aujourd'hui; *Iron* **we are honoured!** quel honneur!; **I'm honoured that you have chosen me** je suis très honoré que vous m'ayez choisi; **our honoured guest** notre invité d'honneur **2** *(bill, signature, cheque etc)* honorer; *(credit card)* accepter

▸▸ *Univ* **honours course** programme *m* d'études approfondies au niveau de la licence; **honours degree** ≃ licence *f*; *Am Mil* **honor guard** garde *f* d'honneur; *(soldier)* soldat *m* de la garde d'honneur; **honours list** *Sch* tableau *m* d'honneur; *Br Admin* = liste *f* des personnes choisies pour recevoir le titre de MBE *etc*; **h. system** = système *m* d'autodiscipline dans les écoles, les prisons, les hôtels etc

honourable, *Am* **honorable** [ˈɒnərəb(ə)l]

ADJ honorable; **he is an h. man** c'est un homme d'honneur; **to receive (an) h. mention** *(in competition)* recevoir une mention spéciale; *Old-fashioned, Hum* **are his intentions h.?** ses intentions sont-elles honorables?; **it's the h. thing to do** c'est la solution la plus honorable

N 1 *Br Parl* **the H., the Hon** = titre *m* donné aux membres du Parlement britannique; **the H. member for Caithness** l'honorable député du Caithness **2** *Br (in aristocracy)* = titre *m* donné aux benjamins des familles nobles britanniques; **her fiancé is an h.** son fiancé est un membre de l'aristocratie

honourably, *Am* **honorably** [ˈɒnərəblɪ] **ADV** honorablement; *(to behave etc)* d'une manière honorable; *(to treat prisoners)* décemment

Hons [ɒnz] *Univ abbr* **Honours,** *see* **honour 5**

hooch [huːtʃ] **N** *Am Sl (drink)* gnôle *f*

hood¹ [hʊd] **N 1** *(of anorak, duffle coat, monk's etc)* capuchon *m*, capuche *f*; *(with eye-holes) (of thief, Ku Klux Klan)* cagoule *f*; *Univ* épitoge *f*; *(over hawk's head)* chaperon *m*; **the kidnappers put a h. over her head** les ravisseurs lui ont couvert la tête avec un sac **2** *(soft top of car)* capote *f*, *Am (bonnet)* capot *m* **3** *(over cooker, fireplace etc)* hotte *f*; *(of hairdryer)* casque *m*; *Phot (over lens)* paresoleil *m*; *(any protective cover, acoustic etc)* couvercle *m*

hood² *esp Am Sl* **1** *(gangster)* truand *m* **2** *(neighbourhood)* **the h.** le quartier

hooded [ˈhʊdɪd] **ADJ 1** *(monk)* encapuchonné; *(executioner, thief)* au visage masqué; *(eyes)* aux paupières tombantes; *(eyelid)* tombant; **h. men** hommes *mpl* en cagoule **2** *(jacket)* avec une cagoule

▸▸ *Orn* **h. crow** corneille *f* mantelée

hoodlum [ˈhuːdləm] **N** *esp Am Fam (delinquent)* voyou *m*; *(gangster)* gangster *m*, truand *m*

hoodoo [ˈhuːduː] **N** *Fam (bad luck)* poisse *f*, guigne *f*; *(person)* porte-malheur *m*; **to put a h. on sb** porter la poisse à qn

hoodwink [ˈhʊdwɪŋk] **VT** *Fam* berner; **I've been hoodwinked** je me suis fait avoir; **to h. sb into believing sth** faire croire qch à qn; **I was hoodwinked into signing** on m'a raconté des bobards pour me faire signer

hooey [ˈhuːɪ] **N** *Fam* **that's all h.** ce ne sont que des sornettes; **don't talk h.** arrête de dire des bêtises

hoof, *pl* **hooves** [huːf, huːvz] **N** *(of horse etc)* sabot *m*; *(of devil)* pied *m* fourchu; **500 cattle on the h.** 500 têtes de bétail sur pied; *Fig* **to do things on the h.** improviser; *Fig* **on the h.** *(on ad hoc basis)* au coup par coup; **I had lunch on the h.** à midi j'ai mangé sur le pouce

VT *Fam* **to h. it** *(walk)* aller à pinces; *(dance)* danser; **to h. sb out** chasser qn à coups de pied

▸▸ *Am Vet* **h. and mouth disease** fièvre *f* aphteuse

hoofbeat [ˈhuːfbiːt] **N hoofbeats** *(of horses)* bruit *m* de la cavalcade

hoofed [huːft] **ADJ** *(animal)* à sabots

hoofer [ˈhuːfər] **N** *Fam Hum* danseur *m*, danseuse *f (de métier)*

hoofprint [ˈhuːfprɪnt] **N** trace *f* de sabot

hoo-ha [ˈhuːhaː] **N** *Fam* raffut *m*; **there was a lot of h. in the press about ...** la presse a fait tout un plat de ...; **the announcement caused a great h. at the school** cette nouvelle a fait beaucoup de bruit à l'école; **when all the h. about the Royal Wedding/government scandal has died down** quand le mariage princier/le scandale au sein du gouvernement ne sera plus à la une de l'actualité; **now that all the h. is over we can get**

down to serious business maintenant que le calme est revenu, nous pouvons nous occuper de choses sérieuses

hook [hʊk] **N 1** crochet *m*; *(for clothes)* patère *f*, *(for meat)* croc *m*; *(on fishing line)* hameçon *m*; *Sewing* **h. and eye** agrafe *f*; *Aviat, Naut* arrester **h.** crosse *f* d'appontage **2** *Boxing* crochet *m*; *Golf* hook *m*; *Boxing* **a left/right h.** un crochet du gauche/droit **3** *Geog* pointe *f* de terre; *(larger)* cap *m* **4** *(phrases)* *Fam* **he swallowed it** *or* **fell for it h. line and sinker** il a tout gobé; *Fam* **he's fallen for her h. line and sinker** il est fou d'elle; **we must do it by h. or by crook** nous devons le faire, coûte que coûte; **to leave the phone off the h.** décrocher le *ou* son téléphone; **your phone was off the h.** tu avais décroché ton téléphone; *(accidentally)* tu avais mal raccroché ton téléphone; **to put the phone back on the h.** reposer le combiné (sur son support); *Fam* **that lets you off the h.** te voilà tiré d'affaire; *Fam* **thanks for getting me off the h.** merci de m'avoir tiré d'affaire; *Fam* **he owned up and got me off the h.** *(vindicated me)* son aveu m'a innocenté; *Am Sl* **to get the h.** *(be sacked)* se faire vider *ou* virer; *Br Sl* **to sling one's h.** foutre le camp; **once she's got her hooks into him ...** une fois qu'elle lui aura mis le grappin dessus ...

VT 1 *(fasten)* accrocher (**to sth** à qch); **to h. the shutters open** accrocher les volets après les avoir ouverts; **to h. the shutters back** ouvrir les volets et les attacher au mur; **he got his sweater hooked on a nail** il a accroché son tricot à un clou; **the two bits of wire had become hooked together** les deux fils de fer s'étaient pris l'un dans l'autre; **he hung with his legs hooked around the trapeze** il se suspendit par les jambes au trapèze; **she had her feet hooked up under her chair** elle avait calé ses pieds sous sa chaise; **h. one end of the wire around ...** fixer une extrémité du fil de fer autour de ...; **to h. a fish** faire mordre le poisson à l'hameçon; *Fam* **she's hooked herself a husband** elle a décroché un mari; *Fam* **she'll never manage to h. him** elle n'arrivera jamais à lui mettre le grappin dessus **2** *Boxing* envoyer un crochet à; **to h. sb to the jaw** envoyer un crochet dans la mâchoire de qn **3** *Rugby (of hooker)* talonner; *Golf* **to h. the ball** faire un hook **4** *Am Fam* **to h. school** faire l'école buissonnière

VI 1 *(of dress etc)* s'agrafer **2** *Boxing* envoyer des crochets; *Golf* faire un/des hook(s) **3** *Am Sl (work as prostitute)* faire le trottoir

▸▸ **H. of Holland** Hoek *m* van Holland

▸ **hook on VI** s'accrocher (**to** à) **VT SEP** *(caravan to car etc)* accrocher (**to** à)

▸ **hook up VI 1** *(of dress etc)* s'agrafer; *(of wires)* se raccorder **2** *TV etc* **we're now going to h. up with ...** nous vous proposons maintenant une émission en duplex avec ...

VT SEP 1 *(dress, bra)* agrafer; **could you h. me up please?** tu peux agrafer ma robe/*etc*? **2** *(trailer etc)* accrocher (**to** à) **3** *Radio, TV* faire un duplex entre; **to h. up two computers** connecter deux ordinateurs

hookah [ˈhʊkə] **N** narguilé *m*

hooked [hʊkt] **ADJ 1** *(nose)* crochu **2** *(having hooks)* à crochets **3** *Fam* **to be h. on** *(drugs etc)* se droguer à, être dépendant de; *(Italian cinema, jazz, tennis etc)* être mordu de, être fana de; *(person)* être fou de; *(novelist etc)* être fana de; **to be h.** *(on drugs)* se droguer; **he's completely h.** il est complètement accro; **one bite and I was h.** une bouchée et j'étais conquis

hooker [ˈhʊkər] **N 1** *Rugby* talonneur *m* **2** *esp Am Fam (prostitute)* putain *f*

hookey ['hʊkɪ] N Am Fam = **hooky**

hook-nosed ['hʊknəʊzd] ADJ au nez crochu

hook-up N TV duplex m; (programme) émission f en duplex; **you can have a direct computer h. with your Paris office** votre ordinateur peut être relié directement à celui de Paris

hookworm ['hʊkwɜ:m] N ankylostome m

hooky ['hʊkɪ] N Am Fam **to play h.** sécher les cours

hooligan ['hu:lɪɡən] N voyou m, hooligan m

hooliganism ['hu:lɪɡənɪz(ə)m] N hooliganisme m

hoop [hu:p] N 1 (on barrel) cercle m; (toy, for skirt, in circus etc) cerceau m; (in croquet) arceau m 2 (coloured ring on plumage, fur etc, stripe) rayure f; (around animal's neck) collier m 3 Am Fam (basketball) **hoop(s)** le basket; **to shoot hoops** jouer au basket 4 (in phrases) **to put sb through the hoops** mettre qn à l'épreuve; **to go through the hoops** passer l'épreuve du feu; **I've really been through the hoops for you** j'ai sué sang et eau pour toi
▸▸ **h. earrings** (anneaux mpl) créoles fpl

hooped [hu:pt] ADJ (skirt) à cerceaux

hoop-la ['hu:plɑ:] N 1 Br (game) jeu m des anneaux 2 Am Fam = **hoo-ha**
▸▸ **h. stall** stand m du jeu des anneaux

hoopoe ['hu:pəʊ] N (bird) huppe f

hooray [hʊ'reɪ] INT, N = **hurrah**
▸▸ Br Fam Pej **H. Henry** = fils m à papa exubérant et bruyant

hoosegow ['hu:sɡaʊ] N Am Sl (prison) taule f

hoot [hu:t] N 1 (of owl) hululement m
2 (mocking) huée f; **hoots of laughter** des hurlements mpl de rire; **she gave a great h. of laughter** elle partit d'un grand éclat de rire
3 Aut coup m de klaxon®; Rail coup de sifflet; Naut coup de sirène; **when you hear three hoots on the factory hooter** quand la sirène de l'usine retentit trois fois
4 Fam **it was a h.!** (hilarious) c'était tordant!; **he's a h.!** il est d'un drôle!
5 Fam **not to give** or **care a h.** or **two hoots about sb/sth** se ficher éperdument de qn/qch; **I don't give a h.** je m'en fiche comme de l'an quarante; **it doesn't matter two hoots** ça n'a strictement aucune importance
VI 1 (of owl) hululer 2 **to h. with laughter** hurler de rire; **they all hooted with** or **in derision** ils poussèrent tous des huées 3 Aut klaxonner, donner un coup/des coups de klaxon®; Rail siffler; Naut donner un coup/des coups de sirène
VT (actor, speaker) huer; (play) siffler; **the speaker was hooted down** l'orateur fut réduit au silence par les huées; **he was hooted off the stage** on lui a fait quitter la scène sous les huées

hootenanny ['hu:tənænɪ] N Am improvisation f collective de musique folklorique

hooter ['hu:tər] N Br 1 Naut, Ind sirène f; Aut klaxon® m 2 Fam (nose) pif m

hooting ['hu:tɪŋ] N 1 (of owl) hululement m
2 (of person) (jeering) huées fpl; (laughter) hurlements mpl de rire 3 (of cars) coups mpl de klaxon

Hoover® ['hu:vər] N aspirateur m
VT (carpet etc) passer l'aspirateur sur; (room) passer l'aspirateur dans
VI passer l'aspirateur
▸ **hoover up** VT SEP enlever avec l'aspirateur; **I'll just h. it up** je vais (y) donner un coup d'aspirateur

hoovering ['hu:vərɪŋ] N **to do the h.** passer l'aspirateur; **when you've finished with the h.** quand tu auras passé l'aspirateur; **there's**

still a lot of h. to do nous n'avons pas/je n'ai pas/etc encore fini de passer l'aspirateur

hooves NPL see **hoof**

hop¹ [hɒp] N Bot houblon m; **hops** (for brewing) houblon
▸▸ Agr **h. field** houblonnière f, Agr **h. grower** houblonnier, -ière; Agr **h. picker** cueilleur, -euse de houblon; Agr **h. picking** cueillette f du houblon

hop² N 1 (jump) saut m; (on one foot) saut à cloche-pied
2 Sport **h. skip and jump** triple saut m
3 Fig Fam **to catch sb on the h.** prendre qn au dépourvu; **to keep sb on the h.** ne pas laisser chômer qn
4 Aviat **it's just a short h. from London to Paris** il n'y a qu'un saut de Londres à Paris
5 Fam (dance) fête f
6 Am Fam (drug) came f
VI 1 (jump) sautiller; **to h. (on one leg)** sauter à cloche-pied
2 **to h. out of bed** sauter du lit; **to h. into bed with sb** coucher avec qn; Fam **h. in!** (into car etc) montez!; **he hopped off the bus/his bike** il sauta du bus/de son vélo; **he hopped on the bus/his bike** il sauta dans le bus/sur son vélo; **I hopped across to France for the weekend** j'ai fait un saut en France pour le week-end; **he hopped onto the first London-bound plane/train** il a sauté dans le premier avion/train pour Londres; Fam **she's just hopped out for a second** elle est sortie deux minutes
VT Fam **h. it!** fiche le camp!; **to h. a ride on a train** voyager en train clandestinement (en sautant dans un wagon de marchandises/sur le toit); **can I h. a ride?** je peux monter avec vous?
▸ **hop off** VI Br Fam (clear off) ficher le camp; **he's hopped off (with the silver)** il a filé (avec l'argenterie)

hope [həʊp] N 1 (no pl) espoir m; **to be full of h.** être plein d'espoir; **to lose** or **to give up h.** perdre (l')espoir; **there is little/no h. of finding it** il y a peu d'espoir/il n'y a aucun espoir de le trouver; **to put one's h. in the future** compter sur l'avenir; **to h. against h. that …** caresser l'espoir que …; Fam **we live in h.!** c'est l'espoir qui fait vivre!; **in the h. of … dans l'espoir de …**
2 (individual instance) **my last h.** mon dernier espoir, ma dernière planche de salut; **to have hopes of doing sth** avoir bon espoir de faire qch; **do you still have hopes of …?** est-ce que vous avez toujours l'espoir de …?; **to have hopes of sth** avoir l'espoir de qch; **to have no hopes of sth/doing sth** n'avoir pas d'espoir ou aucun espoir de qch/faire qch; **to have hopes of doing sth** avoir l'espoir de faire qch; **I'm not getting my hopes up** je ne veux pas (commencer à) me faire des idées; **these events have raised hopes of a peaceful solution** ces événements ont fait naître l'espoir d'une solution pacifique; **the team's hopes were high** les espoirs de l'équipe étaient grands; **they had high hopes for their daughter** ils avaient de grandes espérances pour leur fille; **to set one's hopes on sb/sth** mettre tout son espoir en qn/qch; Iron **what a h.!, some h.!** (si vous) comptez là-dessus!; **she hasn't got a h.** or Fam **a h. in hell of winning** elle n'a aucun espoir de gagner
VI espérer; **to h. for sth** espérer qch; **don't h. for too much** n'en attends pas trop; **we'll just have to h. for the best** nous n'avons plus qu'à espérer que tout aille pour le mieux; **to h. for better days** attendre des jours meilleurs; **we must h. against h.** il faut espérer malgré tout; **hoped-for victory** victoire espérée ou désirée
VT **I h. to see you again** j'espère vous revoir; **I h. (that) your brother is better** j'espère que

votre frère va mieux; **I h. you are right** je souhaite que vous ayez raison; Fam **I h. to God** or **to hell that …** je prie le ciel que … + sub; **I h. and pray that …** je prie Dieu que … + sub; **I h. so** j'espère que oui, j'espère bien; **I h. not** j'espère que non; **I should h. so!** j'espère bien!; **I should h. not!** j'espère bien que non!; **hoping to hear from you** (in letter) dans l'attente (d'avoir) de vos nouvelles VOIR GRAMMAIRE A48
▸▸ Am **h. chest** coffre m à trousseau; Fig trousseau m (de mariage)

hopeful ['həʊpfʊl] ADJ 1 (person) plein d'espoir; **we must remain h.** il faut continuer d'espérer; **to be h. that …** avoir bon espoir que … 2 (promising) **the situation looks more h.** la situation est plus encourageante ou porte à l'optimisme
N Fam (person) (looking for a job) candidat m; **young h.** jeune espoir mf

hopefully ['həʊpfʊlɪ] ADV 1 (to speak, wait etc) avec bon espoir, avec optimisme 2 Fam (with luck) **h. the sun will shine tomorrow** espérons qu'il fera du soleil demain; **do you think he'll come? – h.** est-ce que vous pensez qu'il viendra? – espérons-le; **h. not** espérons que non

hopefulness ['həʊpf(ʊ)lnɪs] N (of person) confiance f, optimisme m

hopeless ['həʊplɪs] ADJ 1 (without hope) (person) sans espoir, désespéré; (situation) désespéré; (project) qui n'a aucune chance de réussir; **to give sth up as h.** renoncer à faire qch (parce ce qu'on a peu de chance de réussir); **it's h.!** ça (ne) sert à rien!; **it is h. to try to …** il est tout à fait inutile de …; **to be in a h. condition** (of patient etc) être dans un état désespéré; **a h. cause** (in politics etc) une cause que l'on sait perdue d'avance; **h. grief** douleur f inconsolable 2 Fam (very bad) **I'm a h. singer** je chante très mal; **you're h.!** espèce d'idiot!; **to be h. at maths/at cooking** être nul en maths/en cuisine; **a h. drunkard** un ivrogne invétéré

hopelessly ['həʊplɪslɪ] ADV 1 (to live) sans espoir; (to sob) plein de désespoir; (to shake one's head, sigh) découragé; (stronger) plein de désespoir 2 (beaten) à plates coutures; (in love) éperdument; **h. lost/out of control** complètement perdu/incontrôlable; **h. drunk** fin soûl; **h. naive** d'une naïveté désespérante; **the government is h. out of touch** le gouvernement a totalement perdu contact (avec le pays)

hopelessness ['həʊplɪsnɪs] N (despair) désespoir m; (of situation) état m désespéré; **a feeling of h.** un sentiment d'impuissance

hophead ['hɒphed] N Am Sl toxicomane mf, drogué, -ée

hopper ['hɒpər] N 1 Fam (insect) sauterelle f; Austr kangourou m 2 Tech trémie f, huche f, hotte f; Agr (for sowing) semoir m; (for feeding poultry) trémie
▸▸ Naut **h. barge** marie-salope f, pl maries-salopes; Rail **h. car** wagon-trémie m, pl wagons-trémies

hopping ['hɒpɪŋ] ADV Fam **to be h. mad** être fou de colère

hopscotch ['hɒpskɒtʃ] N marelle f

Horatian [hə'reɪʃən] ADJ Liter d'Horace

horde [hɔ:d] N (of barbarians), Fig horde f

Attention: ne pas confondre avec **hoard**.

horizon [hə'raɪz(ə)n] N horizon m; **on the h.** à l'horizon; **studying has opened up new horizons for her** les études lui ont ouvert des horizons nouveaux; **reading broadened my horizons** la lecture a élargi mes horizons; Astron, Aviat, Naut **celestial h.** horizon astronomique
▸▸ Aviat, Naut **h. bar** barre f d'horizon

horizontal [hɒrɪ'zɒnt(ə)l] **ADJ** horizontal, -aux; *Am* **a h. increase in salaries of 10%** une augmentation uniforme de 10% sur toutes les rétributions; *Fam* **I was h. for a few days with the flu** je suis resté couché *ou* au lit pendant quelques jours avec la grippe
N horizontale *f*
▸▸ *Sport* **h. bar** barre *f* fixe; *Fin* **h. equity** équité *f* horizontale; *Mktg* **h. integration** intégration *f ou* concentration *f* horizontale; *Comput* **h. justification** justification *f* horizontale; **h. market** marché *m* horizontal; *Comput* **h. orientation** (format *m*) paysage *m*; *Fin* **h. spread** écart *m* horizontal

horizontally [hɒrɪ'zɒntəlɪ] **ADV** horizontalement

hormonal [hɔː'məʊn(ə)l] **ADJ** *Physiol* hormonal, -aux

hormone ['hɔːməʊn] **N** *Physiol* hormone *f*
▸▸ *Med* **h. replacement therapy** traitement *m* hormonal substitutif

horn [hɔːn] **N 1** (*of cattle, ram, snail etc*) corne *f*, (*of stag beetle*) antenne *f*, (*of owl*) aigrette *f*; **horns** (*of deer*) bois *mpl*; *Fig* **to draw in one's horns** restreindre son ardeur, rabattre (de) ses prétentions; (*economize*) se serrer la ceinture, faire des économies, diminuer ses dépenses; **to be (caught) on the horns of a dilemma** être en proie à un dilemme **2** (*of moon*) corne *f*, (*of estuary*) branche *f*; **Cape H., the H.** le cap Horn **3** (*material*) corne *f*; **h. comb** peigne *m* en corne **4** *Mus* cor *m Sl* (*brass or woodwind instrument*) trompette *f*, **English/French h.** cor anglais/d'harmonie; **to sound** *or* **blow the h.** sonner du cor; *Am Fig* **to blow one's own h.** se vanter; **the h. section, the horns** les cors **5** *Br Sl* (*erection*) érection *f*, **to have the h.** avoir la trique *ou* le gourdin; **to give sb the h.** (*arouse*) exciter qn **6** *Am Fam* (*telephone*) bigophone *m*; **to get on the h. to sb** passer un coup de fil *ou* de bigophone à qn **7** (*on car*) klaxon *m*; **to sound one's h.** klaxonner **8** (*of loudspeaker*) pavillon *m*
VT (*gore*) encorner, donner un coup de corne à
▸▸ **the H. of Africa** la corne de l'Afrique; *Mus* **h. player** corniste *mf*; *Lit* **h. of plenty** corne d'abondance
▸ **horn in** **VI** *Am Sl* (*interrupt, intrude*) intervenir sans façon, ramener sa fraise *or*; **don't want him horning in on this deal** je veux pas qu'il fourre son nez dans cette affaire

hornbeam ['hɔːnbiːm] **N** (*tree*) charme *m*

hornbill ['hɔːnbɪl] **N** (*bird*) calao *m*

horned [hɔːnd] **ADJ** (*animal*) à cornes

hornet ['hɔːnɪt] **N** (*insect*) frelon *m*; *Fig* **to stir up a h.'s nest** mettre le feu au poudre

hornpipe ['hɔːnpaɪp] **N** *Naut, Mus* matelote *f*

horn-rimmed **ADJ** (*spectacles*) à monture lourde, à grosse monture

horny ['hɔːnɪ] **ADJ 1** (*like horn*) corné; (*beak etc*) de corne, en corne; (*hand etc*) calleux; **to grow h.** se racornir **2** *Sl* **to be h.** (*sexually aroused*) être tout excité; **to get h.** s'exciter **3** *Br Sl* (*sexy*) bandant

horology [hɒ'rɒlədʒɪ] **N 1** (*clockmaking*) horlogerie *f* **2** (*measuring time*) horométrie *f*

horoscope ['hɒrəskəʊp] **N** horoscope *m*; **to cast sb's h.** faire *ou* dresser l'horoscope de qn; **my h. said that ...** (*in newspaper etc*) d'après mon horoscope ...

horrendous [hɒ'rendəs] **ADJ** affreux, horrible

horrendously [hɒ'rendəslɪ] **ADV** *Fam* (*expensive etc*) affreusement, horriblement

horrible ['hɒrəb(ə)l] **ADJ 1** horrible, affreux, atroce; (*noise*) épouvantable; (*weather*) abominable; **how h.!** quelle horreur! **2** (*unkind*) atroce; **to be h. to sb** être méchant *ou* horrible avec qn; **to say h. things about sb** dire des horreurs *ou* des choses terribles sur qn

horribly ['hɒrɪblɪ] **ADV** horriblement, affreusement; (*to behave*) de façon abominable

horrid ['hɒrɪd] **ADJ 1** horrible, affreux; **he's such a h. little man!** c'est un affreux petit bonhomme; **h. sight** chose *f* horrible à voir **2** *Fam* (*unkind*) méchant, ignoble; **to be h. to sb** être ignoble envers qn, être odieux avec qn; **to say h. things about sb** dire des méchancetés de qn

horridly ['hɒrɪdlɪ] **ADV** *Fam* (*to behave*) méchamment, de façon odieuse *ou* ignoble

horrific [hɒ'rɪfɪk, hə-] **ADJ** horrible; **h. injuries** blessures *fpl* horribles

horrify ['hɒrɪfaɪ] **VT** horrifier

horrifying ['hɒrɪfaɪɪŋ] **ADJ** horrifiant

horror ['hɒrər] **N** (*feeling, terrifying thing*) horreur *f*, **paralysed with h.** glacé d'horreur; **to my h.** à ma grande horreur; **to have a h. of sth/doing sth** avoir horreur de qch/faire qch; **he had a h. of being seen naked** il avait horreur qu'on le voie nu; *Fam* **it gives me the horrors** cela me donne le frisson; *Fam* **that child's a little h.** cet enfant est un petit monstre
▸▸ **h. film, h. movie** film *m* d'horreur; **h. story** histoire *f* d'horreur; *Fig Fam* **h. stories about hotels where nothing worked** histoires terribles sur des hôtels où rien ne marchait

horror-stricken, horror-struck ADJ saisi *ou* glacé *ou* frappé d'horreur

horse [hɔːs] **N 1** cheval *m*, -aux; *Horseracing* **to put some money on the horses** jouer aux courses; **draught h.** cheval de trait; **to fall off one's h.** tomber de cheval; *Fig* **to get up on one's high h.** monter sur ses grands chevaux (**about sth** à propos de qch); *Fam* **to eat like a h.** manger comme quatre; **I could eat a h.!** j'ai une faim de loup!; *Fig* **to hear sth from the h.'s mouth** apprendre qch de source sûre; *Fam* **hold your horses!** ne t'emballe pas!, doucement!, du calme! **2** (*in breeding*) cheval *m* mâle, cheval entier; **stud h.** étalon *m*; **to take a mare to h.** faire couvrir une jument **3** *Mil, Hist* (*pl*) cavalerie *f*, troupes *fpl* montées; **regiment of h.** régiment *m* de cavalerie; *Br* **the (Royal) H. Guards** la Garde Royale (à cheval) **4** *Gym* (*vaulting*) **h.** cheval(-sautoir) *m*; **pommel h.** cheval d'arçons **5** (*for sawing*) chevalet *m*, tréteau *m*, chèvre *f* **6** *Tech Fam* = **horsepower** **7** *Sl* (*heroin*) héro *f*, blanche *f*
▸▸ *Mil, Hist* **h. artillery** artillerie *f* montée; **h. blanket** couverture *f* de cheval; **h. brass** médaillon *m* de bronze (*fixé à une martingale*); *Bot* **h. chestnut** (*tree*) marronnier *m* (d'Inde); (*nut*) marron *m* (d'Inde); **h. collar** collier *m* de cheval (*fixé sur le harnachement du cheval*); *Fam* **h. doctor** vétérinaire *mf*; **h. fair** foire *f* aux chevaux; **h. laugh** gros rire *m* bruyant; **h. meat** viande *f* de cheval; *Am Cin, TV Fam* **h. opera** western *m*; **h. racing** courses *fpl* (de chevaux); *Br* **h. riding** équitation *f*, *Fam* **h. sense** (gros) bon sens *m*; **h. show** concours *m* hippique; **h. trader** maquignon *m*; *also Fig* **h. trading** maquignonnage *m*; **h. trailer** van *m* à chevaux
▸ **horse about, horse around** **VI** (*play roughly*) faire l'imbécile

-horse [hɔːs] **SUFF** **one/two-h.** à un cheval/deux chevaux; *see* **one-horse**

horseback ['hɔːsbæk] **N** **on h.** à (dos de) cheval; **to ride on h.** aller à cheval

horsebox ['hɔːsbɒks] **N** (*trailer*) van *m*; *Rail* wagon *m* à chevaux

horsebreaker ['hɔːsbreɪkər] **N** dresseur, -euse de chevaux

horse-drawn ADJ tiré par des chevaux
▸▸ **h. vehicle** véhicule *m* attelé

horseflesh ['hɔːsfleʃ] **N 1** (*horses*) chevaux *mpl*; **to be a good judge of h.** bien s'y connaître en chevaux **2** (*meat*) chair *f ou* viande *f* de cheval

horsefly ['hɔːsflaɪ] **N** taon *m*

horsehair ['hɔːsheər] **N** crin *m* (de cheval); *Tex* tissu *m* de crin; **h. mattress** matelas *m* de crin

horseman, *pl* **horsemen** ['hɔːsmən] **N** cavalier *m*, écuyer *m*; **to be a good h.** bien monter à cheval, être bon cavalier; **the four horsemen of the apocalypse** les quatre cavaliers de l'apocalypse

horsemanship ['hɔːsmənʃɪp] **N** équitation *f*, art *m* de monter à cheval; **we admired her h.** nous avons admiré l'art avec lequel elle montait à cheval, nous avons admiré son talent de cavalière

horseplay ['hɔːspleɪ] **N** **they were having a bit of h. in the pool** ils faisaient les imbéciles dans la piscine; **it's just harmless h.** c'est une bagarre pour rire; **no h.!** jeux de mains, jeux de vilains!

horsepower ['hɔːspaʊər] **N** *Tech etc* puissance *f* en chevaux; (*measurement*) cheval-vapeur *m*, *pl* chevaux-vapeur; **actual h.** puissance effective en chevaux

horseradish ['hɔːsrædɪʃ] **N** (*plant*) raifort *m*
▸▸ *Culin* **h. sauce** sauce *f* au raifort

horseshoe ['hɔːsʃuː] **N** fer *m* à cheval; **h. brooch/table** broche *f*/table *f* en (forme de) fer à cheval

horsewhip ['hɔːswɪp] **N** cravache *f*
VT (**-pp-**) (*person*) cravacher

horsewoman, *pl* **horsewomen** ['hɔːswʊmən, -wɪmɪn] **N** cavalière *f*, amazone *f*, écuyère *f*, **she's a good h.** elle est bonne cavalière, elle monte bien

horsy, horsey ['hɔːsɪ] **ADJ** (*appearance*) chevalin; (*keen on horses*) fou/folle de chevaux; **she's terribly h.** elle ne parle que chevaux; **h. face** figure *f* chevaline

horticultural [hɔːtɪ'kʌltʃər(ə)l] **N** (*implement*) horticole, d'horticulture
▸▸ **h. show** exposition *f* horticole *ou* d'horticulture

horticulture ['hɔːtɪkʌltʃər] **N** horticulture *f*

horticulturist [hɔːtɪ'kʌltʃərɪst] **N** horticulteur, -trice

hose [həʊz] **N 1** (*pl* **hoses**) (*pipe*) tuyau *m*; *Tech* (**flexible**) **h.** tuyau flexible; (*in car*) durite *f*, **air h.** tuyau d'air flexible; **garden h.** tuyau d'arrosage **2** (*no pl*) *Com* (*stockings etc*) (*for women*) bas *mpl*; *Hist* (*for men*) chausses *fpl*, **half h.** chaussettes *fpl* (*d'hommes*)
VT 1 (*car etc*) laver au jet **2** (*lawn*) arroser (au jet d'eau)
▸▸ *Aut* **h. clip** collier *m* de durite; **h. reel** dévidoir *m*
▸ **hose down** **VT SEP** = **hose VT**
▸ **hose out** **VT SEP** (*clean out*) laver au jet

hosepipe ['həʊzpaɪp] **N** tuyau *m*, flexible *m*
▸▸ **h. ban** = interdiction *f* d'utiliser les tuyaux d'arrosage pendant les périodes de sécheresse

hosier ['həʊzɪər] **N** *Com* bonnetier, -ière

hosiery ['həʊzɪərɪ] **N** *Com* (*stockings and socks*) bas *mpl* et chaussettes *fpl*, **h. counter** *or* **department** rayon *m* des bas (et chaussettes); **h. trade** bonneterie *f*

hospice ['hɒspɪs] N hospice m; (for terminally ill) hospice (pour malades en phase terminale); (part of hospital) pavillon m des incurables

hospitable [hɒs'pɪtəb(ə)l] ADJ (climate) hospitalier, accueillant; (person) accueillant

hospitably [hɒs'pɪtəblɪ] ADV avec hospitalité

hospital ['hɒspɪt(ə)l] N **1** hôpital m, -aux; **to be in h.** être à l'hôpital; **she had to go (in)to** Br **h.** or Am **the h.** elle a dû aller à l'hôpital; **to send sb to** Br **h.** or Am **the h.** hospitaliser qn VOIR GRAMMAIRE A7 **2 Chelsea H.** l'hôpital m de Chelsea (pour les vieux soldats); **Greenwich H.** l'Hospice m de Greenwich (pour les invalides de la marine)
▸▸ **h. bed** lit m d'hôpital; **h. radio** radio f diffusant dans les hôpitaux; **h. ship** navire-hôpital m, pl navires-hôpitaux; **h. staff** personnel m hospitalier; **h. train** train m sanitaire; **h. treatment** traitement m hospitalier

hospitality [hɒspɪ'tælɪtɪ] N hospitalité f, Old-fashioned Euph **to enjoy His/Her Majesty's h.** faire de la prison
▸▸ **h. business** hôtellerie f, **h. industry** industrie f hôtelière; **h. management** gestion f hôtelière; **h. tray** plateau m de courtoisie

hospitalization [hɒspɪtəlaɪ'zeɪʃən] N hospitalisation f

hospitalize ['hɒspɪtəlaɪz] VT (sick person) hospitaliser; **a couple of thugs hospitalized him** deux voyous l'ont envoyé à l'hôpital

host¹ [həʊst] N **1** (in private house) hôte m; Com (in hotel etc) hôtelier m; (in pub) aubergiste m; TV etc (of chat show, gameshow) animateur, -trice; **he was the perfect h.** il a été un hôte parfait **2** Biol hôte m **3** Comput (of website) hébergeur m
VT **1** (party) donner; TV etc (programme) présenter; (gameshow) animer **2** (website) héberger
. ▸▸ Comput **h. computer** ordinateur m principal; (in network) serveur m; Comput **h. file** fichier m serveur; Biol **h. organism** m; Comput **h. system** système m serveur ou hôte

host² N **1** (great number) **a (whole) h.** (of servants etc) (toute) une armée; **a h. of good restaurants** une quantité de bons restaurants **2** Arch, Lit (throng) armée f, multitude f

host³ N Rel (consecrated bread) hostie f

hostage ['hɒstɪdʒ] N otage m; **as (a) h.** en otage, pour otage; **to take sb h.** prendre quelqu'un en otage; **she is being held h.** elle est gardée en otage; Fig **that's a h. to fortune** c'est la porte ouverte à tous les ennuis
▸▸ **h. taker** preneur, -euse d'otage; **h. taking** prise f d'otage(s)

hostel ['hɒstəl] N (for the homeless, students) foyer m; **youth h.** auberge f de jeunesse

hosteller, Am **hosteler** ['hɒstələr] N (youth) **h.** ajiste mf

hostelling, Am **hosteling** ['hɒstəlɪŋ] N (youth) **h.** ajisme m

hostelry ['hɒstəlrɪ] N Arch hostellerie f, Br Hum pub m, bar m

hostess ['həʊstɪs] N **1** (in private house, night club) hôtesse f; (hotel-keeper etc) hôtelière f; TV etc (of chat show etc) animatrice f **2** Aviat (air) **h.** hôtesse f de l'air

hostile ['hɒstaɪl, Am 'hɒst(ə)l] ADJ (attitude, climate, environment) hostile; (act) d'hostilité; **to be h. to sb/sth** (opposed) être hostile à qn/qch
N Am ennemi m
▸▸ Mil **h. forces** forces fpl ennemies; Com **h. takeover bid** OPA f hostile

hostility [hɒs'tɪlɪtɪ] N **1** hostilité f (**to** contre); **to feel no h. towards sb** n'avoir aucune animosité contre qn **2 hostilities** (war) hostilités fpl

hosting N Comput (of website) hébergement m

HOT [hɒt]

ADJ	chaud **1, 5** ▪ fort **2** ▪ épicé **2**
	▪ tout frais **3** ▪ violent **5** ▪ super **6**
	▪ intense **7** ▪ recherché **8**

ADJ (**hotter, hottest**) **1** chaud; (sun) ardent; (fire) vif; Nucl radioactif; **boiling h.** bouillant; **burning h.** brûlant; **to be very h.** (of person) avoir très chaud; (of water, plate etc) être très chaud; (of weather) faire très chaud; **it was a h. day** il faisait chaud; **to get** or **become h.** (of person) commencer à avoir chaud; (of water, plate etc) devenir chaud, chauffer; (of weather) commencer à faire chaud; **to keep a dish h.** tenir un plat au chaud; Fam **to get all h. and bothered** devenir tout rouge; Fam **to get h. under the collar** (with embarrassment) être embarrassé; (with anger) se mettre en colère; Fam **it's all h. air** ce ne sont que des balivernes; Fam **he's full of h. air** il ne raconte que des foutaises; **to sell like h. cakes** se vendre comme des petits pains; **a h. meal** un repas chaud; Fig Fam **to be in h. water** être dans le pétrin; Fig Fam **to get into h. water** s'attirer ou se créer des ennuis **2** Culin (spicy etc) (pepper) fort; (mustard) piquant, fort; (food) épicé; **not all Indian food is h.** la cuisine indienne n'est pas nécessairement relevée **3** (fresh, recent) tout frais; **news h. from the press** nouvelles de dernière heure; **a book h. from the press** un livre qui sort tout juste de l'imprimerie; **h. gossip/news** les tous derniers cancans/les toutes dernières nouvelles **4** (close) **to be h. on the scent** or **trail** être sur la bonne piste; **to be in h. pursuit of sb** suivre qn de près; **you're getting h.** (in guessing game) tu brûles **5** (fiery) violent; **to have a h. temper** s'emporter facilement; **the political climate has become noticeably hotter in recent weeks** le climat politique est devenu sensiblement plus chaud depuis quelques semaines **6** (intense) intense, profond **7** Fam (good) super; **that record wasn't so h.** ce disque n'était pas super; **that isn't such a h. idea** ce n'est pas terrible ou fameux comme idée; **I'm not very h. on history** (knowledgeable about) je ne suis pas très calé en histoire; **they're very h. on formal qualifications** (attach importance to) ils insistent beaucoup sur les diplômes; **they're not very h. on hygiene** (fussy about) ils ne sont pas très portés sur l'hygiène; **to be h. stuff** (sexy) (of woman) être canon; (of man) être super; **he's h. stuff at tennis** au tennis, c'est un as; **how are you? – not so h.** comment ça va? – pas terrible ou fameux **8** Fam (dangerous, difficult) (stolen goods etc) recherché par la police; **the place was getting too h. for me** je me trouvais dans un véritable guêpier; **the situation was too h. to handle** la situation était trop délicate pour qu'on s'en mêle; **to make things** or **it too h. for sb** rendre la vie infernale à qn; **the presence of the army made things h. for the smugglers** la présence de l'armée a rendu les choses très difficiles pour les contrebandiers
ADV **to blow h. and cold** (of person) changer d'avis sans cesse; (in moods) être d'humeur changeante; **she's blowing h. and cold over him** un jour, elle l'aime, un jour, elle ne l'aime pas
▸ **hot up** Fam VT SEP Aut (engine) gonfler; **to h. up the pace** (increase) forcer l'allure
VI (of campaign etc) s'échauffer; (of competi-

tion, love affair, discussion) s'intensifier; (of race) s'animer; **things are beginning to h. up** l'affaire se corse
▸▸ Br **h. cross bun** = brioche f à la canelle; **h. desking** = pratique f qui consiste à ne pas assigner de bureaux individuels aux employés, ces derniers étant libres de s'installer à n'importe quel poste de travail inoccupé; Br Sport **h. favourite** grand(e) favori, -ite; Br **h. flush,** Am **h. flash** bouffée f de chaleur; Comput **h. key** touche f personnalisée; Tel **h. line** numéro m d'urgence; Pol (between US and Kremlin) téléphone m rouge; Comput **h. link** lien m hypertexte; Fam **h. money** (stolen) argent m volé; Fin capitaux mpl flottants ou fébriles; Am **h. pad** dessous-de-plat m inv; **h. pants** mini short m (très court et moulant); Fam Fig **h. potato** sujet m brûlant et délicat; Fam **to drop sb like a h. potato** laisser tomber qn comme une vieille chaussette ou savate; Ir **h. press** (airing cupboard) = placard m chauffé où l'on fait sécher le linge; Am Fam **h. seat** (electric chair) chaise f électrique; Fig **to be in the h. seat** (be responsible) avoir toute la responsabilité; (have to answer difficult questions) être sur la sellette; **the man in the England h. seat** (manager of football team etc) l'homme qui a la tâche difficile de diriger l'équipe d'Angleterre; **h. spot** (dangerous area) point m chaud ou névralgique; Fam (night club) boîte f de nuit; Tech point m chaud; **h. spring** source f chaude; **h. tip** tuyau m de première

hot-air balloon N montgolfière f, ballon m à air chaud

hotbed ['hɒtbed] N **1** Fig (of rebellion, intrigue etc) foyer m **2** (in gardening) couche f

hot-blooded ADJ ardent, passionné; **to be h.** avoir le sang chaud; **the Italians are a h. race** les Italiens sont un peuple qui a le sang chaud

hotchpotch ['hɒtʃpɒtʃ] N mélange m confus; **this book's a bit of a h.** (good and bad) ce livre est de qualité inégale; (mixture) ce livre est un patchwork

hotdog ['hɒtdɒg] N Culin hot-dog m

hot-dog VI Ski faire du ski acrobatique

hot-dogging ['hɒtdɒgɪŋ] N Ski ski m acrobatique

hotel [həʊ'tel] N hôtel m; **at** or **in my h.** à mon hôtel; **to stay at a h.** descendre dans un hôtel; **private** or **residential h.** = pension f de famille; **h. and catering industry** industrie f de l'hôtellerie et de la restauration
▸▸ **h. accommodation** hébergement m en hôtel; **h. administration** gestion f hôtelière; **h. bed** lit m d'hôtel; **h. bedroom** chambre f d'hôtel; **the h. business** l'hôtellerie f, **h. chain** chaîne f d'hôtels; **h. clerk** employé m d'hôtel; **h. group** groupe m hôtelier; **the h. industry** l'industrie f hôtelière, l'hôtellerie f, **h. keeper** hôtelier, -ière; **h. keeping** hôtellerie f, **h. lobby** hall m d'hôtel, hall d'entrée d'un hôtel; **h. management** (training) gestion f hôtelière; (people) direction f (de l'hôtel); **h. manager** gérant, -ante d'hôtel, directeur, -trice d'hôtel; **h. occupancy** taux m d'occupation des hôtels; **h. reception** réception f d'hôtel; **h. receptionist** réceptionniste mf d'hôtel; **h. register** agenda m ou livre m de réservation; **h. school** école f hôtelière; **h. tax** taxe f sur l'hôtellerie; **h. taxi** taxi m d'hôtel; **the h. trade** l'industrie hôtelière, l'hôtellerie; **h. transfer** transfert m (de la gare/l'aéroport à l'hôtel)

hotelier [həʊ'telɪeɪ] N hôtelier, -ière

hotfoot ['hɒtfʊt] ADV (to set off, arrive) à toute vitesse, en (toute) hâte
VT Fam **to h. it** galoper, aller à toute allure

hothead ['hɒthed] N exalté, -ée

hot-headed ADJ *(rash)* exalté, impétueux; *(quick-tempered)* emporté, violent

hothouse ['hɒthaʊs] N serre *f* chaude; *Fig (of new talent etc)* pépinière *f*
▸▸*Fig* **h. plant** plante *f* de serre (chaude); *Fig (person)* plante de serre

hotlist ['hɒtlɪst] N *Comput* liste *f* de signets

hotly ['hɒtlɪ] ADV **1** *(to reply, protest)* vivement; **h. contested** âprement disputé **2** *(to pursue)* avec acharnement

hotplate ['hɒtpleɪt] N *(for cooking)* plaque *f* chauffante; *(on table)* chauffe-plat *m*, *pl* chauffe-plats

hotpot ['hɒtpɒt] N *esp Br Culin* = ragoût *m* de viande aux pommes de terre cuit à l'étuvée

hotrod ['hɒtrɒd] N *Aut Fam* bolide *m*, voiture *f* gonflée

hots [hɒts] NPL *Sl* **to have the h. for sb** *(of woman)* mouiller pour qn; *(of man)* bander pour qn

hot-shoe N *Phot* sabot-contact *m*

hotshot ['hɒtʃɒt] *Fam* ADJ magnifique, terrible; **a h. chess player** un joueur d'échecs super-doué; **they've hired some h. lawyer** ils ont pris un as du barreau
N *(expert)* as *m*, crack *m*; *Br (VIP)* gros bonnet *m*; *Am Pej (self-important person)* = personne *f* qui a la grosse tête

hot-tempered ADJ colérique, coléreux

Hottentot ['hɒt(ə)ntɒt] ADJ hottentot
N Hottentot, -ote

hottie ['hɒtɪ] N *Am Fam (attractive woman)* canon *m*; *(attractive man)* beau mec *m*

hot-water bottle N bouillotte *f*

hound [haʊnd] N **1** *(in hunting)* chien *m* de meute; *Fam (dog)* chien; **the hounds** *(pack)* la meute *f*; **as if all the hounds of hell were after him** comme s'il avait tous les diables de l'enfer à ses trousses; **to ride to hounds** chasser à courre **2** *Sport (in paper chase)* coureur *m*, poursuivant *m* **3** *Old-fashioned Fam (contemptible person)* canaille *f*
VT *Fig* **she was hounded by the press** elle était traquée *ou* poursuivie par la presse; **hounded from place to place** pourchassé d'un endroit à un autre; **he was hounded out of France** il fut chassé de France
▸ **hound down** VT SEP *(person)* traquer jusqu'à la capture; **wherever you are we'll h. you down** où que vous soyez, on vous aura; **he's been hounded down** il s'est fait prendre

hour ['aʊər] N **1** *(period)* heure *f*; **an h. and a half** une heure et demie; **half an h.**, *esp Am* **a half h.** une demi-heure; **a quarter of an h.** un quart d'heure; **h. by h.** d'heure en heure; **to pay sb by the h.** payer qn à l'heure; **to be paid £5 an h.** être payé 5 livres de l'heure; *Ind etc* **output per h.** rendement *m* à l'heure; **there's a train every h. on the h.** il y a un train toutes les heures (à l'heure juste); **to take hours over sth** mettre des heures à faire qch; *Fam* **we've been waiting (for) hours** ça fait des heures que nous attendons VOIR GRAMMAIRE A80-1; B60
2 *(in timetables)* **office hours** heures *fpl* de bureau; **what are your hours?**, **what hours do you work?** quels sont vos horaires de travail?; **to keep late hours** rentrer à des heures indues; *(go to bed late)* se coucher très tard; **they keep odd** *or* **unusual hours** ils ont des horaires bizarres; **to work long hours** faire de longues journées (de travail); **after hours** *(of office)* après les heures de travail; *Br (of pub)* après l'heure de la fermeture
3 *(time of day)* **at this h.?!** à cette heure-ci?!; **in the small** *or* **early hours** en pleine nuit; **well on into the small hours** très avant dans la nuit; **people come and go at all hours** les gens vont et viennent à toute heure; **till all hours** jusqu'à des heures impossibles
4 *(moment)* heure *f*, moment *m*; **in the h. of**

need/death à l'heure du besoin/de la mort; **his h. has come** son heure est venue; **I thought my final h. had come** j'ai cru ma dernière heure arrivée; **her last hours** ses dernières heures; **he was the man of the h.** c'était l'homme du moment
▸▸**h. hand** petite aiguille *f*

-hour ['aʊər] SUFF **one/two**/*etc*-**h.** d'une/de deux/*etc* heure(s); **an eight-h. day** une journée de travail de huit heures; **a 30-h. week** une semaine de trente heures; **a three-h. delay** un retard de trois heures; **to put a twenty-four-h. watch/guard on sb/sth** surveiller qn/qch vingt-quatre heures sur vingt-quatre

hourglass ['aʊəɡlɑːs] N sablier *m*
▸▸**h. figure** taille *f* de guêpe

hourlong ['aʊəlɒŋ] ADJ *(meeting)* d'une heure

hourly ['aʊəlɪ] ADJ de toutes les heures; *(train service etc)* à chaque heure; *(output, yield, wage)* horaire, à l'heure; **at h. intervals** toutes les heures; **there is an h. train from platform 8** il y a un train toutes les heures sur le quai numéro 8
ADV toutes les heures
▸▸**h. rate** taux *m* horaire

-hourly ['aʊəlɪ] SUFF **two/three**/*etc*-**h.** toutes les deux/trois/*etc* heures

house[1], *pl* **houses** [haʊs, 'haʊzɪz] N **1** maison *f*, **at his h.** chez lui; **we invited him to our h.** nous l'avons invité chez nous; **from h. to h.** de porte en porte; **to keep h. for sb** tenir *ou* diriger la maison de qn; **they keep open h.** on est toujours les bienvenus chez eux; **to set up h.** s'installer; *(of young unmarried couple)* se mettre en ménage; *Fig* **the government should put** *or* **set its own h. in order before criticizing others** le gouvernement devrait balayer devant sa porte avant de critiquer les autres; *Fam* **they got on like a h. on fire** ils se sont immédiatement entendus à merveille; *Fam* **he's progressing like a h. on fire** il a fait des progrès du feu de Dieu; *Fam* **it's coming on like a h. on fire** ça marche du feu de Dieu; *Br Fam* **the bus goes all round the houses** le bus fait tout le tour de la ville; *Fig Fam* **to go all round the houses** *(avoid being direct in talking)* tourner autour du pot; **the son/daughter of the h.** le fils/la fille de la maison; **to move h.** déménager
2 *(institution)* **the h. of God** *(church)* la maison de Dieu; **h. of prayer** *or* **worship** église *f*, *(Protestant)* temple *m*; *Br* **the H.** *(parliament)* le Parlement; *(the Stock Exchange)* la Bourse (de Londres)
3 *Com etc (company)* maison *f*, **banking h.** établissement *m* bancaire; **publishing h.** maison d'édition; **in h.** dans les locaux de la compagnie; *see* **in-house**
4 *(restaurant etc)* **to have a drink on the h.** prendre une consommation aux frais du patron *ou* de la maison
5 *Br Sch* = groupe *m* d'élèves qui rivalise avec un autre pour les activités sportives *etc*
6 *Astrol* maison *f*
7 *(of crane)* cabine *f*, *Naut (on deck)* rouf *m*; *(at helm)* kiosque *m*
8 *(household)* maison *f*, *(dynasty)* famille *f*, maison; **the H. of Stuart/Bourbon** les Stuarts *mpl*/les Bourbons *mpl*; **the whole h. was down with flu** toute la maisonnée avait la grippe
9 *Theat* salle *f*, auditoire *m*, assistance *f*, **is there a doctor in the h.?** y a-t-il un médecin dans la salle?; **a full h.** une salle pleine; **h. full** complet; **to play to an empty h.** jouer devant des banquettes vides, jouer devant une salle vide; **to play to packed houses** jouer devant une salle comble, faire salle comble; **there wasn't a dry eye in the h.** tout le monde pleurait dans la salle; *Cin Old-*

fashioned **the first h.** la première séance
▸▸*Br* **h. agent** agent *m* immobilier; *Am Fam* **h. ape** *(child)* môme *mf*, chiard *m*; **h. arrest** assignation *f* à domicile *ou* à résidence; *Fin* **h. bill** double *m* de connaissance, lettre *f* de change creuse; *also Fig* **h. of cards** château *m* de cartes; **the H. of Commons** la Chambre des communes; **h. detective** responsable *m* de la sécurité, détective *m* de l'hôtel; *Naut* **h. flag** pavillon *m* d'armateur *ou* de compagnie (de navigation); **h. guest** invité, -ée; *Theat* **h. lights** lumières *fpl* *ou* éclairage *m* de la salle; **the H. of Lords** la Chambre des lords; **h. magazine** journal *m* interne, bulletin *m*; *Theat* **h. manager** directeur, -trice de théâtre; *Orn* **h. martin** hirondelle *f* de fenêtre; **h. painter** peintre *m* en bâtiment; *Br Parl* **Houses of Parliament** Parlement *m*; **h. party** *(social occasion)* fête *f* de plusieurs jours *(dans une maison de campagne)*; *(guests)* invités *mpl* *(dans une maison de campagne)*; **h. phone** *(in hotel)* téléphone *m* intérieur; **h. physician** médecin *m* de garde; **h. plant** *Bot* plante *f* d'intérieur, plante d'appartement; *Parl* **the H. of Representatives** la Chambre des représentants *(aux États-Unis)*; **h. rule** règle *f* de la maison; *(in games)* règle *f* du jeu particulière; **h. special**, **h. specialty** *(in restaurant)* spécialité *f* (de la) maison; *Br Typ, Journ* **h. style** style *m* maison; *Med* **h. surgeon** chirurgien *m* de garde; *Br* **h. wine** vin *m* de la maison

House of Commons

La Chambre des communes britannique est composée de 659 députés ("MPs") élus pour cinq ans et qui siègent environ 175 jours par an. Les députés du parti majoritaire s'assoient d'un côté de la Chambre (les "government benches"), tandis que les députés de l'opposition s'assoient de l'autre côté (sur les "opposition benches"). Si un projet de loi n'obtient pas l'approbation de la majorité des députés dans la Chambre des communes, il est renvoyé à la Chambre des lords, et doit par ailleurs obtenir l'assentiment du souverain avant de devenir loi.

House of Lords

La Chambre des lords est composée de pairs et d'hommes d'Église. Il s'agit de la plus haute cour au Royaume-Uni (en excluant l'Écosse). Elle a le pouvoir d'amender certains projets de loi qui ont été votés par la Chambre des communes. Le gouvernement travailliste de Tony Blair, élu en 1997, a entrepris des réformes visant à réduire les pouvoirs de la Chambre des lords.

House of Representatives

La Chambre des représentants constitue, avec le Sénat, l'organe législatif américain; ses membres sont élus par le peuple, en proportion de la population de chaque État.

house[2] [haʊz] VT **1** *(person)* loger, héberger; *(population)* pourvoir au logement de; **a building that can h. ten families** un bâtiment qui peut loger dix familles **2** *(of museum etc) (collection)* contenir; *(locomotive)* mettre à l'abri *ou* à couvert; **the gears are housed in a steel case** l'engrenage est contenu dans un carter d'acier; **this section houses the main engines** dans cette section se trouvent les moteurs principaux

houseboat ['haʊsbəʊt] N house-boat *m*, *pl* house-boats, péniche *f* (aménagée)

housebound ['haʊsbaʊnd] **ADJ** obligé de rester à la maison; (invalid) immobilisé à la maison

housebreaker ['haʊsbreɪkər] **N** (burglar) cambrioleur m

housebreaking ['haʊsbreɪkɪŋ] **N** (burglary) cambriolage m, vol m avec effraction

housecoat ['haʊskəʊt] **N** (woman's) robe f d'intérieur

housefly ['haʊsflaɪ] **N** mouche f domestique ou commune

houseful ['haʊsfʊl] **N to have a h. of guests** avoir sa maison pleine d'invités

household ['haʊshəʊld] **N 1** (people in house) (membres mpl de la) maison f; (economically, statistically) ménage m; **there are five people in this h.** (in house) cinq personnes habitent dans cette maison; (in family) cette famille compte cinq personnes; **h. chores** or **duties** or **tasks** tâches fpl ménagères, travaux mpl ménagers; **not for h. use** (on industrial cleaner etc) usage industriel uniquement; **she's a h. name** son nom est connu de tous; **to be a h. name** être connu de tous **2** (servants) domestiques mfpl **3** Br **the H.** la Maison du souverain; **the H. troops** la Garde

▸▸**h. appliances** électro-ménager m; **h. articles** articles mpl pour le ménage; **h. budget** budget m du ménage; **h. consumption** consommation f des ménages; **h. expenses** frais mpl de ou du ménage; **h. goods** articles mpl pour le ménage, produits mpl ménagers; **h. unit** foyer m

householder ['haʊshəʊldər] **N** (owner) propriétaire mf d'une/de la maison; (tenant) locataire mf

househusband ['haʊshʌzbənd] **N** homme m au foyer

housekeeper ['haʊskiːpər] **N** femme f de charge; (of priest etc) gouvernante f; (at castle etc) économe f, intendante f; (in hotel) gouvernante f; **to be a good h.** (at home) être une bonne maîtresse de maison

housekeeping ['haʊskiːpɪŋ] **N** (art) économie f domestique; (work) soins mpl du ménage; Comput (file management) aménagement m; **h. (allowance** or **money)** argent m du ou pour le ménage; **she knows nothing about h.** ce n'est pas une femme d'intérieur

▸▸**h. book** carnet m de dépenses

housemaid ['haʊsmeɪd] **N** Old-fashioned bonne f, femme f de chambre

▸▸Med Fam **h.'s knee** hygroma m du genou

houseman, pl **housemen** ['haʊsmən] **N** Br Med (at hospital) interne m; (in hotel) homme m de ménage

housemaster, **housemistress** ['haʊsmɑːstər, -mɪstrɪs] **N** Br Sch (in boarding school) = professeur m chargé de la surveillance d'un internat; (in day school) = professeur chargé d'un groupe d'élèves

house-proud **ADJ she is very h.** c'est une femme d'intérieur méticuleuse, Pej c'est une véritable maniaque du ménage

houseroom ['haʊsruːm] **N** place f (pour loger qn, qch); Fam **I wouldn't give it h.** je n'en voudrais pas même si on m'en faisait cadeau

house-sit **VI to h. for sb** s'occuper de la maison de qn pendant son absence

house-sitter **N** = personne f qui garde une maison en l'absence de ses occupants

house-style book **N** guide m du style maison; (for design) charte f graphique; (editorial) charte rédactionnelle

house-to-house **ADJ** (enquiry, selling etc) à domicile; **the police made a h. search** la police a fait une fouille maison par maison, la police a perquisitionné maison après maison

▸▸Mktg **h. canvassing** porte-à-porte m inv, démarchage m

housetop ['haʊstɒp] **N** toit m; Fig **to shout** or **proclaim sth from the housetops** crier qch sur tous les toits

house-train **VT** Br (dog etc) dresser à la propreté; **house-trained** (dog etc) propre; Fam Hum **she got him (properly) house-trained** (taught clean habits) elle lui a appris la propreté; (taught basic housekeeping) elle lui a appris à se débrouiller à la maison

house-warming **N to give** or **have a h.** pendre la crémaillère

▸▸**h. party** pendaison f de crémaillère, soirée f pour pendre la crémaillère

housewife, pl **housewives** **N 1** ['haʊswaɪf, -waɪvz] femme f au foyer **2** ['hʌzɪf, -vz] Br Old-fashioned (sewing kit) trousse f de couture

housewifely ['haʊswaɪflɪ] **ADJ** de femme au foyer

housewifery ['haʊswɪf(ə)rɪ] **N** Old-fashioned économie f domestique; (work) soins mpl du ménage

housework ['haʊswɜːk] **N** travaux mpl domestiques ou de ménage; **to do the h.** faire le ménage

Attention: ne pas confondre avec **homework**, qui signifie **devoirs à faire à la maison**.

housey-housey ['haʊsɪ'haʊsɪ] **N** Br (jeu m de) loto m

housing ['haʊzɪŋ] **N 1** (of people) logement m; **the h. problem** or **shortage** la crise du logement **2** (for machine, mechanism etc) boîtier m; (bigger) coffre m; (of gears, differential) carter m

▸▸**h. association** = association f britannique à but non lucratif qui construit ou rénove des logements pour les louer à ses membres; Br **h. benefit** Admin = allocation f de logement versée par l'État aux individus justifiant de revenus faibles; Br **h. estate** grand ensemble m, Pej cité f; **h. market** marché m de l'immobilier; Br **h. project** grand ensemble m, Pej cité f; (plan) plan m d'aménagement immobilier; Am **h. starts** = mise f en chantier de logements; **h. stock** parc m immobilier

hove **PT**, **PP** see **heave**

hovel ['hɒv(ə)l] **N** Pej taudis m, masure f

hover ['hɒvər] **VI 1** (of bird, insect) planer, se balancer; (of helicopter) effectuer un vol stationnaire; **the helicopter hovered just above us** l'hélicoptère s'immobilisa au-dessus de nos têtes

2 Fig (of person) tourner en rond; (waiting to pounce, do sth) guetter; **danger is hovering over him** le danger le menace; **a waitress was hovering near our table** une serveuse tournait autour de notre table; **I don't like him hovering over me** je n'aime pas qu'il soit sur mon dos; **don't just h. in the background** ne reste pas dans ton coin; **to h. between two courses of action** hésiter entre deux possibilités; **a smile hovered on his lips** l'ombre d'un sourire passa sur ses lèvres; **she hovered between life and death** elle oscilla ou resta entre la vie et la mort; **he seemed to be hovering on the brink of saying something** il semblait hésiter à dire quelque chose

▸**hover around** **VT INSEP** (move about, near) **to h. around sb** errer ou rôder autour de qn; **prices are hovering around the £3.50 mark** les prix oscillent autour de 3 livres 50 **VI** (move about nearby) tourner

hovercraft ['hɒvəkrɑːft] **N INV** aéroglisseur m, Fam hovercraft m

hoverport ['hɒvəpɔːt] **N** hoverport m, gare f des aéroglisseurs

hovertrain ['hɒvətreɪn] **N** aérotrain m

HOW [haʊ]

ADV comment **1, 3** ▪ comme **4** ▪ que **4, 5** **N** comment

ADV 1 (in what manner) comment; **h. do you spell this word?** comment écrit-on ce mot?; Fam **h. the devil …?, h. on earth …?, h. in the world …?** comment diable …?; **h. did they find out?** comment est-ce qu'ils l'ont su ou appris?; **tell me h. he did it** dites-moi comment il (l')a fait; **h. was she dressed?** comment est-ce qu'elle était habillée?, qu'est-ce qu'elle portait?; **h. is it that …?** comment se fait-il que …?; **h. so?** comment ça?; Fam **h. come?** comment cela se fait-il?, et comment ça se fait?; **h. come she didn't tell you?** comment ça se fait qu'elle ne te l'ait pas dit?; **h.'s that?** (how can that be?) comment ça?; (repeat that?) pardon?; Cr = appel m à l'arbitre, pour savoir si le guichet est sauf ou si la balle a été bien attrapée; **suppose I offer you another £500, h.'s that?** et si je t'offre 500 livres en plus, qu'est-ce que tu en dis?; **h.'s that for a sandwich?** qu'est-ce que tu dis de ce sandwich?; **h.'s that for size?** (of jacket etc) ça va comme taille?; Fam **and h.!** et comment!; **h. could you?** (shame on you) vous n'avez pas honte?; **I don't know h. he can say that!** je ne sais pas comment il peut dire une chose pareille!; **to learn h. to do sth** apprendre à faire qch; **h. do you like this wine?** comment trouvez-vous ce vin?; **h. do you like your steak?** comment voulez-vous votre steak?; **here's h.!** (toast) santé! VOIR GRAMMAIRE A74–5

2 (to what extent) **h. much/many** combien (de); **h. many times?, h. often?** combien de fois?; **h. many are there of you?** vous êtes combien (de personnes)?; **h. long have you been here?** depuis combien de temps êtesvous là?; **h. long is the flight?** quelle est la durée du vol?; **you know h. useful he is to me** vous savez à quel point il m'est utile; **you don't know h. right you are** vous ne savez pas combien vous dites vrai, vous ne savez pas à quel point vous avez raison; **h. early would you like to be woken?** à quelle heure voulez-vous qu'on vous réveille?; **h. wide is this room?** quelle est la largeur de cette pièce?; **h. old are you?** quel âge avezvous?; **h. likely is that to happen?** quelle est la probabilité d'un tel événement?; **h. keen are you on fish?** aimez-vous le poisson?;

3 (greetings, enquiries after health etc) **h. are you?** comment allez-vous?, Fam comment ça va?; **h. do you do?** (when being introduced) enchanté (de faire votre connaissance); (hello) bonjour; Fam **h. are things?** comment ça va?; Fam **h. are you doing?** comment vas-tu?; Fam **h.'s it going?** comment ça se passe?; **h.'s your leg?** et (comment va) ta jambe?; **h.'s business?** comment vont les affaires?; Fam **h.'s life?** comment vas-tu?

4 (in exclamations) comme, que; **h. pretty she is!** comme elle est jolie!; **h. disgusting!** quelle horreur!; **h. kind (of you)!** comme ou que c'est gentil (de votre part); **h. she has changed!** comme elle a changé!; **h. I wish I could!** si seulement je pouvais!; **h. surprised he was when …!** quelle ne fut pas sa surprise lorsque …!

5 Fam (introducing indirect statement) que; **I told him h. there had been a great storm** je lui ai dit qu'il y avait eu un gros orage

6 h. about …? (making suggestion) et si …?; **h. about a game of cards/going out for a meal?** et si on faisait une partie de cartes/allait au restaurant?; **h. about you?** et vous?

N the hows, whys and wherefores les comment et les pourquoi, tous les détails

howdy ['haʊdɪ] **INT** *Am Fam* salut!

how-d'ye-do [haʊdjə'du:] **N** *Old-fashioned Fam* here's a (fine) **h.!** en voilà une histoire!, quelle histoire!

however [haʊ'evər] **ADV 1** *(on the other hand)* toutefois, cependant, pourtant; **if, h., you don't agree** si toutefois cela ne vous convient pas; **there are more important matters, h.** il y a des problèmes plus importants, pourtant

2 *(in whatever degree)* quelque … que … + *sub,* si … que … + *sub,* **h. poor** si pauvre qu'il soit/qu'elle soit/*etc,* **h. good his work is** si excellent que soit son travail; **h. hard she tried, she couldn't do it** elle a eu beau faire (tout ce qu'elle a pu), elle n'y est pas parvenue; **h. much I try/you cry** même si j'essaie/tu pleures; **h. much it rains** même s'il pleut des cordes VOIR GRAMMAIRE A75

3 *(in whatever way)* de quelque manière que … *sub,* **h. that may be** quoi qu'il en soit; **h. did she find out?** comment est-ce qu'elle l'a su? VOIR GRAMMAIRE A75

howitzer ['haʊɪtsər] **N** *Mil* obusier *m*

howl [haʊl] **N** *(of person, wolf etc)* hurlement *m*; *(of baby)* braillement *m*; *(of wind)* mugissement *m*; *Electron* hurlement d'amplificateur; **to give a h. of pain/rage** hurler de douleur/rage; **there were howls of laughter** on riait à gorge déployée

VI *(of animals, people)* hurler; *(of wind)* mugir, rugir; *Electron (of loudspeaker)* hurler; **to h. with laughter** rire à gorge déployée; **to h. with pain/rage** hurler de douleur/rage

VT *(shout)* hurler

▸ **howl down** **VT SEP** *(person)* faire taire en poussant des huées; *Fig (suggestion)* rejeter; **the speaker was howled down** sous les huées, l'orateur fut contraint de se taire

howler ['haʊlər] **N** *Fam (mistake)* grosse gaffe *f,* bourde *f* énorme; **schoolboy h.** perle *f (d'écolier)*

▸▸ *Zool* **h. monkey** (singe *m*) hurleur *m,* alouate *m*

howling ['haʊlɪŋ] **ADJ ATTRIB 1** *(baby, wolf)* qui hurle; *(crowd)* hurlant; *(gale, wind)* furieux; **I'm not going out in this h. gale** je ne sortirai pas sous un vent pareil **2** *Fam (very great)* énorme; *(success)* **h.** folle

N hurlement *m*; *(of baby)* braillement *m*; *(of wind, gale)* mugissement *m*

hoyden ['hɔɪd(ə)n] **N** *Pol Old-fashioned Pej* garçon *m* manqué

hoydenish ['hɔɪd(e)nɪʃ] **ADJ** *Pol Old-fashioned Pej* garçonnier, -ière

HP, hp [eɪtʃ'pi:] **N 1** *Tech (abbr* **horsepower)** CV *m* **2** *Br Com abbr* **hire-purchase**

HQ, hq [eɪtʃ'kju:] **N** *Mil (abbr* **headquarters)** QG *m*

HR [eɪtʃ'ɑ:r] **N** *(abbr* **human resources)** ressources *fpl* humaines, RH *fpl*; **HR department** direction *f* des ressources humaines, DRH *f*

hr *(abbr* **hour)** h.

HRH [eɪtʃɑ:'reɪtʃ] *Br (abbr* **His/Her Royal Highness)** SAR

HRM [eɪtʃɑ:r'em] **N** *(abbr* **human resource management)** GRH *f*

HRT [eɪtʃɑ:'ti:] **N** *Med (abbr* **hormone replacement therapy)** HTS *f*

HT N *(abbr* **high tension)** HT *f*; **HT cable** fil *m* HT

ht *abbr* **height**

HTML [eɪtʃti:em'el] **N** *Comput (abbr* **Hyper Text Markup Language)** HTML *m*

▸▸ **H. editor** éditeur *m* HTML

HTTP [eɪtʃti:ti:'pi:] **N** *Comput (abbr* **HyperText Transfer Protocol)** protocole *m* HTTP

▸▸ **H. server** serveur *m* Web

hub [hʌb] **N 1** *(of wheel, propeller)* moyeu *m*

2 *Fig* centre *m* d'activité; **the h. of the universe** le centre de l'univers; **h. and spoke system** système *m* d'aéroports central et d'apport extérieur

▸▸ **h. airport** aéroport *m* important *(qui sert de plaque tournante)*

hubbub ['hʌbʌb] **N** remue-ménage *m,* vacarme *m*; **h. of voices** brouhaha *m* de voix

hubby ['hʌbɪ] **N** *Br Fam* (petit) mari *m*

hubcap ['hʌbkæp] **N** *Aut* enjoliveur *m*

hubris ['hju:brɪs] **N** *Lit* orgueil *m* démesuré

huckleberry ['hʌk(ə)lberɪ] **N** *Am (fruit)* airelle *f,* myrtille *f*

huckster ['hʌkstər] **N 1** *Old-fashioned (hawker)* colporteur *m* **2** *(profiteer)* mercanti *m,* profiteur *m*; **political h.** politicien *m* magouilleur

HUD [eɪtʃju:'di:] *abbr* **1** *Mil, Aviat* **head-up display 2** *Am Admin Formerly (abbr* **(Department of) Housing and Urban Development)** ministère *m* de la Ville

huddle ['hʌd(ə)l] **N** *(of things)* tas *m* confus; *(of people)* (petit) groupe *m*; *Fig* **to go into a h.** se réunir en petit comité

VI 1 se blottir; **to h. in a corner/round the fire** se blottir dans un coin/autour du feu **2** *Am Fam (meet and confer)* se réunir en petit comité

VT = huddle up VT SEP

▸ **huddle together** **VI** *(of people, animals)* s'entasser, se serrer les uns contre les autres

VT SEP **houses huddled together** maisons blotties les unes contre les autres

▸ **huddle up** **VI** *(of person)* se pelotonner

VT SEP *(usu pass)* **huddled up in bed** couché en chien de fusil; **huddled up in a corner** blotti dans un coin

Hudson Bay [hʌdsən'beɪ] **N** la baie d'Hudson

hue¹ [hju:] **N** *(colour)* teinte *f,* nuance *f*

hue² **N h. and cry** clameur *f* de haro; **a h. and cry was raised against this reform** cette réforme provoqua un tollé général

huff [hʌf] **N** *Fam* **to be in a h.** être froissé *ou* fâché; **to get into a h.** prendre la mouche, s'offusquer; **he went off in a h.** il prit la mouche et s'en alla

VI he huffed and puffed il soufflait et haletait; *(showed annoyance)* il ronchonnait

VT *Am Sl (glue, solvents)* sniffer

huffily ['hʌfɪlɪ] **ADV** *Fam* d'un air pincé

huffy ['hʌfɪ] **ADJ** *Fam (annoyed)* fâché, vexé

hug [hʌg] **N 1** *(sign of affection)* étreinte *f*; **to give sb a h.** serrer qn dans ses bras, étreindre qn; **give me a h.** prends-moi dans tes bras **2** *(in wrestling)* prise *f,* *(of bear)* étreinte *f*

VT (-gg-) **1** *(person)* étreindre, embrasser, serrer; **she hugged the child to her** elle a serré l'enfant sur son cœur; **clothes that h. the figure** vêtements qui moulent la silhouette; *Fig* **to h. sb to death** embrasser qn jusqu'à l'étouffer; *Fig* **to h. oneself for doing sth** se féliciter d'avoir fait qch **2** *(of bear)* étouffer, enserrer **3** *(keep close to) (wall)* longer, serrer; **to h. the ground** raser le sol; *Naut* **to h. the coast** suivre la côte de près; *Aut* **to h. the kerb** serrer le trottoir

huge [hju:dʒ] **ADJ** immense, énorme; *(success)* immense, formidable; *(man)* colossal, -aux; *(difference)* énorme, capital, -aux; **h. undertaking** vaste entreprise

hugely ['hju:dʒlɪ] **ADV** énormément; *(amusing)* extrêmement

hugeness ['hju:dʒnɪs] **N** énormité *f,* immensité *f*

huggable ['hʌgəbl] **ADJ** trognon

hugger-mugger ['hʌgəmʌgər] **ADJ** *Old-fashioned (confused) (collection)* sans ordre; *(arrangement)* confus

-hugging ['hʌgɪŋ] **SUFF** **hip/figure/etc-h.** *(of clothes)* qui moule les hanches/la silhouette/*etc*

Huguenot ['hju:gənəʊ] **N** *Rel, Hist* Huguenot, -ote

hulk [hʌlk] **N 1** *Naut* carcasse *f* de navire; *Hist (prison ship)* ponton *m* **2** *Fig (person)* mastodonte *m*

hulking ['hʌlkɪŋ] **ADJ ATTRIB** gros, lourd; **h. great man** mastodonte *m,* colosse *m*

hull [hʌl] **N 1** *(of ship, flying boat, tank)* coque *f, (in marine insurance)* corps *m* **2** *(of pea, bean)* cosse *f,* gousse *f* **3** *(of strawberry, raspberry)* calice *m*

VT 1 *(peas)* écosser; *(oats)* baller; *(rice, barley)* décortiquer **2** *Naut (ship)* percer la coque de

▸▸ **h. insurance** assurance *f* sur corps

hullabaloo [hʌləbə'lu:] **N** tintamarre *m,* vacarme *m*

hullo [hʌ'ləʊ] **INT = hello**

hum¹ [hʌm] **N 1** *(of bee)* bourdonnement *m*; *(of machine)* ronflement *m*; *(of plane, top)* vrombissement *m*; *(of voices)* bruit *m* sourd, murmure *m*; *(of conversation)* rumeur *f*; *Radio etc* bourdonnement, ronflement **2** *Br Sl (bad smell)* puanteur *f*

VI (-mm-) **1** *(of person)* fredonner, chantonner; *(of insect etc)* bourdonner; *(of top)* ronfler, vrombir; *(of aircraft)* vrombir; *Radio (of set)* ronronner, ronfler; **town humming with activity** ville bourdonnante d'activité; *Fig* **to make things h.** faire marcher rondement les choses **2** *(say 'hum')* dire hum; **to h. and haw** *(mumble)* bredouiller, bafouiller; *(hesitate)* hésiter *(à prendre un parti)* **3** *Br Sl (smell bad)* chlinguer, puer

VT *(tune)* fredonner, chantonner

hum² **INT** hmm!, hum!

human ['hju:m(ə)n] **ADJ** *(body, race etc)* humain; **he's only h.** il est humain après tout; **it's only h.** c'est humain; **not fit for h. consumption** impropre à la consommation, non comestible; **not fit for h. habitation** inhabitable

N être *m* humain; **humans** les humains *mpl,* les êtres humains

▸▸ **h. being** être *m* humain; *Econ* **h. capital** capital *m* humain; **h. cloning** clonage *m* humain; **h. error** erreur *f* humaine; *Br* **H. Fertilization and Embryology Authority** = organisme *m* chargé de réglementer les traitements de la stérilité et la recherche en embryologie; **the H. Genome Project** le Projet génome humain; *Med* **h. growth hormone** hormone *f* somatotrope *ou* de croissance, somatotrophine *f,* *esp Journ* **h. interest story** histoire *f,* **h. nature** nature *f* humaine; *Admin* **h. resources** ressources *fpl* humaines; **h. resource(s) management** gestion *f* des ressources humaines; **h. resource(s) manager** gestionnaire *m* des ressources humaines; **h. rights** droits *mpl* de l'homme; **h. shield** bouclier *m* humain

> Attention: ne pas confondre avec **humane**.

humane [hju:'meɪn] **ADJ 1** *(kind)* humain **2** *(killing)* qui évite de faire souffrir, humain

▸▸ **h. society** *(for animals)* société *f* protectrice des animaux; *(for good works)* société *f* *ou* association *f* humanitaire

> Attention: ne pas confondre avec **human**.

humanely [hju:'meɪnlɪ] **ADV** humainement, avec humanité

humanism ['hju:mənɪz(ə)m] **N** *Phil* humanisme *m*

humanist ['hju:mənɪst] **N** *Phil* humaniste *m*

humanistic [hjuːmə'nɪstɪk] ADJ *Phil* humaniste

humanitarian [hjuːmænɪ'teərɪən] ADJ, N humanitaire *mf*

humanity [hjuː'mænɪtɪ] N **1** humanité *f*, *Fam* **the club was packed with sweaty h.** le club était plein d'une foule transpirante **2** *Univ* **the humanities** les humanités *fpl*, les lettres *fpl*, les sciences *fpl* humaines

humanize ['hjuːmənaɪz] VT humaniser

humankind [hjuːm(ə)n'kaɪnd] N humanité *f*

humanly ['hjuːm(ə)nlɪ] ADV humainement; **to do everything h. possible** faire tout ce qui est humainement possible

humanoid ['hjuːmənɔɪd] ADJ, N humanoïde *mf*

humble ['hʌmb(ə)l] ADJ **1** *(meek)* humble; **to offer a h. apology** faire de plates excuses; **in my h. opinion** à mon humble avis; **h. prayer** humble prière *f*, *Old-fashioned* **Your h. servant** *(ending letter)* je reste votre humble serviteur **2** *(unpretentious) (cottage, background)* modeste; **to be of h. origin** être d'origine modeste; *Fig* **to eat h. pie** admettre son erreur; **to be forced to eat h. pie** être forcé de se rétracter

▪ VT *(person)* humilier, mortifier; *(sb's pride)* rabattre; **to h. oneself** s'humilier

humblebee ['hʌmb(ə)lbiː] N *(insect)* bourdon *m*

humbleness ['hʌmb(ə)lnɪs] N humilité *f*

humbling ['hʌmb(ə)lɪŋ] ADJ *(experience)* humiliant

▪ N *(of person)* humiliation *f*

humbly ['hʌmb(ə)lɪ] ADV **1** *(meekly)* humblement, avec humilité; **if I may h. suggest ...** si je peux me permettre de suggérer ... **2** *(to live etc)* modestement

humbug ['hʌmbʌg] N **1** *Fam (nonsense)* bêtises *fpl*, *(deceptive, insincere)* foutaises *fpl*, **h.!** c'est du pipeau! **2** *Fam (person) (hypocrite, impostor)* charlatan *m* **3** *Br (sweet)* berlingot *m*, ≃ bêtise *f* de Cambrai

humdinger ['hʌm'dɪŋər] N *Fam* quelque chose d'extraordinaire *ou* de fantastique; **a h. of a speech** un discours formidable *ou* sensationnel

humdrum ['hʌmdrʌm] ADJ monotone, banal, -als; *(existence)* monotone; **h. daily life** train-train *m* quotidien

▪ N *(of existence etc)* monotonie *f*

humerus, *pl* **humeri** ['hjuːmərəs, -aɪ, -iː] N *Anat* humérus *m*

humid ['hjuːmɪd] ADJ humide

humidifier [hjuː'mɪdɪfaɪər] N humidificateur *m*

humidify [hjuː'mɪdɪfaɪ] VT *(air)* humidifier

humidity [hjuː'mɪdɪtɪ] N humidité *f*

humidor ['hjuːmɪdɔːr] N boîte *f* à cigares (pourvue d'un humidificateur)

humiliate [hjuː'mɪlɪeɪt] VT humilier

humiliating [hjuː'mɪlɪeɪtɪŋ] ADJ humiliant, mortifiant

humiliation [hjuːmɪlɪ'eɪʃən] N humiliation *f*

humility [hjuː'mɪlɪtɪ] N humilité *f*

humming ['hʌmɪŋ] ADJ bourdonnant; **h. noise** bourdonnement *m*

▪ N **1** = **hum** N **1 2 h. and hawing** hésitation *f*
▸ ▸ **h. top** toupie *f* ronflante

hummingbird ['hʌmɪŋbɜːd] N colibri *m*, oiseau-mouche *m*, *pl* oiseaux-mouches

hummock ['hʌmək] N **1** *(in ground)* tertre *m*, mamelon *m*, monticule *m* **2** *(in ice field)* hummock *m*

humor ['hjuːmər] N, VT *Am* = **humour**

humorist ['hjuːmərɪst] N *(writer)* écrivain *m* humoristique, humoriste *m*; *(comedian)* humoriste, comique *m*; *(joker)* farceur *m*

humorous ['hjuːm(ə)rəs] ADJ comique, drôle; *(writer etc)* humoriste, humoristique; *(drawing, remark etc)* humoristique

humorously ['hjuːm(ə)rəslɪ] ADV avec humour

humour, *Am* **humor** ['hjuːmər] N **1** *(funniness)* humour *m*; **the h. of the situation** le côté comique de la situation **2 (sense of) h.** sens *m* de l'humour; **to have no sense of h.** ne pas avoir le sens de l'humour; **to have a good sense of h.** avoir le sens de l'humour **3** *Fml (mood, temper)* humeur *f*, disposition *f*, **to be in the h. for doing sth** être disposé à faire qch; **good h.** bonne humeur

▪ VT *(indulge)* se prêter *ou* se plier à tous les caprices de; *(be nice to)* ménager; **are you only saying that just to h. me?** est-ce que tu dis ça simplement pour me faire plaisir?

> When translating the English word **humour**, note that the French words **humour** and **humeur** are not interchangeable. **Humour** is used as a translation when referring to somebody's sense of humour or to the humorous quality of something, while **humeur** is used when referring to somebody's mood or temperament.

humourless, *Am* **humorless** ['hjuːməlɪs] ADJ dépourvu d'humour

hump [hʌmp] N **1** *(on flat surface, of hunchback, camel)* bosse *f*, **to have a h.** être bossu; **h. in the road** dos *m* d'âne; *Fig* **we're over the h. now** *(past the worst)* le plus difficile est passé maintenant **2** *Br Fam* **to have the h.** *(be sulking)* faire la tête, bouder; **what's he got the h. about?** pourquoi est-ce qu'il fait la tête?

▪ VT **1** *Fam (carry) (load)* porter sur son dos **2** *Sl (have sexual intercourse with)* sauter, baiser

▪ VI *Sl (have sexual intercourse)* baiser

humpback ['hʌmpbæk] N = **hunchback**
▸ ▸ *Br* **h. bridge** pont *m* en dos d'âne; **h. whale** baleine *f* à bosse

humpbacked ['hʌmpbækt] ADJ bossu
▸ ▸ **h. bridge** pont *m* en dos d'âne

humph [hʌmf, hm] INT hum! hmm!

humus ['hjuːməs] N *(soil)* humus *m*; *(with fertilizer)* terreau *m*

Hun [hʌn] N **1** *Fam (in First World War)* Boche *m* **2** *Hist* **the Huns** *(from Asia)* les Huns *mpl*

hunch [hʌntʃ] N **1** *(intuition)* **to have a h.** avoir un pressentiment **2** *(hump)* bosse *f*

▪ VT **to h. one's back** arrondir le dos; **to h. one's shoulders** voûter les épaules

▪ VI **to h. up** se tenir le dos rond
▸ **hunch up** VT SEP = **hunch**; **to sit hunched up** se tenir le dos rond

hunchback ['hʌntʃbæk] N bossu, -ue; **to have a h.** être bossu; **the H. of Notre-Dame** le bossu de Notre-Dame

hunchbacked ['hʌntʃbækt] ADJ bossu

hundred ['hʌndrəd] ADJ, N VOIR GRAMMAIRE A12–13; B58–9 **1** *(numeral)* cent *m*; **one** *or* **a h.** cent; **a h. and one** cent un; **about a h. houses** une centaine de maisons; **two h. apples** deux cents pommes; **to live to be a h.** vivre jusqu'à cent ans; **they were dying in (their) hundreds** ils mouraient par centaines; **the temperature was in the hundreds** il faisait plus de 40°; **to drive at a h. kilometres an hour** faire du cent à l'heure; **one** *or* **a h. per cent** cent pour cent; **to be a h. per cent certain** être sûr à cent pour cent; **I'm not feeling a h. per cent** je ne me sens pas dans mon assiette; **I'm not feeling a h. per cent yet** je ne suis pas encore complètement remis; **to sell by the h.** *(of new product)* se vendre par centaines; *Sport* **the h. metre race, the h. metres** le cent mètres

2 *Fam (large number)* **not a h. miles away** pas si loin d'ici; **a h. and one details** mille et

un détails; **I've told you hundreds of times** je vous l'ai dit je ne sais combien de fois; **a h. to one it will be a failure** ça fera un four à coup sûr
▸ ▸ *Culin* **hundreds and thousands** vermicelles *mpl (en sucre)*; *Hist* **H. Years' War** guerre *f* de cent ans

hundredfold ['hʌndrədfəʊld] ADJ centuple; **to increase a h.** centupler

hundredth ['hʌndrədθ] ADJ centième; **the two h. anniversary of ...** le bicentenaire de ...; *Theat* **h. performance** centième *f*, *Fam* **for the h. time, no!** pour la centième fois, c'est non!

▪ N **1** *(person, thing)* centième *mf* **2** *(fraction)* centième *m*; **three hundredths** trois centièmes

hundredweight ['hʌndrədweɪt] N **1** *Br* poids *m* de 112 livres, = 50,8 kg, *Can* = quintal *m*; **two h., two hundredweights** = un quintal, *Can* = deux quintaux **2** *Am* poids *m* de 100 livres, = 45,36 kg

hung PT, PP *see* **hang** VT, VI
▪ ADJ *Sl* **to be well h.** *(man)* être bien membré; **h. like a horse** être bien monté
▸ ▸ *Pol, Law* **h. jury** jury *m* sans majorité; **it was a h. jury** le jury ne parvenait pas à se départager; **h. parliament** parlement *m* sans majorité

Hungarian [hʌŋ'geərɪən] ADJ hongrois
▪ N **1** Hongrois, -oise **2** *Ling* hongrois *m*

Hungary ['hʌŋgərɪ] N Hongrie *f*

hunger ['hʌŋgər] N faim *f*, **to have a h. for sth** avoir un ardent désir de qch, avoir soif de qch
▪ VI *esp Lit* avoir faim
▸ ▸ **h. pains, h. pangs** tiraillements *mpl* d'estomac; **h. strike** grève *f* de la faim; **to go on h. strike** faire la grève de la faim; **h. striker** gréviste *mf* de la faim
▸ **hunger after, hunger for** VT INSEP *esp Lit* être affamé de qch, avoir soif de

hungover [hʌŋ'əʊvər] ADJ *Fam* **to be h.** avoir la gueule de bois

hungrily ['hʌŋgrɪlɪ] ADV avidement, voracement; **she eyed the food h.** elle regardait la nourriture d'un air vorace; *Fig* **they stared h. at the women** ils fixaient les femmes avec avidité

hungry ['hʌŋgrɪ] ADJ **1** affamé, qui a faim; **to be** *or* **feel h.** avoir faim; **to be ravenously h.** *or* **as h. as a wolf** *or Am* **a bear** avoir une faim de loup; **I was getting h.** je commençais à avoir faim; **to look h.** avoir l'air affamé; **it's h. work** ça donne faim **2** *Fig (look, eye)* avide; **to be h. for knowledge** être avide de connaissances; **to be h. for love** avoir soif d'amour

hung-up ADJ *Fam* coincé; **to be h. on sb/sth** être obsédé par qn/qch; **to be h. about sth** *(personal problem)* être complexé par qch; *(sexual matters)* être coincé quand il s'agit de qch

hunk [hʌŋk] N **1** *(of bread)* quignon *m*; *(of meat, cheese etc)* gros morceau *m* **2** *Fam (attractive man)* beau mec *m*, mec bien foutu

hunky ['hʌŋkɪ] ADJ *Fam (man) (with good body)* bien foutu; *(big and strong)* (bien) baraqué

hunky-dory ['hʌŋkɪ'dɔːrɪ] ADJ *Fam* excellent, au poil

hunt [hʌnt] N **1** *Sport (activity)* chasse *f*, *(people)* équipage *m* de chasse; *(area)* terrain *m* de chasse; **fox/tiger h.** chasse au renard/au tigre **2** *(search)* recherche *f*, **he continued his h. for work** il continuait à chercher un emploi; **local people joined in the h. for the child** des gens de la région se sont joints aux recherches pour retrouver l'enfant; **I've had a good h. for my gloves** j'ai cherché mes gants partout; **the h. is on for ...** on recherche ...

vi *Sport* chasser; **to h. for sth/sb** *(search for)* chercher (à découvrir) qch/qn; **to h. for treasure** aller à la recherche d'un trésor; **to h. high and low for sth** chercher partout qch

vt **1** *(fox, deer etc)* chasser; *(whales)* pêcher, chasser; **to h. a criminal** *(try to locate)* poursuivre un criminel, être à la recherche d'un criminel; **h. the slipper** *(game)* jeu *m* de cache-cache **2** *(ride, walk over) (piece of land)* parcourir, battre **3** *(use in hunting) (horse)* monter à la chasse; *(pack)* diriger, conduire

▸▸ *Br* **h. saboteur** = personne *f* qui tente d'arrêter une chasse

▸ **hunt about, hunt around** vi *(search)* chercher partout; **to h. about for sth** chercher qch partout

▸ **hunt down** vt sep **1** *(chase) (animal)* traquer, forcer; *(person)* traquer **2** *(find)* dénicher

▸ **hunt out** vt sep *(find) (person)* débusquer; *(object)* déterrer, dénicher (à force de recherches); **I've hunted out her phone number for you** je t'ai trouvé son numéro de téléphone

▸ **hunt up** vt sep *(find)* dénicher

hunted ['hʌntɪd] ADJ **he had a h. look** il avait l'air persécuté

hunter ['hʌntər] N **1** *Sport (person)* chasseur *m* **2** *(horse)* cheval *m* de chasse, hunter *m* **3** *(watch)* (montre *f* à) savonnette *f*; **half h.** montre à guichet

hunting ['hʌntɪŋ] N **1** *Sport* chasse *f*; *(of game)* poursuite *f*; *(science)* vénerie *f*; **fox h.** chasse au renard; **the Happy H. Grounds** le Paradis des Peaux-Rouges **2** *Aut (engine surge)* pompage *m*

▸▸ **h. dog** chien *m* de chasse; *Sport, Fig* **h. ground** terrain *m* de chasse; **a happy h. ground for collectors** un paradis pour les collectionneurs; *Hunt* **h. horn** cor *m* ou trompe *f* de chasse; *Hunt* **h. lodge** pavillon *m* de chasse; **h. man** fervent *m* de la chasse à courre, grand chasseur *m*

Hunting

Depuis plusieurs années, la chasse à courre au renard constitue pour le gouvernement britannique un dossier controversé. En effet, une partie de plus en plus importante de la population s'oppose à ce type de chasse, considéré comme barbare; mais il existe également en face un groupe de pression pro-chasse très actif qui s'oppose à toute réforme et qui met l'accent sur les conséquences néfastes qu'une interdiction de la chasse au renard aurait sur le mode de vie rural et sur l'emploi dans les campagnes.

Huntington's chorea ['hʌntɪŋtənzkɒ'rɪə] N *Med* chorée *f* de Huntington

huntress ['hʌntrɪs] N chasseuse *f*, *Lit* chasseresse *f*

huntsman, *pl* **huntsmen** ['hʌntsmən] N chasseur *m* (à courre); *(in charge of hounds)* veneur *m*, piqueur *m*

hurdle ['hɜːd(ə)l] N **1** *(in athletics), Horse-racing* haie *f*; **400-metre hurdles** 400 mètres haies *fpl* **2** *Fig (obstacle)* obstacle *m*; **to overcome a h.** franchir un obstacle; **the next h. will be to persuade the managing director** le prochain obstacle sera de persuader le directeur général **3** *(fence)* claie *f*, clôture *f*

vt **1** *(jump over) (obstacle)* sauter; *Sport (fence)* franchir **2** *(surround with fences)* entourer de claies

vi *Sport* courir une course de haies

▸▸ **h. race** course *f* de haies

hurdler ['hɜːdlər] N *(athlete)* coureur, -euse de haies; *(horse)* sauteur *m*

hurdling ['hɜːd(ə)lɪŋ] N *(in athletics), Horse-racing* course *f* de haies; *(part of competition)* courses de haies; **the world 400m h. champion** le champion du monde du 400m haies

hurdy-gurdy ['hɜːd'gɜːdɪ] N *Mus* orgue *m* de Barbarie

hurl [hɜːl] vt *(object)* lancer avec force ou violence (**at** contre); *(insults)* lancer (**at sb** à qn); **to h. oneself at sb** se ruer sur qn; **he hurled himself off the bridge** il s'est jeté du pont; **to h. oneself into the fray** se jeter à corps perdu dans la mêlée; **to h. abuse** vociférer des injures

vi *Fam (vomit)* dégobiller, gerber

▸ **hurl back** vt sep **1** *(object)* relancer avec force ou violence **2** *Lit (repulse) (enemy)* refouler, repousser

▸ **hurl down** vt sep jeter

hurley ['hɜːlɪ] N = **hurling**

hurling ['hɜːlɪŋ] N *Sport (Irish game)* = variété *f* de jeu de hockey

hurly-burly ['hɜːlɪ'bɜːlɪ] N *Fam* charivari *m*, tohu-bohu *m*

hurrah [hʊ'rɑː], **hurray** [hʊ'reɪ] INT, N hourra *m*; **h. for the holidays!** vive(nt) les vacances!

hurricane ['hʌrɪkən, -keɪn] N *Met* ouragan *m*; *(in West Indies)* hurricane *m*; **it was blowing a h.** le vent soufflait en ouragan

▸▸ **h. lamp** lampe-tempête *f*, *pl* lampes-tempête; *Met* **h. warning** avis *m* d'ouragan

hurried ['hʌrɪd] ADJ *(step)* pressé, précipité; *(work)* fait à la hâte; **a few h. words** *(written)* quelques mots écrits à la hâte; *(spoken)* quelques mots dits à la hâte; **to have a h. conversation** échanger rapidement quelques mots; **to make a h. decision** décider à la va-vite; **a h. departure** un départ précipité; **a h. meal** un repas pris à la hâte

hurriedly ['hʌrɪdlɪ] ADV à la hâte, en toute hâte, précipitamment

HURRY ['hʌrɪ] N hâte *f*, précipitation *f*; **to be in a h.** être pressé; **to do sth in a h.** faire qch à la hâte; **to leave in a h.** sortir à la hâte ou en courant; **in her h. she forgot her keys** dans sa précipitation, elle a oublié ses clefs; **they were in a h. to complete the work** ils étaient pressés de terminer le travail; **there's no h.** rien ne presse, ça ne presse pas; **to be in no h.** ne pas être pressé, avoir tout le temps; **he was in no h. to leave** il n'était pas pressé de partir; **you won't see her again in a h.** vous ne la reverrez pas de sitôt; **I won't do that again in a h.** je ne suis pas près de recommencer; **I won't recommencerai pas de sitôt**; **are you in a h. for it?** c'est urgent?; **so what's the h.?** qu'est-ce qui presse tant?; **what's your h.?** pourquoi est-ce que vous êtes aussi pressé?

vt *(person)* presser; *(work)* hâter, activer, presser; **don't h. him** ne le presse pas; **she was hurried to hospital** elle a été transportée à l'hôpital en (toute) hâte; **work that cannot be hurried** travail qui demande du temps; **it can't be hurried** il faut le temps; **don't h. your meal** ne mangez pas trop vite

vi **1** se dépêcher, se hâter, se presser (**to do** de faire); **don't h.** ne vous pressez pas; **there's no need to h.** nous avons tout le temps

2 *(go quickly)* presser le pas; **she hurried home** elle s'est dépêchée de rentrer; **to h. into/out of a room** entrer dans une pièce/sortir d'une pièce en toute hâte; **to h. after sb** courir après qn

▸ **hurry along** vi marcher d'un pas pressé; **h. along please** *(we're closing)* dépêchez-vous, s'il vous plaît

vt sep *(person)* faire se dépêcher; *(work)* accélérer; **he hurried them along** *(walking)* il les a fait marcher plus vite; **h. him along!** dis-lui de se presser!

▸ **hurry away** vi partir précipitamment

vt sep **he hurried the children away from the scene of the accident** il a vite éloigné les enfants du lieu de l'accident

▸ **hurry back** vi revenir ou retourner à la hâte; **she'll soon come hurrying back** elle reviendra vite; **promise to h. back afterwards** promets de revenir vite après

▸ **hurry off** vi partir précipitamment

vt sep **they hurried her off to hospital** ils l'ont emmenée à l'hôpital en (toute) hâte

▸ **hurry on** vi *(proceed quickly)* continuer à la hâte; **she hurried on with the housework** elle a continué le ménage à la hâte

vt sep *(person)* faire hâter le pas à; *(work)* activer

▸ **hurry up** vi se dépêcher, se hâter; **h. up!** dépêche-toi!; **h. up and get dressed** dépêche-toi de t'habiller; **h. up with that packing** dépêche-toi de faire ces bagages; **h. up with the iron** dépêche-toi avec le fer

vt sep *(person)* faire se dépêcher; *(work)* activer, accélérer; **I'll go and h. them up** je vais leur dire de se dépêcher

hurt [hɜːt] N **1** *(physical)* mal *m*

2 *(emotional harm)* **to cause h. to sb** blesser qn, faire de la peine à qn; **what h. can it do you?** quel tort cela peut-il vous faire?

ADJ *(look, feelings)* blessé

vt *(pt, pp* **hurt)** **1** *(cause physical pain or injury to) (person)* faire (du) mal à, blesser; **to h. oneself** se faire (du) mal; **to h. one's foot** se blesser au pied; **to get h.** se blesser; **are you h.?** êtes-vous blessé?; *Fig* **it wouldn't h. him to have to wait for a change** ça ne lui ferait pas de mal de devoir attendre pour changer; **the scandal will h. their prospects** le scandale nuira à leurs chances

2 *(emotionally)* faire de la peine à; **to h. sb's feelings** blesser qn, peiner qn, offenser qn; **it h. me when they did that** ça m'a fait de la peine quand ils ont fait ça; **he is easily h.** il s'offense facilement; **the thing that hurts me most** ce qui me fait le plus mal

vi **1** *(cause physical pain)* faire mal; **it hurts** ça fait mal; **where does it h.?** où est-ce que ça vous fait mal?; **my foot hurts** mon pied me fait mal; *Fam* **I h. all over** j'ai mal partout; *Fig* **just one drink won't h.** juste un verre ne te fera pas de mal; **it wouldn't h. to make a few more photocopies** ça ne fera pas de mal de faire quelques photocopies de plus

2 *(emotionally)* faire souffrir; **it hurts when you say that ...** ça fait mal de t'entendre dire que ...

hurtful ['hɜːtfʊl] ADJ *(remark)* blessant, offensant; **what a h. thing to say!** comme c'est blessant de dire une chose pareille!; **he was very h.** il a été très blessant

hurtle ['hɜːt(ə)l] vi **to h. along** *(of car, person etc)* aller à toute vitesse; **a girl on roller skates hurtled into me** une fille en patins à roulettes m'est rentrée dedans; **the rocks hurtled down** les rochers ont dévalé la pente avec fracas

vt *(throw) (rocks etc)* lancer

husband ['hʌzbənd] N mari *m*, époux *m*; **h. and wife** les (deux) époux, les conjoints *mpl*; **h. and wife run the hotel together** les deux époux s'occupent ensemble de l'hôtel; **to live as h. and wife** vivre maritalement

vt *Fml (resources, strength)* ménager, économiser; *(resources)* bien gérer

husband-and-wife ADJ **h. business** entreprise *f* appartenant à deux époux ou à un couple marié; **h. team** équipe *f* formée par deux époux

husbandry ['hʌzbəndrɪ] N **1** *Agr* agronomie *f*, économie *f* rurale, agriculture *f*, **animal h.** élevage *m* **2** *Fml (management)* gestion *f*

hush [hʌʃ] N *(quiet)* silence *m*, calme *m*;

there was a h. when *or* as ... il y a eu un silence quand ...;
 VT *(baby, child)* calmer, faire taire; *(person)* imposer silence à; *Fam* **I wish you'd h. your mouth** j'espère que tu vas te taire
 VI se taire, faire silence
 INT chut!, silence!
 ► ► *Fam* **h. money** pot-de-vin *m*, *pl* pots-de-vin *(pour acheter le silence de quelqu'un)*; *Fam* **he wanted h. money** il exigeait de l'argent pour se taire
 ► **hush up VT SEP** *(scandal etc)* étouffer

hushed [hʌʃt] **ADJ** **to talk in h. tones** chuchoter, parler à voix basse; **a h. silence** un silence profond; **they stared in h. amazement** frappés de stupeur, ils regardaient sans (pouvoir) rien dire; **h. conversation** conversation étouffée *ou* discrète

hush-hush ADJ *Fam* top-secret, -ète, ultra-secret, -ète

husk [hʌsk] **N** *(of seed, grain)* tégument *m*, pellicule *f*; *(of peas etc)* cosse *f*, gousse *f*; *(of nuts)* brou *m*; *(of chestnut)* hérisson *m*; *(of coffee bean)* coque *f*; *(of corn on the cob)* enveloppe *f*, **husks** *(of grain)* vannure *f*
 VT *(seed)* vanner; *(peas)* écosser; *(rice, barley)* perler, monder; *(corn)* éplucher

huskily [ˈhʌskɪlɪ] **ADV** *(to speak)* d'une voix rauque; *(because of sore throat)* d'une voix enrouée

huskiness [ˈhʌskɪnɪs] **N** **the h. of her voice** *(because of sore throat)* sa voix enrouée; *(natural)* sa voix rauque

husky [ˈhʌskɪ] **ADJ 1 h. voice** *(because of sore throat)* voix *f* enrouée *ou* voilée; *(naturally)* voix rauque **2** *(strong)* fort, *Fam* costaud

husky **N** *(dog)* chien *m* de traîneau, husky *m*

hussar [hʊˈzɑ:r] **N** *Mil* hussard *m*

hussy [ˈhʌsɪ] **N** *Old-fashioned Fam* coquine *f*, friponne *f*, **you little h.!** petite coquine!

hustings [ˈhʌstɪŋz] **NPL** plate-forme *f* électorale; **to be (out) on the h.** faire des discours électoraux sur le terrain; **he's hopeless on the h.** comme orateur sur le terrain, il est nul

hustle [ˈhʌs(ə)l] **N** *(energetic activity)* grande activité *f*, effervescence *f*, **h. and bustle** tourbillon *m* d'activité; **the h. and bustle of London** l'activité incessante de Londres
 VT 1 *(shove, push)* bousculer, pousser, presser; **to be hustled away** être emmené précipitamment; **I was hustled into a small room** on m'a fait entrer précipitamment dans une petite pièce **2** *(hurry)* **to h. things on** faire avancer les choses, *Fam* faire activer les choses; **to h. sb into a decision** forcer qn à se décider (sans lui donner le temps de respirer); **I won't be hustled** je ne veux pas qu'on me bouscule
 VI 1 *(hurry)* se dépêcher, se presser **2** *(shove)* **to h. through the crowd** se frayer un passage à travers la foule **3** *Am Sl (swindle)* arnaquer **4** *Am Sl (of prostitute)* faire le trottoir

hustler [ˈhʌslər] **N 1** *Fam (energetic person)* *(with lots of business activities)* brasseur *m* d'affaires; *(problem-solver etc)* débrouillard *m* **2** *esp Am Sl (swindler)* arnaqueur *m* **3** *Am Sl (prostitute)* prostituée *f*

hut [hʌt] **N** hutte *f*, cabane *f*

hutch [hʌtʃ] **N 1** *(for rabbit)* clapier *m*, lapinière *f* **2** *Am (cupboard)* vaisselier *m*

hutments [ˈhʌtmənts] **NPL** *Mil* baraquements *mpl*

hyacinth [ˈhaɪəsɪnθ] **N 1** *(flower)* jacinthe *f*, **wood** *or* **wild h.** jacinthe des bois **2** *(colour)* bleu jacinthe *m inv*, bleu violet *m inv*; **a h. dress** une robe bleu violet **3** *Miner* hyacinthe *f*

hyaena [haɪˈiːnə] **N** = **hyena**

hybrid [ˈhaɪbrɪd] **N 1** *Biol, Ling etc* hybride *m* **2** *(bicycle)* vélo *m* tout chemin, VTC *m*
 ADJ hybride

hybridism [ˈhaɪbrɪdɪz(ə)m] **N** *Biol* hybridisme *m*

hybridization [haɪbrɪdaɪˈzeɪʃən] **N** *Biol* hybridation *f*

hybridize [ˈhaɪbrɪdaɪz] **VT** hybrider
 VI s'hybrider

hydra [ˈhaɪdrə] **N 1** *(pl* **hydrae** [ˈhaɪdriː]*)* *(animal)* hydre *f* **2** *Myth* **H.** Hydre *f* de Lerne; *Fig* **h.-headed** à plusieurs têtes

hydrangea [haɪˈdreɪndʒə] **N** *(shrub)* hortensia *m*

hydrant [ˈhaɪdrənt] **N** prise *f* d'eau; **fire h.** bouche *f* d'incendie

hydrate [ˈhaɪdreɪt] *Chem* **N** hydrate *m*
 VT hydrater

hydration [haɪˈdreɪʃən] **N** *Med* hydratation *f*

hydraulic [haɪˈdrɒːlɪk] **ADJ** *(force, brake, power etc)* hydraulique
 ► ► **h. cylinder** vérin *m* hydraulique; **h. engineering** technique *f* hydraulique, hydraulique *f*, *Aut, Tech* **h. jack** *(for lifting car)* cric *m* hydraulique; **h. ram** vérin *m* hydraulique

hydraulics [haɪˈdrɒːlɪks] **N** hydraulique *f* VOIR GRAMMAIRE A10

hydro [ˈhaɪdrəʊ] **N 1** *Br (centre for hydrotherapy)* établissement *m* hydrothérapique **2** *Can Fam (power)* énergie *f* hydraulique; *(power station)* centrale *f* hydraulique; **to pay the h. bill** payer la note d'électricité

hydrocarbon [haɪdrəʊˈkɑːbən] **N** *Chem* hydrocarbure *m*

hydrochloric [haɪdrəʊˈklɒrɪk] **ADJ** *Chem (acid)* chlorhydrique

hydrochloride [haɪdrəʊˈklɒːraɪd] **N** *Chem* chlorhydrate *m*

hydrodynamics [haɪdrəʊdaɪˈnæmɪks] **N** hydrodynamique *f* VOIR GRAMMAIRE A10

hydroelectric [haɪdrəʊɪˈlektrɪk] **ADJ** hydroélectrique
 ► ► **h. dam** barrage *m* hydroélectrique; **h. power** énergie *f* hydroélectrique

hydroelectricity [haɪdrəʊɪlekˈtrɪsɪtɪ] **N** hydroélectricité *f*

hydrofoil [ˈhaɪdrəfɔɪl] **N** hydrofoil *m*

hydrogen [ˈhaɪdrədʒən] **N** *Chem* hydrogène *m*
 ► ► *Mil, Nucl* **h. bomb** bombe *f* à hydrogène; **h. engine** moteur *m* hydrogène; *Chem* **h. peroxide** eau *f* oxygénée

hydrography [haɪˈdrɒgrəfɪ] **N** hydrographie *f*

hydrolastic suspension [haɪdrəˈlæstɪk] **N** suspension *f* hydro-élastique

hydrolysis [haɪˈdrɒlɪsɪs] **N** *Chem* hydrolyse *f*

hydrometer [haɪˈdrɒmɪtər] **N** hydromètre *m*

hydrometry [haɪˈdrɒmɪtrɪ] **N** *Phys* hydrométrie *f*

hydropathy [haɪˈdrɒpəθɪ] **N** hydropathie *f*

hydrophobia [haɪdrəˈfəʊbɪə] **N** *Med* **1** *(rabies)* hydrophobie *f* **2** *(fear)* phobie *f* de l'eau

hydrophobic [haɪdrəˈfəʊbɪk] **ADJ** hydrophobe

hydroplane [ˈhaɪdrəpleɪn] **N 1** *(boat)* hydroglisseur *m* **2** *esp Am (seaplane)* hydravion *m*

hydroponics [haɪdrəʊˈpɒnɪks] **N** culture *f* hydroponique VOIR GRAMMAIRE A10

hydrostat [ˈhaɪdrəʊstæt] **N** hydrostat *m*

hydrostatics [haɪdrəʊˈstætɪks] **N** hydrostatique *f* VOIR GRAMMAIRE A10

hydrotherapy [haɪdrəʊˈθerəpɪ] **N** *Med* hydrothérapie *f*

hydroxide [haɪˈdrɒksaɪd] **N** *Chem* hydroxyde *m*, hydrate *m*

hyena [haɪˈiːnə] **N** *(animal)* hyène *f*, **laughing h.** hyène rieuse; **to laugh like a h.** rire comme un bossu

hygiene [ˈhaɪdʒiːn] **N** hygiène *f*

hygienic [haɪˈdʒiːnɪk] **ADJ** hygiénique

hygienically [haɪˈdʒiːnɪklɪ] **ADV** hygiéniquement

hymen [ˈhaɪmen] **N 1** *Anat* hymen *m* **2** *Myth* **H.** Hyménée *f*

hymn [hɪm] **N 1** *Rel* hymne *m ou f*, cantique *m*; **there will be h. singing** on chantera des hymnes **2** *(anthem, poem etc)* hymne *m*
 ► ► **h. book** livre *m* de cantiques

hymnal [ˈhɪmn(ə)l] **N** *Fml* livre *m* de cantiques

hype [haɪp] **N 1** *Fam Pej (publicity)* battage *m* publicitaire, matraquage *m* publicitaire; **it's all h.** c'est du matraquage **2** *Sl (hypodermic needle)* aiguille *f* hypodermique
 VT *Fam* **to h. a product** faire du matraquage publicitaire pour un produit
 ► **hype up VT SEP** *Fam (publicize)* **to h. sth up** faire de la publicité à outrance pour qch; **to h. up a new film/rock group** lancer un nouveau film/groupe de rock à grand renfort de publicité; **it's been so hyped up in the media** on a fait un tel battage médiatique; **I don't want to h. it up too much, but ...** *(overstate)* je ne voudrais pas exagérer mais ...

hyped up [haɪpˈtʌp] **ADJ 1** *Fam (heavily publicized)* lancé à grand renfort de publicité **2** *Fam (excited)* tout excité **3** *Sl (on drugs)* camé

hyper [ˈhaɪpər] **ADJ** *Fam (over-excited)* tout excité; *(generally overactive etc)* hyperdynamique

hyper- [ˈhaɪpər] **PREF** hyper-

hyperacidity [haɪpərəˈsɪdɪtɪ] **N** hyperacidité *f*

hyperactive [haɪpəˈræktɪv] **ADJ** hyperactif

hyperbola [haɪˈpɜːbələ] **N** *Math* hyperbole *f*

hyperbole [haɪˈpɜːbəlɪ] **N** *Liter* hyperbole *f*

hyperbolic(al) [haɪpəˈbɒlɪk, -ɪk(ə)l] **ADJ** *(in rhetoric)*, *Math* hyperbolique

hypercritical [haɪpəˈkrɪtɪkəl] **ADJ** hypercritique

hyperemotivity [haɪpərɪməʊˈtɪvɪtɪ] **N** hyperémotivité *f*

hyperglycaemia [haɪpəglaɪˈsiːmɪə] **N** *Med* hyperglycémie *f*

hyperglycaemic [haɪpəglaɪˈsiːmɪk] **ADJ** *Med* hyperglycémique; *(drug)* hyperglycémiant

hyperinflation [haɪpərɪnˈfleɪʃən] **N** hyperinflation *f*

hyperlink [ˈhaɪpəlɪŋk] **N** *Comput* hyperlien *m*

hypermarket [ˈhaɪpəmɑːkɪt] **N** *Br* hypermarché *m*, grande surface *f*

hypersensitive [haɪpəˈsensɪtɪv] **ADJ** très *ou* trop susceptible

hypersensitivity [haɪpəsensɪˈtɪvɪtɪ] **N** *(emotional)* *(extrême)* susceptibilité *f*

hypertension [haɪpəˈtenʃən] **N** *Med* hypertension *f*

hypertext [ˈhaɪpətekst] **N** *Comput* hypertexte *m*
 ► ► *Comput* **h. link** lien *m* hypertexte

hyperthyroid [haɪpəˈθaɪrɔɪd] **ADJ** *Med* hyperthyroïdien, -ienne

hyperthyroidism [haɪpəˈθaɪrɔɪdɪz(ə)m] **N** *Med* hyperthyroïdie *f*

hyphen [ˈhaɪf(ə)n] **N** trait *m* d'union

hyphenate [ˈhaɪfəneɪt] **VT** *(word)* mettre un trait d'union à; **hyphenated word** mot *m* composé; **is that hyphenated?** est-ce que ça prend un trait d'union?; *Am* **hyphenated**

American étranger naturalisé *(Germano-Américain, Hispano-Américain etc)*

hyphenation [haɪfə'neɪʃən] **N** syllabation *f*, *(in printing)* césure *f*, coupure *f* des mots
▸▸ *Comput* **h. help** aide *f* à la césure; *Comput* **h. logic** logique *f* de césure; *Comput* **h. menu** menu *m* de césure; *Comput* **h. program** programme *m* de césure, logiciel *m* de syllabation

hypnosis [hɪp'nəʊsɪs] **N** hypnose *f*, **under h.** sous hypnose

hypnotic [hɪp'nɒtɪk] **ADJ** *Psy, Pharm* hypnotique; **in a h. trance** en état d'hypnose; **to have a h. effect on sb** hypnotiser qn; **she had a h. fascination for him** il était totalement fasciné par elle; **h. state** état *m* d'hypnose

hypnotism ['hɪpnətɪz(ə)m] **N** hypnotisme *m*

hypnotist ['hɪpnətɪst] **N** hypnotiseur, -euse

hypnotize ['hɪpnətaɪz] **VT** hypnotiser

hypo- ['haɪpəʊ] **PREF** hypo-

hypoallergenic [haɪpəʊælə'dʒenɪk] **ADJ** hypoallergénique, anallergique

hypocalorific [haɪpəkæləˈrɪfɪk] **ADJ** hypocalorique, hypoénergétique

hypochondria [haɪpə'kɒndrɪə] **N** *Med* hypocondrie *f*

hypochondriac [haɪpə'kɒndrɪæk] **N** hypocondriaque *mf*, malade *mf* imaginaire
ADJ hypocondriaque
▸▸ **h. region** *(of abdomen)* hypocondre *m*

hypocrisy [hɪ'pɒkrɪsɪ] **N** hypocrisie *f*

hypocrite ['hɪpəkrɪt] **N** hypocrite *mf*, tartufe *m*

hypocritical [hɪpə'krɪtɪk(ə)l] **ADJ** hypocrite

hypocritically [hɪpə'krɪtɪklɪ] **ADV** hypocritement

hypodermic [haɪpə'dɜːmɪk] **ADJ 1** *(injection, syringe, needle etc)* hypodermique **2** *Anat* sous-cutané
N *(syringe)* seringue *f* hypodermique; *(needle)* aiguille *f* hypodermique; *(injection)* piqûre *f* hypodermique

hypoglycaemia [haɪpəʊglaɪ'siːmɪə] **N** *Med* hypoglycémie *f*

hypoglycaemic [haɪpəʊglaɪ'siːmɪk] **ADJ** *Med* hypoglycémique; *(drug)* hypoglycémiant

hypoid ['haɪpɔɪd] **ADJ** *Tech* hypoïde

hyponym ['haɪpənɪm] **N** hyponyme *m*

hypotenuse [haɪ'pɒtənjuːz] **N** *Math* hypoténuse *f*

hypothalamus [haɪpə'θæləməs] **N** hypothalamus *m*

hypothermia [haɪpəʊ'θɜːmɪə] **N** *Med* hypothermie *f*

hypothesis [haɪ'pɒθəsɪs] **N** hypothèse *f*, **working h.** hypothèse de travail VOIR GRAMMAIRE A14

hypothesize [haɪ'pɒθəsaɪz] **VI** faire *ou* formuler des hypothèses
VT **to h. that ...** admettre comme hypothèse que ...

hypothetical [haɪpə'θetɪk(ə)l] **ADJ** hypothétique, supposé

hypothetically [haɪpə'θetɪklɪ] **ADV** hypothétiquement, par hypothèse

hypothyroid [haɪpəʊ'θaɪrɔɪd] **ADJ** *Med* hypothyroïdien, -ienne

hypothyroidism [haɪpəʊ'θaɪrɔɪdɪz(ə)m] **N** *Med* hypothyroïdie *f*

hypotonic [haɪpəʊ'tɒnɪk] **ADJ** hypotonique

hysterectomy [hɪstə'rektəmɪ] **N** *Surg* hystérectomie *f*, **to have a h.** subir une hystérectomie

hysteria [hɪs'tɪərɪə] **N 1** crise *f* de nerfs; *Med* hystérie *f* **2** *Fam (great amusement)* fou rire *m*

hysteric [hɪs'terɪk] **N** *Med* hystérique *mf*

hysterical [hɪs'terɪk(ə)l] **ADJ 1** *Med* hystérique **2** *(very emotional)* en proie à une crise de nerfs; *(laughter)* nerveux, énervé; *(reaction)* hystérique; **she was h.** elle était dans tous ses états; **h. sobbing** sanglots *mpl* convulsifs **3** *Fam (very amusing)* écroulant, tordant **4** *Fam (very amused)* **h. laughter** fou rire *m*
▸▸ *Am Psy* **h. pregnancy** grossesse *f* nerveuse

hysterically [hɪs'terɪklɪ] **ADV 1** *(very emotionally)* sans pouvoir maîtriser ses émotions; **he was waving his arms h.** il agitait ses bras de façon incontrôlée; **to weep h.** avoir une crise de larmes; **to laugh h.** être pris d'un rire nerveux **2** *Fam* **h. funny** écroulant, tordant **3** *Fam* **to laugh h.** *(with great amusement)* avoir le fou rire

hysterics [hɪs'terɪks] **NPL 1** *Med* hystérie *f* **2** *(emotional reaction)* crise *f* de nerfs; **to go into h.** avoir une crise de nerfs **3** *Fam (great amusement)* fou rire *m*; **to be in h.** être écroulé de rire; **she had us in h.** elle nous a fait tordre de rire; **to send sb into (a fit of) h.** faire tordre qn de rire

I¹, i [aɪ] N *(letter)* I, i *m*; **two i's** deux i

I² PERS PRON VOIR GRAMMAIRE A27; B18 **1** *(unstressed)* je, *(preceding vowel)* j'; **I sing** je chante; **I accuse** j'accuse; **here I am** me voici; **what have I said?** qu'ai-je dit? **2** *(stressed)* moi; **he and I both like jazz** lui et moi, nous aimons le jazz; **I too have a twin sister** moi aussi, j'ai une jumelle
N **another I** un autre moi(-même)

Ia *abbr* Iowa

IAEA [aɪeɪiː'eɪ] N *(abbr* **International Atomic Energy Agency)** AIEA *f*

iambic [aɪ'æmbɪk] *Liter* ADJ *(verse)* iambique
N *(line, poem)* iambe *m*
▸▸ **i. foot** iambe *m*; **i. pentameter** pentamètre *m* iambique

IAP [aɪeɪ'piː] N *Comput (abbr* **Internet Access Provider)** fournisseur *m* d'accès Internet

IASC [aɪeɪes'siː] N *Fin (abbr* **International Accounting Standards Committee)** comité *m* international des normes comptables

IATA [aɪ'ɑːtə, iː'ɑːtə] N *Aviat (abbr* **International Air Transport Association)** IATA *f*

IBA [aɪbiː'eɪ] N *Formerly (abbr* **Independent Broadcasting Authority)** = organisme *m* qui contrôle les chaînes de télévision et les stations de radio privées britanniques, ≃ CSA *m*

IBC [aɪbiː'siː] N *(abbr* **inside back cover)** troisième *f* de couverture

I-beam N *Comput* pointeur *m* en I

Iberia [aɪ'bɪərɪə] N *Hist* Ibérie *f*

Iberian [aɪ'bɪərɪən] ADJ *(people)* ibérien, ibérique
N Ibère *mf*
▸▸ **the I. Peninsula** la péninsule ibérique

ibex, *pl* **ibexes** ['aɪbeks, -eksɪz] N bouquetin *m* des Alpes

ibid ['ɪbɪd] ADV *(abbr* **ibidem)** ibid

ibis, *pl* **ibises** ['aɪbɪs, -ɪsɪz] N ibis *m*

IBM-compatible [aɪbiːemkəm'pætɪb(ə)l] N, ADJ compatible *m* IBM

IBOR ['aɪbɔːr] N *(abbr* **interbank offered rate)** TIO *m*

IBRD [aɪbiːɑː'diː] N *(abbr* **International Bank for Reconstruction and Development)** BIRD *f*

IBS [aɪbiː'es] N *Med (abbr* **irritable bowel syndrome)** colite *f*

IC [aɪ'siː] N *Comput (abbr* **integrated circuit)** circuit *m* intégré
▸▸ **IC card** carte *f* à circuits intégrés

ICAO [aɪsiːeɪ'əʊ] N *Aviat (abbr* **International Civil Aviation Organization)** OACI *f*

ICC [aɪsiː'siː] N **1** *(abbr* **International Chamber of Commerce)** CCI *f* **2** *Law (abbr* **International Criminal Court)** CPI *f*

ice [aɪs] N **1** *(frozen water)* glace *f*, *Met (on road)* verglas *m*; **my feet are as cold as i.** j'ai les pieds glacés; **with i.?** *(in drink)* avec des glaçons *ou* de la glace?; *Fig* **to be on** *or* **skate on thin i.** être sur *ou* toucher à un sujet délicat; *Fig* **to put a project on i.** mettre un projet en veilleuse; **that cuts no i. with me** ça ne marche pas avec moi **2** *Br Culin (ice-cream)* glace *f*, **strawberry i.** glace à la fraise **3** *Sl (diamonds)* cailloux *mpl*
VT **1** *Culin (cake)* glacer **2** *Sl (kill)* refroidir
▸▸ **i. age** période *f* glaciaire; **i. bucket** seau *m* à glace; *Sport* **i. climbing** escalade *f* de murs de glace; **i. cube** glaçon *m*; *Sport* **i. dancer** danseur, -euse sur glace; *Sport* **i. dancing** danse *f* sur glace; **i. floe** glace *f* flottante; *Sport* **i. hockey** hockey *m* sur glace; **i. house** glacière *f*, *Br* **i. lolly** glace *f* à l'eau; **i. machine** distributeur *m* de glaçons; *esp Am* **i. man** livreur *m* de glace; **i. pack** *(pack ice)* banquise *f*, *(ice bag)* sac *m* à glaçons; *Med* poche *f* à glace; **i. pick** pic *m* à glace; *Sport* **i. rink** patinoire *f*, **i. scraper** *(for car window)* raclette *f* *(antigivre)*; **i. show** spectacle *m* sur glace; **i. skate** patin *m* (à glace); **i. skater** patineur, -euse; **i. skating** patinage *m* (sur glace); *Am* **i. water** eau *f* glacée
▸ **ice over** VI *(of pond)* geler; *(of road)* se couvrir de verglas
▸ **ice up** VI *(of windscreen, propeller)* se givrer

iceberg ['aɪsbɜːg] N **1** iceberg *m*; *Fig* **this is just the tip of the i.** ce n'est que la partie visible de l'iceberg **2** *Fig (unemotional person)* glaçon *m*
▸▸ **i. lettuce** = salade *f* aux feuilles serrées et croquantes

icebound ['aɪsbaʊnd] ADJ *(ship, port)* bloqué par les glaces

icebox ['aɪsbɒks] N **1** *(for storing food)* glacière *f*, *(in fridge)* compartiment *m* à glace, freezer *m* **2** *Am Old-fashioned (fridge)* réfrigérateur *m*

icebreaker ['aɪsbreɪkər] N *Naut* brise-glace *m*; *Fig* **if you're looking for an i.** si tu veux briser la glace

icecap ['aɪskæp] N calotte *f* glaciaire

ice-cold ADJ *(water, house)* glacé; *(wind)* glacial, -als *ou* -aux

ice-cream N glace *f*, **strawberry/chocolate i.** glace à la fraise/au chocolat
▸▸ **i. cone, i. cornet** cornet *m*; **i. man** marchand *m* de glaces; *esp Am* **i. parlor** salon *m* de dégustation de glaces; **i. van** = camionnette *f* de vendeur de glaces

iced [aɪst] ADJ **1** *(very cold) (coffee, tea)* glacé **2** *(decorated) (cake)* glacé
▸▸ **i. water** eau *f* avec glaçons

Iceland ['aɪslənd] N Islande *f*

Icelander ['aɪsləndər] N Islandais, -aise

Icelandic [aɪs'lændɪk] ADJ islandais
N *Ling* islandais *m*

ice-skate VI faire du patin à glace

ichthyology [ɪkθɪ'ɒlədʒɪ] N ichtyologie *f*

ichthyosaurus [ɪkθɪə'sɔːrəs] N ichtyosaure *m*

icicle ['aɪsɪk(ə)l] N stalactite *f*, glaçon *m*

icily ['aɪsɪlɪ] ADV **1** *(to say, reply etc)* d'un ton glacial; *(to look at)* d'un air glacial; **we were greeted i.** nous avons eu un accueil glacial **2** *(bitterly)* **it's i. cold** il fait un froid glacial

iciness ['aɪsɪnɪs] N *(of wind, water)* température *f* glaciale; **because of the i. of the steps** parce que les marches étaient verglacées; *Fig* **the i. of her voice** son ton glacial

icing ['aɪsɪŋ] N **1** *esp Br Culin (action, decoration)* glaçage *m*; *Fig* **the i. on the cake** *(final touch)* la cerise sur le gâteau **2** *Aviat (formation of ice)* givrage *m*
▸▸ *Br Culin* **i. sugar** sucre *m* glace

ICJ [aɪsiː'dʒeɪ] N *(abbr* **International Court of Justice)** CIJ *f*

icky ['ɪkɪ] ADJ *Fam (repulsive)* dégoûtant; *(sticky)* collant; *(sentimental)* mièvre, à la guimauve

icon ['aɪkɒn] N *Rel, Comput* icône *f*, *Fig* **a 60's i.** le symbole des années soixante
▸▸ *Comput* **i. bar** barre *f* d'icônes; *Comput* **i. drag** glisser *m inv* d'icônes; *Comput* **i. drag and drop** glisser-lâcher *m inv* d'icônes; *Comput* **i. drop** lâcher *m* d'icônes; *Comput* **i. editor** éditeur *m* d'icônes

iconize ['aɪkɒnaɪz] VT *Comput* représenter en icône

iconoclast [aɪ'kɒnəklæst] N iconoclaste *mf*

iconoclastic [aɪkɒnə'klæstɪk] ADJ iconoclaste

iconography [aɪkə'nɒgrəfɪ] N iconographie *f*, *Cin* symbolique *f*

ICT N *abbr* **information and communications technology)** informatique *f*

ICTR [aɪsiːtiː'ɑːr] N *(abbr* **International Criminal Tribunal for Rwanda)** TPIR *m*

ICTY [aɪsiːtiː'waɪ] N *(abbr* **International Criminal Tribunal for the former Yugoslavia)** TPIY *m*

ICU [aɪsiː'juː] N *Med abbr* **intensive care unit**

icy ['aɪsɪ] ADJ **1** *(covered in ice)* couvert de glace; *(road)* verglacé **2** *(very cold) (water, wind)* glacial, -als *ou* -aux; *(hands)* glacé **3** *Fig (welcome, stare, tone of voice)* glacial, -als *ou* -aux

ID ['aɪ'diː] N *(abbr* **identification)** **1** pièce *f* d'identité; **have you got any ID?** est-ce que vous avez une pièce d'identité?; **ID card** carte *f* d'identité **2** *Comput* numéro *m* d'identification
VT *(abbr* **identify)** identifier

I'd [aɪd] CONTR **1** = **I had**, *see* **have 2** = **I would**, *see* **would**

Ida *abbr* Idaho

IDE [aɪdiː'iː] N *Comput (abbr* **intelligent disk enhancement)** IDE

idea [aɪ'dɪə] N **1** *(individual notion)* idée *f*, **I can't bear the i. (of it)** je ne supporte pas cette idée; **a bright i.** une idée lumineuse; **whose i. was it to do that?** qui a eu l'idée de faire cela?; **what a funny i.!** quelle drôle d'idée!; **what a good i.!** quelle bonne idée!; **I've got a good i.** j'ai une idée; **to be full of ideas** être *ou* avoir plein d'idées; **I got the i. from a film** c'est en voyant un film que l'idée m'est venue; **to get ideas into one's head** se faire des idées; **what put that i. into your head?** qu'est-ce qui vous a donné cette idée?; **don't say that, you'll give her ideas!** ne dis pas ça, tu vas lui donner des idées!; **what an i.!** en voilà une idée!; **the (very) i.!** quelle idée!; **get the i.?** vous comprenez?; **what's the (big) i.?** qu'est-ce qui te prend?

2 *(conception)* conception *f*; **it's not my i. of fun** je ne trouve pas ça drôle; **her i. of a joke is** ... le genre de plaisanterie qu'elle aime c'est ...; **if this is your i. of a joke** si tu trouves que c'est drôle; **you've got a funny i. of loyalty** tu as une conception bizarre de la loyauté

3 *(understanding, impression)* **I have an i. that I've seen him before** j'ai l'impression de l'avoir déjà vu; **I had no i. that** ... je ne savais pas que ...; **you have no i. how anxious I was** tu ne peux pas t'imaginer à quel point j'étais inquiet; **can you give me an** *or* **some i.?** *(of how much it will be, how long it will take etc)* est-ce que vous pouvez me donner une idée?; **he has some i. of chemistry** il a des notions de chimie; **you don't have much i. about women, do you?** tu ne connais pas grand-chose aux femmes, hein?; **to get the i. that** ... s'imaginer que ...

4 *(plan)* **I had some i. of going as far as Paris** j'avais dans l'idée de pousser jusqu'à Paris; **I thought the i. was for them to come here** il n'était pas prévu que ce serait eux qui viendraient ici?; **ideas person** boîte *f* à idées

5 *(aim)* **the general i. is to** ... l'idée est de ...; **the i. is to get the ball into the net** le but est de mettre le ballon dans le panier

▸▸ **i. chairman** *(at group discussion)* directeur *m* de réunion de groupe synectique; **i. committee** comité *m* synectique

ideal [aɪ'diːəl] **ADJ** idéal, -als *ou* -aux; **it's i.!** c'est l'idéal!, c'est le rêve!; **in an i. world** dans l'idéal

N 1 *(perfect example)* idéal *m*, *pl* -als *ou* -aux; **the i. of beauty** l'idéal de la beauté **2** *(principle)* idéal *m*, *pl* -als *ou* -aux; **a man with no ideals** un homme sans idéaux; **with such high ideals you'll never be satisfied** si tu es aussi idéaliste, tu ne seras jamais satisfait

idealism [aɪ'dɪəlɪz(ə)m] **N** idéalisme *m*

idealist [aɪ'dɪəlɪst] **N** idéaliste *mf*

idealistic [aɪdɪə'lɪstɪk] **ADJ** idéaliste

idealize [aɪ'dɪəlaɪz] **VT** idéaliser

ideally [aɪ'diːəlɪ] **ADV 1** *(in ideal case)* dans l'idéal **2** *(extremely well)* *(qualified, suited)* parfaitement; **the flat is i. situated** l'appartement est extrêmement bien situé; **they're i. matched** ils vont parfaitement bien ensemble; **she's i. positioned to benefit from the situation** elle est dans une position idéale pour tirer parti de la situation

ident ['aɪdent] **N** *TV, Radio* indicatif *m*, identification *f*

identical [aɪ'dentɪk(ə)l] **ADJ** identique **(to** à**)**
▸▸ **i. twins** *(boys)* vrais jumeaux *mpl*; *(girls)* vraies jumelles *fpl*

identically [aɪ'dentɪk(ə)lɪ] **ADV** identiquement

identifiable [aɪdentɪ'faɪəb(ə)l] **ADJ** identifiable; **he is i. by** ... on peut l'identifier grâce à ...

identification [aɪdentɪfɪ'keɪʃən] **N 1** *(of body, criminal)* identification *f* *(où l'on demande à un témoin de reconnaître une personne)* **2** *(documents)* papiers *mpl* d'identité; **have you got any i.?** avez-vous une pièce d'identité?; *(to person claiming to be police*

officer, gas man etc) est-ce que vous avez de quoi prouver votre identité? **3** *(association)* **i. of sth with sth** identification *f* de qch avec qch

▸▸ *Aviat, Naut* **i. marks** (lettres *fpl* et numéros *mpl* d')immatriculation *f*; **i. papers** papiers d'identité; *Br* **i. parade** séance *f* d'identification *(au cours de laquelle on demande à un témoin de reconnaître une personne)*

identifier [aɪ'dentɪfaɪər] **N** *Comput* identificateur *m*

identify [aɪ'dentɪfaɪ] **VT 1** *(recognize, put a name to)* *(body, person, bird, plant etc)* identifier; *(car, wallet etc)* reconnaître **2** *(associate)* **to i. sth with sth** identifier qch à qch; **to be identified with sth** être associé à qch; **to i. oneself with a cause** s'identifier à *ou* avec une cause, s'assimiler à une cause

VI s'identifier **(with** sb à qn**)**; **I can't i. with the way she feels** je ne peux pas me mettre à sa place; **I can't i. with his problems** j'ai du mal à comprendre ses problèmes de l'intérieur

identifying [aɪ'dentɪfaɪɪŋ] **ADJ**
▸▸ **i. marks** signes *mpl* particuliers

Identikit® [aɪ'dentɪkɪt] **N** portrait-robot *m*, *pl* portraits-robots
▸▸ **I. picture** portrait-robot

identity [aɪ'dentɪtɪ] **N 1** identité *f*; **to prove one's i.** établir son identité; **mistaken i.** erreur *f* sur la personne, quiproquo *m* **2** *(quality of being identical)* identité *f*
▸▸ **i. bracelet** bracelet *m* d'identité; **i. card** carte *f* d'identité; *Psy* **i. crisis** crise *f* d'identité; *Mil* **i. disc** plaque *f* d'identité; **i. papers** papiers *mpl* d'identité; *Br* **i. parade** séance *f* d'identification *(au cours de laquelle on demande à un témoin de reconnaître une personne)*

ideogram ['ɪdɪəgræm], **ideograph** ['ɪdɪəgræf] **N** idéogramme *m*

ideological [aɪdɪə'lɒdʒɪk(ə)l] **ADJ** idéologique

ideologically [aɪdɪə'lɒdʒɪk(ə)lɪ] **ADV** i., **they are poles apart** en termes d'idéologie, ils sont aux antipodes; **an i. motivated attack** une attaque qui a des motifs idéologiques

ideologist [aɪdɪ'ɒlədʒɪst] **N** idéologue *mf*

ideologue ['aɪdɪəlɒg] **N** idéologue *mf*

ideology [aɪdɪ'ɒlədʒɪ] **N** idéologie *f*

ides [aɪdz] **NPL** *Hist* ides *fpl*

idiocy ['ɪdɪəsɪ] **N 1** *(stupidity)* idiotie *f*, stupidité *f* **2** *Old-fashioned (mental backwardness)* **(congenital)** i. idiotie *f* (congénitale)

idiolect ['ɪdɪəlekt] **N** *Ling* idiolecte *m*

idiom ['ɪdɪəm] **N 1** *(expression)* locution *f*, expression *f* idiomatique **2** *(dialect)* dialecte *m*, idiome *m* **3** *Art, Mus* style *m*

idiomatic [ɪdɪə'mætɪk] **ADJ** idiomatique; **i. expression** expression *f* idiomatique

idiomatically [ɪdɪə'mætɪklɪ] **ADV** *(to express oneself)* de façon idiomatique

idiosyncrasy [ɪdɪəʊ'sɪŋkrəsɪ] **N** particularité *f*, petite manie *f*

idiosyncratic [ɪdɪəʊsɪŋ'krætɪk] **ADJ** particulier

idiot ['ɪdɪət] **N 1** imbécile *mf*, idiot, -ote; **what an i. I've been!** comme j'ai été bête!; **you i.!** espèce d'imbécile *ou* d'idiot!; **some i. has forgotten to lock the door!** il y a un imbécile qui a oublié de fermer la porter à clé; **to make sb look like an i.** faire passer qn pour un imbécile **2** *Old-fashioned (mentally retarded person)* idiot, -ote, imbécile *mf*
▸▸ *TV Fam* **i. board** téléprompteur *m*; *Fam Pej* **i. box** télé *f*, téloche *f*

idiotic [ɪdɪ'ɒtɪk] **ADJ** bête, idiot; **that's i.**

c'est stupide, c'est idiot; **don't be i.!** ne sois pas bête!

idiotically [ɪdɪ'ɒtɪklɪ] **ADV** bêtement, idiotement

idiotism ['ɪdɪətɪz(ə)m] **N** *Am (of language)* idiotisme *m*

idle ['aɪd(ə)l] **ADJ 1** *(unoccupied)* *(person)* inoccupé, oisif, désœuvré; *(machinery)* à l'arrêt; **to be** *or* **stand i.** *(of person)* ne rien faire; *(of machine)* ne pas servir; **to lie i.** *(of money)* dormir; **in my i. moments** à mes heures perdues; **when you've got an i. moment, could you** ... quand tu auras un moment, pourrais-tu ...

2 *(lazy)* paresseux, fainéant, indolent

3 *(futile)* *(threat, suggestion)* en l'air; *(gossip, rumour)* sans fondement; *(boast)* mal placé; **it is i. to speculate** il est vain de spéculer; **i. talk** paroles *fpl* en l'air, balivernes *fpl*

4 *(casual)* *(glance)* en passant; *(remark)* fait en passant; **out of i. curiosity** par simple curiosité

VI 1 *Aut (of engine)* tourner au ralenti **2** *(be lazy)* fainéanter, musarder
▸▸ **i. capital** capital *m* improductif; **i. period** période *f* d'inactivité; **the i. rich** les riches *mpl* désœuvrés; *Aut* **i. screw** vis *f* de ralenti; *Aut* **i. speed** vitesse *f* *ou* régime *m* de ralenti

▸ **idle away** **VT SEP** *(waste)* **to i. one's time away** passer son temps à ne rien faire; **we idled away the afternoon chatting** nous avons passé l'après-midi à discuter tranquillement

idleness ['aɪd(ə)lnɪs] **N 1** *(of person)* *(inaction)* inaction *f*, désœuvrement *m*; *(laziness)* paresse *f*, fainéantise *f* **2** *(futility)* *(of threat, boast)* futilité *f*

idler ['aɪdlər] **N 1** *(lazy person)* paresseux, -euse **2** *Tech (wheel)* roue *f* folle; *(pulley)* poulie *f* folle

idling ['aɪdlɪŋ] **N 1** *(time-wasting)* fainéantise *f*; **that's more than enough i. for one day** assez fainéanté pour aujourd'hui **2** *(of engine)* (marche *f* au) ralenti *m*
▸▸ **i. speed** *(of engine)* ralenti *m*

idly ['aɪd(ə)lɪ] **ADV 1** *(not working)* sans rien faire, sans travailler; **to stand i. by** rester là à ne rien faire **2** *(lazily)* paresseusement; *(casually)* nonchalamment; **to do sth i.** faire qch pour passer le temps **3** *(futilely)* inutilement; *(to speculate etc)* vainement

idol ['aɪd(ə)l] **N** idole *f*; **to make an i. of wealth** idolâtrer l'argent

idolater, idolatress [aɪ'dɒlətər, -trɪs] **N 1** *Rel* idolâtre *mf* **2** *Fig* adorateur, -trice **(of** de**)**

idolatrous [aɪ'dɒlətrəs] **ADJ** *(worship, beliefs etc)* idolâtre

idolatry [aɪ'dɒlətrɪ] **N** *Rel, Fig* idolâtrie *f*

idolize ['aɪdəlaɪz] **VT** idolâtrer

idolizing ['aɪdəlaɪzɪŋ] **ADJ** plein d'adoration **N** idolâtrie *f*

idyll ['ɪdɪl] **N 1** *(scene)* scène *f* bucolique **2** *(poem)* idylle *f*

Note that the French word **idylle** is rarely a translation for the English word **idyll**. Its most common meaning is **romance**.

idyllic [ɪ'dɪlɪk, aɪ-] **ADJ** idyllique

ie ['aɪ'iː] *(abbr* **id est)** c.-à-d.

IEEE [aɪiːiː'iː] *Comput (abbr* **Institute of Electronic and Electrical Engineers)** IEEE

IF [ɪf] **CONJ 1** si; **if not** sinon; **if he does it, he will be punished** s'il le fait, il sera puni; **let him do it if he dare(s)!** qu'il ose seulement!; **if a child can do it so can I** si un enfant peut le faire, je peux le faire aussi; **if I know Sophie, she won't have done it!** comme *ou* telle que je connais Sophie, elle ne l'aura pas fait!; **if (it is) necessary** s'il le faut, si c'est nécessaire, au besoin; **if (it is) possible** si (c'est) possible; **if (it be) so** s'il en est ainsi; **if so, when?** si oui, quand?; **modifications, if any,** will have to be made later les modifications éventuelles devront être apportées plus tard; **go and see her, if only to please me** allez la voir, ne serait-ce que pour me faire plaisir; **if and when they arrive we will decide what to do** s'ils arrivent et seulement à ce moment-là, nous déciderons ce que nous ferons; **if I were** *or* **was you** si j'étais toi, à ta place; **if it were so** même s'il en était ainsi; **even if he did say so** même s'il a dit cela; **what if I did/she has?** et alors?; **if I had only known!** si seulement j'avais su!; **if only he comes in time!** pourvu qu'il vienne à temps!; **if only!** si seulement!; **as if by chance** comme par hasard; **he looks as if he is drunk** on dirait qu'il est soûl; **he said he would do it – as if!** il a dit qu'il le ferait – mon œil!; **as if I would allow it!** comme si j'allais le permettre! VOIR GRAMMAIRE A52–3; B34 **2** *(concessive)* **pleasant weather, if rather cold** temps agréable, bien qu'un peu froid; **it is well-paid, if uninteresting work** c'est un travail bien payé à défaut d'être intéressant; **if anything it's better/worse** en fait c'est mieux/pire **3** *(introducing a noun clause)* si; **I asked if it was true** j'ai demandé si c'était vrai **4** *(for second occurrence in a clause)* que; **if he agrees and (if) we have time** s'il est d'accord et que nous avons le temps **N** si *m inv*; **the agreement is full of ifs and buts** l'accord n'est qu'une suite de conditions; **if … and it's a very big if, …** si … et il n'y a rien de moins sûr, …

IFA [aɪefˈeɪ] N *(abbr* **independent financial adviser)** conseiller *m* financier indépendant

IFC [aɪefˈsiː] N *(abbr* **inside front cover)** deuxième *f* de couverture

iffy [ˈɪfɪ] ADJ *Fam* **1** *(uncertain) (situation)* aléatoire; **the picnic/project is looking very i.** le pique-nique/projet semble très compromis; **the car's a bit i. these days** la voiture n'est pas très fiable ces jours-ci; **I'm still a bit i. about the whole thing** *(haven't made my mind up)* j'hésite encore; **that sky looks a bit i.** le ciel est un peu menaçant; **the ice is a bit i.** *(on pond)* la glace n'a pas l'air très sûre; **it's still a bit i. but I think I will be going to the conference** je ne suis pas complètement sûr mais je pense que j'irai à la conférence **2** *(suspect) (person, appearance)* louche; **it all sounded rather i.** tout ça m'avait l'air plutôt louche

if-then operation N *Comput* opération *f* 'si-alors'

IGC [aɪdʒiːˈsiː] N *(abbr* **Intergovernmental Conference)** CIG *f*

igloo [ˈɪgluː] N igloo *m*

igneous [ˈɪgnɪəs] ADJ éruptif, igné

ignite [ɪgˈnaɪt] VT *(fuel etc)* enflammer, mettre feu à; *(explosive charge)* allumer; *Fig (situation, conflict)* enflammer **VI** prendre feu, s'enflammer; *Fig (of situation, conflict)* s'enflammer

ignition [ɪgˈnɪʃən] N **1** *Aut* allumage *m*; **to switch off the i.** couper l'allumage; **the key was still in the i.** la clé était encore sur le contact **2** *(of explosive charge etc)* ignition *f* ▸▸ *Aut* **i. cable** fil *m* d'allumage *ou* de bougie; **i. coil** bobine *f* d'allumage; **i. cycle** cycle *m* d'allumage; **i. key** clef *f* de contact; **i. lead** fil d'allumage *ou* de bougie; **i. lock** antivol-contact *m, pl* antivols-contact; **i. spark** étincelle *f* d'allumage; **i. switch** contact *m*; **i. system** circuit *m* d'allumage

ignoble [ɪgˈnəʊb(ə)l] ADJ ignoble, vil

ignominious [ɪgnəˈmɪnɪəs] ADJ ignomi-nieux, honteux

ignominiously [ɪgnəˈmɪnɪəslɪ] ADV igno-minieusement, honteusement

ignominy [ˈɪgnəmɪnɪ] N ignominie *f*, hon-te *f*

ignoramus [ɪgnəˈreɪməs] N ignorant, -ante, ignare *mf*

ignorance [ˈɪgnərəns] N **1** ignorance *f*, **out of** *or* **through i.** par ignorance; **to keep sb in i. of sth** laisser qn dans l'ignorance de qch; **I am in complete i. of his intentions** j'ignore tout de ses intentions; **in a situation like this, i. is bliss** dans ce genre de situation, il vaut mieux ne pas savoir; *Law* **i. of the law is no excuse** nul n'est censé ignorer la loi **2** *(ill manners)* manque *m* d'éducation

ignorant [ˈɪgnərənt] ADJ **1** *(lacking knowledge) (person)* ignorant; *(question, remark)* qui trahit l'ignorance; **to be i. of sth** ignorer qch; *Fml* **he is i. of the world** *(unworldly, naïve)* il ne connaît pas les choses du monde; **i. people like him** des ignorants de son espèce **2** *(ill-mannered) (person, remark)* grossier

> Note that the French word **ignorant** never means **ill-mannered**.

ignorantly [ˈɪgnərəntlɪ] ADV *(to believe)* par ignorance; *(to talk)* avec ignorance

ignore [ɪgˈnɔːr] VT *(take no notice of) (person, instructions)* ignorer; *(facts)* méconnaî-tre; *(letter, invitation)* ne pas répondre à; *(insult)* ne pas relever; *(order, advice)* ne tenir aucun compte de; *(signal, red light)* ne pas respecter; **just i. him!** ne fais pas atten-tion à lui!; **I'll i. that!** *(what you said)* je ferai comme si je n'avais rien entendu!

> Note that the French verb **ignorer** also means **not to know**.

iguana [ɪˈgwɑːnə] N iguane *m*

ikon [ˈaɪkɒn] N *Rel, Comput* icône *f*

ilex [ˈaɪleks] *(pl* **ilexes** [ˈaɪleks, -leksɪz] N ilex *m*

ilium [ˈɪlɪəm] N *Anat* os *m* iliaque

ilk [ɪlk] N **1** *Scot* **Moray of that i.** Moray du domaine de Moray **2** **of that i.** de ce genre, *Pej* de cette espèce

Ill *abbr* **Illinois**

ill¹ [ɪl] ADJ **1** *(unwell)* malade; **to be i.** être malade; **to look i.** avoir mauvaise mine; **to feel i.** ne pas se sentir bien; **it makes me feel i.** ça me rend malade; **to fall** *or* **be taken i.** tomber malade; **he was seriously i. last year** il a été gravement malade l'année dernière; **a very i. woman** une femme très malade **2** *(bad) (repute)* mauvais; *(deed, nature etc)* méchant, mauvais; *Prov* **it's an i. wind that blows nobody any good** à quelque chose malheur est bon; **to be in i. health** ne pas être en bonne santé; **he retired due to i. health** il a pris sa retraite pour raisons de santé; **house of i. repute** maison *f* close; **wo-man of i. repute** femme *f* de mauvaise vie; **he hasn't suffered any i. effects** *(after eating, drinking sth)* il n'a pas été malade; *(from being imprisoned etc)* il n'a pas eu de séquel-les **ADV** mal; *Lit* **to take sth i.** prendre qch en mauvaise part; **to be i. provided with sth** être mal pourvu de qch; **I can i. afford the expense** je peux difficilement me permettre cette dépense; **it i. becomes you to …** il vous sied mal de …, vous êtes mal venu de …; **to be** *or* **feel i. at ease** *(uncomfortable)* être mal à l'aise; *(anxious)* être *ou* se sentir inquiet *(about au sujet de)* **N 1** *(evil)* mal *m*; **to speak/think i. of sb** dire/penser du mal de qn **2** *(wrong)* dommage *m*, tort *m*; **I have suffered no i. at his hands** il ne m'a fait aucun tort **3** *(misfortune)* **ills** maux *mpl*, malheurs *mpl* ▸▸ **i. breeding** manque *m* de savoir-vivre; **i.**

feeling ressentiment *m*, animosité *f*, **i. for-tune, i. luck** malchance *f*, **i. will** malveil-lance *f*

ill² *abbr* **illustration**

I'll [aɪl] CONTR **1** = **I will**, *see* **will²** **2** = **I shall**, *see* **shall**

ill-advised [-ədˈvaɪzd] ADJ *(person)* mala-visé *(* **to do** de faire*)*; *(action)* peu judicieux

ill-assorted ADJ disparate

ill-behaved ADJ qui se conduit *ou* se tient mal

ill-bred [-ˈbred] ADJ mal élevé; **an i. young man** un malappris

ill-concealed ADJ mal dissimulé

ill-considered ADJ *(action, view etc)* peu réfléchi; *(measure etc)* hâtif

ill-defined [-dɪˈfaɪnd] ADJ mal défini

ill-disposed ADJ **1** *(unfriendly, unhelpful)* **to be i. towards sb** être mal disposé envers qn; **to be i. towards an idea/a proposal** ne pas être favorable à une idée/une proposi-tion **2** *(disinclined)* **to be i. to do sth** être peu disposé à faire qch

illegal [ɪˈliːg(ə)l] ADJ illégal, -aux; *(immi-grant)* clandestin; *(parking)* interdit; *Comput (file name, character)* non autorisé; **it is i. to …** il est illégal de … **N** *(illegal immigrant)* immigré, -ée clandes-tin(e)

illegality [ɪlɪˈgælɪtɪ] N illégalité *f*

illegally [ɪˈliːg(ə)lɪ] ADV illégalement

illegible [ɪˈledʒɪb(ə)l] ADJ illisible

illegibly [ɪˈledʒɪblɪ] ADV illisiblement

illegitimacy [ɪlɪˈdʒɪtɪməsɪ] N illégitimité *f*

illegitimate [ɪlɪˈdʒɪtɪmət] ADJ *(child, con-clusion, act)* illégitime

illegitimately [ɪlɪˈdʒɪtɪmətlɪ] ADV illégi-timement

ill-equipped ADJ mal équipé; *Fig* **to be i. to do sth** ne pas être apte à faire qch

ill-fated ADJ *(person)* infortuné; *(day, mis-sion)* fatal, -aux, fatidique; **the i. expedition** l'expédition frappée par le destin

ill-fitting ADJ *(garment, lid, window)* mal ajusté

ill-founded [-ˈfaʊndɪd] ADJ *(rumour)* mal fondé, sans fondement

ill-gotten [-ˈgɒt(ə)n] ADJ ▸▸ **i. gains** biens *mpl* mal acquis *ou* acquis malhonnêtement

ill-humoured, *Am* **ill-humored** [-ˈhjuː-məd] ADJ de mauvaise humeur

illiberal [ɪˈlɪbər(ə)l] ADJ peu libéral, -aux; *(narrow-minded)* borné; *(ungenerous)* peu généreux, mesquin

illiberality [ɪlɪbəˈrælɪtɪ] N *(in opinions)* étroitesse *f* d'esprit; *(lack of generosity)* manque *m* de libéralité

illicit [ɪˈlɪsɪt] ADJ illicite ▸▸ **i. still** alambic *m* clandestin

illicitly [ɪˈlɪsɪtlɪ] ADV illicitement

illimitable [ɪˈlɪmɪtəb(ə)l] ADJ illimité

ill-informed ADJ **1** *(having the wrong infor-mation) (person)* mal renseigné **2** *(having in-sufficient information)* peu informé; **we continue to be i. about their intentions** nous ne sommes toujours pas sûrs de savoir quelles sont leurs intentions; **he made an i. attack on the government** il a attaqué le gouvernement en utilisant des arguments sans fondement

ill-intentioned [-ɪnˈtenʃənd] ADJ malin-tentionné *(* **towards** envers*)*

illiquid [ɪˈlɪkwɪd] ADJ peu liquide ▸▸ *Fin* **i. assets** actif *m* non-disponible *ou* immobilisé

illiquidity [ɪlɪˈkwɪdɪtɪ] N illiquidité *f* ▸▸ *Fin* **i. premium** prime *f* d'illiquidité

illiteracy [ɪ'lɪt(ə)rəsɪ] N analphabétisme m

illiterate [ɪ'lɪt(ə)rət] ADJ **1** (unable to read or write) illettré, analphabète **2** (lacking culture) (person) qui n'a aucune culture; (usage, style) incorrect
▪ N illettré, -ée, analphabète mf

ill-judged [-'dʒʌdʒd] ADJ (action) malavisé, peu sage

ill-mannered ADJ grossier, malappris; **to be i.** être mal élevé

ill-matched ADJ mal assorti

ill-natured [-'neɪtʃəd] ADJ (person) d'un mauvais caractère, désagréable; (remark, criticism etc) désagréable; **to be i.** avoir mauvais caractère

illness ['ɪlnɪs] N maladie f VOIR GRAMMAIRE A7

illogical [ɪ'lɒdʒɪk(ə)l] ADJ illogique

illogicality [ɪlɒdʒɪ'kælɪtɪ] N manque m de logique, illogisme m

illogically [ɪ'lɒdʒɪk(ə)lɪ] ADV sans logique; **the i. ordered universe** l'univers désordonné

ill-prepared ADJ mal préparé

ill-starred ADJ Lit (person) infortuné; (day) malheureux, néfaste

ill-suited [-'suːtɪd] ADJ (couple) mal assorti; **such clothes were i. to a hot climate** ces vêtements n'étaient pas adaptés à un climat chaud; **arts graduates are i. to this job** les diplômés en lettres ne sont pas aptes à ce travail

ill-tempered ADJ (person) (in general) grincheux; (on specific occasion) de mauvaise humeur, grincheux; **to be i.** (in general) avoir mauvais caractère; **why must he always be so i.?** pourquoi faut-il qu'il soit toujours d'aussi mauvaise humeur?

ill-timed [-'taɪmd] ADJ (remark) mal à propos, hors de propos, inopportun; (arrival) inopportun

ill-treat VT (person, dog) maltraiter

ill-treatment N mauvais traitement m

illuminate [ɪ'luːmɪneɪt] VT **1** (room etc) éclairer; (building) illuminer **2** Fig (subject, question) éclairer, élucider **3** Art (manuscript) enluminer

illuminated [ɪ'luːmɪneɪtɪd] ADJ **1** (sign) lumineux **2** Art (manuscript) enluminé

illuminating [ɪ'luːmɪneɪtɪŋ] ADJ (speech, interview) qui éclaire la situation; (comparison, remark, example) éclairant; **the programme was very i.** l'émission m'a appris beaucoup de choses
▪ N **1** (of building) illumination f **2** Art (of manuscript) enluminure f

illumination [ɪluːmɪ'neɪʃən] N **1** (of room etc) éclairage m; (of building) illumination f, esp Br **illuminations** (decorative outdoor lights) illuminations **2** Art (of manuscript) enluminure f **3** Opt (of lens etc) éclat m; Phys (degree of) i. éclairement m **4** Rel etc (enlightenment) illumination f

illuminator [ɪ'luːmɪneɪtər] N Art enlumineur, -euse

illumine [ɪ'luːmɪn] VT Lit illuminer

ill-use¹ [-'juːs] N mauvais traitement m

ill-use² [-'juːz] VT **1** (physically) maltraiter **2** (behave badly towards) ne pas bien traiter; **he feels he's been ill-used** il a le sentiment qu'il n'a pas été bien traité

illusion [ɪ'luːʒən] N illusion f; **to be under the i. that ...** s'imaginer que ...; **I have no illusions or am under no i. on that score** je ne me fais aucune illusion à ce sujet

illusionist [ɪ'luːʒənɪst] N illusionniste mf

illusory [ɪ'luːs(ə)rɪ] ADJ illusoire, trompeur

illustrate ['ɪləstreɪt] VT **1** (book, newspaper) illustrer; **illustrated by Cruikshank** (on title page etc) illustré par ou illustrations de Cruikshank; **illustrated magazine** (journal m ou magazine m) illustré m **2** (explain, give example of) illustrer; **to i. my point** pour illustrer ce que je veux dire; **the lecture will be illustrated by slides** la conférence sera accompagnée de diapositives

illustration [ɪləs'treɪʃən] N **1** (picture) (in book etc) illustration f, gravure f; **illustrations** (in book) iconographie f **2** (publishing process) illustration f; **he works in i.** il est illustrateur **3** Fig (of principle etc) illustration f, exemple m; **to be an i. of sth** illustrer qch; **by way of i.** à titre d'exemple

illustrative ['ɪləstr(ə)tɪv] ADJ illustratif; **this incident is i. of his state of mind** cet incident reflète bien son état d'esprit

illustrator ['ɪləstreɪtər] N illustrateur, -trice

illustrious [ɪ'lʌstrɪəs] ADJ illustre, célèbre

illustriously [ɪ'lʌstrɪəslɪ] ADV de façon illustre

ILO [aɪe'ləʊ] N Ind (abbr International Labour Organization) OIT f

I'm [aɪm] CONTR = **I am**, see **be**

image ['ɪmɪdʒ] N **1** (copy) image f; **God created man in his own i.** Dieu créa l'homme à son image; **he's the (very or living or Fam spitting) i. of his father** c'est le portrait de son père, Fam c'est son père tout craché **2** (representation) portrait m; (sculpture) image f (sculptée); (of god etc) représentation f, statue f; (for worship) idole f **3** (mental picture) image f **4** (of politician, party etc) image f, **its i. is that of a dirty industrial city** cette ville a la réputation d'être une ville industrielle sale; **he/it needs a bit of i. building** il a besoin de rehausser un peu son image de marque; **the company is suffering from an i. problem** l'entreprise a un problème d'image **5** Liter image f, métaphore f **6** Comput, Opt image f
▸▸ Comput **i. bank** banque f d'images; Phys **i. converter** convertisseur m d'image(s); Electron, TV **i. distortion** distorsion f d'image; Comput **i. editing** édition f d'images; Comput **i. editing program, i. editor** logiciel m d'édition d'images, éditeur m d'images; Opt, Phot **i. enhancement** correction f de l'image, retouche f d'images; Opt, Phot **i. enhancer** correcteur m d'images; Comput **i. file** fichier m vidéo ou image; Comput **i. format** format m graphique; Comput **i. manipulation** manipulation f d'images; Comput **i. map** image cliquable; Mktg **i. pricing** fixation f de prix en fonction de l'image; Comput **i. processing** traitement m des images; Comput **i. processor** unité f de traitement d'images; **i. refresh rate** taux m de rafraîchissement d'images

image-conscious ADJ qui se soucie de son image

image-maker N Mktg responsable mf des relations publiques

imager ['ɪmɪdʒər] N Comput imageur m

imagery ['ɪmɪdʒ(ə)rɪ] N Liter, Cin images fpl

imagesetter ['ɪmɪdʒsetər] N Typ photocomposeuse f

imaginable [ɪ'mædʒɪnəb(ə)l] ADJ imaginable; **the finest thing i.** la plus belle chose qu'on puisse imaginer

imaginary [ɪ'mædʒɪn(ə)rɪ] ADJ imaginaire

imagination [ɪmædʒɪ'neɪʃən] N imagination f, **to have no i.** n'avoir aucune imagination; **it's your i.!** tu te fais des idées!; **use your i.!** fais preuve d'un peu d'imagination!; **it's all in your i.** tout ça c'est dans ta tête

imaginative [ɪ'mædʒɪnətɪv] ADJ (person, story etc) imaginatif; (solution, excuse, reason) plein d'imagination

imaginativeness [ɪ'mædʒɪnətɪvnɪs] N (of person) imagination f, esprit m inventif; (of story, solution, reason, excuse etc) caractère m imaginatif

imagine [ɪ'mædʒɪn] VT **1** (picture in one's mind) imaginer; **I can just i. her saying/doing that** je la vois très bien dire/faire ça; **I just can't i. you in that hat** je ne t'imagine ou te vois pas du tout avec ce chapeau; **I can't i. living anywhere else** je n'imagine pas vivre ailleurs; **to be always imagining things** se faire des idées; **I was beginning to i. all sorts of things!** je commençais à m'imaginer des tas de choses; **you're imagining things** tu rêves; **that child is always imagining things** c'est un enfant très imaginatif; **you must have imagined it** tu as dû rêver; **as may (well) be imagined** comme on peut (se) l'imaginer; Fam **i. meeting you here!** ça alors, toi ici!; **just i. my despair** tu imagines à quel point j'étais désespéré; **you can't i. it!** vous n'avez pas idée!; **well, what did you i.?** qu'est-ce tu croyais?, qu'est-ce que tu t'imaginais?
2 (suppose) imaginer; **I i. them to be fairly rich** j'imagine qu'ils sont assez riches; **don't i. that I'm satisfied** n'allez pas croire que je sois satisfait; **I i. that you must be very tired** j'imagine ou je suppose que vous devez être fatigué
▪ VI **he ate all of it, can you i.?** il a tout mangé, tu t'imagines?; **I can i.** je veux bien le croire!, j'imagine!

imagined [ɪ'mædʒɪnd] ADJ imaginé, imaginaire

imaging device ['ɪmɪdʒɪŋ] N Comput imageur m

imaginings [ɪ'mædʒɪnɪŋz] NPL **the i. of a fevered mind** les élucubrations d'un esprit enfiévré

imam [ɪ'mɑːm] N imam m

IMAX® ['aɪmæks] N (procédé m) Imax m
▸▸ **I. cinema** cinéma m Imax

imbalance [ɪm'bæləns] N déséquilibre m

imbecile ['ɪmbɪsiːl] N Med, Old-fashioned, Fam imbécile mf
▪ ADJ ATTRIB imbécile

imbecilic [ɪmbɪ'sɪlɪk] ADJ imbécile

imbecility [ɪmbɪ'sɪlɪtɪ] N **1** Fam (stupidity) stupidité f, imbécillité f **2** Med Old-fashioned imbécillité f

imbibe [ɪm'baɪb] VT Fml (of person) (knowledge, ideas) absorber, assimiler; (drink) boire, avaler; **to i. the atmosphere** s'imprégner de l'atmosphère
▪ VI Fam Hum boire trop, Fam picoler

imbroglio [ɪm'brəʊlɪəʊ] N Lit imbroglio m

imbue [ɪm'bjuː] VT Lit (person) imprégner (**with an idea** d'une idée); **to be imbued with melancholy/hope** (of novel etc) être empreint de mélancolie/d'espoir

IMF [aɪem'ef] N Econ (abbr International Monetary Fund) FMI m

imitable ['ɪmɪtəb(ə)l] ADJ imitable

imitate ['ɪmɪteɪt] VT **1** (copy) (person) imiter, copier; **to i. sb's style** imiter le style de qn **2** (mimic) (person) singer, mimer; (call of bird etc) imiter; **to i. its surroundings** (of insect etc) prendre l'aspect de son milieu

imitation [ɪmɪ'teɪʃən] N **1** (action) imitation f, **in i. of sb/sth** à l'imitation de ou imitant qn/qch; Prov **i. is the sincerest form of flattery** l'imitation est la flatterie la plus sincère qui soit **2** (copy) copie f, imitation f; Com imitation; **beware of imitations** méfiez-vous des contrefaçons; **in i. marble/crocodile skin** en imitation marbre/crocodile
▸▸ **i. jewellery** bijoux mpl (de) fantaisie; **i. leather** imitation f cuir, similicuir m; **i. pearls** fausses perles fpl

imitative ['ɪmɪtətɪv] ADJ (sound etc) imitatif; **manner/style i. of sb** manière f/style m qui imite qn

▸▸*Mktg* **i. product** produit m d'imitation

imitator [ˈɪmɪteɪtər] N *(copier)* imitateur, -trice; **the Beatles had their imitators** les Beatles ont eu des imitateurs

immaculate [ɪˈmækjʊlət] ADJ **1** *(dress, desk, room)* impeccable; *Lit (snow, white)* immaculé; *Fig* **her attendance record is i.** elle n'a pas été absente une seule fois **2** *(morally pure) (reputation)* sans tache

▸▸*Rel* **the I. Conception** l'Immaculée Conception f

immaculately [ɪˈmækjʊlətlɪ] ADV *(dressed)* impeccablement; **the children behaved i.** les enfants se sont admirablement bien tenus

immanent [ˈɪmənənt] ADJ *Phil* immanent

immaterial [ɪməˈtɪərɪəl] ADJ **1** *(unimportant, irrelevant)* sans importance; **that fact is (quite) i.** cela n'a aucune importance **2** *(ghost etc)* immatériel, incorporel

immature [ɪməˈtjʊər] ADJ **1** *(young, undeveloped) Biol* immature; *(fruit etc)* (qui n'est) pas mûr **2** *(childish)* immature, qui manque de maturité; **stop being so i.!** arrête de te comporter comme un gamin!; **i. work** œuvre f de jeunesse ou d'apprenti

immaturity [ɪməˈtjʊərɪtɪ] N **1** *(youth, lack of development) (of person), Biol* immaturité f **2** *(childishness)* immaturité f, manque m de maturité; *(of work of art)* manque de maturité

immeasurable [ɪˈmeʒərəb(ə)l] ADJ *(space, complexity etc)* incommensurable; *(time)* infini; **to have an i. influence on sth** avoir une influence énorme sur qch

immeasurably [ɪˈmeʒərəblɪ] ADV *(difficult, painful, bad)* extrêmement, *Lit* incommensurablement; **she influenced her contemporaries i.** elle a énormément influencé ses contemporains

immediacy [ɪˈmiːdɪəsɪ] N caractère m immédiat *(of* de); *(of danger)* imminence f, *(of need)* urgence f

immediate [ɪˈmiːdɪət] ADJ **1** *(urgent, imminent) (need)* pressant, urgent; *(danger)* imminent; **my i. objective** mon objectif premier; **what are your i. plans?** que proposez-vous de faire d'abord?; **I have no i. plans to retire** je n'ai pas l'intention de prendre ma retraite dans un futur proche **2** *(instant) (answer, delivery etc)* immédiat; **house for sale with i. possession** maison à vendre avec jouissance immédiate **3** *(closest) (neighbour, surroundings)* immédiat, proche; **the i. family** les proches parents; **in the i. future** dans un avenir immédiat

immediately [ɪˈmiːdɪətlɪ] ADV **1** *(without delay)* immédiatement, tout de suite; **he is i. recognizable** on le reconnaît immédiatement ou tout de suite; **the distinction isn't i. obvious** la distinction n'est pas évidente tout de suite; **please send … i.** veuillez (bien) envoyer immédiatement ou d'urgence …; **i. after** aussitôt après **2** *(directly)* immédiatement, directement; **it does not affect me i.** cela ne me touche pas directement **3** *(in space)* juste; **i. after the traffic lights** juste après le feu

CONJ *Br* dès que; **i. I saw her I knew …** dès que je l'ai vue j'ai su que …

immemorial [ɪmɪˈmɔːrɪəl] ADJ *Lit* immémorial, -aux; **from time i.** depuis des temps immémoriaux

immense [ɪˈmens] ADJ *(expanse, success, satisfaction etc)* immense; *(quantity)* énorme; **of i. size** de taille immense

immensely [ɪˈmenslɪ] ADV *(large, rich)* immensément; *(to enjoy oneself)* énormément; **to be i. successful** avoir énormément

de succès; **i. entertaining** extrêmement divertissant; **she is i. fat** elle est absolument énorme

immensity [ɪˈmensɪtɪ] N **1** *(of universe, fortune etc)* immensité f **2** *(of problem, task)* énormité f

immerse [ɪˈmɜːs] VT **1** *(in liquid)* plonger; *Rel* baptiser par immersion **2 to i. oneself in sth** *(become absorbed by)* se plonger dans qch; **to be immersed in one's work/thoughts** être plongé ou absorbé dans son travail/ses pensées

immersion [ɪˈmɜːʃən] N **1** *(in liquid)* immersion f; *Rel* baptême m par immersion **2** *(mental)* absorption f *(in* dans); **to learn a language by i.** apprendre une langue par immersion

▸▸**i. course** cours m de langue intensif *(dans lequel seule la langue apprise est utilisée)*; **i. heater** chauffe-eau m inv à immersion

immigrant [ˈɪmɪgrənt] ADJ, N *(in the process of emigrating)* immigrant, -ante; *(who has emigrated)* immigré, -ée; **i. families** familles fpl immigrées

▸▸**i. worker** travailleur m immigré

immigrate [ˈɪmɪgreɪt] VI immigrer

immigration [ɪmɪˈgreɪʃən] N immigration f; **to go through i.** *(at port, airport etc)* passer à l'immigration

▸▸**i. control** contrôle m de l'immigration; **i. department** service m de l'immigration; **i. laws** lois fpl sur l'immigration; **i. officer** agent m du service de l'immigration; **i. quotas** quotas mpl d'immigration

imminence [ˈɪmɪnəns] N imminence f *(of* de)

imminent [ˈɪmɪnənt] ADJ *(danger, disaster, arrival etc)* imminent

immobile [ɪˈməʊbaɪl] ADJ immobile

immobility [ɪməˈbɪlɪtɪ] N immobilité f

immobilize [ɪˈməʊbɪlaɪz] VT *(wounded limb, traffic etc), Fin* immobiliser

immobilizer [ɪˈməʊbɪlaɪzər] N *(for vehicle)* antidémarrage m codé

immoderate [ɪˈmɒd(ə)rət] ADJ *(drinking)* immodéré; *(feeling, attitude, display of grief)* exagéré, excessif; *(behaviour)* excessif; *(thirst)* anormal, -aux; *(gaiety)* exagéré

immoderately [ɪˈmɒd(ə)rətlɪ] ADV immodérément

immodest [ɪˈmɒdɪst] ADJ **1** *(indecent) (person, dress, behaviour)* impudique **2** *(vain)* présomptueux

immodestly [ɪˈmɒdɪstlɪ] ADV **1** *(indecently)* impudiquement **2** *(vainly)* présomptueusement

immolate [ˈɪməʊleɪt] VT *Lit* immoler

immoral [ɪˈmɒrəl] ADJ immoral, -aux; *(novel etc)* contraire à la morale; *Law* **for i. purposes** aux fins de débauche; *Law* **living on i. earnings** *(of pimp)* proxénétisme m

immorality [ɪməˈrælɪtɪ] N immoralité f, *(sexual)* débauche f

immorally [ɪˈmɒrəlɪ] ADV immoralement, de façon immorale

immortal [ɪˈmɔːt(ə)l] ADJ immortel; **the i. memory of …** le souvenir impérissable de …

N immortel, -elle

immortality [ɪmɔːˈtælɪtɪ] N immortalité f

immortalize [ɪˈmɔːtəlaɪz] VT *(person, author's name, sb's memory etc)* immortaliser

immovable [ɪˈmuːvəb(ə)l] ADJ *(object)* (qui est) impossible à déplacer; *Fig (opposition)* inébranlable; *(person)* inflexible; *Fig* **they were i.** ils sont restés inflexibles

NPL *Law* **immovables** immeubles mpl; biens mpl immobiliers

▸▸*Rel* **i. feast** fête f fixe; *Law* **i. property** biens immeubles ou immobiliers

immune [ɪˈmjuːn] ADJ **1** *Med* immunisé (**to** contre) **2** *Fig* **i. to criticism** imperméable à la critique; **no-one was i. from criticism** personne n'a échappé aux critiques; **i. from taxation** exempt d'impôts; **i. from prosecution** à l'abri de poursuites judiciaires

▸▸*Med* **i. deficiency** immunodéficience f; *Physiol* **i. system** système m immunitaire

immunity [ɪˈmjuːnɪtɪ] N **1** *Med* immunité f (**to** contre) **2** *(exemption)* exemption f (**from** de); **they were guaranteed i. from prosecution** on leur a assuré qu'ils seraient à l'abri de poursuites judiciaires

immunization [ɪmjʊnaɪˈzeɪʃən] N *Med* immunisation f (**against** contre)

immunize [ˈɪmjʊnaɪz] VT *Med* immuniser (**against** contre)

immunodeficiency [ɪmjʊnəʊdɪˈfɪʃənsɪ] N *Med* immunodéficience f

immunoglobulin [ɪmjʊnəʊˈglɒbjʊlɪn] N *Med* immunoglobuline f

immunological [ɪmjʊnəʊˈlɒdʒɪk(ə)l] ADJ *Med* immunologique

immunology [ɪmjʊˈnɒlədʒɪ] N *Med* immunologie f

immunosuppressant [ɪmjʊnəʊsəˈpresənt] N *Med* immunosuppresseur m

immunosuppression [ɪmjʊnəʊsəˈpreʃən] N *Med* immunosuppression f

immunosuppressive [ɪmjʊnəʊsəˈpresɪv] ADJ *Med* immunosuppresseur

immunotherapy [ɪmjʊnəʊˈθerəpɪ] N *Med* immunothérapie f

immure [ɪˈmjʊər] VT *Arch, Lit* **1** *(shut away) (person)* enfermer, cloîtrer; **he had immured himself in the library** il s'était enfermé dans la bibliothèque; **immured in silence** cloîtré dans le silence **2** *(wall up) (victim)* emmurer

immutability [ɪmjuːtəˈbɪlɪtɪ] N *Fml* immutabilité f, caractère m immuable

immutable [ɪˈmjuːtəb(ə)l] ADJ immuable

immutably [ɪˈmjuːtəblɪ] ADV immuablement

imp [ɪmp] N diablotin m, lutin m; *Fam* **(little) i.** *(boy)* petit garnement m, galopin m; *(girl)* petite coquine f

impact [ˈɪmpækt] N **1** *(shock)* choc m; *(of bullet)* impact m; **on i.** *(of projectile)* au moment de l'impact **2** *Fig (of speech, play, advertising campaign etc)* impact m; **the play has lost none of its i.** la pièce n'a pas du tout perdu de son impact; **he seems to have made quite an i. on you** il semble avait fait une forte impression sur vous

▸▸*Br* **i. adhesive** colle f instantanée; *Aut* **i. bar** barre f de renfort; *St Exch* **i. day** = jour m où l'on annonce une nouvelle émission d'actions; *Comput* **i. printer** imprimante f à impact; *Aut* **i. test** essai m au choc

▸ **impact on** VT INSEP *(trade figures, section of population etc)* avoir un impact sur, affecter

impacted [ɪmˈpæktɪd] ADJ *Surg (fracture)* avec impaction ou incongruence

▸▸**i. tooth** dent f barrée

impair [ɪmˈpeər] VT *(sight, hearing, mental faculties)* affaiblir; *(strength)* faire perdre, diminuer; *(relations, person's authority, chances)* compromettre; **his health has been (seriously) impaired by the expedition** sa santé s'est (gravement) détériorée à la suite de l'expédition

impairment [ɪmˈpeəmənt] N *(of sight, hearing, memory)* affaiblissement m; *(of health, relations)* dégradation f, *(of strength)* diminution f, **without i. of quality** sans perte de qualité

impala [ɪmˈpɑːlə] N *(antelope)* impala m

impale [ɪm'peɪl] **VT** empaler; **to be impaled** *(on railings etc)* être empalé, s'empaler

impalpable [ɪm'pælpəb(ə)l] **ADJ 1** *(intangible)* impalpable, intangible **2** *(to the mind)* insaisissable

impanel [ɪm'pænəl] **VT** = **empanel**

impart [ɪm'pɑːt] **VT** *Fml* **1** *(lend) (courage etc)* donner; *(movement)* imprimer, communiquer (**to** à); *(heat, light)* transmettre **2** *(transmit) (knowledge)* communiquer; *(news)* faire connaître, annoncer; *(secret)* confier; *(truth)* transmettre (**to** à)

impartial [ɪm'pɑːʃəl] **ADJ** *(person, conduct)* impartial, -aux (**towards** envers); **to be i.** être impartial *ou* équitable

impartiality [ɪmpɑːʃɪ'ælɪtɪ] **N** impartialité *f* (**towards** envers)

impartially [ɪm'pɑːʃəlɪ] **ADV** impartialement, avec impartialité; *(to judge)* équitablement

impassable [ɪm'pɑːsəb(ə)l] **ADJ** *(river, barrier, pass)* infranchissable; *(road)* impraticable

impasse ['æmpɑːs] **N** impasse *f*, **we have reached an i.** nous sommes dans une *ou* l'impasse

impassioned [ɪm'pæʃənd] **ADJ** *(orator, speech, defence etc)* passionné, *(style)* chaleureux

impassive [ɪm'pæsɪv] **ADJ** *(person, face)* impassible

impassively [ɪm'pæsɪvlɪ] **ADV** impassiblement

impatience [ɪm'peɪʃəns] **N** impatience *f* (**to do** de faire); **i. to leave** hâte *f* de partir; **there was a note of i. in his voice** on sentait l'impatience dans sa voix; *Fml* **he was known for his i. of sloppy work** il avait la réputation de mal supporter le travail brouillon

impatient [ɪm'peɪʃənt] **ADJ** *(person, tone)* impatient; *(reply)* vif, emporté; **to get** *or* **grow i.** s'impatienter; **to get i. with sb** s'impatienter contre qn; **I am getting so i. with this photocopier!** je perds complètement patience avec cette photocopieuse!; **to be i. for change/reform** avoir soif de changement/réforme; **to be i. to do sth** être impatient *ou* brûler de faire qch; *Lit* **he was i. of those less intelligent than himself** il supportait mal ceux qui étaient moins intelligents que lui

impatiently [ɪm'peɪʃəntlɪ] **ADV** *(to wait)* avec impatience; *(to answer)* sur un ton *ou* d'un ton d'impatience

impeach [ɪm'piːtʃ] **VT 1** *Law (accuse)* accuser (**of** *or* **with a crime** d'un crime); *Br* **to i. sb for high treason** inculper qn pour haute trahison; *Am* **to i. a public official** = mettre un haut fonctionnaire en accusation devant le Congrès **2** *Fml (call into question) (truth, sb's integrity)* attaquer, mettre en doute; *Law (witness)* récuser, reprocher; *(evidence)* révoquer

impeachable [ɪm'piːtʃəb(ə)l] **ADJ** *Am Law* = passible d'une mise en accusation devant le Congrès

impeachment [ɪm'piːtʃmənt] **N** *Law (of minister etc)* mise *f* en accusation; *Am* impeachment *m*

impeccable [ɪm'pekəb(ə)l] **ADJ** *(house, room etc)* impeccable; *Fig (conduct, management, manners)* irréprochable; **he speaks i. English** il parle un anglais impeccable

impeccably [ɪm'pekəblɪ] **ADV** *(to behave)* irréprochablement; *(dressed)* impeccablement

impecunious [ɪmpɪ'kjuːnɪəs] **ADJ** *Fml* impécunieux

impedance [ɪm'piːdəns] **N** *Elec* impédance *f*

impede [ɪm'piːd] **VT** *(progress, activity, sb's efforts etc)* entraver, gêner; *(traffic)* gêner; **to i. the enemy's movements** gêner les déplacements de l'ennemi; **she was impeded by her skirt** sa jupe entravait ses mouvements

impediment [ɪm'pedɪmənt] **N** obstacle *m* (**to** à); **speech i.** défaut *m* de prononciation

impedimenta [ɪmpedɪ'mentə] **NPL** *Mil, Fig* impedimenta *mpl*

impel [ɪm'pel] **VT** (**-ll-**) **1** *(motivate, oblige)* obliger, forcer (**sb to do sth** qn à faire qch) **2** *(push)* projeter (en avant)

impeller [ɪm'pelər] **N** *Tech* rotor *m*; *(of water pump)* turbine *f*, *(of converter)* roue *f* pompe

impending [ɪm'pendɪŋ] **ADJ** *(danger, arrival, downfall etc)* imminent

impenetrability [ɪmpenɪtrə'bɪlɪtɪ] **N** impénétrabilité *f*

impenetrable [ɪm'penɪtrəb(ə)l] **ADJ** *(defences, mystery, mist)* impénétrable; *(jargon)* incompréhensible

impenitence [ɪm'penɪtəns] **N** *Fml* impénitence *f*

impenitent [ɪm'penɪtənt] **ADJ, N** *Fml* impénitent, -ente

impenitently [ɪm'penɪtəntlɪ] **ADV** sans repentir

imperative [ɪm'perətɪv] **ADJ 1** *(need etc)* urgent; **it is i. that he should come** il est impératif qu'il vienne **2** *(tone)* impérieux, péremptoire **3** *Gram (mood)* impératif **N** *Gram* (mode *m*) impératif *m*; **in the i.** à l'impératif VOIR GRAMMAIRE A40; B34–5

imperceptible [ɪmpə'septɪb(ə)l] **ADJ** *(movement, difference, improvement etc)* imperceptible; *(sound, difference)* insaisissable

imperceptibly [ɪmpə'septɪblɪ] **ADV** imperceptiblement

imperfect [ɪm'pɜːfɪkt] **ADJ 1** *(not perfect)* imparfait; *Com (goods)* qui a un défaut; **it's slightly i.** *(of item for sale)* il a un léger défaut **2** *Gram (tense)* imparfait **N** *Gram* imparfait *m*; **verb in the i.** verbe *m* à l'imparfait SEE GRAMMAR B30

imperfection [ɪmpə'fekʃən] **N 1** *(flaw)* imperfection *f*, défectuosité *f* **2** *(state of being imperfect)* caractère *m* imparfait

imperfectly [ɪm'pɜːfɪktlɪ] **ADV** imparfaitement

imperial [ɪm'pɪərɪəl] **ADJ 1** *(government, crown etc)* impérial, -aux; **His/Her I. Majesty** Sa Majesté Impériale **2** *Br (weights and measures)* = relatif au système de mesure utilisé traditionellement dans les pays anglo-saxons **3** *(commanding)* majestueux, altier

imperialism [ɪm'pɪərɪəlɪz(ə)m] **N** impérialisme *m*

imperialist [ɪm'pɪərɪəlɪst] **ADJ, N** impérialiste *mf*

imperialistic [ɪmpɪərɪə'lɪstɪk] **ADJ** impérialiste

imperially [ɪm'pɪərɪəlɪ] **ADV 1** *Pol* impérialement **2** *(in a commanding manner)* impérieusement

imperil [ɪm'perɪl] **VT** (**-ll-**, *Am* **-l-**) *(sb's life etc)* mettre en danger; *(one's reputation)* compromettre

imperious [ɪm'pɪərɪəs] **ADJ** *(person, tone, character)* impérieux, dictatorial, -aux

imperiously [ɪm'pɪərɪəslɪ] **ADV** *(to speak, act)* impérieusement

imperishable [ɪm'perɪʃəb(ə)l] **ADJ** impérissable

impermanent [ɪm'pɜːmənənt] **ADJ** impermanent

impermeable [ɪm'pɜːmɪəb(ə)l] **ADJ** imperméable

impersonal [ɪm'pɜːsən(ə)l] **ADJ 1** *(style etc)* impersonnel **2** *Gram (verb)* impersonnel SEE GRAMMAR B29–30
▸▸ *Fin* **i. accounts** comptes *mpl* impersonnels

impersonally [ɪm'pɜːsən(ə)lɪ] **ADV** impersonnellement, de façon impersonnelle

impersonate [ɪm'pɜːsəneɪt] **VT** *(pretend to be)* se faire passer pour; *Theat, TV etc (imitate)* imiter

impersonation [ɪmpɜːsə'neɪʃən] **N** *(pretence of being)* usurpation *f* d'identité (**of** de); *Theat, TV etc (imitation)* imitation *f*; **to do an i. of sb** imiter qn

impersonator [ɪm'pɜːsəneɪtər] **N** *(imposter)* imposteur *m*; *Theat, TV etc (mimic)* imitateur, -trice

impertinence [ɪm'pɜːtɪnəns] **N** impertinence *f*, insolence *f*; **an i., a piece of i.** une impertinence

impertinent [ɪm'pɜːtɪnənt] **ADJ 1** *(person, remark)* impertinent, insolent (**to sb** envers qn) **2** *esp Jur (not relevant)* non pertinent

impertinently [ɪm'pɜːtɪnəntlɪ] **ADV 1** *(to say, look at sb)* de façon impertinente, impertinemment **2** *esp Jur* de façon non pertinente

imperturbable [ɪmpə'tɜːbəb(ə)l] **ADJ** imperturbable

impervious [ɪm'pɜːvɪəs] **ADJ 1** insensible (**to criticism** à la critique); **she is i. to reason** on ne peut pas la raisonner **2** *(material etc)* **to be i. to light/water** ne pas laisser passer la lumière/être imperméable

impetigo [ɪmpɪ'taɪɡəʊ] **N** *Med* impétigo *m*; **to have i.** avoir un impétigo

impetuosity [ɪmpetjʊ'ɒsɪtɪ] **N** = **impetuousness**

impetuous [ɪm'petjʊəs] **ADJ** *(person, character, action)* impétueux; *(decision)* hâtif

impetuously [ɪm'petjʊəslɪ] **ADV** impétueusement, avec impétuosité

impetuousness [ɪm'petjʊəsnɪs] **N** *(of person, action)* impétuosité *f*

impetus ['ɪmpɪtəs] **N 1** élan *m*; **to give an i. to sth** donner de l'élan à qch; **to gain i.** prendre *ou* gagner de l'importance; **to lose i.** perdre de son élan **2** *Phys* vitesse *f* acquise

impiety [ɪm'paɪətɪ] **N** impiété *f*

▸**impinge on** [ɪm'pɪndʒ] **VT INSEP 1** *(affect)* affecter; **it impinges in a big way on all our lives** ça affecte énormément notre vie à tous; **to i. on sb's conscious mind** venir à la conscience de qn; **it didn't even i. on his consciousness** il ne s'en est même pas rendu compte; **in so far as it impinges on our department** dans la mesure où cela affecte *ou* a des répercussions sur notre service **2** *(infringe on) (sb's rights etc)* empiéter sur

impingement [ɪm'pɪndʒmənt] **N** *(on sb's rights etc)* empiètement *m*

impious ['ɪmpɪəs] **ADJ** impie

impiously ['ɪmpɪəslɪ] **ADV** avec impiété

impish ['ɪmpɪʃ] **ADJ** *(laughter, face)* de petit diable, d'espiègle; *(child, remark)* espiègle, malicieux

impishly ['ɪmpɪʃlɪ] **ADV** comme un petit diable

impishness ['ɪmpɪʃnɪs] **N** espièglerie *f*

implacable [ɪm'plækəb(ə)l] **ADJ** implacable (**towards** à, pour, à l'égard de)

implacably [ɪm'plækəblɪ] **ADV** implacablement

implant¹ ['ɪmplɑːnt] **N** *Surg* implant *m*

implant² [ɪm'plɑːnt] **VT 1** *(insert), Surg* implanter (**in** dans) **2** *Fig (opinion, principle)* inculquer (**in sb** à qn); *(idea)* implanter (**in sb** dans la tête de qn); **from his youth this**

ideal had been implanted in his mind dès sa jeunesse cet idéal lui avait été inculqué

implausible [ɪmˈplɔːzɪb(ə)l] **ADJ** peu plausible, invraisemblable

implausibly [ɪmˈplɔːzɪblɪ] **ADV** invraisemblablement; **to end i.** *(of book, film etc)* se terminer de façon peu vraisemblable

implement¹ [ˈɪmplɪmənt] **N** outil *m*, instrument *m*; **gardening implements** outils de jardinage; **kitchen implements** ustensiles *mpl* de cuisine

implement² [ˈɪmplɪmənt] **VT** *(treaty, plan, agreement, technique, decision)* mettre en application; *(promise)* exécuter; *(change)* introduire

implementation [ɪmplɪmenˈteɪʃən] **N** *(of treaty, plan, agreement, technique, decision)* mise *f* en œuvre; *(of promise)* exécution *f*; *(of change)* introduction *f*
▸▸ *Mktg* **i. stage** *(of product development)* phase *f* de mise en œuvre

implicate [ˈɪmplɪkeɪt] **VT 1** impliquer, mêler (**sb in a crime** qn dans un crime); **without implicating anyone** sans compromettre personne **2** *Fml (imply)* impliquer, renfermer

implication [ɪmplɪˈkeɪʃən] **N** implication *f*; **by i.** implicitement; **the full i. of what he said was not lost on us** nous avons tout de suite vu ce que ses paroles impliquaient

implicit [ɪmˈplɪsɪt] **ADJ 1** *(implied) (condition, meaning etc)* implicite; *(recognition)* tacite **2** *(absolute) (obedience)* absolu; **i. faith** confiance *f* aveugle (**in** dans)

implicitly [ɪmˈplɪsɪtlɪ] **ADV 1** implicitement; **to i. recognize a country** reconnaître un pays de manière tacite **2** *(absolutely) (to obey)* aveuglément; **to trust sb i.** faire totalement confiance à qn

implied [ɪmˈplaɪd] **ADJ** implicite; **i. meaning** sous-entendu *m*, *pl* sous-entendus

implode [ɪmˈpləʊd] **VI** imploser

implore [ɪmˈplɔːr] **VT** *(person)* implorer, supplier (**to do sth** de faire qch); *(forgiveness)* implorer

imploring [ɪmˈplɔːrɪŋ] **ADJ** *(look, tone)* implorant, suppliant

imploringly [ɪmˈplɔːrɪŋlɪ] **ADV** *(to say)* d'un ton suppliant; *(to look at sb)* d'un air suppliant

implosion [ɪmˈpləʊʒən] **N** implosion *f*

imply [ɪmˈplaɪ] **VT 1** *(of person)* sous-entendre; **you seem to i. that ...** ce que vous dites laisse supposer que ...; **are you implying that I stole the money?** est-ce que tu sous-entends que j'ai volé l'argent?; **your silence implies that you are guilty** votre silence laisse à penser que vous êtes coupable **2** *(of circumstance) (presuppose)* impliquer; **the new deadline implies a lot of hard work** les nouvelles échéances impliquent qu'il va falloir travailler dur

impolite [ɪmpəˈlaɪt] **ADJ** impoli (**to, towards** envers)

impolitely [ɪmpəˈlaɪtlɪ] **ADV** impoliment

impoliteness [ɪmpəˈlaɪtnɪs] **N** impolitesse *f*

impolitic [ɪmˈpɒlɪtɪk] **ADJ** peu judicieux

imponderability [ɪmpɒndərəˈbɪlɪtɪ] **N** pondérabilité *f*

imponderable [ɪmˈpɒndərəb(ə)l] **ADJ** *(reasons, motives)* impondérable
N impondérable *m*

import¹ [ˈɪmpɔːt] **N 1** *Com (item)* article *m* d'importation, importation *f*; *(activity)* importation; **i. and export** l'importation et l'exportation *f*; **imports** importations *f*; *Fig* **the art of lacemaking was an i. from France** l'art de la (fabrication de la) dentelle nous est venu de France **2** *Fml (meaning) (of word)*

sens *m*, signification *f*; *(of document etc)* teneur *f* **3** *Fml (importance) (of event, discovery)* importance *f*; *(of remark)* portée *f*; **a matter of great i.** une affaire de première importance
▸▸ **i. agent** commissionnaire *mf* importateur(trice), agent *m* importateur; **i. ban** interdiction *f* d'importation; **to impose an i. ban on sth** interdire qch d'importation; **i. bonus** prime *f* d'importation; **i. controls** contrôles *mpl* à l'importation; **i. duty** droit *m* d'entrée, taxe *f* d'importation; **i. goods** marchandises *fpl* à l'import; **i. licence** licence *f* d'importation; **i. list** liste *f* des importations; *(of prices)* tarif *m* d'entrée; **i. permit** permis *m* d'importer, permis d'importation; **i. price** prix *m* à l'importation, prix (à l')import; **i. quotas** contingents *mpl* d'importation; **i. restrictions** restrictions *fpl* à l'importation; **i. tariff** tarif *m* import; **i. trade** commerce *m* d'importation; **i. wholesaler** grossiste *m* importateur

import² [ɪmˈpɔːt] **VT 1** *Com (goods)* importer (**from** de); **imported goods** marchandises *fpl* importées *ou* d'importation **2** *Comput* importer (**from** depuis) **3** *Fml (mean)* signifier, vouloir dire

importance [ɪmˈpɔːtəns] **N** importance *f*; **to be of i.** avoir de l'importance; **of vital/strategic i.** d'une importance capitale/stratégique; **it is of the utmost i. to remember that ...** il est absolument essentiel de se rappeler que ...; **it is of no great i.** cela importe peu; **a detail of no i.** un détail sans importance; **to attach i. to sth** mettre *ou* attacher de l'importance à qch; *Pej* **to be full of one's own i.** être imbu de sa personne; *Mktg* **i.-performance analysis** analyse *f* importance-performance

important [ɪmˈpɔːtənt] **ADJ** important; *(difference)* considérable; **what is more i.?** qu'est-ce qui est le plus important?; **to become i.** *(of issue, nation etc)* prendre de l'importance; **it is i. to know that ...** il est important de savoir que ...; **it is i. for you to know that ..., it is i. that you should know that ...** il est important que vous sachiez que ...; **his children/hobbies are very i. to him** ses enfants/passe-temps sont très importants pour lui; *Pej* **he was trying to look i.** il essayait de se donner l'air important

importantly [ɪmˈpɔːtəntlɪ] **ADV** *(to look at)* d'un air important; *(to say)* d'un ton important; **but, more i. ...** mais, ce qui est plus important ...

importation [ɪmpɔːˈteɪʃən] **N 1** *(of goods)* importation *f* **2** *(imported article)* importation *f*, article *m* d'importation **3** *Comput* importation *f*

importer [ɪmˈpɔːtər] **N** *(person)* importateur, -trice; *(country)* pays *m* importateur; **an oil i.** un pays importateur de pétrole; **Japan is still a net i. of technology** le Japon est toujours un importateur net de technologie
▸▸ **i. margin** marge *f* de l'importateur

import-export **N** import-export *m*
▸▸ **i. trade** import-export

importing [ˈɪmpɔːtɪŋ] **ADJ** *(country)* importateur, -trice
N *(of goods)* importation *f*

importunate [ɪmˈpɔːtjʊnɪt] **ADJ** *Fml (creditor, visitor)* importun

importune [ɪmˈpɔːtjuːn] **VT** *Fml* importuner

importunity [ɪmpɔːˈtjuːnɪtɪ] **N** *Fml* importunité *f*

impose [ɪmˈpəʊz] **VT** *(silence, one's will, restrictions etc)* imposer (**on sb** à qn); **his bearing imposes respect** il en impose; **to i. a ban on sth** interdire qch; **the EU is in favour of imposing a ban on tobacco advertising** l'UE

est en faveur d'interdire la publicité pour le tabac; **to i. a tax on sugar** taxer le sucre; **to i. a fine on sb** condamner qn à (payer) une amende; **to i. the maximum penalty provided** appliquer le maximum de la peine; **to i. oneself on a situation/a political party** *(exert strong influence over)* s'imposer dans une situation/un parti politique
VI *(take advantage)* abuser; **I hope I'm not imposing** *(by staying)* j'espère que je ne m'impose pas; **to i. on** *or* **upon sb** abuser de l'amabilité de qn; **to i. on** *or* **upon sb's kindness** abuser de la bonté de qn

imposing [ɪmˈpəʊzɪŋ] **ADJ** *(air, tone)* imposant; *(spectacle, building)* impressionnant

imposition [ɪmpəˈzɪʃən] **N 1** *(of task, tax)* imposition *f*; *(of fine)* fait *m* d'infliger **2** *(abuse)* **I told him I thought it was a bit of an i. asking me to ...** je lui ai dit que je trouvais qu'il abusait un peu de ma bonté en me demandant de ... **3** *(tax)* imposition *f*, impôt *m*, taxe *f* **4** *Br Sch Old-fashioned (punishment)* punition *f*

impossibility [ɪmpɒsɪˈbɪlɪtɪ] **N** impossibilité *f*; **it's a physical i.** c'est matériellement impossible

impossible [ɪmˈpɒsɪb(ə)l] **ADJ 1** *(task, demand)* impossible; **it is i. for me to do it** il m'est impossible de le faire; **to make it i. for sb to do sth** mettre qn dans l'impossibilité de faire qch; **it's not i. that ...** il n'est pas impossible que ...; **(it's) i. to say** *or* **tell** c'est impossible à dire **2** *(unbelievable) (story, account)* invraisemblable **3** *Fam (intolerable) (life, person)* impossible; **you're i.!** vous êtes impossible!
N impossible *m*; **to attempt the i.** tenter l'impossible

impossibly [ɪmˈpɒsɪblɪ] **ADV** *(long, difficult)* incroyablement; **he's i. stupid** est-il possible d'être aussi stupide!; *Fam* **the children were behaving i.** les enfants étaient vraiment impossibles

impostor [ɪmˈpɒstər] **N** imposteur *m*

imposture [ɪmˈpɒstʃər] **N** imposture *f*, tromperie *f*

impotence [ˈɪmpətəns] **N 1** *(powerlessness)* impuissance *f*; *(weakness)* faiblesse *f*, impotence *f* **2** *(sexual)* impuissance *f*

impotent [ˈɪmpətənt] **ADJ 1** *(sexually)* impuissant **2** *(powerless)* impuissant; *(weak)* faible

> Note that the French word **impotent** is a false friend. It means **infirm**.

impound [ɪmˈpaʊnd] **VT 1** *Law (confiscate)* confisquer, saisir **2** *(put in pound) (animal, car etc)* mettre en fourrière

impounding [ɪmˈpaʊndɪŋ] **N 1** *Law (of goods)* arrêt *m*, saisie *f* **2** *(putting in pound) (of animals, cars etc)* mise *f* en fourrière

impoverish [ɪmˈpɒvərɪʃ] **VT** *(person, country, soil)* appauvrir

impoverished [ɪmˈpɒvərɪʃt] **ADJ** appauvri, pauvre

impoverishment [ɪmˈpɒvərɪʃmənt] **N** appauvrissement *m*

impracticability [ɪmpræktɪkəˈbɪlɪtɪ] **N** impraticabilité *f*

impracticable [ɪmˈpræktɪkəb(ə)l] **ADJ** infaisable, impraticable

> Attention: ne pas confondre avec **impractical**.

impractical [ɪmˈpræktɪk(ə)l] **ADJ** *(person)* qui n'a pas le sens *ou* l'esprit pratique; *(project, suggestion)* peu réaliste; **he's completely i.** il n'a aucun sens pratique

Attention: ne pas confondre avec **impracticable**.

imprecation [ɪmprɪ'keɪʃən] N imprécation f

imprecise [ɪmprɪ'saɪs] ADJ imprécis, vague

imprecision [ɪmprɪ'sɪʒən] N imprécision f, manque m de précision

impregnable [ɪm'pregnəb(ə)l] ADJ 1 (fortress) imprenable; **i. to attack** imprenable 2 Fig (truth, argument) invincible

impregnate ['ɪmpregneɪt] VT 1 Biol féconder 2 Tech imprégner, imbiber (**sth with sth** qch de qch); **allow the oil to i. the wood** laissez le bois s'imprégner d'huile

impregnation [ɪmpreg'neɪʃən] N 1 Biol fécondation f 2 Tech (of fabric, wood etc) imprégnation f

impresario [ɪmpre'sɑːrɪəʊ] N impresario m

impress¹ ['ɪmpres] N Fml, Lit 1 (imprint) empreinte f, impression f 2 Fig (distinctive style etc) marque f distinctive

impress² [ɪm'pres] VT 1 (create strong impression on) impressionner, faire une impression à; **I was deeply impressed by it** j'ai été très impressionné, cela m'a fait une grande impression; Fam **I'm not impressed!** c'est pas terrible!; **she wasn't impressed by my excuse** mon excuse ne l'a pas vraiment convaincue; **he impressed me favourably** il m'a fait bonne impression; **she impressed me as hard-working** elle m'a fait l'impression d'être travailleuse

2 (make understood) faire bien comprendre (**sth on** or **upon sb** qch à qn); (idea) inculquer (**on** or **upon sb** à qn); **you must i. on him that ...** il faut bien lui faire comprendre que ...

3 (imprint) **to i. sth on** or **upon sth** imprimer qch sur qch; **to i. sth with a seal** faire une impression sur qch avec un cachet; Fig **to i. sth on the mind** graver qch dans la mémoire; Fig **to i. sb with the idea that ...** inculquer à qn l'idée que ...

VI (of person, remark) faire impression

impression [ɪm'preʃən] N 1 (effect) impression f; **to make an i.** faire impression; **to make a good/bad i.** faire bonne/mauvaise impression (**on** sur); **my argument was making no i. on her** (having no effect) mon argument ne lui faisait aucun effet

2 (idea, opinion) impression f; **I'm under the i. that I've seen him before** j'ai l'impression de l'avoir déjà vu; **I don't know where she got that i. from** je ne sais pas où elle est allée chercher ça; **I had the i. that you liked her** j'avais l'impression que tu l'aimais bien; **to create** or **give the i. that ...** donner ou produire l'impression que ...; **my first i. wasn't favourable** ma première impression n'a pas été favorable

3 (imprint) (of seal) empreinte f, impression f; **to take an i. of sth** prendre l'empreinte ou l'impression de qch

4 (reprint) (of book etc) tirage m

5 (imitation) imitation f; **to do impressions** faire des imitations; **this is my i. of you eating** je t'imite en train de manger

▸ **i. cylinder** cylindre m de rotative

impressionable [ɪm'preʃənəb(ə)l] ADJ (person) influençable

Note that the French word **impressionnable** is a false friend. It means **easily upset**.

impressionism [ɪm'preʃənɪz(ə)m] N Art impressionnisme m

impressionist [ɪm'preʃənɪst] ADJ Art impressionniste

N 1 impressionniste mf 2 (mimic) imitateur, -trice

impressionistic [ɪmpreʃə'nɪstɪk] ADJ impressionniste

impressive [ɪm'presɪv] ADJ (spectacle, language) impressionnant

impressively [ɪm'presɪvlɪ] ADV d'une manière impressionnante

imprest ['ɪmprest] N Fin avance f

▸▸ **i. account** compte m d'avances (à montant fixe); **i. fund** fonds m de caisse à montant fixe; **i. system** comptabilité f de prévision

imprimatur [ɪmprɪ'mɑːtər] N imprimatur m

imprint¹ ['ɪmprɪnt] N 1 (of seal, animal's feet etc) empreinte f; **to take an i. of a credit card** passer une carte de crédit dans la facturette; **the events left their i. on her mind** les événements sont restés gravés dans son esprit 2 (publisher's) i. (mark) marque f de l'éditeur; **XYZ books is an i. of JMG Publishers** XYZ books fait partie des Éditions JMG; **published under the Pentagon i.** édité chez Pentagon

▸▸ **i. page** (of book) page f portant l'adresse bibliographique

imprint² [ɪm'prɪnt] VT imprimer; **to i. sth with sth** marquer ou empreindre qch de qch; **the shape of an animal's foot was imprinted in the earth** l'empreinte du pied d'un animal était restée dans la terre; **to i. sth on the memory** graver ou fixer qch dans la mémoire

imprinter ['ɪmprɪntər] N (for credit card payment) pressographe m

imprison [ɪm'prɪzən] VT emprisonner, mettre en prison; **to keep sb imprisoned** garder qn prisonnier

imprisonment [ɪm'prɪzənmənt] N emprisonnement m; **ten days' i.** dix jours d'emprisonnement ou de prison

improbability [ɪmprɒbə'bɪlɪtɪ] N improbabilité f

improbable [ɪm'prɒbəb(ə)l] ADJ improbable; **it's highly i. that he'll come** il est très improbable ou très peu probable qu'il vienne

improbably [ɪm'prɒbəblɪ] ADV invraisemblablement; **quite i., he won** contre toute attente, il a gagné; **he was wearing an i. large hat** il portait un chapeau d'une grandeur invraisemblable

impromptu [ɪm'prɒmptjuː] ADV (to do sth) sans préparation, impromptu

ADJ (poem, speech) impromptu; **to make an i. speech** improviser un discours

N Theat, Mus impromptu m

improper [ɪm'prɒpər] ADJ 1 (incorrect) (use, purpose) impropre 2 (indecent) (suggestion, remark) indécent, inconvenant 3 (not fitting) (behaviour, dress) déplacé; **it would be i. to refuse** il serait de mauvaise grâce de refuser

▸▸ Math **i. fraction** expression f fractionnaire; **i. practices** pratiques fpl irrégulières

improperly [ɪm'prɒpəlɪ] ADV 1 (incorrectly) (to use a tool, one's power) improprement 2 (indecently) (to behave) d'une manière inconvenante, avec indécence 3 (inappropriately) (to speak, behave) d'une façon déplacée; **to be i. dressed** ne pas porter une tenue convenable

impropriety [ɪmprə'praɪətɪ] N 1 (unsuitable expression, gesture etc) inconvenance f, indécence f; **to be guilty of improprieties** avoir commis des inconvenances 2 (incorrectness) (of language etc) impropriété f, (of behaviour) inconvenance f, indécence f

improve [ɪm'pruːv] VT (one's French, the flavour, translation etc) améliorer; (wine etc) bonifier; (one's knowledge) étendre, élargir; (one's taste) affiner; Agr (soil) bonifier, enri-

chir; **to i. the appearance of sb/sth** embellir qn/qch; esp Hum **to i. one's mind** se cultiver

VI (of situation, sb's health etc) s'améliorer; (of wine etc) s'améliorer, se bonifier; Com (of prices, markets) monter; **business is improving** les affaires reprennent

▸ **improve on, improve upon** VT INSEP (make better) améliorer; Com **to i. on sb's offer** offrir plus que qn

improved [ɪm'pruːvd] ADJ (situation etc) amélioré; (invention) perfectionné; Com (offer) supérieur

improvement [ɪm'pruːvmənt] N 1 (in situation, health etc) amélioration f (**in** de); (of invention) perfectionnement m; **to be an i. on sb/sth** surpasser qn/qch; **the weather is a bit of an i. on what it was yesterday** il fait légèrement meilleur aujourd'hui qu'hier; **we should see something of an i. in the weather tomorrow** le temps devrait s'améliorer demain; **my new car is a great i. on the old one** ma nouvelle voiture est bien supérieure à l'ancienne; **the cakes were an i. on my first attempt** les gâteaux étaient mieux réussis que la première fois; **her new boyfriend's a bit of an i.** son nouveau petit ami est un peu mieux que le(s) précédent(s) 2 (usu pl) Constr etc improvements améliorations fpl, embellissements mpl; **we're making some improvements to the house** nous rénovons la maison

▸▸ Br **i. grant** = subvention f pour la rénovation d'une maison

improvidence [ɪm'prɒvɪdəns] N 1 (rashness) imprévoyance f 2 (carelessness with money) prodigalité f

improvident [ɪm'prɒvɪdənt] ADJ 1 (rash) imprévoyant 2 (careless with money) prodigue

improvidently [ɪm'prɒvɪdəntlɪ] ADV 1 (rashly) de façon imprévoyante 2 (to spend money) de façon prodigue

improving [ɪm'pruːvɪŋ] ADJ (book etc) édifiant; (influence, environment) bénéfique

improvisation [ɪmprəvaɪ'zeɪʃən] N improvisation f

improvise ['ɪmprəvaɪz] VT improviser; **hastily improvised** sommairement organisé; **improvised speech** discours improvisé ou impromptu; **they improvised bandages from bedsheets** ils ont fait des bandages de fortune avec des draps; **improvised raft** radeau m de fortune

VI improviser; **to i. on the piano** improviser au piano; **you will have to i.** (make do) il faudra que vous vous débrouilliez avec ce qu'il y a

improviser ['ɪmprəvaɪzər] N improvisateur, -trice

imprudence [ɪm'pruːdəns] N imprudence f, (with money) manque m de prévoyance

imprudent [ɪm'pruːdənt] ADJ imprudent; **i. with money** imprudent dans ses dépenses; **she's rather i. in her choice of friends** elle choisit mal ses amis

imprudently [ɪm'pruːdəntlɪ] ADV imprudemment

impudence ['ɪmpjʊdəns] N impudence f, insolence f

impudent ['ɪmpjʊdənt] ADJ impudent, insolent; **he's an i. fellow** c'est un insolent

impudently ['ɪmpjʊdəntlɪ] ADV avec impudence ou insolence

impugn [ɪm'pjuːn] VT Fml (sb's honour, motives) mettre en doute ou en question; Law (sb's evidence) récuser

impulse ['ɪmpʌls] N 1 (desire) envie f, Psy (sexual etc) pulsion f; **to feel an i. to do sth** avoir une soudaine envie de faire qch; **a sudden i. made me start running** instinctivement, j'ai commencé à courir; **to act on i.**

agir spontanément *ou* sur le coup d'une impulsion; **I did it on i.** j'ai fait ça sur un coup de tête **2** *(stimulation, force)* impulsion *f*; *Fig* **to give an i.** to trade donner une impulsion au commerce **3** *Phys* quantité *f* de mouvement; *Elec* **electrical impulses** impulsions *fpl* électriques; *Physiol* **nerve i.** signal *m* nerveux
► ► *Mktg* **i. buy** achat *m* d'impulsion; **i. buyer** acheteur, -euse impulsif(ive); **i. buying** achats *mpl* d'impulsion; **i. goods** produits *mpl* d'achat impulsif

impulsion [ɪmˈpʌlʃən] **N** impulsion *f*

impulsive [ɪmˈpʌlsɪv] **ADJ 1** *(person, gesture, decision, remark)* impulsif; **i. action** acte *m* impulsif, coup *m* de tête; **i. buy** achat *m* d'impulsion; **i. buyer** acheteur, -euse impulsif(ive) **2** *Tech* impulsif, propulsif
► ► *Tech* **i. force** force *f* impulsive *ou* projective

impulsively [ɪmˈpʌlsɪvlɪ] **ADJ** *(to act)* par impulsion, de façon impulsive

impulsiveness [ɪmˈpʌlsɪvnɪs] **N** caractère *m* impulsif

impunity [ɪmˈpjuːnɪtɪ] **N** impunité *f*; **to do sth with i.** faire qch impunément *ou* en toute impunité

impure [ɪmˈpjʊər] **ADJ** impur

impurity [ɪmˈpjʊərɪtɪ] **N** *(of water etc)*, *Fig* *(of thoughts)* impureté *f*

imputation [ɪmpjuːˈteɪʃən] **N** imputation *f*

impute [ɪmˈpjuːt] **VT** *(action etc)* imputer, attribuer (**to sb** à qn)

IN [ɪn]

PREP	dans **1, 2, 5, 9, 11** ▪ en **1, 5, 6, 8–10, 13–16, 20** ▪ à **1, 10** ▪ chez **2** ▪ sur **4** ▪ de **5**
CONJ	puisque
ADV	à la maison **1** ▪ à l'intérieur **2** ▪ dedans **2**
ADJ	à la mode **1**

PREP VOIR GRAMMAIRE A70; B54–7 **1** *(of place)* en, à, dans; **in France** en France; **in Japan** au Japon; **in the United States** aux États-Unis; **in Paris** à Paris; **in the provinces** en province; **to be in town/in the country** être en ville/à la campagne; **in his country** dans son pays; **in prison** en prison; **in church** à l'église; **in bed** au lit; **in the house/city** dans la maison/ville; **in the water** dans l'eau; **the key is in the door** la clef est sur la porte; **in this book** dans ce livre; **in my hand** dans ma main; **with a cigar in his mouth** un cigare à la bouche; **in the distance** au loin; **in your place** à votre place; **wounded in the shoulder** blessé à l'épaule
2 *(among)* **in the crowd** dans la foule; **the temperature was in the nineties** la température était dans les 30 degrés; **this illness is rare in men** cette maladie est rare chez les hommes; **this is a common theme in Shakespeare's work** c'est un thème fréquent dans les œuvres de Shakespeare
3 *(regarding)* **an expert in economics** un expert en économie politique; **two metres in length** long de deux mètres; **in certain respects he was right** à certains égards il avait raison
4 *(of ratio)* **one in ten** un sur dix; **once in ten years** une fois tous les dix ans
5 *(of time, age)* **in 1997** en 1997; **in the thirties** dans les années trente; **in the night** pendant la nuit; **in the afternoon/evening** l'après-midi/le soir; **at four o'clock in the afternoon** à quatre heures de l'après-midi; **the baby usually goes for a sleep in the afternoon** d'habitude le bébé dort (dans) *ou* pendant l'après-midi; **in spring/summer/autumn/winter** au printemps/en été/en automne/en hiver; **in (the month of) April** au mois d'avril, en avril; **in the future** à l'avenir;

never in my life have I met … jamais de ma vie je n'ai rencontré …; **in my time** de mon temps; **he's in his sixties** il a la soixantaine; **to do sth in three hours** *(within)* faire qch en trois heures; **he'll be here in three hours** il sera là dans trois heures; **in a little while** dans un petit moment; **I haven't seen you in years** je ne t'ai pas vu depuis des années, ça fait des années que je ne t'ai pas vu
6 *(introducing a gerund)* en; **in crossing the river** en traversant la rivière; **we had no problem/difficulty in doing it** nous n'avons eu aucun problème/aucune difficulté à le faire
7 *(of condition, state)* **in good health** en bonne santé; **in a good mood** de bonne humeur
8 *(clothed in, surrounded by)* **in his shirt** en chemise; **in slippers** en pantoufles; **dressed in white** habillé de *ou* en blanc; **the man in black** l'homme en noir; **wrapped in paper** enveloppé de papier; *Culin* **beef in a red wine sauce** bœuf dans une sauce au vin rouge; **fish in breadcrumbs** poisson pané
9 *(of weather, light)* en, dans; **to go out in the rain/snow** sortir par la pluie/la neige; **in this warm weather** par ce temps chaud; **to work in the rain** travailler sous la pluie; **in the sun** au soleil; **in the dark** dans l'obscurité
10 *(engaged in)* **in politics** en politique; **to be in politics** être dans la politique; **killed in action** tué au combat; **in the navy** dans la marine; **she's been in a lot of films** elle a joué dans beaucoup de films; **he wasn't in that race** il n'a pas pris part à cette course
11 *(due to)* dans; **in their hurry/panic** dans leur hâte/panique; **the fence blew down in the storm** la barrière est tombée pendant la tempête
12 *(of manner)* **in a gentle voice** d'une voix douce; **in a businesslike manner** d'une façon professionnelle; **in the French style** à la française; **to be in fashion** être à la mode
13 *(of medium)* **to write in French** écrire en français; **in writing** par écrit; **to talk in whispers** parler en chuchotant; **they were paid in gold/cash** ils étaient payés en or/liquide
14 *(of arrangement)* **to stand in a circle** se tenir en cercle; **in alphabetical order** par ordre alphabétique; **line up in twos** mettez-vous par deux
15 *(of form)* **I've nothing in your size** je n'ai rien à *ou* dans votre taille; **do you have it in a 5?** est-ce que vous l'auriez dans le 38?; **in the form of a pill** sous forme de pilule; **she was curled up in a ball** elle était roulée en boule; **do you have it in red/silk?** est-ce que vous l'avez en rouge/soie?
16 *(of degree, extent)* **in large quantities** en grandes quantités; **in part** en partie; **in places** par endroits
17 *(of purpose)* **in reply to …** en réponse à …; **in honour of …** en l'honneur de …; **in search of …** à la recherche de …; **in the cause of humanity** pour la cause de l'humanité
18 *(with reflexive pronoun)* **this product is not a poison in itself** ce produit n'est pas un poison en soi
19 *(of character, ability)* **I didn't think she had it in her** je ne l'en croyais pas capable; **he had it in him to be cruel** il était capable de cruauté; **it's not in her nature to be cruel** ce n'est pas dans sa nature d'être cruelle
20 *Mus* en; **symphony in B minor** symphonie en si mineur
CONJ in that parce que, puisque, vu que; **in so far as** dans la mesure où
ADV 1 *(inside building, room, boundary etc)* *(at home)* à la maison, chez soi; *(in one's office etc)* dans son bureau *etc*; **is he in?** est-ce qu'il est là?; **is your mother in?** est-ce que votre mère est à la maison?; **we've got the builders in** nous avons des ouvriers à la mai-

son; *Fam* **what's he in for?** *(in prison)* pourquoi est-ce qu'il fait de la tôle?; *(in hospital)* pourquoi est-ce qu'il est à l'hôpital?; *Agr* **the harvest is in** la moisson est rentrée; **to be in** *(of bus, plane etc)* être arrivé; **the train is in** le train est en gare *ou* est arrivé; *Tennis* **the ball is in** la balle est bonne
2 *(indoors, inside)* à l'intérieur, dedans; **in with you!** *(come in)* allons, rentrez!; *(go in)* allez-y!
3 *(in a situation)* **the Liberals were in** *(in power)* le parti libéral était au pouvoir; **stripes are in this year** *(in fashion)* les rayures sont à la mode cette année; *Fam* **to be (well) in with sb** *(in favour)* être en bons termes avec qn, être dans les petits papiers de qn; **my luck is in** je suis en veine; *Cr* **to be in** battre la balle, *Fam* être à la batte
4 *(phrases)* **I'm in for a thousand pounds** *(have invested etc)* j'ai engagé mille livres; **we're in for a storm** nous aurons sûrement de l'orage; **he's in for a surprise** il va être surpris, il va avoir une surprise; *Fam* **he's in for it** qu'est-ce qu'il va prendre!; *Fam* **to have it in for sb** avoir une dent contre qn; **to be in at the start/end of sth** assister au début/à la fin de qch; **to be in on a secret** être dans le secret; **I wasn't in on it** je n'étais pas dans le coup; **to go in and out** entrer et sortir; **she and I were always in and out of each other's house** nous étions tout le temps fourrées l'une chez l'autre; **to be all in** *(exhausted)* être complètement crevé
ADJ 1 *(fashionable)* **it's the in thing these days** c'est la mode aujourd'hui; **the in people** *or* **crowd** les gens à la mode *ou Fam* dans le coup
2 *(exclusive)* **an in joke** une plaisanterie de coterie
N 1 *Fam* **to know the ins and outs of a matter** connaître une affaire dans tous ses détails
2 *Am Fam* *(influence)* **to have an in** avoir de l'influence; **he has an in with the senator** il a ses entrées chez le sénateur
3 *(where film clip begins)* entrée *f*

inability [ɪnəˈbɪlɪtɪ] **N** incapacité *f* (**to do sth** de faire qch); *(powerlessness)* impuissance *f* (**to do sth** à faire qch)

inaccessibility [ɪnæksesɪˈbɪlɪtɪ] **N** inaccessibilité *f*

inaccessible [ɪnækˈsesɪb(ə)l] **ADJ** *(place, poetry, person)* inaccessible (**to** à); **senior civil servants are i. to the public** le public n'a pas accès auprès des hauts fonctionnaires

inaccuracy [ɪnˈækjʊrəsɪ] **N** *(of rifle, storyteller)* imprécision *f*, manque *m* de précision; *(of report, account)* inexactitude *f*, manque de précision; *(of translation)* infidélité *f*; **full of inaccuracies** *(work)* plein d'inexactitudes

inaccurate [ɪnˈækjʊrət] **ADJ** *(calculation, idea)* inexact; *(account, translation)* inexact, infidèle

inaccurately [ɪnˈækjʊrətlɪ] **ADV** *(to calculate, judge, quote, translate etc)* inexactement, de façon inexacte

inaction [ɪnˈækʃən] **N** inaction *f*

inactive [ɪnˈæktɪv] **ADJ** *(person, volcano, money, account)* inactif; *(mind)* inerte

inactivity [ɪnækˈtɪvɪtɪ] **N** inactivité *f*

inadequacy [ɪnˈædɪkwəsɪ] **N** *(of income)* insuffisance *f*; *(of system etc)* imperfection *f*; *Psy* *(of person)* complexe *m* d'infériorité; *Fml* **because of his i. to the task** en raison de son incapacité à faire ce travail

inadequate [ɪnˈædɪkwət] **ADJ** *(not enough)* *(funds, salary, preparations, ventilation etc)* insuffisant; *(unsuitable)* *(diet, precautions)* inadéquat; **that is an i. explanation of his behaviour** cela ne suffit pas à justifier son comportement; **to be i.** *(of thing)* être insuffisant (**for** pour); **she makes me feel i.** elle me donne des complexes; **I feel so i. in a situation like this** dans une situation comme celle-ci je me sens tellement peu à la hauteur

inadequately [ɪn'ædɪkwətlɪ] ADV *(ventilated, informed, supplied)* insuffisamment; **they were i. equipped for climbing a mountain** ils n'avaient pas l'équipement adéquat pour faire une ascension; **the vehicle was felt to perform i. on rough terrain** la performance du véhicule sur terrain accidenté a été jugée insuffisante

inadmissible [ɪnəd'mɪsɪb(ə)l] ADJ *(theory, claim)* inadmissible; *Law (evidence)* irrecevable

inadvertence [ɪnəd'vɜːtəns] N inattention *f*, **through i.** par inadvertance

inadvertent [ɪnəd'vɜːtənt] ADJ *(mistake etc)* involontaire

inadvertently [ɪnəd'vɜːtəntlɪ] ADV par inadvertance

inadvisability [ɪnədvaɪzə'bɪlɪtɪ] N *(of action)* imprudence *f*

inadvisable [ɪnəd'vaɪzəb(ə)l] ADJ déconseillé

inalienable [ɪn'eɪlɪənəb(ə)l] ADJ *(property, right)* inaliénable

inane [ɪ'neɪn] ADJ *(person, action)* inepte, stupide; *(smile)* bête, niais; *(answer)* inepte, saugrenu; **i. remark** ineptie *f*

inanely [ɪ'neɪnlɪ] ADV bêtement, stupidement

inanimate [ɪn'ænɪmət] ADJ *(body, style etc)* inanimé, sans vie

inanition [ɪnə'nɪʃən] N *Med* inanition *f*

inanity [ɪ'nænɪtɪ] N *(of remark)* inanité *f*, *(of person)* stupidité *f*

inapplicable [ɪn'æplɪkəb(ə)l] ADJ inapplicable (**to** à); **'delete where i.'** 'rayez la mention inutile'

inappropriate [ɪnə'prəʊprɪət] ADJ *(behaviour, music)* peu approprié, qui ne convient pas (**to** à); *(word)* impropre; *(speech, joke, remark)* déplacé; **his clothes were i. to the climate** ses vêtements n'étaient guère appropriés au climat; **her dress was i. to this formal occasion** sa robe convenait mal au caractère officiel de l'occasion

inappropriately [ɪnə'prəʊprɪətlɪ] ADV *(to behave)* de façon inconvenante; **to be i. dressed** ne pas porter des vêtements appropriés

inapt [ɪn'æpt] ADJ *(inappropriate)* peu approprié (**to** à)

inaptitude [ɪn'æptɪtjuːd] N *(inability)* incapacité *f*

inarticulate [ɪnɑː'tɪkjʊlɪt] ADJ **1** *(person)* qui manque de facilité à s'exprimer; *(sound)* inarticulé; *esp Lit (desire)* inexprimé; **he's so i.** il a tellement de mal à s'exprimer; **i. with rage** bégayant de colère; **I was seized by an i. rage** j'ai été pris d'une rage telle que je pouvais à peine m'exprimer **2** *Biol (without joints)* inarticulé

inartistic [ɪnɑː'tɪstɪk] ADJ *(production of play, arrangement of flowers etc)* peu artistique; *(person)* dépourvu de sens artistique; **I'm fairly i.** je n'ai pas beaucoup de sens artistique

inasmuch [ɪnəz'mʌtʃ] CONJ *Fml* **i. as** dans la mesure où

inattention [ɪnə'tenʃən] N inattention *f*, manque *m* d'attention; **i. to detail** inattention aux *ou* manque d'attention pour les détails

inattentive [ɪnə'tentɪv] ADJ *(audience, child at school)* inattentif, distrait; *(husband, waiter etc)* peu attentionné, peu prévenant (**to**,

towards sb à l'égard de qn), inattentif (**to sb's needs** aux besoins de qn); **to be i. to** *(detail, consequences of one's action, comfort of guests)* ne pas faire attention à

inattentively [ɪnə'tentɪvlɪ] ADV sans prêter attention, distraitement

inaudible [ɪn'ɔːdɪb(ə)l] ADJ inaudible; *(sound)* imperceptible, inaudible

inaudibly [ɪn'ɔːdɪblɪ] ADV de manière inaudible

inaugural [ɪ'nɔːgjʊrəl] ADJ *(meeting)* inaugural, -aux; *(speech)* inaugural, -aux, d'inauguration

N *Am (speech)* discours *m* inaugural *ou* d'inauguration

inaugurate [ɪ'nɔːgjʊreɪt] VT *(building)* inaugurer; *(conference, exhibition)* ouvrir; *Fig (new era)* inaugurer, commencer; *(new system, tradition etc)* instaurer; *(head of state)* faire prêter serment à *(lors de la prise de fonctions)*; **he will be inaugurated today** il prêtera serment aujourd'hui

inauguration [ɪnɔː'gjʊ'reɪʃən] N *(of building etc)* inauguration *f*, *(of new system etc)* instauration *f*

▸▸ **i. ceremony** *(for building, bridge etc)* cérémonie *f* d'inauguration; **I. Day** = jour *m* de l'investiture du président des États-Unis (le 20 janvier)

inauspicious [ɪnɔː'spɪʃəs] ADJ *(circumstances)* défavorable; *(moment)* malencontreux; **an i. sign** un mauvais signe; **the project got off to an i. start** le projet a mal commencé

inauspiciously [ɪnɔː'spɪʃəslɪ] ADV de façon peu propice

inauthentic [ɪnɔː'θentɪk] ADJ inauthentique

in-between ADJ intermédiaire

N **but what happens if you're an i.?** et qu'est-ce qu'on fait si on est entre les deux?

inborn ['ɪn'bɔːn] ADJ *(instinct, merit)* inné, naturel; *Med* congénital, -aux

inbound ['ɪnbaʊnd] ADJ *(flight, passenger)* à l'arrivée

▸▸ **i. tourism** tourisme *m* récepteur *ou* réceptif; **i. travel** tourisme récepteur *ou* réceptif

in-box N *Comput (for e-mail)* boîte *f* de réception, corbeille *f* d'arrivée

inbred ['ɪn'bred] ADJ **1** *(dog, horse etc)* consanguin; **they are so i. that …** la consanguinité chez eux est telle que … **2** *(innate)* inné

inbreed ['ɪn'briːd] VI *(pt, pp inbred)* se reproduire entre eux

inbreeding ['ɪn'briːdɪŋ] N *(of animals)* accouplement *m* d'animaux consanguins; *(of people)* unions *fpl* consanguines

in-built ADJ = **built-in**

Inc [ɪŋk] *Am Com (abbr Incorporated)* ≃ SARL

Inca ['ɪŋkə] N Inca *mf*
ADJ inca *inv*

incalculable [ɪn'kælkjʊləb(ə)l] ADJ *(consequences, harm)* incalculable; *(loss, help)* inestimable

incalculably [ɪn'kælkjʊləblɪ] ADV de façon inestimable

in camera ADV, ADJ *Law* à huis clos

incandescence [ɪnkæn'desəns] N incandescence *f*

incandescent [ɪnkæn'desənt] ADJ incandescent; *(light, light bulb etc)* à incandescence

incantation [ɪnkæn'teɪʃən] N incantation *f*

incapability [ɪnkeɪpə'bɪlɪtɪ] N incapacité *f*

incapable [ɪn'keɪpəb(ə)l] ADJ *(unable)* incapable (**of** de); **I'm not i.!** je ne suis pas impo-

tent!; **i. of movement** *(of person)* incapable de bouger; *Fml* **the essay is i. of improvement** *(cannot be improved upon)* cette dissertation ne peut pas être améliorée, tant elle est parfaite; *Law* **declared i. of managing his own affairs** en état d'incapacité légale; *Law* **i. of succeeding to an estate** incapable de prendre la succession d'un domaine

incapacitate [ɪnkə'pæsɪteɪt] VT **1** rendre incapable (**for work** de travailler); *(vehicle)* mettre hors d'état de marche; **the alcohol had temporarily incapacitated him** l'alcool avait temporairement inhibé ses facultés **2** *Law* frapper d'incapacité

incapacity [ɪnkə'pæsɪtɪ] N **1** incapacité *f*, incompétence *f* **2** *Law* incapacité *f*

in-car ADJ *Aut*
▸▸ **i. listening** = écoute *f* de la radio, de cassettes ou de CD en voiture; *Br* **i. stereo** autoradio *m*

incarcerate [ɪn'kɑːsəreɪt] VT *Fml* incarcérer

incarceration [ɪnkɑːsə'reɪʃən] N *Fml* incarcération *f*, emprisonnement *m*

incarnate[1] [ɪn'kɑːneɪt] ADJ incarné; **the devil i.** le diable incarné; **perfection/wisdom i.** la perfection/la sagesse incarnée

incarnate[2] ['ɪnkɑːneɪt] VT incarner

incarnation [ɪnkɑː'neɪʃən] N *Rel, Fig (of Christ, an idea)* incarnation *f*, **to be the i. of wisdom** *(of person)* être l'incarnation de la sagesse; **in a previous i.** dans une vie antérieure; *Fig* **in a previous i. he was an MP** à une époque il était député

incautious [ɪn'kɔːʃəs] ADJ imprudent; *(remark etc)* inconsidéré; **in an i. moment** dans un moment d'inattention

incautiously [ɪn'kɔːʃəslɪ] ADV imprudemment

incendiary [ɪn'sendɪərɪ] ADJ *(bomb, device)*, *Fig (remarks, speech)* incendiaire

N **1** *(arsonist)* incendiaire *mf*, *Fig (agitator)* trublion *m*, agitateur, -trice **2** *(bomb)* bombe *f* incendiaire

incense[1] ['ɪnsens] N encens *m*
▸▸ **i. bearer** thuriféraire *m*; **i. burner** encensoir *m*; **i. stick** bâtonnet *m* d'encens

incense[2] [ɪn'sens] VT rendre furieux

> Note that the French verb **encenser** is a false friend and is never a translation for the English verb **to incense**. It means **to praise lavishly**.

incensed [ɪn'senst] ADJ furieux; **to become** *or* **get i.** être furieux (**with** contre, **about** au sujet de)

incentive [ɪn'sentɪv] N encouragement *m*; *Com, Ind (payment)* prime *f*, *Mktg* stimulation *f*, *Fam* stim *f*, *(reduction, freebie)* stimulant *m*, stimulateur *m*; **there is no i. for students here to work hard** il n'y a rien ici qui incite *ou* encourage les étudiants à travailler dur; **i. to buy** incitation *f ou* stimulation à l'achat

▸▸ *Br Com* **i. bonus** prime de rendement *ou* d'encouragement; **i. company** *(in tourism)* agence *f* spécialisée dans le voyage de stimulation; **i. fare** tarif *m* de stimulation; **i. marketing** marketing *m* de stimulation; *Com, Ind* **i. pay** primes de rendement; **i. scheme** *(for buyers)* programme *m* de stimulation; *(for workers)* système *m* de primes; **i. tourism** tourisme *m* de stimulation; **i. travel** voyages *mpl* de motivation *ou* de stimulation; **i. trip** voyage *m* de motivation *ou* de stimulation

inception [ɪn'sepʃən] N *Fml (of company, scheme etc)* commencement *m*, début *m*

incessant [ɪn'sesənt] ADJ *(noise)* incessant, continuel; *(worry)* éternel

incessantly [ɪn'sesəntlɪ] ADV sans cesse, sans relâche, continuellement

> Note that the French word **incessamment** is a false friend. It means **very shortly**.

incest ['ɪnsest] N inceste m

incestuous [ɪn'sestjʊəs] ADJ incestueux; *Fig* **the i. world of writers** le monde très fermé *ou* en vase clos des écrivains

inch [ɪntʃ] N *(measurement)* pouce m (= 2,54 cm); **he's every i. a** *or* **the soldier** il a tout du militaire; **she won't give (way) an i.** elle ne reculera pas d'une semelle; **by inches, i. by i.** peu à peu, petit à petit; **I know every i. of the neighbourhood** je connais le quartier comme ma poche; **give her an i. and she'll take a mile** tu lui en donnes jusqu'au coude, elle en demande long comme le bras; **to be within an i. of doing** être à deux doigts de faire; **to beat sb to within an i. of their life** battre qn en le laissant pour mort; **I'll beat him to within an i. of his life!** je vais l'étrangler!
▸ **inch along, inch forward** VI avancer tout doucement
 VT SEP faire avancer tout doucement; **she inched her way along the window ledge** elle se déplaça tout doucement le long du rebord de la fenêtre

incidence ['ɪnsɪdəns] N **1** *(frequency) (of thefts, crime etc)* taux m; *(of disease)* incidence f; **the i. of cancer has increased** les cas de cancer se sont multipliés **2** *Opt, Electron, Aviat etc* **angle of i.** angle m d'incidence

incident ['ɪnsɪdənt] N incident m; **a journey full of incident(s)** un voyage mouvementé
 ADJ **1** *Opt, Electron (light beam etc)* incident **2** *Fml (related)* inhérent (**to** à)

incidental [ɪnsɪ'dent(ə)l] ADJ *(minor) (event, circumstance, effect)* secondaire; *(extra, supplementary) (advantage, benefit)* supplémentaire; **to be i. to sth** être occasionné par *ou* découler de qch; **the disruption i. to the reorganization** le désordre occasionné par la restructuration
 N détail m; **incidentals** *(expenses)* faux frais mpl
▸▸ **i. costs, i. expenses** faux frais mpl; **i. music** *(for film)* musique f de film; *(for play)* musique de scène

incidentally [ɪnsɪ'dentəlɪ] ADV **1** *(by the way)* soit dit en passant *ou* entre parenthèses; **i., how is he?** au fait, comment va-t-il? **2** *(accidentally, secondarily)* incidemment

> Note that the French word **incidemment** only means **accidentally**.

incinerate [ɪn'sɪnəreɪt] VT incinérer

incineration [ɪnsɪnə'reɪʃən] N incinération f

incinerator [ɪn'sɪnəreɪtər] N *Ind etc* incinérateur m; *(in crematorium)* four m crématoire

incipient [ɪn'sɪpɪənt] ADJ naissant, dans ses débuts; **i. madness** folie naissante

incise [ɪn'saɪz] VT *Art etc (inscription etc)* graver

incision [ɪn'sɪʒən] N incision f; **to make an i. in sth** inciser qch, pratiquer une incision dans qch

incisive [ɪn'saɪsɪv] ADJ *(remark, style)* incisif; *(mind)* pénétrant

incisively [ɪn'saɪsɪvlɪ] ADV de façon incisive

incisor [ɪn'saɪzər] N *Anat* incisive f

incite [ɪn'saɪt] VT inciter (**to sth** à qch; **to do sth** à faire qch); **to i. racial hatred** inciter à la haine raciale; **to i. sb to crime/violence** inciter *ou* pousser qn au crime/à la violence

incitement [ɪn'saɪtmənt] N *(of people, actions)* incitation f, encouragement m (**to sth** à qch)

incivility [ɪnsɪ'vɪlɪtɪ] N *Fml* incivilité f

incl 1 *(abbr* **inclusive)** inclus; **from 14th to 23rd November i.** du 14 au 23 novembre inclus; **i. of gas and electricity** gas et électricité compris **2** *(abbr* **including)** avec

inclemency [ɪn'klemənsɪ] N *Fml* inclémence f, rigueur f

inclement [ɪn'klemənt] ADJ *Fml (weather)* inclément

inclination [ɪnklɪ'neɪʃən] N **1** *(desire)* envie f (**for sth** de qch; **to do** de faire); **to have an i. for sth** avoir un penchant pour qch; **she had no i. to help him** elle n'avait pas du tout envie de l'aider; **to have lost all i. for sth** n'avoir plus envie de qch; **to show little i. to do sth** se montrer peu enclin à faire qch; **to follow one's inclinations** faire ce à quoi on est naturellement enclin **2** *(tendency)* tendance f (**towards sth** à qch; **to do** à faire); **my i. would be to ...** j'aurais tendance à ..., je serais porté à ...; **my i. would be to say yes, but ...** je serais enclin à dire oui, mais ...; **she is by i. a cautious person** c'est quelqu'un de très prudent par nature **3** *(angle) (of head, body)* inclination f; *Math (of plane)* inclinaison f

incline¹ ['ɪnklaɪn] N pente f

incline² [ɪn'klaɪn] VT **1** *(motivate, cause)* inciter; **this inclines me to believe them** ceci me porte *ou* m'encourage à les croire; **her remarks don't i. me to be sympathetic** ses remarques ne m'incitent pas à être compréhensif **2** *(head)* incliner, pencher
 VI **1** *(of person)* avoir un penchant (**to sth** pour qch, **to do** à faire), avoir tendance (**to sth** à faire); **to i. to the belief that ...** être porté *ou* avoir tendance à croire que ... **2** *(of thing)* s'incliner, pencher (**to** à; **towards** vers)

inclined [ɪn'klaɪnd] ADJ **1** *(person) (temporarily)* disposé (**to** à); *(permanently)* enclin (**to** à); **to feel** *or* **be i. to do sth** *(tend to)* avoir tendance à faire qch; *(have desire to)* avoir envie de faire qch; **I am i. to think that he's right** je suis porté *ou* j'ai tendance à croire qu'il a raison; **to be well i. towards sb** être bien disposé envers qn; **if ever you should feel so x.** si jamais l'envie vous en prenait; **prices are i. to fall** les prix ont tendance à baisser; **he's i. to put on weight** il a tendance à grossir; **i. to laziness** *or* **to be lazy** enclin à la paresse; **I'm not musically i.** *(I don't like music)* je ne suis pas très porté sur la musique; *(I have no talent)* je n'ai pas de talent musical; **if you're that way i.** *(if you want to)* si cela vous dit; *Fam* **he's the other way i.** *(in his sexual orientation)* il est de l'autre bord **2** *Math (plane)* incliné

include [ɪn'kluːd] VT inclure, comprendre; **the speech included several references to Soviet history** le discours comportait plusieurs références à l'histoire de l'Union Soviétique; **the committee includes politicians from all parties** le comité comprend des politiciens de tous les partis; **men over seventy are not included** les hommes de plus de soixante-dix ans ne sont pas compris; **the price does not i. accommodation** le prix ne comprend pas l'hébergement; **if you i. Christmas Day** en comptant le jour de Noël; **to i. sb among one's friends** compter qn parmi *ou* au nombre de ses amis
▸ **include out** VT SEP *Fam Hum* **i. me out** ne compte pas sur moi

included [ɪn'kluːdɪd] ADJ *(y)* compris; **all his property was sold, his house i.** tous ses biens furent vendus, y compris sa maison; **i. in the price are two excursions** deux excursions sont comprises dans le prix; **ser-**

vice i. *(on bill)* service compris; **batteries not i.** les piles ne sont pas comprises

including [ɪn'kluːdɪŋ] PREP y compris; **i. me** moi y compris; **there are five of us, not i. the children** nous sommes cinq, sans compter les enfants; **up to and i. ...** jusqu'à ... inclus

inclusion [ɪn'kluːʒən] N inclusion f

inclusive [ɪn'kluːsɪv] ADJ **1** **five i. of the driver** cinq y compris le chauffeur; **from the 4th to the 12th February i.** du 4 au 12 février inclusivement; **i. price** *(at hotel etc)* (prix m) tout compris; **i. of costs** frais inclus; **i. of tax** toutes taxes comprises, TTC; **i. of VAT** TVA comprise **2** *(all-embracing) (policy)* non discriminatoire; **the party needs to be more i.** il faut que le parti adopte une politique moins discriminatoire

inclusively [ɪn'kluːsɪvlɪ] ADV inclusivement

incognito [ɪnkɒg'niːtəʊ] ADJ, ADV **to be/travel i.** être/voyager incognito
 N *(name, disguise)* incognito m; **to travel under an i.** voyager incognito

incoherence [ɪnkəʊ'hɪərəns] N incohérence f

incoherent [ɪnkəʊ'hɪərənt] ADJ *(speech, reasoning)* incohérent; *(style)* décousu; **to be i.** *(of person)* tenir des propos incohérents

incoherently [ɪnkəʊ'hɪərəntlɪ] ADV d'une manière incohérente

incombustible [ɪnkəm'bʌstɪb(ə)l] ADJ incombustible

income ['ɪnkəm] N **1** revenu m, revenus mpl; **source of i.** source f de revenu; **their combined i.** leurs revenus additionnés; **i. from investments** revenu(s) provenant de placements; **to have a private i. of £15,000 a year** avoir quinze mille livres de rente; **to be on a low/high i.** avoir un faible revenu/un revenu élevé **2** *Com (receipts)* recettes fpl, revenus mpl, rentrées fpl
▸▸ *Acct* **i. account** compte m de produits; **i. bracket** tranche f de salaire *ou* de revenu; *Econ* **i. elasticity** élasticité f par rapport au revenu; *Acct* **i. and expenditure account** compte de dépenses et recettes; *Acct* **i. from operations** produits mpl de gestion courante, produits d'exploitation; **incomes policy** politique f des revenus; **i. smoothing** manipulations fpl de revenu; *Am Acct* **i. statement** compte de résultat; *Am St Exch* **i. stocks** valeurs fpl de rendement; *Fin* **i. stream** flux m de revenus; *Br Admin* **i. support** = prestation f complémentaire en faveur des personnes justifiant de faibles revenus, ≃ revenu m minimum d'insertion; *Fin* **i. tax** impôt m sur le revenu (des personnes physiques); *Fin* **i. tax allowance** déduction f avant impôt, déduction fiscale; *Fin* **i. tax inspector** inspecteur m des contributions directes *ou* des impôts; *Fin* **i. tax return** déclaration f de revenus, feuille f d'impôt; *Fin* **i. velocity of capital** vitesse f de circulation du capital en revenus; *Fin* **i. velocity of circulation** vitesse de circulation de la monnaie en revenus

incomer ['ɪnkʌmər] N nouvel(le) arrivant, -ante

incoming ['ɪnkʌmɪŋ] ADJ *(government)* nouveau; *(plane, missile)* entrant; *(fax, e-mail)* en entrée; *(tide)* montant; **the i. president** le président élu
 NPL *Com, Fin* **incomings** recettes fpl, revenus mpl, rentrées fpl; **incomings and outgoings** dépenses fpl et recettes
▸▸ *Tel* **i. call** appel m de l'extérieur; **this telephone takes i. calls only** ce téléphone ne permet que de recevoir des appels; **i. mail** courrier m (du jour); **i. message** message m entrant; **i. tide** marée f montante; **i. tour operator** voyagiste m de réceptif

incommensurable [ɪnkə'menʃərəb(ə)l] ADJ incommensurable (**with** avec); *Math (number)* irrationnel

incommensurate [ɪnkə'menʃərət] ADJ pas en rapport, pas en proportion (**with** avec)

incommode [ɪnkə'məʊd] VT *Fml* incommoder, déranger

incommodious [ɪnkə'məʊdɪəs] ADJ *Fml* incommode

incommunicado [ɪnkəmjuːnɪ'kɑːdəʊ] ADV **to be held i.** être (gardé) au secret

in-company ['ɪnkʌmpənɪ] ADJ **i. training** formation *f* sur le lieu de travail

incomparable [ɪn'kɒmpərəb(ə)l] ADJ incomparable, sans pareil

incomparably [ɪn'kɒmpərəblɪ] ADV incomparablement; **i. beautiful** d'une beauté incomparable

incompatibility [ɪnkəmpætɪ'bɪlɪtɪ] N *(of people, theories, medication etc)* incompatibilité *f* (**with** avec; **between** entre)

incompatible [ɪnkəm'pætɪb(ə)l] ADJ incompatible (**with** avec)

incompetence [ɪn'kɒmpɪtəns] N *also Jur* incompétence *f*

incompetent [ɪn'kɒmpɪtənt] ADJ **1** *(person)* incompétent, incapable **2** *Law (judge, court) (to hear case, carry out act)* incompétent; **I am i. to act** je n'ai pas qualité pour agir N incompétent, -ente

incomplete [ɪnkəm'pliːt] ADJ *(not complete)* incomplet, ète; *(not finished)* inachevé

incompletely [ɪnkəm'pliːtlɪ] ADV incomplètement

incompleteness [ɪnkəm'pliːtnɪs] N *(of novel, painting etc)* inachèvement *m*; *(of collection of works)* état *m* incomplet

incomprehensible [ɪnkɒmprɪ'hensɪb(ə)l] ADJ *(situation, speech, person)* incompréhensible; *(writing)* indéchiffrable

incomprehensibly [ɪnkɒmprɪ'hensɪblɪ] ADV de manière incompréhensible

incomprehension [ɪnkɒmprɪ'henʃən] N incompréhension *f*

inconceivable [ɪnkən'siːvəb(ə)l] ADJ inconcevable

inconceivably [ɪnkən'siːvəblɪ] ADV inconcevablement

inconclusive [ɪnkən'kluːsɪv] ADJ *(reasoning, evidence)* peu concluant; **it was all very i.** cela n'a donné aucun résultat

inconclusively [ɪnkən'kluːsɪvlɪ] ADV d'une manière peu concluante

incongruity [ɪnkɒŋ'gruːɪtɪ] N incongruité *f*

incongruous [ɪn'kɒŋgrʊəs] ADJ *(behaviour, remark, building)* incongru; *(combination)* bizarre; **the bright red is very i. in this room** le rouge vif détonne fortement dans cette pièce; **they are such an i. couple** ils sont tellement bizarrement assortis

incongruously [ɪn'kɒŋgrʊəslɪ] ADV de manière incongrue, incongrûment

inconsequence [ɪn'kɒnsɪkwəns] N inconséquence *f*

inconsequent [ɪn'kɒnsɪkwənt] ADJ = **inconsequential**

inconsequential [ɪnkɒnsɪ'kwenʃəl] ADJ **1** *(unimportant) (matter, remarks)* sans importance **2** *(not following) (reasoning, ideas)* décousu

inconsiderate [ɪnkən'sɪdərɪt] ADJ *(person)* qui manque d'égards (pour les autres); *(remark, action)* déplacé; **it was most i. of you to do that** tu n'as guère fait preuve de considération en faisant cela; **don't be so i.** pense un peu aux autres

inconsiderately [ɪnkən'sɪdərɪtlɪ] ADV **to behave i. to sb** manquer d'égards *ou* de

considération envers qn; **he had i. locked the door** il avait fermé la porte à clef sans se soucier des autres

inconsistency [ɪnkən'sɪstənsɪ] N **1** *(lack of logicality) (of person, argument)* incohérence *f* **2** *(inconsistent argument, action)* incohérence *f*; **his book is full of inconsistencies** son livre est bourré d'incohérences **3** *(uneven quality) (of artist's work etc)* irrégularité *f*, manque *m* de régularité

inconsistent [ɪnkən'sɪstənt] ADJ **1** *(remark)* en contradiction, contradictoire (**with** avec); **his words are i. with his conduct** ce qu'il dit est en contradiction *ou* ne cadre pas avec ce qu'il fait **2** *(person)* incohérent; **you're being i.** *(in saying that)* tu te contredis; *(in doing that)* tu n'es pas cohérent; **they're i. in what they say** leurs dires sont contradictoires **3** *(irregular) (work)* irrégulier; **his films are very i. in quality** la qualité de ses films est très irrégulière

> Note that the French word **inconsistant** is a false friend. It means **thin, runny** or **vacuous**, depending on the context.

inconsistently [ɪnkən'sɪstəntlɪ] ADV *(to behave)* de façon incohérente; *(to assert)* de façon contradictoire

inconsolable [ɪnkən'səʊləb(ə)l] ADJ inconsolable

inconspicuously [ɪnkən'spɪkjʊəslɪ] ADV de manière discrète

inconspicuous [ɪnkən'spɪkjʊəs] ADJ *(person)* discret, -ète, qui passe inaperçu; *(error, spot)* qui passe inaperçu; **to remain i.** rester dans l'ombre; **I tried to look i.** j'ai essayé de me faire discret

inconstancy [ɪn'kɒnstənsɪ] N *(of person, character)* inconstance *f*; *(of weather etc)* instabilité *f*, caractère *m* changeant

inconstant [ɪn'kɒnstənt] ADJ *(person, character)* inconstant, volage

incontestable [ɪnkən'testəb(ə)l] ADJ incontestable, indéniable

incontestably [ɪnkən'testəblɪ] ADV incontestablement

incontinence [ɪn'kɒntɪnəns] N *Med* incontinence *f*

> ► **i. pads** couches *fpl* pour adultes

incontinent [ɪn'kɒntɪnənt] ADJ *Med* incontinent

incontrovertible [ɪnkɒntrə'vɜːtɪb(ə)l] ADJ *(truth)* incontestable; *(evidence)* irrécusable; *(argument)* irréfutable

inconvenience [ɪnkən'viːnjəns] N dérangement *m*; *(more serious)* désagrément *m*; **to cause i. to sb, to be an i. to sb** incommoder qn, déranger qn; **I'm putting you to a great deal of i.** je vous donne beaucoup d'embarras; **without the slightest i.** sans le moindre dérangement; **we apologize for any i.** nous vous prions de nous excuser pour tout dérangement éventuel; **the i. of living so far from town** les inconvénients qu'il y a à vivre si loin de la ville

VT déranger, causer du dérangement à

inconvenient [ɪnkən'viːnjənt] ADJ *(time)* inopportun; *(visitor)* gênant; *(house)* incommode, malcommode; **this isn't an i. time, is it?** tu es sûr que je ne te dérange pas?; **it's a bit i. just now, could you call back later?** je n'ai pas vraiment le temps tout de suite, tu pourrais me rappeler plus tard?; **if it is not i. to you** si cela ne vous gêne *ou* dérange pas; **Friday's a bit i.** vendredi ne me convient pas tellement; **it's very i. living so far from town** c'est très incommode d'habiter aussi loin de la ville; **the house is very i. for the shops** la maison est mal située par rapport aux commerces

inconveniently [ɪnkən'viːnjəntlɪ] ADV *(to arrive)* à un moment inopportun; **the announcement was i. timed** le moment de l'annonce a été mal choisi; **i. located** mal situé

inconvertible [ɪnkən'vɜːtɪb(ə)l] ADJ *Fin* inconvertible

incorporate [ɪn'kɔːpəreɪt] VT **1** *(include, add)* inclure, incorporer (**with** à, avec; **in** dans); **to i. a paragraph in(to) a chapter** incorporer un paragraphe dans un chapitre; **her work incorporates all the latest discoveries** ses travaux incluent toutes les découvertes les plus récentes **2** *Com (company)* constituer en société commerciale; *(banks)* réunir en société **3** *(merge)* regrouper pour former un tout; **these organizations were incorporated into a national fire brigade** ces organismes ont été regroupés pour constituer une brigade nationale de pompiers

VI **1** s'incorporer **2** *Com* se constituer en société commerciale

incorporated [ɪn'kɔːpəreɪtɪd] ADJ *Am Com* **Sanders I.** ≃ Sanders SARL
> ► **i. company** association *f* constituée en société commerciale, société *f* par actions

incorporation [ɪnkɔːpə'reɪʃən] N **1** *Com (of company)* constitution *f* en société commerciale **2** *(inclusion)* incorporation *f* (**with** à, avec; **in(to)** dans)

incorrect [ɪnkə'rekt] ADJ **1** *(statement, account etc)* inexact; *(figures)* faux, *f* fausse; *(translation)* incorrect **2** *(style, behaviour etc)* incorrect

incorrectly [ɪnkə'rektlɪ] ADV **1** *(reported, stated)* inexactement; *(to speak)* incorrectement; *(invoiced)* indûment; **i. addressed** *(letter)* mal adressé **2** *(to behave etc)* incorrectement

incorrigible [ɪn'kɒrɪdʒɪb(ə)l] ADJ *(child, laziness etc)* incorrigible

incorruptible [ɪnkə'rʌptɪb(ə)l] ADJ *(metal, judge)* incorruptible

incoterms ['ɪnkəʊtɜːmz] NPL *Com* termes *mpl* commerciaux, incoterms *mpl*

increase[1] ['ɪnkriːs] N **1** *(in price, takings, salary, speed etc)* augmentation *f*; *(in pain, population)* accroissement *m*; *(in zeal, attention)* renouvellement *m*; **i. in the cost of living** augmentation du coût de la vie; **sales have shown an i. over the last six months** les ventes ont progressé ces six derniers mois; **i. in value** *(of property etc)* plus-value *f*; **I've had an i. in salary** j'ai été augmenté; **to be on the i.** être en augmentation *ou* en hausse **2** *Knitting* augmentation *f*

increase[2] [ɪn'kriːs] VI *(of prices, speed, unemployment etc)* augmenter; *(of noise, dissatisfaction)* grandir, s'agrandir; *(of pain, population)* s'accroître; **to i. in size** s'agrandir; **to i. in price** augmenter; **to i. in value** prendre de la valeur; **his paintings have increased in value fivefold** la valeur de ses tableaux a quintuplé; **to i. in volume** *(of substance)* augmenter de volume; **the volume of traffic increases every year** le volume de la circulation augmente chaque année

VT **1** *(speed, production, salaries)* augmenter; *(number, expenses)* grossir, augmenter; *(one's wealth)* accroître, augmenter; *(prices)* majorer, augmenter; *(distance)* allonger, augmenter; *(dissatisfaction)* accentuer, augmenter; **to i. sb's salary** augmenter (le salaire de) qn; **to i. the dose** *(of medicine)* augmenter la dose; **to i. one's efforts** redoubler d'efforts; **increased cost of living** augmentation *f* du coût de la vie; **to i. the size of sth** agrandir qch **2** *Knitting* **i. two in the next row** augmenter de deux mailles au rang suivant

increasing [ɪnˈkriːsɪŋ] **ADJ** *(numbers, use, difficulty)* croissant; **an i. number of people are opting for ...** de plus en plus de gens choisissent ...
▸▸ *Fin* **i. rate** tarif *m* progressif

increasingly [ɪnˈkriːsɪŋlɪ] **ADV** *(difficult, big etc)* de plus en plus; **i., people are saying that ...** de plus en plus, les gens disent que ...

incredible [ɪnˈkredɪb(ə)l] **ADJ 1** *(unbelievable)* incroyable; **I find it i. that she didn't know** je n'arrive pas à croire qu'elle n'était pas au courant **2** *Fam (excellent)* incroyable, époustouflant

incredibly [ɪnˈkredɪblɪ] **ADV** incroyablement; **he's i. stupid** il est d'une sottise incroyable; **i., she agreed** elle a consenti, ce qui est incroyable

incredulity [ɪnkrɪˈdjuːlɪtɪ] **N** incrédulité *f*

incredulous [ɪnˈkredjʊləs] **ADJ** incrédule (**of** à l'égard de); *(smile)* d'incrédulité

incredulously [ɪnˈkredjʊləslɪ] **ADV** *(to look at sb)* d'un air incrédule; *(to say)* d'un ton incrédule

increment [ˈɪnkrɪmənt] **N** augmentation *f*, **to rise in annual increments of £1,000** *(of salary)* augmenter de mille livres par an; **unearned i.** *(of land, shares)* plus-value *f*

incremental [ɪnkrɪˈment(ə)l] **ADJ 1** *(increasing)* croissant; **i. increases** augmentations *fpl* régulières **2** *Comput* incrémentiel
▸▸ *Fin* **i. cash flow** cashflow *m* marginal; *Comput* **i. compiler** compilateur *m* incrémentiel; *Fin* **i. cost** coût *m* marginal; *Comput* **i. plotter** traceur *m* par pas

incriminate [ɪnˈkrɪmɪneɪt] **VT** *(implicate)* incriminer, mettre en cause; **I don't want to i. myself** je ne veux rien dire qui me fasse apparaître comme coupable; **you've just incriminated yourself** vous venez de vous compromettre

incriminating [ɪnˈkrɪmɪneɪtɪŋ] **ADJ** *(circumstance, statement etc)* compromettant

incrimination [ɪnkrɪmɪˈneɪʃən] **N** mise *f* en cause, incrimination *f*

incriminatory [ɪnˈkrɪmɪnətərɪ] **ADJ** compromettant

incrustation [ɪnkrʌsˈteɪʃən] **N** *(action)* entartrage *m*; *(deposit)* tartre *m*, dépôt *m* calcaire

incubate [ˈɪnkjʊbeɪt] **VT** *(eggs)* couver, incuber
VI *(of eggs)* incuber; *(of disease)* couver

incubation [ɪnkjʊˈbeɪʃən] **N** incubation *f*
▸▸ **i. period** (période *f* d')incubation

incubator [ˈɪnkjʊbeɪtər] **N** *(for eggs, bacteria)* incubateur *m*; *(for premature babies)* couveuse *f*

incubus [ˈɪnkjʊbəs] **N** *Myth* incube *m*; *Fig Lit* cauchemar *m*

in-cue **N** *TV, Radio* signal *m* de départ

inculcate [ˈɪnkʌlkeɪt] **VT** inculquer; **to i. sth in sb, to i. sb with sth** inculquer qch à qn

inculcation [ɪnkʌlˈkeɪʃən] **N** inculcation *f*

incumbent [ɪnˈkʌmbənt] **N 1** *(of administrative position)* titulaire *mf* **2** *Rel* bénéficiaire *m*, titulaire *m* (d'une charge)
ADJ *(necessary)* **to be i. on sb to do sth** incomber *ou* appartenir à qn de faire qch **2** *(official)* en place

incunabulum, *pl* **incunabula** [ɪnkjuːˈnæbjʊləm, -jʊlə] **N** incunable *m*

incur [ɪnˈkɜːr] **VT** *(-rr-)* *(risk)* courir; *(blame)* encourir; *(loss)* subir; *(sb's anger, hatred)* s'attirer; *(debts)* contracter; *(costs, expenses)* engager; **late payments will i. interest of 4%** en cas de retard de paiements, vous serez redevable d'intérêts au taux de 4%

incurable [ɪnˈkjʊərəb(ə)l] **ADJ** *(disease)* in-

curable, inguérissable; *Fig (optimist, bigot)* invétéré, incorrigible; **an i. romantic** un romantique incorrigible

incurably [ɪnˈkjʊərəblɪ] **ADV** **to be i. ill** avoir une maladie incurable; *Fig* **i. lazy/optimistic** d'une paresse/d'un optimisme incorrigible; **I'm i. romantic** je suis un romantique incorrigible

incurious [ɪnˈkjʊərɪəs] **ADJ** sans curiosité

incursion [ɪnˈkɜːʃən] **N** incursion *f* (**into** dans)

Ind 1 *(abbr* **Independent)** indépendant **2** *abbr* **Indiana**

indebted [ɪnˈdetɪd] **ADJ 1** *(owing money)* endetté; **to be heavily i. to sb** devoir une forte somme à qn **2** *Fig* redevable (**to sb for sth** à qn de qch); **I am i. to Mr Martin for this information** c'est à M. Martin que je dois ce renseignement

indebtedness [ɪnˈdetɪdnɪs] **N** endettement *m*; *Fig* dette *f* (**to** envers)

indecency [ɪnˈdiːsənsɪ] **N** indécence *f*, *Law* **(public act of) i.** *(assault)* attentat *m* à la pudeur; *(exposure)* outrage *m* public à la pudeur

indecent [ɪnˈdiːsənt] **ADJ** indécent; *Fam Fig (sum of money, salary)* scandaleux; **to do sth with i. haste** faire qch avec une rapidité scandaleuse
▸▸ *Law* **i. assault** attentat *m* à la pudeur; **i. behaviour** attentat aux mœurs; **i. exposure** outrage *m* public à la pudeur

indecently [ɪnˈdiːsəntlɪ] **ADV** de manière indécente; *Fig Fam (rich)* scandaleusement

indecipherable [ɪndɪˈsaɪfərəb(ə)l, -frə-b(ə)l] **ADJ** indéchiffrable

indecision [ɪndɪˈsɪʒən] **N** indécision *f*

indecisive [ɪndɪˈsaɪsɪv] **ADJ 1** *(argument)* peu concluant; *(battle, election)* indécis **2** *(person)* indécis, irrésolu; **she was i. about whether to go or stay** elle ne savait pas si elle devait partir ou rester

indecisiveness [ɪndɪˈsaɪsɪvnɪs] **N** indécision *f*

indeclinable [ɪndɪˈklaɪnəb(ə)l] **ADJ** *Gram* indéclinable

indecorous [ɪnˈdekərəs] **ADJ** *(person)* inconvenant; *(departure, retreat etc)* peu digne

indecorously [ɪnˈdekərəslɪ] **ADV** *(to behave)* de manière incorrecte *ou* inconvenante; *(to retreat, leave)* de façon peu digne

indecorum [ɪndɪˈkɔːrəm] **N** incorrection *f*, inconvenance *f*

indeed [ɪnˈdiːd] **ADV 1** *(certainly)* en effet, vraiment; **he was i. a man of genius** c'était vraiment un homme de génie; **I may i. be wrong** il se peut toutefois que j'aie tort
2 *(intensive)* **I am very glad i.** je suis très très content; **thank you very much i.** merci infiniment, merci mille fois
3 *(what is more)* même, à vrai dire; **I think so, i. I am sure of it** je le pense et même j'en suis sûr
4 *(with affirmation or negation)* **you've been to Venice haven't you? – i. I have!** tu es allé à Venise, n'est-ce pas? – oui, j'y suis allé; **you haven't been to Venice – i. I have!** tu ne les jamais allé à Venise – si, j'y suis déjà allé!; **yes i.!** mais certainement!, pour sûr!; **i. not!** certes non!; **it does i.!, i. it does!** *(surprise me, mean that etc)* certainement!
5 *(interrogatively)* **I have lived in Paris – i.?** j'ai vécu à Paris – vraiment?; **have you i.?** *(expressing doubt, lack of interest, mockery)* ah oui?

indefatigable [ɪndɪˈfætɪgəb(ə)l] **ADJ** infatigable

indefatigably [ɪndɪˈfætɪgəblɪ] **ADV** infatigablement

indefensible [ɪndɪˈfensɪb(ə)l] **ADJ** *(theory, argument)* indéfendable; *(behaviour)* inexcusable

indefinable [ɪndɪˈfaɪnəb(ə)l] **ADJ** *(feeling, quality etc)* indéfinissable

indefinite [ɪnˈdefɪnɪt] **ADJ 1** *(period of time, number)* indéterminé; *(leave, strike)* illimité **2** *(ideas, promises etc)* indéfini, vague **3** *Gram (article, pronom)* indéfini **VOIR GRAMMAIRE A5–6; B4–5**

indefinitely [ɪnˈdefɪnɪtlɪ] **ADV** *(to postpone sth)* indéfiniment; **I could go on i.** je pourrais continuer à l'infini

indelible [ɪnˈdelɪb(ə)l] **ADJ** *(ink)* indélébile, ineffaçable; *Fig (mark, memory)* indélébile

indelibly [ɪnˈdelɪblɪ] **ADV** de façon indélébile; *Fig* **i. printed on her mind** à jamais gravé dans son esprit

indelicacy [ɪnˈdelɪkəsɪ] **N** *(of person)* indélicatesse *f*, manque *m* de délicatesse; *(of remark, behaviour)* inconvenance *f*

indelicate [ɪnˈdelɪkət] **ADJ** *(person)* indélicat, qui manque de délicatesse; *(remark, behaviour)* inconvenant

indelicately [ɪnˈdelɪkətlɪ] **ADV** de façon inconvenante

indemnification [ɪndemnɪfɪˈkeɪʃən] **N 1** *(action)* indemnisation *f*, dédommagement *m* (**of sb for sth** de qn de qch) **2** *(money)* indemnité *f*, dédommagement *m*

indemnify [ɪnˈdemnɪfaɪ] **VT 1** *(protect)* garantir (**from, against** contre) **2** *(compensate)* indemniser, dédommager (**for a loss** d'une perte)

indemnity [ɪnˈdemnɪtɪ] **N 1** *(protection) (against loss etc)* garantie *f*, assurance *f* **2** *(compensation)* indemnité *f*, dédommagement *m*

indent¹ [ˈɪndent] **N 1** *Typ* alinéa *m* **2** *Br Com Old-fashioned* commande *f* de marchandises **3** *(notch)* entaille *f*, *(in metal)* bosselure *f*

indent² [ɪnˈdent] **VT 1** *Typ (line)* renfoncer, mettre en retrait *ou* à l'alinéa; **indented line** ligne *f* en alinéa *ou* en retrait; **indented paragraph** paragraphe *m* en retrait **2** *(put notches in)* denteler, entailler; *(surface)* bosseler, bossuer; *Carp (beam)* endenter **3** *Br Com Old-fashioned* **to i. sb for sth** facturer qch à qn
VI *Br Com Old-fashioned* **to i. on sb for sth** commander qch à qn

indentation [ɪndenˈteɪʃən] **N 1** *(made in sand by wheels etc)* trace *f*, impression *f* **2** *(action) (of edges of sth)* découpage *m* **3** *(notched, jagged edge)* dentelure *f*, *(notch)* entaille *f* **4** *Typ* alinéa *m*

indenture [ɪnˈdentʃər] *Jur* **N** contrat *m* synallagmatique, contrat bilatéral; **indentures** *(of apprentice)* contrat d'apprentissage
VT 1 *(bind by contract)* lier par contrat **2** *Arch (of parent or guardian)* mettre en apprentissage (**to sb** chez qn); *(of employer)* engager par un brevet d'apprentissage

independence [ɪndɪˈpendəns] **N** indépendance *f* (**from** à l'égard de); *(of state)* indépendance, autonomie *f*
▸▸ **I. Day** fête *f* nationale de l'Indépendance *(aux États-Unis)*

independent [ɪndɪˈpendənt] **ADJ** *(person, inquiry, record label, cinema etc)* indépendant; *(state, country)* indépendant, autonome; **to be i. of sb/sth** ne pas dépendre de qn/qch; **person of i. means** rentier, -ière *f*; **an i. thinker** un libre-penseur; **his children are i. now** ses enfants peuvent maintenant pourvoir eux-mêmes à leurs besoins
N *Pol etc* indépendant, -ante
▸▸ *Fin* **i. financial adviser** conseiller, -ère financier(ère) indépendant(e); **i. income** revenus *mpl* indépendants, rentes *fpl*; **i. radio** radio *f* privée; **i. retailer** détaillant, -ante in-

dépendant(e); *Br* **i. school** école *f* privée; *Aut* **i. suspension** suspension *f* indépendante

independently [ɪndɪ'pendəntlɪ] **ADV 1** *(to behave etc)* avec indépendance; **to live i.** être indépendant **2** *(without being connected)* indépendamment; **i. of that** indépendamment de cela

in-depth **ADJ** *(study etc)* approfondi, en profondeur; **i. article** article *m* de fond

indescribable [ɪndɪ'skraɪbəb(ə)l] **ADJ** *(anger, poverty)* indescriptible; *(joy)* indicible

indescribably [ɪndɪ'skraɪbəblɪ] **ADV** *(angry, painful etc)* atrocement; *(happy)* indiciblement; **it was i. awful** c'était absolument affreux

indestructible [ɪndɪ'strʌktəb(ə)l] **ADJ** indestructible

indeterminable [ɪndɪ'tɜːmɪnəb(ə)l] **ADJ** indéterminable

indeterminate [ɪndɪ'tɜːmɪnət] **ADJ** *(space etc)*, *Math (quantity)* indéterminé

indeterminately [ɪndɪ'tɜːmɪnətlɪ] **ADV** *(to continue)* de façon indéterminée; **an i. long period** une période indéterminée; **an i. large number of factors** un nombre de facteurs indéterminé

index ['ɪndeks], *pl* **indexes**, **indices** ['ɪndeksɪz, 'ɪndɪsiːz] **N 1** *(pl* **indexes**) *(of book)* index *m*, table *f* alphabétique
  2 *(pl* **indexes**) *(catalogue)* fichier *m*, répertoire *m*
  3 *(pl* **indices**) *Math etc* indice *m*; *(exponent)* exposant *m*
  4 *(pl* **indices**) *(finger)* index *m*
  5 *(pl* **indices**) *Fig (sign)* indice *m*, signe *m* (indicateur)
  6 *Typ (pl* **indices**) *(cross-reference)* renvoi *m*
  VT 1 *(create index of) (book)* dresser l'index de; *Comput (database)* indexer
  2 *(put into index) (article etc)* répertorier, classer
  3 *(wages, pension)* indexer; **indexed to inflation** indexé sur l'inflation
  ►► *Am St Exch* **i. arbitrage** arbitrage *m* sur indice; **i. card** fiche *f*; **i. finger** index *m*; *St Exch* **i. fund** fonds *m* à gestion indicielle, fonds indiciel; **i. number** *(in statistics)* indice; *St Exch* **i. option** option *f* sur indice; *Opt* **i. of refraction** indice *m* de réfraction

indexation [ɪndek'seɪʃən] **N** indexation *f*
  ►► *Fin* **i. clause** clause *f* d'indexation

indexing ['ɪndeksɪŋ] **N** *Comput* indexation *f*

index-link **VT** *(wages, pension)* indexer; **to i. a pension to the cost of living** indexer une retraite sur le coût de la vie

index-linked **ADJ** *(wages, pension)* indexé

index-linking **N** *(of wages, pension)* indexation *f*

India ['ɪndɪə] **N** Inde *f*
  ►► *Am* **I. ink** encre *f* de Chine; **I. paper** papier *m* bible; *Br* **I. rubber** *(substance)* caoutchouc *m*; *(eraser)* gomme *f*

Indian ['ɪndɪən] **ADJ 1** *(of, from India)* de l'Inde, indien **2** *(of Native Americans) (customs, handicrafts etc)* indien, amérindien; *(leader, chief)* indien; *Am Pej* **to be an I. giver** = demander la restitution de quelque chose qu'on a donné
  N 1 *(inhabitant, native of India)* Indien, -ienne **2** *(Native American)* Indien, -ienne (d'Amérique), Amérindien, -ienne
  ►► **I. club** massue *f* (pour la gymnastique); *Am Agr* **I. corn** maïs *m*; **I. elephant** éléphant *m* d'Asie; **I. file** file *f* indienne; *Br* **I. hemp** chanvre *m* indien, cannabis *m*; *Br* **I. ink** encre *f* de Chine; **the I. Ocean** l'océan *m* Indien; **I. reserve** réserve *f* indienne; **I. summer** été *m* de la Saint-Martin, été indien; *Fig* vieillesse *f* heureuse

indicate ['ɪndɪkeɪt] **VT 1** *(point to, show)* indiquer, montrer; **to i. sth with one's hand** in-

diquer qch de la main; **at the time indicated** à l'heure dite *ou* indiquée; *Aut* **to i. a left/right turn** mettre son clignotant pour indiquer que l'on va tourner à gauche/droite
  2 *(denote)* indiquer, dénoter; **an expression that indicated determination** un visage plein de détermination
  3 *(state)* *(opposition, intention to do sth)* faire connaître; **he has indicated that ...** il a fait savoir que ...
  4 *(need)* *Med* **plenty of rest is indicated** il est recommandé de bien se reposer; **strong measures were clearly indicated** il était évident que la situation exigeait des mesures rigoureuses
  VI *Aut* mettre son clignotant

indication [ɪndɪ'keɪʃən] **N 1** *(act of pointing out)* indication *f* (**of sth to sb** de qch à qn)
  2 *(sign)* indice *m*, signe *m*, indication *f*; **there is every i. that he was speaking the truth** tout porte à croire qu'il disait vrai; **there is no i. of a struggle** il n'y a aucun signe de lutte; **all the indications are that ...** tout porte à croire que ...; **he gave early indications of his talent** son talent se révéla de bonne heure; **to take sth as an i. that** interpréter qch comme une indication du fait que
  3 *(warning, statement)* **to give clear i. of one's intentions** faire connaître clairement ses intentions

indicative [ɪn'dɪkətɪv] VOIR GRAMMAIRE A40
  N *Gram* indicatif *m*; **in the i.** à l'indicatif
  ADJ *(suggestive)* révélateur, -trice (**of** de)
  ►► *Gram* **i. mood** mode *m* indicatif, indicatif

indicator ['ɪndɪkeɪtər] **N 1** *(on instrument, gauge etc)* index *m*, aiguille *f*; *Aut* clignotant *m*; *(LED, on machine)* indicateur *m*; *Naut, Aviat (for speed etc)* indicateur, compteur *m*
  2 *(indication, guide)* indicateur *m*, indice *m*
  ►► *Rail etc* **i. board** tableau *m* *ou* indicateur *m* des arrivées et des départs; **i. light** signal *m* lumineux; *(on monitor)* voyant *m*

indict [ɪn'daɪt] **VT** *Law* inculper (**for** pour)

indictable [ɪn'daɪtəb(ə)l] **ADJ** *Law (person)* passible de poursuite en justice
  ►► **i. offence** délit *m*

indictment [ɪn'daɪtmənt] **N** *Law* **1** *(of person)* inculpation *f*; *(by public prosecutor)* réquisitoire *m*; *Fig* **it is an i. of our education system that the illiteracy rate is so high** le taux d'analphabétisme élevé en dit long sur notre système éducatif **2** *(document)* acte *m* d'accusation

indie ['ɪndɪ] *Fam* **N** *(music)* indie-rock *m*
  ADJ indépendant
  ►► **i. music** indie-rock

Indies (the) [ðɪ'ɪndɪz] **NPL** *Hist (South and Southeast Asia)* les Indes *fpl*

indifference [ɪn'dɪfrəns, -fərəns] **N 1** *(lack of interest)* indifférence *f* (**to** *ou* **towards sth/sb** pour qch/à l'égard de qn); **it's a matter of complete i. to me** cela m'est parfaitement indifférent **2** *(of talent etc)* médiocrité *f*

indifferent [ɪn'dɪfrənt, -fərənt] **ADJ 1** *(not interested)* indifférent (**to** à); **I am** *or* **feel i. about him** il m'est indifférent **2** *(meal, cooking, painter)* médiocre

indifferently [ɪn'dɪfrəntlɪ] **ADV 1** *(disinterestedly)* avec indifférence **2** *(to cook, paint etc)* médiocrement

indigence ['ɪndɪdʒəns] **N** *Fml* indigence *f*

indigenous [ɪn'dɪdʒɪnəs] **ADJ** *(plant, product, population etc)* indigène (**to** à)

indigent ['ɪndɪdʒənt] **ADJ** *Fml* indigent

indigestible [ɪndɪ'dʒestɪb(ə)l] **ADJ** indigeste

indigestion [ɪndɪ'dʒestʃən] **N** indigestion *f*; **to have (an attack of) i.** avoir une indigestion

indignant [ɪn'dɪgnənt] **ADJ** *(person, air)* in-

digné; *(shout)* d'indignation; **to be** *or* **feel i. at sth** être indigné *ou* s'indigner de qch; **to make sb i.** indigner qn

indignantly [ɪn'dɪgnəntlɪ] **ADV** avec indignation; *(to look)* d'un air indigné

indignation [ɪndɪg'neɪʃən] **N** indignation *f*

indignity [ɪn'dɪgnɪtɪ] **N** indignité *f*; **to suffer indignities** souffrir des affronts; **the i. of it!** quelle honte!

indigo, *pl* **indigo**, **indigoes** ['ɪndɪgəʊ, 'ɪndɪgəʊz] **N 1** *(dye, colour)* indigo *m* **2** *Bot (plant)* indigotier *m*
  ADJ indigo *inv*
  ►► **i. blue** *(colour)* indigo; *Bot* **i. plant** indigotier

indirect [ɪndɪ'rekt] **ADJ** *(influence, result, answer)* indirect; *(route, approach, ways)* détourné; *Fin (costs, tax)* indirect
  ►► *Fin* **i. investment** investissement *m* indirect; *Gram* **i. object** objet *m* indirect; *Mktg* **i. promotional expenditure** coûts *mpl* de promotion indirects; *Mktg* **i. selling** vente *f* indirecte; *Gram* **i. speech** discours *m* indirect VOIR GRAMMAIRE A21

indirectly [ɪndɪ'rektlɪ] **ADV** indirectement

indiscernible [ɪndɪ'sɜːnɪb(ə)l] **ADJ** *(not visible)* indiscernable; *Fig (reason)* obscur; *(difference)* imperceptible

indiscipline [ɪn'dɪsɪplɪn] **N** indiscipline *f*

indiscreet [ɪndɪ'skriːt] **ADJ** indiscret, -ète; **an i. admission** une indiscrétion

indiscreetly [ɪndɪ'skriːtlɪ] **ADV** indiscrètement; *(to behave)* imprudemment

indiscretion [ɪndɪ'skreʃən] **N 1** *(lack of discretion)* manque *m* de discrétion, indiscrétion *f* **2** *(unwise act)* écart *m* de conduite; *(unwise remark)* indiscrétion *f*; **to be guilty of an i.** *(blunder)* commettre une inconséquence; *(sexual)* se compromettre

indiscriminate [ɪndɪ'skrɪmɪnɪt] **ADJ** *(revenge)* aveugle, qui ne fait pas de distinction; **he's an i. reader** il lit tout ce qui lui tombe sous la main; **he was i. in his praise** il a distribué des compliments sans discernement; **i. slaughter** tuerie *f* générale

indiscriminately [ɪndɪ'skrɪmɪnɪtlɪ] **ADV** *(to hit, blame, kill)* sans distinction; **he reads i.** il lit tout ce qui lui tombe sous la main; **to fire i. into the crowd** tirer dans la foule sans faire de distinction

indispensable [ɪndɪ'spensəb(ə)l] **ADJ** *(person, thing)* indispensable

indisposed [ɪndɪ'spəʊzd] **ADJ** *Fml* **1** *(ill)* indisposé, souffrant; **to be** *or* **feel i.** être indisposé *ou* souffrant **2** *(not inclined)* peu enclin, peu disposé (**to do sth** à faire qch)

indisposition [ɪndɪspə'zɪʃən] **N** *Fml* **1** *(illness)* indisposition *f* **2** *(lack of inclination)* peu *m* d'inclination (**to do sth** à faire qch)

indisputable [ɪndɪ'spjuːtəb(ə)l] **ADJ** incontestable, indiscutable; **it is the i. truth** c'est incontestable

indisputably [ɪndɪ'spjuːtəblɪ] **ADV** indiscutablement, incontestablement

indissoluble [ɪndɪ'sɒljʊb(ə)l] **ADJ** *(union, friendship)* indissoluble

indistinct [ɪndɪ'stɪŋkt] **ADJ** *(object, noise etc)* indistinct, peu distinct; *(sound)* confus; *(memory)* vague

indistinctly [ɪndɪ'stɪŋktlɪ] **ADV** *(to see, talk)* indistinctement; *(to feel)* vaguement

indistinguishable [ɪndɪ'stɪŋgwɪʃəb(ə)l] **ADJ** que l'on ne peut distinguer (**from** de), indiscernable; **the forgery was i. from the real thing** le faux et l'original étaient indiscernables, on ne pouvait distinguer le faux de l'original; **the two insects are i.** les deux insectes ne peuvent pas être distingués

individual [ɪndɪ'vɪdjʊəl] **ADJ 1** *(for a single*

person or thing) individuel; **his pupils get i. attention** il s'occupe de ses élèves individuellement; **every room has its own i. shower** chaque chambre est équipée de sa propre douche **2** *(taken separately)* **i. animals vary in size** la taille varie selon les individus; **i. cases will be decided on their merits** chaque cas sera étudié individuellement **3** *(unique)* personnel; **she always has a very i. hairstyle** elle est toujours coiffée de façon très personnelle

N individu *m*; **a private i.** un simple particulier

▸▸ *Fin* **i. company accounts** comptes *mpl* sociaux, comptes d'entreprise individuelle; *Am Fin* **i. retirement account** plan *m* d'epargne retraite personnel; *Fin* **i. savings account** plan d'epargne en actions; **i. tuition** cours *mpl* particuliers

individualism [ɪndɪˈvɪdjʊəlɪz(ə)m] **N** individualisme *m*

individualist [ɪndɪˈvɪdjʊəlɪst] **N** individualiste *mf*

individualistic [ɪndɪvɪdjʊəˈlɪstɪk] **ADJ** individualiste

individuality [ɪndɪvɪdjʊˈælɪtɪ] **N** individualité *f*

individualize [ɪndɪˈvɪdjʊəlaɪz] **VT** *(to make distinctive)* individualiser; *(adapt to individual needs)* adapter aux besoins de chaque individu

individually [ɪndɪˈvɪdjʊəlɪ] **ADV** individuellement, séparément; **he spoke to us all i.** il nous a parlé à tous un par un

indivisible [ɪndɪˈvɪzɪb(ə)l] **ADJ** indivisible

Indochina [ˈɪndəʊˈtʃaɪnə] **N** Indochine *f*

indoctrinate [ɪnˈdɒktrɪneɪt] **VT** endoctriner; **to i. sb with an idea** inculquer une idée à qn

indoctrination [ɪndɒktrɪˈneɪʃən] **N** endoctrinement *m*

Indo-European [ˈɪndəʊ-] **ADJ** indo-européen
N 1 Indo-Européen, -enne **2** *Ling* indo-européen *m*

indolence [ˈɪndələns] **N** indolence *f*

indolent [ˈɪndələnt] **ADJ** indolent

indolently [ˈɪndələntlɪ] **ADV** indolemment

indomitable [ɪnˈdɒmɪtəb(ə)l] **ADJ** indomptable; *(courage etc)* invincible

Indonesia [ɪndəʊˈniːzɪə, -ʒə] **N** Indonésie *f*

Indonesian [ɪndəʊˈniːzɪən, -ʒ(ə)n] **ADJ** indonésien
N 1 Indonésien, -ienne **2** *Ling* indonésien *m*

indoor [ˈɪndɔːr] **ADJ** *(plant)* d'appartement; *(photography)* en intérieur; *(swimming pool, tennis court)* couvert
▸▸ **i. aerial** antenne *f* intérieure; **i. athletics** athlétisme *m* en salle; **i. games** *(sports)* jeux *mpl* pratiqués en salle; *(board games, charades etc)* jeux d'intérieur; *Cin, TV* **i. scene** scène *f* tournée en intérieur; **i. visitor attraction** centre *m* d'intérêt couvert

Attention: ne pas confondre avec l'adverbe **indoors**.

indoors [ɪnˈdɔːz] **ADV** *(inside house)* à la maison; *(inside building)* à l'intérieur; **to go i.** (r)entrer; **to stay i.** rester à l'intérieur; **don't stay i., go out and play!** ne reste donc pas enfermé, va jouer dehors!; **this job's better, at least it's i.** ce poste est mieux, au moins je/tu/il/*etc* travaille(s) à l'intérieur; *Br Sl* **her i.** *(wife)* la bourgeoise

Attention: ne pas confondre avec l'adjectif **indoor**.

indorse [ɪnˈdɔːs] **VT** = **endorse**

indrawn [ˈɪndrɔːn] **ADJ** *(air)* aspiré; **i. breath** aspiration *f*, **he watched with i. breath** il regardait en retenant son souffle

indubitable [ɪnˈdjuːbɪtəb(ə)l] **ADJ** indubitable

indubitably [ɪnˈdjuːbɪtəblɪ] **ADV** indubitablement

induce [ɪnˈdjuːs] **VT 1** *(persuade)* persuader (**to do** à faire); **nothing will i. him to change his mind** rien ne le fera changer d'idée **2** *(bring about)* *(sleep, vomiting, feeling)* provoquer; *Elec etc (current etc)* amorcer, induire; **a drug-induced state** un état provoqué par la drogue **3** *Obst* **to i. labour** provoquer l'accouchement, déclencher le travail; **she's had to be induced** on a dû lui faire une piqûre pour provoquer l'accouchement *ou* déclencher le travail **4** *(in logic), Math* induire

inducement [ɪnˈdjuːsmənt] **N** *(incentive)* **the company was offered several inducements to relocate in the area** l'entreprise s'est vu offrir plusieurs avantages pour l'inciter à se relocaliser dans la région; **what inducements were used to persuade him to co-operate?** comment l'a-t-on incité à coopérer?; **fears for his daughter's safety will be enough of an i.** le fait qu'il craint pour la sécurité de sa fille sera une motivation suffisante; **an i. of $10,000** *(bribe)* un pot de vin de 10 000 dollars

induct [ɪnˈdʌkt] **VT 1** *(install in office)* installer dans sa charge; *Rel (minister)* mettre en possession d'un bénéfice **2** *(initiate)* initier (**into** à); **he was inducted into the Freemasons** il a été initié à la franc-maçonnerie **3** *Am Mil* **to be inducted** *(into the army)* être appelé sous les drapeaux

inducted gas [ɪnˈdʌktɪd] **N** *Aut* gaz *m* aspiré

induction [ɪnˈdʌkʃən] **N 1** *(of minister, official)* installation *f* **2** *Obst (of labour)* déclenchement *m* **3** *(in logic), Math* induction *f* **4** *Elec* induction *f*
▸▸ *Elec* **i. coil** bobine *f* d'inductance; **i. loop** circuit *m* d'induction

inductive [ɪnˈdʌktɪv] **ADJ 1** *(reasoning)* inductif, par induction **2** *Elec (current etc)* inducteur, -trice

indulge [ɪnˈdʌldʒ] **VT 1** *(person)* être trop gentil avec; *(spoil)* gâter; *(hope)* nourrir; *(passion)* se livrer à, donner libre cours à; **they indulged his every whim** ils lui cédaient tous ses caprices; **to i. oneself** se faire plaisir **2** *Com (payer of bill of exchange)* accorder un délai à
VI to i. in *(activity)* s'adonner à, se livrer à; **to i. in a cigar** se permettre un cigare; **to i. in a glass of port** s'offrir un verre de porto; **to i. in speculation** se laisser aller à des spéculations *(on, about sur)*; **I used to drink a lot but nowadays I rarely i.** je buvais beaucoup mais maintenant c'est rare que je me le permette; *Fam* **thanks, but I don't i.** *(drink, smoke)* merci, mais je ne bois/fume pas

indulgence [ɪnˈdʌldʒəns] **N 1** *(doting, leniency)* indulgence *f* (**to** envers), *Pej* complaisance *f* (**to** envers) **2** *(act, activity)* **because of his i. in his favourite pastime** parce qu'il s'adonnait *ou* se livrait à son passe-temps préféré; **i. in rich food** excès *mpl* de table **3** *(treat)* **Belgian chocolates are my only i.** les chocolats belges sont mon seul péché mignon; **I allow myself the occasional i.** de temps en temps je me fais plaisir **4** *Cathol* indulgence *f*

indulgent [ɪnˈdʌldʒənt] **ADJ** indulgent (**to** envers, pour); **over-i. father** père *m* trop indulgent

indulgently [ɪnˈdʌldʒəntlɪ] **ADV** avec indulgence

industrial [ɪnˈdʌstrɪəl] **ADJ** *(area, city, activity etc)* industriel; *(conflict)* ouvrier, du travail; **for i. use only** usage industriel uniquement; **in i. quantities** en quantités industrielles
▸▸ **i. accident** accident *m* du travail; **i. accident insurance** assurance *f* contre les accidents du travail; *Br* **i. action** grève(s) *f(pl)*; **i. arbitrator** ≃ prud'homme *m*; *Am Sch* **i. art** = cours *m* technique où l'on apprend le maniement des machines propres à une industrie particulière; **i. bank** banque *f* industrielle; **i. centre** centre *m* industriel; **i. complex** complexe *m* industriel; **i. disease** maladie *f* professionnelle *ou* du travail; **i. espionage** espionnage *m* industriel; *Br* **i. estate** zone *f* industrielle; **i. injuries benefit** indemnité *f* pour accidents du travail; **i. injury** accident *m* du travail; **i. marketer** spécialiste *mf* en marketing; **i. marketing** marketing *m* industriel; **i. medicine** médecine *f* du travail; *Econ* **i. production** production *f* industrielle; **i. relations** relations *fpl* entre le patronat et les travailleurs; *Hist* **the I. Revolution** la révolution industrielle; *St Exch* **i. shares** valeurs *mpl* industrielles; **i. statistics** statistiques *fpl* sur l'industrie; *Br, Austr Law* **i. tribunal** ≃ conseil *m* de prud'hommes; **i. unit** atelier *m*; **i. unrest** agitation *f* ouvrière

Note that the French adjective **industriel** never refers to the relationship between employers and employees.

industrialism [ɪnˈdʌstrɪəlɪz(ə)m] **N** industrialisme *m*

industrialist [ɪnˈdʌstrɪəlɪst] **N** industriel *m*

industrialization [ɪndʌstrɪəlaɪˈzeɪʃən] **N** industrialisation *f*

industrialize [ɪnˈdʌstrɪəlaɪz] **VT** industrialiser
VI s'industrialiser

industrialized [ɪnˈdʌstrɪəlaɪzd] **ADJ** **i. countries, i. nations** pays *mpl* industrialisés

industrializing [ɪnˈdʌstrɪəlaɪzɪŋ] **ADJ** *(country, economy)* en voie d'industrialisation

industrials [ɪnˈdʌstrɪəlz] **NPL** *St Exch* valeurs *fpl* industrielles *ou* des sociétés industrielles

industrial-strength **ADJ** *(adhesive, bleach etc)* à usage industriel; *Hum (coffee)* hyper-costaud

industrious [ɪnˈdʌstrɪəs] **ADJ** industrieux, travailleur

industriously [ɪnˈdʌstrɪəslɪ] **ADV** assidûment

industriousness [ɪnˈdʌstrɪəsnɪs] **N** assiduité *f* (au travail), application *f*

industry [ˈɪndʌstrɪ] **N 1** industrie *f*, **i. has declined in this country** l'industrie a décliné dans ce pays; **heavy/light i.** l'industrie lourde/légère; **2** *(diligence)* assiduité *f* (au travail), application *f*
▸▸ **i. expert** expert *m* de l'industrie; **i. forecast** prévision *f* de l'industrie; **i. sector** secteur *m* industriel *ou* secondaire

industry-standard **ADJ** normalisé

Indy [ˈɪndɪ] **ADJ**
▸▸ **I. car** = type de voiture de course, aux États-Unis; **the I. 500** = course *f* automobile qui se déroule à Indianapolis, aux États-Unis

inebriate[1] [ɪnˈiːbrɪət] *Fml* **ADJ** ivre; **in his i. state** dans son état d'ébriété *ou* d'ivresse
N ivrogne *mf*

inebriate[2] [ɪnˈiːbrɪeɪt] **VT** enivrer

inebriated [ɪnˈiːbrɪeɪtɪd] **ADJ** ivre

inebriation [ɪniːbrɪˈeɪʃən] **N 1** *(act of ma-*

king drunk) enivrement *m* **2** *(drunkenness)* ivresse *f*, ébriété *f*

inedible [ɪnˈedɪb(ə)l] **ADJ** non comestible; *(too disgusting to eat)* immangeable

ineducable [ɪnˈedjʊkəb(ə)l] **ADJ** inéducable

ineffable [ɪnˈefəb(ə)l] **ADJ** *Fml (joy etc)* ineffable, indicible

ineffective [ɪnɪˈfektɪv] **ADJ** *(means, remedy, speech, leader)* inefficace; *(speaker)* terne; *(style)* plat, terne

ineffectively [ɪnɪˈfektɪvlɪ] **ADV** *(to protest, plead)* vainement; *(to chair a meeting)* de manière inefficace; **the dart bounced i. off the rhino's hide** la flèche a rebondi sur la peau du rhinocéros sans produire aucun effet

ineffectual [ɪnɪˈfektjʊəl] **ADJ** *(effort, reasoning, person)* inefficace

inefficacious [ɪnefɪˈkeɪʃəs] **ADJ** *Fml* inefficace

inefficacy [ɪnˈefɪkəsɪ] **N** inefficacité *f*

inefficiency [ɪnɪˈfɪʃənsɪ] **N** *(of method, machine, organization, person)* manque *m* d'efficacité, inefficacité *f*

inefficient [ɪnɪˈfɪʃənt] **ADJ** *(measure, person etc)* inefficace

inefficiently [ɪnɪˈfɪʃəntlɪ] **ADV** inefficacement

inelastic [ɪnɪˈlæstɪk] **ADJ** sans élasticité; *Fig* rigide, raide

inelegant [ɪnˈelɪɡənt] **ADJ** inélégant

inelegantly [ɪnˈelɪɡəntlɪ] **ADV** inélégamment

ineligible [ɪnˈelɪdʒɪb(ə)l] **ADJ** *(candidate)* inéligible; **to be i. for sth** ne pas avoir droit à qch; **he's i. to vote** il n'a pas le droit de voter; **i. for military service** inapte au service militaire

ineluctable [ɪnɪˈlʌktəb(ə)l] **ADJ** *Lit* inéluctable

inept [ɪnˈept] **ADJ** inepte

ineptitude [ɪnˈeptɪtjuːd] **N** ineptie *f*

ineptly [ɪnˈeptlɪ] **ADV** de façon inepte

inequality [ɪnɪˈkwɒlɪtɪ] **N** *(social, economic)* inégalité *f*

inequitable [ɪnˈekwɪtəb(ə)l] **ADJ** inéquitable

ineradicable [ɪnɪˈrædɪkəb(ə)l] **ADJ** indéracinable, inextirpable

inert [ɪˈnɜːt] **ADJ** inerte; *Chem* **the i. gases** les gaz *mpl* inertes

inertia [ɪˈnɜːʃɪə] **N** *Phys, Fam (of person)* inertie *f*
▸▸ *Br Mktg* **i. selling** vente *f* forcée; *Phys* **i. switch** contacteur *m* à inertie

inertia-reel seat-belt **N** *Aut* ceinture *f* (de sécurité) à enrouleur

inescapable [ɪnɪˈskeɪpəb(ə)l] **ADJ** incontournable

inessential [ɪnɪˈsenʃəl] **ADJ** non essentiel **N** chose *f* superflue; **that's one of the inessentials** ça fait partie du superflu

inestimable [ɪnˈestɪməb(ə)l] **ADJ** *(value, benefit etc)* inestimable

inevitability [ɪnevɪtəˈbɪlɪtɪ] **N** caractère *m* inévitable

inevitable [ɪnˈevɪtəb(ə)l] **ADJ** *(unavoidable)* inévitable; *(conclusion)* incontournable; **his promotion is i.** il va de soi qu'il sera promu; **the i. conclusion** *(of a play, novel)* le dénouement fatal **N the i.** l'inévitable *m*

inevitably [ɪnˈevɪtəblɪ] **ADV** inévitablement; **he's i. late** il est immanquablement en retard

inexact [ɪnɪɡˈzækt] **ADJ** *(lacking clarity)* imprécis; *(inaccurate)* inexact; **it's an i. science** ce n'est pas une science exacte

inexactitude [ɪnɪɡˈzæktɪtjuːd] **N** *(inaccuracy)* inexactitude *f*; *(lack of clarity)* imprécision *f*

inexactly [ɪnɪɡˈzæktlɪ] **ADV** *(inaccurately)* inexactement; *(with a lack of clarity)* de façon imprécise

inexactness [ɪnɪɡˈzæktnɪs] **N** *(inaccuracy)* inexactitude *f*; *(lack of clarity)* imprécision *f*

inexcusable [ɪnɪkˈskjuːzəb(ə)l] **ADJ** inexcusable, impardonnable; **that was i. of you** tu es impardonnable

inexcusably [ɪnɪkˈskjuːzəblɪ] **ADV** inexcusablement, impardonnablement; **i. rude/slow** d'une grossièreté/lenteur inexcusable

inexhaustible [ɪneɡˈzɔːstɪb(ə)l] **ADJ** inépuisable; *(source)* intarissable; *(patience)* inépuisable, sans limite; **she had an i. supply of jokes** elle avait un stock de blagues inépuisable

inexorable [ɪnˈeksərəb(ə)l] **ADJ** inexorable

inexorably [ɪnˈeksərəblɪ] **ADV** inexorablement

inexpedient [ɪnɪkˈspiːdɪənt] **ADJ** inopportun, malavisé

inexpensive [ɪnɪkˈspensɪv] **ADJ** peu coûteux, bon marché *inv*; **i. to run** *(house, car)* économique

inexpensively [ɪnɪkˈspensɪvlɪ] **ADV** bon marché, à bas prix; *(to live)* économiquement, à peu de frais

inexperience [ɪnɪkˈspɪərɪəns] **N** inexpérience *f*

inexperienced [ɪnɪkˈspɪərɪənst] **ADJ** **1** *(person)* inexpérimenté, sans expérience; **she is still i.** elle manque encore d'expérience; **he's i. in handling staff** il n'a pas l'habitude de diriger le personnel **2** *(eye, ear)* inexercé

inexpert [ɪnˈekspɜːt] **ADJ** inexpert; **he was i. in such matters** il ne connaissait pas grand-chose dans ce domaine; **her i. handling of the situation** la façon maladroite dont elle a géré l'affaire

inexpertly [ɪnˈekspɜːtlɪ] **ADV** maladroitement, de façon maladroite

inexpiable [ɪnˈekspɪəb(ə)l] **ADJ** *Fml* inexpiable

inexplicable [ɪnɪkˈsplɪkəb(ə)l] **ADJ** inexplicable

inexplicably [ɪnɪkˈsplɪkəblɪ] **ADV** inexplicablement

inexpressible [ɪnɪkˈspresɪb(ə)l] **ADJ** *(pleasure)* inexprimable

inexpressive [ɪnɪkˈspresɪv] **ADJ** inexpressif, sans expression

inextinguishable [ɪnɪkˈstɪŋɡwɪʃəb(ə)l] **ADJ** inextinguible

in extremis [ɪnɪkˈstriːmɪs] **ADV 1** *(as a last resort)* en dernier recours **2** *esp Rel (at the point of death)* sur le point de mourir, à l'article de la mort

inextricable [ɪnekˈstrɪkəb(ə)l] **ADJ 1** *(situation)* inextricable **2** *(ties, links)* indissoluble

inextricably [ɪnekˈstrɪkəblɪ] **ADV 1** inextricablement **2** *(tied, linked)* indissolublement

infallibility [ɪnfælɪˈbɪlɪtɪ] **N** *Rel etc* infaillibilité *f*

infallible [ɪnˈfælɪb(ə)l] **ADJ** infaillible, immanquable

infallibly [ɪnˈfælɪblɪ] **ADV** infailliblement, immanquablement

infamous [ˈɪnfəməs] **ADJ** *(person)* infâme; *(behaviour)* abominable, infâme; *(place)* mal famé

infamously [ˈɪnfəməslɪ] **ADV** *(to behave)* de manière infâme

infamy [ˈɪnfəmɪ] **N** infamie *f*

infancy [ˈɪnfənsɪ] **N 1** *(early childhood)* pe-

tite enfance *f*; *Fig (of an art, industry)* débuts *mpl*; **from i.** dès la plus tendre enfance; *Fig* **science was in its i.** la science en était à ses balbutiements **2** *Law (minority)* minorité *f*

infant [ˈɪnfənt] **N 1** *(until the age of two)* nourrisson *m*; *Br (under the age of seven)* jeune enfant *mf* **2** *Law (minor)* mineur, -eure **ADJ** *(child)* en bas âge; *Fig* **an i. science** une science naissante
▸▸ *Br Sch* **i. class** classe *f* enfantine; **i. mortality** mortalité *f* infantile; **i. mortality rate** taux *m* de mortalité infantile; **i. prodigy** enfant prodige; *Br Sch* **i. school** école *f* maternelle *(5–7 ans)*

infanticide [ɪnˈfæntɪsaɪd] **N 1** *(crime)* infanticide *m* **2** *(person)* infanticide *mf*

infantile [ˈɪnfəntaɪl] **ADJ 1** *(of infants) (mind, imagination)* d'enfant; *Med (illness)* infantile **2** *Pej (childish) (reasoning, remark etc)* puéril
▸▸ *Old-fashioned* **i. paralysis** paralysie *f* infantile

infantilism [ɪnˈfæntɪlɪz(ə)m] **N** *Fml* infantilisme *m*

infantry [ˈɪnfəntrɪ] **N** *Mil* infanterie *f*, *(foot soldiers)* fantassins *mpl*

infantryman, *pl* **infantrymen** [ˈɪnfəntrɪmən] **N** *Mil* soldat *m* d'infanterie, fantassin *m*

infarct [ˈɪnfɑːkt] **N** *Med* infarctus *m*

infarction [ɪnˈfɑːkʃən] **N** *Med* infarctus *m*

infatuated [ɪnˈfætjʊeɪtɪd] **ADJ** entiché (**with** de); **to become i. with sb/sth** s'enticher de qn/de qch

infatuation [ɪnfætjʊˈeɪʃən] **N** engouement *m*, *Fam* toquade *f*; **to have an i. for sb** s'enticher de qn; **it's just (an) i.** ce n'est qu'une toquade

infect [ɪnˈfekt] **VT 1** *(water supply, area, food)*, *Med (person)* contaminer; *(wound, limb, disk)* infecter; **to i. sb with a disease** *(involuntarily)* transmettre une maladie à qn; *(voluntarily)* inoculer une maladie à qn; *Fig* **to i. sb with one's enthusiasm** communiquer son enthousiasme à qn **2** *Fig (corrupt, taint) (air, morals etc)* corrompre, vicier

infected [ɪnˈfektɪd] **ADJ** *(clothing, food, area)* contaminé; *(wound, limb, disk)* infecté; **to become i.** *(of wound)* s'infecter

infection [ɪnˈfekʃən] **N** *Med (with disease)* contamination *f*, *(in part of body)* infection *f*; **source of i.** foyer *m* d'infection; **to spread/prevent i.** répandre/empêcher l'infection

infectious [ɪnˈfekʃəs] **ADJ** *Med (disease)* infectieux, contagieux; *Fam (person)* contagieux; *Fig (laughter, optimism, pessimism etc)* communicatif

infectiousness [ɪnˈfekʃəsnɪs] **N 1** *Med (of disease)* nature *f* infectieuse **2** *Fig (of enthusiasm, hope etc)* caractère *m* communicatif

infelicitous [ɪnfɪˈlɪsɪtəs] **ADJ** *Lit (remark, event)* malheureux

infelicity [ɪnfɪˈlɪsɪtɪ] **N** *Lit* **1** *(remark)* expression *f* malheureuse **2** *(unhappiness)* malheur *m*

infer [ɪnˈfɜːr] **VT** **(-rr-) 1** inférer, déduire, conclure (**sth from sth** qch de qch; **that** que) **2** *Fam* = **imply**

inference [ˈɪnfərəns] **N 1** *(method)* inférence *f*, **by i.** par déduction **2** *(conclusion)* déduction *f*, conclusion *f*

inferior [ɪnˈfɪərɪər] **ADJ** inférieur; *(work)* de second ordre; **the expensive screwdriver was i. to the cheap one** le tournevis cher était de moins bonne qualité que celui qui était bon marché; **her second novel is a much i. work** son deuxième roman est bien moins bon; **to be in an i. position** être dans une position inférieure *ou* subordonnée **N 1** inférieur, -eure; **one's inferiors** les per-

sonnes *fpl* inférieures à soi **2** *Typ* petite lettre *f* inférieure
▸▸ *Typ* **i. letter** petite lettre inférieure; *Astron* **i. planet** planète *f* inférieure; **i. quality** qualité *f* inférieure

inferiority [ɪnfɪərɪˈɒrɪtɪ] **N** infériorité *f* (**to** par rapport à)
▸▸ *Psy* **i. complex** complexe *m* d'infériorité

infernal [ɪnˈfɜːn(ə)l] **ADJ 1** *Fam (diabolical)* infernal, -aux, diabolique; **that i. little man!** cet homme infernal *ou* insupportable! **2** *Fam (extreme) (noise, heat etc)* infernal, -aux; **it's an i. nuisance** c'est diablement embêtant **3** *(of hell)* infernal, -aux; **the i. regions** l'enfer *m*

infernally [ɪnˈfɜːn(ə)lɪ] **ADV** *Fam* diablement; **it's i. hot** il fait une chaleur d'enfer *ou* à crever

inferno, *pl* **infernos** [ɪnˈfɜːnəʊ, ɪnˈfɜːnəʊz] **N 1** *(hell)* enfer *m*; *Liter* **Dante's I.** l'Enfer de Dante **2** *(fire)* brasier *m*; **the house was a raging i.** la maison était un véritable brasier

infertile [ɪnˈfɜːtaɪl] **ADJ** *(person, ovum)* stérile; *(land)* stérile, infertile

infertility [ɪnfəˈtɪlɪtɪ] **N** *(of person)* stérilité *f*; *(of soil)* infertilité *f*, stérilité
▸▸ *Med* **i. clinic** = service *m* qui s'occupe des problèmes de stérilité dans un établissement hospitalier

infest [ɪnˈfest] **VT** *(of vermin etc)* infester; **to be infested by rats/cockroaches** être infesté de rats/cafards

infestation [ɪnfesˈteɪʃən] **N** *Med* infestation *f*, *Bot (of plants by parasites etc)* invasion *f*

-infested [ɪnˈfestɪd] **SUFF** **rat-/cockroach-i.** infesté de rats/cafards

infidel [ˈɪnfɪdəl] **ADJ, N** infidèle *mf*

infidelity [ɪnfɪˈdelɪtɪ] **N 1** *(of spouse, lover)* infidélité *f* **2** *(disloyalty) (of servant etc)* infidélité *f*, déloyauté *f*

infighting [ˈɪnfaɪtɪŋ] **N** *(within group)* querelles *fpl* intestines; *Boxing* corps à corps *m*; **political i.** querelles politiques intestines

infill [ˈɪnfɪl] **N** *Constr* remplissage *m*

infiltrate [ˈɪnfɪltreɪt] **VT 1** *Pol etc (of subversives etc) (trade union)* noyauter; *(enemy)* s'infiltrer chez **2** *(cause to enter) (liquid etc)* faire pénétrer (**into** dans); **we've infiltrated someone into the party** l'un des nôtres a réussi à s'infiltrer dans le parti **3** *(of liquid) (substance)* s'infiltrer *ou* pénétrer dans, imprégner
VI *(of fluid, spies etc)* s'infiltrer (**into** dans; **through** à travers)

infiltration [ɪnfɪlˈtreɪʃən] **N 1** *(by spies, troops etc)* infiltration *f*, *Pol* **the i. of the Labour Party by Trotskyists** le noyautage du Parti travailliste par les Trotskistes **2** *(of liquid etc)* infiltration *f* (**into** dans, **through** à travers)

infiltrator [ˈɪnfɪltreɪtər] **N** *(of political party etc)* agent *m* qui s'infiltre

infinite [ˈɪnfɪnɪt] **ADJ** infini; **of i. importance** d'une extrême importance; **to go to i. pains to do sth** se donner infiniment de mal pour faire qch; *Rel, Hum* **in his i. wisdom** dans son infinie sagesse
N the i. l'infini *m*

infinitely [ˈɪnfɪnɪtlɪ] **ADV** infiniment

infinitesimal [ɪnfɪnɪˈtesɪməl] **ADJ** *(quantity)* infinitésimal, -aux; *(majority)* infime
▸▸ **i. calculus** calcul *m* infinitésimal

infinitive [ɪnˈfɪnɪtɪv] **N** *Gram* infinitif *m*; **in the i.** à l'infinitif VOIR GRAMMAIRE A40–2; B35–7

infinity [ɪnˈfɪnɪtɪ] **N 1** *(of space etc)* infinité *f* **2** *Math etc* infini *m*; **to i.** à l'infini; *Phot* **to focus on** *or* **for i.** mettre au point sur l'infini

infirm [ɪnˈfɜːm] **ADJ 1** *(person)* infirme, débile **2** *Fml (mind, judgement)* irrésolu

infirmary [ɪnˈfɜːmərɪ] **N 1** *(hospital)* hôpital *m*, -aux **2** *(in school, prison etc)* infirmerie *f*

infirmity [ɪnˈfɜːmɪtɪ] **N 1** *(weakness) (of body)* infirmité *f* **2** *(affliction)* infirmité *f*; **the infirmities of old age** les infirmités de la vieillesse **3** *(lack of resolve)* **i. of purpose** irrésolution *f*

in flagrante delicto [ɪnfləˈɡræntɪdɪˈlɪktəʊ] **ADV** *Law* en flagrant délit

inflame [ɪnˈfleɪm] **VT 1** *(stir up) (desire)* allumer; *(quarrel)* envenimer; *(crowd)* enflammer **2** *Med (wound)* enflammer
VI *Med (of wound, tissue)* s'enflammer

inflamed [ɪnˈfleɪmd] **ADJ 1** *Med (wound, eye etc)* enflammé; **to become i.** s'enflammer **2** *Fig* enflammé (**with** de); **i. with passion** brûlant d'amour

inflammable [ɪnˈflæməb(ə)l] **ADJ** *(substance etc)* inflammable; *Fig (person, crowd)* prompt à s'échauffer; *Fig* **the situation is highly i.** la situation est explosive

inflammation [ɪnfləˈmeɪʃən] **N** *Med* inflammation *f*

inflammatory [ɪnˈflæmətərɪ] **ADJ 1** *(speech, leaflet)* incendiaire **2** *Med (disease)* inflammatoire

inflatable [ɪnˈfleɪtəb(ə)l] **ADJ** *(balloon etc)* gonflable; *(raft)* pneumatique
N *(boat)* canot *m* pneumatique

inflate [ɪnˈfleɪt] **VT 1** *(fill with air) (balloon, tyre, sail)* gonfler; **to i. the lungs with air** *(one's own)* remplir ses poumons d'air; *(when giving artificial respiration)* souffler dans les poumons **2** *Fin (prices)* faire monter; *Com (account)* grossir, charger; *(expense account, figures)* gonfler; *Econ* **to i. the currency** accroître artificiellement la circulation fiduciaire
VI se gonfler; *Fig* **to i. with pride** se gonfler d'orgueil

inflated [ɪnˈfleɪtɪd] **ADJ 1** *(balloon, tyre etc)* gonflé; **to become i.** *(with air etc)* se gonfler; *Fig* **i. with pride** bouffi d'orgueil; *Fig* **to have an i. opinion of oneself** avoir une opinion trop flatteuse *ou* surfaite de soi-même **2** *Fin (price)* exagéré **3** *Liter (style)* enflé
▸▸ *Econ* **i. currency** inflation *f* monétaire

inflation [ɪnˈfleɪʃən] **N 1** *Econ* inflation *f*, **rate of i.** taux *m* d'inflation; **i. now stands at 5%** l'inflation est maintenant à 5%; **i.-proof** *(pension etc)* protégé contre les effets de l'inflation **2** *(of balloon, tyre etc)* gonflage *m*
▸▸ *Fin* **i. tax** impôt *m* à la production

inflationary [ɪnˈfleɪʃənərɪ] **ADJ** *Econ* inflationniste
▸▸ **i. spiral** spirale *f* inflationniste

inflect [ɪnˈflekt] **VT 1** *Gram (noun, adjective)* décliner; *(verb)* conjuguer **2** *(voice)* moduler; *Mus (note)* altérer **3** *Opt (light beam)* infléchir
VI *Gram* prendre une marque flexionnelle

inflected [ɪnˈflektɪd] **ADJ** *Ling (language)* à flexions, flexionnel; *(vowel)* infléchi

inflection [ɪnˈflekʃən] **N** = **inflexion**

inflexibility [ɪnfleksɪˈbɪlɪtɪ] **N** *(of person, government etc)* inflexibilité *f*, *Tech* rigidité *f*

inflexible [ɪnˈfleksɪb(ə)l] **ADJ** *(person, government etc)* inflexible; *Tech* rigide; **i. code of morals** morale *f* rigide *ou* inflexible

inflexion [ɪnˈflekʃən] **N 1** *Gram (of word)* flexion *f* **2** *(of voice)* inflexion *f*, *Mus (of note)* altération *f* **3** *Opt, Math* inflexion *f*

inflict [ɪnˈflɪkt] **VT** *(suffering, losses)*, *Law (punishment)* infliger (**sth on sb** qch à qn); *(wound)* faire (**on** à); *(unhappiness)* causer, occasionner (**on** à); *Fam Hum* **to i. oneself on sb** s'imposer

infliction [ɪnˈflɪkʃən] **N** *(action)* action *f* d'infliger; **to take pleasure in the i. of pain** prendre le plaisir à infliger de la douleur

in-flight **ADJ** *Aviat* en vol
▸▸ **i. catering** restauration *f* aérienne; **i. entertainment** distractions *fpl* en vol; **i. magazine** magazine *m* distribué dans les avions; **i. meal** plateau-repas *m*, *pl* plateaux-repas; **i. service** service *m* à bord (d'un avion)

inflorescence [ɪnfləˈresəns] **N** *Bot* inflorescence *f*

inflow [ˈɪnfləʊ] **N** *(act of flowing in) (of water)* arrivée *f*, *(of people, goods, cash)* afflux *m*; *(of new ideas)* flot *m*; **i. of capital** afflux de capitaux; **i. of money** rentrée *f* d'argent
▸▸ **i. pipe** *(for water)* arrivée d'eau

influence [ˈɪnflʊəns] **N** influence *f* (**upon, on** sur); **to exert** *or* **exercise an i. on sb** exercer une influence sur qn, influencer qn; **to be a good/bad/great i. on sb** avoir une bonne/mauvaise/grande influence sur qn; **to use one's i. with sb** user de son influence auprès de qn; **man of i.** homme *m* influent; **he owes his position to i.** il doit sa situation à des personnalités influentes; **to have i.** avoir de l'influence; **to have great i. over sb** avoir beaucoup d'influence sur qn; **to be under sb's i.** être sous l'influence de qn; **under the i. of drink,** *Fam* **under the i.** sous l'empire de la boisson
VT influencer; **she's too easily influenced** elle se laisse influencer trop facilement

influencer [ˈɪnflʊənsər] **N** *Mktg* préconisateur *m*

influential [ɪnflʊˈenʃəl] **ADJ** influent; **to be i.** *(of person)* avoir de l'influence, *Fam* avoir le bras long; *(of factor etc)* avoir du poids, jouer un rôle; **he was i. in getting her a job** il a fait jouer son influence pour l'aider à obtenir du travail

influenza [ɪnflʊˈenzə] **N** *Med* grippe *f*, influenza *f*

influx [ˈɪnflʌks] **N** *(of water etc)* arrivée *f*, *(of people, goods, cash)* afflux *m*; *(of gas)* afflux; *(of new ideas)* flot *m*; **a sudden i. of tourists** un soudain afflux de touristes; *Econ* **i. of gold** entrée *f* *ou* afflux d'or

info [ˈɪnfəʊ] **N** *Fam* renseignements *mpl*, tuyaux *mpl*

infobahn [ˈɪnfəʊbɑːn] **N** *Comput* autoroute *f* de l'information

infohighway [ɪnfəʊˈhaɪweɪ] **N** *Comput* autoroute *f* de l'information

infomercial [ɪnfəʊˈmɜːʃəl] **N** *TV* infomercial *m*

inform [ɪnˈfɔːm] **VT 1** *(tell)* **to i. sb of sth** informer qn de qch; **to i. sb about sth** *(provide with information)* renseigner qn sur qch; **to keep sb informed of what is happening** tenir qn au courant de ce qui se passe; **why was I not informed (of this)?** pourquoi est-ce que je n'en ai pas été informé?; **to i. the police** avertir la police; **we are writing to i. you of the dispatch of …** nous vous avisons de l'envoi de …; **I regret to have to i. you that …** j'ai le regret de vous annoncer que …; **we are informed that …** on nous fait savoir que … **2** *Lit (pervade) (literary work etc)* imprégner
VI *Law* **to i. against** *or* **on sb** dénoncer qn

informal [ɪnˈfɔːməl] **ADJ 1** *(person, manner, attitude)* simple, décontracté; *(speech, language, words)* familier; *(clothes)* décontracté; *(reception, dinner)* sans cérémonie; **he's very i. for a prime minister** il est très décontracté pour un premier ministre; **British offices tend to be more i. than German ones** en Grande-Bretagne l'ambiance dans les bureaux tend à être plus décontractée qu'en Allemagne; **dress:** *(on invitation)* tenue de ville **2** *(unofficial) (meeting)* non-officiel; *(arrangement)* officieux; **I had an i. chat with the boss** j'ai discuté un peu avec le patron;

the two leaders had i. **talks** les deux dirigeants ont eu des entretiens non-officiels
▸▸ *Econ* i. **economy** travail *m* au noir

informality [ɪnfɔ:'mælɪtɪ] N *(of person)* simplicité *f*, décontraction *f*; *(of occasion)* absence *f* de formalité *ou* de cérémonie; *(of talks)* caractère *m* non-officiel

informally [ɪn'fɔ:məlɪ] ADV **1** *(to dine)* sans cérémonie, sans formalités; *(to dress)* simplement; i. **known as …** familièrement connu sous le nom de … **2** *(to discuss)* officieusement, à titre non-officiel

informant [ɪn'fɔ:mənt] N informateur, -trice; I **have it from a reliable i.** je le tiens de source sûre

informatics [ɪnfɔ:'mætɪks] N informatique *f* **VOIR GRAMMAIRE A10**

information [ɪnfə'meɪʃən] N **1** *(news, facts etc)* renseignement(s) *m(pl)*, information(s) *f(pl)*; a **bit** or **piece of i.** un renseignement, une information; I'm **afraid your i. is wrong** je crains qu'on vous ait mal renseigné; **to ask for i. on** or **about sb/sth** demander des renseignements sur qn/qch; **for further i. write to …** pour de plus amples informations écrire à …; **why don't you ask at i.?** pourquoi est-ce que tu ne demandes pas aux renseignements?; **for my own i.** pour ma propre information; I **am sending you this brochure for your i.** je vous envoie cette brochure à titre d'information; **for your i., I'm not stupid** sachez que je ne suis pas complètement idiot; **for your i., I've done the dishes for the past week!** je t'apprendrai que j'ai fait la vaisselle toute cette semaine!; **his head is full of useless i.** il encombre sa mémoire de choses inutiles; I **can't retain i. as well as I could** ma mémoire n'est pas aussi bonne qu'avant
2 *Comput* information *f*
3 *Law* dénonciation *f* (**against sb** contre qn), délation *f* (**against sb** de qn); **to lay i. against sb with the police** dénoncer qn à la police, informer contre qn
4 *Am Tel* renseignements *mpl*
▸▸ *Br* i. **bureau** bureau *m ou* service *m* des renseignements; i. **carrier** support *m* d'information; i. **copy** *(of document)* copie *f* pour information; i. **desk** *(in hotel etc)* bureau des renseignements; i. **gathering** collecte *f* d'informations; *Comput* i. **highway** autoroute *f* de l'information, *Can* inforoute *f*; i. **market** marché *m* des informations; i. **overload** surinformation *f*; i. **pack** dossier *m* d'information; *Comput* i. **processing** *(action)* traitement *m* de l'information; *(domain)* informatique *f*; i. **retrieval** recherche *f* documentaire; *Comput* recherche d'information; *Comput* i. **retrieval system** système *m* de recherche documentaire; *Comput* i. **science** science *f* de l'information; *Comput* i. **scientist** informaticien, -ienne; i. **sheet** fiche *f* explicative; *Comput* i. **society** société *f* de l'information; i. **storage** mémorisation *f* des informations; *Comput* i. **system** système *m* informatique; *Comput* i. **technology** technologie *f* de l'information, informatique; i. **theory** théorie *f* de l'information

informative [ɪn'fɔ:mətɪv] ADJ *(programme, book, lecture)* instructif; *(book)* éducatif; **he wasn't very i.** il ne nous a pas appris grand-chose
▸▸ *Mktg* i. **advertising** publicité *f* informative

informed [ɪn'fɔ:md] ADJ *(person)* bien renseigné *ou* informé; **the i. opinion is that …** les experts pensent que …; **the i. consumer** le consommateur averti; **an i. estimate/decision** une évaluation faite/une décision prise en connaissance de cause

informer [ɪn'fɔ:mər] N *Pej* indicateur *m*; **to turn i.** dénoncer ses complices

infotainment [ɪnfəʊ'teɪnmənt] N *TV* émissions *fpl* d'information divertissantes

infraction [ɪn'frækʃən] N *Fml* = infringement

infra dig ['ɪnfrə'dɪg] ADJ *Fam* rabaissant; **it would be i. for us to reply** ce serait au-dessous de nous de répondre, ce serait se rabaisser que de répondre

infrared [ɪnfrə'red] ADJ *Phys* infrarouge
▸▸ *Comput* i. **keyboard** clavier *m* à infrarouge; *Med* i. **lamp** lampe *f* à rayons infrarouges; *Comput* i. **mouse** souris *f* à infrarouge; i. **radiation**, i. **rays** radiation *f* infrarouge, infrarouge *m*; i. **remote control** télécommande *f* (à) infrarouge

infrastructure ['ɪnfrəstrʌktʃər] N infrastructure *f*

infrequency [ɪn'fri:kwənsɪ] N rareté *f*

infrequent [ɪn'fri:kwənt] ADJ rare, peu fréquent

infrequently [ɪn'fri:kwəntlɪ] ADV rarement; **not i.** assez souvent

infringe [ɪn'frɪndʒ] VT *(law, rule)* enfreindre, violer, transgresser; **to i. (an author's) copyright** empiéter sur les droits d'un auteur
▸ **infringe on** VT INSEP *(person's rights)* empiéter sur

infringement [ɪn'frɪndʒmənt] N *(of rule)* infraction *f*, *(of law, right)* violation *f*; i. **of sb's rights** infraction *ou* atteinte *f* aux droits de qn; i. **of copyright** non-respect *m* des droits *f* d'auteur

infuriate [ɪn'fjʊərɪeɪt] VT rendre furieux, enrager

infuriated [ɪn'fjʊərɪeɪtɪd] ADJ furieux

infuriating [ɪn'fjʊərɪeɪtɪŋ] ADJ exaspérant; **at times I find him i.** quelquefois il me met hors de moi; **it's i. the way she's always right** ça me met hors de moi qu'elle ait toujours raison

infuriatingly [ɪn'fjʊərɪeɪtɪŋlɪ] ADV *(to answer)* d'une façon exaspérante; **to be i. slow/difficult** être d'une lenteur/difficulté exaspérante

infuse [ɪn'fju:z] VT **1** *(instil) (energy, new life, courage)* insuffler (**into sb** à qn) **2** *(soak) (tea, herbs)* infuser, faire infuser
VI *(of tea)* infuser

infuser [ɪn'fju:zər] N infusoir *m*

infusion [ɪn'fju:ʒən] N **1** *(liquid) (of camomile etc)* tisane *f*, infusion *f*; *Pharm* infusé *m* **2** *(action) (of tea, herbs)* infusion *f*; *(of energy, new life etc)* injection *f*

ingenious [ɪn'dʒi:nɪəs] ADJ *(person, device)* ingénieux

> Attention: ne pas confondre avec **ingenuous**.

ingeniously [ɪn'dʒi:nɪəslɪ] ADV ingénieusement

ingenuity [ɪndʒɪ'nju:ɪtɪ] N *(of person, invention)* ingéniosité *f*

> Attention: ne pas confondre avec **ingenuousness**.

ingenuous [ɪn'dʒenjʊəs] ADJ **1** *(naive)* ingénu, candide, naïf, *f* naïve **2** *(frank)* franc, *f* franche, sincère

> Attention: ne pas confondre avec **ingenious**.

ingenuously [ɪn'dʒenjʊəslɪ] ADV **1** *(naively)* ingénument, naïvement, avec candeur **2** *(frankly)* franchement, sincèrement

ingenuousness [ɪn'dʒenjʊəsnɪs] N **1** *(naivety)* ingénuité *f*, naïveté *f*, candeur *f* **2** *(frankness)* franchise *f*, sincérité *f*

> Attention: ne pas confondre avec **ingenuity**.

ingest [ɪn'dʒest] VT *Physiol (food)* ingérer

ingestion [ɪn'dʒestʃən] N *Physiol* ingestion *f*

inglenook ['ɪŋg(ə)lnʊk] N coin *m* du feu

inglorious [ɪn'glɔ:rɪəs] ADJ *(shameful) (defeat etc)* déshonorant, honteux

ingloriously [ɪn'glɔ:rɪəslɪ] ADV *(to retreat)* sans gloire; *(to be defeated)* honteusement

ingot ['ɪŋgət] N *(of gold, silver)* lingot *m*

ingrained [ɪŋ'greɪnd] ADJ **1** i. **with dirt** encrassé; i. **dirt** crasse *f* **2** *(deep-seated) (prejudice, distrust, belief etc)* enraciné; *(habit)* invétéré, enraciné; **certain habits are i. in one's nature** certaines habitudes sont enracinées dans la nature de chacun

ingratiate [ɪn'greɪʃɪeɪt] VT **to i. oneself with sb** s'insinuer dans les bonnes grâces de qn

ingratiating [ɪn'greɪʃɪeɪtɪŋ] ADJ doucereux; **to act/speak in an i. manner** agir/parler d'une manière doucereuse

ingratiatingly [ɪn'greɪʃɪeɪtɪŋlɪ] ADV d'une manière doucereuse

ingratitude [ɪn'grætɪtju:d] N ingratitude *f*

ingredient [ɪn'gri:dɪənt] N ingrédient *m*; *Fig* **what are the ingredients of her success?** qu'est-ce qui fait son succès?

ingress ['ɪngres] N *Law* entrée *f*

ingrowing ['ɪngrəʊɪŋ], **ingrown** ['ɪngrəʊn] ADJ
▸▸ *Med* i. **toenail** ongle *m* incarné

inhabit [ɪn'hæbɪt] VT *(house, town)* habiter, habiter dans; **a fictitious world inhabited by strange people** un monde fictif peuplé de gens étranges

inhabitable [ɪn'hæbɪtəb(ə)l] ADJ habitable

> Note that the French word **inhabitable** is a false friend and is never a translation for the English word **inhabitable**. It means **uninhabitable**.

inhabitant [ɪn'hæbɪtənt] N habitant, -ante

inhabited [ɪn'hæbɪtɪd] ADJ habité, peuplé

> Note that the French word **inhabité** is a false friend and is never a translation for the English word **inhabited**. It means **uninhabited**.

inhalant [ɪn'heɪlənt] N *Med* produit *m* à prendre en inhalation

inhalation [ɪnhə'leɪʃən] N **1** *(of chloroform etc)* inhalation *f* **2** *(of perfume)* aspiration *f*

inhale [ɪn'heɪl] VT *Med (ether etc)* inhaler; *(perfume)* aspirer, humer; *(cigarette smoke)* respirer, avaler
VI respirer; *(in smoking)* avaler la fumée

inhaler [ɪn'heɪlər] N **1** *Med (device)* inhalateur *m* **2** *(smoker)* = fumeur *m* qui avale la fumée de sa cigarette

inhaling [ɪn'heɪlɪŋ] N inhalation *f*

inherent [ɪn'hɪərənt, -'herənt] ADJ inhérent, propre (**in** à); **an i. fault in the design** une anomalie inhérente à la conception; **power i. in an office** pouvoir *m* inhérent à une fonction
▸▸ i. **stability** *(of plane, ship etc)* stabilité *f* propre; *Com* i. **vice** vice *m* inhérent

inherently [ɪn'hɪərəntlɪ, -'herəntlɪ] ADV fondamentalement; i. **lazy** né paresseux

inherit [ɪn'herɪt] VT *(house, money etc)*, *Fig (character, looks)* hériter (de); **to i. sth from sb** hériter (de) qch de qn
VI **to i. equally** hériter de parts égales; **to i. jointly** cohériter

inheritance [ɪn'herɪtəns] N **1** *(act of inheriting)* succession *f*; **the title came to him by right of i.** il a hérité du titre de plein droit; **law of i.** droit *m* successif **2** *(money, jewels etc)*, *Fig* patrimoine *m*, héritage *m*; *Biol (ge-*

netic) patrimoine; **to come into an i.** faire un héritage

▸▸ *Fin* **i. tax** droits *mpl* de succession

inherited [ɪn'herɪtɪd] **ADJ** *(property, characteristic, taste, wealth)* hérité

inhibit [ɪn'hɪbɪt] **VT 1** *(progress, growth etc)* entraver **2** *Psy (feeling)* inhiber **3** *Med (secretion etc)* inhiber **4** *Law etc* **to i. sb from doing sth** interdire *ou* défendre à qn de faire qch

▸▸ *Comput* **i. code** code *m* inhibiteur

inhibited [ɪn'hɪbɪtɪd] **ADJ** inhibé; **i. person** inhibé, -ée; **she's not i.** elle n'a pas d'inhibitions

inhibiting [ɪn'hɪbɪtɪŋ] **ADJ** *(influence etc)* inhibiteur, -trice

inhibition [ɪn(h)ɪ'bɪʃən] **N 1** *Med, Psy* inhibition *f*; **to have no inhibitions** avoir aucune inhibition **(about confessing** pour ce qui est d'avouer) **2** *Law etc* défense *f* expresse, prohibition *f*

inhibitive [ɪn'hɪbɪtɪv] **ADJ** *Med* inhibiteur, -trice

inhibitor [ɪn'hɪbɪtər] **N** *Mktg, Aut, Med* inhibiteur *m*

inhibitory [ɪn'hɪbɪt(ə)rɪ] **ADJ 1** *(nerve, reflex)* inhibiteur, -trice **2** *(warrant)* prohibitif

in-home placement testing **N** *Mktg* test *m* à domicile par des consommateurs-témoins

inhospitable [ɪnhɒ'spɪtəb(ə)l, ɪn'hɒs-] **ADJ** *(person, climate, region etc)* inhospitalier

inhospitably [ɪnhɒ'spɪtəblɪ] **ADV** d'une manière inhospitalière

in-house **ADJ** interne *(à une entreprise)*; **to have an i. accountant** avoir un comptable sur place

ADV **to do sth i.** faire qch sur place; **to keep a job i.** faire un travail sur place

▸▸ **i. magazine** revue *f* d'entreprise, magazine *m* interne; **i. newspaper** journal *m* d'entreprise *ou* interne; **i. publication** publication *f* interne; **i. staff** personnel *m* permanent; **i. training** formation *f* interne

inhuman [ɪn'hju:mən] **ADJ** inhumain; *(custom)* barbare

inhumane [ɪnhju:'meɪn] **ADJ** inhumain, cruel

inhumanity [ɪnhju:'mænɪtɪ] **N** *(of person, action)* inhumanité *f*, cruauté *f*, barbarie *f*; **man's i. to man** la cruauté de l'homme envers son prochain

inimical [ɪ'nɪmɪk(ə)l] **ADJ** *(people)* ennemi, hostile; *(conditions)* défavorable, contraire **(to** à)

inimitable [ɪ'nɪmɪtəb(ə)l] **ADJ** inimitable

inimitably [ɪ'nɪmɪtəblɪ] **ADV** d'une manière inimitable

iniquitous [ɪ'nɪkwɪtəs] **ADJ** inique

iniquitously [i'nɪkwɪtəslɪ] **ADV** iniquement

iniquity [ɪ'nɪkwɪtɪ] **N** iniquité *f*

initial [ɪ'nɪʃəl] **ADJ** initial, -aux, premier; **her i. delight** son plaisir initial; **the disease is only in the i. stages** la maladie n'en est qu'à son stade initial; **the i. difficulties** les difficultés du début; *Ling* **in i. position** en position initiale

N 1 initials initiales *f*, *(to alteration of cheque etc)* paraphe *m*; *(of supervisor etc)* visa *m*; *(on garment etc)* monogramme *m* **2** *Typ* lettre *f* initiale, lettrine *f*

VT *(-ll-, Am -l-)* *(treaty, correction etc)* parapher; *(legal document)* viser, mettre son paraphe au bas de

▸▸ **i. letter** initiale *f*, *St Exch* **i. margin** dépôt *m* initial *ou* de marge; *Am St Exch* **i. public offering** introduction *f* en Bourse; *Com* **i. stock** stock *m* de départ; *Fin* **i. value** valeur *f* de départ

initialization [ɪnɪʃəlaɪ'zeɪʃən] **N** initialisation *f*

initialize [ɪ'nɪʃəlaɪz] **VT** *Comput* initialiser

initially [ɪ'nɪʃəlɪ] **ADV** au départ, au début

initiate¹ [ɪ'nɪʃɪeɪt] **VT 1** *(begin) (negotiations etc)* commencer, ouvrir; *(project etc)* lancer, amorcer; *(measures etc)* instaurer; *(new policy etc)* inaugurer; *(reform)* être l'initiateur de; *Law* **to i. proceedings against sb** entamer des poursuites contre qn **2** *(induct)* initier; **to i. sb into a secret society** admettre qn dans une société secrète

initiate² [ɪ'nɪʃɪət] **N** initié, -ée

initiated [ɪ'nɪʃɪeɪtɪd] **ADJ** initié
NPL the i. les initiés *mpl*

initiation [ɪnɪʃɪ'eɪʃən] **N 1** *(induction)* initiation *f* (**into** à) **2** *(beginning) (of undertaking)* commencement(s) *m(pl)*, début(s) *m(pl)*

▸▸ **i. ceremony** cérémonie *f* d'initiation

initiative [ɪ'nɪʃɪətɪv, ɪ'nɪʃətɪv] **N** initiative *f*; **to take the i.** prendre l'initiative **(in doing sth** de faire qch); **to do sth on one's own i.** faire qch de sa propre initiative; **to show/lack i.** faire preuve/manquer d'initiative; **use your i.!** fais preuve d'un peu d'initiative!; **we need sb with i.** nous avons besoin de quelqu'un qui a de l'initiative

initiator [ɪ'nɪʃɪeɪtər] **N** initiateur, -trice

inject [ɪn'dʒekt] **VT** *(drug)*, *Fig (capital)* injecter **(into** dans); *(give injection to)* faire une piqûre à **(with sth** de qch); **to i. sb with morphine** faire une piqûre de morphine à qn; **to i. a fluid into a cavity, to i. a cavity with a fluid** injecter un liquide dans une cavité; **to i. drugs** *(of addict)* s'injecter de la drogue, se piquer; *Fig* **to i. new life into sth** donner un nouvel essor à qch; **she tried to i. a little humour into the meeting** elle a essayé d'introduire une note d'humour dans la réunion

injectable [ɪn'dʒektəb(ə)l] **ADJ** *(drug)* injectable

injection [ɪn'dʒekʃən] **N** *(action)* injection *f*, *Med* **an i.** une injection, une piqûre; **tetanus/polio i.** piqûre *f* *ou* vaccin *m* antitétanique/antipoliomyélitique; **to give sb an i.** faire une injection *ou* une piqûre à qn; *Fig* **i. of capital into a business** injection *ou* apport *m* de capital dans une entreprise

▸▸ *Tech* **i. moulding** moulage *m* par injection; **i. pump** *Constr* pompe *f* à injection; *Aut* pompe d'injection (de carburant)

injector [ɪn'dʒektər] **N** *Aut* injecteur *m*

injudicious [ɪndʒʊ'dɪʃəs] **ADJ** peu judicieux, malavisé

injudiciously [ɪndʒʊ'dɪʃəslɪ] **ADV** d'une façon peu judicieuse

Injun ['ɪndʒən] **N** *Am Offensive Fam* Indien, -ienne (d'Amérique); **honest I.!** vrai de vrai!, sans blague!

injunction [ɪn'dʒʌŋkʃən] **N 1** *Law* arrêt *m* de suspension, arrêt de sursis; **to take out an i. against sb** faire une demande d'injonction contre qn; **I shall ask for an i.** je vais demander un sursis **2** *(command)* injonction *f*, ordre *m*, recommandation *f*; **to give sb strict injunctions to do sth** enjoindre formellement à qn de faire qch

injure ['ɪndʒər] **VT 1** *(physically)* blesser; **to i. oneself** se blesser, se faire du mal; **she injured her head** elle s'est blessée à la tête; *Fig* **to i. sb's pride** blesser qn dans son amour-propre **2** *(harm) (person)* nuire à, faire tort à, léser; *Law* porter préjudice à; *(sb's reputation)* nuire à, faire du tort à; *(sb's interests)* compromettre; **to i. one's health** s'abîmer la santé

Note that the French verb **injurier** is a false friend and is never a translation for the verb **to injure**. It means **to insult, to abuse**.

injured ['ɪndʒəd] **ADJ 1** *(physically)* blessé; **badly/slightly i.** gravement/légèrement blessé **2** *Fig (offended)* offensé, outragé; *(deceived)* trompé, trahi; **the i. party** l'offensé, -ée; *Law* la partie lésée; **in an i. (tone of) voice** d'une voix offensée; **i. pride** orgueil *m* blessé

NPL the i. les blessés *mpl*

injurious [ɪn'dʒʊərɪəs] **ADJ 1** *(harmful)* nuisible, préjudiciable **(to** à); **i. to (the) health** nuisible à la santé **2** *Fml (language)* injurieux, offensant

injury ['ɪndʒ(ə)rɪ] **N 1** *(physical) (to body)* blessure *f*, *Spec* lésion *f*, **to do oneself an i.** se blesser, se faire du mal; **wearing a seat belt can prevent i.** le port de la ceinture de sécurité peut éviter des blessures; **he escaped without i.** il n'a pas été blessé **2** *(wrong)* tort *m*, préjudice *m*; *Law* lésion *f*, **to do sb an i.** faire du tort à qn

▸▸ *Sport* **i. time** arrêts *mpl* de jeu

Note that the French word **injure** is a false friend. It means **insult**.

injustice [ɪn'dʒʌstɪs] **N 1** *(of law, system etc)* injustice *f* **2** *(unjust act, remark)* injustice *f*, **you do him an i.** vous êtes injuste envers lui

ink [ɪŋk] **N 1** encre *f*, **written in i.** écrit à l'encre; **2** *(of squid, octopus)* noir *m*, encre *f*
VT *Typ (letters, plate)* encrer

▸▸ **i. bag** *(of squid, octopus)* glande *f* *ou* poche *f* du noir; **i. bottle** bouteille *f* d'encre; **i. cartridge** cartouche *f* d'encre; *Comput* **i. channel** *(in printer)* canal *m* encreur; **i. pad** tampon *m* (encreur); **i. pot** encrier *m*; **i. sac** *(of squid, octopus)* glande *ou* poche du noir; **i. stain** tache *f* d'encre

▸ **ink in** **VT SEP** *Art* **1** *(pencil lines)* tracer à l'encre **2** *(drawing)* mettre à l'encre

▸ **ink out** **VT SEP** *(word etc)* oblitérer *ou* rayer *ou* biffer à l'encre

inkblot ['ɪŋkblɒt] **N** *(on paper)* pâté *m*; *Psy (in Rorschach test)* tache *f* d'encre

▸▸ **i. test** test *m* de Rorschach *ou* des taches d'encre

inking ['ɪŋkɪŋ] **N** *Typ (of rollers)* encrage *m*

ink-jet, ink-jet printer **N** imprimante *f* à jet d'encre

inkling ['ɪŋklɪŋ] **N** soupçon *m*; **to give sb an i. of sth** faire entrevoir qch à qn; **she gave me no i. of her intentions** elle ne m'a aucunement communiqué ses intentions; **could you give me an i. of what it's about?** est-ce que tu pourrais me donner une idée de ce dont il s'agit?; **he had an i. of the truth** il entrevoyait la vérité; **he has no i. of the matter, he doesn't have an i.** il ne se doute de rien; **she had no i. of what they were up to** elle ne se doutait pas le moins du monde de ce qu'ils préparaient

inkstand ['ɪŋkstænd] **N** (grand) encrier *m*

inkwell ['ɪŋkwel] **N** encrier *m* (de pupitre)

inky ['ɪŋkɪ] **ADJ 1** *(stained with ink)* taché d'encre; *(blotted with ink)* barbouillé d'encre **2** **i. (black)** comme (de) l'encre; **the night was i. black** il faisait nuit noire

inlaid [ɪn'leɪd] **ADJ** *(furniture, brooch etc)* incrusté (**with** de); *(with wood)* marqueté; *(floor)* parqueté; **i. work** *(wood)* marqueterie *f*, **i. enamel work** nielle *f*

inland ['ɪnlənd, 'ɪnlænd] **ADJ 1** *(away from sea)* intérieur **2** *Br (mail)* intérieur; **i. postage rates** (tarif *m* d')affranchissement *m* en régime intérieur

ADV vers l'intérieur, dans les terres; **to go i.** pénétrer vers l'intérieur *ou* dans les terres; **the town is situated a few miles i.** la ville est située à quelques kilomètres dans les terres

▸▸ **i. clearance depot** dépôt *m* de dédouanement intérieur; **i. freight** fret *m* intérieur;

i. haulage transport m routier; **i. navigation** navigation f fluviale; Br **the I. Revenue** ≃ le fisc, la Direction Générale des Impôts; **i. waterway** voie f navigable ou fluviale; **i. waterway transport** transport m fluvial

in-law N parent m par alliance; **in-laws** (mother and father of spouse) beaux-parents mpl; (family of spouse) belle-famille f

inlay¹ ['ɪnleɪ] N 1 (of mother-of-pearl etc) incrustation f; (piece of marquetry) marqueterie f 2 (in dentistry) (of metal, ceramic etc) inlay m, incrustation f

inlay² ['ɪnleɪ, ɪn'leɪ] VT (pt, pp inlaid) incruster (**with** de); (table etc) (with wood) marqueter; **to i. with enamel** nieller; **table inlaid with mother-of-pearl** table incrustée de nacre

inlet ['ɪnlet] N 1 (in shore etc) petit bras m de mer; (small bay) crique f, anse f 2 Tech (opening) (for air etc) (orifice m d')entrée f, (orifice d')admission f; (of ventilator etc) ouïe f
▸▸ **i. manifold** conduits mpl d'admission, collecteur m d'admission; **i. pipe** tuyau m d'arrivée; **i. valve** soupape f d'admission; (of fuel pump) soupape d'alimentation

in-line ADJ
▸▸ Aut **i. engine** moteur m en ligne; **i. skates** patins mpl in-line

inmate ['ɪnmeɪt] N (in prison) détenu, -ue; (in mental hospital) interné, -ée

in memoriam [ɪnmɪ'mɔːrɪəm] PREP en mémoire de

inmost ['ɪnməʊst] ADJ le plus profond; **our i. thoughts** nos pensées les plus secrètes; **our i. feelings** nos sentiments les plus intimes; **our i. being** le plus profond de nous-mêmes

inn [ɪn] N 1 auberge f 2 Eng Jur **Inns of Court** = les quatre Écoles de droit de Londres qui seules confèrent le droit d'être avocat

innards ['ɪnədz] NPL (of person, animal) entrailles fpl, intestins mpl; (of machine) entrailles

innate [ɪ'neɪt] ADJ inné; **i. common sense** bon sens m naturel ou foncier; Phil **i. ideas** idées fpl innées

inner ['ɪnər] ADJ (chamber, courtyard, calm, lining) intérieur; (layer), Anat (ear etc) interne; **i. suburbs** première couronne f, **i. London** Londres intra-muros; **i. conviction** conviction f intime; **i. harbour** arrière-port m, pl arrière-ports;
N (of target) = premier cercle m autour de la mouche
▸▸ **i. circle** cercle m intime (d'amis); (of political party) groupe m dirigeant; **i. city** = quartier m défavorisé dans le centre d'une grande ville; Rel **the i. man** (soul) l'âme f, Hum **here's something for the i. man** (stomach) voilà de quoi boucher un trou; **i. tube** (of tyre) chambre f à air

inner-city ADJ **i. children** enfants mpl des quartiers pauvres; **i. crime** = crimes mpl se produisant dans les quartiers pauvres

innermost ['ɪnəməʊst] ADJ = inmost

inning ['ɪnɪŋ] N Baseball tour m de batte

innings ['ɪnɪŋz] N INV Cr tournée f, tour m de batte (de chaque équipe ou de chaque membre de l'équipe); Fig **she had a good i.** elle a vécu longtemps

innit ['ɪnɪt] Br Fam ADV 1 (isn't it) hein?; **it's great, i.?** c'est super, hein? 2 (general question tag) hein?; **that was a kicking night out, i.** on a passé une super soirée, hein?

innkeeper ['ɪnkiːpər] N aubergiste mf, hôtelier, -ière

innocence ['ɪnəsəns] N 1 (of defendant) innocence f 2 (inexperience, naïveté) naïveté f, innocence f; **to lose one's i.** perdre son innocence; **to take advantage of sb's i.** abuser de l'innocence de qn; **in all i.** en toute innocence

innocent ['ɪnəsənt] ADJ 1 (not guilty) innocent; **i. of a crime** innocent d'un crime; **an i. person** un(e) innocent(e); **the bomb killed several i. bystanders** la bombe a tué plusieurs innocents qui se trouvaient là; Fam **to act all i.** faire l'innocent
2 (pure) innocent; **as i. as a newborn babe** innocent comme l'enfant qui vient de naître
3 (naïve) naïf, f naïve
4 (harmless) (game, fun) innocent; (remark, question etc) sans malice, innocent
5 Fml (devoid) dépourvu (**of** de)
N innocent, -ente; **I was a real i. then** j'étais vraiment innocent à l'époque; **don't come the i. with me** ne fais pas l'innocent avec moi; Cathol **Holy Innocents' Day** la fête des saints Innocents

innocently ['ɪnəsəntlɪ] ADV innocemment, en toute innocence

innocuous [ɪ'nɒkjʊəs] ADJ inoffensif; **an i. remark** une remarque anodine

innocuously [ɪ'nɒkjʊəslɪ] ADV (to remark etc) de façon inoffensive ou anodine

innocuousness [ɪ'nɒkjʊəsnɪs] N (of remark, joke etc) caractère m anodin; Med innocuité f

innovate ['ɪnəveɪt] VI innover (**in** à, en, dans)

innovating company N Mktg entreprise f innovatrice

innovation [ɪnə'veɪʃən] N innovation f

innovative ['ɪnəveɪtɪv, -vətɪv] ADJ (in)novateur, -trice

innovator ['ɪnəveɪtər] N (in)novateur, -trice

innuendo, pl **innuendos, innuendoes** [ɪnjuˈendəʊ, -əʊz] N 1 (insinuation) insinuation f; **to discredit sb by i.** discréditer qn par sous-entendus 2 (in jokes) allusion f grivoise; **the play is full of i.** la pièce est pleine de sous-entendus 3 Law insinuation f, mot m couvert (destiné à atteindre qn dans son honneur)

innumerable [ɪ'njuːmərəb(ə)l] ADJ innombrable, sans nombre; **the successes have been i.** les réussites ne se comptent plus

innumeracy [ɪ'njuːmərəsɪ] N fait m de ne pas savoir compter

innumerate [ɪ'njuːmərət] ADJ qui ne sait pas compter

inoculate [ɪ'nɒkjʊleɪt] VT Med inoculer, vacciner (**contre** against); **to i. sb with a virus** inoculer un virus à qn

inoculation [ɪnɒkjʊ'leɪʃən] N Med inoculation f

inoffensive [ɪnə'fensɪv] ADJ 1 (odour etc) qui n'a rien de désagréable; (remark, humour etc) qui n'a rien d'offensant 2 (harmless) (animal, person) inoffensif

inoperable [ɪn'ɒpərəb(ə)l] ADJ 1 Med inopérable 2 (system) qui ne peut pas être exploité, inexploitable

inoperative [ɪn'ɒpərətɪv] ADJ inopérant

inopportune [ɪn'ɒpətjuːn] ADJ inopportun, intempestif

inopportunely [ɪn'ɒpətjuːnlɪ] ADV inopportunément, mal à propos

inordinate [ɪn'ɔːdɪnət] ADJ démesuré, excessif, immodéré

inordinately [ɪn'ɔːdɪnətlɪ] ADV démesurément, excessivement; **to wait an i. long time** attendre excessivement longtemps

inorganic [ɪnɔː'gænɪk] ADJ inorganique

in-patient N Med patient, -ente hospitalisé(e)

in-plant agency N Am (travel agency) implant m

inpoint ['ɪnpɔɪnt] N (on tape, film) point m d'entrée

input ['ɪnpʊt] N 1 (of factory) besoins mpl (en personnel, matières premières etc), Spec intrant m; (of machine) consommation f; Elec, Electron (current etc) puissance f à l'entrée ou d'alimentation; (terminal) entrée f
2 Comput (of data) entrée f, introduction f; (data) données fpl introduites, données en entrée; **i./output** entrée/sortie f
3 (contribution to discussion etc) contribution f
VT Comput (data) entrer
▸▸ Comput **i. box** case f de saisie; Comput **i. buffer** mémoire f tampon de saisie; Comput **i. data** données introduites, données en entrée; Comput **i. device** périphérique m d'entrée; Comput **i. file** fichier m d'entrée; Comput **i. mask** masque m de saisie; Comput **i./output port** port m d'entrée/sortie; Comput **i. port** port d'entrée; Comput **i. program** programme m d'introduction; **i. socket** (for power) prise f d'alimentation; Fin **i. tax** TVA f récupérée; Comput **i. terminal** terminal m d'entrée (de données); Elec **i. transformer** courant m ou transformateur m d'entrée

inquest ['ɪnkwest] N enquête f, Fig (into reasons for failure of project etc) analyse f

inquire [ɪn'kwaɪər] VT s'informer de (**of sb** auprès de qn); **to i. of sb what is happening** s'informer auprès de qn de ce qui se passe
VI se renseigner (**about** sur); **I'd like to i. about …** je voudrais des renseignements sur …; **i. within** s'adresser ici
▸ **inquire after** VT INSEP (person) demander des nouvelles de; **to i. after sb's health** s'informer de la santé de qn
▸ **inquire into** VT INSEP faire des recherches sur; Law (affair) enquêter ou faire une enquête sur; **to i. into the reasons for sth** chercher à connaître les raisons de qch

inquiring [ɪn'kwaɪərɪŋ] ADJ (mind) curieux; (look) interrogateur, -trice

inquiringly [ɪn'kwaɪərɪŋlɪ] ADV (to look up, to raise one's eyebrows) d'un air interrogateur; (to say) d'un ton interrogateur; **to look i. at sb** interroger qn du regard

inquiry [ɪn'kwaɪərɪ] N 1 (official investigation) recherche f, investigation f, (by police) enquête f; **a man is helping the police with their inquiries** la police est en train d'interroger un individu; **to conduct** or **hold an i. into sth** procéder à une enquête sur qch
2 (request for information) demande f de renseignements; **to make inquiries** se renseigner; **to make inquiries about sb** prendre des renseignements sur qn; (less official) s'informer ou se renseigner sur qn; **to make inquiries after sb** s'enquérir de qn; **to make inquiries into sth** faire des recherches sur qch; **with reference to your i. of 5 May,…** (in letter) en réponse à votre demande du 5 mai,…; **as a result of her inquiries** à la suite de ses recherches; **on i.** renseignements pris; Br (private) **i. agent** détective m (privé); **inquiries** bureau m de renseignements
▸▸ **i. desk, i. office** bureau de renseignements

inquisition [ɪnkwɪ'zɪʃən] N Rel, Hist **the I.** l'Inquisition f; Fam **the interview turned into an i.** l'entrevue s'est transformée en inquisition

inquisitive [ɪn'kwɪzɪtɪv] ADJ 1 (mind, child) curieux; (look) plein de curiosité 2 Pej (prying) indiscret; (gaze) inquisiteur

inquisitively [ɪn'kwɪzɪtɪvlɪ] ADV (with curiosity) avec curiosité; (to look) d'un œil inquisiteur; (to say sth) sur un ton inquisiteur

inquisitiveness [ɪn'kwɪzɪtɪvnɪs] N curiosité f

inquisitor [ɪnˈkwɪzɪtər] **N1** *Law* enquêteur, -euse **2** *Rel, Hist, Fig Fam* inquisiteur *m*

inquisitorial [ɪnkwɪzɪˈtɔːrɪəl] **ADJ** inquisitorial, -aux

inroad [ˈɪnrəʊd] **N** *USU* **PL1 to make inroads into** *(capital, savings)* entamer, ébrécher; *(opposition's support)* entamer; **they were making inroads into the cheese** ils avaient attaqué le fromage **2** *Mil (attack)* incursion *f*

inrush [ˈɪnrʌʃ] **N** *(of water, air etc)* irruption *f*, *(of passengers etc)* afflux *m*

ins 1 *(abbr* **insurance)** asse. **2** *(abbr* **inches)** pouces, ppo.

insalubrious [ɪnsəˈluːbrɪəs] **ADJ** insalubre, malsain

insane [ɪnˈseɪn] **ADJ1** *(person)* fou, *f* folle; **to become** *or* **go i.** perdre la raison; **to drive sb i.** rendre qn fou; **to be i. with grief/jealousy** être fou de douleur/jalousie **2** *Fam (desire, scheme etc)* insensé, fou, *f* folle; **an i. idea** une idée folle
NPL the i. les aliénés *mpl*
▸▸*Am* **i. asylum** hospice *m ou* asile *m* d'aliénés

insanely [ɪnˈseɪnlɪ] **ADV** comme un fou/une folle/des fous/*etc*; **he was i. jealous** *(by nature)* il était d'une jalousie maladive; **he became i. jealous every time he saw ...** il devenait fou de jalousie chaque fois qu'il voyait ...

insanitary [ɪnˈsænɪt(ə)rɪ] **ADJ** insalubre, malsain

insanity [ɪnˈsænɪtɪ] **N 1** *Med* folie *f*, démence *f*, *Fml* aliénation *f* mentale **2** *Fam (of course of action etc)* folie *f*; **it's sheer i. doing that** c'est de la folie pure et simple (que) de faire cela

insatiable [ɪnˈseɪʃ(ɪ)əb(ə)l] **ADJ** *(appetite, desire etc)* insatiable

insatiably [ɪnˈseɪʃ(ɪ)əblɪ] **ADV** insatiablement

inscribe [ɪnˈskraɪb] **VT** *(carve)* inscrire, graver (**sth on stone** qch sur la pierre); *(write)* écrire, *Fig* graver (**in sb's memory** dans la mémoire de qn); **to i. a tomb with a name** graver un nom sur un tombeau

inscription [ɪnˈskrɪpʃən] **N1** *(of name etc)* inscription *f* **2** *(message) (on monument etc)* inscription *f*, *(on coin)* inscription, légende *f*, *(in book etc)* dédicace *f*

inscrutability [ɪnskruːtəˈbɪlɪtɪ] **N** inscrutabilité *f*

inscrutable [ɪnˈskruːtəb(ə)l] **ADJ** *(look, face)* impénétrable, énigmatique; *(remark)* énigmatique; **to remain i.** *(of person)* rester impassible

insect [ˈɪnsekt] **N** insecte *m*
▸▸**i. bite** piqûre *f* d'insecte; **i. eater** insectivore *m*; **i. powder** poudre *f* insecticide; **i. repellent** produit *m* insectifuge

insecticide [ɪnˈsektɪsaɪd] **ADJ, N** insecticide *m*

insectivore [ɪnˈsektɪvɔːr] **N** insectivore *m*

insectivorous [ɪnsekˈtɪvərəs] **ADJ** insectivore

insecure [ɪnsɪˈkjʊər] **ADJ 1** *(person)* qui manque d'assurance (sur le plan affectif); **to feel i.** *(because of circumstances)* éprouver un sentiment d'insécurité **2** *(unstable) (government)* fragile; *(job, arrangement, future)* précaire; **financially i.** financièrement vulnérable **3** *(place)* exposé **4** *(not solid, tight etc) (fastening, border)* peu sûr; *(grip, hold)* lâche

insecurity [ɪnsɪˈkjʊərɪtɪ] **N** insécurité *f*, *(of job, future)* précarité *f*, *esp Mil (of position)* caractère *m* exposé; **to have a feeling of i.** éprouver un manque d'assurance *ou* un sentiment d'insécurité

inseminate [ɪnˈsemɪneɪt] **VT** inséminer

insemination [ɪnsemɪˈneɪʃən] **N** *Biol* insémination *f*

insensate [ɪnˈsenseɪt] **ADJ** *Lit* **1** *(insensitive)* insensible **2** *(senseless)* insensé

insensibility [ɪnsensɪˈbɪlɪtɪ] **N 1** *(unconsciousness)* inconscience *f* **2** *(indifference)* insensibilité *f* (**to** à), indifférence *f* (**to** pour)

insensible [ɪnˈsensɪb(ə)l] **ADJ** *Fml* **1** *(indifferent)* insensible (**to** à) **2** *(unaware)* inconscient (**of** de); **he was quite i. of the danger he was in** il ne se doutait pas du danger qui le menaçait **3** *(unconscious)* sans connaissance, inconscient; **to become i.** perdre connaissance

insensitive [ɪnˈsensɪtɪv] **ADJ** *(person, approach)* dur, insensible; *(remark)* indélicat; **he can be amazingly i.** il peut manquer de tact *ou* de délicatesse à un point incroyable; **to be i. to sth** être insensible à qch

insensitiveness [ɪnˈsensɪtɪvnɪs], **insensitivity** [ɪnsensɪˈtɪvɪtɪ] **N** insensibilité *f*

inseparable [ɪnˈsep(ə)rəb(ə)l] **ADJ** inséparable (**from** de)

inseparably [ɪnˈsep(ə)rəblɪ] **ADV** inséparablement

insert[1] [ˈɪnsɜːt] **N1** *Cin* scène-raccord *f*, *pl* scènes-raccords; *(in magazine etc)* encart *m* **2** *Typ etc (in proofs)* insertion *f* **3** *Comput* insertion *f* **4** *Sewing* incrustation *f*
▸▸*Comput* **i. key** touche *f* d'insertion; *Typ* **i. mark** signe *m* d'insertion; *Comput* **i. mode** mode *m* (d')insertion; *Comput* **i. point** point *m* d'insertion

insert[2] [ɪnˈsɜːt] **VT1** *(key in lock etc)* introduire, enfoncer; *(page in book, scene in film etc)* insérer; *(clause in contract etc)* insérer, introduire, apposer; **to i. an ad (in the newspaper)** mettre une petite annonce dans le journal **2** *Typ (line)* intercaler **3** *Comput* insérer

insertion [ɪnˈsɜːʃən] **N1** *(act of inserting)* insertion *f*, introduction *f* (**of sth into sth** de qch dans qch); *(of advert in newspaper)* insertion **2** *(thing inserted) Typ* insertion *f*, *Sewing* incrustation *f*, *(of lace etc)* entre-deux *m inv*
▸▸**i. mark** signe *m* d'insertion; *Typ* **i. point** point *m* d'insertion

inset[1] [ˈɪnset] **N1** *(in bookbinding) (of four or eight pages)* encart *m*, carton *m*; *(leaf, advertisement)* encartage *m* **2** *Typ (map etc)* hors-texte *m inv*, médaillon *m*; *TV, Cin* médaillon **3** *Sewing* incrustation *f*

inset[2] [ˈɪnset] **VT** *(pt, pp* **inset** *or* **insetted) 1** *(in bookbinding) (leaves, advertisements)* encarter **2** *Typ* insérer en cartouche *ou* en médaillon **3** *Sewing (piece of fabric etc)* insérer; *(lace etc)* faire des incrustations de **4** *Typ (indent) (line, new paragraph)* renfoncer

inshore [ˈɪnˈʃɔːr] *Naut* **ADV** près de la côte; *(to head)* vers la côte; **to keep close i.** naviguer près de la côte
ADJ *(navigation, fishing)* côtier
▸▸**i. waters** eaux *fpl* près de la côte; **i. wind** vent *m* de mer

INSIDE

N	intérieur **1**
ADJ	intérieur
ADV	à l'intérieur **1** ▪ dedans **1**
PREP	à l'intérieur de **1** ▪ dans **1** ▪ en moins de **2**

N [ˈɪnsaɪd] **1** *(of garment etc)* côté *m*) intérieur *m*; *(of house etc)* intérieur *m*; **the door opens from (the) i.** la porte s'ouvre de l'intérieur; **the door had been locked from the i.** la porte était verrouillée de l'intérieur; **on the i.** à l'intérieur; **a scar on the i. of his leg** une cicatrice sur la face interne de sa jambe; **to walk on the i. (of the pavement)** marcher loin de la chaussée; **a motorbike was coming up on the i.** une moto arrivait sur la droite *ou (driving on left)* la gauche; *Fam* **to know the i. of an affair** connaître les dessous d'une affaire
2 *Fam* **insides** *(internal organs)* entrailles *fpl*, **to have pains in one's inside(s)** avoir mal au ventre
3 i. out *(sweater etc)* à l'envers; **to turn sth i. out** mettre qch à l'envers; *Fig* **to turn everything i. out** mettre tout sens dessus dessous; *Fig* **to know sth i. out** savoir qch à fond; *Fig* **to know Paris i. out** connaître Paris comme sa poche
ADJ [ˈɪnsaɪd] *(wall, door, pocket etc)* intérieur; *Constr (measurement, stair etc)* dans œuvre; *(diameter)* interne; *Horseracing* **to be on the i. track** tenir la corde; **it's an i. job** *(of burglary etc)* c'est un coup monté par quelqu'un de la maison; **to have an i. accomplice** avoir un complice à l'intérieur; **I speak with i. knowledge** ce que je dis je le sais de bonne source; **the i. pages** *(of newspaper)* les pages intérieures; **to know the i. story** connaître les dessous de l'histoire
ADV [ɪnˈsaɪd] **1** à l'intérieur; **he took the box and looked i.** il a pris la boîte et a regardé dedans *ou* à l'intérieur; **there's nothing i.** il n'y a rien dedans *ou* à l'intérieur; **i. she was angry** intérieurement elle était en colère; **i. and out** au dedans et au dehors, à l'intérieur et à l'extérieur; **to push sb i.** pousser qn à l'intérieur *ou* dedans; **come i.!** entrez!; *Sl* **to put sb/be i.** *(in prison)* mettre qn/être en tôle *ou* taule
2 *(of time) (within)* **i. of three hours** en moins de trois heures
PREP [ɪnˈsaɪd] **1** *(of place) (house etc)* à l'intérieur de, dans; **i. the country/company** au sein du pays/de la société; **the telephone is just i. the door** le téléphone est juste derrière la porte; *Fam* **get this i. you** avale-ça; *Fam* **to get right i. a part** *(of actor)* entrer dans la peau d'un personnage
2 *(of time)* **i. a week/an hour** en moins d'une semaine/d'une heure
▸▸**i. back cover** troisième *f* de couverture; **i. centre** *(in rugby)* premier centre *m*; **i. front cover** deuxième *f* de couverture; **i. information** renseignements *mpl* privés; **the i. lane** *(in athletics)* la corde, le couloir intérieur; *(of road, driving on left)* la voie de gauche; *(driving on right)* la voie de droite; *Ftbl* **i. left** intérieur gauche; **i. leg measurement** entrejambe *m*; *Typ* **i. margin** marge *f* de reliure, *(blanc m de)* petit fond *m*

insider [ɪnˈsaɪdər] **N** initié, -ée
▸▸*Fin* **i. dealing, i. trading** délit *m ou* opération *f* d'initié

insidious [ɪnˈsɪdɪəs] **ADJ** insidieux

insidiously [ɪnˈsɪdɪəslɪ] **ADV** insidieusement

insight [ˈɪnsaɪt] **N1** *(perspicacity)* perspicacité *f*, **i. into character** finesse *f* psychologique; **to have a lot of i.** être très perspicace **2** *(understanding)* aperçu *m*; **to get an i. into sth** avoir un aperçu de qch; **the book offers several valuable insights into ...** le livre donne un bon aperçu de ...

insightful [ˈɪnsaɪtfʊl] **ADJ** perspicace

insignia [ɪnˈsɪgnɪə] **NPL** *(of royal family etc)* insignes *mpl*, *Mil* **i. of rank** insignes du grade

insignificance [ɪnsɪgˈnɪfɪkəns] **N** insignifiance *f*, **my problems fade into i. beside yours** mes problèmes semblent totalement insignifiants à côté des tiens

insignificant [ɪnsɪgˈnɪfɪkənt] **ADJ** insignifiant

insincere [ɪnsɪnˈsɪər] **ADJ** peu sincère, faux, *f* fausse, *Lit* insincère

insincerity [ɪnsɪn'serɪtɪ] N manque m de sincérité, fausseté f

insinuate [ɪn'sɪnjʊeɪt] VT **1** (suggest indirectly) insinuer; **are you insinuating that …?** est-ce que vous insinuez que …? **2** Fml (manoeuvre) **to i. one's hand/body into an opening** glisser sa main/se glisser dans une ouverture; **to i. oneself into a room** s'introduire dans une pièce; **to i. oneself into sb's favour** s'insinuer dans les bonnes grâces de qn

insinuation [ɪnsɪnjʊ'eɪʃən] N **1** (indirect suggestion) insinuation f **2** Fml (of hand, body) introduction f

insipid [ɪn'sɪpɪd] ADJ (food) insipide, fade; (style, conversation) fade, plat, insipide; (person) insipide

insipidity [ɪnsɪ'pɪdɪtɪ], **insipidness** [ɪn'sɪpɪdnɪs] N insipidité f, fadeur f

insist [ɪn'sɪst] VI insister (**on doing** pour faire); **to i. on a point** insister ou appuyer sur un point; **I won't i.** je n'insiste pas; **very well, if you i.** très bien, si tu insistes; **he insists on your coming** il insiste pour que vous veniez; **he insisted on paying** il a tenu à payer; **let me pay for the meal, I i. (on it)!** laisse-moi payer l'addition, j'insiste!; **show me what you've got there, I i.!** montre-moi ce que tu as dans les mains, je l'exige!; **to i. upon one's innocence** affirmer son innocence avec insistance; **to i. on one's rights** revendiquer ses droits; **i. on the best** exigez la meilleure qualité

▪ VT **1** (maintain) soutenir, maintenir; **people insisted that they had seen him** des gens affirmaient l'avoir vu; **he insisted that it was so** il maintenait qu'il en était ainsi **2 I i. that you let me pay** j'insiste, laisse-moi payer; **I i. that you show me what you have in your hand** j'exige que tu me montres ce que tu as dans la main

insistence [ɪn'sɪstəns] N insistance f, because of his i. **on paying** parce qu'il tenait à payer; **he did it at her i.** il l'a fait parce qu'elle a insisté; **her i. that she was telling the truth didn't convince me** quoi qu'elle ait bien insisté qu'elle disait la vérité, elle ne m'a pas convaincu

insistent [ɪn'sɪstənt] ADJ qui insiste, insistant; (demands) instant; (noise) incessant; **to be i. about sth** insister sur qch; **to be very i.** insister beaucoup; **don't be too i.** n'insistez pas trop

insistently [ɪn'sɪstəntlɪ] ADV instamment, avec insistance

in situ [ɪn'sɪtjuː] ADV in situ

insofar [ɪnsəʊ'fɑːr] ADV Am **i. as** dans la mesure où

insole ['ɪnsəʊl] N (of shoe) (inner sole) première semelle f; (separate piece) (of cork, felt etc) semelle intérieure

insolence ['ɪnsələns] N insolence f (**to** envers)

insolent ['ɪnsələnt] ADJ insolent (**to** envers); **an i. boy** un (jeune) insolent

insolently ['ɪnsələntlɪ] ADV insolemment

insolubility [ɪnsɒljʊ'bɪlɪtɪ] N insolubilité f

insoluble [ɪn'sɒljʊb(ə)l] ADJ (salt etc) insoluble **2** (problem) insoluble, qu'on ne peut pas résoudre

insolvency [ɪn'sɒlvənsɪ] N insolvabilité f

insolvent [ɪn'sɒlvənt] ADJ (debtor, company) insolvable; **to declare oneself i.** se déclarer insolvable; Com déposer son bilan ▪ N (person) débiteur m insolvable; (company) société f insolvable

insomnia [ɪn'sɒmnɪə] N insomnie f

insomniac [ɪn'sɒmnɪæk] N insomniaque mf

insomuch [ɪnsəʊ'mʌtʃ] ADV **=inasmuch**

inspect [ɪn'spekt] VT **1** (examine) examiner, regarder de près; **my mother inspected our hands (to see if they were clean)** ma mère a regardé si nos mains étaient propres **2** (carry out official inspection of) (school etc) inspecter; (accounts of business, machine etc) contrôler, vérifier **3** Mil (regiment) passer en revue; **to be inspected** (of troops) être passé en revue

inspecting officer N inspecteur, -trice

inspection [ɪn'spekʃən] N **1** (of documents etc) examen m, vérification f; (of tickets, goods etc) contrôle m; **on close** or **closer i.** en y regardant de plus près **2** (of school, factory etc) (by official) (visite f d')inspection f; (of head, hands etc) (by nurse) inspection; (of machinery, vehicle) contrôle m, vérification f; **tour of i.** visite d'inspection; **sanitary i.** contrôle m sanitaire; **medical i.** visite médicale; **3** Mil revue f; **to make** or **hold an i.** passer une revue

▪▪ **i. copy** (in publishing) spécimen m; Tech **i. hole** orifice m ou trou m ou regard m de visite; Tech **i. panel** panneau m de visite; Aut **i. pit** fosse f (de réparations); Tech **i. port** orifice ou trou ou regard de visite

inspector [ɪn'spektər] N (of schools, police, mines) inspecteur, -trice; Br (on train, bus etc) contrôleur, -euse

▪▪ Br **i. of taxes** ≃ inspecteur, -trice des impôts

inspectorate [ɪn'spektərət] N **1** (inspectors) corps m d'inspecteurs **2** (post) inspectorat m

inspiration [ɪnspɪ'reɪʃən] N **1** (stimulus) inspiration f; **he is the i. of the movement** c'est l'âme du mouvement; **she's an i. to us all** elle est notre modèle à tous; **to lack i.** (of poet etc) manquer d'inspiration; **to provide the i. for sth** fournir l'inspiration pour qch; **to have a sudden i.** avoir une inspiration subite **2** Fml (inhalation) inspiration f

inspirational [ɪnspɪ'reɪʃənəl] ADJ **1** (inspiring) qui inspire, inspirant **2** (inspired) inspiré

inspire [ɪn'spaɪər] VT **1** (stimulate) inspirer; **to i. a thought/a feeling in sb** inspirer une pensée/un sentiment à qn; **to i. sb with confidence** inspirer (de la) confiance à qn; **to i. sb with hope** donner de l'espoir à qn; **inspired with hope** animé d'espoir; **the programme inspired her to study biology** l'émission l'a poussée à étudier la biologie; **her example inspired us to …** son exemple nous a incités à …; **I don't know what inspired me to turn back** je ne sais pas ce qui m'a poussé à revenir sur mes pas; Iron **what inspired you to do that?** qu'est-ce qui t'a pris de faire ça? **2** Fml (inhale) inspirer

inspired [ɪn'spaɪəd] ADJ (poet, cook etc) inspiré, plein d'inspiration; (decision) inspiré; Fam **no one was (feeling) i.** personne n'était très inspiré; **to make an i. guess** bien tomber, tomber juste; **it was just an i. guess** c'était un coup de chance

inspiring [ɪn'spaɪərɪŋ] ADJ (speech, example etc) qui inspire, inspirant; Fam **the menu wasn't very i.** le menu n'avait rien de bien tentant

inst [ɪnst] Com Old-fashioned (abbr **instant**) (in letter) **on the 5th i.** le 5 courant

instability [ɪnstə'bɪlɪtɪ] N (of government, economy etc) instabilité f; Tech déséquilibre m; Met instabilité (atmosphérique); (of bridge etc) manque m de solidité; (of character) mobilité f, instabilité

install, Am **instal** [ɪn'stɔːl] VT **1** (machine, electricity, software) installer **2** (settle) **she installed herself in an armchair/in front of the TV** elle s'est installée dans un fauteuil/devant la télé **3** Rel, Fml (bishop, person in position) installer

installation [ɪnstə'leɪʃən] N **1** (of central heating, machine, bishop, software) installation f **2** (thing installed) installation f

▪▪ Comput **i. disk** disquette f d'installation; Comput **i. manual** manuel m d'installation; Comput **i. program** programme m d'installation

installer [ɪn'stɔːlər] N Comput disquette f d'installation

instalment, Am **installment** [ɪn'stɔːlmənt] N **1** Com etc (part payment) versement m; **to pay in** or **by instalments** payer par versements, échelonner ou fractionner les paiements; **payable in monthly instalments** payable par mensualités; **final i.** paiement m pour solde **2** (of work published in parts) fascicule m, livraison f; (of work published in periodical), Radio, TV (of soap opera etc) épisode m

▪▪ Fin **i. loan** prêt m à tempérament ou à remboursements échelonnés; Am **i. plan** vente f à tempérament; Am **to buy sth on the i. plan** acheter qch à crédit

instance ['ɪnstəns] N **1** (example) cas m; **in many instances** dans bien des cas; **in the present i., in this i.** dans le cas présent; **for i.** par exemple **2 in the first i.** en (tout) premier lieu **3** Fml (urging) **to do sth at sb's i.** or **at the i. of sb** faire qch à ou sur la demande de qn

▪ VT citer en exemple; **his cruelty is well instanced by …** sa cruauté est bien illustrée par …

> Note that the French noun **instance** is a false friend: it never means **example**.

instant ['ɪnstənt] ADJ **1** (action, dislike etc) immédiat; (solution) instantané; Fml **this calls for i. remedy** il faut y remédier tout de suite ou sur-le-champ **2** (quickly prepared) (coffee) instantané; **i. mash** purée f en flocons/en poudre **3** Lit (urgent) pressant, urgent **4** Old-fashioned (in letter) (of current month) courant

▪ N **1** (moment) instant m, moment m; **come this i.!** venez immédiatement!; **I just arrived this (very) i.** j'arrive à l'instant; **not an i. too soon** juste à temps; **in an i.** dans un instant; **the i. I saw him** dès que je l'ai vu **2** Fam (instant coffee) café m instantané

▪▪ Phot **i. camera** appareil m photo à développement instantané; Comput **i. message** message m instantané; Comput **i. messaging** messagerie f instantanée; TV **i. replay** = répétition f immédiate d'une séquence; (in slow motion) ralenti m

instant-access ADJ (bank account) à accès immédiat

instantaneous [ɪnstən'teɪnɪəs] ADJ instantané

▪▪ Mktg **i. audience** audience f instantanée; Phot **i. exposure** pose f instantanée, instantané m

instantaneously [ɪnstən'teɪnɪəslɪ] ADV instantanément

instantly ['ɪnstəntlɪ] ADV tout de suite, immédiatement, sur-le-champ; **she would have died i.** elle serait morte immédiatement; **i. recognizable** immédiatement reconnaissable

instead [ɪn'sted] ADV **1** (in place of sth) à la place; (in sb's place) à ma/sa/etc place; **if John can't come, take me i.** si Jean ne peut pas venir, emmenez-moi à sa place; **use the hammer i.** utilise le marteau à la place **2 i. of** (thing) au lieu de; (person) à la place de; **i. of doing sth** au lieu de faire qch

instep ['ɪnstep] N (of foot) cou-de-pied m, pl cous-de-pied; (of shoe) cambrure f; **to have a high i.** (of person) avoir le pied très cambré

instigate ['ɪnstɪgeɪt] VT (of person) (inquiry,

negotiations, changes, rebellion etc) être à l'origine de; *(of event, development etc) (rebellion, change)* provoquer; *(incite) (person)* inciter, pousser (**to do** à faire)

instigation [ɪnstɪ'geɪʃən] **N** instigation *f*, incitation *f*; **at sb's i.** à l'instigation de qn

instigator ['ɪnstɪgeɪtər] **N** instigateur, -trice

instil, *Am* **instill** [ɪn'stɪl] **VT** (*Br* **instils,** *Am* **instills,** *Br & Am* **instilled, instilling**) *(courage, pride)* inspirer (**in** à); *(doubt, jealousy)* instiller (**in** à); *(idea)* inculquer (**into** à)

instinct ['ɪnstɪŋkt] **N** instinct *m*; **by** *or* **from i.** d'instinct, par instinct; **to follow one's instincts** suivre son instinct; **my i. was to run away** mon instinct m'a dit de fuir; **to have an i. for business** avoir le sens des affaires; **she has a strong business i.** elle a vraiment le sens des affaires

instinctive [ɪn'stɪŋktɪv] **ADJ** instinctif

instinctively [ɪn'stɪŋktɪvlɪ] **ADV** instinctivement, d'instinct

institute ['ɪnstɪtjuːt] **N** institut *m*; **i. for the blind** établissement *m* pour aveugles
VT 1 *(set up) (order, law)* instituer, établir; *(club etc)* fonder, constituer **2** *(initiate) (search)* lancer; *Law (enquiry)* ordonner, instituer; **to i. (legal) proceedings against sb** entamer *ou* engager des poursuites contre qn
▸▸ *Br* **i. of education** école *f* formant des enseignants; *Br* **I. for Public Policy Research** = groupe *m* d'experts de centre gauche à l'origine de plusieurs grandes politiques du gouvernement travailliste

institution [ɪnstɪ'tjuːʃən] **N 1** *(organization, society) (for education etc)* institution *f*; *(public, financial etc)* établissement *m*; *(for old people)* hospice *m*; *(for mental patients)* asile *m* **2** *(action) (of enquiry etc)* établissement *m*; *(of law etc)* institution *f*; *(of committee)* constitution *f*; *(of state)* création *f*; *(of search)* lancement *m* **3** *(established practice etc)* institution *f*; *Fig* **to become a national i.** *(of person, event etc)* devenir une institution nationale; **the i. of marriage is under threat** le mariage est une institution menacée

institutional [ɪnstɪ'tjuːʃən(ə)l] **ADJ** institutionnel; **he needs i. care** il a besoin d'être hospitalisé; **i. life** la vie en collectivité
▸▸ *Com* **i. advertising** publicité *f* institutionnelle; *Com* **i. buying** achats *mpl* institutionnels; **i. food** nourriture *f* de cantine; *Fin* **i. investment** investissement *m* institutionnel; *Com* **i. investor** investisseur *m* institutionnel; *Fam* **i. zinzin** *m*; *Fin* **i. savings** épargne *f* institutionnelle

institutionalize [ɪnstɪ'tjuːʃənəlaɪz] **VT 1** *(put in a home etc)* placer dans un établissement spécialisé **2** *(turn into an institution)* institutionnaliser

institutionalized [ɪnstɪ'tjuːʃənəlaɪzd] **ADJ 1** *(person)* marqué par la vie en collectivité; **after years in a psychiatric hospital, she had become completely i.** après des années en hôpital psychiatrique, elle était devenue complètement dépendante; **things are less i. in this establishment** cet établissement a un caractère moins institutionnel **2** *(practice)* établi

in-store ADJ
▸▸ *Mktg* **i. advertising** PLV *f*, publicité *f* sur le lieu de vente; *Mktg* **i. advertising space** espace *m* de PLV, espace de publicité sur le lieu de vente; **i. demonstration** démonstration *f* sur le lieu de vente; **i. promotion** promotion *f* sur le lieu de vente

instruct [ɪn'strʌkt] **VT 1** *(teach, train)* **to i. sb in sth** enseigner qch à qn **2** *(command)* ordonner (**to do** de faire); **I am instructed by the Board to inform you that …** la Direction me charge de vous faire savoir que … **3** *Br*

Law **to i. a solicitor** donner ses instructions à un avoué; **to i. counsel** constituer avocat **4** *Fml (inform)* informer (**that** que)

instruction [ɪn'strʌkʃən] **N 1** *(no pl) (training)* instruction *f*, enseignement *m*; **we received i. in using the machines** on nous a appris comment utiliser les machines **2** *(usu pl)* **instructions** *(orders)* instructions *fpl*, directives *fpl*; *(to sentry etc)* consigne *f*; *(to representative etc)* mandat *m*; *Comput (in program)* instructions; **instructions (for use)** *(for machine, cleaning product etc)* mode *m ou* notice *f* d'emploi; **to give sb instructions to do sth** ordonner à qn de faire qch; **strict instructions** des instructions formelles, des ordres formels; **I gave strict instructions that I wasn't to be disturbed** j'ai donné l'ordre formel qu'on ne me dérange pas; **to carry out instructions** exécuter des ordres; **to act in accordance with/contrary to instructions** se conformer/ne pas se conformer aux instructions reçues; **our instructions were to arrest him** nous avions reçu l'ordre de l'arrêter; **to follow sb's instructions** suivre les instructions de qn; **to obey sb's instructions** obéir aux ordres de qn; *Com* **we await your instructions** nous attendons vos instructions; *Br Law* **to give instructions to a solicitor** donner ses instructions à un avoué
▸▸ **i. book, i. booklet** livret *m* d'instruction(s); *Comput* **i. code** code *m* d'instruction; **i. manual** manuel *m* (d'utilisation et d'entretien); *Comput* guide *m* de l'utilisateur; *Comput* **i. set** jeu *m* d'instructions

instructive [ɪn'strʌktɪv] **ADJ** instructif

instructor [ɪn'strʌktər] **N** enseignant, -ante, professeur *m*; *Am Univ* assistant, -ante; *Mil* instructeur, -trice; *Ski, Aut* moniteur, -trice; **swimming/judo/riding i.** professeur *m* de natation/de judo/d'équitation

instructress [ɪn'strʌktrɪs] **N** maîtresse *f*, professeur *m*; *Ski, Aut* monitrice *f*

instrument ['ɪnstrəmənt] **N 1** *Tech, Surg, Mus etc* instrument *m*; **aircraft instruments** instruments de bord; **flying/landing on instruments, i. flying/landing** vol *m*/atterrissage *m* aux instruments *ou* sans visibilité; *Aviat, Aut* **i. board** *or* **panel** *or* **display** tableau *m* de bord **2** *Fml (means, agent)* instrument *m*; **to serve as the i. of sb's vengeance** servir d'instrument à la vengeance de qn **3** *Law (legal document)* instrument *m*, acte *m* juridique; **i. of incorporation** statut *m*, acte de constitution; *Com* **i. to order** papier *m* à ordre
VT 1 *Mus (opera etc)* orchestrer, instrumenter **2** *Tech (workshop etc)* équiper *ou* munir d'outils
VI *Law* instrumenter

instrumental [ɪnstrə'ment(ə)l] **ADJ 1** *(contributing)* **to be i. in doing sth** contribuer à faire qch, jouer un rôle décisif dans qch **2** *Tech* **by i. means** avec des instruments de mesure **3** *Mus* instrumental, -aux
N *Mus* version *f* instrumentale
▸▸ *Tech* **i. error** erreur *f* due aux instruments

instrumentalist [ɪnstrə'mentəlɪst] **N** *Mus* instrumentiste *mf*

instrumentation [ɪnstrʊmən'teɪʃən] **N** *Mus, Aut* instrumentation *f*

insubordinate [ɪnsə'bɔːdɪnət] **ADJ** insubordonné, insoumis

insubordination [ɪnsəbɔːdɪ'neɪʃən] **N** insubordination *f*, insoumission *f*

insubstantial [ɪnsəb'stænʃəl] **ADJ 1** *(thin, flimsy) (reason)* qui manque de substance; *(argument)* vide, creux; *(book etc)* creux, qui manque de substance; **an i. breakfast** un petit déjeuner frugal **2** *(unreal) (fear)* imaginaire

insufferable [ɪn'sʌfərəb(ə)l] **ADJ** insupportable, intolérable

insufferably [ɪn'sʌfərəblɪ] **ADV** insupportablement, intolérablement

insufficiency [ɪnsə'fɪʃənsɪ] **N** insuffisance *f*

insufficient [ɪnsə'fɪʃənt] **ADJ** *(amount, resources, justification etc)* insuffisant; *(facilities)* inadéquat; **the sum is i. to cover our costs** la somme ne suffit pas à couvrir nos frais
▸▸ *Fin* **i. capital** insuffisance *f* de capitaux; **i. evidence** preuves *fpl* insuffisantes; *Fin* **i. funds** provision *f* insuffisante, insuffisance de provision

insufficiently [ɪnsə'fɪʃəntlɪ] **ADV** insuffisamment

insular ['ɪnsjʊlər] **ADJ 1** *(narrow) (mind)* étroit, borné; **to be very i. in one's views** être très étroit d'esprit **2** *Geog (climate etc)* insulaire

Note that the French word **insulaire** is a false friend. It always means **pertaining to an island**.

insularity [ɪnsjʊ'lærɪtɪ] **N** *Pej (of country)* manque *m* d'ouverture sur l'extérieur; **the i. of their views** leur étroitesse *f* d'esprit

insulate ['ɪnsjʊleɪt] **VT** *Elec (wire etc)* isoler; *(pipe, water tank etc)* calorifuger; *Radio etc (soundproof)* insonoriser; **to i. against vibration** protéger contre les vibrations; *Fig* **insulated from the outside world** protégé contre le monde extérieur

insulated ['ɪnsjʊleɪtɪd] **ADJ** *Elec* isolé; *(handle, screwdriver etc)* isolant; *(against loss of heat)* calorifugé; *(soundproofed)* insonorisé

insulating ['ɪnsjʊleɪtɪŋ] **ADJ** isolant; *(against loss of heat)* calorifuge; *(soundproofing)* insonore
▸▸ *Elec* **i. material** isolant *m*; **i. properties** propriétés *fpl* isolantes; **i. tape** ruban *m* isolant, chatterton *m*

insulation [ɪnsjʊ'leɪʃən] **N 1** *(action, state) (of wires etc)* isolation *f*; **heat** *or* **thermal i.** isolation thermique; **sound i.** *(of room etc)* insonorisation *f* **2** *(substance) (for wires, against heat loss etc)* isolant *m*

Attention: ne pas confondre avec le terme anglais **isolation**, qui signifie **isolement**.

insulator ['ɪnsjʊleɪtər] **N** *Elec, Constr (substance)* isolant *m*; *Elec (device)* isolateur *m*

insulin ['ɪnsjʊlɪn] **N** *Med* insuline *f*
▸▸ **i. treatment** insulinothérapie *f*

insulin-dependent **ADJ** *Med* insulinodépendant

insult[1] ['ɪnsʌlt] **N** *(abuse)* insulte *f*, *(affront)* affront *m*, insulte; **and to add i. to injury …** et comme si ça ne suffisait pas …; **it's an i. to the intelligence** c'est une insulte à l'intelligence

insult[2] [ɪn'sʌlt] **VT** *(abuse)* insulter; *(affront)* faire affront *ou* injure à, insulter; **to i. sb's intelligence** *(of book, film etc)* être une insulte à l'intelligence de qn; *(of person)* prendre qn pour un/une imbécile; **to feel insulted** se sentir insulté

insulting [ɪn'sʌltɪŋ] **ADJ** *(gesture, expression)* insultant, offensant, injurieux; *(person)* injurieux; **it is i. to suggest that …** il est insultant de suggérer que …; **it's i.!** c'est une insulte!; **to use i. language** employer un langage injurieux; **to be guilty of i. behaviour towards sb** s'être conduit insolemment à l'égard de qn; *Law (to magistrate, policeman)* être coupable d'outrages à qn

insultingly [ɪn'sʌltɪŋlɪ] **ADV** d'une façon insultante *ou* offensante

insuperable [ɪn'su:pərəb(ə)l] ADJ *(difficulty, obstacle etc)* insurmontable

insuperably [ɪn'su:pərəblɪ] ADV **i. difficult** impossible

in-supplier N *Mktg* fournisseur *m* agréé

insupportable [ɪnsə'pɔ:təb(ə)l] ADJ insupportable

insurable [ɪn'ʃʊərəb(ə)l, ɪn'ʃɔ:r-] ADJ assurable
▸▸ **i. interest** intérêt *m* pécuniaire

insurance [ɪn'ʃʊərəns, -ʃɔ:rəns] N **1** *Com* assurance *f*; **to take out i. on sth** prendre une assurance sur qch; **to take out i. against a risk** prendre une assurance *ou* s'assurer contre un risque; **he's in i.** il est dans les assurances; **i. against loss of trade** assurance contre la perte d'affaires, assurance perte de l'exploitation **2** *(premium)* prime *f* d'assurance; **to pay the i. on a car** payer l'assurance d'une voiture **3** *Fig (protection)* garantie *f*; **to buy gold as (an) i. against inflation** acheter de l'or pour se prémunir contre l'inflation
▸▸ **i. adviser** assureur-conseil *m*, *pl* assureurs-conseils; **i. agent** agent *m* d'assurance(s); **i. banker** bancassureur *m*; **i. broker** courtier, -ière d'assurances; **i. certificate** certificat *m* d'assurance; **i. claim** demande *f* d'indemnité; *(for more serious damage)* déclaration *f* de sinistre; **i. company** société *f* d'assurances; **i. cover** couverture *f* d'assurance; **i. group** groupe *m* d'assurance; **i. inspector** inspecteur, -trice d'une société d'assurances; **i. policy** police *f* d'assurance, contrat *m* d'assurance; **i. portfolio** portefeuille *m* d'assurances; **i. premium** prime *f* d'assurance; **i. value** valeur *f* d'assurance

insure [ɪn'ʃʊər, -ʃɔ:r] VT **1** *(of insurance company) (car, valuables etc)* assurer; *(of client) (goods etc)* (faire) assurer; **I'm insured** je suis assuré; **to i. one's life** s'assurer *ou* se faire assurer sur la vie **2** *esp Am* = **ensure**
▸ **insure against** VT INSEP *(risk, theft, fire)* s'assurer *ou* se faire assurer contre; *(danger)* se garantir de; **to i. against loss** couvrir une perte

insured [ɪn'ʃʊəd, -ʃɔ:d] ADJ assuré
N **the i.** *(person)* l'assuré, -ée
▸▸ **i. value** valeur *f* assurée

insurer [ɪn'ʃʊərər, -ʃɔ:rər] N assureur *m*

insurgent [ɪn'sɜ:dʒənt] ADJ insurgé, révolté
N insurgé, -e, révolté, -ée

insurmountable [ɪnsə'maʊntəb(ə)l] ADJ *(difficulty, obstacle)* insurmontable

insurrection [ɪnsə'rekʃ(ə)n] N insurrection *f*

insurrectionary [ɪnsə'rekʃənərɪ] ADJ insurrectionnel
N insurgé, -ée

insurrectionist [ɪnsə'rekʃənɪst] N insurgé, -ée

intact [ɪn'tækt] ADJ intact

intaglio [ɪn'ta:lɪəʊ] N *(gem)* intaille *f*
▸▸ **i. engraving** gravure *f* en creux

intake ['ɪnteɪk] N **1** *(opening) (for water, electricity)* prise *f*; *(for steam)* arrivée *f*, adduction *f*, admission *f*; *(in engine) (for air)* arrivée, prise; *Min* galerie *f* d'appel d'air; *Tech* aire *f* d'alimentation; **he gave a sharp i. of breath when he heard the news** il a eu le souffle coupé quand il a entendu la nouvelle **2** *(of alcohol, calories etc)* consommation *f* **3** *Sch (of pupils, students)* admission(s) *f(pl)*; *Mil (of recruits)* contingent *m*
▸▸ *Aut* **i. pipe** conduit *m* d'admission

intangible [ɪn'tændʒɪb(ə)l] ADJ *(benefit)* intangible; *(quality)* indéfinissable
NPL *Acct, Fin* **intangibles** valeurs *fpl* immatérielles, actif *m* incorporel
▸▸ *Acct, Fin* **i. assets** valeurs immatérielles, actif incorporel; *Acct, Fin* **i. fixed assets** immobilisations *fpl* incorporelles; *Law* **i. property** biens *mpl* incorporels

integer ['ɪntɪdʒər] N *Math* (nombre *m*) entier *m*

integral ['ɪntɪgr(ə)l] ADJ **1** *(essential)* indispensable (**to** pour); **to be** *or* **form an i. part of sth** faire partie intégrante de qch **2** *Tech (forming a part)* incorporé (**with** à), qui fait partie intégrante (**with** de)
N *Math* intégrale *f*
▸▸ *Math* **i. calculus** calcul *m* intégral; *Math* **i. number** nombre *m* entier; **i. power supply** accumulateur *m* incorporé

integrate ['ɪntɪgreɪt] VT **1** *(incorporate) (minority)* intégrer (**into** à); *Am* **to i. a school** imposer la déségrégation raciale dans une école **2** *(bring together)* regrouper (**into** en), combiner **3** *Math (function)* intégrer
VI *(social milieu, ethnic group etc)* s'intégrer; *Am (carry out racial integration)* pratiquer la déségrégation raciale

integrated ['ɪntɪgreɪtɪd] ADJ **1** intégré; **an i. transport system** un système de transports cohérent **2** *(school)* qui pratique la déségrégation raciale
▸▸ *Electron* **i. circuit** circuit *m* intégré; *Electron* **i. circuit card** carte *f* à circuit intégré; *Comput* **i. package** logiciel *m* ou progiciel *m* intégré, intégré *m*; *Comput* **i. software** logiciel intégré

integration [ɪntɪ'greɪʃən] N **1** intégration *f*; **the i. of ethnic minorities** l'intégration des minorités ethniques; **racial i.** déségrégation *f* raciale **2** *Math* **i. by parts** intégration *f* par parties

integrative growth ['ɪntɪgreɪtɪv] N *Com* croissance *f* par intégration

integrator ['ɪntɪgreɪtər] N *Comput* intégrateur *m*

integrity [ɪn'tegrɪtɪ] N **1** *(honesty) (of person)* intégrité *f*, honnêteté *f*, probité *f*; *(of motive)* honnêteté; **woman/man of i.** femme *f*/homme *m* intègre **2** *(wholeness) (of text, computer data)* intégrité *f*

integument [ɪn'tegjʊmənt] N *Biol* tégument *m*

intellect ['ɪntɪlekt] N intelligence *f*, intellect *m*; **a man of i.** un homme intelligent; **he was one of the best intellects of his time** c'était un des plus grands esprits de son époque

intellectual [ɪntɪ'lektjʊəl, -tʃʊəl] ADJ intellectuel
N intellectuel, -elle
▸▸ *Law* **i. property** propriété *f* intellectuelle

intellectually [ɪntɪ'lektjʊəlɪ, -tʃʊəlɪ] ADV intellectuellement

intelligence [ɪn'telɪdʒəns] N **1** *(mental capacity)* intelligence *f*; *(mind)* esprit *m*; **a person of some i.** une personne assez intelligente; **use your i.!** réfléchis un peu **2** *Mil, Pol (information)* renseignements *mpl*
▸▸ *Mil, Pol* **i. officer** officier *m* de renseignements; **i. quotient** quotient *m* intellectuel; *Mil, Pol* **I. service** service *m* de renseignements; *Psy* **i. test** test *m* d'aptitude intellectuelle

intelligent [ɪn'telɪdʒənt] ADJ intelligent

intelligently [ɪn'telɪdʒəntlɪ] ADV intelligemment, avec intelligence

intelligentsia [ɪntelɪ'dʒentsɪə] N intelligentsia *f*

intelligibility [ɪntelɪdʒɪ'bɪlɪtɪ] N intelligibilité *f*

intelligible [ɪn'telɪdʒɪb(ə)l] ADJ intelligible; **he was hardly i.** on le comprenait à peine

intelligibly [ɪn'telɪdʒɪblɪ] ADV intelligiblement

intemperance [ɪn'temp(ə)rəns] N intempérance *f*

intemperate [ɪn'temp(ə)rɪt] ADJ *Fml (person)* intempérant; *(climate)* rude; **person of i. habits** personne *f* intempérante; *(excessive drinker)* personne qui s'adonne à la boisson

intend [ɪn'tend] VT **1** *(plan)* **to i. to do sth** avoir l'intention de faire qch, compter faire qch; **was that intended?** était-ce fait à dessein?, était-ce intentionnel?; **the play was intended to shock** la pièce voulait choquer; **that's exactly what I intended** c'était exactement mon intention; **what the author intended and what his readers understood** ce que l'auteur a voulu dire et ce que ses lecteurs ont compris; **I i. to be obeyed** je veux qu'on m'obéisse; **I didn't i. her to see it yet** je ne voulais pas qu'elle la voie déjà; **I intended it as a compliment** mon intention était de vous/lui/*etc* faire un compliment
2 *(aim, destine)* **a book intended for students** un livre destiné aux étudiants; **this remark is intended for you** cette observation s'adresse à vous

intended [ɪn'tendɪd] ADJ **1** *(hoped-for)* voulu **2** *(intentional)* intentionnel
N *Old-fashioned, Hum* **his/her i.** sa fiancée/son fiancé, sa future/son futur

intense [ɪn'tens] ADJ *(feeling, anxiety)* vif, *f* vive; *(heat, book, colour, activity etc)* intense; *(pain)* vif, intense; *(bombardment, campaign)* intensif; *(hatred)* profond; **i. expression** expression *f* concentrée; **she's too i.** elle est trop sérieuse

intensely [ɪn'tenslɪ] ADV **1** *(greatly) (amusing, entertaining, boring etc)* extrêmement; **it was i. hot** il faisait une chaleur intense; **i. blue eyes** yeux *mpl* d'un bleu intense **2** *(to look at)* avec intensité, intensément

intensification [ɪntensɪfɪ'keɪʃən] N *(of sound etc)* intensification *f*; *Phot (of negative)* renforcement *m*

intensifier [ɪn'tensɪfaɪər] N *Ling* intensif *m*; *Phot* renforçateur *m*

intensify [ɪn'tensɪfaɪ] VT *(feeling)* intensifier, augmenter, accroître; *(colour)* renforcer
VI s'intensifier, augmenter

intensity [ɪn'tensɪtɪ] N **1** *(of passion, anger)* intensité *f*; *(of pain)* violence *f* **2** *Phys (of sound, current etc)* intensité *f*; *Chem (of reaction)* énergie *f*; *Phot (of negative)* densité *f*

intensive [ɪn'tensɪv] ADJ intensif; *Sch etc* **i. course** cours *m* accéléré
▸▸ *Med* **i. care** soins *mpl* intensifs; *Med* **to be in i. care** être dans le service de soins intensifs; *Med* **i. care unit** service *m* de soins intensifs; *Mktg* **i. distribution** distribution *f* intensive; *Mktg* **i. distribution strategy** stratégie *f* de distribution intensive; **i. farming** culture *f* intensive

intensively [ɪn'tensɪvlɪ] ADV intensivement

intent [ɪn'tent] N intention *f*, dessein *m*, but *m*; **with good i.** dans une bonne intention; *Law* **with i. to defraud** dans l'intention de frauder; **declaration of i.** déclaration *f* d'intention; **to all intents (and purposes)** quasiment
ADJ **1** **to be i. on doing sth** *(determined)* être résolu *ou* déterminé à faire qch; **they left i. on murder** ils sont partis, déterminés à commettre un meurtre; **a woman i. on success** une femme déterminée à réussir **2** **to be i. on sth** *(engrossed in)* être tout entier à *ou* absorbé par qch **3** *(intense) (look)* intense

intention [ɪn'tenʃən] N intention *f*; **I had no i.** *or* **not the slightest i. of accepting** je n'avais nullement l'intention d'accepter; **to have every i. of doing sth** être résolu à faire qch, avoir la ferme intention de faire qch; **I have every i. of calling her!** *(I won't forget)* j'ai bien l'intention de l'appeler; **was (it) your i. to ...?** est-ce qu'il était de ton intention de ...?; **he acted with the best and most honourable intentions** il a agi en tout bien (et) tout honneur; **her intentions were good** elle avait de bonnes intentions; *Old-fashioned* **his intentions are honourable** *(towards her)* il a l'intention de l'épouser; *Mktg* **i. to buy** intention *f* d'achat; **i.-to-buy scale** échelle *f* des intentions d'achat

intentional [ɪn'tenʃən(ə)l] **ADJ** intentionnel, voulu; **it wasn't i.** je ne l'ai pas/il ne l'a pas/*etc* fait exprès

intentionally [ɪn'tenʃən(ə)lɪ] **ADV** intentionnellement; **he didn't do it i.** il ne l'a pas fait exprès *ou* intentionnellement; **I i. didn't invite her** c'est intentionnellement que je ne l'ai pas invitée

intently [ɪn'tentlɪ] **ADV** *(to listen, look at, study)* attentivement; *(to think)* profondément

inter [ɪn'tɜːr] **VT** (**-rr-**) *Fml (bury)* inhumer, enterrer

interact [ɪntər'ækt] **VI** *(of chemicals)* interagir; *esp Psy* **to encourage a child to i. with its environment** encourager les échanges d'un enfant avec son environnement; **a situation in which therapist and patient i.** une situation où il y a interaction entre le thérapeute et son patient; **a person who doesn't i. well with others** une personne qui a du mal dans ses rapports avec les autres; **the way the two characters in the novel i.** l'interaction entre les deux personnages dans ce roman

interaction [ɪntər'ækʃən] **N** interaction *f*

interactive [ɪntər'æktɪv] **ADJ** interactif
▶▶*Comput* **i. CD** CD-I *m*, disque *m* compact interactif; **i. CD-ROM** CD-ROM *m* interactif; **i. learning** apprentissage *m* interactif; **i. marketing** marketing *m* interactif; **i. television** télévision *f* interactive; *Comput* **i. terminal** terminal *m* (informatique) interactif; **i. video** vidéo *f* interactive

interactiveness, interactivity [ɪntər'æktɪvnɪs, ɪntəræk'tɪvɪtɪ] **N** interactivité *f*

inter alia **ADV** *Fml* entre autres

interbank ['ɪntəbæŋk] **ADJ ATTRIB** interbancaire
▶▶**i. deposit** dépôt *m* interbancaire; **i. loan** prêt *m* de banque à banque *ou* entre banques; **i. market** marché *m* interbancaire; **i. money** argent *m* de gré à gré entre banques; **i. offered rate** taux *m* interbancaire offert; **i. transfer** virement *m* interbancaire

interbreed [ɪntə'briːd] *(pt, pp* **interbred)** **VT 1** *(breed from same stock)* croiser *(des animaux consanguins)* **2** *(crossbreed)* croiser
VI 1 *(in same family group)* se reproduire entre eux **2** *(crossbreed)* se reproduire par croisement, se croiser

interbreeding [ɪntə'briːdɪŋ] **N 1** *(in same family)* reproduction *f* entre membres d'une même famille; *(of animals)* reproduction par accouplements consanguins **2** *(crossbreeding)* croisement *m*

intercede [ɪntə'siːd] **VI** intercéder (**with sb** auprès de qn; **for sb, on sb's behalf** en faveur de qn, pour qn)

intercept [ɪntə'sept] **VT** *(letter, enemy plane, person)*, *Ftbl (pass)* intercepter
VI *Ftbl* intercepter une passe
▶▶*Mktg* **i. interview** entretien *m* spontané

interception [ɪntə'sepʃən] **N** *(of letter, message etc)*, *Ftbl* interception *f*

interceptor [ɪntə'septər] **N 1** *(person)* *(of message etc)* personne *f* qui intercepte **2** *Aviat, Mil (aircraft)* avion *m* d'interception, intercepteur *m*
▶▶*Aviat, Mil* **i. aircraft** avion *m* d'interception, intercepteur

intercession [ɪntə'seʃən] **N** intercession *f*

interchange[1] ['ɪntətʃeɪndʒ] **N 1** *(of compliments, things, ideas)* échange *m* **2** *Constr (on motorway)* échangeur *m*

interchange[2] [ɪntə'tʃeɪndʒ] **VT** *(compliments etc)* échanger (**with** avec); *(two parts of machine etc)* intervertir; **all parts of these machines can be interchanged** toutes les pièces de ces machines sont interchangeables

interchangeable [ɪntə'tʃeɪndʒəb(ə)l] **ADJ** interchangeable

interchangeably [ɪntə'tʃeɪndʒəblɪ] **ADV** *(to use)* indifféremment

intercharacter spacing [ɪntə'kærəktə] **N** *Typ* espacement *m* entre les caractères

inter-city [ɪntə'sɪtɪ] *Br Rail* **ADJ** *(service, train)* de grandes lignes; **i. travel** déplacements sur les grandes lignes
N *(train)* train *m* de grandes lignes

intercom ['ɪntəkɒm] **N** *Tel Fam* interphone *m*; **to speak over the i.** parler dans l'interphone

intercommunicate [ɪntəkə'mjuːnɪkeɪt] **VI** *(of rooms etc)* communiquer

intercommunion [ɪntəkə'mjuːnjən] **N** *Rel* intercommunion *f*

intercompany [ɪntə'kʌmpənɪ] **ADJ** inter-entreprise

interconnect [ɪntəkə'nekt] *Elec, Comput* **VT** *(circuits, computers)* interconnecter
VI être interconnectés

interconnecting doors [ɪntəkə'nektɪŋ] **NPL** portes *fpl* de chambres communiquantes

interconnection [ɪntəkə'nekʃən] **N** *Elec, Comput* interconnexion *f*

intercontinental [ɪntəkɒntɪ'nent(ə)l] **ADJ** intercontinental, -aux
▶▶*Mil* **i. ballistic missile** missile *m* balistique intercontinental

intercooled ['ɪntəkuːld] **ADJ** *(engine)* refroidi

intercooler ['ɪntəkuːlər] **N** *Aut* intercooler *m*, refroidisseur *m* intermédiaire

intercostal [ɪntə'kɒst(ə)l] **ADJ** *Anat* intercostal, -aux

intercourse ['ɪntəkɔːs] **N 1** *(sexual)* **i.** rapports *mpl* sexuels; **to have i. with sb** avoir des rapports sexuels avec qn **2** *Old-fashioned (dealings)* commerce *m*, relations *fpl*, rapports *mpl*; **social i.** la fréquentation du monde

intercut [ɪntə'kʌt] **VT** *TV, Cin* insérer
▶▶**i. shot** plan *m* de coupe

interdenominational ['ɪntədɪnɒmɪ'neɪʃən(ə)l] **ADJ** *Rel* interconfessionnel

interdepartmental ['ɪntədiːpɑːt'ment(ə)l] **ADJ** *(in company)* entre différents services; *(in university)* entre différents départements

interdependence [ɪntədɪ'pendəns] **N** interdépendance *f*

interdependent [ɪntədɪ'pendənt] **ADJ** interdépendant

interdict[1] ['ɪntədɪkt] **N 1** *Law* défense *f*, interdiction *f* **2** *Rel* interdit *m*

interdict[2] [ɪntə'dɪkt] **VT 1** *Law* interdire, prohiber **2** *Rel (town)* frapper d'interdit; *(priest)* interdire, frapper d'interdit

interdiction [ɪntə'dɪkʃən] **N 1** *(action)* interdiction *f* **2** *(result)* *Law* interdiction *f*, *Rel* interdit *m*

interdisciplinary [ɪntə'dɪsɪplɪnərɪ] **ADJ** interdisciplinaire

INTEREST ['ɪnt(ə)rɪst] **N 1** *(curiosity)* intérêt *m* (**in** à); **to take/have an i. in sb/sth** s'intéresser à qn/qch; **to show an i. in sth** montrer un intérêt pour qch; **her i. in Latin America** son intérêt pour l'Amérique latine; **to take no further i. in sth, to lose i. in sth** se désintéresser de qch; **two people have shown an i. in (buying) the house** deux personnes sont intéressées par la maison; **there's little**

i. in these old chairs nowadays on ne s'intéresse pas beaucoup à ces vieilles chaises de nos jours
2 *(interesting aspect)* intérêt *m*; **this may be of i. to you** ceci peut vous intéresser; **what he does is of no i. to me** ça ne m'intéresse pas de savoir ce qu'il fait; **there was little of i. on television** il n'y avait pas grand-chose d'intéressant à la télévision; **buildings of historical/architectural i.** bâtiments d'intérêt historique/architectural; **a little garlic will give i. to a stew** l'ail donnera un peu de piquant aux ragoûts
3 *(activity, subject of interest)* **I have many interests** beaucoup de choses m'intéressent; **her interests include skiing and photography** le ski et la photographie font partie de ses centres d'intérêt
4 *(participation)* intérêt *m*, participation *f*; **to have a direct i. in sth** être concerné directement par qch; **I have no financial i. in the business** je ne suis pas intéressé dans cette entreprise; **to have a controlling i. in a company** avoir une participation majoritaire dans une société; **his i. in the company is £10,000** il a une commandite de 10 000 livres
5 *(group)* **the oil/steel interests in the country** l'industrie pétrolière/sidérurgique du pays
6 *(benefit)* intérêt *m*, avantage *m*; **the public i.** l'intérêt public; **it would not be in the public i.** ça ne serait pas dans l'intérêt public; **to act in/against one's (own) interest(s)** agir dans/contre son propre intérêt; **to act in sb's best interest(s)** agir dans l'intérêt de qn; **we look after British interests** nous défendons les intérêts britanniques; **it's in my i. to do it** c'est dans mon intérêt de le faire; **it's not in their i. to offend her** ça n'est pas dans leur intérêt de l'offenser, ils n'ont pas intérêt à l'offenser; **in the interests of justice/peace** dans l'intérêt de la justice/paix; **in the interests of safety/hygiene** par mesure de sécurité/d'hygiène; **in the interests of accuracy** pour être tout à fait précis
7 *Fin* intérêt(s) *m(pl)*; **i. on arrears** intérêt de retard; **i. on capital** rémunération *f* de capital; **to pay i. on a loan** payer des intérêts sur un prêt; **to bear** *or* **yield i.** porter intérêt *ou* des intérêts; **to yield 5% i.** rapporter du 5% *ou* un intérêt de 5%; **i. accrued** fraction *f* d'intérêt; **i. due** intérêts dus *ou* exigibles; **i. due and payable** intérêts exigibles; **i. paid** intérêts versés; **i. payable** intérêt exigible; **i. received** produits financiers, intérêts perçus; *Fig* **to repay an injury with i.** rendre le mal avec usure
VT intéresser; **we couldn't i. her in the idea** nous ne sommes pas parvenus à susciter son intérêt pour cette idée; **we couldn't i. her in a game of cards** nous n'avons pas r éussi à la convaincre de venir jouer aux cartes avec nous; **can I i. you in a drink?** puis-je vous proposer un verre?; **it might i. you to learn** *or* **know that ...** ça t'intéressera peut-être d'apprendre *ou* de savoir que ...
▶▶*Fin* **i. charges** intérêts (à payer); *Banking (on overdraft)* agios *mpl*; *Fin* **i. days** jours *mpl* d'intérêt; *Fin* **i. and dividend income** produits *mpl* financiers; **i. group** groupe *m* d'intérêt; *Fin* **i. payment date** date *f* d'échéance des intérêts; *Fin* **i. rate** taux *m* d'intérêt; *St Exch* **i. rate differential** différentiel *m* de taux; *St Exch* **i. rate swap** échange *m* de taux d'intérêt

interest-bearing **ADJ** *Banking* productif d'intérêts, qui produit des intérêts
▶▶*Banking* **i. account** compte *m* rémunéré; **i. capital** capital *m* productif d'intérêts; **i. loan** prêt *m* à intérêt; *St Exch* **i. securities** titres *mpl* qui produisent des intérêts

interested ['ɪnt(ə)rɪstɪd] **ADJ 1** *(curious)* intéressé; **to be i. in painting/music** s'intéresser à la peinture/à la musique; **I am not i.** cela ne m'intéresse pas; **he wasn't i.** *(in the offer, suggestion)* il n'était pas intéressé, ça ne l'intéressait pas; **anyone i.?** il y en a que ça intéresse?, est-ce que quelqu'un est intéressé?; **I should be i. to hear the end of the story** je serais curieux d'apprendre la fin de l'histoire **2** *(involved)* intéressé; **to act from i. motives** agir par calcul

▸▸ *Law* **i. party** ayant droit *m, pl* ayants droit; **the i. parties** les parties *fpl* intéressées

interest-free ADJ *(credit)* gratuit; *(loan)* sans intérêt

interesting ['ɪnt(ə)rɪstɪŋ] ADJ *(book, job etc)* intéressant

interestingly ['ɪnt(ə)rɪstɪŋlɪ] ADV de façon intéressante; **i. enough ...** ce qui est intéressant c'est que ...; **i., a number of her supporters voted against her** il est intéressant de noter qu'un certain nombre de ses partisans ont voté contre elle

interface ['ɪntəfeɪs] N *Comput, Fig* interface *f*; **the patient-doctor i.** les relations médecin-patient; **the extent of the i. between these two subjects** l'étendue des rapports entre ces deux sujets

VI *Comput* avoir une interface (**with** avec); **this device interfaces with most PCs** ce dispositif permet une interface avec la plupart des ordinateurs individuels

VT *Comput (two computers)* mettre en interface, interfacer

▸▸ *Comput* **i. bus** bus *m* d'interface; *Comput* **i. cable** câble *m* de connexion; *Comput* **i. card** carte *f* d'interface; *Comput* **i. switching** *(on laser printer)* commutation *f* d'interface

interfacing ['ɪntəfeɪsɪŋ] N **1** *Comput* interfaçage *m* **2** *Sewing* entoilage *m*

interfere [ɪntə'fɪər] VI **1** *(of person)* s'ingérer, s'immiscer, intervenir (**in a matter** dans une affaire); *(in quarrel)* s'interposer; **to i. in sb's affairs** se mêler des affaires de qn; **don't i. in what doesn't concern you** ne vous mêlez pas de ce qui ne vous regarde pas; **he's always interfering** il fourre son nez partout, il est toujours à se mêler de ce qui ne le regarde pas; **do not i. with the doors** ne pas gêner la fermeture des portes; **someone has interfered with the clock** on a touché à la pendule; *Euph* **was she interfered with?** *(sexually)* est-ce qu'on a abusé d'elle?

2 *(of thing)* **to i. with** *(sb's plans)* gêner, contrarier; *(traffic, person's movements)* gêner, entraver; *(progress of business)* entraver; **pleasure should not be allowed to i. with business** il ne faut pas que les plaisirs empiètent sur les affaires

3 *Phys etc* interférer; *Chem* perturber; *Electron, Radio* **to i. with a signal** brouiller *ou* parasiter un signal

interference [ɪntə'fɪərəns] N **1** *(by person)* intervention *f*, intrusion *f*, ingérence *f* (**in** dans); *Sport (from opponent)* obstruction *f* **2** *Phys* interférence *f*, *Chem* perturbation *f*, *Electron, Radio* interférence(s), parasite(s) *m(pl)*, brouillage *m*

▸▸ *Opt* **i. figure, i. pattern** figure *f* d'interférence

interfering [ɪntə'fɪərɪŋ] ADJ *(person)* importun, qui se mêle de ce qui ne le regarde pas; **he's so i.** il fourre son nez partout

interferon [ɪntə'fɪərɒn] N *Biol* interféron *m*

interim ['ɪntərɪm] N **in the i.** entre-temps

ADJ *(government, report etc)* intérimaire; **the i. period** l'intérim *m*

▸▸ *Acct* **i. accounts** comptes *mpl* semestriels; *Fin* **i. dividend** dividende *m* intérimaire; *Law* **i. order** avant faire-droit *m inv*; *Acct* **i. profit and loss statement** compte *m* de résultat prévisionnel; **i. report** rapport

m intérimaire; *Acct* **i. statement** bilan *m* intérimaire

interior [ɪn'tɪərɪər] ADJ *(side, trade)* intérieur; *(regions etc)* de l'intérieur; *Math (angle)* interne

N **1** *(of country, region, building)* intérieur *m* **2** *Art* (tableau *m* d')intérieur *m* **3** *Cin, TV* intérieur *m*

▸▸ **i. decoration** décoration *f* (d'intérieurs); **i. decorator** décorateur, -trice (d'intérieurs); *Liter* **i. monologue** monologue *m* intérieur; *TV, Cin* **i. shot** intérieur, scène *f* d'intérieur; *Aut* **i. trim** habillage *m* intérieur

interior-sprung ADJ *(mattress)* à ressorts

interject [ɪntə'dʒekt] VT *(remark etc)* lancer; *(protest)* émettre

interjection [ɪntə'dʒekʃən] N **1** *(action)* *(of remark etc)* action *f* de lancer; *(of protest)* action d'émettre **2** *(word, phrase)* interjection *f*

interlace [ɪntə'leɪs] VT *(wires, branches)* entrecroiser; *(speech etc)* entremêler (**with** de)
VI s'entrelacer, s'entrecroiser

interlaced [ɪntə'leɪst] ADJ *Comput (display, monitor)* entrelacé

interlard [ɪntə'lɑːd] VT *(speech, story)* entrelarder (**with** de)

interleave [ɪntə'liːv] VT *(book)* interfolier; *(sheets)* intercaler

interlibrary [ɪntə'laɪbrərɪ] ADJ interbibliothèque

interline [ɪntə'laɪn] VT **1** *Typ (document, manuscript)* interligner **2** *Sewing* mettre une doublure intermédiaire à

▸▸ *Typ* **i. spacing** interligne *m*

interlinear [ɪntə'lɪnɪər] ADJ *(text)* interlinéaire

interlining ['ɪntəlaɪnɪŋ] N *Sewing* doublure *f* intermédiaire

interlock [ɪntə'lɒk] VT *(mechanism)* enclencher; *(cogs)* engrener; *(parts of mechanism)* emboîter; *(fingers)* entrelacer
VI *(of mechanism)* s'enclencher; *(of parts)* s'emboîter

interlocking [ɪntə'lɒkɪŋ] ADJ *(parts)* emboîtable; *Tech (gears)* qui s'engrènent *ou* s'enclenchent

interlocutor [ɪntə'lɒkjʊtər] N *Fml* interlocuteur, -trice

interloper ['ɪntələʊpər] N intrus, -use

interlude ['ɪntəluːd] N *Theat, Fig* intermède *m*; *TV* interlude *m*; **musical i.** interlude *ou* intermède musical

intermarriage [ɪntə'mærɪdʒ] N *(between families etc)* mariage *m* (entre les membres de différentes familles, castes, races, etc); *(within a family)* mariage consanguin

intermarry [ɪntə'mærɪ] VI *(between families etc)* se marier (entre membres de différentes familles/castes/races/etc); *(within a family)* se marier entre membres d'une même famille; **they began to i.** ils commencèrent à se marier entre eux

intermediary [ɪntə'miːdɪərɪ] N intermédiaire *mf*; **to act as i.** servir d'intermédiaire
ADJ intermédiaire

intermediate [ɪntə'miːdɪət] ADJ *(size etc)* intermédiaire; *Sch (class etc)* (de niveau) moyen;

▸▸ *Fin* **i. broker** intermédiaire *mf*, remisier *m* (en Bourse); *Fin* **i. credit** crédit *m* à moyen terme; *Elec* **i. frequency** fréquence *f* moyenne; **i. goods** biens *mpl* intermédiaires; **i.-range nuclear forces** forces *fpl* nucléaires intermédiaires; **i. stops** *(during journey)* arrêts *mpl* intermédiaires; **i. technology** technologie *f* intermédiaire

interment [ɪn'tɜːmənt] N enterrement *m*, inhumation *f*

intermezzo [ɪntə'metsəʊ] N *Mus, Theat* intermezzo *m*

interminable [ɪn'tɜːmɪnəb(ə)l] ADJ interminable

interminably [ɪn'tɜːmɪnəblɪ] ADV interminablement

intermingle [ɪntə'mɪŋg(ə)l] VT entremêler (**with** de); *(colours)* mélanger
VI se mêler (**with** à), se mélanger (**with** avec)

intermission [ɪntə'mɪʃən] N **1** *Cin, Theat, Mus etc* entracte *m* **2** *(pause)* interruption *f*, pause *f*; *Med (in fever)* intermission *f*; **without i.** sans arrêt

intermittent [ɪntə'mɪtənt] ADJ intermittent;

▸▸ *Aut* **i. facility** *(of wipers)* intermittence *f*

intermittently [ɪntə'mɪtəntlɪ] ADV par intermittence, de façon intermittente

intermodal [ɪntə'məʊdəl] ADJ *Can (transport etc)* intermodal, -aux

▸▸ **i. travel** voyages *mpl* par différents moyens de transport

intern[1] ['ɪntɜːn] N *Am (in hospital)* interne *mf*, *(in company)* stagiaire *mf*

intern[2] [ɪn'tɜːn] VT interner

internal [ɪn'tɜːn(ə)l] ADJ **1** intérieur, interne; *Med (haemorrhage, organ, ear etc)* interne; *(disorder)* organique; **the i. workings of the mind** les opérations *fpl* secrètes de l'esprit **2** *(within a country) (trade)* intérieur; *(legislation)* national, -aux, interne; *(within a company)* interne **3** *(value, proof)* intrinsèque

▸▸ **i. affairs** affaires *fpl* intérieures; *Fin* **i. audit** audit *m* interne; *Fin* **i. auditor** audit interne, auditeur, -trice interne; *Tel* **i. cable** câble *m* d'immeuble; *Tech* **i. combustion engine** moteur *m* à combustion interne, moteur à explosion; *Comput* **i. command** commande *f* interne; **i. company document** document *m* interne à l'entreprise; *Comput* **i. drive** unité *f* (de disque) interne; *Univ* **i. exam** examen *m* propre à une université; *Univ* **i. examiner** examinateur, -trice *(faisant passer un examen dans son propre établissement)*; *Pol* **i. exile** exil *m*; **i. flight** vol *m* intérieur; **i. injuries** lésions *fpl* internes; **i. mail** courrier *m* interne; **i. marketing** marketing *m* interne; *Comput* **i. modem** modem *m* interne; **i. promotion** promotion *f* interne; *Fin* **i. rate of return** taux *m* de rentabilité interne; *Fin* **i. revenue** recettes *fpl* fiscales; **i. security** sécurité *f* intérieure; **i. student** étudiant, -ante d'une université; **i. telephone** téléphone *m* intérieur; **i. travel** voyages *mpl* à l'intérieur d'un même pays

internalize [ɪn'tɜːnəlaɪz] VT intérioriser

internally [ɪn'tɜːn(ə)lɪ] ADV intérieurement; *Pharm* **not to be taken i.** à usage externe

international [ɪntə'næʃən(ə)l] ADJ international, -aux

N **1** *Sport (player)* (joueur, -euse) international, -ale; *(match)* match *m* international **2** *Pol, Hist* **the I.** l'Internationale *f*

▸▸ **I. Air Transport Association** Association *f* internationale de transport aérien; *Law* **I. Chamber of Commerce** chambre *f* de commerce internationale; **I. Court of Justice** cour *f* internationale de justice; *Law* **I. Criminal Court** Cour *f* pénale internationale; **the I. Date Line** la ligne de changement de date; *Br* **i. dialling code**, *Am* **i. dial code** indicatif *m* du pays; *Ind* **I. Labour Organization** Organisation *f* internationale du travail; *Law* **i. law** droit *m* international; *Fin* **I. Monetary Fund** Fonds *m* monétaire international; *Fin* **i. monetary reserves** réserves *fpl* monétaires internationales; *Fin* **i. money market** marché *m* monétaire international; *Fin* **i. money order** mandat *m* international; **i. reply coupon**

coupon-réponse *m* international, *pl* coupons-réponse internationaux; **i. socialism** socialisme *m* international; **the I. Standards Organization** l'organisation *f* internationale de normalisation; **i. tourism destination** destination *f* touristique internationale; *Am* **I. Trade Commission** = organisme *m* fédéral américain traitant de questions de commerce international; **i. trade fair** foire *f* internationale; **I. Trade Organization** Organisation internationale du commerce; *Com* **i. trading corporation** société *f* de commerce international, SCI *f*

internationalism [ɪntə'næʃənəlɪz(ə)m] **N** internationalisme *m*

internationalize [ɪntə'næʃənəlaɪz] **VT** internationaliser

internationally [ɪntə'næʃənəlɪ] **ADV** internationalement; **an i. recognized qualification** un diplôme reconnu sur le plan international

internaut ['ɪntənɔːt] **N** *Comput* internaute *mf*

interne ['ɪntɜːn] **N** *Am* = **intern¹**

internecine [ɪntə'niːsaɪn] **ADJ** de destruction réciproque

internee [ɪntɜː'niː] **N** interné, -ée

Internet ['ɪntənet] **N** *Comput* Internet *m*; **on the I.** sur Internet
▸▸ **I. access** accès *m* (à l') Internet; **I. access provider** fournisseur *m* d'accès à l'Internet; **I. account** compte *m* Internet; **I. address** adresse *f* Internet; **I. banking** banque *f* par Internet, services *mpl* bancaires en ligne; **I. café** cybercafé *m*; **I. chat room** site *m* de bavardage, salon *m*; **I. connection** connexion *f* à l'Internet; **I. number** numéro *m* Internet; **I. phone** téléphone *m* Internet; **I. presence provider** = fournisseur d'accès à l'Internet proposant l'hébergement de sites Web; **I. protocol** protocole *m* Internet; **I. relay chat** service *m* de bavardage Internet, canal *m* de dialogue en direct; **I. service provider** fournisseur d'accès à l'Internet; **I. Society** = organisation *f* non gouvernementale chargée de veiller à l'évolution de l'Internet; **I. surfer** internaute *mf*; **I. surfing** navigation *f* sur l'Internet; **I. telephone** téléphone Internet; **I. telephony** téléphonie *f* sur l'Internet; **I. TV** télévision *f* par Internet; **I. user** internaute *mf*

internist [ɪn'tɜːnɪst] **N** *esp Am Med* spécialiste *mf* des maladies organiques

internment [ɪn'tɜːnmənt] **N** internement *m*
▸▸ **i. camp** camp *m* d'internement

internship ['ɪntɜːnʃɪp] **N** *Am Med (position)* internat *m*

interpenetrate [ɪntə'penɪtreɪt] **VI** s'interpénétrer

interpenetration [ɪntəpenɪ'treɪʃən] **N** interpénétration *f*

interpersonal [ɪntə'pɜːsən(ə)l] **ADJ** interpersonnel

interplanetary [ɪntə'plænɪt(ə)rɪ] **ADJ** interplanétaire

interplay ['ɪntəpleɪ] **N** interaction *f*

Interpol ['ɪntəpɒl] **N** Interpol *m*

interpolate [ɪn'tɜːpəleɪt] **VT 1** *(insert) (remark, question)* glisser; *(word, passage)* intercaler; **interpolated sheet** *(in bookbinding)* feuille *f* intercalaire **2** *(change) (text)* altérer par interpolation

interpolation [ɪntɜːpə'leɪʃən] **N** *(remark)* remarque *f* glissée dans un discours; *(question)* question *f* glissée dans un discours; *(word, passage)* mot *m*/passage *m* intercalé dans un texte; *(intended to change meaning)* interpolation *f*

interpose [ɪntə'pəʊz] **VT** interposer; **to i. a remark** *(in conversation)* faire une observation

interpret [ɪn'tɜːprɪt] **VT** interpréter; **to i. sb's words as a threat** interpréter les paroles de qn comme une menace
VI faire l'interprète; **can you i. for me?** est-ce que vous pouvez me servir d'interprète?

interpretation [ɪntɜːprɪ'teɪʃən] **N** interprétation *f*; **to put the wrong i. on sth** donner une fausse interprétation à qch; **she wasn't sure what i. to put on the remarks** elle ne savait pas trop comment elle devait interpréter ces remarques;
▸▸ *Can* **i. centre** *(at historic site etc)* = centre *m* d'accueil et de documentation pour les visiteurs d'un site touristique

interpretative [ɪn'tɜːprɪtətɪv] **ADJ** interprétatif

interpreter [ɪn'tɜːprɪtər] **N 1** *(person)* interprète *mf*; **to act as i.** servir d'interprète **2** *Comput (program)* interpréteur *m*

interpreting [ɪn'tɜːprɪtɪŋ] **N** *(occupation)* interprétation *f*

interpretive [ɪn'tɜːprɪtɪv] **ADJ** interprétatif
▸▸ **i. centre** = centre *m* d'accueil et de documentation pour les visiteurs d'un site touristique

interracial [ɪntə'reɪʃəl] **ADJ** *(marriage, conflict etc)* entre des races différentes

interregnum [ɪntə'regnəm] *pl* **interregnums, interregna** [-əmz, -ə] **N** interrègne *m*

interrelated [ɪntərɪ'leɪtɪd] **ADJ** *(facts)* étroitement liés, en corrélation; **i. costs** coûts *mpl* interdépendants; **i. demand** demande *f* en rapport

interrelation [ɪntərɪ'leɪʃən] **N** corrélation *f*

interrogate [ɪn'terəgeɪt] **VT** *(person)* interroger, questionner; *(of police)* faire subir un interrogatoire à; *Comput (database)* interroger

interrogation [ɪntərə'geɪʃən] **N** interrogatoire *m*; *Comput (of database)* interrogation *f*; **under i.** en train de subir un interrogatoire;
▸▸ *Mil* **i. centre** *(for prisoners of war)* centre *m* d'interrogatoires; *Gram* **i. mark**, *Am* **i. point** point *m* d'interrogation

Note that the primary sense of **interrogation** in English, as in a police interrogation, is translated by **interrogatoire** and not **interrogation**.

interrogative [ɪntə'rɒgətɪv] **ADJ 1** *(tone, look etc)* interrogateur, -trice **2** *Gram (pronoun etc)* interrogatif
N *Gram (pronoun etc)* interrogatif *m*; *(symbol)* point *m* d'interrogation VOIR GRAMMAIRE A31–2; B16–18

interrogatively [ɪntə'rɒgətɪvlɪ] **ADV** interrogativement; d'un air interrogateur

interrogator [ɪn'terəgeɪtər] **N** interrogateur, -trice

interrogatory [ɪntə'rɒgətərɪ] **ADJ** *(tone, look etc)* interrogateur, -trice

interrupt¹ [ɪntə'rʌpt] **VT 1** *(stop) (action, conversation etc)* interrompre; **am I interrupting something?** est-ce que je vous dérange?; **to i. sb** interrompre qn, couper la parole à qn **2** *(block) (rail etc services)* interrompre; *(communications, supplies)* couper; *(electrical circuit)* interrompre; *(rhythm)* rompre; *(view)* gêner
VI interrompre; **don't i.!** *(when I'm talking)* ne me coupe pas la parole!, ne m'interromps pas!; *(when sb is talking)* ne coupe pas la parole aux gens!, n'interromps pas les gens!; **I'm sorry to i.** *(intrude)* je suis désolé de vous interrompre

interrupt² ['ɪntərʌpt] **N** *Comput* interruption *f*
▸▸ **i. function** fonction *f* d'interruption

interruption [ɪntə'rʌpʃən] **N** interruption *f*; **without i.** sans interruption; **I want no more**

interruptions *(let me finish speaking)* je ne veux plus qu'on m'interrompe; *(leave me in peace)* je ne veux plus être dérangé

interscholastic [ɪntəskə'læstɪk] **ADJ** interscolaire, inter-écoles

intersect [ɪntə'sekt] **VT** *(of street)* croiser; **Maple Street is intersected by Elm Avenue** Maple Street et Elm Avenue se croisent; **line that intersects another** ligne qui en coupe une autre; **to i. one another** *(of lines, surfaces)* se couper, s'entrecroiser
VI *(of lines)* se couper; *(of streets)* se croiser

intersection [ɪntə'sekʃən] **N 1** *Math (of two planes etc)* intersection *f*; **(point of) i.** point *m* d'intersection **2** *esp Am (of roads)* croisement *m*

interspace [ɪntə'speɪs] **VT** *Typ* espacer

intersperse [ɪntə'spɜːs] **VT** parsemer (**with** de); **to i. a speech with quotations** émailler un discours de citations; **plain-clothes officers were interspersed in the crowd** des policiers en civil étaient dispersés dans la foule; **carnations are interspersed among the roses** les roses sont parsemées d'œillets; **there will be sunshine interspersed with showers** il y aura une alternance d'averses et d'éclaircies

interstate ['ɪntəsteɪt] **ADJ** *(commerce etc) (in United States, Australia etc)* entre États
N *Am Aut* autoroute *f*
▸▸ **i. carrier** transporteur *m* inter-État

interstellar [ɪntə'stelər] **ADJ** *Astron* interstellaire

interstice [ɪn'tɜːstɪs] **N** interstice *m*

intertextual [ɪntə'tekstjʊəl] **ADJ** intertextuel

intertextuality [ɪntətekstjʊ'ælətɪ] **N** intertextualité *f*

intertribal [ɪntə'traɪb(ə)l] **ADJ** entre tribus

intertwine [ɪntə'twaɪn] **VT** entrelacer; **his fate seemed intertwined with hers** son destin semblait lié au sien
VI s'entrelacer; **she found them intertwined** elle les a trouvés enlacés dans les bras l'un de l'autre

interurban [ɪntər'ɜːbən] **ADJ** interurbain

interval ['ɪntəvəl] **N 1** *(time)* intervalle *m*; *esp Br Theat, Cin* entracte *m*; *Ftbl etc* mi-temps *f inv*, pause *f*; **it rained at intervals** il a plu par intervalles; **I completed the job at intervals over a period of two months** j'ai effectué le travail en plusieurs fois sur une période de deux mois; **I saw him at intervals during my stay** je l'ai vu de temps en temps au cours de mon séjour; **at regular intervals** à intervalles réguliers; **at five-minute intervals, at intervals of five minutes** toutes les cinq minutes; **rainy weather with bright intervals** temps pluvieux avec éclaircies; **after an i. of time** après un certain temps; **an hour's i. between two lectures** une heure de battement entre deux conférences **2** *(space)* écart *m*, espace *m*, intervalle *m*; **at two-metre intervals** à deux mètres d'écart, à un intervalle de deux mètres; **there are trees growing at regular intervals along the road** des arbres jalonnent la route **3** *Mus* intervalle *m*

intervene [ɪntə'viːn] **VI 1** *(take action)* intervenir (**in** dans); **the government intervened to save the company** le gouvernement est intervenu pour sauver l'entreprise **2** *(of event)* survenir; **the war intervened** la guerre est survenue; **ten years intervened** dix ans s'écoulèrent

intervening [ɪntə'viːnɪŋ] **ADJ** *(period)* intermédiaire; **during the i. period** entre-temps; **the i. events** les événements qui survinrent entre-temps *ou* dans l'intervalle; **during the i. week** pendant la semaine qui s'écoula entre-temps

intervention [ɪntə'venʃən] N *(by government, individual etc)* intervention f
▸▸*Econ* **i. price** prix m d'intervention; *Fin* **i. rate** taux m d'intervention

interventionism [ɪntə'venʃənɪz(ə)m] N interventionnisme m

interventionist [ɪntə'venʃənɪst] ADJ interventionniste
N interventionniste mf

interview ['ɪntəvjuː] N **1** *(for job, place at university etc)* entrevue f, entretien m; *(in survey etc)* entretien; **a job i., an i. for a job** un entretien pour un emploi; **to invite sb to an** *or* **for (an) i.** convoquer qn à un entretien **2** *Journ, TV* interview f; **he rarely gives interviews** il donne *ou* accorde rarement des interviews
VT **1** *(for job, place at university etc)* faire passer un entretien *ou* une entrevue à; *(in survey)* interroger, enquêter; *(criminal, suspect etc)* interroger; **who interviewed you?** qui t'a fait passer l'entretien?; **she's being interviewed tomorrow** elle est convoquée pour un entretien demain **2** *Journ, TV* interviewer
VI **1** *(of job interviewer etc)* faire passer des entretiens; **he doesn't i. well** *(of job candidate etc)* il n'est pas très bon aux entretiens **2** *Journ, TV* **the new Minister interviews well** le nouveau ministre passe bien aux interviews

interviewee [ɪntəvjuː'iː] N *Journ, TV* personne f interviewée; *(for job)* candidat, -ate *(à qui l'on fait passer un entretien)*

interviewer ['ɪntəvjuːər] N *Journ, TV etc* interviewer m, intervieweur, -euse; *(for research, in canvassing)* enquêteur, -euse; **her skills as an i.** *(of job applicants)* ses qualités pour faire passer les entretiens *ou* pour examiner les candidats

inter-war ['ɪntə'wɔːr] ADJ **the i. years** *or* **period** l'entre-deux-guerres m; **i. politics** la politique de l'entre-deux-guerres

interweave [ɪntə'wiːv] *(pt* **interwove** [ɪntə'wəʊv]*, pp* **interwoven** [ɪntə'wəʊv(ə)n]*)* VT **1** *Tex (gold thread with wool etc)* tisser ensemble; *(branches etc)* entrelacer; **material interwoven with gold threads** tissu broché d'or **2** *Fig (stories)* mêler; **to i. sth into sth** mêler qch à qch; **closely interwoven systems** systèmes étroitement liés l'un à l'autre
VI *(of branches)* s'entrelacer; *Fig (of stories, narratives)* s'entremêler

interword spacing [ɪntə'wɜːd] N *Typ* espacement m entre les mots

intestate [ɪn'testeɪt] *Jur* ADJ intestat *inv*; **she died.** elle est morte intestat; **i. estate** *or* **succession** succession f ab intestat
N intestat mf

intestinal [ɪntes'taɪn(ə)l, ɪn'testɪn(ə)l] ADJ *Anat* intestinal, -aux

intestine [ɪn'testɪn] N *Anat* intestin m; **the large i.** le gros intestin; **the small i.** l'intestin grêle

intimacy ['ɪntɪməsɪ] N **1** intimité f; **in the i. of the family** dans l'intimité de la famille **2** *(intimate remark etc)* familiarité f **3** *Fml (sexual intercourse)* rapports mpl sexuels; **evidence that i. took place** preuves fpl de relations intimes

intimate¹ ['ɪntɪmɪt] ADJ *(friendship, friend, restaurant etc)* intime; **they're very i.** ils sont très intimes; **a few i. friends** quelques intimes; **the i. nature of their conversation** la nature intime de leur conversation; **to be i. with sb** *(know well)* être intime avec qn; *Fml (have sexual intercourse)* avoir des relations intimes avec qn; **to have an i. knowledge of sth** avoir une connaissance approfondie de qch
N intime mf

intimate² ['ɪntɪmeɪt] VT **1** *(suggest, hint at)* laisser entendre *(sth to sb* qch à qn*)* **2** *Fml (make known) (order)* intimer; *(one's intentions)* signifier; **to i. sth to sb** notifier qch à qn

intimately ['ɪntɪmətlɪ] ADV intimement; **i. connected** étroitement lié; **to know sb i.** *(well)* connaître qn intimement

intimation [ɪntɪ'meɪʃən] N **1** *Fml (hint)* indication f; **she gave me no i. of her intentions** elle ne m'a rien laissé entrevoir de ses intentions; **they had no i. of the difficulties ahead** ils étaient loin de se représenter les difficultés qui les attendaient **2** *Arch (notice)* **an i. of death** un avis de décès

intimidate [ɪn'tɪmɪdeɪt] VT intimider; **I'm not going to be intimidated by her** je ne vais pas me laisser intimider par elle; **to i. sb into doing sth** intimider qn pour qu'il fasse qch

intimidating [ɪn'tɪmɪdeɪtɪŋ] ADJ intimidant

intimidation [ɪntɪmɪ'deɪʃən] N intimidation f, *Law* menaces fpl

into ['ɪntʊ, 'ɪntə] PREP VOIR GRAMMAIRE A70–1 **1** *(motion, direction)* dans; **to go i. a house** entrer dans une maison; **to fall i. the hands of the enemy** tomber entre les mains de l'ennemi *ou* aux mains de l'ennemi; **the door opens i. the garden** la porte donne sur le jardin; **to come i. a property** *(by inheritance)* hériter d'un bien; **to get i. difficulties** s'attirer des ennuis; **to walk i. a door/sb** rentrer dans une porte/qn; **to cut i. a piece of cheese** couper dans un morceau de fromage; **to speak i. a microphone** parler dans un micro; **I'd like to get i. television** j'aimerais bien rentrer *ou* entrer à la télévision **2** *(change, result)* en; **to change sth i. sth** changer *ou* transformer qch en qch; **to grow i. a man** devenir un homme; **to divide i. four** diviser en quatre; **to break sth i. pieces** briser qch en morceaux; **to burst i. tears** fondre en larmes; **to go i. a coma** tomber dans le coma; **they cajoled her i. agreeing** ils lui ont arraché son accord à force de cajoleries **3** *(with time, age etc)* **to work far i. the night** travailler très tard dans la nuit; **he was well i. his sixties before he retired** il avait la soixantaine bien sonnée quand il est parti à la retraite; **it was well i. January before we got any snow** le mois de janvier était bien entamé quand nous avons eu la première neige **4** *Math* **three i. six goes two** six divisé par trois font deux **5** *Fam* **to be i. sb/sth** *(like)* bien aimer qn/qch; **he's i. drugs** *(uses)* il se drogue; **he's really i. her/jogging/French cooking** il est fou d'elle/de jogging/de cuisine française; **she's i. the green movement** elle est à fond *ou* elle donne à fond dans le mouvement écolo; **I'm not i. computers/wearing ties** l'informatique/les cravates, ce n'est pas mon truc; **I'm not really i. that sort of thing** ces choses-là, ce n'est pas mon truc; **I'm not i. computers the way you are** je ne suis pas aussi amateur d'informatique que toi; **we're not i. cheating people** *(that's not our style)* nous ne cherchons pas à rouler les gens; **if that's what you're i.!** si c'est ton truc! **6** *Am (in debt to)* **he's i. them for $5,000** il leur doit cinq mille dollars

intolerable [ɪn'tɒlərəb(ə)l] ADJ intolérable, insupportable

intolerably [ɪn'tɒlərəblɪ] ADV *(boring, vain)* insupportablement; **it was i. hot** il faisait une chaleur intolérable *ou* insupportable; **they are i. rude** ils sont d'une grossièreté intolérable *ou* insupportable

intolerance [ɪn'tɒlərəns] N intolérance f *(of, towards* à l'égard de*)*; *Med* **i. of a drug/**

foodstuff intolérance à un remède/un aliment

intolerant [ɪn'tɒlərənt] ADJ intolérant *(of* à l'égard de*)*; **to be very i.** être d'une extrême intolérance; *Med* **to be i. of a drug** ne pas tolérer *ou* supporter un médicament

intolerantly [ɪn'tɒlərəntlɪ] ADV avec intolérance, de façon intolérante

intonation [ɪntə'neɪʃən] N intonation f

intone [ɪn'təʊn] VT **1** *(speak)* débiter **2** *Rel (litany)* psalmodier

intoxicate [ɪn'tɒksɪkeɪt] VT *(make drunk)* enivrer, rendre ivre; *Fig* griser

intoxicated [ɪn'tɒksɪkeɪtɪd] ADJ *(drunk)* ivre; **to become i.** s'enivrer *(* with *de)*; *Fig* **i. with power** ivre de pouvoir; **i. by their first taste of freedom** grisés par leur première expérience de la liberté

intoxicating [ɪn'tɒksɪkeɪtɪŋ] ADJ *(wine, perfume)* enivrant; *Fig (experience, freedom)* grisant
▸▸**i. liquor** boisson f alcoolisée

intoxication [ɪntɒksɪ'keɪʃən] N **1** *(drunkenness)* ivresse f, *Fig* griserie f **2** *Med* intoxication f

intra-Community ['ɪntrəkə'mjuːnɪtɪ] ADJ ATTRIB intracommunautaire
▸▸**i. trade** échange m intracommunautaire

intra-company [ɪntrə'kʌmpanɪ] ADJ intra-entreprise

intractability [ɪntræktə'bɪlɪtɪ] N *(of person)* opiniâtreté f, inflexibilité f; *(of illness, problem)* caractère m rebelle

intractable [ɪn'træktəb(ə)l] ADJ *Fml (person) (about specific question)* intraitable; *(child)* insoumis; *(illness)* rebelle; *(problem)* très difficile

intramural [ɪntrə'mjʊərəl] ADJ interne à l'établissement; **i. athletics competition** = épreuves fpl d'athlétisme entre membres d'un même établissement scolaire

intramuscular [ɪntrə'mʌskjʊlər] ADJ *(injection)* intramusculaire

Intranet ['ɪntrənet] N *Comput* Intranet m

intransigence [ɪn'trænsɪdʒəns] N intransigeance f

intransigent [ɪn'trænsɪdʒənt] ADJ, N intransigeant, -ante

intransitive [ɪn'trænsɪtɪv] *Gram* ADJ *(verb)* intransitif
N intransitif m

intransitively [ɪn'trænsɪtɪvlɪ] ADV intransitivement

intra-state carrier [ɪntrə'steɪt] N transporteur m intra-État

intrauterine [ɪntrə'juːtəraɪn] ADJ *Anat* intra-utérin
▸▸**i. device** stérilet m

intravenous [ɪntrə'viːnəs] ADJ *Med* intraveineux
▸▸**i. drip** perfusion f intraveineuse; **i. injection** (injection f) intraveineuse f

intravenously [ɪntrə'viːnəslɪ] ADV *Med* par voie intraveineuse

in-tray N bac m du courrier à traiter *ou* du courrier reçu

intrepid [ɪn'trepɪd] ADJ intrépide

intrepidity [ɪntre'pɪdɪtɪ] N intrépidité f

intrepidly [ɪn'trepɪdlɪ] ADV intrépidement

intricacy ['ɪntrɪkəsɪ] N complexité f; **the intricacies of the law** les complexités de la loi

intricate ['ɪntrɪkət] ADJ *(mechanism, drawing, design)* compliqué; *(question, plot)* complexe

intricately ['ɪntrɪkətlɪ] ADV d'une manière compliquée; **an i. detailed drawing** un dessin extrêmement détaillé

intrigue¹ ['ɪntriːg] N **1** *(plot, plotting)* intrigue f **2** *Old-fashioned (love affair)* aventure f

intrigue² [ɪn'tri:g] ᴠᴛintriguer; **I'm greatly intrigued by the idea** l'idée m'intrigue énormément
ᴠɪintriguer (**against sb** contre qn)

intriguing [ɪn'tri:gɪŋ] ᴀᴅᴊintrigant; **I find all this very i.** tout cela m'intrigue beaucoup

intrinsic [ɪn'trɪnsɪk] ᴀᴅᴊintrinsèque
▸▸*St Exch* **i. value** valeur *f* intrinsèque

intrinsically [ɪn'trɪnsɪklɪ] ᴀᴅᴠ intrinsèquement

intro ['ɪntrəʊ] ɴ*Fam* = **introduction 2**

introduce [ɪntrə'dju:s] ᴠᴛ **1** *(present)* présenter (**to sb** à qn); **to i. oneself** se présenter; **I don't think we've been introduced** je ne crois pas que nous ayons été présentés; **we've introduced ourselves** nous nous sommes déjà présentés; *Cin* **introducing Carlos Bernard** et pour la première fois à l'écran Carlos Bernard; **to be introduced to society** *(of debutante)* faire son entrée dans le monde
2 *(radio or TV programme)* présenter
3 *(initiate)* **to i. sb to sth** faire connaître qch à qn; **he introduced me to Greek** il m'a initié au grec; **they introduced me to drugs/Rabelais** ils m'ont fait connaître la drogue/Rabelais
4 *(put in, bring in)* *(key into lock, new species, disease)* introduire; **to i. a subject** mettre une question sur le tapis; **to i. sb into sb's presence** introduire qn auprès de qn
5 *(have adopted)* *(law, usage)* établir, faire adopter; *(fashion, new machinery, methods etc)* introduire; *Parl* **to i. a bill** déposer un projet de loi
6 *Gram (of conjunction, adverb)* *(phrase)* introduire
7 *Com (product)* lancer; *St Exch (shares)* introduire

introduce-a-friend scheme ɴ *Mktg* offre-ami *f*, *pl* offres-ami

introduction [ɪntrə'dʌkʃən] ɴ **1** *(presentation)* présentation *f* (**of sb to sb** de qn à qn); **to make the introductions** faire les présentations
2 *(of book)* avant-propos *m inv*, introduction *f*, *Mus* introduction *f*
3 *(book for beginners)* introduction *f* (**to** à); *(to chemistry, biology etc)* manuel *m* élémentaire (**to** de), introduction (**to** à)
4 *(act of initiation)* introduction *f*, premier contact *m* (**to sth** avec qch); **this was my i. to Shakespeare** ça a été mon premier contact avec Shakespeare; **this record would be a good i. to her work** ce disque constituerait une bonne introduction à son œuvre
5 *(act of bringing in, putting in)* *(of new species, disease, key into lock)* introduction *f*
6 *(of custom etc)* introduction *f*, **the sport is a recent i. from the United States** ce sport est récemment arrivé des États-Unis
7 *Parl (of bill)* introduction *f*
8 *Com (of product)* lancement *m*, *St Exch (of shares)* introduction *f* au marché hors cote

introductory [ɪntrə'dʌktərɪ] ᴀᴅᴊ (qui sert) d'introduction; *(page, paragraph)* liminaire; **after a few i. words** après quelques mots d'introduction
▸▸ **i. music** introduction *f* musicale, musique *f* d'ouverture; *Com* **i. offer** offre *f* de lancement; *Com* **i. price** prix *m* de lancement

intro-ident ɴ *TV etc* identification *f* d'intro

introit ['ɪntrɔɪt] ɴ *Rel* introït *m*

introspection [ɪntrə'spekʃən] ɴ introspection *f*

introspective [ɪntrə'spektɪv] ᴀᴅᴊ introspectif

introversion [ɪntrə'vɜːʃən] ɴ *Psy* introversion *f*

introvert ['ɪntrəvɜːt] ᴀᴅᴊ, ɴ introverti, -ie

introverted ['ɪntrəvɜːtɪd] ᴀᴅᴊ introverti; **she's become very i. since the accident** elle est devenue très renfermée depuis l'accident

intrude [ɪn'tru:d] ᴠɪ I hope I'm not intruding j'espère que je ne vous dérange pas *ou* que je ne suis pas importun; **to i. on sb's privacy** s'ingérer dans la vie privée de qn; **she didn't want her work to i. on her family life** elle ne voulait pas que son travail empiète sur sa vie de famille; **a supermarket would i. on the character of the village** un supermarché gâcherait le caractère pittoresque du village
ᴠᴛ *(opinion)* imposer; **to i. a note of caution into the discussion** introduire une note de prudence dans la discussion

intruder [ɪn'tru:dər] ɴ *(on other people)* intrus, -use, importun, -une; *(burglar)*, *Comput* intrus *m*; **she felt like an i.** elle se sentait de trop
▸▸ *Comput* **i. detection** détection *f* des intrus

intrusion [ɪn'tru:ʒən] ɴ intrusion *f*, **I hope I am not guilty of an i.** j'espère que je ne suis pas indiscret *ou* que je ne dérange pas

intrusive [ɪn'tru:sɪv] ᴀᴅᴊ *(person)* importun, indiscret; *(noise, presence)* gênant; *Ling* intrusif

intubate ['ɪntjʊbeɪt] ᴠᴛ *Med* intuber

intuit [ɪn'tju:ɪt] ᴠᴛ *Fml* deviner intuitivement *ou* par intuition

intuition [ɪntjuː'ɪʃən] ɴ intuition *f*, **I have an i. that …** j'ai l'intuition que …, mon intuition me dit que …

intuitive [ɪn'tju:ɪtɪv] ᴀᴅᴊ intuitif

intuitively [ɪn'tju:ɪtɪvlɪ] ᴀᴅᴠ intuitivement, par intuition

Inuit ['ɪnjuːɪt] ɴ Inuit *m inv*
ᴀᴅᴊ inuit *inv*

inundate ['ɪnʌndeɪt] ᴠᴛ inonder (**with** de); *Fig* **to be inundated with letters** être submergé de lettres; **to be inundated with phone calls** recevoir une quantité énorme de coups de téléphone

inundation [ɪnʌn'deɪʃən] ɴ inondation *f*

inure [ɪ'njʊər] ᴠᴛ habituer (**to** à)

invade [ɪn'veɪd] ᴠᴛ *(country)*, *Ftbl (pitch etc)* envahir; **to i. sb's privacy** violer l'intimité de qn
ᴠɪ envahir

invader [ɪn'veɪdər] ɴ envahisseur *m*

invading [ɪn'veɪdɪŋ] ᴀᴅᴊ *(army)* d'invasion

invalid¹ [ɪn'vælɪd] ᴀᴅᴊ *(argument, objection, ticket etc)* non valable; *Law (marriage)* invalide, non valide; *(decision)* nul et non avenu; *Comput* invalide; **your position is morally i.** d'un point de vue moral votre position ne tient pas
▸▸ *Comput* **i. character** caractère *m* invalide; *Comput* **i. file name** nom *m* de fichier invalide

invalid² ['ɪnvəlɪd] ɴ *(ill person)* malade *mf*, *(disabled person)* invalide *mf*, infirme *mf*, **I'm not an i.!** je ne suis pas infirme!
ᴀᴅᴊ *(chronically ill)* malade; *(disabled)* invalide, infirme; **she has an i. sister** *(disabled)* elle a une sœur infirme; *(in poor health)* elle a une sœur d'une santé délicate
▸▸ **i. car** voiture *f* d'infirme; **i. carriage** véhicule *m* spécial pour handicapé; **i. chair** fauteuil *m* roulant
▸ **invalid out** ᴠᴛ ꜱᴇᴘ *esp Br Mil* **to be invalided out (of the army)** être réformé pour raisons médicales

invalidate [ɪn'vælɪdeɪt] ᴠᴛ **1** *(theory, hypothesis etc)* infirmer **2** *Law (will)* invalider, rendre nul; *(document, contract)* vicier; *(verdict)* casser, infirmer

invalidation [ɪnvælɪ'deɪʃən] ɴ *(of theory etc)*, *Law (of document, contract)* invalidation *f*, *Law (of verdict)* infirmation *f*, cassation *f*

invalidity [ɪnvə'lɪdɪtɪ] ɴ **1** *(disability)* invalidité *f* **2** *(of passport, contract etc)* invalidité *f*, *(of argument)* manque *m* de fondement
▸▸ *Br Formerly* **i. benefit** prestation *f* d'invalidité *(aujourd'hui remplacée par l'"'incapacity benefit'")*; *Br* **i. pension** pension *f* d'invalidité

invaluable [ɪn'væljʊəb(ə)l] ᴀᴅᴊ extrêmement utile; *(help, assistance)* inestimable; **her help was i. (to us)** elle nous a été d'une aide inestimable *ou* très précieuse

> Attention: ne pas confondre avec l'adjectif **valueless**, qui signifie **sans valeur**.

invariable [ɪn'veərɪəb(ə)l] ᴀᴅᴊ invariable; *(routine)* immuable

invariably [ɪn'veərɪəblɪ] ᴀᴅᴠ invariablement; **he would i. arrive late** il arrivait immanquablement en retard

invariant [ɪn'veərɪənt] ᴀᴅᴊ *Fml* constant

invasion [ɪn'veɪʒən] ɴ **1** *Mil*, *Fig (by army, by tourists)* invasion *f*, **these invasions of my privacy** ces intrusions *fpl* dans mon intimité **2 i. of sb's rights** violation *f* des droits de qn

invasive [ɪn'veɪsɪv] ᴀᴅᴊ *Med* invasif
▸▸ *Med* **i. surgery** chirurgie *f* invasive *ou* effractoire

invective [ɪn'vektɪv] ɴ invective *f*, **a torrent of i.** un flot d'invectives *ou* d'injures *fpl*

inveigh [ɪn'veɪ] ᴠɪ invectiver (**against** contre)

inveigle [ɪn'veɪg(ə)l, -viː] ᴠᴛ *(person)* entortiller; **to i. sb into doing sth** entortiller qn pour qu'il fasse qch

invent [ɪn'vent] ᴠᴛ *(machine, story etc)* inventer; *Fig* **he invented a movie-star mother** il s'est inventé une mère star de cinéma; **recently invented** d'invention récente

invention [ɪn'venʃən] ɴ **1** *(something invented)* invention *f*, *(lie)* invention, mensonge *m*; **this is pure i.** c'est une pure invention **2** *(ability to invent)* esprit *m* inventif, inventivité *f* **3** *(act of inventing)* *(of machine etc)* invention *f*, **a story of his own i.** une histoire de son cru

inventive [ɪn'ventɪv] ᴀᴅᴊ inventif

inventiveness [ɪn'ventɪvnɪs] ɴ esprit *m* inventif, inventivité *f*

inventor [ɪn'ventər] ɴ inventeur, -trice

inventory ['ɪnvənt(ə)rɪ] ɴ **1** *(list)* inventaire *m*; **to draw up** *or* **take an i.** dresser *ou* faire un inventaire **2** *(stock)* stock(s) *m(pl)*
ᴠᴛ *(property, stock)* inventorier, dresser l'inventaire de
▸▸ *Fin* **i. account** compte *m* de stock; **i. balance** balance *f* d'inventaire; **i. control** contrôle *m* des stocks; **i. of fixtures** état *m* des lieux; **i. level** niveau *m* des stocks; **i. management** gestion *f* des stocks; **i. turnaround, i. turnover** rotation *f* des stocks; **i. turnaround rate, i. turnover rate** vitesse *f* de rotation des stocks; **i. valuation** valorisation *f* des stocks; **i. value** valeur *f* d'inventaire

inverse [ɪn'vɜːs] ᴀᴅᴊ inverse; **in i. order** en sens inverse; **in i. ratio/proportion** en raison/proportion inverse (**to** de)
ɴ inverse *m*, contraire *m* (**of** de)
▸▸ *Math* **i. function** fonction *f* inverse

inversely [ɪn'vɜːslɪ] ᴀᴅᴠ inversement

inversion [ɪn'vɜːʃən] ɴ **1** *(of image)* renversement *m*; *Mus* **i. of a chord** *(action)* renversement d'un accord; *(result)* accord *m* dérivé **2** *Gram (of words in phrase)*, *Math (of integral)* inversion *f* VOIR GRAMMAIRE A78; B62 **3** *Chem (of sugar etc)* inversion *f* **4** *Psy* **(sexual) i.** inversion *f* sexuelle

invert¹ ['ɪnvɜ:t] **ADJ** (sugar) inverti
N Psy inverti, -ie

invert² [ɪn'vɜ:t] **VT 1** (object) (turn upside down) renverser, retourner; Mus (chord) renverser **2** (reverse) (order, positions) invertir, intervertir, renverser; Gram (subject etc) inverser **3** Chem (sugar) invertir

invertebrate [ɪn'vɜ:tɪbrɪt] **ADJ, N** Zool invertébré m

inverted [ɪn'vɜ:tɪd] **ADJ 1** (upside down), Mus (chord) renversé **2** (reversed) (word order etc), Opt (image) renversé **3** Psy (instinct) inverti
▸ ▸ Br i. **commas** guillemets mpl; Sewing i. **pleat** pli m inverti ou creux; i. **snob** = personne f qui fait preuve de snobisme à l'envers; i. **snobbery** snobisme m à l'envers

invest [ɪn'vest] **VT 1** Fin (money) placer, investir; (capital), Fig (time etc) investir; **to i. money in real estate** faire des placements dans l'immobilier; **capital invested** mise f de fonds, capital m engagé ou investi
2 Lit (install) (bishop, Pope) introniser; (president) installer
3 Lit (provide) (person) investir (**with authority**/etc de l'autorité/etc); **to i. a subject with interest** rendre un sujet intéressant; **his novels i. criminality with too much glamour** ses romans donnent une image trop séduisante du monde du crime
VI investir, faire des placements, placer son argent; **to i. in property** faire des placements dans l'immobilier; **we're going to i. in three new machines** nous allons investir dans trois nouvelles machines; Fam **you should i. in a good dictionary** tu devrais t'offrir ou te payer un bon dictionnaire

investigate [ɪn'vestɪgeɪt] **VT** (question) examiner, étudier; (crime) faire une enquête sur, enquêter sur
VI I'll **go and i.** je vais voir ce qui se passe

investigating [ɪn'vestɪgeɪtɪŋ] **ADJ**
▸ ▸ i. **committee** commission f d'enquête; i. **officer** officier m chargé de l'enquête

investigation [ɪnvestɪ'geɪʃən] **N** investigation f, (by police, tax authority etc) enquête f (**of** sur); **to conduct** or **carry out an i.** conduire ou effectuer une enquête; **the question is under i.** la question est à l'étude; **on further i.** en poursuivant les recherches; **on further i., the ruins turned out to be …** des recherches plus approfondies ont révélé que les ruines étaient …; **to make investigations** faire des investigations; (of police) procéder à une enquête

investigative [ɪn'vestɪgətɪv] **ADJ**
▸ ▸ i. **journalism** journalisme m d'investigation ou d'enquête; i. **journalist** journaliste mf d'investigation; i. **report** reportage m d'investigation; i. **reporter** reporter m d'investigation; i. **team** équipe f d'investigation

investigator [ɪn'vestɪgeɪtər] **N** enquêteur, -euse ou -trice; (**private**) i. détective m privé

investiture [ɪn'vestɪtʃər] **N** (installation in office) investiture f, (of bishop etc) intronisation f

investment [ɪn'vestmənt] **N** Fin placement m, investissement m; (money invested) investissement, mise f de fonds; **good** or **safe i.** placement sûr; **long-/short-term i.** placement à long/court terme
▸ ▸ Banking i. **account** compte m d'investissement; i. **advice** conseil m en placements; i. **adviser** conseiller, -ère en placements; i. **analyst** analyste mf en placements; i. **bank** banque f d'affaires; i. **banker** banquier, -ière d'affaires; i. **banking** banque f d'affaires; i. **capital** capital-investissement m; i. **company** société f de portefeuille ou d'investissement; i. **consultancy** société de conseil en investissement; i. **curve** courbe f d'investissement; i. **fund** fonds m commun de place-

ment, fonds d'investissement; i. **grant** subvention f d'investissement; i. **house** société f financière; i. **incentives** encouragements mpl à l'investissement; i. **income** revenu m provenant d'investissements; i. **institution** société d'investissements; i. **instrument** instrument m de placement; i. **management** gestion f des investissements; i. **plan** plan m d'investissement; i. **policy** politique f d'investissement; i. **portfolio** portefeuille m d'investissements; i. **securities** valeurs fpl en portefeuille ou de placement; i. **services** services mpl d'investissement; i. **stock** valeurs m en portefeuille ou de placement; i. **subsidy** prime f à l'investissement; i. **trust** société de placement, trust m de placement

investor [ɪn'vestər] **N** investisseur m; **investors in the company** les personnes qui ont investi dans l'entreprise

inveterate [ɪn'vetərɪt] **ADJ** (drunkard, gambler, smoker) invétéré; (opponent) acharné; (liar) incorrigible, impénitent

invidious [ɪn'vɪdɪəs] **ADJ 1** (unpleasant) pénible; (task) ingrat, peu agréable; **to be in an i. position** être dans une position peu enviable **2** (comparison) inéquitable

invigilate [ɪn'vɪdʒɪleɪt] Br Sch, Univ **VI** surveiller les candidats (à un examen)
VT (exam) surveiller

invigilator [ɪn'vɪdʒɪleɪtər] **N** Br Sch, Univ surveillant, -ante (des candidats à un examen)

invigorate [ɪn'vɪgəreɪt] **VT** (of air, walk, holiday etc) vivifier; **she invigorates an otherwise lifeless production of Hamlet** elle donne un souffle de vie à un Hamlet plutôt morne

invigorating [ɪn'vɪgəreɪtɪŋ] **ADJ** vivifiant

invincibility [ɪnvɪnsɪ'bɪlɪtɪ] **N** invincibilité f, (of belief, faith) caractère m inébranlable

invincible [ɪn'vɪnsɪb(ə)l] **ADJ** (army) invincible; (faith, conviction) inébranlable

inviolability [ɪnvaɪələ'bɪlɪtɪ] **N** inviolabilité f

inviolable [ɪn'vaɪələb(ə)l] **ADJ** inviolable

inviolably [ɪn'vaɪələblɪ] **ADV** inviolablement

inviolate [ɪn'vaɪəlɪt] **ADJ** Fml inviolé

invisibility [ɪnvɪzɪ'bɪlɪtɪ] **N** invisibilité f

invisible [ɪn'vɪzɪb(ə)l] **ADJ** invisible; i. **to the naked eye** invisible à l'œil nu
▸ ▸ Fin i. **earnings** gains mpl invisibles; i. **exports** exportations fpl invisibles; i. **imports** importations fpl invisibles; i. **ink** encre f invisible ou sympathique; i. **mending** stoppage m; i. **trade** commerce m de services

invisibly [ɪn'vɪzɪblɪ] **ADV** invisiblement; **he had it i. mended** (hole, garment) il l'avait fait stopper

invitation [ɪnvɪ'teɪʃən] **N** invitation f (**to do sth** à faire qch); (card) carte f d'invitation; **at sb's i.** sur l'invitation de qn; **an i. to lunch** une invitation à déjeuner; **by i. only** uniquement sur invitation; Fig **the speech was an i. to criticism** ce discours ne pouvait pas manquer de provoquer la critique; **that's an i. to burglars** c'est une invitation aux cambrioleurs;
▸ ▸ i. **card** carte d'invitation

invite¹ [ɪn'vaɪt] **VT 1** (ask to come) inviter (**to** à); **to i. sb in** inviter qn à entrer; **to i. oneself** s'inviter soi-même; **the invited guests** les invités mpl **2** (request) inviter (**sb to do sth** qn à faire qch); **to i. bids** or **tenders** faire un appel d'offres; **applications are invited for the position** toute personne intéressée est invitée à déposer un dossier de candidature **3** (arouse) (danger, criticism) (of person) s'exposer à; (of action) provoquer; **to i. trouble** aller au-devant des ennuis

▸ **invite back, invite in, invite round** etc = **ask back, ask in, ask round** etc

invite² ['ɪnvaɪt] **N** Fam invitation f

inviting [ɪn'vaɪtɪŋ] **ADJ** attrayant; (dish) appétissant; **her eyes were dark and i.** ses yeux étaient sombres et attirants; **not very i.** peu attrayant; **the water looks i.** l'eau donne envie de se baigner

invitingly [ɪn'vaɪtɪŋlɪ] **ADV** (arranged, displayed) d'une manière attrayante; (to smile, beckon) en guise d'invitation

in vitro [ɪn'vi:trəʊ] **ADJ**
▸ ▸ i. **fertilization** fécondation f in vitro

invocation [ɪnvə'keɪʃən] **N** invocation f

invoice ['ɪnvɔɪs] **N** Com facture f, **to make out an i.** établir une facture; **to settle an i.** régler une facture; **as per i.** conformément à la facture; **within 30 days of i.** dans les 30 jours après la facturation; **payable against i.** à payer à réception de la facture
VT (goods, person) facturer; **who do I i.?** à qui dois-je adresser la facture?; **to i. sb for sth** facturer qch à qn; **invoiced sales** ventes fpl facturées
▸ ▸ Com i. **clerk** facturier, -ière; i. **date** date f de facturation; i. **of origin** facture originale; i. **price** prix m facturé; i. **value** valeur f de facture

invoiceable ['ɪnvɔɪsəb(ə)l] **ADJ** facturable

invoicing ['ɪnvɔɪsɪŋ] **N** (of goods etc) facturation f
▸ ▸ i. **address** adresse f de facturation; i. **instructions** instructions fpl de facturation; i. **software** logiciel m de facturation

invoke [ɪn'vəʊk] **VT 1** (God, sb's memory, law etc) invoquer; **to i. sb's aid** appeler qn à son secours; **to i. a blessing on an undertaking** demander à Dieu de bénir une entreprise **2** (summon up) (spirit) évoquer

involuntarily [ɪn'vɒlənt(ə)rɪlɪ] **ADV** involontairement

involuntary [ɪn'vɒləntərɪ] **ADJ** involontaire

involve [ɪn'vɒlv] **VT 1** (in crime, scandal etc) impliquer (**in** dans); (in quarrel) mêler (**in** dans); **he is involved in the plot** il est compromis dans le complot; **over 200 people were involved in planning the event** plus de 200 personnes ont participé à la préparation de l'événement; **he's involved in high finance/language teaching** il est dans la haute finance/l'enseignement des langues; **when I first became involved in teaching** quand j'ai commencé à enseigner; **he's getting involved with the school orchestra** il commence à prendre part aux activités de l'orchestre de l'école; **I'm getting really involved in this job** je commence à trouver ce travail vraiment intéressant; **the novel doesn't really i. the reader** le lecteur ne se sent pas impliqué dans ce roman; **they didn't want to get involved in another war** ils ne voulaient pas s'engager dans un autre conflit; **the police became involved** la police est intervenue; **no one wanted to get involved** personne n'a voulu s'en mêler; **he doesn't want to get involved** il ne veut pas s'engager; **don't get involved!** (in other people's problems, argument etc) ne t'en mêle pas!; **I'm too emotionally involved** cela me concerne de trop près ou me touche trop; **he got involved with his friend's wife** il a eu une liaison avec la femme de son ami
2 (include, entail etc) impliquer, entraîner; **my job involves a lot of travel** je dois beaucoup voyager dans mon travail; **it involves learning new techniques** cela implique l'apprentissage de nouvelles techniques; **what exactly is involved in carrying out a project like this?** qu'est-ce que ça implique exactement la réalisation d'un tel projet?; **it involves getting to London by 5.30 in the**

morning ça veut dire qu'il faut arriver à Londres à 5h 30 le matin; **all it involves is sitting by the phone** tout ce qu'il y a à faire, c'est de rester assis à côté du téléphone
3 *(have to do with)* concerner; **this discussion doesn't i. you** cette discussion ne vous concerne pas; **there's been a theft – how much money is involved?** il y a eu un vol – de combien d'argent s'agit-il?

involved [ɪn'vɒlvd] **ADJ** *(complicated)* *(style, discours)* compliqué; *(story, plot)* complexe, compliqué

involvement [ɪn'vɒlvmənt] **N 1** *(participation)* participation *f* (**in** à); *(in crime)* implication *f* (**in** dans); **his i. of his sister in the fraud is unforgivable** il est impardonnable qu'il ait impliqué sa sœur dans cette fraude; **I've had no further i. with him since** je n'ai plus jamais eu affaire à lui depuis; **her i. with this man** sa liaison avec cet homme; **our country's i. in this war** la participation de notre pays à cette guerre **2** *(complexity)* complexité *f*

invulnerability [ɪnvʌlnərə'bɪlɪtɪ] **N** invulnérabilité *f*

invulnerable [ɪn'vʌlnərəb(ə)l] **ADJ** *(person)* invulnérable; *(position etc)* inattaquable

inward ['ɪnwəd] **ADJ 1** *(intimate)* *(thoughts, feelings etc)* intérieur **2** *(directed to the inside)* (orienté *ou* se dirigeant) vers l'intérieur
ADV = **inwards**
▸▸ *Customs* **i. customs clearance** entrée *f* en douane; *Fin* **i. investment** investissements *mpl* étrangers; *Acct* **i. payment** paiement *m* reçu

inward-looking [-lʊkɪŋ] **ADJ** introspectif

inwardly ['ɪnwədlɪ] **ADV** intérieurement; **I was i. pleased** dans mon for intérieur j'étais content

inwards ['ɪnwədz] **ADV** vers l'intérieur; *Com, Naut* pour l'importation

in-your-face **ADJ 1** *(uncompromising)* *(documentary, film)* sans fard **2** *(aggressive)* *(attitude, personality)* agressif

I/O ['aɪ'əʊ] **N** *Comput* *(abbr* **input/output***)* E/S; **I/O port** port *m* d'E/S

IOC [aɪəʊ'siː] **N** *(abbr* **International Olympic Committee***)* CIO *m*

iodine [*Br* 'aɪədiːn, *Am* -daɪn] **N** *Chem* iode *m*; *Pharm* **(tincture of) i.** teinture *f* d'iode

iodize ['aɪədaɪz] **VT** *Med, Phot* ioder

iodoform [aɪ'ɒdəfɔːm] **N** *Chem, Pharm* iodoforme *m*

ion ['aɪən] **N** *Phys, Chem, Elec* ion *m*; **hydrogen i.** ion d'hydrogène
▸▸ **i. beam** faisceau *m* ionique

Ionian [aɪ'əʊnɪən] **N the I. (Sea)** la mer Ionienne

Ionic [aɪ'ɒnɪk] **ADJ** *Archit, Liter* *(order, verse)* ionique; *Ling, Mus* *(dialect, mode)* ionien

ionic [aɪ'ɒnɪk] **ADJ** *Phys, Chem, Elec* ionique

ionization [aɪənaɪ'zeɪʃən] **N 1** *Phys, Elec* ionisation *f* **2** *Med* (traitement *m* par) ionisation *f*

ionize ['aɪənaɪz] *Phys, Elec* **VT** *(air, gas)* ioniser
VI *(of acid etc)* s'ioniser

ionosphere [aɪ'ɒnəsfɪər] **N** ionosphère *f*

iota [aɪ'əʊtə] **N 1** *(in Greek alphabet)* iota *m* **2** *(tiny amount)* iota *m*; **she hadn't changed an or one i.** *(looked the same)* elle n'avait pas changé d'un iota; **not an i. of truth** pas un brin de vérité

IOU, *pl* **IOUs** [aɪəʊ'juː, -'juːz] **N** *(abbr* **I owe you***)* reconnaissance *f* (de dette)

IP [aɪ'piː] **N** *Comput* *(abbr* **Internet Protocol***)* **IP address** adresse *f* IP; **IP number** numéro *m* IP

IPA [aɪpiː'eɪ] **N** *(abbr* **International Phonetic Alphabet***)* API *m*

IPO [aɪpiː'əʊ] **N** *Am St Exch* *(abbr* **initial public offering***)* introduction *f* en Bourse

IPPR [aɪpiːpiː'ɑːr] **N** *(abbr* **Institute for Public Policy Research***)* = groupe *m* d'experts de centre gauche à l'origine de plusieurs grandes politiques du gouvernement travailliste britannique

ipso facto ['ɪpsəʊ'fæktəʊ] **ADV** ipso facto

IQ [aɪ'kjuː] **N** *(abbr* **intelligence quotient***)* QI *m*; **to have an IQ of ...** avoir un QI de ...

IRA [aɪɑː'reɪ] **N** *(abbr* **Irish Republican Army***)* IRA *f*

IRA

L'IRA est une organisation qui lutte pour la réunification de l'Irlande. En 1969, elle s'est scindée en deux factions: la "Provisional IRA", qui a recours à la violence, et la "Official IRA", qui privilégiait un réglement politique du conflit en Irlande du Nord. En 1995, au début du processus de paix qui a abouti à l'accord de 1998 (le "Good Friday Agreement") la "Provisional IRA" a déclaré un cessez-le-feu. Cependant, quelques groupes dissidents, notamment la "Continuity IRA" et la "Real IRA", ont poursuivi les actes terroristes.

Iran [ɪ'rɑːn, ɪ'ræn] **N** Iran *m*

Iranian [ɪ'reɪnɪən] **ADJ** iranien
N 1 Iranien, -ienne **2** *Ling* iranien *m*

Iraq [ɪ'rɑːk, ɪ'ræk] **N** Irak *m*

Iraqi [ɪ'rɑːkɪ] **ADJ** irakien, iraquien
N Irakien, -ienne, Iraquien, -ienne

irascibility [ɪræsɪ'bɪlɪtɪ] **N** irascibilité *f*

irascible [ɪ'ræsɪb(ə)l] **ADJ** *(person)* irascible, coléreux; *(temperament)* colérique

irascibly [ɪ'ræsɪblɪ] **ADV** *(to say etc)* sur un ton irrité

irate [aɪ'reɪt] **ADJ** *(person, telephone call)* furieux

IRC [aɪɑː'siː] **N** *Comput* *(abbr* **Internet relay chat***)* IRC *m*, service *m* de bavardage Internet, canal *m* de dialogue en direct
▸▸ **I. channel** canal IRC, canal de dialogue en direct

ire ['aɪər] **N** *Lit* courroux *m*, colère *f*

Ireland ['aɪələnd] **N** Irlande *f*; **Northern I.** l'Irlande du Nord; **the Republic of I.** la République d'Irlande

iridescence [ɪrɪ'desəns] **N** *Lit* *(of plumage, fabric etc)* irisation *f*, chatoiement *m*

iridescent [ɪrɪ'desənt] **ADJ** *Lit* iridescent, chatoyant

iris ['aɪrɪs], *pl* **irides** ['aɪrɪdiːz] *Anat*, *pl* **irises** ['aɪrɪsɪz] *(flower)* **N 1** *Anat* iris *m* (de l'œil) **2** *(flower)* iris *m*; **yellow i.** iris jaune *ou* des marais **3** *Myth* **I.** Iris *f* **4** *Phot* iris *m*, diaphragme *m*

Irish ['aɪrɪʃ] **ADJ 1** *(people, government, legend etc)* irlandais, d'Irlande **2** *Br Fam* *(stupid, illogical)* stupide; **that's a bit I.** c'est un peu bête
N *Ling* irlandais *m*
NPL the I. les Irlandais *mpl*
▸▸ **I. American** Américain, -aine d'origine irlandaise; **I. bull** proposition *f* absurde car contradictoire; **I. coffee** Irish coffee *m*, = café *m* noir au whiskey irlandais couronné de crème fraîche; **I. joke** = histoire *f* drôle aux dépens des Irlandais, ≃ histoire belge; **I. Sea** mer *f* d'Irlande; **I. setter** setter *m* irlandais; **I. stew** ragoût *m* à l'irlandaise; **I. wolfhound** lévrier *m* irlandais

Irishism ['aɪrɪʃɪz(ə)m] **N** expression *f* irlandaise

Irishman, *pl* **Irishmen** ['aɪrɪʃmən] **N** Irlandais *m*

Irishwoman, *pl* **Irishwomen** ['aɪrɪʃwʊmən, -wɪmɪn] **N** Irlandaise *f*

irk [ɜːk] **VT** agacer

irksome ['ɜːksəm] **ADJ** agaçant

iron ['aɪən] **N 1** *(metal)* fer *m*; **(made of) i.** de ou en fer; *Fig* **i. discipline** discipline *f* de fer; **he has an i. constitution** il a une santé de fer; **man of i.** homme dur *ou* sans pitié; **will of i.** volonté *f* de fer; **an i. fist** *or* **hand in a velvet glove** une main de fer dans un gant de velours; **the i. and steel industry** l'industrie *f* sidérurgique, la sidérurgie
2 *(in diet)* fer *m*
3 *(device, implement)* *(for laundry)* fer *m* à repasser; **electric/steam i.** fer (à repasser) électrique/à vapeur; *Fig* **to have several irons in the fire** avoir plusieurs affaires en route; *Fig* **to have too many irons in the fire** courir trop de lièvres à la fois
4 *Horseriding* *(of stirrup)* étrier *m*
5 *Golf* *(crosse f* en) fer *m*
6 *Arch* *(for prisoner)* **irons** fers *mpl*, chaînes *fpl*
7 *Med* **irons** *(supports)* attelles *fpl*
VT & VI *(clothes)* repasser; **I've been ironing all morning** j'ai repassé *ou* fait du repassage toute la matinée
▸▸ **the I. Age** *m* du fer; **i. bar** barre *f* de fer; **i. bridge** pont *m* en fer; **the I. Curtain** le rideau de fer; *Med* **i. deficiency** carence *f* en fer; **i. filings** limaille *f* de fer; **i. foundry** fonderie *f (de fonte)*; *Am Hist* **the I. horse** = la locomotive; *Br Pol* **the I. Lady** la Dame de Fer; *Med* **i. lung** poumon *m* d'acier; *Chem* **i. nitride** nitride *m* de fer; *Miner* **i. ore** minerai *m* de fer; *Golf* **i. shot** coup *m* de fer; **i. will** volonté de fer
▸ **iron out** **VT SEP** *(crease)* faire disparaître au fer (chaud); *Fig* *(resolve)* *(problem)* résoudre; **to i. out the difficulties** aplanir les difficultés; **have you ironed out your differences?** est-ce que vous avez résolu vos différends?

ironclad ['aɪənklæd] **ADJ 1** *Arch* *(ship)* cuirassé **2** *Fig* *(alibi, assurance, guarantee)* à toute épreuve
N *Naut, Hist* cuirassé *m*

iron-grey **ADJ** gris (de) fer

ironic(al) [aɪ'rɒnɪk, -ɪk(ə)l] **ADJ** ironique

ironically [aɪ'rɒnɪklɪ] **ADV** ironiquement; *(to talk)* avec ironie; **i., the box was empty** l'ironie, c'est que la boîte était vide

ironing ['aɪənɪŋ] **N** repassage *m*; **I've got a lot of i. to do** j'ai beaucoup de repassage à faire
▸▸ **i. board** planche *f ou* table *f* à repasser

ironmonger ['aɪənmʌŋgər] **N** *Br* quincaillier *m*; **i.'s (shop)** quincaillerie *f*

ironmongery ['aɪənmʌŋgərɪ] **N** *Br* *(goods, shop)*, *Hum* *(medals, jewellery)* quincaillerie *f*

iron-on transfer **N** transfert *m* (appliqué au fer à repasser)

ironstone ['aɪənstəʊn] **N** *(clay)* **i.** minerai *m* de fer (argileux)

ironware ['aɪənweər] **N** ferronnerie *f*

ironwork ['aɪənwɜːk] **N 1** *(work in wrought iron)* ferronnerie *f*, *(parts made of iron)* ferrure(s) *f(pl)* **2** *(often with sing verb)* **ironworks** *(for smelting)* fonderie *f* de fonte; *(for casting)* usine *f* sidérurgique, forges *fpl*

irony ['aɪrənɪ] **N** ironie *f*; **the i. is that ...** l'ironie c'est que ...; **i. of fate** ironie du sort; **in one of life's little ironies** par une ironie du sort

IRR [aɪɑː'ɑːr] **N** *Fin* *(abbr* **internal rate of return***)* taux *m* de rentabilité interne

irradiate [ɪ'reɪdɪeɪt] **VT 1** *(of light, heat)* (the

earth etc) irradier; *(of light, rays) (surface)* illuminer **2** *(subject to radiation) (substance etc)* irradier; *Med (patient)* traiter par irradiation; **irradiated food** aliments *mpl* irradiés

irradiation [ɪreɪdɪ'eɪʃən] N **1** *Phys, Opt etc* irradiation *f*, *(of surface by light)* illumination *f* **2** *Nucl* irradiation *f*, *Med* (traitement *m* par) irradiation, radiothérapie *f*

irrational [ɪ'ræʃən(ə)l] ADJ **1** *(person, behaviour, fear)* irrationnel; **don't be so i.!** soyez un peu plus rationnel! **2** *Math (number)* irrationnel
   N **the i.** l'irrationnel *m*

irrationally [ɪ'ræʃən(ə)lɪ] ADV *(to behave)* de façon irrationnelle

irreconcilable [ɪrekən'saɪləb(ə)l] ADJ **1** *(enemy)* irréconciliable; *(hatred)* implacable **2** *(belief, idea)* incompatible, inconciliable (**with** avec)

irrecoverable [ɪrɪ'kʌvərəb(ə)l] ADJ *(debt)* irrécouvrable; *(loss)* irrémédiable; *(object)* irrécupérable

irrecoverably [ɪrɪ'kʌvərəblɪ] ADV *(lost)* pour toujours

irredeemable [ɪrɪ'diːməb(ə)l] ADJ **1** *(fault)* irréparable; *(disaster etc)* irrémédiable; *Rel* **no sinner is i.** on peut tous se racheter **2** *Fin (funds)* irremboursable; *(bill)* non convertible

irredeemably [ɪrɪ'diːməblɪ] ADV irrémédiablement

irreducible [ɪrɪ'djuːsɪb(ə)l] ADJ irréductible

irrefutable [ɪrɪ'fjuːtəb(ə)l] ADJ *(evidence)* irréfutable, irrécusable; *(statement)* irréfutable

irregular [ɪ'regjʊlər] ADJ **1** *(not conforming to rule)* (behaviour, attendance etc), *Gram (plural, verb)* irrégulier; *(life)* déréglé; **this is highly i.** c'est contraire aux règles **2** *(uneven)* *(outline, shape etc)* irrégulier; *(surface)* irrégulier, inégal, -aux; **i. features** traits *mpl* irréguliers **3** *(pulse, breathing)* irrégulier
   N *(usu pl)* *Mil* **irregulars** troupes *fpl* irrégulières, irréguliers *mpl*
   ▸▸ *Mil* **i. troops** troupes *fpl* irrégulières, irréguliers *mpl*

irregularity [ɪregjʊ'lærɪtɪ] N irrégularité *f*, *Admin etc* **irregularities** *(in accounts etc)* irrégularités

irregularly [ɪ'regjʊlərlɪ] ADV irrégulièrement, de façon irrégulière

irrelevance [ɪ'reləvəns], **irrelevancy** [ɪ'reləvənsɪ] N **1** *(state of being inapplicable)* inapplicabilité *f* (**to** à); *(inappropriateness)* manque *m* d'à-propos **2** *(remark)* remarque *f* sans rapport avec la question; *(action)* action *f* sans rapport avec la question; **the defence of the frontier has become an i.** la défense de la frontière n'a plus de raison d'être; **irrelevancies** points *mpl* qui n'ont rien à voir avec la question

irrelevant [ɪ'reləvənt] ADJ non pertinent; *(remark etc)* hors de propos; **that is i.** cela n'a aucun rapport *ou* n'a rien à voir avec la question; **the monarchy had become i.** la monarchie n'avait plus de raison d'être, la monarchie avait perdu sa raison d'être; **it's i. now whether he changes his mind or not** maintenant ça ne fait plus rien qu'il change d'avis ou non

irreligious [ɪrɪ'lɪdʒəs] ADJ irréligieux

irremediable [ɪrɪ'miːdɪəb(ə)l] ADJ *(evil, loss etc)* irrémédiable; *(fault)* incorrigible

irremediably [ɪrɪ'miːdɪəblɪ] ADV irrémédiablement

irremovable [ɪrɪ'muːvəb(ə)l] ADJ *(stain)* indélébile; *(official)* inamovible

irreparable [ɪ'repərəb(ə)l] ADJ *(damage)* irréparable; *(loss)* irrémédiable, irrécupérable

irreparably [ɪ'repərəblɪ] ADV *(damaged)* irréparablement; *(lost)* irrémédiablement

irreplaceable [ɪrɪ'pleɪsəb(ə)l] ADJ irremplaçable

irrepressible [ɪrɪ'presɪb(ə)l] ADJ *(urge)* irrésistible, irrépressible; *(yawn)* irrépressible; *(good humour)* que rien n'entame, à toute épreuve; **i. laughter** fou rire *m*; **he's i.** rien ne peut l'abattre

irrepressibly [ɪrɪ'presɪblɪ] ADV **i. optimistic/enthusiastic/good humoured** d'un optimisme/un enthousiasme/une bonne humeur à toute épreuve

irreproachable [ɪrɪ'prəʊtʃəb(ə)l] ADJ irréprochable

irreproachably [ɪrɪ'prəʊtʃəblɪ] ADV irréprochablement, de façon irréprochable

irresistible [ɪrɪ'zɪstɪb(ə)l] ADJ irrésistible

irresistibly [ɪrɪ'zɪstɪblɪ] ADV irrésistiblement

irresolute [ɪ'rezəluːt] ADJ indécis, irrésolu

irresolutely [ɪ'rezəluːtlɪ] ADV d'un air irrésolu

irresoluteness [ɪ'rezəluːtnɪs], **irresolution** [ɪrezə'luːʃən] N indécision *f*, irrésolution *f*

irrespective [ɪrɪ'spektɪv] ADV **i. of sth** indépendamment *ou* sans tenir compte de qch; **we'll go ahead i. of whether you agree or not** nous allons le faire que tu sois d'accord ou non

irresponsibility [ɪrɪspɒnsɪ'bɪlɪtɪ] N irresponsabilité *f*

irresponsible [ɪrɪ'spɒnsɪb(ə)l] ADJ irresponsable; **he was behaving like an i. idiot** il se comportait en irresponsable

irresponsibly [ɪrɪ'spɒnsɪblɪ] ADV de façon irresponsable

irretrievable [ɪrɪ'triːvəb(ə)l] ADJ *(loss)* irrémédiable; *(money)* irrécupérable; *(mistake, situation)* irréparable; **because of the i. breakdown of their marriage** parce que leur mariage était irrémédiablement brisé

irretrievably [ɪrɪ'triːvəblɪ] ADV *(lost)* irrémédiablement, à tout jamais; **to break down i.** *(of marriage)* se briser irrémédiablement

irreverence [ɪ'revərəns] N irrévérence *f* (**towards** envers, pour)

irreverent [ɪ'revərənt] ADJ irrévérencieux

irreverently [ɪ'revərəntlɪ] ADV irrévérencieusement

irreversible [ɪrɪ'vɜːsɪb(ə)l] ADJ **1** *(decision, step etc)* irrévocable **2** *(process)* irréversible

irrevocable [ɪ'revəkəb(ə)l] ADJ irrévocable; **i. letter of credit** lettre *f* de crédit irrévocable, crédit *m* documentaire irrévocable

irrevocably [ɪ'revəkəblɪ] ADV irrévocablement

irrigable [ɪ'rɪgəb(ə)l] ADJ *(land)* irrigable

irrigate [ɪ'rɪgeɪt] VT *Agr, Med (fields, wound)* irriguer

irrigation [ɪrɪ'geɪʃən] N *Agr, Med (of fields, wound)* irrigation *f*, *Agr* **i. canal** *or* **ditch** canal *m* d'irrigation

irritability [ɪrɪtə'bɪlɪtɪ] N irritabilité *f*

irritable [ɪ'rɪtəb(ə)l] ADJ irritable
   ▸▸ *Med* **i. bowel syndrome** syndrome *m* du côlon irritable

irritably [ɪ'rɪtəblɪ] ADV *(to say, answer)* d'un ton irrité, avec humeur

irritant [ɪ'rɪtənt] ADJ, N *Med* irritant *m*; *Fig* **at least we can be an i.** au moins nous pouvons jouer les empêcheurs de tourner en rond

irritate [ɪ'rɪteɪt] VT **1** *(person)* irriter, agacer; *(animal)* exciter, agacer **2** *Med* irriter

irritating [ɪ'rɪteɪtɪŋ] ADJ **1** irritant, agaçant; **i. little habits** des petites manies agaçantes **2** *Med* irritant

irritatingly [ɪ'rɪteɪtɪŋlɪ] ADV *(to say, behave)* de façon agaçante; **i. slow/jolly** d'une lenteur/bonne humeur exaspérante

irritation [ɪrɪ'teɪʃən] N **1** irritation *f*, **state of nervous i.** état *m* d'énervement **2** *Med (of throat etc)* irritation *f*

IRS [aɪɑːr'es] N *Am (abbr* **Internal Revenue Service)** **the I.** ≃ le fisc

is [ɪz] *see* be

IS [aɪ'es] N *(abbr* **information system)** système *m* informatique

ISA ['aɪsə] N *Br (abbr* **individual savings account)** ≃ PEA *m*, plan *m* d'épargne en actions

ISBN [aɪesbiː'en] N *(abbr* **International Standard Book Number)** ISBN *m*

ISDN [aɪesdiː'en] *Comput* N *(abbr* **integrated services digital network)** RNIS *m*
   VT *Fam* **to I. sth** envoyer qch par RNIS
   ▸▸ **I. card** carte *f* RNIS; **I. line** ligne *f* RNIS; **I. modem** modem *m* RNIS *ou* Numéris

-ish [ɪʃ] SUFF **1** *(with adjective)* blueish bleuâtre; shortish plutôt petit **2** *(with noun)* girlish de petite fille; wolfish de loup **3** *(with time, numbers etc)* around eightish vers huit heures, aux environs de huit heures; **he's fortyish** il a la quarantaine

isinglass ['aɪzɪŋglɑːs] N *(in wine-making)* ichtyocolle *f*, *Culin* gélatine *f*

Islam ['ɪzlɑːm] N *(religion)* islam *m*; *(people)* l'Islam, le monde musulman; **to go over to I.** se convertir à l'islam

Islamic [ɪz'læmɪk] ADJ islamique

island ['aɪlənd] N **1** *Geog* île *f*, *(small)* îlot *m*; **the Pacific Islands** les îles du Pacifique **2** *Fig (in road)* îlot *m*; *(for pedestrians)* refuge *m*; *(of houses etc)* groupe *m*; *(in supermarket)* gondole *f*, **i. of resistance** îlot *m* de résistance; **an i. of calm** un havre de paix
   ▸▸ *Rail* **i. platform** quai *m* d'entre-voie, quai entre voies

islander ['aɪləndər] N *(in general)* insulaire *mf*, *(of specific island)* habitant, -ante de l'île

isle [aɪl] N *(poetic except in certain proper names)* île *f*, **the I. of Man** l'île de Man

islet ['aɪlɪt] N îlot *m*

ism ['ɪz(ə)m] N *Fam usu Pej* doctrine *f*, idéologie *f*

isn't ['ɪz(ə)nt] CONTR = **is not**, *see* be

ISO [aɪes'əʊ] N *(abbr* **International Standards Organization)** ISO *f*

isobar ['aɪsəʊbɑːr] N *Met, Phys* isobare *f*

ISOC [aɪesəʊ'siː] N *Comput (abbr* **Internet Society)** = organisation *f* non gouvernementale chargée de veiller à l'évolution de l'Internet

isolate ['aɪsəleɪt] VT *Med, Pol etc (person)*, *Chem (substance)*, *Biol (culture)* isoler (**from** de, d'avec); **she isolated herself from other people** elle s'est isolée des autres gens

isolated ['aɪsəleɪtɪd] ADJ isolé; **i. case** *or* **instance** cas *m* isolé; *Fin* **i. post allowance** prime *f* d'éloignement

isolation [aɪsə'leɪʃən] N **1** *(state, action)* isolement *m*; *Fam* **these problems do not exist in i.** *(from one another)* ces problèmes n'existent pas isolément; **to look at sth in i.** considérer qch isolément **2** *Med (of patient)* isolement *m*
   ▸▸ *Med* **i. hospital** hôpital *m* d'isolement; *Med* **i. ward** service *m* des contagieux

> Attention: ne pas confondre avec le nom anglais **insulation**, qui signifie **isolation**.

isolationism [aɪsə'leɪʃənɪz(ə)m] N isolationnisme *m*

isolationist [aɪsə'leɪʃənɪst] ADJ, N isolationniste mf

isosceles [aɪ'sɒsɪliːz] ADJ Geom (triangle) isocèle

isotherm ['aɪsəʊθɜːm] N Met isotherme f

isotonic [aɪsəʊ'tɒnɪk] ADJ isotonique

isotope ['aɪsəʊtəʊp] N Chem, Phys isotope m

ISP [aɪes'piː] N Comput (abbr Internet Service Provider) fournisseur m de services Internet

I-spy N Br = jeu m pour enfants où un des joueurs donne la première lettre d'un mot et où les autres doivent deviner l'objet auquel il pense

Israel ['ɪzreɪ(ə)l] N Israël m

Israeli [ɪz'reɪlɪ] ADJ israélien
 N Israélien, -ienne

Israelite ['ɪzr(ɪ)əlaɪt] ADJ israélite
 N Israélite mf

ISSUE ['ɪʃ(j)uː]

N question **1** ▪ émission **2**
▪ distribution **2** ▪ publication **2**
▪ délivrance **2** ▪ prêt **2** ▪ numéro **3**
VT émettre ▪ publier ▪ distribuer
▪ délivrer ▪ prêter

N **1** (subject) problème m, question f; an important i. une question importante; the issues of the day les questions du jour; I don't want to make an i. of it je ne veux pas en faire toute une affaire; to join i. with sb discuter l'opinion de qn (about sth au sujet de qch); the point at i. is the effect it has on the environment le problème n'est l'effet que cela a sur l'environnement; to be at i. with sb être en désaccord avec qn; I would like to take i. with you on that point je voudrais débattre ce point avec vous; I would take i. with that je ne suis pas d'accord là-dessus; that's not the i. ce n'est pas (là) le problème; to evade or avoid the i. prendre la tangente; to confuse the i. compliquer les choses; Law i. (of fact/of law) (matter) question ou point m de fait/de droit; (conclusion) conclusion f
 2 (act of issuing) Admin, Fin (of banknotes, money orders, stamps etc) émission f; Admin, Mil etc (of equipment etc) distribution f; (of book) parution f, publication f; Rail etc (of tickets etc) délivrance f; (in library) (of books) prêt m; Mil etc i. boots/shirts bottes fpl/chemises fpl réglementaires; Mil i. of orders publication f des ordres
 3 (copy) (of magazine) numéro m; the November i. le numéro de novembre
 4 Med (of blood, pus) décharge f
 5 Fml (offspring) descendance f; to die without i. mourir sans (laisser de) descendance
 VI **1** (of blood, water) s'écouler (from de); (of smoke) s'échapper (from de); (of smell) se dégager (from de)
 2 Fml (of children) provenir (from de); the children issuing from this marriage les enfants issus de ce mariage
 VT (banknotes etc) émettre; (bill) créer; (new edition, prospectus etc) publier; Fin (letter of credit) fournir; Mil (order) publier, donner; Law (judgement) rendre; (provisions etc) distribuer; (train tickets etc) délivrer; (of library) (books) prêter; to i. sb with sth délivrer qch à qn; each man will be issued with two uniforms chaque homme recevra deux uniformes; no books will be issued after 8 p.m. le service de prêt se termine à huit heures; to i. a statement faire une déclaration; Law to i. a summons décerner ou lancer une citation
 ▶▶ Fin i. premium prime f d'émission; Fin i. price prix m d'émission, valeur f d'émission

Note that the French word **issue** is a false friend and is never a translation for the English word **issue**. It means exit.

issued ['ɪʃ(j)uːd] ADJ Fin émis
 ▶▶ i. capital capital-action m émis; i. securities titres mpl émis; i. share capital capital-action émis

issueless ['ɪʃ(j)uːlɪs] ADV Fml to die i. mourir sans laisser de descendance

issuer ['ɪʃ(j)uːər] N Fin i. of a draft émetteur m d'une traite

issuing ['ɪʃ(j)uːɪŋ] ADJ esp Fin émetteur, -trice
 N (of loan, banknotes) émission f; (of provisions) distribution f; (in library) (of books) prêt m
 ▶▶ Br i. bank banque f d'émission ou émettrice; i. company société f émettrice; i. house banque d'émission ou émettrice

Istanbul [ɪstæn'buːl] N Istanbul

isthmus, pl **isthmuses** ['ɪsməs, -məsɪz] N Geog isthme m

IT [aɪ'tiː] N (abbr information technology) technologie f de l'information; she's our IT expert c'est notre spécialiste en informatique

it [ɪt]

PERS PRON il/elle **1** ▪ le/la **2** ▪ lui **3**
▪ ce **7, 8** ▪ il **8** ▪ en **10**

PERS PRON VOIR GRAMMAIRE A27–9; B18–21 (referring to inanimate objects, animals and children, but in French taking the gender of the noun for which it stands) **1** (subject) il, elle; the house is small but it's my own c'est une petite maison mais elle est à moi; where is your hat? – it's in the cupboard où est votre chapeau? – il est dans l'armoire SEE GRAMMAR B66
 2 (direct object) le, la; (before vowel) l'; I don't believe it je ne le crois pas
 3 (indirect object) lui; fetch the dog and give it something to eat allez chercher le chien et donnez-lui à manger
 4 Fam (stressed) he thinks he's it il se croit sorti de la cuisse de Jupiter; this book is absolutely it! c'est un livre épatant!; this is it – it's now or never! cette fois-ci c'est la bonne – c'est maintenant ou jamais!; this is it, the moment we've all been waiting for! nous y voilà, c'est le moment que nous attendons tous!; that's it, we're in for it now! ça y est, on est foutu; that's it for today (we have no more time etc) c'est fini pour aujourd'hui
 5 (as unspecified object of a verb) to face it faire front; blast it! zut!
 6 (as unspecified object of a preposition) now for it! et maintenant allons-y!; there is nothing for it but to run il n'y a qu'une chose à faire, c'est de filer; Fam he's (in) for it! qu'est-ce qu'il va prendre!; to have a bad time of it en voir de rudes
 7 (as complement) who is it? qui est-ce?; that's it c'est bien ça; (as encouragement) c'est bien
 8 (as subject of impersonal verb) it frightens me cela me fait peur; it doesn't matter cela ne fait rien; it's raining il pleut; it's ten o'clock il est dix heures; it's Monday c'est lundi SEE GRAMMAR B29–30
 9 it's nonsense talking like that c'est ou il est absurde de dire ça; it's impossible to work in this heat c'est ou il est impossible de travailler par cette chaleur; it says in ... on lit dans ...; the fog made it difficult to see le brouillard réduisait beaucoup la visibilité; I find it hard to understand why je trouve difficile de comprendre pourquoi; you may rely upon it that he will do his best vous pouvez être sûr qu'il fera de son mieux SEE GRAMMAR B66
 10 (with prepositions) to consent to it y consentir; above it, over it au-dessus, dessus; below it, under(neath) it au-dessous,

dessous; as we walked away from it tandis que nous nous en éloignions; he's not bad, far from it il n'est pas méchant, loin de là; give me half of it donnez-m'en la moitié; think of it pensez-y; don't tread on it ne marchez pas dessus; the Committee has devoted much care to the task before it le comité a accordé beaucoup d'attention à la tâche qui lui incombait; I cracked his head with it je lui ai fendu la tête avec
 N (in children's games) you're it! c'est toi qui y es ou qui t'y colles!

Italian [ɪ'tæljən] ADJ italien; (embassy, ambassador, history) d'Italie; (teacher, lesson, dictionary) d'italien
 N **1** Italien, -ienne **2** Ling italien m
 ▶▶ I. Switzerland Suisse f italienne

italic [ɪ'tælɪk] Typ ADJ (character) italique
 N italic(s) italique m; to print in italic(s) imprimer en italique; the italics are mine les italiques sont de moi

italicization [ɪtælɪsaɪ'zeɪʃən] N (putting into italics) mise f en italique(s)

italicize [ɪ'tælɪsaɪz] VT Typ imprimer ou mettre en italique; italicized words mots mpl en italique

Italo- [ɪ'tæləʊ] PREF italo-; I.-American italo-américain

Italy ['ɪtəlɪ] N Italie f

ITC [aɪtiː'siː] N **1** Br (abbr Independent Television Commission) = commission f de surveillance des télévisions britanniques privées **2** Am abbr International Trade Commission

itch [ɪtʃ] N démangeaison f; I've got an awful i. on my back mon dos me démange horriblement; Fig to have an i. for sth/to do sth avoir envie de qch/de faire qch; Fig Fam if you've got an i., scratch it si ça te dit, vas-y
 VI **1** (of person) éprouver des démangeaisons; my hand itches la main me démange; where does it i.? où est-ce que cela vous démange?; these bites really i. ce que ces piqûres me démangent!; Fig to have an itching palm être cupide **2** Fam to be itching to do sth brûler d'envie de faire qch; I was itching to speak la langue me démangeait; she is itching to be off ça la démange de partir

itching ['ɪtʃɪŋ] N démangeaison f
 ▶▶ i. powder poil m à gratter

itchy ['ɪtʃɪ] ADJ I've got an i. hand j'ai la main qui me démange; Fig to have i. feet brûler d'envie de partir; I've always had i. feet j'ai toujours eu la bougeotte

it'd ['ɪt(ə)d] CONTR **1** = it would, see would **2** = it had, see have

item ['aɪtəm] N Com article m; (in bookkeeping) écriture f, article, poste m; Comput (on menu) élément m; Journ (very brief) entrefilet m; (longer) article; Radio, TV (news item) point m ou sujet m d'actualité; i. of expenditure article ou chef m de dépense; the second i. of the contract l'article deux du contrat; the items on the agenda les questions fpl à l'ordre du jour; Theat etc the last i. on the programme le dernier numéro du programme; Journ news items nouvelles fpl; there was an i. on the news about it yesterday ils en ont parlé aux informations hier; Fam they're an i. ils sortent ensemble
 ADV Old-fashioned (when listing) item
 ▶▶ Am Pol i. veto veto m partiel

itemize ['aɪtəmaɪz] VT (bill) détailler; itemized billing, itemized invoicing facturation f détaillée

iterate ['ɪtəreɪt] VT réitérer, répéter (constamment); Comput, Math itérer

iteration [ɪtə'reɪʃən] N itération f

iterative ['ɪt(ə)rətɪv] ADJ Comput itératif

itinerant [ɪˈtɪnərənt, aɪ-] ADJ *(salesman, comedian, musician)* ambulant; *(preacher, worker)* itinérant

itinerary [aɪˈtɪnərərɪ] N itinéraire *m*

it'll [ˈɪt(ə)l] CONTR = **it will,** *see* **will** [2]

ITN [aɪtiːˈen] N *Br (abbr* **Independent Television News)** = service *m* produisant le journal télévisé d'ITV

ITO [aɪtiːˈəʊ] N *(abbr* **International Trade Organization)** OMC *f*

its [ɪts] VOIR GRAMMAIRE A30; B21–2   POSS ADJ son, sa, *pl* ses; *(in the f before a vowel sound)* son; **i. nose, mouth, and eyes** *(of animal)* son nez, sa bouche, et ses yeux; **the jug has lost its handle** le pichet n'a plus de poignée; **a charm of i. own** un charme qui n'appartient qu'à lui/à elle

POSS PRON le sien, la sienne, *pl* les sien(ne)s

> Attention: ne pas confondre avec **it's,** qui est la forme abrégée de **it is.**

it's CONTR **1** = **it is,** *see* **be 2** = **it has,** *see* **have**

> Attention: ne pas confondre avec l'adjectif et le pronom possessifs **its.**

itself [ɪtˈself] PERS PRON VOIR GRAMMAIRE A29–30

1 *(emphatic)* lui-même, elle-même, soi-même; **it is simplicity i.** c'est tout ce qu'il y a de plus simple; **she is kindness i.** elle est la bonté même **2** *(reflexive)* **the dog hurt i.** le chien s'est fait mal SEE GRAMMAR B28–9 **3** *(after prepositions)* **the child was left by i.** l'enfant était laissé(e) tout(e) seul(e); **the thing in i.** la chose en elle-même; **in i. it's not a bad idea** en soi l'idée n'est pas mauvaise

ITV [aɪtiːˈviː] N *Br (abbr* **Independent Television)** = une des chaînes de télévision privées britanniques

IUD [aɪjuːˈdiː] N *Med (abbr* **intra-uterine device)** stérilet *m*

IV [aɪˈviː] *Med (abbr* **intravenous)** IV

I've [aɪv] CONTR = **I have,** *see* **have**

IVF [aɪviːˈef] N *Med (abbr* **in vitro fertilization)** FIV *f*

ivory [ˈaɪvərɪ] N **1** *(substance)* ivoire *m*; *(object)* (objet *m* d')ivoire; **a collection of ivories** une collection d'ivoires; *Fig Fam* **ivories** *(teeth)* dents *fpl*; *(piano keys)* touches *fpl* **2** *(colour)* ivoire *m*

ADJ *(made of ivory)* d'ivoire, en ivoire
▸▸**I. Coast** Côte *f* d'Ivoire; **i. tower** tour *f*

d'ivoire; **i. trade** commerce *m* de l'ivoire

ivory-white [ˈaɪvərɪˈwaɪt] ADJ *(teeth)* d'une blancheur d'ivoire

ivy [ˈaɪvɪ] N *(plant)* lierre *m*
▸▸**the I. League** = groupe *m* des huit universités les plus prestigieuses du nord-est des États-Unis

> ### Ivy League
> On désigne ainsi un groupe de huit universités du nord-est des États-Unis: Brown, Columbia, Cornell, Dartmouth, Harvard, l'Université de Pennsylvanie, Princeton et Yale. Ces universités se caractérisent par une forte proportion d'étudiants de troisième cycle, des moyens financiers importants et la réputation d'excellence de leurs universitaires. Si à l'origine, "Ivy League" servait à promouvoir les rencontres sportives entre les universités qui la composaient, elle est depuis devenue synonyme d'un enseignement prestigieux très compétitif, réservé à l'élite.

IYHF [aɪwaɪeɪtʃˈef] N *(abbr* **International Youth Hostel Federation)** FIAJ *f*

J, j [dʒeɪ] N *(letter)* J, j *m*; **two j's** deux j

jab [dʒæb] N **1** *(with sharp object)* coup *m* (sec); **a j. with an elbow/a knife** un coup de coude/de couteau; **she gave him a sharp j. in the ribs (with her elbow)** elle lui a mis un coup de coude dans les côtes **2** *Br Fam (injection)* injection *f*, piqûre *f*; **to give sb a j.** faire une injection *ou* une piqûre à qn; *(for TB, malaria etc)* vacciner qn; **have you had all the necessary jabs?** est-ce qu'on t'a fait tous les vaccins nécessaires? **3** *Boxing* coup *m* droit, direct *m*

VT (-bb-) **1** *(poke, prick)* **to j. sb/sth** piquer qn/qch (**with sth** avec qch, du bout de qch); **to j. sb with one's elbow/a knife** donner un coup de coude/couteau à qn; **she jabbed him in the eyes with her fingers** elle lui a planté ses doigts dans les yeux **2** *(thrust)* enfoncer, planter (d'un coup sec) (**into** dans); **she jabbed a finger at him to emphasize her point** elle a pointé le doigt dans sa direction pour appuyer ses propos

VI **1** *(poke, prick)* **to j. at sb/sth** piquer qn/qch (**with sth** avec qch, du bout de qch); **to j. at sb with a knife/an umbrella** donner un coup de couteau/de parapluie à qn **2** *Boxing* envoyer un coup droit *ou* un direct (**at** à)

jabber [ˈdʒæbər] *Fam* N **1** *(noise)* brouhaha *m* **2** *(chat)* conversation *f*, *Pej* jacasseries *fpl*; **to have a j.** bavarder, tailler une bavette

VI **1** *(talk fast, unclearly)* baragouiner; **what are you jabbering about?** qu'est-ce que tu baragouines? **2** *(chatter)* bavarder, tailler une bavette, *Pej* jacasser

VT *(excuse, explanation)* bafouiller, bredouiller; **to j. a few words in French/etc** baragouiner quelques mots de français/etc

▶ **jabber away, jabber on** VI baragouiner

▶ **jabber out** VT SEP *(excuse, explanation etc)* bafouiller, bredouiller

jabbering [ˈdʒæbərɪŋ] N **1** *(incomprehensible)* baragouinage *m* **2** *(chattering)* bavardage *m*, *Pej* jacasseries *fpl*

jacaranda [dʒækəˈrændə] N *(shrub)* jacaranda *m*

Jack [dʒæk] N **before you could say J. Robinson** sans qu'on ait eu le temps de dire ouf; *Br Fam* **I'm all right, J.** ça marche très bien pour moi (et les autres, je m'en fiche); *Fam* **an 'I'm all right, J.' attitude** une attitude je-m'en-foutiste

▶▶ **J. Frost** le Bonhomme Hiver

jack [dʒæk] N **1** *(person)* **every man j. (of them)** absolument tout le monde; **j. of all trades** touche-à-tout *m*, *Prov* **j. of all trades, master of none** propre à tout, propre à rien **2** *(lifting device)* *Aut* cric *m*; *Tech* vérin *m* **3** *Cards* valet *m*; **the j. of spades** le valet de pique **4** **jacks** *(game)* (jeu *m* d')osselets *mpl* **5** *(in bowling)* cochonnet *m* **6** *Tel* prise *f*, **microphone/headphone j.** prise de microphone/de casque

▶▶ *Tech* **j. plug** prise *ou* fiche *f* mâle, jack *m*; *Zool* **j. rabbit** = gros lièvre *m* d'Amérique; *Elec* **j. socket** prise *ou* fiche femelle; *Old-fashioned Fam* **j. tar** matelot *m*

▶ **jack around** *Am Sl* VT SEP **to j. sb around** *(treat badly)* se ficher de qn; *(waste time of)* faire perdre son temps à qn

VI *(waste time)* glander, glandouiller

▶ **jack in** VT SEP *Br Sl (job, project, girlfriend)* plaquer, laisser tomber

▶ **jack off** *Vulg* VT SEP **to j. sb off** branler qn

VI se branler, se palucher

▶ **jack up** VT SEP **1** *Aut, Tech* soulever (avec un cric/un vérin) **2** *Fam (increase)* (price, salaries) relever

VI *Br Sl (inject oneself)* s'injecter, se piquer

jackal [ˈdʒækɔːl, -k(ə)l] N *(animal)* chacal *m*

jackaroo [dʒækəruː] N *Austr Fam* = apprenti *m* dans un ranch

jackass [ˈdʒækæs] N **1** *(male donkey)* âne *m*, *Fam* baudet *m* **2** *Fam (person)* idiot, -ote, imbécile *mf* **3** **laughing j.** *(bird)* dacélo *m*

jackboot [ˈdʒækbuːt] N *Mil* botte *f* de cavalier; *Fig* **life under the j. of a military dictatorship** la vie sous la botte de la dictature militaire

jackdaw [ˈdʒækdɔː] N *(bird)* choucas *m*

jacket [ˈdʒækɪt] N **1** *(man's coat)* veste *f*, veston *m*; *(woman's)* veste, jaquette *f* **2** *Culin* **j. potatoes, potatoes cooked in their jackets** pommes *fpl* de terre en robe des champs *ou* en robe de chambre **3** *(of record, computer diskette)* pochette *f*; *(for documents)* chemise *f*, *Tech (of boiler, pipe)* chemise, enveloppe *f*, *(dust)* **j.** *(of book)* jaquette *f*

VT *Tech (cylinder, boiler etc)* garnir *ou* envelopper d'une chemise, chemiser

jackhammer [ˈdʒækhæmər] N marteau-piqueur *m*

jacking point [ˈdʒækɪŋ-] N point *m* de levage, emplacement *m* prévu pour le cric

jack-in-the-box, *pl* **jack-in-the-boxes** N diable *m* à ressort, boîte *f* à surprise(s); *Fam* **to jump up and down like a j.** ne pas tenir en place; **stop jumping up and down like a j.** arrête de sauter dans tous les sens comme ça

jackknife, *pl* **jackknives** [ˈdʒæknaɪf, -naɪvz] N **1** couteau *m* de poche, canif *m* **2** *Swimming (dive)* saut *m* de carpe

VI **1** *Aut (of articulated vehicle)* se mettre en portefeuille **2** *Swimming* faire un saut de carpe

▶▶ *Swimming* **j. dive** saut *m* de carpe

jack-o'-lantern [ˈdʒækəˈlæntən] N *Am (Hallowe'en lantern)* = lanterne *f* faite dans une citrouille sur laquelle on a creusé un visage

jackpot [ˈdʒækpɒt] N **1** *Cards (in poker etc)* pot *m* **2** *(in competition)* gros lot *m*; **to hit or win the j.** gagner le gros lot; *Fig* **to hit the j.** *(be successful)* *(of person)* gagner le gros lot, décrocher la timbale; *(of book, record etc)* faire un malheur *ou* un tabac

jacksie [ˈdʒæksɪ] N *Br Sl (buttocks)* fesses *fpl*, popotin *m*; *(anus)* troufignon *m*

Jacobean [dʒækəˈbɪən] ADJ de l'époque de Jacques 1er (1603-1625); **the J. period** l'époque *f* de Jacques 1er

Jacobite [ˈdʒækəbaɪt] ADJ, N *Hist* jacobite *m*

Jacuzzi® [dʒəˈkuːzɪ] N *(bath, pool)* jacuzzi *m*

jade [dʒeɪd] N **1** *Miner* jade *m* **2** *(colour)* vert jade *m inv*

ADJ **1** *(made of jade)* de *ou* en jade **2** *(colour)* vert jade *inv*

jaded [ˈdʒeɪdɪd] ADJ *(person) (tired)* las, fatigué; *(performance, piece of writing, cliché)* faiblard; **to be or feel j. with sth** être las de qch; **to become j. with sth** se lasser de qch; **I was served a rather j. piece of beef** on m'a servi un morceau de bœuf tout flétri

▶▶ **j. palate** palais *m* blasé; *Fig* appétit *m* fatigué

Jag [dʒæg] N *Fam (Jaguar® car)* Jag *f*

jag [dʒæg] N **1** *Sl (drinking bout)* soûlerie *f*, **to go on a (drinking) j.** se soûler, prendre une cuite **2** *Sl* **to have a crying j.** avoir une crise de larmes **3** *Br Fam (injection)* piquouze *f*

jagged [ˈdʒægɪd] ADJ *(coastline, mountain top)* déchiqueté, découpé; *(edge)* déchiqueté, découpé, dentelé; *(line, tear)* irrégulier; *(knife, blade)* entaillé, ébréché; *(rock)* pointu, dentelé; **the j. outline of the coast** les dentelures *fpl* *ou* découpures *fpl* de la côte

jaggy [ˈdʒægɪ] N *(on printed character)* courbe *f* en escalier

jaguar [*Br* ˈdʒægjʊər, *Am* ˈdʒægwɑːr] N *(animal)* jaguar *m*

jail [dʒeɪl] N *(place, imprisonment)* prison *f*, **to be in j.** être en prison; **to put in j., to send to j.** mettre en prison; **to go to j.** aller en prison, faire de la prison; **he was sent to j. or went to j. for ten years** il a été condamné à dix ans de prison; **she was in j. for ten years, she went to j. for ten years** elle a fait dix ans de prison; **to break out of j.** s'évader de prison; **open j.** prison ouverte

VT mettre en prison, emprisonner; **to j. sb for theft** condamner qn à la prison pour vol; **he was jailed for ten years** il a été condamné à dix ans de prison

jailbait [ˈdʒeɪlbeɪt] N *Sl (girl)* mineure *f* *(avec qui les relations sexuelles sont interdites)*

jailbird [ˈdʒeɪlbɜːd] N *Fam (actually in prison)* taulard, -arde; *(constantly going to prison)* cheval *m* de retour

jailbreak [ˈdʒeɪlbreɪk] N évasion *f* de prison; **to do a j.** s'évader; **to attempt a j.** essayer de s'évader

jailbreaker [ˈdʒeɪlbreɪkər] N évadé, -ée

jailer [ˈdʒeɪlər] N geôlier, -ière

jailhouse, *pl* **jailhouses** [ˈdʒeɪlhaʊs, -haʊzɪz] N *Am* prison *f*

jailor ['dʒeɪlər] N = jailer

Jakarta [dʒə'kɑːtə] N Djakarta

jake [dʒeɪk] N Br Sl (cannabis cigarette) joint m

jalop(p)y [dʒə'lɒpɪ] N Fam (vieille) bagnole f, (vieux) tacot m, (vieille) guimbarde f

jam¹ [dʒæm] N 1 Aut (congestion) bouchon m, embouteillage m, encombrement m

2 (crowd of people) there was a great j. of people outside the theatre il y avait une foule énorme devant le théâtre

3 (in pipe, machine etc) engorgement m; (in printer) bourrage m

4 Fam (difficult situation) to be in/get into a (bit of a) j. être/se mettre dans le pétrin; to get out of/get sb out of a j. se tirer/tirer qn du pétrin

5 Mus Fam bœuf m, jam-session m, pl jam-sessions

vt (-mm-) 1 (pack, cram) (en)tasser (into dans); (thrust, put forcefully) enfoncer, fourrer (into dans); it had been jammed with goodies il avait été rempli à ras bords de bonnes choses; to j. one's foot on the brake(s) écraser le frein ou la pédale de frein

2 (squeeze, wedge) coincer; she got her hand jammed or she jammed her hand in the drawer elle s'est coincé la main dans le tiroir; to j. a door open with a book maintenir une porte ouverte à l'aide d'un livre

3 (immobilize, stop from working) (window, shutter etc) coincer, bloquer; (weapon, mechanism) enrayer, bloquer; (pipe) boucher; the drawer is jammed le tiroir est coincé ou bloqué; to be jammed in the ice être bloqué par les glaces

4 (of people, vehicles) (street, corridor etc) encombrer, bloquer; (building, town) envahir; the hall was jammed (with people) people jammed the hall la salle était pleine à craquer ou bondée

5 Radio (broadcast, station) brouiller

6 Tel (of calls etc) (lines) encombrer; (switchboard) faire sauter; the switchboard was jammed le standard était saturé

vi 1 (of drawer, window, lift etc) se coincer, se bloquer; (of gun, machine) s'enrayer, se bloquer; (of brake, wheel, paper in printer) se bloquer 2 (crowd) s'entasser (into dans)

▶ jam in vt sep 1 (wedge in) coincer; the crowd was jamming him in il était coincé par la foule; her car was being jammed in by a large truck un gros camion était en train de la coincer 2 (pack or press tightly in) (passengers etc) (en)tasser; (objects) bourrer; he had jammed as many quotations as he could find into the essay il avait farci sa dissertation de toutes les citations qu'il avait trouvées

vi (crowd in) s'entasser; they all jammed in (into train) ils s'y entassèrent tous; we won't all be able to j. in at once nous n'allons jamais tous tenir à la fois

▶ jam on vt sep 1 Aut to j. on the brakes écraser le frein ou la pédale de frein 2 (put on forcefully or solidly) (lid, hat etc) enfoncer

▶▶ Mus Fam j. session bœuf m, jam-session f, pl jam-sessions

jam² N Culin confiture f; strawberry j. confiture de fraises; Br Fig what do you want, j. on it? ça ne te suffit pas?, que veux-tu de plus?; j. jar pot m de confiture(s)

▶▶ j. jar pot à confiture; Br Fam Hum j. sandwich (police car) voiture f de police; j. tart tarte f à la confiture

Jamaica [dʒə'meɪkə] N Jamaïque f

Jamaican [dʒə'meɪkən] ADJ jamaïquain, jamaïcain, de la Jamaïque

N Jamaïquain, -aine, Jamaïcain, -aine

jamb [dʒæm] N (side post) (of door, window, chimney) chambranle m, jambage m, montant m

jamboree [dʒæmbə'riː] N 1 (scouts' meeting) jamboree m 2 Fam (celebration, party) fête f, réunion f; (festivities) réjouissances fpl (tapageuses); village j. fête f de village

jammies ['dʒæmɪz] NPL (in children's language) pyjama m

jamming ['dʒæmɪŋ] N 1 Radio brouillage m (délibéré) 2 Tel (of lines) encombrement m

jammy ['dʒæmɪ] ADJ 1 (covered with jam) plein de confiture 2 Br Fam (lucky) veinard, verni; he's a j. devil quel veinard, celui-là!, il est verni, celui-là! 3 Br Fam (easy) facile; j. job filon m, bonne planque f

jam-packed ['dʒæm'pækt] ADJ (suitcase, bag etc) plein à craquer, bourré (with de); j. (with people) (hall, bus etc) plein à craquer, bondé; (street) noir de monde, bondé; this magazine is j. with interesting articles ce magazine est truffé ou regorge d'articles intéressants

jams [dʒæmz] NPL Am (shorts) bermuda m

Jan abbr January

Jane [dʒeɪn] N Am Sl (woman) nana f

▶▶ Am J. Doe (average person) l'Américaine f moyenne, ≃ Madame Dupont; (unidentified woman under arrest) inconnue f; (corpse) morte f non identifiée

jangle ['dʒæŋg(ə)l] N (of metal objects, keys etc) cliquetis m; (of bell) bruit m discordant

vi (of metal objects, keys etc) cliqueter; (of bells) retentir d'un bruit discordant; it jangled on my nerves cela me mettait les nerfs en pelote

vt 1 (keys etc) faire cliqueter; (bells) faire retentir d'un bruit discordant 2 (upset) jangled nerves nerfs en pelote

jangling ['dʒæŋg(ə)lɪŋ] N = jangle N

janitor ['dʒænɪtər] N Am, Scot (caretaker) concierge mf

January ['dʒænjʊərɪ] VOIR GRAMMAIRE A81–2; 860–2 janvier m; in J. au mois de janvier, en janvier; (on) the first/the seventh of J. le premier/le sept janvier

Jap [dʒæp] Offensive Fam N Japonais, -aise

ADJ japonais

Japan [dʒə'pæn] N Japon m

Japanese [dʒæpə'niːz] ADJ japonais; (embassy, ambassador, history) du Japon; (teacher, lesson, dictionary) de japonais

N 1 Japonais, -aise; the J. les Japonais mpl 2 Ling japonais m

▶▶ J. lantern lanterne f vénitienne

jape [dʒeɪp] N Old-fashioned tour m, blague f; to play japes on sb jouer des tours à qn, faire des blagues à qn

japonica [dʒə'pɒnɪkə] N Bot cognassier m du Japon

jar¹ [dʒɑːr] N (jolt, shock), Fig choc m, secousse f; his fall/the news gave him a nasty j. sa chute/la nouvelle l'a fortement ébranlé ou beaucoup secoué; he gave his wrist a j. when he fell il s'est cogné le poignet en tombant

vi (-rr-) 1 (make an unpleasant sound) rendre un son discordant; Mus (of note) détonner 2 (of colours, furniture) détonner, jurer (with avec); (of ideas, styles, remarks) détonner, être incompatible, ne pas s'accorder (with avec); to j. (with each other) (of colours, ideas) se heurter, détonner; to j. on sb's feelings froisser qn

vt (window pane, building) ébranler; (table, microphone) faire bouger; (wrist, ankle etc) se cogner; (of news) ébranler, secouer; someone jarred my elbow quelqu'un m'a cogné le coude

▶ jar on, jar upon vt insep (of noise) (the ears) écorcher; his voice jars (up)on my nerves sa voix me tape sur les nerfs ou me crispe

jar² N 1 (container) pot m; (for storing oil etc) jarre f, (glass) j. pot m; (large) bocal m 2 Br Fam (beer) pot m; to have a j. prendre un pot; we had a few jars on a pris un pot ou deux

jargon ['dʒɑːgən] N Pej (specialized language) jargon m; legal j. jargon juridique, langage m du Palais; to talk (in) j. parler en jargon, jargonner

jarring ['dʒɑːrɪŋ] ADJ 1 (noise, voice etc) discordant; Mus (note) qui détonne; Fig (incident, behaviour) qui produit une sensation désagréable 2 (blow) qui ébranle tout le corps

jasmine ['dʒæzmɪn, 'dʒæs-] N (shrub) (common or white) j. jasmin m (commun ou blanc); winter j. jasmin d'hiver; j. perfume (essence f de) jasmin

▶▶ j. tea thé m au jasmin

jaundice ['dʒɔːndɪs] N 1 Med jaunisse f, ictère m 2 Fig (bitterness) amertume f

jaundiced ['dʒɔːndɪst] ADJ 1 Med ictérique, bilieux 2 Fig (bitter) aigri, amer; (jealous) jaloux; to look on the world or on things with a j. eye (bitterly) voir tout en noir; (jealously) tout regarder d'un œil jaloux; to take a j. view of a situation voir une situation d'un mauvais œil

jaunt [dʒɔːnt] N (petite) excursion f, balade f, sortie f; on a j. en excursion, en balade; to go on or for a j. faire une (petite) excursion ou une balade

jauntily ['dʒɔːntɪlɪ] ADV (to remark) (casually) d'une manière désinvolte, avec désinvolture; (cheerfully) gaiement, avec entrain, d'un air enjoué; (to walk) d'un pas guilleret; (to wear one's hat) d'une façon désinvolte; (of woman, stylishly) coquettement

jauntiness ['dʒɔːntɪnɪs] N (carefreeness) désinvolture f, insouciance f; (cheerfulness) enjouement m, vivacité f; the j. of his step son pas guilleret

jaunty ['dʒɔːntɪ] ADJ (carefree) désinvolte, insouciant, dégagé; (cheerful, lively) enjoué; with a j. air d'un air dégagé; j. step pas m guilleret; he wore his cap at a j. angle sa casquette était négligemment posée sur sa tête

Java ['dʒɑːvə] N 1 Geog (île f de) Java f 2 Comput Java® Java® m

▶▶ Comput J. script Javascript® m, langage m Javascript®

java ['dʒɑːvə] N Am Fam (coffee) caoua m, café m

Javanese [dʒɑːvə'niːz] ADJ javanais

N 1 Javanais, -aise; the J. les Javanais mpl 2 Ling javanais m

javelin ['dʒævlɪn] N (weapon), Sport javelot m; Sport the j. (event) l'épreuve f de javelot

▶▶ j. thrower lanceur, -euse de javelot; j. throwing lancement m du javelot

jaw [dʒɔː] N 1 Anat mâchoire f; the lion opened its jaws le lion a ouvert la gueule; Fig her j. dropped (in surprise) elle en est restée bouche bée, les bras lui en sont tombés; Fig to set one's j. (show determination) décider de s'accrocher

2 Fig the jaws of a valley/cave l'entrée f d'une vallée/grotte; the jaws of a volcano la bouche d'un volcan; the jaws of hell les portes fpl de l'enfer; to snatch sb from the jaws of death/the enemy arracher qn des griffes de la mort/de l'ennemi

3 (of pincer, wrench etc) mâchoire f, mors m

4 Fam (moralizing talk) sermon m; to have a (good) j. tailler une bavette, bavarder; he's all j. and no action il parle beaucoup, mais au moment d'agir …

vi Fam (chat) bavarder (about de); (moralize) prêcher, moraliser; she's been jawing away on the phone all morning elle n'a pas arrêté de papoter au téléphone de toute la matinée

jawbone ['dʒɔːbəʊn] **N** (os m) maxillaire m, mâchoire f

jawbreaker ['dʒɔːbreɪkər] **N 1** *Fam (word)* mot m imprononçable; *(name)* nom m à coucher dehors **2** *(sweet)* bonbon m (très dur)

-jawed [dʒɔːd] **suff** round/long/etc-j. à la mâchoire ronde/allongée/etc; *Boxing etc Fam* glass-j. à la mâchoire fragile

jay [dʒeɪ] **N** *(bird)* geai m (des chênes); **blue j.** geai bleu

jaywalk ['dʒeɪwɔːk] **VI** = traverser la rue d'une manière imprudente ou en dehors des passages pour piétons

jaywalker ['dʒeɪwɔːkər] **N** = piéton m qui traverse en dehors des passages cloutés

jaywalking ['dʒeɪwɔːkɪŋ] **N** = fait de traverser en dehors des passages cloutés

Jaz® [dʒæz] **N**
▸▸ *Comput* J. disk cartouche f Jaz®; **J. drive** lecteur m Jaz®

jazz [dʒæz] **N 1** *Mus* jazz m; **2** *Am Sl (talk)* baratin m; **she gave me a lot of j. about it** elle m'a fait tout un baratin là-dessus; **what's (all) this j. about your leaving?** qu'est-ce que c'est que cette histoire comme quoi tu t'en vas? **3** *Sl* **and all that j.** et tout le tremblement *ou* bazar
▸▸ **the J. Age** = l'âge m d'or du jazz américain; **j. band** orchestre m de jazz
▸ **jazz up VT SEP** *Fam* **1** *Mus* adapter pour le jazz **2** *Fig (enliven) (clothes, room, style)* égayer; *(party)* animer, mettre de l'entrain dans; *(taste)* relever; *(building)* retaper

jazzy ['dʒæzɪ] **ADJ** *Fam (tune)* aux rythmes jazz; *Fig (flashy)* tapageur, voyant; *(non-pejorative sense)* sympa

JCB® [dʒeɪsiː'biː] **N** *Br* = pelle f hydraulique automotrice

jealous ['dʒeləs] **ADJ 1** *(fearful of rivals)* jaloux, -ouse; **a j. woman** une femme jalouse, une jalouse; **I don't see why you're getting so j.** je ne sais pas pourquoi tu fais une telle crise de jalousie **2** *(envious)* jaloux (**of** de); **to be j. of sb** être jaloux de qn, jalouser qn **3** *(vigilant, possessive)* jaloux (**of** de); **with a j. eye** d'un œil jaloux; **j. of one's good name** jaloux de sa réputation

jealously ['dʒeləslɪ] **ADV 1** *(enviously)* jalousement, avec jalousie **2** *(vigilantly)* avec un soin jaloux; **a j. guarded secret** un secret jalousement gardé

jealousy ['dʒeləsɪ] **N** jalousie f

jeans [dʒiːnz] **NPL** **(pair of) j.** jean(s) m(pl); **blue j.** blue-jean m

Jeep® [dʒiːp] **N** *Aut* jeep® f

jeepers (creepers) ['dʒiːpəz('kriːpəz)] **INT** *Old-fashioned Am Fam* ça alors!

jeer [dʒɪər] **N** raillerie f, moquerie f; **the jeers of the crowd** *(boos)* les huées fpl de la foule
VI *(boo)* huer, conspuer; *(mock)* railler
VT **to j. sb** *(boo)* huer qn, conspuer qn; *(mock)* se moquer de qn, railler qn
▸ **jeer at VT INSEP** = **jeer VT**

jeering ['dʒɪərɪŋ] **ADJ** railleur, moqueur; *(laughter)* moqueur
N railleries fpl, moqueries fpl; *(shouts)* cris mpl railleurs *ou* moqueurs; *(of crowd)* huées fpl

jeez [dʒiːz] **INT** *Fam* mon Dieu!

Jehovah [dʒɪ'həʊvə] **N** *Bible* Jéhovah; *Rel* J.'s **Witness** témoin m de Jéhovah

jejune [dʒɪ'dʒuːn] **ADJ** *Lit* naïf, f naïve

jejunum [dʒɪ'dʒuːnəm] **N** *Anat* jéjunum m

Jekyll and Hyde [dʒekələnd'haɪd] **N** **he's a (real) J.** c'est un vrai docteur Jekyll; **to have a J. personality** faire un dédoublement de la personnalité

jell [dʒel] **VI 1** *(of liquid)* se gélifier, prendre (en gelée) **2** *Fig (of ideas)* prendre corps *ou* forme; *(of plans)* prendre tournure *ou* forme *ou* corps; *(of team, cabinet)* parvenir à la cohésion; **they have jelled very well** ils sont parvenus à une excellente cohésion

jellied ['dʒelɪd] **ADJ** *Culin (eel etc)* en gelée

jello® ['dʒeləʊ] **N** *Am Culin* gelée f

jelly ['dʒelɪ] **N 1** gelée f; **my knees were like j.** j'avais les jambes en coton **2** *Br Culin (dessert)* gelée f **3** *Am Culin (aspic)* confiture f **4** *Br Sl (gelignite)* dynamite f
VT *Culin* gélifier, mettre en gelée
▸▸ *Br* **j. baby** bonbon m gélifié *(en forme de bébé)*; *Am* **j. roll** (gâteau m) roulé m

jellybean ['dʒelɪbiːn] **N** bonbon m mou *(couvert de sucre dur et en forme de haricot)*

jellyfish, pl **jellyfish** or **jellyfishes** ['dʒelɪfɪʃ] **N** méduse f

jemmy ['dʒemɪ] *Br* **N** *(burglar's)* j. pince-monseigneur, fpl pinces-monseigneur
VT **to j. a door (open)** forcer une porte à la pince-monseigneur

jenny ['dʒenɪ] **N** *(female bird or animal)* j. **wren** roitelet m femelle; **j. donkey** ânesse f

jeopardize ['dʒepədaɪz] **VT** *(health, future, sb's business)* compromettre, mettre en danger *ou* en péril; *(chances, career)* compromettre; *(one's business)* laisser péricliter

jeopardy ['dʒepədɪ] **N** danger m, péril m; **to be in j.** *(of person, one's life)* être en danger *ou* en péril; *(of one's happiness, career, future etc)* être menacé *ou* compromis; **his business is in j.** son affaire périclite; **to put in j.** *(health, future, sb's life)* compromettre, mettre en danger *ou* en péril; *(chances, career)* compromettre; *(one's business)* laisser péricliter; **to put sb in j.** mettre qn en danger *ou* en péril

jerbil ['dʒɜːbɪl] **N** *(rodent)* gerbille f

jerk[1] [dʒɜːk] **N 1** *(sudden pull, push etc)* secousse f, saccade f, coup m sec; **she gave the rope a j.** elle a donné une secousse à la corde, elle a tiré un coup sec sur la corde; **to move by jerks** *or* **in jerks** *or* **in a series of jerks** *(of vehicle etc)* avancer par saccades *ou* par à-coups, cahoter
2 *(sudden start, jump)* sursaut m; **to wake up with a j.** se réveiller en sursaut
3 *Sport (in weightlifting)* jeté m
VT *(pull, push etc suddenly)* donner une secousse *ou* une saccade à; *(repeatedly)* donner des secousses *ou* des saccades à, secouer; *(pull)* tirer d'un coup sec; **they jerked the washing machine across the floor** ils ont déplacé la machine à laver à travers la pièce par à-coups; **to j. sth out of sb's hands** arracher qch (d'un coup sec) des mains de qn; **to j. forward/back** *(of collision etc) (sb's head, body)* rejeter en avant/en arrière; **she jerked her head** *(in car crash etc)* sa tête a été rejetée en arrière
VI 1 *(shake)* secouer; **to j. (along** *or* **forward)** *(of vehicle)* avancer par saccades *ou* par à-coups, cahoter; **to j. forward/back** *(of head, body)* être rejeté en avant/en arrière; **she jerked forward then slid back** elle se jeta en avant puis se glissa vers l'arrière; **to j. to a halt** *(of vehicle, train)* s'arrêter brusquement (avec des secousses)
2 *(start, jump)* sursauter
3 *(of muscle)* se contracter, avoir un spasme/des spasmes; *Anat* avoir un réflexe *ou* des réflexes
▸ **jerk off** *Vulg* **VT SEP** **to j. sb off** branler qn
VI se branler
▸ **jerk out VT SEP** *(words, excuses etc)* balbutier, dire d'une façon saccadée

jerk[2] **N** *Fam Pej (fool)* crétin, -ine, abruti, -ie; *(obnoxious person)* con(n)ard m; **don't be a j.** ne fais pas le con

jerkily ['dʒɜːkɪlɪ] **ADV** *(to move)* par saccades, par à-coups; *(to walk)* d'un pas saccadé; *(to write, speak)* d'une manière saccadée *ou* hâchée

jerky ['dʒɜːkɪ] **ADJ** *(movement)* saccadé; *(voice, style, speech etc)* saccadé, heurté, hâché; **he took his first j. steps at the age of ten months** il a fait ses premiers pas un peu saccadés à l'âge de dix mois; **in j. French** dans un français heurté *ou* hâché

jerrican ['dʒerɪkæn] **N** jerrycan m, bidon m

Jerry ['dʒerɪ] **N** *Old-fashioned Fam Pej (soldier)* Boche m, Fritz m; *(the Germans)* les Boches

jerry-built ['dʒerɪbɪlt] **ADJ** *Pej (house)* en carton-pâte, construit comme une cabane à lapins

jerry can N = **jerrican**

Jersey ['dʒɜːzɪ] **N 1** *(island)* Jersey f; **in J.** à Jersey **2** *(cow)* vache f de Jersey *ou* jersiaise

jersey ['dʒɜːzɪ] **N 1** *(garment)* tricot m (de laine); *Sport* maillot m **2** *(material)* jersey m; **j. wool/silk, wool/silk j.** jersey de laine/ de soie

Jerusalem [dʒə'ruːsələm] **N** Jérusalem mf
▸▸ *Bot, Culin* J. **artichoke** topinambour m

jessie ['dʒesɪ] **N** *Scot Fam (feeble man)* mauviette f; **stop pretending you're hurt, you big j.!** arrête de faire semblant d'avoir mal, espèce de mauviette!

jest [dʒest] **N** *(joke)* plaisanterie f, *(witty remark)* mot m d'esprit; **in j.** *(to say, speak etc)* en plaisantant, pour rire, par plaisanterie; **(only) half in j.** en ne plaisantant qu'à moitié; **to act in j.** plaisanter; *Prov* **(there is) many a true word spoken in j.** on dit souvent la vérité sous le couvert d'une plaisanterie
VI *(joke)* plaisanter (**about** sur); *(make witty remarks)* faire des mots d'esprit; **he's not a person to j. with** on ne plaisante pas ou on ne badine pas avec lui

jester ['dʒestər] **N** *(joker)* farceur, -euse; *Hist* **(court) j.** bouffon m *ou* fou m (du roi)

jesting ['dʒestɪŋ] **ADJ** *(remark etc)* fait pour plaisanter *ou* pour rire
N *(jokes)* plaisanteries fpl; *(witty remarks)* mots mpl d'esprit

jestingly ['dʒestɪŋlɪ] **ADV** en plaisantant; **j. known as …** désigné par le terme farceur de …

Jesuit ['dʒezjʊɪt] **N** *Rel, Fig Pej* jésuite m
ADJ *Rel (missionary, theologian)* jésuite; *(college, seminary)* de jésuites

Jesuitical [dʒezjʊ'ɪtɪk(ə)l] **ADJ** *Fig Pej* jésuitique

Jesus ['dʒiːzəs] **N** Jésus m; *Rel* **J. Christ** Jésus-Christ m
INT *Sl* **J. (Christ)!** nom de Dieu!; *Br* **J. wept!** bon sang!; *Am* **J. Holy Christ** nom de Dieu!
▸▸ *Fam* **J. freak** chrétien, -ienne hippie

jet[1] [dʒet] **N 1** *(aircraft)* avion m à réaction, jet m; **to travel by j.** voyager en jet *ou* en avion à réaction; *Mil* **fighter j.** chasseur m à réaction **2** *(of liquid, steam etc)* jet m **3** *(nozzle)* jet m, ajutage m, buse f; *(on printer)* buse; *(of stove)* brûleur m; *Aut* gicleur m; **(water) j.** *(in whirlpool, bath etc)* gicleur
VI (-tt-) **1** *(of liquid)* sortir en jet, gicler **2** *Aviat Fam* voyager en jet *ou* en avion à réaction; **she jets round the world** elle parcourt le monde en jet
▸▸ **j. engine** moteur m à réaction; *Mil* **j. fighter** chasseur à réaction; **j. fuel** kérosène m; **j. lag** = fatigue f due au décalage horaire; **I'm still suffering from j. lag** je suis encore sous le coup du décalage horaire; **j. plane** avion m à réaction; **j. propulsion** propulsion f par réaction; *Fam* **j. set** jet-set m *ou* f, **j. ski** scooter m des mers, jet-ski m; **j. stream** jet-stream m, pl jet-streams, courant-jet m, pl courants-jets; **j. trail** traînée f de condensation

▶jet in VI arriver par avion

▶jet off VI s'envoler (**to** pour)

jet² N Miner jais m

ADJ (colour) noir comme (du) jais, (noir) de jais

▶▶**j. black** noir m de jais

jetfoil ['dʒetfɔɪl] N hydroglisseur m

jet-lagged ['dʒetlægd] ADJ fatigué à cause du décalage horaire; **in my current j. state** fatigué comme je le suis (à cause du décalage horaire)

jet-powered [dʒet'paʊəd], **jet-propelled** [dʒetprə'peld] ADJ (engine, aircraft) à réaction

jetsam ['dʒetsəm] N (no pl) Naut, Fig épaves fpl

jetsetter ['dʒetsetər] N membre m de la jet-set

jet-skiing N scooter m des mers, jet-ski m

jettison ['dʒetɪs(ə)n] VT Naut (cargo) jeter à la mer ou par-dessus bord, se délester de; Aviat (bombs, fuel etc) larguer; Fig (hope, plan, tradition etc) abandonner, renoncer à

jetty ['dʒetɪ] N 1 (breakwater) jetée f, môle m 2 (for landing) embarcadère m, débarcadère m, appontement m

Jew [dʒuː] N Juif m, Juive f, Mus J.'s harp guimbarde f

Jew-baiting ['dʒuːbeɪtɪŋ] N persécution f des Juifs

jewel ['dʒuːəl] N 1 (piece of jewellery) bijou m, joyau m; (gem) pierre f précieuse; Fig (person) perle f, (thing of value) perle, bijou 2 (of watch) rubis m

▶▶**j. box** coffret m à bijoux; **j. case** (for gems) coffret à bijoux; (for compact disc) coffret

jewelled, Am **jeweled** ['dʒuːəld] ADJ (tiara, brooch) orné de pierres précieuses; (watch) monté sur rubis

jeweller, Am **jeweler** ['dʒuːələr] N bijoutier, -ière, joaillier, -ière; **j.'s (shop)** bijouterie f, bijouterie-joaillerie f

jewellery, Am **jewelry** ['dʒuːəlrɪ] N bijoux mpl, joyaux mpl; **a piece of j.** un bijou

Jewess ['dʒuːes, -ɪs] N Juive f

Jewish ['dʒuːɪʃ] ADJ juif, f juive

Jewry ['dʒuːərɪ] N la communauté juive, les Juifs mpl

JFK [dʒeɪef'keɪ] N 1 abbr John F. Kennedy 2 = aéroport m de New York

jib [dʒɪb] N 1 Naut (sail) foc m 2 Tech (of crane, derrick) flèche f, bras m 3 Old-fashioned Fig **I don't like the cut of his j.** son allure ne me plaît guère

VI (-bb-) 1 (of person) se rebiffer, regimber, rechigner (**at sth** devant qch); **to j. at doing** rechigner à faire 2 (of horse) regimber, se dérober

jibe¹ [dʒaɪb] N, VI = gibe

jibe² VI Am (agree) s'accorder (**with** avec)

jiffy ['dʒɪfɪ] N Fam **to do sth in a j.** faire qch en un rien de temps ou en moins de deux; **in (half) a j.** en un instant, en un clin d'œil; **I'll be back/there in a j.!** je reviens/j'arrive tout de suite ou dans un instant!

▶▶**J. bag**® enveloppe f ou pochette f matelassée

jig [dʒɪg] N (dance, music) gigue f

VI (-gg-) 1 (dance) danser la gigue 2 (shake) **to j. up and down), to j. about** or **around** se trémousser (en dansant), sautiller

jigger¹ ['dʒɪgər] N (measure for whisky) = 42 ml

jigger² VT Fam (damage) esquinter

jiggered ['dʒɪgəd] ADJ Br 1 Old-fashioned (surprised) étonné; **well I'm j.!, well, I'll be j.!** zut alors!; **I'm** or **I'll be j. if …** (confounded) que le diable m'emporte si … 2 Old-fashioned Sl (tired) crevé, claqué 3 Fam

(broken) (TV etc) naze, déglingué, foutu; **my ankle/back is j.** je me suis niqué la cheville/le dos

jiggery-pokery ['dʒɪgərɪ'pəʊkərɪ] N Br Fam manigances fpl, micmacs mpl; **there was some sort of j. going on** il y avait des manigances ou des micmacs dans l'air

jiggle ['dʒɪg(ə)l] VT **to j. (about** or **around)** remuer légèrement

VI **to j. (about** or **around)** être légèrement secoué; (of earrings) se balancer; **try not to let it j. about** fais en sorte qu'il ne soit pas trop secoué; **I can feel something jiggling about** je sens quelque chose qui remue; **her breasts j. when she runs** ses seins ballottent quand elle court; **stop jiggling about!** arrête de gigoter!

jiggy ['dʒɪgɪ] ADJ esp Am Fam **to get j. (with it)** (have sex) s'envoyer en l'air

jigsaw ['dʒɪgsɔː] N 1 Carp scie f à chantourner 2 (game) puzzle m; Fig **the pieces of the j. were beginning to fall into place** peu à peu tout devenait clair

▶▶**j. puzzle** puzzle m

jihad [dʒɪ'hæd] N (Muslim holy war) djihad m

jilt [dʒɪlt] VT (lover, girlfriend etc) laisser tomber, Fam plaquer

jimjams ['dʒɪmdʒæmz] NPL Fam 1 pyjama m 2 Hum **to have the j.** (fear) avoir les chocottes; (revulsion) avoir la chair de poule; (anxiety) avoir les nerfs en pelote

jimmy ['dʒɪmɪ] N, VT Am = jemmy

jingle ['dʒɪŋg(ə)l] N 1 (of bells) tintement m; (of keys etc) tintement, cliquetis m; (of spurs) cliquetis 2 (catchy tune) ritournelle f, (for children) comptine f, Radio, TV (in advertisement) jingle m

VI (of bells) tinter, tintinnabuler; (of keys, coins etc) tinter, cliqueter

VT (coins, keys etc) faire tinter ou cliqueter; (bells) faire tinter ou tintinnabuler

jingling ['dʒɪŋglɪŋ] N = jingle N 1

ADJ **j. sound** (of bells) tintement m; (of keys) cliquetis m

jingo ['dʒɪŋgəʊ] N Old-fashioned Fam chauvin, -ine; **by j.!** nom d'une pipe!

jingoism ['dʒɪŋgəʊɪz(ə)m] N Pej chauvinisme m

jingoistic ['dʒɪŋgəʊ'ɪstɪk] ADJ Pej chauvin

jinks [dʒɪŋks] NPL Fam **high j.** la rigolade; **we had high j.** on a eu une séance de rigolade, on s'est bien marrés; **stop the high j.!** trêve de rigolade!; **that's enough high j. for today** assez rigolé pour aujourd'hui; Iron **there'll be high j. when my parents find out** ça va barder ou chauffer quand mes parents l'apprendront

jinx [dʒɪŋks] Fam N (person, object) porte-malheur m inv, porte-guigne m inv; (spell, curse) maléfice m, (mauvais) sort m; (bad luck) guigne f; **to have a j.** avoir la guigne; **to put a j. on** porter la guigne à; **to break the j.** échapper à la guigne

VT Fam (usually passive) (person, project etc) porter la guigne à; **to be jinxed** avoir la guigne

JIT [dʒeɪaɪ'tiː] ADJ Com (abbr just-in-time) juste à temps, JAT

▶▶**J. distribution** distribution f JAT; **J. manufacturing** production f JAT; **J. production** production JAT; **J. purchasing** achat m JAT

jitterbug ['dʒɪtəbʌg] N (dance) jitterbug m

VI (-gg-) danser le jitterbug

jitters ['dʒɪtəz] NPL Fam **the j.** (anxiety) la frousse, la trouille; **to have** or **get the j.** avoir la frousse (**about** de); **she's got the j. about her exam** elle a la trouille à cause de son examen; **it gives me the j.** ça me fiche la trouille ou la frousse

jittery ['dʒɪtərɪ] ADJ Fam (anxious) (très)

nerveux; **to be j., to get j.** avoir la frousse, être (très) nerveux

jiujitsu [dʒuː'dʒɪtsuː] N jiu-jitsu m

jive [dʒaɪv] N 1 (music, dance) swing m 2 Am Sl (deceiving talk) baratin m; (foolish talk) foutaises fpl 3 (slang) **j. (talk)** = argot m des musiciens de jazz noirs américains de Harlem dans les années trente

VI 1 (dance) danser le swing 2 Am Sl (talk nonsense) déconner

VT Am Sl (mislead) baratiner

jive-ass ADJ Am Sl à la noix

Jnr (abbr junior) Jr

Joan [dʒəʊn] N Jeanne f; **J. of Arc** Jeanne d'Arc

joanna [dʒəʊ'ænə] N Br Sl piano m

Job [dʒəʊb] N Job m; **to have the patience of J.** avoir la patience d'un ange; **you're a J.'s comforter** vous n'êtes pas d'un grand réconfort

---

JOB [dʒɒb]

N travail 1–3, 6 ▪ tâche 1 ▪ emploi 3 ▪ mal 4
VI faire des petits travaux 1 ▪ travailler à la tâche 2

N 1 (piece of work, task) travail m, tâche f; **to do its j.** (of medicine, alcohol etc) faire son effet; **to do the j.** faire l'affaire; **if that ointment doesn't do the j.** si cette pommade n'a pas d'effet; **the garage/hairdresser did a good j. on her** le garage/coiffeur a fait un bon travail; **to make a good** or **successful j. of sth** bien réussir qch; **it's quite a (difficult) j.** c'est tout un travail (**to do** sth que de faire qch); Fig **to lie down** or **fall down on the j.** (avoid working) tirer au flanc; **on a j.** en déplacement; Fam **to be on the j.** (sexually) faire une partie de jambes en l'air; **this shelf isn't strong** or **good enough for the j.** cette étagère ne tiendra pas le coup; **to do odd jobs** faire des petits travaux, bricoler à droite et à gauche; Ind **it's a precision j.** c'est un travail de précision; Fam **the car has had a paint j.** la bagnole a été repeinte; **he's done a good j. of work** il a fait du bon boulot

2 (responsibility, duty) travail m; **they are only doing their j.** ils ne font que leur travail; **I was given the j. of breaking the bad news** c'est à moi que la tâche est revenue ou c'est moi qui ai été chargé d'annoncer la mauvaise nouvelle; **it's my j. to …** je suis chargé de …, c'est mon travail de …; **it's my j. to remind her** c'est à moi de le lui rappeler; **that's not your j.** ce n'est pas votre travail, ce n'est pas à vous de faire ça; **I make it my j. to …** je me charge de …; **I'll have the j. of clearing it all up later** c'est moi qui serai obligé de ranger ou qui devrai ranger tout ça plus tard; **this muscle has the j. of …** le rôle de ce muscle est de …; **that's not part of his j.** ça n'entre pas dans ses fonctions, ça ne fait pas partie de son travail ou de ses attributions

3 (employment, post) emploi m, travail m, Fam boulot m, Fam job m; **to create (new) jobs** créer des emplois, créer de nouveaux emplois; **she knows her j.** elle connaît son travail ou son affaire ou son métier ou Fam son boulot; **to give up one's j., to resign from one's j.** démissionner; Ind etc **500 jobs were lost** or **axed** il y a eu 500 suppressions d'emplois, 500 emplois ou postes ont été supprimés; **it's more than my j. is worth** ça serait risquer de perdre mon emploi, ça ne vaut pas la peine de perdre mon emploi pour ça; **on-the-j. training** formation f sur le tas; **to be out of a j.** être sans travail; Br Fam **to give jobs to the boys** placer ses copains; **it's jobs for the boys** les boulots vont directement aux copains

4 (difficulty, trouble) **to have (quite) a j.** or **a**

difficult j. doing *or* to do sth avoir du mal à faire qch; **it was quite a j. getting her to come at all** ça a déjà été difficile de la convaincre de venir; *Fam* **she had the devil** *or Sl* **a hell of a j. doing it** elle a eu tout le mal du monde *ou* un mal de tous les diables *ou* un mal fou à faire cela; *Fam* **they've got a real j. on their hands with that baby** ils ont du pain sur la planche avec ce bébé; **it's a j. and a half** c'est un sacré boulot (**doing** pour faire)

5 *Sl (crime)* coup *m*; **to do a j.** monter un coup; **they did that bank j.** ils ont monté le coup de la banque

6 *Comput* travail *m*; **j. control** gestion *f* des travaux

7 *Fam (manufactured object)* **that TV is a really nice j.** cette télé, c'est du beau travail; **his car is the red j. parked on the corner** sa voiture, c'est le bel engin rouge qui est garé au coin; **a souped-up j.** *(car or motorcycle)* une bagnole/une moto au moteur gonflé

8 *Br Fam (excrement)* caca *m*; **the baby has done a big j.** le bébé a fait un gros caca

9 *Fig (phrases)* *Br* **it's** *or* **what a good j. (that) …!** heureusement que … + *ind*, c'est heureux que … + *sub*, *Br Fam* **he got what he deserved, (and) a good j. too!** il a eu ce qu'il méritait, et c'est tant mieux *ou* c'est bien fait pour lui *ou* j'en suis très heureux!; **that's just the j.** c'est exactement ce qu'il faut; *Fam* **to do a j. on a car** *(wreck)* bousiller une voiture; *Fam* **to do a j. on sb** *(beat up)* tabasser qn; **that journalist did a real j. on him** ce journaliste l'a descendu en flammes *ou* vraiment soigné; **the make-up department did a good j. (on him)** les maquilleurs se sont surpassés

vi (**-bb-**) **1** *(do small jobs)* faire des petits travaux, bricoler

2 *(do piecework)* travailler à la tâche *ou* à la pièce

▸▸ **j. creation** création *f* d'emplois; **j. creation scheme** programme *m* de création d'emplois; **j. description** description *f* de poste; *Admin* **j. evaluation** analyse *f* des postes; **j. hunter** demandeur, -euse d'emploi; **j. hunting** recherche *f* d'un emploi; **to go j. hunting** aller à la recherche d'un emploi; **j. losses** suppressions *fpl* d'emplois; *Br Com* **j. lot** lot *m*; **a j. lot of books** des livres en vrac, un lot de livres; **to buy/sell sth as a j. lot** acheter/vendre qch en lot *ou* en vrac; **j. offer** offre *f* d'emploi; **j. opportunities** perspectives *fpl* d'emploi, débouchés *mpl*; **j. satisfaction** satisfaction *f* professionnelle; **j. security** sécurité *f* de l'emploi; **j. seeker** demandeur, -euse d'emploi; **j. sharing** partage *m* d'emploi; **j. title** titre *m* (de fonction)

jobbery ['dʒɒbərɪ] **N** *Br Fam* micmacs *mpl*, trafics *mpl*

jobbing ['dʒɒbɪŋ] *Br* **ADJ** *(worker)* (qui travaille) à la tâche *ou* à la pièce; **j. gardener** jardinier, -ière à la journée

N 1 *(piecework)* travail *m* à la tâche *ou* à la pièce **2** *(odd jobs)* bricolage *m*

Jobcentre ['dʒɒbsentər] **N** *Br* ≃ agence *f* nationale pour l'emploi, ANPE *f*

jobless ['dʒɒblɪs] **ADJ** sans travail, au chômage

NPL the j. les chômeurs *mpl*, les demandeurs *mpl* d'emploi; **the j. figures** le nombre des chômeurs *ou* des demandeurs d'emploi

job-share **N** partage *m* du travail; **we could do it as a j.** nous pourrions nous partager le travail; **they applied for the post as a j.** ils se sont présentés pour le poste en proposant de se partager le travail

vi partager le travail; **we could apply to j.** nous pourrions nous présenter en proposant de nous partager le travail

job-shop specialist **N** *Mktg* spécialiste *m* de production à la commande

jobsworth ['dʒɒbzwɜːθ] **N** petit chef *m* qui ne veut pas se mouiller ni se fatiguer

Jock [dʒɒk] **N** *Sl (Scot)* Écossais; **hello, J.!** salut, l'Écossais!

jock [dʒɒk] **N** *Am Univ Fam (sportsman)* sportif *m*

jockey ['dʒɒkɪ] **N** *Horseracing (man)* jockey *m*; *(woman)* femme *f* jockey; **amateur j.** jockey amateur, gentleman(-rider) *m*

vi *(scheme)* manœuvrer, intriguer **(for a job/etc** pour obtenir *ou* se faire donner un poste/etc); **to j. for position** manœuvrer *ou* intriguer pour se placer avantageusement

vt *(persuade forcefully, deceive)* **to j. sb into doing sth** emberlificoter qn pour qu'il fasse qch; **to j. sb out of a job** évincer *ou* chasser qn d'un poste

▸▸ **j. cap** casquette *f* de jockey; **Jockey®** **shorts** caleçon *m*

jockstrap ['dʒɒkstræp] **N** slip *m* à coquille

jocose [dʒə'kəʊs] **ADJ** facétieux

jocular ['dʒɒkjʊlər] **ADJ** *(humorous)* facétieux, amusant, jovial, -als *ou* -aux; *(jolly)* enjoué; **in (a) j. vein** *(to say, reply etc)* d'un ton facétieux *ou* amusant *ou* rieur

jocularity [dʒɒkjʊ'lærɪtɪ] **N** *(humour)* humour *m*; *(jollity)* jovialité *f*; **an atmosphere of j.** une atmosphère joviale

jocularly ['dʒɒkjʊlərlɪ] **ADV** *(humorously)* facétieusement; *(with jollity)* jovialement; **he was j. known as 'the Walrus' by his pupils** ses élèves lui donnaient le surnom facétieux du 'Morse'

jocund ['dʒɒkənd] **ADJ** *Lit* jovial, -als *ou* aux, enjoué

jodhpurs ['dʒɒdpəz] **NPL** pantalon *m ou* culotte *f* de cheval, jodhpurs *mpl*

Joe [dʒəʊ] **N** *Am Fam (man, fellow)* mec *m*, type *m*; **he's an ordinary J.** c'est un mec comme les autres

▸▸ *Br* **J. Bloggs** Monsieur *m* Tout-le-monde, ≃ Monsieur Dupont; *Am, Austr* **J. Blow** Monsieur Tout-le-monde, ≃ Monsieur Dupont; **J. Public** Monsieur Tout-le-monde, ≃ Monsieur Dupont,

joey ['dʒəʊɪ] **N** *Austr Fam (kangaroo)* petit kangourou *m*

jog [dʒɒg] **N 1** *(push)* poussée *f*, coup *m* sec; *(shake)* secousse *f*, *(with elbow)* coup de coude; *Fig* **to give sb's memory a j.** rafraîchir la mémoire de *ou* à qn **2** *(slow run)* jogging *m*; *Horseriding* petit trot *m*; **at a j.** au petit trot; **to break into a j.** *(of person, horse)* se mettre à trotter; *Sport* **to go for a j.** aller faire un jogging

vt (**-gg-**)*(push)* pousser (d'un coup sec); *(shake)* secouer; **she jogged my elbow** elle m'a poussé le coude; *Fig* **to j. sb's memory** rafraîchir la mémoire de *ou* à qn; *Fig* **to j. sb into doing sth** inciter qn à l'action; **to j. sb out of it** secouer qn; **to j. sb out of their complacency** tirer qn de sa complaisance

vi *Sport* faire du jogging; **to go jogging** aller faire un jogging

▸▸ **j. trot** petit trot; **at a j. trot** au petit trot

▸**jog along** **vi** *(of vehicle etc)* cahoter; *(of person)* trotter; *Fig (of person, factory, country etc)* aller tant bien que mal; *Fig* **I'm jogging along quite happily** je vais mon petit bonhomme de chemin

jogger ['dʒɒgər] **N** *Sport* **1** *(person)* jogger *m*, joggeur, -euse; *Med Fam* **j.'s nipple** irritation *f* des tétons due au frottement contre les vêtements **2** *(shoe)* chaussure *f* de jogging

jogging ['dʒɒgɪŋ] **N** *Sport* jogging *m*; **to like j.** aimer faire du jogging, aimer le jogging

▸▸ **j. bottoms** pantalon *m* de jogging *ou Fam* de survêt; **j. shoes** chaussures *fpl* de jogging; **j. suit** tenue *f* de jogging, jogging

joggle ['dʒɒg(ə)l] **N** légère secousse *f*

vt secouer légèrement; **to j. sth around** re-

muer qch; **he joggled his daughter on his knee** il faisait sauter sa fille sur ses genoux

vi *(shake)* être secoué; **they joggled up and down in the back** ils étaient secoués *ou* bringuebalés à l'arrière

jog-trot **vi** (**-tt-**) *(of horse)*, *Fig (of person)* aller au petit trot

Johannesburg [dʒəʊ'hænɪzbɜːg] **N** Johannesburg

John [dʒɒn] **N 1** Jean *m*; **(Saint) J. the Baptist** saint *m* Jean-Baptiste **2** *Br Fam (term of address)* chef; **got a light, J.?** t'as du feu, chef?

▸▸ **J. Bull** John Bull *(personnification de la nation anglaise, du peuple anglais)*; *Am* **J. Doe** *(average person)* l'Américain *m* moyen, ≃ Monsieur *m* Dupont; *Fam (unidentified man) (under arrest)* inconnu *m*; *(corpse)* mort *m* non identifié; **J. Dory** saint-pierre *m inv*; *Am Fam* **J. Hancock, J. Henry** sa signature, son gribouillis; *Am Fam* **J. Q. Public** Monsieur Tout-le-Monde; *Fam* **J. Thomas** *(penis)* zizi *m*, zob *m*

john [dʒɒn] **N 1** *Am Fam* **the j.** *(lavatory)* le petit coin, les cabinets *mpl* **2** *Am Sl (prostitute's client)* micheton *m*

johnny ['dʒɒnɪ] *Fam* **N 1** *Old-fashioned (man)* gars *m* **2** *(condom) (rubber)* **j.** capote *f*; ▸▸ *Hum* **J. Foreigner** étranger, -ère; *Hist* **J. Reb** soldat *m* confédéré

Johnny-come-lately **N** *Fam (new arrival)* nouveau venu *m*; *Pej (upstart)* parvenu *m*

JOIN [dʒɔɪn]

N raccord **1** ▪ joint **1** ▪ couture **1**
VT joindre **1** ▪ unir **1** ▪ relier **1** ▪ raccorder **1** ▪ rejoindre **2–4** ▪ se joindre à **2** ▪ s'inscrire à **5** ▪ entrer dans **5** ▪ adhérer à **5** ▪ s'engager dans **5**
VI se joindre **1** ▪ se raccorder **1** ▪ se rejoindre **3** ▪ devenir membre **4**

N *(in wallpaper, masonry, tape etc)* raccord *m*; *Tech (junction between elements)* joint *m*; *(in fabric)* couture *f*

vt 1 *(unite) (planks, pieces of material etc)* joindre, unir; *(connect, link) (towns, words, points etc)* relier; *(edges of a wound etc)* rapprocher, réunir; *(pipes, electric wires)* raccorder; **to j. two things end to end** joindre deux choses bout à bout; **the Siamese twins are joined at the thigh** les frères siamois sont rattachés (l'un à l'autre) par la cuisse; **to j. in marriage** *or* **in matrimony** unir par le mariage; *Mil, Fig* **to j. battle** engager le combat (**with** avec); *Fig* **we shall j. forces** nous unirons nos forces; *Fig* **to j. forces** *or* **hands (with sb) to do** *or* **in doing** se joindre *ou* s'unir (à qn) pour faire; **we joined hands** nous nous sommes pris par la main, nous nous sommes donné la main

2 *(catch up with, meet) (person)* rejoindre, retrouver; *(associate oneself with) (person)* se joindre à (**in doing** pour faire); *(take part in) (game)* prendre part à; **to j. a discussion** se joindre à *ou* prendre part à une discussion; **to j. sb in** *or* **for a drink** prendre un verre avec qn, se joindre à qn pour prendre un verre; **will you j. us?** voulez-vous vous joindre à nous?; **may I j. you?** puis-je me joindre à vous?; **why don't you j. (us at) our table?** venez donc vous asseoir à notre table!; **we are joined in the studio by … …** vient nous rejoindre *ou* vient se joindre à nous dans notre studio

3 *(go to, return to)* rejoindre; *Mil, Naut* **to j. one's regiment/ship** rejoindre son régiment/son bâtiment; **we shall soon j. the motorway** nous rejoindrons bientôt l'autoroute

4 *(intersect with, flow into)* rejoindre; **to j. the sea** *(of river)* rejoindre la mer, se jeter dans la mer

5 *(become a member of) (club, political party)* s'inscrire à, entrer dans, adhérer à; *(class, course)* s'inscrire pour *ou* à; *(company, group, religious order)* entrer dans; *(the army, navy, police)* s'engager dans, s'enrôler dans, entrer dans; **to j. a religious order/the newspaper** entrer dans les ordres/au journal; **to j. the queue** se mettre à la queue; **I'm looking for a well-paid and interesting job – j. the queue!** je cherche un travail bien payé et intéressant – bienvenue au club!

VI 1 *(of pieces of fabric, planks etc)* se toucher, se joindre; *(of pipes, wires)* se raccorder

2 to j. with sb *(associate oneself with)* se joindre à qn, s'associer à qn (**in doing** pour faire); **we j. with you in your sorrow** nous compatissons à votre douleur

3 *(of roads, lines, rivers)* se rejoindre

4 *(enrol in club, political party etc)* s'inscrire, devenir membre

▸ **join in** VI *(take part)* se mettre de la partie, participer, prendre part; **I'll sing first and then you (all) j. in** je chanterai d'abord et ensuite vous vous joindrez à moi

VT INSEP *(take part in) (game, activity)* prendre part à, participer à; *(discussion)* prendre part à, se joindre à, participer à; **to j. in the protest(s)** s'associer aux protestations, joindre sa voix aux protestations; **to j. in the singing** chanter; **you'll all j. in the chorus** vous chanterez tous le refrain en chœur

▸ **join on** VT SEP *(fasten)* attacher (**to** à); *(add)* ajouter (**to** à)

VI *(fasten)* s'attacher (**to** à); **the paragraph joins on here** le paragraphe vient s'ajouter ici; **they joined on at the end of the parade** ils se sont mis à la queue du défilé

▸ **join together** VT SEP = **join** VT **1**

VI = **join** VI **1, 2**

▸ **join up** VI **1** *Mil* s'engager; *(for class etc)* s'inscrire

2 *(of pieces of fabric etc)* se toucher, se joindre; *(of pipes, wires)* se raccorder

3 to j. up with sb *(catch up with, meet)* rejoindre qn, retrouver qn; **the three friends always j. up over Christmas** les trois amis se retrouvent toujours à Noël; **to j. up with the motorway** rejoindre l'autoroute

VT SEP *(planks, pieces of material etc)* joindre, assembler; *(pipes, electric cables)* raccorder; *(two machines)* accoupler

joined-up [dʒɔɪnd-] ADJ **can you do j. writing yet?** tu sais lire les lettres?

joiner ['dʒɔɪnər] N **1** *Br (carpenter)* menuisier m **2** *Fam (person who likes joining clubs etc)* = personne f qui aime participer à des activités et s'inscrire à des clubs

joinery ['dʒɔɪnərɪ] N *Br* menuiserie f, **piece of j.** article m *ou* pièce f de menuiserie

joint [dʒɔɪnt] N **1** *Anat* articulation f, jointure f, **out of j.** déboîté; **to put one's arm/shoulder out of j.** se démettre *ou* se disloquer *ou* se déboîter le bras/l'épaule; *Br Fig* **to put sb's nose out of j.** *(make envious)* rendre qn jaloux

2 *Tech* joint m, jointure f, *Carp* assemblage m; **(soldered** *or* **welded) j.** soudure f

3 *Br Culin* rôti m; **j. of beef** rôti de bœuf; **j. of lamb** *(leg)* gigot m d'agneau; *(shoulder)* épaule f d'agneau

4 *Fam Pej (nightclub)* boîte f, *(restaurant)* restau m, gargote f, *(place)* endroit m; **(gambling) j.** tripot m

5 *Sl (cannabis cigarette)* joint m

VT *Culin (chicken etc)* découper aux jointures

ADJ **1** *(united, combined)* conjugué, commun; **to take j. action** mener une action commune; **thanks to their j. efforts...** grâce à leurs efforts conjugués...

2 *(shared, collective)* joint, commun; *(contract) (between two parties)* bilatéral, -aux; *(between more than two parties)* collectif

▸▸ *Banking* **j. account** compte m joint, compte conjoint; **j. author** coauteur m; *Fin* **j. beneficiary** bénéficiaire mf conjoint(e); *Mil* **the J. Chiefs of Staff** = organe m consultatif du ministère américain de la Défense, composé des chefs d'état-major des trois armées; **j. commission** commission f mixte; **j. committee** commission mixte; *Ind* comité m paritaire; *Law* **j. custody** garde f conjointe; *Fin* **j. debtor** codébiteur, -trice; **j. enterprise** tarif m commun; *Fin* **j. financing** financement m conjoint; **j. heir** cohéritier m; **j. holder** *(of record, trophy etc)* codétenteur, -trice; **j. management** cogestion f; *Br* **j. owner** *(of property)* copropriétaire mf; *Br* **j. ownership** copropriété f, **j. partnership** coassociation f, **j. passport** passeport m conjoint; **j. policy** police f conjointe; **j. production** coproduction f, **j. purchase** coacquisition f, **j. report** rapport m collectif; *Fin* **j. and several debtor** débiteur m solidaire; *Fin* **j. and several guarantor** garant m solidaire; *Fin* **j. and several liability** responsabilité f solidaire et indivise; **j. signature** signature f collective; *Fin* **j. stock** capital m social; **j. tenancy** location f commune; **j. undertaking, j. venture** entreprise commune; *(company)* coentreprise f, société f en participation; **j. venture agreement** accord m de partenariat

jointed ['dʒɔɪntɪd] ADJ *(puppet, limb etc)* articulé; **a j. chicken** un poulet découpé

jointing tape ['dʒɪntɪŋ] N *TV etc* bande f de collure

jointly ['dʒɔɪntlɪ] ADV conjointement (**with** avec); *Law* **j. liable** *or* **responsible** *(debtors etc)* solidaire; *Law* **to act j.** *(of several parties)* agir solidairement; **j. and severally** conjointement et solidairement; **to own/manage j.** coposséder/cogérer

joint-stock ADJ

▸▸ *Br Fin* **j. bank** banque f de dépôt; **j. company** société f (anonyme) par actions

joist [dʒɔɪst] N *Constr* solive f

jojoba [həʊ'həʊbə] N *Bot* jojoba m

joke [dʒəʊk] N **1** *(remark)* plaisanterie f, *Fam* blague f, **to make** *or* **tell** *or* **crack a j.** faire une plaisanterie (**about sth** de qch, à propos de qch); **a dirty j.** une histoire cochonne; **to say/do sth for a j.** dire/faire qch histoire de rire *ou* pour rire; **he's always ready with a j.** il a toujours le mot pour rire; **the j. is on me** je suis le dindon de la farce; **she can't take a j.** elle ne comprend pas la plaisanterie; **he didn't see the j.** *(didn't appreciate something funny)* il n'a pas trouvé ça drôle; *(didn't understand somebody's joke)* il n'a pas compris la plaisanterie; **to make a j. about** *(laugh at)* se moquer de; **to make a j. of everything** prendre tout à la plaisanterie *ou Fam* à la blague *ou* à la rigolade; **he tried to make a j. of it** il a essayé d'en rire; **to make jokes about sth** faire des blagues sur *ou* à propos de qch; **the j. is that ...** le comique de l'histoire, c'est que ...; **what a j.!** *(how ridiculous)* quelle blague!; *(how funny)* ce que c'est amusant *ou* drôle!; *Fam* **that's** *or* **it's no j.!** *(not easy)* ce n'est pas de la tarte!; *(serious)* ce n'est pas de la blague!; **it's no j. waiting for hours** ce n'est pas amusant *ou* drôle d'attendre des heures; **it's getting beyond a j.** ça commence à ne plus être drôle, ça dépasse le stade de la plaisanterie

2 *(prank, trick)* **(practical) j.** farce f, plaisanterie f, tour m, *Fam* blague f, **to play a (practical) j. on sb** faire une farce *ou* une plaisanterie *ou Fam* une blague à qn, jouer un tour à qn

3 *Fam (person or thing inspiring ridicule)* plaisanterie f, **to be a j.** *(of novel, so-called planning, festival etc)* être lamentable; **their economic policy is nothing more than a j.**

leur politique économique n'est qu'une vaste plaisanterie; **to regard sb as a j.** considérer qn comme un objet de risée; **he treats the rules as a j.** il se moque du règlement; **this is turning into a j.** *(is getting annoying)* c'est en train de tourner à la farce

VI plaisanter, *Fam* blaguer (**about** sur, à propos de); **to j. about** *(laugh at)* se moquer de; **we were able to j. about it afterwards** après nous avons pu en rire; **to j. with sb** plaisanter avec qn; **I was only joking** ce n'était qu'une plaisanterie, je plaisantais; **you're joking!, you must be** *or* **you've got to be joking!** vous voulez rire!, sans blague!; **I'm not joking!** je ne plaisante pas!

joker ['dʒəʊkər] N **1** *(making or playing jokes)* farceur, -euse, *Fam* blagueur, -euse, *Pej* plaisantin m **2** *Fam Pej (person)* type m, individu m; *(stupid person)* abruti m **3** *Cards* joker m; *Fig* **that's the j. in the pack** c'est la grande inconnue; *Fig* **she's the j. in the pack** c'est la grande inconnue

jokey ['dʒəʊkɪ] ADJ = **joky**

jokily ['dʒəʊkɪlɪ] ADV en plaisantant

joking ['dʒəʊkɪŋ] ADJ *(tone)* moqueur, de plaisanterie; *(comment, response)* moqueur

N *(no pl)* plaisanteries fpl, *Fam* blagues fpl; **the j. must stop** assez plaisanté *ou Fam* blagué; **j. apart** *or* **aside** toute plaisanterie mise à part, *Fam* blague à part

jokingly ['dʒəʊkɪŋlɪ] ADV en plaisantant

joky ['dʒəʊkɪ] ADJ *(person)* qui aime raconter des plaisanteries; *(mood, conversation etc)* jovial, -als *ou* -aux; *(remark)* moqueur; *(present etc)* farfelu

jollies ['dʒɒlɪz] NPL *Am Fam* **to get one's j. (from)** doing sth *(get pleasure from)* prendre son pied à faire qch

jollification [dʒɒlɪfɪ'keɪʃən] N *Fam (merrymaking)* réjouissances fpl

jolliness ['dʒɒlɪnɪs], **jollity** ['dʒɒlɪtɪ] N *(cheerfulness)* jovialité f, gaieté f, *(merrymaking)* réjouissances fpl

jolly ['dʒɒlɪ] *Fam* ADJ *(cheerful)* jovial, -als *ou* -aux, gai, joyeux; *(pleasant)* agréable; **j. hockey sticks** = expression qui se réfère à une jeune fille *ou* à une femme éduquée dans le privé, adorant le sport, terriblement boute-en-train mais peu intellectuelle

ADV *Br Old-fashioned (very)* drôlement, rudement; **it serves him j. well right!** c'est drôlement *ou* rudement bien fait pour lui!; **yes, I j. well did do it!** oui, je l'ai bel et bien fait!; **j. good!** formidable!; **and a j. good job too!** et c'est tant mieux!

VT amadouer, enjôler; **I jollied him into accepting** je l'ai amadoué *ou* enjôlé tant et si bien qu'il a fini par accepter

▸▸ **J. Roger** pavillon m noir, drapeau m de pirate

> Note that the French word **joli** is a false friend and is never a translation for the English word **jolly**. It means *pretty*.

▸ **jolly along** VT SEP = **jolly** VT

jolt [dʒɒlt] N **1** *(shake)* secousse f, *(of vehicle)* cahot m, secousse, à-coup m, pl à-coups; *(of engine)* à-coup, secousse; **to wake up with a j.** se réveiller en sursaut **2** *Fig (shock, surprise)* choc m; **it gave me a bit of a j.** ça m'a fait un choc *ou* un coup

VI *(shake)* secouer; **to j. along** *(of vehicle)* cahoter, tressauter, avancer en cahotant *ou* par à-coups; **to j. forward** *(of vehicle, train)* s'ébranler avec une secousse; **his head jolted forward/back** *(on impact)* sa tête a été rejetée en avant/en arrière; **to j. to a stop** *(of vehicle, train)* s'arrêter en cahotant *ou* avec des à-coups

VT **1** *(shake)* secouer; *(of vehicle) (passengers)* cahoter, secouer; **to j. forward/back** *(of collision etc) (sb's head)* rejeter en avant/en arrière; *(passenger, suitcase)* projeter en avant/en arrière; **to j. sth off the roof** faire tomber qch du toit **2** *Fig (shock, surprise)* secouer, donner un choc à; *Fig* **to j. sb into action** secouer (les puces à) qn; *Fig* **the nation was jolted into action by the news** cette nouvelle a poussé le pays à entrer en action; *Fig* **to j. sb out of a depression** faire sortir qn de son état dépressif d'un seul coup; *Fig* **that jolted him out of his smugness!** ça lui a fait perdre sa belle suffisance d'un seul coup!

jolting ['dʒəʊltɪŋ] N *(of vehicle)* cahots mpl; *(of plane)* secousses fpl

Jonah ['dʒəʊnə] N *Bible* Jonas; *Fig (jinx)* porte-malheur m inv

jonquil ['dʒɒŋkwɪl] N *(flower)* jonquille f

Jordan ['dʒɔːd(ə)n] N *(country)* Jordanie f; **the J.** *(river)* le Jourdain

Jordanian [dʒɔːˈdeɪnɪən] ADJ jordanien; *(embassy, ambassador)* de Jordanie
▸ N Jordanien, -ienne

josh [dʒɒʃ] *Fam* N *(joke)* blague f
▸ VT *(tease)* chambrer, vanner (**about** sur), mettre en boîte (**about** à cause de)
▸ VI *(joke)* blaguer; **only joshing!** je blaguais!

joss [dʒɒs] N
▸ ▸ **j. stick** bâton m d'encens

jostle ['dʒɒs(ə)l] N *(push)* bousculade f
▸ VI *(push each other)* se bousculer; *(use one's elbows)* jouer des coudes (**for sth** pour obtenir qch); **to j. against sb** bousculer qn; *Fig* **to j. for jobs** jouer des coudes pour décrocher un emploi; *Fig* **to j. for position** essayer de bien se placer
▸ VT bousculer; **to be jostled, to get (oneself) jostled** se faire bousculer (**by** par); **to j. sb out of the way** écarter qn à coups de coudes ou en jouant des coudes; **to j. one's way (through)** se frayer un chemin à coups de coude

jostling ['dʒɒs(ə)lɪŋ] N *(of crowd)* bousculade(s) f(pl)

jot [dʒɒt] N *(in negatives)* **he doesn't care a j.** il n'en a rien à faire, il ne s'en soucie pas du tout; **there isn't a j. of truth in what you say** il n'y a pas la moindre parcelle de vérité dans ce que vous dites
▸ **jot down** VT SEP noter, prendre note de, prendre en note; **to j. down (some) notes** prendre des notes

jotter ['dʒɒtər] N *(notepad)* bloc-notes m, pl blocs-notes; *Sch (exercise book)* cahier m

jottings ['dʒɒtɪŋz] NPL notes fpl (prises à la hâte); **she made a few j. of ideas** elle a noté quelques idées à la hâte

joule [dʒuːl] N *Phys* joule m
▸ ▸ **J. effect** effet m Joule

journal ['dʒɜːn(ə)l] N **1** *(periodical)* revue f, journal m **2** *(record of events)* journal m; *Com (for transactions)* livre m de comptes **3** *Tech (bearing)* palier m (de tourillon)
▸ ▸ *Tech* **j. bearing** palier m (de tourillon); *Com* **j. entry** écriture f comptable, contre-passation f, pl contre-passations

Note that the most common meaning of the French word **journal** is **newspaper**.

journalese [dʒɜːnəˈliːz] N *Pej Fam* style m ou jargon m journalistique

journalism ['dʒɜːnəlɪz(ə)m] N journalisme m

journalist ['dʒɜːnəlɪst] N journaliste mf

journalistic [dʒɜːnəˈlɪstɪk] ADJ journalistique

journey ['dʒɜːnɪ] N voyage m; *(of short distance)* trajet m; **it was quite a j. to get here** ça a été toute une épopée pour arriver jusqu'ici; **it is a two-day j. by car** c'est à deux journées de route en voiture; **Bradford is on-**

ly a short j. away (from here) Bradford est tout près d'ici; **to make a j.** faire un voyage; **to set off** *or* **out on a j.** partir en voyage; **it's not wise to set out on such a j. at this time of year** ce n'est pas prudent d'entreprendre un tel voyage en cette période de l'année; **to go (away) on a j.** partir en voyage; **to get to** *or* **reach the end of one's j.** arriver à destination, arriver à la fin de son voyage ou trajet; **have a good j.!** bon voyage!; **to have an hour's j. to work** avoir une heure de trajet pour se rendre à son travail; **to go on a train j.** prendre le train, voyager par le train; **the return j., the j. home** *or* **back** le voyage de retour, le retour; *(from work)* le trajet de retour; **the outward j.** le voyage d'aller, l'aller m
▸ VI *Lit* voyager; **to j. on** continuer son voyage
▸ ▸ **j. time** durée f du voyage; *(shorter distance)* durée du trajet

Note that the French word **journée** is a false friend and is never a translation for the English word **journey**. It means **day**.

journeyman, pl **journeymen** ['dʒɜːnɪmən] N *(craftsman)* compagnon m, ouvrier m; **j. baker** ouvrier boulanger; **j. carpenter** compagnon charpentier

journo ['dʒɜːnəʊ] N *Fam* journaliste mf

joust [dʒaʊst] *Hist, Fig* N joute f
▸ VI *Hist* jouter (**with** contre); *Fig* batailler

jousting ['dʒaʊstɪŋ] N *Hist, Fig* joutes fpl; **a j. match** une bataille

jovial ['dʒəʊvɪəl] ADJ jovial, -als ou -aux, enjoué; **she's in a j. mood** elle est d'humeur joviale; **to feel j.** être enjoué

joviality [dʒəʊvɪˈælɪtɪ] N jovialité f, enjouement m

jovially ['dʒəʊvɪəlɪ] ADV jovialement

jowl [dʒaʊl] N **1** *(jaw)* mâchoire f **2** *(hanging flesh on cheek)* bajoue f; **he had heavy jowls** il avait de grosses bajoues

-jowled [dʒaʊld] SUFF **long/square/etc-j.** à la mâchoire allongée/carrée/etc; **a heavy-j. face** un visage aux grosses bajoues

joy [dʒɔɪ] N **1** *(happiness)* joie f; **to jump** *or* **leap/weep** *or* **cry for j.** sauter ou bondir/pleurer de joie; **wild with j., beside oneself with j.** fou ou ivre de joie; **to our great j.** à notre grande joie; **I wish you (great) j.** je vous souhaite beaucoup de bonheur; *Iron* **I wish you j. (of it)!** je vous souhaite bien du plaisir!, vous m'en voyez fort aise!
2 *(pleasure)* plaisir m; **the joys of marriage/of spring** les joies ou plaisirs du mariage/du printemps; **full of the joys of spring** au comble du bonheur; **the joys of having children** les joies qu'apportent les enfants; **the joys of having a car** les joies d'avoir une voiture; **her style is a j. to watch** son style est un plaisir pour les yeux; **she's a j. to work for** c'est un plaisir de travailler pour lui; **our new car is a j. to drive** avec notre nouveau modèle la conduite est un plaisir; **she's a j. to be with, it's a j. to be with her** c'est un plaisir d'être à ses côtés; **our grandchildren are an absolute j.** nos petits-enfants sont très mignons
3 *Br Fam (no pl) (success)* succès m; **(did you have** *or* **get) any j.?** ça a marché?, tu as réussi?; **no j.!** ça n'a rien donné!, ça n'a pas marché!; **you won't get any j. from him** tu n'arriveras à rien avec lui

joyful ['dʒɔɪfʊl] ADJ *(person, face, news etc)* joyeux

joyfully ['dʒɔɪfəlɪ] ADV joyeusement, avec joie; *(to celebrate, be reunited)* dans la joie

joyfulness ['dʒɔɪfʊlnɪs] N *(grande)* joie f, allégresse f

joyless ['dʒɔɪlɪs] ADJ triste, sans joie; *(face, grin)* triste

joylessly ['dʒɔɪlɪslɪ] ADV tristement, sans joie

joyous ['dʒɔɪəs] ADJ *esp Lit (occasion, person etc)* joyeux; *(news)* heureux

joyously ['dʒɔɪəslɪ] ADV *esp Lit* joyeusement, avec joie; *(to celebrate)* dans la joie

joypad ['dʒɔɪpæd] N *Comput* joypad m

joyride ['dʒɔɪraɪd] N *(in stolen car)* virée f (dans une voiture volée); **to go for a** *or* **on a j.** faire une virée (dans une voiture volée); *Fig* **it's no j. working with him** travailler avec lui, ce n'est pas une partie de plaisir
▸ VI *(pt* **joyrode** [-rəʊd], *pp* **joyridden** [-rɪd(ə)n])* faire une virée (dans une voiture volée); **to go joyriding** faire une virée (dans une voiture volée)

joyrider ['dʒɔɪraɪdər] N voleur, -euse *(qui prend une voiture pour faire une virée)*

joystick ['dʒɔɪstɪk] N *Aviat* manche m à balai; *Comput* manette f *(de jeu)*, manche m à balai

JP [dʒeɪˈpiː] N *Br Law (abbr* **justice of the peace**) juge m de paix

JPEG ['dʒeɪpeg] N *Comput (abbr* **Joint Photographic Experts Group**) (format m) JPEG m

Jr *(abbr* **Junior**) **Thomas Smith, Jr** Thomas Smith fils

jubilant ['dʒuːbɪlənt] ADJ *(shouts)* de joie; *(expression)* épanoui, radieux; *(crowd)* exultant; *(party, celebration)* joyeux; **to be j.** *(of person)* déborder de joie, jubiler, exulter; **to be j. at** *or* **about** *or* **over the news** être transporté de joie par la nouvelle

jubilantly ['dʒuːbɪləntlɪ] ADV avec jubilation

jubilation [dʒuːbɪˈleɪʃən] N *(of person)* *(grande)* joie f, exultation f, jubilation f; **to be a cause for (great) j.** être l'occasion de *(grandes)* réjouissances; **scenes of j.** scènes de réjouissance

jubilee ['dʒuːbɪliː] N **(golden) j.** jubilé m, *(fête f du)* cinquantième anniversaire m *(de mariage etc)*; **silver/diamond j.** *(fête du)* vingt-cinquième/soixantième anniversaire

Judaea [dʒuːˈdiːə] N Judée f

Judaic [dʒuːˈdeɪɪk] ADJ judaïque

Judaism ['dʒuːdeɪɪz(ə)m] N *Rel* judaïsme m

Judas ['dʒuːdəs] N **1** *Bible* Judas; **J. Iscariot** Judas Iscariote **2** *(traitor)* judas m
▸ ▸ **J. kiss** baiser m de Judas; **J. tree** arbre m de Judée, gainier m

judas ['dʒuːdəs] N *(peephole)* judas m
▸ ▸ **j. hole** judas; **j. window** judas

judder ['dʒʌdər] *Br* N vibrations fpl; *(of brakes)* trépidation f, *(of clutch, tool)* broutage m, broutement m
▸ VI vibrer; *(of brakes)* trépider; *(of clutch, tool)* brouter; **to j. to a halt** *(of train, vehicle)* s'arrêter avec de violentes secousses

judge [dʒʌdʒ] N **1** *Law, Sport etc* juge m; *(of contest)* juge, membre m du jury; *Law* **the judges (the bench)** la magistrature assise; *Bible* **(the Book of) Judges** le livre des Juges
2 *Fig* juge m, connaisseur m; **good j.** *(of cars, horses, wine)* spécialiste mf *(of* en); **she fancies herself as a good j. of men** elle croit savoir juger les hommes; **I'm not sure he's the best j. of such things** je ne suis pas sûr qu'il soit très bon juge en la matière; **to be a good** *or* **keen j. of character** être bon ou fin psychologue; **I'll let you be the j. of that** je vous en fais juge, je vous laisse juge; **I will be the j. of that** c'est moi qui jugerai de cela
▸ VT **1** *Law, Sport etc (try, give decision about)* juger; *Law* **to j. a case** juger une affaire
2 *(assess critically) (person, situation, text etc)* juger; *(estimate, evaluate) (distance, speed, weight, price etc)* estimer, évaluer; **her latest novel has been judged a failure by the critics** les critiques ont estimé que

son dernier roman était mauvais; **to j. sb by** or **on sth** juger qn sur ou d'après qch; **to j. people by appearances** juger les apparences; **to j. sth at its true** or **proper value/on its merits** juger ou apprécier qch à sa juste valeur/selon ses mérites

3 (think, consider) juger (**that** que; **if, whether** si); **to j. it necessary to ...** juger nécessaire de ...

VI (assess, estimate, pass judgement), Law, Rel juger; **to j. by appearances** juger d'après les apparences; **as far as I can j.** autant que je puisse en juger; **to j. for oneself** (en) juger par soi-même; **judging by** or **from his letter/my first impressions** à en juger par ou d'après sa lettre/mes premières impressions; **who will be judging?** (in competition) qui va faire fonction de juge?

judg(e)ment, Am **judgment** ['dʒʌdʒmənt] **N1** Law, Rel, Fig jugement m; Law **to pass** or **give** or **deliver j.** prononcer ou rendre un jugement (**on** sur); Law **to sit in j.** (of court) siéger; Fig **to sit in j. on** or **over sb, to pass j. on sb** porter un jugement sur qn, juger qn; Fig **to sit in j., to pass j.** porter des jugements, juger (les gens); Rel **the Last J.** le Jugement dernier

2 (no pl) (discernment) jugement m; **political/financial j.** discernement m en matière de politique/finances; **to have/lack (good** or **sound) j.** avoir du/manquer de jugement; **to have very sound j.** avoir une grande sûreté de jugement, avoir un jugement très sûr; **this decision shows good j.** cette décision montre du discernement; **to trust sb's j.** s'en remettre au jugement de qn

3 (opinion) avis m, opinion f; **to give one's j. on** donner ou exprimer son avis sur; **to form a j.** se faire une opinion; **in my j.** à mon sens; **against my better j.** tout en sachant que je me trompe/trompais sans doute

▸▸Rel **J. Day** le Jugement dernier; Mktg **j. sample** échantillon m discrétionnaire; Mktg **j. sampling** échantillonnage m discrétionnaire

judg(e)mental, Am **judgmental** [dʒʌdʒ'ment(ə)l] **ADJ** (person, book etc) critique; **I don't want to seem j. but ...** je ne veux pas avoir l'air de critiquer mais ...

▸▸Mktg **j. forecasting** prévision f par estimation; Mktg **j. method** méthode f estimative

judicature ['dʒuːdɪkətʃər] **N** Law (administration of justice) justice f; (system) organisation f judiciaire; (judges) magistrature f

judicial [dʒuː'dɪʃ(ə)l] **ADJ** Law (inquiry, power, proceedings) judiciaire

▸▸**j. inquiry** enquête f judiciaire; **j. murder** assassinat m légal ou juridique; Am **j. review** (of ruling) examen m d'une décision de justice (par une juridiction supérieure); (of law) examen de la constitutionnalité d'une loi; **j. separation** séparation f de corps

judicially [dʒuː'dɪʃəlɪ] **ADV** Law judiciairement

judiciary [dʒuː'dɪʃɪərɪ] Law **ADJ** judiciaire **N** (judges) magistrature f; (branch of government) pouvoir m judiciaire; (system of courts) organisation f judiciaire

judicious [dʒuː'dɪʃəs] **ADJ** (person, mind, thought etc) judicieux

judiciously [dʒuː'dɪʃəslɪ] **ADV** judicieusement

judiciousness [dʒuː'dɪʃəsnɪs] **N** (of person, mind) discernement m, bon sens m; (of thought, remark) bon sens

judo ['dʒuːdəʊ] **N** judo m

judy, Judy ['dʒuːdɪ] **N** Old-fashioned Br Sl (girl, woman) nana f

jug [dʒʌg] **N1** Br (for cream, milk, water) pot m; (for wine) pichet m; **coffee j.** cafetière f;

Fam Hum **his ears are like j. handles** il a les oreilles décollées **2** Old-fashioned Sl (prison) taule f, tôle f; **in (the) j.** au trou, en taule ou tôle **3** Sl **jugs** (breasts) nichons mpl, lolos mpl

▸▸**j. kettle** = bouilloire f électrique haute; Am **j. wine** vin m ordinaire

jugful ['dʒʌgfʊl] **N** (of cream, milk, water) (plein) pot m; (of wine) (plein) pichet m

jugged [dʒʌgd] **ADJ**

▸▸Culin **j. hare** civet m de lièvre

juggernaut ['dʒʌgənɔːt] **N1** Br (lorry) (gros) poids m lourd, Fam mastodonte m **2** Fig (destructive force) vague f de fond, vague déferlante, raz-de-marée m inv

juggins ['dʒʌgɪnz] **N** Old-fashioned Br Fam (simpleton) nigaud, -aude, cruche f

juggle ['dʒʌg(ə)l] **VI** (with balls, figures) jongler

VT (balls, figures) jongler avec

juggler ['dʒʌglər] **N** jongleur, -euse

juggling ['dʒʌglɪŋ] **N** jonglerie f, art m du jongleur; (trickery) fourberie f

Jugoslav ['juːgəʊslɑːv] **ADJ, N** = **Yugoslav**

Jugoslavia [juːgəʊ'slɑːvɪə] **N** = **Yugoslavia**

Jugoslavian [juːgəʊ'slɑːvɪən] **ADJ, N** = **Yugoslavian**

jugular ['dʒʌgjʊlər] Anat **ADJ** jugulaire **N** (veine f) jugulaire f; Fig **to go for the j.** attaquer toutes griffes dehors ou tous azimuts

juice [dʒuːs] **N1** (of fruit, vegetables, meat) jus m; (of plant) suc m; Physiol **gastric** or **digestive juices** sucs gastriques ou digestifs **2** Fam (electricity) jus m, courant m; (gas) gaz m; (petrol) essence f **3** Am Fam (popularity, recognition) succès m; **to have a lot of j.** faire un tabac

VT (apple, orange etc) extraire le jus de

▸▸**j. bar** = bar m où l'on sert des jus de fruit; Br **j. extractor** centrifugeuse f (pour faire des jus de fruit)

▸**juice up VT SEP** Am Sl **1** (liven up) (party) mettre de l'animation ou de l'ambiance dans; (add power to) (engine) gonfler **2 to get juiced up** (drunk) se soûler

juiced [dʒuːst] **ADJ** Am Fam (drunk) pété, bourré

juicer ['dʒuːsər] **N1** (for fruit) centrifugeuse f (électrique) **2** Am Fam (alcoholic) alcolo mf, poivrot, -ote

juiciness ['dʒuːsɪnɪs] **N** (of meat) juteux m; Fig (of story, detail) piquant m, (côté m) croustillant m; **the j. of these melons** ces melons bien juteux

juicy ['dʒuːsɪ] **ADJ** (fruit) juteux; (meat) plein de jus, qui rend du jus; Fig (story, detail) croustillant, piquant; **the j. part of the story** le plus croustillant de l'histoire; Fam **a j. deal** (lucrative) une affaire juteuse; **a nice j. morsel** (of meat etc) un morceau de choix bien succulent; **a nice j. scandal** un scandale bien juteux; Br Sl **she's a j. bit** (sexy) elle est très excitante, c'est une sacrée allumeuse

jujitsu [dʒuː'dʒɪtsuː] **N** jiu-jitsu m

juju ['dʒuːdʒuː] **N** (charm, fetish) gri(s)-gri(s) m

jukebox ['dʒuːkbɒks] **N** juke-box m, pl juke-boxes

Jul abbr **July**

julep ['dʒuːlɪp] **N** (drink) **(mint) j.** bourbon m frappé à la menthe

Julian ['dʒuːlɪən] **ADJ** (calendar etc) julien

Julius Caesar ['dʒuːljəs] **N** Jules César

July [dʒuː'laɪ, dʒʊ'laɪ] **N** VOIR GRAMMAIRE A81-2; B60-2 juillet m; **in J.** au mois de juillet, en juillet; **(on) the first/the seventh of J.** le premier/le cinq juillet

jumble ['dʒʌmb(ə)l] **N1** (disorder) fouillis m, pagaïe f, méli-mélo m, Fig (of ideas etc) méli-

mélo, fouillis, fatras m; (of words) fatras m; **in a j.** (papers etc) en pagaïe, en fouillis; Fig (ideas etc) en pagaïe **2** Br (unwanted articles) bric-à-brac m inv

VT (documents, toys, books etc) mélanger, mettre la pagaïe dans; (clothes, shoes etc) mélanger; Fig (ideas, details, words etc) (em)brouiller, mélanger; **the pages got all jumbled** les pages se sont complètement mélangées; **the clothes lay jumbled on the floor** les vêtements gisaient pêle-mêle sur le sol; **everything was jumbled** tout était mélangé; **he jumbled the details** il s'est emmêlé ou embrouillé dans les détails

▸▸Br **j. sale** = vente f de charité où sont vendus des articles d'occasion et des produits faits maison

▸**jumble together, jumble up VT SEP** = **jumble VT**

jumbo ['dʒʌmbəʊ] Fam **ADJ 1** (giant-sized) géant, énorme **2** Am Fin (loan) géant **N** (pl **jumbos**) **1** (person, animal, thing) mastodonte m; Aviat jumbo-jet m, pl jumbo-jets, (avion m) gros porteur m **2** (elephant) = surnom typique donné aux éléphants

▸▸Aviat **j. jet** (avion) gros porteur; St Exch **j. trade** opération f jumbo

JUMP [dʒʌmp]

N saut **1, 5**	▪ bond **1**	▪ obstacle **2**
▪ hausse **3**	▪ sursaut **4**	
VI sauter **1, 2, 4**	▪ faire un bond **3, 4**	
▪ sursauter **4**		
VT sauter **1, 3**	▪ faire sauter **2**	

N1 (leap) saut m, bond m; (by parachute) saut (en parachute); **to take** or **make a j.** faire un saut ou un bond, sauter; **in** or **at one j.** d'un (seul) bond; Fam **go take a j.!** va te faire voir (ailleurs)!, va te faire cuire un œuf!; Fig **to be one j. ahead of** avoir une longueur d'avance sur; Fam **to have the j. on sb** (have a head start) avoir pris une longueur d'avance sur qn dès le départ

2 (on racecourse etc) obstacle m; **to put a horse over a j.** faire sauter un obstacle à un cheval

3 (in temperature, unemployment etc) hausse f (soudaine) (**in** de); **the j. in prices** la flambée des prix, la hausse (soudaine) des prix; **to take a (sudden) j.** faire un bond

4 (sudden movement, start) sursaut m; **that gave me a j.** cela m'a fait sursauter ou tressauter

5 Comput saut m, branchement m

VI1 (leap) (of person, animal etc) sauter; (from aircraft) sauter (en parachute); **j.!** (to child, dog) allez, hop!, saute!; **to j. to one's feet** se (re)lever d'un bond; **to j. to the ground** sauter à terre; **to j. for joy** (feel elated, leap in the air) sauter de joie; **to j. (down) from a wall/tree** sauter (du haut) d'un mur/arbre; **to j. from a train/vehicle** sauter d'un train/d'un véhicule; **to j. across a ditch** franchir un fossé d'un bond, sauter un fossé

2 (go directly) sauter; **to j. from one subject to another** or **to the next** sauter d'un sujet à l'autre; **I jumped to the third chapter** je suis passé directement au troisième chapitre; **the film then jumps to the present** puis le film fait un saut jusqu'au présent; **to j. from the bottom to the top of the list** remonter toute la liste d'un seul coup

3 (of profit, temperature etc) faire un bond; (of price) flamber, faire un bond

4 (make a sudden movement) (of person) sursauter, tressauter; (of heart) faire un bond, bondir; (of record player needle, chisel, drill) sauter; **we nearly jumped out of our skins** (from surprise) nous avons failli sauter au plafond; (from fear, shock) ça nous a fait *ou Fam* fichu un de ces coups; **the sight of her (nearly) made me j. out of my skin** ça m'a fait *ou Fam* fichu un de ces coups de la voir

5 *Fig (phrases)* **to j. at an offer/a chance/a suggestion** sauter sur une offre/une occasion/une proposition; **you should j. at it** vous devriez sauter dessus; **to j. to conclusions** tirer des conclusions prématurées *ou* hâtives; **to j. to the conclusion that ...** conclure prématurément que ...; **and j. to it!** et que ça saute!; **let's wait and see which way she jumps** attendons de voir sa réaction, attendons de voir comment elle va réagir; *Fam* **to j. down sb's throat** *(reply sharply to)* rabrouer qn, rembarrer qn, envoyer qn paître *ou* promener; *(criticize)* engueuler qn; *Am Fam* **to j. all over sb** *(scold, criticize)* passer un savon à qn, engueuler qn

6 *Fam* **to be (really) jumping** *(of party, nightclub)* être très animé

VT 1 *(hedge, ditch etc)* franchir d'un bond, sauter (par-dessus); *Fig (skip) (paragraph, word, page etc)* sauter; *Sch* **to j. a class** sauter une classe; **to j. a** *or* **the groove** *(of record player needle)* sauter

2 *(cause to jump) (horse)* faire sauter; *Sport* **to j. a horse over a hurdle** faire sauter une haie à un cheval

3 *Am* **to j. rope** sauter à la corde

4 *(escape from, pass, leave illegally etc) Law* **to j. bail** se dérober à la justice *(alors qu'on jouit de la liberté provisoire)*; *Aut* **to j. the lights** griller *ou* brûler le feu rouge *ou* les feux; *Br* **to j. the queue** passer avant son tour, resquiller; **to j. the rails** *(of train)* dérailler; *Naut* **to j. ship** *(of sailor)* déserter (le navire)

5 *Rail Fam* **to j. a train** *(get on)* sauter dans un train (**to** à destination de); *(without paying)* voyager sans billet

6 *Fam (attack, ambush, take over)* **to j. sb** sauter *ou* tomber sur (le paletot de) qn; **to j. a train** *(of bandits etc)* attaquer un train; *Am* **to j. a claim** s'emparer illégalement d'une concession

▸▸ *Cin* **j. cut** faux *m* raccord, saut *m* de montage; *Br Aviat* **j. jet** avion *m* à décollage vertical; *Br* **j. leads** câbles *mpl* de démarrage; *Am* **j. rope** corde *f* à sauter; *Br* **j. seat** strapontin *m*; **j. suit** *(clothing)* combinaison-pantalon *f, pl* combinaisons-pantalons; *(for baby)* grenouillère *f*

▸ **jump about, jump around** VI sautiller; *Fig (of story, film etc)* partir dans toutes les directions

▸ **jump back** VI *(of person, vehicle)* faire un bond en arrière, reculer d'un bond; **the story then jumps back twenty years** à ce moment-là l'histoire fait un saut de vingt ans en arrière

▸ **jump down** VI *(from wall etc)* sauter (à terre); **to j. down from a wall/tree** sauter (du haut) d'un mur/arbre

▸ **jump forward** VI *(of person, vehicle)* faire un bond en avant; **at this point the film jumps forward two years** à ce moment-là le film fait un saut de deux années en avant; **if I can briefly j. forward to ...** si je peux anticiper brièvement sur ...

▸ **jump in** VI *(into pool, river etc)* sauter (dedans); *(into vehicle, train)* monter (vite); *(into conversation)* intervenir; *Aut* **j. in!** montez!; *Fig* **to j. in at the deep end** se jeter tête baissée dans les problèmes

VT INSEP = **jump into**

▸ **jump into** VT INSEP *(river, ditch etc)* sauter dans; *(car etc)* sauter *ou* monter dans; **to j. into bed with sb** coucher avec qn

▸ **jump off** VI **1** *(from wall, train etc)* sauter (**from** de)

2 *Horseriding* faire un barrage

VT INSEP *(bicycle, train etc)* sauter de; **to j. off a wall/etc** sauter (du haut) d'un mur/*etc*

▸ **jump on** VI *(on to vehicle, train)* monter; *(on to bicycle)* sauter dessus

VT INSEP **1** *(bus, train etc)* monter *ou* sauter dans; *(bicycle)* sauter sur

2 *Fam* **to j. on sb** *(reprimand)* passer un savon à qn; **you should j. on that kind of thing at once** tu devrais couper court à ce genre de choses

▸ **jump out** VI *(from vehicle, train etc)* sauter (**of, from** de); **I'll j. out at the traffic lights** je vais descendre au feu rouge; **to j. out of bed** (à bas) du lit; **to j. out of the window** sauter par la fenêtre; **to j. out of the bushes/one's hiding place** bondir d'entre les buissons/de sa cachette; *Fig* **to j. out at sb** *(of mistake etc)* sauter aux yeux de qn

▸ **jump over** VT INSEP *(hedge, ditch etc)* franchir d'un bond, sauter (par-dessus)

VI sauter (par-dessus)

▸ **jump up** VI **1** *(to one's feet)* se (re)lever d'un bond; **up she jumped** d'un bond, elle se (re)leva *ou* elle fut debout; **to j. up and down** sautiller

2 *Fam (increase suddenly)* = **jump** VI **3**

jumped-up [dʒʌmp'tʌp] ADJ *Br Fam Pej (recently promoted, arrogant)* récemment promu (et qui a la grosse tête); *(upstart)* parvenu; **some j. little salesman/civil servant** un petit péteux de vendeur/fonctionnaire

jumper¹ ['dʒʌmpər] N **1** *Br (sweater)* pull(-over) *m* **2** *Am (sleeveless dress)* robe *f* chasuble

jumper² N **1** *(horse, athlete)* sauteur, -euse; **to be a good j.** être bon sauteur, bien sauter

2 *Am Aut* **jumpers** câbles *mpl* de démarrage

3 *Comput (pin)* cavalier *m*

▸▸ *Am Aut* **j. cables** câbles de démarrage

jumpily ['dʒʌmpɪlɪ] ADV *(nervously)* nerveusement

jumpiness ['dʒʌmpɪnɪs] N *(of person)* nervosité *f*, *St Exch (of markets)* nervosité, fébrilité *f*

jumping ['dʒʌmpɪŋ] ADJ **1** *(insect)* sauteur **2** *Fam (party, nightclub)* hyper animé

N *(leaps)* sauts *mpl*, *Horseriding (show jumping)* jumping *m*, concours *m* hippique

▸▸ *Bot* **j. bean** pois *m* sauteur; **j. jack** *(firework)* pétard *m* mitraillette; *(puppet)* pantin *m*

jumping-off N **j. place** *or* **point** *(for journey)* point *m* de départ (**for** pour); *Fig (for talks, in one's career)* tremplin *m*, point de départ

jumpmaster ['dʒʌmpmæstər] N *Am Mil* moniteur, -trice de parachutisme

jump-off N *Horseriding* barrage *m*

jump-start N **to give a j. to** = **jump-start** VT

VT *(car) (push)* faire démarrer en poussant; *(with jump leads)* faire démarrer au moyen de câbles de démarrage; *Fig* **to j. the economy** relancer l'économie

jumpy ['dʒʌmpɪ] ADJ **1** *(nervous) (person, gestures etc)* nerveux; *St Exch (market)* nerveux, fébrile **2** *(fitful, jerky) (style, gestures etc)* saccadé

Jun *abbr* **June**

junction ['dʒʌŋkʃən] N **1** *(in roads, railway lines)* embranchement *m*, bifurcation *f*, jonction *f*; *(between two roads)* jonction; *(in rivers)* confluent *m*; *(in pipes)* embranchement, jonction, raccordement *m*; *(crossroads)* carrefour *m*; *(station)* gare *f* de jonction *ou* de raccordement; *(weld)* soudure *f*, *Elec* connexion *f*, *Elec (of wires)* branchement *m*; *Br* **j. 5** *(on motorway) (exit)* la sortie 5; *(entrance)* l'entrée *f* 5

2 *Fml (no pl) (joining)* jonction *f*

▸▸ *Br Elec* **j. box** boîte *f* de dérivation

Attention: ne pas confondre avec **juncture**.

juncture ['dʒʌŋktʃər] N *esp Fml* **1** *(critical point in time)* **at this j.** en ce moment même, dans ces circonstances; *(in past)* à ce moment même; **we have reached a critical j.** nous sommes dans une situation critique **2** *Anat* jonction *f*

Attention: ne pas confondre avec **junction**.

June [dʒuːn] N VOIR GRAMMAIRE A81–2; B60–2 juin *m*; **in J.** au mois de juin, en juin; **(on) the first/the seventh of J.** le premier/le sept juin

▸▸ **J. beetle, J. bug** hanneton *m*

jungle ['dʒʌŋg(ə)l] N *(forest)*, *Fig (competitive environment)* jungle *f*; **a j. animal/plant** une bête/plante de la jungle; *Fig* **a j. of red tape** une montagne de paperasseries

▸▸ *Old-fashioned Offensive Sl* **j. bunny** nègre, *f* négresse; **j. fever** paludisme *m*; *Am* **j. gym** cage *f* à poules *(jeu)*; *Br Fam* **j. juice** gnôle *f*, **j. warfare** combat *m* de jungle

junior ['dʒuːnjər] ADJ **1** *(younger person)* cadet, plus jeune; **to be j. to sb** être plus jeune que qn; **she's three years j. to me, she's j. to me by three years** elle a trois ans de moins que moi; **Hudson J.** *or* **Jnr** *or* **Jr** *or* **Jun** *(the son)* Hudson fils *ou* junior *ou* Jr; *(one of two or more brothers)* Hudson junior *ou* Jr

2 *(in rank)* subalterne; **to be j. to sb** être au-dessous de qn

3 *(small)* petit; **j. portions available** *(in restaurant)* menu enfant

N **1** *(younger person)* cadet, -ette; *esp Am Fam* **where's j.?** où est le petit/la petite?; **to be sb's j.** être le cadet de qn, être plus jeune que qn; **she's three years my j., she's my j. by three years** elle est ma cadette de trois ans, elle est plus jeune que moi de trois ans

2 *(subordinate)* *(employé, -ée)* subalterne *mf*, *Fam Pej* sous-fifre *m*; **he's our office j.** *(performing general duties)* c'est notre factotum

3 *Br Sch (between 7 and 11)* élève *mf* du cours élémentaire *ou* du cours moyen; *Am Sch, Univ* élève/étudiant, -ante d'avant-dernière année; *Br* **to go to the juniors, to attend the juniors** *(junior school)* aller à l'école primaire

4 *Sport (between 13 and 15)* minime *mf*, *(between 15 and 17)* cadet, -ette; *(between 17 and 21)* junior *mf*

▸▸ *Br Sch* **j. classes** petites classes *fpl*; **j. clerk** commis *m* ordinaire, jeune employé, -ée, employé, -ée subalterne; *Am Univ* **j. college** = institut *m* universitaire du premier cycle; *Br Univ* **j. common room** salle *f* des étudiants; *Br Law* **j. counsel** jeune avocat, -ate; **j. executive** jeune cadre *m*; *Am* **j. high school** ≃ collège *m* d'enseignement secondaire; **j. minister** sous-secrétaire *m* d'État, *pl* sous-secrétaires d'État (**in** à); **j. miss** *(clothes size)* fillette *f*; **j. partner** associé, -ée adjoint(e); *Br* **j. school** école *f* élémentaire *(pour les enfants de 7 à 11 ans)*; *Com* **j. sizes** petites tailles *fpl*; **j. teacher** jeune professeur *m*; *Am Sch, Univ* **j. year** avant-dernière année *f*

juniper ['dʒuːnɪpər] N *(tree)* genévrier *m*, genièvre *m*

▸▸ **j. berries** baies *fpl* *ou* grains *mpl* de genièvre; **j. oil** essence *f* de genièvre **j. tree** genévrier, genièvre

junk¹ [dʒʌŋk] N *(no pl)* **1** *(unwanted objects)* bric-à-brac *m inv*, *(outdated objects)* vieilleries *fpl*; *(old iron)* ferraille *f*, *(inferior goods)* camelote *f*, pacotille *f*, *Fam* cochonnerie(s) *f(pl)*, saleté(s) *f(pl)*; **clear your j. off the table** retire tout ton bazar de la table

2 *Fig Fam (bad-quality book, play etc)* navet

m, foutaise *f*, *Sl (nonsense)* foutaises *fpl*, conneries *fpl*; **she eats nothing but j.** elle mange que des saloperies

3 *Sl (heroin etc)* came *f*; **to be on j.** se camer **VT** *Fam (get rid of, discard) (old furniture, documents etc)* balancer, mettre à la poubelle; *(ideas, plan)* laisser tomber, balancer

▸▸ *StExch* **j. bond** junk bond *m (obligation à haut rendement mais à haut risque)*; **j. dealer** brocanteur, -euse; *Comput* **j. e-mail** messages *mpl* publicitaires; *Fam* **j. food** nourriture *f* de mauvaise qualité; **j. heap** dépotoir *m*; *(in garden etc)* tas *m* de détritus; *(old car)* tas *m* de ferraille; *Fig* **to throw sth/sb on the j. heap** mettre qch/qn au rebut; *Fig* **young people who end up on the j. heap** les jeunes qui finissent sous les ponts; *Am* **j. jewelry** bijoux *mpl* (de) fantaisie; **j. mail** courrier *m* publicitaire; **j. room** pièce *f* de débarras; **j. shop** magasin *m* de brocante

junk² **N** *(Chinese boat)* jonque *f*

junker ['dʒʌŋkə(r)] **N** *Am Fam (old car)* vieille bagnole *f*

junket ['dʒʌŋkɪt] **1** *Culin* lait *m* caillé *(souvent parfumé)* **2** *Fam (feast)* festin *m*, banquet *m* **3** *(pleasure trip)* plaisir *m*, voyage *m* d'agrément; *Pej (by public official)* voyage *m* d'agrément aux frais de la princesse *ou* du contribuable

VI 1 *(feast)* banqueter, festoyer **2** *Am (travel)* faire un voyage d'agrément; *Pej (of public official)* voyager aux frais de la princesse *ou* du contribuable

junketing ['dʒʌŋkɪtɪŋ] **N** voyages *mpl* aux frais de la princesse *ou* du contribuable

junkie ['dʒʌŋkɪ] **N** *Sl (drug addict)* drogué, -ée, camé, -ée; *Fig* **a chocolate/sugar j.** un fou/une folle de chocolat/sucre, un(e) accro du chocolat/sucre; *Fig* **a football/chess j.** un(e) fana de football/d'échecs

junkman, *pl* **junkmen** ['dʒʌŋkmæn, -men] **N** *Am* chiffonnier *m*, brocanteur *m*

junky ['dʒʌŋkɪ] **ADJ** *Fam (goods)* de camelote; *(novel, film etc)* nul, à la manque

N *Sl* = **junkie**

junkyard ['dʒʌŋkjɑːd] **N** *(for metal)* dépôt *m* de ferrailleur; *(for rags, discarded objects)* dépôt *m* de chiffonnier; *Fig* **their garden is a real j.** leur jardin est un véritable dépotoir

Juno ['dʒuːnəʊ] **N** *Myth, Astron* Junon *f*, *Fig* déesse *f*

Junoesque [dʒuːnəʊˈesk] **ADJ** d'une grâce souveraine

junta ['dʒʌntə] **N** *Mil, Pol usu Pej* junte *f*

Jupiter ['dʒuːpɪtər] **N** *Myth* Jupiter *m*; *Astron* Jupiter *f*

Jurassic [dʒuːˈræsɪk] **ADJ, N** *Geol* jurassique *m*

juridical [dʒʊˈrɪdɪk(ə)l] **ADJ** juridique

jurisdiction [dʒʊərɪsˈdɪkʃən] **N 1** *Law* juridiction *f*, **area within** *or* **under the j. of …** territoire soumis à l'autorité judiciaire *ou* à la juridiction de …; **to come** *or* **fall within** *or* **under the j. of a court** *(of question etc)* tomber sous *ou* relever de une juridiction d'une cour; **to recognize the j. of the Court** reconnaître l'autorité judiciaire du tribunal

2 *(general authority)* autorité *f*, **to have j. over sb** avoir autorité sur qn; **he has no j. over his brother's activities** il n'a aucune emprise *ou* aucun pouvoir sur ce que fait son frère

3 *Fig (field of activity)* compétence *f*, ressort *m*; **this matter does not come within** *or* **is not in** *or* **falls outside our j.** cette affaire ne relève pas de notre compétence, cette affaire n'est pas de notre ressort

jurisprudence [dʒʊərɪsˈpruːdəns] **N** jurisprudence *f*

jurist ['dʒʊərɪst] **N** *Fml (expert)* juriste *mf*, légiste *m*; *(writer)* juriste *m*; *Am (lawyer)* avocat, -ate; *(student)* étudiant, -ante en droit

juror ['dʒʊərər] **N 1** *Law* juré, -ée *f* **2** *(in competition etc)* membre *m* du jury

jury ['dʒʊərɪ] **N** VOIR GRAMMAIRE A11 **1** *Law* jury *m*; **to be** *or* **serve** *or* **sit on the j.** faire partie *ou* être membre du jury, *Fam* être du jury; **to pack** *or* **rig** *or* **stack a** *or* **the j.** composer un jury partisan; **foreman of the j.** président *m* du jury; **ladies and gentlemen of the j.!** mesdames et messieurs les jurés!; **the j. is out** le jury est en délibération; *Fig Fam* **the j. is still out on that (one)** *(final decision has not been made)* rien de définitif n'a été décidé; *Am Law* **(federal) grand j.** = tribunal *m* (fédéral) se prononçant sur la mise en accusation; **special jury** jury spécial

2 *(for examination, competition)* jury *m*

▸▸ *Law* **j. box** sièges *mpl* des jurés; **j. duty** devoir *m* de participation au jury; **to do (one's) j. duty** s'acquitter de son devoir de participation au jury; **to be called (up) for j. duty** être convoqué comme juré; *Br Sl* **j. nobbling** corruption *f* de jurés; **j. rigging** = composition *f* d'un jury partisan; **j. service** devoir *m* de participation au jury; **to do (one's) j. service** s'acquitter de son devoir de participation au jury; **to be called (up) for j. service** être convoqué comme juré

juryman, *pl* **jurymen** ['dʒʊərɪmən] **N** juré *m*

jurywoman, *pl* **jurywomen** ['dʒʊərɪwʊmən, -wɪmɪn] **N** femme *f* juré, jurée *f*

just¹ [dʒʌst] **ADJ 1** *(fair) (person, criticism etc)* juste **(to, towards** envers, à l'égard de)

2 *(legitimate) (cause, anger, claim)* juste, légitime; *(reward, punishment, law, peace, war)* juste; **to get one's j. deserts** avoir ce qu'on mérite; **it's only j. that …** ce n'est que justice que … + *sub*; **it's only j. to ask such questions** il est tout à fait normal de poser de telles questions; **as (it) is only j.** comme de juste; **to show j. cause for concern, to have j. cause to be concerned** avoir de bonnes raisons de s'inquiéter

3 *(observation, account etc)* juste

NPL the j. les justes *mpl*, *Lit* **to sleep the sleep of the j.** dormir du sommeil du juste

JUST²

juste **1–3, 6, 7, 10**	▪ exactement **1**
▪ seulement **6**	▪ simplement **8**
▪ absolument **11**	

ADV 1 *(exactly, precisely)* juste, justement, exactement, précisément; **he's j. the man you are looking for** c'est juste *ou* exactement *ou* tout à fait l'homme qu'il vous faut; **that's j. what happened** c'est justement *ou* exactement *ou* bien ce qui est arrivé; **how many are there?** combien y en a-t-il au juste *ou* exactement?; **j. why does she do it?** pour quelles raisons exactement le fait-elle?, pourquoi exactement le fait-elle?; **that's j. why she did it** c'est précisément *ou* exactement pour cela qu'elle l'a fait, c'est justement pourquoi elle l'a fait; **j. as you wish** (c'est) comme tu veux; **I left the books j. as they were** *or* **j. the way they were** j'ai laissé les livres exactement comme *ou* tels que je les ai trouvés, j'ai laissé les livres tels quels; **that's j. it** *or* **j. the point!** précisément!, justement!, voilà!; **j. so** *(like this)* exactement comme ça!; *Br (that's right)* exactement!, précisément!, voilà!; **he set the vase down j. so** *(carefully)* il a posé le vase avec soin; *Fam usu Pej* **her house is always j. so** sa maison est toujours archiimpeccable; **it's** *or* **that's j. like him!** *(typical of him)* c'est bien de lui!; **isn't that j. my luck!** c'est bien ma chance!; **I have j. the same problem** j'ai exactement le même problème; **j.**

the same *(nevertheless)* cela n'empêche, tout de même

2 *(with place)* juste; **j. here** juste ici, ici même

3 *(with time: exactly)* juste; **j. then, j. at that moment** juste à ce moment, à ce moment précis; **it's j. ten o'clock** *or* **ten o'clock** il est dix heures juste(s) *ou* pile, il est tout juste dix heures; **j. when** *or* **as the door was opening** au moment même où la porte s'ouvrait; **j. as** *or* **when I was leaving** juste comme *ou* juste quand *ou* au moment même où je partais; **she's j. in time for a drink** elle arrive pile pour *ou* elle arrive juste à temps pour prendre un verre

4 *(with time: at this moment)* **he's busy j. now** il est occupé en ce moment *ou* pour l'instant; **I'm not ready j. now** *or* **j. yet** je ne suis pas encore prêt, je ne suis pas prêt pour le moment; **she's j. leaving, she's leaving j. now** elle part *(tout ou juste à l'instant)*; **she's not leaving j. now** *or* **j. yet** elle ne part pas encore, elle ne part pas tout de suite; **to be j. about to do sth** être sur le point de faire qch; **(I'm) coming!, I'm coming j. now!** j'arrive!; **my hair is j. turning grey** *or* **is j. beginning to turn grey** mes cheveux commencent juste à grisonner

5 *(with time: a short while ago, recently)* **to have j. arrived/woken up/written a letter** venir d'arriver/de se réveiller/d'écrire une lettre; **I've only j. seen him and I haven't had time yet to …** je viens seulement de le voir et je n'ai pas encore eu le temps de …; **I've (only) j. seen him going downstairs** je viens de le voir à l'instant qui descendait; **I saw him j. now, I've j. (now) seen him** je l'ai vu à l'instant, je viens de le voir; **I've only j. this minute seen him** je viens de le voir à l'instant, je l'ai vu à l'instant; **I saw him j. yesterday, I j. saw him yesterday** je l'ai vu pas plus tard qu'hier; **he has j. (now) left school** il sort du lycée; **'j. picked/cooked'** *(newly)* 'cueilli/cuit du jour'; **'j. arrived'** 'fraîchement arrivé' VOIR GRAMMAIRE B31

6 *(only, no more than)* seulement, juste; **I have come j. to see you** je viens seulement *ou* juste *ou* uniquement pour vous voir; **we have j. a few copies left** il nous (en) reste quelques exemplaires seulement *ou* juste quelques exemplaires; **I've got j. one left** il ne m'en reste qu'un; **she's j. a baby** ce n'est qu'un bébé; **it costs j. ten dollars** ça ne coûte que dix dollars, ça coûte dix dollars seulement; **it's j. ten o'clock** il est seulement dix heures, il n'est que dix heures; **(wait) j. a moment!** (attendez) un petit instant!, un instant!; **j. a minute, aren't you supposed to be somewhere else?** une seconde, tu n'es pas censé être ailleurs?; **give me j. a tiny bit** donnez-m'en (juste) un petit peu

7 *(only a little, slightly)* juste, (un) peu; **j. a little more/less/better** juste un peu plus/moins/mieux; **j. in front/behind/above/below** juste devant/derrière/au-dessus/au-dessous; **j. over/under fifty pounds** un tout petit peu plus de/moins de cinquante livres; **it's j. before ten (o'clock)** il est presque dix heures; **we go to bed j. before ten (o'clock)** nous nous couchons juste avant *ou* peu avant dix heures; **j. after my birthday** juste après *ou* peu après mon anniversaire

8 *(merely, simply)* simplement; **tell him j. to wait** dites-lui qu'il n'a qu'à attendre; *Fam* **I'll j. pop in** je ne ferai qu'entrer et sortir; **j. ask if you need money** vous n'avez qu'à demander si vous avez besoin d'argent; **they won't accept j. to please me** ils n'accepteront pas uniquement pour *ou* rien que pour me faire plaisir à moi; **we j. can't understand it** nous n'arrivons vraiment pas à comprendre; **why not? – because I j. don't** pourquoi pas? – parce que c'est comme ça; **I j. don't want to** je ne veux pas, un point c'est tout

9 *(easily)* **I can j. see him as a doctor** je le vois très bien médecin; **I can j. smell the sea air, looking at these photos** rien qu'en regardant ces photos je sens l'air de la mer **10** *(by a narrow margin, barely)* **(only) j.** de justesse; **he (only) j. (about) managed to catch the train** c'est tout juste s'il a eu le train; **they (only) j. missed the train** ils ont manqué le train de peu; **I have (only) j. enough** *or* **j. about enough to live on** j'ai tout juste de quoi vivre; **she caught the train but (only) j.** elle a eu le train mais de justesse; **you're (only) j. in time** vous arrivez à temps, mais c'est de justesse **11** *(utterly, completely)* absolument; **it was j. splendid!** c'était absolument merveilleux!, c'était merveilleux, ni plus ni moins!; **it was j. a nightmare** c'était un véritable cauchemar; *Br* **do you remember? – don't I j.!** vous vous en souvenez? – et comment (que je m'en souviens) *ou* vous pensez (si je m'en souviens)! **12** *(in comparisons)* **j. as, j. about as** tout aussi; **that's j. (about) as good as** c'est tout aussi bien, c'est tout comme; **that will do j. as well** ça fera aussi bien l'affaire **13** *(in threats, orders, exhortations)* **j. (you) try!** essaie donc un peu!; **j. (you) wait!** tu n'as qu'à attendre!; *(threat)* attends, tu vas voir!, tu ne perds rien pour attendre!; **j. (you) read this!** lisez donc cela!; **j. think** réfléchis donc un peu!; **j. look!** regarde-moi ça!; **j. be quiet, will you!** veux-tu bien te taire!; **j. who do you think you are?** pour qui vous prenez-vous, au juste? **14 j. about** *(approximately)* plus ou moins, à peu près; *(almost)* quasiment; **it's j. about ten (o'clock)** il est plus ou moins *ou* à peu près dix heures; **j. about!** plus ou moins!, à peu près!; *Fam* **that j. about does it** *(I'm leaving)* ça suffit comme ça *ou* amplement *ou* largement; **I've j. about had enough of this** j'en ai vraiment par dessus la tête de ça **15** *(indicating preference)* **I would j. as soon stay here** j'aimerais tout autant rester ici; **he would j. as soon that …** il aimerait tout autant que … + *sub* **16 it's j. as well (that) …** *(fortunate)* heureusement que …; **and (it was) j. as well** et

c'était une chance, et tant mieux; **I might j. as well have remained silent** j'aurais (tout) aussi bien fait de garder le silence; **they could j. as well do without it** ils feraient (tout) aussi bien de s'en passer

justice ['dʒʌstɪs] N **1** *(no pl)* *(power of law)* justice *f*; **to administer** *or* **dispense/exercise j.** rendre/exercer la justice; **to demand/obtain j.** demander/obtenir justice; **to bring sb to j.** traduire qn en justice **2** *(no pl)* *(fairness)* *(of cause, claim, decision etc)* légitimité *f*; *(of reward, punishment)* justice *f*; **in all j.** en toute justice; **in (all) j. to her, we should say …** pour être juste envers elle *ou* pour lui rendre justice, on devrait dire …; **to do sb j., to do j. to sb** *(of photo, garment, hairstyle etc)* avantager qn, mettre qn en valeur; **to do j. to a meal** faire honneur à un repas; **to do oneself j.** se mettre en valeur, se montrer sous son meilleur jour; *Fml* **with j.** *(with good reason)* avec juste raison, à juste titre **3** *(judge in Supreme Court)* juge *m*; **Mr J. Long** *(title)* Monsieur le juge Long; **Mrs J. Long** Madame le juge Long
► ► *Am* **the J. Department** ≃ le ministère de la Justice; **J. of the Peace** juge de paix

justifiable ['dʒʌstɪfaɪəb(ə)l] ADJ justifié, légitime
► ► *Law* **j. homicide** *(killing in self-defence)* homicide *m* justifiable; *(state execution)* application *f* de la peine de mort

justifiably ['dʒʌstɪfaɪəblɪ] ADV légitimement, à juste titre; **they acted quite j.** ils ont agi en toute légitimité

justification [dʒʌstɪfɪ'keɪʃən] N **1** justification *f* **(for** de, pour); **in j. of** comme justification de; **there's no j. for behaviour like that!** rien ne peut justifier un tel comportement!; **what's her j. for this?** comment justifie-t-elle ceci?; **with some j., I might add** à juste titre, ajouterais-je; **that's no j.!** ce n'est pas une raison! **2** *Typ, Comput* justification *f*, **left/right j.** justification à gauche/droite

justify ['dʒʌstɪfaɪ] VT **1** *(person, decision, action, sb's behaviour etc)* justifier; **to j. oneself in the eyes of sb** se justifier aux yeux de qn; **that does not j. your voting for my rival** cela

n'est pas une raison suffisante pour que vous votiez pour mon rival; **to be justified in doing sth** *(have a good reason to)* avoir de bonnes raisons pour faire qch, être fondé à faire qch; **a fully justified decison/fear** une décision/une crainte bien fondée *ou* qui se justifie; **am I justified in thinking that …?** ai-je raison de croire que …? **2** *Typ, Comput* justifier; **left/right justified** justifié à gauche/droite

just-in-time ADJ *Com* juste à temps
► ► **j. distribution** distribution *f* juste à temps; **j. manufacturing** production *f* juste à temps; **j. production** production juste à temps; **j. purchasing** achat *m* juste à temps

justly ['dʒʌstlɪ] ADV **1** *(fairly, rightly)* avec justice, justement **2** *(accurately, deservedly)* à juste titre; **j. famous** célèbre à juste titre

justness ['dʒʌstnɪs] N **1** *(of cause, demand)* légitimité *f* **2** *(accuracy)* *(of idea, remark etc)* justesse *f*

► **jut out** [dʒʌt] (**-tt-**) VI *(of balcony, rock etc)* faire saillie, être en saillie; **to j. out over sth** *(overhang)* surplomber qch, avancer sur qch; **the headland juts (out) into the sea** le cap avance (en saillie) dans la mer; **something is jutting out of your pocket** quelque chose dépasse de votre poche; **his chin juts out** il a un menton en galoche
VT SEP *(chin)* avancer

jute [dʒuːt] N *(plant, fibre)* jute *m*

juvenile ['dʒuːvɪnaɪl, *Am* -'n(ə)l] ADJ **1** *Pej (childish)* *(behaviour, ideas etc)* puéril; **don't be so j.!** ne sois pas si puéril *ou* gamin! **2** *(for young people)* *(books, games etc)* pour enfants, pour la jeunesse; *(hobbies, activities)* d'enfant(s); *Fml (youthful)* juvénile
N *Fml* jeune *mf*, adolescent, -ente
► ► **j. court** tribunal *m* pour enfants *(10-16 ans)*; **j. delinquency** délinquance *f* juvénile; **j. delinquent** jeune délinquant, -ante, mineur, -e délinquant(e); **j. offender** accusé, -ée mineur(e)

juvenilia [dʒuːvɪ'nɪlɪə] NPL œuvres *fpl* de jeunesse; **a piece of Mozart j.** une œuvre de jeunesse de Mozart

juxtapose [dʒʌkstə'pəʊz] VT juxtaposer

juxtaposition [dʒʌkstəpə'zɪʃən] N juxtaposition *f*, **to be in j.** se juxtaposer

K, k [keɪ] N 1 (letter) K, k m; two k's deux k 2 Comput (abbr kilobyte) K, Ko; how many k are left? combien de Ko reste-t-il?; 720k diskette disquette f de 720 Ko 3 (abbr thousand) K 4 Fam (abbr thousand pounds) he earns 30K il gagne 30 000 livres 5 Fam (abbr kilometre(s)) kilomètre(s) m(pl); a 10K race une course de dix kilomètres

kabuki [kə'buːkɪ] N kabuki m

Kabul ['kɑːbʊl] N Kaboul

kaffeeklatsch ['kæfeɪ'klætʃ] N Am = réunion f de femmes qui bavardent en prenant le café

Kaffir ['kæfər] ADJ 1 (pertaining to the ethnic group) caf(f)re mf 2 Offensive Sl nègre ▶ N 1 (member of the ethnic group) Caf(f)re mf 2 Offensive Sl nègre m, négresse f

Kafkaesque [kæfkə'esk] ADJ kafkaïen

kaftan ['kæftæn] N kaftan m

kalashnikov [kə'læʃnɪkɒv] N kalachnikov m

kale, kail [keɪl] N (cabbage) (curly) k. chou m frisé

kaleidoscope [kə'laɪdəskəʊp] N kaléidoscope m

kaleidoscopic [kəlaɪdə'skɒpɪk] ADJ kaléidoscopique

kamikaze [kæmɪ'kɑːzɪ] ADJ, N kamikaze m

Kampuchea [kæmpʊ'tʃɪə] N Formerly Kampuchéa m

kangaroo [kæŋgə'ruː] N 1 (animal) kangourou m 2 St Exch Fam valeur f australienne ▶▶ k. court tribunal m illégal; (held by strikers, prisoners etc) ≃ tribunal populaire

Kan(s) abbr Kansas

kaolin ['keɪəlɪn] N kaolin m

kapok ['keɪpɒk] N kapok m ▶▶ k. tree kapokier m

Kaposi's sarcoma [kæ'pəʊsɪzsɑː'kəʊmə] N Med sarcome m de Kaposi

kaput [kə'pʊt] ADJ Fam fichu, foutu

karakul ['kærəkʊl] N (sheep, fur) karakul m, caracul m

karaoke [kærɪ'əʊkeɪ] N Mus karaoké m ▶▶ k. machine karaoké

karate [kə'rɑːtɪ] N Sport karaté m ▶▶ k. chop coup m de karaté (donné avec le tranchant de la main)

karma ['kɑːmə] N Hindu Rel karma m

kart [kɑːt] N kart m ▶▶ k. racing karting m

karting ['kɑːtɪŋ] N karting m; to go k. faire du karting

kasbah ['kæzbɑː] N casbah f

Kashmir [kæʃ'mɪər] N Geog Cachemire m

Kashmiri [kæʃ'mɪərɪ] N 1 (person) Cachemirien, -enne 2 Ling kashmiri m ▶ ADJ cachemirien

Katmandu [kætmæn'duː] N Katmandou

kayak ['kaɪæk] N (canoe) kayac m, kayak m

Kazak(h)stan [kæzæk'stɑːn] N Kazakhstan m

kazoo [kə'zuː] N 1 (instrument) mirliton m 2 Am Fam (buttocks) derrière m, arrière-train m; Fig to have problems/debts up the k. avoir des problèmes/des dettes jusqu'au cou

KB [keɪ'biː] N Comput (abbr kilobyte) Ko m

KBE [keɪbiː'iː] N Br (abbr Knight (Commander of the Order) of the British Empire) Chevalier m de l'Ordre de l'Empire britannique

Kbps [keɪbiːpiː'es] Comput (abbr kilobytes per second) ko/s

KCB [keɪsiː'biː] N Br (abbr Knight Commander (of the Order) of the Bath) Chevalier m Commandeur de l'Ordre du Bain

kebab [kə'bæb] N Culin brochette f, shish k. chiche-kébab m

kecks [keks] NPL Br Fam (trousers) fute m, falzar m

kedge [kedʒ] Naut N ancre f à jet ▶ VT (boat) haler, touer sur une ancre à jet ▶ VI se touer sur une ancre à jet ▶▶ k. anchor ancre f à jet

kedgeree [kedʒə'riː] N Culin = mets m de riz accommodé avec du beurre, des œufs durs et du poisson fumé

keel [kiːl] N 1 Naut, Aviat quille f; on an even k. Naut sans différence de tirant d'eau ou de calaison; Fig to be back on an even k. (of situation etc) être de nouveau stable, s'être stabilisé; (of person) avoir retrouvé son égalité d'âme; to put a company/the economy (back) on an even k. (re)mettre une entreprise/l'économie d'aplomb 2 Bot (of leaf, petal etc) carène f ▶ VT (boat) mettre en carène ▶ keel over VI (of boat) chavirer; Fam (of person) (unconscious) tomber dans les pommes; (dead) tomber raide mort; (of structure, hut etc) se renverser; to k. over backwards tomber à la renverse ▶ VT SEP (boat) faire chavirer

keelhaul [ˈkiːlhɔːl] VT 1 Naut, Hist (sailor) faire passer sous la quille 2 (rebuke) réprimander sévèrement, Fam passer un savon à

keen¹ [kiːn] ADJ 1 (enthusiastic) (yachtsman, follower) ardent, assidu; (reader) passionné; (at school, work) zélé; as a k. reader of your articles, I … lecteur assidu de vos articles, je …; I'll come with you, but I'm not k. j'y vais avec toi, mais je n'en brûle pas d'envie; look, I'm really not k. écoute, je n'en ai vraiment pas envie ou je n'y tiens vraiment pas; she's very k. for us to do it elle tient beaucoup à ce que nous le fassions; he seemed very k. at first (on idea, proposal etc) au départ il avait l'air très enthousiaste; to be as k. as mustard déborder d'enthousiasme, brûler d'ardeur; to be k. on doing sth avoir très envie de faire qch; to be k. on sth (on golf, politics, novel) adorer qch; (idea, proposal) être plein d'enthousiasme pour qch; he wasn't k. on the idea l'idée ne l'emballait pas; she's k. on him il lui plaît; she's k. on sport le sport la passionne, elle adore le sport; to take a k. interest in sth suivre qch avec un intérêt vif; a k. desire for peace un désir ardent de paix; k. competition concurrence f acharnée ou âpre; there is a k. demand for these stocks ces fonds sont activement recherchés; Br Com k. prices prix mpl au plus bas, prix étudiés; k. golfer mordu m ou passionné de golf; k. sportsman ardent sportif m; a k. advocate of … un partisan fervent de … 2 (perceptive) (eye, look) perçant, pénétrant, vif; (mind) fin, pénétrant, vif; to have a k. eye for a bargain être prompt à reconnaître une bonne affaire; to have a k. ear avoir l'oreille ou l'ouïe fine; to have a k. ear for a tune/for accents reconnaître facilement les mélodies/les accents; a k. sense of smell un odorat très développé; to have a k. awareness of a problem être profondément conscient d'un problème 3 (intense) (sorrow) aigu, f aiguë; (regret) poignant; (remorse) cuisant; k. appetite rude appétit m; to have a k. appetite for success avoir un appétit de succès dévorant; k. pleasure vif plaisir m 4 (cold) (wind, air) vif, piquant 5 (sharp) (knife, blade) affilé, aiguisé; Fig (sound) aigu; k. edge fil m tranchant; k. edged bien affilé, aiguisé, tranchant 6 Am Sl (very good) génial, -aux

keen² [kiːn] VI (at funeral) chanter une mélopée (en veillant un corps)

keenly ['kiːnlɪ] ADV 1 (enthusiastically) avec enthousiasme; to be k. interested in … s'intéresser vivement à …; a k. contested competition/election/etc une compétition/des élections/etc âprement disputée(s) 2 (intensely) profondément; (to regret) amèrement; to feel sth k. être profondément affecté par qch 3 the wind was blowing k. il faisait un vent âpre

keenness ['kiːnnɪs] N 1 (of person) enthousiasme m; (at school, work) zèle m; (of troops) mordant m; k. on doing sth grand désir m de faire qch 2 (of sight) acuité f; (of hearing, sense of smell) finesse f; (of mind) pénétration f, finesse f 3 (of feeling, emotion etc) intensité f; (of grief, sense of remorse) acuité f 4 (of blade) tranchant m 5 (of the cold) âpreté f, rigueur f

KEEP [kiːp]

VT	garder 1–3, 5, 7 ▪ retenir 1
	▪ maintenir 3 ▪ entretenir 5 ▪ tenir 6, 8, 9 ▪ élever 6 ▪ observer 8
VI	rester 1 ▪ se tenir 1 ▪ aller 1
	▪ continuer 2 ▪ se conserver 3

N 1 (food) nourriture f; (money) frais mpl de subsistance; to pay for one's k. payer sa pension; do you give your parents any money for your k.? est-ce que tu donnes de l'argent à tes parents pour payer ta pension?; **she can only just afford to pay for her k.** elle arrive tout juste à se nourrir et à se loger; **to earn one's k.** *(earn a living)* subvenir à ses besoins; *(pay one's way) (of employee)* mériter son salaire; *(of lodger etc)* rendre de menus services pour payer sa pension; **to earn its k.** *(of equipment)* être rentable; **the van may be old but it still earns its k.** la camionnette est vieille mais elle nous rend encore bien service

2 *(of castle)* donjon *m*

3 *Fam* **for keeps** pour de bon

VT *(pt & pp* **kept** [kept]*)* **1** *(retain) (something)* garder; *(sb's attention)* retenir; **you can k. the book I lent you** vous pouvez garder le livre que je vous ai prêté; **to k. sth for sb** garder qch pour qn; **I asked them to k. it for me** je leur ai demandé de me le garder; **to k. sth from sb** *(not inform of)* ne pas révéler qch à qn; **to k. sth for later** garder *ou* conserver *ou* réserver qch pour plus tard; **to k. the best for** *or* **until last** garder le meilleur pour la fin; **to k. sth in reserve** *or* **in store** garder qch en réserve; **to k. a seat for sb** garder une place à qn; **to k. one's figure** garder la ligne; **to k. its shape/colour** *(of garment)* conserver sa forme/couleur; **to k. one's job** garder *ou* conserver son emploi

2 *(store) (provisions, letters etc)* garder; **the cupboard where I k. the crockery** l'armoire où je mets la vaisselle; **k. medicines out of the reach of children** ranger les médicaments hors de la portée des enfants

3 *(maintain) (order)* maintenir; *(silence, secret)* garder; **to k. one's composure** garder son sang-froid; **to k. one's course** continuer *ou* poursuivre son chemin; **he keeps himself to himself** il est très réservé; **he prefers to k. himself to himself** il évite les contacts; **they k. themselves to themselves** ils font bande à part

4 *(maintain in a condition)* **to k. sth clean/ secret** tenir qch propre/secret; **k. dry** craint l'humidité; *Fam* **k. it clean!** *(no vulgarity)* pas de grossièretés!; **to k. oneself warm** *(by staying in the warmth)* se tenir au chaud; *(by dressing warmly)* s'habiller chaudement; **to k. the door open/shut** garder *ou* laisser la porte ouverte/fermée; **the noise kept me awake** le bruit m'a empêché de dormir; **to k. sb wondering** laisser qn se poser des questions; **to k. sb waiting** faire attendre qn; **troops were kept on the alert** les soldats ont été maintenus en état d'alerte; **to k. one's hands in one's pockets** garder les mains dans ses poches

5 *(look after, tend) (sheep, herds)* garder; *(garden etc)* entretenir; *(person)* subvenir aux besoins de; *(mistress)* entretenir; **well/ badly kept road** route bien/mal entretenue; **he doesn't earn enough to k. himself** il ne gagne pas de quoi vivre; **he has his parents to k.** il a ses parents à (sa) charge; **I've got a family to k.** j'ai une famille à nourrir

6 *(possess) (bees, poultry etc)* élever; *(shop)* tenir

7 *(detain) (at home, in hospital, prison)* garder; **the doctor kept him in bed** le médecin l'a obligé à garder le lit; **there was nothing to k. me in England/with that firm** rien ne me retenait en Angleterre/dans cette entreprise; **what kept you?** qu'est-ce qui t'a retardé?; *Iron* comment tu as fait pour aller si vite?; **don't let me k. you** *(from your work etc)* je ne veux pas te retenir

8 *(observe) (the law, a rule)* observer, suivre; *(promise)* tenir, remplir; *(vow)* rester fidèle à; *(treaty)* tenir, respecter, observer; *(date, appointment)* ne pas manquer à; **to k. late hours** se coucher tard; **to k. one's word** tenir (sa) parole; *Rel* **to k. the commandments** observer les commandements; **if you cannot**

k. the appointment si vous ne pouvez pas être présent au rendez-vous

9 *(diary, accounts), Com (the books)* tenir; **to k. a record of events** prendre les événements en note; **to k. a note of sth** noter qch

10 *(protect)* préserver; **k. sb from evil** qn du mal); **God k. (you)!** Dieu vous garde!; **God k. his soul!** (que) Dieu ait son âme!; *Sport* **to k. goal** être gardien de but; *Cr* **to k. wicket** garder le guichet

11 *(celebrate) (festival, feast day)* célébrer

VI 1 *(remain, stay)* rester, se tenir; **to k. well** *(stay)* rester en bonne santé; **are you keeping well?** vous vous portez bien?; **she doesn't k. well** elle ne jouit pas d'une bonne santé; **how are you keeping?** comment allez-vous?; **to k. quiet** se tenir *ou* rester tranquille; **to k. awake/calm** rester éveillé/ calme; **the weather is keeping cool/fine** le temps reste frais/se maintient au beau

2 *(continue)* continuer; **to k. straight on** continuer tout droit; **k. (to the) left/right** serrez à gauche/droite; **to k. doing sth** ne pas cesser *ou* ne pas arrêter de faire qch; **to k. working** continuer de travailler; **to k. smiling** garder le sourire; **don't k. asking questions** ne posez pas tout le temps des questions; **I wish you wouldn't k. saying that** j'aimerais bien que tu arrêtes de répéter cela; **I don't know how she keeps going on so little sleep** je ne sais pas comment elle arrive à tenir le coup en dormant si peu; **it's amazing the firm has kept going for so long** c'est incroyable que l'entreprise soit parvenue à se maintenir aussi longtemps

3 *(of food etc)* se garder, se conserver; **the story will k.** *(you can tell it to me later)* l'histoire n'y perdra rien; **what I've got to tell you won't k. till tomorrow** ce que j'ai à te dire n'attendra pas jusqu'à demain; **will it k. till later?** *(news etc)* est-ce que ça peut attendre?

▸ **keep at VT INSEP 1** *(continue to work at) (one's homework etc)* travailler; **to k. hard at it** travailler sans relâche

2 *(nag)* **to k. at sb to do sth** harceler qn *ou Fam* être toujours sur le dos de qn pour qu'il fasse qch

VT SEP to k. sb at it *(working)* faire travailler qn

▸ **keep away VI** ne pas approcher (**from** de); **she told the children to k. away from the river** elle a dit aux enfants de ne pas s'approcher de la rivière; **k. away (from me)!** n'approchez pas!; **I can't k. away from chocolates** je ne peux pas résister quand je vois des chocolats; **to k. away from drugs/alcohol** ne pas toucher à la drogue/à l'alcool

VT SEP k. that dog away (from me)! tenez ce chien loin de moi!; **the wind will k. the rain away** le vent empêchera la pluie; **to k. matches away from the children** tenir les allumettes hors de la portée des enfants; **the rain kept a lot of spectators away** la pluie a dissuadé bien des spectateurs de venir

▸ **keep back VI** ne pas approcher; **k. back!** n'approche pas!

VT SEP 1 *(crowd)* contenir, retenir; *(tears)* refouler, retenir; **he tried desperately to k. back his laughter** il s'efforça désespérément de se retenir *ou* s'empêcher de rire

2 *(withhold)* **to k. a sum back from sb's wages** retenir une somme sur le salaire de qn; **you're keeping something back from me** tu me caches quelque chose

3 *Sch (pupil)* garder en retenue; *(oblige to repeat a year)* faire redoubler; **to be kept back a year** redoubler

4 *(delay)* retenir; *(of strong wind etc)* retarder

5 *(prevent from making progress) (of lack of qualifications etc)* handicaper

▸ **keep down VI** se baisser

VT SEP 1 *(head, voice)* baisser; **to k. the noise (level) down** faire moins de bruit; *Fig* **to k. one's head down** garder un profil bas; **I can't**

k. my food down je rejette tout ce que je mange

2 *(repress)* garder le contrôle sur, avoir la mainmise sur; *(prices)* empêcher d'augmenter; **they were kept down by a repressive government** ils étaient contrôlés par un gouvernement répressif; *Prov* **you can't k. a good man down** les hommes de bien sont toujours récompensés

▸ **keep from VT SEP 1** *(conceal)* **to k. sth from sb** cacher qch à qn

2 *(prevent)* **to k. sb from doing sth** empêcher qn de faire qch

3 *(distract)* **to k. sb from his/her work** empêcher qn de travailler

VT INSEP *(refrain)* **to k. from doing sth** se retenir de faire qch

▸ **keep in VT SEP** *(person)* empêcher de sortir; *Sch (pupil)* garder en retenue; *(fire)* entretenir; **the police/the doctor kept him in overnight** la police/le docteur l'a gardé pour la nuit; *Fig* **to k. one's hand in** garder la main

VT SEP *(keep supplied with)* **to k. sb in sth** *(of person)* approvisionner qn en qch; **to k. sb in clothes/food** fournir de l'habillement/de la nourriture à qn; **to k. sb in beer/cigarettes** payer sa bière/ses cigarettes à qn; **to k. sb in luxury** permettre à qn de vivre dans le luxe; **his pocket money just about kept him in beer** son argent de poche lui servait tout juste à payer sa bière; **the grant barely keeps me in food** ma bourse me permet tout juste de me payer de quoi manger

▸ **keep in with VT INSEP** *Fam* **to k. in with sb** cultiver qn, rester en bons termes avec qn

▸ **keep off VI** *(stay away)* ne pas approcher

VT INSEP k. off the grass! défense de marcher sur le gazon!; **would you please k. off those flower beds** s'il vous plaît, ne marchez pas sur ces parterres de fleurs; **if you don't k. off my property ...** si vous pénétrez dans ma propriété ...

VT SEP 1 k. your hands off that! n'y touchez pas!; **k. your hands off me** bas les mains *ou Fam* les pattes!

2 to k. one's coat off rester sans (son) manteau; **the wind will k. the rain off** le vent empêchera la pluie

▸ **keep on VI 1** continuer; **to k. on doing sth** continuer à faire qch, ne pas cesser de faire qch; **don't k. on asking questions** ne posez pas tout le temps des questions

2 *(annoyingly, naggingly)* **don't k. on so!** arrête!; **I can't stand the way he keeps on about it** je ne supporte pas qu'il insiste tout le temps là-dessus; **he just keeps on and on about it** il n'arrête pas d'en parler

VT SEP 1 *(continue to wear) (coat etc)* garder

2 *(not turn off)* **to k. the central heating on** maintenir le chauffage central; **to k. the lights/TV on** laisser les lumières/la télé allumée(s)

3 *(continue to employ)* garder; **he was kept on by the firm** l'entreprise l'a gardé

▸ **keep on at VT INSEP** *Fam* **to k. on at sb (to do sth)** harceler qn *ou Fam* être toujours sur le dos de qn (pour qu'il fasse qch)

▸ **keep out VI** *(avoid, stay away from)* ne pas entrer (**of** dans); **to k. out of danger** rester à l'abri du danger; **try to k. out of trouble** essaie de ne pas t'attirer d'ennuis; **to k. out of an argument** rester en dehors d'une dispute; **k. out** *(sign)* défense d'entrer; **k. out of this!** mêlez-vous de ce qui vous regarde!

VT SEP *(prevent from entering)* empêcher d'entrer

▸ **keep to VT INSEP 1** *(adhere to) (promise)* tenir; **to k. to a subject** s'en tenir à un sujet; **to k. to the script** *(of actors)* s'en tenir au script

2 *(remain in, on)* rester dans; *(the left, the right)* tenir; **to k. to one's bed** garder le lit; **to k. to main roads** rester sur les grandes routes

VT SEP 1 *(hold)* **to k. sb to a promise** faire tenir une promesse à qn; **to k. delays/costs to**

a minimum minimiser les délais/les coûts **2** *(not reveal)* **to k. sth to oneself** garder qch pour soi, taire qch; **to k. one's impressions/opinions to oneself** garder ses impressions/opinions pour soi; **you can k. your remarks to yourself!** tes remarques, tu peux te les garder!; **k. your hands to yourself!** bas les mains *ou Fam* les pattes!

▸ **keep up** VI **1** *(of rain, snow etc)* continuer **2** *(remain level, go at same speed)* tenir le rythme

VT SEP **1** *(maintain) (building, road etc)* entretenir

2 *(continue) (custom)* conserver; *(correspondence, one's French etc)* entretenir; **we must k. it up** il nous faut continuer nos efforts; **k. it up!** continuez!; **k. up the good work!** continuez à bien travailler!

3 *(stop from falling or waning) (building, interest etc)* soutenir; *(courage)* soutenir, maintenir; **to k. up appearances** garder *ou* sauver les apparences

4 *(stop from going to bed)* empêcher d'aller se coucher; *(stop from sleeping)* empêcher de dormir; **worry had kept her up all night** l'inquiétude l'avait tenue éveillée toute la nuit

▸ **keep up with** VT INSEP **1** *(remain level with, go at same speed as)* **to k. up with sb** aller à la même allure que qn; **I can't k. up with you** vous marchez/parlez/*etc* trop vite pour moi; **he couldn't k. up with the rest of the children in his class** il n'arrivait pas à suivre dans sa classe; **I can barely k. up with her** *(she changes so much)* ça change tellement vite avec elle que j'ai du mal à suivre; *Fam* **to k. up with the Joneses** rivaliser de standing avec ses voisins; **to k. up with events** suivre les événements; **to k. up with the times** être à la page

2 *(remain in contact)* **to k. up with sb** rester en contact avec qn

keeper ['kiːpər] N *(person)* garde *m*; *(in zoo, of park, lighthouse)* gardien, -ienne; *(of museum etc)* conservateur, -trice; *(of herds)* gardien, -ienne, gardeur, -euse; *(gamekeeper)* garde-chasse *m*, *pl* gardes-chasse(s); *Ftbl Fam* goal *m*, gardien, -ienne de but; **I'm not my brother's k.** je ne suis pas responsable de mon frère

keep-fit N culture *f* physique, gymnastique *f* (d'entretien); **to do k.** faire de la gymnastique
▸▸ **k. class** cours *m* de gymnastique

keeping ['kiːpɪŋ] N *(of rule, promise)* observation *f*; *(of feast day)* célébration *f*; **to have sb/sth in one's k.** avoir qn/qch en garde *ou* sous sa garde; **in God's k.** à la garde de Dieu; **in k. with ...** en accord avec ...; **in k. with their commitment** conformément à leur engagement; **it is in k. with his principles** c'est conforme à *ou* en accord avec ses principes; **it's in k. with everything I have been told about her** cela concorde avec tout ce qu'on m'a dit sur elle; **out of k. with ...** en désaccord avec ...; **it was rather out of k. with the spirit of the occasion** cela détonnait avec l'esprit de l'occasion; **good k. qualities** *(of food)* bonnes qualités de conservation

keepsake ['kiːpseɪk] N souvenir *m*; **as a k. of his visit** en souvenir de sa visite

keg [keg] N **1** *(of beer)* barillet *m*; *(of water)* tonnelet *m*; *(of herring)* caque *f* **2** *(beer)* bière *f* pression
▸▸ **k. beer** bière pression

keister ['kiːstər] N *Am Fam (buttocks)* fesses *fpl*, derrière *m*

kelp [kelp] N *(seaweed)* varech *m*

Ken *abbr* Kentucky

ken [ken] N *Lit* **within sb's k.** dans les connaissances *ou* la compétence de qn; **beyond sb's k.** hors de la compétence de qn
VT *Scot, Dial* = **know** VT, VI

kennel ['ken(ə)l] N **1** *(of guard dog etc)* niche *f*; *(of hunting dog)* chenil *m*; **kennels** établissement *m* d'élevage de chiens; **to put a dog into kennels** mettre un chien en pension **2** **the k.** *(hounds)* la meute **3** *(of fox)* terrier *m*

kennelmaid ['ken(ə)lmeɪd] N employée *f* d'éleveur de chiens *ou* de chenil

Kenya ['kenjə, 'kiːn-] N Kenya *m*

Kenyan ['kenjən] ADJ kenyan
N Kenyan, -ane

kept [kept] ADJ *Old-fashioned, Hum* **a k. woman** une femme entretenue
PT, PP *see* **keep** VT, VI

keratosis [kerə'təʊsɪs] N kératose *f*

kerb [kɜːb] N **1** *Br (on pavement)* bordure *f ou* bord *m* de trottoir; **to draw up at the k.** s'arrêter le long du trottoir; **2** *St Exch Fam* **to buy/sell on the k.** acheter/vendre après la clôture officielle de la Bourse; **business done on the k.** opérations effectuées en coulisse, après clôture de Bourse
▸▸ *St Exch Fam* **k. broker** coulissier *m*, courtier, -ière hors Bourse; **k. drill** précautions *fpl* pour traverser la rue; *St Exch Fam* **k. market** marché *m* hors cote; **k. weight** poids *m* à vide

kerbcrawl ['kɜːbkrɔːl] VI = longer le trottoir en voiture à la recherche d'une prostituée

kerbcrawler ['kɜːbkrɔːlər] N = personne *f* qui longe le trottoir en voiture à la recherche d'une prostituée

kerbcrawling ['kɜːbkrɔːlɪŋ] N = recherche *f* d'une prostituée en voiture

kerbstone ['kɜːbstəʊn] N **1** *Br (of pavement)* pierre *f* de bordure
▸▸ *St Exch Fam* **k. market** marché *m* hors cote, coulisse *f*

kerchief ['kɜːtʃɪf] N *Old-fashioned (for head)* mouchoir *m* de tête; *(for neck)* fichu *m*

kerfuffle [kə'fʌf(ə)l] N *esp Br Fam* remueménage *m*, tohu-bohu *m*

kern [kɜːn] VT *Typ* créner, rapprocher

kernel ['kɜːn(ə)l] N **1** *(of nut)* intérieur *m*; *(in stone)* amande *f*; *(of pine cone)* pignon *m*; *(of cereal)* grain *m* **2** *Fig (of problem etc)* fond *m*, essentiel *m*; **a k. of truth** un fond de vérité

kerning ['kɜːnɪŋ] N *Typ* crénage *m*, rapprochement *m* de caractères

kerosene ['kerəsiːn] N **1** *Aviat* kérosène *m* **2** *Am (paraffin)* pétrole *m* lampant
▸▸ **k. lamp** lampe *f* à pétrole

kestrel ['kestrəl] N *(bird)* faucon *m* crécerelle *f*

ketch [ketʃ] N *Naut* ketch *m*, dundee *m*, dindet *m*

ketchup ['ketʃəp] N *(tomato)* **k.** ketchup *m*

kettle [ket(ə)l] N *(for boiling water)* bouilloire *f*; *(for cooking)* chaudron *m*; **to boil a k. of water** mettre une bouilloire d'eau à bouillir; **has the k. boiled?** est-ce que l'eau a bouilli?; **I'll put the k. on** je mets l'eau à chauffer pour le thé *etc*; *Fam* **here's a pretty** *ou* **a fine k. of fish!** nous voilà dans de beaux draps!; *Fam* **that's quite a different k. of fish** ça c'est une autre affaire

kettledrum ['ket(ə)ldrʌm] N *Mus* timbale *f*

key [kiː] N **1** *(of lock, door etc)* clef *f*, clé *f*; **to turn the k. (in the door)** donner un tour de clef (à la porte); *Old-fashioned Fig* **to have the k. of the door** *(have reached one's majority)* avoir atteint sa majorité

2 *Fig* **the k. to happiness/economic success** la clé du bonheur/de la réussite économique; **the k. to good health** les secrets *mpl* d'une bonne santé; *Fig* **it was the k. to his success** cela lui a ouvert les portes du succès; *Fig* **the k. to understanding sth** la clé permettant de comprendre qch; *Fig* **education is the k. to the nation's progress** l'éducation est la clé du progrès de la nation

3 *(answers) (to mystery, code etc)* clef *f*, *(of map etc)* légende *f*, *Sch* corrigé *m*, *(to exercises)* solutions *fpl*, *Comput (of sort, identification etc)* indicatif *m*, critère *m*

4 *Mus* ton *m*; **major/minor k.** ton majeur/mineur; **the k. of C** le ton d'ut; **to be off** *or* **out of k.** chanter/jouer faux

5 *Art etc (of painting)* caractéristique *f* de luminosité; **picture painted in a low k.** tableau peint dans les tons sombres

6 *(button etc) (of piano, organ, typewriter, computer, telephone etc)* touche *f*, *Elec* manette *f*, *Mus (of wind instrument)* clef *f*

7 *(turning device)* clef *f*, carotte *f*, *(of clock, mechanical toy etc)* remontoir *m*

8 *Constr (roughness of surface)* rappointis *m*
ADJ ATTRIB *(most important)* clé, clef; **k. factor** facteur clé; **remaining competitive is k. to our success** le maintien de la compétitivité est essentiel à notre succès; **one of the k. issues in the election** un des enjeux fondamentaux de ces élections; **k. person** *(in organization)* cheville *f* ouvrière, pilier *m*, pivot *m* (in de)
VT *Comput* taper; *(data, text)* taper, saisir; **to k. to disk** saisir
▸▸ **k. bar** *(in shop)* stand *m* de clef-minute; **k. card** *(for hotel room)* carte-clé *f*, *pl* cartesclés; **k. case** porte-clés *m inv*; *Am* **k. club** = club *m* privé dont les membres possèdent chacun une clef; *Comput* **k. combination** combinaison *f* de touches; *Cin* **k. grip** technicien, -ienne en chef *(chargé(e) de l'installation des décors et des rails de caméra au cinéma)*; **k. industries** industries *fpl* clés, industries-clés *fpl*; **k. money** pas *m* de porte; **k. numbers** *(on squared map)* numéros *mpl* de repérage; *Comput* **k. punch** perforatrice *f* à clavier; *Comput* **k. rack** *(in hotel etc)* tableau *m* (des clés); **k. ring** porte-clés *m inv*; *Mus* **k. signature** armature *f*, armure *f*, *Br Sch* **k. stage** étape *f* clé de la scolarité

▸ **key in** VT SEP *Comput etc* = **key** VT
▸ **key up** VT SEP **1** *(usu passive) (make tense)* **the crowd was keyed up for the match** la foule était tendue dans l'attente du match; **to be all keyed up** être crispé *ou* tendu **2** *Comput* = **key** VT

key-account N *Mktg* compte-clé *m*
▸▸ **k. management** gestion *f* de comptesclés; **k. sales** ventes *fpl* aux comptes-clés

keyboard ['kiːbɔːd] N **1** *(of piano, typewriter, computer)* clavier *m* **2** *Mus* **keyboards** claviers *mpl*; **on k.** aux claviers
VT *Comput (text, data)* taper, saisir
VI *Comput* introduire des données par clavier
▸▸ *Comput* **k. buffer** mémoire *f* tampon de clavier; **k. instrument** instrument *m* à clavier; *Comput* **k. layout** disposition *f* de clavier; *Comput* **k. map** schéma *m* de clavier; *Comput* **k. operator** claviste *mf*, *Mus* **k. player** joueur, -euse de synthétiseur/piano; *Comput* **k. shortcut** raccourci *m* clavier; *Comput* **k. skills** compétences *fpl* de claviste; *Comput* **k. template** réglette *f* de clavier

keyboarder ['kiːbɔːdər] N *Comput* claviste *mf*, opérateur, -trice de saisie

keyboarding ['kiːbɔːdɪŋ] N *Comput (of data)* frappe *f*, saisie *f*
▸▸ **k. accuracy** précision *f* de frappe; **k. error** faute *f* de frappe; **k. problems** problèmes *mpl* au niveau de la frappe; **k. skills** compétences *fpl* de claviste; **k. speed** vitesse *f* de frappe

keyboardless computer ['kiːbɔːdlɪs] N ordinateur *m* sans clavier

keyhole ['kiːhəʊl] N trou *m* de serrure; **to look through the k.** regarder par le trou de la serrure
▸▸ *Carp* **k. saw** scie *f* à guichet; *Med* **k. surgery** chirurgie *f* endoscopique

keying ['kiːɪŋ] N **1** *Comput (of data)* frappe *f*, saisie *f* **2** *Mus (of piano)* accordage *m*

▸▸ *Comput* **k. error** faute *f* de frappe; *Comput* **k. speed** vitesse *f* de frappe

keyless entry ['ki:lɪs] N *(to room)* ouverture *f* sans clé

Keynesian ['keɪnzɪən] ADJ keynésien

keynote ['ki:nəʊt] N *Mus* tonique *f*, *(of speech, approach)* idée *f* dominante; *(of policy)* mot *m* d'ordre
▸ VT mettre l'accent sur
▸▸ **k. speaker** orateur *m* qui prononce le discours d'ouverture; **k. speech** discours *m* introductif *ou* liminaire

keynoter ['ki:nəʊtər] N *Am* orateur *m* qui prononce le discours d'ouverture

keypad ['ki:pæd] N *Comput* pavé *m*

keystone ['ki:stəʊn] N *Archit* clef *f* de voûte; *Fig (of policy)* clef de voûte, pivot *m*

keystroke ['ki:strəʊk] N *Comput* frappe *f* (de touche); **keystrokes per minute/hour** vitesse *f* de frappe à la minute/à l'heure

keyword ['ki:wɜːd] N *also Comput* mot-clé *m*, *pl* mots-clés, mot-clef *m*, *pl* mots-clefs

KG [keɪ'dʒiː] N *Br abbr* **Knight of the Order of the Garter**

kg *(abbr* **kilogram)** kg

KGB [keɪdʒiː'biː] N *Formerly* KGB *m*
▸▸ **K. agent** agent *m* du KGB; **K. officer** officier *m* du KGB

khaki ['kɑːkɪ] N *(colour, fabric)* kaki *m*
▸ ADJ kaki *inv*

Khartoum [kɑː'tuːm] N Khartoum

kHz *(abbr* **kilohertz)** kHz

kibbutz, *pl* **kibbutzim** [kɪ'bʊts, kɪ'bʊtsiːm] N *Agr* kibboutz *m*, *pl* kibboutzim

kibitz ['kɪbɪts] VI *Am Fam* donner des conseils non sollicités, ramener son grain de sel

kibitzer ['kɪbɪtsər] N *Am Cards etc Fam* celui/celle qui donne des conseils non sollicités, donneur, -euse d'avis; *(meddler)* mouche *f* du coche

kibosh ['kaɪbɒʃ] N *Sl* **to put the k. on** *(hopes, plans)* réduire en poussière; *(holidays, new car etc)* faire tomber à l'eau

KICK [kɪk] N **1** *(with foot)* coup *m* de pied; *(of horse etc)* ruade *f*; **to give sb/sth a k.** donner un coup de pied à qn/qch; **to have a powerful k.** *(of footballer, horse)* avoir un coup de pied puissant; *(of swimmer)* avoir un battement de pied puissant; *Fam* **she just needs a k. up the backside** *or* **in the pants** elle a juste besoin d'un coup de pied au derrière
2 *Fam (vigour)* vigueur *f*, énergie *f*; **a drink with a k. in it** une boisson qui donne un coup de fouet; **to get a k. out of sth/doing sth** prendre plaisir à qch/à faire qch; **to do sth for kicks** faire qch pour s'amuser; **to get one's kicks doing sth** prendre son pied à faire qch; *Sl* **he's on a jazz/tennis k. at the moment** son truc en ce moment c'est le jazz/tennis
3 *(recoil) (of gun)* recul *m*, réaction *f*, *(of mechanism etc)* cahot *m*, secousse *f*
4 *(of engine)* retour *m* en arrière
▸ VI **1** *(once)* donner un coup de pied; *(several times)* donner des coups de pied; *(of animal)* ruer; *Sport (of athlete)* démarrer; *(of gun)* reculer, repousser
2 *Am Fam (die)* calancher, passer l'arme à gauche
▸ VT *(once)* donner un coup de pied à; *(several times)* donner des coups de pied à; *(push with foot)* pousser du pied; *(of horse etc)* détacher un coup de pied à; *Ftbl (ball)* botter; *(goal)* marquer; **to get kicked** *(once)* recevoir un coup de pied; *(several times)* recevoir des coups de pied; *Fig Fam* **to get kicked in the teeth** recevoir un coup en vache; *Fam* **to k. sb's behind** flanquer à qn un coup de pied au derrière; *Sl* **to k. the bucket** casser sa pipe, crever; *Fig* **to k. a man when he's**

down donner le coup de pied de l'âne à qn; *Fig* **to k. sb upstairs** = donner une promotion à qn dont on veut se débarrasser; **I could have kicked myself** je me serais donné des gifles; **I could k. myself!** quel imbécile je fais!; **to k. a bad habit** se défaire d'une mauvaise habitude; **to k. the habit** *(of smoker)* arrêter (de fumer); *(of drug addict)* décrocher, arrêter (la drogue)
▸▸ **k. boxer** tireur, -euse, personne *f* pratiquant la boxe française; **k. boxing** boxe *f* française; **k. pleat** *(in skirt)* pli *m* d'aisance; **k. turn** *(in skiing, skateboarding)* conversion *f*

▸ **kick about, kick around** VI *Fam (hang around)* traîner; *(travel around)* rouler sa bosse; **there are plenty of people like that kicking around** des gens comme ça, ce n'est pas ça qui manque; **you don't find many of these kicking around nowadays** des comme ça, ça ne court pas les rues de nos jours
▸ VT SEP **1** *(play with) (ball)* taper dans; *Fam (idea etc)* tester
2 *(mistreat)* traiter sans ménagements; **you shouldn't let yourself be kicked around like that** tu ne devrais pas te laisser traiter comme ça
▸ VT INSEP *Fam (spend time in)* **to k. around the world/Africa** rouler sa bosse *ou* traîner ses guêtres autour du monde/en Afrique; *Br* **is my purse kicking around the kitchen somewhere?** est-ce que mon porte-monnaie traîne quelque part dans la cuisine?

▸ **kick against** VT INSEP *Fam (rebel against)* regimber contre; *Fig* **to k. against the pricks** *(against fate)* s'en prendre au destin

▸ **kick aside** VT SEP *(ball, piece of paper)* écarter d'un coup de pied; *(pieces of paper)* écarter à coups de pied

▸ **kick away** VT SEP repousser du pied

▸ **kick away at** VT INSEP *(door)* mettre des coups de pied dans

▸ **kick back** VI *(recoil) (of engine)* donner des retours en arrière; *(of gun)* reculer, repousser
▸ VT SEP **1** *(return by kicking) (ball)* relancer
2 *(person)* rendre un coup de pied à; **I immediately kicked him back** je lui ai tout de suite rendu son coup de pied

▸ **kick in** VT SEP *(break open) (door etc)* enfoncer à coups de pied; *Fam* **to get one's head kicked in** se faire casser la tête

▸ **kick off** VT SEP *(shoes)* enlever d'un coup de pied
▸ VI **1** *Ftbl* donner le coup d'envoi; *Fig Fam (start)* démarrer, débuter
2 *Br Fam (become violent)* **it's going to k. off** ça va bastonner

▸ **kick out** VT SEP *(person)* chasser à coups de pied; *Fam (of job, house, pub etc)* mettre à la porte; *Ftbl (ball)* renvoyer; **to be kicked out** *(of job, house, pub etc)* être mis à la porte
▸ VI **1** *(of horse etc)* ruer; *(of person) (once)* donner un coup de pied; *(several times)* donner des coups de pied; **she would k. out at anyone who came near** elle donnait des coups de pied à tous ceux qui s'approchaient
2 *(swim vigorously)* s'élancer avec des battements vigoureux

▸ **kick over** VT SEP *(overturn)* renverser d'un coup de pied; **to k. over the traces** secouer le joug

▸ **kick up** VT SEP *Fam (cause)* **to k. up a fuss** faire des histoires; **to k. up a row** *or* **a racket** faire du tapage *ou* du boucan

kickback ['kɪkbæk] N *Fam Pej (payment)* dessous-de-table *m inv*, pot-de-vin *m*, *pl* pots-de-vin

kicker ['kɪkər] N **1** *Rugby* botteur *m*
2 *(horse, mule)* cheval *m*/mulet *m* qui rue
3 *TV (light)* projecteur *m* de décrochement, contre-jour *m*, *pl* contre-jours
4 *Am Fam (hidden drawback)* os *m*, hic *m*

5 *Am Fam (worst part of situation)* **the work's tough and the k. is the pay's lousy** le travail est dur, et en plus de ça, c'est payé avec un lance-pierres
▸▸ *TV* **k. light** projecteur de décrochement, contre-jour, *pl* contre-jours

kicking ['kɪkɪŋ] *Br Fam* N **to give sb a k.** tabasser qn à coups de latte; **to get a k.** se faire tabasser à coups de latte
▸ ADJ *(party, nightclub)* hyper animé

kickoff ['kɪkɒf] N *Ftbl* coup *m* d'envoi; *Fig Fam* démarrage *m*; *Ftbl* **k. at two o'clock** la partie commence *ou* le coup d'envoi sera donné à deux heures; *Fam* **for a k.** pour commencer

kickstand ['kɪkstænd] N *(of bicycle)* béquille *f*

kick-start N *(on motorbike)* démarreur *m* au pied, kick *m*
▸ VT *(motorbike, engine)* démarrer au kick; *Fig (economy)* relancer, donner un sérieux coup de pouce à

kick-starter N *(on motorbike)* démarreur *m* au pied, kick *m*

kid [kɪd] N **1** *Fam (child)* gamin, -ine, gosse *mf*; *Am* **say k.!** dis-moi, mon petit/ma petite; **my k. brother** mon petit frère; **it's k.'s stuff** *(easy)* c'est facile à faire; *(childish)* c'est (bon) pour les gosses **2** *(animal)* chevreau *m*, chevrette *f*, *(skin)* (peau *f* de) chevreau, cabron *m*
▸ VT *Fam* en conter à, faire marcher; **you're kidding us** tout ça c'est des blagues, tu veux nous faire marcher; **who do you think you're trying to k.?** et tu crois que je vais avaler ça?; **to k. sb that ...** faire croire à qn que ...; **to k. oneself** se faire des illusions; **I k. you not** je ne plaisante pas; **she's just kidding that she's hurt** elle fait semblant d'avoir mal
▸ VI *Fam* **(I was) only kidding** je plaisantais; **daddy's not really hurt, he's just kidding** papa n'est pas blessé pour de vrai, il fait semblant; **no kidding!** sans blague!; **are you kidding?** *(that's a ridiculous suggestion)* tu plaisantes?
▸▸ **k. gloves** gants *mpl* de chevreau

▸ **kid on** VT SEP, VI = **kid** VT, VI

kiddie, kiddy ['kɪdɪ] N *Fam* petit(e) gosse *mf*

kiddo ['kɪdəʊ] N *Fam* **are you ready, k.?** tu es prêt(e), mon grand/ma grande?

kidglove ['kɪdglʌv] ADJ **to give sb the k. treatment** ménager qn, traiter qn avec ménagement

kidnap ['kɪdnæp] VT (-pp-) kidnapper

kidnapper ['kɪdnæpər] N kidnappeur, -euse, ravisseur, -euse

kidnapping ['kɪdnæpɪŋ] N *Law* kidnapping *m*, enlèvement *m*, rapt *m*

kidney ['kɪdnɪ] N **1** *Anat* rein *m* **2** *Culin* rognon *m* **3** *Br Lit (temperament)* nature *f*, caractère *f*, *Old-fashioned* **people of that k.** les gens de cette espèce
▸▸ **k. bean** *(red)* haricot *m* rouge; *(white)* haricot de Soissons; **k. donor** donneur, -euse de rein; **k. failure** insuffisance *f* rénale; **k. machine** rein artificiel; **k. stone** calcul *m* rénal; *Med* **k. tray** cuvette *f* à pansements réniforme; *Bot* **k. vetch** (anthyllide *f*) vulnéraire *f*

kidney-shaped ADJ *(bean etc)* en forme de haricot, réniforme

kidology [kɪ'dɒlədʒɪ] N *Br Fam* **it's all k.** ce ne sont que des histoires

kill [kɪl] N **1** *(in hunting) (of fox, deer etc)* mise *f* à mort; *(animals killed)* gibier *m* tué, tableau *m* de chasse; **to be in at the k.** assister à la mise à mort; *Fig* assister au dénouement de qch (et en tirer profit)
2 *Mil (of enemy aircraft)* descente *f*, *(of enemy warship)* coulée *f*

vt 1 *(person, animal, microbes)* tuer; *(plant)* faire mourir; *Mil (enemy)* détruire; *(partridge)* tuer, descendre; *(of butcher) (cow etc)* abattre, tuer; *(nerve of tooth)* tuer; *(in hunting) (animal)* servir; **to be killed by gunshots/in an accident** être tué à coups de fusil/dans un accident; **to be killed by the radiation/a mysterious illness** mourir des radiations/d'une maladie mystérieuse; **to k. oneself** se suicider; *Fam (overexert oneself)* se tuer (**doing** à faire); *Fam (with laughing)* être mort de rire; *Iron* **don't k. yourself, will you** surtout, ne te surmène pas *ou* ne te fatigue pas trop!; **to k. oneself with work** se tuer à (force de) travailler; **the shock would k. her** le choc la tuerait; *Fam* **I'll k. you!** *(if you do that again etc)* je t'étrangle!; *Fam* **this one'll k. you** *(of joke)* ça va te faire mourir de rire; **this superstition will be hard to k.** cette superstition aura la vie dure; *Prov* **to k. two birds with one stone** faire d'une pierre deux coups, faire coup double; **to k. sb with kindness** faire du mal à qn par un excès de bonté; *Fam* **my feet/these shoes are killing me** mes pieds/ces chaussures me font atrocement souffrir; *Fam* **the heat is killing me!** j'étouffe!, je meurs de chaud!

2 *Fig (time)* tuer; *(ambition)* éteindre; *(love, sense of humanity etc)* détruire, étouffer; *Pol (bill)* couler; *Journ etc (passage, story)* supprimer; *(file)* effacer; *(printer)* arrêter; *(pain)* atténuer; *(smells)* neutraliser; *Tech (sound)* amortir; **to k. time** tuer le temps; **k. that light!** éteignez-moi ça tout de suite!

3 *Ftbl (ball)* bloquer; *Tennis (balle)* tuer, massacrer

vi tuer; **k. or cure remedy** remède *m* de cheval; **k. or be killed** tuer ou se faire tuer; *Fam* **I'd k. for a beer** je me damnerais pour une bière

▸ **kill off vt sep** tuer; *(whole population)* exterminer; *(hope)* anéantir; *(small businesses)* faire disparaître; **to k. off a character** *(of author etc)* faire mourir un personnage

killer ['kɪlər] **N 1** *(person)* tueur, -euse; *(murderer)* meurtrier, -ière **2** *Fam (difficult question)* colle *f*; **the exam was a real k.** cet examen n'était pas piqué des hannetons; **that dance was a k.!** cette danse m'a tué!; **that walk was a k.!** cette promenade était vraiment crevante; **the real k. is that ...** le comble c'est que ...; **this one's a k.** *(joke)* celle-là est à mourir de rire

▸ *Comput Fam* **k. app** application *f* phare, killer app *f*; **k. disease** maladie *f* meurtrière; *Fig* **k. instinct** agressivité *f*; **he lacks the k. instinct** il manque d'agressivité *ou* de combativité, il a trop de scrupules; *Zool* **k. whale** épaulard *m*, orque *f*

killing ['kɪlɪŋ] **ADJ 1** *(blow)* meurtrier, assassin **2** *Fam (exhausting) (work, dance)* tuant, crevant **3** *Fam (very amusing)* crevant; **it's too k. for words** c'est à mourir de rire, c'est à se tordre

N *(of animal for meat)* abattage *m*; *(of person)* meurtre *m*; *Mil (of enemy)* destruction *f*; **the k. of 500 seal pups** le massacre de 500 bébés phoques; *Fam* **to make a k.** *(on Stock Exchange etc)* faire un bénéfice énorme *ou* une affaire à tout casser

-killing ['kɪlɪŋ] **SUFF** -icide; **germ-k.** bactéricide

killingly ['kɪlɪŋlɪ] **ADV** **it's k. funny** c'est à mourir de rire

killjoy ['kɪldʒɔɪ] **N** rabat-joie *m inv*

kiln [kɪln] **N** four *m* (céramique); *(for drying)* séchoir *m*, sécherie *f*, étuve *f*; **k. drying** *or* **seasoning** séchage *m* au four, étuvage *m*; *(in brewing)* touraillage *m*

kilo ['kiːləʊ] **N** kilo *m*

kilobaud ['kɪləbɔːd] **N**

kilobit ['kɪləbɪt] **N** *Comput* kilobit *m*

kilobyte ['kɪləbaɪt] **N** *Comput* kilo-octet *m*

kilocalorie ['kɪləʊkælərɪ] **N** *Phys* kilocalorie *f*

kilocycle ['kɪləsaɪk(ə)l] **N** *Phys, Elec* kilocycle *m*

kilogram(me) ['kɪləgræm] **N** kilogramme *m*

kilohertz ['kɪləhɜːts] **N** kilohertz *m*

kilometre, *Am* **kilometer** ['kɪləmiːtər, kɪ'lɒmɪtər] **N** kilomètre *m*; **distance in kilometres** distance *f* kilométrique

kilometric [kɪlə'metrɪk] **ADJ** kilométrique

kilovolt ['kɪləvəʊlt] **N** *Elec* kilovolt *m*

kilowatt ['kɪləwɒt] **N** *Elec* kilowatt *m*

kilowatt-hour **N** *Elec* kilowatt-heure *m, pl* kilowatt-heures

kilt [kɪlt] **N** kilt *m* (écossais)

kilted ['kɪltɪd] **ADJ 1** *(person)* en kilt **2** *(pleated)* **k. skirt** kilt *m*

kilter ['kɪltər] **N** *Fam* **out of k.** *(of machine part)* détraqué; *(out of balance) (of schedule, budget etc)* déséquilibré; **this is running out of k. with the rest of the machine** c'est en décalage par rapport au reste de la machine

kimono [kɪ'məʊnəʊ] **N** kimono *m*

kin [kɪn] **N** *Fml* parents *mpl*; **his k.** ses parents, sa parenté; **to be k. to sb** être parent de qn, être apparenté avec qn; **he's no k. of mine** il n'est pas de ma famille

KIND¹ [kaɪnd] **N 1** *(class, sort)* genre *m*, espèce *f*, sorte *f*; **what k. is it?** de quelle sorte *ou* de quel genre (est-ce)?; **what k. of tree is this?** quelle sorte *ou* quel genre d'arbre est-ce?; **what k. of woman is she?** quel genre *ou* quelle sorte de femme est-ce?; **people of all kinds** des gens de toutes sortes; **the worst k. of people** des gens de la pire espèce; **it's a k. of fish** c'est une espèce de poisson; **they have so many different kinds of bread** ils ont tellement de sortes de pain différentes; **they did have some flour, but it wasn't the right k.** ils avaient bien de la farine, mais ce n'était pas la bonne; **something of the k.** quelque chose de ce genre; **nothing of the k.** rien de la sorte; **she's terribly boring – she's nothing of the k.!** elle est terriblement ennuyeuse – pas du tout! loin de là!; **in a k. of a way** en quelque façon; **this k. of woman,** *Fam* **these k. of women** ce genre de femmes; **he's not the understanding k.** il n'est pas du genre compréhensif; **I know your k.!** je connais les gens de ton espèce!; **she's more the stay-at-home k.** elle est plus du genre à rester à la maison; **well, it's beer of a k., I suppose** oui, on peut appeler ça de la bière, je suppose; **he speaks French – of a k.** il parle français – plus ou moins; **we're two of a k.** nous sommes de la même espèce *ou* race; **it's the only one of its k.** c'est le seul en son genre; **what k. of person do you think I am!** pour quel genre de personne me prends-tu?; **he's that k. of person** il est comme ça; **this is my k. of party** c'est le genre de soirée que j'aime; **you're my k. of girl** tu es mon type de femme, tu es le type de femme que j'aime; **I'm not that k. of girl** ce n'est pas mon genre; **is this the k. of thing you're looking for?** est-ce que c'est quelque chose de ce genre que vous cherchez?; **that's not the k. of thing I meant** ce n'est pas exactement ce que je voulais; **this is not the k. of thing you can do overnight** ce n'est pas le genre de chose qu'on fait du jour au lendemain; *Fam* **it was a k. of saucer-shaped thing** c'était une espèce de truc en forme de soucoupe; *Fam* **there's a k. of bump just here** il y a comme une bosse ici; *Fam* **I heard a k. of thump** j'ai entendu une espèce de cognement *ou* comme un cognement **VOIR GRAMMAIRE A13**

2 *(nature, character)* **difference in k.** différence *f* spécifique; **payment in k.** paiement

m en nature; **to repay sb in k.** *(as opposed to cash)* rembourser qn en nature; *(for an injury, disservice)* rendre à qn la monnaie de sa pièce

3 *Fam* **k. of** *(with adjectives and verbs)* un peu, plutôt; **you look k. of tired** tu as l'air un peu *ou* plutôt fatigué; **it's k. of late** il est un peu tard; **I'm k. of worried** je suis un peu inquiet; **I've k. of changed my mind** je crois bien que j'ai changé d'avis; **I k. of expected it** je m'y attendais un peu; **I k. of like it** *(like it a little)* j'aime plus ou moins ça; *(quite a bit)* j'aime bien ça; **do you like it? – k. of** tu aimes ça? – plus ou moins, ça va, couci-couça; **do you agree? – k. of** tu es d'accord? – plus ou moins

kind² **ADJ** gentil; **to be k. to sb** se montrer gentil avec qn, se montrer bon pour *ou* envers qn; **it's very k. of you to ...** c'est bien aimable de votre part *ou* à vous de ...; *Fml* **(would you) be k. enough to** *or* **so k. as to ...** ayez la bonté de ..., veuillez (bien) ...; **you are really too k.** vous êtes vraiment trop aimable; **k. to the skin** *(of detergents etc)* qui n'irrite pas la peau; **by k. permission of ...** avec l'aimable autorisation de ...; **give him my k. regards** faites-lui mes amitiés; **k. words** paroles *fpl* bienveillantes

kinda ['kaɪndə] *Fam* = **kind of,** *see* **kind¹** 3

kindergarten ['kɪndəgaːt(ə)n] **N** *Sch* école *f* maternelle

kind-hearted ['kaɪnd'haːtɪd] **ADJ** *(person)* qui a bon cœur; *(action, response)* bienveillant; **that was very k. of you** c'était très gentil de votre part; **he's very k.** il a très bon cœur, il a le cœur sur la main

kindle ['kɪnd(ə)l] **vt 1** *(flame, fire)* allumer; *(coal, wood)* enflammer, embraser **2** *(hatred)* allumer; *(emotions, passions)* faire naître, susciter; *(desires)* enflammer; *(suspicions, sorrow)* aviver; *(enthusiasm)* exciter

vi *(of fire, wood, passions etc)* s'allumer, s'enflammer

kindliness ['kaɪndlɪnɪs] **N** gentillesse *f*, bonté *f*

kindling ['kɪndlɪŋ] **N** bois *m* d'allumage, petit bois

▸▸ **k. wood** bois d'allumage, petit bois

kindly ['kaɪndlɪ] **ADV** gentiment, avec bonté; **she spoke very k. of you** elle a dit des choses très aimables *ou* gentilles à votre égard; **to be k. disposed towards sb/sth** être bien disposé envers qn/qch; **the council k. agreed to let us use the town hall** le conseil nous a aimablement autorisés à utiliser l'hôtel de ville; **(will you) k. close the window** voudriez-vous avoir la bonté *ou* la gentillesse de fermer la fenêtre?; *Com* **k. remit by cheque** prière de nous couvrir par chèque; **not to take k. to sb/sth** ne pas aimer qn/qch

ADJ *(person)* gentil, bon; *(tone, advice)* bienveillant

kindness ['kaɪndnɪs] **N 1** gentillesse *f*, amabilité *f* (**towards sb** envers qn), bonté *f* (**towards sb** pour qn); **thanks for your k.** merci de votre gentillesse *ou* amabilité; **to repay sb's k.** payer qn de sa gentillesse; **to show k. to sb** témoigner de la bonté à qn; *Fml* **would you have the k. to ...?** voulez-vous avoir la bonté *ou* gentillesse de ...?; **to do sth out of the k. of one's heart** faire qch par gentillesse; *Iron* **and I suppose it was out of the k. of your heart that you did that?** et je suppose que c'est ton bon cœur qui t'a poussé à faire ça?

2 **a k.** un service *(rendu)*; **to do sb a k.** rendre service à qn; **would you at least do me the k. of listening to my proposal?** me ferez-vous au moins l'amabilité d'écouter ma proposition?

kindred ['kɪndrɪd] **N** *Old-fashioned (relationship)* parenté *f*; *(family)* famille *f*, parents *mpl*

ADJ *(related)* apparenté; *(similar)* similaire, analogue
▸▸ **k. spirits** âmes *fpl* sœurs

kinematic [kɪnəˈmætɪk, kaɪn-] **ADJ** *Phys* cinématique

kinematics [kɪnəˈmætɪks, kaɪn-] **N** *Phys* cinématique *f* VOIR GRAMMAIRE A10

kinetic [kɪˈnetɪk, kaɪ-] **ADJ** *Phys, Art* cinétique

kinetics [kɪˈnetɪks] **N** *Phys* cinétique *f* VOIR GRAMMAIRE A10

kinfolk [ˈkɪnfəʊk] **NPL** *Am* parents *mpl* et alliés *mpl*

king [kɪŋ] **N 1** *(person)* roi *m*; *Ind etc* magnat *m*; **the kings and queens of England** les souverains *mpl* d'Angleterre; *Fig* **the k. of (the) beasts** le roi des animaux; *Fig* **the fast-food k.** le roi *ou* magnat de la restauration rapide; *Bible* **K. of Kings** Roi des rois; *Bible* **the three Kings** les Rois *mpl* Mages; *Bible* **(the Book of) Kings** le livre des Rois; **a k.'s ransom** une fortune
2 *Chess, Cards* roi *m*; *(in draughts)* dame *f*
▸▸ *Zool* **k. cobra** cobra *m* royal, hamadryade *f*, *Zool* **k. crab** limule *f*, crabe *m* des Moluques; *Bot, Culin* **K. Edward** *(potato)* (pomme *f* de terre) King Edward *f*, *Orn* **k. penguin** manchot *m* royal; *Br Zool* **k. prawn** (grosse) crevette *f*

kingcup [ˈkɪŋkʌp] **N** *Bot* **1** *(buttercup)* bouton *m* d'or **2** *(marsh marigold)* populage *m*, souci *m* d'eau

kingdom [ˈkɪŋdəm] **N 1** royaume *m*; **the k. of heaven** le royaume des cieux **2** *(animal)* règne *m*; **in the animal k.** chez les animaux **3** *Rel* règne *m*; **Thy k. come** que Ton règne vienne; *Fam* **k. come** le paradis; *Fam* **to send sb to k. come** expédier qn dans l'autre monde; *Fam* **until k. come** jusqu'à la fin des temps

kingfisher [ˈkɪŋfɪʃər] **N** martin-pêcheur *m*, *pl* martins-pêcheurs

kingly [ˈkɪŋlɪ] **ADJ** *Lit* de roi; *(royal)* royal, -aux

kingpin [ˈkɪŋpɪn] **N 1** *Aut* axe *m* de rotule *ou* de fusée, pivot *m* de fusée; *Fig (of organization, company)* cheville *f* ouvrière **2** *(in ten-pin bowling)* quille *f* du milieu

kingship [ˈkɪŋʃɪp] **N** royauté *f*

king-size(d) [ˈkɪŋsaɪz, -d] **ADJ** *(bed, mattress)* (très) grand format; *(cigarette)* long (longue); *(packet, container)* géant; *Fam Fig* **I've got a k. hangover** j'ai une gueule de bois carabinée
▸▸ **k. bed** lit *m* king size

kink [kɪŋk] **N 1** vrillage *m*; *(in felt)* grigne *f*, *(of hair)* crêpelure *f*, *Tex* vrille *f*, boucle *f*, **the rope's got a k. in it** il y a un vrillage dans la corde **2** *(in character)* déséquilibre *m*, aberration *f*, **it's one of her little kinks** c'est l'une de ses petites manies
VI *(of rope)* se nouer, se tortiller, vrillonner; *(of thread)* vriller

kinkiness [ˈkɪŋkɪnɪs] **N** *(sexual) (tastes)* goûts *mpl* bizarres; **no k.!** pas de trucs bizarres!

kinky [ˈkɪŋkɪ] **ADJ 1** *(hair)* crêpelé, crépu **2** *Sl (person) (sexually)* qui a des goûts sexuels excentriques; *Fam (eccentric)* extravagant; *Fam (clothes etc) (strange)* bizarre, extravagant; *(erotic, pornographic)* pervers

kinsfolk [ˈkɪnzfəʊk] **NPL** = kinfolk

kinship [ˈkɪnʃɪp] **N** parenté *f*

kinsman, *pl* **kinsmen** [ˈkɪnzmən] **N** *Lit* parent *m*

kinswoman, *pl* **kinswomen** [ˈkɪnzwʊmən, -wɪmɪn] **N** *Lit* parente *f*

kiosk [ˈkiːɒsk] **N** kiosque *m*

kip [kɪp] *Br Fam* **N 1** *(sleep)* **to have a k.** piquer un roupillon; **to get some k.** roupiller; **an hour's k.** un roupillon d'une heure **2** *(bed)* pieu *m*, plumard *m*; **to be still in one's k.** être encore au plumard

VI *(-pp-)* *(sleep)* roupiller
▸ **kip down** **VI** *Br Fam* pieuter

kipper [ˈkɪpər] *Culin* **N** hareng *m* légèrement salé et fumé, kipper *m*
VT *(herring)* saler et fumer; **kippered herring** hareng *m* légèrement salé et fumé; *Fig Fam* **to k. one's lungs** s'enfumer les poumons

kir [kɪər] **N** *(drink)* kir *m*, blanc *m* cassis
▸▸ **k. royale** kir *m* royal

kirby-grip [ˈkɜːbɪ-] **N** *Br* pince *f* à cheveux

Kirg(h)izia [kɜːˈgiːzɪə], **Kirg(h)izstan** [kɜːgɪzˈstæn] **N** le Kirghizistan

kirk [kɜːk] **N** *Scot* église *f*, **the K.** l'Église (presbytérienne) d'Écosse

kiss [kɪs] **N** baiser *m*; **to give/blow sb a k.** donner/envoyer un baiser à qn; **give mummy a k.!** *(to child)* fais une bise à maman!; *Med* **to give sb the k. of life** faire le bouche-à-bouche à qn; *Fig* **to be the k. of death for sb/sth** *(of act, decision)* être fatal pour qn/qch
VT 1 *(person)* donner un baiser à, embrasser; *(forehead or hand, holy object)* baiser; *(ceremonially) (person)* donner l'accolade à; **to k. sb on the cheek/lips** embrasser qn sur la joue/les lèvres; **they kissed each other** ils se sont embrassés; **mummy will k. it better** maman va te faire un bisou et tu n'auras plus mal; **to k. the book** baiser la Bible (pour prêter serment); *Lit* **to k. the dust** mordre la poussière; **to k. sb goodbye** dire au revoir à qn en l'embrassant; *Fam* **you can k. that promotion goodbye** tu peux dire au revoir à cet avancement; *Br Vulg* **(you can) k. my arse!** va te faire foutre!
2 *(touch lightly)* frôler; *Billiards (of ball)* frapper par contrecoup
VI 1 *(of two people)* s'embrasser; **to k. and make up** se réconcilier; **he's the k. and tell type** il est du genre à aller le crier sur tous les toits quand il a une aventure; **how much did she get for her k. and tell story?** combien on l'a payée pour raconter les détails de son aventure avec lui?
2 *(of two objects)* se frôler; *Billiards (of balls)* se frapper par contrecoup
▸▸ *Br* **k. curl** accroche-cœur *m*, *pl* accroche-cœurs
▸ **kiss away** **VT SEP** **to k. away sb's tears** sécher les larmes de qn en l'embrassant
▸ **kiss off** *Am Fam* **VT SEP 1** *(dismiss)* envoyer promener **2** *(kill)* descendre, buter **3** *(give up hope of)* faire une croix sur, dire adieu à; **you can k. off your promotion!** tu peux faire une croix sur *ou* dire adieu à ta promotion!
VI **k. off!** va te faire voir!

kisser [ˈkɪsər] **N 1** *(person)* embrasseur, -euse; **to be a great k.** bien embrasser **2** *Sl (mouth)* gueule *f*

kiss-off [ˈkɪsɒf] **N** *Am Fam* **to give sb the k.** *(of girlfriend etc)* plaquer qn; *(of employer)* virer qn

kissogram [ˈkɪsəgræm] **N** = message *m* délivré par une personne déguisée et accompagné d'un baiser; **a k. girl** = une fille qui délivre des messages et est chargée d'embrasser le destinataire

kit [kɪt] **N 1** *(equipment)* matériel *m*, équipement *m*; *Mil etc* petit équipement **2** *Sport (clothes)* tenue *f*, *Fam* **to get one's k. off** se déshabiller **3** *(set of parts)* to buy sth in k. form acheter qch en prêt-à-monter *ou* en pièces détachées; **to make sth from a k.** faire qch à partir de pièces détachées
VT *(-tt-)* = kit out, kit up
▸▸ **k. inspection** revue *f* de détail
▸ **kit out, kit up** **VT SEP** *esp Br (soldier etc)* équiper, fournir son équipement à; **(all)** kitted out complètement équipé; *Mil* **to be kitted out** toucher son paquetage

kitbag [ˈkɪtbæg] **N** sac *m* (de) marin; *Mil* sac *m* à paquetage, sac à grande monture

kitchen [ˈkɪtʃɪn] **N** cuisine *f*
▸▸ **k. cabinet** *(furniture)* buffet *m* (de cuisine); *Br Pol* = conseillers *mpl* proches du chef du gouvernement; **k. foil** aluminium *m* ménager, papier *m* d'aluminium *ou* d'alu; **k. hand** aide *mf* de cuisine; **k. knife** couteau *m* de cuisine; **k. paper** essuie-tout *m inv*; **k. roll** essuie-tout; **k. sink** évier *m*; **k. sink drama** = théâtre et cinéma *m* réalistes des années 50–60 dépeignant l'ennui et la misère des gens ordinaires; **k. stove** cuisinière *f*, **k. unit** élément *m* (de cuisine); **k. utensils** batterie *f* de cuisine

kitchenette [kɪtʃɪˈnet] **N** coin-cuisine *m*, *pl* coins-cuisines, cuisinette *f*

kitchenware [ˈkɪtʃɪnweər] **N** vaisselle *f* de cuisine

kite [kaɪt] **N 1** *(toy)* cerf-volant *m*, *pl* cerfs-volants; *Fam* **as high as a k.** *(drunk)* ivre, soûl; *(drugged)* drogué, camé; *(very excited)* tout fou, *f* toute folle **2** *Fin Fam* traite *f* en l'air, billet *m* de complaisance; **to fly** *or* **to send up a k.** tirer en l'air *ou* à découvert **3** *Br Fam (aeroplane)* avion *m*, taxi *m* **4** *(bird)* milan *m*
▸▸ **k. balloon** ballon *m* observateur

kith [kɪθ] **N** **our k. and kin** nos parents et amis; **to have neither k. nor kin** être seul sur la terre

kiting [ˈkaɪtɪŋ] **N** *Fin Fam* tirage *m* en l'air, tirage à découvert

kitsch [kɪtʃ] **N** kitsch *m*; **a piece of k.** du kitsch
ADJ kitsch *inv*

kitschy [ˈkɪtʃɪ] **ADJ** kitsch *inv*; **it's k.** c'est du kitsch

kitten [ˈkɪt(ə)n] **N** *(young cat)* chaton *m*, petit(e) chat(te); *(term of endearment)* ma petite, ma mignonne; **a cat and her kittens** une chatte et ses petits; *Br Fam* **he'll have kittens** *(of person)* il va se mettre dans tous ses états; **to be having kittens** *(of person)* être dans tous ses états
▸▸ **k. heels** talons *mpl* bobine

kittenish [ˈkɪtənɪʃ] **ADJ** *(playful)* enjoué; *(flirtatious)* coquet

kittiwake [ˈkɪtɪweɪk] **N** *(bird)* mouette *f* tridactyle

kitty[1] [ˈkɪtɪ] **N** *Fam (cat)* minou *m*, minet *m*; *(kitten)* chaton *m*; **here k., k.** minou, minou, viens

kitty[2] **N 1** *Cards etc* cagnotte *f*, *(of group)* cagnotte, caisse *f* commune **2** *(at bowls)* cochonnet *m*

kiwi [ˈkiːwiː] **N 1** *(bird)* aptéryx *m*, kiwi *m* **2** *Fam (New Zealander)* **K.** Néo-Zélandais, -aise **3** *(fruit)* kiwi *m*
▸▸ **k. fruit** kiwi

KKK [keɪkeɪˈkeɪ] **N** *abbr* Ku Klux Klan

kleptomania [kleptəˈmeɪnɪə] **N** kleptomanie *f*

kleptomaniac [kleptəˈmeɪnɪæk] **ADJ, N** kleptomane *mf*

klieg light [kliːg] **N** *Am Cin* lampe *f* à arc

klutz [klʌts] **N** *Am Fam* brise-tout *m inv*

km *(abbr* **kilometre)** km

km/h *(abbr* **kilometres per hour)** km/h

knack [næk] **N** talent *m*, chic *m*; *(esp physical)* tour *m* de main; **to have the k. of** *or* **a k. for doing sth** avoir le talent de *ou* le chic pour faire qch; *(esp physically)* avoir le coup *ou* le tour de main pour faire qch; **to have lost the k. of sth** n'avoir plus l'habitude de qch; **there's a k. to it** il y a un truc; **there's a k. to opening this door** il y a un truc pour ouvrir la porte; **you have a k. for telephoning me at exactly the wrong moment** tu as le chic pour me téléphoner précisément au mauvais moment

knacker [ˈnækər] *Br* **N 1** *(of horses)* équarrisseur *m*, **k.'s yard** chantier *m* d'équarrissage, équarrissoir *m* **2** *(of buildings)* entrepreneur *m* de démolitions; *(of ships)* démolisseur *m*

de vieux navires **3** *Vulg* **knackers** *(testicles)* couilles *fpl*
vt *Fam (person)* crever, tuer; *(machine etc)* bousiller

knackered ['nækəd] **ADJ** *Br Fam (tired) (person)* crevé, mort; *(broken) (machine etc)* foutu, naze

knackering ['nækərɪŋ] **ADJ** *Br Fam* crevant

knapsack ['næpsæk] **N** *Old-fashioned* havresac *m*, sac *m* à dos; *Mil* sac d'ordonnance, havresac

knave [neɪv] **N 1** *Cards* valet *m*; **k. of clubs** valet de trèfle **2** *Old-fashioned (scoundrel)* fripon *m*, coquin *m*

knavery ['neɪvərɪ] **N** *Old-fashioned* friponnerie *f*, coquinerie *f*

knead [ni:d] **vt 1** *(dough, clay)* pétrir, malaxer, travailler **2** *Med (muscles)* masser, pétrir

knee [ni:] **N 1** genou *m*, -oux; **these trousers are out at the k.** ce pantalon est troué au genou; **to sit on sb's k.** *or* **knees** s'asseoir sur les genoux de qn; **to put sb over one's k.** *(spank)* donner une fessée à qn; **she put him over her k. and spanked him** elle l'a attrapé sur ses genoux et lui a donné une fessée; **he learnt the song at his mother's k.** il a appris la chanson sur les genoux de sa mère; **to fall** *or* **drop to one's knees** tomber à genoux; **on your knees!** à genoux!; **to go down on one's knees** s'agenouiller; *Fig* se mettre à genoux; *Lit* **to bend** *or* **bow the k. to** *or* **before sb** fléchir le genou devant qn, s'incliner devant qn; *Fig* **to ask for sth on one's (bended) knees** *or* **on bended k.** demander qch à genoux; *Fig* **to bring sb to his knees** obliger qn à capituler; *Fig* **the crisis brought the government to its knees** la crise a mis le gouvernement à genoux; **the famine has brought the country to its knees** la famine a entraîné le pays au bord de la ruine; *Vet* **broken knees** *(of horse)* couronnement *m* **2** *Tech, Constr* raccord *m* coudé, coude *m*; *(in naval architecture)* courbe *f* (de consolidation)
vt *(hit)* donner un coup de genou à; **she kneed him in the groin** elle lui a donné un coup de genou dans les parties; **she kneed the door open** *(push)* elle poussa la porte du genou; **he kneed the box out of the way** il écarta la boîte du genou
▸▸ *Tech* **k. bracket** console-équerre *f*, *pl* consoles-équerres; **k. jerk** réflexe *m* patellaire *ou* rotulien; **k. plate** gousset *m* (de charpente); **k. reflex** réflexe patellaire *ou* rotulien; *Carp* **k. timber** bois *m* courbant *ou* coudé

kneecap ['ni:kæp] **N** *Anat* rotule *f*
vt **to k. sb** tirer dans les rotules de qn

kneecapping ['ni:kæpɪŋ] **N** **it was the third k. that week** c'était la troisième fois de la semaine que quelqu'un se faisait tirer dans les rotules

knee-deep **ADJ** *(mud, water)* jusqu'aux genoux; **to be k. in mud** être enfoncé dans la boue jusqu'aux genoux; *Fig* **to be k. in paperwork** être dans la paperasse jusqu'au cou

knee-high **ADJ, ADV** à hauteur du genou; **the snow/water was k.** la neige/l'eau arrivait à hauteur du genou; **to go k. into the water** entrer dans l'eau jusqu'aux genoux; *Fam* **when I was k. to a grasshopper** quand j'étais haut comme trois pommes

kneejerk ['ni:dʒɜːk] **ADJ** *(reflex)* automatique
▸▸ *Fig Pej* **k. reaction** réflexe *m*, automatisme *m*; *Pol* **k. support** soutien *m* systématique *ou* inconditionnel

kneel [ni:l] **vi** *(pt, pp* **knelt** [nelt], *occ* **kneeled)** s'agenouiller, se mettre à genoux; *Fig Lit,* **to k. to sb** se mettre à genoux devant qn

knee-length **ADJ** *(dress)* qui descend jus-

qu'aux genoux; *(boot, socks)* qui monte jusqu'aux genoux

kneeler ['ni:lər] **N** *(cushion) (in church)* agenouilloir *m*

kneeling ['ni:lɪŋ] **ADJ** agenouillé, à genoux
N agenouillement *m*

kneepad ['ni:pæd] **N** genouillère *f*

kneeroom ['ni:rʊm] **N** espace *m* aux genoux

knees-up ['ni:zʌp] **N** *Br Fam* java *f*; **to have a k.** faire la java; **there was a bit of a k. in the pub** on a un peu fait la java au pub

knee-trembler [tremblər] **N** *Br Fam Hum* **to have a k.** faire l'amour debout

knell [nel] **N** glas *m*; **to toll the (death) k.** sonner le glas; *Fig* **this news/refusal rang the death k. of her hopes** cette nouvelle/ce refus sonnait le glas de ses espérances

knelt **PT, PP** *see* **kneel**

knew **PT** *see* **know**

knickerbocker glory ['nɪkəbɒkər] **N** *Culin* coupe *f* de glace avec fruits et crème Chantilly

knickerbockers ['nɪkəbɒkəz] **NPL** culotte *f* (bouffante), knickerbockers *mpl*

knickers ['nɪkəz] **NPL** VOIR GRAMMAIRE A10 **1** (petite) culotte *f* (de femme); *Old-fashioned Fam* **k.!** *(nonsense)* balivernes!; *Vulg* **to get into sb's k.** s'envoyer qn, culbuter qn; *Br Fam* **to get one's k. in a twist** paniquer (**about** à cause de) **2** *Am (breeches)* = **knickerbockers**

knick-knack ['nɪknæk] **N** *Fam* colifichet *m*, babiole *f*, bibelot *m*

knife, *pl* **knives** [naɪf, naɪvz] **N 1** couteau *m*; *Surg (with narrow blade)* bistouri *m*; **k. and fork** couverts *mpl*; *Old-fashioned Fam* **before you could say k.** en un rien de temps, en moins de deux; **to go through sth like a k. through butter** entrer dans qch comme dans du beurre; **this k. wouldn't cut butter** ce couteau ne coupe que ce qu'il voit *or* ne coupe rien; *Fig* **it was an atmosphere you could have cut with a k.** l'atmosphère était extrêmement tendue; *Fig* **to get** *or* **have one's k. into sb** en vouloir à qn; *Fig* **the knives are out for him** on ne donne pas cher de sa peau; **it was war to the k. between them** ils étaient à couteaux tirés; *Med Fam* **to go under the k.** passer sur le billard; *Med Fam* **he was under the k. for two hours** *(in operation)* il a passé deux heures sur le billard **2** *(blade) (on machine)* lame *f*; *(of guillotine)* couperet *m*
vt *(stab)* donner un coup de couteau à, poignarder; **he's been knifed** il a reçu un coup de couteau, il a été poignardé
▸▸ **k. attack** attaque *f* à coups de couteau; **k. grinder** *(person)* rémouleur *m*, repasseur *m* de couteaux; *(instrument)* meule *f* à aiguiser; *Tech* **k. sharpener** aiguisoir *m* (pour couteaux); **k. wound** blessure *f* à coups de couteau

knife-edge **N** *Fig* **he had been on a k. all day** *(nervous)* il avait été sur les nerfs toute la journée; *Fig* **the situation/game/***etc* **was balanced on a k.** la situation/la partie/*etc* ne tenait qu'à un fil
ADJ **trousers with a k. crease** pantalon au pli cassant

knife-point **N** pointe *f* de couteau; **to be robbed at k.** se faire voler sous la menace d'un couteau

knife-rest **N** porte-couteau *m*, *pl* porte-couteaux

knifing ['naɪfɪŋ] **N** attaque *f* au couteau

knight [naɪt] **N 1** chevalier *m* **2** *Chess* cavalier *m*
vt faire *ou* créer chevalier
▸▸ **k. errant** chevalier errant, paladin *m*; *Br* **K. of (the Order of) the Garter** chevalier de

l'Ordre de la Jarretière; *Liter* **the Knights of the Round Table** les Chevaliers de la Table Ronde; *Hist* **k. service** service *m* de haubert

knighthood ['naɪthʊd] **N** *(title)* **he has just been given a k.** il vient d'être fait *ou* créé chevalier

knightly ['naɪtlɪ] **ADJ** *(conduct etc)* chevaleresque, de chevalier

knit [nɪt] *(pt, pp* **knitted** *or* **knit)** **vt 1** *(sweater etc)* tricoter; **k. two, purl two** deux à l'endroit, deux à l'envers **2** **to k. one's brows** froncer les sourcils
vi 1 tricoter, faire du tricot; *(as opposed to purl)* tricoter à l'endroit **2** *Med (of bones)* se souder
▸ **knit together** **vi** *Med (of bones)* se souder
vt SEP *(join)* **their experience k. them together more tightly than ever** l'expérience qu'ils ont vécue les a liés plus que jamais
▸ **knit up** **vt SEP** assembler (en le tricotant)

knitted ['nɪtɪd] **ADJ 1** tricoté, de *ou* en tricot; *(lace)* au tricot; **a k. jumper** un tricot **2** **k. eyebrows** sourcils *mpl* froncés
▸▸ **k. fabric** tricot *m*; **k. goods** tricots *mpl*, articles *mpl* en tricot

knitter ['nɪtər] **N** tricoteur, -euse

knitting ['nɪtɪŋ] **N 1** *(activity)* tricotage *m*; *(work)* tricot *m*; **to do some k.** tricoter; **I've brought my k.** j'ai apporté mon tricot **2** *(of bones)* soudure *f*
▸▸ **k. machine** machine *f* à tricoter; **k. needle** aiguille *f* à tricoter; **k. pattern** modèle *m* de tricot; **k. wool** laine *f* à tricoter

knitwear ['nɪtweə(r)] **N** lainages *mpl*

knob [nɒb] **N 1** *(on cane, bannisters)* pomme *f*, *(on door, drawer etc)* poignée *f*, *(on radio etc)* bouton; *(on surface, forehead etc)* bosse *f*, protubérance *f*, *Br Fam* **it comes with all the knobs on** *(with all refinements etc)* il est équipé de tous les accessoires possibles et imaginables; *Br Fam* **the same to you with knobs on!** c'est celui qui le dit qui l'est! **2** *(piece)* **a k. of butter** une noix de beurre **3** *Br Vulg (penis)* bite *f*, *(man)* trou *m* du cul

knobbed [nɒbd] **ADJ** *(stick)* à pommeau

knobbly ['nɒblɪ] **ADJ** couvert de bosses; *(tree)* noueux; **k. knees** genoux *mpl* bossués

KNOCK [nɒk]

N coup **1, 2** ▪ cognement **3**
VT frapper **1** ▪ heurter **1** ▪ cogner **1**
VI frapper **1** ▪ cogner **2**

N 1 *(blow)* coup *m*; **to give sb a k. on the head** porter à qn un coup à la tête; *(and make unconscious)* assommer qn d'un coup sur la tête; **to get a nasty k.** prendre un vilain coup; *Fam* **his pride took a bit of a k.** sa fierté en a pris un coup; **to give sb's chances/hopes a k.** miner les chances/espoirs de qn; **to be brought up in the school of hard knocks** être élevé à la dure; *Fam* **he's had a few knocks** *(in business, life)* il en a vu de dures; **k.-for-k. insurance** = assurance *f* entraînant le remboursement séparé des clients par leurs compagnies respectives **2 k. at the door** coup *m* à la porte; **to hear a k.** entendre frapper; **to give a loud k.** frapper très fort; **k., k.!** toc, toc!; **a k., k. joke** = blague *f* dont la première ligne du dialogue est 'toc, toc!' **3** *Tech etc (sound)* cognement *m*, cliquetis *m*; *(of fuel in engine)* détonation *f*
vt 1 *(hit)* frapper, heurter, cogner; **to k. sb on the head** frapper qn sur la tête; **to k. sb unconscious** assommer qn; **to k. sb flying** envoyer valdinguer qn; **to k. one's head against sth** se cogner la tête contre qch; **to k. a nail into a wall** enfoncer un clou dans un mur; **to k. a hole in** *or* **through sth** faire un trou dans qch

2 Fig (phrases) **to k. holes in an argument** démolir un argument; **to k. an idea/a scheme on the head** abandonner ou laisser tomber une idée/un projet; **our plans have been knocked on the head** nos projets sont tombés à l'eau; Br Fam **k. it on the head, will you!** c'est pas bientôt fini?; **to k. some sense into sb** apprendre à vivre à qn; **that'll k. a bit of sense into her!** ça lui apprendra!; **to k. sb into shape** mettre qn au pas; **the army soon knocked his enthusiasm out of him** l'armée a eu tôt fait de tuer en lui toute trace d'enthousiasme; **to k. sb sideways** or **for six** (amaze) abasourdir ou stupéfier qn; **to k. sb dead** (impress) en mettre plein la vue à qn; **Kylie knocked them dead last night** hier soir, Kylie a fait un tabac

3 Fam (criticize) débiner; **don't k. it until you've tried it** ne crache pas dessus avant d'avoir essayé

VI **1** frapper (**at** à); **to k. at the door** frapper à la porte; **to k. against sth** se donner un coup ou se cogner contre qch; **she knocked against him** elle s'est cognée contre lui; **he felt his foot k. against a hard object** il a senti son pied cogner contre ou rencontrer quelque chose de dur; **his knees were knocking** ses genoux s'entrechoquaient

2 (of engine) cogner, cliqueter; (of bearings) tambouriner

▸ **knock about, knock around** VT SEP **1** (mistreat) (person) bousculer, maltraiter, malmener; **he knocks his wife about** il bat sa femme; **the furniture has been badly knocked about** les meubles ont été fort maltraités

2 Fam (discuss) (idea, suggestion) débattre

VI Fam **1 to k. about with sb** fréquenter qn; **they knocked about together at school** ils se fréquentaient à l'école

2 (hang around) traîner; **has anyone seen my keys knocking about?** quelqu'un a vu traîner mes clés dans un coin?; **that's what I wear to k. about in** ce sont mes vêtements d'intérieur; **he's knocked about quite a bit** il a pas mal roulé sa bosse

VT INSEP Fam **to k. about the world/countryside** rouler sa bosse; **she's been knocking about Glasgow for years** ça fait des années qu'elle traîne à Glasgow; **your keys are knocking about the kitchen somewhere** tes clés traînent dans un coin de la cuisine

▸ **knock back** VT SEP Fam **1** (drink) **to k. back a drink** s'enfiler ou s'envoyer un verre

2 (cost) coûter; **it knocked me back £200** ça m'a coûté 200 livres

3 (reject) (idea, proposal) rejeter; (candidate) refuser

4 (surprise) abasourdir, sidérer

▸ **knock down** VT SEP **1** renverser; (person) mettre à terre; (wall, building etc) abattre; **he was knocked down by a car** il a été renversé par une voiture

2 (at auction) adjuger, vendre; **to k. sth down to sb** adjuger qch à qn

3 Fam (reduce) (price) baisser; (reduce price of) solder; **it's been knocked down to £50** ça a été soldé à 50 livres; **she wanted £15 but I knocked her down to 10** elle demandait 15 livres mais j'ai réussi à la faire descendre jusqu'à 10

▸ **knock off** VT SEP **1** (cause to fall off) faire tomber; **he was knocked off his bike by a car** une voiture l'a fait tomber de son vélo; **to k. a book off the table** faire tomber un livre de la table; Fam **to k. sb's head** or **block off** casser la tête à qn; Fig **to k. sb off their pedestal** or **perch** faire tomber qn de son piédestal; Fig **I managed to get something knocked off the price** j'ai réussi à faire baisser un peu le prix

2 Fam (steal) piquer, faucher; **to k. off a bank** se faire une banque

3 Fam (kill) zigouiller

4 Fam **k. it off!** (stop it) arrêtez!, ça suffit!

5 Fam (produce quickly) (letter, report, song etc) expédier

VI (at end of day) finir; **let's k. off for a coffee** arrêtons-nous pour prendre un café

▸ **knock out** VT SEP **1** (remove) retirer, enlever; Fam **to k. sb's brains/teeth out** casser la tête/les dents à qn

2 (make unconscious) assommer raide; Boxing mettre knock-out

3 Sport (in tournament etc) **to be knocked out** être éliminé

4 Mil (tank etc) détruire

5 Am Fam **to k. oneself out** (indulge oneself) se faire plaisir; **there's plenty of food left, k. yourself out!** il reste plein de nourriture, sers-toi autant que tu veux!

▸ **knock over** VT SEP **1** (cause to fall) faire tomber; (overturn) renverser

2 Am Fam (rob) braquer

▸ **knock together** VT SEP **1** (make hastily) (shelter, raft etc) assembler en vitesse; **we knocked together a rough shelter** on s'est fabriqué une espèce d'abri

2 (hit together) entrechoquer; Fig **they should have their heads knocked together** il faudrait les secouer un bon coup

VI (of knees, two objects) s'entrechoquer

▸ **knock up** VT SEP **1** (make hastily) (shed etc) construire en vitesse; (meal) improviser; **I'll k. us up some spaghetti** je vais nous préparer des spaghetti en vitesse

2 Br (wake) réveiller

3 Cr **to k. up a century** faire cent points

4 Sl (make pregnant) mettre en cloque; **to get knocked up** se faire mettre en cloque

VI Tennis faire des balles (avant la partie, pour se faire la main)

knockabout ['nɒkəbaʊt] ADJ (game etc) pour rire; **a k. comedian** un bateleur, bouffon; **a k. comedy** une (grosse) farce

N **1** (game) partie f pour rire **2** Naut petit voilier m

knockback ['nɒkbæk] N Br Fam (rejection) veste f; **to get a k.** prendre une veste

knockdown ['nɒkdaʊn] ADJ **1** (forceful) **a k. blow** un coup à assommer un bœuf; **a k. argument** un argument massue **2** (easy to dismantle) démontable; **sold in k. form** vendu en kit

▸▸ Br Fam **k. price** (at auction) prix m minimum; Br **for sale at k. prices** (reduced) en vente à des prix imbattables ou défiant toute concurrence; **I got it for a k. price** je l'ai eu pour trois fois rien

knocker ['nɒkər] N **1** (door) **k.** marteau m (de porte), heurtoir m **2** Sl **knockers** (breasts) nichons mpl **3** Fam (critic) critiqueur m

knocking ['nɒkɪŋ] N **1** (noise) bruit m de coups, cognement m **2** (of engine) cognement m

▸▸ **k. copy** publicité f comparative

knocking-off time N Fam heure f de sortie

knocking-shop N Br Sl bordel m

knock-kneed [-'niːd] ADJ (person) cagneux

knock-knees [-niːz] NPL genoux mpl cagneux

knock-on effect N répercussions fpl; **businesses are feeling the k. of a strong pound** les entreprises subissent le contrecoup d'une livre forte

knockout ['nɒkaʊt] N **1** Boxing knock-out m inv, K-O m; Fig coup m de grâce; **to win by a k.** gagner par K-O **2** Fam (sensation) **to be a k.** être sensationnel ou génial; **she's a k.!** (beautiful) elle est canon! **3** (at auction) entente f (entre concurrents pour baisser les prix) **4** Sport tournoi m (par élimination directe)

▸▸ Boxing **k. blow** coup m qui met K-O; Fig coup m de grâce; **to deliver the k. blow** Boxing mettre K-O; Fig donner le coup de grâce;

Fam **k. drops** soporifique m, somnifère m (surtout ajouté à une boisson)

knock-up N Tennis **to have a k.** faire quelques balles (avant la partie, pour se faire la main)

knoll [nəʊl] N tertre m, monticule m, butte f, mamelon m

knot [nɒt] N **1** (with rope, string) nœud m; **to tie/untie a k.** faire/défaire un nœud; **k. of hair** chignon m; Fam Fig **to tie the k.** (get married) se marier; Fam Fig **to tie oneself in knots** s'embrouiller

2 (in wood) nœud m

3 Naut (unit of speed) nœud m; **to make 10 knots** (of ship) filer 10 nœuds; Fam **at a rate of knots** à toute vitesse; Fig Fam **she was spending her money at a rate of knots** elle jetait l'argent par les fenêtres

4 (group) (of people) groupe m; (of trees) bouquet m

5 (in muscle) raideur f; **to have a k. in one's stomach** avoir l'estomac noué

VT (-tt-) (piece of string) (make one knot) faire un nœud à; (make several knots) faire des nœuds à; **k. the end of the string around the door handle** nouez le bout de la corde à la poignée de la porte; Br Fam **get knotted!** va te faire voir!

VI (of string) se nouer, faire des nœuds; **her stomach knotted with fear** la peur lui nouait l'estomac

▸ **knot together** VT SEP **k. them together** noue-les ensemble

knotty ['nɒtɪ] ADJ **1** (rope, hair etc) plein de nœuds **2** (problem etc) épineux, embrouillé; (question) difficile, épineux **3** (wood etc) noueux, raboteux; (hands) noueux

KNOW [nəʊ]

VT	connaître **1, 4** ▪ savoir **1, 2, 4**
	▪ reconnaître **3** ▪ distinguer **3**
VI	savoir

N Fam **to be in the k.** être au courant (de l'affaire); Sport etc (have inside information) avoir des tuyaux; **those in the k.** les initiés mpl

VT (pt knew [njuː], pp known [nəʊn]) **1** (be acquainted with) (person, place) connaître; (poverty, happiness etc) savoir ce que c'est que; **to get** or **come to k. sb** faire la connaissance de qn; **when I first knew her** quand j'ai fait sa connaissance; **to have known happiness/poverty** avoir connu le bonheur/la pauvreté; **I've never known anything like it** je n'ai jamais rien vu de semblable; **I don't k. her to speak to** je ne la connais que de vue; **I k. him to say hello to** nous nous saluons; **I'd like to get to k. him better** j'aimerais bien le connaître mieux; **knowing him, he'll probably want to** tel que je le connais, il voudra certainement; **he is well known to the police** il est bien connu de la police

2 (to have knowledge of) savoir; **I k. that** ça je le sais; **to get to k. sth** apprendre qch; **to k. sth by heart** savoir qch par cœur; **how was I to k. you were saving it?** comment est-ce que je pouvais savoir que tu l'avais mis de côté?; **to k. more than one is telling** en savoir plus long qu'on n'en dit; **the end of civilisation as we k. it** la fin de la civilisation en tant que telle; **well, what do you k.!** sans blague!, tiens, tiens!; **she thinks she knows all the answers** elle croit tout savoir; Fig Fam **to k. a thing or two, to k. one's way about** or **around** être malin ou roublard; **he knows his own mind** il sait ce qu'il veut; **I'll have you k. that ...** sachez que ...; **everyone knows that ...** personne n'ignore que ...; **I knew (that) she had talent** je lui connaissais du talent; **how do you k. (that) he will come?** qui vous dit qu'il viendra?; **do you k. when .../why ...?** savez-vous quand .../pourquoi ...?; **heaven** or **God (only) knows when I shall**

get back Dieu (seul) sait quand je serai de retour; **she didn't quite k. what to say** elle ne savait trop que dire; **I don't k. that I do** (agree etc) je n'en suis pas sûr; **I k. him to be a liar** je sais que c'est un menteur; **she is known to be a keen photographer** on sait qu'elle aime beaucoup la photographie; **please let us k. whether …** veuillez nous faire savoir si …; **I don't want it known/ widely known** je ne veux pas que cela se sache/que tout le monde l'apprenne; **he let it be known that he was available** il a fait savoir qu'il était disponible; **that has been known (to happen)** c'est une chose qu'on a vue se produire, ça c'est vu; **I have never known him tell a lie** à ce que je sache, il n'a jamais menti; **I've never known him (to) be this late** je ne l'ai jamais vu y être aussi en retard; **she doesn't k. what fear is** elle ne sait pas ce que c'est que d'avoir peur; **to k. what it's like to be happy/poor** savoir ce que c'est que d'être heureux/pauvre; **nobody knows anything about it** personne n'en sait rien; **to k. all about cars** être très calé sur les voitures; **we k. all about her!** si nous la connaissons? et comment!; **we knew nothing about** or **of it** nous l'ignorions; **I'll be back before you k. it** je serai bientôt de retour; **it'll be Christmas before we k. it** le temps va passer vite jusqu'à Noël

3 (recognize) reconnaître; (distinguish) distinguer (**from** de, d'avec); Fam **he doesn't k. one end of a car from another** il n'y connaît absolument rien en voitures; **don't you k. me?** vous ne me reconnaissez pas?; **I'd k. him anywhere** je le reconnaîtrais n'importe où; **I knew her by her walk** je l'ai reconnue à son allure ou à sa démarche; **I knew him for a troublemaker** j'ai deviné que c'était un agitateur; **to k. good from evil** distinguer le bien du mal; **I didn't k. the one from the other** je ne pouvais pas les distinguer l'un de l'autre

4 (understand) savoir; (subject) connaître; **I don't k. much about it** je ne sais pas grand-chose là-dessus; **she knows German** elle sait parler allemand; **do you k. anything about physics?** est-ce que tu connais quelque chose en physique?; **what do you k.?** qu'est-ce que tu en sais?; **to k. what one is talking about** savoir de quoi on parle; **to k. how to read/swim/do sth** savoir lire/nager/ faire qch; **to k. how to behave** savoir se conduire

5 Fam **don't I k. it!** à qui le dites-vous!; **wouldn't you k. it!** comme par hasard!; **not if I k. Jean-Luc!** tel que je connais Jean-Luc, sûrement pas!; **she is pretty and doesn't she k. it!** elle est jolie et elle le sait bien!

6 to k. better than to … bien se garder de …; **I k. better (than that)** je m'y connais mieux que ça; (I won't be caught out) on ne m'y prendra pas, Fam pas si bête!; **he is old enough to k. better** à son âge il devrait être plus raisonnable; **you can't blame him, he doesn't k. any better** on ne peut pas lui en vouloir, il ne se rend pas compte; **you k. best** vous en êtes le meilleur juge; **you k. best what should be done** vous savez mieux que personne ce qu'il faut faire

7 Bible (sexually) connaître

vi know; **had I known** si j'avais su; **as far as I k., for all I k.** autant que je sache; **I don't want to k.** je ne veux pas le savoir; **when I mentioned that he just didn't want to k.** quand je l'ai mentionné ça n'a rien voulu savoir; Fam **I wouldn't k.** (I don't know) je ne saurais dire; Fam **you k.** (sentence filler) vous voyez; **k. what I mean?** tu vois ce que je veux dire?; **as everyone knows** comme tout le monde le sait; **who knows?** qui sait?; **to k. about sth** être informé de qch, être au courant de qch; **I don't k. about that** (I'm not certain) je n'en suis pas sûr; **to k. of sb** avoir

entendu parler de qn; **to get to k. of sth** apprendre qch; Fam **not that I k. of, not as far as I k.** pas que je sache

know-all N Fam je-sais-tout mf inv; **he's/ she's a bit of a k.** c'est un peu monsieur/madame je-sais-tout

know-how N Fam savoir-faire m; (technical) connaissances fpl techniques

knowing ['nəʊɪŋ] ADJ (intelligent, educated) intelligent, instruit; (cunning) fin, malin, rusé; (smile) entendu

N **there's no k.** c'est impossible à dire; **there's no k. what will happen** on ne peut pas savoir ce qui va se passer

knowingly ['nəʊɪŋlɪ] ADV (with knowledge of the facts) sciemment, en connaissance de cause; (cunningly) finement, d'un air rusé; (to smile) d'un air entendu; Com **never k. undersold** si vous trouvez moins cher, avertissez-nous

know-it-all N esp Am Fam je-sais-tout mf inv

knowledge ['nɒlɪdʒ] N **1** (of fact) connaissance f; **it has come to my k. that …** il est venu ou parvenu à ma connaissance que …, j'ai appris que …; **I had no k. of it** je ne le savais pas, je l'ignorais; **lack of k.** ignorance f (of de); **it is (a matter of) common k. that …** c'est un fait notoire que …; **to (the best of) my k.** à ma connaissance, (autant) que je sache; **not to my k.** pas que je sache; **without my k.** à mon insu; **to speak with full k. (of the facts)** parler en connaissance de cause ou en pleine connaissance des faits

2 (learning) savoir m, connaissance(s) f(pl); **to have a k. of several languages** savoir parler plusieurs langues; **he has a little k. or a working k. of Latin** il a quelques connaissances en latin; **her k. is immense** ses connaissances sont très étendues; **k. of the world** connaissance du monde; Prov **k. is power** savoir c'est pouvoir; **to show off one's k.** étaler sa science

3 carnal k. connaissance f charnelle
▸▸ Comput **k. base** base f de connaissances; **k. economy** économie f de la connaissance; Comput **k. engineer** cogniticien, -ienne

knowledgeable ['nɒlɪdʒəb(ə)l] ADJ (about situation) bien informé; **she's very k. about cars** elle s'y connaît en voitures

knowledge-based system N Comput système m basé sur les connaissances

known [nəʊn] PP see know

ADJ **1** (notorious) connu; notoire; **he's a k. drugs dealer** c'est un revendeur de drogue notoire **2** (recognized) reconnu; **she's a k. expert in the field** c'est un expert reconnu ou qui fait autorité dans ce domaine; **it's a k. fact** c'est un fait établi; **to make oneself k.** se faire connaître; **to let it be k.** faire savoir

knuckle ['nʌk(ə)l] N **1** (of human) articulation f ou jointure f (du doigt); (of animal) première phalange f; **I grazed my knuckles on the wall** je me suis écorché les doigts contre le mur; Fam **that was a bit near the k.** (joke, remark) c'était assez limite **2** Culin (joint of meat) jarret m
▸▸ Fam **k. sandwich** coup m de poing; **he'll get a k. sandwich if he's not careful** il va se prendre un coup de poing dans la tronche s'il ne fait pas gaffe
▸ **knuckle down** VI Fam (begin working hard) s'y mettre sérieusement; **to k. down to sth** se mettre à qch
▸ **knuckle under** VI Fam (give in) mettre les pouces

knuckle-duster N coup-de-poing m (américain), pl coups-de-poing

knurl [nɜːl] N **1** (in wood) nœud m **2** (in metalworking) moletage m; (tool) molette f, godronnoir m
VT (in metalworking) molet(t)er, godronner

KO, pl **KO's** ['keɪ'əʊ, 'keɪ'əʊz] Boxing etc Fam K-O m
VT (3rd person pr **KO's** ['keɪ'əʊz], prp **KO'ing;** pp, pt **KO'd**) mettre K-O

koala [kəʊ'ɑːlə] N Zool koala m
▸▸ **k. bear** koala

Koch's bacillus [kɒxsbə'sɪləs] N Med bacille de Koch m

kohlrabi [kəʊl'rɑːbɪ] N chou-rave m, pl choux-raves, turnep(s) m

kola ['kəʊlə] N (plant) cola m, kola m;
▸▸ **k. nut** noix f de cola ou de kola; **k. tree** kolatier m

kook [kʊk] N Am Fam drôle m d'oiseau

kookaburra ['kʊkəbʌrə] N dacélo m

kopeck ['kəʊpek] N kopeck m

Koran (the) [ðəkɒ'rɑːn] N Rel le Koran, le Coran

Koranic [kɒ'rænɪk] ADJ Rel coranique

Korea [kə'rɪə] N Corée f, **North/South K.** Corée du Nord/du Sud

Korean [kə'rɪən] ADJ coréen
N **1** Coréen, -enne **2** Ling coréen m

korma ['kɔːmə] N Culin **chicken/prawn k.** poulet m/crevettes fpl korma

kosher ['kəʊʃər] ADJ Rel cascher inv, kascher inv; Fam (legitimate) légitime, comme il faut, impec

kowtow [kaʊ'taʊ] VI **1** Fam (act obsequiously) **to k. to sb** faire des courbettes devant qn **2** (bow) se prosterner (**to** devant)

KP ['keɪ'piː] N Am Mil Sl (abbr kitchen police) **to do KP (duty)** être de corvée de patates

kph ['keɪpiː'eɪtʃ] (abbr kilometres per hour) km/h

kraft [krɑːft] N papier m d'emballage fort, papier Kraft

Krakow ['krɑːkɒf] N Cracovie f

Kraut [kraʊt] N Offensive Sl boche mf

Kremlin (the) [ðə'kremlɪn] N le Kremlin; Fam **K. watcher** spécialiste mf du Kremlin, kremlinologiste mf

Kremlinologist [kremlɪ'nɒlədʒɪst] N kremlinologiste mf

krill [krɪl] N krill m

krona ['krəʊnə] N Fin (Swedish currency) couronne f

krone ['krəʊnə], pl **kroner** ['krəʊnə(r)] N Fin (Danish, Norwegian currency) couronne f

Kt abbr knight

kudos ['kjuːdɒs] N (prestige) prestige m; (fame) célébrité f; **to get the k. for sth** recevoir toute la gloire pour qch; **to receive k.** être acclamé

Ku Klux Klan ['kuː'klʌks'klæn] N Ku Klux Klan m

kumquat ['kʌmkwɒt] N kumquat m

kung fu ['kʌŋ'fuː] N kung-fu m; **a k. expert** un expert en kung-fu

Kurd [kɜːd] ADJ kurde
N Kurde mf

Kurdish ['kɜːdɪʃ] ADJ kurde
N Ling kurde m

Kurdistan [kɜːdɪ'stɑːn] N Kurdistan m

Kuwait [kʊ'weɪt, kjuː-] N Koweït m

Kuwaiti [kʊ'weɪtɪ, kjuː-] ADJ koweïtien
N Koweïtien, -ienne

kV (abbr kilovolt) kV

kvetch [kvetʃ] VI Am Fam geindre, se plaindre

kW (abbr kilowatt) kW

kWh (abbr kilowatt-hour) kWh

Ky abbr Kentucky

Kyrie ['kɪrɪeɪ] N Rel **K. (eleison)** Kyrie (eleison) m inv

L, l [el] N (letter) L, l m; **two l's** deux l

l [el] **1** (abbr **litre**) l. **2** (abbr **length**) longueur, long. **3** (abbr **line**) ligne **4** (abbr **left**) gauche

LA [el'eɪ] N abbr Los Angeles

La abbr Louisiana

la [lɑː] N Mus la m; **sing it to 'la'** chante-le en la

laager ['lɑːgər] N Pol (esp in South Africa) camp m

Lab Br Pol (abbr **Labour**) see **labour** N 3

lab [læb] N Fam (abbr **laboratory**) labo m

labcoat ['læbkəʊt] N blouse f de laboratoire

label ['leɪb(ə)l] N **1** (on parcel, bottle etc) étiquette f, **sticky l.** étiquette gommée

2 Com (indication of brand) label m, étiquette f, **to record on the Motown l.** (of singer, musician etc) enregistrer sous le label Motown; **designer l.** (on clothes) marque f, griffe f

3 Comput (of tape, file) label m

4 Fig (of person) étiquette f, **the l. 'reactionary' stayed with him all his life** l'étiquette de réactionnaire lui est restée toute sa vie

5 Chem marque f

VT (-ll-, Am -l-) **1** (tie label to) étiqueter; (stick label on) coller une étiquette sur; **a bottle labelled poison** une bouteille marquée poison; **all luggage must be clearly labelled** tous les bagages doivent être clairement étiquetés

2 to l. sb a liar etc qualifier qn de menteur etc

3 Chem marquer

labelling ['leɪb(ə)lɪŋ] N étiquetage m

labellum, pl **labella** [lə'beləm, -ə] N Bot labelle m

labial ['leɪbɪəl] ADJ labial, -aux
N Ling labiale f
▸▸Ling **l. consonant** consonne f labiale

labialize ['leɪbɪəlaɪz] VT Ling labialiser

labiate ['leɪbɪeɪt] Bot ADJ labié
N labiée f

labiodental [leɪbɪəʊ'dent(ə)l] ADJ Ling labiodental

labium, pl **labia** ['leɪbɪəm, -ə] N Anat **labia** (of vulva) labia mpl, lèvres fpl

labor, labored etc Am = **labour, laboured** etc

laboratory [lə'bɒrətrɪ, esp Am 'læbrətɔːrɪ] N laboratoire m; **dental l.** laboratoire de prothèse dentaire
▸▸**l. assistant** laborantin, -ine; **l. equipment** matériel m de laboratoire; **l. experiment** expérience f en laboratoire

laboratory-tested ADJ testé en laboratoire

laborious [lə'bɔːrɪəs] ADJ **1** pénible, fatigant; (task) laborieux **2** (style) laborieux

laboriously [lə'bɔːrɪəslɪ] ADV péniblement

laboriousness [lə'bɔːrɪəsnɪs] N **1** (of task, ascent etc) pénibilité f **2** (of literary style) caractère m laborieux

labour, Am **labor** ['leɪbər] N **1** (work) travail m, labeur m; **manual l.** travail manuel; **division of l.** division f du travail

2 (workers) main-d'œuvre f, **male/female l.** main-d'œuvre masculine/féminine; **cost of l.** prix m de la main-d'œuvre; **capital and l.** le capital et la main-d'œuvre; Br Formerly **Minister of L.** ministre m du Travail

3 Pol **L.** les travaillistes mpl

4 (task) **the twelve labours of Hercules** les douze travaux mpl d'Hercule; **I'm not doing this as a l. of love** je ne fais pas ça pour le plaisir

5 Obst travail m; **premature l.** accouchement m avant terme; **woman in l.** femme en couches; **to be in l.** être en train d'accoucher; **she went into l. at 3 o'clock** le travail a commencé à 3 heures; **to induce l.** provoquer l'accouchement; **it was a difficult l.** ça a été un accouchement difficile

VI **1** (of person) travailler, peiner; **to l. for sth** se donner de la peine pour obtenir qch; **he laboured all his life for peace** il a travaillé toute sa vie pour la paix; **to l. at** or **over sth** peiner ou trimer sur qch; **to l. up a hill** gravir péniblement une côte; **to l. under great difficulties** être aux prises avec de grandes difficultés; **to l. under a sense of injustice** nourrir un sentiment d'injustice; **to l. under a misapprehension** être dans l'erreur, être (la) victime d'une erreur

2 (of engine) fatiguer, peiner; (of ship) bourlinguer, fatiguer; **to l. uphill** (of car) peiner dans les côtes

VT **I won't l. the point** je ne m'étendrai pas là-dessus

▸▸**l. camp** camp m de travail; Am **l. contract** contrat m de travail; Am **L. Day** fête f du travail; **l. dispute** conflit m du travail; Br, Can Formerly **l. exchange** agence f pour l'emploi, **l. force** (in country) population f active; (in company) main-d'œuvre f; **l. laws** législation f du travail; Pol **L. leader** dirigeant, -ante (du parti) travailliste; **l. market** marché m du travail; **L. Member (of Parliament)** député m travailliste; Obst **l. pains** douleurs fpl de l'accouchement; **the L. Party** le parti travailliste; Ind **l. relations** relations fpl sociales; **l. shortage** pénurie f ou crise f de main-d'œuvre; **l. supply** main-d'œuvre disponible; **l. turnover** rotation f du personnel; Am **l. union** syndicat m (ouvrier); **l. unrest** agitation f ouvrière; Obst **l. ward** salle f d'accouchement

laboured, Am **labored** ['leɪbəd] ADJ **1** (breathing) laborieux **2** (style etc) trop travaillé, trop élaboré; (joke) laborieux

labourer, Am **laborer** ['leɪbərər] N travailleur m; Ind manœuvre m; Prov **the l. is worthy of his hire** toute peine ou tout travail mérite salaire; **unskilled l.** ouvrier m non spécialisé; **agricultural l.** ouvrier agricole

labouring, Am **laboring** ['leɪbərɪŋ] ADJ **the l. class** la classe ouvrière; **a l. job** un travail manuel

labour-intensive, Am **labor-intensive** ADJ qui demande une main-d'œuvre importante

Labourite, Am **Laborite** ['leɪbəraɪt] N Pol travailliste mf

labour-saving, Am **labor-saving** ADJ (device, invention) qui simplifie la tâche; **l. device** (in household) appareil m ménager; **computers are not always l. devices** les ordinateurs ne font pas toujours gagner du temps

Labrador ['læbrədɔːr] N **1** Geog Labrador m **2** (dog) labrador m

laburnum [lə'bɜːnəm] N (tree) cytise m (à grappes)

labyrinth ['læbərɪnθ] N **1** Archit etc labyrinthe m, dédale m **2** Anat (of the ear) labyrinthe m

labyrinthine [læbə'rɪnθaɪn] ADJ Archit en labyrinthe; Fig (procedures, structure) extrêmement compliqué, labyrinthique

lac [læk] N gomme f laque, laque f

lace [leɪs] N **1** Tex dentelle f, **bobbin** or **pillow l.** dentelle aux fuseaux ou au coussin; **l. curtain** rideau m en ou de dentelle **2** (of shoe) lacet m **3** (braid) **gold/silver l.** galon m d'or/d'argent

VT **1** (shoes) lacer; **to l. sth with sth** entrelacer qch de ou avec qch **2** Fam **to l. a drink** ajouter de l'alcool à une boisson; **milk laced with rum** lait au rhum; **she laced his cup of tea with poison** elle ajouta du poison à sa tasse de thé; Fig **he laced his story with salacious details** il ajoutait des détails salaces à son histoire; **her account was laced with scandalous lies** son récit était plein de mensonges effrontés

VI (of boots etc) se lacer

▸ **lace into** VT INSEP Fam (attack) s'en prendre à; (physically) rosser, s'en prendre à

▸ **lace up** VT SEP (shoes) lacer
VI **shoes that l. up** chaussures à lacets; **they l. up at the sides** elles se lacent ou s'attachent sur le côté

lacemaker ['leɪsmeɪkər] N fabricant, -ante de dentelles; (woman only) dentellière f

lacemaking ['leɪsmeɪkɪŋ] N dentellerie f

lacerate ['læsəreɪt] VT lacérer, déchirer

lacerated ['læsəreɪtɪd] ADJ (hand, skin) lacéré; **to be l. by pain** être transpercé par la douleur; **l. feelings** sentiments profondément blessés

laceration [læsə'reɪʃən] N **1** (action) lacération f, déchirement m **2** (tear) déchirure f

lace-up N (shoe) chaussure f à lacets
ADJ (shoe) à lacets

lacewing ['leɪswɪŋ] N Entom hémérobe m
▸▸**l. fly** hémérobe

lacework ['leɪswɜːk] N *(art)* dentellerie f
▸▸ **l. objects** objets *mpl* en dentelle

lachrymal ['lækrɪm(ə)l] ADJ *Anat* lacrymal, -aux
▸▸ **l. duct** conduit *m* lacrymal; **l. gland** glande *f* lacrymale

lachrymose ['lækrɪməʊs] ADJ larmoyant

lacing ['leɪsɪŋ] N **1** milk with a l. of rum lait avec un petit goût de rhum **2** *(on uniform)* galon *m*

lack [læk] N manque *m* (**of** de); **l. of judgment/time** manque de jugement/temps; **l. of money** pénurie *f* d'argent; **she was tired from l. of sleep** elle était fatiguée de n'avoir pas assez dormi; **for l. of …** faute de …
▸ VT *(experience, skill, humour etc)* manquer de; **what the country lacks in modern tourist amenities it more than makes up for in natural beauty** la beauté naturelle du paysage compense largement le manque de structures touristiques; **we l. nothing** nous ne manquons de rien, il ne nous manque rien
▸ VI *(of time)* manquer; **time was lacking** on manquait de temps; **he's lacking in purpose** il lui manque un but; **to be lacking in confidence/experience** manquer de confiance/d'expérience; **they l. for nothing** ils ne manquent de rien; *Fam* **to be lacking** *(mentally)* être (un peu) simplet

lackadaisical [lækə'deɪzɪk(ə)l] ADJ *(person, manner etc)* apathique, *Fam* je-m'en-foutiste; **to take a l. approach to one's work** prendre son travail avec désinvolture

lackey ['lækɪ] N *Pej* larbin *m*

lacklustre, *Am* **lackluster** ['læklʌstər] ADJ *(eyes, gaze)* terne, sans brillant; *(performance)* médiocre

laconic [lə'kɒnɪk] ADJ *(person, answer etc)* laconique

laconically [lə'kɒnɪklɪ] ADV laconiquement

lacquer ['lækər] N *(for wood, hair etc)* laque f, *(coloured)* peinture f laquée; **a red l. screen** un écran recouvert de laque rouge
▸ VT laquer; **a lacquered box** une boîte en laque

lacquerwork ['lækəwɜːk] N laque(s) *m(pl)*

lacrimal ['lækrɪm(ə)l] ADJ = **lachrymal**

lacrosse [lə'krɒs] N *Sport* lacrosse *m*

lacrymal ['lækrɪm(ə)l] ADJ = **lachrymal**

lactate [læk'teɪt] VI produire du lait

lactation [læk'teɪʃən] N lactation f

lacteal ['læktɪəl] ADJ lactaire

lactic ['læktɪk] ADJ *Chem* lactique
▸▸ **l. acid** acide *m* lactique

lactose ['læktəʊz] N *Chem* lactose *m*

lacuna, *pl* **lacunae, lacunas** [læ'kjuːnə, -iː, -əz] N *(in knowledge, manuscript)* lacune f

lacustrine [lə'kʌstraɪn] ADJ *(plant etc)* lacustre

lacy ['leɪsɪ] ADJ *(made of lace)* de dentelle; *(resembling lace)* fin comme de la dentelle

lad [læd] N **1** *Fam (young man)* jeune gars *m*; *(boy)* garçon *m*; **he's only a l.** ce n'est qu'un gosse; **the doctor's l.** *(son)* le fils du docteur; **come on, lads!** allons, les gars!; **he's a bit of a l.** *or* **quite a l.** c'est un gaillard; **one of the lads** un des gars; **listen, my l.** écoute, mon petit gars **2** *Br Horseracing* **(stable) l.** lad *m*
▸▸ *Fam* **l. mag** = magazine *m* destiné à un public d'hommes jeunes

ladder ['lædər] N **1** échelle f; **it's unlucky to walk under a l.** ça porte malheur de passer sous une échelle; *Fig* **the social l.** l'échelle sociale; *Fig* **to get one's foot on the l.** mettre un pied dans le circuit; *Fig* **to reach the top of the l.** atteindre le sommet de l'échelle; **fish** *or* **salmon l.** échelle à saumons **2** *esp Br*

(in stocking) échelle f; **I've got a l.** j'ai une échelle à mon collant, mon collant est filé
▸ VT *esp Br (stocking)* filer
▸ VI *esp Br (of stocking)* se démailler, filer

ladder-proof ADJ *esp Br (stockings)* qui ne filent pas

laddie ['lædɪ] N *Scot Fam* garçon *m*; *(term of endearment)* mon petit gars

laddish ['lædɪʃ] ADJ *Br Fam* = typique d'un style de vie caractérisé par de fréquentes sorties entre copains, généralement copieusement arrosées, un comportement arrogant et macho et un goût prononcé pour le sport et les activités de groupe

laden ['leɪd(ə)n] ADJ chargé (**with** de); **I was l. with shopping** j'avais les bras chargés de commissions; **fully l. ship** navire en pleine charge; **heavily l. tree** arbre chargé de fruits

ladette [læ'det] N *Br Fam* jeune femme f délurée *(qui se revendique l'égale des hommes pour ce qui est des sorties, de la vulgarité, etc)*

la-di-da, la-de-da ['lɑːdɪ'dɑː] ADJ *Fam (air, voice)* affecté, maniéré

ladies ['leɪdɪz] N toilettes *fpl* (des dames); *(as sign)* dames; **can you tell me where the l. is?** pouvez-vous m'indiquer où sont les toilettes?

lading ['leɪdɪŋ] N **1** *(action) (of ship)* chargement *m*; *(of merchandise)* mise f à bord **2** *(cargo)* chargement *m*

ladle ['leɪd(ə)l] N **1** *(soup)* **l.** louche f **2** *Ind* puisoir *m*; *Metal* **foundry l.** poche f de fonderie
▸ VT **to l. (out) the soup** servir le potage (avec une louche); *Fam* **to l. out advice** prodiguer des conseils

ladleful ['leɪd(ə)lfʊl] N pleine louche f (**of** de)

lady, *pl* **ladies** ['leɪdɪ, -ɪz] N **1** dame f; **l. doctor** femme f médecin; **she's a real l.** c'est une femme très comme il faut; **she's no l.** ce n'est pas une femme comme il faut; **a l. and a gentleman** une dame et un monsieur; **a young l.** une jeune fille; *(married)* une jeune dame; **an old l.** une vieille dame; **how are you, young l.?** *(to child)* comment allez-vous, jeune fille?; **listen to me, young l.** écoute un peu, jeune fille; **ladies and gentlemen!** *(at meeting etc)* mesdames, mesdemoiselles, messieurs!; **come in, ladies!** entrez donc, mesdames!; **he's a ladies' man** c'est un homme à femmes; **the l. of the house** la maîtresse de maison; **painted l.** *(butterfly)* belle-dame f, *pl* belles-dames; **ladies' tailor** tailleur *m* pour dames; **l.'s watch** montre pour dames
2 *Rel* **Our L.** Notre-Dame f, la sainte Vierge
3 *(title)* **L. Browne** lady Browne; **the l. of the manor** la châtelaine; *Fam* **stop behaving like L. Muck** arrête de jouer les grandes dames
4 *Old-fashioned (wife)* femme f, épouse f; **how's your good l.?** comment va votre dame?; **this is my l. wife** voici mon épouse; **my young l.** *(fiancée)* ma fiancée, ma future
▸▸ **l. of the bedchamber** *(at court)* dame d'atours; *Pej* **L. Bountiful** = dame patronnesse; **L. Chapel** chapelle f de la Sainte Vierge; **L. Day** *(fête f de)* l'Annonciation f *(le 25 mars)*; **ladies' fingers** *(vegetable)* gombo(s) *m(pl)*; **l.'s maid** femme de chambre; **ladies' night** *(in bar)* = soirée f où les femmes ont droit à des réductions; *Am* **ladies' room** toilettes *fpl* des dames

ladybird, *Am* **ladybug** ['leɪdɪbɜːd, -bʌg] N *Entom* coccinelle f, *Fam* bête f à bon Dieu

ladyfinger ['leɪdɪfɪŋgər] N *Culin* boudoir *m*

lady-in-waiting N *(at court)* dame f d'honneur

lady-killer N *Fam* bourreau *m* des cœurs, don Juan *m*

ladylike ['leɪdɪlaɪk] ADJ *(woman)* comme il

faut, bien élevée; *(air, behaviour)* distingué; **climbing trees isn't very l.** les vraies demoiselles ne grimpent pas aux arbres; **it's not a l. thing to say** ce n'est pas beau dans la bouche d'une jeune fille

ladyship ['leɪdɪʃɪp] N her **l., your l.** madame (la comtesse *etc*); *Iron* her **l. doesn't feel like it** madame n'en a pas envie

lady's-slipper [leɪdɪz'slɪpər] N *(orchid)* sabot *m* de Vénus

lag[1] [læg] N *(delay)*, *Elec* retard *m*; *Ind etc* **time l.** décalage *m*
▸ VI (-gg-) être à la traîne
▸ **lag behind** VI *(of people, walkers, company industry)* être à la traîne; **don't l. behind** ne reste pas à la traîne; **salaries are still lagging behind** les salaires sont restés à un niveau inférieur; **she always lags behind on the way to school** sur le chemin de l'école elle est toujours à la traîne
▸ VT INSEP **to l. behind the others** être à la traîne par rapport aux autres

lag[2] N *esp Br Sl* **an old l.** *(jailbird)* un repris de justice, un récidiviste

lag[3] VT *(boiler etc)* calorifuger, isoler

lager ['lɑːgər] N bière f blonde
▸▸ *Br Fam* **l. lout** = jeune *m* qui, sous l'influence de l'alcool, cherche la bagarre ou commet des actes de vandalisme

lagered (up) ['lɑːgəd] ADJ *Br Fam* bourré à la bière; **he gets l. with his mates every Friday night** il se bourre la gueule à la bière avec ses potes tous les vendredi soir

laggard ['lægəd] N **1** *(in race)* traînard, -arde; **the laggards in the class** ceux qui apprennent plus lentement que les autres **2** *Mktg (product)* innovateur *m* tardif

lagging ['lægɪŋ] N **1** *(action) (of boiler)* garnissage *m*, calorifugeage *m* **2** *(material) (for boiler)* revêtement *m* calorifuge

lagoon [lə'guːn] N *Geog* **1** *(of atoll)* lagon *m* **2** *(with sand, shingle etc)* lagune f

lah [lɑː] N *Mus* = **la**

lah-di-dah ['lɑːdɪ'dɑː] ADJ = **la-di-da**

laid PT, PP *see* **lay**[1] VT

laid-back [leɪd-] ADJ *Fam (person, atmosphere)* relax, décontracté

lain PP *see* **lie**[2] VI

lair [leər] N *(of big cat)* tanière f, repaire *m*, *esp Litt* antre *m*; *Fig (room etc)* antre; **brigands' l.** repaire de brigands

laird [leəd] N *Scot* propriétaire *m* (foncier)

lairy ['leərɪ] ADJ *Br Fam* culotté

laisser-faire, laissez-faire [leseɪ'feər] N *esp Econ* laisser-faire *m*
▸▸ **l. policy** politique f du laisser-faire

laity ['leɪtɪ] N **the l.** les laïques *mpl*

lake[1] [leɪk] N lac *m*; sel; **ornamental l.** bassin *m*, pièce f d'eau décorative; **the Great Lakes** les Grands Lacs; **the Lakes** le Lake District, la région des lacs *(dans le nord-ouest de l'Angleterre)*; *Fig* **wine l.** surplus *m* de vin; *Sl* **go jump in the l.** va te faire voir; **l. front** bord *m* de lac; **they live on the l. front** ils habitent au bord du lac
▸▸ **the L. District** le Lake District, la région des lacs *(dans le nord-ouest de l'Angleterre)*; **l. dwelling** habitation f lacustre; **L. Geneva** le lac Léman, le lac de Genève; **the L. poets** les *(poètes mpl)* lakistes *mpl*

lake[2] N *(pigment)* laque f, **crimson l.** laque carminée

Lakeland ['leɪklənd] N la région des lacs *(au nord-ouest de l'Angleterre)*

lakeshore ['leɪkʃɔː], **lakeside** ['leɪksaɪd] N rive f d'un lac; **they live on the l.** ils habitent au bord du lac
▸ ADJ au bord du lac

lam[1] [læm] N *Am Sl (flight)* fuite f, **to be on**

the l. être en cavale; **to take it on the l.** partir en cavale

lam² vi (-mm-) *Fam* **to l. into sb** (*hit*) rosser qn, étriller qn; (*verbally*) étriller qn

lama ['lɑːmə] N *Rel* lama *m*; **the Dalai** or **Grand L.** le dalaï-lama

lamb [læm] N agneau *m*; **ewe l.** agnelle *f*, **ewe with l.** brebis *f* pleine; *Rel* **L. (of God)** Agneau (de Dieu); *Fam* **to be a l.** (*of person*) être gentil comme tout; **she accepted my decision like a l.** elle a accepté ma décision sans broncher; *Fam* **my l.** (*term of endearment*) mon petit; **poor l.** (*person*) pauvre petit(e); *Prov* **to go like lambs to the slaughter** être comme du bétail que l'on mène à l'abattoir; *Culin* **l. cutlet** or **chop** côtelette *f* d'agneau; *Bot* **l.'s lettuce** mâche *f*, *Fam* **l.'s tails** (*of hazel tree*) chatons *mpl*
vi (*of ewe*) agneler, mettre bas

lambada [læm'bɑːdə] N lambada *f*

lambast [læm'bæst], **lambaste** [læm'beɪst] vt (*person*) réprimander, *Lit* fustiger

lambing ['læmɪŋ] N agnelage *m*; **the l. season** l'agnelage

lambskin ['læmskɪn] N peau *f* d'agneau; (*fur*) agnelin *m*

lambswool ['læmswʊl] N laine *f* d'agneau, lambswool *m*
ADJ en laine d'agneau, en lambswool

lame [leɪm] ADJ 1 (*person, horse*) boiteux; (*through accident etc*) estropié; **l. leg** jambe boiteuse; **to be l.** boiter; **to be l. in one leg** boiter d'une jambe; **to be completely l.** être handicapé des deux jambes; **to go l.** se mettre à boiter; *Fig* **l. excuse** excuse boiteuse; **l. argument** argument boiteux ou qui ne tient pas debout; *Liter* **l. verses** vers boiteux ou qui boitent 2 *Am Fam* (*conventional*) vieux jeu *inv*, (*stupid*) cloche, nouille
vt (*person, horse*) estropier; **to be lamed by an accident/illness** rester boiteux à la suite d'un accident/d'une maladie; **she had been lamed by polio** elle est restée boiteuse à cause de la polio
▸▸ *Fig* **l. duck** canard *m* boiteux; *Am Pol* = candidat *m* sortant non réélu qui attend l'arrivée de son successeur

lamé ['lɑːmeɪ] N *Tex* lamé *m*; **gold/silver l.** lamé d'or/d'argent; **a gold l. dress** une robe en lamé d'or

lamebrain ['leɪmbreɪn] N *Fam* idiot, -ote, abruti, -ie

lamely ['leɪmlɪ] ADV (*to apologize*) faiblement

lameness ['leɪmnɪs] N claudication *f*, (*of horse*) boiterie *f*, *Fig* (*of excuse etc*) faiblesse *f*

lament [lə'ment] N 1 lamentation *f* 2 *Mus* complainte *f*
vt se lamenter sur, pleurer; (*person*) pleurer; **I was lamenting my lost youth** je pleurais ma jeunesse perdue; **the nation did not l. the death of the dictator** le pays n'a pas pleuré la mort du dictateur; **it's to be lamented** c'est à regretter
vi se lamenter (**over sth** sur qch), pleurer (**over sb/sth** qn/qch)

lamentable [lə'məntəb(ə)l] ADJ (*loss, failure*) déplorable; (*pathetic*) (*performance etc*) lamentable; **it's l.!** c'est déplorable!

lamentably [lə'məntəblɪ] ADV déplorablement; (*pathetically*) lamentablement

lamentation [læmən'teɪʃən] N lamentation *f*, *Bible* **the Lamentations of Jeremiah** les Lamentations de Jérémie

lamented [lə'mentɪd] ADJ **the late l. Mr Jones** le regretté M. Jones

laminate ['læmɪneɪt] N stratifié *m*
vt 1 (*bond*) laminer, lamifier; (*glass*) feuilleter; (*plastic*) stratifier; (*wood*) contreplaquer 2 (*split*) diviser en lamelles 3 (*cover*) (*paper etc*) plastifier

vi 1 (*bond*) se laminer 2 (*split*) se diviser en lamelles

laminated ['læmɪneɪtɪd] ADJ 1 (*glass*) feuilleté; (*wood*) contreplaqué 2 (*paper etc*) plastifié
▸▸ **l. jacket** (*of book*) jaquette *f* plastifiée; *Ind* **l. plastics** plastique *m* stratifié; **l. plate glass** verre *m* (de sécurité) feuilleté; **l. spring** ressort *m* à lames (superposées)

Lammas ['læməs] N le premier août
▸▸ **L. Day** le premier août

lammergeier ['læməgaɪər] N (*bird*) gypaète *m* barbu

lamp [læmp] N 1 lampe *f*; **bicycle l.** (*fixed*) phare *m* de bicyclette; (*detachable*) lampe de bicyclette; **portable l., inspection l.** (*in garage etc*) baladeuse *f*; **street l.** réverbère *m*; **hanging l.** suspension *f* 2 **neon l.** lampe au néon; **ultraviolet l.** lampe à ultra-violets

lampblack ['læmpblæk] N noir *m* de fumée

lamplight ['læmplaɪt] N lumière *f* de la lampe; **to work by l.** travailler à la lampe

lamplit ['læmplɪt] ADJ éclairé

lampoon [læm'puːn] N pamphlet *m*, libelle *m*
vt (*person*) brocarder, railler

lampoonist [læm'puːnɪst] N satiriste *m*, pamphlétaire *m*

lamppost ['læmppəʊst] N (*in street*) réverbère *m*

lamprey, *pl* **lampreys** ['læmprɪ, -ɪz] N (*eel*) lamproie *f*

lampshade ['læmpʃeɪd] N abat-jour *m inv*

lampstand ['læmpstænd] N pied *m* de lampe

LAN [læn] N *Comput abbr* **local area network**

lance [lɑːns] N (*weapon*) lance *f*, *Arch, Lit* **to break a l. with sb** rompre une lance avec qn
vt *Med* (*abscess*) percer, inciser
▸▸ *Br* **l. corporal** ≃ caporal *m*, *Suisse* ≃ appointé *m*

lanceolate(d) ['lɑːnsɪəleɪt(ɪd)] ADJ *Bot* lancéolé

lancer ['lɑːnsər] N 1 *Mil* lancier *m* 2 (*dance*) **lancers** (quadrille *m* des) lanciers *mpl*

lancet ['lɑːnsɪt] N 1 *Med* lancette *f* 2 *Archit* (*arch*) lancette *f*
▸▸ *Archit* **l. arch** lancette; **l. window** fenêtre *f* en ogive

Lancs *abbr* **Lancashire**

LAND [lænd] N 1 (*as opposed to sea*) terre *f*, **on l.** sur terre; **to travel by l.** voyager par voie de terre; *Naut* **to make l.** reconnaître la terre; *Fig* **to see how the l. lies** tâter le terrain; *Mil etc* (**to attack**) **by l., sea and air** (attaquer) par terre, par mer et par air
2 (*earth, soil*) terre *f*, sol *m*; **arable l.** terre arable; **man lives off the l.** c'est la terre qui nourrit les hommes; **to live off the l.** (*of farmers*) vivre en autarcie; (*of army*) subsister sans ravitaillement
3 (*country*) pays *m*, terre *f*; **the best in the l.** le meilleur du pays; **to be still in the l. of the living** être encore de ce monde; *Prov* **a l. flowing with milk and honey** un pays où coulent le lait et le miel; **a l. of opportunity** un pays où tout est possible; **the l. of dreams/Nod** le pays des rêves/de Morphée
4 (*property*) terre(s) *f(pl)*; **private l.** terrain privé; **a piece of l.** un terrain; **the farmer wouldn't allow campers on his l.** le fermier n'acceptait pas de campeurs sur ses terres; **to buy l.** acheter des terres
vt 1 (*put on land*) (*from ship, plane*) débarquer; *Com* (*merchandise*) décharger
2 *Aviat* (*bring down to land*) (*plane*) faire atterrir; **they landed him on the deck of the ferry** ils l'ont fait atterrir sur le pont du ferry; **to l. a man on the moon** faire alunir un homme
3 *Zool* (*fish*) amener à terre

4 *Fam* (*win, obtain*) se dégoter; **they landed all the prizes** ils ont raflé tous les prix; **he's just landed a good job** il vient juste de dégoter un bon boulot
5 *Fam* (*in phrases*) **that will l. you in prison** tu vas te retrouver en prison; **you've landed us in a nice mess!** vous nous avez mis dans de beaux draps!; **to be landed with sth** rester avec qch sur les bras; **I've been landed with the job of telling him** c'est à moi qu'il est revenu de le lui dire
vi 1 (*from ship, plane*) débarquer; (*of aircraft, pilot*) atterrir; (*on deck of aircraft carrier*) apponter; **to l. on the moon** alunir; **to l. on the sea** amerrir; *Aviat* **when do we l.?** quand est-ce que nous atterrissons?
2 (*jumping off wall etc*) se recevoir; (*from great height, parachutist*) atterrir; **he slipped and landed in a puddle** il a glissé et a atterri dans une flaque d'eau; **to l. flat on one's back** se retrouver les quatre fers en l'air; **to l. on one's feet** retomber sur ses pieds; (*of cat*) retomber sur ses pattes; *Fig Fam* **he always manages to l. on his feet** il arrive toujours à retomber sur ses pattes
3 *Sport* (*after jumping*) (*of gymnast, ski-jumper, horse*) se réceptionner
▸▸ *Law* **l. act** loi *f* agraire; **l. agent** (*administrator*) régisseur *m*, intendant, -ante; *Br* (*estate agent*) agent *m* immobilier; **l. army** armée *f* de terre; **l. bank** crédit *m* foncier; **l. breeze** brise *f* de terre; **l. bridge** isthme *m*; *Acct* **l. charge** dette *f* foncière; **L.'s End** la pointe des Cornouailles; **l. forces** armée *f* de terre; *Br* **l. girl** fille *f* de ferme (*pendant la Deuxième Guerre mondiale*); *Tel* **l. line** ligne *f* terrestre; **the l. of the midnight sun** le pays du soleil de minuit; **l. mine** mine *f* terrestre; **l. reform** réforme *f* agraire; **l. register** cadastre *m*; **l. route** voie *f* de terre; **l. tax** impôt *m* foncier, contribution *f* foncière; **l. warfare** guerre *f* sur terre

▸ **land up** vi *Fam* (*in a ditch, hospital, jail etc*) se retrouver; **I landed up having to dance with him** il a fallu que je danse avec lui; **I always landed up with the worst jobs** je me retrouvais toujours avec les tâches les plus ingrates à faire

landau ['lændɔː] N (*carriage*) landau *m*, *pl* landaus

landed ['lændɪd] ADJ ATTRIB foncier
▸▸ *Fin* **l. costs** coûts *mpl* fonciers; **l. estate** propriété *f* foncière; **the l. gentry** la petite noblesse; **l. immigrant** résident, -ente permanent(e); **l. property** propriété foncière ou territoriale; **l. proprietor** propriétaire *mf* terrien(ienne)

landfall ['lændfɔːl] N *Naut* (*arrival*) atterrissage *m*; (*sight of land*) arrivée *f* en vue de terre; **to make (a) l.** (*arrive*) atterrir; (*sight land*) arriver en vue de terre

landfill ['lændfɪl] N remblai *m*; **to use sth as l.** utiliser qch pour remblayer ou comme remblai
▸▸ **l. site** décharge *f* publique

landing ['lændɪŋ] N 1 *Naut* débarquement *m*; *Com* débarquement *m*
2 *Aviat* (*of aircraft*) (*on land*) atterrissage *m*; (*on sea*) amerrissage *m*; (*on deck of ship*) appontage *m*; *Aviat* **blind/instrument l.** atterrissage sans visibilité/aux instruments; **visual l.** atterrissage à vue; **forced** or **emergency l.** atterrissage forcé
3 *Constr* (*of staircase*) palier *m*, (*corridor*) couloir *m*
4 (*of fish*) prise *f*
5 (*of gymnast, ski-jumper*) réception *f*
▸▸ **l. card** carte *f* de débarquement; **l. certificate** certificat *m* de déchargement; **l. craft** navire *m* de débarquement; **l. field** terrain *m* d'atterrissage; **l. flap** volet *m* d'atterrissage; *Mil, Naut* **l. force** troupes *fpl* de débarquement; *Aviat* **l. gear** train *m* d'atterrissage; **l.**

lights *(on plane)* phares *mpl* d'atterrissage; *(at airport)* balises *fpl* (d'atterrissage); **l. net** épuisette *f(filet)*; *Naut* **l. operation** opération *f* de débarquement; *Naut* **l. order** permis *m* de débarquement; *Mil, Naut* **l. party** compagnie *f* de débarquement; *Com* **l. and port charges** frais *mpl* de débarquement et de port; **l. stage** débarcadère *m*; **l. strip** piste *f* d'atterrissage; **l. wheels** train d'atterrissage; *Mil, Aviat* **l. zone** zone *f* d'atterrissage *(des troupes aéroportées)*

landlady ['lændleɪdɪ] **N 1** *(from whom one rents accommodation) (owner)* propriétaire *f*, *(living on premises)* logeuse *f* **2** *Br (of pub) (owner)* propriétaire *f*, *(manageress)* gérante *f* **3** *(of small hotel)* aubergiste *f*, hôtelière *f*, **seaside l.** propriétaire *f* d'une auberge au bord de la mer

landlegs ['lændlegz] **NPL** *Fam (of sailor)* **to get one's l.** se familiariser de nouveau avec la terre

landless ['lændlɪs] **ADJ** sans terre; **l. peasants** paysans qui ne sont pas propriétaires

landlocked ['lændlɒkt] **ADJ** *(country)* sans accès à la mer; *(port etc)* entouré de terre; **l. sea** mer *f* intérieure

landlord ['lændlɔːd] **N 1** *(of property)* bailleur *m*; *(from whom one rents accommodation) (owner)* propriétaire *m*; *(living on premises)* logeur *m* **2** *Br (of pub) (owner)* propriétaire *m*; *(manager)* gérant *m*; *(form of address)* patron **3** *(landowner)* propriétaire *m* (foncier)

landlubber ['lændlʌbər] **N** *Naut Fam Hum* marin *m* d'eau douce

landmark ['lændmɑːk] **N 1** *(building, statue etc)* (point *m* de) repère *m*; *Aviat* repère, point de repérage (au sol); *Naut* amer *m*, indice *m* (à terre), point à terre; **that clump of trees is a natural l.** ce groupe d'arbres est un repère naturel **2** *(important event)* point *m* décisif, événement *m* marquant; **to be a l.** *(of event)* faire date **3** *(boundary marker)* borne *f* limite
▸▸**l. building** bâtiment *m* reconnaissable; **l. decision** décision *f* qui fait date

landmass ['lændmæs] **N** *Geog* masse *f* de terre

landowner ['lændəʊnər] **N** propriétaire *m* foncier

landowning ['lændəʊnɪŋ] **ADJ the l. classes** la classe des propriétaires fonciers

landscape ['lændskeɪp] **N** *(land, painting)* paysage *m*; **to print sth in l.** *Comput* imprimer qch en (mode) paysage; *Typ* imprimer qch à l'italienne
ADV *(to print)* *Comput* en paysage; *Typ* à l'italienne
VT *(area)* aménager en parc; **they had their garden landscaped** ils ont employé un jardinier paysagiste pour aménager leur propriété
▸▸**l. architect** architecte *mf* paysagiste; **l. architecture** architecture *f* de paysage; **l. design** architecture de paysage; **l. designer** paysagiste *mf*; **l. gardener** jardinier, -ière paysagiste; **l. gardening** paysagisme *m*; *Comput* **l. mode** mode *m* paysage; *Art* **l. painter** (peintre *m*) paysagiste

landscaping ['lændskeɪpɪŋ] **N** paysagisme *m*

landslide ['lændslaɪd] **N 1** éboulement *m*, affaissement *m*, glissement *m* (de terrain) **2** *Pol* raz-de-marée *m inv* électoral; **to win the elections by a l.** gagner les élections avec une écrasante majorité
▸▸**l. majority** majorité *f* écrasante; **l. victory** victoire *f* écrasante

landslip ['lændslɪp] **N** = **landslide 1**

landward ['lændwəd] **ADV (to) l.** du côté de la terre, vers la terre

ADJ on the l. side vers l'intérieur, du côté de la terre

lane [leɪn] **N 1** *(in country)* petite route *f* de campagne; *(in town)* ruelle *f*, passage *m* **2** *Naut* route *f* de navigation **3** *Aut etc* **(traffic) l.** voie *f*; **four-l. road** route à quatre voies (de circulation); **don't change lanes** ne change pas de voie; **traffic is reduced to two lanes** la circulation ne se fait plus que sur deux files; **stay in l.** restez dans votre file; **get in(to) l.** mettez-vous sur la bonne file **4** *Sport (for runner, swimmer)* couloir *m*
▸▸**l. markings** *(on road)* signalisation *f* au sol *ou* horizontale des voies; *Sport (on track)* lignes *fpl* de marquage des couloirs; *(in swimming pool)* lignes d'eau

langlauf ['lɑːnlaʊf] **N** ski *m* de fond
▸▸**l. skier** skieur, -euse de fond

language ['læŋgwɪdʒ] **N 1** *(of a people)* langue *f*; **the English l.** la langue anglaise; **foreign languages** langues étrangères; **I never learned to speak the l.** je n'ai jamais appris à parler la langue; *Fig* **we don't talk the same l.** nous ne parlons pas le même langage VOIR GRAMMAIRE A8; B4
2 *(vocabulary)* langage *m*; **the l. of flowers** le langage des fleurs; **bad l.** langage grossier, grossièretés *fpl*; **to use bad/foul l.** parler grossièrement; **(mind your) l.!** surveille votre langage!; **code l.** langage convenu, code *m*; **business l.** langage *ou* langue *f* des affaires; *Comput* **computer l., machine l.** langage machine
▸▸**l. course** cours *m* de langues; **l. exchange holiday** échange *m* linguistique; **l. laboratory** laboratoire *m* de langues; **l. learning** apprentissage *m* de langues; **l. studies** études *fpl* de langues; **l. teaching** enseignement *m* de langues

When translating **language**, note that **langue** and **langage** are not interchangeable. **Langue** is used when talking about a specific language used in a country or region, while **langage** refers to the concept of language in general or to a set of vocabulary or terminology.

languid ['læŋgwɪd] **ADJ** languissant, langoureux

languidly ['læŋgwɪdlɪ] **ADV** *(to move)* languissamment, langoureusement; *(to say)* d'une voix langoureuse

languidness [læŋgwɪdnɪs] **N** langueur *f*

languish ['læŋgwɪʃ] **VI** languir; *(of plant)* dépérir; **to l. for sb/sth** languir après *ou* pour qn/qch; *Fam* **it languished in my intray for a week** c'est resté dans ma corbeille à courrier pendant une semaine; **to l. in prison** moisir en prison; **she spends her day languishing on the sofa** elle passe ses journées langoureusement allongée sur le canapé

languishing ['læŋgwɪʃɪŋ] **ADJ** languissant, langoureux

languor ['læŋgər] **N** langueur *f*

languorous ['læŋgərəs] **ADJ** langoureux

languorously ['læŋgərəslɪ] **ADV** langoureusement

lank [læŋk] **ADJ l. hair** cheveux plats

lankness ['læŋknɪs] **N** *(of hair)* aspect *m* terne et sans vigueur

lanky ['læŋkɪ] **ADJ** *(person)* grand et filiforme, dégingandé

lanolin(e) ['lænəlɪn] **N** *Chem, Pharm* lanoline *f*
▸▸**l. shampoo** shampooing *m* à la lanoline

lantern ['læntən] **N 1** lanterne *f*, falot *m*; *Naut* fanal *m*, -aux; **Chinese l.** lanterne véni-

tienne; *Hist* **magic l.** lanterne magique **2** *Archit (of dome)* lanterne *f*, lanternau *m*
▸▸**l. jaws** joues *fpl* creuses; **l. slides** plaques *fpl* de lanterne magique

lantern-jawed [læntən'dʒɔːd] **ADJ** aux joues creuses

lanyard ['lænjɑːd, -jəd] **N** *Naut* aiguillette *f*, *(for rigging)* ride *f*, *(of knife etc)* amarrage *m*

Laos [laʊs] **N** Laos *m*

Laotian ['laʊʃɪən] **ADJ** laotien
N Laotien, -ienne

lap¹ [læp] **N** *(of seated person)* genoux *mpl*, *Lit* giron *m*; **to sit on sb's l.** s'asseoir sur les genoux de qn; **it's in the l. of the gods** c'est entre les mains des dieux; **it's not going to fall into your l.** *(you'll have to work for it)* ça ne va pas te tomber tout cuit (dans le bec); **it dropped in(to) my l.** c'est tombé du ciel; **to live in the l. of luxury** vivre dans le luxe; *Fig* **to drop sth in sb's l.** coller qch à qn
▸▸*Aut* **l. belt** ceinture *f* ventrale; **l. dancing** = type *m* de danse exécutée par une entraîneuse nue pour un client; *Aut* **l. and shoulder belt** ceinture trois points

lap² **N 1** *Sport (of track, circuit)* tour *m*; **to do three laps** faire trois tours de circuit; **they're on the third l.** ils en sont au troisième tour; *Fig* **to be on the last l.** en être à la dernière étape; **l. of honour** tour d'honneur **2** *Tech* recouvrement *m*; *Constr (of tiles, slates)* chevauchement *m*, recouvrement *m* **3** *(of wire around cylinder etc)* tour *m*
VT *(-pp-)* **to l. an opponent** prendre un tour d'avance sur un concurrent; **runners being lapped should move to the outside** les coureurs qui ont un tour de retard doivent s'écarter; **to l. the course** faire un tour de circuit
2 *(wrap)* **to l. sth round sth** enrouler qch autour de qch
3 *Constr (planks)* enchevaucher, poser à recouvrement; *(tiles)* donner du recouvrement à; **to l. a joint with sheet metal** chaperonner un assemblage
VI 1 *Sport (of runner)* faire le tour du stade; *(of car)* faire le tour du circuit **2** **to l. over sth** dépasser *ou* recouvrir qch; *(of tiles etc)* chevaucher qch
▸▸*Tech* **l. joint** enchevauchure *f*, assemblage *m* par recouvrement; **l. weld, l. welding** soudure *f* par recouvrement

lap³ **N** *(of waves)* clapotement *m*, clapotis *m*
VT *(of animal) (milk)* laper
VI *(of waves)* clapoter

▸ **lap up** **VT SEP 1** *(milk)* laper **2** *Fig Fam (book)* dévorer; **he laps up everything she says** il boit toutes ses paroles; **it was sheer flattery but he lapped it all up** c'était de la flatterie pure et simple mais il a tout gobé *ou* avalé

laparoscope ['læpərəskəʊp] **N** *Med* laparoscope *m*

laparoscopy [læpə'rɒskəpɪ] **N** *Med* laparoscopie *f*

laparotomy [læpə'rɒtəmɪ] **N** *Surg* laparotomie *f*

lapdog ['læpdɒg] **N** chien *m* d'appartement; *Fig* marionnette *f*

lapel [lə'pel] **N** *(on jacket)* revers *m*

lapidary ['læpɪd(ə)rɪ] **ADJ, N** lapidaire *m*

lapis lazuli ['læpɪs'læzʊlɪ] **N** *(stone, colour)* lapis(-lazuli) *m inv*

Lapland ['læplænd] **N** Laponie *f*

Laplander ['læplændər] **N** Lapon, -one

Lapp [læp] **ADJ** lapon
N 1 Lapon, -one **2** *Ling* lapon *m*

lapping ['læpɪŋ] **N** *(of waves)* clapotement *m*, clapotis *m*

lapse [læps] **N 1** *(mistake)* erreur *f*, faute *f*, *(fault)* faute, défaillance *f*, *(in behaviour)* écart *m* de conduite; *(in standards etc)* baisse *f* (**in** de); (*in security*) défaillance; **l. of memory** défaillance *ou* absence *f* de mémoire, oubli *m*; **it was a l. in good manners** il/elle/*etc* a temporairement oublié ses bonnes manières; **a l. in (good) taste** une faute de goût; **a l. in concentration/vigilance** un écart de concentration/vigilance; **it was just a temporary l.** ce n'était qu'une défaillance temporaire; **moral l.** faux pas *m*; (*sexual infidelity*) écart *m*

2 (*passage*) (*of time*) cours *m*, marche *f*; **a time l.** un laps de temps; **after a l. of three months** après un laps de temps de trois mois

3 (*expiry*) expiration *f*

vi 1 (*make mistake, err*) **he only lapsed once** il n'a fait qu'une seule erreur; **his concentration lapsed for a split second** il a relâché sa concentration pendant une fraction de seconde; **if standards of education are allowed to l.** si on laisse baisser les niveaux scolaires

2 (*fall, go*) **to l. into silence** se taire; **to l. into unconsciousness** sombrer dans l'inconscience; **he's lapsing back into his old ways** il retombe dans ses vieilles habitudes; **it's too easy to l. back into English** c'est trop facile de revenir à l'anglais

3 (*morally*) être coupable d'un écart de conduite; (*more serious*) manquer à ses devoirs; **he tried to give up drinking but he would all too often l.** il essayait d'arrêter de boire mais trop souvent retombait dans son travers

4 *Law* (*of right, passport etc*) périmer, se périmer; (*of estate*) devenir disponible; (*of legacy*) devenir caduc; (*of law*) tomber en désuétude; (*of insurance policy etc*) cesser d'être en vigueur; *Rel* (*of person*) cesser de pratiquer; **to allow a right to l.** laisser périmer *ou* laisser tomber un droit; **my club membership has lapsed** ma carte de membre du club a expiré

lapsed [læpst] ADJ **1** *Rel* déchu **2** (*postal order etc, right*) périmé; (*inheritance*) tombé en dévolu; (*contract, inheritance*) caduc, *f* caduque; (*insurance policy, membership*) expiré

laptop ['læptɒp] N *Comput* portable *m*

lapwing ['læpwɪŋ] N (*bird*) vanneau *m* (huppé)

larceny ['lɑːsənɪ] N *Law* vol *m*; **petty l.** vol simple, vol minime; *Am* **grand l.** vol qualifié

larch [lɑːtʃ] N (*tree*) mélèze *m*

lard [lɑːd] N saindoux *m*; *esp Am Fam* **he's a tub of l.** c'est un sac de graisse

vt *Culin* (*meat*) larder, barder; *Fam Pej* **to l. one's writings with quotations** larder ses écrits de citations

> Note that the French word **lard** is a false friend. Its most common meaning is **bacon**.

lardarse ['lɑːdɑːs], *Am* **lardass** ['lɑːdæs] N *Sl Pej* (*man*) gros *m* plein de soupe; (*woman*) grosse vache *f*

larder ['lɑːdər] N garde-manger *m inv*

lardy ['lɑːdɪ] ADJ *Fam Pej* gros, *f* grosse

large [lɑːdʒ] ADJ **1** (*physical size*) grand; (*bulky*) (*package, meal, portion*) gros, *f* grosse; (*person*) (*tall*) grand; (*fat*) gros; **l. audience** public *m* nombreux; **a l. company** une grosse entreprise; **to grow** *or* **get larger** (*of town, deficit*) s'agrandir; (*of person, amount*) grossir; **to make sth larger** agrandir qch; **there she is, as l. as life** la voilà, en chair et en os; **larger than life** hors pair; **the l. size** (*packet etc*) la grande taille; **have you this dress in a l. size?** avez-vous cette robe en grande taille?; **to have a l. following** avoir un public nombreux; **a l. family** une famille nombreuse; **a l. parcel** un gros paquet, un paquet volumineux; **a l. sum** une grosse *ou*

forte somme; **l. town** grande ville; **l. whisky** double whisky *m*

2 (*extensive, significant*) **to a l. extent, in l. part** en grande partie; **a l. part of my time/ job/day** une grande partie de mon temps/ mon travail/ma journée; **in l. measure** dans une large mesure; **to take a larger part in sth** prendre une plus grande part à qch; **to trade on a l. scale** faire les affaires en grand; **l. powers** (*comprehensive*) pouvoirs larges *ou* étendus; **l. views** (*liberal*) idées larges

ADV 1 by and l. en gros; **by and l. they vote Conservative** ils votent conservateur pour la plupart **2** *Br Fam* (*to a large extent*) **Arsenal got thrashed l.** Arsenal s'est fait ratatiner *ou* s'est fait battre à plates coutures; **we got drunk l. last night** on s'est pris une cuite maison hier soir

N to set a prisoner at l. élargir *ou* relaxer un prisonnier; **to be at l.** être libre *ou* en liberté; **the murderer is still at l.** l'assassin court toujours; **he was acting as the UN's ambassador at l.** il a joué le rôle de médiateur auprès des Nations Unies; **people at l.** (*in general*) le grand public, la grande masse du public; **teachers at l.** la masse des professeurs; **at l.** (*in detail*) tout au long, en détail; **to talk at l.** parler au hasard

▸▸ *Fin* **l. denominations** grosses coupures *fpl*; *Anat* **the l. intestine** le gros intestin

> Note that the most common meaning of the French adjective **large** is **wide**, **broad**.

large-handed [lɑːdʒ'hændɪd] ADJ généreux

large-hearted [lɑːdʒ'hɑːtɪd] ADJ au grand cœur

largely ['lɑːdʒlɪ] ADV en grande partie, pour une grande part; **his job is l. administrative** son travail est surtout administratif; **it's l. the case that people ...** dans la plupart des cas les gens ...; **it's l. a case of finding the right people** il s'agit surtout de trouver les gens qu'il faut

> Note that the French word **largement** is a false friend. It means **widely** or **generously**, depending on the context.

large-minded ADJ aux idées larges, à l'esprit large

largeness ['lɑːdʒnɪs] N (*of body*) grosseur *f*, (*of profits, majority etc*) grandeur *f*, importance *f*, (*of power*) étendue *f*, (*of ideas*) largeur *f*, (*of soul*) grandeur

large-print ADJ **l. book** livre *m* en gros caractères

large-scale ADJ (*undertaking, farmer*) gros; (*map*) à grande échelle; **l. disaster** grande catastrophe *f*

▸▸ *Comput* **l. integration** intégration *f* à grande échelle

largess(e) [lɑː'ʒes] N largesse *f*

largish ['lɑːdʒɪʃ] ADJ assez grand, assez gros

largo, *pl* **largs** ['lɑːgəʊ, -z] ADV, N *Mus* largo *m inv*

lariat ['lærɪət] N **1** *Am* lasso *m* **2** (*for tethering animals*) corde *f* à piquet

lark¹ [lɑːk] N (*bird*) alouette *f*, **to rise** *or* **get up** *or* **be up with the l.** se lever au chant du coq; **she sings like a l.** elle chante comme un rossignol

lark² N *Fam* (*joke etc*) farce *f*, rigolade *f*, blague *f*; **to do sth for a l.** faire qch histoire de rire *ou* de rigoler; **what a l.!** quelle farce!; **I'd like to know what his little 'l. is** je me demande ce qu'il mijote; **I don't want any more of the 'I lost my homework' l.** ne me faites plus le coup du 'j'ai perdu mes devoirs'; **I don't like this fancy dress l.** je n'aime pas du tout cette histoire de bal masqué; **are**

you still at the teaching l.? tu fais toujours ce foutu métier de prof?

▸ **lark about, lark around** VI *Fam* (*play jokes*) faire des farces; (*have good time*) rigoler; **some children were larking around with an old tyre** des enfants s'amusaient avec un vieux pneu

larkspur ['lɑːkspɜːr] N (*plant*) pied-d'alouette *m*, *pl* pieds-d'alouette

larva, *pl* **larvae** ['lɑːvə, -viː] N *Entom* larve *f*

larval ['lɑːv(ə)l] ADJ *Entom* larvaire

laryngitis [lærɪn'dʒaɪtɪs] N *Med* laryngite *f*, **to have l.** avoir une laryngite

laryngoscope [lə'rɪŋgəskəʊp] N laryngoscope *m*

larynx ['lærɪŋks] N *Anat* larynx *m*

lasagne [lə'sænjə] N *Culin* lasagnes *fpl*

lascivious [lə'sɪvɪəs] ADJ lascif

lasciviously [lə'sɪvɪəslɪ] ADV lascivement

lasciviousness [lə'sɪvɪəsnɪs] N lasciveté *f*

laser ['leɪzər] N laser *m*

▸▸ **l. beam** rayon *m ou* faisceau *m* laser; **l. checkout** (*in supermarket*) caisse *f* munie de lecteurs laser; **l. disk** disque *m* laser; **l. pointer** pointeur *m* laser; **l. printer** imprimante *f* (à) laser; **l. printing** impression *f* laser; **l. printout** imprimé *m* laser, copie *f* laser; *Comput* **l. quality** qualité *f* laser; **l. surgery** chirurgie *f* (au) laser

laser-guided ADJ guidé au laser

lash¹ [læʃ] N **1** (*blow with whip*) coup *m* de fouet; (*end of whip*) lanière *f* (de fouet); **the l.** (*punishment*) le (supplice du) fouet; **to receive ten lashes** recevoir dix coups de fouet; **he felt the l. of the Prime Minister's tongue** il a été durement critiqué par le Premier ministre

2 *Anat* cil *m*

vt 1 (*with whip*) (*horse etc*) fouetter, cingler; (*person*) fouetter, flageller; (*of rain*) (*windows, sb's face*) fouetter; (*of waves*) (*shore*) battre, fouetter; **the wind/storm lashed the sea into a fury** le vent/l'orage s'abattit sur la mer qui se déchaîna; **he lashed the crowd into a frenzy** il a soulevé la foule jusqu'à l'hystérie

2 (*verbally*) cingler; **to l. sb with one's tongue** adresser à qn des paroles cinglantes

3 (*move from side to side*) **to l. its tail** (*of cat, lion etc*) fouetter l'air de la queue

vi to l. against the windows (*of rain*) fouetter les vitres; **the rain** *or* **it was lashing down** il pleuvait dru; **to l. against the shore** (*of waves*) battre *ou* fouetter le rivage; **the rain lashed down on the tent** la pluie fouettait la tente

▸ **lash about** VI (*in pain*) se débattre (de douleur)

▸ **lash back** VI (*reply strongly*) répondre violemment

▸ **lash out** VI **1 to l. out at sb** (*physically*) envoyer un coup à qn; (*verbally*) s'en prendre violemment à qn; **he lashed out at me with his fists/feet** il m'a envoyé des coups de poing/coups de pied

2 *Fam* (*spend extravagantly*) faire une folie *ou* des folies; **I'm going to l. out on a new coat** je vais faire des folies et me payer un nouveau manteau; **they really lashed out on their daughter's wedding** ils ont dépensé une fortune pour le mariage de leur fille

vt sep *Fam* **I lashed out £10 on a bottle of wine** j'ai claqué 10 livres sur une bouteille de vin

lash² VT (*tie*) lier, attacher; *Naut* amarrer; **to l. down a load on a trailer** lier une charge sur une remorque

lashing¹ ['læʃɪŋ] ADJ (*rain*) cinglant

N 1 (*with whip*) coups *mpl* de fouet **2** *Old-fashioned* (*tongue*) l. verte réprimande *f*, **to**

give sb a tongue l. réprimander qn sévèrement **3** Br Fam **lashings of sth** des tas de qch; **apple pie with lashings of cream** de la tarte aux pommes avec une tonne de crème

lashing² N (rope) câble m

lass [læs] N esp Scot, North Eng jeune fille f; **country l.** jeune campagnarde f

Lassa ['lɑːsə] N Med **L. fever** fièvre f de Lhassa

lassie ['læsɪ] N esp Scot fillette f; **a wee l.** une petite fille

lassitude ['læsɪtjuːd] N lassitude f

lasso [læ'suː] N lasso m
VT prendre au lasso

LAST¹ [lɑːst] ADJ **1** (final) dernier; **the l. guest to arrive** le dernier des invités à arriver; **the l. but one** l'avant-dernier, pl les avant-derniers; **the l. syllable but one** l'avant-dernière syllabe; **the l. but three** le troisième à partir de la fin; **this is your l. chance** c'est votre dernière chance; **in the l. resort, as a l. resort** en dernière ressource, en dernier recours; **you are my l. hope** vous êtes mon dernier espoir; **in the l. place** enfin, pour finir; **in the l. analysis** au bout du compte; **to have the l. word** (come after other speakers) parler le dernier; (in argument) avoir le dernier mot; **the l. word in comfort/luxury** (hotel etc) le summum du confort/luxe; **this model is the l. word in car design** ce modèle est le dernier cri de la conception automobile; **I'm down to my l. pound** il ne me reste plus qu'une livre; **every l. scrap of bread had been eaten** on avait mangé jusqu'à la dernière miette; **at the l. moment** or **minute** au dernier moment; **the l. day of the month** le dernier jour du mois; **to do sth l. thing at night** faire qch juste avant d'aller se coucher VOIR GRAMMAIRE A26

2 (most recent) **l. Tuesday, Tuesday l.** mardi dernier; **l. January** en janvier dernier; **the l. time I saw him** la dernière fois que je l'ai vu; **l. week** la semaine dernière, la semaine passée; **l. night** (during the night) la nuit dernière; (in the evening) hier (au) soir; **I slept badly l. night** j'ai mal dormi cette nuit; **I haven't been to church for the l. few weeks** je ne suis pas allé à l'église ces dernières semaines; **in the l. fifty years** pendant les cinquante dernières années; **this day l. week** il y a huit jours aujourd'hui; **this day l. year** l'an dernier à la même date; **l. financial year** exercice m écoulé

3 (least likely) **you're the l. one to criticize** tu es vraiment mal placé pour critiquer; **you're the l. person I expected to see here** tu es bien la dernière personne que je pensais rencontrer ici; **he's the l. person I'd ask to help me** c'est (bien) la dernière personne à qui je demanderais de l'aide; **that's the l. thing that's worrying me** ça c'est le cadet de mes soucis; **that's the l. thing I'd do in your position** c'est (bien) la dernière chose que je ferais si j'étais à ta place

N **1** (person) **the l.** le dernier, la dernière; **am I the l.?** (to arrive) suis-je le dernier?; **l. in, first out** dernier entré, premier sorti; Bible **the l. shall be first** les derniers seront les premiers

2 (end) **we'll never hear the l. of it** on n'a pas fini d'en entendre parler; **we haven't heard the l. of this problem** tôt ou tard ce problème va refaire surface; **I think we've heard the l. of him** je pense qu'on n'en entendra plus parler; **that's the l. I saw of him** je ne l'ai pas revu depuis; **that's the l. of the wine** (that's all there is left) c'est tout ce qui reste comme vin; (that's the last drop gone) il n'y a plus de vin maintenant; or **till the l.** jusqu'au bout, jusqu'à la fin; **faithful to the l.** fidèle jusqu'au bout; **at l., at long l.** enfin; **now at l. I understand** enfin, je comprends;

Lit **to look one's l. on sth** voir qch pour la dernière fois; Lit **to breathe one's l.** rendre le dernier soupir; Lit **to be near one's l.** (death) être proche de sa fin; **towards the l.** vers la fin de sa vie

ADV **1** (in time) **when I l. saw him, when I saw him l.** la dernière fois que je l'ai vu; **I can't remember when I l. ate** je ne sais pas depuis quand je n'ai pas mangé

2 (in order) **he spoke l.** il a parlé le dernier; **she came** or **finished l.** (in exam) elle a été dernière; (in race) elle est arrivée dernière

3 l., I would have to say ... et pour finir, je voudrais dire ...; **l. but not least** enfin et surtout; **l. but not least on the list we have Mr ...** et enfin sur la liste, je ne voudrais pas oublier M ...

VI durer, se maintenir; **it's too good to l.** c'est trop beau pour durer; **if the good weather lasts** si le beau temps se maintient; **cream doesn't l. long** (deteriorates quickly) la crème fraîche ne se conserve pas longtemps; **cakes never l. long in this house** (they get eaten quickly) les gâteaux ne durent jamais très longtemps ou Fam ne font jamais long feu dans cette maison; **the supplies will not l. two months** les vivres ne feront pas deux mois; **their friendship won't l. long** leur amitié ne durera pas; **he won't l. long in that job** il ne tiendra pas très longtemps à ce poste, Fam il ne fera pas long feu à ce poste

VT **it will l. me a lifetime** j'en ai pour la vie; **it has lasted him well** ça lui a fait de l'usage; **she couldn't l. the pace** elle n'a pas pu tenir le rythme

▸▸**the L. Judgment** le Jugement dernier; **l. name** nom m de famille; **l. rites** derniers sacrements mpl; St Exch **l. trading day** dernier jour m de cotation

▸**last out** VT SEP **to l. sb out** (of person) survivre à qn; **he'll l. us all out** il nous survivra tous; **to l. the year out** (of person) survivre jusqu'à la fin de l'année; (of supplies etc) suffire pour l'année; **my overcoat will l. the winter out** mon pardessus fera encore l'hiver; **I don't know if I'll be able to l. out the afternoon without any coffee** je ne sais pas si j'arriverai à tenir tout l'après-midi sans café; **the doctor doubted whether she would l. out the night** le docteur n'était pas sûr qu'elle passerait la nuit

VI (of person) tenir le coup

last² N (for shoe) forme f (à chaussure)

last-ditch ADJ ultime; **a l. effort** un ultime effort

lasting ['lɑːstɪŋ] ADJ durable; (material etc) résistant; **l. peace** paix durable

lastly ['lɑːstlɪ] ADV pour finir, en dernier lieu

last-minute ADJ (decision) de dernière minute

lat (abbr **latitude**) latitude, lat.

latch [lætʃ] N **1** loquet m; (small, for shutters etc) loqueteau m; (of vehicle door etc) pêne m, gâche f; **to leave the door on the l.** fermer la porte sans la verrouiller **2** Tech (of lever, moving mechanical part) verrou m
VT **1** (door) fermer au loquet **2** Tech (lever, moving part) verrouiller, bloquer

▸**latch on** VI Fam **1** (attach oneself) **to l. on to sb/sth** s'accrocher à qn/qch **2** (understand) piger; **to l. on to sth** piger qch; **it took him a while to l. on** il a mis un moment pour piger

latchkey ['lætʃkiː] N clef f de maison, clef de porte d'entrée; **l. child** or Fam **kid** = enfant mf dont les parents travaillent et qui doit rentrer seul après l'école

late [leɪt] ADJ **1** (after the appointed time) en retard; (delayed) retardé; **to be l. (for sth)** être en retard (pour qch); **she was too l. to help** elle est arrivée trop tard pour apporter son aide; **it was too l. to do anything about it** il était trop tard pour faire quoi que ce soit;

am I too l. to register? est-il trop tard pour que je m'inscrive?; **it's never too l.** il n'est jamais trop tard; **the train is l./is ten minutes l.** le train a du retard/a dix minutes de retard; **we apologize for the l. running of the train** veuillez nous excuser pour ce retard; **her baby was five days l.** son bébé est né avec cinq jours de retard

2 (far on in the day etc) tard; **it is l.** il est tard; **it is getting l.** il se fait tard; **it is too l.** il est trop tard; **I was l. going to bed** je me suis couché tard; **to keep l. hours** être un couche-tard; **at this l. hour** à l'heure qu'il est

3 (towards the end of a period of time) **why have they left it to this l. hour before informing us?** pourquoi ont-ils attendu la dernière minute pour nous en informer?; **in the l. afternoon** tard dans l'après-midi; **in l. summer** vers la fin de l'été; Fig **it's a bit l. in the day (to start making changes)** il est un peu tard (pour commencer à faire des modifications); **to be in one's l. thirties** avoir entre trente-cinq et quarante ans, Fam avoir la trentaine bien tassée; **in the l. (nineteen) nineties** vers la fin des années 1990; **a l. marriage** un mariage sur le tard

4 (fruit etc) tardif

5 Fml (deceased) feu, défunt, décédé; **my l. father** feu mon père; **the l. queen** feu la reine, la feue reine

ADV **1** (after the appointed time) en retard; **to arrive too l.** arriver trop tard; Prov **better l. than never** mieux vaut tard que jamais

2 (far on in the day etc) tard; **he came home very l.** il est rentré fort tard; **to work l.** travailler tard; **to go to bed l.** se coucher tard; **to sleep** or **stay in bed l.** faire la grasse matinée; **l. into the night** jusqu'à une heure avancée de la nuit; **l. in the year** vers la fin de l'année; **l. in life** sur le tard; **to marry l. in life** se marier tard ou sur le tard

3 (recently) **as l. as last week** pas plus tard que la semaine dernière

4 (formerly) esp Fml **l. of this address** dernièrement domicilié à cette adresse; **Sir Geoffrey, l. of the Diplomatic Corps** Sir Geoffrey, qui fut anciennement membre du Corps diplomatique

5 Lit = **lately**

N **of l.** récemment; **as events of l. have shown ...** comme les récents événements l'ont montré ...

▸▸ Mktg **l. adopter** utilisateur m tardif; **l. arrival** (at hotel) arrivée f tardive; **he will be a l. arrival** il arrivera tard; **l. availability** (of holiday, seat) disponibilité f de dernière minute; **l. cancellation** (of flight) annulation f de dernière minute; **l. edition** (of a newspaper) dernière édition f; Mktg **l. entrant** concurrent, -ente tardif(-ive); **l. entry** (in competition) inscription f de dernière minute; Mktg lancement m tardif; **Denmark only came into the tournament as a l. entry** le Danemark s'est inscrit au tournoi en toute dernière minute; **l. frosts** gelées tardives ou printanières; Mktg **l. majority** majorité f conservatrice; Fin **l. payment** retard m de paiement; Fin **l. payment penalty** pénalité f de retard; Journ **l. story** nouvelle f de dernière minute; **l. tackle** (in rugby) plaquage m à retardement; (in football) tacle m à retardement; St Exch **l. trading** opérations fpl de clôture

latecomer ['leɪtkʌmər] N retardataire mf; Fig **to be a l. to business/politics** arriver tardivement dans les affaires/en politique

lately ['leɪtlɪ] ADV dernièrement, récemment, ces derniers temps; **what have you been doing l.?** qu'avez-vous fait ces derniers temps?; **it is only l. that the matter has become known** la chose n'a été sue que ces jours-ci

latency ['leɪtənsɪ] N latence f, état m latent
▸▸ **l. period** temps m de latence

lateness ['leɪtnɪs] N **1** (of fruit etc) tardiveté f, (of person) retard m; **I will not tolerate l.** je ne tolérerai aucun retard **2 the l. of the hour** l'heure avancée

late-night ADJ **a l. bar/disco** un bar/une discothèque qui ferme très tard; **a l. party** une soirée qui commence tard; **l. showing** (of film) séance f de minuit

latent ['leɪtənt] ADJ (disease, homosexuality, possibility) latent
▸▸ Bot **l. bud** œil m dormant; **l. defect** vice m caché; **l. heat** chaleur f latente; **l. period** Med incubation f, Psy latence f, état m latent, temps m de latence

later ['leɪtər] (comp of late) ADJ ultérieur; (of two variants) (edition, version, model etc) dernier; **I caught a l. train** j'ai pris un autre train plus tard; **l. events proved that ...** la suite des événements a démontré que ...; **at a l. meeting** dans une séance ultérieure; **l. investigations revealed that ...** les enquêtes ultérieures ou qui ont suivi ont révélé que ...; **his l. novels** (of dead person) les romans qu'il a écrits vers la fin de sa carrière; (of living person) ses romans les plus récents; **in l. life she ...** plus tard dans sa vie, elle ... VOIR GRAMMAIRE A25
ADV plus tard; **l. (on) we went to the cinema** plus tard nous sommes allés au cinéma; **sooner or l.** tôt ou tard; **no l. than tomorrow** demain au plus tard; **a moment l.** l'instant d'après; **this happened l. (on)** cela est arrivé après ou plus tard ou ultérieurement; **a few days l.** quelques jours plus tard, Lit à quelques jours de là; **three pages l.** trois pages plus loin; **as we shall see l.** comme nous le verrons plus tard ou par la suite; Fam **see you l.!** à plus tard!

lateral ['læt(ə)rəl] ADJ latéral, -aux; **he's good at l. thinking** il sait trouver des approches originales
▸▸ Tech **l. motion** mouvement m latéral; Tech **l. play** jeu m latéral

laterally ['læt(ə)rəlɪ] ADV latéralement

latest ['leɪtɪst] ADJ (superl of late) dernier; **this author's l. work** le dernier ouvrage de cet auteur; **his l. views on the subject** ses vues les plus récentes sur ce sujet; **the very l. improvements** les tout derniers perfectionnements; **the very l. news** les informations de toute dernière heure; **the l. edition** la dernière édition; **l. date** (deadline) date f limite; Com, Law terme m de rigueur, délai m de rigueur; **the l. fashions** la dernière mode; Com **l. novelties** dernières nouveautés fpl VOIR GRAMMAIRE A25
N **have you heard the l.?** savez-vous la dernière?; **the l. I can come would be four o'clock** je ne pourrai pas venir après quatre heures; **the l. she could leave the decision until was this evening** elle ne pouvait pas remettre la décision à plus tard que ce soir; **at the l.** au plus tard; **Wednesday at the l.** mercredi au plus tard

latex ['leɪteks] N latex m

lath [læθ] N **1** Constr latte f, **l.-and-plaster partition** cloison lattée et plâtrée **2** (of Venetian blind) lame f

lathe [leɪð] N tour m; **precision l.** tour de précision; **capstan** or **turret l.** tour (à) revolver; **polishing l.** touret m à polir ou de polisseur
▸▸ **l. bed** banc m ou bâti m de tour

lather ['lɑːðər] N **1** mousse f de savon; **to make a l.** (of soap) mousser **2** (on horse) écume f, **horse all in a l.** cheval couvert d'écume; Fam **to work oneself** or **get into a l.** se mettre dans tous ses états (**about sth** à propos de qch); **don't get into such a l.** ce n'est pas la peine de te mettre dans tous tes états
VT **1** savonner (**sb's chin** le menton à qn); **to l. one's face** se savonner le visage; (in order

to shave) se mettre du savon à barbe sur le visage **2** Old-fashioned Fam (thrash) rosser
VI (of soap) mousser

lathe-turned ['leɪðɜːnd] ADJ fait au tour, tourné

Latin ['lætɪn] ADJ latin; **the L. races** les races latines
N **1** (Southern European) Latin, -ine **2** Ling latin m; **written in L.** écrit en latin
▸▸ **L. America** Amérique f latine; **L. American** latino-américain, pl latino-américains; **the L. Quarter** (in Paris) le Quartier latin

latinize ['lætɪnaɪz] VT latiniser

Latino [læ'tiːnəʊ] N Am latino mf

latish ['leɪtɪʃ] ADJ **1** (after the appointed time) un peu en retard **2** (far on in the day etc) un peu tardif; **at a l. hour** à une heure assez avancée
ADV (see adj) **1** un peu en retard **2** un peu tard

latitude ['lætɪtjuːd] N **1** Geog latitude f, **in northern/southern latitudes** dans les latitudes boréales/australes; **at a l. of 30° north** par 30° (de) latitude nord; **in these latitudes** sous ces latitudes **2** (freedom) **to allow sb the greatest l.** laisser à qn la plus grande latitude ou la plus grande liberté d'action; **it doesn't give us much l.** (of deadline, budget etc) cela ne nous donne pas une grande marge de manœuvre; **they are given a lot of l.** on leur donne beaucoup de liberté

latrine [lə'triːn] N esp Mil latrines fpl

latte ['lætei] N café m au lait

latter ['lætər] ADJ **1** (of two) dernier VOIR GRAMMAIRE A77 **2** (belonging to the end) dernier; **the l. years of her life** les dernières années de sa vie; **the l. half** or **part of June** la deuxième moitié de juin VOIR GRAMMAIRE A25
N **the l.** (of two) le dernier, la dernière, pl les derniers, les dernières VOIR GRAMMAIRE A77

latter-day ADJ **1** moderne, d'aujourd'hui **2** Rel **the L. Saints** les Mormons mpl

latterly ['lætəlɪ] ADV **1** (recently) récemment **2** (towards the end of a period) vers la fin

lattice ['lætɪs] N treillis m, treillage m
▸▸ Constr etc **l. beam, l. girder** poutre f en treillis ou à croisillons; **l. window** fenêtre f à croisillons

latticed ['lætɪst] ADJ treillissé, treillagé; Fig (branches) entrecroisé

latticework ['lætɪswɜːk] N treillage m, treillis m

Latvia ['lætvɪə] N Lettonie f

Latvian ['lætvɪən] ADJ letton
N **1** Letton, -one **2** Ling letton m

laud [lɔːd] VT Lit louer

laudable ['lɔːdəb(ə)l] ADJ louable, digne de louanges

laudably ['lɔːdəblɪ] ADV louablement; **she was l. restrained** sa retenue était digne de louanges

laudanum ['lɔːd(ə)nəm] N Pharm laudanum m

laudatory ['lɔːdət(ə)rɪ] ADJ (speech, remarks etc) élogieux, louangeur, -euse

LAUGH [lɑːf] N rire m; **to burst into a (loud) l.** éclater de rire, partir d'un éclat de rire; **to give a short l.** avoir un petit rire; **with a l.** en riant; **he likes a (good) l.** il aime bien rire; **to have the last l.** avoir sa vengeance; **to raise a l.** faire rire; **look outside if you want a l.** regarde dehors si tu veux rigoler; Fam **to do sth for a l.** faire qch pour rire; **what a l.!** quelle rigolade!; Iron **that's a l.!** quelle blague!, la bonne blague!; **the l.'s on us** on a été refait; **these old films are usually good for a l.** ces vieux films sont généralement drôles
VI rire; **to l. at** or **over** or **about sth** rire de

qch; **there's nothing to l. about** il n'y a pas de quoi rire; **to l. at sb** se moquer de qn; **to l. to oneself** rire tout seul; **to l. and cry at the same time** pleurer et rire en même temps; **I didn't know whether to l. or cry** je ne savais pas si je devais rire ou pleurer; **to l. till one cries** or **till the tears come** rire (jusqu')aux larmes; **to l. up one's sleeve** rire dans sa barbe; **to l. in sb's face** rire au nez de qn; Fam **if I get that job I'll be laughing** si j'obtenais ce travail ça serait génial; Fam **if you've already done this before, you're laughing** si tu as déjà fait ça c'est un jeu d'enfant; Fam **when his granny dies, he'll be laughing** quand sa grand-mère mourra, il vivra comme un prince ou il pourra mettre les doigts de pied en éventail; Fam **you've already got your visa, you're laughing** toi, tu as déjà ton visa, tu n'as pas de problèmes; Fam **don't make me l.** laissez-moi rire!; Fam **I soon made him l. on the other side of his face** je lui ai bientôt fait passer son envie de rire; Fam **you'll l. on the other side of your face one of these days** un de ces jours tu vas rire jaune; Fam **to l. all the way to the bank** s'en mettre plein les poches; Prov **he who laughs last laughs longest, he laughs best who laughs last** rira bien qui rira le dernier
VT **he laughed a bitter l.** il eut un rire amer; **to l. oneself silly** rire comme un bossu ou une baleine; **his suggestion was laughed out of court** sa suggestion fut rejetée catégoriquement; **I'd be laughed out of court** je me couvrirais de ridicule
▸ **laugh down** VT SEP (proposal) tourner en ridicule
▸ **laugh off** VT SEP **he laughed the matter off** il tourna la chose en plaisanterie; Fam **to l. one's head off** être mort de rire

laughable ['lɑːfəb(ə)l] ADJ risible, ridicule

laughably ['lɑːfəblɪ] ADV risiblement; (easy) ridiculement

laughing ['lɑːfɪŋ] ADJ (face) riant; (eyes, expression) rieur; **it's no l. matter** il n'y a pas de quoi rire; **I'm in no l. mood** je n'ai pas envie de rire
N rires mpl; **we could hear the sound of l.** nous entendions des rires
▸▸ **l. gas** gaz m hilarant; Br Fam **l. gear** bouche f, clapet m; **l. hyena** hyène f tachetée; Orn **l. jackass** martin-chasseur m (d'Australie), pl martins-chasseurs, kookaburra m; **l. stock** risée f, **to make a l. stock of oneself** se couvrir de ridicule; **to be a l. stock** être la risée de tous; **to make sb a l. stock** couvrir qn de ridicule; **to make sb the l. stock of the village** faire de qn la risée du village

laughingly ['lɑːfɪŋlɪ] ADV **1** (to say) en riant **2 that's l. called art** on a le culot d'appeler ça de l'art

laughter ['lɑːftər] N rire(s) m(pl); **to cause l.** provoquer les rires ou l'hilarité; **there was l. at her words** ce qu'elle dit provoqua des rires; **to receive a proposal with l.** accueillir une proposition par des rires; **everything I say is received with l.** on rit de tout ce que je dis

launch [lɔːntʃ] N **1** (boat, of warship) chaloupe f, **(motor) l.** vedette f **2** (of ship, rocket, missile, new product etc) lancement m
VT (ship, torpedo, rocket) lancer; (ship's boats) mettre à l'eau; (person, business, enquiry, new product) lancer; Mil (offensive) déclencher; **to l. sb on a career** lancer qn dans une carrière; **once he is launched on the subject** une fois lancé sur le sujet
▸▸ Astron **l. pad** rampe f ou plate-forme f de lancement, pl plates-formes de lancement; **l. party** réception f (pour le lancement d'un produit, d'un livre etc); Astron **l. site** base f de lancement; Astron **l. vehicle** fusée f de lancement

▶ **launch into** VT INSEP to l. into abuse of sb se répandre en invectives contre qn; **to l. into a story** se lancer dans une histoire; **to l. into a complaint** se mettre à se plaindre
▶ **launch out** VI to l. out into a new market se lancer sur un nouveau marché; **to l. out on one's own** (in business) faire cavalier seul

launcher ['lɔːntʃər] N (vehicle) lanceur m; (launching pad) rampe f ou plate-forme f de lancement; (for planes) catapulte f de lancement; Mil **grenade l.** lance-grenades m inv (à fusil)

launching ['lɔːntʃɪŋ] N (of ship) lancement m; (of small boat, ship's barge etc) mise f à l'eau; (of torpedo, projectile, rocket) lancement; Com, Fin (of product, loan) lancement; Mil (of attack, offensive) déclenchement m, lancement
▶▶ Aviat **l. catapult** catapulte f de lancement; Mil, Astron **l. pad**, **l. platform** (for rockets, missiles) plate-forme f de lancement, pl plates-formes de lancement; Aviat **l. ramp** rampe f de lancement; Astron **l. site** base f de lancement

launder ['lɔːndər] VT (clothes) blanchir; Fig **to l. money** blanchir de l'argent

launderette [lɔːndə'ret] N Br laverie f automatique

laundering ['lɔːndərɪŋ] N (of clothes) blanchissage m; Fig (of money) blanchiment m

laundress ['lɔːndres] N blanchisseuse f

laundrette [lɔːn'dret] N Br laverie f automatique

Laundromat® ['lɔːndrəʊmæt] N Am laverie f automatique

laundry ['lɔːndrɪ] N **1** (place) blanchisserie f, (in house) buanderie f; **to send sth to the l.** envoyer qch à la blanchisserie **2** (clothes) lessive f, (clean) linge m propre; (dirty) linge sale; **to do the l.** faire la lessive
▶▶ **l. bag** sac m de blanchisserie; **l. basket** panier m à linge; **l. list** liste f de blanchissage; **l. room** buanderie f; **l. service** service m de blanchissage

laureate ['lɔːrɪət] ADJ lauréat; Br Poet **L.**, pl **Poets Laureate** poète m lauréat (dignité conférée par la Couronne)
N lauréat, -ate

laurel ['lɒrəl] N (tree) laurier m; Fig **to win laurels** se couvrir de lauriers; Fig **to rest on one's laurels** se reposer sur ses lauriers; Fig **he must look to his laurels** il est en passe d'être éclipsé
▶▶ **l. wreath** couronne f de lauriers

LAUTRO ['laʊtrəʊ] N Formerly (abbr **Life Assurance and Unit Trust Regulatory Organization**) = organisme m britannique chargé d'établir des codes de conduite à l'usage des compagnies d'assurance-vie et des sociétés d'investissement, et de veiller à leur respect

lav [læv] N Br Fam (abbr **lavatory**) petit coin m, cabinets mpl

lava ['lɑːvə] N lave f, **l. stream** or **flow** coulée f de lave

lavabo pl **lavabos** [lə'veɪbəʊ, -əʊz] N Rel lavabo m

lavalier [læ'vælje] N (clip mike) micro m cravate

lavatorial [lævə'tɔːrɪəl] ADJ (humour) scatologique

lavatory ['lævətrɪ] N (room, object) W.-C. mpl, toilettes fpl; **public l.** W.-C. publics, toilettes publiques
▶▶ Br **l. humour** humour m scatologique; **l. pan** cuvette f de W.-C.; Br **l. paper** papier m hygiénique

lavender ['lævɪndər] N (shrub) lavande f
ADJ (colour) lavande inv
▶▶ **l. water** eau f de lavande

lavish ['lævɪʃ] ADJ **1** (person) prodigue; **to be l. with one's money** dépenser sans compter; **to be l. with the cream/sugar** ne pas pleurer la crème/le sucre; **to be l. in one's praise** être prodigue d'éloges **2** (gift, house etc) somptueux; (praise) dithyrambique; (meal) plantureux; (spending) extravagant; **to live in a l. style** mener la grande vie
VT **to l. money on sb** dépenser des fortunes pour qn; **to l. praise on sb** se répandre en éloges sur qn; **to l. care on sb** prodiguer des soins à qn; **to l. care on sth** être extrêmement soigneux avec qch

lavishly ['lævɪʃlɪ] ADV **1** avec prodigalité; **to spend l.** dépenser de l'argent sans compter; **to praise sb l.** se répandre en éloges sur qn; **we were l. entertained by them** ils se sont royalement occupés de nous **2** (to furnish) somptueusement

lavishness ['lævɪʃnɪs] N **1** (of person) prodigalité f **2** (of furnishings etc) somptuosité f

law [lɔː] N **1** (rule) loi f; Phil principe m; Parl **to pass/repeal a l.** voter/abroger une loi; **there's no l. against it** aucune loi ne l'interdit; Phys **the laws of gravity** les lois de la pesanteur; Econ **l. of diminishing returns** loi des rendements décroissants; **l. of supply and demand** loi de l'offre et de la demande; **by the l. of averages** par la loi des probabilités
2 (set of rules) **the l.** la loi; Sport **the off-side l.** les règles ou le règlement du hors-jeu; **it's the l.** c'est la loi; **it's against the l.** c'est contre la loi (**to do sth** de faire qch); **to carry out the l.** appliquer la loi; **to keep/break the l.** respecter ou observer/enfreindre la loi; **l. and order** ordre m public; **to have the force of l.** avoir force de loi; **his word is l.** sa parole a force de loi; **he thinks he's above the l.** il se croit tout permis; **no-one is above the l.** personne n'est au-dessus des lois; **to be a l. unto oneself** n'en faire qu'à sa tête; **there's one l. for the rich and another for the poor** il y a une loi pour les riches et une pour les pauvres; Rel **the L.**, **the l. of Moses** la loi mosaïque
3 Law (system of justice) droit m; **civil l.** ≃ droit civil; **common l.** (as opposed to statute law) droit coutumier; (of general application) droit civil; **criminal l.** droit pénal ou criminel, législation f criminelle; **l. of contract** ≃ droit des obligations; **Roman l.** droit romain; **judgment quashed on a point of l.** arrêt cassé pour vice de forme; **Bachelor/Doctor of Laws** ≃ licencié(e)/docteur en droit; **to read** or **study l.** étudier le droit, faire son droit; **to practise l.** exercer la profession d'avocat, être avocat
4 (justice) **to go to l.** avoir recours à ou recourir à la justice; **to hand sb over to the l.** remettre qn à la justice; **to be at l.** être en procès; **to take the l. into one's own hands** faire justice soi-même; Fam **the l.** (police) la police; Fam **run! here's the l.!** barre-toi! voilà les flics; Fam **I'll have the l. on you if you don't stop that!** si vous n'arrêtez pas tout de suite, j'appelle les flics; Prov **the long arm of the l.** le bras de la justice
▶▶ **l. costs** frais mpl de procédure; **l. enforcement** application f de la loi; **l. enforcement agency** organisme m chargé de faire respecter la loi; **l. enforcement officer** agent m de police; **l. firm** cabinet m d'avocats, cabinet juridique; Br **l. lord** membre m juriste de la Chambre des Lords; **l. officer** conseiller, -ère juridique; **l. reports** rubrique f juridique (donnant des détails juridiques sur des procès d'un intérêt particulier) ; **l. school** faculté f de droit; **l. student** étudiant, -ante en droit

law-abiding ADJ respectueux des lois, qui observe la loi; **l. people** gens qui respectent les lois

lawbreaker ['lɔːbreɪkər] N transgresseur m de la loi

lawbreaking ['lɔːbreɪkɪŋ] N infraction f à la loi

lawcourt ['lɔːkɔːt] N cour f de justice, tribunal m

lawful ['lɔːfʊl] ADJ (owner, activities) légal, -aux; (right, wife, child etc) légitime; (contract) valide; (claim etc) juste; **to go about one's l. business** vaquer à ses occupations; **l. trade** commerce m licite

lawfully ['lɔːfʊlɪ] ADV légalement, légitimement

lawgiver ['lɔːgɪvər] N Lit législateur m

lawless ['lɔːlɪs] ADJ (country, society) sans loi; (times) d'anarchie; **l. behaviour** comportement débridé

lawlessness ['lɔːlɪsnɪs] N (of times) anarchie f, (of conduct) caractère m débridé; **the town was in a state of utter l.** la ville était plongée dans l'anarchie la plus totale

lawmaker ['lɔːmeɪkər] N législateur m

lawn¹ [lɔːn] N Tex linon m

lawn² N (grass) pelouse f, (parterre m de) gazon m; **do not walk on the l.** ne pas marcher sur la pelouse; **to mow** or **cut the l.** tondre le gazon
▶▶ **l. fertilizer**, **l. food** engrais m à gazon; **l. sprinkler** arrosoir m de pelouse; (spinning) tourniquet m arroseur; **l. tennis** tennis m sur gazon

lawnmower ['lɔːnməʊər] N tondeuse f (à gazon)

Lawrence of Arabia ['lɒrəns] N Lawrence d'Arabie

lawsuit ['lɔːs(j)uːt] N procès m, action f judiciaire; **to bring a l. against sb** intenter un procès à qn

lawyer ['lɔːjər] N (provides advice, appears in court) avocat, -e; (authenticates documents) notaire m; (in company) conseiller, -ère juridique; **we'll have to see a l.** il nous faudra consulter un avocat

lax [læks] ADJ **1** (conduct, principles) relâché; (person) laxiste; (discipline) lâche; **l. morals** morale laxiste; **to be l. in (carrying out) one's duties** ne pas toujours assurer ses devoirs **2** (vague, imprecise) vague; **l. use of the term 'paranoid'** emploi peu précis du mot 'paranoïaque' **3** Med **l. bowels** intestins relâchés

laxative ['læksətɪv] ADJ, N Med laxatif m

laxity ['læksɪtɪ], **laxness** ['læksnɪs] N (of morals, security) relâchement m; (of discipline) laxisme m; **l. in performing one's duties** laxisme dans l'accomplissement de ses devoirs

LAY¹ [leɪ]

| VT coucher 1 ▪ poser 2, 8 ▪ mettre 2 ▪ pondre 4 ▪ miser 5 ▪ soumettre 6 ▪ porter 6 ▪ imposer 7 ▪ tendre 8 ▪ préparer 8 |
| VI pondre 2 |

N **1 l. of the land** configuration f du pays ou du terrain; Fig **to find out the l. of the land** tâter le terrain
2 Sl **she's an easy l.** c'est une fille facile; **he's a good l.** il baise bien
VT (pt, pp **laid** [leɪd]) **1** (make horizontal) coucher; (of wind, rain) (corn) coucher, abattre; **to l. sb/sth flat** coucher ou étendre qn/qch (par terre); **to l. sb flat** (with punch) terrasser qn, abattre qn; **laid low by sickness** terrassé par la maladie
2 (place) mettre, placer, poser (**sth on sth** qch sur qch); **to l. a book on the table** poser un livre sur la table; **to l. one's hand on sb's shoulder** mettre la main sur l'épaule de qn;

to l. the blame (for sth) on sb faire porter la responsabilité (de qch) à qn; **he laid particular emphasis** *or* **stress on the importance of security** il a particulièrement insisté sur la sécurité; **if you l. a finger on her** si tu touches à un cheveu de sa tête; **to have nowhere to l. one's head** ne pas avoir où reposer la tête; *Fam* **to l. eyes on sb/sth** voir qn/qch; *Fam* **to l. one on sb** en mettre une à qn; **to l. sb to rest** enterrer qn; **to l. sth bare** (*one's feelings, sb's motives*) mettre qch à nu; **to l. oneself open to criticism/the charge that …** s'exposer à la critique/l'accusation selon laquelle …

3 (*cause to subside*) (*dust etc*) fixer; (*ghost*) exorciser, conjurer; **to l. sb's fears to rest** ôter toutes les inquiétudes de qn

4 (*of hen etc*) (*egg*) pondre; *Fig* **he nearly laid an egg** (*in surprise*) il a failli en faire une jaunisse

5 *Sport* (*bet*) faire; (*sum of money*) parier, miser

6 *esp Fml* (*present*) (*question, request*) soumettre (**before sb** devant qn); **he laid all the facts before me** il me présenta tous les faits; *Law* **to l. a complaint** déposer une plainte, porter plainte; **to l. a matter before the court** saisir le tribunal d'une affaire; *Law* **to l. information** présenter une information; **to l. claim to sth** prétendre à qch; **the town lays claim to being the place where golf was invented** les gens de cette ville prétendent que c'est ici que le golf fut inventé

7 (*impose*) (*penalty*) imposer (**upon sb** à qn); (*fine etc*) infliger (**on sb** à qn); **to l. a curse on sb/sth** jeter un sort à qn/qch

8 (*dispose, arrange*) (*foundations*) poser, jeter, asseoir; (*bricks*) ranger; (*railway, cable*) poser; (*concrete*) couler; (*carpet*) poser, tendre; (*fire*) préparer; *Naut* (*mine*) poser, mouiller; (*trap*) dresser, tendre; (*ambush*) tendre; **they laid plans to evacuate the city** ils ont prévu un plan d'évacuation de la ville; **they had laid plans to send their money abroad** ils avaient pris toutes les dispositions nécessaires pour envoyer leur argent à l'étranger; *Br* **to l. the table** mettre *ou* dresser la table; **to l. the table for three** mettre la table pour trois personnes, mettre trois couverts

9 *Sl* (*have sex with*) **to l. a girl** s'envoyer une fille; **to get laid** s'envoyer en l'air

vi 1 *Sl* (*incorrectly used for* lie) **to l. in bed** rester couché

2 (*of bird*) pondre

3 *Sl* **to l. about one** (*hit out*) frapper de tous côtés

▸▸ *Com* **l. day** jour *m* de planche; **l. days** jours *mpl* de planche, estarie *f*

Attention: ne pas confondre avec le verbe **to lie**, qui signifie **être couché** ou **être posé à plat**.

▸ **lay aside** VT SEP (*prejudices, reservation*) mettre de côté, oublier; (*work, document, money*) mettre de côté; **it's best to have something laid aside for emergencies** il est préférable d'avoir de l'argent de côté en cas de pépins

▸ **lay away** VT SEP (*money etc*) mettre de côté
▸ **lay back** VT SEP (*of horse*) (*ears*) rabattre, coucher
▸ **lay by** VT SEP mettre de côté
▸ **lay down** VT SEP **1** (*deposit*) déposer, poser; **to l. down one's arms** rendre *ou* déposer les armes

2 (*place horizontally*) (*person*) coucher, étendre; **to l. oneself down** se coucher

3 (*abandon*) (*one's duties, one's responsibilities for sth*) quitter, se démettre de; **to l. down one's life** sacrifier sa vie, faire le sacrifice de sa vie (**for** pour)

4 *Naut* (*ship*) mettre en chantier *ou* sur cale

5 (*establish*) (*principle, rule*) poser, imposer, établir; (*conditions*) fixer; (*duties*) spécifier; (*rule of behaviour*) indiquer, prescrire; **to l. down that …** stipuler que …; **to l. down the law** dicter sa loi (**to sb** à qn; **about** sur)

6 (*store*) (*wine*) mettre en cave *ou* sur chantier

VI *Sl* = **lie down**

▸ **lay in** VT SEP faire provision de, s'approvisionner en; **to l. in provisions** faire des provisions; **we've laid in plenty of food for the weekend** nous avons prévu beaucoup de nourriture pour le week-end; *Com* **to l. in goods** *or* **stock** faire provision de marchandises

▸ **lay into** VT INSEP *Fam* **to l. into sb** (*hit*) rosser qn; (*verbally*) passer un savon à qn

▸ **lay off** VT SEP **1** (*workers*) licencier; (*temporarily*) mettre en chômage technique

2 (*in insurance*) **to l. off a risk** effectuer une réassurance; *Horseracing etc* **to l. off a bet** faire la contrepartie d'un pari

3 *Sport* **to l. the ball off for sb** placer le ballon en bonne position pour qn

VT INSEP **1** *Fam* (*abstain from*) s'abstenir de; **to l. off the drink** arrêter de boire; **l. off it, will you!** laisse tomber, tu veux!

2 *Sl* **to l. off sb** (*leave alone*) ficher la paix à qn; **I told her to l. off my husband** je lui ai dit de laisser mon mari tranquille

VI *Sl* **l. off!** (*leave me alone*) fiche-moi la paix!

▸ **lay on** VT SEP **1** *Br* (*install*) (*gas, electricity, water*) installer

2 *Fam* (*organize*) (*party, entertainment etc*) organiser; **I'll l. on the drinks/food** je m'occuperai de la boisson/la nourriture; **I'll l. on a car for you at the station** j'enverrai une voiture vous chercher à la gare

3 (*apply*) (*coat of plaster etc*) étendre, coucher, appliquer; *Art* **to l. on the paint** peindre dans la pâte *ou* en pleine pâte; *Fam* **to l. it on (thick)** *or* **with a trowel** (*flatter*) flatter grossièrement; (*exaggerate*) exagérer, y aller un peu fort

▸ **lay out** VT SEP **1** (*arrange, display*) (*objects*) arranger, disposer; (*merchandise*) étaler, déployer; (*meal*) servir; **to l. out one's reasons** exposer ses raisons

2 (*dead body*) faire la toilette de

3 *Fam* (*knock down*) (*person*) étendre d'un coup, coucher par terre *ou* sur le carreau; *Boxing* envoyer au tapis

4 **to l. out money** dépenser *ou* débourser de l'argent; **to l. oneself out to help sb** se mettre en quatre pour aider qn; **he's not going to l. himself out** il ne fera pas d'effort, *Fam* il ne va pas se fouler

5 (*plan, design*) (*gardens etc*) tracer; (*physically*) disposer; *Typ* (*text*) mettre en page

▸ **lay over** VI *Am* (*during journey*) faire (une) halte

▸ **lay up** VT SEP **1** (*store*) mettre en réserve; (*supplies*) accumuler, amasser; **you're laying up a lot of trouble for yourself** tu vas t'attirer beaucoup d'ennuis

2 (*take out of service*) (*ship*) désarmer, déséquiper, mettre en rade; (*car*) mettre sur cales

3 **to be laid up** (*with illness*) être alité, être obligé de garder le lit

---

lay² ADJ **1** (*non-clerical*) laïque **2** (*not professional*) profane, non spécialiste; **to the l. mind it seems complicated** aux yeux du profane cela semble compliqué

▸▸ *Rel* **l. brother** frère *m* lai; *Art* **l. figure** mannequin *m*; *Rel* **l. preacher, l. reader** prédicateur *m* laïque; *Rel* **l. sister** sœur *f* converse

lay³ N *Arch* (*song, poem*) lai *m*

lay⁴ PT *see* **lie²** VI

layabout ['leɪəbaʊt] N *Fam* paresseux, -euse

lay-away plan N *Am Com* vente *f* réservée *ou* à terme

lay-by N *Br* (*on road*) espace *m* de stationnement (*sur le bas-côté de la route*); (*on motorway*) aire *f* de stationnement

layer ['leɪər] N **1** (*of paint, chocolate, clouds, clothes etc*) couche *f*, (*of dung*) lit *m*; *Constr* (*of cement, bricks etc*) assise *f*, lit; *Geol* (*of rocks etc*) couche, strate *f*, **the upper layers of the atmosphere** les couches supérieures de l'atmosphère **2** (*hen etc*) **good l.** bonne pondeuse *f* **3** (*of plant*) marcotte *f*

VT **1** poser *ou* disposer en couches; (*hair*) dégrader; **I'd like my hair layered** j'aimerais un dégradé; **a layered cut** une coupe en dégradé **2** (*rosebush etc*) marcotter

▸▸ **l. cake** génoise *f* (*à la crème*); **l. cut** (*haircut*) coupe *f* en dégradé

layette [leɪ'et] N layette *f*

laying ['leɪɪŋ] N **1** (*of rails, pipes, cables, carpet etc*) pose *f*, (*of foundations*) assise *f*, (*of underwater cable*) immersion *f*, (*of mines*) mouillage *m* **2** (*of eggs*) ponte *f*

▸▸ **l. down** (*of principle, rule etc*) établissement *m*; (*of sewage system, cable*) pose *f*, (*of ship*) mise en chantier *ou* sur cale; (*of arms*) dépôt *m*; **l. hen** poule *f* pondeuse; **l. off** (*of workers*) licenciement *m*; *Rel* **l. on of hands** imposition *f* des mains; **l. out** (*of dead body*) toilette *f*

layman, *pl* **laymen** ['leɪmən] N **1** *Rel* laïque *m* **2** *Fig* personne *f* non initiée, profane *m*

lay-off N **1** *Ind* (*action*) licenciement *m*; (*temporary*) mise *f* en chômage *m* technique **2** *Ftbl* petite passe *f* de côté

▸▸ *Am* **l. pay** indemnité *f* de licenciement

layout ['leɪaʊt] N **1** (*plan*) (*of building, town*) tracé *m*; (*of gardens*) dessin *m* **2** (*arrangement*) (*of house, building etc*) plan *m*, agencement *m*; (*of piece of machinery*) agencement *ou* disposition *f* des pièces **3** *Typ* (*of text etc*) mise *f* en page, disposition *f*

▸▸ *Typ* **l. artist** maquettiste *mf*; *Typ* **l. card** (*for pages*) plan de maquette; *Typ* **l. compositor** maquettiste *m*; *Typ* **l. sheet** (*for pages*) maquette *f*, trame *f* de maquette

layover ['leɪəʊvər] N *Am* escale *f*

layperson ['leɪpɜːsən] = **layman, laywoman**

laywoman, *pl* **laywomen** ['leɪwʊmən, -wɪmɪn] N **1** *Rel* laïque *f* **2** *Fig* personne *f* non initiée, profane *f*

Lazarus ['læzərəs] N *Bible* Lazare *m*

laze [leɪz] VI **to l. (about** *or* **around)** paresser, fainéanter; **you've spent the whole morning lazing around** tu as passé la matinée entière à traînasser; **to l. on the beach** faire le lézard sur la plage; **to l. in bed** traînasser au lit, faire la grasse matinée; **to l. away a couple of hours in the sun** passer quelques heures à paresser au soleil

lazily ['leɪzɪlɪ] ADV paresseusement

laziness ['leɪzɪnɪs] N paresse *f*, fainéantise *f*

lazy ['leɪzɪ] ADJ **1** (*person*) paresseux, fainéant; **a l. person** un paresseux, une paresseuse; **a l. smile** un sourire nonchalant; **I feel too l. to do it** je n'ai pas l'énergie de le faire; **to have a l. eye** avoir un œil paresseux **2** (*moments*) de paresse; **we spent a l. afternoon in the garden** nous avons passé l'après-midi à paresser dans le jardin; **these l. summer days** ces journées d'été où l'on ne fait rien; **to go for a l. sail around the islands** faire une croisière relax autour des îles

▸▸ **l. Susan** (*on table*) plateau *m* tournant

lazybones ['leɪzɪbəʊnz] N *Fam* paresseux, -euse, fainéant, -ante

lb (*abbr* libra) livre, lb

LBO [elbiː'əʊ] N *Fin* (*abbr* **leveraged buy-out**) OPA *f* à crédit

L/C N *Com* (*abbr* **letter of credit**) l/c *f*

LCD [elsi:'di:] N *Comput* (*abbr* **liquid crystal display**) affichage *m* à cristaux liquides, LCD *m*
▶▶ **L. screen** écran *m* LCD

LCL *Com* (*abbr* **less than container load**) conteneur *m* chargé en partie

LEA [eli:'eɪ] N *Br Admin* (*abbr* **Local Education Authority**) = organisme *m* chargé de l'enseignement au niveau régional

lea [li:] N *Lit* prairie *f*, pâturage *m*

leach [li:tʃ] VT (*liquid*) filtrer; (*ore*) lessiver; **to l. away** *or* **out salts** extraire des sels par lessivage
VI (*of liquid*) filtrer (**through** à travers); **fertilizers have been leaching into the water supply** des engrais ont infiltré la réserve d'eau

LEAD¹ [li:d]

| Ⓝ tête **1** ▪ exemple **2** ▪ indice **3** ▪ rôle principal **5** ▪ laisse **6** ▪ fil **7** ▪ gros titre **8** ▪ mener **1, 3, 5** ▪ amener **2, 7** ▪ diriger **4** |
| Ⓥ mener **1, 2** |

N **1 to take the l.**, **to go** *or* **move into the l.** prendre la tête, prendre la première place; **to take the l. over sb** prendre le pas *ou* les devants sur qn; **to have a l. of 10 metres** avoir une avance de 10 mètres; **she's hanging on to the l.** (*in race*) elle conserve la tête de la course; (*in points table etc*) elle conserve la tête du classement; **she's hanging on to her l.** (*in race*) elle conserve son avance; (*in points table etc*) elle conserve son avance au classement; **he's opened up a tremendous l.** il a pris une avance considérable; **to be in the l.** être en tête; **to lose one's l.** ne plus être en tête; **the company has lost its l. in portables** la société n'est plus le premier producteur de portables

2 (*example*) **to follow sb's l.** suivre l'exemple de qn; **to give a l. (to sb)** donner l'exemple (à qn)

3 (*clue*) indice *m*; **the police have no leads** la police n'a aucune piste; **to give sb a l.** mettre qn sur la voie; **to be following up an important l.** être sur une piste importante

4 *Cards* **to have the l.** jouer le premier; **your l.!** à vous de jouer!; **is it my l.?** c'est mon tour?, c'est à moi de jouer?; **to follow the l. in clubs** fournir à trèfle

5 *Theat, Cin* (*role*) rôle *m* principal; (*actor*) premier rôle masculin; (*actress*) premier rôle féminin; **juvenile l.** jeune premier, jeune première; **to sing the l.** chanter le rôle principal; **to play the l.** jouer le premier rôle

6 (*for dog etc*) laisse *f*; **dogs must be kept on a l.** les chiens doivent être tenus en laisse

7 *Elec* fil *m* électrique, câble *m ou* branchement *m* de canalisation, amenée *f* de courant

8 *Journ* (*main story*) gros titre *m*; **it'll be** *or* **make the l. in tomorrow's papers** ce sera à la une des journaux demain; **the Telegraph has a l. on the Middle East crisis** le Telegraph consacre sa une à la crise au Proche-Orient
VT (*pt, pp* **led** [led]) **1** (*guide*) mener, conduire, guider (**sb to a place** qn à un endroit); (*blind person etc*) conduire, guider par la main; **to l. the conversation round to the subject of …** amener la conversation sur le sujet de …; **that leads me to another point I wanted to make** ceci m'amène à un autre point que je voulais soulever; (*horse*) mener par la bride; (*dog*) tenir en laisse; *Prov* **you can l. a horse to water (but you cannot make it drink)** on ne fait pas boire un âne qui n'a pas soif; *Law* **to l. a witness** poser des questions tendancieuses à un témoin; **to l. the way** marcher le premier *ou* en tête;

to l. a team to victory mener une équipe à la victoire; **to l. the conversation back to a subject** ramener la conversation sur un sujet; *Fig* **he is easily led** il est très influençable; **she led them to safety** elle les a conduits en lieu sûr; *Rel* **l. us not into temptation** ne nous soumets pas à la tentation

2 (*cause*) amener, porter (**sb to do sth** qn à faire qch); **that leads me to believe that …** cela m'amène à croire que …; **I was led to the conclusion that …** on m'a amené à la conclusion que …; **what led you to apply for this job?** qu'est-ce qui vous a conduit *ou* amené à postuler?

3 (*happy life, sad life*) mener; **to l. sb a dog's life** faire une vie de chien à qn

4 (*be leader of*) (*team, government*) diriger; (*army*) commander; **leading his troops** à la tête de ses troupes; **to l. a party** être chef de parti; **to l. an orchestra** diriger un orchestre; **to l. the congregation in prayer** diriger la congrégation à la prière

5 (*be ahead of*) **to l. the field** mener; *Fig* **to l. the field in …** être au premier rang en matière de …; **to l. sb by eight points** avoir une avance sur qn de huit points; **she leads the class in maths** elle est la première de sa classe en maths; **we l. the world in …** nous sommes les leaders mondiaux de …

6 *Cards* **to l. clubs** jouer trèfle

7 *Tech* (*water to a place*) amener; (*actually install*) installer; (*rope through a pulley*) faire passer
VI **1** (*of road*) mener, conduire (**to** à); **road that leads to the town** route qui mène *ou* va à la ville; **door that leads into the garden** porte qui communique avec le jardin *ou* qui donne accès au jardin; **to l. to a good result** aboutir à un bon résultat, produire un heureux effet; **to l. to a discovery** conduire *ou* aboutir à une découverte; **drinking too much can l. to violence** l'excès d'alcool peut conduire à la violence; **one thing leads to another** une chose en amène une autre; **to l. to nothing** n'aboutir *ou* ne mener à rien; **to l. to a misunderstanding** conduire à un malentendu; **action which led to criticism** action qui a motivé des critiques; **this led to several of them losing their jobs** à cause de cela, plusieurs d'entre eux ont perdu leur emploi

2 (*go first*) (*in competition, race, dance etc*) mener; **you l. and I'll follow** vas-y, je te suis; *Boxing, Cards* ouvrir le jeu, jouer le premier, entamer; **he leads with the left** il est gaucher; **he led with a left** il a donné un coup du gauche; **to l. with** (*of newspaper*) titrer en première page, faire ses gros titres *ou* sa première page sur

3 (*of barrister*) être l'avocat principal; **he led for the prosecution** avocat principal, il dirigea l'accusation
▶▶ *Journ* **l. article** article *m* de tête; *Banking, StExch* **l. manager** chef *m* de file; **l. reins** (*of horse*) grandes guides *fpl*; **l. time** *Ind* délai *m* de préparation; *Com* délai *m* de livraison; *Mktg* **l. user** utilisateur, -trice pilote
▶ **lead away** VT SEP (*prisoner etc*) emmener
▶ **lead back** VT SEP ramener
VI ramener
▶ **lead off** VI **1** (*begin*) commencer, débuter (**with** par); (*in debate*) entamer les débats; (*in game*) jouer le premier; *Billiards* donner l'acquit; (*at dance*) ouvrir le bal

2 **several doors/corridors l. off the hall** il y a plusieurs portes/couloirs qui donnent dans le hall
VT SEP **1** (*discussion*) amorcer; (*attack*) lancer

2 (*prisoner etc*) emmener
▶ **lead on** VT SEP **to l. sb on to talk (about)** encourager qn à parler (de); **try and l. him on to the subject of football** essaie de l'aiguiller sur le sujet du football *ou* *Fam* le

brancher sur le football; *Fam* **to l. sb on** (*deceive*) tromper qn, duper qn
VI **l. on!** en avant!
▶ **lead up** VI **to l. up to a subject** amener sujet; **I was just leading up to that** j'allais justement y venir; **I couldn't see what he was leading up to** je ne voyais pas où il voulait en venir; **the chords that l. up to the final movement** les accords qui introduisent le dernier mouvement; **the period leading up to the war** la période précédant la guerre; **there's a path leading up to the ski lift** il y a un chemin qui mène au téléski
VT SEP (*troops, class etc*) faire avancer; **he led us up (a staircase)** il nous a fait monter (un escalier)

lead² [led] N **1** (*metal*) plomb *m*; *Fam* **to go down like a l. balloon** tomber à plat; *Sl* **they pumped him full of l.** ils l'ont truffé *ou* farci de plomb

2 *Br Constr* **roof leads** plombs *mpl* de couverture; **window leads** plombs de vitrail *ou* de vitraux

3 (*for pencil*) mine *f*

4 *Naut* (*plomb m de*) sonde *f*; *Fam* **to swing the l.** tirer au flanc

5 *Fishing* plomb *m*

6 *Typ* réglette *f*
VT (*pt, pp* **leaded** ['ledɪd], *cont* **leading** ['ledɪŋ]) **1** *Constr* (*roof*) plomber; (*windows*) enchâsser dans les plombs

2 *Fishing* (*line, net*) plomber

3 *Typ* (*lines of type*) interligner
▶▶ **l. content** (*of fuel*) indice *m* de plomb; **l. crystal** verre *m* de *ou* au plomb; **l. ore** minerai *m* de plomb; **l. paint** peinture *f* à base de plomb; **l. pencil** crayon *m* noir *ou* à papier *ou* à mine de plomb; **l. pipe** tuyau *m* de plomb; **l. poisoning** *Med* intoxication *f* par le plomb, saturnisme *m*; *Am Fam* (*death*) mort *f* par balle(s); (*injury*) blessure *f* par balle(s); **l. shot** grenaille *f* de plomb
▶ **lead out** VT SEP *Typ* (*lines of text*) augmenter l'interlignage de

leaded ['ledɪd] ADJ
▶▶ **l. petrol** essence *f* au plomb; **l. window** fenêtre *f* avec verre cathédrale

leaden ['led(ə)n] ADJ (*made of lead*) de plomb; (*complexion*) plombé; **l.-eyed** aux yeux ternes; **l.-footed** à la démarche pesante; **l. limbs** membres inertes; **a l. sky** un ciel de plomb; **the l. calm of the sea** la mer grise et immobile

leader ['li:dər] N **1** (*of expedition, group, organization etc*) chef *m*; *Mil* (*of unit*) commandant *m*; (*of riot*) meneur *m*; *Pol* leader *m*; *Br Mus* premier violon *m*; *Am Mus* chef *m* d'orchestre; *Br Law* avocat *m* principal; **to be a born l.** être fait pour donner des ordres *ou* commander; *Sport* **team l.** chef d'équipe; **a major group, a l. in its field** un groupe important, un leader dans sa branche

2 (*in race*) **he's still the l.** il mène toujours; **the three leaders** les trois premiers

3 (*in horse team*) cheval *m* de tête; (*in dog team*) chien *m* de tête; **the leaders** l'attelage *m* de devant

4 (*of tape, film*) (*bande*) amorce *f*

5 *Journ* (*main item*) article *m* principal; (*article*) article de fond; *Br* (*editorial*) éditorial *m*, -aux

6 *Am Com* (*loss leader*) produit *m* d'appel

7 *Mktg* (*product*) numéro un *m* (*sur le marché*); (*company*) chef *m* de file, leader *m*
▶▶ *Br* **L. of the House of Commons** chef de la majorité à la Chambre des Communes; *Br Journ* **l. writer** éditorialiste *mf*

leaderboard ['li:dəbɔ:d] N (*in golf*) leaderboard *m*; *Fig* **to be top of the l.** être en tête du classement

leadership ['li:dəʃɪp] N **1** (*qualities shown*) qualités *fpl* de chef; **no one showed any l.**

personne n'a montré des qualités de chef; **the organization lacks l.** l'organisation manque d'un vrai chef; **to be under sb's l.** être sous la conduite de qn **2** *(position) (of party, union etc)* direction *f*; *(duties as leader)* fonctions *fpl* de chef; *Mil* commandement *m* **3** *(leaders)* dirigeants *mpl*
▸▸ **l. battle, l. contest** bataille *f* pour la direction; *Pol* **l. election** élections *fpl* pour la position de leader; **l. potential** qualités *fpl* de chef

lead-free [led'friː] **ADJ** *(petrol, paint)* sans plomb
N *(petrol)* essence *f* sans plomb

lead-in ['liːdɪn] **N 1** *(introduction), Mus* introduction *f*; *Elec, Tel etc (of cable)* entrée *f* **2** *Radio etc (to aerial)* descente *f* d'antenne
▸▸ **l. groove** *(on record)* sillon *m* initial

leading¹ ['liːdɪŋ] **ADJ 1** *(chief)* premier, principal, -aux; **a l. authority in the field** un grand spécialiste du domaine; **the l. statesmen of Europe** les hommes d'État dirigeants de l'Europe; **a l. shareholder** un des principaux actionnaires; **he's one of Britain's l. novelists** c'est l'un des plus grands romanciers contemporains de Grande-Bretagne; **she's a l. light in local politics** c'est une personnalité très influente de la politique locale **2** *(in front) (car)* de tête
N *(of horses etc)* conduite *f*, menage *m*
▸▸ *Journ* **l. article** *Br* éditorial *m*; *Am* article *m* leader *ou* de tête; **l. axle** *(of vehicle)* essieu *m* porteur d'avant; *Cards* **l. card** première carte *f*; *Elec* **l. current** courant *m* déphasé en avant; *Aviat* **l. edge** *(of wing)* bord *m* d'attaque; **to be on the l. edge of technology** être à la pointe de la technologie; **l. edge technology** technologie *f* de pointe; *Cin, Theat* **l. lady** premier rôle *m* (féminin); *Cin, Theat* **l. man** premier rôle (masculin); *Cin, Theat* **l. part** premier rôle; *Mil* **l. patrol** patrouille *f* de tête; **l. question** question f orientée; *Law* = question posée au témoin de manière à suggérer la réponse; **l. rein** *(for horse)* longe *f*, *Br* **l. reins** *(for child)* harnais *m*; *Cin, Theat* **l. role** premier rôle; **to play a l. role in a matter** jouer un rôle prépondérant dans une affaire; **l. shoot** *(of plant)* pousse *f* principale; *Am* **l. strings** harnais *(pour enfant)*; *Comput* **l. zeroes** zéros *mpl* à gauche

leading² ['ledɪŋ] **N** *Typ* interligne *f*

lead-out **N** *Elec, Tel (of wire etc)* sortie *f*
▸▸ **l. groove** *(of record)* sillon *m* de sortie

lead-up **N** veille *f*; **in the l. to independence** dans la période qui a précédé l'indépendance

leadwork ['ledwɜːk] **N** *Archit (of window)* plombs *mpl*

leaf, *pl* **leaves** [liːf, liːvz] **N 1** *(of plant, tree)* feuille *f*; **to put out leaves, to come into l.** feuiller; **the trees have already started coming into l.** les arbres commencent déjà à avoir des feuilles; **in l.** couvert de feuilles, en feuilles; **to shake like a l.** trembler comme une feuille
2 *(of book)* feuillet *m*; **single l.** *(in bookbinding)* carton *m* de deux pages; *Fig* **to turn over a new l.** *(of person)* changer de conduite; *Fig* **to take a l. out of sb's book** prendre exemple *ou* modèle sur qn
3 *(of gold, silver etc)* feuille *f*
4 *(of door)* battant *m*, vantail *m*, *pl* -aux; *(of shutter)* battant; *(of spring)* lame *f*, feuille *f*, feuillet *m*; *(of table) (inserted)* rallonge *f* (de table); *(hinged)* battant *m*
▸▸ **l. bud** bourgeon *m* à feuille; **l. green** vert prairie *m inv*; **l. insect** phyllie *f*, **l. mould** terreau *m* de feuilles; **l. tobacco** tabac *m* en feuilles
▸ **leaf through** **VT INSEP** *(book)* feuilleter

leaflet ['liːflɪt] **N** *Com etc* prospectus *m*; *Pol* tract *m*; **instruction l.** mode *m* d'emploi

VT **to l. an area** distribuer des prospectus dans un quartier
▸▸ **l. drop** distribution *f* de prospectus

leafstalk ['liːfstɔːk] **N** *Bot* pétiole *m*

leafy ['liːfɪ] **ADJ** *(tree)* feuillu; **a l. lane** *or* **street** une rue bordée d'arbres; **a l. suburb** une banlieue verte; **a l. canopy** un dais de feuillage *ou* de verdure

league¹ [liːg] **N 1** *(association)* ligue *f*, **everyone is in l. against them** tout le monde est ligué contre eux; **to be in l. with sb** être de connivence avec qn; *Fam* être de mèche avec qn **2** *Fig* **I'm not in your l., I'm not in the same l. as you** je ne suis pas de votre niveau; **they're not in the same l.** ils ne sont pas du même niveau; **I thought I was good but he's in another l.** je pensais que j'étais bon mais il est bien meilleur que moi
▸▸ *Sport* **l. champions** champion *m*; *Sport* **l. leaders** leader *m* du championnat; *Sport* **l. match** match *m* de championnat; *Hist* **the L. of Nations** la Société des Nations; *Br Sport* **l. table** *(classement m* du) championnat *m*
▸ **league together** **VI** faire alliance (**with** avec); **to l. together against sb/sth** se liguer contre qn/qch

league² **N** *Hist (measurement)* lieue *f*

leak [liːk] **N 1** *(of liquid, gas, secrets)* fuite *f* **2** *(entry) (of water etc)* infiltration *f*, rentrée *f*, *Naut* voie *f* d'eau; **to spring a l.** *(of ship)* faire eau, avoir une voie d'eau; *(of shoes)* prendre l'eau **3** *Sl* **to take** *or* **have a l.** *(urinate)* pisser un coup
VI *(of tank etc)* avoir une fuite, fuir; *(of ship etc)* faire eau, avoir une voie d'eau; **roof that leaks** toit qui laisse entrer la pluie; **my shoes l.** mes chaussures prennent l'eau **2** *(of liquid)* fuir, couler; *(of gas)* fuir; *(of truth, news etc)* s'ébruiter, transpirer
VT 1 **the bucket/pipe was leaking water** l'eau coulait du seau/du tuyau; **the pipe had been leaking gas** le tuyau de gaz avait une fuite; **the radiator had been leaking water everywhere** le radiateur avait fui et il y avait de l'eau partout **2** *Fam (information etc)* divulguer
▸ **leak out** **VI** *(of water, gas etc)* fuir; *Fig (of truth, information etc)* filtrer; **the acid was leaking out of the battery** de l'acide fuyait de la batterie

leakage ['liːkɪdʒ] **N 1** *(of water, gas, official secrets)* fuites *fpl* **2** *(loss of stock) (in a business)* coulage *m*

leaky ['liːkɪ] **ADJ** *(barrel)* qui coule, qui fuit; *(boat)* qui fait eau; *(shoes)* qui prennent l'eau; *(tap, roof)* qui fuit; *Fig Fam* **this department is very l.** il y a plein de fuites dans ce service

lean¹ [liːn] **ADJ 1** *(person, dog)* svelte; *(face)* mince; *(too thin) (animal)* efflanqué; *Fig* **the company is now fitter and leaner than it was before** l'entreprise se porte mieux depuis que sa structure a été allégée
2 *(meat)* maigre
3 **a l. year/period** une année/une période de vaches maigres; **we had a l. time** nous avons eu une période de vaches maigres; **a l. harvest** une mauvaise *ou* maigre récolte
4 *(fuel, mixture)* pauvre
N *(on meat)* maigre *m*

lean² **N** *(inclined position)* inclinaison *f*
VI *(pt, pp* **leaned** [liːnd] *or* **leant** [lent]) *(of person)* s'appuyer (**against** contre, à; **on** sur, à); **to l. on one's elbow(s)** s'accouder; **leaning against a wall** appuyé à *ou* contre un mur; **to l. back in one's chair** s'appuyer contre le dossier de sa chaise; *Fig* **to l. on sb** *(for support)* se reposer sur qn; *Fam (to pay money etc)* faire pression sur qn; **she still leans on her father for advice** elle a toujours recours aux conseils de son père; **to l. forward/out of the window** se pencher en

avant/à la fenêtre; **to l. over/towards sth** se pencher sur/vers qch; **that wall is leaning towards the right** ce mur penche vers la droite; **to l. towards a theory** être plutôt partisan d'une théorie; **I think I'm leaning towards the opinion that you were right after all** je commence à penser qu'en fin de compte tu avais raison; **to l. towards socialism** pencher vers le socialisme; *Fam* **to l. over backwards to do sth** se mettre en quatre pour faire qch
VT *(ladder etc)* appuyer (**against** contre); **to l. sth against sth** adosser qch à *ou* contre qch

lean-burn engine **N** moteur *m* Lean Burn

leaning ['liːnɪŋ] **ADJ** penché; *(wall)* qui penche
N *(tendency)* inclination *f* (**towards** pour), penchant *m* (**towards** pour, vers), tendance *f* (**towards** à); **to have leanings towards communism** être de tendance communiste, pencher vers le communisme; **to have artistic leanings** avoir des dispositions artistiques
▸▸ **the L. Tower of Pisa** la tour de Pise

leanness ['liːnnɪs] **N** maigreur *f*

leant **PT, PP** *see* **lean**² **VI, VT**

lean-to **N** appentis *m*
▸▸ **l. garage** = garage *m* attenant à la maison, avec un toit incliné; **l. roof** comble *m* en appentis

leap [liːp] **N** *(jump)* saut *m*, bond *m*; *Fig* **to take a l. in the dark** faire un saut dans l'inconnu; **a l. of faith** un acte de foi; **his heart gave a l.** son cœur bondit, son cœur fit un bond; *Fig* **to advance by leaps and bounds** avancer à pas de géant; **his French had improved by leaps and bounds** il avait fait des progrès phénoménaux en français; **with one l. she cleared the ditch** d'un saut *ou* d'un bond elle franchit le fossé; **the company has taken a great l. forward** la société a fait un grand bond en avant
VI *(pt, pp* **leaped** [liːpt] *or* **leapt** [lept]) **1** sauter, bondir; **to l. to one's feet** se lever brusquement; **to l. over a ditch** sauter un fossé; **to l. at the opportunity** sauter sur l'occasion; **to l. for joy** sauter *ou* bondir de joie; **her heart leapt for joy** elle bondit de joie; **she nearly leapt out of her skin** elle a sauté au plafond **2** *(of flame etc)* jaillir
VT 1 *(ditch)* sauter, franchir d'un saut **2** *(cause to leap)* **to l. a horse over a ditch** faire sauter *ou* faire franchir un fossé à un cheval
▸▸ **l. day** jour *m* intercalaire; **l. year** année *f* bissextile
▸ **leap up** **VI 1** *(of person)* bondir (**to do** pour faire); *(get to one's feet)* se lever brusquement; **their dog leapt up at me** leur chien m'a sauté dessus **2** *(of flame)* jaillir

leapfrog ['liːpfrɒg] **N** **to play l.** jouer à saute-mouton
VT (-**gg**-) **1** **to l. sth** sauter par-dessus qch à saute-mouton **2** *Fig (stage in process)* sauter; **he leapfrogged several of his more senior colleagues to get the post** il a obtenu le poste en passant devant plusieurs de ses collègues d'un échelon supérieur

leapt **PT, PP** *see* **leap** **VI, VT**

learn [lɜːn] *(pt, pp* **learnt** [lɜːnt], *occ* **learned** [lɜːnd]) **VT 1** *(French, maths etc)* apprendre; **to l. to read/drive** apprendre à lire/conduire; **she's learning the violin** elle apprend à jouer du violon, elle étudie le violon; *Fig* **he has learnt his lesson** ça lui servira de leçon; **when will she l. her lesson?** quand est-ce qu'elle comprendra? **2** *(hear about) (news, test results etc)* apprendre; **we are sorry to l. that …** nous sommes désolés d'apprendre que … **3** *Arch, Sl (teach)* **to l. sb sth** apprendre qch à qn; *Sl* **that'll l. him!** ça lui apprendra!
VI apprendre; **they're learning about Victorian times** ils étudient l'époque Victorienne;

to **l.** from one's mistakes tirer un enseignement de ses erreurs; **it is never too late to l.** on apprend à tout âge

▸ **learn of** VT INSEP apprendre

learned ['lɜːnɪd] ADJ *(person)* savant, érudit; *(style)* savant; *Law* **my l. friend** mon éminent confrère; **l. journal** journal savant; **l. profession** profession *f* intellectuelle; **l. treatise** traité savant

learner ['lɜːnər] N **1** apprenant, -ante; **learners of English** les apprenants d'anglais, les gens qui apprennent l'anglais; **advanced l.** personne *f* d'un bon niveau; **intermediate l.** personne d'un niveau intermédiaire; **to be a quick/good l.** apprendre vite/facilement; **she's a slow/bad l.** elle n'apprend pas vite/facilement **2** *(beginner)* élève *mf*, débutant, -ante; *Aut (driver)* apprenti *m* conducteur

▸▸ *Aut* **l. driver** apprenti conducteur

learning ['lɜːnɪŋ] N **1** *(act of learning)* apprentissage *m*; *Am* **to be l. disabled** avoir des difficultés scolaires **2** *(knowledge)* instruction *f*, savoir *m*, connaissances *fpl*; **seat** *or* **centre of l.** centre *m* intellectuel; **a man of great l.** un homme de grand savoir

▸▸ **l. capacity** capacités *fpl* d'apprentissage; **l. curve** courbe *f* d'assimilation; **l. disability** difficultés *fpl* d'apprentissage

learnt PT, PP *see* learn

lease [liːs] N *Law* bail *m*, *pl* baux; *(of equipment)* location *f*; *(of house to let)* bail (à loyer); *(of farming land)* bail à ferme; *(document)* (contrat *m* de) bail; **to sign a l.** signer un bail; **long l.** bail à long terme *ou* à longue échéance; **to take on a new l.,** to renew the **l. of a house** renouveler le bail d'une maison; *Fig* **to take on a new l. of life** *(of person)* renaître à la vie; *(of industry, town, football club)* retrouver un nouveau souffle; **meeting Sarah has given him a new l. of life** sa rencontre avec Sarah lui a redonné goût à la vie; **it's like a new l. of life** on se sent renaître; **cleaning the engine will give the car a new l. of life** ça va retaper la voiture de nettoyer le moteur

VT **1** *(of owner)* **to l. (out)** *(house)* louer, donner à bail; *(land)* affermer **2** *(of tenant)* *(house)* louer, prendre à bail; *(of person)* *(equipment, vehicle)* louer; *(land)* affermer

▸▸ *Acct* **l. charges** charges *fpl* locatives; **l. contract** *(for property)* contrat de bail; *(for equipment)* contrat en location; *Fin* **l. financing** leasing *m*, location avec option d'achat; *Acct* **l. revenue** loyers *mpl*

▸ **lease back** VT SEP louer dans le cadre d'une cession-bail

leaseback ['liːsbæk] N cession-bail *f*

leased line [liːst] N *Comput* ligne *f* louée

leasehold ['liːshəʊld] N **1** tenure *f* à bail *(en particulier tenure en vertu d'un bail emphytéotique)* **2** *(property)* propriété *f* *ou* immeuble *m* loué(e) à bail

ADJ tenu à bail

leaseholder ['liːshəʊldər] N locataire *mf*

lease-purchase N crédit-bail *m*

▸▸ **l. contract** contrat *m* de crédit-bail

leash [liːʃ] N laisse *f*; **to put a dog on the l.** mettre une laisse à un chien; *Fig* **to keep sb on a tight l.** tenir la bride haute à qn; **to keep one's emotions on a tight l.** avoir étroitement en mains les rênes de ses émotions

leasing ['liːsɪŋ] N *(of house)* location *f* à bail; *(of land)* affermage *m*; *Ind, Com (of equipment etc)* location; *(on lease-purchase)* location-bail *f*; *(system)* location avec option d'achat, LOA *f*, crédit-bail *m*

LEAST [liːst]

ADJ le moindre ▪ le moins de
N le moins **1** ▪ au moins **2**
ADV le moins

ADJ *(smallest)* **(the) l.** (le *ou* la) moindre, (le *ou* la) plus petit(e); **to get upset at the l. thing** se fâcher pour un rien; **the government clamps down on the l. sign of opposition** le gouvernement serre la vis au moindre signe d'opposition; **the l. mention of religion was absolutely forbidden** la moindre référence à la religion était interdite; **I'm not the l. bit musical** je ne suis pas musicien pour un sou; **I'm not the l. bit tired** je ne suis pas du tout fatigué; **she has the l. money out of all of us** c'est elle qui a le moins d'argent d'entre nous tous

N **1 (the) l.** (le) moins; **to say the l. (of it)** le moins qu'on puisse dire; **she was not very polite, to say the l.** le moins qu'on puisse dire, c'est qu'elle n'a pas été très polie; **it's the l. I can do** c'est la moindre des choses; **that's the l. of my worries** c'est le dernier de mes soucis

2 **at l.** *(tout)* au moins; **at l. as old/expensive as …** au moins aussi vieux/cher que …; **I can at l. try** je peux toujours essayer; **it cost at l. £1,000** cela lui a coûté 1 000 livres au bas mot; **she's at l. seventy** elle a au moins soixante-dix ans; **at the very l. they should pay your expenses** ce serait vraiment la moindre des choses qu'ils remboursent tes dépenses

3 not in the l. pas du tout, *Fml* aucunement, nullement; **it doesn't matter in the l.** cela n'a pas la moindre importance; **I'm not in the l. upset** je ne suis fâché en aucune manière

ADV **(the) l.** (le) moins; **the l. unhappy** le moins malheureux; **he deserves it l. of all** il le mérite moins que personne; **we didn't expect to win any prizes, l. of all this one** nous ne nous attendions pas à gagner un prix, et en tout cas, certainement pas celui-là; **it always happens when you are l. expecting it** ça arrive toujours au moment où tu t'y attends le moins

leastways, *Am* **leastwise** ['liːstweɪz, -waɪz] ADV *Fam* au (tout) du moins …

leather ['leðər] N **1** cuir *m*; **l. shoes** chaussures *fpl* en cuir; **fancy l. goods** maroquinerie *f* **2** *Br Fam (clothes)* **leathers** cuir *m* **3** *(of pump, valve etc)* cuir *m*; **stirrup l.** étrivière *f*

VT *Fam (person)* tanner le cuir à

leather-bound ADJ *(book)* relié (en) cuir

leathercloth ['leðəklɒθ] N toile *f* cuir

Leatherette® [leðə'ret] N *Old-fashioned* similicuir *m*

leathering ['leðərɪŋ] N *Fam* **to give sb a l.** tanner le cuir à qn

leatherjacket ['leðədʒækɪt] N *Entom* larve *f* de la tipule

leatherneck ['leðənek] N *Am Fam* soldat *m* de l'infanterie de marine

leatherwork ['leðəwɜːk] N **1** *(activity)* travail *m* du cuir **2** *(products)* articles *mpl* de cuir; **fancy l.** maroquinerie *f*

leathery ['leðərɪ] ADJ *(skin)* tanné; *(food)* coriace

LEAVE [liːv]

N permission **1** ▪ congé **2, 3**
VT quitter **1** ▪ laisser **2–4** ▪ oublier **2**
▪ léguer **4**

N **1** *(permission)* permission *f*, autorisation *f*; **to ask l. to do sth** demander la permission de faire qch; **to grant** *or* **give sb l. to do sth** donner *ou* accorder à qn la permission de faire qch; *Arch, Fml* **by** *or* **with your l.** avec votre permission; **without so much as a by your l.** sans même en demander la permission **2** *Admin, Mil etc (holiday)* congé *m*; *(in civil service etc)* congé exceptionnel; **to be on l.** être en congé; **to take two weeks' l.** prendre deux semaines de congé

3 *(farewell)* adieux *mpl*, congé *m*; **to take one's l.** prendre congé; **to take (one's) l. of sb** faire ses adieux à qn; **to take l. of one's senses** perdre l'esprit

VT *(pt, pp* left [left]*)* **1** *(depart from)* *(place, person)* quitter; *(room)* quitter, sortir de; **he has left London** il est parti de Londres, il a quitté Londres; **he left Oxford without finishing his studies** il a quitté Oxford sans avoir terminé ses études; **she left school at 16** elle a quitté l'école à 16 ans; **she never leaves the house** elle ne sort jamais de la maison; *Sch* **may I l. the room?** puis-je sortir?; **his eyes never left her** il ne la quittait pas des yeux; **to l. the table** se lever de table; **to l. one's job** quitter son emploi; *Mil etc* **to l. the service** quitter le service; *Naut* **to l. harbour** sortir du port; **to l. one's wife** quitter sa femme; **to be left behind** *or* **standing** être dépassé *ou* distancé (par ses concurrents); **to l. the rails** *(of train)* dérailler; **the car left the road** la voiture a quitté la route

2 *(put, deposit)* **to l. sth somewhere** *(deliberately)* laisser qch quelque part; *(by mistake)* oublier *ou* laisser qch quelque part; **to l. things (lying) about** laisser traîner des choses; *Fam* **take it or l. it** c'est à prendre ou à laisser; **to l. a message for sb** laisser un mot *ou* un message *ou* un billet pour qn

3 *(allow to remain)* laisser; **to l. the door open** laisser la porte ouverte; **to l. sth unfinished** laisser qch inachevé; **he left his supper untouched** il ne toucha pas à son dîner; **to l. a page blank** laisser une page en blanc; **l. me alone!** laissez-moi tranquille!; **left to oneself** livré à soi-même; **his work/attitude leaves much to be desired** son travail/attitude laisse beaucoup à désirer; **it leaves me cold** ça me laisse froid; **nothing was left to chance** on avait paré à toutes les éventualités; **to l. hold** *or* **go of sth** lâcher qch; **to l. sb for dead** laisser qn pour mort; *Fig (in race etc)* clouer qn sur place; **to l. sb to do sth** laisser qn faire qch, laisser à qn le soin de faire qch; **to l. sb in charge of sth** confier la responsabilité de qch à qn; **he was left in charge of cooking the food** c'est lui qui s'est occupé de faire à manger; **let's l. it at that, we'll l. it at that** *(not do any more work)* arrêtons-nous là; *(not argue any more)* n'en parlons plus; **to l. sb with sth** confier qch à qn; *Fig* **I'll l. it with you** *(let you make decision etc)* je te laisse t'en occuper; **l. it with me** laisse-moi m'en occuper; **I'll l. it to you to decide** je m'en remets à vous; **I l. it to you to decide** je vous laisse le soin de décider; **l. it to me** laisse-moi faire, je m'en occupe

4 *(after dying)* **to l. a wife and three children** laisser une femme et trois enfants; **to l. one's money to sb** laisser *ou* léguer sa fortune à qn; **she had been left a widow at thirty** elle s'était retrouvée veuve à l'âge de trente ans

5 **to be left** *(remain)* rester; **there are no strawberries left** il ne reste plus de fraises; **how many are there left?** combien est-ce qu'il en reste?

6 *Math* **three from seven leaves four** sept moins trois égale quatre

VI partir; **we l. tomorrow** nous partons demain; **we are leaving for Paris** nous partons pour Paris; **I was just leaving when …** j'étais sur le point de partir lorsque …

▸▸ **l. of absence** congé (exceptionnel); *(without pay)* congé sans solde; *Mil* permission exceptionnelle

▸ **leave behind** VT SEP **1** *(forget)* *(one's hat etc)* oublier

2 *(leave in a place)* laisser; **he left his family behind in Manchester and …** il a laissé sa famille à Manchester et …; **they left me behind** ils sont partis sans moi

3 *(in race etc)* **he's left the other runners**

(well) behind il a pris beaucoup d'avance sur les autres concurrents, *Fam* il a largué tous les autres concurrents; **she left the other pupils behind** elle est passée première devant tous les autres élèves

▸**leave in** VT SEP *(section of text etc)* inclure, retenir

▸**leave off** VT INSEP *Fam* **to l. off doing sth** cesser de faire qch; **to l. off work** cesser le travail; **why can't you l. off the subject for a day?** et si tu arrêtais de parler de ça pendant une journée?; *Fam* **l. off pestering me!** arrête de m'embêter!

VT SEP **1** *(not replace) (lid etc)* ne pas (re)mettre; **to l. sb off a list** *(accidentally)* oublier qn dans une liste; *(deliberately)* exclure qn d'une liste

2 l. the light off n'allume pas; **l. the telly off for a bit** éteins la télé un petit moment; **I left the heating off** je n'ai pas mis le chauffage VI s'arrêter; **where did we l. off?** *(in reading etc)* où en sommes-nous restés?; *Sl* **l. off!** ça suffit comme ça!, arrête!

▸**leave on** VT SEP *(coat, gloves etc)* garder; **to l. the light/TV on** laisser la lumière/la télé allumée

▸**leave out** VT SEP **1** *(omit) (a line etc)* omettre **2** *(not involve)* **l. her out of this!** laissez-la en dehors de ça!; **to l. sb out of one's plans** exclure qn de ses projets; **to feel left out** se sentir de trop

3 *(leave ready, available)* **I'll l. your dinner out on the table for you** je te laisse ton dîner sur la table; **l. the disks out where I can see them** laisse les disquettes en évidence

4 *(not put away)* **we l. the car out on the street** nous laissons la voiture dehors dans la rue; **who left the milk out overnight?** qui a oublié de mettre le lait au frigo hier soir?

5 *Sl* **l. it out!** *(stop it)* arrête!

▸**leave over** VT SEP **1 what's left over?** qu'est-ce qui reste?; **you can keep what is left over** vous pouvez garder le surplus

2 *(postpone)* remettre à plus tard

leaved [li:vd] ADJ feuillé, feuillu

-leaved [li:vd] SUFF **three-l.** *(screen etc)* à trois panneaux; **broad-l. tree** arbre à larges feuilles; **ivy-l.** à feuilles de lierre

leaven ['lev(ə)n] N *Culin, Fig* levain *m* VT *(bread, dough)* faire lever; *Fig* **her account is leavened with interesting anecdotes** elle a agrémenté son récit d'anecdotes intéressantes

leavening ['levənɪŋ] N = **leaven**

leaver ['li:vər] N *(school)* **leavers** élèves *mpl* sortants

leave-taking N adieux *mpl*

leaving ['li:vɪŋ] N départ *m*

leavings ['li:vɪŋz] NPL *(from meal)* restes *mpl*

Lebanese [lebə'ni:z] ADJ libanais N Libanais, -aise

Lebanon ['lebənən] N Liban *m*

▸**lech after** [letʃ] VT INSEP *Fam* reluquer

lecher ['letʃər] N débauché *m, Fam* coureur *m* de jupons

lecherous ['letʃərəs] ADJ *(person)* lubrique, débauché; *(look, smile)* lubrique

lecherously ['letʃərəslɪ] ADV lubriquement

lechery ['letʃərɪ] N lubricité *f*

lecithin ['lesɪθɪn] N lécithine *f*

lectern ['lektən] N *(in church etc)* lutrin *m; (in library)* pupitre *m*

lector ['lektɔ:r] N *Univ (for foreign languages)* lecteur, -trice

lecture ['lektʃər] N **1** conférence *f, Univ* cours *m* magistral (**on** sur); **to give/attend a l.** *(public)* donner/assister à une conférence; *(university)* donner/assister à un cours magistral; **history l.** cours *m* d'his-

toire; **l. on Napoleon** cours sur Napoléon **2** *Fam (reprimand)* sermon *m*, semonce *f*; **to give** *or* **read sb a l.** faire la morale à qn; *(for wrongdoing)* semoncer qn, sermonner qn
VI donner une conférence *ou* des conférences; *Univ* donner un cours magistral (**on** sur); **he lectured on Eastern affairs** il a donné une conférence sur l'Orient; **she lectures in Economics** elle donne des cours d'économie à l'université, elle est maître-assistant en économie; **he lectures at Stirling** il est maître-assistant à l'université de Stirling
VT *(person)* faire la morale à; *(for wrongdoing)* sermonner, semoncer

▸▸**l. hall, l. theatre** salle *f* de cours, amphithéâtre *m*

> Note that the French word **lecture** is a false friend and is never a translation for the English word **lecture**. It means **reading**.

lecturer ['lektʃərər] N **1** conférencier, -ière **2** *Univ* **(junior** *or* **assistant) l.** ≃ maître-assistant *m;* **(senior) l.** ≃ maître *m* de conférences; **to be a maths l.** être assistant *m* en maths; **is she a good l.?** est-ce qu'elle est bon professeur?

lectureship ['lektʃəʃɪp] N *Univ* poste *m* de maître-assistant; **she got a l.** elle a été nommée maître-assistante

LED [eli:'di:] N *Comput (abbr* **light-emitting diode)** DEL *f* LED *f*

▸▸**L. display** affichage *m* (par) LED

led PT, PP *see* **lead¹** VT, VI

ledge [ledʒ] N **1** rebord *m*, saillie *f*, *(on wall, building)* corniche *f* **2** *Geol* **l. of rock** plateforme *f* rocheuse; *(awash or under water)* banc *m* de rochers

ledger ['ledʒər] N *(in bookkeeping)* grand livre *m*

▸▸*Mus* **l. line** ligne *f* supplémentaire *(à la portée)*

lee [li:] N **1** *Naut (side)* côté *m* sous le vent **2** *(shelter)* **in** *or* **under the l. of a rock** abrité par un rocher

▸▸**l. shore** terre *f* sous le vent

leeboard ['li:bɔ:d] N *Naut* aile *f ou* semelle *f* de dérive

leech [li:tʃ] N **1** *(animal)* sangsue *f* **2** *Fam Pej (person)* sangsue *f*, crampon *m;* **to cling** *or* **stick to sb like a l.** se cramponner à qn comme une sangsue

▸**leech onto** VT INSEP *Fam* se cramponner à

leek [li:k] N *(vegetable)* poireau *m*

leer [lɪər] N *(sexual)* regard *m* lubrique; *(cruel)* regard sadique
VI **to l. at sb** *(sexually)* regarder *ou Fam* reluquer qn d'un air lubrique; *(cruelly)* regarder qn d'un air sadique

leering ['lɪərɪŋ] ADJ *(sexual)* concupiscent, lubrique; *(cruel)* sadique

leery ['lɪərɪ] ADJ *Fam* **to be l. of sb/sth** se méfier de qn/qch; **why are you so l. of showing your emotions?** pourquoi as-tu si peur de montrer tes émotions?

lees [li:z] NPL *(in wine)* lie *f*

leeward ['li:wəd] *Naut* ADJ, ADV sous le vent N côté *m* sous le vent; **to pass to l. of a ship** passer sous le vent d'un navire

▸▸**L. Islands** *(in South Pacific or West Indies)* les îles *fpl* sous le Vent

leeway ['li:weɪ] N **1** *(freedom)* liberté *f* d'action; *(safety margin)* marge *f* de sécurité **2** *Naut* dérive *f;* **to make l.** dériver (à la voile); *Fig Fam* **he has a lot of l. to make up** il a un fort retard à rattraper

left¹ [left] ADJ gauche; **on my l. hand** à ma gauche; *Fam* **to have two l. feet** s'emmêler les pinceaux; *esp Am Fam* **to be way out in**

l. field être complètement excentrique; *esp Am Fam* **to come out of l. field** surgir de l'ombre

ADV *(to turn etc)* à gauche; *Typ* **l. justified** justifié à gauche; *Mil* **l. turn!** à gauche, gauche!; **eyes l.!** tête (à) gauche!

N gauche *f, Boxing* gauche *m;* **on the l., to the l.** à gauche; *Aut etc* **to keep (to the) l.** tenir la gauche; *Pol* **the L.** la gauche

▸▸*Comput* **l. arrow** flèche *f* vers la gauche; *Comput* **l. arrow key** touche *f* de déplacement vers la gauche; **l. margin** marge *f* de gauche; *TV, Cin* **l. pan** panoramique *m* horizontal DG; **l. wing** *Pol, Mil* gauche *f, Sport (position)* aile *f* gauche; *(player)* ailier *m* gauche; *Sport* **to play on the l. wing** être ailier gauche

left² PT, PP *see* **leave** VT, VI

▸▸*Br* **l. luggage** *(cases)* bagages *mpl* en consigne; *(office)* consigne *f,* **l. luggage lockers** consigne automatique; **l. luggage office** consigne

left-click *Comput* VT cliquer avec le bouton gauche de la souris sur
VI cliquer avec le bouton gauche de la souris (**on** sur)

left-hand ADJ **1** *(pocket, margin etc)* de gauche; **on the l. side** à gauche; **l. turn** virage *m* à gauche **2** *Tech (lock, screw, drill)* à gauche

▸▸*Aut* **l. drive** conduite *f* à gauche; **to have l. drive** avoir le volant à gauche; *Tech* **l. thread** filetage *m* à gauche

left-handed ['left'hændɪd] ADJ **1** *(person)* gaucher, -ère; *(golf club etc)* pour gaucher; **l. blow** coup *m* de la main gauche **2** *Tech* = **left-hand 2**
ADV **to play tennis l.** jouer au tennis de la main gauche

▸▸*Fam* **l. compliment** compliment *m* peu flatteur

left-hander ['left'hændər] N *(person)* gaucher, -ère; *Boxing* coup *m* du gauche

leftie ['leftɪ] N *Pol Fam* gauchiste *mf*

leftist ['leftɪst] *Pol* N gauchiste *mf*
ADJ gauchiste; *(person)* de gauche

leftover ['leftəʊvər] ADJ **there was some l. chicken** il restait du poulet; **I made a curry with the l. chicken** j'ai fait un curry avec le reste du poulet; **you could use the l. paint/wallpaper** tu pourrais utiliser la peinture/le papier peint qu'il reste
N **1** *Com, Culin* **leftovers** restes *mpl* **2** *(from the past)* survivance *f* (**from** de)

▸▸*Com* **l. stock** restes *mpl*

left-wing ADJ *Pol* de gauche; **they are very l.** ils sont très à gauche; **he has slightly l. ideas** il a des idées gauchisantes

left-winger N **1** *Pol (in party, union)* homme/femme de gauche; *(in Parliament)* député *m* de la gauche; **the left-wingers** la gauche **2** *Sport* ailier *m* gauche

leg [leg] N **1** *(of person, horse)* jambe *f, (of dog, bird, insect, reptile)* patte *f,* **wooden l.** jambe de bois; *Fig* **you don't have a l. to stand on** vos arguments ne tiennent pas debout; **you won't have a l. to stand on if they find this letter** s'ils trouvent cette lettre, vous êtes fichu; *Fig* **to be on one's last legs** *(to be tired)* ne plus pouvoir mettre un pied devant l'autre; *(to be dying)* avoir un pied dans la tombe; **the business is on its last legs** la société est au bord de la faillite *ou* mal en point; **after 10 miles we were on our last legs** après 10 mil(l)es nous n'en pouvions plus; **the government is on its last legs** le gouvernement est mal en point; **the car/TV is on its last legs** la voiture/la télé a fait son temps; *Fam* **to have legs** *(last a long time) (of rumour, theory)* avoir la vie dure; *(of film, play)* qui marche beaucoup mieux que prévu; **to give sb a l. up** *(over a wall, fence etc)* faire la courte échelle à qn; *(into* the saddle) aider qn à monter en selle; *Fam (in job etc)* donner un coup de pouce à qn; *Fam* **to pull sb's l.** faire marcher qn; *Fam* **show** *or* **shake a l.!** *(it's time to get up)* debout!; *Sl* **to get one's l. over** *(have sex)* s'envoyer en l'air

2 *Culin (of chicken)* cuisse *f*, *(of veal)* cuisseau *m*; **roast l. of pork** cuissot *m* de porc rôti; **l. of lamb** gigot *m*; **frogs' legs** cuisses de grenouille

3 *(of trousers)* jambe *f*, *(of stocking etc)* tige *f*; **these trousers are a bit short in the l.** ce pantalon est un peu court au niveau des jambes

4 *(of table, chair)* pied *m*; *(of tripod etc)* jambe *f*, *(of trestle)* montant *m*

5 *Cr (when the batsman is right-handed)* côté *m* gauche du terrain; *(when the batsman is left-handed)* côté droit du terrain

6 *(of journey, race)* étape *f*, *(in relay race)* relais *m*

vt (-gg-) *Fam* **to l. it** *(walk)* faire la route à pied; *(hurry)* marcher *ou* courir vite

▸▸ *Med* **l. iron** appareil *m* orthopédique; **l. rest** appui-jambes *m inv*; *Med* étrier *m*; *Fam* **l. show** revue *f* légère; *Cr* **l. side** *(when the batsman is right-handed)* côté *m* gauche du terrain; *(when the batsman is left-handed)* côté droit du terrain

legacy ['legəsɪ] *n Law* legs *m*; **to come into a l.** faire un héritage; **to leave sb a l.** laisser un héritage *ou* quelque chose en héritage à qn; *Fig* **this desk is a l. from my predecessor** j'ai hérité ce bureau de mon prédécesseur; **the l. of the war was a divided Europe** l'héritage de la guerre fut une Europe divisée; **the crisis left a l. of bitterness** la crise a créé un climat d'amertume

legal ['liːg(ə)l] **ADJ 1** *(lawful)* légal, -aux; *(commerce)* licite; **to be l. currency** *or* **tender** avoir cours (légal)

2 *(error)* judiciaire; *(mind, affairs)* juridique; **by l. process** par voies légales, par voies de droit; **to go into the l. profession** faire une carrière juridique; **to take l. advice** ≃ consulter un avocat; **to have a l. claim to sth** avoir légalement droit à qch

3 *Comput (character etc)* autorisé

4 *Am (paper format)* légal, -aux

▸▸ **l. action** action *f* en justice; **to take l. action against sb** intenter une action contre qn; **l. adviser** conseil *m* juridique; **l. aid** aide *f* juridique; **l. charges** frais *mpl* judiciaires; **l. department** *(in bank, company)* (service *m* du) contentieux *m*; **l. dispute** litige *m*; **l. document** acte *m* authentique; **l. entity** personne *f* morale; **l. expert** expert *m* juridique, avocat *m* conseil; **l. holiday** jour *m* férié, fête *f* légale; **l. limit** *(of alcohol)* taux *m* d'alcoolémie autorisé; **l. manager** responsable *mf* juridique; **l. owner** propriétaire *mf* légitime; *Am* **l. pad** bloc-notes *m*, *pl* blocs-notes; **l. proceedings** poursuites *fpl* judiciaires; **to initiate l. proceedings against sb** engager des poursuites judiciaires contre qn; **l. recourse** recours *m* contentieux; **l. redress** recours *m* à la justice; **l. reserve** réserve *f* légale; **l. security** caution *f* judiciaire; **l. separation** séparation *f* de corps; **l. status** statut *m* légal, statut juridique; **l. technicality** vice *m* de forme; **l. year** année *f* civile

legalese [liːgə'liːz] **n** *Fam* jargon *m* juridique

legalism ['liːgəlɪz(ə)m] **n** légalisme *m*

legalistic [liːgə'lɪstɪk] **ADJ** formaliste

legality [lɪ'gælɪtɪ] **n** légalité *f*

legalization [liːgəlaɪ'zeɪʃən] **n** légalisation *f*

legalize ['liːgəlaɪz] **vt** *(drug, document)* légaliser; *(deed)* rendre légal, autoriser

legally ['liːgəlɪ] **ADV** légalement; **l. respon-**

sible responsable en droit; **l. binding contract** contrat qui engage les personnes devant la loi

legate ['legɪt] **n** *Rel, Antiq* légat *m*

legatee [legə'tiː] **n** légataire *mf*

legation [lɪ'geɪʃən] **n** légation *f*

legato [lɪ'gɑːtəʊ] **ADV** *Mus* legato

legend ['ledʒənd] **n** *(story, inscription etc)* légende *f*; **to be/become a l. in one's own lifetime** être/devenir une légende vivante

legendary ['ledʒənd(ə)rɪ] **ADJ** légendaire

legerdemain [ledʒədə'meɪn] **n** *Lit Fig* tour *m* de passe-passe

-legged ['legɪd, legd] **SUFF** **short/bare/etc -l.** aux jambes courtes/nues *etc*; **two-l.** *(person)* à deux jambes; *(animal)* à deux pattes

leggings ['legɪŋz] **NPL** *(for dancers)* jambières *fpl*, *(for women)* caleçon *m*

leggy ['legɪ] *(person)* aux longues jambes; *(plant)* étiolé; **a l. girl** une fille tout en jambes

Leghorn ['leghɔːn] **n** *Geog* Livourne

legibility [ledʒɪ'bɪlɪtɪ] **n** *(of handwriting)* lisibilité *f*

legible ['ledʒɪb(ə)l] **ADJ** *(handwriting)* lisible, net

legibly ['ledʒɪblɪ] **ADV** *(to write)* lisiblement

legion ['liːdʒ(ə)n] **n** légion *f*; **the Foreign L.** la Légion étrangère; **the L. of honour** la Légion d'honneur

ADJ *Lit (many)* **their name is l.** ils sont légion; **the difficulties were l.** les difficultés étaient innombrables

legionary ['liːdʒənərɪ] **ADJ** de la légion

n légionnaire *m*

legionnaire [liːdʒə'neər] **n** légionnaire *m*; **l.'s disease** maladie *f* du légionnaire

legislate ['ledʒɪsleɪt] **vi** faire des *ou* les lois, légiférer; **we can't l. for all possible situations** nous ne pouvons pas prévoir des lois pour tous les cas de figure possibles; **to l. against sth** instaurer une loi contre qch; **child labour had been legislated out of existence by 1900** grâce à la législation, le travail des enfants fut interdit à partir de 1900

legislation [ledʒɪs'leɪʃən] **n** *(laws)* législation *f*, *(action)* élaboration *f* des lois; **further l. may be needed** il faudrait renforcer la législation; **to bring in l. to ...** créer une loi *ou* des lois pour ...; **piece of l.** loi *f*

legislative ['ledʒɪslətɪv] **ADJ** législatif

▸▸ **the L. Assembly** l'Assemblée *f* législative; **l. power** pouvoir *m* législatif

legislator ['ledʒɪsleɪtər] **n** législateur, -trice

legislature ['ledʒɪslətʃər] **n** corps *m* législatif

legit [lɪ'dʒɪt] **ADJ** *Fam* réglo; **this deal is strictly l.** cette affaire est parfaitement réglementaire

legitimacy [lɪ'dʒɪtɪməsɪ] **n** *(of child, opinion etc)* légitimité *f*

legitimate¹ [lɪ'dʒɪtɪmət] **ADJ** *(child, authority, reason, government etc)* légitime; **l. expenditure** dépenses *fpl* justifiées; **it's l. to assume that ...** on peut légitimement penser que ..., il est légitime de penser que ...; **the l. stage** le théâtre traditionnel

legitimate² [lɪ'dʒɪtɪmeɪt] **vt** *(child)* légitimer

legitimately [lɪ'dʒɪtɪmətlɪ] **ADV** légitimement

legitimatize [lɪ'dʒɪtɪmətaɪz], **legitimize** [lɪ'dʒɪtɪmaɪz] **vt** légitimer

legless ['leglɪs] **ADJ 1** **l. cripple** cul-de-jatte *m*, *pl* culs-de-jatte **2** *Br Fam (drunk)* bourré, beurré

legman, *pl* **legmen** ['legmæn, -mən] **n** *Am* **1**

Journ = reporter *m* qui fait la chronique des chiens écrasés **2** *(errand boy etc)* garçon *m* de courses, coursier *m*

leg-of-mutton **ADJ** **l. sleeves** manches *fpl* gigot

leg-pull **n** *Fam* blague *f*

leg-puller [-pʊlər] **n** *Fam* blagueur, -euse, farceur, -euse

legroom ['legrʊm] **n** place *f* pour les jambes; **these little cars don't give you any l.** dans ces petites voitures, on n'a aucune place pour les jambes

legume ['legjuːm] **n** *(vegetable)* légumineuse *f*, **legumes** *(plants)* légumineuses *fpl*

leguminous [lɪ'gjuːmɪnəs] **ADJ** *Bot* légumineux; **l. plant** légumineuse *f*

legwarmer ['legwɔːmər] **n** *(usu pl)* **legwarmers** jambières *fpl*

legwork ['legwɜːk] **n** *Fam* **there's a lot of l. in this job** c'est un travail où l'on marche beaucoup; **I'm the one that gets all the l.** c'est toujours moi qui me déplace ici

Leics *abbr* **Leicestershire**

leisure ['leʒər, *Am* 'liːʒər] **n** loisir(s) *m(pl)*; **to have enough l. for reading** avoir le loisir *ou* le temps de lire; **to do sth at one's l.** faire qch à loisir *ou* dans ses moments de loisir

▸▸ **l. activities** activités *fpl* de loisir; **l. break** court séjour *m* de détente; **l. centre** centre *m* de loisirs; **l. club** club *m* de loisirs; **l. hours** heures *fpl* de loisir; **l. industry** industrie *f* des loisirs; **l. market** marché *m* des loisirs; **l. time** temps *m* libre; **l. tourism** tourisme *m* de loisir, tourisme *m* ludique; **l. wear** vêtements *mpl* sport

leisured ['leʒəd] **ADJ 1** *(life etc)* de loisir **2** *(person)* qui a des loisirs; **the l. classes** les rentiers *mpl*

leisureliness ['leʒəlɪnɪs] **n** *(of pace)* caractère *m* mesuré; *(of weekend)* caractère détendu; **the l. of sea travel** la détente apportée par une croisière

leisurely ['leʒəlɪ] **ADJ** *(person)* qui n'est jamais pressé; *(pace)* tranquille; *(weekend)* détendu, relax; *(journey)* par petites étapes; **progress had been all too l.** nous progressions/ils progressaient beaucoup trop lentement; **they moved with a l. grace** ils se déplaçaient avec grâce et lenteur; **to go for a l. stroll** aller se promener tranquillement; **we had a l. time of it at the beach** nous nous sommes bien reposés à la plage; **to do sth in a l. fashion** faire qch sans se presser

ADV *(without haste)* sans se presser

lemming ['lemɪŋ] **n** lemming *m*; **to follow sb like lemmings** suivre qn comme des moutons (de Panurge)

lemon ['lemən] **n 1** *(fruit, colour)* citron *m*; *Fam* **they squeezed him like a l.** ils l'ont pressé comme un citron **2** *Fam (awkward person)* idiot, -ote; **what a l.!** quelle cruche!; *Fam* **I felt like a real l.** j'ai eu l'air vraiment malin **3** *Fam (useless object)* **it's a l.** c'est de la camelote; **she got sold a l.** elle s'est fait rouler

ADJ **l.(-coloured)** *(jaune)* citron *inv*

▸▸ *Bot* **l. balm** mélisse *f*, citronnelle *f*, *Culin* **l. curd** pâte *f* à tartiner au citron; **l. grass** citronnelle *f*, lemon-grass *m*; **l. juice** jus *m* de citron; *(squash)* sirop *m* de citron; *(freshly squeezed drink)* citron *m* pressé; **l. meringue pie** tarte *f* au citron meringuée; **l. sole** limande-sole *f*, *Br* **l. squeezer** presse-citron *m*, *pl* presse-citrons; **l. tea** thé *m* au citron; **l. tree** citronnier *m*; **l. verbena** verveine *f* citronnelle

lemonade [lemə'neɪd] **n** *(carbonated)* limonade *f*, *(freshly sqeezed)* citronnade *f*

lemony ['lemənɪ] **ADJ** *(smell, taste)* citronné

lemur ['liːmər] **n** maki *m*

lend [lend] *(pt, pp* **lent** [lent]*)* **vt 1** prêter (**sth**

to sb, sb sth qch à qn); **to l. money at interest** prêter de l'argent à intérêt

2 *(give)* **to l. sb a (helping) hand** donner un coup de main à qn; **to l. an ear** *or* **one's ear to …** prêter l'oreille à …; **to l. one's name to a project** donner son nom à un projet; **to l. dignity to an occasion** rehausser le prestige d'un événement; **to l. weight to an argument** donner du poids à un argument; **to l. credibility/drama to a story** rendre une histoire crédible/dramatique; **the bloodstains on his trousers lent support to his story** les taches de sang sur son pantalon accréditèrent son histoire; **distance lends enchantment to the view** tout paraît beau (vu) de loin; **to l. oneself** *or* **itself to sth** se prêter à qch; **the story doesn't l. itself to dramatization** l'histoire ne se prête pas à une dramatisation

VI *Fin* **to l. against securities** prêter sur titres; **to l. at 12%** prêter à 12%

▸ **lend out VT SEP** prêter

lender ['lendər] **N** *(person)* prêteur, -euse; *Fin (institution)* organisme *m* de crédit

lending ['lendɪŋ] **N** *(of money, item)* prêt *m*
▸▸ *Fin* **l. bank** banque *f* de crédit; **l. country** pays *m* créancier; **l. library** bibliothèque *f* de prêt; *Fin* **l. limit** plafond *m* de crédit; **l. policy** *(of bank, country)* politique *f* de prêt; *Fin* **l. rate** taux *m* de prêt

lend-lease **N** *(no pl)* *Econ, Hist* prêt-bail *m*

length [leŋθ] **N 1** *(in space), Swimming* longueur *f*; **to swim a few lengths** faire quelques longueurs; **it's 4.50m in l.** ça fait 4,50m de long; **to win by a l./half a l.** *(in race)* gagner d'une longueur/d'une demi-longueur; **to wander the l. and breadth of the country** errer dans tout le pays; **I fell full l. on the ground** je suis tombé de tout mon long

2 *(in time)* durée *f*; *(of book, journey etc)* longueur *f*; **about 300 pages/30,000 words in l.** *(book)* d'une longueur d'environ 300 pages/30 000 mots; **his essay was a bit under l.** sa dissertation était un peu trop courte; **l. of service** *(in post)* ancienneté *f*; **the l. of time required to do sth** le temps qu'il faut pour faire qch; **at (great) l.** *(to talk)* longuement; *(to explain sth)* en détail

3 to go to the l. of doing sth aller jusqu'à faire qch; **to go to great lengths to do sth** se donner beaucoup de mal à *ou* pour faire qch; **he would go to any lengths (to do sth)** il ne reculerait devant rien (pour faire qch); **I never dreamed that they would go to such lengths** je n'aurais jamais imaginé qu'ils iraient si loin

4 *(of vowel, syllable)* longueur *f*
5 *Tennis, Cr* longueur *f* de balle
6 *(of string etc)* morceau *m*, bout *m*; *(of material)* pièce *f*, coupon *m*; *(of wood)* morceau; *(of pipe)* tronçon *m*; *Sewing* **dress/ trouser l.** coupon de robe/pantalon; *Sewing* **what l. do I need for …?** quel métrage faut-il pour …?

lengthen ['leŋθən] **VT** *(skirt, chain etc)* allonger, rallonger; *(interval)* prolonger; *(vowel, account)* allonger
VI *(of days etc)* allonger, rallonger; *(of intervals etc)* augmenter; *(of shadows)* s'allonger

lengthening ['leŋθənɪŋ] **N** allongement *m*

lengthily ['leŋθɪlɪ] **ADV** longuement

lengthways *Am* **lengthwise** ['leŋθweɪz, -waɪz] **ADV** dans le sens de la longueur, longitudinalement

lengthy ['leŋθɪ] **ADJ** *(speech, report)* long, *f* longue, plein de longueurs; *(process, description)* long

leniency ['li:nɪənsɪ] **N** indulgence *f* **(to, towards** envers)

lenient ['li:nɪənt] **ADJ** indulgent **(to, towards** envers); *(punishment)* peu sévère; *Law* **a l. sentence** un jugement clément

leniently ['li:nɪəntlɪ] **ADV** *(to judge)* avec clémence; *(to mark, treat etc)* avec indulgence

Lenin ['lenɪn] **N** Lénine *m*

Leningrad ['lenɪngræd] **N** *Hist* Léningrad

Leninism ['lenɪnɪz(ə)m] **N** *Pol* léninisme *m*

Leninist ['lenɪnɪst] **ADJ, N** *Pol* léniniste *mf*

lenitive ['lenɪtɪv] **ADJ, N** *Med* lénitif *m*

lens [lenz] **N 1** *Opt* lentille *f*; *(of spectacles)* verre *m*; **converging/diverging l.** lentille *f* convergente/divergente; **concave/convex l.** lentille concave/convexe **2** *Phot* objectif *m* (photographique); *Electron* **electron l.** lentille *f* électronique; **mirror l.** objectif à lentille spéculaire **3** *Anat* **(crystalline) l.** *(of the eye)* cristallin *m*
▸▸ *Phot* **l. attachment** accessoire *m* d'objectif; *Phot* **l. cap** bouchon *m* d'objectif; **l. cleaning fluid** produit *m* de nettoyage pour lentilles; *Phot* **l. holder** étui *m* à objectif; *Phot* **l. hood** pare-soleil *m* inv

Lent [lent] **N** *Rel* Carême *m*; **to keep L.** faire carême; **to give up sth for L.** renoncer à qch pour le Carême

lent **PT, PP** *see* **lend**

lentil ['lentɪl] **N** *Bot, Culin* lentille *f*; **l. soup** soupe *f* aux lentilles

Leo ['li:əʊ] **N** *Astrol* Lion *m*; **to be (a) L.** être (du) Lion

leonine ['li:ənaɪn] **ADJ** *Lit* léonin

leopard ['lepəd] **N** léopard *m*; *Fig Fam* **a l. cannot change its spots** on ne se refait pas
▸▸ **l. skin** peau *f* de léopard; **a l.-skin coat** un manteau en léopard

leotard ['li:ətɑːd] **N** maillot *m* (de danseur), justaucorps *m*

leper ['lepər] **N** *Med, Fig* lépreux, -euse; **l. hospital** *or* **colony** léproserie *f*

lepidopteran [lepɪ'dɒptərən] **ADJ, N** *Entom* lépidoptère *m*

leprechaun ['leprəkɔːn, -hɔːn] **N** *Myth* farfadet *m*, lutin *m*

leprosy ['leprəsɪ] **N** *Med* lèpre *f*; **to have l.** avoir la lèpre

leprous ['leprəs] **ADJ** *Med* lépreux

lesbian ['lezbɪən] **ADJ** lesbien
N lesbienne *f*

lesbianism ['lezbɪənɪz(ə)m] **N** lesb(ian)isme *m*

lesbo ['lezbəʊ] **N** *Sl Pej (lesbian)* gouine *f*

lesion ['li:ʒən] **N** *Law, Med* lésion *f*

Lesotho [lɪ'suːtuː] **N** le Lesotho

LESS [les]

ADJ	moins de **1**
PREP	moins
PRON	moins
ADV	moins **1** ▪ de moins en moins **1**
	▪ encore moins **1** ▪ rien de moins **2**
	▪ pas moins de **2** ▪ moins que **2**

ADJ *(comp* **lesser) 1** *(not so much)* moins de; **we have l. time/money than we thought** nous avons moins de temps/d'argent que nous ne pensions; **l. trouble/difficulty** moins de peine/difficulté; **it's l. than a week's work** cela représente moins d'une semaine de travail; **he has even l. idea about cars than I do** il s'y connaît encore moins que moi en matière de voiture; **he is l. than thirty** il a moins de trente ans; **l. than (sign)** *(signe m)* inférieur à, signe plus petit que VOIR GRAMMAIRE A25-6
2 *(smaller)* **the distance is l. than I thought** la distance est moindre que je ne le pensais
PREP moins; **a year l. two days** une année moins deux jours; **I've £50, l. what I spent on records** j'ai 50 livres, moins ce que j'ai dépensé en disques

PRON moins; **the l. you know the better** le moins tu en sais, le mieux c'est; **I don't think any (the) l. of you** tu n'as pas baissé dans mon estime; **I see l. of her nowadays** je la vois moins ces temps-ci; **in l. than an hour** en moins d'une heure; **in l. than no time** en un rien de temps; **I can't sell it at l. than cost price** je ne peux pas le vendre à moins du prix de revient; **the l. said about it the better** moins on en parle mieux cela vaut; *Fam* **l. of that!** ça suffit!

ADV VOIR GRAMMAIRE A76; B13 **1** moins; **l. (well) known** moins (bien) connu; **she is l. musical than her sister** elle est moins musicienne que sa sœur; **I'm l. happy with that** ça me satisfait *ou* plaît moins; **one person l.** une personne de moins; **one mouth l. to feed** une bouche de moins à nourrir; **not a penny l.** pas un sou de moins; **l. and l.** de moins en moins; **no more, no l.** ni plus ni moins; **still l., even l.** encore moins

2 *(in negative constructions)* **nothing l. than** *(at the very least)* rien (de) moins que; **I want nothing l.** je ne veux rien de moins; **there's nothing I want l. than to hurt him** je ne veux surtout pas le blesser; **he was nothing l. than overjoyed at the news** il fut absolument ravi de la nouvelle; **it's nothing l. than monstrous!** c'est absolument monstrueux!; **this wall is no l. than a metre thick** ce mur n'a pas moins d'un mètre d'épaisseur; **he eats less than he used to** il mange moins qu'avant; **no l. a person than the headmistress** *(came to see me etc)* la directrice en personne; **(had signed the letter etc)** la directrice elle-même; **the letter was signed by Vincent, no l.** la lettre était signée de Vincent, lui-même et en personne; **she was driving a Rolls, no l.** elle conduisait une Rolls, tu te rends compte!; **I expected no l. from you** je n'en attendais pas moins de vous; **they don't own a fridge, much l. a freezer** ils n'ont pas de réfrigérateur, en-core moins de congélateur; **the news of his death came as no l. of a shock for being expected** on avait beau s'y attendre, la nou-velle de sa mort n'en fut pas moins un choc

-less [lɪs] **SUFF** sans; **roofless** sans toit; **penniless** sans le sou; **sleeveless** sans manches

lessee [le'siː] **N** *Law (of premises etc)* locataire *mf* (à bail); *(of casino etc)* tenancier, -ière; *(of farm)* fermier *m*

lessen ['les(ə)n] **VI** s'amoindrir, diminuer; *(of symptoms etc)* s'atténuer
VT *(costs etc)* diminuer; *(importance, severity of sth)* amoindrir; *(noise)* atténuer; *(activity)* ralentir; *(fervour, enthusiasm)* calmer

lessening ['les(ə)nɪŋ] **N** amoindrissement *m*, diminution *f*

lesser ['lesər] **ADJ** VOIR GRAMMAIRE A26 **1** *(in size)* petit **2** *(in importance)* moindre; *Prov* **to choose the l. of two evils** choisir le moindre; **to a l. extent** *or* **degree** dans une moindre mesure, à un degré moindre

lesson ['les(ə)n] **N 1** *(instruction)* leçon *f*; *Sch* cours *m*; *(in primary school)* leçon; **Spanish l.** cours d'espagnol; **swimming l.** cours de natation; **to be an object l. to sb** servir d'exemple à qn; **to learn a l. from sth** tirer une leçon de qch; **he has learnt his l.** il a compris; **let that be a l. to you!** que cela vous serve de leçon!; **it'll teach him a l.** ça lui servira de leçon **2** *Rel (reading from Bible)* lecture *f* de l'Écriture sainte
▸▸ **l. plan** plan *m* de cours

lessor [le'sɔːr] **N** *Law* bailleur, -eresse

lest [lest] **CONJ 1** de peur *ou* de crainte que … (ne) + *subj*, **l. we forget** pour ne pas oublier VOIR GRAMMAIRE A75 **2** *Arch (after verbs of fearing)* **I feared l. he should fall** je craignais qu'il (ne) tombât

LET¹ [let] **vt** (*pt, pp* **let**; *prp* **letting**) **1** VOIR GRAMMAIRE A41; B35 *(allow)* permettre, laisser; **to l. sb do sth** laisser qn faire qch, permettre à qn de faire qch; **the police would not l. anyone pass** la police ne laissait passer personne *ou* ne permettait à personne de passer; **to l. oneself be guided** se laisser guider; **l. me tell you that …** permettez-moi de vous dire que …; **it wasn't easy, l. me tell you!** ça n'a pas été facile, crois-moi!; **to l. sth fall** laisser échapper qch; **l. me go with them** laissez-moi partir avec eux; **he l. go the rope** il a lâché la corde; **someone has l. the dog loose** quelqu'un a lâché le chien; **to l. sb know sth** faire savoir qch à qn, faire part de qch à qn; **l. me know when …** faites-moi savoir quand …; **l. me know if …** préviens-moi si …; **I will l. him know you are here** je vais le prévenir que vous êtes ici; **l. me hear the story** racontez-moi l'histoire; **to l. sth pass** passer sur qch; **we couldn't l. it pass any longer** nous n'avons pas pu laisser passer ça; **to l. sth get one down** se laisser abattre à cause de qch; **to l. sth get to one** se laisser affecter par qch; **to l. things get on top of you** se laisser submerger

2 *Br (house etc)* louer; **(house) to l.** maison à louer

3 *Med Arch* **to l. blood** pratiquer une saignée

v AUX *(supplying 1st & 3rd person of imperative)* **l.'s hurry!** dépêchons-nous!; **l.'s not have an argument about it!** on ne va pas se disputer pour ça!; **why don't we go to the beach on Saturday? – oh yes, l.'s!** et si on allait à la plage samedi? – oh oui! oui!; **l. us pray** prions; **l. there be light** que la lumière soit; **don't l.'s leave yet** ne partons pas tout de suite; **now, don't l.'s have any nonsense!** allons, pas de bêtises!; *Fml* **l. him do it at once!** qu'il le fasse tout de suite!; *Math* **l. AB be equal to CD** supposons que AB soit égal à CD; **l. me see!** voyons un peu!; **l. them all come!** qu'ils viennent tous!; **don't l. me see you here again!** que je ne vous retrouve plus ici! VOIR GRAMMAIRE A40; B34–5

N *Br (of property)* location *f,* **short l.** location de courte durée

▸ **let by vt sep** **to l. sb by** laisser passer qn

▸ **let down vt sep 1** *(blinds etc)* baisser; **to l. one's hair down** laisser tomber ses cheveux; *Fig* se détendre, se laisser aller

2 *Sewing (dress etc)* rallonger

3 *Fam (disappoint) (person)* décevoir; **to l. sb down gently** ménager qn; **I won't l. you down** vous pouvez compter sur moi; **he has been badly l. down** il a été gravement déçu; **the car l. us down again** la voiture nous a encore lâchés; **you've l. everyone down, most of all yourself** tu as fait du tort à tout le monde, à commencer par toi-même; **I've been l. down by the babysitter** la babysitter m'a laissé tomber; **to l. the side down** manquer à ses obligations

4 *(tyre etc)* dégonfler

▸ **let in vt sep 1** *(person)* laisser entrer; *(air, rain, draught)* laisser entrer; **to l. in the light** laisser entrer *ou* passer la lumière; **he's got a key, so he can l. himself in** puisqu'il a une clef, il peut entrer; **my shoes l. in water** mes chaussures prennent l'eau

2 **to l. sb in on a secret** dire un secret à qn; **to l. sb in on a plan** mettre qn au courant d'un projet

3 *Sewing etc (section)* ajouter, introduire

4 *Fam* **I didn't know what I was letting myself in for** je ne savais pas à quoi je m'exposais; **we're letting ourselves in for a lot of work** nous allons avoir beaucoup de travail; **to l. oneself in for a lot of problems** s'exposer à beaucoup de problèmes

▸ **let into vt sep 1** *(person to house etc)* laisser *ou* faire entrer dans

2 **to l. sb into a secret** dévoiler un secret à qn, mettre qn dans le secret

3 *Sewing etc* **to l. a piece into a skirt** mettre *ou* ajouter une pièce à une jupe

▸ **let off vt sep 1** *(explode, fire) (explosive device)* faire partir; *(firework)* tirer, faire partir

2 *(release) (steam)* lâcher, laisser échapper; *Fig* **to l. off steam** se défouler

3 *(excuse)* **to l. sb off from sth/doing sth** dispenser qn de faire qch; **to l. sb off lightly** ne pas être sévère avec qn; **you l. him off too easily** vous n'avez pas été assez sévère avec lui; **I'll l. you off this time** je ferme les yeux pour cette fois; **to be l. off with a fine** en être quitte pour une amende

4 *(permit to leave) (from school, work)* laisser partir

5 *(from vehicle)* laisser (descendre)

vi *Fam (fart)* péter

▸ **let on vi 1** *(tell)* dire; **don't l. on that I was there** n'allez pas dire que j'y étais; **he didn't l. on that he saw her** *(didn't tell anyone)* il n'a pas dit qu'il l'avait vue; *(didn't acknowledge her)* il a fait semblant de ne pas la voir; **don't l. on!** pas un mot!

2 *(claim)* **he wasn't as ill as he l. on** il n'était pas aussi malade qu'il voulait bien le faire croire

▸ **let out vt sep 1** *(release) (person)* laisser sortir; *(bird)* laisser échapper; *(prisoner)* élargir; *(secret)* révéler, divulguer; **the porter l. me out** le gardien m'a ouvert la porte; **I'll l. myself out** ce n'est pas la peine de me raccompagner; **can you l. yourself out?** faut-il vous raccompagner *ou* reconduire?; *Fig* **that lets me out** *(it couldn't have been me)* me voilà soulagé; *(I can't do it)* je suis tranquille; **to l. out the air from** laisser échapper l'air de; *(balloon etc)* dégonfler; **to l. out the bath water** vider la baignoire; **to l. out a yell** laisser échapper un cri

2 *(expand) (jacket, trousers etc)* élargir, agrandir; *(sail)* larguer

3 *(fire etc)* **who l. the fire out?** qui a laissé le feu s'éteindre?

4 *Br (rent out)* louer

▸ **let through vt sep** *(person, water, light)* laisser passer

▸ **let up vi** *(of rain, pressure of business etc)* se calmer; **once he's started he never lets up** une fois lancé il ne s'arrête plus; **the arguing never lets up** ils n'arrêtent pas de se disputer **vt sep l. him up** *(from the ground)* laisse-le se relever

let² conj l. alone sans parler de, encore moins; **we haven't been to England, l. alone Scotland** nous n'avons pas été en Angleterre, pas plus qu'en Écosse

let³ n *Tennis f* balle let; **l.!** let!; **to play a l.** remettre une balle let
▸▸ *Tennis* **l. ball** balle let

let⁴ n *Law* **without l. or hindrance** en toute liberté

let-down n *Fam* déception *f*

lethal ['li:θ(ə)l] ADJ mortel; *Fam* **that vodka's l.!** cette vodka est mortelle!; **l. injury** blessure *f* mortelle
▸▸ **l. dose** dose *f* mortelle *ou* létale; **l. weapon** arme *f* meurtrière

lethally ['li:θəlɪ] ADV **the knife glinted l. in the sun** la lame assassine brillait au soleil; **a l. effective sub-machine gun** une mitraillette d'une efficacité redoutable; **a l. effective debater** un argumentateur d'une efficacité redoutable; **a l. biting wit** un humour mordant redoutable

lethargic [lɪ'θɑ:dʒɪk] ADJ *(person)* léthargique; *(movement, attempt, voice)* mou, *f* molle

lethargically [lɪ'θɑ:dʒɪklɪ] ADV d'une manière léthargique; **to move l.** se déplacer mollement

lethargy ['leθədʒɪ] N léthargie *f*

let-out n *Fam (excuse)* excuse *f*
▸▸ **l. clause** échappatoire *f*

letter [letər] N **1** *(communication)* lettre *f,* **I've had a l. from him** j'ai reçu une lettre de lui; **are there any letters for me?** y a-t-il du courrier pour moi?; **to notify sb by l.** informer qn par lettre; **your l. of …** votre lettre en date du …; **business l.** lettre d'affaires; **rejection l.** lettre de refus; **letters to the editor** courrier *m* des lecteurs

2 *(of alphabet)* lettre *f; Typ* lettre, caractère *m*; **to have letters after one's name** avoir des titres; **according to the l. of the law** selon la lettre de la loi; **to obey to the l.** obéir à la lettre

3 *Am (paper size)* lettre *f*

4 *Lit* letters (belles-)lettres *fpl,* littérature *f,* **man of letters** homme *m* de lettres

vt marquer avec des lettres; *(engrave)* graver des lettres sur
▸▸ **l. of acknowledgement** accusé *m* de réception; **l. of advice** lettre d'avis; *St Exch* **l. of allotment** avis *m* d'attribution *ou* de répartition, lettre d'allocation; **l. of apology** lettre d'excuse; **l. of application** *(for job)* lettre de demande d'emploi; *St Exch (for shares)* lettre de souscription; **l. bomb** lettre piégée; **l. box** boîte *f* à *ou* aux lettres; **l. card** carte-lettre *f,* *pl* cartes-lettres; *Journ* **letters column** rubrique *f* courrier des lecteurs; **l. of complaint** lettre de réclamation; **l. of confirmation** lettre de confirmation; *Com* **l. of credit** lettre de crédit *ou* de créance; **l. of dismissal** lettre de licenciement; *Com* **l. of exchange** lettre de change; **l. of guarantee** lettre de garantie; *Fin* **l. of guaranty** lettre d'aval; *Fin* **l. of indemnity** cautionnement *m,* lettre de garantie (d'indemnité); *Fin* **l. of intent** lettre d'intention; **l. opener** coupe-papier *m inv;* **letters patent** lettres *fpl* patentes; **l. rate** tarif *m* lettres; **l. of reference** lettre de recommandation; **l. scales** pèse-lettre *m,* *pl* pèse-lettres; **l. tray** corbeille *f ou* panier *m* à courrier

lettered ['letəd] ADJ **1** *Fml (person)* lettré **2** *(object)* marqué avec des lettres; **a briefcase l. with my initials** une mallette gravée à mes initiales

letterhead ['letəhed] N en-tête *m inv;* *(paper)* papier *m* à en-tête

lettering ['letərɪŋ] N **1** *(action)* lettrage *m* **2** *(result)* caractères *mpl*

letterpress ['letəpres] N **1** *Typ (method)* impression *f* typographique **2** *(text)* texte *m* *(accompagnant une illustration)*
▸▸ **l. printing** typographie *f*

letter-quality N *Comput* qualité *f* courrier
▸▸ **l. printer** imprimante *f* qualité courrier

letting ['letɪŋ] N *Br (renting out) (of house etc)* location *f*
▸▸ **l. agency** agence *f* de location

lettuce ['letɪs] N laitue *f*

let-up N *Fam (in conflict etc)* trêve *f,* *(in pressure)* diminution *f* (**in** de); *(in weather)* accalmie *f,* *(in efforts, fighting)* relâchement *m*; **to work fifteen hours without a l.** travailler quinze heures d'affilée; **there's been no l. in the rain since this morning** il n'a pas arrêté de pleuvoir depuis ce matin

leucocyte ['lu:kəsaɪt] N *Med* leucocyte *m*

leucocytosis [lu:kəsaɪ'təusɪs] N leucocytose *f*

leukaemia, *Am* **leukemia** [lu:'ki:mɪə] N *Med* leucémie *f,* **to have l.** avoir une leucémie

leukaemic, *Am* **leukemic** [lu:'ki:mɪk] ADJ *Med* leucémique

leukocyte ['lu:kəsaɪt] N *Med* leucocyte *m*

Levant [lɪ'vænt] N **the L.** le Levant

Levantine [lə'væntaɪn] ADJ levantin
N Levantin, -ine

levee ['levɪ] **N** *Am Constr (of river)* levée *f*, digue *f*

LEVEL ['lev(ə)l]

N niveau **1** ▪ taux **1** ▪ hauteur **1**		
ADJ horizontal **1** ▪ de/à niveau **1** ▪ plat **1** ▪ à la hauteur de **2** ▪ égal **3**		
ADV à l'horizontale		
VT niveler **1** ▪ aplanir **1**		

N 1 *(height) (of prices, the sea etc)* niveau *m*; *(in surveying), Geog* altitude *f*, niveau; *(quantity) (of alcohol etc)* taux *m*; **at eye l.** à (la) hauteur des yeux; **to maintain prices at a high l.** maintenir les prix à un niveau élevé; **to be on a l. with sb** être du même niveau que qn, être sur un pied d'égalité avec qn; **on a l. with sth** au niveau *ou* à la hauteur de qch, de niveau avec qch; **her ambition is on a l. with mine** son ambition est du même ordre que la mienne; **to come down to sb's l.** se mettre au niveau *ou* à la portée de qn; **to sink to** *or* **be brought down to sb's l.** tomber au niveau de qn; *Comput* **l. of access** niveau d'accès; *Phys* **l. energy l.** niveau énergétique; **at ministerial l.** à l'échelon ministériel; **noise l.** *(of engine etc)* niveau de bruit; *Tech* **oil l.** niveau d'huile; **radiation l.** niveau de radiation

2 *(flat ground)* terrain *m* de niveau; **to be dead l.** être parfaitement de niveau; **on the l.** *(built etc)* sur un terrain plat; *Fam (person)* honnête; *Fam* **is he on the l.?** est-ce qu'on peut lui faire confiance?; *Fam* **it's completely on the l.** c'est tout à fait légal

3 *Carp (tool)* niveau *m*; *(rule)* latte *f ou* règle *f* de niveau

ADJ 1 *(not sloping)* horizontal, -aux; *(ground)* horizontal, à niveau; *(road, pitch etc) (flat)* plat; *Fig* **to create a l. playing field** créer une situation qui soit juste pour tout le monde *ou* qui ne défavorise personne

2 l. with ... au niveau de ..., à (la) hauteur de ...; **l. with the ground** au ras du sol, à ras de terre; **they are about l. in ability** leurs compétences se valent; **to do one's l. best** faire tout son possible, faire de son mieux; **it's l. pegging** *(between the two)* il y a égalité; **they're l. pegging** ils sont à égalité; **a l. spoonful** une cuillerée rase

3 *(steady) (tone etc)* égal, -aux; **to keep a l. head** garder son sang-froid

ADV à l'horizontale; **hold the tray l.** tenez le plateau à l'horizontale ou bien à plat; *Aviat* **to fly l.** voler en palier; *Sport, Fig* **to draw l. with ...** arriver à la hauteur de ...; *(in rowing)* venir bord à bord avec ...

VT **(-ll-,** *Am* **-l-) 1** *(surface)* niveler, aplanir; *(land etc)* araser; **to l. a town (to the ground)** raser une ville

2 *(aim) (rifle)* pointer; *(canon)* braquer; *(telescope)* diriger (**at** sur); **to l. one's gun at sb** ajuster *ou* viser qn avec son fusil, mettre qn en joue; **to l. criticism at sb** émettre des critiques sur qn; **to l. accusations at sb** lancer des accusations contre qn; **to l. a blow at sb** porter un coup à qn

3 *(in surveying) (region)* effectuer des opérations de nivellement dans, niveler

VI *Fam* **to l. with sb** parler franchement à qn

▸▸ *Br, Can* **l. crossing** passage *m* à niveau; *Aviat* **l. flight** vol *m* horizontal; *Carp* **l. rule** latte *f ou* règle *f* de niveau

▸ **level down** **VT SEP** *esp Pol* niveler par le bas

▸ **level off, level out** **VT SEP** *(ground, surface)* aplanir

VI 1 *(of prices etc)* se stabiliser, plafonner; **demand levels off at this time of year** la demande se stabilise à cette époque de l'année

2 *Aviat* attaquer le palier, voler en palier

▸ **level up** **VT SEP** *esp Pol* accroître le niveau moyen

---

level-headed **ADJ** pondéré

leveller, *Am* **leveler** ['lev(ə)lər] **N** *Pol* égalitaire *mf*; **death is a great l.** tous les hommes sont égaux devant la mort

lever ['liːvər, *Am* 'levər] **N** levier *m*; *Tech* levier, manette *f*

VT **to l. sth open** ouvrir qch avec un levier; **he levered the box open with a piece of wood** il a ouvert la caisse avec un morceau de bois; *Fig* **he has levered himself into a very strong position** il s'est hissé à un poste très important

▸ **lever off** **VT SEP** *(lid, top, tyre)* enlever (avec un levier); *(padlock)* faire sauter

▸ **lever out** **VT SEP** *(object)* extraire; *Fig (person)* évincer; **he has been levered out of his job** on l'a évincé de son emploi

▸ **lever up** **VT SEP** *(lid etc)* soulever (avec un levier); **he levered himself up onto his elbow** il s'est soulevé en s'aidant de son coude

leverage ['liːvərɪdʒ] **N 1** *Tech (power)* force *f ou* puissance *f ou* effet *m* de levier; **to bring l. to bear on sth** *(on door etc)* faire pression sur qch **2** *Fig* influence *f*, *(through manœuvre)* effet *m* de levier; **to exert some l. on sb** exercer de l'influence sur qn; **we have no l. we could bring to bear on him** nous n'avons pas de prise sur lui

VT *Com* tirer profit de

leveraged ['liːvərɪdʒd] **ADJ** *Com* **the company is highly l.** la société est fortement endettée

▸▸ **l. buy-out** rachat *m* d'entreprise financé par l'endettement; **l. management buy-out** rachat d'entreprise par les salariés

lever-arch file **N** classeur *m* à levier

leveret ['levərɪt] **N** levraut *m*

leviathan [lɪ'vaɪəθ(ə)n] **N 1** *Bible* **L.** Léviathan *m* **2** *esp Lit (something huge)* monstre *m*

Levis® ['liːvaɪz] **NPL** Levis® *m*; **a pair of L.** un Levis

levitate ['levɪteɪt] **VI** se soulever (par lévitation)

VT soulever (par lévitation)

levitation [levɪ'teɪʃən] **N** lévitation *f*

levity ['levɪtɪ] **N** légèreté *f*

levy ['levɪ] **N 1** *(tax)* impôt *m*, contribution *f*; **to impose a l. on sugar imports** taxer les importations de sucre; **capital l.** prélèvement *m* sur le capital; **import l.** taxe *f* à l'importation **2** *(action) (of tax, troops)* levée *f*

VT 1 *(tax)* lever, percevoir; *(fine)* infliger; **to l. a duty on goods** imposer des marchandises; **to l. a fine on sb** frapper qn d'une amende **2** *Mil (troops)* lever

levying of taxes ['levɪɪŋ] **N** levée *f* des impôts

lewd [luːd] **ADJ** *(behaviour, gesture, joke)* obscène; *(smile, look)* lubrique

lewdly ['luːdlɪ] **ADV** de façon obscène, lubriquement

lewdness ['luːdnɪs] **N** *(of joke, behaviour, gesture)* obscénité *f*, *(of smile, look)* lubricité *f*

lexical ['leksɪk(ə)l] **ADJ** lexical, -aux

lexicalize ['leksɪkəlaɪz] **VT** lexicaliser

lexicographer [leksɪ'kɒɡrəfər] **N** lexicographe *mf*

lexicographical [leksɪkə'ɡræfɪk(ə)l] **ADJ** lexicographique

lexicography [leksɪ'kɒɡrəfɪ] **N** lexicographie *f*

lexicology [leksɪ'kɒlədʒɪ] **N** lexicologie *f*

lexicon ['leksɪkən] **N** lexique *m*

lexis ['leksɪs] **N** lexique *m*

lez [lez], **lezzy** ['lezɪ] **N** *Sl Pej (lesbian)* gouine *f*

lh [el'eɪtʃ] *Mus etc (abbr* **left hand***)* main gauche

---

liabilities [laɪə'bɪlɪtɪz] **NPL** *Com, Fin* passif *m*; *(in bankruptcy)* masse *f* passive; **assets and l.** actif *m* et passif; **to meet one's l.** faire face à ses engagements

liability [laɪə'bɪlɪtɪ] **N 1** *Law (responsibility)* responsabilité *f*; **employer's l.** *(for accidents at work)* responsabilité patronale; **civil l.** responsabilité civile; **limited l. company** société *f* à responsabilité limitée; **her firm wouldn't accept l. for the accident** son entreprise refusa d'endosser la responsabilité de l'accident

2 *(disadvantage)* désavantage *m*, handicap *m*; **your brother is a l. to us** ton frère ne nous attire que des problèmes

3 *(likelihood)* disposition *f*, tendance *f* (**to sth** à qch; **to do sth** à faire qch); **l. to a fine** risque *m* d'amende; **l. for military service** obligations *fpl* militaires; **l. to explode** *(of product etc)* danger *m* d'explosion

4 *Acct* dette *f*

5 *Com (on bills of exchange)* encours *m*

liable ['laɪəb(ə)l] **ADJ 1** *Law (responsible)* responsable (**for** de); **you are l. for the damage** vous êtes responsable du dommage; **l. party** responsable *mf*

2 *(subject)* assujetti, tenu, astreint (**to** à); **l. to a tax** assujetti à un impôt, redevable d'un impôt; **l. to tax** passible de taxe *ou* d'impôts; **person l. to tax** assujetti *m*; **l. to a fine** passible d'une amende; **l. to customs duty** passible de droits de douane; **l. to military service** astreint au service militaire

3 *(likely)* **to be l. to do sth** *(of person, thing)* risquer de faire qch; **she's l. to make mistakes** elle est susceptible de faire des fautes; **when he gets angry he is l. to do anything** quand il se met en colère, il est capable de tout

liaise [liː'eɪz] **VI** **to l. with sb about sth** *(be in contact with)* être en contact avec qn à propos de qch; *(work together with)* collaborer avec qn; **the two parties have agreed to l. with head office** les deux parties ont accepté de collaborer; **the successful applicant will be required to l. with head office** le candidat retenu sera en contact direct avec le siège

liaison [lɪ'eɪzɒn] **N 1** *(cooperation)* coopération *f* **2** *(love affair)* liaison *f* (amoureuse)

▸▸ *Mil etc* **l. agent** agent *m* de liaison; **l. officer** officier *m* de liaison

liana [lɪ'ɑːnə] **N** *Bot* liane *f*

liar ['laɪər] **N** menteur, -euse; **you l.!** espèce de menteur!

Lib [lɪb] *Pol (abbr* **Liberal***)* libéral

lib [lɪb] **N** *Fam* = **liberation**; = **women's l.** MLF *m*

libation [laɪ'beɪʃən] **N** libation *f*

Lib Dem = **Liberal Democrat**

libel ['laɪb(ə)l] **N** diffamation *f*, *Law* diffamation (par écrit), écrit *m* diffamatoire; **to utter a l. against sb** publier un article *ou* un écrit diffamant qn; **action for l.** procès *m* en diffamation; **to sue sb for l.** poursuivre qn en justice pour diffamation; **that's l.!** c'est une calomnie *ou* de la diffamation!

VT **(-ll-,** *Am* **-l-)** *(person)* calomnier; *Law* diffamer par écrit

▸▸ **l. action, l. case** procès en diffamation; **l. laws** législation *f* en matière de diffamation

libellous, *Am* **libelous** ['laɪbələs] **ADJ** *(document etc)* diffamatoire

liberal ['lɪb(ə)rəl] **ADJ 1** *(idea etc)* libéral, -aux; *(person)* d'esprit large; **a l. education** une éducation libérale

2 *(generous)* libéral, -aux, généreux; **l. with one's money** prodigue *ou* un peu trop large avec son argent

3 *(abundant)* ample; **a l. supply of food** une nourriture abondante; **a l. helping** une portion généreuse

4 *Pol* centriste; **L.** libéral, -aux

N *Pol* centriste *mf*; **L. libéral, -ale**
▸▸ *Br Pol* **L. Democrat** *(party member)* = membre *m* du parti libéral démocrate

liberalism ['lɪb(ə)rəlɪz(ə)m] N libéralisme *m*

liberality [lɪbə'rælɪtɪ] N **1** *(of views)* libéralisme *m* **2** *(with money etc)* libéralité *f*, générosité *f*

liberalize ['lɪb(ə)rəlaɪz] VT libéraliser

liberally ['lɪb(ə)rəlɪ] ADV libéralement, généreusement

liberal-minded ADJ large d'esprit

liberate ['lɪbəreɪt] VT **1** libérer **2** *Chem (gas)* libérer, dégager **3** *Fin* **to l. capital** libérer des capitaux

liberated ['lɪbəreɪtɪd] ADJ *(person)* libéré; *(ideas, views, opinions)* progressiste; **a l. woman** une femme libérée; **these are l. times** on vit à une époque libérée; **her ideas aren't l.** elle n'est pas libérée

liberating ['lɪbəreɪtɪŋ] ADJ libérateur

liberation [lɪbə'reɪʃən] N **1** libération *f*, *Hist* **after the l.** après la Libération; **she doesn't believe in women's l.** elle ne croit pas à la libération de la femme **2** *Chem, Phys (of gas, heat)* dégagement *m* **3** *Fin* **l. of capital** mobilisation *f* de capitaux
▸▸ **l. movement** mouvement *m* de libération

liberator ['lɪbəreɪtər] N libérateur, -trice

Liberia [laɪ'bɪərɪə] N Liberia *m*

Liberian [laɪ'bɪərɪən] ADJ libérien
N Libérien, -ienne

libertarian [lɪbə'teərɪən] N libertaire *mf*
ADJ *(philosophy, idea, tendency etc)* libertaire

libertine ['lɪbətiːn] ADJ, N libertin, -ine

liberty ['lɪbətɪ] N liberté *f*, **l. of conscience** liberté de conscience; **at l.** *(free)* libre; **to be at l. to do sth** être libre de faire qch; **Statue of L.** statue *f* de la Liberté; **to take the l. of doing** *or* **to do sth** se permettre *ou* prendre la liberté de faire qch; *Fam* **what a l.!** quel culot!; **civil liberties** libertés civiques; **to take liberties with sb** prendre *ou* se permettre des libertés avec qn; **the government is taking liberties** le gouvernement se fiche du monde; **to take liberties with a translation** se permettre des libertés dans une traduction; *Fam Pej* **it's l. hall in this house** chacun fait ce qui lui plaît *ou* c'est la pétaudière dans cette maison
▸▸ **l. bodice** chemise *f* américaine; *Naut* **l. ticket** permission *f* de terre *ou* d'aller à terre

libidinous [lɪ'bɪdɪnəs] ADJ libidineux

libido [lɪ'biːdəʊ, -'baɪ-] N *Psy* libido *f*

LIBOR ['laɪbɔːr] N *Br Fin (abbr* **London Inter-Bank Offer Rate)** ≃ TIOP *m*

Libra ['liːbrə] N *Astrol* Balance *f*; **to be (a) L.** être (de la) Balance

librarian [laɪ'breərɪən] N bibliothécaire *mf*

Note that the French word **libraire** is a false friend and is never a translation for the English word **librarian**. It means **bookseller**.

librarianship [laɪ'breərɪənʃɪp] N *(subject)* bibliothéconomie *f*

library ['laɪbrərɪ] N *(of books), Comput (of programs)* bibliothèque *f*; *(of tapes, CDs)* discothèque *f*; *(series of films, videos)* collection *f*; *Br* **mobile l.** bibliobus *m*; **photographic l.** photothèque *f*; **film l.** cinémathèque *f*; **music l.** discothèque; **record l.** discothèque; *Fam* **he's a walking l.** c'est une encyclopédie vivante
▸▸ **l. book** livre *m* de bibliothèque; **l. card** carte *f* de bibliothèque; **l. film** film *m* d'archi-

ves; **l. footage** images *fpl* d'archives; **l. science** bibliothéconomie *f*, **l. steps** *(stepladder)* escabeau *m* de bibliothèque; **l. ticket** carte *f* de bibliothèque

Note that the French word **librairie** is a false friend and is never a translation for the English word **library**. It means **bookshop**.

librettist [lɪ'bretɪst] N *Theat* librettiste *mf*

libretto, *pl* **libretti, librettos** [lɪ'bretəʊ, -iː, -əʊz] N libretto *mpl* librettos, livret *m* *(d'opéra)*

Libya ['lɪbɪə] N Libye *f*

Libyan ['lɪbɪən] ADJ libyen; **the L. Desert** le désert de Libye
N Libyen, -yenne

lice *see* **louse**

licence, *Am* **license** ['laɪsəns] N **1** permis *m*, autorisation *f*, *Com (to manufacture, sell)* licence *f*; **under l. from the inventor** avec l'autorisation de l'inventeur; **l. to sell alcohol** licence des débits de boissons; **made/manufactured under l.** construit/fabriqué sous licence; **dog l.** taxe *f* sur les chiens; *Br* **(driving) l.,** *Am* **driver's l.** permis de conduire; **gun l.** permis de port d'arme(s); **import/export l.** licence d'importation/d'exportation; *Am* **liquor l.** licence des débits de boissons; **manufacturing l.** brevet *m* *ou* licence de fabrication; **marriage l.,** *Br* **special l.** = dispense *f* de bans; *Br* **they were married by special l.** ils se sont mariés avec dispense de bans; *Aviat* **pilot's l.** brevet de pilote; **shooting l.** permis de chasse; *Br* **television l.** *(fee)* redevance *f* télévisuelle; **trading l.** carte *f* de commerce
2 *esp Pej (freedom)* licence *f*
▸▸ *Comput* **l. agreement** licence *f*, *Br* **l. fee** *(for television)* redevance *f* télévisuelle; **l. holder** licencié, -ée *m*; **l. number** *(on vehicle)* numéro *m* d'immatriculation; *(on driving licence)* numéro de permis de conduire; **l. plate** plaque *f* minéralogique *ou* d'immatriculation

Note that the French noun **licence** also means **bachelor's degree**.

license ['laɪsəns] VT **to l. sth to sb** accorder une licence à qn pour qch; **to l. sb to sell drink/practise medicine** autoriser qn à tenir un débit de boissons/exercer la médecine; *Com* **to l. sb to manufacture/sell** accorder une licence à qn pour fabriquer/vendre; **to l. a car** *(of owner)* acheter une vignette pour une voiture; **licensed to sell beer, wines and spirits** autorisé à vendre de l'alcool, *Can* licencié à vendre des boissons alcoolisées; **to be licensed to carry a gun** avoir un permis de port d'arme(s)
N *Am* = **licence**

licensed ['laɪsənst] ADJ *(produit)* sous licence; *Admin* autorisé, patenté; *Aviat (pilot)* breveté
▸▸ **l. brand name** nom *m* de marque sous licence; **l. hotel** hôtel *m* ayant la licence des débits de boissons; **l. house, l. premises** débit *m* de boissons; **l. restaurant** restaurant *m* ayant la licence des débits de boissons; *Fml* **l. victualler** débitant *m* de boissons

licensee [laɪs(ə)n'siː] N concessionnaire *mf*, détenteur, -trice d'une patente *ou* d'un permis; *(for manufacturing)* détenteur d'une licence; *(of pub etc)* gérant, -ante, propriétaire *mf*

licensing ['laɪsənsɪŋ] N
▸▸ **l. agreement** accord *m* de licence; **l. hours** *(in UK)* = heures *fpl* d'ouverture des pubs; **l. laws** *(in UK)* = lois *fpl* réglementant la vente d'alcools

licensor N concédant *m*

licentiate [laɪ'senʃɪət] N *Univ* diplômé, -ée

licentious [laɪ'senʃəs] ADJ licencieux

licentiousness [laɪ'senʃəsnɪs] N licence *f*

lichen ['laɪkən, 'lɪtʃən] N lichen *m*

lichgate ['lɪtʃgeɪt] N = porche *m* d'entrée de cimetière surmonté d'un petit toit

licit ['lɪsɪt] ADJ licite

licitly ['lɪsɪtlɪ] ADV licitement

lick [lɪk] N **1** coup *m* de langue; **to give sth/sb a l.** lécher qch/qn; **give me a l. of your ice cream** laisse-moi goûter ta glace; *Old-fashioned Fam* **a l. and a promise** *(wash)* un brin de toilette
2 *Fam (small amount)* **a l. of paint** un petit coup de peinture; **a few licks of paint** deux ou trois coups de pinceau; **l. (of hair)** mèche *f*
3 *Fam (speed)* **at (a) great l., at full l.** à toute allure, à toute vitesse
4 **salt l.** *(provided for cattle)* pain *m* de sel; *(place)* terrain *m* salifère *(où les bêtes viennent lécher le sol)*
VT **1** lécher; *Fig* **to l. one's lips** *or Fam* **one's chops** se lécher *ou* se pourlécher les babines; *Fig* **to l. one's wounds** panser ses blessures; *Fam* **to l. sb's boots** lécher les bottes à qn; *Vulg* **to l. sb's arse** lécher le cul de qn; *Fam* **to l. sb into shape** dresser qn; **to l. sth up** *(of animal)* laper qch; *Fig Fam* **to l. the plate clean** ne pas laisser une miette dans son assiette
2 *Fam (defeat) (opponent)* mettre une raclée à; *(beat physically) (person)* battre, rosser; **he's got them licked** *(is certain to beat)* il va les écraser; **when it comes to marketing, they've got us licked** pour ce qui est du marketing, on ne leur arrive pas à la cheville; **I've got the problem licked** j'ai surmonté le problème; **this one has got me licked** *(of problem)* ça me dépasse

lickety-split ['lɪkɪtɪ'splɪt] ADV *Am Fam* à toute vitesse, *Fam* à toute berzingue

licking ['lɪkɪŋ] N *Fam (of opponent)* raclée *f*, *(physical beating)* raclée *f*, rossée *f*; **they gave the other team a l.** ils ont mis une raclée à l'autre équipe

lickspittle ['lɪkspɪt(ə)l] N *Old-fashioned* lèche-bottes *m inv*

licorice ['lɪkərɪs] N *Am* = **liquorice**

lid [lɪd] N **1** *(of box, pan etc)* couvercle *m*; *Br Fig* **that puts the (tin) l. on it!** ça c'est le comble!; **this put the l. on her hopes of winning** cela a anéanti ses espoirs de gagner; **to take the l. off sth** ôter le couvercle de qch; *Fig* mettre qch au grand jour; *Fam* **to keep the l. on a piece of information** garder une information pour soi **2** *(eyelid)* paupière *f*

lidded ['lɪdɪd] ADJ *(box etc)* à couvercle

lidless ['lɪdlɪs] ADJ *(eyes)* sans paupières

lido ['li:dəʊ] N *Br (swimming pool)* piscine *f* en plein air

lie[1] [laɪ] N *(untruth)* mensonge *m*; **it's all lies** *or* **a pack of lies!** c'est un tissu de mensonges!; **to tell a l.** dire un mensonge; *Fam* **in 2001, no, I tell a l., it was 2002** en 2001, non, je dis une bêtise, c'était en 2002; *Prov* **there are lies, damned lies and statistics** on fait dire ce que l'on veut aux chiffres; **to give the l. to sb** donner tort à qn; **to give the l. to an argument** démentir un argument

VI *(pt, pp* lied [laɪd], *prp* lying ['laɪɪŋ]) *(tell untruth)* mentir (**to sb** à qn); **to l. about one's age** mentir sur son âge; **to l. through one's teeth** mentir effrontément

VT **she lied her way into the building** elle a pénétré dans l'immeuble grâce à quelques mensonges; **he always lies his way out of difficulties** il se sort toujours des difficultés en mentant

▸▸ **l. detector** détecteur *m* de mensonges; **to take a l. detector test** passer au détecteur de mensonges

LIE[2] N **1** *(of land)* disposition *f*, **l. of the land** configuration *f ou* disposition du terrain, topographie *f*; *Fig* **to find out the l. of the land** tâter le terrain

2 *Golf (of ball)* position *f*, assiette *f*

VI *(pt* lay [leɪ], *pp* lain [leɪn], *prp* lying ['laɪɪŋ]) **1** *(of person, animal) (be in lying position)* être couché (à plat); *(go into lying position)* s'allonger; **he was lying down on the floor** il était allongé *ou* couché par terre; **to l. on one's back/side** être couché sur le dos/côté; **to be lying ill in bed** être (malade et) alité; **we found him lying dead** nous l'avons trouvé mort; **here lies ...** *(on gravestone)* ci-gît ...; **to l. in bed** rester au lit; **I lay awake all night** je n'ai pas pu dormir de la nuit; **I lay awake until 5.30** je suis resté sans pouvoir dormir jusqu'à 5h30; **to l. hidden** rester caché; **to l. in wait for sb** guetter l'arrivée de qn; **the gamekeeper lay in wait all night for the poacher** le garde-chasse est resté tapi toute la nuit à attendre le braconnier

2 *(of object)* être, se trouver; **the papers lay on the table** les papiers étaient sur la table; **all her clothes were lying on the floor** tous ses vêtements étaient étalés par terre; **town lying in a valley** ville située dans une vallée; **a vast plain lay before us** une vaste plaine s'étendait devant nous; **our way lies through the woods** notre chemin passe par les bois; **to l. in ruins** *(of building)* être en ruines; *(of career etc)* être détruit; **the obstacles that l. in our way** les obstacles qui bloquent notre chemin; **these hills l. between us and the sea** ces collines sont entre nous et la mer; *Naut* **ship lying at her berth** navire mouillé *ou* amarré à son poste; **the money is just lying in the bank doing nothing** l'argent dort à la banque; **the snow did not l.** la neige n'a pas tenu; **to l. dormant** *(of volcano)* être en sommeil *ou* au repos; **to l. (heavy) on one's stomach** *(of food)* peser sur l'estomac

3 *(of abstract thing)* **sins that l. heavy on the conscience** péchés qui pèsent sur la conscience; **the onus of proof lies with them** c'est à eux qu'incombe la charge de la preuve; **the responsibility lies with the author** la responsabilité incombe à l'auteur; **to know where one's interests lie** savoir où se trouvent ses intérêts; **the difference lies in this, that ...** la différence réside dans le fait que ...; **the fault lies with you** c'est de votre faute; **a brilliant future lies before her** un brillant avenir s'ouvre devant elle; **what lies behind this uncharacteristic generosity?** qu'y a-t-il derrière cette générosité inhabituelle?; **my talents do not l. in that direction**

je n'ai pas de dispositions *ou* de talent pour cela

4 *Law (of action, appeal)* être recevable

> Attention: ne pas confondre avec le verbe **to lay**, qui signifie **poser à plat**.

▸ **lie about** VI *(of thing, person)* traîner; **to leave one's papers lying about** laisser traîner ses papiers

▸ **lie back** VI se coucher sur le dos; *(in armchair)* se renverser; **just l. back and relax** *(literally)* allongez-vous et détendez-vous; **when you've finished you can l. back and take things easy** quand tu auras fini tu pourras te reposer

▸ **lie down** VI se coucher, s'étendre; **go and l. down** va t'allonger; **to l. down on one's bed** s'allonger sur son lit; **to l. down on the ground** se coucher *ou* s'allonger par terre; **l. down!** *(to dog)* couché!; *Fig* **to take an insult lying down** ne pas relever une insulte; *Fig* **he won't take it lying down** il ne se laissera pas faire

▸ **lie in** VI faire la grasse matinée

▸ **lie off** VI *(of ship)* rester au large

▸ **lie over** VI *(of thing)* être remis à plus tard; **to let a bill l. over** différer l'échéance d'un effet

▸ **lie to** VI *(of ship)* être à la cape, tenir la cape

▸ **lie up** VI **1** *(because of illness)* garder le lit, garder la chambre; *(hide)* se cacher **2** *(of car)* être en panne; *(of ship)* désarmer

Liechtenstein ['lɪktənstaɪn] N le Liechtenstein

lie-down N **to have a l.** faire une sieste *ou* un petit somme

lief [li:f] ADV *Arch* **I would as l. ...** j'aimerais autant ...

liege [li:dʒ] N *Hist* suzerain *m*; **my l.!** sire!

lie-in N **to have a l.** faire la grasse matinée

lien [li:(ə)n] N *Law (on property)* privilège *m*, droit *m* de rétention; **to have a l. on a cargo** avoir un recours sur un chargement; *Fin* **l. on shares** nantissement *m* d'actions

lieu [ljuː, luː] N *Fml* **in l. of ...** au lieu de ...; **to stand in l. of ...** tenir lieu de ...; **I'll take something else in l.** je prendrai quelque chose d'autre à la place; **two weeks salary in l. of notice** deux semaines de salaire en guise de préavis; **time off in l.** repos *m* compensateur

Lieut *Mil (abbr* **Lieutenant)** Lieut, Lt.

Lieut-Col *Mil (abbr* **Lieutenant-Colonel)** Lieut.-Col.

lieutenant [lef'tenənt, *esp Am* luː'tenənt] N *Mil, Fig* lieutenant *m*; *Naut* lieutenant de vaisseau

▸▸ **l. colonel** lieutenant-colonel *m*, *pl* lieutenants-colonels; **l. commander** capitaine *m* de corvette; **l. general** *(in army)* général *m* de corps d'armée; *(in US airforce)* général de corps aérien; **l. governor** *(in Canada)* lieutenant, -ante gouverneur(e); *(in US)* gouverneur, -eure adjoint(e)

LIFE, *pl* lives [laɪf, laɪvz] N **1** *(existence)* vie *f*, **to take sb's l.** tuer qn; **to take one's own l.** se suicider; **to give l. to sb** donner la vie à qn; **to come to l. again** revenir à la vie; **it is a matter of l. and death** c'est une question de vie ou de mort; **to be hovering between l. and death** être entre la vie et la mort; **to believe in l. after death** croire à la vie après la mort; **to risk one's l., to risk l. and limb** risquer sa peau; **to escape with one's l.** avoir la vie sauve; **to lose one's l.** perdre la vie, périr; **no lives were lost** il n'y a eu aucune victime, on ne déplore aucune victime; **100 lives were lost** il y a eu 100 morts; **run for your lives!** sauve qui peut!; **a cat has nine lives** un chat a neuf vies; *Fam* **get a l.!** t'as rien de

mieux à faire de ton temps?; *Br Fam* **my l.!** c'est pas vrai!; *Fam* **not on your l.!** jamais de la vie!; **he was rowing for dear l.** il ramait de toutes ses forces; **she can't sing to save her l.** elle est totalement incapable de chanter; *Fam* **I couldn't for the l. of me think what he wanted** je ne pouvais absolument pas imaginer ce qu'il voulait; *Art* **to draw from l.** dessiner d'après nature; **characters taken from l.** caractères pris sur le vif; **that's her to the l.** *(in that portrait, play etc)* c'est elle toute crachée; **animal/vegetable l.** la vie animale/végétale; **bird l.** la vie des oiseaux

2 *(period of existence) (of person)* vie *f*, **a l. of Tolstoy** une biographie de Tolstoï; **(useful) l.** *(of machine)* vie *ou* durée futile; **to work all one's l.** travailler durant toute sa vie; **never in (all) my l.** jamais de la vie; **in his early l.** quand il était jeune; **to be given a l. sentence,** *Fam* **to get l.** être condamné à vie; **appointed for l.** nommé à vie; *Fam* **to be in for l.** *(in prison)* en avoir pris pour la vie; **to mate for l.** *(of animal, bird)* s'unir pour la vie; *Nucl* **average** *or* **mean l.** *(of atom, isotope)* vie moyenne

3 *(mode of existence)* vie *f*, *Fam* **to live** *or* **lead the l. of Riley** se la couler douce; **to make a new l. for oneself** refaire sa vie; **to depart this l.** quitter ce monde; **the man/woman in one's l.** l'homme/la femme de sa vie; **way of l.** manière *f* de vivre, (train *m* de) vie; **the American way of l.** le style de vie américain; **dieting has become a way of l. with some people** certaines personnes passent leur vie à faire des régimes; **to see l.** se frotter à la vie, partir à l'aventure; **he has seen l.** il sait ce que c'est que la vie; **you really see l. as a cop** quand on est flic, on en voit de toutes les couleurs; **he makes her l. a misery** il lui rend la vie impossible; **to make l. worth living** donner un sens à l'existence; **l. is worth living when I'm with her** avec elle la vie vaut la peine d'être vécu; *Fam* **how's l.?** comment ça va?; **what a l.!** quelle vie!; **such is** *or* **that's l.!** c'est la vie!; **this is the l.!** voilà ce que j'appelle vivre!; **the good l.** la belle vie; **he led** *or* **lived a good l.** il a eu une vie exemplaire

4 *(liveliness)* **to come to l.** *(of person, place, play etc)* s'animer; **to bring a party to l.** *(of person)* animer une fête; **to bring sb to l.** *(of play, book etc)* faire vivre qn; **full of l.** *(person)* plein de vie *ou* d'entrain; *(street etc)* plein de mouvement *ou* d'animation; **to put new l. into** *(person, company etc)* ranimer; **the l. and soul of the party** le boute-en-train de la soirée; **there's no l. in this place** ça manque d'entrain ici; **he may be 80 but there's l. in the old dog yet** il a peut-être 80 ans mais il est encore vif; **the critics say I'm finished but there's l. in the old dog yet** les critiques disent que je suis fini mais je n'ai pas dit mon dernier mot; **there's l. in the old car yet** elle marche toujours, la vieille bagnole

▸▸ **l. annuity** pension *f* viagère; *Br* **l. assurance** assurance-vie *f*, *pl* assurances-vie; **l. belt** bouée *f* de sauvetage; **l. buoy** bouée de sauvetage; *Fin* **l. capitalization** capitalisation *f* viagère; **l. class** cours *m* de dessin avec modèle nu; **l. cycle** cycle *m* de vie; **l. expectancy** *(of human, animal)* espérance *f* de vie; *(of machine, product)* durée *f* (utile) de vie; **l. force** élan *m* vital; **l. form** forme *f* de vie; **the L. Guards** = régiment *m* de cavalerie de la garde royale britannique; **l. imprisonment** prison *f* à vie; **l. insurance** assurance-vie *f*, **l. interest** usufruit *m*; *(of possession)* viager *m*; **l. jacket** gilet *m* de sauvetage; **l. member** membre *m* à vie; **l. membership** adhésion *f* à vie; *Br* **l. peer** pair *m* à vie; **l. pension** rente *f* viagère; *Am* **l. preserver** *(life belt)* bouée de sauvetage; *(life jacket)* gilet de sauvetage; **l. raft** radeau *m* de sauvetage; **the l. sciences** les sciences *fpl* de la vie; **l. span** *(of human, animal)* espérance *f* de la vie; *(of machine, product)* durée de vie; **l. story** biographie *f*, **l. subscription** abonnement *m* à vie

---

life-and-death ADJ **a l. situation** une question de vie ou de mort; **a l. struggle** une lutte désespérée; *(literally)* une guerre à mort

lifeblood ['laɪfblʌd] N *(of company etc)* âme *f*, *Lit (of person)* sang *m*; **the government are draining the l. from small businesses** le gouvernement est en train de saigner les petites entreprises; **the l. of the economy** le pivot de l'économie

lifeboat ['laɪfbəʊt] N **1** *(launched from coast)* canot *m* de sauvetage **2 (ship's) l.** embarcation *f* de sauvetage
▸▸ **l. station** poste *m* de sauvetage

lifeboatman, *pl* **lifeboatmen** ['laɪfbəʊtmən] N sauveteur *m*

life-cycle chart N *Mktg (of product)* courbe *f* du cycle de vie

life-giving ADJ vivifiant; *(sun, water)* nourricier

lifeguard ['laɪfgɑːd] N *(at the seaside)* surveillant, -ante de baignade; *(at swimming pool)* maître *m* nageur; **to be on l. duty** surveiller la baignade

lifeless ['laɪflɪs] ADJ sans vie; *(style, gestures, acting etc)* mou, *f* molle; *(expression)* vide; *(performance)* mort; **she fell l. to the floor** elle est tombée raide sur le sol

lifelessly ['laɪflɪslɪ] ADV sans vie

lifelessness ['laɪflɪsnɪs] N *(of party etc)* manque *m* d'animation; *(of gestures)* mollesse *f*, *(of paintings)* froideur *f*

lifelike ['laɪflaɪk] ADJ *(portrait etc)* vivant, qui a de la vie; **it's very l.** c'est très réaliste

lifeline ['laɪflaɪn] N **1** *Naut* ligne *f* de sauvetage; *(aboard ship)* garde-corps *m inv*; attrape *f*, sauvegarde *f*; *(of diver)* corde *f* de communication; *Fig* **to throw sb a l.** venir à l'aide de qn; *Fig* **for us it was a financial l.** cet argent a permis notre survie **2** *(in palmistry)* ligne *f* de vie

lifelong ['laɪflɒŋ] ADJ ATTRIB *(friendship etc)* de toute la vie; **a l. friend** un ami de toujours; **a l. ambition** une ambition de toujours
▸▸ **l. learning** éducation *f* permanente

lifer ['laɪfər] N *Fam* condamné, -ée à perpétuité

life-saver N **1** *(person)* sauveteur *m* **2** *Fig* planche *f* de salut; **that cup of tea was a l.!** cette tasse de thé m'a redonné vie; **you're a l.** tu me sauves la vie!

life-saving N **l. apparatus** appareils *mpl ou* engins *mpl* de sauvetage; **l. vaccine** vaccin *m* qui sauve la vie

life-size(d) ADJ *(portrait etc)* grandeur nature

lifestyle ['laɪfstaɪl] N style *m* de vie, mode *m* de vie
▸▸ *Mktg* **l. analysis** analyse *f* du style de vie; *Mktg* **l. data** données *fpl* de style de vie; *Mktg* **l. group** sociostyle *m*; *Mktg* **l. segmentation** segmentation *f* par styles de vie

life-support ADJ
▸▸ *Med* **l. machine** respirateur *m*; **l. system** *Med* respirateur *m*; *Astron* équipement *m* de survie; *Med* **to be on a l. system** *or* **machine** être sous assistance respiratoire; *Med* **to switch off the l. system** *or* **machine** arrêter le respirateur *ou* la respiration artificielle

life-threatening ADJ *(disease)* qui peut être mortel; **it's not l.** ce n'est pas mortel; **in a l. situation, the fish ...** quand il se sent en danger de mort, le poisson ...

lifetime ['laɪftaɪm] N *(of person)* vie *f*, *(of lamp, machine)*, *Fin (of option)* durée *f*, vie;

Nucl (of atom, isotope) durée de vie, longévité *f*, *St Exch (of an option)* durée de vie; **in** *or* **during one's l.** de son vivant; **such a bill is unlikely within the l. of this parliament** un tel projet de loi est peu probable tant que ce parlement est en place; **a l. of happiness** toute une vie de bonheur; **it's the chance** *or* **opportunity of a l.** cette chance n'arrive qu'une fois dans la vie; **the holiday of a l.** des vacances sensationnelles; **a l. supply** une réserve pour la vie; **he's bought enough envelopes to last him a l.** il a acheté suffisamment d'enveloppes pour tenir jusqu'à la fin de ses jours

LIFFE [laɪf, 'lɪfɪ] N *(abbr* **London International Financial Futures Exchange)** = marché *m* à terme d'instruments financiers, MATIF *m*

LIFO ['liːfəʊ] *Com (abbr* **last in, first out)** DEPS

lift [lɪft] N **1** *(raising device) Br* ascenseur *m*; *Br* **(goods) l.** monte-charge *m inv*, élévateur *m*; **ski l.** remontée *f* mécanique

2 *esp Br (car ride)* **to give sb a l.** prendre *ou* emmener qn en voiture; **could you give me a l. to the station?** *(it's on your way)* est-ce que tu peux me déposer à la gare?; *(make special trip)* est-ce que tu peux m'emmener à la gare?; **can I give you a l.?** est-ce que je peux vous conduire *ou* déposer quelque part?; **I'll try to arrange a l. for anyone who hasn't got a car** je ferai en sorte que tout le monde ait une place dans une voiture; **we've been waiting over two hours for a l.** cela fait deux heures que nous attendons que quelqu'un veuille bien nous prendre; **we got a great l. yesterday, all the way to Lyons** on a eu de la chance hier, il y a quelqu'un qui nous a emmenés jusqu'à Lyon

3 *Fam* **to give sb a l.** *(cheer up)* remonter le moral à qn

4 *(extent of rise) (of crane etc)* hauteur *f* de levage; *(of pump)* hauteur d'élévation; *Tech (of valve, cam)* levée *f*, *(of millrace)* (hauteur de) chute *f*, *(between bearings etc)* différence *f* de niveau

5 *(raising power) (of balloon, gas)* force *f* ascensionnelle; *Aviat* portance *f*, poussée *f* (aérodynamique), sustentation *f*

VT **1** *(weight)* lever, soulever; *(one's head)* lever, dresser; *(one's eyes, arm)* lever; **to l. weights** *(as exercise)* faire des haltères; **he never lifts a finger to help** il ne lève *ou* bouge jamais le petit doigt pour aider; **she has only to l. a finger and everyone comes running** elle n'a qu'à lever le petit doigt et tout le monde accourt; **to l. sth (up) again** soulever qch, relever qch; **to l. sb (up)** *(who has fallen)* aider qn à se relever; **to l. a child up** *(take in one's arms)* prendre un enfant dans ses bras; *Lit* **to l. (up) one's voice in prayer** adresser une prière au ciel; **to l. sth down** *(from a shelf etc)* descendre qch; **the wind lifted him off his feet** il a été soulevé par le vent

2 *(potatoes, bulbs etc)* arracher; *Com (goods)* enlever

3 *Cr, Golf (ball)* donner de l'essor à; *Tennis (shot)* lifter

4 *Fam (take, steal)* voler, *Fam* piquer; **he had his wallet lifted** il s'est fait piquer son portefeuille; **to l. a passage from an author/a book** piquer un passage chez un auteur/dans un livre

5 *Br Fam (arrest)* agrafer, alpaguer

6 *(remove) (embargo)* lever; *(mortgage)* déshypothéquer

VI **1** *(of valve etc)* se lever, se soulever; *(of floor) (as a result of damp etc)* se soulever **2** *(disperse) (of fog)* se lever, se dissiper; *Am (of rain)* cesser **3** *Naut (of vessel)* s'élever à la lame
▸▸ *Br* **l. attendant** liftier *m*; *Ski* **l. pass** forfait

m de remontées mécaniques; *Br* **l. shaft** cage *f* d'ascenseur
▸ **lift off** VI *(of aircraft, rocket)* décoller
  VT SEP *(lid etc)* soulever
▸ **lift out** VT SEP *(from box etc)* sortir (**from** de); *Mil (troops)* évacuer (par avion *ou* hélicoptère)
▸ **lift up** VT SEP = **lift** VT

liftboy ['lɪftbɔɪ] N *Br* liftier *m*

liftgate ['lɪftgeɪt] N *Am Aut* hayon *m* arrière

lifting ['lɪftɪŋ] N **1** *(of potatoes, bulbs)* arrachage *m* **2** *(of embargo)* levée *f*, *(of mortgage, ban)* mainlevée *f*
▸▸ **l. capacity** puissance *f* de levage; *Aviat* **l. force** force *f* de sustentation, puissance ascensionnelle; *Aut* **l. platform** pont *m* élévateur; *Aviat* **l. power** force de sustentation, puissance ascensionnelle; *Aut* **l. ramp** pont élévateur

liftoff ['lɪftɒf] N *(of rocket)* décollage *m*; **we have l.** lancement réussi

lift-operator N *Br* liftier *m*

ligament ['lɪgəmənt] N *Anat* ligament *m*; **to tear a l.** se déchirer un ligament

ligature ['lɪgətʃər] N **1** *Surg* ligature *f* **2** *Typ* ligature **3** *Mus* liaison *f*
  VT **1** *Surg (vein)* ligaturer, barrer **2** *Typ (two vowels)* ligaturer; **o e ligatured** e dans l'o

---

LIGHT¹ [laɪt]

N	lumière **1, 3, 7** ▪ jour **1** ▪ feu **3, 5**
	▪ phare **4** ▪ fenêtre **6**
VT	allumer **1** ▪ éclairer **2**
ADJ	clair **1, 2**

N **1** lumière *f*, **artificial/electric l.** lumière artificielle/électrique; **by the l. of the moon** au clair *ou* à la clarté de la lune; **the l. of day** la lumière du jour, le jour; **things will look different in the cold l. of day** demain tu verras les choses sous un autre aspect; **it's getting l.** le jour se lève; **to bring sth to l.** *(of investigations)* mettre qch en évidence, révéler qch; **to come to l.** *(of crime etc)* être découvert; **to see the l.** *(realise the truth)* être convaincu *ou* converti; **to (first) see the l. of day** *(of person)* naître, voir le jour; **to be in sb's l.** faire de l'ombre à qn; *Phys* **infrared/ultraviolet l.** lumière infrarouge/ultraviolette; **source of l.** source *f* lumineuse; **against the l., with one's back to the l.** à contre-jour; **good/bad l.** bon/mauvais éclairage *m*; **to act according to one's lights** agir conformément à ses idées

2 *(figurative senses)* **in a bad l.** sous un mauvais angle; **in a positive/favourable l.** sous un angle positif/favorable; **in a poor l. he could pass for 40** dans la pénombre on pourrait penser qu'il a 40 ans; **in a good l. he could pass for 40** avec un bon éclairage on pourrait penser qu'il a 40 ans; **to throw** *or* **shed** *or* **cast l. on sth** faire la lumière sur qch, éclaircir qch; **to see sb/sth in a new l./ in their/its true l.** voir qn/qch sous un jour nouveau/sous son vrai jour; **to see sth in a different l.** voir qch sous un jour différent *ou* sous un autre angle; **the question should be considered in the l. of these facts** on devrait considérer la question à la lumière de ces faits; **in the l. of ...** *(considering)* prenant en considération *ou* en compte ...

3 *(object) (in room etc)* lumière *f*, *(on car, train, ship etc)* feu *m*; *Cin, TV* projecteur *m*; **lights out** l'extinction *f* des feux; **to put** *or* **turn on the l.** allumer; **to put** *or* **turn off the l.** éteindre (la lumière); *Fam* **to go out like a l.** *(fall asleep quickly)* s'endormir aussitôt couché; *(faint, become unconscious)* s'évanouir; *Fam Hum* **the lights are on but there's nobody home** c'est pas une lumière; **(traffic) lights** feux *mpl* de circulation *ou* de signalisation routière, *Fam* feu rouge; **turn**

right at the **(traffic) lights** tournez à droite au feu rouge; *Aut* **dip your lights** roulez en code; **she was showing no lights** *(of ship)* il naviguait *ou* faisait route tous feux éteints; *Tech* **control** or **warning l.** voyant *m* lumineux

4 *(lighthouse)* phare *m*

5 *(flame)* feu *m*; **to set l. to sth** mettre le feu à qch; **could I have a l.?** est-ce que tu peux me donner du feu?; **have you got a l.?** vous avez du feu, s'il vous plaît?

6 *Archit (window)* fenêtre *f, (small round)* lucarne *f, (of mullioned window)* jour *m; (of greenhouse)* carreau *m*

7 *Art, Phot* lumière *f*, clair *m*; **l. and shade** les ombres et la lumière

VT *(pt, pp* lit [lɪt], *occ* lighted**) 1** *(lamp, fire etc)* allumer; **to l. a fire** allumer un feu; *Fig* **to l. sb's fire** exciter qn

2 *(room, street)* éclairer, illuminer; **to l. the way for sb** éclairer qn

ADJ 1 *(room etc)* clair, (bien) éclairé; **it is/ will soon be l.** il fait/fera bientôt jour

2 *(hair, complexion)* blond; *(colour)* clair; **painted in l. tones** peint en tons clairs *ou* lumineux; **l. blue** bleu clair *inv*

▸▸ **l. beam** faisceau *m* lumineux; **l. box** table *f* lumineuse; **l. bulb** ampoule *f* (électrique); *TV* **l. cue** signal *m* lumineux; **l. effects** effets *mpl ou* jeux *mpl* de lumière; **l. flare** fusée *f* éclairante; **l. meter** posemètre *m*; *Comput* **l. pen** crayon *m* optique; **l. ray** rayon *m* lumineux; **l. source** source *f* lumineuse; **l. switch** interrupteur *m*; **l. table** *(for viewing negatives, film)* table *f* lumineuse; **l. wave** onde *f* lumineuse; *Astron* **l. year** année-lumière *f, pl* années-lumière; *Fig* **they are l. years ahead** ils ont des années-lumière d'avance

▸ **light into** *VT INSEP Fam (attack verbally or physically)* tomber dessus, rentrer dedans; **she really lit into him** elle lui est carrément tombée dessus *ou* rentrée dedans

▸ **light on** *VI INSEP (find) (solution, correct method, cure etc)* trouver; **his eyes lighted on the picture** ses yeux se posèrent sur le tableau

▸ **light out** *VI Am Fam* décamper

▸ **light up** *VI (put lights on)* allumer, mettre la lumière; *Fam (of smoker)* allumer sa cigarette/sa pipe/etc; **his eyes lit up** ses yeux se sont animés; **the whole sky lit up** le ciel entier s'illumina

VT SEP 1 *(room)* éclairer; *(cigarette, pipe)* allumer; **the house was lit up** la maison était illuminée; **a smile lit up her face** un sourire a illuminé son visage

2 *Br Sl* **to be lit up** *(drunk)* être éméché

LIGHT² **ADJ 1** *(load, blow etc)* léger; *(soil)* meuble; *(deficient) (weight)* faible; **with a l. step** d'un pas léger; *(of painter, author, film director)* finesse *f*; **she's got a very l. touch with pastry** les pâtisseries qu'elle fait sont très légères; **to be l. on one's feet** avoir le pas léger; **as l. as a feather** léger comme une plume; **to have a l. meal** prendre un repas léger; **to be a l. sleeper** avoir le sommeil léger; **l. showers** ondées *fpl*

2 *(not of full weight, size etc) (aircraft, engine)* léger; *(not fully loaded) (ship)* lège; *Typ (type)* maigre; **l. crop** faible récolte *f*

3 *(not strenuous) (job)* facile; **a little l. housework** un petit peu de ménage mais sans vous forcer; **l. punishment** peine *f* légère; **l. work** petits travaux *mpl*, travail peu fatigant

4 *(not serious) (comedy, style, music etc)* léger; **to make l. of sth** traiter qch à la légère; *(of accusation)* attacher peu d'importance à qch; **l. talk** propos *mpl* frivoles *ou* légers

ADV légèrement; **to travel l.** voyager léger

▸▸ **l. aircraft** avion *m* de tourisme; **l. artillery** artillerie *f* légère *ou* de petit calibre; **l.**

beer bière *f* légère; **l. breeze** petite brise *f*, brise légère; *(on Beaufort scale)* légère brise; *Metal* **l. castings** petites pièces *fpl* de fonderie; *Mil* **l. duty** service *m* réduit; **l. entertainment** variétés *fpl*; **it's not exactly l. entertainment** *(of job)* ce n'est pas ce qu'on fait de plus divertissant; *(of music, play etc)* ce n'est pas ce qu'il y a de plus léger; **l. infantry** infanterie *f* légère; **l. reading** lecture(s) *f(pl)* récréative(s) *ou* délassante(s); *Mktg* **l. user** faible utilisateur, -trice; **l. van** fourgonnette *f*; **l. verse** poésie *f* facile

light-coloured, *Am* **light-colored ADJ** clair

light-emitting diode [laɪtɪmɪtɪŋ] **N** diode *f* électroluminescente

lighten¹ [ˈlaɪt(ə)n] **VT 1** *(light up) (darkness, face)* éclairer; *(house etc)* rendre plus clair **2** *(colour, sky)* éclaircir

VI s'éclairer, s'illuminer; **her face lightened** son visage s'éclaira

lighten² **VT** *(reduce weight of)* alléger; *(ship)* délester; *Fig* **to l. sb's load** *(make work or life easier)* décharger qn

VI **my heart lightened** j'ai été soulagé

▸ **lighten up** *VI esp Am Fam* se dérider; **come on, l. up!** tu ne peux pas parler de choses moins sérieuses?

lighter¹ [ˈlaɪtər] **N** allume-gaz *m inv, (for cigarettes)* briquet *m; (in car)* allume-cigare *m, pl* allume-cigares

▸▸ **l. flint** pierre *f* à briquet; **l. fluid, l. fuel** essence *f* à briquet

lighter² **N** *Naut* allège *f*, gabare *f*

lighterage [ˈlaɪtərɪdʒ] **N** *Naut (unloading)* déchargement *m* par allèges *ou* par gabares, gabarage *m; (fee)* droits *mpl ou* frais *mpl* d'allège *ou* de gabarage

lighter-than-air **ADJ** *(aircraft)* plus léger que l'air

light-face *Typ* **N** *(caractère m)* maigre *m*

ADJ maigre

light-fingered [laɪtˈfɪŋɡəd] **ADJ** *Fam* **he's l.** c'est un voleur; *Fam* il a la main leste

light-footed **ADJ** agile, leste, au pied léger

light-headed **ADJ 1** *(dizzy)* **to feel l.** *(through lack of food etc)* se sentir un peu étourdi **2** *(frivolous)* écervelé; *(excited)* excité; **the realization that she had won made her feel quite l.** elle était tout excitée de réaliser qu'elle avait gagné

light-hearted [ˈlaɪthɑːtɪd] **ADJ** *(person)* allègre; *(remark, discussion)* léger

lighthouse [ˈlaɪthaʊs] **N** phare *m*

▸▸ **l. keeper** gardien *m* de phare

lighting [ˈlaɪtɪŋ] **N 1** *(of stage set etc)* éclairage *m; (lights themselves)* lumières *fpl* **2** *(of painting)* éclairage *m*, exposition *f*

▸▸ **l. angle** angle *m* d'éclairage; **l. board** pupitre *m* d'éclairage; *Theat, Cin* **l. cameraman** directeur, -trice de la photographie, chef opérateur *m* cadreur; **l. effects** effets *mpl* d'éclairage *ou* de lumière; **l. engineer** éclairagiste *m; Fam* **l. conductor**, *Am* **l. rod** éclairo *m; Br Admin* **l. up time** heure *f* d'éclairage

lightly [ˈlaɪtlɪ] **ADV 1** légèrement; *(to walk)* d'un pas léger; **to sleep l.** *(generally)* avoir le sommeil léger; *(on one occasion)* dormir d'un sommeil léger; **to cook sth l.** faire cuire qch légèrement; **her responsibilities sit l. on her** ses responsabilités ne lui pèsent pas; **to get off l.** s'en tirer à bon compte **2** *(to say)* d'un ton léger; **to speak l. of sth** parler de qch à la légère; **to take a decision l.** prendre une décision à la légère

lightness¹ [ˈlaɪtnɪs] **N** *(brightness)* clarté *f*

lightness² **N** *(in weight etc)* légèreté *f*, **l. of foot** agilité *f*, **l. of heart** gaieté *f* de cœur, **l. of touch** *(of pianist, tennis player)* légèreté;

(of artist) légèreté *f* de pinceau; *(of writer)* légèreté de style

lightning [ˈlaɪtnɪŋ] **N** éclairs *mpl*, foudre *f*, **a flash of l.** un éclair; **struck by l.** frappé par la foudre; **as quick as l., with l. speed,** *Fam* **like greased l.** rapide comme l'éclair; *Prov* **l. never strikes twice in the same place** la foudre ne frappe jamais deux fois au même endroit

▸▸ **l. attack** attaque *f* éclair; *Am* **l. bug** luciole *f*, **l. conductor**, *Am* **l. rod** paratonnerre *m*; **l. strike** *(by workers)* grève *f* surprise *(inv)*; **l. visit** visite *f* éclair

lightproof [ˈlaɪtpruːf] **ADJ** opaque

lights [laɪts] **NPL** *Culin (of cow etc)* mou *m*

light-sensitive **ADJ** *Phys* photosensible

lightship [ˈlaɪtʃɪp] **N** *Naut* bateau-feu *m,pl* bateaux-feux, bateau-phare *m, pl* bateaux-phares

lightweight [ˈlaɪtweɪt] **N** *Boxing* poids *m* léger; *Pej (unimpressive person)* personne *f* qui manque d'envergure; **intellectual/political l.** personne qui manque d'envergure intellectuelle/politique

ADJ *(garment etc)* léger

lignite [ˈlɪɡnaɪt] **N** *Miner* lignite *m*

likable [ˈlaɪkəb(ə)l] **= likeable**

LIKE [laɪk] **ADJ** semblable, pareil; **they are of l. temperament** ils ont le même tempérament; **they are as l. as two peas (in a pod)** ils se ressemblent comme deux gouttes d'eau

PREP 1 *(similar to)* **to be l. sb/sth** être semblable à qn/à qch, ressembler à qn/à qch; **we're l. sisters** nous sommes comme des sœurs; **to taste l. sth** avoir le même goût que qch; **to look l. sth/sb** ressembler à qch/qn; **l. want to find one l. it** je veux trouver le/la même; **people l. you** des gens comme vous; **what's the weather l.?** quel temps fait-il?; **you know what she's l.** vous savez comme elle est; **he was l. a father to me** il a été comme un père pour moi; **when I hear things l. that** quand j'entends des choses pareilles; **I know plenty of people l. that** je connais pas mal de gens comme ça; **something very much l. it** quelque chose qui y ressemble beaucoup; **it costs something l. £10** cela coûte environ 10 livres; **it will cost more l. £20** ça coûtera plutôt dans les 20 livres; **that's more l. it** voilà qui est mieux; **we don't have anything l. as many people as we need** on est loin d'avoir tout le monde qu'il nous faut; **it's just l. (at) home** c'est comme à la maison; *Fam* **that's something l. it!** voilà qui est réussi!; **there's nothing l. it** il n'y a rien de mieux; **she is nothing l. as intelligent as you** elle est loin d'être aussi intelligente que vous; **that's not l. him** *(not his way of behaving etc)* ce n'est pas lui ressemble pas; **that's just l. him!** c'est bien de lui!; **that's just l. a woman/a man!** c'est typiquement féminin/ masculin!; **l. father, l. son** tel père, tel fils

2 *(in the manner of)* comme; **I think l. you** je pense comme vous; **just l. anybody else** comme tout le monde; **to speak French l. a native** parler français comme un natif; *Fam* **to run l. blazes** *or* **hell** *or* **mad** courir comme un dératé; *Fam* **be l. that then!** puisque c'est ça, fais comme tu veux!; **don't be l. that about it, he didn't mean what he said** ne le prends pas mal, ce n'est pas ce qu'il voulait dire; **l. this?** *(am I doing it correctly?)* comme ça?; **whisk the egg whites gently, l. this** battez les blancs délicatement, comme ceci; **don't talk l. that** ne parlez pas comme ça; **I'm sorry to keep bothering you l. this** je suis désolé de vous déranger continuellement comme ça

3 *(such as)* tel que; **take more exercise, l. jogging** fais plus d'exercice, du jogging par exemple

ADV *Fam* **l. enough, (as) l. as not** probablement, vraisemblablement; *Sl* **he looked**

angry, l. il était comme en colère; *Sl* **he just came up behind me, l.** il est arrivé derrière moi, comme ça

CONJ *Fam* **1** (= **as**) comme; **do l. l do** faites comme moi; **l. l said** comme je l'ai dit

2 (= **as if**) **he behaved l. he was scared** il s'est conduit comme s'il avait peur; **he looked l. he'd seen a ghost** on aurait dit qu'il avait vu un fantôme

N (*person*) semblable *mf*, pareil, -eille; **he and his l.** lui et ses semblables; **it's too good for the likes of me** c'est trop bien pour des gens comme moi; **the likes of you** des gens comme toi, *Pej* des gens de ton acabit; **music, painting and the l.** la musique, la peinture, et autres choses du même genre; **musicians, painters and the l.** musiciens, peintres et compagnie; **I've never seen the l.** (**of it**) *or* **its l.** je n'ai jamais vu une chose pareille; **it was music, the l. of which I had never heard** c'était de la musique comme je n'en avais jamais entendue

NPL **likes** (*tastes*) goûts *mpl*, préférences *fpl*; **likes and dislikes** préférences *fpl*; **I don't think she has any very strong likes or dislikes** je ne pense pas qu'elle ait des préférences très marquées

VT **1** (*person*) aimer bien; **I l. him** je l'aime bien, il me plaît bien; **I don't l. him** je ne l'aime pas, il ne me plaît pas; **how do you l. him?** comment le trouvez-vous?; **she is well liked** elle est très appréciée

2 (*enjoy*) aimer (bien); **he likes school** il aime l'école; **do you l. tea?** aimez-vous le thé?; **I don't l. it at all** (*situation etc*) cela ne me plaît pas du tout; **if he doesn't l. it he can go elsewhere** si ça ne lui plaît pas il peut aller ailleurs; **whether she likes it or not** que cela lui plaise ou non; **these plants don't l. the damp** ces plantes craignent l'humidité; **I l. to see them now and again** j'aime les voir de temps à autre; *Fam Iron* (**well**) **I l. that!** en voilà une bonne!, elle est bien bonne, celle-là!

3 (*to want*) aimer (**to do** (à) faire); **he doesn't l. people to talk about it** il n'aime pas qu'on en parle; **I would very much l. to go** j'aimerais beaucoup y aller; **would you l. me to go with you?** voulez-vous que je vous accompagne?; **I would l. to know whether ...** je voudrais bien savoir si ...; **I would l. time to consider it** j'aimerais avoir le temps d'y réfléchir; **I would l. some tea** je prendrais bien une tasse de thé; **would you l. a cigarette?** voulez-vous une cigarette?; **I would l. nothing better** je ne demande pas mieux; **I would l. nothing better than a hot bath** il n'y a rien qui me ferait autant plaisir qu'un bon bain chaud; **as you l.** comme vous voudrez; **to do just as one likes** n'en faire qu'à sa tête; **I can do as I l. with it** j'en fais ce que je veux; **he thinks he can do anything he likes** il se croit tout permis; **she is free to do as she likes** elle est libre d'agir à sa guise *ou* de faire comme il lui plaira; **if you l.** si vous voulez; **when you l.** quand il vous plaira; **as much as you l.** tant que vous voudrez; **I didn't l. to mention it** j'ai préféré ne pas le mentionner; **I wanted to ring you but I didn't l. to** (*I would have disturbed you, upset you etc*) je voulais te téléphoner mais j'ai préféré ne pas le faire

▸▸*Elec* **l. poles** pôles *mpl* semblables *ou* de même nom; *Math* **l. quantities** quantités *fpl* semblables; *Math* **l. terms** termes *mpl* semblables

likeable ['laɪkəb(ə)l] ADJ (*person*) agréable, sympathique

likeableness ['laɪkəb(ə)lnɪs] N (*of person*) amabilité *f*

likelihood ['laɪklɪhʊd] N vraisemblance *f*, probabilité *f*, apparence *f*; **there is little l. of his succeeding** il y a peu de chances qu'il

réussisse; **there's a strong l. that ...** il y a une forte probabilité pour que ... + *subj*; **there is every l. that ...** il y a toutes les chances que ... + *subj*; **in all l.** selon toute probabilité, selon toute vraisemblance

likely ['laɪklɪ] ADJ **1** (*probable*) vraisemblable, probable; **it's not a very l. scenario** ce scénario n'est pas très vraisemblable; **the pub is a l. place to find him** le pub est probablement l'endroit où le trouver; *Fam Iron* **that's a l. story!** la belle histoire!, en voilà une bonne!; **it's more than l.** c'est plus que probable; **it's not very l.** c'est peu probable; **it's l. to rain** il y a des chances pour qu'il pleuve; **she is quite l. to do it** il y a des chances qu'elle le fasse; **books l. to interest young people** ouvrages susceptibles d'intéresser les jeunes; **this plan is most l. to succeed** ce projet a beaucoup de chances de réussir; **are the neighbours l. to object?** y a-t-il des chances que les voisins s'y opposent?

2 (*promising*) prometteur; *BrDial* **a l. lad** un gars qui promet; **a l. candidate/horse** un candidat/cheval susceptible *ou* qui a des chances de gagner; **this looked a l. spot to find what they were looking for** l'endroit semblait tout indiqué pour trouver ce qu'ils cherchaient

ADV **most l., very l.,** *Am Fam* **l.** vraisemblablement, très probablement; **as l. as not** vraisemblablement; *Fam* **not l.!** jamais de la vie!

like-minded ADJ du même avis; (*having same tastes*) qui ont les mêmes goûts

liken ['laɪk(ə)n] VT comparer (**to** à)

likeness ['laɪknɪs] N **1** (*similarity*) ressemblance *f* (**between** entre; **to** à); **God created man in his own l.** Dieu a créé l'homme à son image; **a close l.** une ressemblance étroite; **family l.** air *m* de famille **2** (*image*) portrait *m*, image *f*; **the portrait is a good l.** le portrait est très ressemblant

likewise ['laɪkwaɪz] ADV (*similarly*) de même, aussi; **to do l.** faire de même, en faire autant; **pleased to meet you – l.!** ravi de vous rencontrer – moi de même!

liking ['laɪkɪŋ] N goût *m*, penchant *m*; **to one's l.** au goût de qn; **is it to your l.?** cela est-il à votre goût?, est-ce que cela vous plaît?; **to have a l. for sth** avoir du goût pour qch, aimer qch; **I have taken a l. to her** elle m'est devenue sympathique; **to acquire a l. for sth** se mettre à aimer qch

lilac ['laɪlək] N (*flower, tree, colour*) lilas *m* ADJ **l.(-coloured)** lilas *inv*

Lilliputian [lɪlɪ'pju:ʃən] ADJ *Lit* lilliputien

Lilo® ['laɪləʊ] N matelas *m* pneumatique

lilt [lɪlt] N **1** (*of verse*) rythme *m*, cadence *f*; **a song with a l.** une chanson au rythme entraînant; **to speak with a Welsh l.** parler avec des intonations galloises **2** *Arch, Scot* chant *m*, air *m*

lilting ['lɪltɪŋ] ADJ (*rythme*) musical, -aux; (*tune*) cadencé, scandé

lily ['lɪlɪ] N (*flower*) lis *m*; **l. of the valley** muguet *m*

▸▸ **l. pad** feuille *f* de nénuphar

lily-livered ['lɪlɪlɪvəd] ADJ couard

lily-white ADJ blanc, *f* blanche comme le lis, d'une blancheur de lis; *Fam* (*character*) blanc comme neige

lima bean ['li:mə'bi:n] N haricot *m* de Lima

limb [lɪm] N **1** (*of body*) membre *m*; **the lower limbs** les membres inférieurs; **to tear an animal l. from l.** mettre un animal en pièces **2** (*of tree*) (grosse) branche *f*, (*of cross*) bras *m*; *Fam* **to be out on a l.** (*be alone*) être en plan; (*be in dangerous position*) être dans une situation délicate; *Fam* **his refusal to compromise left him out on a l.** son refus

d'accepter un compromis l'a mis dans une situation délicate; *Fam* **to go out on a l.** prendre des risques

-limbed [lɪmd] SUFF **loose-l.** souple; **strong-l.** aux membres solides, solide

limber¹ ['lɪmbər] *Mil* N (*of gun carriage*) avant-train *m*, *pl* avant-trains

VT **to l. a gun** attacher une pièce de canon à l'avant-train

limber² ADJ souple

▸ **limber up** VI *Sport* s'échauffer

VT SEP *Sport* (*muscles*) se chauffer; **to l. up one's fingers** (*of pianist etc*) s'échauffer les doigts

limbering-up exercises [lɪmbərɪŋ'ʌp] NPL exercices *mpl* d'assouplissement

limbless ['lɪmlɪs] ADJ (*person*) à qui il manque un membre/plusieurs membres; (*with no arms or legs*) sans membres; **l. ex-servicemen** grands mutilés *mpl* de guerre

limbo ['lɪmbəʊ] N **1** *Rel* les limbes *mpl*; *Rel, Fig* **to be in l.** être dans les limbes **2** (*dance*) limbo *m*

▸▸ **l. dancer** danseur, -euse de limbo

lime¹ N (*fruit*) lime *f*, citron *m* vert; (*fruit tree*) limettier *m*

▸▸ **l. green** vert *m* jaune; **a l.-green coat** un manteau vert vif; **l. juice** jus *m* de citron vert

lime² N (*linden tree*) tilleul *m*

lime³ N **1** (*substance*) chaux *f* **2** (*for catching birds*) glu *f*

VT **1** *Agr* (*soil*) chauler **2** (*twigs*) **to l. birds** prendre des oiseaux à la glu *ou* au gluau

▸▸ **l. pit** (*quarry*) fosse *f* à chaux; (*in tanning*) pelain *m*; **l. twig** gluau *m*

limeade ['laɪmeɪd] N = jus *m* de citron vert additionné de sucre et d'eau gazeuse

limekiln ['laɪmkɪln] N four *m* à chaux

limelight ['laɪmlaɪt] N **in the l.** sous les feux de la rampe, très en vue; **she doesn't like the l.** elle n'aime pas sentir les projecteurs braqués sur elle; **an actor who's never out of the l.** un acteur très en vue; **to seek the l.** rechercher la vedette; **to steal the l.** voler la vedette

limerick ['lɪmərɪk] N limerick *m*, = poème *m* en cinq vers, burlesque et grivois

limestone ['laɪmstəʊn] N *Geol* calcaire *m*

limey ['laɪmɪ] *Am, Austr Sl* N Anglais *m*

ADJ anglais

limit ['lɪmɪt] N **1** (*boundary*) limite *f*, borne *f*, *Tech* (*of elasticity etc*) limite; (*in insurance*) plein *m*; **to fix** *or* **set a l.** *or* **limits** fixer *ou* mettre une limite *ou* des limites (**to** à); **within a ten kilometre l.** dans un rayon de dix kilomètres; **within limits** dans une certaine mesure; **I like jazz but within limits** j'aime le jazz mais jusqu'à un certain point; **the limits of decency** les limites de la décence; **time l.** (*for speaker etc*) limite de temps; (*for payment etc*) délai *m*; (*on special privilege etc*) durée *f*; **to be over the (legal) l.** (*of drunken driver*) avoir bu plus qu'il n'est permis au volant; *Fin* **credit l.** limite *ou* plafond *m* du crédit; **what is the l. on this road?** (*speed*) quelle est la limitation de vitesse sur cette route?; **to fix a l.** (*in insurance*) fixer les pleins; **there's a l. to everything!** il y a une limite à tout!; **there's no l. to her ambition** son ambition est sans limites; **to know no limits** ne connaître aucune limite; **his arrogance knows no limits** son arrogance ne connaît pas de limites; **that's the l.!** ça c'est le comble!; **he's the l.!** il est impossible!; **off limits** (*place*) inaccessible; *Mil* consigné à la troupe; **to be off limits to sb** (*of place*) être inaccessible à qn; *Mil* **to put a bar off limits** consigner un bar

2 *Tech* (*tolerance*) tolérance *f*

VT (*somebody, something*) limiter, borner, restreindre; **I have to l. my calorie intake** je dois limiter ma consommation de calories; **to l. oneself to …** *(in speaking)* se borner à …; **to l. oneself to the bare necessities** se restreindre au strict nécessaire; **to l. oneself to two whiskies** se limiter à deux whiskies; **I will l. myself to observing that …** je me bornerai à observer que …

▸▸**l. gauge** *(device)* calibre *m* de tolérance; *(external)* bague *f* à tolérance; *(internal)* bouchon *m* à tolérance

limitation [lɪmɪ'teɪʃən] N limitation *f*, **to know one's limitations** connaître ses limites

limited ['lɪmɪtəd] ADJ *(number, intelligence, skills etc)* limité, restreint; *Com (market)* étroit, restreint

▸▸**l. circulation** circulation *f* restreinte; **l. company** ≃ société *f* à responsabilité limitée, SARL *f*; **l. edition** édition *f* à tirage limité; **l. liability** responsabilité *f* limitée; *Fin* **l. partner** commanditaire *m*; *Fin* **l. partnership** société *f* en commandite (simple); **l. stop bus** bus *m* à nombre d'arrêts limité; **l. stop train** train *m* à nombre d'arrêts limité

limiter ['lɪmɪtər] N *Radio, TV* limiteur *m*

limitless ['lɪmɪtlɪs] ADJ sans bornes, illimité

limousine [lɪmə'ziːn], *Fam* **limo** ['lɪməʊ] N *Aut* limousine *f*

limp[1] [lɪmp] N boitement *m*, *Lit* claudication *f*, **to walk with a l., to have a l.** boiter vI boiter, *Lit* claudiquer; **to l. home** *Sport* terminer la course tant bien que mal; *Fig* rentrer tant bien que mal; **to l. along** aller en boitant *ou Fam* clopin-clopant; *(of ship etc)* avancer péniblement; **she limped along the corridor** elle remonta le couloir en boitant

limp[2] ADJ mou, *f* molle, flasque; **to go l.** *(of person)* s'affaisser; **let your arm go l.** relâche ton bras; **to feel l.** *(of person)* se sentir mou *ou* sans énergie; **l. with the heat** abattu par la chaleur; **the heat makes me feel l.** je suis abattu par la chaleur

▸▸**l. binding** *(of book)* cartonnage *m* souple

limpet ['lɪmpɪt] N patelle *f*, arapède *m*; *Fam (person)* crampon *m*; **to stick to sb like a l.** ne pas lâcher *ou* cramponner qn

▸▸**l. mine** mine-ventouse *f*, *pl* mines-ventouses

limpid ['lɪmpɪd] ADJ *Fml (water, style)* limpide

limply ['lɪmplɪ] ADV *(without firmness)* mollement, flasquement; *(without energy)* mollement, sans énergie

limpness ['lɪmpnɪs] N mollesse *f*, manque *m* d'énergie

limp-wristed ['lɪmp'rɪstəd] ADJ *Fam* efféminé

linage ['laɪnɪdʒ] N *(for newspaper ad)* lignage *m*

linchpin ['lɪntʃpɪn] N esse *f*, cheville *f* d'essieu; *Fig (of organization etc)* cheville ouvrière

Lincs *Br abbr* Lincolnshire

linctus ['lɪŋktəs] N *Pharm* sirop *m*

linden ['lɪndən] N tilleul *m*
▸▸**l. tree** tilleul

LINE[1] [laɪn]

N ligne **1, 2, 4–8, 10, 12, 13** ▪ trait **1**	
▪ ride **1** ▪ rang **2** ▪ file **2** ▪ queue **2**	
▪ chaîne **3** ▪ corde **4** ▪ voie **7**	
▪ vers **8** ▪ mot **8** ▪ lignée **10**	
▪ branche **11**	
VT border **2**	

N **1** *(mark)* ligne *f*, trait *m*; *(of shore, face)* contours *mpl*; *(of car etc)* lignes *f*; *Geog Fam* **the L.** *(equator)* la Ligne (de l'Équateur);

---

straight l. (ligne) droite *f*, **broken/wavy l.** trait discontinu; **to put a l. through sth** barrer qch; *Tennis* **on the l.** sur la ligne; *Aut* **white l., Am yellow l.** *(in centre of road)* ≃ ligne blanche, bande *f* médiane; **the lines of the hand** les lignes de la main; **the lines on one's forehead** les rides *fpl* de son front; **his face was covered with lines** son visage était plein de rides; **the hard lines of his face** ses traits durs; **to draw a l. under sth** *(underline it)* souligner qch; *Fig* **you have to draw the l. somewhere** il y a une limite à tout; **he doesn't know where to draw the l.** il ne sait pas où s'arrêter; **that's where I draw the l.** pour moi c'est la à ne pas dépasser; *(warning another person etc)* ça va trop loin; **I draw the l. at lying** je refuse de mentir; *(referring to other people)* je ne tolère pas le mensonge

2 *(row of people or things) (side by side)* ligne *f*, rangée *f*, *(one behind the other)* file *f*, *Am (queue)* queue *f*, **twenty cars in a l.** *(one behind the other)* vingt voitures à la file; **l. of traffic** colonne *f* de véhicules; **to put objects in a l.** aligner des objets; **to stand in a l.** *(of person in a queue)* faire la queue; *(of children)* être en rang; *Am* **to stand in l.** faire la queue; **to fall** *ou* **get into l., to form a l.** *(of people)* se mettre en ligne; *(of children)* se mettre en rang; *(of soldiers)* former les rangs; **out of l.** désaligné; **to be out of l. with sb** *(in opinions)* être en désaccord avec qn; **to be out of l. with** *(policy etc)* ne pas être conforme avec; *Fig* **to be out of l.** *(in what one does, says)* dépasser les bornes; **to get out of l.** se désaligner; *Fig (of political group)* se désolidariser; *(of individual)* faire cavalier seul; **your decision is not in l.** *or* **is out of l. with government policy** votre décision n'est pas conforme à *ou* n'est pas en accord avec la politique du gouvernement; **in l. with my decision** conformément à ma décision; **he's in l. for promotion** il est sur la liste des promotions (futures); **to overstep the l.** dépasser la mesure; **to fall into l. with sb's ideas** se conformer aux idées de qn; **to be on the l.** *(of one's job, reputation etc)* être en jeu; **to put one's job/reputation on the l.** mettre son travail/sa réputation en jeu; **to lay one's reputation/life on the l. (for sb/sth)** mettre sa réputation/vie en jeu (pour qn/qch); **to lay it on the l.** mettre les choses au point; **to lay it on the l. to sb** parler franchement à qn

3 *Ind* **(assembly) l.** chaîne *f* de montage; **(production) l.** chaîne de production

4 *(cord etc), Naut* ligne *f*, corde *f*, cordage *m*; *(for mooring)* amarre *f*, *(for clothes)* corde *ou* fil *m* à linge; *Fishing* ligne (de pêche); *(in surveying), Constr* cordeau *m*; *Elec* **high-tension l.** ligne à haute tension; *Elec, Tel* **overhead/underground l.** ligne aérienne/souterraine; **your clothes are out on the l.** tes vêtements sont sur le fil

5 *Tel* **l. shared** *or* **party l.** ligne partagée; **hold the l. please** restez en ligne s'il vous plaît, ne quittez pas; **the l.'s very bad** la communication est mauvaise; **I have Bill on the l.** j'ai Bill en ligne *ou Fam* au bout du fil; **she's on the other l.** elle est sur l'autre ligne; **all the lines to London are busy** toutes les lignes pour Londres sont occupées; *TV, Radio* **the lines are open from 8 o'clock** *(for viewers and listeners to express their views)* les standards sont ouverts à partir de 8 heures

6 *Mil etc* ligne *f*, **lines** lignes *(de fortification etc)*; **the front/rear lines** le front/l'arrière *m*; **to be in the front l.** *Mil* être au front; *Fig* être en première ligne; *Mil etc* **fighting l., l. of battle** ligne de combat *ou* de bataille; **l. of conduct** ligne de conduite; **to be killed in the l. of duty** *(of policeman)* mourir dans l'exercice de ses fonctions; *(of soldier)* mou-

---

rir au champ d'honneur; *Fig* **to win all along the l.** gagner sur toute la ligne

7 *(direction)* *(of march, communication, route)* ligne *f*, *(of communication)*, *Rail (track)* voie *f*, *Mil etc* **l. of advance** direction *f* de marche; **l. of argument** raisonnement *m*; **l. of attack** ligne d'attaque; **l. of fire** *(of gun)* ligne de tir; **l. of sight** ligne de visée; *(on rifle)* ligne de mire; **l. of thought** raisonnement; **l. of vision** ligne de mire; **to work on the same lines as sb** travailler dans la même direction que qn; **to be working on the right lines** être en bonne voie; **what l. are you going to take?** quel parti allez-vous prendre?; **we must take a firm l. with such people** il nous faut être ferme avec des gens comme ça; **along the lines of** dans le genre *ou* style de

8 *(of text)* ligne *f*, *(of poetry)* vers *m*; **first l. of a paragraph** alinéa *m*; **new l.** *(in dictating)* à la ligne; **opening/closing lines of a play** premières/dernières répliques d'une pièce; *Theat* **not to know one's lines** ne pas savoir son rôle; **to learn one's lines** apprendre son rôle; **to forget one's lines** oublier son texte, *Fam* avoir un trou; *Fam* **just a l. to tell you …** deux mots pour vous dire …; *Fam* **I'll drop you a l.** je vous enverrai un petit mot; **to read between the lines** lire entre les lignes

9 *(information) Fam* **to get a l. on sb** se renseigner sur qn; **I wish I could get a l. on him** j'aimerais avoir des renseignements sur lui; *Fam* **to get a l. on sth** obtenir des tuyaux sur qch; *Fam* **to give sb a l. on sth** tuyauter qn sur qch; *Fam* **don't hand me that l.!** à d'autres!

10 *(family)* lignée *f*, ligne *f*, **male/female l.** ligne masculine/féminine; **long l. of ancestors** longue suite d'ancêtres; **he comes from a long l. of politicians** il descend d'une longue lignée d'hommes politiques; **in (a) direct l.** en ligne directe; **to be descended in (a) direct l. from sb** descendre en droite ligne de qn

11 *Fam (job etc)* métier *m*; **l. of business** genre *m* d'affaires, branche *f*; **what l. (of business) are you in?** dans quelle branche est-ce que tu travailles?; **that's not my l.** ce n'est pas mon rayon; **that's more (in) my l.** *(what I'm good at)* cela est plus dans mes compétences *ou Fam* mes cordes; *(what I like)* je préfère cela, *Fam* c'est plus mon truc

12 *Com (of goods)* ligne *f*, **a new l. in menswear** une nouvelle ligne pour hommes; **they've brought out a new l. in perfume** ils ont sorti une nouvelle ligne de parfum; *Fam* **a rice pudding or something in that l.** un gâteau de riz ou quelque chose dans ce genre(-là)

13 *(company) (of steamers etc)* ligne *f*, compagnie *f*

VT **1** *(piece of paper)* faire des lignes sur; **to become lined** *(of forehead, face)* se rider

2 *(border)* border; **to l. the roads with troops** aligner des troupes sur les routes; **the crowd lined the street** la foule s'alignait le long du trottoir; **lined with trees** bordé d'arbres

▸▸*Mktg* **l. addition** ajout *m* à la ligne; *Comput* **l. break** saut *m* de ligne; **l. caption** légende *f*, *Comput* **l. command** ligne de commande; *Fin* **l. of credit** ligne de crédit, ligne de découvert; **l. dancing** = danse *f* de style country effectuée en rangs; *Mktg* **l. differentiation** différenciation *f* de ligne; **l. drawing** dessin *m* au trait; *Typ, Comput* **l. end** fin *f* de ligne; *Typ, Comput* **l. end hyphen** tiret *m* de fin de ligne; **l. engraving** gravure *f* au trait; *Mktg* **l. extension** extension *f* de ligne; *Comput* **l. feed** changement *m* de ligne; **to do a l. feed** aller à la ligne; *Mktg* **l. filling** consolidation *f* de ligne; **l. fishing** pêche *f* à la ligne; *Com* **l. management** organisation *f* hiérarchique; *Com* **l. manager** chef *m* hiérarchique; **l. noise** parasites *mpl*; *Comput* **l.**

printer imprimante *f* ligne à ligne; *Comput* **l. printout** imprimé *m* ligne à ligne; *Theat* **l. rehearsal** lecture *f* collective; *Tel* **l. rental** abonnement *m*; *Typ, Comput* **l. space** interligne *m*; *Typ, Comput* **l. spacing** interlignage *m*, espacement *m* de lignes; *Typ, Comput* **l. width** longueur *f* de ligne

▶ **line up** VT SEP **1** *(people, objects)* aligner, mettre en ligne

2 *Fam (plan)* prévoir, avoir en vue; **have you got anyone lined up for the job?** avez-vous quelqu'un en vue pour le poste?; **what have you got lined up for us?** qu'est-ce que vous nous préparez?

VI *(of people)* s'aligner, se mettre en ligne, se ranger; *(form queue)* faire la queue

line² VT **1** *Sewing etc (coat, jacket etc)* doubler (**with** de); **fur-lined gloves** gants fourrés; *Fig Fam* **to l. one's own pockets** se servir, se remplir les poches; **to l. a box with paper** tapisser une boîte de papier; **you need something to l. your stomach** tu dois avaler quelque chose avant; *Culin* **to l. a tin with pastry** foncer un moule de pâte; **nest lined with moss** nid garni de mousse; **the walls were lined with books** les murs étaient couverts de livres

2 *Tech (bearing)* garnir, recouvrir; *(wall, furnace)* revêtir, incruster (**with** de); *(well)* cuveler; **to l. a shaft with metal** blinder un puits

lineage¹ ['lɪnɪɪdʒ] N lignée *f*, lignage *m*; **to boast an ancient l.** se vanter d'une longue généalogie; **to trace one's l.** retracer sa généalogie

lineage² ['laɪnɪdʒ] N *(for newspaper ad)* lignage *m*

lineal ['lɪnɪəl] ADJ linéal, -aux; *(descendant, succession)* en ligne directe

lineaments ['lɪnɪəmənts] NPL *Lit* traits *mpl*, linéaments *mpl*

linear ['lɪnɪər] ADJ linéaire
  ▶ ▶ **l. equation** équation *f* linéaire; *Phys* **l. expansion** dilatation *f* linéaire; **l. measure** mesure *f* linéaire, mesure de longueur; **l. metre** mètre *m* linéaire; *Comput* **l. programming** programmation *f* linéaire

lined¹ [laɪnd] ADJ *(paper)* réglé, rayé; **deeply l. forehead** front creusé de rides

lined² ADJ **1** *(coat)* doublé; *(glove)* fourré; *Fig Fam* **well l. purse** bourse bien garnie **2** *Aut (brake)* garni; **steel-l.** *(cylinder)* chemisé d'acier

linen ['lɪnɪn] N **1** linge *m*; *Old-fashioned (underwear)* petit linge; **dirty l.** linge sale; *Fig Fam* **don't wash your dirty l. in public** il faut laver son linge sale en famille **2** *Tex* toile *f* (de lin); **l. dress** robe en lin; **the l. industry** l'industrie *f* linière *ou* toilière; **l. sheets** draps *fil*
  ▶ ▶ **l. basket** corbeille *f* à linge; **l. cupboard** armoire *f* à linge; **l. paper** papier *m* toilé; **l. room, l. store** lingerie *f*

line-oriented ADJ *Comput* orienté ligne

line-out N *Rugby* touche *f*, remise *f* en jeu

liner¹ ['laɪnər] N *Naut (paquebot m)* transatlantique *m*

liner² N *(of cylinder)* fourreau *m*

linesman, pl **linesmen** ['laɪnzmən] N *Tennis* juge *m* de lignes; *Ftbl* juge *m* de touche

line-up N **1** *Am (queue)* queue *f* (de personnes); *(for identity parade)* rangée *f* de personnes *(assemblées par la police pour l'identification d'un suspect)* **2** *Sport* formation *f* *(d'une équipe sur le terrain)*; *Radio, TV etc* **this evening's l.** *(of guests, stars)* nos invités ce soir

linework ['laɪnwɜːk] N *Art* dessin *m* au trait

ling¹ [lɪŋ] N *(fish)* lingue *f*

ling² N *Bot* bruyère *f* commune

linger ['lɪŋɡər] VI **1** *(of person)* s'attarder, traîner (**over** sur); *(of custom, memory)* subsister; **to l. over a meal** s'attarder sur un repas; **a doubt still lingered** un doute subsistait encore dans mon *ou* son *etc* esprit **2** *(of invalid)* **to l. (on)** languir, traîner

lingerie ['lænʒərɪ] N lingerie *f*

lingering ['lɪŋɡərɪŋ] ADJ **1** *(look)* prolongé; *(doubt)* qui subsiste encore; **I had l. doubts/regrets** je gardais un doute/des regrets; **there was a l. hope that …** on conservait un vague espoir que … **2** *(illness)* qui traîne, chronique; *(death)* lent; **she died a l. death** la mort l'a emportée lentement

lingo, pl **lingoes** ['lɪŋɡəʊ, -əʊz] N *Fam* **the l. of the country** *(its language)* la langue du pays; **technical/scientific l.** jargon *m* technique/scientifique

lingua franca ['lɪŋɡwə'fræŋkə] N langue *f* de communication, langue véhiculaire

linguist ['lɪŋɡwɪst] N *(student of linguistics)* linguiste *mf*; **to be a good/no l.** être/ne pas être doué pour les langues

linguistic [lɪŋ'ɡwɪstɪk] ADJ linguistique
  ▶ ▶ **l. atlas** atlas *m* linguistique

linguistically [lɪŋ'ɡwɪstɪklɪ] ADV linguistiquement

linguistics [lɪŋ'ɡwɪstɪks] N linguistique *f*
  VOIR GRAMMAIRE A10

liniment ['lɪnɪmənt] N liniment *m*

lining ['laɪnɪŋ] N *(of coat, jacket, dress)* doublure *f*; *(of hat)* coiffe *f*; *Tech (of brakes, bearing)* garniture *f*, fourrure *f*; *(of furnace, pump)* chemise *f*; *(of well)* cuvelage *m*; *(of tunnel)* paroi *f*; *(of stomach)* paroi
  ▶ ▶ **l. paper** *(for drawer)* papier *m* pour tiroirs; *(for shelves)* papier pour recouvrir les étagères

link [lɪŋk] N **1** *(of chain)* chaînon *m*, maillon *m*, maille *f*; *Naut (of chain)* paillon *m*
  2 *Fig (connection)* lien *m*, liaison *f* (**between** entre); *Comput* lien *m*; **there's a l. between your health and your job** il y a un lien entre votre santé et votre travail; **air/radio l.** liaison *f* aérienne/radiophonique; **he is a l. between the old world and the new** il sert de trait d'union entre le vieux monde et le nouveau; **he was an unwitting l. in a chain of events which …** sans le savoir, il était le maillon d'une chaîne d'événements qui …; **this l. in the chain of events** cet épisode de la série d'événements; **the weak l.** le maillon faible
  3 *Tech etc* pièce *f* de liaison, tige *f* d'assemblage

VT *(two machines, two cities, two river banks etc)* relier; **a tunnel linking Britain and France** un tunnel reliant la Grande-Bretagne à la France; **the two companies are in no way linked** il n'y a aucun lien entre les deux sociétés; **closely linked** *(of companies, theories etc)* étroitement lié; **to l. negotiations to a discussion of Palestine** lier des négociations à une discussion sur la Palestine; **I always l. him with my stay in …** je l'associe toujours dans mon esprit à mon séjour à …; **his name has been linked with several well-known actresses** son nom a été associé à plusieurs actrices bien connues; **it's all linked together** tout cela se tient; **wages linked to the cost of living** salaires indexés sur le coût de la vie; **to l. hands/arms** se donner la main/le bras

VI **to l. on to sth** s'attacher à qch; *Comput* **to l. to sth** *(of device)* être relié à qch
  ▶ ▶ *TV etc* **l. man** speaker *m*; *Comput* **l. program** programme *m* éditeur de liens; **l. road** route *f* de jonction

▶ **link up** VI *(of motorways, spaceships, travellers)* se rejoindre (**with** à); *(of cables)* se raccorder (**with** à); *(of TV stations)* établir une liaison; *(of two companies)* s'associer;

(of climbers) *(with rope)* s'attacher (**with** à); **we'll l. up with you in Paris** nous nous rejoindrons à Paris; **that links up with what we were saying earlier about …** cela rejoint ce que nous disions précédemment à propos de …; **the space rocket will l. up with the orbiting satellite** la navette spatiale rencontrera le satellite en orbite; *TV* **we'll be linking up with Germany at 10 o'clock** nous serons en liaison directe avec l'Allemagne à 10 heures; **we'll be linking up with a French company for this project** nous serons associés à une entreprise française pour ce projet

VT SEP *(to network, cabling system etc)* rattacher (**to** à); *(two computers, broadcasting stations)* relier; **the computers are all linked up** les ordinateurs sont tous rattachés les uns aux autres; **they haven't been linked up to the network yet** ils n'ont pas encore été reliés au réseau; **it's all linked up with what's happening at …** ça a un lien avec ce qui se passe à …

linkage ['lɪŋkɪdʒ] N lien *m*

linked [lɪŋkt] ADJ lié

linking ['lɪŋkɪŋ] N enchaînement *m*, liaison *f*

links [lɪŋks] NPL *(usu with sing verb)* **(golf) l.** terrain *m ou* parcours *m* de golf

link(-)up N lien *m*, liaison *f* (**between** entre); **a satellite l.** une liaison satellite

linnet ['lɪnɪt] N linotte *f* (mélodieuse)

linoleum [lɪ'nəʊlɪəm], *Fam* **lino** ['laɪnəʊ] N linoléum *m*

Linotype® ['laɪnəʊtaɪp] N *Typ* Linotype® *f*

linseed ['lɪnsiːd] N graine *f* de lin
  ▶ ▶ **l. oil** huile *f* de lin

lint [lɪnt] N **1** *Med* pansement *m* ouatiné **2** *(of cotton, duster)* peluche *f*

lintel ['lɪnt(ə)l] N *Constr (of door, window)* linteau *m*

lint-free ADJ *(cloth)* sans peluches

lion ['laɪən] N **1** *(animal)* lion *m*; *Fig* **the l.'s share** la part du lion; *Fig* **to put one's head into the l.'s mouth** se fourrer dans la gueule du loup **2** *Old-fashioned (famous person)* personnage *m* en vue; **a literary l.** sommité *f* littéraire; **the l. of the day** la célébrité du jour
  ▶ ▶ **l. cub** lionceau *m*; **l.'s den, lions' den** antre *m* du lion; **l. house** *(at zoo)* fauverie *f*, **l. hunter** chasseur *m* de lions; **l. tamer** dompteur, -euse (de lions)

lioness ['laɪənes] N *(animal)* lionne *f*

lionheart ['laɪənhɑːt] N *Hist* **(Richard) the L.** Richard Cœur de Lion

lion-hearted ['laɪənhɑːtɪd] ADJ au cœur de lion

lionize ['laɪənaɪz] VT *(person)* porter aux nues

lip [lɪp] N **1** *(of person)* lèvre *f*; *(of animal)* babine *f*; **to do** *or* **pay l. service to sth** faire semblant de s'intéresser à qch; **the company is paying l. service to the need for a crèche** l'entreprise prétend s'intéresser à la nécessité d'une crèche; *Fam* **to keep one's l. buttoned (up)** ne pas souffler mot; **button your l.!** pas un mot!; **to smack** *or* **lick one's lips** se lécher les babines; **no complaint ever passes his lips** il ne se plaint jamais; **to read sb's lips** lire sur les lèvres de qn; *Fam* **read my lips** *(believe what I say)* écoutez-moi bien
  2 *Fam (impudence)* effronterie *f*, insolence *f*; **none of your l.!, don't give me any of your l.!** ne fais pas l'insolent
  3 *Med (of wound)*, *Bot* lèvre *f*; *(of orchid)* labelle *m*
  4 *(rim) (of cup, cavity)* bord *m*, rebord *m*; *(of well)* margelle *f*; *(of crater)* bord; *(projection)* rebord, saillie *f*, **pouring l.** *(of jug)* bec *m*
  ▶ ▶ **l. gloss** brillant *m* à lèvres; **l. salve** pommade *f ou* baume *m* pour les lèvres

lip-flap N *(in dubbing)* lèvres *fpl* non-synchro

lipid ['lɪpɪd] N *Med* lipide *m*

lipoma [lɪ'pəʊmə] N lipome *m*

lipoprotein [lɪpəʊ'prəʊtiːn] N lipoprotéine *f*

liposuction ['laɪpəʊsʌkʃən] N liposuccion *f*

-lipped [lɪpt] SUFF red-l. aux lèvres rouges

lippy ['lɪpɪ] *Fam* N *Br (lipstick)* rouge *m* à lèvres
  ADJ effronté; **don't get l. with me!** il faudrait voir à changer de ton!

lip-read VI lire sur les lèvres
  VT **she can l. what you're saying** elle peut lire sur vos lèvres

lip-reader N **to be a good l.** bien savoir lire sur les lèvres

lip-reading N lecture *f* sur les lèvres

lipstick ['lɪpstɪk] N rouge *m* à lèvres

lip-sync(h) ['lɪpsɪŋk] N play-back *m*
  VT *(song)* chanter en play-back
  VI *(of singer)* chanter en play-back

liquefaction [lɪkwɪ'fækʃən] N liquéfaction *f*

liquefied ['lɪkwɪfaɪd] ADJ **l. natural/petroleum gas** gaz *m* naturel/de pétrole liquéfié

liquefy ['lɪkwɪfaɪ] VT *(gas etc)* liquéfier
  VI *(of gas etc)* se liquéfier

liqueur [liː'kɜːr, lɪ'kjʊər] N **1** liqueur *f* (de dessert) **2** *(in winemaking)* liqueur *f* d'expédition
  ▸▸ **l. brandy** fine *f*; **l. chocolates** bonbons *mpl* à la liqueur; **l. glass** verre *m* à liqueur

liquid ['lɪkwɪd] ADJ **1** liquide; *(sound)* doux, *f* douce, clair; *Hum* **to have a l. lunch** boire de l'alcool en guise de déjeuner **2** *Fin* liquide, disponible **3** *Ling (consonant)* liquide
  N **1** liquide *m* **2** *Ling* (consonne *f*) liquide *f*
  ▸▸ *Acct* **l. assets** actif *m* liquide, disponibilités *fpl*, liquidités *fpl*; **l. crystal** cristal *m* liquide; **l. crystal display** affichage *m* à cristaux liquides; **l. diet** régime *m* ne comprenant que des liquides; *Spec* diète *f* hydrique; **l. measure** mesure *f* de capacité pour les liquides; **l. oxygen** oxygène *m* liquide; **L. paper®** correcteur *m* liquide; **l. paraffin** huile *f* de paraffine; **l. securities** valeurs *fpl* liquides

liquidate ['lɪkwɪdeɪt] VT **1** *Fin (company, debt)* liquider; *(capital)* mobiliser; *St Exch* **to l. a position** liquider une position **2** *(kill)* liquider

liquidation [lɪkwɪ'deɪʃən] N *Fin (of company, debt)* liquidation *f*, *(of capital)* mobilisation *f*; **to go into l.** *(of company)* entrer en liquidation

liquidator ['lɪkwɪdeɪtər] N *(of company in liquidation)* liquidateur, -trice

liquidity [lɪ'kwɪdɪtɪ] N **1** *(of substance)* liquidité *f* **2** *Fin* liquidité *f*
  ▸▸ *Fin* **l. ratio** ratio *m* de liquidité, coefficient *m* de liquidité

liquidize ['lɪkwɪdaɪz] VT **1** *Culin* passer au mixeur

liquidizer ['lɪkwɪdaɪzər] N *Culin* mixeur *m*

liquor ['lɪkər] N **1** *Am* alcool *m*; **he can't hold** *or* **take his l.** il ne supporte pas l'alcool; **to be the worse for l.** être ivre **2** *Culin* Old-fashioned *(of roast)* jus *m*; *(of oysters)* eau *f*
  ▸▸ *Am* **l. store** magasin *m* de vins et spiritueux
  ▸ **liquor up** *Am Sl* VI se soûler
  VT SEP soûler; **to be all liquored up** être soûl

liquorice, *Am* **licorice** ['lɪkərɪs] N réglisse *f*

lira ['lɪrə] *(pl* **lire** ['lɪrə]*)* N **1** *(Turkish currency)* lire *f* **2** *Formerly (Italian currency)* lire *f*

LISA [elaɪɛs'eɪ] N *Br Fin (abbr* **long-term individual savings account)** plan *m* de retraite en actions

Lisbon ['lɪzbən] N Lisbonne *f*

lisle [laɪl] N *Tex (thread)* fil *m* d'Écosse
  ▸▸ **l. stockings** bas *mpl* de fil; **l. thread** fil d'Écosse

lisp [lɪsp] N zézaiement *m*; **to have a l., to speak with a l.** zézayer, avoir un cheveu sur la langue
  VT dire en zézayant
  VI zézayer, parler avec un cheveu sur la langue

lissom ['lɪsəm] ADJ *Lit* souple, agile, leste

list¹ [lɪst] N liste *f*, *Admin etc* bordereau *m*; **l. of names** liste nominative; *Fig* **it's (at the) top of my l.** *(I'll do it first)* c'est la première chose que je doive faire; **a fridge is top of my l.** *(to buy)* la première chose que je doive acheter, c'est un frigidaire; **a diamond necklace is top of my l.** *(as gift)* le cadeau que je préférerais avoir est un collier de diamants; **top of the l. for the government is the appointment of ...** ce qui figure en tête des priorités du gouvernement c'est de nommer ...; *Fig* **it's (at the) bottom of the l.** *(least important)* ce n'est pas à faire en priorité; **you're/your name's not on the l.** vous ne figurez pas sur la liste; **to make out** *or* **draw up a l.** établir *ou* dresser une liste; **to enter sth on a l.** porter qch sur une liste
  VT **1** *(enter in list)* enregistrer; *(names etc)* inscrire *ou* porter sur une liste; **his phone number isn't listed (in the directory)** son numéro de téléphone ne figure pas dans l'annuaire; **to l. on the Stock Exchange** introduire en Bourse; **to be listed on the Stock Exchange** être coté en Bourse
  2 *(display as list)* **to l. names in alphabetical order** faire une liste des noms par ordre alphabétique; **you can l. the data in various ways** on peut faire apparaître les données de différentes manières
  3 *(recite, enumerate)* énumérer; **the striking workers listed their demands** les ouvriers en grève énumérèrent leurs revendications
  ▸▸ *Fin* **l. of investments** (bordereau *m* de) portefeuille *m*; *St Exch* **l. of quotations** bulletin *m* des cours; *Com* **l. price** prix *m* du catalogue

list² N *Naut (leaning)* bande *f*, gîte *f*; **to have a l.** donner de la bande, prendre de la gîte; **l. to starboard** gîte à tribord
  VI donner de la bande (**to starboard** à tribord), prendre de la gîte

list³ N *Hist* **lists** *(for tournament)* lice *f*, *Fig* **to enter the lists** entrer en lice (**against sb** contre qn)

listed ['lɪstɪd] ADJ **l. on the Stock Exchange** coté en Bourse
  ▸▸ *Br* **l. building** bâtiment *m* classé; *Br St Exch* **l. company** société *f* cotée en Bourse; *Br* **l. monument** monument *m* classé; *St Exch* **l. securities, l. stock** valeurs *fpl* admises *ou* inscrites à la cote (officielle)

listen ['lɪs(ə)n] VI **1** écouter; **to l. to sb/sth** écouter qn/qch; **to l. with half an ear** n'écouter que d'une oreille; **you're not listening to a word I'm saying!** tu n'écoutes pas un traître mot de ce que je dis!; **we listened to their daughter singing** nous avons écouté chanter leur fille; **I listened to her singing** je l'ai écoutée chanter
  2 *(pay attention)* faire attention, écouter; **he wouldn't l.** il n'a rien voulu savoir; **to l. to reason** écouter la voix de la raison; **don't l. to him, make up your own mind** n'écoute pas ce qu'il te dit, prends la décision toi-même; **l.! I've got an idea** écoutez, j'ai une idée
  3 **will you l. (out) for the phone?** peux-tu surveiller le téléphone?; **to l. out for the postman/doctor** tendre l'oreille pour entendre l'arrivée du facteur/docteur; **will you l. out for the baby?** si le bébé pleure est-ce que tu peux aller voir?; **he listened for the**

sound of the car driving off il tendit l'oreille pour être sûr d'entendre la voiture quand elle partirait; **she tapped on the wall, listening for a hollow sound** elle cherchait à quel endroit le mur était creux en tapant avec ses doigts
  ▸ **listen in** VI *Radio* écouter la radio; **to l. in to other people's conversations** écouter les conversations d'autrui; **I'd like to l. in on the discussion** j'aimerais assister à cette discussion

listener ['lɪsnər] N **1 to be a good l.** savoir écouter **2** *Radio* auditeur, -trice

listening ['lɪsnɪŋ] N écoute *f*, *(in language learning)* compréhension *f* orale
  ▸▸ **l. post** poste *m* d'écoute; **l. time** heure *f* d'écoute; *(length of time)* durée *f* d'écoute

listeriosis [lɪstɪərɪ'əʊsɪs] N *Med* listériose *f*

listing ['lɪstɪŋ] N *(action)* listage *m*; *(position)* classement *m*; *Comput* listing *m*; **the listings** *(in newspapers)* la rubrique des spectacles; *TV* le programme télévisé; *Am Tel* **do you have a J. Smith?** est-ce que vous avez un J. Smith dans vos fichiers?
  ▸▸ **listings magazine** magazine *m* de spectacles; **l. paper** papier *m* continu, papier listing

listless ['lɪstlɪs] ADJ apathique, sans énergie

listlessly ['lɪstlɪslɪ] ADV sans énergie; **to stare l. into space** regarder dans le vague; **he watched l. as they took away his furniture** il assistait à la saisie de ses meubles le regard vide

listlessness ['lɪstlɪsnɪs] N apathie *f*

lit PT, PP *see* **light¹** VT

litany ['lɪtənɪ] N *Rel* litanies *fpl*, *Fig (of complaints etc)* litanie *f*

litchi ['liːtʃiː, 'laɪ-] N = **lychee**

liter ['liːtər] N *Am* = **litre**

literacy ['lɪtərəsɪ] N alphabétisation *f*; **there's a l. problem in this country** il y a dans ce pays un problème d'alphabétisation; **we want to achieve 90% l. before ...** nous nous fixons comme objectif un taux d'alphabétisation de 90% avant ...; **adult l. classes** cours *m* d'alphabétisation pour adultes
  ▸▸ **l. campaign** campagne *f* d'alphabétisation; **l. level** degré *m* d'instruction *ou* d'alphabétisation; **l. test** test *m* pour mesurer le niveau d'alphabétisation

literal ['lɪtərəl] ADJ **1** *(translation)* littéral, -aux, mot à mot; **he's very l.-minded** il prend tout au pied de la lettre; **in the l. sense of the word** au sens propre du mot; **to take sth in a l. sense** prendre qch au pied de la lettre; **it meant l. starvation for thousands of farmers** cela signifiait que des milliers de fermiers allaient littéralement mourir de faim **2** *Math (coefficient)* littéral, -aux
  N *Typ* coquille *f*
  ▸▸ *Typ* **l. error** coquille

literally ['lɪtərəlɪ] ADV **1** *(to translate)* littéralement, mot à mot; **l. speaking** à proprement parler; **to take sth l.** prendre qch au pied de la lettre **2** *Fam (as intensifier)* littéralement

literary ['lɪtərərɪ] ADJ *(work, agent, criticism etc)* littéraire; **l. man** homme *m* de lettres

literate ['lɪtərɪt] ADJ **1** qui sait lire et écrire; **computer l.** qui sait utiliser l'informatique **2** *(educated)* lettré

literature ['lɪtərɪtʃər] N **1** littérature *f*; **French l.** la littérature française **2** *(giving information)* documentation *f*, *Com etc* prospectus *mpl*, brochures *fpl*; **the l. of a subject** la littérature publiée sur une question

lithe [laɪð] ADJ agile

lithium ['lɪθɪəm] N *Chem* lithium *m*

lithograph ['lɪθəgrɑːf] N lithographie f **vt** lithographier

lithographer [lɪ'θɒgrəfə(r)] N lithographe mf

lithographic [lɪθə'græfɪk] ADJ lithographique

lithography [lɪ'θɒgrəfɪ] N lithographie f, procédés mpl lithographiques

Lithuania [lɪθjʊ'eɪnɪə] N Lituanie f

Lithuanian [lɪθʊ'eɪnɪən] ADJ lituanien N **1** Lituanien, -ienne **2** Ling lituanien m

litigant ['lɪtɪgənt] Law ADJ **l. parties** parties fpl plaidantes ou en litige N plaideur, -euse

litigate ['lɪtɪgeɪt] Law **vi** plaider **vt** (matter, property) contester, mettre en litige

litigation [lɪtɪ'geɪʃən] N Law litige m; **in l.** en litige; **to go to l.** (of person) aller en justice; (of matter) être porté en justice

litigious [lɪ'tɪdʒəs] ADJ **1** Law litigieux **2** Fml Pej (person) chicaneur

litmus ['lɪtməs] N Chem tournesol m ▸▸ **l. paper** papier m de tournesol; **l. test** réaction f au tournesol; Fig test m décisif; **this will be a l. test of the government's will** ce sera un test décisif pour juger de la détermination du gouvernement

litre, Am **liter** ['liːtər] N litre m

litter ['lɪtər] N **1** (in public place) détritus mpl, immondices fpl; (from people eating) papiers mpl gras; **please clear up your l.** (in park) veuillez nettoyer vos ordures; **dropping l. is forbidden, no l.** (on sign) défense de déposer des ordures **2** (of animal) portée f, **five young at a l.** or **in one l.** cinq petits d'une portée **3** (for carrying wounded) civière f; Hist (conveyance) litière f, **to be carried in a l.** être porté en litière **4** Agr (of straw etc) litière f, (of stable etc) fumier m; (for cat) litière f **vt 1** (of person) (streets etc) couvrir de détritus ou d'immondices; (room etc) mettre en désordre; (of objects) couvrir, joncher; **he litters his room with dirty socks** il parsème sa chambre de chaussettes sales; **the streets were littered with bottles** les rues étaient couvertes ou pleines de bouteilles vides; **table littered with papers** table encombrée de papiers; **her works are littered with allusions to the classics** ses écrits sont encombrés d'allusions aux auteurs classiques; **the pages of the book are littered with obscenities** le livre est un tissu d'obscénités; Fig **beaches littered with tourists** des plages jonchées de touristes **2 to l. (down) a horse** faire la litière à un cheval; **to l. (down) a stable** étendre de la paille dans une écurie **vi** (of animal) mettre bas, avoir une portée ▸▸ **l. basket** (in street) poubelle f, boîte f à ordures; Br **l. bin** poubelle, boîte à ordures; **throw it in the l. bin** jette-le à la poubelle; Br Fam **l. lout** = personne f qui jette des papiers ou des détritus par terre

litterbug ['lɪtəbʌg] N Fam personne f qui jette des papiers ou des détritus par terre

LITTLE ['lɪt(ə)l]

┌─────────────────────────────┐
ADJ petit **1** ▪ peu de **2**
N pas grand chose **1** ▪ peu à peu **1**
▪ un peu **2**
ADV peu **1**
└─────────────────────────────┘

ADJ **1** (comp **smaller**, Fam **littler**, superl **smallest**, Fam **littlest**) (small) petit; **l. girl** petite fille f, fillette f; **l. things like that matter** les petits détails comme cela ont leur importance; **poor l. girl!** pauvre petite!; Fam **a tiny l. house** une toute petite maison; **wait a l.**

while! attendez un petit moment!; **a l. something** (gift) une babiole; (to eat) un petit quelque chose VOIR GRAMMAIRE A17

2 (comp **less**, superl **least**) (not much) peu de; **l. money** peu d'argent; **a l. money** un peu d'argent; **I could do with a l. lunch** je mangerais bien un petit quelque chose pour déjeuner; **to gain l. advantage from sth** ne tirer que peu d'avantages de qch; **there is l. point in complaining** ça ne vaut pas vraiment la peine de porter plainte; **it makes l. sense** ça n'a pas beaucoup de sens; **we're only a l. way into the discussion** nous venons juste d'entamer la discussion; Fam **be it ever so l.** si peu que ce soit; **with what l. French I knew** avec le peu de français que je connaissais

3 Pej (mind) mesquin; Prov **l. things please l. minds** à petits esprits, peu n'en faut N **1** (comp **less**; superl **least**) peu m; **to eat l. or nothing** manger peu ou pas du tout; **he knows very l.** il ne sait pas grand-chose; **he has done l. for us** il n'a pas fait grand-chose pour nous; **I see very l. of her** je ne la vois guère; **given the l. that I know about this subject** étant donné le peu de connaissances que j'ai dans ce domaine; **to think l. of sb** ne pas avoir une haute opinion de qn; **to make** or **think l. of sth** faire peu de cas de qch; Prov **every l. helps** les petits ruisseaux font les grandes rivières; **I can only give you half an hour – every l. helps** je ne peux t'accorder qu'une demi-heure – c'est mieux que rien; **l. by l.** peu à peu, petit à petit

2 a l. more encore un peu; **a l. more and he would have died** il est passé à deux doigts de la mort; **a l. hot** un peu chaud; **for/after a l.** (time) pendant/après un certain temps; **he helped him a l.** il l'a aidé un peu; **I was not a l. afraid** j'avais très peur; Prov **a l. of what you fancy does you good** il n'y a pas de mal à se faire du bien; **wait a l.!** attendez un peu!

ADV **1** (comp **less**; superl **least**) (hardly) peu; **l. known** peu connu; **l. more than an hour ago** il y a à peine une heure; **that's l. less than bribery** ça frise la corruption; **l. short of disgusting/outrageous** quand même un peu dégoûtant/scandaleux; **he studied too l.** il a étudié trop peu, il n'a pas assez étudié; **l. as it matters** même si ça n'a pas l'air important ...; **I realized how l. I knew him** je me suis rendu compte à quel point je le connaissais peu; **if you think how l. money they actually have** quand on pense au peu d'argent dont ils disposent; **how l. it really matters in the end!** tout cela est tellement peu important au bout du compte

2 he l. knows or **thinks** or **suspects** ... il ne se doute guère ...; **l. did I think that** ... je ne pensais pas du tout que ...; **I l. expected him to come** je ne m'attendais guère à ce qu'il vienne VOIR GRAMMAIRE A78

3 l. enough assez peu; **you eat l. enough as it is** tu manges déjà assez peu comme ça ▸▸ **l. Englander** Hist isolationniste mf (hostile à l'expansion de l'empire britannique); (chauvinistic) = anglais m chauvin et xénophobe; **l. finger** petit doigt m; Fam **he has you (twisted) round his l. finger** il fait ce qu'il veut de toi; **l. hand** (of clock) petite aiguille f, **the l. man** (the average person) les petites gens fpl; **l. ones** (children) enfants mpl; (of animal) petits mpl; Fam esp Irish **the l. people** les lutins mpl; **l. toe** petit orteil m, doigt m de pied; Br Hum **the l. woman** ma/sa bourgeoise; **I'm fed up with the l. woman role** j'en ai marre d'être la petite femme soumise

littoral ['lɪtərəl] Geog ADJ littoral, -aux N littoral m

liturgical [lɪ'tɜːdʒɪk(ə)l] ADJ liturgique

liturgy ['lɪtədʒɪ] N liturgie f

livable ['lɪvəb(ə)l] ADJ = **liveable**

live¹ [laɪv] ADJ **1** (animal, person) vivant, en vie; (coal) ardent; **a l. issue** un sujet brûlant; **a restaurant where you order your fish l.** un restaurant où on choisit son poisson vivant; Fam **a real l. filmstar** une vedette de cinéma en chair et en os

2 TV, Radio (broadcast, commentary) en direct; TV **recorded before a l. audience** enregistré en public; **a l. performance** un spectacle (en direct); **I never saw a l. performance by the Beatles** je n'ai jamais vu les Beatles en concert; **Sinatra l. at the Palladium** Sinatra en concert au Palladium

3 Mil (ammunition) actif; (bomb) actif, amorcé, armé; (cartridge) à balle, réel

4 Tech (load) roulant, mobile

ADV TV, Radio **to be broadcast l.** être diffusé en direct; **to play/perform l.** (of band, comedian) faire de la scène; **the band hasn't performed l. for nearly ten years** le groupe n'a pas fait de scène depuis presque dix ans; **the show comes l. from New York City** le spectacle nous arrive en direct de New York; **an astronaut speaking l. from the moon** un astronaute parlant en direct de la lune ▸▸ Tech **l. axle** essieu m moteur, pont m; **l. bait** appât m vivant, vif m; **l. birth** enfant m né vivant; Comput **l. cam** caméra f Internet; **l. end** (of studio) salle f de direct; **l. entertainment** spectacle m; (broadcast) spectacles mpl en direct; **nobody goes to see l. entertainment any more** plus personne ne va au spectacle de nos jours; **the theatre and other forms of l. entertainment** le théâtre et autres formes de divertissement; **l. music** musique f live; **l. weight** (of animal for slaughter) poids m vif ou vivant; Elec **l. wire** fil m sous tension; Fam **she's a l. wire** elle est très énergique, Fam **elle pète la forme**

LIVE² [lɪv] **vi 1** (exist, be alive) vivre; **as long as my father lived there was no question of selling** tant que mon père était vivant il n'était pas question de vendre; **she lived in the 20th century** elle vécut au 20ème siècle; **we l. in interesting times** nous vivons une époque intéressante; **she'll l. to be 100** elle vivra jusqu'à 100 ans, elle sera centenaire; **she has only a few months to l.** il ne lui reste plus que quelques mois à vivre; **long l. the king!** vive le roi!; **as long** or **so long as I l.** tant que je vivrai; Fam **you'll l.!** tu survivras!; Prov **you l. and learn** on apprend à tout âge; Prov **l. and let l.** il faut que tout le monde vive; **this is what I call living!** c'est ce que j'appelle vivre!; **if you've never been to Venice, you haven't lived** si tu n'es jamais allé à Venise tu n'as pas vraiment vécu; **I want to l. a little** je veux profiter de la vie; **his name will l.** son nom restera ou sera immortalisé; **this day will l. in history** ce jour fera date dans l'histoire; **he lives by his writing** il vit de sa plume; **he lives by buying and selling antiques** il vit en faisant du commerce d'antiquités; **to l. by one's wits** (of smuggler etc) vivre d'expédients; (of people in hardship) se débrouiller pour survivre; **to l. by one's beliefs** vivre selon ses croyances; **to l. well** vivre bien; **to l. like a king** or **a lord** vivre comme un prince; **to l. in style** mener grand train; **to l. in poverty/fear** vivre dans la pauvreté/peur; **she lived only for her husband** elle n'a vécu que pour son mari; **we're living for the day we emigrate** nous vivons dans l'attente du jour où ous émigrerons; **she was living for the chance of revenge** la perspective de vengeance était sa raison de vivre; **you'll always l. with the guilt** la culpabilité vous poursuivra toute la vie; **you'll just have to l. with the idea!** il faudra que tu te fasses à cette idée!, il faudra que tu t'y fasses; **it's not ideal but I can l. with it** ce n'est pas l'idéal mais je m'y ferai

2 (reside) habiter, vivre; **to l. in Paris** habiter (à) Paris, vivre à Paris; **to l. in France** vivre en France; **to l. in a flat/house** vivre en appartement/dans une maison; **she lives in a fifth floor flat** elle vit dans un appartement au cinquième étage; **to l. at Number 10** habiter au numéro 10; **to l. in the country** habiter ou vivre à la campagne; **where do you l.?** où est-ce que vous habitez?; **fish l. in water** les poissons vivent dans l'eau; **the house doesn't seem to be lived in** la maison ne paraît pas habitée; **to l. with** (boyfriend, parents) vivre avec; (friend, parents) habiter avec; **he lives with his wife and daughter** il vit avec sa femme et sa fille; **he's difficult/ easy to l. with** il est difficile/facile à vivre

VT to l. a happy life mener une vie heureuse; **to l. a life of luxury** mener la grande vie; **life is not worth living** la vie ne vaut pas d'être vécue; **it makes life worth living** cela donne une raison de vivre; **to l. a lie** vivre sur un mensonge; Theat **to l. a part** entrer dans la peau d'un personnage

▸ **live down** VT SEP **to l. down one's past** faire oublier son passé; **this is awful, I'll never l. it down!** c'est terrible, je n'arriverai jamais à faire oublier ça!

▸ **live in** VI **1** (of student) **I'll be living in next year** je serai interne l'année prochaine **2** (of housekeeper etc) habiter sur place

▸ **live off** VT INSEP **to l. off sth** vivre de qch; **to l. off sb** vivre aux crochets de qn

▸ **live on** VI (continue to live) continuer à vivre; **he lived on for another three years** il vécut encore trois ans; **his memory will l. on** sa mémoire lui survivra

VT INSEP (depend on) **to l. on vegetables** se nourrir de légumes; **to l. on one's capital** vivre sur son capital; **it's not enough to l. on** ce n'est pas suffisant pour vivre; **to earn enough to l. on** gagner de quoi vivre; **they lived on her salary** ils ont vécu sur son salaire

▸ **live out** VI (of student) être externe; (of servant) ne pas coucher au domicile de ses patrons

VT SEP (period, one's life) passer; **they lived out their lives in poverty** ils vécurent toute leur vie dans la pauvreté; **he won't l. out the year** il ne passera pas l'année; **to l. out one's dreams/fantasies** vivre ses rêves/fantasmes

▸ **live through** VT INSEP (war, hard times etc) vivre; (survive) (war, drought) survivre à; **anyone who has lived through times like these will know that …** quiconque a vécu cette époque sait que …; **he's unlikely to l. through the winter** il est peu vraisemblable qu'il passe l'hiver

▸ **live together** VI vivre ensemble, être en ménage

▸ **live up** VT SEP Fam **to l. it up** faire la fête

▸ **live up to** VT INSEP **to l. up to expectations** (of person, party, film etc) tenir ses promesses; **his brother has given him a lot to l. up to** son frère a placé la barre très haut; **it's too much for me to l. up to** on m'en demande trop; **to l. up to one's principles** vivre selon ses principes; **to l. up to one's reputation** ne pas faillir à sa réputation; **to l. up to one's promise** tenir sa promesse

liveable ['lɪvəb(ə)l] ADJ **1** (life) supportable **2 l. in** (house, room) (habitable) habitable; (acceptable) vivable **3 l. with** (person) avec qui on peut vivre; **he's l. with** c'est quelqu'un avec qui on peut vivre

lived-in ['lɪvdɪn] ADJ (house, flat) accueillant; Fam (face) mûr; **to have a l. feel (to it)** être accueillant

live-in ADJ (chauffeur, nanny etc) logé et nourri

▸▸ **l. accommodation** (for staff) logement m à demeure; Hum **l. lover** compagnon m/ compagne f (avec qui l'on vit)

livelihood ['laɪvlɪhʊd] N moyens mpl d'existence, gagne-pain m inv; **to earn or gain one's l.** gagner sa vie ou son pain; **tourism is our l.** le tourisme est notre gagne-pain; **to lose one's l.** perdre ses moyens de subsistance

liveliness ['laɪvlɪnɪs] N vivacité f, Fin (of market) animation f

livelong ['lɪvlɒŋ] ADJ Lit **the l. day** toute la journée, tout le long du jour; **the l. night** toute la nuit

lively ['laɪvlɪ] ADJ **1** (person) vivant, plein de vie; (cheerful) gai; (colour) vif; (music) gai; (performance) vivant; (imagination) fertile; (town, description, party, conversation) animé; **you're very l. today** tu es en forme aujourd'hui; Fam **to make it** or **things l. for sb** rendre la vie dure à qn; **things are getting l.** (in discussion, meeting etc) ça chauffe; **to take a l. interest in sth** s'intéresser vivement à qch **2** (car, engine) nerveux; (horse) fougueux; (boat) rapide; **that's quite a l. clutch** c'est un embrayage plutôt sensible

ADV Fam **look l.!** grouille-toi!

▸ **liven up** ['laɪv(ə)n] VT SEP (person, meeting etc) animer, égayer; (proceedings) activer; **to l. up the conversation** ranimer la conversation; **you need to l. up your style** vous devriez mettre plus de dynamisme dans votre style; **some pictures would l. up the text a bit** quelques photos égaieraient un peu le texte

VI s'animer, s'activer, Fam se décoincer

liver[1] ['lɪvər] N Anat, Culin foie m

▸▸ Culin **l. pâté** pâté m de foie

liver[2] N (person) **fast l.** viveur, -euse, noceur, -euse; **loose l.** libertin m, débauché m

liveried ['lɪvərɪd] ADJ en livrée

liverish ['lɪvərɪʃ] ADJ Fig Fam (irritable) irritable; **to be** or **feel l.** avoir une crise de foie

Liverpudlian [lɪvə'pʌdlɪən] ADJ de Liverpool

N personne f originaire de Liverpool; (inhabitant) habitant, -ante de Liverpool

liverwurst ['lɪvəwɜːst] N Am saucisse f de foie

livery ['lɪvərɪ] N (uniform) livrée f, **full l.** grande livrée; **in l.** en livrée

▸▸ Br **l. company** confrérie f (de la cité de Londres); **l. horse** cheval m de louage; **l. stables** écuries fpl de chevaux de louage

livestock ['laɪvstɒk] N bétail m VOIR GRAMMAIRE A11

livid ['lɪvɪd] ADJ **1** (angry) furieux; **to be l. with anger**, Fam **to be absolutely l.** être fou de rage; **it makes me l.!** ça me met en rage! **2** (complexion) livide, blême; (sky) plombé; **a l. bruise** un bleu très marqué

living ['lɪvɪŋ] ADJ (person) vivant; **did she have any l. relatives?** avait-elle encore de la famille?; **she is our finest l. artist** c'est notre meilleure artiste contemporaine; **while she was l.** de son vivant; **there is not a l. soul to be seen** on ne rencontre pas âme qui vive ou Fam pas un chat; **he has done more for them than any man l.** il a fait plus pour eux que n'importe qui; **a l. death** une vie pire que la mort; **to make sb's life a l. hell** faire de la vie de qn un enfer; **within l. memory** de mémoire d'homme; **the sculpture had been carved out of the l. rock** la sculpture avait été taillée à même le roc

N **1** (way of life) vie f, **l. in the country** la vie à la campagne; **to be fond of good l.** être un bon vivant; **fast l. will do him no good** ça ne lui vaut rien de mener une vie débridée

2 (livelihood) vie f, **to earn one's l.** gagner sa vie; **to work for one's** or **a l.** travailler pour gagner sa vie; **to write for a l.** vivre de sa plume; **what does he do for a l.?** qu'est-ce qu'il fait?, quel est son métier?; **to make a l.**

gagner sa vie; **she makes a l. out of it** elle en vit

3 the l. (pl) les vivants mpl, **still in the land of the l.** encore vivant ou de ce monde

4 Br Rel bénéfice m, cure f

▸▸ **l. allowance** indemnité f de séjour; **l. conditions** conditions fpl de vie; **l.-flame gas fire** = chauffage m au gaz à flammes réelles, imitant un feu de charbon; **l. fossil** espèce f fossile; Fig (person) vieux fossile m; **l. language** langue f vivante; **l. proof** preuve f vivante; **l. quarters** (for servants) logements mpl, (on ship) partie f habitée; **l. room** (salle f de) séjour m; **l. space** espace m vital; **l. standards** niveau m de vie; **l. wage** minimum m vital; **l. will** = testament m dans lequel le testateur exprime sa volonté de ne pas être maintenu en vie artificiellement s'il sombre dans un état végétatif irréversible à la suite d'une maladie ou d'un accident

Livy ['lɪvɪ] N Tite-Live m

lizard ['lɪzəd] N lézard m; **l. (skin) handbag** sac m à main en lézard

llama ['lɑːmə] N lama m

LLB [elel'biː] N (abbr Legum Baccalaureus) ≃ Bachelier en Droit

LLD [elel'diː] N (abbr Legum Doctor) ≃ Docteur en Droit

Lloyd's name [lɔɪdz-] N Br = membre m du syndicat d'assurances Lloyds

LMBO [elembiː'əʊ] N Fin (abbr leveraged management buy-out) = rachat m d'entreprise par les salariés

LNG [elen'dʒiː] N (abbr liquefied natural gas) GNL m

lo [ləʊ] INT Arch, Lit voici, voilà; Hum **lo and behold, there he was** et voilà qu'il était là

loach [ləʊtʃ] N loche f

load [ləʊd] N **1** (burden) fardeau m; (of lorry, ship etc) charge f, chargement m; (contents of vehicle) (of gravel etc) camion m, tombereau m; (of wood) charge f; **useful l.** charge utile; **that's a l. off my mind!** cela m'enlève un poids!; **to share** or **spread the l.** (the work) répartir le travail; **to shed its l. on the motorway** (of lorry) répandre son chargement sur l'autoroute

2 Fam (a lot) **a l. of rubbish** or **nonsense** (novel, theory etc) c'est n'importe quoi; Sl **it's a l. of crap** or **bullshit** c'est des conneries; Fam **get a l. of that!** (look) vise un peu!; (listen) écoute un peu ça!; Fam **he's got loads of them** il en a des quantités ou des tas; Fam **loads of money** plein de fric; Fam **we've done it loads of times** on l'a fait plein de fois; Fam **we've got loads of time** nous avons largement le temps

3 Tech, Elec charge f, **safe l.** charge de sécurité; **machine working at full l.** machine qui fonctionne ou travaille à pleine charge; **under l.** en charge; Elec **to shed the l.** délester

VT 1 (lorry, ship, camera, gun, film, shell, program) charger; **to l. passengers** (of bus) prendre des voyageurs; **to l. a washing machine/dishwasher** mettre du linge dans le lave-linge/de la vaisselle dans le lave-vaisselle, remplir le lave-linge/lave-vaisselle; **to l. a program into a computer** entrer un programme dans un ordinateur; **he was loaded with shopping** il avait les bras chargés de courses; **loaded with cares** accablé de soucis; **I'm going to l. some more work onto you** je vais vous confier encore un peu de travail; **I don't think it's fair to l. all the work onto one person** je trouve que ce n'est pas juste de donner tout le travail à une seule personne

2 Tech (spring) serrer, bander

3 (dice) piper; Fig **the dice were loaded in our favour** la situation nous a été favorable

4 (in insurance) (premium) majorer

VI Comput (of software etc) se charger; (of

lorry) prendre un chargement; (of ship) prendre une cargaison; Aut no loading or unloading between 9am and 4pm (on sign) chargement ou déchargement interdits entre 9h et 16h

▸▸ l. bed (of truck) plateau m de chargement; l. box (on vehicle) soute f; l. factor (of plane) coefficient de remplissage; Elec facteur m ou coefficient de charge; Tech facteur de charge; Naut l. line ligne f de charge; l. restraint mesh filet m de retenu de charge; Elec l. shedding délestage m; l. space coffre m; (of lorry) plancher m de chargement; l. unit unité f de chargement

▸load down VT SEP to l. sb down with (packages, work, responsibility) surcharger qn de; to be loaded down with worry être accablé de soucis; to be loaded down with anxiety être rongé d'anxiété

▸load up VT SEP (lorry etc), Comput charger VI (of lorry) prendre une cargaison; (of lorry etc) prendre un chargement

loadable ['ləʊdəb(ə)l] ADJ (software etc) qui peut se charger, chargeable

loaded ['ləʊdɪd] ADJ 1 (lorry, ship, camera, gun etc) chargé 2 (dice) pipé; the situation was l. against me la situation m'a été défavorable; a l. question une question insidieuse; a l. word un mot trop connoté 3 Sl (person) (wealthy) richissime; (drunk) soûl; (on drugs) drogué, camé; to get l. (drunk) se soûler; (on drugs) se camer

loader ['ləʊdər] N 1 (person) chargeur m 2 (device) chargeuse f, Constr chargeur m

loading ['ləʊdɪŋ] N (of lorry, ship, plane, camera, gun) chargement m; (on ship) délai d'embarquement

▸▸ l. bay aire f de chargement; l. charges coût m d'affrètement; l. procedure procédure f de chargement; l. ramp rampe f de chargement; l. time délai m de chargement; (on ship) délai d'embarquement

loaf, pl loaves [ləʊf, ləʊvz] N 1 Culin pain m; a l. of bread un pain; Prov half a l. is better than none or than no bread faute de grives on mange des merles 2 Fam (head) to use one's l. faire marcher son ciboulot; use your l. fais un peu marcher ton ciboulot

▸loaf about, loaf around VI traîner

loafer ['ləʊfər] N 1 (person) fainéant, -ante 2 (shoe) mocassin m

loam [ləʊm] N Agr, Geol terreau m

loamy ['ləʊmi] ADJ (soil) riche en terreau

loan [ləʊn] N (money, object) (from borrower's point of view) emprunt m; (from lender's point of view) prêt m; l. of money prêt ou avance f d'argent; it was very generous of you to give me a l. of that money c'était très généreux de ta part de me prêter cet argent; it's a l., you can have it as a l. je vous le prête; can I have the l. of …? puis-je emprunter …?; to give sb a l. of sth prêter qch à qn; on l. from the Louvre prêt du Louvre; to have sth on permanent l. disposer de qch en prêt permanent; she's on l. from Head Office elle est détachée du bureau central; the video you want is out on l. la vidéo que vous voulez est sortie; to raise a l. on an estate emprunter de l'argent sur une terre; to take out a l. faire un emprunt; to apply for a l. demander un prêt; to repay a l. rembourser un emprunt; long/short-term l. prêt/emprunt à long/court terme; secured l. prêt/ emprunt gagé ou garanti; unsecured l. prêt/emprunt sans garantie; without security prêt/emprunt à découvert; Fin l. at call, l. repayable on demand prêt remboursable sur demande; Fin l. on collateral prêt sur gage ou sur nantissement; Fin l. at interest prêt m à intérêts; Fin l. at notice prêt à terme; Fin l. on overdraft prêt découvert; l. to value = rapport m entre le capital restant dû et la valeur du bien

financé; Acct loans and advances to customers créances fpl clients

VT (sth to sb qch à qn); loaned by the Louvre prêt m du Louvre

▸▸ Banking l. account compte m de prêt; Fin l. agreement contrat m de prêt; Fin l.-back facility (in insurance) possibilité f d'emprunt sur le montant de son assurance-vie; Fin l. capital capital m sur prêt ou d'emprunt; Fin l. certificate titre m de prêt; Fin l. company société f de crédit, maison f de prêt; Fin l. insurance assurance f crédit; Fin l. maturity échéance f emprunt; Fin l. note titre d'obligation, titre de créance; Fin l. office organisme m de crédit, maison de prêt; Acct loans outstanding encours m; Fin l. risk cover couverture f du risque de crédit; Fam Pej l. shark usurier, -ière; Fin l. stock emprunt m obligataire; Ling l. word mot m d'emprunt

loath [ləʊθ] ADJ to be l. to do sth hésiter à faire qch; esp Lit nothing l. sans hésiter

loathe [ləʊð] VT détester, exécrer; I l. milk j'ai horreur du lait, je déteste le lait; to l. doing sth détester faire qch

loathing ['ləʊðɪŋ] N dégoût m, répugnance f (for pour); to feel l. for sb éprouver du dégoût pour qn; to fill sb with l. remplir qn de dégoût, dégoûter qn; to have a l. for milk avoir horreur du lait

loathsome ['ləʊðsəm] ADJ (person) répugnant; (habit) détestable; (smell) nauséabond; that was a l. thing to do/say! c'était vraiment dégoûtant de faire/dire ça!

loathsomeness ['ləʊðsəmnɪs] N nature f repoussante ou dégoûtante

lob [lɒb] N Sport lob m, chandelle f
VT 1 Tennis, Ftbl lober 2 Fam (throw) balancer; l. that over! balance-moi ça!

lobby ['lɒbi] N 1 (corridor) couloir m, antichambre f, vestibule m; (of court) promenoir m; (of theatre) entrée f, (of hotel) hall m 2 the l. of the House (in Parliament) = la salle des pas perdus; Parl division lobbies = vestibules mpl où passent les députés lorsqu'ils se divisent pour voter 3 Pol etc (pressure group) lobby m, groupe m de pression; the anti-abortion l. le groupe de pression contre l'avortement
VI (of pressure group) faire pression (in favour of/against en faveur de/contre); they're lobbying for tax reform ils font pression pour obtenir une réforme fiscale
VT esp Pol (person) faire pression sur
▸▸ Br Pol l. correspondent journaliste mf parlementaire

lobbying ['lɒbɪŋ] N Pol etc lobbying m, lobbysme m

lobbyist ['lɒbɪɪst] N Pol etc lobbyiste mf, membre m d'un groupe de pression

lobe [ləʊb] N 1 Anat (of ear etc) lobe m 2 Bot lobe m

lobelia [ləʊ'biːlɪə] N Bot lobélie f

lobotomize [lə'bɒtəmaɪz] VT Surg lobotomiser

lobotomy [lə'bɒtəmi] N Surg lobotomie f

lobster ['lɒbstər] N homard m; spiny l. langouste f
▸▸ l. boat homardier m; (for spiny lobster) langoustier m; l. pot casier m à homards; (for spiny lobster) casier à langoustes

local ['ləʊk(ə)l] ADJ local, -aux; the l. doctor le médecin du quartier; a matter of l. politics une question de politique locale; they voted for the l. man ils ont voté pour le candidat local
N 1 the locals (people) les gens mpl ou les habitants mpl du coin 2 Med, Fam (anaesthetic) anesthésie f locale 3 Fam the l. (pub) le bar du coin; this is my l. c'est le bar où je vais régulièrement 4 Am Journ (item) nouvelle f locale

▸▸ Med l. anaesthetic anesthésie f locale; to give sb a l. anaesthetic faire une anesthésie f locale; Comput l. area network réseau m local; Pol l. authorities autorités fpl locales ou régionales; Fin, Com l. bill effet m sur place; Comput l. bus bus m local; Comput l. bus card carte f de bus local; Comput l. bus disk disque m connecté au bus local; Tel l. call communication f locale; l. channel canal m local, chaîne f locale; l. colour couleur f locale; l. currency monnaie f locale; l. edition édition f locale; l. government administration f municipale; l. news informations fpl régionales; l. paper journal m local; l. radio radio f locale; l. radio station station f de radio locale; l. showers averses fpl éparses; Am Fin l. taxes impôts mpl locaux; l. television télévision f locale; l. time heure f locale; 6am l. time 6 heures du matin heure locale; l. train (train m) omnibus m; l. wine vin m du pays

locale [ləʊ'kɑːl] N (of events) lieu m; the l. for a film le lieu de tournage d'un film

locality [ləʊ'kælɪtɪ] N (neighbourhood) endroit m, lieu m; in our l. (part of town) dans notre quartier; (out of town) dans notre région; in the general l. of the incident sur les lieux de l'incident; a man was seen in the l. at around 8 o'clock un homme a été vu dans les environs vers 8 heures

localize ['ləʊkəlaɪz] VT (epidemic etc) localiser; to become localized (of disease, pain) se localiser (in dans)

localized ['ləʊkəlaɪzd] ADJ localisé

locally ['ləʊkəlɪ] ADV localement; (to live, be well known, work etc) dans le quartier; l. produced wine vin du pays; we get them printed l. nous les faisons imprimer sur place; I prefer to shop l. je préfère faire mes courses dans le quartier; he set up in business l. il a monté une affaire sur place

locate [ləʊ'keɪt] VT 1 (to find) localiser, situer; Elec (fault etc) repérer, localiser; to l. sth on a map situer qch sur une carte; Naut to l. a ship déterminer la position d'un navire (en mer) 2 (to situate) situer; the new shopping centre is located in the old market square le nouveau centre commercial est situé sur la place du vieux marché
VI (of company etc) s'installer

location [ləʊ'keɪʃən] N 1 (site, place) emplacement m 2 Cin lieu m de tournage; to be on l. tourner en extérieur; filmed on l. filmé en extérieur 3 (finding) localisation f, Elec (of fault etc) repérage m 4 Comput adresse f URL
▸▸ Comput l. box zone f adresse; Cin l. marks (in studio) points mpl de repère au sol; Mktg l. pricing fixation f des prix selon l'endroit; Cin l. shot plan m en extérieur; l. shots extérieurs mpl

> Note that the French word **location** is a false friend and is never a translation for the English word **location**. It means **renting**.

locative ['lɒkətɪv] ADJ, N Gram locatif m

loch [lɒx] N Scot lac m; sea l. bras m de mer, fjord m

LOCK¹ [lɒk]

N	serrure 1	▪ verrouillage 1
▪ verrou 2	▪ clef 4	▪ braquage 5
▪ écluse 6		
VT	fermer à clef 1	▪ verrouiller 1, 2
▪ enfermer 1	▪ bloquer 2	
VI	se bloquer 1	

N 1 (on door etc) serrure f, (padlock) cadenas m; Comput (in network) verrouillage m, blockage m; under l. and key sous clef; (of person) sous les verrous
2 Tech verrou m, pl -ous

3 *(on gun)* platine *f*; **we sold it l. stock and barrel** nous avons tout vendu sans exception; **we bought the whole estate l. stock and barrel** nous avons acheté toute la propriété; **he swallowed the story l. stock and barrel** il a tout avalé; **the motion was rejected l. stock and barrel** la motion a été rejetée en bloc

4 *(in wrestling)* étreinte *f*, clef *f*; **arm l.** clef de bras

5 *Aut etc* (rayon *m*) de braquage; **on full l.** braqué au maximum

6 *(on canal)* écluse *f*

7 *Rugby* avant *m* de deuxième ligne

vt 1 fermer à clef, verrouiller; **behind locked doors** à huis clos; **to l. sb in a room** enfermer qn dans une chambre; **to l. sth (away) in a drawer** enfermer qch dans un tiroir; **to l. valuables (away) in a safe** mettre des objets de valeur dans un coffre

2 *(steering wheel)* *(disable)* bloquer; *(put on full lock)* braquer à fond; *(machine parts)* enclencher; *(computer, keyboard, files)* verrouiller; *(mobile phone)* bloquer; **his jaws were tightly locked** il avait les dents serrées; **to be locked in each other's arms** se tenir étroitement enlacés; **to be locked in a passionate embrace** être passionnément enlacés; *Fig* **to be locked in sb's deadly embrace** être pris dans les griffes de qn; **to be locked (together) in a struggle** *(of people)* être engagés corps à corps dans une lutte; **to be locked in negotiation/dispute** être enfermé dans une négociation/un conflit; *Fig* **to l. horns with the enemy** livrer bataille avec l'ennemi; *Fig* **they have locked horns** *(of people)* ils sont en désaccord

vi 1 *(of wheels etc)* se bloquer; **the door locks on the inside** la porte se ferme de l'intérieur; **the door locks automatically** la porte se verrouille automatiquement; **the parts l. into each other** les parties s'enclenchent l'une dans l'autre

2 *Aut* **to l. left/right** braquer à gauche/à droite

►► **l. chamber** *(on canal)* sas *m* (d'écluse); *Rugby* **l. forward** avant *m* de deuxième ligne; **l. gate** *(on canal)* porte *f* d'écluse; *Comput* **l. inhibit** contre-verrou *m*, *pl* contre-verrous; *Br Aut* **l. ring** jonc *m* d'arrêt

► **lock in** vt sep **1** *(person)* enfermer à clef, mettre sous clef; **to get locked in** se faire enfermer; **to l. oneself in** s'enfermer

2 **to be locked in** *(to pension scheme etc)* ne pas avoir la possibilité de changer; *(to contract)* être lié; **to be locked into a company** *(as a source of supply etc)* être totalement dépendant d'une société; *St Exch, Fin* **to l. in a hedge** immobiliser une couverture

► **lock off** vt sep *Typ, Comput* débloquer; *(bad sector)* interdire l'accès à; **this key locks the caps on and off** cette touche bloque et débloque les majuscules

► **lock on** vt sep *Typ, Comput* bloquer, verrouiller; **l. the caps on before you start typing** bloque les majuscules avant de commencer à taper

► **lock on to** vt insep *(of radar etc), Fig* s'accrocher à

► **lock out** vt sep **1** **to l. sb out** enfermer qn dehors; **I found myself locked out** en rentrant j'ai trouvé la porte fermée (à clef); **I've locked myself out (of my room)** je me suis enfermé dehors

2 *Ind (workforce)* lock-outer

► **lock up** vt sep **1** *(something)* mettre sous clef; *(somebody, something)* enfermer; *(in jail)* mettre sous les verrous; *(house)* fermer à clef; **to l. a house up for the winter** barricader une maison pour l'hiver; **he should be locked up!** il faudrait l'enfermer!

2 *Fin (capital)* immobiliser, bloquer, engager

vi **it's time to l. up** c'est l'heure de fermer; **to**

l. up for the night fermer le soir jusqu'au lendemain

lock² N *(of hair)* mèche *f*, boucle *f*, *Arch, Lit* **locks** cheveux *mpl*, chevelure *f*

locked-in syndrome [ˈlɒkt] N *Med* locked-in syndrome *m*, syndrome *m* d'enfermement

locker [ˈlɒkər] N *(for luggage, in school)* casier *m*; *Naut* coffre *m*; *Aviat* **overhead l.** coffre à bagage
►► *Am* **l. room** vestiaire *m (avec casiers)*; **l.-room jokes** plaisanteries grossières; **l.-room language** langage grossier

locket [ˈlɒkɪt] N médaillon *m*

locking [ˈlɒkɪŋ] ADJ ATTRIB
►► *Aut* **l. bar** barre *f* antivol; *Comput* **l. connector** connecteur *m* autobloquant; *Comput, Tech etc* **l. device** dispositif *m* de verrouillage; *Tech etc* **l. mechanism** mécanisme *m* de verrouillage; *Electron* **l. on** *(of radar etc)* accrochage *m* ; **l. up** mise *f* sous clef; *(of house, room)* fermeture *f*, *Fin (of capital)* immobilisation *f*

lockjaw [ˈlɒkdʒɔː] N tétanos *m*; **to have l.** avoir le tétanos

lock-keeper N *(on canal)* gardien *m* d'écluse, éclusier *m*

locknut [ˈlɒknʌt] N contre-écrou *m*, *pl* contre-écrous

lock-out N lock-out *m inv*

locksmith [ˈlɒksmɪθ] N serrurier *m*

lock-to-lock ADV *Aut* de butée à butée

lockup [ˈlɒkʌp] N **1** *Br (for storage)* remise *f*, *(garage)* box *m* **2** *Fam (police cells)* violon *m*, bloc *m* **3** *Aut (of wheel)* lock-up *m*; *(gear)* rapport *m* bloqué
►► *Aut* **l. clutch** embrayage *m* de prise directe; **l. garage** box *m*

loco¹ [ˈləʊkəʊ] N *Fam (train)* loco *f*

loco² ADJ *Am Fam (mad)* fou, *f* folle, *Fam* dingue

loco³ ADV *Com* loco; **the prices are l. Hull** les prix incluent le transport jusqu'à Hull

locomotion [ləʊkəˈməʊʃən] N locomotion *f*

locomotive [ləʊkəˈməʊtɪv] ADJ locomotif; *Anat* locomoteur, -trice
N *Rail* locomotive *f*

locum [ˈləʊkəm] N *Br (for doctor, cleric)* remplaçant, -ante; **to take a l. job** faire un remplacement, prendre un emploi de remplaçant; **she's working as a l. in a hospital in London** elle fait un remplacement dans un hôpital de Londres
►► *Br* **l. tenens** *(for doctor, cleric)* remplaçant, -ante

locus, *pl* **loci** [ˈləʊkəs, ˈləʊsaɪ, ˈləʊsiː] N **1** *Math* lieu *m* géométrique **2** *Biol (of gene)* locus *m*

locust [ˈləʊkəst] N **1** *Entom* locuste *f*, sauterelle *f* **2** *(carob tree)* caroubier *m*; *(false acacia)* robinier *m*
►► **l. bean** caroube *f*, **l. tree** *(carob tree)* caroubier *m*; *(false acacia)* robinier *m*

locution [ləʊˈkjuːʃən] N locution *f*

lode [ləʊd] N *Geol, Min* filon *m*, veine *f*

lodestar [ˈləʊdstɑːr] N **1** étoile *f* directrice; **the l.** l'étoile polaire **2** *Fig* référence *f*

lodestone [ˈləʊdstəʊn] N *Miner* aimant *m* naturel

lodge [lɒdʒ] N **1** *(for concierge etc)* loge *f*, **keeper's l.** maison *f* de garde-chasse; **(gate) l.** *(to estate)* pavillon *m* d'entrée, pavillon du garde; *Univ* **master's l.** résidence *f* du directeur du collège; **shooting l.** pavillon *m* de chasse **2** *(freemasons')* loge *f*, atelier *m*; *(meeting)* tenue *f*, **the Grand L. of France** le Grand Orient (de France) **3** *(of otter)* terrier *m*; *(of beaver)* hutte *f* **4** *(of Native Americans)* hutte *f*, wigwam *m*

vt 1 *(accommodate)* loger, héberger **2** *(de-*

posit) déposer, remettre; *(money)* consigner, déposer (**with sb** chez qn); *(bonds)* déposer (**with a bank** dans une banque); **securities lodged as collateral** titres déposés *ou* remis en nantissement; *Law* **to l. an appeal** interjeter appel, faire appel; **to l. a complaint** déposer une plainte; **to l. a complaint against sb** porter plainte contre qn

vi 1 *(of person)* loger; **to l. with sb** *(rent room from)* louer une chambre *ou* des chambres chez qn; *(have meals provided)* être en pension chez qn **2** *(of thing)* rester, se loger; **a fishbone lodged in his throat** il s'est coincé une arête dans le gosier; **a bullet lodged close to his spine** il a reçu une balle qui est allée se loger près de sa colonne vertébrale; **the words had lodged in her memory** les mots étaient gravés dans sa mémoire
►► **l. keeper** portier *m*; **l. meeting** *(of freemasons)* tenue *f*

lodger [ˈlɒdʒər] N locataire *mf (en meublé)*; *(who has meals provided)* pensionnaire *mf*; **to take (in) lodgers** louer des chambres; *(provide meals too)* prendre des pensionnaires

lodging [ˈlɒdʒɪŋ] N **1** *(room etc)* logement *m*; **to find a night's l.** trouver où coucher pour la nuit **2** *(usu pl)* **lodgings** logement *m*, appartement *m* meublé, *Arch* logis *m*; **to live** *or* **be in lodgings** loger *ou* habiter en garni *ou* en (hôtel) meublé **3** *(of money, securities etc)* dépôt *m*, consignation *f*, remise *f*, *Law (of complaint)* déposition *f*, *(of appeal)* interjection *f*
►► **l. house** garni *m*; *Am* **l. industry** industrie *f* hôtelière

loft [lɒft] N *(attic)* grenier *m*, soupente *f*, *(in church, hall etc)* galerie *f*, tribune *f*
vt *(ball)* donner de la hauteur à
►► **l. conversion** combles *mpl* aménagés, loft *m*; **we're thinking of doing a l. conversion** nous avons l'intention d'aménager le grenier

loftily [ˈlɒftɪlɪ] ADV **1** *(situated)* en hauteur **2** *Pej (to reply)* de manière hautaine

loftiness [ˈlɒftɪnɪs] N **1** *(of mountain etc)* hauteur *f* **2** *Pej (of person)* arrogance *f*, hauteur *f*

lofty [ˈlɒftɪ] ADJ **1** *(mountain, tree, building etc)* haut, élevé **2** *Pej (person, manner)* hautain **3** *(aim, desire etc)* noble; *(style)* relevé, soutenu; **the l. words in which the argument is expressed** le style relevé de l'argumentation
N *Fam (tall person)* **hello, l.!** salut, mon grand!

log¹ [lɒg] N **1** *(of wood)* bûche *f*, *(esp for building)* rondin *m*; *Fig* **to sleep like a l.** dormir comme une souche **2** *(record)* carnet *m* de route *ou* de bord; *Naut* journal *m*, *pl* -aux; *Aviat* carnet de vol; **ship's l.** journal de bord; **to write up the l.** noter les détails du voyage **3** *Naut (for measuring speed)* loch *m*
vt 1 *(order, in accounts)* enregistrer; *Naut etc* porter au journal; *(results etc)* noter sur un registre; *(of computer)* enregistrer; **the ship's arrival at Southampton was logged at 0800 hours** l'arrivée du bateau à Southampton a été portée au journal à 0800 heures; *Aviat* **to l. (up) 1,000 hours** inscrire 1 000 heures de vol **2** *(wood)* tronçonner, débiter en bûches **3** **the ship logged 15 knots** le navire filait à 15 nœuds
►► **l. cabin** cabane *f* en rondins; *Comput* **l. file** fichier *m* compte-rendu; **l. fire** feu *m* de bois; **l. hut** hutte *f* en rondins, cabane en bois; **l. jam** *(in river)* embâcle *m* de bûches; *Fig (deadlock)* impasse *f*, *Naut* **l. line** ligne *f* de loch; **l. running** flottage *m* du bois; **l. transporter** fardier *m*

► **log in** VI, VT SEP *Comput* = **log on**

► **log off** VI *Comput (of user)* sortir, se déconnecter

  VT SEP faire sortir

► **log on** VI *Comput (of user)* entrer, ouvrir une session; *(to remote system)* entrer en communication; **to l. to a system** se connecter à un système; **to l. on to a data base** entrer dans une base de données

  VT SEP faire entrer

► **log out** VI, VT SEP *Comput* = **log off**

log[2] N *Math Fam* logarithme *m*

  ►► **l. table** table *f* de logarithmes

loganberry ['ləʊɡənberɪ] N *(fruit)* ronce-framboise *f, pl* ronces-framboises

logarithm ['lɒɡərɪð(ə)m] N logarithme *m*

logarithmic [lɒɡə'rɪðmɪk] ADJ *(curve)* logarithmique; *(paper)* à divisions logarithmiques

  ►► **l. table** table *f* de logarithmes

logbook ['lɒɡbʊk] N **1** *(record)* registre *m*; *Aviat* carnet *m* de vol; *Aut (personal record)* carnet de route; *Naut* journal *m* de bord; *(of machine)* journal de travail; *Radio* carnet d'écoute **2** *Br Aut (official documents)* ≃ carte *f* grise

logger ['lɒɡər] N bûcheron *m*

loggerheads ['lɒɡəhedz] N *Fam* **to be at l. with sb** avoir un différend avec qn (**about** au sujet de); **they were constantly at l.** ils se disputaient tout le temps; **his views were at l. with ...** ses opinions étaient en contradiction avec ...

loggia ['lɒdʒɪə] N *Archit* loge *f*, loggia *f*

logging ['lɒɡɪŋ] N **1** *(of details, events)* inscription *f* dans un journal; *Comput* enregistrement *m*; **l. of an order** enregistrement *m* d'une commande **2** *(felling timber etc)* exploitation *f* forestière

  ►► **l. camp** camp *m* forestier

logic ['lɒdʒɪk] N logique *f*, **I don't see the l. of it** je ne vois pas la logique (dans tout cela)

  ►► *Comput* **l. analyser** analyseur *m* logique; *Comput* **l. board** carte *f* logique; *Comput* **l. bomb** bombe *f* logique *ou* à retardement; *Comput* **l. card** carte *f* logique; *Comput* **l. chip** puce *f* logique; *Comput* **l. circuit** circuit *m* logique; *Comput* **l. gate** porte *f* logique; *Comput* **l. operator** opérateur *m* logique; *Comput* **l. seeking** recherche *f* logique

logical ['lɒdʒɪk(ə)l] ADJ *(conclusion, person)*, *Comput* logique; **do be l.!** essaie d'être logique!

  ►► *Comput* **l. access control** contrôle *m* d'accès logique; *Comput* **l. access protection** protection *f* d'accès logique; *Comput* **l. drive** unité *f* logique; *Comput* **l. file** fichier *m* logique; *Comput* **l. log** journal *m* logique; *Comput* **l. operator** opérateur *m* logique

logically ['lɒdʒɪklɪ] ADV logiquement

logic-chopper N ergoteur, -euse

logic-chopping N ergotage *m*

login ['lɒɡɪn] N *Comput* ouverture *f* de session

  ►► **l. name** nom *m* d'utilisateur, nom de login

logistic [lɒ'dʒɪstɪk], **logistical** [lɒ'dʒɪstɪk(ə)l] ADJ logistique

logistics [lɒ'dʒɪstɪks] N *Mil* logistique *f*, **the l. of the situation** les données logistiques de la situation VOIR GRAMMAIRE A10

logo ['ləʊɡəʊ] N sigle *m*, logo *m*

  ►► **l. page** *(of software package)* page *f* d'accueil; **l. screen** *(of software package)* écran *m* d'accueil

logoff ['lɒɡɒf] N **l. timed at ...** fin de session enregistrée à ...

logon ['lɒɡɒn] N ouverture *f* de session; **l. timed at ...** ouverture de session prévue à ...

---

logrolling ['lɒɡrəʊlɪŋ] N **1** transport *m* des billes à la rivière **2** *Am Pol* alliance *f* politique dans un but intéressé

logwood ['lɒɡwʊd] N *(wood)* (bois *m* de) campêche *m*; *(tree)* campêcher *m*

loin [lɔɪn] N **1** *Anat, Lit* **loins** reins *mpl; Lit* **sprung from the loins of ...** sorti des reins de ... **2** *Culin (of mutton, veal)* filet *m*; *(of veal)* longe *f, (of mutton)* carré *m*; *(of beef)* aloyau *m* et faux-filet; *(of pork)* échine *f*, filet

  ►► **l. chop** côtes *fpl* premières

loincloth ['lɔɪnklɒθ] N pagne *m*

loiter ['lɔɪtər] VI *(suspiciously)* rôder; *(delay)* s'attarder (en route); **stop loitering and hurry up** arrête de flâner, dépêche-toi; *Law* **to l. (with intent)** rôder (d'une manière suspecte dans un endroit fréquenté)

loitering ['lɔɪtərɪŋ] N *Law* **l. with intent** délit *m* d'intention

LOL *Comput (abbr* **laughing out loud)** MDR

loll [lɒl] VI **1** *(of person)* être étendu (paresseusement); **lolling back in an armchair** affalé dans un fauteuil **2** *(of tongue)* **to l. (out)** pendre

► **loll about, loll around** VI *(of person)* paresser, fainéanter

lollipop ['lɒlɪpɒp] N *(candy)* sucette *f, (ice)* glace *f* à l'eau; *(chocolate)* esquimau® *m*

  ►► *Br Fam* **l. lady** = contractuelle *f* qui aide les écoliers à traverser la rue; *Br Fam* **l. man** = contractuel *m* qui aide les écoliers à traverser la rue

lollop ['lɒləp] VI *esp Br Fam* **to l. along** courir lourdement; **the rabbit lolloped off** le lapin s'éloigna en bondissant

lolly ['lɒlɪ] N **1** *Fam (candy)* sucette *f, (ice)* glace *f* à l'eau; *(chocolate)* esquimau® *m* **2** *Austr Fam (sweet)* bonbon *m* **3** *Br Sl (money)* fric *m*, flouze *m*

Lombard rate ['lɒmbɑːd] N *Banking* taux *m* Lombard

London ['lʌndən] N Londres; **a L. street** une rue de Londres; **a L. bus/taxi** un bus/taxi londonien

  ►► *Bot* **L. pride** saxifrage *f* ombreuse; *Br* **L. weighting** = indemnité *f* de vie chère venant compléter certains salaires londoniens

Londoner ['lʌndənər] N Londonien, -ienne; **a L. born and bred** un Londonien pure souche

lone [ləʊn] ADJ *esp Lit (person, thing)* solitaire, seul; *(place)* isolé, désert; **a l. parent** un parent isolé; *Fig* **to play a l. hand** agir tout seul, être seul contre tous

  ►► **the L. Star State** = surnom *m* donné au Texas; *Fig* **l. wolf** solitaire *mf*; **to be a bit of a l. wolf** être un peu solitaire

loneliness ['ləʊnlɪnɪs] N *(of house, person, village, political position)* isolement *m; (feeling)* solitude *f*; **with only the l. of old age to look forward to** avec la seule perspective de vieillir dans la solitude

lonely ['ləʊnlɪ] ADJ *(person)* seul; *(life, job)* solitaire; *(place, farmhouse)* isolé; **a l. figure** une silhouette; *Fig (politician etc)* une figure isolée; *Fig* **to travel a l. road** avoir un parcours solitaire; **to feel very l.** se sentir bien seul; **are you feeling l.?** vous vous sentez seul?; **life is very l. since the children left home** la vie est bien morne depuis que les enfants ont quitté la maison

  ►► **l. hearts club** club *m* de rencontres; **l. hearts column** rubrique *f* rencontres *(des petites annonces)*

loner ['ləʊnər] N solitaire *mf*

lonesome ['ləʊnsəm] ADJ *Am* solitaire, seul; **to feel l.** se sentir seul

  N *Fam* **to be on one's l.** être seul avec soi-même; **to do sth all on one's l.** faire qch tout seul

---

[lɒŋ] (**longer** ['lɒŋɡər], **longest** ['lɒŋɡɪst]) ADJ **1** *(in size)* long, *f* longue; **how l. is the table?** quelle est la longueur de la table?; **to make sth longer** allonger qch, rallonger qch; **to be six metres l.** faire six mètres de long; **a 20 foot l. swimming pool** une piscine de 6 mètres de long; *Fam* **to be l. on charm/good ideas** *etc* être plein de charme/bonnes idées *etc*; **l. in the leg** aux longues jambes; *Fam* **l. in the tooth** *(old)* vieux, *f* vieille; **to go the l. way round** *(to a place)* prendre le chemin le plus long; *Fig* **the best by a l. way** de loin le meilleur; **a l. face** un visage allongé; *Fig* **to have a l. face, to pull a l. face** faire la tête, faire une tête de six pieds de long; **patience is not my l. suit** la patience n'est pas mon fort

2 *(in time)* long, *f* longue; **it will take a l. time** cela prendra longtemps, ce sera long; **a l. time ago** il y a (bien) longtemps; **it's a l. time since I was (last) in Paris** ça fait longtemps que je ne suis pas allé à Paris; **I've been wanting to go for a l. time** ça fait longtemps que j'ai envie d'y aller; **to wait for a l. time** attendre longtemps; **it's been a l. night** la nuit a été longue; **we've all had a l. day** nous avons tous eu une longue journée; **we're going away for a l. weekend** nous partons pour un week-end prolongé *ou* long *ou* grand week-end; **the days are getting longer** les jours rallongent; **three days at the longest** trois jours (tout) au plus; **it was a l. haul** *(of journey)* le voyage a été long; *Fig (to complete this project, make a full recovery from illness etc)* c'était un travail de longue haleine; **it looks like being a l. job** cela va prendre du temps; **to take the l. view of sth** voir qch à long terme; **in the l. term** *or* **run** à long terme, à longue échéance; **it'll all be all right in the l. run** tout s'arrangera avec le temps; **to have a l. memory** avoir (une) bonne mémoire; **to have a l. talk with sb** parler longuement avec qn; **he took a l. drink from the flask** il but une longue gorgée à la bouteille; **to take a l. hard look at sth** fixer longuement qch

  N **1** **the l. and the short of the matter is that ...** le fin mot de l'affaire c'est que ...; **that's the l. and the short of it!** un point c'est tout! **2** *St Exch (bill)* effet *m* à longue échéance

  ADV **1** *(for a long period)* longtemps; **I didn't wait l.** je n'ai pas attendu longtemps; **l. live the King/Queen!** vive le roi/la reine!; **as l. as** *(for the same length of time as)* aussi longtemps que; *(during the time that)* tant que; *(provided that)* du moment que; *(since, seeing that)* puisque; **I followed him for as l. as I could** je l'ai suivi aussi longtemps que j'ai pu; **as l. as I am alive** tant que je vivrai; **I'll never forget that day for as l. as I live** jamais de ma vie je n'oublierai ce jour; **as l. as you're happy** *(provided that)* du moment que tu es heureux; **you can take my car so l. as you're careful** tu peux prendre ma voiture du moment que tu es prudent; **to look at sb/sth l. and hard** fixer qn/qch longuement; *Fig* **to look at sth l. and hard** se pencher longuement sur qch; **I've thought l. and hard about this and ...** j'y ai longuement réfléchi et ...; **he was not l. in coming** il n'a pas tardé à venir; **before l.** avant peu, sous peu; **for l.** pendant longtemps; **I won't stay for l.** je ne resterai pas longtemps; **it won't take l.** cela ne prendra pas longtemps, cela ne sera pas long; **she won't be l.** *(will be here soon)* elle ne tardera pas; *(will soon have finished)* elle a bientôt fini; **is he going to be l.?** *(in arriving, finishing)* il en a pour longtemps?; **are you going to be much longer?** tu en as encore pour longtemps?; *Fam* **so l.!** au revoir!, à bientôt! VOIR GRAMMAIRE B31–2

2 *(since sometime in the past)* depuis longtemps; **I have l. been convinced of it** j'en suis convaincu depuis longtemps; **they have l.**

since left England ça fait longtemps qu'ils ont quitté l'Angleterre **3 how l.?** combien de temps?; **how much longer will he be?** (until ready etc) il en a encore pour longtemps?; (until he arrives) dans combien de temps sera-t-il là?; **how l. have you known her?** depuis combien de temps est-ce que tu la connais? **4 l. before/after** longtemps avant/après; **not l. before/after** peu de temps avant/après; **l. before I met you** longtemps avant que je te rencontre; **l. ago** il y a longtemps; **not (very) l. ago** il n'y a pas longtemps; **in the days of l. ago** autrefois, Lit jadis **5** (for the duration of) **all day/night l.** tout le long du jour/de la nuit, pendant toute la journée/la nuit; **all winter l.** tout au long de l'hiver **6 I could no longer hear him** je ne l'entendais plus; **she no longer lives here** elle n'habite plus ici; **I couldn't wait any longer** je ne pouvais plus attendre; **five minutes longer** cinq minutes de plus; **I'll wait five minutes but no longer** je veux bien attendre cinq minutes mais pas plus

▸▸Fin **l. credit** crédit m à long terme; Typ **l. dash** trait m; Math **l. division** division f posée; **l. drink** long drink m; (non-alcoholic) = grand verre m de jus de fruits, de limonade etc; Com **l. dozen** treize; Com **l. hundred** cent vingt; Fam **l. johns** caleçon m long, caleçons mpl longs; Sport **l. jump** saut m en longueur; Sport **l. jumper** sauteur, -euse en longueur; **l. lease** bail m emphytéotique; Old-fashioned **l. player** (record) longue durée f, St Exch **l. position** position f acheteur ou longue; **to take a l. position** acheter à la hausse, prendre une position longue; **l. service award** prime f d'ancienneté; **l. shot** (competitor, racehorse etc) outsider m; (bet) pari m risqué; Cin **l. shot** plan m éloigné; Fig entreprise f hasardeuse; **it's a bit of a l. shot but ...** il n'y a pas de grandes chances que ça marche mais ...; **not by a l. shot** loin de là; Med **l. stay** (lit m de) long séjour m; **l. trousers** pantalon m long; Univ **l. vacation** les grandes vacances fpl; Radio **l. wave** grandes ondes fpl

long² vi **to l. to do sth** avoir bien envie de faire qch, être impatient de faire qch, rêver de faire qch; **to l. for sth** désirer qch fortement ou ardemment; **he longed to be free** il avait hâte d'être libre; **I'm longing for the weekend/the holidays** j'ai hâte d'être en week-end/vacances; **I l. for you** tu me manques beaucoup; **I'm longing for home** (native land) mon pays me manque; (my house) ma maison me manque; **to l. for sb's return** attendre impatiemment le retour de qn; **we're longing for them to leave** nous avons hâte qu'ils partent; **a much longed-for baby** un bébé très désiré; **a longed-for holiday** des vacances très attendues

long³ [lɒŋ] Geog (abbr **longitude**) long

long-awaited ['lɒŋəweɪtɪd] ADJ (event, birth etc) très attendu

longboat ['lɒŋbəʊt] N Naut chaloupe f, (of Vikings) drakkar m

longbow ['lɒŋbəʊ] N Mil, Hist arc m (d'homme d'armes)

long-dated ADJ Fin à longue échéance
▸▸**l. securities** titres mpl longs, obligations fpl longues

long-distance ADJ Tel longue distance; Tel Fam **is it l.?** est-ce que c'est un appel longue distance?
ADV **to telephone l.** faire un appel longue distance
▸▸**l. call** communication f hors circonscription; **l. footpath** sentier m de grande randonnée; Br **l. lorry driver** conducteur, -trice de poids lourd; Sport **l. race** course f de fond; Sport **l. runner** coureur, -euse de fond

long-drawn-out ADJ (sigh etc) prolongé; (story, explanation etc) interminable; **l. tale** récit m prolongé ou à n'en plus finir; **a l. scream** un cri prolongé

long-established ADJ établi depuis longtemps

longevity [lɒnˈdʒevɪtɪ] N longévité f

long-forgotten ADJ oublié depuis longtemps

longhair ['lɒŋheər] Am ADJ **1** (cat, dog) à poil(s) long(s) **2** Old-fashioned Fam (for intellectuals) pour les intellos
N Fam **1** Old-fashioned (intellectual) intello mf **2** (hippie) chevelu m

longhaired ['lɒŋheəd] ADJ **1** (cat, dog etc) à poil(s) long(s); (person) aux cheveux longs **2** Am Fam = **longhair**

longhand ['lɒŋhænd] N écriture f ordinaire ou courante ou non abrégée; **in l.** (written) en clair, écrit à la main

long-haul ADJ Aviat long-courrier, pl longs-courriers; **a l. carrier** un long-courrier

longing ['lɒŋɪŋ] N désir m, grande envie f (**for** de); **to be filled with l. to do sth** être plein d'un ardent désir de faire qch
ADJ **to cast l. looks at sth** jeter des regards pleins d'envie à qch

longingly ['lɒŋɪŋlɪ] ADV avec envie; **to look l. at sth** couver qch des yeux; **she was looking l. out of the window** elle regardait langoureusement par la fenêtre

longish ['lɒŋɪʃ] ADJ assez long, plutôt long

longitude ['lɒndʒɪtjuːd] N Geog longitude f

longitudinal [lɒndʒɪˈtjuːdɪn(ə)l] ADJ longitudinal, -aux
▸▸Constr **l. beam** longeron m

longitudinally [lɒndʒɪˈtjuːdɪn(ə)lɪ] ADV longitudinalement

long-legged ['lɒŋˈlegɪd] ADJ (person) aux jambes longues; (horse) haut sur pattes; (bird) à longues pattes

long-life ADJ (battery) longue durée; (milk, juice) longue conservation

long-lived ['lɒŋˈlɪvd] ADJ (person) qui vit longtemps; **we're a very l. family** dans la famille on vit très vieux
▸▸Acct **l. assets** actifs mpl à long terme, actifs à longue durée de vie

long-lost ADJ (manuscript, painting etc) perdu depuis longtemps; **she has been reunited with her l. brother** elle a retrouvé son frère dont elle avait été séparée depuis très longtemps; **I'm seeking some l. cousins** je suis à la recherche de cousins que j'ai perdu de vue depuis longtemps; **he welcomed me like a l. friend** il m'a accueilli comme si on avait été des amis qui ne s'étaient pas vus depuis des années

long-playing ADJ
▸▸**l. record** disque m (de) longue durée, (disque) microsillon m

long-range ADJ (plane) long-courrier; (gun, radar) à longue portée
▸▸**l. camera** appareil m de photo longue portée; Met **l. forecast** prévisions fpl météorologiques à long terme; Mil **l. missile** missile m longue portée

long-running ADJ (film, play) qui tient l'affiche; (TV/radio programme) qui est diffusé depuis longtemps

long-service ADJ
▸▸Mil **l. men** engagés mpl à long terme

longship ['lɒŋʃɪp] N (of Vikings) drakkar m

longshoreman, pl **longshoremen** ['lɒŋˌʃɔːmən] N Am Naut débardeur m

long-sighted ADJ **1** Opt hypermétrope; (in old age) presbyte **2** Fig (policy, decision) prévoyant

long-sightedness [lɒŋˈsaɪtɪdnɪs] N **1** hy-

permétropie f, (in old age) presbytie f **2** Fig (of policy, decision) prévoyance f

long-sleeved ADJ (dress, pullover) à manches longues

long-standing ADJ (arrangement, friendship etc) de longue date
▸▸Fin **l. accounts** vieux comptes mpl

long-stay ADJ
▸▸Med **l. bed** lit m (de) long séjour; **l. car park** parking m longue durée

long-suffering ADJ patient, endurant; (tolerant) indulgent

long-term ADJ **1** (detainee, prisoner) qui subit un emprisonnement de longue durée; **the l. unemployed** les chômeurs de longue durée **2** Fin (loan, policy etc) à long terme
▸▸Fin **l. bond** obligation f à long terme; Acct **l. borrowings** emprunts mpl à long terme; Acct **l. capital** capitaux mpl permanents; Fin **l. credit** crédit m (à) long terme; Fin **l. debt** dette f à long terme; Br Fin **l. individual savings account** plan m de retraite en actions; Fin **l. investments** placements mpl à long terme; (on balance sheet) immobilisations fpl financières; Fin **l. liabilities** dettes fpl ou passif m à long terme; **l. planning** planification f à long terme; **l. unemployment** chômage m de longue durée

longways ['lɒŋweɪz] ADV = **lengthways**

long-winded [lɒŋˈwɪndɪd] ADJ Pej (story) interminable; (speaker, speech) verbeux

loo [luː] N Br Fam **the l.** les toilettes fpl, les cabinets mpl; **to go to the l.** aller aux toilettes; **in the l.** aux toilettes, aux cabinets
▸▸Br Fam **l. paper** papier m hygiénique; Br Fam **l. seat** siège m des toilettes ou des W.-C.

loofah ['luːfə] N (for washing), Bot loofa(h) m, luffa m

LOOK [lʊk]

> ■ N coup d'œil **1** ▪ regard **2** ▪ air **4** ▪ mode **4** ▪ beauté **5**
> ■ VI regarder **1** ▪ chercher **2** ▪ avoir l'air **3** ▪ écouter **4** ▪ chercher à **5**
> ■ VT regarder

N **1 to have** or **take a l. at sth** regarder qch; (quickly) jeter un coup d'œil sur qch; Fam **let's have a l.** (show me) fais voir; **to take a good l. at sb/sth** bien examiner qn/qch; **I didn't get a good l.** je n'ai pas bien vu comment il était; **did you get a good l. at him?** vous l'avez vu clairement?; **to have a l. round the town** faire un tour dans la ville; **to have a l. through some magazines** jeter un coup d'œil sur des magazines **2** (with eyes) regard m; **a suspicious/nasty/angry l.** un regard soupçonneux/mauvais/méchant; **he shot me a poisonous l.** il m'a lancé un regard foudroyant; **he has a strange l. in his eyes** il a un drôle de regard dans les yeux; **we were getting some very odd looks** nous attirions des regards très étonnés; Prov **if looks could kill ...** si ses yeux étaient des revolvers ... **3** (search) **to have a l. for sth** chercher qch; **have you had a good l. for it?** est-ce que tu as bien cherché?; **let's have a quick l. for it** on va jeter un coup d'œil pour essayer de le trouver **4** (appearance) (of object) aspect m, air m, apparence f, (of person) tête f, **she has the l. of a troublemaker** elle a une tête à faire des histoires; **it has the l. of a successful marriage** cela a l'air d'un mariage heureux; **I don't like the l. of this at all!** cela ne me plaît pas du tout; **the business has a suspicious l. about it** l'affaire paraît suspecte ou louche; **I like the l. of him** il me plaît; **I don't like the l. of him** (he seems suspicious) sa tête ne me revient pas; **I don't like the l. of the weather** le temps a l'air inquiétant; **she has the l. of** her grandfather about her elle a des airs de son grand-père; **the New L.** *(fashion)* le new-look; **this year's new l.** la nouvelle mode de cette année; **the new-l. format/Ford Fiesta**® le format/la Ford Fiesta® nouvelle version

5 **good looks** beauté *f*; **to lose one's looks** perdre ses charmes; **looks don't matter** l'apparence ne compte pas; **she's got her mother's looks** elle a la beauté de sa mère

vi **1** regarder; **to l. through** *or* **out of the window** regarder par la fenêtre; **to l. down a list** parcourir une liste du regard; **to l. the other way** *(avert one's gaze)* détourner les yeux; *Fig* regarder ailleurs; **to l. into sb's eyes** regarder qn dans les yeux; **I'm just looking, thank you** *(to shop assistant)* je ne fais que regarder, merci; *Prov* **l. before you leap** il faut réfléchir avant d'agir; **to l. on the bright side** voir les choses du bon côté; **the house looks south** la maison est exposée au sud; **to l. to** *or* **towards the future** penser à l'avenir

2 *(search)* chercher; **we've looked everywhere** nous avons cherché partout

3 *(seem, appear)* avoir l'air, paraître, sembler; **to l. old** avoir l'air *ou* faire vieux; **to l. ill** avoir l'air malade, avoir mauvaise mine; **to l. well** *(of person)* avoir bonne mine; **that dress looks well on you** cette robe vous va bien; **she looks tired** elle a l'air fatigué(e); **she's not as stupid as she looks** elle est moins bête qu'elle n'en a l'air; **he doesn't l. his age** on ne lui donnerait pas son âge; **to l. like sb** ressembler à qn; **what does she l. like?** comment est-elle?; **it looks like an elephant** on dirait un éléphant; **things are looking bad** *or* **black** les choses prennent une mauvaise tournure; **things are looking good** ça a l'air d'aller *ou* de bien se passer; **the crops l. promising** la récolte s'annonce bien; **you l. as if you've slept badly** vous avez l'air d'avoir mal dormi; **it looks as if he didn't want to go** il semble qu'il ne veuille pas y aller; **he looks the part** il est fait pour ce rôle; **she looks like winning, it looks like she'll win** on dirait qu'elle va gagner; **it looks like rain** on dirait qu'il va pleuvoir

4 *(expressing annoyance, desiring attention etc)* **l. here!** écoutez donc!, dites donc!; **(now)** l. écoute; *Fam* **l. sharp!** fais gaffe!

5 *(intend)* chercher à; **to be looking to do sth** chercher à faire qch; **she'll be looking to improve on her previous best time** elle cherchera à améliorer son meilleur temps; **I'm not looking to cause any trouble** je ne veux pas causer de problème; **they're looking to appoint a new headmaster** ils envisagent d'engager un nouveau directeur

vt to l. sb *(full* or *straight)* **in the face** regarder qn (bien) en face *ou* dans les yeux; **I can never l. her in the face again** je ne pourrai plus jamais la regarder en face; **to l. sb up and down** regarder qn de haut en bas, toiser qn; **l. what you've done!** regarde ce que tu as fait!; **l. where you're going!** fais attention où tu vas!

▸ **look about** = **look around**

▸ **look after** **vt insep** *(a sick person etc)* veiller sur, soigner; *(possessions, an object)* faire attention à; *(one's health, teeth etc)* surveiller, faire attention à; *(one's interests)* prendre soin de; **can you l. after the house for us?** peux-tu garder *ou* faire attention à la maison?; **could you l. after my things while I go to ...?** pourriez-vous surveiller mes affaires pendant que je vais à ...?; **granny's looking after the children this weekend** mamie garde les enfants ce week-end; **he needs a lot of looking after** il a bien besoin qu'on s'occupe de lui; **l. after yourself!** prends bien soin de toi!; **you're well looked after** on s'occupe de vous; **he can l. after himself** *(at home etc)* il peut se débrouil-

ler *(tout seul)*; *(in fight etc)* il sait se débrouiller *(tout seul)*; **the garden needs a lot of looking after** c'est un jardin qui a besoin d'être entretenu; **the car has been well looked after** la voiture est bien entretenue

▸ **look around** **vi 1** *(turn head around)* regarder derrière soi

2 *(have a look)* regarder autour de soi; *(in town, museum etc)* faire un tour; **can I just l. around?** *(in shop)* puis-je jeter un coup d'œil?

3 *(search)* regarder partout; **to l. around for sth** chercher qch; **I'll go upstairs and l. around** je monte jeter un coup d'œil

vt insep **to l. around the house** *(out of interest)* jeter un coup d'œil dans la maison; *(search)* chercher partout dans la maison; **to l. around town** *(have a look)* faire un tour en ville; **to l. around the shops** faire le tour des boutiques

▸ **look at** **vt insep 1** regarder; **what are you looking at?** qu'est-ce que vous regardez?; **just l. at that!** regardez-moi ça!; *Fam* **she won't l. at a man** les hommes, elle ne leur jette même pas un regard; **I haven't looked at another woman in the last forty years** en quarante ans, je n'ai pas regardé une autre femme; **they won't l. at our offer** ils ne font aucun cas de notre offre; **what's he like to l. at?** de quoi a-t-il l'air?; **she's not much to l. at** ce n'est pas une beauté; **he's not much to l. at** il n'est pas très beau; **if you l. at the result** si vous considérez le résultat; **I don't like his way of looking at things** je n'aime pas la manière dont il voit les choses; **I don't l. at it that way at all** je ne le vois pas de cet œil-là; **just l. at the mess we're in!** regarde les ennuis qu'on a!; **just l. at you!** *(you look awful, a mess etc)* mais regarde-toi donc!

2 *(examine)* **brakes, tooth etc)** regarder, jeter un coup d'œil sur

▸ **look away** **vi** tourner la tête

▸ **look back** **vi** regarder en arrière; **to l. back on the past** se retourner sur le passé; *Fig* **he has never looked back since that day** depuis ce jour sa situation n'a cessé de s'améliorer

▸ **look down** **vi** *(from a height)* regarder en *ou* vers le bas; *(lower one's eyes)* baisser les yeux; **don't l. down!** ne regarde pas en bas!; **she looked down on the town below her** elle regarda la ville en bas; **the chalet looks down on the valley** le chalet donne sur la vallée

▸ **look down on** **vt insep** *(think little of, despise)* mépriser

▸ **look for** **vt insep** chercher; **go and l. for him** allez le chercher; **he's looking for trouble** il cherche les ennuis

▸ **look forward** **vi** *(to the future)* regarder vers l'avenir

▸ **look forward to** **vt insep** attendre avec plaisir; **I'm looking forward to seeing her again** il me tarde de la revoir; **I'm looking forward to the weekend** vivement le week-end!; **he hasn't got much to l. forward to in life** il n'a pas grand-chose à attendre de la vie; **they don't exactly l. forward to a visit to the dentist** ils appréhendent d'aller chez le dentiste; **I'm not exactly looking forward to going** je n'ai pas vraiment envie d'y aller; **I'm so looking forward to seeing you all again** j'aimerais tant vous revoir, ça me ferait tellement plaisir de vous revoir; **I'm not looking forward to it at all** je n'y tiens pas du tout; **I l. forward to hearing from you** *(at end of letter)* dans l'attente de vous lire

▸ **look in** **vi 1** *(at window etc)* regarder (à l'intérieur), jeter un coup d'œil (à l'intérieur)

2 *(visit)* entrer en passant; **I'll l. in again tomorrow** je repasserai demain; **to l. in on sb** aller *ou* passer voir qn

▸ **look into** **vt insep** *(investigate)* examiner, étudier; *(allegations)* prendre en considération; **it needs a bit of looking into** il faut étudier la question

▸ **look on** **vi** regarder, être spectateur; **while a crowd looked on** sous les regards de la foule

vt insep *(consider)* considérer, envisager; **I l. on him as a friend** je le considère comme un ami

▸ **look onto** **vt insep** *(of room)* *(garden, street etc)* donner sur

▸ **look out** **vi 1** *(through window etc)* regarder (à l'extérieur), jeter un coup d'œil (à l'extérieur)

2 *(be careful)* prendre garde, être sur ses gardes; **l. out!** attention!, prenez garde!

vt sep trouver, *Fam* dénicher

▸ **look out for** **vt insep 1** *(look for)* guetter (l'arrivée de)

2 *(be on guard for)* *(person, pickpockets, errors etc)* faire attention à

3 *esp Am (take care of)* prendre soin de

▸ **look out onto** **vt insep** *(of room)* *(garden, street etc)* donner sur

▸ **look over** **vt insep** *(have a look at)* jeter un coup d'œil sur; *(papers)* parcourir; *(house for sale)* visiter

▸ **look round** **vi, vt insep** = **look around**

▸ **look through** **vt insep 1** *(papers etc)* parcourir, examiner rapidement

2 *(not see)* **she just looked straight through me** *(deliberately)* elle m'a ignoré; *(not deliberately)* elle m'a regardé sans me voir

vi *(at window, lock etc)* regarder par la fenêtre/la serrure *etc*

▸ **look to** **vt insep 1** *(rely on)* compter sur; **we're looking to you to help us** *or* **for help** nous comptons sur vous pour nous aider; **you can't always l. to your parents for money** on ne peut pas toujours s'en remettre à ses parents pour l'argent

2 *(ensure)* **l. to it that you ...** faites en sorte de ...; **l. to it that he ...** faites en sorte qu'il ... + *sub*; *Old-fashioned* **l. to your daughter** faites attention à *ou* surveillez votre fille

▸ **look up** **vt sep 1** *(word in a dictionary etc)* chercher

2 *(go to visit) (person)* aller voir, passer chez; **l. me up** venez me voir

vi 1 *(from below)* regarder en haut; *(raise one's eyes)* lever les yeux; **if you could all l. up at this picture here** si vous regardez tous le tableau du haut

2 *Fig* **to be looking up** *(of business)* reprendre; *(of shares)* remonter; **things are looking up** la situation s'améliore; **things are looking up for her** sa situation s'améliore

▸ **look upon** **vt insep** = **look on** **vt insep**

▸ **look up to** **vt insep** *(respect)* respecter, estimer

lookalike ['lʊkəlaɪk] **n** *(person)* sosie *m*; **she's a Princess Diana l.** c'est un sosie de la Princesse Diana; **it's just another Renault l.** c'est la copie conforme de la Renault

looker ['lʊkər] **n** *Fam (good)* **l.** *(of a woman)* belle femme *f*; *(younger)* beau brin *m* de fille; *(of a man)* bel homme *m*

looker-on, *pl* **lookers-on** **n** spectateur, -trice (**at** de), *Pej* badaud *m*

look-in **n** *Fam (chance)* **he won't have** *or* **get a l.** il n'a pas la moindre chance; **everyone gets a l.** tout le monde a sa chance

looking-glass ['lʊkɪŋglɑːs] **n** *Old-fashioned* miroir *m*, glace *f*

looking room **n** *TV* salle *f* de visionnage

lookout ['lʊkaʊt] **n 1** *(post)* poste *m* d'observation *ou* de vigie

2 *(person)*, *Mil* guetteur *m*; *Naut* homme *m* de veille *ou* de vigie

3 *(action)* surveillance *f*, observation *f*, *Naut* veille *f*; **to keep a l.** être aux aguets; *Naut* veiller, être en *ou* de vigie; **to be on the l. for** *(person)* guetter; *(something)* être à la recherche de; **to be on l. duty** être de guet

4 *Fam* **that's a poor l. for him** c'est de mau-

vais augure pour lui; **that's your l.!** ça c'est ton affaire *ou Fam* tes oignons!
▸▸ **l. post** poste *m* d'observation *ou* de vigie

lookover ['lʊkəʊvər] N **to give sth a (quick) l.** jeter un coup d'œil sur qch

look-see N *Fam* **to go and have** *or* **take a l.** aller jeter un coup d'œil

look-up table N *Comput* table *f* de recherche *ou* de référence

loom[1] [luːm] N *Tex* métier *m* à tisser

loom[2] VI apparaître indistinctement *(comme une menace)*; **dangers looming ahead** dangers qui menacent; **to l. (large)** *(of event etc)* paraître imminent, être tout proche; **it looms large in his view of things** cela joue un rôle important dans sa manière de voir les choses
▸ **loom up** VI *(of ship, person in authority etc)* surgir

loon [luːn] N **1** *(bird) Am* plongeon *m*, *Can* huart *m* **2** *Fam (fool)* imbécile *mf*; *(crazy)* fada *m*

loony ['luːnɪ] *Fam* N dingue *mf*
ADJ dingue, timbré
▸▸ *Hum* **l. bin** maison *f* de fous; *Br Pej* **the l. left** les gauchos

loop [luːp] N *(of ribbon, film etc)* boucle *f*, *(of fingerprint)* anse *f*, *(of river)* méandre *m*, boucle; *(in skating)* croisé *m*; *(of spiral, spool)* tour *m*; *(contraceptive coil)* stérilet *m*; *Aviat* boucle, looping *m*; *Rail (line)* voie *f* d'évitement, voie de raccordement; *(at terminus)* boucle d'évitement; *Am Fam* **to knock** *or* **throw sb for a l.** abasourdir qn; *Am Fam* **to be out of the l.** ne pas être dans le coup; *Fam* **to cut sb out of the l.** mettre qn aux oubliettes **2** *Elec* boucle *f*, bouclage *m*; *Nucl (of reactor)* boucle, circuit *m*; *Comput* boucle d'itération; *Tel* circuit (branché), ligne *f* dérivée
VT **1** *(piece of string etc)* faire une boucle *ou* des boucles à; **to l. sth around sth** enrouler qch autour de qch **2** *Aviat* **to l. the l.** faire un looping, boucler la boucle **3** *Elec* boucler
VI **1** faire une boucle **2** *Comput* tourner sur une boucle
▸▸ *Electron* **l. aerial**, **l. antenna** cadre *m* d'antenne; *Elec* **l. circuit** circuit *m* bouclé; *Elec* **l. current** courant *m* circulant dans un circuit bouclé; *Rail* **l. line** voie *f* d'évitement, voie de raccordement; *(at terminus)* boucle d'évitement; *Sewing* **l. stitch** point *m* de bouclette
▸ **loop back** VI *(of river etc)* faire une boucle; *Comput (of program)* faire une boucle pour retourner (**to** à)
VT SEP *(curtain)* retenir avec une embrasse

loophole ['luːphəʊl] N **1** *(in law, regulations etc)* point *m* faible; **to find a l.** trouver une échappatoire; **a legal l.** un vide juridique **2** *(gap)* trou *m*, ouverture *f*, *(in fortified wall)* meurtrière *f*

looping ['luːpɪŋ] N *Aviat* **l. the loop** looping *m*

loopy ['luːpɪ] ADJ *Fam (crazy)* toqué, timbré, maboul

LOOSE [luːs] ADJ **1** *(not fastened or attached) (screw, nail, brick, part)* qui se détache *ou* se défait; *(page)* détaché; *(knot)* défait, délié; *(floorboard)* désajusté; *(tooth)* qui bouge; *Elec (connection)* desserré; *(cable)* volant; *Com (goods)* en vrac; **to come l.**, **to get l.** se dégager, se détacher; *(of knot)* se défaire, se délier; *(of screw)* se desserrer; *(of iron bar etc)* se desceller; **to work l.** *(of machine parts)* se desserrer, prendre du jeu; *(of tooth)* se déchausser; *(of hair in bun etc)* se dénouer; **to let the riot police l. on the crowd** lâcher les CRS sur la foule; **I'm dying to be let l. on the garden** je crève d'envie de pouvoir m'en donner à cœur joie dans le jardin;

to let a dog l. lâcher un chien; **they let their dog run l. in the fields** ils ont laissé leur chien courir en liberté dans les champs; **to let l. a torrent of abuse** lâcher un torrent d'injures; *Fig* **to be at a l. end** se trouver désœuvré, n'avoir rien à faire; *Fig* **to tie up the l. ends** régler les derniers détails
2 *(slack)* détendu; *(cable)* mou, *f* molle; *(knot)* lâche; *(skin)* flasque; *(piece of clothing)* ample; *(coat)* flottant; **this skirt is much too l. at the waist** cette jupe est bien trop large au niveau de la taille; **to have l. bowels** avoir la diarrhée
3 *(in structure, arrangement) Tex (weave)* lâche, à claire-voie; *Mil (order)* dispersé
4 *(imprecise)* vague, peu exact; *(style)* lâche, décousu; *(translation)* approximatif
5 *(immoral)* dissolu, débauché; *(woman)* de mauvaise vie
N **to be on the l.** *(of prisoner)* être en cavale; *(of escaped tiger etc)* être en liberté; **there's a horde of louts on the l. in town** il y a une horde de voyous en vadrouille dans la ville; *Hum* **her husband's on the l. tonight** son mari est en vadrouille ce soir
ADV **to hang l.** *(of rope etc)* pendre, flotter; *esp Am Fig Fam (relax)* se relaxer, se détendre; *(not panic)* rester calme
VT **1** *(set free)* délier, détacher; **to l. one's hold** lâcher prise
2 *(untie) (knot etc)* délier, dénouer, défaire; *(hair)* dénouer, détacher; *Naut (mooring rope)* larguer; *(sail)* déferler
3 *(fire) (arrow)* décocher
▸▸ **l. ball** *Cr* balle *f* mal lancée; *Tennis* balle qui traîne; **l. cannon** personne *f* incontrôlable; **l. cash**, **l. change** menue monnaie *f*, **l. chippings** gravillons *mpl*; *Med* **l. cough** toux *f* grasse; *Br* **l. cover** *(for armchair, sofa)* housse *f*; **l. end** *(of a rope)* bout *m* qui pend; *Sport* **l. horse** cheval *m* sauvage; **l. insert** *(in newspaper, magazine)* encart *m* libre; **l. living** débauche *f*, vie *f* dissolue; **l. morals** mœurs *fpl* relâchées; **l. talk** des propos *mpl* lestes
▸ **loose off** VI *Mil Fam (with machine gun etc)* tirer (**at** sur); *Fig Fam* **to l. off at sb** *(tell off)* engueuler qn
VT SEP *(fire) (a few rounds)* tirer, lâcher

loose-fitting ADJ *(item of clothing)* ample, large

loose-leaf ADJ *(album)* à feuilles mobiles, à feuillets rechargeables
▸▸ **l. binder** classeur *m* (à feuilles mobiles); **l. paper** feuillets *mpl* mobiles

loose-limbed ADJ souple

loosely ['luːslɪ] ADV **1** *(to hold sth)* sans serrer; **to be l. fixed** être mal serré *ou* mal ajusté, avoir du jeu; **her dress hung l. on her body** elle flottait dans sa robe **2** *(to speak)* sans précision; **l. translated** traduit approximativement; **the word is often used l.** le mot est souvent employé de façon imprécise; **l. connected** *or* **related** vaguement lié

loosen ['luːs(ə)n] VT *(slacken) (knot)* défaire, délier, desserrer; *(nut)* desserrer, dégager, décoller; *(rope)* relâcher, détendre; *(necktie, item of clothing)* desserrer; *(restrictions)* assouplir; **to l. sb's bonds** desserrer les liens de qn; **to l. one's grip** relâcher son étreinte; **to l. sb's tongue** délier *ou* dénouer la langue à qn; *Med* **to l. the bowels** avoir un effet laxatif
VI *(of knot etc)* se délier, se défaire; *(of screw etc)* se desserrer; *(of rope)* se relâcher
▸ **loosen up** VI *(of person) (relax)* se mettre à l'aise; *(of athlete etc)* s'assouplir; **he always loosens up after a few drinks** il est toujours plus décontracté après un verre ou deux; **she loosens up once you get to know her** elle perd de sa froideur une fois qu'on la connaît
VT SEP *(muscles)* relâcher

looseness ['luːsnɪs] N **1** *(of tooth, stone etc)* déchaussement *m*; *(of pin, bolt etc)* jeu *m*; *(of skin)* flaccidité *f*, *(of rope)* relâchement *m*; *(of piece of clothing)* ampleur *f* **2** *(of terminology)* imprécision *f* **3** *(of discipline, morals etc)* relâchement *m*

loosestrife ['luːsstraɪf] N *(plant)* **(purple) l.** salicaire *f* commune

loot [luːt] **1** N **1** *(goods)* butin *m*; **soldiers on the l.** soldats qui se livrent à des pillages **2** *Fam (money)* flouze *m*, fric *m*
VT *(city etc)* piller, mettre à sac; *(shops)* piller; *(goods)* voler
VI se livrer au pillage

looter ['luːtər] N pilleur, -euse, pillard, -arde

looting ['luːtɪŋ] N pillage *m*

lop [lɒp] VT **(-pp-)** *(tree)* élaguer, ébrancher
▸ **lop off** VT SEP *(branch)* couper, élaguer

▸ **lope along** [ləʊp] VI *(of person)* avancer à grandes enjambées; *(of leopard etc)* courir tout en puissance; *(of hare)* avancer en bondissant

▸ **lope off** VI *(of person)* partir d'une démarche élastique; **the tiger loped off into the jungle** le tigre pénétra dans la jungle de sa démarche souple

lop-eared ['lɒpɪəd] ADJ *(rabbit, dog etc)* aux oreilles pendantes

lopsided [lɒp'saɪdɪd] ADJ qui manque de symétrie, asymétrique; *(picture)* de guingois, de travers; **a l. grin** un sourire en coin; **a l. group with twice as many women as men** un groupe déséquilibré comptant deux fois plus de femmes que d'hommes; **a l. account of the conflict** une description partiale du conflit

loquacious [lɒ'kweɪʃəs] ADJ loquace

loquaciousness [lɒ'kweɪʃəsnɪs], **loquacity** [lɒ'kwæsɪtɪ] N loquacité *f*

lord [lɔːd] N **1** seigneur *m*; **l. of the manor** châtelain *m*; **our sovereign l. the king** notre seigneur souverain, le roi; *(in Middle Ages etc)*, *Hum* **her l. and master** son seigneur et maître **2** *Rel* **the L.** le Seigneur; **in the year of our L. …** en l'an de grâce …; *Fam* **(good) L.!**, **O L.!** mon Dieu!; *Fam* **L. knows if …** Dieu sait si … **3** *Br (title)* lord *m*; **L. Hailsham said that …** Lord Hailsham a dit que …; *Pol* **the House of Lords, the Lords** la Chambre des Lords
VI *Fam* **to l. it** mener la grande vie; **to l. it over sb** traiter qn de haut
▸▸ **L.'s Day Observance Society** = Société *f* pour l'Observance du Jour du Seigneur; **L. God Almighty** Seigneur Dieu Tout-puissant; **lords and ladies** *(flower)* arum *m* maculé, pied-de-veau *m*, *pl* pieds-de-veau; **the L. Mayor** le Lord Maire; **the L.'s Prayer** le Pater

lordly ['lɔːdlɪ] ADJ **1** noble, de grand seigneur **2** *Pej (arrogant)* hautain; **his l. airs** ses airs de grand seigneur; **in a l. manner** avec hauteur

lordship ['lɔːdʃɪp] N **1** *(authority)* suzeraineté *f* **2** **Your L.** *also Hum* votre Seigneurie; *(to nobleman)* monsieur le comte *etc*; *(to judge)* votre honneur

lordy ['lɔːdɪ] INT *esp Am Fam* Seigneur!

lore [lɔːr] N science *f*, savoir *m*; **country l.** connaissance *f* des choses de la campagne

lorgnette [lɔː'njet] N *(spectacles)* face-à-main *m*, *pl* faces-à-main; *(opera glasses)* jumelles *fpl* (de théâtre) à manche

lorry ['lɒrɪ] N *Br* camion *m*; *Euph Hum* **it fell off the back of a l.** *(is stolen)* je l'ai trouvé
▸▸ **l. driver** camionneur, -euse

LOSE [luːz] [*pt, pp* **lost** [lɒst], *prp* **losing** ['luːzɪŋ]]

VT	perdre **1–4** ▪ coûter **6**
VI	perdre **1** ▪ retarder **2**

VT 1 *(money, right etc)* perdre; *(mislay)* perdre, égarer; *(through death, injury) (one's father, baby, arm, voice etc)* perdre; **you will l. nothing by waiting** vous ne perdrez rien à attendre; **to have nothing to l.** n'avoir rien à perdre; **the expression loses something in translation** l'expression perd quelque chose à la traduction; **to l. one's heart to sb** tomber amoureux de qn; **to l. one's reason** perdre la raison; **to l. one's reputation** se perdre de réputation; **to l. one's nerve** ne pas avoir le courage; **he had lost interest in his work** son travail ne l'intéressait plus; **the patient is losing strength** le malade s'affaiblit; **many lives were lost in the disaster** la catastrophe a coûté la vie à de nombreuses personnes; **to be lost at sea** périr en mer; **to l. one's way, to get lost** perdre son chemin, se perdre, s'égarer; *Sl* **get lost!** fiche-moi le camp!; **to l. one's balance** perdre l'équilibre; **to l. share** *(of market)* perdre des parts de marché; **to l. sight of sb** perdre qn de vue; **to l. sight of the reason for doing sth** perdre de vue la raison pour laquelle on fait/a fait qch; *Fig Fam* **I'm lost!, you've lost me!** je suis largué, je ne vous suis plus; *Fam Fig* **you lost me when you started using technical terms** j'ai perdu le fil quand tu as commencé à employer des termes techniques; *Fam* **to l. one's head** perdre la tête; *Fam* **to l. it** *(go mad)* perdre la boule; *(lose one's temper)* piquer une crise, péter les plombs; *Br Fam* **to l. the plot** perdre la boule

2 *(deliberately)* **to l. weight** perdre du poids; **I've lost 10 kilos** j'ai perdu 10 kilos, j'ai maigri de 10 kilos; **to l. oneself in the crowd** se perdre dans/se mêler à la foule; **to l. one's pursuers** *(of sb being chased)* larguer ses poursuivants; **to l. oneself in a book** se plonger dans un livre

3 *(fail to win) (match, race, battle, trial)* perdre; **the motion was lost** *(in debate)* la motion a été rejetée

4 *(waste) (time)* gaspiller, perdre; **the joke was lost on him** la plaisanterie lui est passée au-dessus de la tête; **American humour is lost on us** nous ne comprenons rien à l'humour américain

5 clock that loses five minutes a day pendule qui retarde de cinq minutes par jour

6 *(bring about loss of)* **the decision will l. us our jobs** la décision nous coûtera nos emplois; **that mistake lost him the match** cette faute lui coûta la partie

VI 1 perdre; **to l. heavily** *(in betting)* perdre une grosse somme; *(by a large margin)* se faire écraser; **both armies lost heavily** les deux armées ont subi de lourdes pertes; **to l. in value** perdre de sa valeur; **our team was losing at half-time** notre équipe perdait à la mi-temps; **we've lost on the sale of the house** nous avons perdu sur la vente de la maison; **it loses in translation** on perd un peu à la traduction

2 *(of clock, watch)* retarder

▶ **lose out** **VI** être (le/la) perdant(e); **British industry is losing out to the Japanese** les Britanniques sont victimes de la concurrence japonaise

▶ **lose out on** **VT INSEP** *Fam* **to l. out on a deal** faire les frais d'une affaire; **to l. out on a contract** *(not get)* laisser échapper un contrat; **they lost out on it** ils ont été perdants

loser ['luːzər] **N** *Sport etc* perdant, -ante; **the winners and the losers** les gagnants et les perdants, les vainqueurs et les vaincus; **to be a good/bad l.** être bon/mauvais joueur; **to back a l.** miser sur un perdant; **you'll be the l.** c'est toi qui y perdras; **he's a born l.** il est toujours perdant, il n'arrive jamais à rien

losing ['luːzɪŋ] **ADJ** perdant; **to fight a l. battle** se livrer à une bataille perdue

d'avance; **the l. side** les vaincus *mpl*; *Sport* l'équipe *f* perdante

loss [lɒs] **N 1** perte *f*; **there have been heavy government losses in the Midlands** *(in election)* le gouvernement a perdu beaucoup de sièges dans les Midlands; **the catastrophe resulted in great l. of life** la catastrophe a fait beaucoup de victimes; *Mil etc* **to sustain or suffer heavy losses** subir de grosses pertes; **she has never recovered from the l. of her mother** elle ne s'est jamais remise d'avoir perdu sa mère; **he is a great l. to the British theatre** c'est une grande perte pour le théâtre britannique; **it's no great l. that they're leaving** leur départ n'est pas une grosse perte; **to feel a sense of l.** ressentir un vide; **without l. of face** sans perdre la face; **l. of sight** perte de la vue

2 *Fin, Com (financial)* déficit *m*; *(in insurance)* sinistre *m*; *(of product being manufactured or transported)* freinte *f*, déperdition *f*; **to make a l.** perdre de l'argent; **to sell at a l.** vendre à perte; **to run at a l.** *(of business)* tourner à perte; **to cut one's losses** faire la part du feu; **l. in transit** freinte *ou* déchet *m* de route; **total l.** perte *f* totale

3 *Fig* **to be at a l.** ne savoir que faire; *(not know what to say)* ne savoir que dire; *(not know what to answer)* ne savoir que répondre; **to be at a (total) l. to explain …** être (totalement) incapable d'expliquer …; **to be at a l. (to know) what to do/say** ne savoir que faire/dire; **she's never at a l. for an answer** elle a *ou* trouve toujours réponse à tout; **he's never at a l. for something to say** il n'est jamais à court (de mots)

▶▶ *Br* **l. adjuster** *Ins* expert *m*; *Naut* dispatcheur *m*; **l. assessment** fixation *f* des dommages; *Law* **l. of civil rights** perte des droits civiques, dégradation *f* civique; **l. of earnings** manque *m* à gagner; *Rel* **l. of grace** amission *f* de la grâce; *Mktg* **l. leader** produit *m* d'appel; **l. leader price** prix *m* d'appel

loss-making **ADJ** *Com* qui tourne à perte, déficitaire

lost [lɒst] **PT, PP** *see* **lose**

  ADJ perdu; **the child was l.** l'enfant s'était perdu; **to give sb/sth up for l.** abandonner tout espoir de retrouver qn/qch; **30 people were reported l. at sea** 30 personnes auraient péri en mer; **to seem** *or* **look l.** avoir l'air dépaysé; *(at party, in lesson)* avoir l'air perdu; **she's l. to the world** le monde n'existe plus pour elle; **she's completely l. in her book** elle est complètement absorbée dans sa lecture; **to be l. in thought** être perdu dans ses pensées; **the joke was l. on them** ils n'ont rien compris à la plaisanterie; **it's l. on me** ça me passe au dessus de la tête, je n'y comprends rien; *Fam* **when they talk shop I'm quite l.** quand ils parlent boutique, je suis complètement largué; **to wander (about) like a l. soul** errer comme une âme en peine; **he looks like a l. sheep without his wife** sans sa femme, il a l'air complètement perdu

▶▶ **l. cause** cause *f* perdue; **l. and found** objets *mpl* trouvés; *Am* **l. and found department** *(bureau m des)* objets trouvés; *Br* **l. property** objets trouvés; *Br* **l. property office** *(bureau des)* objets trouvés; *Am* **l. river** rivière *f* souterraine; **l. soul** âme *f* perdue, âme damnée

LOT [lɒt]

N	beaucoup **1** ▪ tirage au sort **2**
	▪ sort **3** ▪ terrain **4** ▪ studio **4** ▪ lot **5**
	▪ paquet **5** ▪ le tout **7**
ADV	beaucoup

N 1 **a l. (of)** beaucoup (de); **what a l. of people!** que de monde!; **such a l. of people** tant de monde; **quite a l. (of sth)** une quantité

considérable (de qch), *Fam* pas mal (de qch); **I saw quite a l. of her in Paris** je l'ai vue assez souvent pendant mon séjour à Paris; **not a l.** pas beaucoup; **what did you think of his speech? – not a l.!** qu'as-tu pensé de son discours? – pas grand-chose!; **a l. of explaining to do** beaucoup d'explications à donner; **we had a l. of fun** nous nous sommes bien amusés; **I would have given a l. to …** j'aurais donné gros pour …; **I've got a l. to do before bedtime** j'ai beaucoup à faire avant ce soir; **I've got a whole l. of things to do** j'ai un tas de choses à faire

2 *(selection)* sort *m*, tirage *m* au sort; **drawn by l.** tiré au sort; **to draw** *or* **cast lots for sth** tirer qch au sort, tirer au sort pour qch

3 *(destiny)* sort *m*, part *f*, partage *m*, destin *m*, destinée *f*; **to be happy/content with one's l.** être content de son sort; **it fell to my l. to decide** c'était à moi de décider; **the poor man's l.** la condition du pauvre; **to throw** *or* **cast in one's l. with sb** partager le sort *ou* la fortune de qn

4 *(land)* *(lot m de)* terrain *m*; *Cin (studio)* **l. studio** *m* (de cinéma); *Am* **parking l.** parking *m*

5 *(at auction) (of merchandise)* lot *m*; *Fin (of bonds, shares)* paquet *m*; **in lots** par lots; **to buy/sell in one l.** acheter/vendre en bloc

6 *(referring to person/people)* **a bad l.** un mauvais sujet, un vaurien; **a nice l. of people** des gens très agréables; *Iron* **you're a nice l., you are!** vous êtes incroyables, vous!; *Fam Pej* **that l. next door** la bande d'à côté; *Fam* **listen, you l.!** écoutez tous; *Fam* **you arrange to get your l. there in time** arrangez-vous pour que votre groupe soit là à l'heure; **the l. tous**, tout le monde; **the whole l. of you** vous tous; **you rotten l.!** espèces de voyous!; **the whole l. of them** toute la bande

7 **the l.** *(everything)* le tout; **I bought the l.** j'ai acheté le tout; *Fam* **the whole damn l.** tout le bazar

  ADV a l. beaucoup; **a l. bigger** beaucoup *ou* bien plus gros; **such a l.** tellement; **times have changed a l.** les temps ont bien changé; **he thought a l. before deciding** il a beaucoup réfléchi avant de se décider; **thanks a l.** merci beaucoup

▶▶ *Fin, St Exch* **l. size** unité *f* de transaction

loth [ləʊθ] **ADJ** = **loath**

lotion ['ləʊʃən] **N** lotion *f*

lots [lɒts] *Fam* **NPL l. (of)** beaucoup (de); **I've got l. of things to do** j'ai beaucoup de *ou* un tas de choses à faire; **he has l. of money** il a énormément d'argent; **he's l. of fun to be with** il est très amusant

  ADV *Fam* beaucoup

lottery ['lɒtərɪ] **N** loterie *f*; *Fig* **it's a bit of a l.** c'est une loterie

▶▶ *Br* **l. funding** = fonds *mpl* provenant de la loterie nationale; *Fin* **l. loan** emprunt *m* à lots; *Fin* **l. loan bond** titre *m* à lots

lotto ['lɒtəʊ] **N** *(game)* loto *m*

lotus, *pl* **lotuses** ['ləʊtəs, -əsɪz] **N** lotus *m*

▶▶ **l. position** position *f* du lotus

lotus-eater **N** *Myth* mangeur *m* de lotus, lotophage *m*

loud [laʊd] **ADJ 1** bruyant, retentissant; *(noise, shout)* grand; *(explosion)* violent; *(laugh)* gros; *(voice)* fort; *(person, behaviour)* bruyant; **to be l. in one's praise of sb/sth** se répandre en louanges sur qn/qch; **to be l. in one's condemnation of sb/sth** condamner qn/qch avec force; **you're too l.!** tu fais trop de bruit!; **in a l. voice** à haute voix; **l. applause** applaudissements vifs; **l. protests** protestations vives; **l. sobs** gros sanglots

2 *(colour etc)* criard, voyant; *(clothes)* voyant; **he wore a l. checked suit** il portait un costume voyant à carreaux

ADV *(to speak)* haut, à haute voix; *(to shout)* fort; **to talk out l.** parler à haute voix; *(in loud voice)* parler (très) fort; **to think out l.** penser tout haut; **to turn the radio/TV up l.** mettre la radio/TV plus fort; **louder!** parlez plus fort!; *Radio* **I hear you l. and clear** je te reçois cinq sur cinq; *Fam (I understand)* j'ai compris

loudhailer ['laʊd'heɪlər] **N** *Br* porte-voix *m inv*

loudly ['laʊdlɪ] **ADV** *(to shout)* haut, fort, à voix haute; *(to laugh)* bruyamment; *(to knock at the door)* rudement; **you're not speaking l. enough** vous ne parlez pas assez fort; **he has always dressed rather l.** il a toujours porté des vêtements assez voyants

loudmouth ['laʊdmaʊθ] **N** *Fam Pej* **to be a l.** être *ou* avoir une grande gueule; *(not be discreet)* avoir une grande langue

loudmouthed ['laʊdmaʊðd] **ADJ** *Fam Pej (who speaks loudly)* gueulard; *(who can't keep a secret)* qui ne sait pas tenir sa langue

loudness ['laʊdnɪs] **N 1** *(of engine, traffic, radio etc)* bruit *m*; **the l. of her voice** sa voix forte **2 the l. of his ties** ses cravates voyantes; **the l. of his behaviour** sa conduite tapageuse

loudspeaker [laʊd'spiːkər] **N** haut-parleur *m, pl* haut-parleurs
▶▶**l. van** camionnette *f* munie d'un haut-parleur

lough [lɒx] **N** *(in Ireland)* lac *m*

Louis ['luːɪ] **N L. the Fourteenth** Louis XIV

Louisiana [luːiːzɪˈænə] **N** Louisiane *f*

lounge [laʊndʒ] **N 1** *(in house, hotel)* salon *m* **2** *Am (sofa)* canapé *m*
VI *(on sofa etc)* s'étendre paresseusement; **I've been lounging in an armchair all afternoon** j'ai passé l'après-midi affalé dans un fauteuil
▶▶*Br* **l. bar** = salon *m* dans un pub (souvent plus confortable et plus cher que le 'public bar'); *Am Rail* **l. car** voiture-salon *f, pl* voitures-salons; *Am* **l. chair** fauteuil *m*; *Old-fashioned Fam* **l. lizard** salonnard *m*; *Br* **l. suit** costume *m* de ville; *(on invitation)* tenue *f* de ville
▶ **lounge about, lounge around** **VI** *usu Pej* flâner
▶ **lounge away** **VT SEP to l. away the time** passer le temps à flâner

lounger ['laʊndʒər] **N 1** *(person)* flemmard, -arde **2** *(sun)* **l.** chaise *f* longue **3** *Am (settee)* canapé *m*

louse [laʊs] **N 1** *(insect)* *(pl* lice*)* pou *m, pl* poux **2** *Sl (person)* *(pl* louses*)* fripouille *f*, salaud *m*
▶ **louse up** **VT SEP** *Sl (ruin, spoil)* bousiller, ficher en l'air

lousewort ['laʊswɜːt] **N** *(plant)* herbe *f* aux poux

lousiness ['laʊzɪnɪs] **N** *Fam (of weather etc)* caractère *m* horrible; *(of service in restaurant etc)* mauvaise qualité *f*

lousy ['laʊzɪ] **ADJ 1** *(full of lice)* pouilleux, plein de poux; *Fig Fam* **this place is l. with ...** ça grouille de ...; *Fam* **to be l. with money** être un gros richard
2 *Fam* affreux *(headache, cold, day, week)* sale, mauvais; *(weather)* sale, de chien; *(hotel, colour etc)* moche; *(holiday, party, meal, book, essay)* minable, nul; *(quality, workmanship)* mauvais; *(computer, car)* qui ne vaut rien, nul; *(raincoat, pen)* qui ne vaut rien; **that's a l. thing to do** *or* **say** c'est dégueulasse *ou* moche de faire *ou* dire une chose pareille; **he's l. to his wife** il est dégueulasse avec sa femme; **a l. trick** un sale tour; **don't buy them, they're l.** n'achetez pas ça, c'est de la camelote; **they made a l. job of it** ils ont salopé le travail; **he's in a l.**

mood il est d'une humeur de chien; **we had a l. time on holiday** nous avons passé des vacances nulles *ou* dégueulasses; **all for a l. £5** tout ça à cause de 5 malheureuses livres; **to feel/look l.** se sentir horriblement mal/avoir l'air horrible; **I'm l. at science** je suis nul en sciences

lout [laʊt] **N** *(oaf)* lourdaud *m*, rustre *m*; *(hooligan)* voyou *m*; **you clumsy l.!** espèce de lourdaud!

loutish ['laʊtɪʃ] **ADJ** rustre, lourdaud; **l. manners** des manières de rustre

louv(e)red ['luːvəd] **ADJ** *(door)* à persiennes; *Naut* muni ou louvre *ou* de louvres; *Aut, Aviat (car bonnet, air inlet)* à persiennes, à volet; *Archit (belfry)* à abat-sons

louvre, *Am* **louver** ['luːvər] **N 1** *Archit (board)* abat-vent *m inv*, abat-son *m, pl* abat-sons *(de clocher)* **2** *(in door, window)* persienne *f; Naut* louvre *m; Aut, Aviat (of ventilation inlet, car bonnet)* persienne, volet *m; Tech (of air intake)* ouïe *f*
▶▶*Archit* **l. board** abat-vent *m inv*, abat-son, *pl* abat-sons *(de clocher)*; **l. door** porte *f* à persiennes

lovable ['lʌvəb(ə)l] **ADJ** *(character, person)* sympathique; *(baby)* adorable; **l. rogue** petit coquin *m*

lovage ['lʌvɪdʒ] **N** *Bot, Culin* ache *f* de(s) montagne(s)

LOVE [lʌv] **N 1** amour *m*; **l. of** *or* **for sb** amour de *ou* pour *ou* envers qn; **l. of** *or* **for sth** amour de qch; **he has a great l. for Scotland** il adore l'Écosse; **there's no l. lost between them** ils ne peuvent pas se sentir; **a teacher with little l. for his pupils** un professeur qui n'a pas beaucoup de sympathie pour ses élèves; **for the l. of God** pour l'amour de Dieu; **give my l. to your parents** faites mes amitiés *fpl* à vos parents; **with l. from ...** *(at end of letter)* affectueuses pensées *fpl* de ...; **Bill sends his l.** Bill vous fait ses amitiés; **give my l. to ...** faites mes amitiés à ...; **I wouldn't do it for l. or money** je ne le ferais pour rien au monde; **to do sth for l.** faire qch pour le plaisir
2 *(between lovers)* amour *m*; **to be/fall in l. with sb** être/tomber amoureux de qn; **head over heels in l.** amoureux fou, éperdument amoureux; **to make l. to sb** faire l'amour avec qn; *Old-fashioned (to court)* faire la cour à qn; **to marry for l.** faire un mariage d'amour; **she's the l. of my life** c'est la femme *ou* l'amour de ma vie; **it was l. at first sight** ce fut le coup de foudre; **his first l.** son premier amour, *Lit* ses premières amours
3 *(term of endearment)* **(my) l.** mon amour; *esp Eng Fam* **more coffee, l.?** tu prends encore du café, mon petit/ma petite?; *esp Eng Fam* **there you are, l.!** voilà, ma petite dame/mon (petit) gars/mon petit monsieur!
4 *Tennis etc* zéro *m*, rien *m*; **l. fifteen/fifteen l.** rien à quinze/quinze à rien; **two sets to l.** deux sets à rien *ou* à zéro
VT 1 *(person)* aimer; **to l. one another** s'aimer; *Prov* **l. me, l. my dog** qui m'aime aime mon chien
2 *(something)* aimer *(passionnément)*; *(music etc)* adorer; **they l. animals** ils aiment les animaux; **to l. to do sth, to l. doing sth** aimer (à) faire qch; **will you come with me? – I'd l. to** voulez-vous m'accompagner? – avec (le plus grand) plaisir; **she'd l. to see you again** elle serait enchantée *ou* ravie de vous revoir; **I'd l. to come** j'aimerais beaucoup venir
▶▶**l. affair** liaison *f (amoureuse); Fig* passion *f;* **l. child** enfant *mf* de l'amour; *Tennis* **l. game** jeu *m* blanc; *Fam Hum* **l. handles** poignées *fpl* d'amour; **l. letter** lettre *f* d'amour, billet *m* doux; **l. life** vie *f* sentimentale; **l. match** mariage *m* d'amour; **l. nest** nid *m*

d'amour; **l. seat** canapé *m* deux places, causeuse *f;* **l. song** chanson *f* d'amour; **l. story** histoire *f* d'amour; **l. triangle** ménage *m* à trois

lovebird ['lʌvbɜːd] **N** *(bird)* perruche *f* inséparable; *Fam Hum* **lovebirds** *(people)* tourtereaux *mpl*

lovebite ['lʌvbaɪt] **N** suçon *m*

loved-up [lʌvd'ʌp] *Fam* **1** *(on drugs)* tout gentil *(sous l'effet de l'ecstasy)* **2** *(in love)* amoureux

love-hate relationship **N** relation *f* qui va de l'amour à la haine

love-in-a-mist **N** *(plant)* nigelle *f* (de Damas), cheveux *mpl* de Vénus

loveless ['lʌvlɪs] **ADJ** sans amour

love-lies-bleeding ['lʌvlaɪz'bliːdɪŋ] **N** *(plant)* amarante *f* à fleurs en queue

loveliness ['lʌvlɪnɪs] **N** beauté *f, (of woman, countryside etc)* charme *m*

lovelorn ['lʌvlɔːn] **ADJ** languissant

lovely ['lʌvlɪ] **ADJ 1** *(attractive, fine)* beau, *f* belle; *(food, smell, idea)* bon, *f* bonne; *(day, weather etc)* beau; **what a l. woman!** quelle femme charmante!; **have a l. time** amusez-vous bien; **it's been l. seeing you again** ça a été charmant de vous revoir; *Fam* **it's l. and warm** il fait une chaleur agréable; **I've made a copy for you – oh! l.!** j'en ai fait une copie pour vous – comme c'est gentil! **2** *(kind, friendly)* très aimable

lovemaking ['lʌvmeɪkɪŋ] **N** rapports *mpl* sexuels; *Old-fashioned (courting)* cour *f (amoureuse);* **his l.** la façon dont il fait l'amour

lover ['lʌvər] **N 1** amant, -ante; *Old-fashioned (suitor)* amoureux *m,* prétendant *m;* **they were lovers** ils étaient amants; **to take a l.** *(of woman)* prendre un amant; *(of man)* prendre une maîtresse **2** *(of nature etc)* amoureux, -euse, fou, *f* folle

loverboy ['lʌvəbɔɪ] **N** *Fam Iron* **1** grand séducteur *m,* le chéri de ces dames; **morning, l.!** *(said by a woman)* bonjour, chéri! **2** *(non-romantic sense)* **we're still waiting for l.!** on attend toujours le petit coco!

lovesick ['lʌvsɪk] **ADJ** qui languit d'amour

lovesickness ['lʌvsɪknɪs] **N** mal *m* d'amour

lovey-dovey ['lʌvɪdʌvɪ] **ADJ** *Sl (talk)* mièvre, à la guimauve; **to get l.** *(of person)* *(get sexy)* s'exciter; **they've gone all l.** ils sont comme deux tourtereaux

loving ['lʌvɪŋ] **ADJ** affectueux; **a l. husband and father** un mari et un père aimant; *Lit* **l. kindness** bonté *f,* **your l. mother** *(at end of letter)* ta mère qui t'aime
▶▶**l. cup** coupe *f* de l'amitié

-loving ['lʌvɪŋ] **SUFF** adventure/danger-**l.** qui aime l'aventure/le danger; home-**l.** casanier, -ière; fun-**l.** qui aime s'amuser

lovingly ['lʌvɪŋlɪ] **ADV** affectueusement, tendrement

LOW¹ [ləʊ] **ADJ 1** *(not high)* bas, *f* basse; **to cook sth over a l. heat** *or* **a l. fire** faire cuire qch à feu doux; **my stocks are rather l.** mes stocks sont un peu dégarnis; **our water supply is getting l.** notre réserve d'eau baisse; **a dress with a l. neckline** une robe décolletée; **to make sb a l. bow** saluer qn très bas; *Cards* **a l. spade** un petit pique; **a l. blow** un coup bas; **l. price** bas prix; **the lowest price** le prix le plus bas; **l. sales** ventes *fpl* faibles; **l. temperature** basse température *f,* **l. tension** basse tension *f,* **l. wages** salaires *mpl* peu élevés
2 *(inferior)* bas, *f* basse, peu élevé; **all the people, high and l.** tous, du haut comme du bas de l'échelle sociale; **to have a l. opinion of sb** avoir une mauvaise opinion de qn; **the lowest of the l.** le dernier des derniers;

that's a l. trick! ça, c'est un sale coup!; **that was rather a l. thing to do** ce n'était pas très joli de faire une chose pareille; **l. company** mauvaise compagnie; **l. cunning** ruse *f* et bassesse *f*

3 to be very l. *or* **in a very l. state** *(of invalid)* être bien bas; **to feel l.**, **to be in l. spirits** *(depressed)* se sentir déprimé, *Fam* avoir le cafard; *Med* **l. physical condition** mauvaise condition *f* physique

4 *(not loud)* bas, *f* basse; *Mus* **l. note** note *f* basse; **l. murmur** faible murmure *m*; **in a l. voice** à voix basse, à mi-voix

ADV 1 *(to hang, aim)* bas; **to bow l.** saluer très bas; **dress cut l. in the back** robe *f* décolletée dans le dos; *Boxing* **to hit l.** frapper bas; **to fly l.** *(of bird, aircraft)* voler bas; **to bring sb l.** humilier qn, abaisser qn; **to lie l.** se tapir, rester tapi

2 the lowest paid employees les employés les moins payés

3 *(to speak)* à voix basse; **turn the music down l.** baisse la musique; *Mus* **to set lower** *(song etc)* baisser d'une ou de deux octaves; **I can't sing that l.** je ne peux pas chanter aussi bas; **we're (running) l. on fuel/food** nous n'avons presque plus de carburant/nourriture; **the fire is burning l.** le feu baisse; **light turned l.** lumière en veilleuse

N 1 *Met* zone *f* de basse pression

2 to reach a new l. descendre encore plus bas; **a record l.** le point le plus bas jamais atteint; **sterling has reached an all-time l.** la livre a atteint son niveau le plus bas, la livre n'avait jamais atteint un niveau aussi bas

► ► **l. birth** basse naissance *f*; *Cards* **the l. cards** les basses cartes *fpl*; **the L. Countries** les Pays-Bas *mpl*, *Met* **l. front** front *m* de basses pressions; **l. gear** rapport *m* inférieur; *(on automatic gearbox)* conduite *f* lente; *Ling* **l. German** bas allemand *m*; *Rel* **L. Mass** messe *f* basse; *Art* **l. relief** bas-relief *m*; **L. Sunday** Pâques *fpl* closes, dimanche *m* de Quasimodo; **l. technology** technologie *f* de base; **l. tide** marée *f* basse

low² VI *(of cattle)* meugler

low-alcohol ADJ *(drink)* peu alcoolisé

low-angle shot N *TV, Cin* contre-plongée *f*

lowboy ['ləʊbɔɪ] N *Am* commode *f*

lowbrow ['ləʊbraʊ] *Pej* ADJ peu intellectuel N personne *f* peu intellectuelle

low-budget ADJ *(film, holiday etc)* à petit budget

low-calorie ADJ *(food, diet)* (à) basses calories; *(diet)* hypocalorique

low-class ADJ *(lower-class)* populaire

low-cost ADJ à bas prix; *(housing, accommodation)* à loyer modéré

low-cut ADJ *(dress)* décolleté

low-density ADJ
► ► **l. housing** zones *fpl* d'habitation peu peuplées

low-down *Fam* ADJ *esp Am (mean)* ignoble; **that's a l. trick** ça, c'est un coup rosse
N **to give sb the l.** tuyauter qn *(on* sur*)*; **to get the l.** se rencarder *(on* sur*)*

low-end ADJ *Mktg* bas de gamme

lower¹ ['ləʊər] ADJ *(less high)* inférieur; *(shelves, rungs)* du bas; **l. part** *(of ladder etc)* bas *m*
VT **1** *(head, eyes, window, blinds)* baisser; *(veil)* abaisser, rabattre; *Theat* **to l. the curtain** baisser le rideau; *Aut* **to l. the hood** décapoter
2 *(reduce)* *(light, one's voice, key)* baisser; *(pressure)* réduire; *(price)* baisser, rabaisser; *(enemy's morale)* déprimer; **to l. one's expectations** viser plus bas; **to l. the quality of sth** nuire à la qualité

de qch; *Med* **to l. sb's resistance** *(of tiredness etc)* diminuer la résistance de qn; **to l. standards** devenir moins exigeant; **to l. oneself** *(degrade)* s'abaisser, se ravaler *(to* à*)*
3 *(reduce in height)* *(object)* diminuer la hauteur de; *(ceiling)* abaisser
4 *(let down)* *(trunk from attic, stretcher into boat)* descendre; **to l. oneself (into/onto sth)** se laisser tomber *(dans/sur* qch*)*; *Naut (mast)* amener, caler; *(ship's boat)* mettre à la mer; **l. away!** laissez aller!; **to l. sb on a rope** *(faire)* descendre qn au bout d'une corde; *Boxing* **to l. one's guard** baisser sa garde; *Fig* relâcher son attention
► ► **the l. Alps** les basses Alpes *fpl*; **the l. animals** les animaux *mpl* inférieurs; *Comput* **l. ASCII** ASCII *m* inférieur; *Anat* **l. back** reins *mpl*; **to have l. back pain** avoir mal aux reins; **the l. classes** *(in society)* le bas peuple; *(in school)* les petites classes *fpl*; **the l. forms** *(in school)* les petites classes; **l. jaw** mâchoire *f* inférieure; *Med* **l. leg** jambe *f*, **the l. ranks** *(in army etc)* les rangs *mpl* inférieurs; **the l. school** les petites classes

lower² ['laʊər] VI **1** *(of person)* se renfrogner; **to l. at sb** regarder qn d'un mauvais œil, menacer qn du regard **2** *(of sky)* se couvrir; *(of storm)* menacer

lower-case ADJ *Typ* minuscule
► ► **l. letter** minuscule *f*

lower-class ADJ *(accent)* populaire; **l. people** prolétaires *mpl*

lower-income group N groupe *m* de contribuables à revenus moyens

lowering¹ ['ləʊərɪŋ] N **1** abaissement *m* **2** *(of prices)* abaissement *m*, diminution *f*, *(of pressure)* réduction *f* **3** *(reducing in height)* diminution *f* de la hauteur; *(of ceiling)* abaissement *m* **4** *(letting down)* *(of ladder etc)* descente *f*, *Naut (of mast)* calage *m*; *(of ship's boat)* mise *f* à la mer

lowering² ['laʊərɪŋ] ADJ *(look, sky)* menaçant

lowest ['ləʊɪst] ADJ
► ► **l. bidder** moins-disant *m*; **l. common denominator** plus petit dénominateur *m* commun

low-flying ADJ *(airplane)* volant à basse altitude

low-grade ADJ **1** *(coal etc)* de qualité inférieure **2** *(official)* de grade inférieur

low-heeled ['ləʊhi:ld] ADJ *(shoe)* à talon plat

low-income ADJ *(family)* à faible revenu

lowing ['ləʊɪŋ] N meuglement *m*

low-interest ADJ *(credit, loan)* à taux réduit

low-key ADJ *(approach, debate, discussion)* modéré; *(film)* au style dépouillé; *(person)* réservé; *(lighting)* de faible intensité; **to keep sth l.** contenir qch, modérer qch

lowland ['ləʊlənd] N plaine *f* (basse); **the Lowlands** *(in Scotland)* les Lowlands *fpl*

low-level ADJ **1** *(radioactivity)* faible **2** *(discussion)* à la base
► ► *Med* **l. infection** infection *f* bénigne; *Comput* **l. language** langage *m* non évolué ou de bas niveau

lowlife ['ləʊlaɪf] N *Sl* crapule *f*; **his l. friends** ses amis pas très recommandables

lowlight ['ləʊlaɪt] N **1** *(in hair)* reflet *m* coloré **2** *Hum* moment *m* décevant

lowliness ['ləʊlɪnɪs] N humilité *f*, modestie *f*

low-loader N camion *m* à plate-forme surbaissée

lowly ['ləʊlɪ] ADJ humble, modeste

low-lying ADJ situé à basse altitude; *(land)* bas, enfoncé

low-maintenance battery N batterie *f* à entretien réduit

low-necked ['ləʊnekt] ADJ *(dress)* décolleté

lowness ['ləʊnɪs] N **1** *(of wall etc)* faible hauteur *f*, *(of island, hills)* faible altitude *f*
2 *(of note)* gravité *f*
3 *(of behaviour)* bassesse *f*
4 l. (of spirits) abattement *m*, découragement *m*

low-octane fuel N carburant *m* à faible indice d'octane

low-pitched ['ləʊpɪtʃt] ADJ **1** *(sound, voice)* grave; *(piano)* accordé à un diapason bas **2** *(roof)* à faible pente

low-pressure ADJ **1** *Met (zone)* de basse pression **2** *(cylinder, machine)* à basse pression ou tension

low-profile ADJ *(politician, company etc)* discret, qui adopte ou garde un profil bas
► ► *Aut* **l. tyre** pneu *m* à profil bas

low-radiation monitor N moniteur *m* à basse radiation

low-rent ADJ **1** *(housing)* à loyer modéré **2** *Fam Pej (low-quality)* bas de gamme

low-resolution ADJ à basse résolution

low-rise N immeuble *m* bas
► ► **l. building** immeuble *m* peu élevé ou bas

low-speed ADJ *(machine)* à petite vitesse

low-spirited ADJ abattu, déprimé

low-tar ADJ *(cigarette)* à taux de goudron faible

low-tech ['ləʊtek] ADJ rudimentaire, *Fam* pas très évolué; **as regards text-processing they're very l.** en matière de traitement de texte, ils ne sont pas très à la page

low-tension circuit N circuit *m* basse tension

low-voltage ADJ à faible voltage, à faible tension

low-wage ADJ
► ► **l. economy** économie *f* où les salaires sont bas

loyal ['lɔɪəl] ADJ **1** *(friend etc)* fidèle, dévoué *(to* à*)*, loyal, -aux *(to* envers*)*; *Mktg* **l. -customer discount** remise *f* de fidélité au client fidèle **2** *(to sovereign)* fidèle au souverain; **to drink the l. toast** porter le toast au souverain

loyalist ['lɔɪəlɪst] ADJ, N loyaliste *mf*

Loyalist
Dans le contexte britannique, le mot "Loyalist" désigne un protestant d'Irlande du Nord souhaitant rester au sein du Royaume-Uni.

---

loyally ['lɔɪəlɪ] ADV fidèlement, loyalement

loyalty ['lɔɪəltɪ] N loyalisme *m*; *(to friends, employer etc)* loyauté *f* *(to* envers*)*; **you'll have to decide where your loyalties lie** il faudra que tu décides de quel côté tu es; **to have divided loyalties** être partagé; **to create customer l.** fidéliser la clientèle
► ► *Mktg* **l. card** carte *f* de fidélité; *Mktg* **l. discount** remise *f* de fidélité; *Mktg* **l. magazine** = magazine *m* publié par une chaîne de magasins, une banque etc, pour ses clients

lozenge ['lɒzɪndʒ] N **1** *Pharm* pastille *f* **2** *Math, Her* losange *m*

Note that the French word **losange** never refers to a medicated tablet.

LP [el'pi:] N *(abbr* **long player***)* 33 tours *m*

L-plate N *Br* = plaque *f* apposée sur une voiture et signalant un apprenti conducteur

L-plate En Grande-Bretagne, la lettre "L" apposée sur l'arrière d'un véhicule indique que le conducteur n'a pas encore son permis mais qu'il est en conduite accompagnée.

LQ [el'kju:] (*abbr* **letter quality**) qualité *f* courrier
▸▸ **LQ printer** imprimante *f* de qualité courrier

LSD [eles'di:] **N 1** (*abbr* **lysergic acid diethylamide**) LSD *m* **2** *Br Formerly abbr* **pounds, shillings and pence**

LSE [eles'i:] **N 1** *Br Univ abbr* **London School of Economics 2** *St Exch abbr* **London Stock Exchange**

L-shaped ADJ en (forme de) L

LSI [ele'sai] **N** *Comput abbr* **large-scale integration**

Lt *Mil* (*abbr* **Lieutenant**) Lt

lt *abbr* **low tension**

LTA [elti'ei] *abbr* **Lawn Tennis Association**

Ltd *Br Com* (*abbr* **limited**) ≃ SARL

lube [lu:b] **N** lubrifiant *m*
VT lubrifier

lubricant ['lu:brikənt] ADJ lubrifiant
N lubrifiant *m*

lubricate ['lu:brikeit] VT lubrifier, graisser; **lubricated condom** préservatif *m* lubrifié; *Fig Fam* **we were all well lubricated** (*drunk*) nous étions tous bien imbibés

lubricating ['lu:brikeitiŋ] **N** lubrification *f*
▸▸ **l. oil** huile *f* de graissage

lubrication [lu:bri'keiʃən] **N** lubrification *f*, graissage *m*; *Fam Hum* (*alcohol*) gnôle *f*
▸▸ **l. nipple** graisseur *m*; **l. oil** huile *f* de lubrification; **l. system** circuit *m* de lubrification

lubricator ['lu:brikeitər] **N** (*device*) graisseur *m*, appareil *m* de graissage; **gravity-feed l.** graisseur par gravité

lubricity [lu:'brisiti] **N** *Lit* (*lewdness*) lubricité *f*

Lucerne [lu:'sɜːn] **N** *Geog* Lucerne; **(the) Lake (of) L.** le lac des Quatre-Cantons

lucerne [lu:'sɜːn] **N** *Br Bot, Agr* luzerne *f*

lucid ['lu:sid] ADJ (*mind, style*) lucide; (*explanation*) clair; *Med* **l. interval** intervalle *m* lucide *ou* de lucidité

lucidity [lu:'siditi] **N** lucidité *f*

lucidly ['lu:sidli] ADV lucidement; (*explained, outlined etc*) avec clarté

Lucifer ['lu:sifər] **N** Lucifer *m*

luck [lʌk] **N** (*chance*) chance *f*; **good l.** bonne chance, bonheur *m*; **bad l.** malchance *f*, mauvaise fortune *f*, *Fam* déveine *f*; **piece or stroke of l.** coup *m* de chance, aubaine *f*, *Fam* coup de bol; **to bring sb bad/good l.** porter malheur/bonheur à qn; **to keep sth for l.** garder qch comme porte-bonheur; **good l. (to you)!** bonne chance!; **good l. with the exams/for Friday** bonne chance pour les examens/pour vendredi; *Iron* **good l. to him!** qu'il le fasse si ça lui chante!; **to wish sb l.** souhaiter bonne chance à qn; **better l. next time** ça ira mieux la prochaine fois; **to be in l.** avoir de la chance *ou Fam* de la veine; **to be out of l.** ne pas avoir de chance; **to be down on one's l.** avoir la guigne; **to try one's l.** tenter sa chance; **don't trust to l.** n'y compte pas trop; (*when you can do something about it*) ne laisse rien au hasard; **her l. has changed** sa chance a tourné; **he has all the l.** c'est lui qui a toute la chance; **to have the l. of the devil** avoir une chance de tous les diables; **just my l.!** c'est bien ma chance!; **with my l. it won't work** avec ma

chance habituelle, ça ne marchera pas; **no such l.!** je n'ai pas (eu) cette chance!, *Fam* tu parles!; **hard l.!** pas de chance!; **I've got to work, worst l.** il faut que je travaille, pas de chance!; **by good l.** par bonheur; **as l. would have it** par bonheur; **as l. would have it, I was there** le hasard a voulu que je sois là; **it's the l. of the draw** c'est le hasard
▸ **luck into** VT INSEP *Fam* **to l. into sth** dégoter qch
▸ **luck out** VI *Am Fam* avoir du pot

luckily ['lʌkɪlɪ] ADV heureusement, par bonheur; **l. for her** par chance pour elle

luckless ['lʌklɪs] ADJ *Fml* **1** (*person*) malheureux, malchanceux **2** (*day*) de malchance

lucky ['lʌkɪ] ADJ (*person*) chanceux; (*time, moment*) propice; **to be l.** (*of person*) avoir de la chance; **you're a very l. person** vous avez beaucoup de chance; **who's the l. man?** (*she's going to marry*) qui est l'heureux élu?; *Fam* **(you) l. devil!, l. beggar!** veinard!; *Iron* **you'll be l.!** tu peux toujours courir!; **to be born l.** être né coiffé; **to have a l. break** avoir un coup de chance *ou* de pot; **to get l.** avoir de la chance; *Sl* (*find sexual partner*) emballer; **l. in love/at cards** heureux en amour/au jeu; **it's l. you came when you did** c'est une chance que tu sois arrivé à ce moment-là; **she's l. to be alive** elle a de la chance d'être en vie; **l. shot** coup *m* de bol *ou* de veine; **my l. number** mon chiffre porte-bonheur; **to make a l. guess** tomber juste; **it's not my l. day** ce n'est pas mon jour de chance; **that was l.** ça a été un coup de chance; **it's l.** (*of thing*) ça porte bonheur
▸▸ **l. charm** porte-bonheur *m inv*; *Br* **l. dip** = jeu *m* consistant à chercher des cadeaux enfouis dans une caisse remplie de sciure ou dans un sac

Lucozade® ['lu:kəzeid] **N** = boisson *f* gazeuse à base de glucose

lucrative ['lu:krətiv] ADJ lucratif

lucre ['lu:kər] **N** *Pej Hum* lucre *m*; **to do sth for** (*filthy*) **l.** agir par amour du gain *ou* du lucre

ludicrous ['lu:dikrəs] ADJ risible, comique, ridicule; **it's l. to ...** c'est ridicule de ...; **he looked faintly l.** il avait l'air assez grotesque

ludicrously ['lu:dikrəslɪ] ADV ridiculement

ludo ['lu:dəʊ] **N** *Br* (*game*) jeu *m* des petits chevaux

luff [lʌf] *Naut* **N 1** (*of sail*) lof *m*, ralingue *f* du vent, chute *f* avant **2** (*of bow*) épaule *f*
VI lof(f)er, faire une aulof(f)ée
VT **to l. the boat (up)** faire loffer la barque

lug¹ [lʌg] (**-gg-**) VT (*sth heavy*) traîner, tirer; **to l. sth along** *or* **away** entraîner qch; **to l. sth about** *or* **with one** promener *ou* trimbaler qch avec soi

lug² **N 1** *Tech* oreille *f* **2** *Fam* (*ear*) esgourde *f*

lug³ **N** *Naut* = **lugsail**

lug⁴ **N** *Zool* = **lugworm**

luge [lu:ʒ] **N** *Sport* luge *f*

luggage ['lʌgɪdʒ] **N** bagage(s) *m(pl)*; **a piece of l.** un bagage
▸▸ *Aviat* **l. bay, l. compartment** soute *f* à bagages; *Naut* **l. hold** soute à bagages; **l. label** étiquette *f* à bagages; **l. locker** consigne *f* automatique; *Br* **l. rack** *Rail* (*shelf*) porte-bagages *m inv*; (*net*) filet *m* (à bagages); *Aut* galerie *f* (de toit); *Naut* **l. room** soute à bagages; **l. trolley** chariot *m* à bagages; *Br Rail* **l. van** fourgon *m* (à bagages)

lugger ['lʌgər] **N** *Naut* lougre *m*

lughole ['lʌghəʊl] **N** *Br Fam* oreille *f*, *Fam* esgourde *f*; **are your lugholes blocked?** est-ce que tu as les portugaises ensablées?

lugsail ['lʌgseil, 'lʌgs(ə)l] **N** *Naut* voile *f* à bourcet

lugubrious [lʊ'gu:brɪəs] ADJ lugubre

lugubriously [lʊ'gu:brɪəslɪ] ADV lugubrement

lugworm ['lʌgwɜːm] **N** *Zool* ariénicole *f*

Luke [lu:k] **N** Luc *m*; **Saint L.** saint Luc

lukewarm ['lu:kwɔːm] ADJ (*water, friendship etc*) tiède; **the critics gave the play a l. reception** les critiques ont accueilli la pièce avec tiédeur; **to become l.** tiédir

lull [lʌl] **N** moment *m* de calme; (*in fighting*) répit *m*; *Naut* accalmie *f*; **the l. before the storm** le calme avant la tempête; **there was a l. in the conversation** la conversation tomba
VT (*person*) (*send to sleep*) bercer, endormir; (*fears*) endormir; **to l. a child to sleep** endormir un enfant en le berçant; **to l. sb into a false sense of security** endormir la vigilance de qn

lullaby ['lʌləbaɪ] **N** *Mus* berceuse *f*

lumbago [lʌm'beigəʊ] **N** *Med* lumbago *m*; **to have l.** avoir un lumbago

lumbar ['lʌmbər] ADJ *Anat* lombaire
▸▸ **l. adjustable seat** siège *m* à réglage lombaire; *Med* **l. puncture** ponction *f* lombaire, rachicentèse *f*

lumber¹ ['lʌmbər] **N 1** *Br* (*useless objects*) objets *mpl* encombrants **2** *Am* (*wood*) bois *m* de charpente *ou* de construction
▸▸ *Br* **l. room** débarras *m*

lumber² VT **1** (*place*) encombrer, embarrasser; **to l. a room with furniture** encombrer une pièce de meubles; *Fam* **to get lumbered with a task** se taper *ou* se coltiner un travail; **to l. sb with sth** flanquer qch à qn; **they've lumbered me with the cooking** c'est moi qui me suis tapé tous les repas; **I was lumbered with him for the whole evening** je l'ai eu sur le dos pendant toute la soirée **2** *Am* (*trees*) abattre; (*wood*) débiter
VI avancer d'un pas pesant
▸ **lumber about** VI se trimbaler çà et là
▸ **lumber along** VI (*of person*) avancer à pas pesants *ou* d'un pas lourd

lumbering ['lʌmbərɪŋ] ADJ lourd, pesant

lumberjack ['lʌmbədʒæk] **N** *esp Am* bûcheron *m*

lumberjacket ['lʌmbədʒækɪt] **N** blouson *m*; (*longer*) canadienne *f*

lumberman, pl lumbermen ['lʌmbəmən] **N** *Am* bûcheron *m*

lumberyard ['lʌmbəjɑːd] **N** *Am* chantier *m* de bois

luminary ['lu:mɪnərɪ] **N** (*person*) lumière *f*, (*of science etc*) sommité *f*

luminescence [lu:mɪ'nesəns] **N** *Phys* luminescence *f*

luminescent [lu:mɪ'nesənt] ADJ *Phys* luminescent

luminosity [lu:mɪ'nɒsɪtɪ] **N** luminosité *f*

luminous ['lu:mɪnəs] ADJ lumineux; (*socks, strip on clothing, roadsign, colours*) fluorescent

lumme, lummy ['lʌmɪ] INT *Br Old-fashioned Fam* nom de Dieu!, mince alors!

lummox ['lʌməks] **N** *Old-fashioned Fam* lourdaud, -aude

lump¹ [lʌmp] **N 1** (*of stone*) gros morceau *m*, bloc *m*; (*of earth, clay*) motte *f*, (*of sugar, cheese etc*) morceau *m*; (*of lead etc*) masse *f*; (*in porridge etc*) grumeau *m*; *Med* (*internal*) grosseur *f*; (*external*) excroissance *f*, (*caused by knock etc*) bosse *f*, *Fig* **to have a l. in one's throat** avoir la gorge serrée; **to pay in a l.** payer en une seule fois; **Parisians, taken in the l., are ...** en général, les Parisiens sont ... **2** *Fam Pej* (*person*) empoté *m*; **great l. of a girl** grosse dondon *f* **3** *Br Fam* **the l.** (*casual workers*) ouvriers *mpl* indépendants (non déclarés)

VT mettre en bloc *ou* en masse *ou* en tas
▸▸ **l. sum** somme *f* forfaitaire, montant *m* forfaitaire

▸ **lump together VT SEP** *(things)* rassembler, mettre ensemble; **to l. people together** considérer des personnes en bloc, *Pej* mettre tout le monde dans le même sac

lump² **VT** *Fam* **if he doesn't like it, he can l. it, he can like it or l. it** que ça lui plaise ou pas, c'est le même prix; **you'll have to l. it!** il faudra que tu fasses avec!, il faudra en passer par là!

lumpectomy [lʌm'pektəmɪ] **N** *Surg* ablation *f* de tumeur mammaire

lumpen ['lʌmpən] **ADJ** grossier; **the l. proletariat** le sous-prolétariat

lumpfish ['lʌmpfɪʃ] **N** lompe *m*, lump *m*

lumpish ['lʌmpɪʃ] **ADJ 1** *(clumsy)* balourd, pataud; **great l. man** lourdaud *m* **2** *(stupid)* stupide

lumpy ['lʌmpɪ] **ADJ** *(sauce)* grumeleux; *(surface, mattress)* bosselé; *(forehead etc)* couvert de bosses

lunacy ['lu:nəsɪ] **N 1** *Fam (action, idea)* action *f*/idée *f* folle; **it's sheer l.** c'est de la folie (pure et simple) **2** *Med* aliénation *f* mentale, folie *f*, *Law* démence *f*

lunar ['lu:nər] **ADJ** *(cycle, module, orbit etc)* lunaire
▸▸ **l. eclipse** éclipse *f* de lune; **l. landing** alunissage *m*

lunaria [lu:'neərɪə] **N** *Bot* lunaire *f*

lunatic ['lu:nətɪk] **ADJ** fou, *f* folle
N fou, *f* folle; *Med Old-fashioned* aliéné, -ée
▸▸ **l. asylum** asile *m* d'aliénés; **the l. fringe** les extrémistes *mpl*

> Note that the French adjective **lunatique** is a false friend and is never a translation for the English word **lunatic**. It means **moody**.

lunch [lʌntʃ] **N** déjeuner *m*, *Can, Belg* dîner *m*; *Am (snack) (eaten at any time)* petit repas *m*, casse-croûte *m inv*; **to have l.** prendre son déjeuner, déjeuner; **they have l. at one o'clock** ils déjeunent à une heure; **what time** *or* **when is l.?** à quelle heure déjeune-t-on?; **what's for l.?** qu'y a-t-il pour le déjeuner?; **we're having trout for l.** il y a de la truite au déjeuner; **let's go out for l.** allons déjeuner dehors; **how long do you get for l.?** combien de temps tu as pour déjeuner?; **what are you doing for l.?** que fais-tu à midi?; **we're having people to l.** nous avons du monde à déjeuner; **she's at l.** *or* **has gone to l.** elle est sortie déjeuner; *esp Am Sl* **to be out to l.** *(be crazy)* débloquer un peu, avoir une case de vide VOIR GRAMMAIRE A7
VI *Fml* déjeuner, *Can, Belg* dîner; **we lunched on sandwiches** nous avons déjeuné de sandwichs
VT *Fml (entertain to lunch)* inviter à déjeuner
▸▸ **l. break** *(in course of working day)* pause *f* du déjeuner; *Am* **l. counter** *(in store)* bar *m* de restauration rapide; **l. hour** heure *f* du déjeuner; **to go shopping during one's l. hour** aller faire des courses à l'heure du déjeuner; **l. menu** menu *m* déjeuner; **l. time** *(noon, one o'clock etc)* moment *m* du déjeuner

lunchbox ['lʌntʃbɒks] **N 1** *(for carrying lunch)* panier-repas *m*, *pl* paniers-repas **2** *Br Fam Hum (man's genitals)* service *m* trois pièces, bijoux *mpl* de famille

lunchbucket ['lʌntʃbʌkɪt] **N** *Am* panier-repas *m*, *pl* paniers-repas

luncheon ['lʌntʃ(ə)n] **N** *Fml* déjeuner *m*
▸▸ **l. meat** = bloc *m* de viande de porc en conserve; *Br* **l. voucher** Ticket-Restaurant® *m inv*

luncheonette ['lʌntʃə'net] **N** *Am* petit restaurant *m*, café-restaurant *m*

lunchpail ['lʌntʃpeɪl] **N** *Am* panier-repas *m*, *pl* paniers-repas

lunchroom ['lʌntʃrʊm] **N** *Am* = pièce *f* où l'on peut manger ses sandwichs etc à l'heure du déjeuner

lung [lʌŋ] **N** poumon *m*; **to shout at the top of one's lungs** crier à tue-tête
▸▸ **l. cancer** cancer *m* du poumon; **l. transplant** greffe *f* du poumon

lunge [lʌndʒ] **N 1** mouvement *m* (brusque) en avant; **she made a l. for the ball** elle s'est jetée sur la balle **2** *Fencing* botte *f*
VI *Fencing* se fendre; **to l. at sb** se jeter sur qn; *Fencing* porter *ou* pousser une botte à l'adversaire

▸ **lunge forward VI** se jeter en avant

lupin, *Am* **lupine** ['lu:pɪn] **N** *(plant)* lupin *m*

lupine ['lu:paɪn] **ADJ** de loup

lupus ['lu:pəs] **N** lupus *m*

lurch¹ [lɜ:tʃ] **N to leave sb in the l.** *(in danger, difficulty etc)* laisser qn dans le pétrin; *(to desert)* planter là qn

lurch² **N** *(of ship)* embardée *f*, coup *m* de roulis; *(of car)* embardée *f*; **with a drunken l.** *(to stagger etc)* en titubant; *(to reach out)* d'un geste d'homme/de femme ivre; **to give a l.** *(of ship, car etc)* faire une embardée; **with a l., the train was off again** le train est reparti avec un à-coup; **a l. to the left/right** un virage à gauche/droite
VI 1 *(of ship, car etc)* faire une embardée **2** *(of person)* tituber

▸ **lurch along VI** *(of person)* marcher en titubant; *(of economy)* progresser tant bien que mal

lurcher ['lɜ:tʃər] **N** *(dog)* lévrier *m* bâtard

lure ['lʊər] **N 1** *(attraction)* attrait *m*; **the l. of the sea** l'attrait de la mer **2** *(in hunting) (decoy)* leurre *m*; *Fig* appât *m*; *(wooden duck)* appât factice
VT 1 *(person)* attirer, séduire; **to be lured into a trap** être attiré dans un piège; **he was lured into it by his friends** il s'y est laissé entraîner par ses amis **2** *(fish, falcon etc)* leurrer

lurid ['lʊərɪd] **ADJ 1** *(sensational) (account, language)* corsé, à sensation; **she gave us a l. description of her operation** elle nous a fait une description de son opération avec force détails; **l. details** détails *mpl* effroyables **2** *(fiery)* cuivré; *(flames)* rougeoyant; *Pej (colour)* criard; **a l. sunset** un coucher de soleil flamboyant **3** *Lit (pale) (light)* blafard; *(complexion)* livide

luridly ['lʊərɪdlɪ] **ADV 1** *(to describe)* de façon sensationnelle **2** *(to glow)* en rougeoyant **3** *Lit (with a pale light)* avec une lueur blafarde

lurk [lɜ:k] **VI** se cacher; **there's a man lurking in the alleyway** il y a un homme qui se cache dans la ruelle; **I'll just l. in the background** je me fondrai dans les décors

lurking ['lɜ:kɪŋ] **ADJ** *(feeling, suspicion etc)* vague; **I have one l. doubt** j'ai encore un léger doute; **if you have any l. doubts** s'il vous reste des doutes; **l. errors in the text** des erreurs qui sont passées inaperçues dans le texte

luscious ['lʌʃəs] **ADJ** succulent; *(fruit)* fondant, succulent; **a l. blonde** une blonde appétissante

lush [lʌʃ] **ADJ 1** *(grass, plant)* plein de sève, luxuriant **2** *(luxurious)* **l. surroundings** environnement *m* luxueux; **a l. sound** un son riche
N *Sl (alcoholic)* poivrot, -ote

lushness ['lʌʃnɪs] **N** *(of grass etc)* luxuriance *f*

lust [lʌst] **N** *(sexual)* désir *m* (charnel *ou* sexuel), *Pej* luxure *f*; **l. for power** soif *f* de pouvoir

▸ **lust after VT INSEP** *(person)* désirer; *(thing)* convoiter

▸ **lust for VT INSEP** *(object)* convoiter; **to l. for power/revenge** avoir soif de pouvoir/de revanche

luster, lusterless etc *Am* = **lustre, lustreless** etc

lustful ['lʌstfʊl] **ADJ** lascif, libidineux

lustfully ['lʌstfʊlɪ] **ADV** lascivement

lustily ['lʌstɪlɪ] **ADV** *(to sing, shout)* à pleine gorge

lustre, *Am* **luster** ['lʌstər] **N 1** *(shine)* éclat *m*, lustre *m*; *(of cloth)* cati *m*, lustre **2** *(of chandelier)* pendeloque *f* **3** *(fabric)* **(cotton) l.** lustrine *f*

lustreless, *Am* **lusterless** ['lʌstələs] **ADJ** terne; *(eyes, hair)* sans éclat

lustreware, *Am* **lusterware** ['lʌstəweər] **N** *Cer* poterie *f* à reflets métalliques, poterie lustrée

lustrous ['lʌstrəs] **ADJ** *(hair, eyes)* brillant; *(fabric)* lustré

lusty ['lʌstɪ] **ADJ** vigoureux, fort, robuste; **l. voices** voix puissantes

lute [lu:t] **N** *Mus* luth *m*
▸▸ **l. maker** luthier *m*; **l. player** joueur, -euse de luth, luthiste *mf*

Lutheran ['lu:θərən] **ADJ, N** *Rel, Hist* luthérien, -ienne

luv [lʌv] **N** *Fam* = **love N 3**

luvvie ['lʌvɪ] **N** *Fam (actor, actress)* comédien, -ienne

luxation [lʌk'seɪʃən] **N** *Med* luxation *f*

Luxemb(o)urg ['lʌksəmbɜ:g] **N the Grand Duchy of L.** le Grand-duché de Luxembourg

luxuriance [lʌg'zjʊərɪəns, lʌk's-] **N** *(of vegetation, style etc)* exubérance *f*, luxuriance *f*

luxuriant [lʌg'zjʊərɪənt, lʌk's-] **ADJ** exubérant, luxuriant; **l. (growth of) hair** chevelure *f* abondante; **l. beard** barbe *f* drue

> Attention: ne pas confondre avec **luxurious**.

luxuriantly [lʌg'zjʊərɪəntlɪ, lʌk's-] **ADV** avec exubérance, en abondance

luxuriate [lʌg'zjʊərɪeɪt, lʌk's-] **VI to l. in a hot bath** se prélasser dans un bain chaud

luxurious [lʌg'zjʊərɪəs, lʌk's-] **ADJ** *(apartment, lifestyle)* luxueux, somptueux; *(tastes)* de luxe

> Attention: ne pas confondre avec **luxuriant**.

luxuriously [lʌg'zjʊərɪəslɪ, lʌk's-] **ADV 1** *(furnished)* luxueusement, avec luxe **2** *(to stretch)* avec volupté

luxuriousness [lʌg'zjʊərɪəsnɪs, lʌk's-] **N** luxe *m*

luxury ['lʌkʃərɪ] **N 1** luxe *m*; **to live in (the lap of) l.** vivre dans le luxe **2** *(object)* objet *m* de luxe; **one of life's little luxuries** un des petits plaisirs de l'existence; **to indulge in the l. of a cigar** se payer le luxe d'un cigare; **it's a l. not to have to cook** c'est un luxe de ne pas avoir à faire la cuisine
ADJ ATTRIB *(car, apartment etc)* de luxe
▸▸ **l. brand** marque *f* de luxe; **l. goods** articles *mpl* de luxe; **l. liner** paquebot *m* de luxe; **l. market** marché *m* du luxe; *Fin* **l. tax** taxe *f* (sur les produits) de luxe

> Note that the French word **luxure** is a false friend and is never a translation for the English word **luxury**. It means **lust**.

LV [el'vi:] *Br abbr* **luncheon voucher**

LW [el'dʌb(ə)lju:] *abbr Radio* **(long wave)** LW

lychee [laɪ'tʃiː] N*(fruit)* litchi *m*
lychgate ['lɪtʃgeɪt] N= **lichgate**
lye [laɪ] N*(of soda, potassium)* lessive *f*
lying ['laɪɪŋ] ADJ *(false) (person)* menteur, -euse; *(account)* mensonger
 N*(falsehoods)* mensonges *mpl*
lying-in N *Med Old-fashioned* couches *fpl*
lymph [lɪmf] N *Physiol* lymphe *f*; **l. node** or *Old-fashioned* **gland** glande *f ou* ganglion *m* lymphatique
lymphangitis [lɪmfæn'dʒaɪtɪs] N lymphangite *f*
lymphatic [lɪm'fætɪk] *Physiol* ADJ lymphatique; **l. node** or *Old-fashioned* **gland** glande *f ou* ganglion *m* lymphatique
 N*(vessel)* lymphatique *m*

lymphocyte ['lɪmfəʊsaɪt] N *Med* lymphocyte *m*
lymphoma [lɪm'fəʊmə] N lymphome *m*
lynch [lɪntʃ] VT lyncher
 ▶ ▶ **l. law** loi *f* de Lynch; **l. mob** lyncheurs *mpl*
lynching ['lɪntʃɪŋ] N lynchage *m*
lynx [lɪŋks] N*(animal)* lynx *m*
lynx-eyed ADJ aux yeux de lynx
Lyons [liːɒn] N Lyon
lyre ['laɪər] N *Mus* lyre *f*
lyrebird ['laɪəbɜːd] N oiseau-lyre *m, pl* oiseaux-lyres, ménure *m*
lyric ['lɪrɪk] ADJ*(poet, drama)* lyrique
 N **1** *(poem)* poème *m* lyrique **2 lyrics**

(of song) paroles *fpl*
 ▶ ▶ **l. writer** parolier *m*
lyrical ['lɪrɪk(ə)l] ADJ **1** *(poetry etc)* lyrique **2** *(expressively formulated)* dit *ou* écrit sur un ton lyrique; *Fam* **she got positively l. about it** elle y a montré un enthousiasme fou; **to wax l. about sth** déborder d'enthousiasme pour qch
lyrically ['lɪrɪklɪ] ADV **1** *Liter* avec lyrisme, lyriquement **2** *(to speak)* avec enthousiasme
lyricism ['lɪrɪsɪz(ə)m] N lyrisme *m*
lyricist ['lɪrɪsɪst] N **1** *(of musical etc)* parolier *m* **2** *(poet)* poète *m* lyrique
lysergic [lɪ'sɜːdʒɪk, laɪ-] ADJ *(acid)* lysergique

M, m [em] N *(letter)* M, m *mf*; **two m's** deux m

m² *(abbr* **metre(s))** m

MA [e'meɪ] N **1** *Univ (abbr* **Master of Arts)** *(degree) Eng* maîtrise *f* de *ou* ès lettres; *Scot* licence *f* de *ou* ès lettres; *(person)* titulaire *mf* d'une maîtrise/licence de *ou* ès lettres; **to have an MA in Russian** avoir une maîtrise/licence de russe; **Susan Long, MA** Susan Long, Maîtrise de lettres/licenciée ès lettres **2** *abbr* **Massachusetts**

ma [mɑː] N *Fam* maman *f*

ma'am [mɑːm] N madame *f*

Mac [mæk] N *Comput* Mac *m*; **available for the M.** disponible en version Mac
▸▸ **M. disk** disquette *f* pour Mac; **M. OS** Mac-OS *m*

mac¹ [mæk] N *Br Fam (raincoat)* imper *m*

mac² N *Am Fam* **hey, m.!** hé, mon vieux *ou* mon pote!

macabre [mə'kɑːbrə] ADJ macabre; **a taste for the m.** le goût du macabre

macadam [mə'kædəm] N *Constr* macadam *m*

macadamize [mə'kædəmaɪz] VT *Constr (road)* macadamiser

macaque [mə'kɑːk] N macaque *m*

macaroni [mækə'rəʊnɪ] N *Culin* macaroni(s) *m(pl)* **VOIR GRAMMAIRE A14**
▸▸ **m. cheese** macaroni(s) au gratin

macaroon [mækə'ruːn] N *Culin* macaron *m*

macaw [mə'kɔː] N *(bird)* ara *m*

Mace® [meɪs] N *(gas)* gaz *m* lacrymogène *ou* incapacitant
VT **to m. sb** asperger qn de gaz lacrymogène *ou* incapacitant

mace¹ [meɪs] N *(weapon, symbol of office)* masse *f*

mace² N *Bot, Culin* macis *m*

macebearer ['meɪsbeərər] N massier *m*

Macedonia [mæsɪ'dəʊnɪə] N Macédoine *f*

Macedonian [mæsɪ'dəʊnɪən] ADJ macédonien
N **1** *(person)* Macédonien, -ienne **2** *Ling* macédonien *m*

macerate ['mæsəreɪt] VT & VI macérer

Mach [mæk] N *Phys* Mach *m*; **at M. 3** à Mach 3
▸▸ **M. number** nombre *m* de Mach

machete [mə'ʃetɪ] N machette *f*

Machiavellian [mækɪə'velɪən] ADJ machiavélique

machination [mækɪ'neɪʃən] N machination *f*, manœuvre *f*

machine [mə'ʃiːn] N **1** machine *f*, **(vending) m.** distributeur *m* (automatique); **m. made** fait à la machine **2** *Fig Pej (person)* automate *m*, robot *m*, machine *f* **3** *Fig (organization)* propaganda **m.** appareil *m* de propagande; **the organization runs like a m.** l'organisation fonctionne très efficacement
VT **1** *Ind (part)* usiner, façonner, travailler à la machine **2** *Sewing* coudre *ou* piquer à la machine
▸▸ *Comput* **m. code** code *m* machine; *Comput* **m. code instruction** instruction *f* de code machine; **m. gun** mitrailleuse *f*, *Mil* **m. gunner** mitrailleur *m*; *Comput* **m. language** langage *m* machine; **m. shop** atelier *m* d'usinage; **m. time** temps-machine *m*; **m. tool** machine-outil *f*, *pl* machines-outils; *Comput* **m. translation** traduction *f* assistée par ordinateur

▸ **machine down** VT SEP *Ind (metal)* amincir

machine-gun VT mitrailler

machine-gunning [-gʌnɪŋ] N *Mil* mitraillage *m*

machine-hour N heure-machine *f*, *pl* heures-machine

machine-readable ADJ *Comput (data)* lisible par ordinateur; **in m. format** dans un format lisible par ordinateur

machinery [mə'ʃiːnərɪ] N **1** *(parts)* mécanisme(s) *m(pl)*; *(machines)* machines *fpl*, machinerie *f* **2** *(of organization)* **the m. of government** les rouages *mpl* du gouvernement; **administrative m.** appareil *m* administratif

machine-time intensive ADJ qui nécessite beaucoup de temps-machine

machinist [mə'ʃiːnɪst] N **1** *Ind (operator)* opérateur, -trice **2** *Sewing* mécanicien, -ienne

machismo [mæ'kɪzməʊ, -'tʃɪz-] N *Fam* machisme *m*; **I'm getting a bit tired of his m.** il commence à m'agacer avec son côté macho

macho ['mætʃəʊ] ADJ *Fam* macho *inv*; **a m. type** un macho

macintosh ['mækɪntɒʃ] N = **mackintosh**

mack [mæk] N *Am Sl* **1** *(pimp)* maquereau *m*, mac *m* **2** *(expert seducer)* tombeur *m*
▸ **mack on** VT INSEP *Am Fam* **to m. on sb** draguer qn

mackerel ['mækrəl] N *(pl* **mackerel** *or occ* **mackerels)** *(fish)* maquereau *m*
▸▸ **m. sky** ciel *m* pommelé

mackintosh ['mækɪntɒʃ] N imperméable *m*

mackle ['mæk(ə)l] *Typ* N maculage *m*
VT mâchurer

mackled ['mæk(ə)ld] ADJ *Typ* bavocheux

macramé [mə'krɑːmɪ] N macramé *m*

macro ['mækrəʊ] N *Comput* macro *m*, macrocommande *f*
▸▸ **m. command** macrocommande; **m. language** macrolangage *m*; **m. virus** virus *m* de macro

macrobiotics [mækrəʊbaɪ'ɒtɪks] N macrobiotique *f* **VOIR GRAMMAIRE A10**

macrocomputing ['mækrəʊkəm'pjuːtɪŋ] N *Comput* macro-informatique *f*

macrocosm ['mækrəkɒzəm] N macrocosme *m*

macroeconomic [mækrəʊiːkə'nɒmɪk] ADJ macroéconomique

macroeconomics [mækrəʊiːkə'nɒmɪks] N macroéconomie *f* **VOIR GRAMMAIRE A10**

macromarketing [mækrəʊ'mɑːkɪtɪŋ] N macromercatique *f*, macro-marketing *m*

macron ['mækrɒn] N *Typ* macron *m*

macroscopic [mækrə'skɒpɪk] ADJ macroscopique

MACRS [emeɪsiːɑː'res] N *Am Acct (abbr* **modified accelerated cost recovery system)** méthode *f* d'amortissement accéléré

mad [mæd] ADJ *(madder, maddest)* **1** *(insane)* fou, *f* folle, *m before vowel or h mute* fol, dément; *Med* aliéné; *(idea, plan)* insensé; *Fam* **as m. as a hatter** *or* **as a March hare** fou à lier; **she's very nice but as m. as a hatter!** elle est très gentille mais elle a un grain!; **it is enough to drive you m.** il y a de quoi devenir fou, c'est à vous rendre fou; **to go m.** devenir fou; **nationalism gone m.** nationalisme forcené; **m. with fear** mort de peur; **m. with desire/envy/etc** fou de désir/jalousie/etc

2 *(enthusiastic)* **to be m. about sb/sth** *(like very much)* être fou de qn/qch; **I'm not m. on Indian food** je ne raffole pas de la cuisine indienne; **to be m. about** *or* **on sport/climbing** être un passionné *ou* mordu de sport/d'escalade, avoir la passion du sport/de l'escalade; **I'm not m. about the idea** ce n'est pas une idée qui m'emballe; **m. for revenge** assoiffé de revanche; *Br* **to be m. for it** *(raring to go)* être prêt à s'éclater

3 *Fam (angry)* furieux, furibond; **that kind of attitude makes me m.** ce genre d'attitude me met hors de moi; **to be m. with** *or* **at sb** être furieux contre qn; **m. bull** taureau furieux *ou* enragé; *Vet* **m. dog** chien *m* enragé

4 *(frantic)* **there was a m. rush for the door** on s'est précipité à la porte; *Fam* **to run/shout/work like m.** courir/crier/travailler comme un fou
ADV *Fam* **m. keen on sb/sth** fou de qn/qch; **to be m. keen on an idea** être emballé par une idée; **I'm not m. keen on Indian food/reggae** je raffole pas de la cuisine indienne/de reggae
▸▸ *Vet* **m. cow disease** maladie *f* de la vache folle

Madagascan [mædə'gæskən] ADJ malgache
N Malgache *mf*

Madagascar [mædə'gæskər] N Madagascar *m*; **they live in M.** ils vivent à Madagascar; **M. is an island** Madagascar est une île

madam ['mædəm] N **1** *(as form of address)* madame *f*; **M. Chairman** Madame la Présidente; **Dear M.** *(in letter)* Madame; *Fam* **that's enough of your cheek, m.!** ça suffit comme ça, petite insolente! **2** *(pl* **madams)** *(in brothel)* tenancière *f* de bordel, maquerelle *f* **3** *Br Fam Pej* **she's a bit of a m.** elle est un peu pimbêche; **she's a proper little m.** c'est une vraie petite pimbêche

madcap ['mædkæp] **ADJ** *(scheme, idea)* insensé
N insensé, -ée

madden ['mæd(ə)n] **VT** *(make angry)* exaspérer, rendre fou

maddening ['mæd(ə)nɪŋ] **ADJ** *(exasperating)* exaspérant; **the really m. thing is that we could so easily have won** ce qui est rageant c'est qu'on aurait facilement pu gagner

maddeningly ['mæd(ə)nɪŋlɪ] **ADV** **a m. long wait** une attente interminable; **he's m. slow/stupid** il est d'une lenteur/bêtise exaspérante; **he was m. calm about the whole thing** il est resté d'un calme horripilant

madder ['mædər] **N 1** *Bot* garance *f* **2** *(in dyeing)* teinture *f* de garance
▸▸*Bot* **m. root** alizari *m*

madding ['mædɪŋ] **ADJ** *Arch, Lit* furieux, déchaîné; **far from the m. crowd** loin de la foule et du bruit

made [meɪd] **PT, PP** *see* **make**
ADJ fait, fabriqué; **m. in France** fabriqué en France; *Fam* **he's a m. man** son avenir est assuré, sa fortune est faite; **she's m., she's got it m.** son avenir est assuré

made-for-TV movie **N** téléfilm *m*

Madeira [mə'dɪərə] **N 1** *Geog* Madère *f*; **to go to M.** aller à Madère **2** *(wine)* vin *m* de Madère, madère *m*
▸▸**M. cake** ≃ quatre-quarts *m inv*

made-up **ADJ 1** *(not true)* faux, *f* fausse; *(intended to deceive)* inventé de toutes pièces **2** *Sewing (garment)* tout fait **3** *(wearing makeup)* maquillé; **heavily m.** très maquillée **4** *Br Fam (thrilled, very happy)* hyper content

madhouse ['mædhaʊs] **N** *Arch (lunatic asylum)* maison *f* de fous; *Fig* **this place is a m.!** c'est une véritable maison de fous ici!

madly ['mædlɪ] **ADV 1** *(to behave)* comme un fou/une folle **2** *Fam (very)* follement; *(to love)* à la folie, éperdument, follement; **m. in love** follement *ou* éperdument amoureux; **I can't say I'm m. interested in it** je ne peux pas dire que ça m'intéresse follement **3** *(desperately)* *(to work, rush, struggle etc)* comme un fou/une folle; **people rushed m. in every direction** les gens couraient comme des fous dans tous les sens

madman, *pl* **madmen** ['mædmən] **N** fou *m*, aliéné *m*, dément *m*; **he's a complete m.!** il est complètement fou!; **like a m.** *(to fight)* comme un forcené, désespérément; *(to shout)* comme un perdu; *(to drive)* comme un fou

madness ['mædnɪs] **N** folie *f*, démence *f*; **in a fit of m.** dans un accès *ou* dans un moment de folie; **it's sheer m.** c'est insensé, c'est de la folie; **it would be m. to …** ce serait de la folie de …

Madonna [mə'dɒnə] **N** *Rel (Mary)* Madone *f*, **M., m.** *(statue, picture)* madone *f*

madras curry **N** curry *m* de Madras

madrigal ['mædrɪg(ə)l] **N** *Mus* madrigal *m*

madwoman, *pl* **madwomen** ['mædwʊmən, -wɪmɪn] **N** folle *f*, aliénée *f*, démente *f*

maelstrom ['meɪlstrəʊm] **N** *(whirlpool)* tourbillon *m*; *Fig* **the m. of modern life** le tourbillon de la vie moderne

maestro, *pl* **maestros, maestri** ['maɪstrəʊ, -trəʊz, -triː] **N** *Mus* maestro *m*, *pl* maestros

Mae West ['meɪ 'west] **N** *Old-fashioned Fam (lifejacket)* gilet *m* de sauvetage

MAFF [mæf] **N** *Br Formerly (abbr* **Ministry of Agriculture, Fisheries and Food)** = ministère *m* de l'Agriculture, de la Pêche et de l'Alimentation

Mafia ['mæfɪə] **N** Mafia *f*

mafioso [mæfɪ'əʊsəʊ] **N** mafioso *m*

mag¹ [mæg] **N** *Fam* = **magazine 1**

mag² **ADJ** *(abbr* **magnetic)**
▸▸**m.** bande *f* magnétique; **m. tape cassette** cassette *f* à bande magnétique; **m. tape reader** lecteur *m* de bandes magnétiques

magalogue ['mægəlɒg] **N** magalogue *m*

magazine [mægə'ziːn] **N 1** *(publication)* magazine *m*, revue *f*; **illustrated m.** revue illustrée, magazine; **sports m.** magazine sportif; **men's/women's magazines** la presse masculine/féminine **2** *Radio, TV (programme)* magazine *m* (télévisé), émission *f* magazine **3** *(for cartridges)* chargeur *m*, magasin *m*; *Phot* magasin **4** *Mil (store) (of arms etc)* magasin *m*, dépôt *m*; **powder m.** *Mil* magasin à poudre, poudrière *f*, dépôt d'explosifs; *Naut* soute *f* aux poudres *ou* à poudre
▸▸*Radio, TV* **m. programme** magazine (télévisé), émission magazine; **m. rack** porte-revues *m inv*; **m. rifle** fusil *m* à répétition *ou* à chargeur

magenta [mə'dʒentə] **N** *(colour)* magenta *m*
ADJ *(colour)* magenta *inv*

maggot ['mægət] **N** ver *m*, asticot *m*

maggoty ['mægətɪ] **ADJ** véreux, plein de vers *ou* d'asticots

Magi ['meɪdʒaɪ] **NPL** *Bible* **the (Three) M.** les (trois) rois mages *mpl*

magic ['mædʒɪk] **N** magie *f*, enchantement *m*; **like m., as if by m.** comme par enchantement; *Fig* **the m. had gone out of their marriage** leur vie conjugale avait perdu tout son charme; **black/white m.** magie noire/blanche
ADJ 1 magique; **to say the m. word** *(say please)* dire s'il vous plaît **2** *Br Fam (excellent)* génial, -aux, super
▸▸**m. carpet** tapis *m* volant; **m. lantern** lanterne *f* magique; *Fam* **m. mushrooms** champignons *mpl* (hallucinogènes); **m. square** carré *m* magique; **m. wand** baguette *f* magique

▸ **magic away** **VT SEP** *(pt, pp* **magicked)** faire disparaître comme par magie *ou* par enchantement

magical ['mædʒɪkəl] **ADJ** magique

magically ['mædʒɪklɪ] **ADV** magiquement; *Fig (to disappear)* (comme) par magie *ou* par enchantement

magician [mə'dʒɪʃən] **N** magicien, -ienne

magisterial [mædʒɪs'tɪərɪəl] **ADJ 1** *(tone, air)* magistral, -aux; *Pej* doctoral, -aux **2** *Law* de magistrat

magistrate ['mædʒɪstreɪt] **N** magistrat *m*, juge *m*; *Eng* **magistrates' court** ≃ tribunal *m* d'instance

magma ['mægmə] **N** *Geol* magma *m*

Magna Carta ['mægnə'kɑːtə] **N** *Hist* la Grande Charte *(de l'année 1215)*

magnanimity [mægnə'nɪmɪtɪ] **N** magnanimité *f*; *(nobility)* grandeur *f* d'âme

magnanimous [mæg'nænɪməs] **ADJ** magnanime; **to be m.** se montrer magnanime

magnanimously [mæg'nænɪməslɪ] **ADV** magnanimement, avec magnanimité

magnate ['mægneɪt] **N** *(of industry etc)* magnat *m*

magnesia [mæg'niːʃə] **N 1** *Chem* magnésie *f* **2** *Pharm* magnésie *f* blanche

magnesium [mæg'niːzɪəm] **N** *Chem* magnésium *m*

magnet ['mægnɪt] **N 1** aimant *m* **2** *Fig (for tourists etc)* pôle *m* d'attraction; *Fam Hum* **his new car's a babe** *or* **chick m.** sa nouvelle voiture est super pour emballer les gonzesses

magnetic [mæg'netɪk] **ADJ 1** *(attraction, field, pole etc)* magnétique **2** *Fig (personality)* magnétique
▸▸*Comput* **m. card** carte *f* magnétique; *Comput* **m. card reader** lecteur *m* de cartes magnétiques; *Comput* **m. character reader** lecteur de caractères magnétiques; *Comput* **m. disk** disque *m* magnétique; *(floppy)* disquette *f* magnétique; *Comput* **m. drive** dérouleur *m* de bande magnétique, unité *f* de bande magnétique; **m. lock** serrure *f* magnétique; **m. media** supports *mpl* magnétiques; **m. needle** aiguille *f* aimantée; **m. north** nord *m* magnétique; *Comput* **m. random access memory** mémoire *f* vive magnétique; *Med* **m. resonance imaging** imagerie *f* par résonance magnétique; **m. soundtrack** bande *f* son magnétique; **m. stripe** piste *f* magnétique; **m. stripe card** carte à piste magnétique; **m. stripe reader** lecteur de pistes magnétiques; **m. tape** bande magnétique; *Comput* **m. tape unit** dérouleur de bande magnétique, unité de bande magnétique

magnetically [mæg'netɪklɪ] **ADV** magnétiquement

magnetism ['mægnɪtɪz(ə)m] **N** *Phys, Fig* magnétisme *m*

magnetization [mægnɪtaɪ'zeɪʃən] **N** aimantation *f*, magnétisation *f*

magnetize ['mægnɪtaɪz] **VT 1** *(needle etc)* aimanter **2** *Fig (person)* magnétiser, attirer *(par magnétisme personnel)*; **he was magnetized by her good looks** il était fasciné par sa beauté
VI *(of iron etc)* s'aimanter

magnetizing ['mægnɪtaɪzɪŋ] **ADJ** *(current, field etc)* magnétisant

magneto [mæg'niːtəʊ] **N** *Elec* magnéto *f*

magneto-electric **ADJ** *Phys* magnéto-électrique

magneto-optical **ADJ** *Comput* magnéto-optique

magnificat [mæg'nɪfɪkæt] **N** *Rel* magnificat *m inv*

magnification [mægnɪfɪ'keɪʃən] **N** *Opt etc* grossissement *f*; *(of sound)* amplification *f*; *Opt* **high m.** fort grossissement

magnificence [mæg'nɪfɪsəns] **N** magnificence *f*

magnificent [mæg'nɪfɪsənt] **ADJ** magnifique; *(meal, wine)* excellent

magnificently [mæg'nɪfɪsəntlɪ] **ADV** magnifiquement

magnifier ['mægnɪfaɪər] **N** verre *m* grossissant

magnify ['mægnɪfaɪ] **VT 1** *(image)* grossir, agrandir; *(sound)* amplifier; *Fig (importance)* grossir, exagérer; **to m. sth out of all proportion** beaucoup exagérer l'importance de qch **2** *Rel, Arch (the Lord)* magnifier

magnifying ['mægnɪfaɪɪŋ] **ADJ**
▸▸**m. glass** loupe *f*, *Opt* **m. power** *(of lens, microscope)* grossissement *m*

magnitude ['mægnɪtjuːd] **N** importance *f*, *Astron* magnitude *f*, *Math* grandeur *f*, valeur *f*, *Astron* **star of the first m.** étoile *f* de première magnitude; *Fig* **of the first m.** de premier ordre; *(mistake)* gravissime

magnolia [mæg'nəʊlɪə] **N** *Bot* magnolia *m*, magnolier *m*; *(colour)* rose *m* pâle
▸▸**m. tree** magnolia, magnolier

magnum, *pl* **magnums** ['mægnəm, -əmz] **N** *(of champagne etc)* magnum *m*

magnum opus **N** *Liter etc* chef-d'œuvre *m*, *pl* chefs-d'œuvre

magpie ['mægpaɪ] **N** *(bird)* pie *f*, *Fig Fam (hoarder)* thésauriseur, -euse

Magyar ['mægjɑːr] **ADJ** magyar
N Magyar, -are

maharajah [mɑːhəˈrɑːdʒə] N maharajah m

maharani [mɑːhəˈrɑːniː] N maharani f

maharishi [mɑːhəˈriːʃɪ] N Rel maharishi m

mahogany [məˈhɒgənɪ] N (tree, wood, colour) acajou m; **m. table** table f en acajou

Mahometan [məˈhɒmətən] ADJ, N Old-fashioned mahométan, -ane

MAI [emeˈaɪ] N Fin (abbr **multilateral agreement on investment**) AMI m

maid [meɪd] N **1** (servant) bonne f, domestique f; **lady's m.** femme f de chambre **2** Arch, Lit (girl) jeune fille f; (virgin) vierge f
▸▸ **m. of all work** bonne à tout faire; **m. of honour** (to queen) demoiselle f d'honneur; (at wedding) première demoiselle d'honneur; Br Culin (cake) petit gâteau m aux amandes; Hist **the M. of Orleans** la Pucelle (d'Orléans); **m. service** (at self-catering apartment) service m de femme de ménage

maiden [ˈmeɪd(ə)n] N **1** Lit (girl) jeune fille f; (virgin) vierge f **2** Cr = série de six balles pendant laquelle aucun point n'est marqué
ADJ ATTRIB (first) premier, -ère
▸▸ **m. aunt** tante f célibataire; **m. flight** premier vol m, vol inaugural; **m. name** nom m de jeune fille; Cr **m. over** = série de six balles pendant laquelle aucun point n'est marqué; Br **m. speech** = premier discours m prononcé par un parlementaire nouvellement élu; **m. voyage** voyage m inaugural

maidenhair [ˈmeɪd(ə)nheər] N (fern) adiante m, cheveu m de Vénus
▸▸ **m. fern** adiante m, cheveu de Vénus

maidenly [ˈmeɪdənlɪ] ADJ virginal, -aux

maidservant [ˈmeɪdsɜːvənt] N Arch domestique f

mail [meɪl] N **1** (letters, parcels) courrier m; **it came in the m.** c'est arrivé au courrier; **was there anything in the m. for me?** est-ce qu'il y avait du courrier pour moi?; **has the m. been yet?** est-ce que le facteur est passé? **2** (postal service) poste f, courrier m **3** Comput courrier m électronique **4** Hist (coach) malle f, malle-poste f, pl malles-poste
VT (letters, parcels) (send) envoyer par la poste, expédier; (put in mailbox) mettre à la poste, poster
▸▸ Comput **m. address** adresse f électronique; **m. bomb** (letter) lettre f piégée; (parcel) colis m piégé; **m. bomber** = personne f qui envoie une lettre ou un colis piégé; Am **m. carrier** facteur, -trice; Hist **m. coach** malle-poste, pl malles-poste; Am **m. drop** boîte f à ou aux lettres; Comput **m. forwarding** réexpédition f du courrier électronique; Comput **m. gateway** passerelle f (de courrier électronique); **m. order** vente f par correspondance; Comput **m. reader** logiciel m de courrier électronique, client m de messagerie électronique; **m. room** service m du courrier; Comput **m. server** serveur m de courrier; **m. train** train m postal; **m. transfer** virement m par courrier; **m. van** Rail wagon-poste m, pl wagons-poste; Aut voiture f ou fourgon m des postes

mail² N (armour) mailles fpl; **coat of m.** cotte f de mailles

mailbag [ˈmeɪlbæg] N sac m postal

mailbot [ˈmeɪlbɒt] N Comput fonction f de réponse automatique

mailbox [ˈmeɪlbɒks] N Am boîte f aux lettres; Comput (**electronic) m.** boîte aux lettres électronique

mailing [ˈmeɪlɪŋ] N (mailshot) publipostage m, mailing m
▸▸ Mktg **m. card** carte f de publicité; **m. list** Mktg liste f de publipostage; Comput liste de diffusion; Mktg **m. shot** mailing, publipostage

mailman, pl **mailmen** [ˈmeɪlmæn, -men] N Am facteur m

mailmerge [ˈmeɪlmɜːdʒ] N Comput publipostage m
▸▸ **m. letter** lettre f envoyée par publipostage; **m. program** programme m de publipostage

mail-order ADJ Com de vente par correspondance, de VPC
▸▸ **m. bride** = nom m donné aux jeunes femmes originaires de pays pauvres cherchant à épouser des occidentaux par le biais d'agences matrimoniales spécialisées; **m. catalogue** catalogue m de vente par correspondance; **m. company, m. firm** maison f de vente par correspondance; **m. goods** marchandises fpl vendues ou achetées par correspondance; **m. organization** vépéciste m; **m. retailing, m. selling** vente f par correspondance; **m. specialist** vépéciste

mailroom [ˈmeɪlruːm] N service m du courrier

mailshot [ˈmeɪlʃɒt] N mailing m, publipostage m
VT envoyer un mailing ou un publipostage à

maim [meɪm] VT (person) estropier, mutiler

main [meɪn] N **1** (pipe) canalisation f ou conduite f maîtresse ou principale; Elec câble m de distribution **2 in the m.** (on the whole) en général, en gros, en somme, généralement (parlant) **3** Arch, Lit **the m.** (ocean) le grand large, l'océan m
ADJ principal, -aux; **the m. body of ...** le gros de ...; **our m. concern** notre préoccupation majeure; **m. idea** (of book, film etc) idée f mère ou maîtresse ou directrice; **m. line of business** activité f principale exercée, APE f; **the m. point** or **thing** l'essentiel, le principal
▸▸ Comput **m. board** carte f principale; Gram **m. clause** proposition f principale; **m. course** plat m principal ou de résistance; Agr **m. crop** culture f principale; Naut **m. deck** pont m principal; **m. dish** plat principal ou de résistance; Am Fam **m. drag** rue f principale, grande rue; **m. entrance** entrée f principale; Rail etc **m. line** voie f principale, grande ligne f; Sl **m. man** (friend) pote m; Br Sl **when it comes to scoring goals, Michael Owen's the m. man** pour ce qui est de marquer des buts, Michael Owen est champion; Naut **m. masts** mâts mpl majeurs; Comput **m. memory** mémoire f principale; Br **m. road** grande route f, route à grande circulation; ≃ nationale f; **m. sewer** égout m collecteur; Fam **m. squeeze** (boyfriend) mec m, jules m; (girlfriend) nana f, gonzesse f; **m. street** rue principale, grande rue

mainbrace [ˈmeɪnbreɪs] N Naut grand bras m de vergue

mainframe [ˈmeɪnfreɪm] N (computer) ordinateur m central
▸▸ **m. computer** ordinateur central

mainland [ˈmeɪnlænd] N (continental land mass) continent m; **you can see the Scottish m.** on voit la côte écossaise; **we live on the m.** (not on island) nous n'habitons pas dans les îles; **the French m., the m. of France** la France continentale

mainline [ˈmeɪnlaɪn] Sl VI se shooter, se piquer
VT se faire un shoot de; (habitually) se shooter à

mainliner [ˈmeɪnlaɪnər] N Sl (drug addict) junkie mf, shooté, -ée

mainly [ˈmeɪnlɪ] ADV principalement, surtout; **the passengers were m. old men** la plupart des passagers étaient des vieux messieurs; **a m. Spanish-speaking population** une population à majorité ou principalement ou surtout hispanophone; **their diet consists m. of insects** ils se nourrissent essentiellement ou principalement ou surtout d'insectes; **she was m. to blame** c'est elle la

principale responsable, c'est surtout de sa faute

mainmast [ˈmeɪnmɑːst, -məst] N Naut grand mât m

mains [meɪnz] NPL secteur m; **the house hasn't been connected to the m.** la maison n'a pas été raccordée au secteur; **electric m.** (cables) canalisations fpl d'électricité; **gas m.** conduites fpl de gaz; **water m.** canalisations ou conduites d'eau
▸▸ **m. adaptor** adaptateur m secteur; **m. electricity** courant m secteur; Radio **m. set** poste m secteur; **m. water** eau f courante

mainsail [ˈmeɪnseɪl, ˈmeɪns(ə)l] N Naut grand-voile f, pl grand(s)-voiles

mainsheet [ˈmeɪnʃiːt] N Naut grand-écoute f, pl grand-écoutes

mains-powered ADJ fonctionnant sur secteur

mainspring [ˈmeɪnsprɪŋ] N **1** Tech grand ressort m; (of clock etc) ressort moteur **2** Fig (force behind sth) moteur m

mainstay [ˈmeɪnsteɪ] N **1** Naut étai m de grand mât **2** (of economy, philosophy, policy) base f, pilier m; (of family) soutien m principal

mainstream [ˈmeɪnstriːm] N courant m principal; **he belongs to the m. of French tradition** il fait partie de la grande tradition française; **a writer who has moved away from the m.** un auteur qui est sorti des sentiers battus
ADJ **m. Hollywood movies** films mpl dans la grande tradition hollywoodienne; **m. politics** courants mpl politiques dominants; **their second album was much more m.** leur deuxième album était beaucoup plus classique
▸▸ Mus **m. jazz** = style m de jazz qui se situe entre le traditionnel et le moderne

maintain [meɪnˈteɪn] VT **1** (keep in good condition) (road, machine, car) entretenir **2** (support) (family etc) entretenir, subvenir aux besoins de, nourrir; (army) entretenir **3** (order, discipline) maintenir; (conversation etc) soutenir; (relations etc) entretenir; (health, advantage, lead) garder, conserver; (attitude, one's silence) garder, observer; (one's rights) défendre; **to m. speed** conserver l'allure **4** (assert) (opinion, fact) soutenir; **to m. that ...** maintenir ou soutenir que ... + ind

maintenance [ˈmeɪntɪnəns] N **1** (of car), Rail, Tel (of lines) entretien m; (of equipment, roads etc) entretien, maintenance f **2** (of law and order) maintien m **3** (of family, troops etc) entretien m **4** Law (alimony) pension f alimentaire **5** (of one's rights) défense f
▸▸ **m. contract** contrat m de maintenance ou d'entretien; **m. costs** frais mpl d'entretien; **m. department** service m de maintenance ou d'entretien; **m. engineer** technicien, -ienne de maintenance; **m. grant** (to student) bourse f d'études; **m. handbook** manuel m d'entretien; **m. kit** trousse f d'entretien; Law **m. order** obligation f alimentaire; **m. man** ouvrier m chargé de l'entretien ou de la maintenance; **m. manual** manuel d'entretien; **m. staff** personnel m d'entretien; **m. vehicle** camion-atelier m, pl camions-ateliers

maintenance-free ADJ qui ne nécessite aucun entretien; **m. battery** batterie f sans entretien

maison(n)ette [meɪzəˈnet] N (appartement m) duplex m

maître d' [metrəˈdiː] N esp Am maître m d'hôtel

maize [meɪz] N esp Br maïs m

Maj Mil abbr **major**

majestic [məˈdʒestɪk] ADJ majestueux; (bearing) majestueux, plein de majesté; (scenery) grandiose

majestically [məˈdʒestɪklɪ] ADVmajestueusement

majesty [ˈmædʒəstɪ] N majesté f; **God in all His m.** Dieu dans toute sa majesté; **His M. (the King)** Sa Majesté le Roi; **Her M. (the Queen)** Sa Majesté la Reine; **Your M.** Votre Majesté; **Br on His/Her M.'s Service** (pour le) service de Sa Majesté (≃ service de l'État); (on envelope) ≃ en franchise; **Her M.'s Prison Service** Br ≃ système m pénitentiaire britannique; **Her M.'s Stationery Office** Br ≃ maison f d'édition publiant les ouvrages ou documents approuvés par le Parlement, les ministères et autres organismes officiels, ≃ l'Imprimerie f nationale

Maj Gen Mil abbr **major general**

major [ˈmeɪdʒər] ADJ **1** (big) grand; (main) le plus grand; (company) de première importance, de premier ordre; (distinction, improvement, changes, difficulties) de taille, grand; (problem, cause, concern, interest, new novel, discovery), Mus majeur; (accident, disaster) grand; **the m. brands** les marques les plus importantes; **it's a m. brand** c'est une des marques les plus importantes; **the m. teams** les plus grandes équipes; **it's of m. importance** c'est de la plus haute importance; **the significance of this event is quite m.** c'est un événement de toute première importance; **the party was a m. disaster** la fête a été une catastrophe absolue; **any problems? – nothing m.** des problèmes? – rien d'important; **he's our m. programmer** c'est notre programmeur principal; **we invested in a m. way** nous avons investi de manière considérable; **he's taken up Spanish in a m. way** il s'est mis à fond à l'espagnol; **he's fallen for Susie in a m. way** il est tombé follement amoureux de Susie; **the m. portion** la majeure partie, la plus grande partie; **m. decision** décision f capitale; **m. illness** maladie f grave; Med etc **m. operation** grosse opération f; **m. repairs** grosses réparations fpl; **to undergo m. surgery** subir une intervention chirurgicale importante

2 Br Sch Old-fashioned **Martin m.** Martin aîné, l'aîné des deux Martin

N **1** Mil (in infantry) chef m de bataillon; (in cavalry etc) chef d'escadron

2 Law (person) majeur, -eure

3 Am Univ (area of study) matière f principale; **physics m.** (student) étudiant, -ante en physique

4 Cin **the Majors** (film companies) ≃ les sociétés fpl de production les plus importantes à Hollywood

VI Am Univ **to m. in a subject** se spécialiser dans une matière

▸▸Mil **m. general** général m de division; Mus **m. key** ton m ou mode m majeur; Am Sport **m. league** première division f, (in baseball) ≃ une des deux principales divisions de baseball professionnel aux États-Unis et au Canada; Mil **m. offensive** vaste offensive f; Phil **m. premise** majeure f; **m. prophets** grands prophètes mpl; **m. road** route f principale ou à grande circulation, ≃ nationale f; Fin **m. shareholder** actionnaire mf de référence; Am Univ **m. subject** matière principale

Majorca [məˈjɔːkə] N Majorque f

Majorcan [məˈjɔːkən] ADJ majorquin
N Majorquin, -ine

major-domo, pl **major-domos** [meɪdʒəˈdəʊməʊ, -əʊz] N majordome m

majorette [meɪdʒəˈret] N Am (drum) m. majorette f

majority [məˈdʒɒrɪtɪ] N **1** (of votes) majorité f; **the m.** (of people etc) la plus grande partie, le plus grand nombre; **a two-thirds m.** une majorité des deux tiers; **to have a m.** avoir la majorité; **to be in a or the m.** être majori-

taire; **elected by a m.** élu à la majorité; **in the m. of cases** dans la majorité des cas VOIR GRAMMAIRE A11 **2** Law (age) majorité f; **to attain** or **reach one's m.** atteindre sa majorité, devenir majeur

▸▸**m. decision** décision f prise à la majorité; **m. government** gouvernement m majoritaire; **m. system of m. government** gouvernement à la majorité absolue, système m majoritaire; Fin **m. holding** participation f majoritaire; **m. party** parti m majoritaire; **m. rule** gouvernement à la majorité absolue, système majoritaire; **m. shareholder** actionnaire mf majoritaire; **m. verdict** verdict m majoritaire; **m. vote** majorité f; **m. world** tiers-monde m, pl tiers-mondes

MAKE [meɪk]

| N | marque **1** |
| VT | faire **1–3, 7, 10** ▪ fabriquer **1** |
| ▪ établir **2** ▪ gagner **3** ▪ faire la fortune de **4** ▪ arriver à **8** |

N **1** Com, Ind (of product) marque f; **cars of all makes** voitures de toutes marques; **what m. is it?** c'est quelle marque?

2 (construction) façon f, fabrication f, construction f; **of French m.** de fabrication française

3 Fam **to be on the m.** (financially) chercher à s'enrichir; (sexually) draguer

VT (pt, pp made [meɪd]) **1** (construct, produce, prepare etc) (bread, tea, meal, bed, hole etc) faire; (machine etc) construire, fabriquer; (paper, box, chair etc) fabriquer, faire; (payment, transaction) effectuer, faire; (a change) opérer, faire, effectuer; (mistake) commettre, faire; (speech, excuses, promise etc) faire; **bread is made (out) of flour** on fait le pain avec de la farine; **the chair is made (out) of wood** la chaise est en bois; **what is it made (out) of?** en quoi est-ce fait?, Fam c'est en quoi?; **to show what one is made of** donner sa mesure, montrer de quoi on est capable; **just let them try to cause trouble and we'll show them what we're made of!** qu'ils essaient de faire des histoires et ils verront de quel bois on se chauffe!; **I'm not made of money** je ne suis pas millionnaire; **do you want to m. something of it?** ça te dérange?; **to m. something of oneself** faire quelque chose de sa vie; **the army will m. a man of him** l'armée fera de lui un homme; **God made man** Dieu a créé l'homme; **the water had made a hole in the rock** l'eau avait percé la roche; **they seem made for each other** ils semblent faits l'un pour l'autre; **to m. trouble** provoquer le désordre; (cause problems) causer des ennuis (for sb à qn); **they made room for one more on the sofa** ils se sont poussés pour (lui) faire une place sur le canapé; **could you m. room for some pudding?** est-ce que tu as encore une petite place pour le dessert?; **to m. time to do sth** trouver le temps de faire qch; **to m. a noise** faire du bruit; **I m. the rules around here** ici, c'est moi qui dirige; **to m. an attempt to do sth** essayer de faire qch; **it makes all the difference** ça change tout; **to m. love/war** faire l'amour/la guerre; **to m. one's escape** s'échapper, se sauver; Knitting **to m. one/two** faire un jeté simple/double

2 (form) établir, assurer (**a connection between** ... le raccordement de ...); Elec (of contact points) (circuit) fermer; **two and two m. four** deux et deux font quatre; **that makes (it) the third time he's been late** c'est ou ça fait la troisième fois qu'il arrive en retard; **they m. a handsome couple** ils font un beau couple

3 (gain) (money) faire; **to m. £400 a week** gagner ou Fam se faire 400 livres par semaine; **to m. one's fortune** faire fortune; **to**

m. a fortune (on a sale etc) gagner une fortune; Fam **to m. a bit on the side** faire de la gratte; **to m. a name for oneself** se faire un nom; **to m. an enemy of sb** se faire un ennemi de qn

4 (cause to be successful) (person) faire la fortune de; **this book made her** or **her name** ce livre l'a rendue célèbre; **this will m. him or break him** cela sera ou son succès ou sa ruine; **it made my day** ça m'a fait très plaisir; Iron **you've made my day** tu m'as fait gagner ma journée

5 (cause to be) **to m. sb happy/rich/sad** rendre qn heureux/riche/triste; **to m. sb hungry/sleepy** donner faim/sommeil à qn; **to m. sb angry** mettre qn en colère, fâcher qn; **he made her a star** il a fait d'elle une star; **to m. sb one's heir** constituer qn son héritier; **to m. sth known** faire connaître qch; **to m. oneself heard** se faire entendre; **to m. oneself ill** se rendre malade; **to m. oneself tired** se fatiguer; **to m. oneself useful** se rendre utile; **to m. oneself comfortable** se mettre à l'aise

6 (cause or compel to do) **to m. sb speak/sleep** faire parler/dormir qn; (stronger) forcer ou obliger ou contraindre qn à parler/dormir; **what makes you say/believe that?** qu'est-ce qui te fait dire/croire ça?; **I made him stop** je l'ai forcé à s'arrêter; **don't m. me laugh!** tu me fais rire!; **her remarks made me feel more cheerful** ses remarques m'ont remonté le moral; **m. them see how important it is** montrez-leur combien c'est important; **he makes playing the violin look easy** à le regarder, on dirait qu'il est facile de jouer du violon; **to m. sb look stupid** faire passer qn pour un idiot; **what made you say that?** qu'est-ce qui vous a fait dire cela?; **you can't m. me!** tu ne peux pas me forcer!; **you made me!** tu m'y as obligé ou forcé!; **it makes my eyes water** ça me fait pleurer VOIR GRAMMAIRE A41

7 (estimate, calculate) **what time do you m. it?** quelle heure avez-vous?; **I make the answer 127** d'après moi, ça fait 127; **I make it $56 each** si je compte bien, ça fait 56 dollars par personne

8 (reach) (station, port etc) arriver à; (catch) (train, flight) avoir; **will we m. the airport in time?** est-ce que nous arriverons à temps à l'aéroport?; **we'll m. Newport before lunch** nous serons à Newport avant le déjeuner; **he'll be lucky to m. 50** il a de la chance s'il atteint 50 ans; **to m. twenty knots** (of ship) faire vingt nœuds

9 Fam (manage to attend on, at) (show, meeting etc) assister à; **I can m. 2 o'clock** je peux être là à deux heures; **can you m. Friday?** est-ce que tu es libre vendredi?; **can you m. lunch on Friday?** peux-tu te libérer pour le déjeuner vendredi?

10 Fam (establish as) **let's m. it a day everyone can come** autant s'arranger pour que ce soit un jour où tout le monde puisse venir; **if we made it a Wednesday ...** si on faisait ça un mercredi ...; **can we m. it your place?** est-ce qu'on peut faire ça chez toi?; **better m. it** or **that two whiskies** mettez-moi un deuxième whisky

11 (become, be) être; **she'd m. a good diver/ singer** elle ferait une bonne plongeuse/ chanteuse; **to m. sb a present of sth** faire cadeau de qch à qn; **you'll never m. a diver/ singer** tu ne seras jamais plongeur/chanteur

12 Sl (have sexual intercourse with) se faire

13 Fam **to m. it** (arrive in time) arriver à temps; (finish in time) finir à temps; (manage to attend) se libérer; (be successful) réussir; **you've got it made** tu n'as plus de soucis à te faire pour ton avenir; **to m. it with sb** (have sexual intercourse) se faire qn; **we'll never m. it** (by that time) nous n'y arriverons jamais; **I made it home for lunch** je suis arrivé à la maison (à temps) pour le déjeuner; **to m. it in politics** réussir en politique

vt 1 to m. as if *or* **as though to do sth** *(get ready to)* s'apprêter à faire qch; *(pretend)* faire semblant *ou* mine de faire qch; **he made as if to speak** il a eu l'air de vouloir parler; **she made (as if) to get up** elle a fait mine de se lever

2 to m. do *(cope)* se débrouiller; **we'll just have to m. do** *(with what we have)* il va falloir faire avec; **we could m. do with ten** *(though we should have more)* nous pourrions nous débrouiller avec dix; **we'll have to m. the milk do** il faut nous contenter du peu de lait que nous avons; **I'll just have to m. that do** il va falloir que je fasse avec

3 they're just making believe *(in playing)* ils font comme si; **let's m. believe that …** *(in playing)* on dirait que …

4 to m. sure *or* **certain of sth** s'assurer de qch; **have you made sure?** tu t'en es assuré?

5 *Fam* **to m. like** *(pretend)* faire semblant *ou* mine de; **he makes like he's the boss** il se conduit comme si c'était lui le patron; **m. like you don't know anything** fais comme si tu savais pas; **m. like you're asleep!** fais semblant de dormir!

▸ **make after vt insep** se lancer à la poursuite de

▸ **make away vi** = **make off**

▸ **make away with vt insep** *Fam* **1** *(steal)* partir avec, voler

2 *(kill)* tuer, supprimer; **to m. away with oneself** se suicider

▸ **make for vt insep 1** *(head towards)* *(place, the door)* se diriger vers; *Naut* faire route sur, mettre le cap sur; **where are you making for?** où allez-vous?; **ship making for Hull** navire à destination de Hull

2 *(contribute to)* *(happiness, wellbeing etc)* contribuer à; **these agreements m. for peace** ces accords favorisent la paix; **it doesn't m. for easy reading** c'est difficile à lire

▸ **make into vt sep** **you could m. this room into an office** tu pourrais transformer cette pièce en bureau, tu pourrais faire de cette pièce un bureau

▸ **make of vt sep 1** *(understand)* **I don't know what to m. of that remark** je ne sais pas comment interpréter cette remarque; **what do you m. of her?** qu'est-ce que tu penses d'elle?; **we couldn't m. much of what he said** nous n'avons pas compris grand-chose à ce qu'il a dit

2 *(attach importance to)* attacher de l'importance à; **you're making too much of this** tu y attaches trop d'importance; **the press has made a lot of this visit** la presse a fait beaucoup de bruit autour de cette visite; **the prosecution made much of this fact** l'accusation a fait grand cas de ce fait; **to m. much** *or* **a lot of** *(be attentive to)* *(person)* être aux petits soins pour; *(child etc)* câliner, choyer; *(flatter)* flatter

▸ **make off vi** *Fam* *(leave)* prendre la fuite, s'enfuir, décamper, filer; **the thieves made off in a van** les bandits se sont enfuis dans une camionnette

▸ **make off with vt insep** *Fam* *(steal)* **to m. off with the cash** filer avec l'argent; **somebody's made off with my overcoat** on m'a volé *ou* chipé mon pardessus

▸ **make out vt sep 1** *(write)* *(list etc)* faire, établir, dresser; *(bill)* établir, dresser, relever; *(cheque)* faire, établir (**to sb** à l'ordre de qn); **to m. out an invoice** libeller une facture; **who do I m. it out to?** *(the cheque)* je le mets à quel ordre?

2 *Fam* *(claim)* **she made out she knew them personally** elle a fait croire qu'elle les connaissait personnellement; **to m. sb out to be richer than he is** faire qn plus riche qu'il ne l'est; **she's not such a fool as people**

m. out elle n'est pas aussi bête qu'on le dit; **he made me out to be a miser** il m'a fait passer pour un avare

3 *(usu with neg)* *(understand, decipher)* *(riddle, problem)* comprendre; *(person's reasons, meaning of sth)* démêler; *(handwriting)* déchiffrer; *(business, matter)* débrouiller; **I can't m. out the address** je n'arrive pas à lire *ou* déchiffrer l'adresse; **I can't m. this guy out** ce type est une énigme pour moi; **I can't m. it out** *(situation, mystery)* je ne m'y retrouve pas, je n'y comprends rien

4 *(discern)* distinguer, discerner; **I can never m. out whether she's being serious or not** je n'arrive jamais à savoir si elle est sérieuse ou non

5 *(conclude)* **how do you m. that out?** comment arrivez-vous à ce résultat *ou* à cette conclusion?

vi 1 *Fam* *(succeed)* se débrouiller; **how is she making out at her new school?** comment ça marche dans sa nouvelle école?; **he's making out very well** ça marche très bien pour lui

2 *Am Sl* *(kiss, fondle)* se peloter; *(have sexual intercourse)* faire l'amour

▸ **make over vt sep** *(transfer)* céder, transférer (**sth to sb** qch à qn); **she has made the estate over to her granddaughter** elle a cédé la propriété à sa petite-fille

▸ **make towards vt insep** *(head for)* se diriger vers; **he made towards the bar** il s'est dirigé vers le bar

▸ **make up vt sep 1** *(invent)* *(story, excuses)* inventer; **he's making the whole thing up** ce qu'il dit est inventé de toutes pièces, il raconte des histoires; **I'm making it up as I go along** j'improvise au fur et à mesure

2 *(compensate for)* *(deficit, loss)* combler; **we made up the time** nous avons rattrapé notre retard; **to m. up lost ground** rattraper; **we've got a lot of ground to m. up on** a beaucoup à rattraper; **I'll m. it up to you** *(for forgetting your birthday etc)* je me rattraperai, je me ferai pardonner; *(for helping me)* je te rendrai ça

3 *(complete)* *(amount)* compléter; **we need two more players to m. up the team** il nous faut deux joueurs de plus pour compléter l'équipe; **another two players would m. it up to eleven** avec deux joueurs de plus, on arriverait à onze; **I was only invited to m. up the numbers** *(in team, for meal etc)* je n'ai été invité que pour compléter l'équipe/la table/etc; **to m. up the difference** parfaire la somme; **I'll m. up your savings up to the price of a new bike** je compléterai tes économies pour que tu puisses acheter un nouveau vélo

4 *(form)* constituer; **all the elements that go to m. up a happy marriage** tout ce qui contribue à faire un bon mariage; **the community is made up primarily of old people** cette communauté est constituée essentiellement de personnes âgées

5 *(prepare, put together)* *(list)* dresser; *(parcel, bed)* faire; *Com* *(clothes)* faire, confectionner; *Com* **to m. up orders** préparer des commandes; **customer's own material made up** on travaille à façon; *Pharm* **to m. up a prescription** préparer les médicaments prescrits sur une ordonnance; **to m. up the fire** préparer le feu; *(add fuel)* alimenter le feu

6 *(in bookkeeping)* *(account)* régler, établir, arrêter; *(the books)* régler, balancer; **to m. up one's accounts** faire ses comptes

7 *(apply make-up to)* maquiller; **to m. one's face** *or* **oneself up** se maquiller; **the actors are being made up** les acteurs se font maquiller

8 to m. it up *(settle quarrel)* se réconcilier (**with sb** avec qn)

9 *Typ* mettre en pages

vi 1 *(end quarrel)* se réconcilier

2 *(catch up)* **he's making up on the leaders** il rattrape ceux qui sont en tête

3 *(apply make-up)* se maquiller

▸ **make up for vt insep** *(losses)* compenser; *(lost time)* rattraper; **that makes up for it** c'est une compensation; **to m. up for the lack of sth** suppléer au manque de qch; **how can I m. up for forgetting your birthday?** comment puis-je me faire pardonner d'avoir oublié ton anniversaire?; **what she lacks in skill she makes up for in enthusiasm** son manque de savoir-faire est compensé par son enthousiasme

▸ **make up to vt insep** *(ingratiate oneself with)* **to m. up to sb** essayer de se faire bien voir de qn

▸ **make with vt insep** *Am Fam* **1** *(produce)* faire; **to m. with the music** faire de la musique; **m. with the French fries** *(to waiter etc)* dépêche-toi de servir les frites; *(to cook)* dépêche-toi de faire les frites

2 *(use)* se servir de; **he made with the food mixer** il s'est servi du mixeur

make-believe N **you shouldn't indulge in m.** tu ne devrais pas te complaire dans des chimères; **what is real and what is m.?** qu'est-ce qui est du domaine du réel et qu'est-ce qui est du domaine de l'invention?; **that's all m.** tout cela est (de la) pure fantaisie; **to live in the land of m.** se faire des illusions, ne pas avoir le sens des réalités

ADJ **a m. world** un monde imaginaire

make-or-break ADJ ATTRIB **it's m. time!** maintenant, ça passe ou ça casse!; **it was one of those m. moments** c'était un moment décisif

makeover ['meɪkəʊvər] N *(of person)* changement *m* de look; *(of building)* transformation *f*

maker ['meɪkər] N **1** *(person)* faiseur, -euse; *Com, Ind* fabricant *m*; *(of machinery, planes, cars etc)* constructeur *m*; **m.'s price** prix *m* de fabrique; **m.'s trademark** cachet *m* de fabrique **2** *Rel* **our M.** le Créateur; **he's gone to meet his M.** il est monté au ciel; **that's between you and your M.** c'est entre toi et le Seigneur

make-ready N *Typ* mise *f* en train

makeshift ['meɪkʃɪft] ADJ de fortune; **a m. shelter** un abri de fortune; **m. equipment** installation *f* de fortune; **it looks a bit m.** ça a l'air un peu rudimentaire; **it's only meant to be m.** ce n'est qu'une solution temporaire

N *(solution etc)* pis-aller *m inv*; expédient *m*; *(object)* pis-aller, moyen *m* de fortune

make-up N **1** *(cosmetics)* maquillage *m*; *Theat* maquillage, fard *m*; *TV etc (department)* *(service m)* maquillage; **she wears far too much m.** elle se maquille beaucoup trop; **she wears m.** elle se maquille; **I'm not wearing any m.** je ne suis pas maquillée; **to put m. on** se maquiller **2** *(composition)* composition *f*, *(of person)* caractère *m*; **it's not in his m. to apologize** ce n'est pas dans son caractère de s'excuser **3** *Typ* mise *f* en pages, imposition *f* **4** *Am Sch (exam)* examen *m* de rattrapage **5** *(putting together, assembly)* fabrication *f*, *(of clothes)* confection *f*

▸▸ **m. artist** maquilleur, -euse; **m. bag** trousse *f* de maquillage; **m. box** boîte *f* à maquillage; *Am Sch* **m. classes** cours *mpl* de rattrapage; *Banking* **m. date** date *f* de situation; *TV etc* **m. department** *(service m)* maquillage; *Theat* **m. girl** maquilleuse *f*; *Theat etc* **m. man** maquilleur *m*; **m. remover** démaquillant *m*; *TV* **m. room** salle *f* de maquillage

makeweight ['meɪkweɪt] N complément *m*; *(stopgap)* bouche-trou *m*, *pl* bouche-trous; **they only asked me to join the team as a m.** ils ne m'ont demandé d'entrer dans l'équipe que pour leur servir de bouche-trou

making ['meɪkɪŋ] N fabrication f, (of clothes) confection f, façon f, (of bridge, machine) construction f, (of film) tournage m; **this ordeal was the m. of him** cette épreuve lui a forgé le caractère; **history in the m.** l'histoire en train de se faire; **a musician/poet in the m.** un musicien/poète en herbe; **the film was three years in the m.** le tournage du film a duré trois ans; **problems of one's own m.** des problèmes qu'on s'est créé soi-même; **Elec m. and breaking** (of circuit) fermeture f et ouverture f

makings ['meɪkɪŋz] NPL **to have the m. of ...** avoir tout ce qu'il faut pour devenir ...; **it has the m. of a good film, but it'll need a lot of work** avec beaucoup de travail, ça pourrait faire un bon film; **he has the m. of a statesman** il a l'étoffe d'un homme d'État

malachite ['mælakaɪt] N Miner malachite f

maladjusted [mælə'dʒʌstɪd] ADJ Psy inadapté, -ée

maladjustment [mælə'dʒʌstmənt] N Psy inadaptation f, **emotional m.** déséquilibre m émotif

maladministration [mælədmɪnɪs'treɪʃən] N mauvaise administration f, mauvaise gestion f

maladroit [mælə'drɔɪt] ADJ maladroit

maladroitly [mælə'drɔɪtlɪ] ADV maladroitement

malady ['mælədɪ] N Fml mal m, maladie f

Malagasy [mælə'gɑːzɪ] N (person) Malgache mf, Ling malgache m
ADJ malgache

malaise [mæ'leɪz] N malaise m

malapropism ['mæləprɒpɪz(ə)m] N pataquès m

malaria [mə'leərɪə] N Med malaria f, paludisme m; **to have m.** avoir la malaria ou le paludisme

malarial [mə'leərɪəl] ADJ paludéen, palustre
▸▸ **m. fever** fièvre f paludéenne

malark(e)y [mə'lɑːkɪ] N Fam ânerie f

Malawi [mə'lɑːwɪ] N Malawi m

Malay [mə'leɪ] ADJ malais; **the M. Peninsula** la presqu'île malaise
N 1 Malais, -aise 2 Ling malais m

Malaya [mə'leɪə] N Malaisie f

Malayan [mə'leɪən] ADJ malais
N Malais, -aise

Malaysia [mə'leɪzɪə] N Malaisie f, Malaysia f

Malaysian [mə'leɪzɪən] N Malais, -aise
ADJ malais

malcontent ['mælkəntent] ADJ, N mécontent, -ente

male [meɪl] ADJ (child, hormone, flower) mâle; (sex, attitude, public) masculin; **a m. friend** un ami; **m. line** (of descent) ligne f masculine; **m. plug** fiche f, prise f mâle; **m. socket** prise f mâle; Comput **m. to female adaptor** adaptateur mâle/femelle m
N Biol, Bot mâle m; esp Fam (man) homme m, Fam mec m; **the average French m.** le Français moyen
▸▸ **m. bonding** amitié f virile; **m. chauvinism** phallocratie f; **m. chauvinist** phallocrate m; **m. chauvinist pig** sale phallocrate; **m. menopause** andropause f, **m. nurse** infirmier m

Note that the French word **mâle** is a not always a translation for the English word **male**.

malediction [mælɪ'dɪkʃən] N Fml malédiction f

malefactor ['mælɪfæktər] N Fml malfaiteur, -trice

malevolence [mə'levələns] N malveillance f (**towards** envers)

malevolent [mə'levələnt] ADJ malveillant

malevolently [mə'levələntlɪ] ADV avec malveillance; (to look at sb) d'un œil malveillant

malformation [mælfɔː'meɪʃən] N Med etc malformation f, difformité f

malformed [mæl'fɔːmd] ADJ difforme

malfunction [mæl'fʌŋkʃən] N fonctionnement m défectueux, mauvais fonctionnement; Med (of organ) dysfonctionnement m
VI mal fonctionner

Mali ['mɑːlɪ] N Mali m

Malian ['mɑːlɪən] ADJ malien
N Malien, -ienne

malice ['mælɪs] N 1 méchanceté f, malveillance f, **out of m.** par méchanceté ou malveillance; **to bear m. to** or **towards sb, to bear sb m.** en vouloir à qn 2 Law intention f criminelle ou délictueuse; **with m. aforethought** avec intention criminelle, avec préméditation

Note that the French word **malice** is a false friend and is never a translation for the English word **malice**. Its most common meaning is **mischief**.

malicious [mə'lɪʃəs] ADJ 1 méchant, malveillant 2 Law fait avec intention criminelle ou délictueuse, criminel
▸▸ Law **m. intent** intention f de nuire ou criminelle

Note that the French word **malicieux** is a false friend and is never a translation for the English word **malicious**. It means **mischievous**.

maliciously [mə'lɪʃəslɪ] ADV 1 (to say, do) méchamment, avec malveillance 2 Law avec intention criminelle, avec préméditation

malign [mə'laɪn] ADJ pernicieux, nuisible
VT calomnier, diffamer; **much maligned man** homme calomnié

malignancy [mə'lɪgnənsɪ] N 1 (of person) malignité f, méchanceté f 2 Med (of disease) malignité f, virulence f; (of tumour) malignité f

malignant [mə'lɪgnənt] ADJ 1 (person) malveillant, méchant 2 Med (tumour etc) malin, f maligne

malignantly [mə'lɪgnəntlɪ] ADV avec malveillance, méchamment

malinger [mə'lɪŋgər] VI faire semblant d'être malade, Fam tirer au flanc

malingerer [mə'lɪŋgərər] N simulateur, -trice, faux malade, f fausse malade; **she's just a m.** c'est une tire-au-flanc

malingering [mə'lɪŋgərɪŋ] N simulation f (de maladie)

mall [mɔːl] N esp Am Com (shopping) m. centre m commercial

mallard ['mælɑːd] N (duck) colvert m

malleability [mælɪə'bɪlɪtɪ] N (of person, metal) malléabilité f

malleable ['mælɪəb(ə)l] ADJ (person, metal) malléable

mallet ['mælɪt] N 1 (hammer) (small) maillet m; (large) mailloche f 2 Sport (in croquet, polo) maillet m

mallow ['mæləʊ] N (plant) mauve f

malnourished ['mæl'nʌrɪʃt] ADJ sous-alimenté

malnutrition [mælnjuː'trɪʃən] N malnutrition f, (lack of food) sous-alimentation f

malodorous [mæ'ləʊdərəs] ADJ Fml malodorant

malpractice [mæl'præktɪs] N (in profes-

sional life) faute f professionnelle; (of doctor) négligence f, incurie f
▸▸ Law **m. insurance** = assurance f souscrite pour parer à des poursuites judiciaires pour négligence; Am Law **m. suit** = procès m pour faute ou négligence professionnelle

malt [mɔːlt] N malt m; (whisky) whisky m de malt
VT (in brewing) (barley) malter; **malted milk** lait m malté
▸▸ **m. extract** extrait m de malt; Am **m. liquor** = boisson f alcoolisée tirée du malt; **m. vinegar** vinaigre m de malt; **m. whisky** whisky de malt

Malta ['mɔːltə] N Malte f

Maltese [mɔːl'tiːz] ADJ maltais
N 1 (person) Maltais, -aise 2 Ling maltais m
▸▸ **M. Cross** croix f de Malte

maltreat [mæl'triːt] VT (person, animal) maltraiter, malmener

maltreatment [mæl'triːtmənt] N mauvais traitement(s) m(pl)

mam [mæm] N Dial maman f

mam(m)a N 1 ['mæmə, Old-fashioned mə'mɑː] (mother) maman f 2 ['mæmə] Am Sl (woman) nana f, **big m.** (object) mastodonte m

mammal ['mæməl] N mammifère m

mammalian [mæ'meɪlɪən] ADJ, N mammifère m

mammary ['mæmərɪ] ADJ Anat mammaire
▸▸ **m. glands** glandes fpl mammaires

mammogram ['mæməgræm] N Med mammographie f

mammography [mæ'mɒgrəfɪ] N Med mammographie f

Mammon ['mæmən] N Bible Mammon m; Fig **the worship of M.** l'adoration f de l'argent

mammoth ['mæməθ] N mammouth m
ADJ énorme, gigantesque, colossal, -aux

mammy ['mæmɪ] N 1 Fam (mother) maman f 2 Am Old-fashioned (black nurse) bonne f d'enfants noire

Man [mæn] N **the Isle of M.** l'île f de Man

MAN, pl **men** [mæn, men] N 1 (adult male) homme m; **men and women** les hommes et les femmes; **m. and wife** mari et femme; **to live as m. and wife** vivre maritalement; **men** (on public convenience) hommes; **an old m.** un vieillard, un vieil homme; **an ambitious m.** un ambitieux; **a dead m.** un mort; **good m.!** bravo, mon gars!; **I've known him m. and boy** je le connais depuis toujours; **a m.'s jacket/bicycle** une veste/bicyclette d'homme; **men's clothes/trousers** vêtements/pantalon pour homme; Com **men's department** rayon m hommes; **soap for men** savon pour homme; **to make a m. of sb** faire un homme de qn; **the army made a m. of him** l'armée a fait de lui un homme; **he took it like a m.** il a pris ça courageusement; **a game that sorts the men from the boys** un jeu qui distingue les hommes des gamins; **he isn't m. enough to tell me** il n'est pas assez courageux pour me le dire; **to talk to sb m. to m.** parler à qn d'homme à homme; **tell me, m. to m.** dismoi, entre nous; **he's just the m. for me** c'est l'homme qu'il me faut; **he's just the m. for the job** c'est l'homme de la situation; **to be one's own m.** être son maître, ne dépendre de personne; **he's a m.'s m.** il préfère la compagnie des hommes; **a m. about town** un mondain; **the m. in the street** l'homme de la rue; **what does the m. in the street think?** que pense l'homme de la rue?; **the m. in the moon** = visage m que l'on peut s'imaginer distinguer lors de la pleine lune; **m. of God** homme m d'église; **a m. of learning** un érudit; **a m. of peace** un homme de paix;

Sport **the m. of the match** le héros du match; **our m. in Rome** *Journ* notre correspondant à Rome; *Com* notre représentant à Rome; *(spy)* notre agent à Rome; *(diplomat)* notre envoyé à Rome; **they took on 200 men** ils ont embauché 200 ouvriers; *Mil* **officers and men** officiers *mpl* et hommes de troupe; *Hum* **a m.'s got to do what a m.'s got to do** (il) faut ce qu'il faut! VOIR GRAMMAIRE A13

2 *(individual, person)* homme *m*; **any m.** n'importe qui; **few men** peu de gens; **they replied as one m.** ils répondirent d'une seule voix; **they rose as one m.** ils se levèrent comme un seul homme; **they were patriots/communists to a m.** ils étaient tous patriotes/communistes; **every m. jack** tous sans exception

3 *(humanity)* l'homme *m*; **iron age m.** l'homme de l'âge de fer; *Prov* **m. proposes, God disposes** l'homme propose et Dieu dispose; **m. does not** *or* **cannot live by bread alone** on ne se nourrit pas que de pain

4 *Br Fam (husband, boyfriend)* mec *m*; **she's got a new m.** elle a un nouveau mec

5 *(type of person)*, *Univ* **a Oxford/a Cambridge m.** un diplômé d'Oxford/de Cambridge; **I'm a whisky m. myself** moi, c'est le whisky que je préfère; **he's a six-pints-a-day m.** il boit ses six pintes par jour

6 *Old-fashioned (manservant)* domestique *m*, valet *m*; *Hist (vassal)* homme *m*

7 *Sport (player)* joueur *m*

8 *(in chess)* pièce *f*, *(in draughts)* pion *m*

9 *esp Am Sl* **hey m.!** *(hello)* salut mon pote!; *(as interjection)* eh! mec!; **m., am I tired!** bon sang, qu'est-ce que je suis crevé!; **you should have seen it, m.!** bon sang tu aurais dû voir ça!

10 *(black American slang)* **the M.** *(whites)* les Blancs *mpl*; *(police)* les flics *mpl*; *(drug peddler)* le dealer

vt (-nn-) 1 *(work at)* **who's manning reception today?** qui assure la réception aujourd'hui?; **reception wasn't manned at the time** personne n'assurait *ou* n'était à la réception à ce moment-là; **someone has to be there to m. the phone** quelqu'un doit être là pour répondre au téléphone; **the campaign office was manned by volunteers** la permanence de la campagne était assurée par des volontaires

2 *(operate)* *(machine)* assurer le fonctionnement de; *(plane, boat etc)* être membre de l'équipage de; *Mil* **to m. a gun** servir *ou* manœuvrer une pièce d'artillerie; **to m. the barricades** défendre les barricades; **the fort was manned by a handful of legionnaires** le fort était tenu par une poignée de légionnaires; **m. the pumps!** armez les pompes!; **m. the boats!** mettez les canots (de sauvetage) à la mer!; **the bomber was manned by a crew of five men** le bombardier avait un équipage de cinq hommes; **the plane was manned by a pilot and a navigator** l'équipage de l'avion consiste en un pilote et un navigateur; **was the spaceship manned?** y avait-il des hommes à bord du vaisseau spatial?; **the machines had to be manned all the time** il fallait quelqu'un continuellement pour assurer le fonctionnement des machines

▶▶**m. Friday** *(servant)* fidèle serviteur *m*; *(office worker)* = employé *m* de bureau affecté à des tâches diverses

---

Note that the French expression **homme du monde** doesn't mean **man of the world**; it means a man who belongs to high society.

-man [mæn] **SUFF** **two-m. toboggan** luge *f* à deux places; **five-m. crew** équipage *m* de cinq hommes

manacle ['mænək(ə)l] **N** *(usu pl)* **manacles** menottes *fpl*

vt mettre *ou* passer les menottes à; **manacled to the wall** attaché au mur par des menottes

manage ['mænɪdʒ] **vt 1** *(run)* *(company, factory, project, bank etc)* diriger; *(estate)* diriger, gérer; *(the economy, one's money, resources, account)* gérer; **to m. sb's affairs** gérer les affaires de qn; **to m. a pop singer/football team** être (le) manager d'un chanteur de pop/d'une équipe de football

2 *(deal with)* *(situation)* gérer; **to know how to m. sb** savoir prendre qn; **she finds it difficult to m. her pupils** elle a du mal à tenir ses élèves

3 *(be able to)* **to m. to do sth** *(succeed)* réussir *ou* arriver *ou* parvenir à faire qch; *Iron (contrive)* s'arranger pour faire qch, réussir à faire qch; **we managed to persuade her** nous avons réussi à la persuader; **I think I can m. it** je crois que je peux le faire *ou* que je peux y arriver; **I shall never m. to learn it** jamais je n'arriverai à l'apprendre; **how do you m. not to dirty your hands?** comment faites-vous pour ne pas vous salir les mains?; **I hope she'll m. to be there** j'espère qu'elle pourra venir

4 *(be able to produce, consume, carry etc)* **£100 is the most that I can m.** je ne peux pas aller au-delà de 100 livres; **can you m. some more pudding?** vous reprendrez bien encore du dessert?; **I can't m. Friday** *(I'm not free)* je ne peux pas me libérer vendredi; **can you m. dinner on Thursday?** est-ce que vous pouvez venir dîner jeudi?; **I can't m. three suitcases** je ne peux pas porter trois valises; **can you m. the stairs?** *(carrying so much, being elderly etc)* est-ce que tu arrives à monter les escaliers?

vi se débrouiller; **she manages well** elle se débrouille bien; **can you m.?** *(with all those suitcases etc)* tu y arriveras?; **we shall m. better next time** nous nous débrouillerons mieux la prochaine fois; **he'll m. all right** il se débrouillera; **we could just m.** *(financially)* on avait juste de quoi vivre; **I don't know how I would have managed without you** je ne sais pas comment j'aurais fait sans toi

manageable ['mænɪdʒəb(ə)l] **ADJ 1** *(thing, vehicle)* maniable; *(hair)* facile à coiffer; **the smaller suitcase is a more m. size** la plus petite valise est plus maniable **2** *(person, child)* facile, docile **3** *(undertaking)* faisable **4** *(company)* gérable

managed ['mænɪdʒd] **ADJ**
▶▶*Fin* **m. currency** devise *f* contrôlée, monnaie *f* dirigée; *Fin* **m. fund** *(in insurance)* fonds *m* géré

management ['mænɪdʒmənt] **N 1** *(action)* *(of company, factory, project etc)* gestion *f*, direction *f*; *(of economy, money, resources)* gestion; **business m.** gestion des affaires; **bad m.** mauvaise gestion; *Com* **under new m.** *(change of ownership)* changement *m* de propriétaire; *(change of manager)* nouvelle direction; **m. by exception** direction par exceptions; **m. by objectives** gestion par objectifs **2** *(with sing or pl verb)* *(managers, employers)* administration *f*, direction *f*; **senior m.** les cadres *mpl* supérieurs; **la Direction**; **representatives of m. and unions** des représentants du patronat et des syndicats

▶▶**m. accountant** contrôleur, -euse de gestion; **m. accounts** comptes *mpl* de gestion; *Fin* **m. buy-in** apport *m* de gestion; *Br Fin* **m. buy-out** rachat *m* d'une société par la direction; **m. committee** comité *m* de direction; **m. consultancy** *(activity)* conseil *m* en gestion (d'entreprise); *(firm)* cabinet *m* (de conseil); **m. consultant** conseiller, -ère en *ou* de gestion (d'entreprise); **m. contract** contrat *m* de gestion; **m. fee** honoraires *mpl* d'un consultant; **m. function** fonction *f*

d'encadrement; **m. information system** système *m* intégré de gestion; **m. report** rapport *m* de gestion; *(accounts statistics)* tableau *m* de bord; **m. skills** qualités *fpl* de gestionnaire; **m. studies** études *fpl* de gestion; **m. style** mode *m* de gestion; **m. summary** résumé *m* managérial; **m. team** équipe *f* dirigeante; **m. technique** méthode *f* de gestion; **m. tool** outil *m* de gestion

manager ['mænɪdʒər] **N 1** *(of bank, company, factory, project)* directeur *m*; *(of café, bar, store)* gérant *m*, patron *m*; *(of department in large store)* chef *m*; *(of funds, money)* gestionnaire *m*; *(of assets)* administrateur *m*; *(of estate)* régisseur *m*; *(of entertainer, rock band, football team etc)* manager *m*; *Pol (of political party)* chef, dirigeant *m*; **I want to see the m.!** je veux le responsable!; **she's a good m.** *(of home etc)* elle est bonne ménagère **2** *Comput (of disk etc)* gestionnaire *m*

manageress [mænɪdʒə'res] **N** *(of bank, company, factory, project)* directrice *f*; *(of café, bar, shop)* gérante *f*, patronne *f*

managerial [mænɪ'dʒɪərɪəl] **ADJ** directorial, -aux; *(position)* de commande; **m. experience** expérience *f* de la direction; **at m. level** au niveau de la direction

▶▶**m. skills** qualités *fpl* de gestionnaire; **m. staff** cadres *mpl*, encadrement *m*

managing ['mænɪdʒɪŋ] **ADJ** directeur, -trice
▶▶**m. director** directeur, -trice général(e), P-DG *m*; **m. editor** rédacteur, -trice en chef

manatee [mænə'ti:] **N** *Zool* lamantin *m*

man-bites-dog story [mænbaɪts'dɒg] **N** *Journ Hum* = article *m* dont le contenu va à l'encontre des idées reçues

Manc [mæŋk] **N** *Br Fam (Mancunian)* = natif *m* de la ville de Manchester

Manchuria [mæn'tʃʊərɪə] **N** Mandchourie *f*

Manchurian [mæn'tʃʊərɪən] **ADJ** mandchou
N Mandchou, -oue

Mancunian [mæŋ'kju:nɪən] **N** habitant, -ante de Manchester; *(by birth)* originaire *mf* de Manchester
ADJ de Manchester

M&A [emən'eɪ] **N** *Fin* *(abbr* **mergers and acquisitions)** fusions et acquisitions *fpl*

Mandarin ['mændərɪn] **N** *Ling* mandarin *m*
▶▶**M. Chinese** mandarin

mandarin ['mændərɪn] **N 1** *(in Chinese history)*, *Fig* mandarin *m* **2** *(fruit)* mandarine *f*; *(tree)* mandarinier *m* **3** *(colour)* mandarine *f inv*
▶▶**m. collar** col *m* Mao; *Orn* **m. duck** *(canard m)* mandarin

mandate ['mændeɪt] **N 1** *(instructions)*, *Pol* mandat *m*; **the government has a m. to …** le gouvernement est mandaté pour …; **his superior had given him a m. to …** son supérieur lui a donné mandat pour … **2** *(territory)* pays *m* sous mandat
▶▶*Fin* **m. form** lettre *f* de signatures autorisées

mandatory ['mændətərɪ] **ADJ** *(obligatory)* obligatoire; *Law* mandataire
▶▶**m. writ** mandement *m*

mandible ['mændɪb(ə)l] **N 1** *(of insect)* mandibule *f* **2** *(of vertebrate)* mâchoire *f* inférieure

mandolin(e) [mændə'lɪn] **N** *Mus* mandoline *f*

mandrake ['mændreɪk] **N** *(plant)* mandragore *f*

mandrel, mandril ['mændrəl] **N** *Tech* mandrin *m*, arbre *m* (de tour)

mandrill ['mændrɪl] **N** *(ape)* mandrill *m*

mane [meɪn] **N** *(of horse, lion etc)*, *Fig* crinière *f*

man-eater, *pl* **man-eaters** N **1** *(animal)* mangeur *m* d'hommes **2** *Fig (woman)* mangeuse *f* d'hommes

man-eating ADJ **1** *(animal)* mangeur d'hommes **2** *(tribe etc)* anthropophage, cannibale
▸▸**m. shark** requin *m* mangeur d'hommes

maneuver, maneuverable *etc Am* = **maneuvre, manoeuvrable** *etc*

manful ['mænfʊl] ADJ vaillant, courageux

manfully ['mænfʊlɪ] ADV vaillamment, courageusement; **he was struggling m. with the suitcases/his second steak** il se démenait vaillamment avec les valises/son deuxième steak

manganese [mæŋgə'niːz] N *Miner, Chem* manganèse *m*
▸▸**m. steel** acier *m* au manganèse

mange [meɪndʒ] N *Vet* gale *f*

mangel-wurzel ['mæŋg(ə)lwɜːz(ə)l] N betterave *f* fourragère

manger ['meɪndʒər] N *Agr* mangeoire *f*, auge *f* d'écurie; *Bible* crèche *f*

mangle¹ ['mæŋg(ə)l] N *(for clothes)* essoreuse *f* (à rouleaux)
VT *(clothes)* essorer *(dans une essoreuse à rouleaux)*

mangle² VT **1** *(mutilate) (person, body)* mutiler; *(piece of meat)* charcuter, massacrer; **their bodies were horribly mangled** leurs corps ont été atrocement mutilés **2** *Fig (quotation)* estropier; *(text)* mutiler, dénaturer

mango, *pl* **mangoes** ['mæŋgəʊ, -əʊz] N *(fruit)* mangue *f*, *(tree)* manguier *m*
▸▸**m. chutney** = condiment *m* à la mangue

mangrove ['mæŋgrəʊv] N manglier *m*, palétuvier *m*
▸▸**m. swamp** mangrove *f*, **m. tree** manglier, palétuvier

mangy ['meɪndʒɪ] ADJ **1** *(dog)* galeux **2** *Fam (furniture etc)* minable, miteux

manhandle ['mænhænd(ə)l] VT **1** *(treat roughly) (person)* brutaliser, malmener **2** *(move by hand) (object)* transporter à la force des bras; *(goods etc)* manutentionner; **they manhandled the piano into position** ils ont poussé le piano pour le mettre à sa place

manhole ['mænhəʊl] N *(for drain)* trou *m* de visite, regard *m*; *(for boiler)* trou d'homme
▸▸**m. cover, m. lid** plaque *f* d'égout

manhood ['mænhʊd] N **1** *(maturity)* âge *m* d'homme, âge viril; **to reach m.** devenir un homme; **he had barely reached m.** il avait à peine atteint l'âge adulte **2** *(masculinity)* virilité *f*; **he felt he had to prove his m.** il pensait devoir prouver sa virilité **3** *(men)* les hommes *mpl*; **British m.** les hommes britanniques **4** *Hum Fam (genitals)* bijoux *mpl* de famille

man-hour N *Ind etc* heure *f* de travail, *Spec* heure-homme *f*, *pl* heures-hommes

manhunt ['mænhʌnt] N chasse *f* à l'homme

mania ['meɪnɪə] N **1** *(passion)* passion *f*, folie *f*, *Pej* manie *f* *(for sth* de qch); **to have a m. for sth** avoir une passion pour qch, avoir la passion *ou* la folie/la manie de qch; **to have a m. for stamp-collecting** avoir la folie des timbres **2** *Psy* manie *f*, **suicidal m.** folie *f* du suicide

maniac ['meɪnɪæk] N *Psy* maniaque *mf*, *Fam (wild person)* fou, *f* folle, cinglé, -ée; *Fam* **a m. driver** un fou du volant; **to drive like a m.** conduire comme un fou; *Fam* **a soccer m.** un fou de football

Note that the French word **maniaque** is most commonly used to describe someone who is obsessive about order and tidiness.

maniacal [mə'naɪək(ə)l] ADJ *(laughter etc)* dément

manic ['mænɪk] ADJ *Psy (wish etc)* qui tient de la folie; *Fig* **she made m. gestures** elle faisait des gestes désordonnés; **at a m. speed** à une vitesse folle
▸▸**m. depression** psychose *f* maniaco-dépressive

manic-depressive ADJ, N *Psy* maniaco-dépressif, -ive

manicure ['mænɪkjʊər] N soin *m* des mains; **to have a m.** se faire faire les mains et les ongles; **to give sb a m.** faire les mains et les ongles de qn; **how much is a m.?** combien coûte un soin des mains et des ongles?
VT *(person)* soigner les mains de, faire les mains et les ongles à; **to m. one's nails** se faire les ongles; **manicured hands** des mains très soignées
▸▸**m. set** trousse *f* de manucure

manicurist ['mænɪkjʊərɪst] N manucure *mf*

manifest ['mænɪfest] ADJ manifeste, évident; **to make sth m.** rendre qch évident; **this makes it m. that …** cela prouve que …
N *Naut, Aviat (document)* manifeste *m*
VT **1** *(display)* manifester, témoigner; **to m. itself** *(of symptom, talent etc)* se manifester, se révéler **2** *Naut (goods)* faire figurer sur le manifeste

manifestation [mænɪfes'teɪʃən] N manifestation *f*

Note that the French word **manifestation** also means **demonstration**.

manifestly ['mænɪfestlɪ] ADV manifestement

manifesto [mænɪ'festəʊ] N *Pol etc* manifeste *m*

manifold ['mænɪfəʊld] ADJ *(numerous)* multiple, nombreux
N *Tech* tubulure *f*, collecteur *m*

manikin ['mænɪkɪn] N = **mannikin**

Manila [mə'nɪlə] N Manille

manil(l)a [mə'nɪlə] ADJ
▸▸**m. envelope** enveloppe *f* en papier kraft; **m. paper** papier *m* kraft; **m. rope** (cordage *m* en) manille *f*

manioc ['mænɪɒk] N **1** *Bot* manioc *m* **2** *Culin* cassave *f*

manipulate [mə'nɪpjʊleɪt] VT **1** *(handle, operate etc) (object)* manipuler; *(mechanical device)* manœuvrer, actionner; *(lever, pedal)* actionner; *Med* **to m. bones** faire des manipulations **2** *Pej (person)* manipuler; *(accounts)* truquer

manipulation [mənɪpjʊ'leɪʃən] N **1** *(of object)* manipulation *f* **2** *Pej (of person)* manipulation *f*, *(of accounts)* trucage *m*

manipulative [mə'nɪpjʊlətɪv] ADJ manipulateur, -trice

manipulator [mə'nɪpjʊleɪtər] N *Pej* tripoteur, -euse, manipulateur, -trice **2** *(of machine etc)* manipulateur, -trice

Man(it) *abbr* **Manitoba**

Manitoba [mænɪ'təʊbə] N Manitoba *m*

mankind [mæn'kaɪnd] N **1** *(the human race)* le genre humain, l'humanité *f*, l'espèce *f* humaine **2** *(men)* les hommes *mpl*

manky ['mæŋkɪ] ADJ *Br Fam* cradingue

manlike ['mænlaɪk] ADJ *(resembling a human)* humain; *(resembling a man)* masculin; *(of woman)* masculin, *Pej* hommasse

manliness ['mænlɪnɪs] N virilité *f*, caractère *m* viril

manly ['mænlɪ] ADJ *(sport, activity)* d'homme, masculin; *(behaviour, character)* mâle, viril

man-made ADJ *(fibre, fabric, product)* synthétique; *(lake, beach)* artificiel; **m. attrac-**

tion *(in tourism)* centre *m* d'intérêt 'non-naturel'; **m. desert** désert *m* créé par l'homme; **m. laws** lois *fpl* faites par l'homme

manna ['mænə] N **1** *Bible etc* manne *f*, *Prov* **it was m. from heaven** c'était un don du ciel **2** *Bot, Pharm etc* manne *f* du frêne

manned [mænd] ADJ *(spacecraft, flight)* habité; *see also* **man** VT

mannequin ['mænɪkɪn] N *(person, dummy), Art* mannequin *m*

manner ['mænər] N **1** *(way, method, style)* manière *f*, façon *f* *(of doing sth* de faire qch); **the m. in which …** la manière dont …; **in a m. of speaking** en quelque sorte, dans un certain sens; *Gram* **adverb of m.** adverbe *m* de manière; **he does it (as if or as) to the m. born** il le fait comme s'il avait fait ça toute sa vie [VOIR GRAMMAIRE A21–2; B12]
2 *(etiquette)* **manners** manières *fpl*; **(good) manners** bonnes manières, savoir-vivre *m*, politesse *f*, **bad manners** mauvaises manières, manque *m* de savoir-vivre, manque d'éducation; **it's bad manners to stare** il est mal élevé de dévisager les gens; **she has bad table manners** elle ne sait pas se tenir à table; *Fig* **I'll teach you some manners, young man!** *(punish for rudeness)* je vais vous apprendre la politesse, jeune homme!; **where are your manners?** *(to child)* en voilà des manières!; **he's got no manners** il est très mal élevé; **I'm forgetting my manners, would you like some tea?** mais où avais-je la tête?, je ne vous ai pas proposé de thé?
3 *(variety)* espèce *f*, sorte *f*, **all m. of people/ things** toutes sortes de gens/choses; *Lit* **what m. of person is she?** quel genre de femme est-ce?; **by no m. of means, not by any m. of means** absolument pas; **they're not rich by any m. of means** ils ne sont absolument pas riches
4 *(attitude, behaviour)* façon *f* d'être; **I do not like his m.** je n'aime pas sa façon d'être; **she's got a very abrasive m.** elle est très acerbe
5 *Lit* **manners** *(customs of a people)* mœurs *fpl*, usages *mpl*

mannered ['mænəd] ADJ *Art, Liter* maniéré; *Pej (person)* maniéré, affecté; *(style)* recherché, précieux

mannerism ['mænərɪz(ə)m] N *Pej (of person)* maniérisme *m*, affectation *f*, *(habit) (of writer etc)* tic *m*; *Art, Liter* maniérisme *m*

mannerly ['mænəlɪ] ADJ poli, courtois

mannikin ['mænɪkɪn] N **1** *(small man)* petit homme *m*; *(dwarf)* nabot *m* **2** *Art, Med, Surg* mannequin *m*

mannish ['mænɪʃ] ADJ *(woman)* hommasse; **she has a m. voice** elle a une voix d'homme; **she looks m.** on dirait un homme

manoeuvrability, *Am* **maneuverability** [mənuːvrə'bɪlɪtɪ] N maniabilité *f*

manoeuvrable, *Am* **maneuverable** [mə'nuːvrəb(ə)l] ADJ *(plane, car etc)* manœuvrable, maniable

manoeuvre, *Am* **maneuver** [mə'nuːvər] N **1** *Mil, Naut etc (action)* manœuvre *f*, **manoeuvres** *(exercise)* manœuvres *fpl*; **troops on manoeuvres** troupes en manœuvres **2** *(action, remark)* manœuvre *f*, **a clever m.** une manœuvre habile; **there wasn't much room for m.** *(between cars etc)* il n'y avait pas beaucoup de place pour manœuvrer *ou* faire une manœuvre; *Fig* il y avait peu de marge de manœuvre; *Pej* **manoeuvres** *(plotting)* menées *fpl*, intrigues *fpl*
VT *Mil, Naut (army, fleet of ships)* manœuvrer, faire manœuvrer; **we manoeuvred the piano through the door** nous avons fait passer le piano par la porte; **she manoeuvred her car into the space** elle a garé sa voiture dans l'emplacement (en manœuvrant); *Fig*

to m. sb into a corner prendre qn au piège, *Fam* coincer qn
VI *Mil, Fig (of troops, politician etc)* manœuvrer; *Naut (of ship)* évoluer

manoeuvring, *Am* **maneuvering** [mə'nu:vrɪŋ] **N** *Mil* manœuvres *fpl, Pej (plotting)* menées *fpl,* intrigues *fpl*

man-of-war, *pl* **men-of-war N 1** *Naut Arch* vaisseau *m ou* bâtiment *m* de guerre **2 (Portuguese) m.** *(jellyfish)* physalie *f,* galère *f*

manometer [mæ'nɒmɪtər] **N** manomètre *m*

manor ['mænər] **N 1** *Hist (estate)* seigneurie *f, (house)* manoir *m;* **the lord of the m.** le châtelain; **the lady of the m.** la châtelaine **2** *Br Sl (of police, criminal)* territoire *m*
▸▸ **m. house** manoir

manorial [mə'nɔːrɪəl] **ADJ** *Hist* seigneurial, -aux

manpower ['mænpaʊər] **N** *Ind etc (labour)* main-d'œuvre *f, Mil* effectifs *mpl*
▸▸ **m. planning** planification *f* de la main-d'œuvre; **m. shortage** manque *m* de main-d'œuvre

manqué ['mɒŋkeɪ] **ADJ** *(placed after noun)* manqué

mansard ['mænsɑːd] **N** *Archit (roof)* toit *m* en mansarde
▸▸ **m. roof** toit en mansarde

manse [mæns] **N** *esp Scot Rel* presbytère *m*

manservant, *pl* **menservants** ['mænsɜːvənt, 'mensɜːvənts] **N** domestique *m; (personal)* valet *m* (de chambre)

mansion ['mænʃən] **N** *(in country)* château *m,* manoir *m; (in town)* hôtel *m* (particulier)
▸▸ **m. house** *(in country)* château, manoir; *(in town)* hôtel (particulier); **the M. House** = la résidence officielle du maire de Londres

mansize(d) ['mænsaɪz(d)] **ADJ** de la grandeur d'un homme; *Fig (handkerchief etc)* pour homme; *(helping of food)* gros, copieux

manslaughter ['mænslɔːtər] **N** *Law (through negligence)* homicide *m* involontaire *ou* par imprudence

mantel ['mænt(ə)l] **N = mantelpiece**

mantelpiece ['mænt(ə)lpiːs] **N** *(shelf)* dessus *m ou* tablette *f* de cheminée; **on the m.** sur la cheminée

mantilla [mæn'tɪlə] **N** *(clothing)* mantille *f*

mantis ['mæntɪs] **N** *(insect)* mante *f*

mantle ['mænt(ə)l] **N** *(covering) (of lava, snow)* manteau *m; (of gas lamp)* manchon *m; Arch (cloak) (of woman)* mante *f,* pèlerine *f, Fig* **to take on the m. of office** assumer les responsabilités qui incombent au poste

man-to-man **ADJ, ADV** *(talk)* d'homme à homme
▸▸ *Ftbl etc* **m. marking** marquage *m* individuel

mantrap ['mæntræp] **N** piège *m* à hommes

manual ['mænjʊəl] **ADJ** *(work, worker etc)* manuel
N 1 *(handbook)* manuel *m* **2** *(car)* voiture *f* à embrayage manuel **3** *(mode of operation)* **to be on m.** être sur commande manuelle **4** *Mus (of organ)* clavier *m*
▸▸ **m. dexterity** dextérité *f,* habileté *f* manuelle; *Aut* **m. gearbox, m. gears** boîte *f* de vitesses mécanique, boîte manuelle *ou* mécanique; *Aut* **m. transmission** transmission *f* mécanique; **m. typewriter** machine *f* à écrire mécanique

manually ['mænjʊəlɪ] **ADV** manuellement, à la main

manufacture [mænjʊ'fæktʃər] **N 1** *(of industrial product)* fabrication *f, (of cars, computers)* construction *f, (of clothing)* confection *f;* **of Italian m.** de fabrication italienne **2 manufactures** *(products)* produits *mpl* manufacturés

VT 1 *(industrial product)* fabriquer; *(car, aircraft, computer)* construire; *(clothing etc)* confectionner; **manufactured product** produit *m* manufacturé **2** *Fig (invent)* inventer (de toutes pièces); **to m. an opportunity to do sth** inventer une occasion de faire qch

manufacturer [mænjʊ'fæktʃərər] **N** fabricant, -ante; *(of cars, aircraft, computers)* constructeur *m;* **send it back to the manufacturers** renvoyez-le au fabricant
▸▸ **m.'s agent** agent *m* exclusif; *Mktg* **m. brand** marque *f* de fabricant; **m.'s instructions** notice *f* du constructeur; **m.'s liability** responsabilité *f* du fabricant; **m.'s recommended price** prix *m* conseillé par le fabricant

manufacturing [mænjʊ'fæktʃərɪŋ] **ADJ** industriel; **the country's m. industry** le secteur industriel du pays
N fabrication *f,* **the decline of m.** le déclin de l'industrie manufacturière
▸▸ **m. company** entreprise *f* industrielle; **m. costs** frais *mpl* de fabrication; **m. defect** vice *m ou* défaut *m* de fabrication; **m. licence** licence *f* de fabrication; **m. plant** usine *f* de fabrication; **m. rights** droits *mpl* de fabrication

manure [mə'njʊər] **N** *Agr* **N** engrais *m;* **farmyard m.** fumier *m* (d'étable); **chemical m.** engrais chimique; **liquid m.** purin *m*
VT *(soil)* engraisser; *(with farmyard manure)* fumer
▸▸ **m. heap** tas *m* de fumier

manuscript ['mænjʊskrɪpt] **N** manuscrit *m;* **in m.** *(book)* sous forme de manuscrit
ADJ manuscrit, écrit à la main

Manx [mæŋks] **ADJ** de l'île de Man
N *Ling* mannois *m*
NPL the M. *(people)* les habitants *mpl* de l'île de Man
▸▸ **M. cat** chat *m* (sans queue) de l'île de Man

many ['menɪ] **ADJ** *(comp* **more,** *superl* **most)** un grand nombre de, beaucoup de, de nombreux, bien des; **m. people** beaucoup *ou* un grand nombre de gens; **m. times** bien des fois, de nombreuses fois; **in m. cases** dans bien des cas, dans de nombreux cas; **in m. ways** de bien des façons; **for m. years** pendant de longues années *ou* de nombreuses années; **m. and varied** nombreux et très variés; **one of his m. acquaintances** une de ses nombreuses relations; **like so m. others** comme tant d'autres; **he told me in so m. words that ...** il m'a fait comprendre que ...; **too m. people** trop de monde; **a few (drinks) too m.** quelques verres de trop; **how m. times?** combien de fois?; **I have as m. books as you** j'ai autant de livres que vous; **four accidents in as m. days** quatre accidents en quatre jours; **a good m. things** pas mal de choses; **a night** *or* **m.'s the night I've done that** j'ai fait ça maintes nuits; **there are only so m. ways you can cook chicken** il n'y a pas une infinité de façons de préparer le poulet; *Prov* **m. hands make light work** à plusieurs, l'ouvrage avance vite **VOIR GRAMMAIRE A5**
PRON beaucoup, un grand nombre; **not (very) m.** pas beaucoup; **m. of us** beaucoup *ou* un grand nombre d'entre nous; **how m.?** combien?; **as m. as you like** autant que vous voulez; **they tried to bring back as m. as possible** ils ont essayé d'en rapporter le plus possible; **as m. again, as m. more, twice as m.** deux fois plus; **too m.** trop; **there are too m.** il y en a trop; **so m.** tant
NPL the m. la foule, la masse; **the sacrifices made by the few for the m.** les sacrifices faits par la minorité pour la masse

many-coloured **ADJ** multicolore

man-year **N** année-personne *f, pl* années-personnes

many-sided **ADJ 1** *(figure)* à plusieurs côtés **2** *(problem)* complexe, compliqué **3** *(person)* aux talents variés

Maoist ['maʊɪst] **ADJ, N** *Pol* maoïste *mf*

Maori ['maʊrɪ] **ADJ** maori
N 1 Maori, -ie **2** *Ling* maori *m*

map [mæp] **N 1** *(plan)* carte *f* (géographique); *(of town, underground, building)* plan *m; (of keyboard)* schéma *m; Fig* **it's off the m.** c'est à l'autre bout du monde; *Fig* **to put a town on the m.** mettre une ville en vedette, faire parler d'une ville; *Fig* **this will put us on the m.** ça va nous faire de la publicité; **the village was wiped off the m.** le village a été rayé de la carte; **he's a good m. reader** il sait bien lire les cartes *ou* les plans **2** *Am Sl (face)* tronche *f,* trombine *f*
VT (-pp-) 1 *(region etc)* dresser une carte de **2** *Math* faire un graphique de **3** *Fig (plot) (progress etc)* consigner
▸▸ **m. maker** cartographe *mf; Aut* **m. pocket** vide-poche *m, pl* vide-poches, bac *m* à cartes; **m. reading** lecture *f* de carte; **m. reference** référence *f* topographique, coordonnées *fpl*
▸ **map out** **VT SEP** *(route)* tracer; *(programme)* dresser, élaborer; **his life had already been mapped out for him** sa vie était déjà toute tracée

maple ['meɪp(ə)l] **N 1** *(tree)* érable *m* **2** *(wood)* (bois *m* d')érable *m*
▸▸ **m. leaf** feuille *f* d'érable; **m. sugar** sucre *m* d'érable; **m. syrup** sirop *m* d'érable; **m. tree** érable

mapping ['mæpɪŋ] **N 1** *(of region)* établissement *m* d'une carte **2** *Comput (in network)* utilité *f* logique **3** *Mktg* mapping *m*

Mar *abbr* **March**

mar [mɑːr] **VT** **(-rr-)** *(pleasure, performance)* gâter, gâcher; *(joy)* troubler; *(beauty of landscape, scenery)* gâcher, gâter, déparer; *(person's beauty)* déparer, gâcher; **to make or m. sb** faire la fortune ou la ruine de qn

marabou ['mærəbuː] **N** *(bird)* marabout *m*

maraca [mə'rækə] **N** *Mus* maraca *f*

maraschino [mærəs'kiːnəʊ] **N** marasquin *m*
▸▸ **m. cherry** cerise *f* au marasquin

marathon ['mærəθən] **N** *(race)* marathon *m; Fig* **m. meeting** conférence-marathon *f,* **m. speech** marathon oratoire
▸▸ **m. race** marathon; **m. runner** coureur, -euse de marathon, marathonien, -ienne

maraud [mə'rɔːd] **VI** marauder, être en maraude; **to go marauding** partir en maraude

marauder [mə'rɔːdər] **N** maraudeur, -euse

marauding [mə'rɔːdɪŋ] **ADJ** maraudeur, -euse; **m. hordes of looters** des hordes de pillards en maraude

marble ['mɑːb(ə)l] **N 1** *(rock)* marbre *m;* **m. floor** sol *m* de *ou* en marbre; **m. statue** statue *f* de marbre **2** *(glass ball)* bille *f,* **to play marbles** jouer aux billes; *Fig Fam* **she's still got all her marbles** elle a encore toute sa tête; *Fig Fam* **to lose one's marbles** perdre la boule **3** *Art (object)* marbre *m*
VT *Tech (in bookbinding)* marbrer, raciner
▸▸ **m. cake** gâteau *m* marbré; **m. cutter** *(person)* marbrier *m;* **m. quarry** marbrière *f,* carrière *f* de marbre

marbled ['mɑːb(ə)ld] **ADJ** marbré

marbling ['mɑːblɪŋ] **N** marbrure(s) *f(pl)*

March [mɑːtʃ] **N** VOIR GRAMMAIRE A81-2; B60-2
mars *m;* **in M.** en mars, au mois de mars; **(on) the first/the seventh of M.** le premier/ le sept mars

march [mɑːtʃ] **N 1** *(by soldiers etc)* marche *f,* **m. in step** marche au pas; **on the m.** en marche; *Fig* **the middle classes are on the m.** la classe moyenne s'est mobilisée; **it is two days' m. from here** c'est à deux jours de marche d'ici **2** *(pace)* pas *m*, allure *f*; **quick m.** pas cadencé; **slow m.** pas de parade **3** *(demonstration)* marche *f*, manifestation *f*; **to go on a m.** participer à une marche **4** *(progress) (of time etc)* marche *f*, progrès *m*; **to be overtaken by the m. of events** être dépassé par les événements **5** *Mus* marche *f*

VI *Mil etc* marcher; **to m. off** se mettre en marche; **he marched off in a rage** il est parti, fou de rage; **to m. by** *or* **past (sb)** défiler (devant qn); **quick m.!** en avant, marche!; **they marched to the town hall to protest** ils ont manifesté jusqu'à la mairie; **time marches on** *(I ought to go)* l'heure tourne; **she marched into his office** elle est entrée dans son bureau d'un pas décidé

VT *(troops)* faire marcher au pas; **he was marched off to prison** il a été emmené en prison

▸▸ **m. past** défilé *m*

marcher ['mɑːtʃər] **N** *(demonstrator)* manifestant, -ante; **peace m.** manifestant, -ante pour la paix

marching ['mɑːtʃɪŋ] **N** *Mil etc* marche *f*, **in m. order** en tenue de campagne; *(in formation)* en formation de marche;

▸▸ *Mil* **m. orders** feuille *f* de route; *Fig Fam* **to give sb his/her m. orders** mettre qn à la porte

marchioness ['mɑːʃənes] **N** marquise *f*

mare¹ [meər] **N 1** *(animal)* jument *f* **2** *Br Fam Pej (woman)* grognasse *f*; **you silly m!** espèce d'andouille!

▸▸ **m.'s nest** illusion *f*

mare² **N** *Br Fam (nightmare)* cauchemar *m*; **it was a total m.!** c'était un vrai cauchemar!

margarine [mɑːdʒəˈriːn] **N** margarine *f*

margarita [mɑːgəˈriːtə] **N** *(drink)* margarita *f*

marge [mɑːdʒ] **N** *Br Fam* margarine *f*

margin ['mɑːdʒɪn] **N 1** *(on paper, page etc)* marge *f*; **to write sth in the m.** écrire qch dans la marge; **there were some notes in the m.** il y avait quelques notes dans la marge; **to set the margins** marger; *(action)* pose *f* de marges

2 *(edge)* bord *m*; *(of forest)* lisière *f*, *(of lake etc)* bord *m*, rive *f*; **on the margin(s) of society** en marge de la société

3 *Com, Fin* marge *f*, *St Exch* acompte *m* *(versé à un courtier)*; *Com* **the margins are very tight** les marges sont très réduites; *Com* **to have a low/high m.** avoir une faible/forte marge; *Com* **we make a 10% m.** nous faisons 10% de marge; **to win by a narrow m.** *(in race etc)* gagner de justesse; **to beat sb by a m. of 20 seconds** battre qn de 20 secondes; **to win by an enormous m.** gagner haut la main; **the election was won by a wide m.** ils ont remporté les élections avec une majorité confortable; **she won the election by a m. of 26 votes** elle a gagné les élections à 26 voix près; **a m. of error** une marge d'erreur; **there is little m. for error** la marge d'erreur est très faible

▸▸ *St Exch* **m. call** appel *m* de couverture *ou* de marge *ou* de garantie; *St Exch* **m. default** défaut *m* de couverture; *Typ* **m. release** déclenche-marge *m inv*; *St Exch* **m. requirement** niveau *m* de dépôt requis, couverture *f* (boursière) obligatoire; *Typ* **m. setting** marge; *(action)* pose *f* de marges; *Typ* **m. stop** margeur *m*

marginal ['mɑːdʒɪn(ə)l] **ADJ 1** *(role, activity)* marginal, -aux; **m. case** cas *m* limite **2** *(note)* marginal, -aux, en marge **3** *(slight) (improvement, increase etc)* léger; **of m. interest/importance** d'un intérêt/d'une importance limité(e); **of m. use** d'un usage restreint **4** *Br Pol (seat, constituency)* à majorité précaire

N *Br Pol* siège *m* *ou* circonscription *f* à majorité précaire

▸▸ *Econ* **m. analysis** analyse *f* marginale; **m. land(s)** terre(s) *f(pl)* pauvre(s); **m. utility** utilité *f* marginale

marginalization [mɑːdʒɪnəlaɪˈzeɪʃən] **N** marginalisation *f*

marginalize ['mɑːdʒɪnəlaɪz] **VT** marginaliser

marginally ['mɑːdʒɪn(ə)lɪ] **ADV** *(slightly)* légèrement

marguerite [mɑːgəˈriːt] **N** *(plant)* grande marguerite *f*, marguerite des champs

marigold ['mærɪgəʊld] **N** *(plant)* souci *m*; **African m.** rose *f* d'Inde; **French m.** œillet *m* d'Inde

marihuana, marijuana [mærɪˈhwɑːnə] **N** marijuana *f*

marina [məˈriːnə] **N** port *m* de plaisance, marina *f*

marinade¹ [mærɪˈneɪd] **N** *Culin* marinade *f*

marinade², **marinate** ['mærɪneɪd, -eɪt] **VT** *Culin* (faire) mariner

marine [məˈriːn] **ADJ** *(life, biology)* marin

N 1 *Mil, Naut (soldier)* ≃ fusilier *m* marin; *Br* **the Royal Marines,** *Am* **the Am M. Corps** ≃ les fusiliers marins; *Fam* **(go) tell it to the marines!** allez raconter ça ailleurs *ou* à d'autres! **2** *Am* **merchant** *or* **mercantile m.** marine *f* marchande

▸▸ **m. architect** ingénieur *m* des constructions navales; **m. artist** peintre *m* de marines; **m. bill of lading** connaissement *m* maritime; **m. engineering** génie *m* maritime; **m. insurance** assurance *f* maritime; **m. insurance policy** police *f* d'assurance maritime; **m. risk** risque *m* maritime

mariner ['mærɪnər] **N** *Naut, Old-fashioned, Lit* marin *m*

marionette [mærɪəˈnet] **N** marionnette *f* à fils

marital ['mærɪt(ə)l] **ADJ** *(relating to marriage)* conjugal, -aux, matrimonial, -aux

▸▸ *Admin* **m. obligations** obligations *fpl* conjugales; **m. status** situation *f* de famille

maritime ['mærɪtaɪm] **ADJ** *(nation, law)* maritime

▸▸ **m. climate** climat *m* maritime

marjoram ['mɑːdʒərəm] **N** *Bot, Culin* marjolaine *f*

Mark [mɑːk] **N** Marc *m*

MARK¹ [mɑːk]

| **N** marque **1, 2, 4** ▪ trace **1, 2** ▪ signe **3** ▪ but **5** ▪ cible **5** ▪ note **6** ▪ série **8** |
| **VT** marquer **1, 4–6** ▪ corriger **3** ▪ célébrer **5** |

N 1 *(scratch, stain etc)* marque *f*, trace *f*
2 *(trace) (of suffering etc)* trace *f*, marque *f*; **to make one's m.** *(succeed)* se faire un nom *ou* une réputation; **he made his m.** *(because he couldn't write)* il a fait une croix; **years of imprisonment had left their m. on him** ses années de captivité avaient laissé des traces
3 *(sign, proof)* signe *m*; **as a m. of respect** en signe de respect
4 *(reference on instrument etc)* marque *f*, repère *m*; *Fam* **he's not up to the m.** *(good enough)* il n'est pas à la hauteur; *Br Fam* **I'm not feeling up to the m.** je ne suis pas dans mon assiette
5 *(target for shooting etc)* cible *f*; *(objective)* but *m*; **unemployment has passed the three million m.** le nombre des chômeurs a passé la barre des trois millions; *Fam* **an easy m.** *(person)* une dupe; *Fig* **to hit the m.** toucher en plein dans le mille; *Fig* **to miss the m.** mettre à côté
6 *Sch (out of twenty etc)* point *m*; *(overall grade)* note *f*, **to give sb/sth marks out of**

ten/twenty noter qn/qch sur dix/vingt; **to get good marks** avoir de bonnes notes; **she got the highest m.** *or* **marks in the class** c'est elle qui a eu la *ou* les meilleure(s) note(s) de la classe; **full marks** *(in a specific subject)* note maximale; **full marks for effort!** bravo d'avoir essayé!; **bad m.** *or* **marks** mauvais point; **(you get) no marks for guessing who did it** tu n'auras aucun mal à deviner qui a fait ça
7 *Sport (starting line)* ligne *f* de départ; **on your marks! get set! go!** à vos marques! prêts! partez!; **to be quick off the m.** *(in race)* démarrer vite; *(to understand)* avoir l'esprit vif; **you were quick off the m.** *(in doing sth)* tu n'as pas perdu de temps; **to be slow off the m.** *(in race)* prendre un mauvais départ; *(to understand)* être long à la détente; **you were too slow off the m.** *(in doing sth)* tu as mis trop de temps
8 *Ind, Mil (of machine etc)* série *f*, **m. II/III** série II/III
9 *(assay)* m. *(on gold, silver)* poinçon *m* de garantie
10 *Culin* **(gas) m. 4** thermostat *m* 4
11 *Sl (victim, target)* pigeon *f*, poire *f*

VT 1 *(put mark on) (linen, silverware, cards etc)* marquer; *(goods)* estampiller; *Tech (jewellery etc)* signer; **her towels were marked with her initials** ses serviettes de bain portaient ses initiales; **face marked by** *or* **with smallpox** visage marqué par la petite vérole; **his face was marked with suffering** son visage était marqué par la souffrance
2 *Com* **to m. (the price of) an article** mettre le prix à un article; *St Exch* **to m. stock** coter des valeurs; *St Exch* **to m. to market** comptabiliser au prix de marché
3 *Sch (homework)* corriger, noter; **to m. sth right/wrong** compter qch comme juste/faux; **to m. exam papers** noter *ou* corriger des copies (d'examen); **marked out of 10** noté sur 10
4 *(indicate)* marquer, indiquer; **to m. a place on the map** indiquer un lieu sur la carte; **stream that marks the boundary of the estate** ruisseau qui marque la limite de la propriété; **X marks the spot** X indique l'endroit; **this decision marks a change in policy** cette décision marque un changement de politique
5 *(show) (one's approval, dissatisfaction)* témoigner, montrer; *(the beat)* accentuer; **to m. time** *Mil* marquer le pas; *Fig* piétiner, faire du sur place, ne pas avancer; **to m. an era** faire époque; **to m. an anniversary** célébrer un anniversaire
6 *Sport, Ftbl etc (opponent)* marquer
7 *(characterize)* caractériser
8 *(pay attention to) (person, thing)* faire attention à; **..., m. you** ..., remarque; **m. what I say** faites bien attention à ce que je dis; **m. my words** c'est moi qui vous le dis

▸ **mark down VT SEP 1** *(write down)* relever
2 they had marked him down as a troublemaker ils l'avaient catalogué comme fauteur de troubles; **he was marked down for the post of ...** il avait été pressenti pour le poste de ...
3 *Com (goods)* baisser le prix de, *Spec* démarquer; **everything has been marked down to half price** tout a été réduit à moitié prix
4 *Sch (homework)* baisser la note de

▸ **mark in VT SEP** noter; *(area on map etc)* hachurer

▸ **mark off VT SEP 1** *(in surveying) (line, road)* jalonner; **to m. off a distance on the map** *(measure)* indiquer une distance sur la carte; **the route was marked off in 1 km sections** le trajet était divisé en tronçons d'un kilomètre
2 *(separate with fence etc) (area)* délimiter

3 *(distinguish)* **to m. sb off from sb** distinguer qn de qn
4 *(with a tick etc)* cocher
▸ **mark out** VT SEP **1** *(distinguish)* distinguer (**from** de); **he was marked out for promotion from ...** il était destiné à occuper un poste important dès ...
2 *(mark with lines) (cricket ground etc)* tracer les lignes de
▸ **mark up** VT SEP **1** *(write up)* noter, inscrire
2 *Com (goods)* augmenter le prix de, *Spec* majorer
3 *Sch (essay)* majorer la note de
4 *(text)* préparer, corriger

mark² N **1** *Formerly (German and Finnish currency)* mark *m* **2 convertible m.** *(Bosnian currency)* mark *m* convertible

markdown ['mɑːkdaʊn] N *Com* réduction *f*

marked [mɑːkt] ADJ **1 badly m. face** *(after accident)* visage balafré **2** *(difference, improvement etc)* marqué, (très) net *f* nette, (très) sensible; *(accent)* prononcé; **the change is becoming more m.** le changement s'accentue
▸▸ **m. card** carte *f* marquée; **m. man** homme *m* marqué; **he's a m. man** il est repéré; *(he's going to be killed)* c'est un homme mort; *Mktg* **m. price** prix *m* marqué

marked-down ADJ *Com* démarqué

markedly ['mɑːkɪdlɪ] ADV de façon marquée *ou* très nette *ou* très sensible; **m. better** nettement meilleur; **m. different** nettement *ou* sensiblement différent

marked-up ADJ *Com* majoré

marker ['mɑːkər] N **1** *Sch* correcteur, -trice; **he's a hard m.** il note sévèrement **2** *(pen)* marqueur *m*, *Ind, Tech (marking device)* marqueur; *(tool)* marquoir *m* **3** *(indicator)* jalon *m*, repère *m*; *(flag)* fanion *m*; *(stick)* piquet *m* d'alignement *ou* de jalonnement; *(for debt)* reconnaissance *f* de dettes; *(biological, genetic)* marqueur *m*, *Aviat etc* (radio)phare *m*, (radio)balise *f* **4** *Ftbl etc* marqueur, -euse
▸▸ *Aviat* **m. beacon** radiobalise *f*, *Naut* **m. buoy** bouée *f* de balisage; **m. pen** marqueur *m*

market ['mɑːkɪt] N **1** *(collection of stalls)* marché *m*; *(large)* foire *f*; **cattle m.** foire aux bestiaux; **fish m.** marché aux poissons **2** *Com, Econ, St Exch* marché *m*; **cotton m.** marché du coton; **to put one's flat on the m.** mettre son appartement en vente; **the most economical car on the m.** la voiture la plus économique du marché; **to come onto the m.** arriver sur le marché; **to take sth off the m.** retirer qch du marché; **to be in the m. for sth** *(of person)* être acheteur de qch; **to find a m. for sth** trouver un débouché *ou* des acheteurs pour qch; **there's no m. for these products** il n'y a pas de marché *ou* de demande pour ces produits, ces produits ne se vendent pas
VT (**-t-**) commercialiser
▸▸ **m. analysis** analyse *f* de marché; **m. analyst** analyste *mf* du marché; **m. appeal** attrait *m* commercial; **m. appraisal** évaluation *f* du marché; **m. behaviour** comportement *m* du marché; *St Exch* **m. capitalization** capitalisation *f* boursière; **m. challenger** challengeur *m*; **m. choice** choix *m* sur le marché; *(product preferred by market)* choix du marché; *St Exch* **m. commentator** chroniqueur *m* boursier; **m. competition** concurrence *f* du marché; **m. conditions** conditions *fpl* du marché; *St Exch* **m. crisis** choc *m* boursier; **m. day** jour *m* de marché; **m. demand** demande *f* du marché; **m. development** développement *m* du marché; **m. economy** économie *f* de marché *ou* libérale; **m. entry** lancement *m* sur le marché; **m. expansion** extension *f* de marché; **m. exploration** prospection *f* du marché; **m. exposure** exposition *f* sur le marché; **m. failure** défaillance *f* du marché; **m. fluctuation** mouvement *m* du

marché; **m. follower** suiveur *m* (sur le marché); **m. forces** les forces *fpl* du marché; **m. forecast** prévisions *fpl* du marché, pronostic *m* du marché; **m. gap** manque *m* sur le marché; *Br* **m. garden** jardin *m* maraîcher; *Br* **m. gardener** maraîcher, -ère; *Br* **m. gardening** culture *f* maraîchère; **m. growth** croissance *f* du marché; **m. indicator** indicateur *m* de marché; **m. intelligence** intelligence *f* marketing, information *f* commerciale; **m. leader** *(product)* premier produit *m* sur le marché; *(firm)* leader *m* du marché; *St Exch* **m. maker** mainteneur *m* *ou* teneur *m* du marché, intermédiaire *mf*; **m. mechanism** mécanisme *m* du marché; **m. minimum** *(base sales)* ventes *fpl* de base; *St Exch* **m. order** ordre *m* au mieux; **m. orientation** orientation *f* marché; **m. participant** intervenant, -ante *ou* acteur *m* sur le marché; **m. penetration** pénétration *f* du marché; **m. penetration pricing** tarification *f* de pénétration du marché; **m. pioneer** pionnier *m*; **m. place** *(market square)* place *f* du marché; *Econ* marché; **the products in the m. place** les produits sur le marché; **m. player** acteur de marché; **m. positioning** positionnement *m* sur le marché; **m. potential** *(of product)* potentiel *m* sur le marché; *(of market)* potentiel du marché; **m. power** pouvoir *m* d'un acheteur sur le marché; **m. price** *Com* prix *m* courant; *St Exch* cours *m* de (la) Bourse; *St Exch* **m. price list** mercuriale *f*; **m. prospects** perspectives *fpl* commerciales; *St Exch* **m. quotation** cotation *f* au cours du marché; *St Exch* **m. rating** cours en Bourse; **m. report** étude *f* de marché, rapport *m* *ou* bilan *m* commercial; **m. research** recherche *f* commerciale; étude *f* *ou* études *fpl* de marché; **m. research company** société *f* d'études de marché; **m. researcher** chargé, -ée d'étude de marché; **m. risk** risque *m* du marché; **m. rollout** élargissement *m* du marché; **m. segment** segment *m* de marché; **m. segmentation** segmentation *f* du marché; **m. share** part de marché; **to lose m. share** voir sa part du marché diminuer; **m. size** *(of product)* part de marché; *(of market)* taille *f* du marché; *St Exch* **m. society** marché boursier; **m. square** place du marché; **m. stall** étalage *m*; **m. structure** structure *f* du marché; **m. study** étude de marché; **m. survey** enquête de marché; **m. test** marché-test *m*, *pl* marchés-tests, test *m* de marché, test de vente; **m. thrust** percée *f* commerciale; **m. town** bourg *m*; *Br* **m. trader** vendeur, -euse qui fait les marchés; *St Exch* **m. trend** conjoncture *f* boursière; **m. value** *Com (of object, product)* valeur *f* marchande; *St Exch (of share)* valeur boursière *ou* en bourse

marketability [mɑːkɪtə'bɪlɪtɪ] N possibilité *f* d'être commercialisé; **we are doubtful about the m. of these machines** nous doutons que ces machines soient commercialisables

marketable ['mɑːkɪtəb(ə)l] ADJ *(goods)* vendable, commercialisable
▸▸ *Fin* **m. securities** valeurs *fpl* de placement, valeurs réalisables

market-driven ADJ déterminé par les contraintes du marché
▸▸ **m. economy** économie *f* de marché

marketeer [mɑːkɪ'tɪər] N **1** *Br Pol* (pro-)M. partisan, -ane du Marché commun **2** *Mktg* mercaticien, -ienne

marketer ['mɑːkɪtər] N *Mktg* mercaticien, -ienne

market-garden ADJ *esp Br* **m. produce** produits *mpl* maraîchers

marketing ['mɑːkɪtɪŋ] N **1** *(of new product)* commercialisation *f*, marketing *m* **2** *(study)* marketing *m*, mercatique *f*

▸▸ **m. agreement** accord *m* de commercialisation; **m. analyst** analyste *mf* mercaticien(ienne); **m. approach** démarche *f* marketing; **m. audit** audit *m* marketing; **m. auditor** audit marketing, auditeur, -trice marketing; **m. campaign** campagne *f* de marketing; **m. channel** circuit *m* de commercialisation *ou* distribution; **m. company** entreprise *f* de marketing; **m. concept** concept *f* de marketing; **m. consultancy** *(service, activity)* conseil *m* en marketing; **m. consultancy firm** société *f* de conseil en marketing; **m. consultant** conseiller, -ère commercial(e), mercaticien, -ienne; **m. costs** frais *mpl* de commercialisation; **m. department** service *m* du marketing; **m. director** directeur, -trice du marketing, dirco *m*, directeur, -trice commercial(e); **m. engineering** marketing informatisé; **m. environment** environnement *m* commercial, environnement marketing; **m. executive** responsable *mf* du marketing, cadre *m* en marketing; **m. expert** mercaticien, -ienne; **m. fit** ajustement *m* stratégique; **m. information system** système *m* d'information marketing; **m. intelligence** intelligence *f* marketing; **m. manager** directeur, -trice du marketing, responsable *mf* du marketing; **m. mix** marchéage *m*, marketing mix *m*, logistique *f* commerciale; **m. network** réseau *m* *ou* circuit de commercialisation; **m. orientation** optique *f* marketing; **m. plan** plan *m* marketing; **m. planner** responsable de planification mercatique; **m. planning** planification *f* mercatique; **m. policy** politique *f* de commercialisation; **m. questionnaire** questionnaire *m* d'étude de marché; **m. spectrum** marchéage *m*; **m. strategy** stratégie *f* marketing; **m. study** étude *f* commerciale, étude marketing; **m. team** équipe *f* commerciale; **m. technique** technique *f* commerciale

marketization [mɑːkɪtaɪ'zeɪʃən] N marchéisation *f*

marketize ['mɑːkɪtaɪz] VT convertir à l'économie de marché

marking ['mɑːkɪŋ] N **1** *(of linen, cattle etc)* marquage *m* **2 markings** *(distinctive marks)* marques *fpl*, *(on animal) (spots)* taches *fpl*, *(stripes)* rayures *fpl*, *Aviat* insignes *mpl* **3** *Sch (of homework)* correction *f*, *(work to be marked)* copies *fpl* (à corriger) **4** *Ftbl etc* marquage *m* **5** *St Exch (of shares)* cotation *f*; **m. to market** comptabilisation *f* au prix de marché
▸▸ **m. ink** encre *f* à marquer; *Sch* **m. scheme** barème *m*

markka ['mɑːkə] N mark *m* finlandais

marksman, *pl* **marksmen** ['mɑːksmən] N tireur *m* d'élite

marksmanship ['mɑːksmənʃɪp] N adresse *f* *ou* habileté *f* au tir

markswoman, *pl* **markswomen** ['mɑːkswʊmən, -wɪmɪn] N tireuse *f* d'élite

mark-up N *Com* majoration *f*; **we operate a 2.5 times m.** nous appliquons une marge de 2,5

marl [mɑːl] N *Agr* marne *f*
▸▸ **m. pit** marnière *f*

marlin ['mɑːlɪn] N *(fish)* poisson *m* épieu

marlin(e)spike ['mɑːlɪnspaɪk] N *Naut* épissoir *m*

marly ['mɑːlɪ] ADJ *(soil)* marneux

marmalade ['mɑːməleɪd] N *Culin* **(orange) m.** confiture *f* d'oranges

marmoset ['mɑːməzet] N *(animal)* ouistiti *m*, marmouset *m*

marmot ['mɑːmɒt] N *(animal)* marmotte *f*

maroon¹ [mə'ruːn] N **1** *(colour)* rouge *m inv* foncé, bordeaux *m inv* **2** *(firework)* fusée *f* de détresse

Note that the French word **marron** is a false friend. When referring to a colour, it means **brown**.

maroon² **VT** abandonner *(sur une île déserte)*

marooned [mə'ru:nd] **ADJ** *Fig* isolé

marquee [ma:'ki:] **N** *(tent)* grande tente *f*

marquess, marquis ['ma:kwɪs] **N** marquis *m*

marquetry ['ma:kɪtrɪ] **N** marqueterie *f*

marram ['mærəm] **N** *Bot* gourbet *m*
▸▸**m. grass** gourbet

marriage ['mærɪdʒ] **N1** mariage *m*; **a happy m.** un ménage heureux; *Fml* **to take sb in m.** épouser qn; *Fml* **to give sb in m.** donner qn en mariage; **uncle by m.** oncle par alliance **2** *Fig* mariage *m*, alliance *f (entre les choses)*; **a m. of minds** une union des esprits
▸▸**m. bed** lit *m* conjugal; **m. broker** agent *m* matrimonial; *Br* **m. bureau** agence *f* matrimoniale; **m. ceremony** cérémonie *f* de mariage; **m. certificate** extrait *m* d'acte de mariage; *Journ* **marriages column** carnet *m* blanc; **m. of convenience** mariage de raison; **m. guidance** conseil *m* conjugal; **m. guidance counsellor** conseiller, -ère conjugal(e); *Old-fashioned Br Fam* **m. lines** extrait *m* d'acte de mariage; **m. settlement** *(dowry)* dot *f*, *(between couple)* ≃ contrat *m* de mariage, ≃ régime *m* matrimonial; **m. vows** vœux *mpl* de mariage

marriageable ['mærɪdʒəb(ə)l] **ADJ** *(daughter)* mariable, à marier; **of m. age** en âge de se marier

married ['mærɪd] **ADJ** marié
▸▸**m. couple** couple *m* marié; **the young/ newly wed. couple** les jeunes/nouveaux mariés *mpl*; **m. life** vie *f* conjugale; **m. name** nom *m* de femme mariée; *Br* **m. quarters** logements *mpl* pour familles

marrow ['mærəʊ] **N1** *(in bone)* moelle *f*; **to be frozen to the m.** être transi de froid, être glacé jusqu'à la moelle **2** *Lit (essence)* essence *f* **3** *Br* **(vegetable)** **m.** courge *f*

marrowbone ['mærəʊbəʊn] **N** os *m* à moelle

marrowfat ['mærəʊfæt] **N** pois *m* carré
▸▸**m. pea** pois carré

marry ['mærɪ] *(pt, pp* **married** ['mærɪd]) **VT1** *(get married to)* se marier avec, épouser; **they've been married for nearly twenty years** cela fait presque vingt ans qu'ils sont mariés; **they're happily married** ils forment un ménage heureux; **will you m. me?** veux-tu m'épouser?; **to get married** se marier; *Fig* **he's married to his job** son travail passe avant tout, il n'y a que son travail qui compte **2** *(of priest, parent)* marier, unir **3** *Fig (combine)* allier, marier
VI se marier; **she never married** elle ne s'est jamais mariée; **to m. beneath oneself** se mésallier; **to m. for money** faire un mariage d'argent; **to m. into money** épouser quelqu'un issu d'une famille riche; **she married into the Smith family/the aristocracy** elle a épousé un membre de la famille Smith/de l'aristocratie; **to m. again** *or* **a second time** se remarier; **he isn't the marrying kind** il n'est pas du genre à se marier; *Prov* **m. in haste, repent at leisure** tel se marie à la hâte qui s'en repent à loisir; *Fig* **the flavours m. well** les parfums se marient bien
▸ **marry off VT SEP** *(dispose of by marriage)* marier; **they were desperate to m. her off** ils voulaient à tout prix la marier
▸ **marry up VT SEP** *(bring together) (two parts)* joindre; *(colours)* marier
VI *(line up, fit)* coïncider, concorder; *(of colours)* aller bien ensemble, se marier; **check that the two parts m. up** vérifier que les deux parties coïncident

Mars [ma:z] **N** *Astron* Mars *f*; *Myth* Mars *m*

marsh [ma:ʃ] **N** marais *m*, marécage *m*
▸▸**m. fever** fièvre *f* des marais, paludisme *m*; **m. gas** gaz *m* des marais, méthane *m*; *Bot* **m. marigold** souci *m* d'eau, populage *m*

marshal ['ma:ʃəl] **N1** *Br Mil, Aviat* **M. of the RAF** ≃ Commandant *m* en Chef des Forces aériennes; **Air Chief Marshal** = général *m* d'armée aérienne; **M. of the Diplomatic Corps** ≃ Chef *m* du Protocole **2** *(at race, demonstration, march)* membre *m* du service d'ordre **3** *Am Law* = fonctionnaire *m* ayant les attributions d'un shérif; *(police officer)* officier *m* de la police fédérale
VT (**-ll-,** *Am* **-l-**) *(people, troops)* rassembler (et placer en ordre/en rang); *(arguments)* passer en revue; *(thoughts)* rassembler; *Rail (trucks, wagons)* trier, manœuvrer; **the children were marshalled into a line** on a fait mettre les enfants en ligne; **he marshalled the children out of the room** il a dirigé les enfants vers la sortie; **to m. facts** rassembler des faits et les mettre en ordre; **we need to m. more support for the project** il nous faut mobiliser plus de monde pour le projet

marshalling yard ['ma:ʃəlɪŋ] **N** *Rail* gare *f* de triage

marshland ['ma:ʃlænd] **N** terres *fpl* marécageuses, marécages *mpl*

marshmallow [ma:ʃ'mæləʊ] **N 1** *Culin* (pâte *f* de) guimauve *f* **2** *(plant)* guimauve *f*, althée *f*

marshy ['ma:ʃɪ] **ADJ** *(ground)* marécageux

marsupial [ma:'su:pɪəl] **ADJ, N** marsupial *m*, -aux

mart [ma:t] **N** centre *m* commercial, marché *m*; **(auction) m.** salle *f* des ventes

marten ['ma:tɪn] **N** *(animal)* mart(r)e *f*

martial ['ma:ʃəl] **ADJ** martial, -aux, guerrier
▸▸**m. arts** arts *mpl* martiaux; **m. law** loi *f* martiale; **to declare m. law** proclamer l'état de siège

Martian ['ma:ʃən] **N** Martien, -ienne

martin ['ma:tɪn] **N** *(bird)* **(house) m.** martinet *m*

martinet ['ma:tɪnet] **N** *Mil* officier *m* à cheval sur la discipline; **to be a m.** être autoritaire

martingale ['ma:tɪŋgeɪl] **N 1** *(part of harness)* martingale *f* **2** *Naut* **m. (guy** *or* **stay)** martingale *f* du beaupré

Martini® [ma:'ti:nɪ] **N** Martini® *m*

Martinican [ma:tɪ'ni:kən] **ADJ** martiniquais
N Martiniquais, -aise

Martinmas ['ma:tɪnməs] **N** la Saint-Martin

martyr ['ma:tər] **N** martyr, -yre; **to die a m. in** *or* **to a cause** mourir martyr d'une cause; **he is a m. to rheumatism** ses rhumatismes lui font souffrir le martyre; *Fam* **my brother's such a m.** mon frère se prend pour un vrai martyr; *Fam* **stop making such a m. of yourself!** arrête de jouer les martyrs!
VT *(person)* martyriser; **a martyred people** un peuple martyr

martyrdom ['ma:tədəm] **N** *Rel, Fig* martyre *m*

martyrize ['ma:təraɪz] **VT** martyriser

marvel ['ma:v(ə)l] **N** merveille *f*; **the marvels of science/the world** les merveilles de la science/du monde; **it would be a m. if she won** ce serait un miracle *ou* un prodige si elle gagnait; **to work marvels** faire des merveilles; *(of treatment etc)* faire merveille; **we're not expecting anybody to work marvels** nous n'attendons de miracle de personne; *Fam* **you're a m.!** tu es un as!; *Iron (you idiot)* espèce d'andouille!
VI (**-ll-,** *Am* **-l-**) *(at splendour, beauty)* s'émerveiller (**at** de); *(at cost)* s'étonner (**at** de)
VT I m. that you are always so calm ton

calme m'impressionne; **I m. that you can be so calm at a time like this** je me demande comment tu peux être aussi calme à un moment pareil; **she marvelled that he had agreed** elle s'est étonnée qu'il ait consenti

marvellous, *Am* **marvelous** ['ma:v(ə)ləs] **ADJ** merveilleux; **it would be m. if …** ce serait merveilleux si …; *Iron* **(isn't it) m.!** ça c'est le bouquet *ou* le comble!

marvellously, *Am* **marvelously** ['ma:v(ə)ləslɪ] **ADV** merveilleusement

Marxian ['ma:ksɪən] **ADJ** *Phil* marxien, -ienne

Marxism ['ma:ksɪz(ə)m] **N** *Pol* marxisme *m*

Marxism-Leninism **N** *Pol* marxisme-léninisme *m*

Marxist ['ma:ksɪst] **ADJ, N** *Pol* marxiste *mf*

Marxist-Leninist **ADJ, N** *Pol* marxiste-léniniste *mf*

Mary Magdalene [meərɪ'mægdəli:n] **N** Marie-Madeleine *f*

Mary Queen of Scots **N** Marie Stuart *f*

Mary Stuart ['stjʊət] **N** Marie Stuart *f*

marzipan ['ma:zɪpæn] **N** *Culin* massepain *m*, pâte *f* d'amandes; **m. fruits** fruits *mpl* en pâte d'amandes

mascara [mæs'ka:rə] **N** mascara *m*
VT **she had heavily mascaraed eyes** elle avait les cils très maquillés

mascot ['mæskət] **N** mascotte *f*, *(on car bonnet)* enjoliveur *m* de capot

masculine ['mæskjʊlɪn] **ADJ 1** masculin, mâle; *(woman)* masculine; *Fam Pej* hommasse **2** *Gram* masculin
N *Gram* masculin *m*; **in the m.** au masculin
SEE GRAMMAR B5–7

masculinity [mæskjʊ'lɪnɪtɪ] **N** masculinité *f*

maser ['meɪzər] **N** *Nucl* maser *m*

MASH [mæʃ] **N** *Am Mil (abbr* **Mobile Army Surgical Hospital)** hôpital *m* de campagne

mash [mæʃ] **N 1** *(pulp)* **to reduce to a m.** *(paper etc)* réduire en pâte *ou* en bouillie **2** *Br Fam (mashed potato)* purée *f* de pommes de terre **3** *Agr (for pigs, poultry)* pâtée *f* **4** *(in brewing)* fardeau *m* (de malt et d'eau chaude)
VT 1 **to m. (up)** broyer, écraser; *Culin* faire une purée de **2** *(in brewing)* brasser, mélanger

mashed [mæʃt] **ADJ**
▸▸**m. potato, m. potatoes** purée *f* (de pommes de terre)

masher ['mæʃər] **N** *Tech (device)* broyeur *m*, écraseur *m*, mélangeur *m*; *Culin* **(potato) m.** presse-purée *m inv*

mashie, mashy ['mæʃɪ] **N** *Golf* mashie *m*

mask [ma:sk] **N 1** masque *m*; *(silk or velvet, for eyes)* loup *m*; **to put on a m.** mettre un masque, se masquer; **with the m. off** à visage découvert; *Fig* **a m. of happiness/confidence** une apparence de bonheur/ confiance trompeuse; *Fig* **the m. had slipped** le masque était tombé; *Fig* **to throw off** *or* **drop the m.** lever le masque, se démasquer **2** *(moulded likeness) (of face)* moulage *m*, masque *m* **3** *Phot* cache *m*, masque *m*
VT 1 *(person)* masquer **2** *(conceal) (one's feelings, thoughts)* cacher, dissimuler, déguiser; *(taste, smell)* dissimuler, masquer; **an apparent cheerfulness masked her deep pessimism** une gaieté apparente masquait son profond pessimisme **3** *Mil etc (battery, beam of light etc)* masquer **4** *Phot* cacher, masquer

masked [ma:skt] **ADJ** *(man, robber, ball)* masqué
▸▸*Mil* **m. battery** batterie *f* masquée; *Comput* **m. ROM** mémoire *f* morte masquée

masking ['mɑːskɪŋ] N
▸▸m. **tape** ruban *m* adhésif *(utilisé pour masquer une surface que l'on ne veut pas peindre)*

masochism ['mæsəkɪz(ə)m] N masochisme *m*

masochist ['mæsəkɪst] N, ADJ masochiste *mf*

masochistic [mæsə'kɪstɪk] ADJ masochiste

mason ['meɪs(ə)n] N **1** maçon *m* **2 M.** *(freemason)* franc-maçon *m, pl* francs-maçons

Masonic [mə'sɒnɪk] ADJ (franc-)maçonnique, des francs-maçons, de la franc-maçonnerie
▸▸**M. lodge** loge *f* maçonnique

masonry ['meɪsənrɪ] N **1** maçonnerie *f* **2 M.** *(freemasonry)* franc-maçonnerie *f*
▸▸m. **drill** foret *m* de maçonnerie

masquerade [mæskə'reɪd] N mascarade *f*
VI **to m. as sb** se faire passer pour qn; **dictatorship masquerading as democracy** dictature qui essaie de se faire passer pour une démocratie

Mass¹ [mæs] N *Rel, Mus* messe *f*; **M. for the dead** messe de requiem, messe des morts; **to celebrate/say M.** célébrer/dire la messe; **to go to M.** aller à la messe

Mass² *abbr* **Massachusetts**

mass [mæs] N **1** *(large number) (of people)* foule *f*, multitude *f*, *Fam* masse *f*, *(of objects, letters)* grande quantité *f*, multitude, *Fam* masse; *Fam* **I've masses (of things) to do** j'ai un tas *ou* des masses de choses à faire; **we've masses of room** nous avons beaucoup de place; **he was a m. of bruises** il était entièrement couvert de bleus; **the (great) m. of the people** la plus grande partie *ou* la majorité de la population; **the masses** les masses *fpl*, le grand public **2** *(body) Phys* masse *f*
VT *(troops etc)* rassembler
VI *(of troops)* se masser; *(of clouds)* s'amonceler
▸▸m. **circulation** grande diffusion *f*, diffusion de masse; **m. communication** communication *f* de masse; **m. consumption** consommation *f* de masse; **m. culture** culture *f* de masse, grande distribution; **m. grave** charnier *m*; **m. hysteria** hystérie *f* collective; **m. market** marché *m* de masse; **m. marketing** marketing *m* de grande consommation, marketing de masse; **m. media** mass media *mpl*; **m. meeting** grand rassemblement *m*; **m. murder** tuerie *f*, **m. murderer** *(serial killer)* tueur, -euse en série; *(tyrant, dictator)* boucher *m*; *Chem* **m. number** nombre *m* de masse; **m. production** fabrication *f* ou production *f* en série; **it goes into m. production next week** la production en série commence la semaine prochaine; **m. protest** protestation *f* en masse; *Comput* **m. storage** mémoire *f* de masse; **m. tourism** tourisme *m* de masse; **m. unemployment** chômage *m* sur une grande échelle

massacre ['mæsəkər] N massacre *m*, tuerie *f*, *Sport etc Fam* **it was a m.** cela a été un massacre *ou* une hécatombe
VT *also Fig* massacrer; *Sport etc Fam* **they were massacred** ils se sont fait massacrer *ou* démolir

massage ['mæsɑːʒam] N massage *m*
VT **1** *(body, scalp)* masser **2** *Fig (manipulate)* **to m. the figures** manipuler *ou* trafiquer les chiffres
▸▸m. **oil** huile *f* de massage; **m. parlour** salon *m* de massage

masseur [mæ'sɜːr] N masseur *m*

masseuse [mæ'sɜːz] N masseuse *f*

massif ['mæsiːf] N *Geog* massif *m*

massive ['mæsɪv] ADJ énorme; *(heart attack,*

stroke) foudroyant; **invasion on a m. scale** invasion massive; **the m. scale of the Mafia's operations** l'échelle massive sur laquelle la Mafia opère; *Pharm etc* **m. dose** dose massive
N *Br Sl (gang)* bande *f*, **the Brighton m.** la bande de Brighton

massively ['mæsɪvlɪ] ADV massivement; *(strong, fat)* extrêmement; **to invest m. in sth** investir massivement dans qch

mass-market ADJ *(products)* de grande consommation

mass-produce VT *Ind* fabriquer en série

mass-produced [-prə'djuːst] ADJ *Ind* produit en série

mast [mɑːst] N **1** *Naut* mât *m*; **the masts** les mâts, la mâture; **to sail before the m.** servir comme simple matelot **2** *Radio, TV, Tel* pylône *m*

mastectomy [mæs'tektəmɪ] N *Surg* mastectomie *f*

-masted ['mɑːstɪd] SUFF *Naut* **three/four/etc-m.** à trois/quatre/*etc* mâts

master ['mɑːstər] N **1** *(man in charge, employer, owner of pet)* maître *m*; *Naut (of merchant ship)* capitaine *m*, commandant *m*; *Univ (esp at Oxford and Cambridge)* directeur *m*, principal *m* *(de certains collèges universitaires)*; **the m. of the house** le maître de (la) maison; **to be m. in one's own house** être maître chez soi; **to be one's own m.** être son (propre) maître; **to be m. of the situation** être maître de la situation; *Prov* **like m. like man** tel maître, tel valet **2** *(skilled person)* maître *m*; **to be a m. of one's art** posséder son art en maître; **she was a m. of the sharp one-liner** elle avait le don de la petite phrase qui tue; **to be a m. of one's brief** connaître son sujet à fond; *Art* **old m.** *(painter)* maître; *(painting)* tableau *m* de maître; **m. carpenter/mason** maître charpentier/maçon **3** *(instructor)* maître *m*; **fencing/dancing m.** maître d'escrime/de danse **4** *esp Br Sch (in primary school)* maître *m*, instituteur *m*; *(in secondary school)* professeur *m*; **French/Geography m.** professeur de français/géographie **5** *Old-fashioned (form of address to small boys)* **M. David Thomas** Monsieur David Thomas; **M. David** *(said by servant)* Monsieur David **6** *Mus (record) (disque m)* original *m*
VT *(person)* se rendre maître/maîtresse de; *(horse, emotions, situation, subject)* maîtriser; *(difficulty)* surmonter, triompher de; **to have mastered a subject** posséder un sujet à fond; **I never really mastered the language** je n'ai jamais eu une maîtrise parfaite de la langue; **to have mastered the violin** être un/une violoniste accompli(e); **to m. one's brief** dominer son sujet
▸▸*Univ* **M. of Arts** ≃ maître ès lettres; **m. bedroom** chambre *f* principale; **m. of ceremonies** *(at reception)* maître des cérémonies; *(on TV show)* présentateur *m*; **m. class** cours *m* de maître; *Mus* master class *m*; *Radio, TV* **m. control room** régie *f* centrale; **m. copy** original *m*; *Comput* **m. disk** disque *m* maître; *Comput* **m. file** fichier *m* principal *ou* maître; **M. of hounds** maître d'équipage, grand veneur *m*; **m. key** passe-partout *m inv*; *Naut* **m. mariner** capitaine *m*; *TV* **m. monitor** récepteur *m* de contrôle final; **m. plan** stratégie *f* globale; **m. race** race *f* supérieure; *Mus* **m. record** *(disque m)* original *m*; *Univ* **M. of Science** ≃ maître ès sciences; *Am Mil* **m. sergeant** ≃ sergent-chef *m, pl* sergents-chefs; *Cin, TV* **m. shot** plan *m* de coupe; **m. soundtrack** mixage *m* magnétique final; *Elec* **m. switch** commutateur *m* ou disjoncteur *m* principal; **m. tape** bande *f* originale;

TV cassette *f* prête à diffuser; *Com* **m. of works** maître d'œuvre

-master ['mɑːstər] SUFF *Naut* **three/four/etc-m.** à trois/quatre-mâts/*etc*

masterbrand ['mɑːstəbrænd] N *Mktg* marque *f* vedette

Mastercard® ['mɑːstəkɑːd] N carte *f* Mastercard®

masterful ['mɑːstəfʊl] ADJ *(tone, voice, performance)* magistral, -aux; **she was wrapped in his m. arms** il l'enveloppait de ses bras puissants; **you're so m.!** quel homme/quelle femme!

masterfully ['mɑːstəfʊlɪ] ADV *(to perform)* magistralement; **he said m.** dit-il d'un ton magistral

masterly ['mɑːstəlɪ] ADJ magistral, -aux, de maître; **m. stroke** coup *m* de maître; **in a m. manner** de main de maître

mastermind ['mɑːstəmaɪnd] N esprit *m* supérieur; *(of undertaking etc)* cerveau *m*; **she was the m. behind the robbery** c'était elle le cerveau du vol
VT *(project etc)* diriger, organiser; *(plot etc)* tramer

masterpiece ['mɑːstəpiːs] N chef-d'œuvre *m, pl* chefs-d'œuvre

master/slave system N système *m* maître/esclave

masterstroke ['mɑːstəstrəʊk] N coup *m* de maître

mastery ['mɑːstərɪ] N **1** *(control)* contrôle *m* *(of de)*, domination *f* *(over sur)* **2** *(knowledge) (of subject)* maîtrise *f*

masthead ['mɑːsthed] N *Naut* tête *f* ou ton *m* de mât, haut *m* du mât; *(of newspaper)* ours *m*
▸▸*Naut* **m. light** feu *m* de tête de mât

mastic ['mæstɪk] N *(resin, cement)* mastic *m*

masticate ['mæstɪkeɪt] VT **1** *(food)* mâcher, mastiquer **2** *Ind (rubber etc)* triturer, malaxer

mastiff ['mæstɪf] N *(dog)* mastiff *m*

mastitis [mæs'taɪtɪs] N *Med* mastite *f*

mastodon ['mæstədɒn] N mastodonte *m*

mastoid ['mæstɔɪd] N *Anat (process)* mastoïde *f*, *Med Fam* **mastoids** mastoïdite *f*
▸▸*Anat* **m. process** apophyse *f* mastoïde

masturbate ['mæstəbeɪt] VI se masturber
VT masturber

masturbation [mæstə'beɪʃən] N masturbation *f*, *esp Med* onanisme *m*

masturbatory [mæstə'beɪtərɪ] ADJ masturbatoire, onaniste

mat¹ [mæt] N *(on floor etc) (of straw, rushes)* natte *f*, *(of wool etc)* (petit) tapis *m*, carpette *f*, *(at entrance)* paillasson *m*, essuie-pieds *m inv*; *Sport (in wrestling)* tapis; **(table) m.** *(for hot dish)* dessous-de-plat *m inv*; *(for vase, ornament)* napperon *m*; **(table or place) m.** *(for plates)* set *m* de table; *Fig Fam* **to be on the m.** *(be in trouble)* être sur la sellette
VT **(-tt-)** *(hair etc)* emmêler
VI *(of hair, fibres etc)* s'emmêler, se coller ensemble

mat² ADJ *(colour, paint, paper)* mat

matador ['mætədɔːr] N matador *m*

[mætʃ] N **1** *(of person)* égal, -ale; **to meet one's m.** trouver son maître; **to be more than a m. for sb** être trop fort pour qn; **they were no m. for the other team** ils n'étaient pas à la hauteur de l'autre équipe; **you're no m. for her** tu n'es pas à sa hauteur; **to be a bad/good m.** *(of things)* aller mal/bien ensemble, être mal/bien assortis; **to find a m. for a wallpaper** *(find curtains etc in suitable colour)* assortir un papier peint; *(find the same)* réassortir un papier peint; **perfect m. of colours** assortiment parfait de couleurs

2 *Sport (of football, rugby, cricket, baseball)* match *m*; *(of golf)* partie *f*; *(of tennis)* match, partie; *(swimming)* compétition *f*
3 *(marriage)* mariage *m*; **to make a good m.** faire un bon mariage; **he's a good m.** c'est un bon *ou* un excellent parti
vt *(person)* égaler, être l'égal de, rivaliser avec; *(colours, gloves, stockings)* assortir; **his jacket doesn't m. his trousers** sa veste ne va pas avec son pantalon; **the music didn't m. her mood** la musique ne correspondait pas à son humeur; **we can't m. their prices** nous ne pouvons pas rivaliser avec leurs prix; **will their deeds m. their words?** est-ce que leurs actes seront à la hauteur de leurs paroles?; **there's nobody to m. him** il n'a pas son pareil; **to m. sb against sb** opposer qn à qn; *Sport* **Scotland has been matched against Brazil** l'Écosse rencontrera le Brésil; **evenly matched** de force égale, bien assortis; **we will try to m. this material for you** *(find something similar to)* nous essayerons de trouver un tissu assorti; **a well-matched couple** un couple bien assorti; **I need a new hat to m. my suit** j'ai besoin d'un nouveau chapeau qui aille avec mon tailleur; **m. the names to the faces** *(in competition)* trouvez les noms correspondant aux visages
vi *(of colours etc) (go well together)* aller (bien) ensemble, être bien assortis; *(be exactly the same)* être exactement les mêmes; *(of fingerprints, descriptions etc)* correspondre; **the carpet doesn't m.** la moquette n'est pas assortie au reste; **I need some shoes to m.** il me faut des chaussures assorties *ou* pour aller avec
▸▸ *Golf* **m. play** match-play *m*, *pl* match-plays, partie *f* par trous; *Tennis* **m. point** balle *f* de match
▸ **match up vt SEP** *(combine)* faire correspondre; **to m. up the names with the faces** faire correspondre les noms et les visages; **to m. up two colours** harmoniser *ou* assortir deux couleurs; **I want to m. up this colour** *(find exact match)* j'aimerais trouver exactement la même couleur
vi *(of fingerprints etc)* correspondre; *(of colours etc) (go well together)* aller (bien) ensemble, être bien assortis; *(be exactly the same)* être exactement les mêmes; **the descriptions didn't m. up** les descriptions ne correspondaient pas; **the suit jacket and trousers don't m. up** la veste et le pantalon ne vont pas ensemble
▸ **match up to vt INSEP to m. up to sb's expectations** répondre aux espérances *ou* à l'attente de qn

---

match² **N** *(for lighting)* allumette *f*; **to put a m. to sth** mettre (le) feu à qch
matchbox ['mætʃbɒks] **N** boîte *f* d'allumettes
matched [mætʃt] **ADJ**
▸▸ *St Exch* **m. bargain** mariage *m*
matching ['mætʃɪŋ] **ADJ** *(hat, colours etc)* assorti; **these pictures are a m. pair** ces tableaux se font pendant
matchless ['mætʃlɪs] **ADJ** incomparable, sans égal, -aux, sans pareil
matchmaker ['mætʃmeɪkər] **N** faiseur, -euse de mariages, marieur, -euse
matchmaking ['mætʃmeɪkɪŋ] **N** entremise *f*
matchstick ['mætʃstɪk] **N** allumette *f*; **to have m. legs** avoir des jambes comme des allumettes; **m. man** *or* **figure** *(drawing)* bonhomme *m* dessiné avec des bâtons
matchwood ['mætʃwʊd] **N** bois *m* d'allumettes; **smashed** *or* **reduced to m.** réduit en miettes
mate¹ [meɪt] **N 1** *(sexual partner) (animal) (male)* mâle *m*; *(female)* femelle *f*; *Fam Hum (husband)* mari *m*; *(wife)* femme *f* **2** *Br Fam*

(friend) (male) copain *m*, pote *m*; *(female)* copine *f*; **thanks, m.** *(to friend)* merci, mon pote; *(to stranger)* merci, m'sieur; **watch where you're going, m.!** eh mec, regarde où tu vas! **3** *(assistant)* assistant, -ante, aide *mf*; **plumber's m.** aide plombier **4** *Naut (on merchant vessel)* officier *m*; **first** *or* **chief m.** second *m*; **second m.** lieutenant *m* **5** *Tech (part)* pièce *f* qui s'accouple *(avec une autre)*; pièce qui s'emboîte *(dans une autre)*
vt *(animals, birds)* accoupler; *Old-fashioned* marier, unir *(sb with sb* qn à qn)
vi *(of birds, animals)* s'accoupler
mate² *Chess* **N** mat *m*
vt *(king)* mettre échec et mat, mater
mater ['meɪtər] **N** *Old-fashioned Br Fam* **(the)** ma mère, maman *f*
material [mə'tɪərɪəl] **N 1** *(substance)* matière *f*, substance *f*; *(for building)* matériau *m*; **raw material(s)** matière(s) première(s); **glass is a brittle m.** le verre est un matériau cassant; **he isn't officer m.** il n'a pas l'étoffe *ou* l'envergure d'un officier **2** *(equipment for specific activity)* matériel *m*; **photographic materials** matériel de photographie **3** *(cloth)* tissu *m*, étoffe *f*; **dress m.** tissu pour robes **4** *(information for a book etc)* matériaux *mpl*; **the m. for a play** les matériaux d'une pièce **5** *(produced by writer, singer etc)* **this singer writes her own m.** cette chanteuse écrit ses propres textes
ADJ 1 *(point of view etc)* matérialiste; *(comfort, interests)*, *Phil, Phys, Rel* matériel; **to have enough for one's m. comfort** *or* **needs** avoir de quoi vivre matériellement **2** *(important)* important, essentiel (**to** pour) **3** *Law (fact, testimony)* pertinent
▸▸ **m. possessions** biens *mpl* matériels; *Law* **m. witness** témoin *m* de fait
materialism [mə'tɪərɪəlɪz(ə)m] **N** matérialisme *m*
materialist [mə'tɪərɪəlɪst] **ADJ, N** matérialiste *mf*
materialistic [mətɪərɪə'lɪstɪk] **ADJ** matérialiste; *(pleasures, mind etc)* matériel
materialize [mə'tɪərɪəlaɪz] **vi** *(of event)* se réaliser; *(of plans)* aboutir, se réaliser; *(of psychic ectoplasm)* apparaître, prendre forme; **the promised computers never materialized** les ordinateurs promis ne se sont jamais matérialisés; **the job he promised me never materialized** le travail qu'il m'avait promis ne s'est jamais matérialisé; **the project failed to m.** le projet n'a jamais abouti; **she promised to lend me a thousand pounds but the money never materialized** elle avait promis de me prêter mille livres mais je n'en ai jamais vu la couleur
materially [mə'tɪərɪəlɪ] **ADV 1** *Phil, Phys, Rel* matériellement; **to benefit m. from sth** bénéficier matériellement de qch **2** *(appreciably)* sensiblement, d'une manière appréciable; **m. different/better** sensiblement différent/meilleur
materiel, matériel [mətɪərɪ'el] **N** *Mil* matériel *m*
maternal [mə'tɜːn(ə)l] **ADJ** maternel
maternally [mə'tɜːn(ə)lɪ] **ADV** maternellement
maternity [mə'tɜːnɪtɪ] **N** maternité *f*
▸▸ **m. benefit** ≃ allocations *fpl* de maternité; **m. dress** robe *f* de grossesse; **m. hospital** maternité; **m. leave** congé *m* (de) maternité; **m. ward** maternité
matey ['meɪtɪ] **ADJ** *Br Fam* copain-copain; **to be m.** *(of people)* être à tu et à toi, être copains; **she's very m. all of a sudden** elle est bien aimable tout d'un coup
math [mæθ] **N** *Am Fam* = **maths**
mathematical [mæθ(ə)'mætɪk(ə)l] **ADJ** *(science, calculation)* mathématique; *(know-*

ledge) en mathématiques; **he's a m. genius** c'est un mathématicien de génie; **victory for the party is now a m. impossibility** mathématiquement, le parti ne peut pas gagner; **I haven't got a m. mind** je n'ai pas l'esprit mathématique
mathematically [mæθ(ə)'mætɪklɪ] **ADV** mathématiquement
mathematician [mæθ(ə)mə'tɪʃən] **N** mathématicien, -ienne
mathematics [mæθ(ə)'mætɪks] **N** VOIR GRAMMAIRE A10 **1** *(subject)* mathématiques *fpl*; **pure/applied m.** mathématiques pures/ appliquées; **m. lesson/teacher** cours *m*/professeur *m* de mathématiques **2** *(calculations)* calculs *mpl*
maths [mæθs] **NPL** *Br Fam* math(s) *fpl*; **m. lesson/teacher** cours *m*/professeur *m* de maths
▸▸ *Comput* **m. co-processor** coprocesseur *m* mathématique *ou* arithmétique
matinée ['mætɪneɪ] **N** *Theat, Cin* matinée *f*
▸▸ *Br* **m. coat** veste *f* (de bébé); *Cin Old-fashioned* **m. idol** = acteur idolâtré par les femmes surtout dans les années 30 ou 40; *Theat, Cin* **m. performance** matinée
matiness ['meɪtɪnɪs] **N** *Br Fam* camaraderie *f*
mating ['meɪtɪŋ] **N** *(of animals, birds)* accouplement *m*
▸▸ **m. call** appel *m* du mâle/de la femelle; **m. instinct** instinct *m* sexuel; **m. ritual** parade *f* nuptiale; **the m. season** la saison des amours
matins ['mætɪnz] **NPL** *Cathol* matines *fpl*; *(in Church of England)* office *m* du matin
matriarch ['meɪtrɪɑːk] **N** femme *f* chef de tribu *ou* de famille
matriarchal ['meɪtrɪɑːk(ə)l] **ADJ** matriarcal, -aux
matriarchy ['meɪtrɪɑːkɪ] **N** matriarcat *m*
matric [mə'trɪk] **N** *Arch Br Fam* = **matriculation**
matricide ['meɪtrɪsaɪd, 'mæ-] **N 1** *(person)* matricide *mf* **2** *(crime)* matricide *m*
matriculate [mə'trɪkjʊleɪt] **vi 1** *(of student)* s'inscrire, se faire inscrire **2** *Br Formerly (pass exam etc)* être reçu à l'examen d'entrée à l'université
matriculation [mətrɪkjʊ'leɪʃən] **N** *Sch* **1** *(enrolment)* inscription *f (comme étudiant)* **2** *Br Formerly (exam)* examen *m* de fin d'études *(pour entrer à l'université)*
▸▸ **m. fee** frais *mpl* d'inscription
matrimonial [mætrɪ'məʊnɪəl] **ADJ** *esp Fml* matrimonial, -aux
matrimony ['mætrɪmənɪ] **N** *esp Fml* mariage *m*; *Rel* **joined in holy m.** unis par les liens sacrés du mariage
matrix, pl matrixes, matrices ['meɪtrɪks, -ɪksɪz, -ɪsiːz] **N 1** *Math etc* matrice *f*; *Fig (of forces, relations etc)* configuration *f* **2** *Geol, Miner* matrice *f*, gangue *f*, gaine *f* **3** *Metal, Typ etc* matrice *f*, moule *m*; *Art, Cer (of plaster moulds etc)* mère *f*
▸▸ *Comput* **m. printer** imprimante *f* matricielle
matron ['meɪtrən] **N 1** *(woman)* matrone *f* **2** *(of institution, boarding school)* intendante *f*; *Old-fashioned (of hospital)* infirmière *f* en chef
▸▸ **m. of honour** *(at wedding)* dame *f* d'honneur
matronly ['meɪtrənlɪ] **ADJ** de matrone
matt [mæt] **ADJ** = **mat²**
matte [mæt] **N** *Cin, TV* cache *m*
matted ['mætɪd] **ADJ** *(cloth)* feutré; *(hair)* emmêlé; **his hair was m. with blood** il avait du sang séché dans les cheveux

MATTER ['mætər]

> **N** matière **1, 7** ▪ affaire **2, 3**
> ▪ question **2** ▪ importer **5**
> **VI** importer

N 1 *(substance)* matière *f*; *Phil etc* form and m. la forme et la matière; **organic/inorganic m.** la matière organique/inorganique
2 *(affair)* affaire *f*, chose *f*; **it's a m. of the utmost importance** c'est une affaire de la plus haute importance; **the m. is closed** le dossier est clos; **let's come back to the m. in hand** revenons à ce qui nous occupe *ou Fam* à nos moutons; **it's an easy/no easy m.** c'est/ce n'est pas facile; **it's no great m.** ce n'est pas grand-chose; **it's no laughing m.** il n'y a pas de quoi rire; **it is a m. for regret** c'est regrettable; **it's a m. for congratulations** cela mérite des félicitations; **that's quite another m.** cela, c'est tout autre chose; **to do sth as a m. of course** faire qch systématiquement; **that's a m. of opinion/taste** c'est une question d'opinion/de goût; **that's a m. for the courts to decide** sur ce point, c'est à la justice de trancher; **it's simply a m. of time** *(is inevitable)* cela arrivera tôt ou tard; *(is a question of time only)* c'est une simple question de temps; **it'll only be a m. of days before they find out** ce n'est qu'une question de jours avant qu'ils découvrent la vérité; **it's just a m. of knowing which button to press** il s'agit juste de savoir sur quel bouton appuyer; **it's just a m. of replacing a few worn-out parts** il suffit de remplacer quelques pièces usées; **it's just a m. of £100** c'est l'affaire de 100 livres; *Iron* **there's the small m. of that money you owe me** il y a cette question de la petite somme que vous me devez; **within a m. of hours** en quelques heures; **for that m.** d'ailleurs; **and so am I for that m.** moi aussi d'ailleurs; **he isn't very well known in London or anywhere else for that m.** il n'est pas très connu à Londres, et nulle part ailleurs en fait; **it's a m. of fact** c'est un fait; **as a m. of fact** en fait
3 as matters stand au point où en sont les choses; **her remarks made matters worse** ses remarques n'ont fait qu'aggraver les choses; **to make matters worse, it had started to rain** pour tout arranger, il s'était mis à pleuvoir; **matters of the heart** affaires *fpl* de cœur *ou* sentimentales; **in matters of religion** en ce qui concerne la religion; **business matters** affaires; **money matters** affaires d'argent
4 *(problem)* **what's the m.?** qu'est-ce qu'il y a?, qu'y a-t-il?; **what's the m. with you?** qu'est-ce que vous avez?, qu'avez-vous?; **what's the m. with the TV?** qu'est-ce qu'elle a, la télé?; **what's the m. with asking her out to the movies?** je ne vois pas ce qu'il y a de mal à lui demander si elle veut aller au cinéma; **I don't know what's the m. with me** je ne sais pas ce que j'ai; **there's something the m.** il y a quelque chose (qui ne va pas), il se passe quelque chose; **there's something the m. with his throat** il a quelque chose à la gorge; **there's nothing the m. with you/the TV** tu n'as/la télé n'a rien; **he went on talking as if nothing was the m.** il continua de parler comme si de rien n'était
5 no m.! n'importe!, peu importe!; **no m. what he does/says** quoi qu'il fasse/dise; **no m. how** par n'importe quel moyen; **no m. how hard I pushed against the door, it wouldn't open** j'avais beau pousser la porte de toutes mes forces, elle ne s'ouvrait pas; **no m. what** quoi qu'il arrive; **no m. when** à n'importe quel moment; **no m. when you ...** peu importe quand tu ...; **no m. who** qui que ce soit; **no m. who gave it to you** peu importe qui te l'a donné; **no m. where** où que ce soit

6 *Med (pus)* pus *m*
7 *Typ* matière *f*, copie *f*
VI avoir de l'importance, être important (**to** pour), *Fml* importer (**to** à); **nothing matters much to him any more since his wife died** plus rien n'a d'importance pour lui depuis la mort de sa femme; **what really matters is that ...** ce qui est vraiment important, c'est que ...; **that is what matters most** c'est le plus important; **it doesn't m.** ce n'est pas important, cela ne fait rien, peu importe; **it doesn't m. how much it costs** peu importe le prix; **it doesn't m. – perhaps not to you, but it matters to me** ce n'est pas important – pour toi, peut-être, mais pour moi, c'est important; **it doesn't m. a bit** cela n'a pas la moindre importance; **it doesn't m. to her what people think** elle se moque de ce que pensent les gens; **what does it m. to you?** qu'est-ce que cela peut bien vous faire?; **nothing else matters** tout le reste est sans importance; **these things m.** ces choses-là comptent; **you need to identify the people who m. in the company** il faut que tu saches qui compte dans l'entreprise

Matterhorn (the) [ðə'mætəhɔːn] **N** le (Mont) Cervin
matter-of-fact **ADJ** *(person, manner, statement etc)* terre-à-terre, prosaïque; **to say sth in a m. tone** dire qch sur un ton neutre
Matthew ['mæθjuː] **N** Mat(t)hieu *m*
matting ['mætɪŋ] **N** *(material)* natte(s) *f(pl)*, paillassons *mpl*
mattins ['mætɪnz] **NPL** = **matins**
mattock ['mætək] **N** *Agr (tool)* hoyau *m*, pioche *f*
mattress ['mætrɪs] **N** matelas *m*; **inflatable** *or* **air m.** matelas pneumatique
maturation [mætjʊ'reɪʃən] **N** *(of fruit, abscess etc)* maturation *f*; *(of wine, whisky)* vieillissement *m*; *(of intelligence etc)* développement *m*
mature [mə'tjʊər] **ADJ 1** *(person, fruit)* mûr; *(animal)* adulte; *Psy (intelligence)* qui dénote beaucoup de maturité; **the more m. trees are slower to come into leaf** les arbres les plus vieux ont des feuilles plus tard que les autres; **to be m. for one's age** *or* **years** être mûr pour son âge; **of m. years** *(person)* d'âge mûr; *Br* **would suit a m. person** *(in job advertisement)* conviendrait à une personne d'âge mûr; **after m. consideration** après mûre réflexion; **m. cheese** fromage *m* fait **2** *Fin (bill)* échu
VT the cheese/wine is matured for five years before it's sold le fromage/vin vieillit pendant cinq ans avant d'être vendu
VI 1 *(of plant)* mûrir; *(of wine)* vieillir; *(of person)* devenir plus mûr, acquérir de la maturité; **she had matured into a sophisticated young woman** elle était devenue une jeune femme sophistiquée; **to let a plan m.** laisser mûrir un projet; **his plans had not yet matured** ses projets n'étaient pas encore mûris *ou* mûrs **2** *Fin (of bill)* échoir, arriver à échéance
▸▸ *Fin* **m. economy** économie *f* en pleine maturité; *Br Univ* **m. student** = étudiant *m* plus âgé que la moyenne ou qui entreprend des études sur le tard, *Can* étudiant, -ante adulte
maturely [mə'tjʊəlɪ] **ADV** *(to decide)* de façon raisonnable; **to behave m.** se comporter en adulte
maturity [mə'tjʊərɪtɪ] **N 1** *(of fruit, wine, cheese etc)* maturité *f*; **to come to** *or* **reach m.** arriver à maturité; **the years of m.** *(of person)* l'âge *m* mûr; **the novels of her m.** les romans qu'elle a écrits à l'âge mûr **2** *Fin* **(date of)** m. *(of bill)* échéance *f*; **payable at m.** payable à l'échéance

▸▸ *Fin* **m. date** date *f* d'échéance; *Fin* **m. value** valeur *f* à l'échéance
maudlin ['mɔːdlɪn] **ADJ** larmoyant, pleurard; *(drunk)* dans un état d'ivresse larmoyante; **m. sentimentality** sentimentalité larmoyante; **to become m.** se mettre à larmoyer *ou* à pleurnicher
maul [mɔːl] **N** *Rugby* maul *m*
VT 1 *(of lion etc)* blesser; *(more seriously)* mutiler; *Fig (author, book, play)* éreinter, tailler en pièces **2** *(grope) (woman)* tripoter
mauling ['mɔːlɪŋ] **N to get a m.** *(from a lion etc)* être blessé; *(more seriously)* être mutilé; *Fam (by enemy troops, opposing team)* être battu à plates coutures, recevoir une raclée; *(from critics)* se faire éreinter
maunder ['mɔːndər] **VI 1** *(in speech)* **to m. (on)** radoter, rabâcher **2** *(dawdle)* **to m. (along)** traîner, errer
Maundy ['mɔːndɪ] **N**
▸▸ *Br* **M. money** = pièces *fpl* de monnaie spéciales offertes par le souverain britannique à certaines personnes âgées le jour du jeudi saint; *Rel* **M. Thursday** jeudi *m* saint
Mauritania [mɒrɪ'teɪnɪə] **N** Mauritanie *f*
Mauritanian [mɒrɪ'teɪnɪən] **N** Mauritanien, -ienne
ADJ mauritanien
Mauritian [mə'rɪʃən] **ADJ** mauricien
N Mauricien, -ienne
Mauritius [mə'rɪʃəs] **N** l'île *f* Maurice
mausoleum [mɔːsə'liːəm] **N** mausolée *m*
mauve [məʊv] **ADJ, N** *(colour)* mauve *m*
maverick ['mævərɪk] **N 1** *(unorthodox person)* non-conformiste *mf*, franc-tireur *m*, *pl* francs-tireurs; **m. MP/salesman** député/vendeur qui fait les choses à sa façon **2** *Am (stray steer)* bouvillon *m* errant sans marque de propriétaire
maw [mɔː] **N 1** *(stomach) (of ruminant)* quatrième poche *f* de l'estomac; *(of bird)* jabot *m*; *Fam (of person)* panse *f* **2** *(mouth) (of animal, fish)* gueule *f*
mawkish ['mɔːkɪʃ] **ADJ** *Pej (person)* d'une sensiblerie outrée, mièvre; *(novel etc)* d'une sentimentalité exagérée, mièvre
mawkishness ['mɔːkɪʃnɪs] **N** *Pej (of person)* sensiblerie *f* outrée, mièvrerie *f*; *(of novel etc)* sentimentalité *f* exagérée, mièvrerie
max [mæks] **N** *(abbr* **maximum**) max *m*; *Am Fam* **to the m.** *(totally)* un max; **did you have a good time? – to the m.!** tu t'es bien amusé? – vachement bien!, un max!
ADV *Fam (at the most)* maxi; **it'll take three days m.** ça prendra trois jours maxi
VT *Am Fam* **to m. an exam** = obtenir le maximum de points à un examen
▸ **max out** **VI** *Fam Am* **to m. out on chocolate** se gaver de chocolat; **to m. out on booze** picoler un max
VT SEP *Am Fam* **to m. out one's credit card** dépenser le maximum autorisé avec sa carte de crédit
maxed [mækst] **ADJ** *Am Fam* **1** *(extremely drunk)* bourré comme un coing, pété à mort **2 to be m. out on one's credit card** avoir dépensé le maximum autorisé avec sa carte de crédit; **to be m. out on chocolate/sci-fi movies** avoir fait une overdose de chocolat/de films de science-fiction
maxi ['mæksɪ] *Fam* **ADJ** *(skirt, coat)* maxi *inv*
N *(skirt)* maxi *f*; *(coat)* maxi *m*
maxim ['mæksɪm] **N** maxime *f*
maximal ['mæksɪməl] **ADJ** *Fml* maximal, -aux
maximization [mæksɪmaɪ'zeɪʃən] **N** maximalisation *f*, maximisation *f*
maximize ['mæksɪmaɪz] **VT** maximiser, maximaliser

maximum, pl **maxima** ['mæksɪməm, -ə] N maximum m, -ums, -a; **at the m.** au (grand) maximum; **to reach one's m.** plafonner
ADJ maximum, maximal, -aux; **we guarantee m. security** nous garantissons une sécurité maximum
▸▸**m. load** charge f maximale ou limite; **m. security prison** prison f de haute sécurité; **m. security unit** quartier m de haute sécurité; **m. speed** (highest possible) vitesse f maximale ou maximum; (highest permitted) vitesse limite; **m. temperatures** températures fpl maximales

May [meɪ] N VOIR GRAMMAIRE A81–2; B60–2 mai m; **in M.** en mai, au mois de mai; **(on) the first/the seventh of M.** le premier/le sept mai
▸▸Entom **M. beetle, M. bug** hanneton m; **M. Day** le Premier mai; **M. Day parade** défilé m du Premier mai; **M. queen** = reine f des festivités du Premier mai

MAY[1] [meɪ] V AUX VOIR GRAMMAIRE A59–60; B39–40 (3rd person sing **may**; pt, cond **might** [maɪt], no pres or past participle) **1** (expressing possibility) **he m.** or **might return at any moment** il peut ou pourrait revenir d'un moment à l'autre; **she m.** or **might not be hungry** elle n'a peut-être pas faim, il se peut qu'elle n'ait pas faim; **we m. remind ourselves at this point that …** il n'est pas inutile de rappeler ici que …; **that m. or m. not be true** cela est peut-être vrai ou peut-être pas; **he m. or might have lost it** peut-être qu'il l'a perdu, il se peut qu'il l'ait perdu; **Queen Anne m. have stayed here** il se peut que la reine Anne ait séjourné ici; **you m. or might see her if you stay another hour** vous la verrez peut-être si vous restez encore une heure; **something I said m. or might have offended him** j'ai peut-être dit quelque chose qui l'a blessé; **it m. or might not be the fastest car in the world, but …** ce n'est peut-être pas la voiture la plus rapide du monde, mais …; **it m. or might be that …** il se peut ou se pourrait bien que + sub …; **you m. or might be wondering why I'm doing that** vous vous demandez peut-être pourquoi je fais cela; **you m. or might well ask!** je me le demande!; **you m. find it funny now, but wait till it's your turn!** tu trouves peut-être ça drôle maintenant mais tu verras quand ce sera ton tour!; **be that as it m. be,** but we can't afford it peut-être, mais nous ne pouvons pas nous le permettre; **but that's as it m. be, it's all history now** enfin, tout ça, c'est du passé; **whatever faults he m.** or **might have he is never dull** quels que soient ses défauts, il n'est jamais ennuyeux; **we m. or might as well stay where we are** autant rester où nous sommes **2** (asking or giving permission) **m. I come in?** est-ce que je peux entrer?; **m. I write to you? – of course you m.** pourrais-je vous écrire? – je vous en prie; **you m. go** vous pouvez partir; (at end of interview) vous pouvez disposer; **if I m. or might be allowed to express an opinion** si je puis me permettre; **if I m. or might say so** si j'ose dire; **m. I?** vous permettez? **3** esp Fml (be allowed to) **passengers m. take only one item of hand luggage** les passagers ne peuvent prendre ou ne sont autorisés à prendre qu'un bagage à main; **candidates m. consult a dictionary** l'utilisation d'un dictionnaire est autorisée pendant l'examen **4** Fml (in clauses expressing purpose, fear etc) **I only hope it m. last!** pourvu que cela ou ça dure!; **I fear you m. be right** j'ai bien peur que tu aies raison; **I pray that you m. be mistaken** j'espère que tu te trompes; **so that others m. sleep in peace** pour que les autres puissent dormir en paix

5 (expressing a wish) **m. she rest in peace!** qu'elle repose en paix!; **m. the best man win!** que le meilleur gagne!; **much good m. it do you!** grand bien vous fasse!

may[2] N (blossom) fleurs fpl d'aubépine
▸▸**m. blossom** fleurs d'aubépine; **m. tree** aubépine f

Maya ['maɪə] N **1** Maya mf **2** Ling maya m

Mayan ['maɪən] ADJ maya
N **1** Maya mf **2** Ling maya m

maybe ['meɪbi:] ADV peut-être; **m. so, but …** peut-être mais …; **m. not, but …** peut-être (pas) mais …; **m. yes, m. no** peut-être bien que oui, peut-être bien que non; **m. she won't accept** peut-être qu'elle n'acceptera pas, elle n'acceptera peut-être pas
N Fam **I don't want any maybes** c'est oui ou non!

Mayday ['meɪdeɪ] N (signal) mayday m, SOS m
INT (distress signal) mayday!
▸▸**M. signal** mayday, SOS

mayfly ['meɪflaɪ] N Entom éphémère m vulgaire

mayhem ['meɪhem] N **1** (chaos) confusion f totale, chaos m; (violent behaviour) grabuge m; **it was m.** c'était le chaos; **to create** or **cause m.** (to cause chaos) semer la pagaille; (to behave violently) faire du grabuge **2** Law (maiming) mutilation f, Am **to commit m. on sb** se livrer à des voies de fait contre qn

mayn't ['meɪənt] CONTR = **may not** see **may**[1]

mayo ['meɪəʊ] N esp Am Fam mayo f

mayonnaise [meɪə'neɪz] N mayonnaise f

mayor [meər] N maire m

mayoress ['meəres] N **1** (mayor) maire m, Old-fashioned mairesse f **2** esp Br (mayor's wife) mairesse f

maypole ['meɪpəʊl] N mât m

maze [meɪz] N labyrinthe m, dédale m; Fig (of streets, regulations etc) dédale

MB Comput (abbr **megabyte**) Mo

Mb Comput (abbr **megabit**) Mb

MBA [embi:'eɪ] N Univ (abbr **Master of Business Administration**) MBA m

MBE [embi:'i:] N Br (abbr **Member of the Order of the British Empire**) (award) Ordre m de l'Empire britannique; (person) membre m de l'Ordre de l'Empire britannique

MBI [embi:'aɪ] N Com (abbr **management buy-in**) apport m de gestion

MBO [embi:'əʊ] N Com **1** (abbr **management buy-out**) rachat m d'une entreprise par la direction **2** (abbr **management by objectives**) gestion f selon objectifs

MBS [embi:'es] N Fin (abbr **mortgage-backed security**) titre m garanti par des créances hypothécaires

MC [em'si:] N (abbr **Master of Ceremonies**) (at formal event) maître m des cérémonies; TV etc animateur m, présentateur m

m-commerce N m-commerce m

MCP [emsi:'pi:] N Fam (abbr **male chauvinist pig**) phallocrate m, macho m

MD [em'di:] N **1** Med (abbr **Doctor of Medicine**) docteur m en médecine **2** Com (abbr **Managing Director**) PDG m **3** (abbr **Mini-Disc®**) MiniDisc® m

Md abbr **Maryland**

MDF [emdi:'ef] N (abbr **medium-density fibreboard**) MDF m, panneaux mpl de fibres de moyenne densité

ME [em'i:] N Med (abbr **myalgic encephalomyelitis**) encéphalo-myélite f myalgique

Me abbr **Maine**

me [unstressed mɪ, stressed mi:] PERS PRON VOIR GRAMMAIRE A27; B18–19 **1** (unstressed) me; (before vowel sound) m'; (with preposition) moi; **he**

knows me il me connaît; **he told me so** il me l'a dit; **listen to me** écoutez-moi; **lend it (to) me** prêtez-le-moi; **she wrote me a letter** elle m'a écrit une lettre; **I'll take it with me** je le prendrai avec moi; **he's younger than me** il est plus jeune que moi; **no-one knows the real me** personne ne sait vraiment qui je suis VOIR GRAMMAIRE A43 **2** (stressed) moi; **you and me** vous et moi; **he was thinking of me** il pensait à moi; **that's for me** ça, c'est pour moi SEE GRAMMAR B20–1 **3** (complement of verb to be) **it's me!** c'est moi!; **is it just me or is there a smell of gas in here?** est-ce que je me fais des idées ou est-ce que ça sent le gaz?; **this jacket isn't really me** cette veste n'est pas vraiment mon style **4** (in int) **silly me! I've forgotten the address** ce que je peux être bête! j'ai oublié l'adresse; **clumsy me! I've spilled my drink!** ce que je peux être maladroit! j'ai renversé mon verre!

mead [mi:d] N (drink) hydromel m

meadow ['medəʊ] N pré m, prairie f
▸▸Bot **m. grass** pâturin m; Orn **m. pipit** pipit m des prés, farlouse f, Br Bot **m. saffron** safran m des prés, colchique m d'automne

meadowland ['medəʊlænd] N prairie(s) f(pl)

meadowsweet ['medəʊswi:t] N (plant) (spirée f) ulmaire f, reine f des prés

meagre, Am **meager** ['mi:gər] ADJ maigre

meagrely, Am **meagerly** ['mi:gəlɪ] ADV maigrement, piètrement; **they exist m.** ils arrivent tout juste à subsister

meal[1] [mi:l] N repas m; **I've had a huge m.** j'ai mangé comme quatre; **to eat between meals** manger entre les repas; **would you like some wine with your m.?** est-ce que vous prendrez du vin (avec votre repas)?; **in Spain the evening m. is later** en Espagne, on dîne plus tard; **to invite sb round for a m.** inviter qn à dîner; **enjoy your m.!** (waiter etc to customers) bon appétit!; Fig Fam **don't make a m. of it!** n'en fais pas toute une histoire!; **she always makes a m. of everything** il faut toujours qu'elle complique tout; Fam **the job is just a m. ticket** ce travail n'est qu'un gagne-pain; Fam **he's just a m. ticket to her** elle n'est avec lui que pour son argent
▸▸**m. tray** plateau m repas

meal[2] N (of oats, rye, corn etc) farine f

meals-on-wheels [mi:lzɒn'wi:lz] N Br Admin = service m de repas (servis) à domicile pour personnes âgées ou handicapées; **she gets m.** on lui livre ses repas à domicile

mealtime ['mi:ltaɪm] N heure f du repas; **they only see each other at mealtimes** ils ne se voient qu'aux heures des repas

mealworm ['mi:lwɜ:m] N Entom ver m de farine

mealy ['mi:lɪ] ADJ **1** (in consistency) farineux **2** (covered in meal) saupoudré de farine, poudreux **3 m. complexion** teint m blême

mealy-mouthed [-'maʊðd] ADJ Pej doucereux, mielleux, patelin

mean[1] [mi:n] N **1** (middle) (juste) milieu m, moyen terme m; **the golden** or **happy m.** le juste milieu **2** Math moyenne f
ADJ (medium, average) moyen
▸▸Comput **m. time between failures** moyenne de temps entre deux pannes

mean[2] ADJ **1** esp Br (with money) avare, Fam radin; **to be m. with one's praise** or **compliments** être avare de compliments; **he's very m. about tipping** il n'aime pas donner de pourboires **2** (low, ignoble) (person, character, action) bas, méprisable, mesquin; (wretched) misérable, pauvre; **even to the meanest intelligence** même pour les esprits les plus obtus; **he has a m. streak** il peut être méchant quand il veut; **a m. trick** un vilain tour, *Fam* un sale coup; **that's m. of her** ce n'est pas chic de sa part; *Fam* **I feel very m. about not going** j'ai honte de ne pas y aller **3** *esp Am Fam (vicious, tough)* méchant, vicieux **4** *(with no)* **no m. …** un très bon …/ une très bonne …; **he's no m. scholar** c'est un grand érudit; **it was no m. feat** ce n'était pas une mince affaire; **it's no m. task (to do sth)** ce n'est pas une mince affaire *ou* ce n'est pas rien (de faire qch) **5** *Fam (excellent)* formidable; **he plays a m. guitar** c'est un guitariste formidable **6** *Am Fam (poorly)* **to feel m.** se sentir mal en train

MEAN³ VT (*pt, pp* **meant** [ment]) **1** *(have intention)* **to m. to do sth** avoir (bien) l'intention de faire qch, (bien) compter faire qch, vouloir faire qch; **what do you m. to do?** que comptez-vous faire?, qu'est-ce que vous avez l'intention de faire?; **I never meant to go** je n'ai jamais eu l'intention d'y aller; **I m. him no harm** je ne lui veux pas de mal; **she didn't m. (to do) it** elle ne l'a pas fait exprès; **without meaning it** sans le vouloir; **I meant to!** *(do what I did)* c'était bien mon intention!; **to m. well by sb** avoir de bonnes intentions à l'égard de qn; **she means well** elle a de bonnes intentions; **I m. to be obeyed** j'entends qu'on m'obéisse; **I m. to succeed** je veux réussir; **I m. to see justice done** je veux que justice soit faite

2 *(intend)* **I meant this book for you** je vous destinais ce livre; **the remark was meant for you** la remarque s'adressait à vous *ou* vous était destinée; **the remark wasn't meant to be overheard** cette remarque n'était pas censée être entendue; **it was meant as a joke/compliment/insult** c'était censé être une blague/un compliment/une insulte; **you weren't meant to open the presents until tomorrow** tu n'étais pas censé ouvrir les cadeaux avant demain; **I have a feeling this was meant to be** *or* **happen** j'ai le sentiment que ça devait arriver; **do you m. him?** est-ce de lui que vous parlez?, est-ce lui à qui vous faites allusion?; **this portrait is meant to be the duke** ce portrait est censé représenter le duc; **we were meant for each other** nous sommes faits l'un pour l'autre

3 *(signify) (of person)* vouloir dire; *(of word, phrase, event etc)* signifier; **what does that word m.?** que signifie ce mot?; **the name means nothing to me** ce nom ne me dit rien; **what is meant by …?** que veut dire …?; **all this means nothing** tout cela ne rime à rien; **it doesn't m. anything** *(what you saw, heard)* cela ne prouve rien; **this means war/the end of our relationship** c'est la guerre/la fin de notre amitié; **what do you m.?** que voulez-vous dire?; **what do you m. by that?** qu'entendez-vous par là?; **I know what you m.!** *(I quite agree)* et comment!; **what, me?, I don't know what you m.!** qui moi?, je ne vois pas ce que vous voulez dire!; **she knew what it meant to be hungry** elle savait ce que c'était que d'avoir faim

4 *(speak sincerely)* **do you think he meant what he said?** pensez-vous qu'il l'ait dit sérieusement?, est-ce que tu crois qu'il parlait sérieusement?; **I didn't m. that** ce n'est pas ce que je voulais dire; **you don't m. it!** vous voulez rire!, vous plaisantez!; **I m. it** je parle sérieusement; **you're my best friend − do you m. that?** tu es mon meilleur ami − tu le penses vraiment?; **when I say no, I m. no** quand je dis non, c'est non; **do you m. to tell me …?** est-ce que tu es en train de me dire que …?; **I m. (to say)!** je veux dire!

5 *(be of importance)* **the price means nothing to him** le prix importe peu pour lui; **doesn't your daughter's education m.**

anything to you? est-ce que l'éducation de ta fille ne t'intéresse pas?; **I cannot tell you what he has meant to me** je ne saurais vous dire tout ce qu'il a été pour moi; **my Sundays m./independence means a lot to me** le dimanche/mon indépendance est sacré(e) pour moi

6 *(imply, involve)* signifier, impliquer; **it would m. the children having to change school again** cela signifierait que les enfants devraient changer d'école une fois de plus; **just because you've been to university doesn't m. you know everything** ce n'est pas parce que tu es allé à l'université que tu sais tout; **it doesn't m. we have to stop seeing each other** ça ne veut pas dire que nous devons cesser de nous voir

meander [mɪˈændər] N *Geog* méandre *m*
VI **1** *(of person)* errer çà et là, flâner; *(in speaking)* divaguer **2** *(of river)* serpenter, faire des méandres

meandering [mɪˈændərɪŋ] ADJ **1** *(speech etc)* sans plan, sans suite **2** *(river)* qui serpente *ou* fait des méandres

meanie [ˈmiːnɪ] N *Fam* **1** *esp Br (miserly person)* rapiat, -ate, pingre *mf* **2** *esp Am (nasty person)* **what a m.!** quel chameau!, qu'il est vache!

meaning [ˈmiːnɪŋ] N signification *f*, sens *m*; *Ling (of term etc)* acception *f*; **what is the m. of this word?** que signifie *ou* que veut dire ce mot?; **what's the m. of this?** *(expressing indignation)* qu'est-ce que cela signifie?; *Fig Fam* **loyalty? you don't know the m. of the word!** tu ne sais pas ce que c'est que la loyauté!; **life had no m. for him** la vie n'avait plus aucun sens pour lui; **to understand sb's m.** comprendre ce que qn veut dire; *Fam* **if you get my m.** si tu vois ce que je veux dire; **a look full of m.** un regard significatif
ADJ *(look, smile)* significatif, qui en dit long

meaningful [ˈmiːnɪŋfʊl] ADJ *(full of meaning)* significatif, éloquent; *(expressive) (look, smile)* significatif, qui en dit long; *esp Pol* **m. talks** conversations *fpl* constructives; **a m. relationship** une relation sérieuse

meaningfully [ˈmiːnɪŋfʊlɪ] ADV *(to sing)* de façon expressive; **he smiled m. at her** le sourire qu'il lui fit en disait long

meaningless [ˈmiːnɪŋlɪs] ADJ dénué *ou* vide de sens, qui ne signifie rien; **a m. act/remark** un non-sens

meanly [ˈmiːnlɪ] ADV **1** *esp Br (in miserly fashion)* en lésinant, chichement **2** *(ignobly) (to act, behave)* peu loyalement, indignement **3** *(wretchedly)* misérablement, pauvrement

meanness [ˈmiːnnɪs] N **1** *esp Br (with money)* avarice *f*, *Fam* radinerie *f* **2** *(nastiness)* mesquinerie *f*, méchanceté *f* **3** *(baseness)* bassesse *f*, petitesse *f*; **the m. of vision expressed in his speech …** l'étroitesse d'esprit que reflétait son discours … **4** *(poor quality, poverty)* médiocrité *f*, pauvreté *f*

means [miːnz] NPL *(often with sing verb)* **1** *(method)* moyen(s) *m(pl)*; **to use every possible m. to do sth** employer tous les moyens pour faire qch; **there is no m. of escape** il n'y a pas d'issue; **by all m.** *(by every possible method)* par tous les moyens (possibles); *(certainly)* mais certainement!, mais oui!; **may I come in? − by all m.!** puis-je entrer? − je vous en prie!; **by no m.** en aucune façon, nullement; **she is not stupid by any (manner of) m.** elle est loin d'être stupide; **by some m. or other** d'une manière ou d'une autre; **by m. of sth** au moyen *ou* à l'aide de qch; **they escaped by m. of a secret passage** ils se sont enfuis par un passage secret; **she succeeded by m. of her own hard work** elle a réussi grâce à son travail acharné; **a m. to an end** un moyen d'arriver à ses fins; *Econ* **m. of pro-**

duction moyens *mpl* de production; **m. of transport** moyen *m* de transport

2 *(income)* moyens *mpl*, ressources *fpl*; *(wealth)* fortune *f*, **according to our m.** selon nos moyens; **to live beyond/within one's m.** vivre au-dessus de/selon ses moyens; **private m.** ressources personnelles; **a man of m.** un homme dont les revenus sont élevés; **to be without m.** *(without resources)* être sans ressources; *(without wealth)* être sans fortune; **they are without the m. to deal with the problem** ils n'ont pas les moyens de résoudre le problème

▸▸ *Admin* **m. test** enquête *f* sur les revenus *(d'une personne désirant bénéficier d'une allocation d'État)*

means-test VT *Admin* **to m. sb** = faire une enquête sur les ressources de qn avant de lui accorder une aide sociale

meant PT, PP *see* **mean³**

meantime, meanwhile [ˈmiːntaɪm, -waɪl] N, ADV **(in the) meantime, meanwhile** dans l'intervalle, pendant ce temps-là, en attendant

measles [ˈmiːz(ə)lz] NPL *(usu with sing verb)* *Med* rougeole *f*; **to have (the) m.** avoir la rougeole; **German m.** rubéole *f*

measly [ˈmiːzlɪ] ADJ *Fam* insignifiant, minable; **keep your m. money!** garde ton sale argent!; **all I got was one m. bar of chocolate** je n'ai eu qu'une misérable tablette de chocolat!

measurable [ˈmeʒərəb(ə)l] ADJ **1** mesurable; **a m. difference** *(m in sb's performance etc)* une différence sensible **2** *Chem etc (constituent)* dosable

measure [ˈmeʒər] N **1** *(measurement)* mesure *f*, *Fig* **to get the m. of sb** prendre la mesure de qn, jauger qn; **to have the m. of sb** savoir comment s'y prendre avec qn **2** *(instrument) (for grain, milk etc)* mesure *f* **3** *(quantity)* dose *f*, mesure *f*, **a m. of whisky** une dose de whisky; **to give sb short m.** donner moins que la mesure à qn; **half m.** demi-mesure *f*, *pl* demi-mesures; *Fig* **there are no half measures with her** avec elle, il n'y a pas de demi-mesure; *Fig* **then she insulted the other man for good m.** elle a aussi insulté l'autre pour ne pas faire de jaloux; **he gave him a couple of kicks for good m.** il lui a donné quelques coups de pied en prime **4** *(degree)* **in some m.** dans une certaine mesure; **she was in great m. to blame for what happened** elle est en grande partie responsable de ce qui s'est passé; **a m. of independence** une certaine indépendance **5** *(limit)* mesure *f*, limite *f*, **beyond m.** outre mesure **6** *(action, step)* mesure *f*, démarche *f*, **to take measures** prendre des mesures; **to take extreme measures** employer les grands moyens **7** *Parl (bill)* projet *m* de loi **8** *(in poetry)* mesure *f* **9** *esp Am Mus* mesure *f*
VT *(distance, time, person etc)* mesurer; *(wall etc)* métrer, mesurer; *(piece of land)* arpenter; *(person for clothes)* mesurer, prendre les mesures de; *Fig* **to m. one's length (on the ground)** *(fall)* s'étaler par terre, tomber de tout son long; *Fig* **to m. one's strength** *or* **oneself with sb** mesurer ses forces avec qn, se mesurer avec *ou* contre qn; *Fig* **to m. one's words** mesurer *ou* peser ses paroles
VI mesurer; **column measuring 10 metres** colonne qui mesure 10 mètres

▸ **measure off** VT SEP *(material etc)* mesurer
▸ **measure out** VT SEP *(corn etc)* mesurer; *(distribute)* répartir, attribuer; **the barman measured out a double whisky** le barman versa un double whisky; **m. out two cups of flour** préparez deux mesures de farine

▶ **measure up** VT SEP *(wood)* mesurer; **to m. sb up for a suit** prendre les mesures de qn pour un costume; **to get measured up for a new suit** se faire prendre ses mesures pour un nouveau costume; *Fig* **they measured each other up** *(before fight etc)* ils se sont jaugés

VI *(of employee etc)* faire le poids, être à la hauteur

▶ **measure up to** VT INSEP **to m. up to one's job** se montrer à la hauteur de sa tâche; **to m. up to sb/sth** être à la mesure de qn/qch; **to m. up to sb's expectations** répondre aux attentes de qn; **the holiday didn't m. up to their expectations** leurs vacances n'ont pas été à la mesure de leurs espérances; **the meal didn't m. up to her usual standards** le repas qu'elle nous a préparé n'était pas aussi bon que d'habitude

measured ['meʒəd] ADJ **1** *(time, distance etc)* mesuré, déterminé **2** *(deliberate) (movement, step)* cadencé; **with m. steps** à pas mesurés *ou* comptés; **m. tread** marche *f* scandée **3** *(language)* modéré; **to speak in m. tones** parler sur un ton modéré **4** *(in poetry) (verse etc)* mesuré

measurement ['meʒəmənt] N *(quantity, length etc)* mesure *f*, *(action)* mesure, mesurage *m*; **the measurements of a room/an object** les dimensions *fpl* d'une pièce/d'un objet; **bust/waist/hip m.** *(of person)* tour *m* de poitrine/taille/hanches; **to take a customer's measurements** prendre les mesures d'un client SEE GRAMMAR B59

▶▶ **m. ton** tonne *f* d'encombrement

measuring ['meʒərɪŋ] N

▶▶ **m. chain** *(in surveying)* chaîne *f* d'arpenteur *ou* d'arpentage; **m. cup** mesure *f*, **m. glass** verre *m* gradué *ou* doseur; **m. jug** mesure; **m. spoon** cuillère *f* à doser; **m. tape** mètre *m* (à) ruban

meat [miːt] N **1** viande *f*, *Old-fashioned* **m. and drink** le manger et le boire; *Fig* **it was m. and drink to them** c'était une véritable aubaine pour eux; *Prov* **one man's m. is another man's poison** on ne discute pas des goûts et des couleurs, ce qui guérit l'un tue l'autre **2** *Fig (substantial content) (of book, film, article etc)* substance *f*

▶▶ **m. broth** bouillon *m* gras; **m. diet** régime *m* carné; **m. hook** crochet *m* de boucherie; **m. loaf** pain *m* de viande; *Br Fam Pej* **m. market** *(nightclub)* = boîte *f* réputée pour être un lieu de drague; *Am Fam* **m. wagon** *(ambulance)* ambulance *f*

meatball ['miːtbɔːl] N **1** *Culin* boulette *f* (de viande) **2** *Am Fam (person)* crétin, -ine, imbécile *mf*

meathead ['miːthed] N *Am Fam* crétin, -ine, imbécile *mf*

meatpacking ['miːtpækɪŋ] N *Am* abattage *m* et boucherie *f*

meaty ['miːtɪ] ADJ **1** *(sausage etc)* riche en viande; *(smell etc)* de viande; *Fig (book etc)* riche **2** *(fleshy)* charnu

Mecca ['mekə] N la Mecque; *Fig* **a M. for antique lovers** un paradis pour les passionnés d'objets anciens

mechanic [mɪˈkænɪk] N mécanicien, -ienne; **I'm not much of a m.** je ne suis pas très mécanicien

Note that the French word **mécanique** is a false friend and is never a translation for the English word **mechanic**. It means **mechanics**.

mechanical [mɪˈkænɪk(ə)l] ADJ **1** *Tech* mécanique; **he has no m. skill** il n'a aucune compétence en mécanique **2** *Fig (reply, smile etc)* machinal, -aux, automatique, mécanique; **to give a m. response** répondre

machinalement; **a m. gesture** un geste machinal; **her playing is very m.** *(of pianist etc)* elle joue d'une façon très mécanique

▶▶ **m. breakdown insurance** assurance *f* panne mécanique; **m. digger** pelleteuse *f* mécanique; **m. drawing** dessin *m* aux instruments; **m. efficiency** rendement *m* mécanique; **m. engineer** ingénieur *m* mécanicien; **m. engineering** génie *m* mécanique; **m. failure** défaillance *f* mécanique, panne *f* mécanique; **m. wear** usure *f* mécanique

mechanically [mɪˈkænɪklɪ] ADV **1** *Tech* mécaniquement; **m. driven** actionné mécaniquement; **I'm not very m. minded** je ne suis pas très doué pour tout ce qui est mécanique **2** *Fig (to reply, smile etc)* machinalement

mechanics [mɪˈkænɪks] N VOIR GRAMMAIRE A10 **1** *(science)* mécanique *f* **2** *(working parts)* mécanisme *m*

mechanism ['mekənɪz(ə)m] N *(device, working parts)*, *Phil, Psy etc* mécanisme *m*

mechanistic [mekəˈnɪstɪk] ADJ *(view of universe, explanation)* mécaniste

mechanization [mekənaɪˈzeɪʃən] N mécanisation *f*

mechanize ['mekənaɪz] VT mécaniser; *(troops)* motoriser

mechanized ['mekənaɪzd] ADJ **m. industry** industrie mécanisée; *Mil* **m. troops** troupes motorisées

Med (the) [ðəˈmed] N *Fam* la Méditerranée

MEd [eˈmed] N *(abbr* **Master of Education)** ≃ CAPES *m*

medal ['med(ə)l] N médaille *f*, **to award a m. to sb** décerner une médaille *ou* une décoration à qn; **to be awarded a m. for bravery** être décoré pour sa bravoure

▶▶ *Am Mil* **M. of Honor** = la plus haute distinction américaine donnée en récompense à un soldat

medallion [mɪˈdæljən] N médaillon *m*

▶▶ *Br Fam Hum* **m. man** = individu *m* entre deux âges à l'allure machiste et vulgaire, qui essaie de passer pour plus jeune qu'il n'est

medallist, *Am* **medalist** ['medəlɪst] N *Sport etc* médaillé, -ée; **gold/silver m.** titulaire *mf* d'une *ou* de la médaille d'or/d'argent

meddle ['med(ə)l] VI *(interfere)* se mêler (**in** de); *(tamper)* toucher (**with** à); **to m. in other people's affairs** se mêler des affaires d'autrui

meddler ['medlər] N **he's a terrible m.** il met son nez partout

meddlesome ['med(ə)lsəm] ADJ qui se mêle de tout

meddling ['medlɪŋ] ADJ = **meddlesome** N *(action)* ingérence *f* (**in** dans)

media ['miːdɪə] NPL **the (mass) m.** les médias *mpl*; **the m. were waiting for her when she flew in** les journalistes l'attendaient à sa descente d'avion VOIR GRAMMAIRE A11

▶▶ **m. advertising** publicité *f* média; **m. analysis** analyse *f* des médias; **m. analyst** analyste *mf* des médias; **m. buyer** acheteur, -euse d'espaces (publicitaires); **m. circus** cirque *m* médiatique; **m. consultant** conseil *m* en communication; **m. coverage** couverture *f* médiatique, médiatisation *f*; **to get too much m. coverage** être surmédiatisé; **m. event** événement *m* médiatique; **m. exposure** *(coverage)* couverture médiatique, médiatisation; *(of product)* exposition *f* dans les médias; **m. group** groupe *m* de médias; **m. hype** battage *m* médiatique; **m. library** médiathèque *f*, **m. mix** mix *m* média; **m. mogul** magnat *m* des médias; **m. overkill** surmédiatisation *f*, médiatisation *f* excessive; **m. person** *(man)* homme *m* de communication; *(woman)* femme *f* de communication; **m. planner** médiaplaneur *m*, média

planner *m*; **m. planning** média planning *m*; **m. release** communiqué *m*; **m. research** médialogie *f*; **m. scrum** ruée *f* de journalistes; **m. studies** = études *fpl* en communication et journalisme

media-conscious ADJ *(politician etc)* médiatique

mediaeval, **mediaevalist** = **medieval**, **medievalist**

media-friendly ADJ médiatique

mediagenic [miːdɪəˈdʒenɪk] ADJ médiatique

medial ['miːdɪəl] ADJ intermédiaire (**to** entre); *(letter)* médial, -aux N *Ling* médiale *f*

median ['miːdɪən] ADJ médian N **1** *Anat (nerve)* nerf *m* médian; *(vein)* veine *f* médiane **2** *(in statistics)*, *Math* médiane *f*

▶▶ *Am Aut* **m. strip** terre-plein *m* central, *pl* terre-pleins centraux, *Belg, Suisse* berme *f* centrale

mediant ['miːdɪənt] N *Mus* médiante *f*

media-shy ADJ qui fuit les médias

mediate ['miːdɪeɪt] VI *(of person)* agir en *ou* servir de médiateur (**between** entre) VT **to m. a peace** intervenir en qualité de médiateur pour amener la paix

mediation [miːdɪˈeɪʃən] N médiation *f*, **to go to m.** recourir à une médiation

mediator ['miːdɪeɪtər] N médiateur, -trice

medic ['medɪk] N *Fam (student)* étudiant, -ante en médecine, carabin *m*; *(doctor)* toubib *m*

Medicaid ['medɪkeɪd] N *Am* = assistance *f* médicale pour les défavorisés

medical ['medɪk(ə)l] ADJ médical, -aux; *(book etc)* de médecine; *(student)* en médecine; **you need m. attention** il faut vous faire soigner par un médecin

N visite *f* médicale; **to have a m.** passer une visite médicale; **he failed the m.** il n'a pas été accepté pour raisons de santé

▶▶ **m. certificate** certificat *m* médical; **m. examination** visite *f* médicale; *Am* **m. examiner** médecin *m* légiste; **m. history** *(patient's file)* dossier *m* médical; *(previous problems)* antécédents *mpl* médicaux; **m. jurisprudence** médecine *f* légale; **M. Officer of Health** directeur, -trice de la santé publique; **m. practitioner** *(médecin)* généraliste *mf*, **the m. profession** *(people)* le corps médical; *(activity)* la profession médicale; **m. record** dossier médical

medically ['medɪklɪ] ADV médicalement; **to be m. examined** subir un examen médical

medicament [meˈdɪkəmənt] N médicament *m*

Medicare ['medɪkeər] N **1** *Am* = assistance *f* médicale pour les personnes âgées et les handicapés **2** *Can* assurance-maladie *f*

medicate ['medɪkeɪt] VT *(patient)* faire suivre un traitement à

medicated ['medɪkeɪtɪd] ADJ *(shampoo)* médical, -aux, traitant; *(soap)* médical, -aux

medication [medɪˈkeɪʃən] N *(medicine, drugs)* médicaments *mpl*; **to take one's m.** prendre ses médicaments; **to be on m.** suivre un traitement

medicinal [meˈdɪsɪn(ə)l] ADJ médicinal, -aux, médicamenteux; *Hum* **it's just for m. purposes** *(having a whisky etc)* c'est mon médicament

▶▶ **m. plants** plantes *fpl* médicinales; **m. properties** vertus *fpl* curatives

medicinally [meˈdɪsɪn(ə)lɪ] ADV *(to use a herb, substance)* médicinalement, comme médicament; *(to treat)* médicalement

medicine ['medsɪn] N **1** *(practice, science)*

médecine *f*, **to practise m.** exercer la médecine; **to study m.** faire des études de médecine, étudier la médecine **2** *(remedy)* médicament *m*; *Fig* **to give sb a taste of his/her
own m.** rendre la pareille à qn; *Fig* **to take
one's m.** avaler la pilule, supporter les
conséquences (de son action)
▸▸**m. ball** medicine-ball *m*, *pl* medicine-
balls, médecine-ball *m*, *pl* médecine-balls;
m. cabinet, m. chest (armoire *f* à) pharmacie
f, **m. man** sorcier *m*, medicine-man *m*

> Note that the French word **médecine**
> never means **remedy**.

medico ['medɪkəʊ] **N** *Fam* = **medic**
medieval [medɪ'iːvəl] **ADJ** du moyen âge,
médiéval, -aux; *Fig (attitudes, person)* rétrograde; **it's m. here** c'est le moyen âge ici
medievalist [medɪ'iːvəlɪst] **N** médiéviste
mf
mediocre [miːdɪ'əʊkər] **ADJ** médiocre
mediocrity [miːdɪ'ɒkrɪtɪ] **N** *(quality)* médiocrité *f*, **a m.** *(person)* un/une médiocre
meditate ['medɪteɪt] **VI 1** *(reflect)* méditer
(**on**, **upon** sur), réfléchir (**on**, **upon** sur, à) **2**
(be in or enter into a state of meditation) méditer; *esp Rel* se recueillir
VT *(project, undertaking)* méditer
meditation [medɪ'teɪʃən] **N 1** *(thinking)*
méditation *f* (**upon** sur) **2** *(state)* recueillement *m* **3** *Liter* **meditations** méditations *fpl*
meditative ['medɪtətɪv] **ADJ** méditatif,
recueilli
meditatively ['medɪtətɪvlɪ] **ADV** d'un air
méditatif
Mediterranean [medɪtə'reɪnɪən] **ADJ** méditerranéen; **the M. Sea** la mer Méditerranée
  N the M. la Méditerranée
medium, *pl* **-a, -ums** ['miːdɪəm, -ə, -əmz] **N**
VOIR GRAMMAIRE A13 **1** *(mid-point)* milieu *m*,
moyen terme *m* (**between** entre) **2** *Art (for
working in)* matériau *m*; *(for advertising)*
support *m*, médium *m*; **marble is her favourite m.** elle préfère travailler le marbre;
opera is his preferred m. l'opéra est son
moyen d'expression favori; **television is a
powerful m.** la télévision est un média *ou*
un moyen de communication *ou* un moyen
de diffusion puissant; **through the m. of the
press** par l'intermédiaire de la presse, par
voie de presse; **French was the m. through
which they communicated** ils communiquaient en français, le français était la langue dans laquelle ils communiquaient;
advertising m. support publicitaire **3** *Phys*
milieu *m*, véhicule *m*; *Biol* culture *f*, bouillon
m de culture **4** *(in spiritualism)* médium *mf*
  ADJ moyen; **of m. height** de taille moyenne;
cook in a m. oven cuire à four moyen; **m.
sized** de grandeur moyenne, de taille
moyenne; **in the m. term** à moyen terme;
m. dry wine vin *m* demi-sec, *pl* vins demi-
secs
  N *(something of medium size)* **this teeshirt's
a m.** ce tee-shirt est une taille moyenne *ou*
un deux; **available in small, m. and large** disponible en petit, moyen et grand
  ▸▸ *Cin* **m. close-up** plan *m* rapproché; *Am
Radio* **m. frequency** ondes *fpl* moyennes;
Cin, TV **m. long shot** plan de demi-en-
semble; *Cin, TV* **m. shot** plan moyen; *Radio*
m. wave ondes moyennes; **on m. wave** sur
ondes moyennes
medium-haul **ADJ** *(flight, route)* moyen-
courrier
medium-range **N**
  ▸▸ **m. ballistic missile** missile *m* balistique
de moyenne portée
medium-rare **ADJ** à point
medium-term **ADJ** *(financing, forecast)* à

moyen terme; **m. financial assistance** aide *f*
financière à moyen terme
  ▸▸ **m. credit** crédit *m* (à) moyen terme; **m.
liabilities** dettes *fpl* à moyen terme; **m. note**
billet *m* à moyen terme (négociable)
medlar ['medlər] **N** *(fruit)* nèfle *f*, *(tree)* néflier *m*
  ▸▸ **m. tree** néflier
medley ['medlɪ] **N** *(of people, objects)* mélange *m*, méli-mélo *m*, *pl* mélis-mélos; *Mus*
pot-pourri *m*, *pl* pots-pourris; *Swimming*
400 metres m. (race) 4 x 100 mètres quatre
nages
medulla [me'dʌlə] **N 1** *Bot* médulle *f*, moelle
f **2** *Anat (of bone)* moelle *f*
meek [miːk] **ADJ** doux, *f* douce, docile; **m.
and mild** doux comme un agneau
meekly ['miːklɪ] **ADV** avec soumission,
docilement
meekness ['miːknɪs] **N** douceur *f* de caractère, soumission *f*, docilité *f*
meerschaum ['mɪəʃəm] **N 1** *Miner* écume *f*
(de mer) **2** *(pipe)* pipe *f* en écume (de mer)
  ▸▸ **m. pipe** pipe en écume (de mer)

MEET[1] [miːt]

> **VT** rencontrer **1, 3, 5, 8** ▪ croiser **1**
> ▪ rejoindre **2** ▪ retrouver **2** ▪ aller
> chercher **2** ▪ faire la connaissance de
> **3** ▪ satisfaire **7**

N 1 *(in hunting)* rassemblement *m* de la
meute
2 *Sport* meeting *m*
3 *esp Am (meeting)* réunion *f*
VT *(pt, pp met* [met]*)* **1** *(by accident) (person)*
rencontrer; **to m. sb on the stairs** croiser qn
dans l'escalier; **to m. another car** croiser
une autre voiture
2 *(by arrangement) (person)* rejoindre, retrouver; **to go to m. sb** aller au-devant de
qn, aller à la rencontre de qn; **to m. sb at
the station** aller chercher qn à la gare; **the
bus meets the train** il y a une correspondance entre le train et l'autobus; **I arranged
to m. him at three o'clock** j'ai pris rendez-
vous avec lui pour trois heures; **I'll m. you
at the crossroads** je te retrouve au croisement
3 *(become acquainted with)* rencontrer,
faire la connaissance de; **I met her at the
Martins'** je l'ai rencontrée chez les Martin;
pleased to m. you ravi de faire votre
connaissance; **have you met my husband?**
vous connaissez mon mari?; **I get to m. a
lot of people in my job** mon travail m'amène
à rencontrer beaucoup de gens; **I like meeting people** j'aime rencontrer des gens; **she's
the nicest person I've ever met** c'est la personne la plus gentille que j'ai jamais rencontrée; **m. Mr Thomas** je vous présente M.
Thomas
4 *(join)* **the stream meets the river** le ruisseau se jette dans la rivière; **where East
meets West** où l'est et l'ouest se rencontrent;
here the road meets the railway c'est ici que
la route rejoint *ou* croise le chemin de fer
5 *(come into contact with)* **his eyes met mine**
nos regards se sont croisés; **he was afraid to
m. her eye** il avait peur de croiser son regard; **her mouth met his** leurs bouches se
rencontrèrent; **her car met an oncoming
lorry and …** sa voiture a percuté un camion
qui arrivait en sens inverse et …
6 *(be perceived by)* **a strange sound met our
ears** nous avons entendu un bruit étrange; **a
remarkable sight met our eyes** nous avons
été témoins d'un spectacle incroyable;
there's more to this than meets the eye on
ne connaît pas les dessous de cette affaire;
there's more to him than meets the eye c'est
quelqu'un de plus complexe qu'il n'y paraît
au premier abord

7 *(satisfy) (a need)* satisfaire, répondre à;
(demands) satisfaire; *(condition, requirement)* satisfaire à; *(objection, criticism)* répondre à; *(cheque)* honorer; *Com (order)*
satisfaire, assurer; *Com (bill of exchange)*
honorer, faire honneur à; **to m. sb's wishes**
combler les désirs de qn; **to m. sb's expectations** répondre à l'attente de qn; **to m. one's
commitments** remplir ses engagements;
Com **to m. demand** répondre à la demande;
to m. expenses supporter les dépenses,
subvenir aux frais; **the cost will be met by
the company** les frais seront pris en charge
par la compagnie
8 *(face) (danger)* affronter; *(the enemy)* rencontrer, affronter; *(difficulty)* se heurter à;
she met her death in an air crash elle a
trouvé la mort *ou* péri dans un accident
d'avion; *Sport* **he will m. the champion in
June** il rencontrera *ou* affrontera le champion en juin
VI 1 *(by accident) (of people)* se rencontrer
(par hasard)
2 *(by arrangement) (of people)* se retrouver;
let's m. for lunch on se retrouve pour le déjeuner?; **where shall we m.?** où se retrouve-
t-on?; **when shall we m. again?** quand nous
reverrons-nous?; **we should m. more often**
on devrait se voir plus souvent
3 *(become acquainted)* se rencontrer, se
connaître; **they met in 1999** ils se sont rencontrés *ou* connus en 1999
4 *(of society, assembly)* se réunir; **the club
meets every other Tuesday** le cercle se réunit un mardi sur deux
5 *(join)* se rencontrer, se rejoindre; *(of rivers)* confluer, se rejoindre; **a country where
East and West m.** un pays où se rencontrent
l'est et l'ouest; **his eyebrows m.** ses sourcils
se touchent
6 *(come into contact)* se rencontrer; **the two
cars met head on** les deux voitures se sont
heurtées de plein fouet; **our eyes met** nos
regards se sont croisés; **their hands met**
leurs mains se rencontrèrent
▸ **meet up** **VI** se rencontrer; **we'll have to m.
up next time I'm in Paris** il faudra qu'on se
voie la prochaine fois que je passerai à Paris; **we met up with an Australian** nous
avons rencontré un Australien
▸ **meet with** **VT INSEP 1 to m. with a refusal**
essuyer un refus; **to m. with difficulties** rencontrer des difficultés; **to m. with failure**
échouer; **the proposal has met with fierce
opposition** la proposition s'est heurtée à
une opposition très vive; **the expedition
met with disaster** l'expédition a tourné au
désastre; **he has met with an accident** il lui
est arrivé un accident; **the plan didn't m.
with her approval** le projet n'a pas reçu son
accord
2 *esp Am (meet) (for discussion)* rencontrer,
retrouver; *(for lunch etc)* retrouver

meet[2] **ADJ** *Arch, Lit* convenable, séant; **it is
m. that …** il convient que …
meet-and-greet **VT** *(guests)* accueillir
meeting ['miːtɪŋ] **N 1** *(encounter)* rencontre
f; **during my first m. with him** lors de notre
première rencontre; *Lit* **m. of minds** communion *f* de pensée **2** *(of society, assembly etc)*
réunion *f*, séance *f*, *(in business, discussion)*
réunion, conférence *f*; **he's in a m.** il est en
conférence *ou* réunion; **at our last m.** lors
de notre dernière réunion; **to hold a m.** tenir
une réunion; **to call a m. of the shareholders**
convoquer les actionnaires; **to open the m.**
déclarer la séance ouverte; **to address the
m.** prendre la parole **3** *Sport* meeting *m*;
Horseracing (réunion *f* de) courses *fpl* **4** *Rel
(of Quakers)* **to go to m.** aller au temple
  ▸▸ *Rel* **m. house** temple *m*; **m. place** *(for
gatherings)* lieu *m* de réunion; *(for rendez-
vous)* (lieu de) rendez-vous *m*; **m. point** *(of*

lines, things) point *m* de jonction; *Math* point de rencontre; *(for people)* lieu de rendez-vous; **meetings secretary** secrétaire *mf* de séance

meg [meg] N *Comput Sl* méga *m*

mega ['megə] ADJ *Fam (tremendous)* super, génial, -aux; *(big)* énorme

mega- ['megə] PREF *Fam* méga-rich/famous/intelligent hyper riche/célèbre/intelligent

megabit N *Comput* mégabit *m*

megabucks ['megəbʌks] N *Sl* un fric fou, une fortune; **her job pays m.** elle gagne une fortune dans son travail

megabyte ['megəbaɪt] N *Comput* méga-octet *m*, *pl* méga-octets, *Fam* méga *m*; **20 m.** memory mémoire *f* de 20 méga-octets

megacycle ['megəsaɪk(ə)l] N *Elec* mégacycle *m*

megadeath ['megədeθ] N mort *f* d'un million de personnes

megaflop ['megəflɒp] N *Comput* mégaflop *m*

megagroup ['megəgruːp] N *Mus* super-groupe *m*

megahertz ['megəhɜːts] N *Elec* mégahertz *m*

megalith ['megəlɪθ] N mégalithe *m*

megalithic [megə'lɪθɪk] ADJ mégalithique

megalomania [megələʊ'meɪnɪə] N mégalomanie *f*

megalomaniac [megələʊ'meɪnɪæk] ADJ, N mégalomane *mf*

megamerger ['megəmɜːdʒər] N *Com* méga-fusion *f*

megaphone ['megəfəʊn] N mégaphone *m*

megapixel ['megəpɪksəl] N mégapixel *m*

megaplex ['megəpleks] N *Am Cin* complexe *m* multisalles, cinéma *m* multisalle *(de plus de 16 salles)*

mega-resort N mégastation *f*, station *f* très importante

megastar ['megəstɑːr] N superstar *f*

megaton ['megətʌn] N mégatonne *f*

megavolt ['megəvɒlt] N *Elec* mégavolt *m*

megawatt ['megəwɒt] N *Elec* mégawatt *m*

megilla [mə'gɪlə] N *Am Fam* **the whole m.** tout le tremblement; **I don't need the whole m., just give me the main points** t'as pas besoin de tout me raconter en détail *ou* par le menu, dis-moi le principal

meiosis [maɪ'əʊsɪs] N **1** *(in rhetoric)* litote *f* **2** *Biol* méiose *f*

melaena [me'liːnə] N *Med* mélæna *m*, méléna *m*

melancholia [melən'kəʊlɪə] N mélancolie *f*

melancholic [melən'kɒlɪk] ADJ mélancolique

melancholy ['melənkəlɪ] N mélancolie *f*, **a bout of m.** un accès de mélancolie
ADJ *(person)* mélancolique; *(news)* triste, attristant

melee ['meleɪ] N mêlée *f*

mellifluous [me'lɪflʊəs] ADJ *(words etc)* mélodieux

mellow ['meləʊ] ADJ **1** *(flavour, taste)* doux, *f* douce; *(wine)* moelleux, velouté; *(fruit)* fondant, mûr; *(voice, sound)* moelleux, doux; *(colour, light)* chaud, doux, velouté; **m. tobacco** tabac doux **2** *(person)* détendu; *Fam (pleasantly drunk)* un peu gris; **to grow m.** *(of person)* s'adoucir
VI **1** *(of flavour, taste, light)* s'adoucir; *(of wine)* mûrir, prendre du moelleux *ou* du velouté; *(of voice, sound)* s'adoucir **2** *(of character)* s'adoucir; **to m. with age** s'adoucir *ou* devenir plus chaud *ou* riche *ou* moelleux, s'adoucir **2** *(of character)* s'adoucir; **to m. with age** s'adoucir *ou* devenir plus accommodant *ou* plus tolérant avec l'âge

VT **1** *(flavour, taste)* rendre plus doux; *(wine)* donner du moelleux *ou* du velouté à **2** *(person's character)* adoucir; **age has mellowed her** l'âge a adouci son caractère

▸ **mellow out** VI *Fam* s'adoucir; **why don't you m. out a bit?** pourquoi est-ce que tu n'essayes pas de te détendre un peu?

mellowing ['meləʊɪŋ] N *(of wine)* maturation *f*, *(of character)* adoucissement *m*

mellowness ['meləʊnɪs] N *(of flavour, light, colour, character)* douceur *f*, *(of wine)* moelleux *m*, velouté *m*; *(of voice, sound)* velouté, moelleux

melodic [mɪ'lɒdɪk] ADJ *Mus* mélodique

melodious [mɪ'ləʊdɪəs] ADJ mélodieux

melodiously [mɪ'ləʊdɪəslɪ] ADV mélodieusement

melodrama ['melədrɑːmə] N mélodrame *m*

melodramatic [melədrə'mætɪk] ADJ mélodramatique

melodramatically [melədrə'mætɪklɪ] ADV d'un air *ou* d'une manière mélodramatique

melody ['melədɪ] N mélodie *f*

melon ['melən] N **1** *(fruit)* melon *m*; **m. seeds** pépins *mpl* de melon **2** *Am Fam (profits, money)* gros bénéfices *mpl* (à distribuer); **to carve** *or* **cut up the m.** distribuer les bénéfices **3** *Sl* **melons** *(breasts)* nichons *mpl*, roberts *mpl*

melt [melt] *(pt, pp* **melted**; *pp adj* **molten** ['məʊlt(ə)n]) VI fondre; *(of solid in liquid)* fondre, se dissoudre; **to m. in the mouth** fondre dans la bouche; **to m. into …** *(of colour etc)* se fondre dans …; *Fig* **my heart** *or* **I melted** j'ai été attendri; **she melted (inside) at his touch** elle fondait sous ses caresses; **to m. into thin air** disparaître
VT *(ice, metal)* fondre; *(salt etc)* (faire) fondre, (faire) dissoudre; **to m. sb's heart** attendrir qn; **m. the butter in a pan** faire fondre le beurre dans une casserole; *Fig Fam* **I'm absolutely melted** *(very hot)* je cuis; **melted snow** neige fondue
N *(sandwich)* **bacon/tuna m.** sandwich *m* au bacon/au thon recouvert de fromage fondu

▸ **melt away** VI **1** *(of snow)* fondre complètement **2** *(of clouds, vapour)* se dissiper; *(of crowd)* se disperser; *(of anger, objections, resistance etc)* se dissiper, s'évanouir

▸ **melt down** VT SEP *(scrap metal etc)* fondre

meltdown ['meltdaʊn] N **1** *Nucl* fusion *f* **2** *Fig* désintégration *f*, *(of Stock Exchange)* dégringolade *f*

melting ['meltɪŋ] ADJ *(wax, neige)* qui fond; *Fig (voice, words etc)* attendrissant
N *(act of melting) (of metal)* fonte *f*, fusion *f*, *(of snow)* fonte *f*
▸▸ **m. point** point *m* de fusion; **m. pot** creuset *m*; *Fig* melting-pot *m*, creuset; *Fig* **everything's in the m. pot** tout est à refaire; *Fig* **the United States is a m. pot** les États-Unis sont un creuset *ou* un melting-pot; **m. temperature** température *f* de fusion

member ['membər] N **1** *(of family, club etc)* membre *m*; *(of party)* adhérent, -ente; **to be a m. of the family** faire partie de la famille; **a m. of the audience** un spectateur, une spectatrice; **a m. of the opposite sex** une personne du sexe opposé **2** *(limb)* membre *m*; **(male) m.** membre (viril) **3** *Math* élément *m*
▸▸ **M. of Congress** membre du Congrès; **m. country** pays *m* membre; **M. of the European Parliament** député *m* européen; *St Exch* **m. firm** société *f* membre; **M. of the House of Representatives** membre de la Chambre des représentants; **M. of the Northern Ireland Assembly** membre de l'Assemblée législative d'Irlande du Nord; **M. of Parliament** membre de la Chambre des communes, ≃ député *m*; **the M. of Parliament**

for Newcastle le député de Newcastle; **M. of the Scottish Parliament** député du parlement écossais; **m. state** État *m* membre; **M. of the Welsh Assembly** membre de l'Assemblée du pays de Galles

membership ['membəʃɪp] N **1** *(state of being a member)* appartenance *f*, **m. of any political party is incompatible with this post** le titulaire de ce poste ne peut adhérer à aucun parti politique; **she resigned her m. of the party** elle a rendu sa carte du parti; **to pay one's m. (fee)** payer sa cotisation; **to renew one's m.** se réinscrire **2** *(members)* membres *mpl*, adhérents *mpl*, *(number of members) (of society etc)* nombre *m* des membres *ou* des adhérents, effectif *m*; **club with a m. of a thousand** club de mille membres; **the majority of our m.** la majorité de nos membres
▸▸ **m. card** carte *f* d'adhérent *ou* de membre; **m. list** liste *f* des membres; **m. number** numéro *m* d'adhérent

membrane ['membreɪn] N *Biol etc* membrane *f*

membranous ['membrənəs] ADJ membraneux

memento, *pl* **mementoes, mementos** [mɪ'mentəʊ, -əʊz] N souvenir *m*

memo ['meməʊ] N note *f* de service
▸▸ *Comput* **m. field** champ *m* mémo; **m. pad** bloc-notes *m*, *pl* blocs-notes

memoir ['memwɑːr] N *(essay) (scientific etc)* étude *f*, monographie *f*, *(biography)* notice *f* biographique; **memoirs** mémoires *fpl*

> Attention: ne pas confondre avec le nom anglais **memory**.

memorable ['memərəb(ə)l] ADJ *(speech, occasion)* mémorable; **a film m. largely for its sex and violence** un film surtout remarqué pour ses scènes de sexe et de violence

memorably ['memərəblɪ] ADV mémorablement, de façon mémorable

memorandum, *pl* **memoranda, memorandums** [memə'rændəm, -də, -dəmz] N **1** *Admin (within office etc)* note *f* de service **2** *(reminder)* note *f* **3** *(in diplomacy)* mémorandum *m* **4** *Law (of sale etc)* mémoire *m*; *(of contract)* mémoire, sommaire *m* des articles; **m. and articles of association** statuts *mpl* de société
▸▸ **m. of association** charte *f* constitutive d'une société à responsabilité limitée, acte *m* de société; **m. book** carnet *m*, calepin *m*, agenda *m*

memorial [mɪ'mɔːrɪəl] ADJ *(statue, festival, tablet, plaque etc)* commémoratif
N **1** *(monument)* monument *m* (commémoratif) **2** *(prize etc)* prix *m* commémoratif
▸▸ **m. service** commémoration *f*

memorize ['meməraɪz] VT apprendre par cœur

memory ['memərɪ] N **1** *(faculty)* mémoire *f*, **to have a good/bad m.** avoir (une) bonne/mauvaise mémoire; **to have a good m. for faces/names** avoir la mémoire des visages/des noms; **to have a bad m. for faces/names** ne pas avoir la mémoire des visages/des noms; *Fam* **m. like a sieve** mémoire de lièvre, très mauvaise mémoire; **loss of m.** perte *f* de mémoire; **if my m. serves me right** si j'ai bonne mémoire; **in** *or* **within living m.** de mémoire d'homme; **from m.** *(to play, recite, paint sth)* de mémoire; **to commit sth to m.** apprendre qch par cœur
2 *(something remembered) (of somebody, something)* souvenir *m*; **I have no m. of you saying any such thing** je ne me souviens pas que tu aies dit cela; **childhood memories** souvenirs *mpl* d'enfance; **I have very pleasant memories of your friend** je garde un

excellent souvenir de votre ami; **her earliest memories are of music** ses plus anciens souvenirs sont des airs de musique; **to take a trip down m. lane** *(visit place)* aller sur les lieux de son passé; **it's a real trip down m. lane hearing that song** cette chanson me rappelle ma jeunesse; **this television programme will take viewers on a trip down m. lane** cette émission rappellera de vieux souvenirs aux téléspectateurs; **to keep sb's m. alive** garder le souvenir de qn; **in m. of ...** à la mémoire de ..., en souvenir de ...

3 *Comput* mémoire *f*

▸▸*Comput* **m. address** adresse *f* de mémoire; *Comput* **m. bank** bloc *m* de mémoire; *Comput* **m. buffer** zone *f* de mémoire tampon; *Comput* **m. capacity** capacité *f* de mémoire; *Comput* **m. card** carte *f* mémoire; *Comput* **m. cell** cellule *f* mémoire; *Comput* **m. chip** puce *f* mémoire; *Comput* **m. expansion card** carte d'extension de mémoire; **m. loss** perte de mémoire; *Comput* **m. management** gestion *f* de mémoire; *Comput* **m. manager** gestionnaire *m* de mémoire; *Comput* **m. mapping** adresses *fpl* mémoire; *Aut* **m. seat** siège *m* à positions mémorisables; **m. typewriter** machine *f* à écrire à mémoire; *Comput* **m. upgrade** ajout *m* de mémoire

> Attention: ne pas confondre avec le nom anglais **memoir**.

memory-intensive ADJ *Comput (application)* qui prend beaucoup de place en mémoire

memory-loadable ADJ *Comput* chargeable en résident

memory-resident ADJ *Comput* résident en mémoire

men [men] *see* **man**

menace ['menɪs] N **1** menace *f*; **there was m. in his voice** il parlait d'un ton menaçant; **to demand money with menaces** réclamer de l'argent en usant de menaces **2** *Fam* **that kid's a m.** cet enfant est une véritable plaie; **he's a m. behind the wheel of a car** c'est un vrai danger au volant; **that carpet's a m.** ce tapis est dangereux
VT menacer

menacing ['menəsɪŋ] ADJ menaçant; **in a m. voice** d'une voix menaçante

menacingly ['menəsɪŋlɪ] ADV *(to look)* d'un air menaçant; *(to say)* d'un ton menaçant

menagerie [mɪ'nædʒərɪ] N ménagerie *f*

mend [mend] N **1** *Fam* **to be on the m.** *(of person)* être en voie de guérison; *(of situation)* s'arranger, s'améliorer **2** *(in fabric etc)* raccommodage *m*; *(darn)* reprise *f*; **the socks have a m. in the heel** les chaussettes ont été raccommodées au talon
VT **1** *(repair) (item of clothing etc)* raccommoder; *(darn) (item of clothing, socks)* repriser; *(fishing net)* rem(m)ailler; *(tool, road, shoes etc)* réparer **2** *(put right)* rectifier, corriger; **to m. one's ways** s'amender, se corriger; **to m. one's manners** s'amender; *Prov* **least said soonest mended** moins on parle, mieux cela vaut
VI *(of broken bones)* se ressouder; *Fam* **you'll/it'll soon m.** tu t'en remettras; **we'll have to make do and m.** il va falloir faire avec

mendacious [men'deɪʃəs] ADJ *Fml (person)* menteur, -euse; *(report)* mensonger

mendacity [men'dæsɪtɪ] N *Fml (characteristic)* propension *f* au mensonge

Mendelian [men'diːlɪən] ADJ *Biol* mendélien

mendicant ['mendɪkənt] ADJ *Lit* mendiant, de mendiant
N **1** *Lit* mendiant, -ante **2** *Rel* moine *m* mendiant

▸▸*Rel* **m. friar** moine mendiant; *Rel* **m. order** ordre *m* mendiant

mending ['mendɪŋ] N **1** *(of clothes etc)* raccommodage *m* **2** *(clothes)* vêtements *mpl* à raccommoder

menfolk ['menfəʊk] NPL **the m.** *(in contrast to women)* les hommes *mpl*; **the women worked alongside their** *or* **the m.** les femmes travaillaient aux côtés des hommes

menial ['miːnɪəl] ADJ *(task)* ingrat; *(job)* subalterne
N *usu Pej* laquais *m*; *(in household)* domestique *mf*

meningitis [menɪn'dʒaɪtɪs] N *Med* méningite *f*; **to have m.** avoir *ou* faire une méningite

meniscus, *pl* **menisci, meniscuses** [mɪ'nɪskəs, -saɪ, -skəsəz] N ménisque *m*

menopausal ['menəpɔːzəl] ADJ ménopausique; *(woman)* à la ménopause

menopause ['menəpɔːz] N *Physiol* ménopause *f*; **to be going through the m.** être en ménopause

mensch [menʃ] N *Am Fam (man)* chic type *m*; *(woman)* brave femme *f*

menses ['mensiːz] NPL *Physiol* menstrues *fpl*

menstrual ['menstrʊəl] ADJ *Physiol (cycle)* menstruel

menstruate ['menstrʊeɪt] VI *Physiol* avoir ses règles

menstruation [menstrʊ'eɪʃən] N *Physiol* menstruation *f*

mensuration [mensʃə'reɪʃən] N **1** *Fml (act of measuring)* mesurage *m*, mesure *f* **2** *Math* mensuration *f*

menswear ['menzweər] N *Com* vêtements *mpl* pour hommes; *(department)* rayon *m* homme

▸▸**m. department** rayon homme

mental ['ment(ə)l] ADJ **1** *(state, age etc)* mental, -aux; **I made a m. note to speak to her about it** je me suis dit qu'il ne fallait pas oublier de lui en parler; **I've made a m. note of it** j'y pense **2** *Sl (mad)* cinglé, dingue; **to go m.** *(go mad)* devenir dingue *ou* cinglé, perdre la boule; *(lose one's temper)* péter les plombs, péter une durite, piquer une crise; *Br* **it was a m. party!** c'était une fête vraiment démente *ou* dingue!

▸▸**m. arithmetic** calcul *m* mental; **m. block** blocage *m* psychologique; **m. breakdown** dépression *f*; **m. cruelty** cruauté *f* mentale; **m. defective** handicapé, -ée mental(e); **m. deficiency** déficience *f* ou débilité *f* mentale; **m. health** santé *f* mentale; **m. home, m. hospital** hôpital *m* ou clinique *f* psychiatrique; **m. illness** maladie *f* mentale; **m. reservation** doute *m*

mentality [men'tælɪtɪ] N *(of person)* mentalité *f*

mentally ['ment(ə)lɪ] ADV mentalement; **m. deficient** *or* **defective** débile mental; **m. ill/handicapped** malade/handicapé mental; **to be m. ill** être un malade mental; **the m. ill/handicapped** les malades/handicapés mentaux

menthol ['menθɒl] N menthol *m*

▸▸**m. cigarettes** cigarettes *fpl* au menthol

mentholated ['menθəleɪtɪd] ADJ *Pharm* mentholé

mention ['menʃən] N *(reference)* référence *f*, mention *f*; **m. was made of ...** on a parlé de ..., on a fait allusion à ...; **I never heard m. of her name again** je n'entendis plus jamais prononcer son nom; **to make no m. of sth** passer qch sous silence, ne pas faire mention de qch; **there is no m. of this extra charge in the brochure** la brochure ne mentionne pas ce supplément; **at the m. of food** quand on parle/a parlé de manger; **at the m.**

of her name he turned white quand il entendit son nom il pâlit; **he gets a brief m. in her autobiography** elle le mentionne brièvement dans son autobiographie; *Mil* **m. in dispatches** citation *f* à l'ordre du jour
VT *(somebody, something)* parler de; *(fact, detail)* relever, mentionner; **the sum mentioned** la somme indiquée; **I had forgotten to m. that ...** j'avais oublié de vous dire que ...; **she mentioned that she had lived in Bristol** elle mentionna qu'elle avait vécu à Bristol; **I shall m. it to him** je lui en parlerai, je lui en toucherai un mot; **too numerous to m.** trop nombreux pour les citer; **I have no money worth mentioning** je n'ai pour ainsi dire pas d'argent; **I didn't think it was worth mentioning** je ne pensais pas que c'était la peine d'en parler; **as mentioned above** comme mentionné ci-dessus; **not to m. ...** sans parler de ...; **I heard my name mentioned** j'ai entendu prononcer mon nom; **did she m. my name?** est-ce qu'elle a parlé de moi?; **to m. sb in one's will** coucher qn sur son testament; *Fam* **don't m. it!** *(after being thanked)* il n'y a pas de quoi!; *(drop the subject)* ne m'en parlez pas!, n'en parlez pas!; *Mil* **to be mentioned in dispatches** être cité à l'ordre du jour

mentor ['mentɔːr] N mentor *m*, guide *m*

menu ['menjuː] N **1** *Culin* menu *m*; **today's m.** la carte du jour **2** *Comput* menu *m*

▸▸*Comput* **m. bar** barre *f* de menu; *Comput* **m. builder** générateur *m* de menus; *Comput* **m. item** élément *m* de menu; *Comput* **m. option** option *f* de menu

menu-controlled ADJ *Comput* contrôlé par menu

menu-driven ADJ *Comput* contrôlé *ou* piloté par menu(s)

MEP [emiː'piː] N *Br (abbr* **Member of the European Parliament)** député *m* du Parlement européen

Merc [mɜːk] N *Fam (abbr* **Mercedes)** Mercedes *f*

mercantile ['mɜːkəntaɪl] ADJ commercial, -iaux, commerçant

▸▸**m. agency** agence *f* commerciale; **m. agent** agent *m* commercial; **m. bank** banque *f* de commerce; **m. law** droit *m* commercial; **m. marine** marine *f* marchande; **m. nation** nation *f* commerçante; **m. operations** opérations *fpl* mercantiles

mercantilism ['mɜːkəntɪlɪz(ə)m] N mercantilisme *m*

mercantilist ['mɜːkəntɪlɪst] ADJ, N mercantiliste *m*

mercenary ['mɜːsɪn(ə)rɪ] ADJ *Pej (person)* intéressé; **for purely m. reasons** uniquement pour l'argent; **must you be so m.?** tu ne penses qu'à l'argent!
N *(soldier)* mercenaire *m*

mercerized ['mɜːsəraɪzd] ADJ *Ind (cotton)* mercerisé

merchandise ['mɜːtʃəndaɪz] N marchandise(s) *f(pl)*
VI faire du commerce *ou* du négoce

merchandiser ['mɜːtʃəndaɪzər] N marchandiseur *m*

merchandising ['mɜːtʃəndaɪzɪŋ] N marchandisage *m*

merchant ['mɜːtʃənt] N **1** *Com esp Old-fashioned (dealer)* négociant, -ante, marchand, -ande; **wine m.** négociant en vins **2** *Fam* **speed m.** chauffard *m*; **gloom m.** pessimiste *mf*, *Br Fam* **rip-off** *or* **con m.** arnaqueur, -euse **3** *Am Com (shopkeeper)* marchand, -ande, boutiquier, -ière
ADJ marchand, de commerce

▸▸**m. bank** banque *f* d'affaires, banque d'investissement; **m. banker** banquier, -ière d'affaires; **m. marine, m. navy** marine *f* marchande; **m. seaman** marin *m* de la marine marchande; **m. ship, m. vessel** navire *m* marchand

merchantman, *pl* **merchantmen** ['mɜː-tʃəntmən] **N** *(ship)* navire *m* marchand, navire de commerce

merciful ['mɜːsɪfʊl] **ADJ** *(God)* miséricordieux (**to** pour); *(judge)* clément (**to** envers); **m. heavens!** grands Dieux!; **death was a m. release from his suffering** la mort fut une délivrance pour lui

mercifully ['mɜːsɪfʊlɪ] **ADV 1** *(showing mercy)* avec clémence **2** *(fortunately)* heureusement

merciless ['mɜːsɪlɪs] **ADJ** impitoyable, sans pitié, sans merci

mercilessly ['mɜːsɪlɪslɪ] **ADV** impitoyablement, sans pitié; **the rain beat down m.** la pluie tombait sans répit

Mercosur ['mɜːkəʊsʊər] **N** *Econ* Mercosur *m*

mercurial [mɜːˈkjʊərɪəl] **ADJ 1** *(lively)* *(temperament, character, person)* vif, *f* vive, éveillé **2** *(changeable)* inconstant, d'humeur changeante **3** *Med, Pharm (product)* mercuriel

Mercury ['mɜːkjʊrɪ] **N** *Myth* Mercure *m; Astron* Mercure *f*

mercury ['mɜːkjʊrɪ] **N** *Chem* mercure *m*
▸▸ **m. poisoning** empoisonnement *m* au mercure

mercy ['mɜːsɪ] **N** pitié *f, Rel* miséricorde *f, Rel* **Lord have m.!** Seigneur prends pitié!; **to show m. to sb** faire preuve de pitié envers qn; **to have m. on sb** avoir *ou* prendre pitié de qn; **to be without m.** être impitoyable *ou* sans pitié; **to call** *or* **beg for m.** demander grâce; **to throw oneself on sb's m.** s'abandonner à la merci de qn; *Old-fashioned* **m.!** grâce!; **at the m. of sb/sth** à la merci de qn/qch; **to be thankful** *or* **grateful for small mercies** être reconnaissant des moindres bienfaits; **what a m.!** quel bonheur!, quelle chance!; **works of m.** œuvres *fpl* de charité
▸▸ **m. flight** vol *m* de secours; **m. killing** *(euthanasia)* euthanasie *f, (individual death)* acte *m* d'euthanasie

mere [mɪər] **ADJ** simple; **a m. coincidence** une coïncidence pure et simple; **it's a m. formality** ce n'est qu'une simple formalité; **it was only by the merest chance that …** ce n'est que par le plus grand des hasards que …; **I shudder at the m. thought of it** je frissonne rien que d'y penser; **he's a m. child** ce n'est qu'un enfant; **he clearly hadn't the merest notion of who I was** il était clair qu'il n'avait pas la moindre idée de mon identité

merely ['mɪəlɪ] **ADV** simplement, seulement; **he m. smiled** il se contenta de sourire; **I mention this m. to draw attention to …** je n'ai dit cela que pour attirer l'attention sur …

meretricious [merɪˈtrɪʃəs] **ADJ** *Fml (style etc)* factice

merge [mɜːdʒ] **VT** *(two systems, classes)* fusionner, amalgamer; *Comput (files)* fusionner; **to m. sth in** *or* **into sth** fondre qch dans qch, amalgamer qch avec qch; **the two regiments were merged (into one)** les deux régiments ont été regroupés
▸ **VI** *Com, Fin (of companies, banks etc)* s'amalgamer, fusionner; *Aut (of lanes, roads etc)* se rencontrer; **the sea and sky merged** le ciel et la mer se confondaient; **the colours/ shapes/voices merged (into each other)** les couleurs/formes/voix se mêlaient; **to m. into the background** *(of building, person)* se fondre dans le décor; **to m. into the shadows** disparaître dans l'ombre
▸ **N** *Comput (of files)* fusion *f*

merger ['mɜːdʒər] **N** *Com, Fin (of several companies)* fusion *f*, fusionnement *m*
▸▸ **m. accounting** = bases *fpl* de prépara-

tion des comptes consolidés où deux sociétés se sont unifiées; **m. talks** discussions *fpl* en vue d'une fusion

meridian [məˈrɪdɪən] **N 1** *Geog* méridien *m* **2** *Astron (of star)* méridien *m*, point *m* culminant
▸ **ADJ** *Astron (altitude, angle etc)* méridien
▸▸ **m. line** *(ligne f)* méridienne *f*

meridional [məˈrɪdɪən(ə)l] **ADJ** méridional, -aux
▸ **N** Méridional, -ale

meringue [məˈræŋ] **N** *Culin* meringue *f*

merino [məˈriːnəʊ] **N** *(sheep, wool)* mérinos *m*

merit ['merɪt] **N 1** *(deserving aspect)* mérite *m*; **according to one's merits** *(to be rewarded)* selon ses mérites; *Law* **the merits of a case** le bien-fondé d'une cause; **to judge a proposal on its merits** juger une proposition pour ce qu'elle vaut; **to stand on its own merits** avoir une valeur en soi; *Rel* **to acquire m.** gagner du mérite; **her remarks at least had the m. of being frank** au moins, ses remarques avaient le mérite d'être franches **2** *(worth)* valeur *f*, mérite *m*; **in order of m.** par ordre de mérite; **these paintings have no m. at all** ces tableaux n'ont aucune valeur artistique
▸ **VT** *(reward, punishment etc)* mériter
▸▸ **m. increase** augmentation *f* au mérite; *Am Admin* **m. system** système *m* d'avancement fondé sur le mérite

meritocracy [merɪˈtɒkrəsɪ] **N** méritocratie *f*

meritocratic [merɪtəˈkrætɪk] **ADJ** méritocratique

meritorious [merɪˈtɔːrɪəs] **ADJ** *Fml (deed, conduct)* méritoire, louable

merlin ['mɜːlɪn] **N** *(bird)* *(faucon m)* émerillon *m*

mermaid ['mɜːmeɪd] **N** *Myth* sirène *f*

merman, *pl* **mermen** ['mɜːmæn, -men] **N** *Myth* triton *m*

Merovingian [merəʊˈvɪndʒɪən] *Hist* **ADJ** mérovingien
▸ **N** Mérovingien, -ienne

merrily ['merɪlɪ] **ADV** gaiement, gaîment, joyeusement

merriment ['merɪmənt] **N** gaieté *f*, gaîté *f*, **there was much m. at the thought of this** l'idée fit beaucoup rire; **sounds of m.** des rires

merry ['merɪ] **ADJ** *(comp* **merrier;** *superl* **merriest) 1** *(happy)* joyeux, gai; **to make m.** se divertir, s'amuser, s'égayer; **M. Christmas!** joyeux Noël!; *Fam* **the weather is playing m. hell with the rail timetables** le mauvais temps a complètement chamboulé l'horaire des trains; *Fam* **my back is giving me m. hell** mon dos me fait souffrir atrocement; *Prov* **the more the merrier** plus on est de fous, plus on rit; **the m. month of May** le gentil mois de mai; **Robin Hood and his m. men** Robin des Bois et ses joyeux *ou* gais lurons **2** *Fam (slightly drunk)* gai, éméché, un peu gris
▸▸ *Arch, Lit* **M. England** l'aimable Angleterre *f*

merry-go-round **N** manège *m, Belg, Suisse* carrousel *m*

merrymaking ['merɪmeɪkɪŋ] **N** réjouissances *fpl*

mescalin(e) ['meskəlɪn] **N** *Pharm* mescaline *f*

mesh [meʃ] **N 1** *(of net, sieve etc)* maille *f* **2** *Tech* prise *f*, engrènement *m*, engrenage *m*; **in m.** en prise
▸ **VI 1** *(coordinate)* concorder **2** *Tech (of teeth, wheels)* engrener, s'engrener; *(be in mesh)* être en prise (**with** avec); *(engage)* se mettre en prise (**with** avec)

▸ **VT** *Tech (of cogwheels)* endenter, engrener
▸▸ **m. stockings** bas *mpl* filet

mesmeric [mezˈmerɪk] **ADJ** *Fml* magnétique, hypnotique

mesmerize ['mezməraɪz] **VT** *Old-fashioned* hypnotiser; *Fig* fasciner

mesmerizing ['mezməraɪzɪŋ] **ADJ** fascinant

meson ['miːzɒn] **N** *Nucl* méson *m*

Mesopotamia [mesəpəˈteɪmɪə] **N** Mésopotamie *f*

mess [mes] **N 1** *(disorder)* désordre *m, Fam* pagaïe *f*, pagaille *f*, *(bungled job etc)* gâchis *m*; **the kitchen's a m.** la cuisine est en désordre, *Fam* la cuisine est un vrai foutoir; **you're** *or* **you look a m.!** tu es dans un triste état!; **my hair's a m.** mes cheveux sont dans un triste état; **to be in a m.** *(of person)* être dans le pétrin *ou* dans de beaux draps; **everything's in a m.** tout est en désordre; **to make a m. of** *(job, translation, repair etc)* gâcher, saboter, *Fam* saloper; **the dentist made a real m. of it** le dentiste a vraiment salopé le travail; **to make a m. of things** tout gâcher; *Fam* **after the fight his face was a terrible m.** après la bagarre il avait le visage tout amoché; *Fam* **he's a m.** *(has complexes)* il est bourré de complexes; *(because of drugs etc)* il est dans un piteux état

2 *(dirt)* saleté *f*; **to make a m. of the tablecloth** salir la nappe; **dog's m.** crotte *f* de chien; **the dog's done a m. on the carpet** le chien a fait ses besoins sur le tapis

3 *Mil (food) (for officers)* popote *f*, *(for men)* ordinaire *m, (room) (for officers)* mess *m*; *(for men)* réfectoire *m*

4 *Bible (food)* **m. of pottage** plat *m* de lentilles
▸ **VT** *(make dirty)* salir, souiller
▸ **VI 1** *Mil etc* manger en commun; **to m. together** manger à la même table

2 *Sl (exaggerate)* **no messing!** sans blagues!; **there were two hundred of them, no messing!** ils étaient deux cents et je n'exagère pas!

3 *Fam (defecate) (of dog, cat)* faire des *ou* ses saletés
▸▸ *Naut* **m. deck** poste *m* d'équipage; **m. jacket** *Mil* veston *m* de tenue de soirée; *(civilian)* veste *f* courte; **m. kit** *Mil (eating equipment)* gamelle *f, Br Fam (clothes)* tenue *f* de soirée; *Br* **m. tin** gamelle

▸ **mess about, mess around VI 1** *(play the fool)* faire l'imbécile; *(waste time)* traîner, glandouiller

2 *(tinker)* tripoter; **don't m. around with something that doesn't belong to you** ne touche pas à ce qui ne t'appartient pas

3 *(sexually)* **to m. around with sb** s'amuser avec qn; **stop messing around with my sister!** laisse ma sœur tranquille!
▸ **VT SEP 1** *(treat badly)* traiter de façon inconsidérée; **I wish you'd stop messing me about and make up your mind** j'aimerais bien que tu arrêtes de te moquer de moi et que tu te décides

2 *(alter)* chambouler

▸ **mess up VT SEP 1** *(put in disorder) (room, clothes etc)* mettre en désordre, semer la pagaïe dans; **you'll m. up my hair!** tu vas me décoiffer!

2 *(ruin) (job)* gâcher, *Fam* saloper; **he's messed everything up** il a tout gâché; **you've messed up all our plans** tu as chamboulé tous nos projets
▸ **VI** *Am Fam (at work, university etc)* tout rater; **to m. up on an exam** merdouiller dans *ou* à un examen

▸ **mess with VT INSEP** *Fam (meddle with)* **don't m. with me!** ne me cherche pas!; **you shouldn't m. with people like that** *(get involved with)* tu ne devrais pas fréquenter des gens comme ça; *(get on wrong side of)* tu ne devrais pas mécontenter ces gens-là;

that's what happens when you m. with drugs! voilà ce qui arrive quand on touche à la drogue!

message ['mesɪdʒ] N **1** message *m*; **to send a m. to sb** envoyer un message à qn; **to leave a m. for sb** laisser un message *ou* un mot à qn; *(when telephoning)* laisser un message à qn; *Comput* laisser un message à qn; *Fam* **have you got the m.?, is the m. getting across?** tu as bien compris?, tu as pigé?; *Fam* **people seem to be getting the m., the m. seems to be getting across** les gens ont l'air de commencer à comprendre; *Comput* **you get the screen m. …** l'écran affiche … **2** *(meaning) (of a book etc)* message *m*; **the film's m. is clear** le message qui ressort du film est clair **3** *Scot (errand)* commission *f*, course *f*
▶▶ **m. board** tableau *m* d'affichage; **m. boy** garçon *m* de courses; **m. form** fiche-message *f*, *pl* fiches-messages; *Comput* **m. handling** messagerie *f* (électronique); *Comput* **m. switching** commutation *f* de messages

messenger ['mesɪndʒər] N messager, -ère; *(in large offices etc)* coursier, -ière; *Mil* coureur *m*; *Admin (in diplomacy)* courrier *m* (diplomatique); *Com* commissionnaire *m*; *Br* **King's/Queen's m.** ≃ courrier *m* d'État; **by m.** par porteur
▶▶ **m. boy** coursier *m*, garçon *m* de courses

Messiah [mɪ'saɪə] N *Rel, Mus, Fig* Messie *m*

messianic [mesɪ'ænɪk] ADJ messianique

messily ['mesɪlɪ] ADV *(to eat)* salement; *Fig* **his first marriage ended rather m.** son premier mariage s'est mal terminé

messmate ['mesmeɪt] N *Mil etc* camarade *mf* de table; *Naut* camarade de plat

Messrs ['mesəz] NPL *(abbr* **Messieurs)** MM

mess-up N *Fam* gâchis *m*, pagaïe *f*

messy ['mesɪ] ADJ **1** *(dirty)* sale; *(untidy) (room, hair, appearance)* en désordre; *(handwriting)* illisible; **to have a m. appearance** avoir l'air peu soigné; **m. eater** personne qui mange salement, cochon *m*; **oranges are a m. fruit (to eat)** les oranges sont difficiles à manger proprement; **it's a m. job** c'est salissant; **this room's so m.** cette pièce est dans un tel désordre! **2** *(unpleasantly complex)* confus, embrouillé; **a m. business** *(criminal etc)* une sale histoire; **the official story is getting messier and messier** l'histoire officielle s'embrouille de plus en plus; **it's a rather m. solution** c'est une solution assez compliquée; **his m. private life** sa vie privée troublée

mestiza [me'sti:zə] N métisse *f*

mestizo, *pl* **mestizos** [me'sti:zəʊ, -əʊz] N métis *m*

met¹ [met] PT, PP *see* **meet¹**

met² ADJ *Br Fam (abbr* **meteorological)** météo
▶▶ **the M. Office** les services *mpl* météorologiques britanniques

metabolic [metə'bɒlɪk] ADJ *Biol* métabolique
▶▶ **m. rate** taux *m* métabolique

metabolism [mɪ'tæbəlɪz(ə)m] N *Biol* métabolisme *m*

metabolize [mɪ'tæbəlaɪz] VT transformer par métabolisme

metacarpal [metə'kɑːp(ə)l] ADJ, N *Anat* métacarpien *m*

metacarpus [metə'kɑːpəs] N *Anat* métacarpe *m*

metal ['met(ə)l] N **1** métal *m* **2** *Typ* caractères *mpl*, métal *m*, plomb *m* **3** *(stones) Rail* ballast *m* (de voie ferrée); **(road) m.** cailloutis *m*, pierraille *f* **4** *(in glassmaking)* verre *m* en fusion
ADJ *(made of metal)* métallique, en métal

VT *(-ll-, Am -l-) Br Constr (road)* empierrer; **metalled road** route *f* empierrée
▶▶ **m. detector** détecteur *m* de métaux; **m. engraver** graveur, -euse sur métaux; **m. polish** produit *m* pour faire briller les métaux

metalanguage ['metəlæŋgwɪdʒ] N métalangage *m*

metallic [mɪ'tælɪk] ADJ *(sound, voice)*, *Chem, Elec etc* métallique; *(taste)* de métal; **m. sheen** éclat *m* métallique; **a m. blue/green** un bleu/vert métallique
▶▶ **m. paint** peinture *f* métallisée

metallurgical [metə'lɜːdʒɪk(ə)l] ADJ métallurgique

metallurgy [me'tælədʒɪ] N métallurgie *f*

metalwork ['met(ə)lwɜːk] N **1** *(practice, technique)* travail *m* des métaux; *Br Sch* **m. teacher/lesson** professeur *m*/cours *m* de travail des métaux **2** *(articles)* métal *m* ouvré; *Art* ferronnerie *f*, **piece of m.** pièce *f* en métal ouvré; *Art* objet *m* en ferronnerie

metalworker ['met(ə)lwɜːkər] N *Ind* (ouvrier *m*) métallurgiste *mf*, **art m.** ferronnier *m ou* serrurier *m* d'art

metamorphic [metə'mɔːfɪk] ADJ *Geol* métamorphique; *Biol* métamorphosique

metamorphose [metə'mɔːfəʊz] VT métamorphoser, transformer (**into** en)
VI se métamorphoser (**into** en)

metamorphosis, *pl* **metamorphoses** [metə'mɔːfəsɪs, -əsiːz] N métamorphose *f*

metaphor ['metəfər] N métaphore *f*, image *f* (**for** symbolisant); **mixed m.** métaphore multiple

metaphoric(al) [metə'fɒrɪk, -ɪk(ə)l] ADJ métaphorique

metaphorically [metə'fɒrɪklɪ] ADV métaphoriquement

metaphysical [metə'fɪzɪk(ə)l] ADJ métaphysique

metaphysics [metə'fɪzɪks] N métaphysique *f* VOIR GRAMMAIRE A10

metatarsal [metə'tɑːs(ə)l] ADJ, N *Anat* métatarsien *m*

metatarsus [metə'tɑːsəs] N *Anat* métatarse *m*

▶ **mete out** [miːt] VT SEP *(punishment)* distribuer, infliger; *(reward)* distribuer, décerner; **to m. out justice** faire justice

metempsychosis ['metəmsaɪ'kəʊsɪs] N métempsychose *f*

meteor ['miːtɪər] N météore *m*
▶▶ **m. shower** pluie *f* d'étoiles filantes, averse *f* météorique

meteoric [miːtɪ'ɒrɪk] ADJ *Astron* météorique; *Fig* **m. rise** ascension *f* fulgurante

meteorite ['miːtɪəraɪt] N météorite *f*, aérolit(h)e *m*

meteorological [miːtɪərə'lɒdʒɪk(ə)l] ADJ météorologique

meteorologist [miːtɪə'rɒlədʒɪst] N météorologiste *mf*, météorologue *mf*

meteorology [miːtɪə'rɒlədʒɪ] N météorologie *f*

meter¹ ['miːtər] N *(device)* compteur *m*; *Aut* parcmètre *m*, *Can* compteur de stationnement; *Aut Fam* **I'm on a m.** je suis garé à un parcmètre
▶▶ *Am Fam* **m. maid** contractuelle *f*, pervenche *f*, *Can* préposée *f* au stationnement; **m. reader** *(person)* releveur, -euse de(s) compteur(s); **m. reading** relevé *m* (de(s) compteur(s))

meter² N *Am* = **metre**

methadone ['meθədəʊn] N *Med* méthadone *f*, **to be on m.** *(of drug addict)* prendre de la méthadone

methane ['miːθeɪn] N *Chem* méthane *m*

methinks [mɪ'θɪŋks] V IMPERS *(pt* **methought** [mɪ'θɔːt]) *Arch, Lit, Hum* il me semble; **you are sad, m.** il me semble que vous êtes triste

method ['meθəd] N *(in research, science)* méthode *f*; **the m. of doing sth** la manière de faire qch; *Admin* **methods of payment** modalités *fpl* de paiement; **to work without m.** travailler sans méthode; **to lack m.** manquer de méthode, ne pas être méthodique; *Prov* **there's m. in his madness** il n'est pas aussi fou qu'il en a l'air
▶▶ *Cin, Theat* **M. acting** la méthode Stanislavski; *Cin, Theat* **M. actor** acteur *m* adepte de la méthode de Stanislavski; *Cin, Theat* **M. actress** actrice *f* adepte de la méthode de Stanislavski; *Ind* **methods engineer** ingénieur *m* des méthodes; *Ind* **methods engineering** étude *f* des méthodes

methodical [mɪ'θɒdɪk(ə)l] ADJ méthodique

methodically [mɪ'θɒdɪklɪ] ADV méthodiquement, avec méthode

Methodism ['meθədɪz(ə)m] N *Rel* méthodisme *m*

Methodist ['meθədɪst] ADJ, N *Rel* méthodiste *mf*

methodology [meθə'dɒlədʒɪ] N méthodologie *f*

meths [meθs] N *Br Fam* alcool *m* à brûler

Methuselah [mə'θjuːzələ] N *Bible* Mathusalem *m*; *Fig* **as old as M.** vieux comme Hérode

methyl ['meθɪl] N *Chem* méthyle *m*
▶▶ **m. alcohol** méthanol *m*, alcool *m* méthylique

methylated ['meθɪleɪtɪd] ADJ
▶▶ **m. spirits** alcool *m* dénaturé, alcool à brûler

methylene ['meθɪliːn] N *Chem* méthylène *m*

meticulous [mɪ'tɪkjʊləs] ADJ méticuleux, minutieux; **with m. attention to detail** avec une attention méticuleuse *ou* minutieuse pour les détails

meticulously [mɪ'tɪkjʊləslɪ] ADV méticuleusement, minutieusement; *(to describe)* dans le détail; **to be m. dressed** être tiré à quatre épingles

meticulousness [mɪ'tɪkjʊləsnɪs] N méticulosité *f*, minutie *f*

metonymic ['metə'nɪmɪk] ADJ métonymique

metonymy [mɪ'tɒnɪmɪ] N métonymie *f*

me-too product N *Mktg* produit *m* tactique

metre,¹ *Am* **meter** ['miːtər] N *Liter (in poetry)* mètre *m*, mesure *f*; **in m.** en vers

metre,² *Am* **meter** N *(measurement)* mètre *m*

metric ['metrɪk] ADJ *(system)* métrique; **to go m.** adopter le système métrique
▶▶ **m. area** métrage *m*; **m. ton** tonne *f*, **m. volume** métrage *m*

metrical ['metrɪk(ə)l] ADJ métrique

metrication [metrɪ'keɪʃən] N adoption *f ou* introduction *f* du système métrique

metrics ['metrɪks] N *(in poetry)* métrique *f* VOIR GRAMMAIRE A10

metro ['metrəʊ] N métro *m*

metronome ['metrənəʊm] N *Mus* métronome *m*

metropolis [mɪ'trɒpəlɪs] N *(city)* métropole *f*

metropolitan [metrə'pɒlɪtən] ADJ *(area etc)* urbain; **m. France** France *f* métropolitaine N *(inhabitant)* habitant, -ante de la métropole *ou* de la capitale; *Rel (bishop)* métropolitain *m*
▶▶ **M. Police** *Br* police *f* londonienne; *Am* police urbaine

mettle ['met(ə)l] N *(courage) (of person)* courage *m*, force *f* d'âme; *(of horse)* fougue *f*; **to be on one's m.** être prêt à donner le meilleur de soi-même; **to show one's m.** montrer de quoi on est capable

mettlesome ['met(ə)lsəm] ADJ *Old-fashioned (person)* plein de courage; *(horse)* fougueux

mew [mju:] N *(of cat)* miaulement *m*
VI *(of cat)* miauler

mewing ['mju:ɪŋ] N miaulement *m*

mews [mju:z] NPL *Br* **1** *(street)* ruelle *f (sur laquelle donnaient des écuries);* **m. cottage, m. house** = maison *f* assez luxueuse aménagée dans une ancienne écurie **2** *Arch (stables)* écuries *fpl*

Mex [meks] *Am Fam Offensive* N Mexicain, -aine
ADJ mexicain

Mexican ['meksɪkən] ADJ mexicain
N Mexicain, -aine

Mexico ['meksɪkəʊ] N Mexique *m*
▸▸ **M. City** Mexico

mezzanine ['metsəni:n] N **1** *Archit* mezzanine *f*, entresol *m* **2** *Theat Am* corbeille *f, Br* premier dessous *m (de la scène)*
▸▸ *Fin* **m. debt** dette *f* subordonnée *ou* mezzanine; **m. finance** = méthode *f* de financement d'une partie du capital nécessaire pour acheter une entreprise *(utilisée principalement par ses employés); Archit* **m. floor** mezzanine, entresol

mezzo ['metsəʊ] *Mus* ADV mezzo
N = **mezzo-soprano**
▸▸ **m. forte** mezzo forte

mezzo-soprano N *Mus (voice)* mezzo-soprano *m, pl* mezzo-sopranos, -ni; *(singer)* mezzo-soprano *f*

mezzotint ['metsəʊtɪnt] N mezzo-tinto *m inv*

mfd *Com (abbr* **manufactured**) fabriqué

mg *(abbr* **milligram(s)**) mg

Mgr *Rel (abbr* **monsignor**) Mgr

MHz *Elec (abbr* **megahertz**) Mhz

MI [e'maɪ] N *Comput (abbr* **machine intelligence**) IA *f*

mi [mi:] N *Mus* mi *m*

MI5 [emaɪ'faɪv] N *Br (abbr* **Military Intelligence Section 5**) MI5 *m*, ≃ DST *f (contre-espionnage)*

MI6 [emaɪ'sɪks] N *Br (abbr* **Military Intelligence Section 6**) MI6 *m*, ≃ DGSE *f (espionnage)*

MIA [emaɪ'eɪ] ADJ, N *Am Mil (abbr* **missing in action**) porté disparu

miaow [mɪ'aʊ] N *(of cat)* miaulement *m*, miaou *m*
INT miaou
VI *(of cat)* miauler

mic [mɪk] N *TV, Radio* micro *m*

mica ['maɪkə] N *Miner* mica *m*

mice *see* **mouse**[1]

Mich *abbr* **Michigan**

Michael ['maɪk(ə)l] N Michel *m; Br Fam* **to take the M. out of sb** se payer la tête de qn; **are you taking the M.?** tu te payes ma/sa tête?

Michaelmas ['mɪkəlməs] N la Saint-Michel
▸▸ *Bot* **M. daisy** aster *m* (d'automne); *Br Univ* **M. term** premier trimestre *m (de l'année scolaire dans certaines universités); Law* session *f* de la Saint-Michel

Michelangelo [maɪkə'læn(d)ʒələʊ] N *Art* Michel-Ange *m*

Michelin man ['mɪtʃlɪn-] N **the M.** le bonhomme Michelin

Mick [mɪk] N *Offensive Sl (Irishman)* Irlandais *m*

Mickey ['mɪkɪ] N *Sl (drugged drink)* = boisson *f* alcoolisée dans laquelle on a versé un sédatif
▸▸ *Sl* **M. Finn** = boisson alcoolisée dans laquelle on a versé un sédatif; **M. Mouse** Mickey *m*

mickey ['mɪkɪ] N *Br Fam* **to take the m. out of sb** se payer la tête de qn; **are you taking the m.?** tu te payes ma/sa tête?

micro ['maɪkrəʊ] N *Comput* micro *m*

micro- ['maɪkrəʊ] PREF micro-

microanalysis [maɪkrəʊə'næləsɪs] N *Chem* microanalyse *f*

microbe ['maɪkrəʊb] N microbe *m*

microbial [maɪ'krəʊbɪəl], **microbic** [maɪ'krəʊbɪk] ADJ microbien

microbiology [maɪkrəʊbaɪ'ɒlədʒɪ] N microbiologie *f*

microbrewery [maɪkrəʊ'brʊərɪ] N microbrasserie *f*

microcamera [maɪkrəʊ'kæmərə] N appareil *m* de micro-photographie

microchannel architecture [maɪkrəʊ-'tʃæn(ə)l] N *Comput* architecture *f* à microcanaux

microchip ['maɪkrəʊtʃɪp] N *Comput* puce *f* (électronique)

microcircuit ['maɪkrəʊsɜ:kɪt] N *Comput* microcircuit *m*

microcircuitry ['maɪkrəʊsɜ:kɪtrɪ] N *Comput* microcircuits *mpl*

microclimate ['maɪkrəʊklaɪmɪt] N *Met* microclimat *m*

micrococcus [maɪkrəʊ'kɒkəs] N *Biol* micrococque *m*, micrococcus *m*

microcode [maɪkrəʊ'kəʊd] N *Comput* microcode *m*

microcomputer ['maɪkrəʊkəm'pju:tər] N micro-ordinateur *m, pl* micro-ordinateurs

microcosm ['maɪkrəʊkɒz(ə)m] N microcosme *m*

microdot ['maɪkrəʊdɒt] N micropoint *m*

microeconomic [maɪkrəʊi:kə'nɒmɪk] ADJ microéconomique

microeconomics [maɪkrəʊi:kə'nɒmɪks] N microéconomie *f* VOIR GRAMMAIRE A10

microeconomy [maɪkrəʊɪ'kɒnəmɪ] N microéconomie *f*

microelectronics [maɪkrəʊelek'trɒnɪks] N micro-électronique *f* VOIR GRAMMAIRE A10

microfibre, *Am* **microfiber** ['maɪkrəʊfaɪbə(r)] N microfibre *m*

microfiche ['maɪkrəʊfi:ʃ] N microfiche *f*

microfilm ['maɪkrəʊfɪlm] N microfilm *m*
VT microfilmer

microfloppy ['maɪkrəʊ'flɒpɪ] N microdisquette *f*

microgroove ['maɪkrəʊgru:v] N microsillon *m*

microlight ['maɪkrəʊlaɪt] N *Aviat* ULM *m*

micromarketing [maɪkrəʊ'ma:kɪtɪŋ] N micromarketing *m*

micromesh ['maɪkrəʊmeʃ] ADJ *(stocking)* à mailles très fines

micrometer [maɪ'krɒmɪtər] N micromètre *m*

micron ['maɪkrɒn] N *(measurement)* micron *m*

Micronesia [maɪkrəʊ'ni:zɪə] N Micronésie *f*

microorganism [maɪkrəʊ'ɔ:gənɪz(ə)m] N micro-organisme *m, pl* micro-organismes

micropayment [maɪkrəʊ'peɪmənt] N *Comput* micropaiement *m*

microphone ['maɪkrəfəʊn] N microphone *m*, micro *m;* **speak into the m.** parlez dans le micro; **a good m. voice** une voix qui passe bien à la radio/à l'enregistrement

microphysics [maɪkrəʊ'fɪsɪks] N microphysique *f* VOIR GRAMMAIRE A10

microprocessor ['maɪkrəʊ'prəʊsesər] N *Comput* microprocesseur *m*

microreader ['maɪkrəʊri:dər] N microliseuse *f*

microscooter ['maɪkrəʊsku:tər] N trottinette *f ou* patinette *f* à moteur

microscope ['maɪkrəskəʊp] N microscope *m;* **under the m.** au microscope; *Fig* **to put sth under the m.** examiner qch à la loupe

microscopic [maɪkrə'skɒpɪk] ADJ **1** *(very small)* microscopique **2** *(examination etc)* au microscope, microscopique

microscopy [maɪ'krɒskəpɪ] N microscopie *f*

microsecond ['maɪkrəʊsekənd] N microseconde *f*

microsegment ['maɪkrəʊsegmənt] N *Mktg* microsegment *m*

microsegmentation [maɪkrəʊsegmən-teɪʃən] N *Mktg* microsegmentation *f*

microspacing ['maɪkrəʊspeɪsɪŋ] N *Comput* micro-espacement *m*

microsurgery [maɪkrəʊ'sɜ:dʒərɪ] N microchirurgie *f*

microtechnology [maɪkrəʊtek'nɒlədʒɪ] N microtechnologie *f*

microwave ['maɪkrəʊweɪv] N **1** *(oven)* (four *m* à) micro-ondes *m inv* **2** *Electron, Radio* micro-onde *f, pl* micro-ondes
VT **to m. sth** faire cuire qch au (four à) micro-ondes; **microwaved food** nourriture *f* cuite au (four à) micro-ondes
▸▸ **m. oven** (four à) micro-ondes

micturition [mɪktjʊ'rɪʃən] N *Med* miction *f*

mid [mɪd] ADJ **in m. ocean** en plein océan, en pleine mer; **from m. June to m. August** de la mi-juin à la mi-août; **m. season** demi-saison *f, pl* demi-saisons; **he stopped in m. sentence** il s'est interrompu au milieu de sa phrase; **m. Wales** le centre du pays de Galles; **the m. 1960s** le milieu des années soixante

midafternoon [mɪdɑ:ftə'nu:n] N milieu *m* de l'après-midi; **we had a m. break** on a fait une pause en milieu de l'après-midi

midair [mɪd'eər] ADJ *(collision)* en plein ciel
N **in m.** en plein ciel

Midas ['maɪdəs] N Midas *m; Prov* **to have the M. touch** transformer tout ce qu'on touche en or

mid-Atlantic ADJ **m. accent** accent mi-américain mi-britannique

midday ['mɪd'deɪ] N midi *m;* **at m.** à midi
▸▸ **m. meal** repas *m* de midi

midden ['mɪd(ə)n] N *Br (dunghill)* (tas *m* de) fumier *m; Scot Fam* **this room is like a m.** cette pièce est une vraie porcherie

middle ['mɪd(ə)l] ADJ du milieu; *(in between)* intermédiaire; **the m. house/sister** la maison/la sœur du milieu; *Fig* **to steer a m. course** adopter une solution intermédiaire; **in the m. distance** au second plan
N **1** milieu *m;* **in the m. of …** au milieu de …; **in the m. of nowhere** dans un coin perdu; **in the m. of the summer** en plein été; **about the m. of August** à la mi-août; **in the m. of the night** en pleine nuit; **I was in the m. of reading/of watching a programme** j'étais en train de lire/de regarder une émission; **he was driving down the m. of the road** il roulait au (beau) milieu de la route; *Fam* **they split the money down the m.** ils ont partagé l'argent en deux parties égales **2** *Fam (waist)* taille *f*, ceinture *f*; **round one's m.** autour de la taille; **the water came up to his m.** l'eau lui arrivait à la taille
▸▸ **m. age** l'âge *m* mûr; **man of m. age** un homme d'âge mûr; **in m. age** vers la cin-

quantaine; **in early m. age he ...** vers la cinquantaine il ... ; **the M. Ages** le Moyen Âge *m*; **M. America** *Geog* Amérique *f* centrale; *Fig (American middle class)* l'Amérique moyenne; *Pej* l'Amérique bien pensante; *Mus* **m. C** do *m inv* du milieu du clavier; **m. classes** bourgeoisie *f, Anat* **m. ear** oreille *f* moyenne; **the M. East** le Moyen-Orient; **M. Eastern** moyen-oriental; **M. England** l'Angleterre *f* moyenne *(aux tendances conservatrices)*; *Pej* **M. Englander** Anglais, -aise moyen(enne); *Ling* **M. English** le moyen anglais; **m. finger** majeur *m*, médius *m*; *Br Fam* **m. finger salute** doigt *m* d'honneur; **to give sb the m. finger salute** faire un doigt d'honneur à qn; **m. ground** *(in picture)* second plan *m*; *Fig* terrain *m* neutre; *Fig* **to occupy the m. ground** *(in political spectrum)* adopter une position intermédiaire; **m. management** cadres *mpl* moyens; **m. manager** cadre *m* moyen; **m. name** deuxième prénom *m*; *Fig* **procrastination is your m. name!** tu remets toujours tout au lendemain; **honesty is her m. name** c'est l'honnêteté même; **laziness is his m. name** c'est un incorrigible paresseux; **generosity isn't exactly his m. name!** on ne peut pas dire qu'il soit particulièrement généreux; **m. neck** *(of beef)* côtes *fpl* découvertes; *St Exch* **m. price** cours *m* moyen; **m. school** *Br* = école *f* pour enfants de 8 ou 9 à 13 ans; *Am* = école pour enfants de 10 à 13 ans, ≃ collège *m*; *Am Geog* **the M. West** le Midwest

middle-aged ADJ *(person)* entre deux âges, d'un certain âge
▸▸ **m. spread** bourrelets *mpl* (qui viennent avec l'âge)

middlebrow ['mɪd(ə)braʊ] ADJ qui ne demande pas trop d'efforts intellectuels

middle-class ADJ bourgeois

middle-income ADJ
▸▸ *Mktg* **m. group** groupe *m* de contribuables à revenus moyens

middleman, *pl* **middlemen** ['mɪd(ə)læn, -men] N *Com* intermédiaire *m*; **m.'s market** marché *m* des intermédiaires

middlemost ['mɪd(ə)məʊst] ADJ le plus proche du milieu

middle-of-the-road ADJ *(policy)* modéré; *Mus Pej* grand public

middle-roader [-rəʊdər] N *Am Pol* modéré, -ée

middle-sized ADJ de taille moyenne

middleweight ['mɪd(ə)lweɪt] N *(boxer)* poids *m* moyen; **m. champion** champion *m* poids moyen

middling ['mɪdlɪŋ] ADJ *(mediocre)* médiocre; *(fairly good)* passable, assez bon; *Fam* **how are you? – m.** comment allez-vous? – comme ci comme ça

middy ['mɪdɪ] N *Naut Fam* midship *m*

Mideast [mɪd'iːst] N *esp Am* **the M.** le Moyen-Orient

midfield [mɪd'fiːld] N *Ftbl etc* milieu *m* de terrain; **to play in m.** jouer au milieu du terrain
▸▸ **m. player** *(joueur m* du) milieu de terrain

midfielder [mɪd'fiːldər] N *Ftbl etc* milieu *m* de terrain

midge [mɪdʒ] N *(insect)* moucheron *m*

midget ['mɪdʒɪt] N *(small person)* nain, *f* naine, nabot, -ote
ADJ miniature

MIDI ['mɪdɪ] N *Comput (abbr* **musical instrument digital interface)** MIDI

midi ['mɪdɪ] ADJ *(skirt, coat etc)* de longueur moyenne, midi *inv*
N *(skirt, coat etc)* jupe *f*/manteau *m*/etc de longueur moyenne
▸▸ **m. system** *(stereo)* chaîne *f* midi

midland ['mɪdlənd] ADJ *(plain etc)* du centre *(d'un pays)*

Midlands (the) [ðə'mɪdləndz] NPL les Midlands *fpl (comtés du centre de l'Angleterre)*; **a M. accent** un accent des Midlands

midlife ['mɪdlaɪf] N quarantaine *f*
▸▸ **m. crisis** *(in professional etc life)* crise *f* à l'abord de la quarantaine; *(in sex life also)* démon *m* de midi; **to be going through a m. crisis** traverser la crise de la quarantaine

midmorning [mɪd'mɔːnɪŋ] N milieu *m* de la matinée; **m. coffee break** pause-café *f* au milieu de la matinée

midnight ['mɪdnaɪt] N minuit *m*; **at m.** à minuit; **to burn the m. oil** travailler tard dans la nuit; **a m. snack** un casse-croûte en plein milieu de la nuit
▸▸ **m. blue** bleu nuit *m inv*; **m. feast** = petit repas *m* pris en cachette la nuit par des enfants, à l'insu de leurs parents; **m. Mass** messe *f* de minuit; **m. sun** soleil *m* de minuit; **the land of the m. sun** le pays du soleil de minuit

mid-range ADJ *Com (computer, car)* de milieu de gamme

midriff ['mɪdrɪf] N *Anat (diaphragm)* diaphragme *m*; *(stomach)* ventre *m*; **bare m.** ventre *m* nu, taille *f* nue

midshipman, *pl* **midshipmen** ['mɪdʃɪpmən] N *Naut* aspirant *m (de marine), Fam* midship *m*

midships ['mɪdʃɪps] ADV *Naut* au milieu du navire, par le travers

midst [mɪdst] N **in the m. of sth** au milieu de qch; **in the m. of winter** au milieu *ou* au cœur de l'hiver, en plein hiver; **in the m. of all this** *(these events)* sur ces entrefaites; **in the m. of the celebration** en plein milieu de la fête; **in our/your/their m.** parmi nous/vous/eux; **there are traitors in our m.** il y a des traîtres parmi nous

midstream [mɪd'striːm] N **in m.** au milieu du courant; *Fig* **she stopped in m.** *(of speaker)* elle s'est arrêtée en plein milieu de son récit

midsummer ['mɪdsʌmər] N *(middle of summer)* milieu *m* de l'été, cœur *m* de l'été; *(solstice)* solstice *m* d'été; **in m.** au milieu *ou* au cœur de l'été, en plein été
▸▸ **M. Day** la Saint-Jean; **m. madness** folie *f* estivale; *Liter* **A M. Night's Dream** le Songe d'une Nuit d'Été

midterm [mɪd'tɜːm] N **1** *Pol Am* milieu *m* du mandat présidentiel, *Br* milieu du mandat du Premier Ministre **2** *Sch, Univ* milieu *m* du trimestre
▸▸ *Sch, Univ* **m. break** vacances *fpl* de milieu de trimestre; *Pol* **m. elections** = aux États-Unis, élections *fpl* législatives qui ont lieu au milieu du mandat présidentiel; *Sch, Univ* **m. exams** examens *mpl* du milieu du trimestre

midway ['mɪdweɪ] ADV à mi-chemin, à mi-distance; **m. up the hill** à mi-côte; **m. between ... and ...** à mi-distance *ou* à mi-chemin entre ... et ...; **a style m. between John's and Paul's** un style intermédiaire entre celui de John et celui de Paul

midweek [mɪd'wiːk] N milieu *m* de la semaine; **I'll see you m.** je te verrai vers le milieu de la semaine; **m. show** spectacle *m* de milieu de semaine

Midwest [mɪd'west] N Midwest *m*

Midwestern [mɪd'westən] ADJ du Midwest *m*

midwife, *pl* **midwives** ['mɪdwaɪf, -waɪvz] N sage-femme *f, pl* sages-femmes, accoucheuse *f*

midwifery ['mɪdwɪfərɪ] N **1** *(profession)* profession *f* de sage-femme **2** *(obstetrics)* obstétrique *f*

midwinter ['mɪd'wɪntər] N *(middle of winter)* milieu *m* de l'hiver, cœur *m* de l'hiver; *(solstice)* solstice *m* d'hiver

mien [miːn] N *Lit* mine *f*, air *m*, contenance *f*

miffed [mɪft] ADJ *Fam* froissé, piqué, fâché

MIG [mɪg] N *Fin (abbr* **minimum income guarantee)** = revenu *m* minimum assuré par l'État britannique aux plus de 60 ans

might[1] [maɪt] N *(strength)* puissance *f*, force(s) *f(pl)*; **with all one's m.** *(to work, push etc)* de toute sa force, de toutes ses forces; *Lit* **with m. and main** de toutes mes/ses/etc forces; **she strove with m. and main to prevent it** elle a fait tout ce qu'elle a pu pour empêcher cela; *Prov* **m. is right** la raison du plus fort est toujours la meilleure

MIGHT[2] V AUX *see* **may**[1] **are you coming? – I m.** tu viens? – peut-être; **she refused, as well she m.** rien d'étonnant à ce qu'elle ait refusé; **when I mentioned his name she blushed, as well she m.** quand j'ai prononcé son nom, elle a rougi, et cela n'a rien d'étonnant; **and who m. you be?** qui êtes-vous, sans indiscrétion?; **and what m. you be doing here?** peut-on savoir ce que vous faites là?; **I wonder what I m. have done to offend him** je me demande ce que j'ai bien pu faire pour le fâcher; **he m. have arrived in time if ...** il aurait pu arriver à temps si ...; **you m. shut the door** vous pourriez fermer la porte!; **all the same, you m. have made less noise!** tout de même vous auriez pu faire moins de bruit!; **I was afraid he m. have done it** j'avais peur qu'il ne l'ait *ou Fml* l'eût fait VOIR GRAMMAIRE A59–60

might-have-been N *Fam (person)* raté, -ée

mightily ['maɪtɪlɪ] ADV **1** *(powerfully)* puissamment, fortement **2** *Fam (extremely)* extrêmement; **to be m. relieved** être vraiment soulagé

mighty ['maɪtɪ] ADJ *(comp* **mightier;** *superl* **mightiest) 1** *(powerful) (nation, army etc)* puissant; *(blow)* grand **2** *(large, imposing)* grandiose, majestueux **3** *esp Am Fam (considerable)* grand; **you're in a m. hurry** vous êtes diablement pressé
ADV *esp Am Fam* rudement; **you're making a m. big mistake** vous commettez là une erreur colossale; **she looked m. pleased with herself** elle avait l'air très contente d'elle

mignonette [mɪnjə'net] N *Bot* réséda *m*

migraine ['miːgreɪn, 'maɪ-] N *Med* migraine *f*, **to suffer from m.** souffrir de migraines; **a bad m.** une forte migraine; **m. sufferer** migraineux, -euse

migrant ['maɪgrənt] ADJ = **migratory**
N *(person, bird etc)* migrateur, -trice
▸▸ **m. worker** *(seasonal)* travailleur, -euse saisonnier, -ière; *(foreign)* travailleur, -euse immigré(e)

migrate [maɪ'greɪt] VI *(of bird)* migrer; *(of person)* émigrer; **to m. south** migrer vers le sud; **people who had migrated from eastern Europe** les gens qui avaient émigré d'Europe de l'est

migration [maɪ'greɪʃən] N *(of birds)* migration *f*, *(of people)* émigration *f*

migratory ['maɪgrətrɪ, maɪ'greɪtərɪ] ADJ *(bird)* migrateur, -trice; *(movement)* migratoire

Mike [maɪk] N *Fam* **for the love of M.** pour l'amour du ciel

mike [maɪk] N *Fam (abbr* **microphone)** micro *m*

milch [mɪltʃ] ADJ
▸▸ **m. cow** vache *f* laitière; *Fig* vache à lait

mild [maɪld] ADJ **1** *(person, remark)* doux, *f* douce; *(answer)* conciliant; *(criticism)* léger, anodin **2** *(punishment)* peu sévère, léger **3**

(climate) doux, *f* douce, tempéré; *(winter)* doux, clément; **the weather is getting milder** le temps s'adoucit **4** *(dish)* peu épicé; *(cigar, tobacco, soap)* doux, *f* douce; *(sedative, medicine)* léger; **m. cheddar** cheddar *m* doux; **a m. curry** un curry peu épicé **5** *Med (illness, infection)* bénin, *f* bénigne; **a m. form of measles** une forme bénigne de rougeole **6** *(slight) (astonishment)* léger; **the joke caused some m. amusement** la plaisanterie a fait sourire; **the play caused a m. sensation** la pièce a fait un peu de bruit; **the play was a m. success** la pièce a obtenu un succès modéré
▸ **N** *Br (beer)* bière *f* brune
▸▸ **m. steel** acier *m* doux

mildew ['mɪldjuː] **N 1** *(fungus) (on wheat etc)* rouille *f; (on vines etc)* mildiou *m* **2** *(stains) (on fabric, leather etc)* moisissure *f*, moisi *m*, piqûres *fpl*

mildewy ['mɪldjuːɪ] **ADJ** *(bread)* moisi; *(wallpaper etc)* piqué par l'humidité, moisi; **m. smell** odeur de moisi; **to go m.** *(of plant)* se rouiller, *(of bread)* moisir, *(of vine)* être atteint par le mildiou; *(of paper etc)* se piquer

mildly ['maɪldlɪ] **ADV 1** *(to say)* doucement, avec douceur **2** *(moderately)* modérément; **it has a m. laxative effect** ça a un léger effet laxatif; **to be m. successful** *(of play)* obtenir un succès modéré; **to put it m.** pour ne pas dire plus; **he's a bastard, and that's putting it m.!** c'est un salaud, et c'est peu dire

mild-mannered **ADJ** placide, imperturbable

mildness ['maɪldnɪs] **N 1** *(of person, weather)* douceur *f, (of criticism)* caractère *m* anodin; *(of punishment)* légèreté *f* **2** *Med (of disease)* bénignité *f*

mile [maɪl] **N** *(distance)* mil(l)e *m;* **five miles** cinq mil(l)es; *Sport* **four-minute m.** mil(l)e couru en quatre minutes; **a 200-m. journey** un voyage de 200 mil(l)es; **miles per hour** mil(l)es par heure; **smaller cars do more miles to the** *or* **per gallon** les petites voitures consomment moins; **you don't see anyone for miles and miles** on parcourt des kilomètres sans voir personne; **m. after m. of sandy beaches** des plages de sable sur des kilomètres et des kilomètres; **people came from miles around** les gens sont venus de kilomètres à la ronde; **it's miles from anywhere** c'est à des kilomètres de tout; **he lives miles away** il habite très loin d'ici; **you'll recognize him a m. off** tu ne risques pas de le rater; **you can smell the factory a m. off** on sent les fumées de l'usine à des kilomètres; **you can tell she's Italian a m. off** elle a vraiment le type italien; *Fam* **to be miles away** *(be daydreaming)* être dans la lune; **someone not a thousand** *or* **million miles from us** une certaine personne qui ne se trouve pas très loin de nous; *Fam* **I feel miles better** je me sens vachement mieux; *Fam* **he's miles better than the others** il est vachement meilleur que les autres; *Fam* **it's miles more interesting** c'est vachement plus intéressant; *Fam* **it sticks out a m.** ça vous crève les yeux, ça se voit comme le nez au milieu de la figure; *Fam* **I can see you coming a m. off!** *(I know what you want)* je te vois venir (avec tes gros sabots)!; *Fam* **he'd run a m.** *(if that happened)* il prendrait ses jambes à son cou; *Fig* **to go the extra m.** faire un petit effort supplémentaire

mileage ['maɪlɪdʒ] **N 1** *(distance travelled)* distance *f* en mil(l)es, *Can* millage *m,* ≃ kilométrage *m; Admin, Com etc (allowance)* indemnité *f* kilométrique; **car with a very low** *or* **small m.** voiture qui a très peu roulé **2** *(per gallon)* ≃ consommation *f* aux cent kilomètres; **what m. do you get?** combien est-ce que la voiture consomme aux cent?; **you**

can improve the m. by keeping the engine clean on consomme moins avec un moteur propre; *Fig Fam* **the opposition got a lot of m. out of the scandal** l'opposition a largement profité de ce scandale, ce scandale a largement profité à l'opposition; *Fig Fam* **there's no m. in it** *(in idea etc)* ça ne nous mènera nulle part, on ne peut rien en tirer
▸▸ *Admin, Com etc* **m. allowance** indemnité kilométrique

milestone ['maɪlstəʊn] **N** borne *f* routière, ≃ borne kilométrique; *Fig* événement *m* important; **this discovery is a m. in medical research** cette découverte marque une étape importante dans la recherche médicale

milieu ['miːljəː] **N** *Fml* milieu *m*

militancy ['mɪlɪtənsɪ] **N** militantisme *m*

militant ['mɪlɪtənt] **ADJ** militant; *Old-fashioned* **the Church m.** l'Église *f* militante
▸ **N** *Pol etc* militant, -ante

militarily ['mɪlɪtərɪlɪ] **ADV** militairement

militarism ['mɪlɪtərɪz(ə)m] **N** militarisme *m*

militarist ['mɪlɪtərɪst] **N** militariste *mf*

militaristic [mɪlɪtə'rɪstɪk] **ADJ** militariste

militarize ['mɪlɪtəraɪz] **VT** militariser

military ['mɪlɪtərɪ] **ADJ** *(aircraft, base etc)* militaire; **a strong m. presence** une forte présence militaire
▸ **NPL** **the m.** les militaires *mpl*, l'armée *f,* **the m. were called in** on a fait venir l'armée
▸▸ **m. academy** école *f* militaire; **m. attaché** attaché, -ée militaire; **m. court** tribunal *m* militaire; **m. government** gouvernement *m* militaire; **the m.-industrial complex** le complexe militaro-industriel; *Br* **m. man** militaire *m;* **m. police** police *f* militaire; **m. rule** régime *m* militaire; **m. service** service *m* militaire; **m. tribunal** tribunal militaire

militate ['mɪlɪteɪt] **VI** *(of fact, reason etc)* militer (**against** contre)

militia [mɪ'lɪʃə] **N** milice *f, Am* ≃ garde *f* nationale

militiaman, *pl* **militiamen** [mɪ'lɪʃəmən] **N** milicien *m*, soldat *m* de la milice, *Am* ≃ garde *m* national

milk [mɪlk] **N 1** lait *m; Culin* **with m.** au lait; *Lit* **land of m. and honey** pays *m* de cocagne; *Prov* **to be full of the m. of human kindness** être la bonté même; **he's not exactly overflowing with the m. of human kindness** *(kind-hearted)* ce n'est pas un tendre; *(generous)* ce n'est pas quelqu'un de particulièrement généreux **2** *(in plant, coconut)* lait *m; Prov* **there's no point in crying over spilt m.** ce qui est fait est fait
▸ **VT 1** *(cow etc)* traire **2** *Fam Pej (exploit) (person)* dépouiller; *(country, colony)* exploiter; **the newspapers milked the story for all it was worth** les journaux ont tiré tout ce qu'ils ont pu de l'histoire; **they just milked all his ideas** ils se sont approprié toutes ses idées
▸▸ **m. bar** milk-bar *m, pl* milk-bars; **m. bottle** bouteille *f* de lait; *Bot* **m. cap** *(fungus)* lactaire *m;* **m. chocolate** chocolat *m* au lait; **m. churn** bidon *m* à lait; **m. diet** régime *m* lacté; **m. duct** canal *m* galactophore; *Br* **m. float** camionnette *f* du laitier; **m. gland** glande *f* lactéale *ou* galactophore; **m. jug** pot *m* à *ou* au lait; *Pharm* **m. of magnesia** magnésie *f* hydratée; **m. powder** lait *m* en poudre; *Br* **m. pudding** entremets *m* au lait; *Br* **m. round** *(for milk delivery)* tournée *f* du laitier; *Univ* ≃ tournée des universités par les employeurs pour recruter des étudiants en fin d'études; *Fam* **m. run** *Aviat* vol *m* sans histoire, partie *f* de rigolade; *(regular journey)* trajet *m* habituel, tournée habituelle; **m. tooth** dent *f* de lait; **m. train** premier train *m* (du matin)

milk-and-water **ADJ** insipide

milker ['mɪlkər] **N** *(cow etc)* **good/bad m.** bonne/mauvaise laitière *f*

milkiness ['mɪlkɪnɪs] **N** *(of liquid etc)* couleur *f* laiteuse, aspect *m* laiteux

milking ['mɪlkɪŋ] **N** *(of cow)* traite *f*
▸▸ **m. machine** machine *f* à traire, trayeuse *f;* **m. pail** seau *m* à traire; **m. parlour** salle *f* de traite

milkmaid ['mɪlkmeɪd] **N** trayeuse *f*, fille *f* de laiterie

milkman, *pl* **milkmen** ['mɪlkmən] **N** *(delivery man)* laitier *m*

milk-shake **N** milk-shake *m, pl* milk-shakes

milksop ['mɪlksɒp] **N** *Old-fashioned Fam Pej* poule *f* mouillée

milkweed ['mɪlkwiːd] **N** *Bot* laiteron *m*, lait *m* d'âne

milk-white **ADJ** d'une blancheur laiteuse

milky ['mɪlkɪ] **ADJ 1** *(containing milk)* qui contient du lait; **I like my coffee m.** *(with lots of milk)* j'aime mon café avec beaucoup de lait **2** *(colour)* laiteux, *Lit* lactescent; *(gem)* laiteux; **m. white** blanc laiteux
▸▸ *Astron* **the M. Way** la Voie lactée

mill [mɪl] **N 1** *(flour)* **m.** moulin *m* (à farine); *(large)* minoterie *f, Fam* **he's been through the m.** il en a bavé; **to put sb through the m.** en faire baver à qn; **coffee/pepper m.** moulin à café/à poivre; **(crushing) m.** broyeur *m*, concasseur *m* **2** *Metal* **(rolling) m.** laminoir *m*, train *m* (de laminage) **3** *(factory)* usine *f,* **cotton m.** filature *f* de coton; **steel m.** aciérie *f*
▸ **VT** *(wheat, flour)* moudre; *Tech (crush)* broyer; *Tech (gears)* fraiser, tailler; *(screw)* moleter; *(coin)* créneler
▸▸ *Old-fashioned* **m. hand** ouvrier, -ière (d'usine); **m. owner** industriel *m*
▸ **mill about, mill around** **VI** *(of crowd)* grouiller

millboard ['mɪlbɔːd] **N** carton-pâte *m inv*

milled [mɪld] **ADJ** *(grain etc)* moulu
▸▸ **m. edge** *(on coin)* crénelage *m*, grènetis *m*

millennial [mɪ'lenɪəl] **ADJ** **m. celebrations** = festivités *fpl* organisées pour marquer l'arrivée du nouveau millénaire

millennium [mɪ'lenɪəm] **N 1** *(thousand years)* millénaire *m*, mille ans *mpl* **2** *Rel, Hist* millénium *m*
▸▸ *Comput* **M. bug** bogue *m* de l'an deux mille; **the M. Dome** = centre *m* d'expositions en forme de dôme construit à Londres à l'occasion de l'an 2000

millepede ['mɪlɪpiːd] **N** mille-pattes *m inv*

miller ['mɪlər] **N** meunier *m; (on large scale)* minotier *m*

millet ['mɪlɪt] **N** *Bot, Culin* millet *m*, mil *m;* **Indian m.** sorgho *m*, millet d'Inde

millibar ['mɪlɪbɑːr] **N** *Met* millibar *m*

milligram(me) ['mɪlɪɡræm] **N** milligramme *m*

millilitre, *Am* **milliliter** ['mɪlɪliːtər] **N** millilitre *m*

millimetre, *Am* **millimeter** ['mɪlɪmiːtər] **N** millimètre *m;* **a 10-m. gap** un espace de 10 millimètres

milliner ['mɪlɪnər] **N** modiste *f*, chapelier, -ière

millinery ['mɪlɪnərɪ] **N** *Old-fashioned* (articles *mpl* de) modes *fpl;* **m. department** *(in shop)* rayon *m* des chapeaux

milling ['mɪlɪŋ] **N 1** *(grinding) (of grain)* mouture *f*, moulage *m* **2** *Metal* fraisage *m; (of screw etc)* moletage *m; (of coin)* cordonnage *m* **3** *(on coin)* cordon *m*, grènetis *m*, tranche *f* cannelée
▸▸ **m. cutter** fraise *f*, fraiseuse *f,* **m. machine** fraiseuse

million ['mɪljən] **N** million *m*; **two m. men** deux millions d'hommes; **half a m.** un demi-million; **worth millions** *(person)* riche à millions; **an actor who gave pleasure to millions** un acteur qui a diverti des millions de gens; *Fam* **I've told him a m. times** je le lui ai dit mille fois; *Fam* **she's one in a m.** elle est unique; *Fam* **thanks a m.!** merci mille fois!; *Iron* eh bien, merci!; *Fam* **I feel like a m. dollars** je me sens en pleine forme; **to look like a m. dollars** être superbe VOIR GRAMMAIRE A12–13

millionaire [mɪljə'neər] **N** millionnaire *mf*, milliardaire *mf*; **to be a m. twice/three times over** être deux/trois fois millionnaire; **I've got a m. uncle** j'ai un oncle millionnaire *ou* milliardaire

millionairess [mɪljə'neəres] **N** millionnaire *f*

millionth ['mɪljənθ] **ADJ** millionième
N 1 *(person, thing)* millionième *mf* **2** *(fraction)* millionième *m*

millipede ['mɪlɪpiːd] **N** mille-pattes *m inv*

millisecond ['mɪlɪsekənd] **N** milliseconde *f*

millpond ['mɪlpɒnd] **N** réservoir *m ou* retenue *f* de moulin; **sea as calm *or* smooth as a m.** mer *f* d'huile

millrace ['mɪlreɪs] **N** *(channel)* bief *m* de moulin; *(water)* courant *m* du bief

millstone ['mɪlstəʊn] **N** meule *f* (de moulin); *Fig* **a m. round my neck** un boulet que je traîne

millstream ['mɪlstriːm] **N** courant *m* du bief

millwheel ['mɪlwiːl] **N** roue *f* de moulin

millwright ['mɪlraɪt] **N** constructeur *m* de moulins

milometer [maɪ'lɒmɪtər] **N** *Aut etc* compteur *m* de mil(l)es, ≃ compteur kilométrique

milt [mɪlt] **N** *(of fish)* laitance *f*, laite *f*

MIME [maɪm] **N** *Comput* (abbr **Multipurpose Internet Mail Extensions**) (protocole *m*) MIME *m*

mime [maɪm] *Theat* **N** *(performance)* mime *m*; *(actor)* mime *mf*; **a version of Hamlet in m.** une version d'Hamlet en mime
VT *(scene)* mimer; *(song)* chanter en play-back
VI mimer; *(of singer)* faire du play-back; **to m. to a song** chanter en play-back
▸▸ **m. artist** mime *mf*

mimeo(graph)® ['mɪmɪəʊ(grɑːf)] **N 1** *(machine)* machine *f* à ronéotyper **2** *(document)* polycopie *f*
VT ronéotyper

mimic ['mɪmɪk] **N** imitateur, -trice
VT *(pt, pp* **mimicked** [mɪmɪkt]) *(imitate)* *(person)* imiter, mimer; *Fam* singer; *(voice, walk, behaviour, nature etc)* imiter

mimicry ['mɪmɪkrɪ] **N 1** imitation *f* **2** *Biol* mimétisme *m*

mimosa [mɪ'məʊzə] **N** *(shrub)* mimosa *m*

min 1 *(abbr* **minute(s))** min. **2** *(abbr* **minimum)** min

minaret [mɪnə'ret] **N** minaret *m*

mince [mɪns] **N** *Br Culin* viande *f* hachée
VT 1 *(chop up)* *(meat etc)* hacher; **minced meat** viande *f* hachée **2** *(always in negative)* **not to m. one's words** *(speak plainly)* ne pas mâcher ses mots, parler net; **not to m. matters** pour parler net
VI 1 *(walk in affected manner)* marcher à petits pas affectés *ou* efféminés **2** *(talk in affected manner)* parler avec une élégance affectée *ou* minaudière
▸▸ **m. pie** = tartelette *f* fourrée avec un mélange de fruits secs et d'épices que l'on sert à Noël en Grande-Bretagne

mincemeat ['mɪnsmiːt] **N** *Culin* = préparation *f* de raisins secs, écorce d'oranges et graisse de bœuf pour tartelettes; *Fam* **to make m. of sb** *(in fist fight, boxing match)* réduire qn en bouillie, démolir qn; *(in football, tennis match)* écraser qn; *(in debate, argument)* démolir qn; **the lawyer made m. of his testimony** l'avocat a démoli son témoignage

mincer ['mɪnsər] **N** *Culin (device)* hachoir *m*

mincing ['mɪnsɪŋ] **ADJ** *(manner, tone)* affecté, minaudier; *(steps, gait)* efféminé

MIND [maɪnd]

N esprit **1, 6, 8** ▪ mémoire **2** ▪ avis **3** ▪ attention **5** ▪ raison **7**
VT faire attention à **1, 2** ▪ garder **4**

N 1 *(thoughts)* esprit *m*; **such a thought had never entered his m.** une telle pensée ne lui était jamais venue à l'esprit; **to have sth on one's m.** avoir qch qui vous préoccupe; **it's all in your m.!** tu te fais des idées!; **it's all in the m.** tout ça, c'est dans la tête; **in the m.'s eye** dans l'imagination; **in her m.'s eye she could see them staring at her** elle se les imaginait la fixant; **to put *or* set sb's m. at rest** rassurer qn; **to be easy/uneasy in one's m.** avoir/ne pas avoir l'esprit tranquille; **I couldn't get it off my m.** je ne pouvais pas m'empêcher d'y penser; **a walk will take my m. off it** une promenade me changera les idées; **it's a problem that is always on my m.** c'est un problème auquel je n'arrête pas de penser; **she couldn't get their faces out of her m.** elle ne pouvait oublier leurs visages; **put it out of your m.** n'y pensez plus

2 *(memory)* mémoire *f*; **to have a m. like a sieve** avoir (une) très mauvaise mémoire; **to bear *or* keep sth in m.** *(think about)* songer à qch; *(take into account)* tenir compte de qch; *(not forget)* ne pas oublier qch, garder qch à l'esprit; **we must bear in m. that she is only a child** il ne faut pas oublier que ce n'est qu'une enfant; **I'll bear it in m.** *(what you suggested)* je m'en souviendrai; **to call sth to m.** se rappeler qch, se souvenir de qch; **it brings *or* calls to m. Beethoven's Fifth** cela rappelle la cinquième de Beethoven; **to put sb in m. of sb/sth** rappeler qn/qch à qn; **it went (completely *or* clean) out of my m.** cela m'est (complètement) sorti de l'esprit

3 *(opinion)* avis *m*, idée *f*; **to change one's m.** changer d'avis *ou* d'idée, se raviser; **I've changed my m. about him** j'ai changé d'avis *ou* d'idée à son égard; **I've changed my m. about moving to London** *(don't want to)* j'ai changé d'avis, je ne veux plus aller vivre à Londres; *(want to)* j'ai changé d'avis, je veux maintenant aller vivre à Londres; *Fam* **I gave him a piece of my m.** je lui ai dit son fait *ou* ses quatre vérités; **to be of one m., to be of the same m.** être du même avis, être d'accord; **to my m.** selon moi, à mon avis; **to speak one's m.** dire ce qu'on pense; **to keep an open m. about sth** réserver son opinion sur qch

4 *(will, wants)* **to know one's own m.** savoir ce qu'on veut; **you've got a m. of your own** tu peux décider toi-même; **the car seemed to have a m. of its own** la voiture semblait faire ce que bon lui semblait; **make up your m.!** décidez-vous!; **to make up one's m.** se décider; **I can't make up your m. for you** je ne peux pas décider à ta place; **to be in two minds about sth** être indécis sur qch; **I'm in two minds about going** je ne sais pas si je vais y aller; **I've a good m. to do it** je suis bien tenté de le faire; **I've half a m. to tell his parents** j'ai presqu'envie de le dire à ses parents; **to set one's m. on sth** vouloir absolument avoir qch, se mettre la tête d'avoir qch; **to set one's m. on doing sth** vouloir absolument faire qch, se mettre en tête de faire

qch; **to have sth in m.** avoir qch en vue; **what kind of party did you have in m.?** à quelle sorte de soirée est-ce que tu pensais?; **I had in m. something smaller** je pensais à quelque chose de plus petit; **the person I have in m.** la personne à laquelle je pense; **who did you have in m. for the job?** à qui pensiez-vous pour le poste?

5 *(attention)* **to give one's whole m. to sth** accorder toute son attention à qch; **to keep one's m. on sth** se concentrer sur qch; **your m. is not on the job** tu n'as pas la tête à ce que tu fais; **I'm sure if you put your m. to it you could do it** je suis sûr que si tu essayais vraiment, tu pourrais le faire

6 *(way of thinking)* attitude *f* of m. manière *f* de penser; **to have a good m.** être intelligent, avoir la tête bien faite; **to have the m. of a three-year-old** avoir l'esprit *ou* l'intelligence d'un enfant de trois ans; **I haven't got a scientific m.** je n'ai pas l'esprit scientifique; **you've got a dirty m.!** tu as l'esprit mal placé!; **you've got a nasty m.** tu vois le mal partout; **it's probably just my suspicious m. but I don't trust him** c'est probablement que je suis trop suspicieux, mais je n'ai pas confiance en lui

7 *(reason)* raison *f*; **to be out of one's m.** avoir perdu la raison *ou* la tête; *Fam (drunk, from drugs)* être parti; **are you out of your m.?, you must be out of your m.!** est-ce que tu as perdu la tête?; *Fam* **he was out of his m. with boredom *or* bored out of his m.** il s'ennuyait à mourir; **to be in one's right m.** avoir toute sa raison *ou* toutes ses facultés

8 *(person)* esprit *m*; **one of the most brilliant minds of this century** l'un des esprits les plus brillants de ce siècle; *Prov* **great minds think alike, (fools seldom differ)** les grands esprits se rencontrent; *Hum* **how about a drink? – great minds think alike!** si on prenait un verre? – les grands esprits se rencontrent!

VT 1 *(pay attention to)* *(somebody, something)* faire attention à, prêter attention à; *(concern oneself with)* *(something)* s'occuper de; **never m. the car** ne t'en fais pas *ou* ne t'inquiète pas pour la voiture; **don't m. him, he's always like that** ne fais pas attention à lui, il est toujours comme ça; *Iron* **don't m. me, I only live here!** je t'en prie, fais comme chez toi!; **don't m. them** ne faites pas attention à eux; **m. you, I've always thought that ... remarquez, j'ai toujours pensé que ...; **but, m. you, it was late** mais, voyez-vous, il était tard; **m. what you're doing!** faites attention à ce que vous faites!

2 *(take care)* **m. you're not late!** faites en sorte de ne pas être en retard!; **m. you write to him!** n'oubliez pas de lui écrire!; **m. you don't fall!** faites attention de ne pas tomber!; **m. the step!** attention à la marche!; **would you m. where you're putting your feet, please?** est-ce que tu peux faire attention où tu mets les pieds, s'il te plaît?; **m. your backs (please)!** attention devant!; **to m. one's language** surveiller son langage; *Br Fam* **m. how you go!** fais attention à toi!; *Fam* **don't be late, m.!** surtout, ne sois pas en retard!

3 *(object to)* **what I m. is ...** ce qui me gêne, c'est que ...; **I don't m. the cold** le froid ne me gêne pas; **I don't m. trying** je veux bien essayer; **do you m. my asking ...?** puis-je vous demander sans indiscrétion ...?; **how much do you earn, if you don't m. my *or* me asking?** combien est-ce que vous gagnez, sans indiscrétion?; **I wouldn't m. a cup of tea** je prendrais volontiers une tasse de thé; **I wouldn't m. having his salary** ça ne me dérangerait pas de gagner autant que lui

4 *(look after)* *(children)* garder, surveiller; *(animals etc)* garder; *(house)* garder, veiller sur; **to m. the shop** s'occuper du magasin

5 *Arch, Dial (remember)* se souvenir de, se rappeler

VI 1 *(object)* **would you m. if …?** est-ce que cela vous gênerait *ou* dérangerait si …?; **do you m.!** *(how dare you)* dites donc!; **if you don't m.** si cela ne vous dérange pas; **I don't m.** *(it doesn't matter to me)* cela m'est égal; *(go ahead)* je veux bien; **if nobody minds** si personne n'y voit d'inconvénient; **do you m. if I smoke?** cela ne vous dérange *ou* gêne pas que je fume?; *Fam* **another drop of wine? – I don't m. if I do** encore un peu de vin? – ce n'est pas de refus

2 *(trouble oneself)* **never m.!** *(it doesn't matter)* ça ne fait rien!, tant pis!; *(don't worry)* ne vous inquiétez pas!; *Fam* **never you m.!** *(don't be nosy)* ça, c'est mon affaire!, ça ne te regarde pas; *(don't get upset)* ne t'en fais pas

▸▸ *Mktg* **m. share** part *f* de notoriété
▸ **mind out VI** *Br* faire attention (**for** à)

─────────

mind-blowing ADJ *Sl (drug)* hallucinant; *(experience)* ahurissant, époustouflant

mind-boggling [-bɒglɪŋ] **ADJ** *Fam* époustouflant

minded ['maɪndɪd] **ADJ** disposé, enclin (**to do sth** à faire qch); **if you were so m.** si vous le vouliez; **commercially m.** qui a le sens du commerce, commerçant; **to be mechanically m.** être bon mécanicien; **she isn't very money-m.** *(money isn't important to her)* elle n'est pas très préoccupée par les questions d'argent

minder ['maɪndər] **N** *(bodyguard)* garde *m*; **(child** *or* **baby) m.** gardienne *f*, *Fam* nounou *f*, *Ind* **(machine) m.** surveillant *m*

mindful ['maɪndfʊl] **ADJ** *esp Fml (keeping in mind)* **to be m. of sth** se souvenir de qch, ne pas oublier qch; **m. of this warning …** ne se souvenant de cet avertissement …; **m. of the danger to her health** soucieuse de sa santé; **he is always m. of others** il pense toujours aux autres

mindless ['maɪndlɪs] **ADJ** *(senseless) (destruction, violence)* gratuit; *(task, job)* stupide, abrutissant

mind-numbing ADJ abêtissant

mind-reader N voyant, -ante; **I'm not a m.!** je ne peux pas lire dans *ou* deviner tes/ses/ *etc* pensées, je ne suis pas devin

mindset ['maɪndset] **N** façon *f* de penser

mine[1] [maɪn] **N 1** *(for coal etc)* mine *f*; **he went down the m. at 16** il est descendu dans la mine à 16 ans; *Fig* **a m. of information** une mine d'informations **2** *Mil, Naut* mine *f*, **(land) m.** mine terrestre; **to lay a m.** *(on land)* poser une mine; *(at sea)* mouiller une mine

VT 1 *(coal seam)* exploiter; *(coal, gold)* extraire **2** *Mil, Naut* miner; **mined area** zone *f* minée

VI *Min* **to m. for coal/gold** extraire du charbon/de l'or

▸▸ **m. detector** détecteur *m* de mines; **m. shaft** puits *m* de mine; **m. workings** chantiers *mpl* d'exploitation minière

mine[2] **POSS PRON** le mien, la mienne, *pl* les miens, les miennes; **this letter is m.** cette lettre est à moi; **this signature is not m.** cette signature n'est pas de moi; **I took her hands in m.** je pris ses mains dans les miennes; **a friend of m.** un(e) de mes ami(e)s, un(e) ami(e) à moi; **it is no business of m.** ce n'est pas mon affaire, ça ne me regarde pas; **everything of m. had been ripped to shreds** toutes mes affaires avaient été réduites en lambeaux; *Fml* **m. was a difficult/thankless task** c'était une tâche difficile/ingrate que la mienne; **what's m. is yours** ce qui est à moi est à toi; **so much money and it's (m.,) all m.!** tant d'argent, et c'est à moi, rien qu'à moi!;

─────────

Fam **m.'s a beer** *(in pub)* pour moi, ce sera une bière VOIR GRAMMAIRE A30; B21–2

POSS ADJ *Arch, Lit* mon, ma, *pl* mes; *Hum* **m. host** l'aubergiste *m*

minefield ['maɪnfiːld] **N** *Mil, Naut* champ *m* de mines; *Fig* terrain *m* miné

minehunter ['maɪnhʌntər] **N** *Naut* chasseur *m* de mines

minelayer ['maɪnleɪər] **N** *Naut* mouilleur *m* de mines

minelaying ['maɪnleɪɪŋ] **N** *Mil* pose *f* de mines; *Naut* mouillage *m* de mines

miner ['maɪnər] **N** *Min* mineur *m*; **m.'s lamp** lampe *f* de mineur

mineral ['mɪn(ə)rəl] **ADJ** *(oil etc)* minéral, -aux

N 1 minéral *m*; **the m. resources of a country** les ressources *fpl* minières d'un pays **2** *Old-fashioned Br* **minerals** *(drinks)* boissons *fpl* gazeuses

▸▸ *Min* **m. deposits** gisements *mpl* miniers *ou* minéraux; **the m. kingdom** le monde minéral; **m. spring** source *f* d'eau minérale; **m. water** eau *f* minérale

mineralogist [mɪnə'rælədʒɪst] **N** minéralogiste *mf*

mineralogy [mɪnə'rælədʒɪ] **N** minéralogie *f*

minestrone [mɪnə'strəʊnɪ] **N** minestrone *m*

minesweeper ['maɪnswiːpər] **N** *Naut* dragueur *m* de mines

minesweeping ['maɪnswiːpɪŋ] **N** *Naut* dragage *m* des mines

ming [mɪŋ] **VI** *Br Fam* puer, schlinguer; **it mings in here!** ça schlingue ici!

minger ['mɪŋər] **N** *Br Fam (unattractive person)* mocheté *f*

minging ['mɪŋɪŋ] **ADJ** *Br Fam (unattractive)* moche; *(of poor quality)* merdique; **that wine is absolutely m.!** ce vin est vraiment dégueulasse!; **is she going out with him? he's m.!** elle sort avec lui? il est moche comme un pou!

mingle ['mɪŋg(ə)l] **VT** *(usu passive)* mélanger (**with** avec); **her tears were mingled with laughter** elle pleurait et riait à la fois; **joy mingled with sadness** joie mêlée de tristesse

VI *(of things)* se mélanger; *(of person)* *(at party)* circuler; **to m. with the crowd** se mêler à la foule

▸ **mingle together VI** se mélanger

mingy ['mɪndʒɪ] **ADJ** *Br Fam (mean) (person)* mesquin, *Fam* radin; *(salary, gift)* minable; *(amount of money)* ridicule; **a m. helping** une portion minuscule; **a m. five pounds** cinq malheureuses livres

mini ['mɪnɪ] **N** *Fam (dress etc)* mini *f*, *(style)* mini *m*

▸▸ **m. system** *(hi-fi)* minichaîne *f*, *Comput* **m. tower** mini-tour *f*, *pl* mini-tours

mini- **PREF** mini(-); **minibiography** mini-biographie *f*, **minirecording studio** mini-studio *m* d'enregistrement

miniature ['mɪnɪtʃər] **N** *(figure, bottle, painting)* miniature *f*, **to paint in m.** peindre en miniature; **Paris in m.** *(model)* Paris en miniature

ADJ en miniature; *(garden, bottle etc)* miniature; *(book etc)* minuscule; *Phot (camera)* (de) petit format

▸▸ **m. golf** golf *m* miniature, minigolf *m*; **m. painter** miniaturiste *mf*, **m. poodle** caniche *m* nain

miniaturist ['mɪnɪtʃərɪst] **N** *Art* miniaturiste *mf*

miniaturize ['mɪnɪtʃəraɪz] **VT** miniaturiser

minibar ['mɪnɪbɑːr] **N** minibar *m*

mini-break N *(holiday)* mini-séjour *m*, *pl* mini-séjours

─────────

minibudget ['mɪnɪbʌdʒɪt] **N** budget *m* auxiliaire *ou* exceptionnel

minibus ['mɪnɪbʌs] **N** minibus *m*; **m. service** service *m* de minibus

minicab ['mɪnɪkæb] **N** *Br* radio-taxi *m*, *pl* radio-taxis; **m. firm** société *f* de radio-taxis

minicomputer [mɪnɪkəm'pjuːtər] **N** mini-ordinateur *m*, *pl* mini-ordinateurs

mini-cruise N mini-croisière *f*, *pl* mini-croisières

MiniDisc® ['mɪnɪdɪsk] **N** MiniDisc® *m*
▸▸ **M. player** lecteur *m* de MiniDiscs

minidish ['mɪnɪdɪʃ] **N** mini antenne *f* parabolique

minidisk ['mɪnɪdɪsk] **N** mini-disquette *f*, *pl* mini-disquettes

mini-floppy N mini-disquette *f*, *pl* mini-disquettes

minigolf ['mɪnɪgɒlf] **N** minigolf *m*

minim ['mɪnɪm] **N** *Br Mus* blanche *f*
▸▸ **m. rest** demi-pause *f*, *pl* demi-pauses

minimal ['mɪnɪm(ə)l] **ADJ 1** *(very small)* minime **2** *(minimum)* minimal, -aux, minimum
▸▸ **m. value** valeur *f* minimale

minimalism ['mɪnɪməlɪz(ə)m] **N** minimalisme *m*

minimalist ['mɪnɪməlɪst] **N, ADJ** minimaliste *mf*

minimization [mɪnɪmaɪ'zeɪʃən] **N** minimisation *f*

minimize ['mɪnɪmaɪz] **VT** *(something, importance of something)* minimiser; *(noise, friction etc)* réduire *ou* limiter au minimum; *Comput (window)* réduire

minimum, *pl* **minima** ['mɪnɪməm, -ə] **N** minimum *m*, *pl* minimums, minima; **a m. of two years' experience** un minimum de deux ans d'expérience; **as a m.** au minimum; **to reduce sth to a m.** réduire qch au minimum; **keep the questions to a m.** essayez de poser le moins de questions possible; **in order to keep mistakes to a m.** de façon à avoir le minimum d'erreurs; **in order to reduce delays to a m.** de façon à réduire l'attente au maximum

ADJ minimum, minimal, -aux

▸▸ **m. charge** charge *f ou* tarif *m* minimum; **m. connecting time** *(when travelling)* temps *m* minimal de correspondance; *Fin* **m. income guarantee** = revenu *m* minimum assuré par l'État britannique aux plus de 60 ans; *Br Fin Formerly* **m. lending rate** taux *m* de base, taux officiel d'escompte; **m. rates** taux *mpl* minima; **m. speed** vitesse *f* minimum *ou* minimale; *Com* **m. stock level** stock *m* d'alerte; **m. wage** salaire *m* minimum *(légal)*, ≃ SMIC *m*

mining ['maɪnɪŋ] **N 1** *Min* exploitation *f* minière; **m. area/town** région *f*/ville *f* minière; **the m. industry** l'industrie *f* minière **2** *Mil, Naut* pose *f* de mines *(of an area* dans une zone), minage *m*

▸▸ **m. engineer** ingénieur *m* des mines

minion ['mɪnjən] **N** *Pej (lackey)* larbin *m*; *Fam Iron (subordinate)* subordonné, -ée; **the minions of the law** les laquais *mpl* de l'ordre établi

minipill ['mɪnɪpɪl] **N** mini-pilule *f*, *pl* mini-pilules

mini-roundabout N mini rond-point *m*, *pl* mini-ronds-points

miniseries ['mɪnɪsɪərɪz] **N** *TV* mini-feuilleton *m*, *pl* mini-feuilletons, mini-série *f*, *pl* mini-séries

miniskirt ['mɪnɪskɜːt] **N** minijupe *f*

minister ['mɪnɪstər] **N 1** *Pol* ministre *m* (d'État); *Br* **M. of State** ministre d'État; *Br* **M. of Defence** ministre de la Défense; **M. for Tourism** ministre du Tourisme **2** *Rel (Pro-*

testant) pasteur *m*, ministre *m*; *(Jesuit)* ministre

vi to m. to sb soigner qn, s'occuper de qn; **to m. to sb's needs** pourvoir *ou* subvenir aux besoins de qn; *Rel* **to m. to a parish** desservir une paroisse

▸▸ *Rel* **m. general** ministre général; **M. Plenipotentiary** ministre plénipotentiaire

ministerial [mɪnɪˈstɪərɪəl] ADJ **1** *Pol* ministériel **2** *Rel* sacerdotal, -aux **3** *Law* exécutif; **m. functions** fonctions *fpl* exécutives

ministering [ˈmɪnɪstərɪŋ] ADJ
▸▸ **m. angel** ange *m* de bonté

ministration [mɪnɪˈstreɪʃən] N **1** *Fml (assistance)* soins *mpl* **2** *Rel* sacerdoce *m*; **to receive the ministrations of a priest** être administré par un prêtre

ministry [ˈmɪnɪstrɪ] N **1** *Pol (department)* ministère *m*; *(government)* ministère, gouvernement *m*; *Br* **the M. of Defence** le ministère de la Défense; **M. of Transport** ministère des Transports **2** *Rel* **the m.** le sacerdoce; **he was intended for the m.** il fut destiné à l'Église

mink [mɪŋk] N **1** *(animal)* **(American) m.** vison *m* **2** *(fur)* vison *m*; *(coat)* (manteau *m* de) vison
▸▸ **m. coat** (manteau de) vison; **m. farm** visonnière *f*, **m. oil** huile *f* de vison; **m. ranch** visonnière *f*

Minn *abbr* **Minnesota**

minnow [ˈmɪnəʊ] N *(fish)* vairon *m*; *(any small fish)* fretin *m*; *Fig* menu fretin

Minoan [mɪˈnəʊən] ADJ minoen

minor [ˈmaɪnər] ADJ **1** *(lesser)* secondaire, mineur; *(unimportant)* petit, peu important; *(detail, repair)* mineur, petit; **the film is a m. classic** le film est un petit chef-d'œuvre; **of m. importance** sans grande importance; **to play a m. part** *or* **role** *Cin, Theat etc* avoir un petit rôle; *Fig* jouer un rôle mineur *ou* accessoire; *Med* **m. operation** petite opération *f*, opération sans gravité **2** *Br Sch Old-fashioned* **Martin m.** Martin junior

N **1** *Law* mineur, -eure **2** *Am Univ* matière *f* secondaire

VI *Am Univ* **to m. in physics** étudier la physique comme matière secondaire
▸▸ *Mus* **m. key** ton *m ou* mode *m* mineur; *Rel* **m. orders** ordres *mpl* mineurs; **m. road** route *f* secondaire; *Fin* **m. shareholder** actionnaire *mf* minoritaire; *Am Univ* **m. subject** matière secondaire

Minorca [mɪˈnɔːkə] N Minorque *f*

Minorcan [mɪˈnɔːkən] ADJ minorquin
N Minorquin, -ine

minority [mɪˈnɒrɪtɪ, maɪ-] N **1** *(of total number)* minorité *f*; **to be in a** *or* **the m.** être en minorité; **to be in a m. of one** être seul de son opinion VOIR GRAMMAIRE A11 **2** *Law (age)* minorité *f*
▸▸ **m. government** gouvernement *m* minoritaire; *Fin* **m. holding, m. interest** participation *f* minoritaire; **m. opinion** opinion *f* d'une minorité; **m. opinion must be respected** on doit respecter l'opinion de la minorité; *Pol* **m. party** parti *m* minoritaire; **m. report** contre-rapport *m*, *pl* contre-rapports *(soumis par une minorité)*; **m. shareholder** actionnaire *mf* minoritaire

Minotaur [ˈmaɪnətɔːr] N *Myth* **the M.** le Minotaure

minster [ˈmɪnstər] N *Br* cathédrale *f*, *(attached to abbey)* église *f* abbatiale; **York M.** la cathédrale d'York

minstrel [ˈmɪnstrəl] N **1** *(in Middle Ages)* ménestrel *m* **2** *Lit (poet)* poète *m*; *(musician)* musicien *m*; *(singer)* chanteur *m* **3** *(actor/singer with blackened face)* acteur *m*/musicien *m* blanc maquillé en noir
▸▸ **m. show** = spectacle *m* de music-hall avec des acteurs blancs déguisés en Noirs

mint¹ [mɪnt] N *(plant)* menthe *f*, *(sweet)* bonbon *m* à la menthe; **m. chocolate** chocolat *m* à la menthe
▸▸ **m. julep** cocktail *m* au bourbon et à la menthe; **m. sauce** sauce *f* à la menthe; **m. tea** *(tea with mint)* thé *m* à la menthe; *(herbal tea)* infusion *f* de menthe

mint² N *Fin* **the (Royal) M.** ≃ (l'hôtel *m* de) la Monnaie; *Fam* **to be worth a m.** *(of person)* rouler sur l'or; *(of thing)* valoir une somme fabuleuse *ou* une fortune; *Fam* **to make a m.** gagner une fortune; **to be in m. condition** être comme neuf *ou* à l'état neuf; *Philat* **m. stamp** timbre non oblitéré *ou* neuf
VT **1** *(coins)* frapper; *Fig Fam* **he must be minting it** il doit rouler sur l'or; **the company was minting it with their latest model** l'entreprise ramassait l'argent à la pelle grâce au nouveau modèle **2** *Lit (word, expression)* inventer, forger, créer

minted [ˈmɪntɪd] ADJ *Br Fam* plein aux as, bourré de fric

minuet [mɪnjʊˈet] N *Mus* menuet *m*

minus [ˈmaɪnəs] PREP moins; **ten m. eight leaves two** dix moins huit égale(nt) deux; **he managed to escape, but m. his luggage** il a réussi à s'échapper, mais sans (ses) bagages; **it's m. twelve degrees** il fait moins douze degrés
ADJ *Math (quantity, number)* négatif; *Sch* **3 m. B** moins; **but, on the m. side, the pay is low** mais le revers de la médaille, c'est que c'est mal payé; **the m. side of a situation** les désavantages d'une situation
N *Math (sign)* moins *m*
▸▸ **m. sign** signe *m* moins, moins

minuscule [ˈmɪnəskjuːl] ADJ minuscule; *Fam (salary)* dérisoire

minute¹ [ˈmɪnɪt] N **1** *(measurement of time)* minute *f*; **it's ten minutes to** *or Am* **of three** il est trois heures moins dix; **ten minutes past** *or Am* **after three** trois heures dix; **to observe a m.'s silence** observer une minute de silence; **at five-m. intervals, at intervals of five minutes** toutes les cinq minutes; **it's five minutes from here** c'est à cinq minutes d'ici; **the town centre is a ten-m. walk/drive from here** le centre-ville est à dix minutes d'ici à pied/en voiture; **a m.'s rest** un moment de repos; **wait a m.!** attendez une minute *ou* un instant!; **go downstairs this m.!** descends immédiatement!; **just a m.** (attendez) un instant *ou* une minute; **he's come in this (very) m.** il vient de rentrer à l'instant, il vient juste de rentrer; **the m. my back was turned she …** j'avais à peine le dos tourné qu'elle …; **he'll be here any m.** il va arriver d'une minute à l'autre; **it'll be ready in a m.** ça sera prêt dans une minute *ou* un instant; **in a few minutes** dans quelques minutes; **I've just popped in for a m.** je ne fais qu'entrer et sortir, je ne fais que passer; **until the last m.** jusqu'à la dernière minute; **at the last m.** à la dernière minute VOIR GRAMMAIRE A80-1; B60 **2** *Math, Astron* minute *f* **3** *(note)* note *f* (de service); **minutes** *(of meeting)* compte rendu *m*, procès-verbal *m*; **to take the minutes of a meeting** faire le compte rendu d'une réunion
VT *(facts, remarks etc)* prendre note de; *(meeting)* dresser le procès-verbal *ou* le compte rendu de
▸▸ **minutes book** registre *m* des procès-verbaux; **m. hand** grande aiguille *f*, aiguille des minutes; **m. steak** entrecôte *f* minute; **m. timer** minuterie *f*

minute² [maɪˈnjuːt] ADJ **1** *(small)* tout petit, minuscule; *(detailed)* **the minutest details** les moindres détails; **he told us about his holiday in m. detail** il nous a raconté ses vacances par le menu **2** *(detailed)* *(examination etc)* minutieux

minutely [maɪˈnjuːtlɪ] ADV *(to examine etc)* minutieusement, en détail

minutiae [maɪˈnjuːʃɪiː] NPL petits détails *mpl* infimes

minx [mɪŋks] N *Fam* friponne *f*, coquine *f*, **you little m.!** petite espiègle!, petite polissonne!

MIPS [mɪps] N *Comput (abbr* **million instructions per second)** MIPS *m*

miracle [ˈmɪrək(ə)l] N *Rel* miracle *m*; *Fig* miracle, prodige *m*; **by a m.** par miracle; **I can't perform miracles** je ne peux pas faire de miracles; **it sounds like a m.** cela tient du miracle; **it's a m. that …** c'est (un) miracle que … + *sub*
▸▸ *Fig* **m. cure** remède *m* miracle; *Pharm* **m. drug** remède miracle; **m. play** miracle *(drame)*; **m. worker** faiseur, -euse de miracles

miraculous [mɪˈrækjʊləs] ADJ *Rel, Fig* miraculeux; **to have a m. escape** s'en sortir indemne comme par miracle; *Iron* **she made a m. recovery as soon as the weekend arrived** comme par miracle, son état de santé s'est amélioré juste avant le week-end

miraculously [mɪˈrækjʊləslɪ] ADV miraculeusement, (comme) par miracle; **m. low prices** des prix incroyablement bas

mirage [ˈmɪrɑːʒ] N mirage *m*

MIRAS [ˈmaɪərəs] N *Formerly (abbr* **Mortgage Interest Relief at Source**) = système *m* par lequel les intérêts dus à une société de crédit immobilier sont déductibles des impôts

mire [ˈmaɪər] N *(bog)* bourbier *m*; *(mud)* boue *f*, bourbe *f*, *Lit* fange *f*; *Fig* **to drag sb through the m.** traîner qn dans la boue
VT **1** *Lit (in debt, difficulty)* empêtrer **2** *(in mud)* embourber

mirror [ˈmɪrər] N glace *f*, miroir *m*; *Aut* **in my/the m.** dans mon/le rétroviseur; *Fig* **to hold a m. to society** refléter l'image d'une société; *Fig* **the press is the m. of public opinion** la presse est le miroir de l'opinion publique
VT *also Fig* refléter; **the steeple is mirrored in the lake** le clocher se reflète *ou* se mire dans le lac; *Fig* **his experience exactly mirrors my own** nous avons eu des expériences identiques
▸▸ **m. finish** fini *m* spéculaire; **m. image** image *f* en miroir, image spéculaire; *Fig* copie *f* conforme; **m. polish** polissage *m* spéculaire; *Comput* **m. site** *(on Internet)* site *m* miroir; **m. writing** écriture *f* spéculaire *ou* en miroir

mirrorball [ˈmɪrəbɔːl] N sphère *f* à facettes de verre

mirth [mɜːθ] N gaieté *f*, allégresse *f*

mirthful [ˈmɜːθfʊl] ADJ *(amused)* gai, joyeux; *(amusing)* amusant

mirthless [ˈmɜːθlɪs] ADJ sans gaieté, peu réjouissant; *(laugh)* forcé, sans joie

MIRV [mɜːv] N *Mil (abbr* **multiple independently targeted re-entry vehicle)** MIRV *m*

miry [ˈmaɪərɪ] ADJ fangeux, bourbeux

MIS [emaɪˈes] N **1** *Comput (abbr* **management information system)** système *m* intégré de gestion **2** *Mktg (abbr* **marketing information system)** système *m* d'information marketing

misadventure [mɪsədˈventʃər] N mésaventure *f*, *(less serious)* contretemps *m*; *Law* **a verdict of death by m.** un verdict de mort accidentelle

misalliance [mɪsəˈlaɪəns] N mésalliance *f*

misanthrope [ˈmɪzənθrəʊp] N misanthrope *mf*

misanthropic [mɪzənˈθrɒpɪk] ADJ *(person)* misanthrope; *(mood etc)* misanthropique

misanthropist [mɪˈzænθrəpɪst] N misanthrope mf

misanthropy [mɪˈzænθrəpɪ] N misanthropie f

misapply [mɪsəˈplaɪ] VT **1** mal employer **2** Fin = **misappropriate**

misapprehend [mɪsæprɪˈhend] VT Fml (somebody, something) mal comprendre; (person's words) mal comprendre, se méprendre sur

misapprehension [mɪsæprɪˈhenʃən] N malentendu m, méprise f; **to be** or **labour under a m.** se méprendre, se tromper; **the Government appears to be (labouring) under the m. that ...** le gouvernement semble s'imaginer que ...

misappropriate [mɪsəˈprəʊprɪeɪt] VT (funds) détourner

misappropriation [ˈmɪsəprəʊprɪˈeɪʃən] N (of funds) détournement m

misbegotten [mɪsbɪˈgɒt(ə)n] ADJ **1** Old-fashioned Fam (badly thought out) mal conçu, Fam biscornu **2** Arch (child) illégitime, bâtard

misbehave [mɪsbɪˈheɪv] VI se conduire mal; (of child) se tenir mal; **he has been misbehaving at school** il n'a pas été sage à l'école

misbehaviour, Am **misbehavior** [mɪsbɪˈheɪvjər] N (bad behaviour) mauvaise conduite f; (more serious) inconduite f

misc (abbr **miscellaneous**) divers

miscalculate [mɪsˈkælkjʊleɪt] VT (amount, distance etc) mal calculer; (sb's response etc) se tromper sur
VI mal calculer; Fig se tromper

miscalculation [mɪskælkjʊˈleɪʃən] N erreur f de calcul; Fig mauvais calcul m

miscarriage [mɪsˈkærɪdʒ] N **1** Obst fausse couche f, Spec interruption f de grossesse spontanée; **to have a m.** faire une fausse couche **2** (failure) (of project) échec m, insuccès m **3** (in post) (of letter, package) égarement m, perte f
▸▸ Law m. of justice erreur f judiciaire

miscarry [mɪsˈkærɪ] VI **1** Obst faire une fausse couche, Spec avorter **2** (of scheme, enterprise) échouer, avorter, ne pas réussir **3** (of letter, parcel) s'égarer, se perdre; (reach wrong address) parvenir à une fausse adresse

miscast [mɪsˈkɑːst] VT (pt, pp **miscast**) Theat, Cin etc **to m. an actor/actress** donner à un acteur/une actrice un rôle qui ne lui convient pas; **he was m. in the part** ce n'était pas un rôle qui lui convenait; **the play/film was m.** les acteurs de la pièce/du film étaient mal choisis

miscegenation [mɪsɪdʒɪˈneɪʃ(ə)n] N Fml métissage m

miscellaneous [mɪsəˈleɪnɪəs] ADJ varié, divers; **the file marked 'm.'** le dossier 'Divers'
▸▸ Journ m. news faits mpl divers

miscellany [mɪˈselənɪ] N **1** (of objects etc) mélange m, collection f **2** Liter recueil m, anthologie f

mischance [mɪsˈtʃɑːns] N mésaventure f; **by m.** par malchance

mischief [ˈmɪstʃɪf] N **1** (naughtiness) bêtises fpl; (esp of very small children) bêtises, sottises fpl; **out of sheer m.** par pure espièglerie; **he's full of m.** il est très espiègle; **to keep sb out of m.** empêcher qn de faire des sottises ou des bêtises; **that'll keep her out of m.** ça l'occupera, pendant ce temps-là elle ne fera pas de bêtises; **I wonder what m. he's up to** je me demande ce qu'il trame ou fricote **2** (trouble) **to make m. (for sb)** créer des problèmes (à qn), faire du tort (à qn); **to make m. between people** semer la

discorde entre les gens **3** Fam (child) fripon, -onne; **little m.** petit(e) espiègle, petit(e) coquin, -ine **4** Fam (injury) **to do oneself a m.** se faire mal, s'esquinter

mischiefmaker [ˈmɪstʃɪfmeɪkər] N brandon m de discorde; (gossip) mauvaise langue f

mischievous [ˈmɪstʃɪvəs] ADJ **1** (naughty) (child) espiègle, malicieux, coquin; **m. trick** or **prank** espièglerie f; **to play a m. trick on sb** jouer un tour ou faire une farce à qn; **as m. as a monkey** malin comme un singe; **a m. grin/wink** un sourire/clin d'œil malicieux **2** (malicious) (person) méchant, malveillant, malfaisant; (remarque) malveillant

mischievously [ˈmɪstʃɪvəslɪ] ADV **1** (naughtily) par espièglerie; (to grin, wink, smile) malicieusement **2** (maliciously) méchamment

mischievousness [ˈmɪstʃɪvəsnɪs] N **1** (naughtiness) (of child) malice f, espièglerie f **2** (malice) méchanceté f

misconceive [mɪskənˈsiːv] VT Fml se méprendre sur

misconceived [mɪskənˈsiːvd] ADJ (idea, scheme) mal conçu

misconception [mɪskənˈsepʃən] N (false idea) conception f erronée, idée f fausse; **a popular** or **common m.** une idée fausse très répandue

misconduct¹ [mɪsˈkɒndʌkt] N mauvaise conduite f; Law (sexual) adultère m; **professional m.** faute f professionnelle

misconduct² [mɪskənˈdʌkt] VT (matter, business) mal diriger, mal gérer; **to m. oneself** mal se conduire

misconstruction [mɪskənˈstrʌkʃən] N Fml fausse interprétation f

misconstrue [mɪskənˈstruː] VT mal interpréter

miscount¹ [ˈmɪskaʊnt] N (miscalculation) erreur f de calcul; (mistake in addition) erreur d'addition; Pol (of votes) erreur dans le dépouillement du scrutin

miscount² [mɪsˈkaʊnt] VT & VI mal compter

miscreant [ˈmɪskrɪənt] ADJ, N Lit scélérat, -ate, misérable mf

Note that the French word **mécréant** is a false friend and is never a translation for the English word **miscreant**. It means **unbeliever.**

misdeal [mɪsˈdiːl] Cards N maldonne f
VT & VI (pt, pp **misdealt** [mɪsˈdelt]) **to m. (the cards)** faire maldonne

misdeed [mɪsˈdiːd] N méfait m, mauvaise action f; Law crime m, délit m

misdemeanour, Am **misdemeanor** [mɪsdɪˈmiːnər] N **1** Law délit m **2** (minor act of misbehaviour) écart m de conduite; (more serious) méfait m

misdiagnose [mɪsˈdaɪəgnəʊz] VT Med **to m. the symptoms/illness/etc** faire une erreur de diagnostic; Fig **to m. the situation** faire une mauvaise analyse de la situation

misdiagnosis [mɪsdaɪəgˈnəʊsɪs] N Med erreur f de diagnostic; Fig **his m. of the situation** sa mauvaise analyse de la situation

misdirect [mɪsdɪˈrekt] VT **1** (person) envoyer au mauvais endroit **2** (letter) envoyer à la mauvaise adresse **3** (blow) mal diriger **4 to m. the jury** mal instruire le jury

misdirected [mɪsdɪˈrektɪd] ADJ **1** (letter, parcel etc) envoyé à la mauvaise adresse **2** (blow) frappé à faux **3** (zeal) mal employé

misdirection [mɪsdɪˈrekʃən] N **1** (on letter) erreur f d'adresse **2** (of resources, talents) mauvais emploi m, mauvais usage m

miser [ˈmaɪzər] N avare mf

miserable [ˈmɪzər(ə)b(ə)l] ADJ **1** (unhappy) malheureux, triste; j'ai le cafard; **don't look so m.!** remets-toi!; **to make sb's life m.** rendre la vie impossible à qn **2** (unpleasant) (condition) misérable, déplorable; (journey) pénible, affreux; **if only I didn't have this m. cold!** si je n'avais pas cet affreux rhume!; **what a m. day** quelle journée épouvantable; **what m. weather!** quel temps épouvantable! **3** (poor, wretched) misérable, pitoyable; (wage, amount) dérisoire; **I've only got a m. £70** je n'ai que 70 malheureuses livres; **a m. failure** (plan etc) un ratage complet ou lamentable; (person) un raté

Note that the French adjective **misérable** never means **unhappy.**

miserably [ˈmɪz(ə)rəblɪ] ADV **1** (unhappily) (to look) d'un air malheureux; (to say) d'un ton malheureux **2** (in poverty) pauvrement; **to live m.** vivre dans la misère **3** (very badly) (to perform) lamentablement; **to be m. paid** avoir un salaire de misère; **to fail m.** échouer lamentablement

Miserere [mɪzəˈrɪərɪ] N Rel **1** (psalm) miséréré m, miserere m **2 m. (seat)** = **misericord 2**

misericord [mɪˈzerɪkɔːd] N Rel **1** (in monastery) miséricorde f **2** (seat) miséricorde f, patience f (de stalle)

miserliness [ˈmaɪzəlɪnɪs] N avarice f, pingrerie f

miserly [ˈmaɪzəlɪ] ADJ (person) avare, pingre

misery [ˈmɪzərɪ] N **1** (unhappiness) détresse f, tristesse f; (suffering) souffrance(s) f(pl); (stronger) supplice m; **to make sb's life a m.** rendre la vie impossible à qn; **to put an animal out of its m.** donner le coup de grâce à un animal; Hum **to put sb out of their m.** mettre fin aux souffrances ou au supplice de qn **2** Br Fam (person) geignard, -arde, grincheux, -euse

Note that the French word **misère** is a false friend and is never a translation for the English word **misery.** Its most common meaning is **extreme poverty.**

misery-guts [-gʌts] N Fam rabat-joie m inv, empêcheur, -euse de tourner en rond

misfire [mɪsˈfaɪər] N (of rifle) raté m (de percussion); (of missile, car) raté d'allumage
VI (of firearm) rater, faire long feu; (of rocket) avoir un raté d'allumage; (of engine) avoir un raté/des ratés; Fig (of joke) manquer son effet, Fam foirer; (of plan) rater, Fam foirer

misfit [ˈmɪsfɪt] N (person) inadapté, -ée; **a social m.** un inadapté social

misfortune [mɪsˈfɔːtʃən] N malheur m, malchance f; **I had the m. to ...** j'ai eu le malheur ou la malchance de ...

misgiving [mɪsˈgɪvɪŋ] N doute m (**about sth** sur qch); **not without misgivings** non sans hésitation; **to have misgivings** avoir des doutes (**about sb** à l'égard de qn; **about sth** au sujet de qch); **to be filled with m.** être en proie au doute; **she had misgivings about allowing them to go** elle hésitait à les laisser y aller

misgovern [mɪsˈgʌvən] VT mal gouverner

misgovernment [mɪsˈgʌvənmənt] N mauvais gouvernement m, mauvaise administration f

misguided [mɪsˈgaɪdɪd] ADJ (person) mal-avisé; (missionary, reformer, politician) mal inspiré; (attempt) malencontreux; (energy, idealism) mal placé; **you would be m. to trust him** vous seriez mal avisé ou inspiré de lui faire confiance; **in the m. belief that ...** croyant à tort que ...

misguidedly [mɪsˈgaɪdɪdlɪ] **ADV** de façon peu judicieuse, malencontreuseument

mishandle [mɪsˈhænd(ə)l] **VT 1** *(machine, appliance)* mal se servir de; *(substance, product)* manipuler sans prendre les précautions nécessaires **2** *(manage badly)* *(situation etc)* mal gérer; *(person)* mécontenter; **if you m. the staff** si vous ne traitez pas le personnel avec considération

mishandling [mɪsˈhændlɪŋ] **N** *(of situation, staff etc)* mauvaise gestion *f*

mishap [ˈmɪshæp] **N** incident *m*, mésaventure *f*, **after many mishaps** après bien des incidents *ou* des mésaventures *ou* des péripéties

mishear [mɪsˈhɪər] **VT & VI** *(pt, pp* **misheard** [mɪsˈhɜːd]*)* mal entendre

mishmash [ˈmɪʃmæʃ] **N** *Fam* méli-mélo *m*, *pl* mélis-mélos

misinform [mɪsɪnˈfɔːm] **VT** mal informer; **to be misinformed** être mal informé

misinformation [mɪsɪnfəˈmeɪʃən] **N** fausse information *f*

misinterpret [mɪsɪnˈtɜːprɪt] **VT** *(person's words)* mal interpréter; *(person)* mal interpréter les paroles de; **this decision should not be misinterpreted as …** cette décision ne doit pas être interprétée comme …

misinterpretation [mɪsɪntɜːprɪˈteɪʃən] **N** mauvaise *ou* fausse interprétation *f*; **open to m.** *(of rules, statement etc)* susceptible d'être mal interprété

misjudge [mɪsˈdʒʌdʒ] **VT** *(somebody)* mal juger, se tromper sur le compte de; *(something)* mal juger (de), se méprendre sur; *(distance)* mal évaluer; **it appears I misjudged you** il semblerait que je vous aie mal jugé

misjudg(e)ment [mɪsˈdʒʌdʒmənt] **N** jugement *m* erroné, erreur *f* de jugement; *(of distance)* mauvaise évaluation *f ou* estimation *f*

miskey¹ [ˈmɪskiː] **N** faute *f* de frappe

miskey² [mɪsˈkiː] **VT** ne pas taper correctement

mislay [mɪsˈleɪ] **VT** *(pt, pp* **mislaid** [mɪsˈleɪd]*)* *(one's umbrella etc)* égarer; **I've just mislaid it somewhere** je l'ai juste mis quelque part, mais je ne me souviens plus où

mislead [mɪsˈliːd] **VT** *(pt, pp* **misled** [mɪsˈled]*)* *(deceive)* *(person)* induire en erreur, tromper **(as to** quant à); **to m. sb into thinking sth** faire croire qch à qn; **her behaviour misled him into thinking her feelings were stronger** sa conduite lui a laissé croire que ses sentiments étaient plus profonds, mais il n'en était rien

misleading [mɪsˈliːdɪŋ] **ADJ** *(advertisement etc)* trompeur; **the description she gave was deliberately m.** elle a fait exprès de donner une fausse description

mismanage [mɪsˈmænɪdʒ] **VT** *(matter, business)* mal administrer, mal diriger, mal gérer

mismanagement [mɪsˈmænɪdʒmənt] **N** mauvaise administration *f*, mauvaise gestion *f*

mismatch [ˈmɪsmætʃ] **N** *Comput* différence *f*, *(between two sets of data)* décalage *m*; **they're a m.** *(of two people)* ils sont mal assortis

misnomer [mɪsˈnəʊmər] **N** terme *m* qui ne convient pas, terme mal approprié; **changes which, by a great m., are called progress** changements auxquels on donne fort mal à propos le nom de progrès

misogynist [mɪˈsɒdʒɪnɪst, maɪ-] **N** misogyne *mf*

misogynistic [mɪsɒdʒɪˈnɪstɪk, maɪ-] **ADJ** misogyne

misogyny [mɪˈsɒdʒɪnɪ, maɪ-] **N** misogynie *f*

misplace [mɪsˈpleɪs] **VT 1** *(one's affections etc)* mal placer; **misplaced remark** remarque déplacée *ou* hors de propos; **misplaced trust** confiance mal placée **2** *(lose temporarily)* *(book etc)* égarer **3** *Ling (tonic accent etc)* placer à faux

misprint¹ [ˈmɪsprɪnt] **N** *Typ* erreur *f* typographique, faute *f* d'impression, *Fam* coquille *f*

misprint² [mɪsˈprɪnt] **VT** imprimer incorrectement; **my name was misprinted in the newspaper** il y a eu une coquille dans mon nom sur le journal

mispronounce [mɪsprəˈnaʊns] **VT** mal prononcer

mispronunciation [mɪsprənʌnsɪˈeɪʃən] **N** *(act)* prononciation *f* incorrecte; *(instance)* faute *f* de prononciation

misquotation [mɪskwəʊˈteɪʃən] **N** citation *f* inexacte

misquote [mɪsˈkwəʊt] **VT** *(something, author)* citer incorrectement *ou* inexactement; **I've been misquoted** *(by the press etc)* on a déformé mes propos

misread [mɪsˈriːd] **VT** *(pt, pp* **misread** [mɪsˈred]*)* *(text etc)* mal lire, mal interpréter; *Comput* ne pas lire correctement; *Fig* **to m. the situation** mal interpréter la situation; **I m. her remarks** j'ai mal interprété ses remarques

misrepresent [mɪsreprɪˈzent] **VT** *(the facts)* dénaturer, présenter sous un faux jour; **I have been misrepresented in the press as …** j'ai été représenté à tort dans la presse comme …

misrepresentation [mɪsreprɪzenˈteɪʃən] **N** *(of the facts etc)* présentation *f* erronée, dénaturation *f*, travestissement *m*; *Law* fausse déclaration *f*

misrule [mɪsˈruːl] **N 1** *(inefficient rule)* mauvais gouvernement *m*, mauvaise administration *f* **2** *(disorder)* désordre *m*, confusion *f*

Miss *abbr* **Mississippi**

MISS¹ [mɪs]

| **VT** | manquer **1, 5, 6** ▪ rater **1** ▪ faillir **1** |
| **VI** | manquer **1, 2** |

N *(shot, stroke etc)* coup *m* manqué; *Billiards* manque *m* de touche; *Fam* **I think I'll give that film/the party a m.** je ne pense pas que j'irai voir ce film/que j'irai à cette soirée; **I'll give the soup a m.** je ne prendrai pas de soupe; **thanks, but I think I'll give it a m.** merci, pas cette fois; *Prov* **a m. is as good as a mile** rater de près ou de loin, c'est toujours rater

VT 1 *(fail to hit, find, attend, catch etc)* manquer, rater; *(opportunity)* manquer, laisser échapper, rater; *(appointment)* manquer; *(meal) (accidentally)* rater; *(skip)* sauter; **to m. one's entrance** *(of actor)* rater son entrée; **to m. one's cue** *(of actor)* manquer sa réplique; **to m. one's way** s'égarer; *Fig Fam* **to m. the boat** *or* **the bus** rater le coche; **I missed him (by two minutes)** je l'ai manqué *ou* raté (de deux minutes); **an opportunity not to be missed** une occasion à ne pas manquer *ou* laisser passer; **a life of missed opportunities** une vie d'occasions manquées; **I've missed my turn** j'ai perdu mon tour; **I missed the first five minutes of the programme** j'ai raté les cinq premières minutes de l'émission; *Fam* **you haven't missed much!** vous n'avez pas perdu au rate grand-chose!; **you don't m. much!** rien ne t'échappe!; *Fam* **you don't know what you're missing** tu ne sais pas ce que tu rates; **he never misses a chance to put other people down** il ne manque jamais une occasion de rabaisser les autres; **he narrowly** *or* **just missed being killed** il a failli se faire tuer; **the boss doesn't m. a thing** rien n'échappe au

patron; **you can't m. the house** vous ne pouvez pas manquer de reconnaître la maison, vous ne pouvez pas rater la maison

2 *(not hear)* *(question, remark etc)* ne pas entendre; *(not understand)* *(joke)* ne pas saisir; **you m. a lot if you read this novel in translation** on perd beaucoup à ne pas lire ce roman dans le texte; **you've missed the point** vous n'avez pas compris; *(in your answer)* vous avez répondu à côté

3 *(omit)* *(word, line)* omettre, sauter; **to m. one's stop** *(of passenger etc)* rater son arrêt

4 *(notice absence of)* **I missed him at the meeting** j'ai remarqué qu'il n'était pas à la réunion; **we are sure to be missed** on va sûrement remarquer notre absence; **they won't m. a few biscuits** quelques biscuits de plus ou de moins, quelle est la différence?

5 *(feel lack of)* **I m. you** tu me manques; **don't you m. your family?** est-ce que ta famille ne te manque pas?; **I m. the countryside/my piano** la campagne/mon piano me manque; **I m. being able to do what I like** ça me manque de ne pas pouvoir faire ce que je veux; **I missed my umbrella** mon parapluie m'aurait été bien utile; **I m. the older version** j'aimais mieux l'ancien modèle; **you can't m. what you've never had** ce que l'on n'a jamais eu ne nous manque pas; **I'm not allowed cigarettes, but I don't m. them** on me défend de fumer, mais ça ne me manque pas

6 *(lack)* *(always in continuous form)* **the table's missing one of its legs** il manque un pied à la table

VI 1 *(miss target)* manquer *ou* rater son coup; **missed!** manqué!, *Fam* raté!

2 *(be absent)* *(always in continuous form)* manquer; **how many members are missing tonight?** combien avons-nous de membres absents *ou* d'absents ce soir?, combien y a-t-il d'absents ce soir?; **nothing is missing** il ne manque rien

▸ **miss out VI** *(not benefit)* **you missed out there** vous avez raté quelque chose

VT SEP *(omit)* *(accidentally)* oublier; *(page, paragraph, passage)* sauter, oublier; *(intentionally)* omettre; **this film/book misses out …** il manque … à ce film/livre; **they decided to m. out the pudding** ils ont préféré de se passer de dessert

▸ **miss out on VT INSEP** *(good film, great party etc)* rater; **a lot of people are missing out on state benefits they are entitled to** bien des gens ne profitent pas des allocations auxquelles ils ont droit

miss² **N 1** **M. Martin** Mademoiselle *f* Martin; *(on envelope)* Mademoiselle *ou* Mlle Martin; *Old-fashioned* **the M. Martins, the Misses Martin** les demoiselles *fpl* Martin; **thank you, M. Martin** merci Mademoiselle; **M.!** *(to waitress etc)* Mademoiselle!, s'il vous plaît!; *(to older woman)* Madame!, s'il vous plaît! **2** *Br Sch Fam* la maîtresse; *(in secondary school)* la prof; **yes M.** *(to woman teacher)* oui, madame **3** *Fam Hum (girl)* **(young) m.** jeune demoiselle *f*

▸ ▸ **M. World** Miss *f* Monde

missal [ˈmɪs(ə)l] **N** *Rel* missel *m*

misshapen [mɪsˈʃeɪpən] **ADJ** *(person, limb etc)* difforme; *(hat)* déformé

missile [ˈmɪsaɪl, *Am* ˈmɪs(ə)l] **N 1** *(projectile)* projectile *m* **2** *Mil* missile *m*

▸ ▸ **m. base** base *f* de missiles; **m. launcher** lance-missiles *m inv*

missing [ˈmɪsɪŋ] **ADJ** *(person etc)* *(not present)* absent; *(object)* égaré, disparu; *(money)* *(stolen)* disparu; *(lacking)* qui manque; **there are two cups m.** il manque deux tasses, il y a deux tasses qui manquent; **here's the m. part** voilà la pièce qui

manquait *ou* qui était perdue *ou* qui avait disparu; **one climber is m.** on est sans nouvelles d'un des alpinistes; *Mil etc* **to report sb m.** porter qn disparu; *Mil* **m. in action** porté disparu au combat; **to go m.** disparaître
▸▸ *also Fig Hum* **m. link** chaînon *m* manquant; **m. person** personne *f* disparue; *Mil* disparu, -ue; **m. persons bureau** service *m* qui s'occupe des personnes disparues

mission ['mɪʃən] N **1** *(task)* mission *f*; **to charge** *or* **entrust sb with a m.** charger qn d'une mission, confier une mission à qn; **m. accomplished** mission accomplie; **minister on a special m.** ministre en mission spéciale; **she thinks her m. is to ...** elle croit avoir pour mission de ...; **reconnaissance m.** mission de reconnaissance **2** *(body of persons)* mission *f*, *Am (permanent)* représentation *f* diplomatique; **military/trade m.** mission *f* militaire/commerciale **3** *Rel* **foreign/home missions** missions *fpl* étrangères/métropolitaines **4** *Rel (place)* mission *f*
▸▸ **m. control** centre *m* de contrôle; **m. statement** ordre *m* de mission; *Rel* **m. station** mission

missionary ['mɪʃənərɪ] N missionnaire *mf*
ADJ *(priest, work)* missionnaire; *(vocation)* de missionnaire
▸▸ **m. position** position *f* du missionnaire; *Mktg* **m. selling** ventes *fpl* de prospection; *also Fig* **m. zeal** prosélytisme *m*

missis ['mɪsɪz] N *Sl* = **missus**

missive ['mɪsɪv] N *Fml* missive *f*

misspell ['mɪs'spel] VT *(pt, pp* **misspelt** ['mɪs'spelt]*)* mal orthographier

misspelling ['mɪs'spelɪŋ] N faute *f* d'orthographe; **the frequent m. of this word** le fait que ce mot soit fréquemment mal orthographié

misspend ['mɪs'spend] VT *(pt, pp* **misspent** ['mɪs'spent]*)* *(money, time)* mal employer, gaspiller; **a misspent youth** une jeunesse dissipée

missus ['mɪsɪs, 'mɪsɪz] N *Fam* **1** *(wife)* **the** *or* **my/his/your m.** la patronne **2** *(woman)* **m.!** M'dame!

mist [mɪst] N *Met* brume *f*; *(on mirror etc)* buée *f*; **to see things through a m.** voir trouble; *Fig* **lost in the mists of time** perdu dans la nuit des temps
▸ **mist over** VI **1** *(of landscape)* disparaître dans la brume **2** *(of mirror)* se couvrir de buée, s'embuer; *(of eyes)* se voiler, s'embuer
▸ **mist up** VT & VI = **mist over 2**

mistakable [mɪs'teɪkəb(ə)l] ADJ **easily m.** facile à confondre (**for** avec)

mistake [mɪs'teɪk] N erreur *f*, faute *f*; **m. in calculation/in the date** erreur de calcul/de date; **grammatical mistakes** fautes de grammaire; **it would be a m. to imagine that ...** ce serait une erreur d'imaginer que ...; **to make a m.** faire *ou* commettre une faute *ou* une erreur, se tromper (**about, over** sur, au sujet de, quant à); **you're making a big m.** tu es en train de commettre une grosse erreur; **to make the m. of doing sth** faire *ou* commettre l'erreur de faire qch; **it's an easy m. to make** c'est une erreur qu'il est facile de faire; **make no m.** que l'on ne s'y trompe pas; **by m.** *(to do sth)* par erreur, par méprise; **there is** *or* **can be no m. about that** il n'y a pas à s'y tromper; **there must be some m.** il doit y avoir une erreur; *Fam* **this is hard work and no m.!** c'est vraiment très dur; **(sorry,) my m.!** je suis désolé, je me suis trompé *ou* j'ai fait erreur!; **my m.** c'est moi qui me suis trompé
VT *(pt* **mistook** [mɪs'tʊk], *pp* **mistaken** [mɪs'teɪkən]*)* *(person's words, intentions)* se méprendre sur; *(confuse)* *(person, object)* confondre (**for sb/sth** avec qn/qch); *(house etc)* se tromper de; **there's no mistaking it** il

n'y a pas à s'y méprendre; **I mistook him for someone else** je l'ai pris pour quelqu'un d'autre, je l'ai confondu avec quelqu'un d'autre

mistaken [mɪs'teɪkən] PP *see* **mistake** VT
ADJ *(opinion)* erroné; *(idea)* faux, *f* fausse; **I must be m.** je dois faire erreur; **if I'm not m.** si je ne me trompe (pas); **in the m. belief that ..., under the m. impression that ...** croyant, à tort, que ...; **it was (a case of) m. identity** il y a eu erreur sur la personne

mistakenly [mɪs'teɪkənlɪ] ADV par erreur, par méprise; **it was m. believed to be ...** on croyait à tort que c'était ...

misted-up [mɪstɪd-] ADJ *(windscreen)* embué

mister ['mɪstər] N *Fam* m'sieur *m*

mistime [mɪs'taɪm] VT *(counterattack, announcement)* faire au mauvais moment; *(entrance on stage)* rater; **to m. a punch/smash/pass** ne pas frapper/smasher/faire une passe au moment opportun; **the launch of the new product had been badly mistimed** le nouveau produit n'avait pas été lancé au moment propice; **he badly mistimed it** il a vraiment choisi le mauvais moment, il a fait une grosse erreur de timing; **she mistimed her entrance/intervention/etc** elle est entrée/intervenue/etc au mauvais moment, elle a mal choisi son moment pour entrer/intervenir/etc

mistimed [mɪs'taɪmd] ADJ *(remark, intervention etc)* inopportun, mal à propos; *(blow)* mal calculé

mistiness ['mɪstɪnɪs] N *(mist)* brouillard *m*, brume *f*

mistlethrush ['mɪs(ə)lθrʌʃ] N *(bird)* (grive *f*) draine *f*

mistletoe ['mɪs(ə)ltəʊ] N *Bot* gui *m*

mistook PT *see* **mistake** VT

mistranslate [mɪstræns'leɪt] VT mal traduire; **it's often mistranslated as ...** c'est souvent traduit à tort par ...

mistranslation [mɪstræns'leɪʃən] N mauvaise traduction *f*, *(mistake in translation)* erreur *f* de traduction

mistreat [mɪs'triːt] VT *(somebody, something)* maltraiter

mistreatment [mɪs'triːtmənt] N mauvais traitement *m*

mistress ['mɪstrɪs] N **1** *(woman in charge)* maîtresse *f*; **to be one's own m.** être indépendante, être sa propre maîtresse; **to be m. of oneself** *or* **of one's emotions** être maîtresse de soi(-même); **she was the m. of the situation** elle était maîtresse de la situation; *Old-fashioned* **the m. of the house** la maîtresse de maison **2** *(owner of pet)* maîtresse *f* **3** *esp Br Sch (woman teacher)* *(in primary school)* maîtresse *f* (d'école), institutrice *f*, *(in secondary school)* professeur *m*; **the French m.** le professeur de français *m* **4** *(lover)* maîtresse *f* **5** *Arch* **M.** *(in titles)* Madame *f*

mistrial [mɪs'traɪəl] N *Law* jugement *m* entaché d'un vice de procédure; *Am (because jury cannot agree)* = procès *m* ajourné, l'unanimité n'ayant pas été atteinte parmi le jury

mistrust [mɪs'trʌst] N méfiance *f* (**of** à l'égard de), défiance *f* (**of** à l'égard de), manque *m* de confiance (**of** en)
VT se méfier de, se défier de, ne pas avoir confiance en

mistrustful [mɪs'trʌstfʊl] ADJ méfiant, défiant (**of sth** à l'égard de qch; **of sb** à l'égard de qn, envers qn)

mistrustfully [mɪs'trʌstfʊlɪ] ADV avec méfiance, avec défiance

misty ['mɪstɪ] ADJ *(place etc)* brumeux, embrumé; *(weather)* brumeux; *(form)* flou,

voilé, estompé; *(memory)* vague, confus; **m. eyes** yeux embués; **m. blue** bleu gris; **it's m.** le temps est brumeux; **the windscreen is all m.** le pare-brise est tout couvert de buée

misunderstand [mɪsʌndə'stænd] *(pt, pp* **misunderstood** [mɪsʌndə'stʊd]*)* VT *(misinterpret) (somebody, something)* mal comprendre; *(misjudge) (somebody)* méconnaître, se méprendre sur le compte de; *(action etc)* mal comprendre, mal interpréter, se méprendre sur; **we misunderstood each other** il y a eu un malentendu entre nous; **don't m. me, I'm as opposed to this plan as you are** comprends-moi bien, je suis aussi opposé à ce projet que toi
VI mal comprendre; **if I have not misunderstood** si j'ai bien compris

misunderstanding [mɪsʌndə'stændɪŋ] N **1** *(misconception)* erreur *f*, *(mistake)* malentendu *m*, méprise *f*, *(confusion of two objects)* quiproquo *m*; **I think there's been a m.** je crois qu'il y a un malentendu *ou* (une) méprise **2** *(disagreement)* malentendu *m*, désaccord *m*, différend *m*

misuse¹ [mɪs'juːs] N *(of something)* mauvais usage *m ou* emploi *m*; *(of authority)* abus *m*; *(of word)* emploi abusif; *Law* **fraudulent m. of funds** détournement *m* de fonds

misuse² [mɪs'juːz] VT *(something)* faire (un) mauvais usage *ou* (un) mauvais emploi de; *(one's authority)* abuser de; *(word)* employer à tort *ou* abusivement

mite [maɪt] N **1** *Arch, Lit (sum of money)* **the widow's m.** le denier de la veuve **2** *(small amount)* *Fam* **it's a m. expensive** c'est un peu cher **3** *Fam (child)* petit(e) gosse *mf*, mioche *mf*, *(animal)* petite bête *f*; **poor little m.!** pauvre petit! **4** *Entom* acarien *m*

miter ['maɪtər] N, VT *Am* = **mitre**

mitigate ['mɪtɪgeɪt] VT *(sb's anger)* adoucir; *(suffering, grief etc)* adoucir, atténuer; *(pain)* apaiser; *(punishment, effects), Law (crime)* atténuer

mitigating ['mɪtɪgeɪtɪŋ] ADJ
▸▸ *Law* **m. circumstances** circonstances *fpl* atténuantes

mitigation [mɪtɪ'geɪʃən] N *Fml (of pain)* adoucissement *m*; *(of punishment)* atténuation *f*; **if you have anything to say in m. of this offence** si vous avez quelque chose à dire pour votre défense; **in m. of this, it should be noted that ...** il faut noter que ... et ceci constitue une circonstance atténuante; **in m. of the accused's crime ...** à la décharge de l'accusé ...

mitral ['maɪtrəl] ADJ
▸▸ *Anat* **m. valve** valvule *f* mitrale

mitre¹, *Am* **miter** ['maɪtər] N *(headdress)* mitre *f*

mitre², *Am* **miter** *Carp* N *(joint)* onglet *m*
VT **1** *(shape) (part)* tailler à onglet **2** *(join) (two parts)* assembler à onglet
▸▸ **m. box** boîte *f* à onglet(s); **m. joint** (assemblage *m* à) onglet; **m. square** équerre *f* à onglet

mitt [mɪt] N **1** = **mitten**; *(in baseball)* gant *m* **2** *Fam (hand)* patte *f*; **keep your mitts off my lunch!** touche pas à mon déjeuner!; **get your mitts off me!** bas les pattes!

mitten ['mɪt(ə)n] N *(glove without separate fingers)* moufle *f*, *Can* mitaine *f*, *(glove with no fingers)* mitaine; *Boxing Fam* **mittens** gants *mpl*

MIX [mɪks] N **1** *(of mortar, plaster)* mélange *m*; *(cake)* **m.** préparation *f* pour gâteaux; **there was a good m. of people at the party** il y avait un mélange intéressant de personnes à la soirée; *Com* **product m.** assortiment *m* de produits, *Spec* mix *m*
2 *Cin, Mus* mixage *m*; **the 12-inch m.** *(record)* le trente centimètres

VT 1 mêler, mélanger (**several things together** plusieurs choses ensemble; **sth with sth** qch à *ou* avec qch); *(drink)* préparer; *(mortar, plaster)* gâcher; *Culin (salad)* retourner; *Am (cards)* battre, mélanger; **to m. business with pleasure** mélanger le travail et les loisirs; **you should never m. your drinks** il ne faut jamais mélanger les alcools; **to m. one's metaphors** confondre deux expressions; *Fam* **to m. it** *(fight)* se bagarrer (**with sb** avec qn); **do you want to m. it?** tu veux te battre?

2 *Cin, Mus* mixer

VI *(of things)* se mélanger (**with** avec, à); **sport and drug-taking don't m.** le sport et l'utilisation de drogue ne font pas bon ménage; **to m. with people** *(of person)* fréquenter des gens; **I don't m. much** je ne fréquente pas beaucoup de gens; **to m. with the crowd** se mêler à la foule; **to m. with the guests** circuler parmi les invités

▸ **mix up** VT SEP **1** *(prepare)* *(drink, medication)* préparer

2 *(put in disorder)* *(one's papers etc)* mettre le désordre dans; **everything got mixed up** tout avait été mélangé

3 *(confuse)* confondre (**with** avec); **I was mixing you up with your brother** je vous confondais avec votre frère; **I was getting all mixed up** je ne savais plus où j'en étais

4 *(involve)* **to be mixed up in an affair** être mêlé à une affaire, être compromis *ou* impliqué dans une affaire; **mixed up in something dishonest** impliqué dans quelque chose de malhonnête

5 *esp Am Sl* **to m. it up** *(fight)* en venir aux coups

mix-down N *TV etc* mixage *m* avec réduction de pistes

mixed [mɪkst] ADJ mélangé; **person of m. blood/race** sang-mêlé *mf inv*; *Fam* **they were a m. bag** *(of people or things)* il y avait de tout; **her resignation was a m. blessing** sa démission avait du bon et du mauvais; **to meet with a m. reception** recevoir un accueil mitigé; **in m. company** en présence de personnes des deux sexes; **m. feelings** sentiments *mpl* contradictoires; **it was with m. feelings that I took up the position** j'ai accepté le poste malgré mes réserves

▸▸ *Sport* **m. doubles** double *m* mixte; **m. economy** économie *f* mixte; **m. farming** agriculture *f* mixte; *Culin* **m. grill** assortiment *m* de grillades, mixed grill *m*; **m. marriage** mariage *m* mixte; **m. metaphor** mélange *m* de métaphores; *Br* **m. school** école *f* mixte; *Pol* **m. system** *(of voting)* scrutin *m* mixte; **m. vegetables** jardinière *f* de légumes

mixed-ability ADJ *USU ATTRIB (classes)* qui regroupe des élèves de niveaux différents

mixed-media ADJ multimédia

mixed-up ADJ *Fam (person)* déboussolé, qui ne sait plus où il en est; **a crazy m. kid** un pauvre gosse un peu paumé

mixer [ˈmɪksər] N **1** *(machine)*, *Ind etc* mélangeuse *f*, agitateur *m*; *TV etc* mixeur *m*, mélangeur *m*; *(tap)* mélangeur; *(tap with single control)* mitigeur *m*; *Culin* **(food) m.** mixeur, mixer *m* **2** **to be a good m.** *(socially)* être très sociable **3** *(drink)* = boisson *f* non-alcoolisée que l'on utilise pour allonger certains alcools **4** *esp Am Univ Fam (party)* = soirée *f* pour permettre aux étudiants de faire connaissance

▸▸ *Br* **m. tap** mélangeur; *(with single control)* mitigeur

mixing [ˈmɪksɪŋ] N **1** mélange *m* **2** *TV etc* mixage *m*, mélange *m* sonore

▸▸ **m. bowl** *(big)* saladier *m*; *(smaller)* bol *m*; **m. chamber** *(in engine)* chambre *f* de mélange *ou* de carburation; **m. console, m. desk**

table *f* de mixage; **m. drum** mélangeur *m* (à tambour); *TV* **m. room** régie *f*

mixture [ˈmɪkstʃər] N **1** *(of objects, people, styles, fuel)* mélange *m*; **their music is a m. of traditional and modern** leur musique est un mélange de moderne et de traditionnel; **(cake) m.** préparation *f* pour gâteaux; **he's an odd m.** c'est un type difficile à cerner, c'est un drôle de type; *Aut* **m. adjusting screw** vis *f* de richesse **2** *Pharm* mixtion *f*, mixture *f*

mix-up N *(confusion)* confusion *f*; *(misunderstanding)* malentendu *m*; *Fam (mess)* pagaïe *f*, pagaille *f*; **there's been a m. with the reservations** ils se sont embrouillés dans les réservations

mizzen [ˈmɪz(ə)n] N *Naut* artimon *m*

▸▸ **m. sail** artimon

mizzenmast [ˈmɪz(ə)nmɑːst] N *Naut* mât *m* d'artimon

ml *(abbr* **millilitre(s))** ml

MLM [emelˈem] N *Mktg (abbr* **multi-level marketing)** VRC *f*

MLR [emeˈlɑːr] N *Br Fin Formerly (abbr* **minimum lending rate)** taux *m* de base

mm *(abbr* **millimetre(s))** mm

MMC N *Com (abbr* **Monopolies and Mergers Commission)** = commission *f* britannique veillant au respect de la législation antitrust

MMFs [emeˈmefs] NPL *St Exch (abbr* **money market funds)** = SICAV *fpl* monétaires

MMS [ememˈes] N *Tel (abbr* **multimedia messaging service)** MMS *m*

MNA [emeˈneɪ] N *Can (in Quebec) (abbr* **Member of the National Assembly)** MAN *m*

mnemonic [nɪˈmɒnɪk] ADJ mnémonique
N moyen *m* mnémotechnique

MO [eˈməʊ] N **1** *Mil etc abbr* **medical officer 2** *(abbr* **modus operandi)** *(of criminal)* façon *f* d'agir **3** *(abbr* **money order)** mandat-poste *m, pl* mandats-poste

mo [məʊ] N *Br Fam* instant *m*, minute *f*; **half a mo!** une petite seconde!

moan [məʊn] N **1** *(sound)* gémissement *m*, plainte *f* **2** *Fam (complaint)* plainte *f*, jérémiades *fpl*; **to have a (good) m.** râler un bon coup

VI 1 *(make sound)* gémir, pousser des gémissements; *(of wind)* mugir, gémir **2** *Fam (complain)* geindre, gémir, *Fam* râler, ronchonner; **to m. about sth** se plaindre de qch; **he's always moaning (and groaning)** il est toujours à gémir *ou* à geindre *ou Fam* à ronchonner; **what are they moaning about now?** de quoi se plaignent-ils maintenant?

VT *(something)* dire en gémissant

moaner [ˈməʊnər] N *Fam* ronchonneur, -euse, râleur, -euse

moaning [ˈməʊnɪŋ] N **1** *(sound)* gémissement(s) *m(pl)* **2** *Fam (complaining)* jérémiades *fpl*; **he's a real m. Minnie** c'est un vrai geignard

moat [məʊt] N fossé(s) *m(pl)*, douves *fpl*

mob [mɒb] N **1** *Pej* **the m.** *(the masses)* la populace, *Fam* le populo **2** *(crowd)* foule *f* (agitée); *(gang)* bande *f*, troupe *f*; *(of reporters etc)* meute *f*; **mobs of drunken hooligans** des hordes de hooligans ivres **3** *Fam (gang)* bande *f*, clique *f*; **the M.** *(Mafia)* la Mafia; **which m. were you in?** *(in forces)* dans quel régiment étais-tu?

VT *(-bb-)* *(of angry crowd) (person)* assaillir, attaquer; *(of fans, reporters etc) (person)* assiéger, se presser autour de; *(place)* prendre d'assaut, assiéger; **the crowds mobbing the entrance** la foule qui se pressait à l'entrée

▸▸ **m. rule** règne *m* de la populace

mobbed [mɒbd] ADJ *Fam (crowded)* bondé

mobile [ˈməʊbaɪl] ADJ mobile; **the patient is m.** le patient peut se déplacer; *Fam* **are you**

m.? *(do you have a car with you?)* vous êtes motorisé?; **he wants to stay professionally m.** il veut être libre de ses mouvements dans son métier; **m. features** physionomie *f* changeante

N **1** *Art* mobile *m* **2** *(phone)* *(téléphone m)* portable *m*, *Belg* GSM *m*, *Suisse* Natel® *m inv*, *Can* cellulaire *m*

▸▸ *TV etc* **m. control room** régie *f* mobile; *Mil* **m. defence** troupes *fpl* mobiles; **m. home** *(caravan)* camping-car *m*, *pl* camping-cars; *(house)* = maison *f* sans fondations qui peut être déplacée; **the m. Internet** l'Internet *m* mobile; *Mil* **m. kitchen** cuisine *f* roulante; **m. library** bibliobus *m*; **m. phone** *(téléphone)* portable, *Belg* GSM, *Suisse* Natel®, *Can* cellulaire; **m. shop** commerce *m* ambulant; *TV* **m. studio** studio *m* mobile; **m. telephony** téléphonie *f* mobile; *Radio, TV* **m. unit** car *m* régie, car de reportage; **m. warfare** guerre *f* de mouvement

mobility [məʊˈbɪlɪtɪ] N mobilité *f*; **she has very little m. in her right arm** elle peut à peine bouger son bras droit; **he values his professional m.** il tient à conserver sa liberté de mouvement dans son métier

▸▸ **m. allowance** indemnité *f* de déplacement *(versée aux personnes handicapées)*

mobilization [məʊbɪlaɪˈzeɪʃən] N *(of troops, capital, support etc)* mobilisation *f*

▸▸ *Mil* **m. order** appel *m* de mobilisation; *(to individual recruit)* ordre *m* de mobilisation

mobilize [ˈməʊbɪlaɪz] VT *(troops, capital, public opinion)* mobiliser
VI *Mil, Fig* se mobiliser

mobster [ˈmɒbstər] N *esp Am* gangster *m*

moby [ˈməʊbɪ] N *Br Fam (mobile phone)* mobile *m*

moccasin [ˈmɒkəsɪn] N *(footwear)* mocassin *m*

mocha [ˈmɒkə] N **1** *(coffee)* moka *m* **2** *(coffee and chocolate flavour)* parfum *m* chocolat-café

▸▸ **m. coffee** *(café m)* moka

mock [mɒk] N *Br Sch, Univ* examen *m* blanc; **to make a m. of sb/sth** se moquer de qn/qch
ADJ *(imitation)* simulé; **m. fight** simulacre *m* de combat; **to indulge in m. heroics** jouer au *ou* se prendre pour un héros; **m. tortoiseshell** *(rims, frame etc)* en imitation écaille; **m. trial/elections** simulacre *m* de procès/d'élections

VT *(ridicule) (person)* se moquer de, *Lit* railler; *(imitate) (person)* imiter en se moquant, ridiculiser

VI to m. at se moquer de, *Lit* railler

▸▸ *Br Sch, Univ* **m. examination** examen blanc; *Bot* **m. orange** seringa *m*; **m. turtle soup** consommé *m* à la tête de veau

▸ **mock up** VT SEP *Br* faire une maquette de

mocker [ˈmɒkər] N **1** *(person)* moqueur, -euse, railleur, -euse **2** *Br Fam* **to put the mockers on sth** *(spoil)* foutre qch en l'air

mockery [ˈmɒkərɪ] N **1** *(action)* moquerie *f*, raillerie *f* **2** *(person, thing)* sujet *m ou* objet *m* de moquerie *ou* de raillerie, objet de risée; **to make a m. of sb** ridiculiser qn; **to make a m. of oneself** se ridiculiser; **to make a m. of sth** faire perdre toute crédibilité à qch **3** *(pretence)* parodie *f*, simulacre *m* (**of** de); **the trial was a mere m.** le procès n'a été qu'un simulacre

mocking [ˈmɒkɪŋ] ADJ moqueur, railleur
N moquerie *f*, raillerie *f*; **she couldn't put up with their m. any more** elle ne pouvait plus supporter leurs railleries

mockingbird [ˈmɒkɪŋbɜːd] N moqueur *m*

mockingly [ˈmɒkɪŋlɪ] ADV *(to say)* d'un ton moqueur *ou* railleur; *(to smile)* d'un air moqueur

Mockney [ˈmɒknɪ] *Br Fam* N = personne *f*

issue d'un milieu aisé qui affecte l'accent cockney

ADJ = caractéristique des personnes issues d'un milieu aisé qui affectent l'accent cockney

mockumentary [mɒkjʊˈment(ə)rɪ] **N** *TV* faux documentaire *m*

mock-up N maquette *f*

MOD [eməʊˈdiː] **N** *Br* (*abbr* **Ministry of Defence**) ministère *m* de la Défense; **M. property** propriété *f* du ministère de la Défense

Mod [mɒd] **N** *Scot Mus* = festival *m* de musique et de littérature dans les Highlands

mod [mɒd] **N** *Br Fam* **mods** = adolescents *mpl* à l'apparence soignée opposés aux rockers pendant les années soixante
▸▸ *Fam* **m. cons** confort *m* moderne; **the car comes equipped with the latest m. cons** la voiture dispose de toutes les options

modal [ˈməʊd(ə)l] VOIR GRAMMAIRE A57-61; B39-40 *Gram* **ADJ** modal, -aux
N verbe *m* modal

modality [məʊˈdælɪtɪ] **N** modalité *f*

mode [məʊd] **N 1** (*manner*) mode *m*, façon *f* (of de); **m. of transport** mode de transport **2** (*fashion*) mode *f* **3** *Mus, Phil, Comput* mode *m*

model [ˈmɒd(ə)l] **N 1** (*small version*) (*built as a hobby*) modèle *m* (réduit), maquette *f*, *Com, Ind* maquette; (*in naval architecture etc*) gabarit *m*; (*in surveying*) plan *m* en relief **2** (*example*), *Com* modèle *m*; **this is our latest m.** c'est notre dernier modèle; *Com, Ind* **there are several different models** il y a plusieurs modèles différents; **Paris models** (*clothing*) modèles de la haute couture parisienne **3** *Econ etc* modèle *m* **4** (*perfect example*) **to take sb as one's m.** prendre modèle sur qn, prendre qn pour modèle; **to be a m. of virtue** être un modèle *ou* un exemple de vertu; **m. pupil** écolier, -ière modèle **5** (*person*), *Art* modèle *m*; (*fashion*) **m.** mannequin *m*, modèle
VT (-ll-, *Am* -l-) **1** *Art* (*figure, group*) modeler (after, up(on) sur); *Fig* **to m. oneself on sb** prendre exemple sur qn, se modeler sur qn **2** (*of fashion model*) (*dress etc*) présenter **3** *Comput* modéliser
VI (*of artist's model*) poser (comme modèle); (*of fashion model*) travailler comme mannequin *ou* modèle
▸▸ **m. aircraft** (*toy*) modèle (réduit) *ou* maquette d'avion; *Ind* maquette d'avion; **m. kit** modèle en pièces détachées; **m. maker** (*as hobby*) modéliste *mf*, *Ind* maquettiste *mf*

modeller, *Am* **modeler** [ˈmɒdələr] **N** modeleur, -euse

modelling, *Am* **modeling** [ˈmɒdəlɪŋ] **N 1** (*occupation*) métier *m* de mannequin; **to get a career in m.** faire une carrière de mannequin **2** (*of dress etc*) présentation *f* **3** *Art* modelage *m* **4** *Comput* modélisation *f*
▸▸ **m. clay** pâte *f* à modeler

modem [ˈməʊdem] *Comput* **N** modem *m*
VT envoyer par modem; **to m. sth to sb** envoyer qch à qn par modem
▸▸ **m. cable** câble *m* du modem; **m. card** carte *f* modem; **m. link** liaison *f* par modem; **m. port** port *m* modem; **m. transmission** transmission *f* par modem

moderate¹ [ˈmɒdərɪt] **ADJ** modéré; (*drinker*) tempéré; (*language*) mesuré; (*price*) modéré, modique, moyen; (*income, size*) moyen; **to express oneself in m. language** s'exprimer en termes modérés; **a m. breeze** une légère brise
N *Pol etc* (*person*) modéré, -ée

moderate² [ˈmɒdəreɪt] **VT 1** (*one's demands, wishes, one's zeal*) modérer; **to be a moderating influence on sb** exercer une influence modératrice sur qn **2** *Fml* (*meeting*) présider; (*discussion*) arbitrer

VI 1 (*of storm*) s'apaiser, se calmer **2** *Fml* (*at meeting*) présider

moderately [ˈmɒdərɪtlɪ] **ADV** (*to eat, drink, like*) modérément; (*fast, well-off*) assez, moyennement; **m. priced** à prix moyen

moderation [mɒdəˈreɪʃən] **N 1** modération *f*, mesure *f*, (*of language*) sobriété *f*; **in m.** avec modération, modérément; **taken in m. alcohol is not harmful** consommé avec modération, l'alcool n'est pas nocif **2** *Univ* (*at Oxford University*) **Moderations** = premier examen *m* pour le grade de Bachelor of Arts

moderator [ˈmɒdəreɪtər] **N 1** (*at meeting*) président, -ente **2** *Univ* (*of exam*) = examinateur *m* qui assure l'harmonisation de la notation **3** *Phys* (*of reactor etc*) modérateur *m*, ralentisseur *m*
▸▸ *Scot Rel* **M. of the General Assembly** modérateur *m ou* président *m* du synode (de l'Église d'Écosse)

modern [ˈmɒdən] **ADJ** moderne
N 1 (*person*) moderne *mf* **2** *Typ* didot *m*
▸▸ **m. art** art *m* moderne; **m. Greek** grec *m* moderne; **m. languages** langues *fpl* vivantes; *Sport* **m. pentathlon** pentathlon *m* moderne; **m. times** les temps *mpl* modernes

modernism [ˈmɒdənɪz(ə)m] **N 1** modernisme *m* **2** *Ling* néologisme *m*

modernist [ˈmɒdənɪst] **N, ADJ** moderniste *mf*

modernity [mɒˈdɜːnɪtɪ] **N** modernité *f*

modernization [mɒdənaɪˈzeɪʃən] **N** modernisation *f*

modernize [ˈmɒdənaɪz] **VT** moderniser
VI se moderniser

modernizer [ˈmɒdənaɪzər] **N** *Pol* modernisateur, -trice

modest [ˈmɒdɪst] **ADJ 1** (*not boastful*) modeste; **to be m. about one's achievements** ne pas se vanter de ses réussites **2** (*moderate*) (*request*) modeste, modéré; (*fortune*) modeste; **to be m. in one's requirements** être peu exigeant; **a m. house** une maison sans prétentions *ou* à l'aspect modeste **3** *Old-fashioned* (*chaste*) pudique

modestly [ˈmɒdɪstlɪ] **ADV 1** (*not boastfully*) modestement, avec modestie **2** (*moderately*) modérément **3** (*in sexual sense*) modestement, pudiquement

modesty [ˈmɒdɪstɪ] **N 1** (*of person*) modestie *f*, (*in all m.*) en toute modestie **2** (*of request*) modération *f*, (*of expense*) modicité *f* **3** *Old-fashioned* (*chasteness*) pudeur *f*

modicum [ˈmɒdɪkəm] **N a m. of ...** un minimum de ..., un petit peu de ..., un brin de ...; **a m. of truth** une petite part de vérité; **she doesn't have even a m. of taste** elle n'a aucun goût

modification [mɒdɪfɪˈkeɪʃən] **N** modification *f*, **to make modifications to sth** apporter des modifications à qch

modifier [ˈmɒdɪfaɪə(r)] **N** *Gram* modificateur *m*
▸▸ *Comput* **m. key** touche *f* de modification

modify [ˈmɒdɪfaɪ] **VT 1** (*alter*) modifier; (*reduce*) (*punishment*) mitiger, atténuer; **she modified her opinion of him in the light of this information** elle a changé d'avis à son égard lorsqu'elle a appris cela **2** *Gram, Ling* (*verb, vowel etc*) modifier

modish [ˈməʊdɪʃ] **ADJ** (*hat etc*) à la mode

modishly [ˈməʊdɪʃlɪ] **ADV** (*dressed*) à la mode

modiste [məʊˈdiːst] **N** modiste *f*

Mods [mɒdz] **NPL** *Univ Fam* (*at Oxford University*) = premier examen *m* pour le grade de Bachelor of Arts

modular [ˈmɒdjʊlər] **ADJ** *Archit, Math etc* modulaire; (*furniture*) modulaire, à éléments (composables)

modulate [ˈmɒdjʊleɪt] **VT** (*one's voice, sound*), *Phys* (*amplitude etc*) moduler; **modulating frequency** fréquence *f* de modulation
VI *Mus* moduler

modulation [mɒdjʊˈleɪʃən] **N** (*of voice*) modulation *f*, inflexion *f*, *Mus, Elec, Electron* modulation

modulator [ˈmɒdjʊleɪtər] **N** *Elec, Electron* modulateur *m*

module [ˈmɒdjuːl] **N** *Archit, Astronaut, Constr etc* module *m*; *Univ* module, unité *f* de valeur; *Comput* (*of RAM chips*) barrette *f*

modulus, *pl* **moduli** [ˈmɒdjʊləs, -aɪ] **N** *Math, Phys* module *m*, coefficient *m*

modus operandi [ˈməʊdəsɒpəˈrændaɪ, -diː] **N** façon *f* de procéder

modus vivendi [ˈməʊdəsvɪˈvendaɪ, -diː] **N** modus *m* vivendi

mofo [ˈməʊfəʊ] **N** *Am Vulg* (*abbr* **motherfucker**) enfoiré *m*

moggy [ˈmɒgɪ] **N** *Br Fam* (*cat*) minou *m*; (*esp male*) matou *m*

Mogul [ˈməʊgəl] **N** *Hist* mogol *m*

mogul¹ [ˈməʊgəl] **N** *Fam* (*powerful person*) gros bonnet *m*, grand manitou *m*, nabab *m*; **movie m.** grand manitou du cinéma

mogul² **N** *Ski* bosse *f*

mohair [ˈməʊheər] **N** mohair *m*; **m. sweater** pull *m* en mohair

Mohammed [məʊˈhæmɪd] **N** *Rel* Mahomet *m*, Mohammed *m*

Mohammedan [məʊˈhæmɪd(ə)n] **ADJ, N** mahométan, -ane

Mohawk [ˈməʊhɔːk] **N** (*native American*) Mohawk *mf*

mohawk [ˈməʊhɔːk] **N** *Am* (*hairstyle*) iroquoise *f*

Mohican [məʊˈhiːkən] **N** (*native American*) Mohican *mf*

mohican [məʊˈhiːkən] **N** *Br* (*hairstyle*) iroquoise *f*

moiré [ˈmwɑːreɪ] **ADJ, N** *Tex* moiré *m*

moist [mɔɪst] **ADJ** humide; (*skin, hand*) moite; (*heat*) moite, humide; (*cake*) moelleux; **eyes m. with tears** yeux mouillés de larmes, yeux embués; **to grow m.** se mouiller, s'humecter

moisten [ˈmɔɪs(ə)n] **VT** mouiller, humecter; **to m. a cloth with sth** imbiber un chiffon de qch
VI (*of eyes*) se mouiller

moistness [ˈmɔɪstnɪs] **N** humidité *f*, (*of skin, palms*) moiteur *f*

moisture [ˈmɔɪstʃər] **N** humidité *f*, (*on mirror etc*) buée *f*

moisturize [ˈmɔɪstʃəraɪz] **VT** humidifier; (*skin*) hydrater

moisturizer [ˈmɔɪstʃəraɪzər] **N** (*for skin*) crème *f ou* lotion *f* hydratante, (lait *m*) hydratant *m*

molar [ˈməʊlər] **N** molaire *f*
ADJ molaire

molasses [məˈlæsɪz] **NPL** (*with sing verb*) mélasse *f*, *Am Fam* **to be as slow as m.** (*in winter*) être d'une lenteur de limace *ou* d'escargot *ou* de tortue

mold, molder etc *Am* = **mould, moulder** etc

Moldavia [mɒlˈdeɪvɪə], **Moldova** [mɒlˈdəʊvə] **N** Moldavie *f*

Moldavian [mɒlˈdeɪvɪən], **Moldovan** [mɒlˈdəʊvən] **N** Moldave *mf*
ADJ moldave

mole¹ [məʊl] **N** (*birthmark*) grain *m* de beauté

mole² **N 1** (*animal*) taupe *f* **2** *Fig* (*spy*) espion *m*, taupe *f*
▸▸ **m. catcher** taupier *m*; **m. trap** taupière *f*

mole[3] N (breakwater) môle m, digue f

mole[4] N Chem mole f

molecular [mə'lekjʊlər] ADJ Phys (mass etc) moléculaire

molecule ['mɒlɪkjuːl] N Chem, Phys molécule f

molehill ['məʊlhɪl] N taupinière f

moleskin ['məʊlskɪn] N 1 (peau f de) taupe f, **m. coat** manteau m en taupe 2 (material) velours m de coton

molest [mə'lest] VT (sexually) faire subir des sévices sexuels à; (physically) (of person) molester, agresser, attaquer; (of dog) attaquer; Old-fashioned (pester) importuner

> Note that the French verb **molester** only means **to rough up**.

molestation [məʊles'teɪʃən] N (physical) agression f, (sexual) attentat m à la pudeur

molester [mə'lestər] N (child) m. coupable mf d'attentat à la pudeur sur un/des enfant(s)

moll [mɒl] N Sl (gangster's) m. poule f ou môme f (d'un gangster)

mollify ['mɒlɪfaɪ] VT (somebody, somebody's anger) calmer, apaiser

mollusc, Am **mollusk** ['mɒləsk] N mollusque m

mollycoddle ['mɒlɪkɒd(ə)l] VT Fam (child) dorloter, élever dans du coton

Molotov ['mɒlətɒf] N
> ▸ **M. cocktail** cocktail m Molotov

molt, molting Am = moult, moulting

molten ['məʊltən] ADJ Metal fondu, en fusion; **m. metal** métal m en fusion

molybdenum [mɒ'lɪbdɪnəm] N molybdène m

mom [mɒm] N Am Fam maman f

moment ['məʊmənt] N 1 moment m, instant m; **at the (present) m.** actuellement, en ce moment; **at this m.** (presently, now) en ce moment; **it was at this m. that …** c'est à cet instant que …; **just at that m.** à ce moment ou cet instant précis; **I have just** ou **only this m. heard about it** je viens de l'apprendre, je l'apprends à l'instant; **at the last m.** à la dernière minute, au dernier moment; **I haven't a m. to spare** je n'ai pas un instant ou une minute de libre; **wait a m.!, just a m.!, one m.!** une seconde!, une minute!, un instant!; **he may return at any m.** il peut revenir d'un instant à l'autre; **I saw her a m. ago** je l'ai vue il y a un instant ou une seconde; **the m. he arrives** dès qu'il arrivera, dès son arrivée; **the m. she saw him** dès l'instant où elle le vit; **I'll be with you in a m.** je suis à vous dans une minute ou dans un instant; **nothing else for the m.** rien de plus pour le moment ou l'instant; **I don't for one m. believe that this will happen** je ne crois pas un instant que ça va se produire; **not a m.'s hesitation** pas une seconde d'hésitation; **without a m.'s hesitation** sans hésiter une seconde; **the man of the m.** l'homme du jour ou du moment; **to live for the m.** profiter du moment présent; **the m. of truth** la minute ou l'heure de vérité; **the film had its moments** il y avait quelques bons moments ou passages dans le film; **she has her moments of being quite pleasant** il y a des moments où elle est assez agréable; **I have my moments, you know** ça m'arrive, des fois! 2 Phys, Math etc moment m 3 (importance) **of great m.** d'une importance considérable, de grande ou haute importance; **of little m.** de peu d'importance; **to be of no m.** n'avoir aucune importance
> ▸ Phys **m. of inertia** moment m d'inertie

momentarily ['məʊməntərɪlɪ] ADV 1 (very briefly) momentanément 2 esp Am (very soon) très bientôt, d'un instant à l'autre

momentary ['məʊməntərɪ] ADJ momentané, passager

momentous [məʊ'mentəs] ADJ (decision) capital, -aux, très important; **on this m. occasion** en cette occasion mémorable

momentousness [məʊ'mentəsnɪs] N importance f capitale; (of an occasion) importance f

momentum, pl **momenta** [məʊ'mentəm, -tə] N 1 Phys force f vive, force d'impulsion; Nucl, Phys (of particle) impulsion f 2 (impetus) vitesse f (acquise), élan m; Fig (of attack etc) force f, Fig **carried away by my own m.** emporté par mon (propre) élan; **to gather m.** (of moving object) acquérir de la force (vive) ou de la vitesse; (of political movement etc) prendre de l'ampleur, s'amplifier; Fig **we'll never get that m. back again** on ne retrouvera jamais ce rythme; **to lose one's m.** être en perte de vitesse; Fig **it was m. for old rope**

Mon abbr Monday

Monaco ['mɒnəkəʊ, mə'nɑːkəʊ] N (principality of) M. (principauté f de) Monaco

monad ['mɒnæd] N Phil, Biol, Chem monade f

monadic [mɒ'nædɪk] ADJ
> ▸ Mktg **m. test** test m monadique; Mktg **m. testing** tests mpl monadiques

Mona Lisa ['məʊnə'liːzə] N Art **the M.** la Joconde

monarch ['mɒnək] N monarque m

monarchic(al) [mɒ'nɑːkɪk, -ɪk(ə)l] ADJ monarchique

monarchist ['mɒnəkɪst] ADJ, N monarchiste mf

monarchy ['mɒnəkɪ] N monarchie f

monastery ['mɒnəstrɪ] N monastère m

monastic [mə'næstɪk] ADJ Rel, Fig monastique, monacal, -aux; (attitude) monacal, -aux; **he's a m. sort of person** il mène une vie monacale ou de moine

monasticism [mə'næstɪsɪz(ə)m] N 1 (way of life) vie f monastique 2 (system) système m monastique, monachisme m

monaural [mɒ'nɔːrəl] ADJ monaural, -aux

Monday ['mʌndɪ] N VOIR GRAMMAIRE A81-2; 861-2 lundi m; **M. 16 November** lundi 16 novembre; **M. morning/evening** lundi matin/soir; **it's M. today** nous sommes lundi aujourd'hui; **on Mondays** le lundi; **she's coming on M.** elle vient lundi; **every M.** tous les lundis; Fam **that M. morning feeling** le cafard du lundi matin ou de l'après-weekend

mondo ['mɒndəʊ] ADV Am Fam vachement

MONEP ['məʊnep] N St Exch MONEP m

monetarism ['mʌnɪtərɪz(ə)m] N Econ monétarisme m

monetarist ['mʌnɪtərɪst] ADJ, N Econ monétariste mf

monetary ['mʌnɪt(ə)rɪ] ADJ (unit etc) monétaire
> ▸ **m. adjustment** alignement m monétaire; **m. aggregate** agrégat m monétaire; **m. area** zone f monétaire; **m. assets** liquidités fpl, **m. compensatory amounts** montants mpl compensatoires monétaires; **m. convention** convention f monétaire; Br **m. policy committee** = comité m formé de quatre membres de la Banque d'Angleterre et de quatre économistes nommés par le gouvernement, dont l'un des rôles est de fixer les taux d'intérêt; **m. reform** réforme f monétaire; **m. reserves** réserves fpl de change; **m. system** système m monétaire

money ['mʌnɪ] N 1 (no pl) argent m; **to do sth for m.** faire qch pour l'argent; **to earn** ou **make m.** gagner de l'argent; **to earn good m.** bien gagner; **the job's boring but the m.'s**

good le travail est ennuyeux mais ça paye bien ou c'est bien payé; **to throw good m. after bad** s'enfoncer davantage dans une mauvaise affaire; **it's throwing m. away, it's m. down the drain** c'est de l'argent gaspillé ou jeté par la fenêtre; **to be worth a lot of m.** (of thing) valoir cher, avoir beaucoup de valeur; (of person) être riche; **to get one's m. back** (get reimbursed) se faire rembourser; (recover one's expenses) rentrer dans ses fonds; **Fam to be made of m.** être plein aux as, rouler sur l'or; **I'm not made of m.** je ne suis pas cousu d'or, je ne suis pas riche comme Crésus; Fam **to be in the m.** être en fonds; St Exch être dans les cours; St Exch **at the m.** à parité; St Exch **out of the m.** hors des cours; **there's m. to be made in this business** il y a de l'argent à gagner dans ce métier; **there's no m. in it** ça ne paye pas; **to have m. to burn** avoir de l'argent à jeter par les fenêtres; **your m. or your life!** la bourse ou la vie!; Fig **it was m. for old rope** ou **for jam** c'était de l'argent facilement gagné; **you've had your m.'s worth** vous en avez eu pour votre argent; **to put m. on a horse** mettre de l'argent sur un cheval; **to put one's m. where one's mouth is** passer aux actes; **for my m. Jackson is the better player** à mon avis, Jackson est le meilleur joueur; Prov **m. is the root of all evil** l'argent est la source de tous les maux; Prov **m. makes m.** l'argent va à l'argent; Prov **m. talks** c'est l'argent qui décide de tout; **m. matters** affaires fpl financières, questions fpl financières 2 (pl moneys, occ monies ['mʌnɪz]) (currency) monnaie f, Law, Arch **moneys, monies** (sums) argent m, fonds mpl, sommes fpl (d'argent); **public moneys** deniers mpl publics
> ▸ **m. of account** monnaie de compte; **m.-back guarantee** garantie f de remboursement intégral; **'m.-back guarantee'** 'satisfait ou remboursé'; **m.-back offer** offre f de remboursement; **m. belt** ceinture f portefeuille; Fin **m. broker** prêteur, -euse sur titre; **m. laundering** blanchiment m d'argent; Am Fin **m. manager** gestionnaire mf de portefeuille; Fin **m. market** marché m monétaire ou financier; Fin **m. market funds** ≃ SICAV fpl monétaires; **m.-off deal** réduction f de prix; **m.-off voucher** bon m de remboursement; Fin **m. order** mandat m (postal); **international m. order** mandat international; Fin **m. rate** taux m de l'argent; Br **m. spider** = petite araignée f censée apporter bonheur et richesse à ceux qu'elle touche; Fin **m. supply** masse f monétaire; Fin **m. trader** cambiste mf

> Note that the French word **monnaie** is a false friend and is rarely a translation for the English word **money**. It means **change** or **currency**, depending on the context.

moneybag ['mʌnɪbæg] N 1 sac m à argent; (of bus conductor etc) sacoche f 2 Old-fashioned Fam (person) **moneybags** richard, -arde, rupin, -ine

moneybox ['mʌnɪbɒks] N Br (child's) tirelire f

moneychanger ['mʌnɪtʃeɪndʒər] N 1 (person) courtier, -ière de change 2 (machine) = distributeur m de monnaie

moneyed ['mʌnɪd] ADJ riche, nanti; **the m. classes** les classes fpl possédantes

money-grubber [-grʌbər] N Fam grippe-sou m, pl grippe-sous, pingre m

money-grubbing [-grʌbɪŋ] ADJ Fam grippe-sou inv

moneylender ['mʌnɪlendər] N (person) prêteur, -euse (à intérêt); (establishment) maison f de prêt

moneymaker ['mʌnɪmeɪkər] N (shop, business, product) magasin m/affaire f/produit m qui rapporte

moneymaking ['mʌnɪmeɪkɪŋ] ADJ *(business etc)* qui rapporte N acquisition f d'argent

Mongol ['mɒŋgəl] ADJ *Geog* mongol N 1 Mongol, -ole 2 *Ling* mongol m

mongol ['mɒŋgəl] ADJ, N *Med Old-fashioned* mongolien, -ienne

Mongolia [mɒŋ'gəʊlɪə] N Mongolie f

Mongolian [mɒŋ'gəʊlɪən] ADJ mongol N 1 Mongol, -ole 2 *Ling* mongol m

mongolism ['mɒŋgəlɪz(ə)m] N *Med Old-fashioned* mongolisme m

mongoloid ['mɒŋgəlɔɪd] ADJ *(features etc)* de mongolien

mongoose, pl **mongooses** ['mɒŋgu:s, -sɪz] N mangouste f

mongrel ['mʌŋgrəl] N *(dog)* bâtard, -arde; *(other animal)* métis, -isse ADJ *(dog)* bâtard; *(other animal)*, Fam Pej *(race)* métis, -isse

moni(c)ker ['mɒnɪkər] N *Sl (name)* nom m; *(nickname)* surnom m

monies ['mʌnɪz] NPL *see* **money 2**

monitor ['mɒnɪtər] N 1 *(person)* surveillant, -ante, contrôleur, -euse; *Tel* opérateur m d'interception; *esp Br Sch Old-fashioned* = élève mf qui a une fonction de surveillant 2 *(device)*, *Radio* appareil m de contrôle ou de surveillance, moniteur m; *TV (screen)* écran m de contrôle; *(speaker on stage)* = enceinte f qui permet aux musiciens de s'entendre jouer 3 *Comput* moniteur m
VT *Radio, Med etc (broadcasts, patient's condition etc)* surveiller; *Tel (conversation)* écouter, être à l'écoute de; *Cin (sound recording)* contrôler; *(level of pollution)* examiner, surveiller, contrôler
▸▸ *TV* **m. screen** écran m de contrôle; **m. speaker** *(on stage)* = enceinte qui permet aux musiciens de s'entendre jouer

monitoring ['mɒnɪtərɪŋ] N *(of broadcasts, phonecalls)* écoute f; *(of conversation)* surveillance f; *(of patient)* surveillance continue, monitorage m
▸▸ *Radio* **m. station** station f ou centre m d'écoute

monk [mʌŋk] N moine m

monkey ['mʌŋkɪ] N 1 *(animal)* singe m; **female m., she-m.** guenon f; *Fig* **you little m.!** *(child)* petit(e) polisson(ne)!, petit(e) espiègle!; **little m. face** petite frimousse espiègle; *Sl* **to make a m. (out) of sb** se payer la tête de qn; *Sl* **I don't give a m.'s** je m'en fous complètement; *Am Sl* **to have a m. on one's back** être accro 2 *Constr etc (of pile-driver)* mouton m 3 *Br Sl* cinq cents livres fpl
▸▸ *Am* **m. bars** cage f d'écureuil; *Fam* **m. business** *(suspect activity)* combines fpl, *(mischief)* bêtises fpl; **m. house** pavillon m des singes; **m. jacket** spencer m *(de garçon de café etc)*; *Br* **m. nut** cacahouète f, cacahuète f; *Bot* **m. puzzle tree** désespoir m des singes, *Spec* araucaria m; *Am (uniform)* uniforme m; *Fig Fam* **m. tricks** espiègleries fpl; **m. wrench** clef f anglaise ou à molette
▸ **monkey about, monkey around** VI *Fam (fool around)* faire des bêtises, faire l'imbécile; **to m. about with sth** *(play with)* tripoter qch, jouer avec qch; **somebody's been monkeying about with the lock** quelqu'un a essayé de forcer la serrure; **to m. about with the brakes on sb's car** saboter les freins de la voiture de qn

monkfish ['mʌŋkfɪʃ] N lotte f, baudroie f

monkish ['mʌŋkɪʃ] ADJ de moine, monacal, -aux

monkshood ['mʌŋkshʊd] N *Bot* (aconit m) napel m

mono ['mɒnəʊ] ADJ mono inv

N 1 *(abbr* **monophony***)* monophonie f; **recorded in m.** enregistré en mono 2 *Am (abbr* **mononucleosis***)* mononucléose f infectieuse

monochrome ['mɒnəkrəʊm] ADJ *Phot* monochrome; *Art* monochrome, en camaïeu; *Comput* **m. monitor** moniteur m monochrome; **m. screen** écran m monochrome N *Art* camaïeu m, *(peinture f)* monochrome m

monocle ['mɒnək(ə)l] N monocle m

monoclonal [mɒnəʊ'kləʊnəl] ADJ ▸▸ *Biol* **m. antibody** anticorps m monoclonal

monocoque ['mɒnəkɒk] N *Aut* monocoque m

monoculture ['mɒnəʊkʌltʃər] N *Agr* monoculture f

monogamous [mɒ'nɒgəməs] ADJ monogame

monogamy [mɒ'nɒgəmɪ] N monogamie f

monogram ['mɒnəgræm] N monogramme m

monogrammed ['mɒnəgræmd] ADJ *(handkerchief)* brodé à mes/ses/etc initiales

monograph ['mɒnəgræf] N monographie f

monokini ['mɒnəki:nɪ] N monokini m

monolingual [mɒnəʊ'lɪŋgwəl] ADJ monolingue

monolith ['mɒnəlɪθ] N monolithe m

monolithic [mɒnə'lɪθɪk] ADJ 1 *(monument)* monolithe 2 *Pol etc* monolithique

monologue ['mɒnəlɒg] N monologue m

monomania [mɒnəʊ'meɪnɪə] N monomanie f

monometallism [mɒnjəʊ'metəlɪz(ə)m] N *Fin* monométallisme m

mononucleosis [mɒnəʊnju:klɪ'əʊsɪs] N *Med* mononucléose f

monophonic [mɒnəʊ'fɒnɪk] ADJ monophonique

monoplane ['mɒnəʊpleɪn] N *Aviat* monoplan m

Monopolies and Mergers Commission N *Com* = commission f britannique veillant au respect de la législation antitrust

monopolist [mə'nɒpəlɪst] N monopoliste mf

monopolistic [mənɒpə'lɪstɪk] ADJ monopoliste, monopolistique
▸▸ **m. competition** concurrence f monopolistique

monopolization [mənɒpəlaɪ'zeɪʃən] N monopolisation f

monopolize [mə'nɒpəlaɪz] VT *Com, Fig* monopoliser, accaparer

monopoly [mə'nɒpəlɪ] N *Com, Fig* monopole m; **to have a m. of sth** *or* **on sth** avoir ou détenir le monopole de qch, monopoliser qch; **no political party has a m. of morality** aucun parti politique ne détient le monopole de la moralité; **to form a m.** truster
▸▸ **m. control** contrôle m monopolistique; **m. market** marché m monopolistique

monopsonist [mə'nɒpsənɪst] N *Econ* = partisan m du monopsone

monopsonistic [mənɒpsə'nɪstɪk] ADJ *Econ* monopsoniste

monopsony [mə'nɒpsənɪ] N *Econ* monopsone m

monorail ['mɒnəʊreɪl] N *Rail etc* monorail m

monoski ['mɒnəʊski:] N monoski m

monosodium glutamate [mɒnəʊ'səʊdɪəm'glu:təmeɪt] N glutamate m de sodium

monospaced [mɒnəʊ'speɪst] ADJ *Comput* non proportionnel

monosyllabic [mɒnəʊsɪ'læbɪk] ADJ monosyllabe, monosyllabique; **he's rather m.** il ne s'exprime que par monosyllabes

monosyllable [mɒnəʊ'sɪləb(ə)l] N monosyllabe m; **he replied in monosyllables** il a répondu par monosyllabes

monotheism ['mɒnəʊθi:ɪz(ə)m] N monothéisme m

monotheistic [mɒnəʊθi:'ɪstɪk] ADJ monothéiste

monotone ['mɒnətəʊn] ADJ monotone N *(in speaking)* débit m monotone; **to speak in a m.** parler d'une voix uniforme ou monotone

monotonous [mə'nɒtənəs] ADJ 1 *(job etc)* monotone 2 *(sound)* monotone, monocorde

monotonously [mə'nɒtənəslɪ] ADV de ou d'une manière ou façon monotone

monotony [mə'nɒtənɪ] N monotonie f; **to relieve** *or* **break the m.** rompre la monotonie

Monotype® ['mɒnətaɪp] N *Typ (machine)* Monotype® f, *Art* monotype m

mono-unsaturated [-ʌn'sætʃəreɪtɪd] ADJ *(fat)* mono-insaturé

monoxide [mɒ'nɒksaɪd] N *Chem* **carbon m.** oxyde m de carbone

Monsignor [mɒn'si:njər] N *Cathol* monseigneur m

monsoon [mɒn'su:n] N *Met* mousson f; **the m. season** la mousson

monster ['mɒnstər] N 1 monstre m; *Fig* **a m. of cruelty** un monstre de cruauté 2 *(large person)* colosse m, géant, -ante; **his last novel was a m.** son dernier roman est un pavé ADJ *Fam (enormous)* monstre, colossal, -aux, énorme

monstrance ['mɒnstrəns] N *Rel* ostensoir m

monstrosity [mɒn'strɒsɪtɪ] N monstruosité f, horreur f

monstrous ['mɒnstrəs] ADJ 1 *(repugnant)* monstrueux; *Old-fashioned* **it is perfectly m. that ...** c'est monstrueux que ... + sub 2 *(enormous)* énorme, monstrueux

monstrously ['mɒnstrəslɪ] ADV monstrueusement

mons veneris [mɒnz'venərɪs] N mont m de Vénus

Mont *abbr* **Montana**

montage [mɒn'tɑ:ʒəm] N *Cin, Phot* montage m

Monte Carlo [mɒntɪ'kɑ:ləʊ] N Monte-Carlo

Montezuma [mɒntɪ'zu:mə] N Moctezuma m, Montezuma m
▸▸ *Fam Hum* **M.'s revenge** la turista f

month [mʌnθ] N mois m; **in the m. of August** au mois d'août; **in the summer/winter months** pendant les mois d'été/d'hiver; **a m. ago today** il y a aujourd'hui un mois; **a thirteen-m.-old baby, a thirteen months' old baby** un bébé de treize mois; **from m. to m.** de mois en mois; **once a m.** une fois par mois; *Fam* **never in a m. of Sundays** jamais de la vie; *Fam* **to see sb once in a m. of Sundays** voir qn une fois tous les trente-six du mois; *Euph* **it's that time of the m.** *(menstruation)* je suis/elle est indisposée **VOIR GRAMMAIRE A81–2; B60–2**

monthly ['mʌnθlɪ] ADJ mensuel; *Com* **m. payment** *or* **instalment** mensualité f, mensualisation f, paiement m mensuel; *Rail etc* **m. season ticket** (billet m d')abonnement m mensuel
ADV mensuellement, tous les mois; **it happens once or twice m.** ça arrive une ou deux fois par mois; **to make payments m.** mensualiser les paiements
N 1 *(publication)* revue f ou publication f

mensuelle **2** *Old-fashioned Fam* **monthlies** *(menstruation)* règles *fpl*
▶▶**m. periods** règles *fpl*

Montreal [mɒntrɪˈɔːl] N Montréal

monument [ˈmɒnjʊmənt] N monument *m* (**to** à); **ancient monuments** monuments historiques

monumental [mɒnjʊˈment(ə)l] ADJ *(statue, literary work, error, stupidity etc)* monumental, -aux; *(ignorance)* prodigieux
▶▶**m. mason** marbrier *m*

monumentally [mɒnjʊˈmentəlɪ] ADV *(important, stupid, conceited etc)* extrêmement

moo [muː] N **1** *(of cow)* meuglement *m*, beuglement *m* **2** *Fam* **silly** *or* **stupid old m.!** (espèce de) vieille bique!
INT m.! meuh!
VI *(of cow)* meugler, beugler

mooch [muːtʃ] *Fam* VT *(cadge)* taper, taxer (**from sb** à qn); **he's always mooching cigarettes (from me)** il est toujours en train de (me) taper des cigarettes
VI *(cadge)* taxer
▶**mooch about, mooch around** VI *Fam* traîner, flemmarder

moocher [ˈmuːtʃər] N *Fam* tapeur, -euse

moocow [ˈmuːkaʊ] N *Fam (in children's language)* vache *f*, meu-meu *f*

mood¹ [muːd] N **1** *(in logic), Gram* mode *m* **VOIR GRAMMAIRE A40; B32–5** **2** *esp Am Mus* mode *m*

mood² N *(state of mind)* humeur *f*, disposition *f*; **as the m. takes her** selon son humeur; **to be in a (bad) m.** être de mauvaise humeur; **to be in a good m.** être de bonne humeur; **to be in a generous m.** être en veine de générosité; **to be in the m. for reading** avoir envie de lire; **he's in no m. for jokes** il n'est pas d'humeur à rire; **I'm not in the m.** ça ne me dit rien; **I wasn't in the m. (for it)** je n'étais pas d'humeur à ça
▶▶**m. music** musique *f* d'ambiance; **m. swing** saute *f* d'humeur

moodily [ˈmuːdɪlɪ] ADV *(to look)* d'un air morose; *(to say)* d'un ton morose *ou* maussade, maussadement; *(to behave)* avec morosité

moodiness [ˈmuːdɪnɪs] N morosité *f*, maussaderie *f*

moody [ˈmuːdɪ] ADJ **1** *(sulky)* chagrin, morose, maussade **2** *(changeable)* d'humeur changeante, lunatique **3** *Br Sl (goods)* volé; *(passport, document)* faux, *f* fausse

moola, moolah [ˈmuːlə] N *Fam (money)* flouze *m*, fric *m*, pognon *m*

moon [muːn] N lune *f*; **to land on the m.** alunir; *Fig* **to ask for the m.** demander la lune; **to promise sb the m.** promettre la lune à qn; *Fam Hum* **many moons ago** il y a bien longtemps; *Fam* **to be over the m.** être enchanté *ou* ravi (**about** de)
VI *Sl (bare one's buttocks)* montrer ses fesses
VT *Sl (somebody)* montrer ses fesses à
▶▶**m. buggy** Jeep® *f* lunaire; **m. landing** atterrissage *m* sur la lune, alunissage *m*; *Astronaut* **m. walk** marche *f* sur la lune
▶**moon about, moon around** VI musarder, flâner
▶**moon over** VT INSEP *(person)* languir pour; *(photograph)* regarder amoureusement

moonbeam [ˈmuːnbiːm] N rayon *m* de lune

moonfaced [ˈmuːnfeɪst] ADJ à la figure toute ronde

moonless [ˈmuːnlɪs] ADJ *(night etc)* sans lune

moonlight [ˈmuːnlaɪt] N clair *m* de lune; **in the m., by m.** au clair de lune, à la clarté *ou* la lumière de la lune
VI *Fam (work illegally)* faire du travail au noir, travailler au noir

▶▶*Br Fam* **m. flit** déménagement *m* à la cloche de bois; **to do a m. flit** déménager à la cloche de bois

moonlighter [ˈmuːnlaɪtər] N *Fam (illegal worker)* travailleur, -euse au noir

moonlighting [ˈmuːnlaɪtɪŋ] N *Fam (illegal work)* travail *m* (au) noir

moonlit [ˈmuːnlɪt] ADJ éclairé par la lune

moonrise [ˈmuːnraɪz] N lever *m* de (la) lune

moonshine [ˈmuːnʃaɪn] N **1** *Am Fam (illegal alcohol)* alcool *m* illicitement distillé **2** *Fam (nonsense)* balivernes *fpl*, fariboles *fpl* **3** *(moonlight)* clair *m* de lune

moonshot [ˈmuːnʃɒt] N *Astronaut* tir *m* lunaire

moonstone [ˈmuːnstəʊn] N *(gem)* adulaire *f*, feldspath *m* nacré, pierre *f* de lune

moonstruck [ˈmuːnstrʌk] ADJ dérangé, *Fam* toqué

moony [ˈmuːnɪ] ADJ *Fam (dreamy)* rêveur; **what are you looking so m. about?** pourquoi est-ce que tu as l'air si rêveur?

Moor [mʊər] N Maure *m*, Mauresque *f*, More *m*, Moresque *f*

moor¹ [mʊər] N lande *f*

moor² *Naut* VT *(ship)* amarrer; *(buoy, mine)* mouiller
VI s'amarrer

moorcock [ˈmʊəkɒk] N *(bird)* lagopède *m* rouge d'Écosse

moorhen [ˈmʊəhen] N **1** *(water bird)* poule *f* d'eau **2** *(red grouse)* lagopède *m* rouge d'Écosse (femelle)

mooring [ˈmʊərɪŋ] N *Naut (place)* poste *m* d'amarrage; **ship at her moorings** navire sur ses amarres
▶▶**m. buoy** corps-mort *m*, *pl* corps-morts, coffre *m* d'amarrage; **m. line** câble *m* d'amarrage

Moorish [ˈmʊərɪʃ] ADJ maure, *f* mauresque, more, *f* moresque

moorland [ˈmʊələnd] N lande *f*

moose [muːs] N *(inv in pl)* **(American)** m. orignal *m*, élan *m* du Canada

moot [muːt] ADJ *(question etc)* sujet à controverse, discutable; **it is a m. point** c'est discutable
VT *(always in passive) Fml* **to be mooted** *(of question)* être soulevé; *(of solution)* être suggéré

mop [mɒp] N *(for floor)* balai *m* à franges; *(sponge mop)* balai-éponge *m*, *pl* balais-éponges; *(for dishes)* lavette *f* (à vaisselle); *Fig* **m. of hair** tignasse *f*
VT *(-pp-)* **to m. the floor** passer un coup de serpillière, laver par terre; **to m. one's brow** s'éponger le front
▶**mop up** VT SEP **1** *(clean up) (water etc)* éponger; **to use a piece of bread to m. up the sauce** saucer son assiette avec un morceau de pain **2** *Mil etc (last remnants)* liquider
VI *(clean floor)* passer un coup de serpillière, laver par terre; *Mil etc* nettoyer, faire une opération de nettoyage

mope [məʊp] VI être triste *ou* mélancolique, broyer du noir
▶**mope about, mope around** VI broyer du noir

moped [ˈməʊped] N *Br* mobylette® *f*, *Fam* mob *f*

moppet [ˈmɒpɪt] N *Fam (child)* gamin, -ine, gosse *mf*

mopping [ˈmɒpɪŋ] N *(of floor etc)* nettoyage *m*
▶▶**m. up** *(of floor etc)* nettoyage; *Mil etc* **m.-up operations** opérations *fpl* de nettoyage

moquette [mɒˈket] N *Tex* moquette *f*

MOR [eməʊˈɑːr] ADJ *esp Mus abbr* **middle-of-the-road**

moraine [mɒˈreɪn] N *Geol* moraine *f*

moral [ˈmɒrəl] ADJ *(person, certainty, victory etc)* moral, -aux; **to give sb m. support** soutenir qn moralement; **young people today have no m. fibre** les jeunes d'aujourd'hui n'ont ni caractère ni moralité; **m. obligation** obligation *f* morale; **m. tale** conte *m* moral
N **1** *(lesson) (of a story)* morale *f*, moralité *f*; **to draw the m. from a story** tirer la morale d'une histoire; **there's a m. to that story** cette histoire a une morale; **story with a m.** conte moral **2** *(usu pl)* **morals** moralité *f*, principes *mpl* moraux; **man of loose morals** homme de mœurs relâchés
▶▶*Am Pol* **M. Majority** = ultra-conservateurs *mpl* aux États-Unis prônant un retour aux valeurs morales; **m. philosophy** morale *f*, éthique *f*; **m. standard** valeur *f* morale; **m. standards** sens *m* moral, valeurs *fpl* morales; **m. values** valeurs morales

> Attention: ne pas confondre avec le nom anglais **morale**.

morale [mɒˈrɑːl] N *(no pl)* moral *m*; **m. is very low/high** le moral est très bas *ou* mauvais/bon; **good for m.** bon pour le moral; **to undermine the m. of the army** saper le moral des troupes, démoraliser les troupes

> Attention: ne pas confondre avec le nom anglais **moral**.

moralist [ˈmɒrəlɪst] N moraliste *mf*

moralistic [mɒrəˈlɪstɪk] ADJ *usu Pej* moraliste

morality [məˈrælɪtɪ] N **1** *(of person, decision, principles)* moralité *f* **moralities** principes *mpl* moraux **2** *Theat (play)* moralité *f*
▶▶*Theat* **m. play** moralité

moralize [ˈmɒrəlaɪz] VI moraliser

moralizing [ˈmɒrəlaɪzɪŋ] ADJ moralisant, moralisateur, -trice
N **I'm tired of your incessant m.!** j'en ai assez que tu me fasses la morale!

morally [ˈmɒrəlɪ] ADV moralement; **m. bound to do sth** moralement obligé de faire qch

morass [məˈræs] N marais *m*, *Fig (of figures etc)* bourbier *m*

moratorium [mɒrəˈtɔːrɪəm] N **1** moratoire *m*, moratorium *m* (**on** sur); **to hold a m. on sth** procéder à un moratoire sur qch **2** *Econ, Fin, Law* moratoire *m*; *(of debt)* moratoire, suspension *f*; **to declare a m.** décréter un moratoire

morbid [ˈmɔːbɪd] ADJ **1** *(idea, curiosity etc)* morbide, malsain **2** *Med (anatomy)* pathologique; *(symptom)* morbide, pathologique

morbidity [mɔːˈbɪdɪtɪ] N morbidité *f*, *(rate)* morbidité
▶▶**m. rate** morbidité

morbidly [ˈmɔːbɪdlɪ] ADV d'une façon morbide *ou* malsaine

morbidness [ˈmɔːbɪdnɪs] N *(of idea, curiosity etc)* caractère *m* morbide *ou* malsain, morbidité *f*

mordant [ˈmɔːd(ə)nt] ADJ *(wit)* mordant, caustique

MORE [mɔːr]

ADJ	plus de	▪ davantage de
N, INDEF PRON	encore	▪ plus
ADV	plus **1–3**	▪ de plus en plus **1**
	▪ davantage **2**	▪ plus que **2, 3**

ADJ *(cars, people, water, time etc)* plus de, davantage de; **he has m. patience than I (have)** il a plus de patience que moi; **one m.** un de plus, encore un; **one or m.** un ou plusieurs; **one m. hour** une heure de plus, encore une heure; **there's only one m. problem to solve** il n'y a plus qu'un problème à résoudre; **(some) m. bread, please!** encore du pain, s'il vous plaît!; **is there any m. bread?** est-ce qu'il reste du pain?; **to have some m. wine** reprendre du vin; **have you (got) any m. books?** avez-vous d'autres livres?; **that's m. than enough** c'est plus qu'il n'en faut; **he is m. than 30** il a plus de 30 ans, il a 30 ans passés; **she's m. of an artist than her sister** elle est plus artiste que sa sœur; **I have no m. money** je n'ai plus d'argent; **no m. soup, thank you** plus de potage, merci

N, INDEF PRON do you want (any or **some) m.?** en voulez-vous encore?, est-ce que vous en revoulez?; **what m. can I say?** que puis-je dire de plus?; **there is nothing m. to be said** il n'y a plus rien à dire, il n'y a rien à ajouter; **I need still m.** il m'en faut encore davantage; **I needn't say m.** pas besoin d'en dire davantage; **m. than that I can't say** je ne peux pas en dire plus; **he knows m. about it than you (do)** il en sait plus (long) que vous; **she doesn't know any m. about it** elle n'en sait pas davantage; **we should see m. of each other** nous devrions nous voir plus *ou* davantage; **the latest budget is just m. of the same** il n'y a rien de nouveau dans le dernier budget; **... and there's (plenty) m. where that came from!** ... et ce n'est pas fini!; **what is m.** (et) qui plus est, de plus; **neither m. nor less** ni plus ni moins; **I have no m.** je n'en ai plus; **I can do no m.** je ne peux pas faire plus; **let us say no m. about it** n'en parlons plus; *Fam* **say no m.!** cela suffit!, n'en dites pas plus!; **he's just a good friend, nothing m.** c'est un bon ami, rien de plus; **the m. you have the m. you want** plus on a, plus on en veut; **the m. I read, the m. I learn** plus je lis, plus j'apprends

ADV 1 *(to form comp)* plus; **m. interesting** plus intéressant; **he became m. and m. drunk** il est devenu de plus en plus ivre; **easily** plus facilement; **this is far m. serious** c'est bien *ou* beaucoup plus grave VOIR GRAMMAIRE A24–6; B11; B13–14

2 *(with verbs) (to eat, exercise etc)* plus, davantage; **this word is used m.** ce mot s'emploie plus *ou* davantage; **it's used m. than that one** il s'emploie plus que celui-là; **I would think m. of her if ...** j'aurais une plus haute opinion d'elle si ...; **(the) m.'s the pity** c'est d'autant plus malheureux *ou* plus regrettable; **he is no m. a lord than I am** il n'est pas plus lord que moi; **no m. can I (ni) moi non plus; I would no m. have suspected him than I would my own mother** je ne l'aurais pas soupçonné davantage que ma propre mère; **it's m. a question of luck** c'est plus une question de chance; **this m. than makes up for it** ça fait plus que compenser

3 *(with adjectives etc)* plus; **he was m. surprised than annoyed** il était plus surpris que fâché; **m. than satisfied** plus que satisfait; **that's m. like it!** ça, c'est mieux!; **m. or less** plus ou moins; **I am all the m. surprised as ...** je suis d'autant plus étonné que ...; **this made things all the m. difficult** ça a rendu les choses d'autant plus difficiles; **it makes me all the m. proud** je n'en suis que plus fier

4 *(in time)* **once m.** encore une fois, une fois de plus; **I can't see her any m.** je ne peux plus la voir; **he doesn't drink any m.** il ne boit plus; *Lit* **he is no m.** il n'est plus, il est mort

5 (the) m. fool you! que tu es bête!; **all the m. reason for going/telling her** raison de plus pour y aller/le lui dire

moreish ['mɔːrɪʃ] **ADJ** *Fam* **this cake is very m.** ce gâteau a un petit goût de revenez-y

morel [mɒ'rel] **N** *(fungus)* morille *f*

morello [mə'reləʊ] **N** griotte *f*
▶ ▶ **m. cherry** griotte

moreover [mɔː'rəʊvər] **ADV** de plus, et qui plus est

mores ['mɔːreɪz] **NPL** *Fml* mœurs *fpl*

morganatic [mɔːgə'nætɪk] **ADJ m. marriage** mariage *m* morganatique

morgue [mɔːg] **N 1** morgue *f*; **it's like a m. here** c'est complètement mort ici **2** *Journ Sl* archives *fpl*

MORI ['mɔːrɪ] **N** *(abbr* **Market and Opinion Research Institute)** = institut *m* de sondage, ≃ IPSOS *m*

moribund ['mɒrɪbʌnd] **ADJ** *Fml* moribond

morish ['mɔːrɪʃ] **ADJ** *Fam* = **moreish**

Mormon ['mɔːmən] **ADJ, N** *Rel* mormon, -one

morn [mɔːn] **N** *Lit* matin *m*

morning ['mɔːnɪŋ] **N** matin *m*; *(whole period)* matinée *f*; **to work from m. till night, to work m., noon and night** travailler du matin au soir; **this m.** ce matin; **tomorrow m.** demain matin; **the next m., the m. after** le lendemain matin; **the m. before** la veille au matin; *Fam* **the m. after (the night before)** *(after drinking bout)* un lendemain de cuite; **I had that m. after feeling** j'avais la gueule de bois; **four o'clock in the m.** quatre heures du matin; **early in the m.** de bon *ou* grand matin; **on Wednesday m.** mercredi matin; **on the m. of Sunday 1st April** le dimanche 1er avril au matin; *Fam* **to be a m. person** du matin; **good m.!, Fam m.!** bonjour!; **in the course of the m.** dans la matinée; **a m.'s work** une matinée de travail; **m. coffee** café *m* (servi le matin); **m. off** matinée *f* de congé SEE GRAMMAR B61
▶ ▶ **m. coat** queue-de-pie *f*, *pl* queues-de-pie; **m. dress** habit *m*; **m. paper** journal *m* du matin; **m. room** petit salon *m*; **m. sickness** nausées *fpl* matinales *ou* du matin; **m. star** étoile *f* du matin

When translating **morning**, note that **matin** and **matinée** are not interchangeable. **Matin** is used to refer to the morning as part of the day as opposed to the evening or the afternoon. For **matinée**, the emphasis is on duration.

morning-after pill **N** pilule *f* du lendemain

morning-glory **N** *(plant)* belle-de-jour *f*, liseron *m*

Moroccan [mə'rɒkən] **ADJ** marocain
N Marocain, -aine

Morocco [mə'rɒkəʊ] **N** Maroc *m*

morocco [mə'rɒkəʊ] **N** *(leather)* maroquin *m*; **m.-bound** relié en maroquin

moron ['mɔːrɒn] **N 1** *Fam (idiot)* idiot, -ote, crétin, -ine **2** *Med* faible *mf* d'esprit

moronic [mə'rɒnɪk] **ADJ** *Fam (stupid)* idiot, crétin

morose [mə'rəʊs] **ADJ** *(person, disposition)* chagrin, morose

morosely [mə'rəʊslɪ] **ADV** d'un air chagrin *ou* morose

moroseness [mə'rəʊsnɪs] **N** morosité *f*, humeur *f* chagrine *ou* morose

morph [mɔːf] *Comput* **VT** *(image)* transformer par morphing
VI **to m. into sth** se transformer *ou* se métamorphoser en qch

morpheme ['mɔːfiːm] **N** *Ling* morphème *m*

Morpheus ['mɔːfɪəs] **N** *Myth* Morphée *m*; *Hum* **in the arms of M.** dans les bras de Morphée

morphine ['mɔːfiːn], **morphia** ['mɔːfɪə] **N** morphine *f*
▶ ▶ **m. addict** morphinomane *mf*; **m. addiction** morphinomanie *f*

morphing ['mɔːfɪŋ] **N** *Comput* morphing *m*

morphological [mɔːfə'lɒdʒɪk(ə)l] **ADJ** morphologique

morphology [mɔː'fɒlədʒɪ] **N** morphologie *f*

morris dance ['mɒrɪs] **N** = danse *f* folklorique anglaise

morrow ['mɒrəʊ] **N** *Arch, Lit (next day)* lendemain *m*; **on the m.** le lendemain

Morse [mɔːs] **N** *Tel (alphabet, code)* morse *m*
▶ ▶ **M. alphabet** (alphabet *m*) morse; **M. code** (code *m*) morse

morsel ['mɔːs(ə)l] **N** (petit) morceau *m*; **choice** *or* **dainty m.** morceau de choix

mortadella [mɔːtə'delə] **N** mortadelle *f*
▶ ▶ **m. sausage** mortadelle

mortal ['mɔːt(ə)l] **ADJ 1** mortel; **all men are m.** tous les hommes sont mortels; **2** *(fatal)* mortel, fatal, -als (**to** à); **m. blow** coup *m* mortel **3** *(very great)* **to be in m. fear of sth** avoir très peur de qch, craindre qch par-dessus tout **4** *Fam (conceivable)* **it's no m. use** ça ne sert absolument à rien
N mortel, -elle; **ordinary mortals like us** des gens comme nous
▶ ▶ **m. combat** combat *m* à mort; **m. enemy** ennemi *m* mortel; **m. remains** dépouille *f* mortelle; **m. sin** péché *m* mortel

mortality [mɔː'tælɪtɪ] **N 1** *(of person etc)* condition *f* mortelle **2** *(death rate)* mortalité *f*
▶ ▶ **m. tables** tables *fpl* de mortalité *ou* de létalité

mortally ['mɔːt(ə)lɪ] **ADV** mortellement; **m. wounded** blessé à mort; **to be m. afraid (of sb)** être mort de peur (devant qn); **they are m. afraid that ...** ils craignent par-dessus tout que ...; **m. offended** très offusqué

mortar ['mɔːtər] **N 1** *Constr* mortier *m* **2** *Pharm, Culin etc* mortier *m*; **m. and pestle** pilon *m* et mortier **3** *Mil* mortier *m*
VT *Constr (stones)* cimenter avec du mortier
▶ ▶ *Mil* **m. attack** attaque *f* au mortier; *Mil* **m. shell** obus *m* de mortier

mortarboard ['mɔːtəbɔːd] **N** *Univ* = coiffure *f* traditionnelle portée par les universitaires en Angleterre et dans d'autres pays anglo-saxons

mortgage ['mɔːgɪdʒ] **N** *Fin (for house purchase)* crédit *m* immobilier; *(raised on property)* hypothèque *f*; **to raise a m.** prendre un crédit immobilier/une hypothèque; **to buy a house on a m.** prendre un crédit immobilier *ou* emprunt-logement pour acheter une maison; **to secure a debt by m.** hypothéquer une créance; **to pay off a m.** purger une hypothèque
VT *Fin (land, house etc)* hypothéquer; *(title deeds)* engager, mettre en gage; *Fam* **we're mortgaged up to the eyeballs** *or* **up to the hilt** on a des crédits jusqu'au cou; *Fig* **to m. one's future** hypothéquer l'avenir
▶ ▶ **m. bank** banque *f* hypothécaire; **m. bond** obligation *f* hypothécaire; **m. broker** courtier, -ière en prêts hypothécaires; **m. charge** affectation *f* hypothécaire; **m. debenture** obligation hypothécaire; **m. deed** acte *m* hypothécaire; **m. lender** prêteur, -euse hypothécaire; **m. loan** emprunt *m ou* prêt *m* hypothécaire, prêt sur hypothèque; **m. payments** remboursements *mpl* d'un emprunt-logement; **m. rate** taux *m* de crédit immobilier; **m. repayments** remboursements d'un emprunt-logement; **m. repossession** mainlevée *f* d'une hypothèque; **m. security** garantie *f* hypothécaire

mortgagee [mɔːgɪ'dʒiː] **N** créancier, -ière hypothécaire

mortgager, mortgagor ['mɔːgɪdʒər] **N** débiteur, -trice hypothécaire

mortice ['mɔːtɪs] **N, VT** = **mortise**

mortician [mɔː'tɪʃən] **N** *Am* entrepreneur *m* de pompes funèbres

mortification [mɔːtɪfɪ'keɪʃən] **N 1** *(humiliation)* humiliation *f, Lit* mortification *f;* **to my (eternal) m.** à ma (grande) honte **2** *Rel (of the flesh)* mortification *f* **3** *Med* nécrose *f*

mortify ['mɔːtɪfaɪ] **VT 1** *(humiliate)* humilier, *Lit* mortifier; *Fam* **I was mortified** j'étais mort de honte **2** *Rel (the flesh)* mortifier **VI** *Med* se gangrener, se nécroser

mortifying ['mɔːtɪfaɪɪŋ] **ADJ** *(experience etc)* humiliant, *Lit* mortifiant

mortise ['mɔːtɪs] *Carp* **N** mortaise *f* **VT** *(cut mortise in)* mortaiser; **to m. two beams (together)** emmortaiser *ou* emboîter deux poutres
▸▸**m. lock** serrure *f* encastrée

mortuary ['mɔːtjʊərɪ] **N** morgue *f* **ADJ** mortuaire

Mosaic [məʊ'zeɪɪk] **ADJ** *Bible (law etc)* mosaïque, de Moïse

mosaic [məʊ'zeɪɪk] **N** *Art etc* mosaïque *f;* **m. floor** dallage *m* en mosaïque

Moscow ['mɒskəʊ] **N** Moscou

Moses ['məʊzɪz] **N** *Bible* Moïse *m* **INT** *Old-fashioned Fam* **Holy M.!** grand Dieu!
▸▸**M. basket** couffin *m*

▸**mosey along** ['məʊzɪ] **VI** *esp Am Fam* flâner, se promener sans se presser; **I'll just m. along to the bar** je vais faire un tour au bar; **I'll be moseying along now** *(leaving)* je vais y aller

Moslem ['mɒzləm] **ADJ, N** musulman, -ane

mosque [mɒsk] **N** mosquée *f*

mosquito, *pl* **mosquitoes** [məs'kiːtəʊ, -əʊz] **N** moustique *m*
▸▸**m. bite** piqûre *f* de moustique; **m. net** moustiquaire *f;* **m. repellent** produit *m* antimoustique

moss [mɒs] **N** *Bot* mousse *f*
▸▸*Miner* **m. agate** agate *f* mousseuse; *Bot* **m. rose** rose *f* mousseuse *ou* mousseuse; *Sewing* **m. stitch** point *m* de riz

mossy ['mɒsɪ] **ADJ** moussu

MOST [məʊst] *(superl of* **many, much)**

ADJ le plus de ▪ la plupart de	
N, INDEF PRON le plus **1** ▪ au plus **1** ▪ la plupart **2** ▪ la plus grande partie **2**	
ADV le plus **1, 3** ▪ bien **2**	

ADJ *(cows, milk etc)* le plus de; **you have made (the) m. mistakes** c'est vous qui avez fait le plus de fautes; **m. women** la plupart des femmes; **in m. cases** dans la majorité *ou* la plupart des cas; **for the m. part** *(in greatest number of cases)* pour la plupart; *(most often)* le plus souvent *ou* la plupart du temps

N, INDEF PRON 1 *(greatest amount)* **the m.** le plus, le maximum; **do the m. you can** faites le plus que vous pourrez; **at the (very) m.** au (grand) maximum, (tout) au plus; **to make the m. of a situation** tirer le meilleur parti d'une situation; **to make the m. of one's talents** tirer le meilleur parti de ses capacités; **she made the m. of her time in Mexico** elle a profité au maximum du temps qu'elle a passé au Mexique; **the opposition made the m. of the scandal** l'opposition a tiré tout ce qu'elle pouvait du scandale; **make the m. of it** profitez-en au maximum **2** *(majority)* **m. of the women/cars** la plupart *ou* la majorité des femmes/des voitures; **m. of the work** la plus grande *ou* la majeure partie du travail; **m. of the time** la plupart du temps; **he is more reliable than m.** on peut compter sur lui plus que sur bien des gens

ADV 1 *(to form superl)* le plus; **the m. beautiful woman** la plus belle femme; **they bought**

the m. expensive (ones) ils ont acheté les plus chers/chères; **those who have answered m. accurately** ceux qui ont répondu le plus exactement VOIR GRAMMAIRE A25–6; B11; B13 **2** *(very)* très, bien; **m. unhappy** bien malheureux; **m. likely** *or* **probably** très probablement; **he has been m. rude** il a été on ne peut plus impoli

3 *(to drink, talk etc)* le plus; **what I want m.** ce que je désire par-dessus tout; **that's what worries me (the) m.** c'est ce qui m'inquiète le plus VOIR GRAMMAIRE A26

mostly ['məʊstlɪ] **ADV 1** *(in the main)* surtout, principalement; **they come m. from Scotland** ils viennent surtout d'Écosse; **a m. young audience** un public composé pour une large part de jeunes, un public composé en majorité de jeunes; **they're m. working-class** ils sont issus de la classe ouvrière pour la plupart **2** *(most often)* le plus souvent, la plupart du temps

MOT [eməʊ'tiː] **N** *Br Admin* **1** *Formerly abbr* **Ministry of Transport 2** *Aut (test)* = contrôle *m* technique **3** *Aut (certificate)* = certificat *m* de contrôle technique; **six months' M.** *(in advertisement)* = certificat *m* de contrôle technique valable pendant six mois

mote [məʊt] **N** *Lit* grain *m* de poussière; *Bible* **the m. in thy brother's eye** la paille dans l'œil du voisin

motel [məʊ'tel] **N** motel *m*

motet [məʊ'tet] **N** *Mus* motet *m*

moth [mɒθ] **N** *(insect)* papillon *m* nocturne *ou* de nuit; **(clothes) m.** mite *f, Fam* **the moths have been at my fur coat** mon manteau de fourrure est tout mangé par les mites

mothball ['mɒθbɔːl] **N** boule *f* de naphtaline; *Fig* **to put a project in mothballs** remettre un projet à plus tard; **to take a project out of mothballs** déterrer un projet; *Fig* **to put a ship in mothballs** retirer un navire du service actif et le couvrir de bâches **VT** *Fig (ship)* retirer du service actif et couvrir de bâches; *(plan)* remettre à plus tard; *(piece of equipment)* entretenir en vue d'une utilisation future

moth-eaten **ADJ 1** mangé des *ou* par les mites, mité **2** *Fam (in poor condition)* miteux, misérable; *(hotel)* miteux

mother ['mʌðər] **N 1** mère *f; Admin, Law* mère de famille; **yes, m.!** oui, maman!; **m. of six** mère de six enfants; *Br Fam* **shall I be m.?** *(pour out tea)* je fais le service?; *Fig Fam* **I've got the m. and father of all headaches** j'ai un mal de tête épouvantable; *Fig Fam* **we had the m. and father of a row!** nous avons eu une de ces empoignades!; **every m.'s son was there!** tout le monde était là, il ne manquait personne; *Rel* **reverend m.** (sœur *f*) supérieure *f; (form of address)* **ma mère 2** *Am Vulg* salaud *m,* fumier *m,* ordure *f* **VT** materner, dorloter
▸▸**m.'s boy** garçon *m* à sa maman; **m. church** église *f* mère; **m. country** (mère) patrie *f, (of colony)* métropole *f;* **M.'s Day** la fête des Mères; **m. hen** mère poule; **m.'s little helper** *(helpful child)* = enfant *m* qui aide sa mère dans les tâches ménagères; *Fig Hum* = alcool *m* ou médicament *m* consommé pour oublier ses soucis; **M. Nature** la Nature; *Geol* **m. rock** roche *f* mère; *Fig Hum* **m.'s ruin** *(gin)* gin *m; Mil* **m. ship** ravitailleur *m; Rel* **M. Superior** Mère *f* supérieure; **m.-to-be** future maman *f;* **m. tongue** langue *f* maternelle; *Chem* **m. of vinegar** mère de vinaigre; **m. wit** bon sens *m*

motherboard ['mʌðəbɔːd] **N** *Comput* carte *f* mère

motherfucker ['mʌðəfʌkər] **N** *Vulg* salaud *m,* fumier *m,* ordure *f;* **the m. won't start** cette saloperie ne veut pas démarrer

motherfucking ['mʌðəfʌkɪŋ] **ADJ ATTRIB** *Vulg* putain de

motherhood ['mʌðəhʊd] **N** maternité *f*

mothering ['mʌðərɪŋ] **N** soins *mpl* maternels
▸▸**m. skills** capacité *f* à s'occuper d'un petit; *Br* **M. Sunday** la fête des Mères

mother-in-law, *pl* **mothers-in-law** **N** belle-mère *f, pl* belles-mères
▸▸*Fam* **m.'s tongue** *(plant)* sansevière *f*

motherland ['mʌðəlænd] **N** patrie *f,* pays *m* natal

motherless ['mʌðəlɪs] **ADJ** sans mère, orphelin (de mère)

motherly ['mʌðəlɪ] **ADJ** maternel, de mère

mother-of-pearl **N** nacre *f,* **m. decoration** décoration *f* en nacre

moth-hole **N** trou *m* de mite

mothproof ['mɒθpruːf] **ADJ** traité à l'antimite **VT** traiter à l'antimite

motif [məʊ'tiːf] **N** *Art, Mus etc* motif *m*

motion ['məʊʃən] **N 1** *Phys etc* mouvement *m; (of vehicle, apparatus)* marche *f,* mouvement; *Phys* **body in m.** corps *m* en mouvement; **car in m.** voiture en marche; **to put** *or* **set a machine in m.** mettre une machine en marche; *Fig* **to put** *or* **set a process in m.** mettre un processus en branle; *Fig* **I'll set things** *or* **the wheels in m.** je vais mettre les choses en route

2 *(of arm etc)* mouvement *m; (sign)* geste *m;* **to go through the motions** agir machinalement; **he's just going through the motions** il fait juste semblant; **you could at least go through the motions** tu devrais au moins le faire pour la forme

3 *(in meeting, debate)* motion *f,* proposition *f;* **to propose a m.** faire une proposition; **to put the m.** mettre la motion *ou* la proposition aux voix; **the m. was carried** la motion fut adoptée

4 *Law (application)* demande *f,* requête *f* **5** *Br (bowel evacuation)* évacuation *f,* **motion(s)** *(faeces)* selles *fpl*

VT to m. sb to do sth faire signe à qn de faire qch; **to m. sb away/in** faire signe à qn de s'éloigner/d'entrer **VI to m. to sb to do sth** faire signe à qn de faire qch
▸▸*Am Cin* **m. picture** film *m;* **the m. picture industry** l'industrie *f* du cinéma; *Tech* **m. study** analyse *f* du mouvement, chronophotographie *f*

motionless ['məʊʃənlɪs] **ADJ** immobile; **to remain m.** ne pas bouger, rester immobile

motivate ['məʊtɪveɪt] **VT** *(decision, employees)* motiver; **to m. sb to do sth** pousser *ou* inciter qn à faire qch; **they were motivated by a desire to help others** ils étaient poussés par un désir d'aider les autres

motivated ['məʊtɪveɪtɪd] **ADJ** motivé; **to be highly m.** être très motivé

motivating ['məʊtɪveɪtɪŋ] **ADJ** motivant

motivation [məʊtɪ'veɪʃən] **N** motivation *f;* **he lacked the m. to succeed** il n'était pas assez motivé pour réussir
▸▸*Mktg* **m. research** recherche *f* de motivation; *Mktg* **m. study** étude *f* de motivation

motivational [məʊtɪ'veɪʃənəl] **ADJ** motivationnel
▸▸*Mktg* **m. research** recherche *f* de motivation; *Mktg* **m. study** étude *f* de motivation

motivator ['məʊtɪveɪtər] **N he's a good m.** il sait motiver les gens

motive ['məʊtɪv] **N 1** *(reason)* motif *m,* raison *f, (for a crime)* mobile *m;* **interest is a powerful m.** l'intérêt est un puissant ressort; **I wonder what his m. is** je me demande pourquoi *ou* pour quelle raison il fait cela; **I**

don't understand what her m. is for refusing to … je ne comprends pas pourquoi *ou* pour quelle raison elle refuse de … **2** *Art (of painting etc)* motif *m*

ADJ moteur, -trice

▶▶ **m. power** force *f* motrice

motley ['mɒtlɪ] **ADJ 1** *(diverse)* varié, hétéroclite; **m. crew** *or* **crowd** bande *f ou* mélange *m* hétéroclite **2** *(of different colours)* bariolé, bigarré

N 1 *(mixture)* mélange *m* hétéroclite **2** *Hist (jester's costume)* costume *m* de bouffon de cour

motocross ['məʊtəʊkrɒs] **N** *Sport* motocross *m*

motor ['məʊtər] **N 1** *(engine)* moteur *m* **2** *Br Fam (car)* bagnole *f*

ADJ *Anat (muscle, nerve)* moteur, -trice

VI *Old-fashioned (travel by car)* voyager en auto *ou* en voiture; **we motored across France** nous avons traversé la France en voiture **2** *Br Fam* **to be motoring** *(going fast)* foncer; *Fig* **now we're motoring!** cette fois on y vient!

▶▶ **m. caravan** camping-car *m, pl* camping-cars; *Rail* **m. carriage** *(voiture f)* motrice *f*, **m. engineer** ingénieur *m* en automobile, motoriste *mf*; **m. fuel** carburant *m*; **m. industry** industrie *f* automobile; **m. insurance** assurance *f* automobile; **m. launch** vedette *f*; *Am* **m. lodge** motel *m*; **m. manufacturer** constructeur *m* automobile; **m. mechanic** mécanicien, -ienne; *Med* **m. neurone disease** maladie *f* de Charcot; *Med* **m. paralysis** paralysie *f* des centres moteurs; **m. race** course *f* automobile; **m. racing** courses *fpl* automobiles; **m. rally** rallye *m* automobile; **m. scooter** scooter *m*; **m. show** salon *m* de l'auto(mobile); *Tech* **m. torque** couple *m* moteur; **the m. trade** l'automobile *f*; **m. vehicle** véhicule *m* automobile; *Naut* **m. vessel** bateau *m* à moteur

motorail ['məʊtəreɪl] **N** *Rail* train(s) *m(pl)* auto-couchettes; **m. service** train(s) auto-couchettes

motor-assisted [-ə'sɪstɪd] **ADJ**

▶▶ **m. bicycle** cyclomoteur *m*

motorbike ['məʊtəbaɪk] **N** moto *f*

motorboat ['məʊtəbəʊt] **N** canot *m* à moteur; *(fast)* vedette *f*

motorcade ['məʊtəkeɪd] **N** cortège *m* de voitures

motorcar ['məʊtəkɑːr] **N** *Br* automobile *f*, voiture *f*

motorcycle ['məʊtəsaɪk(ə)l] **N** motocyclette *f*, moto *f*, **m. wheel** roue *f* de moto

▶▶ **m. accident** accident *m* de moto; **m. combination** moto et sidecar *m*; **m. courier** coursier, -ière, porteur, -euse; **m. gang** bande *f* de motards; **m. policeman** agent *m* motocycliste, motard *m*; **m. rider** motocycliste *mf*, motard

motorcycling ['məʊtəsaɪklɪŋ] **N** motocyclisme *m*

motorcyclist ['məʊtəsaɪklɪst] **N** motocycliste *mf*

motor-driven **ADJ** à moteur; *(device)* actionné *ou* commandé par un moteur

motor-home **N** *Am* auto-caravane *f*, *pl* auto-caravanes, camping-car *m*, *pl* camping-cars

motoring ['məʊtərɪŋ] **N** conduite *f* (automobile); **school of m.** auto-école *f*, *pl* auto-écoles

▶▶ **m. correspondent** chroniqueur, -euse automobile; *Old-fashioned* **m. holiday** virée *f* en voiture; **m. offence** infraction *f* au code de la route; **m. organization** association *f* d'automobilistes

motorist ['məʊtərɪst] **N** automobiliste *mf*

motorization [məʊtəraɪ'zeɪʃən] **N** motorisation *f*

motorize ['məʊtəraɪz] **VT** motoriser; **motorized** motorisé; **motorized bicycle** vélomoteur *m*

motorman, *pl* **motormen** ['məʊtəmæn, -men] **N** *Am (on tram)* wattman *m*; *(on subway)* conducteur *m*

motormouth ['məʊtə'maʊθ] **N** *Fam* **he's a bit of a m.** c'est un véritable moulin à paroles

motorway ['məʊtəweɪ] **N** *Br* autoroute *f*

▶▶ **m. accident** accident *m* sur autoroute; **m. driving** conduite *f* sur autoroute; **m. exit** sortie *f* d'autoroute; **m. madness** la folie de l'autoroute; **m. network** réseau *m* autoroutier; **m. police** police *f* de l'autoroute; **m. restaurant** restauroute *m*, restoroute *m*; **m. services** services *mpl* autoroutiers

Motown® ['məʊtaʊn] **N 1** *Am Fam* = surnom de la ville de Détroit **2** *Mus* style *m* Motown

mottled ['mɒt(ə)ld] **ADJ** *(fabric)* tacheté, moucheté; *(skin)* marbré; *(wood)* madré

motto, *pl* **mottoes** ['mɒtəʊ, -əʊz] **N 1** devise *f*, **that's my m.** voilà ma devise **2** *Her* devise *f* **3** *Typ* épigraphe *f* **4** *Mus* motif *m* **5** *Br (in Christmas cracker) (riddle)* devinette *f*, *(funny saying)* phrase *f* amusante

mould¹, *Am* **mold** [məʊld] **N** *(fungus)* moisi *m*, moisissure *f*

mould², *Am* **mold** **N 1** *Art, Cer etc* moule *m*; *Typ (of character)* matrice *f*, *Culin* **(jelly) m.** moule *m* à gelée; *Lit* **to be cast in a heroic m.** être de la trempe des héros; **he is cast in his father's m.** il est fait dans le même moule que son père; **people cast in the same m.** des gens sortis du même moule; **a star in the John Wayne m.** une star du style John Wayne; *Fig* **to break the m.** rompre avec la tradition **2** *(template), Constr etc* calibre *m*, profil *m*; *Naut, Aviat* gabarit *m* **3** *Culin* **rice m.** gâteau *m* de riz **4** *Archit* moulure *f*

VT 1 *(make from a mould)* mouler; **the bucket is moulded in plastic** le seau est moulé dans du plastique **2** *(shape)* mouler; *(person's character)* façonner, former; **to m. clay/etc into sth** façonner l'argile/etc pour en faire qch; *Fig* **she moulded them into a team** elle a fait d'eux une équipe; *Fig* **public opinion has been moulded by the media** l'opinion publique a été façonnée par les médias **3** *(adhere closely to)* **the dress moulded her figure** la robe moulait ses formes

mould³, *Am* **mold** **N** *(earth)* terre *f* meuble; **vegetable m.** terreau *m*, humus *m*

moulded, *Am* **molded** ['məʊldɪd] **ADJ** *(plastic)* moulé

moulder, *Am* **molder** ['məʊldər] **VI** *(of wood)* tomber en poussière, s'effriter; *(of food)* moisir; *(of building etc)* se désagréger; *Fig (of person)* moisir

▶ **moulder away,** *Am* **molder away** **VI** = **moulder**

moulding, *Am* **molding** ['məʊldɪŋ] **N 1** *Metal etc* moulage *m* **2** *Fig (of character, public opinion)* formation *f*, façonnement *m* **3** *Archit (ornament)* moulure *f*, *(edging strip)* baguette *f*, **drip** *or* **weather m.** *(on window, door)* jet *m* d'eau; *(on wall)* larmier *m*; **plain m.** listeau *m*, listel *m*; **grooved m.** moulure à gorge

mouldy, *Am* **moldy** ['məʊldɪ] **ADJ** moisi; **to smell m.** sentir le moisi

moult, *Am* **molt** [məʊlt] **N** mue *f*

VI *(of cat, dog)* perdre ses poils; *(of bird, reptile)* muer; *Hum* **I must be moulting!** je perds mes poils!

moulting, *Am* **molting** ['məʊltɪŋ] **ADJ** en mue

N mue *f*

mound [maʊnd] **N** *(artificial)* tertre *m*, monticule *m*, butte *f*, *Constr etc* remblai *m*; *(of*

stones etc) monceau *m*, tas *m*; *(natural)* monticule

mount¹ [maʊnt] **N 1** *(mountain)* mont *m* **2** *(in palmistry)* mont *m*

▶▶ **M. Sinai** le mont Sinaï

mount² **N 1** *(support), Tech* montage *m*, support *m*; *Mil etc* affût *m*, trépied *m*; *(of lens, prism)* monture *f*

2 *Art etc (of painting etc)* carton *m* de montage

3 *(horse)* cheval *m*, monture *f*, *Horseracing (ride)* monte *f*

VT 1 *(climb onto) (bicycle, horse)* monter sur, enfourcher; **to m. the scaffold** monter sur l'échafaud; **to m. the throne** monter sur le trône; **to m. the pavement** *(of car etc)* monter sur le trottoir

2 *(mate with)* couvrir, monter

3 *(climb) (stairs, hill)* monter, gravir; *(ladder)* monter à

4 *(set on)* **to m. sb (on a horse)** hisser qn sur un cheval; **to m. a squadron of cavalry** monter un escadron de cavalerie; **they were mounted on grey horses** ils chevauchaient des chevaux gris

5 *Tech* installer; *(precious stone)* monter, sertir; *Art, Phot, Cin (painting, photograph, film reel)* monter; *Mil etc (cannon)* mettre sur (son) affût; *(machine, engine etc)* monter, installer

6 *(prepare)* **to m. a play/an exhibition** monter une pièce/une exposition; *Mil* **to m. an offensive** lancer une offensive; *Mil* **to m. guard** monter la garde

VI 1 *Horseriding* se mettre en selle

2 *(rise, climb)* monter; **the blood mounted to his head** le sang lui est monté à la tête; **the cost was mounting** le coût augmentait

▶ **mount up** **VI** monter, augmenter; **the bill was mounting up** la facture augmentait; **her savings soon mounted up** ses économies augmentèrent rapidement; **it all mounts up** ça finit par chiffrer

mountain ['maʊntɪn] **N** montagne *f*, **range of mountains** chaîne *f* de montagnes; **to spend one's holidays in the mountains** passer ses vacances à la montagne; *Fig* **a m. of work** un travail monstre; *Fig* **a m. of evidence** des quantités de preuves; *Fig* **mountains of papers to mark** des tas de copies à corriger; **butter/beef m.** *(surplus)* montagne de beurre/bœuf; *Fig* **to make a m. out of a molehill** faire une montagne d'un rien; **m. scenery/stream** paysage *m*/ruisseau *m* de montagne

▶▶ **m. ash** *(rowan)* sorbier *m* des oiseleurs *ou* des oiseaux; *(eucalyptus)* eucalyptus *m*; **m. bike** VTT *m*, vélo *m* tout-terrain; **m. biking** VTT, vélo tout-terrain; **m. chain** chaîne de montagnes; **m. climbing** alpinisme *m*; **m. lion** puma *m*, cougouar *m*; **m. pass** col *m*, défilé *m*; **m. pine** pin *m* de montagne; **m. range** chaîne de montagnes; **m. rescue** secours *m* en montagne; **m. rescue service** service *m* de secours en montagne; **m. resort** station *f* de montagne, station montagnarde; **m. sickness** mal *m* des montagnes; **m. side** flanc *m ou* versant *m* de montagne; *Am* **M. Standard Time** heure *f* normale des montagnes Rocheuses; **m. top** sommet *m* de montagne; **m. tribe** tribu *f* montagnarde; **m. troops** chasseurs *mpl* alpins

mountaineer [maʊntɪ'nɪər] **N** alpiniste *mf*

VI faire de l'alpinisme

mountaineering [maʊntɪ'nɪərɪŋ] **N** alpinisme *m*

mountainous ['maʊntɪnəs] **ADJ** *(country etc)* montagneux; *Fig* **m. seas** vagues gigantesques

mountebank ['maʊntɪbæŋk] **N** *Lit* charlatan *m*

mounted ['maʊntɪd] **ADJ**

▸▸ **the m. police** la police montée; **m. policeman** policier *m* à cheval

Mountie ['maʊntɪ] N *Fam* = membre *m* de la Gendarmerie Royale du Canada

mounting ['maʊntɪŋ] N *(support)*, *Tech* support *m*; *Tech (of machine, engine)* bâti *m*, socle *m*; *(of rifle etc)* monture *f*, garniture *f*; *(of precious stone)* monture, sertissage *m*; *Mil (of machine gun)* affût *m*, trépied *m*; *Tech* **engine mountings** pièces *fpl* d'assemblage de moteur

ADJ m. **costs/death toll** coût/nombre des morts en augmentation; **there is m. evidence against her** il y a de plus en plus de preuves contre elle

▸▸ **m. bracket** support de montage; **m. point** *(for seatbelt)* point *m* d'ancrage

mounting-block N *Horseriding* montoir *m*

mourn [mɔːn] VT *(somebody, something, sb's death)* pleurer; **there's no point mourning what might have been** cela ne sert à rien de se lamenter sur ce qui aurait pu se passer
 VI être en deuil

▸ **mourn for** VT INSEP **to m. for sb** pleurer (la mort de) qn; **to m. for sth** pleurer qch, déplorer qch

▸ **mourn over** VT INSEP = **mourn for**

mourner ['mɔːnər] N **1** *(at funeral)* personne *f* qui suit le cortège funèbre; **the mourners** le convoi, le cortège funèbre **2** *(person grieving)* personne *f* endeuillée, personne qui porte le deuil

mournful ['mɔːnfʊl] ADJ triste, mélancolique

mournfully ['mɔːnfʊlɪ] ADV tristement

mourning ['mɔːnɪŋ] N deuil *m*; *(clothing)* (vêtements *mpl ou* habits *mpl* de) deuil; **to be in m.** être en deuil; **to wear m.** porter le deuil; **to go into m.** se mettre en deuil, prendre le deuil; **house of m.** maison *f* endeuillée

mouse [maʊs] ¹, *pl* **mice** [maɪs] N **1** *(animal)* souris *f*; **young m.** souriceau *m*; **m. grey, m. colour(ed)** gris *m* souris **2** *Fam (timid person)* timide *mf*; **are you a man or a m.?** t'es un homme ou quoi? **3** *Comput* souris *f*
 ▸▸ *Comput* **m. ball** boule *f* de la souris; *Comput* **m. button** bouton *m* de souris; *Comput* **m. click** clic *m* de souris; *Comput* **m. driver** programme *m* de commande de la souris; **m. hole** trou *m* de souris; *Comput* **m. keys** touches *fpl* souris; *Comput* **m. mat, m. pad** tapis *m* de souris; *Comput* **m. port** port *m* souris

mouse ² [maʊz] VI *(of cat etc)* chasser les souris

mouser ['maʊzər] N *(cat etc)* souricier *m*; **she's a good m.** elle attrape bien les souris

mousetrap ['maʊstræp] N souricière *f*, tapette *f*; *Fam (cheese)* fromage *m* ordinaire, *Can* fromage à souris
 ▸▸ *Fam* **m. cheese** fromage ordinaire, *Can* fromage à souris

moussaka [mʊˈsɑːkə] N moussaka *f*

mousse [muːs] N *(for hair)*, *Culin* mousse *f*; **chocolate m.** mousse au chocolat

moustache [məˈstɑːʃ], *Am* **mustache** ['mʌstæʃ] N moustache(s) *f(pl)*; **short m., clipped m.** moustache courte *ou* en brosse

mousy ['maʊsɪ] ADJ **1** *(colour)* gris sale; *Fam (hair)* châtain terne *inv* **2** *(timid)* timide **3** *(smell etc)* de souris

mouth ¹ [maʊθ] N *(pl* **mouths** [maʊðz]*)* **1** *(of person, horse)* bouche *f*; *(of other animal)* gueule *f*; **to have one's m. full** avoir la bouche pleine; **don't speak with your m. full** ne parle pas (avec) la bouche pleine; **to have seven mouths to feed** avoir sept bouches à nourrir; *Fig* **big m.** *(person)* gueulard *m*, grande gueule *f*; **to be** *or* **have a big m.** être *ou* avoir une grande gueule; **you had to**

open your big m., didn't you! il a fallu que tu ouvres ta grande gueule!; **me and my big m.!** pourquoi faut-il toujours que je l'ouvre!; *Fam* **he's all m.** parler, c'est tout ce qu'il sait faire; *Fam* **keep your m. shut about this** garde ça pour toi; **to put words into sb's m.** *(misquote)* faire dire à qn ce qu'il ne dit pas; **I don't want to put words into your m. but ...** dites-moi si je me trompe mais ...; *Fig Fam* **to be all mouth and (no) trousers** être une grande gueule **2** *(opening etc)* *(of tunnel, cave)* ouverture *f*, entrée *f*; *(of river)* embouchure *f*
 ▸▸ **m. organ** harmonica *m*; **m. ulcer** aphte *m*

mouth ² [maʊð] VT **1** *(say without sincerity)* dire de façon mécanique, dire mécaniquement **2** *(say silently) (words)* former; **she mouthed something to me** elle a essayé de me dire quelque chose en remuant les lèvres silencieusement
 VI *esp Am (grimace)* grimacer, faire des grimaces

▸ **mouth off** VI *Fam (brag)* se vanter, crâner; *(talk impudently)* la ramener; *(talk indiscreetly)* parler à tort et à travers

mouthful ['maʊθfʊl] N **1** bouchée *f*, *(of soup, wine etc)* gorgée *f*; **to swallow sth in** *or* **at one m., to make one m. of sth** ne faire qu'une bouchée de qch; *(soup, wine)* avaler qch d'une seule gorgée; **I swallowed** *or* **got a m. (of water)** *(when swimming etc)* j'ai bu la *ou* une tasse; *esp Am Fam* **you said a m.** *(were right)* tu as bien parlé; *Br Fam* **to give sb a m.** *(insult)* traiter qn de tous les noms **2** *Fam (long word, phrase)* mot *m*/phrase *f* difficile à prononcer; *(person's name)* nom *m* à coucher dehors; **cerebral thrombosis is quite a m.** thrombose cérébrale est vraiment difficile à prononcer

mouthpiece ['maʊθpiːs] N **1** *(of loudhailer)* embout *m*; *(of pipe)* tuyau *m*, bout *m*; *Mus (of clarinet etc)* bec *m*; *Mus (of horn etc)* embouchure *f*; *Tel* microphone *m* **2** *(person, magazine) (of party etc)* porte-parole *m inv*, *Am Sl (lawyer)* avocat *m* (au criminel)

mouth-to-mouth ADJ
 ▸▸ **m. resuscitation** bouche-à-bouche *m inv*; **to give sb m. resuscitation** faire du bouche-à-bouche à qn

mouthwash ['maʊθwɒʃ] N *Pharm* bain *m* de bouche; *(for teeth)* eau *f* dentifrice

mouthwatering ['maʊθwɔːtərɪŋ] ADJ alléchant, qui fait venir l'eau à la bouche

mouthy ['maʊðɪ] ADJ *Fam* gueulard, grande gueule

movable ['muːvəb(ə)l] ADJ **1** mobile **2** *Law* mobilier, meuble
 NPL *Law* **movables** biens *mpl* meubles
 ▸▸ *Rel* **m. feast** fête *f* mobile; *Law* **m. property** biens *mpl* meubles

MOVE [muːv]

N	mouvement 1	▪ démarche 2
▪ déménagement 3	▪ coup 4	
VT déplacer 1	▪ déménager 1	
▪ bouger 2	▪ pousser 3	▪ émouvoir 4
▪ proposer 5		
VI se déplacer 1	▪ bouger 1, 2	
▪ avancer 3	▪ agir 4	▪ déménager 5
▪ jouer 7		

N 1 *(motion)* mouvement *m*; **to make a m. towards sth** faire un mouvement vers qch; **there was a general m. towards** *or* **for the door** tout le monde s'est dirigé vers la porte; *Fam* **to make a m.** *(leave)* y aller, bouger; *Fam* **it's late, I ought to be making a m.** il se fait tard, il faut que j'y aille *ou* que je parte; **don't make a m.!** *(or I'll shoot, they'll see us etc)* ne bouge pas!; **the police were watching her every m.** la police surveillait ses

moindres gestes; **on the m.** en marche; **to be always on the m.** ne jamais rester en place; *Fam* **to get a m. on** se grouiller, se manier *ou* magner (le train)
 2 *Fig (action, step)* démarche *f*, action *f*, manœuvre *f*; **smart m.** manœuvre habile; **at one time there was a m. to ...** à un moment, on avait envisagé de ...; **what's the next m.?** qu'est-ce qu'il faut faire maintenant?; *Fam* **to make a m. on sb** faire des avances à qn; **to make the first m.** faire le premier pas; **don't make a m. without contacting me** *(don't do anything)* ne fais rien sans me contacter; **when would the enemy make his m.?** quand l'ennemi allait-il se décider à agir?; **the Government has made moves towards resolving ...** le gouvernement a pris des mesures pour résoudre ...
 3 *(from home, office etc)* déménagement *m*; **after ten years in the job she needed a m.** après dix ans passés à faire le même travail, elle avait besoin de changement
 4 *Chess etc* coup *m*; **mate in four moves** (échec et) mat en quatre coups; **to have first m.** commencer la partie; **to make a m.** jouer; **(it's) your m.** à vous de jouer, c'est votre tour; **to learn the moves** apprendre comment les pièces se déplacent
 5 *Comput (of text block etc)* déplacement *m*
 VT 1 *(shift) (furniture, troops etc)* déplacer, changer de place; *(employee)* muter (**to** à); *(drive) (wheels etc)* entraîner; *Chess etc (piece)* jouer; *Comput (text block etc)* déplacer; *Com* vendre; **to m. sth from its place** changer qch de place; **could you m. your feet/bag (out of the way) please?** est-ce que tu peux pousser tes pieds/ton sac s'il te plaît?; **to m. one's position** changer de place; **to m. one's chair near the fire** approcher son fauteuil du feu; **he was moved to London** on l'a muté à Londres; **to m. house/premises** déménager; **to m. heaven and earth** remuer ciel et terre; **come on, m. yourself! we're going to be late!** allez, remue-toi! on va être en retard!
 2 *(stir) (one's head etc)* remuer, bouger; *(of wind etc) (branches etc)* agiter, remuer; *(set in motion)* mouvoir, animer, mettre en mouvement; *Med* **to m. one's bowels** aller à la selle
 3 *Fig (sway)* ébranler la résolution de; **you won't m. me** tu ne me feras pas changer d'avis; **I won't be moved** je ne changerai pas d'avis; **nothing will m. him** il est inflexible; **to m. sb to do sth** pousser *ou* inciter qn à faire qch
 4 *(affect emotionally) (somebody)* émouvoir, toucher; **easily moved** émotif; **to m. sb to anger** provoquer la colère de qn; **to m. sb to tears** émouvoir qn (jusqu')aux larmes; **to m. sb to pity** exciter la pitié de qn
 5 *(in debate etc) (resolution)* proposer; **to m. that ...** proposer que ... + *sub*
 6 *Com (sell)* écouler, vendre; **we must m. these goods quickly** nous devons vendre ces marchandises rapidement
 VI 1 *(stir)* bouger; *(change one's position)* se déplacer; **they won't m. on the question of compensation** ils ne fléchiront pas sur la question des compensations; **to m. to another seat** changer de place; **to m. in high society** fréquenter la haute société; **don't m.!** ne bougez pas!; **I'm stuck, I can't m.** je suis coincé, je ne peux pas bouger; **I can't get it to m.** je n'arrive pas à le/la faire bouger; **could you m. so that we can get in?** pourriez-vous pousser que nous puissions entrer?; **the way the dancers m.** la façon de se mouvoir *ou* de bouger des danseurs; **she moves like a model** elle marche comme un mannequin; **I saw the curtains m.** j'ai vu les rideaux bouger; **something moved in the bushes** quelque chose a bougé dans les buissons; *Fam* **come**

on, m.! *(hurry)* allez, magne-toi le train *ou* remue-toi!; **wait till the car stops moving** attends que la voiture soit arrêtée

2 *(of machine parts etc)* bouger; **this part is meant to m.** cette partie est censée bouger; **what makes it m.?** qu'est-ce qui le fait tourner/avancer/descendre/*etc*?; **to m. upwards** monter; **to m. downwards** descendre; **to m. freely** *(of part)* jouer librement; *(of dissident, prisoner)* se déplacer librement

3 *(progress, advance)* avancer; **the earth moves round the sun** la terre tourne autour du soleil; **it moves in an elliptical orbit** il/elle décrit une ellipse; **to m. towards a place** se diriger *ou* s'avancer vers un endroit; **the traffic was only just moving** les voitures avançaient à peine; **things are moving slowly** les choses avancent lentement; **that's really moving!** *(that's fast)* ça fonce!; *(referring to work)* ça avance!, ça progresse!; **it's time we were moving, we must be moving** il est temps de partir

4 *(act)* agir; **it is for him to m. first in the matter** c'est à lui d'agir le premier dans cette affaire

5 *(to new home, office etc)* déménager; **we have moved to new premises** nous avons déménagé dans de nouveaux locaux; **to m. to the country** aller s'installer à la campagne

6 *Com (sell)* se vendre, s'écouler; **this product's not moving** *(not selling)* ce produit ne se vend pas

7 *Chess etc* jouer

▶ **move about, move around** VI bouger, remuer; *(travel and move house)* bouger; **I heard someone moving about** j'ai entendu quelqu'un se déplacer; **he finds it difficult to m. about** il a du mal à se déplacer; **he moves around a lot** *(in job etc)* il est toujours en déplacement

VT SEP *(furniture etc)* déplacer, changer de place; **they keep moving her around from one department to another** ils n'arrêtent pas de la faire passer d'un service à l'autre

▶ **move along** VT SEP *(of police officer)* *(onlookers, beggars etc)* faire circuler

VI **1** *(to make room)* se déplacer, se pousser; **m. along and let the old lady sit down** poussez-vous un peu pour laisser la vieille dame s'asseoir

2 *(leave)* partir, s'en aller; **I ought to be moving along** il faut que je m'en aille; **the policeman told us to m. along** le policier nous a dit de circuler; **m. along (please)!** circulez, s'il vous plaît!

3 *(continue)* moving along to my next question pour passer à ma question suivante

▶ **move away** VT SEP *(something)* écarter, éloigner (**from** de)

VI **1** *(go away)* s'éloigner, s'écarter, s'en aller

2 *(go to new home etc)* déménager; **they've moved away from here** ils ont déménagé

▶ **move back** VT SEP **1** *(to more distant position)* *(people)* (faire) reculer; *(things)* mettre en retrait; **could you m. your car back?** pourriez-vous reculer?

2 *(to former position)* remettre en place

VI **1** *(retreat)* (se) reculer

2 *(to former position)* retourner, revenir

3 *(to former home etc)* retourner; **they have moved back to London** *(come)* ils sont revenus habiter à Londres; *(gone)* ils sont repartis habiter à Londres; **to m. back to one's old job** reprendre son ancien travail

▶ **move down** VT SEP **1** *(change position of)* *(something)* descendre; *Typ etc* **m. this section down** mettez cette section plus bas

2 *(demote)* rétrograder; **to m. sb down three places** rétrograder qn de trois places; *Sch* **to be moved down (a class)** descendre de classe

VI *(be demoted)* descendre; **the team**

moved down to the fourth division l'équipe est descendue en quatrième division

▶ **move forward** VT SEP *(object, date etc)* avancer; *(troops)* faire avancer

VI (s')avancer

▶ **move in** VT SEP **1** *(send)* *(troops)* envoyer; **troops were moved in by helicopter** les troupes ont été transportées par hélicoptère

2 *(install)* *(furniture)* installer

VI **1** *(take up residence)* emménager; **he has moved in with his girlfriend** il est allé s'installer chez sa petite amie

2 *(enter situation)* entrer en scène, faire son apparition; **the market changed when the multinationals moved in** le marché a changé quand les multinationales ont fait leur apparition

3 *(advance)* s'avancer; **troops moved in to quell the riots** les troupes sont intervenues pour réprimer les émeutes

▶ **move into** VT INSEP *(diversify into)* se reconvertir dans

▶ **move off** VI **1** *(go away)* s'éloigner, s'en aller, partir

2 *(start journey)* *(of train, army etc)* se mettre en marche; *(of car etc)* démarrer

▶ **move on** VT SEP *(crowd etc)* faire circuler

VI **1** *(go further on journey etc)* avancer, continuer son chemin; **can we m. on to the next item on the agenda?** pouvons-nous passer à la question suivante de l'ordre du jour?; **time's moving on** il se fait tard; **it's time we were moving on** il est temps que nous partions

2 *(make progress)* *(of science)* faire des progrès, évoluer; **women have moved on** les femmes ont évolué *ou* changé

▶ **move out** VT SEP *(remove)* *(something)* sortir; *(somebody)* faire sortir; **the troops will be moved out** les troupes se retireront; **people were moved out (of their homes) to make way for the new road** les gens ont dû quitter leur maison pour permettre la construction de la nouvelle route

VI **1** *(leave home etc)* déménager

2 *Mil (withdraw)* se retirer

▶ **move over** VI se ranger, se pousser; **m. over!** pousse-toi!; **they moved over to a market economy** ils sont passés à une économie de marché

▶ **move up** VT SEP **1** *(change position of)* *(object)* monter; *Typ etc* **m. this section up** mettez cette section plus haut; **the regiment was moved up to the front** on a envoyé le régiment au front

2 *(promote)* promouvoir; **they've moved her up to be assistant manager** on l'a promue directrice-adjointe; *Sch* **to be moved up (a class)** passer dans la classe supérieure

VI **1** *(advance)* s'avancer, avancer

2 *(be promoted)* être promu; *Sch* passer dans la classe supérieure; *St Exch (of shares)* se relever; **shares moved up three points today** les actions ont gagné trois points aujourd'hui; **he has moved up in my estimation** il est monté dans mon estime

3 *(to make room)* se pousser; **m. up so I can sit down** pousse-toi (un peu) que je m'assoie

moveable ['mu:vəb(ə)l] ADJ = movable

movement ['mu:vmənt] N **1** *(change of place)* mouvement *m*; *(on stock exchange)* activité *f*, *(of vehicles, goods, capital)* mouvement *m*, circulation *f*, *Mil etc* mouvement, manœuvre *f*, *(of prices etc)* mouvement; **there was a general m. towards the door** tout le monde s'est dirigé vers la porte; **to watch sb's movements** *(of police etc)* surveiller les faits et gestes *ou* les allées et venues de qn; *Fig* **there had been little m. in the negotiations** les négociations n'avaient pas beaucoup avancé; **free m. of labour** libre

circulation de la main-d'œuvre **2** *(motion)* *(of one's arm etc)* mouvement *m*, geste *m* **3** *(group, tendency)* *(political, literary, artistic etc)* mouvement *m* **4** *(mechanism of clock)* mouvement *m* **5** *Mus (of symphony etc)* mouvement *m* **6** *Physiol* **to have a (bowel) m.** aller à la selle

mover ['mu:vər] N **1** *(in debate)* auteur *m* d'une motion, motionnaire *mf* **2** *Am (removal firm, person)* déménageur *m* **3** **he's a beautiful** *or* **lovely m.** *(footballer etc)* il a une démarche superbe; *(dancer)* il est superbe quand il danse **4** *Fam* **movers and shakers** les grands pontes *mpl*

movie ['mu:vɪ] N *esp Am* film *m*; **the movies** *(cinema)* le cinéma; **to go to the movies** aller au cinéma; **she's in the movies** elle travaille dans le cinéma

▶▶ **m. actor** acteur *m* de cinéma; **m. actress** actrice *f* de cinéma; **m. archives** archives *fpl* cinématographiques; **m. buff** cinéphile *mf*, **m. camera** caméra *f*, **m. channel** chaîne *f* de cinéma; **m. clip** extrait *m* de film; **m. critic** critique *mf* de cinéma; **m. director** metteur *m* en scène; *Am* **m. house** (salle *f* de) cinéma *m*; **the m. industry** l'industrie *f* cinématographique *ou* du cinéma; **m. library** cinémathèque *f*, **m. premiere** première *f*, **m. producer** producteur, -trice de cinéma; **m. review** critique *f* cinématographique; **m. reviewer** critique *mf* de cinéma; **m. star** vedette *f* de cinéma; *Am* **m. theater** cinéma *m*

moviegoer ['mu:vɪɡəʊər] N *esp Am* cinéphile *mf*, amateur *m* de cinéma

movie-maker N *esp Am* cinéaste *mf*

moving ['mu:vɪŋ] ADJ **1** *(in motion)* en mouvement, mouvant; *(train, vehicle)* en marche; *(part etc)* mobile **2** *(force etc)* moteur, -trice; **the m. spirit** *(in a venture)* l'âme *f* **3** *(touching)* *(scene, story etc)* émouvant, touchant

N mouvement *m*; *(being moved)* déplacement *m*; *(from house etc)* déménagement *m*

▶▶ *Phys* **m. body** corps *m* en mouvement; **m. in** *(into house, premises)* emménagement *m*; **m. out** *(from house etc)* déménagement; **m. pavement** trottoir *m* roulant; *Old-fashioned* **m. picture** film *m*; *Am* **m. sidewalk** trottoir roulant; **m. staircase** escalier *m* roulant, escalator *m*; *Mil* **m. target** cible *f* mobile; *Am* **m. van** camion *m* de déménagement

movingly ['mu:vɪŋlɪ] ADV d'une manière émouvante *ou* touchante

mow [məʊ] VT & VI *(pt* **mowed** [məʊd]*, pp* **mown** [məʊn]*)* **1** *(lawn)* tondre **2** *Agr (corn, field)* faucher

▶ **mow down** VT SEP *(slaughter)* faucher

mower ['məʊər] N **1** *(machine)*, *Agr* faucheuse *f*, **(lawn)** *m*. tondeuse *f* (à gazon) **2** *Agr (person)* faucheur, -euse

mowing ['məʊɪŋ] N **1** *(of lawn)* tonte *f* **2** *Agr (of hay etc)* fauchage *m*

mown PP *see* mow

Mozambican [məʊzæm'bi:kən] N Mozambicain, -aine

ADJ mozambicain

Mozambique [məʊzæm'bi:k] N Mozambique *m*

MP [em'pi:] N **1** *Br Parl (abbr* **Member of Parliament***)* député *m* **2** *Mil (abbr* **Military Police***)* police *f* militaire; *(abbr* **Military Policeman***)* membre *m* de la police militaire

MP3 [empi:'θri:] N *Comput (abbr* **MPEG1 Audio Layer***)* (format *m*) MPEG *m*; **MP3 file** fichier *m* MP3; **MP3 player** lecteur *m* de MP3

MPC [empi:'si:] N *Br Fin (abbr* **monetary policy committee***)* = comité *m* formé de quatre membres de la Banque d'Angleterre et de quatre économistes nommés par le gouvernement, dont l'un des rôles est de fixer les taux d'intérêt

MPEG ['empeg] N *Comput (abbr* **Moving Pictures Expert Group)** (format *m*) MPEG *m*

mpg [empi:'dʒi:] N *(abbr* **miles per gallon)** mil(l)es au gallon; **what sort of m. do you get?** combien faites-vous au cent?

mph [empi:'eɪtʃ] N *(abbr* **miles per hour)** mil(l)es à l'heure, ≃ kilomètres à l'heure

MPhil [em'fɪl] N *(abbr* **Master of Philosophy)** ≃ DEA *m*

MPV [empi:'vi:] N *Aut (abbr* **multi-purpose vehicle)** véhicule *m* multifonction, véhicule à usages multiples

Mr ['mɪstər] N *(form of address, not used without name)* **Mr Thomas** Monsieur Thomas; *(on envelope)* Monsieur *ou* M. Thomas; **Mr President** Monsieur le Président
▸▸ *Fam* **Mr Big** le cerveau de l'affaire; *Fam* **Mr Right** l'homme *m* idéal

MRAM [em'ræm] N *Comput (abbr* **magnetic random access memory)** MRAM *f*

MRC [ema:'si:] N *Br (abbr* **Medical Research Council)** Comité *m* pour la recherche médicale

MRI [ema:'raɪ] N *Med (abbr* **magnetic resonance imaging)** IRM *f*

mrp [ema:'pi:] N *Com (abbr* **manufacturer's recommended price)** prix *m* conseillé par le fabricant

Mrs ['mɪsɪz] N *(form of address, not used without name)* **M. Long** Madame Long; *(on envelope)* Madame *ou* Mme Long

MS, [1] **ms,** *pl* **MSS, mss** *(abbr* **manuscript)** manuscrit *m*

MS [2] [em'es] N *(abbr* **multiple sclerosis)** sclérose *f* en plaques

Ms [mɪz] N *(form of address, not used without name)* **Ms Martin** *(unmarried)* Mademoiselle Martin; *(married)* Madame Martin; *(on envelope)* Madame *ou* Mme Martin

MSc [emes'si:] N *(abbr* **Master of Science)** *(degree)* maîtrise *f* de *ou* ès sciences; *(person)* titulaire *mf* d'une maîtrise

MS-DOS [emes'dɒs] N *Comput (abbr* **Microsoft Disk Operating System)** MS-DOS *m*

MSG [emes'dʒi:] N *(abbr* **monosodium glutamate)** glutamate *m* de sodium

MSP [emes'pi:] N *(abbr* **Member of the Scottish Parliament)** député *m* du parlement écossais

MST [emes'ti:] N *abbr* **Mountain Standard Time**

Mt *(abbr* **Mount)** Mt

MTBF [emti:bi:'ef] N *Comput (abbr* **mean time between failures)** moyenne *f* de temps entre deux pannes

MUCH [mʌtʃ]

ADJ	beaucoup de ▪ combien (de) ▪ tant de
ADV	beaucoup
PRON	beaucoup ▪ autant de

ADJ *(usu only with neg and interr)* beaucoup de; *Fml* **m. care** beaucoup de soin; *Iron* **m. good may it do you!** grand bien vous fasse!; **how m. money?** combien d'argent?; **too m. money** trop d'argent; **so m. money** tellement *ou* tant d'argent; **as m. money as** autant d'argent que

ADV beaucoup; **I don't like them m., I don't m. like them** je ne les aime pas beaucoup; **(very) m. better** beaucoup mieux; **m. worse** bien pire; **it doesn't matter m.** cela n'a pas beaucoup d'importance; **m. more/less pleasant** beaucoup plus/moins agréable; **the largest** de beaucoup le plus grand, le plus grand de beaucoup; **m. too small** beaucoup trop petit; **we are m. obliged to you for …** nous vous sommes très obligés de *ou* pour …; **thank you very m. (for …)** merci beau-

coup *(de ou pour …)*; **it's (pretty or very) m. the same thing** c'est à peu près la même chose; **he's m. the same** *(of somebody ill)* son état n'a pas changé; **that's m. how I felt** c'est à peu près ce que j'ai ressenti, moi aussi; **m. to my astonishment** à mon grand étonnement; *Fam Iron* **he doesn't like beer, does he? – not m. he doesn't!** il n'aime pas la bière, non? – et comment, il aime ça! VOIR GRAMMAIRE A22-3

PRON 1 beaucoup; **m. remains to be done** il reste beaucoup à faire; **m. has happened while you have been away** il s'est passé bien des choses pendant votre absence; **there is not m. of it** il n'y en a pas beaucoup; **it's not worth m.** *or Fam* **not up to m.** cela ne vaut pas grand-chose; **to make m. of sth** accorder beaucoup d'importance à qch; **I'll say this m. for him** je dirai ceci en sa faveur; **there's not (all) that m.** il n'y en a pas tellement *ou* tant que ça; **I don't think m. of it** je n'aime pas beaucoup ça; **it wasn't m. of a surprise** ce n'était pas une grande surprise; **she isn't m. of a singer** comme chanteuse, elle n'est pas terrible; **it wasn't m. of a joke** ce n'était pas terrible comme plaisanterie

2 *(phrases)* **m. as I'd like to** *(I can't accept, be there etc)* bien que je le veuille; **m. as I'd like to, I can't come** je voudrais bien, mais je ne peux pas venir; **m. as I like him** quelle que soit mon affection pour lui; **m. as I try, I can't succeed** j'ai beau essayer, je n'y arrive pas; **the result was m. as I expected** le résultat correspondait bien à ce que j'attendais; **as m. autant**; **as m. again** encore autant; **twice as m.** deux fois autant; **I expected as m.** je m'y attendais; **I suspected** *or* **guessed** *or* **thought as m.** je m'en doutais; **as m. as** autant que; **as m. as possible** autant que possible; **quite as m. as …** tout autant que …; **not quite as m. as …** pas tout à fait autant que …; **it is as m. your fault as (it is) mine** c'est autant de votre faute que de la mienne; **it is as m. as he can do to read** c'est tout juste s'il sait lire; **it was as m. as we could do to stand upright** nous avions le plus grand mal à nous tenir debout; **he looked at me as m. as to say …** il me regarda avec l'air de (vouloir) dire …; **as m. as that?** (au)tant que cela?; **do you love her as m. as that?** vous l'aimez donc tant *ou* à ce point-là?; **he went away without so m. as saying goodbye** il est parti sans même dire au revoir; **I would not so m. as raise a finger to help him** je ne lèverais pas même le petit doigt pour l'aider; **so m.** tant; **tellement**; **he has drunk so m. that …** il a tellement bu que …; **so m. the better** tant mieux; **so m. so that …** au point que …, à tel point que …; **not so m. a …, more a …** pas vraiment un …, mais plutôt un …; **so m. for his friendship!** et voilà ce qu'il appelle l'amitié!; **so m. per cent** tant pour cent; **so m. a kilo** tant le kilo; **too m.** trop; **m. too m.** beaucoup trop; **£10 too m.** 10 livres de trop; **to cost too m.** coûter trop cher; **this is (really) too m.!** c'est vraiment trop fort!; *Fam* **that's a bit m.!** c'est un peu fort!; **you can't have too m. of a good thing** abondance de biens ne nuit pas

muchness ['mʌtʃnɪs] N *Fam* **they're much of a m.** *(of pictures, books, people etc)* ils se ressemblent beaucoup; *(of two candidates)* ils se valent; **it's (all) much of a m.** *(doesn't really matter)* ça revient au même

muck [mʌk] N 1 *(dung)* fumier *m* 2 *(dirt)* saleté *f*; *(from the streets)* saletés 3 *Br Fam (rubbish, unhealthy food, obscene book etc)* cochonnerie *f*; *(unappetizing food)* saloperie *f*; *(worthless objects)* camelote *f* 4 *Br Fam (mess)* **to make a m. of sth** saloper qch
▸▸ *Agr* **m. spreader** épandeur *m*
▸ **muck about, muck around** VI, VT SEP *Br Fam* = **mess about, mess around**

▸ **muck in** VI *Br Fam* **to m. in with sb** *(share room)* crécher avec qn; *(join in)* partager le boulot avec qn; **everyone mucked in** *(helped out)* tout le monde s'y est mis
▸ **muck out** VT SEP *(stables etc)* nettoyer
VI nettoyer l'écurie/les écuries/*etc*
▸ **muck up** VT SEP *Br Fam* 1 *(make dirty)* saloper 2 *(make a mess of)* ficher en l'air; *(job)* bousiller; *(plans)* flanquer par terre

mucker ['mʌkə(r)] N *Br Fam* 1 *(friend)* pote *m* 2 *(term of address)* vieux *m*; **alright, me old m.!** salut vieux!, salut mon pote!

muckheap ['mʌkhi:p] N tas *m* de fumier *ou* d'ordures

muckraker ['mʌkreɪkər] N *Fam* journaliste *mf* à l'affût des scandales, *Sl* fouille-merde *m inv*

muckraking ['mʌkreɪkɪŋ] N *Fam* révélation *f* de scandales

mucky ['mʌkɪ] ADJ *Br Fam* sale; **m. books** *(obscene)* des livres cochons; **you're a m. pup!** que tu es sale!

mucous ['mju:kəs] ADJ muqueux
▸▸ *Anat* **m. membrane** muqueuse *f*

mucus ['mju:kəs] N 1 *Physiol* mucus *m*, mucosité *f* 2 *Bot* mucosité *f*

mud [mʌd] N boue *f*, gadoue *f*, *(in swamp)* bourbe *f*, **(river) m.** vase *f*, **to get stuck** *or* **to sink in the m.** s'embourber; *(of ship)* s'envaser; *Fig* **to drag sb's name in the m.** traîner qn dans la boue; *Fig* **to fling** *or* **sling** *or* **throw m. at sb** couvrir qn de boue; *Fam* **his name is m.** il est mal vu; *Old-fashioned Fam* **here's m. in your eye!** à votre santé!, à la vôtre!; *Fam* **as clear as m.** clair comme du jus de boudin
▸▸ *Med* **m. bath** bain *m* de boue; **m. hut** case *f* en pisé *ou* en terre; **m. pie** *(made of mud)* pâté *m* (de sable); *(cake)* = sorte de gâteau au chocolat; **m. wrestling** catch *m* dans la boue

mudbank ['mʌdbæŋk] N *(in river)* banc *m* de vase

muddle ['mʌd(ə)l] N confusion *f*, *Fam* embrouillamini *m*; **to be in a m.** *(of things)* être en désordre *ou* en pagaille *ou* en pagaïe; *(of person)* ne plus savoir où l'on en est; **to get into a m.** s'embrouiller; *(about sth* au sujet de qch); **to make a m. of sth** faire qch de travers
VT 1 *(put in disorder) (story)* embrouiller, brouiller; *(matter, affair)* gâcher 2 *(bewilder) (person)* embrouiller; **to get muddled** s'embrouiller
▸ **muddle along** VI *(cope haphazardly)* faire son chemin *ou* se débrouiller tant bien que mal
▸ **muddle through** VI *(get through haphazardly)* se débrouiller *ou Fam* se dépatouiller *ou* s'en tirer tant bien que mal
VT INSEP **to m. through a crisis** traverser une crise tant bien que mal; **to m. through an exam** passer un examen tant bien que mal
▸ **muddle up** VT SEP 1 *(mix up)* mélanger; **I've muddled the dates up** j'ai mélangé les dates 2 *(bewilder) (somebody)* embrouiller

muddled ['mʌd(ə)ld] ADJ 1 *(objects)* en désordre, *Fam* en pagaille *ou* pagaïe 2 *(person, ideas)* confus, embrouillé

muddleheaded [mʌd(ə)l'hedɪd] ADJ *(person)* à l'esprit confus, brouillon, -onne; **m. ideas** idées confuses *ou* embrouillées

muddler ['mʌdlər] N brouillon, -onne, esprit *m* brouillon

muddy ['mʌdɪ] ADJ 1 *(path)* boueux, bourbeux; *(stream)* bourbeux, vaseux; *(jacket etc)* crotté, couvert de boue; **to taste m.** avoir un goût de vase 2 *(liquid, wine etc)* trouble; *(colour)* sale; *(complexion)* brouillé, terreux; **m. brown** couleur (de) terre
VT 1 *(one's clothes etc)* crotter 2 *(water)* trou-

bler; *Fig* **to m. the waters** semer la confusion

mudflap ['mʌdflæp] **N** pare-boue *m inv*

mudflat ['mʌdflæt] **N** banc *m* de boue

mudguard ['mʌdgɑːd] **N** *Br* garde-boue *m inv*

mudlark ['mʌdlɑːk] **N** *Old-fashioned Fam* gamin, -ine des rues

mudpack ['mʌdpæk] **N** masque *m* à l'argile

mudskipper ['mʌdskɪpər] **N** (*fish*) gobie *m* des marais

mudslinger ['mʌdslɪŋər] **N** *Fam* calomniateur, -trice

mudslinging ['mʌdslɪŋɪŋ] *Fam* **N** calomnies *fpl*
   ADJ diffamatoire

mud-stained **ADJ** taché de boue

muesli ['mjuːzlɪ] **N** muesli *m*

muezzin [muːˈezɪn] **N** muezzin *m*

muff[1] [mʌf] **VT** *Br Fam* (*bungle*) rater, louper; *Golf etc* (*stroke*) manquer, rater

muff[2] **N 1** (*for hands*) manchon *m* **2** *Vulg* (*female sex organs*) touffe *f*, chatte *f*, **m.-diving** descente *f* au barbu

muffin ['mʌfɪn] **N** *Culin* muffin *m*

muffle ['mʌf(ə)l] **VT 1** (*deaden sound of*) (*oars, bell etc*) assourdir, étouffer; *Mus* (*drum*) assourdir **2** (*wrap*) emmitoufler; **to m. oneself up** s'emmitoufler

muffled ['mʌf(ə)ld] **ADJ 1** (*sound, footstep*) étouffé, assourdi; (*oar*) assourdi; (*voice*) étouffé; *Mus* **m. drums** tambours voilés **2** (*wrapped*) **m. (up)** emmitouflé

muffler ['mʌflər] **N 1** (*scarf*) cache-nez *m inv*; cache-col *m*, *pl* cache-col(s) **2** *Am Aut* silencieux *m*; *Tech* (**exhaust**) **m.** gueule-deloup *f*, *pl* gueules-de-loup **3** *Mus* (*on piano*) étouffoir *m*

Mufti ['mʌftɪ] **N** *Rel* mufti *m*, muphti *m*

mufti ['mʌftɪ] **N** *Mil etc Sl* tenue *f* civile; **in m.** en civil

mug [mʌg] **N 1** (*for beer*) chope *f*, pot *m*; (*for tea etc*) grande tasse *f*; (*made of metal*) quart *m* **2** *Fam* (*face*) gueule *f*, trombine *f*, bouille *f*, *esp Am* (*photo of criminal*) photo *f* (*d'un criminel*); **ugly m.** sale gueule, gueule d'empeigne; **shut your (ugly) m.!** ferme ta sale gueule! **3** *Br Fam* (*gullible person*) poire *f*, andouille *f*, **it's a m.'s game** c'est bon pour les poires; **the lottery's a m.'s game** le loto, c'est un attrape-couillons
   VT *Fam* (*attack*) (*person*) attaquer, agresser
   VI faire des grimaces
   ▸ *esp Am* **m. shot** photo (*d'un criminel*)
   ▸ **mug up** *Br Sch Fam* **VI** (*study, revise*) plancher, bûcher; **to m. up on sth** plancher sur qch
   VT SEP (*subject*) potasser

mugful ['mʌgfʊl] **N** (*of beer*) chope *f*, pot *m*; (*of coffee, tea*) grande tasse *f*

mugger ['mʌgər] **N** *Fam* agresseur *m*

mugging ['mʌgɪŋ] **N** *Fam* agression *f*

muggins ['mʌgɪnz] **N** *Br Fam* idiot, -ote, nouille *f*, (*oneself*) mézigue, ma pomme; **I suppose m. will have to do it!** je suppose que c'est ma pomme qui va s'y coller!; **m. (here) paid the bill as usual** comme d'habitude c'est mézigue qui a payé l'addition

muggy ['mʌgɪ] **ADJ** (*weather*) lourd

mugwump ['mʌgwʌmp] **N** *Am Pol Fam* (*independent*) non-inscrit, -ite; (*neutral*) neutre *mf*

mulatto [mjuːˈlætəʊ] *Old-fashioned* **ADJ** mulâtre
   N mulâtre *mf*, mulâtresse *f*

mulberry ['mʌlbərɪ] **N** (*fruit*) mûre *f*, **m. (bush** or **tree)** mûrier *m*

mulch [mʌltʃ] **N** paillis *m*
   VT pailler

mulct [mʌlkt] **VT 1** *Law* frapper d'une amende **2** (*cheat*) **to m. sb of sth** extorquer qch à qn

mule[1] [mjuːl] **N 1** (*he*) **m.** mulet *m*; (*she*) **m., m. mare** mule *f*; **as stubborn as a m.** têtu comme une mule **2** *Fam* (*stubborn person*) tête *f* de mule **3** *Sl* (*drug smuggler*) mule *f* **4** *Tex* renvideur *m*
   ▸▸ **m. driver** muletier *m*; *Tex* **m. jenny** renvideur; **m. path** chemin *m* ou sentier *m* muletier; *Am Fam* **m. skinner** muletier; **m. train** caravane *f* de mules

mule[2] **N** (*slipper*) mule *f*

muleteer [mjuːlɪˈtɪər] **N** muletier *m*

mulish ['mjuːlɪʃ] **ADJ** entêté, têtu (comme une mule)

mulishness ['mjuːlɪʃnɪs] **N** entêtement *m*

mull [mʌl] **VT** (*wine, beer*) chauffer avec des épices
   ▸ **mull over VT SEP** (*consider*) (*idea*) ruminer, retourner dans sa tête; **I've been mulling it over** j'y ai réfléchi

mulled [mʌld] **ADJ**
   ▸▸ **m. wine** vin *m* chaud épicé

mullered ['mʊləd] **ADJ** *Br Fam* (*drunk*) bourré, pété

mullet ['mʌlɪt] **N 1** (*fish*) grey **m.** muge *m* (capiton), mulet *m*; **red m.** rouget(-barbet) *m* **2** *Fam* (*hairstyle*) = coupe *f* de cheveux longue sur la nuque, courte sur les côtés et en brosse longue sur le dessus

mulligatawny [mʌlɪgəˈtɔːnɪ] **N m.** (**soup**) potage *m* au curry

mullion ['mʌlɪən] **N** *Archit* meneau *m* (vertical)

mullioned ['mʌlɪənd] **ADJ** *Archit* (*window*) à meneau(x)

multi- ['mʌltɪ] **PREF** multi-

multiaccess [mʌltɪˈækses] **ADJ** *Comput* à accès multiple

multiangle ['mʌltɪæŋgəl] **ADJ** multiangle

multibrand ['mʌltɪbrænd] **N** *Mktg* marque *f* multiple, multimarque *f*
   ▸▸ **m. store** point *m* de vente multimarque

multicast ['mʌltɪkɑːst] **N** *Comput* multi-diffusion *f*

multi-centre holiday **N** vacances *fpl* en circuit

multichannel [mʌltɪˈtʃæn(ə)l] **ADJ** multicanal, -aux

multicoloured ['mʌltɪkʌləd] **ADJ** multicolore

multicriterion sorting [mʌltɪkraɪˈtɪərɪən] **N** *Comput* classement *m* multicritère

multicultural [mʌltɪˈkʌltʃər(ə)l] **ADJ** multiculturel

multicurrency [mʌltɪˈkʌrənsɪ] **ADJ** multidevise

multidirectional [mʌltɪdɪˈrekʃən(ə)l] **ADJ** multidirectionnel

multifaceted [mʌltɪˈfæsɪtɪd] **ADJ** qui a plusieurs facettes

multifarious [mʌltɪˈfeərɪəs] **ADJ** *Fml* varié, divers

multiform ['mʌltɪfɔːm] **ADJ** multiforme

multi-fuel engine **N** moteur *m* polycarburant

multi-functional **ADJ** *Comput* multifonction(s)
   ▸▸ **m. key** touche *f* multifonction(s); **m. keyboard** clavier *m* multifonction(s)

multi-function display **N** affichage *m* multifonction(s)

multi-grade oil **N** huile *f* multigrade

multilateral [mʌltɪˈlæt(ə)rəl] **ADJ** multilatéral, -aux; **m. diplomacy** diplomatie *f* multilatérale

multilevel [mʌltɪˈlev(ə)l] **ADJ** *Comput* multiniveaux
   ▸▸ *Mktg* **m. marketing** marketing *m* de réseau, vente *f* par réseau coopté

multilingual [mʌltɪˈlɪŋgwəl] **ADJ** (*person*) polyglotte; (*country*) plurilingue

multimedia [mʌltɪˈmiːdɪə] **ADJ** multimédia
   N multimédia *m*
   ▸▸ **m. computer** ordinateur *m* multimédia; **m. group** groupe *m* multimédia

multimillionaire [mʌltɪmɪlɪəˈneər] **ADJ, N** multimillionnaire *mf*

multimodal operator [mʌltɪˈməʊd(ə)l] **N** opérateur *m* de transport multimodal, OTM *m*

multinational [mʌltɪˈnæʃ(ə)n(ə)l] **ADJ** multinational, -aux
   N multinationale *f*
   ▸▸ **m. company** entreprise *f* multinationale; **m. corporation** société *f* multinationale; **m. marketing** marketing *m* multinational

multi-ownership **N** multipropriété *f*

multi-part stationery **N** papier *m* multiple

multiparty [mʌltɪˈpɑːtɪ] **ADJ** *Pol* (*state*) pluripartite

multi-plate clutch **N** embrayage *m* à disques multiples

multiple ['mʌltɪp(ə)l] **ADJ** multiple; *Elec* **batteries in m.** accumulateurs *mpl* en parallèle
   N 1 *Math* multiple *m*; **lowest** or **least common m.** plus petit commun multiple **2** *Tel* multiplage *m* **3** *Com* (*chain store*) magasin *m* à succursales (multiples)
   ▸▸ *Tel* **m. circuit** accumulateurs *mpl* en parallèle; *Cin* **m. image** image *f* multiple; **m. injuries** blessures *fpl* multiples; **m. occupancy** (*by tenants*) colocation *f*, (*by owners*) copropriété *f*, **m. ownership** multipropriété *f*, *Psy* **m. personality** personnalité *f* multiple; *Elec, Radio* **m. reception** réception *f* multiple; *Med* **m. sclerosis** sclérose *f* en plaques; **m. store** magasin *m* à succursales (multiples); *Tel* **m. switchboard** multiple (téléphonique)

multiple-choice **ADJ** (*question, exam*) à choix multiple

multiplex ['mʌltɪpleks] **N 1** (*cinema*) complexe *m* multisalles **2** *Radio, Tel, TV* multiplex *m*
   VT multiplexer
   ▸▸ **m. broadcast** transmission *f* en multiplex; **m. cinema** complexe multisalles

multiplexer [mʌltɪpleksər] **N** *Radio, Tel, TV* multiplexeur *m*

multiplexing ['mʌltɪpleksɪŋ] **N** *Radio, Tel, TV* multiplexage *m*

multiplication [mʌltɪplɪˈkeɪʃən] **N** *Math etc* multiplication *f* VOIR GRAMMAIRE A77; B59
   ▸▸ **m. table** table *f* de multiplication

multiplicity [mʌltɪˈplɪsɪtɪ] **N** multiplicité *f*

multiplier ['mʌltɪplaɪər] **N** *Math, Comput, Elec* multiplicateur *m*

multiply ['mʌltɪplaɪ] **VT** *Math, Fig* multiplier; **to m. 2 by 6** multiplier 2 par 6
   VI 1 (*of species, difficulties etc*) se multiplier **2** *Math* multiplier, faire une/des multiplication(s)

multi-point fuel-injected engine **N** moteur *m* à injection multipoint

multiprocessing ['mʌltɪprəʊsesɪŋ] **N** *Comput* multitraitement *m*

multiprocessor [mʌltɪˈprəʊsesər] **N** *Comput* multiprocesseur *m*

multipurpose [mʌltɪˈpɜːpəs] **ADJ** (*tool, vehicle*) à usages multiples, polyvalent

multiracial [mʌltɪˈreɪʃəl] **ADJ** multiracial, -aux

multiscan monitor ['mʌltɪskæn] N moniteur *m* à balayage multiple

multiscreen ['mʌltɪskriːn] N **1** *(cinema)* complexe *m* multisalles, cinéma *m* multisalle **2** *TV* écran-mosaïque *m*, *pl* écrans-mosaïques, multi-écran *m*, *pl* multi-écrans
▸▸ *TV* **m. channel** canal *m* mosaïque; **m. cinema** complexe multisalles, cinéma multisalle

multisector ['mʌltɪsektər] ADJ multisectoriel
▸▸ **m. journey** voyage *m* multi-secteur; **m. ticketing** délivrance *f* de billets multisecteurs

multi-spreadsheet N *Comput* multifeuille *f*

multistage ['mʌltɪsteɪdʒ] ADJ *Elec, Tech (amplifier, compressor)* à plusieurs étages
▸▸ *Aut* **m. converter** convertisseur *m* multiétagé; *Astronaut* **m. rocket** fusée *f* composite à étages multiples

multi-station ADJ *Comput* multipostes

multistorey, *Am* **multistory** [mʌltɪ'stɔːrɪ] ADJ *(building)* à plusieurs étages
N *(car park)* parc *m* de stationnement *ou* parking *m* à plusieurs niveaux
▸▸ **m. car park** parc de stationnement *ou* parking à plusieurs niveaux

multisyllabic [mʌltɪsɪ'læbɪk] ADJ polysyllabique

multi-talented ADJ aux talents multiples

multitasking [mʌltɪ'tɑːskɪŋ] N **1** = capacité *f* à mener plusieurs tâches de front **2** *Comput* multitâche *m*

multitrack [mʌltɪ'træk] ADJ *(recording)* multipiste

multitracking [mʌltɪ'trækɪŋ] N *(in recording)* enregistrement *m* multipiste

multitude ['mʌltɪtjuːd] N **1** *(large number) (of reasons etc)* multitude *f*, multiplicité *f*; *Fig* **to cover** *or* **hide a m. of sins** *(of carpet, woodwork etc)* ça cache des horreurs invraisemblables; *esp Hum (of job title, definition)* ça englobe des tas de choses **2** *Fml, Lit (crowd)* multitude *f*, foule *f*

multitudinous [mʌltɪ'tjuːdɪnəs] ADJ *Fml* nombreux, innombrable

multi-user ADJ *Comput* pour utilisateurs multiples
▸▸ **m. software** logiciel *m* multi-utilisateur; **m. system** système *m* multi-utilisateur

multi-valve ADJ multisoupape

multivision ['mʌltɪvɪʒən] N multivision *f*

multivitamin ['mʌltɪvɪtəmɪn, *Am* 'mʌltɪvaɪtəmɪn] N multivitamine *f*

mum[1] [mʌm] N *Br Fam (mother)* maman *f*

mum[2] *Fam* N **m.'s the word!** motus (et bouche cousue)!
ADJ **to keep m.** ne pas souffler mot (**about sth** de qch)

mumble ['mʌmb(ə)l] N marmonnement *m*, marmottement *m*; **to say in a m.** dire en marmonnant
VT marmonner, marmotter; **he mumbled a few words** il a marmonné quelques mots
VI marmonner, parler entre ses dents *ou* dans sa barbe, manger ses mots

mumbo jumbo ['mʌmbəʊ'dʒʌmbəʊ] N *Fam (nonsense)* âneries *fpl*, *(words etc)* charabia *m*; *(ritual phrases etc)* bla-bla *m*; **astrology is just a load of m.** l'astrologie, c'est du pipeau

mummer ['mʌmər] N *Theat* mime *mf*

mummery ['mʌmərɪ] N *Theat* momerie *f*

mummification [mʌmɪfɪ'keɪʃən] N mommification *f*

mummify ['mʌmɪfaɪ] VT momifier
VI se momifier

mummy[1] ['mʌmɪ] N *(embalmed body)* momie *f*

mummy[2] N *Br Fam (mother)* maman *f*, *Pej* **m.'s boy** fils *m* à maman

mumps [mʌmps] NPL *(usu with sing verb)* *Med* oreillons *mpl*; **to have m.** avoir les oreillons

munch [mʌntʃ] VT mâcher, mâchonner
▸ **munch at** VT INSEP mastiquer
▸ **munch away** VI mastiquer; **he was munching away at an apple** il mastiquait (bruyamment) une pomme
▸ **munch on** VT INSEP = munch at
▸ **munch out** VI *Am Fam* se goinfrer, s'empiffrer

Munchausen ['mʌntʃaʊzən] N *Med*
▸▸ **M. by proxy** syndrome *m* de Münchhausen par procuration; **M. Syndrome** syndrome de Münchhausen

munchies ['mʌntʃɪz] NPL *Fam (snacks)* petites choses *fpl* à grignoter; **to have the m., to have an attack of the m.** *(desire to eat)* avoir la fringale

mundane [mʌn'deɪn] ADJ banal, -als, ordinaire

Note that the French adjective **mondain** is a false friend and is never a translation for the English word **mundane**. It refers to people or events in high society.

municipal [mjuː'nɪsɪp(ə)l] ADJ municipal, -aux
▸▸ *Am Fin* **m. bond** obligation *f* de collectivité locale; **m. buildings** ≃ mairie *f*, *(in large town)* ≃ hôtel *m* de ville; *Can, Austr* **m. district** ≃ municipalité *f*

municipality [mjuːnɪsɪ'pælɪtɪ] N municipalité *f*

munificence [mjuː'nɪfɪsəns] N munificence *f*

munificent [mjuː'nɪfɪsənt] ADJ munificent, généreux

munitions [mjuː'nɪʃənz] NPL munitions *fpl*
▸▸ **m. dump** dépôt *m* de munitions; **m. factory** fabrique *f* de munitions; **m. worker** = personne *f* qui travaille dans une usine de munitions

muppet ['mʌpɪt] N *Br Fam* andouille *f*

mural ['mjʊərəl] *Art* ADJ mural, -aux; **m. paintings** peintures *fpl* murales
N peinture *f* murale

murder ['mɜːdər] N meurtre *m*; *Law* homicide *m* volontaire; *Law* **premeditated m.,** *Am* **m. in the first degree** assassinat *m*; **to commit (a) m.** commettre un meurtre/assassinat; **the m. weapon** l'arme *f* du crime; *Fig* **it's (sheer** *or* **downright) m. in the rush hour** c'est (absolument) cauchemardesque *ou* infernal aux heures de pointe; **it's m. trying to park in the town centre** c'est cauchemardesque *ou* infernal d'essayer de se garer dans le centre-ville; *Fig* **he gets away with m.** il peut tout se permettre, personne ne lui dit quoi que ce soit; **their kids get away with m.** leurs gosses font absolument tout ce qu'ils veulent
VT **1** *(kill)* assassiner; *Fig Fam* **I'll m. you (for that)!** je vais te tuer! **2** *Fig Fam (destroy) (song, tune etc)* massacrer, saboter **3** *Fig Fam (defeat heavily)* battre à plates coutures **4** *Br Fig Fam (drink, eat)* **I could m. a beer/pizza** je taperais bien une bière/une pizza
VI commettre un meurtre
▸▸ **m. case** affaire *f* de meurtre; **m. trial** procès *m* pour meurtre; **m. weapon** arme *f* du crime

murderer ['mɜːdərər] N meurtrier *m*, assassin *m*

murderess ['mɜːdərɪs] N meurtrière *f*

murderous ['mɜːdərəs] ADJ meurtrier, assassin; **with m. intent** dans une intention homicide; **a m.-looking knife** un couteau à

l'apparence particulièrement menaçante; **to give sb a m. look** lancer un regard meurtrier à qn

murk [mɜːk] N obscurité *f*, ténèbres *fpl*

murky ['mɜːkɪ] ADJ obscur, ténébreux; *(sky)* brouillé; *(details)* sordide; **m. past** passé *m* obscur *ou* ténébreux

murmur ['mɜːmər] N **1** *(of voices, waves)* murmure *m*; *Med* **heart m.** souffle *m* (au cœur) **2** *(of approval, discontent etc)* murmure *m*; **without a m.** *(to do something)* sans murmurer, sans broncher; **in a m.** à voix basse
VI murmurer, susurrer; *(complain)* murmurer (**against** contre)
VT *(something)* murmurer, dire à voix basse

murmuring ['mɜːmərɪŋ] N murmure *m*; **murmurings** *(complaints)* murmures (**against** contre)

Murphy ['mɜːfɪ] N
▸▸ *Am* **M. bed** lit *m* escamotable; *Fam* **M.'s Law** loi *f* de l'emmerdement maximum

muscatel [mʌskə'tel] N muscat *m*

muscle ['mʌs(ə)l] N **1** *Anat* muscle *m*; **she didn't move a m.** elle n'a pas bronché; **he has plenty of m.** il est bien musclé **2** *Fig (political, financial)* pouvoir *m*; **it would give our campaign more m.** cela donnerait plus de force à notre campagne
▸▸ **m. fibre** fibres *fpl* musculaires; *Med* **m. strain** élongation *f*
▸ **muscle in** VI *Fam (force one's way in)* s'immiscer, s'imposer (**on sth** dans qch); **a lot of big companies are muscling in** de nombreuses grosses sociétés arrivent en force; **to m. in on sb's territory** marcher sur les platesbandes de qn; **we don't want them muscling in** nous ne voulons pas qu'ils marchent sur nos plates-bandes

musclebound ['mʌs(ə)lbaʊnd] ADJ très musclé

muscleman, *pl* **musclemen** ['mʌs(ə)lmæn, -men] N *(strongman)* Monsieur *m* Muscle

muscovado (sugar) [mʌskə'vɑːdəʊ] N cassonade *f*

Muscovite ['mʌskəvaɪt] ADJ moscovite
N Moscovite *mf*

muscular ['mʌskjʊlər] ADJ **1** *Anat (system, tissue, action)* musculaire **2** *(man)* musclé
▸▸ *Med* **m. dystrophy** myopathie *f*

musculature ['mʌskjʊlətʃər] N *Anat* musculature *f*

Muse [mjuːz] N **1** *Myth* Muse *f*; **the (nine) Muses** les Muses **2** *(of poet)* **the m.** les muses *fpl*

muse [mjuːz] VI songer, rêver
VT **that's queer, he mused** voilà qui est bien étrange, songea-t-il
▸ **muse on** VT INSEP songer à

museum [mjuː'zɪəm] N musée *m*
▸▸ **m. piece** pièce *f* de musée; *Fig Hum* **his car's a m. piece** sa voiture est une pièce de musée

mush [mʌʃ] N **1** *Fam (pulp)* bouillie *f*, purée *f* **2** *esp Am Culin* bouillie *f* de farine de maïs **3** *Fam (sentimentality)* sentimentalité *f* (à l'eau de rose)

mushroom ['mʌʃrʊm] N **1** *(fungus)* champignon *m*; **cultivated** *or* **button mushrooms** champignons de couche *ou* de Paris; **m. soup** potage *m* aux champignons **2** *Sewing* boule *f* à repriser
VI **1** *(gather mushrooms)* faire la cueillette des champignons; **to go mushrooming** aller aux champignons **2** *(grow rapidly)* pousser comme un champignon/des champignons; *(proliferate)* se multiplier, proliférer; **profits/costs have mushroomed in the past year** les profits/coûts ont considérablement augmenté durant l'année passée
▸▸ **m. cloud** champignon *m* atomique; **m.**

farm champignonnière *f*; **m. grower** champignonniste *mf*; **m. town** ville *f* champignon

mushrooming ['mʌʃrʊmɪŋ] **N 1** (*gathering of mushrooms*) cueillette *f* des champignons **2** (*rapid growth*) croissance *f* rapide; (*proliferation*) multiplication *f* rapide, prolifération *f*

mushy ['mʌʃɪ] **ADJ 1** (*food etc*) en bouillie; (*ground etc*) détrempé; (*pear etc*) blet, *f* blette **2** *Fam* (*sentimental*) sentimental, -aux, à l'eau de rose, à la guimauve; **m. sentimentality** sentimentalité *f* à l'eau de rose *ou* à la guimauve

▸▸ **m. peas** purée *f* de petits pois

music ['mju:zɪk] **N** musique *f*; **to set words to m.** mettre des paroles en musique; (**sheet**) **m.** partition *f*; **I can't play without m.** je ne peux pas jouer sans partition; *Fig* **those words were m. to his ears** il était ravi d'entendre ces mots, ces mots le remplirent d'aise

▸▸ **m. box** boîte *f* à musique; **m. case** portemusique *m inv*; *Old-fashioned* **m. centre** chaîne *f* (midi); *TV* **m. channel** chaîne musicale; **m. critic** critique *m* musical; *esp Br* **m. hall** music-hall *m*, *pl* music-halls; **m. lover** mélomane *mf*; **m. paper** papier *m* à musique; **m. piracy** piratage *m* musical; **m. press** presse *f* musicale; **m. publishing** édition *f* musicale; **m. stand** pupitre *m* (à musique); **m. station** station *f* musicale; **m. video** clip *m* (vidéo)

musical ['mju:zɪk(ə)l] **ADJ 1** musical, -aux; **to be m.** (*of person*) être (bon) musicien/ (bonne) musicienne **2** (*sound, voice*) harmonieux, mélodieux

N *Cin, Theat* comédie *f* musicale

▸▸ *Br* **m. box** boîte *f* à musique; **m. chairs** chaises *fpl* musicales; *also Fig* **to play m. chairs** jouer aux chaises musicales; **m. comedy** comédie *f* musicale, musical *m*; **m. evening** soirée *f* musicale; **m. instrument** instrument *m* de musique

musician [mju:'zɪʃən] **N** musicien, -ienne

musicianship [mju:'zɪʃənʃɪp] **N** qualités *fpl* de musicien/musicienne

musicologist [mju:zɪ'kɒlədʒɪst] **N** musicologue *mf*

musicology [mju:zɪ'kɒlədʒɪ] **N** musicologie *f*

musing ['mju:zɪŋ] **ADJ** songeur, pensif, rêveur

N musings rêverie(s) *f(pl)*

musk [mʌsk] **N** (*substance, smell, plant*) musc *m*

▸▸ *Zool* **m. cat** civette *f*; *Zool* **m. deer** portemusc *m*, *pl* porte-muscs; *Zool* **m. ox** bœuf *m* musqué, ovibos *m*; **m. plant** musc; *Bot* **m. rose** (*flower*) rose *f* musquée; (*bush*) rosier *m* musqué

musket ['mʌskɪt] **N** *Mil, Hist* mousquet *m*

musketeer [mʌskɪ'tɪər] **N** *Mil, Hist* mousquetaire *m*; **the Three Musketeers** Les Trois Mousquetaires

musketry ['mʌskɪtrɪ] **N** *Mil* tir *m* au fusil

muskrat ['mʌskræt] **N 1** (*North American*) rat *m* musqué, ondatra *m* **2** (*European*) desman *m* musqué

musky ['mʌskɪ] **ADJ** musqué, de musc

Muslim ['mʊzlɪm] **ADJ, N** = **Moslem**

muslin ['mʌzlɪn] **N** *Tex* mousseline *f*, *Am* calicot *m*

muso ['mju:zəʊ] **N** *Br Fam* (*musician*) musico *m*

musquash ['mʌskwɒʃ] **N 1** (*animal*) rat *m* musqué, ondatra *m* **2** (*fur*) rat *m* musqué

muss [mʌs] **VT** *Am Fam* = **muss up**

▸ **muss up VT SEP** *Am Fam* (*hair*) déranger; (*dress*) froisser, chiffonner

mussel ['mʌs(ə)l] **N** moule *f*; **m. bank** *or* **bed** banc *m* de moules; (*man-made*) moulière *f*

MUST¹ [mʌst] **N** *Fam* **1** (*necessity*) nécessité *f*, chose *f* indispensable; **the ability to speak Russian is a m.** il est indispensable de savoir parler russe, une bonne connaissance du russe est un must; **sunglasses are a m.** les lunettes de soleil sont indispensables **2** (*thing not to be missed, that must be done*) chose *f* à ne pas manquer/à faire à tout prix; **this film's a m.** c'est un film à ne pas manquer

MODAL AUX V INV   VOIR GRAMMAIRE A60; B39
(**must not** *is often contracted into* **mustn't**) **1** (*expressing obligation*) **you m. be ready at four o'clock** vous devez *ou* devrez être prêt à quatre heures, il faut *ou* faudra que vous soyez prêt à quatre heures; **you m. hurry up** il faut vous dépêcher; **you mustn't tell anyone** vous ne devez le dire à personne, il ne faut le dire à personne; **you mustn't touch it!** il ne faut pas y toucher!; **we mustn't be late** il ne faut pas que nous soyons en retard; **they mustn't find out** il ne faut pas qu'ils le sachent; **plant that m. have continual attention** plante qui demande des soins continuels; **I simply m. see him** il faut absolument que je le voie; **he is stupid, I m. say** il est stupide, je dois l'avouer; **I m. say I thought it was rather good** je dois dire que c'était très bien; *Iron* **very clever, I m. say!** je dois dire que c'est très astucieux!; **if you m.** si c'est vraiment nécessaire; **m. you be so silly?** qu'est-ce que tu peux être bête!; **why m. you always be so unhelpful?** pourquoi faut-il toujours que tu sois si peu serviable?; **if you m. drink so much, what do you expect?** si tu t'entêtes à boire autant, il ne faut pas t'étonner!

2 (*suggesting, inviting*) **you m. come and visit us** il faut que vous veniez nous voir; **we m. go out for a drink** il faut que nous allions boire un verre

3 (*expressing probability*) **you m. be hungry after your walk** vous devez avoir faim après votre promenade; **it m. be interesting working there** ça doit être intéressant de travailler là; **you m. be joking** tu plaisantes!; *Fam* **she mustn't be very happy** elle ne doit pas être très heureuse; **I m. have made a mistake** j'ai dû me tromper; **she m. have been talking about somebody else** elle devait parler de quelqu'un d'autre; **if he says so it m. be true** si c'est lui qui le dit c'est que c'est vrai; **was it her? – it m. have been** est-ce que c'était elle? – oui, je pense; **I saw that he m. have suspected something** j'ai bien vu qu'il avait dû se douter de quelque chose

---

must² **N** (*in winemaking*) moût *m*

must³ **N** (*mould*) moisi *m*, moisissure *f*

mustache ['mʌstæʃ] **N** *Am* = **moustache**

mustang ['mʌstæŋ] **N** (*horse*) mustang *m*

mustard ['mʌstəd] **N** *Bot, Culin* moutarde *f*; **French m.** ≃ moutarde de Dijon; *Am Fig Sl* **to cut the m.** se montrer à la hauteur

▸▸ **m. bath** bain *m* sinapisé; **m. and cress** moutarde blanche et cresson *m* alénois; **m. gas** gaz *m* moutarde, ypérite *f*; **m. plaster** sinapisme *m*; **m. pot** moutardier *m*, pot *m* à moutarde; **m. powder** farine *f* de moutarde; **m. seed** graine *f* de moutarde

muster ['mʌstər] **N** (*action of gathering*) rassemblement *m*; (*meeting*) assemblée *f*, réunion *f*; (*roll call*), *Naut etc* appel *m*; *Mil* contrôles *mpl*; *Fig* **to pass m.** passer, être passable, être acceptable

VT 1 (*supporters, funds*) rassembler; **society that musters a hundred members** association qui compte cent membres; **she mustered all her strength** elle a rassemblé toutes ses forces; **to m. one's courage** rassembler son courage, prendre son courage à deux mains; **we need all the help we can m.** nous avons besoin de toute l'aide que

---

nous pouvons trouver **2** *Naut* (*men*) faire l'appel de; (*crew*) assembler

VI s'assembler, se rassembler

▸▸ **m. roll** feuille *f* d'appel

▸ **muster up VT SEP** = **muster VT 1**

musty ['mʌstɪ] **ADJ** (*taste, smell*) de moisi; (*books, room*) qui sent le moisi; **to smell m.** sentir le moisi; (*of room etc*) sentir le renfermé

mutability [mju:tə'bɪlɪtɪ] **N** mutabilité *f*

mutable ['mju:təb(ə)l] **ADJ 1** variable, mutable **2** *Ling* sujet à mutation

mutant ['mju:tənt] **ADJ, N** mutant *m*

mutate [mju:'teɪt] **VI** subir une mutation; **to m. into sth** se transformer en qch
VT faire subir une mutation à

mutation [mju:'teɪʃən] **N** altération *f*, changement *m*; *Biol* mutation *f*; **m. of type** métatypie *f*

mute [mju:t] **ADJ 1** (*person, appeal etc*) muet, -ette; **she stood m. with wonder** elle restait muette d'étonnement **2** *Ling* muet, -ette; (*consonant*) sourd
N 1 (*dumb person*) muet, -ette **2** *Mus* sourdine *f*
VT 1 (*muffle*) amortir, étouffer, assourdir **2** *Mus* mettre une sourdine à, assourdir

muted ['mju:tɪd] **ADJ** (*sound, voice etc*) assourdi, sourd; (*colour*) sourd; (*protest, criticism etc*) voilé; *Mus* (*trumpet etc*) en sourdine; **to discuss in m. tones** discuter à voix basse

mutely ['mju:tlɪ] **ADV** silencieusement, en silence

mutilate ['mju:tɪleɪt] **VT** (*person*) mutiler, estropier; (*statue, play*) mutiler; *Fig* (*passage, quotation*) tronquer

mutilation [mju:tɪ'leɪʃən] **N** mutilation *f*

mutineer [mju:tɪ'nɪər] **N** mutiné *m*, mutin *m*

mutinous ['mju:tɪnəs] **ADJ** rebelle, mutiné, mutin; (*crew*) mutiné, insurgé

mutiny ['mju:tɪnɪ] **N** révolte *f*, mutinerie *f*
VI se révolter, se mutiner (**against** contre)

mutism ['mju:tɪz(ə)m] **N** mutisme *m*

mutt [mʌt] **N** *Fam* **1** (*dog*) clebs *m*, clébard *m* **2** (*idiot*) idiot, -ote, andouille *f*; **poor m.!** pauvre mec!

mutter ['mʌtər] **N** murmure *m*; **a m. of discontent** un murmure de mécontentement
VT marmonner, marmotter; (*say unclearly*) dire dans sa barbe; **a muttered protest** un marmottement de protestation; **he muttered something to himself** (*angrily*) il a murmuré quelque chose entre ses dents
VI marmonner, marmotter; (*speak unclearly*) parler dans sa barbe; (*complain*) murmurer

muttering ['mʌtərɪŋ] **N** marmottement *m*, grommellement *m*; **mutterings** (*complaints*) murmures *mpl* de mécontentement

mutton ['mʌt(ə)n] **N** *Culin* mouton *m*; **leg of m.** gigot *m*; **m. chop** *or* **cutlet** côtelette *f* de mouton; *Fam* **m.-chop whiskers** favoris *mpl* en côtelette; *Fig* **m. dressed as lamb** = femme *f* qui essaie de faire plus jeune que son âge

muttonchops ['mʌt(ə)ntʃɒps] **NPL** (*whiskers*) favoris *mpl* en côtelette

muttonhead ['mʌt(ə)nhed] **N** *Fam* andouille *f*, cornichon *m*

mutual ['mju:tʃʊəl] **ADJ 1** (*reciprocal*) (*feelings etc*) mutuel, réciproque; *Elec* (*attraction*) mutuel; **the feeling is m.** c'est réciproque **2** (*shared*) commun; **a m. friend** un ami commun

▸▸ *Fin* **m. benefit society** société *f* de secours mutuel; *Fin* **m. fund** fonds *m* commun de placement, FCP *m*; *Fin* **m. insurance** (assurance *f*) mutuelle *f*; *Fin* **m. insurance company** société de crédit mutuel, société de mutualité; *Fin* **m. investment fund** fonds commun de placement, FCP

mutually ['mjuːtʃʊəlɪ] **ADV** mutuellement, réciproquement; **to be m. exclusive** s'exclure l'un(e) l'autre

Muzak® ['mjuːzæk] **N** musiquette *f*

muzzle ['mʌz(ə)l] **N 1** *(mouth of animal)* museau *m* **2** *(device) (for dog etc)* muselière *f*; *(for horse)* bâillon *m* **3** *(of gun)* bouche *f*, gueule *f*
▸ **VT** *(dog)* museler; *Fig (press etc)* museler, bâillonner
▸▸ **m. velocity** vitesse *f* initiale

muzzle-loader **N** *Mil* pièce *f* se chargeant par la bouche

muzzy ['mʌzɪ] **ADJ** *Fam (ideas)* confus; *(outline, picture)* flou, estompé; **I feel m.** *(slightly unwell)* je me sens tout drôle; **my head feels a bit m.** j'ai la tête qui tourne; **she was m. about what it really meant** elle ne comprenait pas bien ce que tout cela signifiait

MV [em'viː] **1** *Elec (abbr* **megavolt(s)**) MV **2** *Naut (abbr* **motor vessel**) bateau *m* à moteur

MW [em'dʌb(ə)ljuː] **1** *Radio (abbr* **Medium Wave**) PO *fpl* **2** *Elec (abbr* **megawatt(s)**) MW

my [maɪ] **POSS ADJ** mon, ma, *pl* mes; *(in the f sing before a vowel sound)* mon; **my hat and gloves** mon chapeau et mes gants; **in my opinion** à mon avis; **one of my friends** un de mes amis, un ami à moi; **my own son** mon propre fils; **my hair is grey** j'ai les cheveux gris; **if you don't mind my asking** si je peux me permettre de vous le demander; **my idea would be to …** mon idée à moi serait de …; **my turn!** à moi! VOIR GRAMMAIRE A30; A43; B21

▸ **INT** *Fam* **my! how you've changed!** mon Dieu, comme vous avez changé!; **my! my! aren't we touchy!** oh là là! que vous êtes susceptible!; **(oh) my!** ça par exemple!

myalgic encephalomyelitis [maɪˈældʒɪ-

kensefələʊmaɪəˈlaɪtɪs] **N** *Med* encéphalomyélite *f* myalgique

mycology [maɪˈkɒlədʒɪ] **N** *Bot* mycologie *f*

myelin ['maɪəlɪn] **N** myéline *f*

myelitis [maɪəˈlaɪtɪs] **N** *Med* myélite *f*

myeloma [maɪəˈləʊmə] **N** *Med* myélome *m*

myna(h) ['maɪnə] **N** *Orn* mainate *m*
▸▸ **m. bird** mainate

myocardial [maɪəʊˈkɑːdɪəl] **N**
▸▸ *Med* **m. infarct, m. infarction** infarctus *m* du myocarde

myopia [maɪˈəʊpɪə] **N** myopie *f*; *Fig* manque *m* de perspicacité

myopic [maɪˈɒpɪk] **ADJ** *(person, eyes, look)* myope; *Fig* qui manque de perspicacité

myriad ['mɪrɪəd] **N** myriade *f*
▸ **ADJ** *Lit* innombrable

myriapod ['mɪrɪəpɒd] **ADJ, N** *Biol* myriapode *m*

myrmidon ['mɜːmɪd(ə)n] **N** *Pej Hum* homme *m* de main

myrrh [mɜːr] **N** myrrhe *f*

myrtle ['mɜːt(ə)l] **N** *(shrub)* myrte *m*; *Am (periwinkle)* pervenche *f* grimpante

myself [maɪˈself] **PERS PRON** VOIR GRAMMAIRE A29 **1** *(emphatic)* moi(-même); **I did it m.** je l'ai fait moi-même; *Fam* **I'm not quite m.** je ne suis pas dans mon assiette; **I m. believe that …** (quant à) moi *ou* pour ma part, je crois que … **2** *(reflexive)* me; *(before vowel sound)* m'; **I've hurt m.** je me suis fait mal; **I was enjoying m. very much** je m'amusais beaucoup SEE GRAMMAR B28–9 **3** *(after preposition)* **I live by m.** je vis tout seul; **I was laughing to m.** je riais tout seul; **I'll keep it for m.** je le garderai pour moi

mysterious [mɪsˈtɪərɪəs] **ADJ** mystérieux
N *(no pl)* **the m.** le mystérieux

mysteriously [mɪsˈtɪərɪəslɪ] **ADV** mystérieusement, de façon mystérieuse

mysteriousness [mɪsˈtɪərɪəsnɪs] **N** caractère *m* mystérieux, mystère *m* (**of** de)

mystery ['mɪstərɪ] **N 1** mystère *m*; **to make a m. of sth** faire (un) mystère de qch; **why make such a m. out of it?** pourquoi (faire) tant de mystères?; **it's a m. to me** pour moi, c'est un mystère; **there's no great m. about it** ça n'a rien de mystérieux; *(it's not a secret)* ce n'est un secret pour personne; **the key to the m.** la clef du mystère **2** *Theat (play)* mystère *m*
▸ **ADJ** *(guest, prize)* surprise; **m. man** mystérieux individu *m*; **who was the m. benefactor?** qui était le mystérieux bienfaiteur?
▸▸ **m. novel** roman *m* à énigmes; *Theat* **m. play** mystère; *Mktg* **m. shopper** client, -ente mystère; *Mktg* **m. shopping** pseudo-achat *m*; **m. tour** = excursion *f* dont la destination est inconnue des participants

mystic ['mɪstɪk] **ADJ** *Rel* mystique; *(rites, arts)* ésotérique; *(power)* occulte
N mystique *mf*

mystical ['mɪstɪk(ə)l] **ADJ** mystique

mysticism ['mɪstɪsɪz(ə)m] **N** mysticisme *m*

mystification [mɪstɪfɪˈkeɪʃən] **N** *(action, result)* mystification *f*; **to our (great) m.** à notre grande perplexité

mystify ['mɪstɪfaɪ] **VT** *(bewilder) (person)* laisser perplexe, déconcerter; **mystified by …** intrigué par …; **I was mystified** j'étais perplexe

> Note that the French verb **mystifier** is a false friend. It means **to fool, to take in**.

mystique [mɪsˈtiːk] **N** mystique *f*

myth [mɪθ] **N** mythe *m*

mythical ['mɪθɪk(ə)l] **ADJ** mythique

mythological [mɪθəˈlɒdʒɪk(ə)l] **ADJ** mythologique

mythology [mɪˈθɒlədʒɪ] **N** mythologie *f*

myxomatosis [mɪksəməˈtəʊsɪs] **N** myxomatose *f*

N¹, n [en] N (*letter*) N, n *m*; **two n's** deux n

N² 1 (*abbr* **North**) N **2** *Phys* (*abbr* **Newton**) N

n/a, N/A *Admin abbr* **not applicable**

NAACP [eneɪeɪsiː'piː] N *Am* (*abbr* **National Association for the Advancement of Colored People**) = association *f* nationale pour la promotion des personnes de couleur

NAAFI ['næfɪ] N *Br Mil* (*abbr* **Navy, Army and Air Force Institutes**) (*organization, canteen, shop*) = coopérative *f* militaire

nab [næb] VT (**-bb-**) *Sl* **1** (*steal*) faucher **2** (*catch doing sth, arrest*) pincer, choper; **to get nabbed** se faire pincer *ou* choper

nabob ['neɪbɒb] N nabab *m*

nacelle [næ'sel] N **1** (*of aircraft*) carlingue *f*, habitacle *m*; (**engine**) **n.** fuseau-moteur *m*, *pl* fuseaux-moteur **2** (*of airship, balloon*) nacelle *f*

nacre ['neɪkər] N nacre *f*

nadir ['neɪdɪər] N nadir *m*; *Fig* point *m* le plus bas

nads [nædz] NPL *Br Sl* (*testicles*) couilles *fpl*

naevus, *Am* **nevus,** *pl* **naevi** ['niːvəs, -aɪ] N *Med* nævus *m*, *pl* nævi

naff [næf] ADJ *Br Sl* **1** (*tasteless*) ringard **2** (*stupid*) nul, *f* nulle; **it was pretty n. of me to do that** j'ai été carrément nul d'avoir fait ça **3** **n. all** que dalle; **I've got n. all money** j'ai que dalle comme argent

▸ **naff off** VI *Br Sl* **n. off!** (*go away*) casse-toi!; (*expressing contempt, disagreement*) va te faire voir!

naffing ['næfɪŋ] *Br Sl* ADJ (*for emphasis*) foutu, sacré; **shut your n. mouth!** ferme-la!, ferme ton clapet!

ADV (*for emphasis*) vachement; **you're so n. stupid!** t'es vraiment débile!

NAFTA ['næftə] N (*abbr* **North American Free Trade Agreement**) ALENA *m*

nag¹ [næg] N *Fam* (*horse*) bidet *m*, bourrin *m*

nag² N (*person*) enquiquineur, -euse; (*woman also*) chipie *f*; **she's a terrible n.** elle n'arrête pas de nous/le/*etc* harceler

VI (**-gg-**) **he's always nagging** il n'arrête pas de me/te/*etc* casser les pieds *ou* harceler

VT (*person*) casser les pieds à, harceler; (*of doubt*) harceler; (*of conscience*) ne pas laisser en paix, tourmenter; **she's always nagging (at) him to get it fixed** elle n'arrête pas de lui casser les pieds *ou Fam* de l'asticoter pour qu'il le fasse réparer; **he nags her to death** il la harcèle sans pitié; **why do I always have to n. you into doing everything?** pourquoi faut-il que je sois toujours après toi pour que tu fasses quoi que ce soit?

▸ **nag at** VT INSEP = **nag²** VT; **her conscience was nagging at her to go to the police** sa conscience l'exhortait sans répit à se rendre à la police

nagger ['nægər] N = **nag²**

nagging ['nægɪŋ] ADJ (*pain*) tenace; (*worry, fear, uncertainty*) tenace, qui persiste; **I've got a n. doubt that …** je n'arrête pas de me demander si …; **I've still got this n. doubt about him** je n'arrête pas de me poser des questions à son sujet; **I've got this n. feeling that …** j'ai cette impression persistante que …; **he has a n. wife** sa femme est une enquiquineuse

N harcèlement *m*; **I've had enough of your n.!** j'en ai assez que tu me harcèles *ou Fam* m'enquiquines!

naiad, *pl* **naiads, naiades** ['naɪæd, -ædz, -ədiːz] N *Myth* naïade *f*

nail [neɪl] N **1** (*for fixing*) clou *m*; *Fig* **another n. in sb's coffin/the coffin of sth** un autre coup funeste à qn/qch; *Fig Fam* **to hit the n. (right) on the head** mettre le doigt dessus **2** (*on finger, toe*) ongle *m*

3 *Fam* **to pay on the n.** payer rubis sur l'ongle; **she demanded cash on the n.** elle a exigé qu'on la paie en argent comptant

VT **1** clouer (**onto** à); **to n. sth shut** clouer qch; **she nailed the plank into place** elle a fixé la planche à l'aide de clous; *Fig* **he stood nailed to the spot** il est resté cloué au sol (**in fear/astonishment** de peur/surprise)

2 (*shoes, door etc*) clouter

3 *Fam* (*catch*) (*person*) attraper, coincer; *Fam* **to n. a lie** exposer un mensonge; **we should n. the lie that unemployment is falling** nous devrions démontrer que la soi-disant baisse du chômage n'est qu'un tissu de mensonges

▸ ▸ **n. bar** salon *m* de manucure; **n. bomb** bombe *f* à fragmentation (*bourrée de clous*); *Am* **n. enamel** vernis *m* à ongles; **n. polish** vernis *m* à ongles; **n. punch** chasse-clou *m*, *pl* chasse-clous; **n. scissors** ciseaux *mpl* à ongles; *Tech* **n. set** chasse-clou *m*, *pl* chasse-clous, chasse-pointe *m*, *pl* chasse-pointes; **n. varnish** vernis à ongles

▸ **nail down** VT SEP **1** (*fasten*) (*lid of a box*) clouer; (*furniture*) fixer à l'aide de clous; *Fig Fam* **you'd better n. that table down or it'll walk** tu ferais bien de cadenasser cette table au sol sinon elle va disparaître **2** *Fam* **we couldn't n. him down to anything definite** nous n'avons pu obtenir aucun engagement précis de sa part; **to n. sb down on a date** obtenir de qn qu'il fixe une date

▸ **nail up** VT SEP (*crate, box*) clouer; (*door, window*) condamner

nail-biter N **1** (*person*) personne *f* qui se ronge les ongles **2** *Fam* (*situation*) situation *f* au suspense insoutenable

nail-biting ADJ *Fam* (*finish, excitement etc*) palpitant; (*film, story*) à suspense

N habitude *f* de se ronger les ongles

nailbrush ['neɪlbrʌʃ] N brosse *f* à ongles

nailfile ['neɪlfaɪl] N lime *f* à ongles

naïve, naive [naɪ'iːv] ADJ (*person, manner etc*) naïf, -ïve; (*ingenuous*) ingénu

▸ ▸ *Art* **n. art** l'art *m* naïf

naïvely, naively [naɪ'iːvlɪ] ADV naïvement

naïveté, naivety [naɪ'iːvtɪ] N naïveté *f*

naked ['neɪkɪd] ADJ **1** (*person*) nu, *Fam* à poil; (*arm, back etc*) découvert, nu; (*wall etc*) nu, dégarni; (*countryside, tree*) dénudé, nu; *Biol* (*stalk, tail etc*) nu; **stark n.** tout nu, *Fam* nu comme un ver; **to strip (oneself) n.** se mettre nu *ou Fam* à poil **2** *Fig* (*sword, flame, lightbulb*) nu; (*aggression, exploitation*) (*not concealed*) non dissimulé; (*outright*) flagrant; **n. facts** faits bruts; **visible to the n. eye** visible à l'œil nu; **the n. truth** la pure vérité, la vérité toute nue

▸ ▸ *Bot* **n. lady** colchique *m* d'automne; *St Exch* **n. option** option *f* d'achat vendue à découvert; **n. sale** vente *f* nue

nakedness ['neɪkɪdnɪs] N nudité *f*

NALGO ['nælgəʊ] N *Br Formerly* (*abbr* **National and Local Government Officers' Association**) = association *f* des fonctionnaires nationaux et régionaux

Nam [nɑːm] N *Am Fam* (*Vietnam*) le Viêt-Nam

namby-pamby ['næmbɪ'pæmbɪ] N (*ineffectual person*) mollasson, -onne

ADJ (*spineless*) (*person*) ramolli, gnangnan *inv*; gnian-gnian *inv*; (*remark, attitude*) faiblard

NAME [neɪm] N **1** (*of person, object, plant etc*) nom *m*; (*of ship*) devise *f*, nom; *Com* (*of company, business*) raison *f* sociale; (*of account*) intitulé *m*; (*of play, novel etc*) titre *m*; **full n.** nom et prénoms *mpl*; **what's your n.?** quel est votre nom?, comment vous appelez-vous?; **my n. is …** je m'appelle …; **a man by the n. of Blenkinsop** un nommé Blenkinsop; **to go by** *or* **under the n. of …** être connu sous le nom de …; **he answers to his n.** (*of dog etc*) il répond quand on l'appelle; **to know sb by n.** connaître qn de nom; **to know sb by another** *or* **a different n.** connaître qn sous un autre nom; **to mention sb/ sth by n.** nommer qn/qch; **you were mentioned by n.** on a cité votre nom, on vous a nommé; **to put a n. to sth** donner un nom à qch, mettre un nom sur qch; **to put a n. to a face** mettre un nom sur un visage; **to take sb's n.** (*of police etc*) prendre le nom de qn; *Ftbl* donner un carton jaune à qn; *Ftbl* **to have one's n. taken** recevoir un carton jaune; **he took his idol's n.** il a pris le nom de son idole; **I'm sorry, I didn't catch** *or* **get your n.** désolé, je n'ai pas bien entendu votre nom; **what n. shall I say?** (*to caller*) qui dois-je annoncer?; **famous n.** (*person*) célébrité *f*; **Pentagon is a huge n. in the publishing business** Pentagon est une entreprise très importante dans le monde de l'édition; **a big n. in the theatre** un nom bien connu dans le monde du théâtre; **to send in one's n.** (*for competition etc*) se faire inscrire; (*have oneself announced*) se faire annoncer; **to put one's n. down** (*in election*) poser sa candidature; (*on list*) s'inscrire (**for sth** pour qch);

list of names liste nominative; **in the n. of ...** au nom de ...; **in the n. of the law/the king** au nom de la loi/du roi; **in the n. of God** or **Heaven, in God's** or **Heaven's n.** pour l'amour de Dieu; *Fam* **what in the n. of God** or **Heaven** or **goodness are you doing?** que diable faites-vous là?; **to be master/prime minister in n. only** n'être maître/premier ministre que de nom; **they are married in n. only** *(marriage hasn't been consummated)* leur mariage est un mariage blanc; *(without love)* ils ne sont mariés que pour la forme; **the PSF is a socialist party in n. only** le PSF n'a de socialiste que le nom; **she was President in all but n.** elle avait tout du Président sauf le nom; **they are married in all but n.** c'est comme s'ils étaient mariés; **to call sb names** insulter qn; **she called me a rude n.** elle m'a insulté; **that's the n. of the game** c'est ce qui compte; **not to have a penny/a decent pair of shoes to one's n.** ne pas avoir un centime/une paire de chaussures convenable à soi; **to have several books to one's n.** être l'auteur de plusieurs livres; **to have several victories/trophies to one's n.** avoir remporté plusieurs victoires/trophées **2** *(reputation)* réputation *f*, renommée *f*; **she has a good/bad n.** elle a (une) bonne/(une) mauvaise réputation; **to get a bad n.** se faire une mauvaise réputation; **she has a n. for honesty** elle est connue *ou* réputée pour son honnêteté; **the firm has established a n. for quality** l'entreprise s'est bâtie une réputation de qualité; **to have a n. for prompt and efficient service** être réputé pour ses services rapides et efficaces; **to make a n. for oneself** se faire un nom *ou* une réputation **(as** de)

VT 1 *(give name to)* *(person, thing)* nommer, donner un nom à; *(ship)* baptiser; **he was named Peter** on lui a donné le nom de Peter, on l'a appelé *ou* nommé Peter; **someone named Thompson** un nommé Thompson; **to n. sb after sb** or *Am* **for sb** donner à qn le nom de qn; **they named her Cathy after the heroine of Wuthering Heights** ils l'ont appelée Cathy, comme l'héroïne des Hauts du Hurlevent **2** *(appoint)* nommer; **he was named (as) President** il a été nommé président; **she was named (as) best supporting actress** elle a été élue pour le meilleur second rôle féminin **3** *(designate, identify by name)* désigner (par son nom); *(example, fact)* citer; *(reveal name of)* révéler le nom de, nommer; **n. the kings of England/these species of birds** donnez les noms des rois d'Angleterre/de ces espèces d'oiseaux; *Law* **to n. sb as a beneficiary** *(in one's will etc)* désigner qn comme bénéficiaire; *Law* **to n. sb as a witness** citer qn comme témoin; *Br Parl* **to n. a member** *(of the Speaker, in House of Commons)* signaler à la Chambre l'indiscipline d'un membre; **to n. names** donner des noms; **naming no names** sans nommer personne; **to n. and shame** dénoncer publiquement les responsables; *Fam* **you n. it, she's done it/got it** tout ce qu'on peut imaginer, elle l'a fait/le possède **4** *(set)* *(day, amount)* fixer; **n. your price** donnez-moi un prix

▸▸ **Com n. brand** marque *f*; **n. day** *(of person)* fête *f*; *St Exch* deuxième jour *m* de liquidation; **n. label** étiquette *f* de nom; *Mktg* **n. licensing** cession *f* de licence de nom; *Br Cin, Theat* **n. part** vrai rôle *m*; *(title role)* = rôle qui donne son titre à la pièce ou au film; *Com* **n. product** marque

---

name-calling N insultes *fpl*

named [ˈneɪmd] ADJ nommé; **on the n. day** le jour fixé

---

name-dropper N **she's a terrible n.** elle ne manque jamais de glisser des noms de personnalités (supposées connues d'elle) dans la conversation

name-dropping N **there was a lot of n. in his speech** il n'a pas arrêté de glisser des noms de personnalités (supposées connues de lui) dans son discours

nameless [ˈneɪmlɪs] ADJ **1** *(unknown)* *(person)* inconnu, obscur; *(anonymous)* *(writer, grave etc)* anonyme; **someone who shall be** or **remain n.** quelqu'un dont je tairai le nom **2** *(dread, grief etc)* indéfinissable, indicible, inexprimable; *(vice etc)* abominable

namely [ˈneɪmlɪ] ADV c'est-à-dire, à savoir

nameplate [ˈneɪmpleɪt] N écusson *m*, médaillon *m* *(portant un nom)*; *(on door etc)* plaque *f*, **manufacturer's n.** *(on machine etc)* plaque du constructeur

namesake [ˈneɪmseɪk] N homonyme *mf*; **my famous n.** la célébrité qui porte le même nom que moi

nametape [ˈneɪmteɪp] N marque *f* à linge

Namibia [nəˈmɪbɪə] N Namibie *f*

Namibian [nəˈmɪbɪən] N Namibien, -ienne ADJ namibien

naming [ˈneɪmɪŋ] N **1** *(giving name)* attribution *f* d'un nom; *(of ship)* baptême *m*; **n. of a product** attribution *f* d'un nom à un produit **2** *(choosing)* *(of official)* nomination *f* **3** *(fixing)* *(of day, amount)* fixation *f*

nan[1], **nana** [ˈnæn, ˈnænə] N *Fam (grandmother)* mamie *f*, grand-maman *f*, mémé *f*

nan[2] [nɑːn] N *Culin* pain *m* nan ▸▸ **n. bread** pain nan

nancy [ˈnænsɪ] *Old-fashioned Pej Sl* N *(effeminate man)* homme *m* efféminé, chochotte *f*; *(homosexual)* tapette *f* ADJ *(behaviour, ways etc)* de chochotte, de tapette ▸▸ **n. boy** *(effeminate man)* homme efféminé, chochotte; *(homosexual)* tapette

nandrolone [ˈnændrɪləʊn] N *Pharm* nandrolone *f*

nanny [ˈnænɪ] N **1** *(nursemaid)* bonne *f* d'enfant, nurse *f*, *(in children's language)* nounou *f* **2** *Fam (grandmother)* mamie *f*, mémé *f* **3** *(goat)* chèvre *f*, *Fam* biquette *f* ▸▸ **n. goat** chèvre, *Fam* biquette; **the n. state** l'État *m* paternaliste

nanoengineering [nænəʊendʒɪˈnɪərɪŋ] N nano-ingénierie *f*

nanosecond [ˈnænəʊsekənd] N nanoseconde *f*

nanotechnology [ˈnænəʊˈteknɒlədʒɪ] N nanotechnologie *f*

nap[1] [næp] N *(sleep)* petit somme *m*; **afternoon n.** sieste *f*; **to take** or **have a n.** faire un petit somme; *(after lunch)* faire la sieste VI (-pp-) faire un petit somme; *(doze)* sommeiller; *Fig* **to be caught napping** *(off guard)* être pris au dépourvu

nap[2] *Tex* N *(of cloth, velvet, felt)* poil *m*; **cloth with raised n.** étoffe molletonnée *ou* tirée à poil *ou* garnie; **against the n.** à rebrousse-poil, à rebours VT *(cloth)* garnir, gratter, lainer; *(wool, cotton)* molletonner

nap[3] N *Cards* **to go n.** demander les cinq levées; *Old-fashioned Fig* **to go n. on sth** être sûr et certain de qch; *Old-fashioned Fig* **to hold a n. hand** avoir en main toutes les cartes pour réussir **2** *Horseracing* tuyau *m* sûr VT *Horseracing Fam* **to n. a winner** donner un tuyau sûr

napalm [ˈneɪpɑːm] N napalm *m* VT bombarder au napalm ▸▸ **n. bomb** bombe *f* au napalm

nape [neɪp] N **n. (of the neck)** nuque *f*

---

naphtha [ˈnæfθə] N *Ind* naphte *m*

naphthalene [ˈnæfθəliːn] N *Chem, Com* naphtaline *f*, naphtalène *m*

napkin [ˈnæpkɪn] N **1** *(table)* n. serviette *f* (de table) **2** *Br Fml (baby's)* n. couche *f* (de bébé) **3** *Am (sanitary)* n. serviette *f* hygiénique ▸▸ **n. ring** rond *m* de serviette

Napoleon [nəˈpəʊlɪən] N Napoléon *m*

Napoleonic [nəpəʊlɪˈɒnɪk] ADJ napoléonien

nappy [ˈnæpɪ] N *Br* couche *f* (pour bébé) ▸▸ **n. rash** érythème *m* fessier

narc [nɑːk] N *Am Sl* = agent *m* de la brigade des stups

narcissism [ˈnɑːsɪsɪz(ə)m] N narcissisme *m*

narcissistic [nɑːsɪˈsɪstɪk] ADJ narcissique

narcissus [nɑːˈsɪsəs], *pl* **narcissi, narcissuses** [nɑːˈsɪsaɪ, -ˈsɪsəsɪz] N *(plant)* narcisse *m*

narcosis [nɑːˈkəʊsɪs] N *Med* narcose *f*

narcotic [nɑːˈkɒtɪk] ADJ narcotique, stupéfiant N narcotique *m*, stupéfiant *m*; *Am* **narcotics agent** agent *m* de la brigade des stupéfiants; *Am* **narcotics (branch)** *(of police force)* brigade *f* des stupéfiants

nark[1] [nɑːk] *Sl* N *(informer)* indic *m*, mouchard *m* VI *(inform)* moucharder; **to n. on sb** balancer qn

nark[2] VT *Br Fam (annoy)* taper sur les nerfs de, énerver; **to get narked** s'énerver, s'exciter; **she's really narked about it** ça s'énerve vraiment

narky [ˈnɑːkɪ] ADJ *Br Fam* de mauvais poil; **to get n.** se mettre en pétard

narrate [nəˈreɪt] VT *(of person)* raconter, relater, narrer; *(of story, book)* raconter, relater; *TV, Cin (film, documentary)* lire *ou* dire le commentaire de; *Radio (play)* narrer

narration [nəˈreɪʃən] N **1** *(of story etc)* narration *f*, *TV, Cin (of film, documentary)* (lecture *f* du) commentaire *m*; *Radio (of play)* narration **2** *(account)* récit *m*, narration *f*

narrative [ˈnærətɪv] N **1** *(story)* récit *m*; *Liter* **the n.** la narration **2** *(art)* (l'art *m* de) la narration ADJ *(style, poem)* narratif ▸▸ **n. writer** narrateur, -trice

narrator [nəˈreɪtər] N narrateur, -trice; *Mus* récitant, -ante

narrow [ˈnærəʊ] ADJ *(path etc)* étroit; *(body, waist, face)* mince; *(valley etc)* resserré; *(passage, channel)* étranglé; *Ling (vowel)* tendu; *(mind)* étroit, borné; *(existence)* limité, circonscrit; **to grow** or **become n.** se rétrécir; **to have n. shoulders** ne pas être large d'épaules, avoir des épaules étroites; **within n. bounds** dans des limites étroites; **to have a n. escape** or *Fam* **squeak** l'échapper belle; **n. bodied aircraft** avion *m* petit porteur; **a n. interpretation** *(of rules etc)* une interprétation au pied de la lettre; **a n. majority** une faible majorité; **by a n. margin** *(to win, lose)* de peu; **they won by the n. margin of two points** ils ont gagné de deux petits points; **to win/lose by the narrowest of margins** gagner/perdre de très peu; **in the narrowest sense** dans le sens le plus strict; **to suffer a n. defeat** être vaincu de peu; **it was another n. victory for the French side** l'équipe française l'a encore emporté de justesse; **to take a n. view of sth** adopter un point de vue étroit sur qch

NPL **narrows** *(of river)* étranglement *m* VT *(road etc)* resserrer, rétrécir; *(space, choice, possibilities, chances)* restreindre, limiter; *(gap)* réduire, resserrer; *(ideas)* rétrécir; **to n. a margin of victory/defeat** réduire l'ampleur d'une victoire/défaite; **narrowed eyes** paupières mi-closes

VI *(of road, path)* devenir plus étroit, se rétrécir; **the gap between rich and poor has narrowed** l'écart entre les riches et les pauvres s'est resserré

▸▸ *Rail* **n. gauge** voie *f* étroite; *St Exch* **n. market** marché *m* étroit; *Fin* **n. money** = ensemble *m* des billets et pièces de monnaie en circulation

▸ **narrow down VT SEP** *(limit)* limiter; *(possibilities)* restreindre, réduire; *(candidates)* réduire le nombre de; **that narrows it down to two suspects** cela nous laisse avec *ou* nous ramène à deux suspects

narrow-boat N péniche *f*

narrowcast ['nærəʊkɑːst] *Radio, TV* **VT** diffuser localement
VI = diffuser des émissions destinées à un public spécialisé

narrowing ['nærəʊɪŋ] N *Med (of artery etc)* rétrécissement *m*

narrowly ['nærəʊlɪ] **ADV 1** *(to interpret)* étroitement, strictement, au pied de la lettre **2** *(only just)* de peu; **he n. missed being run over** il a failli se faire écraser; **they n. escaped being caught** ils ont failli se faire prendre; **the missile just n. missed them** le missile les a ratés de peu

narrow-minded **ADJ** *(person)* (d'un esprit) borné, à l'esprit étroit; *(views, opinions)* borné; *(approach, outlook)* étroit, limité; **to be n. about politics/sex** être borné en ce qui concerne la politique/le sexe

narrow-mindedness [-maɪndɪdnɪs] N *(of person)* étroitesse *f ou* petitesse *f* d'esprit; *(of views, outlook)* caractère *m* borné

narrowness ['nærəʊnɪs] N *(of path, shoulders, passage etc)* étroitesse *f*, *(of sb's waist)* minceur *f*, *(of space etc)* petitesse *f*, exiguïté *f*; *(of gap, difference)* caractère *m* limité; *(of existence, intelligence etc)* limitations *fpl*; **n. of mind** étroitesse d'esprit

narw(h)al, narwhale ['nɑːwəl] N narval *m*, *pl* narvals

NASA ['næsə] N *Astronaut (abbr* **National Aeronautics and Space Administration**) NASA *f*

nasal ['neɪz(ə)l] **ADJ** *Anat, Ling etc* nasal, -aux; **the n. cavities** les fosses *fpl* nasales; **to have a n. voice** parler du nez
N *Ling* nasale *f*

nasalize ['neɪzəlaɪz] **VT** *(syllable etc)* nasaliser

nasally ['neɪzəlɪ] **ADV** par le nez; **to speak n.** parler du nez, nasiller

nascent ['neɪsənt, 'næs-] **ADJ** *Fml (talent, discontent, suspicion etc)* naissant; *Chem (body, element)* à l'état naissant

NASDAQ® ['næzdæk] N *St Exch (abbr* **National Association of Securities Dealers Automated Quotation**) Nasdaq *m* *(Bourse américaine des valeurs technologiques)*

nastily ['nɑːstɪlɪ] **ADV 1** *(unpleasantly)* désagréablement **2** *(maliciously)* méchamment **3** *(indecently)* indécemment

nastiness ['nɑːstɪnɪs] N **1** *(of smell, taste)* caractère *m* désagréable; *(of surroundings, building)* caractère *m* répugnant; **the n. of the weather** le mauvais temps **2** *(of person)* méchanceté *f*, *(of remark)* méchanceté, malveillance *f*, **the n. of his behaviour** son comportement malveillant **3** *(of book, film etc)* ignominie *f*, bassesse *f*, *(of crime, rape)* atrocité *f*, abjection *f*

nasturtium [nə'stɜː∫(ə)m] N *(plant)* capucine *f*

nasty ['nɑːstɪ] **ADJ 1** *(unpleasant, bad)* désagréable; **his behaviour left (me with) a n. taste in the mouth** sa conduite m'a laissé un arrière-goût désagréable; **to give sb a n. fright** faire une sale peur à qn; **he had a n. surprise** il a eu une mauvaise surprise; **n. corner** tournant dangereux; **n. accident** ac-

cident *m* grave; **n. cold/rash** méchant(e) rhume/éruption; **it gave her a n. shock** ça lui a donné un sale coup; **n. wound** vilaine blessure; **she's had a n. attack of bronchitis** elle a fait une mauvaise bronchite; **he's had quite a n. blow to the head** il a pris un mauvais coup sur la tête; **n. weather** sale *ou* mauvais temps; **the weather turned n.** le temps s'est dégradé

2 *(malicious) (person)* méchant, mauvais, déplaisant, *Fam* rosse; **to turn n.** devenir méchant; **to be n. to sb** être méchant envers qn; **that was a really n. thing to do** c'est vraiment méchant d'avoir fait ça; **n. trick** vilain tour, *Fam* sale tour; **what a n. little mind you've got!** que tu es méchant *ou* horrible!; *Fam* **he's a n. piece of work** c'est un sale individu *ou* un sale type

3 *(indecent) (book, film etc)* ignoble; *(crime, rape)* ignoble, atroce; **n. word** vilain mot

4 *Am Fam (excellent)* super, génial, -aux; **she makes a n. pizza** elle fait super bien la pizza

natal ['neɪt(ə)l] **ADJ** natal, -als, de naissance

natality [nə'tælɪtɪ] N *esp Am (birth rate)* natalité *f*

natch [næt∫] **INT** *Fam* sûr

nation ['neɪ∫ən] N **1** *(state)* nation *f*, *Pol* **United Nations (Organization)** (Organisation *f* des) Nations *fpl* Unies **2** *(people)* pays *m*; **the whole n. rose in arms** tout le pays se souleva; **the Prime Minister addressed the n.** le Premier Ministre s'est adressé à la nation; **to serve the n.** servir l'État

national ['næʃən(ə)l] **ADJ** national, -aux; *(custom)* du pays; *Journ* **the n. dailies** les quotidiens nationaux
N **1** ressortissant, -ante (d'un pays); **a French n.** un(e) Français(e); **foreign nationals** ressortissants de pays étrangers **2** *(newspaper)* journal *m ou* quotidien *m* national

▸▸ **n. anthem** hymne *m* national; *Br* **the N. Audit Office** ≃ la Cour des comptes; *Tel* **n. call** appel *m* national; *Fin* **n. debt** dette *f* publique, dette de l'État; *Econ* **n. demand** demande *f* intérieure; **n. grid** *Br Elec* réseau *m* national d'électricité; *Geog* réseau; *Br* **N. Health Service** ≃ Sécurité *f* sociale; **to get treatment on the N. Health (Service)** se faire soigner sous le régime de la Sécurité sociale; *Horseracing* **n. hunt** courses *fpl* d'obstacles; *Br* **N. Insurance** = système *m* britannique de sécurité sociale (maladie, retraite) et d'assurance chômage; **n. insurance contributions** cotisations *fpl* à la Sécurité sociale; **n. interest** intérêt *m* national; **N. Missile Defence** projet *m* NMD *(programme de défense antimissiles américain)*; **n. newspaper** journal à diffusion nationale; **n. park** parc *m* national; *Fin* **n. product** produit *m* national; **n. readership survey** étude *f* nationale sur le lectorat; **n. scenic area** = zone *f* protégée pour la beauté de son paysage; *Br* **n. service** service *m* militaire; *Econ* **n. treatment** traitement *m* national; *Br* **the N. Trust** = organisme *m* non gouvernemental britannique assurant la conservation de certains paysages et monuments historiques

---

National Health Service

Le National Health Service ou NHS fut créé par le gouvernement travailliste en 1948, donnant accès à chacun aux soins médicaux gratuits. Cependant, suite notamment aux coupes budgétaires réalisées dans les années 80, le système de santé britannique est aujourd'hui en crise. Au cours des dernières années, la polémique autour du National Health Service s'est intensifiée et est devenue un enjeu majeur lors des élections en Grande-Bretagne.

---

nationalism ['næʃənəlɪz(ə)m] N nationalisme *m*

nationalist ['næʃənəlɪst] N nationaliste *mf*
ADJ nationaliste; **N. China** la Chine nationaliste

nationalistic [næʃənə'lɪstɪk] **ADJ** nationaliste

nationality [næʃə'nælɪtɪ] N nationalité *f*, **what n. are you?** de quelle nationalité êtes-vous?, quelle est votre nationalité?; **to take** *or* **adopt British n.** prendre la nationalité britannique VOIR GRAMMAIRE A18–19; B11–12

nationalization [næʃənəlaɪ'zeɪʃən] N **1** *(of industry etc)* nationalisation *f* **2** *(of foreigner)* naturalisation *f*

nationalize ['næʃənəlaɪz] **VT 1** *(industry etc)* nationaliser **2** *(foreigner)* naturaliser

nationalized ['næʃənəlaɪzd] **ADJ** *(industry etc)* nationalisé

nationally ['næʃənəlɪ] **ADV** nationalement; **to be n. renowned** avoir une renommée nationale

nation-state N *Pol* état-nation *m*, *pl* états-nations

nationwide ['neɪʃənwaɪd] **ADJ** *(opinion)* répandu dans tout le pays; *(campaign, survey)* au niveau national
ADV *(to advertise etc)* au niveau national; *(to be known)* dans tout le pays

native ['neɪtɪv] N **1** *(person) (of country, town)* originaire *mf*, *(in colonial sense)* indigène *mf*, **she was a n. of Scotland** elle était originaire d'Écosse; **n. of Australia** Australien, -ienne de naissance; **she speaks English like a n.** elle parle anglais comme une Anglaise; **to go n.** adopter la manière de vivre des habitants, *Hum* adopter les mœurs des indigènes **2** *(plant, animal)* indigène *mf*, **the koala is a n. of Australia** le koala est originaire d'Australie
ADJ 1 *(country etc)* natal, -als, de naissance; **he returned to his n. London** il est revenu à Londres, sa ville natale **2** *(plant, inhabitant etc)* indigène (**to** de, à) **3** *(qualities etc)* naturel, inné **4** *(metals, minerals)* (à l'état) natif

▸▸ **N. American** Indien, -ienne d'Amérique, Amérindien, -ienne; **n. costume** costume *m* national; **n. labour** main d'œuvre *f* indigène; **n. land** pays *m* natal; **n. language** langue *f* maternelle; *Ling* **n. speaker** locuteur, -trice natif(ive); **n. wit** esprit *m* naturel

native-born **ADJ** indigène, natif; **a n. German** un(e) Allemand(e) de naissance

nativism ['neɪtɪvɪz(ə)m] N *esp Am Pol* exclusivisme *m* en faveur des autochtones

nativist ['neɪtɪvɪst] *esp Am Pol* N = partisan *m* de l'exclusivisme en faveur des autochtones
ADJ qui favorise les autochtones

Nativity [nə'tɪvɪtɪ] N *Rel* nativité *f*, **the (festival of the) N.** la Nativité

▸▸ **N. play** = pièce *f* jouée par des enfants et représentant l'histoire de la Nativité; **N. scene** crèche *f*, *Art* nativité

Nato, NATO ['neɪtəʊ] N *(abbr* **North Atlantic Treaty Organisation**) OTAN *f*

▸▸ **N. forces** les forces *fpl* de l'Otan

natter ['nætər] *esp Br Fam* N causerie *f*, causette *f*, **to have a n.** bavarder, jacter
VI bavarder, jacter; **what were you two nattering about?** de quoi étiez-vous en train de bavarder, tous les deux?

natty ['nætɪ] **ADJ** *Fam* **1** *(person, dress etc)* chic *inv* **2** *(gadget etc)* astucieux

natural ['nætʃərəl] **ADJ 1** *(colour, taste)* naturel; **the n. world** le monde physique; **the n. order (of things)** l'ordre *m* des choses; **death from n. causes** mort *f* naturelle; **a n. blonde** une vraie blonde; **in the n. state** à l'état naturel *ou* primitif; **for the rest of one's n. life**

or Fam **one's n.** pour le reste de sa vie; **n. gift** *or* **talent (for sth/doing sth)** don *m* naturel (pour qch/faire qch); **and that brings us to a n. break** et ceci nous amène tout naturellement à une pause; **n. rate of unemployment** taux *m* de chômage naturel **2** *(normal, to be expected)* naturel, normal, -aux; **it is n. for a woman to ...** il est dans *ou* de la nature de la femme de ...; **it's n. (enough) (that) ...** il est (bien) naturel que ... + *sub*; **it's only n. that ...** il est *ou* c'est tout à fait normal que ... + *sub*; **as is (only) n.** comme de raison; **n. consequence** conséquence *f* naturelle; **n. inclination** penchant *m* naturel, inclination *f* naturelle; **my n. inclination would be to ...** j'inclinerais naturellement à ...; **one's** *or* **the n. reaction is to ...** la réaction instinctive est de ...; **I'm sure there's a perfectly n. explanation for it** je suis sûr qu'on peut l'expliquer de façon tout à fait naturelle; **to be a n. dancer/orator/leader** être un danseur/orateur/dirigeant né **3** *(unaffected)* naturel; **be** *or* **act n.!** soyez naturel!; **that'll look more n.** ça fera plus naturel **4** *Arch (illegitimate) (child)* naturel

N 1 as an actor, he's a n. c'est un acteur né; **she's a n. for the part** elle est faite pour ce rôle **2** *Mus (note)* (note *f*) naturelle *f*, *(sign)* bécarre *m*
▸▸ **n. childbirth** accouchement *m* naturel; **n. disaster** catastrophe *f* naturelle; *Phys, Elec* **n. frequency** fréquence *f* propre; **n. gas** gaz *m* naturel; **n. history** histoire *f* naturelle; **n. justice** droits *mpl* naturels; **n. language** langage *m* naturel, langue *f* naturelle; **n. law** loi *f* naturelle; **n. medicine** médecine *f* douce *ou* naturelle, phytothérapie *f*, *Econ* **n. monopoly** monopole *m* naturel; **n. mother** mère *f* naturelle; *Mus* **n. note** (note) naturelle; *Phys Old-fashioned* **n. philosophy** physique *f*, **n. resources** ressources *fpl* naturelles; *Mus* **n. scale** gamme *f* naturelle; **n. sciences** sciences *fpl* naturelles; **n. selection** sélection *f* naturelle; **n. size** grandeur *f* nature; *Radio, TV* **n. sound** son *m* naturel; *Econ, Ind* **n. wastage** départs *mpl* volontaires et en retraite; **n. wavelength** longueur *f* d'onde propre

natural-born ADJ *(singer, leader etc)* né; **n. Frenchwoman** Française de naissance

naturalism ['nætʃərəlɪz(ə)m] N *Liter, Phil* naturalisme *m*

naturalist ['nætʃərəlɪst] ADJ, N *Bot, Zool* naturaliste *mf*

naturalistic [nætʃərə'lɪstɪk] ADJ *Liter etc* naturaliste

naturalization [nætʃərəlaɪ'zeɪʃən] N **1** *(of alien, foreign word)* naturalisation *f* **2** *(of plant, animal)* acclimatation *f*

naturalize ['nætʃərəlaɪz] VT **1** *(alien, word)* naturaliser; **to become naturalized** *(of person)* se faire naturaliser **2** *(plant, animal)* acclimater
VI *(of plant etc)* s'acclimater

naturally ['nætʃərəlɪ] ADV **1** naturellement; *(to speak)* naturellement, sans affectation; *(to behave)* avec naturel; *(to die)* de mort naturelle; **n. occurring** naturel; **n. curly hair** cheveux qui frisent naturellement; **he's n. shy/funny/cheerful** il est timide/drôle/enjoué de nature; **she has a n. optimistic disposition** elle est d'un naturel optimiste; **it comes n. to him** c'est un don chez lui; **it comes n. to him to ...** il a une facilité innée pour ...; **although it didn't come n., he forced himself to ask questions** bien que cela ne lui vienne pas naturellement, il se força à poser des questions **2 n. (enough)** *(of course)* naturellement, bien entendu

naturalness ['nætʃərəlnɪs] N **1** *(of acting)* caractère *m* naturel **2** *(of person)* naturel *m*

nature ['neɪtʃər] N **1** *(character) (of thing)* nature *f*, caractère *m*; *(of person)* nature, naturel *m*, tempérament *m*; **it is in the n. of things that ...** il est dans l'ordre *ou* la nature des choses que ...; **a jealous n.** un naturel *ou* caractère jaloux; **to have a** *or* **to be of a happy n.** être d'un heureux naturel; **it's not in her n.** ce n'est pas dans sa nature (**to do** faire); **by n.** par tempérament, de (sa) nature, naturellement; **shy by n.** timide de nature, d'un naturel timide **2** *(sort)* genre *m*, sorte *f*, **things of this n.** les choses de ce genre; **something in the n. of a ...** une espèce *ou* une sorte de ...; **something of that n., anyway** quelque chose dans le genre *ou* de cette espèce, en tout cas; **that was in the n. of being a compliment, coming from him** c'était plutôt un compliment, venant de lui; *Fml* **what is the n. of your complaint?** quelle est la nature de votre réclamation?; *Admin* **n. of contents** désignation *f* du contenu **3** *(the natural world)* nature *f*, **to let n. take its course** laisser faire la nature; **the n. versus nurture debate** le débat nature/culture; *Hum Fam* **to answer a call of n.** satisfaire un besoin naturel; **to draw/paint from n.** dessiner/peindre d'après nature; **to go against n.** aller contre la nature; **return to n.** retour à l'état de nature
▸▸ **n. lover** amoureux, -euse de la nature; **n. reserve** réserve *f* naturelle; *Sch* **n. study** sciences *fpl* naturelles, histoire *f* naturelle; **n. trail** sentier *m* écologique

naturism ['neɪtʃərɪz(ə)m] N naturisme *m*

naturist ['neɪtʃərɪst] N naturiste *mf*

naught [nɔːt] N **1** *Arch, Lit (nothing)* rien *m*; **to come to n.** *(of plans etc)* échouer, n'aboutir à rien; **to bring to n., to set at n.** anéantir **2** *Am Math* zéro *m*

naughtily ['nɔːtɪlɪ] ADV **to behave n.** se conduire mal, ne pas être sage, être vilain; **rather n., I spread rumours about her private life** j'ai fait courir des rumeurs sur sa vie privée, ce qui est un peu vilain

naughtiness ['nɔːtɪnɪs] N **1** *(of child etc)* mauvaise conduite *f* **2** *(mild indecency)* grivoiserie(s) *f(pl)*

naughty ['nɔːtɪ] ADJ **1** *(child)* vilain, méchant; **it was very n. of you** c'était très vilain de ta part; **you n. child!** petit vilain!; **he's been a n. boy** *or* **n.** il a été vilain *ou* méchant, il n'a pas été sage **2** *Fam (indecent) (story)* grivois, cochon; *(song)* gaillard, paillard; *(book, picture, person)* cochon
▸▸ *Br Euph* **n. bits** parties *fpl* honteuses

nausea ['nɔːsɪə] N **1** *Med* nausée *f*, envie *f* de vomir; **to be overcome with n.** avoir mal au cœur, avoir des nausées **2** *(disgust)* dégoût *m*, nausée *f*, écœurement *m*

nauseate ['nɔːsɪeɪt] VT **1** *Med* donner des nausées à, donner mal au cœur à **2** *(disgust)* donner la nausée à, écœurer, dégoûter

nauseating ['nɔːsɪeɪtɪŋ] ADJ **1** *Med* nauséeux **2** *(disgusting)* dégoûtant, écœurant; **I find him n.** il m'écœure, il me dégoûte; **in n. detail** avec des détails écœurants *ou* à donner la nausée

nauseatingly ['nɔːsɪeɪtɪŋlɪ] ADV d'une façon dégoûtante *ou* écœurante; **he made it look so n. easy** il l'a fait avec une facilité écœurante; **he's n. clever/good-looking** il est tellement intelligent/beau que c'en est écœurant

nauseous ['nɔːsɪəs, *Am* 'nɔːʃəs] ADJ **1** *Med* nauséeux; **to feel n.** avoir mal au cœur, avoir des nausées **2** *(disgusting)* nauséabond, écœurant

nautical ['nɔːtɪk(ə)l] ADJ nautique, marin; *(term, expression)* de navigation, de marine; **he had a n. air/bearing** il avait l'air/l'allure

d'un marin; **he comes from a n. background** il vient d'une famille de marins
▸▸ **n. almanac** éphémérides *fpl* nautiques; **n. club** club *m* nautique; **n. mile** mille *m* marin

nautilus, *pl* **nautiluses, nautili** ['nɔːtɪləs, -əsɪz, -aɪ] N *(mollusc)* nautile *m*

NAV [enei'viː] N *Fin (abbr* **net asset value***)* = valeur *f* d'actif net

naval ['neɪv(ə)l] ADJ *(attaché, base, battle etc)* naval, *pl* -als; *(power)* maritime
▸▸ **n. architect** architecte *mf* naval(e); *(for warships)* ingénieur *m* du génie maritime *ou* en construction navale; **n. architecture** construction *f* navale; **n. college** école *f* navale; **n. dockyard** arsenal *m* maritime; **n. hospital** hôpital *m* naval; **n. officer** officier *m* de marine; **n. station** base *f* navale; **n. stores** *(depot)* entrepôts *mpl* maritimes; *(supplies)* approvisionnements *mpl ou* matériel *m ou* fournitures *fpl* de navires; **n. vessel** navire *m*

nave[1] [neɪv] N *(of wheel)* moyeu *m*

nave[2] N *Archit (of church)* nef *f*

navel ['neɪv(ə)l] N *Anat* nombril *m*, ombilic *m*; *Fig* **to contemplate one's n.** se regarder le nombril, faire du nombrilisme
▸▸ **n. orange** navel *f*

navel-gazing [-'geɪzɪŋ] N nombrilisme *m*

navigability [nævɪgə'bɪlɪtɪ] N *(of river, vessel)* navigabilité *f*, *(of balloon)* dirigeabilité *f*

navigable ['nævɪgəb(ə)l] ADJ *(river, vessel)* navigable; *(balloon)* dirigeable; **ship in n. condition** vaisseau en état de prendre la mer *ou* de naviguer

navigate ['nævɪgeɪt] VI **1** *(find one's way)* naviguer; *Aut* **I'll drive if you n.** je conduis si vous me dirigez **2** *Comput* naviguer
VT **1** *(seas)* naviguer dans *ou* sur; **this river is difficult to n.** la navigation est difficile sur ce fleuve; **to n. a ship** *(steer)* gouverner *ou* diriger un navire; *(plot path of)* naviguer; *Fam* **to n. one's way to the door** *(through crowd)* se frayer un chemin jusqu'à la porte; **the drunk navigated his way to the door** le soûlard a réussi à trouver son chemin jusqu'à la porte **2** *Comput* naviguer sur; **to n. the Net** naviguer sur Internet

navigating officer ['nævɪgeɪtɪŋ] N officier *m* de navigation, officier navigateur

navigation [nævɪ'geɪʃən] N **1** navigation *f*, *(of ship, balloon)* conduite *f* **2** *Comput (on the Internet)* navigation *f*
▸▸ **n. aids** aides *fpl* à la navigation; **n. bar** barre *f* de navigation; **n. button** bouton *m* de navigation; **n. lights** *Aviat* feux *mpl* de position; *Naut* fanaux *mpl*, feux de bord *ou* de route; **n. officer** officier *m* de navigation, officier navigateur

navigational [nævɪ'geɪʃənəl] ADJ *(instrument etc)* de navigation; *(aids)* à la navigation

navigator ['nævɪgeɪtər] N **1** *Naut, Aviat* (officier *m)* navigateur *m*; *Aut* navigateur **2** *Hist (explorer)* navigateur *m*

navvy ['nævɪ] N *Br (worker)* terrassier *m*

navy ['neɪvɪ] N **1** *(service)* marine *f*, **to serve in the n.** servir dans la marine *ou* sur mer; **2** *(warships collectively)* marine *f* de guerre; *(fleet)* flotte *f*
ADJ de la marine
▸▸ **N. Cut®** tabac *m* haché fin; **n. yard** arsenal *m* maritime

navy, navy blue N bleu *m* marine *inv*
ADJ bleu marine *inv*

nay [neɪ] ADV *Arch, Lit, Dial* non; *Lit (introducing a more emphatic statement)* (et) même, qui plus est, voire; **I am astounded, n., disgusted** j'en suis ahuri, voire révolté

N *Arch, Lit* non *m*; **ayes and nays** *(in voting)* voix *fpl* pour et contre; **I was one of the n.-sayers** j'étais un de ceux qui ont voté contre

Nazarene [ˈnæzəriːn] ADJ, N *Bible* nazaréen, -éenne; **the N.** le Nazaréen

Nazi [ˈnɑːtsɪ] ADJ nazi; *(persecution, seizure of power)* par les nazis
N nazi, -ie

Nazism [ˈnɑːtsɪz(ə)m] **N** nazisme *m*

NB [enˈbiː] **1** *(abbr* **nota bene)** NB **2** *(abbr* **New Brunswick)** NB

NBC [enbiːˈsiː] **N** *TV (abbr* **National Broadcasting Company)** = chaîne *f* de télévision américaine

NBG, nbg [enbiːˈdʒiː] ADJ *Fam (abbr* **no bloody good)** *(person)* nul, bon à rien; *(book etc)* nul

NBV [enbiːˈviː] **N** *Fin (abbr* **net book value)** valeur *f* comptable nette

NC *abbr* **North Carolina**

NC-17 *Am Cin* = indique qu'un film est interdit aux moins de 17 ans

NCB [ensiːˈbiː] **N** *Br Formerly (abbr* **National Coal Board)** = direction *f* des charbonnages britanniques

NCO [ensiːˈəʊ] **N** *Mil (abbr* **noncommissioned officer)** sous-officier *m*, *pl* sous-officiers

ND *abbr* **North Dakota**

NDP [endiːˈpiː] **N** *Econ (abbr* **net domestic product)** produit *m* intérieur net

Neandert(h)al [nɪˈændətɑːl] ADJ **1** *(during Stone Age)* néandertalien **2** *Fig Pej (attitude etc)* primaire
N *Fig Pej (uncultured man)* primate *m*
▸▸ **N. man** *(in anthropology)* l'homme *m* de Néanderthal

neap [niːp] ADJ faible
N morte-eau *f*, *pl* mortes-eaux
▸▸ **n. tide** marée *f* de morte-eau

Neapolitan [nɪəˈpɒlɪt(ə)n] ADJ napolitain
N Napolitain, -aine
▸▸ **N. ice cream** tranche *f* napolitaine

NEAR [nɪər]

ADV	près **1** ▪ proche **1**
PREP	près de **1, 3, 4** ▪ sur le point de **3** ▪ proche de **4**
ADJ	proche **1, 3**
VT	approcher de

ADV 1 *(in space or time)* près; *(closely connected by kinship or intimacy)* proche; **she lives quite n.** elle habite tout près; **to come** or **draw n.** (s')approcher (**to sb/sth** de qn/qch); **come nearer** venez plus près, approchez-vous; **the time is drawing n.** l'heure approche; **to bring sth nearer** rapprocher qch (**to** de); **nearer and nearer** de plus en plus près; **n. at hand** *(of thing)* tout près, à proximité; *(of event)* tout proche; **keep** or **stay n. to me** restez près de moi; **he was standing n. to the table** il se tenait près de la table; **those n. and dear to him** ceux qui le touchent de près, ses proches; **no, it took nearer to three days** non, ça a pris plutôt trois jours
2 *(in extent)* **as n. as I can remember** autant que je puisse m'en souvenir; **they came n. to blows/to splitting up** ils en sont presque venus aux coups/à se séparer; **they were n. to giving up** ils étaient sur le point d'abandonner; **I came n. to crying** j'ai été sur le point de pleurer; **he's nowhere n. so** or **as strong as you** il est loin d'être aussi fort que vous; **she's nowhere n. finished** elle est loin d'avoir fini; **as n. as makes no difference** à peu de chose près; **50 or n. enough, 50 or as n. as makes no difference** 50 ou peu s'en faut, à peu de chose près 50; **a n. total failure** un échec presque total
3 *Arch, Lit* presque, à peu près

PREP **1** *(in space)* près de; **n. the village** près du village; **bring your chair near(er) the fire** (r)approchez votre chaise du feu; **to come** or **draw n. (to) sb/sth** (s')approcher de qn/qch
2 *(in time)* **it is n. Christmas** Noël approche, on approche de Noël; **we're getting n. that stage** on approche ou se rapproche de cette phase; **it was n. the time when he had his accident** c'était à l'époque de son accident
3 *(in extent)* près de, sur le point de; **n. death** sur le point de mourir; **he came n. (to) being run over** il a failli être écrasé; **n. to tears/despair** au bord des larmes/du désespoir
4 *(in resemblance)* **to be** or **to come n. sb/sth** ressembler à qn/qch; **language that is nearer Latin than Italian** langue qui est plus près ou proche du latin que de l'italien; **nobody can come anywhere n. her** il n'y a personne à son niveau; **he's nowhere n. it!** *(with guess etc)* il n'y est pas du tout!; **perhaps your definition comes n. it** or **the mark** votre définition s'approche peut-être de la vérité

ADJ **1** *(relative)* proche; **I felt very n. to her when she said that** je me suis senti très proche d'elle quand elle a dit cela; **we grew n. to one another** nous sommes devenus intimes; **our n. relations** nos proches (parents)
2 *(referring to side)* **n. foreleg** *(of horse etc)* pied *m* du montoir
3 *(place, time, event)* proche; **go to the nearest chemist's** allez à la pharmacie la plus proche; **in the n. future** dans un proche avenir; **give the measurements to the nearest metre** donnez les mesures au ou à un mètre près
4 **it was a n. thing** *(we only just escaped, attempt nearly succeeded)* il s'en est fallu de peu; *(nearly hit target)* il ne manquait pas grand-chose; **this is the nearest thing we have to a conference room** c'est ce que nous avons qui ressemble le plus à une salle de conférence; **it's the nearest you'll get to a bookshop in these parts** c'est ce que vous trouverez de mieux en matière de librairie par ici; **the nearest equivalent** l'équivalent le plus proche; **it's quite n. the original** *(of translation)* c'est assez proche de l'original
NPL *often Hum* **one's nearest and dearest** ses plus proches parents
VT (s')approcher de; **as we were nearing Oxford** comme nous approchions d'Oxford; **the road is nearing completion** la route est près d'être achevée; **we are nearing our goal** nous touchons au but; **he seemed to be nearing a breakdown/a crisis/a turning point** il semblait au bord de la dépression/d'une crise/d'un tournant; *Lit* **he's nearing his end** il approche de la fin
▸▸ **the N. East** le Proche-Orient; *Comput* **n. letter quality** qualité *f* courrier; **n. letter quality printer** imprimante *f* de qualité courrier; **n. miss** coup *m* qui a raté de peu; *(between planes, vehicles etc)* collision *f* évitée de justesse; **it was a n. miss** *(answer)* la réponse était presque bonne; *(accident)* on a frôlé l'accident; **that was a n. miss!** *(escape)* on l'a échappé belle!; **n. money** quasi-monnaie *f*, *pl* quasi-monnaies; *St Exch* **n. month** échéance *f* proche

near- [nɪər] PREF **n.-perfect** presque parfait; **a n.-disaster** un désastre évité de peu

nearby ADV [nɪəˈbaɪ] tout près; **is it n.?** est-ce que c'est près d'ici?; **to live n.** habiter dans les parages; **in a house n.** dans une maison voisine; **they stood n., watching** ils se tenaient à proximité et regardaient
ADJ [ˈnɪəbaɪ] proche; **a n. house** une maison voisine ou avoisinante

near-death experience **N** expérience *f* aux frontières de la mort

nearly [ˈnɪəlɪ] ADV **1** *(almost)* presque; **it's n.**

midnight il est presque ou bientôt minuit; **we're n. there** nous y sommes presque; **I've got n. all of them** je les ai presque ou à peu près tous; **I'm n. forty** j'ai près de ou presque quarante ans; **it cost n. ten pounds** cela a coûté près de ou presque dix livres; **very n.** peu s'en faut; **I very n. resigned on the spot** il s'en est fallu de peu pour que je ne démissionne sur le champ; **I very n. fell/burst out laughing** j'ai bien failli tomber/éclater de rire; **he very n. died** il a frôlé la mort; **she's not n. as old as me** elle est loin d'être aussi âgée que moi **2** *(closely)* (de) près
▸▸ *Fam* **n. man** ≃ éternel second *m*

nearly-new ADJ presque neuf

nearness [ˈnɪənɪs] **N** *(of time, place)* proximité *f*; *(of place)* voisinage *m*; *(of friends)* intimité *f*; **their growing n. to one another** leur intimité grandissante

nearside [ˈnɪəsaɪd] *Br* **N** *(of horse)* côté *m* gauche; *Aut (when driving on left)* *(of road)* gauche *f*, *(of vehicle)* côté gauche; *(when driving on right)* *(of road)* droite *f*, *(of vehicle)* côté droit
ADJ *Aut (when driving on left)* gauche; *(when driving on right)* droit; **keep to the n. lane** serrez *(when driving on left)* à gauche ou *(when driving on right)* à droite

near-sighted ADJ myope; *Fig (policy, government etc)* obtus

near-sightedness [-saɪtɪdnɪs] **N** myopie *f*; *Fig* imprévoyance *f*

neat [niːt] ADJ **1** *(tidy)* *(person)* ordonné, qui a de l'ordre; *(in one's appearance)* soigné, net, *f* nette; *(room, drawer etc)* bien rangé, en ordre; *(exercise book etc)* bien tenu, propre; *(garden)* bien tenu, *Fam* propret, -ette; *(way of dressing, handwriting)* soigné; **he's a n. worker** son travail est très soigné; **his clothes are always very n.** ses vêtements sont toujours très nets
2 *(elegant, well-formed)* *(turn of phrase, answer etc)* bien tourné, adroit; *(idea, solution)* ingénieux; **she is small and n.** elle est petite et bien faite; *esp Am* **a n. plan** un plan bien pensé; **a n. little gadget** un petit gadget bien conçu; **that's a n. trick** c'est malin; **a n. manoeuvre** une manœuvre adroite; **a n. piece of work** un ouvrage bien exécuté; **she made a n. job of it** elle a fait du bon travail; **the surgeon made a n. job of those stitches** le chirurgien a bien soigné ces points de suture
3 *(tight)* étroit; **it's rather n. across the shoulders/around the waist** c'est un peu étroit au niveau des épaules/à la taille
4 *(undiluted)* pur, sans eau; **to take** or **drink one's whisky n.** boire son whisky sec
5 *Am Fam (good)* super; **that's really n.** c'est vraiment super

neaten [ˈniːt(ə)n] VT = **neaten up**
▸ **neaten up** VT SEP *(clothes)* ajuster; *(hair, garden)* arranger; *(hair, by trimming etc)* rafraîchir; *(room)* ranger; *(presentation)* fignoler, peaufiner; **go and n. yourself up a bit** va t'arranger un peu

neatly [ˈniːtlɪ] ADV **1** *(to put away etc)* d'une manière soignée ou ordonnée, avec ordre; **n. written** écrit soigneusement; **n. set out** disposé avec soin; **everything is n. in its place** tout est soigneusement rangé à sa place **2** *(cleverly etc)* adroitement; **n. phrased** bien tourné; **that is n. put** c'est joliment dit; **that brings us n. back to my opening question** cela nous ramène justement à ma question de départ

neatness [ˈniːtnɪs] **N 1** *(of handwriting, clothes)* netteté *f*; *(of garden)* apparence *f* soignée; *(of room etc)* bon ordre *m*; *(of exercise book etc)* propreté *f*; **the n. of her appearance** son allure ou apparence soignée; **personal n. is essential** il est essentiel d'avoir une apparence soignée **2** *(skill, cleverness)* adresse *f*, habileté *f*; *(of solution, idea)* ingéniosité *f*; *(of phrase)* tournure *f* adroite

nebula, *pl* **nebulæ** *or* **nebulas** ['nebjʊlə, -iː] N *Astron* nébuleuse *f*

nebulous ['nebjʊləs] ADJ *(vague)*, *Astron* nébuleux

necessaries ['nesɪsərɪz] NPL **the n.** *(food, money etc)* ce qu'il faut pour vivre; *Law (means to live)* le nécessaire; **we haven't got enough for the n.** nous n'avons pas assez pour nous payer le strict nécessaire

necessarily [nesɪ'serəlɪ] ADV **1** nécessairement; **it's not n. the case** ce n'est pas nécessairement *ou* forcément vrai **2** *(inevitably)* inévitablement, forcément

necessary ['nesɪsərɪ] ADJ **1** *(indispensable)* nécessaire (**to** *or* **for sb/sth** à qn/qch); **the time/space/resources n.** le temps/l'espace/les ressources nécessaire(s); **everything n.** tout ce qui est nécessaire; **it is n. to do something** il est nécessaire de faire quelque chose, il faut faire quelque chose; **it is n. for him to return** il faut qu'il revienne; **I find it n. to …** je juge nécessaire de …; **it is n. that …** il est nécessaire *ou* il faut que … + *sub*; **it's not n. to be rude** ce n'est pas la peine d'être impoli; **to make all n. arrangements** prendre toutes les dispositions utiles *ou* nécessaires; **to make it n. for sb to do sth** mettre qn dans l'obligation de faire qch; **if n.** si cela est nécessaire, s'il le faut, le cas échéant, au besoin; **whenever n.** chaque fois qu'il le faudra; **as and when n.** quand c'est/ce sera nécessaire; **to do what is n.** faire le nécessaire; **not to do more than is absolutely n.** ne faire que le strict nécessaire *ou* l'essentiel
2 *(inevitable) (result, conclusion, etc)* nécessaire, inévitable; **a n. evil** un mal nécessaire ▸ N *Fam* **the n.** *(things, action required)* le nécessaire; *(money)* les fonds *mpl*; **his father will provide the n.** *(money)* son père fournira le nécessaire; **to do the n.** faire le nécessaire

necessitate [nɪ'sesɪteɪt] VT nécessiter, rendre nécessaire

necessitous [nɪ'sesɪtəs] ADJ *Fml* nécessiteux, dans le besoin; **their present n. state** leur indigence actuelle

necessity [nɪ'sesɪtɪ] N **1** *(abstract need)* nécessité *f*; **by** *or* **from** *or* **out of n.** par nécessité, par la force des choses; **of n.** nécessairement, forcément; *Prov* **n. is the mother of invention** en cas de besoin on trouve toujours une solution
2 *(specific need)* nécessité *f*, besoin *m* (**of doing sth** de faire qch); **the n. for sth** le besoin de qch; **if the n. arose** *or* **should arise** si le besoin s'en faisait sentir; **in case of n.** au besoin, en cas de besoin; **case of absolute n.** cas *m* de force majeure; **there's no n. to be rude** ce n'est pas la peine d'être impoli; **is there any real n. for such haste?** une telle hâte est-elle nécessaire *ou* indispensable?
3 *(usu pl)* **necessities** *(things needed)* le nécessaire; **the bare necessities** le strict nécessaire; **the necessities of life** les nécessités *fpl* de la vie; **a car is not one of life's necessities** une voiture n'est pas indispensable; **a washing machine is a n.** une machine à laver est indispensable
4 *Fml (poverty)* dénuement *m*; **the family live in dire n.** la famille vit dans le dénuement le plus complet

neck [nek] N **1** *(of person, animal)* cou *m*; **to throw** *or* **fling one's arms round sb's n.** sauter *ou* se jeter au cou de qn; *Fig* **to be up to one's n. in work** avoir du travail par-dessus la tête, être débordé de travail; *Fam Fig* **he's in it up to his n.** il y est jusqu'au cou; *Fig* **to stick one's neck out** prendre des risques; *(and say sb will win etc)* s'engager; *Fam Fig* **to risk/save one's n.** risquer/sauver sa peau;

Fam **to get it in the n.** en prendre pour son grade; *Horseracing* **to win by a n.** gagner d'une encolure; **to finish n. and n.** arriver à égalité; **it's n. or nothing** il faut risquer *ou* jouer le tout pour le tout; *Fam* **what are you doing in this n. of the woods?** qu'est-ce que tu fais dans le coin?
2 *Br Sl (cheek)* culot *m*; **to have a (brass) n.** avoir du culot; **to have the (brass) n. to do sth** avoir le culot de faire qch
3 *(of dress, shirt)* encolure *f*; **square/round n.** encolure carrée/ronde; **V-n.** encolure en pointe *ou* en V; **high n.** col *m* montant; **low n.** décolleté *m*
4 *Culin (of lamb)* collier *m*, collet *m*; *(of beef)* collier
5 *(of bottle)* goulot *m*, col *m*; *(of vase)* col; *(of pipe)* rétrécissement *m*, étranglement *m*; *Anat (of uterus, bone)* col; *(of land)* langue *f*; *(of string instrument)* manche *m*, collet *m* ▸ VI *Sl (of couple)* se bécoter; **he was necking with her** ils se bécotaient
▸ ▸ **n. microphone** micro *m* cravate

neckband ['nekbænd] N *(ribbon etc)* tour *m* de cou; *(on shirt)* col *m*

neckerchief ['nekətʃɪf] N *Old-fashioned* foulard *m*, tour *m* de cou

necklace ['neklɪs] N collier *m*

necklet ['neklɪt] N collier *m* *(de fourrure etc)*

neckline ['neklaɪn] N encolure *f*, **dress with a plunging n.** robe au décolleté plongeant

necktie ['nektaɪ] N *Am* cravate *f*

neckwear ['nekweər] N *Com* cols *mpl*, cravates *fpl* et foulards *mpl*

necrology [ne'krɒlədʒɪ] N *Fml* **1** *(list of deaths)* nécrologie *f*, *Rel* nécrologe *m* **2** *(obituary)* nécrologie *f*

necromancer ['nekrəʊmænsər] N nécromancien, -ienne

necromancy ['nekrəʊmænsɪ] N nécromancie *f*

necrophilia [nekrəʊ'fɪlɪə] N nécrophilie *f*

necrophobia [nekrəʊ'fəʊbɪə] N nécrophobie *f*

necropolis [ne'krɒpəlɪs] N nécropole *f*

necrosis [ne'krəʊsɪs] N *Med* nécrose *f*

nectar ['nektər] N **1** *Myth, Bot* nectar *m* **2** *(fruit juice)* nectar *m*

nectarine ['nektəriːn] N brugnon *m*, nectarine *f*
▸ ▸ **n. tree** brugnonier *m*

ned [ned] N *esp Scot Fam* casseur *m*; **he's a bit of a n.** il est du genre casseur

NEDC [eniːdiː'siː] N *Br Admin Formerly* (*abbr* **National Economic Development Council**) = agence *f* nationale pour le développement économique

Neddy ['nedɪ] N *Br Admin Formerly Fam* = **NEDC**

née [neɪ] ADJ née; **Mrs Thomas, n. Long** Mme Thomas, née Long

NEED [niːd] N **1** *(requirement)* besoin *m*; **to feel/satisfy a n.** éprouver/satisfaire un besoin; **if need(s) be, in case of n.** en cas de besoin, au besoin, s'il (en) est besoin, si besoin (en) est; **n. for sth/sb** besoin de qch/qn; **there is no n. to …** il n'est pas nécessaire de …, ce n'est pas la peine de …; **(there's) no n. to wait** (il est) inutile d'attendre, ce n'est pas la peine d'attendre; **without the n. for sth** sans nécessiter qch; **the information will be made available on a n.-to-know basis** les informations ne seront fournies qu'à ceux qui en ont besoin; **the boss works on a n.-to-know basis** le patron ne dit que ce qu'on a besoin de savoir; **to be in n.** *or* **have n. of sth** avoir besoin de qch; **to be badly in n. of repair** avoir bien *ou* grand besoin d'être réparé; **she is in n. of a rest** elle a besoin de se reposer *ou* de repos; **to attend to sb's needs**

pourvoir aux besoins de qn; **that will meet my needs** cela fera mon affaire; **my most pressing n. is (for) a …** ce dont j'ai le plus besoin dans l'immédiat est de …; **whenever/wherever there's a n. for it** chaque fois que/partout où c'est nécessaire
2 *(difficulty)* adversité *f*, difficulté *f*; *(financial difficulty)* besoin *m*, indigence *f*; **in times** *or* **in the hour of n.** dans les moments difficiles; **in my hour of n.** au moment où j'en ai eu besoin; **to be in n.** être dans la nécessité *ou* dans le besoin; **their n. is greater than mine** ils en ont plus besoin que moi
3 *Mktg* **needs analysis** analyse *f* des besoins; **needs assessment** estimation *f* des besoins; **needs-based market** marché *m* fondé sur les besoins; **needs-based segmentation** segmentation *f* fondée sur les besoins; **needs study** étude *f* des besoins; **needs-and-wants exploration** exploration *f* des besoins et des désirs
▸ VT VOIR GRAMMAIRE A61 *(3rd person sing pr ind* needs; *pt, pp* needed*) (of person)* avoir besoin de; *(of thing)* exiger, nécessiter, demander; **my bike needs a few repairs** mon vélo a besoin de quelques réparations; **his hair needs cutting** il a besoin de se faire couper les cheveux; **they n. to be oiled/covered in plastic** il faut les graisser/couvrir d'un plastique; **this soup needs more salt/pepper** cette soupe manque de sel/poivre; **to n. rest** avoir besoin de repos; **I work because I n. the money** je travaille par besoin d'argent; **these facts n. no (further) comment** ces faits se passent de commentaire; **a much needed lesson** une leçon dont on avait grand besoin; **what he needs is a thrashing** ce dont il a besoin, c'est d'une bonne raclée, ce qu'il lui faudrait c'est une bonne raclée; **you'll n. to take more money** il va falloir que tu prennes plus d'argent; **the baby needs changing** il faut changer le bébé; **he needs to do more work on it/to see a doctor** il faut qu'il y travaille davantage/qu'il voie un docteur; **they n. to be told everything** il faut qu'on leur dise tout; **I didn't n. to be reminded of it** je n'avais pas besoin qu'on me le rappelle; **he didn't n. to be told twice** il ne s'est pas fait dire deux fois; **you only needed to ask** vous n'aviez qu'à demander; *Iron* **that's all I n.!** j'avais bien besoin de ça!; **the last thing we n. is someone like him snooping about the place** la dernière chose qu'il nous faut, c'est bien que quelqu'un comme lui vienne fouiner par ici; **who needs two cars anyway?** comme si on avait besoin d'avoir deux voitures!; **it needs a great deal of skill to do it properly** il faut beaucoup d'habileté pour le faire correctement; **it needs more patience than I have** cela exige *ou* requiert plus de patience que je n'en ai

▸ MODAL AUX V VOIR GRAMMAIRE A41 *(3rd person sing pr ind* need; *pt* need; *no prp; no pp)* **adults only n. apply** seuls les adultes peuvent postuler; **you needn't trouble yourself** (vous n'avez) pas besoin de vous déranger; **we needn't have bothered after all** nous n'aurions pas dû nous déranger après tout; **you needn't bother!** ne prends pas cette peine!; **n. you go yet?** est-ce qu'il faut que tu partes déjà?; **n. I go on?** faut-il que je continue?; **you needn't wait** il est inutile que vous attendiez, inutile (pour vous) d'attendre; **I n. hardly tell you how grateful I am** il n'est pas besoin de vous dire combien je vous suis reconnaissant; **it n. not necessarily be true** ce n'est pas nécessairement vrai
▸ ▸ *Mktg* **n. identification** identification *f* des besoins; *Mktg* **n. level** niveau *m* des besoins; *Mktg* **n. market** marché *m* des besoins; *Mktg* **n. recognition** reconnaissance *f* des besoins; *Mktg* **n. set** ensemble *m* de besoins

needful ['ni:dfʊl] ADJ *Old-fashioned* nécessaire (**to** à; **for** pour)
■ N *Fam* **to do the n.** faire le nécessaire; *(pay, provide money)* casquer

neediness ['ni:dɪnɪs] N indigence *f*

needle ['ni:d(ə)l] N **1** *(for sewing etc)* aiguille *f*, *Bot* **(pine) n.** aiguille *f* de pin; **it's like looking for a n. in a haystack** c'est comme chercher une aiguille dans une botte de foin; **hypodermic n.** aiguille pour injections hypodermiques; *Fam* **I hate needles!** j'ai horreur des piqûres!; *Sl* **to be on the n.** *(take drugs)* se shooter, se piquer
2 *Br Fam* **to give sb the n.** *(irritate)* taper sur les nerfs à qn, agacer qn; *(deliberately)* faire enrager qn; *(anger)* mettre qn en rogne; **she's got the n.** elle est en rogne (**with** contre); **a bit of n. has crept into the match** les joueurs commencent à s'énerver *ou* disputent le match avec plus d'âpreté
3 *Tech (of record player, compass, speedometer etc)* aiguille *f*, *Aut (in float)* pointeau *m*; *(of scales)* aiguille, langue *f*, languette *f*, **compass** n. aiguille aimantée; *Art* **engraving n.** pointe *f* pour taille douce, pointe sèche
4 *Archit* obélisque *m*; *Geol, Geog* aiguille *f* (rocheuse); *Chem, Miner* **crystalline needles** aiguilles cristallines
■ VT *Fam (irritate)* agacer, taper sur les nerfs à; *(deliberately)* faire enrager; *(anger)* mettre en rogne; **to n. sb about not having a girlfriend** narguer qn parce qu'il n'a pas de petite amie; **to n. sb about his/her exam results** narguer qn à propos de ses résultats à un examen
■ VI *Sl (inject drugs)* se shooter, se piquer
▸▸ *Br* **n. bank** distributeur-échangeur *m* de seringues, *pl* distributeurs-échangeurs de seringues; **n. exchange scheme** programme *m* d'échange de seringues; *Br Fam* **n. match** match *m* âprement disputé; **n. noise** *(on record player)* bruit *m* d'aiguille; **n. scratch** *(on record player)* bruit d'aiguille; *Sewing* **n. threader** filifère *m*, enfile-aiguilles *m inv*; **n. valve** soupape *f* à pointeau

needlecord ['ni:d(ə)lkɔ:d] N *Tex* velours *m* mille-raies

needlecraft ['ni:d(ə)lkrɑ:ft] N travail *m* à l'aiguille, travaux d'aiguille

needle-nosed pliers N pince *f* à bec fin

needlepoint ['ni:d(ə)lpɔɪnt] N *(embroidery)* tapisserie *f* à l'aiguille

needless ['ni:dlɪs] ADJ inutile; *(remark)* déplacé; **n. to say, we shall refund the money** il va de soi que nous rembourserons l'argent

needlessly ['ni:dlɪslɪ] ADV *(to be rude, pedantic, to worry)* inutilement; *(to die, suffer, work)* pour rien

needletime N *(for broadcasting records)* durée *f* de passage à l'antenne

needlewoman, *pl* **needlewomen** ['ni:d(ə)lwʊmən, -wɪmɪn] N *(seamstress)* couturière *f*, **I'm no n.** je ne sais pas coudre

needlework ['ni:d(ə)lwɜ:k] N travaux *mpl* d'aiguille; *(school subject)* couture *f*, **she's good at n.** elle coud bien

needs [ni:dz] ADV *Old-fashioned (used only with* **must***)* de toute nécessité; **if n. must ...** s'il le faut absolument...; **ah well! n. must!** ah! il le faut bien; *Prov* **n. must when the devil drives** nécessité fait loi

need-to-know ADJ **information is given on a n. basis** les renseignements ne sont donnés qu'aux personnes concernées

needy ['ni:dɪ] ADJ *(person)* nécessiteux, indigent; **to be emotionally n.** manquer d'affection
■ NPL **the n.** les nécessiteux *mpl*

ne'er [neər] ADV *Lit* (ne ...) jamais; **n. the less** néanmoins

ne'er-do-well N, ADJ propre *mf* à rien

nefarious [nɪ'feərɪəs] ADJ *(person, purpose etc)* infâme, scélérat

nefariously [nɪ'feərɪəslɪ] ADV d'une manière infâme

nefariousness [nɪ'feərɪəsnɪs] N *(of deed, crime, behaviour)* infâmie *f*, *(of person)* scélératesse *f*

neg [neg] N, ADJ *(abbr* **negative***)* négatif *m*

negate [nɪ'geɪt] VT **1** *esp Fml (deny)* nier **2** *(nullify) (effect)* annuler; *(efforts, work)* anéantir; *(law etc)* annuler **3** *Gram* mettre au négatif

negation [nɪ'geɪʃən] N **1** *(denial)* (*of fact, proposition etc)* négation *f* **2** *(nullification)* *(of sb's work, efforts)* anéantissement *m*

negative ['negətɪv] ADJ *(reply, result, virtue etc)*, *Math, Elec, Phot* négatif; **don't be so n.** ne sois pas aussi négatif; **he's a very n. sort of person** il est très négatif
■ N **1** *(reply)* négative *f*, *Gram* négation *f*, *Math* valeur *f ou* quantité *f* négative; **to answer in the n.** répondre négativement *ou* par la négative; *Math* **two negatives make a positive** moins moins égale plus; *Gram* **to put a statement into the n.** mettre une affirmation à la forme négative VOIR GRAMMAIRE A47–8; B62–3 **2** *Phot (cliché m)* négatif *m*; *Elec (of battery)* plaque *f* négative
■ ADV *(in answer to a question)* non
■ VT **1** *(plan, project)* s'opposer à, rejeter **2** *(hypothesis, theory)* réfuter; *(report)* contredire, nier
▸▸ *Fin* **n. amortization** amortissement *m* négatif; *Phot* **n. cutter** monteur *m* négatif; *Fin* **n. equity** plus-value *f* immobilière négative, = situation *f* où l'acquéreur d'un bien immobilier reste redevable de l'emprunt contracté alors que son logement enregistre une moins-value; **n. (income) tax** impôt *m* négatif; *Fin* **n. interest** intérêt *m* négatif; **n. sign** signe *m* moins *ou* négatif

negatively ['negətɪvlɪ] ADV négativement

negativism ['negətɪvɪz(ə)m] N négativisme *m*

negativity [negə'tɪvɪtɪ] N négativité *f*, be**cause of the n. of his attitude** à cause de son attitude négative; **to feel a lot of n. towards sb** avoir beaucoup de sentiments négatifs contre qn

neglect [nɪ'glekt] N *(of person)* négligence *f*, *(of machine, property etc)* mauvais entretien *m*; **n. of one's duties/responsibilities** manquement *m* à ses devoirs/responsabilités; **out of** *or* **from** *or* **through n.** par négligence; **his n. of his children led to a court case** le fait qu'il néglige ses enfants a donné lieu à un procès; **to die in total n.** mourir complètement abandonné *ou* dans l'abandon le plus total; **to die of n.** mourir à cause d'un manque de soins; **to suffer n.** souffrir d'un manque de soins; **the equipment was allowed to fall into n.** le matériel n'a pas été entretenu
■ VT **1** *(not look after) (children, health etc)* négliger; **to n. oneself** négliger sa personne, se négliger; **the garden looks neglected** le jardin est mal tenu *ou* à l'abandon; **are you feeling neglected?** est-ce que vous avez l'impression qu'on vous néglige?
2 *(ignore) (duties)* négliger, oublier; *(one's responsibilities)* manquer à; *(one's post)* délaisser, abandonner; **to n. to do sth** omettre de faire qch; **he chooses to n. my advice** il choisit de ne pas tenir compte de mon conseil

neglectful [nɪ'glektfʊl] ADJ négligent; **to be n. of sth/sb** négliger qch/qn; **n. of one's duty** oublieux de son devoir; **to be n. of one's responsibilities/obligations** manquer à ses responsabilités/obligations

negligé, negligée ['neglɪʒeɪ] N négligé *m*, déshabillé *m*

negligence ['neglɪdʒəns] N *(lack of care)*, *Law* négligence *f*, **through n.** par négligence; **n. of one's duties/responsibilities** manquement *m* à ses devoirs/ responsabilités

negligent ['neglɪdʒənt] ADJ **1** *(neglectful)* négligent; **to be n. of sth** négliger qch; *(of one's duties, responsibilities etc)* être oublieux de qch, manquer à qch **2** *(casual)* *(air, tone)* nonchalant, insouciant

negligently ['neglɪdʒəntlɪ] ADV **1** *(neglectfully)* avec négligence; **to fail n. to do sth** avoir la négligence de faire qch **2** *(casually)* négligemment, nonchalamment

negligible ['neglɪdʒɪb(ə)l] ADJ *(amount)* négligeable

negotiability [nɪgəʊʃə'bɪlɪtɪ] ADJ *Fin* négociabilité *f*

negotiable [nɪ'gəʊʃəb(ə)l] ADJ **1** *Fin etc (bill, document, demands, fee etc)* négociable; **not n.** non-négociable; *(on cheque)* non à ordre **2** *(barrier, obstacle etc)* franchissable; *(path etc)* praticable; **the path was not easily n.** le chemin n'était guère praticable
▸▸ *Fin* **n. instrument** instrument *m* négociable; *Fin* **n. paper** papier *m* négociable; *Fin* **n. stock** titres *mpl* négociables

negotiate [nɪ'gəʊʃɪeɪt] VT **1** *(business deal, marriage)* négocier, traiter; *(loan, treaty, fee)* négocier; *(peace)* traiter; *Fin (bill, document)* négocier, trafiquer; **price to be negotiated** prix *m* à débattre **2** *(obstacle etc)* franchir; *Fig (difficulty)* surmonter; *Aut (bend)* négocier, prendre; *(minefield)* traverser; *(rapids)* passer
■ VI négocier; **to be negotiating with sb for sth** être en traité *ou* en marché avec qn pour qch; **to n. for peace** entreprendre des pourparlers de paix; **to n. about sth** négocier qch

negotiating table [nɪ'gəʊʃɪeɪtɪŋ] N table *f* des négociations; **to sit round the n.** s'asseoir à la table des négociations

negotiation [nɪgəʊʃɪ'eɪʃən] N **1** *(of treaty, loan etc)* négociation *f*, **under n.** en négociation; **to be in n. with sb** être en pourparler(s) avec qn; **to break off/resume negotiations** rompre/reprendre les négociations; **pay/ redundancy negotiations** négociations sur les salaires/les licenciements; **peace negotiations** pourparlers *mpl* de paix **2** *(of obstacle)* franchissement *m*; *(of corner)* prise *f*

negotiator [nɪ'gəʊʃɪeɪtər] N négociateur, -trice

Negress ['ni:grɪs] N Noire *f*, *(in anthropology)*, *Pej* négresse *f*

Negro, *pl* **Negroes** ['ni:grəʊ, -z] ADJ noir, nègre; **the N. race** la race noire *ou* nègre
■ N Noir *m*; *(in anthropology)*, *Pej* nègre *m*
▸▸ **N. spiritual** (negro) spiritual *m*

Negroid ['ni:grɔɪd] ADJ, N *(in anthropology)* négroïde *m*

neigh [neɪ] N hennissement *m*
■ VI hennir

neighbour, *Am* **neighbor** ['neɪbər] N **1** *(person, country)* voisin, -ine; **to be a good n.** être bon voisin **2** *Bible etc (fellow human being)* prochain *m*; **love thy n. as thyself** aime ton prochain comme toi-même
▸ **neighbour on,** *Am* **neighbor on** VT INSEP *(adjoin)* avoisiner, être contigu à; *(of country)* être limitrophe à

neighbourhood, *Am* **neighborhood** ['neɪbəhʊd] N **1** *(vicinity)* **in the n. of** *(place)* aux alentours de, dans les environs de; **to live in the (immediate) n. of ...** demeurer à proximité de ...; **anyone in the n. of the crime should contact the police** quiconque se trouvait à proximité du lieu du crime doit contacter la police; **in the n. of 10** environ 10, dans les 10; **a figure in the n. of £2000**

un chiffre avoisinant les 2 000 livres **2** *(district)* voisinage *m*, quartier *m*; **I was in the n.** j'étais dans le coin *ou* dans le quartier *ou* dans le voisinage; **the whole n. is talking about it** tout le voisinage *ou* le quartier en parle; **a very friendly n.** un quartier très sympa; **a good/bad n.** un bon/mauvais quartier; **she's the n. gossip** c'est la commère du quartier *ou* du voisinage

▸▸ *Br* **n. watch** = système *m* par lequel les habitants d'un quartier s'entraident pour en assurer la surveillance et la sécurité

neighbouring, *Am* **neighboring** ['neɪbərɪŋ] ADJ avoisinant, voisin

neighbourliness, *Am* **neighborliness** ['neɪbəlɪnɪs] N (relations *fpl* de) bon voisinage *m*, bons rapports *mpl* entre voisins; **an act of n.** un acte de bon voisinage; **to show a little n.** se montrer bon voisin; **the n. of the family next door** l'obligeance *f* de la famille d'à-côté

neighbourly, *Am* **neighborly** ['neɪbəlɪ] ADJ *(person)* obligeant, bon voisin; *(action, behaviour etc)* de bon voisin; *(visit)* de bon voisinage; **it was very n. of them** c'était très obligeant de leur part; **to be n. with sb** entretenir des rapports de bon voisinage avec qn; **people used to be more n.** autrefois les gens entretenaient de meilleurs rapports avec leurs voisins

neighing ['neɪɪŋ] N hennissement(s) *m(pl)*

neither ['naɪðər, 'niːðər] VOIR GRAMMAIRE A37
ADV **n. ... nor ...** ni ... ni ...; **he will n. eat nor drink** il ne veut ni manger ni boire; **n. (the) one nor the other** ni l'un ni l'autre; **that's n. here nor there** *(irrelevant)* ça n'a rien à voir
CONJ non plus; **n. do I** (ni) moi non plus; **if you don't go n. will I** si vous n'y allez pas je n'irai pas non plus; **I haven't read it, n. do I intend to** je ne l'ai pas lu et d'ailleurs je n'en ai pas l'intention; **the funding wasn't available and n. was the necessary expertise** ni les fonds ni les compétences nécessaires n'étaient disponibles VOIR GRAMMAIRE A73–4
ADJ **n. driver was injured** ni l'un ni l'autre des conducteurs n'a été blessé; **on n. side** ni d'un côté ni de l'autre
PRON **which do you want? – n.** lequel voulez-vous? – ni l'un(e) ni l'autre; **n. of my two brothers can come** aucun de mes deux frères ne peut venir; **n. of us is satisfied** nous ne sommes satisfaits ni l'un ni l'autre

nelly ['nelɪ] N *Br Sl* **not on your n.!** jamais de la vie!

nelson ['nelsən] N *(in wrestling)* nelson *m*; **double** *or* **full n.** double nelson

nematode ['nemətəʊd] N nématode *m*

Nemesis ['nemɪsɪs] N *Myth* Némésis *f*, *Fig* **this/he was my n.** cela/il a été ma ruine

neo- ['niːəʊ] PREF néo-

neoclassic(al) [niːəʊ'klæsɪk, -ɪk(ə)l] ADJ néoclassique; **neoclassical economics** économie *f* néoclassique

neoclassicism [niːəʊ'klæsɪsɪz(ə)m] N néoclassicisme *m*

neocolonialism [niːəʊkə'ləʊnɪəlɪz(ə)m] N néocolonialisme *m*

neofascism [niːəʊ'fæʃɪz(ə)m] N néofascisme *m*

neofascist [niːəʊ'fæʃɪst] ADJ, N néofasciste *mf*

neogothic [niːəʊ'gɒθɪk] ADJ, *Archit* néogothique *m*

neolithic [niːəʊ'lɪθɪk] ADJ néolithique; **the N. age** l'âge *m* de la pierre polie, le néolithique

neologism [nɪ'ɒlədʒɪz(ə)m] N néologisme *m*

neon ['niːɒn] N *Chem* néon *m*
▸▸ *Elec* **n. light** lumière *f* au néon; **n. sign**

enseigne *f* lumineuse (au néon); **n. tube** tube *m* fluorescent *ou* au néon

neonatal [niːəʊ'neɪt(ə)l] ADJ néonatal, -als

neonazi [niːəʊ'nɑːtsɪ] ADJ, N néonazi, -ie

neophyte ['niːəʊfaɪt] N *Rel etc* néophyte *mf*

neoplasm ['niːəʊplæz(ə)m] N *Med* néoplasme *m*

neorealism [niːəʊ'rɪəlɪz(ə)m] N *Cin* néoréalisme *m*

Nepal [nɪ'pɔːl] N Népal *m*

Nepalese [nepə'liːz], **Nepali** [ne'pɔːlɪ] ADJ népalais
N **1** Népalais, -aise **2** *Ling* népalais *m*

nephew ['nefjuː] N neveu *m*

nephrite ['nefraɪt] N *Miner* néphrite *f*

nephritic [ne'frɪtɪk] ADJ *Med* néphrétique

nephritis [ne'fraɪtɪs] N *Med* néphrite *f*; **to have n.** avoir une néphrite

nephron ['nefrɒn] N *Anat* néphron *m*

nepotism ['nepətɪz(ə)m, 'niː-] N népotisme *m*

Neptune ['neptjuːn] N *Astron* Neptune *f*; *Myth* Neptune *m*

nerd [nɜːd] N *Pej Fam* ringard, -arde

nerdy ['nɜːdɪ] ADJ *Pej Fam* ringard

Nereid ['nɪərɪɪd] N *Myth* Néréide *f*

Nero ['nɪərəʊ] N *Antiq* Néron *m*

nerve [nɜːv] N **1** *Anat* nerf *m*; **to take the n. out of a tooth** *(of dentist)* dévitaliser une dent; **to be in a state of nerves** être sur les nerfs; **we're living on our nerves** nous vivons sur les nerfs; **it's her nerves** c'est les nerfs; **my nerves won't stand it** mes nerfs vont lâcher; **to get on sb's nerves** taper sur les nerfs à qn, énerver qn; **she's got nerves of steel** elle a des nerfs d'acier; **war of nerves** guerre des nerfs

2 *(courage)* courage *m*; *(coolness)* sang-froid *m*; **his n. failed him, he lost his n.** le courage lui a manqué; **a pilot who has lost his n.** un pilote qui n'est plus mentalement en état de voler; **he never regained his n.** il n'a jamais retrouvé son courage

3 *Fam (cheek)* culot *m*; **to have the n. to do sth** avoir le toupet *ou* le culot de faire qch; **what a n.!** quel culot!; **you've got a n.!** tu es gonflé!

4 *Bot, Entom, Archit* nervure *f*

VT **to n. oneself to do sth** s'armer de courage pour faire qch; **to n. sb for sth** encourager qn pour qch, donner du courage à qn pour qch

▸▸ **n. cell** cellule *f* nerveuse; **n. centre** *Anat* centre *m* nerveux; *Fig (headquarters)* centre névralgique; **n. ending** terminaison *f* nerveuse; **n. fibre** fibre *f* nerveuse; **n. gas** gaz *m* neurotoxique; **n. impulse** influx *m* nerveux; *Med* **n. specialist** neurologue *mf*

nerveless ['nɜːvlɪs] ADJ **1** *(calm) (person)* calme, plein de sang-froid; *(courage, bravery)* imperturbable **2** *(lacking strength) (person, limb etc)* inerte; *(style etc)* sans vigueur, languissant; **the cup fell from her n. fingers** la tasse a échappé à ses doigts engourdis

nerve-racking, nerve-wracking [-rækɪŋ] ADJ *(experience)* éprouvant; *(wait, suspense)* angoissant

nerviness ['nɜːvɪnɪs] N **1** *Br Fam (tension)* nervosité *f* **2** *Am Fam (cheek)* culot *m*

nervous ['nɜːvəs] ADJ **1** nerveux; *(timid)* craintif; **to be n.** *(before a performance, an exam etc)* avoir le trac; *(before going to the dentist etc)* avoir peur; **to be n. about sth** s'inquiéter à propos de qch; **are you n. about the exams?** est-ce que tu appréhendes les examens?; **he's n. about flying** il appréhende *ou* a peur de voyager en avion; **to be n. about doing sth** avoir peur *ou* appré-

hender de faire qch; **I was a bit n. about lending him the car** j'avais un peu d'appréhension à l'idée de lui prêter ma voiture; **the bank was n. about making the loan** la banque hésitait à accorder le prêt; **I'm still a little n. about taking on this contract** j'hésite encore un peu à accepter ce contrat; **if you're n. about offering him the job** *(are worried)* si vous craignez de lui proposer l'emploi; *(are uncertain)* si vous hésitez à lui proposer l'emploi; **he gets terribly n. every time he has to make a speech** chaque fois qu'il doit faire un discours il a un trac terrible *ou* il devient terriblement nerveux *ou* anxieux; **I feel** *or* **am n. in his presence** sa présence me rend nerveux; **airports make me n.** les aéroports me rendent nerveux; **he makes me n.** *(is intimidating)* il m'intimide; **don't hold your glass like that, you're making me n.** tu me tiens pas ton verre comme ça, tu me rends nerveux *ou* tu me fais peur **2** *Anat (exhaustion etc)* nerveux

▸▸ **n. breakdown** dépression *f* nerveuse; **to have a n. breakdown** faire une dépression nerveuse; **n. disorder** maladie *f* nerveuse; **n. energy** énergie *f* nerveuse; **the n. system** le système nerveux

nervously ['nɜːvəslɪ] ADV nerveusement; **he wondered n. if ...** il se demanda, avec une certaine nervosité, si ...

nervousness ['nɜːvəsnɪs] N **1** *(timidity)* timidité *f*, *(before performance)* trac *m* **2** *(tension, anxiety)* nervosité *f*

nervy ['nɜːvɪ] ADJ **1** *Br Fam (tense)* nerveux; **to feel n.** avoir les nerfs en pelote **2** *Am Fam (cheeky)* qui a du culot

nest [nest] N *(of bird, wasps etc)* nid *m*; *(nestful) (of fledglings)* nichée *f*, couvée *f*; *(of eggs)* couvée; *Fig (of bandits, machine guns etc)* repaire *m*, nid; *Fig* **the children have all left** *or* **flown the n.** les enfants ont tous quitté le nid; **n. of tables** tables *fpl* gigognes
VI *(of bird etc)* (se) nicher, faire son nid; *(of tables etc)* s'emboîter
VT **1** *(pipes etc)* emboîter **2** *Comput, Typ* imbriquer
▸▸ **n. box** *(in henhouse)* pondoir *m*; *(in birdhouse)* nichoir *m*; **n. egg** économies *fpl*, bas *m* de laine, pécule *m*

nested ['nestɪd] ADJ *Comput, Typ* imbriqué

nestful ['nestfʊl] N *(of fledglings)* nichée *f*, couvée *f*; *(of eggs)* couvée

nesting ['nestɪŋ] ADJ *(bird)* nicheur; *(time, instinct)* de (la) nidification
N **1** *(building nests)* nidification *f*, **to go (bird) n.** aller dénicher des œufs/des oisillons **2** *Comput, Typ* imbrication *f*
▸▸ **n. box** *(in henhouse)* pondoir *m*; *(in birdhouse)* nichoir *m*; **n. time** saison *f* de la ponte

nestle ['nes(ə)l] VI se pelotonner, se blottir; *(of house, tree)* être blotti; **to n. (up) close to sb** se pelotonner *ou* se blottir *ou* se serrer contre qn; **to n. (up) against sb's shoulder** se blottir contre l'épaule de qn; **village nestling in a valley** village blotti *ou* tapi dans une vallée
VT **to n. one's face against sb's shoulder** se blottir contre l'épaule de qn

nestling ['neslɪŋ] N oisillon *m*

Net [net] N *Comput* **the N.** le Net, l'Internet *m*
▸▸ **N. user** internaute *mf*, utilisateur, -trice du Net

net¹ [net] N **1** filet *m*; **to haul in a n.** relever un filet; *Fig* **to be caught in the n.** être pris au piège *ou* au filet; *Fig* **to slip through the n.** passer à travers les mailles du filet; *Ftbl* **to put the ball in the n.** envoyer la balle dans le filet **2** *Tex* tulle *m* **3** *Tel, TV (national)* réseau *m*; *(channel)* chaîne *f*

VT (-tt-) **1** *(capture) (fish, hares)*, *Fig (criminals etc)* prendre au filet; *Fig (tax evaders, drugs etc)* mettre la main sur; *Fig* **the charity ap-**

peal **netted several large donations** l'appel caritatif a rapporté plusieurs dons importants **2** *(river)* tendre des filets dans **3** *Ftbl* **he netted the ball twice** *(scored two goals)* il a marqué deux buts **4** *(in gardening) (peas etc)* protéger avec un filet

▸▸ **n. curtain** rideau *m* (de tulle *ou* en filet), voilage *m*; *Sport* **n. play** jeu *m* au filet

net² ADJ *(weight, price)* net, *f* nette; **n. proceeds of a sale** (produit *m*) net *m* d'une vente; **terms strictly n.** sans déduction

N *(income, profit, weight)* net *m*

ADV **n. of tax** net d'impôt; **n. of VAT** hors TVA

VT *Fin (sum of money) (of person)* toucher net, gagner net; *(of enterprise etc)* rapporter net; **we netted over $10,000** nous avons réalisé un bénéfice net de plus de 10 000 dollars; **he nets £20,000 a year** il gagne 20 000 livres net par an

▸▸ *Fin* **n. amount** somme *f* nette, montant *m* net; *Fin* **n. assets** actif *m* net; *Br Formerly* **the N. Book Agreement** = accord *m* entre maisons d'édition et libraires stipulant que ces derniers n'ont le droit de vendre aucun ouvrage à un prix inférieur à celui fixé par l'éditeur; *Fin* **n. book value** valeur *f* comptable nette; *Fin* **n. capital expenditure** mise *f* de fonds nette, dépenses *fpl* nettes d'investissement; *Fin* **n. cash flow** cash-flow *m* net, *pl* cash-flows nets; *Fin* **n. cost** prix *m* de revient; *Fin* **n. current assets** actif circulant net; *Fin* **n. dividend** dividende *m* net; *Fin* **n. domestic product** produit intérieur net; *Fin* **n. earnings** *(of company)* bénéfices *mpl* nets; *(of worker)* salaire *m* net; *Fin* **n. income** *(in accounts)* produit net; *(of individual)* revenu *m* net; *Fin* **n. interest income** net financier; *Fin* **n. loss** perte *f* nette; *Fin* **n. margin** marge *f* nette; *Fin* **n. national income** revenu national net; *Fin* **n. national product** produit national net; *Fin* **n. operating profit** rentabilité *f* nette d'exploitation; **n. payable** net à payer; *Fin* **n. present value** valeur actuelle nette; *Fin* **n. present value rate** taux *m* d'actualisation; *Fin* **n. profit** bénéfice *m* net, net commercial; *Fin* **n. profit margin** marge commerciale nette; *Fin* **n. profit ratio** ratio *m* de rentabilité nette, taux *m* de profit net; *Fin* **n. realizable value** valeur réalisable nette; *Fin* **n. receipts** recettes *fpl* nettes; *Fin* **n. result** résultat *m* final; *Fin* **n. return** rendement *m* net, résultat net; *Fin* **n. salary** salaire net; *Comput* **n. storage capacity** capacité *f* nette de stockage; *Fin* **n. tangible assets** actif corporel net; **n. tonnage** *(of ship)* tonnage *m* net; *Fin* **n. total** montant net; *Fin* **n. variance** écart *m* net; *Fin* **n. working capital** fonds *m* de roulement net; *Fin* **n. worth** situation *f* nette, valeur nette

.net [dɒt'net] *Comput* = abréviation *f* désignant les organismes officiels de l'Internet dans les adresses électroniques

netball ['netbɔ:l] N *Sport* netball *m*

nethead ['nethed] N *Comput Fam* accro *mf* de l'Internet

nether ['neðər] ADJ inférieur, bas, *f* basse; **the n. regions** *Lit* l'enfer *m*, les régions *mpl* infernales; *Hum (of body)* les parties *fpl* basses; **the n. regions of the rue St. Denis** le bas de la rue St. Denis

Netherlands ['neðələndz] NPL **the N.** les Pays-Bas *mpl*; **in the N.** dans les *ou* aux Pays-Bas

netiquette ['netɪket] N *Comput Fam* netiquette *f*

netizen ['netɪzən] N *Comput* internaute *mf*

netspeak ['netspi:k] N *Comput* langage *m* du Net, cyberjargon *m*

nett [net] ADJ, N, ADV, VT = **net²**

netting ['netɪŋ] N *(nets) (for protection, camouflage)* filet(s) *m(pl)*; *(around tennis court*

etc) grillage *m*; *Tex* tulle *m*

nettle ['net(ə)l] N *(weed)* ortie *f*, *Fig* **to grasp the n.** prendre le taureau par les cornes; **to grasp the n. of reorganisation** s'attaquer au problème épineux de la réorganisation

VT *(irritate)* irriter, énerver

▸▸ **n. rash** urticaire *f*

NetWare® loadable module ['netweər] N *Comput* module *m* logiciel téléchargeable

network ['netwɜ:k] N **1** *(of canals, streets, contacts, users etc)* réseau *m*; **electricity n.** réseau électrique **2** *Comput, TV, Radio* réseau *m*; *TV (channel)* chaîne *f*

VT **1** *(to cover)* parcourir; **the country was networked with canals** le pays était parcouru de canaux; **to n. the country with railway lines/motorways** construire un réseau ferroviaire/autoroutier à travers le pays **2** *TV, Radio* diffuser sur l'ensemble du réseau; **networked programmes** émissions *fpl* diffusées en réseau **3** *Comput* mettre en réseau; **networked systems** systèmes *mpl* en réseau

VI *(establish contacts)* établir un réseau de contacts

▸▸ *Comput* **n. access** accès *m* au réseau; *Comput* **n. access costs** coûts *mpl* d'accès au réseau; *Comput* **n. adaptor** carte *f* réseau; *Comput* **n. adaptor card** carte-adaptateur *f* réseau, *pl* cartes-adaptateurs réseau; *Comput* **n. administrator** administrateur, -trice de réseau; *Comput* **n. architecture** architecture *f ou* topologie *f* de réseau; *Comput* **n. card** carte réseau; *Comput* **n. computer** ordinateur *m* de réseau; *TV* **n. controller** contrôleur *m* de réseau, directeur *m* d'antenne ou de chaîne; *Comput* **n. driver** gestionnaire *m* de réseau; **n. management** administration *f* de réseau; **n. manager** gestionnaire de réseau; *Comput* **n. operating system** système *m* d'exploitation réseau; *Comput* **n. server** serveur *m* de réseau; *Comput* **n. software** logiciel *m* de réseau; **n. station** station *f* réseau; **n. supervisor** superviseur *m* de réseau; **n. television** réseau (de télévision) national; *Comput* **n. traffic** trafic *m* de réseau

networking ['netwɜ:kɪŋ] N **1** *Comput* travail *m* en réseau; *(connecting as network)* mise *f* en réseau; **n. capabilities** *(of terminal)* offrir la possibilité d'intégration à un réseau **2** *(establishing contacts)* établissement *m* d'un réseau de contacts

neural ['njʊərəl] ADJ *Anat* neural, -aux

▸▸ *Comput* **n. network** réseau *m* neuronal

neuralgia [njʊ'rældʒə] N *Med* névralgie *f*, **to have n.** avoir une névralgie

neuralgic [njʊ'rældʒɪk] ADJ *Med* névralgique

neurasthenia [njʊərəs'θi:nɪə] N *Med* neurasthénie *f*

neurasthenic [njʊərəs'θenɪk] ADJ, N *Med* neurasthénique *mf*

neuritis [njʊ'raɪtɪs] N *Med* névrite *f*

neurobiology [njʊərəbaɪ'ɒlədʒɪ] N neurobiologie *f*

neurochemistry [njʊərə'kemɪstrɪ] N neurochimie *f*

neurological [njʊərə'lɒdʒɪk(ə)l] ADJ neurologique

neurologist [njʊə'rɒlədʒɪst] N neurologue *mf*

neurology [njʊə'rɒlədʒɪ] N neurologie *f*

neuromuscular [njʊərəʊ'mʌskjuːlər] ADJ neuromusculaire

neuron ['njʊərɒn] N *Physiol* neurone *m*

neurone ['njʊərəʊn] N *Biol* neurone *m*

neuropathology [njʊərəʊpə'θɒlədʒɪ] N neuropathologie *f*

neuropsychiatrist [njʊərəʊsaɪ'kaɪətrɪst] N neuropsychiatre *mf*

neuropsychologist [njʊərəʊsaɪ'kɒlədʒɪst]

N neuropsychologue *mf*

neuroscience ['njʊərəʊsaɪəns] N neuroscience *f*

neurosis, *pl* **neuroses** [njʊ'rəʊsɪs, -si:z] N névrose *f*

neurosurgeon [njʊərəʊ'sɜ:dʒən] N neurochirurgien, -ienne

neurosurgery [njʊərəʊ'sɜ:dʒərɪ] N neurochirurgie *f*

neurosurgical [njʊərəʊ'sɜ:dʒɪk(ə)l] ADJ neurochirurgical, -aux

neurotic [njʊ'rɒtɪk] ADJ **1** *(person)* névrosé; *Fig Fam* **he's positively n. about it** c'est une obsession chez lui; **to be n. about losing one's keys** avoir une peur obsessionnelle de perdre ses clés; **she gets very n. if everything isn't exactly as she left it** elle pique des crises folles si elle ne trouve pas tout exactement comme elle l'a laissé; **I think I'm getting a bit n. about it** je crois que je suis en train d'en faire une obsession **2** *(relating to a neurosis)* névrotique

N névrosé, -ée

neurotically [njʊ'rɒtɪklɪ] ADV de façon obsessionnelle; **to be n. obsessed with sth** avoir une obsession névrotique de qch

neuroticism [njʊ'rɒtɪsɪz(ə)m] N névrose *f*

neurotransmitter [njʊərəʊtrænz'mɪtər] N *Biol* neurotransmetteur *m*

neuter ['nju:tər] ADJ **1** *Gram* neutre **2** *Biol* neutre, asexué

N **1** *Gram* neutre *m*; **in the n.** au neutre **2** *(animal)* animal *m* châtré; *(bee)* abeille *f* asexuée *ou* ouvrière

VT *Vet (cat etc)* châtrer

neutraceutical [nju:trə'sju:tɪk(ə)l] N alicament *m*

neutral ['nju:tr(ə)l] ADJ *(colour)*, *Pol etc* neutre; **to remain n.** rester neutre; *Pol* rester neutre, garder la neutralité

N **1** *(nation)* (État *m ou* pays *m*) neutre *m*; *(person)* ressortissant, -ante d'un État neutre **2** *(person) (in an argument, politics etc)* personne *f* neutre **3** *Aut* point *m* mort; **in n.** au point mort

neutralism ['nju:trəlɪz(ə)m] N neutralisme *m*

neutralist ['nju:trəlɪst] ADJ, N neutraliste *mf*

neutrality [nju:'trælɪtɪ] N *Pol etc* neutralité *f*, *Chem (of salt)* neutralité, indifférence *f*

neutralization [nju:trəlaɪ'zeɪʃən] N neutralisation *f*

neutralize ['nju:trəlaɪz] VT *(opposition, country)* neutraliser; **to n. one another** *(of chemical agents)* se neutraliser; *(of forces)* se neutraliser, s'annuler

neutrino [nju:'tri:nəʊ] N *Phys* neutrino *m*

neutron ['nju:trɒn] N *Nucl* neutron *m*;

▸▸ **n. bomb** bombe *f* à neutrons; **n. star** étoile *f* à neutrons

Nev *abbr* Nevada

never ['nevər] ADV **1** (ne …) jamais; **I n. there** je n'y vais jamais; **n. again!** plus jamais!; **I'll n. go there again, n. again will I go there** je n'irai plus jamais; **he n. came back** il n'est jamais revenu; **he's n. yet been beaten** il n'a encore jamais été battu; **I've n. yet understood why** je n'ai jamais compris pourquoi; **n. in (all) my life, in all my born days** jamais de la vie; **that n.-to-be-forgotten day** ce jour inoubliable; **n. say die!** accroche-toi!; **n. fear!** n'aie pas peur!, ne t'en fais pas! VOIR GRAMMAIRE A21; A78 **2** *(emphatic neg)* **I n. expected him to come** je ne m'attendais pas du tout à ce qu'il vienne; **she n. said a word** elle n'a pas dit un mot; **this will n. do!** c'est inacceptable!; **n. ever do that again!** ne refais jamais cela!; **they n. even wrote back** ils n'ont même pas répondu; **n. a one** pas un seul; *Fam* **you n. left him all alone!** ne me dites pas que vous l'avez laissé tout seul! **3** *Lit* **be he n. so brave** quelque courageux qu'il soit, si courageux soit-il

INT *Br Fam* **n.!** *(incredulity)* pas possible!; **he n. did!** ça alors!; *esp Old-fashioned*, **well I n.!** ça par exemple!

never-ending ADJ perpétuel, éternel, sans fin; *(complaints, noise)* incessant; *(job, sermon, evening)* interminable; **my problems seem to be n.** mes problèmes semblent ne pas en finir; **a n. supply of funny stories** un stock inépuisable d'histoires drôles; **housework is n.** le ménage n'est jamais fini

never-failing ADJ inépuisable, intarissable

nevermore [nevə'mɔːr] ADV *Lit* (ne …) plus jamais, (ne …) jamais plus; **n.!** jamais plus!, plus jamais!

never-never N *Br Fam (hire purchase)* **to buy sth on the n.** acheter qch à crédit *ou* à tempérament

ADJ imaginaire, chimérique

▶▶ **n. land** pays *m* de cocagne; **you're living in n. land if you believe that …** tu rêves si tu crois que …

nevertheless [nevəðə'les] ADV néanmoins, cependant; **I love him n.** je l'aime quand même *ou* malgré tout

nevus ['niːvəs] N *Am* = **naevus**

NEW [njuː] ADJ nouveau, -elle; *(before masculine noun beginning with vowel or silent h)* nouvel; *(not used)* neuf, *f* neuve; **I need a n. car** *(different)* il me faut une nouvelle voiture; **I'd prefer a new car** *or* **a car that's n.** *(which has not been used)* je préférerais une voiture neuve *ou* qui soit neuve; **we visited a n. country** *(one we did not know)* nous avons visité un nouveau pays; **America was a n. country** *(just developing)* l'Amérique était un pays neuf; **I felt a n. man** je me sentais un homme nouveau *ou* neuf; **she's got a n. man** elle a un nouveau mec; **it's made a n. man of him** cela a fait de lui un autre homme *ou* un homme neuf *ou* un nouvel homme; **would you like a n. glass?** *(for a different wine)* désirez-vous un autre verre?; **what's n.?** quoi de neuf *ou* de nouveau?; **that's nothing n.!** rien de nouveau à cela!; **it's quite n. to me** c'est tout nouveau *ou* neuf pour moi; *Fam* **that's a n. one on me!** c'est la première fois que j'entends/je vois cela!; **she's n. to this work** elle débute dans ce travail; **I'm n. to this town** je suis nouveau venu dans cette ville; **to be wearing n. clothes** être habillé de neuf; *Com* **in n. condition, as n.** à l'état (de) neuf; **to do sth up like n.** remettre qch à neuf; **n. ideas** *(modern ideas)* idées neuves; **a completely n. idea** une idée tout à fait nouvelle *ou* neuve; **the subject is quite n.** le sujet n'a pas encore été traité; *Sch* **the n. boys** les nouveaux; *Mktg* **n. and improved** nouveau et meilleur; **n. business** nouvelles affaires *fpl*; *(new company)* nouvelle entreprise *f*; **to look for n. business** faire de la prospection

ADV *(used to form compound adj)* nouvellement; **n. blown** *(flower)* fraîchement *ou Lit* frais épanoui; **n.-cut grass** herbe fraîchement coupée; **n.-found** *(confidence, happiness)* tout neuf; *(friend etc)* nouveau; **n.-laid egg** œuf fraîchement pondu; **n.-made** *or* **n.-baked bread** pain frais; **n. mown hay** foin fraîchement *ou Lit* frais coupé

▶▶ **n. account manager** responsable *mf* des nouveaux comptes-clients; **N. Age** new age *m*, nouvel âge *m*; *Fam* **n. blood** sang *m* neuf; **N. Brunswick** le Nouveau-Brunswick; *Mktg* **n. buy situation** situation *f* de nouvel achat; **N. Caledonia** Nouvelle-Calédonie *f*; **n. classical economics** nouvelle économie *f* classique; **N. England** Nouvelle-Angleterre *f*; *Mil* **the n. guard** la garde montante; **N. Guinea**

Nouvelle-Guinée *f*; *St Exch* **n. issue** nouvelle émission *f*; *St Exch* **n. issue market** marché *m* des nouvelles émissions, marché primaire; **N. Labour** = nouveau nom *m* donné au parti travailliste britannique vers le milieu des années 90 dans le souci d'en moderniser l'image; *Pol* **the N. Left** la nouvelle gauche; **N. Man** homme *m* moderne *(qui participe équitablement à l'éducation des enfants et aux tâches ménagères)*; **n. maths** maths *fpl* modernes; **the n. media** les nouveaux médias *mpl*; **N. Mexico** le Nouveau-Mexique; **n. moon** nouvelle lune *f*; **N. Orleans** La Nouvelle-Orléans; **n. potatoes** pommes *fpl* de terre nouvelles; *Com, Mktg* **n. product** nouveau produit *m*; *Com, Mktg* **n. product development** développement *m* de nouveaux produits; *Com, Mktg* **n. product marketing** marketing *m* de nouveaux produits; **the n. rich** les nouveaux riches *mpl*; *Pol* **the N. Right** la nouvelle droite; *Fin* **n. shares** actions *fpl* nouvelles; **n. technology** nouvelle technologie *f*, technologie de pointe; *Bible* **N. Testament** Nouveau Testament *m*; *Br* **n. town** ville *f* nouvelle; *Med* **n. variant CJD** nouveau variant *m* de la maladie de Creutzfeld-Jacob; **n. wave** *(in cinema)* nouvelle vague *f*, *(in pop music)* new wave *f*; **n. wine** vin *m* primeur; **the N. World** le Nouveau Monde; **N. Year** Nouvel An *m*; **N. Year's Day** jour *m* de l'an; **N. Year's Eve** Saint Sylvestre *f*; **N. York** New York; **N. Yorker** New-Yorkais, -aise; **N. Zealand** Nouvelle-Zélande *f*; **N. Zealander** Néo-Zélandais, -aise

newbie ['njuːbɪ] N *Comput Fam* internaute *mf* novice

newborn ['njuːbɔːn] ADJ nouveau-né, *f* nouveau-née

▶▶ **n. baby** nouveau-né, -née, *pl* nouveaunés, -nées

newcomer ['njuːkʌmər] N nouveau venu *m*, nouvelle venue *f* (**to** dans)

newel ['njuːəl] N *Constr etc* **1** *(of spiral staircase)* noyau *m* (d'escalier) **2** *(of bannister)* pilastre *m*

▶▶ **n. post** pilastre *m*

newfangled ['njuːfæŋg(ə)ld] ADJ *Pej* nouveau genre *inv*; *(word, idea etc)* moderne; **n. gadgets** gadgets *mpl* à la dernière mode

Newfie ['njuːfɪ] N *Can Fam* Terre-Neuvien, -ienne

▶▶ **N. joke** = plaisanterie *f* sur les Terre-Neuviens, ≃ histoire *f* belge

Newfoundland ['njuːfəndlænd, -lənd, -'faʊndlənd] N **1** *Geog* Terre-Neuve *f* **2** *(dog)* terre-neuve *m inv*

ADJ terre-neuvien

▶▶ **N. dog** terre-neuve *m*

Newfoundlander ['njuːfəndlændər, njuː-'faʊndləndər] N *(native)* Terre-Neuvien, -ienne; *(inhabitant)* habitant, -ante de Terre-Neuve

newish ['njuːɪʃ] ADJ *Fam (car, dress etc)* assez neuf, *f* assez neuve

newly ['njuːlɪ] ADV *(usu hyphenated in conjunction with attributive adj before n)* récemment, nouvellement, fraîchement; **n.-dug** fraîchement creusé; **n.-formed** récemment formé; **n.-discovered/returned** qui vient d'être découvert/de rentrer; **n.-elected MPs** députés nouvellement élus; **n.-painted wall** mur qui vient d'être peint

▶▶ **n.-industrialized country** nouveau pays *m* industrialisé; **n.-industrialized economy** économie *f* nouvellement industrialisée; **n.-industrializing country** pays en voie d'industrialisation

newlyweds ['njuːlɪwedz] NPL jeunes mariés *mpl*

newness ['njuːnɪs] N *(of idea etc)* nouveauté

f, *(of piece of clothing etc)* état *m* neuf; *(of bread etc)* fraîcheur *f*, *(of wine)* jeunesse *f*; **her n. to** *or* **in the job** le fait qu'elle soit nouvelle à ce poste

news [njuːz] NPL *(usu with sing verb)* **1** nouvelle(s) *f(pl)*; **what's the n.?** quelles nouvelles?, quoi de nouveau *ou* de neuf?; **there's been no n. so far** on n'a pas encore de nouvelles; **I've got some n. for you** j'ai une nouvelle à vous annoncer; **have you heard the n.?** est-ce que vous avez appris la nouvelle?; **a sad piece of n., sad n.** une triste nouvelle; **good/bad n.** bonne/mauvaise nouvelle; *Prov* **no n. is good n.** pas de nouvelles, bonnes nouvelles; *Prov* **bad n. travels fast** les mauvaises nouvelles vont vite; **I've got some good n. and some bad n.** j'ai deux nouvelles, une bonne et une mauvaise; **have I got n. for you!** j'ai quelque chose à vous annoncer!; **that's n. to me!** première nouvelle!

2 the n. *Radio, TV* les informations *fpl*, *TV (bulletin)* le (télé)journal; **to be in the n.** faire parler de soi dans la presse, *esp Pej* défrayer la chronique; **a city that is in the n. a lot these days** une ville dont on parle beaucoup ces jours-ci; **he's always in the n.** on parle toujours de lui dans la presse; **I heard it on the n.** je l'ai entendu aux informations; **financial n.** chronique financière; **sports n.** chronique des sports; **local/national/world n.** informations locales/nationales/internationales; **n. in brief** faits *mpl* divers

3 *(person, event etc)* sujet *m* propre au reportage; **to make n.** faire sensation; **she's no longer n.** on ne parle plus d'elle; **the fact that she's leaving is bad n. for the company** son départ est mauvais pour la société; *Fam* **he's bad n.** *(is unpopular etc)* c'est un enquiquineur

▶▶ **n. agency** agence *f* de presse; *Am Radio, TV* **n. analyst** commentateur, -trice; **n. blackout** black-out *m inv* sur l'actualité, censure *f* de l'actualité; **to impose a n. blackout on sth** empêcher la divulgation de qch; **the government has imposed a n. blackout** le gouvernement a fait le blackout; **n. broadcasting** diffusion *f* des informations; **n. bulletin** bulletin *m* d'informations; **n. centre** salle *f* de rédaction télévision; **n. channel** chaîne *f* d'information continue; **n. conference** conférence *f* de presse; **n. content** contenu *m* d'informations; **n. coverage** reportage *m* d'actualités; **n. desk** (salle *f* de) rédaction *f*; **n. editor** rédacteur, -trice en chef des actualités; **n. gathering** collecte *f* de l'information; **n. headlines** titres *mpl* de l'actualité; **n. item** nouvelle, information *f*, **n. magazine** news magazine *m*; **n. programme** magazine *m* d'actualités; **n. report** bulletin *m* d'informations; **n. reporter** reporter *m*; **n. satellite** satellite *m* d'informations; *Am* **n. service** = agence de presse qui publie ses informations par le biais d'un syndicat de distribution; **n. sheet** bulletin d'information; **n. short** brève *f*, **n. stand** kiosque *m* à journaux; **n. story** sujet *m*; **n. value** intérêt *m* médiatique; **n. vendor** marchand, -ande de journaux; **n. writer** rédacteur, -trice d'actualités

newsagent ['njuːzeɪdʒənt] N *Br* marchand, -ande de journaux; *(shopkeeper also selling papers)* dépositaire *mf* de journaux; **n.'s** *(shop)* maison *f* de la presse

newscast ['njuːzkɑːst] N *Radio, TV* informations *fpl*

newscaster ['njuːzkɑːstər] N *Radio, TV* présentateur, -trice du journal

newscasting ['njuːzkɑːstɪŋ] N *Radio, TV* présentation *f* du journal

newsdealer ['njuːzdiːlər] N *Am* = **newsagent**

newsfilm ['njuːzfɪlm] N film *m* d'actualités

newsflash ['njuːzflæʃ] N *Radio, TV* flash *m* d'information(s)

newsgroup ['njuːzgruːp] N *Comput* newsgroup *m*, forum *m ou* groupe *m* de discussion

newshawk, newshound ['njuːzhɔːk, -haʊnd] N *Fam* reporter *m*, chasseur *m* de copie

newsie ['njuːzɪ] N *Am Fam (newspaper vendor)* vendeur, -euse de journaux; *(journalist)* journaleux, -euse

newsletter ['njuːzletər] N bulletin *m* (d'informations), circulaire *f*

newsman, *pl* **newsmen** ['njuːzmən] N journaliste *m*

newspaper ['njuːzpeɪpər] N journal *m*; **daily n.** (journal) quotidien *m*; **weekly n.** (journal) hebdomadaire *m*; **to work for** *or* **on a n.** travailler dans *ou* pour un journal; **to wrap sth in/line a drawer with n.** emballer qch dans/tapisser un tiroir de (papier) journal ▸▸ **n. ads** petites annonces *fpl* des journaux; **n. advertisement** publicité *f* presse; **n. advertising** publicité presse; **n. article** article *m* de presse *ou* journal; **n. artist** *(for layout)* maquettiste *mf*; **n. clippings** coupures *fpl* de journaux; **n. cuttings** coupures de journaux; **n. editor** rédacteur, -trice *m* de journal; **n. group** groupe *m* de presse; **n. kiosk** kiosque *m* à journaux; **n. office** bureau *m* de la presse; **n. photographer** photographe *mf* de presse; **n. publisher** éditeur *m* de presse; **n. rack** porte-journaux *m inv*; **n. report** reportage *m*; **n. reporter** reporter *m* (de la presse écrite); **n. stand** kiosque à journaux

newspaperman, *pl* **newspapermen** ['njuːzpeɪpəmən] N **1** *Journ (reporter)* journaliste *m*; *(proprietor)* propriétaire *m* de journal **2** *Br (vendor)* marchand de journaux

newspaperwoman, *pl* **newspaperwomen** ['njuːzpeɪpəwʊmən, -wɪmɪn] N **1** *Journ (reporter)* journaliste *f*, *(proprietor)* propriétaire *f* de journal **2** *Br (vendor)* marchande *f* de journaux

newsprint ['njuːzprɪnt] N papier *m* (de) journal; **I got my hands covered in n.** *(ink)* je me suis mis de l'encre plein les mains

newsreader ['njuːzriːdər] N *Radio, TV* présentateur, -trice du journal

newsreel ['njuːzriːl] N *Cin* actualités *fpl*

newsroom ['njuːzruːm] N *Journ, TV* salle *f* de rédaction des informations

newswoman, *pl* **newswomen** ['njuːzwʊmən, -wɪmɪn] N journaliste *f*

newsworthiness ['njuːzwɜːðɪnɪs] N intérêt *m* médiatique

newsworthy ['njuːzwɜːðɪ] ADJ d'un intérêt médiatique

newsy ['njuːzɪ] ADJ *Fam (letter)* plein de nouvelles

newt [njuːt] N triton *m*; *Br Sl* **pissed as a n.** soûl comme une bourrique, beurré comme un petit lu

new-to-the-company product N *Mktg* produit *m* nouveau dans la compagnie

new-to-the-world product N *Mktg* produit *m* nouveau dans le monde

NEXT [nekst]

ADJ d'à côté **1** ▪ prochain **2, 3**	
▪ suivant **2**	
ADV après **1, 3** ▪ ensuite **1** ▪ la	
prochaine fois **2** ▪ à côté de **3**	
▪ presque **3**	

ADJ 1 *(in location)* d'à côté; **the n. room** la pièce voisine *ou* d'à côté; **it's the n. house** c'est la maison voisine *ou* d'à côté; **the girl (from) n. door** la jeune fille d'à côté; **he lives n. door (to us)** il habite à côté (de chez nous); **he's the boy-n.-door type** c'est un bon petit gars; **n.-door neighbours** voisins *mpl* d'à côté *ou* immédiats; **we are n.-door neighbours** nous sommes voisins; *Fig* **it's n. door to madness** cela confine à la folie; **this has left us n. door to the poorhouse** cela nous a mis quasiment sur la paille

2 *(in time) (in future)* prochain; *(in past or in listing events)* suivant; **I leave n. month** je pars le mois prochain; *Fam* **see you n. week** à la semaine prochaine; **the n. thing I remember is …** la première chose dont je me rappelle après ça c'est …; **the n. week it rained** la semaine d'après *ou* suivante il a plu; **the n. month was awful** le mois suivant fut terrible; **in the n. few weeks we will discover …** dans les semaines à venir *ou* qui vont venir nous allons découvrir …; **in the n. four weeks we were to discover that …** dans les quatre semaines suivantes *ou* qui suivirent nous devions découvrir que …; **this time n. year** d'ici un an; **n. Friday, (on) Friday n.** vendredi prochain; **the n. day** le lendemain, le jour d'après; **the n. day but one** le surlendemain; **(the) n. morning** le lendemain matin; **n. Easter** à Pâques prochain; **n. summer** l'été prochain; **the week/ year after n.** dans deux semaines/ans; **from one moment to the n.** d'un instant à l'autre

3 *(in order)* prochain; **it's the n. station** c'est la prochaine gare; **the n. turning on the right** le prochain tournant à droite; **the n. chapter/page** le chapitre/la page suivant(e); **(the) n. time I see him** la prochaine fois que je le verrai; **ask the n. person you meet** demandez à la première personne que vous rencontrerez; **the n. thing is to …** maintenant il s'agit de …; **your name is n. on the list** votre nom est le suivant *ou* prochain sur la liste; **n. (person) please** au suivant, s'il vous plaît; **who's n.?, whose turn is it n.?** à qui le tour?, c'est à qui?; **you're n.** après c'est ton tour; **(the) n. to speak is …** la parole est maintenant à …; **(the) n. to arrive was Penelope** Penelope est arrivée à la suite; **your train is the n. but one** ton train n'est pas le prochain, mais celui d'après; **the n. size up/ down** la taille au-dessus/au-dessous

ADV 1 *(afterwards)* ensuite, après; **what shall we do n.?** qu'est-ce que nous allons faire maintenant?; **what did you do n.?** qu'avez-vous fait après *ou* ensuite?; *Fam* **you'll be asking me to give up my job (for you) n.!** tu n'as qu'à me demander de laisser tomber mon travail pendant que tu y es!; *Fam* **whatever n.!** par exemple!, et quoi encore!; *Fam* **what (ever) will they think of n.!** que ne vont-ils pas inventer!; *Fam* **what will he do n.!** qu'est-ce qu'il va bien pouvoir faire maintenant?

2 *(again)* la prochaine fois; **when I n. saw him, when n. I saw him** quand je l'ai revu; **when shall we meet n.?** quand nous reverrons-nous?; **we had no idea when we would n. meet** nous ignorions complètement quand nous allions nous revoir

3 n. to à côté de; **her room is n. to mine** sa chambre est à côté de la mienne; **I can't bear wool n. to my skin** je ne supporte pas la laine à même la peau; **I got n. to last loaf** j'ai eu l'avant-dernière baguette; **n. to my dog I like my sister best** après mon chien, c'est ma sœur que je préfère; **I got it for n. to nothing** je l'ai eu pour presque rien *ou* pour une bouchée de pain; **there's n. to nothing left** il ne reste presque rien; **there is n. to no evidence** il n'y a pour ainsi dire pas de preuves; **in n. to no time** en un rien de temps; *Am Fam* **to get n. to sb** *(friendly with)* se mettre bien avec qn; *(emotionally involved with)* se lier avec qn; *(have sex with)* coucher avec qn

4 *(with superlatives)* **the n. best thing would be to …** à défaut, le mieux serait de …; **the n. fastest after the Ferrari was …** la voiture la plus rapide après la Ferrari était …; **the n. highest building in the world is …** le deuxième immeuble dans le monde pour la hauteur, c'est …; **Mark is the n. oldest/youngest** *(second oldest/youngest of all of them)* Mark est le second par ordre d'âge; **who is the n. oldest/youngest after Mark?** qui est le suivant *ou* le prochain par ordre d'âge après Mark?

next-day delivery N *Com* livraison *f* lendemain

next-of-kin N *(relative)* parent *m* le plus proche; *(used as pl)* famille *f*; **to inform the n.** prévenir la famille

NGO [endʒiː'əʊ] N *(abbr non-governmental organization)* ONG *f*

NG take [en'dʒiː] N *TV, Cin* mauvaise prise *f*

NH *abbr* New Hampshire

NHI [eneɪtʃ'aɪ] N *Br (abbr* **National Health Insurance***)* ≃ Sécurité *f* sociale

NHS [eneɪtʃ'es] N *Br (abbr* **National Health Service***)* ≃ Sécurité *f* Sociale

NI [e'naɪ] N *Br (abbr* **National Insurance***)* = système *m* britannique de sécurité sociale (maladie, retraite) et d'assurance chômage

Niagara [naɪ'æg(ə)rə] N Niagara *m* ▸▸ **N. Falls** les chutes *fpl* du Niagara

nib [nɪb] N **1** *(of fountain pen)* (bec *m* de) plume *f*; **broad n.** grosse plume, plume à gros bec; **fine n.** plume fine, plume à bec fin **2** *Tech (of tool etc)* pointe *f*

nibble ['nɪb(ə)l] N **1** *(action)* grignotement *m*; **to have a n. at the cake** grignoter le gâteau **2** *Fishing* touche *f*; **I didn't get** *or* **have a n. all day** le poisson n'a pas mordu *ou* je n'ai pas fait une seule touche de toute la journée **3** *(of biscuit etc)* petit morceau *m*; **to have a n.** grignoter quelque chose; **I feel like a n. of something** j'ai envie de grignoter un petit morceau; *Fam* **nibbles** amuse-gueules *mpl* ▪ **VT** grignoter; **to n. sb's ear** mordiller l'oreille à qn ▪ **VI** *(of fish), Fam (of person)* mordre à l'hameçon

▸ **nibble at** VT INSEP *(biscuit etc)* grignoter; **she was nibbling at his ear** elle lui mordillait l'oreille; **to n. at the bait** *(of fish), Fam (of person)* mordre à l'hameçon; **they're nibbling at our offer** notre offre les séduit

▸ **nibble away** VT SEP *(remove)* grignoter entièrement

▸ **nibble away at** VT INSEP *(biscuit, carrot)* grignoter; *Fig (value of money etc)* écorner, entamer

▸ **nibble on** VT INSEP *(biscuit etc)* grignoter

nibbler ['nɪblər] N grignoteur, -euse; **he's a compulsive n.** il n'arrête pas de grignoter

nibs [nɪbz] N *Fam Iron* **his/her n.** son altesse

NIC [enaɪ'siː] N **1** *(abbr* **newly-industrialized country***)* NPI *m* **2** *(abbr* **newly-industrializing country***)* pays *m* en voie d'industrialisation **3** *(abbr* **national insurance contribution***)* cotisation *f* à la Sécurité sociale **4** *Comput (abbr* **network interface card***)* carte *f* (d')interface réseau

NiCad battery [nɪ'kæd] N accumulateur *m* au cadmium nickel

NICAM, Nicam ['naɪkæm] N *(abbr* **near-instantaneous companded audio multiplex***)* Nicam *m*

Nicaragua [nɪkə'rægjʊə] N Nicaragua *m*

Nicaraguan [nɪkə'rægjʊən] ADJ nicaraguayen

N Nicaraguayen, -enne

nice [naɪs] ADJ **1** *(pleasant) (person)* gentil, *f* gentille, agréable, aimable; *(car, house, shirt, park, trip etc)* joli, beau, *f* belle; *(meal, idea, hotel etc)* bon, *f* bonne; *(view)* beau;

(evening, smell, taste) bon, agréable; *(place)* agréable; **it's n. here** c'est bien, ici; **to have a n. time** bien s'amuser; **sending flowers was a n. gesture** c'était gentil d'envoyer des fleurs; **to be n. to sb** se montrer gentil *ou* aimable envers qn; **it is n. of you to …** c'est gentil de votre part de …, vous êtes bien aimable de …; **it's not n. of you to make fun of him** ce n'est pas gentil *ou* bien de vous moquer de lui; **it's not a n. thing to happen to anyone** ce n'est pas agréable quand ça arrive; **he's a n. chap** il est gentil, c'est un gentil garçon; **have a n. day!** bonne journée!; **it's turned out n. again** il fait encore beau; **the garden is beginning to look n.** le jardin commence à être joli; *Fam* **n. one!** bien joué!, bravo!

2 *(intensive)* **n. and handy** bien commode; **it's n. and cool** il fait bien frais; **it's n. and easy** c'est très facile; **a n. cold drink** une boisson bien fraîche; **to have a n. long chat** faire une bonne petite causette

3 *(respectable)* **n. people** des gens bien; **he's such a n. boy** il est tellement bien, ce garçon; **it's not n.** ce n'est pas bien; **it's not a n. story** c'est une histoire peu édifiante

4 *Iron* **we are in a n. mess!** nous voilà dans de beaux draps!; **that's a n. way to behave!** en voilà des manières!; **that's a n. way to talk to your mother/father/sister!** en voilà une manière de parler à ta mère/ton père/ta sœur!; **you're a n. one to talk about being punctual!** tu peux bien parler d'être ponctuel!

5 *Fml (delicate, subtle) (question etc)* délicat; *(taste etc)* subtil, fin, recherché; *(distinction)* subtil; **it's a n. point** c'est délicat

6 *Old-fashioned (scrupulous)* scrupuleux

nice-looking [-lʊkɪŋ] **ADJ** beau, *f* belle, joli

nicely ['naɪslɪ] **ADV 1** *(pleasantly, kindly)* gentiment; *(well)* bien; **ask n.!** demande poliment!; **sit n., Jessica!** tiens-toi bien, Jessica!; **to be coming along** *or* **doing n.** *(of roast, cake etc)* être bien en train de cuire; *(of garden)* commencer à prendre tournure; *(of investments)* bien se porter; *(of invalid, pupil)* faire de bons progrès; **to do n.** *(for oneself)* bien s'en sortir; **everything was n. done** tout était bien fait; **those will do (very) n.** ceux-là feront très bien l'affaire; **he spoke very n. about you** il m'a parlé de vous en très bons termes **2** *(accurately) (judged)* exactement, avec justesse; *(scrupulously)* minutieusement, scrupuleusement; **a n. turned phrase** une phrase bien tournée; **that's n. put** voilà qui est bien dit **3** *(respectably)* **n. brought up** bien élevé

niceness ['naɪsnɪs] **N 1** *(pleasantness) (of person)* gentillesse *f*, amabilité *f*; *(of house, hotel etc)* caractère *m* agréable; **the n. of the weather** le temps agréable **2** *Fml (delicacy, subtlety) (of question)* délicatesse *f*; *(of taste, distinction)* subtilité *f*

nicety ['naɪsɪtɪ] **N 1** *(of calculation etc)* exactitude *f*, précision *f*; *(of judgement)* finesse *f*; *(of question)* subtilité *f*, délicatesse *f*; **to a n.** exactement, à la perfection **2 niceties** *(subtleties)* subtilités *fpl*; **social niceties** règles *fpl* de la politesse

niche [niːʃ] **N** *(recess)* niche *f*; *Fig* **to find one's n.** trouver sa voie; *Fig* **to carve out** *or* **make a n. for oneself** *(trouver à)* se caser
▸▸ **n. broadcasting** = diffusion *f* d'émissions destinées à un public restreint; *Com, Mktg* **n. market** niche, créneau spécialisé; *Com, Mktg* **n. marketing** marketing *m* de créneau, marketing ciblé; *Com, Mktg* **n. player** acteur *m* sur un segment de marché; *Com, Mktg* **n. product** produit *m* ciblé; *TV* **n. programming** = programmation *f* d'émissions destinées à un public restreint; **n. publish-**

ing = publication *f* d'ouvrages destinés à un public restreint

nicher ['niːʃər] **N** *Mktg* spécialiste *mf* dans une niche

niching ['niːʃɪŋ] **N** *Mktg* segmentation *f* en niches

Nick [nɪk] **N** *Fam* **Old N.** le diable

nick [nɪk] **N 1** *(in wood)* entaille *f*, encoche *f*; *(in blade)* brèche *f*; *(on chin, in finger etc)* entaille, coupure *f*; **to give oneself a n.** se couper **2 in the n. of time** juste à temps; **you've come just in the n. of time** vous tombez bien **3** *Br Fam (condition)* état *m*; **in good/bad n.** en bon/mauvais état; **he's in pretty good n. for his age** il est en bonne forme pour son âge **4** *Br Sl (prison)* taule *f*; *(police station)* poste *m* (de police)

VT 1 *(stick etc)* entailler, encocher; *(blade)* ébrécher; *(cards)* biseauter; **to n. oneself** se couper; **to n. one's finger/chin** s'entailler *ou* se couper le doigt/le menton **2** *esp Br Sl (arrest)* pincer, choper, épingler; **to get nicked** se faire pincer *ou* choper *ou* épingler; **you're nicked!** tu es fait! **3** *esp Br Sl (steal)* piquer, faucher; **it was nicked last week** quelqu'un l'a piqué *ou* fauché la semaine dernière **4** *Am Sl (overcharge)* **they've nicked me for 50 dollars** je me suis fait avoir de 50 dollars; **how much did they n. you for that?** combien ils t'ont fait payer ça?

nickel ['nɪk(ə)l] **N 1** *Metal* nickel *m* **2** *Am (coin)* pièce *f* de cinq cents; *Fam* **it's not worth a plugged n.** ça vaut pas un clou
VT (**-ll-**, *Am* **-l-**) nickeler
▸▸ **n. plating** nickelage *m*

nickel-and-dime **ADJ** *esp Am (business operation)* de quatre sous

nickel-cadmium battery **N** batterie *f* au nickel-cadmium

nickel-plate **VT** nickeler

nicker ['nɪkər] **N** *(no pl)* *Br Sl* livre *f* (sterling); **five n.** cinq livres

nickname ['nɪkneɪm] **N** surnom *m*
VT surnommer

nicotine ['nɪkətiːn] **N** nicotine *f*; **n.-stained** *(fingers, teeth)* jauni de nicotine
▸▸ **n. addict** accro *mf* à la nicotine; **n. addiction** tabagisme *m*; **n. patch** patch *m ou* timbre *m* anti-tabac; **n. poisoning** tabagisme, intoxication *f* nicotinique

nicotinism ['nɪkətiːnɪz(ə)m] **N** *Med* nicotinisme *m*, tabagisme *m*

niece [niːs] **N** nièce *f*

Nielsen ['niːlsən] **N**
▸▸ *Am TV* **N. Ratings** ≃ l'Audimat® *m*

niff [nɪf] **N** *Br Sl* **N** puanteur *f*; **there's a bit of a n. in here** ça pue là-dedans
VI puer

niffy ['nɪfɪ] **ADJ** *Br Sl* puant, qui pue; **it's a bit n. in here** ça pue là-dedans

nifty ['nɪftɪ] **ADJ** *Fam* **1** *(clever) (person)* adroit, débrouillard; *(thing)* commode; **he's pretty n.** il se débrouille bien; **that was a n. piece of driving** ça c'est de la conduite!; **a n. piece of footwork** un beau jeu de jambes; **a n. idea** une idée géniale; **it's a very n. little car** c'est une petite voiture très commode *ou* pratique **2** *Am (attractive) (dress etc)* coquet, pimpant

Niger [niː'ʒeər] **N 1** *(river)* Niger *m* **2** *(country)* (République *f* du) Niger *m*

Nigeria [naɪ'dʒɪərɪə] **N** Nigeria *m*

Nigerian [naɪ'dʒɪərɪən] **ADJ** nigérian
N Nigérian, -ane

niggard ['nɪgəd] **N** *Old-fashioned* pingre *mf*, avare *mf*

niggardliness ['nɪgədlɪnɪs] **N** *(of person)* avarice *f*, pingrerie *f*; *(of sum, salary)* maigreur *f*

niggardly ['nɪgədlɪ] **ADJ** *(person)* avare, pingre, mesquin; *(sum, portion)* maigre; *(budget)* étroit; *(acknowledgement)* mesquin; **don't be so n. with the wine/caviare!** ne sois pas aussi regardant sur le vin/caviar!; **she's quite n. with her compliments/thanks** elle est assez avare de compliments/de remerciements

nigger ['nɪgər] **N** *Offensive Sl* nègre *m*, négresse *f*; *Old-fashioned Fam* **there's a n. in the woodpile** il y a anguille sous roche; *Old-fashioned Fam* **he's the n. in the woodpile** le problème, c'est lui

niggle ['nɪg(ə)l] **VI** *(be overfussy)* couper les cheveux en quatre; **he always has something to n. about** *(complain)* il a toujours quelque chose à redire; **don't n. about details** ne chipote pas sur les détails; **he's been niggling on at** *or* **away at me all week** il m'a cassé les pieds toute la semaine (**about** à propos de)
VT *(of doubt etc)* triturer l'esprit à, tracasser; *(annoy)* embêter; **he keeps niggling me to get it done** il n'arrête pas de m'embêter *ou* de me casser les pieds pour que je le fasse
N 1 *(minor criticism)* petit reproche *m*; **I've just one or two little niggles about …** il y a juste une ou deux petites choses à revoir au niveau de … **2** *(worry)* tracasserie *f*, doute *m* **3** *(complaint)* protestation *f*; **to have a little n. about sth** ronchonner à propos de qch

niggler ['nɪglər] **N** *(who annoys people)* enquiquineur, -euse; *(who worries about details)* coupeur, -euse de cheveux en quatre

niggling ['nɪg(ə)lɪŋ] **ADJ** *(details etc)* insignifiant; *(pain)* persistant; *(doubt, worry)* insinuant; **I've got a n. feeling that I left the light on** je n'arrête pas de me demander si je n'ai pas laissé la lumière allumée

nigh [naɪ] *Arch, Lit, Dial* **ADV** près, proche; **n. unto death** près de mourir; **the end is n.!** la fin est proche!
PREP près de

night [naɪt] **N 1** *(hours of darkness)* nuit *f*; *(evening)* soir *m*; **at n.** (à) la nuit; *(in the evening)* le soir; **in the n.** (pendant) la nuit; **last n.** *(in the evening)* hier soir; **the n. before** la veille (au soir); **I saw him on Thursday n.** je l'ai vu jeudi soir; **ten o'clock at n.** dix heures du soir; **it was a warm n.** la nuit était douce; **all n. long** toute la nuit; **good n.!** *(when going to bed)* bonne nuit!; *(when leaving)* bonsoir!; **to have a good/bad n.** bien/mal dormir; **to have a late/an early n.** se coucher tard/tôt; **too many late nights can be bad for you** se coucher tard trop souvent peut nuire à la santé; **to work day and n.** *or* **n. and day** travailler nuit et jour; **to have a n. off** avoir une soirée libre; **to travel by n.** *or* **at n.** voyager de nuit *ou* la nuit; **we stayed the n. (there)** nous y avons passé la nuit; **to spend the n. together/with sb** passer la nuit ensemble/avec qn; **the n. sky, the sky at n.** le ciel nocturne; **n. is falling** la nuit tombe, il commence à faire nuit; **n. boat/train/flight** bateau *m*/train *m*/vol *m* de nuit

2 *(evening's entertainment)* soirée *f*; **to have a n. out** sortir; **that was a great n. last n.** on a passé une super soirée hier; **to make a n. of it** faire la fête toute la nuit; *Theat* **first n.** première *f*; **Wagner n.** soirée Wagner
▸▸ **n. bird** *Orn* oiseau *m* nocturne *ou* de nuit; *Fig (person)* noctambule *mf*, oiseau de nuit; **n. blindness** héméralopie *f*; **n. clerk** *(in hotel)* réceptionniste *mf* de nuit; **n. clothes** vêtements *mpl* de nuit; **n. driving** conduite *f* de nuit; **n. editor** rédacteur, -trice de nuit *(dans un journal)*; *Mil, Aviat* **n. fighter** chasseur *m* de nuit; *Cin* **n. filter** filtre *m* pour effet de nuit; **n. light** lampe *f* veilleuse, veilleuse *f*; **n. manager** directeur, -trice de nuit; **n. nurse** infirmier, -ière de nuit; *Fam* **n. owl** couche-tard *mf inv*, oiseau de nuit; **n. porter**

portier, -ère de nuit; *Fin* **n. rate** tarif *m* de nuit; *Banking* **n. safe** coffre(-fort) *m* de nuit, *pl* coffres(-forts) de nuit; **n. school** cours *mpl* du soir; **n. shift** *(work force)* équipe *f* de nuit; *(period of duty)* poste *m* de nuit; **n. soil** fumier *m (d'excréments humains)*; *Am* **n. stick** *(of policeman)* matraque *f*, **n. storage heater** radiateur *m* à accumulation; *Am* **n. table** table *f* de chevet; **n. watch** *(period, guards)* garde *f* de nuit; *Naut* quart *m* de nuit; **n. watchman** veilleur *m* de nuit; **n. work** travail *m* de nuit

nightcap ['naɪtkæp] **N 1** *(drink)* = boisson *f* prise avant de se coucher; **would you like a n.?** prendrez-vous quelque chose avant de vous coucher? **2** *(hat)* bonnet *m* de nuit

nightclub ['naɪtklʌb] **N** boîte *f* de nuit

nightclubbing ['naɪtklʌbɪŋ] **N to go n.** sortir en boîte

nightdress ['naɪtdres] **N** chemise *f* de nuit

nightfall ['naɪtfɔːl] **N** tombée *f* du jour *ou* de la nuit; **at n.** à la nuit tombante

nightgown ['naɪtgaʊn] **N** chemise *f* de nuit

nighthawk ['naɪthɔːk] **N** *Am Fam (person)* noctambule *mf*, *Hum* oiseau *m* de nuit

nightie ['naɪtɪ] **N** *Fam* = **nightdress**

nightingale ['naɪtɪŋgeɪl] **N** rossignol *m*

nightjar ['naɪtdʒɑːr] **N** *(bird)* engoulevent *m* (d'Europe)

nightlife ['naɪtlaɪf] **N** vie *f* nocturne; **what's the n. like?** qu'est-ce qu'on peut faire le soir?; **there's not much n.** il n'y a pas grand-chose à faire le soir

night-light **N** veilleuse *f*

nightlong ['naɪtlɒŋ] **ADJ** *(party, wake etc)* qui dure toute la nuit

nightly ['naɪtlɪ] **ADJ** de toutes les nuits; *(in the evening)* de tous les soirs; **it's a n. occurrence** c'est comme ça toutes les nuits/tous les soirs; **there are n. flights** il y a des vols toutes les nuits; **he would take his n. stroll** il faisait sa promenade nocturne
ADV toutes les nuits; *(in the evening)* tous les soirs; **performances n.** représentations tous les soirs
▸▸ **n. performance** *(sign)* représentation tous les soirs

nightmare ['naɪtmeər] **N** *also Fig* cauchemar *m*; **to give sb nightmares** donner des cauchemars à qn; **getting to work was an absolute n.** se rendre au travail était un véritable cauchemar; **the journey/experience was a n.** ça a été un voyage/une expérience cauchemardesque

nightmarish ['naɪtmeərɪʃ] **ADJ** cauchemardesque

night-night **INT** *Fam* bonne nuit

nightrobe ['naɪtrəʊb] **N** *Am* chemise *f* de nuit

nights [naɪts] **ADV** *(to work)* de nuit

nightshade ['naɪtʃeɪd] **N** *Bot* **(black) n.** morelle *f* noire

nightshirt ['naɪtʃɜːt] **N** chemise *f* de nuit

nightstand ['naɪtstænd] **N** *Am* table *f* de nuit

night-time **N** nuit *f*; **at n.** la nuit
ADJ nocturne; **n. television** télévision *f* de nuit

nightwear ['naɪtweər] **N** vêtements *mpl* de nuit

nihilism ['naɪ(h)ɪlɪz(ə)m] **N** nihilisme *m*

nihilist ['naɪ(h)ɪlɪst] **N** nihiliste *mf*

nihilistic [naɪ(h)ɪ'lɪstɪk] **ADJ** nihiliste

Nikkei index ['nɪkeɪ] **N** indice *m* Nikkei

nil [nɪl] **N** rien *m*; *(on report sheet etc)* néant *m*; *Sport* zéro *m*; *Fin* **the balance is n.** le solde est nul; **they won three n.** ils ont gagné par trois à zéro **VOIR GRAMMAIRE A77**

Nile [naɪl] **N** Nil *m*

---

nimble ['nɪmb(ə)l] **ADJ** *(person, fingers etc)* agile, souple; *(leap, movement)* leste, agile; *(mind, thinking etc)* vif, *f* vive; **n.-fingered** aux doigts agiles *ou* souples *ou* de fée; **n.-footed** aux pieds agiles *ou* légers

nimbleness ['nɪmb(ə)lnɪs] **N** *(of person, limbs etc)* agilité *f*, souplesse *f*; *(of movement, leap)* agilité; *(of mind etc)* vivacité *f*

nimbly ['nɪmb(ə)lɪ] **ADV** *(to move, leap)* agilement, avec légèreté; **she n. unpicked the knot** elle a défait le nœud de ses doigts agiles *ou* souples

nimbus, *pl* **nimbi, nimbuses** ['nɪmbəs, -aɪ, -əsɪz] **N 1** *Met* nimbus *m* **2** *(of saint) (cloud)* nuage *m* lumineux; *(halo)* halo *m* **3** *Art* nimbe *m*, auréole *f*

NIMBY, nimby ['nɪmbɪ] **N** *Fam (abbr* **not in my back yard)** = personne *f* qui est favorable à un projet (construction d'autoroute, offre d'asile etc) à condition qu'il ne soit pas mis en œuvre près de chez elle

nimrod ['nɪmrɒd] **N** *Am Fam (fool)* crétin, -ine, andouille *f*

nincompoop ['nɪŋkəmpuːp] **N** *Fam* nigaud, -aude, andouille *f*; **you stupid n.!** bougre d'andouille!

nine [naɪn] **N** neuf *m*; **n. and four are thirteen** neuf et quatre font treize; **it's n. o'clock** il est neuf heures; **to be n.** *(in age)* avoir neuf ans; *Cards* **the n. of diamonds** le neuf de carreau; *Fam* **dressed up to the nines** sur son trente et un; **to work n. to five** travailler de 9 à 5; **I couldn't stand a n.-to-five job** je ne supporterais pas de travailler de 9 à 5; **9/11** *(11 September 2001)* le 11 septembre; **there must never be another 9/11** les événements du 11 septembre ne doivent plus jamais se reproduire
PRON neuf; **I need n. (of them)** il m'en faut neuf, j'en ai besoin de neuf
NUM ADJ neuf; **n. times out of ten** neuf fois sur dix; **to have n. lives** *(of cat)* avoir neuf vies; *(of person)* avoir l'âme chevillée au corps; **to dial** *Br* **999** *or Am* **911** appeler les urgences

ninefold ['naɪnfəʊld] **ADJ there's been a n. increase in …** … a été multiplié par neuf
ADV to increase n. (se) multiplier par neuf

ninepin ['naɪnpɪn] **N 1 ninepins** *(game)* (jeu *m* de) quilles *fpl* **2** *(pin)* quille *f*; *Fam* **to go down like ninepins** tomber comme des mouches

nineteen [naɪn'tiːn] **NUM ADJ, N** dix-neuf *m*; **she is n.** elle a dix-neuf ans; *Br Fam* **to talk n. to the dozen** bavarder comme une pie

nineteenth [naɪn'tiːnθ] **ADJ** dix-neuvième
N 1 *(person, thing)* dix-neuvième *mf* **2** *(fraction)* dix-neuvième *m*
▸▸ *Hum* **the n. hole** *(of golf course)* le bar du golf

1922 Committee [naɪntiːnˈtwentɪˈtuː] **N** *Br Pol* = comité *m* rassemblant les députés de base du parti conservateur

ninetieth ['naɪntɪɪθ] **ADJ** quatre-vingt-dixième
N 1 *(person, thing)* quatre-vingt-dixième *mf* **2** *(fraction)* quatre-vingt-dixième *m*

ninety ['naɪntɪ] **NUM, ADJ, N** quatre-vingt-dix *m*, *Belg, Suisse* nonante; **n.-one/n.-nine** quatre-vingt-onze/quatre-vingt-dix-neuf, *Belg, Suisse* nonante-et-un/nonante-neuf; **the nineties** *(decade)* les années quatre-vingt-dix; **temperatures in the nineties** des températures autour de trente-cinq degrés; **she's in her nineties** elle est nonagénaire; *Law* **n.-nine years' lease** bail *m* emphytéotique de quatre-vingt-dix-neuf ans

ninny ['nɪnɪ] **N** *Old-fashioned Fam* niais, -aise, nigaud, -aude

ninth [naɪnθ] **ADJ** neuvième
N 1 *(person, thing)* neuvième *mf* **2** *(fraction)* neuvième *m* **3** *Mus* neuvième *f*

Nip [nɪp] **N** *Br Offensive Sl (Japanese)* jap *mf*

nip¹ [nɪp] **N 1** *(pinch)* pincement *m*; **to give sb a n.** pincer qn **2** *(of frost, cold)* morsure *f*; *(frost)* coup *m* de gelée; **the n. of the early morning air** le froid *ou* le piquant du petit jour; *Fam* **there's a n. in the air** ça pince, l'air est piquant
VT (-pp-) 1 *(pinch)* pincer; **to n. one's finger** se pincer le doigt **2** *(remove)* *(buds etc)* pincer, éborgner; *Fig Fam* **to n. sth in the bud** écraser *ou* étouffer qch dans l'œuf **3** *(of cold, frost)* *(face, fingers etc)* pincer, piquer; *(buds etc)* brûler; *Bot* **nipped by the frost** brûlé par la gelée
VI *Br Fam (go quickly)* **just n. across** *or* **along** *or* **down to the baker's** cours vite chez le boulanger, fais donc un saut chez le boulanger; **he nipped back to see if she was alright** il est repassé pour voir si elle allait bien; **to n. in and out of the traffic** se faufiler adroitement parmi les voitures; **I'll n. through to Glasgow next week** je ferai un saut à Glasgow la semaine prochaine
▸ **nip in VI** *Br Fam* **I just nipped in to see him** je suis entré juste un instant pour le voir; **if you're passing, do n. in and see us** si vous passez par ici, rendez-vous donc une petite visite; **she saw a parking place and quickly nipped in** elle a vu une place libre et elle s'est empressée de la prendre; **could I just n. in in front of you?** *(in queue etc)* pourrais-je passer devant vous?; **he always nips into the pub on the way home** il fait toujours un petit détour par le pub en rentrant chez lui; **he nipped into the doorway** il s'engouffra dans l'entrée
▸ **nip off VI** *Br Fam* filer; *(to avoid sb/sth)* s'esquiver
VT SEP to n. sth off enlever *ou* couper qch (en le pinçant)
▸ **nip out VI** *Br Fam* sortir; **he's just nipped out for a second** *(from house, office etc)* il est sorti un instant; **I'll n. out and buy a paper** je sors acheter un journal

nip² **N** *Fam (drink) (of brandy etc)* goutte *f*, petit verre *m*, doigt *m*; **to have** *or* **take a n.** boire *ou* prendre une goutte

nipper ['nɪpər] **N 1** *Br Fam (child)* gamin, -ine, gosse *mf*; **I've lived here since I was a n.** j'habite ici depuis que je suis tout(e) gamin(e) *ou* gosse **2** *(of lobster etc)* pince *f* **3 (pair of) nippers** *(tool)* pince(s) *f(pl)*; *(de serrage)*, tenaille(s) *f(pl)*

nipple ['nɪp(ə)l] **N 1** *Anat* mamelon *m*, bout *m* de sein; *(of feeding bottle)* tétine *f* **2** *Geog* mamelon *m* **3** *(grease)* **n.** graisseur *m*

nippy ['nɪpɪ] **ADJ** *Fam* **1** *Br (nimble)* vif, *f* vive; *(quick)* rapide; **look n.!** grouille-toi!; **a n. little car** une petite voiture nerveuse **2** *(wind etc)* froid, piquant; **it's a bit n. today** il fait un froid/un vent vif *ou* mordant aujourd'hui **3** *(flavour)* fort

nirvana [nɪəˈvɑːnə] **N** *Rel* nirvana *m*

nisi ['naɪsaɪ] **ADJ** *Law (decree, order)* provisoire; *(decision)* rendu sous condition

Nissen ['nɪs(ə)n] **N**
▸▸ *Br Mil* **N. hut** abri *m* (en tôle ondulée)

nit [nɪt] **N 1** *Entom* lente *f*; **to have nits** avoir des poux **2** *Br Fam (person)* nigaud, -aude, andouille *f*; **you silly n.!** andouille!; **don't be such a n.!** ne sois pas aussi bête!

niter ['naɪtər] **N** *Am* = **nitre**

nitery ['naɪtərɪ] **N** *Am Fam* boîte *f* de nuit

nit-pick VI *Fam* chercher la petite bête, ergoter, chinoiser

nit-picker N *Fam* chipoteur, -euse

nit-picking N *Fam* chipotage *m*, chinoiserie *f*
ADJ *(attitude etc)* chipoteur, chicanier; **I'm tired of his n. criticisms of everything I do** j'en ai assez qu'il critique tout ce que je fais avec autant de chicanerie

nitrate ['naɪtreɪt] N Chem (of silver etc) nitrate m; **potassium n.** nitrate de potassium, salpêtre m; Agr **n. fertilizers, nitrates** engrais mpl azotés

nitre ['naɪtər] N salpêtre m

nitric ['naɪtrɪk] ADJ Chem
▸▸ **n. acid** acide m nitrique; **n. oxide** oxyde m nitrique

nitro ['naɪtrəʊ] N Sl = **nitroglycerin(e)**

nitrogen ['naɪtrədʒən] N Chem azote m; **to fix n.** (of plant) fixer l'azote
▸▸ **n. dioxide** dioxyde m d'azote

nitroglycerin(e) [naɪtrəʊ'glɪsəri:n] N nitroglycérine f

nitrous ['naɪtrəs] ADJ (oxide etc) nitreux, d'azote

nitty-gritty ['nɪtɪ'grɪtɪ] N Fam (of a matter) aspects mpl pratiques; **when you get down to the n.** quand on considère les aspects pratiques de la chose

nitwit ['nɪtwɪt] N Fam idiot, -ote, imbécile mf; **don't be such a n.!** arrête de faire l'idiot ou l'imbécile!

nix [nɪks] Am Fam N (nothing) rien m (du tout), Sl que dalle
▸ INT rien à faire!
▸ VT (project, proposal) refuser, rejeter

NJ abbr New Jersey

NLM [enel'em] N Comput (abbr **netware loadable module**) module m logiciel téléchargeable

NLQ N Comput (abbr **near letter quality**) qualité f courrier

NM abbr New Mexico

NMD [enem'di:] N (abbr **National Missile Defense**) projet m NMD (programme de défense antimissiles américain)

NMR [ene'ma:r] N Med (abbr **nuclear magnetic resonance**) RMN f

NNTP [enenti:'pi:] N Comput (abbr **Network News Transfer Protocol**) NNTP m

---

NO [nəʊ]

ADJ	pas de **1** ▪ ne… pas **2**
ADV	ne… pas **1** ▪ ne… plus **1** ▪ non **2**
N	non

ADJ VOIR GRAMMAIRE A35; B62–3 **1** (not any) pas de, aucun, -une (with **ne** expressed or understood); **he has no bread** il n'a pas de pain; **this fact is of no importance whatever** ce fait n'a aucune importance; **I have no intention of doing it** je n'ai aucune intention de le faire; **it's no distance** ce n'est pas loin; **I am in no way surprised** je n'en suis aucunement étonné; **no nonsense!** pas de bêtises!; **no smoking** défense de fumer; esp Lit **no father was ever more indulgent** jamais père ne fut plus indulgent
2 (not at all) ne … pas (du tout); **it's no easy job** ce n'est pas une tâche facile; **he's no artist** ce n'est pas un artiste, il n'est pas artiste; **he's no friend of mine** il ne fait pas partie de mes amis, tant s'en faut; Cr **no ball** balle nulle; Fam **no way!** pas question!; Fam **no way am I going to work on Saturday** il n'est pas question que je travaille samedi; **no way can I get him to admit he was wrong** il n'y a pas moyen de lui faire admettre qu'il a eu tort
3 (with gerund) **there's no pleasing him** il n'y a pas moyen de le satisfaire; **there's no getting out of it** impossible de s'en tirer
▸ ADV **1** (with comparatives) ne … plus, ne … pas; **I'm no taller than he (is)** je ne suis pas plus grand que lui; **how is she? – no better** comment va-t-elle? – pas mieux; **no less than £100** pas moins de 100 livres; **he's no longer here** il n'est plus ici
2 (answer) non; **no, no, you're wrong!** mais

non, mais non, vous vous trompez!; **to say no** dire non; (deny) dire que non SEE GRAMMAR B63
3 Arch, Lit, Scot (not) **pleasant or no, it's true** agréable ou non ou pas, c'est vrai; **whether or no** que cela soit ou non
4 Scot Fam (not) **it's no bad** c'est pas mal!; **I'm no going** j'y vais pas
▸ N (pl **noes**) non m inv; **she won't take no for an answer** elle n'acceptera pas de refus; **ayes and noes** (in voting) voix fpl pour et contre; **the noes have it** c'est le non qui l'emporte

No., no (abbr **number**) No, no

Noah ['nəʊə] N Bible Noé m
▸▸ Bible **N.'s ark** l'arche f de Noé

nob¹ [nɒb] N Sl (head) caboche f

nob² N esp Br Sl (upper-class person) aristo mf; **the nobs** les rupins mpl, les aristos mpl

nobble ['nɒb(ə)l] VT Br Fam **1** Horseracing doper (avant la course); Fig **to n. sb's chances of doing sth** bousiller ou saboter les chances que qn a de faire qch **2** (bribe) (witness etc) soudoyer, acheter **3** (steal) faucher, piquer **4** (grab) (thief) pincer, choper, épingler; (person) attraper (au passage); **a journalist nobbled him in the corridor** un journaliste l'a coincé dans le couloir

Nobel [nəʊ'bel] ADJ
▸▸ **N. laureate** lauréat, -ate du prix Nobel; **N. Peace Prize** prix m Nobel de la paix; **N. prize** prix Nobel; **N. prize for Literature** prix Nobel de littérature; **N. prizewinner** lauréat, -ate du prix Nobel

nobility [nəʊ'bɪlɪtɪ] N **1** (of rank, heart etc) noblesse f **2** **the n.** (nobles) la noblesse

noble ['nəʊb(ə)l] ADJ **1** (birth, person) noble; **to be of n. descent** ou **birth** être de naissance noble **2** (sentiment etc) noble; Fam Hum **I'll be n. and let you have the last piece of cake** je vais me montrer grand seigneur et te laisser le dernier morceau de gâteau; Fam Hum **that's very n. of you** c'est très généreux ou charitable de ta part; **to have a n. soul** avoir de la grandeur d'âme **3** (building, proportions, sight etc) majestueux; (mountain) altier, imposant; **4** Chem (gas, metal) noble
▸ N noble mf, aristocrate mf
▸▸ Chem **n. gas** gaz m rare; **n. rot** pourriture f noble; **n. savage** bon sauvage m; **n. soul** grande âme f, **n. wine** vin m noble, grand vin

nobleman, pl **noblemen** ['nəʊb(ə)lmən] N noble m, aristocrate m

nobleminded [nəʊb(ə)l'maɪndɪd] ADJ (person) magnanime, aux nobles sentiments; (sentiment, action, commitment) noble

nobleness ['nəʊb(ə)lnɪs] N **1** (of birth etc) noblesse f **2** (of mind, action etc) noblesse f, (of soul) grandeur f **3** (of statue, horse etc) proportions fpl superbes ou magnifiques; (of building etc) aspect m majestueux

noblewoman, pl **noblewomen** ['nəʊb(ə)lwʊmən, -wɪmɪn] N (femme f) noble f, aristocrate f

nobly ['nəʊb(ə)lɪ] ADV **1** noblement; **n. born** noble de naissance; Fam Hum **he n. gave up his weekends** il a magnanimement renoncé à ses week-ends; **she n. offered him the last piece of cake** elle s'est montré grand seigneur et lui a offert le dernier morceau de gâteau **2** (splendidly) (proportioned etc) magnifiquement, superbement

nobody ['nəʊbədɪ] PRON personne (with **ne** expressed or understood); **n. spoke to me** personne ne m'a parlé; **who's there? – n.** qui est là? – personne; **n. knows it** personne ne le sait; **n.'s perfect** nul ou personne n'est parfait; **n. was more surprised than me** ou **than I (was)** personne n'a été plus étonné que moi; **n. who was there heard anything** aucun de ceux ou personne parmi tous ceux

qui étaient là n'a entendu quoi que ce soit; **there was n. there** or **about** il n'y avait personne; **n. else** personne d'autre; Fam **like n.'s business** comme personne, comme pas un; Fam **the dogs were barking like n.'s business** les chiens aboyaient à vous rompre les tympans; **she's n.'s fool** elle n'est pas folle; **when he was n.** alors qu'il était encore inconnu; **as far as they're concerned, if you don't have money, you're n.** pour eux si tu n'as pas d'argent tu es un zéro ou un moins que rien SEE GRAMMAR B62–3
▸ N (person) nullité f, zéro m; **they're (mere) nobodies** ce sont des gens de rien; **some n. of a journalist** un journaliste à la manque

no-brainer [-breɪnər] N Am Fam (person) crétin, -ine; (question, problem) jeu m d'enfant

no-claim(s) ADJ
▸▸ **n. bonus** (in car insurance) bonus m

nocturnal [nɒk'tɜ:n(ə)l] ADJ nocturne

nocturne ['nɒktɜ:n] N **1** Mus nocturne m **2** Art effet m de nuit

nod [nɒd] N **1** inclination f de la tête; (of consent) signe m d'assentiment, signe de tête affirmatif; (greeting) signe de la tête; **to answer with a n.** répondre d'un signe de tête; **she gave me a n.** elle m'a fait un petit signe de la tête; Fig **to give sb the n.** donner le feu vert à qn; Fam **on the n.** sans débats; **a n. in sb's direction** un signe de tête à l'intention de qn; **these terms are a n. in the direction of Marxist scholars** ces termes sont des renvois ou références aux intellectuels marxistes; Prov **a n. is as good as a wink** = pas besoin d'en dire davantage ou plus (on a compris) **2** **the land of N.** le pays des songes; Hum **to be in the land of N.** être dans les bras de Morphée
▸ VT (-dd-) **to n. one's head** faire un signe de tête (de haut en bas); **she nodded her head in agreement** elle a fait un signe de tête affirmatif; **he nodded his head in agreement at the proposal** il accepta la proposition d'un signe de tête; **to n. one's agreement/approval** consentir/approuver d'un signe de tête
▸ VI **1** **to n.** (in agreement/approval) consentir/approuver d'un signe de tête; **to n. to sb** (in greeting) faire un signe de tête à qn **2** (in sleep) dodeliner (de) la tête **3** (of plumes etc) ballotter, danser
▸ **nod off** VI Fam s'endormir

nodal ['nəʊd(ə)l] ADJ Opt, Phys nodal, -aux

nodding ['nɒdɪŋ] N **I'm on n. terms with my neighbours** mes voisins et moi, nous nous saluons; **we are on n. terms, we have a n. acquaintance** nous nous saluons; **we still only have a n. acquaintance** nous nous saluons et c'est tout; Fig **she had only a n. acquaintance with the town's history** elle n'avait qu'une vague connaissance de l'histoire de la ville

noddle ['nɒd(ə)l] N esp Br Fam (head, intelligence) caboche f; **use your n.!** fais marcher ta caboche ou ton ciboulot!

node [nəʊd] N Astron, Math, Phys (of orbit, curve etc) nœud m, point m nodal; Bot (of tree trunk etc) nœud m; Med nœud, nodosité f; Comput noyau m

nodular ['nɒdjʊlər] ADJ Geol, Med etc nodulaire

nodule ['nɒdju:l] N Geol, Med, Bot nodule m

Noël [nəʊ'el] N **1** (Christmas) Noël m **2** Arch (carol) Noël m

no-fly zone N zone f d'exclusion aérienne

no-frills ADJ (airline, travel) sans prestation de services; (insurance policy etc) de base; (car, bicycle etc) sans gadgets; (service, wedding) sans chichis, tout simple

noggin ['nɒgɪn] N **1** (container) (petit) pot

m; **to have a n.** *(drink)* prendre un verre **2** *Fam (head)* caboche *f*

no-go ADJ
▶▶ **n. area** zone *f* interdite; **this neighbourhood is a n. area for the police** la police n'ose pas s'aventurer dans ce quartier

no-good *esp Am Fam* ADJ bon, *f* bonne à rien
N bon *m* à rien, bonne *f* à rien

no-hoper [-ˈhəʊpər] N tocard *m*

nohow [ˈnəʊhaʊ] ADV *Am Sl* pas question

noise [nɔɪz] N **1** bruit *m*; **a loud n.** un gros bruit; **to make a n.** faire du bruit; *Fig (complain, make a fuss)* protester (**about sth** au sujet de qch); **he made a lot of n. about improving working conditions** *(talked about it)* il a fait beaucoup de bruit au sujet d'une éventuelle amélioration des conditions de travail; *Fam* **the big n.** *(in company etc)* le grand manitou; *Fam* **she's a big n. in publishing** c'est quelqu'un d'important dans le monde de l'édition; *Fam* **shut** *or* **hold your n.!** ferme-la!
2 *(sound)* bruit *m*, son *m*; *Radio, Electron etc* bruit, parasite(s) *m(pl)*; **she's making noises about retiring** elle donne à entendre qu'elle va prendre sa retraite; **to make encouraging noises** dire des choses encourageantes; **to make the right noises** se montrer compréhensif; **clicking n.** cliquetis *m*; **tinkling n.** tintement *m*
▶▶ **n. abatement** lutte *f* contre le bruit; **n. abatement campaign** campagne *f* ou lutte contre le bruit; **n. insulation** insonorisation *f*, **n. level** niveau *m* de bruit

noise-absorbing ADJ insonorisé

noiseless [ˈnɔɪzlɪs] ADJ *(machine, movement etc)* silencieux; **with n. tread** à pas feutrés

noiselessly [ˈnɔɪzlɪslɪ] ADV sans bruit, silencieusement

noiselessness [ˈnɔɪzlɪsnɪs] N silence *f*

noisily [ˈnɔɪzɪlɪ] ADV bruyamment, à grand bruit

noisiness [ˈnɔɪzɪnɪs] N caractère *m* bruyant; **because of the n. of the street** à cause du bruit qu'il y a dans la rue; **I can't stand their n.** je ne peux pas supporter le bruit qu'ils font

noisome [ˈnɔɪsəm] ADJ *Fml* **1** *(offensive)* *(smell)* fétide; *(sight, behaviour, person)* répugnant **2** *(harmful)* *(plant, germ)* nocif, nuisible

noisy [ˈnɔɪzɪ] ADJ bruyant; **to be n.** *(of person)* faire du bruit; **the TV is a bit n.** la télé est un peu forte

no-load fund N *St Exch* fonds *m* sans frais d'acquisition, fonds qui ne prélève pas une commission

nomad [ˈnəʊmæd] ADJ, N nomade *mf*

nomadic [nəʊˈmædɪk] ADJ nomade

no-maintenance battery N batterie *f* sans entretien

no man's land N terrains *mpl* vagues; *Mil, Fig* no man's land *m*, zone *f* neutre; *Fig (intellectual, psychological etc)* zone floue

no-mark N *Fam (pathetic person) (male)* nul *m*, pauvre type *m*; *(female)* nulle *f*

nom de plume, *pl* **noms de plume** [ˈnɒmdəˈpluːm] N pseudonyme *m* *(d'un auteur)*

nomenclature [nəʊˈmɛnklətʃər] N nomenclature *f*

nominal [ˈnɒmɪn(ə)l] ADJ **1** *(in name only)* *(owner, leader)* de nom (seulement), nominal, -aux; *(ownership, leadership)* nominal; **to be the n. head** n'être chef que de nom **2** *(negligible)* insignifiant, nominal, -aux; **a n. amount** une somme insignifiante **3** *(token)* symbolique; **a n. contribution of one pound**

a year une contribution symbolique d'une livre par an
▶▶ *Acct* **n. account** compte *m* d'exploitation générale; *Fin* **n. capital** capital *m* nominal; *Law* **n. damages** dommages-intérêts *mpl* symboliques; *Fin* **n. interest rate** taux *m* d'intérêt nominal; *Acct* **n. ledger** grand-livre *m* général, *pl* grands-livres généraux; *Fin* **n. partner** associé, -ée fictif(ive); *Fin* **n. price** prix *m* nominal; **n. rent** loyer *m* insignifiant; *Fin* **n. value** valeur *f* nominale; *Fin* **n. wages** salaire *m* nominal; *Fin* **n. yield** taux *m* nominal

nominally [ˈnɒmɪn(ə)lɪ] ADV *(in name)* nominalement

nominate [ˈnɒmɪneɪt] VT *(appoint)* nommer, désigner; *(propose)* proposer, présenter la candidature de; *(for award)* sélectionner, nominer; **to n. sb to a post** nommer *ou* désigner qn à un poste; **to n. sb for a post** proposer qn pour un poste; **to n. sb as president** nommer qn président; **the film was nominated for an Oscar** le film a été sélectionné *ou* nominé pour un oscar

nomination [nɒmɪˈneɪʃən] N **1** *(proposal)* *(of candidate etc)* proposition *f*, *(for an award)* nomination *f*; **the three nominations for best actor are …** les trois nominés pour le prix du meilleur acteur sont …; **the film got three Oscar nominations** le film a obtenu trois nominations aux oscars **2** *(appointment)* *(of candidate)* nomination *f*, *(of president, judge etc)* investiture *f*
▶▶ *Pol* **n. papers** dossier *m* de candidature

nominative [ˈnɒmɪnətɪv] *Gram* N nominatif *m*; **in the n.** au nominatif
ADJ nominatif

nominator [ˈnɒmɪneɪtər] N his nominators ceux qui ont proposé sa nomination

nominee [nɒmɪˈniː] N **1** *(proposed)* candidat, -ate **2** *(appointed)* personne *f* désignée; **the government nominees on the commission** les membres de la commission nommés par le gouvernement
▶▶ *St Exch* **n. account** compte *m* d'intermédiaire; **n. company** prête-nom *m*, *pl* prête-noms; *Fin* **n. name** nom *m* de l'intermédiaire; *St Exch* **n. shareholding** actionnariat *m* intermédiaire

non- [nɒn] PREF non-

nonabsorbent [nɒnəbˈzɔːbənt] ADJ non absorbant

nonacceptance [nɒnəkˈsɛptəns] N *(of bill, treaty)* refus *m* d'acceptation

non-adopter N *Mktg* = consommateur *m* qui n'essaie jamais de nouveaux produits

nonagenarian [nəʊnədʒɪˈnɛərɪən] ADJ, N nonagénaire *mf*

nonaggression [nɒnəˈgrɛʃən] N *Pol* non-agression *f*
▶▶ **n. pact** pacte *m* de non-agression

nonalcoholic [nɒnælkəˈhɒlɪk] ADJ *(drink)* non-alcoolisé

nonaligned [nɒnəˈlaɪnd] ADJ *Pol (country)* non aligné

nonalignment [nɒnəˈlaɪnmənt] N *Pol* non-alignement *m*

no-name product N *Mktg* produit *m* sans nom

nonappearance [nɒnəˈpɪərəns] N *(of person)* *Law* non-comparution *f*; **I put his n. down to the fact that …** j'ai pensé qu'il n'était pas venu parce que …

nonarrival [nɒnəˈraɪv(ə)l] N non-arrivée *f*

non-ASCII character N *Comput* caractère *m* non ASCII

nonattendance [nɒnəˈtɛndəns] N absence *f* (**at** à)

non-bank ADJ non-banque

non-business marketing N marketing *m* non-commercial

nonce¹ [nɒns] N *Old-fashioned* **for the n.** pour la circonstance, pour l'occasion
▶▶ *Ling* **n. word** mot *m* créé pour l'occasion

nonce² N *Br Sl (sex offender)* délinquant *m* sexuel *(s'attaquant en particulier aux enfants)*

nonchalance [ˈnɒnʃələns] N nonchalance *f*

nonchalant [ˈnɒnʃələnt] ADJ nonchalant

nonchalantly [ˈnɒnʃələntlɪ] ADV nonchalamment

noncombatant [nɒnˈkɒmbətənt] ADJ, N *Mil* non-combattant *m*, *pl* non-combattants

noncommissioned [ˈnɒnkəˈmɪʃənd] ADJ *Mil* sans brevet
▶▶ **n. officer** sous-officier *m*, *pl* sous-officiers

noncommittal [nɒnkəˈmɪt(ə)l] ADJ *(answer etc)* qui n'engage à rien; **to be n.** *(when answering)* ne pas s'engager; **why are you being so n.?** pourquoi est-ce que tu ne veux pas t'engager?

non-competition clause N clause *f* de non-concurrence

noncompletion [nɒnkəmˈpliːʃən] N *(of job)* non-achèvement *m*; *(of contract)* non-exécution *f*

noncompliance [nɒnkəmˈplaɪəns] N refus *m* (de consentement); **n. with an order** refus d'obéissance à un ordre

nonconductor [nɒnkənˈdʌktər] N *Phys* non-conducteur *m*, *pl* non-conducteurs, mauvais conducteur *m*; *Elec* isolant *m*

nonconformism [nɒnkənˈfɔːmɪz(ə)m] N non-conformisme *m*

nonconformist [nɒnkənˈfɔːmɪst] ADJ, N non-conformiste *mf*, *pl* non-conformistes

nonconformity [nɒnkənˈfɔːmɪtɪ] N non-conformité *f*

noncontributory [nɒnkənˈtrɪbjʊt(ə)rɪ] ADJ *(pension scheme)* sans versements de la part des bénéficiaires

nonconvertible [nɒnkənˈvɜːtəb(ə)l] ADJ inconvertible

non-cumulative ADJ *Fin* non cumulatif

non-current liabilities NPL *Acct* passif *m* non exigible

noncustodial [nɒnkʌsˈtəʊdɪəl] ADJ *(sentence)* n'entraînant pas l'emprisonnement

nondescript [ˈnɒndɪskrɪpt] ADJ *(person, object)* quelconque; *(colour)* neutre, *Pej* fade; **a very n. looking person** une personne d'apparence très quelconque

nondestructive [nɒndɪˈstrʌktɪv] ADJ *(test)* non destructif

nondetachable [nɒndɪˈtætʃəb(ə)l] ADJ inamovible

nondirectional [nɒndəˈrɛkʃən(ə)l, -dɪ-] ADJ *Electron, Radio* non directionnel

non-DOS disk N *Comput* disque *m* à format incompatible avec DOS

non-drip ADJ *(paint)* qui ne coule pas

non-dutiable N *Com* exempt de droits de douane

NONE [nʌn] PRON VOIR GRAMMAIRE A35; B62–3 **1** *(not any)* aucun, -une; **n. of you can tell me** aucun d'entre vous *ou* personne ne peut me le dire; **n. of this concerns me** rien de ceci ne me regarde; **any news today? – n.** pas de nouvelles aujourd'hui? – aucune(s); **n. at all** pas un(e) seul(e); **n. of these books are** *or* *esp Fml* **is worth keeping** tous ces livres sont bons à jeter; **n. of the milk was fresh** tout le lait avait tourné; **how much of the wood did you use? – n. of it** quelle quantité du bois avez-vous utilisée? – pas un seul morceau; **n. of the money/the water was left** il ne restait rien de l'argent/de l'eau; **n. of your impudence!** pas d'insolences!; *Fam* **n. of that!** pas de ça!; *Arch, Hum* **answer came**

there n. de réponse il n'en arriva point
2 (no-one) personne, nul; **the visitor was n. other than the king** le visiteur n'était (nul) autre que le roi; **she is aware, n. better, that …** elle sait mieux que personne que …
3 Admin (in schedules etc) néant
ADV 1 I like him n. the better/worse for that je ne l'en aime pas plus/moins
2 he is n. too bright il est loin d'être brillant; **she was n. too happy about it** elle n'en était pas trop contente; **his position is n. too secure** sa position est loin d'être assurée

non-equity share N St Exch action f sans privilège de participation

non-EU country N pays m hors Union européenne

nonentity [nɒ'nentɪtɪ] N (person) personne f insignifiante; **she's a bit of a n.** elle est plutôt insignifiante

non-erasable memory N Comput mémoire f non-effaçable

nonessential [nɒnɪ'senʃəl] ADJ non essentiel
N (usu pl) **nonessentials** superflu m, accessoire m; **if you're travelling light forget the nonessentials** si tu voyages avec peu de bagages, n'emporte rien de superflu

nonetheless [nʌnðə'les] ADV = **nevertheless**

nonevent [nɒnɪ'vent] N Fam bide m; **the press conference was pretty much a n.** la conférence de presse ne valait pas le déplacement

nonexecutive [nɒnɪg'zekjʊtɪv] N
▸▸ **n. director** administrateur m consultant

nonexistence [nɒnɪg'zɪstəns] N non-existence f

nonexistent [nɒnɪg'zɪstənt] ADJ non existant, inexistant

nonferrous [nɒn'ferəs] ADJ non ferreux

non-fiction N ouvrages mpl généraux
▸▸ **n. section** (of bookshop) rayon m des ouvrages généraux

non-floating exchange rate N Econ taux m de change fixe

non-fulfilment, Am **non-fulfillment** N (of contract) non-exécution f

non-governmental organization N organisation f non gouvernementale

non-impact printer N imprimante f sans impact

non(in)flammable [nɒn(ɪn)'flæməb(ə)l] ADJ ininflammable

non-interlaced display N Comput affichage m non entrelacé

nonintervention [nɒnɪntə'venʃən] N Pol non-intervention f

noninterventionist [nɒnɪntə'venʃənɪst] Pol N non-interventionniste mf, pl non-interventionnistes
ADJ (policy) non-interventionniste, de non-intervention

non-iron ADJ (clothing) lavé-repassé inv

non-judgmental ADJ objectif; **to try to be n.** s'efforcer de ne pas porter de jugements

non-linear ADJ non linéaire

nonmalignant [nɒnmə'lɪgnənt] ADJ Med bénin, f bénigne

non-member N (at club etc) invité, -ée; **open to non-members** ouvert au public; **non-members of the EU** pays mpl non membres de l'UE

non-negotiable ADJ (bill, demands etc) non négociable

non-nuclear ADJ (country) non nucléarisé; (war, defence, policy) non nucléaire

no-no N Fam **that's a n.** c'est défendu; **that subject is a n.** ce sujet est tabou; **criticizing**

his cooking is a n. critiquer sa cuisine est fortement déconseillé

non-observance N (of laws, Lent etc) inobservance f

no-nonsense ADJ (approach) direct; **she's a very n. kind of person** c'est quelqu'un qui ne plaisante pas; **she told him so in her usual n. way** elle le lui a dit très directement, comme à son habitude; **his n. handling of the unrest** la fermeté avec laquelle il a fait face aux troubles

nonpareil ['nɒnpəreɪl] Old-fashioned, Lit N (person) prodige m; (object) chose f sans pareille
ADJ incomparable, sans égal, -aux

non-participating ADJ St Exch (share) sans droit de participation

non-partisan ADJ neutre, impartial, -aux

non-payment N non-paiement m; **for n.** faute de paiement

non-performance N (of contract) non-exécution f, inexécution f

non-performing loan N Banking prêt m en souffrance

non-person N Pol proscrit, -ite; Fam **I felt like a n.** je me suis senti une non-valeur

nonplus [nɒn'plʌs] VT (-ss-) interloquer

non-poisonous ADJ non toxique; (snake) non venimeux; (mushroom) non vénéneux

nonpolluting [nɒnpə'luːtɪŋ] ADJ non polluant, propre

non-printable character N caractère m non imprimable

non-probability method N Mktg (of sampling) méthode f non probabiliste

non-probability sample N Mktg échantillon m non probabiliste

non-probability sampling N Mktg échantillonnage m non probabiliste

non-procedural language N Comput langage m non procédural

non-productive N (capital) improductif

non-profit-making, Am **nonprofit** [nɒn'prɒfɪt] ADJ (association) sans but lucratif; **on a n. basis** sur une base non lucrative

non-proliferation N Mil non-prolifération f
▸▸ **n. treaty** traité m de non-prolifération

non-racist ADJ non raciste

non-random ADJ
▸▸ Mktg **n. sample** échantillon m empirique; Mktg **n. sampling** échantillonnage m empirique

non-recoverable N Comput (file, data) non récupérable

nonrecurring [nɒnrɪ'kɜːrɪŋ] ADJ exceptionnel, extraordinaire
▸▸ **n. expenditure** frais mpl ou dépenses fpl extraordinaires

non-reflecting ADJ anti-reflet

non-refundable packaging N Com emballage m perdu

nonresident [nɒn'rezɪdənt] N non-résident, -ente; Sch externe mf, (in hotel) client, -ente de passage; **open to nonresidents** (hotel) ouvert aux hôtes de passage
ADJ non résident

nonreturnable [nɒnrɪ'tɜːnəb(ə)l] ADJ (bottle) non consigné; (deposit for holiday etc) non remboursable; Com sans réserve de retour

non-return valve N Tech clapet m anti-retour

nonscheduled [nɒn'ʃedjuːld] ADJ (flight) spécial, -aux
▸▸ **n. stop** étape f non prévue

nonsectarian [nɒnsek'teərɪən] ADJ non sectaire

nonsense ['nɒns(ə)ns] N bêtises fpl, idioties fpl; **a piece of n.** une bêtise, une absurdité; **to talk (a lot of) n.** dire des bêtises ou des idioties; **I don't think we'll get any more n. from them** je pense qu'ils vont arrêter leurs bêtises; **I've translated all the words, but the result is absurd** j'ai traduit tous les mots, mais le résultat est complètement absurde; **it's n. to think that …** il est absurde de penser que …; **to make a n. of sth** (undo, go against etc) ôter tout sens à qch; **I won't stand for any n.** je ne supporterai aucune imbécillité; **there's no n. about her** elle ne plaisante pas
INT **n.!** n'importe quoi!
▸▸ N. **verse** vers mpl amphigouriques; **n. word** mot m qui ne veut rien dire, non-sens m

nonsensical [nɒn'sensɪk(ə)l] ADJ (speech, reason etc) absurde, qui n'a pas de sens

nonsensically [nɒn'sensɪklɪ] ADV absurdement

non sequitur [nɒn'sekwɪtər] N **his conversation was full of non sequiturs** il n'y avait pas de suite dans sa conversation; **that's a n.** ça manque de suite

non-sexist ADJ non sexiste
N personne f non sexiste

nonshrink [nɒn'ʃrɪŋk] ADJ irrétrécissable

nonskid [nɒn'skɪd] ADJ antidérapant
▸▸ **n. tyre** (pneu m) antidérapant m

non-smoker N **1** non-fumeur, -euse; **she's been a n. all her life** elle n'a jamais fumé de sa vie **2** Rail (compartment) compartiment m non-fumeurs

non-smoking ADJ (carriage, area) non-fumeurs; (seat) non-fumeur

non-speaking part N Cin, TV rôle m muet

non-specialist N non-spécialiste mf, pl non-spécialistes
ADJ non spécialisé

nonstandard [nɒn'stændəd] ADJ (size etc) spécial, -aux; Ling d'usage non général; **it's a n. usage** ce n'est pas un usage général

nonstarter [nɒn'stɑːtər] N Sport, Horseracing etc non-partant m, pl non-partants; Fam **the project's a n.** le projet est fichu d'avance

nonstick ['nɒn'stɪk] ADJ (frying pan etc) avec revêtement anti-adhésif, qui n'attache pas; (surface) anti-adhésif

non-stop ADJ Rail (train) direct; (journey) sans arrêt; Aviat (flight) sans escale; Cin (show) permanent; (films, cartoons) en continu; **n. music programme** programme m musical en continu
ADV (to talk) sans arrêt; (to work) sans interruption; **we flew to Sydney n.** nous avons fait un vol sans escale jusqu'à Sydney

non-synchronous ADJ Cin, TV non-synchrone

nontaxable [nɒn'tæksəb(ə)l] ADJ non imposable

nontransferability [nɒntrænsfərə'bɪlɪtɪ] N (of property, right) incessibilité f

nontransferable [nɒn'trænsfərəb(ə)l] ADJ (property, right) incessible; (share) nominatif

non-U ADJ Old-fashioned Br Fam = pas classe

non-union ADJ (labour) non syndiqué; (company, firm) qui ne reconnaît pas de syndicat en son sein
▸▸ **n. worker** non-syndiqué m, pl non-syndiqués

non-user N non utilisateur m

nonverbal [nɒn'vɜːb(ə)l] ADJ non verbal, -aux

nonvintage [nɒn'vɪntɪdʒ] ADJ (wine) non millésimé

nonviolence [nɒn'vaɪələns] N non-violence f

nonviolent [nɒn'vaɪələnt] ADJ non violent

nonvoting [nɒn'vəʊtɪŋ] ADJ Fin (share) sans
droit de vote

non-wasting ADJ (asset) indéfectible

non-White ADJ (in South Africa) de couleur
N personne f de couleur

noodle ['nuːd(ə)l] N 1 Culin (usu pl) noodles
nouilles fpl 2 Old-fashioned Fam (simpleton)
nouille f, nigaud, -aude 3 Fam (head) caboche f

nook [nʊk] N (corner) coin m, recoin m; (in
room) renfoncement m; (retreat) refuge m;
nooks and crannies coins et recoins

nooky, nookie ['nʊkɪ] N Sl Hum (sex) crac-
crac m; **he wants his n.** il veut s'envoyer en
l'air

noon [nuːn] N midi m; **it is twelve n.** il est midi; **about n.** vers midi; **the n. train** le train de
midi

noonday ['nuːndeɪ], Old-fashioned **noon-
tide** ['nuːntaɪd] N Lit midi m; **the n. sun** le soleil de midi

no-one ['nəʊwʌn] PRON = **nobody**

noose [nuːs] N nœud m coulant; (for trapping animals) lacet m, lacs m, collet m; (lasso) lasso m; Fig **to put one's head in a n.**
signer son arrêt de mort; **(hangman's) n.**
corde f (de potence)

nope [nəʊp] ADV Fam non

nor [nɔːr] CONJ VOIR GRAMMAIRE A73 **1** (continuing the force of a negative) ni; **he has neither father n. mother** il n'a ni père ni mère, il
n'a pas de père ni de mère; **he neither drinks
n. smokes** il ne boit ni ne fume; **neither she
n. her mother is at home** ni sa mère ni elle ne
sont chez elles
2 (and not) **I do not know, n. can I guess** je
n'en sais rien et je ne peux pas le deviner; **n.
was this all** et ce n'était pas tout; **I haven't
read it, n. do I intend to** je ne l'ai pas lu et
d'ailleurs je n'en ai pas l'intention; **he hasn't
any, n. have I** il n'en a pas, ni moi non plus ou
et moi non plus; **n. do I/does his wife** moi/sa
femme non plus VOIR GRAMMAIRE A78

Norah ['nɔːrə] N Br Fam **flaming N.!** punaise!, purée!; **bloody N.!** putain!

Nordic ['nɔːdɪk] Geog ADJ nordique, scandinave
N Nordique mf, Scandinave mf

nordic ['nɔːdɪk] ADJ Ski nordique

nor'east [nɔː'riːst] Naut = **northeast**

nor'easterly [nɔː'riːstəlɪ] Naut = **northeasterly**

nor'eastern [nɔː'riːstən] Naut = **northeastern**

nork [nɔːk] N Br, Austr Sl (breast) nichon m

norm [nɔːm] N norme f; **according to the n.**
selon la norme; **to deviate from the n.** sortir
de la norme; **it's the n.** c'est la règle

normal ['nɔːm(ə)l] ADJ (person, situation,
behaviour, development, result) normal,
-aux; Math (line etc) normal (**to** à); Chem (solution etc) normal, titré; **it's n. to react/feel
like that** c'est normal de réagir/se sentir
comme ça; **he arrived at the n. time** il est arrivé à l'heure habituelle; **any n. person
would have ...** toute personne normalement constituée aurait ...; **n. temperature**
température f moyenne ou normale; **n.
working** or **running** (of engine etc) régime
m normal
N 1 état m normal, condition f normale;
Math normale f, perpendiculaire f; **temperature above n.** température f au-dessus de la
normale; **things quickly got back to n. after
the strike** les choses rentrèrent rapidement
dans l'ordre après la grève; **he'll soon be
back to n.** tout rentrera bientôt dans l'ordre
2 Geom normale f

▶▶ **n. distribution** distribution f normale; **n.
distribution curve** courbe f de distribution
normale

normal-angle lens N Phot objectif m à focale fixe

normality [nɔː'mælɪtɪ], Am **normalcy**
['nɔːməlsɪ] N normalité f; **a return to n.** un retour à la normale; **to return to n.** redevenir
normal

normalization [nɔːməlaɪ'zeɪʃən] N normalisation f

normalize ['nɔːməlaɪz] VT normaliser
VI se normaliser, redevenir normal

normally ['nɔːməlɪ] ADV normalement; **n. I
would have offered you a lift, but ...** je vous
aurais bien proposé de vous emmener, mais
...; **I wouldn't n. ask you, but everyone else
is away** cela m'ennuie de vous le demander,
mais tous les autres sont partis

Norman ['nɔːmən] ADJ 1 Geog, Hist normand
2 Archit roman (anglais)
N 1 (person) Normand, -ande 2 Ling normand m
▶▶ Hist **the N. Conquest** la conquête normande (de l'Angleterre); Ling **N. French** normand m

Normandy ['nɔːməndɪ] N Normandie f; **in N.**
en Normandie
▶▶ Hist **the N. landings** le débarquement

normative economics ['nɔːmətɪv] N économie f normative

nor'nor'east [nɔːnɔː'riːst] Naut = **north-
northeast**

nor'nor'west [nɔːnɒː'west] Naut = **north-
northwest**

Norse [nɔːs] ADJ (Scandinavian) scandinave,
nordique; (Norwegian) norvégien
N 1 Hist **the N.** (Norwegians) les Norvégiens
mpl; (Vikings) les Vikings mpl 2 Ling nordique m, norrois m; **Old N.** vieux norrois
▶▶ **N. legends** légendes fpl scandinaves; **N.
mythology** mythologie f scandinave

Norseman, pl **Norsemen** ['nɔːsmən] N Hist
Scandinave m

north [nɔːθ] N nord m; **the house faces n.** la
maison est exposée au nord; **in the n.** au
nord, dans le nord (**of** de); **to live in the n.
of England** habiter dans le nord de l'Angleterre; **true n.** nord vrai ou géographique;
magnetic n. nord magnétique; Hist **the N.**
(in American Civil War) = les États mpl anti-
esclavagistes du nord des États-Unis; (affluent countries) **the n.** hémisphère m nord; **the
(Canadian) Far N.** le Grand Nord Canadien;
the N.-South divide la division nord-sud
ADV au nord; **to travel n.** voyager vers le
nord; **it's n. of here** c'est au nord d'ici; **I'm going up n.** (to northern part of country) je vais
dans le nord; **n. by east/by west** nord-quart-
nord-est/nord-quart-nord-ouest
ADJ nord inv; (wind) du nord; (wall, window)
exposé au nord; **n. side** côté m nord; **on the
n. side** du côté nord; **the n. coast** la côte nord
▶▶ **N. Africa** Afrique f du Nord; **N. African**
nord-africain, -aine; **N. America** Amérique f
du Nord; **N. American** nord-américain,
-aine; Econ **N. American Free Trade Agreement** Accord m de libre-échange nord-américain; **N. Carolina** la Caroline du Nord; **the
N. Country** (in England) l'Angleterre f du
Nord; (in America) = l'Alaska f, le Yukon et
les Territoires du Nord-Ouest; **he has a
strong N. Country accent** il a un accent du
nord prononcé; **N. Island** l'île f du Nord; **N.
Korea** Corée f du Nord; **the N. Pole** le pôle
Nord; **the N. Sea** la mer du Nord; **the N. Star**
l'étoile f Polaire; **n. transept** (in church)
transept m septentrional; **N. Vietnam** le
Viêt-Nam du Nord

Northants abbr **Northamptonshire**

northbound ['nɔːθbaʊnd] ADJ (traffic) en

direction du nord; (lane, carriageway) du
nord; (road) vers le nord; **n. traffic is subject
to delays** la circulation est ralentie dans le
sens nord; **there's a jam on the n. carriageway** il y a un bouchon en direction du nord

northeast [nɔːθ'iːst] N nord-est m; Naut
nordé m
ADJ 1 Geog nord-est inv; du nord-est; **in n.
Scotland** dans le nord-est de l'Écosse 2
(wind) de nord-est, du nord-est
ADV au nord-est; (to travel) vers le nord-est;
it's 20 miles n. of Birmingham c'est à 32 kilomètres au nord-est de Birmingham

northeaster [nɔːθ'iːstər] N (wind) vent m de
nord-est

northeasterly [nɔːθ'iːstəlɪ] ADJ 1 Geog
nord-est inv; du nord-est; **to travel in a n. direction** aller vers le nord-est; Naut **to steer a
n. course** faire route vers le nord-est; (when
setting out) mettre le cap au nord-est 2
(wind) de nord-est, du nord-est
ADV vers le nord-est
N vent m de nord ou est; Naut nordé m,
nordet m

northeastern [nɔːθ'iːstən] ADJ nord-est inv;
du nord-est; (wind) de nord-est, du nord-est;
the n. suburbs la banlieue nord-est

northerly ['nɔːðəlɪ] ADJ 1 Geog nord inv; du
nord; **to travel in a n. direction** aller vers le
nord; **n. point** point situé au nord ou vers le
nord; **a room with a n. aspect** une pièce exposée au nord; Naut **to steer a n. course** faire
route vers le nord; (when setting out) mettre
le cap au nord 2 (wind) de nord, du nord
ADV vers le nord

northern ['nɔːðən] ADJ 1 Geog nord inv; du
nord; **she has a n. accent** elle a un accent
du nord; **the n. wing of the castle** l'aile nord
du château; **in n. Mexico** dans le nord du
Mexique; **the n. migration of swallows in
spring** la migration printanière des hirondelles vers le nord 2 (wind) de nord, du nord
3 Hist (in American Civil War) nordiste
▶▶ **n. hemisphere** l'hémisphère m nord ou
boréal; **N. Ireland** Irlande f du Nord; **n. lights**
aurore f boréale

> ### Northern Ireland
> L'Irlande du Nord désigne la partie de
> l'Irlande à majorité protestante restée
> rattachée à la Grande-Bretagne lors de
> la partition du pays, en 1921. Les émeu-
> tes sanglantes qui ont éclaté en 1969 à
> la suite de manifestations revendi-
> quant l'égalité des droits pour la mino-
> rité catholique ont marqué le début de
> trente ans de conflit entre catholiques
> et protestants. Ce conflit vit s'affronter
> les nationalistes de l'IRA, favorables à
> un rattachement avec la République
> d'Irlande, différents groupes paramili-
> taires protestants anti-catholiques, et
> l'armée et la police, sous contrôle bri-
> tannique. Le processus de paix,
> amorcé en 1994 et qui aboutit au "Good
> Friday Agreement" de 1998 marqua une
> nouvelle étape dans l'histoire de l'Ir-
> lande du Nord.

northerner ['nɔːðənər] N 1 habitant, -ante
du nord; **he's a n.** il vient du nord 2 Hist (in
American Civil War) nordiste mf

north-facing ADJ (house, wall) (exposé)
au nord

north-north-east N nord-nord-est m inv
ADJ nord-nord-est inv
ADV au nord-nord-est; (to travel) vers le
nord-nord-est

north-north-west N nord-nord-ouest m
ADJ nord-nord-ouest inv
ADV au nord-nord-ouest; (to travel) vers le
nord-nord-ouest

North-Sea gas N gaz *m* de la mer du Nord

Northumb *abbr* Northumberland

northward ['nɔːθwəd] ADJ vers le nord, en direction du nord
   N nord *m*
   ADV = **northwards**

northwards ['nɔːθwədz] ADV vers le nord, en direction du nord

northwest [nɔːθ'west] N nord-ouest *m*
   ADJ 1 *Geog* nord-ouest *inv*, du nord-ouest 2 *(wind)* de nord-ouest, du nord-ouest
   ADV au nord-ouest; *(to travel)* vers le nord-ouest; **n. by west** nord-ouest-quart-ouest; **n. by north** nord-ouest-quart-nord

northwester [nɔːθ'westər] N *(wind)* vent *m* de *ou* du nord-ouest; *Naut* noroît *m*

northwesterly [nɔːθ'westəlɪ] ADJ 1 *Geog* nord-ouest *inv*, du nord-ouest; **to travel in a n. direction** aller vers le nord-ouest; *Naut* **to steer a n. course** faire route vers le nord-ouest; *(when setting out)* mettre le cap au nord-ouest 2 *(wind)* de nord-ouest, du nord-ouest
   ADV vers le nord-ouest
   N = **northwester**

northwestern [nɔːθ'westən] ADJ nord-ouest *inv*, du nord-ouest

Norway ['nɔːweɪ] N Norvège *f*
   ▸ ▸ **N. lobster** langoustine *f*

Norwegian [nɔː'wiːdʒən] ADJ norvégien
   N 1 Norvégien, -ienne 2 *Ling* norvégien *m*

nor'west [nɔː'west] *Naut* = **northwest**

nor'westerly [nɔː'westəlɪ] *Naut* = **northwesterly**

nor'western [nɔː'westən] *Naut* = **northwestern**

nose [nəʊz] N 1 *(of person, animal)* nez *m*; **her n. is bleeding** elle saigne du nez; **to blow one's n.** se moucher; **to hold one's n.** se boucher le nez; **to speak through one's n.** parler du nez, nasiller; **to have one's n. in a book** avoir le nez dans un livre; **the parson's or pope's n.** *(of fowl)* le croupion; *Fig* **he can't see any further than the end of his n.** il ne voit pas plus loin que le bout de son nez; **it's under your n.** vous l'avez sous le nez; **I did it under his very n.** *or* **right under his n.** je l'ai fait sous son nez; **to poke one's n. into other people's business** fourrer *ou* mettre son nez dans les affaires des autres; **to turn up one's n. at sth** dédaigner qch; **to look down one's n. at sb** regarder qn de haut en bas; *Fig (despise)* mépriser qn; **she walked by with her n. in the air** elle passa avec un air dédaigneux *ou* supérieur; *Prov* **to cut off one's n. to spite one's face** se punir soi-même; **that's cutting off your n. to spite your face** c'est toi le perdant; **to lead sb by the n.** mener qn par le bout du nez; *Fam* **to pay through the n. for sth** payer qch une fortune *ou* les yeux de la tête; **to win by a n.** gagner d'un nez; *Fam* **to rub sb's n. in it** retourner le couteau dans la plaie; *Fam* **to have a n. (a.)round** faire un tour d'inspection; **to get up sb's n.** *(of person)* taper sur les nerfs de qn; **it really gets up my n. that …** ça me met en boule que …; *Fig* **to keep one's n. clean** se tenir à carreau
   2 *(of wine etc)* bouquet *m*; **to have a good n.** *(of person)* avoir bon nez *ou* le nez fin *ou* l'odorat fin; *Fig* **to have a n. for sth** *(of person)* avoir du flair pour qch
   3 *Tech (of vehicle, plane etc)* nez *m*, avant *m*; *(of engine)* nez; *(of tool)* bec *m*, nez; *(of bullet, missile)* pointe *f*, ogive *f*; *Naut (of torpedo)* cône *m* de choc
   VT **the ship nosed her way through the fog** le navire avançait à l'aveuglette à travers le brouillard; **the car nosed its way forward/ out of the garage** la voiture avança prudemment/sortit prudemment du garage

   VI **the ship nosed through the fog** le navire avançait à l'aveuglette à travers le brouillard
   ▸ ▸ **n. cone** *(of missile)* ogive *f*, *(of aircraft)* nez *m*; *Aviat* **n. dive** *(vol m)* piqué *m*; *Fam* **to take a n. dive** *(of prices)* faire un plongeon, piquer du nez; **n. drops** gouttes *fpl* nasales *ou* pour le nez; *Fam* **n. job** = intervention *f* esthétique de chirurgie sur le nez; **to have a n. job** se faire refaire le nez; **n. ring** *(of bull)* anneau *m* nasal, nasière *f*, *(of person)* anneau de nez

▸ **nose about, nose around** VI fureter, fouiner; **what are you nosing around here for?** pourquoi est-ce que tu fouines par ici?
   VT INSEP *(office, room, garden)* fureter dans, fouiner dans; **a policeman was nosing around the car/dustbin** un agent de police fouinait *ou* furetait autour de la voiture/ poubelle

▸ **nose out** VT SEP 1 *(of dog)* *(game)* flairer 2 *Fam (secret)* découvrir, éventer; *(person)* dépister, dénicher; *(good restaurant, bargain)* dénicher
   VI *(of car, driver)* sortir prudemment; **the car nosed out into the traffic** la voiture s'est prudemment faufilée entre les autres; **the van nosed through the crowds/up the ramp** la camionnette a traversé la foule/monté la rampe prudemment *ou* tout doucement

▸ **nose through** VT INSEP *(papers etc)* fouiller dans

nosebag ['nəʊzbæg] N musette *f* (mangeoire)

noseband ['nəʊzbænd] N *(on harness)* muserolle *f*

nosebleed ['nəʊzbliːd] N saignement *m* de nez; **to have a n.** saigner du nez

nose-dive VI *Aviat* piquer du nez, descendre en piqué; *Fam (of prices)* faire un plongeon, piquer du nez

nosegay ['nəʊzgeɪ] N petit bouquet *m* (de fleurs)

nose-to-tail ADJ *(traffic)* pare-choc(s) contre pare-choc(s)

nosey ['nəʊzɪ] ADJ *Fam* = **nosy**

nosh [nɒʃ] *Sl* N *(food)* bouffe *f*; **time for some n.!** c'est l'heure de bouffer *ou* de la bouffe!
   VI *(eat)* bouffer

no-show N *(at airport, for travel)* désistement *m*, défection *f*, no-show *m*, *pl* no-shows

nosh-up N *Br Sl (meal)* boustifaille *f*

nosily ['nəʊzɪlɪ] ADV *Fam* indiscrètement

nosiness ['nəʊzɪnəs] N *Fam* indiscrétion *f*, curiosité *f*

no-smoking ADJ *(carriage, area)* non-fumeurs; *(seat)* non-fumeur

nostalgia [nɒs'tældʒɪə] N nostalgie *f*

nostalgic [nɒs'tældʒɪk] ADJ nostalgique; **a n. moment** un moment de nostalgie

nostalgically [nɒs'tældʒɪklɪ] ADV avec nostalgie, nostalgiquement

nostril ['nɒstrɪl] N *(of person)* narine *f*, *(of horse, ox etc)* naseau *m*

nostrum ['nɒstrəm] N *Old-fashioned usu Pej*, *Fig* panacée *f*, *(quack medicine)* remède *m* de charlatan

nosy ['nəʊzɪ] ADJ *Fam* curieux, fouinard; *(questions)* indiscret, -ète; **don't be so n.!** ne soyez pas si curieux!; **I don't mean to be n. but …** je ne veux pas me mêler de ce qui ne me regarde pas mais …
   ▸ ▸ *Br Fam Pej* **n. parker** fouine *f*

NOT [nɒt]

ADV	ne… pas **1, 3** ▪ non **2, 7** ▪ pas **2, 4, 5**		

ADV VOIR GRAMMAIRE A23–4 **1** *(following the aux verb informally affixed as* **n't***)* ne … pas;

I don't *or* **do n. know** je ne sais pas; **he won't** *or* **will n. come** il ne viendra pas; **is she coming? – no, she isn't** *or* **she's n.** est-ce qu'elle vient? – non, (elle ne vient pas); **don't move** ne bougez pas; **I'm n. in the least surprised** je ne suis nullement étonné; **you understand, don't you?** vous comprenez, n'est-ce pas?; **she would n. wear a hat!** *(stressed)* un chapeau, elle n'en porterait pas! VOIR GRAMMAIRE A47–8
   2 *(elliptically in answers etc)* **n. at all, n. a bit (of it)** pas du tout; **n. in any way, n. in the least** pas le moins du monde; **thank you so much! – n. at all!** merci beaucoup! – je vous en prie; **n. if I've got anything to do with it** pas si j'ai mon mot à dire; **n. likely!** jamais de la vie!; **whether he likes it or n.** que cela lui plaise ou non; **little or n. at all** peu ou pas, peu ou point; **I think/hope n.** je crois/j'espère que non; **n. always** pas toujours; **n. any more** *or* **longer** plus maintenant; **n. even in France** (non) pas même en France; **n. just** *or* **simply** pas seulement; **n. so** pas du tout; **n. yet** pas encore
   3 *(with a non-finite verb)* **n. wishing to be seen, I drew the curtain** comme je ne désirais pas être vu, j'ai tiré le rideau; **n. including …** sans compter …; **n. to mention …** pour ne pas parler de …; *Fam* **n. to worry!** ne vous en faites pas!; **she asked me n. to do it** elle m'a demandé de ne pas le faire VOIR GRAMMAIRE A47–8
   4 *(in contrasts)* **she's n. my mother but my aunt** ce n'est pas ma mère, c'est ma tante; **he is respected but n. loved** il est respecté mais (non) pas aimé; **n. only … but also …** non seulement … mais encore …
   5 *(with pronoun or noun)* **n. I** pas moi; **n. one replied** pas un(e) n'a répondu; *Old-fashioned* **he'll never pay, n. he!** il ne paiera jamais, c'est sûr!; **n. everyone was so enthusiastic** tout le monde n'était pas aussi enthousiaste; **n. a word was spoken** on n'a pas dit un mot; **who will believe it? – n. a soul** qui le croira? – personne
   6 *(understatement)* **I wasn't sorry to go** j'étais bien content de partir; **a n. inconsiderable sum of money** une somme non négligeable; **n. without reason/regret** non sans raison/regrets; **they were annoyed, n. to say furious** ils étaient ennuyés, pour ne pas dire furieux; *Fam* **n. half!** et comment!, tu parles!
   7 *(with adverb or adjective)* non; **n. far from the town** non loin de la ville; **n. guilty** non coupable; **n. negotiable** non négociable
   8 *Arch, Lit (following the verb)* **I know n.** je ne sais point; **fear n.!** n'ayez crainte!
   9 *Sl* **the party was fantastic, n.!** la fête ne cassait rien du tout; **he's really gorgeous, n.!** c'est pas exactement un Apollon!
   CONJ **n. that …** ce n'est pas que … + *sub*, non (pas) que … + *sub*; **n. that I can remember** pas autant que je m'en souvienne
   ▸ ▸ **n. equals sign** signe *m* différent de

notability [nəʊtə'bɪlɪtɪ] N *Old-fashioned (person)* notabilité *f*, notable *m*; *(state)* prééminence *f*

notable ['nəʊtəb(ə)l] ADJ *(person, thing)* notable, insigne, remarquable; *(person)* éminent; **with a few n. exceptions** avec quelques exceptions et non des moindres; **in a speech n. only for its length** dans un discours qui n'avait de remarquable que sa longueur; **the town is chiefly n. for …** la ville se distingue essentiellement par …
   N *Fml* notable *m*

notably ['nəʊtəblɪ] ADV *(particularly)* notamment, particulièrement

notarize ['nəʊtəraɪz] VT authentifier; **notarized contract/deed** contrat *m*/acte *m* notarié

notary ['nəʊtərɪ] N *Law* notaire *m*; **signed in**

the presence of a n. signé par-devant notaire; ▶▶**n. public** notaire

notation [nəʊˈteɪʃən] N *Mus etc* notation *f*; *Math* numération *f*

notch [nɒtʃ] N **1** *(in wood)* entaille *f*, encoche *f*; *(in belt, rack)* cran *m*; *(of toothed wheel)* cran, dent *f*; *(in blade etc)* brèche *f*; *Sewing* cran; *(in diskette)* encoche; **to cut a n.** faire une entaille *ou* une encoche; **to take one's belt in a n.** resserrer sa ceinture d'un cran; *Fig* se serrer la ceinture; *Fig* **a n. on the bedpost** une conquête **2** *Fig (grade, level)* **to be a n. above the rest** être dans la catégorie supérieure; **it raised their spirits a n. or two but** … cela leur a quelque peu remonté le moral mais … **3** *Am (in mountain)* défilé *m*, gorge *f*
▪ VT *(stick etc)* entailler, encocher; *(wheel)* denteler, créneler; *(blade)* ébrécher
▶**notch up** VT SEP *(point)* marquer; *(victory)* remporter

note [nəʊt] N **1** *(in writing)* note *f*; *(on a text)* note, annotation *f*, remarque *f*; *(letter)* mot *m*; *Univ* **lecture notes** notes (de cours); **to make notes, to take (down) notes** prendre des notes; **to take** *or* **make a n. of sth** prendre note de qch; **I must make a n. of it** il faut que je m'en souvienne; **they have no n. of any such meeting** ils n'ont aucune trace de cette réunion; **without notes** *(to speak, lecture)* sans notes; **to speak from notes** parler d'après des notes; **to write** *or* **make notes on a text** annoter un texte; **diplomatic n.** note *f* diplomatique, mémorandum *m*; *Acct* **notes to the accounts** annexes *fpl*
2 *Mus* note *f*; *(of piano etc)* touche *f*; **to sing** *or* **play a false n.** faire une fausse note; **there was a n. of impatience in her voice** il y avait une pointe d'impatience dans sa voix; **to introduce a n. of discord/optimism** introduire une note discordante/optimiste; **speech that strikes the right n.** discours dans la note voulue; **to end on a more serious/a lighter n.** … pour conclure sur une note plus sérieuse/gaie, …
3 *Fin, Com* billet *m*; *(money)* billet (de banque); **n. of hand** reconnaissance *f* (de dette), billet simple; **credit/debit n.** note *f ou* bordereau *m* de crédit/de débit; **hundred-euro notes** billets *ou* coupures *fpl* de cent euros
4 *(distinction)* distinction *f*, marque *f*, renom *m*; **a man of n.** un homme de qualité *ou* de marque; **nothing of n.** rien d'extraordinaire *ou* de spécial
5 to take n. of sth noter qch
▪ VT *(notice)* noter, remarquer; *(error)* relever; *(fact)* constater; **it should be noted that** … il est à noter que …; **we duly n. that** … nous prenons bonne note (de ce) que …; *Law* **which fact is hereby duly noted** dont acte
▶**note down** VT SEP prendre note de

notebook [ˈnəʊtbʊk] N carnet *m*, calepin *m*; *(larger)* cahier *m*; *(for shorthand etc)* bloc-notes *m*, *pl* blocs-notes, notebook *m*; *(computer)* notebook *m*, ordinateur *m* bloc-notes
▶▶**n. computer** notebook, ordinateur bloc-notes

notecase [ˈnəʊtkeɪs] N *Br Old-fashioned* portefeuille *m*

noted [ˈnəʊtɪd] ADJ *(person)* distingué, éminent; *(thing)* fameux **(for sth** pour qch), remarquable **(for sth** par qch); **the area is n. for its cheese** la région est célèbre *ou* fameuse pour son fromage

notelet [ˈnəʊtlət] N carte-lettre *f*, *pl* cartes-lettres

notepad [ˈnəʊtpæd] N *(for notes)* bloc-notes *m*, *pl* blocs-notes; *(for letters)* bloc *m* de papier à lettres

notepaper [ˈnəʊtpeɪpər] N papier *m* à lettres

note-taking N prise *f* de notes

noteworthy [ˈnəʊtwɜːðɪ] ADJ *(fact etc)* remarquable; **it is n. that** … il convient de noter que …

not-for-profit ADJ *Am* = **non-profit-making**

NOTHING [ˈnʌθɪŋ] PRON rien; **n. at all** rien du tout; **he does n.** il ne fait rien; **I saw n.** je n'ai rien vu; **what are you doing? – n.** que faites-vous? – rien; **it's better than n.** c'est mieux que rien; **n. can beat French cooking** il n'y a rien de mieux que la cuisine française; **a cheese sandwich is better than n.** un sandwich au fromage, c'est mieux que rien *ou* c'est toujours ça; **n. could be simpler** rien de plus simple, c'est tout ce qu'il y a de plus simple; **you can't live on n.** on ne peut pas vivre de rien; **he let me have it for almost** *or* **next to n.** il me l'a cédé pour presque rien *ou* pour une bouchée de pain; **they pay him next to n.** ils le paient trois fois rien; **it looks like n. on earth** c'est ridicule; **as if n. had happened** comme si de rien n'était; **say n. about it** n'en dites rien; **to say n. of** … sans parler de …; **she gets angry about n.** elle se fâche pour un rien; **there's n. in these rumours** ces bruits sont sans fondement; *Fam* **there's n. to it** *(it's easy)* c'est simple comme bonjour; **there's n. in it** *(no difference)* il n'y a aucune différence; *(in choosing between two candidates etc)* ils se valent, il n'y a aucune différence entre eux; *(in race)* ils sont à égalité; **he was n. if not discreet** il était surtout discret, il était discret avant tout; **n. new/remarkable** rien de nouveau/de remarquable; **that's n. new** ce n'est pas nouveau; **that's n. unusual** cela n'a rien d'anormal; **n. much** pas grand-chose; **there is n. more to be said** il n'y a plus rien à dire; **I have n. to do** je n'ai rien à faire; **to have n. to do with sb/sth** n'avoir rien à voir avec qn/qch; **that's n. to do with you** ce n'est pas votre affaire, cela ne vous regarde pas; **these people will stop at n.** ces gens ne reculent devant rien; **there's n. to cry/worry about** il n'y a pas de quoi pleurer/s'inquiéter; **to have n. on** *(no engagement)* être libre; *(no clothes)* être tout nu; **as a pianist he is n. on his brother** comme pianiste il n'arrive pas à la cheville de son frère; **he has n. of his father in him** il n'a rien de son père; **n. but** … rien que …; **n. but the best will satisfy her** seul ce qu'il y a de meilleur la satisfait; **n. but the truth** rien que la vérité; **n. else** rien d'autre; **n. else matters** tout le reste n'est rien, rien d'autre n'a d'importance; **there's n. else for it** c'est inévitable; **there's n. like a cold bath in the mornings** il n'y a rien de tel qu'un bain froid le matin; **to do sth for n.** *(in vain)* faire qch pour rien; *(free of charge)* faire qch gratuitement; **it's not for n. that** … ce n'est pas pour rien *ou* sans raison que …; **to come to n.** ne pas aboutir; *(of hopes etc)* s'anéantir; *(of scheme etc)* s'effondrer; **all my efforts came to n.** tous mes efforts se sont révélés inutiles; **to count for n.** ne compter pour rien; **he is n. to her** *(she doesn't care for him)* il lui est indifférent; *(she is much better than he is)* elle est bien meilleure que lui; **£1000 is n. to her** 1000 livres ne sont rien pour elle; **that's n. to what mum will say** ce n'est rien par rapport à ce que Maman va dire; **in those days it was n. to see** … en ce temps-là on voyait facilement …; **it's n. to me either way** cela m'est égal; **to think n. of doing sth** *(not hesitate to do)* ne pas hésiter à faire qch; **she thinks n. of walking 10 km** pour elle 10 km à pied, ce n'est rien; **to think n. of sb** avoir peu d'estime pour qn; **I can make n. of it** je n'y comprends rien du tout; *Fam* **n. doing** rien à faire, pas question; *Fam*

to do sth in n. flat faire qch en deux temps trois mouvements; *Prov* **n. ventured, n. gained** qui ne risque rien n'a rien SEE GRAMMAR B62–3

N **1** *(nonexistence)* néant *m*, rien *m*
2 *(trifle)* bagatelle *f*, rien *m*; *(person)* zéro *m*, nullité *f*; **a hundred euros? – a mere n.!** cent euros? – une bagatelle!; **to whisper sweet nothings to sb/in sb's ear** chuchoter des mots doux à qn/à l'oreille de qn
3 *Math* zéro *m*
▪ ADV **n. like** *or* **near so** *or* **as big** loin d'être aussi grand; **London is n. like as near as that** Londres est bien plus loin que ça; **she looks n. like her sister** elle ne ressemble pas du tout *ou* en rien à sa sœur; **it's n. less than** *or* **short of madness** c'est de la folie ni plus ni moins; **it's n. less than scandalous that** … c'est ni plus ni moins un scandale que …

nothingness [ˈnʌθɪŋnɪs] N néant *m*; **a feeling** *or* **sense of n.** un sentiment de vide

NOTICE [ˈnəʊtɪs]

N avis **1** ▪ préavis **1** ▪ congé **1** ▪ démission **1** ▪ affiche **2** ▪ pancarte **2** ▪ critique **3** ▪ annonce **3** ▪ attention **4**		
VT remarquer		
VI remarquer		

N **1** *(notification)* avis *m*, notification *f*; *(warning)* préavis *m*, avertissement *m*; *(served by bailiff)* exploit *m* (d'huissier); **to give sb n. of sth** prévenir *ou* avertir qn de qch; **to give official n. that** … donner acte que …; **n. is hereby given that** … le public est avisé que …; **without (prior) n.** sans préavis; **until further n.** jusqu'à nouvel ordre *ou* nouvel avis; **public n.** avis au public; **important n.** avis important; *Rel* **the weekly notices** les annonces *fpl* de la semaine; *Com* **n. of claim** déclaration *f* de sinistre; **n. of a/ the meeting** convocation *f*; **n. to pay** avertissement *m*; **at short n.** dans un bref délai; **to give sb short n.** prendre qn de court; **that's rather short n.** c'est un peu court comme délai; **at a moment's** *or* **a minute's n.** sur-le-champ; **without a moment's n.** sans crier gare; **to require three months' n.** exiger un préavis de trois mois; **deposit at seven days' n.** dépôt *m* à sept jours de préavis; **next time give me a bit more n.** la prochaine fois prévenez-moi un peu plus à l'avance; **n. (to quit)** *(avis de)* congé *m*; **to be under n. to quit** avoir reçu son congé; **what n. do you require?** quel est le terme du congé?; **to give sb n.** *(of landlord, employer)* congédier qn, donner son congé à qn; *(of employer)* licencier qn; **to give sb a week's n.** donner ses huit jours à qn; **to give n., to give** *or* **hand in one's n.** *(of tenant, employee)* donner *ou* demander (son) congé; *(of employee)* donner sa démission, démissionner
2 *(poster)* affiche *f*, placard *m*; *(sign, card etc)* écriteau *m*, pancarte *f*
3 *(in newspaper etc)* annonce *f*; *(review)* *(of play, work etc)* critique *f*; **they put a birth n. in the local paper** ils ont passé un faire-part de naissance dans le quotidien régional; **the play got good notices** la pièce a eu de bonnes critiques
4 *(attention)* **to take n. of** faire attention *ou* prêter attention à; *(warning)* tenir compte de; **to take not the slightest n. of sth** ne pas prêter la moindre attention à qch; **nobody took any n. of me** personne n'a fait attention à moi; **I warned him but he took no n. (of me)** je l'ai prévenu mais il n'a pas prêté la moindre attention à ce que je lui ai dit; **I should take no n.** *or* **I shouldn't take any n. of it if I were you** je n'y ferais pas attention à ta place; **it has come to my n. that** … il est venu à ma connaissance que …; **to attract**

n. *(of author etc)* commencer à être connu *ou* à percer; *(of performance, publication etc)* être remarqué; **to avoid n.** se dérober aux regards; **the fact escaped everyone's n.** ce fait a échappé à tout le monde; **to bring** *or* **call sth/sb to sb's n.** appeler *ou* porter *ou* attirer l'attention de qn sur qch/qn; **the baby is beginning to take n.** le bébé commence à avoir conscience des choses

vt remarquer, s'apercevoir de; *(errors)* relever; **didn't anybody n. him leaving?** est-ce que personne n'a remarqué qu'il partait?; **without his noticing it** sans qu'il s'en aperçoive; **she's beginning to get herself noticed** elle commence à être connu *ou* à percer; **to be noticed** *or* **to get oneself noticed by sb** attirer l'attention de qn (sur soi)

vi remarquer; **nobody will ever n.** personne ne s'en apercevra *ou* ne le remarquera jamais; **what happened? – I don't know, I didn't n.** qu'est-ce qui s'est passé? – je ne sais pas, je ne m'en suis pas rendu compte

▸▸ *Law* **n. of appeal** intimation *f* d'appel; *Com* **n. period** période *f* de préavis; *Com* **n. of receipt** accusé *m* de réception; *Banking, Fin* **n. of withdrawal** avis *m* de retrait de fonds

> Note that the French word **notice** is a false friend and is never a translation for the English word **notice**. Its most common meaning is **directions (for use)**.

noticeable ['nəʊtɪsəb(ə)l] ADJ *(perceptible)* perceptible; *(difference, improvement, change)* sensible; **it was very n. that she didn't speak to her husband** on ne pouvait pas ne pas remarquer qu'elle ne parlait pas à son mari

noticeably ['nəʊtɪsəblɪ] ADV sensiblement

noticeboard ['nəʊtɪsbɔːd] N panneau *m* d'affichage; *(in schools, clubs etc)* tableau *m* d'affichage; *(on house for sale etc)* écriteau *m*

notifiable [nəʊtɪ'faɪəb(ə)l] ADJ *(disease)* dont la déclaration aux autorités est obligatoire

notification [nəʊtɪfɪ'keɪʃən] N *(of fact etc)* avis *m*, notification *f*; *(of birth etc)* déclaration *f*; **letter of n.** lettre *f* notificative

notify ['nəʊtɪfaɪ] VT annoncer, notifier; *(birth)* déclarer; **to n. sb of sth** avertir *ou* aviser qn de qch; **to n. the authorities of a fact** saisir l'administration d'un fait; **to n. the police of sth** signaler qch à la police; **have you notified the police?** avez vous prévenu la police?; **to be notified of sth** recevoir notification de qch, être avisé de qch; *Com* **to send sth n.** expédier qch 'notify'

notion ['nəʊʃən] N 1 *(idea)* notion *f*, idée *f*; **to have no n. of sth** ne pas avoir la moindre notion de qch; **to have no n. of time** n'avoir pas la notion *ou* le sens de l'heure; **I haven't the first n. about it** je n'en ai pas la moindre idée; **I haven't the first n. about physics/French** je n'y connais absolument rien en physique/français; **I have a n. that …** j'ai dans l'idée que …; **she has some pretty strange notions** elle a de drôles d'idées 2 *(whim)* caprice *m*; **as the n. takes him** comme il en a envie; **to have a n. to do sth** avoir envie de faire qch 3 *Phil (concept)* notion *f*, concept *m* 4 *Am* **notions** *(ribbons, needles etc)* (articles *mpl* de) mercerie *f*

notional ['nəʊʃən(ə)l] ADJ *(abstract)* hypothétique; *(income)* fictif; *Phil* spéculatif; *(imaginary) (things, relations etc)* imaginaire

notoriety [nəʊtə'raɪətɪ] N notoriété *f*; **to seek n.** chercher à se faire remarquer; **this action gained** *or* **earned him some n.** cette action lui a valu une certaine notoriété

notorious [nəʊ'tɔːrɪəs] ADJ d'une triste notoriété; *(criminal, thief)* notoire; *(place)* mal

famé; *(liar)* fieffé; **Mexico City is n. for being one of the world's most polluted cities** Mexico est réputée pour être *ou* a la triste notoriété d'être l'une des villes les plus polluées du monde; **to be n. for being late/one's lack of tact** être réputé pour arriver en retard/son manque de tact

notoriously [nəʊ'tɔːrɪəslɪ] ADV notoirement; **n. cruel** connu pour sa cruauté; **to be n. difficult/dangerous** être bien connu pour sa difficulté/ses dangers

Notts *abbr* Nottinghamshire

notwithstanding [nɒtwɪθ'stændɪŋ] PREP malgré, en dépit de, *Fml* nonobstant

ADV quand même, tout de même, néanmoins

nougat ['nuːgɑː] N nougat *m*

nought [nɔːt] N 1 *Math* zéro *m*; *Br* **noughts and crosses** *(game)* ≃ morpion VOIR GRAMMAIRE A77 2 = **naught 1**

noun [naʊn] N *Gram* substantif *m*, nom *m*; **common/proper n.** nom commun/propre VOIR GRAMMAIRE A9–17; B5–8
▸▸ **n. clause** proposition *f*, **n. phrase** groupe *m ou* syntagme *m* nominal

nourish ['nʌrɪʃ] VT 1 *(person, plant, wood, leather)* nourrir; **to n. sb on** *or* **with sth** nourrir qn de qch; **to be well nourished** être bien nourri 2 *Old-fashioned (feeling, hope etc)* nourrir, entretenir

nourishing ['nʌrɪʃɪŋ] ADJ nourrissant, nutritif

nourishment ['nʌrɪʃmənt] N 1 *(food)* nourriture *f*, aliments *mpl*; *(nourishing quality)* richesse *f* nutritive; **to take (some) n.** se nourrir, s'alimenter; **you're not getting enough n.** tu ne t'alimentes pas bien; **to receive n.** être nourri; *(of plants)* trouver sa nourriture; **it's full of n.** c'est très nourrissant *ou* nutritif 2 *(action)* alimentation *f*

nous [naʊs] N *Br Sl* bon sens *m*; *(know-how)* savoir-faire *m*; **she's got a lot of n.** elle a beaucoup de bon sens, elle est très sensée; **anyone with any n.** n'importe qui doté d'un minimum de bon sens

Nov *abbr* November

nova, *pl* **novae** *or* **novas** ['nəʊvə, -iː] N *Astron* nova *f*, *pl* novae
▸▸ **N. Scotia** Nouvelle-Écosse *f*

novel [¹ ['nɒv(ə)l] N roman *m*

> Note that the French noun **nouvelle** is a false friend. It means **short story**.

novel [² ADJ nouveau, *f* nouvelle, original, -aux; **that's a n. idea!** voilà qui est original!

novelette [nɒvə'let] N *(short novel)* nouvelle *f*, *(sentimental story)* petit roman *m* à l'eau de rose

novelist ['nɒvəlɪst] N romancier, -ière

novelization [nɒvəlaɪ'zeɪʃən] N *(of film)* novélisation *f*

novella [nəʊ'velə] N nouvelle *f*

novelty ['nɒvəltɪ] N 1 *(quality)* nouveauté *f*; **the n. will soon wear off** l'attrait de la nouveauté ne tardera pas à s'estomper; **there was no n. in it any more** cela n'avait plus rien de nouveau; **the n. of this scheme is that …** ce que ce programme a de nouveau *ou* d'innovateur c'est que … 2 *(thing)* nouveauté *f*, *Com (article m* de) nouveauté, fantaisie *f*; **such ideas are a n.** ces idées sont complètement nouvelles; **as the only Chinese child, he was something of a n.** seul enfant chinois, il faisait figure de nouveauté; **to have n. value** avoir l'attrait de la nouveauté

November [nəʊ'vembər] N VOIR GRAMMAIRE A81–2; B60–2 novembre *m*; **in N.** au mois de novembre, en novembre; **(on) the first/the seventh of N.** le premier/le sept novembre

novena [nəʊ'viːnə] N *Cathol* neuvaine *f*

novice ['nɒvɪs] N apprenti, -ie, débutant, -ante; *Rel* novice *mf*; **to be a n. in** *or* **at sth** être novice en qch; **I'm still a bit of a n. at this** je suis encore un peu novice; **he was something of a sexual n.** il était pour ainsi dire novice en matière de sexe

noviciate, **novitiate** [nəʊ'vɪʃɪət] N *Rel* 1 *(state, period)* noviciat *m* 2 *(living quarters)* noviciat *m*, maison *f* des novices

NOW [naʊ]

ADV	maintenant **1** ▪ alors **1** ▪ or **2**
CONJ	maintenant que

ADV **1** *(this instant)* maintenant *(at present)* maintenant, à présent; *(nowadays)* actuellement, à l'heure actuelle; *(in narrative)* alors, à ce moment-là; **what shall we do n.?** qu'est-ce que nous allons faire maintenant?; *Fam* **it's (a case of) n. or never** c'est le moment ou jamais; **n. or never!**, **n. for it!** allons-y!; **goodbye for n.!** à bientôt!; **that'll do for n.** ça suffit pour le moment; **it's two years n. since his mother died** ça fait maintenant deux ans que sa mère est morte; **he won't be long n.** il ne va plus tarder; **even n., I don't understand** même maintenant je ne comprends pas; **and n. I must go** sur ce je vous quitte; **n. is the time to …** c'est le bon moment pour …; **right n.** *(immediately)* tout de suite; **I'm not in a position right n. to decide** je ne peux rien décider pour le moment; **all was n. ready** dès lors tout était prêt; **he was even n. on his way** il était déjà en route; **just n.** *(past)* il y a un instant; *(present)* en ce moment; **she left just n.** elle vient de partir; **(every) n. and then**, **(every) n. and again** de temps en temps, de temps à autre; **n. one thing, n.** *or* **then another** tantôt une chose, tantôt l'autre; **n. here n. there** tantôt ici tantôt là; **up to n.** jusqu'ici; **from n. on** à partir de maintenant, dorénavant; **it should be finished in three days from n.** cela devrait être fini d'ici trois jours; **I'm leaving in three days from n.** je pars dans trois jours; **he ought to be here by n.**, **he ought to have been here before n.** il devrait déjà être arrivé; **until n.** jusqu'ici; **and n. for some music** et maintenant, un peu de musique VOIR GRAMMAIRE A19; A21

2 *(without temporal significance) (explanatory or in development of an argument)* or; **n. to come back to what we were saying** pour revenir à ce que nous disions; **n. it happened that …** *(in story)* or il advint que …; **n. what's the matter with you!** qu'avez-vous donc?; **come n.!** voyons!; **n., n.! stop quarrelling!** voyons, voyons! assez de querelles!; **well n.!** eh bien!; **n. then, stop fighting** allons, arrêtez de vous battre; **n. then, listen to what I have to say!** allons *ou* bon, écoutez ce que j'ai à vous dire!; **n. then, what's all the noise about?** eh bien alors, qu'est-ce que c'est que tout ce bruit?

CONJ maintenant que, à présent que; **n. (that) I'm older I think differently** maintenant que je suis plus âgé je pense autrement

ADJ *Fam* **1** *(current)* actuel; **the n. president** le président actuel **2** *(fashionable)* branché

nowadays ['naʊədeɪz] ADV aujourd'hui, de nos jours, à l'heure actuelle; **where's she working n.?** où travaille-t-elle actuellement?

nowhere ['nəʊweər] ADV nulle part; **she was n. to be found** on ne la trouvait nulle part, elle était introuvable; **we're getting n. fast** nous n'avançons pas d'un poil; **that kind of attitude will get you n. fast** ce genre d'attitude ne t'avancera *ou* ne te servira à rien du tout; **qualifications alone will get you n.** les diplômes seuls ne suffisent pas; **it's n. near the shopping centre** ce n'est pas du tout dans les parages du centre commercial; **it's n. near enough** c'est loin d'être suffisant; **he's n. near as intelligent as his sister** il est loin d'être aussi intelligent que sa sœur; **we're n. near ready** on est loin d'être prêt; **the rest are n.** (in race, sales etc) les autres ne sont plus dans le coup; **she finished n.** elle a fini loin derrière VOIR GRAMMAIRE A62–3

N a small place in the middle of n. un petit trou perdu; **he seemed to come from n.** il est apparu tout d'un coup; **the money won't just come from n.** l'argent ne va pas tomber du ciel; **he came from n. to win the race** il a fait une remontée spectaculaire et a gagné la course; **the Greens came from n. to win nearly 15% of the vote** les Verts sont partis de rien et ont remporté près de 15% des votes

nowt [naʊt] PRON, N EngDial (ne …) rien m; **I don't do owt for n.** je ne fais rien pour rien

noxious ['nɒkʃəs] ADJ nocif; (gas, fumes) délétère, nocif

nozzle ['nɒz(ə)l] N Tech (of pipe) ajutage m, jet m; (of fire hose etc) lance f; (of syringe) canule f; (of bellows) bec m, tuyau m, buse f; (of vacuum cleaner) suceur m; (of injector, turbine) tuyère f, ajutage; (for icing) douille f; (of petrol pump) pistolet m

NPD [enpi:'di:] N Mktg (abbr new product development) développement m de nouveaux produits

NPV [enpi:'vi:] N Acct (abbr net present value) VAN f, valeur f actuelle nette
▶▶ **N. rate** taux m d'actualisation

NRS [ena:r'es] N (abbr national readership survey) étude f nationale sur le lectorat

NS abbr Nova Scotia

ns (abbr nanosecond) ns

NSPCC [enespi:si:'si:] N Br (abbr National Society for the Prevention of Cruelty to Children) = comité m national pour la prévention des mauvais traitements envers les enfants

nth [enθ] ADJ 1 Fam énième; **to the n. degree** au énième degré; **for the n. time** pour la énième fois 2 Math **to the n. power** à la puissance n

nuance ['nju:ɒns] N nuance f; **a n. of meaning** une nuance; **I detected a n. of uncertainty in his voice** j'ai décelé une note d'incertitude dans sa voix

nuanced ['nju:ɒnst] ADJ nuancé; **finely n.** subtilement nuancé

nub [nʌb] N 1 (protuberance) bosse f, protubérance f 2 **the n. of the matter** or **issue** le cœur du sujet

nubile ['nju:baɪl] ADJ 1 (sexually attractive) désirable 2 Fml (marriageable) nubile

nuclear ['nju:klɪər] ADJ 1 Phys, Mil nucléaire 2 Biol nucléaire
▶▶ **n. bomb** bombe f atomique; **n. energy** énergie f nucléaire; **n. family** famille f nucléaire; **n. fission** fission f nucléaire; **n. fusion** fusion f nucléaire; **n. magnetic resonance** résonance f magnétique nucléaire; **n. magnetic resonance scanner** scanner m de résonance magnétique nucléaire; **n. physics** physique f nucléaire; **n. power** nucléaire m, énergie nucléaire; **n. power plant** centrale f nucléaire; **n. powers** puissances fpl nucléaires; **n. power station** centrale nucléaire; **n. war(fare)** guerre f nucléaire; Mil **n. weapon** arme f nucléaire; **n. winter** hiver m nucléaire

nuclear-free ADJ
▶▶ **n. zone** zone f anti-nucléaire

nucleic [nju:'kli:ɪk] ADJ Chem (acid) nucléique

nucleus, pl **nuclei** ['nju:klɪəs, -ɪaɪ] N 1 Phys,

Biol, Astron noyau m 2 Fig (of organization etc) noyau m; (of argument etc) cœur m; **the n. of a library** (beginnings) un commencement de bibliothèque; **the n. of a fine sales team** les premiers éléments d'une bonne équipe de vente

nuddy ['nʌdɪ] N Br Fam Hum **in the n.** tout nu, à poil

nude [nju:d] ADJ (person) nu
N 1 Art **a n.** un nu; **the n.** (genre) le nu; **to draw/paint from the n.** dessiner/peindre des nus ou des académies 2 **in the n.** tout nu

nudge [nʌdʒ] N coup m de coude; Fam **he didn't come home last night, n. n., wink wink** il n'est pas rentré hier soir, si tu vois ce que je veux dire
VT pousser du coude, donner un coup de coude à; **to n. one's way through a crowd** jouer des coudes pour se frayer un chemin à travers la foule; **we nudged the sofa forward a few inches** nous avons avancé le sofa de quelques centimètres
▶▶ Aut **n. bar** barre f de calandre

nudie ['nju:dɪ] ADJ Fam porno
▶▶ **n. book** magazine m porno

nudism ['nju:dɪz(ə)m] N nudisme m, naturisme m

nudist ['nju:dɪst] N nudiste mf, naturiste mf
▶▶ **n. camp** camp m de nudistes; **n. colony** camp de nudistes

nudity ['nju:dɪtɪ] N nudité f

nugatory ['nju:gətərɪ] ADJ Lit, Fml sans valeur

nugget ['nʌgɪt] N (of gold) pépite f, Fig **a n. (of useful information)** une information très utile; **a n. (of wisdom)** une perle; **chicken nuggets, nuggets of chicken** morceaux mpl de poulet

nuisance ['nju:səns] N 1 (person) casse-pieds mf inv, **go away, you('re a) n.!** va-t'en, tu m'embêtes ou tu me casses les pieds!; **she's a bit of a n.** elle est un peu casse-pieds; **he's being a n.** (of child, drunk) il m'embête/l'embête/etc; **to make a n. of oneself** embêter le monde; **theTV won't work – it's a real n.** la télé ne marche pas – c'est vraiment embêtant; **long skirts are a n.** les jupes longues sont gênantes; **this keyboard/pen is a n.** ce clavier/stylo est embêtant; **it's a n. for me to have to …** cela me gêne ou Fam m'embête de devoir …; **what a n.!, that's a n.!** que c'est embêtant ou agaçant!; **at least we won't have the n. of going through customs** au moins nous ne serons pas embêtés à douane; **to have n. value** être un élément gênant 2 Law dommage m; (to public at large) atteinte f portée aux droits du public; (to individual) atteinte portée aux droits privés des voisins
▶▶ Tel **n. call** appel m anonyme; Tel **n. caller** auteur m d'appels anonymes

NUJ [enju:'dʒeɪ] N Br (abbr National Union of Journalists) = syndicat m national des journalistes

nuke [nju:k] Fam N (bomb) bombe f nucléaire
VT 1 (bomb) atomiser 2 (microwave) faire cuire au four à micro-ondes 3 (defeat) ratatiner, battre à plates coutures

null [nʌl] ADJ Law etc (decree, act etc) nul, f nulle; (legacy) caduc, f caduque; **n. and void** nul et non avenu; **to render n.** (decree, will) annuler, infirmer, invalider
▶▶ Comput **n. modem cable** câble m de connexion sans modem; **n. set** ensemble m vide; Comput **n. string** chaîne f vide

nullification [nʌlɪfɪ'keɪʃən] N annulation f, invalidation f

nullify ['nʌlɪfaɪ] VT (contract, result) annuler, rendre nul; (act) infirmer; (decree) invalider; **his marriage was nullified** son mariage a été déclaré nul

nullity ['nʌlɪtɪ] N Law (of marriage) nullité f, invalidité f; (of inheritance) caducité f
▶▶ **n. suit** demande f en nullité de mariage

NUM [enju:'em] N Br (abbr National Union of Mineworkers) = syndicat m national des mineurs

numb [nʌm] ADJ (limb) engourdi, gourd; (mind) engourdi; **to go n.** s'engourdir; **hands n. with cold** mains engourdies par le froid; **to be n. with shock/grief** être hébété par le choc/la douleur; **n. with terror** glacé d'horreur; **to become n. to sth** devenir insensible à qch
VT (limbs, mind etc) engourdir; **she was numbed by her father's death** elle était sous le choc après la mort de son père, la mort de son père l'a laissée sous le choc

NUMBER ['nʌmbər]

N nombre **1, 3, 4, 6** ▪ chiffre **2** ▪ numéro **5**	
VT numéroter **1** ▪ compter **2, 3**	

N 1 (quantity), Math nombre m; **three-figure n.** nombre de trois chiffres; **even/odd/prime n.** nombre pair/impair/premier; **the n. of people present** le nombre des présents; **we were in equal numbers** or **equal in n.** nous étions en nombre égal; **they are few in n.** ils sont peu nombreux; Fml **without n.** sans nombre, innombrable; **a n. of …** un certain nombre de …; **she is one of a n. of people who …** elle figure parmi les personnes qui …; **a large n. of men** were killed un grand nombre d'hommes a été tué ou ont été tués; **any n. of …** un grand nombre de …, bon nombre de …; **to be present in small numbers/in (great) numbers** être présents en petit nombre/en grand nombre; **they are coming in ever-increasing numbers** ils sont de plus en plus nombreux à venir; **one of their n.** (l')un d'entre eux; Bible **(the Book of) Numbers** le Livre des Nombres, les Nombres VOIR GRAMMAIRE A76–7; B58–60

2 (symbol) chiffre m; **the n. eight** le chiffre huit

3 (of house, page, telephone etc) numéro m; (of soldier etc) (numéro) matricule m; **I live at n. 40** j'habite au (numéro) 40; Fam **to do a n. one** (in children's language) faire pipi, faire la petite commission; Fam **to do a n. two** (in children's language) faire la grosse commission; Fam **to look after n. one** tirer la couverture à soi; **he's only interested in n. one** tout ce qui l'intéresse c'est sa pomme; **my n. one priority** la première de mes priorités; Fam **to be at n. one** (of record) être (le) numéro un; Fam **he's my n. two** c'est mon adjoint; Aut **registration n.** numéro d'immatriculation; Fig Fam **I've got your n.!** je sais ce que tu as en tête!; **to draw a lucky n.** (at lottery etc) tirer un bon numéro; Fam **his n.'s up** il a son compte, il est fichu

4 Gram nombre m

5 Theat numéro m; **for my next n. I'd like to sing …** j'aimerais vous chanter maintenant …; **instrumental n.** morceau m instrumental

6 Journ (of newspaper etc) numéro m; (of work appearing in editions) livraison f, fascicule m; **current n.** numéro du jour/de la semaine/du mois, dernier numéro; **back n.** vieux numéro

7 Fam (thing, person) **she's a good-looking n.** c'est une jolie nénette; **that car/dress is a nice little n.** elle est pas mal, cette voiture/robe

8 Fam **a cushy n.** (job) une bonne planque; **she's got a nice little n. there** (situation) elle s'est dégoté un bon plan
VT 1 (give number to) numéroter
2 (count) compter; **his days are numbered**

ses jours sont comptés; **to n. sb among one's friends** compter qn au nombre de *ou* parmi ses amis

3 *(amount to)* **they numbered no more than twenty** ils n'étaient pas plus de vingt; **the town/the army numbers thirty thousand** la ville/l'armée compte trente mille habitants/trente mille hommes

▸▸*Comput* **n. crunching** calculs *mpl* (rapides); *Comput* **n. key** touche *f* numérique; *Comput* **n. lock** verrouillage *m* du clavier numérique;*Comput* **n. lock key** touche de verrouillage du clavier numérique; **n. plate** plaque *f* minéralogique *ou* d'immatriculation; **N. Ten Downing Street** = résidence *f* officielle du Premier ministre britannique

▸ **number off** VI *Mil* se numéroter

number-coded ADJ codé en chiffres

number-crunch VT *Comput Fam* faire subir des calculs rapides à

number-cruncher [-krʌntʃər] N *Comput* super-ordinateur *m*, *pl* super-ordinateurs

numbering ['nʌmbəriŋ] N *(of houses, pages etc)* numérotage *m*

▸▸**n. machine** numéroteur *m*; **n. system** système *m* de numérotation

numberless ['nʌmbəlis] ADJ innombrable, sans nombre

number-one ADJ numéro un

numberplate ['nʌmbəpleit] N *Br Aut* plaque *f* minéralogique *ou* d'immatriculation

numbly ['nʌmli] ADV *(to react, say)* mollement; *(to look, stare)* d'un air engourdi

numbness ['nʌmnis] N *(of fingers etc)* engourdissement *m*; *(of emotions etc)* torpeur *f*

numbskull ['nʌmskʌl] N *Fam* nigaud, -aude, bêta, -asse; **stop behaving like such a n.!** arrête de faire le nigaud comme ça!

numeracy ['nju:m(ə)rəsi] N degré *m* d'aptitude en calcul

numeral ['nju:m(ə)r(ə)l] N chiffre *m*, nombre *m*; **Roman numerals** chiffres romains; **the cardinal numerals** les numéraux *mpl* cardinaux

ADJ *(word, letter etc)* numéral, -aux

numerate ['nju:mərət] ADJ qui a le sens de l'arithmétique; **applicants should be highly n.** les candidats doivent avoir des compétences élevées en calcul; **to be barely n.** savoir à peine compter

numeration [nju:mə'reiʃən] N *Math* numération *f*; **binary n.** numération binaire

numerator ['nju:məreitər] N *Math* numérateur *m*

numeric [nju:'merik] *Comput* ADJ numérique

NPL **numerics** chiffres *mpl ou* caractères *mpl* numériques

▸▸**n. coding** codage *m* numérique; **n. field** champ *m* numérique; **n. keypad** pavé *m* numérique

numerical [nju:'merik(ə)l] ADJ *(value, superiority, order etc)* numérique; **to have a n. advantage** avoir l'avantage du nombre

▸▸**n. control** contrôle *m* numérique; **n. data** données *fpl* numériques; *Mktg* **n. distribution** distribution *f* numérique; *Comput* **n. keypad** pavé *m* numérique

numerically [nju:'merikli] ADV numériquement

numerous ['nju:m(ə)rəs] ADJ nombreux; **to grow more n.** devenir de plus en plus nombreux

numismatic [nju:miz'mætik] ADJ numismatique

numismatics [nju:miz'mætiks] N numismatique *f* VOIR GRAMMAIRE A10

numismatist [nju:'miz(ə)mətist] N numismate *mf*

num lock *Comput* *(abbr* **numbers lock)** verr num; **the n. is on** le pavé numérique est verrouillé

▸▸**n. key** touche *f* de verrouillage du pavé numérique

numpty ['nʌmpti] N *Scot Fam (idiot)* crétin, -ine, andouille *f*

numskull ['nʌmskʌl] N *Fam* = **numbskull**

nun [nʌn] N *Rel* religieuse *f*, *Fam* bonne sœur; **to become a n.** se faire religieuse, prendre le voile, entrer en religion

nuncio, *pl* **nuncios** ['nʌnʃiəu, -z] N *Rel* nonce *m*

nunnery ['nʌnəri] N *Old-fashioned* couvent *m* de religieuses

nuptial ['nʌpʃəl] *Lit* ADJ nuptial, -aux; **their n. day** le jour de leurs noces

NPL **nuptials** noces *fpl*

NUR [enju:'ɑ:r] N *Br Formerly (abbr* **National Union of Railwaymen)** = syndicat *m* national des employés des chemins de fer

nurse [nɜ:s] N **1** *(in hospital)* infirmier, -ière; *(privately employed)* infirmier, -ière, garde-malade *mf*, *pl* gardes-malades; **thank you, n.** merci mademoiselle/madame; **n. will take out the stitches** l'infirmière retirera les points de suture; **(male) n.** infirmier *m*

2 *(looking after children)* nurse *f*, bonne *f* d'enfant; **(wet) n.** nourrice *f*

3 *Entom (of bees, ants)* ouvrière *f*

VT **1** *(sick person)*, *Fam (a cold)* soigner; **she nursed him back to health** elle lui a fait recouvrer la santé grâce à ses soins

2 *(suckle) (baby)* nourrir (de son lait), allaiter

3 *Fig (plants etc)* soigner; *(horse, team etc)* ménager en vue du dernier effort à donner; *(feeling, hope etc)* nourrir, entretenir; *(project)* mitonner, mijoter; **he nursed the damaged plane back to base** il a réussi à ramener l'avion endommagé jusqu'à la base; **they nursed the family business through the worst of the recession** ils ont maintenu l'entreprise familiale sur pied au pire de la récession; *Br Pol* **to n. one's constituency** chauffer ses électeurs; **to n. an old grievance** entretenir un grief

4 *(clasp) (child)* bercer, dorloter; *(whisky, drink)* siroter; **to n. one's knee** tenir son genou dans ses mains

VI **1** *(as profession)* être infirmier, -ière; **she spent a few years nursing** elle a travaillé pendant quelques années comme infirmière **2** *(of baby)* téter

nursemaid ['nɜ:smeid] N bonne *f* d'enfants, nurse *f*, *Fig* **I'm not your n.!** je ne suis pas votre bonne!

nursery ['nɜ:s(ə)ri] N **1** *(room) (in house)* chambre *f* des enfants *ou* d'enfants; *(in hospital)* pouponnière *f* **2** *(establishment) (school)* (école *f*) maternelle *f*, **(day) n.** crèche *f*, garderie *f* **3** *(for plants, trees)*, *Fig* pépinière *f*

▸▸**n. education** enseignement *m* de l'école maternelle; **n. garden** pépinière; **n. gardener** pépiniériste *mf*; **n. nurse** puéricultrice *f*; **n. rhyme** comptine *f*; **n. school** (école) maternelle; **n. school teacher** instituteur, -trice de maternelle; *Br* **n. slopes** pistes *fpl* pour débutants

nurseryman, *pl* **nurserymen** ['nɜ:s(ə)rimən] N pépiniériste *m*

nursing ['nɜ:siŋ] ADJ **1** *Med* d'infirmier; **the n. staff** le personnel soignant **2** *(suckling)* allaitant

N **1** *(suckling) (of baby)* allaitement *m* **2** *(care given by a nurse)* soins *mpl* **3** *(profession)* profession *f* d'infirmier/d'infirmière; **to go into n.** devenir infirmier/infirmière

▸▸**n. auxiliary** aide-soignant, *pl* aide-soignants, *f* aide-soignante, *pl* aide-soignan-

tes; **n. home** *(for aged)* maison *f* de retraite; *(for convalescents)* maison de repos; *(for mentally ill)* maison de santé; *Br (private clinic)* hôpital *m* privé, clinique *f* privée; **n. mother** mère *f* qui allaite; *Br* **n. officer** infirmier, -ière en chef; **n. staff** *(in hospital)* personnel *m* soignant, infirmiers, -ières

nurture ['nɜ:tʃər] N éducation *f*, *(of plant)* soins *mpl*

VT **1** *(feed) (children, plants etc)* nourrir; *(feelings etc)* nourrir, entretenir; *(plan, scheme)* préparer, élaborer **2** *(bring up)* élever, faire l'éducation de

nurturing ['nɜ:tʃəriŋ] ADJ attentionné, maternel

NUS [enju:'es] N *Br (abbr* **National Union of Students)** = syndicat *m* étudiant, ≃ UNEF *f*

NUT [enju:'ti:] N *Br (abbr* **National Union of Teachers)** = syndicat *m* d'enseignants, ≃ FEN *f*

nut [nʌt] N **1** = terme générique pour les amandes, noisettes, noix etc; **a bag of nuts and raisins** un sachet de fruits secs mélangés; **fruit and n. (chocolate)** chocolat *m* aux fruits et aux noisettes/amandes/*etc*; *Fam* **tough** *ou* **hard n. to crack** *(problem)* problème *m* difficile à résoudre; **a hard** *ou* **tough n.** *(person)* personne *f* difficile *ou* peu commode

2 *Fam (head)* caboche *f*; **to be off one's n.** être timbré *ou* toqué, avoir perdu la boule; **to go off one's n.** *(go mad)* perdre la boule; *(become angry)* piquer une crise; *Br* **to do one's n.** péter les plombs, piquer une crise

3 *Fam (mad person)* dingue *mf*, barjo *mf*; **don't be a n.** arrête de dérailler *ou* débloquer; **a jazz/tennis n.** un(e) dingue *ou* fana de jazz/de tennis

4 *Tech* écrou *m*; **butterfly** *ou* **wing n.** écrou à oreilles, écrou (à) papillon; *Fig* **the nuts and bolts of the problem** les détails pratiques du problème; *Fig* **the nuts and bolts of a language** les éléments de base d'une langue

5 *Br Com, Min* **n. coal, nuts** gailletin *m*, têtes *fpl* de moineau

6 *Sl* **nuts** *(testicles)* couilles *fpl*

▸▸**n. cutlet** côtelette *f* végétarienne *(à base de noix, noisettes etc)*; **n. roast** rôti *m* végétarien

nutball ['nʌtbɔ:l] N *Am Fam* dingue *mf*, cinglé, -ée

nut-brown ADJ *(couleur)* noisette *inv*; *(hair)* châtain; *(skin)* brun

nutcase ['nʌtkeis] N *Fam* dingue *mf*, cinglé, -ée; **he's a complete n.** il est complètement dingue *ou* cinglé *ou* timbré

nutcracker ['nʌtkrækər] N **(pair of) nutcrackers** casse-noisette(s) *m inv*, casse-noix *m inv*

nuthatch ['nʌthætʃ] N *(bird)* sittelle *f*

nuthouse ['nʌthaus] N *Fam* maison *f* de fous

nutmeg ['nʌtmeg] N *(nut)* (noix *f* de) muscade *f*, *(tree)* muscadier *m*

▸▸**n. grater** râpe *f* à muscade; **n. tree** muscadier

nutrient ['nju:triənt] ADJ nutritif

N substance *f* nutritive

nutriment ['nju:trimənt] N *Fml* nourriture *f*

nutrition [nju:'triʃən] N nutrition *f*

nutritional [nju:'triʃənəl] ADJ *(science, research)* nutritionnel; *(value, disorder, process)* nutritif

▸▸*Com* **n. labelling** étiquetage *m* de l'apport nutritionnel

nutritionist [nju:'triʃənist] N nutritionniste *mf*

nutritious [nju:'triʃəs] ADJ nutritif, nourrissant

nutritive ['nju:trɪtɪv] ADJ = nutritional

nuts [nʌts] *Fam* ADJ *(mad)* cinglé; **to go n.** *(go mad)* perdre la boule; *(get angry)* péter les plombs, piquer une crise; **that noise is driving me n.** ce bruit me rend dingue; **to be n. about sb/sth** être fou/folle de qn/qch, raffoler de qn/qch

INT *esp Am* zut!; **n. to that!** plutôt crever!

nutshell ['nʌtʃel] N coquille *f* de noix/de noisette/*etc*; *Fig* **that's the whole thing in a n.** voilà toute l'affaire (résumée) en un mot *ou* en deux mots; *Fig* **(to put it) in a n. ...** pour résumer ..., bref ...

nutso ['nʌtsəʊ] ADJ *Am Fam* **to go n.** *(go mad)* perdre la boule; *(get angry)* péter les plombs, piquer une crise; **that noise is driving me n.** ce bruit me rend dingue; **to be n. about sb/sth** être fou/folle de qn/qch, raffoler de qn/qch

nutter ['nʌtər] N *Br Fam* dingue *mf*, toqué, -ée

nutty ['nʌtɪ] ADJ **1** *(in taste)* au goût de noisette; *(taste, flavour)* de noisette; *(containing nuts)* aux noisettes/noix/*etc* **2** *Fam (mad)* dingue; **as n. as a fruitcake** complètement dingue; **to be n. about sb/sth** raffoler de qn/qch

nuzzle ['nʌz(ə)l] VT & VI **to n. (against)** sb's shoulder *(of dog, horse)* fourrer son nez sur l'épaule de qn; *(of person)* se blottir dans le creux de l'épaule de qn; **to n. sb's hand** fourrer son nez dans la paume de la main de qn; **he nuzzled her neck** il lui caressait le cou de ses lèvres; **the dog nuzzled up to my leg** le chien me reniflait la jambe

NY *abbr* New York

NYC *abbr* New York City

nylon ['naɪlɒn] N *Tex* nylon® *m*; **n. sheets** draps *mpl* en nylon; **n. stockings** bas *mpl* nylon; **n. thread** fil *m* de nylon

NYMEX [enwaɪemi:'eks] N *St Exch* (*abbr* New York Mercantile Exchange) = marché *m* à terme des produits pétroliers de New York

nymph [nɪmf] N **1** *Myth* nymphe *f*; **tree** *or* **wood n.** hamadryade *f*; **sea n.** néréide *f*; **water n.** naïade *f* **2** *Entom* nymphe *f*

nymphet ['nɪmfɪt] N nymphette *f*

nympho, *pl* **nymphos** ['nɪmfəʊ, -z] ADJ, N *Fam* = nymphomaniac

nymphomania [nɪmfəʊ'meɪnɪə] N *Med* nymphomanie *f*

nymphomaniac [nɪmfəʊ'meɪnɪæk] ADJ, N nymphomane *f*

NYSE [enwaɪes'i:] N *abbr* New York Stock Exchange

NZ *abbr* New Zealand

O¹, o [əʊ] N **1** (letter) O, o m; **two o's** deux o **2** Tel etc zéro m VOIR GRAMMAIRE A77

O² INT (vocative) O, ō

O³ abbr Ohio

oaf, pl **oafs** [əʊf, -əʊfs] N rustre m; **you clumsy o.!** espèce de gros empoté!

oafish ['əʊfɪʃ] ADJ rustre

oak [əʊk] N **1** (tree) chêne m **2** (wood) (bois m de) chêne m; **o. furniture** meubles mpl de ou en chêne; **dark o. (colour)** couleur f vieux chêne **3** Br Univ Old-fashioned = porte f extérieure d'un appartement dans les universités d'Oxford et Cambridge; **to sport one's o.** fermer sa porte aux visiteurs
▸ ▸ **o. apple** noix f de galle; **o. grove** chênaie f, **o. leaf** feuille f de chêne; **o. tree** chêne; **o. wood** (material) (bois de) chêne; (forest) bois de chênes, chênaie

oaken ['əʊk(ə)n] ADJ de ou en chêne

oakum ['əʊkəm] N étoupe f (noire), filasse f, **to pick o.** démêler ou tirer l'étoupe

OAP [əʊeɪ'piː] N Br (abbr old age pensioner) retraité, -ée

oar [ɔːr] N aviron m, rame f, (as opposed to scull) aviron de nage; Fig Fam **to put** or **stick one's o. in** mettre son grain de sel; **good o.** (rower) bon rameur, bonne rameuse

oarlock ['ɔːlɒk] N Am tolet m

oarsman, pl **oarsmen** ['ɔːzmən] N rameur m

oarswoman, pl **oarswomen** ['ɔːzwʊmən, -wɪmɪn] N rameuse f

OAS [əʊeɪ'es] N (abbr Organization of American States) OEA f

oasis, pl **oases** [əʊ'eɪsɪs, -iːz] N oasis f, Fig **an o. of calm** une oasis de calme

oast [əʊst] N séchoir m (à houblon)

oasthouse ['əʊsthaʊs] N sécherie f (de houblon)

oat [əʊt] N (plant) avoine f (commune); **oats** (food) avoine; (porridge) **oats** flocons mpl d'avoine; Br Sl **to get one's oats** (have sex) baiser, prendre son pied; Fam **to sow one's wild oats** faire des fredaines, jeter sa gourme; Fam **to be off one's oats** avoir perdu l'appétit; (be off form) être patraque; Fam **to be feeling one's oats** (be self-important) ne plus se sentir; (be cheerful) avoir la pêche

oatcake ['əʊtkeɪk] N Culin galette f d'avoine

oath, pl **oaths** [əʊθ, əʊðz] N **1** (pledge) serment m; **o. of allegiance** serment d'allégeance; **to take an o.,** Law **to take the o.** prêter serment; **he took** or **swore an o. to avenge his father's death** il a juré de venger la mort de son père; Law **to be on** or **under o.** être sous serment, être assermenté; Law **to put sb on** or **under o.** faire prêter serment à qn; **she swore on her o. that …** elle a juré sous serment que … **2** (swearword) juron m, gros mot m

oatmeal ['əʊtmiːl] N farine f d'avoine; (colour) beige m; Culin **o. porridge,** Am **o.** bouillie f d'avoine, porridge m

OAU [əʊeɪ'juː] N Formerly (abbr Organization of African Unity) OUA f

OB [əʊ'biː] N Br TV (abbr outside broadcast) émission f en extérieur; **OB unit** car m régie, unité f mobile; **OB van** car de reportage

obduracy ['ɒbdjʊrəsɪ] N entêtement m, obstination f

obdurate ['ɒbdjʊrɪt] ADJ (stubborn) (person) entêté, obstiné, têtu; (refusal, attitude etc) inflexible; **to remain o.** ne pas fléchir, rester inflexible; **to be o. in the face of pressure** ne pas fléchir sous la pression; **an o. sinner** un pécheur impénitent

obdurately ['ɒbdjʊrɪtlɪ] ADV (stubbornly) avec entêtement; (to resist) inflexiblement; **to remain o. silent** garder un silence obstiné ou têtu; **to refuse o.** refuser obstinément, s'entêter à refuser

OBE [əʊbiː'iː] N Br abbr Officer of the Order of the British Empire

obedience [ə'biːdɪəns] N **1** obéissance f (to sb à qn; to the law à la loi); **to show o. to sb** se montrer obéissant envers qn **2** Rel **the Roman o.** l'obéissance f de Rome

> Note that the French word **obédience** is a false friend and is not normally used to translate the English word **obedience**.

obedient [ə'biːdɪənt] ADJ obéissant; (animal, child) obéissant, docile; **to be o. to sb** être obéissant envers qn; Arch **Your o. servant** (in letter) votre serviteur dévoué

obediently [ə'biːdɪəntlɪ] ADV docilement; **she had o. done everything which had been asked of her** elle s'était docilement exécutée

obelisk ['ɒbəlɪsk] N **1** Archit obélisque m **2** Typ croix f, obèle m; **double o.** diésis m

obese [əʊ'biːs] ADJ obèse

obeseness [əʊ'biːsnɪs] N obésité f

obesity [əʊ'biːsɪtɪ] N obésité f

obey [ə'beɪ] VT (person, order) obéir à; **to o. the law** obéir à la loi; **his legs refused to o. him** ses jambes refusaient d'obéir
VI obéir

obfuscate ['ɒbfʌskeɪt] VT obscurcir

obfuscation [ɒbfə'skeɪʃən] N obscurcissement m

obituary [ə'bɪtjʊərɪ] N nécrologie f, notice f nécrologique; Journ **the obituaries** la nécrologie, la rubrique nécrologique
▸ ▸ Journ **o. column** nécrologie, rubrique f nécrologique; **o. list** registre m des morts, nécrologe m; **o. notice** notice nécrologique

object¹ ['ɒbdʒɪkt] N **1** (thing) objet m **2** (subject etc) objet m; **o. of pity/contempt** objet de pitié/mépris; **to be an o. of ridicule** être en butte au ridicule; **she was the o. of his desires** elle était l'objet de ses désirs; **o. of a contract** objet d'un contrat

3 (purpose) but m, objectif m, fin f, **to have sth for** or **as an o.** avoir qch pour objectif ou pour but; **with this o. (in view)** dans cette intention, à cette fin; **with the sole o. of doing sth** à seule fin de faire qch; **what's the o. of the exercise** or **all this?** ça sert à quoi?, quel est le but de tout ceci?; **what is the o. of all this noise?** pourquoi tout ce bruit?; **to defeat one's o.** manquer son but; **the o. of the exercise** le but de l'exercice; **to succeed in** or **attain one's o.** atteindre son but

4 (obstacle) **expense is no o.** peu importe le prix, le prix n'est pas un obstacle; **distance is no o.** la distance importe peu

5 Gram **direct/indirect o.** complément m d'objet direct/indirect VOIR GRAMMAIRE A78–9; B52–3
▸ ▸ Comput **o. code** code m objet; **o. finder** (of microscope) chercheur m d'objet; **o. lesson** (example) démonstration f, illustration f (d'un principe); Sch leçon f de choses; Comput **o. linking and embedding** incorporation f d'objets liés

object² [əb'dʒekt] VI faire une/des objection(s); **to o. to sth** faire objection à qch; (of demonstrators etc) protester contre qch; **he objected to being asked to help** il a protesté parce qu'on lui a demandé d'aider; **I o. to being treated like a child** je n'aime pas qu'on me prenne pour un gamin; **to o. to doing sth** se refuser à faire qch; **I o. to the fact that …** ce qui me dérange (vraiment), c'est que …; **to o. to sb** avoir des objections à faire contre qn; **I don't o. to his** or **him coming here but …** je ne vois pas d'objection à ce qu'il vienne ici mais …; **he objects (to it)** il s'y oppose; **I o.!** je ne suis pas d'accord!, je proteste!; **if no one objects** si personne n'y voit d'objection(s); Law **to o. to a witness** récuser un témoin

objectify [əb'dʒektɪfaɪ] VT objectiver

objection [əb'dʒekʃən] N **1** (protest) objection f, **no objections were raised at the time** cela n'avait soulevé aucune objection à l'époque; **to make no o. to** or **against sth** ne pas voir d'objection à qch; **I have no o. to her doing so** je n'ai pas d'objection à ce qu'elle le fasse; **I have no o. to him** je n'ai rien contre lui; **if you have no o.** si vous n'y voyez pas d'inconvénient; **to raise an o.** soulever une objection; Law **o. to a witness** récusation f de témoin; **does anyone have any objection(s)?** est-ce que quelqu'un a une objection ou Fam quelque chose contre?; **does anyone have any objections if I open the window?** est-ce que quelqu'un verrait un inconvénient à ce que j'ouvre la fenêtre? **2** (reason for objecting) inconvénient m; **the chief o. to your plan is its cost** le plus grand inconvénient de votre projet, c'est son coût; **I see no o. (to it)** je n'y vois pas d'inconvénient

objectionable [əb'dʒekʃənəb(ə)l] ADJ (unpleasant) désagréable; (person) insupportable; (view, state of affairs) inacceptable; (language etc) choquant

objective [əb'dʒektɪv] ADJ **1** objectif; **let's be o.** soyons objectifs; **it is an o. fact that ...** le fait est que ... **2** *Gram (case)* accusatif

N **1** *(aim, goal)* objectif *m*, but *m*; **to achieve one's objectives** atteindre ses objectifs; **the committee has set out its objectives** le comité a fixé ses objectifs; **our o. for this year is to increase sales by 10%** nous avons pour objectif d'augmenter nos ventes de 10% au cours de l'année prochaine **2** *Opt* objectif *m* **3** *Gram* cas *m* régime, cas accusatif

objectively [əb'dʒektɪvlɪ] ADV objectivement, d'une manière objective

objectivism [əb'dʒektɪvɪz(ə)m] N objectivisme *m*

objectivity [ɒbdʒek'tɪvɪtɪ] N objectivité *f*

objector [əb'dʒektər] N *Pol etc* opposant *m*, personne *f* qui émet des objections; **the objectors to the plan** les personnes qui s'opposent au projet

object-orientated [-'ɔːrɪənteɪtɪd] ADJ *Comput* orienté objet
▸▸ **o. language** langage *m* à objets; **o. programming** programmation *f* par objets

oblate ['ɒbleɪt] ADJ *Math etc* aplati (aux pôles), raccourci

obligate ['ɒblɪgeɪt] VT **to o. sb to do sth** mettre qn dans l'obligation de faire qch; **to feel obligated to help** se sentir dans l'obligation d'aider; **to be obligated to do sth** avoir l'obligation de faire qch; **to feel obligated to sb** se sentir redevable envers qn

obligation [ɒblɪ'geɪʃən] N obligation *f*; **to put sb/to feel under an o. to ...** mettre qn/ se sentir dans l'obligation de ...; **moral o.** obligation morale; **to be under an o. to do sth** être dans l'obligation de faire qch; **I am under no o. to go with them** rien ne m'oblige à les accompagner; *Com* **without o.** sans engagement; **to do sth out of (a sense of) o.** faire qch parce que l'on s'y sent obligé; **to be under an o. to sb** avoir une dette de reconnaissance envers qn; **I am under a great o. to him** je lui suis redevable de beaucoup; *Com* **to meet one's obligations** faire face à ses engagements VOIR GRAMMAIRE A60–1; B39

obligatory [ɒ'blɪgət(ə)rɪ] ADJ obligatoire; **after the o. exchange of greetings** après les salutations de rigueur; **ties are o.** la cravate est obligatoire

oblige [ə'blaɪdʒ] VT **1** *(compel)* obliger, astreindre (**sb to do sth** qn à faire qch); **to be obliged to do sth** être obligé *ou* tenu de faire qch; *Admin* être astreint à faire qch; **I feel obliged to tell him** je me vois contraint de lui dire **2** *(do a favour for)* rendre service à, *Fml* obliger; **he did it to o. us** il l'a fait pour nous rendre service *ou* par complaisance **3** *(make indebted) (usu passive)* **to be obliged to sb** être reconnaissant à qn (**for sth** pour qch); *Fam* **much obliged** merci beaucoup; **I would be obliged if you would ...** je vous serais reconnaissant de bien vouloir ...

VI **he did it to o.** il l'a fait pour rendre service *ou* par complaisance; **to be always willing to o.** être très obligeant *ou* toujours prêt à rendre service; **anything to o.** tout ce que vous voudrez pour vous faire plaisir; **I'm sorry, I can't o.** je suis désolé, je ne peux pas

obliging [ə'blaɪdʒɪŋ] ADJ obligeant, serviable; **that's very o. of you** c'est très aimable de votre part

obligingly [ə'blaɪdʒɪŋlɪ] ADV obligeamment, complaisamment, complaisance; *also Iron* **they had very o. left the door open** ils avaient été assez aimables pour laisser la porte ouverte

oblique [ə'bliːk] ADJ *(line, angle)* oblique (**to** à); *(indirect) (reference, hint etc)* indirect; **o. glance** regard *m* en biais

N *(line)* (ligne *f*) oblique *f*, *Geom (figure)* figure *f* oblique *f*, *Anat (muscle)* oblique *m*; *Typ* barre *f* transversale *ou* oblique
▸▸ *Gram* **o. case** cas *m* indirect *ou* oblique

obliquely [ə'bliːklɪ] ADV obliquement, de biais, obliquement; *(indirectly) (to refer)* d'une façon indirecte; *(to glance)* de *ou* en biais

obliqueness [ə'bliːknɪs], **obliquity** [ə'blɪkwɪtɪ] N *also Geom* obliquité *f*, *(indirectness)* caractère *m* indirect

obliterate [ə'blɪtəreɪt] VT *(erase) (figures, footprints, traces etc)* effacer; *(the past, a culture)* annihiler; *(a stamp)* oblitérer; *(destroy) (buildings, town, evidence etc)* détruire; **the town had been all but obliterated during the war** la ville avait été quasiment rayée de la carte pendant la guerre

obliteration [əblɪtə'reɪʃən] N *(erasing) (of figures, footprints, traces etc)* effacement *m*; *(of the past, a culture etc)* anéantissement *m*; *(destruction) (of buildings, town, evidence etc)* destruction *f*

oblivion [ə'blɪvɪən] N oubli *m*; **to fall** *or* **sink into o.** tomber dans l'oubli; **to consign to o.** condamner à l'oubli

oblivious [ə'blɪvɪəs] ADJ oublieux (**of, to** de); **I was o. of** *or* **to what was going on** je n'étais pas conscient *ou* je n'avais pas conscience de ce qui se passait; **he was o. to danger** il était inconscient du danger

obliviously [ə'blɪvɪəslɪ] ADV *(to carry on etc)* en toute inconscience

oblong ['ɒblɒŋ] ADJ oblong, -ongue; *(face etc)* allongé
N rectangle *m*

obloquy ['ɒbləkwɪ] N *Fml* opprobre *m*

obnoxious [əb'nɒkʃəs] ADJ *(person, action etc)* odieux; *(smell etc)* repoussant

oboe ['əʊbəʊ] N *Mus* hautbois *m*; **o. player** hautboïste *mf*

oboist ['əʊbəʊɪst] N *Mus* hautboïste *mf*

obscene [əb'siːn] ADJ *(indecent) (song, telephone call, word etc)* obscène; *Fig (profits, prices, demands etc)* scandaleux; **it's o. that they are so rich when people are starving** il est scandaleux *ou* révoltant qu'ils soient aussi riches alors qu'il y a des gens qui meurent de faim

obscenely [əb'siːnlɪ] ADV d'une manière obscène; **o. rich** scandaleusement riche

obscenity [əb'senɪtɪ] N obscénité *f*, **disgusted by the o. of such profits/salaries** dégoûté par ces bénéfices/salaires scandaleux; **the o. of people earning millions while others starve** le caractère scandaleux *ou* révoltant d'une situation où certains gagnent des millions tandis que d'autres meurent de faim
▸▸ **o. laws** lois *fpl* concernant les outrages à la pudeur

obscurantism [ɒbskjʊ'ræntɪz(ə)m] N obscurantisme *m*

obscurantist [ɒbskjʊ'ræntɪst] ADJ, N obscurantiste *mf*

obscure [əb'skjʊər] ADJ **1** *(unclear) (speech, book etc)* obscur; **for some o. reason he thought it would help** il pensait, pour d'obscures raisons, que ça serait utile **2** *(little known) (birth, background)* obscur; *(author, book)* inconnu, peu connu, obscur; *(village etc)* inconnu, ignoré **3** *(vague) (feeling)* vague, obscur **4** *(dark)* obscur, sombre, ténébreux; **to grow** *or* **become o.** s'obscurcir, s'assombrir

VT **1** *(hide from view)* cacher; **to o. sth from sb's view** cacher qch à qn **2** *(make unclear) (argument, facts, truth)* obscurcir **3** *(overshadow)* éclipser, voiler **4** *(darken)* obscurcir, assombrir

obscurely [əb'skjʊəlɪ] ADV **1** *(to speak)* de façon obscure *ou* mystérieuse **2** *(to feel, see)* vaguement, obscurément

obscurity [əb'skjʊərɪtɪ] N obscurité *f*, *Fig* **to sink back into o.** retomber dans l'oubli

obsequies ['ɒbsɪkwɪz] NPL obsèques *fpl*, funérailles *fpl*

obsequious [əb'siːkwɪəs] ADJ obséquieux

obsequiously [əb'siːkwɪəslɪ] ADV obséquieusement

obsequiousness [əb'siːkwɪəsnɪs] N obséquiosité *f*

observable [əb'zɜːvəb(ə)l] ADJ observable; *(change, difference, improvement)* perceptible; **it was o. that ...** on a pu observer que ...

observance [əb'zɜːvəns] N **1** *(of law, custom etc)* observation *f*, observance *f* **2** *(practice)* **religious observances** pratiques *fpl* religieuses

observant [əb'zɜːvənt] ADJ observateur, -trice (**of** de); **that's very o. of you** tu es bien observateur

observation [ɒbzə'veɪʃən] N **1** observation *f*, *Mil (of terrain, enemy)* surveillance *f*, **to put/keep under o.** *(house, premises)* mettre/tenir en observation; *(person)* mettre/tenir sous surveillance; **this fact has not escaped his o.** ce fait n'a pas échappé à sa vigilance; *Med* **to keep sb in hospital for o.** garder qn en observation à l'hôpital; **to take an o.** *(in surveying)*, *Astron* faire une observation; *Naut* faire le point **2** *(remark)* observation *f*, remarque *f*, **to make an o.** faire une observation *ou* une remarque (**about sb/ sth** sur qn/qch)
▸▸ **o. aircraft** avion *m* de reconnaissance; *Rail* **o.car, o. coach** voiture *f* panoramique; **o. deck** terrasse *f* panoramique; **o. point** point *m* d'observation; *Mil* **o. post** poste *m* d'observation; **o. satellite** satellite *m* d'observation; *Med* **o. ward** salle *f* d'observation

observational research [ɒbzə'veɪʃən(ə)l] N étude *f* par observation

observatory [əb'zɜːvət(ə)rɪ] N observatoire *m*

observe [əb'zɜːv] VT **1** *(stars etc)* observer; **to o. the enemy's movements** surveiller les mouvements ennemis **2** *(notice) (fact etc)* remarquer, noter; **he didn't o. her leaving** il ne l'a pas vue partir **3** *(say)* to o. that ... observer *ou* faire remarquer que ... **4** *(respect, follow) (the law, the proprieties, a fast)* observer; *(the Sabbath)* respecter, observer; *(order)* se conformer à; **to o. silence** observer le silence; **a two minutes' silence was observed** on observa/ils observèrent/*etc* deux minutes de silence

observer [əb'zɜːvər] N **1** *(watcher)* observateur, -trice; **to be a close o. of sth** observer qch de près; **to be a keen o. of sth** suivre qch attentivement **2** *(expert)* expert *m*, spécialiste *mf* (**of** de); **political observers** experts *ou* spécialistes en politique

obsess [əb'ses] VT obséder; **to be obsessed with** *or* **by an idea** être obsédé *ou* hanté par une idée; **to be obsessed with sb** être obsédé par qn

obsession [əb'seʃən] N obsession *f* (**with** de); **to have an o. with sb/an idea** être obsédé par qn/une idée; **it's becoming a bit of an o.** ça tourne à l'obsession; **cleanliness is an o. with her** c'est une maniaque de la propreté

obsessional [əb'seʃən(ə)l] ADJ obsessionel; **to be o. about sth/sb** être obsédé par qch/qn

obsessive [əb'sesɪv] ADJ *(person)* à tendances obsessionnelles; *(behaviour, hatred,* *fear)* obsessionnel; *(idea, image)* obsédant; **he was becoming quite o. about it** ça devenait une obsession chez lui; **she never struck me as the o. type** elle ne m'a jamais semblé être du genre obsessionnel

▪ N **he's a bit of an o.** il est du genre obsessionnel; **our boss is a real o. when it comes to punctuality** la ponctualité est une véritable obsession chez notre patron; **you're turning into an o.** ça tourne à l'obsession chez toi

▸▸ *Psy* **o. compulsive disorder** névrose *f* obsessionnelle

obsessively [əb'sesɪvlɪ] ADV de manière obsessionnelle; **he's o. concerned with his appearance** il est obsédé par son apparence; **to be o. afraid of sth** avoir une peur maladive de qch; **he is o. tidy** c'est un maniaque de la propreté; **she is almost o. interested in birds/politics** son intérêt pour les oiseaux/la politique frise l'obsession

obsolescence [ɒbsə'les(ə)ns] N *(of law, ideas)* caractère *m* désuet; *(of word, term)* vieillissement *m*; *Ind etc (of equipment)* obsolescence *f*; **to fall into o.** tomber en désuétude; *Ind* **planned o.** obsolescence prévue; *Ind, Com* **built-in o.** obsolescence programmée

obsolescent [ɒbsə'les(ə)nt] ADJ *(equipment)* obsolescent; *(falling into disuse)* qui tombe en désuétude; *(word, term)* qui vieillit, qui a vieilli

obsolete ['ɒbsəliːt] ADJ *(word, idea, law)* désuet, -ète, tombé en désuétude; *(design etc)* démodé, dépassé; *(technique, equipment)* obsolète, périmé; *(ship)* déclassé; *(institution)* caduc, -ucque

obstacle ['ɒbstək(ə)l] N obstacle *m*; **to be an o. to sth** faire obstacle à qch; **to put obstacles in sb's way** faire obstacle à qn

▸▸ **o. course** parcours *m* d'obstacles; *Fig* parcours du combattant; **it's only one part of the o. course of finding a job** ce n'est qu'un bout du parcours du combattant qu'il faut suivre pour trouver un emploi; **o. race** course *f* d'obstacles

obstetric(al) [ɒb'stetrɪk, -ɪk(ə)l] ADJ obstétrical, -aux

obstetrician [ɒbste'trɪʃən] N médecin *m* accoucheur, obstétricien, -ienne

obstetrics [ɒb'stetrɪks] N obstétrique *f* VOIR GRAMMAIRE A10

obstinacy ['ɒbstɪnəsɪ] N *(of person)* obstination *f*, entêtement *m*; *(of resistance)* ténacité *f*; *Med (of disease)* persistance *f*

obstinate ['ɒbstɪnɪt] ADJ 1 *(person, refusal)* obstiné *(in doing sth* à faire qch*)*; *(resistance etc)* tenace; **to be o.** s'entêter, s'obstiner 2 *(illness, cold, spot)* tenace, coriace; *(stain, grease)* rebelle

obstinately ['ɒbstɪnɪtlɪ] ADV obstinément; *(to resist)* avec acharnement; **to behave o.** se montrer obstiné

obstreperous [əb'strepərəs] ADJ *(rebellious)* rebelle; *(noisy)* bruyant, tapageur; **don't get o. with me!** ne me faites pas d'histoires!; **to get o. about sth** faire un scandale de qch

obstreperously [əb'strepərəslɪ] ADV *(rebelliously) Fam* en rouspétant; *(noisily)* bruyamment, tapageusement; **to behave o.** faire des histoires

obstreperousness [əb'strepərəsnɪs] N *(of crowd, children)* caractère *m* tapageur; *(of sb's tone)* agressivité *f*; **I won't put up with your o. any longer** j'en ai assez de tes caprices et de ton agressivité

obstruct [əb'strʌkt] VT 1 *(block) (road etc)* obstruer, encombrer; *(pipe etc)* boucher; *Med (intestine)* oblitérer, obstruer; *(view)* boucher, cacher; **her view was obstructed**

by a tall man un homme de haute taille lui bouchait *ou* cachait la vue 2 *(hinder progress) (person's movements, attempts)* gêner, entraver; *(traffic, shipping)* entraver; *(reforms, inquiry, investigation)* faire obstruction à; **to o. sb's path** barrer le chemin à qn; *Law* **to o. the course of justice** entraver le cours de la justice; **to o. sb in the execution of his duty** gêner qn dans l'exercice de ses fonctions; *Sport* **to o. another player** faire obstruction; *Parl* **to o. a bill** faire obstruction

▪ VI *Sport* faire obstruction

obstruction [əb'strʌkʃən] N 1 *(action) (of road etc)* obstruction *f*; *(of pipe etc)* engorgement *m*; *Med (of intestine)* obstruction, oblitération *f*; *(of traffic, person in their affairs etc)* entravement *m*; *Sport, Pol* obstruction 2 *(blockage) (in road)* encombrement *m*; *(to shipping)* entrave *f*, *(in pipe)* engorgement *m*; **to cause an o.** *(on road)* entraver la circulation; *Rail* **an o. on the line** un obstacle sur la voie

obstructionism [əb'strʌkʃənɪz(ə)m] N *Pol* obstructionnisme *m*

obstructionist [əb'strʌkʃənɪst] ADJ, N *Pol* obstructionniste *mf*

obstructive [əb'strʌktɪv] ADJ *(person)* qui fait de l'obstruction, qui met des bâtons dans les roues; *(tactic, attitude)* d'obstruction; *Med* obstructif, obstruant; *Parl etc* **to be o.** faire de l'obstruction, être obstructionniste

obtain [əb'teɪn] VT *(information, money etc)* obtenir; **to o. sugar from beet** extraire du sucre de la betterave; **I obtained permission to see him** j'ai obtenu la permission de le voir

▪ VI *Fml (of practice etc)* avoir cours; *(of rules)* être en vigueur

obtainable [əb'teɪnəb(ə)l] ADJ easily **o.** facile à obtenir; **this model is only o. in America** on ne peut se procurer ce modèle qu'en Amérique

obtrude [əb'truːd] *Fml* VT mettre en avant; **to o. one's opinions on others** imposer ses opinions à autrui; **to o. oneself** s'imposer

▪ VI 1 *(of person)* s'imposer 2 *(of object)* dépasser *(from* de*)*

obtrusion [əb'truːʒən] N intrusion *f*

obtrusive [əb'truːsɪv] ADJ 1 *(person, behaviour, question)* importun, indiscret, -ète 2 *(smell etc)* pénétrant

obtrusively [əb'truːsɪvlɪ] ADV importunément; *(to behave)* indiscrètement; **the lights were o. bright** l'éclairage ôtait tout sentiment d'intimité

obtrusiveness [əb'truːsɪvnɪs] N 1 *(of behaviour, presence)* importunité *f* 2 *(of smell)* caractère *m* pénétrant

obtuse [əb'tjuːs] ADJ 1 *(person, mind)* obtus; *(behaviour, remark)* stupide; **you're being deliberately o.** tu fais exprès de ne pas comprendre 2 *(blunt-ended)* obtus, émoussé

▸▸ *Geom* **o. angle** angle *m* obtus

obtuseness [əb'tjuːsnɪs] N *(of person, behaviour, remark)* stupidité *f*

obverse ['ɒbvɜːs] N *(of medal)* avers *m*, face *f*; *(of truth etc)* opposé *m*

▸▸ **o. side** *(of medal)* avers, face

obviate ['ɒbvɪeɪt] VT *(difficulty etc)* parer à, obvier à; *(objection)* répondre à; **this obviates the need to …** ceci pare à la nécessité de …

obvious ['ɒbvɪəs] ADJ évident, clair, manifeste; *(lie, displeasure)* manifeste; *(feature)* frappant; **it's quite o. that she is lying** il est évident *ou* clair *ou* manifeste qu'elle ment, elle ment, cela saute aux yeux; **you were too o.** *(unsubtle)* tu n'as pas été très subtil; **it was the o. thing to do** c'était tout indiqué,

cela s'imposait; **an o. comparison would be with the French Revolution** la première comparaison qui vient à l'esprit est la révolution française; **his patriotism is a little (too) o.** son patriotisme sonne faux; **there was a very o. stain in the middle** il y avait une tache bien visible en plein milieu; **there are several o. objections to the plan** ce projet présente plusieurs inconvénients on ne peut plus évidents

▪ N **to state the o.** enfoncer une porte ouverte; **it would be stating the o. to say that we were surprised by the news** il va sans dire que ces nouvelles nous ont surpris; **to miss the o.** passer à côté de l'essentiel

▸▸ *Com* **o. defect** vice *m* apparent

obviously ['ɒbvɪəslɪ] ADV 1 *(in an obvious way)* manifestement; **he's so o. English** il est si manifestement anglais; **he did it so o.** il l'a fait si ostensiblement; **they are different, but not o.** ils sont différents, mais ça ne saute pas aux yeux; **he wasn't o. the right choice but …** au premier abord il n'était pas évident que c'était le bon choix mais … 2 *(of course)* évidemment; **do you prefer this? – o.** préférez-vous cela? – bien sûr; **o. not!** bien sûr que non!, évidemment non!; **I'll have to turn the offer down** il va sans dire que je vais devoir refuser l'offre

obviousness ['ɒbvɪəsnɪs] N évidence *f*, clarté *f*; *(of lie)* caractère *m* manifeste; **the o. of his displeasure** son mécontentement manifeste

OC [əʊ'siː] N *Mil (abbr* **Officer Commanding***)* chef *m* de corps

ocarina [ɒkə'riːnə] N *Mus* ocarina *m*

occasion [ə'keɪʒən] N 1 *(time)* occasion *f*, **on this o.** en cette occasion; **this is not the o. to discuss such matters** les circonstances sont peu appropriées pour parler de ces choses; *Fml* **on the o. of my daughter's marriage** à l'occasion du mariage de sa fille; **I am prepared to overlook it on this o., but …** je veux bien fermer les yeux cette fois-ci, mais …; **on one o.** une fois; **on another o.** une autre fois; **on several occasions** à plusieurs reprises; **on rare occasions** rarement; **on such an o.** en pareille occasion; **on great occasions** dans les grandes occasions; **words appropriate to the o.** paroles de circonstance; **to dress to suit the o.** mettre la tenue appropriée; **she could have dressed to suit the o.** elle aurait pu faire l'effort de s'habiller un peu mieux

2 on o. *(occasionally)* parfois, de temps en temps

3 *(event)* événement *m*; **her wedding was quite an o.** son mariage a été un grand événement ou n'a pas été une petite affaire; **an o. to remember** un événement mémorable; **we'll make this an o. to remember** nous allons fêter ça dans les règles; **there was a real sense of o.** il y avait une vraie atmosphère de célébration; **he has no sense of o.** *(for celebration)* il n'a pas le sens de la fête; *(for serious event)* il n'a pas le sens des convenances

4 *(opportunity)* occasion *f*; **I'll speak to him on the first o.** je lui parlerai à la première occasion; **should the o. arise** si l'occasion se présente, s'il y a lieu, le cas échéant

5 *Fml (cause)* sujet *m*, cause *f*; **to have o. to suspect sb/to be angry** avoir lieu de soupçonner qn/d'être en colère; **there's** *or* **you have no o. to be alarmed** il n'y a pas lieu de vous inquiéter; **this action was the o. of great suffering** cette action a donné lieu à de grandes souffrances

▪ VT *Fml (fear, inconvenience, surprise etc)* causer; *(response)* susciter, provoquer

occasional [ə'keɪʒ(ə)nəl] ADJ 1 *(visit)* espacé, occasionnel; *(incident)* qui se produit de temps en temps, occasionnel; **o. sho-**

wers averses *fpl* éparses *ou* occasionnelles; **I still get the o. twinge in my back** mon dos m'élance toujours un peu de temps en temps; **I have the o. cigarette/glass of wine** il m'arrive de fumer une cigarette/de boire un verre de vin; **he is an o. smoker** il ne fume qu'occasionnellement **2** *(play, verse etc)* de circonstance
▸▸ **o. chair** chaise *f* volante; *Br* **o. table** table *f* d'appoint

occasionally [ə'keɪʒən(ə)lɪ] ADV de temps en temps, parfois, occasionnellement; **we only see them very o. nowadays** nous ne les voyons que très occasionnellement *ou* de loin en loin ces temps-ci

occident ['ɒksɪdənt] N occident *m*, couchant *m*; *Pol etc* **the O.** l'Occident

occidental [ɒksɪ'dent(ə)l] ADJ occidental, -aux

occipital [ɒk'sɪpɪt(ə)l] ADJ, N *Anat* occipital *m*

occiput ['ɒksɪpʌt] N *Anat* occiput *m*

occlude [ə'kluːd] VT *Fml (opening etc)* occlure, fermer, boucher; *(eyelids)*, *Chem (gas)* occlure

occlusion [ə'kluːʒən] N **1** *(of pipe etc)*, *Chem (of gas)* occlusion *f* **2** *(of tooth)* occlusion *f* (molaire/etc)

occlusive [ə'kluːsɪv] N *Ling (consonne f)* occlusive *f*
▸▸ **o. consonant** consonne occlusive

occult [ɒ'kʌlt, 'ɒkʌlt] ADJ occulte, secret, -ète; **the o. sciences** les sciences *fpl* occultes
N **the o.** l'occulte *m*

occultism ['ɒkʌltɪz(ə)m] N occultisme *m*

occupancy ['ɒkjʊpənsɪ] N **1** *Law* possession *f* à titre de premier occupant **2** *(of building)* occupation *f*, habitation *f*
▸▸ **o. forecast** *(in hotels)* prévision *f* du taux d'occupation; **o. level** *(in hotel)* niveau *m* d'occupation

occupant ['ɒkjʊpənt] N *(of house etc)* occupant, -ante; *Law* premier occupant; *(of car etc)* occupant *m*; *(of job)* titulaire *mf*; *(of seat on board, of position)* détenteur, -trice

occupation [ɒkjʊ'peɪʃən] N **1** *(activity)* occupation *f*, *(profession)* métier *m*, profession *f*, *(on form)* qualité *f*; **a leisure o.** un loisir SEE GRAMMAR B5 **2** *(of house, land)* occupation *f*, **to be in o. of a house** occuper une maison; **how long have they been in o.?** cela fait combien de temps qu'ils occupent les lieux?; **fit for o.** *(house)* habitable; **army/ troops of o.** armée *f*/troupes *fpl* d'occupation; **they decided to organize an o. of the Embassy** ils ont décidé d'organiser l'occupation de l'Ambassade; *Hist* **the Roman o. of Britain** l'occupation de la Grande-Bretagne par les Romains; *Hist* **the O.** *(of France)* l'Occupation *f*

occupational [ɒkjʊ'peɪʃən(ə)l] ADJ
▸▸ **o. disease** maladie *f* professionnelle; **o. hazard** risque *m* professionnel *ou* du métier; **o. illness** maladie professionnelle; **o. medicine** médecine *f* du travail; **o. therapist** ergothérapeute *mf*; **o. therapy** ergothérapie *f*

occupied ['ɒkjʊpaɪd] ADJ **1** *(house)*, *Mil (territory)* occupé; **this seat is o.** cette place est prise; **in o. France** dans la France occupée *ou* de l'Occupation **2** *(busy)* **to be o. in** *or* **with doing sth** être occupé à faire qch; **he was o. with thoughts of ...** il était occupé à penser à ...; **to keep sb o.** occuper qn; **to keep one's mind o.** s'occuper l'esprit

occupier ['ɒkjʊpaɪər] N *(tenant)* locataire *mf*, *(of house)* occupant, -ante, habitant, -ante; **to the o.** *(on letter)* à l'attention de l'occupant

occupy ['ɒkjʊpaɪ] VT **1** *(house etc)* occuper, habiter; *(land)* occuper; *(position)* occuper, remplir; *Mil (enemy country)* occuper; *(stra-*

tegic point) s'emparer de; **the workers have occupied the building** les ouvriers ont occupé le bâtiment **2** *(room, space, attention)* occuper; **to o. one's time (in** *or* **with) doing sth** occuper son temps à faire qch; **her work occupies all her time** son travail occupe tout son temps; **it occupied two hours of the afternoon** cela a pris deux heures dans l'après-midi; **to o. one's mind** s'occuper l'esprit

occur [ə'kɜːr] VI (**-rr-**) **1** *(happen) (of event etc)* avoir lieu, arriver, se produire; *(of opportunity, vacancy)* se présenter; *(of accident)* avoir lieu, se produire; **this seldom occurs** cela arrive rarement; **I hope it will not o. again** j'espère que cela ne se répétera pas **2** *(be present) (of objects, types etc)* se rencontrer, se trouver, se présenter; **this word occurs twice in the letter** on trouve *ou* on rencontre ce mot deux fois dans la lettre **3** *(of idea etc)* venir à l'esprit; **this thought has occurred to me** cela m'est déjà venu à l'esprit; **it didn't o. to them that she might be lying** il ne leur est pas venu à l'esprit que peut-être elle mentait

occurrence [ə'kʌrəns] N **1** two hours before its o. deux heures avant que cela eût lieu; *Fml* **to be of frequent o.** arriver *ou* se produire fréquemment; **the o. of two murders on the same day** le fait que deux meurtres aient été commis le même jour; **the o. of leukaemia in this community is twice ...** le nombre des cas de leucémie dans cette communauté est le double de ...; **the o. of storms** *(frequency)* la fréquence des tempêtes; **to prevent the o. of violence** combattre (le phénomène de) la violence **2** *(event)* fait *m*, événement *m*; **an everyday o.** un fait quotidien; **a singular o.** un fait étrange; **this was the first o. of its kind** c'était la première fois qu'un événement de cette espèce se produisait

OCD [əʊsiː'diː] N *Psy (abbr* **obsessive compulsive disorder)** névrose *f* obsessionnelle

ocean ['əʊʃən] N océan *m*; **the Atlantic O.** l'océan Atlantique; *Fig* **an o. of sand** une mer de sable; *Fig* **we've got oceans of time** nous avons énormément de temps
▸▸ **o. current** courant *m* océanique; **o. floor** fond *m* de l'océan; **o. freight** fret *m* maritime; **o. liner** paquebot *m*

ocean-going ADJ *(ship)* au long cours, de haute mer

Oceania [əʊʃɪ'eɪnɪə] N Océanie *f*

oceanic [əʊʃɪ'ænɪk] ADJ *(voyage, climate)* océanique

oceanographer [əʊʃə'nɒɡrəfər] N océanographe *mf*

oceanography [əʊʃə'nɒɡrəfɪ] N océanographie *f*

ocelot ['ɒsəlɒt] N ocelot *m*

ochre, *Am* **ocher** ['əʊkər] N *Miner* ocre *f*, **red o.** ocre rouge; **yellow o.** jaune *m* d'ocre, ocre jaune
ADJ **o.(-coloured)** ocre *inv*

ocker ['ɒkər] N *Austr Fam (boor)* beauf *m*
ADJ *(boorish)* beauf

o'clock [ə'klɒk] ADV **one o.** une heure; **two/ three o.** deux/trois heures; **at four o.** à quatre heures; **the seven o. train** le train de sept heures VOIR GRAMMAIRE A80; B60

OCR [əʊsiː'ɑːr] N *Comput* **1** *(abbr* **optical character reader)** lecteur *m* (à reconnaissance) optique de caractères, lecteur OCR **2** *(abbr* **optical character recognition)** reconnaissance *f* optique des caractères
▸▸ **O. font** fonte *f* reconnue optiquement; **O. software** logiciel *m* d'OCR

Oct *abbr* **October**

octagon ['ɒktəɡən] N *Geom* octogone *m*

octagonal [ɒk'tæɡən(ə)l] ADJ *Geom* octogonal, -aux

octahedral [ɒktə'hiːdrəl, -'hed-] ADJ *Geom* octaédrique

octahedron, *pl* **octahedrons, octahedra** ['ɒktə'hiːdrən, -'hed-, -ənz, -ə] N *Geom* octaèdre *m*

octane ['ɒkteɪn] N *Chem* octane *m*; **o. number** *or* **rating** indice *m* d'octane

octave ['ɒktɪv] N *Rel, Mus, Fencing* octave *f*, *(in poetry)* huitain *m*; *Mus* **an o. apart** à une octave de différence

octavo [ɒk'teɪvəʊ] N *Typ* in-octavo *m inv*

octet [ɒk'tet] N **1** *Mus* octuor *m* **2** *(in poetry)* huitain *m* **3** *Chem* octet *m*

October [ɒk'təʊbər] N VOIR GRAMMAIRE A81–2; B60–2 octobre *m*; **in O.** au mois d'octobre, en octobre; **(on) the first/seventh of O.** le premier/sept octobre

octogenarian [ɒktədʒɪ'neərɪən] ADJ, N octogénaire *mf*

octopod ['ɒktəpɒd] ADJ, N octopode *m*

octopus ['ɒktəpəs] N poulpe *m*, pieuvre *f*

octosyllabic [ɒktəsɪ'læbɪk] ADJ *(verse, word)* octosyllabe, octo-syllabique

octuple ['ɒktjuːp(ə)l] ADJ, N octuple *m*

ocular ['ɒkjʊlər] ADJ *(nerve etc)* oculaire
N *Opt (of microscope etc)* oculaire *m*

oculist ['ɒkjʊlɪst] N oculiste *mf*

OD [əʊ'diː] N **1** *Fam (abbr* **overdose)** overdose *f* **2** *(abbr* **overdraft)** découvert *m*
VI *(pt, pp* **OD'd)** *Fam (abbr* **overdose)** prendre une overdose (**on** de); *Fig Sl* **I think I'm rather OD'd on pizzas** je crois que j'ai un peu forcé sur les pizzas; **they OD'd on soap operas** ils se sont pris une overdose de séries télévisées

ODA [əʊdiː'eɪ] N *(abbr* **Official Development Assistance)** aide *f* publique au développement

odalisk, **odalisque** ['əʊdəlɪsk] N odalisque *f*

odd [ɒd] ADJ **1** *(strange)* bizarre; **the o. thing about it is that ...** le curieux de l'affaire *ou* ce qui est bizarre c'est que ...; **it's o. your not knowing about it** c'est drôle *ou* bizarre que vous n'en sachiez rien; **it would look o. to refuse** ça ferait drôle si tu refusais/on refusait/etc; **how o. that he should have forgotten it!** comme c'est drôle *ou* bizarre qu'il l'ait oublié!; **(well,) that's o.!** voilà qui est bizarre *ou* singulier!, c'est curieux!; **an o. way of saying sorry** une drôle de manière *ou* une curieuse manière de s'excuser; *Com* **o. size** taille *f* peu courante
2 *Math etc (number)* impair
3 *(one of a set)* dépareillé; *(one of a pair)* déparié, dépareillé; **o. socks** chaussettes dépareillées; **to be the o. man out** être en trop; *Fig* être à part; **she was the o. woman out, not being German** n'étant pas allemande, elle faisait figure d'exception; **which of these books is the o. one out?** lequel de ces livres n'a rien à voir avec les autres?, trouvez l'intrus
4 *(occasional)* **they got the o. tin of food** on leur servait des boîtes de conserve de temps en temps *ou* par-ci par-là; **he scores the o. goal** il marque un but de temps en temps *ou* par-ci par-là; **at o. times** par-ci par-là; **at o. moments** dans mes/ses/etc moments perdus; **we get the o. visitor** nous avons de la visite de temps en temps nobody, apart from the o. anthropologist ... personne, à part quelques (rares) anthropologues ...
5 *(odd uses)* **a hundred o. sheep** cent et quelques moutons; **twenty o. pounds** un peu plus de vingt livres; **a few o. things to do** quelques petites choses à faire; **an o. any o. piece of cloth** un bout d'étoffe quelconque; **o. jobs about the house** petits travaux dans la maison

▸▸ **o. lot** *Com* lot *m* dépareillé; *St Exch (of shares)* lot de moins de cent actions; *Comput* **o. parity** parité *f* impaire

oddball ['ɒdbɔːl] *Fam* **N** allumé, -ée, farfelu, -ue

ADJ *(ideas, friends)* farfelu, loufoque

oddbod ['ɒdbɒd] **N** *Fam* original, -ale

odd-even ADJ

▸▸ *Comput* **o. check** contrôle *m* de parité; *Mktg* **o. price** prix *m* magique; *Mktg* **o. pricing** fixation *f* des prix magiques

oddity ['ɒdɪtɪ] **N 1** *(strangeness)* singularité *f*, bizarrerie *f*; **he has some little oddities** il a quelques petits travers **2** *(thing)* chose *f* bizarre, curiosité *f*; **she's a bit of an o.** *(odd)* elle est un peu bizarre; *(sticks out)* c'est un cas à part; **I'm sick of people treating me like an o.** j'en ai marre qu'on me traite comme si j'étais anormal; **this movie is an o.** *(weird)* c'est un film bizarre; *(unusual)* c'est un film à part

odd-job man, odd-jobber ['ɒd'dʒɒbmæn, -ɒbər] **N** homme *m* à tout faire

odd-looking ADJ (à l'apparence) bizarre

oddly ['ɒdlɪ] **ADV** bizarrement, étrangement; **o. enough nobody knew anything about it** chose curieuse, personne n'en savait rien; **an o. shaped face** un visage aux contours bizarrement irréguliers; **I find her o. attractive** je la trouve étrangement attirante

oddment ['ɒdmənt] **N** *(one of a set)* article *m* dépareillé; *(sale item)* fin *f* de série; *(piece of material)* coupon *m* d'étoffe; **remnants and oddments** soldes *mpl* et occasions *fpl*

oddness ['ɒdnɪs] **N** étrangeté *f*, bizarrerie *f*

odds [ɒdz] **NPL 1** *(probability)* chances *fpl*; **what are the o. on his getting the job?** quelles chances a-t-il d'avoir le poste?; **the o. are that she was lying** il y a de grandes chances pour qu'elle ait menti; **the o. are against him/in his favour** il y a peu de chance(s)/de grosses chances qu'il réussisse; **the o. are that he'll succeed** il y a gros à parier qu'il réussira; **it's against all the o.** c'est fort peu probable; **they fought** *or* **struggled against great o. to win the election** bien que les chances de succès étaient extrêmement minces, ils ont réussi à remporter l'élection; **we're always fighting against enormous o.** nous nous battons toujours contre des montagnes; **what are the o. that she'll remember?** quelles chances y a-t-il qu'elle s'en souvienne?; *Br Fam* **what's the o.?** *(what does it matter?)* qu'est-ce que ça fait?; *Br Fam* **it makes no o.** ça ne fait rien, cela n'a pas d'importance; **it makes no o. what she says** ce qu'elle dit n'a pas d'importance **2** *Horseracing etc* cote *f*, **o. on** *or* **against a horse** cote d'un cheval; **short/long o.** faible/forte cote; **the o. are (at) ten to one** la cote est à dix contre un; *Sport* **to give sb o. of ten to one** proposer à qn un pari à dix contre un

3 to be at o. with sb *(be in disagreement)* ne pas être d'accord avec qn; *(be on bad terms)* être brouillé avec qn *(over à propos de)*; **his latest statement is at o. with his earlier account** sa dernière déclaration ne concorde pas avec son premier récit des faits

4 o. and ends *or Br Fam* **sods** *(miscellaneous articles)* bricoles *fpl*; *(of cloth)* bouts *mpl*; **I've still a few o. and ends to do** j'ai encore quelques bricoles *ou* petites choses à faire

odds-on ADJ **it's o. that he won't notice** il y a gros à parier qu'il ne le remarquera pas

▸▸ **o. bet** pari *m* inégal; **o. favourite** grand favori *m*

ode [əʊd] **N** *Liter* ode *f*

odious ['əʊdɪəs] **ADJ** odieux **(to à)**

odiously ['əʊdɪəslɪ] **ADV** odieusement

odiousness ['əʊdɪəsnɪs] **N** caractère *m* odieux, abjection *f*

odium ['əʊdɪəm] **N** haine *f*, **to bring** *or* **cast o. upon sb** rendre qn odieux (aux yeux des autres)

odometer [əʊ'dɒmɪtər] **N** *Am* compteur *m* (kilométrique)

odontology [ɒdɒn'tɒlədʒɪ] **N** odontologie *f*

odor ['əʊdər] **N** *Am* = **odour**

odorless ['əʊdəlɪs] **ADJ** *Am* = **odourless**

odorous ['əʊdərəs] **ADJ 1** odorant, qui exhale une odeur (agréable) **2** *Fam (bad-smelling)* malodorant

odour, *Am* **odor** ['əʊdər] **N** odeur *f*, *(pleasant smell)* odeur (agréable), parfum *m*; *Fam (bad smell)* mauvaise odeur; *Fig Fml* **to be in good/bad o. with sb** être bien/mal vu de qn; **you're not in good o. with the boss** tu n'es pas en odeur de sainteté auprès du patron; *Rel* **o. of sanctity** odeur de sainteté

odourless, *Am* **odorless** ['əʊdəlɪs] **ADJ** inodore, sans odeur

Odyssey ['ɒdɪsɪ] **N** *Myth* **the O.** l'Odyssée *f*, *Fig* **a spiritual odyssey** une odyssée spirituelle

OECD [əʊiːsiː'diː] **N** *(abbr* **Organization for Economic Co-operation and Development)** OCDE *f*

oedema, *Am* **edema** [ɪ'diːmə] **N** œdème *m*

Oedipal ['iːdɪpəl] **ADJ** *Psy* Œdipien, -ienne

Oedipus ['iːdɪpəs] **N** *Myth* Œdipe *m*

▸▸ **O. complex** complexe *m* d'Œdipe

OEM [əʊiː'em] **N** *Comput (abbr* **original equipment manufacturer)** constructeur *m* de systèmes originaux

o'er [ɔːr, 'əʊər] **PREP, ADV** *Lit* = **over**

oesophagus, *Am* **esophagus,** *pl* **esophagi, esophaguses** [iː'sɒfəgəs, -gaɪ, -gəsɪz] **N** *Anat* œsophage *m*

oestrogen, *Am* **estrogen** ['iːstrədʒən] **N** *Biol, Chem* œstrogène *m*

oestrous, *Am* **estrous** ['iːstrəs] **ADJ** *Biol (cycle etc)* œstral, -aux

oestrus, *Am* **estrus** ['iːstrəs] **N** *Biol* œstrus *m*

OF [ɒv, *unstressed* əv] **PREP 1** *(belonging to)* de; **the name of the country/city** le nom du pays/de la ville; **the names of the districts** le nom des régions; **citizen of London** citoyen, -enne de Londres; **he is a friend of mine** c'est un de mes amis VOIR GRAMMAIRE A15–16

2 *(indicating separation, origin, cause)* de; **south of** au sud de; **within a mile of** à moins d'un mil(l)e de; **free of** libre de; **of noble birth** de naissance noble; **works of Shakespeare** œuvres de Shakespeare; **to ask a favour of sb** demander une faveur à qn; **of my own choice** de mon propre choix; **she died of grief** elle mourut de chagrin; **proud of sth** fier de qch; **I'm sick of it** j'en ai assez

3 *(indicating agency)* de; **it is very good** *or* **kind of you** c'est bien aimable de votre part, c'est très gentil à vous; **how clever of her** comme c'est intelligent de sa part; *Arch* **beloved of all** aimé de tout le monde

4 *(indicating material)* de, en; **made of wood** fait de *ou* en bois; **wall of stone** mur en *ou* de pierre; **full of water** plein d'eau

5 *(concerning, in respect of)* **to think of sb** penser à qn; **what do you think of him?** que pensez-vous de lui?; **to warn sb of sth** avertir qn de qch; **of President Taylor it was said that …** il a été dit du Président Taylor que …; **guilty of** coupable de; **doctor of medicine** docteur en médecine; **well, what of it?** et bien?, et après?

6 *(in description)* **the city of Rome** la ville de Rome; **man of genius** homme de génie; **people of foreign appearance** gens à l'air étranger; **child of ten** enfant (âgé(e)) de dix ans; **his wife of twenty years** la femme avec

qui il est marié depuis vingt ans; **that fool of a sergeant** cet imbécile de sergent; **all of a tremble** tout tremblant

7 *(with grammatical subject)* de; **the love of a mother** l'amour d'une mère

8 *(with grammatical object)* de; **the fear of God** la crainte de Dieu; **great drinker of whisky** grand buveur de whisky

9 *(partitive)* **three quarters of the crowd** trois quarts de la foule; *Fam* **no more of that!** plus de ça!; **how much of it do you want?** combien en voulez-vous?; **many/several of us** beaucoup/plusieurs d'entre nous; **there were two/several of us** nous étions deux/plusieurs; **she is one of us** elle est des nôtres; **one of the best** un des meilleurs; **the best of men** le meilleur des hommes; **the bravest of the brave** le brave des braves; **he, of all men** *or* **people** lui entre tous; **this day of all days** ce jour entre tous; **you, of all people, should know …** toi, plus que tout le monde, devrais savoir que …

10 *(with expressions of time)* **of late years** *(pendant)* ces dernières années; **of late** dernièrement, récemment; *Fam* **of an evening** le soir

ofay [əʊ'feɪ] **N** *Am Fam Offensive* sale Blanc *m*, sale Blanche *f*

Ofcom ['ɒfkɒm] **N** *Br* = organisme *m* chargé de réglementer le secteur des communications

OFF [ɒf] **ADV 1** *(away)* **house a mile o.** maison à un mil(l)e de distance; **some way o.** à quelque distance; **far o.** au loin, dans le lointain; **to go** *or* **be o.** *(leave)* s'en aller, partir; **isn't it time you were o. to bed?** n'est-il pas l'heure que tu ailles te coucher?; **I'm o. to London** je pars pour Londres; **I must be o.** (il faut que) je me sauve, il faut que je m'en aille; **be o. with you!** sauve-toi!, va-t-en!; **o. you go, you'll be late!** sauve-toi *ou* vas-y, tu vas être en retard!; **they're o.!** *(of racers, racehorses etc)* ils sont partis!, ils ont pris le départ!; **to go o. (to sleep)** s'endormir; *Theat* **to speak o.** parler depuis les coulisses; **he's o. again!** *(complaining etc)* le voilà qui remet ça!; **o. we go again!** nous voilà repartis!

2 *(indicating separation, removal)* **to take o. one's coat** retirer *ou* ôter son manteau; **with his jacket/trousers o.** sans sa veste/son pantalon; **a button has come o.** un bouton a sauté; **could you take two centimetres o.?** *(off sleeves etc)* est-ce que vous pourriez enlever deux centimètres?; **to cut sb's head o.** couper *ou* trancher la tête à qn, décapiter qn; **o. with her head!** qu'on lui coupe la tête!; **o. with those wet clothes!** retire(-moi) *ou* enlève(-moi) ces vêtements humides!; **hands o.!** bas les pattes!

3 *(not functioning, turned off)* **the light/radio is o.** la lumière/radio est éteinte; **the gas/electricity/water is o.** le gaz/l'électricité/l'eau est coupé(e); **the ignition is o.** l'allumage est coupé

4 *(in price)* **20%/£5 o.** 20%/5 livres de réduction *ou* de remise, réduction *f ou* remise *f* de 20%/5 livres

5 *(indicating completion)* **to finish o. a piece of work** finir *ou* terminer un travail

6 *(away from work etc)* **have you any time o. during the week?** avez-vous des heures libres pendant la semaine?; **he's o. today** il ne travaille pas aujourd'hui; **to take some time o.** se libérer; **day o.** jour de congé; **to give the staff a day o.** donner un jour de congé à son personnel; **to arrange to take two days o.** prendre deux jours de congé; **I get two hours o. for lunch** j'ai deux heures de libres pour le déjeuner

7 *(in phrases)* **o. and on, on and o.** par intervalles; *(from time to time)* de temps en temps; *Fam* **right** *or* **straight o.** immédiatement, sur-le-champ, tout de suite

PREP **1** *(from)* de; **to fall o. sth** tomber de qch; **to take a ring o. one's finger** ôter une bague de son doigt; **to cut a slice o. sth** couper une tranche de qch; **we dined o. a leg of lamb** nous avons dîné d'une tranche de gigot; *Elec* **to work o. the mains** se brancher sur secteur; **get that knife o. him!** prends-lui son couteau!; *Fam* **to borrow money/buy sth o. sb** emprunter de l'argent/ acheter qch à qn; *Fam* **I caught a cold o. my brother** mon frère m'a passé son rhume; **o. the top of one's head** *(to say, answer etc)* comme ça; **o. the cuff** *(to make a speech)* au pied levé; **(get) o.!** enlevez-vous de là!; **o. the sofa!** *(don't stand on it)* descends du canapé!; *(don't sit on it)* lève-toi du canapé!

2 *(indicating reduction in price etc)* **a third o. everything** rabais d'un tiers sur toute la marchandise; *Com* **10%/£20 o. a price** 10%/ 20 livres de réduction *ou* de remise sur un prix; **that's 2 seconds o. the record** c'est 2 secondes de moins que le record

3 *(away from, outside of)* écarté de, éloigné de; **village o. the beaten track** village dans un coin reculé; **street o. the main road** rue qui donne sur la grande route; **it's just o. Regent Street** c'est tout près de Regent Street

4 *(on vacation)* **to have time o. work** avoir du temps (de) libre; *see also* **off** ADV **6**

5 *(not liking)* **to be o. one's food** ne pas avoir d'appétit; **I'm o. coffee at the moment** ces temps-ci je n'ai pas envie de boire de café; *(because of doctor's orders)* en ce moment, je n'ai plus le droit au café; **he's o. drugs/drink** il ne se drogue/boit plus; *Fam* **I'm o. her** je ne l'aime plus

6 *Naut* **o. the Cape** au large du Cap; *(at latitude of)* à la hauteur du Cap; **o. the coast of Spain** au large de la côte espagnole; **to sail o. the wind** naviguer vent largue

ADJ **1** *(not functioning)* **o. position** position *f* arrêt; *(of lever)* position de repos; *(on scale)* position 'zéro'; *(of brakes)* position de desserrage; **o. switch** bouton *m* d'arrêt

2 *(on vacation, not working)* en congé, en vacances; **to be o. sick** être absent parce qu'on est malade, être malade; **he's o. today** il n'est pas là aujourd'hui; **are you o. tomorrow?** tu travailles demain?; *(no school)* tu (n')as (pas d')école demain?; *(no college)* tu (n')as (pas) cours demain?; **when are you o. this afternoon?** à quelle heure tu finis cet après-midi?; **I'm o. from 3 to 5** je ne travaille pas entre 3 et 5 heures

3 *(cancelled, finished)* *(marriage, trip, meeting)* annulé; *(engagement)* rompu; **it's all or the whole thing is o.** *(of relationship)* tout est fini; *(of deal)* la transaction est annulée *ou* ne se fera pas, *Fam* l'affaire est tombée à l'eau; **the lamb is o.** *(in restaurant)* il n'y a plus d'agneau

4 *(not fresh)* **to be o.** *(of food)* ne plus être frais; *(of meat)* être avarié; *(of milk, orange juice etc)* être tourné; **this beer's o.** cette bière est éventée

5 *(inaccurate, unsuccessful)* **his timing was a bit o.** *(when he asked for a rise etc)* il n'a pas choisi un très bon moment; **an o. day** un jour où l'on n'est pas en forme *ou* en train; *(with bad luck)* un jour sans

6 *Fam* **that's a bit o.!** *(improper, unfair)* c'est pas un truc à faire!; *(not nice)* ça c'est pas sympa!

7 to be well/badly o. *(financially)* être à l'aise/dans le besoin *ou* la gêne; **to be badly o. for sth** être à court de qch; **how are we o. for money/time?** combien d'argent/de temps avons-nous?; **how are we o. for coffee/bread?** est-ce qu'il y a encore du café/ pain?; **he is better o. where he is** il est bien mieux où il est; **you'd be better o. accepting their offer** tu ferais mieux d'accepter leur offre

N *Horseracing* **the o.** le départ; **to be ready for the o.** être prêt pour le départ

VT *Sl (kill)* descendre, zigouiller

▸▸ *Horseriding* **o. leg** jambe *f* de dehors; *Cr* **o. side** *(when the batsman is right-handed)* côté *m* droit du terrain; *(when the batsman is left-handed)* côté gauche du terrain

off-air ADJ, ADV hors antenne

offal ['ɒf(ə)l] N *(of animal) (edible)* abats *mpl*

off-balance sheet ADJ hors bilan
▸▸ **o. item** poste *m ou* élément *m* hors bilan; **o. transactions** opérations *fpl* de hors bilan

offbeat ['ɒfbiːt] N *Mus* temps *m* faible
ADJ *Fam (person, clothes, music)* original, -aux, excentrique

off-Broadway [-brɔːdweɪ] ADJ *Am Theat (production)* en dehors de Broadway

off-camera ADJ, ADV hors caméra

off-centre, off-centred, *Am* off-center, off-centered [ɒf'sentər, -təd] ADJ décentré, décalé; *Cin* décadré; *Fig (analysis, description)* légèrement inexact, pas tout à fait exact; *(humour, style)* excentrique, saugrenu

off-chance N **on the o.** à tout hasard; **I went on the o. that they would be there** j'y suis allé au cas peu probable où ils y seraient; **they had waited for hours on the o. of meeting their hero** ils avaient attendu pendant des heures dans l'espoir de rencontrer leur héros

off-colour, *Am* off-color ADJ **1** *Br (unwell)* **to be** *or* **feel o.** ne pas se sentir dans son assiette; **to look o.** ne pas avoir l'air dans son assiette **2** *Old-fashioned (joke)* d'un goût douteux

off-course ADJ *(bet)* effectué hors des champs de course

offcut ['ɒfkʌt] N *(from wooden plank, cloth, carpet)* chute *f*, *(for animals)* rognures *fpl*; **offcuts** *(of meat)* restes *mpl* du découpage

off-duty ADJ qui n'est pas de service

offence, *Am* offense [ə'fens] N **1** *Law etc (minor)* infraction *f*, *(more serious)* délit *m*; **petty** *or* **minor o.** contravention *f* (de simple police); **second o.** récidive *f* **2** *(no pl) (annoyance, displeasure)* blessure *f* faite à la susceptibilité de qn; **to take o.** s'offenser, se froisser (**at** de qch); **to take o. at the slightest thing** s'offenser d'un rien; **to cause** *or* **to give o. to sb** *(of person, personal remarks)* offenser *ou* blesser *ou* froisser qn; *(of film, book, programme)* heurter la sensibilité de qn; **I meant no o., I didn't mean to cause o.** je ne voulais offenser personne; **his speech caused a great deal of o. to the Catholic church** son discours a profondément déplu à l'église catholique; **it's an o. to the eye** cela choque la vue *ou* les regards **3** *Mil (attack)* attaque *f*, agression *f* **4** ['ɒfens] *Am Sport* attaque *f*

offend [ə'fend] VT *(person)* offenser, blesser, froisser; *(the Lord, Islam etc)* offenser; **to be offended at** *or* **by sth** se froisser *ou* s'offenser de qch; **to be easily offended** être très susceptible, se froisser facilement; **I hope you won't be offended if I …** j'espère que vous ne vous froisserez pas si je …; **to o. the eye** choquer les regards *ou* la vue; **harsh sound that offends the ear** son dur qui écorche *ou* heurte l'oreille

VI **1** *(cause offence)* **I didn't mean to o.** *(give offence to the general public)* je ne voulais offenser personne; *(give offence to you)* je ne voulais pas t'offenser *ou* te froisser **2** *Law* commettre une infraction, *(more serious)* commettre un délit; **to o. a second time** récidiver

▸ **offend against** VT INSEP *(law, principle)* violer, enfreindre; *(common sense)* choquer;

(good taste) heurter; **his behaviour offends against good manners** son comportement est un outrage aux bonnes manières

offended [ə'fendɪd] ADJ **1** *(insulted)* blessé, offensé, froissé; **in an o. tone of voice** d'une voix offensée **2** *Law* **the o. party** l'offensé, -ée

offender [ə'fendər] N malfaiteur *m*; *Law* délinquant, -ante; *Law* **first o.** délinquant, -ante primaire

offending [ə'fendɪŋ] ADJ fautif

offense [ə'fens] N *Am* = offence

offensive [ə'fensɪv] ADJ **1** *(word, action)* blessant, offensant, choquant; *(spectacle)* choquant, repoussant; *(smell)* repoussant, nauséabond; **morally o.** book livre moralement choquant; **these remarks were o. to many people** ces remarques ont choqué de nombreuses personnes; **to be o. to sb** *(of person)* se montrer blessant envers qn; **in an o. tone** d'un ton injurieux **2** *Mil etc* offensif

N *Mil, Sport, Fig* offensive *f*; **to take the o.** prendre l'offensive; **to be on the o.** être sur l'offensive

offensively [ə'fensɪvlɪ] ADV **1** *(shockingly)* d'une manière blessante *ou* choquante; *(to say)* d'un ton injurieux **2** *Mil, Sport* offensivement

offensiveness [ə'fensɪvnɪs] N *(of sight, behaviour)* nature *f* offensante *ou* choquante; *(of smell)* nature nauséabonde; *(of remark etc)* nature injurieuse; **the o. of her tone** son ton injurieux

offer ['ɒfər] N offre *f*, proposition *f*; **I had several offers of help** plusieurs personnes m'ont proposé de m'aider; **we need somebody to help, any offers?** nous avons besoin de quelqu'un pour nous aider, est-ce qu'il y a des volontaires?; **I've had the o. of a job** on m'a fait une offre d'emploi, on m'a offert un emploi; **I've had the o. of a car for the weekend** on m'a proposé une voiture pour le week-end; *Com* **to make an o. for sth** faire une offre pour qch; *Com* **on o.** *(on sale)* en vente; **what is on o. in the negotiations?** qu'est-ce qui est proposé dans les négociations?; **£500 or nearest o.** = prix *m* à débattre autour de 500 livres; *Com* **special o.** promotion *f*, **on special o.** en promotion; **job offers** offres d'emploi; **o. of marriage** demande *f* en mariage; **to make sb an o.** faire une offre *ou* une proposition à qn; *esp Hum* **to make sb an o. they can't refuse** faire à qn une proposition à laquelle il est impossible de dire non; *St Exch* **o. by prospectus** offre publique de vente; *Fin* **o. to purchase** offre publique d'achat; *Fin* **o. for sale** mise *f* sur le marché

VT *(something, one's services)* offrir; *(excuses)* présenter; *(one's hand)* tendre; *(remark, criticism, description)* faire; *(opinion)* avancer; *(advice, chance, explanation)* donner; *(definition)* proposer; *(of scheme etc)* *(difficulties, advantages)* présenter; **to o. sb sth** offrir qch à qn; **he was offered a job** on lui a offert un emploi; **he offered her his car for the weekend** il lui a proposé (de lui prêter) sa voiture pour le week-end; **house offered for sale** maison mise en vente; **the conditions that we are able to o. you** les conditions que nous sommes à même de vous faire; **they're offering two weeks' skiing for £200** ils proposent deux semaines aux sports d'hiver pour 200 livres; **to o. to do sth** offrir de faire qch; **this offers a glimpse of things to come** ceci donne une petite idée de ce qui va suivre; *Law* **to o. a plea** exciper d'une excuse; **to o. resistance** offrir de la résistance

VI if occasion offers si une belle occasion se présente

▸▸ **o. price** *St Exch* cours *m ou* prix vendeur; *Mktg* prix vendeur, prix offert

▸ **offer up** VT SEP *(prayers, thanks to God)* offrir

offering ['ɒfərɪŋ] N **1** *(thing offered)* offre *f*; *Rel* offrande *f*; **this year's offerings from Hollywood** ce qu'Hollywood nous propose cette année; **his latest o. is a poem entitled …** sa dernière production est un poème intitulé …; **let's hope this essay is better than your last o.** espérons que cette dissertation sera meilleure que votre dernier chef-d'œuvre; **and this, I believe, was your o., Smith** et voici votre torchon, Smith **2** *(action)* offre *f*; **the o. of thanks/congratulations** les remerciements/félicitations

offertory ['ɒfət(ə)rɪ] N *Rel* **1** *(of mass)* offertoire *m* **2** *(of collection)* quête *f*; *(amount collected)* montant *m* de la quête

▸▸ **o. box** tronc *m*

off-exchange ADJ *St Exch (transaction, contract, market)* hors Bourse, hors cote

offhand ['ɒf'hænd] ADV *(immediately)* **I don't know** o. comme ça de but en blanc, je ne le sais pas; **nonsense! o. I can think of six** n'importe quoi! je peux en nommer six sur-le-champ

ADJ *(casual)* cavalier, -ière, désinvolte; *(brusque)* brusque; **to be o. with sb** se montrer désinvolte *ou* cavalier à l'égard de qn; **to treat sb in an o. manner** traiter qn cavalièrement *ou* avec désinvolture

offhanded ['ɒf'hændɪd] ADJ = **offhand** ADJ

offhandedly ['ɒf'hændɪdlɪ] ADV *(casually)* avec désinvolture; **I didn't like the way she o. assumed that …** je n'ai pas aimé la désinvolture avec laquelle elle a supposé que …

offhandedness ['ɒf'hændɪdnɪs] N *(casualness)* désinvolture *f*; *(brusqueness)* brusquerie *f*

off-highway ADJ, ADV tout-terrain, hors-route

off-hook, **offhook** ['ɒf'hʊk] ADJ

▸▸ *Comput* **o. signal** signal *m* de réponse *ou* de décrochage

office ['ɒfɪs] N **1** bureau *m*; *(of solicitor)* étude *f*, *(of lawyer)* cabinet *m*; *Am (of doctor, dentist)* cabinet (de consultation); **to work in an o., to have an o. job** avoir un emploi de bureau; **to stay late at the o.** rester tard au bureau; **the whole o. knows** tout le monde le sait au bureau, tout le bureau le sait; **for o. use only** *(on form)* (cadre) réservé à l'administration **2** *Pol etc (position)* charge *f*, fonctions *fpl*; **the o. of Prime Minister** la fonction de premier ministre; **high o.** fonctions hautes; **public o.** fonction publique; **to be in o., to hold o.** être en fonction; *(of government, politician)* être au pouvoir; **he has never held high o.** il n'a jamais occupé de poste élevé; **to be out of o.** ne plus être au pouvoir; **to take o., to come into o.** entrer en fonctions; *(of government)* arriver au pouvoir; **to seek o.** chercher à se faire élire **3** *Fml (service)* **through** *or* **owing to the good offices of a friend** grâce aux bons offices *ou* par les bons soins d'un ami; **to offer one's good offices to sb** proposer ses bons offices à qn **4** *Rel* **o. of the day** office *m* du jour; **o. for the dead** office des morts; **last offices** *(for the dead)* derniers devoirs *mpl*; *(funeral)* obsèques *fpl* **5** *Fml* **offices** *(of a house)* communs *mpl* et dépendances *fpl*

▸▸ *Fin* **o. account** compte *m* commercial; **o. address** adresse *f* au bureau; **o. automation** bureautique *f*, **o. block** immeuble *m* de bureaux; *Old-fashioned* **o. boy** garçon *m* de bureau; **o. building** immeuble de bureaux; *Br* **O. of the Deputy Prime Minister** = service

m du vice-Premier ministre; **o. equipment** matériel *m* de bureau; **o. expenses** frais *mpl* de bureau; **the O. of Fair Trading** = organisme *m* britannique de défense des consommateurs et de régulation des pratiques commerciales; **o. furniture** mobilier *m* de bureau; **o. hours** heures *fpl* de bureau; *Comput* **o. IT** bureautique; **o. manager** chef *m* de bureau; *Br* **O. for National Statistics** ≃ INSEE *m*; **o. party** = réception *f* organisée dans un bureau à l'occasion des fêtes de fin d'année; **o. politics** = jeux *mpl* d'alliances, antipathies etc au sein d'une entreprise; **o. romance** liaison *f* au bureau; **o. staff** personnel *m* de bureau; **o. work** travail *m* de bureau; **o. worker** employé, -ée de bureau

officeholder ['ɒfɪshəʊldər] N employé, -ée de l'État, fonctionnaire *mf*

officer ['ɒfɪsər] N **1** *(official)* fonctionnaire *mf*; **municipal o.** officier *m* municipal; *Admin* **clerical o.** secrétaire *mf* d'administration; **administrative o.** ≃ administrateur, -trice civil(e); **customs o.** douanier, -ière; **police o.**, *Am* **o.** agent *m ou* officier de police; *Am* **O. Smith** officier Smith; **yes, o.** oui, monsieur/ madame l'agent **2** *Mil etc* officier *m*; *(in Salvation Army)* officier, -ière **3** **high o.** *(of an order)* grand dignitaire *m*

▸▸ *Mil* **o. of the day** officier *m* de permanence

official [ə'fɪʃəl] ADJ *(statement, visit, strike etc)* officiel; *(language)* *(officially recognized)* officiel; *(bureaucratic)* administratif; **to act in one's o. capacity** agir dans l'exercice de ses fonctions; **she was speaking in her o. capacity as General Secretary** elle parlait en sa qualité de Secrétaire général; **the o. organist** le/la titulaire de l'orgue

N responsable *mf*, *(of government)* fonctionnaire *mf*, *Pej* bureaucrate *mf*; *(at sports meeting etc)* commissaire *mf*; *Am Sport (referee)* arbitre *m*; **minor officials** petits fonctionnaires

▸▸ *Fin* **o. exchange rate** cours *m* officiel; **o. letter** pli *m* officiel *ou* de service; *St Exch* **O. List** cote *f* officielle; *Fin* **o. market** marché *m* officiel; **o. opening** *(of new factory, museum etc)* inauguration *f*, *St Exch* **o. quotation** cours officiel; *Banking* **o. rate** taux *m* officiel d'escompte; *Br* **o. receiver** administrateur, -trice judiciaire; *Br* **o. receivership** liquidation *f* judiciaire; *Sport* **o. record** record *m* homologué; **the O. Secrets Act** = loi britannique sur le secret Défense

officialdom [ə'fɪʃəldəm] N *(no pl) (officials)* administration *f*, *Pej (bureaucracy)* bureaucratie *f*, fonctionnarisme *m*

officialese [əfɪʃə'liːz] N *Fam* jargon *m* administratif

officially [ə'fɪʃəlɪ] ADV officiellement

officiate [ə'fɪʃɪeɪt] VI *Rel* **to o. at a service** officier à un office; **to o. at a church** desservir une église; **officiating minister** (pasteur *m*) officiant *m*

officious [ə'fɪʃəs] ADJ trop zélé

officiously [ə'fɪʃəslɪ] ADV avec trop de zèle; **to behave o. towards sb** faire l'empressé auprès de qn

offie ['ɒfɪ] N *Br Fam (abbr* **off-licence***)* magasin *m* de vins et spiritueux

offing ['ɒfɪŋ] N **in the o.** en perspective, en vue; **there is an election in the o.** une élection est en perspective *ou* en vue; **there could be some changes in the o.** il se pourrait qu'il y ait des changements en perspective; **there's a dispute in the o.** il y a de la dispute dans l'air; **Christmas is in the o.** Noël se profile à l'horizon

off-key ADV *Mus* faux

ADJ **1** *Mus* **he/the lead trumpet was o.** il/la première trompette n'était pas dans le ton **2**

Fig (remark, comment etc) inopportun, déplacé

off-licence N *Br* **1** *(premises)* = magasin *m* de vins et spiritueux **2** *(licence)* = licence *f* permettant la vente de boissons alcoolisées à emporter

off-line ADJ *Comput* non connecté; *(processing)* en différé; *(printer)* déconnecté; **to be o.** ne pas être connecté; **to go o.** se déconnecter

▸▸ **o. backup** sauvegarde *f* externe; *Aviat* **o. connection** *(changing plane with different airline)* correspondance *f* avec changement de compagnie aérienne; *TV* **o. editing** montage *m* 'off-line'; *TV* **o. editor** monteur *m* 'off-line'; **o. mode** mode *m* autonome; **o. operation** opération *f* autonome *ou* indépendante; **o. reader** lecteur *m* non connecté

offload [ɒf'ləʊd] VT **1** *(unload)* décharger; *(from boat)* débarquer **2** *Fig (get rid of)* fourguer *(* **onto** à); **he offloads most of his work on(to) his colleagues** il se décharge de la plus grande partie de son travail sur ses collègues; **we offloaded the kids onto my parents for the weekend** nous avons fourgué les gosses à mes parents pour le week-end; **to o. the blame/responsibility onto sb** rejeter le blâme/la responsabilité sur qn; **he tried to o. the blame for these decisions onto his civil servants** il a essayé de mettre ces décisions sur le dos de ses fonctionnaires

offloading [ɒf'ləʊdɪŋ] N *(unloading)* déchargement *m*

off-message ADJ qui ne respecte pas scrupuleusement la ligne du parti

off-peak ADJ *(holidays, accommodation etc)* en basse saison

▸▸ *Mktg* **o. buying** achats *mpl* aux heures creuses; **o. electricity** électricité *f* consommée pendant les heures creuses; *Rail etc* **o. fare** = tarif *m* réduit valable en dehors des heures de pointe; **o. hours** heures *fpl* creuses; *Elec* **o. rate** tarif *m* de nuit

off-piste ADJ, ADV *Ski* hors-piste

offprint ['ɒfprɪnt] N *Phot* tirage *m* à part, tiré *m* à part

off-putting ADJ *Br Fam (person)* peu engageant; *(smell)* répugnant; *(appearance, manner, prospect)* rébarbatif; *(experience)* démoralisant

off-ramp N *(from motorway)* bretelle *f* de sortie

off-road ADJ

▸▸ *Aut* **o. driving** conduite *f* tout-terrain; **o. vehicle** véhicule *m* tout-terrain

off-roader [-'rəʊdər] N *Aut* tout-terrain *m inv*

off-sales NPL *Br* = vente *f* de boissons alcoolisées à emporter

offscreen ['ɒfskriːn] *Cin* ADV **1** *(out of sight)* hors champ, off **2** **o., he's really charming** dans la vie de tous les jours c'est un homme tout à fait charmant

ADJ **1** *(out of sight)* hors champ, off; **o. narration** commentaire *m* en voix off **2** *(life)* privé; **their o. relationship mirrored their love affair in the film** la liaison qu'ils entretenaient dans la vie reflétait celle du film

off-season ADJ *(rate etc)* hors-saison *inv*; de basse saison; **to go on an o. holiday** partir en vacances hors saison *ou* en basse saison

offset ['ɒfset] N **1** *Fin (compensation)* compensation *f* **2** *Tech (of wheel)* désaxage *m*, décentrement *m*, déport *m* **3** *Typ (process)* offset *m*; **printed in o.** tiré en offset **4** *Bot (of plant)* rejeton *m*

VT *(pt, pp* **offset***; prp* **offsetting***)* **1** *Fin (compensate for) (losses, increasing cost etc)* compenser; **to o. one thing against another** compenser quelque chose par quelque chose d'autre; **to o. losses against tax** déduire le montant de ses pertes de ses impôts **2** *Tech (wheel)* désaxer, décentrer; *(part)* déporter, décaler **3** *Typ (print) (book)* imprimer en offset

▸▸ *Fin* **o. agreement** accord *m* de compensation; *Typ* **o. lithography** lithographie *f* offset; *Typ* **o. plate** plaque *f* offset

offshoot ['ɒfʃuːt] N *(of tree)* rejeton *m*; *Fig (of family)* branche *f*, *(of language)* dérivé *m*; *(of political party, artistic movement etc)* ramification *f*

offshore ['ɒfʃɔːr] ADV *Petr (to live, drill etc)* en mer, au large

ADJ *(near coast)* côtier, -ière, littoral, -aux; *(far from coast)* éloigné de la côte; *Petr (exploration, drilling)* en mer, off-shore; *Banking, Fin* offshore

▸▸ *Banking* **o. banking** opérations *fpl* bancaires offshore; **o. company** société *f* offshore; **o. fishing** pêche *f* côtière; *Banking, Fin* **o. fund** fonds *m* offshore; *Petr* **o. installations** installations *fpl* pétrolières marines *ou* off-shore; *Banking, Fin* **o. investment** placement *m* offshore; *Petr* **o. oilfield** champ *m* (pétrolifère) en mer *ou* offshore; **o. wind** vent *m* de terre ou d'aval

off-shot ADJ, ADV *TV, Cin* hors plan

offside ['ɒf'saɪd] N *Aut (when driving on left)* côté *m* droit; *(when driving on right)* côté gauche

ADJ **1** *Sport* hors jeu **2** *Aut (when driving on left)* du côté droit; *(when driving on right)* du côté gauche

ADV *Sport* hors jeu

▸▸ *Sport* **the o. rule** la règle du hors-jeu

offspring ['ɒfsprɪŋ] N *(no pl) (of animal)*, *Hum (children)* progéniture *f*; **none of her o. were there** sa progéniture n'était pas là; **bring the o.** amenez votre progéniture

offstage [ɒf'steɪdʒ] *Theat* ADV *(to hear voices etc)* derrière la toile; **his life o.** *(of actor)* sa vie privée; **o., he is really charming** dans la vie de tous les jours c'est un homme tout à fait charmant

ADJ *(life)* privé; *(noises)* derrière la toile

off-street ADJ

▸▸ **o. parking** place *f* de parking *(située ailleurs que dans la rue)*

off-the-cuff ADJ *(remark, opinion)* impromptu; *(speech)* improvisé

off-the-peg, *Am* **off-the-rack** ADJ *(clothes)* de prêt-à-porter

off-the-record ADJ *(comment, briefing)* officieux; **on the understanding that it is strictly o.** à titre strictement officieux

off-the-shelf ADJ *Com (goods)* prêt à l'usage

off-the-wall ADJ *Fam* bizarroïde

off-topic ADJ *Comput* hors sujet

off-white ADJ blanc cassé *inv*

N blanc *m* cassé

OFGAS ['ɒfgæs] N *Br Formerly (abbr* **Office of Gas Supply***)* = organisme *m* chargé de contrôler les activités des sociétés de distribution de gaz en Grande-Bretagne

Ofgem ['ɒfdʒem] N *Br (abbr* **Office of Gas and Electricity Markets***)* = organisme *m* chargé de réglementer les secteurs de la fourniture de gaz et d'électricité en Grande-Bretagne

OFSTED ['ɒfsted] N *Br (abbr* **Office for Standards in Education***)* = organisme *m* chargé de veiller au maintien du niveau des élèves dans l'enseignement public en Grande-Bretagne

oft [ɒft] ADV *Arch, Lit* souvent; **many a time and o.** maintes et maintes fois

oft- [ɒft] PREF *Arch, Lit* **o.-visited/-quoted** souvent visité/cité

OFTEL ['ɒftel] N *Br (abbr* **Office of Telecommunications***)* = organisme *m* chargé de contrôler les activités des sociétés de télécommunications en Grande-Bretagne

often ['ɒf(ə)n, 'ɒft(ə)n] ADV souvent, fréquemment; **I don't see her very o. now** je ne la vois plus très souvent; **how o.?** *(how many times)* combien de fois?; *(at what intervals)* tous les combien?; **how o. have I told you!** combien de fois ne vous l'ai-je pas dit!; **I visited her as o. as I could** je lui rendais visite aussi souvent que je le pouvais; **as o. as not** assez souvent; **more o. than not** le plus souvent; **every so o.** de temps en temps, de temps à autre; **it cannot be repeated too o.** on ne saurait trop le répéter; **once too o.** une fois de trop VOIR GRAMMAIRE A21

OFWAT ['ɒfwɒt] N *Br Com (abbr* **Office of Water Services***)* = organisme *m* chargé de contrôler les activités des sociétés de distribution d'eau en Grande-Bretagne

ogle ['əʊg(ə)l] VT lorgner, guigner, reluquer

O-grade N *Sch Formerly Scot* ≃ BEPC *m*

ogre ['əʊgər] N ogre *m*

ogress ['əʊgrɪs] N ogresse *f*

oh [əʊ] INT oh; *(expressing doubt)* ah?; **oh, what a surprise!** oh, quelle surprise!; **oh no!** oh non!; **oh yes you will!** mais si!; **oh really?** ah oui?; **oh damn!** et merde!, oh merde!, et zut!

ohc [əʊɪtʃ'siː] N *(abbr* **overhead camshaft***)*

▸▸ **o. engine** moteur *m* ACT

ohm [əʊm] N *Elec* ohm *m*

OHMS [əʊəɪtʃem'es] *Br (abbr* **On His/Her Majesty's Service***)* = tampon *m* apposé sur le courrier administratif britannique

oho [əʊ'həʊ] INT *(expressing triumph)* ah ah!

OHP [əʊeɪtʃ'piː] N *(abbr* **overhead projector***)* rétroprojecteur *m*

oi [ɔɪ] INT *Fam* hé!

OID [əʊaɪ'diː] N *Fin (abbr* **original issue discount bond***)* obligation *f* à prime d'émission

oik [ɔɪk] N *Br Sl* prolo *mf*

oil [ɔɪl] N **1** *(in general)* huile *f*; **to cook sth in oil** *(faire)* cuire qch à l'huile; **fried in o.** frit à l'huile; **to paint in oils** peindre à l'huile; *Fig* **to pour o. on troubled waters** apaiser les esprits **2** *Ind (petroleum)* pétrole *m*; *(for lubricating etc)* huile *f* (de graissage); *Aut* huile; **to check the o.** vérifier le niveau d'huile; *StExch* **o. shares** valeurs *fpl* pétrolières **3** **essential o.** essence *f*, huile *f* essentielle

VT *(machine)* huiler, graisser, lubrifier; **to o. one's skin** s'enduire la peau d'huile; **to o. the wheels** graisser les roues; *Fig* faciliter les choses

▸▸ **o. cake** tourteau *m* (pour bétail); **o. change** vidange *f*, **to have an o. change** faire faire la vidange; **o. company** compagnie *f* pétrolière; **o. cooling** refroidissement *m* par huile; **o. crisis** choc *m* pétrolier; **o. drain hole** orifice *m* d'écoulement d'huile; **o. drain plug** bouchon *m* de vidange; **o. drum** bidon *m* à pétrole; **o. filter** filtre *m* à huile; **o. gauge** *(for measuring level)* jauge *f* ou indicateur *m* de niveau d'huile; *(for measuring pressure)* indicateur *m* de pression d'huile; **o. gland** glande *f* uropygienne; **o. heating** chauffage *m* au mazout; **o. industry** industrie *f* pétrolière; **o. lamp** *(burning oil)* lampe *f* à huile; *(burning paraffin)* lampe *f* à pétrole; **o. paint** peinture *f* à l'huile *(substance)*; **o. painting** peinture à l'huile; **o. pressure** pression *f* d'huile; **o. prices** prix *mpl* pétroliers; **o. pump** pompe *f* à huile; **o. refinery** raffinerie *f* de pétrole; **o. rig** *(onshore)* derrick *m*; *(offshore)* plate-forme *f* pétrolière, *pl* plates-formes pétrolières; *Fin* **o. royalty** redevance *f* pétrolière; **o. seal** joint *m* d'huile; **o. slick** *(on sea)* nappe *f* de pétrole; *(on beach)* ma-

rée *f* noire; **o. sump** carter *m* d'huile; **o. tanker** *(ship)* pétrolier *m*, tanker *m*; *(lorry)* camion-citerne *m*, *pl* camions-citernes *(pour l'essence)*; **o. temperature gauge** indicateur de température d'huile; **o. well** puits *m* de pétrole

oil-bearing ADJ *Geol* pétrolifère

oilcan ['ɔɪlkæn] N *(for applying oil)* burette *f*, *(large container)* bidon *m* à huile

oilcloth ['ɔɪlklɒθ] N toile *f* cirée

oil-cooled [-kuːld] ADJ refroidi par huile

oiled [ɔɪld] ADJ huilé; *Fig Fam* **to be well o.** *(drunk)* être soûl; **to get well o.** se soûler

▸▸ **o. silk** taffetas *m* imperméable

oiler ['ɔɪlər] N *Naut (tanker)* pétrolier *m*

oilfield ['ɔɪlfiːld] N gisement *m* ou champ *m* pétrolifère

oil-fired [-faɪəd] ADJ

▸▸ **o. central heating** chauffage *m* central au mazout

oiliness ['ɔɪlɪnɪs] N **1** *(of clothes, rags etc)* aspect *m* graisseux; *(of dish, sauce)* caractère *m* huileux **2** *Pej (of person)* onctuosité *f*

oilpaper ['ɔɪlpeɪpər] N papier huilé

oil-producing ADJ **1** *(shale etc)* pétrolifère; *(country)* producteur, -trice de pétrole **2** *(plant)* oléifère; *(substance etc)* oléifiant

oilrich ['ɔɪlrɪtʃ] ADJ *(countries)* enrichi par le pétrole

oilskin ['ɔɪlskɪn] N *(fabric)* toile *f* cirée; *(garment)* ciré *m*

oilstone ['ɔɪlstəʊn] N *(for sharpening)* pierre *f* à huile

oily ['ɔɪlɪ] ADJ **1** *(hands, rag)* graisseux; *(food)* huileux **2** *Pej (manner etc)* onctueux; *(voice)* gras, *f* grasse

oink [ɔɪŋk] VI *(of pig)* grogner

N *(of pig)* grognement *m*

ointment ['ɔɪntmənt] N onguent *m*, pommade *f*

OK, okay ['əʊ'keɪ] *Fam* INT OK! OK!, bon!, d'accord!; **OK?** OK?, d'accord?; **OK, if I could have your attention for a moment …** bon, si je pouvais avoir votre attention pour un instant …; **OK, it wasn't a great movie but I've seen worse** bon, d'accord, ce n'était pas un film super mais j'ai vu pire

ADJ **1** *(in order, fine)* correct, exact; **everything's OK** tout est en règle *ou* OK; **to be OK** *(unhurt)* aller bien; **are you OK?, did I hurt you/are you upset?** ça va?, je ne t'ai pas fait mal/tu es fâché?; **I'll be OK when I get home** ça ira une fois que je serai à la maison; **but is the car OK?** mais est-ce que la voiture n'a rien?; **that's OK by *or* with me** d'accord!; **is that OK by *or* with your mother** est-ce que ta mère est d'accord?; **is it OK to bring my friend?** est-ce que ça vous dérange si je viens avec mon ami?; **no, it is not OK** pas question; **clothes like that are OK for a party** des vêtements comme ça, ça va bien pour une soirée

2 *(acceptable) (meal, film etc)* pas mal; *(candidate, singer etc)* pas mauvais, pas mal; **how are things? – OK** comment ça va? – ça peut aller; **the meal/her performance was more than OK** le repas/sa prestation était au-dessus de la moyenne; **was I OK?** comment j'étais?; **an OK computer** un ordinateur pas mal

3 *(understanding)* **she was OK about it** elle n'a pas fait d'histoires; **are you sure he'll be OK about letting us use the car?** tu es sûr qu'il ne fera pas d'histoires pour nous laisser la voiture?

4 *(likeable etc) (person)* **he's an OK sort of guy** c'est un type plutôt bien; **she's OK but … ** elle est assez sympa mais …

5 to be OK for work/money *(have enough of)* avoir assez de travail/d'argent; **is every-**

body **OK for drink?** est-ce que tout le monde a à boire?

N to give one's OK to sth approuver qch; **to give the OK** donner le feu vert; **the doctor's given me the OK to use my arm again** le docteur m'a dit que je pouvais recommencer à me servir de mon bras

VT *Fam (give permission or approval to)* approuver; *(course of action)* donner le feu vert à

okapi [əʊˈkɑːpɪ] **N** *(animal)* okapi *m*

okay [ˈəʊˈkeɪ] *Fam* = **OK**

okey-doke, okey-dokey [əʊkɪˈdəʊk, -kɪ] **INT** *Fam* d'accord

Okie [ˈəʊkɪ] **N** *Am Fam Pej (inhabitant)* habitant, -ante de l'Oklahoma; *Hist (migrant worker from Oklahoma)* = un des nombreux petits fermiers qui ont quitté le Midwest dans les années 30 pour chercher du travail dans d'autres états

Okla *abbr* **Oklahoma**

okra [ˈɒkrə] **N** *(vegetable)* okra *m*

OLD [əʊld]

ADJ	vieux **1, 5** ▪ âgé de **2** ▪ ancien **3**
NPL	vieux

ADJ 1 *(aged) (person)* vieux, *f* vieille, âgé; *(in sing before a qualified noun beginning with a vowel or h mute)* vieil; *(car, furniture, food etc)* vieux; **you're as o. as you feel** on a l'âge de ses artères; **she married a man who was o. enough to be her father** elle s'est mariée avec un homme qui aurait pu être son père; **to grow** *or* **get older** vieillir; **to be growing** *or* **getting o.** vieillir, prendre de l'âge; **an o. man** un homme âgé, un vieillard, *Fam* un vieux; **an o. woman** une femme âgée, une vieille femme, *Fam* une vieille; **o. people, o. folk(s)** *(in general)* les personnes âgées, *Fam* les vieux *mpl*; **the o. people next door** le couple âgé qui habite à côté, *Fam* les vieux qui habitent à côté; **my o. friend** mon vieil ami; **he's an o. friend of mine** c'est un de mes vieux amis; **an o. debt** une dette de longue date; **that's an o. trick** c'est un coup classique; **an o. story** une vieille histoire; **that's an o. one!** *(of joke)* celle-là est connue; **o. memories** vieux souvenirs *mpl*; **as o. as the hills** *(of person, joke etc)* vieux comme le monde; **as o. as Methuselah** *(of person)* vieux comme Hérode *ou* Mathusalem; *Fig* **a boss/politician of the o. school** un patron/homme politique de la vieille école; **to go over o. ground** revenir sur le passé; **to be o. hat** être démodé **VOIR GRAMMAIRE A17**

2 *(with specific age)* **how o. are you?** quel âge avez-vous?; **the oldest of the tribe** l'aîné, -ée de la tribu; **to be five years o.** avoir cinq ans, être âgé de cinq ans; **she is older than I am** elle est plus âgée *ou* vieille que moi; **when you're older** *(to child)* quand tu seras plus grand; **at six years o.** à l'âge de) six ans; **a two-year-o. (child)** un(e) enfant (âgé(e)) de deux ans; **to be o. enough to do sth** être assez grand pour faire qch, être d'âge à faire qch

3 *(former)* ancien; **my o. house/school** mon ancienne maison/école; **in the o. days** autrefois

4 *Fam (intensifier)* **any o. how** n'importe comment; **any o. thing** n'importe quoi; **it's a strange o. world** c'est un drôle de monde; **we had a fine o. time** nous avons passé un sacré bon moment

5 *Fam (expressing familiarity or affection)* vieux, *f* vieille, brave; **o. Jack wants to speak to you** le vieux Jack veut te parler; **good o. Frank!** ce vieux Frank!; **o. Fred** le Fred **VOIR GRAMMAIRE A17**

6 *Lit* **in days of o.** autrefois, au temps jadis; **I know him of o.** je le connais depuis longtemps

NPL the o. les vieux *mpl*; **popular with o. and young** apprécié des jeunes et des moins jeunes

▸▸ **o. age** la vieillesse; *Br* **o. age pension** *(pension f* de) retraite *f; Br* **o. age pensioner** retraité, ée *mf*; **the O. Bailey** = la cour d'assises de Londres; *Br Sl* **the O. Bill** les flics *mpl*, les poulets *mpl; Br* **o. boy** *(former pupil)* ancien élève *m; Fam (old man)* vieux *m; Old-fashioned Fam (form of address)* mon vieux; **the O. Country** le pays; **they kept in close touch with events in the O. Country** ils suivaient de près ce qui se passait au pays; *Br Fam* **o. dear** *(elderly woman)* grand-mère *f*, *pl* grand(s)-mères; *(mother)* vieille *f*; **O. English sheepdog** bobtail *m; Ling* **O. English** vieil anglais *m*; **o. flame** ancien(enne) amoureux/amoureuse, *Fam* ancien flirt *m*; **O. French** ancien français *m; Br* **o. girl** *(former pupil)* ancienne élève *f, Fam (old woman)* vieille *f, Old-fashioned Fam (form of address)* ma chère, chère amie; *Am* **O. Glory** = surnom du drapeau américain; **o. gold** *(colour)* vieil or *m inv; Pol etc* **o. guard** vieille garde *f, Fig* **one of the o. guard** un vieux de la vieille; **o. hand** vieux routier *m*, vétéran *m*; **to be an o. hand at sth** être rompu à faire qch; *Fam* **old lady** *(wife)* patronne *f*, bourgeoise *f*; *(mother)* vieille *f; Br Fam* **o. lag** truand *m;* **o. maid** vieille fille *f, Fam* **old man** *(husband)* homme *m;(father)* vieux *m; Old-fashioned (term of address)* mon vieux, mon pote; *Am* **O. Man River** = surnom donné au Mississippi; **o. master** *(painter)* grand maître *m* (de la peinture); *(painting)* tableau *m* de maître; **o. money** *(before decimalization)* ancien système *m* monétaire; *(in UK)* ancienne monnaie *f*; **it's o. money** *(of old wealthy family)* c'est une vieille fortune; *Fam* **O. Nick** Satan *m*, Lucifer *m*; **o. pupil** ancien(enne) élève *mf*; **o. rose** *(colour)* vieux rose *m; Br* **o. school tie** = la franc-maçonnerie des écoles privées et des universités; *Bible* **O. Testament** Ancien Testament *m*; **o. wine** un vieux vin; **o. wives' tale** conte *m* de bonne femme; *Fam* **old woman** *(wife)* patronne, bourgeoise; *(mother)* vieille *f*; **to be (a bit of) an o. woman** avoir des manies de vieille fille; **he was being a bit of an o. woman about it** il en faisait tout un cinéma; **the O. World** l'ancien monde *m*

olden [ˈəʊld(ə)n] **ADJ** *Lit* **in o. times, in the o. days** au temps jadis

old-established **ADJ** ancien, établi depuis longtemps

olde-worlde [ˈəʊldɪˈwɜːldɪ] **ADJ** *Hum, Pej (house, village etc)* qui a un aspect vieillot factice

old-fashioned [-fæʃənd] **ADJ** *(dress) (outdated)* démodé, passé de mode; *(from former times)* d'autrefois, de l'ancien temps; *(person)* démodé, vieux jeu *inv; (manners)* de l'ancien temps; *(atmosphere, charm, air)* vieillot; *(ideas)* arriéré, vieillot, vieux jeu; **I like to do things the o. way** j'aime bien faire les choses à l'ancienne; **he's rather o. in his views/attitudes** il a des opinions/attitudes un peu vieillottes *ou* vieux jeu; **you can call me o. but ...** tu vas peut-être me trouver vieux jeu, mais ...; **o. Christmas** Noël à l'ancienne; *Fam* **o. look** *(glance)* regard de travers

N *Am* = cocktail *m* composé de whisky, d'amers, de sucre et d'eau de seltz

oldie [ˈəʊldɪ] **N** *Fam* **1** *(old thing)* vieillerie *f*, antiquaille *f*, *(song)* vieux tube *m*; **that's a real o.** *(song, joke etc)* il ne date pas d'aujourd'hui celui-là!; **oldies but goldies** *(songs)* bons vieux tubes; *(jokes)* bonnes vieilles blagues *fpl* **2** *(old person)* vieillard, -arde

oldish [ˈəʊldɪʃ] **ADJ** assez vieux, *f* assez vieille

oldster [ˈəʊldstər] **N** *Am Fam* vieillard *m*, vieille *f*

old-style **ADJ** à l'ancienne (mode); *Hist* **the o. calendar** le calendrier ancien style

old-time **ADJ ATTRIB** du temps jadis
▸▸ **o. dancing** danses *fpl* anciennes

old-timer **N** *Fam* **1** ancien, -ienne *m;* *(experienced person)* vieux *m* de la vieille **2** *esp Am (form of address) (old man)* vieux *m*

old-world **ADJ** *(of former times)* de l'ancien temps, d'autrefois; *Geog, Hist* de l'ancien monde

OLE [əʊelˈiː] **N** *Comput (abbr* **object linking and embedding)** OLE *m*

ole [əʊl] **ADJ** *Fam* vieux, *f* vieille

oleaginous [əʊlɪˈædʒɪnəs] **ADJ** oléagineux; *Fig Lit* mielleux

oleander [əʊlɪˈændər] **N** *(shrub)* oléandre *m*, laurier-rose *m*, *pl* lauriers-rose(s)

olfactory [ɒlˈfæktərɪ] **ADJ** *(bulb, nerve etc)* olfactif

O-level **N** *Sch Formerly (in England, Wales, Northern Ireland)* ≃ BEPC *m*

oligarchic(al) [ɒlɪˈgɑːkɪk, -ɪk(ə)l] **ADJ** oligarchique

oligarchy [ˈɒlɪgɑːkɪ] **N** oligarchie *f*

oligopoly [ɒlɪˈgɒpəlɪ] **N** *Econ* oligopole *m*

oligopsony [ɒlɪˈgɒpsənɪ] **N** *Econ* oligopsone *m*

olive [ˈɒlɪv] **N 1** *(fruit)* olive *f* **2** *(tree)* olivier *m; Fig* **to hold out the o. branch** proposer la paix (**to sb** à qn) **3** *(wood)* (bois *m* d')olivier *m* **4** *(colour)* (vert *m*) olive *m inv*

ADJ *(complexion etc)* olivâtre
▸▸ *Am* **o. drab** *(colour)* gris-vert *m* (olive); *(cloth)* toile *f* gris-vert (olive); *(uniform)* uniforme *m* gris-vert *(surtout celui de l'armée des États-Unis)*; **in his o. drabs** dans son treillis; **o. green** (vert) olive; **o. grove** oliv(er)aie *f*, **o. grower** oléiculteur, -trice; **o. oil** huile *f* d'olive; **o. plantation** oliv(er)aie *f*, **o. tree** olivier *m*; **o. wood** (bois d')olivier

Olympiad [əˈlɪmpɪæd] **N** *Sport* olympiade *f*

Olympian [əˈlɪmpɪən] **ADJ** *(air, calm etc)* olympien; *(god)* de l'Olympe
N Olympien, -ienne

Olympic [əˈlɪmpɪk] **ADJ** *Antiq, Sport (stadium, record etc)* olympique
NPL the Olympics les Jeux *mpl* olympiques
▸▸ **the O. flame** la flamme olympique; **the O. Games** les Jeux *mpl* olympiques

Olympus [əˈlɪmpəs] **N** l'Olympe *m*

O & M [əʊənˈdem] **N** *(abbr* **organization and methods)** **O. department** bureau *m* des méthodes

Oman [əʊˈmɑːn] **N** Oman *m*

Omani [əʊˈmɑːnɪ] **N** Omanais, -aise
ADJ omanais

ombudsman, pl ombudsmen [ˈɒmbʊdzmən] **N** ombudsman *m*, médiateur *m* *(entre individus et instances gouvernementales), Can* protecteur *m* du citoyen

omega [ˈəʊmɪgə] **N** *(in Greek alphabet)* oméga *m*

omelette, Am omelet [ˈɒmlɪt] **N** *Culin* omelette *f*, **ham/cheese/mushroom o.** omelette au jambon/au fromage/aux champignons; *Prov* **you can't make an o. without breaking eggs** on ne fait pas d'omelette sans casser d'œufs

omen [ˈəʊmen] **N** présage *m*, augure *m*, auspice *m*; **to take sth as a good/a bad** *or* **an ill o.** prendre qch comme un bon/mauvais augure; **all the omens seemed good** tous les présages paraissaient favorables

ominous [ˈɒmɪnəs] **ADJ** *(event)* de mauvais augure; *(look)* lourd de sens; *(sign, lack of enthusiasm, news, silence)* inquiétant; **o.-**

looking sky ciel menaçant; **an o. silence** *(implying disaster)* un silence lourd de menaces; **I heard an o. crack** j'entendis un craquement qui ne présageait rien de bon; **an emergency meeting? – that sounds o.** une réunion d'urgence? – ça ne présage rien de bon

ominously ['ɒmɪnəslɪ] ADV *(to say sth)* d'une voix qui ne présage rien de bon; **it was o. quiet** il régnait un calme inquiétant; **o., there was no answer when they rang** le téléphone ne répondait pas, ce qui ne présageait rien de bon; **the deadline was drawing o. close** la date limite se rapprochait dangereusement

omission [əʊ'mɪʃən] N omission *f*, *Typ* bourdon *m*; *Rel* omission *f*; *Rel* **sin of o.** péché *m ou* faute *f* d'omission; **to sin by o.** pécher par omission

omit [əʊ'mɪt] VT **(-tt-) 1** *(details, word etc)* omettre; **to o. any mention of** *or* **reference to sb/sth** omettre toute mention de *ou* référence à qn/qch **2** **to do sth** omettre de faire qch; **not to o. to do sth** ne pas manquer de faire qch

omnibus, *pl* **omnibuses** ['ɒmnɪbəs, -bəsɪz] N **1** *(book)* recueil *m*; **Edgar Allan Poe o.** recueil d'œuvres d'Edgar Allan Poe; **detective o.** recueil de romans policiers **2** *Arch (vehicle)* **(horse) o.** omnibus *m*; **(motor) o.** autobus *m*
▸▸ **o. edition** *TV, Radio* = rediffusion *f* hebdomadaire des épisodes d'un feuilleton diffusés pendant la semaine; *(of stories, poems)* gros recueil *m*; *Mktg* **o. survey** enquête *f* omnibus; **o. volume** *(of stories, poems etc)* gros recueil

omnidirectional ['ɒmnɪdɪ'rekʃən(ə)l] ADJ *(aerial, microphone)* omnidirectionnel

omnipotence [ɒm'nɪpətəns] N omnipotence *f*, toute-puissance *f*

omnipotent [ɒm'nɪpətənt] ADJ omnipotent, tout-puissant, *pl* tout-puissants N *Lit* **the O.** le Tout-Puissant

omnipresence [ɒmnɪ'prezəns] N omniprésence *f*

omnipresent [ɒmnɪ'prezənt] ADJ omniprésent

omniscience [ɒm'nɪsɪəns] N omniscience *f*

omniscient [ɒm'nɪsɪənt] ADJ omniscient

omnium ['ɒmnɪəm] N *St Exch* omnium *m*

omnivore ['ɒmnɪvɔːr] N omnivore *m*

omnivorous [ɒm'nɪvərəs] ADJ omnivore; *Fig (reader)* qui lit de tout

omnivorously [ɒm'nɪvərəslɪ] ADV *(to read)* de tout

ON [ɒn]

PREP	sur **1, 2, 7** ▪ à **1, 4** ▪ en **1, 4, 6** ▪ par rapport à **10**
ADV	en marche **4** ▪ allumé **4** ▪ ouvert **4** ▪ de garde **11** ▪ de service **11**

PREP **1** *(indicating position)* sur; **on the table** sur la table; **on Arran/the Isle of Wight** sur Arran/l'île de Wight; **on Corsica/Crete** en Corse/Crète; **on Majorca/Minorca** à Majorque/Minorque; **on the other side of the page** de l'autre côté de la page; **on page four** à la quatrième page, à la page quatre; **house on the main road** maison sur la grande route; *Am* **she lives on Sixth Avenue** elle habite dans la Sixième Avenue; **room on the second floor** chambre au second (étage); **on the right/left** à droite/gauche; **on this side** de ce côté; **don't tread on it** ne marchez pas dessus; **the post with the seagull on it** le poteau sur lequel il y a la mouette; **on the high seas** en haute mer; **on the train** dans le train; **on foot/horseback** à pied/cheval; **on a bicycle** à bicyclette; **hanging on the wall** pendu au mur; **on the ceiling** au plafond; **he has a ring on his finger** il a une bague au doigt; **he had his rucksack on his back** il portait son sac sur le dos; **have you any money on you?** avez-vous de l'argent sur vous?; **on (the) television/radio** à la télévision/radio; **what's on the other channel?** qu'est-ce qu'il y a sur l'autre chaîne?

2 *(indicating direction)* **on(to)** sur; **to fall on(to) sth** tomber sur qch; **to climb on(to) a wall** grimper sur un mur; **to march on London** avancer vers *ou* sur Londres

3 *(indicating membership)* **to be on the committee** être membre du comité; **to be on a jury** être membre d'un jury; **to be on a newspaper** *(work for)* travailler dans un journal; **he's on the Guardian now** il travaille *ou* il est au Guardian à présent

4 *(in expressions of time)* **on Sunday** dimanche; **on Sundays** le dimanche; **on the day of my arrival** le jour de mon arrivée; **on the following day** le lendemain; **on April 3rd** le trois avril; **on a fine day in June** par une belle journée de juin; **on and after the fifteenth** à partir du quinze; **on or about the twelfth** vers le douze; **on the hour** à l'heure juste; **on that occasion** à cette occasion; **on the death of his mother** à la mort de sa mère; **on my arrival** à mon arrivée; **on my first/last/etc visit** lors de ma première/dernière/*etc* visite; **on (my) entering the room** quand je suis entré *ou* en entrant dans la pièce, à mon entrée dans la pièce; **on realizing what he had done** quand il s'est rendu compte de ce qu'il avait fait; **on completing the test candidates should ...** quand ils auront fini l'examen les candidats devront ...; **on the count of three** à trois; **on the third stroke** au troisième coup; **on time** ponctuel, à l'heure; **just on a year ago** *(approximately)* il y a près d'un an

5 *(indicating manner)* **on the cheap** à bon marché; **on the sly** en cachette, *Fam* en douce

6 *(indicating state)* en; **on sale** en vente

7 *(about, concerning)* sur; **a book on France** un livre sur la France; **a lecture on history** une conférence d'histoire; **you should read Watson on toxicology** vous devriez lire les écrits de Watson sur la toxicologie; **what have you got on him?** qu'est-ce que vous avez sur lui?; **the police have nothing on him** la police n'a rien sur lui

8 *(indicating activity)* **I am here on business/on a mission of mercy** je suis ici pour affaires/pour remplir une mission de charité; **could I speak to you on a matter of some delicacy?** pourrais-je vous parler d'une affaire assez délicate?; **on tour** en tournée; **on holiday** en vacances; **to be working on sth** travailler à qch

9 *(indicating source of support)* **to live on one's private income/a student grant** vivre de ses rentes/d'une bourse d'études; **to retire on a pension of £5,000 a year** prendre sa retraite avec une pension de 5 000 livres par an; **many live on less than that** beaucoup vivent avec moins que ça; **to be on the dole** toucher le chômage; **this round (of drinks) is on me** c'est moi qui paie cette fois-ci; **he's on insulin/heroin** il prend de l'insuline/de l'héroïne; **to be on drugs** se droguer; **what was he on?** *(drug)* qu'est-ce qu'il avait pris?; **she's on the pill** elle prend la pilule; **it runs** *or* **works on gas/electricity/etc** ça marche au gaz/à l'électricité/*etc*; **to travel on a British passport** voyager avec un passeport britannique

10 *(compared with)* **prices are up on last year** les prix ont augmenté par rapport à l'année dernière

11 *Horseracing etc* **to put money on a horse** parier *ou* miser sur un cheval; **he's got £500**

on me going the full ten rounds il a parié 500 livres que je vais faire les dix tours

ADV **1** *(indicating direction, position)* **to put the cloth on** mettre la nappe; **to put the kettle on** mettre la bouilloire à chauffer; **it's not on properly** *(lid, covering etc)* il n'est pas bien mis; **to be on** *(of actor)* être en scène; **we're on in ten minutes** c'est à nous dans dix minutes; **to put on one's clothes** s'habiller; **put something on** *(clothing)* mets quelque chose; **what had she got on?** *(clothes)* qu'est-ce qu'elle portait?, comment était-elle habillée?; **to have nothing on** *(be naked)* être tout nu

2 *(expressing continuation)* **to go on** continuer (**doing** à faire); **to march/work/battle on** continuer sa marche/son travail/la lutte; **to drive/sail/talk on** continuer à rouler/naviguer/parler; **on, on, we must keep on!** en avant, en avant, il faut continuer!; **the speech/he went on and on** le discours/il n'en finissait plus *ou* pas; *Fam* **he's always on about the war/teenagers/etc** il n'arrête pas de déblatérer sur la guerre/les adolescents/*etc*; *Fam* **what was he on about?** qu'est-ce qu'il racontait *ou* rabâchait?; *Fam* **he's always on at** *or* **to me** *(nagging)* il s'en prend toujours à moi (**to do** pour que je fasse); *Fam* **why is he always getting on at them about their hair?** pourquoi est-ce qu'il s'en prend toujours à leur coiffure?; *Fam* **I've been on at them for months to get it fixed** cela fait des mois que je suis sur leur dos pour qu'ils le fassent réparer; **and so on** ainsi de suite; **on with the show!** que le spectacle continue!

3 *(in time)* **later on** plus tard; **from that day on** à partir *ou* dater de ce jour; **well on in years** d'un âge avancé

4 *(in operation) (machine, engine)* en marche; *(light, television, radio)* allumé; *(gas, tap)* ouvert; *(alarm)* enclenché; **the brakes are on** les freins sont serrés; **is the electricity on?** est-ce que l'électricité est mise?

5 *(taking place)* **the meeting is on right now** la réunion est en train de se dérouler; **the play was on for weeks** la pièce a tenu l'affiche pendant des semaines; **what's on tonight?** *(on TV etc)* qu'est-ce qu'il y a ce soir?; *(what are we doing?)* qu'est-ce qu'on fait ce soir?; *TV, Radio* **there's nothing good on** il n'y a rien de bien; **it's not on today** *(programme)* ça ne passe pas aujourd'hui; **what's on at the cinema?** qu'est-ce qu'on donne *ou* joue au cinéma?; **it's on at the Filmhouse** il passe au Filmhouse; **have you anything on this evening?** est-ce que vous avez quelque chose de prévu *ou* en vue pour ce soir?; **is the party still on?** est-ce que la soirée se fait toujours?; **it's (still) on** *(hasn't been cancelled)* ça tient toujours

6 *Fam (in agreement)* **are you still on for dinner tonight?** ça marche toujours pour le dîner de ce soir?; **you're on!** d'accord!, c'est bon!; **shall we say £10? you're on!** disons 10 livres? d'accord *ou* tope là!

7 *Fam (acceptable)* **that sort of behaviour isn't on** cette sorte de comportement n'est pas admissible; **it's not on, charging £10 a ticket!** faire payer un billet 10 livres, ça dépasse les bornes!; **it's not on!** ça va pas du tout!

8 **to be on to sth** *(understand)* comprendre *ou* saisir *ou Fam* piger qch; **they were on to him at once** *(saw what he was up to)* ils ont tout de suite vu clair dans son jeu; **to be on to a good thing** être sur une bonne affaire; **the police are on to her** la police est sur sa piste; **I'll put you on to her** *(on phone)* je vais vous la passer

9 *Horseracing* **to put a bet on** faire un pari; **I have a bet on** j'ai fait un pari

10 **on and off** *see* **off 7**

11 *(on duty) (in hospital, surgery etc)* de

garde; *(in shop, administration etc)* de service; **I'm on at three o'clock, then off at nine o'clock** je commence à trois heures et je finis à neuf heures

ADJ 1 on position position *f* marche; *(of brakes)* position de serrage; **on/off switch** interrupteur *m* marche/arrêt; *Fig* **an on-off romance/relationship** une idylle/relation qui marche par à-coups; **it's a bit of an on-off relationship** ils passent leur temps à casser et à se remettre ensemble

2 *Cr* **on side** *(when the batsman is right-handed)* côté *m* gauche du terrain; *(when the batsman is left-handed)* côté *m* droit du terrain

3 *Fam* **it was not one of his on days** il n'était pas dans un de ses meilleurs jours

on-air ADJ, ADV à l'antenne; **o. (warning) light** voyant *m* de passage à l'antenne

onanism ['əʊnənɪz(ə)m] N onanisme *m*

on-board ADJ

▸▸ *Comput* **o. RAM** RAM *f* sur carte; *Fin* **o. surcharge** surcharge *f* "on-board"

on-camera ADJ, ADV à l'image

once [wʌns] ADV **1** *(one time only)* une fois; **not o.** pas une seule fois, jamais; **he's never o. said he was sorry** il ne s'est jamais excusé, il ne s'est pas excusé une seule fois; **o. only** une seule fois; **more than o.** plus d'une fois; **o. a week** une fois par semaine; **o. or twice** une ou deux fois, une fois ou deux; **o. in a while** une fois de temps en temps; **o. more, o. again** une fois de plus, encore une fois; **o. too often** une fois de trop; **o. and for all** une fois pour toutes; **you may do so this o.** *or* **just for (this)** je vous le permets pour une seule fois pour cette fois(-ci); **for o. you are right** pour une fois tu as raison; **a o.-in-a-lifetime opportunity** une occasion qui ne se présente qu'une fois

2 *(formerly)* autrefois; **o. upon a time there was a princess, there was o. a princess** il était une fois une princesse; **o. (upon a time) children used to respect their elders** il fut un temps où les enfants respectaient leurs aînés; **I knew him o.** je l'ai connu autrefois *ou* dans le temps; **o. it would have all been so easy** il fut un temps où ça aurait été si facile; **a o.-flourishing company** une entreprise autrefois prospère

3 at o. *(immediately)* tout de suite, immédiatement; *(at the same time)* à la fois, en même temps; **all at o. we were home** tout à coup nous étions arrivés à la maison; **to do several things at o.** faire plusieurs choses à la fois *ou* en même temps; **it all happened at o.** tout est arrivé en même temps

CONJ *(when)* **o. he reached home, he collapsed** une fois arrivé chez lui, il s'effondra; **o. you master this, everything will be …** dès que *ou* quand vous aurez maîtrisé cela, tout sera …

once-over N *Fam* **to give sb/sth the o.** jeter un coup d'œil (scrutateur) sur qn/qch; **to give a room a o.** *(with duster)* passer un coup de chiffon dans une chambre

oncology [ɒŋ'kɒlədʒɪ] N oncologie *f*

oncoming ['ɒnkʌmɪŋ] ADJ *(approaching)* approchant, qui approche; **the o. traffic** *(for vehicle)* les véhicules venant en sens inverse; *(for pedestrian)* les véhicules qui approchent

▸▸ *Ind* **o. shift** poste *m* entrant

oncosts ['ɒnkɒsts] NPL *Com* frais *mpl* généraux

OND [əʊən'diː] N *Br (abbr* **Ordinary National Diploma)** ≃ diplôme *m* d'études techniques

ONE [wʌn]

ADJ	un/une **1** ▪ seul **2** ▪ même **2**
N	un/une **1, 2**
INDEF PRON	un **1** ▪ on **3**

ADJ **1** un; **twenty-o. apples** vingt et une pommes; **to have a thousand** *or* **a million and o. things to do** avoir des tas de choses à faire; **o. or two people saw it** une ou deux personnes l'ont vu; **o. day out of two, o. day in every two** un jour sur deux; **o. stormy evening in January** par une soirée de janvier où il faisait de l'orage; **o. man in a hundred** un homme sur cent; **for o. thing I'm short of cash** entre autres raisons je suis à court d'argent; **o. thing at a time** chaque chose en son temps; **o. thing you'll need to know is …** il y a quelque chose qu'il vous faudra savoir: …; *Fam* **it was o. hell of a journey** ça a été un voyage épouvantable; **o. way and another** *(on balance)* à tous (les) points de vue; **o. way or another** d'une manière ou d'une autre

2 *(single)* seul; **my o. and only suit** mon seul et unique complet; **my o. and only daughter** *(only child)* ma fille unique; *(only daughter)* ma seule fille; **the o. and only Marilyn Monroe** la seule et l'unique Marilyn Monroe; **o. price** prix *m* unique; **her o. worry** son seul *ou* unique souci; **they were of o. mind on the subject** ils partageaient le même avis sur le sujet; **no o. man can do it** il n'y a pas d'homme qui puisse le faire à lui seul *ou* tout seul; **they cried out with o. voice** *or* **as o. man** ils s'écrièrent d'une seule voix *ou* comme un seul homme; **all in o. direction** tous dans la même direction; **o. and the same thought** une seule et même pensée; *Fam* **it's all o.** cela revient au même; *Fam* **it's all o. to me** ça m'est égal

N **1** un *m*; **chapter o.** chapitre un, chapitre premier; *Sport* **o., two, three, go!** un(e), deux, trois, partez!; **o. fifty** *(a hundred and fifty)* cent cinquante; *(one pound and fifty pence)* une livre cinquante (pence); *(one dollar fifty cents)* un dollar cinquante (cents); *(time)* deux heures moins dix, une heure cinquante; **it's o. o'clock** il est une heure; *Horseracing* **the odds are (at) ten to o.** la cote est à dix contre un; *Fam* **it's ten to o. that** *or* **Am o. will get you ten that he's at the office** je parie (à) dix contre un qu'il est au bureau

2 *(individual thing, person)* **there's only o. left** il n'en reste qu'un; **I was the only o. there** j'étais le seul à me trouver là; **she's the only o. you need to worry about** c'est la seule personne de qui *ou* dont tu doives te préoccuper; **the top/bottom stair but o.** l'avant-dernière marche; **to arrive in ones and twos** arriver un par un ou deux par deux; **two for the price of o.** deux pour le prix d'un; **two volumes in o.** deux volumes en un; **chauffeur and gardener in o.** *or* **rolled into o.** chauffeur et jardinier en un; **to be at o. with sb** être d'accord avec qn; *Fam* **there's o. born every minute** comment peut-on être aussi stupide!; *Fam* **I landed him o.** je lui ai flanqué un marron; *Sl* **to give sb o.** *(have sex with)* en glisser une paire à qn; **o. for the road** *(drink)* le coup de l'étrier; *Br* **to go into o.** *(lose one's temper)* péter les plombs, péter une durite; **to have had o. too many** *(drink)* avoir bu un verre de trop; *Sport* **to be o. up on an opponent** être en avance d'un point/d'un jeu/ d'un but/*etc* sur un concurrent; *Fam* **to be o. up on sb** *(have advantage)* avoir l'avantage sur qn

3 *Knitting* **to make o.** faire une augmentation, augmenter d'une maille

4 *St Exch* unité *f*; **to issue shares in ones** émettre des actions en unités

DEM PRON **this o.** celui-ci, celle-ci; *Fam* **these ones** ceux-ci, celles-ci; **that o.** celui-là, celle-là; *Fam* **those ones** ceux-là, celles-là; **which o. do you prefer?** lequel/laquelle préférez-vous?; **the o.** I spoke of celui/celle dont j'ai parlé; **to pick the ripe plums and leave the green ones** cueillir les prunes mûres et laisser les vertes; **the big/silly/blonde o.** *(woman)* la grosse/l'imbécile/la blonde; **the right/wrong o.** le bon/mauvais; **the ones with the long sleeves** ceux avec les manches longues; **the scheme was a good o. on paper** le plan était excellent en théorie; **that's a good o.!** *(story, joke)* elle est bonne, celle-là!; **have you heard the o. about …?** est-ce que tu as déjà entendu celle de …?; **that's a hard o.** *(a difficult question)* vous me posez une colle; **our loved** *or* **dear ones** ceux qui nous sont chers; *(our dead friends, relatives)* nos chers disparus; **the little ones** *(children)* les petits enfants; **he's a strange o., that boy** il est bizarre ce garçon VOIR GRAMMAIRE A30–1; B13–14

INDEF PRON **1** *(pl* some, any*)* **I haven't a pencil, have you got o.?** je n'ai pas de crayon, en avez-vous un?; **this question is o. of extreme delicacy** ce problème est délicat entre tous; **o. of them** l'un d'entre eux, l'un d'eux; **give me o. of them** donnez-m'en un; *Old-fashioned Fam* **I think he's o. of them** *(homosexual)* je crois qu'il en est; **o. of these days** un de ces jours; **she is o. of the family** elle fait partie de la famille, elle est de la famille; **he is o. of us** il est des nôtres; **o. of my friends** un de mes amis, un ami à moi; **any o. of us** n'importe lequel d'entre nous; **o. and all** tous sans exception; **Merry Christmas to o. and all** Joyeux Noël à tous; *Prov* **o. for all and all for o.** un pour tous et tous pour un; **(the) o. … the other** l'un … l'autre; **you can't have o. without the other** l'un ne va pas sans l'autre; **o. after the other** l'un après l'autre; **o. at a time** un à la fois; **o. by o.** un à un, un par un

2 *(particular person)* **I want the opinion of o. better able to judge** je voudrais avoir l'opinion de quelqu'un qui soit plus capable de juger; **o. Anne Martin** une certaine Anne Martin; **I, for o., do not believe it** pour ma part je n'en crois rien; **I'm not o. to complain** je ne suis pas du genre à me plaindre; **I'm not much of a o. for sweets** je ne suis pas grand amateur de bonbons; **he's a great o. for letting you know exactly what he thinks** il n'a pas son pareil pour vous faire savoir ce qu'il pense; **she's a great o. for foreign travel** elle adore voyager à l'étranger; *Old-fashioned* **you are a o.!** vous êtes fameux *ou* impayable, vous! VOIR GRAMMAIRE A37–8

3 *esp Fml (people in general) (subject)* on; *(direct and indirect object)* vous; **o. cannot always be right** on ne peut pas toujours avoir raison; **if o. wanted to do it** si l'on voulait le faire; **it is enough to make o. weep** il y a de quoi vous faire pleurer; **o.'s** son, sa, *pl* ses; *(object)* votre, *pl* vos; **if o. loses o.'s** *or* **Am his …** si on perd son … VOIR GRAMMAIRE A28–9; B16

4 o. another l'un l'autre, l'une l'autre, *pl* les uns les autres, les unes les autres; **to look at o. another** se regarder

one-act ADJ ATTRIB

▸▸ **o. play** pièce *f* en un (seul) acte

one-armed ADJ *(person)* manchot

▸▸ **o. bandit** machine *f* à sous

one-day ADJ *Sport (cricket, international, match etc)* d'un jour; *(cricket)* = matches *mpl* de cricket d'un jour

one-eyed ADJ *(person)* borgne; **o. man/woman** borgne *mf*

one-horse ADJ

▸▸ *Fam* **o. town** petite ville *f* de rien du tout, trou *m* perdu

one-legged ADJ unijambiste; **o. man/woman** unijambiste *mf*

one-liner N bon mot *m*

one-man ADJ ATTRIB *(job etc)* pour un seul homme

▸▸ **o. band** homme-orchestre *m, pl* hommes-orchestres; *Com* **o. company** société *f* à une seule personne *ou* à personne unique *ou* unipersonnelle; **o. show** *(by artist)* exposition *f* individuelle; *(by performer)* spectacle *m* solo, **one-man-show** *m inv*; *Fig* entreprise *f* individuelle

oneness ['wʌnɪs] N *(unity)* unité *f*; *(of opinions)* accord *m*

one-night ADJ
▸▸**o. stand** *Theat* représentation *f* unique; *Mus* unique concert *m*; *Fam (sexual encounter)* histoire *f ou* rencontre *f* sans lendemain

one-off *Br* ADJ *Com (item)* spécial, -aux, hors série; *(order, job)* unique; *(situation)* exceptionnel; **a o. design** un modèle exclusif N *(object)* objet *m*/exemplaire *m* unique; *(order)* commande *f* unique; *(job)* tâche *f* unique; **he was a o.** c'était quelqu'un d'unique; **the mistake was a o.** cette erreur ne se reproduira pas; **her success was a o.** son succès sera sans lendemain; **I promise you, this is a o.** c'est exceptionnel, je vous le promets; **as a o., you can have it for just £50** à titre exceptionnel, je vous le laisse pour 50 livres

one-one, one-on-one ADJ, ADV *Am* = **one-to-one**

one-parent ADJ
▸▸**o. family** famille *f* monoparentale

one-party ADJ ATTRIB *(state etc)* à parti unique
▸▸**o. rule** = régime *m* à parti unique; **o. system** *(of government)* système *m* du parti unique

one-piece ADJ d'une seule pièce; *Tech (casting)* monobloc *inv*
▸▸**o. swimsuit** maillot *m* une pièce

oner ['wʌnər] N *Br Fam* **to do sth in a o.** faire qch d'un seul coup; **to down a drink in a o.** faire cul sec; **he got it in a o.** *(understood)* il a tout de suite pigé; *(got answer)* il a tout de suite trouvé la solution

onerous ['ɒnərəs, 'əʊ-] ADJ *(tax, task, responsibility)* lourd; **he's finding all this responsibility rather o.** il trouve que toutes ces responsabilités sont plutôt lourdes à porter

Note that the French word **onéreux** is a false friend and is never a translation for the English word **onerous**. It means **expensive**.

oneself [wʌn'self] PRON VOIR GRAMMAIRE A29-30; B28 **1** *(reflexive)* se; **to wash/feed/flatter o.** se laver/se nourrir/se flatter; **to look after o.** *(when ill) (generally)* se soigner, s'occuper de soi; **to speak of o.** parler de soi; **to keep o. to o.** être peu sociable, ne pas se mêler aux autres; **to feel o. again** se sentir complètement rétabli **2** *(emphatic)* soi-même; *Fml* **one must do it o.** il faut le faire soi-même; **to do sth all by o.** faire qch tout seul

one-sided ADJ *(unfair) (contest)* inégal, -aux; *(contract)* inégal, inéquitable; *(judgment)* partial, -aux; *(relationship)* à sens unique

one-step N *(dance)* one-step *m*, *pl* one-steps

one-stop ADJ
▸▸*Com, Mktg* **o. buying** achats *mpl* regroupés (dans un seul magasin); *Com* **o. shop** magasin *m* où l'on trouve de tout; *Com, Mktg* **o. shopping** achats regroupés (dans un seul magasin); *Com* **o. store** magasin où l'on trouve de tout

one-time ADJ ancien; **Mr Martin, o. mayor** M. Martin, ancien maire

one-to-one ADJ *(correspondence, connection, relationship between figures etc)* univoque; *(relationship between people)* exclusif; *(conversation, meeting)* seul à seul,

en tête à tête; **the first time I met her in a o. situation** la première fois que je l'ai rencontrée en tête à tête *ou* seul à seul
ADV *(to talk, meet)* seul à seul, en tête à tête; *(to correspond)* de manière univoque, exclusivement
▸▸**o. marketing** marketing *m* one to one; **o. tuition** cours *mpl* particuliers

one-track mind N **to have a o. mind** avoir une idée fixe; *(be obsessed with sex)* ne penser qu'à ça *ou* qu'à une chose; **will you stop going on about work, you're developing a o. mind** vas-tu arrêter de parler de travail, ça devient une idée fixe chez toi

one-upmanship [-'ʌpmənʃɪp] N *Fam* art *m* de se montrer supérieur aux autres; **this is no time for o.** ce n'est pas le moment d'essayer de démontrer sa supériorité; **that's a nice piece of o.** voilà une belle démonstration de supériorité

one-way ADJ **1** *(ticket)* simple; *Com (packaging)* perdu **2** *(street, traffic)* à *ou* en sens unique; **their relationship was all o.** leurs rapports étaient à sens unique
▸▸*Tech* **o. valve** clapet *m* anti-retour

ongoing ['ɒŋgəʊɪŋ] ADJ **1** *(continuing, permanent)* continuel; **for them it's an o. state of affairs** pour eux c'est une situation courante *ou* habituelle **2** *(happening now) (research, discussions, restructuring)* en cours, actuel; *(work)* en cours; **is it o. at the moment?** est-ce que c'est en train de se faire?

on-hook, onhook ADJ
▸▸*Comput* **o. signal** signal *m* de fin de communication *ou* de raccrochage

onion ['ʌnjən] N **1** oignon *m*; **string of onions** chapelet *m* d'oignons; *Culin* **o. soup** soupe *f* à l'oignon **2** *Br Sl* **she knows her onions** elle connaît son affaire, elle s'y connaît

onionskin ['ʌnjənskɪn] N *(paper)* pelure *f* d'oignon

oniony ['ʌnjənɪ] ADJ *(in smell)* qui sent l'oignon; *(in taste)* qui a un goût d'oignon

on-line, online ADJ **1** *Comput* connecté, en ligne; *(with a connection set up)* connecté; **to be o.** être connecté à qch; **to be o. to sb/sth** *(by modem)* être en ligne avec qn/qch; **to go o.** se connecter; **to put the printer o.** connecter l'imprimante; **o. backup** sauvegarde *f* en ligne; **o. bank** banque *f* en ligne; **o. banking** banque par Internet, services *mpl* bancaires en ligne; *St Exch* **o. broker** courtier, -ière électronique; **o. cash desk** terminal *m* de paiement connecté; **o. catalogue** catalogue *m* en ligne; *TV* **o. editing** montage *m* "on-line", conformation *f*; *TV* **o. editor** monteur, -euse "on-line"; **o. forum** forum *m ou* groupe *m* de discussion; **o. help** aide *f* en ligne; **o. interviewing** enquête *f* téléphonique "en ligne"; *Fin* **o. investing** investissement *m* en ligne; *Fin* **o. investor** investisseur, -euse en ligne; **o. marketing** marketing *m* électronique; **o. mode** mode *m* connecté; **o. newspaper** journal *m* en ligne; **o. operation** opération *f* en ligne; **o. programming** programmation *f* en ligne; **o. registration** inscription *f* en ligne; **o. retailer** société *f* de commerce en ligne; **o. retailing** commerce *m* électronique; **o. selling** vente *f* en ligne, vente électronique; **o. service** service *m* en ligne; **o. shop** magasin *m* électronique; **o. shopping** achats *mpl* par Internet; **o. terminal** terminal *m* de paiement connecté; **o. test** test *m* en ligne; **o. time** durée *f* de connexion; *St Exch* **o. trading** transactions *fpl* boursières électroniques
2 o. area *(area where carrier has right to operate)* zone *f* autorisée

onlooker ['ɒnlʊkər] N spectateur, -trice; *(at accident, incident)* badaud *m*

ADJ seul = unique
ADV seulement = ne... que
CONJ mais

ADJ seul, unique; **o. son/daughter** *(sole child)* fils/fille unique; *(sole son/daughter)* seul(e) fils/fille; **his o. answer was to laugh** pour toute réponse il a ri; **we are the o. people who know it** nous sommes les seuls à le savoir; **you are not the o. one** vous n'êtes pas le seul; **the o. thing is that it's rather expensive** seulement ça coûte cher; **Boston is the o. place to live** Boston est la ville idéale pour vivre

ADV seulement, ne ... que, ne ... rien que; **she has o. one brother** elle n'a qu'un (seul) frère; **it's o. a scratch** c'est seulement une égratignure, ce n'est (rien) qu'une égratignure; **o. half an hour more** plus qu'une demi-heure; **one man** *o.* un seul homme; **(entrance for) season ticket holders o.** entrée réservée aux abonnés; **o. an expert could advise us** seul un expert pourrait nous conseiller; **I o. touched it** je n'ai fait que le toucher; **he has o. to ask for it** il n'a qu'à le demander; **I will o. say that I disagree** je me bornerai à dire que je ne suis pas de cet avis; **I shall be o. too pleased to come** je ne serai que trop heureux de venir; **o. if you agree** seulement si tu es d'accord; **o. think what pleasure it gave me** imaginez un peu le plaisir que cela m'a fait; **if o. I knew where he was!** si seulement je savais où il est!; **if o. they knew!, if they o. knew!** si (seulement) ils savaient!; **not o. useful but also decorative** non seulement utile, mais aussi décoratif; **she left o. yesterday** elle n'est partie qu'hier; **o. last week he appeared to be quite happy** la semaine dernière encore, il semblait parfaitement heureux; **I saw her/used it o. yesterday** je l'ai vue/m'en suis servi pas plus tard qu'hier; **o. just** à peine; **it's o. me** *(wanting to come in, speak to you etc)* ce n'est que moi VOIR GRAMMAIRE A22

CONJ mais; **the book is interesting, o. rather too long** le livre est intéressant, mais un peu long; **I would do it o. I can't spare the time** je le ferais si j'avais le temps
▸▸**o. child** enfant *mf* unique

only-begotten [-bɪ'gɒt(ə)n] ADJ, N *Rel* **the o. (Son) of the Father** le Fils unique du Père

on-message ADJ qui respecte scrupuleusement la ligne du parti

o.n.o. [əʊen'əʊ] ADV *Com (abbr* **or nearest offer)** à débattre

on/off switch N bouton *m* marche-arrêt

onomatopoeia [ɒnəmætə'piːə] N onomatopée *f*

onomatopoeic [ɒnəmætə'piːɪk] ADJ onomatopéique

on-pack ADJ
▸▸*Mktg* **o. offer** prime *f* différée; *Mktg* **o. promotion** promotion *f* on-pack

on-ramp N *(to motorway)* bretelle *f* d'accès

on-road ADJ, ADV *(performance)* sur route

onrush ['ɒnrʌʃ] N *(of people)* ruée *f*; *(of water)* torrent *m*; *(of emotions, desire)* flot *m*, vague *f*; *(of pain, grief)* vague *f*

ONS [əʊen'es] N *Br* ≃ INSEE *m*

on-screen ADJ **1** *Comput* à l'écran **2** *Cin, TV* à l'écran; **her o. character bears a close resemblance to her real-life personality** le personnage qu'elle joue à l'écran ressemble beaucoup à ce qu'elle est en réalité
ADV **1** *Comput* sur (l')écran; **to work o.** travailler sur écran **2** *Cin, TV* à l'écran
▸▸*Comput* **o. graphics** graphiques *mpl* affichés; *Comput* **o. help** aide *f* en ligne

onset ['ɒnset] N **1** *(beginning) (of winter, ill-*

ness, war) début *m*, commencement *m*; **the o. of a disease** la première attaque d'une maladie **2** *(attack)* assaut *m*, attaque *f*

onshore ['ɒnʃɔːr] ADJ **1** *(wind etc)* du large **2** *(oil rig etc)* à terre

on-site ADJ, ADV *(supervision, maintenance)* sur site

onslaught ['ɒnslɔːt] N assaut *m*, attaque *f*, *(of policies etc)* attaque

on switch N bouton *m* de marche

Ont *abbr* Ontario

on-target earnings NPL *Com* salaire *m* de base plus commissions

on-the-job ADJ *(training, experience)* sur le tas

on-the-spot fine N amende *f* immédiate

onto ['ɒntʊ, *unstressed* 'ɒntə] PREP = **on to**, *see* **on**

ontological [ɒntə'lɒdʒɪk(ə)l] ADJ *Phil* ontologique

ontology [ɒn'tɒlədʒɪ] N *Phil* ontologie *f*

onus ['əʊnəs] N responsabilité *f*, obligation *f*; **the o. is on the government to compensate the victims** il incombe au gouvernement d'indemniser les sinistrés; **the o. is now on United to attack** United se doit maintenant d'attaquer; **the o. is on you to lodge a complaint** il tient à toi de déposer une plainte; *Law* **o. of proof** charge *f* de la preuve; **the o. of proof lies with you** c'est à vous qu'il incombe d'en apporter la preuve

onward ['ɒnwəd] ADV = **onwards** ADJ *(motion etc)* en avant; **we wish you a pleasant o. journey** nous vous souhaitons une bonne continuation pour votre voyage ►► **o. connection** correspondance *f*, **o. flight** correspondance

onwards ['ɒnwədz] ADV en avant, plus loin; **from tomorrow/then o.** à partir de demain/de ce moment-là; **from this time o.** désormais, dorénavant

onyx ['ɒnɪks] N *Miner* onyx *m*

oodles ['uːd(ə)lz] NPL *Fam* **there's o. of it** il y en a un tas *ou* des tas *ou* une tapée; **to have o. of money** avoir un paquet *ou* une tonne de fric; **o. of cream** des tonnes de crème; **o. of time/space** plein de temps/d'espace

ooh [uː] INT *(expressing surprise, awe, pleasure)* oh!

oolite ['əʊəlaɪt] N *(rock)* oolithe *m*

oomph [ʊmf] N *Fam* **1** *(energy)* énergie *f*, **to have plenty of o.** *(person)* avoir la pêche, avoir du punch; *(song, plot etc)* avoir du punch; **their new album lacks the o. of the last one** leur nouvel album n'a pas la pêche du précédent **2** *(sex appeal)* sex-appeal *m*

oops [uːps] INT **1** *(to child who has fallen down)* houp-là! **2** *(after sb has made a mistake)* oh là là!

oops-a-daisy INT = **oops**

ooze [uːz] N **1** *(mud)* vase *f*, limon *m* **2** *(flow) (of liquid)* suintement *m*
VI suinter **(from** de**)**; **the wound was oozing with pus/blood** du pus/sang suintait de la plaie; **water that oozes out from the rock** eau qui sourd du rocher; **the walls were oozing with water** les murs suintaient, l'eau suintait des murs; **the mud oozed up between her toes** la boue sourdait lentement entre ses orteils; *Fig* **to o. with confidence** déborder d'assurance
VT **the wound was oozing pus/blood** du pus/sang suintait de la plaie; *Fig* **to o. confidence** déborder d'assurance; **to o. charm** déborder de charme; *Fig* **this place just oozes wealth** cet endroit sue l'opulence

op¹ [ɒp] N *Surg, Mil Fam (abbr* **operation**) opération *f*

op² ADJ *Art* **op art** op art *m*

opacity [əʊ'pæsɪtɪ] N opacité *f*, *Fig (of writing etc)* caractère *m* obscur, obscurité *f*

opal ['əʊp(ə)l] N **1** *(mineral)* opale *f*, **o. necklace** collier *m* d'opale **2** *(colour)* opale *m inv* **3** *(glass)* verre *f* opale, opaline *f* ►► **o. glass** verre opale, opaline

opalescence [əʊpə'lesəns] N opalescence *f*

opalescent [əʊpə'lesənt] ADJ opalescent; *(hue)* opale *inv*; *(haze etc)* opalisé

opaline ['əʊpəlaɪn] ADJ opalin N *(glass)* opaline *f*

opaque [əʊ'peɪk] ADJ **1** opaque; **to become o.** s'opacifier **2** *Fig (words, comments, style)* obscur

opaqueness [əʊ'peɪknɪs] N = **opacity**

OPEC ['əʊpek] N *(abbr* **Organization of Petroleum-Exporting Countries**) OPEP *f*, **O. countries/prices** pays *mpl*/prix *mpl* de l'OPEP

op-ed ['ɒped] N *Journ (in newspaper)* page *f* face éditoriale; **an o. piece** un article d'opinion *(situé sur la page faisant face à l'éditorial)*

OPEIC [əʊpiːiːə'siː] N *Fin (abbr* **open-ended investment company**) SICAV *f*, société *f* d'investissement à capital variable

OPEN ['əʊp(ə)n]

ADJ ouvert **1**, **3–5**, **7** ▪ découvert **2** ▪ franc **3** ▪ libre **5** ▪ non résolu **6**	
VT ouvrir **1** ▪ déboucher **1** ▪ commencer **3** ▪ engager **3**	
VI s'ouvrir **1**, **3**, **4** ▪ ouvrir **2** ▪ commencer **4**	

ADJ 1 *(box, door, book, shop etc)* ouvert; *Fig* **my door is always o.** ma porte t'est/vous est/*etc* toujours ouverte; **half o.** *(door, window)* entrouvert, entrebâillé; **o. to the public** *(museum etc)* ouvert *ou* accessible au public; **o. late** ouvert en nocturne; **o. all night** ouvert (toute) la nuit; *Law* **in o. court** en plein tribunal; **career o. to very few** carrière accessible à très peu de gens *ou* très fermée **2** *(not enclosed)* découvert, non couvert; *(coast, position)* exposé **(to** à**)**; **o. country** *(not offering protection)* terrain *m* découvert; **in (the) o. country** *(not wooded)* en pleine *ou* rase campagne; **in the o. country-side** en pleine campagne, en rase campagne; **there's a lot of o. countryside** c'est la pleine campagne; **to work in the o. fields** travailler dans les champs; **in the o. air** au grand air, à ciel ouvert; **to sleep in the o. air** coucher à la belle étoile; **the o. sea** la haute mer, le large; **the city was designed with lots of o. spaces** la ville a été conçue de manière très aérée; **the wide o. spaces** les grands espaces; **o. view** vue *f* dégagée; **o. to the elements/to the winds** exposé aux intempéries/aux quatre vents; **o. to doubt** douteux; **o. to ridicule** qui prête au ridicule; **o. to criticism** critiquable; **o. to question** contestable; **she is still o. to persuasion on the issue** on peut encore lui faire changer d'avis sur la question; **the Government has left itself o. to the criticism that …** le gouvernement a prêté le flanc à la critique de …; **o. to any reasonable offer** disposé à considérer toute offre raisonnable; **to be o. to suggestions** être ouvert à toute suggestion; *Ftbl* **to leave the goal o.** dégarnir ses buts **3** *(frank) (person, personality)* ouvert, franc, *f* franche; *(conflict, disagreement)* ouvert; *(preference, favouritism)* manifeste, public, *f* -ique; **to be o. in one's affection** témoigner ouvertement son affection; **to be o. with sb** parler franchement à qn, être franc avec qn; **he is o. about his homosexuality** il ne cache pas son homosexualité; **her o. dislike** son aversion déclarée; **they are in o. revolt** ils sont en révolte ouverte

4 *(flower, lips, hand)* ouvert; **o. at the neck** *(of dress)* échancré; **his shirt was o. at the neck** le col de sa chemise était ouvert; **with eyes o. wide** les yeux écarquillés; **to welcome with o. arms** *(person)* accueillir à bras ouverts; *(proposal, development etc)* accueillir avec enthousiasme **5** *(clear, unobstructed)* libre, non obstrué; **road o. to traffic** route ouverte à la circulation; **to keep one's bowels o.** aller à la selle régulièrement; *(of diet)* faciliter le transit intestinal; **to keep a day o. for sb** réserver un jour pour qn; **the job is still o.** la place est toujours vacante; **membership o. to anyone over 18** inscription ouverte à toute personne de plus de 18 ans; **two courses/choices are o. to us** deux moyens/choix s'offrent à nous; **an o. border** une frontière ouverte **6** *(unresolved)* non résolu; *(question, case)* pendant; **to keep an o. mind on sth** réserver son opinion sur qch; **to leave the matter o.** ne pas prendre de décision *ou* ne pas trancher sur la question; **I want to leave the return date o.** *(on ticket)* je ne veux pas réserver le retour tout de suite **7** *Sport (play) (free-flowing)* ouvert, dégagé N **1 in the o.** *(outdoors)* dehors; *(to go for a stroll, work etc)* au grand air, dehors; *(not hidden)* au grand jour; **to sleep in the o.** dormir à la belle étoile; *Fig* **to bring sth out into the o.** mettre qch au grand jour; **their mutual dislike was out in the o.** ils affichaient ouvertement l'antipathie qu'ils avaient l'un pour l'autre; *Fig* **let's get all this out in the o.** jouons cartes sur table; **to come out into the o. about sth** révéler qch **2** *Sport* open *m* ADV **to fling the door wide o.** ouvrir la porte toute grande; **the door flew o.** la porte s'ouvrit brusquement; **to cut o.** couper, ouvrir; **to force sth o.** forcer qch; **to smash/lever sth o.** ouvrir qch en le fracassant/à l'aide d'un levier

VT **1** *(door, book, parcel, hand, eyes etc)* ouvrir; *(bottle)* ouvrir, déboucher; *(letter)* ouvrir, décacheter; *(post)* ouvrir, dépouiller; *(institution, establishment)* inaugurer; *(legs etc)* écarter; **to o. the door wide** ouvrir la porte toute grande; *Med* **to o. the bowels** aller à la selle; **to o. one's shop** *(in morning etc)* ouvrir son magasin; **to o. a new shop** *ou* monter un nouveau magasin; **to o. a park to the public/a road (to traffic)** ouvrir un parc au public/une route à la circulation; **to o. one's heart** ouvrir son cœur, s'ouvrir **(to sb** à qn**)**; **that opens new prospects for me** cela m'ouvre de nouveaux horizons; **to o. Parliament** ouvrir la session du Parlement **2** *(make) (tunnel)* creuser; *(hole)* faire **3** *(begin)* commencer; *(negotiations, conversation, debate)* entamer, engager; *(performance)* ouvrir; *(fire, hostilities)* ouvrir; **to o. an account in sb's name** ouvrir un compte à qn; **to o. a line of credit** ouvrir un crédit; *Law* **to o. the case** exposer les faits VI **1** s'ouvrir; **to half o.** *(of door etc)* s'entrebâiller, s'entrouvrir; **door that opens into the garden** porte qui donne sur le jardin; **o. wide!** *(said by doctor, dentist etc)* ouvrez grand la bouche! **2** *(of shop, museum)* ouvrir; **to o. late** *(of shop)* ouvrir en nocturne; **as soon as the season opens** dès l'ouverture de la saison **3** *(of view, prospects)* s'étendre; *(of flower)* s'épanouir, s'ouvrir **4** *(begin)* commencer; **the play opens with a death scene** la pièce s'ouvre sur une scène de mort; *Cin* **the film opens next week** le film sort la semaine prochaine; *St Exch* **the FTSE opened at 1083** l'indice FT a ouvert à 1083

►► *Banking* **o. account** compte *m* ouvert; **o. carriage** voiture *f* découverte; *Golf, Tennis* **o.**

championship championnat *m* open *inv ou* ouvert; *Banking* **o. cheque** chèque *m* ouvert *ou* non barré; *St Exch* **o. contract** position *f* ouverte; *Fin* **o. credit** crédit *m* à découvert; **o. enemy** ennemi *m* déclaré; **o. hostilities** guerre *f* ouverte; **o. inquiry** enquête *f* publique; **o. invitation** invitation *f* permanente; **it's an o. invitation to tax-dodgers/ thieves** c'est une invitation à la fraude fiscale/aux voleurs; **o. letter** lettre *f* ouverte; **o. market** marché *m* libre; *St Exch* **o. outcry system** système *m* de criée; *St Exch* **o. position** position ouverte; **o. prison** prison *f* ouverte; **o. sandwich** tartine *f*, **o. season** saison *f*, *Br* **o. secret** secret *m* de Polichinelle; *Ind* **o. shop** *Br (open to non-union members)* = entreprise *f* ne pratiquant pas le monopole d'embauche; *Am (with no union)* établissement *m* sans syndicat; **o. side** *(in rugby)* grand côté *m*, côté ouvert; **o. space** *(park)* espace *m* vert; *Mus* **o. string** corde *f* à vide; **o. ticket** billet *m* open; *Sport* **o. tournament** (tournoi *m*) open *m*; *Br* **O. University** = enseignement *m* universitaire par correspondance doublé d'émissions de télévision ou de radio; *Law* **o. verdict** verdict *m* de décès sans cause déterminée; *Ling* **o. vowel** voyelle ouverte; **o. wound** *(gaping)* plaie *f* béante; *(not healed)* plaie non cicatrisée

▸ **open out** VI **1** *(of flower)* s'ouvrir; *(of wings)* se déployer; *(of view, prospects)* s'ouvrir, s'étendre

2 *(become wider)* s'élargir (**into** pour donner dans)

3 *Fig (of person)* s'ouvrir

VT SEP **1** *(unfold) (sheet of paper, map)* ouvrir, déplier

2 *(develop) (company)* développer

3 *(widen) (hole)* élargir, agrandir; *(mouth of pipe)* évaser

▸ **open up** VI **1** *(of flower)* s'ouvrir

2 *(of view, prospects)* s'ouvrir, s'étendre; **new markets are opening up** de nouveaux marchés sont en train de s'ouvrir

3 *(of shopkeeper etc)* ouvrir; **this is the police, o. up!** police! ouvrez!

4 *(of new shop etc)* ouvrir

5 *Fig (of person)* s'ouvrir (**to sb** à qn)

6 *Mil* ouvrir le feu

VT SEP **1** *(letter, parcel, box, newspaper)* ouvrir

2 *(make accessible) (a country to trade, mine)* ouvrir; *(path)* ouvrir, frayer, rendre praticable; **this remote area is being opened up for development** cette région reculée commence à être exploitée

3 *(possibility of something)* ouvrir; **to o. up opportunities** donner des chances

4 *(start)* **to o. up a business, to o. up shop** ouvrir *ou* monter une affaire

open-air ADJ *(restaurant, market, cinema, life etc)* en plein air; *(swimming pool)* découvert

open-and-shut ADJ **it was an o. case** tout était clair comme de l'eau de roche; **this may not be such an o. case as it first appears** ce n'est peut-être pas aussi simple que cela paraît au premier abord

opencast ['əʊpənkɑːst] ADJ *Br (mining)* à ciel ouvert, au jour

open-date ticket N billet *m* open *inv ou* ouvert

open-door ADJ

▸▸ **o. policy** *(for immigrants)* politique *f* d'ouverture des frontières; *(of university etc)* politique d'ouverture

open-ended [-'endɪd] ADJ *(credit, contract)* à durée indéterminée; *(question)* ouvert; **it's a bit too o.** c'est un peu trop vague; **can we leave it o. for the time being?** est-ce nous pouvons ne pas tout fixer tout de suite?; **avoid o. commitments** évite de t'engager

sans fixer de limites; **o. discussion** libre discussion *f*; **could we keep the arrangement o.?** pourrions-nous garder une certaine flexibilité au niveau de notre arrangement?

▸▸ *Fin* **o. investment company, o. investment trust** SICAV *f*, société *f* d'investissement à capital variable; **o. spanner** clé *f* ouverte

opener ['əʊpənər] N **1** *Theat (item on programme)* premier numéro *m*; *Fam* **for openers** pour commencer **2** *(device) (bottle) o.* décapsuleur *m*; **(can or tin) o.** ouvre-boîtes *m inv* **3** *Cr* premier batteur *m*

open-eyed ADJ qui a les yeux ouverts; **to look at sb in o. astonishment** regarder qn les yeux écarquillés de surprise

open-handed [-'hændɪd] ADJ généreux; **to be o.** être généreux, avoir la main sur le cœur

open-heart ADJ *(surgery)* à cœur ouvert

open-hearted [-'hɑːtɪd] ADJ *(kind)* charitable

open-hearth ADJ

▸▸ *Metal* **o. furnace** four *m* Martin

opening ['əʊpənɪŋ] N **1** *(of door, shop, account, one's heart etc)* ouverture *f*; **formal o.** inauguration *f*; **the o. of Parliament** l'ouverture du Parlement; *Com* **late o. Friday** ≃ nocturne le vendredi **2** *(beginning) (of play, new era)* commencement *m*, début *m*; *(of negotiations)* ouverture *f*, *(start of letter)* formule *f* de début; *Law (speech by lawyer)* exposition *f* des faits **3** *(open space) (in wall)* ouverture *f*, trou *m*; *(for door, window)* embrasure *f*, baie *f*, *(in forest)* clairière *f*, *(man-made also)* percée *f*, *(between the trees)* échappée *f* **4** *(mouth, entrance) (of cave, tunnel)* entrée *f*, *(of sack)* ouverture *f* **5** *(opportunity)* occasion *f* favorable; *(job)* poste *m*, place *f* (**as** de); *Com (for goods)* débouché *m*; **we have exploited an o. in the market** nous avons exploité une ouverture sur le marché; **this could be your big o.** ça pourrait être la chance de ta vie

ADJ **o. address** *or* **speech** discours *m* d'ouverture; *Theat* **the o. lines** les premières lignes; *Cin, Theat* **the o. scene** la scène d'ouverture

▸▸ *Acct* **o. balance** solde *m* d'ouverture; *Acct* **o. balance sheet** bilan *m* d'ouverture; *Cr* **o. batsman** premier batteur *m*; *Cards* **o. bid** annonce *f* d'entrée *ou* d'indication; **o. bracket** parenthèse *f* ouvrante; **o. ceremony** cérémonie *f* d'inauguration; *Cin, TV* **o. credits** générique *f* de début; *St Exch* **o. day** jour *m* d'ouverture; *Acct* **o. entry** écriture *f* d'ouverture; *Com* **o. hours** heures *fpl* d'ouverture; *Theat* **o. night** première *f*, *St Exch* **o. price** *(at start of trading)* cours *m* d'ouverture, premier cours; *(of new shares)* cours d'introduction; **o. quotation marks** guillemets *mpl* ouvrants; *Fin* **o. session** séance *f* d'ouverture; *Fin* **o. stock** stock *m* initial *ou* d'ouverture; *Com* **o. time** heure *f* d'ouverture; *Cin* **o. weekend** premier week-end *m* d'exploitation

openly ['əʊpənlɪ] ADV ouvertement; *(publicly)* publiquement; *(in front of everyone)* au vu (et au su) de tous; *(to speak)* sans réticence; **to be o. critical of sb** critiquer qn ouvertement; **to act o.** agir à découvert *ou* cartes sur table, jouer franc jeu

open-minded ADJ qui a l'esprit ouvert; **to be o. on** *or* **about sth** ne pas avoir de parti pris *ou* d'idée préconçue sur qch; **her parents are very o.** ses parents sont des gens très ouverts

open-mouthed [-'maʊðd] ADJ **to stand o.** *or* **in o. astonishment** rester bouche bée

openness ['əʊpənnɪs] N **1** *(frankness)* franchise *f*, **I was surprised by the o. with which they expressed their criticism** cela m'a sur-

pris qu'ils expriment leurs critiques aussi ouvertement **2** *(of mind)* largeur *f*, ouverture *f* **3** *(of coastline etc)* situation *f* exposée; *(of terrain)* aspect *m* découvert; **the o. of the countryside** les grands horizons

open-plan ADJ *(office)* paysager; *(flat)* sans cloison; **we've gone o.** nous avons maintenant un bureau paysager

open-top ADJ décapotable

open-topped bus N autobus *m* à impériale

openwork ['əʊpənwɜːk] N *(piece of embroidery)* ouvrage *m* ajouré *ou* à jour; *(holes)* jours *mpl*, ajours *mpl*

▸▸ **o. stockings** bas *mpl* ajourés *ou* à jour

opera ['ɒp(ə)rə] N opéra *m*; *(company)* (compagnie *f* d')opéra; **comic o.** opéra bouffe *ou* comique

▸▸ **o. bouffe** opéra bouffe *ou* comique; **o. glasses** jumelles *fpl* de théâtre; **o. goer** amateur *m* d'opéra; **o. house** opéra, *m*; **o. singer** chanteur, -euse d'opéra

operable ['ɒp(ə)rəb(ə)l] ADJ **1** *Surg (disease, tumour)* opérable **2** *(system etc)* utilisable

operand ['ɒpərænd] N opérande *m*

operate ['ɒpəreɪt] VI **1** *(of machine)* fonctionner; *(of burglar, company etc)* opérer, travailler; **the wage increase will o. from the first of January** l'augmentation des salaires prendra effet à partir du premier janvier **2** *Surg* opérer; **to o. (on sb) for appendicitis** opérer (qn) de l'appendicite; **to be operated on** subir une opération *ou* une intervention chirurgicale, se faire opérer

VT **1** *(of person) (machine)* manœuvrer; *(brakes)* actionner; *(of part of machine)* commander, actionner; **operated by electricity** actionné par l'électricité **2** *Com (rail or bus service, business)* exploiter

operatic [ɒpə'rætɪk] ADJ d'opéra

NPL **operatics** *(amateur)* opéra *m* d'amateurs

▸▸ **o. society** groupe *m* d'opéra d'amateurs

operating ['ɒpəreɪtɪŋ] ADJ ATTRIB

▸▸ *Am Fin* **o. account** compte *m* d'exploitation; *Acct* **o. assets** actif *m* d'exploitation; *Acct* **o. budget** budget *m* d'exploitation, budget de fonctionnement; *Am* **o. capital** capital *m* d'exploitation, capital de roulement; *Acct* **o. cash flow** cash-flow *m* disponible, *pl* cash-flows disponibles; **o. cost** charge *f* opérationnelle; *Acct* **o. costs** frais *mpl ou* coûts *mpl* d'exploitation; *Fin* **o. deficit** déficit *m* d'exploitation; *Acct* **o. expenses** frais d'exploitation; **o. income** produits *mpl* d'exploitation; **o. instructions** mode *m* d'emploi; *Fin* **o. leverage** levier *m* d'exploitation; *Acct, Fin* **o. loss** perte *f* d'exploitation; *Acct, Fin* **o. margin** marge *f* (nette) d'exploitation; *Acct, Fin* **o. profit** bénéfice *m* d'exploitation; *Acct* **o. ratio** coefficient *m ou* ratio *m* d'exploitation; *Am* **o. room** salle *f* d'opération, bloc *m* opératoire; *Comput* **o. speed** vitesse *f* d'exécution; *Fin* **o. statement** compte *ou* rapport *m* d'exploitation; *Comput* **o. system** système *m* d'exploitation; *Comput* **o. system command** commande *f* du système d'exploitation; **o. table** table *f* d'opération; *Br* **o. theatre** salle d'opération, bloc opératoire

operation [ɒpə'reɪʃən] N **1** *(functioning) (of appliance, machine)* fonctionnement *m*, marche *f*, *(of mechanism)* jeu *m*; **in o.** *(machine)* en marche, en fonctionnement; *(law)* en application, en vigueur; **to come into o.** *(of machine)* commencer à fonctionner; *(of law)* entrer en application *ou* en vigueur; *(of curfew, rationing)* être imposé **2** *(controlling) (of machine etc)* manœuvre *f*, commande *f*, *(of reactor, ship, transport system, business)* exploitation *f*

3 *(process)* opération *f*, *(element) (of manu-*

facture etc) unité f; **it's a tricky o.** c'est une opération délicate; **(mathematical) o.** opération (mathématique); Comput **(computer) o.** opération (machine); **a firm's operations** les activités fpl d'une entreprise; **the company is moving its soft drinks o.** la société déménage sa branche de boissons non alcoolisées
 4 Mil etc opération f; **O. Snow** opération Neige
 5 Surg opération f, intervention f (chirurgicale); **an o. to have one's appendix out** une opération de l'appendicite; **to perform an o. on sb** opérer qn (**for** de); **to undergo** or **have an o.** se faire opérer, subir une opération ou une intervention chirurgicale (**for** de); **a throat o.** une opération de la gorge
 ▸▸**operations manager** directeur, -trice des exploitations; **operations research** recherche f opérationnelle; **operations room** salle f d'opérations (d'un état-major)

operational [ɒpəˈreɪʃən(ə)l] ADJ **1** Mil etc opérationnel **2** (machine) opérationnel, en état de marche ou de fonctionnement; **the new power station should be o. next year** la nouvelle centrale électrique devrait être opérationnelle l'an prochain **3** Com (costs, requirements) d'exploitation
 ▸▸Acct **o. audit** audit m opérationnel; Acct **o. cost accounting** comptabilité f analytique d'exploitation; Acct **o. cost centre** centre m d'analyse opérationnel; **o. marketing** marketing m opérationnel; Com **o. planning** planification f des opérations; Mktg **o. research** recherche f opérationnelle; Mil **o. training** instruction f tactique, entraînement m au combat

operative [ˈɒpərətɪv] ADJ **1** (law, rule etc) en vigueur; **to become o.** (of law) entrer en vigueur, prendre effet; **the o. word** le mot clé **2** Surg (method) opératoire
 N **1** (worker) ouvrier, -ière; (of machine etc) opérateur, -trice **2** Am (detective) détective m **3** (secret agent) agent m secret

operator [ˈɒpəreɪtər] N **1** (person) (of machine) opérateur, -trice; (of business) exploitant, -ante; **the o. of the service, British Airways …** la compagnie qui assure le service, British Airways …; **(tour) o.** tour opérateur m, voyagiste m; Fam **he's a pretty slick o.** c'est un petit débrouillard, il se débrouille plutôt bien; **he's a pretty quick o.** il va vite en besogne **2** Tel téléphoniste mf; Com (in hotel etc) standardiste mf; **radio** or **wireless o.** (opérateur, -trice de) radio m; Tel **switchboard o.** standardiste **3** Math (of logarithm, logical) opérateur m **4** St Exch opérateur m

operetta [ɒpəˈretə] N Mus opérette f

ophthalmic [ɒfˈθælmɪk] ADJ (nerve, complaint) ophtalmique; (hospital) ophtalmologique
 ▸▸**o. optician** opticien, -ienne (optométriste)

ophthalmologist [ɒfθælˈmɒlədʒɪst] N Med ophtalmologiste mf, ophtalmologue mf

ophthalmology [ɒfθælˈmɒlədʒɪ] N Med ophtalmologie f

opiate [ˈəʊpɪɪt] N Pharm opiacé m; Fig Pej **the o. of television** la télévision, cette drogue abrutissante

opine [əʊˈpaɪn] VT Am Old-fashioned, Lit (be of opinion) être d'avis (**that** que + sub); (state opinion) exprimer l'avis (**that** que + ind)

opinion [əˈpɪnjən] N opinion f; **in my o.** à mon avis; **in the o. of experts** de l'avis ou au dire des experts, suivant ou selon l'opinion des experts; **to be of the o. that …** être d'avis ou estimer que …; **to be of the same o. as sb** être du même avis que qn, avoir la même opinion que qn; **to have a high/low o. of sb** avoir une bonne/mauvaise opinion

de qn; **to express** or **put forward an o.** exprimer une opinion; **to ask sb's o.** demander l'avis de qn, consulter qn; **I'd like your o.** j'aimerais avoir ton opinion ou savoir ce que tu en penses; **that's my o., for what it's worth** c'est mon humble avis; **to form an o. of sb/sth** se faire une opinion sur ou de qn/qch; **I have no strong opinion(s) on the matter** je n'ai pas d'opinion très arrêtée sur la question; **what is your o. of him/on the situation?** que pensez-vous de lui/de la situation?; **opinions differ** les avis sont partagés; **o. is divided on the subject** les avis divergent sur le sujet; **that's a matter of o.** chacun ses opinions; **it's a matter of o.** c'est discutable; **it is the o. of the court that …** la cour est d'avis que …; **you ought to have a second o.** Med vous devriez consulter un autre médecin; (generally) vous devriez consulter quelqu'un d'autre
 ▸▸Mktg **o. former, o. leader** leader m d'opinion; Mktg **o. measurement** sondage m d'opinion; Mktg **o. measurement technique** technique f de sondage d'opinion; Mktg **o. poll** sondage (d'opinion), enquête f (d'opinion); Mktg **o. pollster** sondeur, -euse (d'opinion); Mktg **o. survey** sondage d'opinion (publique), enquête (d'opinion)

opinionated [əˈpɪnjəneɪtɪd] ADJ Pej (tone) dogmatique; (person) qui a des idées très arrêtées; **he can be quite o. on the subject** il a des idées très arrêtées sur le sujet

opium [ˈəʊpɪəm] N opium m
 ▸▸**o. addict** opiomane mf; **o. den** fumerie f d'opium; **o. poppy** pavot m (somnifère)

Oporto [əˈpɔːtəʊ] N Porto

opossum [əˈpɒsəm] N (animal) opossum m

opp (abbr **opposite**) en face

opponent [əˈpəʊnənt] N (of reform, deregulation, in argument, match) adversaire mf; (of government) opposant, -ante (**of** à)

opportune [ˈɒpətjuːn] ADJ (time) opportun; (action) à propos; **you have come at an o. moment** vous arrivez à propos, vous tombez bien

opportunely [ɒpəˈtjuːnlɪ] ADV opportunément; (to arrive) opportunément, en temps opportun

opportunism [ɒpəˈtjuːnɪz(ə)m] N opportunisme m

opportunist [ɒpəˈtjuːnɪst] ADJ, N opportuniste mf

opportunistic [ɒpətjuːˈnɪstɪk] ADJ (person, policy, disease) opportuniste

opportunity [ɒpəˈtjuːnɪtɪ] N occasion f (**for** or **of doing sth, to do sth** de faire qch); **at every o.** à la moindre occasion; **at the first** or **earliest o.** à la première occasion; **I would go if I were you, it's the o. of a lifetime** à ta place j'irais, c'est la chance de ta vie; **if I get an o.** si l'occasion se présente, si j'en ai l'occasion; **to miss an o.** laisser passer ou perdre une occasion; **I'd like to take this o. to thank everyone** j'aimerais profiter de cette occasion pour remercier tout le monde; **a job with opportunities** un emploi qui offre des perspectives; Mktg **o. and issue analysis** analyse f des attraits et des atouts; Mktg **o. and threat analysis** analyse des opportunités et des menaces; Mktg **o. to hear** occasion d'entendre; Mktg **o. to see** occasion de voir

oppose [əˈpəʊz] VT **1** (resist) (person) s'opposer à, résister à; (reform, act etc) faire obstacle ou opposition à; **to be opposed to sth** être opposé à qch; Law **to o. an action/a marriage** s'opposer à un acte/un mariage **2** (contrast) opposer; (two colours etc) mettre en opposition ou en contraste

opposed [əˈpəʊzd] ADJ opposé; **as o. to** par opposition à; **I'd say he was 'robust' as o. to**

simply **'fat'** je dirais qu'il était 'costaud' plutôt que simplement 'gros'

opposing [əˈpəʊzɪŋ] ADJ (armies, characters, viewpoints) opposé; (party) opposant; **o. team** équipe f adverse

opposite [ˈɒpəzɪt] ADJ (characters) opposé; (opinion) contraire; (end of room etc) autre; (wall) d'en face, opposé; **to be of the o. opinion** être d'opinion contraire ou d'un avis contraire; **in the o. direction** en sens inverse, dans le sens opposé; **they went in o. directions** ils prirent des directions opposées; **the diagram on the o. page** la figure ci-contre
 N contraire m; **the exact o.** exactement le contraire
 ADV en face; **the house o.** la maison (d')en face; **the page o.** la page ci-contre
 PREP en face de, vis-à-vis (de); **to stand/sit o. sb** être (debout)/être assis en face de qn, faire vis-à-vis à qn; **a house o. the church** une maison en face de l'église ou qui fait face à l'église; **we live o. them** nous habitons en face de chez eux; Theat, Cin **she played o. many famous stars** elle a eu beaucoup de grandes vedettes comme partenaires
 ▸▸Aut **o. lock** contre-braquage m, pl contre-braquages; **to apply o. lock** contrebraquer; **o. number** homologue mf; **the o. sex** l'autre sexe m

opposition [ɒpəˈzɪʃən] N opposition f, résistance f; Com (competitors) concurrence f; **to act in o. to public opinion** agir contrairement à l'opinion publique; **to meet with fierce o.** rencontrer une farouche opposition; **to break down all o.** vaincre toutes les résistances; **the o.** le camp adverse; Br Pol **the O.** l'opposition; Pol **to be in o.** être dans l'opposition; Astron **in o.** en opposition

oppress [əˈpres] VT (conquered race, poor etc) opprimer; (the mind) oppresser, opprimer

oppressed [əˈprest] ADJ (people) opprimé
 NPL **the o.** les opprimés mpl

oppression [əˈpreʃən] N oppression f

oppressive [əˈpresɪv] ADJ **1** (law, régime) oppressif, opprimant **2** (atmosphere) lourd, étouffant; (heat) oppressant, accablant, étouffant **3** (mental burden, excessive attentiveness, affection) oppressant

oppressively [əˈpresɪvlɪ] ADV **1** (to rule) d'une manière oppressive **2 it was o. hot** il faisait une chaleur accablante ou étouffante **3** (with excessive affection) d'une manière oppressante ou étouffante

oppressiveness [əˈpresɪvnɪs] N **1** (of law, regime) caractère m oppressif **2** (of weather) lourdeur f; **the o. of the heat** la chaleur accablante ou étouffante **3** (emotional) caractère m oppressant

oppressor [əˈpresər] N oppresseur m

opprobrious [əˈprəʊbrɪəs] ADJ Fml injurieux, outrageant

opprobrium [əˈprəʊbrɪəm] N Fml opprobre m; **to incur sb's o.** s'attirer le mépris de qn

opt [ɒpt] VI opter (**for** pour; **between** entre); **to o. to do sth** choisir de faire qch
 ▸**opt in** VI (join) choisir de participer
 ▸**opt into** VT INSEP (join) **to o. into an association/the European Union/etc** entrer dans une association/l'Union européenne/etc
 ▸**opt out** VI choisir de ne plus participer (**of** à); **to o. out of one's responsibilities/an agreement** se désengager de ses responsabilités/d'un accord; Br **to o. out (of local authority control)** (of school, hospital etc) devenir autonome; **to o. out of society** se mettre en marge de la société; **I'm opting out** pour moi, c'est terminé

optative [ˈɒptətɪv] ADJ, N Gram optatif m

optic ['ɒptɪk] **ADJ** optique
N *Br* **Optic®** = mesure *f* transparente *(utilisée dans les bars)*
▶▶ *Comput* **o. drive** lecteur *m* optique; *Anat* **o. nerve** nerf *m* optique; *Comput* **o. scanner** scanneur *m* optique

optical ['ɒptɪk(ə)l] **ADJ** optique; *(instrument)* d'optique
▶▶ **o. axis** *(of lens)* axe *m* optique; **o. centre** *(of lens)* centre *m* optique; *Comput* **o. character reader** lecteur *m* optique de caractères; *Comput* **o. character recognition** reconnaissance *f* optique de caractères; *Comput* **o. disk** disque *m* optique; *Comput* **o. drive** lecteur *m* optique; **o. fibre** fibre *f* optique; **o. fibre cable** câble *m* à fibre optique; **o. fibre technology** fibre optique; **o. illusion** illusion *f ou* effet *m* d'optique; *Comput* **o. mouse** souris *f* optique; *Comput* **o. scanner** scanneur *m* optique

optician [ɒp'tɪʃən] **N** opticien, -ienne

optics ['ɒptɪks] **N** optique *f* VOIR GRAMMAIRE A10

optimal ['ɒptɪm(ə)l] **ADJ** optimal, -aux
▶▶ *Mktg* **o. price** prix *m* optimum; *Mktg* **o. pricing** fixation *f* du prix optimal; *Mktg* **o. psychological price** prix psychologique optimum

optimism ['ɒptɪmɪz(ə)m] **N** optimisme *m*

optimist ['ɒptɪmɪst] **N** optimiste *mf*; **ever the o.** l'éternel optimiste

optimistic [ɒptɪ'mɪstɪk] **ADJ** optimiste; **things are looking quite o.** les choses se présentent plutôt bien

optimistically [ɒptɪ'mɪstɪklɪ] **ADV** d'une manière optimiste, avec optimisme; **they o. predicted record profits** ils se sont montrés optimistes et ont prédit des bénéfices record

optimize ['ɒptɪmaɪz] **VT** *Comput* optimiser

optimizer ['ɒptɪmaɪzər] **N** *Comput* optimiseur *m*

optimum, *pl* **optima** ['ɒptɪməm, -ɪmə] **N** optimum *m*
ADJ o. conditions conditions *fpl* optimums *ou* optima

option ['ɒpʃən] **N 1** *(choice)* option *f*, choix *m*; **I can see no other o.** je ne vois pas d'autre solution; **the military o.** l'option militaire; **to have the o. of doing sth** avoir la possibilité *ou* le choix de faire qch; **we have the o. of staying here** nous avons la possibilité de rester ici; **to give** *or* **allow sb the o. of doing sth** donner à qn la possibilité de faire qch; **he didn't give me much o.** il ne m'a pas vraiment donné le choix; **we have no o. but to agree** nous ne pouvons rien faire d'autre que donner notre accord; **I haven't got any o., I've got no o.** je n'ai pas le choix; **do I have any o.?** est-ce que j'ai le choix?; **you leave me no o. but to phone the police** vous ne me laissez pas d'autre choix que celui d'appeler la police; *Law* **imprisonment without the o. of a fine** emprisonnement sans substitution d'amende; **which of them is the best o.?** lequel est le meilleur choix?; **there was no soft o.** il n'y avait pas de solution facile; **it's no soft o.** ce n'est pas une partie de plaisir; **they always go for the soft o.** ils choisissent toujours la solution de facilité; **it's best to leave** *or* **keep your options open** il est préférable d'envisager toutes les possibilités; **to consider** *or* **review one's options** considérer toutes les lignes d'action possibles **2** *Com, St Exch etc* option *f*, *(marché m à)* prime *f*; **o. on shares** option sur actions; **o. to double** option du double; **o. to buy** option d'achat; **o. to sell** option de vente; **to take an o. on sth** prendre une option sur qch; *St Exch* **buyer's/seller's o.** prime acheteur/vendeur; *St Exch* **to take up an o.** lever une prime

VT *Cin (book)* prendre une option sur les droits de
▶▶ *Comput* **o. box** case *f* d'option; *Comput* **o. button** case d'option; *St Exch* **o. date** jour *m* d'option; *St Exch* **o. day** (jour de la) réponse *f* des primes; *St Exch* **o. deal** opération *f* à prime; **options desk** desk *m* d'options; *Comput* **o. key** touche *f* Option; *St Exch* **options market** marché à options *ou* à primes; *St Exch* **o. money** (montant *m* de la) prime; *St Exch* **o. price** prix *m* de l'option; *St Exch* **o. spread** écart *m* de prime; *St Exch* **options trading** négociations *fpl* à prime

optional ['ɒpʃən(ə)l] **ADJ** facultatif; **evening dress is o.** la tenue de soirée n'est pas de rigueur; **o. retirement at sixty** préretraite *f* à soixante ans
▶▶ **o. extras** accessoires *mpl* en option; *Mktg* **o.-feature pricing** fixation *f* du prix en fonction des options; *Sch* **o. subjects** *(one must be chosen)* matières *fpl* à option *ou* optionnelles; *(possible to choose none)* matières facultatives

optionee [ɒpʃə'niː] **N** *St Exch* bénéficiaire *mf* d'options

optomagnetic [ɒptəmæg'netɪk] **ADJ** magnéto-optique

optometrist [ɒp'tɒmɪtrɪst] **N** optométriste *mf*

opt-out ADJ ATTRIB *(clause, provisions)* de désengagement
N désengagement *m*

opulence ['ɒpjʊləns] **N** *(wealth)* opulence *f*, richesse *f*

opulent ['ɒpjʊlənt] **ADJ 1** *(wealthy)* opulent **2** *(plentiful)* généreux, opulent

opulently ['ɒpjʊləntlɪ] **ADV** *(to dress, decorate, dine etc)* avec opulence; *(to live)* dans l'opulence

opus, *pl* **opuses** *or* **opera** ['əʊpəs, 'ɒp-, -əsɪz, 'ɔpərə] **N** opus *m*

or [ɔːr, *unstressed* ər] **CONJ** ou; *(with neg)* ni; **do you want beef or ham?** voulez-vous du bœuf ou du jambon?; **either one or the other** soit l'un soit l'autre, l'un ou l'autre; **either come in or (else) go out** entrez ou (bien) sortez; **don't move or (else) I'll shoot** pas un geste ou je tire; **either you or he has done it** c'est vous ou (c'est) lui qui l'a fait; **without money or luggage** sans argent ni bagages; **in a day or two** dans un ou deux jours; **a mile or so** environ un mil(l)e; **did she do it or not?** est-ce qu'elle l'a fait ou pas?; **we could go to the beach or we could go to the zoo** nous pourrions aller soit à la plage soit au zoo; *Fam* **do it now or else** fais-le tout de suite ou sinon … (ça va aller mal) VOIR GRAMMAIRE A74

oracle ['ɒrək(ə)l] **N** oracle *m*; *(priest, priestess)* oracle; **the Delphic o.** l'oracle de Delphes; **to consult the o.** consulter les oracles

oracular [ɒ'rækjʊlər] **ADJ 1** *(relating to an oracle)* oraculaire **2** *Fig (wise)* prophétique; *(mysterious)* sibyllin

oracy ['ɒrəsɪ] **N** *Fml* facultés *fpl* orales

oral ['ɔːrəl] **ADJ** *(agreement, tradition, contraceptive)* oral, -aux; *(vaccine)* buccal, -aux; *(administration of medication)* par la bouche, par voie orale
N *Sch* (examen *m*) oral *m*
▶▶ *Anat* **o. cavity** cavité *f* orale *ou* buccale; *Sch* **o. examination** (examen) oral; **o. sex** rapports *mpl* bucco-génitaux; *(fellatio)* fellation *f*, *(cunnilingus)* cunnilingus *m*

Attention: ne pas confondre avec *aural*.

orally ['ɔːrəlɪ] **ADV** oralement, de vive voix; *Pharm* par la bouche, par voie orale

Orange ['ɒrɪndʒ] **N 1** *Geog* **the O. (River)** l'Orange *m* **2** *Hist* **the Prince of O.** le prince d'Orange; **William of O.** Guillaume d'Orange

orange ['ɒrɪndʒ] **N 1** *(fruit)* orange *f* **2** *(tree)* oranger *m* **3** *(colour)* orange *m*, orangé *m*
ADJ *(colour)* orangé, orange *inv*
▶▶ **o. blossom** fleur *f ou* fleurs *fpl* d'oranger; **o. flower water** eau *f* de fleur d'oranger; **O. Free State** l'État *m* libre d'Orange; **o. grove** orangeraie *f*, **o. juice** jus *m* d'orange; **o. marmalade** marmelade *f* d'orange, confiture *f* d'orange *ou* d'oranges; **O. Order** ordre *m* des Orangistes; **o. peel** écorce *f ou* peau *f* d'orange; *Fig (cellulite)* peau d'orange; **o. red** rouge *m* orangé; **o. segment** quartier *m* d'orange; **o. squash** boisson *f* à l'orange; **o. stick** bâtonnet *m* (de) manucure; **O. Walk** = défilé *m* des Orangistes, le 12 juillet; **o. tree** oranger *m*

Orange marches

Depuis des siècles, les Orangistes défilent dans les villes d'Irlande du Nord pour commémorer les dates clés de l'histoire du protestantisme en Irlande. L'événement le plus important fut la bataille de la Boyne en 1690 où le protestant Guillaume d'Orange l'emporta sur Jacques II, roi catholique déposé. Les Orangistes sont farouchement attachés à la Couronne britannique et s'opposent à tout rapprochement avec la République d'Irlande. Leurs défilés annuels donnent souvent lieu à de violents affrontements, notamment quand ils traversent les quartiers catholiques.

---

orangeade [ɒrɪn'dʒeɪd] **N** *(fizzy)* soda *m* (à l')orange, boisson *f* gazeuse à l'orange

Orangeman, *pl* **Orangemen** ['ɒrɪndʒmən] **N** *Br* = Orangiste *m* (du parti protestant de l'Irlande du Nord)

orangery ['ɒrɪndʒərɪ] **N** orangerie *f*

orang-outang, orang-utan [ɔːræŋuːˈtæŋ, -'tæn] **N** *(ape)* orang-outan(g) *m*, *pl* orangs-outan(g)s

oration [ɔːˈreɪʃən] **N** allocution *f*, discours *m*; **funeral o.** oraison *f* funèbre

orator ['ɒrətər] **N** orateur, -trice

oratorical [ɒrə'tɒrɪk(ə)l] **ADJ** *(style, talent)* oratoire; **o. emphasis** accent *m* oratoire

oratorio [ɒrə'tɔːrɪəʊ] **N** *Mus* oratorio *m*

oratory [1] ['ɒrət(ə)rɪ] **N** *(art)* art *m* oratoire; *(speaking skill)* éloquence *f*, **powers of o.** facultés *fpl* oratoires; **a brilliant piece of o.** brillant spécimen d'art oratoire; **flight of o.** envolée *f* éloquente

oratory [2] **N** *Rel* oratoire *m*

orb [ɔːb] **N** globe *m*, sphère *f*, *(of regalia)* globe *m*; *Arch, Lit (planet etc)* orbe *m*; **the o. of the sun** le globe du soleil; **the o. and the sceptre** l'orbe et le sceptre

orbit ['ɔːbɪt] **N 1** *(of planet, space vehicle)*, *Fig (of country)* orbite *f*, **in o.** en orbite; **to enter** *or* **go into o.** se mettre *ou* se placer en orbite; **to send a satellite into o.** lancer un satellite en orbite, mettre un satellite sur orbite; *Fig* **the family o.** le cercle familial; *Fam* **to go into o.** *(get angry)* entrer en furie **2** *Anat (of eye)* orbite *f* **3** *Fig (scope)* domaine *m*; **such matters don't come within the o. of my department** ces affaires-là ne sont pas du domaine de mon service *ou* ne relèvent pas de mon service
VT to o. the sun décrire une orbite *ou* orbiter autour du soleil
VI *(of satellite etc)* être en orbite, décrire une orbite

orbital ['ɔːbɪt(ə)l] **ADJ 1** *Astron etc* orbital, -aux **2** *Anat (cavity etc)* orbitaire
N *Br (road)* périphérique *m*
▶▶ *Br* **o. road** périphérique

Orcadian [ɔːˈkeɪdɪən] **N** habitant, -ante des

îles Orcades; *(native)* originaire *mf* des îles Orcades
ADJ des îles Orcades

orchard ['ɔːtʃəd] **N** verger *m*; **apple o.** pommeraie *f*

orchestra ['ɔːkɪstrə] **N** *Mus* orchestre *m*; *Am Theat* **the o.** les fauteuils *mpl* d'orchestre
VOIR GRAMMAIRE A11
▸▸ **o. pit** fosse *f* d'orchestre; **o. stalls** fauteuils d'orchestre

orchestral [ɔːˈkestr(ə)l] **ADJ** orchestral, -aux

orchestrate ['ɔːkɪstreɪt] **VT** *(symphony etc)*, *Fig (press campaign etc)* orchestrer

orchestration [ɔːkɪsˈtreɪʃən] **N** orchestration *f*

orchid ['ɔːkɪd] **N** *(plant)* orchidée *f*, *(wild)* orchis *m*

orchis ['ɔːkɪs] **N** *(plant)* orchis *m*

ordain [ɔːˈdeɪn] **VT 1** *(decree)* ordonner, fixer; *(measure)* décréter; **fate ordained *or* it was ordained that we should meet** il était écrit que nous nous rencontrerions, le sort a voulu que nous nous rencontrions **2** *Rel (priest)* ordonner; **to be ordained** être ordonné, recevoir les ordres

ordeal [ɔːˈdiːl] **N 1** épreuve *f*; **to go through a terrible o.** subir *ou* passer par une terrible épreuve; **it is an o. for me to make a speech** je suis au supplice quand je dois faire un discours; **they spoke of their o.** ils ont évoqué le supplice *ou* l'épreuve qu'ils ont vécu(e) **2** *Law, Hist* épreuve *f* judiciaire, ordalie *f*; **o. by fire** épreuve du feu

ORDER ['ɔːdər]

N ordre **1, 3, 4, 7–10** ▪ commande **2**
▪ mandat **3** ▪ état **5** ▪ classe **10**
VT ordonner **1, 4** ▪ commander **2**
▪ classer **3**
VI commander

N 1 *(instruction)* ordre *m*; *Mil* ordre, consigne *f*; **I have orders to remain here** j'ai ordre de rester ici; **to give orders/an o.** donner des ordres/un ordre; **he gave orders for the trunks to be packed** il donna l'ordre de boucler les malles; **to obey *or* follow orders** obéir aux ordres, suivre la consigne; **our orders are to ...** nous avons l'ordre de ...; **to be under orders from the President** tenir ses ordres du Président; **and that's an o.!** c'est un ordre!; **orders are orders** les ordres sont les ordres; *Fig* **I don't take (my) orders from him** je ne suis pas à ses ordres; **until further orders** jusqu'à nouvel avis *ou* ordre; **by o. of the King** par ordre du roi, de par le roi **2** *(in restaurant)*, *Com* commande *f*; **to place an o. with sb, to give sb an o.** passer une commande à qn, commander qch à qn; **to fill an o.** exécuter une commande; **to deliver an o.** livrer une commande; **your o. has now arrived** votre commande est arrivée; **as per o.** conformément à votre commande; **another firm got the o.** ils ont passé la commande auprès d'une autre compagnie; **it's on o.** c'est commandé; **made to o.** fabriqué sur commande; *(suit)* fait sur mesure; **I can't do it to o.** ça ne se commande pas; **have you given your o.?** *(in restaurant)* est-ce que vous avez commandé?; **have they taken your o.?** est-ce qu'on a pris votre commande?; *Am* **an o. of French fries** une portion de frites **3** *(document)* ordre *m*; *Com, Admin* bon *m*; *Fin* mandat *m*; **deportation o.** arrêté *m* d'expulsion; *Fin* **pay to the o. of J. Martin** payez à l'ordre de J. Martin; **pay J. Martin o.** payez à J. Martin ou à son ordre; **by o. and for account of J. Martin** d'ordre et pour compte de J. Martin; **cheque to o.** chèque *m* à ordre **4** *(peace, harmony)* ordre *m*; **to keep or**

maintain o. in a town assurer *ou* maintenir l'ordre dans une ville; *Sch* **to keep o. in class** maintenir la discipline dans une classe; **to establish/restore o.** mettre de/rétablir l'ordre **5** *(condition)* **machine in (good) working o.** machine *f* en (bon) état de fonctionnement *ou* de marche; **out of o.** *(mechanism)* détraqué, dérangé; *(telephone)* en dérangement; *(lift, machine)* en panne **6** *(in meeting etc)* **to rule a question out of o.** statuer qu'une interpellation n'est pas dans les règles; *Br Fam* **you're out of o.!** tu as dépassé les bornes!; **to call sb to o.** rappeler qn à l'ordre; *Parl* **o.! o.!** de l'ordre!; *Law* **o. in court!** silence dans la salle! **7** *(tidiness, organization)* ordre *m*; **in o.** *(as it should be)* en ordre; *(document)* en règle, conforme à la règle; **to put things in o.** mettre les choses en ordre; **to put *or* set one's affairs in o.** mettre ses affaires en ordre, régler ses affaires; *Fig* **to set one's house in o.** remettre de l'ordre dans ses affaires **8** *(system)* ordre *m*; **the old o. is changing** l'ancien ordre des choses devient caduc; **it's not in the natural o. of things** ce n'est pas dans l'ordre des choses; **I think a celebration is in o.** je pense que ça mérite d'être fêté; **it's perfectly in o. for them to ask for your papers** ils ont parfaitement le droit de vous demander vos papiers **9** *(sequence)* ordre *m*; **in the correct *or* right/wrong o.** dans le bon ordre/le désordre; **in alphabetical/chronological o.** en *ou* par ordre alphabétique/chronologique; **in o. of age** par rang d'âge; *Theat, Cin* **in o. of appearance** par ordre d'apparition; **o. of battle** ordre de bataille **10** *(class)* classe *f*, *Biol* ordre *m*; **the higher/lower orders (of society)** les classes supérieures/inférieures; **workmanship of the highest o.** travail *m* de premier ordre; **population of *or* in *or* *Am* on the o. of 100,000** population *f* de l'ordre de 100 000 habitants; **o. of magnitude** ordre de grandeur; **a disaster/a project/investment of this o. (of magnitude)** un désastre/un projet/des investissements de cette envergure; *Archit* **Ionic/Doric o.** ordre ionique/dorique; *Rel* **to take holy orders** entrer dans les ordres; **to be in (holy) orders** être prêtre/moine/religieuse; **monastic o.** ordre monastique; **o. of knighthood** ordre de chevalerie **11** **in o. to do sth** afin de *ou* pour faire qch; **in o. that they understand** afin *ou* pour qu'ils comprennent VOIR GRAMMAIRE A75
VT 1 **to o. sb to do sth** ordonner à qn de faire qch; **she ordered them into her office/off the premises** elle leur a ordonné d'entrer dans son bureau/de quitter les lieux; **he's been ordered to report tomorrow** il a reçu l'ordre de se présenter demain; **he ordered them into battle** il leur a donné l'ordre de livrer bataille; *Law* **to be ordered to pay costs** être condamné aux dépens **2** *(in restaurant)*, *Com* commander; **to o. goods from Paris** commander des marchandises à Paris; **we can o. it for you** nous pouvons vous le commander; **to o. a taxi** (faire) appeler un taxi; **what have you ordered for dessert?** qu'est-ce que vous avez commandé comme dessert? **3** *(arrange) (furniture etc)* arranger; *(papers, books etc)* classer, ranger; *(one's life)* ordonner, agencer; *(one's thoughts)* mettre de l'ordre dans; **to o. sth according to author/size** classer *ou* ranger qch par auteur/taille; **to o. one's affairs** mettre ses affaires en ordre; *Mil* **o. arms!** reposez armes! **4** *Med (treatment)* prescrire, ordonner; *Fig* **that's just what the doctor ordered** c'est exactement ce qu'il me fallait
VI *(in restaurant)* commander
▸▸ *Com* **o. book** carnet *m* de commandes;

o. in council = décret *m* du gouvernement, arrêté ministériel; *(statutory order)* décret-loi *m*, *pl* décrets-lois; *Law* **o. of the court** injonction *f* de la cour; *Com* **o. cycle time** durée *f* du cycle de commande; *Mil, (in meeting etc)* **o. of the day** ordre du jour; *Fig* **simplicity/optimism was the o. of the day** la simplicité/l'optimisme était de rigueur; **promiscuity/extravagance was the o. of the day in Ancient Rome** la promiscuité sexuelle/un faste somptuaire était monnaie courante dans la Rome antique; *Com* **o. department** service *m* des commandes; **o. form** bon de commande; **the O. of the Garter** l'ordre de la Jarretière; **the O. of Merit** l'ordre du Mérite; *Com* **o. number** numéro *m* de commande; *Pol* **o. paper** (feuille *f* de l') ordre du jour; **o. to pay, o. for payment** ordonnance *f* de paiement; *Com* **o. processing** traitement *m* des commandes; *Com* **o. to remittance cycle** cycle *m* commande-livraison-facturation; **o. to sell** ordre de vente; *Rel* **o. of service** office *m*; *Com* **o. taking** prise *f* de commande; **o. to view** permis *m* de visiter *(une maison à vendre)*
▸ **order about, order around VT SEP** *(person)* commander; **he likes ordering people about** il aime commander les autres; **you can't o. me about!** je n'ai pas d'ordres à recevoir de toi
▸ **order in VT SEP** *(supplies, food)* commander; *(police, troops)* faire venir
▸ **order off VT SEP** *Sport (player)* expulser *(du terrain)*
▸ **order out VT SEP** *(from room etc)* mettre dehors
▸ **order up VT SEP 1** *(troops, air support etc)* faire monter
2 *(stationery supplies, round of drinks etc)* commander

order-driven **ADJ** *St Exch (market)* dirigé par les ordres

ordered ['ɔːdəd] **ADJ** ordonné; *(in good order)* en bon ordre; **an o. life** une vie régulière *ou* réglée

orderer ['ɔːdərər] **N** acheteur *m*

orderliness ['ɔːdəlɪnɪs] **N 1** *(methodical nature)* méthode *f*, *(of existence)* caractère *m* rangé *ou* réglé; **the o. of her records/room/papers/etc** le bon ordre dans lequel se trouvaient ses dossiers/sa chambre/ses papiers/etc **2** *(discipline)* *(of crowd, football supporters etc)* discipline *f*, *(of pupils)* bonne conduite *f*

orderly ['ɔːdəlɪ] **ADJ 1** *(arrangement)* ordonné, méthodique; *(room etc)* en ordre, ordonné, rangé; *(life)* réglé, rangé, régulier; *(mind)* méthodique; **to be very o.** *(of person)* avoir beaucoup de méthode; **to do sth in an o. way *or* manner** faire qch avec beaucoup de méthode **2** *(crowd)* discipliné; **leave the building in an o. fashion** quittez l'immeuble dans l'ordre et avec calme; **an o. retreat/withdrawal** une retraite/un repli ordonné(e)
N 1 *Mil* planton *m*; **to be on o. duty** être de planton **2** **hospital o., medical o.** aide-infirmier, -ière, *pl* aides-infirmiers, -ières; *Mil* infirmier *m*, ambulancier *m*
▸▸ *Br Mil* **o. officer** officier *m* de permanence; *Mil* **o. room** salle *f* des rapports

ordinal ['ɔːdɪn(ə)l] **ADJ** *(number)* ordinal, -aux VOIR GRAMMAIRE A76; B59
N *(number)* nombre *m* ordinal

ordinance ['ɔːdɪnəns] **N** *Fml (decree)* ordonnance *f*, règlement *m*

ordinand ['ɔːdɪnænd] **N** *Rel* ordinand *m*

ordinarily ['ɔːdɪn(ə)rɪlɪ, *Am* ɔːdɪˈneːrɪlɪ] **ADV 1** *(in an everyday manner)* normalement; **he was quite o. dressed** il était habillé de façon tout à fait banale; **a more than o. gifted/stupid child** un enfant d'une intelligence/stupidité supérieure à la normale; **a more than o. attractive woman** une femme d'une beauté exceptionnelle **2** (usually) d'habitude, ordinairement, d'ordinaire; **did he seem nervous? – not more than he o. is** est-ce qu'il avait l'air nerveux? – pas plus que d'habitude ou qu'à l'ordinaire

ordinary [ˈɔːdɪn(ə)rɪ] ADJ ordinaire; **she was just an o. tourist** c'était une touriste comme une autre; **this is no o. house/car** ce n'est pas une maison/voiture ordinaire; **in the o. course of events, in the o. run of things** d'ordinaire; Pej **a very o. kind of man** un homme tout à fait ordinaire ou quelconque; **an o. Englishman** un Anglais moyen ou typique

▸ N**1** ordinaire m; **out of the o.** exceptionnel, qui sort de l'ordinaire; **nothing out of the o. happened** il n'est rien arrivé d'inhabituel ou d'exceptionnel **2** Rel **the O. (of the Mass)** l'Ordinaire m (de la messe)

▸▸**o. activities** Com activités fpl ordinaires; Acct (balance sheet item) opérations fpl courantes; Fin **o. creditor** créancier, -ière ordinaire; Br Sch Formerly **O.-level,** Scot **O.-grade** = examen m qui sanctionnait autrefois la fin des études au niveau de la seconde, ≃ BEPC m; **o. seaman** matelot m breveté; Br St Exch **o. share** action f ordinaire; Br St Exch **o. share capital** capital m en actions ordinaires

ordinate [ˈɔːdɪnɪt] N Math ordonnée f

ordination [ɔːdɪˈneɪʃən] N Rel ordination f

ordnance [ˈɔːdnəns] N**1** Mil (unit) (service m du) matériel m; Br **Royal Army O. Corps** Service m du Matériel; **o. and supplies** les ravitaillements mpl **2** Mil (artillery) artillerie f, **piece of o.** bouche f à feu, pièce f d'artillerie

▸▸**o. factory** usine f d'artillerie; Am **O. Service** Service du Matériel; Br **O. Survey** service m national de cartographie, ≃ IGN m

ordure [ˈɔːdjʊər] N Lit ordure f

ore [ɔːr] N minerai m; **iron/aluminium o.** minerai de fer/d'aluminium; **rich** or **high-grade o.** minerai à ou de haute teneur

▸▸**o. deposit** gisement m de minerai

Ore(g) abbr **Oregon**

oregano [ɒrɪˈɡɑːnəʊ] N Bot, Culin origan m

.org [dɒtˈɔːɡ] Comput = abréviation f désignant les organisations à but non lucratif dans les adresses électroniques

organ [ˈɔːɡən] N**1** Mus orgue m; Rel orgues fpl; **grand o.** grand orgue, grandes orgues; **choir o.** orgue du chœur; **American o.** orgue de salon; **street o.** orgue de Barbarie **2** Anat (of human body, plant) organe m; Euph (penis) membre m; **o. of hearing** organe de l'ouïe; **the vocal organs** l'appareil m vocal **3** Fig (instrument) (of government) organe m; (newspaper) (of government, party) organe, porte-parole m inv; **an efficient o. of propaganda** un organe de propagande efficace; **the official o.** l'organe officiel

▸▸**o. builder** facteur m d'orgues; **o. gallery, o. loft** tribune f d'orgue; **o. pipe** tuyau m d'orgue; **o. stop** jeu m d'orgue; **o. transplant** transplantation f d'organe

organdie [ˈɔːɡəndɪ] N Tex organdi m; **o. dress** robe f d'organdi

organ-grinder N joueur, -euse d'orgue de Barbarie; Fig **I want to speak to the o., not the monkey** je veux parler au responsable, pas au sous-fifre

organic [ɔːˈɡænɪk] ADJ**1** organique; (fertilizer) organique, biologique; Ecol (food, farming, gardening etc) biologique **2** (structural) organique; (fundamental) organique, fondamental, -aux; **an o. whole** un ensemble systématique, un tout intégré; **o. growth/change** croissance f/changement m natu-

rel(elle) ou spontané(ée); **an o. part** une partie intégrante

▸▸**o. chemist** organicien, -ienne; **o. chemistry** chimie f organique

> Note that the French word **organique** is never used in relation to food or farming.

organically [ɔːˈɡænɪklɪ] ADV**1** organiquement; (to farm, garden) avec un engrais organique; **o. grown foods** produits mpl biologiques **2** Fig **to change/grow o.** changer/grandir naturellement ou spontanément; Fig **to be o. linked** être fondamentalement lié

organigram [ɔːˈɡænɪɡræm] N organigramme m

organism [ˈɔːɡənɪz(ə)m] N organisme m

organist [ˈɔːɡənɪst] N organiste mf

organization [ɔːɡənaɪˈzeɪʃən] N**1** (action) organisation f, Ind **o. and methods** organisation f scientifique du travail; Ind **o. and methods department** bureau m des méthodes **2** (association) organisation f, organisme m; **charity o.** organisation charitable, œuvre f de charité; **youth o.** mouvement m de jeunesse **3** Ind (of labour) syndicalisation f

▸▸**o. chart** organigramme m; **o. tree** organigramme m en arborescence

organizational [ɔːɡənaɪˈzeɪʃən(ə)l] ADJ (defect, skills etc) d'organisation, de structure, organisationnel

▸▸**o. buyer** acheteur, -euse (pour une organisation); **o. marketer** mercaticien, -ienne au sein d'une organisation

organizationally [ɔːɡənaɪˈzeɪʃən(ə)lɪ] ADV du point de vue de l'organisation; **he doesn't get involved o. in the project** il n'est pas impliqué au niveau de l'organisation du projet

organize [ˈɔːɡənaɪz] VT**1** (sort out, put into groups etc) organiser; **to o. people into work groups** répartir les gens dans des groupes de travail

2 (arrange, bring about) (concert, party etc) organiser; (transport, food, accommodation) s'occuper de; (money) s'occuper de trouver; (one's time) organiser, aménager; Fam (a day off etc) se faire accorder; **she organized it so that we got in free** elle s'est arrangée pour que nous puissions entrer sans payer; **I'll just go and o. something to eat** (do it myself) je vais préparer quelque chose à manger; **don't worry, it's all organized** ne t'inquiète pas, tout est organisé

3 Ind (workers) syndiquer

▸ VI **1** s'organiser **2** Ind (of workers) se syndiquer

organized [ˈɔːɡənaɪzd] ADJ (society, person, files) organisé

▸▸**o. crime** le crime organisé; Sch **o. games** jeux mpl dirigés; **o. labour** main-d'œuvre f syndiquée, pl mains-d'œuvre syndiquées; **o. religion** religion f organisée

organizer [ˈɔːɡənaɪzər] N (person) organisateur, -trice; (diary etc) organiseur m; (electronic) agenda m (électronique); (software) organiseur m; **she's a born o.** elle a le sens de l'organisation, c'est une organisatrice née

organizing [ˈɔːɡənaɪzɪŋ] ADJ ATTRIB (ability, committee) d'organisation

orgasm [ˈɔːɡæz(ə)m] N Physiol orgasme m; **to have an o.** avoir un orgasme, jouir; Fig Sl **they were having orgasms** ça les faisait bander, ils ont trouvé ça jouissif ou bandant

orgasmic [ɔːˈɡæzmɪk] ADJ Physiol orgastique; Sl (pleasure, experience etc) jouissif

orgiastic [ɔːdʒɪˈæstɪk] ADJ orgiaque

orgy [ˈɔːdʒɪ] N (sexual), Fig (of colour) orgie f; (of violence) déchaînement m; **orgies** (in an-

cient Greece, Rome) orgies, bacchanales fpl; **drunken o.** beuverie f, Fam soûlerie f

oriel [ˈɔːrɪəl] N Archit oriel m

▸▸**o. window** oriel m

orient[1] [ˈɔːrɪənt] N orient m; **the O.** l'Orient m

orient[2] [ˈɔːrɪənt] VT = **orientate**

oriental [ɔːrɪˈent(ə)l] ADJ oriental, -aux N **O.** (person) Oriental, -ale

▸▸**o. rug** tapis m d'Orient

orientalist [ɔːrɪˈentəlɪst] N orientaliste mf

orientate [ˈɔːrɪənteɪt] VT (map) orienter; **to o. oneself** (physically, psychologically) s'orienter

orientation [ɔːrɪənˈteɪʃən] N orientation f

▸▸esp Am **o. course** cours m d'introduction

oriented [ˈɔːrɪəntɪd] ADJ orienté

-oriented [ˈɔːrɪəntɪd] SUFF **profit-o.** axé sur le profit; **youth-o.** qui s'adresse à la jeunesse; Comput **computer-o. language** langage orienté machine; **export-o.** (company, industry) tourné vers l'exportation

orienteering [ɔːrɪənˈtɪərɪŋ] N Sport course f d'orientation

orifice [ˈɒrɪfɪs] N orifice m

origami [ɒrɪˈɡɑːmɪ] N (art m du) pliage m, origami m

origin [ˈɒrɪdʒɪn] N**1** origine f; **to trace an event back to its o.** remonter à l'origine d'un événement; **to have its origins in …** tirer son origine de …; **the custom has its o.** or **origins in …** l'origine de cette coutume est …; Archit **point of o.** (of curve etc) point m d'origine; **word/woman of Greek o.** mot m/ femme d'origine grecque; **a man of humble o.** un homme d'humble origine ou extraction; Com **country of o.** pays m d'origine; Com **certificate of o.** certificat m d'origine **2** Anat (of muscle) attache f

▸▸Com **o. of goods label** marque f d'origine

original [əˈrɪdʒɪn(ə)l] ADJ**1** (first) (suggestion, idea etc) premier, initial, -aux; (manuscript, painting) original, -aux; **the o. colour** la couleur d'origine; **the o. members of the band** les premiers membres du groupe; TV etc **based on an o. idea by …** d'après une idée originale de …; **the o. meaning of a word** le sens premier d'un mot; **in the o. Chinese** dans le texte original en chinois/dans le texte chinois d'origine; **to translate from the o. German** traduire d'après le texte allemand original **2** (innovative) (writer, style, idea, approach etc) original, -aux

N**1** (of painting, invoice etc) original m; Fin (of bill of exchange) primata m; **to copy sth from the o.** copier qch sur l'original; **to read the classics in the o.** lire les classiques dans le texte **2** Fam (person) original, -ale

▸▸Fin **o. capital** capital m d'origine; Fin **o. cost** coût m initial; Com **o. defect** vice m originaire; Acct **o. document** pièce f comptable; **o. edition** édition f originale; **o. guarantee** garantie f d'origine; Fin, Com **o. invoice** facture f originale; Com **o. packaging, o. packing** emballage m d'origine; Rel **o. sin** péché m originel; Fin **o. value** valeur f initiale ou d'origine; Cin **o. version** version f originale, VO f

> When translating **original**, note that the French words **originel** and **original** are not interchangeable.

originality [ərɪdʒɪˈnælɪtɪ] N originalité f

originally [əˈrɪdʒɪn(ə)lɪ] ADV**1** (initially, to begin with) à l'origine, au départ; **the building was o. used as a warehouse** à l'origine ou au départ, l'immeuble servait d'entrepôt; **o. we come from Hampshire** nous sommes originaires du Hampshire; **where do you come from o.?** d'où êtes-vous originaire?; **that's what I o. thought** c'est ce que je pensais au début *ou* au départ; **I o. heard about it in Spain** c'est en Espagne que j'en ai entendu parler pour la première fois **2** *(in an innovative way)* d'une façon originale, avec originalité

originate [əˈrɪdʒɪneɪt] **VI** *(of person)* être originaire (**from** de); *(of language)* dériver, provenir (**from** de); *(of river)* prendre sa source (**in** dans); **the fire originated under the floor** le feu a pris naissance sous le plancher; **the scheme originated with me** je suis à l'origine de ce projet, je suis l'auteur *ou* l'initiateur de ce projet; **the custom originated in France** cette coutume est née en France; **originating airline** compagnie *f* aérienne de départ
  VT donner naissance à, être l'auteur de; *(proposal)* être l'auteur de; *(reform, project etc)* être à l'origine de, être l'auteur *ou* l'initiateur, -trice de

originator [əˈrɪdʒɪneɪtər] **N** créateur, -trice; *(of proposal)* auteur *m*; *(of scheme)* auteur, initiateur, -trice

oriole [ˈɔːrɪəʊl] **N** *(bird)* loriot *m*, *Can* oriole *m*; **golden o.** loriot (jaune d'Europe)

Orkneys (the) [ðɪˈɔːknɪz] **NPL** les Orcades *fpl*

ormolu [ˈɔːməluː] **N** similor *m*

ornament[1] [ˈɔːnəmənt] **N 1** *(vase etc)* ornement *m* **2** *(no pl) (decoration) (of style, architecture etc)* ornements *mpl*; *(on dress etc)* garniture *f*, **by way of o.** pour ornement **3** *Mus* ornement *m*

ornament[2] [ˈɔːnəmənt] **VT** *(room etc)* orner, ornementer (**with** de); *(dress etc)* agrémenter, embellir (**with** de); *(one's style)* orner (**with** de)

ornamental [ɔːnəˈment(ə)l] **ADJ** décoratif, ornemental, -aux; **o. tree/plant** arbre *m*/plante *f* d'ornement; **o. lake** *or* **pond** pièce *f* d'eau

ornamentation [ɔːnəmenˈteɪʃən] **N** ornementation *f*

ornate [ɔːˈneɪt] **ADJ** orné, ornementé, *Pej* chargé; **o. style** style *m* imagé *ou* fleuri

ornately [ɔːˈneɪtlɪ] **ADV** de façon très ornementée, *Pej* avec une surabondance d'ornements; *(written)* dans un style très fleuri

ornery [ˈɔːnərɪ] **ADJ** *Am Fam (unpleasant)* désagréable; *(bad-tempered)* rouspéteur, -euse; *(stubborn)* têtu

ornithological [ɔːnɪθəˈlɒdʒɪk(ə)l] **ADJ** ornithologique

ornithologist [ɔːnɪˈθɒlədʒɪst] **N** ornithologue *mf*, ornithologiste *m*

ornithology [ɔːnɪˈθɒlədʒɪ] **N** ornithologie *f*

orotund [ˈɒrəʊtʌnd] **ADJ** *esp Lit (sound)* plein, riche; *(writing) (pompous)* emphatique, pompeux

orphan [ˈɔːfən] **N 1** orphelin, -ine; **to be left an o.** devenir orphelin; **war o.** pupille *mf* de la Nation **2** *Typ* orpheline *f*
  ADJ an o. child un orphelin, une orpheline
  VT he had been orphaned at the age of six il est devenu orphelin à l'âge de six ans; **they were orphaned by the war** ils ont perdu leurs parents pendant la guerre
  ▸▸ *Pharm* **o. drug** médicament *m* orphelin

orphanage [ˈɔːf(ə)nɪdʒ] **N** orphelinat *m*

Orpheus [ˈɔːfjuːs] **N** *Myth* Orphée *m*

orthodontics [ɔːθəˈdɒntɪks] **N** orthodontie *f* VOIR GRAMMAIRE A10

orthodontist [ɔːθəˈdɒntɪst] **N** orthodontiste *m*

orthodox [ˈɔːθədɒks] **ADJ 1** *Rel* orthodoxe; **the O. Church** l'Église *f* orthodoxe **2** *(historian etc)* traditionaliste, orthodoxe; *(method, opinion etc)* orthodoxe
  NPL *Rel* **the o.** *(people)* les orthodoxes *mpl*

---

orthodoxy [ˈɔːθədɒksɪ] **N 1** *(of doctrine, person's opinions)* orthodoxie *f* **2** *(in Jewish religion)* judaïsme *m* rabbinique

orthogonal [ɔːˈθɒɡən(ə)l] **ADJ** *Math* orthogonal, -aux

orthographic(al) [ɔːθəˈɡræfɪk, -ɪk(ə)l] **ADJ** orthographique

orthographically [ɔːθəˈɡræfɪklɪ] **ADV** orthographiquement

orthography [ɔːˈθɒɡrəfɪ] **N 1** *(spelling)* orthographe *f* **2** *Math* projection *f* orthogonale

orthopaedic, *Am* **orthopedic** [ɔːθəˈpiːdɪk] **ADJ** *Med (treatment, device)* orthopédique
  ▸▸ **o. surgeon** (chirurgien, -ienne) orthopédiste *mf*; **o. surgery** chirurgie *f* des os

orthopaedics, *Am* **orthopedics** [ɔːθəˈpiːdɪks] **N** *Med* orthopédie *f* VOIR GRAMMAIRE A10

orthopaedist, *Am* **orthopedist** [ɔːθəˈpiːdɪst] **N** *Med* orthopédiste *mf*

orthoptist [ɔːˈθɒptɪst] **N** orthoptiste *mf*

ortolan [ˈɔːtələn] **N** ortolan *m*
  ▸▸ **o. bunting** ortolan

Orwellian [ɔːˈwelɪən] **ADJ** orwellien

oryx [ˈɒrɪks] **N** *(antelope)* oryx *m*

OS [əʊˈes] **N** *Comput (abbr* **operating system**) système *m* d'exploitation

Oscar [ˈɒskər] **N** *Cin* oscar *m*; **the Oscars, O. night** *(ceremony)* la cérémonie des oscars, les oscars; **O.-winning film** film *m* primé aux oscars; **in her O.-winning role** dans le rôle qui lui a valu l'oscar

OSCE [əʊessiːˈiː] **N** *(abbr* **Organization for Security and Cooperation in Europe**) OSCE *f*

oscillate [ˈɒsɪleɪt] **VI** *Phys, Radio* osciller; *Fig* **to o. between two opinions** osciller *ou* balancer *ou* hésiter entre deux opinions

oscillating [ˈɒsɪleɪtɪŋ] **ADJ** *(electron)* oscillateur, -trice

oscillation [ɒsɪˈleɪʃən] **N** *(of pendulum etc)* oscillation *f*

oscillator [ˈɒsɪleɪtər] **N** oscillateur *m*; **o. valve** *or* **tube** lampe *f* oscillatrice

oscillatory [ˈɒsɪleɪt(ə)rɪ] **ADJ** oscillant, oscillatoire

oscillogram [ɒˈsɪləɡræm] **N** oscillogramme *m*

oscillograph [ɒˈsɪləɡræf] **N** oscillographe *m*

oscilloscope [ɒˈsɪləskəʊp] **N** *Elec* oscilloscope *m*

osculate [ˈɒskjuleɪt] **VI 1** *Fml, Hum (kiss)* s'embrasser **2** *Geom* **curve that osculates with a line** courbe osculatrice à une ligne (**at a point** en un point)

osculation [ɒskjuˈleɪʃən] **N** *Geom* osculation *f*; **point of o.** point *m* d'attouchement

osier [ˈəʊzɪər, ˈəʊʒər] **N** osier *m*; **o. basket** panier *m* d'osier
  ▸▸ **o. bed** oseraie *f*

osmosis [ɒzˈməʊsɪs] **N** *Chem, Physiol, Fig* osmose *f*

osmotic [ɒzˈmɒtɪk] **ADJ** *Chem, Physiol* osmotique

osprey [ˈɒspreɪ] **N 1** *(bird)* balbuzard *m* pêcheur *ou* fluviatile, *Can* aigle *m* pêcheur **2** *(feather)* aigrette *f*

ossicle [ˈɒsɪk(ə)l] **N** *Anat (of ear)* osselet *m*

ossification [ɒsɪfɪˈkeɪʃən] **N** ossification *f*

ossified [ˈɒsɪfaɪd] **ADJ** *(cartilage)* ossifié; *Fig (mind, ideas, social system)* sclérosé; *(person)* à l'esprit sclérosé; **the o. old fools who run this country** les vieux fossiles abrutis qui dirigent ce pays

ossify [ˈɒsɪfaɪ] **VI** *(of cartilage)* s'ossifier; *Fig (of person)* se fossiliser; *(of government, mind)* se scléroser

---

VT *(cartilage)* ossifier; *Fig* amener *ou* entraîner la sclérose de

ossuary [ˈɒsjʊərɪ] **N** ossuaire *m*

Ostend [ɒsˈtend] **N** Ostende

ostensible [ɒsˈtensɪb(ə)l] **ADJ** prétendu; **the o. justification for their action was …** la raison qu'ils ont avancée pour justifier leur acte était …

> Note that the French adjective **ostensible** is a false friend and is never a translation for the English adjective **ostensible**. It means **conspicuous**.

ostensibly [ɒˈstensɪblɪ] **ADV** en apparence, prétendument; **while the Confederation is o. a single state, …** alors qu'en apparence *ou* qu'officiellement la Confédération est un état unique, …; **he went out o. to buy some tobacco** il sortit sous prétexte d'acheter du tabac *ou* soi-disant pour acheter du tabac; **he married her o. for love** il l'a soi-disant épousée par amour

> Note that the French adverb **ostensiblement** is a false friend and is never a translation for the English adverb **ostensibly**. It means **conspicuously**.

ostentation [ɒstenˈteɪʃən] **N** ostentation *f*

ostentatious [ɒstenˈteɪʃəs] **ADJ** plein d'ostentation; *(person, attitude)* prétentieux, ostentatoire

ostentatiously [ɒstenˈteɪʃəslɪ] **ADV** avec ostentation, d'une manière ostentatoire; **to display sth o.** faire ostentation de qch; **to be o. rich** faire ostentation de sa richesse

ostentatiousness [ɒstenˈteɪʃəsnɪs] **N** = **ostentation**

osteoarthritis [ɒstɪəʊɑːˈθraɪtɪs] **N** *Med* arthrose *f*; **to have o.** avoir de l'arthrose

osteomyelitis [ɒstɪəʊmaɪˈlaɪtɪs] **N** *Med* ostéomyélite *f*

osteopath [ˈɒstɪəpæθ], *Am* also **osteopathist** [ɒstɪˈɒpəθɪst] **N** *Med* (médecin *m*) ostéopathe *mf*

osteopathy [ɒstɪˈɒpəθɪ] **N** *Med* ostéopathie *f*

osteoplasty [ˈɒstɪəʊˈplæstɪ] **N** ostéoplastie *f*

osteoporosis [ɒstɪəʊpɔːˈrəʊsɪs] **N** *Med* ostéoporose *f*

ostler [ˈɒslər] **N** *Hist* valet *m* d'écurie, garçon *m* d'écurie

ostracism [ˈɒstrəsɪz(ə)m] **N** ostracisme *m*; **to suffer the o. of the press** être frappé d'ostracisme par la presse

ostracize [ˈɒstrəsaɪz] **VT** frapper d'ostracisme, mettre au ban de la société; *(country, company)* frapper d'ostracisme; **she's been ostracized at work** on l'a mise en quarantaine au travail

ostrich [ˈɒstrɪtʃ] **N** autruche *f*; *Fig* **o. policy** politique *f* de l'autruche

OT [əʊˈtiː] **1** *(abbr* **Old Testament**) AT *m* **2** *abbr* **occupational therapy; occupational therapist**

OTC [əʊtiːˈsiː] **N 1** *Br Sch (abbr* **Officers' Training Corps**) corps *m* de formation des officiers **2** *St Exch (abbr* **over-the-counter**) hors cote
  ▸▸ *St Exch* **O. market** marché *m* hors cote

OTE [əʊtiːˈiː] **NPL** *Com (abbr* **on-target earnings**) salaire *m* de base plus commissions

OTH [əʊtiːˈeɪtʃ] *Mktg (abbr* **opportunity to hear**) ODE *f*

OTHER [ˈʌðər] **ADJ** autre; **the o. one** l'autre *mf*, **every o. day/week** un jour/une semaine sur deux, tous les deux jours/toutes les deux semaines; **the o. day** l'autre jour; **the o. four** les quatre autres; **potatoes and o. ve-**

getables pommes de terre et autres légumes; **o. people have seen it** d'autres l'ont vu; **o. people's property** le bien d'autrui; **any o. book** tout autre livre; *Acct* **o. debtors** (*item on balance sheet*) créances *fpl* diverses; *Br Mil* **o. ranks** = ensemble *m* des militaires non gradés; **no one o. than he knows it** nul autre que lui ne le sait, il n'y a que lui qui le sache; **somebody o. than me/you/her/***etc* quelqu'un d'autre; **all verbs o. than those in -er** tous les verbes autres que ceux en -er; **some woman or o.** une femme quelconque; **the o. woman/man** (*in relationship*) l'autre VOIR GRAMMAIRE A36–7; B15

PRON autre *mf*; **one after the o.** l'un après l'autre; **the others** les autres; **all the others are there** tous les autres sont là; **some ... others ...** les uns ... les autres ...; **have you got any others?** (*any more*) en avez-vous encore?; (*any different ones*) en avez-vous d'autres?; **I have no o.** je n'en ai pas d'autre; **for this reason, if for no o.** pour cette raison, à défaut d'une autre; **no** *or* **none o. than the great actress Greta Garbo** nulle autre que la grande Greta Garbo; **one or o. of us will see to it** l'un de nous y veillera; **others** (*other people*) les autres; (*not as grammatical subject*) autrui *m*; **to see oneself as others see one** se voir comme les autres nous voient; **they prefer you to all others** ils vous préfèrent à tout autre; **the property of others** le bien d'autrui; **someone or o. said ...** quelqu'un a dit ...; **something or o. I said** quelque chose que j'ai dû dire; **somehow or o.** d'une façon ou d'une autre; **to be somewhere or o.** être dans les parages VOIR GRAMMAIRE A36–7; B16

ADV autrement; **to see things o. than as they are** voir les choses autrement qu'elles ne le sont; **o. than that everything is fine** à part ça *ou* autrement, tout va bien; **she never speaks of them o. than admiringly** c'est toujours avec admiration qu'elle parle d'eux

N *Hum* **your significant o.** l'homme/la femme de ta vie; **to talk about this, that and the o.** parler de ci et ça; *Br Fam Hum* **to have a bit of the o.** (*sex*) s'envoyer en l'air

otherwise ['ʌðəwaɪz] ADV **1** (*differently*) autrement (**than** que); **he could not do o.** il n'a pas pu faire autrement; **to think o.** penser différemment *ou* autrement; **if she's not o. engaged** si elle n'est pas occupée à autre chose; (*socially*) si elle n'a pas d'autres obligations; **except where o. stated** sauf indication contraire; **all people rich or o.** tout le monde, riches et pauvres **2** (*apart from that*) à part cela *ou* ça, autrement; **o. he is quite sane** à part cela il est complètement sain d'esprit

ADJ **the facts were o.** les faits étaient différents *ou* autres; *Fml* **should it be o.** s'il en était autrement

CONJ autrement, sans quoi, sans cela; **do what I tell you, o. everything will go wrong** faites ce que je vous dis, autrement *ou* sans quoi *ou* sans cela tout ira de travers

otherworldly [ʌðə'wɜːldlɪ] ADJ détaché de ce monde

otic ['əʊtɪk] ADJ *Anat* otique

otitis [əʊ'taɪtɪs] N *Med* otite *f*

OTS [əʊtiː'es] *Mktg* (*abbr* **opportunity to see**) ODV *f*

OTT [əʊtiː'tiː] ADJ *esp Br Sl* (*abbr* **over the top**) exagéré; **there was no need to be quite so O. about it** ce n'était pas la peine d'en faire toute une histoire; **the house is nice, but the decor's a bit O.** la maison est bien, mais la décoration est un peu lourdingue

otter ['ɒtər] N (*animal*) loutre *f*; **sea o.** loutre de mer *ou* marine

▸▸**o. hound** chien *m* pour la chasse aux loutres

Ottoman ['ɒtəmən] *Hist* ADJ ottoman

N Ottoman, -ane

ottoman ['ɒtəmən] N (*furniture*) ottomane *f*

OU [əʊ'juː] N *Br Univ* (*abbr* **Open University**) = organisme *m* d'enseignement universitaire par correspondance doublé d'émissions de télévision et de radio éducatives

ouch [aʊtʃ] INT (*expressing pain*) aïe!, ouille!

ought[1] [ɔːt] V AUX VOIR GRAMMAIRE A60–1; B39 (*with present and past meaning; inv; ought not is frequently abbreviated to* **oughtn't**) **1** (*obligation*) **this o. to have been done before** on aurait dû *ou* il aurait fallu le faire avant; **to behave as one o.** se conduire comme il convient; **to drink more than one o.** boire plus que de raison; **I thought I o. to let you know about it** j'ai cru devoir vous en faire part; **one o. never to be unkind** il ne faut *ou* on ne doit jamais être malveillant **2** (*desirability*) **you o. to go and see it** vous devriez aller le voir; **you o. not to have waited** vous n'auriez pas dû attendre; **I o. to be going** il me faut partir; **you o. to have seen it!** tu aurais dû *ou* il fallait voir ça! **3** (*probability*) **they o. to be in Paris by now** ils doivent être à Paris maintenant; **you o. to be able to get £50 for it** tu devrais pouvoir en tirer 50 livres; **your horse o. to win** votre cheval devrait gagner; **you o. to know** vous êtes bien placé pour le savoir, vous devriez le savoir

ought[2] N *Arch, Lit* = **aught**

Ouija® ['wiːdʒə] N **O. (board)** oui-ja *m*

ounce[1] [aʊns] N (*measurement*) once *f*, = 28,35g.; (**troy**) **o.** (*of gold, silver*) = 31,1035g.; *Fig* **an o. of intelligence/humanity/***etc* une once *ou* un tant soit peu d'intelligence/d'humanité/etc; **if you had an o. of sense** si tu avais un gramme de bon sens; *Fig* **he hasn't an o. of courage** il n'a pas un sou de courage, il n'est pas courageux pour deux sous

ounce[2] N (*animal*) once *f*, panthère *f* des neiges

our ['aʊər] POSS ADJ VOIR GRAMMAIRE A30; A43; B21 notre, *pl* nos; **o. father and mother** notre père et mère, nos père et mère; **o. friends** nos ami(e)s; **o. two** les deux nôtres; *Com* **o. Mr Martin** M. Martin de notre maison

ours ['aʊəz] POSS PRON VOIR GRAMMAIRE A30; B21–2 le nôtre, la nôtre, *pl* les nôtres; **your house is larger than o.** votre maison est plus grande que la nôtre; **this is o.** ceci est à nous, ceci nous appartient; **o. is a nation of travellers** nous sommes une nation de voyageurs; **a friend of o.** un(e) de nos ami(e)s, un(e) ami(e) à nous; **it's no business of o.** cela ne nous regarde pas

ourself [aʊə'self] PERS PRON (*said by monarch, editor etc*) nous-même

ourselves [aʊə'selvz] PERS PRON PL VOIR GRAMMAIRE P. 29–30 **1** (*emphatic*) nous-mêmes; **we o. do not believe it** nous, pour notre part, ne le croyons pas **2** (*reflexive*) nous; **we are enjoying o. very much** nous nous amusons bien SEE GRAMMAR B28 **3** (*after preposition*) nous, nous-mêmes; **we say to o.** nous nous disons; **we shouldn't talk about o.** on ne doit pas parler de soi; **instead of fighting among o.** au lieu de nous battre entre nous

ousel ['uːz(ə)l] N = **ouzel**

oust [aʊst] VT **1** évincer; **the ousted ruler** le dirigeant évincé; **to o. sb from his post** déloger qn de son poste **2** *Law* (*deprive*) déposséder, évincer (**of** de)

OUT [aʊt] ADV **1** (*outside*) dehors; **to go** *or* **walk o.** sortir; **to run/stagger o.** sortir en courant/chancelant; **it's colder inside than o.** il fait plus froid à l'intérieur qu'à l'extérieur; **what's it** *or* **the weather like o.?** quel

temps fait-il dehors?; **where are you going – o.** où allez-vous? – dehors; **o. you go!** sortez!, hors d'ici!, allez, hop!; **voyage o.** voyage *m* d'aller

2 (*not in, not at home, released*) **I was only o. for a minute** je ne suis sorti qu'une minute; **my father is o.** mon père est sorti; **she's o. a lot in the daytime** elle est souvent absente pendant la journée; **we've been o. a lot recently** (*to theatres, restaurants etc*) nous sommes beaucoup sortis ces temps-ci; (*not been at home*) nous avons été beaucoup absents ces temps-ci; **he's o. in September** (*of prisoner*) il sort en septembre; **he is o. and about again** il est de nouveau sur pied; **she loves getting o. and about in her pushchair** elle aime beaucoup qu'on la promène en poussette; **she's o. picking mushrooms** elle est sortie (pour aller) cueillir des champignons; **the men are o.** (*on strike*) les ouvriers sont en grève; **to bring the workforce o.** appeler le personnel à la grève; **you'll have everybody o. if you're not careful** tu vas provoquer une grève générale si tu ne fais pas attention; **the jury was o. for two hours** le jury s'est retiré pendant deux heures pour délibérer; **the tide is o.** la marée est basse

3 (*distant*) **a long way o.** loin, éloigné; **o. at sea** en mer, au large; **four days o. from Rio** à quatre jours de Rio; **o. there** là-bas; **she does not live far o.** (*of the town*) elle n'habite pas loin de la ville; **o. in the country** dans la campagne

4 (*uncovered, in the open*) découvert, exposé; (*secret*) connu; (*flower*) épanoui; **he's been o. for years** (*openly homosexual*) cela fait des années qu'il ne cache plus son homosexualité; **he's not o.** il n'a pas révélé son homosexualité; **the tulips are o. early this year** les tulipes ont fleuri de bonne heure cette année; **the cherry tree is o.** le cerisier est en fleur; **the sun is o.** il fait soleil; **the moon is/the stars are o.** on voit la lune/les étoiles; *Fam* **the best game o.** le meilleur jeu qui soit; **the book is o.** (*published*) le livre est paru; (*borrowed*) le livre est en prêt; **to be o. at the elbows** (*of garment*) être troué *ou* percé aux coudes; **to whip o. a revolver** tirer *ou* sortir vivement son revolver; **o. loud** tout haut, à haute voix; **to say sth straight** *or* **right o.** dire qch carrément *ou* sans détours; *Fam* **o. with it!** allons, dites-le!, expliquez-vous!; **truth will o.** tôt ou tard la vérité se saura

5 (*indicating aim*) **he's simply o. for money** tout ce qui l'intéresse c'est l'argent; **she was o. for a good time** elle cherchait à s'amuser; **he's only o. for what he can get** il ne cherche qu'à servir ses propres intérêts; (*sexually*) tout ce qu'il veut, c'est s'envoyer en l'air; **to be o. to get sb** en avoir après qn; **I am not o. to reform the world** je n'ai pas entrepris de réformer le monde; **I'm o. for big results** je vise (à) de grands résultats

6 (*not in place*) **I've put my shoulder o.** (*of joint*) je me suis luxé l'épaule; *Pol* **the party that's o.** (*of power*) le parti qui n'est pas au pouvoir; **long skirts are o. this year** les jupes longues ne sont plus à la mode cette année; **the players who are o.** (*of the game*) les joueurs qui sont hors jeu *ou* ont été éliminés; *Cr* **not o.** = encore au guichet (*à la fin de l'innings, de la journée*); **to be o. for ten** avoir marqué dix

7 (*inaccurate*) **to be o.** être dans l'erreur; **I was £25 o.** je m'étais trompé de 25 livres; **to be o. in one's calculations** s'être trompé dans ses calculs; **I was not far o.** je ne me trompais pas de beaucoup; **the shot was only a centimetre o.** le coup n'a manqué le but que d'un centimètre; *Fam* **he was miles o.** il était totalement à côté

8 (*not functioning*) **the fire/gas is o.** le feu/

gaz est éteint; **the light was o.** la lumière était éteinte

9 *(indicating completion)* **before the week is o.** avant la fin de la semaine; *Radio* **o.!** terminé!

10 *(unconscious)* **to be o. cold** être K-O; **to be o. for seven seconds** *(of boxer)* rester au plancher pendant sept secondes; *Fam* **to be o. on one's feet** tomber de fatigue; **I went** *or* **was o. like a light** *(fell asleep)* je me suis endormi comme une bûche

11 o. of *(outside)* hors de, en dehors de; **o. of danger** hors de danger; **o. of sight** hors de vue; **to be o. of the country** être à l'étranger; **o. of doors = outdoors** ADV, **hardly were the words o. of my mouth** à peine avais-je prononcé ces mots; **I'm glad I'm o. of the whole business** je suis content de ne plus rien avoir à faire avec ça; **to feel o. of it** se sentir de trop; **to go o. of the house** sortir de la maison; *Fam* **I'm o. of here** je me casse; *Fam* **let's get o. of here** allez, on se casse; **is there a way o. of it?** y a-t-il (un) moyen d'en sortir?; **to throw sth/to jump o. of the window** jeter qch/sauter par la fenêtre; **from o. of the open window came bursts of laughter** par la fenêtre ouverte arrivaient des éclats de rire; **Gladiator by Monarch o. of Gladia** *(in breeding)* Gladiateur par *ou* issu de Monarch et Gladia; **to drink o. of a glass** boire dans un verre; **to drink o. of the bottle** boire à (même) la bouteille; **to copy sth o. of a book** copier qch dans un livre; **the firemen are paid o. of the rates** on paie les pompiers sur le budget de la ville; **she paid them o. of her own pocket** elle les a payés de sa poche; **choose one o. of these ten** choisissez-en un parmi les dix; **three days o. of four** trois jours sur quatre; **one o. of every three** un sur trois; **hut made o. of a few old planks** cabane faite de quelques vieilles planches; **o. of friendship/curiosity** par amitié/curiosité; **to act o. of fear** *(habitually)* agir sous l'emprise de la peur; *(on precise occasion)* agir sous le coup de la peur; **to be o. of tea/ideas** être à court de thé/d'idées; **o. of cash** démuni d'argent; *Com* **I'm o. of this item** je n'ai plus cet article pour le moment

INT **1 o. (with you)!** sortez!, hors d'ici!

2 *Tennis* out!

ADJ *(outward)* **the o. door** la (porte de) sortie

N **1** *esp Am Fam (from difficult situation)* échappatoire *f*, **always leave yourself an o.** garde-toi toujours une porte de sortie *ou* une échappatoire

2 *Tennis* balle *f* (qui tombe) en dehors des limites

3 *TV, Cin (point where clip ends)* sortie *f*

PREP **to go o. the door** sortir par la porte; **to look o. the window** regarder par la fenêtre

VT **to o. sb** *(reveal to be homosexual)* révéler que qn est homosexuel

▶▶ *Comput* **o. box, o.tray** *(for e-mail)* corbeille *f* de départ; *TV, Radio* **o. words** mots *mpl* en trop (dans une séquence)

out- PREF **the government is attempting to out-Tory the Tories** le gouvernement essaie d'être plus conservateur que les conservateurs eux-mêmes

outage ['aʊtɪdʒ] N **1** *Com (amount lost)* perte(s) *f(pl)*; quantité *f* perdue; **stock o.** rupture *f* de stock **2** *Elec* coupure *f*, *(of machine)* panne *f*

out-and-out ADJ *(liar, villain)* fieffé, achevé; *(republican etc)* convaincu; *(disaster, failure)* total, -aux; *(scandal, disgrace)* véritable; *(success, triumph)* éclatant

outasight ['aʊtə'saɪt] ADJ, INT *esp Am Sl* fantastique

outback *Austr* N ['aʊtbæk] **the o.** l'intérieur *m*

ADV [aʊt'bæk] à l'intérieur

outbid [aʊt'bɪd] VT *(pt* **outbid;** *pp* **outbid, -bidden** [-'bɪdən]) *(at auction)* **to o. sb** enchérir sur qn et emporter la vente; **they were easily o. by the Getty Museum** le musée Getty n'a eu aucun mal à surenchérir et emporter la vente

outboard ['aʊtbɔːd] *Naut* N *(motor)* moteur *m* hors-bord

▶▶ **o. motor** moteur hors-bord

outbound ['aʊtbaʊnd] ADJ en partance

▶▶ **o. tourism** tourisme *m* émetteur

outbox ['aʊtbɒks] VT boxer mieux que; **he was completely outboxed** il a été complètement dominé

outbreak ['aʊtbreɪk] N *(of hostilities)* déclenchement *m*, début *m*, commencement *m*; *(of violence)* déclenchement; **there's been an o. of flu** il y a eu de nombreux cas de grippe; **there has been another o. of cholera** de nouveaux cas de choléra ont été enregistrés; **precautions against an o. of typhus** précautions contre une épidémie de typhus; **in order to prevent another o.** *(epidemic)* pour empêcher une autre épidémie; **o. of fire** incendie *m*; **at the o. of war** quand la guerre a éclaté

outbuilding ['aʊtbɪldɪŋ] N bâtiment *m* extérieur; **outbuildings** dépendances *fpl*

outburst ['aʊtbɜːst] N éclat *m*; *(of generosity)* élan *m*; *(of hatred etc)* déchaînement *m*, éruption *f*; *(of energy)* accès *m*; *(of activity, enthusiasm)* débordement *m*; *(of violence, gunfire)* explosion *f*, **an o. of laughter** un grand éclat de rire; **o. of temper** accès *ou* éclat de colère; **she apologized for her o.** elle s'est excusée de l'éclat qu'elle venait de faire

outcast ['aʊtkɑːst] N banni, -ie, proscrit, -ite; **an o. of society, a social o.** un paria

outclass [aʊt'klɑːs] VT *(competitor)* surclasser

outcome ['aʊtkʌm] N résultat *m*, issue *f*, **the o. of our labours** le fruit de nos travaux; **I don't know what the o. will be** je ne sais pas ce qui en résultera

outcrop ['aʊtkrɒp] N **1** *Geol* affleurement *m*, pointement *m* **2** *(projecting part)* saillie *f*

outcry ['aʊtkraɪ] N *(protest)* protestations *fpl*, tollé *m*; **there was a public o. when the hospital was closed** un tollé général s'est élevé contre la fermeture de l'hôpital; **to raise an o. against sb/sth** crier haro sur qn/qch; *St Exch* **by open o.** à la criée

out-cue N *TV, Cin* signal *m* de sortie; *(video)* point *m* de sortie

outdated [aʊt'deɪtɪd] ADJ *(clothes, furniture)* démodé; *(custom, beliefs)* désuet, -uète, démodé; *(word, expression)* vieilli, démodé; *(textbook, theory)* démodé, périmé

outdistance [aʊt'dɪstəns] VT distancer, dépasser

outdo [aʊt'duː] VT *(pt* **outdid** [aʊt'dɪd], *pp* **outdone** [aʊt'dʌn]) l'emporter *ou* renchérir sur, surpasser (**sb in sth** qn en qch); **we don't want to be outdone when it comes to quality** nous ne voulons surtout pas être surpassés en ce qui concerne la qualité; **they are all anxious to o. each other** c'est à qui fera le mieux; **not to be outdone** pour ne pas être en reste (**in** de)

outdoor ['aʊtdɔːr] ADJ *(life)* au grand air, en plein air, de plein air; *(swimming pool)* en plein air, découvert; *(games, activities)* de plein air; **she's an o. person** c'est une personne qui aime le grand air *ou* qui aime être dehors; **he's not an o. person** il n'aime pas spécialement le grand air

▶▶ **o. advertising** publicité *f* extérieure; **o. aerial** antenne *f* extérieure; **o. clothes** *(warm)* vêtements *mpl* chauds; *(waterproof)* vêtements de pluie; *Mktg* **o. network** réseau

m d'affichage; *Cin, TV* **o. scene** extérieur *m*; *Cin* **o. set** décor *m* en extérieur; **o. shoes** *(warm)* grosses chaussures *fpl*, *(waterproof)* chaussures imperméables; *(for walking)* chaussures de marche; **leave your o. shoes at the door** laissez vos chaussures à la porte; *Cin, TV* **o. shot** extérieur *m*; **o. work** travail *m* (à l')extérieur *ou* en plein air

┌─────────────────────────────────┐
│ Attention: ne pas confondre avec l'ad- │
│ verbe **outdoors**. │
└─────────────────────────────────┘

outdoors [aʊt'dɔːz] ADV dehors; *(in open air)* en plein air; **to sleep o.** coucher à la belle étoile; **to sow o.** *(in gardening)* semer en pleine terre

N **the o.** la vie au grand air *ou* en plein air; **the great o.** la nature à l'état sauvage; **she's an o. person** c'est une personne qui aime le grand air *ou* qui aime être dehors

┌─────────────────────────────────┐
│ Attention: ne pas confondre avec l'adjec- │
│ tif **outdoor**. │
└─────────────────────────────────┘

outer ['aʊtər] ADJ ATTRIB *(walls, covering)* extérieur; *(surface)* externe, extérieur; **the secretary in the o. office** le secrétaire qui se trouve dans le bureau à l'extérieur; **just within the o. limits of what is acceptable** tout juste à la limite de l'acceptable

▶▶ *Archit* **o. door** avant-portail *m*, *pl* avant-portails; **o. garments** vêtements *mpl* de dessus; **O. Mongolia** Mongolie-Extérieure *f*, **o. space** espace *m* intersidéral, cosmos *m*

outermost ['aʊtəməʊst] ADJ **1** *(closest to outside)* le plus à l'extérieur; **the o. layer was waterproofed** la première couche était imperméable; **make sure the coloured side is o.** assure-toi que le côté coloré se trouve à l'extérieur **2** *(most remote)* le plus reculé *ou* écarté; **to the o. parts of the earth** jusqu'aux extrémités de la terre

outfall ['aʊtfɔːl] N *(of pipe)* embouchure *f*

outfit ['aʊtfɪt] N **1** *(clothes)* ensemble *m*; *Mil* tenue *f*, *(for child to play with)* panoplie *f* **2** *(equipment)* équipement *m* **3** *Fam (organization, company etc)* boîte *f*, *(of workers)* équipe *f* d'ouvriers; *Mil (unit)* unité *f*, *(rock band etc)* groupe *m*

VT *(person, expedition, ship)* équiper (**with** de)

outfitter ['aʊtfɪtər] N **1** *esp Br (for clothes)* spécialiste *mf* de la confection **2** *Am (for hunting etc equipment)* fournisseur *m*

outflank [aʊt'flæŋk] VT **1** *Mil (enemy position)* déborder, tourner; **outflanking movement** mouvement *m* débordant *ou* tournant **2** *Fig (person)* circonvenir

outflow ['aʊtfləʊ] N *(of liquid)* écoulement *m*; *(of lava)* coulée *f*, *(from sewer)* décharge *f*, *Fin (of gold, currency)* sortie *f*

outfox [aʊt'fɒks] VT *(person)* se montrer plus rusé que; *(security system)* déjouer

outgoing ['aʊtgəʊɪŋ] ADJ **1** *(departing)* (tenant, official) sortant; *(minister)* sortant; *(resigning)* démissionnaire; *(train, boat, plane)* en partance; *Tel (call)* sortant **2** *(sociable)* sociable; *(extrovert)* extraverti

NPL **outgoings** *Fin* dépenses *fpl*, débours *mpl*, sorties *fpl* de fonds

▶▶ *Com* **o. inventory** inventaire *m* de sortie; **o. mail** courrier *m* à expédier; *Ind* **o. shift** équipe *f* sortante *ou* relevée; **o. tide** marée *f* descendante

outgrow [aʊt'grəʊ] VT *(pt* **outgrew** [aʊt'gruː], *pp* **outgrown** [aʊt'grəʊn]) **1** *(one's clothes etc)* devenir trop grand pour **2** *(habit)* perdre avec le temps *ou* en vieillissant; **I would have thought he'd have outgrown all that by now** j'aurais pensé qu'il aurait dépassé tout ça à présent; **to have outgrown one's friends** ne plus avoir grand-chose en commun avec ses amis **3** *(grow larger than)* *(person, thing)* croître plus vite que, devenir plus grand que

outgrowth ['aʊtɡrəʊθ] N excroissance f

outguess [aʊt'ɡes] VT *(person)* déjouer les intentions de

outgun [aʊt'ɡʌn] VT avoir une puissance de feu supérieure à

out-Herod VT *Lit* to o. **Herod** se montrer plus cruel qu'Hérode

outhouse ['aʊthaʊs] N bâtiment m extérieur, dépendance f; *Am (outside lavatory)* toilettes fpl extérieures

outing ['aʊtɪŋ] N **1** *(excursion)* excursion f, sortie f; *(drive)* sortie, excursion, promenade f en voiture; *(walk)* promenade; *Sport (of footballer etc)* match m; **his first o. this season** *(of horse)* son premier concours de la saison; **day's o.** *(in a car etc)* sortie pour la journée; **school o.** sortie scolaire **2** *(of homosexual person)* révélation f de l'homosexualité

outlandish [aʊt'lændɪʃ] ADJ incongru, bizarre

outlast [aʊt'lɑːst] VT *(object)* durer plus longtemps que; *(person)* survivre à; **it has outlasted ten centuries of war, weather and vandalism** cela a résisté à dix siècles de guerres, d'intempéries et de vandalisme; **the theory has outlasted all its critics** cette théorie a résisté à l'assaut de tous les critiques

outlaw ['aʊtlɔː] N hors-la-loi m inv; **to declare sb an o.** déclarer qn hors la loi

VT **1** *Hist (person)* mettre hors la loi, proscrire **2** *(custom etc)* proscrire, bannir

outlay ['aʊtleɪ] N frais mpl, dépenses fpl, débours mpl; **to get back** *or* **recover one's o.** rentrer dans ses fonds; **without any great o.** *(by company)* sans grande mise de fonds; *(by individual)* à peu de frais

outlet ['aʊtlet] N **1** *Tech* orifice m (d'émission); *(for air, gas)* sortie f; *(for steam)* échappement m; *(of pipe)* débouché m **2** *Fig* exutoire m; **an o. for one's energy** un exutoire pour son trop-plein d'énergie **3** *Com (for goods)* débouché m; **(retail) o.** point m de vente **4** *esp Am Elec* prise f de courant

▸▸ *Tech* **o. drain, o. pipe** tuyau m d'écoulement; *Com* **o. village** = centre m commercial spécialisé dans les marques à prix réduit

outline ['aʊtlaɪn] N **1** *(form)* **outline(s)** *(of hill, building, boat etc)* contour(s) m(pl), profil m; *(of person, building)* silhouette f; *(of car)* ligne f **2** *(drawing)* dessin m au trait, tracé m; *(in text processing)* plan m de document; *Fig (of play, novel)* argument m, canevas m; *(of plan, policy etc)* grandes lignes fpl, grands traits mpl; **drawn in o.** dessiné au trait; **in o.** en gros, dans les grandes lignes; **rough o.** premier jet m; **main** *or* **general** *or* **broad outlines** *(of project)* ébauche f; **a fairly detailed o. of the plan** une description assez détaillée du projet; **could you give us a quick o. of your plans?** pourriez-vous nous décrire les grandes lignes de votre projet?; **an o. of French history** un résumé de l'histoire de France; **outlines of astronomy** éléments mpl d'astronomie

VT **1** *(the shape of sth)* silhouetter **2** *(plot of a novel etc)* esquisser; *(plan, project)* esquisser, tracer les grandes lignes de; *(plan of action)* ébaucher, indiquer; **I briefly outlined my objections/what needed to be done** j'ai donné un bref aperçu de mes objections/de ce qui devait être fait

▸▸ **o. agreement** protocole m d'accord; **o. drawing** dessin au trait; *Comput* **o. font** police f vectorielle; **o. plan** plan schématique *ou* d'ensemble; *Cin, TV* **o. script** scénario m indicatif

outliner ['aʊtlaɪnər] N *Comput* outliner m

outlive [aʊt'lɪv] VT *(person)* survivre à; **he will o. us all** il nous enterrera tous; **to have outlived its usefulness** *(of machine, theory etc)* ne plus servir (à rien); **he had outlived the era which had need of him** l'époque qui avait besoin de lui était maintenant révolue

outlook ['aʊtlʊk] N **1** *(view)* vue f, perspective f; **the political/economic o.** l'horizon m politique/économique; **the o. is gloomy** *(for industry, economy, weather etc)* les perspectives ne sont pas réjouissantes **2** *(attitude)* façon f de voir les choses; **we need a fresh o. on the matter** nous avons besoin d'un nouveau regard sur le sujet; **o. on life** conception f de la vie **3** **to be on the o. for sth** être à l'affût de qch

outlying ['aʊtlaɪɪŋ] ADJ ATTRIB éloigné, isolé; **o. areas** régions fpl périphériques

outmanoeuvre, *Am* **outmaneuver** [aʊtmə'nuːvər] VT *Mil (the enemy)* l'emporter sur en tactique; *Fig (person)* déjouer les tactiques de; **we've been outmanoeuvred** nos tactiques ont été déjouées

outmatch [aʊt'mætʃ] VT surclasser, dominer

outmoded [aʊt'məʊdɪd] ADJ *(custom, beliefs)* désuet, -uète, démodé; *(furniture, theory, word)* démodé

outnumber [aʊt'nʌmbər] VT *(the enemy etc)* l'emporter en nombre sur; **we were heavily outnumbered** nous étions très minoritaires; **they outnumbered us three to one** ils étaient en majorité de trois à un par rapport à nous

out-of-body experience N expérience f hors du corps, EHC f, autoscopie f

out-of-court ADJ *(settlement)* à l'amiable

out-of-doors ADV = **outdoors** ADV

out-of-focus ADJ flou

out-of-phase ADJ *TV, Cin* déphasé

out-of-pocket ADJ

▸▸ **o. expenses** menues dépenses fpl, frais mpl

out-of-shot ADJ *TV, Cin* en dehors du champ

out-of-sync ADJ désynchronisé, hors synchronisation

out-of-the-way ADJ **1** *(place etc)* écarté, loin de tout et de tous **2** *(unusual)* peu ordinaire, peu commun, insolite; **it was nothing o.** cela n'avait rien d'extraordinaire

out-of-town ADJ *(shopping centre, retail park)* situé en dehors du centre-ville

out-of-towner [-'taʊnər] N *Am Fam* étranger, -ère à la ville; **he's an o.** il n'est pas d'ici

outpace [aʊt'peɪs] VT *(competitor etc)* dépasser, distancer; **demand has outpaced production** la demande a dépassé la production

outpatient ['aʊtpeɪʃənt] N malade mf qui vient consulter à l'hôpital; **he was being treated as an o.** il était traité en consultation externe

▸▸ **outpatients' clinic, outpatients' department** service m des consultations externes; **o. treatment** traitement m ambulatoire

outplacement ['aʊtpleɪsmənt] N = licenciement m accompagné d'aide et de conseils fournis par l'employeur pour trouver un autre emploi

outplay [aʊt'pleɪ] VT *(person)* jouer mieux que; **she was outplayed** son adversaire a joué mieux qu'elle

outpoint [aʊt'pɔɪnt] N *(on tape, film)* point m de sortie

outpost ['aʊtpəʊst] N *Mil* poste m avancé; **the last o. of civilization** le dernier bastion de la civilisation

outpouring ['aʊtpɔːrɪŋ] N *(of feelings)* épanchement m, effusion f; *(of ideas, literary creativity)* déluge m, flux m; **outpourings of the heart** épanchements, effusions

output ['aʊtpʊt] N **1** *(of factory, worker)* production f, rendement m; *(of machine)* débit m, rendement m; **o. of an author** production littéraire d'un auteur; **he kept up a phenomenal o. throughout his writing career** il a produit à un rythme phénoménal tout au long de sa carrière littéraire; **our o. is not keeping pace with demand** notre production est insuffisante pour répondre à la demande **2** *Tech etc (of engine)* puissance f, rendement m; *Elec (of generator)* débit m; *Elec* **power o.** puissance débitée *ou* de sortie **3** *Comput (of data, information)* sortie f, *(of data processing operation)* résultat(s) m

VT *(pt, pp* output) **1** *(of factory etc)* produire **2** *Comput (data)* sortir (to)

▸▸ *Comput* **o. buffer** mémoire f tampon de sortie; *Comput* **o. card** carte f sortie, carte résultat; *Comput* **o. device** périphérique m de sortie; *Comput* **o. file** fichier m de sortie; *Comput* **o. formatting** mise f en forme de sortie; *Econ* **o. gap** écart m de production; *Comput* **o. port** port m de sortie; *Tech* **o. shaft** arbre m de sortie; *Acct* **o. tax** TVA f encaissée, impôt m à la consommation; *Tech* **o. torque** couple m en sortie; *Elec* **o. voltage** tension f de sortie

outrage ['aʊtreɪdʒ] N **1** *(vicious act)* atrocité f, *(violation of decency)* scandale m; **to commit an o. on** *or* **against sb** commettre une atrocité sur qn; **$200 a ticket?!, it's an o.!** 200 dollars un billet?!, c'est un scandale!; **o. against humanity/society** crime m contre l'humanité/la société *ou* de lèse-humanité/de lèse-société; **bomb o.** *(in headline)* attentat m à la bombe **2** *(indignation)* indignation f (at contre)

VT **1** *(public decency, feelings etc)* outrager, faire outrage à **2** *(make indignant) (person)* scandaliser, outrer; **she's easy to o.** elle se scandalise facilement; **I am outraged** je suis scandalisé *ou* outré

outrageous [aʊt'reɪdʒəs] ADJ *(cruelty)* atroce; *(price, conduct)* scandaleux; *(statement, accusation)* outrageant; **it's/he's o.!** cela/il dépasse toutes les bornes!; **he enjoys being o.** il aime scandaliser; *Fam* **an o. get-up** une tenue extravagante

outrageously [aʊt'reɪdʒəslɪ] ADV *(cruel)* atrocement; *(expensive)* scandaleusement; *(to behave)* d'une façon scandaleuse; *(to dress)* de façon extravagante

outrageousness [aʊt'reɪdʒəsnɪs] N *(of behaviour)* caractère m scandaleux; *(of clothes, hairstyle)* extravagance f; **the o. of the prices** les prix scandaleux

outrank [aʊt'ræŋk] VT **1** *(be of higher rank than)* être supérieur en grade à; **he was outranked by most of those present** la plupart des personnes présentes avaient un grade supérieur au sien **2** *(take precedence over)* avoir *ou* prendre le pas sur; **to be outranked by** donner *ou* céder le pas à

outreach ['aʊtriːtʃ] N *Admin* = activité f visant à encourager les gens à profiter des avantages sociaux

▸▸ **o. worker** = employé, ée dans un bureau d'aide sociale

outrider ['aʊtraɪdər] N *(on horseback)* cavalier m d'escorte; **(motor-cycle) o.** motard m d'escorte

outrigger ['aʊtrɪɡər] N **1** *(in rowing)* portenage m inv en dehors; *(boat)* outrigger m **2** *(on canoe)* balancier m

outright ADV [aʊt'raɪt] **1** *(completely)* complètement; *(immediately)* du premier coup, sur le coup; **to buy sth o.** acheter qch (au) comptant; **he was killed o.** il fut tué sur le coup *ou* net **2** *(bluntly)* sans ménagement;

(frankly) franchement, carrément; *(to deny)* carrément; **to refuse o.** refuser tout net **ADJ ATTRIB** ['aʊtraɪ] *(failure)* total, -aux; *(refusal)* net; **it's o. wickedness** c'est de la pure méchanceté; **an o. disaster** un vrai désastre; **the o. winner** le vainqueur incontesté ▸▸**o. gift** don *m* pur et simple; **o. payment** somme *f* forfaitaire; **o. sale** vente *f* au comptant

outrival [aʊt'raɪv(ə)l] **VT** *(-ll-, Am -l-)* *(person)* surpasser, l'emporter sur

outrun [aʊt'rʌn] **VT** *(pt* outran [aʊt'ræn]*, pp* outrun; *prp* outrunning) **1** *(go faster than)* **to o. sb** gagner de vitesse; **he can o. the rest of the team** il court plus vite que le reste de l'équipe **2** *(exceed)* **his zeal outruns his discretion** son ardeur l'emporte sur son jugement

outs [aʊts] **NPL** *Am Fam* **to be on the o. with sb** être brouillé avec qn; **they're on the o.** ils sont brouillés

outsell [aʊt'sel] **VT** *(pt, pp* outsold [aʊt'səʊld]*)* *(object)* se vendre mieux que; *(competitors)* vendre plus que; **we are being outsold by the competition** nos concurrents vendent plus que nous

outset ['aʊtset] **N** commencement *m*; **at the o.** au départ, au début; **from the o.** dès le début

outshine [aʊt'ʃaɪn] **VT** *(pt, pp* outshone [aʊt'ʃɒn]*)* **1** *(shine brighter than)* briller plus que **2** *Fig (surpass)* surpasser, éclipser; **I don't like being outshone** je n'aime pas qu'on m'éclipse *ou* me surpasse

N	extérieur ▪ dehors
ADJ	extérieur **1** ▪ maximum **2**
ADV	dehors
PREP	à l'extérieur de **1** ▪ devant **1** ▪ en dehors de **3**

N [aʊt'saɪd] *(of book, building etc)* extérieur *m*; **on the o. of sth** à l'extérieur de qch; **from the o.** de l'extérieur, du dehors; **the fruit is yellow on the o.** le fruit est jaune à l'extérieur; **friends on the o.** *(of prisoner)* des amis dehors; **to open a door on the o.** ouvrir une porte du dehors *ou* de l'extérieur; **at the o.** *(at most)* tout au plus, au maximum; **to come up on the o.** *(in race)* arriver sur l'extérieur

ADJ ['aʊtsaɪd] **1** *(influence)* extérieur; *(help)* de l'extérieur; **the o. world** le monde extérieur

2 *(price, odds, amount etc)* maximum; **there's an o. chance** *(remote)* ce n'est pas exclu (**of** … que … + *sub*); **I think we have an o. possibility** je pense que nous avons une toute petite chance

ADV [aʊt'saɪd] dehors, à l'extérieur, au dehors; **to go o.** sortir, aller dehors; **to run/ dash/etc o.** sortir en courant/à toute vitesse/etc; **the taxi is o.** le taxi vous attend dehors; **seen from o.** vu de dehors *ou* de l'extérieur; *Fam* **o. of** à l'extérieur de, en dehors de; *Fam* **o. of a few friends nobody knows anything about it** sauf *ou* à part quelques amis, personne n'en sait rien

PREP [aʊt'saɪd] **1** *(in space)* en dehors de, hors de, à l'extérieur de; **o. my bedroom** *(at the door)* à la porte de ma chambre; *(below the windows)* sous les fenêtres de ma chambre; **I'll meet you o. the cinema** je vous retrouverai devant le cinéma; **o. the town** en dehors de la ville

2 *(not part of)* **o. working hours** en dehors des heures de travail; **he's o. the family** il n'appartient pas à la famille; **that's o. our agreement** ça ne fait pas partie de notre accord; **that's o. our terms of reference** cela n'entre pas dans nos attributions; **it's o. our**

range *(of gun, tank etc)* c'est hors de (notre) portée; *(of aircraft)* ce n'est pas dans notre rayon d'action; *(too expensive)* ce n'est pas dans nos prix

3 *(apart from)* en dehors de; **o. a few friends** en dehors de quelques amis ▸▸**o. aerial** antenne *f* extérieure; *TV* **o. broadcast** émission *f* réalisée en dehors des studios; *TV* **o. broadcasting** émissions réalisées en dehors des studios; *TV* **o. broadcasting vehicle** car *m* régie, unité *f* mobile de tournage; *St Exch* **o. broker** courtier, -ière marron *ou* libre; *Rugby* **o. centre** deuxième centre *m*; *Rugby* **o. half** demi *m* d'ouverture; *Rugby* **o. diameter** diamètre *m* extérieur; **o. interests** intérêts *mpl* en dehors de son travail/de sa famille; **o. lane** *(driving on left)* file *f ou* voie *f* de droite; *(driving on right)* file *ou* voie *f* de gauche; *Sport* **o. left** ailier *m* gauche; *Tel* **o. line** ligne *f* extérieure; *St Exch* **o. market** marché *m* hors cote *ou* en coulisse; *Constr* **o. measurements** dimensions *fpl* hors d'œuvre; *Sport* **o. right** ailier droit; **o. work** travail *m* extérieur *ou* à l'extérieur; *(in open air)* travail au grand air *ou* en plein air; **o. worker** *(at home)* ouvrier, -ière à domicile

outsider [aʊt'saɪdər] **N 1** *(socially)* étranger, -ère; **he had always been a bit of an o.** il avait toujours été un peu à l'écart **2** *(in election), Horseracing, Sport etc* outsider *m* **3** *St Exch* coulissier *m*

outsize ['aʊtsaɪz] **N** *Com (large size)* très grande taille *f*; *(in men's clothes)* très grand patron *m*

outsize(d) ['aʊtsaɪz(d)] **ADJ** USU ATTRIB **1 o. dress** robe en très grande taille **2** *(packet etc)* géant; *(appetite, ego)* démesuré

outskirts ['aʊtskɜːts] **NPL** limites *fpl*, (a)bords *mpl*, *(of forest)* orée *f*, lisière *f*; *(of town)* faubourgs *mpl*, *(of city)* banlieue *f*, périphérie *f*

outsmart [aʊt'smɑːt] **VT** *Fam (person)* surpasser en finesse; **they had been outsmarted once again** une fois de plus ils avaient trouvé plus malin qu'eux

outsource ['aʊtsɔːs] **VT** externaliser; **computer maintenance has been outsourced to another company** l'entretien du matériel informatique a été externalisé

outsourcing ['aʊtsɔːsɪŋ] **N** externalisation *f*

outspend [aʊt'spend] **VT** dépenser plus que

outspoken [aʊt'spəʊkən] **ADJ** *(person)* franc, *f* franche, carré; **to be o.** parler franc, ne pas mâcher ses mots; **o. criticism** critique *f* franche

outspokenly [aʊt'spəʊkənlɪ] **ADV** franchement, carrément, rondement

outspokenness [aʊt'spəʊkənnɪs] **N** franchise *f*, franc-parler *m*, *pl* francs-parlers

outspread [aʊt'spred] **ADJ** étendu, étalé, déployé; **with wings o., with o.** ['aʊtspred] **wings** les ailes déployées; **with o. arms, with arms o.** les bras grand ouverts

outstanding [aʊt'stændɪŋ] **ADJ 1** *(remarkable)* remarquable, exceptionnel, hors du commun; **a man of o. talents/merits/intelligence** un homme aux talents/mérites exceptionnels/à l'intelligence exceptionnelle; **a matter of o. importance** une affaire de première importance; **she plays o. tennis** c'est une joueuse de tennis exceptionnelle *ou* remarquable **2** *(main, prominent) (feature)* marquant **3** *(unresolved) (business)* en suspens, en cours de règlement; *(problem)* pas encore résolu **4** *Fin (amount, account)* impayé, à recouvrer, à percevoir; *(payment)* arriéré, en retard; *(invoice)* en souffrance; *(interest)* échu, arriéré ▸▸*Fin* **o. balance** solde *m* à découvert;

Banking **o. cheques** chèques *mpl* en circulation; *Fin* **o. debts** créances *fpl* à recouvrer, recouvrements *mpl*

outstandingly [aʊt'stændɪŋlɪ] **ADV** éminemment, exceptionnellement

outstay [aʊt'steɪ] **VT** *(person)* rester plus longtemps que; **I hope I haven't outstayed my welcome** j'espère ne pas avoir abusé de votre hospitalité

outstretched ['aʊtstretʃt] **ADJ** *(wing)* déployé; *(leg, arm)* tendu; **with arms o., with o. arms** *(to welcome sb)* les bras grand ouverts; **to lie o.** être allongé de tout son long

outstrip [aʊt'strɪp] **VT** *(-pp-)* *(person when running)* devancer, dépasser; *Sport (competitor)* distancer; *Fig (expectations, budget)* dépasser; *(surpass)* surpasser (**sb in sth** qn en qch)

out-supplier **N** *Com* fournisseur *m* potentiel

outta ['aʊtə] **PREP** *Fam (out of)* **let's get o. here!** allez, on se casse!; **you must be o. your mind!** mais t'es complètement dingue!; *Am* **o. sight** *(excellent)* dingue, dément

outtake ['aʊteɪk] **N** *Cin, TV* coupure *f*, prise *f* non-utilisée, coupe *f*

outvote [aʊt'vəʊt] **VT** *(usu in pass)* *(person, government)* mettre en minorité; *(proposal)* rejeter à la majorité des voix; **we were outvoted** nous avons été mis en minorité, la majorité des voix a été contre nous

outward ['aʊtwəd] **ADJ 1** **in an o. direction** vers l'extérieur; **o. journey** voyage *m* aller **2** *(appearance)* extérieur; **o. form** extérieur *m*, dehors *m* **ADV = outwards**; *Naut* **o.-bound** *(ship)* en partance; *(for foreign destination)* en route pour l'étranger; **O.-Bound®** **course** école *f* d'endurance (en plein air) ▸▸**o. half** *(of ticket)* billet *m* aller; *Econ* **o. investment** investissement *m* à l'étranger

outwardly ['aʊtwədlɪ] **ADV** en apparence; **she was o. calm** en apparence elle était calme

outwards ['aʊtwədz] **ADV** vers l'extérieur; **to turn one's feet o.** tourner les pieds en dehors

outwear [aʊt'weər] **VT** *(pt* outwore [aʊt'wɔːr]*, pp* outworn [aʊt'wɔːn]*)* **the system has outworn its usefulness** le système est désormais périmé

outweigh [aʊt'weɪ] **VT 1** *(be more important than)* l'emporter sur; **these arguments were outweighed by considerations of security** les questions de sécurité l'ont emporté sur ces arguments **2** *(weigh more than)* peser plus que

outwit [aʊt'wɪt] **VT** *(-tt-)* *(person)* se montrer plus malin que; *(thwart plans of)* déjouer les intentions *ou* les menées de; **once again he had been outwitted** une fois de plus il avait trouvé plus malin que lui

outwith [aʊt'wɪθ] **PREP** *Scot* **= outside 3**

outworn ['aʊt'wɔːn] **ADJ** *(custom, idea)* périmé

ouzel ['uːz(ə)l] **N** *(bird)* **ring o.** merle *m* à plastron *ou* à collier; **water o.** cincle *m* plongeur, merle d'eau

oval ['əʊv(ə)l] **ADJ** (en) ovale; *Am Pol* **the O. Office** = le bureau du Président des États-Unis; **he has decided to make a bid for the O. Office** il a décidé de se présenter à la Maison-Blanche **N** ovale *m*

ovarian [əʊ'veərɪən] **ADJ** *Anat, Bot* ovarien

ovariectomy [əʊvərɪ'ektəmɪ] **N** *Surg* ovariectomie *f*

ovary ['əʊvərɪ] **N** *Anat, Bot* ovaire *m*

ovate ['əʊveɪt] **ADJ** *Biol* ové, ovale

ovation [əʊˈveɪʃən] N ovation f, **to give sb an o.** faire une ovation *ou* un triomphe à qn; **to give sb a standing o.** se lever pour applaudir qn; **the performers received a standing o.** tout le monde s'est levé pour applaudir les acteurs

oven [ˈʌv(ə)n] N four m; *Ind* four, étuve f, **electric/gas o.** four électrique/à gaz; **to put sth in the o.** mettre qch au four; **to cook sth in a slow/quick o.** cuire qch à four doux/vif; **it's like an o. in here** on se croirait dans un four ici; **to put one's head in the o.** se suicider (au gaz); **o. gloves** *or* **mitts** gants *mpl* isolants

oven-proof ADJ (*dish*) allant au four

oven-ready ADJ (*meal, dish*) prêt à mettre au four; (*chicken, meat*) prêt à rôtir

ovenware [ˈʌv(ə)nweər] N vaisselle f allant au four

OVER [ˈəʊvər]

PREP sur **1, 2** ▪ par-dessus **1** ▪ au-dessus de **2** ▪ à propos de **3** ▪ plus de **5**	
ADV encore **2** ▪ plus **7**	
ADJ fini	

PREP 1 (*on surface of, on top of*) sur; **to spill ink o. the table** répandre de l'encre sur la table; **to spread a cloth o. sth** étendre une toile sur *ou* par-dessus qch; **all o. the north of England** sur tout le nord de l'Angleterre; **to search all o. Paris** chercher dans tout Paris; **famous all o. the world** célèbre dans le monde entier; **to glance o. sth** parcourir qch des yeux *ou* du regard; **length o. all** longueur totale *ou* hors tout; *Fam* **to be all o. sb** (*be excessively polite*) faire l'empressé auprès de qn; (*be excessively physical*) accaparer qn; (*the top of*) **sth** par-dessus qch; **to throw sth o. the wall** jeter qch par-dessus le mur; **to read o. sb's shoulder** lire par-dessus l'épaule de qn; **with his coat o. his shoulder** le manteau sur l'épaule; **he wore an old coat o. his uniform** il portait un vieux manteau par-dessus son uniforme; **to stumble** *or* **trip o. sth** buter contre qch

2 (*above*) **directly o. our heads** juste au-dessus de nos têtes; **bending o. his work** courbé sur son travail; **to have a chat o. a glass of wine** bavarder tout en prenant un verre de vin; **to discuss sth o. lunch** discuter de qch pendant le déjeuner; **I couldn't hear her o. the noise of the machine** je ne pouvais pas l'entendre à cause du bruit de la machine; **with his hat o. his eyes** le chapeau enfoncé jusqu'aux yeux; *Math* **12 o. 3** 12 divisé par 3; **to have an advantage o. sb** avoir un avantage sur qn; **to reign/govern o. a country** régner sur/gouverner un pays VOIR GRAMMAIR A72

3 (*about*) à propos de; **to laugh o. sth** rire (à propos) de qch; **to cry o. sb/sth** pleurer qn/qch; **we had trouble o. the tickets** nous avons eu des ennuis à propos de *ou* au sujet des billets; **to fight o. sth** se battre à cause de *ou* au sujet de qch; (*in order to obtain it*) se battre pour (obtenir) qch

4 (*across*) **to cross o. the road** traverser la rue; **the house o. the way** la maison d'en face; **o. the border** de l'autre côté *ou* au-delà de la frontière; **to live o. the river** habiter de l'autre côté de la rivière; **from o. the seas** de par delà les mers; **the bridge o. the river** le pont qui enjambe la rivière VOIR GRAMMAIRE A72

5 (*in excess of*) **numbers o. a hundred** numéros au-dessus de cent; **o. ten pounds** plus de dix livres; **not o. 250 grams** (*in post office*) jusqu'à 250 grammes; **to be o. the limit** dépasser la limite; (*of drunk driver*) avoir dépassé le taux légal d'alcoolémie; **children o. five (years of age), the o. fives** les enfants au-dessus de *ou* de plus de cinq

ans; **he's o. fifty** il a (dé)passé la cinquantaine; **he spoke for o. an hour** il a parlé pendant plus d'une heure; **he receives tips o. and above his wages** il reçoit des pourboires en sus de son salaire

6 (*in the course of*) **o. the last three years** au cours des trois dernières années; **o. Christmas** pendant la période de Noël *ou* des fêtes; **I'll do it o. the weekend** je le ferai pendant le week-end; **o. a period of several weeks** pendant plusieurs semaines; **let's spread it o. a period of weeks** étalons-le sur une période de plusieurs semaines

7 (*recovered from the effects of*) **I'm/you're/ she's/etc o.** le plus mauvais moment est passé; **to be o. a cold** être guéri d'un rhume; **she's o. the disappointment** elle est remise de sa déception; **don't worry, you'll be o. her soon** ne t'en fais pas, bientôt tu n'y penseras plus

ADV 1 (*everywhere*) **famous the world o.** célèbre dans le monde entier; **to ache all o.** avoir mal partout; **that's him all o.** c'est tout lui

2 (*indicating repetition*) encore; **I've had to do it all o. again** j'ai dû tout refaire, j'ai dû le faire de *ou* à nouveau; **ten times o.** dix fois de suite; **twice o.** à deux reprises; **o. and o. (again)** à de nombreuses reprises, *esp Lit* maintes et maintes fois, *esp Lit* à maintes reprises; **he did it o. and o. (again) until …** il a recommencé des dizaines de fois jusqu'à ce que …

3 (*over the top of sth*) par-dessus, dessus; **throw it o.!** (*over the wall etc*) lance-le par-dessus!; *Fam* (*throw it to me*) lance-le-moi!; **Concorde flew o.** le Concorde est passé

4 (*down*) **to knock sth o.** renverser qch; **and o. I went** et me voilà par terre

5 (*to other side*) **please turn o.!** voir au dos!, tournez s'il vous plaît!; **to turn sth o. and o.** tourner et retourner qch; **to bend sth o.** plier qch

6 (*across*) **he led me o. to the window** il m'a conduit à la fenêtre; **to cross o.** (*street etc*) traverser; (*the Channel etc*) faire la traversée; **o. here** ici, de ce côté; **o. there** là-bas; **ask him o.** demandez-lui de venir (chez nous); **our friends are coming o. tomorrow** nos amis vont venir nous voir demain; **to deliver sth o. to sb** remettre qch à qn; **to hand sth o. to sb** remettre qch entre les mains de qn; *Radio* **o.** à vous; *Radio* **o. and out** à vous, terminé; **o. to you** (*it's your turn*) c'est votre tour, c'est à vous; **now o. to our Cardiff studio** nous passons maintenant l'antenne à nos studios de Cardiff

7 (*with specific figure or amount*) plus; **articles costing £100 or o.** les articles de 100 livres et plus

8 (*in excess*) en plus, en excès; **allow five minutes o.** ajoutez-y cinq minutes; **children of fourteen and o.** les enfants de quatorze ans et plus; **three into seven goes twice and one o.** sept divisé par trois donne deux, et il reste un; **you will keep what is (left) o.** vous garderez l'excédent *ou* le surplus; **I have one card left o.** il me reste une carte

9 (*excessively*) (*easy, difficult, expensive*) trop; **we're not o. busy** nous n'avons pas trop à faire; **he didn't look o. cheerful** il n'était pas d'une gaieté folle

10 (*until later*) **to hold o.** (*decision*) remettre (à plus tard)

ADJ (*finished*) fini, terminé; **the danger is o.** le danger est passé; **the rain is o.** la pluie s'est arrêtée *ou* a cessé; **the game is o.** la partie est finie; **the war was just o.** la guerre venait de finir *ou* de s'achever; **when the strike is o.** quand la grève sera finie; **it is (all) o.** c'est fini; **it is all o. with me** c'en est fait de moi; **it's all o. between us** tout est fini entre nous; **that's o. and done with** voilà qui est fini et bien fini

N 1 *Com* **shorts and overs** déficits *mpl* et excédents *mpl*; **overs** (*in publishing*) exemplaires *mpl* de passe
2 *Cr* série f de six balles

overabundance [əʊvərəˈbʌndəns] N surabondance f

overabundant [əʊvərəˈbʌndənt] ADJ surabondant

overachieve [əʊvərəˈtʃiːv] VI (*exceed expectations*) faire mieux que prévu; **parents shouldn't push their children to o.** les parents ne devraient pas pousser leurs enfants à en faire trop

overachiever [əʊvərəˈtʃiːvər] N *esp Sch* personne f qui en fait trop; (*successful person*) surdoué, -ée

overact [əʊvərˈækt] VI (*of actor*) forcer son jeu

overactive [əʊvərˈæktɪv] ADJ trop actif; *Med* **to have an o. thyroid** faire de l'hyperthyroïdie

overaffectionate [əʊvərəˈfekʃənət] ADJ affectueux à l'excès

over-age ADJ au-dessus de l'âge limite

overall ADJ [ˈəʊvərɔːl] **1** (*from one end to the other*) total, -aux, hors tout **2** (*taken as a whole*) général, -aux
▪ ADV [əʊvərˈɔːl] dans l'ensemble, globalement; **England came third o.** au classement général l'Angleterre a fini troisième; **yacht measuring … o.** yacht dont la longueur totale *ou* hors tout est de …
▪ N [ˈəʊvərɔːl] (*garment*) blouse f, (*child's*) tablier m, blouse; **overalls** combinaison f (de travail), salopette f, *Fam* bleus *mpl* (de travail)
▸▸ **o. budget** budget m global; **o. consumption** consommation f totale; **o. demand** demande f globale; **o. efficiency** (*total efficiency*) rendement m total; (*efficiency in general*) rendement global

overanxious [əʊvərˈæŋkʃəs] ADJ **1** (*excessively worried*) trop inquiet; **you're being o. about her** tu t'inquiètes beaucoup trop pour elle; **he is o. about getting up to follow the regulations** sa grande préoccupation c'est de nous faire suivre le règlement **2** (*excessively eager*) **o. to please** trop soucieux de plaire

overarm [ˈəʊvərɑːm] ADV **to serve o.** (*in tennis, badminton*) servir par en dessus; *Cr* **to bowl o.** servir par en dessus
▸▸ *Cr* **o. bowling** service m au-dessus de la tête; **o. service** (*in tennis, badminton*) service au-dessus de la tête; *Swimming* **o. stroke** brasse f indienne, nage f (à l') indienne

overassess [əʊvərəˈses] VT *Fin* (*for tax*) surimposer

overassessment [əʊvərəˈsesmənt] N *Fin* (*for tax*) surimposition f

overawe [əʊvərˈɔː] VT intimider; (*of prospect, difficulty, surroundings*) impressionner; **don't be overawed by him** ne te laisse pas intimider par lui, ne sois pas intimidé par lui

overbalance [əʊvəˈbæləns] VI (*of person*) perdre l'équilibre; (*of thing*) se renverser
▪ VT (*knock over*) renverser

overbearing [əʊvəˈbeərɪŋ] ADJ autoritaire; **in an o. manner** autoritairement

overblown [əʊvəˈbləʊn] ADJ (*flower*) trop épanoui *ou* ouvert; (*style, book*) ampoulé; (*praise*) excessif

overboard [ˈəʊvəbɔːd] ADV *Naut* par-dessus bord; **to be washed o.** être enlevé par une lame; **to throw sb/sth o.** (*into water*) jeter qn/qch par-dessus bord *ou* à la mer; *Fig* **to throw sb/sth o.** se débarrasser de qn/abandonner qch; **to fall o.** tomber à la mer; **man o.!** un homme à la mer!; *Fam* **to go o.** (*be enthusiastic*) s'emballer (**for sb/sth** pour qn/qch)

overbook [əʊvəˈbʊk] VT & VI (of airline etc) surréserver, surbooker; **this flight was overbooked** il y a eu surréservation sur ce vol

overbooking [əʊvəˈbʊkɪŋ] N surréservation f, surbook(ing) m, surlocation f

overboot [ˈəʊvəbuːt] N couvre-chaussure m, pl couvre-chaussures

overborrow [əʊvəˈbɒrəʊ] VI Fin (of company) emprunter de façon excessive

overborrowing [əʊvəˈbɒrəʊɪŋ] N Fin (of company) surendettement m

overbought [əʊvəˈbɔːt] ADJ St Exch (market) surévalué, suracheté

overburden [əʊvəˈbɜːd(ə)n] VT (with work, responsibility) surcharger, accabler (**with** de); **he is not overburdened with principles** ce ne sont pas les principes qui l'étouffent

overcapacity [ˈəʊvəkəˈpæsɪti] N Ind surcapacité f

overcapitalization [əʊvəkæpɪtəlaɪˈzeɪʃən] N Fin surcapitalisation f

overcapitalize [əʊvəˈkæpɪtəlaɪz] VT Fin surcapitaliser

overcast [ˈəʊvəkɑːst] ADJ (sky, weather) couvert, nuageux; (day) nuageux; Fig (face) assombri; (expression, look) sombre; **it will become o. later** cela se couvrira plus tard; **it's looking a bit o.** ça a l'air un peu couvert

overcautious [əʊvəˈkɔːʃəs] ADJ trop prudent (**about** à propos de)

overcautiously [əʊvəˈkɔːʃəslɪ] ADV avec trop de prudence, avec une prudence excessive

overcharge [əʊvəˈtʃɑːdʒ] VT **1** Com faire payer trop cher à; **to o. sb for** or **on sth** faire payer qch trop cher à qn; **he overcharged me by a pound** il m'a fait payer une livre en trop **2** Fig (overload) (battery) surcharger
VI (of shopkeeper etc) faire payer trop cher

overcoat [ˈəʊvəkəʊt] N pardessus m

overcome [əʊvəˈkʌm] VT (pt **overcame** [əʊvəˈkeɪm], pp **overcome**) **1** (one's opponents etc) triompher de, vaincre; (difficulty, problem) venir à bout de, avoir raison de; (one's reluctance, fears etc) dominer, maîtriser; (obstacle) surmonter, vaincre; **to o. a disability** surmonter un handicap **2 to be o. with** or **by** (grief) être accablé de; (sleep, tears) être gagné par; (emotion, heat) succomber à; (fumes) être asphyxié par; **I was quite o.** j'ai été bouleversé

overcompensate [əʊvəˈkɒmpenseɪt] VI surcompenser; **to o. for sth** surcompenser qch

overcomplicated [əʊvəˈkɒmplɪkeɪtɪd] ADJ trop ou excessivement compliqué

overconfidence [əʊvəˈkɒnfɪdəns] N confiance f exagérée (**in** en); **to be guilty of o.** faire preuve d'une confiance exagérée

overconfident [əʊvəˈkɒnfɪdənt] ADJ **1** (about winning, finding a job etc) trop confiant; **you're being o. about her reaction/the exam** tu présumes un peu trop de sa réaction/de ta réussite à l'examen **2** (self-important) présomptueux

overcook [əʊvəˈkʊk] VT (faire) trop cuire

over-correction N (of air/fuel ratio etc) sur-correction f

overcritical [əʊvəˈkrɪtɪk(ə)l] ADJ trop critique

overcrowd [əʊvəˈkraʊd] VT (bus etc) trop remplir, surcharger; (city, region etc) surpeupler

overcrowded [əʊvəˈkraʊdɪd] ADJ trop rempli (**with** de); (with people) surchargé, bondé; (city, region etc) surpeuplé; (classroom) surchargé

overcrowding [əʊvəˈkraʊdɪŋ] N (of bus) remplissage m excessif; (of room etc) en-

combrement m; (of city) surpeuplement m; **o. is a problem in our schools** les sureffectifs sont un problème dans nos écoles

overdemand [əʊvədɪˈmɑːnd] N demande f excédentaire

overdeveloped [əʊvədɪˈveləpt] ADJ Phot etc trop développé

overdo [əʊvəˈduː] VT (pt **overdid** [əʊvəˈdɪd], pp **overdone** [əʊvəˈdʌn]) **1** (exaggerate) (welcome, praise) exagérer; **to o. one's enthusiasm** manifester un enthousiasme un peu forcé; **he overdoes the charm** il fait un peu trop le charmeur
2 (do or have too much of) forcer ou exagérer sur; **don't o. the chocolates** ne te gave pas de chocolats; **you've overdone the salt/cream** tu as un peu forcé sur le sel/la crème; **she overdoes the jogging** elle force un peu trop sur le jogging; **to o. the telly-watching** trop regarder la télé; Fam **to o. it** or **things** (work too hard) en faire trop, se surmener; **you've been overdoing it** or **things** (you need a rest) tu en as trop fait; Iron **don't o. it!** surtout ne te surmènes pas!
3 Culin trop cuire

overdose [ˈəʊvədəʊs] N dose f excessive, surdose f, overdose f; **to take an o.** prendre une dose excessive ou une surdose ou une overdose de drogue; (commit suicide) prendre une dose massive de barbituriques/etc; **to die of an o.** mourir d'overdose
VI **he overdosed on heroin** (took too much) il a pris une overdose ou surdose d'héroïne; (died) il est mort d'une overdose ou surdose d'héroïne; Fig **to o. on chocolate** exagérer sur le chocolat; **to o. on TV** se prendre une overdose de télé

overdraft [ˈəʊvədrɑːft] N Banking découvert m, solde m débiteur; **to have an o.** avoir un découvert; **to allow** or **give sb an o.** accorder à qn un découvert; **to pay off an/one's o.** rembourser un/son découvert
►► **o. facility** autorisation f de découvert, facilités fpl de caisse; **o. limit** plafond m de découvert; **o. loan** prêt m à découvert

overdraw [əʊvəˈdrɔː] (pt **overdrew** [əʊvəˈdruː], pp **overdrawn** [əʊvəˈdrɔːn]) Banking VT **to o. one's account** mettre un compte à découvert; **overdrawn account** compte m à découvert ou désapprovisionné, compte débiteur; **to be overdrawn** être à découvert; **your account is overdrawn** votre compte est débiteur; **to be £100 overdrawn** avoir un découvert de 100 livres; **to go overdrawn** passer en découvert
VI tirer à découvert

overdress [əʊvəˈdres] VI (dress too elegantly) s'habiller de façon trop élégante; (wear too many clothes) trop se couvrir; **to be overdressed** être habillé de façon trop élégante/être trop couvert

overdrive [ˈəʊvədraɪv] N Aut vitesse f surmultipliée, overdrive m; **in o.** en surmultipliée; Fig **to go into/be in o.** passer/être passé (à) la vitesse supérieure

overdub [əʊvəˈdʌb] VT (sound) doubler

overdubbing [əʊvəˈdʌbɪŋ] N doublage m, voice over m

overdue [əʊvəˈdjuː] ADJ (amount, account) en souffrance; (interest) qui n'a pas été payé à l'échéance; (person, train, library book) en retard; (reform, law, improvement etc) qui fait défaut; **to be long o.** (of law, reform etc) faire défaut depuis longtemps; **changes to the law on divorce were long o.** ça faisait longtemps qu'on aurait dû apporter des modifications à la loi sur les divorces; **the baby was two weeks o.** le bébé avait deux semaines de retard; **she's o.** (of pregnant woman) elle a dépassé le terme

overeat [əʊvəˈriːt] VI (pt **overate** [əʊvəˈret],

pp **overeaten** [əʊvəˈriːt(ə)n]) trop manger, manger avec excès

overeating [əʊvəˈriːtɪŋ] N excès mpl alimentaires ou de table

overelaborate [əʊvərɪˈlæbərət] ADJ (style, ideas, design) trop recherché; (proposal) trop compliqué

overemphasis [əʊvərˈemfəsɪs] N accentuation f excessive

overemphasize [əʊvərˈemfəsaɪz] VT trop accentuer; **it would be impossible to o. it** on ne saurait en exagérer l'importance

overemployment [əʊvərɪmˈplɔɪmənt] N suremploi m

overenthusiastic [əʊvərɪnθjuːzɪˈæstɪk] ADJ (par) trop enthousiaste

overestimate [əʊvərˈestɪmeɪt] VT (cost, person's talent, difficulty) surestimer, surévaluer; (danger) exagérer; (one's strength) trop présumer de; Com (assets) majorer; **to o. one's own importance** surestimer sa propre importance

overexcite [əʊvərekˈsaɪt] VT surexciter

overexcited [əʊvərekˈsaɪtɪd] ADJ surexcité

overexcitement [əʊvərekˈsaɪtmənt] N surexcitation f

overexert [əʊvəregˈzɜːt] VT **to o. oneself** trop se fatiguer, se surmener

overexertion [əʊvəregˈzɜːʃən] N surmenage m

overexpose [əʊvəreksˈpəʊz] VT Phot surexposer

overexposed [əʊvəreksˈpəʊzd] ADJ **1** Phot surexposé **2** Pej (person) trop présent dans les médias

overexposure [əʊvəreksˈpəʊʒər] N Phot surexposition f, Fig (on the media) surmédiatisation f, **to suffer from o.** faire trop parler de soi; **because of people's o. to advertising** parce que les gens sont bombardés de publicité

overextend [əʊvəreksˈtend] VT Fin **to o. oneself** s'engager au-dessus de ses moyens

overfamiliar [əʊvəfəˈmɪlɪər] ADJ **to be o. with sb** (too friendly etc) se montrer trop familier ou prendre des libertés excessives avec qn; **I'm not o. with the rules** les règlements ne me sont pas tellement familiers; **I'm not o. with what's been going on here** je ne suis pas très au courant de ce qui s'est passé ici

overfeed [əʊvəˈfiːd] VT suralimenter; **to be overfed** être suralimenté
VI se suralimenter, trop manger

overfishing [əʊvə(r)ˈfɪʃɪŋ] N surpêche f

overflow[1] [ˈəʊvəfləʊ] N **1** (action) débordement m **2** (excess liquid) débordement m; Comput dépassement m de capacité; Fig (of population) surplus m **3** (outlet) trop-plein m, pl trop-pleins
►► **o. pipe** (from sink, cistern) trop-plein; (large-scale) déversoir m

overflow[2] [əʊvəˈfləʊ] VI (of liquid, cup, heart) déborder; (of gutter, stream) déborder, dégorger; **a room overflowing with people** une salle qui regorge de monde; **the guests overflowed into the other rooms** les invités se sont répandus dans les autres pièces; Fig esp Lit **her heart overflowed with joy** son cœur débordait de joie
VT **to o. its banks** (of river) sortir de son lit

overflowing [əʊvəˈfləʊɪŋ] ADJ (water, river etc) qui déborde; (container) plein à déborder; (joy, gratitude) débordant
N **full to o.** plein à déborder

overfly [əʊvəˈflaɪ] VT (pt **overflew** [əʊvəˈfluː], pp **overflown** [əʊvəˈfləʊn]) survoler

overfond [əʊvəˈfɒnd] ADJ trop attaché (**of**

à); **I'm not o. of oranges** je ne raffole pas des oranges

overfull [əʊvə'fʊl] ADJ trop plein (**of, with** de); **to be o.** (after eating too much) être gavé

overgear [əʊvə'gɪər] VT Fin (company) surendetter; **to be overgeared** être surendetté

overgearing [əʊvə'gɪərɪŋ] N Fin surendettement m

overgrown [əʊvə'grəʊn] ADJ **1** (re)couvert (**with** de qch); **o. with weeds** (re)couvert de ou envahi par les mauvaises herbes; **o. with ivy** (re)couvert de ou tapissé de ou envahi de lierre **2** **he's like an o. schoolboy** il est resté très gamin; **you great big o. baby you!** espèce de grand bébé!

overhang[1] ['əʊvəhæŋ] N surplomb m; Constr **to have an o.** porter à faux; **a balcony with an o. of three feet** un balcon avec une saillie d'un mètre

overhang[2] [əʊvə'hæŋ] (pt, pp overhung [əʊvə'hʌŋ]) VT (of balcony, rocks etc) surplomber, faire saillie au-dessus de

VI (of balcony, rocks etc) surplomber, être en surplomb, faire saillie; (of wall) être en surplomb, déverser

overhanging [əʊvə'hæŋɪŋ] ADJ (rocks, balcony) en surplomb; (wall) en surplomb, déversé

overhaul[1] ['əʊvəhɔːl] N **1** (examination) (of machine etc) révision f, vérification f, complete o. révision complète **2** (repairs) (of vehicle, machine) révision f, remise f en état; Fig (of organization, theory, schedule) remaniement m

overhaul[2] [əʊvə'hɔːl] VT **1** (examine) (machine) réviser, vérifier **2** (repair) (machine) remettre en état; Fig (organization, theory, schedule) remanier **3** (overtake) dépasser

overhead ADV [əʊvə'hed] au-dessus; **the stars o.** les étoiles dans le ciel

ADJ ['əʊvəhed] (cable etc) aérien

N ['əʊvəhed] Com charge f opérationnelle; Am **o.**, Br **overheads** frais mpl généraux; **to reduce overheads** réduire les frais généraux ▸▸Fin **o. budget** budget m des charges; Tech **o. camshaft** arbre m à cames en tête; Com **o. charges** frais généraux; Constr, Rail **o. crossing** croisement m supérieur; Com **o. expenses** frais généraux; **o. lighting** éclairage f vertical; **o. projector** rétroprojecteur m; **o. railway** chemin m de fer aérien; Cin, TV **o. shot** plan m en plongée; Tennis **o. valve** soupape f en dessus ou en tête; Tennis **o. volley** volée f rattrapée au-dessus de la tête

overhead-valve engine N moteur m à soupapes en tête

overhear [əʊvə'hɪər] (pt, pp overheard [əʊvə'hɜːd]) VT (conversation etc) surprendre, entendre (par hasard); **they were overheard discussing it** ils ont été surpris en train d'en parler; **I couldn't help overhearing what you were saying** je n'ai pas pu m'empêcher d'entendre ce que vous disiez

VI **I couldn't help overhearing** je n'ai pas pu m'empêcher d'entendre ce que vous disiez/ce qu'il disait/etc

overheat [əʊvə'hiːt] VT (oven etc) surchauffer, trop chauffer; (economy) provoquer la surchauffe de

VI (of engine etc) chauffer; (of economy) entrer en surchauffe

overheated [əʊvə'hiːtɪd] ADJ (engine, room) surchauffé; (economy) en surchauffe; **to get o.** (of engine, brakes etc) chauffer; (of economy) entrer en surchauffe; Fig (of person) (become agitated) (trop) s'échauffer

overheating [əʊvə'hiːtɪŋ] N surchauffe f, Tech échauffement m (anormal)

overhype [əʊvə'haɪp] VT faire tout un tabac sur; (counter-productively) faire trop de battage sur

overindulge [əʊvərɪn'dʌldʒ] VT (person) montrer trop d'indulgence envers; (spoil) gâter; (own predilections etc) accorder une place excessive à; **to o. oneself** se faire plaisir; (eating, drinking) exagérer (sur la nourriture/la boisson), faire un excès (de table); **she tends to o. her taste for fine food** elle aime la bonne chère et elle ne se prive pas

VI (to eat, drink too much) faire des excès (de table); **to o. in chocolate/champagne** forcer sur le chocolat/le champagne

overindulgence [əʊvərɪn'dʌldʒəns] N **1** indulgence f excessive (**of sb** envers qn) **2** (in food, drink) excès mpl, abus m

overinvest [əʊvərɪn'vest] Fin VT trop investir

VI trop investir, surinvestir (**in** dans)

overinvestment [əʊvərɪn'vestmənt] N Fin surinvestissement m

overjoyed [əʊvə'dʒɔɪd] ADJ ravi, enchanté (**at** de), transporté de joie (**at** par); **he was o. to meet her** il était ravi ou enchanté de la rencontrer

overkeen [əʊvə'kiːn] ADJ empressé (**to do** de faire); **he wasn't o. on her/the idea** elle/l'idée ne lui plaisait pas outre mesure

overkill ['əʊvəkɪl] N Mil surcapacité f de tuer; Fig **it's o.** c'est exagéré, c'est trop; **don't you think we could be accused of o.?** ne croyez-vous pas qu'on pourrait nous accuser d'exagérer?; **so many police for such a demonstration was o.** le nombre d'agents de police était complètement disproportionné face à une telle manifestation; **media o.** médiatisation f excessive, surmédiatisation f

overladen [əʊvə'leɪd(ə)n] ADJ surchargé (**with** de)

overland ADV [əʊvə'lænd] par voie de terre

ADJ ['əʊvəlænd] par voie de terre; **o. journey** voyage m par voie de terre; **o. route** voie f de terre; Aviat trajet m survolant la terre

overlap[1] ['əʊvəlæp] N **1** (act, state of overlapping) recouvrement m; Constr (of tiles etc) chevauchement m; **an o. of two inches** un chevauchement de 5 cm; **there is some o. between philosophy and religion** il y a des points communs entre la philosophie et la religion; **the o. between two departments** les activités communes à deux départements **2** (overlapping part) partie f chevauchante

overlap[2] [əʊvə'læp] VT & VI (-pp-) recouvrir (partiellement); (of categories etc) avoir un domaine commun; (in time) coïncider; (of theories, evidence) avoir des points communs; **to o. (one another)** (of tiles, slates) se chevaucher; **our holidays will o. by a week** nos vacances vont coïncider pendant une semaine

overlapping [əʊvə'læpɪŋ] ADJ (tiles, planks etc) qui se chevauchent; (responsibilities) qui se recoupent; (holidays) qui coïncident

overlay[1] ['əʊvəleɪ] N **1** (of paint, varnish) couche f **2** Comput recouvrement m ▸▸Comput **o. program** programme m à recouvrement

overlay[2] [əʊvə'leɪ] VT (pt, pp overlaid [əʊvə'leɪd]) **1** recouvrir, couvrir (**with** de) **2** TV, Cin incruster, superposer

overleaf [əʊvə'liːf] ADV au dos (de la page); **see o.** voir au verso ou au dos

overlie [əʊvə'laɪ] VT (pt overlay [əʊvə'leɪ], pp overlain [əʊvə'leɪn]) recouvrir, couvrir

overload[1] ['əʊvələʊd] N **1** Elec surcharge f, surélévation f d'intensité; (of engine) excès m d'injection; **o. running** marche f en surcharge **2** (of vehicle) (excess weight) (poids m en) surcharge f

overload[2] [əʊvə'ləʊd] VT (lorry, machine, market) surcharger; (person) surmener; **to o. sb with work/responsibility** surcharger qn de travail/responsabilités

overlong [əʊvə'lɒŋ] ADV trop longtemps

ADJ trop long, f trop longue

overlook [əʊvə'lʊk] VT **1** (look out over) avoir vue sur, donner sur; **the castle/hill overlooks the town** le château/la colline surplombe la ville; **the window overlooks the street** la fenêtre donne sur la rue; **we are overlooked by our neighbours** nos voisins ont vue sur nous **2** (fail to notice) (detail, fact) négliger; (opportunity) négliger, laisser échapper; **I overlooked the fact** ce fait m'a échappé **3** (disregard) (contribution, project) ne pas prendre en compte; (breaches of procedure) fermer les yeux sur; (mistake) laisser passer; **I cannot o. this insolence** je ne peux pas laisser passer cette insolence; **he had been overlooked for promotion once again** une fois de plus quelqu'un d'autre avait été promu à sa place

overlord ['əʊvəlɔːd] N Hist suzerain m

overly ['əʊvəlɪ] ADV trop, excessivement; **not o.** pas trop

overlying [əʊvə'laɪɪŋ] ADJ superposé; (stratum) surjacent

overmanned [əʊvə'mænd] ADJ **to be o.** avoir un personnel trop nombreux; Ind avoir un surplus de main-d'œuvre

overmanning [əʊvə'mænɪŋ] N surplus m de personnel ou Ind de main-d'œuvre

overmuch [əʊvə'mʌtʃ] ADV (par) trop, outre mesure; **she didn't seem to mind o.** ça ne semblait pas trop la déranger, ça ne semblait pas la déranger outre mesure

overnight ADV [əʊvə'naɪt] (pendant) la nuit; (to change etc) du jour au lendemain; **to stay o.** passer la nuit; **leave to soak o.** laisser tremper toute la nuit; **he became famous/rich o.** il est devenu célèbre/riche du jour au lendemain

ADJ ['əʊvənaɪt] d'une nuit; **to be an o. success** devenir célèbre du jour au lendemain ▸▸**o. bag** sac m ou nécessaire m de voyage; **o. case** mallette f; **o. guest** ami, -ie qui passe la nuit (chez qn); (in hotel) client, -ente qui passe la nuit; Sport **o. leader** leader m du jour; Fin **o. loan** prêt m du jour au lendemain; Fin **o. rate** taux m de l'argent au jour le jour; **o. stay** séjour m d'une nuit; (in hotel) nuitée f, **to stay o.** arrêt m pour la nuit

overoptimism [əʊvə'rɒptɪmɪz(ə)m] N optimisme m exagéré; **to suffer from** or **be guilty of o.** être excessivement ou par trop optimiste

overoptimistic [əʊvərɒptɪ'mɪstɪk] ADJ excessivement ou par trop optimiste (**about** quant à); **I am not o. about their chances** je ne crois pas qu'ils aient de grandes chances

over-packaging N Mktg suremballage m

overpaid [əʊvə'peɪd] ADJ surpayé, trop payé

overparticular [əʊvəpə'tɪkjʊlər] ADJ (par) trop exigeant; **he's not o. about these things** il se moque un peu de ces choses-là

overpass ['əʊvəpɑːs] N (for pedestrians) passerelle f surélevée; (road) autopont m, pont m autoroutier

overpay [əʊvə'peɪ] VT (pt, pp overpaid [əʊvə'peɪd]) (person) surpayer, trop payer

overpayment [əʊvə'peɪmənt] N **1** (of taxes, on bill) trop-perçu m, pl trop-perçus **2** (of employee) rémunération f excessive

overplay [əʊvə'pleɪ] VT **to o. one's hand** Cards annoncer au-dessus de ses moyens; Fig présumer de ses chances (de réussite)

overpolite [əʊvəpə'laɪt] ADJ trop poli

overpopulated [əʊvə'pɒpjʊleɪtɪd] ADJ surpeuplé

overpopulation [əʊvəpɒpjʊ'leɪʃən] N surpeuplement m, surpopulation f

overposition [əʊvəpə'zɪʃən] VT *Mktg* surpositionner

overpositioning [əʊvəpə'zɪʃənɪŋ] N *Mktg* surpositionnement *m*

overpower [əʊvə'paʊər] VT *(person)* maîtriser; **to be overpowered by superior numbers** succomber sous *ou* être écrasé par le nombre

overpowering [əʊvə'paʊərɪŋ] ADJ *(grief, heat etc)* accablant; *(smell, taste)* (unpleasant) effroyable; *(much stronger than others)* prédominant; *(desire etc)* irrésistible; **I find him o.** je le trouve par trop imposant

overprice [əʊvə'praɪs] VT demander un prix excessif pour

overpriced [əʊvə'praɪst] ADJ trop cher, d'un prix excessif

overpricing [əʊvə'praɪsɪŋ] N fixation *f* d'un prix trop élevé

overprint[1] ['əʊvəprɪnt] N 1 *Typ* impression *f* en surcharge; *(on postage stamp etc)* surcharge *f; Phot* surimpression *f* 2 *(postage stamp)* timbre-poste *m* surchargé, *pl* timbres-poste surchargés

overprint[2] [əʊvə'prɪnt] VT *Typ (correction)* imprimer en surcharge; *Comput* surimprimer; *(postage stamp)* surcharger; *Phot* tirer en surimpression
▶ VI *Comput* surimprimer

overprinting [əʊvə'prɪntɪŋ] N *Typ* impression *f* en surcharge; *Comput* surimpression *f, Phot* (tirage *m* en) surimpression

overproduce [əʊvəprə'djuːs] VT & VI surproduire

overproduction [əʊvəprə'dʌkʃən] N surproduction *f*

overrate [əʊvə'reɪt] VT *(person's abilities, person)* surévaluer, surestimer; *(restaurant, film)* surfaire; **I think he's overrated as an actor** j'estime que sa réputation en tant qu'acteur est surfaite; **sex is overrated** le sexe, n'est pas aussi formidable qu'on le dit

overrated [əʊvə'reɪtɪd] ADJ *(film, book)* surfait; *(actor)* à la réputation surfaite

overreach [əʊvə'riːtʃ] VT **to o. oneself** trop présumer de ses forces
▶ VI *(of horse)* (s')attraper

overreact [əʊvərɪ'ækt] VI réagir de façon excessive (**to** à; **against** contre); **I don't want to o. but I do think something has to be done** sans vouloir dramatiser je crois vraiment qu'on devrait faire quelque chose

overreaction [əʊvərɪ'ækʃən] N réaction *f* trop forte *ou* excessive; **to accuse sb of o.** accuser qn de réagir de façon excessive

override [əʊvə'raɪd] N *Tech* forçage *m* en mode manuel; **manual o.** *(on automatic camera, lift etc)* commande *f* de passage en mode manuel
▶ VT *(pt* **overrode** [əʊvə'rəʊd], *pp* **overridden** [əʊvə'rɪd(ə)n]) 1 *(disregard) (objections, protest, rules, decision)* passer outre à 2 *(take precedence over)* avoir plus d'importance que, avoir la priorité sur; **decision that overrides a former decision** décision qui annule une décision antérieure; **this duty overrode all her other commitments** cette tâche a pris la priorité sur tous ses autres engagements 3 *(automated process)* annuler 4 *(horse)* surmener

overriding [əʊvə'raɪdɪŋ] ADJ *(ambition, factor)* principal, -aux; *(importance)* capital, -aux; *(objection)* majeur; *(principle)* premier; **it was not an o. factor** ce n'a pas été un facteur décisif; **to have an o. desire to do sth** être en proie à un irrésistible désir de faire qch; **but there are o. reasons** mais il y a des raisons d'ordre majeur

overripe [əʊvə'raɪp] ADJ trop mûr; *(cheese)* trop fait

overrule [əʊvə'ruːl] VT *(proposal, advice)* rejeter; *Law (decision)* annuler, casser; *Law (claim, objection)* rejeter; **she was overruled by her boss** son patron a rejeté ce qu'elle avait proposé; *Am Law* **objection overruled** objection rejetée

overrun[1] ['əʊvərʌn] N 1 *Typ (at end of line)* chasse *f, (at end of page)* report *m,* ligne(s) *f(pl)* à reporter 2 *Com* **(cost) overruns** dépassement *m* du coût estimé
▶▶ *Comput* **o. error** perte *f* d'informations par engorgement; *Aut* **o. valve** limiteur *m* de régime

overrun[2] [əʊvə'rʌn] *(pt* **overran** [əʊvə'ræn], *pp* **overrun;** *prp* **overrunning)** VT 1 *(of invaders) (country)* envahir; **a garden o. with weeds** un jardin envahi par les mauvaises herbes; **a house o. with mice** une maison infestée de souris 2 *(allotted time)* dépasser; *Rail (signal)* dépasser; **to o. a budget** dépasser un budget 3 *Typ (word)* reporter à la ligne/à la page suivante; **words that o. the line** mots qui chassent
▶ VI *TV, Radio* déborder; **words that o. (into the margin)** mots qui chassent; **the TV programme/the speech overran** le programme télévisé/le discours a duré plus longtemps que prévu; **you mustn't o.** vous ne devez pas dépasser le temps qui vous est imparti; **the project has o. by three weeks** le projet a dépassé la date limite de trois mois

oversale ['əʊvəseɪl] N *Am* surlocation *f*

overseas ADJ ['əʊvəsiːz] *(colony, trade)* d'outre-mer; *(branch, office of business)* à l'étranger; *(market)* étranger
▶ ADV [əʊvə'siːz] à l'étranger, *Lit* par delà les mers; **from o.** d'outre-mer
▶▶ **o. investment** investissement *m* extérieur

oversee [əʊvə'siː] VT *(pt* **oversaw** [əʊvə'sɔː], *pp* **overseen** [əʊvə'siːn]) *(workshop, site etc)* surveiller

overseer ['əʊvəsiːər] N surveillant, -ante; *Ind* contremaître, -esse; *Constr* chef *m* de chantier

oversell ['əʊvəsel] VT *(pt, pp* **oversold** [əʊvə'səʊld]) 1 *(praise too highly)* vanter les mérites de 2 *Com (sell too much of)* vendre trop de; **the flight/concert had been oversold** trop de billets avaient été vendus par rapport au nombre de places pour le vol/concert

oversensitive [əʊvə'sensɪtɪv] ADJ hypersensible; **you're just being o.** tu es trop susceptible; **to be a bit o. about criticism** être un peu trop sensible aux critiques

oversew ['əʊvəsəʊ] VT *(pt* **oversewed** ['əʊvəsəʊd], *pp* **oversewn** ['əʊvəsəʊn]) *Sewing* surjeter; *(edge)* surfiler

oversexed [əʊvə'sekst] ADJ qui a une libido démesurée; **you're o.** tu es un obsédé sexuel, tu ne penses qu'à ça

overshadow [əʊvə'ʃædəʊ] VT 1 *(spread shadow over)* ombrager, couvrir de son ombre 2 *Fig (of atmosphere)* planer sur; **the negotiations were overshadowed by gloom** une atmosphère morose planait sur les négociations; **his success had been overshadowed by his father's death** sa réussite avait été assombrie par la mort de son père 3 *Fig (eclipse)* éclipser; **he had always been overshadowed by his brother** son frère l'avait toujours éclipsé

overshoe ['əʊvəʃuː] N couvre-chaussure *m, pl* couvre-chaussures; *(with wooden soles)* galoche *f,* **rubber overshoes** caoutchoucs *mpl*

overshoot [əʊvə'ʃuːt] *(pr, pp* **overshot** [əʊvə'ʃɒt]) VT *(of shot, gun)* porter au delà de; **to o. the mark** dépasser le but; *Fig* dépasser les bornes; *Aviat* **to o. the run-**way dépasser la piste; *(deliberately)* survoler la piste; **to o. a production target** dépasser *ou* excéder un objectif de production
▶ VI *(of plane, pilot)* dépasser la piste

overshot ['əʊvəʃɒt] ADJ *Tech (wheel)* mû par en dessus

oversight ['əʊvəsaɪt] N 1 *(omission)* oubli *m,* omission *f,* **through** *or* **by an o.** par mégarde, par inadvertance, par oubli 2 *(supervision)* surveillance *f*

oversimplification [əʊvəsɪmplɪfɪ'keɪʃən] N simplification *f* excessive

oversimplify [əʊvə'sɪmplɪfaɪ] VT & VI simplifier à outrance

oversized ['əʊvəsaɪzd] ADJ trop grand; *(class)* surchargé; *Fam (very big)* énorme; **you great o. oaf!** espèce de grosse brute!

oversleep [əʊvə'sliːp] VI *(pt, pp* **overslept** [əʊvə'slept]) ne pas se réveiller à temps, *Fam* avoir une panne d'oreiller; **in order to stop him from oversleeping** pour qu'il se réveille à temps, *Fam* pour qu'il n'ait plus de pannes d'oreiller

oversleeve ['əʊvəsliːv] N manchette *f*

oversold [əʊvə'səʊld] ADJ *St Exch (market)* sousévalué

overspend [əʊvə'spend] *(pt, pp* **overspent** [əʊvə'spent]) VI dépenser trop; **to o. by ...** dépenser ... de trop
▶ VT *(budget)* dépasser

overspending [əʊvə'spendɪŋ] N dépense *f* excessive; *Fin* dépassement *m* budgétaire

overspill ['əʊvəspɪl] N *(population)* surplus *m ou* déversement *m* de population
▶▶ **o. population** surplus *ou* déversement de population; **o. town** = ville *f* servant à décongestionner une agglomération surpeuplée

overstaffed [əʊvə'stɑːft] ADJ qui a un excédent de personnel

overstaffing [əʊvə'stɑːfɪŋ] N excédents *mpl* de personnel, sureffectifs *mpl*

overstate [əʊvə'steɪt] VT *(facts etc)* exagérer; **I am neither overstating nor understating the case** je n'exagère ni dans un sens ni dans l'autre; **it would not be overstating the problem to say that ...** on pourrait dire sans exagérer que ...

overstay [əʊvə'steɪ] VT **to o. one's welcome** abuser de l'hospitalité de ses hôtes; *Mil* **to o. one's leave** dépasser la durée de sa permission

oversteer[1] ['əʊvəstɪər] N *Aut* comportement *m* survireur, survirage *m*

oversteer[2] [əʊvə'stɪər] VI *Aut* survirer; **a car which oversteers** une voiture survireuse

overstep [əʊvə'step] VT *(-pp-)* *(limit, boundary, one's powers)* outrepasser; *Fig* **to o. the mark** dépasser les bornes

overstock [əʊvə'stɒk] VT *(outlet)* munir de stocks excessifs; *(market)* encombrer; *(farm)* mettre trop de bétail dans; *(pond)* mettre trop de poissons dans; **to be overstocked** *(of shop)* avoir des stocks excessifs

overstocking [əʊvə'stɒkɪŋ] N *Com* stockage *m* excessif

overstrike ['əʊvəstraɪk] N *(in printing)* surimpression *f*

oversubscribe [əʊvəsəb'skraɪb] VT *Fin (share issue)* sursouscrire

oversubscribed [əʊvəsəb'skraɪbd] ADJ *Fin* sursouscrit

oversubscription [əʊvəsəb'skrɪpʃən] N *Fin (of share issue)* sursouscription *f*

overt [əʊ'vɜːt] ADJ évident, manifeste; **do you have to be quite so o. about it?** dois-tu absolument le montrer aussi clairement?
▶▶ *Law* **o. act** acte *m* manifeste

overtake [əʊvə'teɪk] VT *(pt* **overtook**

[əʊvə'tʊk], *pp* **overtaken** [əʊvə'teɪk(ə)n]) **1** *esp Br (go past) (competitor, car)* doubler, dépasser; *(previous level)* dépasser; **demand has overtaken supply** la demande a dépassé l'offre **2** *(of fate etc)* s'abattre sur; **their plans/we were overtaken by fate** le sort s'est joué de leurs projets/nous; **overtaken by events** dépassé *ou* devancé par les événements; **darkness overtook us** la nuit nous surprit

overtaking [əʊvə'teɪkɪŋ] **N** *esp Br Aut* dépassement *m*; **no o.** défense de doubler ▸▸ **o. lane** *(when driving on right)* voie *f* de gauche; *(when driving on left)* voie de droite

overtax [əʊvə'tæks] **VT 1** *Fin (nation)* accabler sous les impôts; *(individual)* surtaxer, surimposer **2** *(overburden) (person)* surmener; *(resources)* peser lourdement sur; **to o. one's strength** se surmener, abuser de ses forces; **to o. sb's patience** abuser de la patience de qn

over-the-counter **ADJ** *(sales)* au comptant; *(medication)* vendu sans ordonnance ▸▸ *St Exch* **o. market** marché *m* hors cote, marché des transactions hors séance

overthrow[1] [ˈəʊvəθrəʊ] **N** *(of empire, government)* renversement *m*; *(of person)* chute *f*

overthrow[2] [əʊvə'θrəʊ] **VT** *(pt* **overthrew** [əʊvə'θru:], *pp* **overthrown** [əʊvə'θrəʊn]) *(person)* défaire, vaincre; *(empire)* renverser, abattre; *(government, established order)* renverser

overtime [ˈəʊvətaɪm] **N 1** *Ind* heures *fpl* supplémentaires; **to do o.** faire des heures supplémentaires; **to get o. (pay)** être payé pour les heures supplémentaires que l'on fait **2** *Am Sport* temps *m* supplémentaire
ADV *Ind* **to work o.** faire des heures supplémentaires; *Fig* **my imagination was working o.** mon imagination galopait *ou* s'emballait ▸▸ *Ind* **o. ban** refus *m* de faire des heures supplémentaires; *Ind* **o. pay** paiement *m* des heures supplémentaires; *Ind* **o. rate** tarif *m* des heures supplémentaires

overtire [əʊvə'taɪər] **VT** *(person)* surmener; **to o. oneself, to get overtired** se surmener, trop se fatiguer; **to be overtired** *(of child)* être trop fatigué

overtiredness [əʊvə'taɪədnɪs] **N** *Med* surmenage *m*

overtly [əʊ'vɜːtlɪ] **ADV** ouvertement

overtness [əʊ'vɜːtnɪs] **N** franchise *f*

overtone [ˈəʊvətəʊn] **N 1** *(suggestion) (of sadness, bitterness)* nuance *f*, soupçon *m*; **there are overtones of racism in her books** il y a des relents de racisme dans ses livres; **the phrase has an o. of disparagement** l'expression comporte un soupçon *ou* un rien de dénigrement; **an o. of criticism** une note critique **2** *Mus* harmonique *m*

overtrade [əʊvə'treɪd] **VI** avoir une marge d'exploitation trop étroite

overture [ˈəʊvətjʊər] **N** *Mus* ouverture *f*; *Fig* **to make overtures to sb** *(sexually)* faire des avances à qn; *(for business purposes)* faire des propositions à qn; **peace overtures** propositions *fpl* de paix

overturn [əʊvə'tɜːn] **VT** *(table, government, status quo)* renverser; *(car)* faire verser; *(boat)* faire chavirer; *(theory)* démonter; **the bill was overturned in the Senate** le projet de loi a été rejeté par le Sénat
VI se renverser; *(of vehicle)* verser, capoter; *(of boat)* chavirer; *(of plane)* capoter

overuse[1] [əʊvə'ju:s] **N** emploi *m* excessif (**of** de); **the phrase has been made meaningless by o.** l'expression a perdu tout son sens à force d'être trop employée

overuse[2] [əʊvə'ju:z] **VT** trop employer

overvaluation [əʊvəvælju:'eɪʃən] **N** surévaluation *f*

overvalue [əʊvə'vælju:] **VT 1** *Com (assets)* surestimer, majorer; *(object)* surestimer, surévaluer **2** *Fig (person's abilities etc)* surestimer, surévaluer, exagérer

overview [ˈəʊvəvju:] **N** *(of situation etc)* vue *f* d'ensemble

overvoltage protection [ˈəʊvəvəʊltɪdʒ] **N** protection *f* contre la surtension

overwater [əʊvə'wɔːtər] **VT** *(plant)* trop arroser

overwatering [əʊvə'wɔːtərɪŋ] **N** *(of plant)* arrosage *m* excessif

overweening [əʊvə'wiːnɪŋ] **ADJ** *(person, attitude)* outrecuidant, présomptueux; *(ambition, vanity)* sans bornes

overweight **ADJ** *(person)* trop gros; *(luggage)* en excédent; **he's a few kilos o.** il a quelques kilos en trop
N [ˈəʊvəweɪt] *(excess weight)* surpoids *m*, poids *m* en excès

overwhelm [əʊvə'welm] **VT** *(the enemy)* écraser, accabler; *(with kindness)* combler; *(with shame)* confondre; **overwhelmed with work** débordé de travail; **overwhelmed with phone calls** submergé d'appels; **I am overwhelmed (by your kindness)** je suis confus (de votre gentillesse); **overwhelmed with joy/grief/despair** au comble de la joie/du malheur/du désespoir; **to be overwhelmed with relief** être profondément soulagé

overwhelming [əʊvə'welmɪŋ] **ADJ** *(need, desire etc)* irrésistible; *(joy, happiness)* débordant; *(grief, sense of guilt)* accablant; *(heat, pressure)* écrasant, accablant; *(defeat, majority)* écrasant; **to have an o. desire to do sth** éprouver le besoin irrésistible de faire qch

overwhelmingly [əʊvə'welmɪŋlɪ] **ADV** *(beaten, defeated)* d'une manière écrasante; **it is o. sad** c'est affreusement triste

overwind [əʊvə'waɪnd] **VT** *(pt, pp* **overwound** [əʊvə'waʊnd]) *(watch etc)* trop remonter

overwork [əʊvə'wɜːk] **N** surmenage *m*; **suffering from o.** surmené
VT *(person)* surmener, surcharger de travail; *(muscle, heart)* surmener; *(idea, metaphor etc)* utiliser à outrance; **to o. oneself** se surmener
VI se surmener

overworking [əʊvə'wɜːkɪŋ] **N** surmenage *m*

overwrite[1] [ˈəʊvəraɪt] **N** ▸▸ *Comput* **o. mode** mode *m* de superposition

overwrite[2] [əʊvə'raɪt] **VT** *Comput (data)* superposer

overwrought [əʊvə'rɔːt] **ADJ** *(with grief)* accablé; **to be o.** *(nervous and upset)* avoir les nerfs à vif, être angoissé; **the child was o.** l'enfant était à bout; **to become o.** s'affliger, se tourmenter

overzealous [əʊvə'zeləs] **ADJ** trop zélé

Ovid [ˈɒvɪd] **N** Ovide *m*

oviduct [ˈəʊvɪdʌkt] **N** *Biol* oviducte *m*

ovine [ˈəʊvaɪn] **ADJ** *(animal etc)* ovin

oviparous [əʊ'vɪpərəs] **ADJ** *Biol* ovipare

ovoid [ˈəʊvɔɪd] **ADJ** ovoïde
N figure *f* ovoïde

ovulate [ˈɒvjʊleɪt] **VI** *Biol* ovuler

ovulation [ɒvjʊ'leɪʃən] **N** *Biol* ovulation *f*

ovule [ˈɒvjuːl] **N** *Biol* ovule *m*

ovum, *pl* **ova** [ˈəʊvəm, ˈəʊvə] **N** *Biol* ovule *m*

ow [aʊ] **INT** aïe!, ouille!

owe [əʊ] **VT** *(pt, pp* **owed** [əʊd]) *(money)* devoir; **to o. sb sth, to o. sth to sb** devoir qch à qn; **the sum owed (to) her by her brother** la somme que son frère lui doit *ou* qui lui est due par son frère; **I still o. you for**

the petrol je vous dois encore l'essence; **what** *or* **how much do I o. you?** qu'est-ce que je te dois?, combien est-ce que je te dois?
2 *Fig (respect, obedience etc)* devoir; **I o. you an apology/an explanation** je vous dois des excuses/une explication; **you o. it to yourself to do your best** vous vous devez à vous-même de faire de votre mieux; **I o. my life to you** je vous dois la vie; **to o. sb a favour** être redevable d'un service à qn; **to what do I o. this honour?** qu'est-ce qui me vaut cet honneur?; **he owes his success to his parents' influence** il doit son succès à l'influence de ses parents

owing [ˈəʊɪŋ] **ADJ 1** **there is £5 o.** 5 livres restent dues; **all the money o. to me** tout l'argent qui m'est dû **2** **o. to** *(because of)* en raison de, à cause de; **o. to a recent bereavement** en raison d'un deuil récent; **o. to the force of circumstances** par la force des choses

owl [aʊl] **N** hibou *m*, *pl* -oux, chouette *f*; *Fig* **a wise old o.** *(person)* un vieux sage; *Fam* **o. glasses** lunettes *fpl* (parfaitement) rondes

owlet [ˈaʊlɪt] **N** jeune hibou *m*, jeune chouette *f*

owlish [ˈaʊlɪʃ] **ADJ** de hibou; **o. look** air *m* de sage

OWN [əʊn]

> **VT** posséder **1**
> **ADJ** propre
> **PRON** le mien/le sien/*etc* **1** ▪ seul **2**

VT 1 *(land, house, car etc)* posséder, être propriétaire de; *(washing machine, stereo, dog etc)* avoir, posséder; **who owns this land?** qui est le propriétaire de cette terre?; **who owns this stereo?** à qui appartient cette chaîne stéréo?; **he behaves as if he owned the place** il se conduit comme en pays conquis; **you don't o. me!** je ne t'appartiens pas!; **company owned by the state** compagnie qui appartient à l'État
2 *Fml (admit)* **I o. that I was wrong** je reconnais que j'ai eu tort, j'ai eu tort, **j'**avoue *ou* je le reconnais; **to o. oneself beaten** s'avouer vaincu; *esp Jur* **to o. a child** *(recognize as one's own)* reconnaître un enfant; *Fam* **I won't o. you!** je ne te connais plus!
VI **to o. to a mistake** reconnaître *ou* avouer une erreur; **he owns to being forty** *(admits he is)* il admet qu'il a quarante ans
ADJ propre; **her o. money** son propre argent; **I saw it with my o. eyes** je l'ai vu de mes propres yeux; **I had my o. table** j'avais ma table à moi; **I do my o. cooking** je fais la cuisine moi-même, je fais ma propre cuisine; **the supermarket does its o. baking** le supermarché cuit son propre pain; **to roll one's o. cigarettes** rouler ses cigarettes; **to score an o. goal** *Ftbl* marquer un but pour l'équipe adverse; *Fig* apporter de l'eau au moulin de l'adversaire; **to be one's o. man/woman** vivre à sa façon *ou* à son idée
PRON 1 **my/his/***etc* **o.** le mien/le sien/*etc*; **one's o.** le sien; **they are my o.** ce sont les miens, ils sont à moi, ils m'appartiennent; **to look after one's o.** *(property)* soigner son bien; *(friends, relatives)* s'occuper des siens; **I have money of my o.** j'ai de l'argent à moi; **a child of his o.** un enfant à lui; **the house is my o.** la maison est à moi *ou* m'appartient; **to make sth one's o.** s'approprier qch; **she took the song and made it her o.** elle s'est approprié la chanson; **she has a copy of her o.** elle a un exemplaire à elle *ou* en propre; **for reasons of his o.** pour des raisons qui le regardent; **his ideas are his o.** ses idées lui sont propres; **a style of one's o.** *or* **all one's o.** un style original *ou* propre *ou* spécifique; *Fam* **to roll one's o.** rouler ses ci-

garettes; **the landscape has a wild beauty of its o.** le paysage a une beauté sauvage qui lui est propre; **may I have it for my (very) o.?** est-ce que je peux l'avoir pour moi seul?; **there's not a thing here that I can call my o.** il n'y a pas ici un objet qui m'appartienne en propre; **my time is my o.** mon temps est à moi *ou* m'appartient, je suis libre de mon temps

 2 to do sth on one's o. *(without company)* faire qch tout seul; *(on one's own initiative)* faire qch sur sa propre initiative *ou* de son propre chef; **to be** *or* **work on one's o.** travailler tout seul; *(be in business alone)* être établi à son propre compte; **I am (all) on my o.** je suis seul; **you're on your o.!** c'est à toi de te débrouiller!

 3 to come into one's o. *(develop fully)* s'épanouir; **to get one's o. back** se venger; **to hold one's o.** *(of patient, in argument, fight etc)* se maintenir

▸ **own up** VI *(confess)* avouer; **to o. up to a crime/to having done sth** avouer un crime/ avoir fait qch

---

own-brand *Mktg* ADJ **our o. butter** du beurre sous notre propre marque
 N marque *f* de distributeur
 ▸▸ **o. label** marque de distributeur; **o. product** produit *m* à marque de distributeur

own-branding N *Mktg* apposition *f* de sa propre marque

owner ['əʊnər] N *(of house, land, car)* propriétaire *mf*; *(of business)* patron, -onne, propriétaire; *(of dog etc)* propriétaire, maître, -esse; **the o. of this stereo** la personne à qui cette chaîne stéréo appartient; **cars parked here at (the) owners' risk** les voitures garées ici le sont aux risques de leurs propriétaires; *Naut* **the owners** *(of ship)* les armateurs *mpl*, l'armement *m*
 ▸▸ *Acct* **o.'s capital account** compte *m* de l'exploitant; *Aut* **o. driver** conducteur, -trice propriétaire

ownerless ['əʊnəlɪs] ADJ sans propriétaire; *(dog)* sans maître

owner-occupancy N fait *m* d'être propriétaire du logement qu'on occupe; **o. has increased** de plus en plus de gens sont propriétaires de leurs logements

owner-occupier N propriétaire-occupant *m*, *pl* propriétaires-occupants

ownership ['əʊnəʃɪp] N possession *f*; *(right)* (droit *m* de) propriété *f*; **to have o. of sth** être en possession de qch; **she wants o. of the car** elle veut être propriétaire de la voiture; **the o. of the house is contested** les droits de propriété sont contestés; **change**

of o. *Com* changement *m* de propriétaire; *Law* mutation *f*; **under new o.** *(notice in shop, restaurant etc)* nouveau propriétaire; **during her o. of the property** pendant qu'elle possédait la propriété; **the bus company is now in private o.** la compagnie de bus est maintenant aux mains du secteur privé

own-label ADJ = **own-brand**

owt [aʊt] PRON *Eng Dial* = **anything**

ox, *pl* **oxen** [ɒks, 'ɒks(ə)n] N bœuf *m*; **ox cart** char *m* à bœufs; *Culin* **ox heart/tongue** cœur *m*/langue *f* de bœuf

oxalic [ɒkˈsælɪk] ADJ *Chem* oxalique

oxblood ['ɒksblʌd] N *(colour)* rouge *m* sang
 ADJ rouge sang *inv*

oxbow ['ɒksbəʊ] N *Geog* bras *m* mort *(d'un cours d'eau)*
 ▸▸ **o. lake** bras mort

Oxbridge ['ɒksbrɪdʒ] N les universités *fpl* d'Oxford et de Cambridge
 ADJ *(graduate etc)* de l'université d'Oxford ou de Cambridge

---

Oxbridge

Oxbridge désigne conjointement les universités d'Oxford et de Cambridge, les plus anciennes et les plus prestigieuses d'Angleterre. Oxford et Cambridge se distinguent des autres établissements d'enseignement supérieur, notamment par leur structure collégiale et leurs conditions d'admission très rigoureuses. De nos jours, Oxbridge est toujours synonyme d'élitisme en dépit des efforts entrepris pour élargir le recrutement des deux universités. Jusqu'à une époque très récente, un diplôme d'Oxbridge était considéré comme indispensable pour accéder à des postes importants dans le monde de la politique ou de la diplomatie.

---

oxen *see* **ox**

oxeye ['ɒksaɪ] N **o. daisy, white o.** *(flower)* marguerite *f* des champs

Oxfam ['ɒksfæm] N *Br* = œuvre *f* de bienfaisance travaillant pour le tiers-monde
 ▸▸ **O. shop** = magasin *m* où l'œuvre de bienfaisance Oxfam vend des articles d'occasion et d'artisanat au profit du tiers-monde

Oxford ['ɒksfəd] N
 ▸▸ **O. bags** *(trousers)* pantalon *m* très large; **O. blue** *(colour)* bleu *m* foncé; *(sportsperson)*

= sportif *m* qui porte ou a porté les couleurs de l'université d'Oxford; **O. shoes** oxfords *mpl*, souliers *mpl* richelieu

oxherd ['ɒkshɜːd] N bouvier, -ière

oxhide ['ɒkshaɪd] N cuir *m* de bœuf

oxidation [ɒksɪˈdeɪʃən] N *Chem* oxydation *f*

oxide ['ɒksaɪd] N *Chem* oxyde *m*

oxidization [ɒksɪdaɪˈzeɪʃən] N *Chem* oxydation *f*

oxidize ['ɒksɪdaɪz] *Chem* VT oxyder
 VI s'oxyder

Oxonian [ɒkˈsəʊnɪən] ADJ oxfordien, -ienne, oxonien, -ienne
 N *Univ* membre *m* de l'université d'Oxford

oxtail ['ɒksteɪl] N *Culin* queue *f* de bœuf
 ▸▸ **o. soup** soupe *f* de queue de bœuf

oxyacetylene [ɒksɪəˈsetɪliːn] N
 ▸▸ **o. burner** chalumeau *m* oxyacétylénique de découpage; **o. cutting** découpage *m* au chalumeau; **o. torch** chalumeau oxyacétylénique de découpage

oxygen ['ɒksɪdʒən] N *Chem* oxygène *m*
 ▸▸ **o. bottle, o. cylinder** bouteille *f* d'oxygène; **o. mask** masque *m* à oxygène; **o. tent** tente *f* à oxygène

oxygenate ['ɒksɪdʒɪneɪt, ɒkˈsɪ-] VT oxygéner

oxygenation [ɒksɪdʒɪˈneɪʃən] N oxygénation *f*

oxygenize ['ɒksɪdʒɪnaɪz] VT oxygéner

oxymoron [ɒksɪˈmɔːrɒn] N oxymoron *m*, oxymore *m*

oyez [əʊˈjeɪ, əʊˈjez] INT **o.! o.!** oyez!

oyster ['ɔɪstər] N huître *f*; **pearl o.** (huître) perlière *f*; *Fig* **the world is your o.** le monde t'appartient
 ▸▸ **o. bank, o. bed** huîtrière *f*, banc *m* d'huîtres; **o. breeder** ostréiculteur, -trice; **o. farm** parc *m* à huîtres; **o. farmer** ostréiculteur, -trice; **o. knife** couteau *m* à huîtres; **o. mushroom** pleurote *f*, **o. park** parc à huîtres; **o. shell** écaille *f* d'huître

oystercatcher ['ɔɪstəkætʃər] N *(bird)* huîtrier *m*

Oz [ɒz] N *Sl* Australie *f*

oz *abbr* **ounce(s)**

ozone ['əʊzəʊn] N *Chem* ozone *m*; *(bracing air)* bon air *m* frais
 ▸▸ **o. depletion** diminution *f* de l'ozone; **o. layer** couche *f* d'ozone; *Met* ozonosphère *f*

ozone-friendly ADJ *(product, aerosol)* qui préserve la couche d'ozone

Ozzie ['ɒzɪ] N *Sl* Australien, -ienne

P

P, p [piː] N **1** *(letter)* P, p *m*; **two p's** deux p; *Mktg* **the four P's** les quatre P, le marketing mix; *Fam* **to mind one's P's and Q's** *(be polite)* se surveiller **2** *Br (abbr* **penny, pence**) penny *m*, *pl* pence; **a 20p stamp** un timbre à 20 pence

p. *(abbr* **page**) p.

P45 [piːfɔːtɪˈfaɪv] N *Br* = document *m* administratif donné à tout employé lorsqu'il quitte un emploi et devant être présenté à tout nouvel employeur, où figurent le total des rémunérations versées par l'employeur ainsi que les sommes payées par l'employé en impôts et cotisations sociales; *Fig* **to be handed one's P45** se faire licencier

PA [ˈpiːˈeɪ] N **1** *(abbr* **public address**) PA (system) *(système m de)* sonorisation *f*, système *m* de haut-parleurs, *Fam* sono *f*, **an announcement over the PA** une annonce par haut-parleurs **2** *(abbr* **personal appearance**) **to do a PA** venir en personne; **a PA has been scheduled to promote their new album** ils vont venir faire la promotion de leur nouvel album en personne **3** *(abbr* **personal assistant**) *(of executive)* assistant, -ante; *(with secretarial duties)* secrétaire *mf* (de direction) **4** *(abbr* **Press Association**) agence *f* de presse britannique **5** *(abbr* **production assistant**) assistant, -ante de production

Pa *abbr* **Pennsylvania**

pa [paː] N *Fam* papa *m*

p.a. [ˈpiːˈeɪ] *(abbr* **per annum**) par an; **£16,000 p.a.** 16 000 livres par an

pace¹ [peɪs] N **1** *(step)* pas *m*; **ten paces off** à dix pas de distance; *Mil etc* **one p. forward!** un pas en avant! **2** *(gait)* allure *f*, *(of horse etc)* amble *m*; **to put a horse through its paces** faire passer un cheval à la montre; **to put a car/machine through its paces** mettre une voiture/une machine à l'épreuve; **to put sb through his/her paces** mettre qn à l'épreuve **3** *(speed)* vitesse *f*, train *m*, allure *f*, **there was a lot of p. on the ball** la balle filait à toute allure; **at a smart p.** à vive allure; **at a slow p.** à petite allure; **at walking p.** au pas; **to keep p. with sb** marcher du même pas que qn, aller à la même allure que qn; *Fig (in activity)* suivre le rythme de qn; **I can't keep p. with today's teenagers** avec les adolescents d'aujourd'hui, je n'arrive pas à suivre; **supply is keeping p. with demand** l'offre suit la demande; **our incomes haven't kept p. with inflation** nos revenus n'ont pas augmenté au même rythme que l'inflation; **the company did not keep p. with developments in the industry** la société n'a pas suivi le rythme des développements dans l'industrie; **it's all happened so fast I can barely keep p. with it** tout est arrivé si vite que j'ai

du mal à suivre le rythme; **to force the p.** forcer le pas *ou* l'allure; **the p. has slackened** l'allure s'est ralentie; **to set the p.** donner le pas; *Sport* donner *ou* régler l'allure; *(of company etc)* mener le train; **to stand the p.** tenir le rythme; **he can't stand the p.** il ne tient pas le rythme

VI marcher à pas mesurés; *(of horse etc)* aller l'amble; **to p. about** *or* **up and down** faire les cent pas

VT *(room, street)* arpenter; *Sport (runner)* tirer; **to p. oneself** *(when running, drinking)* trouver son rythme; *(when eating)* garder de la place pour la suite

▸▸ **p. bowler** *(in cricket)* lanceur *m* rapide *ou* puissant

▸ **pace off, pace out** VT SEP *(distance)* mesurer au pas

pace² [ˈpɑːtʃeɪ] PREP *Fml* n'en déplaise à

pacemaker [ˈpeɪsmeɪkər] N **1** *Sport (of runner)* meneur, -euse de train **2** *Med (device)* stimulateur *m* (cardiaque), pacemaker *m* **3** *Anat* nœud *m* sinusal cardiaque

pacesetter [ˈpeɪssetər] N *Sport* meneur, -euse de train; *Fig* **to be a p.** mener le train

pacey [ˈpeɪsɪ] ADJ = **pacy**

pachyderm [ˈpækɪdɜːm] N *(animal)* pachyderme *m*

pacific [pəˈsɪfɪk] ADJ **1** *Geog* **the P. (Ocean)** l'océan *m* Pacifique, le Pacifique **2** *Fml (not aggressive)* pacifique; *(peaceful)* paisible

pacifically [pəˈsɪfɪklɪ] ADV pacifiquement

pacification [pæsɪfɪˈkeɪʃən] N *Pol (of country etc)* pacification *f*, *(of person)* apaisement *m*

pacifier [ˈpæsɪfaɪər] N **1** *esp Am (for babies)* sucette *f*, tétine *f* **2** *(person)* pacificateur, -trice

pacifism [ˈpæsɪfɪz(ə)m] N pacifisme *m*

pacifist [ˈpæsɪfɪst] N, ADJ pacifiste *mf*

pacify [ˈpæsɪfaɪ] VT *(crowd, country etc)* pacifier; *(person, sb's anger)* apaiser, calmer; *(sb's demands)* apaiser; **she refused to be pacified** elle n'a jamais voulu se calmer

PACK [pæk]

| N paquet **1** ▪ sac à dos **1** ▪ bande **2** |
| ▪ meute **2** |
| VT empaqueter **1** ▪ entasser **2** |
| ▪ remplir **3** ▪ bourrer **3** |
| VI faire sa valise **1** ▪ s'entasser **2** |

N **1** *(bundle etc) (of goods)* paquet *m*, ballot *m*; *(backpack)* sac *m* à dos; *(of beast of burden)* bât *m*; *esp Am (of cigarettes)* paquet *m*; **an economy p. of washing powder** un paquet de lessive de taille économique; **a four-/six-p. of beer** un pack de quatre/six; **a p. of lies** un tissu de mensonges; *Med* **wet/cold p.** enveloppement *m* humide/froid **2** *(group) (of people, thieves)* groupe *m*, bande *f*, *(of wolves, foxhounds)* meute *f*, *(of*

staghounds) équipage *m*; *(of cub scouts, Brownies)* meute; **wolves hunt in packs** les loups chassent en meutes; **p. of fools** bande *ou* tas *m* d'imbéciles; *Rugby* **the p.** le pack **3** *(set) (of playing cards)* jeu *m* **4** *Geog (ice)* **p.** banquise *f*

VT **1** *(put into box, carton etc)* emballer, empaqueter; *(put into suitcase etc)* mettre dans sa valise/son sac/sa malle/*etc*, *(in cotton wool, newspaper etc)* emballer, envelopper; *Com* emballer, conditionner; **did you p. any towels?** est-ce que tu as mis des serviettes dans les bagages?; *esp Am* **shall I p. these for you?** *(in supermarket)* je vous emballe vos achats? **2** *(cram) (passengers into a train etc)* entasser; *(earth into a hole etc)* tasser; **we were packed in like sardines** nous étions serrés comme des harengs (en caque) *ou* comme des sardines; *Naut* **to p. on all sail** mettre toutes voiles dehors **3** *(fill)* remplir, bourrer *(* **sth with sth** qch de qch); *Constr, Min etc (trench)* remblayer; **to p. one's case/one's bags** faire sa valise/ses bagages; *Fig* **to p. one's bags** *(leave)* plier bagages; **we're not packed** nous n'avons pas fait nos bagages; *Theat* **the show packed the house** le spectacle a fait salle comble, le spectacle s'est joué à guichets fermés **4** *esp Am (carry in a backpack)* transporter dans un sac à dos; **to p. a pistol** porter un revolver; *Fam* **to p. a punch** *(of person)* cogner dur; *(of drink)* donner un coup de fouet **5** *Tech (packing box)* garnir, étouper **6** *(rig)* **to p. a jury** se composer un jury favorable; **to p. a meeting** s'assurer un nombre prépondérant de partisans à une réunion; *Cards* **to p. the cards** apprêter les cartes **7** *Comput (database)* condenser, compacter

VI **1** *(prepare luggage)* faire sa/ses valise(s) *ou* ses bagages; **a tent that packs easily** une tente facile à emballer; *Fam* **to send sb packing** envoyer promener qn **2** *(crush) (of person, animal)* s'entasser *(* **into** dans) **3** *Rugby* former le pack

▸▸ **p. animal** bête *f* de somme; *Mil* **p. drill** exercice *m* avec paquetage *(à titre de punition)*; **p. ice** pack *m*, banquise *f*; *TV, Cin* **p. shot** pack shot *m*; **p. train** convoi *m* de bêtes de somme

▸ **pack away** VT SEP **1** *(store)* ranger; *(bed)* replier **2** *Fam* **I've never seen anyone p. it away like him/p. away the beer like he does** je n'ai jamais vu personne engouffrer de la nourriture comme lui/avaler autant de bière que lui; **she can really p. away the food when she gets going** ce qu'elle peut engouffrer quand elle s'y met

VI *(of bed)* se replier; **this tent packs away easily** cette tente se replie *ou* se range facilement

▸ **pack down** VT SEP *(earth, snow etc)* tasser; VI **1** *(be compacted)* **to p. down hard** *(of snow etc)* se tasser **2** *Rugby* former la mêlée

▸ **pack in** VT SEP **1** *(cram in)* entasser; **I couldn't p. anything more in** je ne pouvais pas en faire rentrer plus; **they packed a lot of sightseeing into their short trip** ils ont visité énormément d'endroits pendant leur bref séjour; **one more thing to be packed into the Christmas period** une chose de plus pour laquelle il va falloir trouver du temps pendant la période de Noël; *Fam* **this movie is packing them in** ce film attire les foules; **we were packed in like sardines** nous étions serrés comme des harengs (en caque) *ou* comme des sardines **2** *Br Fam (stop, give up)* arrêter; *(job)* laisser tomber, plaquer; **to p. in smoking** arrêter de fumer; **to p. in jogging** laisser tomber le jogging; **p. it in!** arrête!, ça suffit! **3** *Fam (finish relationship with)* larguer, plaquer **4** *Am (bring in)* **if you p. it in, p. it out** = remmenez vos ordures VI **1** *(crowd in)* entrer en foule *ou* en masse **2** *Fam (stop working) (of machine etc)* tomber en panne; *(of person)* arrêter; **the photocopier's just packed in on me** la photocopieuse vient de me lâcher

▸ **pack off** VT SEP *Fam (send)* expédier; **to p. the kids off to school/bed** expédier *ou* envoyer les enfants à l'école/au lit; **his father packed him off to America/to boarding school** son père l'a expédié en Amérique/en pension

▸ **pack out** VT SEP *Fam (fill completely) (room)* remplir à craquer; **the pub was packed out** le bar était plein à craquer *ou* comble *ou* bondé; **the theatre had been packed out for weeks** le théâtre faisait salle comble depuis des semaines; **the event was completely packed out** il n'y avait plus un seul billet pour ce spectacle

▸ **pack up** VT SEP *(suitcase)* faire; *(belongings)* emballer; *(at end of class, work etc) (books, tools)* ranger VI **1** *(before moving house)* emballer ses affaires **2** *(store things away at end of class, work etc)* ranger ses affaires, *Fam* remballer **3** *Fam (stop working) (of machine etc)* tomber en panne; **my car's packed up** ma voiture m'a lâché; **her heart has packed up** son cœur a lâché *ou* cédé

package ['pækɪdʒ] N **1** *(parcel)* paquet *m*, colis *m* **2** *Comput (software)* logiciel *m* **3** *Com (offer)* offre *f*; **the employment p. includes ...** les avantages accompagnant ce poste sont ...; **the p. includes a company car** l'offre comprend une voiture de société; **I didn't know this would be extra, I thought we were buying a p.** je ne savais pas que ce serait en supplément, je pensais que tout était compris; **you get all these services in a complete p.** tous ces services sont inclus dans le contrat **4** *TV (of channels)* bouquet *m*

VT *Com etc* emballer, conditionner; *Fam* **to p. sb** *(pop star, candidate etc)* créer l'image de marque de qn; **she has packaged herself as a sex symbol** elle s'est créé *ou* fabriqué une image de sex-symbol

▸▸ **p. deal** transaction *f* globale, accord *m* global; **p. holiday** vacances *fpl* à prix forfaitaire; *Am* **p. store** = magasin *m* qui vend des boissons alcoolisées (à emporter); **p. tour** voyage *m* à prix forfaitaire; **p. tourism** tourisme *m* organisé

packager ['pækɪdʒər] N *(in publishing)* packager *m*

packaging ['pækɪdʒɪŋ] N *(action)* emballage *m*, conditionnement *m*; *(materials)* emballage; *Fam (of pop star, candidate etc)*

image *f (fabriquée autour d'une personnalité publique)*; **the p. of the project is all wrong** la façon dont on a présenté le projet ne marche pas du tout; **p. charges** *or* **costs** frais *mpl* d'emballage

packed [pækt] ADJ **p.** *(with people) (bus, train etc)* bondé; *(hall etc)* plein à craquer, comble, bondé; **p. with tourists** plein de touristes; **the book was p. with information** le livre était truffé *ou* bourré de renseignements; *Theat etc* **to play to a p. house** faire salle comble

▸▸ **p. lunch** panier-repas *m*, *pl* paniers-repas, casse-croûte *m inv*

packer ['pækər] N **1** *Com etc (person)* emballeur, -euse, empaqueteur, -euse; **fruit p.** emballeur, -euse de fruits **2** *(device)* machine *f* à emballer *ou* à empaqueter; *(for tamping down)* bourroir *m*

packet ['pækɪt] N **1** *(of tea, cigarettes etc)* paquet *m*; *Comput (of data)* paquet; **I made the sauce from a p.** j'ai fait la sauce à partir d'un sachet; **pay p.** *(envelope)* enveloppe *f* de paie; *(money)* paie *f*, **wage p.** *(envelope)* enveloppe *f* de salaire; *(money)* salaire *m*; **(postal) p.** colis *m* (postal), paquet poste; *Sl* **to make** *or* **earn a p.** gagner un fric fou; *Sl* **that'll cost a p.** ça va coûter les yeux de la tête **2** *Old-fashioned (boat)* paquebot *m* **3** *Sl (male genitals)* = contour *m* des parties génitales masculines moulées dans un pantalon; **what a p.!** quel entrejambe!

▸▸ *Old-fashioned* **p. boat** paquebot *m*; **p. soup** soupe *f* en sachet; *Comput* **p. switching** commutation *f* de paquets; *Comput* **p.-switching network** réseau *m* à commutation de paquets

packhorse ['pækhɔːs] N cheval *m* de somme; *Fam* **I'm not your p.!** je ne suis pas ton porteur

packing ['pækɪŋ] N **1** *Com etc (material, act)* emballage *m*; **postage and p.** frais *mpl* d'emballage et d'envoi **2** *(for holiday etc)* **to do one's p.** faire sa/ses valise(s), faire ses bagages; **there isn't much p. (to do)** il n'y a pas beaucoup de bagages à faire **3** *(material, object added or inserted)*, *Constr (for trench etc)* remblai *m*

▸▸ *Tech* **p. box** presse-étoupe *m*, *pl* presse-étoupe(s); **p. case** caisse *f* d'emballage; **p. charges, p. costs** frais d'emballage; **p. list** liste *f* de colisage; **p. materials** matériaux *mpl* d'emballage; *Tech* **p. ring** *(of cylinder)* rondelle *f ou* bague *f* de garniture; *(of piston)* segment *m*, bague, garniture *f*; *Com* **p. slip** bon *m* de livraison

packsaddle ['pæksæd(ə)l] N bât *m*

pact [pækt] N pacte *m*; **to make a p. with sb** faire un pacte avec qn, pactiser avec qn (**to do sth** pour faire qch)

pacy ['peɪsɪ] ADJ *(film, novel)* mouvementé, vivant; *(sportsperson)* rapide

pad [pæd] N **1** *(for protection, to prevent chafing etc)* coussinet *m*; *(for brake)* plaquette *f*; *(keypad)* bloc *m*; *Sport* **shin pads**, *Cr* **pads** jambières *fpl*; **shoulder p.** *(in dress, jacket)* épaulette *f* **2** *Med* tampon *m*, compresse *f*, *(for feminine hygiene)* serviette *f* hygiénique **3** *(on body) (of finger, toe)* pulpe *f*; *(of dog, fox, hare etc)* coussinet *m* **4** *(writing paper)* bloc *m*; *(on desktop)* sous-main *m inv*; **(inking) p.** tampon *m* encreur **5** *Aviat etc (for helicopters)* aire *f* de décollage et d'atterrissage; **launching p.** aire *ou* plate-forme *f* de lancement **6** *Sl (home)* baraque *f*, casbah *f*; **let's go to my p.** allons chez moi; **you can crash at my p.** tu peux pieuter chez moi **7** *(sound) (of animal)* pas *mpl* sourds; *(of person)* pas feutrés; **the p. of his footsteps**

ses pas feutrés; **she heard the p. of feet in the corridor** elle a entendu quelqu'un qui marchait à pas feutrés dans le couloir

VT **(-dd-) 1** *(armchair, door, wall)* capitonner **2** = **pad out** VI **to p. (along)** *(of dog etc)* trotter; **to p. about** *(of person)* aller et venir à pas feutrés; **he padded downstairs in his slippers** il descendit l'escalier en pantoufles; **stop padding about in your bare feet** ne marche pas pieds nus

▸ **pad out** VT SEP *(fill out) (speech, essay etc)* étoffer; **they included two old songs to p. the album out** ils ont inclu deux vieilles chansons pour étoffer l'album; **they padded out the meal with some rice** ils ont complété le repas avec du riz

padded ['pædɪd] ADJ *(door, wall etc)* capitonné; *(garment)* matelassé, ouatiné; *(envelope)* rembourré

▸▸ **p. bra** soutien-gorge *m* à bonnets renforcés, *pl* soutiens-gorge; **p. cell** cellule *f* capitonnée; **p. shoulders** *(of dress, jacket)* épaulettes *fpl*

padding ['pædɪŋ] N **1** *(material) (for cushion etc)* bourre *f*, rembourrage *m*, *(for seat, jacket etc)* rembourrage; *(on walls, door)* capitonnage *m* **2** *(in speech, essay etc)* délayage *m*

paddle ['pæd(ə)l] N **1** *(for canoe)* pagaie *f*, **double p.** pagaie à double pale **2** *(blade) (of paddleboat, waterwheel)* aube *f*, pale *f*, palette *f* **3** *(of turtle, penguin, cetacean)* nageoire *f*, *(of duck)* patte *f* **4** *(table-tennis bat)* raquette *f* de ping-pong **5** *(walk in water)* **to go for a p.** aller patauger dans l'eau

VT **1** **to p. a/the/one's canoe** pagayer; *Prov* **to p. one's own canoe** *(get by on one's own)* se débrouiller (tout seul), arriver par soi-même **2** *Am Fam (hit)* donner une fessée à VI **1** *(in canoe)* pagayer; *(in rowing boat)* tirer en douce; *(of duck)* nager **2** *(walk in water)* patauger; *(in mud etc)* patauger, patouiller

▸▸ **p. boat** bateau *m* à aubes *ou* à roues; **p. steamer** bateau à aubes *ou* à roues; *Naut* **p. wheel** roue *f* à aubes

paddling pool ['pædlɪŋ] N pataugeoire *f*

paddock ['pædək] N *(field for horse)*, *Horse-racing* paddock *m*; *Austr (field)* champ *m*

Paddy ['pædɪ] N *Fam (Irishman)* Irlandais *m*; **hey, P.!** hé, l'Irlandais

paddy ['pædɪ] N **1** *Com (rice)* paddy *m* **2** *Br Fam* **to be/get in a p.** être/se mettre en rogne (**about** pour)

▸▸ **p. field** rizière *f*, *Am Fam* **p. wagon** panier *m* à salade

padlock ['pædlɒk] N cadenas *m* VT *(door)* cadenasser, fermer au cadenas; **he padlocked his bike to the fence** il a cadenassé son vélo à la grille

padre ['pɑːdreɪ] N *Rel* prêtre *m*; *Mil* aumônier *m* (militaire)

paean ['piːən] N *Fml* péan *m*, pæan *m*

paediatric, Am pediatric [piːdɪ'ætrɪk] ADJ *(hospital, care etc)* de pédiatrie; *(specialist)* en pédiatrie

▸▸ **p. surgery** chirurgie *f* pédiatrique

paediatrician, Am pediatrician [piːdɪə'trɪʃən] N pédiatre *mf*

paediatrics, Am pediatrics [piːdɪ'ætrɪks] N pédiatrie *f* VOIR GRAMMAIRE A10

paedology, Am pedology [piː'dɒlədʒɪ] N pédologie *f*

paedophile, Am pedophile ['piːdəʊfaɪl] N pédophile *mf*

paedophilia, Am pedophilia [piːdəʊ'fɪlɪə] N pédophilie *f*

pagan ['peɪgən] ADJ, N païen, -ïenne

paganism ['peɪgənɪz(ə)m] N paganisme m

page[1] [peɪdʒ] N page f; **on p. 6** à la page 6; **continued on p. 6/on back p.** suite f (en) page 6/en dernière page; **the sports/business pages** (in newspaper) la section sport/économie; Fig **a glorious p. in our history** une page glorieuse de l'histoire de notre pays

VT (book) paginer
▶▶ Comput **p. break** saut m de page; Comput **p. break character** caractère m de changement de page; Typ **p. bromide** bromure m de page; Typ **p. depth** hauteur f de page; Comput **p. description language** langage m de description de page; Typ, Comput **p. design** mise f en page; Comput **p. down** page suivante; Typ, Comput **p. down key** touche f page suivante; Typ, Comput **p. format** format m de page; Comput **p. layout** mise en page; Typ **p. length** longueur f de page; Typ **p. make-up** mise en page; Typ **p. number** numéro m de page; Typ **p. numbering** numérotage m des pages, pagination f; Journ **p. one** la une; Typ **p. plan** plan m de mise en page, chemin m de fer; Comput **p. preview** aperçu m avant l'impression; Comput **p. printer** imprimante f page par page, imprimante par pages; Comput **p. printer language** langage d'imprimante par pages; Typ **p. proofs** épreuves fpl en pages; Comput **p. scanner** lecteur m de pages; Comput **p. setup** format de page; Journ **p. three** = page sur laquelle une femme pose seins nus dans certains quotidiens de la presse populaire britannique; Journ **p. three girl** = jeune femme f posant seins nus dans certains quotidiens de la presse populaire britannique; Comput **p. up** page précédente; Comput **p. up key** touche page précédente
▶ **page down** VI Comput feuilleter en avant
▶ **page off** VT SEP Typ paginer
▶ **page up** VI Comput feuilleter en arrière

page[2] N (at hotel) jeune chasseur m; (at wedding) page m (d'honneur); (attending person of rank) page
VT (call) **to p. sb** (of pageboy) appeler qn; (by loudspeaker) appeler qn par haut-parleur; (by sending messenger) envoyer chercher qn par un chasseur; (by paging device) biper qn; **I'm having her paged** je la fais appeler; **paging Mr Wilson** on demande M. Wilson

pageant ['pædʒənt] N (display) spectacle m grandiose ou majestueux; (of historical events) cortège m historique; Fig **the rich p. of our country's history** la riche galerie de tableaux de l'histoire de notre pays

pageantry ['pædʒəntrɪ] N apparat m, pompe f

pageboy ['peɪdʒbɔɪ] N 1 (hairstyle) coiffure f à la Jeanne d'Arc **2** = **page**[2] N
▶▶ **p. style** (hairstyle) coiffure à la Jeanne d'Arc

pager ['peɪdʒər] N Tel récepteur m d'appel ou de poche

page-turner N Fam (book) livre m passionnant ou captivant

paginate ['pædʒɪneɪt] VT (make into pages) mettre en pages; (number pages in) paginer

pagination [pædʒɪ'neɪʃən] N (page make-up) mise f en pages; (numbering) pagination f

pagoda [pə'gəʊdə] N Archit pagode f

pah [pɑː] INT pouah!

paid [peɪd] PT, PP see **pay** VT, VI
ADJ **1** (person, work) rétribué, rémunéré; **to get p. sick/maternity leave** avoir droit aux congés de maladie/de maternité **2** Com (goods, bill) payé; **p.** (on bill) pour acquit **3 to put p. to sb's chances/hopes** réduire les chances/espoirs de qn en poussière; **well,**

that's put p. to that! et voilà, tout tombe à l'eau!
▶▶ **p. holidays** congés mpl payés

paid-out ADJ ATTRIB
▶▶ **p. form** bon m de décaissement; **p. voucher** bon de débours

paid-up ADJ **1** (fully) **p. member** (of party) membre m qui a payé sa cotisation **2** Fin (capital) versé; (shares) libéré; **fully p. policy** police f d'assurance dont les primes sont à jour; **to make a life assurance policy p.** cesser de cotiser à une assurance-vie (sans l'annuler)
▶▶ Fin **p. share capital** capital m appelé et libéré

pail [peɪl] N (bucket) seau m

pailful ['peɪlfʊl] N plein seau m

pain [peɪn] N **1** (physical) douleur f, (mental) peine f, douleur f; **I have a p. in my leg** j'ai une douleur à la jambe; **there was a lot of p. in his right arm** son bras droit lui faisait très mal ou le faisait terriblement souffrir; **to cause sb p.** (physical) faire mal à qn, faire souffrir qn; (mental) faire de la peine à qn; **to be in great p.** souffrir beaucoup; **he was carried from the field in great p.** il souffrait beaucoup quand on l'a transporté hors du terrain; **the p. was unbearable** la douleur était insupportable; **to put a wounded animal out of its p.** achever un animal blessé; **shooting pains** élancements mpl, douleurs lancinantes; **labour pains** douleurs de l'accouchement

2 Fam (nuisance) **he's a p.** (in the neck or Vulg arse) il est casse-pieds ou emmerdant ou chiant; **working can be a p. sometimes** il y a des fois où c'est vraiment casse-pieds d'avoir à travailler

3 (trouble) (usu pl) **pains** peine f, **to take pains** or **be at great pains** or **go to great pains to do sth** se donner de la peine ou du mal pour faire qch; **as she was at pains to explain** ce qu'elle se donnait du mal à expliquer; **to take pains over sth** se donner du mal pour qch; **to have nothing for one's pains** en être pour sa peine

4 Fml **on** or **under p. of death** sous peine de mort
VT **1** (mentally) faire de la peine à, peiner, attrister; **it pained her to see them quarrel** ça lui faisait de la peine ou ça la peinait de les voir se disputer; **it pains me to have to tell you that …** je regrette infiniment d'avoir à vous dire que …

2 Old-fashioned (physically) faire souffrir, faire mal à; **the wound still pained her** la blessure la faisait encore souffrir ou lui faisait encore mal
▶▶ **p. barrier** seuil m de douleur; **p. relief** soulagement m; **aspirin for fast p. relief** aspirine pour soulager rapidement la douleur

pained [peɪnd] ADJ **p. expression** air m affligé ou peiné; **to look p.** avoir l'air affligé ou peiné

painful ['peɪnfʊl] ADJ **1** (wound, part of the body) douloureux; **I find walking p.** j'ai mal quand je marche; **to become p.** (of limb etc) devenir douloureux, s'endolorir; **that looked p.!** ça a dû faire mal!

2 (unpleasant) (spectacle, effort, subject) pénible; **a p. memory** un souvenir désagréable; **it was p. to see (it)** c'était pénible à voir; **the expensive shops were a p. reminder of their poverty** les boutiques chères leur rappelaient péniblement leur pauvreté **3** (difficult) (task) laborieux, pénible **4** Fam (bad) (performance, singing) atroce

painfully ['peɪnfʊlɪ] ADV **1** (with physical pain) douloureusement; **her head throbbed p.** elle sentait une douleur lancinante à la tête; **she fell p.** elle s'est fait mal en tombant **2** (shy, embarrassing) atrocement, pénible-

ment; **it was p. obvious** c'était tellement évident que c'en était embarrassant **3** (with difficulty) (to climb etc) laborieusement

painkiller ['peɪnkɪlər] N calmant m, analgésique m

painkilling ['peɪnkɪlɪŋ] ADJ calmant, analgésique

painless ['peɪnlɪs] ADJ indolore, sans douleur; Fam Fig **replacing the fan belt was fairly p.** remplacer la courroie de ventilateur n'a pas posé trop de problèmes; **the p. way to pay your bills** la manière commode de payer vos factures

painlessly ['peɪnlɪslɪ] ADV (without pain) sans douleur; Fam Fig (effortlessly) sans effort, sans problème

painstaking ['peɪnzteɪkɪŋ] ADJ (person) soigneux, appliqué, assidu; (labour) soigné; (investigation) poussé; (accuracy, attention to detail) extrême

painstakingly ['peɪnzteɪkɪŋlɪ] ADV avec (grand) soin; **to be p. accurate/detailed in one's work** faire preuve d'une extrême précision/attention aux détails dans son travail

paint [peɪnt] N peinture f, Art couleur f, Med badigeon m; Fam (face make-up) fard m; **wet p.!** (on sign) attention, peinture fraîche!; **box of paints** boîte f de couleurs; **tube of p.** tube m de peinture ou de couleur
VT **1** Art peindre; **to p. a portrait in oils** peindre un portrait à l'huile; **to p. a picture** peindre un tableau; **to p. (a picture of) sb** faire le portrait de qn

2 (coat with paint) (room, door etc) peindre (green en vert); Med (throat) badigeonner; **the kitchen needs painting** la cuisine a besoin d'être repeinte; Theat **to p. the scenery for a play** brosser les décors d'une pièce; **to p. one's nails** se vernir les ongles; Fam **to p. one's face** (put on make-up) se maquiller, se farder; Fig **to p. the town red** faire la noce ou la bringue

3 (depict) dépeindre; **to p. a favourable/an unfavourable picture of a situation** brosser un tableau favorable/défavorable de la situation; **to p. everything in rosy colours** peindre tout en rose
VI Art faire de la peinture; **to p. in watercolours/in oils** faire de l'aquarelle/de la peinture à l'huile; **I've always wanted to p.** j'ai toujours voulu faire de la peinture; **I wish I could p. like that!** si seulement je pouvais peindre comme cela!
▶▶ **p. gun** pistolet m à peinture; Br **p. pot** pot m de peinture; Comput **p. program** programme m de dessin bitmap; **p. roller** rouleau m à peinture; **p. shop** magasin m de couleurs; Ind (in factory etc) atelier m de peinture; **p. stick** palette f de bois (utilisée pour mélanger la peinture)

paintball ['peɪntbɔːl] N paintball m

paintbox ['peɪntbɒks] N boîte f de couleurs

paintbrush ['peɪntbrʌʃ] N pinceau m

painter[1] ['peɪntər] N **1** Art peintre m; (of toys etc) coloriste mf; **landscape/portrait p.** paysagiste mf/portraitiste mf **2** (house) p. peintre m (en bâtiments); **J. Smith, painters and decorators** J. Smith, peintre et décorateur

painter[2] N Naut (rope) bosse f, **to cut the p.** couper l'amarre

painting ['peɪntɪŋ] N **1** (picture) tableau m, peinture f **2** (of house, picture etc) peinture f, **to study p.** étudier la peinture; **landscape/portrait p.** peinture de paysages/portraits; **(house) p.** peinture en bâtiment

paintwork ['peɪntwɜːk] N peinture(s) f(pl); (on car etc) peinture f

pair [peər] N **1** (of shoes, scissors, vases, legs etc) paire f; (of horses) attelage m; (man and woman, male and female animal) couple m; (in rowing) deux m; **in pairs** deux par deux;

the p. of you vous deux; **they can go to bed without their supper, the p. of them!** qu'ils aillent au lit sans manger tous les deux!; **what a p.!** (of two people) quelle paire!; **a p. of trousers** un pantalon; Old-fashioned **a p. of scales** une balance; **p. of step(ladder)s** escabeau m; **these two pictures are a p.** (match) ces deux tableaux se font pendant; **socks that are not a p.** chaussettes dépareillées; **where is the p. of this glove?** où se trouve l'autre gant de cette paire?; **a p. of aces/tens** une paire d'as/de dix VOIR GRAMMAIRE A10

2 Br Parl (two MPs from opposing parties) = deux membres mplde partis adverses qui se sont associés (pour un vote); (MP from opposing party) = membre du parti adverse avec qui on peut s'associer

vi faire la paire (**with sb/sth** avec qn/qch); (of birds etc) s'accoupler, s'apparier (**with** avec); Br Parl s'associer (**with sb** avec qn)

vt (socks etc) appareiller, assortir; (birds etc) accoupler, apparier; Mktg **paired comparison** comparaison f par paire

▸▸ Cards **p. royal** brelan m

▸ **pair off vi** (of people) former un/des couple(s)

vt sep (objects) arranger deux par deux; (people) mettre deux par deux; **they were paired off by their hostess** leur hôtesse les a mis ensemble; **he's trying to get them paired off** (in a relationship) il essaie de les mettre ensemble

▸ **pair up vi** s'associer, se mettre ensemble; **to p. up with sb** s'associer avec qn, se mettre avec qn

paisley ['peizli] **N p. scarf** foulard m à dessin cachemire

▸▸ Tex **p. pattern** (dessin m) cachemire m

pajamas [pə'dʒɑːməz] **NPL** Am = **pyjamas** VOIR GRAMMAIRE A10

Paki ['pæki] **N, ADJ** Br Offensive Sl pakistanais, -aise mf; (corner shop) épicerie f tenue par un/des Pakistanais

Paki-basher [-bæʃər] **N** Br Offensive Sl = raciste mf qui attaque les gens issus du sous-continent indien

Paki-bashing N Br Offensive Sl = persécution f des gens issus du sous-continent indien

Pakistan [pɑːkɪ'stɑːn] **N** Pakistan m

Pakistani [pɑːkɪ'stɑːnɪ] **ADJ** pakistanais **N** Pakistanais, -aise

pakora [pə'kɔːrə] **NPL** Culin = beignets mpl de légumes/poisson/etc

pal [pæl] **N** Fam copain m, copine f, **be a p. and make me a coffee!** sois gentil, tu voudrais bien me faire un café?; **watch where you're going p.!** regarde où tu vas mon vieux ou (more aggressively) mon coco!

▸ **pal about, pal around vi** Fam **to p. about** or **around with sb** copiner avec qn, être pote avec qn; **they p. about together** ils sont toujours fourrés ensemble

▸ **pal up vi** Fam (become friends) (of two people) devenir copains/copines; **to p. up with sb** devenir copain/copine avec qn

palace ['pælɪs] **N 1** palais m; **bishop's/archbishop's p.** palais épiscopal/archiépiscopal **2** Br **the P., Buckingham P.** (royal entourage) Buckingham m; **the P. raised no objections to the visit** Buckingham n'a élevé aucune objection concernant la visite; **a P. spokesperson** un porte-parole de Buckingham

▸▸ **p. guard** (person) garde m du palais; (all guards) garde f du palais; **p. revolution** révolution f de palais

---

Note that the French word **palace** is a false friend and is never a translation for the English word **palace**. It means **luxury hotel**.

---

paladin ['pælədɪn] **N** Hist, Lit paladin m

palaeographer [pælɪ'ɒɡrəfər] **N** paléographe mf

palaeography [pælɪ'ɒɡrəfɪ] **N** paléographie f

Palaeolithic [pælɪəʊ'lɪθɪk] **ADJ** paléolithique; **the P. age** le paléolithique, l'âge m de la pierre taillée

palaeontologist [pælɪɒn'tɒlədʒɪst] **N** paléontologiste mf, paléontologue mf

palaeontology [pælɪɒn'tɒlədʒɪ] **N** paléontologie f

palatable ['pælətəb(ə)l] **ADJ** (meal) d'un goût agréable, agréable au palais; (wine) qui se laisse boire; Fig (doctrine, suggestion etc) acceptable (**to** aux yeux de)

palatal ['pælət(ə)l] **ADJ** Anat, Ling palatal, -aux **N** Ling palatale f

palatalize ['pælətəlaɪz] **vt** Ling palataliser, mouiller

palate ['pælɪt] **N** Anat palais m; **hard p.** palais (dur), voûte f du palais, voûte palatine; **soft p.** voile m du palais; **to have a good p.** avoir le palais fin

palatial [pə'leɪʃəl] **ADJ** (building) magnifique, grandiose; (dimensions, scale) monumental, -aux

palatinate [pə'lætɪnɪt] **N** Hist palatinat m; **the Rhineland p.** le palatinat du Rhin

palaver [pə'lɑːvər] **N 1** Fam (fuss) histoires fpl; **what's all the p. about?** qu'est-ce qui cloche? **2** Old-fashioned (discussion) palabre m ou f; **after a long p.** après de longs ou longues palabres

pale¹ [peɪl] **ADJ** pâle; (because ill, angry, afraid etc) blême, pâle; (colour) pâle, clair; **a p. blue dress** une robe bleu pâle; **p. as death, deathly** pâle comme un mort, d'une pâleur mortelle; **to grow** or **become p.** pâlir; **to turn p. with fright** pâlir de terreur; **by the p. light of the moon** à la lumière blafarde de la lune; Fig **a p. reflection/imitation of sth** un pâle reflet/une pâle copie de qch **vi** (of person) pâlir, blêmir; Fig **my adventures p. beside yours** mes aventures semblent bien pâles auprès des vôtres; Fig **to p. into insignificance** devenir insignifiant

▸▸ **p. ale** pale-ale f, pl pale-ales, bière f blonde légère

pale² **N 1** (of fence) pieu m **2 beyond the p.** (behaviour, remarks) inacceptable; (of person) pas fréquentable

paleface ['peɪlfeɪs] **N** visage m pâle

pale-faced ['peɪlfeɪst] **ADJ** au visage ou au teint pâle; **they looked p.** leurs visages étaient pâles

paleness ['peɪlnɪs] **N** pâleur f

Palestine ['pælɪstaɪn] **N** Palestine f; **the P. Liberation Organization** l'Organisation f de libération de la Palestine

Palestinian [pælɪ'stɪnɪən] **ADJ** palestinien **N** Palestinien, -ienne

palette ['pælɪt] **N** Art palette f

▸▸ **p. knife** Art couteau m (à palette); Culin spatule f

palimony ['pælɪmənɪ] **N** Fam = pension f alimentaire versée au concubin/à la concubine

palimpsest ['pælɪmpsest] **ADJ, N** palimpseste m

palindrome ['pælɪndrəʊm] **N** palindrome m

paling ['peɪlɪŋ] **N** (fence) palissade f, palis m; (stake) pieu m

palisade [pælɪ'seɪd] **N 1** palissade f **2** Am palisades (cliffs) falaises fpl abruptes

pall¹ [pɔːl] **N 1** (over coffin) poêle m **2** Fig (of smoke etc) voile m; (of snow, darkness, gloom etc) manteau m

pall² **vi** (become uninteresting) perdre son attrait (**on sb** pour qn); **it never palls** on ne s'en lasse pas

pallbearer ['pɔːlbeərər] **N** porteur m (du cercueil)

pallet¹ ['pælɪt] **N** (straw mattress) paillasse f, Lit (poor bed) grabat m

pallet² ['pælɪt] **N 1** Com palette f **2** Art = **palette**

▸▸ **p. truck** chariot m élévateur, transpalette m

palletizable [pælɪ'taɪzɪb(ə)l] **ADJ** Com palettisable

palletization [pælɪtaɪ'zeɪʃən] **N** Com palettisation f

palletize ['pælɪtaɪz] **vt** Com palettiser

palletizer ['pælɪtaɪzər] **N** Com palettiseur m

palliasse ['pælɪæs] **N** paillasse f

palliate ['pælɪeɪt] **vt** Fml (make less severe) pallier; (illness) lénifier; (fears) apaiser; (offence) pallier, atténuer; **her words had a palliating effect** ses paroles ont eu un effet lénifiant

palliative ['pælɪətɪv] **ADJ, N** palliatif m; **to have a p. effect** (of medicine) avoir un effet palliatif ou lénifiant; (of words) avoir un effet lénifiant; **p. care** soins mpl palliatifs

pallid ['pælɪd] **ADJ** (person, face, complexion etc) pâle, blême, blafard; (skin, hands) pâle; (light, moon) blafard; Fig (performance) fade, insipide; **a p. reflection/imitation of sth** un pâle reflet/une pâle copie de qch

pallidness ['pælɪdnɪs], **pallor** ['pælər] **N** pâleur f

pally ['pælɪ] **ADJ** Fam **to be p. with sb** être copain/f copine avec qn

palm [pɑːm] **N 1** (of hand) paume f, (of glove) empaumure f, **to read sb's p.** lire les lignes de la main à qn; Fam **to grease sb's p.** graisser la patte à qn; Fam **to have** or **hold sb in the p. of one's hand** avoir qn dans sa poche **2** (tree) palmier m **3** (branch) palme f, Rel rameau m, buis m (bénit); Fig **to bear** or **win** or **carry off the p.** remporter la palme

vt (conceal) (coin, brooch, card etc) escamoter; **to p. a card** (in conjuring) filer une carte

▸▸ Br **p. court orchestra** = petit orchestre m jouant dans le salon d'un hôtel (décoré de palmiers); **p. grove** palmeraie f, **p. leaf** feuille f de palmier; **p. oil** huile f de palme; **p. plantation** palmeraie; Rel **P. Sunday** le dimanche des Rameaux, les Rameaux mpl; **p. tree** palmier; **p. wine** vin m de palme

▸ **palm off vt sep 1** (dispose of something unwanted) faire passer, Fam refiler (**sth on sb** qch à qn); **they're palming the children off on us for the weekend** ils vont nous refiler les enfants pour le week-end **2** (give something worthless to) **when I complained, they palmed me off with a standard letter** quand je me suis plaint, ils se sont contentés de me refiler une lettre toute faite; **she tried to p. me off with some ridiculous excuse** elle a essayé de me faire avaler une excuse ridicule

palmist ['pɑːmɪst] **N** chiromancien, -ienne

palmistry ['pɑːmɪstrɪ] **N** chiromancie f

palmtop ['pɑːmtɒp] **N** (computer) ordinateur m de poche

▸▸ **p. computer** ordinateur de poche

palmy ['pɑːmɪ] **ADJ p. days** (of country etc) époque f florissante; **in his p. days** dans ses beaux jours

palpable ['pælpəb(ə)l] **ADJ** (tangible) palpable, que l'on peut toucher; Fig (obvious) (lack of enthusiasm, interest) manifeste; (lie) évident; (difference) sensible, manifeste

palpably ['pælpəblɪ] **ADV** manifestement

palpate ['pælpeɪt] **vt** Med palper

palpation [pæl'peɪʃən] **N** Med palpation f, palper m

palpitate ['pælpɪteɪt] **VI** palpiter

palpitating ['pælpɪteɪtɪŋ] **ADJ** palpitant

palpitation [pælpɪ'teɪʃən] **N** palpitation *f*, **to get** *or* **have palpitations** avoir des palpitations

palsied ['pɔːlzɪd] **ADJ** *Med* paralysé; *Lit (step, grip)* tremblant

palsy ['pɔːlzɪ] **N** *Med Old-fashioned* paralysie *f*

palsy-walsy ['pælzɪ'wælzɪ] **ADJ** *Fam* **to be p. with sb** être comme cul et chemise avec qn, être à tu et à toi avec qn; **they're very p. all of a sudden** ils sont très potes *ou* copain-copain tout d'un coup

paltry ['pɔːltrɪ] **ADJ** *(amount, sum)* misérable, dérisoire; **p. excuses** piètres excuses *fpl*

pampas ['pæmpəz] **N** *Geog* **the P.** la Pampa
▸▸ **p. grass** herbe *f* de la pampa

pamper ['pæmpər] **VT** *(person)* choyer, dorloter; **a hotel where you will be pampered** un hôtel où l'on sera à vos petits soins; **to p. oneself** se faire plaisir; **pampered tastes** goûts *mpl* difficiles

pamphlet ['pæmflɪt] **N** brochure *f*, *(literary, scientific)* opuscule *m*; *(libellous, scurrilous)* pamphlet *m*

> Note that the French word **pamphlet** always refers to a satirical tract.

pamphleteer [pæmflɪ'tɪər] **N** auteur *m* de brochures; *(scurrilous)* pamphlétaire *mf*

Pan [pæn] **N** *Myth* Pan

pan [pæn] **N 1** *(for cooking)* casserole *f*
2 *(of scales)* plateau *m*; *Min (for gold)* batée *f*, **(toilet) p.** cuvette *f* (de W.-C.); *Fam* **to go down the p.** s'en aller en fumée; **that's six months' work down the p.!** voilà six mois de travail qui s'en vont en fumée!
3 *Geol etc* cuvette *f*, bassin *m* de déposition *ou* de sédimentation; **salt p.** marais *m* salant, saline *f*, salin *m*
4 *TV, Cin* panoramique *m*
VT (-nn-) 1 *Min (gravel etc)* laver à la batée
2 to p. the camera faire un panoramique, panoramiquer; **to p. the camera across the room** prendre la salle en panoramique, faire un panoramique de la salle
3 *Fam (criticize adversely) (film, play etc)* éreinter, esquinter
VI 1 *Min* laver le gravier/*etc* à la batée; **to p. for gold** laver le gravier/*etc* à la batée pour en extraire l'or
2 *TV, Cin* panoramiquer; **the camera pans around the bay** la caméra prend la baie en panoramique *ou* fait un panoramique de la baie; **to p. across the room** prendre la salle en panoramique, faire un panoramique de la salle; **a panning shot** une prise panoramique, un panoramique
▸▸ *TV, Cin* **p. down** panoramique vers le bas; *Scot* **p. loaf** pain *m* de mie; **p. scourer** éponge *f* à récurer les casseroles; *TV, Cin* **p. up** panoramique vertical
▸ **pan down VI** *TV, Cin* faire un panoramique vers le bas
▸ **pan out VI** *Fam (turn out)* **it didn't p. out (well)** cela n'a pas marché; **it depends how things p. out** ça dépend de comment les choses vont s'arranger
VT SEP *Min (wash)* laver à la batée
▸ **pan up VI** *TV, Cin* faire un panoramique vers le haut

panacea [pænə'sɪə] **N** panacée *f*

panache [pə'næʃ] **N** *(style)* panache *m*

Pan-African ADJ panafricain

Pan-Africanism [-'æfrɪkənɪz(ə)m] **N** panafricanisme *m*

Panama ['pænəmɑː] **N 1** *(country)* Panama *m*; **the P. Canal** le canal de Panama **2 p. (hat)** panama *m*
▸▸ **p. hat** panama *m*

Panamanian [pænə'meɪnɪən] **ADJ** panaméen
N Panaméen, -enne

Pan-American ADJ panaméricain; **the P. Highway** la route panaméricaine

Pan-Americanism N panaméricanisme *m*

panatella [pænə'telə] **N** panatel(l)a *m*
▸▸ **p. cigar** panatel(l)a

panavision ['pænəvɪʒən] **N** panavision *f*

pancake ['pænkeɪk] **N 1** *Culin* crêpe *f* **2** *Aviat* atterrissage *m* brutal **3** *(make-up)* fond *m* de teint
VI *Aviat* faire un atterrissage brutal
▸▸ *Br* **P. Day** mardi *m* gras; *Aviat* **p. landing** atterrissage brutal; **p. make-up** fond de teint; *Br* **P. Tuesday** mardi gras

panchromatic [pænkrəʊ'mætɪk] **ADJ** *Phot* panchromatique

pancreas ['pæŋkrɪəs] **N** *Anat* pancréas *m*

pancreatic [pæŋkrɪ'ætɪk] **ADJ** pancréatique

pancreatitis [pæŋkrɪə'taɪtəs] **N** pancréatite *f*

panda ['pændə] **N** panda *m*; **giant p.** panda géant
▸▸ *Br* **p. car** voiture *f* de police

pandemic [pæn'demɪk] *Med* **ADJ** pandémique
N pandémie *f*

pandemonium [pændɪ'məʊnɪəm] **N** **it's p.** c'est la confusion la plus totale, c'est un désordre indescriptible; **their entire household was in p.** c'était un véritable cirque chez eux quand je suis arrivé

pander ['pændər] **VI** **these films p. to our worst instincts** ces films font appel à nos pires instincts; **to p. to sb** encourager bassement qn; **to p. to a vice** encourager un vice; **to p. to sb's whims** se prêter aux exigences de qn

Pandora [pæn'dɔːrə] **N** *Myth* Pandore; **P.'s box** boîte *f* de Pandore

pane [peɪn] **N** *(of window)* vitre *f*, carreau *m*; *(of computer screen)* panneau *m*; **a p. of glass** un carreau, une vitre

panegyric [pænɪ'dʒaɪrɪk] **ADJ, N** *Fml* panégyrique *m*

panel ['pæn(ə)l] **N 1** *(on wall, of door)* panneau *m*; *(in ceiling)* caisson *m*; *(of altarpiece)* panneau; *(of cartoon strip)* case *f*, *Sewing* panneau; *Archit, Constr* entre-deux *m inv*
2 *(list of jury members)* tableau *m* *ou* liste *f* du jury; *(of committee members)* liste des membres d'un comité *ou* d'une commission; *(group) (of enquiry etc)* comité *m*, commission *f*, *(working party)* groupe *m* de travail; *(round table)* table *f* ronde; **the p.** *Radio, TV* les invités *mpl*; *Scot Law (the accused)* l'accusé, -ée, *pl* les accusé(e)s; **p. of experts** comité *ou* commission d'experts; *Mktg (for market research)* panel *m*; *Mktg* **p. of expert opinion** panel de spécialistes
3 *Radio, TV (mixing desk, console)* pupitre *m*
VT (-ll-, *Am* **-l-)** recouvrir de panneaux; *(wall)* lambrisser; *(surface)* plaquer
▸▸ *Br Aut* **p. beater** carrossier *m*, tôlier *m*; **p. discussion** débat *m*, table ronde; *Br* **p. game** *Radio* jeu *m* radiophonique; *TV* jeu télévisé; **p. light** lampe *f* *ou* éclairage *m* de tableau de bord; **p. member** *(jury member)* juré, -ée; *(in radio or TV quiz)* invité, -ée; *(in public debate)* panéliste *mf*; *(of committee)* membre *m* du comité; *Br* **p. pin** pointe *f* à tête d'homme, clou *m* à panneau; **p. research** recherches *fpl* par panel; *Am Aut* **p. truck** camionnette *f*, fourgonnette *f*

panelled, *Am* **paneled** ['pæn(ə)ld] **ADJ** *(room, wall)* recouvert *ou* revêtu de boiseries, lambrissé

panelling, *Am* **paneling** ['pæn(ə)lɪŋ] **N 1** *(wall covering)* lambris *m*, boiseries *fpl*, placage *m*; **oak p.** lambris *mpl* de chêne **2** *(material)* panneaux *mpl*

panellist, *Am* **panelist** ['pæn(ə)lɪst] **N** *(jury member)* juré, -ée; *(of committee)* membre *m* du comité; *(of working party)* membre du groupe de travail; *(in radio or TV quiz)* invité, -ée

pang [pæŋ] **N** **pangs of jealousy** tourments *mpl* de la jalousie; **to feel a p.** sentir un pincement au cœur; **a p. of conscience** un soubresaut de conscience; **to feel** *or* **have pangs of remorse** être tiraillé par les remords; **pangs of hunger** tiraillements *mpl* d'estomac

panhandle ['pænhænd(ə)l] *Am* **N 1** *Geog* langue *f* de terre; **the Texas p.** = langue de terre correspondant à la partie nord-ouest du Texas **2** *TV, Cin* manche *m* (de tête de caméra)
VI *Fam* mendier
VT *Fam* essayer de taper

panhandler ['pænhændlər] **N** *Am Fam* mendiant, -ante

panic[1] ['pænɪk] **N** panique *f*, *Fam* **there's no p.** il n'y a pas le feu; **to create** *or* **cause (a) p.** causer un mouvement de panique; **to throw the crowd/the stockmarkets into a p.** affoler la foule/les marchés; **in a p.** paniqué, affolé; **to get into a p. over** *or* **about sth** s'affoler à cause de qch; *Fam* **it was p. stations** c'était la panique totale *ou* l'affolement général
VT (pt, pp panicked) *(person, crowd etc)* remplir de panique, paniquer, affoler; *(horse)* affoler; **the news panicked the government into action** la panique provoquée par cette nouvelle a poussé le gouvernement à l'action; **she was panicked into resigning** sous le coup de la panique, elle a démissionné
VI être pris de panique, s'affoler, paniquer (**about** à propos de); **don't p.!** ne t'affole pas!, ne panique pas!
▸▸ **p. attack** crise *f* de panique; **p. button** signal *m* d'alarme; *Fam Fig* **to hit the p. button** paniquer; **p. buying** = achats *mpl* massifs provoqués par la crainte de la pénurie; *St Exch* achats de précaution; **p. measures** mesures *fpl* dictées par la panique; **p. reaction** réaction *f* de panique

panic[2] **N** *Bot* panic *m* (d'Italie)
▸▸ **p. grass** panic (d'Italie)

panicky ['pænɪkɪ] **ADJ** *Fam (feelings)* paniqué; *(person)* sujet à la panique; *(reaction, response)* affolé; *(market etc)* enclin à la panique; **a p. decision** une décision prise sous le coup de la panique; **don't get p.!** ne paniquez pas!, ne vous affolez pas!

panic-stricken ADJ pris de panique, affolé; *(reaction, response, look)* affolé

panjandrum [pæn'dʒændrəm] **N** *Lit* gros bonnet *m*

pannier ['pænɪər] **N** *(basket)* panier *m*; *(on motorbike or bicycle)* sacoche *f*, *(of beast of burden)* panier de bât

panning ['pænɪŋ] **N** *TV, Cin* panoramique *m*
▸▸ *TV, Cin* **p. handle** poignée *f* de panoramique; *TV, Cin* **p. shot** prise *f* panoramique

panoply ['pænəplɪ] **N** panoplie *f*

panorama [pænə'rɑːmə] **N** panorama *m*

panoramic [pænə'ræmɪk] **ADJ** *(view etc)* panoramique
▸▸ *Cin* **p. screen** écran *m* panoramique

panpipes ['pænpaɪps] **NPL** *Mus* flûte *f* de Pan

pansy ['pænzɪ] **N 1** *(flower)* pensée *f* **2** *Offensive Sl (male homosexual)* pédale *f*, tante *f*

pant [pænt] N souffle m pantelant ou haletant

VI 1 (gasp) haleter; (of animal) battre du flanc; **to p. for breath** chercher à reprendre haleine; **she panted up the hill** elle a monté la côte en haletant ou soufflant **2** Fam (be eager) **he's panting to do it** il a tellement envie de le faire

VT listen to me, she panted écoute-moi, dit-elle d'une voix haletante

▶ **pant out** VT SEP (say) dire en haletant

pantechnicon [pæn'teknɪkən] N Br Old-fashioned (van) camion m de déménagement

pantheism ['pænθɪɪz(ə)m] N panthéisme m

pantheist ['pænθɪɪst] ADJ, N panthéiste mf

pantheistic [pænθɪ'ɪstɪk] ADJ panthéiste

pantheon ['pænθɪən] N panthéon m

panther ['pænθər] N panthère f; Am (puma) couguar m, puma m; Am Pol **Black P.** Panthère f noire; **the (Black) Panthers** = mouvement m politique fondé par des militants noirs américains dans les années soixante

panties ['pæntɪz] NPL culotte f, slip m (de femme)

pantihose ['pæntɪhəʊz] NPL Am collant m

panting ['pæntɪŋ] N halètement m

panto ['pæntəʊ] N Br Theat Fam = **pantomime 1**

pantograph ['pæntəgrɑːf] N **1** Art pantographe m, singe m **2** Elec (of electric train) pantographe m

pantomime ['pæntəmaɪm] N **1** Br Theat (traditional winter show) = revue-féerie f à grand spectacle (présentée aux environs de Noël) **2** (dumb show) pantomime f **3** Br Fam (ridiculous situation) cirque m, sérénade f; **there was a bit of a p. over who should pay** ça a été une sérénade pour savoir qui devait payer

> Note that the French word **pantomime** is a false friend and is never a translation for the English word **pantomime**. It means **mime**.

Pantomime

Le genre typiquement britannique de la "pantomime" est très conventionnel; certains personnages-types ("pantomime dame", "principal boy") et certaines rengaines ("Behind you!", "Oh yes he is! – Oh no he isn't!") apparaissent dans toutes les pièces. Ces pièces, qui se jouent au moment des fêtes de fin d'année, sont généralement inspirées d'un conte de fées.

pantry ['pæntrɪ] N (cupboard) (grand) placard m à provisions, dépense f

pants [pænts] NPL VOIR GRAMMAIRE A10 **1** Br (underwear) slip m; (boxer shorts) caleçon m **2** esp Am (trousers) pantalon m; Fam **to give sb a kick in the p.** donner un coup de pied au derrière à qn; Fam **to beat the p. off sb** mettre une sacrée volée à qn; Fam **to scare the p. off sb** faire une peur ou trouille bleue à qn; Fam **to bore the p. off sb** barber qn comme ce n'est pas permis; Fam **to be caught with one's p. down** être pris dans une situation des plus embarrassantes; Fam **to wear the p.** porter la culotte; Fam **it's clear who wears the p. around here** il n'y a pas de doute sur qui porte la culotte ici

ADJ Br Fam (of poor quality) nul

INT Br Fam zut!, mince!

panty ['pæntɪ] N

▶▶ **p. girdle** gaine-culotte f, pl gaines-culottes; **p. liner** protège-slip m, pl protège-slips

pantyhose ['pæntɪhəʊz] NPL Am collant m

panzer ['pænzər] N panzer m; **a p. division** une division blindée

Pap [pæp] N Med **P. test** or **smear** frottis m vaginal

pap [pæp] N (baby food) bouillie f; Pej (nonsense) idioties fpl, stupidités fpl

papa [pə'pɑː] N Old-fashioned papa m

papacy ['peɪpəsɪ] N papauté f

papadum ['pæpədəm] N = **poppadom**

papal ['peɪp(ə)l] ADJ papal, -aux

▶▶ **p. bull** bulle f papale; **p. interdict** interdit m papal; **p. nuncio** nonce m du Pape; **p. throne** trône m pontifical

paparazzi [pæpə'rætsɪ] NPL Journ, Phot Pej paparazzi mpl

papaw [pə'pɔː] N Bot **1** (asimina triloba) (fruit) asimine f, (tree) asiminier m **2** = **papaya**

papaya [pə'paɪə] N (carica papaya) papaye f; (tree) papayer m

paper ['peɪpər] N **1** papier m; (for wall) papier peint; **a sheet/a piece of p.** une feuille/un morceau de papier; **a pile of p.** une pile de papier; **to put sth down on p.** mettre qch par écrit; **on p. it is an army of 300,000** sur le papier ou en théorie, c'est une armée de 300 000 hommes; **it's a good plan on p.** ce projet est excellent en théorie; **the p. industry** l'industrie f papetière, la papeterie

2 (document) écrit m, document m; Fin etc papier m valeur; (banknotes) billets mpl de banque; **private** or **personal papers** papiers personnels; **(identity) papers** papiers (d'identité); Fin **long/short p.** papier à long/court terme

3 Sch (examination) **p.** épreuve f écrite; (questions) questions fpl d'examen; (answer) copie f; **the Shakespeare/history p.** l'épreuve (écrite) sur Shakespeare/d'histoire

4 (scholarly study, report) article m; **to read** or **give a p.** faire un exposé

5 (newspaper) journal m, -aux; Am Fam **go peddle your papers!** va voir ailleurs si j'y suis!

VT (room) tapisser

▶▶ **p. advance** (of printer) entraînement m du papier; **p. aeroplane** avion m en papier; **p. bag** sac m en papier; **p. bin** (of printer) bac m à papier; **p. blockage** (of printer) bourrage m de papier; **p. chase** rallye-papier m, ≃ jeu m de piste; Fig **education has become an academic p. chase** l'éducation est devenue une véritable course aux diplômes; Fin **p. company** société f d'investissement; **p. cup** gobelet m en carton; **p. currency** papier-monnaie m, pl papiers-monnaies; **p. dart** avion m en papier; Comput, Typ **p. feed** alimentation f du papier; **p. folding machine** machine f à plier les documents; Comput, Typ **p. format** format m de papier; **p. guide** (of printer) guide-papier m, pl guides-papier; **p. handkerchief** mouchoir m en papier; **p. handling** (of printer) gestion f du papier; Fam **p. hankie** mouchoir en papier; **p. input** (of printer) entrée f de papier; **p. jam** (of printer) bourrage de papier; Fin **p. loss** moins-value f, pl moins-values; **p. mill** usine f à papier; (on small scale) fabrique f de papier; Fin **p. money** papier-monnaie m, pl papiers-monnaies, monnaie f fiduciaire; **p. out indicator** (of printer) indicateur m de fin du papier; **p. out light** (of printer) voyant m de fin du papier; **p. out warning** (of printer) avertissement m de fin du papier; **p. park function** (of printer) fonction f de parcage de l'imprimante; **p. path** (of printer) chemin m du papier; **p. plate** assiette f en carton; **p. profits** profits mpl fictifs; **p. release arm** (of printer) levier m de dégagement du papier; **p. round** livraison f de journaux; **to have** or **do a p. round** distribuer les journaux; Fin **p.** securities titres mpl fiduciaires, papiers valeurs; Br **p. shop** marchand m de journaux; Comput **p. tape** bande f perforée; Comput **p. tape reader** lecteur m de bandes de papier; **p. tiger** tigre m de papier; **p. tissue** mouchoir en papier; **p. towel** serviette f en papier; **p. transaction** jeu m d'écritures; **p. tray** (of printer) bac à feuilles

▶ **paper over** VT SEP **to p. sth over** (with wallpaper) masquer qch en le tapissant; Fig **to p. over the cracks** (disguise faults) masquer les défauts; (disguise disagreements) masquer les mésententes

paperback ['peɪpəbæk] N livre m de poche; **available in p.** disponible en livre de poche; **p. sales** ventes fpl de livres de poche

ADJ p. book/edition livre m/édition f de poche

paperboard ['peɪpəbɔːd] N carton m

paperboy ['peɪpəbɔɪ] N (deliverer) livreur m de journaux; (seller) vendeur m de journaux

paperclip ['peɪpəklɪp] N trombone m

papergirl ['peɪpəgɜːl] N (deliverer) livreuse f de journaux; (seller) vendeuse f de journaux

paperhanger ['peɪpəhæŋər] N **1** (decorator) peintre m décorateur **2** Am Sl (counterfeiter) faux-monnayeur m, pl faux-monnayeurs

paperknife ['peɪpənaɪf] N coupe-papier m inv

paperless ['peɪpəlɪs] ADJ

▶▶ **p. office** bureau m entièrement informatisé; St Exch **p. trading** marché m ou cotation f électronique

paperweight ['peɪpəweɪt] N presse-papiers m inv

paperwork ['peɪpəwɜːk] N paperasseries fpl; (official documents) papiers mpl; **to do the p.** s'occuper du travail de bureau; **I'm drowning in p.** je suis dans la paperasserie jusqu'au cou

papery ['peɪpərɪ] ADJ qui ressemble à du papier; (thin) mince comme du papier; **p. skin** peau f parcheminée

papier-mâché ['pæpjeɪ'mæʃeɪ] N carton-pâte m, pl cartons-pâtes

papilloma [pæpɪ'ləʊmə] N Med papilloma m

papist ['peɪpɪst] N, ADJ Pej papiste mf

papistry ['peɪpɪstrɪ] N Pej papisme m

paprika [pə'priːkə] N paprika m

Papua ['pæpjʊə] N Hist Papouasie f

▶▶ **P. New Guinea** Papouasie-Nouvelle-Guinée f

Papuan ['pæpjʊən] ADJ papou

N Papou, -oue

papyrus, pl **papyri** [pə'paɪrəs, -raɪ] N papyrus m

par [pɑːr] N **1** (equality) pair m, égalité f; **to be on a p. with sb/sth** être au niveau de qn/qch; **they're on a p.** ils sont au même niveau **2** above/below **p.** au-dessus/au-dessous du pair; **at p.** au pair; **to issue shares at p.** émettre des actions au pair; **close to p.** au voisinage de la parité **3** (average) moyenne f; above/below **p.** au-dessus/au-dessous de la moyenne; Fam **to feel below p., not to feel up to p.** ne pas être dans son assiette; **the film wasn't really up to p.** le film n'est pas aussi bon qu'on aurait pu s'y attendre **4** Golf par m; **to be under/over p.** être en dessous/au-dessus du par; **a p.-three (hole)** un par trois; Fam Fig **that's about p. for the course** c'est ce à quoi il faut s'attendre; **his behaviour was about p. for the course** son comportement n'a rien eu de vraiment surprenant

▶▶ Fin, St Exch **p. bond** obligation f émise au pair; Fin, St Exch **p. of exchange** pair du change; *Fin, St Exch* **p. value** valeur *f* au pair *ou* nominale

para ['pærə] N **1** (*abbr* **paragraph**) par. **2** *Mil Fam* (*abbr* **paratrooper**) para *m*

parable ['pærəb(ə)l] N parabole *f*; **teaching in parables** enseignement *m* en paraboles

parabola [pə'ræbələ] N *Math* parabole *f*

parabolic [pærə'bɒlɪk] ADJ *Math etc* (*curve, mirror*) parabolique
▸▸ *TV* **p. dish** antenne *f* parabolique, parabole *f*

paracetamol [pærə'si:təmɒl] N paracétamol *m*; **take two p.** *or* **paracetamols** prenez deux cachets de paracétamol

parachute ['pærəʃu:t] N parachute *m*; **to drop sb/sth by p.** larguer qn/qch par parachute, parachuter qn/qch; **brake** *or* **tail p.** parachute de freinage (à l'atterrissage)
VI sauter en parachute
VT (*person, supplies*) parachuter, larguer par parachute
▸▸ **p. descent** descente *f* en parachute; **p. flare** fusée *f* (éclairante) à parachute; **p. harness** ceinture *f* ou harnais *m* de parachute; **p. jump** saut *m* en parachute; **to make a p. jump** sauter en parachute; **p. pack** (*parachute*) parachute (plié et prêt à servir); (*container*) enveloppe *f* ou sac *m* de parachute
▸ **parachute in** VT SEP (*troops, supplies etc*) parachuter, envoyer par parachute; *Fig* (*new manager, candidate etc*) parachuter
VI être parachuté; **I'll p. in** je vais me faire parachuter, je vais descendre en parachute

parachuting ['pærəʃu:tɪŋ] N (*activity*) parachutisme *m*; (*of person, supplies*) parachutage *m*

parachutist ['pærəʃu:tɪst] N parachutiste *mf*

parade [pə'reɪd] N **1** *Mil* (*exercise*) exercice *m*; **church p.** (*of battalion etc*) rassemblement *m* pour assister à l'office du dimanche; **on p.** à l'exercice
2 (*procession*) défilé *m*; *Rel* procession *f*; **fashion p.** défilé de mannequins; *Mil* **to go on p.** défiler
3 (*display*) parade *f*; *Pej* **to make a p. of one's knowledge/feelings** étaler sa culture/ses sentiments; **a street where you'll see all the new fashions on p.** une rue où l'on arbore toutes les dernières créations de la mode; **all the world leaders were on p.** il y avait tout une panoplie de chefs d'états
4 (*along beach*) boulevard *m*; **a p. of shops** une rangée de magasins
5 *Fencing* parade *f*
VT **1** *Mil* (*troops*) faire parader, faire défiler; (*assemble*) (*battalion*) rassembler **2** (*riches*) faire parade *ou* étalage de; (*knowledge, feelings, opinions*) afficher, faire étalage de; **to p. one's dislike of sb** montrer clairement son antipathie à l'égard de qn
VI **1** *Mil* (*for exercise, inspection*) parader; **to p. through the streets** défiler dans les rues **2** *Fig* (*show off*) se pavaner; **young people parading up and down the beach with next to nothing on!** des jeunes gens qui se pavanent sur la plage avec presque rien sur le dos!
▸▸ *Mil* **p. ground** terrain *m* d'exercices *ou* de manœuvres

paradigm ['pærədaɪm] N paradigme *m*

paradigmatic [pærədɪg'mætɪk] ADJ paradigmatique

paradise ['pærədaɪs] N *Rel, Fig* paradis *m*; **an earthly p.** un paradis sur terre; **to go to p.** aller au paradis; **bird of p.** paradisier *m*, oiseau *m* de paradis

paradisiac [pærə'dɪzɪæk], **paradisiacal** [pærədɪ'zaɪək(ə)l] ADJ paradisiaque

paradox ['pærədɒks] N paradoxe *m*

paradoxical [pærə'dɒksɪk(ə)l] ADJ paradoxal, -aux

paradoxically [pærə'dɒksɪklɪ] ADV paradoxalement

paraffin ['pærəfɪn] N paraffine *f*; (*fuel*) pétrole *m* (lampant), kérosène *m*; *Pharm* **liquid p.** huile *f* de paraffine; **to coat with p.** paraffiner
▸▸ **p. lamp** lampe *f* à pétrole; **p. oil** (*fuel*) pétrole (lampant), kérosène; **p. wax** paraffine

paragliding ['pærəglaɪdɪŋ] N *Sport* parapente *m*

paragon ['pærəgən] N (*of virtue, beauty*) modèle *m*

paragraph ['pærəgrɑ:f] N paragraphe *m*, alinéa *m*; *Journ* (*short article*) entrefilet *m*; *Typ* (*mark*) pied *m* de mouche; **new p.** (*when dictating*) à la ligne; **to start a new p.** aller à la ligne
VT (*piece of writing*) diviser en paragraphes
▸▸ **p. indent** alinéa *m*; *Typ* **p. mark** pied de mouche

Paraguay ['pærəgwaɪ] N Paraguay *m*

Paraguayan [pærə'gwaɪən] ADJ paraguayen
N Paraguayen, -enne

parakeet ['pærəki:t] N (*bird*) perruche *f*

parallel ['pærəlel] ADJ **1** *Math etc* parallèle (**to** *or* **with sth** à qch); **to be** *or* **run p. to sth** être parallèle à qch **2** (*analogous*) pareil, semblable; (*case, situation*) analogue (**to** *or* **with sth** à qch); **the two cases are exactly p.** les deux cas sont analogues
N **1** *Math* (*ligne f*) parallèle *f*, *Geog, Astron* parallèle *m*; *Mil* (*trench*) (tranchée *f*) parallèle *f*, *Typ* **parallels** barres *fpl* **2** *Elec* **in p.** (*connected*) en parallèle, en dérivation; **out of p.** (*of dynamo*) déphasé, hors de phase, hors de synchronisme **3** (*analogy*) parallèle *m*, comparaison *f*; **to draw a p. between two things** établir un parallèle *ou* une comparaison entre deux choses; **without p.** sans pareil
VT (-l-) **1** (*be similar to*) être analogue à **2** (*be equal to*) égaler; **the victory has not been paralleled** cette victoire est restée sans égal
▸▸ *Gym* **p. bars** barres parallèles; *Elec* **p. circuits** circuits *mpl* parallèles; *Elec* **p. connection** couplage *m* ou montage *m* en parallèle *ou* en dérivation; **p. importing** importations *fpl* parallèles; *Comput* **p. input** entrée *f* parallèle; *Comput* **p. interface** interface *f* parallèle; **p. lines** lignes *fpl* parallèles; *Comput* **p. output** sortie *f* parallèle; **p. parking** stationnement *m* en créneau; *Comput* **p. port** port *m* parallèle; *Comput* **p. printer** imprimante *f* en parallèle; *Comput* **p. printer cable** câble *m* d'imprimante parallèle; *Comput* **p. printer port** port d'imprimante parallèle; *Comput* **p. processing** traitement *m* en parallèle *or* en simultanéité; *Fin* **p. rate of exchange** cours *m* parallèle; **p. rule, p. ruler** règle *f* à (tracer des) parallèles, parallèle *m*; *Mktg* **p. selling** vente *f* parallèle; *Comput* **p.-to-serial converter** convertisseur *m* parallèle-série; *Ski* **p. turn** virage *m* en parallèle

parallelism ['pærəlelɪz(ə)m] N parallélisme *m*

parallelogram [pærə'leləgræm] N parallélogramme *m*

paralyse, *Am* **paralyze** ['pærəlaɪz] VT *Med, Fig* paralyser; **paralysed in one leg** paralysé d'une jambe; *Fig* **laws that p. industry** lois qui paralysent l'industrie; **paralysed with fear** paralysé par l'effroi, glacé d'effroi

paralysing, *Am* **paralyzing** ['pærəlaɪzɪŋ] ADJ *Med, Fig* (*poison, fear etc*) paralysant

paralysis [pə'ræləsɪs] N *Med, Fig* paralysie *f*

paralytic [pærə'lɪtɪk] ADJ **1** *Med* paralytique **2** *Br Fam* (*very drunk*) ivre mort
N *Med* paralytique *mf*
▸▸ *Med* **p. stroke** attaque *f* de paralysie

paralytically [pærə'lɪtɪklɪ] ADV *Br Fam* **p. drunk** ivre mort

paralyze, paralyzing *Am* = **paralyse, paralysing**

paramedic [pærə'medɪk] N auxiliaire *mf* médical(e)
ADJ (*skills, qualification*) paramédical, -aux

parameter [pə'ræmɪtər] N *Math, Comput etc* paramètre *m*; **to set the parameters of** paramétrer; *Fig* **within the parameters of the enquiry** dans les limites fixées par les paramètres de l'enquête

paramilitary [pærə'mɪlɪtrɪ] ADJ paramilitaire
N membre *m* d'une formation paramilitaire

paramount ['pærəmaʊnt] ADJ (*chief, leader*) suprême; (*necessity, consideration, interest*) primordial, -aux; **it is of p. importance** c'est d'une importance primordiale; **it is p. that we do this** il est primordial que nous fassions ceci

paramour ['pærəmʊər] N *Old-fashioned, Lit* amant, -ante

paranoia [pærə'nɔɪə] N paranoïa *f*, *Fam Fig* **you're suffering from p.** tu es parano

paranoiac [pærə'nɔɪɪk] ADJ, N paranoïaque *mf*; **he's an absolute p.** il est complètement paranoïaque

paranoid ['pærənɔɪd] ADJ paranoïaque; (*delirium, madness*) paranoïde; *Fig* **he's p. about being cheated** il est obsédé par l'idée qu'on cherche à le avoir; **you're being p.** tu es parano; **I know it'll sound p., but …** je suis sûr que tu vas me trouver parano mais …

paranormal [pærə'nɔ:məl] ADJ (*experience, phenomenon etc*) paranormal, -aux
N **the p.** le paranormal

parapet ['pærəpet] N **1** *Mil* (*in fortress*) parapet *m*; (*of trench*) berge *f* **2** (*wall*) parapet *m*; (*railing*) garde-fou *m*, *pl* garde-fous; (*of bridge*) garde-corps *m inv*

paraphernalia [pærəfə'neɪlɪə] NPL (*things*) affaires *fpl*; (*equipment*) attirail *m*; **and all the other p.** et tout le bazar

paraphrase ['pærəfreɪz] N paraphrase *f*
VT paraphraser

paraplegia [pærə'pli:dʒə] N *Med* paraplégie *f*

paraplegic [pærə'pli:dʒɪk] ADJ, N *Med* paraplégique *mf*

parapsychology [pærəsaɪ'kɒlədʒɪ] N parapsychologie *f*, métapsychique *f*

parasite ['pærəsaɪt] N (*animal, plant*), *Fig* parasite *m*; **to be a p. on society** (*of person*) parasiter la société

parasitic [pærə'sɪtɪk] ADJ (*insect, plant, person*) parasite (**on** de); (*existence*) de parasite; **to be p. on an organism/on society** parasiter un organisme/la société
▸▸ *Electron etc* **p. noise** (bruit *m*) parasite *m*

parasitism ['pærəsaɪtɪz(ə)m] N parasitisme *m*

parasitize ['pærəsɪtaɪz] VT parasiter

parasitology [pærəsaɪ'tɒlədʒɪ] N parasitologie *f*

parasol ['pærəsɒl] N (*over table etc*) parasol *m*; (*ladies'*) ombrelle *f*
▸▸ *Bot* **p. mushroom** coulemelle *f*, lépiote *f*, **p. pine** pin *m* parasol

paratrooper ['pærətru:pər] N *Mil* parachutiste *m*

paratroops ['pærətru:ps] NPL *Mil* parachutistes *mpl*

paratyphoid [pærə'taɪfɔɪd] N *Med* paratyphoïde *f*

parboil ['pɑ:bɔɪl] VT *Culin* faire cuire à demi (dans l'eau)

parcel ['pɑ:s(ə)l] N **1** (*bundle, packet*) paquet *m*, colis *m* **2** (*of land*) parcelle *f* **3** *St Exch* (*of bonds*) paquet *m*; *Com* (*batch*) lot *m*
VT (-ll-, *Am* -l-) emballer, empaqueter

▶▶**parcel(s) office** bureau *m* des messageries, messageries *fpl*; **p. post** service *m* de colis postaux; **parcels service** *(courier)* messagerie *f*; *Aut* **p. shelf** tablette *f*

▶**parcel out** VT SEP *(distribute) (inheritance)* parceller, partager; *(land)* lotir, morceler; *(provisions, books)* répartir

▶**parcel up** VT SEP *(wrap)* empaqueter, emballer

parch [pɑːtʃ] VT *(of sun) (grass, earth etc)* dessécher; *(cereal crops)* rôtir, griller, sécher

parched [pɑːtʃt] ADJ *(earth, grass etc)* desséché; *(lips, throat etc)* sec, *f* sèche; *Fam* **to be** *or* **feel p.** *(be thirsty)* mourir de soif

parchment ['pɑːtʃmənt] N parchemin *m*
▶▶**p. paper** papier *m* parchemin *ou* parcheminé

pardon ['pɑːd(ə)n] N **1** **(I beg your) p.?** *(asking sb to repeat sth)* pardon?, comment?; **I beg your p.!** *(in disapproval, shock etc)* je vous demande pardon!, *Fam* pardon?, hein? **2** *Law* grâce *f*, *(document)* lettre *f* de grâce; **free p.** grâce; **to grant sb a free p.** *(of monarch)* faire grâce à qn; **to receive the King's/Queen's p.** être gracié; **general p.** amnistie *f* VT **1** *(fault etc)* pardonner, excuser; **p. my contradicting you, p. me for contradicting you** pardonnez (-moi) si je vous contredis **2** **to p. sb** pardonner à qn; **to p. sb for sth** pardonner qch à qn; **you could be pardoned for thinking so** il est facile de croire cela; **p. me!** *(in apology)* je vous demande pardon!; *Am* **p. me?** *(asking sb to repeat sth)* pardon?; *Iron* **p. me for speaking!** hou là là, excuse-moi d'avoir osé m'exprimer!; **p. me for breathing!** hou là là, excuse-moi d'exister! **3** *Law* gracier, amnistier; *Rel* **to p. sb sth** absoudre qn de qch

pardonable ['pɑːdənəb(ə)l] ADJ **1** pardonnable, excusable **2** *Law* graciable

pardonably ['pɑːdənəblɪ] ADV de façon bien pardonnable *ou* excusable; **he was p. late** il est bien pardonnable *ou* excusable qu'il soit arrivé en retard

pare [peər] VT *(vegetable etc)* éplucher; *(finger nails)* rogner; *(horseshoe)* parer; **expenses have been pared to the bone** les frais généraux ont été réduits *ou* ramenés au strict minimum

▶**pare down** VT SEP *(expenditure etc)* réduire; **the budget has been pared down to the bone** le budget a été réduit *ou* ramené au strict minimum

parent ['peərənt] N père *m*, mère *f*, *pl* parents *mpl*; **when you first become a p.** quand on devient père/mère; **the p.-child relationship** la relation parents-enfant; **each p. should …** le père et la mère devraient …; **if neither p. can …** si ni le père ni la mère ne peuvent … ADJ **the p. plant** la plante mère; **the p. tree** l'arbre d'origine; **the p. birds feed their young** les parents nourrissent leurs oisillons

▶▶*Com* **p. company** société *f ou* maison *f* mère; *Sch* **p. power** pouvoir *m* de décision des parents d'élèves; *Sch* **p.-teacher association** = association *f* regroupant parents d'élèves et enseignants

parentage ['peərəntɪdʒ] N origine *f*; **of unknown p.** de parents inconnus

parental [pə'rent(ə)l] ADJ *(authority etc)* des parents, parental, -aux

parenthesis, *pl* **parentheses** [pə'renθəsɪs, -iːz] N parenthèse *f*; **in parentheses** entre parenthèses

parenthesize [pə'renθəsaɪz] VT *(words)* mettre entre parenthèses

parenthetical [pærən'θetɪk(ə)l] ADJ entre parenthèses
▶▶*Gram* **p. clause** incidente *f*

parenthetically [pærən'θetɪklɪ] ADV entre

parenthèses, par parenthèse; **could I just say p. …** je voudrais dire entre parenthèses que …

parenthood ['peərənthʊd] N *(fatherhood)* paternité *f*, *(motherhood)* maternité *f*

parenting ['peərəntɪŋ] N *(art)* art *m* d'être parent; *(activity)* métier *m* de parent; **to benefit from good p.** bénéficier d'une bonne éducation parentale
▶▶**p. skills** capacités *fpl* à élever des enfants

pariah [pə'raɪə] N paria *m*
▶▶**p. dog** (chien *m*) paria

paring ['peərɪŋ] N *(usu pl)* **parings** *(of vegetables etc)* épluchures *fpl*, *(of nails)* rognures *fpl*, *(of metal)* cisaille *f*
▶▶**p. knife** couteau *m* à légumes

pari passu [pærɪ'pæsʊ] ADV **1** *Lit* **to go p. with …** marcher de pair avec … **2** *Fin, St Exch* pari passu (**with** avec)

Paris ['pærɪs] N Paris *m*; **the P. basin** le bassin parisien

parish ['pærɪʃ] N *Rel* paroisse *f*; *Br Admin* **(civil) p.** commune *f*
▶▶**p. boundary** limites *fpl* de la paroisse; **p. church** église *f* paroissiale; **p. council** ≃ conseil *m* municipal *(d'une petite commune, en Angleterre)*; **p. hall** salle *f* paroissiale; **p. priest** *(Catholic)* curé *m*; *(Protestant)* pasteur *m*; **p.-pump issue** histoire *f* de clocher; **p.-pump politics** politique *f* d'intérêts de clocher; **p. register** registre *m* paroissial; **p. school** école *f* communale

parishioner [pə'rɪʃənər] N paroissien, -ienne

Parisian [pə'rɪzɪən] ADJ parisien
N Parisien, -ienne

parity ['pærɪtɪ] N **1** *(equality) (of status, rank etc)* égalité *f*, *(of pay)* égalité, parité *f*; **to achieve p. of productivity with Japan** atteindre le niveau de productivité du Japon; **ambulance staff want p. with firemen** les ambulanciers veulent obtenir l'égalité de statut avec les pompiers

2 *Fin* parité *f*; **the two currencies were at p.** les deux monnaies étaient à parité; **euro-dollar p.** parité euro-dollar

3 *Comput* parité *f*; **odd p./even p./no p.** parité impaire/parité paire/pas de parité

4 **p. of reasoning** raisonnement *m* analogue

▶▶*Comput* **p. bit** bit *m* de parité; *Comput* **p. check** contrôle *m* de parité; *Comput* **p. error** erreur *f* de parité; *Econ, Fin* **p. of exchange** parité de change; **p. ratio** rapport *m* de parité; **p. table** table *f* des parités; *Fin* **p. value** valeur *f* au pair

park [pɑːk] N **1** parc *m*; *(in hunting)* réserve *f*; **(public) p.** jardin *m* public, parc; **deer p.** parc *(clôturé)* réservé aux cerfs; **national p.** parc national; *Ind, Com* **business/industrial p.** zone *f* commerciale/industrielle; *Br* **car p.** parc de stationnement, parking *m*

2 *Aut (gear)* stationnement *m*
VT **1** *(car)* garer, parquer; **to be double parked** *(of car, driver)* être garé en double file; *Fam* **she parked her bags in the hall** a laissé ses sacs dans l'entrée; *Fam* **to p. oneself beside sb/on sth/etc** se poser *ou* poser ses fesses à côté de qn/sur qch/etc

2 *(sheep)* parquer

3 *Mil (artillery etc)* mettre en parc

4 *Comput (hard disk)* parquer; **to be parked** être en parquage **5** *St Exch* mettre en attente
VI *(of car, driver, aircraft etc)* stationner, se garer

▶▶*Br* **p. keeper** *(of large park)* gardien, -ienne de parc; *(of smaller park)* gardien de jardin public; **p. officer** gardien de parc

parka ['pɑːkə] N *(coat)* parka *m ou f*

park-and-ride N = système *m* de contrôle

de la circulation qui consiste à garer les voitures à l'extérieur des agglomérations dans des parkings prévus à cet effet, puis à prendre un autobus vers le centre-ville

parked [pɑːkt] ADJ *(car, plane etc)* en stationnement, garé

parker ['pɑːkər] N **she's a good p.** elle sait très bien faire les créneaux

parking ['pɑːkɪŋ] N **1** *(of cars, planes etc)* stationnement *m*; **p. is a problem in town** il est difficile de se garer *ou* de stationner en ville; **no p.** défense de stationner; **p. prohibited** stationnement interdit; **double p.** stationnement en double file; **to get a p. ticket** avoir une contravention pour stationnement illégal **2** *St Exch* mise *f* en attente

▶▶**p. area** aire *f* de stationnement, parking *m*; **p. attendant** *(in car park)* gardien, -ienne; *(at hotel)* voiturier *m*; **p. bay** aire de stationnement; *Am* **p. brake** frein *m* à main; **p. fees** tarif *m* de stationnement; **p. fine** amende *f* de stationnement; **p. lights** feux *mpl* de position; **p. lock** *(on automatic gearbox)* position *f* parking; *Am* **p. lot** parking, parc *m* de stationnement; **p. meter** parcmètre *m*, parcomètre *m*, *Can* compteur *m* de stationnement; *Astronaut* **p. orbit** orbite *f* d'attente; **p. place** *(for one vehicle) (in street, car park)* place *f* de parking; **p. space** *(for one vehicle) (in street, car park)* place de parking; **there's more p. space behind the restaurant** il y a encore des places de parking derrière le restaurant

Parkinson ['pɑːkɪnsən] N **1** *Med* **P.'s disease** maladie *f* de Parkinson; **to have P.'s disease** avoir la maladie de Parkinson *ou* un parkinson **2** *Hum* **P.'s law** = plus on a de temps pour accomplir une tâche plus on prend de temps pour l'accomplir

parkland ['pɑːklænd] N espace *m* vert

parkway ['pɑːkweɪ] N *Am Aut* = grande voie *f* de communication

parky ['pɑːkɪ] ADJ *Br Fam (weather)* frisquet

parlance ['pɑːləns] N langage *m*, parler *m*; **in common p.** dans la langue de tous les jours, en langage courant; **in legal/civil service/football p.** en termes juridiques *ou* de pratique/administratifs/de football; **in the p. of the EU** dans le langage de l'UE

parley ['pɑːlɪ] N conférence *f*, *Mil (with enemy)* pourparlers *mpl*; **to hold a p.** parlementer (**with**)
VI être en pourparlers, parlementer (**with the enemy** avec l'ennemi); *(begin discussions)* entrer en pourparlers, parlementer

parliament ['pɑːləmənt] N parlement *m*; **P.** le Parlement; **in P.** au Parlement VOIR GRAMMAIRE A11

parliamentarian [pɑːləmen'teərɪən] N *(member of parliament)* parlementaire *mf*, membre *m* du Parlement; *(expert in parliamentary procedures)* expert *m* en procédures parlementaires

parliamentary [pɑːlə'ment(ə)rɪ] ADJ *(government, rule)* parlementaire
▶▶**p. candidate** candidat *m* aux (élections) législatives; *Br* **p. committee** commission *f* parlementaire; **p. election** élection *f* législative; **p. majority** majorité *f* parlementaire; **p. private secretary** = en Grande-Bretagne, député *m* qui assure la liaison entre un ministre et la Chambre des communes; **p. privilege** immunité *f* parlementaire; *Br* **p. question** = question *f* posée au cours d'un débat parlementaire; **p. reporter** journaliste *mf* parlementaire; *Br* **p. secretary** ≃ sous-secrétaire *m* d'État, *pl* sous-secrétaires; **p. sovereignty** souveraineté *f* parlementaire

parlour, *Am* **parlor** ['pɑːlər] N *Old-fashioned (living room)* salon *m*; *(of convent)* parloir *m*; **beauty p.** salon de beauté; *Am* **beer p.**

bar *m* (où l'on sert de la bière); **funeral p.** entreprise *f* de pompes funèbres; *Am* **ice-cream p.** salon de dégustation de glaces
► ► **p. games** petits jeux *mpl* de salon *ou* de société

parlourmaid ['pɑːləmeɪd] **N** bonne *f (affectée au service de table)*

parlous ['pɑːləs] **ADJ** *Lit, Hum (state)* précaire; *(situation)* périlleux

Parma ['pɑːmə] **N** Parme
► ► **P. ham** jambon *m* de Parme

Parmesan [pɑːmɪ'zæn] **N** *(cheese)* parmesan *m*
► ► **P. cheese** parmesan

Parnassus [pɑː'næsəs] **N** Parnasse *m*

parochial [pə'rəʊkɪəl] **ADJ** *Rel* paroissial, -aux; *Fig Pej* provincial, -aux; **p. outlook** esprit *m* de clocher
► ► *Am* **p. school** école *f* religieuse

parochialism [pə'rəʊkɪəlɪz(ə)m] **N** *Pej* esprit *m* de clocher; *(of approach, attitude)* provincialisme *m*

parodist ['pærədɪst] **N** parodiste *mf*

parody ['pærədɪ] **N** parodie *f*, pastiche *m*; *(of justice)* parodie; *(of truth)* travestissement *m*
VT parodier, pasticher

parole [pə'rəʊl] **N** *Law (from jail)* libération *f* conditionnelle; **prisoner on p.** prisonnier, -ière *(de droit commun)* libéré(e) conditionnellement; *Mil* prisonnier sur parole; **to be put on p.** être mis en liberté conditionnelle, être libéré conditionnellement; **to break one's p.** manquer à sa parole; **day p.** libération conditionnelle de jour
VT *Law* libérer conditionnellement, mettre en liberté conditionnelle; *Mil* libérer sur parole; **paroled inmate** prisonnier, -ière libéré(e) conditionnellement, libéré, -ée conditionnel(elle)
► ► **p. supervisor** surveillant, -ante de liberté conditionnelle

parolee [pərəʊ'liː] **N** *Am* prisonnier, -ière en liberté conditionnelle

paroxysm ['pærəksɪz(ə)m] **N** *Med (of fever)* paroxysme *m*; *(of anger, guilt)* accès *m*; *(of jealousy, grief)* crise *f*; **to be in paroxysms of laughter** avoir le fou rire; **to send sb into paroxysms of laughter** donner le fou rire à qn; **to be in a p. of delight** être absolument ravi

parquet ['pɑːkeɪ] **N 1** *(floor)* parquet *m* **2** *Am Theat* premiers rangs *mpl* du parterre
► ► **p. floor** parquet; **p. flooring** parquet

parricide ['pærɪsaɪd] **N 1** *(person)* parricide *mf* **2** *(crime)* parricide *m*

parrot ['pærət] **N** *(bird)*, *Fig (person)* perroquet *m*; *Fam* **I was as sick as a p.** ça m'a rendu malade
VT répéter comme un perroquet

parrot-fashion **ADV** *Fam* **to repeat sth p.** répéter qch comme un perroquet; **to learn sth p.** *(by repetition)* apprendre qch en le répétant; **he learnt it p.** *(by mimicking sounds)* il est capable de le répéter comme un perroquet

parrotfish ['pærətfɪʃ] **N** perroquet *m* de mer

parry ['pærɪ] **N** *Fencing, Boxing* parade *f*
VT *Fencing, Boxing etc (blow)* parer; *Fig (question)* se dérober à, éluder
VI *Fencing* **to p. and thrust** parer et tirer

parse [pɑːz] **VT 1** *Gram (word)* faire l'analyse (grammaticale) de; *(sentence)* faire l'analyse logique de **2** *Comput* analyser
► ► *Comput* **p. error** erreur *f* d'analyse (syntaxique)

Parsee ['pɑːsiː, pɑː'siː] **ADJ, N** parsi, -ie

parser ['pɑːzər] **N** *Comput* analyseur *m* syntaxique

parsimonious [pɑːsɪ'məʊnɪəs] **ADJ** parci-

monieux; **to be p. with one's money** dépenser son argent avec parcimonie

parsimoniously [pɑːsɪ'məʊnɪəslɪ] **ADV** parcimonieusement

parsimony ['pɑːsɪmənɪ] **N** *esp Fml* parcimonie *f*; **this is not a time for p.** ce n'est guère l'occasion de se montrer parcimonieux

parsing ['pɑːzɪŋ] **N 1** *Gram (of word)* analyse *f* grammaticale; *(of sentence)* analyse logique **2** *Comput* analyse *f* syntaxique

parsley ['pɑːslɪ] **N** *Bot* persil *m*
► ► *Culin* **p. sauce** sauce *f* au persil

parsnip ['pɑːsnɪp] **N** *Bot, Culin* panais *m*

parson ['pɑːs(ə)n] **N** *(clergyman)* ecclésiastique *m*; *(Protestant priest)* pasteur *m*; **the p.'s nose** *(of chicken etc)* le croupion

parsonage ['pɑːsənɪdʒ] **N** *Old-fashioned* ≃ presbytère *m*, cure *f*

PART [pɑːt]

> **N** partie **1, 3, 5** ▪ pièce **1** ▪ rôle **2**
> ▪ épisode **6**
> **VT** séparer ▪ entrouvrir
> **VI** s'entrouvrir ▪ se quitter ▪ céder

N 1 *(portion, component)* partie *f*, *Ind etc* pièce *f*; **(a) p. of the house is to let** une partie de la maison est à louer; **good in parts** bon en partie; **it's not bad in parts** il y a des parties qui ne sont pas mal; **the funny/odd p. about it is that ...** ce qu'il y a de comique/d'étrange c'est que ...; **the best/worst p. was when he started laughing** le mieux/le pire ça a été quand il s'est mis à rire; **the hard p. is remembering** le plus dur c'est de se souvenir; **that was the easy p.** ça c'était le plus facile; **in the early p. of the week** au début *ou* dans les premiers jours de la semaine; **for the best** *or* **greater p. of five years** *(to wait, last etc)* presque cinq ans; **the greater p. of the population** la plus grande partie de la population; **(one) p. of her wanted to agree with them** une partie d'elle-même voulait être d'accord avec eux; **to be** *or* **form p. of sth** faire partie de qch; **it's become (a) p. of our daily routine** ça fait maintenant partie de notre routine quotidienne; **it's all p. of growing up** c'est ce qui se passe quand on grandit; **it is p. and parcel of ...** c'est une partie intégrante *ou* essentielle de ...; **to contribute to the expenses p.** pour partie aux frais; **this is due in p. to inflation** c'est en partie dû à l'inflation; **for the most p.** pour la plupart; *Culin etc* **ten parts of water to one of milk** dix mesures d'eau pour une mesure de lait; **the parts of the body** les parties du corps **SEE GRAMMAR B21** ; **(spare) parts** pièces détachées *ou* de rechange

2 *(active role)* part *f*, *Theat, Cin etc* rôle *m*; **to play a p.** *Theat* avoir un rôle; *Fig (act, pretend)* jouer la comédie; *Theat etc* **small p.** petit rôle; *Theat* **she took** *or* **played the p. of Esmeralda** elle a joué le rôle d'Esmeralda; **to play a p. in sth** *(be involved in, contribute to)* jouer un rôle dans qch; **to have** *or* **play a large/small p. in sth** avoir *ou* jouer un rôle important/peu important dans qch; **she played a large p. in persuading the company to relocate** c'est surtout elle qui a persuadé l'entreprise de se relocaliser; **to take p. in sth** prendre part à qch, participer à qch; **to take p. in the conversation** prendre part à *ou* se mêler à la conversation; **she takes an active p. in decision-making** elle participe activement au processus de prise de décision; *TV etc* **those taking p. were ...** avec le concours de ...; **to take no p. in sth** ne pas prendre part à qch, ne pas participer à qch; **I had no p. in it** je n'y suis pour rien; **I want no p. of** *or* **in it** *(I don't want to be involved)* je ne

veux rien avoir à faire là-dedans; **to dress/look the p.** mettre une tenue de circonstance/avoir la tête de l'emploi

3 *Mus (for specific instrument or voice)* partie *f*; *(of song, fugue)* voix *f*; *(written score)* partition *f*; **a two-p. song** une mélodie à deux voix

4 *(side)* parti *m*; **to take sb's p.** prendre parti pour qn, prendre fait et cause pour qn; **an indiscretion on the p. of ...** une indiscrétion de la part de ...; **for my p.** pour ma part; **to keep one's p. of the agreement** respecter sa part de l'accord

5 *(region)* **in that p. of the world** dans cette partie du monde; **in those parts** dans cette région-là, *Fam* dans ce coin-là; **they are not from our p. of the world** ils ne sont pas de chez nous; **in these parts** par ici; **what are you doing in these parts?** qu'est-ce que vous faites ici *ou* dans ces parages?

6 *(in publishing, of part work)* fascicule *m*, livraison *f*; **p. two** *(of book, TV programme)* deuxième partie *f*, *Radio, TV* **a serial in four parts** un feuilleton en quatre épisodes

7 **to take sth in good/bad p.** prendre qch en bonne/mauvaise part, prendre qch du bon/mauvais côté

8 *Fml (usu pl)* **parts** *(abilities)* moyens *mpl*, facultés *fpl*; **a man of many parts** un homme à facettes

9 *Am (parting in hair)* raie *f*

ADV partiellement, en partie; **I'm p. Spanish** je suis en partie espagnol; **p. silk, p. cotton** mi-soie mi-coton; **a mythical creature, p. woman, p. fish** une créature mythique mi-femme, mi-poisson; **p. one and p. the other** moitié l'un moitié l'autre; **will you take it in p. exchange?** voulez-vous le reprendre?

VT séparer (**sth from sth** qch de qch); *(rock etc)* séparer en deux; *(curtains)* entrouvrir; *(two people)* séparer; *(of bodyguard) (crowd)* ouvrir un passage dans; **to p. one's hair** se faire une raie (dans les cheveux); **to p. one's hair in the middle/at the side** se faire la raie au milieu/sur le côté; **his hair was parted on the left/in the middle** il avait la raie à gauche/au milieu; **they can't bear to be parted** ils ne supportent pas d'être séparés; **to p. company** *(of associates, friends)* se séparer; *(become detached) (of one object from another)* se détacher (**from** de); *Hum* **to p. company with one's horse/bike** *(fall off)* tomber de son cheval/vélo; **this is where we p. company** *(I'm going in the opposite direction)* c'est ici que nous nous quittons; *(where I begin to disagree with you)* c'est là que nos points de vue divergent, c'est là que je ne suis plus d'accord

VI *(of crowd etc)* se diviser; *(of two people)* se quitter, se séparer; *(of roads)* diverger; *(of cable etc)* rompre, céder; **her lips parted in a smile** ses lèvres s'entrouvrirent dans un sourire; **the curtains parted** les rideaux s'entrouvrirent; **to p. good friends** se quitter bons amis; **let us p. (as) friends** séparons-nous (en) bons amis; **to p. from sb** quitter qn; *(separate)* se séparer de *ou* d'avec qn; **to p. with sth** *(get rid of)* se débarrasser *ou* se défaire de qch; *(give up)* céder qch; *Law (right, possession)* aliéner qch; **he hates to p. with (his) money** il n'aime pas débourser
► ► *Com* **p. consignment** expédition *f* partielle; **parts and labour warranty** garantie *f* pièces et main-d'œuvre; **parts list** nomenclature *f*, *Com* **p. load** chargement *m* partiel; **p. music** musique *f* d'ensemble; **p. owner** copropriétaire *mf*; **p. ownership** copropriété *f*; *Com* **p. shipment** expédition *f* partielle; **p. singing** chant *m* polyphonique *ou* à plusieurs voix; **p. song** chant polyphonique *ou* à plusieurs voix; *Gram* **parts of speech** parties du discours; *Br* **p. work** ouvrage *m* à fascicules

partake [pɑːˈteɪk] **VI** (pt **partook** [pɑːˈtʊk], pp **partaken** [pɑːˈteɪkən]) Fml **to p. in sth** participer à qch (**with sb** avec qn); **to p. of the nature of sth** relever de qch; **it partakes of a certain grandeur** c'est empreint d'une certaine grandeur; Old-fashioned **to p. of a meal** prendre un repas; Old-fashioned, Hum **do you p.?** (would you like a drink?) vous prendrez bien un petit verre?; **I no longer p.** (don't drink) je ne bois plus; Rel **to p. of the Sacrament** s'approcher des sacrements

parterre [pɑːˈteə(r)] **N** Am (in theatre) parterre m

parthenogenesis [pɑːθənəʊˈdʒenɪsɪs] **N** Biol parthénogénèse f

Parthian [ˈpɑːθɪən] **ADJ**
▸▸**P. shot** flèche f du Parthe

partial [ˈpɑːʃəl] **ADJ 1** (biased) partial, -aux (**towards sb** envers qn); (unjust) injuste **2** Fam **to be p. to sb/sth** (like) avoir un faible ou une prédilection pour qn/qch, avoir un penchant pour qn/qch; **I am rather p. to a spot of whisky after dinner** je bois volontiers un petit verre de whisky après dîner **3** (in part) partiel
▸▸**p. disability** incapacité f partielle; **p. eclipse** éclipse f partielle; Ins **p. loss** perte f partielle, sinistre m partiel; Fin **p. payment** paiement m partiel

> When translating the English word **partial**, note that the French words **partial** and **partiel** are not interchangeable. **Partial** means **biased** and **partiel** is the opposite of **complete**.

partiality [pɑːʃɪˈælɪtɪ] **N 1** (bias) partialité f (**towards** envers, en faveur de); (favouritism) favoritisme m **2** (liking) prédilection f, penchant m, faible m (**for** pour)

partially [ˈpɑːʃəlɪ] **ADV 1** (with bias) avec partialité **2** (partly, in part) partiellement, en partie; **p. sighted** malvoyant; **the p. sighted** (npl) les malvoyants mpl

participant [pɑːˈtɪsɪpənt] **ADJ, N** participant, -ante (**in** à)

participate [pɑːˈtɪsɪpeɪt] **VI** (of person) prendre part, participer (**in sth** à qch); Lit **to p. in sb's joy** s'associer à la joie de qn

participating [pɑːˈtɪsɪpeɪtɪŋ] **ADJ** participant
▸▸Fin **p. interest** intérêt m de participation; **to hold a p. interest in a company** avoir un intérêt de participation dans une société

participation [pɑːtɪsɪˈpeɪʃən] **N** participation f (**in sth** à qch); **thank you for your p.** merci de votre participé
▸▸St Exch **p. certificate** titre m ou bon m de participation; St Exch **p. rate** taux m d'activité

participial [pɑːtɪˈsɪpɪəl] **ADJ** Gram participial, -aux

participle [ˈpɑːtɪsɪp(ə)l] **N** Gram participe m; **present/past p.** participe présent/passé
VOIR GRAMMAIRE A44–6; B37–9

particle [ˈpɑːtɪk(ə)l] **N 1** (of matter) particule f, (of metal) paillette f, (of sand) grain m; Nucl particule, corpuscule m; **there's not a p. of truth in the story** il n'y a pas une ombre de vérité dans ce récit **2** Gram particule f
▸▸Phys **p. accelerator** accélérateur m de particules; Constr **p. board** panneau m d'aggloméré, panneau de particules; **p. physics** physique f des particules

parti-coloured, Am **parti-colored** [ˈpɑːtɪ-] **ADJ** esp Lit bigarré, bariolé

particular [pəˈtɪkjʊlər] **ADJ 1** (specific) particulier; **that p. book** ce livre-là, ce livre en particulier; **is there any p. time you'd like to come?** y a-t-il une heure qui vous convienne en particulier?; **they didn't have this p. brand** ils n'avaient pas cette marque-

là; **which p. thing/person did you have in mind?** à quoi/qui pensiez-vous en particulier?; **this one is a p. favourite of mine** j'affectionne tout particulièrement celui-ci; **he is a p. friend of mine** c'est l'un de mes meilleurs amis; **why did you insist on this p. one?** pourquoi as-tu insisté sur celui-là en particulier?; **in my p. field (of study/research)** dans ma spécialité; **my own p. feelings** mes sentiments personnels; **to take p. care over doing sth** faire qch avec un soin (tout) particulier; **to take p. care to do sth** mettre un soin (tout) particulier à faire qch; **to do sth for no p. reason** faire qch sans raison précise; **I didn't notice anything (in) p.** je n'ai rien remarqué de particulier; **in p.** en particulier
2 Old-fashioned, Fml (detailed) (account etc) détaillé, circonstancié
3 (person) (exacting) méticuleux, minutieux, soigneux; (about rules etc) pointilleux; (about choice of friends, methods used etc) difficile, exigeant; **I have to be quite p. about what I eat** je dois faire très attention à ce que je mange; **it had to be pure silk, he was most p. about it** il fallait que ce soit de la soie pure, il a insisté; **to be p. about one's food** (demanding) être exigeant pour la nourriture; (difficult) être difficile pour la nourriture; **to be p. about one's dress** soigner sa mise ou sa tenue; Fam **I'm not p. (about it)** (I don't care) je n'y tiens pas plus que ça; **he's not p. about where the goods come from** l'origine des marchandises lui importe peu
N détail m; **alike in every p.** semblables en tout point; **they differ in several particulars** ils diffèrent en plusieurs points; **to go into particulars** entrer dans les détails; **to give particulars of sth** donner les détails de qch; **to ask for fuller particulars about sth** demander des précisions ou des détails supplémentaires sur qch; **to take down sb's particulars** prendre les coordonnées de qn; **for further particulars apply to …** pour plus amples détails ou renseignements s'adresser à …
▸▸Fin **p. lien** privilège m spécial

particularity [pətɪkjʊˈlærɪtɪ] **N 1** (special quality) particularité f **2** (exacting nature) méticulosité f, (detailed nature) (of description etc) minutie f

particularize [pəˈtɪkjʊləraɪz] Fml **VT** spécifier
VI entrer dans les détails, préciser

particularly [pəˈtɪkjʊləlɪ] **ADV** particulièrement, en particulier; **it's cold here, p. at night** il fait froid ici, particulièrement ou spécialement la nuit; **note p. that …** notez en particulier que …; **be p. careful** faites particulièrement attention; **she's not p. rich** elle n'est pas tellement riche

particulate emissions [pɑːˈtɪkjʊlɪt] **NPL** émission f de particules

parting [ˈpɑːtɪŋ] **N 1** (division) séparation f, (of the waters) partage m; Fig **to be at or to have come to the p. of the ways** être à la croisée des chemins **2** (leave-taking) séparation f, **it was a painful p.** la séparation a été douloureuse; **p. kiss** baiser m d'adieu; **p. words** mots mpl d'adieu **3** Br (in hair) raie f, **centre/side p.** raie au milieu/sur le côté
▸▸Fig **p. shot** flèche f du Parthe

partisan [pɑːtɪˈzæn] **N** (supporter, resistance fighter) partisan m
ADJ 1 partisan; **to act in a p. spirit** (of politician etc) faire preuve d'esprit de parti; (be prejudiced) faire preuve de parti pris **2** Mil partisan

partisanship [pɑːtɪˈzænʃɪp] **N** partialité f, (of politician etc) esprit m de parti

partition [pɑːˈtɪʃən] **N 1** (dividing) division f, découpage m; (of conquered country, inheritance etc) (division) partition f, (sharing out) partage m **2** (screen) séparation f, cloisonnage m; (wall) cloison f, (of ship's hold etc) compartiment m; Constr **internal p., p. wall** cloison **3** Comput partition f
VT 1 (divide) diviser; (inheritance etc) partager; (conquered country) démembrer, partager **2** = **partition off 3** Comput (hard disk) découper
▸**partition off VT SEP** (room) cloisonner; (part of a room) séparer par une cloison

> Note that the French word **partition** never means **wall**.

partitive [ˈpɑːtɪtɪv] **ADJ, N** Gram partitif m
SEE GRAMMAR B5

partly [ˈpɑːtlɪ] **ADV** partiellement, en partie; **wholly or p.** en tout ou en partie; **p. by force, p. by persuasion** moitié par la force, moitié par la persuasion; **a p. eaten sandwich** un sandwich à moitié mangé; **she was only p. convinced** elle n'était qu'à moitié convaincue
▸▸Fin **p. paid-up capital** capital m non entièrement versé; St Exch **p. paid-up shares** actions fpl non entièrement libérées; Fin **p. secured creditor** créancier, -ière partiellement nanti(e)

partner [ˈpɑːtnər] **N** Com etc associé, -ée (**with sb in sth** de qn dans qch); (in tennis, driving etc) partenaire mf, (in dancing) cavalier, -ière, partenaire; (of cowboy, bank robber etc) acolyte m; (person one lives with) compagnon m, compagne f, (boyfriend, girlfriend) ami m, amie f, **our European partners** nos partenaires européens; **partners should consider each other's moods** chacun au sein du couple doit prendre les humeurs de l'autre en considération; **they became partners** ils se sont associés; **to be sb's p. in a crime** être associé à qn dans un crime; Cards **to cut or draw for partners** = faire les rois
VT Com etc (be partner of) être associé à ou avec; (become partner of) s'associer à ou avec; (in games) être le/la partenaire de; (in dancing) être le cavalier/la cavalière de

partnership [ˈpɑːtnəʃɪp] **N 1** association f (**in sth with sb** avec qn dans qch); **p. in crime** association dans le crime; Com etc **to enter or go into p. with sb** s'associer avec qn; **to take sb into p.** prendre qn comme associé(e) **2** Com etc (company) = société f en nom collectif
▸▸**p. agreement** accord m de partenariat; EU **P. and Cooperation Agreements** Accords mpl de partenariat et de coopération; **p. marketing** marketing m de partenariat; St Exch **p. share** part f d'association; **p. sponsoring** parrainage-partenariat m

partridge [ˈpɑːtrɪdʒ] **N** (pl **partridges, partridge**) perdrix f, Culin perdreau m

part-time **ADJ** (job, work) à temps partiel, à mi-temps; **on a p. basis** à temps partiel, à mi-temps; **p. worker/employee** ouvrier, -ière/employé, -ée qui travaille à temps partiel ou à mi-temps; **p. contract** contrat m à temps partiel
ADV (to work) à temps partiel, à mi-temps

parturition [pɑːtjʊˈrɪʃən] **N** Med parturition f

partway [ˈpɑːtweɪ] **ADV** **they were p. through the rehearsal** ils avaient commencé à répéter depuis déjà un moment; **I'm only p. through it** (the book, the task) je ne l'ai pas encore fini; **they had gone p. towards an agreement** ils s'acheminaient vers un accord; **we were p. there** (in project etc) nous en avions fait une bonne partie; **this will go p. towards covering the costs** cela couvrira une bonne partie des coûts

party ['pɑːtɪ] N **1** Pol parti m; **a p. member, a member of the p.** un membre du parti; **p. quarrels** querelles fpl partisanes; **p. spirit** esprit m de parti; **he's just making a p. political point** son argument ne relève que de la politique politicienne; **to follow** or **toe the p. line** obéir aux directives du parti

2 (gathering) fête f; (evening celebration) soirée f; (reception) réception f; **dinner p.** dîner m; Fam **he's caught the p. spirit** il s'est abandonné aux joies de la fête

3 (group) (of tourists etc) groupe m, bande f; Min (of miners, workers etc) brigade f, équipe f, groupe; Mil etc détachement m; **the official p.** le groupe des officiels, les officiels mpl; **will you join our p.?** voulez-vous être des nôtres?; **we're a small p.** nous sommes peu nombreux; **I was one of the p.** j'étais de la partie; **the wedding/funeral p.** les invités au mariage/le cortège funéraire

4 (participant), Law (to a suit, to a dispute) partie f; **the parties to the case** les parties en cause; **to be p. to a suit** être en cause; Com etc **parties to a bill of exchange** intéressé(e)s à une lettre de change; **to be/become (a) p. to a crime** être/se rendre complice d'un crime; **I would never be (a) p. to such a thing** je ne me ferais jamais complice d'une chose pareille, je ne m'associerais jamais à une chose pareille

5 Fam (person) individu m, type m

VI Fam faire la bringue, faire la fête; **let's p.!** faisons la bringue ou la fête!; **to p. the night away** faire la bringue ou la fête toute la nuit

▸▸ Fam **p. animal** fêtard, -arde; **she's a real p. animal** elle adore faire la fête; **p. convention** Congrès m du parti; **p. dress** robe f habillée; **p. games** = jeux mpl auxquels on joue dans les soirées ou les fêtes; **p. leader** chef m de parti; **p. line** Tel ligne f commune (à plusieurs abonnés); Pol ligne du parti; Pol **p. machine** machine f du parti; Pol **p. man** homme m de parti; Br Fam **p. piece** numéro m (à l'occasion d'une fête); Iron **that's his p. piece** c'est son numéro habituel; TV, Radio **p. political broadcast** émission f reservée à un parti politique; **that was a p. political broadcast on behalf of the Labour P.** vous venez de voir/d'entendre une émission du parti travailliste; **p. politics** politique f politicienne; Fam **p. pooper** rabat-joie m inv; **p. system** système m des partis; Constr **p. wall** mur m mitoyen

partygoer ['pɑːtɪɡəʊər] N habitué, -ée des soirées; (on one occasion) invité, -ée; **the streets were full of partygoers** les rues étaient pleines de gens se rendant à des soirées

party-list system N Pol (of voting) scrutin m de liste

PASCAL [pæ'skæl] N Comput PASCAL m

paschal ['pæsk(ə)l] ADJ pascal, -aux

pashmina [pæʃ'miːnə] N (wool, garment) pashmina m

PASS [pɑːs]

N	col **1** ▪ laissez-passer **2**
	▪ moyenne **3** ▪ passe **4**
VT	passer devant **1** ▪ dépasser **1**
	▪ passer **1, 4-6, 9** ▪ être reçu à **2**
	▪ voter **4**
VI	passer **1, 3, 4, 6** ▪ se passer **2, 5**
	▪ être adopté **8**

N **1** (in mountains) col m

2 (permit) permis m, laissez-passer m inv; Mil permission f; **(free) p.** Rail etc titre m ou carte f de circulation; Theat etc (free ticket) billet m gratuit ou de faveur

3 Sch, Univ (in examination) moyenne f, mention f passable; **to obtain** or **get a p.** être reçu

4 (movement) (of footballer, magician etc)

passe f; Fencing passe, passade f, botte f; **the aircraft made two low passes over the village** l'avion a effectué deux passages à basse altitude au-dessus du village; Fam **to make a p. at sb** draguer qn, faire des propositions à qn

5 (in data analysis) examen m (through de); (of read head) passage m; **to make a p. over sth** passer sur qch

6 Old-fashioned Fam (situation) **things have come to a pretty p.!** voilà donc où en sont les choses!; **things came to such a p. that ...** les choses en vinrent à ce point ou à tel point que ...

VT **1** (go past) (window, building etc) passer devant; (person) croiser; (destination) dépasser; (frontier) passer, franchir; Naut (headland) dépasser, doubler; (overtake) (person, another ship) dépasser, rattraper; (another car, runner) doubler, dépasser; (in league table) passer devant; **not a word about it had passed her lips** elle n'en avait pas dit un mot; Lit **to p. understanding** dépasser l'entendement

2 (succeed in) (exam) être reçu ou admis à; **to p. a test** (of vehicle, product) subir une épreuve avec succès; (of person) réussir une épreuve, subir une épreuve avec succès

3 (be accepted by) **bill that has passed the House of Commons** projet de loi qui a été voté par la Chambre des communes; **to p. the censor/the customs** être accepté par la censure/la douane

4 (approve) (invoice) approuver, admettre, apurer; (expenditure) allouer; Parl etc (bill, resolution) passer, voter, adopter; **to p. a bill through Parliament** faire adopter une loi par le Parlement; **to p. a dividend of 5%** (of company) approuver un dividende de 5%; **the censor has passed the play/the film** en censeur a accordé le visa; **to p. for press** donner le bon à tirer; Sch **to p. a candidate** recevoir un candidat, admettre un candidat; Mil etc **to be passed fit** être reconnu apte

5 (give, transfer) (faire) passer; (counterfeit banknote etc) (faire) passer, écouler, Fam refiler; **to p. sth from hand to hand** passer qch de main en main; **p. me the salt, please** passez-moi le sel, s'il vous plaît; Ftbl etc **to p. the ball** passer le ballon

6 (put) passer; **to p. one's hand between the bars** passer ou glisser sa main à travers les barreaux; **to p. a rope round sth** passer une corde autour de qch; **to p. a sponge over sth** passer l'éponge sur qch; **to p. one's hand over one's brow** se passer la main sur le front

7 Mil **to p. troops in review** passer des troupes en revue

8 Fin **to p. a dividend** conclure un exercice sans payer de dividende

9 **to p. the time** (of person) passer le temps; **it passes the time** cela fait passer le temps

10 (utter) **to p. criticism on sth** faire la critique de qch; **to p. remarks** faire des commentaires ou des observations (**on sth** sur qch); Law **to p. sentence** prononcer le jugement; **to p. judgement on sb** porter un jugement sur qn, juger qn

11 Physiol **to p. water** uriner; Med **to p. blood** avoir du sang dans les urines; **has he passed anything?** est-ce qu'il a uriné ou été à la selle?

VI **1** (go past) passer; Aut (overtake) doubler, dépasser; Cards passer, renoncer, passer parole; (at dominoes) bouder; **we p. on the stairs every morning** nous nous croisons tous les matins dans l'escalier; **the tourists passed into the dining hall** les touristes sont passés dans le réfectoire; **words passed between them** ils ont eu une altercation; **to p. along a street** passer par une rue; **the procession passed slowly** le cortège passa ou

défila lentement; **everyone smiles as he passes** tout le monde sourit à son passage; **the motorway passes close to the village** l'autoroute passe tout près du village; **to let sb p.** or **allow sb to p.** laisser passer qn; **they shall not p.!** ils ne passeront pas!; Rail etc **p. along** or **down the car!** avancez!, dégagez la portière!; **to p. unobserved** passer inaperçu; **I can't allow such a mistake to p. unremarked** je ne peux pas permettre qu'une telle erreur ne soit pas relevée; **let it p.!** passe pour cela!, Fam laisse courir!; **I'd like to say in passing** soit dit en passant; Aut **no passing** défense de doubler; Cards, Fig **p.!** je passe!; Fig **I think I'll p. on the onions** je le voudrais sans les oignons; **can I p. on the mountain climbing this afternoon?** est-ce que je peux être dispensé d'escalade cet après-midi?

2 (of time) (se) passer, s'écouler; **when five minutes had passed** au bout de cinq minutes; **it seemed like no time at all had passed since I had last seen her** on aurait dit que pas une minute ne s'était écoulée depuis la dernière fois que je l'avais vue; **how time passes!** comme le temps passe (vite)!; **to let the opportunity p.** laisser passer l'occasion

3 (be transferred) **water passes from a liquid to a solid state when it freezes** l'eau passe de l'état de liquide à celui de solide quand il gèle; **the expression has passed into the language** l'expression est passée dans la langue; **his fortune passed to his brother** sa fortune est revenue à son frère

4 (go away) passer; (of clouds etc) s'en aller; **I was about to say something witty, but the moment passed** j'allais dire quelque chose de spirituel, mais j'ai laissé passer l'occasion

5 Old-fashioned (take place) avoir lieu, se passer; **I don't know what passed between them** je ne sais pas ce qui s'est passé entre eux; Arch, Lit **to come to p.** arriver, avoir lieu; Arch, Lit **it came to p. that ...** or il arriva ou advint que ...

6 (be accepted) **it would p. in certain circles** cela passerait dans certains milieux; Fam **you'd p. in a crowd!** tu n'es pas si mal que ça!; **she could p. for an Italian** elle pourrait passer pour une Italienne

7 (succeed in examination) être reçu

8 Pol **to p. through Parliament** (of bill) être adopté par le Parlement

▸▸ Banking **p. book** livret m de banque; **p. laws** = lois fpl qui anciennement restreignaient la liberté de mouvement de la population noire en Afrique du Sud; Br Sch **p. mark** moyenne f; **to get a p. mark** avoir la moyenne

▸ **pass away** VI **1** Euph (die) s'éteindre **2** (disappear) disparaître

▸ **pass by** VI **1** (go past) passer; (carry on without stopping) continuer son chemin; **luckily a taxi was passing by** heureusement un taxi passait par là **2** (of time) passer

VT INSEP (go past) (house etc) passer devant

VT SEP (ignore) ignorer; **life is passing me by** je n'ai pas l'impression de vivre une vie épanouissante; **life has passed her by** elle n'a pas vraiment vécu; **whenever a chance comes, don't let it p. you by** quand une occasion se présente, ne la laissez pas échapper

▸ **pass down** VT SEP **1** (hand down) passer; **p. me down that cup** passez-moi cette tasse **2** (knowledge, story etc) transmettre; (clothing etc) passer (**from ... to** de ... en)

▸ **pass off** VI **1** (take place) **everything passed off well** tout s'est bien passé **2** (end) (of pain) passer, disparaître; **is the nausea passing off?** est-ce que la nausée se passe?

VT SEP **1** (pretend to be) **to p. oneself off as an artist** se faire passer pour (un) artiste; **she passed him off as a duke** elle l'a fait passer pour un duc; **to p. sth off as sth** faire passer qch pour qch **2** (dismiss) **to p. sth off as a**

joke *(accept as a joke)* prendre qch en riant *ou* comme une plaisanterie; *(claim to be a joke)* dire qu'on a fait/dit qch pour rire
▸ **pass on** VI **1** *Euph (die)* décéder, s'éteindre **2** *(proceed) (on journey)* continuer son chemin *ou* sa route; **to p. on to another subject** passer à un autre sujet; **passing on to the question of cost, …** si nous passons maintenant à la question du coût, …
VT SEP *(tell or give to other people)* faire circuler; *(give to other people)* (faire) passer; **read this and p. it on** lisez ceci et faites circuler; **these price increases have been passed on to the consumer** ces hausses des coûts ont été répercutées sur le consommateur; **these cost reductions have been passed on to the consumer** le consommateur a bénéficié de ces réductions des coûts
▸ **pass out** VI **1** *(faint)* s'évanouir **2** *(leave)* sortir (**of** de); **don't let this document p. out of your hands** gardez soigneusement ce document **3** *Sch etc (after final examination)* sortir; **cadets passing out** élèves sortants; **passing-out list** classement *m* de sortie
VT SEP *(distribute)* distribuer
▸ **pass over** VT SEP **1 to p. sb over** *(for promotion)* passer par-dessus le dos à qn; **he's been passed over again** on lui a encore passé par-dessus le dos **2 to p. one's eye over sth** jeter un coup d'œil à qch
VT INSEP **1** *(cross) (river etc)* traverser, franchir; *(obstacle)* franchir, passer sur **2** *(ignore)* passer sous silence; *(difficulty etc)* passer sur, glisser sur; **they passed over the subject in silence** ils ont passé la question sous silence
VI **1** *(end) (of storm)* se dissiper, finir **2 to p. over to the enemy** passer à l'ennemi
▸ **pass round** VT SEP faire passer; **p. the cakes round** faites passer les gâteaux; *Fig* **to p. round the hat** faire une quête
▸ **pass through** VI *(travel through)* passer; **I was just passing through** je ne faisais que passer; **the bullet passed right through** la balle a traversé; **the bus doesn't stop in Hull, it just passes through** le bus ne s'arrête pas à Hull, il ne fait que traverser la ville
VT INSEP *(travel through) (country etc)* traverser; **he was only passing through Paris** il n'était que de passage à Paris **2** *(experience) (crisis)* traverser
▸ **pass up** VT SEP **1** *Fam (not take)* (offer of a job etc) refuser; *(chance)* laisser passer **2** *(hand up)* passer; **p. (me) up that hammer** passe-moi ce marteau

---

Note that the French expression **passer un examen** does not mean **to pass an exam**. It means **to sit an exam**.

---

passable ['pɑːsəb(ə)l] ADJ **1** *(of acceptable quality)* passable, assez bon; **it's p.** ce n'est pas trop mal; **a very p. soufflé** un soufflé plutôt bien réussi **2** *(river, forest etc)* traversable, franchissable; *(road)* praticable

passably ['pɑːsəblɪ] ADV passablement, assez; **to perform p.** offrir une performance passable

passage ['pæsɪdʒ] N **1** *(act of passing) (journey)* passage *m; esp Naut* traversée *f; Pol (of bill)* adoption *f;* **with the p. of time** avec le temps; **bird of p.** oiseau *m* de passage; *Naut* **to have a bad** *or* **rough p.** avoir *ou* faire une mauvaise traversée; *Naut* **to work one's p.** gagner son passage (en travaillant à bord); **to force a p.** se forcer un passage; *Law* **right of p.** droit *m* de passage
2 *(corridor)* couloir *m*, corridor *m; (alley, at end of street)* passage *m*, ruelle *f*, **underground p.** passage souterrain; *Geog* **the North-West/North-East p.** le passage Nord-Ouest/Nord-Est

3 *Tech* canalisation *f*, conduit *m*, conduite *f;* **air p.** conduit d'aérage, conduit(e) d'air; *Anat* **air passages** voies *fpl* aérifères; *Anat* **the back p.** le rectum
4 *(from book, piece of music etc)* passage *m;* **selected passages** morceaux *mpl* choisis

passageway ['pæsɪdʒweɪ] N **1** *(space)* passage *m;* **to leave a p.** laisser le passage libre **2** *(alley)* passage *m*, ruelle *f*, *(corridor)* couloir *m*, corridor *m*

passé ['pæseɪ] ADJ *(outdated)* qui n'est plus à la mode, dépassé

passel ['pæs(ə)l] N *Am Fam (of people etc)* tas *m*

passenger ['pæsəndʒər] N **1** *(on train)* voyageur, -euse; *(on ship, aircraft, in car)* passager, -ère **2** *esp Br Fam (non-contributing member)* non-valeur *f*, *pl* non-valeurs, poids *m* mort; **we can't carry passengers** on ne peut pas traîner de poids morts
▸▸ *Rail* **p. car** voiture *f ou* wagon *m* de voyageurs; **p. and cargo plane** avion *m* mixte; **p. and cargo ship** bateau *m* mixte; *Rail* **p. carriage** voiture *ou* wagon de voyageurs; **p. compartment** *(of car)* habitacle *m;* **p. kilometre** kilomètre-passager *m, pl* kilomètres-passagers; **p. load factor** *(in transport)* taux *m* d'occupation des places; *Aut* **p. safety cage** habitacle de sécurité; *Aut* **p. survival cell** cellule *f* de survie; *Aut* **p. wagon** voiture familiale

passe-partout [pæspɑː'tuː] N **1** *(key)* (clef *f*) passe-partout *m inv* **2** *Art, Phot (method of framing)* encadrement *m* sous verre; *(gummed paper)* bande *f* de papier de bordure

passer-by ['pɑːsəbaɪ], *pl* **passers-by** ['pɑːsəbaɪ] N passant, -ante

passim ['pæsɪm] ADV passim

passing ['pɑːsɪŋ] ADJ *(hour, minute etc)* qui passe/passait; *(remark)* en passant; *(whim, fancy)* passager, éphémère; **he is growing stronger with each p. day** il devient de plus en plus fort avec chaque jour qui passe; **flag down a p. car** fais signe à une voiture de s'arrêter; **she flagged down a p. car** elle a fait signe à une voiture qui passait de s'arrêter; *Lit* **the p. hour** l'heure *f* fugitive
N **1** *(going past) (of train, birds etc)* passage *m;* *(overtaking) (of another car)* dépassement *m*, doublement *m; Com (of dividend)* passation *f*, **in p.** *(incidentally)* en passant
2 *(of time)* écoulement *m; (of sb's beauty)* disparition *f*, *esp Fml (death)* mort *f*
3 *(approval) Pol etc (of resolution)* adoption *f*, *(of law)* vote *m; Fin, Com (of accounts)* approbation *f*
4 *(giving) (of message etc)* transmission *f; Law (of judgement)* prononcé *m; Ftbl etc (of the ball)* passes *fpl*
ADV *Arch, Lit* **p. fair** de toute beauté
▸▸ *Literary* **p. bell** glas *m;* **p. customer** client, -ente de passage; **p. place** *Aut (on narrow road)* aire *f* de croisement; *(in general)* endroit *m* pour doubler; *Rail* voie *f* d'évitement *ou* de dédoublement; **p. shot** *Tennis* passing-shot *m, pl* passing-shots; *Cin, TV* = plan *m* avec déplacement d'un personnage ou d'un objet devant la caméra fixe ou vice versa; *Com* **p. trade** clients *mpl ou* clientèle *f* de passage

passion ['pæʃən] N **1** passion *f*, **to have a p. for sb** aimer qn passionnément; *Fig* **to have a p. for music/painting/cars** avoir la passion de la musique/de la peinture/des voitures; **to have a p. for Chinese cooking** adorer la cuisine chinoise; *Law* **crime of p.** crime *m* passionnel
2 *(anger)* colère *f*, emportement *m;* **a fit of p.** un accès de colère; **to be in a p. about sth** être fou de colère à cause de qch; **to fly into a p.** s'emporter

3 *(strong emotion)* passion *f*, **passions are running high on this issue** ce sujet déchaîne les passions; **to sing/speak with great p.** chanter/parler avec passion; **imagine getting into such a p. about a football match!** se mettre dans un tel état à propos d'un match de foot!; **to hate sb/sth with a p.** avoir horreur de qn/qch
4 *Rel* **the P. (of Christ)** la Passion (de Jésus-Christ)
▸▸ **p. fruit** fruit *m* de la Passion; *Rel* **p. play** mystère *m* de la Passion; *Rel* **P. Sunday** le dimanche de la Passion; *Rel* **P. week** la semaine de la Passion

passionate ['pæʃənɪt] ADJ **1** *(speech)* véhément; *(advocate, believer)* fervent, ardent; **a p. plea for justice** un véhément appel à la justice **2** *(love, lover)* passionné, ardent; *(embrace, kiss)* passionné; *(relationship)* passionnel; **to make p. love** faire l'amour avec passion; **a p. weekend** un week-end de passion

passionately ['pæʃənɪtlɪ] ADV *(to love, defend sth)* passionnément, ardemment, avec passion; *(to believe, be committed to)* ardemment, avec ferveur; *(to speak)* avec passion, avec véhémence; *(to sing)* avec passion; **to be p. in love with sb** aimer qn passionnément; **to be p. fond of sth/doing sth** adorer qch/faire qch

passionflower ['pæʃənflauər] N *(plant)* passiflore *f*

passionless ['pæʃənlɪs] ADJ sans passion

passive ['pæsɪv] VOIR GRAMMAIRE A54–5; B39
ADJ **1** passif; *Metal, Elec (iron, electrode etc)* passif **2** *Gram* passif; **the p. voice** la voix passive **3** *Com (debts)* ne portant pas d'intérêt
N *Gram* **the p.** la voix passive, le passif; **in the p.** au passif
▸▸ *Psy* **p. aggressivity** comportement *m* passif-agressif; *Comput* **p. matrix screen** écran *m* à matrice passive; **p. resistance** résistance *f* passive; **p. smoking** tabagisme *m* passif

passive-aggressive ADJ *Psy* passif-agressif

passively ['pæsɪvlɪ] ADV **1** passivement **2** *Gram* au passif, à la forme passive

passiveness ['pæsɪvnɪs], **passivity** [pæ'sɪvɪtɪ] N *(of mind, metal etc)* passivité *f*

passkey ['pɑːskiː] N (clef *f*) passe-partout *m inv*

Passover ['pɑːsəuvər] N *Rel* la Pâque

passport ['pɑːspɔːt] N passeport *m; ship's* **p.** permis *m* de navigation; *Fig* **this job was her p. to fame** ce travail a été son passeport pour la célébrité; **money is a p. to anything** l'argent ouvre toutes les portes
▸▸ **p. control** contrôle *m* des passeports; **p. number** numéro *m* de passeport

passport-sized photograph N photo *f* d'identité

password ['pɑːswɜːd] N *Mil, Comput etc* mot *m* de passe
▸▸ *Comput* **p. protection** protection *f* par mot de passe

password-protected ADJ *Comput* protégé par mot de passe

past [pɑːst] ADJ passé; **the time for negotiating is p.** l'heure n'est plus à la négociation; **those days are p.** ces temps sont révolus; **in p. times, in times p.** autrefois, *Lit* au temps jadis; **p. chairmen** *(former chairmen)* anciens présidents; **she's a p. master at it** elle est experte en la matière; **she's a p. master at doing it** elle est experte maître dans l'art de le faire; **the p. week** la semaine dernière *ou* passée; **the p. two months** les deux derniers mois; **for some time p.** depuis quelque temps; *Gram* **in the p. tense** au passé
N **1** **the p.** le passé; **in the p.** autrefois; **it is a**

thing of the p. *(no longer exists) (of institution, custom)* ça n'existe plus; *(of relationship)* c'est du passé; *(is old-fashioned)* c'est périmé; **those days are a thing of the p.** cette époque est révolue; **to live in the p.** vivre dans le passé **2** *(background) (of person)* passé *m*; **woman with a p.** femme *f* qui a vécu *ou* qui a un passé; **town with a p.** ville *f* historique; **our country's glorious p.** le glorieux passé de notre pays **3** *Gram* passé *m*; **in the p.** au passé VOIR GRAMMAIRE A49–50; B30

PREP *(beyond)* au delà de; **a little p. the bridge** un peu plus loin que le pont, un peu au delà du pont; **to walk p. the house** passer devant la maison; **it is p. four (o'clock)** il est quatre heures passées; **half/a quarter p. four** quatre heures et demie/et quart; *Br* **ten (minutes) p. four** quatre heures dix; **it is half p.** il est la demie; **this bread is p. its sell-by date** ce pain a dépassé sa date limite de vente; **to be p. all understanding** dépasser toute compréhension; **that's p. all belief** c'est incroyable; **I'm p. work** *(too old)* je ne suis plus d'âge à travailler; *(too ill)* je ne peux plus travailler; **I'm p. caring** *(what happens, what you or they have done etc)* je n'en ai plus rien à faire; *Fam* **to be p. it** *(of person)* être trop vieux *(pour travailler, pour jouer au tennis etc)*; *(of car, machine)* avoir son compte; *Fam* **I wouldn't put it p. her** elle en est bien capable; **I wouldn't put anything p. this government** ce gouvernement est capable de tout *ou* du pire

ADV to walk/go p. passer; **to run p.** passer en courant

▸▸ *Gram* **p. historic** passé simple; *Gram* **p. participle** participe *m* passé; *Gram* **p. perfect** plus-que-parfait *m*, *pl* plus-que-parfaits

pasta ['pæstə] **N** *Culin* pâtes *fpl* (alimentaires)

paste [peɪst] **N 1** *(malleable substance)* pâte *f*; *Cer* **hard/soft p.** pâte dure/tendre **2** *(glue)* colle *f* **3** *Culin (for pastry)* pâte *f* (à pâtisserie); **fish p.** = mousse *f* de poisson; **liver p.** = sorte de pâté de foie; **meat p.** = sorte de pâté **4** *(jewellery)* stras(s) *m*; **it's only p.** ce n'est que du stras(s); **p. jewellery** bijoux *mpl* en stras(s)

VT 1 *(glue) (poster, picture etc)* coller (**on** sur; **in** dans); *(wallpaper)* encoller; *Comput* coller (**into/onto** dans) **2** *Fam (beat up)* rosser, casser la figure à; *(defeat heavily)* mettre la pâtée à

▸▸ **p. pot** pot *m* de colle

▸ **paste up VT SEP 1** *(notice)* afficher; *(bill, advert)* coller, monter **2** *Typ (page)* monter

pasteboard ['peɪstbɔːd] **N** carton *m*

pastel ['pæst(ə)l] **N** *Art (crayon)* (crayon *m*) pastel *m*; *(drawing)* pastel; **drawing in p.** (dessin *m* au) pastel; **p. blue** bleu pastel *m inv*

▸▸ **p. drawing** (dessin au) pastel; **p. shades** tons *mpl* pastel

pastern ['pæstən] **N** pâturon *m*, paturon *m*

paste-up N *(in publishing)* maquette *f*

pasteurization [pæstʃəraɪ'zeɪʃən] **N** pasteurisation *f*

pasteurize ['pæstʃəraɪz] **VT** pasteuriser; **pasteurized milk** lait *m* pasteurisé

pastiche [pæ'stiːʃ] **N** pastiche *m*

pastille ['pæstɪl] **N 1** pastille *f*, **fruit pastilles** = pâtes *fpl* de fruits **2** *(for fumigating the air)* pastille *f* à brûler

pastime ['pɑːstaɪm] **N** passe-temps *m inv*

pastiness ['peɪstɪnɪs] **N 1** *(of face)* teint *m* terreux **2** *(of bread etc)* consistance *f* pâteuse

pasting ['peɪstɪŋ] **N 1** *(gluing) (of poster etc)* collage *m*; *(of wallpaper)* encollage *m* **2** *Fam (beating)* rossée *f*, raclée *f*; **to give sb a p.**

mettre une raclée à qn, rosser qn; *Sport* **to get a p.** être battu à plate(s) couture(s); *Sport* **to give sb a p.** mettre la pâtée à qn

pastor ['pɑːstər] **N** *Rel* pasteur *m*

pastoral ['pɑːstərəl] **ADJ 1** *(rural)* pastoral, -aux; **a p. people** un peuple de bergers **2** *Rel* pastoral, -aux **3** *Sch (care)* qui concerne la santé physique et spirituelle des élèves

N 1 *Liter, Mus, Art, Theat* pastorale *f* **2** *Rel* (letter *f*) pastorale *f*

▸▸ **p. land** pâturages *mpl*; *Rel* **p. letter** (lettre) pastorale

pastrami [pə'strɑːmɪ] **N** *Culin* = bœuf *m* fumé et épicé

pastry ['peɪstrɪ] **N** pâte *f*, *(cake)* pâtisserie *f*, **short(-crust) p.** pâte brisée; **flaky** *or* **puff p.** pâte feuilletée

▸▸ **p. board** planche *f* à pâtisserie; **p. brush** pinceau *m* (à pâtisserie); **p. case** croûte *f*, **p. cutter** emporte-pièce *m inv*

pastrycook ['peɪstrɪkʊk] **N** pâtissier, -ière

pasturage ['pɑːstʃərɪdʒ] **N 1** *(right)* (droit *m* de) pâturage *m ou* pacage *m* **2** *(land)* = **pasture N**

pasture ['pɑːstʃər] **N** *(land)* (lieu *m* de) pâture *f*, pâturage *m*, herbage *m*; **to be put out to p.** *Agr* être mis au pré *ou* au pâturage; *Fig* être mis à la retraite *ou* au vert; *Fig* **to move on to pastures new** *or* **greener pastures** aller vers de nouveaux horizons

VI paître, pâturer, pacager

VT *(of shepherd) (animals)* (faire) paître; *(of animals) (field)* pâturer

▸▸ **p. land** (lieu de) pâture, pâturage, herbage

pasty 1 ['peɪstɪ] **ADJ 1** *(face, complexion)* terreux; *(person)* qui a le teint terreux; **p.-faced** au teint terreux **2** *(texture)* pâteux

pasty 2 ['pæstɪ] **N** *Br Culin* = (petit) pâté *m* en croûte *(cuit sans moule)*; **Cornish p.** = pâté (en croûte) qui contient du bœuf, des pommes de terre et autres légumes

pat 1 [pæt] **VT** (-tt-) *(tap)* tapoter; *(animal)* caresser, flatter (de la main); **to p. one's hair** se tapoter les cheveux; **she patted the boy's head** elle a tapoté la tête du petit garçon; **to p. sb on the back** donner une tape dans le dos à qn; *Fig (congratulate)* féliciter qn; *Fig* **to p. oneself on the back** se féliciter

N 1 *(tap)* petite tape *f*; *(on animal)* petite tape, caresse *f*; **to give sb a p. on the back** donner une tape dans le dos à qn; *Fig (congratulate)* féliciter qn; *Fig* **to give oneself a p. on the back** se féliciter **2** *(lump) (of butter)* rondelle *f*, médaillon *m*; **cow p.** bouse *f* de vache

ADJ *(answer, solution)* facile; *(explanation)* simple

ADV his answer came p. il a répondu du tac au tac; **to know** *or* **have sth off p.** savoir qch par cœur; **he had his explanation off p.** il avait une explication toute prête; **to stand p.** *Cards* jouer d'autorité; *esp Am (not give in)* refuser de bouger

▸ **pat down VT SEP** *(soil, cement etc)* tasser (doucement)

pat 2 1 *(abbr* **patent)** brev. **2** *(abbr* **patented)** breveté

Patagonia [pætə'gəʊnɪə] **N** Patagonie *f*

patch [pætʃ] **N 1** *(of cloth)* pièce *f* (pour raccommoder un vêtement); *(on garment)* pièce (rapportée); *(on sail)* placard *m*; *(for bromide corrections)* cache *m*; *Med (nicotine, drug treatment)* timbre *m*, patch *m*; *Comput (correction)* correction *f*; *Aut etc* (rubber) p. *(for inner tube)* rustine *f*, **to put a p. on a garment** mettre une pièce à *ou* rapiécer un vêtement; *Fam* **his last novel isn't a p. on the others** son dernier roman est loin de valoir les autres; **(eye) p.** couvre-œil *m*, *pl* couvre-œils

2 *(of colour, light)* tache *f*, *(of fog, mist)* nappe *f*, *(of oil)* flaque *f*, *(of ice)* plaque *f*, **p. of blue sky** pan *m ou* coin *m ou* échappée *f* de ciel bleu; **rough patches** *(on wood, metal etc)* aspérités *fpl*; **the book was good in patches** le livre contient de bons passages; *Fam* **to be going through** *or* **to have struck a bad p.** traverser une mauvaise période

3 *(of land)* lopin *m*, parcelle *f*, *(of vegetables)* carré *m*; *Fam (of prostitute, salesperson, police officer)* secteur *m*; *Fam* **keep off my p.!** *(territory)* ne mets pas les pieds sur mon territoire!

VT *(piece of clothing)* mettre une pièce à, rapiécer; *(inner tube)* poser une rustine à; *Naut (sail)* placarder

▸▸ *Tel* **p. board** tableau *m* de raccordement; *Elec, Tel* **p. cord** cordon *m* de commutation; *Sewing* **p. pocket** poche *f* plaquée

▸ **patch together VT SEP** *Fam (temporary shelter, something broken)* assembler; *(business plan, team, government)* mettre sur pied; **they patched together a documentary** ils ont monté un documentaire tant bien que mal; **we are beginning to p. together an understanding of ...** petit à petit nous commençons à nous faire une idée de ...; *Pej* **the whole thing is a bit patched together** tout ça est un peu mal fichu

▸ **patch up VT SEP** *Fam (repair temporarily) (object)*, *Fig (marriage)* rafistoler; *Med Fam (person)* retaper; **I managed to p. the car up** j'ai réussi à retaper la voiture; **we've patched things up** *(after quarrel, argument)* nous avons réussi à arranger les choses; **they patched up their differences** ils ont réglé leurs différends

patching ['pætʃɪŋ] **N** *(of piece of clothing)* rapiéçage *m*, rapiècement *m*; **we can use that old jacket for p.** nous pouvons utiliser cette vieille veste pour faire du rapiècement *ou* rapiéçage

patchwork ['pætʃwɜːk] **N** *Sewing, Fig* patchwork *m*; *Fig* **a p. team** une équipe disparate *ou* hétéroclite; **a p. of measures** un ensemble de mesures hétéroclites; *Fig* **a p. of fields** une campagne bigarrée

▸▸ **p. quilt** couverture *f* en patchwork

patchy ['pætʃɪ] **ADJ** *(paintwork etc)*, *Fig (novel etc)* inégal, -aux

pate [peɪt] **N** *Arch, Hum (head)* caboche *f*, **bald p.** crâne *m* chauve

pâté ['pæteɪ] **N** *Culin* pâté *m*; **liver p.** pâté de foie; **p. sandwich** sandwich *m* au pâté

patella, *pl* **patellae, patellas** [pə'telə, -iː, -əz] **N** *Anat* rotule *f*

paten ['pæt(ə)n] **N** *Rel* patène *f*

patent ['peɪtənt, 'pætənt] **ADJ 1** *(protected by patent)* breveté **2** *Law* **letters p.** lettres *fpl* patentes *ou* de noblesse; *(of inventor)* lettres patentes, brevet *m* d'invention *ou* d'inventeur **3** *(evident) (lack of concern, disrespect)* manifeste; *(fact)* évident; **that's a p. lie!** c'est un mensonge éhonté!

N 1 *(right)* brevet d'invention; *(invention)* invention *f*/fabrication *f* brevetée; **to take out a p. for an invention** faire breveter une invention; **p. applied for, p. pending** demande de brevet déposée; **infringement of a p.** contrefaçon *f* **2** *(grant of nobility)* lettres *fpl* patentes; **p. of nobility** lettres d'anoblissement *ou* de noblesse

VT *(invention) (of authorities)* protéger par un brevet, breveter; *(of inventor)* faire breveter, prendre un brevet pour; **patented** breveté

▸▸ **p. agent** agent *m* en brevets; **p. application** demande *f ou* dépôt *m* de brevet; *Am* **p. attorney** conseil *m* en matière de brevets; **p. goods** articles *mpl* brevetés; **p. leather** cuir *m* verni, vernis *m*; **p.-leather shoes** chaussures *fpl* vernies; **p. medicine** médicament *m* vendu sans ordonnance; *Pej (cure-all)* élixir *m* universel, remède *m* de charlatan; **P. Office** ≃ Institut *m* national de la propriété industrielle; **p. rights** propriété *f* industrielle

patentable ['peɪtəntəb(ə)l] ADJ brevetable

patentee [peɪtən'tiː] N détenteur, -trice d'un/du brevet

patently ['peɪtəntlɪ] ADV manifestement; **he was p. lying** il était manifeste qu'il mentait; **it was p. obvious that …** il était absolument évident que …

patentor ['peɪtəntər] N organisme *m* délivrant un brevet

pater ['peɪtər] N *Old-fashioned Br Fam* **(the) p.** le paternel

paterfamilias [peɪtəfə'mɪlɪæs] N *Fml* chef *m* de famille

paternal [pə'tɜːnəl] ADJ *(love, attention)* paternel; *(role, responsibilities)* de père; *Lit* **under the p. roof** dans la maison paternelle
▸▸ **p. grandparents** grands-parents *mpl* paternels

paternalism [pə'tɜːnəlɪz(ə)m] N paternalisme *m*

paternalist [pə'tɜːnəlɪst] ADJ paternaliste
N personne *f* à tendances paternalistes

paternalistic [pətɜːnə'lɪstɪk] ADJ paternaliste

paternalistically [pətɜːnə'lɪstɪklɪ] ADV *(to govern)* avec paternalisme; *(to say)* d'un ton paternaliste; *(to smile)* d'un air paternaliste

paternally [pə'tɜːnəlɪ] ADV paternellement

paternity [pə'tɜːnɪtɪ] N paternité *f*; **there are doubts about his p.** on n'est pas sûr de l'identité de son père
▸▸ **p. leave** congé *m* de paternité; *Law* **p. suit** action *f* en recherche de paternité

path, *pl* **paths** [pɑːθ, pɑːðz] N **1** *(through forest etc)* chemin *m*, sentier *m*; *(in garden)* allée *f*, *Fig (in research etc)* voie *f*; *(of inquiry, investigation)* ligne *f*; *Comput (of paper in printer)* chemin; *Comput (of directory structure)* chemin (d'accès); *Fig* **the p. of glory** le chemin de la gloire; **this was a certain p. to disaster** cela menait tout droit au désastre **2** *(course) (of moving body)* trajet *m*, course *f*; *(of projectile, particle, planet)* trajectoire *f*; *(of ray of light)* passage *m*, trajet; *(of sun)* route *f*; **p. of a bullet** *(through the air)* trajectoire d'une balle; *(through the body)* trajet *ou* sillon *m* d'une balle; **he killed everyone in his p.** il a tué tout le monde sur son chemin *ou* passage; **in the p. of a vehicle** sur le chemin *ou* passage d'un véhicule; **a tree blocked his p.** un arbre lui bloquait le passage *ou* chemin; **their paths had crossed before** leurs chemins s'étaient déjà croisés

pathetic [pə'θetɪk] ADJ **1** *(touching) (sight etc)* touchant, attendrissant; **she looked rather p.** elle était touchante **2** *Fam (weak, poor, useless) (excuse, game, person etc)* lamentable, pitoyable; **you're p.!** tu es lamentable!; **how p.!, it's p.!, isn't it p.?** c'est (vraiment) lamentable! **3** *Liter* **the p. fallacy** l'attribution *f* des caractéristiques humaines à la nature

Note that the French word **pathétique** never means **appalling**.

pathetically [pə'θetɪklɪ] ADV **1** *(touchingly)* pitoyablement; **they wept p.** ils pleuraient d'une façon pitoyable; **she looked at him p.** elle lui jeta un regard pitoyable **2** *Fam (atrociously)* lamentablement; **p. bad** *(performance, speech etc)* lamentable; **p. easy** si facile que c'en est ridicule; **that's a p. weak excuse** c'est une excuse lamentable; **they performed p.** ils ont offert une performance lamentable *ou* pitoyable; **he's so p. arrogant** il est si arrogant que c'en est ridicule

pathfinder ['pɑːθfaɪndər] N **1** *(scout)* éclaireur, -euse; *(pioneer)* pionnier, -ière **2** *(aircraft)* avion *m* éclaireur

pathname ['pɑːθneɪm] N *Comput* chemin *m* d'accès

pathological [pæθə'lɒdʒɪk(ə)l] ADJ *(hatred, liar etc)* pathologique

pathologically [pæθə'lɒdʒɪklɪ] ADV pathologiquement; **to be p. afraid of sth** avoir une peur pathologique de qch

pathologist [pə'θɒlədʒɪst] N pathologiste *mf*; **(forensic) p.** médecin *m* légiste

pathology [pə'θɒlədʒɪ] N pathologie *f*

pathos ['peɪθɒs] N pathétique *m*

pathway ['pɑːθweɪ] N sentier *m*

patience ['peɪʃəns] N **1** patience *f*; **to try** *or* **tax sb's p.** éprouver la patience de qn; **my p. is exhausted** *or* **is at an end** ma patience est à bout, je suis à bout de patience; **you've exhausted my p.** tu as abusé de ma patience; **(have) p.!** (prenez) patience!; **to lose p.** perdre patience; **I've no p. with him** il m'énerve, il m'agace **2** *Br Cards* réussite *f*; **to play p.** faire des réussites

patient ['peɪʃənt] ADJ patient; **to be p.** *(naturally)* être patient, avoir de la patience; *(on specific occasion)* être patient, patienter, prendre patience; **you will have to be p.** il vous faudra être patient
N malade *mf*, patient, -ente; *(after operation)* opéré, -ée; **a doctor and his patients** un médecin et ses clients *ou* patients
▸▸ **p. care** soins *mpl* administrés aux patients

patiently ['peɪʃəntlɪ] ADV patiemment; **a long illness, p. borne** une longue maladie, endurée avec patience

patina ['pætɪnə] N patine *f*, **to take on a p.** *(of bronze)* se patiner

patio ['pætɪəʊ] N patio *m*
▸▸ **p. doors** porte-fenêtre *f*, *pl* portes-fenêtres

patriarch ['peɪtrɪɑːk] N *Rel etc* patriarche *m*

patriarchal [peɪtrɪ'ɑːk(ə)l] ADJ patriarcal, -aux

patriarchy ['peɪtrɪɑːkɪ] N patriarcat *m*, système *m* patriarcal

patrician [pə'trɪʃən] ADJ, N *Antiq etc* patricien, -ienne

patricide ['pætrɪsaɪd] N **1** *(person)* parricide *mf* **2** *(crime)* parricide *m*

patrimony ['pætrɪmənɪ] N **1** *(inheritance)* patrimoine *m* **2** *(of church)* biens-fonds *mpl*, revenu *m*

patriot ['peɪtrɪət, 'pæ-] N patriote *mf*

patriotic [peɪtrɪ'ɒtɪk, pæ-] ADJ *(person)* patriote; *(speech, feeling etc)* patriotique

patriotically [peɪtrɪ'ɒtɪklɪ, pæ-] ADV patriotiquement, avec patriotisme

patriotism ['peɪtrɪətɪz(ə)m, 'pæ-] N patriotisme *m*

patrol [pə'trəʊl] N patrouille *f*; *(of police)* patrouille (de surveillance); *(of nightwatchman, police officer on foot)* ronde *f*; **to be on p.** être en patrouille, patrouiller
VI **(-ll-)** patrouiller, être en patrouille
VT *(area etc)* patrouiller dans, faire une patrouille dans; *(border)* patrouiller à; **the border is heavily patrolled** de nombreuses patrouilles surveillent la frontière
▸▸ **p. bomber** patrouilleur *m* de bombardement, bombardier *m* patrouilleur; **p. car** voiture *f* de police; *Naut* **p. craft** patrouilleur, vedette *f* de surveillance; **p. leader** chef *m* de patrouille; *Naut* **p. vessel** patrouilleur, vedette de surveillance

patrolman, *pl* **patrolmen** [pə'trəʊlmən] N **1** *Br (employee of AA, RAC etc)* patrouilleur *m* **2** *Am (policeman)* agent *m* de police (en service de ronde)

patrolwoman, *pl* **patrolwomen** [pə'trəʊlwʊmən, -wɪmɪn] N *Am* femme *f* agent de police (en service de ronde)

patron ['peɪtrən] N **1** *(of artists, the arts etc)* protecteur, -trice, mécène *m*; *(of charity)* patron, -onne; *Rel, Hist (of living)* patron *m*, collateur *m* **2** *Com (of shop)* client, -ente; *(regular)* habitué, -ée
▸▸ **p. saint** *(saint)* patron, *(sainte)* patronne

Note that the French word **patron** is a false friend and is never a translation for the English word **patron**. It means **boss**.

patronage ['pætrənɪdʒ] N **1** *(support etc)* patronage *m*, protection *f*; *(of arts)* mécénat *m*; *(of charity)* patronage; *Pej (condescension) (towards sb)* attitude *f* condescendante *(* **of** envers); **concert under the p. of …** concert patronné par … **2** *(of hotel etc)* clientèle *f* **3** *Church of Eng* droit *m* de présentation (à un bénéfice) **4** *Pol* népotisme *m*; **yet another p. appointment** encore une nomination qui tient du népotisme

patroness ['peɪtrənɪs] N *Old-fashioned (of the arts etc)* protectrice *f*; *(of charity)* (dame *f*) patronnesse *f*

patronize ['pætrənaɪz] VT **1** *(artist etc)* patronner; *(art)* encourager; *(hospital etc)* subventionner; *(charitable institution)* souscrire à **2** *Pej (treat in a patronizing way)* traiter avec condescendance; **don't p. me!** je n'ai pas besoin de ta condescendance! **3** *Com (company, shop)* accorder sa clientèle à; *(cinema, restaurant etc)* être un(e) habitué(e) de, fréquenter; **a restaurant patronized by the famous** un restaurant fréquenté par des gens célèbres

patronizing ['pætrənaɪzɪŋ] ADJ *(person, tone etc)* condescendant; **to be p. towards sb** se montrer condescendant envers qn, traiter qn avec condescendance

patronizingly ['pætrənaɪzɪŋlɪ] ADV *(to look)* d'un air condescendant; *(to say)* d'un ton condescendant; *(to treat sb)* avec condescendance

patronymic [pætrə'nɪmɪk] ADJ patronymique
N patronyme *m*, nom *m* patronymique

patsy ['pætsɪ] N *Am Sl (dupe)* gobeur *m*, jobard *m*

patten ['pæt(ə)n] N socque *m* *(pour protéger les chaussures de la boue)*

patter[1] ['pætər] N *(of footsteps)* petit bruit *m*; *(of mice)* trottinement *m*; *(of rain)* crépitement *m*; *(gentler)* tambourinement *m*; *Hum* **soon we'll be hearing the p. of tiny feet** la famille s'élargira bientôt
VI *(walk)* trottiner, marcher à petits pas rapides; *(of rain)* crépiter; *(more gently)* tambouriner
▸ **patter about** VI *(walk, run)* trottiner çà et là

patter[2] N *(of sales person)* baratin *m*, boniment *m*; *(of comedian)* bagout *m*; *(chatter)* bavardage *m*
VI *(chatter)* bavarder sans arrêt, caqueter
▸▸ *Fam* **p. merchant** baratineur *m*

pattern ['pæt(ə)n] N **1** *(design) (on wallpaper, fabric etc)* motif *m*; *(of hit marks on a target, on the ground etc)* groupement *m*; *Comput (of perforations)* combinaison *f*; **streets arranged in an orderly p.** rues établies suivant un plan ordonné
2 *(of events, behaviour etc)* **the normal p. of trade** la tendance normale du marché; **some clear patterns emerge from the statistics** des tendances nettes ressortent des statistiques; **the evening followed the usual p.** la soirée s'est déroulée selon le schéma habi-

tuel; **a typical p. of events** une suite d'événements type; **patterns of behaviour** comportements *mpl* types; **there was a certain p. in his behaviour** son comportement suivait un certain schéma

3 *(model)* modèle *m*, dessin *m*; *Sewing etc (paper cutout)* patron *m*; *Knitting* modèle *m*; *Metal* modèle *m*, gabarit *m*, calibre *m*; **machines all built to one p.** machines construites *ou* fabriquées toutes sur le même modèle; *Sewing* **to cut out a shirt from a p.** tailler une chemise sur un patron

4 *(example)* modèle *m*, exemple *m*; **to set a p.** créer un modèle; **this opening debate set the p. for ...** ce débat d'ouverture a donné le ton *ou* la note de ...

5 *Com (sample)* échantillon *m*
vt 1 *(draw patterns on)* tracer des motifs sur; *(decorate with patterns)* orner de motifs **2** *(model)* **to p. sth after** *or* **(up)on sth** modeler qch sur qch
▸▸ *Mil* **p. bombing** bombardement *m* systématique; *Com* **p. book** livre *m* d'échantillons; *Com* **p. card** carte *f* d'échantillons; *Ind* **p. designer** dessinateur, -trice de patrons; *Sch* **p. drill** exercice *m* d'apprentissage des structures grammaticales; **p. maker** modeleur, -euse; *Comput* **p. recognition** reconnaissance *f* de formes

patterned ['pætənd] **ADJ** à dessins, à motifs

patty ['pætɪ] **N** *Culin* pâté *m* (en croûte)

paucity ['pɔːsɪtɪ] **N** *(of information, proof etc)* manque *m*; *(of money, food, materials, talent etc)* manque, pénurie *f*

paunch [pɔːntʃ] **N** *(of person)* ventre *m*, *Fam* bide *m*, bedaine *f*; *(of ruminant)* panse *f*, rumen *m*; **to develop a p.** prendre du ventre *ou Fam* du bide

paunchy ['pɔːntʃɪ] **ADJ** *Fam* ventru, pansu

pauper ['pɔːpər] **N** indigent, -ente; **to die a p.** mourir dans l'indigence; **p.'s grave** fosse *f* commune

pause [pɔːz] **N 1** pause *f*, arrêt *m*; *(on recording)* blanc *m* sonore; *(in conversation etc)* silence *m*; **to have a p.** faire une pause **2** *(in poetry)* repos *m*; *(caesura)* césure *f* **3** *Mus* point *m* d'orgue; *(over a rest)* point d'arrêt **4** *esp Lit* **to give sb p.** faire hésiter qn; *(make sb think)* donner à réfléchir à qn
vi 1 *(stop) (when working)* faire une pause; *(when speaking)* s'interrompre, faire une pause; *(when leaving etc)* marquer un temps d'arrêt, s'arrêter; **to p. for breath/thought** faire une pause pour reprendre son souffle/réfléchir **2** *(hesitate)* hésiter; **to make sb p.** faire hésiter qn; *(make sb think)* donner à réfléchir à qn **3 to p. on a word** s'arrêter sur un mot; *Mus* **to p. on a note** tenir une note
▸▸ *Comput* **p. key** touche *f* pause

pave [peɪv] **vt** *(road etc)* paver; *Fig* **to p. the way** préparer le terrain (**for sth** pour qch); **the streets here aren't paved with gold** on ne roule pas sur l'or ici

pavement ['peɪvmənt] **N 1** *esp Br (path beside street)* trottoir *m* **2** *Am (roadway)* chaussée *f* **3** *(material)* pavé *m*
▸▸ *Br* **p. artist** artiste *mf* de rue (qui dessine sur les trottoirs); **p. café** café *m*, terrasse *f* d'un café

pavilion [pə'vɪlɪən] **N** *Br Sport, Archit etc* pavillon *m*

paving ['peɪvɪŋ] **N 1** *(action)* pavage *m*; *(with tiles)* carrelage *m*; *(with slabs)* dallage *m* **2** *(surface)* pavé *m*; *(made of bigger slabs)* dalles *fpl*
▸▸ **p. stone** pavé *m*; **p. tile** carreau *m* (de pavage); *(bigger)* dalle *f* (de pavage)

Pavlova [pæv'ləʊvə] **N** *Culin* vacherin *m*; **raspberry P.** vacherin à la framboise

Pavlovian [pæv'ləʊvɪən] **ADJ** *Psy (treatment, reaction, response)* pavlovien

paw [pɔː] **N** *(of animal)*, *Fam (of person)* patte *f*, *Fam* **paws off!** bas les pattes!; *Fam* **you're not getting your dirty** *or* **sweaty paws on my new bike!** il n'est pas question que tu touches à mon nouveau vélo!
vt 1 *(of animal)* donner un/des coup(s) de patte à; **to p. the ground** *(of horse)* gratter (la terre) du pied **2** *Fam (of person)* tripoter, peloter

pawky ['pɔːkɪ] **ADJ** *Scot (witty)* pince-sans-rire

pawl [pɔːl] **N** *Tech etc (of catch)* cliquet *m*; **p. and ratchet wheel** roue *f ou* encliquetage *m* à rochet

pawn¹ [pɔːn] **N 1** *(object pawned)* gage *m*, nantissement *m* **2 in p.** en gage; **to put one's watch in p.** mettre sa montre en gage *ou* au mont-de-piété *ou Fam* au clou; **to get sth out of p.** dégager qch (du mont-de-piété)
vt mettre en gage *ou* au mont-de-piété *ou Fam* au clou, engager; *Fig (one's life, honour)* engager
▸▸ **p. ticket** reconnaissance *f* du mont-de-piété

pawn² **N** *Chess* pion *m*; *Fig* **to be sb's p.** être le jouet de qn

pawnbroker ['pɔːnbrəʊkər] **N** prêteur, -euse sur gage(s)

pawnbroking ['pɔːnbrəʊkɪŋ] **N** prêt *m* sur gage(s)

pawnshop ['pɔːnʃɒp] **N** bureau *m* de prêt sur gage(s), mont-de-piété *m*, *pl* monts-de-piété

pawpaw ['pɔːpɔː] **N = papaw**

pax [pæks] **INT** *Br Sl (truce)* pouce!

PAY [peɪ]

N	salaire ▪ paie ▪ traitement
VT	payer **1**, **2** ▪ régler **1**
VI	payer **1**, **2** ▪ régler **1**

N salaire *m*, paie *f*, paye *f*, *(of domestic staff)* gages *mpl*; *(of civil servant)* traitement *m*, salaire; *(of member of parliament)* indemnité *f*; *Mil* solde *f*; **to get an extra £10 a week in one's p.** toucher 10 livres de salaire en plus par semaine; **the p.'s good/terrible** ça paie bien/mal; *Pej* **to be in sb's p.** être à la solde *ou* aux gages de qn
vt *(pt, pp* **paid** [peɪd]*)* **1** *(account, invoice)* payer, régler; *(fine)* payer; *(dividend)* distribuer; *(debt)* payer, liquider, régler, acquitter; *(creditor)* rembourser; *(money)* verser; *(premium)* verser, acquitter; **to p. sb £100** payer 100 livres à qn; **how much do you p. for tea?** combien est-ce que vous payez le thé?; **I paid £5 for it** je l'ai payé cinq livres; **I expect to p. my way** je m'attends à payer mon écot; **to be paid in four instalments** payable en quatre versements; **to p. cash (down)** *or* **ready money** payer (argent) comptant, payer au comptant; **p. self, p. cash** *(on cheque)* payez (à l'ordre de) moi-même; **to p. money into an account** alimenter un compte, approvisionner un compte; **to p. money into sb's account** verser de l'argent au compte de qn; **to p. something on account** verser une somme à titre de provision; *Fam* **to make sb p. through the nose** écorcher qn; *Fig* **they paid a heavy price for this mistake** cette erreur leur a coûté cher
2 *(employees)* payer; **to be paid by the hour/the week** être payé à l'heure/la semaine; **badly paid job** travail *m* mal payé; **to p. sb to do sth** payer qn pour faire qch; **I wouldn't do it if you paid me** je ne le ferais pas même si on me payait
3 *(give)* **to p. tribute** *or* **homage to sb** rendre hommage à qn; **to p. one's respects to sb** présenter ses respects à qn; **to p. one's (last) respects to sb** rendre les derniers devoirs à qn; **to p. a visit to sb** rendre visite à

qn; **we paid a visit to the Louvre** nous avons visité le Louvre; **p. attention to what you are doing** faites attention à ce que vous faites
4 *(profit)* **it will p. you to do it** c'est dans votre intérêt de le faire
vi 1 payer; **who's paying?** qui paie?; **p. at the gate** *or* **door** entrée payante; *Admin Br* **p. as you earn,** *Am* **p. as you go** retenue *f* (de l'impôt sur le revenu) à la base *ou* à la source; **how would you like to p.?** comment souhaitez-vous régler?; **to p. by cheque** payer *ou* régler par chèque
2 *Com, Fin etc* **to p. in advance** payer d'avance; **to p. on delivery** payer à la livraison; **to p. in full** payer intégralement *ou* en totalité; **to p. on demand** payer à vue *ou* à présentation; **p. to the order of ...** payez à l'ordre de ...; *Fin* **p. to bearer** payez au porteur
3 *(be profitable)* **business that doesn't p.** affaire qui ne rapporte pas *ou* qui n'est pas rentable; **it wouldn't p.** cela ne serait pas rentable; **it pays to advertise** la publicité rapporte; **it pays to be honest** l'honnêteté est toujours récompensée; **it doesn't always p. to tell the truth** on n'a pas toujours intérêt à dire la vérité
▸▸ **p. award** augmentation *f* de salaire; *Br* **p. bed** lit *m* payant; *Mil* **p. book** livret *m* de solde; *TV* **p. channel** chaîne *f* à péage *ou* payante; **p. cheque,** *Am* **p. check** chèque *m* de règlement de traitement *ou* de salaire; **p. deductions** retenues salariales; **p. desk** caisse *f*, **p. dirt** *(earth)* gisement *m*; *Fam (discovery)* trouvaille *f*, *Fam* **to hit p. dirt** trouver un bon filon; **p. and display** *(car park)* parking *m* à horodateur; **p. dispute** conflit *m* salarial; **p. formula** formule *f* de paie; **p. freeze** gel *m ou* blocage *m* des salaires; **p. increase** augmentation *f* de salaire; **p. ledger** livre *m* de paie; *Br* **p. packet** *(envelope)* enveloppe *f* contenant le salaire; *(money)* paie, salaire; **p. phone** téléphone *m* public; *(enclosed)* cabine *f* téléphonique; **p. rise** augmentation de salaire; **p. slip** bulletin *m* de paie; **p. television, p. TV** télévision *f* à péage, télévision payante
▸ **pay back vt sep 1** *(loan, person)* rembourser
2 *Fig (have revenge on)* **to p. sb back in his own coin** rendre la pareille à qn, rendre la monnaie de sa pièce à qn; **I'll p. you back for this!** je te le revaudrai!, tu me le paieras!
▸ **pay for vt insep** *(something)* payer; **his uncle paid for his schooling** son oncle a payé ses études; *Fig Fam* **he'll p. for this!, I'll make him p. for this!** il me le payera!; *Fig Fam* **you'll p. for this tomorrow** *(for drinking too much etc)* tu vas en subir les conséquences demain; **it's all paid for** *(someone has paid for everything)* tout a été réglé; *(I've paid for everything)* c'est à mes frais; **a free holiday with everything paid for** des vacances gratuites tout compris
▸ **pay in vt sep** *(cheque, money)* verser sur son compte; **to p. in a cheque** déposer un chèque, *esp Fml* remettre un chèque à l'encaissement
vi faire un versement
▸ **pay off vt sep 1** *(finish paying) (debt etc)* liquider, régler; *(creditor)* rembourser; *(mortgage)* purger; **to p. sth off over three years** acheter *ou* payer qch en trois ans; **I'm still paying it off** je n'ai pas encore fini de le payer
2 *(dismiss) (worker, troops)* licencier; *(sailors)* débarquer; *(servant)* congédier
3 *Fam (bribe)* soudoyer, donner des pots de vin à
vi *(of deal etc)* être payant *ou* rentable *ou* fructueux; *(of efforts etc)* porter ses *ou* des fruits; **all these years of work have paid off at last** nous sommes enfin récompensés

après toutes ces années de travail; **it paid off** ça a valu la peine

▸ **pay out VT SEP 1** (*spend*) payer, débourser; **I've had to p. out a lot on car repairs this year** j'ai eu beaucoup à débourser pour les réparations de voiture cette année **2** (*salaries*) payer **3** (*pt, pp* **payed**) *Naut* (*cable*) (laisser) filer **VI** payer

▸ **pay up VI** (*pay debt*) payer, *Fam* s'exécuter; **I finally made him p. up** j'ai finalement réussi à le faire payer *ou* débourser; **p. up!** allez, l'argent!, *SI* aboule! **VT SEP** (*pay*) payer

payable ['peɪəb(ə)l] **ADJ 1** payable; **rates p. by the tenant** = impôts à la charge du locataire; *Com* **p. at sight/to order/to bearer** payable à vue/à ordre/au porteur; *Com* **p. at thirty days** exigible: trente jours; **p. in cash** payable comptant; **p. on delivery/with order** payable à la livraison/à la commande; **to make a bill p. to sb** établir un billet à l'ordre de qn; **cheque p. to bearer** chèque *m* au porteur; **please make your cheque p. to Miss Johnston** veuillez libeller votre chèque à l'ordre de Miss Johnston; **bonds made p. in euros** bons libellés en euros **2** *Min* (*seam etc*) exploitable

NPL payables *Am* factures *fpl* à payer

pay-as-you-earn N *Br* prélèvement *m* de l'impôt à la source

pay-as-you-go N facturation *f* à la durée; *Tel* paiement *m* par carte prépayée

pay-as-you-view TV N télévision *f* à la carte

payback ['peɪbæk] **N 1** *Fin* récupération *f* du capital investi **2** *esp Am* (*revenge*) revanche *f*; **it's p. time** c'est le moment de la revanche ▸▸ **p. period** délai *m* de récupération, période *f* de remboursement

payday ['peɪdeɪ] **N** jour *m* de paie, paie *f*, *Mil* jour de solde; *St Exch* jour de liquidation *ou* de règlement

PAYE [piːeɪwaɪˈiː] **N** *Br* (*abbr* **pay as you earn**) retenue *f* (de l'impôt sur le revenu) à la base *ou* à la source; **P. and NIC return** déclaration *f* sociale

payee [peɪˈiː] **N** (*of postal order, cheque etc*) bénéficiaire *mf*; *Com* (*of bill*) porteur *m*, preneur *m*

payer ['peɪər] **N** payeur, -euse; **they're slow payers** ils ne paient pas vite

paying ['peɪɪŋ] **N** paiement *m*; *Fin* **p. up of a share** libération *f* d'une action **ADJ 1** (*student etc*) payant **2** (*business etc*) rémunérateur, -trice, profitable, qui rapporte; **it's not a p. proposition** ce n'est pas une proposition intéressante ▸▸ *Com* **p. agent** domiciliataire *m*; **p. agent for commercial bills** domiciliation *f* d'effets de commerce **p. back** (*of loan*) remboursement *m*; *Fin* **p. bank** domiciliataire, établissement *m* payeur, domiciliation bancaire; **p. guest** hôte *m* payant, pensionnaire *mf*, **p. in** (*of money, cheque etc*) (*into one's account*) versement *m*, encaissement *m*; **p.-in book** carnet *m* de versements; **p.-in date** date *f* d'encaissement; **p.-in slip** bordereau *m* de versement *ou* de remise; **p. off** (*of debt*) liquidation *f*, règlement *m*; (*dismissal*) (*of workers*) licenciement *m*; (*of sailors*) débarquement *m*; (*of servants*) congédiement *m*

payload ['peɪləʊd] **N** (*of vehicle*) charge *f* payante *ou* utile; (*of missile*) charge utile; *Aviat* poids *m* utile

paymaster ['peɪmɑːstər] **N** intendant *m*, caissier *m*, payeur *m*; *Mil* trésorier *m*; *Naut* commissaire *m*; **the terrorists' p.** le commanditaire des terroristes ▸▸ **the P. General** le Trésorier-payeur-général britannique

payment ['peɪmənt] **N 1** (*act or fact of paying*) (*of money*) paiement *m*, versement *m*; (*of debt*) paiement, liquidation *f*, règlement *m*, acquittement *m*; (*of fine*) paiement; (*of invoice*) paiement, règlement; (*of creditor*) remboursement *m*; **to make a p.** effectuer un versement; **to stop p. on a cheque** faire opposition sur un chèque; **(hire purchase) p.** paiement par traites; **I'm behind on the payments** j'ai du retard dans les paiements; **non p.** défaut de paiement; **to present a bill for p.** présenter un effet au paiement *ou* à l'encaissement; **on p. of £100** contre paiement de 100 livres; **p. against documents** paiement contre documents; **p. by cheque** paiement par chèque; **p. by electronic transfer** paiement électronique; **p. on account** acompte *m*; **to make a p. on account** donner un acompte; **p. in advance** paiement anticipé *ou* par anticipation *ou* d'avance; **p. in arrears** paiement arriéré; **p. in cash** paiement comptant, règlement au comptant; **p. on delivery** livraison *f* contre remboursement; **p. in full** paiement intégral; **p. by instalments** paiement par acomptes; **p. of a dividend** passation *f ou* distribution *f* d'un dividende; **p. in kind** paiement *ou* avantages *mpl* en nature; **p. at maturity** paiement à échéance; **p. at sight** paiement à vue **2** (*remuneration*) paiement *m*, rémunération *f*, **as (a) p. for your services** en rémunération de vos services; **they offered their services without p.** ils ont offert leurs services à titre gracieux; **she would not accept p.** elle n'a pas voulu accepter de paiement; **you can expect little but gratitude in p. for your efforts** ne vous attendez pas à beaucoup plus que de la gratitude en retour de vos efforts; **p. received** (*stamped on invoice*) pour acquit

▸▸ **p. advice** avis *m* de paiement; **p. card** carte *f* de paiement; **p. day** jour *m* de paiement, jour de règlement; **p. facilities** facilités *fpl* de paiement; **p. method** mode *m* de paiement; **p. order** ordre *m* de paiement; **p. period** délai *m* de paiement; **p. schedule** échéancier *m* de paiement; **p. term** délai de paiement

payoff ['peɪɒf] **N 1** (*final payment*) règlement *m*; *Fin* rentabilité *f* **2** *Fam* (*bribe*) pot-de-vin *m*, *pl* pots-de-vin **3** *Fam* (*ending*) dénouement *m* **4** (*reward*) récompense *f*

payola [peɪˈəʊlə] **N** *Fam* (*bribe*) pot-de-vin *m*, *pl* pots-de-vin

pay-per-view *TV* **N** système *m* de télévision à la carte *ou* à la séance **ADJ** (*channel*) à péage; (*film, programme*) à la carte, à la séance

payroll ['peɪrəʊl] **N 1** (*list of employees*) liste *f* du personnel; *Mil* feuille *f ou* état *m* de solde; **to be on the p.** être salarié; **how many do you have on the p.?** combien d'employés avez-vous?; **she's been on our p. for over twenty years** elle fait partie de notre personnel depuis plus de vingt ans; *Pej* **he's on our p.** (*we're bribing him*) on l'a acheté **2** (*money paid*) masse *f* salariale ▸▸ *Fin* **p. ledger** journal *m ou* livre *m* de paie; *Fin* **p. tax** impôt *m* sur la masse salariale

PBX [piːbiːˈeks] **N** *Tel* (*abbr* **private branch exchange**) autocommutateur *m* privé

PC ['piːˈsiː] **N 1** *Br* (*abbr* **Police Constable**) = agent *m* de police **2** (*abbr* **personal computer**) PC *m*, ordinateur *m* individuel; **P. disk** disquette *f* pour PC **ADJ** (*abbr* **politically correct**) politiquement correct

pc ['piːˈsiː] **N** (*abbr* **postcard**) carte *f* postale

PCB [piːsiːˈbiː] **N 1** *Chem* (*abbr* **polychlorinated biphenyl**) PCB *m* **2** *Electron* (*abbr* **printed circuit board**) carte *f* à *ou* de circuits imprimés

PC-compatible **ADJ** compatible PC

PCI [piːsiːˈaɪ] **N** *Comput* (*abbr* **peripheral component interface**) PCI *m*

PCMCIA [piːsiːˈemsiːaɪˈeɪ] *Comput* (*abbr* **PC memory card international association**) PCMCIA

PD ['piːˈdiː] *Am* (*abbr* **Police Department**) service *m* de police

PDA [piːdiːˈeɪ] **N** *Comput* (*abbr* **personal digital assistant**) agenda *m* électronique de poche, assistant *m* numérique de poche

PDF [piːdiːˈef] **N** *Comput* (*abbr* **portable document format**) (format *m*) PDF *m*

pdq [piːdiːˈkjuː] **ADV** *Fam* (*abbr* **pretty damn(ed) quick**) illico presto, rapido **N** (*abbr* **processes data quickly**) (*machine*) terminal *m* électronique de paiement, TEP *m*

PDSA [piːdiːˈesˈeɪ] **N** *Br* (*abbr* **People's Dispensary for Sick Animals**) ≃ SPA *f*

PE ['piːˈiː] **N** *Sch* (*abbr* **physical education**) EPS *f*, **PE lesson/teacher** cours *m*/professeur *m* d'EPS

pea [piː] **N** pois *m*; *Culin* (**green** *or* **garden**) **peas** petits pois; **like two peas in a pod** comme deux gouttes d'eau; **p. soup** soupe *f* aux pois; (**thick**) purée *f* de pois (cassés) ▸▸ **p. green** vert pomme *m inv*; **p. jacket** caban *m*; **p. pod** cosse *f* de pois

peace [piːs] **N 1** (*absence of war, conflict*) paix *f*, (*treaty*) traité *m* de paix; **at p.** en paix (**with** avec); **to live in p. with one's neighbours** (*of person, tribe, country*) vivre en paix ou en harmonie avec ses voisins; **in time of p.** en temps de paix; **to make (one's) p. with sb** faire la paix *ou* se réconcilier avec qn; **we come in p.** nous venons en amis; *Hist* **the P. of Amiens** la Paix d'Amiens **2** (*public order*) **to keep the p.** (*of citizen*) ne pas troubler l'ordre public; (*of police, troops*) veiller à l'ordre public; **to break** *or* **disturb the p.** troubler *ou* violer l'ordre public; (*at night*) faire du tapage nocturne **3** (*tranquillity*) (*of soul, night etc*) tranquillité *f*, **for the sake of p. and quiet** pour avoir la paix; **to leave sb in p.** laisser qn tranquille *ou* en paix; **he gave me no p. until I agreed** il ne m'a pas laissé tranquille *ou* en paix tant que je n'ai pas accepté; *esp Rel* **go in p.!** allez en paix!; **p. of mind** tranquillité d'esprit; **it will give you p. of mind** ça te tranquillisera; **to be at p.** (*of dead person*) reposer en paix; **to hold** *or* **keep one's p.** se taire ▸▸ *Br* **p. campaigner** militant, -ante pour la paix; **P. Corps** = organisation *f* américaine de coopération avec les pays en voie de développement; **p. dividends** dividendes *mpl* de la paix; **p. formula** formule *f* de paix; **p. initiative** initiative *f* de paix; **p. movement** mouvement *m* pour la paix; **p. negotiations** négociations *fpl* pour la paix; **p. offering** offrande *f* de paix; **p. pipe** calumet *m* (de la paix); **p. plan** plan *m* de paix; **p. process** processus *m* de paix; **p. studies** = discipline *f* universitaire consistant à étudier les rapports stratégiques entre pays, le rôle de l'armée et la promotion de la paix dans le monde; **p. talks** pourparlers *mpl* de paix; **p. treaty** traité de paix

peaceable ['piːsəb(ə)l] **ADJ** pacifique, qui aime la paix; **a p. man** un homme de paix; **p. means** moyens pacifiques

peaceably ['piːsəblɪ] **ADV** pacifiquement

peaceful ['piːsfʊl] **ADJ 1** (*calm*) paisible, calme, tranquille; (*death*) paisible; (*colour*) doux, *f* douce **2** (*not warlike or aggressive*) pacifique; **p. settlement of a dispute** règlement *m* pacifique d'un litige

peacefully ['piːsfʊlɪ] **ADV** (*to sleep, die*) paisiblement, tranquillement; (*to demonstrate, resolve differences*) pacifiquement; **p. situ-**

ated situé dans un lieu paisible; **p., at home** (in death notice) mort dans son lit

peacefulness ['piːsfʊlnɪs] N tranquillité f, paix f; **the organizers have guaranteed the p. of the demonstration** les organisateurs ont garanti que la manifestation se déroulerait dans le calme

peacekeeping ['piːskiːpɪŋ] N maintien m de la paix
▸▸ Mil **p. force** force f de maintien de la paix

peace-loving ADJ pacifique

peacenik ['piːsnɪk] N Fam Pej pacifiste mf

peacetime ['piːstaɪm] N temps m de paix; **in p.** en temps de paix

peach [piːtʃ] N pêche f; (tree) pêcher m; **p. (colour)** pêche f inv; **a peaches and cream complexion** un teint de pêche; Fam **she's a p.** c'est une jolie fille; Fam **it's a p.** c'est magnifique; **a p. of a goal/dress** un but/une robe magnifique
vi Old-fashioned Sl **to p. on sb** (inform on) moucharder qn
▸▸ **p. melba** pêche melba; **p. tree** pêcher

peachy, peachy keen ['piːtʃɪ(kiːn)] ADJ Am Fam super, génial, -aux, grand

peacock ['piːkɒk] N (bird) paon m; (colour) bleu canard m inv
▸▸ **p. blue** bleu canard; **p. butterfly** paon de jour

peahen ['piːhen] N paonne f

peak [piːk] N 1 (of mountain) pic m, cime f, sommet m; (mountain) pic; **the highest peaks** les plus hauts sommets; Culin **whisk the egg white until it forms stiff peaks** battre les blancs en neige jusqu'à ce qu'ils forment des becs 2 (maximum point) maximum m; (of graph, load) pointe f; Med (of fever) pointe, poussée f; Phys (of wave) crête f; **prosperity was at its p.** la prospérité était à son apogée ou à son maximum; **in p. condition** dans une forme excellente 3 (of cap) visière f; (of bicycle saddle, anchor etc) bec m; (of roof) pointe f
vi (of curve etc) passer par son apogée; **inflation peaked at 10%** l'inflation a fait une pointe à 10%; Sport **she peaked in time for the Olympics** (of athlete) elle a atteint le maximum de sa forme juste à temps pour les Jeux olympiques
▸▸ **p. demand** demande f maximum; **p. hours** (for traffic) heures fpl de pointe; (in shop etc) heures d'affluence; **p. load** charge f maximum; (of generator) débit m maximum; **p. period** (for traffic) heures de pointe; (in shop etc) heures d'affluence; St Exch **p. price** prix m maximum; **p. rate** tarif m heures pleines; **p. sales** ventes fpl maximales; Br TV **p. time** heures de grande écoute, prime time m; Br TV **p. time advertisement** publicité f aux heures de grande écoute ou en prime time; Br TV **p. time advertising** publicité aux heures de grande écoute ou en prime time; Br TV **p. viewing hours** heures de grande écoute; Br TV **p. viewing time** heures f de grande écoute
▸ **peak out** vi (reach top limit) atteindre son maximum

peaked [piːkt] ADJ (cap) à visière

peaky ['piːkɪ] ADJ Fam **to look p.** ne pas avoir l'air dans son assiette; **to feel p.** ne pas se sentir dans son assiette

peal [piːl] N (bells) carillon m; (noise) carillon, carillonnement m; (of organ) grondement m; (of thunder) coup m, grondement m; **to ring a p.** sonner un carillon, carillonner; **peals of laughter** éclats mpl de rire; **to go** or **break into peals of laughter** lancer de grands éclats de rire
vi (of bells) (chime) carillonner; (ring out loudly) sonner à toute volée; (of thunder, of the organ) retentir, gronder; (of laughter) ré-

sonner; **to p. with laughter** éclater de rire
vt (bells) sonner à toute volée; (tune) carillonner
▸ **peal out** vi = **peal** vi

peanut ['piːnʌt] N cacahuète f; Fam **they pay us peanuts** (small sum of money) ils nous paient trois fois rien; **that's peanuts to him** pour lui, c'est rien
▸▸ **p. butter** beurre m de cacahuètes; Am Fam **p. gallery** (in theatre) poulailler m; **p. oil** huile f d'arachide

pear [peər] N poire f; (tree) poirier m
▸▸ **p. tree** poirier

peardrop ['peədrɒp] N bonbon m parfumé à la poire

pearl¹ [pɜːl] N perle f; (cultured) perle de culture; Prov **to cast pearls before swine** jeter des perles aux cochons ou aux pourceaux; **he comes out with some real pearls** (amusing comments etc) il sort de vraies perles; **pearls of dew** perles de rosée; **pearls of wisdom** perles de sagesse; Iron inepties fpl; **p. button** bouton m de nacre; **p. necklace** collier m de perles
vi 1 (of moisture etc) perler, former des gouttelettes 2 (dive for pearls) pêcher des perles
▸▸ **p. barley** orge m perlé; **p. diver** pêcheur, -euse de perles; **p. grey** gris perle m inv; **p. lightbulb** ampoule f opale; **p. oyster** huître f perlière

pearl² N, vt Knitting = **purl**

pearly ['pɜːlɪ] ADJ perlé; **p. (white) teeth** dents fpl perlées ou de perle
▸▸ Fam **the P. Gates** les portes fpl du paradis; **p. king** = marchand m des quatre saisons de Londres portant une tenue traditionnelle couverte de boutons de nacre; Zool **p. nautilus** (mollusc) nautile m, nautilus m; **p. queen** = marchande f des quatre saisons de Londres portant une tenue traditionnelle couverte de boutons de nacre

pear-shaped ADJ en forme de poire; (female figure) qui s'épaissit au niveau des hanches; Br Fam **to go p.** (go wrong) partir en eau de boudin

peasant ['pezənt] N paysan, -anne, Pej péquenaud, -aude, rustre mf; **p. ways** mœurs fpl paysannes

peasantry ['pezəntrɪ] N (people) paysannerie f, paysans mpl

pease [piːz] N
▸▸ Culin **p. pudding** = purée f de pois au jambon

peashooter ['piːʃuːtər] N petite sarbacane f

peasouper ['piːˈsuːpər] N esp Br Fam (fog) purée f de pois

peat [piːt] N tourbe f; turf or sod or block of p. motte f de tourbe; **to cut** or **dig p.** tourber
▸▸ **p. bog** tourbière f; **p. cutter** tourbier, -ière; **p. cutting, p. digging** tourbage m; Bot **p. moss** sphaigne f

peaty ['piːtɪ] ADJ (soil) tourbeux; (taste) de fumée de tourbe

pebble ['peb(ə)l] N 1 caillou m, -oux; (big, smooth and rounded) galet m; Fam **you're not the only p. on the beach** il n'y a pas que toi au monde; **p. beach** plage f de galets 2 Opt (crystal) cristal m de roche; (lens) lentille f en cristal de roche
▸▸ Constr **p. dash** crépi m (moucheté); **p.-dash finish** crépi

pebble-dash vt Constr (wall) crépir

pebbly ['peblɪ] ADJ caillouteux; (beach) de galets

pecan ['piːkən, pɪˈkæn] N (nut) noix f de pecan, Can pacane f; (tree) pacanier m
▸▸ **p. nut** noix de pecan, Can pacane f; Culin **p. pie** tourte f aux noix de pecans ou Can aux pacanes; **p. tree** pacanier

peccadillo [pekəˈdɪləʊ] N peccadille f

peccary ['pekərɪ] N (animal) pécari m

peck¹ [pek] N 1 (of bird) coup m de bec; **to have a p. at sth** picoter qch 2 Fam (kiss) bise f, bécot m; **to give sb a p.** faire une bise à qn
vt 1 (of bird) (something) picoter, becqueter; (person) donner un coup de bec à 2 Fam (to kiss) faire une bise à
vi **to p. (at sth)** (of bird) picoter (qch), donner des coups de bec (à qch)

peck² N (measure) (of oats etc) picotin m

pecker ['pekər] N 1 Fam (bird) pic m vert 2 Br Sl **keep your p. up!** (du) courage! 3 esp Am Vulg (penis) bite f

peckerwood ['pekəwʊd] N Am Sl **to be a p.** être génial ou super

pecking ['pekɪŋ] N
▸▸ **p. order** (among birds) hiérarchie f du becquetage; Fig hiérarchie sociale; (in business etc) hiérarchie

peckish ['pekɪʃ] ADJ Fam **to be** or **feel p.** avoir un creux

pecs [peks] NPL Fam (pectorals) pectoraux mpl

pectin ['pektɪn] N Chem pectine f

pectoral ['pektər(ə)l] ADJ Anat, Med etc pectoral, -aux
N 1 Rel, Hist pectoral m 2 Anat (muscle m) pectoral m
▸▸ **p. cross** (of bishop) croix f pectorale; **p. fin** (of fish) nageoire f pectorale

peculate ['pekjʊleɪt] vi détourner des fonds
vt (funds) détourner

peculation [pekjʊˈleɪʃən] N malversation f

peculiar [pɪˈkjuːlɪər] ADJ 1 (strange) bizarre, curieux; (eccentric) original, -aux; **well, that's p.** tiens, c'est bizarre ou curieux!, voilà qui est singulier!; **he/she is a little p.** il/elle est un peu bizarre 2 (characteristic) particulier; **her singing style is p. to her** son style de chant lui est particulier; **this species is p. to Scandinavia** cette espèce n'existe qu'en Scandinavie 3 (special) spécial, -aux, particulier; **of p. interest** d'un intérêt tout particulier

peculiarity [pɪkjuːlɪˈærɪtɪ] N 1 (strangeness) bizarrerie f, singularité f; (eccentricity) originalité f; **one of her little peculiarities** une de ses petites manies 2 (distinctive feature) particularité f

peculiarly [pɪˈkjuːlɪəlɪ] ADV 1 (strangely) singulièrement 2 (specially) particulièrement

pecuniary [pɪˈkjuːnɪərɪ] ADJ Fml pécuniaire; **p. difficulties** embarras mpl pécuniaires ou financiers, ennuis mpl d'argent

pedagogic(al) [pedəˈgɒdʒɪk, -ɪk(ə)l] ADJ pédagogique

pedagogue ['pedəgɒg] N pédagogue m, Pej pédant, -ante

pedagogy ['pedəgɒdʒɪ] N pédagogie f

pedal ['ped(ə)l] N (of bicycle, car, machine, musical instrument etc) pédale f; Mus (note) (note f de) pédale; **soft p.** (of piano) pédale douce, sourdine f; **loud p.** pédale forte
ADJ Anat (relating to foot) pédieux
vi (-ll-, Am -l-) 1 Cycling etc pédaler; **she had pedalled around France when she was a teenager** adolescente, elle avait parcouru la France à vélo; **he pedalled off** il est parti (à vélo) 2 Mus (in playing organ) jouer sur le pédalier; (in playing piano) mettre la pédale
vt (bicycle) appuyer sur les pédales de; **to p. a bicycle around Europe** parcourir l'Europe à vélo ou à bicyclette; **he pedalled his bike up the hill** il a pédalé jusqu'en haut de la côte sur son vélo
▸▸ Br **p. bin** poubelle f à pédale; **p. boat** pédalo® m; **p. car** voiture f à pédales; **p. keyboard** (of organ) pédalier m; Mus **p. note**

(note de) pédale; *Aut* **p. pressure** pression *f* sur la pédale; **p. pushers** (pantalon *m*) corsaire *m*

pedalo, *pl* **pedalos, pedaloes** ['pedələʊ, -əʊz] N pédalo® *m*

pedal-operated [-ɒpəreɪtɪd] ADJ *Tech etc* commandé par pédale(s)

pedant ['pedənt] N *Pej* pédant, -ante; **don't be such a p.!** ne sois pas aussi pédant!

pedantic [pɪ'dæntɪk] ADJ pédant

pedantically [pɪ'dæntɪklɪ] ADV avec pédantisme; *(to say)* d'un ton pédant

pedantry ['pedəntrɪ] N pédantisme *m*, pédanterie *f*

peddle ['ped(ə)l] VI faire du colportage; *(with drugs)* faire du trafic de drogues
VT *(goods), Fig (ideas, theories)* colporter; **to p. drugs** faire du trafic de drogues

peddler ['pedlər] N **1 (drug) p.** trafiquant, -ante de drogues **2** *Am* = **pedlar**

pederast ['pedəræst, 'pi:-] N pédéraste *m*

pederasty ['pedəræstɪ, 'pi:-] N pédérastie *f*

pedestal ['pedɪst(ə)l] N *Archit, Art etc* piédestal *m*, -aux; *Fig* **to put sb on a p.** mettre qn sur un piédestal
▸▸ **p. table** guéridon *m*; **p. washbasin** lavabo-colonne *m*, *pl* lavabos-colonnes

pedestrian [pɪ'destrɪən] ADJ *(on foot)* pédestre; *Fig (style etc)* prosaïque, terre à terre *inv*; *(pace, rhythm)* lourd
N piéton, -onne
▸▸ *Br* **p. crossing** passage *m* clouté *ou* piétons; **p. precinct** zone *f* piétonnière

pedestrian-controlled crossing N passage *m* piéton à bouton d'appel

pedestrianization [pɪdestrɪənaɪ'zeɪʃən] N *(of area)* aménagement *m* en zone piétonnière; **in favour of p.** en faveur de l'aménagement de zones piétonnières

pedestrianize [pɪ'destrɪənaɪz] VT *(road)* aménager en zone piétonnière

pediatric, pediatrician *etc Am* = **paediatric, paediatrician** *etc*

pedicure ['pedɪkjʊər] N **1** *(activity)* soins *mpl* des pieds, *Spec* pédicurie *f*; **to have a p.** se faire soigner les pieds, aller chez le/la pédicure **2** *(person)* pédicure *mf*
VT *(feet)* soigner

pedigree ['pedɪgri:] N **1** *(of dog etc)* pedigree *m*; **to have a p.** *(of dog)* être un chien de race, avoir un pedigree **2** *(background)* passé *m*, antécédents *mpl*; **she had an impeccable political p.** ses antécédents politiques étaient irréprochables **3** *(person's ancestry)* ascendance *f*, généalogie *f* **4** *(genealogical table)* arbre *m* généalogique
ADJ *(dog etc)* de (pure) race; *(person)* de bonne lignée

pediment ['pedɪmənt] N *Archit* fronton *m*

pedlar ['pedlər] N colporteur *m*, marchand *m* ambulant

pedology N *Am* = **paedology**

pedometer [pɪ'dɒmɪtər] N podomètre *m*

pedophile, pedophilia *Am* = **paedophile, paedophilia**

pee [pi:] N *Fam* pipi *m*; **to go and have a p.** aller faire pipi; **he was desperate for a p.** il avait énormément envie de faire pipi; **cat's p.** pipi de chat
VI *Fam* faire pipi; **it's peeing down** *(raining)* il pleut comme vache qui pisse
▸ **pee off** VT SEP *Sl (annoy)* **to p. sb off** faire chier qn; **to be peed off** être fumasse *ou* furibard; **to be peed off at sb/about sth** être en pétard contre qn/à cause de qch; **to be peed off with sb/sth** *(have had enough of)* en avoir ras le bol de qn/qch

peek [pi:k] N regard *m* furtif, coup *m* d'œil (furtif); **to take** *or* **have a p. (at sth/sb)** jeter

un coup d'œil (furtif) (à *ou* sur qch/qn)
VI jeter un regard *ou* un coup d'œil furtif (**at** sur); risquer un coup d'œil; **no peeking!** on ne regarde pas!

peekaboo ['pi:kəbu:] INT coucou!
ADJ *Am (blouse etc) (see-through)* transparent; *(with holes)* avec *ou* en broderie(s) ajourée(s)

peel [pi:l] N *(of apple etc)* pelure *f*, épluchure *f*, *(of potato etc)* épluchure; *(of orange, lemon)* écorce *f*, *Culin* zeste *m*
VT *(fruit)* peler, éplucher; *(potatoes etc)* éplucher; *(oak, almonds)* décortiquer; **to p. the bark/skin** enlever l'écorce/la peau; **to keep one's eyes peeled** ouvrir l'œil; **we were all keeping our eyes peeled for a pub** nous guettions tous un pub, nous étions tous à l'affût d'un pub
VI *(of paint etc)* s'écailler; *(of nose, back etc)* peler; *Med* se desquamer; *(of bark)* se détacher; *(of wall)* se décrépir; **you're peeling** tu pèles; **the skin on his back was starting to p.** son dos commençait à peler
▸ **peel off** VT SEP *(rind, skin, shirt, vest)* enlever; **to p. off one's clothes** se déshabiller
VI **1** *(become detached) (of paint, nail varnish etc)* s'écailler; *(of skin)* se détacher; *Med* se desquamer; *Aviat* se détacher de la formation; **the skin on my nose is peeling off** mon nez pèle **2** *Fam (undress)* se déshabiller

peeler ['pi:lər] N **1** *Culin (device)* éplucheur *m*; **potato p.** économe *m* **2** *Br Arch (policeman)* agent *m* de police

peeling ['pi:lɪŋ] N **1** *Med (of skin)* desquamation *f* **2 peelings** *(of potato etc)* épluchures *fpl*
ADJ *(nose, back etc)* qui pèle/pelait

peep¹ [pi:p] N **1** *(furtive glance)* coup *m* d'œil furtif; **to have** *or* **take a p. at sth** jeter un regard furtif sur qch; **to get a p. at sth** entrevoir qch **2** *(of light)* rayon *m*
VI *(glance furtively)* jeter un coup d'œil; **to p. at sb/sth** regarder qn/qch à la dérobée, jeter un coup d'œil furtif sur qn/qch; **to p. through the door** jeter un coup d'œil (furtif) par la porte; **I saw you peeping through the keyhole** je vous ai vu regarder par le trou de la serrure; **someone was peeping at her from behind the curtains** quelqu'un l'observait, caché derrière les rideaux; **no peeping!** on ne regarde pas!; **a Peeping Tom** un voyeur
▸ **peep out** VI *(be visible)* se laisser entrevoir, se montrer; *(of flower)* percer, pointer; **his feet were peeping out from beneath the curtains** ses pieds dépassaient de derrière les rideaux; **her big toe was peeping out through a hole in her sock** son gros doigt de pied pointait par un trou de sa chaussette

peep² N *(sound) (of bird)* pépiement *m*, piaulement *m*; *(of mouse)* cri *m*; *Fam* **if I hear so much as a p. out of you** si tu fais le moindre bruit; *Fam* **we haven't heard a p. from him for months** ça fait des mois qu'il n'a pas donné le moindre signe de vie
VI *(of bird)* pépier, piauler; *(of mouse)* crier

peep-bo [-bəʊ] INT coucou!
N **to play (at) p.** jouer à cache-cache *(avec un enfant)*

peepers ['pi:pəz] N *Sl (eyes)* mirettes *fpl*

peephole ['pi:phəʊl] N **1** *(in door)* judas *m* **2** *Tech etc (trou m de)* regard *m*

peepshow ['pi:pʃəʊ] N *(pictures)* vues *fpl* stéréoscopiques; *(erotic, with live model)* peepshow *m*

peer¹ [pɪər] N **1** *(equal)* pair *m*; **you will not find his p.** vous ne trouverez pas son pareil; **he is without p.** il n'a pas son pareil; **she does not have many peers** peu l'égalent; *Law* **a jury of one's peers** un jury de ses pairs **2** *(noble)* pair *m*; *Br* **p. of the realm** pair du Royaume-Uni; *Br* **life p.** pair à vie

▸▸ **p. group** pairs; **p. pressure** influence *f* des pairs *ou* du groupe

peer² VI **to p. at sb/sth** scruter qn/qch du regard; **he peered at the writing** il fixa son regard sur ce qui était écrit; **he peered (out) into the night** il cherchait à percer l'obscurité; **to p. round the corner** risquer un coup d'œil au coin de la rue; **he was peering through the curtains** il guettait entre les rideaux; **he was peering into the bottom of his glass** il scrutait le fond de son verre; **several pairs of eyes were peering at her** plusieurs paires d'yeux étaient braquées sur elle

peerage ['pɪərɪdʒ] N **1** *(noble title, rank)* pairie *f*, **life p.** pairie à vie; **to confer a p. on sb, to raise sb to the p.** élever qn à la pairie **2** *(no pl)* **the p.** *(peers)* les pairs *mpl* **3** *(book)* (almanach *m*) nobiliaire *m*

peeress ['pɪərɪs] N pairesse *f*

peerless ['pɪəlɪs] ADJ *Lit* sans pareil, sans égal, hors pair

peer-to-peer ADJ peer-to-peer

peeve [pi:v] VT *Fam* mettre en boule, irriter; **to be peeved** être fâché *ou* irrité; **to be peeved at sb for not doing sth** être fâché contre qn parce qu'il n'a pas fait qch; **I was peeved at his behaviour/the decision** son comportement/cette décision m'a mis en boule *ou* m'a irrité

peevish ['pi:vɪʃ] ADJ maussade, irritable; *(response)* maussade; *(child)* grognon

peevishly ['pi:vɪʃlɪ] ADV *(to say)* avec mauvaise humeur, d'un ton irrité; *(to respond)* d'un air maussade

peevishness ['pi:vɪʃnɪs] N *(of person)* maussaderie *f*, mauvaise humeur *f*; *(of response, behaviour)* maussaderie

peewit ['pi:wɪt] N *(bird)* vanneau *m* (huppé)

peg [peg] N **1** *(pin, bolt) (wooden)* cheville *f*, *(metal)* fiche *f*, *(of barrel)* fausset *m*, fosset *m*; *Tech* clavette *f*, goupille *f*, *(for tent)* piquet *m*; *Mus (on violin)* cheville; *Br* **(clothes) p.** pince *f* à linge; **(hat** *or* **coat) p.** patère *f*, *esp Br Com* **a suit off the p.** un costume de confection; **off the p. clothing** prêt-à-porter *m*, *pl* prêts-à-porter; *Fig* **to take sb down a p. (or two)** remettre qn à sa place; **that's a p. to hang a grievance on** ce n'est pas qu'un prétexte pour se plaindre; **we can use this as a p. to hang our story on** nous pouvons centrer notre article là-dessus **2** *Br (of whisky etc)* doigt *m*
VT *(-gg-)* **1** *(structure, joint)* cheviller; **to p. sth in place** cheviller qch; **to p. clothes on the line** accrocher du linge sur la corde *(avec des pinces à linge)* **2** *St Exch, Fin (prices) (fix)* fixer; *(stabilize)* stabiliser; **to p. sth to the rate of inflation** indexer qch sur le taux de l'inflation; **oil was pegged at $20 a barrel** le prix du pétrole était fixé à 20 dollars le baril; **export earnings are pegged to the exchange rate** le revenu des exportations varie en fonction du taux de change
▸▸ *Fam* **p. leg** *(wooden leg)* jambe *f* de bois, pilon *m*; *(artificial leg)* jambe artificielle; *(person)* = personne *f* qui a une jambe de bois ou une jambe artificielle
▸ **peg away** VI *Fam (work hard)* bosser (**at sth** à qch); **to p. away at one's algebra** piocher *ou* bûcher son algèbre
▸ **peg down** VT SEP *(fix) (net etc)* fixer avec des piquets; *Fig* **to p. sb down to a price** obliger qn à s'engager sur un prix
▸ **peg out** VT SEP **1** *(mark with pegs) (plot of land)* piqueter, jalonner, borner; *(line)* jalonner **2** *(hang)* **to p. out clothes on the line** accrocher du linge sur la corde *(avec des pinces à linge)*
VI **1** *Sl (die)* casser sa pipe **2** *(in croquet)* toucher le piquet final (et se retirer de la partie)

pegboard ['pegbɔːd] N **1** *(for hanging things)* panneau *m* alvéolé **2** *(for game)* table *f* à trous

pegging ['pegɪŋ] N **1** *St Exch, Fin (of prices etc) (fixing)* fixation *f*, *(stabilizing)* stabilisation *f*, *(to rate of inflation etc)* indexation *f* **2** *Br Sport, Fig* it's level p. ils sont à égalité

PEI [piːiːˈaɪ] N *Geog (abbr* **Prince Edward Island)** IPE *f*

pejorative [prˈdʒɒrətɪv] ADJ péjoratif N *(mot m)* péjoratif *m*

pejoratively [prˈdʒɒrətɪvlɪ] ADV péjorativement

peke [piːk] N *Fam* (chien *m*) pékinois *m*

Pekinese [piːkɪˈniːz] ADJ pékinois N **1** *(person)* Pékinois, -oise **2** *(dog)* (chien *m*) pékinois *m*

Peking [piːˈkɪŋ] N Pékin

Pekingese [piːkɪŋˈiːz] ADJ, N = **Pekinese**

pelagic [prˈlædʒɪk] ADJ pélagique

pelargonium [peləˈgəʊnɪəm] N *(plant)* pélargonium *m*

pelican ['pelɪkən] N *(bird)* pélican *m*
▸▸ *Br* p. crossing = passage *m* piétons à commande manuelle

pellagra [peˈlægrə, -ˈleɪ-] N *Med* pellagre *f*

pellet ['pelɪt] N *(of paper, bread, clay etc)* boulette *f*, *(of dung)* bille *f*, *(in shotgun cartridge)* grain *m* de plomb; *Pharm* pilule *f*, grain; *Orn (regurgitated food of owl etc)* boulette (d'aliments regurgités), bol *m* alimentaire; *Metal, Chem* boulette

pell-mell ['pel'mel] ADV pêle-mêle; *(to run)* à la débandade

pellucid [peˈluːsɪd] ADJ *Lit* pellucide, transparent; *Fig (mind etc)* lucide; *(style)* clair, limpide

pelmet ['pelmɪt] N lambrequin *m*

Peloponnese (the) [ðəpeləpəˈniːs] N le Péloponnèse

Peloponnesian [peləpəˈniːsɪən] ADJ péloponnésien, du Péloponnèse

pelota [pəˈlɒtə] N *(game)* pelote *f* basque

pelt[1] [pelt] N **1** *(skin) (of sheep, goat)* peau *f*, fourrure *f* **2** *(in tanning) (with hair on)* peau *f* verte; *(without hair)* peau en tripe

pelt[2] VT to p. sb with stones/snowballs bombarder qn de pierres/boules de neige; he pelted abuse at them il les a criblés d'injures; to p. sb with criticism mitrailler *ou* accabler qn de critiques
VI **1** *(of rain etc)* tomber à verse; it was pelting with rain la pluie tombait à verse, il pleuvait à verse; pelting rain pluie *f* battante **2** *(go fast)* aller à toute vitesse *ou* à toute allure, *Fam* foncer; he came pelting round the corner il a débouché du coin à toute allure; the kids pelted off down the street les gosses ont descendu la rue à toute allure *ou* ventre à terre; he pelted upstairs il est monté comme une flèche *ou* ventre à terre; she's really pelting through her work elle abat son travail à toute allure; he pelted through the exam il a passé l'examen à toute allure *ou* à toute vitesse
N (at) full p. *(to run, flee)* à toute vitesse, ventre à terre
▸ pelt down VI *(of rain etc)* tomber à verse; the rain *or* it was pelting down la pluie tombait à verse, il pleuvait à verse

pelvic ['pelvɪk] ADJ *Anat* pelvien
▸▸ p. bone ilion *m*; p. fins *(of fish)* pelviennes *fpl*, p. floor plancher *m* pelvien; p. girdle ceinture *f* pelvienne; p. inflammatory disease syndrome *m* inflammatoire pelvien

pelvis ['pelvɪs] N *Anat* **1** bassin *m*, pelvis *m* **2** *(of kidney)* bassinet *m*

pen[1] [pen] N stylo *m*; fountain p. stylo à plume, stylo-plume *m*, *pl* stylos-plumes;

ball(point) p. stylo à bille, stylo-bille *m*, *pl* stylos-billes; felt(-tip) p. *(crayon m ou* stylo) feutre *m*; drawing *or* mapping p. plume *f* à dessin; stroke of the p. trait *m* de plume; to put p. to paper prendre la plume; to live by one's p. vivre de sa plume; *Prov* the p. is mightier than the sword la plume blesse souvent plus que l'épée
VT (-nn-) *(letter, article etc)* écrire, rédiger
▸▸ p. drawing dessin *m* à la plume *ou* à l'encre; *Br* p. friend correspondant, -ante *(épistolaire)*; p.-and-ink drawing dessin à la plume *ou* à l'encre; p. name nom *m* de plume, pseudonyme *m*; *Fam* p. pal correspondant *(épistolaire)*; *Comput* p. plotter traceur *m* à plumes

pen[2] N *(for sheep etc)* parc *m*, enclos *m*; *(for bulls)* toril *m*; *(for pigs)* porcherie *f* **2** *Naut (for submarine)* abri *m* **3** *Am Sl (penitentiary)* tôle *f*, taule *f*, trou *m*; in the p. en tôle *ou* taule, au trou; he spent ten years in the p. il a fait dix ans de tôle *ou* taule
VT (-nn-, *Lit* pent) *(sheep etc)* parquer
▸ pen in, pen up VT SEP *(sheep etc)* parquer; we were penned up in the room for weeks nous sommes restés parqués dans la pièce pendant des semaines; we spent the week penned up in a caravan nous avons passé toute la semaine enfermés dans une caravane

pen[3] N *(female swan)* cygne *m* femelle

penal ['piːn(ə)l] ADJ *Law (laws, code)* pénal, -aux; *(offence)* qui comporte *ou* entraîne une pénalité
▸▸ p. colony colonie *f* pénitentiaire; *Fin* p. rate taux *m* d'usure; p. servitude travaux *mpl* forcés, bagne *m*; p. settlement colonie pénitentiaire

penalization [piːnəlaɪˈzeɪʃən] N infliction *f* d'une peine *(* of sb à qn); *Sport* pénalisation *f*

penalize ['piːnəlaɪz] VT **1** *(impose a penalty on) (person)* sanctionner; *Sport (competitor, player)* pénaliser **2** *(attach a penalty to) (crime)* attacher une peine à **3** *(disadvantage)* désavantager, pénaliser; to p. sb for doing sth désavantager *ou* pénaliser qn parce qu'il a fait qch; this penalizes those living in the country ceci défavorise *ou* désavantage les gens qui habitent à la campagne

penalty ['penltɪ] N **1** *(punishment)* peine *f*, pénalité *f*; *Com (for late delivery etc)* amende *f*; *Admin* sanction *f* (pénale); to impose penalties prendre des sanctions; on *or* upon *or* under p. of death sous peine de mort; the p. for this is death/excommunication la peine encourue pour ce crime est la mort/l'excommunication; to pay the p. of one's foolishness subir les conséquences *ou* être puni de sa sottise; one of the penalties of fame/wealth un des désavantages dont la gloire/la richesse s'accompagne; to pay the p. of fame payer la rançon de la gloire **2** *Sport* pénalisation *f*, pénalité *f*, *(kick) (in football)* penalty *m*, *pl* penalties; *(in rugby)* pénalité
▸▸ *Ftbl* p. area surface *f* de réparation; p. box *Ftbl* surface de réparation; *(in ice hockey)* banc *m* de pénalité; *Law* p. clause clause *f* pénale; *Fin* p. interest pénalité de retard, intérêts *mpl* moratoires; p. kick *(in football)* penalty; *(in rugby)* (coup *m* de pied de) pénalité; *Ftbl* p. shootout épreuve *f* des penalties; *Ftbl* p. spot point *m* de réparation; *Golf* p. stroke coup *m* d'amende; *Sport* p. throw penalty

penance ['penəns] N *Rel* pénitence *f*; to do p. faire pénitence *(* for de, pour); to do sth as a p. faire qch par pénitence

pence [pens] *see* **penny**

pencil ['pens(ə)l] N **1** crayon *m*; to mark/

write sth in p. *or* with a p. marquer/écrire qch au crayon; drawing in p. (dessin *m* au crayon, crayonnage *m* **2** *Geom (of curves etc)* faisceau *m*; *Opt* p. of light rays faisceau de lumière
VT (-ll-, *Am* -l-) *(mark with a pencil)* marquer au crayon; *(draw, sketch in pencil)* dessiner/ esquisser au crayon, crayonner; *(write) (note)* écrire au crayon, crayonner; to p. one's eyebrows se faire les sourcils (au crayon); pencilled eyebrows sourcils *mpl* dessinés au crayon
▸▸ p. case trousse *f* (à crayon, crayonnage; p. drawing (dessin au) crayon, crayonnage; p. lead mine *f* de crayon; p. mark trait *m* ou marque *f* de ou au crayon; p. sharpener taille-crayon *m*, *pl* taille-crayon(s); p. sketch croquis *m* au crayon
▸ pencil in VT SEP *(write)* écrire au crayon; the date has been pencilled in on a fixé provisoirement la date; p. me in for Friday inscrivez-moi provisoirement pour vendredi; *Fig* en principe, vous pouvez compter sur moi vendredi

pendant ['pendənt] N **1** *(necklace)* pendentif *m* **2** *(ornamental piece) (of necklace)* pendentif *m*; *(on bracelet)* breloque *f*, *(of chandelier)* pendeloque *f*

pending ['pendɪŋ] ADJ *(trial)* pendant, en instance; *(negotiations)* en cours; *Admin, Com (documents)* en souffrance, en attente
PREP en attendant
▸▸ *Br* p. tray corbeille *f* des dossiers en attente

pendulous ['pendjʊləs] ADJ *(breasts, lip, ear etc)* pendant

pendulum ['pendjʊləm] N *Phys* pendule *m*; *(in clockmaking)* balancier *m*, pendule
▸▸ p. ball, p. bob lentille *f* de pendule *ou* de balancier; p. clock horloge *f* à pendule *ou* à balancier

penetrable ['penɪtrəb(ə)l] ADJ **1** *(material, defences)* pénétrable; easily p. facile à pénétrer **2** *(prose etc)* barely p. difficilement compréhensible

penetrate ['penɪtreɪt] VT pénétrer; darkness that the eye could not p. ténèbres que l'œil ne pouvait percer; to p. sb's mind voir clair dans l'esprit de qn
VI pénétrer; *(of ideas, beliefs)* s'implanter; the water is penetrating everywhere l'eau pénètre *ou* s'introduit partout; to p. through sth passer à travers qch; to p. into a forest pénétrer dans une forêt; the custom has not penetrated to this part of the country cette coutume n'est pas parvenue jusqu'à cette partie du pays; it hasn't penetrated *(hasn't been understood)* ça n'a pas fait le tour, ça n'est pas rentré

penetrating ['penɪtreɪtɪŋ] ADJ *(wind, cold)* pénétrant; *(sound, voice, scream)* perçant; *(bullet, shell)* perforant; *(mind, analysis)* pénétrant; to have a p. eye avoir des yeux perçants; a p. stare un regard pénétrant *ou* perçant
▸▸ p. oil dégrippant *m*

penetration [penɪˈtreɪʃən] N pénétration *f*
▸▸ *Mktg* p. price prix *m* de pénétration

penetrative ['penɪtrətɪv] ADJ *(sex)* avec pénétration; *(questioning)* approfondi

penguin ['peŋgwɪn] N manchot *m*, gorfou *m*, *Fam* pingouin *m*
▸▸ *Br Fam Hum* p. suit costard *m* chic

penholder ['penhəʊldə] N porte-plume *m inv*

penicillin [penɪˈsɪlɪn] N pénicilline *f*

peninsula [prˈnɪnsjʊlə] N péninsule *f*, presqu'île *f*

peninsular [prˈnɪnsjʊlə] ADJ péninsulaire

penis, *pl* **penes** ['piːnɪs, -niːz] N *Anat* pénis *m*, verge *f*
▸▸ *Psy* p. envy envie *f* du pénis

penitence ['penɪtəns] N pénitence f, repentir m; **to perform p.** faire pénitence; **to show (one's) p. for one's actions** se repentir ou faire pénitence de ses actions; **to be without p.** ne pas se repentir

penitent ['penɪtənt] ADJ pénitent, repentant; **to be** or **feel p.** se repentir, faire pénitence
N pénitent, -ente

penitential [penɪ'tenʃəl] ADJ pénitentiel
N (book) pénitentiel m

penitentiary [penɪ'tenʃərɪ] N **1** Am (prison) pénitencier m **2** Cathol (person) pénitencier m; (tribunal) pénitencerie f
ADJ Am (crime) puni de réclusion dans un pénitencier ou une centrale

penitently ['penɪtntlɪ] ADV d'un air contrit; (to say etc) d'un ton contrit; (to act, behave) avec contrition

penknife ['pennaɪf] N canif m

penmanship ['penmənʃɪp] N (calligraphy) calligraphie f

Penn(a) abbr Pennsylvania

pennant ['penənt] N flamme f, banderole f, Naut flamme, guidon m

penniless ['penɪlɪs] ADJ sans le sou; **to be p.** être sans le sou, ne pas avoir le sou; **to leave sb p.** laisser qn sans le sou

Pennines (the) [ðə'penaɪnz] NPL la chaîne Pennine, les Pennines fpl

pennon ['penən] N flamme f, banderole f

Pennsylvania [pensɪl'veɪnɪə] N Pennsylvanie f

penny ['penɪ] N VOIR GRAMMAIRE A13 **1** Br (coin) (pl usu pennies) penny m, pl pennies; **they haven't a p.** (to their name or Old-fashioned to bless themselves with) ils sont sans le sou ou sans un sou vaillant; **pennies from heaven** une aubaine; Prov **take care of the pennies and the pounds will take care of themselves** les petits ruisseaux font les grandes rivières; **to count every p.** compter ses sous; **it was worth every p.** je n'ai/nous n'avons/etc pas regretté le prix que je l'ai/nous l'avons/etc payé; **you'd better start saving (up) your pennies** tu ferais mieux de commencer à mettre de l'argent de côté; **not a p. more** pas un sou de plus; Fam **the p.'s dropped** (I understand now) j'y suis, ça y est; (he's understood) il y est, ça y est

2 Br (value) (pl pence [pens]) penny m, pl pence; **I paid 60 pence for it** je l'ai payé 60 pence; **a ten/fifty pence piece** une pièce de dix/cinquante pence; **to buy ten pence worth of sweets** acheter pour dix pence de bonbons; **(new) p.** = nouveau penny; **(old) p.** (before 1971) = ancien penny; Fig **they're two** or **ten a p. nowadays** c'est monnaie courante à l'heure actuelle; **a p. for your thoughts** or **for them** à quoi rêvez-vous ou pensez-vous?; Prov **in for a p. in for a pound** quand le vin est tiré il faut le boire; esp Br Fam **a bad p.** (rogue, worthless person) bon m à rien, bonne f à rien; **it didn't cost them a p.** ça ne leur a pas coûté un centime; **that'll cost a p. or two** cela va coûter de l'argent; **to earn** or **turn an honest p.** gagner honnêtement sa vie

3 Am, Can (cent) cent m
▸▸ Philat **p. black** = premier timbre-poste m britannique; **p. farthing** (bicycle) vélocipède m; Br St Exch **p. shares** actions fpl d'une valeur de moins d'une livre sterling; Fin, St Exch **p. stock** = actions d'une valeur de moins d'un dollar; **p. whistle** pipeau m

penny-dreadful N Old-fashioned Fam roman m à deux sous ou à sensation

penny-in-the-slot ADJ Old-fashioned (machine) à sous

penny-pincher [-pɪntʃər] N pingre mf, radin, -ine

penny-pinching [-pɪntʃɪŋ] ADJ (person) radin, pingre, qui fait des économies de bouts de chandelle; (action, step) mesquin; (lifestyle, measures) de lésine, d'économie de bouts de chandelle
N pingrerie f (with, on sur)

penny-wise ADJ Prov **to be p. and pound-foolish** chipoter sur les petites dépenses sans regarder aux grandes

pennyworth ['penɪwɜːθ] N **to buy a p. of sweets** acheter pour un penny de bonbons; Fig **not a p.** rien du tout

penology [piː'nɒlədʒɪ] N pénologie f

penpusher ['penpʊʃər] N Fam Pej grattepapier m inv; scribouillard, -arde

penpushing ['penpʊʃɪŋ] Fam Pej ADJ (job etc) de gratte-papier
N paperasse f, paperasserie f

pension N **1** ['penʃən] (payment) retraite f, pension f, **government** or Br **state p.** pension sur l'État; **to be on a p.** (of elderly person) vivre de sa retraite ou d'une pension; **to retire on a p.** prendre sa retraite; **(retirement** or **old age) p.** (pension de) retraite **2** ['pɒnsɪɒn] (hotel) pension f de famille; **en p.** (at hotel) en pension
▸▸ Br **p. book** ≃ titre m de pension (carnet permettant de retirer sa pension de retraite); **p. contribution** cotisation f vieillesse; **p. fund** caisse f de retraite, fonds m de pension; **p. plan** plan m de retraite; **p. scheme** caisse de retraite

▸ **pension off** VT SEP mettre à la retraite; Fam (something) mettre au rebut

pensionable ['penʃənəb(ə)l] ADJ (person) qui a droit à une pension ou à sa retraite; (injury, job etc) qui donne droit à une pension
▸▸ **p. age** âge m de la mise à la retraite

pensioner ['penʃənər] N pensionné, -ée; **(old-age) p.** retraité, -ée

Note that the French term **pensionnaire** is never a translation for the English word **pensioner**.

pensive ['pensɪv] ADJ pensif, (music, silence) méditatif

pensively ['pensɪvlɪ] ADV pensivement, d'un air pensif

pent [pent] PT, PP see pen² VT

pentagon ['pentəgən] N Geom pentagone m; Am Mil **the P.** le Pentagone

pentagonal [pen'tægən(ə)l] ADJ pentagonal, -aux

pentameter [pen'tæmɪtər] N (in poetry) pentamètre m

Pentateuch (the) [ðə'pentətjuːk] N Bible le Pentateuque

pentathlete [pen'tæθliːt] N Sport pentathlonien, -ienne

pentathlon [pen'tæθlən] N Sport pentathlon m

Pentecost ['pentɪkɒst] N Rel Pentecôte f

pentecostal [pentɪ'kɒst(ə)l] ADJ Rel de la Pentecôte; **the P. Church** l'église pentecôtiste

penthouse ['penthaʊs] N **1** (apartment) = appartement m de standing au dernier étage d'un immeuble **2** (shed) appentis m
▸▸ **p. suite** (in hotel) suite f avec terrasse

Pentium® ['pentɪəm] N Comput Pentium® m

pent-up ADJ (emotion, frustation, desire) refoulé; (energy, rage) contenu

penultimate [pe'nʌltɪmɪt] ADJ pénultième, avant-dernier

penumbra [pe'nʌmbrə] N pénombre f

penurious [pe'njʊərɪəs] ADJ Fml (poor) indigent; **reduced to a p. condition** réduit à l'indigence

penury ['penjʊrɪ] N **1** (poverty) indigence f **2** (dearth) manque m (of de)

peony ['piːənɪ] N (plant) pivoine f

PEOPLE ['piːp(ə)l]

| N gens **1** ▪ personnes **1** ▪ peuple **2–4** ▪ nation **2** |
| VT peupler |

N VOIR GRAMMAIRE A11 (with pl verb) **1** gens mpl; **there were five p. in the room** il y avait cinq personnes dans la pièce; **young p.** les jeunes gens; **old p.** les personnes fpl âgées, Fam les vieux mpl; **old p.'s home** maison f de retraite pour personnes âgées; **there were not many p.** il n'y avait pas beaucoup de gens ou de monde; **most p.** la plupart des gens; **rich p.** les (gens) riches; **homeless p.** les sans-abris mpl; **blind/deaf p.** les aveugles mpl/les sourds mpl; **stop annoying p.** arrête d'embêter le monde; **he's one of those p. who ...** il est de ceux qui ..., c'est un homme qui ...; **you of all p. should know better!** tu devrais bien être le dernier/la dernière à faire pareille erreur!; **I met Janet of all p. at the theatre** Janet était bien la dernière personne que je m'attendais à rencontrer au théâtre; **it's a question of knowing the right p.** il faut avoir des relations; **we're having p. to dinner tonight** nous avons des invités ou du monde à dîner ce soir; **p. don't like being told they're wrong** les gens n'aiment pas qu'on leur dise qu'ils ont tort; **p. say that ...** on dit que ...; **she's a p. person** elle est très sociable

2 (nation) peuple m, nation f, **the French p.** les Français mpl; **the Sikhs/Russians are a proud p.** les Sikhs/les Russes sont un peuple fier; **English-speaking peoples** peuples ou nations de langue anglaise

3 (citizens) peuple m, citoyens mpl (d'un État); **the common p.** le peuple, Pej la populace; **a man of the p.** un homme sorti du peuple; **a king and his p.** un roi et ses sujets ou son peuple; **to go to the p.** (call an election) en appeler au peuple

4 (population) peuple m, habitants mpl; **the p. of Paris** les habitants de Paris; **town p.** gens mpl de la ville, citadins mpl; **country p.** gens de la campagne, campagnards mpl

5 (employees) employés, -ées; (workers) ouvriers, -ières; **I'll get one of my p. to do it** un de mes employés/ouvriers le fera; **our p. in Moscow** (representatives) nos représentants à Moscou; (compatriots) nos compatriotes installés à Moscou; **the p. in accounts** les gens de la comptabilité

6 Old-fashioned Fam (family) famille f, **how are your p.?** comment va votre famille?

VT peupler (with de); **a country peopled by many different races** un pays multiracial
▸▸ **p. carrier** (car) monospace m; **p. meter** (for viewing figures) audimètre m; **p. mover** (car) monospace; **p. power** pouvoir m populaire; **p.'s republic** république f populaire

PEP [pep] N Formerly (abbr personal equity plan) PEA m

pep [pep] N Fam entrain m, allant m, fougue f, **full of p.** plein d'entrain ou d'allant
▸▸ **p. pill** stimulant m, excitant m; **p. talk** discours m d'encouragement

▸ **pep up** VT SEP (-pp-) Fam (person) ragaillardir, revigorer; (dish, punch etc) relever; (presentation, style) égayer; (plant) revigorer; **to p. up a business** dynamiser une entreprise

pepper ['pepər] N **1** (spice) poivre m; (plant) poivrier m; **black/white p.** poivre noir ou gris/blanc **2** (vegetable) **(sweet) p.** piment m doux, poivron m; **green/red/yellow p.** poivron vert/rouge/jaune
VT **1** (meat etc) poivrer **2** Fig **to p. with bullets** cribler de balles; **peppered with swear-**

words pimentée de jurons; **peppered with spelling mistakes** parsemé de fautes d'orthographe

▸▸**p. mill** moulin *m* à poivre; **p. plant** poivrier; **p. pot** poivrier, poivrière *f*, *Br Culin* **p. steak** steak *m* au poivre

pepper-and-salt ADJ *(hair)* poivre et sel; *(jacket etc)* marengo

peppercorn ['pepəkɔːn] N grain *m* de poivre
▸▸*Br* **p. rent** loyer *m* modique

peppermint ['pepəmɪnt] N **1** *(plant)* menthe *f* poivrée; *(flavour)* menthe poivrée, peppermint *m* **2** *(sweet)* bonbon *m* à la menthe, pastille *f* de menthe

peppery ['pepərɪ] ADJ **1** *(dish etc)* poivré **2** *(person)* irascible, coléreux, colérique

peppy ['pepɪ] ADJ *Fam (person)* plein d'entrain *ou* d'allant

pepsin ['pepsɪn] N *Chem, Physiol* pepsine *f*

peptic ['peptɪk] ADJ *Physiol* peptique
▸▸**p. ulcer** ulcère *m* gastro-duodénal *ou* de l'estomac

peptide ['peptaɪd] N *Biol, Chem* peptide *m*

peptone ['peptəʊn] N *Biol, Chem* peptone *f*

Péquiste [peɪ'kiːst] N *Can (member, supporter of Parti québécois)* péquiste *mf*

per [pɜːr] PREP *Com etc* par; **sent p. carrier** envoyé par messagerie; **p. day** par jour; **100 km p. hour** cent kilomètres à l'heure; **ten euros p. kilo** dix euros le kilo; **as p. invoice** suivant facture; **as p. your instructions** conformément à vos instructions; **as p. sample** conformément à l'échantillon; *Fam* **as p. usual** comme d'habitude
▸▸**p. annum** ['ænəm] par an; **p. capita** ['kæpɪtə] par personne; **p. capita consumption** consommation *f* par tête; **the highest p. capita income in Europe** le revenu par habitant le plus élevé d'Europe; **p. cent = per cent**; **p. pro signature** signature *f* par procuration; **p. se** [seɪ] en soi; **it is not a bad idea p. se** en soi, ce n'est pas une mauvaise idée

peradventure [pɜːrəd'ventʃər] ADV *Arch (by chance)* par aventure, par hasard

perambulate [pə'ræmbjʊleɪt] VT *Fml (one's garden etc)* parcourir, se promener dans

perambulator [pə'ræmbjʊleɪtər] N *Arch, Fml* landau *m*

p/e ratio [piːˈiː] N *Acct (abbr* **price/earnings ratio**) ratio *m* cours-bénéfice

perceive [pə'siːv] VT **1** *(notice) (sound, light, smell)* percevoir; *(person)* apercevoir; *(difference)* percevoir, distinguer; *(become aware of)* s'apercevoir de; **he perceived that he was being watched** il s'aperçut qu'on l'observait **2** *(understand) (the truth etc)* percevoir **3** *Mktg (product, brand)* percevoir

perceived [pə'siːvd] ADJ
▸▸*Mktg* **p. performance** résultats *mpl* perçus; *Mktg* **p. quality** qualité *f* perçue; **p. risk** risque *m* perçu; *Mktg* **p. service** service *m* perçu; *Mktg* **p. value** valeur *f* perçue; *Mktg* **p. value pricing** tarification *f* en fonction de la valeur perçue

percent [pə'sent] N pourcentage *m*; **10 p.** 10 pour cent; **what p. of people ...?** combien de personnes ...?; *(speaking statistically)* quel pourcentage de personnes ...?; **50 p. of the staff** la moitié du personnel; *(speaking statistically)* 50 pour cent du personnel
ADJ **a 5 p. increase** une augmentation de 5 pour cent; **thirty p. solution** solution à trente pour cent
ADV **a hundred p. efficient** cent pour cent efficace; **I'm ninety p. sure** je suis sûr à quatre-vingt dix pour cent
▸▸**p. sign** signe *m* pour cent

percentage [pə'sentɪdʒ] N **1** *(proportion)* pourcentage *m*; **p. of acid/alcohol** teneur *f*

en acide/en alcool; **to express sth as a p.** exprimer qch en pourcentage; **what p. of tenants own a car?** combien de locataires ont une voiture?; *(speaking statistically)* quelle est la proportion de locataires qui ont une voiture?; **in a high/tiny p. of cases** dans une vaste/petite proportion des cas **2** *Com* pourcentage *m*; **to allow a p. on all transactions** allouer un pourcentage *ou* un tantième sur toutes les opérations; *Fam* **what's my p.?** quel pourcentage est-ce que je touche?; *Fig Fam* **there's no p. in it** il n'y a rien à gagner

percentile [pə'sentaɪl] N centile *m*

perceptibility [pəseptɪ'bɪlɪtɪ] N perceptibilité *f*

perceptible [pə'septɪb(ə)l] ADJ perceptible; *Phil* cognoscible; *(difference)* sensible; **p. to the eye** visible; **p. to the ear** perceptible à l'oreille, audible

perceptibly [pə'septɪblɪ] ADV sensiblement

perception [pə'sepʃən] N **1** *(act of perceiving)* perception *f*; **organs of p.** organes *mpl* percepteurs **2** *(ability to perceive)* sensibilité *f*, **powers of p.** facultés *fpl* perceptives **3** *(understanding)* perception *f*; **the public's p. of the government's role** la façon dont l'opinion publique perçoit le rôle de l'État; **to have different perceptions of a situation** percevoir une situation différemment

perceptive [pə'septɪv] ADJ **1** *(perspicacious) (person, remark)* perspicace; *(analysis, article)* qui témoigne de clairvoyance **2** *(able to perceive)* perceptif; **p. faculties** facultés *mpl* perceptives

perceptively [pə'septɪvlɪ] ADV *(to write, comment)* avec perspicacité

perceptiveness [pə'septɪvnɪs] N *(perspicacity)* perspicacité *f*

perceptoscope [pə'septəskəʊp] N *Mktg Old-fashioned* perceptoscope *m*

perceptual [pə'septjʊəl] ADJ **1** *(organ)* percepteur **2** *Mktg* perceptuel
▸▸*Mktg* **p. map** carte *f* perceptuelle

perch¹ [pɜːtʃ] N **1** *(for bird)* perchoir *m*; *Fam* **to knock sb off his/her p.** *(depose)* détrôner qn; *(force to abandon pretensions)* rabattre son caquet à qn **2** *Arch (measurement)* perche *f*
VI *(of bird)* se percher *(*on *sur)*; *(of person)* se percher, se jucher; *Orn* **perching bird** oiseau *m* percheur
VTA **castle perched on a hill** un château perché sur (le sommet d')une colline; **with his glasses perched on the end of his nose** avec ses lunettes perchées sur le bout du nez; **to p. oneself on sth** se percher *ou* se jucher sur qch

perch² N *(fish)* perche *f*

perchance [pə'tʃɑːns] ADV *Arch, Lit (perhaps)* peut-être

percipient [pə'sɪpɪənt] ADJ *Fml (faculty)* percepteur, -trice; *(person)* perspicace

percolate ['pɜːkəleɪt] VI *(of liquid)* s'infiltrer; *(of coffee etc)* filtrer, passer; *Fig (of information, news)* filtrer
VT *(of liquid) (sand etc)* filtrer à travers, s'infiltrer dans; *(of person, with filter etc) (liquid)* filtrer; *(coffee)* passer

percolator ['pɜːkəleɪtər] N cafetière *f* à pression; *(for large quantities)* percolateur *m*

percussion [pə'kʌʃən] N **1** *Mus (section)* percussions *fpl* **2** *(in firearm)* percussion *f*
▸▸**p. drill** perceuse *f* à percussion; **p. gun** fusil *m* à percussion; *Mus* **p. instruments** instruments *mpl* de *ou* à percussion; *Mil* **p. pin** rugueux *m* (de fusée); *Mus* **p. player** percussionniste *mf*; *Mus* **p. section** percussions

percussionist [pə'kʌʃənɪst] N percussionniste *mf*

percussive [pə'kʌsɪv] ADJ percutant

perdition [pə'dɪʃən] N *Lit* perte *f*, ruine *f*, *Rel* perdition *f*

peregrination [perɪgrɪ'neɪʃən] N *Lit* pérégrination *f*

peregrine falcon ['perɪgrɪn] N faucon *m* pèlerin

peremptorily [pə'remptərɪlɪ] ADV *(to order etc)* péremptoirement, de façon péremptoire

peremptory [pə'remptərɪ] ADJ péremptoire; *(refusal)* absolu, sans appel; *(tone, person)* péremptoire, impérieux
▸▸*Br Law* **p. writ** assignation *f* à comparaître en personne

perennial [pə'renɪəl] ADJ *(problems, worries)* continuel, perpétuel; *(beauty, hope)* perpétuel, éternel; *(interest)* continuel; *(plant)* vivace
N plante *f* vivace

perennially [pə'renɪəlɪ] ADV *(worried, dissatisfied etc)* continuellement, perpétuellement; *(beautiful)* éternellement

perestroika [perə'strɔɪkə] N perestroïka *f*

perfect¹ ['pɜːfɪkt] ADJ **1** parfait; **a p. example of ...** un parfait exemple de ...; **a p. piece of work** un travail impeccable *ou* parfait; **her behaviour was far from p.** son comportement a beaucoup laissé à désirer; **to be in p. condition** *(of thing)* être impeccable; *(of person)* être en excellente forme; **her English is p.** son anglais est impeccable *ou* parfait; **no one's p.** personne n'est parfait; **p.!** parfait!; **the p. gift** le cadeau idéal; **the p. opportunity** l'occasion idéale *ou* rêvée; **a wine that is the p. accompaniment for fish** un vin qui accompagne parfaitement le poisson; **it was a p. day** *(weather)* il faisait un temps magnifique; *(activities)* nous avons passé une excellente journée
2 *(complete)* **he's a p. stranger to me** il m'est tout à fait inconnu; **I have a p. right to be here** j'ai parfaitement le droit d'être ici; **it makes p. sense (to me)** cela me semble être une excellente idée; *Fam* **he's a p. idiot** c'est un parfait imbécile; **he's being a p. nuisance** il est carrément empoisonnant
3 *Math (number, square)* parfait; *Mus (interval)* juste; *(chord)* parfait; **to have p. pitch** avoir l'oreille absolue
N *Gram* le passé composé, le parfait; **a verb in the p.** un verbe au passé composé *ou* au parfait VOIR GRAMMAIRE A50; B30
▸▸**p. binding** *(in bookbinding)* reliure *f* sans couture; *Mus* **p. cadence** cadence *f* parfaite; *Gram* **p. tense** le passé composé, le parfait

perfect² [pə'fekt] VT *(make perfect) (method)* perfectionner, parfaire; *(invention, design)* mettre au point

perfectibility [pəfektɪ'bɪlɪtɪ] N perfectibilité *f*

perfectible [pə'fektɪb(ə)l] ADJ perfectible

perfection [pə'fekʃən] N **1** *(state)* perfection *f*; **it was sheer p.** c'était absolument parfait; **p. itself** la perfection même; **to attain p.** toucher *ou* arriver à la perfection; **to do sth to p.** faire qch à la perfection **2** *(action) (of job etc)* perfectionnement *m*

perfectionism [pə'fekʃənɪz(ə)m] N perfectionnisme *m*

perfectionist [pə'fekʃənɪst] N perfectionniste *mf*; **she's such a p.** elle est tellement perfectionniste
ADJ perfectionniste

perfective [pə'fektɪv] *Gram* ADJ perfectif
N aspect *m* perfectif

perfectly ['pɜːfɪktlɪ] ADV *(symmetrical, flat, harmless)* parfaitement; *(idiotic, meaningless, useless)* complètement; *(to know sth)* à fond; *(to do sth)* à la perfection; **she's p. right**

elle a parfaitement raison; **to be p. honest/ frank with you** pour être tout à fait honnête/ franc avec vous; **I'm p. capable of doing it** je suis tout à fait *ou* parfaitement capable de le faire; **you know p. well** *(what I mean)* tu le sais parfaitement bien *ou* très bien; **it would be p. pointless** cela ne servirait à rien du tout

perfecto [pəˈfektəʊ] N *Am (cigar)* = cigare *m* effilé aux deux bouts

perfidious [pəˈfɪdɪəs] ADJ *Lit* perfide
▶▶ **p. Albion** la perfide Albion

perfidiously [pəˈfɪdɪəslɪ] ADV *Lit* perfidement

perfidiousness [pəˈfɪdɪəsnɪs], **perfidy** [ˈpɜːfɪdɪ] N *Lit* perfidie *f*

perforate [ˈpɜːfəreɪt] VT *(pierce)* perforer, percer, transpercer; *(metal sheet, ticket)* poinçonner; *Tech (paper) (with line of holes)* perforer en pointillé
VI *Med (of ulcer)* déterminer une perforation

perforated [ˈpɜːfəreɪtɪd] ADJ perforé; *(stamps)* dentelé; *Med (eardrum)* crevé; **tear along the p. line** détachez suivant le(s) pointillé(s)
▶▶ *Comput* **p. paper** papier *m* à bandes perforées; *Comput* **p. tape** bande *f* perforée; *Med* **p. ulcer** perforation *f* ulcéreuse

perforation [pɜːfəˈreɪʃən] N **1** *(action)* perforage *m*, perçage *m*; *(of stamps)* perforage **2** *(hole)* perforation *f*, *(petit)* trou *m*; *Med* perforation; *(for counterfoils etc)* (perforation(s) en) pointillé *m*; *(of postage stamp)* dentelure *f*, **tear along the perforations** déchirer selon le(s) pointillé(s)
▶▶ *Philat* **p. gauge** adontomètre *m*; *Comput* **p. skip** saut *m* de perforation

perforce [pəˈfɔːs] ADV *Lit* forcément

perform [pəˈfɔːm] VT **1** *(ritual)* célébrer; *(miracle)* faire; *(one's duty)* remplir; *(actions)* effectuer, réaliser; *(task)* accomplir; **to p. a contract** exécuter un contrat; *Surg* **to p. an operation on sb** opérer qn **2** *Theat etc (play)* jouer, représenter; *(dance)* exécuter; *(piece of music)* exécuter, jouer; *Fig (rôle)* tenir, remplir
VI **1** *(of machine)* marcher, fonctionner; **it performs well in all conditions** *(of vehicle, machine etc)* elle donne de bonnes performances en toutes conditions; **to p. well/ badly** *(of student etc)* avoir de bons/mauvais résultats; **how are your shares performing?** comment vos actions se tiennent-elle?; **the Miami branch is not performing well** les résultats de la succursale de Miami ne sont pas très satisfaisants; **how did the company p. in the first quarter?** comment la société a-t-elle fonctionné au premier trimestre?; **how does he p. in bed?** comment est-il au lit?; **I couldn't p.** *(sexually)* je n'ai pas pu **2** *Theat etc (of theatre company)* donner une/des représentation(s), jouer; *(of actor, instrumentalist, orchestra)* jouer; *(of singer)* chanter; *(of dancer)* danser; *(of mime artist etc)* exécuter un/des numéro(s); **to p. in a play** tenir un rôle *ou* jouer dans une pièce; **he performed well in the role of Claudius** il a bien joué *ou* interprété le rôle de Claudius; **to p. on the flute** jouer de la flûte

performance [pəˈfɔːməns] N **1** *(action) (of contract)* exécution *f*, *(of task, duty)* accomplissement *m*; *(of rite)* célébration *f*
2 *(quality, ability)*, *Sport etc* performance *f*, *(of actor)* interprétation *f*, *(of musician)* exécution *f*, interprétation; *(of dancer)* exécution; *(of pupil, economy, exports)* résultats *mpl*, performances; *(in bed)* performance sexuelle; *(of employee, plane, engine, piece of equipment)* rendement *m*, performance; *(of shares)* rendement; *(at work)* productivité *f*, *Ind* cadence *f* (de travail); *Tech (of machine)* fonctionnement *m*, marche *f*, *(of*

material) comportement *m*, tenue *f*, **to put up a good p.** *(of team etc)* accomplir une bonne performance; *(in exam, interview, court case)* bien s'en tirer; **a good/poor p. in exams** de bons/mauvais résultats à des examens; *Theat, Mus* **she gave a superb p.** son interprétation était fantastique
3 *(event)*, *Theat etc (of play etc)* représentation *f*, *(at cinema)* séance *f*, **first p.** première *f*, **there is no p. tonight** il y a relâche ce soir; *Fig* **he made such a p. about having to wash his hair** il a fait toute une histoire parce qu'il devait se laver les cheveux; *Fig* **what a p.!** quel spectacle!; *Fig* **it's such a p. cooking Christmas dinner!** c'est toute une histoire de préparer un dîner de Noël!
▶▶ **p. appraisal** *(system)* système *m* d'évaluation; *(individual)* évaluation *f*, **p. art** performance, action *f*, **p. artist** = artiste *mf* spécialisé(e) dans la performance; **p. bonus** prime *f* de rendement *ou* de performance; *Aut* **p. car** voiture *f* puissante, voiture haute performance; **p. indicator** indice *m* de performance; *Fin* **p. ratio** coefficient *m* *ou* ratio *m* d'exploitation; **p. statistics** statistiques *fpl* de performance

> Note that the French word **performance** never means *show*.

performance-enhancing [-enˈhɑːnsɪŋ] ADJ *(drug)* qui améliore les performances

performance-related ADJ *(pay)* au rendement

performative [pəˈfɔːmətɪv] ADJ, N *Ling* performatif *m*

performer [pəˈfɔːmər] N *Mus* exécutant, -ante, artiste *mf*, interprète *mf*; *Theat* acteur, -trice, artiste *mf*; **he has been a consistent p.** *(in sport)* il a toujours été régulier; **an accomplished p. on the flute** un joueur de flûte accompli; **a good/bad p.** *(student)* un bon/ mauvais élève; *(car)* une voiture performante/peu performante

performing [pəˈfɔːmɪŋ] ADJ *(dog, seal)* savant
N *(of symphony etc)* exécution *f*, interprétation *f*
▶▶ **p. arts** arts *mpl* du spectacle; **p. rights** *Theat* droits *mpl* de représentation; *Mus* droits d'exécution

perfume¹ [ˈpɜːfjuːm, *Am* pəˈfjuːm] N parfum *m*
▶▶ **p. counter** *(in shop)* rayon *m* parfumerie

perfume² [pəˈfjuːm] VT parfumer; **to p. the air** embaumer l'air

perfumed [ˈpɜːfjuːmd] ADJ *(soap etc)* parfumé

perfumery [pəˈfjuːmərɪ] N parfumerie *f*

perfunctorily [pəˈfʌŋktrɪlɪ] ADV *(to examine)* superficiellement; *(to order, instruct)* sommairement; *(to read)* mécaniquement; *(to greet sb)* négligemment

perfunctory [pəˈfʌŋkt(ə)rɪ] ADJ *(examination, glance)* rapide; *(smile)* mécanique; *(letter, style, instructions)* sommaire; **it was just a p. enquiry** il/elle/*etc* m'a juste demandé pour la forme; **her p. manner** ses manières négligentes; **he greeted me with a p. nod** il m'a salué de façon automatique d'un petit signe de la tête

pergola [ˈpɜːgələ] N pergola *f*

perhaps [pəˈhæps, præps] ADV peut-être; **p. (so)/not** peut-être (bien) que oui/que non; **p. he's forgotten** peut-être qu'il a oublié; **p. we shall come back tomorrow** peut-être reviendrons-nous demain; **p. you would like to try it on** voulez-vous l'essayer?

perigee [ˈperɪdʒiː] N *Astron* périgée *m*

perihelion [perɪˈhiːlɪən] N *Astron* périhélie *m*

peril [ˈperɪl] N péril *m*, danger *m*; **in p.** en danger, en péril; **in p. of one's life** en danger de mort; **to do sth at one's (own) p.** faire qch à ses risques et périls; **peril(s) of the sea** *(in marine insurance)* fortune(s) *f(pl)* de mer

perilous [ˈperɪləs] ADJ périlleux, dangereux

perilously [ˈperɪləslɪ] ADV dangereusement; **p. close to the edge of the cliff** dangereusement proche du bord de la falaise; **he came p. close to getting himself sacked** il a bien failli se faire mettre à la porte

perimeter [pəˈrɪmɪtər] N périmètre *m*
▶▶ *Mktg* **p. advertising** publicité *f* périphérique; **p. alarm** alarme *f* périmétrique; *Mktg* **p. board** panneau *m* publicitaire *(autour d'un terrain de sport)*; **p. fence** grillage *m*

perinatal [perɪˈneɪt(ə)l] ADJ *Med (treatment, care, death)* périnatal, -als *ou* -aux

perineum [perɪˈniːəm] N *Anat* périnée *m*

period [ˈpɪərɪəd] N **1** période *f*, *(stage)* moment *m*, époque *f*, stade *m*; *Astron* cycle *m*, période; *Phys* période; **for a p. of three months** pendant une période de trois mois; **during** *or* **for the p. of their stay here** pendant (la durée de) leur séjour ici; **a long p. of illness** de longs ennuis de santé; **p. of notice** délai-congé *m*, *pl* délais-congés; **within the agreed p.** dans les délais convenus; *Banking* **deposit for a fixed p.** dépôt *m* à terme fixe; *Met* **clear periods** éclaircis *fpl*, **sunny periods** intervalles *mpl* ensoleillés
2 *Sch* heure *f* de cours; **a French/maths p.** un cours de français/maths; **a free p.** une heure de libre
3 *(menstruation)* **(monthly) period(s)** règles *fpl*, **I've got my p.** j'ai mes règles; **when you have your first p.** la première fois que tu auras tes règles
4 *(age)* époque *f*, *(era)* ère *f*, **p. play/novel/ drama** comédie *f*/roman *m*/drame *m* historique
5 *esp Am Gram, Typ (full stop)* point *m*; *Am Fam* **he's no good at math! – he's no good, p.!** il est nul en math! – il est nul tout court!; *Am Fam* **you're not going to the party, p.!** tu n'iras pas à cette soirée, un point c'est tout!
6 *Liter (sentence)* phrase *f*, *Mus* phrase complète
▶▶ *Fin* **p. bill** effet *m* à terme; **p. costume** toilette *f* d'époque; **p. detail** détail *m* historique; **p. dress** *(costume)* costume(s) *m(pl)* de l'époque; *(woman's garment)* robe *f* de style; **p. furniture** meubles *mpl* de style *ou* d'époque; *Fin* **p. of grace** délai *m* de grâce; *Banking* **p. money** dépôts à terme; **p. pains** règles douloureuses; **p. piece** *(object, antique)* objet *m* d'époque; *(film)* film *m* historique; *(play)* pièce *f* historique

periodic [pɪərɪˈɒdɪk] ADJ périodique
▶▶ *Fin* **p. inventory** inventaire *m* périodique; *Chem* **p. table** classification *f* périodique (des éléments), tableau *m* de Mendeleïev

periodical [pɪərɪˈɒdɪk(ə)l] ADJ périodique
N *(publication f)* périodique *m*; **the p. room** la salle des périodiques

periodically [pɪərɪˈɒdɪklɪ] ADV périodiquement

periodontal [perɪəˈdɒnt(ə)l] ADJ parodontal, -aux

peripatetic [perɪpəˈtetɪk] ADJ ambulant, itinérant; *(teacher)* en poste sur plusieurs établissements

peripheral [pəˈrɪfərəl] ADJ **1** *(area, vision etc)* périphérique; **of purely p. importance** d'une importance purement accessoire; **this issue is p. to the central debate** ce problème est accessoire au débat principal **2** *Comput* périphérique
N *Comput* périphérique *m*
▶▶ *Comput* **p. device** unité *f* périphérique;

Comput **p. equipment** matériel *m* périphérique, périphériques; *Comput* **p. interchange program** logiciel *m* de commutation de périphérique; *Comput* **p. unit** unité périphérique

periphery ['pə'rɪfərɪ] N périphérie *f*; **on the p. of one's vision** à la périphérie de son champ de vision; **on the p. of the crowd** en bordure de la foule; **on the p. of society** en marge de la société

periphrasis, *pl* **periphrases** [pə'rɪfrəsɪs, -iːz] N *Liter* périphrase *f*

periphrastic [perɪ'fræstɪk] ADJ *Liter* périphrastique

periscope ['perɪskəʊp] N périscope *m*
  ▶▶ *TV, Cin* **p. shot** plan *m* en contre-plongée

perish ['perɪʃ] VI **1** *(of person)* périr; *Fam* **p. the thought!** loin de moi cette pensée!; **if, p. the thought, you should die …** si, Dieu nous en préserve, vous deviez mourir … **2** *(of rubber, leather)* se détériorer; *(of fresh food)* s'avarier
  VT *(rubber, leather)* détériorer; *(fresh food)* avarier

perishability [perɪʃə'bɪlɪtɪ] N *Com* périssabilité *f*

perishable ['perɪʃəb(ə)l] ADJ périssable
  NPL **perishables** denrées *fpl* périssables

perished ['perɪʃt] ADJ détérioré, usé; *Fam* **I'm p.** *(very cold)* je meurs de froid

perisher ['perɪʃər] N *Br Sl (pest)* saligaud *m*; **little p.** petit coquin *m*

perishing ['perɪʃɪŋ] ADJ **1** *Fam (very cold)* très froid; **it's p.** il fait un froid de canard; **I'm p.** je meurs de froid **2** *Br Sl (intensifier)* sacré; *(car, machine)* satané; **p. idiot** sacré idiot; **it's a p. nuisance** c'est sacrément ennuyeux

peristalsis [perɪ'stælsɪs] N péristaltisme *m*

peristyle ['perɪstaɪl] N *Archit* péristyle *m*

peritoneum [perɪtə'niːəm] N *Anat* péritoine *m*

peritonitis [perɪtə'naɪtɪs] N *Med* péritonite *f*; **to have p.** avoir une péritonite

periwig ['perɪwɪg] N *Hist* perruque *f*

periwinkle[1] ['perɪwɪŋk(ə)l] N *(plant)* (petite) pervenche *f*, *(colour)* bleu pervenche *m inv*
  ▶▶ **p. blue** bleu pervenche

periwinkle[2] N *(mollusc)* bigorneau *m*

perjure ['pɜːdʒər] VT *Law* **to p. oneself** faire un faux témoignage

perjurer ['pɜːdʒərər] N *Law* faux témoin *m*

perjury ['pɜːdʒərɪ] N *Law* faux témoignage *m*; **to commit p.** faire un faux témoignage; **the penalty for p.** la peine encourue quand on fait un faux témoignage

perk[1] [pɜːk] N *Br Fam* à-côté *m*, *pl* à-côtés, avantage *m*; **perks include …** les avantages acquis comprennent …; **free tickets are one of the perks of the job** un des avantages de ce travail est que l'on peut obtenir des billets gratuits; **clean air is a p. of working in the country** l'air pur est un des avantages du travail à la campagne

perk[2] *Fam* VI *(of coffee)* passer
  VT *(coffee)* faire
  ▶ **perk up** VI *(become more cheerful, after illness)* se requinquer; *(of party)* s'animer; **I don't know what to do to make him p. up** je ne sais pas quoi faire pour lui remonter le moral
    VT SEP **1** *(revive) (person)* requinquer, ragaillardir; *(cheer up)* remonter le moral à; **the coffee perked her up** le café l'a requinquée *ou* ravigotée **2** *(raise)* **to p. up its ears** *(of dog)* dresser les oreilles

perkily ['pɜːkɪlɪ] ADV d'un air animé; *(to answer, say)* d'un ton dégagé *ou* désinvolte

perky ['pɜːkɪ] ADJ *(lively)* plein d'entrain, animé; *(cheerful)* guilleret; *(tone)* dégagé, désinvolte; *(remark)* désinvolte

perm[1] [pɜːm] N *(in hair)* permanente *f*, **to have a p.** se faire faire une permanente
  VT **to p. sb's hair** faire faire une permanente à qn; **to have one's hair permed** se faire faire une permanente

perm[2] N *Br (in football pools)* permutation *f*

permafrost ['pɜːməfrɒst] N *Geol* permafrost *m*

permanence ['pɜːmənəns] N permanence *f*

permanency ['pɜːmənənsɪ] N permanence *f*

permanent ['pɜːmənənt] ADJ permanent; *(residence, address)* fixe; *(ink, stain)* indélébile; **p. hearing loss** perte *f* définitive de l'ouïe; **she was in a p. state of depression** elle était continuellement déprimée
  N *(in hair)* permanente *f*
  ▶▶ *Fin* **p. credit** accréditif *m* permanent; *Ins* **p. health insurance** assurance *f* longue maladie; *Com* **p. inventory** stock *m* de sécurité, stock stratégique, inventaire *m* permanent; **p. press** *(for clothes)* plissé *m* permanent; *Pol* **p. representation** représentation *f* permanente; *Pol* **p. representative** représentant, -ante permanent(e); **p. site** *(caravan site)* terrain *m* de caravaning permanent; **p. wave** permanente *f*; *Br* **p. way** voie *f* ferrée

permanganate [pə'mæŋgəneɪt] N *Chem* permanganate *m*

permeability [pɜːmɪə'bɪlɪtɪ] N perméabilité *f*

permeable ['pɜːmɪəb(ə)l] ADJ perméable

permeate ['pɜːmɪeɪt] VT **1** *(penetrate)* filtrer *ou* passer à travers; **the soil was permeated with water** le sol était saturé d'eau; **a smell of flowers permeated the room** des fleurs embaumaient la pièce; **his clothes were permeated by a smell of napthalene** ses vêtements étaient imprégnés d'une odeur de naphtaline; **the house was permeated by damp** la maison était imprégnée d'humidité **2** *Fig (of feeling, idea etc)* imprégner; **this attitude permeated 18th-century thought** la pensée du 18e siècle a été imprégnée par cette attitude; **the country was permeated with fear** le pays était plongé dans la peur; **doubt had permeated the organization** le doute s'était infiltré dans l'organisation
  VI passer; **to p. through sth** filtrer *ou* passer à travers qch; **water permeates everywhere** l'eau s'infiltre partout

Permian ['pɜːmɪən] ADJ *Geol* permien

permissible [pə'mɪsɪb(ə)l] ADJ admissible, acceptable

permission [pə'mɪʃən] N permission *f*, autorisation *f*; **to ask/give/refuse sb p. to do sth** demander/donner/refuser à qn la permission *ou* l'autorisation de faire qch; **with your p.** avec votre permission *ou* autorisation; **you have my p.** je te donne la permission, je t'y autorise; **published by kind p. of …** publié avec l'aimable autorisation de …; *St Exch* **p. to deal** visa *m* *(de la COB)* VOIR GRAMMAIRE A58–9; B39–40

permissive [pə'mɪsɪv] ADJ *(tolerant)* permissif
  ▶▶ **p. society** société *f* permissive

permissively [pə'mɪsɪvlɪ] ADV de manière permissive

permissiveness [pə'mɪsɪvnɪs] N permissivité *f*

permit[1] ['pɜːmɪt] N permis *m*; *(allowing entry)* laissez-passer *m inv*; *(at Customs)* acquit-à-caution *m*, *pl* acquits-à-caution, passavant *m*; **export p.** autorisation *f* d'exporter; **work p.** permis de travail; **p. holders only** *(on sign)* réservé aux personnes autorisées

permit[2] [pə'mɪt] (-tt-) VT permettre; **to p. sb to do sth** permettre à qn de faire qch, autoriser qn à faire qch; **larger telescopes p. us to …** des télescopes plus performants nous permettent de …; **if I may be permitted** si vous me le permettez; **p. me to tell you …!** *(angrily)* laissez-moi vous dire que …!; *Br Admin* **permitted hours** *(for selling alcohol)* = heures *fpl* légales de vente des boissons alcoolisées
  VI **if time permits** si j'ai/nous avons/*etc* le temps; **weather permitting** si le temps le permet
  ▶ **permit of** VT INSEP *Fml (admit possibility of)* admettre; **this permits of only one explanation** ceci n'admet qu'une explication

permutation [pɜːmjʊ'teɪʃən] N permutation *f*

permute [pə'mjuːt] VT *Ling, Math* permuter

pernicious [pə'nɪʃəs] ADJ pernicieux
  ▶▶ *Med* **p. anaemia** anémie *f* pernicieuse

perniciously [pə'nɪʃəslɪ] ADV pernicieusement

pernickety [pə'nɪkɪtɪ] ADJ *Fam (person)* tatillon, pointilleux; *(job)* délicat, minutieux; **to be p. about one's food** être difficile sur la nourriture; **soufflé can be rather a p. thing to make** le soufflé est un plat assez délicat à préparer

perorate ['perəreɪt] VI *Fml* **1** *(conclude speech)* faire la péroraison **2** *(speak at length)* discourir longuement

peroration [perə'reɪʃən] N *Fml* **1** *(conclusion)* péroraison *f* **2** *(long speech)* long discours *m*, discours de longue haleine

peroxide [pə'rɒksaɪd] N *Chem* peroxyde *m*
  VT *(hair)* (faire) blondir à l'eau oxygénée
  ▶▶ *Pej* **p. blonde** *(woman)* blonde *f* décolorée

perp [pɜːp] N *Am Sl (perpetrator)* auteur *m*

perpendicular [pɜːpən'dɪkjʊlər] ADJ perpendiculaire (**to** à); *(wall etc)* vertical, -aux; *(upright, straight)* à plomb; *(cliff)* à pic; **line p. to another** ligne perpendiculaire à une autre
  N **1** *(plumb line)* fil *m* à plomb; **out of (the) p.** hors d'aplomb, hors d'équerre **2** *Geom* perpendiculaire *f*
  ▶▶ *Archit* **p. style** style *m* (gothique) perpendiculaire

perpendicularly [pɜːpən'dɪkjʊlərlɪ] ADV perpendiculairement; *(to rise, fall, drop)* verticalement, à la verticale; *(to be built)* d'aplomb; **the cliff rose p.** la falaise s'élevait tout droit

perpetrate ['pɜːpɪtreɪt] VT *(crime)* commettre, perpétrer; *(fraud, error)* commettre

perpetration [pɜːpɪ'treɪʃən] N *(of crime)* perpétration *f*, *(of fraud, deception)* accomplissement *m*

perpetrator ['pɜːpɪtreɪtər] N *(of crime)* auteur *m*; **the p.** l'auteur du délit

perpetual [pə'petjʊəl] ADJ *(eternal)* perpétuel, éternel; *(incessant)* sans fin, continuel, incessant
  ▶▶ *Chess* **p. check** échec *m* perpétuel; *Fin* **p. inventory** stock *m* stratégique; *Fin* **p. loan** emprunt *m* perpétuel; **p. motion** mouvement *m* perpétuel; **p. snow** neiges *fpl* éternelles

perpetually [pə'petjʊəlɪ] ADV *(eternally)* perpétuellement, éternellement; *(ceaselessly)* sans cesse; *(continually)* continuellement, perpétuellement

perpetuate [pə'petjʊeɪt] VT perpétuer; **to p. the species** perpétuer l'espèce

perpetuation [pəpetjʊ'eɪʃən] N perpétuation *f*

perpetuity [pɜːpɪ'tjuːɪtɪ] N **1** perpétuité *f*, **in** *or* **for p.** à perpétuité **2** *Law (of property)* jouissance *f* à perpétuité; **(annuity in) p.** rente *f* perpétuelle

perplex [pə'pleks] **VT** laisser *ou* rendre perplexe; **she was perplexed by his lack of enthusiasm** son manque d'enthousiasme la laissait *ou* rendait perplexe

perplexed [pə'plekst] **ADJ** perplexe

perplexing [pə'pleksɪŋ] **ADJ** *(problem etc)* troublant; *(book, play etc)* difficile (à comprendre); *(person)* déconcertant; **it's very p.** on n'y comprend rien; **I find his attitude most p.** son attitude me laisse totalement perplexe

perplexity [pə'pleksɪtɪ] **N** perplexité *f*

perquisite ['pɜːkwɪzɪt] **N** *Br Fml* = **perk**[1]

perry ['perɪ] **N** *(drink)* poiré *m*

persecute ['pɜːsɪkjuːt] **VT** persécuter; **to be persecuted in the press** faire l'objet d'attaques répétées dans la presse

persecution [pɜːsɪ'kjuːʃən] **N** persécution *f*; *Psy* **p. complex** *or* **mania** complexe *m* de persécution

persecutor ['pɜːsɪkjuːtər] **N** persécuteur, -trice

perseverance [pɜːsɪ'vɪərəns] **N** persévérance *f*

persevere [pɜːsɪ'vɪər] **VI** persévérer (**with** *or* **in** dans qch; **with sb** avec qn); **to p. in one's belief that …** persister à croire que …; **to p. in doing sth** persister à faire qch

persevering [pɜːsɪ'vɪərɪŋ] **ADJ** persévérant; **thanks to our p. staff** grâce à la persévérance de notre personnel

Persia ['pɜːʃə] **N** Perse *f*

Persian ['pɜːʃən] **ADJ** persan; *Antiq* perse; *(cat, horse)* persan; *(carpet)* de Perse ▪ **N 1** *(person)* Persan, -ane; *Antiq* Perse *mf* **2** *(cat)* chat *m* persan **3** *Ling* perse *m*

Persian Gulf (the) **N** le Golfe persique

persimmon [pɜː'sɪmən] **N 1** *(fruit)* plaquemine *f*, *(from Japan)* kaki *m* **2** *(tree)* plaqueminier *m*

▸▸ **p. tree** plaqueminier *m*

persist [pə'sɪst] **VI 1** persister, s'obstiner (**in doing sth** à faire qch); **to p. in one's opinion** persister *ou* s'obstiner dans son opinion; **to p. in one's belief that …** persister à croire que … **2** *(of fog, fever etc)* persister, continuer; *(of belief)* persister

persistence [pə'sɪstəns] **N 1** persistance *f*, ténacité *f*, obstination *f* (**in doing sth** à faire qch) **2** *(of fog, fever, belief etc)* persistance *f*

persistent [pə'sɪstənt] **ADJ** *(person)* persistant, opiniâtre, tenace; *(doubts, problems, pain etc)* continuel, incessant; *(rumours)* persistant; *(rain)* continuel, qui s'obstine; **to be in p. pain** souffrir continuellement; **to have a p. belief in sth** persister à croire à qch; *Com* **p. demand for …** demande suivie *ou* soutenue pour …

▸▸ **p. offender** récidiviste *mf*; *Med* **p. vegetative state** état *m* végétatif chronique

persistently [pə'sɪstəntlɪ] **ADV** avec persistance; *(to fail, refuse, warn)* à plusieurs reprises; *(to be late, short of funds)* continuellement; **she p. offended** elle récidivait sans cesse

persnickety [pə'snɪkɪtɪ] **ADJ** *Am Fam* = **pernickety**

person ['pɜːs(ə)n] **N 1** personne *f*, *Pej* individu *m*, type *m*; **what's he/she like as a p.?** il/ elle est comment sur le plan personnel?; **I like her as a p.** je l'aime bien en tant que personne; **he/she is a kind/strange p.** c'est une personne gentille/étrange, c'est quelqu'un de gentil/d'étrange; **a coffee/football p.** un amateur de café/de foot; **are you a cat p. or a dog p.?** est-ce que tu préfères les chats ou chiens?; **there is no p. of that name here** il n'y a personne de ce nom ici; *Law* **some p. or**

persons unknown un certain quidam; **in p.** en propre, en personne; **he came in p.** il est venu en personne; **to deliver sth in p.** remettre qch en main(s) propre(s); **help came, in the p. of Amanda** on a trouvé de l'aide, en la personne d'Amanda; **to carry weapons on one's p.** porter des armes sur soi; **to be one's own p.** vivre à sa façon *ou* à son idée; *Tel* **p. to p. call** appel *m* avec préavis *ou* de personne à personne

2 *Gram* verb in the first **p.** verbe *m* à la première personne; **the second p. plural** la deuxième personne du pluriel; **the story is told in the first p.** l'histoire est racontée à la première personne

3 *Rel* **(one) God in three Persons** la Trinité

persona [pə'səʊnə] **N** *also Psy* personnage *m*; **p. grata/non grata** persona grata/non grata; *Fig* **you'll be p. non grata unless you bring a present** tu ne seras pas bien vu si tu n'apportes pas de cadeau; **to be p. non grata with sb** ne pas être dans les petits papiers de qn

personable ['pɜːsənəb(ə)l] **ADJ** bien (fait) de sa personne; **he's a very p. young man** c'est un jeune homme qui présente très bien

personage ['pɜːsənɪdʒ] **N** personnage *m*

personal ['pɜːsən(ə)l] **ADJ** personnel; **to be careless about one's p. appearance** négliger sa tenue; **to make a p. appearance** venir *ou* paraître en personne; **for p. reasons** pour des raisons personnelles; **don't be p., don't make p. remarks** ne faites pas d'allusions personnelles; **it's nothing p. but … ça** n'a rien de personnel mais …; **to do sb a p. favour** rendre un service à qn à titre personnel; **it's a p. matter** c'est une affaire privée *ou* personnelle; **my p. opinion** *or* **view is that …** à mon avis …; **this is not my p. opinion** ce n'est pas mon opinion personnelle; **to give a p. touch to sth** donner une touche personnelle à qch; **I want it for my p. use** j'en ai besoin pour mon usage personnel; **articles for p. use** *(at customs)* objets à usage personnel

▸▸ **p. accident insurance** assurance *f* contre les accidents corporels; **have you got any p. accident insurance?** est-ce que vous avez une assurance contre les accidents?; **p. account** *Banking* compte *m* personnel; *St Exch* compte de tiers; *Acct* compte propre; *Law* **p. action** *(relating to property)* action *f* mobilière; *Fam* **p. ad** petite annonce *f* *(pour rencontres)*; *Banking* **p. assets** patrimoine *m*; *Banking* **p. assets profile** profil *m* patrimonial; **p. assistant** *(of executive)* assistant, -ante; *(with secretarial duties)* secrétaire *mf* de direction; *Sport* **p. best** record *m* personnel; **3 mins 22 secs is my p. best** mon record *(personnel)* est 3 min 22; **p. column** petites annonces *(pour rencontres)*; **p. computer** ordinateur *m* individuel *ou* personnel, PC *m*; **p. data** données *fpl* nominatives; **p. effects** effets *mpl* personnels; *Br Fin Formerly* **p. equity plan** ≃ plan *m* d'épargne en actions; **p. estate** biens *mpl* mobiliers personnels; **p. financial statement** état *m* de fortune; **p. friend** ami, -ie personnel(elle); *Comput* **p. home page** page *f* personnelle, page perso; **p. hygiene** hygiène *f* corporelle; *Banking* **p. identification number** code *m* confidentiel *(d'une carte bancaire)*; **p. liberty** liberté *f* individuelle; **p. loan** prêt *m* personnel, prêt personnalisé; *Mktg* **p. observation** observation *f* en situation; **p. organizer** organiseur *m*; *(electronic)* agenda *m* électronique, organiseur; *Gram* **p. pronoun** pronom *m* personnel; **p. property** biens mobiliers personnels; **p. property insurance** assurance sur les objets personnels; *Mktg* **p. selling** ventes *fpl* personnelles; **p. shopper** acheteur, -euse personnel(elle); **p. stereo** Walkman® *m*, baladeur *m*; **p. trainer** entraîneur, -euse per-

sonnel(elle); *Acct* **p. wealth statement** état *m* de fortune

personality [pɜːsə'nælɪtɪ] **N 1** *(character)* personnalité *f*; **he's got no p.** il n'a aucune personnalité **2** *(well-known person)* personnalité *f*; **TV/sports p.** personnalité célèbre de la télévision/du monde du sport **3** *Old-fashioned (personal remark)* **to indulge in personalities** faire des remarques personnelles

▸▸ **p. cult** culte *m* de la personnalité; **p. disorder** trouble *m* de la personnalité; **p. profile** profil *m* de personnalité; *Mktg* **p. promotion** promotion *f* par une personnalité; **p. test** test *m* de personnalité, *Spec* test projectif

personalize ['pɜːsənəlaɪz] **VT** personnaliser; **a personalized shirt** une chemise personnalisée; **personalized letter** lettre *f* personnelle; **I don't want to p. the issue** je ne veux pas donner un tour personnel à ce problème

personally ['pɜːsən(ə)lɪ] **ADV** personnellement; *(to intervene, see sb)* en personne; **to attend to sth p.** s'occuper de qch en personne *ou* personnellement; **p. I think …** pour ma part je pense …; **that belongs to me p.** cela m'appartient en propre; **to deliver sth to sb p.** remettre qch à qn en main(s) propre(s); **don't take it p.** *(what was said, done)* n'en faites pas une affaire personnelle, ne le prenez pas personnellement; **I didn't mean it p.** ma remarque n'avait rien de personnel

personalty ['pɜːsənltɪ] **N** *Law* biens *mpl* meubles, biens mobiliers

personification [pɜːsɒnɪfɪ'keɪʃən] **N** personnification *f*; **to be the p. of meanness** être l'avarice même *ou* l'avarice personnifiée *ou* l'avarice en personne; **he is the p. of this new trend in English fiction** il incarne cette nouvelle tendance de la fiction anglaise

personify [pə'sɒnɪfaɪ] **VT** personnifier; **he's meanness personified** il est *ou* c'est l'avarice même *ou* l'avarice personnifiée *ou* l'avarice en personne

personnel [pɜːsə'nel] **N** personnel *m*; **I work in p.** *(the department)* je travaille au service du personnel; *(the field)* je suis dans la branche du personnel

▸▸ *Mil* **p. carrier** *(vehicle* *m* de) transport *m* de troupes; *(aircraft)* avion *m* de transport de personnel; **p. consultant** conseiller, -ère du travail; **p. department** service *m* du personnel; **p. director** directeur, -trice du personnel; **p. file card** fiche *f* signalétique; **p. files** fichiers *mpl* des salariés; **p. management** direction *f* ou administration *f* du personnel; **p. manager** directeur du personnel; **p. representative** délégué, -ée du personnel

perspective [pə'spektɪv] **N 1** *Math, Art* perspective *f*; **to draw an object in/out of p.** dessiner un objet en perspective/en faussant la perspective **2** *Fig (relative importance)* **to see a matter in its true p.** voir une affaire sous son vrai jour; **to put sth in(to) p.** remettre qch à sa (vraie) place; **let's keep things in p.** n'exagérons rien; **to see events in a historical p.** voir des événements dans une perspective *ou* optique historique **3** *Fml (view), Fig (prospect)* perspective *f*; **a fine p. opened out before his eyes** une belle perspective s'ouvrit devant ses yeux

▪ **ADJ** *Art (drawing etc)* en perspective, perspectif; **p. lines of a picture** fuyants *mpl* d'un tableau

Perspex® ['pɜːspeks] **N** plexiglas(s)® *m*

perspicacious [pɜːspɪ'keɪʃəs] **ADJ** *Fml (person)* perspicace; *(comment, analysis etc)* clairvoyant, lucide, fin

perspicaciously [pɜːspɪ'keɪʃəslɪ] **ADV** *Fml* avec perspicacité *ou* clairvoyance *ou* discernement

perspicacity [pɜːspɪ'kæsɪtɪ] N *Fml* perspicacité *f*

perspicuity [pɜːspɪ'kjuːɪtɪ] N *Fml (of person)* perspicacité *f*, *(of style etc)* clarté *f*, netteté *f*, lucidité *f*

perspicuous [pə'spɪkjʊəs] ADJ *Fml* clair, net, *f* nette, lucide

perspicuously [pə'spɪkjʊəslɪ] ADV *Fml* clairement, nettement

perspiration [pɜːspə'reɪʃən] N 1 *(sweat)* transpiration *f*, sueur *f*; **beads of p.** gouttes *fpl* de sueur; **bathed in** or **dripping with p.** trempé de sueur, en nage 2 *(act)* transpiration *f*, perspiration *f*

perspire [pə'spaɪər] VI transpirer

persuadable [pə'sweɪdəb(ə)l] ADJ **easily p.** facile à persuader

persuade [pə'sweɪd] VT persuader, convaincre (**to do** de faire); **to p. sb not to do sth** dissuader qn de faire qch; **to p. sb that ...** persuader qn que ... + *ind*; **nothing could p. her** aucun argument n'a pu la convaincre; **she persuaded herself that everything would work out** elle s'est persuadée ou convaincue elle-même que tout marcherait bien
▪ VI *Fml* **the argument fails to p.** cet argument n'est pas très convaincant

persuasion [pə'sweɪʒən] N 1 *(act of persuading, ability to persuade)* persuasion *f*; **powers of p.** force *f* ou pouvoir *m* de persuasion; **the art of p.** l'art *m* de la persuasion 2 *(beliefs)* **(religious) p.** *(religion)* religion *f*, confession *f*; **political p.** opinions *fpl* politiques; **he was of a different political p. altogether** ses opinions politiques étaient complètement différentes; **to be of the Catholic p.** être de religion catholique; *Hum* **a person of the male/female p.** un homme/ une femme; *Old-fashioned* **it's my p. that ...** je suis persuadé ou convaincu que ...

persuasive [pə'sweɪzɪv, -sɪv] ADJ *(person)* persuasif; *(argument)* convaincant

persuasively [pə'sweɪzɪvlɪ, -sɪvlɪ] ADV *(to say)* d'un ton persuasif; *(to argue, write)* de façon convaincante

persuasiveness [pə'sweɪzɪvnɪs, -sɪv-] N *(of person)* force *f* persuasive ou de persuasion; *(of argument)* caractère *m* convaincant; **the p. of her tone** son ton persuasif

pert [pɜːt] ADJ 1 *(cheeky)* effronté 2 *(of clothing)* *(stylishly neat)* pimpant 3 *(nose, breasts)* pointu; *(bottom)* petit et ferme

pertain [pə'teɪn] VI *Fml* 1 *(belong)* appartenir (**to sth** à qch); **the house and the land pertaining to it** la maison et le terrain qui font partie de la propriété 2 *(have reference)* **to p. to sth** se rapporter à qch, avoir un rapport avec qch, avoir rapport à qch

pertinacious [pɜːtɪ'neɪʃəs] ADJ *Fml* obstiné, opiniâtre

pertinaciously [pɜːtɪ'neɪʃəslɪ] ADV *Fml* obstinément, opiniâtrement

pertinence ['pɜːtɪnəns] N *(of question, criticism)* pertinence *f*, à-propos *m inv*; *(of remark)* pertinence, à-propos, justesse *f*

pertinent ['pɜːtɪnənt] ADJ *(question, criticism)* pertinent; *(remark)* pertinent, juste; **to be p. to** *(question)* avoir un rapport avec, avoir rapport à

pertinently ['pɜːtɪnəntlɪ] ADV d'une manière pertinente, avec à-propos

pertly ['pɜːtlɪ] ADV 1 *(cheekily)* avec effronterie 2 *(in a lively way)* d'un air guilleret

pertness ['pɜːtnɪs] N 1 *(cheekiness)* effronterie *f* 2 *(liveliness)* air *m* guilleret 3 **the p. of her breasts** ses petits seins bien fermes

perturb [pə'tɜːb] VT 1 *(worry)* troubler, inquiéter; **to be perturbed** être troublé ou inquiet; **if you are perturbed by this idea** si

cette idée vous inquiète 2 *Lit (put into confusion)* *(kingdom etc)* jeter le désordre ou la perturbation dans 3 *Astron (star)* dévier; *Phys (compass needle)* affoler

perturbation [pɜːtə'beɪʃən] N 1 *Fml (of mind)* agitation *f*, inquiétude *f*, trouble *m* 2 *Phys (of magnetic needle)* affolement *m*

perturbed [pə'tɜːbd] ADJ troublé, inquiet

Peru [pə'ruː] N Pérou *m*

perusal [pə'ruːz(ə)l] N *Fml* lecture *f*; **for your p. and approval** pour que vous l'étudiez et l'approuviez; **for your p. when you have time** pour que vous y jetiez un coup d'œil, quand vous en aurez le temps

peruse [pə'ruːz] VT 1 *(read carefully)* lire attentivement, prendre connaissance de 2 *(read quickly)* *(magazine, newspaper)* feuilleter; *(letter, article)* survoler

Peruvian [pə'ruːvɪən] ADJ péruvien
▪ N Péruvien, -ienne

perv [pɜːv] N *Fam* = **pervert**[1]

pervade [pɜː'veɪd] VTs'infiltrer dans, se répandre dans; **the scent of pine trees pervaded the air** l'air était embaumé de l'odeur des pins; **the novel is pervaded by a sense of gloom** le roman est imprégné d'une atmosphère lugubre; **minor errors p. the entire dictionary** le dictionnaire est parsemé de petites erreurs; **such attitudes p. British business** ces attitudes sont omniprésentes dans ou se retrouvent à tous les niveaux dans les entreprises britanniques

pervading [pɜː'veɪdɪŋ] ADJ *(smell)* pénétrant; *(all-)p.* qui se répand partout; *(influence, feeling etc)* dominant; **the p. nostalgia of his work** la nostalgie qui est omniprésente dans son œuvre

pervasive [pɜː'veɪsɪv] ADJ qui se répand partout; *(gloom, smell)* envahissant

perverse [pə'vɜːs] ADJ 1 *(wicked)* pervers, perverti; *(stubborn)* entêté; *(contrary)* contrariant; **to take a p. pleasure in doing** prendre un malin plaisir à faire; **then it would be p. to deny that ...** *(illogical)* alors ce serait illogique de nier que ... 2 *(sexually deviant)* pervers

> Note that the French word **pervers** never means **stubborn** or **contrary**.

perversely [pə'vɜːslɪ] ADV *(wickedly)* perversement, avec perversité; *(contrarily)* d'une manière contrariante; **to p. believe that ...** s'entêter à croire que ...

perverseness [pə'vɜːsnɪs] N *(wickedness)* perversité *f*, *(contrariness)* esprit *m* contraire ou contrariant; *(cantankerousness)* caractère *m* revêche ou acariâtre

perversion [pə'vɜːʃən] N 1 *(act of corrupting)* pervertissement *m*; *(perverted action, form)* perversion *f*; **a p. of the truth** un travestissement de la vérité 2 *(sexual)* perversions perversions *fpl* sexuelles

perversity [pə'vɜːsɪtɪ] N = **perverseness**

pervert[1] ['pɜːvɜːt] N *Psy (sexual)* p. pervers, -erse (sexuel(elle)); *Fam* **your brother is such a p.!** ton frère est un véritable obsédé!

pervert[2] [pə'vɜːt] VT *(corrupt morally)* *(person)* pervertir; *(distort)* *(facts)* altérer, dénaturer; *Law* **to p. the course of justice** entraver le bon fonctionnement de la justice; **to p. the truth** déformer la vérité

perverted [pə'vɜːtɪd] ADJ pervers

pervious ['pɜːvɪəs] ADJ perméable *(à l'eau etc)*

pervy ['pɜːvɪ] ADJ *Br Fam* pervers

peseta [pə'seɪtə] N *Formerly (Spanish currency)* peseta *f*

pesky ['peskɪ] ADJ *esp Am Fam* embêtant, empoisonnant; **what are those p. kids up**

to now? que font ces maudits ou sacrés gosses maintenant?

peso ['peɪseʊ] *(pl* **pesos**) N *(Mexican currency)* peso *m*

pessary ['pesərɪ] N *Med* ovule *m*

pessimism ['pesɪmɪz(ə)m] N pessimisme *m*; **there is growing p. about the prospects for peace** on est de plus en plus pessimiste quant aux chances de paix

pessimist ['pesɪmɪst] N pessimiste *mf*; **don't be such a p.!** ne sois pas si pessimiste!

pessimistic [pesɪ'mɪstɪk] ADJ pessimiste

pessimistically [pesɪ'mɪstɪklɪ] ADV avec pessimisme

PEST [pest] N *Mktg (abbr* **political economic sociological technological**) = facteurs *mpl* politiques, économiques, sociaux et technologiques (considérés comme les aspects les plus importants lors de l'analyse de l'environnement d'une entreprise)

pest [pest] N 1 *(animal, insect, plant)* animal *m*/insecte *m*/plante *f* nuisible; **rabbits are a p. here** ici les lapins sont un fléau 2 *Fam (nuisance)* **stop being a p.!** arrête d'embêter le monde!; **he's a perfect p.!** c'est un vrai poison!; **having to take the dog for a walk is a real p.** c'est vraiment embêtant d'avoir à promener le chien
▪ ▪ **p. control** *(action)* *(of rats)* dératisation *f*, *(of insects)* désinsectisation *f*, *(department)* *(for rats)* service *m* de dératisation; *(for insects)* service de désinsectisation

> Note that the French word **peste** also means **plague**.

pester ['pestər] VT tourmenter, importuner; **to p. sb to do sth** harceler qn pour qu'il fasse qch; **to p. sb with questions** importuner ou assommer ou harceler qn de (ses) questions; **to p. sb for money** harceler qn pour obtenir de l'argent

pesticide ['pestɪsaɪd] N pesticide *m*

pestiferous [pe'stɪfərəs] ADJ *Lit (air)* pestilentiel; *(doctrine)* pernicieux

pestilence ['pestɪləns] N *Lit* peste *f*

pestilential [pestɪ'lenʃəl] ADJ *Med (disease)* pestilentiel; *(smell)* pestilentiel, infect; *Fam (irritating)* assommant, empoisonnant

pestle ['pes(ə)l] N *Culin* pilon *m*

pet[1] [pet] N 1 *(animal)* animal *m* domestique ou familier ou de compagnie; **do you have any pets?** est-ce que tu as un animal?; **a p. monkey/budgerigar** un singe/une perruche apprivoisé(e) 2 *(favourite child)* enfant *mf* gâté(e); **mother's/teacher's p.** le chouchou de sa maman/du professeur; **my p.!** mon chéri!, mon petit chou!; **my p. hate** ma bête noire; **p. subject** sujet *m* de prédilection
▪ VT *(-tt-)* 1 *(make a pet of)* *(person)* choyer, chouchouter 2 *(stroke, pat)* *(person, dog etc)* caresser, câliner
▪ VI *Fam (sexually)* se caresser, *Fam* se peloter
▪ ▪ **p. food** aliments *mpl* pour animaux *(domestiques)*; **p. name** surnom *m* affectueux; **p. passport** = sorte de passeport pour animal domestique, visant à éviter la période de quarantaine après un séjour à l'étranger; **p. shop** magasin *m* d'animaux domestiques, animalerie *f*

pet[2] N *Old-fashioned Fam* **to be in a p.** *(to sulk)* faire la tête, être de mauvaise humeur *(about* à cause de); **to go in a p.** faire la tête

petal ['pet(ə)l] N 1 *(of flower)* pétale *m* 2 *Fam (term of affection)* **thanks p.** merci mon chou

petard [pe'tɑːd] N **to be hoist with one's own p.** être pris à son propre piège

Pete [piːt] N *Fam* **for P.'s sake!** pour l'amour du ciel!

Peter ['piːtər] **N he's a real P. Pan** c'est un vrai gosse
▸▸ **P. Pan collar** col *m* Claudine

peter ['piːtər] **N 1** *Sl (safe)* coffre-fort *m*, *pl* coffres-forts **2** *Am Sl (penis)* quéquette *f*, zizi *m*
▸ **peter out** VI *Fam (of conversation, interest, enthusiasm etc)* tarir; *(of scheme, plan)* n'aboutir à rien; *(of path, stream)* disparaître; *(of flame etc)* mourir; **the party gradually petered out** les gens ont quitté la fête peu à peu

peterman ['piːtəmæn] **N** *Sl (safe-breaker)* casseur *m* de coffres-forts

petersham ['piːtəʃəm] **N** *Tex* gros-grain *m*, *pl* gros-grains

petite [pə'tiːt] **ADJ** *(woman)* menu

petition [pɪ'tɪʃən] **N 1** *(request)* requête *f*, supplique *f*; *(document)* pétition *f*; **to grant a p.** faire droit à une pétition; **to hand in/ sign a p.** remettre/signer une pétition; **to get up a p.** faire signer une pétition **2** *Law* **p. for mercy** recours *m* en grâce; **p. for a divorce** demande *f* en divorce; **p. in bankruptcy** *(made by creditors)* requête *f* des créanciers; *(made by bankrupt)* requête du négociant insolvable **3** *(to God)* prière *f*
▸ VT *(court, sovereign etc)* adresser *ou* présenter une pétition à
▸ VI *(with document)* pétitionner; **to p. for sth** *(collect signatures)* faire signer une pétition pour qch; *(present petition)* adresser une pétition pour qch; *Fml* **to p. for mercy** se pourvoir *ou* recourir en grâce; *Law* **to p. for divorce** faire une demande de divorce

petitioner [pɪ'tɪʃənər] **N** pétitionnaire *mf*; *Law* requérant, -ante

petrel ['petrəl] **N** *(bird)* pétrel *m*

petrifaction [petrɪ'fækʃən], **petrification** [petrɪfɪ'keɪʃən] **N** pétrification *f*

petrified ['petrɪfaɪd] **ADJ** *(wood etc)* pétrifié; *Fam* **p. with fear** pétrifié *ou* paralysé de terreur; *Fam* **I was p. he would shoot me** j'étais mort de peur à l'idée qu'il me tire dessus

petrify ['petrɪfaɪ] **VT** *(wood etc)* pétrifier; *Fam (with fear)* pétrifier, paralyser
▸ VI se pétrifier

petrifying ['petrɪfaɪɪŋ] **ADJ** *Fam (frightening)* paralysant

petrochemical [petrəʊ'kemɪk(ə)l] **ADJ** *(industry etc)* pétrochimique
▸ NPL **petrochemicals** produits *mpl* pétrochimiques

petrocurrency ['petrəʊkʌrənsɪ] **N** pétromonnaies *fpl*

petrodollar ['petrəʊdɒlər] **N** pétrodollar *m*

petrol ['petrəl] **N** *Br Aut* essence *f*, *Suisse* benzine *f*; **to fill up with p.** faire le plein d'essence; **to run out of p.** tomber en panne d'essence; **high-grade** *or* **four-star p.** = supercarburant *m*, *Fam* super *m*
▸▸ **p. bomb** cocktail *m* Molotov; **p. can** bidon *m* d'essence; **p. cap** bouchon *m* d'essence; **p. company** compagnie *f* pétrolière; **p. filler cap** bouchon d'essence; **p. filler pipe** tuyau *m* de remplissage d'essence; **p. gauge** jauge *f* à essence; **p. pump** *(at service station)* pompe *f* à essence; **p. station** station-service *f*, *Aut* **p. tank** réservoir *m* (d'essence); **p. tanker** *(lorry)* camion-citerne *m*, *pl* camions-citernes; *(ship)* pétrolier *m*, tanker *m*

Note that the French word **pétrole** is a false friend and is never a translation for the English word **petrol**. It means *oil*.

petrol-bomb VT jeter des cocktails Molotov sur

petroleum [pə'trəʊlɪəm] **N** pétrole *m*

▸▸ **p. industry** industrie *f* pétrolière; *Br* **p. jelly** vaseline *f*

petrolhead ['petrəlhed] **N** *Br Fam* dingue *mf* de bagnoles

petrology [pe'trɒlədʒɪ] **N** pétrologie *f*

petticoat ['petɪkəʊt] **N** *(skirt length)* jupon *m*; *(full length)* combinaison *f*
▸▸ *Fam* **p. government** gouvernement *m* de femmes

pettifogging ['petɪfɒgɪŋ] **ADJ** *Old-fashioned (detail)* insignifiant; *(objection)* de pure chicane; *(person)* chicanier; **p. lawyer** avocassier, -ière

pettiness ['petɪnɪs] **N** *(insignificance)* insignifiance *f*; *(small-mindedness)* mesquinerie *f*

petting ['petɪŋ] **N** *Fam* pelotage *m*; **heavy p.** attouchements *mpl*

pettish ['petɪʃ] **ADJ** *(person)* de mauvaise humeur, maussade, irritable; *(behaviour, reaction)* maussade, morose

pettishly ['petɪʃlɪ] **ADV** avec mauvaise humeur

petty ['petɪ] **ADJ 1** *(insignificant, minor)* petit, insignifiant; **p. annoyances** tracasseries *fpl*, petits ennuis *mpl* **2** **p.(-minded)** mesquin
▸▸ **p. cash** petite caisse *f*; **p. cash book** livre *m* de petite caisse; **p. cash box** petite caisse; **p. cash voucher** bon *m* de petite caisse; **p. crime** actes *mpl* délictueux; **p. larceny** larcin *m*; **p. offences** contraventions *fpl*; *Br Naut* **p. officer** ≃ second maître *m*

petty-mindedness [petɪ'maɪndɪdnɪs] **N** mesquinerie *f*

petulance ['petjʊləns] **N** irascibilité *f*, mauvaise humeur *f*; **an outburst of p.** un accès de mauvaise humeur

petulant ['petjʊlənt] **ADJ** irritable, susceptible; *(frown)* irrité; **he became quite p.** il s'est montré vraiment susceptible; **you're in a p. mood today!** tu es vraiment susceptible aujourd'hui!

Note that the French word **pétulant** is a false friend and is never a translation for the English word **petulant**. It means *exuberant*.

petulantly ['petjʊləntlɪ] **ADV** *(to look at)* d'un air irrité; *(to say)* d'un ton irrité; *(to react)* avec humeur

petunia [pɪ'tjuːnɪə] **N** *(plant)* pétunia *m*

pew [pjuː] **N** banc *m* d'église; *Fam* **take** *or* **have a p.!** assieds-toi!

pewter ['pjuːtər] **N** étain *m*; **p. (ware)** étains, vaisselle *f* d'étain; **I like p. (ware)** j'aime les étains

PFI [piːef'aɪ] **N** *(abbr* private finance initiative*)* partenariat *m* public-privé

PG [piː'dʒiː] **ADJ** *Br Cin (abbr* parental guidance*)* *(film)* = qui exige une autorisation parentale

PGCE [piːdʒiːsiː'iː] **N** *Br Sch (abbr* Postgraduate Certificate in Education*)* = diplôme *m* d'enseignement

PgDn *Comput (abbr* page down*)* PgSv

PGP [piːdʒiː'piː] **N** *Comput (abbr* Pretty Good Privacy*)* (logiciel *m* de chiffrement) PGP *m*

PgUp *Comput (abbr* page up*)* PgPr

pH [piː'eɪtʃ] **N** *Chem* pH *m*; **a pH of 9** un pH de 9

phalanx ['fælæŋks] **N 1** *(pl usu* phalanxes ['fælæŋksɪz]*)* *(in ancient armies)*, *Fig* armée *f* **2** *Anat, Bot (pl usu* phalanges [fə'lændʒiːz]*)* phalange *f*

phallic ['fælɪk] **ADJ** phallique
▸▸ **p. symbol** symbole *m* phallique

phallocentric [fæləʊ'sentrɪk] **ADJ** phallocentrique

phallus ['fæləs] **N** phallus *m*

phantasm ['fæntæz(ə)m] **N** *Lit (illusion)* illusion *f*; *(ghost)* apparition *f*

phantasmagoria [fæntæzmæ'gɒrɪə] **N** *Lit* fantasmagorie *f*

phantasy ['fæntəsɪ] **N** = **fantasy**

phantom ['fæntəm] **N** fantôme *m*, spectre *m*
▸▸ *Tel* **p. circuit** circuit *m* fantôme; *Med* **p. limb** membre *m* fantôme; *Br* **p. pregnancy** grossesse *f* nerveuse; **p. ship** vaisseau *m* fantôme

Pharaoh ['feərəʊ] **N** *Antiq* pharaon *m*

Pharisee ['færɪsiː] **N** *Antiq*, *Fig* pharisien, -ienne

pharmaceutical [fɑːmə'sjuːtɪk(ə)l] **ADJ** pharmaceutique; **p. rep(resentative)** visiteur, -euse médical(e)
▸ NPL **pharmaceuticals** *(medicines)* produits *mpl* pharmaceutiques; *(industry)* industrie *f* pharmaceutique; **I'm in pharmaceuticals** je suis dans l'industrie pharmaceutique
▸▸ **pharmaceuticals company** société *f* pharmaceutique

pharmacist ['fɑːməsɪst] **N** pharmacien, -ienne

pharmacological [fɑːməkə'lɒdʒɪk(ə)l] **ADJ** pharmacologique

pharmacologist [fɑːmə'kɒlədʒɪst] **N** pharmacologiste *mf*, pharmacologue *mf*

pharmacology [fɑːmə'kɒlədʒɪ] **N** pharmacologie *f*

pharmacopoeia [fɑːməkəʊ'piːə] **N** *(book)* pharmacopée *f*, *(collection of drugs)* pharmacopée *f*, pharmacie *f*

pharmacy ['fɑːməsɪ] **N** pharmacie *f*

pharyngitis [færɪn'dʒaɪtɪs] **N** *Med* pharyngite *f*

pharynx ['færɪŋks] **N** *Anat* pharynx *m*

phase [feɪz] **N** *(of phenomenon, process, moon etc)* phase *f*; **it's still in the development p.** c'est encore en cours de développement; **initial/final p.** phase initiale/finale; *Rugby* **second p.** deuxième temps *m*; **to enter upon a new p.** entrer dans une nouvelle phase; **it's just a p. (he's/she's going through)** ça lui passera; *Phys, Tech* **in p.** en phase (**with sth** avec qch); **out of p.** *Phys, Tech* hors de phase, déphasé; *Fig* déphasé; *Elec* **single/two/three-p. current** courant *m* monophasé/diphasé/triphasé
▸ VT **1** *(changes, new methods)* introduire progressivement; *(project)* développer en phases successives; *(schedule, introduction of technology etc)* échelonner; **the negotiations have to be properly phased** les diverses phases des négociations doivent être correctement planifiées **2** *Elec etc* mettre en phases, caler en phase
▸▸ *TV* **p. distortion** déphasage *m*
▸ **phase in** VT SEP *(changes, new methods etc)* introduire progressivement; *(new systems, equipment etc)* mettre en place progressivement
▸ **phase out** VT SEP **1** *(get rid of gradually)* *(methods, equipment, jobs etc)* éliminer progressivement; *Hum (boyfriend)* faire sortir de sa vie; **the system is being phased out** ce système est en cours d'abandon **2** *(get rid of)* éliminer; **that's all been phased out now** ça n'existe plus maintenant

phased [feɪzd] **ADJ 1** par phases, progressif; *(evacuation)* progressif **2** *Elec* phasé; *(light)* cohérent

phasing ['feɪzɪŋ] **N 1** *(planning)* planification *f* par phases; *(of manufacturing schedule etc)* échelonnement *m*; *(phasing in) (of measures, new methods)* introduction *f* progressive **2** *Elec etc* mise *f* en phase, calage *m* en phase

▶▶ **p. in** (of new methods) adoption f ou introduction progressive; (of new systems, new equipment) mise en place progressive; **p. out** (of old methods, systems, equipment etc) abandon m progressif; (of jobs) suppression f progressive

phat [fæt] ADJ Am Sl super, génial, -aux

PhD [piːeɪtʃ'diː] N Univ (abbr **Doctor of Philosophy**) (diploma) = doctorat m; (person) docteur m, titulaire mf d'un doctorat; **to have a P. in Maths** avoir un doctorat en maths

pheasant ['fezənt] N faisan m; **cock p.** (coq m) faisan; **hen p.** (poule f) faisane f; **young p.** faisandeau m
  ▶▶ **p. poult** faisandeau; **p. shoot** faisanderie f, **p. shooting** chasse f au faisan

phenix ['fiːnɪks] N Am Myth = **phoenix**

phenobarbitone [fiːnəʊ'baːbɪtəʊn] N Pharm phénobarbital m

phenol ['fiːnɒl] N Chem phénol m

phenomenal [fɪ'nɒmɪn(ə)l] ADJ (very great) phénoménal, -aux, prodigieux; Phil phénoménal

phenomenally [fɪ'nɒmɪn(ə)lɪ] ADV prodigieusement; **he's p. rich/stupid** il est phénoménalement riche/d'une insondable bêtise

phenomenological [fənɒmənə'lɒdʒɪk(ə)l] ADJ phénoménologique

phenomenologist [fənɒmə'nɒlədʒɪst] N phénoménologue mf

phenomenology [fənɒmə'nɒlədʒɪ] N phénoménologie f

phenomenon, pl **phenomena** [fɪ'nɒmɪnən, -mɪnə] N phénomène m

pheromone ['ferəməʊn] N phérormone f, phéromone f

phew [fjuː] INT (when hot) pfff!; (disgust) pouah!; (relief) ouf!

phial ['faɪəl] N fiole f, flacon m, ampoule f

Phil abbr **Philadelphia**

Philadelphia [fɪlə'delfɪə] N Philadelphie f

philander [fɪ'lændər] VI Lit Pej courir le jupon

philanderer [fɪ'lændərər] N Pej coureur m de jupons

philandering [fɪ'lændərɪŋ] Pej N **she had had enough of his p.** elle en avait assez qu'il coure le jupon
ADJ (ways, habits) de coureur de jupon; **her p. husband** son coureur de mari

philanthropic [fɪlən'θrɒpɪk] ADJ philanthropique; (person) philanthrope

philanthropist [fɪ'lænθrəpɪst] N philanthrope mf

philanthropy [fɪ'lænθrəpɪ] N philanthropie f

philatelic [fɪlə'telɪk] ADJ philatélique

philatelist [fɪ'lætəlɪst] N philatéliste mf

philately [fɪ'lætəlɪ] N philatélie f

-phile [faɪl] SUFF -phile; **Anglop.** anglophile mf, **Francop.** francophile mf

philharmonic [fɪlə'mɒnɪk] ADJ philharmonique
N philharmonie f, société f philharmonique

-philia ['fɪlɪə] SUFF -philie; **necrop.** nécrophilie f, **anglop.** anglophilie f

Philippine [fɪlɪpiːn] ADJ philippin
N **the Philippines** les (îles fpl) Philippines fpl VOIR GRAMMAIRE A12

philistine ['fɪlɪstaɪn] N Art, Liter béotien, -ienne, philistin m; Bible **P.** Philistin m
ADJ Art, Liter béotien, philistin

philistinism ['fɪlɪstɪnɪz(ə)m] N philistinisme m

Phillips® ['fɪlɪps] ADJ
  ▶▶ **P. screw** vis f à empreinte cruciforme; **P. screwdriver** tournevis m à empreinte cruciforme

philodendron [fɪlə'dendrən] N (plant) philodendron m

philological [fɪlə'lɒdʒɪk(ə)l] ADJ philologique

philologist [fɪ'lɒlədʒɪst] N philologue mf

philology [fɪ'lɒlədʒɪ] N philologie f

philosopher [fɪ'lɒsəfər] N philosophe mf; **the p.'s stone** la pierre philosophale

philosophic(al) [fɪlə'sɒfɪk, -ɪk(ə)l] ADJ Phil philosophique; Fig (person, attitude) philosophe; **she was p. about her defeat** elle a pris sa défaite en philosophe ou avec philosophie

philosophically [fɪlə'sɒfɪklɪ] ADV Phil philosophiquement; Fig (to react etc) en philosophe, avec philosophie

philosophize [fɪ'lɒsəfaɪz] VI philosopher

philosophy [fɪ'lɒsəfɪ] N philosophie f, **a personal p.** une philosophie personnelle; **one's own p. about sth** sa conception personnelle de qch; **my p. is ...** ma philosophie c'est ...; **with p.** (to endure hardship) avec philosophie, en philosophe

philtre, Am **philter** ['fɪltər] N philtre m

phiz [fɪz], **phizog** ['fɪzɒg] N esp Br Old-fashioned Sl (face) binette f, tronche f

phlebitis [flɪ'baɪtɪs] N Med phlébite f, **to have p.** avoir une phlébite

phlegm [flem] N **1** (mucus) flegme m, pituite f (bronchiale); **to cough up p.** tousser gras **2** Fml (composure) flegme m, calme m

phlegmatic [fleg'mætɪk] ADJ flegmatique

phlegmatically [fleg'mætɪklɪ] ADV flegmatiquement

phlox [flɒks] N (plant) phlox m

-phobe [fəʊb] SUFF -phobe mf

phobia ['fəʊbɪə] N phobie f, **to have a p. about sth** avoir une phobie pour qch

-phobia ['fəʊbɪə] SUFF -phobie f

phobic ['fəʊbɪk] ADJ, N Med phobique mf; Fig **he's really p. about tidiness** c'est un vrai maniaque du rangement

-phobic ['fəʊbɪk] SUFF -phobe

Phoenician [fɪ'niːʃən] Antiq ADJ phénicien N **1** Phénicien, -ienne **2** Ling phénicien m

phoenix, Am **phenix** ['fiːnɪks] N Myth phénix m; **to rise, p.-like, from ...** renaître, tel un phénix, de ...

phone¹ [fəʊn] N téléphone m; **to be on the p.** (talking) être au téléphone; (have a telephone) avoir le téléphone; Fam **to give sb a p.** donner un coup de téléphone ou de fil à qn; **he was on the p. for an hour** il a passé une heure au téléphone; **he's on the p.** (in office) il est en ligne; **quiet, Mummy's on the p.** tais-toi, maman a quelqu'un au bout du fil; **I've got Mummy on the p.** j'ai Maman au bout du fil; **to get on the p. to sb** téléphoner à qn; **I couldn't get her on the p.** je n'ai pas réussi à l'avoir au téléphone ou à la joindre; **could you get Maria on the p. for me?** est-ce que tu pourrais m'appeler Maria (au téléphone)?; **get off the p.!** raccroche!; **to speak to sb on** or **over the p.** parler à qn au téléphone
VT **1** to **p. sb** téléphoner à qn, appeler qn au téléphone, donner un coup de téléphone ou Fam de fil à qn; **to p. the office/police** téléphoner au bureau/à la police **2** to **p. a piece of news** téléphoner une nouvelle
VI téléphoner; **to p. home** téléphoner à la maison
  ▶▶ **p. bill** facture f de téléphone; **p. book** annuaire m (téléphonique); **p. booth** cabine f téléphonique; Br **p. box** cabine téléphonique; **p. call** coup m de téléphone, appel m (téléphonique); **p. number** numéro m de téléphone; **p. tap** écoute f téléphonique; **p. tapping** écoutes téléphoniques

▶ **phone in** VI téléphoner; **to p. in sick** téléphoner pour dire qu'on est malade
▶ **phone up** VT SEP = **phone VT**

phone² N Ling phonème m

-phone [fəʊn] SUFF -phone; **Anglop./Francop.** anglophone/francophone

phonecard ['fəʊnkaːd] N Br Tel télécarte f, carte f téléphonique

phone-in N **p. (programme)** émission f à ligne ouverte, émission au cours de laquelle les téléspectateurs/auditeurs peuvent intervenir par téléphone

phoneme ['fəʊniːm] N Ling phonème m

phonemic [fə'niːmɪk] ADJ phonémique

phonetic [fə'netɪk] ADJ phonétique
  ▶▶ **p. alphabet** alphabet m phonétique

phonetically [fə'netɪklɪ] ADV phonétiquement

phonetician [fəʊnə'tɪʃən] N phonéticien, -ienne

phonetics [fə'netɪks] N VOIR GRAMMAIRE A10 **1** (science) phonétique f **2** (symbols) phonétique f

phoney, esp Am **phony** ['fəʊnɪ] Fam ADJ (comp **phonier;** superl **phoniest**) faux, f fausse; (story, excuse etc) bidon; **he's p. (Am as a two-dollar bill)** il est faux comme un jeton, il est faux jeton
N (impostor) imposteur m; (insincere person) faux jeton m; (fake object) faux m
  ▶▶ Hist **p. war** drôle f de guerre

phonic ['fɒnɪk, 'fəʊnɪk] ADJ phonique

phonograph ['fəʊnəgræf] N Am phonographe m

phonology [fə'nɒlədʒɪ] N phonologie f

phony ['fəʊnɪ] ADJ, N esp Am Fam = **phoney**

phooey ['fuːɪ] INT peuh!

phosgene ['fɒzdʒiːn] N Chem phosgène m

phosphate ['fɒsfeɪt] N Chem phosphate m; **p. of lime, calcium p.** phosphate de chaux; **p. mine** or **works** phosphaterie f

phosphide ['fɒsfaɪd] N Chem phosphure m

phosphite ['fɒsfaɪt] N Chem phosphite m

phosphoresce [fɒsfə'res] VI être phosphorescent, luire par phosphorescence

phosphorescence [fɒsfə'resəns] N phosphorescence f

phosphorescent [fɒsfə'resənt] ADJ phosphorescent

phosphoric [fɒs'fɒrɪk] ADJ Chem phosphorique

phosphorous ['fɒsfərəs] ADJ Chem phosphoreux

phosphorus ['fɒsfərəs] N Chem phosphore m

photo ['fəʊtəʊ] N photo f, **to take good photos** prendre de bonnes photos; **to take a good p. (be photogenic)** être photogénique
  ▶▶ **p. album** album m de photos; Cin, TV **p. call** séance f de photos; Comput **p. CD** CD-Photo m inv, Photo-CD m inv; Comput **p. editing** retouche f d'images; **p. finish** Sport arrivée f groupée; Fig partie f serrée; **p. library** photothèque f, **p. opportunity** séance de photo; **p. shoot** séance photos

photo- ['fəʊtəʊ] PREF photo-

photobooth ['fəʊtəʊbuːð] N Photomaton® m

photocard ['fəʊtəʊkaːd] N carte f portant une photo d'identité du titulaire

photocell ['fəʊtəʊsel] N photocellule f

photocompose [fəʊtəʊkəm'pəʊz] VT photocomposer

photocomposer [fəʊtəʊkəm'pəʊzər] N (person) photocompositeur, -trice

photocomposition [fəʊtəʊkɒmpə'zɪʃən]

N photocomposition f
▸▸ **p. machine** photocomposeuse f

photocompositor [fəʊtəʊkəm'pɒzɪtər] N (machine) photocomposeuse f

photocopier ['fəʊtəʊkɒpɪər] N photocopieur m, photocopieuse f

photocopy ['fəʊtəʊkɒpɪ] N photocopie f; **to take** or **make a p. of sth** faire une photocopie de qch, photocopier qch
VT photocopier
VI **these pictures won't p. very well** ces dessins ne donneront pas de bonnes photocopies; **to do some photocopying** faire des photocopies

photoelectric [fəʊtəʊɪ'lektrɪk] ADJ photoélectrique
▸▸ **p. cell** cellule f photoélectrique

photoelectron [fəʊtəʊɪ'lektrɒn] N Phys photoélectron m

photoengraving [fəʊtəʊɪn'greɪvɪŋ] N photogravure f

Photofit® ['fəʊtəʊfɪt] N (picture) portrait-robot m, pl portraits-robots
▸▸ **P. picture** portrait-robot

photogenic [fəʊtə'dʒenɪk] ADJ photogénique

photograph ['fəʊtəgrɑːf] N photo f, photographie f, **in the p.** sur la photo; **to have a p. of sth** avoir qch en photo; **to take sb's p.** prendre une photo de qn; **he had his p. taken** il s'est fait photographier; **she takes a good p.** (is photogenic) elle est photogénique
VT photographier, prendre en photo
VI **to p. well** (be photogenic) être photogénique; **it won't p. well in this light** cela ne fera pas une bonne photo dans cette lumière
▸▸ **p. album** album m de photos; **p. library** photothèque f

Note that the French word **photographe** is a false friend and is never a translation for the English word **photograph**. It means **photographer**.

photographer [fə'tɒgrəfər] N photographe mf; **she's a good/bad p.** elle prend de bonnes/mauvaises photos

photographic [fəʊtə'græfɪk] ADJ (process, description etc) photographique; **to have a p. memory** avoir une mémoire photographique
▸▸ **p. agency** agence f photographique; **p. library** photothèque f, **p. paper** papier m photo

photographically [fəʊtə'græfɪklɪ] ADV photographiquement

photography [fə'tɒgrəfɪ] N photographie f

photogravure [fəʊtəʊgrə'vjʊər] N photogravure f

photojournalism [fəʊtəʊ'dʒɜːnəlɪz(ə)m] N photoreportage m

photojournalist [fəʊtəʊ'dʒɜːnəlɪst] N reporter m photographe, photojournaliste mf

photolithograph [fəʊtəʊ'lɪθəʊgrɑːf] N photolithographie f

photolithography [fəʊtəʊlɪ'θɒgrəfɪ] N photolithographie f

photoluminescence [fəʊtəʊluːmɪ'nesəns] N photoluminescence f

photometer [fəʊ'tɒmɪtər] N Phys photomètre m

photometry [fəʊ'tɒmɪtrɪ] N Phys photométrie f

photomontage [fəʊtəʊmɒn'tɑːʒ] N photomontage m

photon ['fəʊtɒn] N Phys photon m

photonovel ['fəʊtəʊnɒv(ə)l] N roman-photo m, pl romans-photos

photosensitive [fəʊtəʊ'sensɪtɪv] ADJ photosensible

photoset ['fəʊtəʊset] VT Br photocomposer

photosetter ['fəʊtəʊsetər] N Br photocomposeuse f, photocompositeur m

photosetting ['fəʊtəʊsetɪŋ] N Br photocomposition f
▸▸ **p. machine** photocomposeuse f

Photostat® ['fəʊtəʊstæt] N photostat m
VT faire un photostat de
VI faire des photostats

photo-story N roman-photo m, pl romans-photos

photosynthesis [fəʊtəʊ'sɪnθɪsɪs] N photosynthèse f

photosynthesize [fəʊtəʊ'sɪnθɪsaɪz] VT photosynthétiser

phototropism [fəʊtəʊ'trəʊpɪz(ə)m] N Biol phototropisme m

phototypesetter [fəʊtəʊ'taɪpsetər] N Br photocompositeur m

phototypesetting [fəʊtəʊ'taɪpsetɪŋ] N Br photocomposition f

photovoltaic [fəʊtəʊvɒl'teɪɪk] ADJ photovoltaïque
▸▸ **p. cell** cellule f photovoltaïque, photopile f; **p. effect** effet m photovoltaïque

phrasal ['freɪzəl] ADJ
▸▸ Gram **p. verb** verbe m à particule, verbe composé VOIR GRAMMAIRE A61–3; B65

phrase [freɪz] N expression f, Mus phrase f, Gram locution f (adverbiale etc), membre m de phrase; **noun p.** syntagme m nominal; **could you describe it for us in a p. or two?** est-ce que vous pourriez nous le décrire en quelques phrases?; **in Voltaire's p.** comme dirait Voltaire
VT **1** (verbally) exprimer, donner un tour à; (letter, invitation, question, answer) tourner; **that is how he phrased it** voilà comment il s'est exprimé, voilà comment il a tourné cela **2** Mus phraser
▸▸ **p. book** manuel m ou guide m de conversation

Note that the French noun **phrase** is a false friend. It means **sentence**.

phraseology [freɪzɪ'ɒlədʒɪ] N phraséologie f

phrasing ['freɪzɪŋ] N **1** (of text) phraséologie f, (of thought) expression f, (of answer, notice etc) tournure f **2** Mus phrasé m

phreaker ['friːkər] N Comput, Tel Fam pirate m du téléphone

phreaking ['friːkɪŋ] N Comput, Tel Fam piratage m du téléphone

phrenic nerve ['frenɪk] N Med nerf m phrénique

phrenology [frɪ'nɒlədʒɪ] N phrénologie f

phthisis ['θaɪsɪs] N Med phtisie f

phut [fʌt] ADV Fam **to go p.** (of business, engine etc) claquer; **the light went p.** la lumière s'est éteinte

phwoar [fwɔːr] INT Fam wouaouh!; **p.! he's a bit of all right** wouaouh! il n'est pas mal

phylactery [fɪ'læktərɪ] N Jewish Rel phylactère m

phylloxera [fɪlɒk'sɪərə] N (insect) phylloxéra m

phylum, pl **phyla** ['faɪləm, -lə] N Biol phylum m

physic ['fɪzɪk] N Arch remède m

physical ['fɪzɪk(ə)l] ADJ **1** (relating to the body) physique; Med (symptoms) somatique; **rugby is a very p. sport** le rugby est un sport dans lequel il y a beaucoup de contacts physiques; **the game got very p.** le jeu est devenu très physique; **it left him**

a p. wreck ça lui a détruit la santé **2** (concrete, material) physique; Geog **p. features** topographie f
N Med Fam visite f médicale; **to have a p.** passer une visite médicale
▸▸ **p. access control** contrôle m d'accès physique; Fin **p. assets** immobilisations fpl non financières; Fin **p. capital** capital m existant; **p. chemistry** chimie f physique; **p. contact** contact m physique; Comput **p. disk cache** cache m disque physique; Mktg **p. distribution** distribution f physique; Mktg **p. distribution management** gestion f de la distribution physique; **p. education** éducation f physique; Med **p. examination** visite médicale; **p. exercises** (exercices mpl de) gymnastique f, **p. fitness** (bonne) forme f physique; **p. geography** géographie f physique; **p. handicap** infirmité f, **p. impossibility** impossibilité f matérielle ou physique; Com **p. inventory** inventaire m effectif; Old-fashioned Br Fam **p. jerks** (exercices de) gymnastique; **p. presence** présence f physique; **p. property** propriété f physique; **p. sciences** sciences fpl physiques; **p. strength** force f physique; **p. training** (exercices de) gymnastique

physically ['fɪzɪklɪ] ADV **1** physiquement; **p. attractive** attirant sur le plan physique; **p. fit** en bonne forme physique; **to be p. handicapped** être handicapé physique **2** (materially) physiquement, matériellement; **seeing it on TV isn't the same as being p. there** le voir à la télévision ce n'est pas la même chose que d'y assister en personne

physician [fɪ'zɪʃən] N médecin m

Note that the French word **physicien** is a false friend and is never a translation for the English word **physician**. It means **physicist**.

physicist ['fɪzɪsɪst] N physicien, -ienne

physics ['fɪzɪks] N physique f VOIR GRAMMAIRE A10

physio ['fɪzɪəʊ] N Med Fam **1** (abbr physiotherapist) kiné mf **2** (abbr physiotherapy) kiné f

physiognomy [fɪzɪ'ɒnəmɪ] N Fml (of person) physionomie f, Geog (of region) configuration f

physiological [fɪzɪə'lɒdʒɪk(ə)l] ADJ physiologique

physiologically [fɪzɪə'lɒdʒɪklɪ] ADV physiologiquement

physiologist [fɪzɪ'ɒlədʒɪst] N physiologiste mf, physiologue mf

physiology [fɪzɪ'ɒlədʒɪ] N physiologie f

physiopathology [fɪzɪəʊpə'θɒlədʒɪ] N Med physiopathologie f

physiotherapist [fɪzɪəʊ'θerəpɪst] N kinésithérapeute mf

physiotherapy [fɪzɪəʊ'θerəpɪ] N kinésithérapie f, rééducation f, **to have p.** faire de la rééducation

physique [fɪ'ziːk] N physique m; **fine p.** beau physique; **poor p.** physique ingrat; **he hasn't the p. for it** il n'a pas le physique de l'emploi

pi [paɪ] N (in Greek alphabet), Math pi m

PIA [piːaɪ'eɪ] N Fin (abbr personal investment authority) = organisme m chargé de surveiller les activités des conseillers financiers indépendants et de protéger les petits investisseurs

pianissimo [pɪə'nɪsɪməʊ] ADV, N pianissimo m

pianist ['pɪənɪst] N pianiste mf

piano[1] [pɪ'ænəʊ], Fml **pianoforte** [pjænəʊ'fɔːtɪ] N piano m; **sonata for p. and violin** sonate pour piano et violon

▶▶**p. accordion** accordéon *m* (à touches); **p. concerto** concerto *m* pour piano; **p. duet** duo *m* pour piano; **p. key** touche *f*, **p. player** pianiste *mf*, **p. stool** tabouret *m* de piano; **p. tuner** accordeur *m* de pianos

piano² [pɪˈɑːnəʊ] ADJ, ADV *Mus* piano

piastre [pɪˈæstər] N *(currency)* piastre *f*

piazza [pɪˈætsə] N *(esp in Italy)* place *f* (publique); *Br (covered)* galerie *f*

PIBOR [ˈpaɪbɔːr] N *(abbr Paris interbank offered rate)* TIOP *m*, PIBOR *m*

pic [pɪk] N *Fam* **1** *(picture)* image *f*, *(photograph)* photo *f* **2** *Br Cin* film *m*; **the pics** *(the cinema)* le ciné, le cinoche

pica [ˈpaɪkə] N *Typ* pica *m*

picador [ˈpɪkədɔːr] N picador *m*

Picardy [ˈpɪkədɪ] N Picardie *f*

picaresque [pɪkəˈresk] ADJ *(novel)* picaresque

piccalilli [pɪkəˈlɪlɪ] N *Culin* pickles *mpl* à la moutarde

piccaninny [pɪkəˈnɪnɪ] N *Old-fashioned Offensive Sl (negro child)* négrillon, -onne

piccolo [ˈpɪkələʊ] N *Mus* piccolo *m*

piccy [ˈpɪkɪ] N *Fam (snapshot)* photo *f*

pick¹ [pɪk] N **1** *(tool)* pic *m*, pioche *f*, **(miner's) p.** pic à main **2** *Mus (plectrum)* plectre *m*, médiator *m*

pick² N **the p.** *(best) (of people)* l'élite *f*, la crème; *(of apples, new films etc)* le meilleur, *pl* les meilleurs; **the p. of the bunch** le meilleur de tous *ou Fam* du lot; *(several people)* le dessus du panier, *Fam* le gratin; **we had first p.** nous avons été les premiers à choisir; **take your p.** choisissez

PICK³ VT **1** *(choose)* choisir, sélectionner; **to p. one's words (carefully)** (bien) choisir ses mots; *Horseracing etc* **to p. a winner** choisir *ou* désigner un gagnant; *Fig* **we've certainly picked a winner in Paul Rodger** nous avons vraiment tiré le bon numéro avec Paul Rodger; **he was picked for Scotland** il a été choisi pour représenter l'Écosse; **to p. one's way through a field** traverser un champ en regardant où on met les pieds; **you picked a fine time to tell me** tu as bien choisi ton moment pour me le dire; **to p. a fight** chercher la bagarre (**with sb** à qn) **2** *(gather) (flowers, fruit etc)* cueillir **3** *(lock)* crocheter; **to p. rags** détisser *ou* effilocher des chiffons; **to p. sb's pocket** faire les poches à qn; **she picked a hole in her jumper** elle a fait un trou à son pull en tirant sur la laine; *Fig* **to p. holes in sth** *(in argument, theory, book etc)* trouver des failles dans qch; *Fam* **she's constantly picking holes (in everything)** elle n'arrête pas de chercher la petite bête; **to p. sb's brains** avoir recours aux lumières de qn; **can I p. your brains a minute?** est-ce que je peux faire appel à tes connaissances une minute?; **to p. a bone** décortiquer un os; *Fig* **to have a bone to p. with sb** avoir un compte à régler avec qn; **to p. one's nose/teeth** se curer le nez/les dents; **to p. a spot/scab** gratter un bouton/une croûte **4** *(of birds) (corn etc)* picoter, becqueter **5** *Mus* **to p. a guitar** pincer la guitare

VI *(choose)* choisir; **you p. first** choisis d'abord; **to p. and choose** faire le/la difficile

▶ **pick at** VT INSEP **to p. at one's food** picorer; **to p. at a scab** gratter une croûte

▶ **pick off** VT SEP **1** *(remove) (flowers, leaves etc)* enlever, ôter; **p. those papers off the ground** ramassez ces papiers qui sont par terre; **to p. the meat off a bone** décortiquer un os; **she picked herself off the floor** elle s'est relevée **2** *(of gunman, sniper)* descendre, abattre; *(several people)* descendre *ou* abattre un à un; *Fig (opponent etc)* éliminer; *(several op-*

ponents) éliminer les uns après les autres

▶ **pick on** VT INSEP **1** *(victimize)* s'en prendre à; **stop picking on her** arrête de t'en prendre à elle; **why p. on me?** pourquoi s'en prendre à moi?; **p. on sb your own size!** ne t'attaque pas à qn de plus faible que toi! **2** *(choose) (person, thing)* choisir; **I always get picked on for the worst jobs** c'est toujours à moi que reviennent les tâches les plus ingrates

▶ **pick out** VT SEP **1** *(remove) (something)* extirper, enlever **2** *(select) (something)* choisir; **he picked out the best peaches** il a choisi les meilleures pêches; **to p. out a criminal** *(in identification parade)* identifier un criminel **3** *(recognize)* repérer; **she was easy to p. out in her orange coat** elle était facilement reconnaissable *ou* facile à repérer avec son manteau orange **4** *(highlight)* picked out in gold rehaussé d'or **5** *Mus* **to p. out a tune** essayer de retrouver un air

▶ **pick over** VT INSEP *(fruit etc)* trier; *Fig (performance, exam, details)* débattre de

▶ **pick up** VT SEP **1** *(lift up)* prendre; *(sth from the ground)* ramasser; *(sth that has fallen over)* relever; *(telephone)* décrocher; *Knitting (stitch)* relever; **to p. up survivors** *(of ship, helicopter)* recueillir des survivants; **to p. up the odd pound here or there** *(earn)* gagner un peu d'argent par ci par là; **to p. up a child** *(in one's arms)* prendre un enfant dans ses bras; *(after falling)* relever un enfant; **to p. oneself up** *(after falling)* se relever; *Fig (recover from crisis)* se remettre; **to p. up the pieces** *(after breaking sth)*, *Fig* ramasser les morceaux; **we were left to p. up the bill** c'est nous qui avons dû casquer; **let me p. up the bill** laisse-moi payer **2** *(collect)* aller prendre *ou* chercher; **I'll p. you up at the station** je viendrai vous chercher *ou* vous chercher à la gare; **the train stops to p. up passengers** le train s'arrête pour prendre des voyageurs **3** *(catch)* **to p. up a cold** ramasser *ou* attraper un rhume **4** *(acquire)* **to p. sth up cheap** acheter qch bon marché; **she's good at picking up bargains** elle a du flair pour les bonnes affaires; **to p. up a parking ticket** attraper un PV **5** *Fam (initiate casual sexual relationship with)* **to p. up a man/woman** lever *ou* emballer un homme/une femme; **he tried to p. her up** il l'a draguée; **to p. up a customer** *(of prostitute)* racoler *ou* raccrocher un client **6** *(arrest) (person)* arrêter **7** *(message)* capter, recevoir; *Radio (station)* capter; *Elec (current)* prendre, capter; *(of searchlight) (plane etc)* repérer; **the police have picked up a trail** la police a trouvé une piste **8** *(learn) (trick, language, fact)* apprendre; *(news, information)* recueillir; **to p. up a habit** prendre une habitude; **I don't know where he's picking up these funny ideas from** je ne sais pas où il va chercher ces idées bizarres; **she seems to have picked up the idea that ...** elle a l'air de s'être mis dans la tête que ... **9** *(notice) (error)* relever **10** *(continue) (discussion)* reprendre; **we soon picked up the road again** nous avons vite retrouvé notre chemin **11** *(reprimand)* **to p. sb up sharply** reprendre qn vertement; **I'd like to p. Chris Jones up on that (point)** *(in debate)* j'aimerais reprendre Chris Jones sur ce point; **to p. sb up for a mistake** réprimander qn pour avoir fait une erreur **12** *Aut etc* **to p. up speed** reprendre de la vitesse; **to p. up strength** *(of person)* reprendre des forces

13 *(make better) (person)* remonter; **that will p. you up** voilà qui vous remontera

VI **1** *(improve)* s'améliorer; *(after illness)* retrouver la santé *ou* ses forces, se rétablir; **business is picking up** les affaires reprennent; **the weather looks like picking up** le temps a l'air de se remettre; **the game certainly picked up in the second half** la partie s'est animée pendant la deuxième mi-temps **2** *(continue) (of conversation, negotiations etc)* reprendre; *(in relationship)* recommencer; **let's p. up where we left off** reprenons là où nous nous étions arrêtés **3** *Sport etc* **to p. up on sb** rattraper qn; **this engine picks up well** ce moteur a de bonnes reprises

pick-a-back ADV, ADJ, N = **piggyback**

pickaninny [pɪkəˈnɪnɪ] N *Old-fashioned Offensive Sl* = **piccaninny**

pickaxe, *Am* **pickax** [ˈpɪkæks] N *(tool)* pioche *f*, pic *m*
VT piocher

picker [ˈpɪkər] N **1** *(of fruit etc)* cueilleur, -euse **2** *(of cotton etc)* démêleur, -euse

pickerel [ˈpɪkərəl] N *(fish)* doré *m*

picket [ˈpɪkɪt] N **1** *Ind etc (of strikers)* piquet *m* de grève; *(one person)* gréviste *mf* en faction **2** *Mil etc (detachment)* piquet *m* (d'hommes); *(one soldier)* factionnaire *m*; **to be on p.** être de piquet **3** *(stake) (of fence etc)* piquet *m*, pieu *m*; *(for horses etc)* piquet d'attache

VT (-t-) **1** *Ind etc* **to p. a factory** mettre un piquet de grève aux portes d'une usine **2** *(fence) (area)* entourer de piquets *ou* de pieux **3** *(fasten) (horses)* mettre au(x) piquet(s)

VI *Ind etc* faire le piquet de grève

▶▶ **p. duty** piquet; **p. fence** clôture *f* de piquets, palissade *f*; **p. line** piquet de grève

picketing [ˈpɪkɪtɪŋ] N *Ind etc* blocage *m* par des piquets de grève

picking [ˈpɪkɪŋ] N **1** *(choosing)* choix *m* **2** *(of fruit, flowers etc)* cueillette *f* **3** *(of lock)* crochetage *m*

▶▶ **p. season** cueillette

pickings [ˈpɪkɪŋz] NPL *(money etc)* bénéfices *mpl*; **to make rich p. from a scheme** tirer de gros bénéfices d'une affaire

pickle [ˈpɪk(ə)l] N **1** pickles pickles *mpl*, conserves *fpl* au vinaigre; **mixed pickles** mélange *m* de pickles **2** *(marinade)* saumure *f* **3** *Fam (predicament)* **to be in a bit of a p.** être dans de beaux draps *ou* dans le pétrin

VT saumurer, conserver (au vinaigre *ou* à la saumure)

pickled [ˈpɪk(ə)ld] ADJ **1** saumuré, en saumure **2** *Fam (drunk)* gris, pompette

▶▶ **p. cabbage** chou *m* rouge au vinaigre; **p. onions** oignons *mpl* au vinaigre

pickling [ˈpɪk(ə)lɪŋ] N saumurage *m*, conservation *f* au vinaigre

▶▶ **p. onions** petits oignons *mpl*

picklock [ˈpɪklɒk] N **1** *(person)* crocheteur *m (de serrures)* **2** *(key)* crochet *m*, rossignol *m*

pick-me-up N *Fam* remontant *m*

pickpocket [ˈpɪkpɒkɪt] N voleur, -euse à la tire, pickpocket *m*

pick-up N **1** *(collection)* ramassage *m*; *Electron, Radio (of signal)* captage *m* **2** *(device) (on record player)* lecteur *m* (phonographique), pick-up *m inv*, *Electron etc (of waves, vibrations)* capteur *m*, détecteur *m* **3** *(truck)* pick-up *m inv*, camionnette *f* à plateau **4** *Fam (man, woman)* conquête *f* **5** *Fam (improvement)* amélioration *f*, *(of business etc)* reprise *f*, *(of optimism)* regain *m*

▸▸ **p. arm** (on record player) pick-up; **p. point** (for passengers on coach journey, goods etc) point m de ramassage; **p. truck** pick-up, camionnette à plateau

picky ['pɪkɪ] ADJ Fam difficile; **to be p. about one's food** être difficile sur la nourriture

picnic ['pɪknɪk] N pique-nique m, pl pique-niques; **to go on a p.** aller faire un pique-nique, aller pique-niquer; Fig Fam **it was no p.** cela n'a pas été une partie de plaisir; **we had a p. lunch** nous avons pique-niqué à midi; **we'll take a p. lunch with us** nous emporterons un pique-nique (pour le déjeuner)

VI (pt, pp **picnicked**) pique-niquer, faire un pique-nique

▸▸ **p. area** aire f de pique-nique; **p. basket, p. hamper** panier m à pique-nique; (filled) panier garni; **p. site** aire de pique-nique

picnicker ['pɪknɪkər] N pique-niqueur, -euse, pl pique-niqueurs -euses

Pict [pɪkt] N Hist Picte mf

Pictish ['pɪktɪʃ] ADJ Hist picte, pictique

pictogram ['pɪktəgræm] N pictogramme m

pictograph ['pɪktəgrɑːf] N pictographe m

pictorial [pɪk'tɔːrɪəl] ADJ (magazine etc) illustré; (representation) en images

N périodique m illustré, journal m illustré

▸▸ **p. dictionary** dictionnaire m en images

pictorially [pɪk'tɔːrɪəlɪ] ADV en images

PICTURE ['pɪktʃər] N **1** (image) (painting) tableau m, peinture f; (drawing) dessin m; (in picture book etc), TV image f; (illustrating text) illustration f; (photograph) photo f; **to paint a p.** faire ou peindre un tableau; **to draw a p.** faire un dessin; **to get one's p. in the paper** avoir sa photo dans le journal

2 Cin Fam (film) film m; **to make a p.** faire un film; Br **to go to the pictures** aller au cinéma

3 Fig **the political/economic p.** la situation politique/économique; Med **we don't know the clinical p.** nous ne savons pas quelle est la situation clinique; **to get a mental p. of sth** se représenter qch; **to paint a bleak p. of the future** présenter une triste image de l'avenir; **this book gives a more accurate p. of the General** ce livre offre un portrait plus fidèle du général; **a clearer p. is emerging of what is taking place in the city** une image plus nette de ce qui se passe dans la ville est en train de se dessiner

4 (phrases) **she's a p., she looks a p.** elle est belle; **he's no p.!** ce n'est pas une beauté!; **she looked an absolute p. in her new dress** elle était à croquer avec sa nouvelle robe; **he's the p. of health** il respire la santé; **she looked a p. of misery** elle faisait pitié; **his face was a p.** il a fait une tête à mourir de rire; **to be in the p.** être au courant ou au fait; **put/keep me in the p.** mets/tiens-moi au courant; **I get the p.** je vois; **to be out of the p.** être dépassé, être en dehors du coup; **it doesn't come into the p.** cela n'entre pas en ligne de compte; **when did he come into the p.?** quand a-t-il commencé à être question de lui?

VT **1** (imagine) **to p. (to oneself)** s'imaginer, se figurer, se représenter; **I can't p. him as a teacher** je ne me l'imagine ou le figure pas professeur; **p. yourself as leader/at 80** imagine-toi dirigeant/à 80 ans

2 (represent, portray) représenter; (in words) dépeindre, décrire; Fig **Orwell pictures a world where …** Orwell décrit ou dépeint un monde où …

▸▸ **p. book** livre m d'images; Cards **p. card** figure f, **p. cheque** image-chèque f, pl images-chèques; Mktg **p. completion** images à compléter; **p. dealer** marchand, -ande de tableaux; Journ **p. desk** bureau m des illustrations; **p. dictionary** dictionnaire m en images; **p. editor** illustrateur, -trice; **p. frame** cadre m (pour tableaux); **p. framer**

encadreur, -euse; **p. gallery** musée m de peinture; **p. hat** capeline f; **p. library** banque f d'images; Comput **p. memory** mémoire f d'images; Tel **p. messaging** envoi m de photos par téléphone portable; Br Old-fashioned **p. palace** cinéma m; Old-fashioned **p. postcard** carte f postale (illustrée); **p. puzzle** rébus m; TV **p. quality** qualité f des images; **p. research** documentation f iconographique; **p. researcher** documentaliste mf iconographique; **p. story** roman-photo m, pl romans-photos; TV **p. tube** tube m image; **p. window** fenêtre f ou baie f panoramique; **p. writing** écriture f idéographique

picturesque [pɪktʃə'resk] ADJ pittoresque; (descriptions etc) imagé; Euph **she told him in p. language to leave** elle lui a ordonné de partir dans un langage assez cru

picturesquely [pɪktʃə'resklɪ] ADV pittoresquement; (to describe, write) de façon imagée

picturesqueness [pɪktʃə'resknɪs] N pittoresque m

piddle ['pɪd(ə)l] Fam VI faire pipi

N pipi m; **to have a p.** faire pipi

piddling ['pɪdlɪŋ] ADJ Fam insignifiant, ridicule

pidgin ['pɪdʒɪn] N Ling pidgin m; **p. English etc** ≃ petit nègre m

pie [paɪ] N (with meat) = pâté m en croûte; (apple etc) **p.** = tourte f (aux pommes etc); esp Am (without top) tarte f (aux pommes etc); **chicken p.** = croustade f de volaille; **cottage or shepherd's p.** hachis m parmentier; **fish p.** = timbale f de poissons; Fam **p. in the sky** des châteaux en Espagne; **easy as p.** simple comme bonjour

▸▸ **p. chart** graphique m circulaire, camembert m; **p. dish** plat m à tarte; (for meat) terrine f; (oven-proof) plat allant au four

piebald ['paɪbɔːld] ADJ (horse) pie

N (cheval m) pie m

PIECE [piːs]

morceau 1	▪ bout 1	▪ parcelle 1
▪ pièce 1–4	▪ article 1	▪ pion 2

N **1** (of paper, bread etc) morceau m, bout m; (of string, ribbon) bout m; (of land) parcelle f; (of cloth) morceau, coupon m; (of glass etc) morceau, fragment m, éclat m; (of machine etc) partie f, pièce f; (of music, poetry) morceau; (in book) passage m; Journ article m, papier m; **to do a p. to camera** s'adresser directement à la caméra (pour un reporter de télévision); **a p. of clothing** un vêtement; **a p. of furniture** un meuble; **a p. of luggage** (suitcase) une valise; (bag) un sac; **how many pieces of luggage do you have?** combien de bagages avez-vous?; **one p. of hand-luggage** un bagage à main; **to do a p. of work** faire un travail; **to show sb a p. of one's work** montrer un échantillon de son travail à qn; **he's a nasty p. of work** c'est un sale type; **a p. of advice** un conseil; **p. of bravery/folly** acte m de bravoure/folie; **a p. of carelessness** une étourderie; **a p. of cruelty** une cruauté; **p. of (good) luck** coup m de chance; **what a p. of luck!** quelle chance!; **a p. of news** une nouvelle; Fig Fam **it was a p. of cake** c'était de la tarte; Fig **everyone wants a p. of the cake** tout le monde veut sa part du gâteau

2 (in games) (in backgammon) dame f; (in dominoes) domino m; (in draughts) pion m; (of jigsaw puzzle), Chess pièce f

3 esp Br (coin) **five-/fifty-pence p.** pièce f de cinq/cinquante pence

4 (weapon) (of artillery) pièce f; (firearm) arme f; Fam **to be carrying a p.** porter une arme, être armé

5 Sl (girl) nana f, **she's a nice or tasty p.** c'est une belle nana ou nénette

6 Metal punched/shaped **p.** pièce f estampée/profilée; **to cast cylinders in one p.** couler des cylindres d'un seul jet ou en bloc; **cast or pressed or made in one p.** monobloc inv

7 esp Am (short distance) **he lives down the road a p.** il n'habite pas loin d'ici; **I'll walk with you down the road a p.** je vais faire un petit bout de chemin avec toi

8 Sl (gun) flingue m

9 (in phrases) **they are all of a p.** (of people) ils sont tous du même genre ou acabit; **it's all of a p. to me** pour moi c'est la même chose ou ça revient au même; **to be still in one p.** (of person, car etc after accident) être encore entier; **all in one p.** (made, constructed) tout d'une pièce, d'un seul morceau, d'un seul tenant; **to give sb a p. of one's mind** dire ses quatre vérités à qn; **to say one's p.** dire ce qu'on a à dire; **p. by p.** morceau par morceau; Com **to sell sth by the p.** vendre qch à la pièce; Fam **to go to pieces** (of person) s'effondrer (complètement), Fam craquer; Sport (of team etc) s'effondrer; **to fall to pieces** (of bicycle, furniture, plans etc) tomber en morceaux; (of house etc) se délabrer, crouler; **my coat is falling to pieces** mon manteau part en morceaux; **her life was falling to pieces** toute sa vie s'effondrait; **to take a machine to pieces** démonter une machine; **to break sth in or to pieces** briser qch, mettre qch en morceaux

▸▸ Tex **p. goods** marchandises fpl ou tissus mpl à la pièce; **p. rate** paiement m à la pièce

▸ **piece together** VT SEP (assemble) (model, jigsaw etc) joindre, assembler les morceaux de; (broken vase, chair, torn letter) recoller les morceaux de; (facts etc) coordonner; **to p. together what happened** reconstituer ce qui s'est passé; **detectives are piecing together a picture of the events** les enquêteurs sont en train de se faire une idée des événements

-piece [piːs] SUFF **one-p. overall** combinaison f, **a three-p. suite** un salon trois pièces; **two-/three-p. suit** costume m deux/trois pièces; **a twenty-four-p. dinner service** un service de table vingt-quatre pièces; **three-p. ensemble** trio m; **a four-p. band** un groupe de quatre éléments; **a twenty-p. orchestra** un orchestre de vingt musiciens ou éléments

piecemeal ['piːsmiːl] ADV par morceaux; (gradually) petit à petit, peu à peu; **the collection was sold p.** les pièces de la collection ont été vendues séparément

ADJ fragmentaire, parcellaire; (work) fait petit à petit; (funding, transformation) morcelé, fragmenté

piecework ['piːswɜːk] N Ind travail m à la tâche ou à la pièce

pieceworker ['piːswɜːkər] N Ind travailleur, -euse à la tâche ou à la pièce

piecrust ['paɪkrʌst] N croûte f de pâté

pied [paɪd] ADJ bigarré, panaché; **the P. Piper of Hamelin** le Joueur de flûte d'Hamelin

pied-à-terre, pl **pieds-à-terre** [pjeɪdɑːˈteər] N pied-à-terre m inv

Piedmont ['piːdmɒnt] N Piémont m

pie-eyed ADJ Sl (drunk) rond, bourré; **to get p.** se saouler

pier [pɪər] N **1** (at seaside resort) jetée f, (of stone) jetée, môle m, digue f, (on piles) estacade f **2** Constr (of stonework) pilier m

pierce [pɪəs] VT percer, transpercer; **to p. a hole in sth** faire ou percer un trou dans qch; **to have one's ears pierced** se faire percer les oreilles; **to p. the darkness** (of light) trouer l'obscurité; **to p. the air with one's cries** percer l'air de ses cris

VI to p. through the enemy's lines pénétrer les lignes de l'ennemi

piercing ['pɪəsɪŋ] ADJ (tool, cry) aigu, perçant; (look) perçant, pénétrant; (cold, wind) pénétrant

pierhead ['pɪəhed] N musoir m

pierrot ['pɪərəʊ] N Theat pierrot m

piety ['paɪətɪ] N piété f

piffle ['pɪf(ə)l] N Fam futilités fpl, bêtises fpl, niaiseries fpl; **to talk p.** dire des futilités ou des bêtises

piffling ['pɪflɪŋ] ADJ Fam (objection, mistake) insignifiant; (sum, wage) ridicule, insignifiant; (occupation, activity) futile; (speech etc) creux; **some p. little assistant** un petit assistant insignifiant

pig [pɪg] N 1 (animal) porc m, cochon m; Am (young pig) cochonnet m, porcelet m; Fam (glutton) goinfre mf, glouton, -onne; **to eat like a p., to make a p. of oneself** s'empiffrer, se goinfrer; Fam **he's a greedy p.** c'est un goinfre; Fig Fam **to buy a p. in a poke** acheter chat en poche; Fig Fam **when pigs fly** quand les poules auront des dents; Br Fam **to make a p.'s ear of sth** saloper qch; **wild p.** sanglier m; Am (piglet) marcassin m, jeune sanglier 2 Fam (unpleasant person) salaud m, salope f, sale type m; Fam (ugly person) mocheté f, Sl Pej (police officer) flic m; Br Fam (unpleasant thing, task) truc m chiant; Fam **you dirty little p.!** petit cochon!; Fam **what a selfish p.!** quel sale égoïste!; Fam **the filing cabinet was a p. to move** ça a été vachement difficile de déplacer le classeur 3 Metal (of casting) gueuse f; (of lead, tin etc) saumon m

VI (-gg-) (of sow) mettre bas, cochonner
VT Fam 1 **to p. oneself** (eat excessively) s'empiffrer, se goinfrer (on sth de qch) 2 **to p. it** (be untidy, dirty) vivre comme des cochons
▸▸ **p. farm** porcherie f, élevage m de porcs; **p. iron** fonte f brute; **P. Latin** = argot m codé utilisé en milieu scolaire, ≃ javanais m

▸ **pig out** VI Fam (eat excessively) s'empiffrer, se goinfrer (on sth de qch)

pigeon ['pɪdʒɪn] N 1 (bird) pigeon m 2 Br Fam **that's not my p.** (concern) ce n'est pas mon truc
▸▸ **p. fancier** colombophile mf; **p. loft** pigeonnier m; **p. post** transport m de dépêches par pigeons voyageurs

pigeon-breasted [-'brestɪd], **pigeon-chested** [-'tʃestɪd] ADJ à la poitrine saillante

pigeonhole ['pɪdʒɪnhəʊl] N 1 (in desk) case f, casier m; Fig **to put sb in a p.** cataloguer qn, étiqueter qn 2 (in dovecote) boulin m
VT 1 (classify) (papers etc) caser, classer; (complaint etc) classer; (file away in memory) reléguer dans sa mémoire 2 (defer) remettre à plus tard; **the scheme had been pigeonholed until further notice** le projet avait été remis jusqu'à nouvel ordre 3 (person) étiqueter, cataloguer, mettre une étiquette à; **I don't like being pigeonholed** je n'aime pas qu'on me catalogue

pigeon-toed ADJ qui marche les pieds tournés en dedans

piggery ['pɪgərɪ] N porcherie f; Fam (gluttony) goinfrerie f

piggish ['pɪgɪʃ] ADJ Fam (person) (dirty) sale, malpropre; (gluttonous) goinfre

piggy ['pɪgɪ] Fam N (in children's language) cochonnet m, petit cochon m; **p. in the middle** (children's game) = jeu m d'enfants dans lequel l'un des participants doit attraper la balle que les autres s'envoient; Fig **I've had enough of being p. in the middle** j'en avais assez d'être pris entre deux feux

ADJ (gluttonous) goinfre; (behaviour) de

goinfre; (eyes) porcin; **that was p. of you!** tu t'es goinfré!
▸▸ **p. bank** tirelire f

piggyback ['pɪgɪbæk] ADV 1 (on one's back) sur le dos; **to ride p. on sb** monter sur le dos de qn 2 Comput **to mount sth p. on sth** superposer qch sur qch
N **to give sb a p.** porter qn sur son dos; **can I have a p.?** est-ce que je peux monter sur ton dos?
▸▸ Comput **p. board** carte f fille

piggybacking ['pɪgɪbækɪŋ] N 1 Com exportation f kangourou 2 Banking portage m

pig-headed ADJ obstiné, entêté

pigheadedly [pɪg'hedɪdlɪ] ADV obstinément

pigheadedness [pɪg'hedɪdnɪs] N obstination f, entêtement m

piglet ['pɪglɪt] N cochonnet m, porcelet m

pigment ['pɪgmənt] N 1 Art etc couleur f, colorant m, pigment m 2 Physiol pigment m
▸▸ **p. cell** cellule f pigmentaire

pigmentation [pɪgmən'teɪʃən] N pigmentation f

pigmented [pɪg'mentɪd] ADJ pigmenté

pigmy ['pɪgmɪ] N, ADJ = **pygmy**

pigpen ['pɪgpen] N Am = **pigsty**

pigskin ['pɪgskɪn] N (leather) peau f de porc; **p. purse** bourse f en peau de porc

pigsty ['pɪgstaɪ] N 1 porcherie f 2 Fig Fam (house, room) porcherie f; **your room is a p.** ta chambre est une vraie porcherie

pigswill ['pɪgswɪl] N pâtée f pour les porcs; Fam (food) pâtée pour chiens

pigtail ['pɪgteɪl] N natte f

pig-thick ADJ Br Fam con comme un balai

pig-ugly ADJ Br Fam moche comme un pou

pike¹ [paɪk] N 1 (weapon) pique f 2 Br Dial (peak in the Lake District) pic m
▸▸ **p. bearer** piquier m

pike² N (fish) brochet m

pike³ N esp Am = **turnpike**

pikestaff ['paɪkstɑːf] N 1 (weapon) bois m ou hampe f de pique 2 (for walking) bâton m à pointe de fer

pikey ['paɪkɪ] N Br Sl casseur m

pilaf(f) ['piːlæf] N Culin pilaf m, pilau m

pilaster [pɪ'læstər] N Archit pilastre m

pilates [pɪ'lɑːteɪz] N Pilates m, méthode f Pilates; **to do p.** pratiquer la méthode Pilates

pilau, pilaw ['piːlaʊ, -ləʊ, -lɔː] N = **pilaf**

pilchard ['pɪltʃəd] N (fish) pilchard m

PILE [paɪl]

N	tas 1 ▪ pile 1, 2 ▪ édifice 3
	▪ pieu 4 ▪ poil 5
VT	entasser ▪ empiler

N 1 (heap) (of wood, stones, rubbish etc) tas m; (of objects, goods etc) tas, amas m, amoncellement m; (of gold) monceau m; (of plates, laundry etc) pile f; **to put in(to) a p., to make a p. of** mettre en tas, empiler; Fam **he made his p. in the fur trade** (fortune) il a fait fortune dans le commerce de fourrure; Fam **she must have made a p. out of that deal** elle a dû gagner une fortune dans ce contrat; Fam **to have piles** or **a p. of ironing/work to do** avoir un tas de repassage/ travail à faire; Fig Fam **to be at the top/bottom of the p.** être favorisé/défavorisé 2 Elec (electric) p. pile f (électrique); Nucl (atomic) **p.** pile, réacteur m (atomique) 3 (building) édifice m; Fam Hum **the family p.** la cabane familiale 4 Constr pieu m; **to drive piles** enfoncer des pieux; **built on piles** bâti sur pilotis 5 Tex (of carpet etc) poil m
VT (earth etc) entasser, amonceler; (objects)

mettre en tas; (wood, books etc) empiler; **they piled food onto my plate** ils ont amoncelé de la nourriture dans mon assiette; **the table was piled high with dishes** des assiettes s'empilaient sur la table
VI Fam **seven of them piled into the car** sept d'entre eux se sont entassés dans la voiture
▸▸ **p. dwelling** habitation f lacustre ou sur pilotis; **p. fabrics** tissus mpl à poil

▸ **pile in** VI Fam (of people) entrer en masse; **p. in everybody!** (into car etc) allez-y, montez tout le monde!
VT SEP Fam (cause to enter in large numbers, quantity) entasser

▸ **pile off** VI Fam descendre en masse

▸ **pile on** VT SEP (give in large numbers, quantity) amonceler; **my plate was full, but they piled on more** mon assiette était pleine mais ils m'ont resservi une platée; **to p. on the pressure** faire monter la pression; **to p. on the agony** dramatiser; **to p. on the runs** marquer un grand nombre de points; Fam **to p. it on** exagérer, en rajouter

▸ **pile out** VI Fam (of people) partir en masse; (from vehicle) sortir en masse; **fifteen people piled out of the compartment** quinze personnes ont quitté le compartiment en masse

▸ **pile up** VI (form into pile(s)) s'amonceler, s'entasser, s'empiler; (of cars) se caramboler; **dirty dishes were piling up** la vaisselle sale s'empilait ou s'amoncelait; **work was piling up on her desk** le travail s'amoncelait sur son bureau; **the clouds are piling up** les nuages s'amoncellent
VT SEP 1 (form into pile(s)) entasser, empiler; **p. the leaves up here** entasse les feuilles ici; **to p. up money** amasser de l'argent 2 Fam (crash, wreck) **to p. up one's plane/a car** bousiller son appareil/une voiture; **ship piled up on the rocks** navire échoué sur les rochers

pile-driver N Constr sonnette f, Fam (blow) coup m d'assommoir; Ftbl shoot m vigoureux

piles [paɪlz] NPL Med hémorroïdes fpl; **to have p.** avoir des hémorroïdes

pile-up N Aut carambolage m, télescopage m en série

pilfer ['pɪlfər] VT & VI chaparder (sth from sb qch à qn)

pilferage ['pɪlfərɪdʒ] N = **pilfering**

pilferer ['pɪlfərər] N chapardeur, -euse

pilfering ['pɪlfərɪŋ] N petits vols mpl, larcins mpl; **the percentage lost through p.** le pourcentage perdu imputable aux petits vols

pilgrim ['pɪlgrɪm] N pèlerin, -ine; **pilgrims to Lourdes/Mecca** les pèlerins de Lourdes/ de la Mecque
▸▸ **the P. Fathers** les (Pères) Pèlerins mpl; Liter **The P.'s Progress** Le Voyage du pèlerin

pilgrimage ['pɪlgrɪmɪdʒ] N Rel, Fig pèlerinage m; **to go on a p., to make a p.** aller en pèlerinage, faire un pèlerinage

pill [pɪl] N Pharm pilule f; **the p.** (contraceptive) la pilule; **she's on the p.** elle prend la pilule; (sugar-coated) **p.** dragée f, Fam **to be a p. popper** se bourrer de médicaments

pillage ['pɪlɪdʒ] Lit N pillage m
VT (town) piller, saccager, mettre à sac
VI se livrer au pillage, piller

pillager ['pɪlɪdʒər] N pilleur, -euse, pillard, -arde

pillar ['pɪlər] N Archit pilier m; (of table, pedestal table) pied m central; Fig **a p. of the Church/of society** un pilier de l'Église/de la société; **to be a p. of strength** être d'un grand appui; **I've been rushing around from p. to post** je n'ai pas arrêté de courir d'un endroit à l'autre ou à droite et à gauche; **p. of**

fire/smoke colonne *f* de feu/fumée; **p. of rock** colonne rocheuse; **p. of salt** statue *f* de sel; *Aut* **door p.** montant *m* de porte
▸▸ *Br* **p. box** boîte *f* à lettres

pillared ['pɪləd] ADJ *Archit* à piliers

pillbox ['pɪlbɒks] N **1** (*for pills*) boîte *f* à pilules **2** (*hat*) petit chapeau *m* rond sans bord **3** *Mil* blockhaus *m*
▸▸ **p. hat** petit chapeau rond sans bord

pillhead ['pɪlhed] N *Sl* accro *mf* aux tranquillisants ou aux speeds

pillion ['pɪljən] N (*seat on motorcycle*) siège *m* arrière, selle *f* tandem, tan-sad *m*, *pl* tan-sads; **to ride p.** monter derrière
▸▸ **p. passenger, p. rider** passager, -ère (de derrière); **p. seat** siège arrière, selle tandem, tan-sad

pillock ['pɪlək] N *Br Sl* (*fool*) abruti *m*, con *m*

pillory ['pɪlərɪ] N pilori *m*
VT *Hist, Fig* (*person*) mettre au pilori; *Fig* (*evil, corrupt practice*) dénoncer

pillow ['pɪləʊ] N oreiller *m*
VT **to p. one's head on one's arms** poser sa tête sur ses bras; **her head was pillowed on a mound of leaves** sa tête reposait sur un oreiller de feuilles
▸▸ **p. fight** bataille *f* de polochons; **p. talk** confidences *fpl* sur l'oreiller

pillowcase, pillowslip ['pɪləʊkeɪs, -slɪp] N taie *f* d'oreiller

pilot ['paɪlət] N **1** *Aviat, Naut* pilote *m* **2** *TV* émission *f* pilote
VT (*ship, plane etc*) piloter; (*person through obstacles*) mener, conduire; **to p. the country through difficult times** aider le pays à traverser une mauvaise passe
▸▸ *Met* **p. balloon** ballon-sonde *m*, *pl* ballons-sondes; **p. boat** bateau-pilote *m*, *pl* bateaux-pilotes; **p. burner** veilleuse *f*, **p. cutter** bateau-pilote; **p. factory** usine-pilote *f*, *pl* usines-pilotes; **p. fish** pilote, poisson-pilote *m*, *pl* poissons-pilotes; **p. flame** veilleuse; *Naut* **p. house** poste *m* de pilotage; **p. jet** veilleuse (au gaz); **p. lamp** veilleuse (électrique); **p. light** veilleuse; *Br Aviat* **p. officer** ≃ sous-lieutenant *m*, *pl* sous-lieutenants; **p. plant** usine-pilote; **p. questionnaire** questionnaire *m* pilote; *Aviat, Ind, Com* **p. run** présérie *f*, *Br* **p. scheme** projet-pilote *m*, *pl* projets-pilotes; *Ind, Com* **p. series** présérie; **p. study** étude *f* pilote, avant-projet *m*, *pl* avant-projets, préétude *f*; **p. survey** enquête-pilote *f*, *pl* enquêtes-pilotes; **p. waters** zone *f* de pilotage

PIM [pɪm] N *Comput* (*abbr* **personal information manager**) gestionnaire *m* d'informations personnelles

pimento [pɪ'mentəʊ] N (*plant*), *Culin* piment *m*

pimp [pɪmp] N souteneur *m*, proxénète *m*, *Sl* maquereau *m*
VI être proxénète *ou* souteneur; **to p. for sb** maquer qn
VT maquer

pimpernel ['pɪmpənel] N (*flower*) mouron *m*; **scarlet p.** mouron rouge

pimple ['pɪmp(ə)l] N (*on skin*) bouton *m*; **to come out in pimples** boutonner, bourgeonner

pimply ['pɪmplɪ] ADJ boutonneux, couvert de boutons

PIMS [pɪmz] N *Mktg* (*abbr* **profit impact of marketing strategy**) IRSM *m*

PIN [pɪn] N (*abbr* **Personal Identification Number**) (*d'une carte bancaire*) code *m* confidentiel
▸▸ **P. number** code confidentiel

PIN [pɪn] N **1** épingle *f*, (*for hair*) épingle (à cheveux); (*brooch*) broche *f*, (**safety**) **p.** épingle de *ou* à nourrice; **you could have heard a p. drop** on aurait entendu voler une

mouche; **as bright** *or* **clean as a new p.** propre comme un sou neuf; **for two pins I'd punch his face** pour un rien je lui casserais la figure; **pins and needles** (*tingling*) fourmillements *mpl*; **I've got pins and needles in my foot** j'ai des fourmis dans le pied
2 *Tech* axe *m*; (*for securing sth*) goupille *f*, clavette *f*, (*of hinge*) gond *m*; *Elec* (*of plug, on connector*) broche *f*, (*of printhead*) aiguille *f*; *Surg* (*for fracture*) broche, clou *m*; (**firing**) **p.** percuteur *m*; (**safety**) **p.** (*of grenade*) goupille
3 *Golf* drapeau *m* de trou; (*at ninepins*) quille *f*
4 *Fam* **pins** (*legs*) quilles *fpl*, cannes *fpl*, **to feel a bit shaky on one's pins** (*after illness etc*) ne pas se sentir très solide sur ses quilles *ou* cannes
VT (*-nn-*) **1** (*fasten with pin*) épingler, attacher avec une/des épingle(s) (**to** à); (*notice to noticeboard, map to wall*) attacher *ou* fixer avec une/des punaise(s), punaiser (**to** à); **to p. papers together** épingler des papiers ensemble
2 *Tech etc* cheviller, goupiller, mettre une goupille à
3 (*hold still*) fixer, clouer; **to p. sb against** *or* **to a wall** clouer *ou* plaquer qn contre un mur; **to p. sb's arms to his sides** coller *ou* plaquer les bras de qn au corps; **to be pinned under a fallen tree** se trouver pris *ou* coincé sous un arbre déraciné; *Fig* **to p. the blame on sb** rejeter la responsabilité sur qn; **you can't p. this on me** tu ne peux pas me mettre ça sur le dos; **to p. one's hopes on sb/ sth** mettre tous ses espoirs en qn/dans qch
4 *Constr* (*wall etc*) étayer, étançonner
▸▸ **p. money** argent *m* de poche; *Arch* (*given to wife*) argent pour le ménage; **p. table** flipper *m*; *Sewing* **p. tuck** nervure *f*, **p. wheel** (*on printer*) roue *f* à picots

▸ **pin back** VT SEP *Surg* recoller; *Fig Fam* **to p. back one's ears** tendre l'oreille; *Fig Fam* **to p. back your ears** ouvrez bien vos oreilles

▸ **pin down** VT SEP **1** (*trap*) coincer; **he pinned me down** (*in fight etc*) il m'a coincé; **they were pinned down by the wreckage** ils ont été coincés dans les décombres; *Mil* **to p. down the enemy** coincer l'ennemi; **pinned down by enemy fire** coincé par le feu de l'ennemi
2 (*force to be definite*) obliger à s'engager; **I tried to p. her down to a time** j'ai essayé de l'obliger à donner une heure précise; **to p. sb down to do sth** obliger *ou* contraindre qn à faire qch; **without pinning himself down to anything** sans s'engager à rien
3 (*identify*) identifier; **we couldn't p. down the source of the noise** nous ne pouvions pas identifier la source du bruit; **a feeling that's difficult to p. down** un sentiment qu'il est difficile de définir; **it's difficult to p. it down** c'est difficile de mettre le doigt dessus

▸ **pin up** VT SEP **1** (*fasten to wall etc*) (*photo etc*) fixer au mur etc, punaiser
2 (*fasten*) **to p. up one's hair** relever ses cheveux; **to p. up a hem** rabattre un ourlet avec des épingles

pinafore ['pɪnəfɔːr] N *esp Br* (*apron*) tablier *m*; (*dress*) robe *f* à bretelles, robe-chasuble
▸▸ **p. dress** robe à bretelles, robe-chasuble, *pl* robes-chasubles

pinball ['pɪnbɔːl] N (*machine, game*) flipper *m*
▸▸ **p. machine** flipper

pincer ['pɪnsər] N (*of crab, insect etc*) pince *f*
▸▸ *Mil* **p. movement** manœuvre *f* *ou* mouvement *m* d'encerclement

pincers ['pɪnsəz] NPL (*tool*) (**pair of**) **p.** pince *f*, tenaille(s) *f (pl)* VOIR GRAMMAIRE A10

pinch [pɪntʃ] N **1** (*action*) pincement *m*; **to give sb a p.** pincer qn; **the p. of hunger** les tiraillements *mpl* de la faim; *Fam* **to feel the**

p. être gêné; **at** *or Am* **in a p.** à la rigueur **2** (*of salt etc*) pincée *f*, (*of snuff*) prise *f*, *Fig* **to take sth with a p. of salt** ne pas prendre qch pour argent comptant
VT **1** (*nip*) (*somebody, somebody's cheek etc*) pincer; **these shoes are pinching my feet** ces chaussures me font mal aux pieds *ou* me blessent; **I had to p. myself** (*I thought I was dreaming*) je me suis pincé **2** *Fam* (*steal*) piquer, faucher (**from sb** à qn); (*arrest*) (*thief etc*) épingler, pincer, choper; **I've had my purse pinched** on m'a piqué *ou* fauché mon porte-monnaie; **who's pinched my pen?** qui est-ce qui m'a chipé *ou* piqué mon stylo?; **to get pinched** (*of thief etc*) se faire pincer *ou* épingler *ou* choper
VI **1** (*nip*) blesser; **a shoe that pinches** une chaussure qui blesse *ou* qui serre; *Fig* **that's where the shoe pinches** c'est là que le bât blesse **2** **to p. and scrape** *or* **save** faire des économies de bouts de chandelle

▸ **pinch off** VT SEP (*remove*) enlever en pinçant; **to p. off a bud** épincer un bourgeon

▸ **pinch out** VT SEP épincer

pinchbeck ['pɪntʃbek] *Lit* N toc *m*
ADJ (*sham*) simili, en toc

pinched [pɪntʃt] ADJ **1** (*face*) tiré, hâve; (*features*) tiré; **to be p. with hunger** être tenaillé par la faim **2** (*restricted*) étroit; **to be (a bit) p. for money/time** être à court d'argent/de temps; **to be (a bit) p. for space** être un peu à l'étroit

pinch-hit VI *Am* **to p. for sb** *Baseball* frapper à la place de qn; *Fig* remplacer qn

pinch-hitter N *Am Baseball* frappeur *m* d'urgence *ou* suppléant

pinch-runner N *Am Baseball* coureur *m* d'urgence *ou* suppléant

pincushion ['pɪnkʊʃən] N pelote *f* à épingles

pine¹ [paɪn] N **1** (*tree*) pin *m* **2** (*wood*) (*bois m de*) pin *m*; **p. furniture** meubles *mpl* en pin
▸▸ **p. cone** pomme *f* de pin, *Can* cocotte *f*, **p. forest** forêt *f* de pins, pinède *f*, **p. kernel** pignon *m*, pigne *f*, **p. marten** martre *f*, **p. needle** aiguille *f* de pin; **p. nut** pignon, pigne; **p. tree** pin

pine² VI languir; **to p. with grief** languir de tristesse

▸ **pine away** VI = **pine²**

▸ **pine for** VT INSEP languir pour *ou* après; **to p. for home/the good old days** avoir la nostalgie du foyer/du bon vieux temps; **he's pining for a good plate of sauerkraut** il meurt d'envie de manger une bonne assiette de choucroute

pineapple ['paɪnæp(ə)l] N ananas *m*; **p. juice** jus *m* d'ananas

ping [pɪŋ] N (*of sth hitting wine glass, small bell etc*) tintement *m*, petit bruit *m* clair; (*of bullet etc*) cinglement *m*
VI (*of sth hitting wine glass, small bell etc*) tinter, faire un petit bruit clair; (*of bullet etc*) cingler

Pinger® ['pɪŋər] N (*timer*) minuteur *m*

Ping-Pong® N ping-pong *m*
▸▸ **P. ball** balle *f* de ping-pong; **P. table** table *f* de ping-pong

pinhead ['pɪnhed] N **1** tête *f* d'épingle **2** *Fam* (*stupid person*) idiot, -ote, abruti, -ie

pinhole ['pɪnhəʊl] N **1** trou *m* d'épingle; *Opt* (*in screen etc*) ouverture *f* minuscule; *Phot* sténopé *m*; **p. source of light** source *f* de lumière punctiforme *ou* ponctuelle **2** *Tech* trou *m* de cheville *ou* de goujon
▸▸ **p. camera** appareil *m* à sténopé

pining ['paɪnɪŋ] N langueur *f*, languissement *m*; (*strong desire*) désir *m* ardent (**for sth** de qch); (*for home*) nostalgie *f*

pinion¹ ['pɪnjən] N *Orn* (*flight feathers*) penne *f*, rémige *f*

vt 1 *(hold)* **to p. sb to the ground/against a wall** clouer qn au sol/contre un mur; **to p. sb's arms** *(tie)* attacher *ou* lier les bras de qn; *(hold)* tenir les bras de qn **2** *(bird)* rogner les ailes à

pinion² N *Tech* pignon *m*
▸▸ **p. wheel** roue *f* à pignon

pink¹ [pɪŋk] **N 1** *(colour)* rose *m*; **in the p. of condition** *or* **health** en excellente *ou* parfaite santé; *(of racehorse etc)* entraîné à fond; **to be in the p.** *(of person)* se porter à merveille **2** *(flower)* œillet *m*; **garden p.** (œillet) mignardise *f*
ADJ 1 *(colour)* rose; **to turn** *or* **go p.** *(with embarrassment etc)* rosir; **to see p. elephants** voir double; **p. eyes** *(of albino)* yeux *mpl* rouges **2** *Fam* = **pinko**
▸▸ **p. champagne** champagne *m* rosé; *Am Fam* **p. collar job** = emploi *m* typiquement féminin; *Am Fam* **p. collar workers** employées *fpl* de bureau; **p. gin** = cocktail *m* à base de gin et d'angustura; **p. lady** = cocktail à base de gin et de grenadine; **the p. pound** = le pouvoir d'achat de la communauté homosexuelle; *Am Fam* **p. slip** lettre *f* *ou* avis *m* de licenciement; **to get one's p. slip** être licencié

pink² VT *Sewing etc (with pinking shears)* denteler, cranter; *(leather etc)* travailler à jour, évider

pink³ VI *(of engine)* cliqueter

pinkeye [ˈpɪŋkaɪ] N *Med* conjonctivite *f* aiguë contagieuse

pinkie [ˈpɪŋkɪ] N *Am, Scot Fam* petit doigt *m*, auriculaire *m*

pinking¹ [ˈpɪŋkɪŋ] N *Sewing etc* découpage *m*, découpure *f*
▸▸ **p. scissors, p. shears** ciseaux *mpl* à cranter *ou* à denteler

pinking² N *(of engine)* cliquetis *m* *(produit par les autoallumages)*

pinkish [ˈpɪŋkɪʃ] ADJ rosé, rosâtre

pinko [ˈpɪŋkəʊ] N, ADJ *Pol Fam* gauchisant, -ante

pinky¹ [ˈpɪŋkɪ] N *Am, Scot Fam* = **pinkie**

pinky² ADJ *Fam* rosé, rosâtre; **p. grey** gris *m inv* rosâtre *ou* rosé

pinnace [ˈpɪnɪs] N *Naut* chaloupe *f*, grand canot *m*

pinnacle [ˈpɪnək(ə)l] **N 1** *(of mountain)* cime *f*, **a p. of rock** un piton rocheux; *Fig* **on the highest p. of fame** à l'apogée *ou* au sommet de la gloire **2** *Archit* pinacle *m*, clocheton *m*; *(of ridge)* couronnement *m*

pinny [ˈpɪnɪ] N *esp Br Fam* tablier *m*

pinout [ˈpɪnaʊt] N *Comput* broche *f* de sortie

pinpoint [ˈpɪnpɔɪnt] N *(tip of a pin)* pointe *f* d'épingle; *(very small point)* point *m* infime *ou* infinitésimal
VT *(point out)* indiquer exactement; *(locate)* *(place, fact, argument, consideration)* localiser *ou* repérer exactement; *(source of rumour, cause of problem)* déterminer, identifier; *Mil (aim at)* viser avec précision; *(fire on, bomb)* effectuer un tir/un bombardement de précision sur; **to p. a problem** isoler un problème, mettre le doigt sur un problème
▸▸ **p. accuracy** haute précision *f*, *Mil* **p. bombing** bombardement *m* de précision

pinprick [ˈpɪnprɪk] N piqûre *f* d'aiguille; *Fam* **pinpricks** *(annoying things)* tracasseries *fpl*

pinstripe [ˈpɪnstraɪp] N *Tex* rayures *fpl* fines; **pinstripes** costume *m* rayé
▸▸ **p. suit** costume rayé

pint [paɪnt] **N 1** *(measurement)* pinte *f* (= 0,568 litre; *Am* = 0,473 litre) **2** *Br Fam* **a p.** *(beer)* une pinte de bière; **I'm going for a p.** je vais prendre une bière
▸▸ **p. mug, p. pot** chope *f* d'une pinte

pinta [ˈpaɪntə] N *Br Fam* pinte *f* de lait

pintail [ˈpɪnteɪl] **N 1** *(wild duck)* pilet *m* **2** *(grouse)* tétras *m* à longue queue, *Can* gelinotte *f* à queue fine

pinto [ˈpɪntəʊ] N *Am (horse)* (cheval *m*) pie *m*
▸▸ *Culin* **p. beans** haricots *mpl* pinto; *Am* **p. horse** (cheval) pie

pint-size(d) ADJ *Fam* minuscule

pin-up N *Fam (woman, picture of woman)* pin-up *f inv*

Pinyin [ˈpɪnˈjɪn] N *Ling* pinyin *m*

pioneer [paɪəˈnɪər] N pionnier, -ière; **a p. researcher in the field of …** un chercheur qui est à l'avant-garde des travaux dans le domaine de …; **her p. work in the study of radioactivity** ses travaux innovateurs dans le domaine de la radioactivité
VT **to p. a new method** être le premier/l'un des premiers à développer une nouvelle méthode; **to p. research into …** être à l'avant-garde de la recherche dans …

pioneering [paɪəˈnɪərɪŋ] ADJ *(work)* innovateur, -trice; *(scientist etc)* qui fait œuvre de pionnier; **to do p. work in a science** faire œuvre de pionnier dans une science, ouvrir la voie dans une science; **in p. days** au temps des pionniers; **p. company** entreprise *f* innovatrice

pious [ˈpaɪəs] ADJ pieux; **p. fraud** pieux mensonge *m*; *Fam (person)* hypocrite *mf*; **p. hope** espoir *m* vain; **these p. hopes** ces vains espoirs

piously [ˈpaɪəslɪ] ADV pieusement, avec piété

piousness [ˈpaɪəsnɪs] N piété *f*

PIP [pɪp] N *Comput (abbr* **peripheral interchange program)** logiciel *m* de commutation de périphérique

pip¹ [pɪp] N *(of fruit)* pépin *m*

pip² **N 1** *(on card, die etc)* point *m* **2** *Br Mil Fam* **to get one's third p.** ≃ recevoir sa troisième ficelle **3** *Radio (sound)* top *m*; *(on radar)* top d'écho; **the pips** *Radio* = les bips *mpl* sonores; *Tel* la tonalité de crédit épuisé

pip³ VT (-pp-) *Fam* **to be pipped at the post** se faire coiffer *ou* battre sur le poteau

pip⁴ N *Old-fashioned Br Fam* **to give sb the p.** embêter qn

pipe [paɪp] **N 1** *(tube)* tuyau *m*, conduit *m*, conduite *f*, canalisation *f*; **pipes and fittings** tuyauterie *f* et accessoires *mpl* de tuyauterie **2** *Mus* chalumeau *m*; *Naut (of boatswain)* sifflet *m*; *(of bird)* chant *m*; **the pipes** *(bagpipes)* la cornemuse
3 *(for smoking)* pipe *f*; **to smoke a p.** fumer une pipe; *Fam* **put that in your p. and smoke it!** mettez ça dans votre poche et votre mouchoir par-dessus!
VI *Mus* jouer du chalumeau; *(play the bagpipes)* jouer de la cornemuse; *(of bird etc)* siffler; *(speak shrilly)* parler d'une voix flûtée; *Naut* donner un coup de sifflet
VT **1** *(house etc)* installer *ou* poser des canalisations dans; *(water, oil etc)* canaliser; **piped water** eau *f* courante; **to p. oil to a refinery** amener le pétrole à une raffinerie par oléduc *ou* par pipeline; *Fam* **piped music** musique *f* de fond
2 *Mus (tune)* jouer au chalumeau; *(on bagpipes)* jouer à la cornemuse; *(sing)* chanter d'une voix flûtée; *Naut (order)* siffler; *Naut* **to p. sb aboard** rendre les honneurs du sifflet à qn
3 *Sewing etc (cushion etc)* passepoiler
4 *Culin (cake)* décorer avec une (poche à) douille
5 *Comput (commands)* chaîner
▸▸ *Mus* **p. band** orchestre *m* de cornemuses; **p. bomb** = bombe *f* artisanale fabriquée à partir d'un morceau de tuyau contenant des explosifs; **p. cleaner** cure-pipe *m*, *pl* cure-pipes; **p. dream** chimère *f*; **p. of peace** calumet *m* de la paix; **p. rack** râtelier *m* à pipes; **p. tobacco** tabac *m* à pipe
▸ **pipe down** VI *Fam* **1** *(make less noise)* faire moins de bruit; **p. down!** moins de bruit! **2** *(not talk so much)* rabattre son caquet; **p. down!** boucle-la!; **he piped down when he realized she knew a lot more about it** il a fermé son clapet quand il s'est rendu compte qu'elle en savait bien plus que lui
▸ **pipe in** VT SEP **to p. in the guests** *(in Scotland)* jouer de la cornemuse en tête de la procession (lors de l'entrée solennelle des invités)
▸ **pipe up** VI *(start to speak)* commencer à parler; **a little voice piped up** une petite voix s'est fait entendre

pipeclay [ˈpaɪpkleɪ] N terre *f* de pipe

pipeline [ˈpaɪplaɪn] **N 1** *(large pipe)* canalisation *f*, conduite *f*; *(for gas)* conduite de gaz naturel, gazoduc *m*; *(for petrol)* oléoduc *m*, pipeline *m* **2** *Fig (for news, technology etc)* canal *m ou* voie *f* d'acheminement; **it's in the p.** c'est en route; **there's a pay rise in the p.** il y a une augmentation de salaire en perspective

piper [ˈpaɪpər] N *Mus* joueur, -euse de chalumeau; *(of bagpipes)* joueur, -euse de cornemuse, cornemuseur *m*, cornemuseux *m*; *Prov* **he who pays the p. calls the tune** c'est celui qui paye qui décide

pipette [pɪˈpet] N *Chem etc* pipette *f*, compte-gouttes *m inv*

piping [ˈpaɪpɪŋ] ADJ *(sound)* flûté, aigu, *f* aiguë; *(voice)* flûté
ADV **p. hot** tout chaud, bouillant
N 1 *(system)* canalisations *fpl*, *(pipes collectively)* conduites *fpl*, tuyaux *mpl*, tuyauterie *f*, canalisations
2 *Mus etc (sound of pipe)* son *m* du chalumeau; *(sound of bagpipes)* son de la cornemuse; *(of birds)* gazouillement *m*, gazouillis *m*; *Naut* coups *mpl* de sifflet
3 *Sewing etc (material)* passepoil *m*
4 *Culin (of cake)* décoration *f* faite à la (poche à) douille
5 *Comput (of commands)* chaînage *m*
▸▸ *Culin* **p. bag** poche *f* à douille; *Culin* **p. nozzle** douille *f*

pipistrelle [pɪpɪˈstrel] N *(bat)* pipistrelle *f*
▸▸ **p. bat** pipistrelle

pipit [ˈpɪpɪt] N *(bird)* pipit *m*

pippin [ˈpɪpɪn] N *(apple)* (pomme *f*) reinette *f*

pipsqueak [ˈpɪpskwiːk] N *Fam (person)* petit bonhomme *m* de rien du tout, gringalet *m*

piquancy [ˈpiːkənsɪ] **N 1** *(of food)* goût *m* piquant **2** *Fig (of tale, affair etc)* sel *m*, piquant *m*

piquant [ˈpiːkənt] ADJ *(flavour, story)* piquant

piquantly [ˈpiːkəntlɪ] ADV d'une manière piquante, avec du piquant

pique [piːk] N dépit *m*, ressentiment *m*; **in a fit of p.** dans un accès de dépit
VT **1** *(offend) (person)* piquer, dépiter; **to feel piqued by sth** être dépité par qch; **to p. sb's pride** piquer *ou* blesser qn dans son orgueil **2** *(arouse) (sb's curiosity, interest)* piquer, exciter

piquet [pɪˈket] N *Cards* piquet *m*

piracy [ˈpaɪrəsɪ] **N 1** *Naut etc* piraterie *f*; **an act of p.** un acte de piraterie; **air p.** piraterie de l'air **2** *(of copyright)* atteinte *f* au droit d'auteur; *(of ideas etc)* pillage *m*, vol *m*; *(of software etc)* piratage *m*; **film p.** piratage de films

piranha [pɪˈrɑːnə] N *(fish)* piranha *m*, piraya *m*

pirate [ˈpaɪrɪt] **N 1** *Naut (person)* pirate *m*;

(ship) navire *m* pirate **2** *Radio (person)* pirate *m* **3** *(of literary work etc)* contrefacteur *m*; *(of ideas etc)* voleur, -euse; *(of software, cassette etc)* pirate *m*
vt 1 *Naut (ship)* s'emparer de **2** *(invention, ideas etc)* s'approprier, voler; *(brand)* contrefaire; *(cassette, film, software etc)* pirater; **to p. a book** *(republish without permission)* republier un livre sans autorisation; *(copy)* contrefaire *ou* démarquer un livre
▸▸ **p. cassette** cassette *f* pirate; **p. edition** édition *f* pirate; **p. program** programme *m* pirate; **p. radio** radio *f* pirate; **p. software** logiciel *m* pirate; **p. station** poste *m ou* émetteur *m* pirate; **p. tape** cassette pirate; **p. video** vidéo *f* pirate

pirated [ˈpaɪrɪtɪd] ADJ pirate; **a p. edition** une édition pirate

piratical [paɪˈrætɪk(ə)l] ADJ **1** *Naut* de pirate **2** *Com (reproduction etc)* de contrefacteur, de contrefaçon

pirating [ˈpaɪrɪtɪŋ] N *(of software etc)* piratage *m*

pirouette [pɪruˈet] N pirouette *f*
vi pirouetter, faire une/des pirouette(s)

Pisa [ˈpiːzə] N Pise *f*

piscatorial [pɪskəˈtɔːrɪəl] ADJ *Fml* halieutique

Pisces [ˈpaɪsiːz] N *Astrol* les Poissons *mpl*; **to be (a) P.** être (des) Poissons

pish [pɪʃ] *Scot* = **piss**

piss [pɪs] *Sl* N pisse *f*; **to have a p.** pisser; **to take the p. out of sb** se foutre (de la gueule) de qn; **to take the p. out of sth** se foutre de qch; **you're taking the p.!** tu te fous de moi!, tu déconnes!; **the artist is taking the p.** cet artiste se fout de la gueule du monde; *Br* **to go on the p.** *(go out drinking)* aller se bourrer la gueule, aller prendre une cuite; **it was p. easy** c'était de la tarte; **p. poor** *(very bad)* complètement nul
vi pisser; **it's pissing (with rain** *or* **down)** il pleut comme vache qui pisse; *Am* **p. on it!** *(forget it)* laisse béton!; *(I'm fed up)* j'en ai plein le cul!; **to p. all over sb** *(defeat)* battre qn à plates coutures
vt *(blood etc)* pisser; **to p. oneself, to p. one's pants** pisser dans son froc; **to p. the bed** pisser au lit; **I almost pissed myself laughing** j'ai tellement rigolé que j'ai failli en pisser dans mon froc
▸▸ *Br* **p. artist** *(drunkard)* poivrot, -ote
▸ **piss about, piss around** vi *Sl (behave foolishly)* faire le con, déconner; *(waste time)* glandouiller; **we don't have time to p. about** on n'a pas de temps à perdre en conneries; **don't p. around with my stuff** arrête de tripoter mes affaires *ou* de foutre le bordel dans mes affaires
vt sep *Sl (waste time of)* **to p. sb about** *or* **around** faire perdre son temps à qn
▸ **piss down** vi *Sl (rain)* **it's pissing down** il pleut comme vache qui pisse
▸ **piss off** *Sl* vi *(go away)* foutre le camp; **p. off!** fous le camp!
vt sep *(annoy)* faire chier; **that really pisses me off** ça me fait vraiment chier; **to be pissed off** en avoir ras le cul; **to be pissed off with sb/sth** *(have had enough of)* en avoir ras le bol de qn/qch; **to be pissed off at sb/about sth** être en pétard contre qn/à cause de qch

pissbucket [ˈpɪsbʌkɪt] N *Sl* **1** *(toilet)* chiottes *fpl* **2** *(person)* ordure *f*, raclure *f*

pissed [pɪst] ADJ **1** *Br Sl (drunk)* soûl, bourré, plein; **to get p.** se soûler la gueule; **as p. as a fart** *or* **a newt, p. out of one's mind** rond comme une queue de pelle **2** *Am Sl (angry)* en rogne, en boule; **to be p. at sb** être en rogne contre qn; **I was pretty p. about it** ça m'a vraiment foutu en rogne

pisser [ˈpɪsər] N *Sl* **1** *(annoying situation)* **what a p.!** quelle merde!; **it was a real p. that the weather wasn't better** c'était vraiment chiant qu'il fasse pas plus beau **2** *Am (remarkable situation)* **what a p.!** c'est génial *ou* super! **3** *Am (annoying person)* emmerdeur, -euse; *(remarkable person)* **to be a p.** être un mec/une nana génial(e)

pisshead [ˈpɪshed] N *Br Sl (drunkard)* soûlard, -arde

pisshole [ˈpɪshəʊl] N *Sl* **his eyes are like pissholes in the snow** il a des petits yeux

piss-take N *Br Sl (joke)* blague *f*, *(parody)* parodie *f*; **this is a p. isn't it?** non mais tu te fous de ma gueule ou quoi?

piss-taker N *Br Sl (mocker)* personne *f* qui se fout du monde; **he's a real p.** il se fout vraiment de la gueule du monde

piss-up N *Br Sl (drinking spree)* **to go on** *or* **have a p.** (aller) se soûler la gueule; **they couldn't organize a p. in a brewery** ils ne sont pas foutus d'organiser quoi que ce soit correctement

pistachio [pɪˈstɑːʃɪəʊ] N *(nut)* pistache *f*, *(tree)* pistachier *m*
▸▸ **p. nut** pistache; **p. tree** pistachier

piste [piːst] N *Ski* piste *f*

pistil [ˈpɪstɪl] N *Bot* pistil *m*

pistol [ˈpɪst(ə)l] N **1** *(gun)* pistolet *m*; **to hold a p. to sb's head** tenir un pistolet braqué contre la tempe de qn; *Fig* mettre le couteau sous la gorge à qn; *Fig* **to make a decision with a p. to one's head** prendre une décision avec le couteau sous la gorge **2** *Tech (of pneumatic tool)* pistolet *m*
▸▸ **p. grip** *(of tool, camera)* crosse *f*; **p. shot** coup *m* de pistolet

pistol-whip vt **(-pp-)** frapper avec un pistolet

piston [ˈpɪstən] N *Tech, Mus (of brass instrument)* piston *m*
▸▸ **p. dwell** temps *m* d'immobilité du piston; **p. engine** moteur *m* à pistons; **p. head** tête *f ou* fond *m* du piston; **p. ring** segment *m* (de piston); **p. walls** parois *fpl* du piston

pit[1] [pɪt] N **1** *(hole in ground)* fosse *f*, puits *m*; *(coal mine)* mine *f*; **to dig a p.** creuser une fosse; *Aut etc* **inspection p.** fosse de visite; *Lit* **the (bottomless) p.** *(hell)* l'enfer *m*, les enfers; **to work in the pits** travailler à la mine; **he went down the pit when he was 16** il est descendu à la mine à 16 ans
2 *Fig Sl* **it's/he's the pits** *(awful)* c'est/il est nul
3 *Theat (seating, spectators)* parterre *m*; *(at Stock Exchange)* corbeille *f*, *(for cock fight)* arène *f*, *(for bears)* fosse *f*, **(orchestra) p.** fosse d'orchestre; *Sport* **the pits** les stands *mpl* de ravitaillement
4 *(mark)* *(on metal, glass etc)* piqûre *f*, alvéole *m*
5 *Med (from smallpox etc)* cicatrice *f*, marque *f*; *Anat* **the p. of the stomach** le creux de l'estomac; *Fig* **her rejection hit him in the p. of his stomach** son rejet lui a fait l'effet d'un coup de poing dans l'estomac
6 *Br Sl (bed)* pieu *m*; **in one's p.** au pieu
7 *Sl (untidy place)* foutoir *m*
vt (-tt-) **1** **to p. sb against sb** mettre qn aux prises avec qn, opposer qn à qn; **to p. oneself against sb** se mesurer à qn; **to p. one's wits against sb** se mesurer avec qn **2** *(of acids etc)* *(metal etc)* piquer, trouer; *Med (of smallpox etc)* *(sb's face)* grêler, marquer
▸▸ **p. pony** cheval *m* de mine; **p. prop** poteau *m ou* étau *m* de mine, étançon *m*

pit[2] N *(stone)* *(of cherry etc)* noyau *m*
vt (-tt-) *(cherries etc)* dénoyauter

pita [ˈpiːtə] N = **pitta**

pit-a-pat ADV **to go p.** *(of rain etc)* crépiter; *(of feet)* trottiner; *(of the heart)* faire toc-toc

N *(of rain)* crépitement *m*; *(of feet)* trottinement *m*; *(of heart)* battement *m*

pitch[1] [pɪtʃ] N **1** *(act of throwing)* *(of stone, ball etc)* lancement *m*
2 *Br (place)* *(in market)* place *f*, emplacement *m*; *(of stallholder, beggar etc)* place habituelle
3 *Sport (for football etc)* terrain *m*; *Cr* terrain entre les guichets
4 *Mus (of note)* hauteur *f*; **to have perfect p.** avoir l'oreille absolue; **to give the orchestra the p.** donner le ton à l'orchestre; **to rise in p.** monter de ton
5 *(degree)* **to such a p. that ...** à tel point que ...; **expectation had reached fever p.** l'attente était fébrile
6 *(talk)* **(sales) p.** baratin *m*, boniment *m* publicitaire; *(of advertising agency)* spéculative *f*; *Am Sl* **to make a p. for** *(express support for)* vanter les mérites de
7 *Cin* présentation *f*, soumission *f*, pitch *m*
8 *Constr (slope)* *(of staircase)* pente *f*, rampant *m*; *(of roof)* pente, inclinaison *f*, *Tech (of plane)* inclinaison, basile *f*
9 *Archit (of ceiling)* hauteur *f*
10 *(of ship, aircraft)* *(type of movement)* tangage *m*; *(instance)* coup *m* de tangage; **angle of p.** angle *m* de tangage
11 *Tech (spacing)* *(of rivets, holes)* espacement *m*, écartement *m*; *(of cogwheel, screw, propeller etc)* *Typ (of characters)* pas *m*
vt 1 *(throw)* *(ball, stone etc)* jeter, lancer; *(in baseball)* lancer; **to p. the hay onto the cart** jeter le foin sur la charrette
2 *(set up)* *(tent)* dresser, monter; *(camp)* établir; *Cr* **to p. wickets** planter *ou* dresser les guichets
3 *Mus* jouer dans une clef donnée; **to p. one's voice higher/lower** hausser/baisser le ton de sa voix
4 *(aim)* **to p. an estimate too low** arrêter un devis trop bas; **to p. one's aspirations too high** viser trop haut; **stories pitched at older children** histoires écrites pour des enfants plus âgés
5 *Cin* présenter, soumettre, pitcher
6 *Fam* **to p. a yarn** raconter des histoires
vi 1 *(in baseball)* lancer **2** *(fall)* tomber; **to p. forward** *(be thrown)* être projeté en avant; *(fall)* piquer du nez; **he pitched into the water** il est tombé dans l'eau; **the ball pitched on a stone** le ballon a rebondi sur une pierre **3** *(of ship, aircraft)* tanguer
▸▸ **p. angle** angle de tangage; *Tech* **p. circle** cercle *m* primitif; *(of wheel)* ligne *f* d'engrènement; *Mus* **p. pipe** diapason *m* *(sifflet)*
▸ **pitch in** vi *(contribute to a task)* s'y mettre; *(contribute money etc)* payer son écot; **they all pitched in to help** ils ont tous donné un coup de main
▸ **pitch into** vt insep *Fam (attack)* *(physically)* attaquer, se lancer sur; *(verbally)* dire son fait à; **to p. into a task** se mettre à une tâche
▸ **pitch on** vt insep *(choose)* choisir
▸ **pitch out** vt sep *(person)* *(from house)* expulser; *(from competition)* éliminer; *(rubbish)* balancer, jeter; **to p. sb out of office** démettre qn de ses fonctions

pitch[2] N *(substance)* poix *f*, *(from coal tar)* brai *m*; **black** *or* **dark as p.** *(hair, eyes)* noir comme le jais; *(room, night)* noir comme dans un four
vt *(coat with pitch)* brayer, enduire de poix *ou* de brai
▸▸ *Bot* **p. pine** pitchpin *m*

pitch-black ADJ noir comme le jais; **her p. hair** ses cheveux noirs de jais; **it's p.** *(I can't see)* il fait noir comme dans un four

pitch-dark ADJ **it's p.** *(outside)* il fait nuit noire; *(in cellar etc)* il fait noir comme dans un four

pitched [pɪtʃt] ADJ
▸▸ *Mil, Fig* **p. battle** bataille *f* rangée

pitcher¹ ['pɪtʃər] N *(jug)* cruche *f*, pichet *m*; *(large)* broc *m*; *esp Am (small jug)* pot *m*; *Prov* **little pitchers have big ears** = pas devant les enfants

pitcher² N *Baseball* lanceur *m*

pitchfork ['pɪtʃfɔːk] N *Agr* fourche *f*, *(two-pronged)* bident *m*
▶ VT *(hay)* lancer avec une fourche; *Fig Fam (force) (person)* parachuter (**into a job** à un poste)

pitching ['pɪtʃɪŋ] N *Naut, Aviat (of ship, plane)* tangage *m*

piteous ['pɪtɪəs] ADJ pitoyable, piteux; **he was a p. sight** il faisait pitié

piteously ['pɪtɪəslɪ] ADV pitoyablement, piteusement

pitfall ['pɪtfɔːl] N *(pit)* trappe *f*, fosse *f*; *Fig (trap)* piège *m*; **the pitfalls of English** les pièges de l'anglais

pith [pɪθ] N **1** *(of orange etc)* peau *f* blanche; *Bot (medulla)* moelle *f* **2** *Fig (of argument, idea etc)* essence *f*, *(piquancy) (of story)* piquant *m*
▶ **p. helmet** casque *m* colonial

pithead ['pɪthed] N *Min* bouche *f* de puits
▶ **p. ballot** vote *m* des mineurs *(de fond)*; **p. baths** bains *mpl*/douches *fpl* de la mine

pithiness ['pɪθɪnɪs] N *(of style etc)* concision *f*

pithy ['pɪθɪ] ADJ **1** *(orange etc)* couvert de peau blanche; *(stem etc)* moelleux **2** *(style etc)* concis; **p. phrase** phrase *f* lapidaire

pitiable ['pɪtɪəb(ə)l] ADJ pitoyable, piteux; *(appearance, object)* minable, lamentable; **she was in a p. state** elle était dans un état à faire pitié, elle était dans un état pitoyable *ou* dans un piteux état

pitiful ['pɪtɪfʊl] ADJ **1** *(arousing pity)* pitoyable; **it's p. to see him like this** ça fait pitié de le voir comme ça **2** *Pej (deplorable)* lamentable, pitoyable

pitifully ['pɪtɪfʊlɪ] ADV **1** *(arousing pity)* pitoyablement; **she was p. thin** elle était d'une maigreur pitoyable **2** *Pej (deplorably)* lamentablement, pitoyablement; **he was p. bad at drawing** il était lamentable en dessin; **she sings p.** elle chante lamentablement mal; **p. small** *(salary)* de misère; *(house etc)* si petit que c'en est lamentable

pitiless ['pɪtɪlɪs] ADJ impitoyable; *(wind, cold)* cruel

pitilessly ['pɪtɪlɪslɪ] ADV impitoyablement, sans pitié; **p. cruel** d'une cruauté impitoyable; **to behave p. towards sb** se montrer impitoyable envers qn

piton ['piːtɒn] N *(in mountaineering)* piton *m*

pitta ['pɪtə] N
▶ **p. bread** pita *m*

pittance ['pɪtəns] N *(wages)* salaire *m* de misère; *(income)* maigre revenu *m*, revenu misérable; **his pension is a p.** sa retraite est dérisoire

Note that the French word **pitance** is a false friend and is never a translation for the English word **pittance**. It means **sustenance**.

pitted ['pɪtɪd] ADJ **1** *(metal etc)* piqué, alvéolé; *(surface of moon)* alvéolé; *(skin) (by smallpox)* grêlé; *(by acne)* couvert de marques **2** *(olives)* dénoyauté

pitter-patter ['pɪtə-] N *(of rain, hail)* crépitement *m*; *(of feet)* trottinement *m*; *(of heart)* battement *m*
▶ ADV **to go p.** *(feet)* trottiner; *(heart)* palpiter; **the rain fell p. on the leaves** la pluie tombait doucement sur les feuilles

pitting ['pɪtɪŋ] N *(on metal surface)* piquage *m*

pituitary [pɪ'tjuːɪt(ə)rɪ] *Anat* N *(gland)* hypophyse *f*, glande *f* pituitaire
▶ ADJ pituitaire
▶ **p. gland** hypophyse, glande pituitaire

pity ['pɪtɪ] N **1** *(compassion)* pitié *f*, **to have** *or* **take p. on sb** avoir pitié de qn, prendre qn en pitié; **to take p. on sb** *(be moved to pity)* s'apitoyer sur qn; **she deserves no p.** elle ne mérite pas qu'on s'apitoie sur elle; **are you entirely without p.?** es-tu incapable du moindre sentiment de pitié?; **to show no p.** ne manifester aucune pitié; **the thought moved him to p.** cette pensée lui inspira de la pitié; **to do sth out of p. for sb** faire qch par pitié pour qn; **for p.'s sake** par pitié **2** *(misfortune)* **what a p.!** quel dommage!; **it's a great p. that ...** il est bien malheureux *ou* dommage que ... + *subj*; **it's no great p. that ...** ce n'est pas si grave que ... + *subj*; *(quite a good thing)* encore heureux que ... + *subj*; **more's the p.** c'est bien dommage
▶ VT *(person)* plaindre, avoir pitié de; **he is to be pitied** il est à plaindre

pitying ['pɪtɪɪŋ] ADJ compatissant; *(look)* compatissant, de pitié

pityingly ['pɪtɪɪŋlɪ] ADV *(to look)* avec pitié, d'un air compatissant; *(to say)* d'un ton compatissant

Pius ['paɪəs] N Pie *m*

pivot ['pɪvət] N **1** *Tech etc* pivot *m*, axe *m*; *(of crane)* pivot; *(of axle etc)* tourillon *m* **2** *Fig (person in company etc)* pivot *m*, cheville *f* ouvrière; *Mil (man)* pivot, guide *m*, homme *m* de base
▶ VI *(-t-)* pivoter, tourner (**on sth** sur qch); **she pivoted on her left leg** elle pivota sur sa jambe gauche; *Fig* **their plans pivoted around her** leurs projets reposaient sur elle
▶ VT *(turn) (something)* faire pivoter; *(set on a pivot) (gun)* monter sur pivot
▶ *Mil* **p. man** pivot, guide, homme de base

pivotal ['pɪvət(ə)l] ADJ *(point)* cardinal, -aux; *Fig (position etc)* clef *inv*; *(importance)* capital, -aux; **she is p. in their plans** elle joue un rôle central dans leurs projets

pix [pɪks] NPL *Fam* = **pics,** *see* **pic**

pixel ['pɪksəl] N *Comput* pixel *m*
▶ **p. density** densité *f* en pixels

pixelated ['pɪksəleɪtəd] ADJ = **pixellated**

pixelation ['pɪksəleɪʃən], **pixelization** ['pɪksəlaɪz'eɪʃən] N *TV (to hide identity)* mosaïquage *m*

pixelize ['pɪksəlaɪz] VT *TV (to hide identity)* mosaïquer

pixellated ['pɪksəleɪtəd] ADJ *Comput (image)* pixélisé, bitmap, en mode point

pixie ['pɪksɪ] N *(elf)* lutin *m*; *(fairy)* fée *f*

pixil(l)ated ['pɪksɪleɪtəd] ADJ *Am Sl (drunk)* bourré, plein

pixy ['pɪksɪ] N = **pixie**

pizza ['piːtsə] N *Culin* pizza *f*
▶ **p. base** pâte *f* à pizza; **p. parlour** pizzeria *f*

pizzazz [pə'zæz] N *Fam* = **pzazz**

pizzeria [piːtsə'riːə] N pizzeria *f*

PJs ['piːdʒeɪz] NPL *Fam (abbr* **pyjamas)** pyjama *m*

Pk *abbr* **Park**

pkg N *abbr* **package**

pkt N *abbr* **packet**

P & L [piːən'el] N **1** *(abbr* **profit and loss)** pertes *fpl* et profits *mpl* **2** *(abbr* **profit and loss account, profit and loss statement)** compte *m* de résultat; **we can see from the P. that developing the product is not a viable option** le compte de résultat montre clairement qu'il ne serait pas rentable de développer ce produit **3** *(abbr* **profit and loss form)** compte *m* d'exploitation

Pl *(abbr* **Place)** = rue

pl *Gram (abbr* **plural)** pl

placard ['plækɑːd] N *(written notice)* écriteau *m*; *(poster)* affiche *f*, *(carried by protester)* pancarte *f*
▶ VT *(wall)* placarder

Note that the French word **placard** is a false friend and is never a translation for the English word **placard**. Its most common meaning is **cupboard**.

placate [plə'keɪt] VT apaiser, calmer

PLACE [pleɪs] ◼

◼ **N** endroit **1** ◼ lieu **1, 3** ◼ place **2, 6–10** ◼ avoir lieu *(to take place)* **4** ◼ maison **5**
◼ **VT** placer **1, 3, 4** ◼ mettre **1**

N 1 *(location)* endroit *m*, lieu *m*; *(in street names)* rue *f*; **an ideal p. for a picnic** un endroit idéal pour pique-niquer; **a good p. to meet people** un bon endroit pour rencontrer des gens; **this is the p.!** *(here we are)* nous voilà arrivés!; **to move from one p. to another** se déplacer d'un endroit à un autre; **the village/museum was an interesting p.** le village/musée était intéressant; **I'm looking for a p. to stay** je cherche un logement; **can you recommend a p. to eat?** pouvez-vous me recommander un restaurant?; **this is no p. for you** ce n'est pas un endroit pour vous; **I've broken my arm in two places** je me suis cassé le bras en deux endroits; **I can't be in two places at once** je ne peux pas être à deux endroits à la fois; **the book was good in places** le livre était bon par endroits; **all over the p.** *(in many different places)* partout; *Fig (in disorder)* dans tous les sens; *Fig Fam* **the team were all over the p.** l'équipe a joué n'importe comment; *Fig Fam* **these figures are all over the p.** *(are inaccurate)* ces chiffres ont été calculés n'importe comment; *Fig Fam* **at the interview he was all over the p.** *(panicking, unclear)* il a raconté n'importe quoi à l'entretien; *Fig Fam* **this paragraph is all over the p.** ce paragraphe a été écrit n'importe comment; *Fig Fam* **to go places** *(succeed)* réussir (dans la vie); *Br Fam* **the other p.** *Univ (at Oxford)* Cambridge; *(at Cambridge)* Oxford; *Parl (in House of Commons)* la Chambre des lords; *(in House of Lords)* la Chambre des communes; **Belmont P.** rue Belmont

2 *(assigned to somebody, something)* place *f*, **everything in its p.** chaque chose à sa place; **in its proper time and p.** en temps et lieu; **to find a p. for sth** trouver une place pour qch; **this town has a special p. in my affections** j'ai une tendresse particulière pour cette ville; **to hold sth in p.** tenir qch en place; **to lose/find one's p.** *(in a book)* perdre/retrouver sa page; **his anger gave p. to pity** sa colère a fait place à un sentiment de pitié; **to take sb's p.** remplacer qn; *(oust)* prendre la place de qn; **a woman's p. is in the home** la place d'une femme est à la maison

3 *(for specific purpose)* **p. of amusement** lieu *m* de divertissement; **p. of payment** lieu de paiement; **p. of refuge** lieu de refuge

4 to take p. *(happen)* avoir lieu; **the marriage will not take p.** le mariage n'aura pas lieu *ou* ne se fera pas; **many changes have taken p.** il y a eu beaucoup de changements; **while this was taking p.** tandis que cela se passait

5 *(residence)* **a little p. in the country** une petite maison à la campagne; *Fam* **nice p. you've got here** c'est bien chez vous!; *Fam* **come round to my p.** venez chez moi; *Fam* **your p. or mine?** on va chez toi ou chez moi?

6 *(seat etc)* **is this p. taken?** est-ce que cette

place est prise?; **to book a p.** réserver une place; **to change places with sb** changer de place avec qn; **to give up** or **offer one's p. to sb** laisser sa place à qn; **if I get there first I'll keep a p. for you** si j'arrive le premier je te garderai une place; **to keep sb's p. in a queue** garder la place de qn dans une file d'attente; **to set** or **lay an extra p. at table** mettre une assiette de plus à table

7 (vacancy etc) **to get a p. at university** être admis à l'université; **the school still has five places left** cette école a encore cinq places de libres

8 this remark is out of p. (inappropriate) cette observation est déplacée ou hors de propos; **to look out of p.** (of person) ne pas être à sa place ou dans son élément; (of thing) ne pas être à sa place; **he didn't look out of p.** il ne déparait pas; **it's not my p. to do it** ce n'est pas à moi de le faire

9 (situation) **put yourself in my p.** mettez-vous à ma place; **if I were in your p. I'd go** à votre place, j'irais

10 (in society, competition etc) place f, rang m; **to keep sb in his p.** montrer à qn où est sa place; **to know one's p.** savoir où est sa place; Iron **I know my p.** je sais où est ma place; Fig **to put sb in his p.** remettre qn à sa place; **in first/second p.** en premier/second lieu; Sport **to finish in second/last p.** finir à la deuxième/dernière place ou en deuxième/dernière position; Horseracing **to back a horse for a p.** jouer un cheval placé; Math **to three decimal places** à trois décimales

11 (parts of an argument etc) **in the first p. ..., in the second p. ...** en premier lieu ..., en second lieu ...; **I don't know why they gave him the job in the first p.** d'ailleurs je ne sais même pas pourquoi ils l'ont embauché

vt 1 (put) placer, mettre; **to p. a book back on a shelf** remettre un livre (en place) sur un rayon; **to p. a book with a publisher** confier un livre à un éditeur; **to p. a matter in sb's hands** mettre une affaire dans les mains de qn; **I p. myself at your disposal** je me mets à votre disposition; **to p. a child in sb's care** confier un enfant à la garde de qn; **to p. a child in care/with foster parents** placer ou mettre un enfant à la DDASS/dans une famille d'accueil

2 the house is well placed (situated) la maison est bien située; **how are we placed for time?** combien de temps avons-nous?; **how are you placed for money?** comment ça va côté finances?; **you're better placed than I am to answer that** tu es mieux placé que moi pour répondre à cela; **British industry is well placed to ...** l'industrie britannique est à même de ...; **strategically placed airfields** des terrains d'aviation stratégiquement situés

3 Com, Fin etc (goods, shares) placer, vendre; (loan) placer, négocier; (invest) (funds) placer; (contract) adjuger, concéder; **to p. an order** passer une commande; **to p. an order for sth** passer commande de qch; **to p. an order with sb** passer commande à qn; **to p. a bet** prendre un pari; **to p. a bet on sb/sth** parier sur qn/qch

4 (find a job for) placer

5 (class), Sch, Sport etc **to be placed third** se classer troisième; **I would p. him among the outstanding biographers of the century** je le classerais parmi les meilleurs biographes du siècle; Horseracing **was your horse placed?** est-ce que votre cheval s'est classé dans les trois premiers?

6 (identify) (sound) localiser; **I know his face but I can't p. him** je l'ai déjà vu mais je n'arrive pas à le remettre

vi Am esp Horseracing se classer entre les trois premiers

▸▸ **p. of birth** lieu de naissance; **p. of business** lieu de travail; **p. card** = carte f marquant la place de chaque convive à table; **p. of death** lieu de décès; Fin **p. of issue** lieu d'émission; Sport **p. kick** coup m de pied placé; **p. mat** set m (de table); **p. name** nom m de lieu; **p. of residence** résidence f, domicile m (réel); Br Law **p. of safety order** = ordonnance f autorisant une personne ou un organisme à garder des enfants maltraités en lieu sûr; **p. setting** couvert m; **p. of work** lieu de travail; **p. of worship** lieu de culte

placebo [plə'siːbəʊ] N Med, Fig placebo m; **the p. effect** l'effet m placebo

placement ['pleɪsmənt] N **1** (putting in place) placement m, mise f en place; (siting) localisation f; (of funds, bet, shares) placement; (of contract) adjudication f; (of order) passage m; (finding job) placement; **the p. of children in care/with foster parents** le placement d'enfants à la DDASS/dans des familles d'accueil **2** (of trainee etc) stage m; **to get a p.** (of trainee) trouver un stage

placenta [plə'sentə] N Anat, Bot placenta m

placid ['plæsɪd] ADJ placide, calme, tranquille

placidity [plə'sɪdɪtɪ], **placidness** ['plæsɪdnɪs] N placidité f, calme m, tranquillité f

placidly ['plæsɪdlɪ] ADV placidement, calmement, tranquillement

placing ['pleɪsɪŋ] N **1** = **placement 1**
2 p. of an order passation f de commande
3 Sport etc (ranking) classement m

placket ['plækɪt] N Sewing patte f

plagiarism ['pleɪdʒərɪz(ə)m] N plagiat m; **student accused of p.** étudiant accusé d'avoir copié

plagiarist ['pleɪdʒərɪst] N plagiaire mf

plagiarize ['pleɪdʒəraɪz] vt (author) plagier; (work) plagier, faire un plagiat de, contrefaire; (student's essay) copier (**from** dans)
vi se livrer à des plagiats

plague [pleɪg] N Med peste f; Bible, Fig (scourge) fléau m, plaie f; **to avoid sb/sth like the p.** éviter qn/qch comme la peste; Arch **a p. on both your houses!** allez tous au diable!; Arch **a p. on you and your statistics!** allez au diable, toi et tes statistiques!; **p. ridden** or **stricken** infesté par la peste
vt (person) tourmenter, harceler; **she was plagued by illness** la maladie la poursuivait sans relâche; **to p. sb's life** empoisonner l'existence de qn; **to p. sb with questions** harceler qn de questions; **our journey was plagued by minor problems** nous avons été accablés de petits ennuis pendant notre voyage; **the team was plagued by injury** l'équipe a collectionné les blessures

plaice [pleɪs] N (fish) carrelet m, plie f (franche)

plaid [plæd, Scot pleɪd] N **1** (material) tartan m, tissu m écossais **2** (part of Highland costume, travelling rug) plaid m

PLAIN [pleɪn]

ADJ clair **1** ▪ simple **2** ▪ nature **2** ▪ uni **3** ▪ quelconque **4**			
ADV simplement **1** ▪ franchement **2**			
N plaine			

ADJ 1 (clear, unambiguous) clair, évident; **to make sth p. to sb** faire comprendre qch à qn; **to make one's feelings p.** exprimer clairement ses sentiments; **they made their contempt for him p.** ils n'ont pas caché leur mépris pour lui; **it's as p. as (plain) can be** or **as p. as a pikestaff** or **as the nose on your face** c'est on ne peut plus clair, c'est clair comme le jour; **it's p. (to see) that you don't like me** il est évident que vous ne m'aimez

pas; **I'll be quite p. with you** je vais être franc avec toi; **in p. English** clairement; **what is that in p. English?** = qu'est-ce que ça veut dire en bon français?; **p. answer** réponse f carrée; **p. speaking** franc parler m; **the p. truth** la pure ou simple vérité

2 (simple) (style, furniture, dress, sewing) simple, sans recherche; (cigarettes) sans filtre; (unadorned) (rice, yoghurt etc) nature; **that's just p. foolishness/ignorance** c'est de la pure bêtise/ignorance; Knitting **one p. one purl** une maille à l'endroit, une maille à l'envers; **p. country people** de simples campagnards; **in p. clothes** en civil; **p. cooking** cuisine f simple; **p. living** vie f simple

3 (uniformly coloured) (wallpaper, carpet, material etc) uni; (paper) non réglé

4 (unattractive) (woman) pas particulièrement belle, plutôt quelconque; **she's rather a p. Jane** c'est une jeune fille plutôt quelconque

ADV Fam **1** (simply) simplement; **he's just p. ignorant** il est tout simplement ignorant

2 (frankly) franchement; **to speak p.** parler franc ou sans détours; **she told him p. what she thought about him** elle lui a dit franchement ou sans détours ce qu'elle pensait de lui

N Geog plaine f; **alluvial p.** plaine alluviale; **the Great Plains** la Prairie (américaine)

▸▸ **p. chocolate** chocolat m noir; **p.-clothes policeman** agent m en civil; **p. flour** farine f (sans levure); **p. knitting** tricot m à l'endroit; **p. paper fax** télécopieur m ou fax m sur papier ordinaire

plainchant ['pleɪntʃɑːnt] N = **plainsong**

plainly ['pleɪnlɪ] ADV **1** (clearly) (to see) clairement, nettement; **to speak p.** (be frank) parler franchement ou sans détours; **I can p. see that I am not welcome here** je vois bien que je ne suis pas le bienvenu ici; **p. visible/audible** qui se voit/s'entend clairement; **p. I was not wanted** il était clair que j'étais de trop; **they were p. exhausted** ils étaient de toute évidence épuisés **2** (simply) (to live) simplement; (to dress) simplement, sans recherche

plainness ['pleɪnnɪs] N **1** (clarity) (of concise language) clarté f, simplicité f, (of frank language) franchise f, rondeur f **2** (simplicity) (of lifestyle etc) simplicité f **3** (lack of beauty) manque m de beauté

plainsong ['pleɪnsɒŋ] N Mus plain-chant m, pl plains-chants

plain-spoken ADJ franc, f franche

plaint [pleɪnt] N Law plainte f

plaintiff ['pleɪntɪf] N Law demandeur, -eresse, plaignant, -ante

plaintive ['pleɪntɪv] ADJ plaintif

plaintively ['pleɪntɪvlɪ] ADV plaintivement

plaintiveness ['pleɪntɪvnɪs] N ton m plaintif

plait [plæt] N (of hair) natte f, tresse f; **she had her hair in plaits** elle avait des nattes
vt (hair etc) natter, tresser

plan [plæn] N **1** (proposal, intention) projet m, plan m; (timetable) planning m; (for the future) projet; **p. of battle** plan de bataille; **p. of campaign** plan d'action; Fin investment **p.** plan d'investissement; Econ **five-year p.** plan quinquennal; Aviat **flight p.** plan de vol; **to change one's plans** changer ses projets; **to have no fixed plan(s)** ne pas avoir de projet bien déterminé; **everything went according to p.** tout a marché comme prévu; **the best p. would be to ...** la meilleure solution serait de ...; **it would be a good p. to ...** ce serait une bonne idée de ...; **what are your plans for the summer?** quels sont vos projets pour cet été?; **I've thought of a p.** j'ai imaginé un plan; **to have other plans** avoir d'autres projets; **they had other plans for us** ils avaient autre chose en vue en ce qui nous concernait

2 *(drawing etc) (of building, town)* plan *m*; *(in surveying) (of area)* plan, levé *m*; *(outline) (of novel etc)* plan; **ground p.** plan géométral **VT (-nn-) 1** *(arrange) (trip)* projeter; *(attack etc)* combiner; *(crime)* comploter, tramer; **everything had been planned down to the last detail** tout avait été planifié dans les moindres détails; **to p. to do sth** projeter de faire qch; **we don't have anything planned tomorrow afternoon** nous n'avons rien de prévu demain après-midi; **things did not go as planned** les choses ne se sont pas passées comme prévu; **this had been planned** cela avait été prévu

2 *(make a plan of)* faire *ou* dessiner le plan de; *Econ (production etc)* planifier; *(new novel etc)* faire *ou* établir *ou* élaborer le plan de; **to p. one's lessons** *(of teacher)* préparer ses cours; **the school was planned for 500 pupils** l'école a été prévue pour 500 élèves **VI** faire des projets; **to p. for the future** faire des projets d'avenir; **they had planned for six** ils avaient prévu pour six personnes

▶ **plan ahead VI** faire des projets; *(for lunch, party)* s'y prendre à l'avance

▶ **plan on VT INSEP** *(have intention of) (something)* prévoir; **to p. on doing sth** prévoir *ou* projeter *ou* avoir l'intention de faire qch; **we're planning on going to Brazil** *or* **on a trip to Brazil** nous projetons *ou* nous avons l'intention de partir au Brésil, nous projetons un voyage au Brésil; **don't p. on being able to persuade him** ne compte pas arriver à le persuader; **we hadn't planned on staying long** nous n'avions pas prévu de *ou* ne comptions pas rester longtemps

▶ **plan out VT SEP** *(make detailed plans for)* prévoir (en détail); **he had planned it all out** il avait tout prévu, il en avait établi tous les détails

plane[1] [pleɪn] **ADJ** *(angle, geometry etc)* plan **N 1** *Geom* plan *m*; **horizontal/vertical p.** plan horizontal/vertical; *Opt* **focal p.** plan focal; *Geol* **fault p.** plan de faille

2 *Fig* plan *m*, niveau *m*; **on the economic p.** sur le plan économique; **a higher p. of intelligence** un niveau intellectuel supérieur

3 *Aviat* **tail p.** plan *m* fixe horizontal

4 *(aeroplane)* avion *m*; **by p.** en avion; **it's just a short p. ride** c'est un court voyage en avion

VI *(of bird, aircraft)* planer; **to p. down** descendre en vol plané *ou* en planant; **to p. along the water** *(of hydroplane)* glisser à la surface de l'eau

▶▶ *Geom* **p. surface** surface *f* plane; **p. ticket** billet *m* d'avion; *Math* **p. trigonometry** trigonométrie *f* rectiligne

plane[2] **N** *(tool)* rabot *m*
VT *Carp etc (wood)* raboter, aplanir, planer; *(metal)* aplanir, planer; **to p. a surface smooth** aplanir une surface; *(also wood)* raboter une surface

plane[3] **N** *(tree)* platane *m*
▶▶ **p. tree** platane

planet ['plænɪt] **N** *Astron* planète *f*; **the biggest country on the p.** le plus grand pays de la planète

planetarium [plænɪ'teərɪəm] **N** planétarium *m*

planetary ['plænɪt(ə)rɪ] **ADJ** *Astron (system, time, movement)* planétaire

plangent ['plændʒənt] **ADJ** *Lit* élégiaque

planing ['pleɪnɪŋ] **N** *Carp etc (of wood)* rabotage *m*, planage *m*, aplanissage *m*; *(of metal)* planage, aplanissage
▶▶ **p. machine** raboteuse *f*

planisphere ['plænɪsfɪər] **N** planisphère *m* céleste

plank [plæŋk] **N 1** *Carp, Constr etc* planche *f* (épaisse), madrier *m*; *Naut* **to walk the p.** passer à la planche **2** *Pol Fig* **this was a main p. in the party platform** c'était un des principaux articles du programme du parti
VT *Constr (floor)* planchéier

▶ **plank down VT SEP** *(put down heavily)* poser brusquement

planking ['plæŋkɪŋ] **N** *(planks)* planches *fpl*, madriers *mpl*

plankton ['plæŋktən] **N** plancton *m*

planned ['plænd] **ADJ 1** prévu, projeté; **the p. meeting never took place** la réunion qui avait été prévue n'a jamais eu lieu; **well/badly p.** bien/mal conçu; *(plot, crime)* bien/mal concerté *ou* organisé; **was it a p. pregnancy?** c'était vraiment votre/leur intention d'avoir un enfant? **2** *Econ etc* planifié; **p. takeover of** projet *m* d'OPA sur
▶▶ *Econ* **p. economy** économie *f* planifiée

planner ['plænər] **N 1** *(person)* planificateur, -trice; **(town)** p. urbaniste *mf* **2** *(on wall of office etc)* planning *m*; *(chart)* chronogramme *m*; *(diary)* agenda *m*

planning ['plænɪŋ] **N 1** *(of project, plot etc)* conception *f*, élaboration *f*; *(of menus)* élaboration; **the expedition will require careful p.** il faudra une organisation minutieuse pour mener à bien cette expédition; **it's still at the p. stage** c'est encore à l'état de projet; **the project was halted at the p. stage** le projet n'a pas dépassé le stade de la planification **2** *Econ* planification *f*, *Fam* planning *m*; *Admin* **to get p. permission to build sth** *or* **for sth** obtenir le permis de construire qch; **town p.** urbanisme *m*; **family p.** planning familial

plant [plɑːnt] **N 1** plante *f*, **flowering p.** plante à fleurs; **pot p., house p.** plante d'appartement; **bedding p.** plant *m* à repiquer

2 *Ind (equipment)* équipement *m*, matériel *m* (industriel); *(facility)* installation *f* (industrielle); *(factory)* usine *f*, **cooling p.** appareil *m* de refroidissement; **(electric) power p., generating p.** centrale *f* électrique

3 *Sl (spy)* taupe *f*; *(from police)* mouchard *m*; *(of magician, memory man)* compère *m*; *(something planted in order to incriminate)* coup *m* monté; **the drugs were a p.** la drogue avait été placée là pour me/le/*etc* mettre en cause

VT 1 *(tree etc)* planter; **to p. a field with wheat** mettre un champ en blé

2 *(insert, place) (stake in the ground etc)* planter; *Mil etc (bomb)* poser; *Fam (spy)* planter; **to p. an idea in sb's mind** implanter une idée dans l'esprit de qn; *Fam* **a well planted blow** un coup bien asséné *ou* bien appliqué; *Fam* **he planted a big kiss on her cheek** il lui planta un gros baiser sur la joue; *Fam* **to p. oneself in front of sb** se planter devant qn; **to p. incriminating evidence on sb** fabriquer de fausses preuves contre qn
▶▶ **p. biology** phytobiologie *f*; **p. breeder** phytogénéticien, -ienne; **p. hire** location *f* de matériel industriel; **p. life** flore *f*, **p. physiology** physiologie *f* végétale; **p. stand** jardinière *f*

▶ **plant out VT SEP** *Agr (seedling)* repiquer

plantain[1] ['plæntɪn] **N** *(plant)* plantain *m*

plantain[2] **N 1** *(fruit)* banane *f* des Antilles **2** *(tree)* bananier *m* du paradis
▶▶ **p. tree** bananier du paradis

plantar ['plæntər] **ADJ** *Anat* plantaire

plantation [plæn'teɪʃən] **N** *(of trees, cotton etc)* plantation *f*

planter ['plɑːntər] **N 1** *(plantation owner, worker)* planteur, -euse; **coffee/sugar/cotton p.** planteur, -euse de café/de sucre/de coton **2** *(tool)* planteuse *f* **3** *(pot for house plant)* cache-pot *m inv*; *(for outside)* jardinière *f*

plaque [plæk] **N 1** *(bronze, marble etc)* plaque *f* (commémorative) **2** *(on teeth)* plaque *f* dentaire

plash [plæʃ] **N** *(of waves, stream etc)* clapotement *m*, clapotis *m*; *(of object falling into water)* flac *m*
VI *(of liquids)* clapoter, faire un clapotis; *(of falling object etc)* faire flac *(sur l'eau etc)*

plasm ['plæz(ə)m] **N** *Biol* protoplasme *m*

plasma ['plæzmə] **N** plasma *m*; **(blood) p.** plasma (sanguin)
▶▶ *Comput* **p. display** affichage *m* à plasma; *Comput* **p. screen** écran *m* (à) plasma

plasmapheresis [plæzmə'ferəsɪs] **N** *Med* plasmaphérèse *f*, échange *m* plasmatique

plaster ['plɑːstər] **N 1** *Constr etc* plâtre *m*; **to put a leg in p.** plâtrer une jambe, mettre une jambe dans le plâtre **2** *Br Med* **(sticking) p.** pansement *m* adhésif, sparadrap *m*; **corn p.** pansement coricide
VT 1 *Constr etc (wall)* plâtrer, enduire de plâtre **2** *Fig* **the wall was plastered with advertisements** le mur était tapissé d'affiches; **plastered with mud** *(person, shoes, car etc)* couvert de boue; **her face was plastered with make-up** elle avait un peu forcé sur le maquillage; **he plastered his hair down** il aplatit ses cheveux; **her name was plastered over the front pages** son nom s'étalait en première page **3** *Med (leg etc)* plâtrer
▶▶ **p. cast** *Med* plâtre; *Art* moule *m* (en plâtre); **p. of Paris** plâtre de Paris *ou* à mouler

plasterboard ['plɑːstəbɔːd] **N** *Constr* Placoplâtre® *m*

plastered ['plɑːstəd] **ADJ** *Fam* beurré, pinté; **to get p.** se beurrer, se pinter

plasterer ['plɑːstərər] **N** plâtrier *m*

plasterwork ['plɑːstəwɜːk] **N** *Constr* plâtres *mpl*

plastic ['plæstɪk] **N 1** plastique *m*; **laminated p.** (plastique) stratifié *m*, lamifié *m*; **moulded p.** plastique moulé; **wrapped in p.** emballé dans du plastique; **the plastics industry** l'industrie *f* des plastiques **2** *Fam (money)* monnaie *f* électronique; **he paid for it with p.** il l'a payé avec une carte de crédit

ADJ 1 *(made of plastic) (bag, cup)* en plastique **2** *Art etc* plastique **3** *(artificial)* synthétique, artificiel; **p. smile** sourire *m* artificiel
▶▶ **the p. arts** les arts *mpl* plastiques; **p. bomb** charge *f* de plastique, bombe *f* au plastique; **to blow up a house with a p. bomb** plastiquer une maison; **p. bullet** balle *f* en plastique; **p. explosive** plastic *m*; *Fam* **p. money** monnaie électronique; **p. surgeon** *(cosmetic)* chirurgien, -ienne esthétique; *(therapeutic)* plasticien, -ienne; **p. surgery** *(cosmetic)* chirurgie *f* esthétique; *(therapeutic)* chirurgie plastique *ou* réparatrice

Plasticine® ['plæstɪsiːn] **N** pâte *f* à modeler

plasticity [plæs'tɪsɪtɪ] **N** plasticité *f*, *Art, Cin* effet *m* plastique

plate [pleɪt] **N 1** *(for food)* assiette *f*, **dinner/soup p.** assiette plate/creuse; *Fig Fam* **to have a lot on one's p.** avoir du pain sur la planche; *Fig Fam* **I've already got far too much on my p.** j'ai déjà largement à faire; *Fig Fam* **I've got enough on my p. without him causing problems** j'ai déjà assez à faire sans qu'il ne crée de problèmes; *Fig Fam* **to hand sth to sb on a p.** apporter qch à qn sur un plateau; *Fig Fam* **he got it handed to him on a p.** on le lui a apporté sur un plateau; *Rel etc* **(collection) p.** plateau *m* de quête; *Rel etc* **to pass round the p.** faire la quête

2 *(small piece) (of metal, glass, plastic etc)* petite plaque *f*, lamelle *f*, *Geol, Med* plaque *f*; **(dental) p.** *(for straightening teeth)* appareil *m* (dentaire); *(dentures)* dentier *m*

3 *Metal (large piece)* plaque *f*, *Ind* (grande) feuille *f*, *(of armour)* plaque, plate *f*; *(of door*

hinge) paumelle *f;* **hot p.** *(on cooker)* plaque chauffante; *(single plate)* réchaud *m;* *(plate warmer)* chauffe-assiettes *m inv;* **name p.** *(on door)* plaque de porte; *(of street)* plaque de rue; *(of machine)* plaque d'identification *ou* de série; *Br Aut etc* **number p.** plaque d'immatriculation

4 *Elec (of battery etc)* plaque *f,* lame *f, Electron (of electron tube)* plaque, anode *f*

5 *(in engraving), Typ* plaque *f; (in engraving), Phot etc* cliché *m; (engraving)* planche *f,* gravure *f,* estampe *f; Phot* **(photographic) p.** plaque *(photographique);* **p. 12 (a)** *(in book)* planche 12 (a)

6 *Constr* **(wall) p.** *(of beam)* plaque *f* d'assise **7** *(plated metal) (gold)* orfèvrerie *f;* **silver p.** argenterie *f,* **it's (only) p.** c'est du plaqué **8** *Sport* coupe *f* (d'or, d'argent donnée en prix)

VT 1 *(protect with plates of metal)* blinder, recouvrir *ou* garnir de plaques **2** *(add layer of metal to)* métalliser; *(with gold)* plaquer en or; *(with silver)* plaquer en argent

▸▸ **p. armour** armure *f (en plaques de fer); Aut* **p. clutch** embrayage *m* à disque *ou* à plateau; *Typ* **p. cylinder** cylindre *m* porte-plaque, *pl* cylindres porte-plaques; **p. glass** verre *m* (à vitres); **p.-glass window** *(of shop)* vitrine *f, (of house)* baie *f* vitrée; **p. rack** égouttoir *m;* **p. service** *(in restaurant)* service *m* à l'assiette; *Geol* **p. tectonics** tectonique *f* des plaques; **p. warmer** chauffe-assiettes

plateau, *pl* **plateaux, plateaus** ['plætəʊ, -əʊz] N *Geog* plateau *m; Fig* **to reach a p.** atteindre un palier

plated ['pleɪtɪd] ADJ **1** *(protected with metal plates)* recouvert *ou* garni de plaques; **armour p.** blindé **2** *(coated with metal)* plaqué; **gold p.** plaqué or; **silver p.** argenté; **chromium p.** chromé

plateful ['pleɪtfʊl] N assiettée *f,* (pleine) assiette *f*

platelayer ['pleɪtleɪə(r)] N *Br Rail* poseur *m* de rails

plateless printing ['pleɪtlɪs] N impression *f* sans presse

platelet ['pleɪtlɪt] N *(in blood)* plaquette *f*

plate-making N *Typ* préparation *f* des plaques offset

platen ['plæt(ə)n] N rouleau *m; Typ* platine *f*

plate-room manager N *Typ* conducteur *m* de presse

platform ['plætfɔːm] N **1** *(raised flat surface)* plate-forme *f, pl* plates-formes; *Rail (where passengers stand)* quai *m; (where train stops)* voie *f, (of weighing machine)* tablier *m; (of crane)* passerelle *f; Petr* **drilling p.** plate-forme de forage; **launching/firing p.** plate-forme de lancement/de tir (de missiles); *Rail* **the train waiting at p. one** le train au départ voie n° 1; *Rail* **to wait on the p.** *(of person)* attendre sur le quai; *Rail* **what p. is it for London?** quel quai est-ce pour Londres?; *Rail* **arrival/departure p.** quai d'arrivée/de départ

2 *(at public meeting)* estrade *f,* tribune *f; Pol Fig (of party)* plate-forme *f, pl* plates-formes, programme *m;* **he used his programme on TV as a p.** for promoting his political views son émission télévisée lui servait de tribune pour promouvoir ses opinions politiques **3** *Comput* plate-forme *f, pl* plates-formes **4 platforms** *(shoes)* chaussures *fpl* à semelles compensées

▸▸ *Am Rail* **p. car** *(wagon m)* plate-forme; **p. shoes** chaussures à semelle compensée; **p. soles** semelles *fpl* compensées; *Rail* **p. ticket** ticket *m* de quai

plating ['pleɪtɪŋ] N **1** *(protective)* blindage *m;* **steel** *or* **armour p.** blindage **2** *(coating with metal)* placage *m; (copper)* cuivrage *m;*

(gold) dorage *m,* dorure *f; (silver)* argentage *m,* argenture *f*

platinum ['plætɪnəm] N platine *m;* **p. blond hair** cheveux blond platiné *ou* blond platine *ou* platinés; **she's a p. blonde** c'est une blonde platinée

ADV **to go p.** *(of record)* devenir disque de platine

▸▸ **p. disc** disque *m* de platine

platitude ['plætɪtjuːd] N *(remark)* platitude *f,* banalité *f,* lieu *m* commun

platitudinous [plætɪ'tjuːdɪnəs] ADJ *(style, speech)* plat, banal, -s

Plato ['pleɪtəʊ] N Platon

Platonic [plə'tɒnɪk] ADJ *(philosophy etc)* platonicien; *(love)* platonique; **he wanted to keep things platonic** il voulait que leur relation reste platonique

platoon [plə'tuːn] N *Mil (in infantry)* section *f, (in tanks)* peloton *m; Fig (of assistants, students)* armée *f*

▸▸ **p. commander** chef *m* de section; *(in tanks)* chef de peloton

platter ['plætə(r)] N **1** *(plate)* plat *m* **2** *esp Am Fam (record)* disque *m*

platypus ['plætɪpəs] N *(animal)* ornithorynque *m*

plaudits ['plɔːdɪts] NPL *esp Lit* (salve *f* d')applaudissements *mpl;* **the new menus on trains have won the p. of passengers** les nouveaux menus servis dans les trains ont été accueillis avec enthousiasme par les passagers

plausibility [plɔːzə'bɪlɪtɪ] N *(of argument, excuse etc)* plausibilité *f;* **the plot is lacking in p.** l'intrigue n'est guère plausible; **I would question the p. of someone doing …** il ne me semble guère plausible que quelqu'un fasse …; **she argued, with some p., that …** elle a avancé, de façon assez convaincante, que …

plausible ['plɔːzəb(ə)l] ADJ **1** *(excuse etc)* plausible, vraisemblable; *(pretext etc)* spécieux **2** *(person, argument)* convaincant

plausibly ['plɔːzəblɪ] ADV plausiblement; *(to argue etc)* de façon convaincante

PLAY [pleɪ]

N	pièce (de théâtre) **1** ▪ jeu **2, 3, 5**
VI	jouer **1–4**
VT	jouer **1–3** ▪ jouer à **1** ▪ jouer de **3**
	▪ mettre **3**

N **1** *Theat* pièce *f* de théâtre; **Shakespeare's plays** les pièces *ou* le théâtre de Shakespeare; **(radio) p.** pièce radiophonique; **(television) p.** dramatique *f*

2 *(movement) (of mechanical part)* course *f; (unwanted slack)* jeu *m; (of light)* jeu, reflets *mpl;* **a complex p. of forces** un rapport de forces complexe; **there's still too much p. in the brakes** il y a encore trop de jeu dans les freins; **to come into p.** entrer en jeu, intervenir; **to bring** *or* **call** *or* **put sth into p.** mettre qch en jeu *ou* en œuvre; *(one's faculties)* exercer qch; *Fam* **to make a p. for sth** jouer le grand jeu pour obtenir qch; *Fam* **to make a p. for sb** *(try to seduce)* jouer le grand jeu à qn, faire des avances à qn; **to give** *or* **allow full p. to one's imagination** donner libre cours à son imagination; **to make great p. of sth** beaucoup insister sur qch

3 *(of children etc)* jeu *m;* **I didn't want to interrupt the children's p.** je ne voulais pas interrompre les enfants alors qu'ils étaient en train de jouer; **at p.** en train de jouer; **the aristocracy at p.** l'aristocratie en train de se détendre; **to say sth in p.** dire qch en plaisantant *ou* pour rire; **p. on words** calembour *m,* jeu de mots

4 *Sport* **p. began at one o'clock** la partie a

commencé à une heure; **after some very boring p. in the first half …** après une première mi-temps très ennuyeuse …; *Tennis* **there was some incredibly fast p. in the final set** il y a eu des échanges très rapides au dernier set; **what a good piece of p.!** quel beau coup!, bien joué!; *Cr* **rain stopped p.** la partie a été interrompue par la pluie; **in p.** *(of ball)* en jeu; **out of p.** hors jeu

5 *(gambling)* jeu *m* (de hasard); **to lose at p.** perdre au jeu

VI **1** *(have fun)* jouer; *(of animals)* jouer, folâtrer, gambader

2 *(participate in game)* jouer; **to p. against sb/a team** jouer contre qn/une équipe; **to p. in goal** être goal; **who plays first?** à qui de commencer?; *(at bowling)* à qui la boule?; *Golf* à qui l'honneur?; **to p. fair** jouer franc jeu; **to p. hard to get** se faire désirer; **to p. for money** *(in gambling)* jouer pour de l'argent; **to p. high** *or* **for high stakes** *(in gambling)* jouer gros (jeu); *Cards* **to p. high/low** jouer une forte/basse carte; **do you p.?** est-ce tu sais jouer?

3 *(move) (of light, colour, fountain)* jouer, chatoyer; **the sun is playing on the water** le soleil joue sur l'eau

4 *Theat etc (act)* jouer; **to p. on the stage** *(of actor)* jouer *ou* se produire sur la scène; **production/film now playing at …** pièce/film qui passe actuellement à …; **to p. to packed houses** jouer *ou* se produire à guichets fermés

5 *Mus (of instrument, musician, band)* jouer; **they always have music playing full blast** ils mettent toujours leur musique plein pot; **I could hear the radio playing in the next room** j'entendais (le son de) la radio dans la pièce à côté

VT **1** *Sport etc (game of tennis etc)* faire, jouer; *(match)* jouer, disputer; *(include on one's team)* inclure dans son équipe; **to p. football/tennis** jouer au football/tennis; **to p. cards/chess** jouer aux cartes/échecs; **to p. sb at chess** faire une partie d'échecs avec qn; **Real Madrid played Dynamo Kiev** le Real de Madrid a affronté *ou* a joué contre le Dynamo de Kiev; *Ftbl etc* **to p. left back** jouer arrière gauche; **the team was playing two substitutes** l'équipe jouait avec deux remplaçant(e)s; *Sport* **to p. a shot/ball** jouer un coup/une balle; *Cards* **to p. a card** jouer une carte; **to p. clubs/spades** jouer trèfle/pique; *Chess etc* **to p. a move** jouer; *Fam* **to p. a hunch** jouer *ou* agir sur une intuition; **I'll p. you for the drinks** le perdant paie les consommations, d'accord?

2 *Theat, Cin (part)* jouer; *(tragedy)* jouer, représenter; **to p. Macbeth** jouer *ou* tenir le rôle de Macbeth; *Fig* **to p. an important part** jouer un rôle important; *Fam* **to p. the fool** faire l'idiot(e) *ou* l'imbécile; *Fam* **don't p. the innocent with me!** ne fais pas l'innocent avec moi!

3 *Mus* **to p. the piano/the flute** jouer du piano/de la flûte; **to p. a piece** jouer un morceau; **to p. a record-player** faire marcher un tourne-disques; **to p. a record/a tape** passer *ou* mettre un disque/une cassette; **can you p. some Pink Floyd?** tu peux mettre quelque chose de Pink Floyd?; **the neighbours were playing loud music** les voisins avaient mis la musique à fond

4 to p. a joke *or* **a trick on sb** jouer un tour à qn

5 *esp Lit* **to p. sb false** trahir qn

6 *(direct)* diriger (**upon, over** sur); **to p. the hose on the fire** diriger la lance sur le feu

▸▸ **p. area** aire *f* de jeux

▸ **play about, play around** VI **1** *(play)* jouer, s'amuser; **stop playing around with that gun!** arrête de jouer avec ce revolver!

2 *(not be serious)* s'amuser; **it's time he stopped playing about and settled down** il est temps qu'il arrête de s'amuser et qu'il se fixe

3 *(consider possibilities)* **to p. around with an idea** retourner une idée dans sa tête; **to p. around with a tune** expérimenter avec un air; **they played around with the words to find a good slogan** ils jonglaient avec les mots pour trouver un bon slogan; **they played around with various names** ils ont envisagé plusieurs noms

4 *(sexually)* avoir des aventures; **to p. around with sb** avoir une aventure avec qn; **you're just playing around (with me)** tu joues avec moi

▸ **play along** VI **1** *(accompany)* **I played the fiddle while he played along on the accordeon** je jouais du violon tandis qu'il m'accompagnait à l'accordéon

2 *(cooperate)* coopérer (**with** avec)
VT SEP *(manipulate)* *(person)* manipuler

▸ **play at** VT SEP INSEP **1 to p. at soldiers** jouer aux soldats; **to p. at keeping shop** jouer au marchand/à la marchande

2 *(dabble in)* **to p. at doing sth** faire qch en amateur; **they played at being revolutionaries** ils jouaient aux petits révolutionnaires; **they're just playing at being married** ils voient le mariage comme un jeu; *Fam* **what do you think you're playing at?** à quoi tu joues?

▸ **play back** VT SEP *(tape)* écouter, passer

▸ **play down** VT SEP *(importance of sth)* minimiser; *(problem)* dédramatiser; **the government is trying to p. down its role** le gouvernement tente de minimiser l'importance de son rôle

▸ **play in** VT SEP **1** *Sport* **to p. oneself in** *(become accustomed)* se faire au jeu

2 *(with music)* accueillir en musique

▸ **play into** VT SEP INSEP **to p. into sb's hands** faire le jeu de qn

▸ **play off** VT SEP *(oppose)* **to p. sb off against sb** opposer qn à qn; **they played their enemies off against each other** ils ont dressé leurs ennemis les uns contre les autres
VI *Sport (attempt to break tie)* faire *ou* jouer la belle

▸ **play on** VI *(continue to play)* continuer à jouer
VT INSEP **1** *(exploit)* **to p. on sb's feelings** jouer sur les sentiments de qn

2 *(pun on)* **to p. on words** jouer sur les mots; **the title plays on a line from Shakespeare** le titre est un jeu de mots sur une phrase de Shakespeare

▸ **play out** VT SEP **1** *(act)* **the events being played out on the world's stage** les événements qui se déroulent dans le monde

2 *Fam (usu passive)* *(exhaust)* **to be played out** *(of person, horse etc)* être vanné *ou* éreinté; *(of idea etc)* être vieux jeu *ou* démodé; *(of story)* avoir perdu tout intérêt

3 *(with music)* **they were played out to the strains of ...** leur départ a été accompagné par l'air de ...

▸ **play up** VI **1** *Br Fam (of car, child, horse etc)* faire des siennes; **my back/war wound is playing up again** mon dos/ma blessure de guerre recommence à me faire souffrir

2 *Fam (flatter)* **to p. up to sb** flatter qn
VT SEP **1** *Br Fam (cause difficulties to)* énerver, *Fam* taper sur le système de; **my rheumatism is playing me up** mes rhumatismes me font souffrir

2 *(emphasize)* faire ressortir; *(incident, scandal)* exploiter

▸ **play upon** VT INSEP = **play on** VT INSEP

▸ **play with** VT INSEP **1** *(to amuse oneself with)* **to p. with a doll/dolls** jouer *ou* s'amuser avec une poupée/jouer à la poupée; **to p. with one's glasses** *(distraitement)* jouer avec ses lunettes; **to be playing with fire** jouer avec le feu; **to p. with sb's affections** jouer avec l'affection de qn; **to p. with words** jouer sur les mots

2 *(to have at one's disposal)* **we've got plenty of time to p. with** nous avons beaucoup de temps à nous; **we don't have a lot of money to p. with** nous n'avons pas beaucoup d'argent à notre disposition

3 *Fam* **to p. with oneself** *(masturbate)* se toucher

playable ['pleɪəb(ə)l] ADJ *(football pitch etc)* praticable; *(shot, ball, music)* jouable

play-act VI *(pretend)* jouer la comédie; *(clown around)* faire le clown

play-acting N **it's just p.** *(pretence)* c'est de la comédie; *(clowning around)* c'est pour rire

playback ['pleɪbæk] N réécoute *f*; *TV etc* présonorisation *f*, play-back *m inv*, présono *f*; **we watched the p. after the programme** nous avons regardé l'enregistrement après l'émission
▸▸ **p. deck** magnétoscope *m* de lecture; **p. head** tête *f* de lecture

playbill ['pleɪbɪl] N *Theat (poster)* affiche *f* (de théâtre); *Am (programme)* programme *m*

playboy ['pleɪbɔɪ] N playboy *m*

player ['pleɪər] N **1** *Sport* joueur, -euse; *(team member)* équipier, -ière, joueur, -euse; **card/billiards p.** joueur, -euse de cartes/billard

2 *Mus* musicien, -ienne; *(of instrument)* joueur, -euse; **a good guitar p.** un(e) bon(ne) guitariste; **the band's piano p.** le pianiste du groupe

3 *(machine)* **record p.** tourne-disque *m*, *pl* tourne-disques; **cassette p.** lecteur *m* de cassettes, magnétophone *m* (à cassettes)

4 *Theat* acteur, -trice; *(of part)* interprète *mf*

5 *Com, Mktg* acteur *m*; **who are the key players in this market?** qui sont les acteurs principaux sur ce marché?
▸▸ **p. piano** piano *m* mécanique

playfellow ['pleɪfeləʊ] N *Old-fashioned* = **playmate**

playful ['pleɪfʊl] ADJ *(person, cat)* espiègle; *(mood)* enjoué, badin; *(remark)* espiègle, enjoué; **she gave him a p. push** elle l'a poussé pour jouer *ou* par espièglerie

playfully ['pleɪfʊlɪ] ADV *(to say, remark)* en badinant, d'un ton enjoué; *(to smile)* d'un air enjoué; *(to push sb etc)* pour jouer, par espièglerie

playfulness ['pleɪfʊlnɪs] N *(of remark)* caractère *m* badin; *(of person, cat)* espièglerie *f*

playgoer ['pleɪgəʊər] N habitué, -ée du théâtre

playground ['pleɪgraʊnd] N *Sch* cour *f* (de récréation); *(outside of school)* parc *m* de jeu; *Fig* **St Tropez is the p. of the rich** St Tropez est le lieu de villégiature des riches

playgroup ['pleɪgruːp] N ≃ (école *f*) maternelle *f*

playhouse ['pleɪhaʊs] N **1** *Theat* théâtre *m* **2** *(for children)* maison *f*

playing ['pleɪɪŋ] N **1** *(by children etc)* jeu *m*; **I'm not in the mood for p.** je ne suis pas d'humeur à jouer **2** *Sport* jeu *m*; **the team's p.** le jeu de l'équipe; **p. is more important than winning** il est plus important de jouer que de gagner **3** *Mus* jeu *m*; **his p. is superb** son jeu est magnifique; **her p. of the sonata was superb** elle a joué la sonate de façon magnifique
▸▸ **p. card** carte *f* à jouer; *Br* **p. field** terrain *m* de sport

playlist ['pleɪlɪst] N *TV etc* liste *f* de disques à programmer

playmaker ['pleɪmeɪkər] N *Sport* meneur, -euse de jeu

playmate ['pleɪmeɪt] N camarade *mf* (de jeu); *(friend)* copain *m*, copine *f*

play-off N *Sport* belle *f*

playout music ['pleɪaʊt] N musique *f* (de générique) de fin

playpen ['pleɪpen] N parc *m* (pour bébé)

playroom ['pleɪruːm] N salle *f* de jeux

playschool ['pleɪskuːl] N ≃ (école *f*) maternelle *f*

plaything ['pleɪθɪŋ] N jouet *m*; *Fam* **she's just his p.** il se sert d'elle comme d'un jouet

playtime ['pleɪtaɪm] N *Sch* récréation *f*, *Fam* récré *f*

playwright ['pleɪraɪt] N auteur *m* dramatique, dramaturge *mf*

plaza ['plɑːzə] N *Am* **1** *(square)* place *f* **2** *(shopping centre)* centre *m* commercial **3** *Aut (service area)* aire *f* de service

plc, PLC [piːel'siː] N **1** *Br Com (abbr public limited company)* ≃ SA *f*; **Smith p.** Smith SA **2** *Mktg (abbr product life-cycle)* cycle *m* de vie du produit

plea [pliː] N **1** *(appeal)* appel *m*; **p. for mercy** appel à la clémence; **to make a p. for tolerance** en appeler à *ou* implorer la tolérance **2** *(excuse)* excuse *f*, prétexte *m* (**for doing sth** pour faire qch); **on the p. that he had a prior engagement** sous prétexte d'un autre engagement; **they did not accept his p. that he had simply forgotten** il a allégué qu'il avait simplement oublié mais ils n'ont pas accepté cette excuse **3** *Law* défense *f*, special plea exception *f* péremptoire; **to enter a p. of guilty/not guilty** plaider coupable/non coupable; **to put forward a p. of insanity** *(of counsel)* plaider la folie
▸▸ *Law* **p. bargaining** = possibilité *f* pour un inculpé de se voir notifier un chef d'inculpation moins grave s'il accepte de plaider coupable

plead [pliːd] *(pt, pp* **pleaded**, *occ Am* **pled** [pled])* VI **1 to p. with sb for sb/sth** intervenir *ou* intercéder *ou* plaider auprès de qn pour qn/qch; **to p. for mercy** implorer la clémence, en appeler à la clémence; **to p. for justice** demander que justice soit faite; **they were pleading with him to stop** ils le suppliaient de s'arrêter **2** *Law* plaider (**for** pour; **against** contre); **to p. guilty/not guilty** plaider coupable/non coupable; **how do you p.?** plaidez-vous coupable ou non coupable?
VT **1** *Law, Fig (case)* plaider; *Fig* **to p. sb's cause with sb** intercéder pour qn auprès de qn, plaider la cause de qn auprès de qn; **to p. insanity** *(of counsel)* plaider la folie **2** *(claim) (ignorance etc)* prétexter; *(excuse)* invoquer, alléguer

pleading ['pliːdɪŋ] ADJ suppliant, implorant
N **1** prières *fpl* (**for sb** en faveur de qn) **2** *Law (speech)* plaidoyer *m*; *(action)* plaidoirie *f*, *(art)* l'art *m* de plaider

pleadingly ['pliːdɪŋlɪ] ADV *(to say)* d'un ton suppliant *ou* implorant; *(to look)* d'un regard suppliant *ou* implorant

pleasant ['plezənt] ADJ agréable; *(person)* agréable, affable, aimable; *(breeze)* brise *f* douce *ou* agréable; **it's a p. day** il fait bon aujourd'hui; **to have a p. day** *(relaxing etc)* passer agréablement la journée; **I had a p. day at the office** tout s'est bien passé au bureau; **to make oneself p. or to be p. (to sb)** se rendre agréable (auprès de qn); **he was very p.** il s'est montré très affable *ou* très gentil; **the account of the trial does not make p. reading** le récit du procès n'est pas une lecture des plus agréables; **p. dreams!** fais de beaux rêves!

pleasantly ['plezəntlɪ] ADV agréablement, d'une manière agréable; **she smiled p. at him** elle lui sourit d'un air affable; **p. situated** agréablement situé, d'une situation agréable; **to be p. surprised** être agréablement surpris

pleasantness ['plezəntnıs] N *(of place etc)* agrément *m*, charme *m*; *(of person, manner etc)* affabilité *f*

pleasantry ['plezəntrı] N 1 *(joke)* plaisanterie *f* 2 **pleasantries** *(polite remarks)* civilités *fpl*

please [pli:z] INT s'il vous plaît/s'il te plaît; **come in, p.** entrez, s'il vous plaît, entrez, je vous prie; **p. don't cry** ne pleurez pas, je vous en supplie; **p., daddy, p.** s'il te plaît, papa; **p. tell me …** voudriez-vous bien me dire …; **may I? – p. do!** vous permettez? – je vous en prie!; **p. sit down** *or* **take a seat** veuillez vous asseoir; **p. don't interrupt!** veuillez bien ne pas m'/nous interrompre; **p. do not walk on the grass** *(on sign)* prière de ne pas marcher sur le gazon; **would you like some cake/to come with me? – yes, p.** est-ce que vous voulez un peu de gâteau/venir avec moi? – oh, oui, avec plaisir; **p. let me win the lottery!** Mon Dieu, j'aimerais tant gagner au loto!; *Sch* **p., sir!** pardon, monsieur!; **(oh) p.!** *(in indignation, disgust etc)* c'est pas vrai!

VT *(give pleasure to)* plaire à, faire plaisir à; *(make content)* contenter, satisfaire; **the news pleased her immensely** cette nouvelle lui a fait immensément plaisir; **to try to p. sb** chercher à faire plaisir à qn; **you can't p. everybody** on ne peut plaire à tout le monde; *Prov* **you can't p. all of the people all of the time** on ne peut pas faire plaisir à tout le monde; **he's hard to p.** il est difficile (à contenter); **she's easy to p., she's easily pleased** elle n'est pas difficile; **music that pleases the ear** musique qui flatte l'oreille; **p. yourself!** faites comme il vous plaira *ou* comme vous voudrez; *Fml* **His Majesty has been graciously pleased to …** il a plu à sa gracieuse Majesté de …

VI 1 *(like)* to do as one pleases agir à sa guise *ou* à son gré; **do as you p.** faites comme vous voudrez; **he will only do as he pleases** il n'en fait jamais qu'à sa tête; **just as you p.** comme vous voudrez; **if you p.** s'il vous/te plaît; **and then, if you p., he blamed me for it!** et le comble c'est qu'il a dit que c'était de ma faute! 2 *(give pleasure)* faire plaisir; **he tries hard to p.** il fait tout pour me/te/*etc* plaire

V IMPERS *Arch, Lit* **may it p. your Majesty** plaise *ou* n'en déplaise à votre Majesté; **p. God!** plaise à Dieu!, Dieu le veuille!

N **without so much as a p. or thank you** sans même dire merci

pleased [pli:zd] ADJ *(satisfied)* satisfait, content; *(happy)* heureux; *(smile)* de satisfaction; **to be p. with sth/sb** être content de qch/qn; **to be p. to do sth** faire qch avec plaisir; **he's very p. with himself** il est très content *ou* fort satisfait de lui-même *ou Pej* de sa petite personne; **I'm very p. (that) she's coming** cela me fait énormément plaisir qu'elle vienne, je suis ravi *ou* très content qu'elle vienne; **I'll be p. to come** je viendrai avec plaisir; **p. to meet you** enchanté de faire votre connaissance; **I'm so p. to see you** je suis très content *ou* cela me fait grand plaisir de vous voir; **she didn't exactly look p. to see me** elle n'avait pas vraiment l'air contente de me voir; **I'm p. to say that …** je suis heureux de pouvoir vous dire que …; *Fml* **I am p. to inform you that …** j'ai le plaisir de vous aviser que …; **to be p. for sb** être content pour qn; *Fam* **he's as p. as Punch** il est heureux comme un roi

pleasing ['pli:zıŋ] ADJ *(news, result)* qui fait plaisir; *(meal, film, conversation etc)* agréable; *(person, manner)* agréable, plaisant

pleasingly ['pli:zıŋlı] ADV agréablement

pleasurable ['pleʒərəb(ə)l] ADJ agréable

pleasurably ['pleʒərəblı] ADV agréablement

pleasure ['pleʒər] N 1 *(contentment)* plaisir *m*; **to take** *or* **find p. in doing sth** éprouver du plaisir à faire qch, prendre *ou* avoir (du) plaisir à faire qch; **it gave me great p.** cela m'a fait énormément plaisir; **her books gave p. to many people** beaucoup de gens ont pris du plaisir à lire ses livres; *Fml* **I have p. in informing you that …** j'ai le plaisir *ou* je suis heureux de vous apprendre que …; **it gives me no p. to inform you that …** j'ai la triste tâche de vous apprendre que …; **it's a real p. to see you looking so cheerful** cela me fait vraiment plaisir de vous voir si gai; **it is a p. to listen to him** on a plaisir à l'écouter; **thank you very much – (it was) a p.** merci beaucoup – de rien; **the p. was all mine** tout le plaisir était pour moi; **I haven't the p. of knowing her** *or* **of her acquaintance** je n'ai pas le plaisir de la connaître; **with p.** avec plaisir, volontiers; **with the greatest (of) p.** avec le plus grand plaisir; *Fml* **Mr Stevens requests the p. of the company of Miss Miller at …** *(invitation)* M. Stevens prie Mlle Miller de lui faire le plaisir d'assister à …

2 *(enjoyment)* plaisir(s) *m(pl)*; **life given up to p., life of p.** vie consacrée aux plaisirs; **to take one's p.** s'amuser, se divertir; **to travel for p.** voyager pour son plaisir

3 *Old-fashioned (will)* volonté *f*, bon plaisir *m*; **at sb's p.** au gré de qn, au bon plaisir de qn; **during the King's p.** pendant le bon plaisir du roi

VT *Arch* faire plaisir à

VI *Arch* se plaire, prendre plaisir (**in sth** à qch; **in doing sth** à faire qch)

▸▸ **p. boat** bateau *m* de plaisance; **p. cruising** navigation *f* de plaisance; **the p. principle** le principe de plaisir; **p. seeker** jouisseur, -euse; **p. seeking** recherche *f* des plaisirs; **p. trip** excursion *f*

pleat [pli:t] *Sewing etc* N pli *m*

VT *(skirt etc)* plisser, faire des plis à

pleated ['pli:tıd] ADJ *(skirt etc)* plissé

pleating ['pli:tıŋ] N *(no pl) (pleats)* plis *mpl*, plissé(s) *m(pl)*

pleb [pleb] N *Fam* prolo *mf*

plebby ['plebı] ADJ *Fam* prolo

plebeian [plə'bi:ən] ADJ, N plébéien, -ienne

plebiscite ['plebısıt] N plébiscite *m*; **to hold a p.** organiser un plébiscite; **to vote for sb/sth by p.** plébisciter qn/qch

plectrum ['plektrəm] N *Mus (for guitar etc)* médiator *m*

pled PT, PP see plead

pledge [pledʒ] N 1 *(oath)* promesse *f*, vœu *m*; **a p. of loyalty/support** une promesse *ou* un serment de loyauté/soutien; **the Opposition has given a p. to repeal this law** l'opposition a fait le serment d'abroger cette loi; *Old-fashioned* **to take** *or* **sign the p.** *(of abstainer)* promettre de s'abstenir d'alcool

2 *(object of value)* gage *m*, nantissement *m*; **to hold in p.** (dé)tenir en gage *ou* en nantissement; **to redeem a p.** retirer un gage; *Fin* **p. over property** gage immobilier

3 *(sign)* **p. of good faith** garantie *f* de bonne foi

VT 1 *(promise) (one's word etc)* engager; **to p. oneself** *or* **one's word to do sth** s'engager à faire qch; **to be pledged to do sth** avoir pris l'engagement de faire qch; **to p. one's loyalty/support** accorder sa loyauté/son soutien; **to p. one's honour** donner sa parole d'honneur, s'engager sur l'honneur (**to do sth** à faire qch); **to p. one's allegiance to the king** vouer obéissance au roi; **to p. money** *(in radio, television appeal)* promettre un don

2 *(give as pledge or security)* donner *ou* mettre en gage, déposer en gage *ou* en nantissement, engager; **to p. one's property** engager son bien; **to p. securities** déposer des titres en garantie

▸▸ *Fin* **p. holder** détenteur, -trice de gage(s)

pledgee [ple'dʒi:] N *Fin* gagiste *mf*

pledgor ['pledʒər] N *Fin* gageur, -euse

pleiad, *pl* **pleiads, pleiades** ['plaıæd, -æz, -ədi:z] N 1 *Liter* pléiade *f* 2 *Myth, Astron* **the Pleiads, the Pleiades** les Pléiades *fpl*

plenary ['pli:nərı] ADJ complet, -ète, entier; ▸▸ **p. assembly** assemblée *f* plénière; **p. power** *(of dictator)* pouvoir *m* absolu; *(of president)* pleins pouvoirs; **p. session** *(at conference)* séance *f* plénière

plenipotentiary [plenıpə'tenʃ(ə)rı] ADJ, N plénipotentiaire *m*

plenitude ['plenıtju:d] N plénitude *f*

plentiful ['plentıful] ADJ abondant, copieux; **to be p.** abonder

plentifully ['plentıfulı] ADV abondamment, copieusement

plenty ['plentı] N abondance *f*, **p. of …** beaucoup de …, *Fam* plein de …; **you've got p. of time** vous avez largement le temps; **to arrive in p. of time** arriver de bonne heure; **to have p. to live on** avoir largement de quoi vivre; **that's p.** *(when being served food, drink)* ça suffit; *Fam* **there's p. more where that came from!** *(food etc)* quand il y en a plus, il y en a encore; **take as much as you like, there's p. more** prenez-en autant que vous voulez, il en reste beaucoup; **land of p.** pays *m* de cocagne; **year of p.** année *f* d'abondance

ADV *Fam* **it's p. big enough** c'est bien assez gros

ADJ *Arch, Am* abondant; **money is p.** l'argent ne manque pas *ou* abonde

pleonasm ['pli:ənæz(ə)m] N pléonasme *m*

pleonastic [pli:ə'næstık] ADJ pléonastique, redondant; **to be p.** *(of word)* être un pléonasme

plethora ['pleθərə] N pléthore *f*, surabondance *f*

pleural ['pluər(ə)l] ADJ *Med* pleural, -aux ▸▸ **p. membrane** plèvre *f*

pleurisy ['pluərısı] N *Med* pleurésie *f*, **to have p.** avoir *ou* faire une pleurésie

plexus ['pleksəs] N 1 *Anat* plexus *m* 2 *Fig (maze)* enchevêtrement *m*

pliability [plaıə'bılıtı] N *(of stem etc)* flexibilité *f*, souplesse *f*, *(of character)* docilité *f*, souplesse

pliable ['plaıəb(ə)l] ADJ pliable, pliant, flexible; *(leather)* souple; *Fig (character etc)* docile, malléable, souple

pliers ['plaıəz] NPL *(tool)* pince(s) *f(pl)*, tenaille(s) *f(pl)*; **a pair of p.** des tenailles VOIR GRAMMAIRE A10

plight[1] [plaıt] N condition *f ou* état *m* critique; **to be in a sorry** *or* **sad p.** *(of person, country, economy)* être dans une mauvaise passe; **she saw my p. and helped me get up** elle a vu que ça n'allait pas et m'a aidé à me relever; **what a p. you're in!** comme vous voilà fait!

plight[2] VT **to p. one's troth to sb** *Arch* donner sa foi à qn; *(promise to marry)* se fiancer à qn

Plimsoll ['plımsəl] N ▸▸ *Naut* **P. line, P. mark** ligne *f* de Plimsoll

plimsolls ['plımsəlz] NPL *Br* (chaussures *fpl* de) tennis *mpl*

plinth [plınθ] N *Archit* plinthe *f*, *(of statue, column)* socle *m*

Pliny ['plını] N **P. the Elder/the Younger** Pline *m* l'Ancien/le Jeune

plip key [plıp] N *Aut* plip *m*

PLO [pi:el'əʊ] N *(abbr* **Palestine Liberation Organization)** OLP *f*, **P. representatives** représentants de l'OLP

plod [plɒd] N 1 *(walking)* démarche *f* lourde *ou* lente; **it's a long p.** il faut marcher longtemps **2** (heavy work) travail m pénible **3** Sl (police officer) flic m, poulet m; **the p.** (the police) les flics, les poulets

VT (-dd-) **1** (walk) marcher lourdement ou péniblement; **to p. on** continuer sa marche pénible; **he plodded home alone** (dejected) seul et malheureux, il est rentré chez lui **2** (work) = **plod away**

VT to p. one's way avancer ou marcher d'un pas lent

▸ **plod along VI 1** (walk slowly) avancer ou marcher d'un pas lent **2** (work slowly) travailler laborieusement (**with** à)

▸ **plod away VI** (work slowly) travailler laborieusement (**at** à), peiner, trimer (**at** sur)

▸ **plod on VI** = **plod along**

▸ **plod through VT INSEP** (work slowly at) travailler laborieusement à; **I'm plodding through a rather boring book just now** j'avance péniblement dans un livre plutôt barbant en ce moment

plodder ['plɒdər] **N** Pej besogneux, -euse

plodding ['plɒdɪŋ] **ADJ** (steps) pesant, lourd

plonk¹ [plɒŋk] **N** (sound) bruit m sourd

VT = **plonk down**

▸ **plonk away VI** Fam **to p. away on the piano** pianoter

▸ **plonk down VT SEP** poser lourdement; **just p. it down there** pose-le par là; **he plonked his glass down** il posa son verre bruyamment; **to p. oneself down in an armchair** se laisser tomber dans un fauteuil

▸ **plonk out VT SEP** Fam **to p. out a tune on a guitar/piano** jouer maladroitement un air à la guitare/au piano

plonk² **N** Br Fam (wine) pinard m; (poor quality wine) piquette f

plonker ['plɒŋkər] **N** Br Sl **1** (penis) bite f, Hum zizi m **2** (fool) branleur m

plook [pluk] **N** Scot, North Eng Fam (pimple) bouton m

plop [plɒp] **N 1** (splash) flac m, plouf m **2** (soft sound) pouf m

ADV to go p. (of sth falling into water etc) faire plouf; (of sth landing softly) faire pouf

VI (-pp-) **1** (splash) faire flac ou plouf, tomber en faisant flac ou plouf **2** (land softly) tomber; **she plopped exhausted onto the bed** épuisée, elle s'est laissée tomber sur le lit

plosive ['pləʊsɪv] Ling **ADJ** (consonant) explosif

N explosive f

plot [plɒt] **N 1** (conspiracy) complot m, conspiration f; **a p. on sb's life** un complot pour tuer qn; **to hatch a p.** tramer ou ourdir un complot

2 Liter, Theat, Cin (of play, novel etc) intrigue f, action f; Fig **the p. thickens** l'affaire se corse

3 Math etc tracé m; (graph) graphe m, graphique m; Aviat, Naut (of ship's or plane's route) tracé, graphe; (on radar) pointé m

4 (land) (parcelle f ou lot m de) terrain m; (small) lopin m de terre; **building p.** terrain à bâtir; (**vegetable**) **p.** (in garden) potager m

VT (-tt-) **1** (plan) (person's downfall) machiner, combiner; **to p. sb's murder** comploter de tuer qn, combiner le meurtre de qn

2 Liter, Cin etc **a well plotted novel/film** un roman/film qui a une bonne intrigue

3 Math, Phys (curve, diagram, graph) tracer; (in surveying etc) (area of land) dresser ou lever le plan de, faire le levé de; (geometric figure) tracer, rapporter; (point on map) marquer, tracer, repérer; (on radar) marquer, relever; Comput tracer; Fig (progress, development) suivre; **to p. a course** (for plane, ship) relever ou tracer une route; Aviat, Naut **to p. the position** faire le point

VI (conspire) comploter, conspirer (**against sb** contre qn)

plotter ['plɒtər] **N 1** (conspirator) conspirateur, -trice, comploteur, -euse **2** (on radar) marqueur, -euse, plotteur m; Comput (device) traceur m

plotting ['plɒtɪŋ] **N** (conspiring) complot(s) m(pl), conspiration(s) f(pl)

▸▸ Comput **p. board, p. table** table f traçante, traceur m de courbes

plough, Am **plow** [plaʊ] **N 1** charrue f; **under the p.** (of land) cultivé; Fig **to put one's hand to the p.** mettre la main à la pâte **2** Astron **the P.** la Grande Ourse

VT 1 (field) labourer; (furrow) tracer, creuser; (of ship) (waves) fendre, sillonner; **to p. the soil** labourer la terre, retourner la terre (à la charrue); **ploughed land** terres fpl labourées **2** Sch Old-fashioned Br Fam **to p. an exam** se planter à un examen; **to be** or **get ploughed in an exam** être recalé ou collé à un examen

VI Agr labourer la terre

▸ **plough back,** Am **plow back VT SEP** Com, Fin réinvestir (**into** dans); **profits ploughed back into the business** bénéfices réinvestis dans l'affaire

▸ **plough in,** Am **plow in VT SEP** (manure etc) enterrer ou enfouir dans le sol en labourant; Com, Fin etc (money etc) investir

▸ **plough into,** Am **plow into VT INSEP 1** (of vehicle) rentrer dans, foncer dans **2** (attack) (physically) se jeter sur; (verbally) s'en prendre à

VT SEP (money etc) investir dans

▸ **plough on,** Am **plow on VI** (continue laboriously) **to p. on with one's work/a book** poursuivre laborieusement son travail/sa lecture; **let's p. on another fifteen minutes** encore un petit effort d'un quart d'heure; **as negotiations p. on** tandis que les négociations se poursuivent laborieusement

▸ **plough through,** Am **plow through VT INSEP** (move laboriously) **to p. through the snow** avancer péniblement dans la neige; Fig **to p. through a book** lire un livre avec peine; **to p. through some work** faire un travail laborieusement; **they were ploughing through their work** ils avançaient laborieusement dans leur travail; **I've got all this to p. through** j'ai tout ça à me taper

VT SEP to p. one's way through the snow avancer péniblement dans la neige; **to p. one's way through a book** lire un livre à grand peine; **I'm ploughing my way through this** (book) je suis en train de lire ce pavé; **he was ploughing his way through a huge plate of spaghetti** il s'efforçait de finir une énorme assiette de spaghettis

▸ **plough up,** Am **plow up VT SEP 1** (turn over), Fig (churn up) (field etc) labourer **2** (remove) (weeds etc) déraciner ou arracher à la charrue

ploughback, Am **plowback** ['plaʊbæk] **N** bénéfices mpl réinvestis

ploughing, Am **plowing** ['plaʊɪŋ] **N** labourage m, labour m; **p. back of profits** réinvestissement m des bénéfices

ploughland, Am **plowland** ['plaʊlænd] **N** (cultivated land) terres fpl cultivées; (ploughed land) terres labourées; (arable land) terre f arable ou labourable

ploughman, Am **plowman,** pl **ploughmen, plowmen** ['plaʊmən] **N** laboureur m

▸▸ Br **p.'s lunch** = plat m à base de pain, de fromage et de pickles

ploughshare, Am **plowshare** ['plaʊʃeər] **N** soc m de charrue

plover ['plʌvər] **N** (bird) pluvier m; **golden p.** pluvier doré; Culin **p.'s eggs** œufs mpl de vanneau

plow, plowland etc Am = **plough, ploughland** etc

ploy [plɔɪ] **N** stratagème m, Fam truc m

pluck [plʌk] **N 1** (courage) cran m, courage m; **she's got plenty of p.** elle a du cran ou du courage, elle a du cœur au ventre **2** (pull) (at guitar string etc) pincement m

VT 1 (pull out) (hair, feathers etc) arracher; (flower) cueillir; Fig **they were plucked from danger by a helicopter** un hélicoptère les a arrachés au danger; Fig **to p. sb from obscurity** faire sortir qn de l'anonymat; Fig **these figures have been plucked from the air** ces chiffres ne reposent sur rien de concret

2 (pull) **to p. sb's sleeve** tirer qn par la manche; Mus **to p. a guitar** pincer les cordes d'une guitare

3 (remove feathers from) (poultry) plumer; **to p. one's eyebrows** s'épiler les sourcils

VI to p. at sb's sleeve tirer qn par la manche

▸ **pluck up VT SEP to p. up** (one's) **courage to do sth** rassembler son courage pour faire qch

pluckily ['plʌkɪlɪ] **ADV** courageusement, avec cran ou courage

pluckiness ['plʌkɪnɪs] **N** cran m, courage m

plucky ['plʌkɪ] **ADJ** courageux; **to be p.** être courageux, avoir du courage ou du cran

plug [plʌg] **N 1** (for sink, bath, tank etc) bonde f; (stopper) bouchon m, tampon m; (dentistry), Surg tampon (d'ouate, de coton); Geol culot m volcanique; **to pull the p. out** (of sink etc) enlever la bonde

2 Elec fiche f, prise f de courant, prise mâle; Tech (for nail, screw in wall) fiche f; (**spark**) **p.** bougie f; Elec **two-/three-pin p.** fiche à deux/trois broches; **to pull the p. out** (disconnect electrical appliance) débrancher; Fig Fam **to pull the p. on sb** couper tous ses moyens à qn; **to pull the p. on a project** annuler un projet

3 Am (fire) **p.** bouche f d'incendie

4 (of toilet) chasse f d'eau; **to pull the p.** tirer la chasse

5 p. of tobacco chique f de tabac

6 Com Fam (publicity) pub f; **the DJ gave the album a p.** l'animateur a fait de la pub pour l'album

VT (-gg-) **1** (block) (opening, pipe) boucher, obturer; (wound) tamponner; (of dentist) (cavity) obturer; **to p. a leak** arrêter une fuite **2** Com Fam (promote) (product) faire du battage ou de la pub pour

3 esp Am Sl (shoot) (person) fusiller, flinguer

▸▸ Comput **p. compatible** compatible au niveau du matériel; **p. socket** prise de courant, prise femelle; Aut **p. spanner** clé f à bougies

▸ **plug away VI** Fam (persevere) persévérer (**at sth** dans qch), s'acharner (**at sth** sur qch)

▸ **plug in** Elec **VT SEP** (lamp etc) brancher; (printer to computer etc) connecter

VI (insert plug) brancher

▸ **plug into VT SEP** Elec (connect) **to p. sth into sth** brancher qch sur qch

VT INSEP Elec (connect) **the TV plugs into that socket** la télé se branche sur cette prise; Fig **to p. into a computer network** avoir accès à un réseau informatique; **to p. into public opinion** se mettre à l'écoute de l'opinion publique

▸ **plug up VT SEP** = **plug VT 1**

plug-and-play ADJ Comput prêt à brancher

plughole ['plʌghəʊl] **N** (in sink, bathtub) bonde f, trou m d'écoulement; Fam **that's £300 down the p.!** voilà 300 livres par la fenêtre!; Fam **his company's going down the p.** sa société se casse la figure

plug-in N Comput module m d'extension

plug-in-and-go ADJ Comput prêt à brancher

plug-ugly ADJ Fam (person) affreux

plum [plʌm] **N 1** (fruit) prune f, (tree) prunier m; **p. jam** confiture f de prunes **2** Fam (job) boulot m en or; (part in play etc) rôle m en or

ADJ *(colour)* prune *inv*
▸▸**p. brandy** (eau *f* de vie de) prune; **p. cake** cake *m*; **p. pudding** pudding *m* de Noël; **p. tomato** olivette *f*, **p. tree** prunier

plumage ['plu:mɪdʒ] **N** plumage *m*

plumb [plʌm] **N 1** *(perpendicular)* aplomb *m*; **out of p.** hors d'aplomb **2** *(of plumb line)* plomb *m*
ADJ droit, vertical, -aux, d'aplomb
ADV perpendiculairement (**with sth** à qch), à la verticale, à l'aplomb (**with sth** de qch); *Fam* au milieu, en plein milieu, au beau milieu; *(of target)* en plein dans le mille; *Am Fam* **p. crazy** complètement fou
VT 1 *(in surveying)* vérifier l'aplomb de; *(wall)* vérifier l'aplomb de, plomber **2** *Naut, Fig* sonder; *Fig* **to p. the depths** toucher le fond
▸▸**p. bob** plomb; **p. line** *Constr* fil *m* à plomb; *Naut* sonde *f*
▸ **plumb in VT SEP** *(install)* *(washing machine etc)* raccorder

plumbago [plʌm'beɪgəʊ] **N 1** *Bot* plumbago *m* **2** *Miner* plombagine *f*

plumber ['plʌmər] **N** plombier *m*; **p.'s mate** aide *m* plombier

plumbing ['plʌmɪŋ] **N 1** *(action, job)* plomberie *f* **2** *(pipes)* plomberie *f*, tuyauterie *f*, tuyaux *mpl*; *(toilets, washbasins etc)* installations *fpl* sanitaires; *Fam Hum* **to inspect the p.** *(urinate)* aller aux toilettes

plume [plu:m] **N 1** *Arch, Lit (feather)* plume *f*, **a p. of smoke** une volute de fumée; **a p. of spray** un jet d'eau; *Fig Lit* **in borrowed plumes** paré des plumes du paon **2** *(ornament)* panache *m*, aigrette *f*, *(on helmet)* plumet *m*, panache
VT 1 *(ornament)* orner *ou* garnir de plumes; **black-plumed** aux plumes noires; **plumed helmet** casque *m* empanaché **2** *(preen)* **to p. itself** *(of bird)* se lisser les plumes; **to p. oneself on sth** *(of person)* se glorifier de qch

plummet ['plʌmɪt] **N** *(weight)* *(of plumb line, fishing line, sounding line)* plomb *m*
VI plonger, tomber à la verticale; *(of morale, popularity, standards)* chuter; *(of prices etc)* s'effondrer; *(of blood pressure etc)* tomber soudainement; **the aircraft plummeted to the ground** l'avion s'est écrasé au sol

plummy ['plʌmɪ] **ADJ** *Br Fam* **1** *usu Pej (voice)* de la haute, snobinard **2** *Old-fashioned (job)* agréable, bien payé

plump [plʌmp] **ADJ** *(person)* grassouillet, -ette, dodu, boulot, -otte, bien en chair; *(baby, chicken, cheeks)* dodu; *(hands)* potelé
VT to p. oneself into an armchair s'affaler dans un fauteuil
▸ **plump down VT SEP** *(suitcase etc)* laisser tomber lourdement; **she plumped herself down on the sofa** elle s'est affalée sur le sofa
▸ **plump for VT INSEP** *Fam (choose)* choisir
▸ **plump out VI = plump up VI**
▸ **plump up VT SEP** *(shake) (pillow)* secouer
VI *(become fat)* devenir dodu

plumpness ['plʌmpnɪs] **N** embonpoint *m*, rondeur *f*, **to be inclined to p.** avoir tendance à prendre de l'embonpoint; **the p. of the baby's arms** les bras potelés du bébé

plunder ['plʌndər] **N** *(booty)* butin *m*; *(act)* pillage *m*
VT *(country etc)* piller, mettre à sac; *Fig (bookshelves, fridge)* faire une descente dans
VI piller

plundering ['plʌndərɪŋ] **ADJ** pillard
N pillage *m*

plunge [plʌndʒ] **N** plongeon *m*; *Fig* baisse *f* radicale, chute *f* (**in** de); **to take a p.** faire un plongeon, plonger (**into** dans); *Fig (of profits etc)* s'effondrer; *Fam* **to take the p.** *(resolve to do sth)* prendre le taureau par

les cornes; *(get married)* se marier
VT *(into water)* plonger, immerger; **to p. a dagger into sb's back** plonger un poignard dans le dos de qn; **plunged in darkness** plongé dans l'obscurité; **to p. sb into despair** plonger qn dans le désespoir
VI *(of person) (into water)* plonger, se jeter (la tête la première); *(into forest etc)* s'enfoncer; *(into affair etc)* se jeter à corps perdu; *(into conversation)* se lancer; *(in gambling)* jouer sans compter *ou* gros jeu; *(of ship)* tanguer, piquer du nez; *(of profits)* s'effondrer; *St Exch (of speculator, investor)* risquer de grosses sommes; **the lorry plunged over the cliff** le camion plongea par-dessus la falaise; **the aircraft plunged to the ground** l'avion s'est écrasé au sol; **the aircraft was plunging to the ground** l'avion tombait en chute libre; **she plunged to her death** elle fit une chute mortelle; **sales have plunged by 30%** les ventes ont chuté de 30%; **necklines have plunged this year** cette année les décolletés sont plus profonds; **to p. forward** s'élancer en avant

plunger ['plʌndʒər] **N 1** *(device) (on pump, in coffee-maker, syringe)* piston *m*; *Aut* piston plongeur; *(in lock)* bonhomme *m* de verrouillage; *(of detonator)* manette *f*, **(rubber) p.** *(for clearing sink etc)* ventouse *f* **2** *Fam (gambler)* flambeur, -euse

plunging ['plʌndʒɪŋ] **ADJ** *(prices)* en chute libre; **p. neckline** décolleté *m* plongeant
N *(of boat)* tangage *m*

plunk [plʌŋk] **VT 1** *(banjo etc)* pincer les cordes de **2** *(drop heavily)* laisser tomber lourdement
▸ **plunk down VT SEP** laisser tomber lourdement

pluperfect ['plu:pɜ:fɪkt] VOIR GRAMMAIRE A50; B30 *Gram* **ADJ** plus-que-parfait
N plus-que-parfait *m*, *pl* plus-que-parfaits; **in the p.** au plus-que-parfait
▸▸**p. subjunctive** plus-que-parfait du subjonctif

plural ['plʊər(ə)l] **ADJ** *Gram* pluriel
N *Gram* pluriel *m*; **in the p.** au pluriel VOIR GRAMMAIRE A9–15; B8
▸▸*Pol* **p. vote** vote *m* plural

pluralism ['plʊərəlɪz(ə)m] **N 1** *Phil etc* pluralisme *m* **2** *(holding of several posts)* cumul *m* de(s) fonctions

plurality [plʊə'rælɪtɪ] **N 1** pluralité *f* **2** *(of functions)* cumul *m* **3** *Am Pol (relative majority)* majorité *f* relative *ou* simple

plus [plʌs] **PREP** plus; **seven p. nine** sept plus neuf; **two floors p. an attic** deux étages plus un grenier; **remember this, p. what she told you** rappelle-toi de ça, en plus de ce qu'elle t'a dit
ADJ on the p. side of the account à l'actif du compte; **on the p. side, the bicycle is very light** la légèreté est l'un des avantages de cette bicyclette; **fifteen p.** *(quantity)* plus de quinze; *(age)* au-dessus de quinze ans
N *(pl* **plusses** ['plʌsɪz]*) Math (symbol)* plus *m*; *(positive quantity)* quantité *f* positive; *Fig (advantage)* avantage *m*, atout *m*; **it's a p.** c'est un plus *ou* avantage *ou* atout
▸▸**p. fours** pantalon *m* de golf; *Comput* **p. key** touche *f* plus; **p. sign** signe *m* plus, plus

plush [plʌʃ] **N** *Tex* peluche *f*
ADJ 1 *Tex* en peluche **2** *Fam (apartment etc)* somptueux, luxueux, *(restaurant, hotel)* de luxe

plushy ['plʌʃɪ] **ADJ** *Fam* = **plush ADJ 2**

Plutarch ['plu:tɑ:k] **N** Plutarque

Pluto ['plu:təʊ] **N 1** *Myth* Pluton **2** *Astron* Pluton *f*

plutocracy [plu:'tɒkrəsɪ] **N** ploutocratie *f*

plutocrat ['plu:təkræt] **N** *often Pej* ploutocrate *mf*

plutocratic [plu:tə'krætɪk] **ADJ** ploutocratique

plutonium [plu:'təʊnɪəm] **N** *Chem* plutonium *m*

pluviometer [plu:vɪ'ɒmɪtər] **N** pluviomètre *m*

ply [plaɪ] **N 1** *(of plywood)* placage *m*, épaisseur *f*, *(of tyre)* pli *m*; **two-p. paper handkerchief** mouchoir *m* en papier double épaisseur
2 *(strand) (of wool, rope)* fil *m*, brin *m*; **three-p. wool** laine *f* trois fils; **what p. is it?** c'est de la laine à combien de fils?
3 *Fam (plywood)* contreplaqué *m*; **three-p.** contreplaqué à trois plis
VT 1 *(use) (tool)* manier vigoureusement; *(needle)* faire courir; *(trade)* exercer
2 *(supply)* **to p. sb with questions** presser qn de questions; **to p. sb with drink** ne pas arrêter de verser à boire à qn, verser force rasades à qn; **to p. sb with food** donner abondamment à manger à qn
3 **to p. an ocean** *(of ship)* faire la traversée; **to p. a route** *(of ship, bus etc)* assurer une liaison
VI *(of ship, bus etc)* faire le service *ou* la navette (**between ... and ...** entre ... et ...); **to p. for hire** *(of taxi etc)* prendre des clients

plywood ['plaɪwʊd] **N** contreplaqué *m*

PM [pi:'em] **N** *Br, Can Pol (abbr* **Prime Minister***)* Premier ministre *m*

pm, p.m. ['pi:em] **ADV** *(abbr* **post meridiem***)* **6 pm** 18h; **10 am or pm?** 10 heures du matin ou du soir? VOIR GRAMMAIRE A80; B60

PMS [pi:em'es] **N** *Med (abbr* **premenstrual syndrome***)* syndrome *m* prémenstruel

PMT [pi:em'ti:] **N** *Med (abbr* **premenstrual tension***)* syndrome *m* prémenstruel

P/N [pi:'en] **N** *Com (abbr* **promissory note***)* billet *m* à ordre

pneumatic [nju:'mætɪk] **ADJ** pneumatique; *Fam (bosom)* plantureux, généreux
▸▸**p. brakes** freins *mpl* à air comprimé; **p. drill** marteau-piqueur *m*, *pl* marteaux-piqueurs; **p. tyre** pneu *m*

pneumatically [nju:'mætɪklɪ] **ADV** **p. operated** *(machine)* à air comprimé

pneumatics [nju:'mætɪks] **N** *Phys* pneumatique *f* VOIR GRAMMAIRE A10

pneumonia [nju:'məʊnɪə] **N** *Med* pneumonie *f*, **to have p.** avoir une pneumonie

PO [pi:'əʊ] **N 1** *(abbr* **Post Office***)* **PO Box** BP **2** *(abbr* **postal order***)* mandat *m* postal **3** *Naut (abbr* **petty officer***)* second maître *m*

po [pəʊ] **N** *Old-fashioned Br Fam* pot *m* de chambre, Jules *m*

POA ['pi:əʊ'eɪ] **N** *(abbr* **Prison Officers' Association***)* = syndicat *m* des agents pénitentiaires en Grande-Bretagne

poach[1] [pəʊtʃ] **VT** *Culin (eggs etc)* pocher; **poached egg** œuf *m* poché

poach[2] **VT** *(steal) (game etc)* braconner; *(steal from) (woods etc)* braconner dans; *Fig (employee)* débaucher
VI braconner; *Ftbl etc* rester près des buts de l'équipe adverse; **to p. on sb's preserves** braconner sur la chasse gardée de qn; *Fig* empiéter sur le domaine de qn

poacher[1] ['pəʊtʃər] **N (egg) p.** pocheuse *f* (à œufs)

poacher[2] **N** *(thief)* braconnier, -ière

poaching ['pəʊtʃɪŋ] **N** *(thieving)* braconnage *m*

pock [pɒk] **N** *Med* pustule *f (de la petite vérole)*

pocket ['pɒkɪt] **N 1** *(of jacket etc)* poche *f*, **waistcoat p.** gousset *m*; **to put one's hands in one's pockets** mettre les mains dans ses poches; **to go through sb's pockets** faire les

poches à qn; *Fam* **to have sb in one's p.** avoir qn dans sa poche; *Fam* **to live in each other's** *or* **one another's pockets** ne pas se lâcher d'une semelle; **prices to suit every p.** des prix à la portée de tout le monde; *Fig Fam* **to line one's pockets** se remplir les poches; *Fig* **he's always got his hand in his p.** il a toujours la main sur le portefeuille, il est toujours à débourser; **to be in p.** y gagner; **to be out of p.** *(over a transaction)* y être de sa poche, ne pas rentrer dans ses fonds; **how much are you out of p.?** combien est-ce que vous avez dépensé?; **to pay for sth out of one's own p.** payer qch de sa poche
  2 *(bag) (for hops, wool)* sac *m*; *Billiards* blouse *f*
  3 *Min (of ore, water, gas)* poche *f*, *(of fire-damp)* nid *m*
  4 *(small area) (of resistance, rebellion etc)* poche *f*
  VT (**-t-**) **1** *(put in pocket)* empocher, mettre dans sa poche; *Pej (steal) Fam* chiper
  2 *(insult)* avaler, encaisser
  3 *(one's feelings)* faire taire; **to p. one's pride** faire taire son amour-propre
  4 *Billiards (ball)* blouser
  ▸▸ **p. battleship** cuirassé *m* de poche; *Br* **p. billiards** *(pool)* billard *m* américain; *Sl Hum* **to play pocket billiards** jouer avec ses cacahuètes; **p. calculator** calculatrice *f* de poche; **p. comb** peigne *m* de poche; **p. computer** ordinateur *m* de poche; **p. dictionary** dictionnaire *m* de poche; **p. handkerchief** mouchoir *m* de poche; **p. modem** modem *m* de poche; *Br* **p. money** argent *m* de poche; **p. notebook** carnet *m*; **p. size** *(in bookbinding)* format *m* de poche

pocketbook ['pɒkɪtbʊk] **N** *Am* **1** *(handbag)* sac *m* à main **2** *(small book)* livre *m* de poche

pocketful ['pɒkɪtfʊl] **N** pleine poche *f*; **pocketfuls of sweets** de pleines poches *ou* des poches pleines de bonbons

pocketknife ['pɒkɪtnaɪf] **N** couteau *m* de poche, canif *m*

pockmark ['pɒkmɑːk] **N** marque *f* de la petite vérole

pockmarked ['pɒkmɑːkt] **ADJ** *(face)* grêlé; *(surface of the moon etc)* plein de trous

pod [pɒd] **N 1** *(of beans, peas etc)* cosse *f*, gousse *f* **2** *(of silkworm)* cocon *m* **3** *Aviat (of jet engine)* nacelle *f*; **engine p.** nacelle-moteur *f*, *pl* nacelles-moteur
  VT (**-dd-**) *(peas)* écosser

podgy ['pɒdʒɪ] **ADJ** *(person)* boulot, -otte; *(finger)* boudiné, rondelet; *(knees)* grassouillet; **to get p.** engraisser

podiatrist [pə'daɪətrɪst] **N** *Am* pédicure *mf*

podium, *pl* **podia** ['pəʊdɪəm, -ɪə] **N** estrade *f*, *(for medallist)* podium *m*

poem ['pəʊəm] **N** poème *m*, poésie *f*

poet ['pəʊɪt] **N** poète *m*
  ▸▸ **p. laureate** poète lauréat

poetaster [pəʊɪ'tæstər] **N** *Pej* mauvais poète *m*, rimailleur, -euse

poetess ['pəʊɪtɪs] **N** *Old-fashioned* femme *f* poète, poétesse *f*

poetic [pəʊ'etɪk] **ADJ** poétique
  ▸▸ **p. justice** justice *f* divine; **p. licence** licence *f* poétique

poetical [pəʊ'etɪk(ə)l] **ADJ** poétique

poetically [pəʊ'etɪklɪ] **ADV** poétiquement; **p. gifted** doué pour la poésie

poetics [pəʊ'etɪks] **N** poétique *f* VOIR GRAMMAIRE A10

poetry ['pəʊɪtrɪ] **N** poésie *f*; **to write p.** écrire des poèmes; **the art of p.** l'art *m* poétique; **it was p. in motion** c'était un vrai plaisir pour les yeux
  ▸▸ **p. reading, p. recital** lecture *f* de poèmes

po-faced [-feɪst] **ADJ** *Fam Pej* avec une tête d'enterrement; **why are you looking so p.** pourquoi fais-tu une telle tête d'enterrement?; **the p. old cow!** elle fait une de ces tronches!

pogo ['pəʊgəʊ] **VI** *(dance)* danser le pogo
  ▸▸ **p. stick** bâton *m* sauteur

pogrom ['pɒgrəm] **N** pogrom(e) *m*

poignancy ['pɔɪnjənsɪ] **N** *(of an emotion etc)* caractère *m* poignant; **a moment of great p.** un moment très poignant

poignant ['pɔɪnjənt] **ADJ** *(feeling)* poignant, vif; *(regret etc)* amer, -ère

poignantly ['pɔɪnjəntlɪ] **ADV** d'une façon poignante

poinsettia [pɔɪn'setɪə] **N** *(plant)* poinsettia *m*

POINT [pɔɪnt]

| **N** point **1, 3, 6–8** ▪ moment **2** ▪ but **4** |
| ▪ virgule **6** ▪ pointe **9** |
| **VT** pointer **1** ▪ diriger **1** ▪ indiquer **2** |
| **VI** montrer du doigt **2** |

N 1 *(in space)* point *m*; **p. of arrival/departure** point d'arrivée/de départ; **at that p. on the road** à cet endroit de la route; **the train goes to Taunton and all points west** le train dessert Taunton et toutes les gares dans cette direction; **p. of contact** point de contact
  2 *(precise moment)* **at this p. in time** en ce moment même; **at this p. the phone rang** c'est alors que le téléphone a sonné, à ce moment-là le téléphone a sonné; **at one p. I thought we would all be killed** à un certain moment, j'ai cru que nous allions tous être tués; **to be on the p. of doing sth** être sur le point de faire qch; **on** *or* **at the p. of death** sur le point de mourir, à l'article de la mort; **to be on the p. of departure** être sur le point de partir; **the p. of no return** le point de non-retour; **a high/low p. in sb's life** un moment fort/difficile de la vie de qn; **when it came to the p.** quand le moment critique est arrivé; **there comes a p. in everyone's life when …** dans la vie de chacun il arrive un moment où …; **up to a (certain) p.** jusqu'à un certain point; **she had reached the p. where she was no longer interested** elle en était arrivée à perdre tout intérêt; **severe to the p. of cruelty** sévère jusqu'à la cruauté
  3 *(of argumentation etc)* point *m*; **the chief p. of an argument** le point essentiel d'un raisonnement; **figures that give p. to his argument** chiffres qui ajoutent du poids à sa thèse; **on that p. we disagree** là-dessus nous ne sommes pas d'accord; **I take your p.** je vois ce que vous voulez dire; **p. taken!** *(agreeing)* très juste!; **OK, OK p. taken!** ça va, ça va, j'ai compris!; **she has a p.** elle a raison; **to make a p.** faire une remarque; **to make a p. of doing sth** ne pas manquer de faire qch; **my p.** *or* **the p. I'm making is that …** là où je veux en venir c'est que …; **you've made your p.!** ça va, j'ai compris!; **the teacher went through the essay p. by p.** le professeur a repris la dissertation point par point; **in p. of fact** en fait, à vrai dire; **p. of grammar/of law** question *f* de grammaire/de droit; **p. of honour** point d'honneur; **the p.** *(subject)* le sujet, la question; **the p. at issue** le sujet dont il est question; **the p. is (that) …** c'est que …; **get** *or* **come to the p.!** *(venons-en)* au fait!; **that's the p.** c'est bien de cela qu'il s'agit; **that's not the p.** il ne s'agit pas de cela; **that's beside the p.!** ce n'est pas le problème *ou* la question; **you're missing the p.** tu n'as pas compris ce que je voulais dire; **on this p.** à cet égard, à ce propos; **this is very much to the p.** c'est bien parlé *ou* bien dit

  4 *(purpose)* but *m*; **what would be the p. (of doing that)?** à quoi bon (faire cela)?; **there is no p. in (doing) it** cela ne servirait à rien; **I can't see the p.** *(of doing it)* je ne vois pas l'intérêt
  5 *(characteristic)* **a p. of interest** un détail intéressant; **a p. of similarity/difference** une similarité/différence; **to have its good points** avoir ses bons côtés; **tact has never been one of your strong points** la délicatesse n'a jamais été ton fort; **its price is a p. in its favour** son prix est un de ses atouts
  6 *Gram* **(full) p.** point *m*; *Math* **(decimal) p.** virgule *f* (décimale); **three p. five (3.5)** trois virgule cinq (3,5)
  7 *(in game, exam etc)* point *m*; **to score so many points** marquer *ou* obtenir tant de points; **you get three points for a correct answer** une bonne réponse vaut trois points; *Cards etc* **to play ten pence a p.** jouer à dix pence le point; *Boxing* **to win on points** gagner aux points; *Boxing* **beaten on points** battu aux points; *Boxing* **a points decision** une décision aux points
  8 *Typ etc (measure)* point *m*; **6-p. type** caractères *mpl* de 6 points; **the thermometer went up/down two points** le thermomètre a monté/a baissé de deux degrés; *St Exch* **rise/fall of one p.** *(of price)* hausse *f*/baisse *f* d'un point
  9 *(sharp end) (of needle, nail, sword, tool etc)* pointe *f*, *(of drill)* mouche *f*, *(of quill pen)* bec *m*; *Geog* pointe, promontoire *m*; **to dance on points** faire des pointes; **on (full) p.** *(of dancer)* sur la pointe; **on demi-p.** *(of dancer)* sur la demi-pointe; **to end in a p.** aller *ou* se terminer en pointe; **to give a p. to a pencil** tailler un crayon; **p. of a joke** piquant *m ou* sel *m* d'une plaisanterie; **points** *(of horse etc)* extrémités *fpl*; *(in hunting) (of deer)* cors *mpl*; *Fig* **not to put too fine a p. on it …** pour dire les choses clairement …
  10 *Br Elec (off mains)* prise *f* de courant; **eight-p. distributor** *(in engine)* distributeur *m* (d'allumage) à huit plots
  11 *Aut* **points** contacts *mpl* de rupteur
  12 *Br Rail* **points** aiguillage *m*
  13 **the points of the compass** les aires *fpl* du vent; **to alter course 16 points** venir de 16 quarts
  14 *(in backgammon)* flèche *f*, pointe *f*, case *f*
  VT 1 *(aim) (gun)* pointer, braquer; *(telescope)* diriger, orienter, braquer (**at** sur); *(finger)* pointer; **to p. one's finger at sb** montrer qu du doigt; *Fig* **to p. the finger at sb** montrer qn du doigt; **to p. a gun at sb** braquer *ou* pointer une arme sur qn; **to p. a camera at sth/sb** braquer un appareil photo sur qch/qn; *Fam* **just p. me in the right direction** dites-moi simplement quelle direction je dois prendre; **she pointed the car/the boat towards home** elle a pris la direction de la maison
  2 *(indicate)* **to p. the way** indiquer *ou* montrer le chemin (**to sb** à qn; **to a place** vers un endroit); *Fig* indiquer la direction à suivre (**towards sth** pour parvenir à qch); **the ship/car was pointing the wrong way** le navire/la voiture était tourné(e) du mauvais côté
  3 *(in ballet)* **to p. the toe** *or* **the foot** pointer le pied
  4 *Constr (wall)* jointoyer
  5 *(of hunting dog) (game)* arrêter
  VI 1 *(indicate)* **the magnetic needle always points north** l'aiguille aimantée est toujours tournée vers le nord; **the hour hand is pointing to 10** la petite aiguille indique 10 heures; **the arrow points in the direction of the entrance** la flèche indique la direction de l'entrée; **this points to the fact that …** ceci montre *ou* indique que …; **everything seems to p. to success** tout semble indiquer

que tout ira bien; **everything points to suicide** tout semble privilégier l'hypothèse du suicide

2 *(with finger etc)* **to p. at sb/sth** montrer *ou* désigner qn/qch du doigt *etc*; **don't p., it's rude** ne montre pas du doigt, ce n'est pas poli
3 *(of hunting dog)* tomber en arrêt
▸▸ *Cycling* **points competition** classement *m* par points; *Br* **p. duty** *(of police officer, traffic warden)* service *m* de la circulation; **policeman on p. duty** agent *m* de circulation; **to be on p. duty** être à la circulation; *Br Rail* **p. lever** levier *m* d'aiguille; *Br* **p. of order** point de procédure; *Mktg* **p. of purchase** lieu *m* d'achat, lieu de vente; *Mktg* **p. of sale** lieu de vente, point de vente; *Typ, Comput* **p. size** corps *m*; **p. source** source *f* ponctuelle; **p. system** *(at school etc)* barème *m*, système *m* de notation *f*, *(in game etc)* système d'attribution des points; **p. of view** *TV, Cin* angle *m* du regard; *(opinion)* point de vue, opinion *f*; **to consider sth from all points of view** considérer qch sous tous ses aspects; **p. work** *(of ballet dancer)* pointes

▸ **point off** VT SEP *Math (decimals)* séparer par une virgule
▸ **point out** VT SEP **1 to p. sb/sth out to sb** montrer qn/qch à qn; *(with one's finger)* montrer *ou* désigner qn/qch du doigt à qn
2 *(indicate, show)* *(error etc)* signaler, relever; *(fact)* faire remarquer; **to p. out sth to sb** attirer l'attention de qn sur qch, signaler *ou* faire remarquer qch à qn; **to p. out to sb that he is wrong** faire remarquer à qn qu'il a tort; **to p. out to sb the advantages of sth** montrer à qn les avantages de qch; **might I p. out that ...?** permettez-moi de vous faire observer *ou* remarquer que ...; **he has been pointed out to me as a capable man** on me l'a signalé comme un homme capable
▸ **point up** VT SEP *(highlight)* mettre en évidence

point-blank ADJ *Mil etc (firing)* direct, à bout portant; *(refusal, denial)* catégorique; **to fire at p. range** tirer à bout portant; **he was shot at p. range** on lui a tiré dessus à bout portant
ADV **to fire p. at sb** tirer sur qn à bout portant; **he asked me p. whether ...** il m'a demandé de but en blanc si ...; **to deny sth p.** nier qch catégoriquement; **to refuse p.** refuser catégoriquement *ou* (tout) net (**to do sth** de faire qch)

point-by-point ADJ **p. analysis** analyse *f* point par point

pointed ['pɔɪntɪd] ADJ **1** *(having a sharp point)* pointu; *(beard)* taillé en pointe **2** *(remark)* sarcastique, mordant; *(allusion, look)* peu équivoque, peu voilé
▸▸ **p.-nose pliers** pince *f* à bec pointu

pointedly ['pɔɪntɪdlɪ] ADV *(to say)* d'un ton sarcastique *ou* mordant; *(to refer)* explicitement, nettement; **not too p.** sans appuyer; **she stared p. at the ceiling during the speech** elle fixa ostensiblement son regard au plafond pendant le discours

pointedness ['pɔɪntɪdnɪs] N *(of remark)* mordant *m*; *(of allusion)* caractère *m* explicite

pointer ['pɔɪntər] N **1** *(of clock)* aiguille *f*, *(of scales)* aiguille, languette *f*; *Sch (at blackboard)* baguette *f*; *Comput* pointeur *m*; **optical** *or* **illuminated p.** *(for slides)* flèche *f* lumineuse
2 *Fam (advice)* tuyau *m*; **to give sb a few pointers on sth** donner à qn quelques indications *ou* tuyaux à propos de qch; **a p. to the future** un signe précurseur
3 *(dog)* pointer *m*
4 *Constr (bricklayer's tool)* pointe *f*

pointillism ['pwæntɪlɪz(ə)m] N *Art* pointillisme *m*

pointing ['pɔɪntɪŋ] N *Constr (of wall)* jointoiement *m*
▸▸ *Comput* **p. device** pointeur *m*

pointless ['pɔɪntlɪs] ADJ *(story etc)* qui ne rime à rien; *(joke)* fade, sans sel; *(remark etc)* qui n'a rien à voir avec la question; *(action, suffering)* inutile; *(violence)* gratuite; *(existence)* sans but; **it would be p.** ce serait inutile, cela ne servirait à rien (**to do** de faire); **it is a p. exercise** ça ne sert à rien

pointlessly ['pɔɪntlɪslɪ] ADV *(to argue, work, die etc)* inutilement, vainement

pointlessness ['pɔɪntlɪsnɪs] N *(of joke etc)* fadeur *f*, *(of remark etc)* manque *m* d'à-propos; *(of action, changes)* inutilité *f*, *(of violence)* gratuité *f*, *(of existence)* futilité *f*

point-of-purchase ADJ *Mktg* sur le point *ou* sur le lieu de vente;
▸▸ **p. advertising** publicité *f* sur le lieu de vente, PLV *f*; **p. competition** concurrence *f* entre points de vente; **p. display** exposition *f* sur le lieu de vente; **p. information** informations *fpl* sur le lieu de vente; **p. material** matériel *m* de publicité sur le lieu de vente, matériel de PLV; **p. promotion** promotion *f* sur le lieu de vente

point-of-sale ADJ *Mktg* sur le point *ou* sur le lieu de vente
▸▸ **p. advertising** publicité *f* sur le lieu de vente, PLV *f*; **p. competition** concurrence *f* entre points de vente; **p. display** exposition *f* sur le lieu de vente; **p. information** informations *fpl* sur le lieu de vente; **p. material** matériel *m* de publicité sur le lieu de vente, matériel de PLV; **points-of-sale network** réseau *m* de points de vente; **p. promotion** communication *f* ou promotion *f* ou publicité sur le lieu de vente, CLV *f*, PLV; **p. terminal** terminal *m* point de vente, TPV *m*

point-of-view shot N *Cin, TV* plan *m* subjectif

pointsman ['pɔɪntsmən] N *Br Rail* aiguilleur *m*

point-to-point ADJ *Br Sport* cross *m* à cheval
▸▸ *Tel* **p. audioconference** audioconférence *f* point à point; *Comput* **p. protocol** protocole *m* point à point; *Br Sport* **p. race** cross à cheval

pointy-headed ['pɔɪntɪ-] ADJ *Am Pej* intello

poise [pɔɪz] N **1** *(balance)* équilibre *m*; *(state of composure)* aplomb *m*; **to recover one's p.** retrouver son aplomb; **to have p.** *(of person)* avoir de la prestance; **a man of p.** un homme pondéré **2** *(of head, body)* port *m*
VT équilibrer; *(in hand)* tenir en équilibre; **to be poised** être en équilibre; *(of person)* être équilibré; **her hand was poised over the telephone** sa main était suspendue au-dessus du téléphone; **she poised herself on the edge of the desk** elle s'assit délicatement sur le bord du bureau; **the cat was poised ready to spring** le chat se tenait prêt à bondir; **Rome was poised to conquer the known world** Rome se tenait prête à conquérir le monde connu; **to be poised on the brink of sth** être à deux doigts de qch

poised [pɔɪzd] ADJ posé; **she's very p. for one so young** elle est très posée pour quelqu'un d'aussi jeune

poison ['pɔɪz(ə)n] N poison *m*; **to take p.** s'empoisonner; *Fam* **what's your p.?** *(drink)* qu'est-ce que tu veux boire?
VT *(of person) (somebody, something)* empoisonner; *(of substance) (somebody)* intoxiquer; *Fig (the mind)* corrompre, pervertir; *(sb's life)* empoisonner; **to p. sb's mind against sb** monter qn contre qn; **poisoned arrow** flèche *f* empoisonnée; *Fig* **poisoned chalice** cadeau *m* empoisonné; **poisoned food** nourriture *f* empoisonnée

▸▸ **p. gas** gaz *m* toxique; *Zool* **p. gland** glande *f* à venin; *Bot* **p. ivy** sumac *m* vénéneux, *Can* herbe *f* à puces *ou* à la puce; **p. pen letter** lettre *f* anonyme *(d'insulte ou de menace)*; *Fin Fam* **p. pill** *(strategy)* pilule *f* empoisonnée

poisoner ['pɔɪzənər] N empoisonneur, -euse

poisoning ['pɔɪzənɪŋ] N *(by person) (of person, food)* empoisonnement *m*; *(by substance) (of person)* intoxication *f*, *(of mind)* corruption *f*

poisonous ['pɔɪzənəs] ADJ *(substance)* toxique, intoxicant; *(gas)* asphyxiant, toxique; *(animal)* venimeux; *(plant)* vénéneux; *Fig (doctrine)* pernicieux; *(remark, allegation)* pernicieux; *(atmosphere)* malfaisant; *(coffee, liquid)* répugnant

> When translating the English word **poisonous**, note that the French words **vénéneux** and **venimeux** are not interchangeable. **Vénéneux** applies to plants whereas **venimeux** applies to animals.

poke[1] [pəʊk] N **1** *(push)* poussée *f*, *(with elbow)* coup *m* de coude; **to give sth a p. with one's finger/a stick** pousser qch du doigt/du bout d'un bâton; **to give sb a p. in the eye** *(with finger)* mettre le doigt dans l'œil à qn; *(with umbrella)* mettre un coup de parapluie dans l'œil à qn; **to give sb a (friendly) p. in the ribs** donner une bourrade (amicale) à qn
2 *Vulg (act of sexual intercourse)* partie *f* de jambes en l'air; **to give sb a p.** sauter qn, tirer un coup avec qn
VT **1 to p. one's finger in sb's eye** mettre le doigt dans l'œil à qn; **he poked his finger at the map** il a pointé le doigt vers la carte; **to p. one's umbrella in sb's eye** mettre un coup de parapluie dans l'œil à qn; **he poked the ice with a stick** il a tâté la glace du bout d'un bâton; **to p. sb in the ribs** *(friendly gesture)* donner une bourrade (amicale) à qn; **to p. a hole in sth** faire un trou dans qch, crever qch
2 *(insert) (finger in cake, thermometer in mouth)* enfoncer, planter; *(finger up nose)* fourrer (**in(to)** dans); **to p. one's head through the window** passer la tête par la fenêtre; *Fam* **to p. one's nose into other people's business** fourrer son nez dans les affaires des autres
3 *(fire)* tisonner, attiser
4 to p. fun at sb/sth se moquer de qn/qch
5 *Vulg (have sexual intercourse with)* sauter, tirer un coup avec qn
VI **to p. at sth** *(with one's finger/a stick)* tâter qch du bout du doigt/d'un bâton; *Fam* **to p. into other people's business** fourrer son nez dans les affaires des autres
▸ **poke about, poke around** VI **1** *(search)* fouiller, fureter; **a dog was poking about in the bushes** un chien fouinait *ou* furetait dans les buissons; **she was poking about in the wardrobe for something to wear** elle fouillait dans l'armoire pour trouver quelque chose à mettre **2** *(make unwanted enquiries)* fourrer son nez partout, fouiner; **that social worker is always poking about** cette assistante sociale est toujours en train de fourrer son nez partout
VT INSEP *(search in) (antique shop etc)* fouiller dans
▸ **poke out** VI *(protrude)* sortir, dépasser (**of, from** de); **her umbrella was poking out (of her bag)** son parapluie sortait *ou* dépassait de son sac; **his stomach was poking out** son ventre dépassait
VT SEP **1** *(push out)* **to p. one's head out (of the window)** passer *ou* sortir la tête par la fenêtre; **to p. one's tongue out** tirer la langue (**at sb** à qn) **2 to p. sb's eye out** éborgner qn

poke² N *Dial esp Scot (bag)* sac *m*, sachet *m*

poker ['pəʊkər] N **1** *(for fire)* tisonnier *m* **2** *Cards* poker *m*
▸▸ **p. dice** dés *mpl* pour jouer au poker d'as; *(game)* poker d'as; **p. face** visage *m* impassible *ou* impénétrable; **p. game** partie *f* de poker; **p. work** pyrogravure *f*

poker-faced [-feɪst] ADJ *(person)* au visage impassible; *(reply, response)* qui ne trahit aucune émotion

poky ['pəʊkɪ] ADJ *(room)* exigu, -uë; **to live in a p. little place** être logé à l'étroit

pol [pɒl] N *Am Fam (abbr* **politician** *)* politicien *m*

Polack ['pəʊlæk] N *Offensive Sl* Polack *mf*

Poland ['pəʊlənd] N Pologne *f*

polar ['pəʊlər] ADJ *Geog, Math, Phys* polaire
▸▸ **p. bear** ours *m* polaire *ou* blanc

polarity [pəʊ'lærɪtɪ] N *Phys* polarité *f*

polarization [pəʊlərɪ'zeɪʃən] N *Phys* polarisation *f*; *esp Pol Fig* radicalisation *f*

polarize ['pəʊləraɪz] VT **1** *Phys (light, iron bar etc)* polariser **2** *(make extreme) (opinions)* radicaliser
VI **1** *Phys* se polariser **2** *(of opinions ec)* se radicaliser

polarizing filter ['pəʊləraɪzɪŋ] N *TV, Cin* filtre *m* polarisant

Polaroid® ['pəʊlərɔɪd] N **1** *Phot (camera)* Polaroïd® *m*; *(photograph)* photographie *f* instantanée **2** *Opt* Polaroïd® *m*; **Polaroids®** *(sunglasses)* lunettes *fpl* de soleil (à verre) polaroïd
ADJ *(camera)* Polaroïd®; *(film)* pour Polaroïd®

polder ['pəʊldə(r)] N polder *m*

Pole [pəʊl] N *(person)* Polonais, -aise VOIR GRAMMAIRE A19

pole¹ [pəʊl] N **1** *(stick, rod)* perche *f*, *(fixed in ground)* poteau *m*; *(for plants)* échalas *m*, rame *f*; *(of scaffolding)* mât *m*; *(for flag)* hampe *f*; *(of stretcher)* bras *m*; *Naut (of mast)* flèche *f*, *(of tent)* piquet *m*; *(of circus tent)* mât; *Br Fam* **to be up the p.** *(mad)* être timbré *ou* toqué; **to be up the p. with worry** être fou *ou* malade d'inquiétude
2 *Arch (measurement)* perche *f*
3 *Vulg (penis)* queue *f*, bite *f*
▸▸ **p. dancing** = style de danse de striptease qui s'exécute autour d'une barre verticale

pole² N *Elec, Geog* pôle *m*; **North P.** pôle Nord, pôle arctique *ou* boréal; **South P.** pôle Sud, pôle antarctique *ou* austral; **magnetic/ true p.** pôle magnétique/géographique; *Fig* **to be poles apart** *(of people)* être aux antipodes l'un de l'autre; *(of views etc)* être diamétralement opposés; **opposite poles** *(of magnet)* pôles contraires
▸▸ **P. Star** *(étoile f)* Polaire *f*

poleaxe, *Am* **poleax** ['pəʊlæks] N merlin *m* VT *(hit) (person)* assommer; *(animal)* abattre avec un merlin; *Fig* **she was poleaxed by the news** la nouvelle l'a abasourdie *ou* assommée

polecat ['pəʊlkæt] N *(animal)* putois *m*

polemic [pə'lemɪk] N polémique *f*
ADJ *Fml* polémique

polemical [pə'lemɪk(ə)l] ADJ polémique

polemicist [pə'lemɪsɪst] N polémiste *mf*

polemics [pə'lemɪks] N polémique *f* VOIR GRAMMAIRE A10

polenta [pə'lentə] N polenta *f*

pole-vault *Sport* VI sauter à la perche
N saut *m* à la perche

pole-vaulter N *Sport* sauteur, -euse à la perche, perchiste *mf*

police [pə'liːs] N INV *(with pl verb)* **the p.** la police; **twenty p. were on duty** vingt agents

mpl (de police) étaient de service; **to be a member of the p.,** **to be in the p.** être de *ou* dans la police; **hours of careful p. work** des heures d'un travail poussé de la part de la police VOIR GRAMMAIRE A11
VT **1** *(the country)* maintenir l'ordre dans; **to p. a football match/demonstration** assurer l'ordre à un match de football/une manifestation; **the area is heavily policed** la zone est sous haute surveillance **2** *Fig (institution etc)* surveiller, contrôler; *(measures etc)* veiller au respect de; **should the press p. itself?** la presse doit-elle être autorisée à s'autoréglementer?
▸▸ *Am* **p. captain** ≃ commissaire *m* de police; **p. car** voiture *f* de police; *Br* **p. constable** ≃ gardien *m* de la paix, ≃ agent *m* (de police); *Am* **the p. department** la Police; **p. dog** chien *m* policier; *Br* **the Police Federation** = syndicat *m* de la police britannique; **p. force** police *f*; **to be a member of the p. force** être de *ou* dans la police; **p. informer** indicateur, -trice; **p. inspector** inspecteur, -trice de police; *Br (in the CID)* commissaire *m* de police; **p. officer** policier, -ière, agent de police; **p. state** État *m* *ou* régime *m* policier; **p. station** *(urban)* poste *m* de police, commissariat *m* (de police); *(rural)* gendarmerie *f*; **p. van** *(for transporting prisoners)* voiture cellulaire; *(for transporting police)* car *m* de police

policeman, *pl* **policemen** [pə'liːsmən] N agent *m* (de police)

policewoman, *pl* **policewomen** [pə'liːswʊmən, -wɪmɪn] N femme *f* agent (de police)

policing [pə'liːsɪŋ] N **1** *(by police)* maintien *m* de l'ordre; **the p. of the match/demonstration was inadequate** le service d'ordre du match/de la manifestation était inadéquat **2** *Fig* **the p. of these regulations** la responsabilité de veiller au respect de cette réglementation
▸▸ **p. policy** politique *f* de maintien de l'ordre

policy¹ ['pɒlɪsɪ] N politique *f*, *(measure)* mesure *f*; **foreign p.** politique étrangère *ou* extérieure; **economic/agricultural p.** politique économique/agricole; **we have the right policies** nous avons les mesures adéquates; **the company's success is essentially down to their inspired marketing p.** le succès de l'entreprise est dû en grande partie à l'intelligence de leur politique de commercialisation; **my p. is not to tell him anything** ma politique, c'est de ne rien lui dire; **sales p.** politique de vente; **changes of p.** changements *mpl* de politique
▸▸ **p. adviser** conseiller, -ère politique; **p. changes** changements de politique; **p. meeting** séance *f* de concertation; **p. paper** = document *m* énonçant une position de principe; **p. position** position *f* de principe; **p. statement** déclaration *f* de principe; **p. unit** comité *m* politique; *Am Pej* **p. wonk** conseiller, -ère politique

policy² N *(in insurance)* police *f* (d'assurance); **(fully) comprehensive** *or* **all-risks p.** police tous risques; **to take out a p.** souscrire à une police d'assurance

policyholder ['pɒlɪsɪhəʊldər] N assuré, -ée

polio ['pəʊlɪəʊ] N *Med* polio *f*; **to have p.** avoir la polio

poliomyelitis [pəʊlɪəʊmaɪə'laɪtɪs] N *Med* poliomyélite *f*

Polish ['pəʊlɪʃ] VOIR GRAMMAIRE A19 ADJ polonais
N *Ling* polonais *m*

polish ['pɒlɪʃ] N **1** *(finish of surface etc)* poli *m*, brillant *m*, lustre *m*; *(of metals)* poli, brunissure *f*; **high p.** poli brillant; **to lose its p.** se dépolir, se ternir; **to take the p. off sth** dépolir qch, ternir qch; **to give the table a p.** cirer la table

2 *(substance)* crème *f* *ou* pâte *f* à polir; **boot** *or* **shoe p.** cirage *m*, crème pour chaussures; **floor p.** encaustique *f* *ou* cire *f* à parquet; **metal p.** produit *m* pour faire briller les métaux; **nail p.** vernis *m* à ongles

3 *Fig (refinement) (of person)* belles manières *fpl*, savoir-vivre *m* inv; *(of novel, style, performance)* élégance *f*; **to have a certain p.** *(of person)* avoir un certain savoir-vivre; *(of novel, style etc)* avoir une certaine élégance; **to lack p.** *(of person)* manquer d'éducation *ou* de savoir-vivre; *(of novel, style etc)* manquer d'élégance; **to give sth a final p.** mettre la dernière main à qch
VT **1** *(wood, metal etc)* polir; *(gold, silver)* brunir; *(shoes)* cirer; *(brass)* astiquer, faire briller; *(stone etc)* lisser; *(parquet floor, tiles)* cirer, encaustiquer; *(rice)* glacer, polir
2 *Fig (make more refined) (person, manners)* polir, dégrossir; *(style, interpretation)* polir, perfectionner; **to p. one's French** perfectionner son français
▸ **polish off** VT SEP *Fam (course, dish)* finir; *(meal, bottle, job)* expédier; *(put finishing touch to) (job)* mettre la dernière main à; *(get rid of, defeat) (rebels, competitor etc)* liquider, régler son compte à; **to p. off one's drink** vider son verre; **such hard work at his age polished him off** un travail aussi dur à son âge l'a achevé
▸ **polish up** VT SEP **1** faire reluire; *(brass objects)* astiquer, brunir, lustrer **2** *(improve) (language)* perfectionner; *(style)* parfaire

polished ['pɒlɪʃt] ADJ **1** poli; *(wood, floor, shoes)* ciré **2** *(manners etc)* poli, distingué **3** *(style etc)* châtié, raffiné

polisher ['pɒlɪʃər] N **1** *(person) (of metals etc)* polisseur, -euse, brunisseur, -euse; *(of brass)* astiqueur, -euse **2** *(tool)* instrument *m* à polir, polissoir *m*; *(for metal)* brunissoir *m*; **electric floor p.** cireuse *f* électrique à parquet

Politburo ['pɒlɪtbjʊərəʊ] N *Pol* Politburo *m*

polite [pə'laɪt] ADJ *(courteous)* poli (**to sb** envers *ou* avec qn); **I was just being p.** j'ai fait/dit ça par politesse; **p. refusal** refus *m* poli
▸▸ **p. society** la bonne société, le beau monde; **this word is not used in p. society** ce mot ne s'utilise pas chez les gens bien élevés

politely [pə'laɪtlɪ] ADV poliment

politeness [pə'laɪtnɪs] N politesse *f*

politic ['pɒlɪtɪk] ADJ **1** *Fml (person, conduct)* politique, avisé, *Pej* rusé, astucieux; **it would not be p. to ...** ce ne serait pas prudent de ... **2 the body p.** le corps politique; *(the state)* l'État *m*

political [pə'lɪtɪk(ə)l] ADJ **1** *Pol (party etc)* politique; **he isn't very p.** il n'a pas une forte conscience politique; **p. beliefs** opinions *fpl* politiques **2** *Fig* **she's a p. animal** c'est quelqu'un de très politisé; **things are getting far too p. in the office** ça devient vraiment intenable au bureau avec toutes ces manigances *ou Fam* magouilles; **it was a p. decision** c'était une décision qui relevait de la politique interne de l'entreprise/du service/*etc*
▸▸ **p. analyst** analyste *mf* politique; **p. asylum** asile *m* politique; **to request/be granted p. asylum** demander/se voir accorder l'asile politique; **p. correctness** le politiquement correct; **p. correspondent** journaliste *mf* politique; **p. economy** économie *f* politique; **p. editor** rédacteur, -trice en chef politique; **p. map** carte *f* politique; **p. prisoner** prisonnier, -ière politique; **p. science** sciences *fpl* politiques; **p. theory** théorie *f* politique

politically [pə'lɪtɪklɪ] ADV **1** politiquement; **p. informed** au courant des choses de la politique; **to be p. aware** avoir une conscience

politique, être politisé; **p. radical** radical sur le plan politique **2** *Fig* **p. that wouldn't be a wise thing to say** du point de vue tactique, ce ne serait pas une chose à dire
▸▸ **p. correct** politiquement correct

politician [pɒlɪ'tɪʃən] **N 1** homme *m*/femme *f* politique; *esp Pej* politicien, -ienne **2** *esp Am Pej (self-interested)* politicard, -arde

politicize [pə'lɪtɪsaɪz] **VT** *(debate, problem, person etc)* politiser

politicking [pɒlɪtɪkɪŋ] **N** activité *f* électorale menée pour obtenir des suffrages; **the issue has been bogged down by last-minute p.** des tractations de politique politicienne ont fait s'enliser la discussion

politico [pə'lɪtɪkəʊ] **N** *esp Am Pej* politicard, -arde

politico-economic **ADJ** politico-économique

politics ['pɒlɪtɪks] **N** politique *f*; **to be interested in p.** s'intéresser à la politique; **to talk p.** parler politique; **his p. are right of centre** (politiquement parlant) il se situe à droite; **what are her p.?** de quel bord est-elle?, politiquement, où est-ce qu'elle se situe?; **foreign p.** politique étrangère; *Fig* **office p.** intrigues *fpl* de bureau [VOIR GRAMMAIRE A10]

polity ['pɒlɪtɪ] **N** *Pol* **1** *(constitution)* constitution *f* politique; *(form of government)* régime *m*; *(state)* État *m* **2** *(management)* administration *f* politique

polka ['pɒlkə] **N** *Mus* polka *f*
▸▸ *Tex* **p. dots** pois *mpl*

polka-dot **ADJ** à pois; **blue p.-dot tie** cravate *f* bleue à pois (blancs)

poll¹ [pəʊl] **N 1** *(voting)* vote *m* (par bulletins), scrutin *m*; **to go to the polls** aller aux urnes; **to head the p.** arriver en tête de scrutin; **heavy/light p.** forte/faible participation *f* électorale; **a 76% p.** un taux de participation de 76%; **to get a large share of the p.** remporter *ou* réunir une grande proportion des voix *ou* suffrages
2 *(survey)* sondage *m*; **(public) opinion p.** sondage d'opinion; **to carry out a p.** faire un sondage; **the latest p. puts the Socialists in the lead** le dernier sondage donne les socialistes en tête
VT 1 *(of polling clerk) (person)* recueillir le bulletin de vote; *(of candidate) (votes)* réunir; **the Conservatives polled 41% nationally** les conservateurs ont remporté 41% des voix *ou* suffrages au niveau national; **to p. a vote for sb** donner sa voix à qn, voter pour qn
2 *(in opinion poll)* sonder; **most of those polled were in favour of the plan** la plupart des personnes sondées étaient favorables au projet
3 *(tree)* étêter, écimer; *(bull)* décorner
4 *Comput* interroger
VI the party polled well le parti a remporté une bonne proportion des suffrages *ou* des voix
▸▸ **p. tax** *(in UK)* = impôt *m* aboli en 1993, regroupant taxe d'habitation et impôts locaux, payable par chaque occupant adulte d'une même habitation; *(in US)* = impôt, aboli en 1964, donnant droit à être inscrit sur les listes électorales; *Hist* capitation *f*

poll² **N** *(animal)* vache *f* etc sans cornes

pollack ['pɒlək] **N** = **pollock**

pollard ['pɒlɑːd] **N** *(tree)* arbre *m* étêté; *(animal)* animal *m* sans cornes
VT *(tree)* étêter, écimer

pollen ['pɒlən] **N** *Bot* pollen *m*
▸▸ **p. count** taux *m* de pollen; **p. sac** sac *m* pollinique

pollinate ['pɒlɪneɪt] **VT** *Bot* polliniser

pollination [pɒlɪ'neɪʃən] **N** *Bot* pollinisa-

tion *f*, fécondation *f*; **self-p.** pollinisation directe; **cross-p.** pollinisation croisée

polling ['pəʊlɪŋ] **N 1** scrutin *m*, élections *fpl* **2** *(for opinion poll)* sondage *m* **3** *Comput (querying)* interrogation *f*
▸▸ **p. booth** isoloir *m*; **p. company** institut *m* de sondage; **p. day** jour *m* des élections *ou* du scrutin; **p. station** bureau *m* de vote

polliwog ['pɒlɪwɒg] **N** *Am (tadpole)* têtard *m*

pollock ['pɒlək] **N** colin *m*

pollster ['pəʊlstər] **N** enquêteur, -euse; **according to the pollsters** selon les sondages

pollutant [pə'luːtənt] **N** polluant *m*

pollute [pə'luːt] **VT** *(river, atmosphere etc)* polluer; *(language, mind)* contaminer

polluted [pə'luːtəd] **ADJ** *Am Fam (drunk)* pété, bourré

polluter [pə'luːtər] **N** pollueur, -euse

pollution [pə'luːʃən] **N 1** *(contamination) (of river, atmosphere)* pollution *f*; *(of language, mind)* contamination *f*; **p. policy** politique *f* antipollution; **atmospheric p., p. of the atmosphere** pollution atmosphérique *ou* de l'air **2** *(pollutants)* polluants *mpl*; **the river is full of p.** la rivière est très polluée

pollution-free **ADJ** non pollué

Polly ['pɒlɪ] **N** *Fam (parrot)* **(pretty) P.** Jacquot *m*

Pollyanna [pɒlɪ'ænə] **N** *esp Am* optimiste *mf*

pollywog ['pɒlɪwɒg] **N** *Am (tadpole)* têtard *m*

polo ['pəʊləʊ] **N** *Sport* polo *m*; **to play p.** jouer au polo
▸▸ *Br* **p. neck** *(collar)* col *m* roulé; *(sweater)* (pull *m* à) col roulé; *Br* **p. neck sweater** pull à col roulé; *Sport* **p. pony** poney *m* de polo; **p. shirt** polo *m (chemise)*; *Sport* **p. stick** maillet *m*

polonaise [pɒlə'neɪz] **N** *Mus* polonaise *f*

poltergeist ['pɒltəgaɪst] **N** esprit *m* frappeur

poly ['pɒlɪ] **N** *Br Formerly Fam* = **polytechnic**

poly- ['pɒlɪ] **PREF** poly-

polyandrous [pɒlɪ'ændrəs] **ADJ** polyandre

polyandry ['pɒlɪændrɪ] **N** polyandrie *f*

polyanthus [pɒlɪ'ænθəs] **N** primevère *f* des jardins

poly bag **N** *Fam* sac *m* en plastique

polychromatic [pɒlɪkrəʊ'mætɪk] **ADJ** polychrome

polychrome ['pɒlɪkrəʊm] **ADJ** polychrome
N *(statue)* statue *f* polychrome; *(colouring)* polychromie *f*

polychromy ['pɒlɪkrəʊmɪ] **N** polychromie *f*

polyclinic [pɒlɪ'klɪnɪk] **N** *Med* polyclinique *f*

polyester [pɒlɪ'estər] **N** *Chem* polyester *m*

polyethylene [pɒlɪ'eθɪliːn] **N** *esp Am Chem* polyéthylène *m*, polythène *m*

polygamist [pə'lɪgəmɪst] **N** polygame *mf*

polygamous [pə'lɪgəməs] **ADJ** polygame

polygamy [pə'lɪgəmɪ] **N** polygamie *f*

polyglot ['pɒlɪglɒt] **ADJ, N** polyglotte *mf*

polygon ['pɒlɪgən] **N** *Geom* polygone *m*

polygonal [pə'lɪgən(ə)l] **ADJ** *Geom* polygonal, -aux

polygraph ['pɒlɪɡrɑːf] **N** détecteur *m* de mensonges; **to take a p. test** subir un test au détecteur de mensonges

polyhedron [pɒlɪ'hiːdrən] **N** *Geom* polyèdre *m*

polymath ['pɒlɪmæθ] **N** esprit *m* universel

polymer ['pɒlɪmər] **N** *Chem* polymère *m*

polymerization [pɒlɪmər'aɪ'zeɪʃən] **N** *Chem* polymérisation *f*

polymorphic [pɒlɪ'mɔːfɪk] **ADJ** *Biol, Chem* polymorphe, polymorphique

polymorphism [pɒlɪ'mɔːfɪz(ə)m] **N** *Biol, Chem* polymorphisme *m*, polymorphie *f*

polymorphous [pɒlɪ'mɔːfəs] **ADJ** = **polymorphic**

Polynesia [pɒlɪ'niːzɪə] **N** Polynésie *f*

Polynesian [pɒlɪ'niːzɪən] **ADJ** polynésien **N** Polynésien, -ienne

polyneuritis [pɒlɪnjʊ'raɪtɪs] **N** *Med* polynévrite *f*

polynomial [pɒlɪ'nəʊmɪəl] **N** *Math* polynôme *m*

polyp ['pɒlɪp] **N** *Zool, Med* polype *m*

polyphase ['pɒlɪfeɪz] **ADJ** *Elec* polyphasé

polyphonic [pɒlɪ'fɒnɪk] **ADJ** *Mus, Ling* polyphonique

polyphony [pə'lɪfənɪ] **N** *Mus, Ling* polyphonie *f*

polypropylene [pɒlɪ'prəʊpɪliːn] **N** *Chem* polypropène *m*, polypropylène *m*

polypus ['pɒlɪpəs] **N** *Med* polype *m*

polysaccharide [pɒlɪ'sækəraɪd] **N** *Chem* polysaccharide *m*, polyoside *m*

polystyrene [pɒlɪ'staɪriːn] **N** *Chem* polystyrène *m*; **p. packaging** emballage *m* en polystyrène

polysyllabic [pɒlɪsɪ'læbɪk] **ADJ** polysyllabe, polysyllabique

polysyllable ['pɒlɪsɪləb(ə)l] **N** polysyllabe *m*

polytechnic [pɒlɪ'teknɪk] **ADJ** *Formerly* polytechnique
N *Br Univ Formerly* ≃ Institut *m* universitaire de technologie

Note that the French noun **Polytechnique** is a false friend and is never a translation for the word **polytechnic**. It is the name of one of France's most prestigious **Grandes écoles**.

polytheism ['pɒlɪθiːɪz(ə)m] **N** polythéisme *m*

polytheistic [pɒlɪθiː'ɪstɪk] **ADJ** polythéiste

polythene ['pɒlɪθiːn] **N** *esp Br* polyéthylène *m*, polythène *m*
▸▸ **p. bag** sac *m* en plastique

polyunsaturated [pɒlɪʌn'sætʃəreɪtɪd] **ADJ** *Chem* polyinsaturé
▸▸ **p. fats** graisses *fpl* polyinsaturées

polyurethane [pɒlɪ'jʊərɪθeɪn] **N** *Chem etc* polyuréthane *m*

polyvalent [pɒlɪ'veɪlənt] **ADJ** *Chem* polyvalent

polyvinyl [pɒlɪ'vaɪnɪl] **N** *Chem* polyvinyle *m*
▸▸ **p. chloride** chlorure *m* de polyvinyle

pom [pɒm] **N** *Austr Fam* Anglais, -aise

pomegranate ['pɒmɪɡrænɪt] **N 1** *(fruit)* grenade *f* **2** *(tree)* grenadier *m*
▸▸ **p. tree** grenadier

Pomerania [pɒmə'reɪnɪə] **N** Poméranie *f*

Pomeranian [pɒmə'reɪnɪən] **N** *(dog)* loulou *m* (de Poméranie)
ADJ de Poméranie
▸▸ **P. dog** loulou (de Poméranie)

pommel ['pɒm(ə)l] **N** *(of sword, saddle)* pommeau *m*
VT (-ll-, *Am* -l-) = **pummel** **VT**
▸▸ **p. horse** cheval-d'arçons *m inv*

pommie, pommy ['pɒmɪ] **N** *Austr Fam* Anglais, -aise; **p. bastard** salaud *m* d'Anglais, sale Anglaise *f*

pomp [pɒmp] **N** pompe *f*, éclat *m*, faste *m*; **p. and circumstance** (grand) apparat *m*

Pompeii [pɒm'peɪiː] **N** Pompéi

pompom, pompon ['pɒmpɒm, -pɒn] **N** *(tuft)* pompon *m*

pom-pom N *Mil* canon-mitrailleuse *m, pl* canons-mitrailleuses (*système Maxim*)

pomposity [pɒm'pɒsɪtɪ] N *Pej (of person)* suffisance *f*, *(of remark, style)* emphase *f*

pompous ['pɒmpəs] ADJ *Pej (person)* plein de suffisance; *(style, remark)* emphatique, pompeux

pompously ['pɒmpəslɪ] ADV *Pej (to behave, talk etc)* avec suffisance; *(to write)* avec emphase

pompousness ['pɒmpəsnɪs] N *Pej (of person)* suffisance *f*, *(of style, remark)* emphase *f*

ponce [pɒns] *esp Br Sl* N **1** *(effeminate man)* gonzesse *f*, pédé *m* **2** *(pimp)* maquereau *m*
  VI *(live off earnings)* vivre aux crochets d'une prostituée
▸ **ponce about, ponce around** VI *Br Sl* **1** *(waste time)* glandouiller **2** *(of effeminate man)* se pavaner
▸ **ponce up** VT SEP *Sl (dress up)* **to get all ponced up** se mettre sur son trente-et-un

poncey ['pɒnsɪ] ADJ *esp Br Sl* = **poncy**

poncho, *pl* **ponchos** ['pɒntʃəʊ, -əʊz] N poncho *m*

poncy ['pɒnsɪ] ADJ *esp Br Sl (effeminate) (manner etc)* efféminé, de gonzesse

pond [pɒnd] N étang *m*; *(in park)* bassin *m*, pièce *f* d'eau; *(in village)* mare *f*, *(for fish)* vivier *m*, réservoir *m*; *(of mill)* réservoir; *Fam* **the P.** *(the Atlantic)* l'Atlantique *m*
  ▸▸ **p. life** la faune des étangs; *Fam Hum Pej (disreputable people)* minables *mpl*

ponder ['pɒndər] VT *(question)* réfléchir sur; *(opinion, proposal)* considérer, peser; *(situation)* méditer (sur), réfléchir à; *(idea)* considérer; **to p. whether …** se demander si …
  VI réfléchir, méditer; **to p. over** *or* **on sth** réfléchir à *ou* méditer sur qch

ponderable ['pɒndərəb(ə)l] ADJ pondérable

ponderous ['pɒndərəs] ADJ **1** *(large)* massif, énorme; *(movements, person)* lourd **2** *(task, work)* laborieux **3** *(style)* lourd, pesant; *(joke, remark)* lourd

ponderously ['pɒndərəslɪ] ADV *(to move)* lourdement; *(to make progress)* laborieusement

pondweed ['pɒndwiːd] N *(plant)* épi *m* d'eau

pone [pəʊn] N *Am* **(corn) p.** *(bread)* pain *m* de maïs
  ▸▸ **p. bread** pain de maïs

pong [pɒŋ] *Br Fam* N *(smell)* puanteur *f*, **what a p.!** ça pue!, ça schlingue!; **there's a terrible p. of fish!** ça pue le poisson à plein nez!
  VI *(smell)* puer, schlinguer; **the room still pongs of cigarettes** la pièce pue encore la cigarette

pongy ['pɒŋɪ] ADJ *Br Fam (smelly)* **it's a bit p. in here** ça pue *ou* schlingue là-dedans

pontiff ['pɒntɪf] N *Rel* pontife *m*; **the sovereign p.** le souverain pontife

pontifical [pɒn'tɪfɪk(ə)l] ADJ *Rel* pontifical, -aux
  N *Rel (book)* pontifical *m*

pontificate¹ [pɒn'tɪfɪkɪt] N *Rel* pontificat *m*

pontificate² [pɒn'tɪfɪkeɪt] VI *Rel, Fig Pej* pontifier; **to p. about sth** pontifier à propos de *ou* sur qch

Pontius Pilate ['pɒntʃəs'paɪlət] N *Bible* Ponce Pilate

pontoon [pɒn'tuːn] N **1** *(float)* ponton *m*; *Aviat (on aeroplane)* flotteur *m* **2** *Br Cards* vingt-et-un *m inv*
  ▸▸ **p. bridge** pont *m* flottant

pony ['pəʊnɪ] N **1** *(animal)* poney *m*; *Am (small horse)* petit cheval *m*; *Am* **cow p.** che-

val de ranch **2** *Br Sl (£25)* vingt-cinq livres *fpl* sterling **3** *Am Sch Fam (in exam)* traduction *f* (juxtalinéaire) **4** *(drinking glass)* petit verre *m* (sans pied)
  ▸▸ **p. trekking** randonnées *fpl* à dos de poney

ponytail ['pəʊnɪteɪl] N *(hairstyle)* queue *f* de cheval; **to wear one's hair in a p.** avoir une queue de cheval

poo [puː] *Fam* N **1** *(excrement)* caca *m*; **to do** *or Br* **have a p.** faire caca **2** *Br (worthless things)* **it's a load of p.** ça vaut pas un clou; **he's talking a load of p.** il raconte n'importe quoi
  VI faire caca

pooch [puːtʃ] N *Sl (dog)* cabot *m*, clebs *m*

poodle ['puːd(ə)l] N caniche *mf*, *Fig (servile follower)* larbin *m*

poof¹ [pʊf] N *Br Offensive Sl* pédé *m*, tante *f*

poof² INT pouf; **and then suddenly, p., it disappeared!** et puis pouf! il a disparu!

poofter ['pʊftər] N *Br Offensive Sl* pédé *m*, tante *f*

poofy ['pʊfɪ] ADJ *Br Offensive Sl* de gonzesse, de pédé; **some p. guy** une espèce de pédé; **it's p. to …** c'est bon pour les gonzesses *ou* les pédés de …; **to look p.** avoir l'air d'un pédé

pooh [puː] INT bah!, peuh!
  N *(in children's language) (faeces)* caca *m*

pooh-pooh¹ N = **pooh** N

pooh-pooh² VT *(idea, warning, piece of advice)* se moquer de, faire peu de cas de

pool¹ [puːl] N *(pond)* mare *f*, *(puddle)* flaque *f* d'eau; *(ornamental)* pièce *f* d'eau; *(left on beach by tide)* bâche *f*, *(in river)* clame *m*; **(swimming) p.** piscine *f*, **lying in a p. of blood** étendu dans une mare de sang; **a p. of light** une flaque de lumière

pool² N **1** *(group etc)* groupe *m*; *Com (of companies)* groupement *m*, pool *m*; *Econ* fonds *m* commun; *(of company cars, computers etc)* parc *m*; *Fig (of ideas, talent etc)* réservoir *m*; **a p. of experience** une mine d'expériences bigarrées; **a p. of experts/advisers** un groupe *ou* une équipe d'experts/ de conseillers; **a p. of funds** un fonds commun; **typing p.** central *m* dactylographique, pool de dactylos
  2 *(in games) (kitty)* cagnotte *f*, *Billiards* poule *f*
  3 *(game)* billard *m* américain
  4 *Br* **football pools,** *Fam* **pools** = concours *m* de pronostics de matchs de football; **to do the pools** faire des concours de pronostics (sur des matchs de football)
  VT *(capital, profits, ideas)* mettre en commun; *(resources)* grouper, mettre en commun; *Com etc (orders)* grouper; **pooled services** services *mpl* en commun
  ▸▸ **p. cue** queue *f* de billard; **p. hall** salle *f* de billard; **p. table** table *f* de billard

pooling of interests ['puːlɪŋ] N *Am Fin* (absorption-)fusion *f, pl* (absorptions-) fusions, unification *f*

poolroom ['puːlrʊm] N salle *f* de billard

poon [puːn], **poontang** ['puːntæŋ] N *Am Vulg* **1** *(female genitals)* chatte *f*, chagatte *f* **2** *(women)* gonzesses *fpl*, meufs *fpl*; **he's gone out looking for p.** il cherche une meuf à se mettre sur le bout

poonani [puː'nænɪ] N *Vulg (female genitals)* chatte *f*, chagatte *f*

poop [puːp] N *Am Fam (excrement)* caca *m*; **to take a p.** faire caca **2** *Naut (deck)* dunette *f*, gaillard *m* d'arrière **3** *Naut (raised part)* poupe *f*
  VI *Am Fam (defecate)* faire caca
  ▸▸ *Naut* **p. deck** (pont de) dunette, gaillard d'arrière

pooped [puːpt] ADJ *esp Am Fam (exhausted)* claqué, vanné

pooper-scooper ['puːpə'skuːpər] N *Fam* ramasse-crottes *m inv*

POOR [pɔːr] ADJ **1** *(having little wealth)* pauvre; **a p. man/woman** un pauvre/une pauvre; **as p. as a church mouse** pauvre comme Job; **I'm poorer by a thousand euros, I'm a thousand euros poorer** j'en suis pour mille euros; **the p. man's champagne** le champagne du pauvre
  2 *(inferior)* mauvais, médiocre; *(quality)* inférieur; *(health)* fragile; *(soil)* maigre, peu fertile; *(weather)* mauvais; **I've a p. memory** je n'ai pas une bonne mémoire; **to have p. sight** avoir une mauvaise vue; **her hearing is very p.** elle entend très mal, elle est très dure d'oreille; **to be p. at maths** être faible en math(s); **his French is very p.** son français est très faible; **to cut a p. figure** faire piètre figure; **the patient had a p. night** le malade a passé une mauvaise nuit; **to be a p. sailor** ne pas avoir le pied marin; **he gave a p. account of himself** il ne s'en est pas très bien tiré; **in p. condition** en mauvais état; **p. excuse** piètre excuse; **p. harvest** mauvaise récolte; **p. light** mauvais éclairage; **p. loser** mauvais perdant; **p. performance** *(of company)* contre-performance *f, pl* contre-performances; **p. reception** *(unwelcoming)* mauvais accueil; *Radio etc* mauvaise transmission; *Com* **p. sales (figures)** mauvais chiffre de ventes; **to come a p. second** *(in race)* se classer deuxième, loin derrière le vainqueur; **in terms of exports, Britain comes a p. second to Japan** en matière d'exportations, la Grande-Bretagne est en deuxième position, loin derrière le Japon; **I come a very p. second in his affections** je n'ai qu'une misérable deuxième place dans son cœur; **it's a p. substitute for the real thing** c'est loin de valoir l'original; **in p. taste** de mauvais goût; **there was a p. turnout** peu de gens sont venus
  3 *(to be pitied)* pauvre; **p. creature!, p. thing!** pauvre petit!, pauvre petite!; **the p. soul!** le pauvre!, la pauvre!; **p. Philippe!** pauvre Philippe!; **I'm so sorry for the p. man** comme je le plains, le pauvre homme; **when p. Alice was alive** du vivant de la pauvre Alice; **p. you, you p. thing** *(to man)* mon pauvre vieux; *(to woman)* ma pauvre vieille
  NPL **the p.** les pauvres *mpl*
  ▸▸ **p. box** tronc *m* des pauvres; *Hist* **p. law** = loi *f* sociale dictant les conditions dans lesquelles les pauvres étaient pris en charge par les communes; **p. relation** parent *m* pauvre; *Am Pej* **p. White** petit blanc, petite blanche

poorhouse ['pɔːhaʊs] N *Hist* asile *m* des pauvres

poorly ['pɔːlɪ] ADV pauvrement; **p. dressed** pauvrement vêtu; **to be p. off** *(financially)* avoir des problèmes d'argent; **p. lit** mal éclairé; **he did p. in his exams** il a eu de mauvais résultats à ses examens; **p. suited to these conditions** mal adapté à ces conditions; **to perform p. at low temperatures** donner de mauvais résultats à basse température
  ADJ PRED *Fam (person)* souffrant, indisposé; **she's looking p.** elle n'a pas l'air bien, elle a mauvaise mine; **I'm feeling p.** je ne suis pas dans mon assiette

poorness ['pɔːnɪs] N **1** *(of person)* pauvreté *f* **2** *(inferiority)* médiocrité *f*

POP ['piːəʊ'piː] N **1** *Comput (abbr* post office protocol) protocole *m* POP **2** *Comput (abbr* point of presence) point *m* de présence, point d'accès **3** *Mktg (abbr* point of purchase) point *m* de vente

pop¹ [pɒp] INT crac!, pan!; **to go p.** éclater,

crever; **p. goes the cork!** paf! le bouchon
saute
N 1 *(sound of cork etc)* bruit *m* sec **2** *Fam (fizzy drink)* boisson *f* gazeuse **3** *Fam* **to take a p. at sb/sth** critiquer qn/qch
VI (-pp-) 1 éclater, péter; *(of cork)* sauter, péter; *(of balloon, corn)* éclater; *(of ears)* se déboucher tout d'un coup
2 *Fam (go quickly)* **to p. over** *or* **across** *or* **down to the grocers** faire un saut (jusque) chez l'épicier; **they popped by** *or* **round to see us** ils sont passés nous voir; **I'm going to p. into town** je vais faire un saut en ville; **to p. into bed** se mettre vite au lit
VT 1 *(balloon)* crever; *(cork)* faire sauter; **to p. corn** faire du pop-corn
2 *(put quickly)* mettre; **to p. sth into a drawer** mettre *ou* glisser qch dans un tiroir; **to p. one's head out of the window** passer la tête par la fenêtre
3 *Fam* **then he popped the question** alors il lui a/m'a demandé de l'épouser
4 *Fam* **to p. pills** se bourrer de comprimés
5 *Old-fashioned Br Sl (pawn)* mettre en gage *ou* au clou
▸ **pop in VI** *Fam* entrer en passant *ou* un instant (**at sb's** chez qn); **I've just popped in** je ne fais que passer; **he popped in to say hello** il est passé (me/nous/etc) dire bonjour
VT SEP porter; **could you p. these trousers in at the dry cleaners?** est-ce que tu peux porter ce pantalon au pressing?
▸ **pop off VI 1** *Fam (leave abruptly)* filer, partir **2** *Br Sl (die)* claquer
▸ **pop out VI** *Fam (go out)* sortir; **I only popped out for five minutes** je ne suis sorti que cinq minutes; **his eyes were popping out of his head** les yeux lui sortaient de la tête
▸ **pop up VI** *Fam* **1** *(rise suddenly)* surgir; **a head popped up through the trap door** une tête a surgi de la trappe **2** *this question has popped up again* cette question est revenue sur le tapis; **he popped up again some years later in Miami** il est réapparu quelques années après à Miami

pop² **ADJ** pop
N *Mus (musique f)* pop *m ou f*
▸▸ **p. art** pop art *m*; **p. music** musique pop, pop music *f*, **p. psychology** psychologie *f* de pacotille; **p. singer** chanteur, -euse de pop; **p. song** chanson *f* pop

pop³ **N** *Am Fam (father)* papa *m*

pop⁴ *(abbr* **population)** pop

popcorn ['pɒpkɔ:n] **N** pop-corn *m inv*

pope [pəʊp] **N** *(in Catholic Church)* pape *m*; *(in Eastern Orthodox Church)* pope *m*; *Fam Hum* **is the P. Catholic?** à ton avis?
▸▸ *Culin* **p.'s nose** croupion *m*

popemobile ['pəʊpməbi:l] **N** *Fam* papamobile *f*

popery ['pəʊpərɪ] **N** *Pej* papisme *m*

popeyed ['pɒpaɪd] **ADJ** *Fam (having protuberant eyes)* aux yeux exorbités; *(with surprise)* aux yeux écarquillés

popgun ['pɒpɡʌn] **N** *(toy) (rifle)* fusil *m* à bouchon; *(handgun)* pistolet *m* à bouchon

popinjay ['pɒpɪndʒeɪ] **N** *Old-fashioned* fat *m*, freluquet *m*

popish ['pəʊpɪʃ] **ADJ** *Pej* papiste

poplar ['pɒplər] **N** *(tree)* peuplier *m*

poplin ['pɒplɪn] **N** *Tex* popeline *f*

popover ['pɒpəʊvər] **N** *Culin* beignet *m*

poppadom, poppadum ['pɒpədəm] **N** *Culin* poppadum *m*

popper ['pɒpər] **N 1** *Br Fam (on clothing, bag etc)* bouton-pression *m*, *pl* boutons-pression **2** *Fam (drug)* **poppers** poppers *mpl*

poppet ['pɒpɪt] **N** *Old-fashioned Fam* **she's a p.** elle est charmante; **my p.** *(to boy, man)*

mon chéri; *(to girl, woman)* ma chérie; *(to boy or girl)* mon (petit) chou
▸▸ **p. valve** soupape *f* à champignon

popping ['pɒpɪŋ] **N** *(of microphone)* saturation *f* acoustique

poppy ['pɒpɪ] **N** *(plant)* pavot *m*; *(flower)* coquelicot *m*; *(worn on Armistice Day)* = coquelicot en papier porté le jour de l'Armistice, vendu au profit des anciens combattants; **p. (coloured), p. red** rouge coquelicot *inv*
▸▸ *Br* **P. Day** = journée *f* de commémoration (le dimanche suivant ou précédant le 11 novembre) pendant laquelle on porte un coquelicot en papier en souvenir des soldats britanniques morts lors des guerres mondiales; **p. seed** graine *f* de pavot

poppycock ['pɒpɪkɒk] **N** *Fam* bêtises *fpl*, inepties *fpl*

Popsicle® ['pɒpsɪk(ə)l] **N** *Am Culin* ≃ Esquimau® *m*

popsy ['pɒpsɪ] **N** *Old-fashioned Br Fam* pépée *f*, nana *f*

populace ['pɒpjʊləs] **N** *Fml* **the p.** le peuple, *Pej* la populace

popular ['pɒpjʊlər] **ADJ 1** *(generally liked)* *(person, action etc)* populaire; *(in vogue)* à la mode, en vogue; *(music, song)* populaire; **to make oneself p.** se rendre populaire (**with** auprès de); **his views have not made him p. with the authorities** à cause de ses opinions, il est mal vu des autorités; **she is p. with her colleagues** elle est très populaire auprès de ses collègues, elle est très appréciée par ses collègues; **this was not a p. decision** cette décision n'était pas populaire
2 *(of or for the people)* populaire, du peuple; **with p. appeal** qui plaît au grand public; **by p. demand** à la demande générale; **contrary to p. belief** contrairement à ce que les gens croient; **p. misconception** idée *f* fausse et très répandue; **p. prices** prix *mpl* à la portée de tous; **p. support** soutien *m* populaire; **to be chosen by p. vote** rencontrer l'adhésion du public; **p. work** *or* **treatise** ouvrage *m* de vulgarisation
▸▸ **p. culture** culture *f* populaire; *Hist* **P. Front** Front *m* populaire; **the p. press** la presse à grand tirage et à sensation

popularity [pɒpjʊ'lærɪtɪ] **N** popularité *f*, *Com (of product etc)* succès *m* auprès du (grand) public; **the president's p. has fallen** *or* **diminished** la popularité du président a baissé; **to experience a rise/fall in p.** voir sa popularité augmenter/baisser; **to grow/decline in p.** devenir plus/moins populaire (**among** parmi); **the sport has gained in p.** le sport est de plus en plus populaire
▸▸ **p. rating** taux *m* de popularité

popularization [pɒpjʊləraɪ'zeɪʃən] **N** popularisation *f*, *(of science etc)* vulgarisation *f*

popularize ['pɒpjʊləraɪz] **VT** *(game, activity, form of music)* populariser; *(knowledge, idea, science etc)* vulgariser; *(method)* propager; *(fashion)* mettre en vogue

popularizer ['pɒpjʊləraɪzər] **N** *(of science, ideas)* vulgarisateur, -trice

popularly ['pɒpjʊləlɪ] **ADV** communément, généralement; **p. known as ...** *(of plant etc)* dont le nom vulgaire est ...; *(of person)* familièrement appelé ...; **it is p. believed that ...** les gens croient que ..., il est communément admis que ...

populate ['pɒpjʊleɪt] **VT** peupler; **densely** *or* **thickly populated country** pays très peuplé; **sparsely populated** *(region)* peu densément peuplé

population [pɒpjʊ'leɪʃən] **N** population *f*, **the town has a p. of 85,000** la ville compte 85 000 habitants; **world p. figures are rising** la population mondiale augmente

▸▸ **p. census** recensement *m* démographique *ou* de la population; **p. control** contrôle *m* démographique; **p. explosion** explosion *f* démographique; **p. growth** croissance *f* démographique; **p. statistics** statistiques *fpl* démographiques

populism ['pɒpjʊlɪz(ə)m] **N** *Pol* populisme *m*

populist ['pɒpjʊlɪst] *Pol* **N** populiste *mf*
ADJ populiste; **p. support** support *m* populaire

populous ['pɒpjʊləs] **ADJ** populeux, très peuplé

pop-up **ADJ** *(toaster)* automatique
▸▸ **p. book** livre *m* en relief; *Comput* **p. menu** menu *m* local; *Aut* **p. sunroof** toit *m* ouvrant dépliant

porcelain ['pɔːs(ə)lɪn] **N** porcelaine *f*, **a p. collection** une collection d'objets en porcelaine; **p. plate** assiette *f* en porcelaine
▸▸ **p. manufacturer** porcelainier, -ière; **p. ware** porcelaine

porch [pɔːtʃ] **N 1** *(over door)* porche *m*; **(glass) p.** *(of hotel etc)* marquise *f* **2** *Am (veranda)* véranda *f*
▸▸ **p. roof** auvent *m*

porchscreen ['pɔːtʃskri:n] **N** *Am* moustiquaire *f (autour d'une véranda)*

porchswing ['pɔːtʃswɪŋ] **N** *Am* balançoire *f (sur une véranda, typique de certaines maisons aux États-Unis)*

porcine ['pɔːsaɪn] **ADJ** porcin, de porc

porcupine ['pɔːkjʊpaɪn] **N** porc-épic *m*, *pl* porcs-épics
▸▸ **p. fish** poisson *m* porc-épic

pore [pɔːr] **N** *Anat, Bot etc* pore *m*
▸ **pore over VT INSEP** *(examine closely)* *(book)* être absorbé par; *(map, contract)* étudier soigneusement; *(problem)* méditer longuement

pork [pɔːk] **N** *Culin* porc *m*
▸▸ *Am Pol Fam* **the p. barrel** = fonds *mpl* alloués par le gouvernement à une circonscription et destinés à s'attirer les bonnes grâces des électeurs; **p. chop** côtelette *f* de porc; **p. pie** ≃ paté *m* en croûte *(à la viande de porc)*; *Br Sl* **to tell p. pies** *(tell lies)* raconter des bobards; **p. scratchings** grattons *mpl*

porker ['pɔːkər] **N** = jeune porc *m* engraissé, destiné à la boucherie

porkpie hat ['pɔːkpaɪ-] **N** = chapeau *m* de feutre rond à forme aplatie

porky ['pɔːkɪ] **ADJ** *Fam* gras, gros
N *Sl (lie)* bobard *m*

porn [pɔːn] *Fam* **N** pornographie *f*, **soft/hard p.** pornographie soft/hard
ADJ porno *inv*
▸▸ **p. dealer** vendeur *m* de matériel pornographique; **p. shop** sex-shop *m*, *pl* sex-shops; *Br* **p. squad** = branche *f* de la police chargée de réprimer la production et la distribution illégales de matériel pornographique

porno ['pɔːnəʊ] **ADJ** porno *inv*

pornographer [pɔː'nɒɡrəfər] **N** pornographe *mf*

pornographic [pɔːnə'ɡræfɪk] **ADJ** pornographique; *Fig* indécent

pornography [pɔː'nɒɡrəfɪ] **N** pornographie *f*
▸▸ **p. dealer** vendeur *m* de matériel pornographique; **p. shop** sex-shop *m*, *pl* sex-shops

porosity [pɔː'rɒsɪtɪ] **N** porosité *f*

porous ['pɔːrəs] **ADJ** poreux

porousness ['pɔːrəsnɪs] **N** porosité *f*

porphyry ['pɔːfɪrɪ] **N** *Miner* porphyre *m*

porpoise ['pɔːpəs] **N** *(animal)* marsouin *m*

porridge ['pɒrɪdʒ] N **1** Culin bouillie f d'avoine, porridge m **2** Br Sl **to do p.** purger sa peine en prison
▸ ▸ **p. oats** flocons mpl d'avoine

porringer ['pɒrɪndʒər] N écuelle f

port¹ [pɔːt] N (harbour, town) port m; **the p. of London** le port de Londres; **in p.** au port; **to put into p.** relâcher; **to call at a p.** faire escale à un port; Prov **any p. in a storm** (any will do) nécessité fait loi; **p. to p. shipment** expédition f port à port
▸ ▸ **p. of arrival** port d'arrivée; **p. authorities** autorités fpl portuaires, administration f portuaire; **p. of call** Naut escale f, Fig arrêt m; **p. charges** droits mpl de port, frais mpl portuaires; **p. of departure** port de départ; **p. of discharge** port d'arrivée; **p. dues** droits de port, frais portuaires; **p. of embarkation** port d'embarquement; **p. of entry** port de débarquement; **p. of loading** port d'embarquement; **p. of refuge** port de refuge; **p. of registry** port d'attache

port² N **1** Naut (opening for loading) sabord m; **p.(-lid)** mantelet m ou panneau m ou volet m de sabord, contre-sabord m, pl contre-sabords; **air** or **ventilation p.** sabord d'aération **2** Tech (of cylinder etc) orifice m, lumière f; **admission** or **inlet p.** orifice ou pipe f d'admission **3** Comput port m; **input/output p.** port entrée/sortie
VT Comput transférer, transporter

port³ N Naut **p. (side)** bâbord m; **land to p.!** la terre par bâbord!; **on the p. bow** par bâbord devant

port⁴ N (wine) porto m
▸ ▸ Old-fashioned **p. wine stain** (birthmark) tache f de vin

portability [pɔːtə'bɪlɪtɪ] N portabilité f

portable ['pɔːtəb(ə)l] ADJ portatif, portable; Fin (pension, mortgage) transférable; Comput (program) portable
N (television) téléviseur m portatif ou portable; (computer) (ordinateur m) portable m

portage ['pɔːtɪdʒ] N Fml **1** (transport) (of goods) transport m, port m; (of canoe etc between waterways) portage m **2** (costs) frais mpl de port ou de transport

Portakabin® ['pɔːtəkæbɪn] N = baraquement m préfabriqué

portal ['pɔːt(ə)l] N **1** Archit (of cathedral) portail m **2** Comput portail m
▸ ▸ Anat **p. vein** veine f porte

Portaloo® ['pɔːtəluː] N toilettes fpl provisoires

portcullis [pɔːt'kʌlɪs] N (of castle) herse f, sarrasine f

portend [pɔː'tend] VT Fml présager, faire pressentir

portent ['pɔːtent] N Fml **1** (sign) présage m **2** (importance) portée f

portentous [pɔː'tentəs] ADJ **1** (prodigious) (event, happening) prodigieux; (ominously so) de mauvais présage ou augure **2** (solemn) solennel; Pej (over-serious) pompeux, pontifiant

portentously [pɔː'tentəslɪ] ADV solennellement; Pej pompeusement

porter ['pɔːtər] N **1** Rail porteur, -euse; (at hotel) chasseur m, garçon m; Am Rail (of sleeper) garçon m **2** esp Br (doorkeeper) (of museum etc) portier, -ière, concierge mf; (of building) concierge m; **p.'s desk** comptoir m du concierge; **p.'s lodge** loge f de concierge; (at entrance to large estate) maisonnette f du portier **3** Br Old-fashioned (beer) bière f brune (anglaise), porter m

porterage ['pɔːtərɪdʒ] N **1** (carrying) transport m, factage m **2** (cost) prix m de transport, factage m

porterhouse ['pɔːtəhaʊs] N

▸ ▸ Culin **p. steak** chateaubriand m, châteaubriant m

portfolio [pɔːt'fəʊlɪəʊ] N **1** (for documents etc) serviette f; (for drawings, prints) carton m; **candidates are asked to bring a p. of their recent work** on a demandé aux candidats d'apporter un dossier contenant leurs travaux récents; **minister's p.** portefeuille m de ministre; **minister without p.** ministre sans portefeuille **2** Fin (of shares) portefeuille m; **securities in p.** valeurs fpl en portefeuille
▸ ▸ **p. analysis** analyse f de portefeuille; **p. diversification** diversification f de portefeuille; **p. insurance** assurance f de portefeuille; **p. management** gestion f de portefeuille; **p. manager** gestionnaire mf de portefeuille; **p. mix** portefeuille d'activités; **p. securities** valeurs de portefeuille; **p. worker** = personne f ayant plusieurs emplois ou travailleur indépendant ayant plusieurs employeurs

porthole ['pɔːthəʊl] N Naut hublot m

portico, pl **porticos, porticoes** ['pɔːtɪkəʊ, -əʊz] N Archit portique m

portion ['pɔːʃən] N **1** (part) partie f, (of inheritance) part f; Culin (of meat etc) portion f; **this p. to be given up** (on ticket) côté m à détacher; Law **p. (of inheritance)** part d'héritage; **(marriage) p.** dot f **2** Lit (destiny) destinée f, sort m
VT = **portion out**
▸ **portion out** VT SEP (property, sum) partager, répartir

portliness ['pɔːtlɪnɪs] N corpulence f

portly ['pɔːtlɪ] ADJ corpulent

portmanteau, pl **portmanteaus, portmanteaux** [pɔːt'mæntəʊ, -əʊz] N Old-fashioned valise f
▸ ▸ **p. word** mot-valise m, pl mots-valises

portrait ['pɔːtreɪt] N **1** Art, Fig portrait m; **to have one's p. painted, to sit for one's p.** se faire peindre **2** Typ, Comput **to print sth in p.** imprimer qch en portrait
ADV (to print) en mode portrait, à la française
▸ ▸ **p. bust** (portrait en) buste m; Comput **p. format** format m portrait; **p. gallery** galerie f de portraits; Comput **p. lens** objectif m pour portraits; Comput **p. mode** mode m portrait; **p. painter** portraitiste mf

portraitist ['pɔːtrətɪst] N portraitiste mf

portraiture ['pɔːtrətʃər] N (art) (art m du) portrait m

portray [pɔː'treɪ] VT **1** (depict) dépeindre, décrire; **in the film the soldiers are portrayed as monsters** dans le film les soldats sont dépeints comme des monstres **2** Arch, Lit (paint portrait of) faire le portrait de

portrayal [pɔː'treɪəl] N **1** (depiction) description f, peinture f; Theat, Cin (by actor, actress) interprétation f **2** Arch, Lit (portrait) portrait m

Portugal ['pɔːtjʊg(ə)l] N Portugal m

Portuguese [pɔːtjʊ'giːz] ADJ portugais
N Portugais, -aise **2** Ling portugais m
▸ ▸ Zool **P. man-of-war** physalie f; **P.-speaking** lusophone

POS [piːəʊ'es] N Mktg (abbr **point of sale**) PDV m

pose [pəʊz] N **1** (of body) pose f, attitude f, (of model) pose; **to strike a p.** (of model) prendre une pose **2** (affectation) pose f, affectation f; **it's just a p.** c'est juste un air qu'il/elle/etc se donne
VT **1** Art (model) faire poser; **to p. sb** faire prendre une pose à qn pour son portrait **2** (problem) poser, soulever; (question, difficulty) soulever; (danger) présenter (**to** pour); **to p. a threat to sth** menacer qch
VI (for one's portrait, as model) poser; (be-

have affectedly) poser, se donner des airs (affectés); **to p. for sb** (as a model) poser pour qn; **young men posing in biker jackets** (affectedly) des jeunes gens se donnant des airs avec leurs blousons de moto; **to p. as a Frenchman/a socialist** se faire passer pour un Français/un socialiste

poser ['pəʊzər] N Fam **1** Pej (person) poseur, -euse **2** (difficult question) colle f; **to give sb a p.** poser une colle à qn

poseur [pəʊ'zɜːr] N Pej = **poser 1**

posh [pɒʃ] Br Fam ADJ (upper-class) très comme il faut, Pej snob; (hotel, restaurant) chic, de luxe; **a p. accent** un accent snob; **a p. area** un quartier chic ou bourgeois; **you do look p.!** comme tu fais chic!; **it looks p.** ça fait bien
ADV **to talk p.** parler comme un snob
N Br Sl (cocaine) coke f

posit ['pɒzɪt] VT Phil etc, Fml (proposition) avancer, poser en principe (**that ...** que ... + ind)

POSITION [pə'zɪʃən]

| N | position **1–4** ▪ place **3** ▪ situation **3–5** ▪ guichet **3** ▪ poste **5** |
| VT | mettre en place **1** ▪ placer **1** ▪ situer **1** |

N **1** (of body) (posture etc) position f, posture f; **in a horizontal/vertical** or **upright p.** en position horizontale/verticale; **in the off/on p.** dans la position arrêt/marche **2** (mental attitude) position f, point m de vue; **to take up an uncompromising p.** adopter une attitude intransigeante (**about sth** à l'égard de qch); **I have no p. on the matter** je n'ai pas d'idée bien arrêtée sur le sujet; **what is the American p. on this issue?** quelle est la position des Américains sur ce problème?; **her p. is that ...** ce qu'elle pense c'est que ..., son point de vue est que ... **3** (place) position f, (of object) place f, (of town etc) situation f, Banking etc (window) guichet m; Aviat, Naut (of plane, ship) position; Mil emplacement m, position; **in p.** en place; **out of p.** déplacé; **to put** or **get sth into p.** mettre qch en place; Aviat, Naut **to fix** or **work out one's p.** faire le point; **to change the p. of sth** changer qch de position; Ftbl **what p. do you play?** en quelle position jouez-vous?, quelle est votre position sur le terrain?; Naut **to take up p. ahead/astern** prendre poste en tête/derrière; Mil **to move into p.** se mettre en place ou en position; **to bring guns into p.** mettre des pièces en batterie ou en position; **p. closed** (in bank etc) guichet fermé **4** (situation) situation f, Old-fashioned (social status) rang m social, condition f, état m; **to be in an awkward p.** se trouver dans une situation difficile ou délicate; **to be in a strong p.** être bien placé; **put yourself in my p.** mettez-vous à ma place; **try to see this from my/their/our p.** essayez de voir ceci de mon/leur/notre point de vue; **to be in a p. to do sth** être à même ou en mesure de faire qch; **you're in no p. to criticize** tu es vraiment mal placé pour faire des critiques; **what is the financial p. of the firm?** quelle est la situation financière de la maison?; **to keep up one's p.** (in society) tenir son rang; **to be in seventh p.** (in race etc) être en septième position **5** esp Fml (job) poste m, emploi m, situation f; **it's a p. of great responsibility** c'est un poste à haute responsabilité; **there were four candidates for the p. of manager** il y avait quatre candidats au poste de directeur; **to work one's way up to a good p.** se faire une belle situation; **p. of trust** poste de confiance

VT **1** (place) (objects) mettre en place, pla-

cer; *(troops)* mettre en position, poster; **to p. oneself** *(of troops, military observer, police etc)* se poster; *(of spectators)* se placer; **the town is positioned on the top of a basalt rock** la ville est située au sommet d'un rocher de basalte; **we are well positioned to take advantage of this opportunity** nous sommes bien placés pour tirer parti de cette opportunité
2 *(locate)* déterminer la position de
3 *Mktg (product)* positionner
▸▸**p. finding** orientation *f*; *Mil* goniométrie *f*; *St Exch* **p. limit** limite *f* de position; *Pol* **p. paper** déclaration *f* de principe; *St Exch* **p. taking** prise *f* de position

positioning [pəˈzɪʃənɪŋ] N *Mktg* positionnement *m*
▸▸*Comput* **p. macro** macro-commande *f* de position, *pl* macro-commandes; *Mktg* **p. study** étude *f* de positionnement

positive [ˈpɒzɪtɪv] ADJ **1** *(affirmative)* positif; *Med* **the test was p.** le test était positif; **p. answer** *(yes)* réponse *f* affirmative; *(indicating willingness to do sth)* réponse positive *ou* favorable; **p. proof, proof p.** preuve *f* formelle; **there was a tremendously p. response to this idea** cette idée a été extrêmement bien accueillie *ou* reçue
2 *Fam (for emphasis)* **a p. miracle** un véritable miracle; **it's a p. shame** c'est une véritable honte
3 *(certain)* certain, sûr (**of** de); **I'm p. on that point** j'en ai aucun doute à ce sujet; **I'm p. (that) I saw him** je suis certain *ou* sûr de l'avoir vu; **are you sure? – p.!** tu es sûr? – absolument!
4 *(constructive)* *(person, philosophy)* positif; *(proposition, help)* constructif; **he described the talks as 'p.'** il a qualifié les discussions de 'positives'; **but on the p. side, ...** mais d'un autre côté, ...
5 *Math, Elec* positif
N **1 to accentuate the p.** mettre l'accent sur le côté positif des choses
2 *Phot* positif *m*, épreuve *f* positive
3 *Gram* degré *m* positif; **in the p.** à la forme affirmative
▸▸**p. action** *(discrimination)* = mesures *fpl* anti-discriminatoires en faveur de l'égalité des races et des sexes, *Can* action *f* positive; *Gram* **p. degree** *(of adjective, adverb)* degré positif; **p. discrimination** = mesures anti-discriminatoires en faveur de l'égalité des races et des sexes, *Can* action positive; *Fin* **p. prescription** prescription *f* acquisitive; *Phot* **p. print** positif *m*, épreuve positive; *Med etc* **p. reaction** réaction *f* positive; **p. thinking** idées *fpl* constructives; **p. vetting** contrôle *m* *ou* enquête *f* de sécurité *(sur un candidat à un poste touchant à la sécurité nationale)*

positively [ˈpɒzɪtɪvlɪ] ADV **1** *(affirmatively)* positivement; **try to think p. about the situation** essaie de voir la situation d'une manière constructive; **people have responded quite p. to our suggestions** nos suggestions ont été fort bien accueillies; **he had been p. vetted on three occasions** il avait fait l'objet de trois enquêtes de sécurité qui s'étaient avérées satisfaisantes; **the body has been p. identified** le corps a été identifié de façon certaine
2 *(for emphasis)* assurément, certainement, sûrement; **I'm p. convinced it was him** je suis absolument convaincu que c'était lui; *Fam* **p. not** absolument pas; **smiling? – she was p. beaming!** souriante? – elle était littéralement radieuse!
3 *Elec* **p. charged** à charge positive; *Tech* **p. driven** à commande directe

positivism [ˈpɒzɪtɪvɪz(ə)m] N *Phil* positivisme *m*

positivist [ˈpɒzɪtɪvɪst] ADJ, N *Phil* positiviste *mf*
posology [pəˈsɒlədʒɪ] N *Med* posologie *f*
poss *abbr* possible
posse [ˈpɒsɪ] N *(of people)* troupe *f*, bande *f*; *Am Hist (under sheriff)* = détachement *m* d'hommes aux ordres du shérif; *Fam (group of friends)* bande; *(entourage)* clique *f*, *(criminal gang)* gang *m*; **he's out with the p.** il est sorti avec ses potes *ou* avec sa bande
possess [pəˈzes] VT **1** *(property etc)* posséder; *(quality, faculty)* avoir, posséder; **all I p.** tout ce que je possède; *Lit* **to be possessed of a property** posséder un bien **2** *(of evil spirit)* posséder; **possessed by fear/rage** pris de terreur/de rage; **what possessed you to do that?** qu'est-ce qui vous a pris de faire cela?; **to be possessed with an idea** être obsédé par une idée; **to scream like one possessed** crier comme un possédé **3** *Lit* **to p. oneself in patience** se munir de patience
possession [pəˈzeʃən] N **1** *(ownership)* possession *f*, jouissance *f* (**of** de); **to have sth in one's p.** avoir qch en sa possession; **to be in p. of sth** être en possession de qch; **how did the car come into your p.?** comment la voiture est-elle entrée en votre possession?; **to take p. of an estate, to come** *or* **enter into p. of an estate** entrer en possession *ou* en jouissance d'un bien; **to take** *or* **get p. of sth** *(forcefully)* s'emparer de qch; **the information in my p.** les renseignements dont je dispose; **in full p. of one's faculties** en pleine possession de ses facultés; **he's been arrested for p.** *(of drugs)* il a été arrêté pour détention de drogue; **sorry, p. is nine points** *or* **tenths of the law!** la possession vaut titre; *Ftbl* **to lose p. of the ball** perdre le ballon; *Sport* **to have p.** être en possession du ballon
2 *(object possessed)* possession *f*, **possessions** possessions, biens *mpl*, *(colonies)* possessions, colonies *fpl*
3 *(by demon)* possession *f*
possessive [pəˈzesɪv] ADJ **1** *(parent etc)* possessif (**about** avec); **she's very p. about her children** elle est une mère très possessive
2 *Gram* **the p. case** le cas possessif VOIR GRAMMAIRE A30; B21–2
N *Gram* adjectif *m*/pronom *m* possessif; **the p.** *(case)* le possessif
▸▸*Gram* **p. adjective** adjectif possessif; **p. pronoun** pronom possessif
possessiveness [pəˈzesɪvnɪs] N possessivité *f* (**about** avec)
possessor [pəˈzesər] N possesseur *m*
possibility [pɒsɪˈbɪlɪtɪ] N **1** *(of event)* possibilité *f*, éventualité *f*; **have you considered the p. of his being dead?** avez-vous envisagé la possibilité qu'il soit mort?; **within the range** *or* **the bounds of p.** dans la limite du possible; **there's a p. that it will rain** il est possible qu'il pleuve; **there's a definite** *or* **a strong p. that he'll say yes** il est fort probable qu'il dise oui; **there is little p. that he will win** il n'a guère de chances de gagner, il est peu probable qu'il gagne VOIR GRAMMAIRE A59–60; B40
2 *(possible event, outcome)* éventualité *f*; **that is a distinct p.** c'est bien possible; **to allow for all possibilities** parer à toute éventualité; **the possibilities are endless!** les possibilités sont innombrables!
3 *(potential)* *(usu pl)* **the plan has possibilities** ce projet offre des chances de succès; **the flat has possibilities** l'appartement a un bon potentiel
POSSIBLE [ˈpɒsɪb(ə)l] ADJ possible; **it's p.** c'est possible; **that's quite p.** c'est très *ou* fort possible; **it's just p. that ...** il y a des chances pour que ... + *subj*; **anything's p.** tout est possible; **it is p. that he will come** il est pos-

sible *ou* il se peut qu'il vienne; **is it p. to see her?** y a-t-il moyen *ou* est-il possible de la voir?; **as cheap/soon as p.** aussi bon marché/tôt que possible; **the best p.** le meilleur possible; **the shortest p. route** l'itinéraire le plus court possible; **to give as many details as p.** donner le plus de détails possible *ou* tous les détails possibles; **what p. interest can you have in it?** mais quel intérêt cela peut-il donc avoir pour vous?; **there's no p. reason why he should have done it** il n'avait absolument aucune raison de le faire; **if p.** *(I will do it)* si possible; **if it's p. to ...** si c'est possible de ...; **whenever/wherever p.** toutes les fois que/partout où c'est possible; **as far as p.** dans la mesure du possible; **the p. nomination of ...** la nomination éventuelle de ...; **to insure against p. accidents** s'assurer contre les accidents éventuels
N **1 it's in the realms of the p.** c'est dans le domaine du possible
2 *Fam (candidate)* candidat, -ate possible *ou* acceptable; **only two of the jobs/flats are possibles** seuls des emplois/appartements sont à considérer
possibly [ˈpɒsɪblɪ] ADV **1** **I can't p. do it** je ne peux vraiment pas le faire, il ne m'est vraiment pas possible de le faire; **I'll do all I p. can** je ferai tout mon possible; **you can't p. mean that!** vous ne pouvez pas dire ça sérieusement!; **I can't p. allow you to do that!** je ne peux vraiment pas vous permettre de faire cela!; **they can't p. have left yet!** il est tout à fait impossible qu'ils soient déjà partis!; **it can't p. cost that much!** c'est absolument impossible que ça coûte aussi cher que ça! **2** *(perhaps)* peut-être (bien); **he has p. heard of you** il se peut qu'il ait entendu parler de vous; **p.!** c'est possible, cela se peut; **p. not** peut-être pas
possum [ˈpɒsəm] N *Fam (animal)* opossum *m*; **to play p.** faire le mort; *(keep low profile)* se tenir coi
post¹ [pəʊst] N **1** *(of fence)* pieu *m*; *(of frame)* montant *m*; *Constr etc* poteau *m*, pilier *m*; *(of door, window)* montant, jambage *m*; *Ftbl* poteau; *(bed)* **p.** colonne *f* de lit; **(telegraph) p.** poteau télégraphique
2 *(starting)* **p.** (poteau *m* de) départ *m*; **(winning) p.** (poteau d')arrivée *f*, *Sport, Fig* **to be left at the p.** rater le départ; *Sport, Fig* **to be beaten** *or Fam* **pipped at the p.** se faire coiffer *ou* battre sur le poteau
VT **1** *(on wall etc)* *(bills, notice etc)* afficher, placarder, coller; **p. no bills** *(on sign)* défense d'afficher; **to p. prices** afficher des prix
2 *(on list)* *(person)* inscrire *ou* porter sur une liste; *(in marine insurance)* *(ship)* porter disparu; **to be posted for night duty** être sur la liste (du personnel) de service de nuit; **to be posted missing** être porté disparu *ou* manquant; *St Exch* **to p. security** déposer des garanties

POST²

Ⓝ courrier 1 ▪ poste 1, 3, 4
Ⓥⓣ poster 1, 5 ▪ affecter 4

N *Br* **1** *(mail)* courrier *m*; *(service)* poste *f*, **by return of p.** par retour du courrier; **when does the next p. go?** à quelle heure est la prochaine levée?; **to miss the p.** manquer la levée; *(in office)* manquer le courrier; **the first p.** la première distribution; **to catch the p.** poster une lettre/un paquet/*etc* à temps *(pour une levée déterminée)*; **there's no p. today** *(no letters for you, no delivery service)* il n'y a pas de courrier aujourd'hui; **to put sth in the p.** mettre qch à la poste; **to send sth by p.** envoyer qch par la poste; **has the p. been yet?** est-ce que le facteur est passé?; **was there any p. for me?** est-ce que j'ai du courrier?

2 *Hist (coach)* (malle-)poste *f, pl* malles-poste(s)

3 *Fml (job)* poste *m*, emploi *m*; **to take up a p.** commencer un travail, débuter dans un poste, *Fml* entrer en fonction

4 *Mil etc* poste *m; Am (permanent station)* camp *m*, fort *m*; *(garrison)* garnison *f*; **to be/die at one's p.** être/mourir à son poste; **advanced** *or* **outlying p.** *(place, group of men)* poste avancé; **lookout p.** poste de guet *ou* d'observation; **frontier p.** poste frontière

5 *Br Mil (bugle call)* **first p.** première partie *f* de la sonnerie de la retraite; **last p.** dernière partie (de la sonnerie); *(for the dead)* sonnerie *f* aux morts; **to sound the last p. (over the grave)** jouer la sonnerie aux morts

VT 1 *Br (letter) (put in the post)* mettre à la poste *ou* à la boîte, poster; *(send)* envoyer par la poste, poster; **I'll p. it to you** je vous l'enverrai par la poste, je vous le posterai

2 *Acct (in bookkeeping)* passer écriture de; *(in computerized accounts)* valider; **to p. an amount** passer un montant

3 *Fam* **I'll keep you posted** *(informed)* je vous tiendrai au courant

4 *(assign), Mil etc* désigner *ou* affecter à un commandement; *Com etc* **to be posted to a different branch** être muté dans une autre succursale; *Mil* **to be posted to a unit/a ship** être affecté à une unité/un navire

5 *Mil etc (position)* poster, placer; *(guard)* poster, placer, mettre en faction; *Fig* **she posted herself at the window** elle s'est postée à la fenêtre

▸▸**p. chaise** chaise *f* de poste; *Hist* **p. coach** (malle-)poste; **p. office** *(place)* (bureau *m* de) poste; *(service)* (service *m* des) postes *fpl*, poste; *Am (game)* = jeu *m* d'enfant dans lequel un des joueurs fait semblant de distribuer des lettres, en échange desquelles il reçoit un baiser; **the P. Office** *(government department)* ≃ la Poste; **p. office account** compte *m* chèque postal; **p. office box** boîte *f* postale; **p. office cheque** chèque *m* postal; **p. office van** ≃ camionnette *f* de la Poste

▸ **post on** **VT SEP** *(forward)* faire suivre; **I'll p. your mail on to you** je te ferai suivre ton courrier

postage ['pəʊstɪdʒ] **N** *(for mail)* affranchissement *m*, port *m*; **add 10% (for) p. and packing** ajouter 10% pour les frais d'emballage et d'expédition; **additional p.** *(on insufficiently stamped letter)* surtaxe *f* (postale); **p. included** port compris; **p. paid** port payé

▸▸**p. rates** tarifs *mpl* postaux; **p. stamp** timbre *m*, timbre-poste *m, pl* timbres-poste

postal ['pəʊst(ə)l] **ADJ 1** postal, -aux **2** *Am Fam* **to go p.** *(get angry)* péter les plombs

▸▸*Am* **p. card** carte *f* postale; **p. charges** *(system of charges)* tarifs *mpl* postaux; *(actually charged)* frais *mpl* d'envoi *ou* de port; *Br* **p. order** mandat *m* postal, mandat poste; **p. rates** tarifs *mpl* postaux; **p. services** services *mpl* postaux; *Mktg* **p. survey** enquête *f* postale

postbag ['pəʊstbæg] **N** *esp Br* sac *m* postal; *Radio, TV etc* **our p. has been heavy this week** vous avez été nombreux à nous écrire cette semaine

postbox ['pəʊstbɒks] **N** *esp Br* boîte *f* aux *ou* à lettres

postcard ['pəʊstkɑːd] **N** carte *f* postale

postcode ['pəʊstkəʊd] **N** *Br* code *m* postal

post-colonial **ADJ** post-colonial, -aux

post-colonialism **N** post-colonialisme *m*

post-colonialist **ADJ, N** post-colonialiste *mf*

postdate ['pəʊst'deɪt] **VT** postdater

postedit ['pəʊst'edɪt] **VT** *(in machine translation)* post-éditer

posted price ['pəʊstɪd] **N** prix *m* affiché

poster ['pəʊstər] **N** affiche *f*; *(decorative)* poster *m*; **to be a p. boy/girl for sth** incarner qch

▸▸*Mktg* **p. advertising** publicité *f* par affichage, publicité par voie d'affiches; *Mktg* **p. campaign** campagne *f* d'affichage; **p. paint** gouache *f*

poste restante ['pəʊstres'tɒnt] **N, ADV** *Br* poste *f* restante

posterior [pɒ'stɪərɪər] **ADJ** *Fml* postérieur (**to** à); *Anat (towards back of body)* dorsal, -aux

N *Fam Hum (person's bottom)* postérieur *m*, derrière *m*

posterity [pɒ'sterɪtɪ] **N** postérité *f*; **to preserve sth for p.** garder qch pour la postérité; **p. will remember her as ...** elle entrera dans la postérité comme ...

postern ['pəʊstɜːn] **N** poterne *f*

postgrad ['pəʊst'græd] **N** *Fam* = **postgraduate N**

postgraduate ['pəʊst'grædjʊɪt] **ADJ** *(degree, student, qualifications)* de troisième cycle; *(club)* pour les étudiants de troisième cycle **N** *(student)* étudiant, -ante de troisième cycle

▸▸**p. studies** = (études *fpl* de) troisième cycle *m*

posthaste ['pəʊst'heɪst] **ADV** en toute hâte

posthumous ['pɒstjʊməs] **ADJ** *(works)* posthume

posthumously ['pɒstjʊməslɪ] **ADV** *(to be awarded a medal)* à titre posthume; *(to publish a book, piece of music etc)* après la mort de l'auteur/du compositeur/*etc*

post-ignition **N** autoallumage *m*

postil(l)ion [pɒ'stɪlɪən] **N** postillon *m*

postimpressionism [pəʊstɪm'preʃənɪz(ə)m] **N** *Art* postimpressionnisme *m*

postimpressionist [pəʊstɪm'preʃənɪst] **ADJ, N** *Art* postimpressionniste *mf*

postindustrial [pəʊstɪn'dʌstrɪəl] **ADJ** post-industriel

posting ['pəʊstɪŋ] **N 1** *(in diplomatic service, army)* affectation *f* (à un poste); **he had been given a p. as sales manager in Eastern Europe** on l'avait envoyé en Europe de l'Est comme directeur des ventes **2** *Com (in bookkeeping)* passation *f* (d'écritures) **3** *Mil (of guards)* mise *f* en faction **4** *Br (putting in the post)* mise *f* à la boîte *ou* à la poste; *(sending by mail)* envoi *m* par la poste

▸▸**p. date** date *f* de la poste

Post-it® **N** Post-it® *m*

postman, *pl* **postmen** ['pəʊstmən] **N** facteur *m*

▸▸**p.'s knock** *(game)* ≃ mariage *m* chinois

postmark ['pəʊstmɑːk] **N** cachet *m* de la poste, (cachet d')oblitération *f*; **date as p.** cachet de la poste faisant foi

VT oblitérer; **the letter was postmarked London** la lettre était timbrée (au départ) de Londres

postmaster ['pəʊstmɑːstər] **N** receveur *m* (des postes); *Comput* maître *m* de poste

▸▸**P. General** ≃ ministre *m* des Postes et Télécommunications; *Can* ministre *m* des Postes

post meridiem [mə'rɪdɪəm] **ADV** *Fml (in the afternoon)* de l'après-midi; *(in the evening)* du soir

post-millennial **ADJ** d'après le passage au troisième millénaire

postmistress ['pəʊstmɪstrɪs] **N** receveuse *f* des postes

postmodern ['pəʊst'mɒdən] **ADJ** *Archit, Art etc* postmoderne

postmodernism ['pəʊst'mɒd(ə)nɪz(ə)m] **N** *Archit, Art etc* postmodernisme *m*

postmodernist ['pəʊst'mɒd(ə)nɪst] **ADJ, N** *Archit, Art etc* postmoderniste *mf*

postmortem ['pəʊst'mɔːtəm] **N** autopsie *f*; *Fig* analyse *f* rétrospective *ou* après coup; *Fig* **please, no postmortems** inutile de revenir sur ce qui est terminé

▸▸**p. examination** autopsie *f*; **to hold a p. examination (on)** faire une autopsie (sur)

postnatal [pəʊst'neɪt(ə)l] **ADJ** postnatal, -als *ou* -aux

▸▸**p. depression** dépression *f* postnatale

post-op **ADJ** postopératoire

N salle *f* de réveil

postoperative [pəʊst'ɒpərətɪv] **ADJ** *Med* postopératoire

post-paid **ADJ** port payé

postpartum [pəʊst'pɑːtəm] **N** *Med* postpartum *m*

postpone [pəʊst'pəʊn] **VT** *(departure, project, decision etc)* remettre, reporter, renvoyer à plus tard; *(deadline)* reculer; *Sport (match)* différer, ajourner, remettre; *(payment)* différer; **to p. a matter for a week** remettre *ou* renvoyer une affaire à huitaine; **the meeting is postponed until next week** la réunion a été remise à *ou* ajournée jusqu'à la semaine prochaine

postponement [pəʊst'pəʊnmənt] **N** *(of meeting, decision etc)* report *m*; *(of match, trial)* ajournement *m*

postposition [pəʊstpə'zɪʃən] **N** *Gram* postposition *f*

postprandial [pəʊst'prændɪəl] **ADJ** *usu Hum* après le repas; **to go for a p. stroll** faire une promenade digestive

postproduction [pəʊstprə'dʌkʃən] **N** *Cin, TV* postproduction *f*; **the film is in p.** le film est en postproduction

▸▸**p. editing** montage *m* de postproduction; **p. mixer** mélangeur *m* de postproduction; **p. studio** studio *m* de postproduction

post-purchase **ADJ** *Mktg* post-achat

▸▸**p. behaviour** comportement *m* post-achat; **p. dissonance** discordance *f* post-achat; **p. evaluation** évaluation *f* post-achat

PostScript® ['pəʊstskrɪpt] **N** *Comput* PostScript® *m*; **PostScript® font** police *f* de caractères PostScript®; **PostScript® printer** imprimante *f* PostScript®

postscript ['pəʊstskrɪpt] **N 1** *(in letter)* post-scriptum *m inv*; **by way of p.** en post-scriptum **2** *(in book)* postface *f*; *Fig (additional events)* suite *f*

post-sync(h)ing ['pəʊstsɪŋkɪŋ] **N** *TV etc* postsynchro *f*

post-synchronization **N** *TV etc* postsonorisation *f*, postsynchronisation *f*

post-test *Mktg* **N** post-test *m, pl* post-tests

VT post-tester

post-traumatic stress disorder **N** *Med* névrose *f* post-traumatique

postulant ['pɒstjʊlənt] **N** *Rel* postulant, -ante

postulate[1] ['pɒstjʊlɪt] **N** *(in logic), Math* postulat *m*

postulate[2] ['pɒstjʊleɪt] **VT 1** *(in logic), Math* postuler, poser en postulat **2** *(put forward existence of)* postuler

posture ['pɒstʃər] **N 1** posture *f*, pose *f*, attitude *f*; **to have good p.** avoir une bonne posture, bien se tenir **2** *Fig (attitude)* attitude *f*, position *f* (**on** en ce qui concerne)

VI *(physically)* poser; *(in behaviour, attitude) (show off)* se donner des airs; *(adopt position) (in negotiations, making threat etc)* user de roublardise

posturing ['pɒstʃərɪŋ] **N** *(physical)* poses *fpl*; *(in behaviour, attitude) (showing off)* affectation *f*, airs *mpl*; *(of politician, negotiator etc)* roublardise *f*

postwar ['pəʊst'wɔːr] ADJ d'après-guerre; **the p. period** l'après-guerre *m*

posy ['pəʊzɪ] N petit bouquet *m*

pot [pɒt] N **1** *(receptacle)* pot *m*; *(for cooking)* marmite *f*; *(saucepan)* casserole *f*; *Sport Sl (trophy)* coupe *f*; **pots and pans** batterie *f* de cuisine; **a p. of tea** un thé (servi dans une théière); **it's (a case of) the p. calling the kettle black** c'est l'hôpital qui se moque de la charité; *Fam* **to go to p.** *(of country, economy)* aller à la ruine; *(of hopes, chances)* tomber en poussière; **his health has gone to p.** sa santé s'est délabrée; **her marriage has gone to p.** ça ne va plus du tout avec son mari; *Sl* **he hasn't got a p. to piss in** il est complètement fauché; *Fam* **to take a p. shot at sb/sth** *(fire at)* tirer à l'aveuglette sur qn/qch; *Fig* **I'll take a p. shot at it** je vais tenter ma chance; **he took a p. shot at the answer** il a répondu au petit bonheur (la chance) *ou* au pif; **to take a p. shot at sb** lancer une critique à qn; **taking a p. shot, I'd say ...** au pif, je dirais ...
2 *Fam* **pots of...** *(a lot of)* des tas de ...; **to have pots of money** rouler sur l'or; **we have pots of time** nous avons tout le temps
3 *Sl (marijuana)* herbe *f*; *(hashish)* hasch *m*
4 *(kitty)* cagnotte *f*
5 *Fam (potbelly)* bedon *m*
6 *(potentiometer)* potentiomètre *m*
VT **(-tt-) 1** *(butter, salted meat etc)* mettre en pot; *(plant)* mettre en pot, empoter; *(baby)* mettre sur son pot; *Billiards (ball)* blouser **2** *(shoot) (rabbit, pheasant etc)* abattre
VI *(shoot)* **to p. at** *(rabbit, pheasant etc)* lâcher un coup de fusil à
▸▸ *Br* **p. plant** plante *f* d'intérieur
▸ **pot on** VT SEP *(plant)* rempoter
▸ **pot up** VT SEP *(plant)* mettre en pot, empoter

potable ['pəʊtəb(ə)l] ADJ *Fml, Hum* potable, buvable

potash ['pɒtæʃ] N potasse *f*

potassium [pə'tæsɪəm] N *Chem* potassium *m*
▸▸ **p. chloride** chlorure *m* de potassium

potato, *pl* **potatoes** [pə'teɪtəʊ, -əʊz] N pomme *f* de terre; **to dig up** *or* **lift potatoes** arracher des pommes de terre
▸▸ *Am* **p. chips,** *Br* **p. crisps** (pommes) chips *fpl*, **p. masher** presse-purée *m inv*; **p. peeler** *(tool)* éplucheur *m*, épluche-légumes *m inv*, (couteau *m*) économe *m*; *(machine)* éplucheuse *f*; **p. salad** salade *f* de pommes de terre

potbellied [pɒt'belɪd] ADJ *Fam* ventru, bedonnant

potbelly ['pɒtbelɪ] N *Fam* gros ventre *m*, bedaine *f*, bedon *m*

potboiler ['pɒtbɔɪlər] N *Fam* œuvre *f* alimentaire

poteen [pɒ'tiːn] N = whisky *m* irlandais distillé en fraude

potency ['pəʊtənsɪ] N *(of argument)* force *f*, puissance *f*; *(of medicine)* efficacité *f*, puissance; *(of alcoholic drink)* force; **sexual p.** puissance sexuelle

potent ['pəʊtənt] ADJ *(drug etc)* efficace, puissant; *(motive etc)* convaincant, décisif; *(argument)* fort, puissant; *(drink)* très fort; *(poison)* violent; *(sexually)* viril

potentate ['pəʊtənteɪt] N potentat *m*

potential [pə'tenʃəl] ADJ *Math etc* potentiel; *(danger)* possible, latent; *(enemy, criminal)* en puissance; *(client)* éventuel
N *Phys, Elec* potentiel *m*; *Gram* **the p.** le potentiel; **human p.** potentiel humain; **to reach** *or* **fulfil one's p.** atteindre son maximum; **to have p.** avoir du potentiel; **the building has a lot of** *or* **considerable p.** le bâtiment offre de grandes possibilités d'aménagement; **this idea has great p.** cette idée ouvre de grandes possibilités; **there is the p. for a major accident** tous les risques d'un grave accident sont réunis
▸▸ *Com, Mktg* **p. buyer** acheteur, -euse éventuel(elle); *Elec, Phys* **p. energy** énergie *f* potentielle; *Econ* **p. GDP** PIB *m* potentiel; **p. market** marché *m* potentiel; *Gram* **the p. mood** le potentiel; *Mktg* **p. user** utilisateur *m* potentiel

potentiality [pətenʃɪ'ælɪtɪ] N potentialité *f*

potentially [pə'tenʃəlɪ] ADV potentiellement

potentiometer [pətenʃɪ'ɒmɪtər] N potentiomètre *m*

pothead ['pɒthed] N *Sl* gros(se) fumeur, -euse de haschisch

pother ['pɒðər] N *Dial (confusion)* agitation *f*, confusion *f*; *(din)* tapage *m*, vacarme *m*

pothole ['pɒthəʊl] N *Geol* marmite *f* torrentielle *ou* de géants; *(in road)* nid *m* de poule, fondrière *f*

potholer ['pɒthəʊlər] N spéléologue *mf*

potholing ['pɒthəʊlɪŋ] N spéléologie *f*; **to go p.** faire de la spéléologie

pothook ['pɒthʊk] N *Culin* crémaillère *f*

pothunter ['pɒthʌntər] N *Sport Fam* coureur, -euse de prix

potion ['pəʊʃən] N potion *f*; **love p.** philtre *m* d'amour

potluck [pɒt'lʌk] N *Fam* **to take p.** choisir au hasard; **it was just p.** c'était un pur hasard; **come round for a meal, but you'll have to take p.** venez manger à la maison, mais ça sera à la fortune du pot

potpourri [pəʊ'pʊərɪ, -pə'riː] N *(dried flowers)* fleurs *fpl* séchées; *Mus, Liter* potpourri *m, pl* pots-pourris

pot-roast N morceau *m* de viande cuit à l'étouffée
VT cuire à l'étouffée

potsherd ['pɒtʃɜːd] N *Archeol* fragment *m* de poterie

pottage ['pɒtɪdʒ] N *Arch* potage *m* (épais); *(with meat and vegetables)* potée *f*; *Bible* **mess of p.** = plat *m* de lentilles

potted ['pɒtɪd] ADJ **1** *Culin* (conservé) en pot, en terrine; *Fam (biography etc)* abrégé, condensé **2** *Am Fam (drunk)* pété, bourré
▸▸ **p. meat** ≃ terrine *f*, **p. palm** palmier *m* en pot; **p. plant** plante *f* verte; **p. shrimps** crevettes *fpl* en conserve

potter [' pɒtər] N *Art* potier, -ière
▸▸ **p.'s clay** terre *f* de potier *ou* à potier; **p.'s wheel** tour *m* de potier

potter VI *Br* **1** *(do odd jobs)* bricoler **2** *(walk about slowly)* traîner, traînasser; **to p. down to the shops** aller faire un tour dans les magasins
▸ **potter about, potter around** VI *Br* **1** *(do odd jobs)* bricoler; **to p. about at odd jobs** bricoler, faire des petits travaux; **to p. about the house** faire des petits travaux *ou* bricoler dans la maison **2** *(move about slowly)* traîner, traînasser; **pottering about in country lanes in her car** en se baladant dans les chemins de campagne au volant de sa voiture
▸ **potter along** VI *(move slowly, work slowly)* *(of person)* aller sans se presser; *(of car)* aller doucement; **he's just pottering along** *(in life)* il va son petit bonhomme de chemin; **he just potters along** *(in job)* il avance tranquillement; **I think I'll p. along to the pub** je crois que je vais aller faire un petit tour au pub

pottery ['pɒtərɪ] N *(art, place)* poterie *f*, **a piece of p.** une poterie; **some p.** des poteries; **a p. vase** un vase en terre *ou* en poterie

potting shed ['pɒtɪŋ] N cabane *f* de jardin

potty ['pɒtɪ] ADJ *Br Fam (crazy)* toqué, timbré, dingue; **to go p.** devenir timbré *ou* dingue; **to be p. about sb/sth** être toqué de qn/qch; **you're driving me p.** tu me rends dingue, tu me fais tourner en bourrique

potty N *(in children's language)* pot *m* (de chambre) *(d'enfant)*; **to p. train one's child** apprendre à son enfant à être propre *ou* à aller sur le pot; **is she p. trained?** est-ce qu'elle est propre?
▸▸ **p. training** apprentissage *m* de la propreté

pouch [paʊtʃ] N **1** *(small bag)* (petit) sac *m*; *(for money)* bourse *f*; *(of dispatch rider, courier)* sacoche *f*; *(for ammunition)* étui *m*; **tobacco p.** blague *f* à tabac **2** *(of marsupial)* poche *f* ventrale

pouf(fe) [puːf] N *(furniture)* pouf *m*

poult [pəʊlt] N *(young chicken)* (jeune) poulet *m*; *(young turkey)* dindonneau *m*; *(young pheasant, partridge)* pouillard *m*

poulterer ['pəʊltərər] N marchand, -ande de volaille, volailler, -ère

poultice ['pəʊltɪs] N *Med* cataplasme *m*

poultry ['pəʊltrɪ] N *(no pl)* volaille *f*
▸▸ **p. dealer** marchand, -ande de volaille, volailler, -ère; **p. farm** ferme *f* de volaille *ou* de volailles; **p. farmer** éleveur, -euse de volaille *ou* de volailles, aviculteur, -trice; **p. farming** élevage de volaille *ou* de volailles, aviculture *f*

pounce [paʊns] N bond *m*; **to make a p. on** *(of bird, animal)* fondre *ou* s'abattre *ou* bondir sur; *Fam (of person)* se précipiter *ou* se jeter sur
VI **1** *(of bird, animal)* bondir, attaquer; **to p. on the prey** fondre *ou* s'abattre *ou* bondir sur la proie **2** *Fam (of person)* se précipiter, se jeter (**on** sur); *(of police etc)* faire une descente (**on** sur); *Fig* **he pounced on her mistake** il a sauté sur son erreur; **to p. on an opportunity** saisir une chance à la volée; **when the shares are low, we'll p.** quand les actions auront baissé, nous attaquerons

pound [paʊnd] N VOIR GRAMMAIRE A13 **1** *(measurement of weight)* livre *f* (= 453,6 grammes); **to sell sth by the p.** vendre qch à la livre; **40 pence a p.** quarante pence à la livre; *Fig* **to demand one's p. of flesh from sb** exiger son dû de qn
2 *(currency unit)* **p. (sterling)** livre *f* (sterling)
▸▸ *Culin* **p. cake** ≃ quatre-quarts *m inv*; **p. coin** pièce *f* d'une livre; *Hist* **p. note** billet *m* d'une livre; **p. sign** (£) symbole *m* de la livre (sterling); *Am (on telephone)* dièse *m*

pound N *(for stray animals, cars)* fourrière *f*

pound VT *Law* saisir

pound VT *(crush etc) (stones etc)* broyer, piler, concasser; *(salt, sugar, drug)* piler, broyer; *(lumps of earth)* casser, briser; *(earth)* pilonner; *(person) (with fists)* battre, rosser; *(in competition)* mettre la pâtée à; *Mil (position)* pilonner, marteler; **to p. sth to pieces** réduire qch en miettes *ou* en morceaux; **to p. sb into submission** s'acharner sur qn jusqu'à ce qu'il se soumette; **to p. the beat** *(of policeman)* patrouiller; **you'll be back to pounding the beat** *(demoted)* on vous remettra à la circulation; **to p. the streets** battre le trottoir
VI frapper *ou* taper dur; *(of heart)* battre à grands coups; *(of drum, music)* résonner; **to p. at** *or* **on sth** cogner dur sur qch; **to p. on the door** donner de grands coups sur la porte; **the waves pounded against the shore** les vagues s'abattaient *ou* se brisaient sur le rivage; **feet were heard pounding on the stairs** on entendit des pas résonner lourdement dans l'escalier; **she pounded down the road after them** elle s'élança derrière eux sur la route

▸**pound along** VI they're really pounding along ils vont à fond de train; he was pounding along after them ils les poursuivait à toute allure

▸**pound away** VI (of waves) se briser (at, against sur); we heard the guns pounding away nous entendions le bruit incessant des canons; the guns pounded away at their position les canons pilonnaient sans relâche leur position; he sat pounding away at the piano il martelait le piano, il jouait du piano comme un forcené; he was pounding away at the typewriter il tapait comme un fou sur la machine à écrire

poundage ['paʊndɪdʒ] N **1** (weight) poids m en livres **2** (tax, commission) taxe f/commission f proportionnelle au poids/à la valeur

-pounder ['paʊndər] SUFF two/three-p. (fish) poisson m de deux/de trois livres (de poids); Mil thirty-p. canon m ou pièce f de trente

pounding ['paʊndɪŋ] N (of heart) battement m frénétique; (of drums) battement; the p. of the waves le martèlement des vagues; to take a p. (of boat) être fortement secoué; (of troops, city etc) être pilonné; Fig (of team etc) être battu à plate(s) couture(s); Fig the economy has taken quite a p. l'économie a subi des coups de boutoir; Fig the euro took a p. l'euro a été attaqué

POUR [pɔːr] VT verser (into dans); Metal couler; to p. sb a drink verser un verre à qn; p. the water down the sink versez l'eau dans l'évier; Fig the government poured money into the industry le gouvernement a investi des sommes énormes dans l'industrie; Fig she looked as if she'd been poured into her jeans elle portait un jean extrêmement moulant

VI **1** it's pouring (with rain), the rain's pouring down il pleut à verse, la pluie tombe à torrents; there were tears pouring down her cheeks son visage était baigné de larmes; blood was pouring from the cut on her forehead le sang s'écoulait en abondance de l'entaille qu'elle avait au front; the sunlight poured into the room les rayons du soleil inondaient la pièce; water was pouring into the cellar l'eau entrait à flots dans la cave; sweat was pouring off him il ruisselait de sueur; reinforcements poured in to the area des renforts sont arrivés en masse dans la région; tourists were pouring into the palace les touristes entraient en foule dans le palais

2 this jug doesn't p. well ce broc ne verse pas bien; shall I p.? puis-je faire le service?

▸**pour down** VI (of rain) tomber à verse; it's been pouring down for days il pleut à verse depuis des jours et des jours

▸**pour in** VI (of water) se déverser, entrer à flots; the crowd came pouring in on entrait à flots ou en foule; invitations came pouring in ça a été une avalanche d'invitations

VT SEP (liquid) verser; Fig the government poured money in le gouvernement a investi des sommes énormes

▸**pour off** VT SEP vider

▸**pour out** VI (of water) se déverser, sortir à flots; (of people) sortir en foule; smoke was pouring out of the window des nuages de fumée s'échappaient de la fenêtre; the words just poured out les mots sont sortis en flots; all his feelings came pouring out il a laissé libre cours à ses émotions

VT SEP (tea, coffee etc) verser; (anger, feelings) donner libre cours à; (of chimney) (clouds of smoke) cracher, vomir; Fig he poured out all his frustrations to me il m'a déballé toutes ses frustrations; to p. out a torrent of abuse at sb déverser un torrent d'injures sur qn; she poured out her feelings to me elle m'a ouvert son cœur; Japanese

products are being poured out onto the market les produits japonais inondent le marché

pouring ['pɔːrɪŋ] ADJ (rain) torrentiel

pout [paʊt] N moue f

VI faire la moue; (sulk) bouder; her pouting lips ses lèvres boudeuses

pouter ['paʊtər] N (pigeon) pigeon m boulant

▸▸ **p. pigeon** pigeon boulant

POV [piːəʊ'viː] N TV, Cin (abbr point of view) angle m du regard

poverty ['pɒvətɪ] N **1** pauvreté f; extreme or abject p. misère f; to live in p. vivre dans la gêne ou ultima la misère **2** (lack) (of food etc) disette f, manque m, pénurie f; (poor quality) (of soil) pauvreté f; p. of ideas pénurie f d'idées

▸▸ **p. line** seuil m de pauvreté; to live below the p. line vivre en-dessous du seuil de pauvreté; **p. trap** = situation f inextricable de ceux qui dépendent de prestations sociales qu'ils perdent pour peu qu'ils trouvent une activité, même très peu rémunérée

poverty-stricken ADJ (person) indigent, réduit à la misère; (dwelling, area etc) misérable; a. p. country un pays souffrant de la misère

POW [piːəʊ'dʌb(ə)ljuː] N (abbr prisoner of war) prisonnier m de guerre

powder ['paʊdər] N poudre f, (gunpowder) poudre, explosif m; to reduce sth to p. réduire qch en poudre, pulvériser qch; Fig (destroy) réduire qch en poussière ou en miettes; (face) p. poudre (de riz); Am Sl to take a p. (disappear) ficher le camp

VT **1** (cake etc) saupoudrer (with de); a landscape powdered with snow un paysage saupoudré de neige; to p. one's face se poudrer (le visage); Fam Euph to go and p. one's nose aller se laver les mains **2** (convert to powder) (milk etc) réduire en poudre

▸▸ **p. blue** bleu m pastel; **p. compact** poudrier m; **p. keg** (of gunpowder) baril m de poudre; Fig poudrière f; **p. puff** houppette f; Euph **p. room** toilettes fpl (pour dames)

powdered ['paʊdəd] ADJ **1** (milk etc) en poudre; (coal etc) pulvérisé; in p. form sous forme de poudre **2** (face) poudré

powdery ['paʊd(ə)rɪ] ADJ poudreux; (crumbly) friable

POWER ['paʊər]

| N pouvoir **1, 2, 6** ▪ faculté **2** ▪ force **3** ▪ puissance **3, 4, 8, 9** ▪ courant **7** |
| VT faire marcher |

N **1** Pol etc (authority, control) pouvoir m, autorité f; to come (in)to p. arriver au pouvoir; to be in/out of p. être/ne pas être au pouvoir; to lose p. perdre le pouvoir; the party in p. le parti au pouvoir; to be voted into/out of p. être nommé au pouvoir/chassé du pouvoir par un vote; to be in sb's p. être à la merci de qn; also Fig to be the real p. behind the throne tirer les ficelles; also Hum the powers that be les autorités fpl; Rel the powers of darkness les puissances des ténèbres; to have sb in one's p. avoir qn à sa merci; absolute/executive/legislative p. pouvoir absolu/exécutif/législatif; they constitute his p. base ils constituent le groupe d'où il tire son pouvoir

2 (capacity) pouvoir m; to have the p. to do sth avoir le pouvoir ou la faculté de faire qch; I'll do everything in my p. je ferai tout ce qui est en mon pouvoir ou tout mon possible; it is beyond my p. ce n'est pas en mon pouvoir; to be at the height or peak of one's powers être à l'apogée de sa puissance; her powers were failing her les forces lui manquaient; mental or intellectual powers fa-

cultés fpl intellectuelles; a man of great mental or intellectual powers un homme doté de grandes facultés intellectuelles; Phys, Chem p. of absorption capacité f d'absorption; p. of observation facultés d'observation; the p. of reason (faculty) la raison; (strength, force) la puissance de la raison; the p. of speech (faculty) la parole; (force) le pouvoir de la parole; powers of concentration facultés de concentration; powers of persuasion dons mpl de persuasion

3 (physical strength) force f, puissance f; Fam more p. to your elbow! allez-y!

4 (nation etc) puissance f, sea/air/industrial/nuclear/world p. (country) puissance maritime/aérienne/industrielle/nucléaire/mondiale; the great powers (countries) les grandes puissances

5 Fam that'll do you a p. of good ça vous fera énormément de bien

6 Law procuration f, mandat m, pouvoir m; p. of life and death droit m de vie et de mort; Law delegation of powers délégation f de pouvoirs; Law to furnish sb with full powers donner pleins pouvoirs à qn; to act with full powers agir de pleine autorité; the police have been given greater powers la police a reçu des pouvoirs plus importants

7 (electricity) courant m; nuclear/wind/hydroelectric p. énergie f nucléaire/éolienne/hydroélectrique; to shut off/turn on the p. couper/mettre le courant

8 Tech (of machine etc) puissance f, (of magnet) force f, Tech etc full p. puissance maximale

9 Math (of a number) puissance f, three to the p. of ten trois (à la) puissance dix

VT (provide with power) (machine) actionner, faire marcher; (propel) propulser; powered by two engines actionné par deux moteurs

VI Fam (move fast) he powered round the bend il avala la courbe à toute allure; she powered into the lead elle accéléra et prit la tête de la course; the rocket powered up into the sky la fusée s'éleva vers le ciel

▸▸ **p. amplifier** amplificateur m de puissance; Law **p. of attorney** procuration f, to give sb p. of attorney donner procuration à qn; Aut **p. box** (for airbag) boîtier m d'alimentation; Aut **p. brakes** freins mpl assistés; **p. broker** décideur, -euse politique; **p. cut** coupure f de courant; Br **p. dressing** = façon f de s'habiller qu'adoptent certaines femmes cadres dans le but de projeter une image d'autorité; she goes in for p. dressing elle s'habille pour donner une image imposante; Tech **p. driven** à propulsion mécanique; **p. failure** panne f de courant; **p. line** ligne f à haute tension; **p. lunch** déjeuner m d'affaires entre personnes importantes; Am **p. outage** rupture f de l'alimentation; Elec **p. pack** bloc m d'alimentation électrique; **p. plant** (factory) centrale f électrique; (generator) groupe m électrogène; (engine) groupe moteur; **p. point** prise f de courant; **p. politics** politique f du coup de force; Comput **p. save mode** mode m repos; **p. station** centrale (électrique); Aut **p. steering** direction f assistée; **p. strike** grève f des employés de l'électricité; Aut **p. stroke** temps m explosion ou détente; **p. structure** (system) hiérarchie f, répartition f des pouvoirs; (people with power) = ensemble m des personnes qui détiennent le pouvoir; **p. struggle** lutte f pour le pouvoir; **p. supply** Elec alimentation f (électrique); Comput transformateur m; **p. switch** bouton m marche-arrêt; **p. tool** outil m électrique; Comput **p. unit** dispositif m d'alimentation; **p. user** gros utilisateur, grosse utilisatrice; Comput = personne f qui sait utiliser au mieux les ressources de son ordinateur

▸**power down** VT SEP mettre hors tension

VI *(of computer, machine)* se mettre hors tension

▸ **power up VT SEP** mettre sous tension
VI *(of computer, machine)* se mettre sous tension, s'allumer

power-assisted [-əsɪstɪd] **ADJ** *Aut (steering)* assisté

power-down **N** *Comput* mise *f* hors tension

-powered ['paʊəd] **SUFF** nuclear-p. à propulsion atomique *ou* nucléaire

powerful ['paʊəfʊl] **ADJ 1** puissant; *(blow)* grand; *(argument, incentive)* puissant, de poids; *(language, prose style)* vigoureux, qui a de l'impact; *(music, passage)* puissant, plein de vigueur; *(speaker, actor)* qui a de la présence, qui en impose; **to become more p.** *(of State, ruler)* devenir plus puissant; *(of hurricane etc)* augmenter en puissance; **p. dose** *(of drug)* forte dose; **a p. new novel/film** un nouveau roman/film très puissant *ou* fort; **a p. image** une image chargée de force, une image-choc; **there's a p. smell of cats in here** ça pue les chats ici
2 *Old-fashioned Fam* **a p. lot of …** un tas de …
ADV *esp Am Fam* **I was p. tired** j'étais rudement fatigué

powerfully ['paʊəfʊlɪ] **ADV** puissamment; *(influenced, affected)* fortement; *(to argue)* vigoureusement; **p. built** *(man)* à forte carrure; **it smells p. of cabbage** ça sent le chou à plein nez

powerhouse ['paʊəhaʊs] **N** *Elec* centrale *f* électrique; *Fam (person)* personne *f* vigoureuse et dynamique; **she's the p. of the organization** c'est le moteur de l'organisation; **he's a p. of new ideas** il ne tarit pas d'idées nouvelles

powerless ['paʊəlɪs] **ADJ** impuissant; **in a p. state** dans un état d'impuissance totale; **p. to act** impuissant à agir; **I am p. to help you** je ne peux *ou* *Fml* puis rien faire pour vous aider

power-on key **N** *Br Comput* touche *f* d'alimentation

powertrain ['paʊətreɪn] **N** *Aut* groupe *m* motopropulseur

power-up **N** *(of computer, machine)* mise *f* sous tension; **on p.** à la mise sous tension

powwow ['paʊwaʊ] **N** *(of American Indians)* assemblée *f*, *Fam (talk, discussion)* palabre *f*, discussion *f*
VI *(of American Indians)* tenir une assemblée; *Fam (talk)* palabrer; *Fam* **to p. about sth** discuter de qch

pox [pɒks] **N** *Med Fam* **the p.** la vérole; *Arch* **a p. on …!** maudit soit …!/maudits soient …!

poxy ['pɒksɪ] **ADJ** *Br Sl (worthless)* merdique; *(unpleasant)* dégueulasse; **he only gave me a p. five pounds for it** il me l'a acheté cinq malheureuses livres

pp [1] [piːˈpiː] *(abbr* **per procurationem)** **ADV** pp **Jane Smith** p.p. Jane Smith
VT shall I pp it? est-ce que je signe à votre/sa place?

pp [2] *(abbr* **pages)** pp; **see pp 44–47** voir pp 44 à 47

p & p [piːənˈpiː] **N** *Br Com (abbr* **postage and packing)** port *m* et emballage

PPB [piːpiːˈbiː] **N** *Acct (abbr* **planning-programming-budgeting system)** système *m* de planification-programmation-budgétisation, rationalisation *f* des choix budgétaires

PPD [piːpiːˈdiː] **N** *Com (abbr* **prepaid)** port payé par le destinataire

PPE [piːpiːˈiː] **N** *Univ (abbr* **philosophy, politics and economics)** études *fpl* de philosophie, sciences politiques et économie

ppi [piːpiːˈaɪ] **N** *Comput (abbr* **pixels per inch)** ppp *mpl*

ppm [piːpiːˈem] **N** *Comput (abbr* **pages per minute)** ppm

PPP [piːpiːˈpiː] **N 1** *Comput (abbr* **point-to-point protocol)** protocole *m* PPP, protocole point à point **2** *(abbr* **public-private partnership)** partenariat *m* public-privé

pps [piːpiːˈes] **N** *(abbr* **post postscriptum)** pps

PQ [piːˈkjuː] **N** *Can* **1** *abbr* **Province of Quebec** **2** *abbr* **Parti québécois**

PR [piːˈɑːr] **N 1** *(abbr* **public relations)** relations *fpl* publiques, RP *fpl*; **we need better PR** il nous faut améliorer nos relations publiques; **a skilful PR man** un homme qui excelle dans les relations publiques **2** *Pol (abbr* **proportional representation)** RP *f*
▸▸ **PR agency** agence *f* conseil en communication; **PR company** société *f* conseil en communication; **PR consultancy** agence conseil en communication; **PR consultant** conseil *m* en communication

practicability [præktɪkəˈbɪlɪtɪ] **N** faisabilité *f*, *(of road etc)* praticabilité *f*

practicable ['præktɪkəb(ə)l] **ADJ 1** *(feasible)* faisable, réalisable; **as far as is p.** autant que possible **2** *(road, ford)* praticable

practical ['præktɪk(ə)l] **ADJ 1** *(mind, solution, clothing, appliance)* pratique; *(proposition)* réalisable; **he's very p.** il a l'esprit pratique; **we must be p.** il faut que nous soyons raisonnables; **the p. thing to do would be to …** il serait raisonnable de …; **I know it's a very boring and p. question** je sais que c'est une question très ennuyeuse et pragmatique; **for all p. purposes** en fin de compte; **of no p. use** *or* **value** inutilisable dans la pratique; **p. application** *(of theory etc)* mise *f* en pratique; *(of invention etc)* réalisation *f* (pratique)
2 *(virtual)* **with p. unanimity** d'un consentement presque unanime; **it's a p. certainty** c'est quasiment certain
N *Sch (lesson)* travaux *mpl* dirigés *ou* pratiques; *(examination)* épreuve *f* pratique
▸▸ **p. joke** farce *f*, **p. joker** farceur, -euse; *Sch* **p. work** travaux dirigés *ou* pratiques

practicality [præktɪˈkælɪtɪ] **N 1** *(feasibility)* aspect *m* pratique, caractère *m* pratique **2** *(of person)* sens *m* *ou* esprit *m* pratique **3** **practicalities** *(details)* détails *mpl* *ou* aspects *mpl* pratiques

practically ['præktɪklɪ] **ADV 1** *(based)* sur la pratique; *(useful)* dans la pratique, en pratique; **to be p. minded** avoir un esprit pratique; **p. speaking** en pratique **2** *(almost)* pour ainsi dire, pratiquement; **there has been p. no snow** il n'y a presque pas *ou* pratiquement pas eu de neige; **p. the whole of the audience** la quasi-totalité de l'auditoire; **we're p. there** nous y sommes presque, nous sommes pratiquement arrivés

practice ['præktɪs] **N 1** *(action)* pratique *f*; **to put one's ideas into p.** mettre ses idées en pratique; **in p.** en *ou* dans la pratique
2 *(of profession etc)* exercice *m*; *(of doctor etc) (surgery)* cabinet *m*; *(patients)* clientèle *f*, *(of solicitor)* étude *f*; **to be in p.** *(of doctor etc)* exercer; **to set up in** *or* **go into p.** commencer à exercer
3 *(custom)* coutume *f*, usage *m*; *Ind etc* technique *f*, méthodes *fpl*; **to make a p. of doing sth** se faire une habitude *ou* une règle de faire qch; **it's the usual p.** c'est l'usage; **in hospitals it's standard p. to throw needles away** dans les hôpitaux, la règle est de jeter les seringues usagées; **it's good/bad p. to do this** il est conseillé *ou* recommandé/déconseillé de faire cela
4 *(exercise, training)* exercice(s) *m(pl)*; *Sport etc* entraînement *m*; **it takes years of p.** cela demande des années de pratique *ou*

Sport etc d'entraînement; **I don't get much p.** *(at driving, playing sport, music etc)* je ne m'exerce pas souvent; **I need more p.** j'ai besoin de plus de pratique *ou Sport etc* de m'entraîner davantage; **to do 2 hours' p. a day** s'entraîner *ou* s'exercer deux heures par jour; **to keep in p.** continuer à s'exercer; *Sport* se maintenir en forme; **I have to get back into p.** il faut que je m'y remette; **to get out of p.** perdre l'habitude *ou* la main, se rouiller; **I'm out of p.** je manque de pratique; *Sport* **Schumacher did 3.25 in p.** Schumacher a fait 3 mn. 25 aux essais; **he refuses to do his piano p.** il refuse de travailler son piano; *Prov* **p. makes perfect** c'est en forgeant qu'on devient forgeron
VT & VI *Am* = **practise**
▸▸ *Sport* **p. match** match *m* d'entraînement

practiced, practicing **ADJ** *Am* = **practised, practising**

practise, *Am* **practice** ['præktɪs] **VT 1** *(carry out) (witchcraft, self-denial etc)* pratiquer; *(method)* suivre; *(principle etc)* mettre en pratique *ou* en action; **to p. what one preaches** mettre en pratique ce que l'on prêche; **to p. a custom** suivre une coutume
2 *(work at) (profession)* pratiquer, exercer; *(medicine)* exercer; *Law* **to p. law** exercer le métier de notaire/d'avocat; **he studied law/medicine, but never practised in it** il a étudié le droit/la médecine, mais n'a jamais exercé
3 *(do exercises etc on) (the piano, flute etc)* travailler, s'exercer à; *Tennis, Billiards etc (shot)* s'exercer à; **to p. one's backhand** travailler son revers; *Mus* **to p. one's scales** faire des gammes; **to p. one's French** pratiquer son français (**on sb** avec qn)
VI 1 *(of doctor, lawyer)* exercer **2** *(do exercises etc)* s'exercer; *Sport* s'entraîner

practised, *Am* **practiced** ['præktɪst] **ADJ** *(teacher, nurse, speaker etc)* expérimenté; *(ear, eye)* exercé; *Pej (charm)* étudié, compassé; **with a p. hand** d'une main exercée *ou* habile; **with p. ease** avec une grande aisance; **p. in the arts of seduction/deception** rompu aux arts de la séduction/tromperie

practising, *Am* **practicing** ['præktɪsɪŋ] **ADJ** *(doctor, solicitor etc)* en exercice; *(Christian, Catholic)* pratiquant; **a p. homosexual** un homosexuel actif, une homosexuelle active

practitioner [prækˈtɪʃənər] **N** médecin, *Fml* praticien, -ienne; **a skilled p. of acupuncture/osteopathy** un acupuncteur/ostéopathe exercé

praetorian [priːˈtɔːrɪən] **ADJ**
▸▸ *Hist, Fig* **p. guard** garde *f* prétorienne

pragmatic [prægˈmætɪk] **ADJ** pragmatique

pragmatism ['prægmətɪz(ə)m] **N** pragmatisme *m*

pragmatist ['prægmətɪst] **N** pragmatiste *mf*

prairie ['preərɪ] **N** *(North American)* prairie *f*, **the Prairies** les Prairies
▸▸ *Zool* **p. dog** chien *m* de prairie; **p. oyster** *(drink)* = boisson *f* à base d'œuf cru *(remède contre les excès d'alcool)*, *(offal)* = délices *mpl* de brebis; *Zool* **p. wolf** coyote *m*

praise [preɪz] **N** *(deserved)* éloge(s) *m(pl)*, louange(s) *f(pl)*, *(adulatory or in worship)* louange(s); **in p. of sb/sth** à la louange de qn/qch; **to be full of p. for sb/sth** ne pas tarir d'éloges sur qn/qch; **to sing the praises of sth/sb** chanter *ou* célébrer les louanges de qch/qn; **to sing one's own praises** chanter ses propres louanges, faire son propre éloge; **I have nothing but p. for him** je n'ai rien pour lui que des éloges *ou* louanges; **she deserves special p.** elle mérite tous les éloges *ou* toutes les louanges; **his conduct is beyond all p.** sa conduite est au-dessus de tout éloge; *Arch* **p. be (to God)!** Dieu soit loué!

VT louer, faire l'éloge de; **to p. sb to the skies** porter qn aux nues; **to p. God** louer *ou* glorifier Dieu

praiseworthiness ['preɪzwɜ:ðɪnɪs] **N** mérite *m*, valeur *f*

praiseworthy ['preɪzwɜ:ðɪ] **ADJ** digne d'éloges, louable, méritoire; **that was very p. of you** c'est très louable de votre part

praline ['prɑ:li:n] **N** *Culin* **1** *(filling)* pralin *m* **2** *(sweet) (almond)* amande *f* pralinée, praline *f*

pram [præm] **N** *Br* landau *m*, voiture *f* d'enfant

prance [prɑ:ns] **VI 1** *(of horse)* caracoler; **a prancing horse** un cheval fringant **2** *(of person) (to strut)* se pavaner; *(to skip)* avancer en sautillant; **to p. in/out** entrer/sortir en se pavanant/en sautillant; **she pranced in and calmly announced that …** elle est entrée d'un pas léger et a annoncé calmement que …
▸ **prance about** **VI** *(of horse)* caracoler; *(of person)* se pavaner

prang [præŋ] *Br Fam* **N** **to have a p.** *(in car)* avoir un accrochage
VT *(aeroplane, car)* amocher

prank [præŋk] **N** *(escapade)* frasque *f*, fredaine *f*, *(practical joke)* tour *m*, farce *f*, **to get up to all sorts of pranks** faire les cent coups; **to play pranks on sb** jouer des tours à qn, faire des farces à qn

prankster ['præŋkstər] **N** farceur, -euse

prat [præt] **N** *Br Sl (idiot)* andouille *f*, imbécile *mf*; **I feel like a right p.** j'ai vraiment l'air d'une andouille *ou* d'un imbécile
▸ **prat about, prat around** **VI** *Br Sl (act foolishly)* faire l'idiot; *(waste time)* glander, glandouiller

prate [preɪt] **VI** *Pej (self-importantly)* débiter des niaiseries *ou* des absurdités; *(chatter)* jaser, bavarder

pratfall ['prætfɔ:l] **N** *Am* **to do a p.** tomber sur les fesses; *Fig* se planter

prattish ['prætɪʃ] **ADJ** crétin, idiot

prattle ['præt(ə)l] **N** *(of children)* babil *m*, babillage *m*; *(of busybodies)* bavardage *m*, papotage *m*
VI *(talk nonsense) (of child)* babiller; *(of adult)* jacasser; *(converse)* bavarder, papoter (**to** avec); **they never stop prattling to one another about …** ils n'arrêtent pas de bavarder *ou* de papoter ensemble à propos de …

prawn [prɔ:n] **N** crevette *f* (rose); *(bigger)* bouquet *m*; **Dublin Bay p.** langoustine *f*; *Austr Fam* **don't come the raw p. with me!** n'essaie pas de m'embobiner!
▸▸ **p. cocktail** cocktail *m* de crevettes; **p. crackers** beignets *mpl* de crevettes

pray [preɪ] **VI 1** prier; **to p. to God** prier Dieu; **to p. for sb** prier pour qn; **to p. for** *(peace, person's safety etc)* prier pour; **they're praying for a child** ils prient pour avoir un enfant; **to p. for rain/good weather** prier pour qu'il pleuve/pour qu'il fasse beau; **to p. for sb's soul** prier pour (le repos de) l'âme de qn; **I've been praying for you to say that** j'espérais de tout mon cœur que tu dises cela; *Fam* **he's past praying for** il est perdu
2 *Arch* **p. be seated** veuillez (bien) vous asseoir; *Lit, Iron* **and what, p., would you have me say?** et que voudrais-tu donc que je dise?; *Lit, Iron* **and what, p., would you suggest I do?** et que suggérerais-tu donc que je fasse?
VT **I prayed that they wouldn't hear me** j'ai prié pour qu'ils ne m'entendent pas; **I p. we are on time** je prie pour que nous arrivions à l'heure

prayer [preər] **N** prière *f*; **p. for the dead** prière pour les morts; **to say one's prayers** faire *ou* dire *ou* réciter ses prières; *Sch* **prayers** la prière du matin en commun; *Church of Eng* **Morning/Evening P.** office *m* du matin/du soir; **his p. was granted** sa prière a été exaucée; **they knelt in p.** ils se sont agenouillés pour prier; **his head was bowed in p.** sa tête était inclinée dans une prière; *Fam* **he doesn't have a p.** il n'a aucune chance
▸▸ **p. beads** chapelet *m*; **p. book** livre *m* de prières; **p. mat** tapis *m* à prières; **p. meeting** réunion *f* de prière; **p. wheel** moulin *m* à prières

praying ['preɪɪŋ] **ADJ** en prières
N prière(s) *f(pl)*
▸▸ *Entom* **p. mantis** mante *f* religieuse

pre- [pri:] **PREF** pré-

preach [pri:tʃ] **VI** prêcher; **to p. to sb** prêcher qn; *Fig* **to p. to the converted** prêcher un converti; **to p. against sb** prêcher contre qn; *Fig Fam* **he's always preaching at me** il est toujours à me faire la leçon *ou* à me sermonner; **stop preaching!** arrête ton sermon!
VT *(sermon)* prononcer; **to p. a new doctrine** prêcher une doctrine nouvelle; **she preaches austerity and lives in luxury** elle prêche l'austérité mais elle vit dans le luxe

preacher ['pri:tʃər] **N** prédicateur *m*; *Am (clergyman)* pasteur *m*; *Fig Pej* prêcheur, -euse; **he's a poor p.** il prêche mal

preachify ['pri:tʃɪfaɪ] **VI** *Fam Pej* faire la morale

preaching ['pri:tʃɪŋ] **ADJ** prêcheur, -euse
N prédication *f*, *Fig Pej* sermons *mpl*

preachy ['pri:tʃɪ] **ADJ** *Fam Pej* prêcheur, -euse, sermonneur, -euse

preamble [pri:'æmb(ə)l] **N 1** *Fml (to legal text)* préambule *m*; *(of book)* introduction *f*, préface *f*, *(of treaty)* préliminaires *mpl*; *(to speech)* préambule, entrée *f* en matière **2** *Law (of bill)* exposé *m*

preamplifier [pri:'æmplɪfaɪər] **N** préamplificateur *m*

prearrange [pri:ə'reɪndʒ] **VT** arranger au préalable *ou* d'avance; **at a prearranged signal** sur un signal convenu

prebend ['prebənd] **N** *Rel (stipend)* prébende *f*, *(person)* prébendier *m*

prebendary ['prebənd(ə)rɪ] **N** *Rel* prébendier *m*

prebill [pri:'bɪl] **VT** *Acct* préfacturer

prebilling [pri:'bɪlɪŋ] **N** *Acct* préfacturation *f*

pre-board **VT** *(unaccompanied children etc)* pré-embarquer

precancerous ['pri:'kænsərəs] **ADJ** précancéreux

precarious [prɪ'keərɪəs] **ADJ** précaire; **to make a p. living** gagner sa vie précairement; **a p. life** une vie précaire

precariously [prɪ'keərɪəslɪ] **ADV** précairement; **p. balanced** dans un équilibre précaire

precariousness [prɪ'keərɪəsnɪs] **N** précarité *f*

precast ['pri:kɑ:st] **ADJ** *(concrete)* prémoulé

precaution [prɪ'kɔ:ʃən] **N** *(act)* précaution *f*, *(attitude)* prévoyance *f*; **to take precautions** prendre des précautions (**against sth** contre qch); *(use contraceptive)* se protéger; **despite all our precautions** en dépit de toutes les précautions que nous avions prises; **as a p.** par mesure de précaution

precautionary [prɪ'kɔ:ʃən(ə)rɪ] **ADJ** *(measure)* préventif (**against** contre)

precede [prɪ'si:d] **VT 1** *(in time)* précéder; **the conference was preceded by a reception** une réception a eu lieu avant la conférence; **she preceded me as secretary** elle m'a précédé au poste de secrétaire **2** *(in space)* précéder, être devant **3** *(take precedence over)* avoir le pas *ou* la préséance sur

precedence ['presɪdəns] **N** *(in rank)* préséance *f*, *(in priority etc)* priorité *f*; **in order of p.** par ordre de préséance; **to have** *or* **take p. over sb** avoir le pas *ou* la préséance sur qn, prendre le pas sur qn; **a duty that takes p. over all others** un devoir qui prime tout; **this job takes p. over everything else** ce travail est à faire en priorité

precedent ['presɪdənt] **N 1** précédent *m*; **to create** *or* **set a p.** créer un précédent; **to break with p.** rompre avec la tradition; **there's no p. for it** il n'y en a pas d'exemple; **according to p.** conformément à la tradition; **without p.** sans précédent **2** *Law* décision *f* judiciaire faisant jurisprudence; **to set p.** faire jurisprudence

preceding [prɪ'si:dɪŋ] **ADJ** précédent; **the p. day** la veille; **in the p. article/chapter** dans l'article/le chapitre ci-avant

precentor [prɪ'sentər] **N** *Rel* maître *m* de chapelle

precept ['pri:sept] **N** précepte *m*

pre-check-in **N** préinscription *f*

precinct ['pri:sɪŋkt] **N 1** *(enclosed area)* enceinte *f*, enclos *m*; **precincts** *(of cathedral etc)* enceinte, enclos; **(shopping) p.** centre *m* commercial *(fermé à la circulation automobile)* **2** *(boundary)* **within the precincts of** dans l'enceinte de **3** *Am (electoral district)* circonscription *f* électorale; *(police district)* circonscription administrative

preciosity [preʃɪ'ɒsɪtɪ] **N** *Fml* préciosité *f*

precious ['preʃəs] **ADJ** *(metals, stones)*, *Pej (affected)* précieux; **we wasted a lot of p. time** nous avons perdu un temps précieux; **a few p. drops of water** quelques précieuses gouttes d'eau; **that photo is very p. to me** je tiens beaucoup à cette photo; *Fam Iron* **you and your p. project!** toi et ton sacré projet!
N *(term of endearment)* **my p.!** mon trésor!, mon amour!
ADV *Fam* **there are p. few of them** il y en a très peu; **there's p. little chance of that happening** il y a très peu de chances que cela se produise
▸▸ **p. stones** *(in raw state)* pierres *fpl* précieuses; *(cut)* pierreries *fpl*, pierres précieuses

precipice ['presɪpɪs] **N** précipice *m*; **to fall over a p.** tomber dans un précipice

precipitance [prɪ'sɪpɪtəns], **precipitancy** [prɪ'sɪpɪtənsɪ] **N** *Fml (suddenness, abruptness)* précipitation *f*, *(haste)* empressement *m*; *(rashness)* irréflexion *f*

precipitant [prɪ'sɪpɪtənt] **ADJ** = **precipitate¹ ADJ**
N *Chem* précipitant *m*

precipitate¹ [prɪ'sɪpɪtɪt] **N** *Chem* précipité *m*; **to form a p.** (se) précipiter
ADJ *Fml (sudden, abrupt, hasty)* précipité; **let's not be p.** ne précipitons pas les choses

> Attention: ne pas confondre avec **pre-cipitous**.

precipitate² [prɪ'sɪpɪteɪt] **VT 1** *(hasten)* *(crisis, person's downfall)*, *Chem (solid substance)* précipiter; **to p. a war/an argument** faire éclater une guerre/une dispute; **to p. matters** précipiter *ou* hâter les choses **2** *(throw)* précipiter
VI *Chem* (se) précipiter; *Met* se condenser

precipitately [prɪ'sɪpɪtɪtlɪ] **ADV** précipitamment

precipitation [prɪsɪpɪ'teɪʃən] **N 1** *Chem* précipitation *f*, *Met* précipitations; *Met* **annual p.** précipitations annuelles **2** *Fml* *(haste)* **to act with p.** agir avec précipitation *ou* précipitamment

precipitous [prɪˈsɪpɪtəs] ADJ **1** *(steep)* escarpé, abrupt; *(sheer)* à pic **2** *(hasty) (departure etc)* précipité

> Attention: ne pas confondre avec **precipitate.**

precipitously [prɪˈsɪpɪtəslɪ] ADV **1** *(steeply) (to rise, fall)* à pic **2** *(hastily)* précipitamment

précis, *pl* **précis** [ˈpreɪsiː, ˈpreɪsiːz] N résumé *m*

VT faire un résumé de
▸▸ **p. writing** compte rendu *m* de lecture

precise [prɪˈsaɪs] ADJ **1** *(exact) (orders, movements, ideas, details)* précis; **there were a few people, five to be p.** il y avait quelques personnes, cinq pour être précis; **at the p. moment when ...** au moment précis où ..., juste au moment où ... **2** *(person) (meticulous); (punctilious)* pointilleux, formaliste

precisely [prɪˈsaɪslɪ] ADV *(to cost, number etc)* précisément, exactement; *(to describe, draw etc)* avec précision; **at six (o'clock) p.** à six heures précises; **p.!** précisément!, exactement!; **that's p. why** c'est précisément pour ça

preciseness [prɪˈsaɪsnɪs] N **1** *(of figure, calculation etc)* précision *f* **2** *(of person) (meticulousness)* méticulosité *f*, *(punctiliousness)* formalisme *m*

precision [prɪˈsɪʒ(ə)n] N précision *f*, **with mathematical p.** avec une précision (toute) mathématique
▸▸ *Mil* **p. bombing** bombardement *m* de précision; **p. engineering** mécanique *f* de précision; **p. instruments** instruments *mpl* de précision; **p. tools** instruments de précision; **p. work** travail *m* de précision

precision-engineered [-endʒɪˈnɪəd] ADJ de haute précision

precision-made ADJ de (haute) précision

preclude [prɪˈkluːd] VT *esp Fml (objection, misunderstanding)* prévenir, empêcher; **to p. sb from doing sth, to p. sb's doing sth** empêcher qn de faire qch

precocious [prɪˈkəʊʃəs] ADJ précoce

precociously [prɪˈkəʊʃəslɪ] ADV précocement, avec précocité

precociousness [prɪˈkəʊʃəsnɪs], **precocity** [prɪˈkɒsɪtɪ] N précocité *f*

precognition [priːkɒgˈnɪʃən] N *Phil etc* connaissance *f* anticipée *ou* antérieure

precombustion [priːkəmˈbʌstʃən] N précombustion *f*

preconceive [priːkənˈsiːv] VT préconcevoir; **preconceived idea** idée *f* préconçue

preconception [priːkənˈsepʃən] N idée *f* *ou* opinion *f* préconçue; *(prejudice)* préjugé *m*; **to free oneself from all preconceptions** se libérer de toute opinion préconçue

precondition [priːkənˈdɪʃən] N condition *f* préalable *(of sth* à qch; *for doing* pour faire)
VT conditionner *(to do sth* à faire qch)

pre-configured [-kənˈfɪgəd] ADJ préconfiguré

pre-contractual negotiations NPL négociations *fpl* précontractuelles

precooked [priːˈkʊkt] ADJ *(food)* précuit

precursor [priːˈkɜːsər] N *(person)* précurseur *m*; *(sign, event)* avant-coureur *m, pl* avant-coureurs; *(of machine, aeroplane etc)* ancêtre *m*

precursory [priːˈkɜːsərɪ] ADJ *Fml* précurseur; *(symptom)* avant-coureur, *pl* avant-coureurs; *(observation)* préliminaire

precut [priːˈkʌt] ADJ *(ham, cheese, bread)* prédécoupé

predate [priːˈdeɪt] VT **1** *(precede) (historical event etc)* précéder **2** *(put earlier date on) (document)* antidater

predator [ˈpredətər] N prédateur *m*; *(bird)* rapace *m*; *Fig* vautour *m*, rapace

predatory [ˈpredət(ə)rɪ] ADJ *(animal)* prédateur, -trice; *Fig (person, attentions etc)* rapace; **p. instincts** instincts de bête de proie, instincts prédateurs; **there was nothing p. in her manner** elle n'avait rien de menaçant
▸▸ *Mktg* **p. price** prix *m* prédateur; *Mktg* **p. pricing** fixation *f* de prix prédateurs

predecease [priːdɪˈsiːs] VT prédécéder, décéder avant

predecessor [ˈpriːdɪsesər] N prédécesseur *m*; *(of dignitary etc)* devancier, -ière; **my (immediate) p. (in the job)** mon prédécesseur (à ce poste); **my new desk is much better than its p.** mon nouveau bureau est bien mieux que le précédent

predestination [priːdestɪˈneɪʃən] N prédestination *f*

predestine [priːˈdestɪn] VT prédestiner *(to* à); **to be predestined to do sth** être prédestiné à faire qch; **the letter was predestined to go astray** la lettre était destinée à se perdre

predetermination [priːdɪtɜːmɪˈneɪʃən] N *Rel, Phil* prédétermination *f*

predetermine [priːdɪˈtɜːmɪn] VT *Rel, Phil* prédéterminer

predetermined [priːdɪˈtɜːmɪnd] ADJ prédéterminé

predicament [prɪˈdɪkəmənt] N *(difficult situation)* situation *f* difficile, conjoncture *f* malheureuse; **to be in an awkward p.** être dans une mauvaise passe, être dans le pétrin; **this is quite a p. you've landed us in** tu nous as fourrés dans un beau pétrin

predicate¹ [ˈpredɪkət] N *Phil* prédicat *m*; *Gram* attribut *m*

predicate² [ˈpredɪkeɪt] VT **1** *(affirm)* affirmer **2 to p. sth on sth** *(base)* baser *ou* fonder qch sur qch; **this view is predicated on ...** ce point de vue est basé *ou* fondé sur ... **3** *Phil (ascribe as a quality)* **to p. a quality of sth** attribuer une qualité à qch

predicative [prɪˈdɪkətɪv] ADJ *(in logic), Gram* prédicatif

predict [prɪˈdɪkt] VT *(forecast) (on basis of instinct, cards etc)* prédire; *(on basis of data)* prévoir

predictable [prɪˈdɪktəb(ə)l] ADJ prévisible; *Fam* **the film was too p.** ce film était sans surprise; **you're so p.** j'étais sûr que tu allais dire/faire ça; *(boring)* avec toi, aucun imprévu!; **am I getting p.?** tu me vois venir?; **that was p.!** c'était à prévoir!; **there was the p. standing ovation** comme on pouvait le prévoir, le public s'est levé pour l'ovationner/les ovationner

predictably [prɪˈdɪktəblɪ] ADV comme on pouvait le prévoir; **to behave p.** se comporter de manière prévisible; **the evening proceeded entirely p.** la soirée s'est déroulée sans surprise aucune

prediction [prɪˈdɪkʃən] N *(based on instinct, cards etc)* prédiction *f*, *(based on data)* prévision *f*

predictive [prɪˈdɪktɪv] ADJ **1** *(anticipating)* de prédiction; *Tel* **p. texting, p. text input** écriture *f* prédictive **2** *Fml (prophetic)* prophétique; **to be p. of sth** être annonciateur de qch; **the p. power of the theory** la capacité de la théorie de prévoir des événements

predigested [priːdɪˈdʒestɪd, priːdaɪ-] ADJ prédigéré; *Fig (idea)* tout fait

predilection [priːdɪˈlekʃən] N prédilection *f (for* pour)

predispose [priːdɪsˈpəʊz] VT prédisposer

(to à); **to p. sb in sb's favour** prédisposer qn en faveur de qn

predisposition [priːdɪspəˈzɪʃən] N prédisposition *f (to* à)

predominance [prɪˈdɒmɪnəns] N prédominance *f*, **there is a p. of women in the profession** il y a une majorité de femmes dans ce métier

predominant [prɪˈdɒmɪnənt] ADJ prédominant

predominantly [prɪˈdɒmɪnəntlɪ] ADV d'une manière prédominante; **cars sold here are p. Italian** la plupart des voitures vendues ici sont italiennes; **a p. Jewish area** un quartier à majorité juive; **to be p. concerned with a particular problem** être essentiellement préoccupé par un problème particulier

predominate [prɪˈdɒmɪneɪt] VI **1** *(prevail)* prédominer, l'emporter *(over* sur) **2** *(be in the majority)* être plus nombreux, prédominer

predominating [prɪˈdɒmɪneɪtɪŋ] ADJ prédominant

pre-election ADJ préélectoral, -aux

preemie [ˈpriːmɪ] N *Am Fam (premature baby)* prématuré, -ée

pre-eminence N prééminence *f*, **this country's sporting p.** la prééminence de ce pays sur le plan sportif; **to achieve p. in the field of ecology** obtenir une place prééminente dans le domaine de l'écologie

pre-eminent ADJ prééminent

pre-eminently ADV essentiellement

pre-empt [-ˈempt] VT **1** *(prevent, frustrate) (person)* devancer; *(plan, decision etc)* anticiper sur, devancer **2** *Law (land, property)* préempter; *Am (occupy) (land)* occuper *(afin d'obtenir un droit d'achat préférentiel)*

pre-emption [-ˈempʃən] N *Law* (droit *m* de) préemption *f*

pre-emptive [-ˈemptɪv] ADJ *Mil (strike, attack)* préventif
▸▸ *Cards* **p. bid** *(in bridge)* annonce *f* de barrage; *Mktg* **p. penetration strategy** stratégie *f* de pénétration préventive; *Law* **p. right** droit *m* de préemption

preen [priːn] VT *(of bird) (feathers)* lisser avec le bec; **to p. itself** *(of bird)* se lisser les plumes; *Fig* **to p. oneself** *(of person)* se faire beau/belle; *Fig* **to p. oneself on one's achievements** s'enorgueillir de ses réussites

pre-establish VT préétablir

pre-established ADJ préétabli

pre-exist VI préexister

pre-existence N préexistence *f*

pre-existent, pre-existing ADJ préexistant

prefab [ˈpriːfæb] N *Fam* préfabriqué *m*

prefabricate [priːˈfæbrɪkeɪt] VT préfabriquer; **prefabricated house** maison *f* préfabriquée *ou* en préfabriqué

preface [ˈprefɪs] N *(of book)* préface *f*, avant-propos *m inv*, *(to speech)* préambule *m*
VT **1** *(introduce)* **to p. one's remarks with an anecdote** faire précéder ses remarques d'une anecdote; **the events that prefaced the crisis** les événements qui ont précédé la crise **2** *(write preface to) (book)* préfacer

prefade [priːˈfeɪd] N *TV etc* pré-fondu *m*

pre-faded ADJ *(denims)* délavé

prefatory [ˈprefətərɪ] ADJ *Fml (remark)* préliminaire, d'introduction

prefect [ˈpriːfekt] N **1** *Br Sch* = élève *mf* des grandes classes chargé(e) de la discipline **2** *Admin (French etc official)* préfet *m*

prefectship [ˈpriːfektʃɪp] N *Br Sch* = responsabilité *f* de maintenir la discipline, attribuée à un(e) élève des grandes classes

prefecture ['priːfektjʊər] N (in France etc) préfecture f

prefer [prɪ'fɜːr] VT (-rr-) **1** (like better) préférer, aimer mieux; **to p. sth to sth** préférer qch à qch, aimer mieux qch que qch; **I p. her to her sister** je la préfère à sa sœur; **which would you p., wine or beer?** tu préfères du vin ou de la bière?; **I p. meat well done** je préfère la viande bien cuite; **I much p. his first film** je préfère de loin ou de beaucoup son premier film; **I would p. to stay at home** j'aimerais mieux ou je préférerais rester à la maison; **I would p. it if you didn't mention it to him** je préférerais que vous ne lui parliez pas de cela; **I would p. that you did not repeat this** je préférerais que tu ne répètes pas ça **2** Law (legal action) intenter; **to p. charges** déposer ou porter plainte (**against** contre); (of police) porter l'affaire en justice **3** esp Rel Fml (appoint) (person to a position) nommer, élever

preferable ['prefərəb(ə)l] ADJ préférable (**to** à)

preferably ['prefərəblɪ] ADV de préférence; **would you like to make the presentations? – p. not** voudriez-vous faire les présentations? – je n'y tiens pas

preference ['prefərəns] N **1** préférence f; **this is my p.** voilà celui que je préfère; **I have no p.** je n'ai pas de préférence; **to give sth p.** donner ou accorder la préférence à qch (**over sth** sur qch); **women will be given p.** les femmes auront la préférence; **in p. to ...** de préférence à ...; **in order of p.** par ordre de préférence; **to express a p.** se prononcer **2** Econ tarif m ou régime m de faveur; (preferential treatment) traitement m préférentiel ou de faveur; **imports entitled to p.** importations bénéficiant d'un régime de faveur **3** St Exch droit m de priorité **4** Comput **preferences** préférences fpl
▸▸ Br St Exch **p. dividend** dividende m privilégié ou prioritaire; Br St Exch **p. shares** actions fpl privilégiées ou de priorité; Mktg **p. test** test m de préférence

preferential [prefə'renʃəl] ADJ (treatment, tariff etc) préférentiel, de faveur; **to get p. treatment** (of people) bénéficier d'un traitement préférentiel ou de faveur
▸▸ Law **p. claim** privilège m; Fin **p. creditor** créancier, -ière privilégié(e); Fin **p. dividend** dividende m privilégié ou de faveur; Customs **p. duty** préférences fpl douanières; Com **p. price** prix m de faveur ou préférentiel; Fin **p. rate** tarif m préférentiel; Law **p. right** privilège; Pol **p. voting** vote m préférentiel

preferment [prɪ'fɜːmənt] N esp Rel Fml (promotion) avancement m, promotion f (**to an office** à une fonction)

preferred [prɪ'fɜːd] ADJ préféré
▸▸ Fin **p. creditor** créancier, -ière privilégié(e); Fin **p. debt** dette f ou créance f privilégiée; Br St Exch **p. share** action f privilégiée; Am St Exch **p. stock** actions fpl privilégiées ou de priorité

prefiguration [priːfɪgə'reɪʃən] N préfiguration f

prefigure [priː'fɪgər] VT préfigurer

pre-financing N Acct préfinancement m

prefix ['priːfɪks] N Gram etc préfixe m; (before name) particule f, (title) titre m
VT préfixer, mettre un préfixe à

preflight ['priːflaɪt] ADJ (inspection etc) avant vol

pre-focus VT mettre au point préalablement

preformatted [priː'fɔːmætɪd] ADJ Comput pré(-)formaté

prefrontal [priː'frʌnt(ə)l] ADJ Anat préfrontal, -aux

preggers ['pregəz] ADJ Br Fam en cloque

pregnancy ['pregnənsɪ] N (of woman) grossesse f, (of animal) gestation f
▸▸ **p. test** test m de grossesse

pregnant ['pregnənt] ADJ **1** (woman) enceinte; (animal) pleine; **she's three months p.** elle est enceinte de trois mois; **to become** or **get p.** tomber enceinte (**by sb** de qn); **to get sb p.** mettre qn enceinte **2** Fig (fertile) fécond (**with** en); (pause, silence) lourd de signification ou de sens; **p. with possibilities** riche de possibilités; **p. with danger** plein de danger; **p. with meaning/tension** chargé de sens/tension

pre-hear circuit N TV, Radio circuit m de pré-écoute

preheat [priː'hiːt] VT préchauffer

pre-heater N Aut dispositif m de préchauffage; **p. warning light** indicateur m de préchauffage

pre-heating N Aut préchauffage m

prehensile [prɪ'hensaɪl] ADJ préhensile

prehistoric [priːhɪs'tɒrɪk] ADJ Hist, Fig préhistorique

prehistory [priː'hɪst(ə)rɪ] N préhistoire f

pre-ignition N (in engine) préallumage m

pre-installed [-ɪn'stɔːld] ADJ pré(-)installé

pre-inventory balance N Acct balance f avant inventaire

prejudge [priː'dʒʌdʒ] VT (issue etc) préjuger de, Lit préjuger; (person) condamner d'avance

prejudice ['predʒʊdɪs] N **1** (preconception) préjugé m, parti m pris (**against** contre; **in favour of** en faveur de); **racial p.** préjugés raciaux; **I have a p. about** or **against that sort of thing** j'ai des préjugés contre ce genre de choses **2** Fml (harm) préjudice m, tort m, dommage m; **to cause p. to** porter préjudice à; Law **without p. (to my rights)** sans préjudice de mes droits; **without p. to the solution of the question** sans préjuger la solution de la question
VT **1** (bias) (person) prévenir, prédisposer (**against** contre; **in favour of** en faveur de) **2** (harm) (reputation, solution etc) nuire à, faire du tort à, porter préjudice à; (interests) nuire à; **without prejudicing my rights** sans préjudice de mes droits

> Note that the French word **préjudice** never means **bias**.

prejudiced ['predʒʊdɪst] ADJ (person) plein de préjugés; (idea, view) préconçu; **to be p.** avoir des préjugés (**in favour of** en faveur de; **against** contre); **racially p.** plein de préjugés raciaux

prejudicial [predʒʊ'dɪʃəl] ADJ préjudiciable, nuisible (**to** à); **to be p.** porter préjudice (**to** à)

prelacy ['preləsɪ] N Rel **1** (office) prélature f **2** (prelates) prélats mpl

prelate ['prelɪt] N Rel prélat m

prelim ['priːlɪm] N Fam **1** Sch examen m blanc **2** Typ **prelims** pages fpl de départ, préliminaires mpl

preliminary [prɪ'lɪmɪnərɪ] ADJ (inquiry, selection, interview, negotiations etc, Med examination) préliminaire; (stage) initial, -aux, premier; Sch préparatoire; **after a few p. remarks** après quelques avant-propos ou remarques préliminaires; Constr etc **p. scheme** or **plan** avant-projet m, pl avant-projets
N **1** (to conversation etc) prélude m; **by way of** or **as a p.** préalablement, en guise d'introduction ou d'avant-propos; **the measure is seen by many as a p. to ...** cette mesure est considérée par beaucoup comme une action préliminaire à ... **2** (of treaty etc) **preliminaries** préliminaires mpl

preloaded [priː'ləʊdɪd] ADJ préchargé

prelude ['preljuːd] N Mus, Fig prélude m (**to** à)
VT préluder à, précéder

premarital [priː'mærɪt(ə)l] ADJ préconjugal, -aux, prénuptial, -aux
▸▸ **p. sex** rapports mpl sexuels avant le mariage

pre-marketing N précommercialisation f, prémarketing m

premature ['premətʃʊər] ADJ (decision, end, death etc) prématuré; (baldness, senility) précoce; **to be two weeks p.** (of baby) être né deux semaines avant terme, être prématuré de deux semaines; Fam **you're being a bit p.!** tu vas trop vite!; **it was a bit p. of him** c'était un peu prématuré de sa part
▸▸ **p. birth** accouchement m prématuré ou avant terme; **p. ejaculation** éjaculation f précoce

prematurely ['premətʃʊəlɪ] ADV (to decide, die) prématurément; (born) avant terme; **to be p. senile/bald** souffrir de sénilité/calvitie précoce

premed ['priːmed] N Med Fam prémédication f

premedicate [priː'medɪkeɪt] VT Med prémédiquer

premedication [priːmedɪ'keɪʃən] N Med prémédication f

premeditate [priː'medɪteɪt] VT préméditer

premeditated [priː'medɪteɪtɪd] ADJ (crime) prémédité

premeditation [priːmedɪ'teɪʃən] N préméditation f

premenstrual [priː'menstrʊəl] ADJ prémenstruel; **I think she's feeling p.** je crois que ses règles ne vont pas tarder à arriver
▸▸ **p. syndrome, p. tension** syndrome m prémenstruel

premier ['premɪər] ADJ (tout) premier
N (prime minister) premier ministre m

première ['premɪeər, 'prem-, Am prɪ'mɪər] N Theat, Cin première f
VT (play, film) donner la première de; **the film was premièred in London** la première du film a eu lieu à Londres
VI **the play premièred in New York** la première de la pièce a eu lieu à New York

premiership ['premɪəʃɪp] N (of prime minister) fonctions fpl de premier ministre; **to be elected to the p.** être élu premier ministre; **during her p.** pendant qu'elle était premier ministre; **he had a successful p.** il a rempli son mandat de premier ministre avec succès

pre-millennial ADJ d'avant le passage au troisième millénaire

premise ['premɪs] N (in logic) prémisse f, **to argue from different premises** discuter à partir de prémisses différentes
VT poser en principe (**that** que); (in logic) poser en prémisse (**that** que); **to be premised on sth** être basé ou fondé sur qch

premises ['premɪsɪz] NPL **1** (property) **the p.** le local, les locaux; **business p.** locaux commerciaux; **drinks to be consumed on/off the p.** boissons à consommer dans/hors de l'établissement; **she's still on the p.** elle est encore dans le bâtiment **2** Law (of document) intitulé m

> Note that the French word **prémices** is a false friend and never refers to a location.

premiss ['premɪs] N = premise N

premium ['priːmɪəm] N **1** (for insurance) prime f, **to pay an additional p.** payer une surprime
2 (additional sum) (on price) supplément m; (on salary) prime f, Fin etc (**exchange**) **p.** agio

m, prix *m ou* prime du change; *St Exch* **to pay a p.** verser *ou* acquitter un premium; **to issue shares at a p.** émettre des actions au-dessus du pair *ou* de leur valeur nominale; **to sell sth at a p.** vendre qch à prime *ou* à bénéfice; **antiques are at a p.** *(are sought after)* les antiquités sont très recherchées; *(sell at high prices)* les antiquités se vendent à prix d'or; **time is at a p.** le temps presse; **her time is at a p.** son temps est précieux; **good translators are at a p.** les bons traducteurs ne courent pas les rues *ou* sont rares; *Fig* **to put** *ou* **place a p. on sth** *(of people, government etc)* accorder beaucoup d'importance à qch; *(of circumstances, nature of work etc)* mettre l'accent sur qch

▸▸*Br* **p. bonds** obligations *fpl* à lots; *Am* **p. fuel**, *Am* **p. gasoline**, *Br* **p. grade petrol** supercarburant *m*, *Fam* super *m*; *Com* **p. price** prix de prestige; *Mktg* **p. product** produit *m* de prestige; *Com* **p. rebate** ristourne *f* de prime; *Mktg* **p. selling** vente *f* avec prime; *Mktg* **p. service** service *m* premier

premium-rate ADJ *Tel (call)* vers un numéro surtaxé; *(number)* surtaxé

premolar [pri:ˈməʊlər] N *Anat* prémolaire *f*
▸▸**p. tooth** (dent *f*) prémolaire

premonition [preməˈnɪʃən, pri:-] N *(of misfortune etc)* prémonition *f*, pressentiment *m*; **to have a p.** avoir un pressentiment; **to have a p. of disaster** pressentir un désastre; **to have a p. that …** avoir le pressentiment que …, pressentir que …

premonitory [prɪˈmɒnɪtərɪ] ADJ prémonitoire

prenatal [pri:ˈneɪt(ə)l] ADJ prénatal, -als *ou* -aux

prenup [ˈpri:nʌp] N *Fam* contrat *m* de mariage

prenuptial [pri:ˈnʌpʃəl] ADJ prénuptial, -aux
▸▸**p. agreement** contrat *m* de mariage

preoccupation [prɪɒkjʊˈpeɪʃən] N préoccupation *f* (**with** à l'égard de); **to have a p. with sth** être préoccupé par qch

preoccupied [prɪˈɒkjʊpaɪd] ADJ préoccupé (**with, by** par); **to be p. with** *or* **by sth** se préoccuper de qch

preoccupy [prɪˈɒkjʊpaɪ] VT *(person, the mind)* préoccuper

preordain [pri:ɔ:ˈdeɪn] VT *(destine)* prédéterminer; **it was preordained** c'était prédestiné

prep [prep] N *Br Sch Fam (esp in private school) (period)* étude *f* (du soir); *(homework)* devoirs *mpl* (du soir)
VT (**-pp-**) *Am Fam* préparer; *Med* **to p. sb for an operation** préparer qn pour une opération
▸▸**p. period** (heure *f* de) permanence *f*; **p. room** (salle *f* d')étude; **p. school** *(in UK)* école *f* primaire privée *(pour enfants de sept à treize ans, préparant généralement à entrer dans une "public school")* ; *(in US)* = école privée qui prépare à l'enseignement supérieur

prepack [pri:ˈpæk] VT *Com* préconditionner, préemballer

prepaid [pri:ˈpeɪd] ADJ prépayé; *Acct* payé *ou* constaté d'avance
▸▸**p. card** carte *f* prépayée; **p. envelope** enveloppe *f* affranchie; **p. income** produit *m* constaté d'avance

preparation [prepəˈreɪʃən] N **1** *(action) (of food, medication etc)* préparation *f*; *(of plane, car etc)* mise *f* en état; **they broke the news to her without any p.** ils lui ont annoncé la nouvelle sans aucune préparation; **p. of accounting entries** précomptabilisation *f*, préimputation *f*; **in p. for the summer holidays** en prévision des vacances d'été

2 preparations *(measures)* préparatifs *mpl*; **preparations for war** préparatifs de guerre; **to make (one's) preparations for sth** prendre ses mesures *ou* ses dispositions en vue de qch, faire des préparatifs en vue de qch; **to make (one's) preparations for a journey** se préparer à *ou* pour un voyage, faire ses préparatifs de voyage

3 *Br Sch (esp in private school) (period)* étude *f* (du soir); *(homework)* devoirs *mpl* (du soir)

4 *(substance) (pharmaceutical etc)* préparation *f*

> When translating the English word **preparation**, note that the French words **préparatifs** and **préparation** are not interchangeable.

preparatory [prɪˈpærətərɪ] ADJ préparatoire; *(steps, measures)* préalable; **p. to** *(departure, invasion etc)* en préparation pour; **p. to going abroad/resigning** avant d'aller à l'étranger/de démissionner
▸▸**p. school** *(in UK)* école *f* primaire privée *(pour enfants de sept à treize ans, préparant généralement à entrer dans une "public school")*; *(in US)* = école privée qui prépare à l'enseignement supérieur

prepare [prɪˈpeər] VT *(meal etc)* préparer; *(attack etc)* monter, préparer; *(plane, car etc)* mettre en état; **to p. a surprise for sb** préparer *ou* ménager une surprise à qn; **to p. the way for negotiations** préparer la voie pour des négociations; **to p. sb for an exam** préparer qn à un examen; **to p. sb for bad news** préparer qn à recevoir une mauvaise nouvelle; **to p. oneself for sth** se préparer à qch; **their training had prepared them for most eventualities** leur entraînement les avait préparés à presque toutes les éventualités; **prepared from the finest ingredients** préparé avec les meilleurs ingrédients
VI se préparer, s'apprêter (**for sth** à qch; **to do sth** à faire qch); **to p. for departure** faire ses préparatifs de départ; **to p. for an examination** préparer un examen

prepared [prɪˈpeəd] ADJ **1** *(willing)* **I am (quite) p. to …** je suis prêt *ou* disposé à …; **he was/was not p. to lie** il était/n'était pas disposé à mentir
2 *(ready)* **to be p. for anything** être prêt à tout; **to be p. for bad news** être préparé à recevoir une mauvaise nouvelle; **be p.** *(Scout's motto)* toujours prêt; **I wasn't p. for this reaction** je ne m'attendais pas à cette réaction
3 *(made)* préparé; **to have a p. excuse/explanation** avoir une excuse/explication toute prête; **a well p. dish** un plat bien préparé; **a p. speech** un discours préparé (à l'avance); **p. timber** bois *m* refait

preparedness [prɪˈpeərɪdnɪs] N état *m* de préparation; **I am unsure of their p. to deal with such an eventuality** je doute qu'ils soient prêts à faire face à une telle éventualité; *Mil* **to be in a state of p.** être en état d'alerte (préventive)

prepay [pri:ˈpeɪ] VT *(pt, pp* prepaid*)* payer *ou* régler d'avance; *(letter etc)* affranchir; **a prepaid envelope** une enveloppe affranchie
▸▸*Tel* **p. package** *(for mobile phone)* coffret *m* avec carte prépayée

prepayment [pri:ˈpeɪmənt] N paiement *m* à l'avance, paiement préalable; *Acct* charge *f* constatée d'avance
▸▸*Acct* **p. and accrued income** compte *m* de régularisation; *Acct* **p. clause** clause *f* de remboursement par anticipation; *Fin* **p. penalty** indemnité *f* de remboursement par anticipation

preponderance [prɪˈpɒndərəns] N prépon-

dérance *f* (**over** sur); **there was a p. of French books on the shelf** il y avait une majorité de livres français sur l'étagère

preponderant [prɪˈpɒndərənt] ADJ prépondérant; **boys tend to be p.** il tend à y avoir une majorité de garçons

preponderantly [prɪˈpɒndərəntlɪ] ADV à un degré prépondérant; **the guests were p. French** les invités étaient pour la majeure partie français

preponderate [prɪˈpɒndəreɪt] VI l'emporter (**over** sur)

preposition [prepəˈzɪʃən] N *Gram* préposition *f*

prepositional [prepəˈzɪʃən(ə)l] ADJ prépositif

prepositionally [prepəˈzɪʃən(ə)lɪ] ADV *(used)* comme préposition

prepossess [pri:pəˈzes] VT *Fml* **1** *(engross)* préoccuper **2** *(influence)* influencer

prepossessing [pri:pəˈzesɪŋ] ADJ *(face)* agréable, avenant; **p. appearance** aspect *m* engageant; *(of person)* air *m* sympathique *ou* avenant; **he's not the most p. of people** ce n'est pas l'homme le plus avenant du monde

preposterous [prɪˈpɒstərəs] ADJ absurde; **that's a p. lie!** c'est complètement absurde!

preposterously [prɪˈpɒstərəslɪ] ADV d'une façon absurde; **it was p. easy** ça a été un jeu d'enfant

preposterousness [prɪˈpɒstərəsnɪs] N absurdité *f*

preppy [prepɪ] *esp Am Fam* ADJ *(look, clothes etc)* ≃ bon chic bon genre, BCBG
N **to be a p.** être *ou* faire très BCBG

pre-press N prépresse *m*

pre-printed form N pré-imprimé *m, pl* pré-imprimés

preproduction [pri:prəˈdʌkʃən] N *TV etc* préproduction *f*; **the film is in p.** le film est en préproduction

preprogram [pri:ˈprəʊgræm] VT *Comput etc* préprogrammer; **humans are preprogrammed to behave in certain ways** les êtres humains sont conditionnés à se comporter d'une certaine façon

preprogrammed [pri:ˈprəʊgræmd] ADJ *Comput etc* préprogrammé

prepubescent [pri:pju:ˈbesənt] ADJ prépubère; *Fig Pej (immature)* puéril

prepublication [pri:pʌblɪˈkeɪʃən] N prépublication *f*

prepuce [ˈpri:pju:s] N *Anat* prépuce *m*

prequel [ˈpri:kwəl] N = film *m* qui reprend des thèmes et des personnages d'un film réalisé plus tôt, mais dont l'action se déroule antérieurement aux événements exposés dans le premier film

Pre-Raphaelite [pri:ˈræfəlaɪt] ADJ, N *Art* préraphaélite *m*

prerecord [pri:rɪˈkɔ:d] VT préenregistrer; *TV, Radio* **prerecorded broadcast** émission *f* en différé; **prerecorded cassette** cassette *f* préenregistrée; **prerecorded telephone message service** audiophone *m*

prerecording [pri:rɪˈkɔ:dɪŋ] N préenregistrement *m*; *TV, Radio* (émission *f* en) différé *m*

preregistration [pri:redʒɪˈstreɪʃən] N *Univ* préinscription *f, pl* avant-premières

prerelease [pri:rɪˈli:s] *Cin* N *(of film)* avant-première *f, pl* avant-premières
▸▸**p. publicity** = publicité *f* qui précède la sortie d'un film, d'un livre, d'un disque etc

prerequisite [pri:ˈrekwɪzɪt] ADJ préalablement nécessaire, indispensable
N condition *f* préalable

prerogative [prɪˈrɒgətɪv] N prérogative *f*,

privilège *m*; **the royal p.** la prérogative royale; **to exercise the royal p.** faire acte de souverain

▸▸ *Pol* **p. powers** = pouvoir *m* de décision d'un chef d'État ne nécessitant pas l'approbation du pouvoir législatif

Pres *Pol etc abbr* **President**

presage¹ ['presɪdʒ] N *Lit (sign)* présage *m*; *(foreboding)* pressentiment *m*; **to be a p. of sth** présager qch, être le présage de qch

presage² ['presɪdʒ, prɪ'seɪdʒ] VT *Lit (catastrophe etc)* présager, faire pressentir

pre-sales service N service *m* pré-vente

Presbyterian [prezbɪ'tɪərɪən] ADJ, N *Rel* presbytérien, -ienne

Presbyterianism [prezbɪ'tɪərɪənɪz(ə)m] N *Rel* presbytérianisme *m*

presbytery ['prezbɪt(ə)rɪ] N *Rel* **1** *(in church)* sanctuaire *m* **2** *Cathol (residence)* presbytère *m* **3** *(in Presbyterian Church) (court)* consistoire *m*

preschool [priː'skuːl] ADJ *(age etc)* préscolaire

prescience ['presɪəns] N *Fml* prescience *f*

prescient ['presɪənt] ADJ *Fml* prescient

prescoring [priː'skɔːrɪŋ] N *(of sound)* pré-enregistrement *m*

prescribe [prɪ'skraɪb] VT **1** prescrire; **prescribed task** tâche *f* imposée; **in the prescribed time** dans le délai prescrit **2** *Med* **to p. sth for sb** prescrire qch à qn

prescription [prɪ'skrɪpʃən] N **1** *(order)* prescription *f* **2** *Med* ordonnance *f*; **available only on (a doctor's) p.** délivré seulement sur ordonnance; **repeat p.** = ordonnance renouvelable

▸▸ **p. charges** frais *mpl* de médicaments *ou* pharmaceutiques; **p. drugs** médicaments *mpl* délivrés uniquement sur ordonnance

prescriptive [prɪ'skrɪptɪv] ADJ **1** *(prescribing action)* normatif **2** *(established by custom)* consacré par l'usage *ou* par la coutume

prescriptivism [prɪ'skrɪptɪvɪz(ə)m] N *Phil* normativisme *m*

preselect [priːsə'lekt] VT *(tracks, channels)* prérégler

pre-selector N *Aut* présélecteur *m*
▸▸ **p. gearbox** boîte *f* à présélection

presence ['prezəns] N **1** présence *f*; **in the p. of ...** en présence de ...; **say nothing about it in his p.** n'en parlez pas devant lui; *Fml* **to be admitted to the p.** *(to see monarch etc)* être admis en présence; **your p. is requested at ...** vous êtes prié d'assister à ...; **the police maintained a discreet p.** *(at demonstration etc)* la police a assuré une surveillance discrète; **the American military p.** la présence militaire américaine; **to make one's p. felt** se faire remarquer, faire sentir sa présence

2 p. of mind présence *f* d'esprit; **to keep one's p. of mind** garder son sang-froid; **to have the p. of mind to do sth** avoir la présence d'esprit de faire qch

3 *(bearing)* présence *f*, prestance *f*; **to have stage p.** avoir de la présence sur scène; **he has p.** il a de la présence *ou* de la prestance, il en impose

present¹ ['prezənt] ADJ **1** *(in attendance)* présent; **to be p. at a ceremony** être présent *ou* assister à une cérémonie; **he cannot be interviewed without a lawyer being p.** on ne peut pas l'interroger sans la présence d'un avocat; **all (those) p. heard it** toute l'assistance l'a entendu; **some of you p. here** quelques-uns d'entre vous, ici présents; **minerals which are p. in the solution** minéraux qui sont présents dans la solution; **p. company excepted** à l'exception des personnes ici présentes, bien sûr

2 *(in time)* actuel; *(under discussion)* en question; **the p. king** le roi actuel; **at the p. time** *or* **moment** *(at this very moment)* en ce moment; *(in this period of time)* actuellement, aujourd'hui; **up to the p. time** jusqu'ici; **in the p. case** dans le cas qui nous occupe; **the p. year** l'année *f* courante

N **1** *(time),Gram* présent *m*; **the p.** le présent; **up to the p.** jusqu'à présent, jusqu'ici; **at p.** *(at this very moment)* en ce moment; *(now)* à présent; *(in this period of time)* actuellement, aujourd'hui; **that's all I can tell you at p.** c'est tout ce que je peux vous dire pour l'instant *ou* pour le moment; **no more at p.** rien de plus pour le moment *ou* pour l'instant; **as things are at p.** *(at the stage things have reached)* au point où en sont les choses; *(nowadays)* par les temps qui courent; **for the p.** pour le moment, pour l'instant

2 *Law* **by these presents** par les présentes

▸▸ *Gram* **p. perfect** passé *m* composé VOIR GRAMMAIRE A50; B30 ; *Gram* **p. subjunctive** présent du subjonctif VOIR GRAMMAIRE A53–4; B32–3 ; *Gram* **p. tense** présent VOIR GRAMMAIRE A49; B30 ; *Acct* **p. value** valeur *f* actuelle *ou* actualisée

present² N *(gift)* cadeau *m*; **to make sb a p. of sth, to give sth to sb as a p.** faire cadeau de qch à qn, donner qch en cadeau à qn; **it's for a p.** *(when buying)* c'est pour offrir

present³ [prɪ'zent] VT **1** *(introduce, put forward)* présenter; **to p. sb to sb** présenter qn à qn; *Fml* **allow me to p. Miss Lorna Johnston** permettez-moi de vous présenter Miss Lorna Johnston; **to p. sb at court** présenter qn à la cour; *Theat* **to p. a play** *(of company etc)* présenter *ou* donner une pièce; *TV, Radio* **to p. a programme** *(of presenter)* présenter une émission; **to p. oneself at** *or* **for an examination** se présenter à *ou* pour un examen; **a good opportunity presents itself** une bonne occasion se présente (**for doing sth** de faire qch); **to p. sb/sth in a good/bad light** présenter qn/qch sous un jour favorable/défavorable; **his attempts to mount the horse presented a strange spectacle** ses tentatives pour se mettre en selle offraient un curieux spectacle

2 *(give) (gift) (award, certificate)* remettre; **to p. sth to sb, to p. sb with sth** donner/remettre qch à qn; **the mayor will be presenting the prizes** le maire distribuera les prix; **to p. one's compliments to sb** présenter ses compliments à qn; **they were presented with an empty goalmouth** ils se trouvèrent devant un but vide; **this presented her with no option but to agree** ceci ne lui a pas laissé d'autre alternative que d'accepter; *Mil, Fig* **to p. sb with an easy target** offrir une bonne cible à qn

3 *Com* **to p. a bill for acceptance** présenter une traite à l'acceptation; *Law* **to p. a plea** introduire une instance; *Com* **to p. invoices** présenter des factures

4 *Parl (bill)* présenter, introduire; **to p. a plan to a meeting** soumettre un plan à une assemblée

5 *Mil* **to p. arms** présenter les armes; **p. arms!** présentez armes!

VI *Obst (of foetus)* se présenter; *Med* **to p. with sth** avoir qch, présenter qch

presentable [prɪ'zentəb(ə)l] ADJ *(person, thing)* présentable; *(garment)* portable, mettable; **am I p.?** je suis présentable?

presentation [prezən'teɪʃən] N **1** *(of person, theory, business plan, sales proposal etc)* présentation *f*; *(of play)* présentation, représentation *f*; *(of thesis, dissertation)* soutenance *f*; **to give a p.** faire un exposé; **p. of accounts for audit** reddition *f* de comptes

2 *(giving) (of gift, medal etc to somebody)* remise *f*, *(gift)* cadeau *m* *(offert à qn)*; **to make**

a p. to sb remettre un cadeau/une médaille/ *etc* à qn

3 *Com* **payable on p. of the coupon** payable contre remise du coupon; **on p. of the invoice** au vu de *ou* sur présentation de la facture; **p. for acceptance** présentation *f* à l'acceptation; **p. for payment** présentation au paiement

4 *Obst (of foetus)* présentation *f*

▸▸ **p. ceremony** cérémonie *f* de remise *(d'un prix)*; **p. copy** *(specimen)* spécimen *m* (gratuit); *(from writer)* exemplaire *m* gratuit; *Fin* **p. date** date *f* de présentation; *Comput* **p. graphics** graphiques *mpl* de présentation; *Mktg* **p. pack** paquet *m* de présentation; **p. slides** diapositives *fpl* de présentation; *Comput* **p. software** logiciel *m* de présentation *ou* de préAO

present-day ADJ ATTRIB actuel; **p. London/ Brazil** le Londres/Brésil d'aujourd'hui

presenteeism [prezən'tiːɪzm] N = fait, pour un employé, de travailler également en dehors des heures de bureau pour se faire bien voir de ses supérieurs

presenter [prɪ'zentər] N *Radio, TV etc* présentateur, -trice

presentiment [prɪ'zentɪmənt] N *esp Fml* pressentiment *m*; **to have a p. of danger** avoir le pressentiment qu'il y a du danger

presently ['prezəntlɪ] ADV **1** *(soon)* bientôt; *(in past)* au bout d'un certain temps **2** *esp Am (now)* actuellement, à présent

Note that the French word **présentement** always means **at present**.

presentment [prɪ'zentmənt] N *Com (of bill of exchange etc)* présentation *f*

preservation [prezə'veɪʃən] N **1** *(maintenance)* conservation *f*, préservation *f*, *(of peace, order)* maintien *m*; *(in laboratory) (of a flower, specimen)* naturalisation *f*; *Com (of goods etc)* traitement *m* avant stockage; **in a good state of p.** en bon état de conservation **2** *(protection)* préservation *f* (**from a danger** d'un danger)

▸▸ *Br* **p. order** classement *m* (à titre de monument historique); **p. society** = association *f* pour la protection des sites et monuments

preservative [prɪ'zɜːvətɪv] N conservateur *m*; *(in foods)* agent *m* de conservation, conservateur, préservateur *m*; **it acts as a p. for the wood** cela conserve le bois

Note that the French word **préservatif** is a false friend and is never a translation for the English word **preservative**. It means **condom**.

preserve [prɪ'zɜːv] N **1** *(apricot etc)* preserve(s) *(jam)* confiture *f* (d'abricots *etc*); **preserves** *(bottled fruit)* conserves *fpl* **2** *(area)* **(game) p.** réserve *f*; *Fig* **engineering is no longer a male p.** le métier d'ingénieur n'est plus réservé aux hommes; **the kitchen is his p. entirely** la cuisine c'est son domaine à lui

VT **1** *(maintain) (custom, sense of humour etc)* conserver, préserver; *(peace etc)* maintenir; *(appearance, illusion)* préserver; *(silence etc)* garder, observer **2** *(leather, wood, building etc)* protéger, préserver; *Culin (fruit etc)* conserver, mettre en conserve; *(in laboratory) (plant, animal)* naturaliser **3** *(protect) (person)* préserver (**from sth** de qch); **saints p. us!** grands dieux!

preserved [prɪ'zɜːvd] ADJ **1** *(fruit)* en conserve; **p. food** conserves *fpl*; *Old-fashioned* **p. meat** conserve *f* de viande **2** **well/ badly p.** *(building etc)* en bon/mauvais état de conservation; **well p.** *(person)* bien conservé

preserver [prɪ'zɜːvər] N *(person) (of traditions etc)* conservateur, -trice

preserving [prɪ'zɜːvɪŋ] N = **preservation**
▸▸ *Old-fashioned* **p. pan** bassine *f* à confitures

preset [priː'set] VT *(pt, pp* **preset;** *prp* **presetting**) *Tech, Electron (machine etc)* prérégler
ADJ préréglé; *Comput* présélectionné

preshrink [priː'ʃrɪŋk] VT *(pt* **preshrank** [-'ʃræŋk]; *pp* **preshrunk** [-'ʃrʌŋk]) *(fabric)* rendre irrétrécissable

preshrunk [priː'ʃrʌŋk] ADJ *(fabric)* irrétrécissable

preside [prɪ'zaɪd] VI présider; **to p. at** *or* **over a meeting** présider une réunion; **the man who presided over the collapse of the company** l'homme qui était président lors de la chute de l'entreprise; **to p. over events** *(direct)* diriger les événements

presidency ['prezɪdənsɪ] N présidence *f*; **to assume the p.** assumer la présidence

president ['prezɪdənt] N président *m*; *(of American company)* président-directeur *m* général, *pl* présidents-directeurs généraux, P.-D.G. *m*; **P. Truman** le président Truman; **Mr P.** Monsieur le Président; *EU* **P. of the Commission** président de la Commission; *Am* **P. of the Senate** président du Sénat

president-elect N *Pol* président *m* élu

presidential [prezɪ'denʃəl] ADJ présidentiel; **to nurse p. ambitions** *or* **aspirations** aspirer à *ou* ambitionner la présidence
▸▸ **p. appointment** = poste *m* à pourvoir sur nomination présidentielle; **p. elections** (élections *fpl*) présidentielles *fpl*; **p. hopeful** présidentiable *mf*

presidium [prɪ'sɪdɪəm, -'zɪd-] N *Pol* présidium *m*

PRESS [pres]

N	pression **1** ▪ presse **2–4**
VT	appuyer sur **1** ▪ presser **1, 3, 4**
	▪ repasser **3**
VI	appuyer **1** ▪ exercer une pression **1**

N **1** *(act of pushing) (of something)* pression *f*; *(crowd)* foule *f*; *Lit (of battle)* mêlée *f*; **at the p. of a button, it …** il suffit d'appuyer sur un bouton pour qu'il …; **give it a slight p.** appuyez légèrement là-dessus; **give your trousers a p.** donne un coup de fer à ton pantalon; **to force one's way through the p.** fendre la foule, se frayer un chemin à travers la foule

2 *(device) (for trousers, tennis racquet, coins etc)* presse *f*; *(for wine, cider, oil)* pressoir *m*; **hydraulic p.** presse hydraulique

3 *Typ (printing)* **p.** presse *f* (d'imprimerie); **to go to p.** être mis sous presse, aller à l'impression; **we go to p. at 5.00** on est mis sous presse à 5.00; *(copy deadline)* on boucle à 5.00; **at the time of going to p.** au moment d'être mis sous presse; **hot** *or* **straight from the p.** tout frais; **ready for p.** prêt à mettre sous presse; **to pass a proof for p.** donner le bon à tirer; **the Conway P.** *(printing firm)* l'Imprimerie *f* Conway; *(publishing firm)* les Éditions *fpl* Conway

4 *Journ* **the p.** *(newspapers)* la presse, les journaux *mpl*; *(journalists)* la presse; **p. freedom, freedom of the p.** la liberté de la presse; **to write for the p.** écrire pour les journaux; **she's a member of the p.** elle a une carte de presse; **to have** *or* **get a good/bad p.** avoir bonne/mauvaise presse; **the story appeared in the p.** on a parlé de cette affaire dans la presse; **they managed to keep her name out of the p.** ils ont réussi à ce que son nom ne paraisse pas dans la presse

5 *(in weightlifting)* développé *m*

6 *Scot (cupboard)* **(linen** *or* **clothes) p.** armoire *f* à linge

VT **1** *(push) (something)* appuyer sur; *(squeeze)* presser, serrer; *(into clay, wet cement etc)* enfoncer; *(grapes)* pressurer; *(with feet)* fouler; **he pressed my hand in his** il a serré ma main dans la sienne; **she pressed the child to her** elle a serré l'enfant contre elle; **she pressed her nose against the window** elle a collé son nez à la vitre; **to p. sth home** enfoncer qch; **to p. sth shut** fermer qch en appuyant dessus; **to p. sth flat** aplatir qch; **to p. sth (back) into shape** rendre sa forme à qch; **to p. a lemon** presser un citron; **to p. flowers** presser des fleurs

2 *Tech* mettre sous presse; *(metal)* matricer, estamper; *(record)* matricer, presser; *(holes)* percer; *(paper)* calandrer

3 *(trousers, skirt)* repasser, donner un coup de fer à; *Sewing* **to p. a seam** rabattre une couture

4 *(put pressure on)* **to p. the enemy hard** *or* **closely** serrer l'ennemi de près, talonner l'ennemi; **to p. sb hard** harceler qn; **pressed by one's creditors** harcelé par ses créanciers; **to be pressed for time/money** être à court de temps/d'argent; **to p. sb for an answer/a decision** presser qn pour qu'il réponde/prenne une décision; **to p. sb to do sth** presser qn de faire qch; **if you p. her she'll tell you** si tu insistes, elle te le dira; **if pressed, he would admit …** quand on insistait *ou* le poussait, il admettait …; **to p. sth into service (as sth)** utiliser qch (comme qch)

5 *(persist with sth)* **to p. an analogy/a comparison too far** pousser une analogie/une comparaison trop loin; **to p. (home) one's advantage** profiter de son avantage; **to p. one's attentions on sb** faire des avances à qn; **to p. a claim** insister sur une demande; **to p. a gift on sb** forcer qn à accepter un cadeau; **can I p. another piece of cake on you?** vous mangerez bien une autre part de gâteau?; **to p. a point** insister sur un point; *Law* **to p. charges** porter plainte

VI **1** *(push)* appuyer, exercer une pression; **don't p. too hard** n'appuyez pas trop fort; **the crowd was pressing forward towards the exit** la foule se pressait pour gagner la sortie; **to p. close against sb** se serrer contre qn; **stop pressing!** *(pushing me)* ne poussez pas!

2 **time is pressing** le temps presse; **nothing presses** rien ne presse; **to p. for an answer** insister pour avoir une réponse immédiate; **to p. for an adjournment/the law to be tightened up** exiger un ajournement/que la loi soit renforcée

▸▸ **p. advertising** publicité *f* dans la presse; **p. agency** agence *f* de presse; **p. agent** attaché, -ée de presse; **p. attaché** attaché, -ée de presse; **p. badge** macaron *m* de presse; **p. baron** magnat *m* de la presse; **p. box** tribune *f* de (la) presse; **p. campaign** campagne *f* de presse; **p. card** carte *f* de presse *ou* de journaliste; **p. clipping** coupure *f* de presse *ou* de journal; *Br* **the P. Complaints Commission** = organisme *m* britannique de contrôle de la presse; **p. conference** conférence *f* de presse; **p. copy** *(of book)* exemplaire *m* de service de presse; **p. corps** journalistes *mpl*; **p. coverage** couverture *f* médiatique; *Br* **p. cutting** coupure de presse *ou* de journal; **p. day** jour *m* de tirage; **p. gallery** tribune de (la) presse; *Hist* **p. gang** enrôleurs *mpl*, racoleurs *mpl*; **p. handout** communiqué *m* de presse; **p. insert** encart *m* presse; **p. kit** dossier *m* de presse *(distribué aux journalistes)*; **p. lord** magnat de la presse; **p. office** service *m* de presse; **p. officer** responsable *mf* des relations avec la presse; **p. pack** dossier de presse; **p. pass** carte de presse; **p. photogra-**

pher photographe *mf* de presse; *Typ* **p. proof** tierce *f*; **p. relations** relations *fpl* presse; **p. release** communiqué de presse; **p. report** reportage *m*; **p. reporter** reporter *m* de la presse écrite; **p. run** tirage *m*; *Pol* **p. secretary** ≃ porte-parole *m inv* du gouvernement; **p. stand** tribune de (la) presse; *Br* **p. stud** bouton-pression *m, pl* boutons-pression, pression

▸ **press down** VT SEP appuyer sur; *(with force)* enfoncer
VI **to p. down on sb** peser sur qn

▸ **press on** VI *(walk faster)* presser *ou* forcer le pas; *(travel faster)* se presser, se dépêcher; *(continue journey)* continuer son chemin; *(persevere with activity)* persévérer, ne pas abandonner; *(continue activity)* continuer; **to p. on** *or* **ahead with one's work** poursuivre son travail; **p. on regardless!** allez-y quand même

▸ **press out** VT SEP **1** *(juice etc)* exprimer
2 *Tech (holes)* percer (**out of** dans); *(shapes, parts)* découper (**out of** dans)

press-button ADJ
▸▸ *Tel* **p. dialling** numérotation *f* à touches

pressed [prest] ADJ
▸▸ *Old-fashioned* **p. beef** = bœuf *m* salé, bouilli et moulé en forme; **p. flowers** fleurs *fpl* pressées; **p. steel** acier *m* embouti

press-gang VT *Hist* **to p. sb into the navy/army** enrôler qn de force dans la marine/l'armée; *Fig Fam* **to p. sb into doing sth** forcer la main à qn pour qu'il fasse qch

pressie ['prezɪ] N *Br Fam* cadeau *m*

pressing ['presɪŋ] ADJ *(danger, invitation)* pressant; *(work, matters)* urgent, pressant; *(debt)* criard; **the matter is p.** il y a urgence; **there is a p. need for action** il faut agir vite
N **1** *(act of pressing) (on something)* pression *f*, *(of grapes)* pressurage *m*; *(with feet)* foulage *m*; *(of record, metal)* estampage *m*, matriçage *m*; *(of paper)* calandrage *m*; *(of clothes)* pressing *m* **2** *(pressed metal piece)* pièce *f* matricée

pressman, *pl* **pressmen** ['presmən] N *(journalist)* journaliste *m*, reporter *m*

pressmark ['presmɑːk] N *(of book in library)* cote *f*

press-up N *Gym* traction *f*, *Fam* pompe *f*; **to do press-ups** faire des tractions *ou Fam* des pompes

pressure ['preʃər] N **1** *(on something, somebody)* pression *f*; **I felt the slight p. of his hand on my arm** j'ai senti la légère pression de sa main sur mon bras; *Fig* **to bring p. to bear** *or* **to put p. on sb** faire pression sur qn; **to act under p.** agir sous la pression des circonstances; **I can't take all this p.** je ne supporte pas d'être sous une telle pression; **he's been under a lot of p. lately** il est très stressé *ou* vraiment sous pression ces derniers temps; **financial p.** pressions financières; **the p. of business/work/modern life** la pression des affaires/du travail/de la vie moderne; **he pleaded p. of work to excuse his absence** il a excusé son absence en invoquant un excès de travail; **to work at high p.** être débordé; **there's no p., don't come if you don't want to** rien ne t'oblige, si tu ne veux pas venir, ne viens pas

2 *Phys, Tech etc* pression *f*; *(of fluid, heavy body)* poussée *f*; *Elec* pression (électrique), tension *f*, voltage *m*; *Met* **high/low-p. area** zone *f* anticyclonique/cyclonique, zone de hautes/basses pressions
VT *(person)* exercer une pression sur; **stop pressuring me!** arrête de me presser comme ça!; **to p. sb to do** *or* **into doing sth** forcer *ou* obliger qn à faire qch, exercer des pressions sur qn pour qu'il/elle fasse qch
▸▸ *Tech* **p. chamber** réservoir *m* d'air comprimé; *Culin* **p. cooker** cocotte-minute®

f, pl cocottes-minute, autocuiseur *m*; **p. gauge** jauge *f* de pression, manomètre *m*; **p. group** groupe *m* de pression; *Physiol* **p. point** *(on artery)* point *m* de compression; **p. pump** pompe *f* à pression; *Med* **p. sore** escarre *f*, **p. suit** scaphandre *m* pressurisé; **p. switch** *(for oil pressure)* manocontact *m*

pressure-charged [-ˈtʃɑːdʒd] ADJ *Aut* suralimenté

pressure-cook VT *Culin* (faire) cuire sous pression *ou* à la cocotte-minute®

pressurization [preʃəraɪˈzeɪʃən] N *Tech* pressurisation *f*, mise *f*/maintien *m* sous pression

pressurize [ˈpreʃəraɪz] VT **1** *Tech* pressuriser; *Aviat, Astronaut* **pressurized cabin/suit** cabine *f*/combinaison *f* pressurisée; *Nucl* **pressurized water reactor** réacteur *m* à eau sous pression **2** *(put moral pressure on) (person)* exercer une pression sur; **to p. sb into doing sth** faire pression sur qn pour qu'il/ elle fasse qch; **don't p. me** ne me force pas; **a pressurized environment** un environnement stressant

Prestel® [ˈprestel] N *Br TV* ≃ Minitel® *m*

prestidigitation [prestɪdɪdʒɪˈteɪʃən] N *Fml, Hum* prestidigitation *f*

prestidigitator [prestɪˈdɪdʒɪteɪtər] N *Fml, Hum* prestidigitateur, -trice

prestige [presˈtiːʒ] N prestige *m*; **it would mean a loss of p.** ce serait déchoir *ou* déroger; **p. flats** appartements *mpl* de grand standing; **a p. job** un poste prestigieux; **the p. value of the address** le caractère prestigieux de l'adresse, l'adresse prestigieuse; **it has p. value** c'est prestigieux ▸▸ *Mktg* **p. advertising** publicité *f* de prestige; **p. goods** produits *mpl* prestigieux; **p. model** modèle *m* de prestige; *Com* **p. price** prix *m* de prestige; *Mktg* **p. product** produit *m* de prestige; *Mktg* **p. promotion** promotion *f* de prestige

prestigious [presˈtɪdʒəs] ADJ prestigieux

presto [ˈprestəʊ] ADJ, ADV, N *Mus* presto *m* INT **hey p.!** et le tour est joué!

prestressed [priːˈstrest] ADJ *(concrete)* précontraint

presumably [prɪˈzjuːməblɪ] ADV vraisemblablement; **p. she will come** il est probable qu'elle vienne, elle viendra vraisemblablement; **p. you told him that …** je suppose que vous lui avez dit que …; **have they left? – p.** ils sont partis? – je pense *ou* vraisemblablement

presume [prɪˈzjuːm] VT présumer; **you're presuming rather a lot** tu es bien présomptueux; **to p. sb innocent** présumer qn innocent *ou* que qn est innocent; **he was presumed dead** *(by family etc)* on le croyait mort; *(by authorities)* on a présumé qu'il était mort, on l'a considéré comme décédé; **I p. (that) you've written to him** je suppose que vous lui avez écrit; **I p. so** je suppose, je présume que oui; *Fml* **I wouldn't p. to question her decision** je n'aurais pas la présomption de mettre sa décision en question; *Fml* **I wouldn't p. so far as to …** je n'aurais pas la présomption de …
VI *Fml* se montrer présomptueux; **to p. on one's friendship with sb** abuser de l'amitié de qn

presumption [prɪˈzʌmpʃən] N **1** *(assumption)* présomption *f*; **to make a p. that …** présumer que …; **I agreed on the p. that …** j'ai dit que j'étais d'accord parce que je supposais que …; **the p. is that she is dead** on présume qu'elle est morte; *Law* **p. of law** présomption légale; *Law* **p. of fact** présomption de fait **2** *Fml (arrogance)* présomption *f*

presumptive [prɪˈzʌmptɪv] ADJ **heir p.** hé-

ritier *m* présomptif, héritière *f* présomptive
▸▸ *Law etc* **p. evidence** (preuve *f* par) présomption *f*

presumptuous [prɪˈzʌmptjʊəs] ADJ présomptueux

presumptuously [prɪˈzʌmptjʊəslɪ] ADV présomptueusement; **she p. assumed that …** elle a eu la présomption de croire que …

presumptuousness [prɪˈzʌmptjʊəsnɪs] N présomption *f*; **her p. in assuming that …** sa présomption à croire que …

presuppose [priːsəˈpəʊz] VT présupposer

presupposition [priːsʌpəˈzɪʃən] N présupposition *f*

pre-tax ADJ avant impôt
▸▸ **p. margin** marge *f* avant impôt; **p. profit** bénéfice *m* avant impôt

pretence, *Am* **pretense** [prɪˈtens] N **1** *(feigning)* faux-semblant *m*, *pl* faux-semblants, simulation *f*; **to make a p. of doing sth** faire semblant de faire qch; **under the p. of friendship** sous prétexte d'amitié; **under the p. that …** sous prétexte que …; **under** *or* **on the p. of consulting me** sous prétexte de me consulter; **she makes no p. to photographic skills** elle ne prétend pas avoir des dons de photographe; **he made no p. of his boredom/his scepticism** il n'a pas caché son ennui/son scepticisme; **she made no p. of being interested/of feeling anything for him** elle n'a aucunement feint d'être intéressée/de ressentir quoi que ce soit envers lui
2 *(pretension)* **devoid of all p.** sans aucune prétention

pretend [prɪˈtend] VT **1** *(feign)* feindre, simuler; **to p. ignorance** simuler l'ignorance, faire l'ignorant(ante); **to p. to be ill** faire semblant d'être malade, faire le/la malade; **to p. to do sth** faire semblant *ou* mine de faire qch; **they pretended that nothing had happened** ils ont fait comme si rien ne s'était passé *ou* comme si de rien n'était; **let's p. that we're astronauts** on dirait qu'on était astronautes; **p. you haven't seen him** fais semblant de ne pas l'avoir vu; **I'll p. I didn't hear that last remark** je vais faire comme si je n'avais pas entendu cette dernière remarque; **it's no use pretending (that) I'm still young** ce n'est pas la peine de prétendre que je suis encore jeune; **he pretended he was a doctor** *(in order to deceive)* il s'est fait passer pour médecin; **pretending that he had a lot of work to do, he left early** sous prétexte d'avoir beaucoup de travail à faire, il est parti de bonne heure
2 *(claim)* prétendre; **she does not p. to be artistic** elle ne prétend pas être artiste
VI **1** *(put on act)* faire semblant, jouer la comédie; **to play at 'let's p.'** jouer à faire semblant; **I can't go on pretending to her like this** je ne peux pas continuer à lui jouer la comédie comme ça; **don't worry, I was only pretending, I still want to do it!** mais non, c'était pour rire, je suis toujours d'accord!; **he appeared interested, but he was just pretending** il s'est montré intéressé mais il faisait semblant *ou* jouait la comédie
2 *Fml (lay claim)* **to p. to sth** prétendre à qch; **I don't p. to great knowledge on the matter/any special expertise** je ne prétends pas savoir grand-chose sur la question/ avoir des connaissances particulières; *Arch* **to p. to the throne** prétendre au trône
ADJ *Fam* **it was only p.!** c'était pour rire!; **a p. slap** une claque pour rire; **it's only p. money/a p. gun** ce n'est pas du vrai argent/un vrai pistolet

---

Note that the French verb **prétendre** is a false friend and is rarely a translation for the English verb **to pretend**. It means **to claim**.

---

pretended [prɪˈtendɪd] ADJ *(emotion, interest)* feint, simulé; *(doctor, wealth, ignorance etc)* soi-disant, prétendu

pretender [prɪˈtendər] N **1** *(person who puts on act)* simulateur, -trice **2** *(claimant)* prétendant, -ante (**to** à); *Hist* **the Old P.** le Prétendant, -ante; *Hist* **the Young P.** le Jeune Prétendant

pretense [prɪˈtens] N *Am* = **pretence**

pretension [prɪˈtenʃən] N **1** *(claim, esp a false one)* prétention *f* (**to** à); **man of no pretension(s)** homme sans prétentions; **to have pretensions to literary taste** se piquer de littérature; **to have social pretensions** vouloir arriver; **I make no pretensions to being impartial** je ne prétends pas être impartial **2** = **pretentiousness**

pretentious [prɪˈtenʃəs] ADJ prétentieux

pretentiously [prɪˈtenʃəslɪ] ADV prétentieusement

pretentiousness [prɪˈtenʃəsnɪs] N prétention *f*

preterite [ˈpretərɪt] N *Gram* prétérit *m*, passé *m* simple VOIR GRAMMAIRE A39

preternatural [priːtəˈnætʃərəl] ADJ *Lit* hors du commun, exceptionnel

pre-test N pré-test *m*, *pl* pré-tests
VT pré-tester

pre-testing N pré-tests *mpl*

pretext [ˈpriːtekst] N prétexte *m*; **to give sth as a p.** alléguer qch comme prétexte; **he came under** *or* **on the p. of consulting his sister** il est venu sous prétexte de consulter sa sœur

Pretoria [prɪˈtɔːrɪə] N Prétoria

prettify [ˈprɪtɪfaɪ] VT *esp Pej* enjoliver

prettily [ˈprɪtɪlɪ] ADV *(decorated, dressed)* joliment; **to smile p.** faire un/des sourire(s) charmeur(s); **she sang very p.** elle a chanté avec beaucoup de charme

prettiness [ˈprɪtɪnɪs] N *(of woman)* charmes *mpl*; *Pej (of style etc)* mignardise *f*; **the p. of her smile** son joli sourire

pretty [ˈprɪtɪ] ADJ *(woman, child)* joli, mignon; *(thing)* joli; **p. picture/song** joli tableau/jolie chanson; *(with pejorative nuance)* joli petit tableau/jolie petite chanson; **as p. as a picture** joli *ou* mignon comme tout; *usu Pej* **his p.-boy good looks** ses charmes de joli garçon; *Pej* **to make p. speeches** dire des gentillesses; **(it was) not a p. sight** ce n'était pas beau à voir; *Iron* **a p. state of affairs!, a p. mess!** c'est du joli *ou* du propre!; *(that we're in)* nous voilà dans de beaux draps!; *Fam* **that'll cost me a p. penny!** ça va me coûter cher!; *Fam* **to make a p. penny out of sth** tirer une petite fortune de qch; *Fam* **I'm not just a p. face** qu'est-ce que tu crois?, il y en a là-dedans!
ADV *(fairly)* assez, passablement; **I was p. certain that …** j'étais à peu près sûr que …; **I'm p. well** ça ne va pas trop mal; **p. good** *(not bad)* pas mal *ou* mauvais; *(very good)* vraiment bon; **it's p. difficult** c'est plutôt difficile; **p. nearly** *or* **much** *or* **well the same thing** à peu près la même chose **2** *Fam* **to be sitting p.** ne pas avoir à s'en faire

▸ **pretty up** VT SEP enjoliver; **to p. oneself up** se faire beau/belle

pretty-pretty ADJ *Pej (actor)* insipide, sans caractère; *(paintings, style)* gentillet; *(dress)* cucul la praline; **his p. good looks** son charme presque efféminé

pretzel [ˈpretz(ə)l] N *Culin* bretzel *m*

prevail [prɪˈveɪl] VI **1** *(come out strongest)* prévaloir, avoir l'avantage; **let us hope that justice/reason prevails** espérons que la justice/la raison l'emportera; **to p. over** *or* **against sb** prévaloir sur *ou* contre qn, avoir l'avantage *ou* l'emporter sur qn **2 to p. on sb**

to do sth (persuade) amener ou décider qn à faire qch; **he was prevailed (up)on by his friends to ...** il se laissa persuader par ses amis de ... **3** (predominate) prédominer, régner; (of theory etc) prédominer, avoir cours; **the conditions prevailing in France** les conditions qui règnent en France

prevailing [prɪ'veɪlɪŋ] ADJ **1** (widespread) (pré)dominant; **the p. opinion** l'opinion la plus répandue **2** (current) actuel; **in the then p. moral climate** dans le climat moral qui régnait alors; **the p. cold** le froid qui règne en ce moment; **p. fashions** la mode actuelle; **p. winds** vents mpl dominants

prevalence ['prevələns] N (of opinion etc) prédominance f; Med prévalence f; **p. of bribery** caractère m généralisé de la corruption; **p. of typhus** fréquence f des cas de typhus

prevalent ['prevələnt] ADJ **1** (widespread) (pré)dominant; (opinion) le plus répandu; **this opinion is p. among teenagers** cette opinion est très répandue parmi les adolescents; **the disease is p. here** la maladie est très répandue ici **2** (current, prevailing) (conditions) actuel; (in the past) de l'époque

prevaricate [prɪ'værɪkeɪt] VI user d'équivoques, tergiverser

prevarication [prɪværɪ'keɪʃən] N tergiversation f

prevaricator [prɪ'værɪkeɪtər] N personne f qui tergiverse ou qui use d'équivoques

prevent [prɪ'vent] VT (wedding etc) empêcher, faire obstacle à; (accident, misfortune etc) empêcher, prévenir, parer à; **to p. sb (from) doing sth, to p. sb's doing sth** empêcher qn de faire qch, empêcher que qn ne fasse qch; **to p. a disease from spreading** empêcher une maladie de s'étendre, éviter qu'une maladie ne s'étende; **there is nothing to p. our doing so** il n'y a rien qui nous en empêche; **to be unavoidably prevented from doing sth** être dans l'impossibilité matérielle de faire qch; **I cannot p. him** je ne peux pas l'en empêcher; **to p. any scandal** pour éviter tout scandale; **the police prevented the murderer from being lynched** la police a empêché que l'assassin ne soit lynché

preventable [prɪ'ventəb(ə)l] ADJ évitable; **it would have been easily p.** ç'aurait été facile à éviter; **a p. disease** une maladie que l'on peut prévenir

preventative [prɪ'ventətɪv] ADJ, N = preventive

prevention [prɪ'venʃən] N prévention f; **p. of accidents** prévention des accidents; **p. of disease** prévention de la maladie; **rust/fire/crime p.** protection f contre la rouille/les incendies/le crime; **society for the p. of cruelty to children/to animals** société f protectrice des enfants/des animaux; Prov **p. is better than cure** mieux vaut prévenir que guérir

preventive [prɪ'ventɪv] ADJ **p. measures** mesures fpl préventives ou de précaution; N (measure) mesure f préventive; (medication) médicament m préventif
▶▶ Br Law **p. detention** détention f préventive; **p. medicine** médecine f préventive, prophylaxie f

preventively [prɪ'ventɪvlɪ] ADV préventivement; **to act p. against sth** prendre des mesures préventives contre qch

preview ['priːvjuː] N Cin, Theat avant-première f, pl avant-premières; (of art exhibition) vernissage m; esp Am Cin (advertising film) bande-annonce f, pl bandes-annonces; **we got a p. of the latest computers** on a eu un aperçu des derniers ordinateurs

VT Cin, Theat (of person) voir en avant-première; (of cinema) donner ou présenter en avant-première; TV etc pré-visionner; (film) passer en avant-première
▶▶ Comput **p. mode** mode m de prévisualisation; TV etc **p. monitor** écran m de preview

previous ['priːvɪəs] ADJ précédent; (in time) antérieur (**to** à); (coming immediately before) précédent; **they have returned to their p. intransigence** ils sont retournés à leur intransigence passée; **my p. belief was that ...** mon sentiment était auparavant que ...; **on a p. occasion** une autre fois; **on the p. occasion we had met** la dernière fois que nous nous étions rencontrés; **the p. day** le jour précédent, la veille; **the p. evening** la veille au soir; **in the days/weeks p. to his departure** pendant les jours/semaines qui ont précédé son départ; **in the programme p. to this one** dans l'émission antérieure à celle-ci; **her p. job** son travail précédent; **tell me about your p. jobs** parlez-moi de vos emplois antérieurs; **in a p. existence** dans une vie antérieure; **have you had any p. experience?** avez-vous de l'expérience dans ce domaine?; **p. engagement** engagement m antérieur; **p. convictions** condamnations fpl antérieures; (for motoring offences) contraventions fpl antérieures; SI **you're being a bit p.!** vous êtes trop pressé!, vous allez trop vite!
ADV **p. to my departure** avant mon départ
N Br SI (previous convictions) casier m judiciaire; **he's got p. for drink-driving** il a déjà été arrêté pour conduite en état d'ivresse

previously ['priːvɪəslɪ] ADV auparavant; **three days p.** trois jours auparavant; **I was going to introduce them, but they'd met p.** j'allais les présenter l'un à l'autre, mais ils s'étaient déjà rencontrés

prewar [priː'wɔːr] ADJ (prices etc) d'avant-guerre; **the p. period/years** l'avant-guerre m/les années fpl d'avant-guerre

prey [preɪ] N proie f; **birds of p.** oiseaux mpl de proie, rapaces mpl; **beasts of p.** bêtes fpl de proie; **to pursue its p.** (of beast) poursuivre sa proie; **to be a p. to** être la proie de; (fear, doubt etc) être en proie à, être la proie de; **to fall p. to temptation** céder à la tentation
▶ **prey on, prey upon** VT INSEP (be predator of) (something, somebody) faire sa proie de; Fig **something is preying on his mind** il y a quelque chose qui le tourmente ou Fam le travaille; **to p. on old people** (of confidence trickster etc) abuser des personnes âgées; **to p. on sb's fears/insecurity** exploiter les craintes/l'insécurité de qn

prezzie ['prezɪ] N Br Fam cadeau m

PRICE [praɪs] N prix m; (of shares) cours m, cote f; Horseracing cote; **to rise** or **increase** or **go up in p.** (of goods) augmenter; **what p. is that article?** quel est le prix de cet article?; **petrol has come down** or **gone down in p.** le prix de l'essence a baissé; **car prices have fallen** le prix des voitures a chuté; **he charges reasonable prices** il pratique des prix raisonnables; **to quote** or **name a p.** faire le prix; **his pictures fetch huge prices** ses tableaux atteignent des sommes phénoménales ou se vendent à prix d'or; **what p. can you put on good health?** la santé n'a pas de prix; **to be beyond** or **without p.** être (d'un prix) inestimable ou hors de prix, ne pas avoir de prix; **you can buy it at a p.** vous pouvez l'acheter en y mettant le prix; **this must be done at any p.** il faut que cela se fasse à tout prix ou coûte que coûte; **not at any p.** à aucun prix; **I got a good p. for it** j'en ai eu un bon prix; Fig **to pay the p. (for sth)** faire les frais (de qch); Fig **the p. paid for progress/fame** la rançon du progrès/de la gloire; Fig **to set a high p. on sth** faire grand

cas de qch; **it's too high a p. (to pay)** c'est trop cher; Fig **c'est** trop cher payé; **to put** or **set a p. on sb's head** mettre la tête de qn à prix; **she's got a p. on her head** sa tête a été mise à prix; **everyone has their p.** il n'y a pas d'homme qu'on ne puisse acheter; Horse-racing **long/short p.** forte/faible cote; Fam **what p. my chances of being appointed?** quelles sont mes chances d'être nommé?; **what p. glory!** pour ce qu'elle rapporte, la gloire!; **p. inclusive of tax** prix taxe comprise SEE GRAMMAR B59

VT **1** (indicate cost of) mettre un prix à; (decide cost of) fixer le prix de; **all goods must be clearly priced** le prix des marchandises doit être clairement indiqué; **the book is priced at £10** le livre est vendu (au prix de) dix livres
2 (of customer) s'informer du prix de
3 Com **to p. competitors out of the market** éliminer la concurrence en pratiquant des prix déloyaux; **to p. oneself out of the market** perdre sa clientèle en demandant des prix inabordables; **we've been priced out of the Japanese market** nous avons perdu le marché japonais à cause de nos prix; **he priced himself out of the job** il n'a pas été embauché parce qu'il a demandé un salaire trop élevé
▶▶ **p. agreement** accord m sur les prix; Fin **p. bid** offre f de prix; **p. break** baisse f de prix; **p. ceiling** plafond m de prix; **p. comparison** comparaison f des prix; **p. competitiveness** compétitivité-prix f, pl compétitivités-prix; **p. control** contrôle m des prix; **p. cut** rabais m, réduction f (des prix), baisse des prix; **p. cutting** baisse de prix; Mktg **p. differential** écart m de prix; **p. discount** remise f sur les prix; **p. discrimination** tarif m discriminatoire; St Exch **p./earnings ratio** ratio m cours-bénéfice; **p. effect** effet m de prix; **p. elasticity** élasticité f des prix; **p. escalation** flambée f des prix; **p. ex-works** prix départ usine; **p. floor** prix plancher; **p. freeze** blocage m des prix, gel m des prix; **p. hike** hausse f de prix; **prices and incomes policy** politique f des prix et des salaires; **p. increase** hausse f des prix, augmentation f des prix; **p. index** indice m de prix; **p. indicator** indicateur m de prix; Fin **p. inflation** inflation f des prix; **p. instability** instabilité f des prix; Mktg **p. label** étiquette f de prix; **p. labelling** étiquetage m des prix; Mktg **p. leader** prix directeur; Mktg **p. leadership** commandement m des prix; **p. level** niveau m de prix; **p. list** tarif, liste f des prix; St Exch **p. maker** inflation f des prix; **p. markup** majoration f de prix; Fin **p. of money** prix ou loyer m de l'argent; Fin **p. plan** plan m prix; Mktg **p. point** prix (de référence); Mktg **p. policy** politique de prix; Mktg **p. positioning** positionnement m de prix; Mktg **p. promotion** promotion f, Mktg **p. proposal** proposition f de prix; **p. range** gamme f ou échelle f des prix; **what is your p. range?** combien voulez-vous mettre?; **it's not in my p. range** ce n'est pas dans mes prix; **p. reduction** réduction f (des prix); **p. regulation** réglementation f des prix; **p. rigging** alignement m des prix; Fin **p. ring** monopole m des prix; Mktg **p. scale** barème m des prix, échelle des prix; Mktg **p. sensitivity** sensibilité f aux prix; Mktg **p. setting** détermination f des prix, fixation f des prix; St Exch **p. spreads** écarts de cours; Mktg **p. stability** stabilité f des prix; Mktg **p. step** écart de prix; Fin **p. structure** structure f des prix; **p. support** soutien m des prix; Mktg **p. survey** enquête f sur les prix; **p. tag** (label) étiquette f de prix; (value) prix, valeur f des prix; Mktg **p. theory** théorie f des prix; Mktg **p. undercutting** gâchage m des prix; **p. war** guerre f des prix
▶ **price down** VT SEP Com baisser le prix de
▶ **price up** VT SEP Com augmenter le prix de

price-conscious ADJ attentif aux prix

priced [praɪst] ADJ **1** high-p. cher, coûteux; low-p. bon marché, à bas prix **2** (marked with price) marqué d'un prix; **everything in the window is p.** tous les prix des articles qui se trouvent dans la vitrine sont indiqués

price-elastic ADJ Mktg au prix élastique

price-fixing N (by companies, cartel) alignement m des prix

price-inelastic ADJ Mktg au prix stable

priceless ['praɪslɪs] N **1** (invaluable) inestimable, qui n'a pas de prix **2** Fam (funny) (joke, person etc) impayable

> Attention: ne pas confondre avec **worthless**, qui signifie **sans aucune valeur**.

price-sensitive ADJ sensible au prix

pricey ['praɪsɪ] ADJ Fam cher, coûteux

pricing ['praɪsɪŋ] N (setting price(s)) fixation f du prix (**of sth** de qch); **anticipatory p.** fixation des prix par anticipation
‣‣ **p. policy** politique f de(s) prix; **p. research** recherche f sur les prix

prick [prɪk] N **1** (of needle etc) piqûre f; **pricks of conscience** remords mpl (de conscience), scrupules mpl; **to have a p. of conscience** être titillé par sa conscience **2** Vulg (penis) bite f, queue f; (man) connard m; **stop making such a p. of yourself!** arrête de faire le con!; **to feel like a spare p. (at a wedding)** tenir la chandelle
VT (make holes in) (sausages, potatoes) piquer; (balloon) crever, percer; (blister) crever; **to p. one's finger** se piquer au ou le doigt; **the nurse pricked my arm with a needle** l'infirmière m'a piqué le bras avec une aiguille; **his conscience is pricking him** sa conscience l'aiguillonne ou le tourmente; **to p. a hole in sth** faire un trou dans qch
VI **his skin was pricking with the heat** sa peau le picotait à cause de la chaleur
‣‣ Vulg **p. teaser** allumeuse f
‣ **prick out** VT SEP (seedlings) repiquer
‣ **prick up** VT SEP **to p. up one's ears** (of animal) dresser les oreilles; (of person) tendre ou dresser l'oreille
VI **his ears pricked up** (of dog) ses oreilles se sont dressées; (of person) il a dressé l'oreille

pricking ['prɪkɪŋ] ADJ piquant; **a p. sensation** un picotement, un fourmillement
N (piercing) piquage m; (sensation) (of skin etc) picotement m, fourmillement m; **prickings of conscience** remords mpl (de conscience)
‣‣ **p. out** (of seedlings) repiquage m

prickle ['prɪk(ə)l] N **1** (of animal) piquant m; (of plant) épine f, piquant m **2** (sensation) (of skin etc) picotement m; Fig (of anticipation, excitement) fourmillement m
VT piquer, picoter, aiguillonner
VI (of skin, parts of body) fourmiller; Fig **to p. with indignation** se hérisser

prickling ['prɪklɪŋ] ADJ (sensation) de picotement, de fourmillement
N picotement m

prickly ['prɪklɪ] ADJ **1** (animal) hérissé de piquants; (plant) épineux, piquant; Fig (reply etc) sec; (person) difficile; Fig **he's very p. today** il est très susceptible ou irritable aujourd'hui **2** (sensation) de picotement, de fourmillement
‣‣ Med **p. heat** fièvre f miliaire, miliaire f, suette f miliaire; **p. pear** (fruit) figue f de Barbarie; (tree) figuier m de Barbarie

pride [praɪd] N **1** (satisfaction) fierté f, orgueil m; (self-esteem) amour-propre m, pl amours-propres, orgueil; Pej (vanity) orgueil, vanité f; **her children were a source of great p. to her** elle était très fière de ses enfants, ses enfants étaient sa grande fierté; **the sin of p.** le péché d'orgueil; **puffed up or** blown up or swollen with p. bouffi d'orgueil; **I have my p.!** j'ai ma fierté!; **to have too much p. to do sth** être trop fier pour faire qch; **to hurt** or **wound sb's p.** blesser l'amour-propre ou l'orgueil de qn; **to take (a) p. in sth** être fier de qch; **to take p. in one's work** mettre tout son amour-propre ou toute sa fierté dans son travail; **he takes great p. in his daughter's achievements** il est très fier des succès de sa fille; Prov **p. comes before a fall** l'arrogance précède la ruine et l'esprit altier la chute
2 (person, thing) fierté f; **he is the p. of the family** il fait la fierté de la famille; **the p. of my collection** le clou de ma collection; **the p. of the fleet** l'orgueil m de la flotte; **she's his p. and joy** elle fait toute sa fierté; **that antique table is her p. and joy** elle est très fière de cette table ancienne
3 to have p. of place avoir ou tenir la place d'honneur
4 (of lions) troupe f
VT **to p. oneself (up)on sth/doing sth** être fier de qch/de faire qch; Pej s'enorgueillir ou se piquer ou se faire gloire de qch/de faire qch; **to p. oneself on one's knowledge of literature** se piquer de littérature

priest [pri:st] N prêtre m; **the priests** (as a body) le clergé; Cathol **parish p.** ≃ curé m; **assistant p.** vicaire m; **to become a p.** devenir prêtre

priestess ['pri:stes] N prêtresse f

priesthood ['pri:sthʊd] N **1** (state) prêtrise f, sacerdoce m; **to enter the p.** entrer dans les ordres, se faire prêtre **2** (priests) **the p.** le clergé

priestly ['pri:stlɪ] ADJ sacerdotal, -aux, de prêtre; **p. duties** fonctions fpl sacerdotales

prig [prɪg] N **he's a real little p.** il fait toujours le petit saint; **don't be such a p.!** ne sois pas aussi bégueule!

priggish ['prɪgɪʃ] ADJ (person) collet monté inv; (objection, criticism) pudibond; **she's very p.** elle est très collet monté ou très bégueule

priggishness ['prɪgɪʃnɪs] N bégueulerie f, pudibonderie f

prim [prɪm] ADJ **1** usu Pej (person) collet monté inv; (manner) guindé, compassé; **she's so p. and proper** (morally) elle est tellement prude ou collet monté; (in appearance, tidiness etc) elle est tellement correcte **2** (garden) méticuleusement entretenu

prima ['pri:mə] ADJ
‣‣ **p. ballerina** danseuse f étoile; **p. donna** (opera singer) prima donna f, pl prime donne ou prima donna; Pej (temperamental person) diva f; Fig **he's a real p. donna** il joue à la star

primacy ['praɪməsɪ] N **1** primauté f, prééminence f **2** Rel primatie f

primaeval [praɪ'mi:v(ə)l] ADJ = **primeval**

prima facie ['praɪmə'feɪʃɪ] ADV de prime abord
ADJ Law **p. case** = affaire f qui, d'après les premiers témoignages, paraît bien fondée; Fig **this is a p. case of ...** à première vue c'est une affaire de ...; Law **p. evidence** commencement m de preuve

primal ['praɪm(ə)l] ADJ **1** (first) primitif, originel **2** (most important) (duty etc) principal, -aux, fondamental, -aux
‣‣ Psy **p. scream** cri m primal

primarily ['praɪmərɪlɪ, praɪ'merɪlɪ] ADV **1** (principally) principalement, essentiellement **2** (originally) à l'origine, originairement

primary ['praɪmərɪ] ADJ (original) primitif, originel; (first) premier; (fundamental, main) premier, principal, -aux; Elec, Phys etc (coil, current, electron etc) primaire; **the p. meaning of a word** le sens premier d'un mot
N **1** Astron planète f principale, grande planète **2** Elec bobine f primaire **3** (colour) couleur f fondamentale **4** Orn (feather) rémige f **5** Am Pol (election) (élection f) primaire f, (assembly) assemblée f primaire
‣‣ **p. cause** cause f première; Elec **p. cell** pile f primaire; **p. colours** couleurs fondamentales; Mktg **p. data** informations fpl primaires, données fpl primaires; Fin **p. dealer** spécialiste mf en valeurs du Trésor; Mktg **p. demand** demande f primaire; Am St Exch **p. earnings per share** bénéfices mpl premiers par action; Sch **p. education** enseignement m primaire; Pol **p. election** (in US) (élection) primaire; Comput **p. file** fichier m primaire ou principal; Econ **p. industries** secteur m primaire; Med **p. infection** primo-infection f, pl primo-infections; Med **p. lesion** lésion f ou accident m primaire; St Exch **p. market** marché m primaire, marché du neuf; Astron **p. planet** planète principale ou primaire; Com **p. product** matière f première, produit m brut; Geol **p. rocks** roches fpl primaires; **p. school** école f primaire; Gram **p. tenses** temps mpl primitifs

> **Primaries**
> Les élections primaires américaines (directes ou indirectes selon les États) aboutissent à la sélection des candidats qui seront en lice pour représenter les deux grands partis nationaux à l'élection présidentielle.

primate ['praɪmeɪt] N **1** Rel primat m; **the P. of All England** l'archevêque m de Cantorbéry **2** Zool primate m

prime[1] [praɪm] ADJ **1** (most important) premier, principal, -aux; **of p. importance** d'importance capitale, de (toute) première importance; **p. motive** principe moteur m (**of** de) **2** (excellent) (wines etc) excellent, de qualité supérieure, de première qualité; (example, condition, building land etc) excellent; **p. quality meat** viande f de premier choix
N **1** (best time) **p. of youth** fleur f de la jeunesse; **in the p. of life, in one's p.** à ou dans la fleur de l'âge; **to be past one's/its p.** ne plus être de la première jeunesse **2** Rel prime f; **to say/sing the p.** dire/chanter prime **3** Math nombre m premier
‣‣ Fin **p. bill** papier m commercial de premier ordre; Fin **p. bond** obligation f de premier ordre; **p. cost** prix m de revient; **p. meridian of Greenwich** méridien m (d')origine de Greenwich; **p. minister** Premier ministre m; **p. ministerial** de/du premier ministre; **p. ministership** poste m de premier ministre; **p. mover** Phys force f motrice; Phil cause f première; Fig (person) instigateur, -trice; Math **p. number** nombre premier; Fin **p. rate** taux m d'escompte bancaire préférentiel, prime rate m; TV **p. time** heures fpl de grande écoute, prime time m

prime[2] VT **1** (warhead, pump, gun etc) amorcer; **to p. oneself for battle/for a fight** se préparer au combat; Fig **to p. the pump** donner son appui (dans un premier temps) **2** (provide with information) (person) renseigner; **to p. sb for a speech** préparer qn à faire son discours; **the witnesses had all been primed by the police** les dépositions des témoins leur avaient été suggérées par la police; **to be well primed (with alcohol)** être bien imbibé **3** (prepare) (surface to be painted) apprêter

primer[1] ['praɪmər] N **1** (of explosive) amorce f **2** (paint) apprêt m
‣‣ **p. detonator** amorce-détonateur f, pl amorces-détonateurs

primer[2] N *Old-fashioned (reading book)* premier livre *m* de lecture; *(for mathematics etc) (junior level)* premier livre; *(more advanced)* introduction *f*

prime-time ADJ *TV* diffusé à une heure de grande écoute *ou* de prime time
▸▸ **p. advertising** publicité *f* aux heures de grande écoute *ou* en prime time

primeval [praɪˈmiːv(ə)l] ADJ primitif

priming [ˈpraɪmɪŋ] N1 *(of pump)* amorçage *m*; *(explosive powder)* amorce *f* 2 *(in painting) (of wood etc)* apprêtage *m*, apprêt *m*; *(paint)* apprêt
▸▸ **p. charge** charge *f* d'amorçage; **p. powder** *(explosive)* amorce

primitive [ˈprɪmɪtɪv] ADJ primitif; *(manners)* grossier, rude; *(understanding)* rudimentaire; **p. language** langue *f* primitive; **the plumbing is very p.** les installations sanitaires sont plutôt rudimentaires
N *Art (painter, picture)* primitif *m*; *(in anthropology)* primitif, -ive; *Math* primitive *f*

primitively [ˈprɪmɪtɪvlɪ] ADV primitivement; *(constructed, equipped)* de manière rudimentaire

primitiveness [ˈprɪmɪtɪvnɪs] N caractère *m* primitif; *(of plumbing, understanding etc)* caractère rudimentaire; *(of manners)* grossièreté *f*, rudesse *f*

primitivism [ˈprɪmɪtɪvɪz(ə)m] N primitivisme *m*

primly [ˈprɪmlɪ] ADV *(to smile, remark)* d'un air collet monté, d'un air guindé; *(to dress, behave)* avec pruderie *ou* pudibonderie, très correctement

primness [ˈprɪmnɪs] N *(of person's behaviour, manner)* pruderie *f*, pudibonderie *f*; *(of person's appearance)* côté *m* très correct, air *m* guindé *ou* compassé; *(of garden)* ordre *m* méticuleux

primogeniture [praɪməʊˈdʒenɪtʃər] N primogéniture *f*; **(right of) p.** droit *m* d'aînesse

primordial [praɪˈmɔːdɪəl] ADJ primordial, -aux, originel

primordially [praɪˈmɔːdɪəlɪ] ADV primordialement, originellement

primp [prɪmp] *Old-fashioned Fam* VI *(dress up)* se mettre sur son trente-et-un; *Pej* s'attifer
VT **to p. oneself up** se mettre sur son trente-et-un; *Pej* s'attifer

primrose [ˈprɪmrəʊz] N *(plant)* primevère *f*; *(yellow)* jaune *m* pâle
▸▸ *Fig Lit* **the p. path** le chemin de la facilité; **p. yellow** jaune pâle

primula [ˈprɪmjʊlə] N *(plant)* primula *f*, primevère *f*

Primus® [ˈpraɪməs] N *(stove)* réchaud *m* portatif
▸▸ **P. stove** réchaud portatif

prince [prɪns] N prince *m*; **to live like a p.** vivre comme un prince; **P. Charles** le Prince Charles; *Hist* **the Black P.** le Prince Noir
▸▸ **p. of the blood** prince du sang; **P. Charming** le Prince Charmant; **p. consort** prince consort; *Fig* **the P. of Darkness** le prince des ténèbres; **P. Edward Island** l'île *f* du Prince-Édouard; **p. regent** prince régent; **the P. of Wales** le Prince de Galles

princeling [ˈprɪnslɪŋ] N principicule *m*

princely [ˈprɪnslɪ] ADJ princier; *(gift)* magnifique; **to get a p. salary** être payé princièrement; **a p. sum** une somme princière

princess [prɪnˈses] N princesse *f*; **P. Anne** la Princesse Anne
▸▸ **p. dress** robe *f* princesse; **the p. royal** la princesse royale *(fille aînée du monarque)*; **the P. of Wales** la Princesse de Galles

principal [ˈprɪnsɪp(ə)l] ADJ principal, -aux; **p. events in one's life** événements *mpl* capitaux de la vie

N1 *(person) (of college)* principal, -ale; *(of school)* directeur, -trice; *Com, Law (in transaction)* mandant, -ante, commettant *m*; *St Exch* donneur, -euse d'ordre; *Law (of crime)* auteur *m*; *Mus* soliste *mf*; *Theat* acteur, -trice qui tient le rôle principal; *Law* **p. and agent** commettant et préposé; **principals in a duel** adversaires *mpl* dans un duel
2 *Fin (of debt)* capital *m*, principal *m*; **p. and interest** principal et intérêts
▸▸ **p. boy** = jeune héros *m* d'une pantomime dont le rôle est traditionnellement joué par une femme; *Gram* **p. clause** (proposition *f*) principale *f*

principality [prɪnsɪˈpælɪtɪ] N principauté *f*

principally [ˈprɪnsɪplɪ] ADV principalement, surtout

principle [ˈprɪnsɪp(ə)l] N1 *(idea)* principe *m*; **fundamental p.** principe premier *ou* fondamental; **in p.** en principe; **to reach an agreement in p.** parvenir à un accord de principe; **machines that work on the same p.** machines qui fonctionnent sur *ou* d'après le même principe
2 *(moral rule)* principe *m*; **to have high principles** avoir des principes; **man of no principles** homme sans principes; **on p.** par principe; **to do sth on p.** faire qch par principe; **to stick to one's principles** rester fidèle à ses principes; **it's the p. of the thing** c'est une question de principe
3 *Phil (law)* loi *f*, **p. of causality** loi de causalité

principled [ˈprɪnsɪp(ə)ld] ADJ *(behaviour)* dicté par des principes; *(person)* qui a des principes; **to be p.** *(of person)* avoir des principes; **it was very p. of her to refuse** elle a démontré de hauts principes en refusant; *Fam* **he doesn't have a p. bone in his body!** il est complètement dépourvu de principes!

print [prɪnt] N1 *(imprint)* empreinte *f*, *(of foot)* marque *f*, trace *f*, **thumb p.** empreinte du pouce
2 *(printed matter)* matière *f* imprimée; **to read several pages of p.** lire plusieurs pages de texte; **to appear in p.** *(of writings)* paraître; *(of author)* se faire imprimer; **to see one's name appear in p.** voir son nom apparaître dans un livre/journal/*etc*; **he refused to believe the story until he saw it in p.** il a refusé de croire à l'histoire tant qu'il ne l'a pas vue publiée; **in p.** édition en vente (courante); **his unguarded comments got into p.** ses propos irréfléchis ont été publiés ou imprimés; **the newspapers had already gone to p.** when the news broke les journaux étaient déjà sous presse lorsque la nouvelle est tombée; **out of p.** épuisé
3 *(characters)* caractères *mpl*; **large/small p.** gros/petits caractères; **the p. was so small I could barely read it** il était imprimé en caractères si petits que j'avais du mal à le lire; **always read the small p.** *(of contract, guarantee etc)* il faut toujours lire ce qu'il y a d'écrit en petits caractères
4 *(engraving etc)* estampe *f*
5 *Phot* épreuve *f*, *Cin* copie *f*, **to take a p. from a negative** tirer une épreuve d'un cliché; **contact p.** épreuve par contact
6 *(material)* indienne *f*, **(cotton) p.** imprimé *m*

VT 1 *(book etc)* imprimer; *(copies)* tirer; *(newspaper)* imprimer, tirer; **the novel is being printed** le roman est sous presse *ou* en cours d'impression; **1,000 copies of the book have already been printed** on a déjà tiré le livre à 1000 exemplaires; **printed in France** imprimé en France; **the story was printed in all the national newspapers** la nouvelle a été relatée par tous les grands quotidiens; **the papers refused to p. the story** les journaux ont refusé de publier cette histoire

2 *(imprint)* imprimer **(sth on sth** qch sur qch**); incidents that p. themselves on the memory** incidents qui se gravent dans la mémoire
3 *(write) (address, name etc)* écrire en lettres d'imprimerie
4 *Phot* **to p. a negative** tirer une épreuve d'un cliché
5 *Tex (cotton etc)* imprimer

VI 1 *(of printer)* imprimer; *(of document)* s'imprimer; *Phot* **the negative hasn't printed very well** le cliché n'a pas donné un très bon résultat au tirage; **the book is now printing** le livre est à l'impression *ou* est actuellement sous presse
2 *(when writing)* écrire en lettres d'imprimerie; **please p.** *(on form etc)* veuillez écrire en lettres d'imprimerie
▸▸ *Mktg* **p. ad, p. advertisement** publicité *f* presse; *Mktg* **p. advertising** publicité *f* presse; *Comput* **p. buffer** mémoire *f* tampon d'imprimante; *Comput* **p. code** code *m* d'impression; *Comput* **p. drum** tambour *m* d'impression; *Comput* **p. file** fichier *m* d'impression; *Comput* **p. format** format *m* d'impression; *Comput* **p. head** tête *f* d'impression; *Comput* **p. job** *(file)* fichier à imprimer; *Comput* **p. list** liste *f* de fichiers à imprimer; **the p. media** la presse écrite et l'édition; *Comput* **p. menu** menu *m* d'impression; *Comput* **p. option** option *f* d'impression; *Comput* **p. preview** prévisualisation *f*, aperçu *m* avant impression; *Comput* **p. quality** qualité *f* d'impression; *Comput* **p. queue** liste de fichiers à imprimer; *Comput* **p. queuing** mise *f* en attente à l'impression; **p. ribbon** ruban *m* d'impression; **p. room** cabinet *m* d'estampes; **p. run** tirage *m*; *Comput* **p. screen** copie *f* d'écran; **to do a p. screen** imprimer un écran; *Comput* **p. screen key** touche *f* d'impression d'écran; **p. shop** imprimerie *f*, *Comput* **p. speed** vitesse *f* d'impression; **the p. unions** les syndicats *mpl* des typographes; **p. wheel** roue *f* d'impression

▸ **print off** VT SEP 1 *(book)* imprimer; *(copy)* tirer; *(magazine)* tirer, imprimer 2 *Phot* tirer
▸ **print out** VT SEP *Comput* imprimer

printable [ˈprɪntəb(ə)l] ADJ publiable, imprimable

printed [ˈprɪntɪd] ADJ imprimé; **such is the power of the p. word** tel est le pouvoir de l'écrit
▸▸ *Elec* **p. circuit** circuit *m* imprimé; *Elec* **p. circuit board** carte *f* de *ou* à circuits imprimés; *Tex* **p. cotton** coton *m* imprimé; **p. directory** annuaire *m* papier; **p. form** imprimé *m*, formulaire *m*; **p. matter** imprimés; **p. paper rate** *(at post office)* tarif *m* imprimés

printer [ˈprɪntər] N1 *Typ etc (person)* imprimeur *m*; *(machine)*, *Comput* imprimante *f*, *Tel* téléscripteur *m*; **it's at the p.'s** c'est chez l'imprimeur *ou* à l'impression 2 *Phot (person)* tireur, -euse d'épreuves; *(machine)* tireuse *f*
▸▸ *Comput* **p. buffer** mémoire *f* tampon d'imprimante; *Comput* **p. cable** câble *m* d'imprimante; **p. carriage** chariot *m* d'imprimante; *Comput* **p. code** code *m* d'imprimante; **p.'s devil** apprenti *m* imprimeur; *Comput* **p. driver** programme *m* de commande d'impression; **p. drum** tambour *m* d'impression; **p. engine** mécanique *f* d'impression; **p.'s error** faute *f* d'impression, coquille *f*, **p. font** fonte *f* imprimante; **p.'s ink** encre *f* d'imprimerie; *Comput* **p. interface** interface *f* d'imprimante; **p. language** langage *m* d'imprimante; **p.'s mark** marque *f* d'imprimeur; **p. output** sortie *f* d'imprimante; **p. paper** papier *m* d'impression; *Comput* **p. port** port *m* d'imprimante; **p.'s proofs** épreuves *fpl* d'imprimerie; **p.'s reader** correcteur,

-trice d'épreuves; **p. sharing** partage *m* d'imprimantes; **p. speed** vitesse *f* d'impression; **p. spooler** spouleur *m* d'imprimante, pilote *m* de mise en attente des fichiers à imprimer; **p. spooling** mise *f* en attente des fichiers à imprimer; **p. stand** table *f* d'imprimante

printing ['prɪntɪŋ] N **1** *(action) (of book)* impression *f*, tirage *m*; *(craft)* imprimerie *f*, typographie *f*; *(writing)* écriture *f* en lettres d'imprimerie; **he works in p.** il travaille dans l'imprimerie; **fourth p.** quatrième impression **2** *Phot* tirage *m* **3** *Tex* **cotton p.** impression *f* sur coton

▸▸ **p. error** erreur *f* typographique; **p. ink** encre *f* d'imprimerie; **p. paper** papier *m* d'impression; **p. press** presse *f* (d'imprimerie)

printout ['prɪntaʊt] N *Comput* impression *f*, sortie *f* (sur) imprimante, copie *f*; *(continuous)* listing *m*, listage *m*

print-through paper N *Comput* papier *m* à effet d'empreinte, liasse *f* carbonnée

prior ['praɪər] ADJ précédent, antérieur; **p. to** avant; **p. to his winning/appointment** avant qu'il ne gagne/ne soit nommé; **to have a p. claim** avoir des prétentions antérieures; **p. engagement** engagement *m* antérieur; **I have a p. engagement** je suis déjà pris; **to have p. knowledge of sth** être déjà au courant de qch
N *Rel* prieur *m*

prioress ['praɪəres] N *Rel* prieure *f*

prioritization [praɪɒrɪtaɪ'zeɪʃən] N **the p. of all these jobs** la définition d'un ordre de priorité pour toutes ces tâches; **they opted for a p. of expansion** ils ont décidé de donner la priorité à l'expansion

prioritize [praɪ'ɒrɪtaɪz] VT **1** *(arrange according to priority) (several tasks etc)* donner un ordre de priorité à; **it depends how you p. them** tout dépend de l'ordre de priorité que tu établis; **it was wrongly prioritized** on a mal jugé de son importance **2** *(give priority to) (one task etc)* donner la priorité à
VI *(evaluate priorities)* établir un ordre de priorités

priority [praɪ'ɒrɪti] N priorité *f*; **to give p. to sb/sth** donner la priorité à qn/qch; **to have p.** *(of job etc)* être prioritaire; *(of person when driving)* avoir la priorité; **to have** *or* **take p. over sb** avoir la préséance *ou* la priorité sur qn; **hygiene has a high p.** l'hygiène est tout à fait prioritaire; **our first p. is to buy the tickets** il faut que nous achetions les billets, c'est une priorité absolue; **p.** *(on message)* urgent; **to have one's priorities right/wrong** savoir/ne pas savoir ce qui est important; **p. of claim** priorité
ADJ ATTRIB **to get p. treatment** *(of task)* être exécuté *ou* fait en priorité

▸▸ **p. booking** réservation *f* prioritaire; **p. holder** prioritaire *mf*; *Law* **p. rights** droits *mpl* de priorité *ou* de préférence; *St Exch* **p. share** action *f* privilégiée, action de priorité

priory ['praɪəri] N *Rel* prieuré *m* *(de couvent)*

prise [praɪz] VT *Br* = **prize**²

prism ['prɪz(ə)m] N prisme *m*
▸▸ **p. binoculars** jumelle(s) *f(pl)* prismatiques *ou* à prismes

prismatic [prɪz'mætɪk] ADJ *(shape, colour etc)* prismatique
▸▸ **p. binoculars** jumelle(s) *f(pl)* prismatiques *ou* à prismes

prison ['prɪz(ə)n] N *also Fig* prison *f*; **to send sb to p., to put sb in p.** mettre qn en prison; **to throw sb into p.** jeter qn en prison; **he's been in p.** il a fait de la prison; *Fig* **to escape from the p. of one's marriage** mettre fin à un mariage qui était devenu une prison VOIR GRAMMAIRE A6

▸▸ **p. camp** camp *m* de prisonniers; **p. officer** gardien, -ienne de prison; **p. visitor** visiteur, -euse de prison; **p. yard** cour *f* de prison

prisoner ['prɪz(ə)nər] N **1** *(captive)* prisonnier, -ière; **to take/hold sb p.** faire/retenir qn prisonnier; **to take prisoners** faire des prisonniers; *Fig* **to take no prisoners** être impitoyable; *Fig* **to be a p. of one's past** être prisonnier de son passé **2** *Law* détenu, -ue; *(after sentence)* détenu, -ue, prisonnier, -ière; **p. at the bar** prévenu, -ue; *(for serious crimes)* accusé, -ée

▸▸ **p. of conscience** prisonnier, -ière d'opinion; **p. of war** prisonnier, -ière de guerre; **p. of war camp** camp *m* de prisonniers de guerre

prissy ['prɪsɪ] ADJ *(person) (fussy)* pointilleux, maniaque; *(prudish)* collet monté *inv*, bégueule; *(language)* pudibond

pristine ['prɪstiːn] ADJ *(spotless)* impeccable, sans tache; **in p. condition** comme neuf

prithee ['prɪðɪ] INT *Arch* je te prie

privacy ['praɪvəsɪ, 'prɪ-] N intimité *f*; **the p. of one's home** l'intimité de son foyer; **a desire for p.** un désir d'échapper aux regards indiscrets; **I like my p.** j'aime avoir un peu d'intimité; **to disturb sb's p.** faire intrusion chez qn; **there is no p. here** on n'est jamais seul ici

▸▸ *Can* **P. Commissioner** Commissaire *m* à la protection de la vie privée

PRIVATE ['praɪvɪt] ADJ **1** *(personal)* privé; **can I talk to you about something p.?** puis-je discuter avec vous de quelque chose de personnel?; **can we go somewhere p.?** est-ce que nous pourrions discuter en privé?; **a p. joke** une plaisanterie entre nous/eux/*etc*; **the p. life of an actor** la vie privée d'un acteur; **in one's p. life** dans la vie privée, dans le privé; **p. motives** motifs *mpl* personnels
2 *(secret)* secret, -ète; **to keep a matter p.** tenir une affaire secrète; **she is a very p. person** c'est quelqu'un de très discret *ou* réservé; **he is very p. about his affairs** il est très réservé *ou* secret pour ce qui est de ses affaires; **p. and confidential** secret et confidentiel; **to mark a letter p.** marquer sur une lettre 'confidentiel' *ou* 'personnel'; **you stay out of this! – it's p. between John and me** reste en dehors de tout ça! – ça ne regarde que John et moi; **to be received in p. audience** être reçu en audience particulière
3 *(for private use)* **p. bathroom** salle *f* de bain particulière; **this is his own p. room** c'est sa pièce à lui; **for my p. use** pour mon usage personnel
4 *(to which public not admitted)* **the funeral will be p.** les obsèques auront lieu dans la plus stricte intimité; **P.** *(on sign)* entrée interdite au public
5 *(not state-run)* privé
N **1** *(in private life)* dans la vie privée; *(with close family)* dans l'intimité; *(with friends etc, not in public)* dans le privé; *(confidentially)* en privé; **married in p.** marié dans l'intimité; **to sit in p.** *(of assembly)* se réunir en séance privée; *Law* **to hear a case in p.** juger une affaire à huis clos; **to speak to sb in p.** parler à qn en privé; **in p. she admitted she was worried** en privé elle a admis qu'elle était inquiète; *(to herself)* dans son for intérieur elle a admis qu'elle était inquiète
2 *Mil* simple soldat *m*; **the privates and the NCOs** la troupe et les gradés; **p. Jones!** soldat Jones!
3 *Fam* **privates** *(genitals)* parties *fpl* (génitales)

▸▸ **p. bank** banque *f* privée; *Tel* **p. branch exchange** autocommutateur *m* privé; **p. bus** bus *m* réservé; **p. car** voiture *f* particulière;

p. citizen simple particulier *m*; **p. company** entreprise *f* *ou* société *f* privée; **p. dance** bal *m* sur invitation; **p. detective** détective *m* privé; **p. education** enseignement *m* privé; **p. enterprise** entreprise *f* privée; *(principle)* libre entreprise; *Fam* **p. eye** *(private detective)* privé *m*; **p. finance initiative** partenariat *m* public-privé; **p. fishing** pêche *f* gardée; **p. function** réception *f* privée; **p. health insurance** assurance *f* maladie privée; **p. house** maison *f* particulière; **p. income** rentes *fpl*; **p. individual** particulier *m*; **p. industry** privé *m*; **p. investigator** détective *m* privé; *Fin* **p. investment** investissement *m* *ou* placement *m* privé; *Fin* **p. investor** investisseur, -euse privé(e); **p. lessons** cours *mpl* particuliers; *Fin* **p. limited company** société à responsabilité limitée; *Tel* **p. line** ligne *f* privée; **p. means** rentes, fortune *f* personnelle; *Parl* **p. member** = simple député *m*; *Parl* **p. member's bill** = proposition *f* de loi faite par un simple député; **p. nursing home** clinique *f* privée; **p. office** cabinet *m* particulier; **p. ownership** propriété *f* privée; *Fam Euph* **p. parts** parties génitales; **p. party** *(gathering)* réunion *f* privée *ou* intime; *(group)* groupe *m* de particuliers; **p. patient** = patient *m* d'un médecin dont les consultations ne sont pas prises en charge par les services de santé; *Fin* **p. pension** retraite *f* complémentaire; **they operate a p. pension scheme** ils ont leur propre caisse de retraite; *Theat* **p. performance** représentation *f* privée; *Med* **p. practice** médecine *f* privée *ou* non conventionnelle; **p. property** propriété privée; **p. road** voie *f* privée; **p. room** *(in hospital)* chambre *f* particulière; **p. sale** vente *f* à l'amiable; **p. school** école *f* privée; *Cin* **p. screening** projection *f* privée, séance *f* privée; **p. secretary** secrétaire *mf* particulier(ière); *Br Pol* = haut fonctionnaire *m* dont le rôle est d'assister un ministre; **p. sector** *(secteur m)* privé *m*; **p. sector salaries** salaires *mpl* du secteur privé; *Cin* **p. showing** projection privée, séance privée; **p. soldier** simple soldat, (soldat de) deuxième classe *m*; *Law* **p. wrong** atteinte *f* aux droits d'un individu

privateer [praɪvə'tɪər] N *Hist (ship)* (bâtiment *m* armé en) corsaire *m*; *(man)* corsaire *m*

private-label brand N *Mktg* marque *f* de distributeur

privately ['praɪvɪtlɪ] ADV **1** *(as/by a private individual) (to act, speak etc)* en simple particulier; *(to sell)* de gré à gré; **to benefit p. from sth** bénéficier personnellement de qch; **p. owned** qui appartient à un particulier; *(hotel)* familial, -aux; *(not state-owned)* du (secteur) privé
2 *(in private)* en privé; **to speak to sb p.** parler à qn en privé *ou* en particulier
3 *(inwardly) (to think, suspect etc)* intérieurement
4 *(not through state system)* **I had it done p.** *(of treatment at doctor's, dentist's etc)* je l'ai fait faire à mes frais; **she was p. educated** elle a fait sa scolarité dans le privé; **he had them p. educated** il les a mis dans une école privée

privation [praɪ'veɪʃən] N privation *f* (**of** de); **to live in p.** vivre dans la privation, vivre de privations

privatization [praɪvɪtaɪ'zeɪʃən] N privatisation *f*

privatize ['praɪvɪtaɪz] VT privatiser

privet ['prɪvɪt] N *(plant)* troène *m*
▸▸ **p. hedge** haie *f* de troènes

privilege ['prɪvɪlɪdʒ] N **1** *also Comput* privilège *m*; **to grant sb certain privileges** octroyer certains privilèges *ou* avantages à qn; **to enjoy the p. of doing sth** jouir du privilège *ou* avoir le privilège de faire qch; **it is**

my p. to introduce ... j'ai le grand honneur *ou* le privilège de vous présenter ...; **it was a p. to have known her** c'est un privilège de l'avoir connue; **I had the p. of knowing him personally** j'ai eu le privilège de le connaître personnellement **2** *Law (of lawyer)* droit *m* de tenir une information secrète; *Parl* immunité *f* parlementaire

▶ **VT** *(usu passive) (person)* privilégier; **I am privileged to be able to present to you ...** j'ai l'honneur *ou* le privilège de vous présenter ...

privileged ['prɪvɪlɪdʒd] ADJ privilégié; **the p. classes** les classes *fpl* privilégiées; **a p. few** quelques privilégiés; **p. information** informations *fpl* confidentielles

▶ **NPL the p.** les privilégiés *mpl*

▶▶ *Fin* **p. debt** dette *f* privilégiée

privily ['prɪvɪlɪ] ADV *Arch* en secret

privy ['prɪvɪ] ADJ *Fml* **to be p. to sth** *(have knowledge of)* avoir connaissance de qch

▶ **N** *Old-fashioned (toilet)* cabinets *mpl* (souvent en dehors de la maison)

▶▶ *Br* **the P. Council** le Conseil privé *(du souverain)*; **the P. Purse** = la cassette du souverain

prize ['praɪz] **N 1** *(award)* prix *m*; *(what is at stake, to be won)* enjeu *m*; *Fam* **no prizes for guessing** ce n'est pas difficile à deviner; **to win the p.,** **to carry off the p.** remporter le prix **2** *(in a lottery)* lot *m*; **to win first p.** gagner le gros lot; **the first p. is a week in London** le premier prix est une semaine à Londres **3** *Naut (ship)* prise *f*, capture *f*

▶ ADJ ATTRIB *(example)* excellent, parfait; *(tulips, sheep etc)* primé; **p. bull** taureau *m* primé; *Fam* **he's a p. idiot** c'est un abruti de première; **it's my p. possession** c'est l'objet que je prise au-dessus de tout

▶ **VT** *(value)* priser; **to p. sth highly** faire grand cas de qch; **her most prized possession** l'objet qu'elle prise au-dessus de tout

▶▶ *Fin* **p. bond** obligation *f* à lots, valeur *f* à lots; **p. draw** tombola *f*, loterie *f*; **p. list** liste *f* des gagnants; **p. money** prix *(en argent)*; **the p. money is £5000** le prix se monte à 5000 livres; **what did you do with the p. money?** qu'est-ce que tu as fait avec l'argent de la récompense?; *Boxing* **p. ring** ring *m (pour la boxe professionnelle)*

prize ['praɪz] VT *Br (force)* **to p. sth up** soulever qch à l'aide d'un levier *etc*; **I managed to p. the plaque off the wall** j'ai réussi à décrocher *ou* détacher la plaque du mur; **to p. a lid open** forcer un couvercle avec un levier *etc*; **they had to p. his hand open to get the key** ils ont dû ouvrir sa main de force pour avoir la clé; **to p. sth out of sb** *(money)* soutirer qch à qn; *(secret, information)* arracher qch à qn; **to p. sth out of sb's grasp** arracher qch à qn

prizefight ['praɪzfaɪt] N match *m* de boxe professionnel

prizefighter ['praɪzfaɪtər] N boxeur, -euse professionnel(elle)

prizefighting ['praɪzfaɪtɪŋ] N boxe *f* professionnelle

prizegiving ['praɪzgɪvɪŋ] N distribution *f* des prix

▶▶ *Sch* **p. day** jour *m* de la distribution des prix

prizewinner ['praɪzwɪnər] N *(in game, lottery etc)* gagnant, -ante *(du prix)*; *Sch, Art etc* lauréat, -ate

prizewinning ['praɪzwɪnɪŋ] ADJ *(novel etc)* primé; *(ticket, number)* gagnant

PRO [piːɑːˈrəʊ] **N 1** *(abbr* **public relations officer***)* responsable *mf* des relations publiques **2** *Br (abbr* **Public Record Office***)* ≃ Archives *fpl* nationales

pro ['prəʊ] **N 1** *Sport etc Fam (professional*

person) pro *mf inv*; **to turn p.** passer pro; **she was a real p.** *(actress, singer etc)* c'était une vraie pro **2** *Sl (prostitute)* professionnelle *f*

pro ADJ, PREP pour; **he was very p. (the idea)** il était tout à fait pour (cette idée)

▶ **NPL the pros and cons** le pour et le contre

pro- ['prəʊ] PREF pro-; **to be p.-hanging/ -abortion** être partisan de la pendaison/ de l'interruption volontaire de grossesse; **a p.-hanging demonstration** une manifestation en faveur de la pendaison; **to be p.- Europe/American** être pro-européen/pro- américain; **the p.-Yeltsin forces** les forces de Yeltsin

proactive [prəʊˈæktɪv] ADJ dynamique, qui prend les devants, plein d'initiative; **you should be more p.** prends plus souvent des initiatives

▶▶ *Mktg* **p. marketing** marketing *m* proactif; *Admin* **p. staffing** dotation *f* par anticipation

pro-am ADJ *Golf (abbr* **professional- amateur***)*

▶▶ **p. tournament** = tournoi *m* opposant des équipes composées chacune d'un professionnel et d'un amateur

prob [prɒb] N *Fam (abbr* **problem***)* problème *m*, blème *m*; *Br* **no probs!** pas de problèmes!

probability [prɒbəˈbɪlɪtɪ] N probabilité *f*, **in all p.** selon toute probabilité *ou* vraisemblance; **the p. is that it will get hotter** il est probable qu'il fasse encore plus chaud; **there is a strong p./not much p. that ...** il est fort probable/il n'est guère probable que ...; **there would be little p. of our succeeding** nous aurions peu de chances de réussir; **there is every p. that events will prove him right** selon toute probabilité les événements lui donneront raison; *Math* **calculation of probabilities, calculus of probabilities** calcul *m* des probabilités; **what is the p. of 10% proving defective?** quelle probabilité y a-t-il que 10% s'avèrent défectueux? VOIR GRAMMAIRE A58–60; B39

▶▶ **p. laws** lois *fpl* des probabilités; *Mktg* **p. method** *(of sampling)* méthode *f* probabiliste; *Mktg* **p. sample** échantillon *m* probabiliste; *Mktg* **p. sampling** échantillonnage *m* probabiliste

probable ['prɒbəb(ə)l] ADJ probable; *(story, excuse)* vraisemblable; **it's p. that he'll come** il est probable qu'il viendra; **p. cause of death** cause *f* probable de la mort

▶ **N** *(likely candidate, participant)* candidat, -ate/participant, -ante qui a de bonnes chances; *esp Am (probable thing, event)* probabilité *f*; **certainties and probables** certitudes *fpl* et probabilités

▶▶ *Math* **p. error** erreur *f* probable

probably ['prɒbəblɪ] ADV probablement; **will they come? – p. not** est-ce qu'ils viendront? – probablement pas

probate ['prəʊb(e)ɪt] N *Law* **1** *(grant of)* **p.** *(for will)* validation *f*, homologation *f*, **to grant p. (of a will)** homologuer un testament; *Am* **p. court, court of p.** tribunal *m* des successions et des tutelles **2** *(will)* testament *m* revêtu de la formule exécutoire

probation [prəˈbeɪʃən] **N 1** *(trial period)* **(period of) p.** période *f* d'essai; *Rel (of novice)* probation *f*, **to be on p.** faire une période d'essai; *Rel* être en probation **2** *Law (mise f en)* liberté *f* surveillée; **he'll probably get p.** on lui accordera probablement la liberté surveillée; **on p.** en liberté surveillée

▶▶ **p. officer** ≃ agent *m* de probation; **p. system** régime *m* de la liberté surveillée

probationary [prəˈbeɪʃən(ə)rɪ] ADJ

▶▶ **p. period** période *f* d'essai; *Rel* probation *f*

probationer [prəˈbeɪʃənər] **N 1** *(person on trial period)* stagiaire *mf*, personne *f* (qui

est) à l'essai; *Rel* novice *mf* **2** *Law* délinquant, -ante en liberté surveillée

probe [prəʊb] **N 1** *(instrument)* sonde *f*, *(act)* coup *m* de sonde; **space p.** sonde spatiale **2** *Fam (enquiry)* enquête *f* (**into** sur)

▶ **VT** *Med (wound etc)* sonder, explorer; *Fig (person)* sonder; *(the past)* fouiller (dans); *(mystery etc)* approfondir, fouiller

▶ **VI to p. into the past** fouiller dans le passé; **to p. deeply into the human heart** *(of novelist)* sonder le cœur humain; **if you'd probed more deeply** *(to journalist etc)* si vous aviez fait des recherches plus approfondies; **to p. into people's private lives** fouiller dans la vie des gens; **to p. into the circumstances surrounding the accident** analyser *ou* explorer les circonstances dans lesquelles l'accident s'était produit

probing ['prəʊbɪŋ] ADJ *(investigation, enquiry)* approfondi; *(eyes, look)* scrutateur; **she felt the doctor's p. fingers on her arm** elle sentait les doigts du docteur qui sondaient son bras

▶ **N** *Med (of wound)* sondage *m*, exploration *f*, *(enquiries, questions)* questions *fpl* (**into** sur); **to do some p.** poser des questions; **I'll do some p. and try to find out why she's so reluctant** je ferai ma petite enquête pour savoir pourquoi elle est si réticente; **no amount of p. will persuade him to reveal the truth** on aura beau insister, rien ne le persuadera à révéler la vérité

probity ['prəʊbɪtɪ] N *Fml* probité *f*, honnêteté *f*

problem ['prɒbləm] N *Math, Fig* problème *m*; **that's your p.** ça, c'est ton problème; **their p. is that they don't have enough time** leur problème c'est qu'ils n'ont pas assez de temps; **money isn't a p.** l'argent n'est pas un problème; **and I thought I had problems!** moi qui pensais que j'avais des problèmes!; **I can't pay until next week – that's not a p.** je ne pourrai pas payer avant la semaine prochaine – ce n'est pas un problème *ou* pas de problème; *Fam* **I haven't got a car – no p., I'll take you** je n'ai pas de voiture – pas de problème, je t'emmènerai; **social problems** problèmes sociaux; **the housing p.** la crise du logement; **it's a p. to know what to do** il est bien difficile de savoir quoi faire; **he's a p.** c'est un cas *ou* c'est un problème, celui-là; **I don't want to be a p.** je ne veux pas causer *ou* créer de problème(s); **what seems to be the p.?** qu'est-ce qu'il y a?, où est le problème?; **has anyone got a p. with that?** est-ce que quelqu'un a une objection?, est-ce que ça dérange quelqu'un?; *Fam* **what's your p.?** tu as un problème ou quoi?; **to have a drink/drug p.** (trop) boire/ se droguer; **to have a weight p.** avoir tendance à prendre du poids; **the LX31 always was a p. car** la LX31 nous/leur/*etc* a toujours posé des problèmes

▶▶ **p. area** *(in town)* quartier *m* à problèmes; *(in project)* source *f* de problèmes; **p. child** *(child)* enfant *mf* à problèmes, enfant difficile; *Mktg (company, product)* dilemme *m*; **p. families** familles *fpl* à problèmes; *Br* **p. page** courrier *m* du cœur; **p. recognition** reconnaissance *f* du problème

problematic(al) [prɒblɪˈmætɪk, -ɪk(ə)l] ADJ *(question, opinion, result etc)* problématique

problematically [prɒblɪˈmætɪklɪ] ADV problématiquement

problem-orient(at)ed ADJ

▶▶ *Comput* **p. language** langage *m* orienté problème

problem-solving N résolution *f* de problèmes

▶▶ **p. skills** capacités *fpl* à résoudre les problèmes

pro bono [-'bəʊnəʊ] ADJ *Am Law (legal work)* à titre gratuit; *(lawyer)* exerçant à titre gratuit

proboscis, *pl* **proboscises** [prəʊ'bɒsɪs, -ɪsɪz] N **1** *(of elephant, insect)* trompe *f* **2** *Hum (nose)* appendice *m*
▸▸ *Zool* **p. monkey** nasique *m*

procedural [prə'siːdʒər(ə)l] ADJ de procédure; *Law* procédural, -aux
▸▸ *Comput* **p. language** langage *m* de procédures

procedure [prə'siːdʒər] N procédure *f*; *Med (for administering treatment etc)* protocole *m*; **the correct p.** la marche à suivre, la bonne procédure; **what's the p. for renewing a passport?** quelle est la marche à suivre pour faire renouveler un passeport?; **in case of fire** marche à suivre en cas d'incendie; **rules** *or* **order of p.** règles *fpl* de procédure; *(of assembly)* règlement *m* intérieur; **code of criminal p.** code *m* de procédure pénale

procedure-orient(at)ed ADJ *Comput* orienté procédure
▸▸ **p. language** langage *m* procédural

proceed [prə'siːd] VI **1** *esp Fml (walk)* marcher; *(drive)* rouler; **in which direction were you proceeding?** dans quelle direction vous dirigiez-vous?; **to p. to a place** *(go to a place)* aller *ou* se rendre à un endroit; *(go towards a place)* se diriger vers un endroit; **to p. with caution** *(go)* avancer prudemment **2** *(act)* procéder; **how shall we p.?** comment allons-nous procéder?; **how does one p.?** quelle est la marche à suivre?, comment procède-t-on?; **to p. with caution** procéder *ou* agir avec prudence **3** **to p. to do sth** *(begin)* se mettre à faire qch, commencer à faire qch; **you may p. to remove the outer casing** vous pouvez maintenant enlever le carter; **to p. to business** *(at meeting etc)* passer aux affaires; **I will now p. to another matter** je passe maintenant à une autre question **4** *(continue)* se poursuivre, (se) continuer; **to p. (on one's way)** continuer son chemin, poursuivre sa route; **the play proceeded without further interruption** la pièce se poursuivit sans autre interruption; **the project is proceeding well** le projet se déroule bien; **negotiations are now proceeding** des négociations sont en cours; **to pay as the work proceeds** payer au fur et à mesure que l'ouvrage avance; **he immediately proceeded to say the opposite** et le voilà qui se met à dire le contraire; **to p. with sth** poursuivre qch, continuer qch; **before we p. any further** avant d'aller plus loin; **she is proceeding with her complaint** elle maintient sa plainte; **p.!** continuez! **5** *Law* **to p. against sb** poursuivre qn (en justice) **6** *(originate)* **sounds proceeding from a room** bruits qui sortent *ou* proviennent d'une pièce; **the social problems proceeding from lack of education** les problèmes sociaux qui découlent du manque d'éducation **7** *Comput (in dialog box)* continuer

proceeding [prə'siːdɪŋ] N **1** *Fml (way of acting)* manière *f* de procéder, façon *f* d'agir **2** *(event, operation)* opération *f*; **proceedings** *(of assembly)* débats *mpl*; *(of conference)* actes *fpl*; **proceedings were interrupted by …** le déroulement des événements a été interrompu par …; **to co-ordinate proceedings** coordonner les opérations; *Admin* **the entire proceedings were disgraceful** toute l'affaire a été menée d'une façon indigne; *Admin* **to conduct the proceedings** diriger les débats; *Admin* **the proceedings were orderly** la réunion s'est déroulée dans le calme **3** *Law* **(legal) proceedings** procès *m*, pour-

suites *fpl* judiciaires *ou* en justice; **to take** *or* **institute proceedings against sb** intenter une action contre qn, intenter un procès à qn, poursuivre qn en justice; **to order proceedings to be taken against sb** instrumenter contre qn

proceeds ['prəʊsiːdz] NPL *(from sale etc)* produit *m*, montant *m*; *(of charity)* bénéfices *mpl*; **all the p. of the album will go to charity** tous les bénéfices faits grâce à cet album iront à des œuvres de bienfaisance

process¹ ['prəʊses] N **1** processus *m*; **it's a slow p.** c'est un processus lent; *(persuading sb, adopting new system etc)* ça va prendre longtemps; **by a p. of elimination/of trial and error** en procédant par élimination/par tâtonnements *ou* approximations successives; **to be in the p. of doing sth** être en train de faire qch; **he lost most of his friends in the p.** il a perdu presque tous ses amis en faisant cela; **but you ruined the carpet in the p.** mais tu as abîmé la moquette par la même occasion; **during the p. of dismantling** au cours du démontage; **the work is in p.** le travail est en cours; **the building is in the p. of construction/of being repaired** le bâtiment est en cours de construction/de réparation; **the peace p.** le processus de paix
2 *Tech (industrial)* procédé *m*; *(chemical)* réaction *f*; *Typ, Phot* procédés photomécaniques; *Comput* procédé, opération *f*, traitement *m*; *Metal* **Bessemer p.** procédé Bessemer
3 *Law* procès *m*, action *f* en justice; *(summons)* sommation *f* de comparaître; **by due p. of law** par voies légales
VT **1** *Ind (raw material, product)* traiter, transformer; *(food)* préparer *ou* confectionner industriellement; *(mail)* acheminer; *Comput (information)* traiter; *Admin (documents, job applications)* traiter; **to p. an order** donner suite à une commande, traiter une commande; **your request is being processed** votre demande est en cours de traitement; **processed cheese** fromage *m* fondu *ou* à tartiner; *(in slices)* fromage en tranches; **processed food** aliment(s) *m(pl)* conditionné(s); *(precooked)* plat(s) *m(pl)* cuisiné(s) industriellement
2 *Law (person)* intenter un procès à, poursuivre (en justice)
3 *Phot* développer
▸▸ *Phot* **p. camera** tireuse *f* optique; *Comput, Typ* **p. colours** impression *f* en quadrichromie; **p. engineering** ingénierie *f* de procédés; **p. printing** impression en couleurs

Note that the French noun **procès** is a false friend. It only means *trial*.

process² [prə'ses] VI *(walk in line)* défiler (en cortège); *Rel* défiler en procession

processing ['prəʊsesɪŋ] N *(of raw material, product)* traitement *m*, transformation *f*; *(of food)* confection *f ou* préparation *f* industrielle; *Comput (of data)* traitement *m*; *Phot (of film)* développement *m*, traitement; *Admin (of application)* traitement *m*; **p. of mail** acheminement *m* du courrier
▸▸ **p. industry** industrie *f* de transformation; *Comput* **p. language** langage *m* de traitement; **p. plant** *(for sewage, nuclear waste etc)* usine *f* de traitement; *Comput* **p. power** puissance *f* de traitement; *Comput* **p. speed** vitesse *f* de traitement; *Comput* **p. time** temps *m* de traitement; *Comput* **p. unit** unité *f* de traitement

procession [prə'seʃən] N *(of people)* cortège *m*, défilé *m*; *(of cars)* file *f*, *(religious)* procession *f*; **to go** *or* **walk in p.** aller en cortège *ou* en procession, défiler; *Fig* **a p. of**

people came through his office throughout the day les gens n'ont pas arrêté de défiler dans son bureau de toute la journée

processional [prə'seʃən(ə)l] ADJ processionnel
N *Rel (book)* processionnal *m*; *(hymn)* hymne *m* processionnel

processor ['prəʊsesər] N *Comput* processeur *m*
▸▸ **p. speed** vitesse *f* du processeur

process-server N *Law* huissier *m* (qui dresse des exploits)

pro-choice ADJ *(pro-abortion)* en faveur du droit à l'avortement

proclaim [prə'kleɪm] VT **1** *(declare)* *(one's innocence, guilt, despair etc)* proclamer; *(one's love)* déclarer; **to p. that one is innocent** proclamer que l'on est innocent; **to p. sb king** proclamer qn roi; **to have sth proclaimed through the town** faire annoncer *ou* faire crier qch par la ville; **to p. a state of emergency/one's independence** déclarer l'état d'urgence/son indépendance **2** *Fig (show)* *(one's guilt, anger, joy)* révéler

proclamation [prɒklə'meɪʃən] N proclamation *f*, déclaration *f* (publique); *(of banns etc)* publication *f*, **to make** *or* **issue a p.** faire une proclamation

proclivity [prə'klɪvɪtɪ] N *esp Fml* penchant *m* (**for sth** pour *ou* à qch)

proconsul [prəʊ'kɒnsəl] N *Hist* proconsul *m*

procrastinate [prəʊ'kræstɪneɪt] VI remettre les choses au lendemain; **stop procrastinating** arrêtez de remettre les choses au lendemain

procrastination [prəʊkræstɪ'neɪʃən] N **I've had enough p.** j'en ai assez qu'on remette toujours tout au lendemain; **there's too much p.** on a trop tendance à remettre les choses au lendemain; *Prov* **p. is the thief of time** il ne faut pas remettre au lendemain ce que l'on peut faire le jour même

procrastinator [prəʊ'kræstɪneɪtər] N **she's a terrible p.** il faut toujours qu'elle remette les choses au lendemain

procreate ['prəʊkrieɪt] VI procréer

procreation [prəʊkri'eɪʃən] N procréation *f*

proctor ['prɒktər] N **1** *Univ (at Oxford, Cambridge)* membre *m* exécutif du conseil de discipline; *Am (invigilator)* = personne *f* chargée de surveiller un/des examen(s) **2** *Law* avoué *m* *(devant une cour ecclésiastique)*; **Queen's/King's p.** procureur *m* de la reine/du roi **3** *Rel* procureur *m*
VT & VI *Am Univ (invigilate)* surveiller

procurable [prə'kjʊərəb(ə)l] ADJ que l'on peut se procurer; **they're easily p.** on peut se les procurer facilement; **it is no longer p.** on ne peut plus s'en procurer

procuration [prɒkjʊ'reɪʃən] N *Law* procuration *f*, **letters of p.** procuration, mandat *m*

procurator ['prɒkjʊəreɪtər] N *Law* fondé, -ée de pouvoir(s)
▸▸ **p. fiscal** = en Écosse, magistrat *m* qui fait office de procureur et qui remplit les fonctions du 'coroner' en Angleterre

procure [prə'kjʊər] VT **1** *(obtain)* obtenir, procurer; **to p. sth for sb** procurer qch à qn; **to p. sth (for oneself)** se procurer qch **2** *(for prostitution) (woman)* offrir les services de
VI faire du proxénétisme

procurement [prə'kjʊəmənt] N *Fml* acquisition *f* (**of** de); *Ind* achat *m*; *(department)* service *m* des achats
▸▸ **p. department** service des achats; *Mil* **p. officer** agent *m* des achats

procurer [prə'kjʊərər] N *Fml* **1** *(of prostitutes)* proxénète *mf* **2** *(one who obtains)* personne *f* chargée des acquisitions

procuress [prə'kjʊərɪs] N *Lit* entremetteuse *f*

procuring [prə'kʊərɪŋ] N **1** *(for prostitution)* proxénétisme *m* **2** *(of supplies)* acquisition *f*; *Ind* achat *m*

Prod [prɒd] N *esp Ir, Scot Offensive Sl* protestant, -ante

prod [prɒd] N **1** *(act)* coup *m* *(donné du bout du doigt etc)*; **to give sb a p.** pousser qn (du doigt/avec un baton/etc); **she gave him an encouraging p. with her elbow** elle l'a poussé du coude pour l'encourager; *Fig Fam* **give him a p.** aiguillonnez-le un peu; *Fig Fam* **he needs an occasional p.** il a besoin qu'on le pousse de temps en temps; **thanks for the p.** *(reminder)* merci de me l'avoir rappelé **2** *(object)* aiguillon *m*
▸ vT **(-dd-)** **1** **to p. sb/sth** pousser qn/qch *(* **with sth** du bout de qch); **2** *Fig Fam (person)* aiguillonner, pousser **(into doing sth** à faire qch); **they were finally prodded into action by the news** cette nouvelle les a finalement poussés *ou* incités à entrer en action; **he needs a lot of prodding** il faut toujours le pousser
▸ vI **to p. at** = **prod** vT **1**

prodigal ['prɒdɪg(ə)l] ADJ prodigue; *Fml* **to be p. with** *or* **of sth** être prodigue de qch
N prodigue *mf*
▸▸ *Bible* **the P. Son** l'enfant *m* prodigue

prodigality [prɒdɪ'gælɪtɪ] N prodigalité *f*

prodigally ['prɒdɪg(ə)lɪ] ADV *(to spend etc)* avec prodigalité

prodigious [prə'dɪdʒəs] ADJ prodigieux

prodigiously [prə'dɪdʒəslɪ] ADV prodigieusement; *(to eat, drink)* énormément

prodigy ['prɒdɪdʒɪ] N prodige *m*, merveille *f*; **child** *or* **infant p.** enfant *mf* prodige

produce[1] ['prɒdjuːs] N *(no pl) Agr (products)* produits *mpl*, denrées *fpl*; **p. of Spain** *(on packaging)* produit d'origine espagnole; **agricultural/dairy p.** produits agricoles/laitiers

PRODUCE[2] [prə'djuːs]

produire **1–5**	▪ fabriquer **1**
▪ rapporter **2**	▪ présenter **3**
▪ fournir **3**	▪ provoquer **4**

▸ vT **1** *(manufacture, make)* produire, fabriquer; *(cheese, sausages)* faire; *(wine)* produire; *(sound)* émettre
 2 *(yield) (profit)* rapporter; *(milk, apples, steam etc)* produire; *Phys (energy)* produire, générer; *Elec (spark)* faire jaillir
 3 *(present) (one's ticket, passport)* présenter, montrer; *(reasons)* fournir, donner; *(objection)* émettre; *Law (documents, alibi)* produire, fournir; *(witness)* faire comparaître; **she produced a ten-pound note/a gun** elle a sorti un billet de dix livres/un revolver
 4 *(create)* créer; *(children)* faire; *(reaction)* produire, provoquer, entraîner; *(denial)* entraîner, provoquer; *(anger, despair, uncertainty)* susciter, provoquer, donner lieu à; *(interest)* susciter; *(effect)* provoquer; **to p. a vacuum** produire *ou* faire le vide; **to p. a sensation** *(of book etc)* faire sensation; **the drug produces a sensation of well-being** cette drogue procure une sensation de bien-être; **this writer has produced about thirty novels** cet auteur a écrit *ou* produit une trentaine de romans; **the publishers produced a special edition** les éditeurs ont publié *ou* sorti une édition spéciale
 5 *Theat (play) (of person) (organize generally)* produire; *Br (direct)* mettre en scène; *(of company)* produire, représenter; *Cin, Radio, TV (film, radio or TV programme, record)* produire; *Theat* **a badly produced play** une pièce mal montée

producer [prə'djuːsər] N **1** *Agr, Ind* producteur, -trice; *(of manufactured goods)* producteur, -trice, fabricant, -ante (**of** de); **the company/country is an important p. of coffee** *or* **coffee p.** cette entreprise/ce pays est un important producteur de café **2** *Theat* producteur, -trice; *Br (director)* metteur en scène; *Cin, Radio, TV* producteur, -trice
▸▸ **p. goods** biens *mpl* de production; *Econ* **p. price index** indice *m* des prix à la production

-producing [prə'djuːsɪŋ] SUFF **coffee/oil-p.** producteur, -trice de café/de pétrole; **oil-p. country** pays producteur de pétrole

product ['prɒdʌkt] N **1** *(result), Com* produit *m*; **the p. of ten years' work** le produit de dix années de travail; **the disaster was the p. of bad planning** ce désastre était le résultat d'une mauvaise organisation; **she was a p. of her age** c'était un pur produit de son époque **2** *Math* produit *m*
▸▸ **p. advertising** publicité *f* de produit; **p. analysis** analyse *f* de produit; **p. attribute** attribut *m* du produit; **p. augmentation** amélioration *f* du produit; **p. awareness** notoriété *f* du produit, mémorisation *f* du produit; **p. awareness advertising** publicité de sensibilisation au produit; **p. awareness level** degré *m* de mémorisation d'un produit; **p. budget** budget *m* de production; **p. bundling** groupage *m* de produits; **p. bundling pricing** fixation *f* des prix par lot; **p. category** catégorie *f* de produit; **p. champion** champion *m* de produit; **p. depth** profondeur *f* de produit; **p. design** conception *f* du produit; **p. development** élaboration *f* du produit; **p. development cost** coût *m* de l'élaboration du produit; **p. development programme** programme *m* de mise au point du produit; **p. differentiation** différenciation *f* du produit; **p. display** présentation *f* du produit; **p. diversification** diversification *f* des produits; **p. features** caractéristiques *fpl* du produit; **p. form** type *m* de produit; **p. group manager** directeur, -trice de groupe de produits; **p. hierarchy** hiérarchie *f* des produits; **p. image** image *f* de produit; **p. improvement** amélioration du produit; **p. information sheet** fiche *f* technique; **p. innovation** innovation *f* de produit; *EU* **p. liability** responsabilité *f* du produit; **p. liability insurance** assurance *f* de responsabilité du produit; **p. life-cycle** cycle *m* de vie du produit; **p. life-cycle curve** courbe *f* du cycle *m* de vie d'un produit; **p. line** ligne *f* de produits; **p. line manager** directeur, -trice de ligne de produits; **p. management** gestion *f* de produits; **p. manager** chef *m* *ou* directeur, -trice de produit, responsable *mf* produit; **p. mapping** carte *f* perceptuelle de produits; **p. market** marché *m* de produit; **p. marketing** marketing *m* du produit; **p. mix** assortiment *m* *ou* mix *m* de produits; **p. mix depth** profondeur *f* de l'assortiment de produits; **p. mix width** largeur *f* de l'assortiment de produits; **p. orientation** optique *f* produit; **p. overheads** frais *mpl* généraux de production; **p. placement** placement *m* de produit; **p. planning** plan *m* de développement des produits; **p. policy** politique *f* de lancement de produit; **p. portfolio** portefeuille *m* de produits; **p. positioning** positionnement *m* du produit; **p. positioning map** carte de positionnement des produits, carte de l'univers des produits; **p. profile** profil *m* du produit; **p. promotion** communication *f* produit; **p. range** gamme *f* de produits; **p. specialist** spécialiste *mf* produit; **p. test** test *m* de produit, essai *m* de produits; **p. testing** essais *ou* tests de produit

production [prə'dʌkʃən] N **1** *(of cars, appliances etc)* production *f*, fabrication *f*; *(of milk, apples etc)* production; **to go into p.**
entrer en production; **to go out of p.** cesser d'être produit; **to take sth out of p.** cesser de produire qch; **when do we go into p.?** quand est-ce que nous lançons la production?; **is it in p. yet?** est-ce qu'on en a commencé la production?; **to move** *or* **shift p.** relocaliser son unité de production; **drop in p.** chute *f ou* baisse *f* de la production
 2 *(presentation) (of documents)* production *f*, présentation *f*; *(of ticket)* présentation
 3 *Phys (of energy)* production *f*, génération *f*
 4 *Cin, Radio, TV, Theat* production *f*; *Br (directing)* mise *f* en scène; *(finished work)* pièce *f*; **the film goes into p. in the autumn** le tournage du film commence en automne; *Fam* **to make a p. (number) (out) of sth** *(make fuss)* faire tout un fromage de qch; *Cin* **a film with high/low p. values** un film à gros/petit budget
▸▸ **p. assistant** assistant, -ante de production; **p. associate** producteur, -trice associé(e); *Ind* **p. budget** budget *m* de production; **p. buyer** responsable *mf* des achats; **p. capacity** capacité *f* de production; **p. car** voiture *f* de série; **p. company** société *f* de production; **p. control** direction *f* de la production; **p. control room** salle *f* de contrôle de production; **p. cost** coût *m* de production; **p. department** service *m* (de) production; **p. designer** directeur, -trice artistique; **p. director** directeur, -trice de production; *Journ* directeur, -trice de la fabrication; *TV* administrateur, -trice de la production; **p. editor** rédacteur, -trice en chef technique; **p. flowchart** organigramme *m* de production; **p. leadtime** délai *m* de production; **p. line** chaîne *f* de fabrication; **to work on a p. line** travailler à la chaîne; **p. manager** directeur, -trice de la production; **p. meeting** conférence *f* de production; **p. mixer** mélangeur *m* (de production); **p. platform** plate-forme *f* de production, *pl* plates-formes; **p. secretary** secrétaire *mf* de production; **p. switcher** mélangeur (de production); **p. talkback system** réseau *m* d'ordres, intercom *m* de production; **p. team** équipe *f* de production

productive [prə'dʌktɪv] ADJ **1** productif; *(discussions)* positif; *(land etc)* productif, fertile; *(mine etc)* qui rend; **p. period of an author** années *fpl* productives d'un auteur; **the meeting wasn't very p.** la réunion n'a pas été très productive **2** *Econ (work)* productif **3** *Fml* **to be p. of** *(give rise to)* engendrer, produire
▸▸ *Econ* **p. labour** travail *m* productif; **p. life** *(of machine)* vie *f* physique

productively [prə'dʌktɪvlɪ] ADV **to use one's time p.** employer son temps de façon efficace

productivity [prɒdʌk'tɪvɪtɪ] N productivité *f*
▸▸ **p. agreement** accord *m* de productivité; **p. bargaining** négociation *f* syndicale d'un contrat de productivité; **p. bonus** prime *f* de rendement; **p. deal** accord de productivité; **p. drive** campagne *f* de productivité

product/market pair N *Mktg* couple *m* produit/marché

product/price policy N *Mktg* politique *f* de produit/prix

Prof *(abbr* **Professor)** *(in title)* Prof

prof [prɒf] N *Fam (at university)* prof *mf*; *(at hospital)* professeur *m*

profanation [prɒfə'neɪʃən] N *Rel* profanation *f*

profane [prə'feɪn] ADJ **1** *(blasphemous) (act)* profane; *(language)* impie, blasphématoire; *(person)* qui blasphème à tout propos **2** *Lit (secular)* profane; **things sacred and p.** le sacré et le profane
▸ vT *(something sacred, one's talent)* profaner

profanity [prə'fænɪtɪ] N **1** (word, remark) blasphème m, juron m; **to utter profanities** blasphémer **2** (of language) grossièreté f; (of text) nature f profane; (of action) impiété f

profess [prə'fes] VT **1** (declare) (one's faith etc) professer, faire profession de; (enthusiasm, hatred, disbelief) professer; **to p. oneself a socialist** se déclarer socialiste, faire profession de socialisme; **to p. oneself satisfied** se déclarer satisfait; **to p. one's ignorance** avouer son ignorance **2** (allege, claim) prétendre; **he professes to be a socialist but …** il se prétend ou se déclare socialiste, mais …; **I do not p. to be a scholar** je ne prétends pas être savant; **to p. a lack of understanding of sth** prétendre ne pas comprendre qch

professed [prə'fest] ADJ **1** (enemy) déclaré; (Marxist etc) déclaré; (pretended) prétendu **2** (monk, nun) profès, -esse

professedly [prə'fesɪdlɪ] ADV (on one's own admission) de son propre aveu; (according to one's claims) soi-disant

profession [prə'feʃən] N **1** (occupation) profession f; **the p.** (people) (les membres mpl de) la profession; **the teaching p.** le corps enseignant, les enseignants mpl; **the (learned) professions** les professions libérales; **writer by p.** écrivain professionnel; **she is a doctor by p.** elle est médecin de (sa) profession; Hum **the oldest p. (in the world)** le plus vieux métier du monde VOIR GRAMMAIRE A6; B5 **2** (declaration) profession f, déclaration f; **p. of faith** profession de foi

professional [prə'feʃən(ə)l] ADJ **1** (paid) (dancer, photographer, footballer etc) professionnel; (soldier, diplomat) de carrière; Fig a **p. liar/hypochondriac** un menteur/un hypocondriaque professionnel; Sport etc **to turn** or **go p.** passer ou devenir professionnel; **p. man/woman** homme m/femme f qui exerce une profession libérale **2** (relating to job) professionnel; **to take a p. interest in sth** s'intéresser professionnellement à qch; **to take p. advice on sth** consulter une personne du métier ou un professionnel sur qch; (on legal, medical matter) consulter un avocat/un médecin à propos de qch; Euph **I think she needs p. help** je pense qu'elle a besoin d'aller voir un psychiatre **3** (competent) professionnel; **she is very p.** elle est très professionnelle; **they made a very p. job of the repair** la réparation qu'ils ont faite est digne de professionnels; **his manner was very p.** il s'est comporté en professionnel ▸ N professionnel, -elle; **it's best to leave such work to the professionals** il vaut mieux laisser ce genre de travail à des professionnels ou à des gens du métier; **a golf/rugby p.** un golfeur/rugbyman professionnel ▸▸ **p. army** armée f de métier; **p. association** association f professionnelle; **p. body** organisme m professionnel; **p. certificate** certificat m d'aptitude professionnelle; **p. code of ethics** déontologie f; **p. football** football m professionnel; Ftbl **p. foul** faute f délibérée; **p. hospitality** industrie f de l'hôtellerie; **p. indemnity insurance** assurance f d'indemnisation professionnelle; **p. misconduct** faute professionnelle

professionalism [prə'feʃənəlɪz(ə)m] N professionnalisme m; **his air of spurious p.** ses airs de faux professionnel

professionally [prə'feʃənəlɪ] ADV **1** (as a job) professionnellement; **to sing/dance/play football p.** être un chanteur/danseur/footballeur professionnel **2** (competently) comme un professionnel, en professionnel; **it was very p. done** c'est du travail de professionnel

professor [prə'fesər] N Univ Br professeur m (de faculté) titulaire d'une chaire; Am enseignant, -ante, professeur (de faculté); **she's a p.** elle est professeur; **he's the p. of German** c'est le professeur titulaire de la chaire d'allemand; **P. Martin** le Professeur Martin; (as address) Monsieur/Madame Martin, Professeur; (as address to medical doctor) Monsieur/Madame le Professeur Martin

professorial [prɒfɪ'sɔːrɪəl] ADJ professoral, -aux

professorship [prə'fesəʃɪp] N Univ chaire f; **a p. in Modern History** une chaire d'histoire moderne; **to get a p.** obtenir une chaire

proffer ['prɒfər] VT (-r-) Fml (advice) offrir, présenter; (opinion, observation) avancer; (resignation) présenter; **to p. one's hand** tendre la main (**to sb** à qn)

proficiency [prə'fɪʃənsɪ] N (in a subject) compétence f, capacités fpl (**in** dans); (in a language) maîtrise f (**in** de)

proficient [prə'fɪʃənt] ADJ compétent; (swimmer) excellent; **to be p. at German** avoir une bonne maîtrise de l'allemand; **to be a p. liar** avoir le mensonge facile

proficiently [prə'fɪʃəntlɪ] ADV avec compétence; (to speak a language) couramment; **to swim p.** être un excellent nageur; **to lie p.** avoir le mensonge facile

profile ['prəʊfaɪl] N (of person, face, mountain) profil m; TV, Journ (of celebrity) portrait m, profil; (of company) profil; Tech (of land, aircraft wing) profil; (on graph) graphique m, courbe f; **she has the right p. for the job** elle a le profil qui convient pour cet emploi; Art **drawn in p.** dessiné de profil; Fig **to keep a low p.** (of person) garder un profil bas; Fig **to have a high p.** (of person) être (très) en vue; (of issue) être d'actualité; Fig **to raise one's p.** se mettre plus en vue; **to raise a party's/sb's p.** promouvoir l'image du parti/de qn ▸ VT (draw in profile) dessiner ou montrer de profil; TV, Journ faire le portrait de; **she was profiled in a TV programme** une émission télévisée a présenté son portrait; **the trees are profiled against the horizon** les arbres se profilent sur l'horizon ▸▸ **p. characteristics** (of tourists) caractéristiques fpl; TV, Cin **p. shot** plan m de profil; TV, Cin **p. spotlight** spot m de profil

profit ['prɒfɪt] N Com bénéfice m, profit m; Fig (advantage) avantage m; **what p. is there in it for her?** quel avantage cela présente-t-il pour elle?, qu'est-ce que cela peut lui rapporter?; **to make a p.** (of seller, company) faire un ou des bénéfice(s); (of goods) rapporter; **we made a p. on the sale of or on selling the house** nous avons fait ou réalisé un bénéfice sur la vente de la maison; **to turn sth to p.** tirer profit ou bénéfice de qch; Com **gross/net p.** bénéfice brut/net; **£100 clear p.** 100 livres de bénéfice net; **p. on a transaction** rendement m d'une opération; **profits were down/up this year** les bénéfices ont diminué/augmenté cette année; **at a p.** (to sell sth) à profit; (to work a mine) avec profit; **to derive (a) p. from sth** retirer un bénéfice ou un profit de qch; **p. and loss** pertes et profits mpl; **p. and loss account, p. and loss statement** compte m de résultat; **p. or loss** résultat m; **p. or loss for the financial year** résultat de l'exercice ▸ VI (-t-) **to p. by** or **from sth** bénéficier de qch, tirer profit de qch; **to p. by** or **from sb's advice** mettre à profit le conseil de qn; **you could well p. by being more careful** vous avez tout intérêt à faire plus attention ▸ VT Lit (person) rapporter ou profiter à ▸▸ Acct **p. balance** solde m bénéficiaire;

Acct **p. centre** centre m de profit; Acct **p.-centre accounting** = comptabilité f par centres de profits; Fin **p. equation** équation f de bénéfice; Mktg **p. impact of marketing strategy** impact m sur la rentabilité de la stratégie marketing; Fin **p. indicator** indice m de profit; Fin **p. margin** marge f bénéficiaire; Fin **p. motive** motivation f par le profit; Fin **p. opportunity** occasion f de profit; Fin **p. optimization** optimisation f du ou des profits; Fin **p. outlook** perspectives fpl de profit; Fin **p. rate** taux m de profit ou de bénéfice; Fin **p. squeeze** compression f des bénéfices, étranglement m des marges; Fin **p. tax** impôt m sur les bénéfices; Fin **p. warning** = annonce f d'une baisse prochaine des bénéfices d'une entreprise

profitability [prɒfɪtə'bɪlɪtɪ] N rentabilité f ▸▸ **p. index** indice m de rentabilité; **p. ratio** ratio m de rentabilité; **p. value** (of a company) valeur f de rendement

profitable ['prɒfɪtəb(ə)l] ADJ (deal, agreement) profitable, avantageux; (speculation, company) rentable, lucratif; **it will be more p. for us to sell it** ce sera plus avantageux pour nous de le vendre; **it would be a more p. use of your time** ça serait pour vous une meilleure manière d'utiliser votre temps

profitably ['prɒfɪtəblɪ] ADV (at a profit) profitablement, avantageusement; (to invest) avec bénéfice; **to sell a house p.** vendre une maison à profit; **to use one's time p.** employer utilement son temps

profit-driven ADJ poussé par les profits

profiteer [prɒfɪ'tɪər] Pej N affairiste mf; **war profiteers** profiteurs mpl de guerre ▸ VI faire des bénéfices immoraux

profiteering [prɒfɪ'tɪərɪŋ] N Pej mercantilisme m, affairisme m

profitless ['prɒfɪtlɪs] ADJ sans profit; **we spent a p. week investigating the possibilities** nous avons perdu une semaine à étudier les diverses possibilités

profit-making ADJ (company) rentable; (association) à but lucratif; **this is supposed to be a p. company** cette entreprise est censée être à but lucratif

profit-sharing N participation f aux bénéfices, intéressement m ▸▸ **p. scheme** plan m de participation aux bénéfices, plan d'intéressement

profit-taking N prise f de bénéfices

profit-volume ratio N Fin rapport m profit sur ventes

profligacy ['prɒflɪgəsɪ] N **1** (debauchery) débauche f **2** (extravagance) prodigalité f

profligate ['prɒflɪgət] ADJ **1** (debauched) débauché **2** (extravagant) prodigue, dissipateur, -trice ▸ N **1** (debauchee) débauché, -ée **2** (extravagant person) prodigue mf

pro forma [-'fɔːmə] ADJ pour la forme ▸ N (invoice) facture f pro forma ▸▸ Fin **p. bill** traite f pro forma; **p. invoice** facture f pro forma

profound [prə'faʊnd] ADJ profond

profoundly [prə'faʊndlɪ] ADV **1** (grateful, deaf, wise) profondément **2** (to write, express sth) avec profondeur

profundity [prə'fʌndɪtɪ] N profondeur f

profuse [prə'fjuːs] ADJ (copious) abondant, Lit profus; **to offer p. thanks** remercier avec profusion; **to be p. in one's apologies** se confondre en excuses; **to be p. in one's praise** se répandre en compliments; **p. bleeding** hémorragie f abondante

profusely [prə'fjuːslɪ] ADV profusément; **to apologize p.** se confondre en excuses; **to bleed p.** saigner en abondance; **to perspire**

p. transpirer abondamment; **to praise sb p.** ne pas tarir d'éloges sur qn; **to thank sb p.** remercier qn avec profusion

profuseness [prə'fju:snɪs] **N** profusion f

profusion [prə'fju:ʒən] **N** (abundance) profusion f, abondance f; **flowers in p.** des fleurs à profusion

prog [prɒg] **N** TV, Radio Old-fashioned Fam émission f

progenitor [prəʊ'dʒenɪtər] **N** (ancestor) ancêtre m, aïeul, -eule, pl aïeux; Fig (forerunner) précurseur m; (founder) fondateur m; Fml, Hum (parent) géniteur, -trice

progeny ['prɒdʒɪnɪ] **N** Fml (offspring) progéniture f, (descendants) descendants mpl; Hum **is this another of your p.?** est-ce que c'est un de tes rejetons?

progesterone [prəʊ'dʒestərəʊn] **N** Biol, Chem progestérone f

prognosis, pl **prognoses** [prɒg'nəʊsɪs, -əʊsi:z] **N 1** Med pronostic m; (art) prognose f **2** (forecast) prévision(s) f(pl), pronostic m; **to make a p.** faire un pronostic ou des prévisions

prognostic [prɒg'nɒstɪk] **ADJ** (test etc) de pronostic
N Med signe m pronostique

prognostication [prɒgnɒstɪ'keɪʃən] **N** prédiction f, présage m

program [ˈprəʊgræm] **N** Comput programme m

VT & VI Comput programmer; **to p. a computer to do sth** programmer un ordinateur pour qu'il fasse qch; **to be programmed to do sth** être programmé pour faire qch

▸▸ **p. card** carte f programme; **p. disk** disquette f programme; **p. error** erreur f de programmation; **p. file** fichier m programme; **p. language** langage m de programmation; **p. library** bibliothèque f de programmes; **p. line** ligne f de programme

program [ˈprɒɡræm] **N, VT** Am = **programme**

programmable [prəʊ'græməb(ə)l] **ADJ** (computer, oven etc) programmable
▸▸ Comput **p. ROM** mémoire f morte programmable

programme, Am **program** ['prəʊgræm] **N 1** (for play, concert, of political party etc) programme m; **what's the p. for today?** quel est le programme aujourd'hui?; **training p.** programme d'instruction ou de formation **2** TV, Radio émission f, programme m; **current affairs p.** émission ou programme d'actualités; **in a change to the advertised p.** contrairement à ce qu'annonçait le programme **3** TV (channel) chaîne f; Radio (station) station f

VT programmer; **to p. sth to do sth** programmer qch pour faire qch; **programmed teaching** or **learning** enseignement m programmé
▸▸ **p. billing** = position f d'un programme dans la grille de programmation; **p. bus** tableau m de programmation; **p. controller** directeur, -trice des programmes ou d'antenne; **p. grid** grille f de programmes; **p. music** musique f à programme; **p. planner** programmateur, -trice; **p. planning** programmation f, **p. schedule** grille f de programmes; **p. scheduler** programmateur, -trice; **p. seller** vendeur, -euse de programmes; **p. supervisor** chef m d'antenne; **p. trail** annonce f de programme

programme-maker **N** TV etc réalisateur, -trice

programmer ['prəʊgræmər] **N 1** (person) Comput programmeur, -euse; TV, Radio, Tech programmateur, -trice **2** (device) programmateur m

programming ['prəʊgræmɪŋ] **N 1** Comput

programmation f **2** TV, Radio programmation f
▸▸ Comput **p. error** erreur f de programmation; Comput **p. language** langage m de programmation

progress [ˈprəʊgres] **N** (no pl) **1** (improvement) progrès mpl; **age of p.** époque f ou siècle m de progrès; **to make p. in one's studies** faire des progrès dans ses études; **he was making slow/rapid p. with the language** il progressait lentement/rapidement dans son apprentissage de la langue; **to make great p.** avancer à pas de géant; (of industry) prendre un grand essor; **negotiations are making good p.** les négociations sont en bonne voie; **the patient is making good p.** le patient donne de bons signes de récupération; Iron **that's p. for you!** c'est ça le progrès!
2 (movement) (of time, disease etc) marche f, (of events) cours m; (of plan, project) déroulement m; (of work) progrès m, avancement m; Chess **the knight's p.** la marche du cavalier; **the work is now in p.** le travail est en cours; **the negotiations in p.** les négociations en cours; **do not enter while a lecture is in p.** défense d'entrer pendant le déroulement d'un cours
▸▸ Ind **p. chart** diagramme m de l'avancement des travaux; Ind **p. payment** paiement m proportionnel (à l'avancement des travaux); **p. report** compte-rendu m, pl comptes-rendus; (on work) rapport m sur l'avancement des travaux; (on patient) bulletin m de santé; (on pupil) bulletin scolaire

progress [prə'gres] **VI 1** (improve) (of person) faire des progrès, progresser; (of project) progresser, avancer; **her English has progressed a lot** elle a fait de gros progrès en anglais, elle a beaucoup progressé en anglais; **to p. with one's studies** progresser dans ses études; **the patient is progressing satisfactorily** le malade fait des progrès satisfaisants **2** (move forwards) (in space, time etc) avancer; **as the inquiry progresses** à mesure que l'enquête avance; **as the year progresses** au fur et à mesure que l'année avance; **to p. towards a place** s'approcher d'un endroit (par étapes successives); **to p. onto more difficult tasks** passer à des tâches plus difficiles; **I never progressed beyond the first lesson** je ne suis jamais allé au-delà de la première leçon
VT esp Com (advance) faire progresser

progression [prə'greʃən] **N** (movement) Math, Mus progression f, (of star) marche f; Mil avance f

progressive [prə'gresɪv] **ADJ 1** (movement) progressif, en avant **2** (forward-looking) (ideas, methods) avancé, progressiste; (literature, music) d'avant-garde; **to be p.** (of person) avoir des idées avancées ou progressistes; Pol **the p. party** le parti progressiste **3** Gram **the p. form** la forme progressive
N 1 Pol progressiste mf **2** Gram (temps m) progressif m VOIR GRAMMAIRE A49–51
▸▸ Med **p. disease** maladie f dégénérative; Mus **p. jazz** jazz m progressif; Fin **p. taxation** imposition f progressive

progressively [prə'gresɪvlɪ] **ADV** progressivement

progressiveness [prə'gresɪvnɪs] **N** progressivité f

prohibit [prə'hɪbɪt] **VT** (forbid) défendre, interdire, prohiber; **it is prohibited by law** c'est interdit ou défendu par la loi; **smoking prohibited** défense de fumer; **to p. sb from doing sth** (of person) défendre ou interdire à qn de faire qch; (of cause, quality etc) empêcher qn de faire qch; **prohibited goods** marchandises fpl prohibées

prohibition [prəʊɪ'bɪʃən] **N** interdiction f, prohibition f (**from doing sth** de faire qch); Hist **P.** la Prohibition
▸▸ Pol **p. party** parti m prohibitionniste

prohibitionist [prəʊɪ'bɪʃənɪst] **ADJ, N** prohibitionniste mf

prohibitive [prə'hɪbɪtɪv] **ADJ** prohibitif; **the price of flowers is p.** les fleurs sont hors de prix
▸▸ **p. price** prix m prohibitif ou inabordable

prohibitively [prə'hɪbɪtɪvlɪ] **ADV p. expensive** à un prix prohibitif

project [ˈprɒdʒekt] **N** projet m; Sch (of pupil, group of pupils) étude f pratique; (for drainage, irrigation etc) travaux mpl; Am (housing) p. lotissement m
▸▸ **p. leader** responsable mf de projet; **p. management** gestion f de projets; Comput **p. management package** gestionnaire m de projets; **p. manager** chef m de projet; Constr maître m d'œuvre; **p. milestones** étapes fpl principales du projet

project [prə'dʒekt] **VT 1** (plan) projeter; **the Minister's projected visit had to be cancelled** la visite que le Ministre avait prévue a dû être annulée
2 (propel) projeter; (missile etc) lancer; **to p. one's voice** projeter sa voix
3 Cin etc (image, film) projeter (**onto a screen** sur un écran); Math (line) projeter; (plane) projeter, tracer la projection de; **he projected himself as France's saviour** il s'est présenté comme le sauveur de la France; **she projects an image of self-confidence** elle donne d'elle-même l'image d'une personne pleine d'assurance; **the country has successfully projected itself as a stable economy** le pays a réussi à donner de lui l'image d'une économie stable
4 (predict) (results) prévoir; **the projected sales figures** le chiffre d'affaires escompté; **he's projecting a 40% slide in May** il prévoit une baisse de 40% au mois de mai
5 (imagine) **to p. oneself into the past/the future** se transporter dans le passé/l'avenir; Psy **to p. one's needs onto other people** projeter ses besoins sur les autres
VI 1 (protrude) déborder, dépasser, faire saillie; **the balcony projects over the pavement** le balcon surplombe le trottoir
2 (with voice) projeter sa voix

projected [prə'dʒektɪd] **ADJ** (legislation, undertaking) en projet, prévu
▸▸ Geom **p. angle** angle m projeté; TV etc **p. background** fond m projeté, transparence f; Com, Fin **p. growth** croissance f prévue; Art **p. shadow** ombre f portée; Fin **p. turnover** chiffre m d'affaires prévisionnel

projectile [prə'dʒektaɪl] **ADJ** (force) impulsif, projectif
N projectile m
▸▸ **p. vomiting** vomissements mpl violents; Mil **p. weapons** armes fpl de jet

projecting [prə'dʒektɪŋ] **ADJ** Archit saillant, en saillie; **p. part of a roof** avancée f d'un toit

projection [prə'dʒekʃən] **N 1** (of image, one's voice etc) projection f, (of projectile) lancement m **2** (in mapmaking) projection f **3** (prediction) prévision f; **demographic projections** projections fpl démographiques **4** Psy projection f **5** (protruding part) saillie f, (of roof etc) avancée f, (of façade) avant-corps m inv
▸▸ Cin **p. booth, p. room** cabine f de projection

projectionist [prə'dʒekʃənɪst] **N** Cin projectionniste mf

projective [prə'dʒektɪv] **ADJ** Math (plane) de projection; (geometry) projectif
▸▸ Psy **p. test** test m projectif

projector [prə'dʒektər] N *Cin* projecteur *m*

prolapse ['prəʊlæps] *Med* N *(of womb etc)* prolapsus *m*
VI *(of organ)* descendre, tomber

prolapsed ['prəʊlæpst] ADJ *Med* prolabé

prole [prəʊl] N *Fam Pej* prolo *mf*

proletarian [prəʊlɪ'teərɪən] ADJ prolétarien, prolétaire
N prolétaire *mf*

proletarianize [prəʊlɪ'teərɪənaɪz] VT prolétariser

proletariat [prəʊlɪ'teərɪət] N prolétariat *m*
VOIR GRAMMAIRE A11

pro-life ADJ
▸▸ **p. movement** mouvement *m* pour le respect de la vie *(adversaire de l'interruption volontaire de grossesse)*

pro-lifer N *Fam* adversaire *mf* de l'interruption volontaire de grossesse

proliferate [prə'lɪfəreɪt] VI proliférer; *(of human beings)* se multiplier

proliferation [prəlɪfə'reɪʃən] N prolifération *f*

prolific [prə'lɪfɪk] ADJ prolifique, fécond, fertile **(in, of** en); *(writer, composer)* prolifique, fécond; **the country has been a p. producer of inventors** le pays a été fécond en inventeurs; **a p. goalscorer** un bon buteur

prolifically [prə'lɪfɪklɪ] ADV *(to write, compose)* abondamment; **she is a p. productive writer** c'est un écrivain prolifique *ou* fécond; **he has been a p. successful goalscorer** il a marqué énormément de buts

prolix ['prəʊlɪks] ADJ *Fml* prolixe, diffus

prolixity [prəʊ'lɪksɪtɪ] N *Fml* prolixité *f*

prologue ['prəʊlɒg] N prologue *m* **(to** de)

prolong [prə'lɒŋ] VT *(life etc)* prolonger; *(line)* continuer, prolonger; **don't p. the agony** ne me/le/*etc* faites pas souffrir plus longtemps

prolongation [prəʊlɒŋ'geɪʃən] N *(of the time sth lasts)* prolongation *f*; *(of line etc)* prolongement *m*

prolonged [prə'lɒŋd] ADJ prolongé

PROM [prɒm] N *Comput (abbr* **Programmable Read Only Memory)** mémoire *f* morte programmable

prom [prɒm] N *Fam* **1** *Br (at seaside)* front *m* de mer **2** *Br Mus (concert)* concert-promenade *m, pl* concerts-promenades; **the Proms** = série *f* de concerts-promenades, qui a lieu au mois de juillet au Albert Hall de Londres **3** *Am Sch (dance)* = bal *m* d'étudiants
▸▸ *Am Sch, Univ* **p. queen** reine *f* du bal

pro-marketeer N *Pol* = partisan *m* de l'appartenance de la Grande-Bretagne au Marché commun

promenade ['prɒmənɑːd] N *(place for walking)* promenade *f*, *Br (at seaside)* front *m* de mer; *Theat Old-fashioned (in pit)* promenoir *m*
VI se promener
VT exhiber
▸▸ **p. concert** concert-promenade *m, pl* concerts-promenade; *Naut* **p. deck** pont *m* promenade

promenader ['prɒmənɑːdər] N *Br Mus Fam* auditeur, -trice d'un concert-promenade

Promethean [prə'miːθɪən] ADJ *Myth* prométhéen

Prometheus [prə'miːθɪəs] N *Myth* Prométhée

prominence ['prɒmɪnəns] N **1** *(of issue, person etc)* éminence *f*; **to bring sth into p., to give sth p.** faire ressortir qch, donner une place importante à qch; **to come** *or* **rise to p.** prendre de l'importance; **she came to international p. with that song** c'est grâce à

cette chanson qu'elle a percé au niveau international; **to occupy a position of some p.** *(of politician etc)* occuper une position éminente; *(of house)* être situé sur une éminence **2** *(of land, feature etc)* proéminence *f*, *(part sticking up)* saillie *f*, protubérance *f*

prominent ['prɒmɪnənt] ADJ **1** *(projecting)* saillant, en saillie, proéminent; *(cheekbone)* saillant; *(nose)* proéminent **2** *(obvious)* saillant, frappant; *(well-known)* éminent; **p. feature** trait *m* saillant; **in a p. position** dans une position éminente; *(house)* situé sur une éminence; **to hold a p. position** occuper une position éminente; **p. people** personnages *mpl* éminents *ou* en vue

prominently ['prɒmɪnəntlɪ] ADV *(to place etc)* bien en vue; **to display sth p.** mettre qch bien en évidence *ou* en vue

promiscuity [prɒmɪ'skjuːɪtɪ] N promiscuité *f* sexuelle

> Note that the French word **promiscuité** is a false friend and is never a translation for the English word **promiscuity**. It means **lack of privacy**.

promiscuous [prə'mɪskjʊəs] ADJ **1** *(behaviour)* dissolu; *(person)* aux mœurs dissolues; **to be p.** *(of person)* coucher avec n'importe qui *ou* tout le monde; *(of society, group)* être permissif **2** *Fml (mixed)* confus, mêlé; *(crowd)* hétérogène

promiscuously [prə'mɪskjʊəslɪ] ADV **1** to behave p. avoir des mœurs dissolues **2** *Fml (in a random or confused way)* confusément

promise ['prɒmɪs] N **1** *(pledge)* promesse *f*, **to make a p.** faire une promesse; **to keep one's p.** tenir sa promesse; **to break one's p.** manquer à sa parole, ne pas tenir sa promesse; **I'm not making any promises but I'll try my best** je ne promets rien, mais je ferai de mon mieux; **a p. is a p.** chose promise, chose due; **promises, promises!** rien que des promesses!; **empty promises** promesses vaines; **to hold out a p. of sth to sb** laisser espérer qch à qn, faire miroiter qch à qn **2** *(potential) (no pl)* **to show p.** être prometteur, promettre; **child who shows p., child full of p.** enfant qui promet; **young man with every p. of a brilliant future** jeune homme promis à un brillant avenir
VT **1** *(make a promise of)* promettre; **to p. sb sth** promettre qch à qn; **to p. (sb) to do sth** promettre (à qn) de faire qch; **he promised me he'd do it** il m'a promis qu'il le ferait *ou* de le faire; **they were promised help** on leur a promis de l'aide; **to p. oneself sth** se promettre qch; *Fam* **you'll be sorry, I p. you** je vous promets que vous le regretterez **2** *(indicate)* promettre; **it promises to be hot** le temps promet d'être *ou* s'annonce chaud
VI promettre; **I'll pay you back, I p.** je te rembourserai; je te le promets *ou* c'est promis; **I'll wait for you – (do you) p.?** je t'attendrai – tu le promets? *ou* promis?; **but you promised!** mais tu avais promis!; **the scheme promises well** le projet s'annonce bien

promised ['prɒmɪst] ADJ promis
▸▸ *Bible, Fig* **the P. Land** la Terre promise

promising ['prɒmɪsɪŋ] ADJ prometteur, -euse, qui promet; **she's made a p. start** elle a fait des débuts prometteurs; **the future looks p.** l'avenir promet, l'avenir s'annonce bien

promisingly ['prɒmɪsɪŋlɪ] ADV d'une façon prometteuse *ou* qui promet

promissory ['prɒmɪsərɪ] ADJ
▸▸ *Com* **p. note** billet *m* à ordre

promo ['prəʊməʊ] N *Fam* **1** *(video)* vidéo *f* promotionnelle; *(for record)* clip *m* **2** *Com (promotion)* promo *f*

promontory ['prɒmənt(ə)rɪ] N promontoire *m*

promote [prə'məʊt] VT **1** *(raise in rank)* promouvoir, donner de l'avancement à; **to be promoted to (the rank of) captain** être promu (au grade de) capitaine, passer capitaine; **to be promoted** être promu, monter en grade; *Ftbl (of team)* passer dans la division supérieure; **to be promoted to the first division** passer *ou* monter en première division **2** *(encourage) (peace, growth, justice, cause)* promouvoir; *(the arts, a project)* encourager; *(success)* favoriser; *(person's interests)* servir; *(result)* amener, contribuer à; *Com (product)* promouvoir, faire la promotion de; *Chem (reaction)* amorcer, provoquer; *Parl* **to p. a bill** prendre l'initiative d'un projet de loi

promoter [prə'məʊtər] N *(of construction project)* promoteur, -trice; *Sport, Theat* organisateur, -trice; *(sponsor)* parrain *m*; **to be a p. of** *(theory, idea, cause)* promouvoir; **the main promoters of this idea** les principaux défenseurs de cette idée; **sales p.** promoteur, -trice de ventes

promotion [prə'məʊʃən] N **1** *(in rank)* promotion *f*, avancement *m*; *Ftbl (of team)* ascension *f*, promotion; **to get p.** être promu, avoir *ou* obtenir de l'avancement; *Ftbl (of team)* passer dans la division supérieure; **to get p. to captain** être promu au grade de capitaine; **to get p. to manager** être promu directeur **2** *Com (of product)* promotion *f*, **to have a Chanel® p.** avoir des produits Chanel® en promotion; **sales p.** promotion des ventes
▸▸ **promotions agency** agence *f* de promotion; **p. budget** budget *m* promotionnel; **p. campaign** campagne *f* de promotion; **p. team** équipe *f* promotionnelle; **p. techniques** techniques *fpl* de promotion des ventes

promotional [prə'məʊʃən(ə)l] ADJ *Com* promotionnel
▸▸ **p. campaign** campagne *f* de promotion; **p. costs** coûts *mpl* de promotion; **p. discount** remise *f* promotionnelle; **p. literature** prospectus *mpl* promotionnels; **p. material** matériel *m* de promotion; **p. offer** offre *f* promotionnelle; **p. policy** politique *f* de communication, politique de promotion; **p. price** prix *m* promotionnel; **p. sample** échantillon *m* promotionnel; **p. target** cible *f* de communication; **p. video** (cassette *f*) vidéo *f* promotionnelle

prompt [prɒmpt] ADJ **1** *(swift)* rapide, prompt; **the article elicited a p. denial** cet article a été promptement démenti; **to take p. action** prendre des mesures immédiates; **her p. action saved his life** la rapidité de sa réaction lui a sauvé la vie; **to be p. to act** être prompt à agir, agir rapidement; **he was always very p. to understand** il comprenait toujours très vite; **p. reply** *(to letter etc)* prompte réponse *f*, réponse rapide; **p. service** service *m* rapide **2** *(on time)* ponctuel
ADV **at three o'clock p.** à trois heures précises
VT **1** *(cause) (reaction, reply)* provoquer; **to p. sb to do sth** pousser *ou* porter qn à faire qch; **what prompted you to come?** qu'est-ce qui vous a donné l'idée de venir?; **these events prompted her to ...** ces événements l'ont poussée à ...; **to be prompted by a feeling of pity** être animé par un sentiment de pitié **2** *(actor, pupil, speaker)* **to p. sb** *Theat* souffler sa réplique à qn; *(provide with correct response, answer)* souffler à qn; **she needed no prompting when asked her opinion on the subject** elle n'avait pas besoin d'encouragement pour donner son opinion sur le sujet; **'where did you go?', the teacher prompted** 'où es-tu allé?' dit le professeur pour

l'encourager à parler; **the teacher prompted him with another question** le professeur lui posa une autre question pour le mettre sur la voie

N 1 *Theat (reminder)* **to give an actor a p.** souffler une réplique à un acteur **2** *Comput* invite *f*, indicatif *m*; *(with wording)* message *m* d'invite; **DOS p.** invite du DOS; **return to the C:\ p.** revenir au message d'attente du DOS

▸▸ *Theat* **p. box** trou *m* (du souffleur); *TV* **p. card** aide-mémoire *m inv*, carton *m* de prompteur; *Theat* **p. copy** exemplaire *m ou* manuscrit *m* du souffleur; *Fin* **p. note** rappel *m* d'échéance; *Com* **p. payment** paiement *m* dans les délais; *Theat* **p. side** *(in UK)* côté *m* cour; *(in US)* côté jardin; **opposite p. side** *(in UK)* côté jardin; *(in US)* côté cour

prompter ['prɒmptər] **N 1** *Theat* souffleur, -euse; **p.'s box** trou *m* du souffleur **2** *TV* téléprompteur *m*

prompting ['prɒmptɪŋ] **N 1** *(persuasion, encouragement)* insistance *f*; **they will not do it without the p. of the international community** ils ne le feront pas si la communauté internationale ne les y pousse pas; **I wonder whose p. lies behind these questions** je me demande qui est à l'origine de ces questions; **to do sth at sb's p.** faire qch sur les instances *ou* à l'instigation de qn; **the promptings of conscience** l'aiguillon *m* de la conscience; **he needed no p.** il n'a pas été nécessaire de le pousser **2** *(of actor, pupil, speaker)* **he needed a lot of p.** *(of actor)* on devait lui souffler tout le temps; **to answer a question without p.** répondre à une question sans que personne ne souffle; *Sch* **no p.!** ne soufflez pas!

promptitude ['prɒmptɪtjuːd] **N** = **promptness**

promptly ['prɒmptlɪ] **ADV 1** *(rapidly)* promptement, rapidement **2** *(punctually)* ponctuellement **3** *(immediately)* sur-le-champ, immédiatement

promptness ['prɒmptnɪs] **N** promptitude *f*

promulgate ['prɒmǝlgeɪt] **VT** *Fml* **1** *(law, edict)* promulguer **2** *(idea, doctrine etc)* propager, répandre

promulgation [prɒmǝl'geɪʃǝn] **N** *Fml* **1** *(of law, edict)* promulgation *f* **2** *(of idea, doctrine)* propagation *f*

prone [prǝʊn] **ADJ 1** *(lying)* *(person, animal etc)* couché sur le ventre, étendu face contre terre; **to be in a p. position** être couché sur le ventre **2** *(inclined)* **p. to sth/do sth** enclin *ou* porté à qch/faire qch; **p. to a disease** prédisposé à une maladie

-prone [prǝʊn] **SUFF** **to be accident-/disaster-p.** être enclin aux accidents/désastres; **a strike-p. industry** une industrie sujette aux grèves

proneness ['prǝʊnnɪs] **N** propension *f* (**to** à); *(to disease)* prédisposition *f*; **he has a certain p. to accidents/to letting himself be influenced** il est assez enclin aux accidents/à se laisser influencer

prong [prɒŋ] **N** *(of fork)* dent *f*; *(on stag's antler)* pointe *f*

pronged [prɒŋd] **ADJ** **two-p. fork** fourchette *f* à deux dents; *Mil* **two/three-p. attack** attaque *f* sur deux/trois fronts; **it's a two-p. argument** c'est un argument qui porte sur deux fronts

pronominal [prǝʊ'nɒmɪn(ǝ)l] **ADJ** *Gram* pronominal, -aux

pronominally [prǝʊ'nɒmɪn(ǝ)lɪ] **ADV** *Gram* pronominalement

pronoun ['prǝʊnaʊn] **N** *Gram* pronom *m*
VOIR GRAMMAIRE A27–38; B14–23

pronounce [prǝ'naʊns] **VT 1** *(word etc)* prononcer; **this letter is not pronounced** cette

lettre ne se prononce pas; **is that how you p. it** *or* **how it's pronounced?** est-ce que c'est comme ça que ça se prononce? **2** *Fml (declare)* déclarer (**that** que); *Law (sentence)* prononcer; *(judgment)* rendre, prononcer; **to p. sb (to be) a genius** déclarer que qn est un génie; **I now p. you man and wife** *(in marriage service)* je vous déclare mari et femme

VI to p. on a subject se prononcer sur un sujet; *(of tribunal)* statuer sur une question; **to p. for** *or* **in favour of sb/against sb** se prononcer *ou* se déclarer pour/contre qn

pronounceable [prǝ'naʊnsǝb(ǝ)l] **ADJ** prononçable; **a barely p. name** un nom tout juste prononçable; **easily p.** facile à prononcer

pronounced [prǝ'naʊnst] **ADJ** *(squint, accent, liking)* prononcé, marqué; *(features)* accusé; *(views, opinions)* arrêté; **the change is becoming more p.** le changement s'accentue; **he walks with a p. limp** il boite de façon prononcée

pronouncement [prǝ'naʊnsmǝnt] **N** *esp Fml* déclaration *f*

pronouncing [prǝ'naʊnsɪŋ] **N** *Law (of sentence)* prononcé *m*

▸▸ **p. dictionary** dictionnaire *m* de prononciation

pronto ['prɒntǝʊ] **ADV** *Fam* illico

pronuclear [prǝʊ'njuːklɪǝr] **ADJ** *(policy, statement etc)* en faveur du nucléaire; **he is p.** il est pour le nucléaire

pronunciation [prǝnʌnsɪ'eɪʃǝn] **N** *(of word, language)* prononciation *f*; **his French p. was good** il avait une bonne prononciation en français

proof [pruːf] **N 1** *(evidence)* preuve *f*; **you have no p.** tu n'as pas de preuve; **positive p., p. positive** preuve patente; **clear p. of guilt** preuve évidente de culpabilité; **to give p. of** *(guilt, innocence)* prouver, démontrer; *(commitment, loyalty)* faire preuve de; *(intelligence)* montrer, indiquer; **this is p. that he is lying** cela prouve qu'il ment; **in p. of** *or* **as a p. of one's good faith** comme preuve *ou* en témoignage de sa bonne foi; **to produce p. to the contrary** fournir la preuve du contraire; *Law* **the onus** *or* **the burden of p. lies with …** la charge de la preuve incombe à …; **p. of one's identity** preuve d'identité **2** *(test)* épreuve *f*; **to put sth/sb to the p.** mettre qch/qn à l'épreuve; *Prov* **the p. of the pudding is in the eating** c'est à l'œuvre que l'on connaît l'artisan **3** *Typ (printer's)* **p.** épreuve *f* (d'imprimerie); **to read proofs** corriger des épreuves; **to pass the proofs** donner le bon à tirer; **at the p. stage** à la correction des épreuves **4** *Phot* épreuve *f* **5** *(of alcoholic drink)* teneur *f* en alcool

ADJ 1 *(resistant)* **p. against sth** résistant à qch, à l'épreuve de qch; **p. against damp** imperméable, étanche; *Tech* hydrofuge; **to be p. against danger/disease** être à l'abri du danger/immunisé contre la maladie; **p. against temptation** *(person)* insensible à la tentation

2 **to be 0.9% p.** *(of alcohol)* contenir 0,9% d'alcool

VT 1 *Typ (take proof from)* tirer une épreuve de **2** *(check proofs of)* corriger **3** *(fabric etc)* imperméabiliser; *(against acid etc)* rendre résistant *ou* inattaquable

▸▸ *Typ* **p. correction marks** signes *mpl* de correction sur épreuve; *Com* **p. of debt** affirmation *f* de créance; **p. of identity** pièce *f* d'identité; **p. of insurance** attestation *f* d'assurance; *Typ* **p. marks** signes de correction sur épreuve; **p. of payment** justificatif *m* de paiement; **p. of purchase** reçu *m*

-proof [pruːf] **SUFF** **bulletp./heatp.** à l'épreuve des balles/de la chaleur

proofing ['pruːfɪŋ] **N 1** *(action) (of fabric etc)* imperméabilisation *f* **2** *(coating)* enduit *m* imperméable **3** *Typ (production)* tirage *m* des épreuves; *(reading)* correction *f* des épreuves

proofread ['pruːfriːd] *Typ* **VI** corriger des épreuves

VT corriger, relire, corriger les épreuves de; **once it's been p.** une fois les épreuves corrigées

proofreader ['pruːfriːdǝr] **N** *Typ* correcteur, -trice

proofreading ['pruːfriːdɪŋ] **N** *Typ* correction *f* d'épreuves

▸▸ **p. mark** signe *m* de correction

prop[1] [prɒp] **N 1** *(support)* appui *m*, support *m*; *(of wall)* étançon *m*, étai *m*; *Rugby (player)* pilier *m*; *Min* **(pit) p.** étai *ou* étançon de mine; *Fig* **he was the p. of his father's old age** c'était lui qui soutenait son père âgé; **this fact serves as a p. to her argument** ce fait étaye son argument; **it is one of the props of his existence** c'est une des choses qui l'aident à vivre **2** *Theat etc* accessoire *m*; **props** *(person)* accessoiriste *mf*; *Fig* **the rock star's guitar was just a p.** la guitare du chanteur de rock n'était qu'un accessoire

VT **(-pp-)** *(support)* appuyer, soutenir; **to p. a ladder/a person against a wall** appuyer une échelle/une personne contre un mur; **she propped her chin on her hand** elle posa son menton sur sa main

▸▸ *Theat etc* **props department** service *m* des accessoires; *Rugby* **p. forward** pilier; *Theat etc* **props person** accessoiriste

▸ **prop open** **VT SEP** maintenir ouvert; **she propped the door open with a chair** elle a calé *ou* bloqué la porte avec une chaise pour qu'elle reste ouverte

▸ **prop up** **VT SEP** *(support) (tunnel, building)* appuyer, soutenir; *(wall)* étançonner, étayer; *Fig (currency, system etc)* soutenir; **propped up on one's elbows** accoudé; **to p. up a patient on his pillow** redresser un malade sur son oreiller; **to p. a ladder/a person up against a wall** appuyer une échelle/une personne contre un mur; **to p. oneself up against sth** s'appuyer contre qch; **propped up by a pile of books** calé par une pile de livres; *Fig* **the régime is being propped up by the military** le régime est maintenu en place par l'armée; *Hum* **a group of boys propping up a wall** un groupe de jeunes appuyés contre un mur; **are you propping up the wall?** tu as peur que le mur s'écroule?; *Br* **he's always propping up the bar** c'est un vrai pilier de bar; **he'll be out propping up a bar somewhere** il doit être dans un bar quelque part

prop[2] **N** *Aviat Fam* = **propeller**

prop[3] *Com (abbr* **proprietor)** propriétaire *mf*

propaganda [prɒpǝ'gændǝ] **N** propagande *f*
▸▸ **p. film** film *m* de propagande

propagandist [prɒpǝ'gændɪst] **N, ADJ** propagandiste *mf*

propagandize [prɒpǝ'gændaɪz] *Fml* **VI** faire de la propagande

VT *(one's ideas, theories)* faire de la propagande pour; *(the masses, one's colleagues etc)* faire de la propagande à

propagate ['prɒpǝgeɪt] **VT** *Bot, Phys etc* propager; *Fig (ideas etc)* propager, disséminer **VI** *(of animal, plant)* se propager

propagation [prɒpǝ'geɪʃǝn] **N** *Bot, Phys, Fig* propagation *f*

propagator ['prɒpǝgeɪtǝr] **N** *(for seedlings)* = mini-serre *f, pl* mini-serres

propane ['prǝʊpeɪn] **N** *Chem* propane *m*

propel [prǝ'pel] **VT** **(-ll-)** *(something)* propulser; *Fig (urge on)* pousser (**towards** vers);

propelled by ambition poussé *ou* animé par l'ambition

propellant, propellent [prə'pelənt] N *(fuel)* combustible *m; (for rocket)* propergol *m;* **liquid/solid (rocket) p.** propergol liquide/solide

ADJ propulseur *(no f)*, propulsif

propeller [prə'pelər] N *Naut, Aviat* hélice *f*
▸▸ **p. blade** pale *f* d'hélice; **p. shaft** *Aviat* arbre *m* porte-hélice; *Naut* arbre d'hélice; *Aut* arbre de transmission

propelling [prə'pelɪŋ] ADJ propulsif
▸▸ **p. pencil** porte-mine *m inv*

propensity [prə'pensɪtɪ] N propension *f* (**to** sth à qch; **to do** *or* **for doing sth** à faire qch)

PROPER ['prɒpər]

| ADJ | vrai **1** ▪ proprement dit **1** |
| ▪ convenable **2** ▪ bon **2** ▪ correct **2** |

ADJ **1** *(true, real)* vrai; **it'll be good to sleep in a p. bed** ça va être agréable de dormir dans un vrai lit; **the p. word** le mot juste; **p. meaning of a word** signification *f* propre d'un mot; **what's its p. name?** comment ça s'appelle au juste?; **to get a p. night's sleep** avoir une bonne nuit de sommeil; **it's more a course in design than in architecture p.** c'est plus un cours de design que d'architecture proprement dite; **we're still not in London p. yet** nous ne sommes pas encore arrivés a Londres même

2 *(most suitable, suited)* convenable; *(behaviour, model etc)* approprié; *(correct in behaviour)* convenable, comme il faut; **is that the p. way to treat your sister?** est-ce que c'est comme ça qu'on traite sa sœur?; **at the p. time** en temps utile, au moment voulu; **to apply to the p. person** s'adresser à qui de droit; **to put sth in the p. place** mettre qch à sa place; **to think it p. to do sth** juger bon *ou* à propos de faire qch; **do as you think p.** faites comme bon vous semblera; *Fam* **to do the p. thing by sb** faire son devoir, faire ce qu'il faut; **the p. way to do it** la bonne façon de le faire; **the p. use of the subjunctive** l'emploi *m* correct du subjonctif; **paid at the p. rate** payé au taux *ou* au prix convenable; **a very p. old lady** une vieille dame très comme il faut; *(very dignified)* une vieille dame très digne; *Fam* **a p. little madam** une vraie petite madame; *Old-fashioned* **it's not the p. thing to do** cela ne se fait pas; **it's not p.** ce n'est pas bien; **that's not the p. way to behave!** en voilà des manières!, tiens-toi convenablement!; **she thanked him, as is only p.** elle l'a remercié, comme il se devait

3 *(characteristic)* **p. use of a drug** emploi *m* rationnel d'un remède; **to put sth to its p. use** utiliser qch correctement *ou* de la bonne façon; *Fml* **p. to sth** propre *ou* particulier à qch

4 *Br Fam (intensifier)* **we're in a p. mess** nous voilà dans de beaux draps!; **he's a p. fool** c'est un parfait imbécile *ou* une vraie andouille; **we gave him a p. kicking** nous lui avons mis une bonne raclée

ADV *Fam* **they got it good and p.** ils ont reçu ce qu'ils méritaient; *Fam* **to talk p.** parler correctement; *Br Dial* **he was p. angry** il était drôlement en colère
▸▸ *Math* **p. fraction** fraction *f* inférieure à l'unité; *Gram* **p. name** nom *m* propre; *Gram* **p. noun** nom propre

Note that the French word **propre** never means **right** or **adequate**. Its most common meaning is **clean**.

properly ['prɒplɪ] ADV **1** *(correctly)* correctement; **p. speaking** proprement dit, à proprement parler; **speak p.!** tu pourrais

t'exprimer convenablement!; **do it p. or not at all** faites-le correctement *ou* comme il faut ou pas du tout; **I haven't been sleeping p.** je dors mal ces temps-ci

2 *(suitably)* convenablement; *(correctly in behaviour)* comme il faut; **he very p. refused** il a refusé, comme il le fallait

3 *Fam (intensive)* **he was p. fed up** il en avait carrément marre

4 *Law (to act)* de bon droit

propertied ['prɒpətɪd] ADJ possédant

property ['prɒpətɪ] N **1** *(possessions)* propriété *f,* biens *mpl; (buildings)* immeuble(s) *m(pl); (land)* propriété (foncière), terrain *m; (house)* propriété; **that's my p.** cela m'appartient; **they have p. in Scotland** *(land)* ils ont des terres en Écosse; **personal p.** affaires *fpl* personnelles, *Lit* effets *mpl* personnels; **damage to p.** dommages *mpl* matériels; **to be on sb's p.** être sur les terres de qn; **get off my p.!** sortez de ma propriété!; **p. is theft** la propriété, c'est le vol; **this television is stolen p.** cette télévision a été volée

2 *Law (right)* (droit *m* de) propriété *f,* **literary/intellectual p.** propriété littéraire/intellectuelle

3 *(quality) (of thing)* propriété *f,* **(inherent) p.** attribut *m;* **plants with healing properties** plantes qui ont des propriétés *ou* des vertus thérapeutiques

4 *Theat etc* accessoire *m*

5 *Comput* **properties** *(of file, drive)* propriétés *fpl*
▸▸ *Br* **p. assets** patrimoine *m* immobilier; **p. developer** promoteur, -trice (immobilier (ière)); **p. development** promotion *f* immobilière; *Acct* **p. improvement cost** impense *f,* *Br* **p. loan** prêt *m* immobilier; *Theat* **p. man** accessoiriste *m;* **p. market** marché *m* immobilier; *Theat* **p. mistress** accessoiriste *f,* **p. owner** propriétaire *mf,* **p. pages** section *f* immobilier; **p. shares** valeurs *fpl* immobilières; **p. speculation** spéculation *f* immobilière; **p. tax** impôt *m* foncier

Attention: ne pas confondre avec **propriety**, qui signifie **bienséance**.

prophecy ['prɒfɪsɪ] N prophétie *f*

prophesy ['prɒfɪsaɪ] VI prophétiser, faire des prophéties; **exactly as she had prophesied** exactement comme elle l'avait prédit
VT *(event)* prophétiser, prédire

prophet ['prɒfɪt] N prophète *m; Bible* **the major/minor prophets** les grands/petits prophètes; **the P.** *(in Islam)* le Prophète (Mahomet); *Prov* **no man is a p. in his own country** nul n'est prophète en son pays; *Fam* **the prophets of doom** les prophètes de malheur

prophetess ['prɒfɪtes] N prophétesse *f*

prophetic [prə'fetɪk] ADJ prophétique; **these deeds were p. of his future greatness** ces actions annonçaient sa grandeur future

prophetically [prə'fetɪklɪ] ADV prophétiquement

prophylactic [prɒfɪ'læktɪk] *Med* ADJ prophylactique
N prophylactique *m; (condom)* préservatif *m*

prophylaxis [prɒfɪ'læksɪs] N *Med* prophylaxie *f*

propinquity [prə'pɪŋkwɪtɪ] N *Fml* **1** *(proximity)* proximité *f* (de lieu); **to live in close p. to sb** habiter tout à proximité de qn **2** *(of blood relationship)* (proche) parenté *f* **3** *(similarity)* affinité *f* (of ideas entre les idées)

propitiate [prə'pɪʃɪeɪt] VT *Fml (person whom one has offended)* apaiser

propitiation [prəpɪʃɪ'eɪʃən] N *Fml (of the gods)* propitiation *f, Fig* apaisement *m*

propitiatory [prə'pɪʃɪət(ə)rɪ] ADJ *Fml* propitiatoire

propitious [prə'pɪʃəs] ADJ *Fml (to person, undertaking)* propice, favorable

propitiously [prə'pɪʃəslɪ] ADV *Fml* d'une manière propice

propman ['prɒpmæn] N *Theat* accessoiriste *m*

proponent [prə'pəʊnənt] N adepte *mf,* partisan *m*

proportion [prə'pɔ:ʃən] N **1** *(relationship)* rapport *m,* proportion *f; Math (arithmetic, geometric)* proportion; **friction in p. to the load** frottement proportionnel à la charge; **the same ingredients in different proportions** les mêmes ingrédients dans des proportions différentes; **in p. to ...** proportionnellement à ...; **out of all p. to ...** sans commune mesure avec ...; **the payment is out of all p. to the work involved** la rétribution n'est pas du tout proportionnelle au travail requis; **it has grown out of all p. to the original design** cela n'a plus aucune commune mesure avec le plan initial; **in perfect p.** en parfaite harmonie (**to** avec); **out of p.** mal proportionné, disproportionné; **he has no sense of p.** il n'a pas le sens de la mesure; **to lose all sense of p.** ne garder aucune mesure; **let's keep a sense of p.** remettons les choses à leur place; **you're getting this all out of p.** tu as une impression complètement déformée de tout cela; **in direct/inverse p. to sth** en rapport direct/inverse à qch SEE GRAMMAR B59

2 *(part) (of ingredient in mixture)* part *f,* portion *f, (of work, time, money etc)* part, partie *f,* **a large p. of them are students** une grande part *ou* partie d'entre eux sont étudiants; **what p. of the group is French?** quelle est la proportion de Français dans le groupe?

3 *(dimensions)* **proportions** *(of building, human body, crisis)* proportions *fpl; (of machine)* dimensions *fpl;* **a Greek temple of classical proportions** un temple grec de proportions classiques
VT proportionner

proportional [prə'pɔ:ʃən(ə)l] ADJ proportionnel (**to** à), en proportion (**to** de); **inversely/directly p. to ...** inversement/directement proportionnel à ...
N *Math* proportionnelle *f*
▸▸ *Admin* **p. assessment** coéquation *f, Typ* **p. font** police *f* proportionnelle; *Pol* **p. representation** représentation *f* proportionnelle; *Typ* **p. spacing** espacement *m* proportionnel; **p. tax** impôt *m* proportionnel

proportionally [prə'pɔ:ʃən(ə)lɪ] ADV en proportion, proportionnellement (**to** à); **they spend p. more of their budget on research than does ...** ils accordent à la recherche une proportion de leur budget supérieure à celle que dépense ...

proportionate [prə'pɔ:ʃənɪt] ADJ proportionné, proportionnel (**to** à); **a p. response** une réponse en conséquence

proportionately [prə'pɔ:ʃənɪtlɪ] ADV proportionnellement, en proportion (**to** à)

proportioned [prə'pɔ:ʃənd] ADJ **well-/badly p.** bien/mal proportionné

proposal [prə'pəʊz(ə)l] N **1** *(offer)* proposition *f,* offre *f,* **to make a p.** faire *ou* formuler une proposition; **p. (of marriage)** demande *f* en mariage; **p. of peace, peace p.** proposition de paix **2** *(plan)* projet *m;* **the p. to turn the building into a museum** le projet de transformer le bâtiment en musée

propose [prə'pəʊz] VT *(candidate, motion)* proposer; **to p. sb for treasurer** proposer qn pour le poste de trésorier; **he proposed that ...** il a proposé que ... + *subj;* **to p. a toast** porter un toast (**to sb** à la santé de qn); **to p. sb's health** porter un toast à la santé de qn; **to p. to do sth** *or* **doing sth** *(in-*

tend) avoir l'intention de *ou Fml* se proposer de faire qch; **they p. making the street one-way** *(suggest)* ils suggèrent de mettre cette rue en sens unique

VI 1 *(make offer of marriage)* faire une demande en mariage; **he proposed to her** il lui a demandé de l'épouser; **when did he p.?** quand a-t-il fait sa demande en mariage? **2** *Prov* **man proposes, God disposes** l'homme propose et Dieu dispose

proposed [prə'pəʊzd] ADJ proposé

proposer [prə'pəʊzər] N auteur *m* d'une offre *ou* d'une proposition; *(at club etc) (of candidate)* parrain *m*, marraine *f*, **p. of a motion** promoteur, -trice d'une motion

proposition [prɒpə'zɪʃən] N 1 *(offer)* proposition *f*, offre *f*; *(sexual)* avances *fpl*; *Fam (matter)* affaire *f*; **that's quite a p.!, it's a tough p.!** ce n'est pas une mince affaire!; **I've got a p. (to put to you)** j'ai une proposition (à te faire); *Fam* **paying p.** affaire rentable *ou* qui rapporte; *Fam* **that's a very different p.** c'est tout à fait autre chose, c'est une autre histoire; *Fam* **he's a tough p.** il n'est pas commode

2 *(in logic), Gram* proposition *f*
VT *(sexually)* faire des avances à

propound [prə'paʊnd] VT *(idea)* émettre; *(programme, theory)* exposer

proprietary [prə'praɪɪt(ə)rɪ] ADJ *(right etc)* de propriété, de propriétaire; *(air, attitude)* possessif
▶▶*Com* **p. article** article *m* de marque (déposée); *Com* **p. brand** marque *f* déposée; **p. medicines** spécialités *fpl* pharmaceutiques; *Com* **p. name** marque déposée

proprietor [prə'praɪətər] N propriétaire *mf*

proprietorial [prəpraɪə'tɔːrɪəl] ADJ *(attitude, rights)* de propriétaire; **he's very p. about it** il est très possessif avec ça

proprietorship [prə'praɪətəʃɪp] N *Fml* **to dispute the p. of sth** disputer la propriété de qch; **under his p.** alors qu'il est/était propriétaire

proprietress [prə'praɪətrɪs] N propriétaire *f*

propriety [prə'praɪətɪ] N 1 *(correctness) (of language, manners, behaviour)* bienséance *f*, correction *f*; *(of action, measure)* opportunité *f* 2 *(standard of behaviour)* **to observe the proprieties** observer les convenances

> Note that the French word **propriété** is a false friend and is never a translation for the English word **propriety**. It means **property**.
>
> Attention: ne pas confondre avec **property**, qui signifie **propriété**.

propshaft ['prɒpʃɑːft] N *Aut* arbre *m* de transmission

propulsion [prə'pʌlʃən] N *Tech* propulsion *f*; **means of p.** moyen(s) *m(pl)* *ou* mode *m* de propulsion

propulsive [prə'pʌlsɪv] ADJ propulsif; *(movement, effort)* de propulsion; *(force)* moteur, -trice

pro rata [-'rɑːtə] ADJ proportionnel, au prorata; **p. payment** paiement *m* proportionnel
ADV proportionnellement, au prorata

prorogation [prəʊrə'geɪʃən] N *Fml* prorogation *f*

prorogue [prə'rəʊg] VT *Fml* proroger

prosaic [prəʊ'zeɪɪk] ADJ *(style, mind etc)* prosaïque

prosaically [prəʊ'zeɪɪklɪ] ADV prosaïquement

proscenium [prəʊ'siːnɪəm] N *Theat* avant-scène *f*, *pl* avant-scènes
▶▶**p. arch** ≃ manteau *m* d'Arlequin

proscribe [prəʊ'skraɪb] VT proscrire

proscription [prəʊ'skrɪpʃən] N proscription *f*

prose [prəʊz] N 1 prose *f*, **poem in p.** poème *m* en prose **2** *Sch, Univ (translation)* thème *m*
VI *Pol Old-fashioned Pej* tenir des discours ennuyeux
▶▶**p. poem** poème en prose; **p. writer** prosateur *m*

prosecute ['prɒsɪkjuːt] VT 1 *Law (person)* poursuivre (en justice); **the prosecuting counsel** *or Am* **attorney** ≃ le Ministère public **2** *Fml (pursue) (claim, activities, war etc)* poursuivre
VI *Law* **to decide to p.** décider d'engager des poursuites judiciaires; **who's prosecuting?** qui plaide pour le Ministère public?

prosecution [prɒsɪ'kjuːʃən] N 1 *Law (proceedings)* poursuites *fpl* judiciaires, accusation *f*; **the p.** *(lawyers)* les plaignants *mpl*; *(in Crown case)* ≃ le Ministère public; **who's appearing for the p.?** qui plaide pour le Ministère public?; **witness for the p.** témoin *m* à charge; **to bring a p. against sb** engager des poursuites judiciaires contre qn **2** *Fml (of activity etc)* poursuite *f*

prosecutor ['prɒsɪkjuːtər] N *Law* plaignant, -ante; **she was p. in several famous trials** elle a plaidé pour le Ministère public dans plusieurs grands procès

proselyte ['prɒsɪlaɪt] N prosélyte *mf*

proselytism ['prɒsɪlɪtɪz(ə)m] N prosélytisme *m*

proselytize ['prɒsɪlɪtaɪz] VT *(person)* convertir, faire un/une prosélyte de
VI faire du prosélytisme *ou* des prosélytes

proselytizing ['prɒsɪlɪtaɪzɪŋ] N prosélytisme *m*

prosodic [prə'sɒdɪk] ADJ prosodique

prosody ['prɒsədɪ] N prosodie *f*

prospect¹ ['prɒspekt] N 1 *(expectation, thought)* perspective *f*, **to open up a new p. to sb** ouvrir une nouvelle perspective à qn; **there is very little p. of it** on ne peut guère y compter; **there is every p. that we shall succeed/of his becoming Prime Minister** tout semble indiquer que nous réussirons/qu'il deviendra Premier ministre; **no p. of agreement** aucune perspective d'accord; **in p.** en perspective

2 *(chance, likelihood)* **future prospects** perspectives *fpl* d'avenir; **prospects of success** chances *fpl* de succès; **his prospects are brilliant** un brillant avenir l'attend; **to have prospects** *(of person)* avoir de l'avenir *ou* un avenir prometteur; **a job with prospects** un poste qui offre des perspectives d'avenir

3 *Com (prospective customer)* client *m* éventuel, prospect *m*

4 *Fml (view)* vue *f*, perspective *f*
▶▶*Mktg* **p. pool** groupe *m* de prospects

prospect² [prə'spekt] VI *Min, Mktg* prospecter; **to p. for gold** chercher de l'or
VT *(land, mine)* prospecter

prospecting [prə'spektɪŋ] N *Min, Mktg* prospection *f*, **oil/gold p.** prospection pétrolière/d'or

prospective [prə'spektɪv] ADJ *(likely)* en perspective; **my p. son-in-law** mon futur gendre; **p. buyer** acheteur, -euse éventuel(elle) *ou* potentiel(elle); **the p. sale of the painting at auction** la possibilité d'une vente aux enchères du tableau; **the p. Conservative candidate** l'éventuel candidat des conservateurs

prospector [prə'spektər] N prospecteur, -trice; **oil p.** chercheur, -euse de pétrole, *(géologue mf)* pétrolier(ière); **gold p.** chercheur, -euse d'or

prospectus, *pl* **prospectuses** [prə'spektəs, -təsɪz] N *Com* prospectus *m*, réclame *f*; *Fin* appel *m* à la souscription publique; *Sch, Univ* brochure *f* d'information

prosper ['prɒspər] VI prospérer, réussir; **how's he doing, still prospering?** comment va-t-il, ça marche toujours bien pour lui?

prosperity [prɒ'sperɪtɪ] N prospérité *f*

prosperous ['prɒspərəs] ADJ 1 *(wealthy)* prospère **2** *Lit (favourable)* favorable; **p. winds** vents *mpl* favorables

prosperously ['prɒspərəslɪ] ADV d'une manière prospère; **he lives quite p.** il vit dans la prospérité

prosperousness ['prɒspərəsnɪs] N prospérité *f*

prostaglandin [prɒstə'glændɪn] N *Physiol* prostaglandine *f*

prostate ['prɒsteɪt] N *Anat* prostate *f*
▶▶**p. gland** prostate

prosthesis ['prɒsθɪsɪs, prɒs'θiːsɪs] N *Surg, Gram* prothèse *f*

prosthetics [prɒs'θetɪks] N prothétique *f*
VOIR GRAMMAIRE A10

prostitute ['prɒstɪtjuːt] N prostituée *f*; **male p.** prostitué *m*
VT *(one's body, talent etc)* prostituer; **to p. oneself** se prostituer

prostitution [prɒstɪ'tjuːʃən] N prostitution *f*

prostrate¹ ['prɒstreɪt] ADJ 1 *(lying down)* couché; *(submissively)* prosterné; **to lie p.** être couché; *(submissively)* être prosterné **2** *(exhausted)* abattu, accablé; *Med* prostré; **p. with grief** terrassé par le chagrin

prostrate² [prɒ'streɪt] VT 1 *(lay down) (on ground)* coucher *ou* étendre par terre; **to p. oneself before sb** se prosterner devant qn **2** *(exhaust)* abattre, accabler; *Med* mettre dans un état de prostration; **prostrated by the heat** accablé de chaleur

prostration [prɒ'streɪʃən] N 1 *(lying down)* prosternation *f* **2** *(exhaustion)* abattement *m*, accablement *m*; *Med* prostration *f*

prosy ['prəʊzɪ] ADJ *Fam (style)* fastidieux; *Old-fashioned (person)* verbeux, ennuyeux

protagonist [prə'tægənɪst] N protagoniste *mf*, *(of idea, view)* partisan *m*

protean [prəʊ'tiːən, 'prəʊtɪən] ADJ *Lit* protéiforme

protease ['prəʊtɪeɪz] N protéase *f*
▶▶*Pharm* **p. inhibitor** antiprotéase *f*, inhibiteur *m* de protéase

protect [prə'tekt] VT 1 protéger; *(person's interests etc)* sauvegarder; **to p. sb/sth from** *or* **against** protéger qn/qch de *ou* contre; *(rain etc)* protéger *ou* abriter qn/qch de; **well protected against the cold** bien protégé contre le froid, bien protégé du froid; **to p. sb against sb's anger** soustraire qn à la colère de qn **2** *Econ (industry)* protéger

protected [prə'tektɪd] ADJ *(area, species etc)* protégé

protection [prə'tekʃən] N 1 protection *f* (**against** contre); *(of person's interests etc)* sauvegarde *f*; *Fam (money)* = argent *m* versé à un racket en échange de sa soi-disant protection; **to be under sb's p.** être sous la protection de qn; **under police p.** sous la protection de la police; **to claim the p. of the law** demander la protection de la loi; **p. against attack** protection en cas d'attaque; **society for the p. of birds** société *f* protectrice des oiseaux; **suntan lotion gives** *or* **provides some p. against the sun** le lait solaire protège du *ou* contre le soleil **2** *Econ* protectionnisme *m*; *(of industry)* protection *f*
▶▶**p. factor** *(of suntan lotion)* indice *m* de protection; *Fam* **p. money** = argent versé à un racket en échange de sa soi-disant protection; **p. racket** racket *m*

protectionism [prə'tekʃənɪz(ə)m] N *Econ* protectionnisme *m*

protectionist [prə'tekʃənɪst] ADJ, N *Econ* protectionniste *mf*

protective [prə'tektɪv] ADJ protecteur, -trice; *(clothing, mask etc)* de protection, protecteur; **he is very p. towards his children** il se montre très protecteur envers ses enfants; **to be p. of one's interests** sauvegarder ses intérêts

▸▸ *Aut* **p. cage** cage *f* de sécurité; *Biol* **p. coloration, p. colouring** mimétisme *m* des couleurs; *Econ* **p. duties** droits *mpl* protecteurs; *Econ* **p. tariff** tarif *m* protecteur

protectively [prə'tektɪvlɪ] ADV d'une manière protectrice; *(with protective gesture)* d'un geste protecteur; **he put an arm p. around her shoulder** il entoura son épaule d'un bras protecteur; **to behave p. towards sb** se montrer protecteur envers qn

protector [prə'tektər] N **1** *(person)* protecteur, -trice **2** *(device) (for machine, equipment etc)* dispositif *m* de protection; **ear p.** protège-oreilles *m inv*

protectorate [prə'tektərɪt] N *Pol* protectorat *m*

protectress [prə'tektrɪs] N protectrice *f*

protégé, protégée ['prɒteʒeɪ] N protégé, -ée

protein ['prəʊtiːn] N protéine *f*

proteinaceous [prəʊtiː'neɪʃəs] ADJ *Med* protéique

protest[1] ['prəʊtest] N **1** protestation *f*; **to make a p.** protester, élever des protestations (**about sth** à propos de qch); **to register a p.** protester (**with** auprès de); **to raise a strong p.** élever des protestations énergiques; **to give rise to protests** *(of action)* soulever des protestations; **to stage a p.** *(demonstration)* organiser *ou* monter une manifestation; **she has strong grounds for p. at the way she was treated** elle a de bons motifs de protester contre la manière dont elle a été traitée; *Law* **p. in writing** réserve *f*, **under p.** *(to do something)* à son corps défendant, en protestant; *(to sign etc)* sous réserve; *Law* **to act under p.** protester de violence; **she resigned in p. (at this decision)** elle a démissionné en signe de protestation (contre cette décision)

2 *Law, Fin* protêt *m*; **p. for non-acceptance** protêt faute d'acceptation

▸▸ **p. march** marche *f* de protestation; **p. meeting** réunion *f* de protestation; **p. singer** chanteur, -euse engagé(e); **p. song** chanson *f* engagée; **p. strike** grève *f* de protestation; **p. vote** vote *m* de protestation

protest[2] [prə'test] VT **1** *(one's innocence etc)* protester de; **to p. that ...** protester en disant que ...; *Fin* **to p. a bill** (faire) protester un effet *ou* une lettre de change **2** *Am (protest against) (decision, measure)* protester contre

VI protester (**against** contre); **the demonstrators protesting against** *or* **about the new tax** les manifestants qui protestent contre le nouvel impôt; **really, I p., that's too much!** non, vraiment, je proteste, c'est trop!

protestable [prə'testəb(ə)l] ADJ *Fin* protestable

Protestant ['prɒtɪstənt] ADJ, N *Rel* protestant, -ante

▸▸ **the P. Church** l'Église *f* protestante *ou* réformée; **P. work ethic** éthique *f* protestante du travail

Protestantism ['prɒtɪstəntɪz(ə)m] N *Rel* protestantisme *m*

protestation [prɒtes'teɪʃən] N protestation *f*, **in spite of his protestations of innocence** en dépit de ses protestations d'innocence; **her reaction provoked protestations of love/loyalty from him** sa réaction l'a poussé à protester de son amour/de sa loyauté

protester [prə'testər] N protestataire *mf*; **anti-nuclear/peace p.** manifestant, -ante contre le nucléaire/pour la paix

protocol ['prəʊtəkɒl] N *(in diplomacy etc), Law, Comput* protocole *m*

proton ['prəʊtɒn] N *Nucl* proton *m*

protoplasm ['prəʊtəplæz(ə)m] N *Biol* protoplasme *m*, protoplasma *m*

prototype ['prəʊtətaɪp] N prototype *m*; **p. aircraft/car** prototype d'avion/de voiture

protozoa [prəʊtə'zəʊə] NPL *Biol* protozoaires *mpl*

protozoan [prəʊtə'zəʊən] N, ADJ *Biol* protozoaire *m*

protract [prə'trækt] VT prolonger; *(matter, business)* faire traîner en longueur

protracted [prə'træktɪd] ADJ prolongé

protraction [prə'trækʃən] N **1** *(of trial etc)* prolongation *f*, *(of procedure etc)* longueur *f* **2** *Anat (of muscle)* protraction *f*

protractor [prə'træktər] N **1** *Geom* rapporteur *m* **2** *Anat (muscle)* (muscle *m*) protracteur *m*

▸▸ *Anat* **p. muscle** (muscle) protracteur

protrude [prə'truːd] VI *(of brick, beam etc)* dépasser; *(of shelf, balcony, rock etc)* dépasser, avancer; **his teeth p. (too far)** il a les dents qui avancent; **there was a notebook protruding from her pocket** un carnet dépassait de sa poche

VT *(faire)* sortir, pousser en avant, avancer

protruding [prə'truːdɪŋ] ADJ en saillie, saillant; *(jaw, teeth)* qui avance; *(eyes)* exorbité, saillant; *(stomach, ribs)* protubérant

protrusion [prə'truːʒ(ə)n] N **1** *(state)* sortie *f*, saillie *f* **2** *(thing)* saillie *f*, protubérance *f*, *Anat* protrusion *f*

protuberance [prə'tjuːbərəns] N protubérance *f*

protuberant [prə'tjuːbərənt] ADJ protubérant

proud [praʊd] ADJ **1** *(justifiably)* fier; **to be p. of sth/of having done sth** être fier *ou* s'enorgueillir de qch/d'avoir fait qch; **to be p. of oneself** être fier de soi; *Iron* **I hope you're p. of yourself!** tu peux être fier de toi!; **I'm p. to have known her** je suis fier de l'avoir connue; **it made me feel p. to be Welsh** cela m'a rendu fier d'être gallois; **we're all p. of you** nous sommes tous fiers de toi; **he's the p. owner of ...** il est l'heureux propriétaire de ...; **it was her proudest possession** c'était ce qu'elle avait de plus précieux; **a p. moment** un moment d'intense fierté; **a picture of the p. parents** une photo des parents, débordants de fierté; **as p. as a peacock** *or* **as Punch** fier comme Artaban

2 *Pej (arrogant)* orgueilleux, fier; **too p. to apologize** trop fier pour s'excuser; **I'll sit here, I'm not p.** je m'assiérai là, je ne suis pas exigeant

3 *(noble)* fier, digne; *(impressive) (city etc)* imposant, magnifique; *Old-fashioned, Hum* **a p. beauty** une beauté orgueilleuse; *Lit* **a p. and noble race** *or* **people** un peuple fier et noble

4 *Tech (protruding)* **to stand p. of a surface** dépasser *ou* déborder d'une surface

ADV *Fam* **to do sb p.** faire honneur à qn; *(entertain lavishly)* se mettre en frais pour qn; **the caterers did us p.** les traiteurs nous ont fait un festin de rois; **they do you p. at that restaurant** on se régale dans ce restaurant; **to do oneself p.** se dépasser

proudly ['praʊdlɪ] ADV **1** *(with justifiable pride)* fièrement; **we p. present the Rolling Stones in concert** nous avons le plaisir *ou* nous sommes heureux de vous présenter les Rolling Stones en concert; **the banners waved p. in the wind** les drapeaux flottaient fièrement dans le vent **2** *Pej (haughtily)* orgueilleusement

prove [pruːv] *(pp proved, esp Am, Scot proven* ['pruːv(ə)n, 'prəʊ-]*)* VT **1** *(demonstrate) (the truth of something)* prouver, démontrer; *(fact)* constater; *(one's identity)* justifier de; *(one's good will)* témoigner de; *Law (a will)* homologuer; **I can't p. it** je ne peux pas le prouver; **to p. that ...** prouver que ...; **the evidence goes to p. that ...** les témoignages concourent à prouver que ...; **she/this assertion was proved wrong** on a prouvé qu'elle avait tort/que cette affirmation était fausse; **subsequent developments proved me right** la suite des événements m'a donné raison; **to p. oneself** faire ses preuves; **what are you trying to p.?** qu'est-ce que tu cherches à prouver?; **to do sth to p. a point** faire qch pour démontrer un point de vue; **that proves my point** ceci confirme ce que je disais; **that doesn't p. anything!** cela ne prouve rien!; *Math* **to p. a sum** faire la preuve d'un calcul **2** *Culin (dough)* faire lever

VI *(of person)* se montrer; **she proved (to be) ideal for the job** elle s'est révélée être la personne idéale pour cet emploi; **if what you say proves (to be) true** si ce que vous dites se confirme; **many of his observations have proved correct** beaucoup de ses observations se sont avérées *ou* révélées justes; **to p. unequal to one's task** se montrer au-dessous de sa tâche

proven ['pruːv(ə)n, 'prəʊ-] PP *esp Am, Scot see* **prove**

ADJ *(demonstrated) (courage, method, remedy etc)* éprouvé; *Scot Law* **a verdict of p./not p.** un verdict de culpabilité prouvée/non prouvée

provenance ['prɒvənəns] N provenance *f*, origine *f*

Provençal [prɒvɒn'saːl] ADJ provençal, -aux N **1** Provençal, -ale **2** *Ling* provençal *m*

provender ['prɒvɪndər] N *Agr* fourrage *m*

proverb ['prɒvɜːb] N proverbe *m*; *Bible* **(the Book of) Proverbs** le livre des Proverbes

proverbial [prə'vɜːbɪəl] ADJ proverbial, -aux; **as happy as the p. sandboy** gai comme le pinson du proverbe

proverbially [prə'vɜːbɪəlɪ] ADV proverbialement

provide [prə'vaɪd] VT **1** *(supply)* fournir; **to p. sb with sth, to p. sth for sb** fournir qch à qn, pourvoir qn de qch; **they were well provided with food** ils étaient bien approvisionnés *ou* ravitaillés; **this provided her with an excuse** ça lui a fourni une excuse; **please write your name and address in the space provided** veuillez écrire vos nom et adresse dans le blanc prévu à cet effet; **to p. an explanation** donner *ou* fournir une explication; **to p. an exit** *(of passage)* offrir une sortie; *(of architect)* ménager une sortie; **to p. a regular bus service** assurer un service d'autobus régulier; **to p. jobs** fournir des emplois; **this factory will p. 500 new jobs** cette usine créera 500 emplois **2** *(stipulate)* stipuler *(that* que); **the law provides that ...** la loi stipule *ou* prévoit que ...

VI **the Lord will p.** Dieu y pourvoira

▸ **provide against** VT INSEP *(attack etc)* se prémunir contre; *(danger)* parer à

▸ **provide for** VT INSEP **1** *(supply needs of)* pourvoir *ou* subvenir aux besoins de; **to p. for oneself** pourvoir *ou* subvenir à ses propres besoins; **to be well** *or* **amply provided for** avoir grandement de quoi vivre; **he provided for everything** il a subvenu à tout; **he left his family well provided for** il laissa sa famille à l'abri du besoin **2** *(allow for)* **to p. for an eventuality** pourvoir à *ou* parer à une éventualité; **expenses provided for in the budget** dépenses prévues au budget; **this has been provided for** on y a pourvu; **they had failed to p. for that possibility** ils ne s'étaient pas prémunis contre cette possibilité

provided [prə'vaɪdɪd] **CONJ p. (that)** pourvu que + *sub*, à condition que + *subj*, **p. there is enough** pourvu qu'il y en ait assez, à condition qu'il y en ait assez, seulement s'il y en a assez

providence ['prɒvɪdəns] **N 1** *Rel* providence *f* (divine); **by a special p.** par une intervention providentielle; **P.** smiled on us la chance *ou* la fortune nous a souri **2** *Old-fashioned (foresight)* prévoyance *f*, prudence *f*

provident ['prɒvɪdənt] **ADJ** prévoyant
▸▸*Br* **p. society** société *f* de prévoyance

providential [prɒvɪ'denʃəl] **ADJ** *(help etc)* providentiel

providentially [prɒvɪ'denʃəlɪ] **ADV** providentiellement

providently ['prɒvɪdəntlɪ] **ADV** avec prévoyance; **he had p. set aside a considerable sum** il avait eu la prévoyance de mettre une somme considérable de côté

provider [prə'vaɪdər] **N** pourvoyeur, -euse; *Com* fournisseur, -euse; **the region was one of the main providers of unskilled labour** cette région était l'une des principales réserves de main-d'œuvre non qualifiée

providing [prə'vaɪdɪŋ] **CONJ = provided**

province ['prɒvɪns] **N 1** *(of country)* province *f*; **in the provinces** en province **2** *Law (of court)* juridiction *f*, ressort *m*, compétence *f*; **that is not (within) my p.** ce n'est pas de mon ressort

provincial [prə'vɪnʃəl] **ADJ** provincial, -aux; *(theatre)* de province
N provincial, -ale

provincialism [prə'vɪnʃəlɪz(ə)m] **N** provincialisme *m*

proving ['pruːvɪŋ] **N** *(of truth of sth)* preuve *f*, démonstration *f*; *(of fact)* constatation *f*; *Law (of a will)* homologation *f*; **the p. of a theory/a hypothesis** la démonstration d'une théorie/d'une hypothèse
▸▸**p. ground** terrain *m* d'essai

provirus ['prəʊvaɪrəs] **N** *Med* provirus *m*

provision [prə'vɪʒən] **N 1** *(supply)* provision *f*, réserve *f*; **provisions** *(food)* provisions (de bouche); **to lay in a store of provisions** faire provision de vivres; **wholesale p. business** maison *f* d'alimentation en gros
2 *(act of supplying)* **p. of capital/services** prestation *f* de capitaux/de services; **the p. of free education is under threat** l'éducation gratuite est menacée; **the p. of food to the refugees** l'approvisionnement des réfugiés en nourriture; **the p. of housing to the refugees** le logement des réfugiés; **there was little p. for education in the budget** la part du budget consacrée à l'éducation était faible
3 *(allowance)* **p. for/against sth** (prise *f* des) dispositions *fpl* nécessaires pour assurer qch/pour parer à qch; **to make p. for sth** pourvoir à qch; **the law makes no p. for a case of this kind** la loi ne prévoit pas un cas semblable; **to make p. for one's family** assurer l'avenir de sa famille; **to make p. against sth** prendre des mesures contre qch, se prémunir contre qch
4 *(stipulation) (of treaty)* article *m*; *(of contract)* clause *f*, stipulation *f*; **provisions of an act** dispositions *fpl* d'une loi; **to come within the provisions of the law** être prévu par la loi
VT *(army, ship etc)* approvisionner
▸▸*Acct* **p. for charges** provision pour frais; *Acct* **p. for depreciation** provision pour dépréciation *ou* amortissement; *Acct* **p. for liabilities** provision pour sommes exigibles

provisional [prə'vɪʒən(ə)l] **ADJ** provisoire;

Law provisionnel; *(finding)* par provision
N *Pol* **the Provisionals** les membres *mpl* de l'IRA provisoire
▸▸*Fin* **p. budget** budget *m* prévisionnel; *Br Aut* **p. driving licence** permis *m* de conduire provisoire; **p. government** gouvernement *m* provisoire; **the P. IRA** l'IRA *f* provisoire

provisionally [prə'vɪʒən(ə)lɪ] **ADV** provisoirement; *Law* provisionnellement; *(to appoint sb)* à titre provisoire

proviso, *pl* **provisos** [prə'vaɪzəʊ, -əʊz] **N 1** *(in document)* clause *f* conditionnelle; *(of contract)* condition *f* **2** *(stipulation)* stipulation *f*, **with the p. that he gives his consent** à condition qu'il soit d'accord

provisory [prə'vaɪzərɪ] **ADJ** conditionnel

Provo ['prəʊvəʊ] **N** *Pol Fam* membre *m* de l'IRA provisoire

provocation [prɒvə'keɪʃən] **N** provocation *f*, **at the slightest p.** à la moindre provocation; **to act under p.** agir en réponse à une provocation; **without p.** sans provocation

provocative [prə'vɒkətɪv] **ADJ** provocateur, -trice, provocant; *(smile, dress etc)* provocant, aguichant; **he's just being p.** il ne fait cela que pour provoquer

provocatively [prə'vɒkətɪvlɪ] **ADV** *(to smile, be dressed)* d'une manière provocante, …, **he said p.**, …, dit-il d'un air provocant; **a p. low-cut dress** une robe au décolleté provocant

provoke [prə'vəʊk] **VT 1** *(person)* provoquer, pousser, inciter **(to do sth** à faire qch); *(irritate)* irriter, agacer, exaspérer; *(dog)* exciter; **to p. sb to anger** mettre qn en colère; **I was provoked** on m'a provoqué *ou Fam* cherché; **don't p. her** ne la provoque *ou Fam* cherche pas **2** *(arouse) (curiosity)* exciter, faire naître; *(gaiety)* provoquer; *(passion, indignation, interest)* soulever; **to p. a reaction** provoquer une réaction

provoking [prə'vəʊkɪŋ] **ADJ** *(irritating)* irritant, agaçant, exaspérant

provost ['prɒvəst] **N 1** *Sch, Univ* principal *m* **2** *Scot Admin* maire *m*
▸▸*Mil* **p. duty** ['prɒvəʊ] service *m* prévôtal, prévôté *f*; *Mil* **p. marshal** ['prɒvəʊ] prévôt *m*

prow [praʊ] **N** *(of ship)* proue *f*

prowess ['praʊɪs] **N 1** *(skill)* talent *m*, habileté *f*, **her p. at tennis** *or* **as a t. player** son talent au tennis; **she has shown great p.** elle a fait de prouesses; **his sexual/intellectual p.** ses prouesses sexuelles/intellectuelles **2** *Lit (courage)* vaillance *f*

prowl [praʊl] **N to go on the p.** *(of lion etc)*, *Fig* partir en chasse; **to be on the p. for sth** être en quête *ou* à la recherche de qch; **let's have a p. around** et si on zyeutait?
VI *(of animal, person)* rôder; **to p. about the streets** rôder dans les rues; **to p. about the shops** tourner dans les magasins
VT to p. the streets rôder dans les rues
▸▸*Am* **p. car** voiture *f* de police en patrouille

prowler ['praʊlər] **N** rôdeur, -euse; **there's a p. in the neighbourhood** il y a quelqu'un qui rôde dans le voisinage

prox [prɒks] **ADV** *Com Old-fashioned (abbr* **proximo)** (du mois) prochain

proximity [prɒk'sɪmɪtɪ] **N** *(closeness)* proximité *f*, **its p. to London** sa situation à proximité de Londres; **in p. to** à proximité de, près de; **in close p. to** juste à proximité *ou* tout près de; *Fig* **p. of blood** proche parenté *f*
▸▸*Mil* **p. fuse** fusée *f* à influence, fusée de proximité; *Pol* **p. talks** négociations *fpl* rapprochées

proximo ['prɒksɪməʊ] **ADV** *Com Old-fashioned* (du mois) prochain

proxy ['prɒksɪ] **N 1** *(power)* procuration *f*,

délégation *f* de pouvoirs, pouvoir *m*, mandat *m* **2** *(person)* mandataire *mf*, fondé, -ée de pouvoir, délégué, -ée; *Com* mandataire; **to make sb one's p.** déléguer ses pouvoirs à qn; **to vote by p.** voter par procuration
▸▸**p. bomb** = bombe *f* amenée sur les lieux par une personne agissant sous la contrainte; *Comput* **p. server** serveur *m* proxy, serveur mandataire *ou* de procuration; **p. vote** vote *m* par procuration

Prozac® ['prəʊzæk] **N** Prozac® *m*

PRP [piːaːˈpiː] **N** *(abbr* **performance-related pay)** salaire *m* au rendement

prude [pruːd] **N** prude *mf*, bégueule *f*, **don't be such a p.!** ne soyez pas si prude *ou* si bégueule!

prudence ['pruːdəns] **N** prudence *f*, *(common sense)* sagesse *f*
▸▸*Acct* **p. concept** principe *m* de prudence

prudent ['pruːdənt] **ADJ** prudent; *(sensible)* sage

prudential [pruːˈdenʃəl] **ADJ**
▸▸*Am* **p. committee** *(of municipality, company)* = comité *m* de surveillance

prudently ['pruːdəntlɪ] **ADV** prudemment

prudery ['pruːdərɪ] **N** pruderie *f*, pudibonderie *f*

prudish ['pruːdɪʃ] **ADJ** prude, pudibond

prudishness ['pruːdɪʃnɪs] **N = prudery**

prune [pruːn] **N** pruneau *m*; *Fig Fam* **old p.** *(old woman)* vieille bique *f* ratatinée
VT 1 *(rose bush, fruit tree)* tailler; *(tree roots)* rafraîchir; *(tree)* émonder; *(branch)* élaguer **2** *Fig (article etc)* faire des coupures dans, élaguer; *(list of tasks, demands)* réduire; *(army, bureaucracy)* dégraisser
▸**prune away, prune off VT SEP** *(branch)* élaguer

Note that the French word **prune** is a false friend and is never a translation for the English word **prune**. It means **plum**.

---

pruning ['pruːnɪŋ] **N 1** *(of rose bush, fruit tree)* taille *f*; *(of tree)* émondage *m*; *(of branch)* élagage *m* **2** *Fig (of article etc)* élagage *m*
▸▸**p. hook** ébranchoir *m*; **p. knife** serpette *f*; **p. shears** cisailles *fpl*

prurience ['prʊərɪəns], **pruriency** ['prʊərɪənsɪ] **N** lasciveté *f*, lubricité *f*

prurient ['prʊərɪənt] **ADJ** (à l'esprit) lascif; **to take a p. interest in sth** porter un intérêt lascif à qch

Prussia ['prʌʃə] **N** Prusse *f*

Prussian ['prʌʃən] **ADJ** prussien
N Prussien, -ienne
▸▸**P. blue** bleu *m* de Prusse

prussic ['prʌsɪk] **ADJ** *Chem (acid)* prussique, cyanhydrique

pry[1] [praɪ] **VI** *(pt, pp* **pried)** *(into particular matter)* fouiller, fureter **(into sth** dans qch); *(generally)* fourrer son nez partout; **I don't mean to p., but why did you do it?** je sais que ça ne me regarde pas, mais pourquoi est-ce que tu as fait ça?; **to p. into a secret** chercher à pénétrer un secret

pry[2] **VT** *(pt, pp* **pried)** *Am* **= prize**[2]
▸**pry loose VT SEP** *Am* décoller, détacher
▸**pry open VT SEP** *Am (door, safe etc)* forcer

prying ['praɪɪŋ] **ADJ** curieux, indiscret, -ète; **safe from p. eyes** à l'abri des regards indiscrets

PS [piːˈes] **N** *(abbr* **postscript)** PS *m*; **to add a PS to a letter** ajouter un PS à une lettre; **PS see you next week** PS à la semaine prochaine

psalm [saːm] **N** psaume *m*; *Bible* **(the Book of) Psalms** (le livre des) Psaumes
▸▸**p. book** livre *m* de psaumes, psautier *m*

psalmist ['sɑ:mɪst] N psalmiste m

psalmody ['sɑ:mədɪ] N psalmodie f

psalter ['sɔ:ltər] N psautier m

PSB [pi:es'bi:] N Am TV (abbr **public service broadcasting**) émissions fpl de service public

PSBR [pi:esbi:'ɑ:r] N Br Econ (abbr **public sector borrowing requirement**) = besoins mpl d'emprunt du secteur public non couverts par les rentrées fiscales

psephological [sefə'lɒdʒɪk(ə)l] ADJ relatif à l'étude scientifique des élections

psephologist [se'fɒlədʒɪst] N spécialiste mf de l'étude des élections

psephology [se'fɒlədʒɪ] N étude f scientifique des élections

pseud [sju:d] N Br Fam Pej crâneur, -euse; P.'s Corner = section f de la revue humoristique Private Eye où des articles prétentieux sont publiés pour l'amusement général

pseudo ['sju:dəʊ] ADJ, PREF Fam faux, f fausse, pseudo-

pseudonym ['sju:dənɪm] N pseudonyme m; to write sth under a p. écrire qch sous un pseudonyme

pseudonymous [sju:'dɒnɪməs] ADJ (writer) qui écrit sous un pseudonyme; (column, article) écrit sous un pseudonyme

pseudy ['sju:dɪ] ADJ Fam Pej prétentieux

pshaw [(p)ʃɔ:] INT Old-fashioned (indicating disgust) peuh!

psi [pi:es'aɪ] Phys (abbr **pounds per square inch**) livres par pouce carré

psittacosis [sɪtə'kəʊsɪs] N Med, Vet psittacose f

psoriasis [sə'raɪəsɪs] N Med psoriasis m

psst [pst] INT (to attract attention) psitt!, pst!; (to warn) chut!

▶ **PST** [pi:es'ti:] N Am (abbr **Pacific Standard Time**) PST

▶ **PSV** [pi:es'vi:] N Formerly (abbr **public service vehicle**) véhicule m de transport en commun

psych out [saɪk] VT SEP Fam = psyche out

psych up VT SEP Fam = psyche up

psyche ['saɪkɪ] N psychisme m; Phil psyché f

▶ **psyche out** [saɪk] VT SEP Fam (unnerve) déstabiliser; (guess) (sb's intentions, motives etc) deviner, percer à jour

▶ **psyche up** VT SEP Fam (prepare) to p. oneself up (for sth/to do sth) se préparer mentalement (à qch/à faire qch); to p. sb up for sth préparer qn mentalement pour qch

psychedelic [saɪkə'delɪk] ADJ psychédélique

psyched-up [saɪkt-] ADJ Fam gonflé à bloc; to get oneself p. se préparer mentalement

psychiatric [saɪkɪ'ætrɪk] ADJ psychiatrique
▶ ▶ Br p. social worker assistant, -ante social(e) en psychiatrie

psychiatrist [saɪ'kaɪətrɪst] N psychiatre mf

psychiatry [saɪ'kaɪətrɪ] N psychiatrie f

psychic(al) ['saɪkɪk, ɪk(ə)l] ADJ psychique; (phenomenon etc) métapsychique; to have p. powers avoir des dons mpl de voyance, être un peu médium; Fam I'm not p.! je ne suis pas devin!
N médium m

psycho ['saɪkəʊ] ADJ, N Fam psychopathe mf

psychoanalyse, Am **psychoanalyze** [saɪkəʊ'ænəlaɪz] VT psychanalyser

psychoanalysis [saɪkəʊə'nælɪsɪs] N psychanalyse f

psychoanalyst [saɪkəʊ'ænəlɪst] N psychanalyste mf

psychoanalytic(al) [saɪkəʊænə'lɪtɪk, -ɪk(ə)l] ADJ psychanalytique

psychoanalyze Am = psychoanalyse

psychobabble ['saɪkəʊbæb(ə)l] N Fam jargon m de psy

psychodrama ['saɪkəʊdrɑ:mə] N psychodrame m, jeu m de rôle

psychographic [saɪkəʊ'græfɪk] N psychographique
▶ ▶ Mktg p. segmentation segmentation f psychographique

psychographics [saɪkəʊ'græfɪks] N psychographie f VOIR GRAMMAIRE A10

psychological [saɪkə'lɒdʒɪk(ə)l] ADJ psychologique
▶ ▶ p. contract contrat m psychologique; the p. moment le moment psychologique; Mktg p. price prix m psychologique ou d'acceptabilité; p. profile profil m psychologique; p. warfare guerre f psychologique

psychologically [saɪkə'lɒdʒɪklɪ] ADV psychologiquement

psychologist [saɪ'kɒlədʒɪst] N psychologue mf; child p. psychologue pour enfants

psychology [saɪ'kɒlədʒɪ] N psychologie f; the p. of the football hooligan la psychologie des hooligans du football; Fam to use p. faire preuve de psychologie

psychometric [saɪkə'metrɪk] ADJ psychométrique

psychomotor ['saɪkəʊməʊtər] ADJ psychomoteur, -trice

psychoneurosis [saɪkəʊnjʊ'rəʊsɪs] N psychonévrose f

psychopath ['saɪkəʊpæθ] N psychopathe mf

psychopathic [saɪkəʊ'pæθɪk] ADJ (person) psychopathe; (condition, personality) psychopathique

psychopathology [saɪkəʊpə'θɒlədʒɪ] N psychopathologie f

psychophysiology [saɪkəʊfɪzɪ'ɒlədʒɪ] N psychophysiologie f

psychosis, pl psychoses [saɪ'kəʊsɪs, -əʊsi:z] N psychose f

psychosomatic [saɪkəʊsə'mætɪk] ADJ psychosomatique

psychotherapist [saɪkəʊ'θerəpɪst] N psychothérapeute mf

psychotherapy [saɪkəʊ'θerəpɪ] N psychothérapie f

psychotic [saɪ'kɒtɪk] ADJ, N psychotique mf

psychotropic [saɪkəʊ'trɒpɪk] ADJ Pharm psychotrope
▶ ▶ p. drug psychotrope m

PT [pi:'ti:] N Old-fashioned (abbr **physical training**) EPS f

PTA [pi:ti:'eɪ] N Sch (abbr **Parent-Teacher Association**) = association f de parents d'élèves et de professeurs

ptarmigan ['tɑ:mɪgən] N (bird) p., Am rock p. lagopède m muet, Can lagopède des rochers

Pte Mil (abbr **private**) simple soldat m

pterodactyl [terəʊ'dæktɪl] N ptérodactyle m

PTO [pi:ti:'əʊ] (abbr **please turn over**) TSVP

ptomaine ['təʊmeɪn] N Chem ptomaïne f
▶ ▶ p. poisoning intoxication f alimentaire

P2P ['pi:tu:'pi:] ADJ (abbr **peer to peer**) P2P

Pty (abbr **proprietary company**) SARL

pub [pʌb] N Br Fam pub m
▶ ▶ p. food, Fam p. grub = nourriture f (relativement simple) servie dans un pub; p. lunch déjeuner m simple (servi dans un pub); to go out for a p. lunch aller déjeuner dans un pub; p. quiz jeu m de culture générale dans un pub

pub-crawl N Br Fam tournée f des bars; to go on a p. faire la tournée des bars, aller de bar en bar, Can Fam partir sur une brosse

puberty ['pju:bətɪ] N Physiol puberté f, at p. à la puberté; to reach p. atteindre l'âge de la puberté

pubescence [pju:'besəns] N **1** Bot pubescence f **2** Physiol puberté f

pubescent [pju:'besənt] ADJ **1** Bot pubescent **2** Physiol pubère

pubic ['pju:bɪk] ADJ Anat pubien
▶ ▶ p. bone symphyse f pubienne; p. hair poils mpl pubiens ou du pubis; (single) poil m pubien ou du pubis

pubis ['pju:bɪs] N Anat pubis m

public ['pʌblɪk] ADJ public, f publique; to go p. (of firm) émettre ou placer des actions dans le public; (reveal information) tout dire ou raconter; to go p. with the story raconter toute l'histoire; to make sth p. rendre qch public; (news etc) publier qch; to make a p. appearance paraître en public; at p. expense aux frais du contribuable; to be in the p. eye être très en vue; to work for the p. good travailler pour le bien public; to be in the p. interest servir le bien public; of p. interest d'intérêt public; p. interest in the matter was flagging l'intérêt du public pour cette affaire faiblissait; it's p. knowledge tout le monde sait cela; to be in p. ownership être nationalisé; in a p. place dans un lieu public; to make a p. protest protester publiquement

N the (general) p. le (grand) public; book aimed at a wide p. livre qui s'adresse à un large public; my p. like the old songs mon public aime les vieilles chansons; there isn't much of a p. for that kind of thing ce genre de choses n'attire pas un grand public; in p. en public, publiquement; Fin to issue shares to the p. placer des actions dans le public VOIR GRAMMAIRE A11

▶ ▶ Am TV p. access channel = chaîne f du réseau câblé sur laquelle des particuliers peuvent diffuser leurs propres émissions; p. accountability transparence f, Br Pol P. Accounts Committee = comité m chargé d'examiner les comptes publics; p. address system sonorisation f, Fam sono f, Am p. assistance aide f sociale; p. authorities pouvoirs mpl publics; Br p. bar salle f de bar (dans un pub qui contient deux bars séparés, l'expression désigne le plus populaire des deux); p. body corporation f de droit public; Am Radio, TV p. broadcaster diffuseur m public; Br p. call box cabine f (téléphonique) publique; p. carrier transporteur m public; p. company ≃ société f anonyme; p. company law loi f sur les sociétés anonymes; Br p. convenience toilettes fpl publiques; Br, Can p. corporation entreprise f publique; p. data network réseau m public de données; Fin p. debt dette f publique ou de l'État; Am Law p. defender avocat m commis d'office; Fin p. deposits = avoirs mpl des différents services du gouvernement britannique à la Banque d'Angleterre; p. domain domaine m public; to be p. domain être dans le domaine public; in the p. domain dans le domaine public; Comput p. domain software logiciel m (du domaine) public, Can publiciel m; p. enemy number one ennemi m public numéro un; p. examination examen m national de l'enseignement public; p. excursion fare tarif m excursion; p. figure personnalité f très en vue; p. foreign debt dette publique extérieure; p. funds fonds mpl publics; p. health official représentant, -ante de la santé publique; p. holiday jour m férié, fête f légale; p. house Br (pub) pub m, bar m, Am (inn) auberge f; Am p. housing logements mpl sociaux, ≃ HLM f inv; p. information broadcast message m de grande cause nationale; Br p. lavatory toilettes publiques; p. lending right = droits mpl que touche un auteur ou un éditeur pour le prêt de ses livres en bibliothèque; **p. liability** responsabilité *f* civile; **p. liability insurance** assurance *f* responsabilité civile; **p. life** la vie publique; **p. limited company** ≃ société anonyme; **p. loan** emprunt *m* public; **p. money** deniers *mpl ou* fonds publics; *St Exch* **p. offering** offre *f* publique; **p. opinion** opinion *f* publique; **p. opinion poll** sondage *m* (d'opinion); **p. park** jardin *m* public; *Br* **P. Record Office** ≃ Archives *fpl* nationales; **p. relations** relations *fpl* publiques; **p. relations consultant** conseil *m* en relations publiques, conseil *m* en communication; **p. relations department** service *m* des relations publiques; **p. relations director** directeur, -trice des relations publiques; **p. relations exercise** opération *f* de relations publiques; **p. relations manager** directeur, -trice des relations publiques; **p. relations officer** responsable *mf* des relations publiques; **p. sales office** (of an airline etc) agence *f* commerciale; **p. school** (in UK) public school *f*, école *f* privée (prestigieuse); (in US) école publique; *Br* **a p.-school education** une scolarité *ou* des études *fpl* dans le privé; *Br* **he's very p.-school** il fait très école privée; **p. sector** secteur *m* public; *Br Econ* **p. sector borrowing requirement** = besoins *mpl* d'emprunt du secteur public non couverts par les rentrées fiscales; **p. sector earnings** revenus *mpl* du secteur public; **p. service** (amenity) service public *ou* d'intérêt général; *Br* (civil service) fonction *f* publique; **the p. services** les services publics; **the organization performs a useful p. service** cette organisation offre un service public fort utile; *Am TV* **p. service broadcasting** émissions *fpl* de service public; **p. service vehicle** véhicule *m* de transport en commun; *St Exch* **p. share offer** offre publique de vente; **p. speaking** art *m* oratoire; *Fin* **p. spending** dépenses *fpl* publiques *ou* de l'État; **p. spirit** sens *m* civique, civisme *m*; **p. transport** transports *mpl* en commun; **p. transport advertising** affichage *m* transport; **p. transport vehicle** véhicule *m* des transports en commun; **p. utility** *Am* (company) = société privée assurant un service public et réglementée par une commission d'État; *Br* (amenity) service public; *Br* **p. utility company** société d'utilité publique; **p. works** travaux *mpl* publics

> Note that the French expression **école publique** is never a translation for the British sense of the expression **public school**. It means **state school**.

Public schools

En Angleterre et au pays de Galles, le terme "public school" désigne une école privée de type traditionnel. Certaines de ces écoles (Eton et Harrow, par exemple) sont très prestigieuses et élitistes. Les "public schools" sont censées former l'élite de la nation. Aux États-Unis et parfois en Écosse, le terme désigne une école publique.

publican ['pʌblɪkən] N *Br* patron, -onne d'un/du pub

publication [pʌblɪ'keɪʃən] N **1** (of book, news, the banns etc) publication *f*, (of order, decree) promulgation *f*, **my article has been accepted for p.** mon article va être publié; **this is not for p.** ceci n'est pas destiné à la publication **2** (published work) publication *f*
▸▸ **p. date** (of book) date *f* de parution *ou* de publication; **p. day** jour *m* de parution

publicist ['pʌblɪsɪst] N publicitaire *mf*

publicity [pʌb'lɪsɪtɪ] N (given to a matter) publicité *f*, *Fam* pub *f*, *Com* publicité, réclame *f*, **the football team has received a**

lot of free p. as a result of this scandal ce scandale a fait beaucoup de publicité (gratuite) à l'équipe de football; **it's another one of his p.-seeking gimmicks** c'est encore un de ses trucs pour se faire de la publicité; **there's no such thing as bad p.** on ne fait jamais trop parler de soi; **they're very p. conscious** ils sont très conscients de leur image
▸▸ **p. agent** agent *m* publicitaire; **p. brochure** brochure *f* publicitaire; **p. budget** budget *m* publicitaire; **p. campaign** (for new product) campagne *f* publicitaire, campagne de publicité; (by government) campagne d'information; **p. department** service *m* de publicité; **p. expenses** dépenses *fpl* de la publicité; **p. manager** chef *m* de (la) publicité; **p. stunt** coup *m* de pub

publicize ['pʌblɪsaɪz] VT (make known) faire connaître au public; *Com* (advertise) (product) faire de la publicité *ou* de la réclame *ou* *Fam* de la pub pour; **her resignation was widely publicized** on a fait beaucoup de battage autour de sa démission; **the launch of their new product has been widely publicized** leur nouveau produit a été lancé à grand renfort de publicité; **she doesn't p. the fact** elle ne le crie pas sur tous les toits

publicly ['pʌblɪklɪ] ADV publiquement, en public; *Econ* **p. owned** nationalisé, d'état

public-spirited ADJ (person) qui a le sens civique; (gesture, response) dicté par le sens civique; **that was very p. of them** ils ont fait preuve par là d'un grand civisme *ou* sens civique

publish ['pʌblɪʃ] VT **1** (of publisher, author) (book) éditer, publier; *Comput* (web page) publier; **we're going to p. it next week** on va le publier la semaine prochaine, ça paraîtra chez nous la semaine prochaine; **who publishes Sartre?** qui édite *ou* publie Sartre?; **it's published by Polygon** c'est édité chez Polygon; **the magazine is published quarterly** la revue paraît tous les trois mois; **just published** (of book) vient de paraître; **she's had two novels published** on a publié deux de ses romans; **he's a published author** ses livres sont publiés **2** (edict, the banns) publier; (news) publier, faire paraître
VI **they decided not to p.** ils ont décidé de ne pas faire publier la nouvelle/leur ouvrage/cet article/etc; **p. and be damned!** publiez si vous voulez et allez au diable!; **we're going to p. and be damned** on publiera, advienne que pourra

publishable ['pʌblɪʃəb(ə)l] ADJ publiable

publisher ['pʌblɪʃər] N **1** éditeur, -trice; (company) maison *f* d'édition; **p.'s reader** lecteur, -trice de manuscrits (dans une maison d'édition) **2** *Am* (newspaper owner) propriétaire *mf* d'un/du journal

publishing ['pʌblɪʃɪŋ] N **1** (of book, report, accounts etc) publication *f*, (profession, business) édition *f*, **to work** *or* **be in p.** travailler dans l'édition **2** (of the banns etc) publication *f*
▸▸ **p. firm, p. house** maison *f* d'édition; **the p. trade** l'édition

puce [pjuːs] ADJ, N puce *m inv*

puck¹ [pʌk] N (elf) lutin *m*, farfadet *m*

puck² N *Sport* (in ice hockey) palet *m*

pucker ['pʌkər] N (in face) (wrinkle) ride *f*, (fold) pli *m*; (in material) faux pli, godet *m*
VT (one's face) rider; (material) froncer, faire goder *ou* godailler; (one's brow, forehead etc) froncer; (one's lips) plisser
VI = **pucker up** VI
▸ **pucker up** VI (of garment, material) faire des faux plis, goder, godailler; **his face puckered up** sa figure s'est crispée; **she puckered up for his kiss** elle tendit les lèvres, se préparant à son baiser
VT SEP (one's lips) tendre

puckish ['pʌkɪʃ] ADJ malicieux, espiègle

pud [pʊd] N *Br Fam* pudding *m*; (dessert) dessert *m*; **what's for p.?** qu'est-ce qu'il y a comme dessert?; **there's ice-cream for p.** il y a de la glace en dessert

pudding ['pʊdɪŋ] N **1** (dish) (suet) p. pudding *m*, pouding *m*; *Sl Hum* **to be in the p. club** (be pregnant) avoir un polichinelle dans le tiroir **2** (dessert) dessert *m*; **what's for p.?** qu'est-ce qu'il y a comme *ou* pour le dessert? **3** *Fam* (chubby person) petit gros *m*, petite grosse *f*, (baby) gros bébé *m*
▸▸ **p. basin, p. bowl** moule *m* à puddings *ou* à poudings; **p. basin haircut, p. bowl haircut** coupe *f* au bol

puddingface ['pʊdɪŋfeɪs] N *Fam* visage *m* empâté

puddinghead ['pʊdɪŋhed] N *Fam* idiot, -ote, andouille *f*

puddingstone ['pʊdɪŋstəʊn] N *Geol* poudingue *m*

puddle ['pʌd(ə)l] N (of water, oil) flaque *f*, (small pool) petite mare *f*, *Fam* **the dog's made a p. on the carpet** le chien a fait pipi sur le tapis
VT *Metal* (iron) puddler

pudenda [pju:'dendə] NPL *Fml* parties *fpl* génitales

pudgy ['pʌdʒɪ] ADJ *Fam* (person) rondelet, dodu

puerile ['pjʊəraɪl] ADJ *Pej* puéril; **he's being utterly p. about it** il a une attitude complètement puérile à cet égard

puerility [pjʊə'rɪlɪtɪ] N *Fml* puérilité *f*

puerperal [pjuː'ɜːpərəl] ADJ *Med* puerpéral, -aux

Puerto Rican [pweətəʊ'riːkən, pwɜːtəʊ-] ADJ portoricain
N Portoricain, -aine

Puerto Rico [pweətəʊ'riːkəʊ, pwɜːtəʊ-] N Porto Rico *m*

puff [pʌf] N **1** (of breath) souffle *m*; (of air) souffle, bouffée *f*, (of smoke, steam) bouffée; **to take a p. at one's pipe** tirer une bouffée de sa pipe; **give me a p.** (of your cigarette) passe-moi une bouffée *ou* *Fam* une taffe; *Fam* **out of p.** essoufflé, à bout de souffle; *Fam* **let me get my p. back** laissez-moi reprendre mon souffle; *Fig Fam* **our ideas went up** *or* **disappeared in a p. of smoke** nos idées sont parties en fumée
2 *Sewing* (of dress) bouillon *m*; (of sleeve) bouffant *m*; *Am* (quilt) édredon *m*
3 (in media) reportage *m* flatteur; *Old-fashioned Fam* (advertisement) pub *f*, réclame *f* (tapageuse); **I managed to get in a p. about my new book** j'ai réussi à faire de la pub *ou* de la réclame pour mon nouveau livre
4 *Culin* cream p. chou *m* à la crème
5 *Br Sl* (marijuana) herbe *f*, beu *f*, (cannabis) shit *m*, hasch *m*
VI (of person) souffler; (of steam engine) lancer des bouffées de vapeur; **to p. and blow** *or* **pant** haleter; **to p. (away) at one's pipe** tirer sur sa pipe, tirer des bouffées de sa pipe; **the steam engine puffed into view** la fumée indiqua l'arrivée du train; **to p. into the station** entrer en gare dans un nuage de fumée
VT **1** (smoke, air) émettre, envoyer; (pipe etc) fumer par petites bouffées; (rice) (faire) gonfler; **to p. smoke into sb's face** envoyer de la fumée à la figure de qn
2 *Old-fashioned Fam* (advertise) (one's wares) pousser, vanter
▸▸ *Zool* **p. adder** vipère *f* heurtante; *Culin* **p. pastry** pâte *f* feuilletée; **p. sleeves** manches *fpl* ballon
▸ **puff out** VT SEP **1** (one's cheeks) gonfler; (sleeve etc) faire ballonner *ou* bouffer; **to p. out one's chest** bomber le torse **2** (emit) (smoke) émettre, envoyer **3** *Fam* (exhaust)

crever; **that walk has puffed me out** cette marche m'a crevé

▶ **puff up** VT SEP *(one's cheeks)* gonfler; **he was puffed up with pride** il était bouffi d'orgueil

Puffa jacket® ['pʌfə] N blouson *m* de rappeur

puffball ['pʌfbɔːl] N *Bot* vesse-de-loup *f, pl* vesses-de-loup

puffed [pʌft] ADJ **1 p. out** *(of skirt etc)* ballonné; **p. up (with pride)** bouffi d'orgueil **2** *Fam* **p. (out)** *(person)* essoufflé, à bout de souffle; *(tired)* fatigué

▶▶ **p. rice** riz *m* gonflé; **p. sleeves** manches *fpl* ballon

puffer ['pʌfər] N *Fam (train)* train *m* à vapeur; *(boat)* bateau *m* à vapeur

puffin ['pʌfɪn] N *(bird)* macareux *m* moine, puffin *m*

puffiness ['pʌfɪnɪs] N *(of face etc)* aspect *m* bouffi

puffy ['pʌfɪ] ADJ **1** *(swollen) (face, clouds)* bouffi, boursouflé; *(eyes)* gonflé, bouffi; **to be p. under the eyes** avoir les yeux bouffis *ou* gonflés **2** *Fam (person) (short-winded)* à l'haleine courte, poussif; *(out of breath)* hors d'haleine

pug [pʌg] N *(dog)* carlin *m*

▶▶ **p. dog** carlin *m*; **p. nose** nez *m* camus

pugilism ['pjuːdʒɪlɪz(ə)m] N *Fml* boxe *f*

pugilist ['pjuːdʒɪlɪst] N *Fml* pugiliste *m*

pugnacious [pʌgˈneɪʃəs] ADJ querelleur, -euse, batailleur, -euse, *Lit* pugnace

pugnaciously [pʌgˈneɪʃəslɪ] ADV d'une manière querelleuse *ou* batailleuse *ou Lit* pugnace; *(to defend sth)* avec pugnacité

pugnacity [pʌgˈnæsɪtɪ], **pugnaciousness** [pʌgˈneɪʃəsnɪs] N caractère *m* querelleur *ou* batailleur, *Lit* pugnacité *f*

pug-nosed [-nəʊzd] ADJ au nez écrasé *ou* camus

puke [pjuːk] *Fam* VT & VI dégobiller, dégueuler; **it makes me p.!** c'est à gerber!; **you make me p.!** tu es dégueulasse!

N *(vomit)* dégueulis *m*; **to have a p.** dégobiller, dégueuler

pukey ['pjuːkɪ] ADJ *Sl (disgusting)* merdique

pukka ['pʌkə] ADJ *Br* **1** *(upper-class, posh)* snob **2** *Old-fashioned, Hum (genuine)* authentique; **a p. Englishman** un vrai Anglais d'Angleterre **3** *Fam (excellent)* génial, -aux, super

pulchritude ['pʌlkrɪtjuːd] N *Lit* beauté *f*

PULL [pʊl]

N	traction **1** ▪ attrait **1** ▪ influence **3**
VT	tirer **1, 2, 6** ▪ se déchirer **1**
	▪ traîner **2** ▪ attirer **3** ▪ arracher **4**

N **1** *(act of pulling)* tirage *m*, traction *f*; *(of magnet)* force *f* d'attraction; *(in rowing)* coup *m* (d'aviron); *Fig (attraction) (of foreign places, high salaries etc)* attrait *m*; **give it a hard** *or* **good p.!** tirez fort!; **to give a p. on the rope** tirer sur la corde; **give it one more p.** tire encore un coup; **a few more pulls and I'll be able to reach it** en tirant encore un peu j'arriverai à l'atteindre; **I felt a p. at my sleeve** j'ai senti qu'on me tirait par la manche; *Br Sl* **to be (out) on the p.** *(looking for sexual partner)* draguer

2 *(gulp) (of beer etc)* gorgée *f*, lampée *f*; **to take a p. at one's pipe** tirer une bouffée de sa pipe

3 *(influence)* influence *f*; **to have plenty of p.** avoir le bras long

4 *(climb, effort etc)* **it's a long p. to the top** la montée est rude jusqu'au sommet; **it was a long p. to the shore** *(in rowing boat)* ça a pris du temps pour regagner la rive

5 *(handle)* poignée *f*; **(bell)** p. cordon *m* de sonnette

6 *Golf, Cr* coup *m* tiré

7 *Typ* première épreuve *f*

8 *(catch) (in jumper etc)* accroc *m*; **my cardigan has a p. in it** j'ai fait un accroc à mon cardigan

VT **1** *(rope, person's hair etc)* tirer; *(muscle etc)* se déchirer; *(oar)* manier; **p.** *(notice on door)* tirez, tirer; **pulled muscle** élongation *f*, **he pulled her closer (to him)** il l'a attirée plus près de lui; **he pulled the knot tight(er)** il a resserré le nœud; **she pulled the box from his hands** elle lui a arraché la boîte des mains; **to p. a door/drawer/window open** ouvrir une porte/un tiroir/une fenêtre; **to p. a door shut** *or* **closed** fermer une porte; **to p. the curtains/blinds** tirer les rideaux/stores; **to p. the trigger** presser sur la détente *ou* la gâchette; **p. your chair up to** *or* **nearer the fire** approchez votre fauteuil du feu; **to p. to pieces** déchirer, mettre en morceaux; *(criticize severely)* démolir; **to p. rank on sb** faire valoir son ancienneté sur qn; *Br Fam* **p. the other one!** *(it's got bells on!)* laisse-moi rire!; **to p. one's hat (down) over one's eyes** enfoncer *ou* rabattre son chapeau sur les yeux; *TV, Cin* **to p. focus** faire la mise au point

2 *(haul) (cart etc)* traîner, tirer; *(of barge etc) (boat)* haler

3 *(attract) (customers, crowd)* attirer; *Sl (pick up) (sexual partner)* lever, emballer

4 *(extract, remove)* **to p. a cork** déboucher une bouteille; **to p. a plant** arracher une plante; **to p. a tooth** arracher *ou* extraire une dent; **to have a tooth pulled** se faire arracher une dent; **it was like pulling teeth** c'était pénible comme tout; **to p. a pint** tirer une bière; **to p. pints** *(for a living)* travailler comme barman/comme serveuse de bar; **to p. a TV programme** retirer une émission de télé; **to p. sth from the files** *(cancel)* retirer qch des fichiers; *Fam* **to p. a gun on sb** mettre un pistolet sous le nez de qn

5 *(do) Fam* **to p. a bank job** se faire une banque; *Fam* **to p. a fast one on sb** avoir qn, rouler qn; **so you thought you could p. a fast one (on me)?** alors comme ça tu voulais me jouer un tour?; **to p. a trick on sb** jouer un tour à qn; **don't ever p. a stunt like that again** ne me/nous/*etc* refais jamais un tour comme ça; **to p. a face** faire une grimace

6 *Typ (proof)* tirer

7 *Sport* **to p. one's shot** envoyer la balle trop loin sur le côté; *Golf* faire un coup tiré

VI **1** tirer; *(in rowing)* ramer, souquer; **she pulled clear of the pack** elle s'est détachée du peloton; **he pulled clear of the traffic and sped on** il est sorti du flot de la circulation et a accéléré; **he pulled sharply to the left** il a viré brutalement sur la gauche; **the lorry pulled slowly up the hill** le camion gravissait lentement la côte; **to p. on** *or* **at a rope** tirer sur un cordage; **to p. at one's pipe** tirer sur sa pipe; **they're pulling in different directions** *(they disagree)* ils ne s'entendent pas, ils ne sont pas d'accord, *Fam* ils tirent à hue et à dia

2 **the engine is pulling heavily** le moteur fatigue *ou* peine; **the brakes p. to the left/right** les freins tirent à gauche/droite

3 *Sport* envoyer la balle trop loin sur le côté; *Golf* faire un coup tiré

4 *Sl (find sexual partner)* faire une touche

▶▶ *Mktg* **p. strategy** stratégie *f* pull; *Comput* **p. technology** recherche *f* individuelle, technologie *f* pull

▶ **pull about** VT SEP *(handle roughly) (object)* tirer dans tous les sens, tirailler; *(person)* malmener; **stop pulling me about!, she said** ne sois pas aussi brutal!, dit-elle

▶ **pull ahead** VI *(in race, election campaign)*

prendre la tête; **to p. ahead of one's rival** distancer son rival

▶ **pull along** VT SEP *(person)* tirer par le bras/par l'épaule/*etc*, *(load etc)* tirer derrière soi

▶ **pull apart** VT SEP **1** *(break up) (object)* mettre en petits morceaux; *(clothing etc)* déchirer; *(dismantle for storage etc)* démonter; *(body, flesh)* déchiqueter; *(separate) (two people fighting)* séparer

2 *(criticize) (person)* éreinter; *(performance, argument etc)* démolir

VI **it pulls apart** c'est démontable, ça se démonte

▶ **pull away** VT SEP *(remove forcefully)* **to p. sth away from sth/sb** arracher qch de qch/des mains de qn; **he pulled his hand away** il retira vivement sa main; **they pulled the distraught father away from the burning car** ils ont arraché le père affolé à la voiture en feu

VI **1** *(of train, car)* partir; **the train pulled away from the station** le train a quitté la gare; **as the train began to p. away** alors que le train s'ébranlait; **to p. away from sb** s'écarter de qn; **she's beginning to p. away** *(in race)* elle commence à prendre de l'avance

2 *(in rowing)* **p. away!** souquez!

▶ **pull back** VI *(hesitate)* hésiter; *(not continue with project etc)* se retirer, refuser de continuer; *Mil* décrocher; **they pulled back from committing themselves fully** ils ont renoncé à s'engager complètement

VT SEP *(curtains)* ouvrir; *(covers)* rejeter en arrière; *Mil* retirer; **his father pulled him back from the fire** son père l'a éloigné du feu; **to p. sb/a company back from the brink** faire refaire surface à qn/une entreprise, tirer qn/une entreprise d'affaire

▶ **pull down** VT SEP **1** *(lower) (blind, skirt etc)* baisser; **to p. one's hat down over one's eyes** enfoncer *ou* rabattre son chapeau sur ses yeux; **he's pulling the whole team down** il fait baisser le niveau de toute l'équipe; **my marks in the oral exam will p. me down** mes notes à l'oral vont baisser *ou* descendre ma moyenne

2 *(demolish) (house etc)* démolir, abattre

3 *(of illness, circumstances) (person)* abattre

4 *Comput (menu)* dérouler

5 *Am Fam (earn) (salary)* toucher; *(money)* gagner; **he doesn't p. down much of a salary** il ne gagne pas *ou* touche pas des masses

▶ **pull in** VT SEP **1** *(fishing net etc)* rentrer; *(money)* gagner, *Fam* se faire; **he pulled me in** *(to swimming pool)* il m'a tiré dedans

2 *(attract) (the public)* attirer; **it's really pulling them in** ça attire les foules

3 *Fam (of police) (suspect)* arrêter; **they pulled him in for questioning** ils l'ont arrêté pour l'interroger; **to be pulled in for speeding** être arrêté pour excès de vitesse

4 *Aut* **to p. one's car in to the kerb** se ranger près du trottoir

5 **to p. oneself** *or* **one's stomach in** rentrer son ventre

6 *Horseriding (hold back) (horse)* retenir, tirer les rênes de

VI **1** *(stop at side of road) (of vehicle, driver)* s'arrêter, se garer; **p. in here** arrête-toi là; **to p. in to the kerb** se ranger près du trottoir; **we'll p. in at** *or* **to the next garage** on s'arrêtera à la prochaine station-service

2 *(arrive) (of train, bus, person)* arriver; **the express pulled in two hours late** l'express est arrivé avec deux heures de retard

▶ **pull into** VT INSEP *(arrive at) (of train, bus, person etc)* arriver à; **the train was pulling into the station** le train entrait en gare; **the bus pulled into view** le bus apparut; *Sport* **to p. into the lead** prendre la tête

▶ **pull off** VT SEP **1** *(remove) (clothes, wrapping etc)* enlever; *(detach)* détacher (**from** de); **to p. sth off sth** *(detach from)* détacher qch de qch; **to p. the sheets off the bed** retirer *ou* enlever les draps du lit

2 *Fam (win) (prize)* décrocher, gagner, remporter; **to p. off a deal** réussir une opération, boucler une affaire; **to p. off a bank raid/a project** réussir un hold-up/un projet; **he pulled it off** il a réussi

VI the lid simply pulls off il suffit de tirer pour enlever le couvercle; **the top pulls off to reveal ...** le dessus se retire et on peut voir ...

▸ **pull on** VT SEP *(sweater, one's hat etc)* mettre; **to p. sth on over sth else** enfiler qch par-dessus qch d'autre

▸ **pull out** VT SEP **1** *(extract) (tooth)* arracher, extraire; **to p. a wallet out of one's pocket** tirer *ou* sortir un portefeuille de sa poche; **to p. a nail out of a plank** arracher un clou d'une planche; **to p. a cork out of a bottle** enlever un bouchon d'une bouteille; **to p. a car out of a ditch** sortir une voiture d'un fossé; **to p. the country/economy out of the recession** faire sortir le pays/l'économie de la récession; **p. me out, I'm stuck in the mud!** sors-moi de là, je suis enlisé dans la boue!; **he was pulled out of the burning car** il a été arraché de la voiture en feu; *Fam* **to p. out all the stops** faire le maximum (**to do sth** pour faire qch)

2 *(withdraw) (troops)* retirer

3 *(drawer) (open)* ouvrir; *(remove)* enlever, dégager; *(leaf of table, shelf)* tirer

VI 1 *Aut (move out to overtake)* déboîter; **to p. out from behind a car** déboîter de derrière une voiture

2 *(leave) (of train, bus, person etc)* partir; **when do we p. out?** quand est-ce qu'on part?

3 *(withdraw) (of troops)* se retirer; *(of firm from project, buyer)* se désister; *(of firm from place)* quitter une/la région/ville/*etc*

4 *(be extendible or detachable) (of drawer)* s'ouvrir; *(of handle) (be telescopic)* s'allonger; *(of map)* se déplier; **the table pulls out to seat ten** avec les rallonges c'est une table de dix personnes; **the sofa pulls out so you can sleep on it** on peut déplier le sofa pour dormir dedans

▸ **pull out of** VT INSEP **1** *(leave) (of train, bus, person etc)* partir de; **the train was pulling out of the station** le train sortait de la gare; *Aviat* **to p. out of a dive** arrêter de piquer; **the country is pulling out of the recession** le pays est en train de sortir de la récession

2 *(withdraw from) (agreement, deal, country)* se retirer de

▸ **pull over** VT SEP **1** tirer; *(cause to fall)* faire tomber; **careful you don't p. that wardrobe over on top of you!** attention de ne pas te faire tomber l'armoire sur la tête!

2 **she pulled her sweater over her head** *(putting it on)* elle a enfilé son pull; *(taking it off)* elle a enlevé son pull

VI she's pulling over to let the other runners past elle se met sur le côté pour laisser passer les autres coureurs; *Aut* **to p. over to the kerb** se ranger le long du trottoir

▸ **pull round** VT SEP *(chair, object)* tourner; *(boat) (turn)* faire tourner; *(turn through 180 degrees)* faire faire demi-tour à; *(person) (help regain consciousness)* ranimer; *(help recover from illness)* remonter, remettre sur pied

VI *(of ship)* tourner; *(through 180 degrees)* faire demi-tour; *(of person) (regain consciousness)* revenir à soi; *(recover from illness)* se remettre

▸ **pull through** VT SEP **1** *(of doctor etc) (person)* remettre sur pied

2 *(help survive difficulty) (person)* tirer d'embarras *ou* d'affaire; **he says his faith pulled him through** il dit que c'est sa foi qui lui a permis de s'en sortir

VI 1 *(recover from illness)* s'en tirer

2 *(survive difficulty)* se tirer d'affaire, s'en tirer, surmonter ses difficultés

▸ **pull to** VT SEP *(door)* tirer, fermer

▸ **pull together** VT SEP *(information)* rassembler, réunir; **he pulled them together into a team** il a réussi à faire d'eux une équipe; **to p. oneself together** *(become calm, more organized)* se ressaisir, se reprendre, reprendre ses esprits; **p. yourself together!** ressaisissez-vous!

VI *(co-operate)* s'entendre; **if we all p. together on this** si nous y mettons tous du nôtre; **p. together!** *(in rowing)* avant partout!

▸ **pull up** VT SEP **1** *(raise) (blind)* hausser, lever; *(one's skirt)* retrousser, relever; *(plant, weeds)* arracher; **p. up a chair!** prends une chaise!; **to p. one's socks up** tirer *ou* remonter ses chaussettes; *Fig Fam* se remuer, s'activer; **his good marks in maths pulled him up again** ses bonnes notes en maths ont remonté sa moyenne

2 *(stop), Horseriding (horse)* arrêter; **to p. oneself up (short)** s'arrêter *(quand on est sur le point de dire ou faire qch d'indiscret)*; **to p. sb up (short)** arrêter qn net

3 *(reprimand) (person)* rembarrer; **he pulled me up for being late** il m'a rembarré parce que j'étais en retard; *Aut* **to be pulled up (by the police)** se faire arrêter (par un agent)

VI 1 *(stop)* s'arrêter; **the horse pulled up lame** le cheval s'est arrêté en boitant

2 *(close gap)* **to p. up (on another competitor)** réduire la distance (qui vous sépare d'un autre concurrent)

pull-back N *(withdrawal) (of troops)* retrait *m*

pull-down ADJ

▸▸ *Comput* **p. menu** menu *m* déroulant; *Comput* **p. window** fenêtre *f* déroulante

pullet ['pʊlɪt] N poulette *f*, *(fattened)* poularde *f*

pulley ['pʊlɪ] N poulie *f*

▸▸ **p. block** palan *m*, moufle *f*; **p. wheel** réa *m*, rouet *m*

pull-in N *Br (café)* = restoroute® *m*; *(for parking)* parking *m* *(surtout près d'un restaurant)*

Pullman ['pʊlmən] N *Rail (carriage)* voiture *f* Pullman

▸▸ **P. car, P. carriage** voiture Pullman

pull-off N *Am Aut (rest area)* aire *f* de repos

pull-out ADJ ATTRIB *(section in magazine)* détachable

N *Journ* supplément *m* détachable

▸▸ **p. leaf** *(on desk, table)* rallonge *f*

pullover ['pʊləʊvər] N pull-over *m*, *pl* pullovers, *Fam* pull *m*

pullulate ['pʌljʊleɪt] VI *Lit* pulluler *(with life* de vie)

pull-up N **1** *(of car etc)* arrêt *m* **2** *(café)* = restoroute® *m* **3** *Gym* traction *f*

pulmonary ['pʌlmənərɪ] ADJ ATTRIB *Anat, Med* pulmonaire

pulp [pʌlp] N *(of fruit)* pulpe *f*, chair *f*; **dental p.** pulpe dentaire; **paper p.** pâte *f ou* pulpe à papier; **to reduce to p.** *(a) (wood etc)* réduire en pulpe *ou* en pâte; *Fam* **to beat sb to a p.** mettre qn en bouillie

VT *(wood etc)* réduire en pulpe *ou* en pâte; *(fruit)* écraser, réduire en purée; *(books)* mettre au pilon; **pulping machine** *(in paper-making)* pilon *m*

▸▸ **p. fiction** romans *mpl* de gare; **p. novels** romans *de ou* à quatre sous; **p. writer** auteur *m* de romans de gare

pulpit ['pʊlpɪt] N *(of minister)* chaire *f*; **condemned from the p.** condamné par l'église

pulpwood ['pʌlpwʊd] N *(for papermaking)* bois *m* à pâte

pulpy ['pʌlpɪ] ADJ pulpeux, charnu

pulsar ['pʌlsər] N *Astron* pulsar *m*

pulsate [pʌl'seɪt] VI palpiter; *(vibrate)* vibrer; *(of heart etc)* *Fig* **his novels p. with life** ses romans bouillonnent de vie

pulsation [pʌl'seɪʃən] N *Physiol, Elec, Astron* pulsation *f*, *(of heart)* battement *m*, pulsation

pulse[1] [pʌls] N **1** *Physiol* pouls *m*; **quick p.** pouls fréquent *ou* précipité; **strong/weak p.** pouls fort/faible; **to feel** *or* **take sb's p.** prendre le pouls à qn; **his p. quickened** son pouls s'est accéléré; *Fig* **to have one's finger on the p.** être à la page; *Fig* **to keep one's finger on the p. of ...** se tenir étroitement au courant de ... **2** *(of heart)* pulsation *f*, battement *m*; *Phys (of light, sound etc)* vibration *f*; *Electron, Radio* impulsion *f*, *Mus* cadence *f*, rythme *m*

VI 1 *(of heart)* battre; *(beat hard)* palpiter; **a vein pulsed above his right eye** une veine se gonflait au-dessus de son œil droit; **to p. through the arteries** *(of blood)* circuler dans les artères par pulsations rythmées **2** *Fig* vibrer *(with energy* d'énergie); **her novels p. with life** ses romans bouillonnent de vie; **the pulsing music** le rythme saccadé de la musique

VT *Elec etc (current)* moduler en impulsions

▸▸ **p. rate** fréquence *f* du pouls

pulse[2] N *(plant)* (plante *f*) légumineuse *f*, légume *m* à gousse; *(lentils, beans etc)* légume sec, *Spec* graine *f* de légumes à gousse

pulverization [pʌlvəraɪˈzeɪʃən] N pulvérisation *f*

pulverize ['pʌlvəraɪz] VT pulvériser, réduire en poudre; *Fam* **to p. sb** *(beat up)* démolir qn; *(defeat heavily)* pulvériser qn; *(criticize severely)* éreinter qn

puma ['pjuːmə] N *(animal)* puma *m*, couguar *m*

pumice ['pʌmɪs] N (pierre *f*) ponce *f*

VT *(surface)* poncer, passer à la pierre ponce

▸▸ **p. stone** (pierre) ponce

pummel ['pʌm(ə)l] VT (-ll-, *Am* -l-) *(person)* battre, rosser; *(door, sb's chest)* battre; *(mixture into dough)* pétrir; **to be pummelled by the waves** être battu par les vagues; **to be pummelled by artillery** être pilonné par les tirs d'artillerie

N = **pommel** N

pummelling, *Am* **pummeling** ['pʌm(ə)lɪŋ] N volée *f* de coups, raclée *f*; **to give sb a good p.** donner une bonne raclée à qn; **to get a p.** *(of boxer)* se faire taper dessus

pump [pʌmp] N **1** *(device)* pompe *f* **2** *(shoe) (for dancing)* escarpin *m*; *(for sports)* (chaussure *f* de) tennis *f*

VT *(water etc)* pomper; **to p. a well dry** assécher *ou* épuiser un puits; **to p. sb's stomach** faire un lavage d'estomac à qn; **to p. air into sb's lungs** insuffler de l'air dans les poumons de qn; **to p. air into a balloon** gonfler un ballon *(à l'aide d'une pompe)*; **to p. water into a cavity** amener de l'eau à la pompe dans une cavité; *Fam* **to p. sb's hand** serrer vigoureusement la main à qn; *Fam* **to p. sb** *(for information)* tirer les vers du nez à qn; *Sl* **to p. water into a boiler** refouler de l'eau dans une chaudière; *Fam* **the athletes were pumped full of drugs** les athlètes étaient complètement dopés; *Sl* **to p. sb full of lead** *(shoot)* trouer la peau à qn; *Fam* **to p. iron** faire de la gonflette; **he looks as if he pumps iron** on dirait un haltérophile; *Fig* **the government pumped money into the region** le gouvernement a injecté des capitaux dans cette région

VI 1 *(of heart, machine etc)* pomper **2** *Br Sl (pass wind)* péter

▸▸ **p. attendant** *(at petrol station)* pompiste

mf; **p. room** *(building)* pavillon *m*; *(room)* buvette *f* *(dans une station thermale)*; **p. water** eau *f* de pompe

▸ **pump in** VT SEP *(water etc)* faire entrer à l'aide d'une pompe; *Fig* **more money will have to be pumped in** il faudra injecter plus d'argent

▸ **pump out** VT SEP *(water etc)* pomper; *Naut* **to p. out the holds** assécher les cales; **to p. out sb's stomach** faire un lavage d'estomac à qn

▸ **pump up** VT SEP *(tyre)* gonfler; *(oil, water)* pomper

pump-action shotgun N fusil *m* à pompe

pumped [pʌmpt] ADJ *Am Fam (excited)* surexcité; *(enthusiastic)* emballé

pumping ['pʌmpɪŋ] N *(of water etc)* pompage *m*
  ▸▸ **p. station** station *f* de pompage

pumpkin ['pʌmpkɪn] N potiron *m*, citrouille *f*
  ▸▸ **p. pie** tarte *f* au potiron

pun [pʌn] N calembour *m*, jeu *m* de mots (**on sth** sur qch); **if you'll forgive** *or* **pardon the p.** pardonnez-moi ce jeu de mots ▸ VI **(-nn-)** faire des calembours *ou* des jeux de mots; **…, he punned** …, plaisanta-t-il

Punch [pʌntʃ] N ≃ Polichinelle *m*, Guignol *m*; **P. and Judy show** ≃ (théâtre *m* de) Guignol

---

Punch and Judy

En Grande-Bretagne, le "Punch and Judy show" est un spectacle pour enfants semblable aux Guignols en France. Il est souvent présenté dans un jardin public ou sur une plage. On y retrouve Punch le bossu, sa femme Judy avec laquelle il se querelle constamment, et leur chien Toby.

---

punch¹ [pʌntʃ] N **1** *(blow)* coup *m* de poing; **I got quite a p.** je me suis pris un sacré coup de poing; **to pack quite a p.** *(hit hard)* cogner dur; *Boxing* avoir du punch; *Fig (of drink)* être corsé; **to pull a p.** retenir un coup; **he didn't pull his punches** *(he hit hard)* il n'y est pas allé de main morte; *Fig (he spoke frankly)* il n'a pas mâché ses mots; *Fig* **a documentary that pulls no punches** un documentaire sans complaisance
  2 *Fam (energy)* punch *m*; **style that has p.** style qui a du punch, style incisif
  3 *Tech etc (tool)* poinçon *m*; *(machine)* poinçonneuse *f*, *(for making holes)* perforatrice *f*; **(ticket) p.** *(of ticket inspector etc)* poinçon *m*; *(for use by passenger)* composteur *m*
  VT **1** *(hit) (person)* donner un/des coup(s) de poing à, cogner sur; *(ball, wall etc)* donner un/des coup(s) de poing à, cogner dans; *(typewriter keys, telephone)* taper sur; *(number)* taper, frapper (**into** sur); **to p. a number into a phone** composer un numéro; **to p. sb on the nose** donner un coup de poing sur le nez de qn; **he punched him on the chin** il lui a donné un coup de poing au menton; **the goalie punched the ball clear** le goal a écarté la balle d'un coup de poing; **to p. the air** lever le bras en signe de victoire; *Am* **to p. cattle** être cowboy
  2 *Tech (with tool)* percer, découper à l'emporte-pièce; *(hole)* faire, percer; *(leather etc)* perforer; *(iron sheet)* estamper, étamper; *Comput (card, tape)* perforer; **to p. a ticket** *(of ticket inspector etc)* poinçonner un billet; *(of passenger)* composter un billet; *Comput* **punched card** carte *f* perforée
  ▸▸ *Comput* **p. card** carte *f* perforée; **p. card reader** machine *f* interprète de cartes perforées; **p. line** chute *f* *(d'une histoire drôle)*; *Ind* **p. operator** mécanographe *mf*; **p. tape** bande *f* perforée

▸ **punch away** VT SEP *(ball etc)* détourner d'un coup de poing
  VI donner des coups de poing

▸ **punch in** VT SEP **1** *(box etc)* cabosser (d'un/de coup(s) de poing); *Fam* **to p. sb's face in** casser la gueule à qn **2** *(enter) (number, details)* taper; **p. your number in** composez votre numéro

▸ **punch out** VT SEP **1** *Tech (pin)* chasser; *(shape, pattern etc)* découper à la matrice **2** **to p. it out with sb** échanger des coups de poing avec qn

punch² N *(drink)* punch *m*

punchbag ['pʌntʃbæg] N *Boxing* punchingbag *m*, *pl* punching-bags; *Fig* souffre-douleur *m inv*

punchball ['pʌntʃbɔːl] N *Boxing* punchingball *m*, *pl* punching-balls

punchbowl ['pʌntʃbəʊl] N **1** bol *m* à punch **2** *Br Geog (between two hills)* cuvette *f*

punch-drunk ADJ *esp Boxing* sonné, abruti (par les coups); *Fig* sonné

puncher ['pʌntʃər] N **1** *Tech (person)* *(of sheet metal etc)* poinçonneur, -euse, perceur, -euse; *Comput (of cards, tapes)* perforeur, -euse; *(in metalworking)* estampeur, -euse **2** *Tech (device) (for sheet metal)* poinçonneuse *f*, *(for cardboard, leather etc)* emporte-pièce *m inv*; *Comput (for cards, tapes)* perforatrice *f* **3** *Boxing* puncheur *m*; *Am* **cow p.** cowboy *m*

punching ['pʌntʃɪŋ] N *Tech (action)* perçage *m*, poinçonnage *m*; **p. (out)** découpage *m* (à l'emporte-pièce)
  ▸▸ *Am* **p. bag** *Sport* sac *m* de sable, punching-bag *m*, *pl* punching-bags; *Fig (victim)* souffre-douleur *m inv*; **p. machine** machine *f* poinçonneuse

punchtape reader ['pʌntʃteɪp] N lecteur *m* de ruban perforé

punch-up N *Br Fam* bagarre *f*; **to have a p.** se bagarrer, se battre; **he looked as if he'd been in a p.** on aurait dit qu'il s'était battu *ou* bagarré

punchy ['pʌntʃɪ] ADJ *Fam* **1** *(slogan etc)* incisif, marquant; *(speech, novel)* plein de punch **2** = **punch-drunk**

punctilious [pʌŋk'tɪlɪəs] ADJ pointilleux, méticuleux

punctiliously [pʌŋk'tɪlɪəslɪ] ADV scrupuleusement, dans les moindres détails

punctiliousness [pʌŋk'tɪlɪəsnɪs] N grande attention *f* portée aux détails, méticulosité *f*

punctual ['pʌŋktjʊəl] ADJ *(person)* ponctuel, à l'heure; *(train, bus etc)* à l'heure; **to make a p. start** partir à l'heure

punctuality [pʌŋktjʊ'ælɪtɪ] N *(of person)* ponctualité *f*, exactitude *f*; *(of train, bus etc)* exactitude

punctually ['pʌŋktjʊəlɪ] ADV *(to arrive) (of person)* ponctuellement, à l'heure; *(of train, bus etc)* à l'heure; **we intend to leave p. at 7.30** nous comptons partir à 7h30 précises

punctuate ['pʌŋktjʊeɪt] VT **1** *(sentence etc)* ponctuer **2** *Fig* **speech punctuated with anecdotes** discours ponctué *ou* agrémenté d'anecdotes; **speech punctuated with applause** discours entrecoupé d'applaudissements; **a landscape punctuated with clumps of trees** un paysage avec çà et là un bouquet d'arbres

punctuation [pʌŋktjʊ'eɪʃən] N ponctuation *f*
  ▸▸ **p. mark** signe *m* de ponctuation

puncture ['pʌŋktʃər] N **1** *(in tyre)* crevaison *f*, *(hole in surface, skin etc)* perforation *f*; **to have a p.** *(action)* crever; *(state)* être crevé **2** *Med (action) (of abscess)* ponction *f*
  VT *(tyre)* crever, perforer; *Mil, Sport (defence)* percer; *Med (blister, abscess)* ponc-

tionner; **a punctured lung** un poumon perforé; *Fig* **to p. sb's pride/self-confidence** entamer la fierté/la confiance en soi de qn; **to p. sb's self-esteem** rabattre le caquet à qn
  VI *(of tyre)* crever
  ▸▸ **p. patch** *(for repairing inner tube)* rustine® *f*, **p. repair kit** trousse *f* de réparation pour crevaisons; *Med* **p. wound** blessure *f* pénétrante

pundit ['pʌndɪt] N **1** *(expert) (political etc)* spécialiste *mf*, expert *m*, *Fam* pontife *m*, ponte *m*; **according to the pundits** si l'on en croit les spécialistes *ou Fam* les grands pontes **2** *(in India)* pandit *m*

pungency ['pʌndʒənsɪ] N **1** *(of spice etc) (in taste)* saveur *f* piquante; *(in smell)* odeur *f* forte *ou* piquante **2** *Fig (of words)* âcreté *f*, aigreur *f*; *(of story)* saveur *f*; *(of style etc)* saveur, causticité *f*

pungent ['pʌndʒənt] ADJ **1** *(smell etc)* fort, âcre, piquant; *(taste)* piquant; **p. sauce** sauce *f* relevée *ou* épicée **2** *(style, wit etc)* mordant, caustique

pungently ['pʌndʒəntlɪ] ADV d'une manière piquante

Punic ['pjuːnɪk] ADJ *Hist* punique

puniness ['pjuːnɪnɪs] N faiblesse *f*

punish ['pʌnɪʃ] VT **1** *(child, wrongdoer, mistake)* punir; **to p. sb with imprisonment** punir qn d'une peine d'emprisonnement; **to p. sb for a crime** punir qn pour un crime; **to p. sb for having done sth** *or* **for doing sth** punir qn pour avoir fait qch; *Law* **to p. sb by** *or* **with a fine** frapper qn d'une amende **2** *Sport etc Fam (boxer) (hit hard)* taper dur sur; *(opponent's mistake)* ne pas pardonner; *(horse)* malmener; *Aut (engine)* fatiguer, forcer; **he really punishes himself in training** il se donne à fond à l'entraînement

punishable ['pʌnɪʃəb(ə)l] ADJ punissable; *Law* délictueux; **p. by a fine/by death** passible d'amende/d'une peine de mort

punishing ['pʌnɪʃɪŋ] ADJ dur; *(blow)* violent; *(game)* rude; *(work)* épuisant, éreintant; **a p. race** une course épuisante; **a p. schedule** un emploi du temps extrêmement serré
  N punition *f*

punishment ['pʌnɪʃmənt] N **1** punition *f*, châtiment *m*; *Law* peine *f*; **as a p. for sth** en punition de qch; **to inflict a p. on sb** donner *ou* infliger une punition à qn; **to escape p.** échapper à la punition; **to make the p. fit the crime** proportionner la punition au crime; **to take one's p. like a man** recevoir sa punition sans broncher **2** *Fam (blows etc)* **to take a lot of p.** *(of boxer etc)* encaisser; *(of army, warship, tank, car, boat etc)* être malmené; *(of shoes, clothes etc)* être soumis à rude épreuve; **it has to be able to take a lot of p.** *(of footwear, paint etc)* il faut que ça soit résistant; *(of car)* il faut qu'elle soit bien solide; **to inflict severe p. on a team** administrer une cruelle défaite à une équipe

punitive ['pjuːnɪtɪv], **punitory** ['pjuːnɪt(ə)rɪ] ADJ répressif; *(taxation)* très sévère
  ▸▸ *Law* **p. damages** dommages et intérêts *mpl* dissuasifs; *Mil* **p. expedition** expédition *f* punitive; *Law* **p. justice** justice *f* répressive

Punjab ['pʌndʒɑːb] N Pendjab *m*

Punjabi [pʌn'dʒɑːbɪ] ADJ du Pendjab
  N **1** habitant, -ante du Pendjab; *(by birth)* originaire *mf* du Pendjab **2** *Ling* pendjabi *m*

punk [pʌŋk] N **1** *(music fan, rebel etc)* punk *mf*; *(music)* le punk (rock) **2** *Am Fam Pej (worthless person)* vaurien *m*, crapule *f*
  ADJ **1** *(music, hairstyle etc)* punk *inv*; **a p. band** un groupe punk **2** *Am Fam (worthless)* nul, qui ne vaut rien
  ▸▸ *Mus* **p. rock** le punk rock

punnet ['pʌnɪt] N *esp Br (for strawberries etc)* petit carton m, barquette f

punster ['pʌnstər] N faiseur, -euse de calembours *ou* de jeux de mots

punt[1] [pʌnt] N *(boat)* bateau m à fond plat
VT *(boat)* conduire à la perche; *(person)* transporter dans un bateau à fond plat
VI **to go punting** faire un tour dans un bateau à fond plat
▸▸ **p. pole** perche f *(pour la conduite d'un bateau à fond plat)*

punt[2] *Ftbl, Rugby* VT *(ball)* envoyer d'un coup de volée
VI donner un coup de pied de volée
N coup m de volée

punt[3] VI **1** *Cards* ponter; **to p. high** ponter gros **2** *Br Horseracing* parier

punt[4] N *Formerly (Irish currency)* livre f irlandaise

punter[1] ['pʌntər] N *Br* **1** *Horseracing* parieur, -euse **2** *Fam (consumer, customer)* client, -ente; **the punters** *(the public)* le public, les gens; **the average p.** l'homme de la rue **3** *Fam (prostitute's client)* miché m, micheton m **4** *St Exch Fam (speculator)* boursicoteur, -euse, boursicotier, -ière **5** *Cards* ponte m

punter[2] N *(in boat)* canotier m *(qui conduit à la perche)*

puny ['pju:nɪ] ADJ *(person)* chétif; *(arms, chest)* frêle, maigre; *(hands)* tout petit; *(effort)* malheureux; *(argument, excuse)* piètre; **a p. little fellow** un petit gringalet; **our p. little guns** nos pauvres *ou* malheureux petits canons; **a p. 50p** cinquante malheureux pence

pup [pʌp] N **1** *(of dog)* jeune chien, -ienne, chiot m; *(of seal)* jeune phoque m; *(of wolf)* louveteau m; *(of rat)* raton m; **a bitch and her pups** une chienne et ses petits; **to be in p.** *(of bitch)* être grosse; *Fig* **to be sold a p.** se faire rouler **2** *Fam (young man) (self-important)* freluquet m; *(impertinent)* petit impertinent m
VI mettre bas

pupa, *pl* **pupae** ['pju:pə, -i:] N *(insect)* nymphe f

pupate [pju:'peɪt] VI *(of insect)* se métamorphoser en nymphe

pupil ['pju:p(ə)l] N **1** *Sch* élève mf **2** *Law* pupille mf **3** *Anat (of eye)* pupille f

pupil(l)age ['pju:pɪlɪdʒ] N *Law* pupillarité f, **child in p.** enfant en pupille *ou* en tutelle

pupilometer [pju:pɪ'lɒmɪtər] N pupillomètre m

puppet ['pʌpɪt] N marionnette f, *Fig (person)* marionnette, fantoche m; **glove** *or* **hand p.** marionnette à gaine
▸▸ *Fig* **p. government** gouvernement m fantoche; **p. play, p. show** (spectacle m de) marionnettes; **p. theatre** théâtre m de marionnettes

puppeteer [pʌpɪ'tɪər] N marionnettiste mf

puppetry ['pʌpɪtrɪ] N art m des marionnettes; *(puppet making)* fabrication f de marionnettes

puppy ['pʌpɪ] N **1** *(dog)* jeune chien, -ienne, chiot m **2** *Fam (young man)* = **pup** N **2**
▸▸ **p. dog** jeune chien, -ienne, chiot; *Br* **p. fat** rondeurs fpl de l'adolescence; **p. love** amourette f, amour m d'adolescent

purblind ['pɜːblaɪnd] ADJ **1** *(almost blind)* presque aveugle **2** *Fml (obtuse)* obtus; *(policy, refusal)* aveugle

purchase ['pɜːtʃɪs] N **1** *(act of buying, thing bought)* achat m; *(of company)* rachat m; **to make some purchases** faire des achats **2** *(grip)* prise f, **to get** *or* **secure a p. on sth** trouver prise sur qch
VT *(object)* acheter, *Fml* acquérir, faire l'ac-

quisition de; *Acct* **to p. a debt** racheter une créance
VI acheter; **now is the time to p.** c'est maintenant qu'il faut acheter
▸▸ *Acct* **p. account** compte m d'achats; *Am Acct* **p. accounting** = méthode f de comptabilité utilisée lors de l'acquistion d'une entreprise, dans laquelle les résultats de la filiale n'apparaissent pas dans le bilan de la société mère; *Mktg* **p. behaviour** comportement m d'achat; *Acct* **p. budget** budget m des approvisionnements; **p. contract** contrat m d'achat; **p. cost** coût m d'achat; *Acct* **p. of debts** rachat des créances; *Mktg* **p. decision** décision f d'achat; *Mktg* **p. diary** relevé m d'achat journalier; *Acct* **p. entry** écriture f d'achats; *Mktg* **p. environment** environnement m d'achat; *Mktg* **p. frequency** fréquence f d'achat; *Acct* **p. invoice** facture f d'achat; *Acct* **p. invoice ledger** journal m factures-fournisseurs; *Acct* **p. ledger** (grand-) livre m d'achats, *pl* grands-livres, journal des achats; *Acct* **p. ledger clerk** facturier, -ière m d'entrée; *Acct* **p. method** méthode d'achat; *Fin* **p. note** bordereau m d'achat; *Mktg* **p. occasion** occasion f d'achat; **p. order** *Fin (for goods, service)* bon m de commande; *St Exch (for shares)* ordre m d'achat; **p. price** prix m d'achat; *Fin* **p. value** valeur f d'achat; *Mktg* **p. volume** volume m d'achat

Note that the French verb **pourchasser** is a false friend and is never a translation for the English word **to purchase**. It means **to chase**.

purchaser ['pɜːtʃəsər] N acheteur, -euse, *Fml* acquéreur, -euse
▸▸ *Mktg* **p. behaviour** comportement m de l'acheteur

purchasing ['pɜːtʃəsɪŋ] N achat m; *(of company)* rachat m; *(department)* service m des achats
▸▸ *Am* **p. agent** acheteur, -euse; *Mktg* **p. behaviour** comportement m d'achat; *Mktg* **p. behaviour model** modèle m de comportement d'achat; **p. co-operative** groupement m d'achat; **p. costs** frais mpl de passation de commande; *Mktg* **p. decision** décision f d'achat; **p. department** service m des achats; **p. manager** chef m des achats; *Mktg* **p. motivator** mobile m d'achat; *Fin* **p. power** capacité f d'achat, pouvoir m d'achat; *Mktg* **p. process** processus m d'achat; **p. rights** droits mpl d'achat

purdah ['pɜːdə] N *Rel* = système m qui astreint les femmes à une vie retirée; *Fig* **to go into p.** se retirer, ne voir personne

pure [pjʊər] ADJ *(unadulterated, morally uncorrupted)* pur; **as p. as the driven snow** pur comme l'enfant qui vient de naître; **p.-minded** pur d'esprit; **the p. and simple truth** la vérité pure et simple; *Bible* **the p. in heart** ceux qui ont le cœur pur; **p. Arab (horse)** (cheval m) arabe m de race pure; **by p. chance** par un pur hasard; **p. English** anglais m pur; *Phil* **p. reason** la raison pure; **p. thoughts** pensées fpl pures; **p. silk/wool** pure soie f/laine f
▸▸ **p. mathematics** les mathématiques mpl pures

pure-blood ADJ *(horse)* pur sang inv
N *(horse)* pur-sang m inv

pure-blooded ADJ *(of animal, person)* pur sang inv

purebred ['pjʊəbred] ADJ *(dog, bull)* de race (pure), pur sang inv
N animal m de race; *(horse)* pur-sang m inv

purée ['pjʊəreɪ] N *Culin* purée f, **tomato p.** concentré m de tomate
VT *(apples, potatoes etc)* réduire *ou* écraser en purée; **puréed potatoes/spinach** purée f de pommes de terre/d'épinards

purely ['pjʊəlɪ] ADV purement; **he is p. concerned with …** il est uniquement préoccupé de …; **p. routine questioning** interrogatoire m de simple routine; **it was p. by chance that we met** notre rencontre n'était qu'un pur hasard; **it was p. accidental** c'était un pur hasard; **p. and simply** purement et simplement

pureness ['pjʊənɪs] N pureté f

purgation [pɜːˈgeɪʃən] N **1** *Med (of intestine)* purge f **2** *Rel (in purgatory)* purgation f de l'âme

purgative ['pɜːgətɪv] ADJ, N *Med* purgatif m

purgatory ['pɜːgət(ə)rɪ] N *Rel* purgatoire m; **the souls in p.** les âmes du purgatoire, les âmes en peine; **to live a life of p.** souffrir les peines du purgatoire de son vivant; *Fig* **it was sheer p.** c'était l'enfer, c'était atroce

purge [pɜːdʒ] N **1** *(drug etc)* purgatif m, purge f **2** *(action) Med* purge f, *Pol etc (of political party etc)* épuration f, nettoyage m, purge
VT *Med (person)* purger; *(political party etc)* nettoyer, épurer; *Rel* **to p. oneself of** *or* **from sin** se laver de ses péchés; *Law* **to p. oneself of a charge** se disculper, se justifier; *Am Law* **to p. one's contempt** faire amende honorable *(pour outrage aux magistrats)*

purging ['pɜːdʒɪŋ] N *Med etc (of body)* purge f, purification f, *(of political party etc)* épuration f

purification [pjʊərɪfɪ'keɪʃən] N purification f, *(of gas, oil, water etc)* épuration f, *Rel* **the Feast of the P. (of the Virgin Mary)** (la fête de) la Purification

purifier ['pjʊərɪfaɪər] N *(for gas, oil etc)* épurateur m; *(for air)* assainisseur m

purify ['pjʊərɪfaɪ] VT *(air etc)* assainir, purifier; *(gas, oil etc)* épurer; *(language)* purifier, épurer; *(blood)* dépurer; *(heart, mind etc)* purifier; **to p. sb of** *or* **from his sins** laver qn de ses péchés

purist ['pjʊərɪst] N puriste mf; **a linguistic p.** un puriste en matière de linguistique

puritan ['pjʊərɪt(ə)n] ADJ, N **1** puritain, -aine **2** *Hist* P. puritain, -aine

puritanical [pjʊərɪ'tænɪk(ə)l] ADJ puritain

puritanism ['pjʊərɪtənɪz(ə)m] N puritanisme m

purity ['pjʊərɪtɪ] N pureté f, **degree of p.** *(of water etc)* (degré m de) pureté; *(of gold)* titre m; **the p. of sb's motives** la pureté des motifs de qn

purl [pɜːl] *Knitting* N maille f à l'envers
VT *(row)* tricoter à l'envers; **knit one, p. one** une maille à l'endroit, une maille à l'envers
▸▸ **p. stitch** maille f à l'envers

purlieus ['pɜːljuːz] NPL *Lit (surrounding area)* alentours mpl, environs mpl; **in the p. of** aux alentours *ou* environs de

purloin [pɜːˈlɔɪn] VT *Fml* voler, dérober

purple ['pɜːp(ə)l] ADJ violet; **he turned** *or* **went p.** il est devenu rouge
N *(colour)* violet m; *(dye)* pourpre f, **born to the p.** né dans la pourpre
▸▸ *Mil* **P. Heart** = médaille f décernée aux blessés de guerre de l'armée américaine; *Pharm Fam* **p. heart** pilule f d'amphétamine; *Liter* **p. patch** morceau m de bravoure; *Liter* **p. prose** prose f héroïque

purplish ['pɜːplɪʃ] ADJ violacé, violâtre; *(face)* cramoisi

purport[1] ['pɜːpɔːt] N *Fml (of document) (intention)* esprit m; *(of argument)* portée f, force f

purport[2] [pɜːˈpɔːt] VT **to p. to be sth** *(of person)* prétendre être qch; *(of thing)* être présenté comme étant qch

purpose ['pɜːpəs] N **1** *(object, aim)* but m, objectif m; **fixed p.** dessein m *ou* objectif bien arrêté; **to gain** *or* **achieve one's p.** atteindre son but *ou* objectif, accomplir son dessein; **for** *or* **with the p. of doing sth** dans l'intention *ou* le but de faire qch; **what is the p. of your visit?** quel est le but *ou* l'objet de votre visite?; **it does not suit her p. to have it widely known** ça ne l'arrangerait pas que ça se sache; **to do sth on p.** faire qch exprès; **to have a sense of p.** être motivé; **his life lacked any real sense of p.** sa vie était dépourvue de but précis; **to give sb a sense of p.** motiver qn; **man of p.** homme *m* résolu *ou* décidé **2** *(use)* *(of object)* but *m*, objet *m*; **the buildings were not built for this p.** ces bâtiments n'ont pas été construits dans ce but *ou* à cette fin; **I've never understood their p.** je n'ai jamais compris à quoi ils servaient; **does it serve any useful p.?** est-ce que ça sert à quelque chose?; **intended p.** *(of building, amount of money)* destination *f*, affectation *f*; **they were never used for their intended p.** ils n'ont jamais servi à l'usage auquel on les destinait; **to serve no p.** ne servir à rien; **once she had served her p. they abandoned her** une fois qu'elle eut tenu son rôle, ils l'abandonnèrent; **this will suit** *or* **serve your p.** cela fera votre affaire; **made for that very p.** fait tout exprès; **for all purposes** à toutes fins, à tous usages; **intended for practical purposes** destiné à des usages pratiques; **to set up a commission for the p. of investigation** former un comité à des fins d'enquête; **for the p. of this article …** *(in lease, contract etc)* au sens du présent article …; **for our purposes we can assume this is true** en ce qui nous concerne, nous pouvons admettre que c'est vrai

3 to speak to the p. parler à propos; **very much to the p.** fort à propos; **to some p.** utilement, avantageusement, efficacement; **all that will have been to no p.** tout cela n'aura servi à rien; **we're (talking) at cross purposes** il y a un malentendu (entre nous), nous ne parlons pas de la même chose/personne; **in order to avoid talking at cross purposes** afin d'éviter tout malentendu

VT *Fml* **to p. to do sth** *or* **doing sth** se proposer de faire qch

purpose-built ADJ *(conference centre, sports complex)* construit (tout) spécialement; **it's not exactly p. but …** ce n'est pas exactement fait pour mais …

purposeful ['pɜːpəsfʊl] ADJ *(determined)* résolu, déterminé

purposefully ['pɜːpəsfʊlɪ] ADV *(determinedly)* *(to act)* résolument, avec détermination; *(to walk out etc)* d'un air résolu *ou* déterminé

> Attention: ne pas confondre avec **purposely**, qui signifie **délibérément**.

purposeless ['pɜːpəslɪs] ADJ *(existence)* sans but; *(lacking determination)* *(atmosphere)* d'indécision; *(attempts, person)* qui manque de conviction; **the p. air which seems to surround this government** le manque de détermination qui semble caractériser ce gouvernement

purposely ['pɜːpəslɪ] ADV exprès, à dessein, délibérément; **he p. looked the other way** il a regardé exprès de l'autre côté; **I came to p. to see her** je suis venu exprès pour la voir

> Attention: ne pas confondre avec **purposefully**, qui signifie **avec détermination**.

purr [pɜːr] N *(of cat)* ronron *m*, ronronnement *m*; *(of machine)* ronflement *m*; *(of car engine etc)* ronronnement; **she's got a very loud p.** *(of cat)* elle ronronne très fort

   VI *(of cat, car, person)* ronronner

purring ['pɜːrɪŋ] ADJ *(cat)* qui ronronne, qui fait ronron

   N = **purr** N

purse [pɜːs] N porte-monnaie *m inv*; *Am (handbag)* sac *m* à main; **the public p.** le Trésor public; *Old-fashioned* **it is beyond my p.** c'est au-dessus de mes moyens; *Sport* **to put up a p.** offrir un prix; *Sport* **how big is the p.?** à combien se monte le prix?; *Fam* **she holds the p. strings** c'est elle qui tient les cordons de la bourse

   VT **to p. (up) one's lips** *or* **mouth** pincer les lèvres; **she pursed her lips in disapproval** elle pinça les lèvres en signe de désapprobation

   ►► *Zool* **p. crab** crabe *m* des cocotiers; *Fishing* **p. net, p. seine** senne *f ou* seine *f* à poche

purser ['pɜːsər] N *Naut (in merchant navy)* commissaire *m*; **p.'s mate** cambusier *m*

pursuance [pə'sjuːəns] N *Fml* exécution *f*; **in p. of one's duty** dans l'exercice de ses fonctions; **in p. of your instructions** conformément à vos instructions

pursuant [pə'sjuːənt] ADV *Fml* **p. to your instructions** conformément à vos instructions

pursue [pə'sjuː] VT **1** *(chase)* *(person, animal)* poursuivre; *(pleasure, happiness)* rechercher; *(aim)* chercher à atteindre; **to be pursued by misfortune** être poursuivi par le malheur **2** *(continue)* *(one's path, studies)* continuer, poursuivre; *(policy)* poursuivre; *(course of action)* suivre; *(trade, profession)* faire, exercer; *(enquiry, matter)* donner suite à, poursuivre; **the subject was pursued no further** on ne s'attacha pas davantage à débattre ce sujet; **to p. a career in medicine/the law/journalism** faire carrière dans la médecine/le droit/le journalisme

pursuer [pə'sjuːər] N **1** poursuivant, -ante **2** *Scot Law* plaignant, -ante

pursuit [pə'sjuːt] N **1** *(chase)* poursuite *f*, *Fig (of pleasure, knowledge, happiness etc)* recherche *f*, quête *f*; **to be in p. of sb** être à la poursuite de qn; **the dogs were in hot p.** les chiens avaient engagé la chasse; **with two policemen in hot p.** avec deux agents à ses/mes/etc trousses; **in p. of his aim** en poursuivant son but; **in p. of happiness** à la poursuite *ou* en quête du bonheur **2** *(occupation)* occupation *f*, **(leisure) p.** passe-temps *m inv*; **literary pursuits** travaux *mpl* littéraires

   ►► *Mil, Aviat* **p. plane** avion *m* de chasse; *Cycling* **p. race** poursuite

purulence ['pjʊərʊləns] N *Med* **1** purulence *f* **2** *(pus)* pus *m*

purulent ['pjʊərʊlənt] ADJ *Med* purulent

purvey [pə'veɪ] VT *Com Fml (provisions)* fournir; **we p. a selection of fine wines** nous offrons une sélection de vins fins; **to p. information** diffuser l'information

purveyance [pə'veɪəns] N fourniture *f* de provisions, approvisionnement *m*

purveyor [pə'veɪər] N *Com Fml* fournisseur, -euse *(de provisions)*, approvisionneur, -euse (**of** en; **to** de)

purview ['pɜːvjuː] N **1** *Law (of a law)* corps *m* **2** *Fml (scope)* *(of inquiry)* limites *fpl*, portée *f*, **it is not within my p. to …** il n'est pas dans mes compétences de …

pus [pʌs] N *Med* pus *m*

PUSH [pʊʃ]

N	poussée **1** ▪ effort **2**
VT	pousser **1, 4** ▪ appuyer sur **1**
	▪ enfoncer **2** ▪ préconiser **3**
VI	pousser **1** ▪ avancer **2**

   N **1** poussée *f*, *Billiards (stroke)* coup *m* queuté; **to give sth/sb a p.** pousser qch/qn; *Fig* **to give sb a p.** pousser qn; **she just needs a little p.** elle a besoin qu'on la pousse un peu; *Fam* **to get the p.** *(from job)* se faire virer, être flanqué à la porte; *(from relationship)* se faire plaquer; *Fam* **to give sb the p.**

(from job) virer qn, flanquer qn à la porte; *(from relationship)* plaquer qn; **to give a car a p. start** faire démarrer une voiture en la poussant

2 *(effort)* effort *m*, coup *m* de collier; *Mil (attack)* attaque *f* en masse; **to make a p. for change** lutter pour le changement; **the club's p. for promotion** les efforts soutenus du club pour être promu; **the final p. for the summit** le dernier effort pour atteindre le sommet

3 *(drive)* dynamisme *m*

4 *Fam (difficult moment)* **at a p.** à la limite; **when it comes to the p., you can always rely on her** aux moments critiques, on peut toujours compter sur elle; **if it comes to the p., he'll choose Sarah not Henry** s'il fallait qu'il choisisse, il prendrait Sarah et pas Henry; **if p. comes to shove** si la situation l'exige

5 *esp Austr Sl (gang)* bande *f*, clique *f (de voyous, de pickpockets)*

   VT **1** *(person, wheelbarrow etc)* pousser; *(button)* appuyer sur; **to p. sb into the room** pousser qn (pour le faire entrer) dans la pièce; **to p. the door shut/open with one's foot** fermer/ouvrir la porte du pied; **don't p. (me)!** ne (me) poussez pas!, ne (me) bousculez pas!; **did he fall or was he pushed?** il est tombé ou on l'a poussé?; **did he leave or was he pushed?** *(from job)* il est parti de lui-même ou on l'y a poussé?; **to p. sb into a corner** acculer qn; **to p. sb out of the way** écarter qn; **to p. one's way through the crowd** se frayer *ou* s'ouvrir un chemin à travers la foule; **to p. one's way in** *(party, conversation etc)* s'immiscer; **to p. an attack home** pousser à fond une attaque; **to p. home one's advantage** tirer le meilleur parti possible de son avantage; *Fig* **to p. oneself** *(make an effort)* forcer; *Fig* **he needs pushing** il faut toujours le pousser

2 *(thrust)* *(knife, stick, hands etc)* enfoncer (**into** dans)

3 *Fig (goods)* faire (de) la réclame pour; *(theory, system)* préconiser; *(drugs)* vendre, fournir; **the government is pushing the idea of people setting up small businesses** le gouvernement favorise la création de petites entreprises; **he's pushing himself as a compromise candidate** il se présente comme le candidat du compromis; **to p. one's demands** revendiquer ses droits; *St Exch* **to p. shares** placer des valeurs douteuses; **to p. the line that …** insister sur le fait que …

4 *(force)* **to p. sb into doing sth** pousser qn à faire qch; **don't p. me!** ne me presse pas!; **her parents didn't p. her into the law** ses parents ne l'ont pas poussée à faire du droit; **to p. sb for payment/an answer** harceler qn pour se faire payer/pour qu'il réponde; **don't p. him too far** ne le poussez pas à bout; **I don't want to p. the comparison too far, but …** je ne veux pas pousser la comparaison trop loin, mais …; *Fam* **to p. one's luck** y aller un peu fort; *Fam* **that's pushing it a bit** tu y vas/il y va/etc un peu fort; **I'm terribly pushed (for time)** je suis très pressé; **to be pushed for money** être à court d'argent

5 *Fam* **he's pushing sixty** il frise la soixantaine

   VI **1** pousser; *(sign on door)* poussez, pousser; **to p. against sth** pousser qch; *Aut* **we'll have to get out and p.** il va falloir descendre pousser; **stop pushing!** arrêtez de pousser!; *Fig* **you have to p. to get your way** pour réussir il faut savoir se mettre en avant

2 *(move forward)* avancer (avec difficulté); **the crowd pushed towards the exits** la foule se pressait vers la sortie; **to p. through the crowd** se frayer *ou* s'ouvrir un chemin à travers la foule; **he pushed past me** il m'a bousculé et m'a passé devant

   ►► **p. button** bouton-poussoir *m*, *pl* boutons-poussoirs; *Com* **p. money** prime *f* au vendeur; *Mktg* **p. strategy** stratégie *f* push; *Billiards* **p. stroke** coup queuté; *Comput* **p. technology** technologie *f* du push de données

▸ **push about, push around** VT SEP *Fam* (*bully*) (*person*) marcher sur les pieds de, mener par le bout du nez; **we're sick and tired of being pushed about** *or* **around** nous en avons marre d'être menés par le bout du nez *ou* de nous faire marcher sur les pieds

▸ **push ahead** VI **1** (*continue*) continuer, persévérer; **to p. ahead with the work** poursuivre les travaux

2 (*advance*) avancer, progresser (**with** dans); **research is pushing ahead** les recherches avancent

▸ **push along** VT SEP (*move by pushing*) (*pram etc*) pousser

VI *Fam* (*leave*) partir, y aller; **I suppose I should be pushing along soon** il va bientôt falloir que j'y aille

▸ **push around = push about**

▸ **push aside** VT SEP (*shove out of way*) écarter

▸ **push away** VT SEP (*shove from oneself*) écarter, repousser

▸ **push back** VT SEP (*shove away*) (*person*) repousser; (*crowd, enemy etc*) faire reculer, refouler; (*attack*) réprimer; (*curtains*) écarter

▸ **push down** VT SEP (*lever, switch*) abaisser; (*prices*) faire baisser; **he pushed down the lid but it wouldn't shut** il a appuyé sur le couvercle mais il ne voulait pas fermer

VI **1** (*of lever etc*) s'abaisser; (*of person*) appuyer

2 (*press down*) (*of weight*) peser (**on** sur)

▸ **push for** VT INSEP faire campagne pour; **the unions are pushing for 10%** les syndicats font pression pour obtenir 10%; **to p. for a decision** exiger qu'une décision soit prise

VT SEP **to p. sb for an answer** presser qn pour qu'il/elle donne une réponse

▸ **push forward** VT SEP (*cause to move*) pousser en avant, (faire) avancer; **he was pushed forward by the crowd** la foule l'a poussé en avant; *Fig* **to p. oneself forward** se mettre en avant, chercher à s'imposer

VI (*move forward*) avancer

▸ **push in** VT SEP (*insert*) enfoncer; **the side of the car was pushed in** le flanc de la voiture était enfoncé; **he was standing by the pool and someone pushed him in** il était au bord de la piscine et quelqu'un l'a poussé dedans; **they opened the door and pushed me in** ils ont ouvert la porte et m'ont poussé à l'intérieur; *Sl* **to p. sb's face in** casser la gueule à qn

VI (*jump queue*) resquiller; **she's always pushing in where she's not wanted** il faut toujours qu'elle s'immisce *ou* s'impose là où on ne veut pas d'elle

▸ **push off** VT SEP **1** (*cause to fall*) faire tomber; **he pushed me off the wall** il m'a fait tomber du mur, il m'a poussé du haut du mur; **they tried to p. her (car) off the road** ils ont essayé de faire sortir sa voiture de la route; **to p. sb off a committee** exclure *ou* écarter qn d'un comité

2 (*remove by pushing*) pousser; **p. the lid off** soulève le couvercle

VI **1** *Fam* (*leave*) partir, se casser; *Naut* pousser au large; *Fam* **p. off!** fiche le camp!, tire-toi!

2 the lid pushes off le couvercle glisse

▸ **push on** VI (*continue with work, journey etc*) continuer; **to p. on to** *or* **as far as a place** pousser jusqu'à un endroit; **it's time to p. on** (*with journey*) il est temps de nous remettre en route; **to p. on with the work** se remettre au travail

VT SEP **1** (*press into place*) (*lid, cover etc*) appuyer sur

2 (*encourage*) encourager

▸ **push onto** VT SEP **to p. sth onto sb** (*blame, work etc*) mettre qch sur le dos de qn

▸ **push out** VT SEP **1** (*cause to leave*) (*physically*) pousser dehors, faire sortir; **he was pushed out of the group** il a été exclu du groupe; **to p. one's way out** se frayer un chemin vers la sortie

2 (*launch*) (*boat*) mettre à l'eau; *Fig Fam* **to p. the boat out** ne pas regarder à la dépense

▸ **push over** VT SEP (*cause to fall*) faire tomber

▸ **push through** VT SEP **1** (*cause to pass through*) faire passer; **to p. sth through sth** faire passer qch à travers qch; *Pol* **to p. a bill through Parliament** faire accepter un projet de loi au parlement

2 *Pol* (*get accepted*) (*bill etc*) faire accepter

3 (*bring to completion*) (*work*) mener à bien, parvenir à terminer

VI (*shove through*) se frayer un chemin

VT INSEP (*shove through*) se frayer *ou* se faire un chemin à travers; **to p. through a crowd** se frayer un chemin dans la foule

▸ **push to** VT SEP (*door, shutters*) pousser, fermer

▸ **push up** VT SEP **1** (*lift by pushing*) (*lid etc*) relever, soulever

2 (*help climb by pushing*) (*person*) aider à monter (en le poussant)

3 (*increase*) (*prices etc*) faire monter

push-bike N *Br Fam* vélo *m*, bécane *f*

push-button ADJ

▸▸ **p. controls** commandes *fpl* automatiques; **p. operation** fonctionnement *m* automatique; **p. telephone** téléphone *m* à touches; **p. war** guerre *f* presse-bouton

pushcart ['pʊʃkɑːt] N voiture *f* à bras, charrette *f* à bras

pushchair ['pʊʃtʃeər] N *Br* (*for baby*) poussette *f*

pusher ['pʊʃər] N **1** *Fam* (*drug*) **p.** dealer *m* **2** (*ambitious person*) ambitieux, -euse, *Pej* arriviste *mf* **3** *Br* (*baby's*) **p.** (*utensil*) raclette *f* **4** *TV* machiniste *m* chargé du travelling

pushiness ['pʊʃɪnɪs] N *Fam* **they didn't like his p.** ils le trouvaient trop ambitieux; **you need a bit of p.** il faut insister un peu, il faut jouer des coudes

pushing ['pʊʃɪŋ] ADJ = **pushy**

N poussée *f*; **no p.!** ne poussez pas!; **there was a lot of p. and shoving** ça poussait et ça se bousculait dans tous les sens

pushover ['pʊʃəʊvər] N **1** *Fam* (*thing*) **it's a p.** c'est un jeu d'enfant, c'est de la tarte **2** *Fam* (*opponent*) adversaire *mf* facile; (*gullible person*) bonne poire *f*; **when it comes to redheads, I'm a p.** quand je rencontre une rousse, je ne peux pas me retenir

pushpin ['pʊʃpɪn] N *Am* (*for drawing board etc*) punaise *f*

push-pull N *Electron* push-pull *m inv*

▸▸ **p. amplifier** amplificateur *m* push-pull; **p. circuit** circuit *m* push-pull; *Aut* **p. hand control** (*for disabled driver*) commande *f* manuelle pousser-tirer; **p. train** train *m* réversible

pushrod ['pʊʃrɒd] N *Aut* (*in engine*) poussoir *m*, tige *f* poussoir *ou* de poussée *ou* de culbuteur

push-start VT *Aut* (*car etc*) faire démarrer en le poussant

push-up N *Gym* traction *f*, *Fam* pompe *f*, **to do push-ups** faire des tractions *ou Fam* des pompes

pushy ['pʊʃɪ] ADJ *Fam* **1** (*self-assertive*) **you have to be pretty p. in this work** il faut savoir insister dans ce travail **2** (*ambitious*) ambitieux, *Pej* arriviste; **I had very p. parents** mes parents m'ont beaucoup poussé

pusillanimity [pjuːsɪləˈnɪmɪtɪ] N *Fml* pusillanimité *f*

pusillanimous [pjuːsɪˈlænɪməs] ADJ *Fml* pusillanime

puss [pʊs] N **1** *Fam* (*cat*) minet *m*, minette *f*, minou *m*; **P. in Boots** le Chat botté **2** *Sl* (*face*) figure *f*

pussy¹ ['pʊsɪ] N **1** *Fam* (*cat*) minet *m*, minette *f*, minou *m* **2** *Vulg* (*female genitals*) chatte *f*; **he hadn't had any p. for months** (*sex*) il n'avait pas baisé depuis des mois

▸▸ *Fam* **p. cat** minet, minette, minou; *Bot* **p. willow** saule *m* blanc

pussy² ['pʌsɪ] ADJ (*containing pus*) suintant

pussyfoot ['pʊsɪfʊt] VI *Fam* (*avoid committing oneself*) ne pas se mouiller; **stop pussyfooting around!** arrête de tergiverser!; **we could do without all this pussyfooting about** on se passerait bien de toutes ces tergiversations

pussy-whipped [-wɪpt] ADJ *Sl* dominé par sa femme

pustule ['pʌstjuːl] N *Med, Vet* pustule *f*

PUT [pʊt] (*pt, pp* **put**; *prp* **putting**)

VT	mettre **1, 4–6** ▪ poser **1, 2**
	▪ soumettre **2** ▪ dire **3** ▪ estimer **4**

VT **1** (*place*) mettre; **p. it on the table** mettez-le *ou* posez-le sur la table; **to p. one's arms around sb/sth** prendre qn/qch dans ses bras; **she p. her head through the window/round the door** elle a passé la tête par la fenêtre/dans l'encoignure de la porte; **to p. a hem on a skirt** faire un ourlet à une jupe; **to p. the telescope to one's eye** porter le télescope à son œil; **to p. a child in a home** placer un enfant dans une maison d'accueil; **to p. sb on the street** (*leave destitute*) mettre qn à la rue; **to p. an advertisement in the paper** mettre *ou* insérer une annonce dans le journal; **to p. a man on the moon** envoyer un homme sur la lune; **to p. a man into orbit** mettre un homme en orbite; **to p. a bowl/a chair into sb's hands** mettre un bol/une chaise entre les mains de qn; **to p. a coin/a letter/a gun into sb's hand** glisser une pièce/une lettre/un revolver dans la main de qn; **to p. a limit/tax on sth** mettre une limite/une taxe sur qch; **to p. a ban on sth** interdire qch; **to p. a ban on sb doing sth** interdire à qn de faire qch; *Fam* **p. it there!** (*shake hands*) touchez là!; **to p. oneself into sb's hands** s'en remettre à qn; **to p. a matter into sb's hands** confier une affaire à qn; *Fig* **to p. sb in his/her place** (*reprimand*) remettre qn à sa place; *Fig* **he didn't know where to p. himself** il ne savait plus où se mettre; **p. yourself in my position** *or* **place** mettez-vous à ma place; **p. it out of your mind** *or* **head** sors-le-toi de la tête; **I had long p. this thought out of my mind** ça faisait longtemps que je m'étais sorti cette idée de la tête; **to p. one's signature to sth** apposer sa signature sur *ou* à qch; **to p. one's name to sth** prêter son nom à qch; **to p. honour before riches** préférer l'honneur à l'argent; **to p. a matter right** arranger une affaire, remettre les choses au point; **to p. sb out of suspense** tirer qn du doute; **to p. sb against sb** monter qn contre qn; **to p. an article on the market** mettre un article en vente *ou* sur le marché; **to p. a play on the stage** monter une pièce; **to p. one's thoughts into words** traduire ses pensées par des mots; **to p. money into an undertaking** mettre de l'argent dans une affaire; **to p. money on a horse** miser *ou* parier sur un cheval; **to p. some energy into finishing a job** mettre de l'énergie à achever une tâche; **to p. a lot of work into sth/doing sth** beaucoup travailler à qch/pour faire qch

2 (*present*) **to p. a question to sb** poser une question à qn; **to p. a case before sb** soumettre un cas à qn; **to p. a resolution to the meeting** présenter une résolution à l'assemblée; *Law* **I p. it to you that …** n'est-il pas vrai que …?; **I p. it to him that it would be better to …** je lui ai suggéré qu'il vaudrait mieux …; **to p. the case clearly** exposer clairement la situation; **what did you p. for question three?** qu'est-ce que tu as mis à la troisième question?

3 *(express)* **to p. it bluntly** pour parler franc; **you could have p. that better** tu aurais pu tourner cela un peu mieux; **if one may p. it in that way** si l'on peut s'exprimer ainsi; **I wouldn't p. it quite like that** je ne dirais pas cela; **I don't know how to p. it** je ne sais comment dire; **to p. it another way, …** en d'autres termes, …; '**to encourage the others', as Voltaire puts it** 'pour encourager les autres' comme dirait Voltaire

4 *(estimate)* estimer, évaluer; **to p. the population at 10,000** estimer *ou* évaluer la population à 10 000; **I would p. her on a par with** *or* **in the same class as Henry James** je la mettrais dans la même catégorie que Henry James; **I wouldn't have p. her age at more than 25** je ne lui aurais pas donné plus de 25 ans; **what would you p. it at?** quelle est votre estimation?

5 **to p. an end to sth** mettre fin à qch; **to p. a stop to sth** mettre un terme à qch

6 *(cause to do, go, be etc)* **to p. sb to do sth** *(to make, have sb do sth)* faire faire qch à qn; *(to designate sb to do sth)* désigner qn pour faire qch; **to p. sb in(to) a good/bad mood** mettre qn de bonne/mauvaise humeur; **to p. a guard on the door** faire surveiller la porte; **to p. a child to bed** mettre un enfant au lit; **to p. sth to (a) good use** faire bon usage de qch, bien employer *ou* utiliser qch; **to p. sb to the test** mettre qn à l'épreuve; **to p. a resolution to the vote** mettre une résolution aux voix; **to p. the enemy to flight** mettre l'ennemi en fuite; **to p. sb to sleep** endormir qn; *Euph* **to have a dog p. to sleep** faire piquer un chien; **I'm putting you to a lot of trouble** je vous cause beaucoup d'ennuis; **to p. sb to work** mettre qn au travail (**on sth** sur qch)

7 *(direct, force)* **to p. a bullet through sb's head** mettre *ou* loger une balle dans la tête de qn; **to p. one's fist through the window** enfoncer la fenêtre d'un coup de poing; *Sport* **to p. the shot** lancer le poids

vi 1 *Naut* **to p. (out) to sea** prendre la mer *ou* le large; **to p. into port** faire escale, relâcher, faire relâche

n 1 *Sport (of shot)* lancer *m*, lancement *m*
2 *St Exch (option)* option *f* de vente, put *m*
▸▸ St Exch p. band période *f* de validité d'une option de vente; *St Exch* **p. bond** emprunt *m* à fenêtre; *St Exch* **p. option** option de vente, put; *St Exch* **p. warrant** warrant *m* à la vente

▸ put about **vt sep 1** *(spread) (rumour)* faire circuler; **to p. it about that …** faire circuler le bruit que …; **it's being p. about by her rivals that …** ses rivaux font circuler le bruit que …; **it is being p. about that …** il paraîtrait que …, le bruit court que …
2 *Naut* **to p. a ship about** virer de bord
3 *Fam (be sexually promiscuous)* **to p. oneself about, to p. it about** coucher avec tout le monde
vi *Naut* virer de bord

▸ put across **vt sep 1** *(communicate) (feeling)* communiquer; *(message, idea)* faire passer; **to p. sth across to sb** faire comprendre qch à qn; **she knows how to p. her ideas across** elle sait bien faire passer ses idées; **he's good at putting himself across at interviews** il sait se faire valoir dans les entretiens; **he p. himself across badly at the interview** il a donné une mauvaise image de lui-même à l'entretien; **it doesn't p.**

across **the sense of size you get from the place** cela ne restitue pas le sentiment d'immensité qu'on ressent à cet endroit
2 *Fam* **to p. one across on sb** *(trick)* rouler qn, avoir qn

▸ put around **vt sep** = **put about vt sep 1**

▸ put aside **vt sep** *(place on one side) (one's book etc)* poser à côté de soi; *(keep)* mettre de côté; *Fig (hope, idea)* renoncer à; *Fig (save) (money etc)* mettre de côté; **if we p. aside the emotional trauma caused** mis à part le choc émotionnel provoqué; **p. aside all gloomy thoughts** oublie toutes ces pensées maussades; **let's try to p. aside our differences** essayons de laisser nos différends de côté

▸ put away **vt sep 1** *(tidy away)* ranger; *(return to its place)* remettre à sa place; *(car)* garer; **p. your money/wallet away** *(I'm paying)* range ton argent/ton portefeuille
2 *(save)* mettre de côté; **to p. something away for one's old age** mettre quelque chose de côté pour sa retraite
3 *Fam (lock up) (in prison)* mettre en taule; *(in asylum etc)* (faire) enfermer
4 *Fam (consume) (food)* avaler, expédier; *(drink)* siffler; **he can really p. it away** *(drink)* il a une bonne descente; *(food)* il a un appétit d'ogre

▸ put back **vt sep 1** *(restore to its position)* remettre à sa place; **to p. sth back where one found it** remettre qch là où on l'a trouvé
2 *(postpone) (meeting etc)* reporter; *(turn back hands of) (clock, watch)* retarder; *Fig* **this decision has p. the clock back** cette décision nous a ramenés en arrière; *Sch* **his absence has p. him back** son absence l'a retardé dans ses études
vi *Naut* retourner *ou* revenir *ou* rentrer au port

▸ put by **vt sep** *(money)* mettre de côté; *(supplies etc)* mettre en réserve; **to have something p. by** *(savings)* avoir des économies

▸ put down **vt sep 1** *(set down)* poser; **to p. sth down on the ground** poser *ou* déposer qch par terre; *Tel* **to p. down the receiver** *or* **the phone** raccrocher; **p. that gun down!** pose ce revolver!; **to p. down passengers** *(of bus etc)* débarquer *ou* déposer *ou* laisser descendre des voyageurs; **to p. the baby down** *(put to bed)* mettre le bébé au lit, coucher le bébé; **to p. down roots** *(of plant)*, *Fig (of person)* s'enraciner; **I couldn't p. it down** *(book)* je l'ai lu d'un trait
2 *(suppress) (revolt, opposition)* réprimer
3 *(close) (umbrella)* fermer
4 *(write)* noter; **to p. sth down in writing** mettre *ou* *Fml* coucher qch par écrit; **to p. down one's name** *(enrol)* s'inscrire, se faire inscrire (**for** pour); *Fam* **p. me down for a ticket/to play** mets-moi sur la liste pour les tickets/des joueurs; **p. me down for £5** inscris-moi pour 5 livres; **p. it down to me** *or* **to my account** inscrivez-le *ou* mettez-le sur mon compte; **we'll have to p. it down to experience** au moins on a appris quelque chose; **to p. sb/sth down as sth** classer qn/qch comme qch; **I should p. her down as thirty** je lui donne trente ans
5 *(attribute)* **to p. sth down to sb/sth** attribuer *ou* imputer qch à qn/qch; **I p. his success down to luck** j'attribue son succès à la chance
6 *(pay)* **to p. some money down** *(as a deposit)* verser *ou* déposer une caution; **how much can you p. down?** combien pouvez-vous verser *ou* déposer en caution?; **I've p. £500 down on my new car** j'ai versé 500 livres d'arrhes pour ma nouvelle voiture
7 *(kill) (animal)* abattre; *Vet* **to have a dog p. down** faire piquer un chien
8 *(say negative things about)* dire du mal de; **you're always putting me down** tu n'arrêtes pas de me critiquer; **you shouldn't p. your-**

self down **tu ne devrais pas te sous-estimer**
9 *esp Parl* **to p. down a motion of censure** déposer une motion de censure
10 *(wine)* mettre en cave
vi *Aviat* atterrir

▸ put forward **vt sep 1** *(suggest) (plan, theory etc)* avancer, mettre en avant; *(claim)* émettre; **to p. sb** *or* **sb's name forward** *(for a post)* suggérer qn *ou* le nom de qn (pour un poste); **to p. oneself forward** *(get oneself noticed)* se mettre en avant; **to p. one's best foot forward** *(walk faster)* presser le pas; *Fig* se mettre en devoir de faire de son mieux
2 *(advance) (clock, time of meeting etc)* avancer

▸ put in **vt sep 1** *(place in)* mettre; **to p. one's contact lenses in** mettre ses lentilles de contact; **to p. one's head in at the window** passer la tête par la fenêtre; **you only get out what you p. in** on ne récolte que ce qu'on sème; **and it was before twelve, she p. in spitefully** et il n'était pas midi, ajouta-t-elle méchamment; **to p. in a (good) word for sb** dire un mot en faveur de qn
2 *(install)* installer; **we're having a new telephone p. in** on nous installe un nouveau téléphone; **the voters p. the Tories in** les électeurs ont mis les conservateurs au pouvoir
3 *(enter)* présenter; **to p. in a claim/an application** déposer une réclamation/une candidature; **we're putting him in for the 500 metres** nous le présentons pour le 500 mètres; **to p. pupils in for an examination** présenter des élèves à un examen
4 *(spend time doing)* **to p. in an hour's work** faire une heure de travail; **she's p. in a lot of time on this project** elle a passé beaucoup de temps sur ce projet; **they've p. in a tremendous amount of work** ils ont fourni une quantité de travail remarquable
vi 1 *Naut* **to p. in at a port** faire escale *ou* relâcher dans un port
2 *(apply)* **to p. in for an election/for a job** poser sa candidature à une élection/à un poste; **to p. in for two days' leave** demander un congé *ou* *Mil* une permission de 48 heures

▸ put off **vt sep 1** *(postpone) (meeting, appointment)* remettre *ou* renvoyer à plus tard, ajourner, repousser; *(decision, payment)* remettre à plus tard, différer; *(work)* remettre à plus tard; *(guests)* décommander; **to p. off doing sth** remettre à plus tard de faire qch; **he p. off telling her for as long as possible** il a repoussé le plus possible le moment de lui dire; **don't keep putting things off** ne remettez pas toujours à plus tard; *Prov* **never p. off till tomorrow what you can do today** il ne faut jamais remettre au lendemain ce que l'on peut faire le jour même; **let's p. lunch off to another time** nous déjeunerons ensemble une autre fois
2 *(make excuses to)* **to p. sb off** donner le change à qn, entortiller qn; **to p. sb off with an excuse** se débarrasser de qn *ou* renvoyer qn avec une excuse; **I won't be p. off any longer** j'en ai assez qu'on m'entortille
3 *(allow to get off bus etc)* laisser descendre; *(force to get off)* faire descendre; **could you p. me off at the High Street?** pourriez-vous me laisser descendre *ou* m'arrêter à High Street?
4 *(switch off) (television, radio etc)* éteindre
5 *(cause dislike in) (person)* dégoûter; **there's something about him that puts me off** il y a quelque chose en lui qui me goûte; **the mere smell of that cheese puts me off** l'odeur de ce fromage suffit à m'écœurer; **don't be p. off by his gruff manner** ne te laisse pas décourager *ou* rebuter par ses manières rébarbatives
6 *(disturb) (person)* déconcerter, dérouter, troubler; **these interruptions p. me off** ces

interruptions me déconcentrent; **the noise was putting her off her tennis** le bruit l'empêchait de bien jouer au tennis; **the worry was putting me off my food** l'inquiétude me coupait l'appétit

vi *Naut* déborder du quai, pousser au large; **to p. off from the shore** quitter la côte, prendre le large

▸ **put on VT SEP 1** *(clothes, shoes)* mettre; **to p. on one's make-up** se maquiller

2 *(assume)* **to p. on an air of innocence** prendre *ou* se donner un air innocent; **to p. on an act** jouer la comédie; **to p. on an accent** prendre un accent; *Fam* **you're putting it on!** tout ça c'est du chiqué!

3 *Fam (deceive)* **she's putting you on** elle te fait marcher

4 *(present) Theat (play)* monter; *TV, Radio (programme)* diffuser, passer; *TV, Radio* **why can't they p. something decent on for a change?** ils ne pourraient pas passer quelque chose d'intéressant pour une fois?

5 *(add to weight, price etc)* **to p. on weight** grossir, prendre du poids; **I've p. on five kilos** j'ai pris cinq kilos, j'ai grossi de cinq kilos; **they've 2p on (the price)** on a augmenté le prix de 2 pence

6 *(switch on) (light, gas)* allumer; *(radio, television)* allumer, mettre; **he p. on some Vivaldi/the news** il a mis du Vivaldi/les informations; **to p. the kettle on** mettre la bouilloire à chauffer; **to p. the potatoes on** *(to cook)* mettre les pommes de terre à cuire; *(to heat up)* faire chauffer les pommes de terre; **to p. on a record/a tape** passer un disque/une cassette; **to p. on the brake(s)** freiner

7 *(put into service) (train)* mettre en service; **to p. on speed** prendre de la vitesse

8 *Horseracing etc (bet)* **to p. on £1** miser 1 livre

9 *(advance) (clock)* avancer

10 *(on telephone)* **could you p. him on, please?** pouvez-vous me le passer, s'il vous plaît?

▸ **put on to VT SEP 1** *(provide with information about)* **to p. sb on to sth** indiquer qch à qn; **who p. you on to it?** *Fam* qui est-ce qui vous a donné le tuyau?; **who p. the police on to me?** qui m'a dénoncé à la police?

2 *Tel* **would you p. me on to Mr Lawrence?** voulez-vous me passer M. Lawrence?

▸ **put out VT SEP 1** *(place outside)* mettre dehors; **to p. the cat out** mettre le chat dehors; **to p. the rubbish out** sortir la/les poubelle(s); *Naut* **to p. out a boat** mettre un canot à l'eau; **to p. one's head out of the window** passer la tête par la fenêtre; **the snail p. out its horns** l'escargot a sorti ses cornes; **to p. out peace feelers** envoyer des sondages de paix; **to p. sb's eyes out** crever les yeux à qn, éborgner qn

2 *(arrange for use)* sortir, préparer; **I've p. your clothes out** je t'ai sorti *ou* préparé tes vêtements

3 *(extend) (one's hand)* avancer, tendre; *(one's arm)* allonger, tendre; **to p. out one's tongue** tirer la langue; **she p. out a foot to trip him up** elle a mis un pied en avant pour le faire trébucher

4 *(issue) (new record, edition, model etc)* sortir; *(appeal, request)* faire; *(statement)* émettre

5 *(extinguish) (candle, fire, light)* éteindre; *(gas)* fermer

6 *(make unconscious) (patient)* endormir

7 *(make angry) (person)* ennuyer, fâcher, contrarier; **to be p. out about sth** être mécontent de qch; **she gets terribly p. out if you don't agree with her** elle s'énerve si on n'est pas d'accord avec elle

8 *(inconvenience) (person)* déranger, incommoder, gêner; **you mustn't p. yourself out for me** il ne faut pas vous déranger pour

moi; **would one more guest p. you out?** est-ce qu'un invité de plus te dérangerait?; **I don't want to p. anyone out** je ne veux pas déranger personne

9 *(dislocate)* **to p. one's back/shoulder out** se démettre le dos/l'épaule

10 to p. a cow out to grass mettre une vache en pâture; **to p. money out (to interest)** placer de l'argent (à intérêt); **to p. work out** *(subcontract)* mettre du travail en soustraitance; **to p. work out to tender** mettre du travail en adjudication

vi 1 *Naut* **to p. out (to sea)** prendre le large *ou* la mer

2 *Am Sl (of woman)* accepter de coucher *(* **for** avec); **did she p. out?** est-ce qu'elle a bien voulu coucher?; **she puts out for anyone** *(is promiscuous)* elle coucherait avec le premier venu

▸ **put over VT SEP 1** *(communicate)* = **put across 1**

2 *Am (postpone)* remettre à plus tard, différer

3 *Fam* **to p. one over on sb** avoir qn

▸ **put through VT SEP 1** *(carry through) (project)* mener à bien, faire aboutir; *(have accepted) (deal)* faire accepter

2 *Tel (connect)* **to p. sb through to sb** mettre qn en ligne avec qn, passer qn à qn; **p. him through, please** mettez-le en ligne *ou* passez-le moi, s'il vous plaît; **I'll p. you through to him** je vous le passe

3 *(cause to suffer)* **you've p. your mother through a lot of worry** tu as causé beaucoup d'inquiétude à ta mère; **I've p. myself through hell for you** j'ai souffert le martyre pour toi; *Fam* **to p. sb through it** *(at interview etc)* mettre qn à l'épreuve; **to p. sb through an ordeal** faire subir une rude épreuve à qn; **have you any idea what you're putting him through?** as-tu la moindre idée de ce que tu lui fais subir?

4 *(subject to)* **to p. sb/sth through sth** soumettre qn/qch à qch, faire subir qch à qn/qch; **to p. oneself through sth** endurer qch

5 she p. herself through university elle s'est payé ses études à l'université

▸ **put to VT SEP** *(only in passive)* **to be hard p. to it to do sth** avoir beaucoup de mal à faire qch

▸ **put together VT SEP 1** *(place side by side) (two objects)* mettre côte à côte; *(facts)* rapprocher, comparer

2 *(assemble) (parts, components)* assembler, mettre ensemble; *(machine etc)* monter, assembler; *(meal)* préparer, confectionner; *(menu)* élaborer; *(report, story, programme)* mettre sur pied; *(team, show)* monter; *(different elements, contrasting things)* réunir, rassembler; **the programme is nicely p. together** ce programme est bien fait; **to p. together a convincing picture of what happened** reconstituer une idée convaincante de ce qui s'est passé; *Fam* **to p. two and two together** tirer ses conclusions; **I'll just p. a few things together (in my bag)** je vais faire rapidement ma valise; **she's got more brains than the rest of them p. together** elle est plus intelligente qu'eux tous mis ensemble

▸ **put up VT SEP 1** *(raise) (one's hair, collar of coat etc)* relever; *(umbrella)* ouvrir; *(rocket, distress flare)* envoyer; **could all those going p. up their hands?** que tous ceux qui y vont lèvent la main; **p. up your hands!, p. your hands up!** haut les mains!; *Fam* **p. them up!** *(in robbery)* haut les mains!; *(before fight)* défends-toi!; **I'm going to p. my feet up for a few minutes** je vais me reposer un peu

2 *(erect) (ladder, tent etc)* dresser; *(house etc)* construire, bâtir; *(monument)* ériger; *(scaffolding)* installer, monter

3 *(attach to wall) (painting)* fixer, accrocher; *(poster) (with paste)* coller; *(notice etc)*

afficher; *(curtain)* poser, accrocher; *(wallpaper)* poser

4 *(increase) (prices)* augmenter

5 *(provide accommodation for)* loger, héberger; **I can't p. you up** je ne peux pas vous loger *ou* vous héberger

6 *(offer) (candidate)* proposer *(* **for the elections** aux élections); **to p. sth up for sale** mettre qch en vente; **to p. a picture up for auction** mettre un tableau aux enchères; **to p. up resistance** *or* **a fight** *or* **a struggle** *(physically)* opposer une résistance; *(morally)* s'opposer; **to p. up a good case for sth** présenter de bons arguments en faveur de qch

7 *(provide) (sum of money)* fournir; **to p. up the money for an undertaking** fournir les fonds d'une entreprise

8 *(sword)* baisser

vi 1 *(stay)* **to p. up at a hotel** descendre dans un hôtel; **I've been putting up at a hotel for three weeks** ça fait trois semaines que je suis à l'hôtel; **where are you putting up?** où est-ce que tu loges?; *(in hotel)* où es-tu descendu?

2 *(of candidate)* **to p. up for the council** poser sa candidature comme conseiller; **to p. up for re-election** se présenter pour être réélu

3 *Fam* **p. up or shut up!** montrez la couleur de votre argent d'abord!

▸ **put upon VT INSEP** **to p. upon sb** *(abuse)* abuser de qn; *(exploit)* exploiter qn; **I won't be p. upon** je refuse qu'on abuse de moi

▸ **put up to VT SEP** **to p. sb up to doing sth** *(incite)* inciter qn à faire qch; **who p. you up to it?** *(put the idea into your head)* qui vous a donné l'idée de faire ça?; *(made you do it)* qui vous a fait faire ça?

▸ **put up with VT INSEP** *(tolerate)* supporter, tolérer; **we'll have to p. up with it** il faut l'accepter *ou* nous y résigner; **I don't know how you p. up with the noise** je ne sais pas comment tu peux supporter tout ce bruit; **I'll have to p. up with him** il faudra bien que je le supporte

putative ['pjuːtətɪv] **ADJ ATTRIB** *Fml* putatif

put-down **N** *Fam* affront *m*

put-in **N** *Rugby* introduction *f*

put-on **ADJ** *(air, smile)* affecté; *(joy)* affecté, feint

N *esp Am Fam (deception)* **it's just a p.** c'est du chiqué, c'est de la comédie; **the whole thing was a p. to gain sympathy** toute l'histoire n'était qu'un subterfuge pour s'attirer de la sympathie

put-put ['pʌtpʌt] **N** *(sound)* teuf-teuf *m*, pl teufs-teufs

vi *(of small engine etc)* faire teuf-teuf

putrefaction [pjuːtrɪ'fækʃən] **N** putréfaction *f*

putrefy ['pjuːtrɪfaɪ] **vt** putréfier, pourrir

vi se putréfier, pourrir, suppurer, s'envenimer; **a putrefying corpse** un cadavre en état de putréfaction

putrescence [pjuː'tresəns] **N** *Fml* putrescence *f*

putrescent [pjuː'tresənt] **ADJ** *Fml* putrescent, en putréfaction

putrid ['pjuːtrɪd] **ADJ 1** putride **2** *Fam (disgusting, horrible)* dégoûtant, dégueulasse

putsch [pʊtʃ] **N** putsch *m*

putt [pʌt] *Golf* **N** putt *m*; **to hole a long p.** rentrer un long putt

vt & vi putter

putter¹ ['pʌtər] **N** *Golf (club)* putter *m*; **good/bad p.** *(person)* joueur, -euse qui putte bien

putter² **vi** *Am* = **potter²**

putting ['pʌtɪŋ] **N** *(game), Golf* putting *m*; **to practise p.** s'exercer à putter

▸▸ **p. green** green *m*; **p. iron** putter *m*

putto, *pl* **putti** ['pʊtəʊ, -tiː] N *Art* putto *m, pl* putti

putty ['pʌtɪ] N mastic *m*; **to fill a hole with p.** boucher un trou au mastic, mastiquer un trou; **my legs felt like p.** j'avais les jambes en coton; **p.-coloured** grisâtre; **she's like p. in my hands** j'en fais ce que je veux
VT *(hole)* mastiquer, boucher au mastic
▸▸ **p. knife** couteau *m* à mastiquer, spatule *f* de vitrier

put-up ADJ
▸▸ *Fam* **p. job** affaire *f* préparée à l'avance; *(trap)* coup *m* monté

put-upon ADJ **she was feeling p.** elle avait l'impression qu'on abusait de sa gentillesse; **a p. expression** une tête de martyr

put-you-up N canapé-lit *m, pl* canapés-lits

putz [pʌts] N *Am Fam* andouille *f*, truffe *f*
▸ **putz around** VI *Am Fam (act foolishly)* faire l'idiot, faire l'imbécile; *(waste time)* glander, glandouiller

puzzle ['pʌz(ə)l] N **1** *(game) (manual)* casse-tête *m inv*; *(mental)* devinette *f* **2** *(mystery)* énigme *f*
VT *(person)* intriguer, laisser perplexe; **puzzled look** air *m* perplexe; **I was puzzled** j'étais perplexe, je ne savais que penser; **he puzzles me** il m'intrigue, c'est une énigme pour moi; **I am puzzled to know why you have done this** ça m'intrigue de savoir pourquoi tu as fait ça; **to p. one's head over sth** se casser la tête sur qch, chercher à comprendre qch
VI **to p. about sth** chercher à comprendre qch
▸▸ **p. book** livre *m* de jeux; *(of crosswords)* livre de mots croisés
▸ **puzzle out** VT SEP *(problem)* résoudre; *(solution, meaning)* trouver; **I'm still trying to p. out how he did it** je cherche toujours à comprendre comment il l'a fait

▸ **puzzle over** VT INSEP *(wonder about)* chercher à comprendre, se casser la tête sur

puzzlement ['pʌz(ə)lmənt] N perplexité *f*; **to look at sb in p.** regarder qn d'un air perplexe; **an expression of p.** un air perplexe; **much to my p.** à ma grande surprise

puzzler ['pʌzlər] N *Fam (mystery)* énigme *f*, **that's a p.!** *(problem)* voilà une question difficile!

puzzling ['pʌzlɪŋ] ADJ curieux, bizarre

PVC [piːviːˈsiː] N *(abbr* **polyvinyl chloride***)* PVC *m*; **a P. belt** une ceinture en PVC

PVS [piːviːˈes] N *(abbr* **persistent vegetative state***)* état *m* végétatif chronique

PW [piːˈdʌb(ə)ljuː] N *(abbr* **policewoman***)* femme *f* policier

PWR [piːdʌb(ə)ljuːˈɑːr] N *Nucl (abbr* **pressurized-water reactor***)* REP *m* (réacteur à eau pressurisée)

PX [piːˈeks] N *Am Mil (abbr* **post exchange***)* foyer *m*

pygmy ['pɪgmɪ] N pygmée *m*
ADJ pygmée

pyjamas [pəˈdʒɑːməz] N *esp Br* **(pair of)** pyjamas pyjama *m*; **he's in pyjamas** il est en pyjama VOIR GRAMMAIRE A10
▸▸ **p. bottoms** pantalon *m* de pyjama; **p. jacket** veste *f* de pyjama; **p. party** = fête *f* où tous les invités portent un pyjama; **p. top** *(jacket)* veste de pyjama; *(pull-on type)* haut *m* de pyjama; **p. trousers** pantalon de pyjama

pylon ['paɪlən] N **1** *(of metal, reinforced concrete)* pylône *m*; **(electricity) p.** pylône (de transformateur électrique) **2** *Archit (gateway)* pylône *m*

pyorrhea [paɪəˈrɪə] N *Med* pyorrhée *f*

pyramid ['pɪrəmɪd] N *Archit, Math* pyramide *f*

▸▸ *Com* **p. scheme** plan *m* commercial en cascade; *Com* **p. selling** vente *f* pyramidale

pyramidal [pɪˈræmɪd(ə)l] ADJ *Fml* pyramidal, -aux

pyre ['paɪər] N **(funeral) p.** bûcher *m* (funéraire)

Pyrenean [pɪrəˈniːən] ADJ pyrénéen, des Pyrénées
▸▸ **P. mountain dog** chien *m ou* berger *m* des Pyrénées

Pyrenees (the) [ðəpɪrəˈniːz] NPL les Pyrénées *fpl*

pyrethrum [paɪˈriːθrəm] N *(plant)* pyrèthre *m*

pyretic [paɪˈretɪk] ADJ *Med* pyrétique

Pyrex® ['paɪreks] N Pyrex® *m*; **P. dish** plat *m* en Pyrex®

pyrites [paɪˈraɪtiːz] N *Miner* pyrite *f*, **iron p.** pyrite de fer, fer *m* sulfuré

pyritic [paɪˈrɪtɪk] ADJ *Miner* pyriteux

pyromaniac [paɪrəʊˈmeɪnɪæk] N pyromane *mf*

pyrotechnic [paɪrəʊˈteknɪk] ADJ USU ATTRIB pyrotechnique; **p. display** feu *m* d'artifice

pyrotechnics [paɪrəʊˈteknɪks] N pyrotechnie *f*, *(fireworks)* feux *mpl* d'artifice; *Fig (of style etc)* fioritures *fpl* VOIR GRAMMAIRE A10

Pyrrhic ['pɪrɪk] ADJ *Antiq* de Pyrrhus
▸▸ *Fig* **P. victory** victoire *f* à la Pyrrhus, victoire désastreuse

Pythagoras [paɪˈθægərəs] N Pythagore *m*

Pythagorean [paɪθægəˈriːən] ADJ pythagoricien

python ['paɪθən] N python *m*

pyx [pɪks] N *Rel* ciboire *m*

pzazz [pəˈzæz] N *Fam (flair)* punch *m*

Q, q[1] [kju:] N (letter) Q, q m; **two Q's** deux Q

q[2] Sch etc (abbr **question**) q.

Qatar [kæ'tɑ:(r)] N le Qatar

Qatari [kæ'tɑ:rɪ] N habitant, -ante du Qatar
ADJ du Qatar

QC [kju:'si:] N Br Law abbr **Queen's Counsel**

QE2 [kju:i:'tu:] N Br Naut (abbr **Queen Elizabeth II**) = le paquebot Queen Elizabeth II

QED [kju:i:'di:] (abbr **quod erat demonstrandum**) CQFD (ce qu'il fallait démontrer)

QIP [kju:aɪ'pi:] N (abbr **quality improvement programme**) programme m d'amélioration de la qualité

QM [kju:'em] N Mil abbr **Quartermaster**

QMG [kju:em'dʒi:] N Mil (abbr **Quartermaster General**) = Directeur m de l'Intendance (militaire)

QMV [kju:em'vi:] N EU (abbr **qualified majority voting**) vote m à la majorité qualifiée

qt, pl **qts** abbr **quart**, pl **quarts**

q.t. [kju:'ti:] N Fam (abbr **quiet**) **to do sth on the q.t.** faire qch en douce; **to tell sb sth on the q.t.** dire qch à qn discrètement ou en confidence; **this is strictly on the q.t.** c'est confidentiel

Q-tip® N Am coton-tige® m, pl cotons-tiges

qty Com abbr **quantity**

qua [kwɑ:] PREP Fml alcohol q. alcohol l'alcool en tant que tel

quack[1] [kwæk] INT **q.! q.!** coin-coin!
N **1** (cry) coin-coin m inv **2** (in children's language) **q.-q.** (duck) canard m
VI **1** (of duck) cancaner, Fam faire coin-coin **2** Fam (of person) jacasser

quack[2] N Pej **1** (charlatan) charlatan m **2** Br, Austr Fam (doctor) toubib m
▸▸ **q. doctor** (unqualified) charlatan; **q. remedy** remède m de charlatan; Fig fausse solution f

quackery ['kwækərɪ] N charlatanisme m, charlatanerie f

quad[1] [kwɒd] N Sch Fam cour f

quad[2] N Fam (child) quadruplé, -ée
▸▸ **q. bike** quad m; **q. biking** quad; **to go q. biking** faire du quad; Comput **q. density** densité f quadruple

quadragenarian [kwɒdrədʒə'neərɪən] ADJ, N quadragénaire mf

Quadragesima [kwɒdrə'dʒesɪmə] N Rel Quadragésime f
▸▸ **Q. Sunday** le dimanche de la Quadragésime

quadrangle ['kwɒdræŋg(ə)l] N **1** Geom figure f quadrangulaire, quadrilatère m **2** (courtyard) (at school, college etc) cour f, Archit cour carrée

quadrangular [kwɒ'dræŋgjʊlər] ADJ quadrangulaire

quadrant ['kwɒdrənt] N Astron, Geom (of circle) quart m de cercle; (of surface), Naut quadrant m

quadraphonic [kwɒdrə'fɒnɪk] ADJ quadriphonique, tétraphonique

quadraphonics [kwɒdrə'fɒnɪks] N SING quadriphonie f, tétraphonie f VOIR GRAMMAIRE A10

quadrasonic [kwɒdrə'sɒnɪk] ADJ tétraphonique

quadratic [kwɒ'drætɪk] ADJ Math (equation) quadratique, du second degré

quadrature ['kwɒdrətʃər] N Math, Astron quadrature f; **q. of the circle** quadrature du cercle

quadrennial [kwɒ'drenɪəl] ADJ quadriennal, -aux

quadri- ['kwɒdrɪ] PREF quadri-

quadrilateral [kwɒdrɪ'lætər(ə)l] Geom etc ADJ quadrilatéral, -aux
N quadrilatère m

quadrille [kwə'drɪl] N Mus quadrille m

quadrillion [kwɒ'drɪlɪən] N Br (10^{24}) quadrillion m; Am (10^{15}) mille billions

quadriplegia [kwɒdrɪ'pli:dʒɪə] N Med tétraplégie f, quadriplégie f

quadriplegic [kwɒdrɪ'pli:dʒɪk] ADJ, N Med tétraplégique mf, quadriplégique mf

quadroon [kwɒ'dru:n] ADJ, N quarteron, -onne

quadruped ['kwɒdrʊped] ADJ, N quadrupède m

quadruple [kwɒ'dru:p(ə)l] ADJ, N quadruple m VT & VI quadrupler

quadruplet [kwɒ'dru:plɪt, 'kwɒdrʊplɪt] N **1** (child) quadruplé, -ée **2** Mus quartolet m

quadruplicate[1] [kwɒ'dru:plɪkət] ADJ quadruple; **in q.** en quatre exemplaires

quadruplicate[2] [kwɒ'dru:plɪkeɪt] VT **1** (multiply by four) quadrupler, multiplier par quatre **2** (make four copies of) (letter etc) faire ou tirer quatre exemplaires de

quaff [kwɒf] VT Lit (wine) boire à longs traits; (glass) vider d'un trait

quagmire ['kwægmaɪər, 'kwɒg-] N (bog) marécage m; Fig (awkward situation) bourbier m

quail[1] [kweɪl] N INV (bird) caille f (des blés), Can colin m; **q.'s eggs** œufs mpl de caille

quail[2] VI Lit (of person) fléchir, faiblir (**before** devant); **his heart quailed** son cœur défaillit

quaint [kweɪnt] ADJ (unusual) curieux; (attractively old-fashioned) suranné, vieillot, -otte; (picturesque) pittoresque; mignon, -onne; **he has this q. hope that he'll find a permanent job** il croit naïvement qu'il va trouver un emploi permanent; **a q. little cottage** une petite chaumière pittoresque

quaintly ['kweɪntlɪ] ADV (unusually) curieusement; (picturesquely) de façon pittoresque; **q. old-fashioned** d'un charme vieillot; **rather q. worded** formulé de façon assez mignonne

quaintness ['kweɪntnɪs] N (unusualness) étrangeté f; (old-fashioned charm) pittoresque m suranné; **the q. of the wording** la façon assez mignonne dont c'était formulé

quake [kweɪk] N **1** Fam (earthquake) tremblement m de terre **2** (shaking) tremblement m
VI (of person) trembler, frémir (**with fear** de crainte); **to q. in one's shoes** trembler de peur; **he was quaking with laughter** il était secoué de rires **2** (of thing) trembler, branler; **quaking grass** brize f

Quaker ['kweɪkər] N Rel quaker m, quakeresse f

Quakerism ['kweɪkərɪz(ə)m] N Rel quakerisme m

qualification [kwɒlɪfɪ'keɪʃən] N **1** (diploma etc) diplôme m, qualification f; **to have the necessary qualifications for a job** (skills etc) avoir les qualités ou les compétences requises pour remplir une fonction; (diplomas) avoir les diplômes requis ou les qualifications requises pour remplir une fonction; **paper or formal qualifications** diplômes; **professional q.** qualification professionnelle; **what are your qualifications?** quels diplômes avez-vous?; **a q. in translation** un diplôme de traduction; **one of the qualifications for this job is a sense of humour** une des qualités requises pour ce poste est le sens de l'humour
2 (successful completion of studies) obtention f d'un diplôme; **on q.** une fois le diplôme obtenu
3 Sport qualification f; **on q. for the World Cup** après s'être qualifié pour la Coupe du monde
4 (reservation) réserve f, restriction f; (condition) condition f; **to accept without q.** (without reservation) accepter sans réserve; (without conditions) accepter sans conditions; **to add a few qualifications** (to a statement, remarks etc) apporter quelques modifications
5 Fml (description) qualification f; **the report's q. of them as 'mercenaries'** le fait que le rapport les qualifiait de mercenaires

qualified ['kwɒlɪfaɪd] ADJ **1** (competent) (for position etc) qualifié, compétent, qui a les capacités requises; (having diploma etc) qualifié, diplômé; (for position etc) qui a les diplômes requis ou les qualifications requises; (pilot etc) breveté; Law capable (**to do** de faire); **she's very highly q.** elle est très qualifiée; **to be q. to do sth** (be competent) avoir les compétences voulues ou les capacités requises pour faire qch; (have diploma etc) avoir les diplômes requis ou les qualifi-

cations requises pour faire qch; **I am q. to speak about it** (*I know about it*) je suis bien placé pour en parler; **to be q. to speak** (*at meeting etc*) avoir voix au chapitre; **q. persons** personnes *fpl* compétentes
2 (*modified*) (*approval, support etc*) modéré; (*praise*) mitigé
▸▸ *EU* **q. majority voting** vote *m* à la majorité qualifiée; *Acct* **q. report** rapport *m* réservé; **q. success** demi-succès *m inv*

qualifier ['kwɒlɪfaɪər] **N 1** *Sport* (*person, team that qualifies*) qualifié, -ée; (*qualifying round*) série f éliminatoire **2** *Gram* qualificatif *m* **3** (*reservation*) restriction f, réserve f, (*condition*) condition f

qualify ['kwɒlɪfaɪ] **VT 1** **to q. sb for sth/for doing** *or* **to do sth** (*of course, training etc*) donner à qn les compétences voulues pour qch/pour faire qch, qualifier qn pour qch/pour faire qch; *Law* donner qualité à qn pour qch/pour faire qch; **my knowledge qualifies me to undertake this work** j'ai les connaissances pour entreprendre cet ouvrage; **what do you think qualifies you for this job?** en quoi vous considérez-vous comme qualifié pour cet emploi?
2 (*modify*) (*consent etc*) apporter des réserves à; (*statement*) apporter des précisions à, préciser; (*enjoyment*) modérer, diminuer
3 *Fml* (*describe*) **to q. sb/sth as sth** qualifier qn/qch de qch
4 *Gram* qualifier
VI obtenir son diplôme; *Sport* se qualifier (**for** pour); **to q. for sth** obtenir les diplômes *ou* les qualifications nécessaires pour qch; **to q. as an engineer/a nurse/an accountant** obtenir son diplôme d'ingénieur/d'infirmière/de comptable; **to q. as a doctor** être reçu médecin; **to q. as a pilot** obtenir son brevet de pilote; **you don't q. for a grant** vous ne remplissez pas les conditions requises pour recevoir une bourse; **that doesn't q. as news** (*nobody is interested*) ça n'intéresse personne; (*the information is out of date*) ça n'a rien de nouveau; **it hardly qualifies as a mountain** on ne peut pas vraiment appeler cela une montagne

qualifying ['kwɒlɪfaɪɪŋ] **ADJ 1** (*modifying*) modificateur, -trice **2** *Gram* (*adjective*) qualificatif; (*adverb*) modificatif
▸▸ **q. examination** (*at end of course*) examen *m* de fin d'études; (*to get onto course*) examen d'entrée; *Sport* **q. round** (épreuve f) éliminatoire f, **q. statement** déclaration f corrective

qualitative ['kwɒlɪtətɪv] **ADJ** qualitatif
▸▸ **q. analysis** analyse f qualitative; *Mktg* **q. forecasting** prévisions *fpl* qualitatives; *Mktg* **q. research** études *fpl* qualitatives; *Mktg* **q. study** étude f qualitative

qualitatively ['kwɒlɪtətɪvlɪ] **ADV** qualitativement

quality ['kwɒlɪtɪ] **N 1** (*degree of excellence*) qualité f; **of good q.** de bonne qualité; **of high/poor q.** de qualité supérieure/inférieure; **high/poor q. goods** marchandises *fpl* de bonne/mauvaise qualité; **a q. service/magazine** un service/magazine de qualité; **q. matters more than quantity** la qualité importe plus que la quantité; **the q. of life** la qualité de la vie; **q./price ratio** rapport *m* qualité/prix; *esp Am* **to spend q. time together** passer de bons moments ensemble
2 (*characteristic*) (*of person*) qualité f, trait *m*; (*of thing*) qualité f; (*of sound, voice*) qualité, timbre *m*; **one of the qualities I look for in a friend** une des qualités que je recherche chez un ami; **moral/intellectual qualities** qualités morales/intellectuelles; **he has many (good) qualities** il a beaucoup de qualités

3 *Fml* **to act in the q. of ...** agir en qualité de ...
4 *Arch* (*high status*) **person of q.** personne f de qualité; **the q.** les gens *mpl* de qualité, *Pej* le beau linge
▸▸ **q. assurance** garantie f de qualité; **q. audit** audit *m* de qualité; *Br* **q. circle** cercle *m* de qualité; **q. control** contrôle *m* de (la) qualité; **q. controller** responsable *mf* du contrôle de (la) qualité, qualiticien, -ienne; *Com* **q. improvement programme** programme *m* d'amélioration de la qualité; *Com* **q. goods** marchandises de qualité; **q. label** label *m* de qualité; **q. management** gestion f qualité; *Br* **q. newspaper** = quotidien *m* ou journal *m* du dimanche de qualité (par opposition à la presse populaire); *Mktg* **q. positioning** positionnement *m* par la qualité; **q. press** presse f de qualité

quality-assurance manager N directeur, -trice de l'assurance-qualité

qualm [kwɑːm] **N 1** (*pang of conscience*) scrupule *m*; **to have no qualms about doing sth** n'avoir aucun scrupule à faire qch; **I sometimes have qualms about what I did** j'ai parfois des remords pour ce que j'ai fait **2** (*premonition*) pressentiment *m* de malheur; (*anxiety*) inquiétude f; **don't you feel any qualms about getting married?** n'éprouves-tu aucune inquiétude à l'idée de te marier?

quandary ['kwɒndərɪ] **N** dilemme *m*; **to be in a q.** (*unable to decide what to do*) ne pas trop savoir que faire; **it put him in a q.** il ne savait que faire, il était face à un dilemme

quango ['kwæŋgəʊ] **N** *Br* (*abbr* **quasi-autonomous non-governmental organization**) = organisme *m* créé par le gouvernement et doté de pouvoirs quasi autonomes

---

Quango
En Grande-Bretagne, un "quango" est un organisme semi-public principalement financé par l'État mais disposant d'une certaine autonomie. Certains de ces organismes ont un rôle purement consultatif. D'autres sont habilités à prendre des décisions, notamment au niveau local, et c'est pourquoi au cours de ces dernières années les "quangos" ont fait l'objet de critiques, car leurs membres sont nommés par le gouvernement et non pas élus.

---

quantifiable [kwɒntɪ'faɪəb(ə)l] **ADJ** quantifiable

quantifier ['kwɒntɪfaɪər] **N** (*in logic*), *Math, Ling* quantificateur *m*

quantify ['kwɒntɪfaɪ] **VT 1** (*losses, damage*) quantifier, calculer; (*influence, contribution*) quantifier, évaluer; **happiness is hard to q.** le bonheur est difficile à quantifier **2** (*in logic*) quantifier

quantitative ['kwɒntɪtətɪv] **ADJ** quantitatif
▸▸ **q. analysis** analyse f quantitative; *Mktg* **q. forecasting** prévisions *fpl* quantitatives; *Mktg* **q. research** études *fpl* quantitatives; *Mktg* **q. study** étude f quantitative

quantitatively ['kwɒntɪtətɪvlɪ] **ADV** quantitativement

quantity ['kwɒntɪtɪ] **N 1** quantité f; **a small q. of** une petite quantité de; **to buy sth in large quantities** acheter qch en grande quantité; **they would drink quantities of beer** ils buvaient des litres et des litres de bière; **negligible q.** quantité négligeable; **to produce sth in q.** produire qch en quantité; *Constr* **bill of quantities** devis *m* SEE GRAMMAR B58–60 **2** (*in prosody*) quantité f
▸▸ **q. discount** remise f *ou* escompte *m* sur la quantité *ou* sur les achats en gros; **q. mark** signe *m* de quantité; **q. surveying** métrage

m; **q. surveyor** métreur, -euse; *Econ* **q. theory** théorie f quantitative

quantum, *pl* **quanta** ['kwɒntəm, -ə] **N** *Maths, Phys* quantum *m*
▸▸ **q. leap** saut *m* quantique; *Fig* bond *m* en avant; **q. mechanics** mécanique f quantique; **q. number** nombre *m* quantique; **q. physics** physique f quantique; **q. theory** théorie f des quanta *ou* quantique

quarantine ['kwɒrəntiːn] **N** quarantaine f; **to be in q.** (*of person, animal*) être en quarantaine
VT (*person, ship*) mettre en quarantaine; *Comput* (*infected file*) mettre en quarantaine

quark [kwɑːk] **N 1** *Nucl* quark *m* **2** (*soft cheese*) ≃ fromage *m* blanc

quarrel ['kwɒr(ə)l] **N** (*dispute*) dispute f, querelle f; **to pick a q. with sb** faire une scène à qn, se quereller avec qn; **to try to pick a q. with sb** chercher querelle *ou* noise à qn; **they've had a q.** ils se sont disputés *ou Fml* querellés; **what was their q. about?** pourquoi se sont-ils disputés?; **to make up a q.** se réconcilier; **I have no q. with him** je n'ai rien à lui reprocher; **my q. with you is that ...** ce que je te reproche c'est que ...; **she has no q. with that** elle n'a rien à redire là-dessus
VI (**-ll-,** *Am* **-l-**) **1** se disputer, *Fml* se quereller (**with sb over** *or* **about sth** avec qn à propos de qch); **they've been quarrelling** ils se sont disputés *ou Fml* querellés; **I don't want to q.** je ne veux pas me disputer *ou Fam* me bagarrer **2** **to q. with sb for doing sth** (*find fault with*) reprocher à qn de faire qch; **to q. with sth** (*take exception to*) ne pas être d'accord avec qch; **I can't q. with that** je n'ai rien à redire à cela; **while I wouldn't q. with your figures ...** bien que je ne conteste pas vos chiffres ...

quarrelling, *Am* **quarreling** ['kwɒr(ə)lɪŋ] **ADJ** querelleur, -euse
N disputes *fpl*, querelles *fpl*

quarrelsome ['kwɒr(ə)lsəm] **ADJ** querelleur, -euse, batailleur, -euse; **in a q. mood** d'humeur batailleuse *ou* querelleuse

quarrier ['kwɒrɪər] **N** = **quarryman**

quarry [¹] ['kwɒrɪ] **N** (*animal, bird*), *Fig* (*person*) proie f

quarry [²] **N** (*for stone, slate etc*) carrière f; **open q.** carrière à ciel ouvert
VT (*stone, slate etc*) extraire
VI exploiter une carrière; **to q. for granite** extraire du granite
▸▸ **q. stone** moellon *m*; **q. tile** carreau *m*
▸ **quarry out** VT SEP (*stone, slate etc*) extraire

quarrying ['kwɒrɪɪŋ] **N** exploitation f de carrières

quarryman, *pl* **quarrymen** ['kwɒrɪmən] **N** (*ouvrier m*) carrier *m*; **slate q.** perrayeur *m*, perrier *m*

quart [kwɔːt] **N** (*liquid measurement*) (*in UK*) = 1,136 litres; (*in US*) = 0,946 litre; *Prov* **you can't fit a q. into a pint pot** à l'impossible, nul n'est tenu

quarte [kɑːt] **N** *Fencing* quarte f

quarter ['kwɔːtər] **N 1** (*portion*) (*of apple, circle, century etc*) quart *m*; (*of orange, moon*) quartier *m*; *Culin* (*of beef, lamb*) quartier; **to divide sth in(to) quarters** diviser qch en quatre; **three quarters** trois quarts; **three and a q.** trois et quart; **a q. (of a pound) of coffee** un quart (de livre) de café, ≃ cent grammes de café; **bottle one q.** *or* **a q. full** bouteille au quart pleine; *Culin* **fore/hind q.** quartier de devant/de derrière; **moon at the first q.** lune au premier quartier; **moon in its last q.** lune dans son dernier quartier *ou* sur son décroît; **I can get it for you for a q. of the price** je peux vous l'avoir pour le quart du prix

2 *(of time) (three-month period)* trimestre *m*; **profits were up during the last q.** les bénéfices ont augmenté au cours du dernier trimestre; **to be paid by the q.** être payé par trimestre; **in the first q. of 2004** pendant le premier trimestre de l'année 2004; **in the first q. of the century** pendant le premier quart du siècle; **a q. to six,** *Am* **a q. of six** six heures moins le quart; **it's a q. to** il est moins le quart; **a q. past six,** *Am* **a q. after six** six heures et quart; **it's a q. past** il est le quart; **there's a train at a q. to and a q. past every hour** il y a un train à moins le quart et au quart; **a q. of an hour** un quart d'heure

3 *Naut (direction)* aire *f* de vent, quart *m*, côté *m*; **the wind is in the right q.** le vent vient du bon côté

4 *(area) (of town)* quartier *m*; **the slum q.** le quartier des taudis; **the residential q.** le quartier résidentiel; **from the four quarters of the globe** des quatre coins du monde; **news from all quarters** des nouvelles de partout; **what is he doing in these quarters?** que fait-il dans ces parages?; **an order from high quarters** un ordre d'en haut; **in some quarters there is talk of rebellion** on parle de rébellion dans certains milieux; **you'll get no help from that q.** vous n'obtiendrez aucune aide de ce côté; **it is rumoured in certain quarters that …** on murmure dans certains milieux que …

5 **quarters** *(lodgings) Mil* quartier *m*, cantonnement *m*, logement *m*; *(for servants)* appartements *mpl* (domestiques); *Aviat* **crew's quarters** locaux *mpl* affectés au personnel de bord

6 *Naut* **quarters** *(stations)* postes *mpl*; *Naut* **to beat** *or* **pipe to quarters** battre *ou* sonner le branle-bas; *Naut* **general quarters** branle-bas de combat

7 *esp Lit (mercy)* quartier *m*, merci *f*; **to give q.** faire quartier, accorder merci; **to give no q.** ne pas faire de quartier

8 *Am (coin)* pièce *f* de vingt-cinq cents; *(sum)* quart *m* de dollar

VT 1 *(apple etc)* diviser en quatre; *(beef etc)* diviser par quartiers, équarrir; *(time, amount)* réduire des trois quarts; *Hist (condemned man)* écarteler; **to q. the ground** *(of hunting dogs)* quêter **2** *Mil (lodge) (troops)* cantonner, caserner, loger; **to be quartered with sb** loger chez qn

▶▶ **q. binding** *(in bookbinding)* demi-reliure *f, pl* demi-reliures; *Br Fin* **q. day** *(jour m* du) terme *m; Am Mus* **q. note** noire *f, Law* **q. sessions** *(in England and Wales)* ≃ cour *f* d'assises *(remplacée en 1972 par la "Crown Court"); (in US)* = dans certains États, tribunal *m* local à compétence criminelle, pouvant avoir des fonctions administratives; *Mus* **q. tone** quart de ton

quarterback ['kwɔːtəbæk] N *Am Ftbl* arrière *m; Fam* **to be a Monday morning q.** être sage a posteriori

quarterdeck ['kwɔːtədek] N *Naut* **1** plage *f* arrière **2** *(no pl)* **the q.** *(officers)* les officiers *mpl*

quarterfinal [kwɔːtə'faɪnəl] N *Sport* quart *m* de finale; **he's in the quarterfinals** il est en quarts de finale, il dispute les quarts de finale

quarterfinalist [kwɔːtə'faɪnəlɪst] N quart-de-finaliste *mf, pl* quart-de-finalistes

quartering ['kwɔːtərɪŋ] N **1** *(division)* division *f* en quatre; *(of beef, tree trunk)* équarrissage *m* **2** *Mil (lodging) (of troops)* logement *m*, cantonnement *m*, stationnement *m*

quarterlight ['kwɔːtəlaɪt] N *Aut* déflecteur *m* de porte avant

quarterly ['kwɔːtəlɪ] ADJ trimestriel; *(subscription)* au trimestre

N publication *f* trimestrielle
ADV trimestriellement, tous les trimestres, tous les trois mois

quartermaster ['kwɔːtəmɑːstər] N *Naut* maître *m* de timonerie; *Mil* commissaire *m*; intendant *m*

▶▶ *Mil* **Q. General** Directeur *m* de l'Intendance *(militaire);* **q.'s store** magasin *m*

quarter-pounder [-'paʊndər] N *Culin* = hamburger *m* d'environ 100 grammes

quarterstaff ['kwɔːtəstɑːf] N *Hist (weapon)* bâton *m*; **to fence with quarterstaffs** jouer du bâton

quarterwindow ['kwɔːtəwɪndəʊ] N *Aut* glace *f* de custode, custode *f*

quartet(te) [kwɔː'tet] N **1** *(players, music, group of four)* quatuor *m; (jazz band)* quartette *m*; **string q.** quatuor à cordes **2** *Liter* tétralogie *f*

quartile ['kwɔːtaɪl] N quartile *m*

quarto ['kwɔːtəʊ] ADJ, N in-quarto *m inv*

quartz [kwɔːts] N *Miner* quartz *m*

▶▶ **q. clock** pendule *f* à quartz; **q. crystal** cristal *m* de quartz; **q. lamp** lampe *f* (à vapeur de mercure) à tube de quartz; **q. watch** montre *f* à quartz

quartz-halogen N halogène *m* à quartz

quartzite ['kwɔːtsaɪt] N *Miner* quartzite *m*

quasar ['kweɪzɑːr] N *Astron* quasar *m*

quash [kwɒʃ] VT **1** *(feeling, plan)* étouffer; *(revolt)* écraser; *Fam* **to q. sb** écraser qn **2** *Law (verdict, decision)* casser, infirmer, annuler; **to q. proceedings** *or* **an action** arrêter les poursuites

quasi- ['kweɪsaɪ, 'kwɑːzɪ] PREF quasi-; **q.-contract** quasi-contrat *m, pl* quasi-contrats; *Fin* **q.-money** quasi-monnaie *f, pl* quasi-monnaies; **q.-scientific** quasi-scientifique, presque scientifique

quatercentenary [kwɒtəsen'tiːnərɪ] N quatrième centenaire *m*

quaternary [kwə'tɜːnərɪ] ADJ *Chem, Geol, Math* quaternaire; *Geol* **the Q. era** l'ère *f* quaternaire
N *Geol* **the Q.** le quaternaire

quatrain ['kwɒtreɪn] N *(of poem)* quatrain *m*

quaver ['kweɪvər] N **1** *Br Mus (note)* croche *f* **2** *(trembling) (in voice)* tremblement *m*, chevrotement *m; Mus* tremolo *m*; **to have a q. in one's voice** parler d'une voix tremblante
VI *(of voice)* chevroter, trembloter; *Mus* faire un tremolo; **quavering voice** voix *f* tremblotante *ou* chevrotante, voix mal assurée
VT **to q. (out)** *(song)* chevroter

quay [kiː] N quai *m*; **alongside the q.** à quai; *Com* **ex-q.** *(goods)* à prendre *ou* livrable à quai

quayside ['kiːsaɪd] N quai *m*; **we walked along the q.** nous nous sommes promenés le long du quai; **on the q.** sur le quai

queasiness ['kwiːzɪnɪs] N *Med* nausées *fpl; Fig* malaise *m*

queasy ['kwiːzɪ] ADJ *(stomach)* délicat; **I feel q.** j'ai la nausée, j'ai mal au cœur; **the drugs make him q.** les médicaments lui donnent des nausées; **the very sight of meat makes her feel q.** la simple vue de la viande lui donne la nausée; **she was looking rather q.** elle avait l'air d'avoir mal au cœur; *Fig* **to feel q. about sth** se sentir mal à l'aise en ce qui concerne qch

Quebec [kwɪ'bek] N Québec *m*; **I'm from Q.** je suis Québécois, -oise, je suis du Québec

Quebecer [kɪ'bekər] N Québécois, -oise

queen [kwiːn] N **1** reine *f*; **the kings and queens of England** les souverains *mpl* d'Angleterre; *Br* **the Q.'s Christmas message** = discours *m* télévisé et radiodiffusé de la reine le jour de Noël; **Q. of heaven** reine du ciel; *esp Iron* **she is the q. of my heart** elle règne sur mon cœur; **the rose is the q. of flowers** la rose est la reine des fleurs

2 *Cards* dame *f, Chess* reine *f*, dame; **Q. of hearts** reine de cœur

3 *(insect) (of ants etc)* reine *f*

4 *Offensive Sl (male homosexual)* tante *f*, folle *f*

VT **1** *Fam* **to q. it** faire la reine *ou* jouer les personnages importants *(over sb avec qn)*
2 *Chess (pawn)* damer
VI *Chess (of pawn)* aller à dame

▶▶ **Q. Anne** = style *m* d'architecture et de mobilier du XVIIIème siècle caractérisé par des lignes sobres; **a Q. Anne house** une maison de l'époque de la reine Anne; *Entom* **q. bee** reine des abeilles; *Fig* **she's the q. bee around here** c'est elle qui commande ici, c'est elle la patronne ici; *Law* **Queen's Bench** = en Angleterre et au pays de Galles, l'une des trois divisions de la High Court, ≃ tribunal *m* de grande instance; *Law* **Queen's Counsel** ≃ bâtonnier *m* de l'ordre *(en Angleterre);* **the Q.'s English** l'anglais *m* britannique correct; **she speaks the Q.'s English** elle s'exprime dans un anglais très soigné; **Q. Mother** reine mère; *Br Parl* **Q.'s Speech** = allocution *f* prononcée par la reine (mais préparée par le gouvernement) lors de la rentrée parlementaire et dans laquelle elle définit les grands axes de la politique gouvernementale

queencake ['kwiːnkeɪk] N *Am* = petit gâteau *m* aux raisins secs

queenly ['kwiːnlɪ] ADJ de reine

queen-size bed N grand lit *m* double

queer ['kwɪər] N **1** *Offensive Sl (male homosexual)* pédé *m*, pédale *f* **2** *Am Sl (counterfeit money)* fausse monnaie *f*
ADJ **1** *(strange)* bizarre, étrange, singulier; **she's a q.-looking person** elle a une drôle de tête; **she has a q.-sounding name** elle a un drôle de nom; **q. ideas** idées *fpl* bizarres *ou Fam* biscornues; *Fam* **q. in the head** toqué, timbré; *Br Fam* **to be in Q. Street** être dans une situation *(financière)* délicate
2 *(suspicious)* suspect, louche
3 *Offensive Sl (homosexual)* pédé, homo
4 *Fam (unwell)* pas bien; **I feel very q.** je me sens tout chose *ou* tout drôle; **to come over** *or* **to be taken q.** avoir un malaise
VT *Fam* **to q. the pitch for sb, to q. sb's pitch** bouleverser *ou* faire échouer les plans de qn
▶▶ *Am Fam* **q. money** *(counterfeit)* fausse monnaie

queer-basher [-bæʃər] N *Br Offensive Sl (assaults on homosexuals)* = individu *m* qui se livre à des violences à l'encontre d'homosexuels

queer-bashing N *Br Offensive Sl (assaults on homosexuals)* chasse *f* aux pédés

queerly ['kwɪəlɪ] ADV bizarrement, étrangement

queerness ['kwɪənɪs] N étrangeté *f*

quell [kwel] VT *Lit (revolt, emotion)* réprimer; *(rioters)* mater; *(person, passion)* dompter

quench [kwentʃ] VT **1 to q. one's thirst** se désaltérer, étancher sa soif **2** *(extinguish) (fire, flame)* éteindre **3** *(cool) (in metalwork) (metal)* tremper; *Fig (person's enthusiasm)* atténuer **4** *(suppress) (desire)* réprimer, étouffer

querulous ['kwerʊləs] ADJ *(person)* qui se plaint toujours, grognon; *(tone)* plaintif, dolent

querulously ['kwerʊləslɪ] ADV d'un ton plaintif *ou* dolent

query ['kwɪərɪ] N *(question)* question *f; Comput* interrogation *f*, **I have a q.** j'ai une question; **to raise a q.** soulever une question; **to settle a q.** résoudre une question;

there was a note of q. in her voice il y avait une note d'interrogation dans sa voix; **q.: is this accurate?** *(in margin of document etc)* question: est-ce exact?

VT 1 *(ask)* **to q. if** *or* **whether ...** demander si ...; **how much is that?, he queried** combien est-ce?, demanda-t-il

2 *(put in doubt) (question, statement)* mettre en question *ou* en doute; *(mark with question mark)* marquer d'un point d'interrogation; *Am (question) (person)* poser des questions à; **she queried the bill** elle a dit qu'ils s'étaient trompés dans l'addition; **I would q. it if I were you** à votre place je vérifierais qu'ils ne se sont pas trompés

3 *Comput* **to q. a database** interroger une base de données

▸▸ *Comput* **q. language** langage *m* d'interrogation

quest [kwɛst] *Lit* **N** quête *f*, recherche *f*; **to go in q. of sb/sth** se mettre *ou* aller *ou* partir à la recherche de qn/qch *ou* en quête de qn/qch; **her q. for justice** sa bataille pour que justice soit faite; **the q. for the Holy Grail** la quête du Graal

VI to q. after *or* **for sth** être à la recherche de qch

QUESTION ['kwɛstʃən]

| **N** question **1, 3** | = doute **2** |
| **VT** interroger **1** | = mettre en doute **2** |

N VOIR GRAMMAIRE A46–7; B63–4 **1** *(interrogation)* question *f*, demande *f*; *(in exam)* question; **to ask sb a q., to ask a q. of sb, to put a q. to sb** poser une question à qn; *Parl* adresser une interpellation à qn; **does anyone have any questions?** quelqu'un a-t-il une question?; **I have a q.** j'ai une question; **the q. is, did she know?** la question est de savoir si elle était au courant; *Gram* **direct/indirect q.** interrogation *f* directe/indirecte; *Sch etc* **list** *or* **set of questions** questionnaire *m*; **a q. and answer session** une séance questions-réponses

2 *(doubt)* doute *m*; **without q.** sans aucun doute, sans contredit; **to obey without q.** obéir aveuglément; **her courage/dedication is beyond q.** son courage/dévouement est indiscutable; **that is beyond q.** c'est incontestable; **his honesty has never been in q.** son honnêteté n'a jamais été mise en doute; **to call sb's honesty into q.** mettre en question l'honnêteté de qn; **there is no q. about it** il n'y a pas de doute là-dessus; **it's open to q. whether ...** on peut se demander si ...; **the wisdom of this decision is open to q.** le bien-fondé de la décision est discutable

3 *(matter, issue)* question *f*; **that's the q.** c'est bien là la question; **that's another** *or* **a different q.** c'est une autre histoire; **that is not the q., that is beside the q.** ce n'est pas là la question, il ne s'agit pas de cela; **the q. is whether ...** il s'agit de savoir si ...; **it is out of the q.** c'est hors de question; **it is quite out of the q. for us to ...** il ne saurait être question pour nous de ...; **there's no q. of you(r) going back to work at the moment** il n'est pas question que vous repreniez le travail pour le moment; **there is no q. of going back now** il n'est pas question de revenir en arrière; **it's not a q. of who's right** la question n'est pas de savoir qui a raison; **the Palestinian q.** la question palestinienne; **a q. of life or death** une question de vie ou de mort; **a q. of money/time** une question d'argent/de temps; **it's only a q. of time before it happens** ça arrivera tôt ou tard; **the matter/person in q.** l'affaire/la personne en question; *Law* **the case in q.** le cas en litige; **there was some q. of ...** il a été question de ...

4 *Hist* **to put sb to the q.** *(torture)* mettre qn

à la question, appliquer la question à qn

VT 1 *(person)* questionner, interroger (**about** sur, à propos de); **to be questioned** être interrogé; *(of suspect)* subir un interrogatoire; **the people questioned in the survey** les personnes interrogées dans le cadre du sondage; **she was questioned on her views** *(in interview etc)* on l'a interrogée sur ses opinions

2 *(cast doubt on)* mettre en question *ou* en doute *ou* en cause, contester; **nobody is questioning your ...** personne ne met en doute *ou* en question votre/vos ...; **I q. whether he will come** je doute qu'il vienne; **I q. whether it would not be better to ...** je me demande s'il ne vaudrait pas mieux ...

▸▸ *Gram* **q. form** forme *f* interrogative; **q. mark** *(punctuation mark)* point *m* d'interrogation; *Mktg (product)* point d'interrogation, dilemme *m*; *Fig* **a q. mark hangs over the project** il y a un point d'interrogation quant au projet; **q. master** meneur, -euse de jeu; *Radio, TV* animateur, -trice *(d'un jeu)*; *Ling* **q. tag** question tag *m*, = tournure *f* interrogative en fin de phrase, équivalent du "n'est-ce pas" français VOIR GRAMMAIRE A47; B64 ; *Parl* **q. time** heure *f* consacrée aux questions; **q. word** mot *m* interrogatif

questionable ['kwɛstʃənəb(ə)l] **ADJ 1** *(doubtful)* contestable, discutable, douteux; **of q. authenticity** *(document etc)* d'une authenticité (fort) douteuse; **this is the most democratic country – that's very q.** c'est le pays le plus démocratique – c'est très discutable **2** *Pej (conduct etc)* suspect, équivoque; **in q. taste** d'un goût douteux

questioner ['kwɛstʃənər] **N** interrogateur, -trice; *(who likes asking questions)* questionneur, -euse; *(calling in to TV programme)* téléspectateur, -trice; *(calling in to radio programme)* auditeur, -trice; *(in studio audience)* spectateur, -trice

questioning ['kwɛstʃənɪŋ] **ADJ** *(look etc)* interrogateur, -trice; **to have a q. mind** avoir un esprit curieux

N questions *fpl*, interrogation *f*; *Mil etc (of prisoner)* interrogatoire *m*; **to be held for q.** *(by police)* être détenu pour un interrogatoire

questioningly ['kwɛstʃənɪŋlɪ] **ADV** *(to look at sb)* d'un air interrogateur; *(to say sth)* d'un ton interrogateur

questionnaire [kwɛstʃə'neər] **N** questionnaire *m*

▸▸ **q. analysis** dépouillement *m* de questionnaire; **q. construction** construction *f* de questionnaire; **q. survey** enquête *f* par questionnaire

quetzal ['kɛtsəl] **N** *(bird)* quetzal *m*, *pl* quetzals

queue [kju:] **N 1** *esp Br (line) (of people)* queue *f*, file *f*; *(of cars)* file; **is this the q.?** *(for tickets etc)* est-ce que c'est la queue?; **to form a q., to stand in a q.** faire la queue; **there is a q., you know!** il faut faire la queue!; **to join the q.** se mettre à la queue; *Fig* **join the q.!** vous n'êtes pas le seul/la seule; **to jump the q.** passer avant son tour **2** *Comput* file *f* d'attente **3** *Arch (of hair, wig)* queue *f*

VI faire la queue; **I spent ages queuing for a bus** j'ai passé des heures à attendre le bus

VT *Comput (print jobs)* mettre en file d'attente

▸ **queue up VI** faire la queue; **people queued up to shake his hand** les gens faisaient la queue pour lui serrer la main; **people are queuing up for a job like yours** les gens se battent pour décrocher un emploi comme le vôtre

queue-jump VI resquiller

queue-jumper N resquilleur, -euse

quibble ['kwɪb(ə)l] **N** argutie *f*, chicane *f* sur les mots

VI *(equivocate)* ergoter, chicaner; *(split hairs)* chipoter, couper les cheveux en quatre; **he didn't q. about the price** il n'a pas chipoté sur le prix

quibbler ['kwɪblər] **N** ergoteur, -euse, chicaneur, -euse

quibbling ['kwɪb(ə)lɪŋ] **N** arguties *fpl*, chicanerie *f*, ergoterie *f*

ADJ qui porte sur des vétilles

quiche [ki:ʃ] **N** *Culin* quiche *f*

quick [kwɪk] **ADJ** *(movement, growth etc)* rapide; *Mus* animé, vif; **that was q.!** ça a été rapide!; **as q. as lightning** *or* **as a flash** aussi vite que l'éclair, en un clin d'œil; **be q. (about it)!** faites vite!, dépêchez-vous!; **he's q.** *(of runner)* il court vite; *(of worker)* il est rapide; *(he understands etc quickly)* il est vif; **q. to act/to anger** prompt à agir/à se fâcher; **she's very q. to take offence** elle se vexe très facilement; **don't be so q. to criticize** ne critique donc pas si vite; **she was q. to realize what had happened** elle s'est vite rendu compte de ce qui s'était passé; **to be q. off the mark** *(in race)* démarrer vite; *(to start sth)* démarrer sans perdre de temps; *(to understand)* avoir l'esprit vif; **he wasn't exactly q. off the mark when it came to ordering drinks** il était plutôt lent à la détente quand il s'agissait de commander les boissons; *Fam* **let's have a q. one** *(drink)* si on prenait un petit verre?; **they've gone upstairs for a q. one** *(sex)* ils sont montés (pour) tirer un petit coup; **the quickest way there** le chemin le plus court (pour y arriver); **what's the q. way to find a job?** comment trouve-t-on un emploi rapidement?; **I'll just have a q. bath** je vais juste prendre un bain en vitesse; **can I ask you a q. question?** je peux vous poser une petite question?; **q. mind** esprit *m* prompt *ou* vif; **q. recovery (from an illness)** prompt rétablissement *m* (d'une maladie); **q. temper** tempérament *m* emporté, irascibilité *f*; **she has a q. temper** elle s'emporte facilement

N 1 *(flesh)* vif *m*; **to bite one's nails to the q.** se ronger les ongles jusqu'au vif; *Fig* **to sting** *or* **cut sb to the q.** le blesser *ou* piquer au vif **2** *Rel* **the q. and the dead** *(pl)* les vivants *mpl* et les morts

ADV 1 *Fam* vite, rapidement; **as q. as possible** aussi vite que possible; **to run quicker** courir plus vite; **he just wants to get rich q.** il ne pense qu'à s'enrichir rapidement; **q.! over here!** vite! par ici!

2 *(in compounds)* **q.-acting, q.-action** *(mechanism)* à action rapide *ou* immédiate; *(drug, medication)* à action rapide; **q.-drying paint** peinture *f* qui sèche rapidement; **q.-firing rifle** fusil *m* à tir rapide; **q.-growing** *(plant etc)* à croissance rapide; *Constr, Culin* **q.-setting** *(cement, jelly)* à prise rapide

▸▸ *Acct* **q. assets** liquidités *fpl*, actif *m* liquide; **q. fix** solution *f* miracle; *Comput* **q. launch bar** barre *f* de lancement rapide; *Acct* **q. ratio** ratio *m* de liquidité immédiate; **q. reference guide** aide-mémoire *m inv*; **q. sale** vente *f* rapide; *Cards* **q. trick** levée *f* assurée

quick-change artiste N *Theat* = acteur *m* qui change de costume souvent au cours d'un spectacle; *Fig* personne *f* versatile

quicken ['kwɪk(ə)n] **VT** *(step, pace)* hâter, presser, accélérer; *Med (pulse)* accélérer; *(stimulate) (imagination)* stimuler; *(interest)* exciter; *(appetite)* aiguiser; *(feelings)* provoquer; *Sport* **to q. the pace** accélérer le pas *ou* le rythme

VI *(of pace, pulse etc)* devenir plus rapide, s'accélérer; *Lit (of nature, hope etc)* s'animer, se ranimer; *(of foetus)* bouger

quickening ['kwɪkənɪŋ] **ADJ** *(pace)* qui s'accélère; *Lit* **her q. hope** ses espoirs grandissants

N *(of pace, pulse)* accélération *f*; *(of nature etc)* renouveau *m*; *Obst* premiers mouvements *mpl* du foetus

quickfire ['kwɪkfaɪər] **ADJ ATTRIB** *(questions, repartee)* rapide, au rythme soutenu

quick-freeze VT *Culin* surgeler

quickie ['kwɪkɪ] **N** *Fam (quick drink)* consommation *f* prise sur le pouce; *(something done quickly)* chose *f* faite à la hâte; **let's have a q.** *(drink)* si on prenait un petit verre?; *(sex)* on fait l'amour en vitesse?; **OK, but make it a q.** si tu veux, mais en vitesse
▸▸ **q. divorce** *m* express

quicklime ['kwɪklaɪm] **N** chaux *f* vive

quickly ['kwɪklɪ] **ADV** vite, rapidement; **q.!** vite!

quickness ['kwɪknɪs] **N 1** *(rapidity)* vitesse *f*, rapidité *f*; *(of pulse)* rythme *m* rapide **2** *(sharpness) (of sight)* acuité *f*, *(of hearing)* finesse *f*, *(of mind)* vivacité *f*; **q. of temper** caractère *m* emporté *ou* irascible

quicksand ['kwɪksænd] **N** sables *mpl* mouvants; **to get caught** *or* **stuck in q.** *or* **in the quicksands** être pris dans des sables mouvants

quickset ['kwɪkset] **N** *Br* haie *f* vive
▸▸ **q. hedge** haie vive

quickshift gear change ['kwɪkʃɪft] **N** changement *m* de vitesse rapide

quicksilver ['kwɪksɪlvər] **N** vif-argent *m*, *pl* vifs-argents; **he's/she's just like q.** c'est du vif-argent

quickstep ['kwɪkstep] **N** *(dance)* fox-trot *m* inv rapide

quick-tempered ADJ emporté, colérique, coléreux, irascible; **to be q.** s'emporter facilement

quick-witted ADJ vif, éveillé, à l'esprit vif

quid[1] [kwɪd] **N** *Br Fam (inv in pl) (pound)* livre *f*, **it cost me 10 q.** ça m'a coûté 100 balles; **to be quids in** être tranquille *ou* peinard

quid[2] **N** *(of tobacco)* chique *f*

quid pro quo [kwɪdprəʊ'kwəʊ] **N** compensation *f*, contrepartie *f*; **what did she get as a q. for her silence?** qu'est-ce qu'elle a reçu en contrepartie de son silence?

quiescence [kwɪ'esəns] **N** *Fml* tranquillité *f*

quiescent [kwɪ'esənt] **ADJ** *Fml* inactif, passif

QUIET ['kwaɪət]

N	tranquillité ▪ calme ▪ silence
ADJ	doux **1, 2** ▪ tranquille **1, 4**
	▪ calme **1, 4** ▪ silencieux **1** ▪ discret
	3 ▪ dans l'intimité **3**

N *(calm)* tranquillité *f*, calme *m*; *(silence)* silence *m*; **to enjoy perfect peace and q.** jouir d'une parfaite tranquillité; **the q. of the night** le calme de la nuit; *Br Fam* **to do sth on the q.** faire qch discrètement, *Pej* faire qch en cachette *ou* à la dérobée

ADJ 1 *(with little sound or motion) (music)* doux, *f* douce; *(voice)* bas, doux; *(neighbour, neighbourhood)* tranquille, calme; *(sea)* calme; *(engine)* silencieux; **can we go somewhere q.?** est-ce que nous pouvons aller dans un endroit tranquille?; **the wind grew q.** le vent s'est apaisé; **to keep q.** *(make no noise)* rester *ou* se tenir tranquille; *(say nothing)* se taire, ne rien dire, garder le silence; **we must keep q. about it** il ne faut pas en parler; **keep it q.** pas un mot; **she was very q. about her background** elle n'a pas dit grand-chose de ses antécédents; **to keep a child q.** faire taire un enfant; **to keep sb q.** tenir qn tranquille; **be q.!** tais-toi!/ taisez-vous!; **q. please!** silence, s'il vous

plaît!; **to be as q. as a mouse** *(of person)* être très silencieux; **the house was as q. as the grave** il n'y avait pas un bruit dans la maison; **it's as q. as the grave here on a Saturday** c'est complètement mort ici le samedi; **could I have a q. word (with you)?** est-ce que je peux vous prendre à part pour vous dire deux mots?

2 *(calm)* doux, *f* douce; **he's a very q. kind of chap** c'est un type très tranquille; **q. disposition** caractère *m* doux *ou* calme; **q. horse** cheval *m* doux *ou* tranquille *ou* sage

3 *(subdued, discreet) (dress, colours etc)* simple, discret, -ète, sobre; **we had a q. laugh over it** nous en avons ri entre nous; **you're very q., is anything wrong?** tu es drôlement silencieux, il y a quelque chose qui ne va pas?; **it's very pretty countryside, in a q. sort of way** c'est un très joli paysage, dans le genre paisible; **q. irony** ironie *f* voilée; **q. optimism** optimisme *m* modéré; **q. wedding** mariage *m* célébré dans l'intimité

4 *(undisturbed)* calme, tranquille, paisible; **to lead a q. life** mener une vie calme; *Fam* **anything for a q. life!** n'importe quoi du moment qu'on me fiche la paix!; *Com* **business is very q.** les affaires ne marchent pas très fort; **it's very q. in here tonight** *(in the pub, shop etc)* c'est très calme ce soir; **to have a q. drink** boire un coup tranquillement; **to spend a q. evening (in)** passer une soirée tranquille; *Fam* **all q. on the western front** à l'ouest rien de nouveau

VT = quieten
▸ **quiet down = quieten down**

quieten ['kwaɪət(ə)n] **VT** *Br (uproar etc)* apaiser, calmer; *(person, one's conscience)* tranquilliser; *(child)* faire taire; *(fears, suspicions)* dissiper; *(pain)* calmer
▸ **quieten down** *Br* **VI 1** *(become silent)* se taire **2** *(become calm) (of person)* se calmer; *(of business)* ralentir
VT SEP 1 *(make silent)* faire taire **2** *(make calm) (person, animal)* calmer

quietly ['kwaɪətlɪ] **ADV 1** *(with little sound or motion)* silencieusement, sans bruit **2** *(calmly)* tranquillement, doucement; **to be q. determined to do sth** être froidement décidé à faire qch **3** *(discreetly) (dressed etc)* simplement, discrètement; **to get married q.** se marier sans cérémonie *ou* dans l'intimité **4** *(with little excitement)* **we live very q.** nous menons une vie très calme

quietness ['kwaɪətnɪs] **N 1** *(lack of sound)* silence *m* **2** *(calmness) (of person)* calme *m* **3** *(of dress, colour etc)* sobriété *f* **4** *(of life)* tranquillité *f*; *(of business)* manque *m* d'activité

quietude ['kwaɪətjuːd] **N** *Lit* quiétude *f*

quietus [kwaɪ'iːtəs] **N** *Lit (death)* mort *f*

quiff [kwɪf] **N** *Br (hairstyle)* banane *f*

quill [kwɪl] **N 1** *(feather)* penne *f*, *(shaft of feather)* tuyau *m*; *(pen)* plume *f* (d'oie) **2** *(of porcupine etc)* piquant *m*
▸▸ **q. feather** penne *f*; **q. pen** plume d'oie

quilt [kwɪlt] **N** couverture *f* piquée *ou* matelassée; *(eiderdown)* édredon *m* piqué; **(continental) q.** couette *f*, *Suisse* duvet *m*
VT 1 *(garment etc)* matelasser, ouater, ouatiner et piquer; **quilted jacket** veste *f* matelassée **2** *(two pieces of material)* piquer
VI faire du matelassage
▸▸ **q. cover** housse *f* de couette

quilting ['kwɪltɪŋ] **N** matelassage *m*

quin [kwɪn] **N** *Br Fam (child)* quintuplé, -ée

quince [kwɪns] **N 1** *(fruit)* coing *m* **2** *(tree)* cognassier *m*
▸▸ **q. jelly** gelée *f* de coings; **q. tree** cognassier

quincentenary [kwɪnsen'tiːnərɪ] **N** cinquième centenaire *m*

quinine [kwɪ'niːn] **N** *Chem* quinine *f*

quinquagenarian [kwɪŋkwədʒə'neərɪən] **ADJ, N** quinquagénaire *mf*

Quinquagesima [kwɪŋkwə'dʒesɪmə] **N** *Rel* Quinquagésime *f*
▸▸ **Q. Sunday** le dimanche de la Quinquagésime

quinsy ['kwɪnzɪ] **N** *Med Old-fashioned* angine *f* phlegmoneuse

quintal ['kwɪnt(ə)l] **N** *(measurement)* quintal *m* métrique *(de 100 kg)*

quinte [kænt] **N** *Fencing* quinte *f*

quintessence [kwɪn'tesəns] **N** *Fml* quintessence *f*

quintessential [kwɪntɪ'senʃəl] **ADJ** *Fml* quintessenciel

quintessentially [kwɪntɪ'senʃəlɪ] **ADV** *Fml* fondamentalement

quintet(te) [kwɪn'tet] **N** *Mus* quintette *m*

quintillion [kwɪn'tɪljən] **N** *Br* (10^{30}) quintillion *m*; *Am* (10^{18}) trillion *m*

quintuple [kwɪn'tjʊp(ə)l] **ADJ, N** quintuple *m*
VT & VI quintupler

quintuplet [kwɪn'tjuːplɪt, 'kwɪntjʊplɪt] **N** *(child)* quintuplé, -ée

quip [kwɪp] **N** *(sarcastic remark)* sarcasme *m*, raillerie *f*; *(witty remark)* trait *m* *ou* mot *m* d'esprit; *(riposte)* repartie *f*
VI (-pp-) *(make sarcastic remark)* railler; *(be witty)* faire des mots d'esprit
VT *(say sarcastically)* dire de façon sarcastique; *(say wittily)* dire avec esprit

quire ['kwaɪər] **N 1 q. of paper** *(24 sheets)* ≃ main *f* de papier *(25 feuilles)* **2** *Typ* **in quires** en feuilles

quirk [kwɜːk] **N** *(of character)* particularité *f*, bizarrerie *f* de caractère; **he's got a lot of little quirks** il y a plein de choses bizarres chez lui; **a q. of fate** un caprice du sort; **by a q. they both went to Rome** par un effet du hasard, ils sont tous les deux allés à Rome

quirky ['kwɜːkɪ] **ADJ** *(sense of humour etc)* bizarre

quisling ['kwɪzlɪŋ] **N** *Pej* collaborateur, -trice

quit [kwɪt] **VI** *(pt, pp quitted, Dial, Am quit; prp quitting)* *(resign)* démissionner; *(in fight)* abandonner; *Comput* sortir; **you can't fire me, I q.!** vous ne pouvez pas me mettre à la porte, je démissionne!; **to receive notice to q.** *(of tenant)* recevoir son congé
VT 1 *(leave) (person, place)* quitter **2** *Comput (database, programme)* sortir de, quitter **3 to q. office** se démettre de ses fonctions **4** *Fam* **to q. one's job** quitter son emploi, démissionner; **to q. doing sth** arrêter *ou* cesser de faire qch; **q. annoying me, will you!** tu vas arrêter de m'ennuyer!; **to q. work** arrêter de travailler, cesser le travail
ADJ *Fml* quitte, libéré; **to be q. of sb/sth** être débarrassé de qn/qch

QUITE [kwaɪt]

vraiment **1** ▪ tout à fait **1** ▪ assez **2**

ADV VOIR GRAMMAIRE A5 **1** *(entirely)* vraiment; **she's q. happy** elle est tout à fait heureuse; **he's q. happy to let others do the work** ça ne le dérange absolument pas de laisser les autres faire le travail; **q. finished** entièrement *ou* complètement fini; *Iron* **have you q. finished?** c'est pas bientôt fini?; **q. recovered** tout à fait *ou* complètement rétabli; **he was q. obviously drunk** il était manifestement ivre; **q. the best story of its kind** sans aucun doute la meilleure histoire de ce genre; **q. as much** autant; **q. enough** bien assez; **that's q. enough of that!** ça suffit comme ça!; **q. apart from the fact that ...**

en dehors du fait que …; **q. right** *(of sum)* parfaitement juste; *(of clock)* bien à l'heure; **you are q. right** vous avez bien *ou* tout à fait raison; **q. (so)!** parfaitement!, d'accord!; **I'm afraid I'll be a bit late – that's q. all right** je crains d'être un peu en retard – ce n'est pas grave; **not q.** pas tout à fait; **not q. 300** pas tout à fait 300; **it's not q. 2 o'clock** il n'est pas tout à fait 2 heures; **q. the opposite** bien au contraire; **I don't q. know what he will do** je ne sais pas trop ce qu'il fera; **you know q. well what I mean** vous savez très bien ce que je veux dire; **I q. understand** je comprends bien, je me rends parfaitement compte; **I don't q. understand** je ne comprends pas bien; **I can't q. remember when it happened** je ne me souviens pas bien *ou* tout à fait quand ça s'est passé; **in q. another tone** sur un tout autre ton; **that's q. another matter!** c'est tout autre chose! **2** *(fairly, rather)* assez; **q. big/small** assez gros/petit; **q. frequently/recently** assez fréquemment/récemment; **this furniture is q. sought after** ces meubles sont assez recherchés; **I q. like him** je l'aime bien; **she is q. happy** elle est assez heureuse; **q. a lot of people/money** un assez grand nombre de gens/une assez grosse somme d'argent; **q. a few people** pas mal de gens **3** *(really)* **q. a beauty** une vraie beauté; **it was q. a surprise** c'était une véritable surprise; **it's been q. a day** quelle journée!; **she's q. a girl** elle est formidable; **that film was q. something** ce film c'était vraiment quelque chose; **it's q. something when …** c'est vraiment quelque chose quand …; **it was q. something (to do sth)** c'était vraiment quelque chose (de faire qch)

quits [kwɪts] **ADJ now we're q.** maintenant nous sommes quittes; **double or q.** quitte ou double; **I'll be q. with him yet** il me le paiera; **let's call it q.** *(agree to end game, dispute)* restons-en là

quittance ['kwɪt(ə)ns] **N** *Fin* quittance *f*, décharge *f*, acquit *m*

quitter ['kwɪtər] **N** *Fam Pej* personne *f* qui abandonne facilement; **she's not a q.** elle n'est pas du genre à abandonner *ou* à se laisser abattre

quiver[1] ['kwɪvər] **N** *(of person)* tremblement *m*, frisson *m*, frémissement *m*; *(of leaves, lips)* frémissement, tremblement; *(of flesh)* palpitation *f*, frémissement; **with a q. in one's voice** d'une voix frémissante *ou* mal assurée
VI *(of person)* trembler, frémir, frissonner; *(of leaves, lips)* frémir, trembler; *(of voice, light)* trembloter; *(of flesh)* palpiter, frémir; **to q. with fear** trembler de peur; **voice quivering with emotion** voix vibrante d'émotion
VT *(of bird)* **to q. its wings** agiter ses ailes

quiver[2] **N** *(arrow holder)* carquois *m*; *esp Lit Fig* **to have an arrow** *or* **a shaft left in one's q.** n'être pas à bout de ressources

quivering ['kwɪvərɪŋ] **ADJ** *(person)* tremblant, frissonnant, frémissant; *(leaves, lips)* frémissant, tremblant; *(flesh)* palpitant, frémissant; **the experience had reduced him to a q. mass** *or* **jelly** l'épreuve l'avait réduit à l'état de loque
N *(of person)* tremblement *m*, frémissement *m*, frissonnement *m*; *(of leaves, lips)* frémissement, tremblement; *(of flesh)* palpitation *f*, frémissement; *(of eyelashes)* battement *m*

qui vive [ki:'vi:v] **N on the q.** sur le qui-vive

Quixote, Don Quixote [dɒn'kwɪksəʊt, -ki:'həʊtɪ] **N** *Liter* Don Quichotte *m*

quixotic [kwɪk'sɒtɪk] **ADJ** *(person)* chimérique; *(plan, idea, character etc)* donquichottesque; *(behaviour)* chimérique, donquichottesque

quixotically [kwɪk'sɒtɪklɪ] **ADV** en Don Quichotte, à la manière de Don Quichotte

quiz [kwɪz] **N 1** *(on radio)* jeu *m* radiophonique; *(on TV)* jeu télévisé; *(in magazine etc)* quiz *m*, questionnaire *m* **2** *(questioning)* interrogatoire *m*; *esp Am Sch* oral
VT **(-zz-)** questionner; *Am Sch (candidate)* faire passer un/l'oral à; **they quizzed me on my political views** ils m'ont interrogé sur mes opinions politiques
▸▸ **q. programme, q. show** *(on radio)* jeu radiophonique; *(on TV)* jeu télévisé

quizmaster ['kwɪzmɑːstər] **N** *Radio, TV etc* animateur, -trice, meneur, -euse de jeu

quizzical ['kwɪzɪk(ə)l] **ADJ** *(look, air)* interrogateur, -trice; *(mocking)* railleur

quizzically ['kwɪzɪk(ə)lɪ] **ADV** d'un air interrogateur; *(mockingly)* d'un air railleur

quod [kwɒd] **N** *Br Sl (prison)* taule *f*; **in q.** en taule

quoin [kɔɪn] **N** *Constr (cornerstone)* pierre *f* d'angle; *(of wall)* coin *m*; *(internal)* encoignure *f*

quoit [kɔɪt] **N** palet *m*; **to play (at) quoits** jouer au palet

quorate ['kwɔːreɪt] **ADJ** *Admin, Fml* **to be q.** être en nombre

Quorn® [kwɔːn] **N** = aliment *m* aux protéines végétales servant de substitut à la viande

quorum ['kwɔːrəm] **N** quorum *m*; **to have a q.** être en nombre; **to form a q.** constituer un quorum

quota ['kwəʊtə] **N** *(stipulated quantity, number)* quota *m*; *(share)* quote-part *f*, *pl* quotes-parts; *Fin* quotité *f*; **import/export quotas** contingents *mpl* *ou* quotas d'importation/d'exportation; **to apportion** *or* **fix quotas for import** déterminer les quotas d'importation; **I've had my q. of bad luck** j'ai eu ma dose *ou* part de malchance; **we've had more than our q. of rain recently** nous avons eu plus que notre quota *ou* dose de pluie dernièrement

▸▸ *Mktg* **q. method** *(of sampling)* méthode *f* des quotas; *Mktg* **q. sample** échantillon *m* par quotas; *Mktg* **q. sampling** échantillonnage *m* par quotas

quotable ['kwəʊtəb(ə)l] **ADJ 1** *(worth quoting)* qui vaut la peine d'être cité, digne d'être cité; *(able to be quoted)* que l'on peut *ou* qu'il est permis de citer; **a very q. phrase** une formule qui vaut la peine d'être citée; **the press find him very q.** les journalistes adorent ses petites phrases **2** *St Exch* cotable

quotation [kwəʊ'teɪʃən] **N 1** *(from author etc)* citation *f* **2** *Com* prix *m*; *(for repair work etc)* devis *m*; *St Exch* cotation *f*, cote *f*, cours *m*, prix; **to ask for a q.** *(for proposed work)* demander un devis; **they gave me a q. of £500** ils m'ont fait un devis de 500 livres; **to seek a share q.** faire une demande d'admission *ou* d'inscription à la cote
▸▸ **q. marks** guillemets *mpl*; **in q. marks** entre guillemets

quote [kwəʊt] **N 1** citation *f*; **a q. from Shakespeare** une citation de Shakespeare **2** **quotes, q. marks** guillemets *mpl*; **in quotes** entre guillemets **3** *Com Fam* = **quotation 2**
VT 1 *(author, passage etc)* citer; *(authority, proof)* alléguer, citer; **he was quoted as saying that …** il aurait dit que …; **she said q. …** et voici exactement ce qu'elle a dit …; **his q. unquote 'friends'** ses amis entre guillemets; **can I q. you on that?** est-ce que je puis vous citer?; **don't q. me (on this) but …** ce n'est pas encore officiel *ou* définitif mais …; **to q. sb as an example** citer qn *ou* en exemple; *Admin, Com* **in reply please q. this number** prière de rappeler ce numéro dans toute correspondance ultérieure **2** *Com (price)* établir, faire; **to q. a price** faire *ou* indiquer un prix; **they quoted me £500 for the work** ils m'ont fait un devis de 500 livres pour ce travail **3** *St Exch (share, expiry)* coter; **stock officially quoted** valeurs *fpl* admises à la cote officielle; **quoted on the Stock Exchange** coté en Bourse; *Br* **quoted company** société *f* cotée en Bourse; **quoted investment** valeur *f* cotée en Bourse; **quoted price** cours *m* inscrit à la cote officielle; **quoted securities** valeurs de Bourse; **quoted share** action *f* cotée, action inscrite à la cote officielle
VI 1 *Com* faire un devis, donner un prix **2** **to q. from a book/an author/memory** citer un livre/un auteur/de mémoire

quoth [kwəʊθ] **VT** *Arch, Hum* **no, q. I** non, dis-je

quotidian [kwɒ'tɪdɪən] **ADJ** *Lit* quotidien

quotient ['kwəʊʃənt] **N** *Math* quotient *m*

qv [kjuː'viː] *(abbr quod vide)* cf

qwerty ['kwɜːtɪ] **N**
▸▸ **q. keyboard** clavier *m* QWERTY

qwertz [kwɜːts] **N**
▸▸ **q. keyboard** clavier *m* QWERTZ

R, r [ɑːr] N *(letter)* R, r *m*; **two r's** deux r; **the three Rs** = la lecture, l'écriture et l'arithmétique *(qui constituent les fondements de l'enseignement primaire)*
ADJ *Am Cin* (*abbr* **Restricted**) interdit aux moins de 17 ans

RA [ɑːˈreɪ] N *Br* (*abbr* **Royal Academy**) = académie *f* royale des beaux-arts

rabbet [ˈræbɪt] N *Carp* feuillure *f*

rabbi [ˈræbaɪ] N *Rel* rabbin *m*; **chief r.** grand rabbin

rabbinic(al) [rəˈbɪnɪk, -ɪk(ə)l] ADJ rabbinique

rabbit [ˈræbɪt] N 1 *(animal, fur)* lapin *m*; *Fig* **they breed like rabbits** ils se reproduisent comme des lapins; **to produce a r. out of a hat** *(of conjuror)* faire sortir un lapin d'un chapeau; *Fig* trouver une solution miracle; **to run like a scared r.** courir *ou* détaler comme un lapin; **young r.** lapereau *m*; **wild r.** lapin de garenne; **I'm fed up with all this r. food** je vais finir par me transformer en lapin avec toutes ces crudités 2 *Culin* lapin *m*; **stewed r.** ragoût *m* de lapin 3 *Sport Old-fashioned (poor performer)* nullard, -arde
▶▶ **r. burrow** terrier *m* (de lapin); *Am* **r. ears** antenne *f* téléscopique; **r. food** aliments *mpl* pour lapins; *Fam Hum Pej (salad, green vegetables)* verdure *f*; **r.'s foot** *(lucky charm)* patte *f* de lapin; **r. hole** terrier de lapin; **r. hutch** clapier *m*, cage *f ou* cabane *f* à lapins; *Br Fam Fig (accommodation)* cage à lapins; **r.'s paw** *(lucky charm)* patte de lapin; **r. punch** coup *m* du lapin; **r. warren** garenne *f*, *Fig* labyrinthe *m*, dédale *m*
▶ **rabbit on** VI *Br Fam (talk)* jacasser, bavasser (**about** à propos de); **what's she rabbiting on about?** qu'est-ce qu'elle raconte *ou* bave?; **do stop rabbitting on** tais-toi un peu

rabbiting [ˈræbɪtɪŋ] N **to go r.** faire la chasse au lapin, chasser le lapin

rabble [ˈræb(ə)l] N 1 *(disorderly mob)* foule *f* 2 *Pol Old-fashioned Pej (lower classes)* **the r.** la populace, la canaille

rabble-rouser [-raʊzər] N agitateur, -trice

rabble-rousing N incitation *f* à la révolte
ADJ *(speech)* incendiaire; *(leader)* qui incite à la révolte

Rabelaisian [ræbəˈleɪzɪən] ADJ *(humour etc)* rabelaisien

rabid [ˈræbɪd, ˈreɪ-] ADJ *Vet (dog etc)* enragé; *Fig (socialist etc)* enragé, fanatique; *(hatred)* farouche

rabies [ˈreɪbiːz] N *Med, Vet* rage *f*; **the dog is a r. carrier** le chien est porteur de la rage; **r. vaccine** vaccin *m* contre la rage

RAC [ɑːreɪˈsiː] N *Br Aut* (*abbr* **Royal Automobile Club**) ≃ Touring-Club *m*

raccoon [rəˈkuːn] N *(animal)* raton *m* laveur; **r. skin hat** toque *f* en raton laveur

race¹ [reɪs] N 1 *Sport* course *f*; **a hundred metres r.** une course sur cent mètres, un cent mètres; **it's anybody's r.** il n'y a pas de favori; *Sport, Fig* **a r. against time** une course contre la montre; *Horseracing* **the races** les courses; **to go to the races** aller aux courses; **he loves the races** c'est un passionné des courses
2 *(channel for water)* canal *m*; **mill r.** bief *m* de moulin
3 *(tide)* raz *m*
VI 1 *(move quickly) (of person, animal)* courir à toute vitesse, galoper; **to r. by** *(of time)* filer; **the weekend just raced by** le weekend a passé très vite; **to r. for a bus/train** courir *ou* galoper pour attraper un bus/train; **to r. down the street** dévaler la rue à toute vitesse; **she raced to answer the door** elle se précipita pour ouvrir la porte; **the ambulance raced to the scene of the accident** l'ambulance fonça sur les lieux de l'accident; **the car was racing along** la voiture allait à toute vitesse; **to r. up the stairs** monter les escaliers quatre à quatre; **he raced through his meal** il a avalé son repas à toute vitesse; **the horse raced towards the winning post** le cheval a foncé vers la ligne d'arrivée; **the work is racing ahead** le travail avance très vite; **the clouds are racing across the sky** les nuages filent dans le ciel
2 *Sport (of cyclist, driver)* participer à une épreuve *ou* à des épreuves de vitesse; *(of jockey)* monter; *(of athlete, horse)* courir; *Horseracing (of owner)* faire courir des chevaux
3 *(of engine)* s'emballer
4 *(of pulse)* être rapide; **my heart is racing** mon cœur bat la chamade
VT 1 *(against person, car etc)* faire la course avec; **I'll r. you home!** le premier arrivé à la maison a gagné!; **come on, r. you!** le premier arrivé là-bas!; **he raced me round the block** il a fait la course avec moi autour du pâté de maisons; **the car raced the bus to the traffic lights** la voiture a fait la course avec le bus pour arriver la première aux feux
2 *(enter for race) (horse)* faire courir; **to r. pigeons** faire des courses de pigeons
3 *(transport quickly)* **he raced me to the airport** il m'a emmené à l'aéroport à toute vitesse
4 *Aut (engine)* emballer
▶▶ *Am* **r. car** voiture *f* de course; *Horseracing* **r. card** programme *m* (des courses); *Am* **r. driver** pilote *m* de course; *Horseracing* **r. meeting** courses; **there's a r. meeting at Newmarket tomorrow** on court *ou* il y a des courses demain à Newmarket

race² N *(species)* race *f*; **the human r.** la race humaine
▶▶ **r. relations** relations *fpl* interraciales; **r. riot** émeute *f* raciale

racecourse [ˈreɪskɔːs] N champ *m* de courses, hippodrome *m*, turf *m*

racegoer [ˈreɪsɡəʊər] N turfiste *mf*

racehorse [ˈreɪshɔːs] N cheval *m* de course

raceme [rəˈsiːm] N *Bot* grappe *f*

racer [ˈreɪsər] N *(person)* coureur, -euse; *(horse, bicycle, car, motorcycle)* cheval *m*/vélo *m*/voiture *f*/moto *f* de course; *(yacht)* yacht *m* de course, racer *m*

racetrack [ˈreɪstræk] N *(for cars)* circuit *m*; *(for bikes)* piste *f*; *Horseracing* champ *m* de courses, hippodrome *m*

raceway [ˈreɪsweɪ] N 1 *(channel for water)* canal *m* 2 *esp Am Elec* conduite *f* pour câbles 3 *(car racing)* circuit *m* 4 *esp Am Horseracing* champ *m* de courses, hippodrome *m* 5 *esp Am Tech (for ball bearings)* chemin *m* de roulement à billes

racial [ˈreɪʃəl] ADJ 1 *(concerning a race)* racial, -aux, ethnique 2 *(between races)* racial, -aux
▶▶ **r. discrimination** discrimination *f* raciale; **r. violence** violence *f* raciale

racialism [ˈreɪʃəlɪz(ə)m] N racisme *m*

racialist [ˈreɪʃəlɪst] ADJ, N raciste *mf*

racially [ˈreɪʃəlɪ] ADV **r. biased policy** politique *f* de discrimination raciale; **they were r. discriminated against** ils ont souffert de discrimination raciale; **a r. slanted article** un article à tendance raciste

raciness [ˈreɪsɪnɪs] N 1 *(liveliness) (of writing, style)* verve *f* 2 *(suggestiveness) (of story, joke)* grivoiserie *f*

racing [ˈreɪsɪŋ] N *Sport* course *f*; *Horseracing* courses *fpl* (de chevaux), hippisme *m*, turf *m*; **motor r.** course automobile
ADJ 1 *Fig* **it's a r. certainty** c'est certain, c'est une certitude; **if anyone is a r. certainty for divorce, it's them!** s'il y a un couple qui est sûr de divorcer, c'est (bien) eux 2 **r. pulse** pouls *m* élevé; **a r. heart may be a warning sign of a heart attack** avoir des palpitations peut être le signal avant-coureur d'une crise cardiaque
▶▶ **r. bicycle** vélo *m* de course; **r. car** voiture *f* de course; *Horseracing.* **r. colours** couleurs *fpl* de l'écurie; **r. driver** coureur, -euse automobile, pilote *m* (de course); **r. man** turfiste *m*; **r. pigeon** pigeon *m* voyageur *(de compétition)*; **r. stable** écurie *f* de courses; **r. tip** pronostic *m*

racism [ˈreɪsɪz(ə)m] N racisme *m*

racist [ˈreɪsɪst] ADJ, N raciste *mf*

rack¹ [ræk] N **to be going to r. and ruin** *(of country, company)* courir à la ruine; *(of house etc)* se délabrer, tomber en ruines; *(of health, economy, business)* aller de mal en pis; **this country/the economy/this house has gone to r. and ruin** ce pays/l'économie/la maison est dans un état lamentable

rack² N 1 *(for hay etc)* râtelier *m*; *(sectioned)* casier *m*; *(set of shelves)* étagère *f*, *(bicycle)* support *m ou* râtelier à vélos; **(bottle) r.** casier à bouteilles; **(display) r.** présentoir *m*; **(luggage) r.** porte-bagages *m inv* 2 *Hist (for torture)* chevalet *m* (de torture); *Fig* **to be on**

the r. être au supplice; **to keep sb on the r., to have sb on the r.** mettre qn au supplice **3** *Comput* châssis *m*; *Tech* crémaillère *f* **4** *Culin* **r. of lamb** carré *m* d'agneau **5** *Am Fam* **to hit the r.** (*go to bed*) se pieuter, se bâcher
VT (*person*) (*of disease, pain, guilt etc*) tourmenter, torturer, faire souffrir le martyre à; **to be racked with pain** être perclus de douleur; **to be racked by doubts** être en proie au doute; **to be racked by guilt** être tourmenté par un sentiment de culpabilité; **her body was racked with sobs** son corps était secoué de sanglots; **to r. one's brains** se creuser la tête *ou Fam* les méninges
▸▸ **r. and pinion** crémaillère *f*; **r. and pinion railway** chemin *m* de fer à crémaillère; **r. railway** chemin de fer à crémaillère; **r. rate** (*in hotel*) plein tarif *m*; **r. slip** fiche *f* de réservation
▸ **rack back** VT SEP *Am Fam* **to r. sb back** passer un savon à qn, remonter les bretelles à qn
▸ **rack up** VT SEP *Sport etc* (*points*) accumuler

racket¹ ['rækɪt] N (*bat*) raquette *f*; **rackets** (*game*) jeu *m* de paume
▸▸ *Sport* **r. cover** housse *f* de raquette; *Sport* **r. press** presse-raquette *m inv*, presse *f*

racket² N *Fam* **1** (*noise*) vacarme *m*, tintamarre *m*, *Fam* boucan *m*; **to make a r.** faire du tapage *ou* du vacarme *ou Fam* du boucan; **will you turn that r. off!** arrêtez ce vacarme! **2** (*criminal activity*) escroquerie *f*, racket *m*; **it's a r.** c'est du racket *ou de* l'escroquerie *ou du* vol; **this lottery is such a r.** cette loterie, c'est de l'arnaque; **he's involved in some money-laundering r.** il trempe dans des affaires de blanchiment d'argent **3** *Hum* (*occupation*) métier *m*; **how did you get into this r.?** comment est-ce que tu es arrivé dans cette branche?; **the teaching r.** le métier d'enseignant

racketeer [rækɪ'tɪər] N racketter *m*, racketteur, -euse

racketeering [rækɪ'tɪərɪŋ] N racket *m*

racking ['rækɪŋ] ADJ (*pain etc*) atroce; (*doubts, guilt*) affreux

rack-rent N loyer *m* excessif *ou* exorbitant

racoon [rə'ku:n] N = **raccoon**

racquet ['rækɪt] N = **racket¹**

racy ['reɪsɪ] ADJ **1** (*lively*) (*description, writing*) piquant **2** (*person*) plein de vie, très vivant; (*style*) plein de verve **3** (*suggestive*) (*story, joke*) osé

rad 1 (*abbr radiation*) (*unit*) rd *f* **2** *esp Am* (*abbr radiator*) radiateur *m*

RADA ['rɑːdə] N *Br* (*abbr* **Royal Academy of Dramatic Art**) = Conservatoire *m* national d'art dramatique

radar ['reɪdɑ:r] N radar *m*; **ground r.** radar au sol
▸▸ **r. detection** détection *f* radar; **r. gun** radar gun *m*; **r. operator** radariste *mf*, opérateur, -trice radar; **r. screen** écran *m* (de) radar; **r. speed trap** contrôle *m* radar; **r. station** station *f* radar; **r. trap** contrôle radar

raddled ['rædəld] ADJ (*face*) (*worn-out*) ravagé; (*over made-up*) peinturluré

radial ['reɪdɪəl] ADJ **1** *Tech, Math* radial, -aux **2** *Anat* (*artery etc*) radial, -aux
N **1** (*tyre*) pneu *m* radial *ou* à carcasse radiale **2** (*line*) rayon *m*
▸▸ **r. engine** moteur *m* en étoile; **r. road** radiale *f*, **r. tyre** pneu radial

radially ['reɪdɪəlɪ] ADV radialement

radiance ['reɪdɪəns] N (*of light, sun*) rayonnement *m*, éclat *m*; (*of beauty, smile*) éclat

radiant ['reɪdɪənt] ADJ **1** (*light, sun*) éclatant **2** (*beauty, smile*) radieux, rayonnant; **a woman of r. beauty** une femme d'une beauté éblouissante; **the bride was r.** la mariée était radieuse *ou* rayonnante; **to be r. with joy** rayonner de joie

N **1** *Phys* point *m* radiant **2** (*of heater*) foyer *m* de rayonnement **3** *Astron* radiant *m*
▸▸ *Phys* **r. energy** énergie *f* de rayonnement; *Phys* **r. heat** chaleur *f* rayonnante; **r. heating** chauffage *m* par rayonnement; **r. point** point radiant

radiantly ['reɪdɪəntlɪ] ADV radieusement; **to be r. beautiful** être rayonnant de beauté; **she smiled r.** elle eut un sourire radieux; **r. happy** rayonnant de bonheur

radiate ['reɪdɪeɪt] VI (*of heat, light*), *Med* (*of pain*) rayonner, irradier
VT (*heat, light*) émettre; **to r. happiness** rayonner de bonheur

radiation [reɪdɪ'eɪʃən] N **1** (*radioactivity*) radiation *f*; **to be exposed to r.** être exposé à des radiations **2** (*heat*) rayonnement *m* **3** (*light*) irradiation *f*, **ultraviolet r.** rayons *mpl* ultraviolets
▸▸ **r. sickness** mal *m* des rayons; **r. therapy** radiothérapie *f*

radiator ['reɪdɪeɪtər] N **1** (*for heating*) radiateur *m* **2** *Aut* radiateur *m*
▸▸ *Aut* **r. cap** bouchon *m* du radiateur; *Aut* **r. core** faisceau *m* de radiateur; *Aut* **r. grille** calandre *f*, *Aut* **r. matrix** faisceau de radiateur

radical ['rædɪk(ə)l] ADJ **1** (*opinion, policy etc*) radical, -aux; **to make a r. alteration in sth** changer qch radicalement **2** *Ling, Math, Bot* radical, -aux
N **1** *Pol* radical, -ale **2** *Chem, Ling, Math* radical *m*
▸▸ **r. chic** ≃ socialisme *m* de salon

radicalism ['rædɪkəlɪz(ə)m] N *Pol* radicalisme *m*

radicalize ['rædɪkəlaɪz] VT radicaliser

radically ['rædɪklɪ] ADV radicalement

radicle ['rædɪk(ə)l] N **1** *Bot* (*embryo*) radicule *f*, (*root*) radicelle *f* **2** *Chem* radical *m*

radio ['reɪdɪəʊ] N **1** (*set*) poste *m* (de radio), radio *f*; **to put** *or* **switch** *or* **turn the r. on/off** allumer/éteindre la radio; **she was on the r. last night** elle est passée à la radio hier soir; **R. Moscow** Radio Moscou **2** (*service, system*) French r. radiodiffusion *f* française **3** *Tel* radio(télégraphie) *f*, (*in taxi, ship etc*) radio *f*, **to communicate by r.** communiquer par radio; **to send a message by r.** envoyer un message radio
VT (*information etc*) envoyer par radio; **to r. a person/ship** contacter une personne/un bateau par radio; **to r. one's position** signaler sa position par radio
VI **to r. for assistance** *or* **help** demander de l'aide par radio
▸▸ *Mktg* **r. advertising** publicité *f* à la radio; **r. alarm** radio-réveil *m*, *pl* radio-réveils; **r. announcer** speaker, -trice de radio; **r. astronomy** radioastronomie *f*, **r. beacon** radiobalise *f*; **r. broadcast** émission *f* de radio; **r. broadcasting** radiodiffusion *f*, **r. bulletin** bulletin *m* radiophonique; **r. button** bouton *m* radio, bouton d'option; **r. car** voiture *f* radio; **r. cassette** radiocassette *f*, **r. communication** contact *m* radio, liaison *f* radio, radiocommunications *fpl*; **r. data system** (*for motorists*) système *m* radio de transmission de données; **r. drama** pièce *f* radiophonique; **r. engineer** ingénieur *m* radio; **r. frequency** fréquence *f* radioélectrique, radiofréquence *f*; **r. ham** radioamateur *m*; **r. journalism** journalisme *m* de radio; **r. journalist** journaliste *mf* de radio; *Tel* **r. link** liaison radio; **r. listener** auditeur, -trice; **r. mast** antenne *f* (radio); **r. message** message *m* radio; **r. microphone** microphone *m* sans fil; **r. navigation** radionavigation *f*, **r. officer** radionavigant *m*; **r. operator** (*on plane*) radio; (*on ship*) radionavigant *m*; **r. play** pièce radiophonique; **r. producer** producteur, -trice d'émissions de radio; **r. programme** programme *m* radiodiffusé *ou* radiophonique, émission de radio; **r. receiver** radiorécepteur *m*; **r. reporter** reporter *m* radio; *Naut* **r. room** poste radio de bord; **r. satellite** satellite *m* radio; **r. set** poste (de radio), radio *f*; **r. signal** signal *m* radiophonique; **r. spectrum** spectre *m* radio *ou* radioélectrique *ou* des fréquences radioélectriques; **r. station** station *f* de radio; **r. taxi** radio-taxi *m*, *pl* radio-taxis; **r. telescope** radiotélescope *m*; **r. transmitter** (poste) émetteur *m* radio; **r. vehicle** véhicule *m* radio; **r. waves** ondes *fpl* hertziennes, ondes radio

Radio
Les principales stations de radio de la BBC sont: Radio 1 (bulletins d'information, musique pop et rock); Radio 2 (variétés); Radio 3 (musique classique); Radio 4 (actualités, reportages, théâtre, programmes éducatifs); Radio 5 Live (sports, reportages éducatifs, musique pop et rock). La BBC comprend également trente-neuf stations locales. Il existe d'autre part plus de cent stations indépendantes.

radioactive [reɪdɪəʊ'æktɪv] ADJ (*substance, material*) radioactif
▸▸ **r. dust** poussières *fpl* radioactives; **r. fallout** retombées *fpl* radioactives; **r. waste** déchets *mpl* radioactifs *ou* nucléaires

radioactivity [reɪdɪəʊæk'tɪvɪtɪ] N radioactivité *f*

radiocarbon [reɪdɪəʊ'kɑːbən] N radiocarbone *m*, carbone *m* 14
▸▸ **r. dating** datation *f* au carbone 14

radio-controlled ADJ télécommandé

radiogram ['reɪdɪəʊgræm] N **1** *Br Old-fashioned* (*radio and record player*) = meuble *m* qui incorpore un poste de radio et un pick-up **2** *Radio* (*message*) radiogramme *m*, radiotélégramme *m* **3** *Med* = **radiograph**

radiograph ['reɪdɪəʊgrɑːf] N *Med* radiographie *f*

radiographer [reɪdɪ'ɒgrəfər] N *Med* radiologue *mf*

radiographic [reɪdɪəʊ'græfɪk] ADJ *Med* radiographique

radiography [reɪdɪ'ɒgrəfɪ] N *Med etc* radiographie *f*

radioisotope [reɪdɪəʊ'aɪsətəʊp] N radioisotope *m*, *pl* radio-isotopes

radiological [reɪdɪəʊ'lɒdʒɪk(ə)l] ADJ radiologique

radiologist [reɪdɪ'ɒlədʒɪst] N radiologue *mf*

radiology [reɪdɪ'ɒlədʒɪ] N radiologie *f*

radio-pager N récepteur *m* d'appel *ou* de poche

radioscopic [reɪdɪəʊ'skɒpɪk] ADJ *Med* radioscopique

radioscopy [reɪdɪ'ɒskəpɪ] N *Med* radioscopie *f*

radiotelegram [reɪdɪəʊ'telɪgræm] N radiotélégramme *m*, radiogramme *m*, *Fam* radio *m*

radiotelephone [reɪdɪəʊ'telɪfəʊn] N radiotéléphone *m*

radiotelephony [reɪdɪəʊtɪ'lefənɪ] N radiotéléphonie *f*, *Old-fashioned* téléphonie *f* sans fil, TSF *f*

radiotherapist [reɪdɪəʊ'θerəpɪst] N radiothérapeute *mf*

radiotherapy [reɪdɪəʊ'θerəpɪ] N radiothérapie *f*

radish ['rædɪʃ] N radis *m*

radium ['reɪdɪəm] N *Chem* radium *m*
▸▸ **r. treatment** curiethérapie *f*

radius, *pl* **radii** ['reɪdɪəs, -ɪaɪ] N **1** (*of circle*) rayon *m*; *Aviat* rayon (d'action), autonomie *f*; **within a r. of ten miles** dans un rayon de seize kilomètres **2** *(of crane)* portée *f* **3** *Anat (bone)* radius *m*

radix, *pl* **radices** ['reɪdɪks, -ɪsiːz] N **1** *Math (in logarithms etc)* base *f* **2** *Ling* radical *m*

radon ['reɪdɒn] N *Chem* radon *m*

RAF [ɑːreɪ'ef] N *Br Mil (abbr* **Royal Air Force)** Armée *f* de l'air britannique

raffia ['ræfɪə] N *Bot* raphia *m*
 ▸▸ **r. mat** tapis *m* en raphia

raffish ['ræfɪʃ] ADJ dissolu; *(look)* canaille

raffle ['ræf(ə)l] N tombola *f*; **I won it in a r.** je l'ai gagné dans une tombola
 VT **to r. (off)** mettre en tombola
 ▸▸ **r. ticket** billet *m* de tombola

raft [rɑːft] N **1** radeau *m*; **(inflatable) life r.** canot *m* (pneumatique) de sauvetage **2** *(in logging)* timber r., *Am* lumber r. train *m* de bois *ou* de flottage **3** *Fam (large quantity)* **I have a r. of papers on my desk** j'ai une montagne de papiers sur mon bureau; **a r. of new measures** un paquet de nouvelles mesures
 VT *(wood)* flotter en trains; **they rafted the logs to the paper mill** ils ont flotté les troncs jusqu'à la papeterie
 VI **to r. across the river** traverser le fleuve sur un radeau

rafter ['rɑːftər] N *Constr* chevron *m*; **main r.** arbalétrier *m*; **the rafters** le chevronnage

rafting ['rɑːftɪŋ] N *Sport* rafting *m*

rag¹ [ræg] N **1** *(piece of cloth)* chiffon *m*; *Fig* **to feel like a wet r.** être lessivé *ou* ramollo *ou* vidé; *Fig Fam* **to lose the** *or* **one's r.** sortir de ses gonds; *Sl* **to be on the r.** *(menstruating)* avoir ses ragnagnas **2** *(old garment)* guenille *f*, **rags** haillons *mpl*, guenilles, loques *fpl*; **to be in rags** être en guenilles *ou* en haillons; **to go from rags to riches** passer de la pauvreté à la richesse; **a rags to riches story** l'histoire d'une réussite sociale fulgurante **3** *Fam Pej (newspaper)* feuille *f* de chou, torchon *m*; **you don't read that r., do you?** tu ne lis pas ce torchon quand même?; **the local r.** le journal du coin
 ▸▸ **r. book** livre *m* en tissu; **r. content** *(of paper)* pourcentage *m* de peille; **r. doll** poupée *f* de chiffon; **r. paper** papier *m* à base de peille; **r. picker** chiffonnier, -ière; **r. rug** catalogne *f*, *Fam* **r. trade** confection *f*; **he's in the r. trade** il est *ou* travaille dans les fringues

rag² VT (-gg-) *Br (tease)* taquiner (**about** sur); *Sch (teacher etc)* chahuter, asticoter, *Fam* mettre en boîte; **to r. sb mercilessly** asticoter qn sans arrêt
 N *Br Old-fashioned (joking etc)* blague *f*, farce *f*, **I did it for** *or* **as a r.** je l'ai fait pour blaguer, c'était une blague
 ▸▸ **r. week** = semaine *f* annuelle du calendrier universitaire où les étudiants organisent des kermesses dont les bénéfices vont à des œuvres de charité

raga ['rɑːgə] N *Mus* raga *m*

ragamuffin ['rægəmʌfɪn] N *(child)* gamin *m* des rues; **you little r.!** petit polisson!

rag-and-bone ADJ
 ▸▸ *Br* **r. man** chiffonnier *m*

ragbag ['rægbæg] N *(jumble) (of things, ideas etc)* fatras *m*, ensemble *m* hétéroclite; **they were a r. team** ils formaient une équipe hétéroclite; **this file's just a r.** ce fichier, c'est un fourre-tout

rage [reɪdʒ] N **1** *(of person)* colère *f*, fureur *f*, rage *f*, **to be in a r.** être furieux *ou* fou de rage; **to get** *or* **fly into a r.** se mettre en colère, piquer une colère; **to have a fit of r.** avoir un accès de fureur; **to weep with r.** pleurer de rage **2** *Fam* **to be all the r.** *(of dance, music etc)* faire fureur, être la grande mode

VI **1** *(of person)* être furieux, rager; **to r. against** *or* **at sb/sth** être furieux *ou* tempêter contre qn/qch **2** *(of river, ocean)* être déchaîné *ou* démonté; *(of epidemic, war)* régner, sévir; *(of battle, fire, storm)* faire rage; *(of wind)* souffler en tempête

ragga ['rægə] N *Mus* ragga *m*

ragged ['rægɪd] ADJ *(garment etc)* en lambeaux, en loques; *(person)* en haillons, en guenilles, déguenillé; **a shirt with r. cuffs** une chemise aux poignets élimés; **she was beginning to look rather r.** elle commençait à avoir l'air dépenaillé; *Mus* **the execution is r.** l'exécution manque d'ensemble; *Fam* **to run oneself r.** s'éreinter; **she's run r. with those kids** les gosses l'épuisent; *Typ* **right/left** non-justifié à droite/à gauche; *Typ* **to print sth r.** imprimer qch sans justification
 ▸▸ *Bot* **r. robin** fleur *f* de coucou *(lychnis)*

ragging ['rægɪŋ] N *(teasing)* taquineries *fpl*; **to give sb a r.** mettre qn en boîte, taquiner qn; **he took a lot of r.** on l'a beaucoup taquiné

raggle-taggle ['ræg(ə)l'tæg(ə)l] ADJ *(army etc)* hétéroclite

raghead ['ræghed] N *Am Fam (Arab)* raton *m*, bicot *m*; *(gypsy)* romanichel, -elle

raging ['reɪdʒɪŋ] ADJ *(person)* furieux, en colère; *(fever)* très fort; *(thirst)* terrible; *(sea)* déchaîné, démonté; *(storm, wind)* déchaîné; **I had a r. headache** j'avais affreusement mal à la tête; **to be in a r. temper** être furieux; **r. toothache** rage *f* de dents
 N *(of person)* colère *f*, fureur *f*, rage *f*; *(of sea, wind)* fureur

raglan ['ræglən] N *(coat)* raglan *m*
 ADJ raglan *inv*
 ▸▸ **r. coat** (manteau *m*) raglan; **r. sleeves** manches *fpl* raglan; **r. sweater** pull *m* raglan

ragman, *pl* **ragmen** ['rægmən] N chiffonnier *m*

ragout [ræ'guː] N *Culin* ragoût *m*

rag-roll VT *(wall etc)* = appliquer de la peinture (sur un mur etc) à l'aide d'un chiffon

ragtag ['rægtæg] N **the r. and bobtail** la racaille
 ADJ hétéroclite

ragtime ['rægtaɪm] N *Mus* ragtime *m*

ragtop ['rægtɒp] N *Am Fam* décapotable *f*

ragweed ['rægwiːd] N *Bot* herbe *f* à poux

ragwort ['rægwɜːt] N *Bot* séneçon *m*, *Fam* herbe *f* de saint-Jacques

rah-rah ['rɑːrɑː] ADJ *Am* enthousiaste; *Fig* **he's very r. about the President** c'est un fervent admirateur du Président

raid [reɪd] N *(on bank etc)* hold-up *m inv*; *Fam* braquage *m*; *(by police)* descente *f*, *St Exch* raid *m*; *Mil, Aviat* raid *m*; *Mil, Aviat* **daylight/night r.** attaque *f* (aérienne) de jour/de nuit
 VT *(attack) (bank, post office)* attaquer, *Fam* braquer; *(bar, club etc) (of police)* faire une descente dans; *Mil* faire un raid *ou* des raids dans; *Aviat* faire un raid *ou* des raids sur; **the terrorists raided the presidential palace** les terroristes ont fait un raid sur le palais présidentiel; *Fig* **the children raided the fridge** les enfants ont fait une razzia dans le frigo

raider ['reɪdər] N *St Exch* raider *m*; *(of banks)* voleur, -euse, *Fam* braqueur, -euse de banques; *Mil (boat)* raider *m*; *(plane)* bombardier *m*; *(soldier)* membre *m* d'un commando

rail¹ [reɪl] N **1** *(for protection, support) (of escalator, stairway)* main *f* courante; *(of balcony)* balustrade *f*; *(banister)* rampe *f*, *Naut* lisse *f*
 2 *(for hanging things)* **curtain r.** tringle *f* à rideaux; **picture r.** cimaise *f*, **towel r.** porte-serviettes *m inv*

3 *Rail (track)* rail *m*; **to travel by r.** voyager en train; **to send goods by r.** envoyer des marchandises par chemin de fer
 4 rails *Horseracing* corde *f*, *Naut* bastingage *m*, garde-corps *m inv*, rambarde *f*; **he was pushed to the rails by the other jockeys** il a été forcé de tenir la corde par les autres jockeys; *Rail* **to jump** *or* **leave the rails** dérailler, sortir des rails; *Fig* **to go off the rails** dérailler; *(morally)* s'écarter du droit chemin; **to get the economy back on the rails** remettre l'économie sur les rails; **I did my best to get him back on the rails after his breakdown** j'ai fait de mon mieux pour le remettre sur pieds après sa dépression nerveuse
 ▸▸ **r. network** réseau *m* ferroviaire *ou* de chemin de fer; **r. pass** carte *f* de train; **r. strike** grève *f* des chemins de fer; **r. transport** transport *m* par chemin de fer *ou* par train; **r. worker** employé, -ée des chemins de fer; *(for track, rolling stock)* cheminot *m*
 ▸ **rail against, rail at** VT INSEP *Fml (person)* s'en prendre à; **to r. against fate** s'en prendre au destin
 ▸ **rail in** VT SEP clôturer, entourer d'une clôture
 ▸ **rail off** VT SEP fermer avec une clôture *ou* une barrière; **the path down to the beach was railed off after the accident** le chemin qui mène à la plage a été fermé après l'accident

rail² N *(bird)* râle *m*; **water r.** râle d'eau

railcar ['reɪlkɑːr] N *Am Rail* autorail *m*

railcard ['reɪlkɑːd] N *Br* carte *f* de chemin de fer

railfreight ['reɪlfreɪt] N **to send r.** envoyer par chemin de fer

railhead ['reɪlhed] N *Rail etc* tête *f* de ligne

railing¹ ['reɪlɪŋ] N *(also* **railings) 1** *(barrier) (of metal)* grille *f*, *(of wood)* palissade *f*, **iron railings** grille **2** *(in dangerous place)* garde-fou *m*, *pl* garde-fous, garde-corps *m inv* **3** *(for support) (on staircase)* rampe *f*, *(on balcony)* balustrade *f*

railing² N *(complaints)* invectives *fpl* (**at, against** contre)

raillery ['reɪlərɪ] N *(teasing)* raillerie *f*

railman, *pl* **railmen** ['reɪlmən] N = **railway-man**

railroad ['reɪlrəʊd] N *Am (system)* chemin *m* de fer; *(track)* voie *f* ferrée; **to travel by r.** voyager en chemin de fer
 VT **1** *Fam (force acceptance of)* **to r. a bill through Parliament** imposer un projet de loi au Parlement **2** *Fam (force into action)* **to r. sb into doing sth** faire pression sur qn pour qu'il fasse qch; **to be railroaded into doing sth** être forcé à faire qch; **I don't want to r. you, but …** je ne voudrais pas te forcer mais …; **she was railroaded into this job** on a fait pression sur elle pour qu'elle prenne ce poste **3** *esp Am Law Fam (convict by false charges)* condamner à l'aide de fausses inculpations; *(hastily)* juger sommairement **4** *Am (transport)* transporter par chemin de fer
 ▸▸ *Am* **r. apartment** = appartement *m* dont les pièces sont en enfilade; **r. car** wagon *m*

railway ['reɪlweɪ] N *Br, Can (system)* chemin *m* de fer; *(track)* voie *f* ferrée; **to travel by r.** voyager en chemin de fer; **to work on the railway(s)** être employé des chemins de fer; **Canadian National Railways** Chemins de fer nationaux du Canada
 ▸▸ **r. bridge** pont *m* ferroviaire; **r. carriage** wagon *m*, voiture *f*, **r. company** société *f* des chemins de fer; **r. crossing** passage *m* à niveau; **r. cutting** traversée *f* en déblai; **r. embankment** remblai *m*; **r. engine** locomotive *f*, **r. engineer** ingénieur *m* des chemins de fer; **r. guide** indicateur *m* des chemins de fer; **r. line** *(route)* ligne *f* de chemin de fer; *(track)* voie ferrée; *(rail)* rail *m*; **r. network**

réseau *m* ferroviaire *ou* de chemin de fer; **r. signal** signal *m* ferroviaire; **r. station** gare *f* (de chemin de fer); *(in France)* gare SNCF; **r. strike** grève *f* des chemins de fer; **r. system** réseau ferroviaire *ou* de chemin de fer; **r. ticket** billet *m* de train; **r. timetable** horaires *mpl* des chemins de fer; *(printed)* fiche *f* horaire; **r. track** voie ferrée; **r. worker** employé, -ée des chemins de fer; *(for track, rolling stock)* cheminot *m*; **r. yard** dépôt *m*

railwayman, *pl* **railwaymen** ['reɪlweɪmən] N *Br, Can (administrative employee)* employé, -ée des chemins de fer; *(technical employee)* cheminot *m*; *Br Formerly* **National Union of Railwaymen** = syndicat *m* des employés de chemins de fer de Grande-Bretagne

raiment ['reɪmənt] N *Arch, Lit* vêtements *mpl*, habits *mpl*

rain [reɪn] N **1** pluie *f*; **in the r.** sous la pluie; **it looks like r.** on dirait qu'il va pleuvoir, le temps est à la pluie; *Br* **it's pouring with r.** il pleut à verse, il pleut des cordes; **they had some r. during their holiday** ils ont eu de la pluie pendant leurs vacances; **a river swollen with r., a r.-swollen river** une rivière gonflée par les pluies; **the rains** la saison des pluies; **(come) r. or shine** *(whatever the weather)* qu'il pleuve ou qu'il vente; *(whatever the circumstances)* quoiqu'il arrive; *Br Fam* **two days in bed and you'll be as right as r.** deux jours au lit et tu seras remis; *Fig* **he doesn't have the sense to come in out of the r.** il n'a pas inventé le fil à couper le beurre; **driving/fine r.** pluie battante/fine; **freezing r.** pluie verglaçante; **heavy r.** forte *ou* grosse pluie; **light r.** pluie fine

2 *Fig (large quantity) (of abuse, blows etc)* pluie *f*, avalanche *f*

V IMPERS pleuvoir; **it rains/is raining** il pleut; **it is raining hard** il pleut à verse; *Br Fam* **it's raining cats and dogs** il tombe des cordes, il pleut comme vache qui pisse; *Prov* **it never rains but it pours** un malheur ne vient jamais seul

VI *(of abuse, blows etc)* pleuvoir **(on** sur**)**

VT **to r. gifts/flowers on sb** couvrir qn de cadeaux/fleurs; **to r. blows on sb** rouer qn de coups

▸ ▸ *Geog* **r. belt** zone *f* des pluies; **r. cape** pèlerine *f*; *Am* **r. check** = bon *m* pour un autre match (ou spectacle) donné par suite d'une annulation à cause de la pluie; *Fam Fig* **I'll take a r. check on that** ça sera pour une autre fois; **r. cloud** nuage *m* de pluie; **r. dance** danse *f* de la pluie; **r. gauge** pluviomètre *m*; **r. hat** capuche *f*, **r. hood** capuche; *(attached to anorak, jacket etc)* capuchon *m*, capuche; **r. shower** averse *f*

▸ **rain down** VI = **rain** VI

VT SEP = **rain** VT

▸ **rain off** VT SEP *Br Sport etc* **to be rained off** *(of match etc)* être annulé à cause du mauvais temps

▸ **rain out** VT SEP *Am* = **rain off**

rainbow ['reɪnbəʊ] N arc-en-ciel *m*, *pl* arcs-en-ciel; **all the colours of the r.** toutes les couleurs de l'arc-en-ciel; **a dress in all the colours of the r.** une robe arc-en-ciel; *Fig* **to chase rainbows** se nourrir d'illusions; **r.-coloured** aux couleurs de l'arc-en-ciel

▸ ▸ *Pol* **r. coalition** = coalition *f* représentant un large éventail de tendances; **r. trout** truite *f* arc-en-ciel

raincoat ['reɪnkəʊt] N imperméable *m*, *Fam* imper *m*

raindrop ['reɪndrɒp] N goutte *f* de pluie

rainfall ['reɪnfɔːl] N *(amount)* précipitations *fpl*; **average r.** précipitations moyennes, taux *m* de pluviosité; **low/high r.** précipitations faibles/importantes

rainforest ['reɪnfɒrɪst] N *(tropical)* **r.** forêt *f* tropicale humide

rainless ['reɪnlɪs] ADJ *(day etc)* sans pluie

rainmaker ['reɪnmeɪkər] N *(magician)* faiseur, -euse de pluie

rainmaking ['reɪnmeɪkɪŋ] ADJ *(ritual etc)* pour faire pleuvoir

rainout ['reɪnaʊt] N *Am Sl* match *m* annulé à cause du mauvais temps

rainproof ['reɪnpruːf] ADJ *(coat, fabric etc)* imperméable

VT *(fabric)* imperméabiliser

rainslicker ['reɪnslɪkə(r)] N *Am* ciré *m*

rainstorm ['reɪnstɔːm] N pluies *fpl* torrentielles

rainwater ['reɪnwɔːtər] N eau *f* de pluie

rainwear ['reɪnweər] N *(clothing)* vêtements *mpl* de pluie

rainy ['reɪnɪ] ADJ *(climate, weather)* pluvieux; **a r. day** un jour de pluie; **it has been very r. recently** il a beaucoup plu récemment; *Fig* **to put something by** *or* **keep something for a r. day** garder une poire pour la soif; *Fig* **she puts by ten pounds a week for a r. day** elle met dix livres de côté par semaine au cas où elle en aurait besoin

▸ ▸ **r. season** saison *f* des pluies

RAISE [reɪz]

> VT lever **1, 6, 13** ▪ soulever **1, 5, 12** ▪ remonter **1** ▪ augmenter **2** ▪ faire monter **2** ▪ élever **8** ▪ cultiver **8**
> N augmentation **1**

VT **1** *(lift, cause to rise)* *(one's hand, eyes, anchor)* lever; *(veil)* relever; *(weight)* lever, soulever; *(blind)* remonter; *(flag)* hisser; *(sunken ship)* renflouer; **to r. a cloud of dust** soulever un nuage de poussière; *Theat* **to r. the curtain** lever le rideau; **to r. an eyebrow** *or* **one's eyebrows** *(in disapproval)* froncer les sourcils, sourciller; *(in surprise)* ouvrir des yeux ronds; **he raised an eyebrow at the news** il eut l'air étonné d'entendre cette nouvelle; **that will r. a few eyebrows** *or* **an eyebrow or two** *(cause surprise)* cela va en surprendre plus d'un; *(cause disapproval)* cela va en faire tiquer plus d'un; **eyebrows were raised yesterday when ...** *(in surprise)* cela en a surpris plus d'un hier quand; *(in disapproval)* la désapprobation s'est lue sur les visages hier quand ...; **to r. one's fist to sb** menacer qn du poing; **to r. one's glass** lever son verre (**to sb** à la santé de qn); **to r. one's glass to one's lips** porter son verre à ses lèvres; **to r. sb's hackles** hérisser qn; **to r. one's hand to sb** lever la main sur qn; **to r. one's hat to sb** soulever son chapeau pour saluer qn; *Fig* tirer son chapeau à qn; **to r. one's head** *(from lowered position)* lever la tête; *(hold erect)* dresser la tête; **to r. a patient to a sitting position** soulever un malade pour l'asseoir; **to r. sb's hopes** donner de l'espoir à qn; **don't r. your hopes too much** n'espère pas trop; *Mil, Fig* **to r. one's sights** viser plus haut; **to r. standards** *(of education, morality)* élever le niveau; *(of cleanliness, safety)* améliorer les conditions; **to r. the standard of living** améliorer le niveau de vie; **to r. sb's spirits** remonter le moral à qn; **to r. the tone** *or* **level of the conversation** élever le niveau de la conversation; **to r. the tone** *or* **level of the neighbourhood** rehausser le prestige du quartier; **to r. the rafters** *(make noise)* faire un foin d'enfer *ou* un boucan de tous les diables; **to r. the roof** *(make noise)* faire un foin d'enfer *ou* un boucan de tous les diables; *(complain)* faire une scène terrible *ou* de tous les diables

2 *(increase in amount)* *(wages, price)* augmenter; *(temperature)* faire monter; **to r. a credit limit** déplafonner un crédit; **to r. production to a maximum** porter la production

au maximum; **to r. the school-leaving age** prolonger la scolarité; **they've raised the age limit to ...** l'âge limite est passé à ...; **to r. the stakes** faire monter les enjeux; **to r. the pass mark** élever le niveau requis; *Fig* **she raised the temperature (of the room) by her condemnation of party policy** les esprits se sont échauffés lorsqu'elle a condamné la politique du parti; *Am* **to r. a cheque** falsifier le montant d'un chèque; *Cards* **I'll r. you ten** *(at poker)* plus dix; *Math* **to r. a number to the ninth power** élever un nombre à la puissance neuf

3 *(increase in height)* **to r. (the level of) a wall** rehausser *ou* surélever un mur; **to r. the level of the ground** rehausser le niveau du sol; **to r. the ceiling on wage increases** augmenter le plafond des salaires; **she raised herself to her full height and replied ...** elle se redressa et, de toute sa hauteur, répondit ...

4 *(increase in intensity)* **to r. sb's consciousness (of sth)** *(inform)* sensibiliser qn (à qch); *(emphasize)* faire prendre conscience à qn (de qch); **to r. one's voice** *(speak more loudly)* élever la voix; *(speak in anger)* hausser le ton; **no one raised their voice (to answer** *or* **speak)** personne ne souffla mot

5 *(create, produce)* *(problem, matter for discussion)* soulever (**with** auprès de); *(fears, doubts, distrust)* susciter; *Br* **to r. a cheque** faire un chèque; **to r. an objection** élever *ou* soulever une objection; **to r. a question** *(make query)* poser une question; **his attitude raises certain questions** son attitude pose *ou* soulève *ou* suscite certaines questions; **his attitude raises questions about his loyalty** son attitude remet en question sa loyauté; *Fam* **to r. hell** *or* **a stink** *(complain)* faire une scène terrible *ou* de tous les diables (**about sth** à propos de qch); **to r. a blush/laugh** faire rougir/rire; **to r. a cheer** *(of people)* crier hourra; *(of announcement, speech etc)* soulever des hourras; **to r. a shout** *(of people)* pousser un cri; **to r. a smile** *(in oneself)* esquisser un sourire; *(in others)* provoquer *ou* faire naître un sourire; **to r. a storm of laughter/protest** déclencher *ou* soulever une tempête de rires/protestations; **to r. the alarm** donner *ou* sonner l'alarme; **to r. a loan** *(of government)* émettre *ou* lancer un emprunt; *(of individual)* faire un emprunt (**on** sur); **to r. steam** *(in boiler)* chauffer la chaudière

6 *(collect together)* *(money)* rassembler; **to r. money for charity** mobiliser des fonds pour une œuvre de bienfaisance; **to r. an army** réunir une armée, mettre une armée sur pied; **to r. funds** *(for charity)* *(of volunteers)* collecter des fonds (**for** pour, au profit de); *(for business, government programme)* se procurer des fonds; **to r. signatures** *(for petition)* rassembler des signatures; **how much (money) did you r. on the car when you sold it?** combien est-ce que tu t'es fait sur la vente de la voiture?; **he wanted a new motorbike but couldn't r. the money** il voulait une moto neuve mais il n'a pas pu trouver l'argent nécessaire; **to r. taxes** lever des impôts

7 *(erect)* *(building, barn etc)* construire; *(statue)* ériger (**to** à l'effigie de)

8 *(rear, grow)* *(children)* élever; *(cattle, poultry etc)* élever, faire l'élevage de; *(wheat, vegetables)* cultiver, faire pousser

9 *(promote)* *Mil, Fig* **to r. sb from the ranks** promouvoir qn; *Mil* **to r. sb to the rank of lieutenant** promouvoir qn lieutenant; **to r. sb from the gutter** sortir qn du caniveau; **to r. sb to the peerage** *(give hereditary title to)* anoblir qn; *(give life title to)* conférer à qn un titre de pair

10 *(contact)* *(by telephone)* *(person)* joindre, contacter; *(by radio)* *(ship)* entrer en contact (radio) avec; *Naut* **to r. land** apercevoir la terre

11 *(awaken, rouse)* **to r. Cain** *(make noise)* faire un foin d'enfer *ou* un boucan de tous les diables; *(complain)* faire une scène terrible *ou* de tous les diables; **to r. the devil** *(complain)* faire une scène terrible *ou* de tous les diables; **to r. sb from his/her bed** faire lever qn, sortir qn du lit; **to r. sb from the dead** ressusciter qn; **to r. a ghost** faire apparaître un fantôme; **to r. a spirit** évoquer un esprit

12 *(stir up) (nation)* soulever; *(rebellion)* provoquer

13 *(end) (blockade, embargo, siege)* lever

N 1 *Am (pay increase)* augmentation *f* (de salaire); **to get a r.** être augmenté, avoir une augmentation

2 *Cards (poker)* relance *f*, *(bridge)* enchère *f*

▸ **raise up VT SEP** lever, soulever; **she raised herself up out of her chair** elle se leva de son fauteuil

---

Attention: ne pas confondre avec le verbe **to rise**, qui n'est jamais suivi d'un complément d'objet.

---

raised [reɪzd] **ADJ 1** *(lifted) (arm etc)* levé; **we could hear r. voices from the next room** on entendait des gens qui se disputaient dans la pièce d'à côté; **to say sth in a r. voice** dire qch en haussant le ton **2** *(elevated) (deck, flowerbed)* surélevé; *(embossed) (design, letter, motif)* en relief **3** *Am Culin* au levain

raiser [ˈreɪzər] **N** *(breeder) (of cattle etc)* éleveur, -euse

raisin [ˈreɪz(ə)n] **N** raisin *m* sec
  ▸▸ **r. bread** pain *m* aux raisins *(miche)*

Note that the French word **raisin** is a false friend and is never a translation for the English word **raisin**. It means **grapes**.

---

raising [ˈreɪzɪŋ] **N 1** *(lifting) (of curtain)* lever *m*; *(of sunken ship)* renflouage *m*; *(of standards)* élévation *f* **2** *(of prices, rents, salaries)* augmentation *f*, **r. of the school-leaving age** prolongation *f* de la scolarité **3** *(of army)* levée *f*, *(collecting) (of funds for charity)* collecte *f*; *(of taxes)* levée *f*; *(of money)* mobilisation de fonds **4** *(of barn, building)* construction *f*; *(of monument, statue)* érection *f* **5** *(of animals)* élevage *m*; *(of children)* éducation *f*; *(of crops)* culture *f* **6** *(of blockade, embargo, siege)* levée *f* **7** **r. of the dead** résurrection *f* des morts
  ▸▸ *Culin* **r. agent** levure *f*

Raj [rɑːdʒ] **N** *Hist* **the R.** l'empire *m* britannique en Inde

rajah [ˈrɑːdʒə] **N** ra(d)ja(h) *m*

rake¹ [reɪk] **N 1** *(for gardener, croupier)* râteau *m* **2** *(for grate)* râble *m*, ringard *m*; **as thin as a r.** maigre comme un clou

VT 1 *(collect or level with rake) (leaves, ground, path)* ratisser **2** *Mil (fire on with machine gun) (enemy forces, trenches)* mitrailler **3** *(search) (with eyes) (group, crowd)* détailler minutieusement; *(with searchlights) (sky, sea)* balayer; **to r. one's memory** fouiller dans ses souvenirs

▸ **rake about, rake around VI** *(search)* fouiller (**among, in** dans)

▸ **rake in VT SEP 1** *Fam (money) (acquire)* amasser; **you must be raking it in!** tu dois t'en mettre plein les poches!; **that shop is raking in a fortune** ce magasin ramasse une fortune **2** *(in garden) (compost)* enfouir au râteau; *(in casino) (stakes)* ratisser

▸ **rake off VT SEP 1** *(remove) (pebbles, leaves)* enlever au râteau **2** *Fam (take)* empocher; **he raked off £50** il a empoché 50 livres, il s'est mis 50 livres dans la poche

▸ **rake out VT SEP** *(remove ashes from)* reti-

rer *ou* enlever les cendres de **2** *Fam (find) (scarf, gloves etc)* dégoter, dénicher (**from** dans)

▸ **rake over VT SEP** *(ground)* ratisser; *Fig* **to r. over the ashes** *or* **the past** *(revive)* remuer le passé

▸ **rake through VT INSEP** *(search) (pockets, drawer)* fouiller dans; **the down-and-out was raking through the dustbins** le clochard fouillait dans *ou* faisait les poubelles

▸ **rake up VT SEP 1** *(collect with rake) (leaves)* ratisser **2** *(revive) (fire)* attiser; *Fig* **to r. up an old quarrel** raviver une ancienne querelle; **to r. up the past** remuer le passé; **to r. up sb's past** fouiller dans le passé de qn **3** *Fam (find with difficulty) (money, story etc)* dégoter, dénicher

rake² **N** *(slope) (of aircraft wings, funnel, mast etc)* (angle m d')inclinaison *f*; *(of stage)* pente *f*, inclinaison; **stage with a steep r.** scène fortement inclinée

VI *(of aircraft wings, funnel, mast etc)* être incliné; *(of stage)* être en pente *ou* incliné **VT** *(funnel, mast etc)* incliner; *(stage)* construire en pente; **a steeply raked stage** une scène fortement inclinée

rake³ **N** *Lit (dissolute man)* coureur *m*, débauché *m*, libertin *m*, *Old-fashioned* roué *m*

rake-off **N 1** *Fam (share of profits) (legal)* commission *f*, *(illegal)* ristourne *f*; **what's her r.?** *(legal)* quelle est sa part?; *(illegal)* combien est-ce qu'elle se met dans la poche? **2** *Am (deduction)* rabais *m*, réduction *f* (**on** sur)

raki [rɑːˈkiː, ˈrækɪ] **N** *(drink)* raki *m*

rakish [ˈreɪkɪʃ] **ADJ 1** *Old-fashioned (dissolute) (behaviour, life)* débauché **2** *(jaunty) (air)* cavalier, désinvolte; **to wear one's hat at a r. angle** porter son chapeau avec désinvolture; **r. charm/smile** charme *f*/sourire *m* canaille; *Naut* **a ship built on r. lines** un navire à la forme élancée *ou* effilée

rakishly [ˈreɪkɪʃlɪ] **ADV** d'un air désinvolte

rally [ˈrælɪ] **N 1** *(meeting)* grand rassemblement *m*; *(protest gathering)* manifestation *f* **2** *(improvement) (in health)* amélioration *f* passagère, mieux *m* momentané; *St Exch* redressement *m*, rally *m* **3** *Sport (in tennis etc)* long échange *m* **4** *(car race)* rallye *m*

VT 1 *(unite, win over) (troops, supporters)* rallier; **to r. support for a cause** s'assurer un soutien pour une cause **2** *(recover) (one's strength)* reprendre; **to r. one's spirits** reprendre courage; **to r. sb's spirits** redonner courage à qn

VI 1 *(unite, support)* se rallier (**to, round** à); **to r. for the attack** se regrouper pour attaquer; **to r. round sb** *(help)* venir en aide à qn; **all the neighbours rallied round to help** tous les voisins sont venus apporter leur soutien; **to r. to sb's defence** accourir au secours de qn **2** *(recover) (of shares)* se redresser; *(of patient)* se remettre momentanément; *(of athlete)* se reprendre, se ressaisir; **the pound rallied in the afternoon** la livre est remontée dans l'après-midi; **the market rallied** les cours ont repris **3** *Sport (enter car rallies)* courir *ou* participer à des rallyes; *Tennis* **they've been rallying for five minutes** l'échange dure depuis cinq minutes
  ▸▸ **r. driver** pilote *m* de rallye

rallycross [ˈrælɪkrɒs] **N** *Aut* rallycross *m*

rallyer [ˈrælɪər] **N** *Sport* concurrent, -ente d'un rallye

rallying [ˈrælɪɪŋ] **N 1** *(of troops, supporters)* ralliement *m* **2** *Sport, Aut* rallyes *mpl*; **to go r.** faire un rallye
  ▸▸ **r. cry** cri *m* de ralliement; **r. point** point *m* de ralliement

ralph [rælf] **VI** *Fam (vomit)* gerber, dégueuler

RAM **N 1** [ræm] *Comput (abbr* **random access**

memory)* mémoire *f* vive; **R.-resident** résident en mémoire vive **2** [ˌɑːreɪˈem] *Br (abbr* **Royal Academy of Music**) = Conservatoire *m* national de musique
  ▸▸ *Comput* **R. chip** puce *f* de mémoire vive; *Comput* **R. disk** mémoire à disque

ram [ræm] **N 1** *(animal)* bélier *m*; *(astrological sign)* Bélier **2** *Tech (part of pile driver)* marteau *m*; *(part of hydraulic press)* (piston *m*) plongeur *m*; **(hydraulic) r.** bélier *m* hydraulique **3** *Hum Sl (sexually active man)* viril *m*, macho *m*

VT (-mm-) 1 *(crash into) (of ship) (another ship, submarine)* entrer en collision avec, aborder; *Hist (galleon)* éperonner; *(of car) (tree, lorry)* heurter, percuter; **he rammed the gates with a lorry** *(knocked down)* il a défoncé le portail avec un camion; **he rammed the trolley into my ankles** il m'a heurté les chevilles avec son caddie® **2** *(force into place)* enfoncer (**into** dans)
  ▸▸ *Aut* **r. air** air *m* forcé; *Aut* **r. air induction** introduction *f* d'air par forçage; **r. cylinder** vérin *m*

▸ **ram down VT SEP** *(compact) (earth)* tasser; *Fig* **to r. one's hat down on one's head** enfoncer son chapeau (sur la tête); **she's always ramming religion down my throat** elle me rebat toujours les oreilles avec sa religion

▸ **ram home VT SEP** *(emphasize)* **(the importance of sth)** insister sur; **he kept ramming it home that we should ...** il n'arrêtait pas de répéter que nous devions ...; *Mil* **to r. home a charge** bourrer un canon *ou* un fusil

▸ **ram into VT SEP** *(force)* **to r. clothes into a suitcase** bourrer une valise de vêtements; **to r. a charge into a gun** bourrer un fusil; *Fig* **the teacher rammed the dates into them** le professeur leur enfonçait *ou* leur faisait entrer les dates dans la tête; **to r. food into one's mouth** se gaver

VT INSEP *(collide with)* emboutir, percuter; **a Jag rammed into the back of me** une Jag a embouti l'arrière de ma voiture; **they rammed into each other** ils se sont percutés

▸ **ram through VT SEP** *(force acceptance of) (appointment)* imposer

Ramadan [ˌræməˈdɑːn] **N** *Rel* ramadan *m*; **during R.** pendant le ramadan

ramble [ˈræmb(ə)l] **N** *(walk) (spontaneous)* balade *f*, grande promenade *f*, *(planned)* randonnée *f*; **to go on** *or* **for a r.** *(spontaneously)* faire une balade *ou* une grande promenade; *(planned)* partir en randonnée

VI 1 *(walk) (spontaneously)* se balader, faire une grande promenade (**over, through** dans); *(planned)* faire une randonnée (**over, through** dans) **2** *(talk in disconnected fashion)* parler sans suite, dire n'importe quoi (**about** de) **3** *(be delirious)* divaguer, *Fam* battre la campagne **4** *(meander) (of stream)* serpenter (**through** dans); **there was ivy rambling all over the ruins** le lierre rampait sur les ruines; **the path that rambles through the fields** le chemin sinueux qui traverse les champs

▸ **ramble on VI** tenir des discours sans fin, discourir; **to r. on about nothing in particular** parler pour ne rien dire; **what are you rambling on about now?** qu'est-ce que tu racontes maintenant?

rambler [ˈræmblər] **N 1** *(hiker)* randonneur, -euse **2** *(rose)* rosier *m* grimpant **3** *Am (house)* ranch *m*

rambling [ˈræmblɪŋ] **ADJ 1** *(conversation, letter, speech etc)* décousu **2** *(path, stream etc)* sinueux; **a r. house** une maison pleine de coins et de recoins; **a r. town** une ville construite au hasard

N 1 *(hiking)* randonnées *fpl*; **to go r.** partir en randonnée **2 ramblings** *(delirium)* divagations *fpl*; **the ramblings of old age**

les radotages *mpl* de la vieillesse
▶▶ **r. rose** rosier *m* sarmenteux

rambunctious [ræm'bʌŋkʃəs] **ADJ** *Am Fam*
1 *(boisterous)* *(behaviour, child)* turbulent,
chahuteur, -euse, tapageur **2** *(noisy)* *(meeting)* bruyant, mouvementé; *(party)* bruyant

RAMC [ɑːreɪem'siː] **N** *Br Mil* (*abbr* **Royal Army Medical Corps**) ≃ service *m* de santé de
l'armée

ramee ['ræmɪ] **N** *Tex* = **ramie**

ramekin, ramequin ['ræmɪkɪn] **N** *Culin* ramequin *m*

ramie ['ræmɪ] **N** *Tex* ramie *f*

ramification [ræmɪfɪ'keɪʃən] **N** ramification *f*

ramify ['ræmɪfaɪ] **VT** ramifier
VI se ramifier

ramjet ['ræmdʒet] **N** *Aviat (engine)* statoréacteur *m*, tuyère *f* thermopropulsive; *(aircraft)*
avion *m* à statoréacteur
▶▶ **r. engine** statoréacteur, tuyère thermopropulsive

rammer ['ræmər] **N** *(for road-making)* dame
f, *(for metal-working)* fouloir *m*, batte *f*, *(for civil engineering)* engin *m* de compactage
du sol

ramp [ræmp] **N 1** *(slope)* rampe *f* **2** *Aut (in garage)* pont *m* élévateur; *(connecting road)*
bretelle *f* (d'accès); *(bump on road)* dos *m*
d'âne; *(difference in level)* dénivellation *f*, dénivellement *m*; *(to slow traffic down)* ralentisseur *m*; *Aviat* **boarding r.** passerelle *f*

rampage¹ ['ræmpeɪdʒ] **N** *Fam* **to be** *or* **go on the r.** *(lose control)* se déchaîner; *(cause damage)* tout saccager; *Hum* **the boss is on the r.** le patron est complètement déchaîné; **the hooligans went on a r.** les hooligans ont tout saccagé sur leur passage

rampage² [ræm'peɪdʒ] **VI to r. (about** *or*
around) se déchaîner; **they were rampaging through the streets** ils saccageaient
tout dans les rues

rampaging [ræm'peɪdʒɪŋ] **ADJ** *(bulls, protestors etc)* déchaîné

rampancy ['ræmpənsɪ] **N** *(of corruption, vice)* prolifération *f*, *(of plant)* exubérance *f*

rampant ['ræmpənt] **ADJ 1** *(corruption, poverty, vice)* qui sévit, endémique; *(plant)* exubérant, luxuriant; **to be r.** *(of corruption etc)*
régner, sévir; *Fam* **he's a bit r. tonight** *(sexually)* il est émoustillé ce soir; **r. inflation** inflation *f* galopante **2** *Her* rampant; **the Lion R.** le Lion rampant

rampart ['ræmpɑːt] **N** *(fortification)*, *Fig* rempart *m*

ram-raid **VT to r. a shop** = dévaliser un magasin après en avoir brisé la vitrine à l'aide
d'un véhicule

ramrod ['ræmrɒd] **N** *(for cleaning rifle)* écouvillon *m*; *(for loading cannon)* refouloir *m*; **to be as stiff as a r.** être raide comme un piquet; **to sit as straight as a r.** *or* **r.-straight**
être raide comme un piquet sur sa chaise

ramshackle ['ræmʃæk(ə)l] **ADJ** *(building, farm)* délabré, qui tombe en ruines; *(economy, government)* qui s'effrite *ou* s'effondre,
délabré; **r. old car** vieille guimbarde *f*

ran [ræn] **PP** *see* **run VT, VI**

ranch [rɑːntʃ] **N** ranch *m*, ferme *f* d'élevage;
cattle/mink r. ferme d'élevage de bétail/du
vison
VI avoir *ou* exploiter *ou* tenir un ranch
VT *(cattle, mink)* élever, faire l'élevage de
▶▶ *Culin* **r. dressing** = mayonnaise *f* crémeuse à l'ail; **r. hand** ouvrier, -ière agricole;
r. house *(bungalow)* maison *f* sans étage; *(on ranch)* maison; *Am* **r. mink** vison *m* d'élevage

rancher ['rɑːntʃər] **N** propriétaire *mf* de
ranch; **cattle/mink r.** éleveur, -euse de bétail/visons

ranching ['rɑːntʃɪŋ] **N** *(of cattle, mink)* élevage *m*

rancid ['rænsɪd] **ADJ** rance; **to go r.** rancir; **to smell r.** sentir le rance

rancidity [ræn'sɪdɪtɪ], **rancidness** ['rænsɪdnɪs] **N** *(of butter, fat etc)* rancidité *f*

rancorous ['ræŋkərəs] **ADJ** *(attitude)* rancunier, plein de rancœur; *(remark)* amer, plein
de rancœur

rancour, *Am* **rancor** ['ræŋkər] **N** rancune *f*,
rancœur *f*, **full of r.** *(remark etc)* amer; **the r. of her remarks/criticisms; he is full of r.** *(permanent condition)* il est aigri; **to be full of r. against sb** avoir beaucoup de rancœur
contre qn

rand [rænd] **N 1** *(South African currency)* rand
m **2** *Geog* **the R.** le Rand

random ['rændəm] **ADJ** *(choice)* fait au hasard; *(sample)* prélevé au hasard; *(pattern)*
irrégulier; *Math (error, number)* aléatoire; **I just made a r. guess** j'ai deviné tout à fait
par hasard; **a r. selection of people were asked if …** on a demandé à des gens choisis
au hasard si …; **a r. shot** une balle perdue;
to be killed by a r. shot *or* **bullet** être tué
par une balle perdue
N at r. au hasard; **to fire at r.** tirer au hasard
ou à l'aveuglette
▶▶ *Comput* **r. access** accès *m* aléatoire;
Comput **r. access file** fichier *m* à accès aléatoire; *Comput* **r. access memory** mémoire *f*
vive; *Mktg* **r. check** contrôle *m* par sondage(s); *Comput* **r. error** erreur *f* aléatoire; **r. killings** tuerie *f* aveugle *ou* au hasard; *Mktg* **r. sample** échantillon *m* aléatoire; *Mktg* **r. sampling** échantillonnage *m* aléatoire; *Mktg*
r. selection sélection *f* au hasard; *Math* **r. variable** variable *f* aléatoire; **r. violence** violence *f* aveugle

randomize ['rændəmaɪz] **VT** randomiser

randy ['rændɪ] **ADJ** *Br Fam* émoustillé, allumé; **to get** *or* **become r.** commencer à s'exciter; **to make sb r.** allumer qn; **to be feeling r.** être excité; **he's a r. devil** c'est un chaud
lapin

ranee ['rɑːnɪ] **N** rani *f*

RANGE [reɪndʒ]

| **N** portée **1** ▪ échelle **3** ▪ étendue **4** ▪ gamme **5** |
| **VT** ranger **1** ▪ parcourir **2** |
| **VI** aller de … à **1** ▪ parcourir **2** |

N 1 *(of missile, telescope, weapon)* portée *f*,
(of car, plane) autonomie *f*, *Mil* **out of r.** hors
de portée (de tir); *Mil* **within r.** à portée de tir;
at point blank r. à bout portant; **at a r. of 1,000 metres** à une distance de 1000 mètres;
to fire at short/long r. tirer à petite/grande
distance *ou* à courte/longue portée; **short/ medium/long-r. aircraft** avion *m/*moyen/long-
courrier *m*; *Met* **short/long-r. forecast** prévisions *fpl* météorologiques à court/long
terme; **to be within hearing r.** être à portée
de voix; **r. of vision** champ *m* visuel
2 *(target practice area)* **rifle** *or* **shooting r.**
Mil champ *m* de tir; *(at funfair)* stand *m* de
tir; **rocket/torpedo r.** zone *f* d'essai de fusées/torpilles
3 *(scale)* *(of prices, salaries)* échelle *f*, éventail *m*; *(of instrument, voice)* étendue *f*, registre *m*, tessiture *f*; **beyond one's r.** *(of price)*
au-dessus de ses moyens; *(of note)* hors de
son registre; **within one's r.** *(of price)* dans
ses prix; *(of note)* dans son registre; **what is your price r.?** quel prix voulez-vous mettre?;
a house at the lower end of the r. une maison bas de gamme; **an actor with a wide r. of expressions** un acteur qui a une gamme
d'expressions très variée
4 *(scope)* *(of knowledge, research)* étendue

f, *(of inquiry, investigation)* domaine *m*; **she has a wide r. of interests** elle s'intéresse à
beaucoup de choses
5 *(collection, series)* *(of colours, feelings, products)* gamme *f*, *(of patterns, sizes)* choix
m; **the shop carries a wide/limited r. of …** le
magasin offre un grand choix/choix limité
de …; **the coat comes in a wide r. of colours/sizes** le manteau existe dans une
gamme variée de couleurs/un grand choix
de tailles; **a top of the r. sports car** une voiture de sport haut de gamme; **to experience the full r. of emotions** passer par toute la
gamme des émotions
6 *(of hills, mountains)* chaîne *f*
7 *(territory)* *(of animal, plant)* habitat *m*; *Am (grazing area)* prairie *f*, pâturages *mpl*
8 *(in surveying)* alignement *m*, direction *f*
9 *(cooker)* **kitchen r.** fourneau *m* de cuisine
VT 1 *(arrange in row)* *(troops, pupils)* faire
aligner; *(tanks along border)* déployer;
(plates, books) ranger (**along** le long de);
Fig **to r. oneself with sb** se ranger du côté
de qn; *(in political, scientific etc matters)* s'aligner sur la position de qn; *Fig* **to r. oneself against sb** s'opposer à qn; **the forces which were ranged against them** les forces alliées
contre eux
2 *(travel)* *(forest, sea)* parcourir, sillonner
(**in search of, looking for** à la recherche de)
3 *(aim)* *(weapon, telescope)* braquer (**on** sur)
4 *Am* **to r. cattle** élever du bétail dans la
prairie
VI 1 *(extend)* *(of ages, colours, marks)* aller
(**from … to** de … à); *(of prices, temperatures)* varier (**from … to** entre … et); **incomes ranging from £12,000 to £15,000** *or*
between £12,000 and £15,000 revenus *mpl*
de l'ordre de 12 000 à 15 000 livres; **their discussions will r. over a great many topics**
leurs discussions couvriront un grand nombre de sujets
2 *(travel)* *(of animals, people)* parcourir; *(of projectiles)* porter (**over a given distance** à
une distance donnée); **these guns r. over six miles** ces canons ont une portée de six
mil(l)es; **they ranged over a large area** *(were found)* leur habitat était très étendu;
(roamed across) ils parcouraient de larges
étendues; *Fig* **his eyes ranged over the audience** il parcourut l'auditoire des yeux
3 *Mil (adjust aim)* régler le tir
▶▶ *Mktg* **r. addition** ajout *m* à la gamme; *Am*
r. cattle bétail *m* élevé dans la prairie; **r. finder** télémètre *m*; **r. finding** télémétrie *f*; **r. pole** *(surveying instrument)* jalon *m*; **r. rod** *(surveying instrument)* jalon; *Mktg* **r. stretching** extension *f* de la gamme

rangefinder ['reɪndʒfaɪndər] **N** télémètre
m

rangeland ['reɪndʒlænd] **N** *Am* prairie *f*

ranger ['reɪndʒər] **N 1** *(in forest, park)* garde
m forestier **2** *Am (State police officer)* ≃ gendarme *m* **3** *Am Mil* ranger *m* **4** **R.** *(senior Girl Guide)* (guide *f*) aînée *f*
▶▶ *Br* **R. Guide** (guide) aînée

ranging ['reɪndʒɪŋ] **ADJ**
▶▶ *Mil* **r. fire** tir *m* de réglage; **r. pole** *(surveying instrument)* jalon *m*; **r. rod** *(surveying instrument)* jalon

rangy ['reɪndʒɪ] **ADJ** *(thin)* élancé

rani ['rɑːnɪ] **N** rani *f*

rank¹ [ræŋk] **N 1** *(position)* *(in army, navy)*
grade *m*; *(in society)* rang *m* (social); *Fin (of debt, mortgage)* rang; *Br* **badge of r.** insigne
m de grade; **officer of high r.** officier *m* supérieur; **to hold the r. of colonel** avoir le grade
de colonel; **to be reduced in r.** rétrograder; *Mil*
the ranks les hommes *mpl* (du rang); *Mil*,
Fig **to have risen from the ranks** être sorti
du rang; **to reduce an NCO to the ranks** cas-

ser un sous-officier; **to have served in the ranks** avoir servi comme simple soldat; *Mil* **all ranks** les militaires *mpl* de tous grades; *Br Mil* **officers and other ranks** gradés et simples soldats; **the higher ranks of the civil service** les hauts fonctionnaires; **person of (high) r.** personne de haut rang; **actor/dancer of the first r.** comédien/danseur de premier ordre; *Br* **a Minister of Cabinet r.** un ministre du cabinet; *Fig* **to pull r. (on sb)** faire jouer son grade (avec qn); *Fig* **the ranks of the homeless/unemployed** les rangs des sans-abri/chômeurs

2 *(row)* *(of trees, on chessboard etc)* rangée *f*; *(of people)* rang *m*; **r. upon r.** *(of objects)* rangée après rangée; *(of people)* rang après rang; **to arrange in ranks** *(objects)* mettre en rangées; *(people)* (faire) mettre en rangs; *Mil* **close ranks!** serrez!; *Mil* **to break/close ranks** rompre/serrer les rangs; *Fig* **to break ranks** se désolidariser (**with** de, d'avec); *Fig* **to close ranks** se montrer solidaire; *Mil* **front r.** premier rang; *Br* **(taxi) r.** station *f* de taxis

VT 1 *(classify)* *(athlete, book etc)* classer (**among** parmi, au nombre de)

2 *Am* *(outrank)* *(in army)* occuper un rang supérieur à; *(in office, organization etc)* être le supérieur de

3 *(arrange in rows)* *(pieces of game)* mettre en rangées; *(troops)* (faire) mettre en rangs

VI 1 *(occupy position)* compter (**among** parmi); **to r. above sb** être le supérieur de *ou* occuper un rang supérieur à qn; **to r. below sb** occuper un rang inférieur à qn; **to r. equally** être au même niveau (**with** que); **to r. with sb** être du même niveau que qn; **in chess, a castle ranks above a bishop** aux échecs, la tour est plus forte que le fou; **this must** *or* **has to r. as the best/biggest/worst** ... ceci doit être le meilleur/plus grand/pire ...; **a car does not r. high in my order of priorities** une voiture ne vient pas en tête de mes priorités

2 *Fin* **to r. before/after sb** *(of creditor, claimant)* prendre rang *ou* passer avant/après qn; **to r. equally (with sb)** prendre *ou* avoir le même rang (que qn); **to r. after sth** *(of share)* être primé par qch; **to r. before sth** *(of share)* avoir la priorité sur qch

3 *Am Mil* *(be most senior)* être le plus haut en grade; *Fig* **he doesn't r.** ce n'est pas quelqu'un d'important

rank² **ADJ 1** *Fml* *(excessive)* *(vegetation, weeds)* envahissant, luxuriant; **to grow r.** pousser (très) rapidement **2** *(foul-smelling)* fétide, qui sent fort; **to be r. with sweat** sentir fort la sueur; **to smell r.** sentir fort **3** *(absolute)* complet, -ète, absolu; *(ignorance, stupidity, incompetence)* crasse; **he's a r. outsider** *(in competition)* c'est un outsider; **r. beginner** parfait(e) novice *mf*; **r. imposter** fieffé imposteur *m*; **r. injustice** injustice *f* flagrante **4** *Br Fam* *(worthless)* merdique; **his last film was totally r.!** son dernier film était complètement merdique!

▸ **rank on** **VT INSEP** *Am Fam* **to r. on sb** agonir qn d'injures, traiter qn de tous les noms

rank-and-file **N 1** *(soldiers)* simples soldats *mpl*; **ten officers and two hundred r.** dix officiers et deux cents hommes **2** *(ordinary members)* *(in political party, union)* base *f*; **r. feelings/opinions** sentiments/opinions des membres *ou* de la base

rank-and-filer **N** *(in army)* simple soldat *m*; *(in political party, union)* membre *m* de la base

ranker ['ræŋkər] **N** *Mil* *(soldier)* simple soldat *m*; *(officer)* officier *m* sorti du rang

ranking ['ræŋkɪŋ] **N** *(classification)* classement *m*; **his r. is number four** il est classé quatrième

ADJ 1 *Am* *(authority, economist)* éminent **2** **high/low r.** *(officer)* de haut grade/grade in-

férieur; *(diplomat, official)* de haut rang/ rang inférieur; **a low r. civil servant** un petit fonctionnaire

▸▸ *Am Mil* **r. officer** officier *m* responsable

rankle ['ræŋk(ə)l] **VI** rester sur le cœur; **it rankled with me** je ne l'ai pas digéré; **what they did still rankles with her** elle n'a toujours pas digéré ce qu'ils ont fait

rankness ['ræŋknɪs] **N 1** *Fml* *(of vegetation)* exubérance *f*, luxuriance *f* **2** *(foul smell)* odeur *f* forte *ou* fétide

ransack ['rænsæk] **VT 1** *(search)* *(room, drawer)* mettre sens dessus dessous **2** *(pillage)* *(store, town)* piller, mettre à sac; *(house)* *(of burglar)* dévaliser

ransom ['rænsəm] **N** *(money)* rançon *f*; **to hold sb to r.** demander une rançon pour la libération de qn; *Fig* **the strikers were holding the country to r.** les grévistes exerçaient un chantage sur le pays

VT *(captive)* racheter

rant [rænt] **VI** déclamer avec véhémence, *Fam* déblatérer (**about, at** contre); **to r. and rave** fulminer, tempêter (**about, at** contre)

▸ **rant on** **VI** = **rant**

ranting ['ræntɪŋ] **ADJ** *(style)* déclamatoire; *(speech)* tonitruant

N **ranting(s)** déclamation *f*; **to listen to sb's r. about sth** écouter qn s'échauffer à propos de qch; **sectarian rantings** propos *mpl* d'un sectarisme hystérique; **r. and raving, rantings and ravings** discours *m* délirant

ranunculus, *pl* **ranunculuses, ranunculi** [rə'nʌŋkjələs, -əsɪz, -aɪ] **N** *Bot* renoncule *f*

rap [ræp] **N 1** *(slight blow)* petit coup *m* sec; **I heard a r. at the door** j'ai entendu frapper à la porte; **to give sb a r. on** *or* **over the knuckles** *(hit)*, *Fig* taper sur les doigts à qn; *Fig* **the saleswoman was given a r. over the knuckles for being rude to a customer** la vendeuse s'est fait taper sur les doigts pour avoir été impolie avec un client

2 *esp Am Sl* *(accusation, charge)* **he's up on a murder/drugs r.** il est accusé de meurtre/ dans une affaire de drogue; **to beat the r.** échapper à la condamnation; **to take the r. for sth** trinquer pour qch; **you let me take the r. for you** tu m'as laissé trinquer à ta place

3 *Am Fam* *(conversation, speech)* **don't give me that r.!** raconte pas n'importe quoi!; **r. session** bavardage *m*; **we had a good r. session** on a discuté pendant un bon bout de temps; **he was laying down some r. about the new model** il était en train de faire un baratin sur le nouveau modèle

4 *Fig Fam* *(small amount)* **he doesn't care** *or* **give a r.** il s'en moque *ou* s'en fiche éperdument **5** *Mus* rap *m*

VT **(-pp-)** *(strike)* *(window, door)* frapper à; **to r. sb's knuckles** *or* **sb on** *or* **over the knuckles** *(hit)*, *Fig* taper sur les doigts à qn; *Am* **to r. sb** *(criticize)* éreinter qn

VI 1 **to r. at/on sth** frapper sur *ou* contre qch **2** *Am Fam* *(talk)* papoter, bavarder

▸▸ *Mus* **r. artist** chanteur, -euse de rap; *Mus* **r. music** rap *m*; *Am Fam* **r. sheet** casier *m* judiciaire

▸ **rap out** **VT SEP 1** *(order, instruction)* lancer **2** **to r. out a message** *(by tapping)* communiquer au moyen de coups

rapacious [rə'peɪʃəs] **ADJ** rapace

rapaciously [rə'peɪʃəslɪ] **ADV** avec rapacité

rapacity [rə'pæsɪtɪ] **N** rapacité *f*

rape¹ [reɪp] **N 1** viol *m*; **to commit r.** violer; *Fig* **the r. of the tropical forests** la destruction des forêts tropicales **2** *Arch* *(abduction)* enlèvement *m*; **the R. of the Sabine Women** l'enlèvement des Sabines

VT *(person)* violer; *Fig* *(forest, environment, region)* détruire

▸▸ **r. crisis centre** centre *m* d'accueil pour femmes violées; **r. suite** pièce *f* réservée aux victimes de viols *(dans un commissariat)*; **r. victim** personne *f* violée, victime *f* d'un viol

rape² **N 1** *Bot* *(crop)* colza *m* **2** *(remains of grapes)* marc *m* (de raisin)

▸▸ **r. oil** huile *f* de colza

rapeseed ['reɪpsiːd] **N** graine *f* de colza

▸▸ **r. oil** huile *f* de colza

raphia ['ræfɪə] **N** *Bot* raphia *m*

ADJ en raphia

rapid ['ræpɪd] **ADJ** *(developments, improvement, progress)* rapide; **a r. pulse** un pouls rapide; **r. strides** longues enjambées *fpl*; *Fig* **we are making r. strides towards a cure for cancer** la recherche contre le cancer fait des progrès rapides; **they have had six children in r. succession** ils ont eu six enfants très rapprochés

▸▸ *Mil* **r. deployment force** force *f* d'intervention rapide; **r. eye movement** mouvements *mpl* oculaires rapides; *Mil* **r. reaction force** forces *fpl* d'action rapide

rapid-fire **ADJ** *Mil* à tir rapide; *Fig* *(questions, jokes)* qui se succèdent à toute allure

rapidity [rə'pɪdɪtɪ] **N** rapidité *f*

rapidly ['ræpɪdlɪ] **ADV** rapidement

rapids ['ræpɪdz] **NPL** *Geog* rapides *mpl*; **to shoot the r.** descendre les rapides

rapier ['reɪpɪər] **N** rapière *f*

▸▸ **r. thrust** coup *m* de rapière; **r. wit** esprit *m* acerbe

rapist ['reɪpɪst] **N** violeur *m*, auteur *m* d'un viol/de viols

▸ **rappel down** [ræ'pel] **VI** *(in mountaineering)* descendre en rappel

rapper ['ræpər] **N** *Mus* chanteur, -euse de rap

rapport [ræ'pɔːr] **N** bons rapports *mpl*, affinités *fpl*; **there was an instant r. between them** ils ressentirent une sympathie immédiate l'un pour l'autre; **he had a r. with his music teacher** il avait des affinités avec son professeur de musique

rapprochement [ræ'prɒʃmɒn] **N** rapprochement *m*; **to effect a r.** se rapprocher (**with sb** de qn)

rapscallion [ræp'skælɪən] **N** *Arch, Hum* garnement *m*

rapt [ræpt] **ADJ** *(attention, interest)* profond; *(look, smile)* ravi, d'extase; **a r. face** un visage attentif; **there was a r. look on her face as she listened** elle écoutait, l'air très absorbé; **to be r. in contemplation** être plongé dans ses pensées, *Litt* s'abîmer dans la contemplation

raptor ['ræptər] **N** *Orn* rapace *m*

rapture ['ræptʃər] **N** ravissement *m*, extase *f*; **to be in raptures** être ravi *ou* enchanté (**with, over** de); **in raptures of delight** transporté de joie; **he was filled with r. at the thought/the idea** il était en extase à cette pensée/cette idée; **to go into raptures** s'extasier (**over** devant); **he goes into raptures over his new grandchild** il s'extasie *ou* il est en extase devant son dernier petit-enfant; **she went into raptures at the prospect of meeting him** elle est tombée en extase à l'idée de le rencontrer

rapturous ['ræptʃərəs] **ADJ** *(cries)* d'extase, de ravissement; *(applause)* frénétique; *(reception, welcome)* enthousiaste; **his face was r. with joy** il rayonnait de joie; **they were r. about their daughter's success** le succès de leur fille les rendait fous de joie

rare [reər] **ADJ 1** *(uncommon)* rare; **very** *or* **extremely r.** très *ou* extrêmement rare, rarissime; **it is r. for him to do that** c'est rare qu'il fasse ça; *Fig* **he's a r. bird** *(strange)* il est bizarre; *Fam* **you're a r. bird in these parts since you got that promotion** vous vous faites rare depuis que vous avez été promu **2** *Culin (meat)* saignant; **medium r.** à point; **very rare** bleu **3** *(lacking oxygen) (air, atmosphere)* raréfié **4** *(exceptional)* rare, exceptionnel; **he has a rare gift** il a un don exceptionnel **5** *(excellent)* super, génial, -aux; **we had a r. night out last night** on a passé une super soirée hier **6** *Fam (extreme)* énorme; **you gave me a r. fright!** tu m'as fait une peur bleue ou une de ces peurs!

▸▸ *Chem* **r. earth** terre *f* rare; *Chem* **r. gas** gaz *m* rare

rarebit ['ræbɪt, 'reəbɪt] N *Culin* **Welsh r.** = tranche *f* de pain grillée recouverte de fromage fondu souvent mélangé à de la moutarde et de la bière

rarefied ['reərɪfaɪd] ADJ *(thin) (air, gas)* raréfié; *Fig* **to live in a r. atmosphere** vivre dans un monde à part

rarefy ['reərɪfaɪ] VT *(air, gas)* raréfier
VI *(of air, gas)* se raréfier

rarely ['reəlɪ] ADV rarement; **r. have I** *or* **I have r. encountered anyone like him** j'ai rarement rencontré quelqu'un comme lui; **she is r. ill** elle est rarement malade, il est rare qu'elle soit malade

rareness ['reənɪs] N *(uncommonness)* rareté *f*

raring ['reərɪŋ] ADJ *(eager)* **r. to start** impatient de commencer; **to be r. to go** *(of person, animal)* trépigner *ou* piaffer d'impatience

rarity ['reərɪtɪ] N *(uncommonness)* rareté *f*; **a fine day is a r. here** une belle journée est un événement rare ici; **wild flowers are becoming (something of) a r.** les fleurs sauvages se font de plus en plus rares

rascal ['rɑːsk(ə)l] N **1** *(child)* coquin, -ine, fripon, -onne; **you little r.!** petit coquin!, petite canaille! **2** *Old-fashioned (scoundrel)* coquin *m*, vaurien *m*

rascally ['rɑːskəlɪ] ADJ *Old-fashioned (behaviour)* de coquin; *(person)* coquin

rase [reɪz] VT = **raze**

rash¹ [ræʃ] N **1** *Med* rougeur *f*, éruption *f* (cutanée); *(caused by allergy)* urticaire *f*, *(caused by chickenpox, measles, scarlet fever)* exanthème *m*, *Fam* boutons *mpl*; **to come out** *or* **break out in a r.** attraper des boutons; *(because of allergy)* avoir une crise d'urticaire; **strawberries bring me out in a r.** les fraises me donnent de l'urticaire; *Fig* **the very thought of him brings me out in a r.!** rien que de penser à lui ça me donne des boutons! **2** *Fig (of anonymous letters, resignations etc)* vague *f*, épidémie *f*

rash² ADJ *(person)* imprudent, téméraire; *(action, words)* imprudent, inconsidéré, irréfléchi; **don't make any r. promises!** ne faites pas de promesses en l'air!; **we decided in a r. moment to …** nous avons décidé dans un moment de folie de …; **that was a bit r. of you** c'était un peu risqué de ta part; *Hum* **don't do anything r., will you?** surtout, ne fais pas de folies!

rasher ['ræʃər] N *Br* tranche *f* de bacon

rashly ['ræʃlɪ] ADV *(to behave, act, speak)* sans réfléchir, imprudemment; *(to agree, decide)* dans un moment de folie

rashness ['ræʃnɪs] N *(of person, action)* imprudence *f*, inconséquence *f*; **I paid for my r.** j'ai payé cher mes imprudences; **the r. of the chairman's statement** la déclaration inconsidérée du président

rasp [rɑːsp] N **1** *(file)* râpe *f* **2** *(sound)* grincement *m*; **the r. in his voice** le ton rauque de sa voix **3** *Scot Fam (abbr* raspberry*)* framboise *f*

VT **1** *(use file on)* râper; *Fig* **the cat rasped its tongue over my face** le chat m'a léché la figure de sa langue râpeuse; **he rasped his hand over his unshaven chin** il frotta sa main sur son menton râpeux **2** *(say hoarsely)* **to r. (out)** dire d'une voix rauque; **to r. out an answer/a plea** répondre/supplier d'une voix rauque

VI **1** *(make hoarse sound)* **her breath rasped in her lungs** elle avait une respiration sifflante **2** *(be irritating)* **to r. on the ears** écorcher les oreilles; **the constant creaking of the door was rasping on their nerves** le grincement constant de la porte leur portait sur les nerfs

raspberry ['rɑːzb(ə)rɪ] N **1** *(fruit, flavour)* framboise *f* **2** *Fam* **to blow** *or* **give sb a r.** *(jeer)* siffler qn; **to get a r.** se faire siffler

▸▸ **r. bush** framboisier *m*; **r. cane** framboisier; **r. jam** confiture *f* de framboise; **r. tart** tarte *f* à la framboise; **r. vinegar** vinaigre *m* de framboise

rasping ['rɑːspɪŋ] N **1** *(noise)* grincement *m*, crissement *m* **2** *(shaved-off piece of metal)* copeau *m*
ADJ *(noise)* grinçant, crissant; *(voice)* rauque, grinçant

raspings ['rɑːspɪŋz] NPL *Culin (breadcrumbs)* chapelure *f*

Rasta ['ræstə] N, ADJ *(abbr* Rastafarian*)* rasta *mf inv*

Rastafarian [ræstə'feərɪən] N, ADJ rastafari *mf inv*

Rastafarianism [ræstə'feərɪənɪz(ə)m] N rastafarianisme *m*

raster ['ræstər] N trame *f*
▸▸ *Comput, Typ* **r. image** image *f* tramée; *Comput, Typ* **r. scan** balayage *m* de trame

rasterize ['ræstəraɪz] VT *Comput, Typ* convertir en mode point à point

rat [ræt] N **1** *(animal)* rat *m*; **to be caught like a r. in a trap** être fait comme un rat; **with her hair all in rats' tails** avec ses mèches collées; *Fig* **I smell a r.** il y a quelque chose de louche; *Am Sl* **I don't give a r.'s ass** je m'en fous pas mal, je m'en balance **2** *Fam Pej (unreliable person)* lâcheur, -euse; **you r.!** salaud!, ordure! **3** *Am Fam Pej (informer)* mouchard, -arde, indic *m* **4** *Fam Pej (strikebreaker)* jaune *mf*, briseur, -euse de grève **5** *Old-fashioned Br Fam* **rats!** *(exclamation of irritation)* zut!

VI **(-tt-)** *Fam Pej (reveal information)* moucharder, cafarder
▸▸ *Am Fam* **r. cheese** fromage *m* ordinaire; **r. pack** *(paparazzi)* paparazzi(s) *mpl*; **r. poison** mort-aux-rats *f inv*; **r. race** foire *f* d'empoigne; **r. run** = rue *f* résidentielle empruntée par les automobilistes qui veulent éviter les bouchons aux heures de pointe

▸ **rat on** VT INSEP *Fam Pej (person) (to friends, parents etc)* dénoncer; *(to police)* balancer; **to r. on a promise** revenir sur une promesse; **they ratted on our deal** ils nous ont laissé tomber dans cette affaire

▸ **rat out** VT SEP *Am Fam* **to r. sb out** balancer qn, moucharder qn

ratable ['reɪtəb(ə)l] ADJ = **rateable**

ratafia [rætə'fiːə] N *(liqueur)* ratafia *m*; *(biscuit)* macaron *m*
▸▸ **r. biscuit** macaron *m*

ratan [ræ'tæn] N = **rattan**

rat-arsed [-ɑːst] ADJ *Br Sl (drunk)* rond comme une queue de pelle

rat-a-tat(-tat) N *(on door)* toc toc *m*; *(on drum)* rantanplan *m*; *(of machine gun)* pétarade *f*, *(of typewriter)* tac-tac-tac *m*
VI **(-tt-)** *(on door)* frapper; *(of machine gun)* pétarader

ratatouille [rætə'tuːiː] N *Culin* ratatouille *f*

ratbag ['rætbæg] N *Sl (obnoxious person)* con *m*, conne *f*, *Hum* **you r.!** petit saligaud, petite garce!

rat-catcher N chasseur, -euse de rats

ratchet ['rætʃɪt] N *Tech* rochet *m*; *Fig* **this had a r. effect on prices** cela a entraîné une augmentation irréversible des prix
▸▸ **r. mechanism** (dispositif *m* d')encliquetage *m*; **r. screwdriver** tournevis *m* à cliquet; **r. wheel** roue *f* à rochet, **r. wrench** clé *f* à rochet

rate [reɪt] N **1** *(of inflation, tax etc)* taux *m*; *Fin* **birth/crime/death r.** taux de natalité/criminalité/mortalité; **pass** *or* **success/failure r.** *(in exam etc)* pourcentage *m* de réussites/d'échecs; **at the r. of** *(amount)* à raison de; **to be paid at the r. of five pounds an hour** être payé (à raison de) cinq livres de l'heure; **to strike for higher rates of pay** faire la grève pour obtenir une augmentation de salaire; **the r. is 60p in the pound** le taux est de soixante pence par livre

2 *(speed)* vitesse *f*, *Comput, Tel* débit *m*; **the fearful r. of technological advance** le rythme effrayant du progrès technologique; **at the r. of …** au rythme de …; *Fam* **at a r. of knots** à toute allure; **at this r.** à ce rythme-là; *(slow speed)* à ce train-là; **at the r. things are going** du train où vont les choses; *Fig* **at any r.** en tout cas

3 *(price, charge)* tarif *m*; **what are your rates?** *(for hotel room, service)* quels sont vos tarifs *ou* prix?; **to pay the full r.** payer plein tarif

4 *Br Formerly (tax) (usu pl)* **rates** impôts *mpl* locaux; **rates and taxes** impôts et contributions; **rates office** recette *f* municipale

VT **1** *(consider)* considérer (**as** comme); *(classify) (athlete, pianist etc)* classer (**among** parmi); *(evaluate) (pupil, concert, film etc)* évaluer; **I r. him among my closest friends** je le compte au nombre de *ou* le considère comme un de mes amis les plus proches; **to r. sb/sth highly** apprécier beaucoup qn/qch; **to be highly rated** être très apprécié; **how do you r. their chances of winning the contract?** à votre avis, quelles sont leurs chances de décrocher le contrat?; **I r. this restaurant very highly** je trouve ce restaurant excellent; *Br Fam* **I don't r. him** je ne l'apprécie pas beaucoup

2 *(deserve)* mériter; **that performance should r. him third place** cette prestation devrait lui assurer la troisième place; **a battle that didn't r. a mention in the history books** une bataille qui n'a pas mérité d'apparaître dans les livres d'histoire

3 *Br (set amount of taxes on) (property)* établir *ou* calculer le montant des impôts locaux sur; **their house has been rated higher this year** leur maison a été classée dans la tranche supérieure cette année

VI *(be classified)* se classer, être classé (**as** comme); **in terms of efficiency, she rates higher than anyone else** en ce qui concerne l'efficacité, elle bat tout le monde; **to r. with** *(impress)* plaire à, impressionner

▸▸ *Mktg* **r. of adoption** *(of product)* taux d'adoption; *Aviat* **r. of climb** vitesse ascensionnelle; *Mktg* **r. of awareness** taux de notoriété; **r. band** plage *f* ou fourchette *f* de taux; *Mktg* **r. of churn** taux de clients passés à la concurrence; *Br Formerly* **r. collector** receveur, -euse municipal(e); *Fin* **r. of depreciation** taux d'amortissement; **r. of exchange** cours *m* ou taux de change; **r. of flow** *(of rivers, turbines)* débit *m*; *Fin* **r. of growth** taux d'accroissement *ou* de croissance; *Fin* **r. of increase** taux d'accroissement; *Fin, Econ* **r. of inflation** taux d'inflation; *Mktg* **r. of penetration** taux de pénétration; **r. of production** taux de production; *Br Formerly* **r. rebate** dégrèvement *m* d'impôts locaux; *Mktg* **r. of renewal** taux de renouvellement; *Fin* **r. of return** *(on investment)* taux de rendement; *Fin* **r. of return pricing** fixation *f* de prix au taux de rendement établi; **r. of uptake** taux de succès

-rate [reɪt] SUFF **first/second -r.** de premier/second ordre

rateable [ˈreɪtəb(ə)l] ADJ *Br Admin (house, property)* imposable
▸▸ **r. value** ≃ valeur *f* locative imposable

rate-cap VT *Br Admin (local authority)* fixer un taux plafond pour les impôts locaux de

rate-capping [-kæpɪŋ] N *Br Admin* plafonnement *m* des impôts locaux

rated [ˈreɪtɪd] ADJ *Tech (load, speed, voltage)* nominal, -aux

rate-of-return analysis N analyse *f* du rendement

ratepayer [ˈreɪtpeɪər] N *Br Formerly (local taxpayer)* contribuable *mf* (assujetti(e) aux impôts locaux)

ratfink [ˈrætfɪŋk] N *Am Pej Sl (obnoxious person)* salaud *m*, ordure *f*

rather [ˈrɑːðər] ADV **1** *(preferably)* plutôt (**than** que); **I'd r. stay** j'aimerais mieux *ou* je préférerais rester (**than** que); **I would r. that you came** je préférerais que vous veniez; **I'd r. not** je n'y tiens pas; **I'd r. you didn't do it** je préférerais que tu ne le fasses pas; **r. than leave/stay** plutôt que de partir/rester; **anything r. than that** tout sauf ça; **r. you than me!** plutôt toi que moi!; **accept? I'd r. die!** accepter? plutôt mourir!
2 *(more precisely)* **or r.** ou plutôt, ou pour être plus précis
3 *(fairly)* plutôt, assez; *(to a degree)* un peu; **she's a r. or r. a beautiful woman** elle est plutôt belle femme; **she is r. plain** elle n'est pas très jolie; **r. a lot of people** pas mal de monde; **I r. think you know him** je crois bien *ou* il me semble que vous le connaissez; **it tastes r. like a pear** *(but I know it's not)* ça rappelle le goût de la poire; *(I'm guessing)* on dirait de la poire; **I am r. inclined to agree with you** je suis plutôt de votre avis; **I r. liked it** ça m'a assez *ou Fam* pas mal plu; **it's r. nice** c'est bien, *Fam* c'est pas mal; **r. more tired** un peu plus fatigué (**than** que) VOIR GRAMMAIRE A5
4 [ˈrɑːˈðɜː] *Old-fashioned (certainly)* *(when accepting offer)* oui alors, et comment; *(when answering question)* et comment

ratification [rætɪfɪˈkeɪʃən] N *(by government)* ratification *f*; *(by sports authorities)* homologation *f*

ratify [ˈrætɪfaɪ] VT *(treaty)* ratifier; *(record)* homologuer; **to r. a contract** approuver un contrat

ratine [ræˈtiːn] N *Tex* ratine *f*

rating [ˈreɪtɪŋ] N **1** *(classification)* classement *m* **2** *(evaluation)* *(of employee, student etc)* appréciation *f*, *(of candidates, politicians)* cote *f* de popularité; *(for credit)* notation *f* **3** *TV* **the ratings** l'indice *m* d'écoute, le taux *m* d'audience, le taux d'écoute; **to boost the ratings** améliorer l'indice d'écoute; **to stand high in the ratings** avoir un indice d'écoute élevé; **ratings success** succès *m* d'audience; **ratings war** guerre *f* de l'audimat®, course *f* à l'audimat® **4** *Br Admin (of property)* *(setting of tax)* calcul *m* du montant des impôts locaux; *(tax)* montant *m* des impôts locaux **5** *Br (sailor)* matelot *m*; **the ratings** les matelots et gradés
▸▸ **r. agency** agence *f* de notation *ou* de rating; *Am Mil* **r. badge** insigne *m* de grade; *Mktg* **r. scale** *(in market research)* échelle *f* de classement; *Cin* **r. system** = système *m* de classement des films en fonction de l'âge du public autorisé

ratio, *pl* **ratios** [ˈreɪʃɪəʊ, -əʊz] N *(proportion,*

relationship) proportion *f*, rapport *m*; **in a r. of 25 to 1** dans une proportion *ou* un rapport de 25 pour 1; **in direct r.** directement proportionnel, en rapport direct (**to** avec), en raison directe (**to** de); **the school has a teacher-pupil r. of 1 to 10** l'école a un rapport professeur-élève de 1 pour 10

ratiocination [rætɪɒsɪˈneɪʃən] N *Fml* raisonnement *m*

ration [ˈræʃən, *Am* ˈreɪʃən] N *(of bread, sugar etc)* ration *f*; **you've had your r. of TV for this evening** tu as eu ta dose de télévision pour ce soir; **rations** *(food supplies)* provisions *fpl*, **to be on short rations** avoir des rations réduites; **to put sb on short rations** réduire les rations de qn; **full rations** rations complètes; *Mil* **to draw rations** toucher sa ration; *Am Mil* **C rations** vivres *mpl*; *Br Mil* **iron rations** vivres de réserve
VT *(bread, sugar etc)* rationner; **I was rationed to ...** ma ration était de ...; **she rations herself to one film a week** elle se limite à un film par semaine; **I'll r. you to an hour's television a day** je ne t'autoriserai à regarder la télévision qu'une heure par jour
▸▸ **r. book** carte *f* de rationnement; **r. card** carte de rationnement

rational [ˈræʃənəl] ADJ **1** *(sensible)* *(behaviour, person)* raisonnable, sensé; **it seemed like the r. thing to do** il me semblait que c'était ce qu'il y avait de plus logique à faire **2** *(sane)* rationnel; *(lucid)* lucide; **to be quite r.** avoir toute sa tête **3** *(based on or using reason)* *(decision)* sensé; *(thought)* rationnel; *(animal, creature)* doué de raison; **she is not quite r. when the subject of divorce comes up** elle ne pense pas très clairement lorsqu'on parle de divorce **4** *Math (number)* rationnel

rationale [ræʃəˈnɑːl] N *(reasoning)* raisonnement *m* (**for** de); *(written or spoken)* exposé *m* raisonné; **what's the r. for the decision?** comment peut-on expliquer cette décision?

rationalism [ˈræʃənəlɪz(ə)m] N rationalisme *m*

rationalist [ˈræʃənəlɪst] ADJ, N rationaliste *mf*

rationalistic [ræʃənəˈlɪstɪk] ADJ rationaliste

rationality [ræʃəˈnælɪtɪ] N *(of decision, thought)* rationalité *f*

rationalization [ræʃənəlaɪˈzeɪʃən] N **1** *(of action, behaviour etc)* justification *f*, rationalisation *f* (**of** de) **2** *Br Ind (of company etc)* rationalisation *f*

rationalize [ˈræʃənəlaɪz] VT **1** *(action, behaviour, dislike, fear etc)* justifier, rationaliser, trouver une explication logique *ou* rationnelle à **2** *Br Ind (company etc)* rationaliser
VI **(do) stop rationalizing!** arrête de chercher des excuses!

rationally [ˈræʃənəlɪ] ADV **1** *(sensibly)* raisonnablement **2** *(sanely)* rationnellement **3** *(using reason)* *(to decide, think)* rationnellement

rationing [ˈræʃənɪŋ, *Am* ˈreɪʃənɪŋ] N *(of bread, sugar etc)* rationnement *m* (**of** de); **(food) r.** rationnement alimentaire

ratlin(e) [ˈrætlɪn] N *Naut* enflèchure *f*

ratrack [ˈrætræk] N *Ski* ratrack *m*

rat-tail N *(file)* (lime *f*) queue-de-rat *f*, *pl* (limes) queues-de-rat

rattan [ræˈtæn] N *Bot* rotang *m*; *(substance)* rotin *m*; **r. furniture** meubles *mpl* en rotin

rat-tat N, VI = **rat-a-tat(-tat)**

ratted [ˈrætɪd] ADJ *Br Sl (drunk)* bourré comme un coing, pété à mort; **to get r.** se péter, se torcher

ratteen [ræˈtiːn] N *Tex* = **ratine**

ratter [ˈrætər] N *(dog)* ratier *m*

rattiness [ˈrætɪnɪs] N *Br Fam (irritability)* irritabilité *f*

ratting [ˈrætɪŋ] N **to go r.** faire la chasse aux rats

rattle [ˈræt(ə)l] N **1** *(for baby)* hochet *m*; *(on pram)* boulier *m*; *(for sports fan)* crécelle *f*; *(of snake)* sonnette *f* **2** *(noise)* *(of bottles, chains, coins, keys)* cliquetis *m*; *(in engine)* bruit *m* (de ferraille); *(of gunfire, hailstones)* crépitement *m*; *(of door, window)* vibration *f*; **(death) r.** râle *m*
VI *(make noise)* faire du bruit; *(of bottles)* cliqueter, s'entrechoquer; *(of chains, coins, keys)* cliqueter; *(of door, window)* vibrer; *(of engine)* faire un bruit de ferraille; *(of gunfire, hailstones)* crépiter; **the door rattled in the wind** le vent faisait vibrer la porte
VT **1** *(make noise with)* *(box)* secouer; *(bottles)* entrechoquer; *(chains, coins, keys)* faire du bruit avec; *(door, window)* ébranler, faire vibrer **2** *Fam (make nervous)* *(person)* démonter, ébranler, faire perdre son sang froid à; **to get rattled** perdre son sang froid; **don't get rattled!** pas de panique!; **we got them rattled** on a semé la panique parmi eux; **she was badly rattled by the news** la nouvelle l'a beaucoup secouée *ou* la complètement démontée; **to be easily rattled** être facilement démonté
▸ **rattle along** VI **1** *(move noisily)* *(of car, train)* rouler dans un bruit de ferraille **2** *(move quickly)* *(in car, train)* rouler à toute allure
▸ **rattle around** VI **he's been rattling around in that enormous house since his wife died** il est perdu dans cette grande maison depuis la mort de sa femme
▸ **rattle away** VI *(talk rapidly)* jacasser
▸ **rattle down** VI *(of stones etc)* tomber avec fracas
▸ **rattle off** VT SEP *(lines, recitation etc)* débiter
▸ **rattle on** VI *(speak at length)* ne pas arrêter de parler (**about** de)
▸ **rattle through** VT INSEP *(homework, task etc)* expédier

rattlebrain [ˈræt(ə)lbreɪn] N *Old-fashioned Fam (foolish person)* cervelle *f* d'oiseau, tête *f* de linotte

rattlesnake [ˈræt(ə)lsneɪk], *Am* **rattler** [ˈrætlər] N serpent *m* à sonnette, crotale *m*

rattletrap [ˈræt(ə)ltræp] N *Old-fashioned Fam (car)* vieille guimbarde *f* ou bagnole *f*

rattling [ˈræt(ə)lɪŋ] N = **rattle** N 2
ADJ **1** *(noisy)* bruyant; **r. noise** cliquetis *m* **2** *(fast)* rapide; **to set a r. pace** imposer un rythme très rapide; *(in race)* mener à une cadence rapide
ADV *Old-fashioned (extremely)* **we had a r. good time** on s'est drôlement amusés; **this book is a r. good read** ce livre est vraiment formidable

rat-trap N **1** *(for animals)* piège *m* à rats, ratière *f* **2** *Am (rundown building)* taudis *m*

ratty [ˈrætɪ] ADJ **1** *Br Fam (irritable)* irritable, grincheux; *(annoyed)* irrité, grincheux; **to get r.** *(of adult)* prendre la mouche; *(of child)* devenir grognon **2** *Am Fam (shabby)* *(building, clothes)* miteux

raucous [ˈrɔːkəs] ADJ **1** *(hoarse)* rauque; **r. voice** voix *f* rauque *ou* éraillée **2** *(loud, rowdy)* **r. laughter** rires *mpl* gras; **a r. party** une soirée tapageuse *ou* bruyante; **things got a bit r. as the evening wore on** la soirée est devenue de plus en plus bruyante

raucously [ˈrɔːkəslɪ] ADV **1** *(to shout etc)* d'une voix rauque **2** *(to celebrate)* bruyamment, de façon tapageuse

raucousness [ˈrɔːkəsnɪs] N **1** *(hoarseness)* raucité *f* **2** *(rowdiness)* **the r. of the party**

was not to his liking il n'aimait pas le côté tapageur *ou* bruyant de la soirée

raunch(iness) [rɔːntʃ, 'rɔːntʃɪnɪs] N *Fam* **1** *(of joke, song)* grivoiserie f **2** *(of dance, voice)* sensualité f

raunchy ['rɔːntʃɪ] ADJ *Fam* **1** *(joke, song) (dirty)* cochon; *(in more light-hearted way)* grivois; **that's much too r. for our viewers** c'est beaucoup trop grivois pour nos téléspectateurs **2** *(sexy) (dance, voice)* sexy *inv*; **there is something a little r. about her** elle a un petit quelque chose de sexy

ravage ['rævɪdʒ] N *(damage) (caused by alcohol, disease, grief, time etc) (usu pl)* **ravages** ravages *mpl*
  VT *(destroy) (crops, region)* ravager, dévaster; *(person)* ravager; **the invading army ravaged the land** l'armée ennemie a mis le pays à feu et à sang; **ravaged face** visage *m* ravagé

rave [reɪv] N **1** *Fam (praise)* éloge *m* enthousiaste; *Br Fam* **to have a r. about sb/sth** parler avec beaucoup d'enthousiasme de qn/qch; **r. notice** *or* **review** critique f *ou* revue f dithyrambique **2** *(party)* rave f
  VI **1** *(be delirious)* délirer **2** *(talk nonsense)* divaguer, délirer *(about* à propos de); **to r. (on)** *(rage)* tempêter *(about,* at contre); **to r. at** *or* **against sb** s'emporter contre qn, être *ou* se mettre en colère contre qn **3** *Fam* **to r. about sb/sth** *(praise)* ne pas tarir d'éloges sur qn/qch, faire l'éloge de qn/qch

raven ['reɪv(ə)n] N *(bird)* corbeau *m*
  ADJ *(colour)* (noir comme de) jais, de jais; **a r.-haired beauty** une beauté aux cheveux noir corbeau *ou* de jais

ravening ['ræv(ə)nɪŋ] ADJ *(hungry)* vorace; *Hum* **the r. hordes** les morfales *mpl*

ravenous ['ræv(ə)nəs] ADJ *(animal)* vorace; *(person)* affamé; *(appetite)* vorace, féroce; **to be r.** avoir une faim dévorante *ou* de loup; *Fig* **to be r. for** *(fame, power)* être assoiffé *ou* avide de

ravenously ['ræv(ə)nəslɪ] ADV *(to eat)* voracement; **to be r. hungry** avoir une faim dévorante *ou* de loup

raver ['reɪvər] N *Br* **1** *Fam (socially active person)* fêtard, -arde, noceur, -euse; **he's a bit of a r.** il est noceur; *(trendy)* il est dans le coup, il est branché **2** *(who goes to raves)* raver *m*

rave-up N *Br Fam (party)* fiesta f, nouba f; **to have a r.** faire la fiesta *ou* nouba; **the neighbours had a right old r. last night** les voisins ont fait une de ces fiestas *ou* noubas hier soir

ravine [rə'viːn] N ravin *m*

raving ['reɪvɪŋ] ADJ ATTRIB **1** *(delirious)* délirant **2** *(angry)* furieux; **a r. lunatic** un fou furieux, une folle furieuse; **I'd have to be a r. lunatic to …** il faudrait que je sois complètement fou pour …; **to be r. mad** *(crazy)* être complètement fou; *Fam (angry)* être furax *(about* au sujet de; *with* contre); *Br Fam* **you are stark r. mad** *or* **bonkers** tu es complètement givré *ou* fêlé; *Fig* **she is a r. beauty** elle est d'une grande beauté; **she is no r. beauty** ce n'est pas une beauté; **to be a r. success** avoir un succès fou
  N **1** *(delirium)* délire *m* **2** *(wild talk)* divagation f; **the ravings of a madman** les divagations d'un fou

ravioli [rævɪ'əʊlɪ] N *(pasta)* ravioli *mpl* VOIR GRAMMAIRE A14

ravish ['rævɪʃ] VT *Fml* **1** *Lit (delight) (person)* enchanter, ravir **2** *(rape)* violenter, violer; *Arch (woman)* enlever, ravir

ravishing ['rævɪʃɪŋ] ADJ *(sight, view)* magnifique, ravissant; **a r. woman, a woman of r. beauty** une femme ravissante *ou* d'une grande beauté

ravishingly ['rævɪʃɪŋlɪ] ADV *(to play, sing)* à ravir; **r. beautiful** d'une beauté ravissante

raw [rɔː] ADJ **1** *(uncooked) (meat, shellfish, vegetables)* cru
  2 *(untreated) (sugar, latex, leather)* brut; *(spirits)* pur; *(cotton, linen)* écru; *(silk)* grège, écru; *(sewage)* non traité
  3 *(unprocessed) (data, statistics)* brut
  4 *(inexperienced)* inexpérimenté; **a r. recruit** un bleu
  5 *(sore) (wound)* à vif; *(skin)* écorché; **her hands were r. with the cold** ses mains étaient bleues à cause du froid; *Fig* **the memory was still r.** le souvenir était encore cuisant *ou* douloureux; *Fig* **my nerves are r.** j'ai les nerfs à vif *ou* à fleur de peau; *Fig* **a r. deal** *(unfair treatment)* traitement *m* injuste; **to give sb a r. deal** être dur avec qn; **he's had a r. deal out of life** il n'a pas été gâté par la vie; **working mothers get a r. deal from the government** les mères qui travaillent sont très défavorisées par le gouvernement; *Fig* **to touch a r. nerve** toucher un point sensible
  6 *(unpleasant) (climate, weather)* âpre, glacial, -als *ou* -aux; **a r. wind** un vent âpre *ou* pénétrant; **it's a r. day** il fait glacial
  7 *Am (frank)* cru, brutal, -aux, réaliste; **the film paints a r. picture of penitentiary life** le film peint la vie carcérale de façon crue *ou* brutale *ou* réaliste
  N **life in the r.** la vie telle qu'elle est; **to get** *or* **touch sb on the r.** piquer *ou* toucher qn au vif; *Fam* **in the r.** *(naked)* nu, tout nu, *Fam* à poil
  ▸▸ **r. edge** *(of material)* bord *m* coupé; **r. material** matière f première; *Fig* **he uses his former colleagues as r. material for his plays** il s'inspire de ses anciens collègues pour ses pièces

rawboned ['rɔːbəʊnd] ADJ *(thin and strong-looking)* mince et vigoureux

rawhide ['rɔːhaɪd] N **1** *(untreated leather)* cuir *m* brut *ou* vert; **r. bag/belt** sac *m*/ceinture f en cuir vert **2** *(whip)* fouet *m* à lanières

Rawlplug® ['rɔːlplʌɡ] N cheville f, tampon *m*

rawness ['rɔːnɪs] N **1** *(inexperience) (of recruit etc)* inexpérience f **2** *(soreness) (of skin)* écorchure f, éraflure f **3** *(unpleasantness) (of climate, weather)* âpreté f, rudesse f, *(of wind)* âpreté f **4** *Am (frankness)* réalisme *m*, brutalité f

ray [reɪ] N **1** *(of light, sun etc)*, *Phys* rayon *m*; *Fig* **that child has brought a r. of sunshine into my life** cet enfant, c'est mon rayon de soleil; *Iron* **you're a real little r. of sunshine, aren't you!** tu as vraiment le mot pour rire, toi! **2** *Fig (of hope, intelligence)* lueur f **3** *(fish)* raie f; **electric r.** torpille f
  ▸▸ **r. gun** pistolet *m* à rayons

rayon ['reɪɒn] N *Tex* rayonne f, **r. dress/shirt** robe f/chemise f en rayonne

raze [reɪz] VT **to r. (to the ground)** *(building)* raser

razor ['reɪzər] N rasoir *m*; **electric r.** rasoir électrique; **lady's r.** rasoir pour femme; **r. edge** fil *m* tranchant; *(mountain ridge)* arête f effilée *ou* aiguë; *Fig* **to be (balanced) on a r.'s edge** *(election, match, fate)* être très incertain; **on a r.'s edge** *(in difficulty)* au bord du précipice *ou* du gouffre; **her life was on a r.'s edge for days** sa vie n'a tenu qu'à un fil pendant plusieurs jours; **she gave him a r. slash across the face** elle lui a donné un coup de rasoir au visage
  ▸▸ **r. blade** lame f de rasoir; *Am Zool* **r. clam** couteau *m*; **r. cut** *(hairstyle)* coupe f au rasoir; *Am* **r. ribbon** barbelés *mpl* tranchants; **r. wire** barbelés tranchants

razorback ['reɪzəbæk] N **1** *(whale)* rorqual *m* **2** *Am (wild pig)* cochon *m* sauvage

razorbill ['reɪzəbɪl] N *(bird)* petit pingouin *m*

razor-cut VT *(hair)* couper au rasoir

razor-sharp ADJ *(knife)* coupant comme un rasoir; *Fig (intelligence, mind)* vif; *(wit, reply)* acerbe

razor-shell N *(Br) (shellfish)* couteau *m*, solen *m*

razz [ræz] VT *Am Fam (tease)* taquiner, railler, tourner en ridicule

razzamatazz ['ræzəmətæz] N = **razzmatazz**

razzle ['ræz(ə)l] N *Br Fam* **to be** *or* **go on the r.** faire la bringue *ou* la fête *ou* la nouba

razzle-dazzle N *Fam (flashy display)* tape-à-l'œil *m inv*; clinquant *m*; *Br* **to be** *or* **go on the r.** faire la bringue *ou* la fête *ou* la nouba

razzmatazz ['ræzmətæz] N *Fam (flashy display)* tape-à-l'œil *m inv*; clinquant *m*

R & B [ɑːrən'biː] N *Mus (abbr* **rhythm and blues)** rhythm and blues *m*

RC [ɑː'siː] N, ADJ *Rel (abbr* **Roman Catholic)** catholique *mf*

RCMP [ɑːsiːem'piː] N *Can (abbr* **Royal Canadian Mounted Police)** GRC f

R & D [ɑːrən'diː] N *(abbr* **research and development)** recherche f et développement; **R. department** bureau *m* d'études; **R. director** directeur, -trice de recherche et développement; **R. expenditure** dépenses *fpl* pour la recherche et le développement

Rd *abbr* **Road**

RDA [ɑːdiː'eɪ] N *(abbr* **recommended daily allowance)** recommandation f quotidienne officielle *(en vitamines, sels, minéraux etc)*

RDBMS [ɑːdiːbiːem'es] N *Comput (abbr* **relational database management system)** SGBDR *m*

RDS [ɑːdiː'es] N *(abbr* **radio data system)** RDS *m*

re[1] [reɪ] N *Mus* ré *m*

re[2] [riː] PREP *(with reference to) (at top of letter)* objet *m*; *(in body of letter etc)* en référence à, suite à
  N *Law* **(in) re Martin v Thomas** dans l'affaire Martin contre Thomas

re- [riː-] PREF **1** *(before consonant)* re-, ré-; **to rebaptize** rebaptiser; **to reheat** réchauffer **2** *(before vowel)* r-, ré-; **to reassure** rassurer; **to readjust** rajuster, réajuster

[riːtʃ]

N	portée **1, 5** ▪ extension **2**
VT	arriver **1, 3** ▪ atteindre **1, 2**
	▪ parvenir à **1** ▪ joindre **2**
VI	s'étendre

N **1** *(accessibility)* atteinte f, portée f; **beyond the r. of the authorities** à l'abri des *ou* hors de la portée des autorités; **he was beyond the r. of human help** on ne pouvait plus rien faire pour lui; **a subject beyond my r.** une matière qui dépasse mon entendement; **out of r.** *(object)* hors de portée; **I'll be out of r. for a week** on ne pourra pas me contacter pendant une semaine; **keep out of the r. of children** *(instruction on medicine bottles, plastic bags etc)* ne pas laisser à la portée des enfants; **within r. of** à portée de; *(near)* à proximité de, proche de; **within arm's r.** à portée de la main; **within easy r.** *(object)* à portée de la main; *(banks, shops etc)* facilement accessible; **within everyone's r.** *(affordable)* à la portée de tous *ou* de toutes les bourses; **fifty pounds for a meal is not within my r.** je ne peux pas me permettre de mettre cinquante livres dans un repas
  2 *(length of arm)* extension f; *Boxing* allonge f; **he has a longer r. than any of the other contenders** il a la meilleure allonge de tous les concurrents
  3 *(action)* **she made a r. for the gun** elle étendit la main pour prendre le revolver

4 *(area, region) (of river)* partie *f*; **the upper reaches of a river** le cours supérieur d'une rivière; **in the further reaches of the empire** au fin fond de l'empire

5 *TV etc (audience size)* portée *f*

VT 1 *(arrive at) (conclusion, destination)* arriver à; *(goal, height)* atteindre; *(of letter, news, parcel)* parvenir à; **to r. (an) agreement** aboutir à un accord (**on** sur); **to r. a decision** prendre une décision; **to r. a ceiling** *(of imports, wages)* plafonner; **to r. the end of one's journey** arriver au bout de son voyage; **which page have you reached?** à quelle page en es-tu?; **it has reached my ears that ...** j'ai entendu dire *ou* appris que ...; **production has reached rock bottom** *or* **an all time low** la production est descendue à son niveau le plus bas; **unemployment is reaching the two million mark** le nombre de chômeurs atteint le seuil des deux millions

2 *(gain access to) (beach, house)* atteindre; *(contact)* joindre, contacter; **to r. sb by telephone** joindre qn par/*ou* au téléphone; **easy/difficult to r.** *(house etc)* facile/difficile d'accès; **the town could only be reached by sea** on ne pouvait accéder à *ou* atteindre la ville que par la mer; *Fig* **nobody can r. him** *(get through to him)* on ne peut pas communiquer avec lui; **the adverts are intended to r. the over-40s** les publicités sont destinées aux *ou* sont à l'intention des plus de 40 ans; **to r. a younger/wider audience** toucher un public plus jeune/large

3 *(stretch as far as) (one's shoulder, waist)* arriver (jusqu')à; **can you r. the ceiling?** est-ce que vous pouvez toucher le plafond?; **are the curtains long enough to r. the floor?** est-ce que les rideaux sont suffisamment longs pour descendre jusqu'au sol?

4 *(hand)* **to r. sb sth** passer qch à qn

5 *Am Fam (corrupt) (witness)* corrompre, suborner

VI *(extend) (of forest, property etc)* s'étendre (**to** jusqu'à); *(of noise, voice)* porter (**to** jusqu'à); **as far as the eye can r.** à perte de vue; **can you r.?** est-ce que tu peux y arriver?; **to r. for sth** *or* **to get sth** allonger *ou* étendre le bras pour prendre qch; **the policeman reached for his gun** l'agent de police mit la main sur son revolver; *Fig* **to r. for the sky** *or* **the stars** être très ambitieux, viser très haut; *Am* **r. (for the sky)!** haut les mains!; **to r. into** *(drawer, pocket)* mettre la main dans (**for** pour prendre)

▸**reach across** VI allonger *ou* (é)tendre le bras (**for** pour prendre)

▸**reach back** VI *Fig (of records, files etc)* remonter (**to** à)

▸**reach down** VI *(of coat, curtains, hair etc)* descendre (**to** jusqu'à); *(of person)* allonger *ou* (é)tendre le bras (**for** pour prendre)

VT SEP *(object) (from cupboard, shelf)* descendre; **can you r. me down that saucepan?** est-ce que tu peux me passer la casserole là-haut?; **he reached it down to her** il le lui a passé

▸**reach out** VI allonger *ou* (é)tendre le bras (**for** pour prendre)

VT SEP **he reached out his hand for the glass** il tendit la main vers le verre

▸**reach over** VI = **reach across**

VT SEP **to r. sb over sth** passer qch à qn; **could you r. me over the salt?** est-ce que tu peux me passer le sel?

▸**reach up** VI *(of person)* lever le bras (**for** pour prendre); *(of snow, water)* monter (**to** jusqu'à); **her boots reached halfway up her legs** ses bottes lui montaient à mi-jambe

VT SEP **to r. sb up sth** passer qch à qn

reachable ['riːtʃəb(ə)l] ADJ *(place, object)* accessible; *(goal, objective)* que l'on peut atteindre; **put it where it won't be r. by the kids** mets-le hors de portée des enfants

---

reach-me-down N *Br Old-fashioned* vieux vêtement *m*

react [rɪ'ækt] VI réagir (**against** contre; **on** sur; **to** à); **to be slow to r.** *(of chemical)* avoir une réaction lente; *(of person)* être lent à réagir; **he reacted well to the treatment** il a bien réagi au traitement; **an acid can r. with a base to form a salt** un acide et une base peuvent réagir ensemble et former un sel

VT *Chem* faire réagir (**sth with sth** qch avec qch)

reactance [rɪ'æktəns] N *Elec* réactance *f*

reactant [rɪ'æktənt] N *Chem* réactif *m*

reaction [rɪ'ækʃən] N **1** *(response) (of chemical, person)* réaction *f*; **to show no r.** rester sans réaction; **what was her r.?** quelle a été sa réaction?, comment a-t-elle réagi?; **in r. to** en *ou* par réaction contre; *Med* **if there is any adverse r.** en cas d'effets indésirables; **the patient's adverse r.** le fait que le malade ait mal réagi **2** *Pol Pej* **the forces of r.** les réactionnaires *mpl*, *Fam* les réacs *mpl*
▸▸*Aviat* **r. engine** moteur *m* à réaction, réacteur *m*; *Aviat* **r. motor** moteur à réaction, réacteur *m*; *Cin, TV* **r. shot** plan *m* de coupe; **r. time** temps *m* de réaction; *Tech* **r. turbine** turbine *f* à réaction

reactionary [rɪ'ækʃən(ə)rɪ] ADJ, N *Pol* réactionnaire *mf*; **the reactionaries** les réactionnaires *mpl*, *Fam* les réacs *mpl*

reactivate [rɪ'æktɪveɪt] VT **1** *(start again) (group, club)* reconstituer, reformer **2** *esp Am Mil (return to active status) (ship)* remettre en service

reactive [rɪ'æktɪv] ADJ *Chem, Phys* réactif; *Elec (load, power)* réactif, déwatté
▸▸*Elec* **r. current** courant *m* réactif; *Mktg* **r. marketing** marketing *m* réactif

reactivity [rɪæk'tɪvɪtɪ] N *Chem, Phys* réactivité *f*

reactor [rɪ'æktər] N *Chem* réacteur *m*; *Nucl* réacteur atomique

read [riːd] N **to have a r.** faire un peu de lecture; *Fam* **just have a r. of this!** lis-moi ça!; *Br Fam* **can I have a r. of your magazine?** est-ce que je peux jeter un coup d'œil à votre magazine?; *Fam* **this book's a good r.** ce livre est agréable à lire; **I've always enjoyed a good r.** j'ai toujours aimé avoir un bon livre à lire; **he was having a quiet r.** il lisait tranquillement; *Theat* **we'll have a r. through this afternoon** nous lirons la pièce cet après-midi
▸▸*Comput* **r. error** erreur *f* de lecture; *Comput* **r. head** tête *f* de lecture

READ² *(pt, pp* **read** [red])

VT	lire **1-4** ■ interpréter **2** ■ étudier **5** ■ indiquer **6**
VI	lire **1, 2**

VT 1 *(newspaper, book, Braille etc)*, *Comput* lire; *(writing, score)* lire, déchiffrer; **have you got anything to r.?** avez-vous de quoi lire *ou* quelque chose à lire?; **have you got enough to r.?** avez-vous assez de lecture?; **to r. sth over and over (again)** lire et relire qch; **I r. Italian** je lis *ou* je peux lire l'italien; **to r. Proust in the original** lire Proust dans le texte; **her novels have been r.** [red] **and enjoyed by millions** ses romans ont été lus et appréciés par des millions de personnes; **to be widely r.** [red] *(of magazine, author etc)* être très lu (**by** parmi); *(of scholar etc)* avoir beaucoup lu; **she is widely r.** [red] **in history** elle a lu beaucoup de livres d'histoire; **for 'least', r. 'lease'** il faut lire 'lease' au lieu de 'least'; **do you r. me?** *Radio* est-ce que vous me recevez?; *Fig* est-ce que tu me comprends?; **I r. you loud and clear** *Radio* je vous reçois cinq sur cinq; *Fig* oui, oui j'ai

compris; **he was reading my lips** il lisait sur mes lèvres; *Fig* **r. my lips!** *(believe me)* je te jure!; *Admin* **r.** [red] **and approved** *(stamp on document)* lu et approuvé; *Fig* **to take sth as r.** [red] *(evident)* considérer qch comme allant de soi; *(agreed upon)* considérer qch comme entendu; *Admin* **to take the minutes as r.** [red] passer sur la lecture du procès-verbal

2 *(interpret) (situation, sb's actions etc)* interpréter; **to r. sb's mind** *or* **thoughts** lire dans les pensées de qn; **to r. the future** lire *ou* prédire l'avenir; **she can r. him like a book** elle sait toujours ce qu'il pense; *Sport* **to r. the game well** anticiper sur les mouvements de l'adversaire; **he r.** [red] **that well** *(of sportsman)* il a bien anticipé; **I r.** [red] **it as 24, but it was actually 224** j'ai vu 24 mais en fait c'était 224; **to r. the temperature/a thermometer** lire la température/un thermomètre; **to r. an electricity meter** relever un compteur d'électricité; **to r. sb's palm** *or* **hand** lire les lignes de la main de qn

3 *(say aloud) (letter, poem)* lire (à haute voix); **to r. sb sth, to r. sth to sb** lire qch à qn; **r. me that last bit again** relis-moi le dernier passage; **to r. a child a bedtime story** lire une histoire à un enfant pour qu'il s'endorme; *Rel* **to r. the lesson** lire un passage de l'Évangile; *Fig* **to r. sb a lesson** *or* **a lecture** faire la leçon à qn; **to r. a paper at a conference** présenter un exposé à une conférence; **to r. the news** *Radio* lire les informations; *TV* présenter le journal; *Law* **to r. a will** exécuter la lecture d'un testament

4 **to r. oneself to sleep** lire jusqu'à ce qu'on s'endorme; **he r.** [red] **me to sleep** il m'a fait la lecture jusqu'à ce que je m'endorme

5 *Br Univ (study) (French, history etc)* étudier; **to r. law/medicine** faire son droit/sa médecine

6 *(show) (of measuring instrument)* indiquer; **the inscription on the monument reads ...** on peut lire sur le monument ...; **the sign on the door r.** [red] **No Entry** sur l'écriteau on pouvait lire 'Défense d'entrer'

VI 1 lire; **she taught her daughter (how) to r.** elle a appris à lire à sa fille; **to r. to sb** faire la lecture à qn; **I'm very fond of reading** j'aime beaucoup lire *ou* la lecture *ou* *Fam* bouquiner; **to r. aloud** lire à haute voix; **r. quietly to yourselves** lisez en silence; **to r. about sb/ sth** lire quelque chose sur qch/qn; **what are you reading about?** qu'est-ce que tu lis?; **we r.** [red] **of his death in the newspaper** nous avons appris sa mort dans le journal

2 *(interpret)* **to r. between the lines** lire entre les lignes; **she r.** [red] **in the cards that I would be famous** elle a lu dans les cartes que je serais célèbre

3 *Br Univ* **to r. for a degree** préparer un diplôme; **to r. for the Bar** faire des études de droit

4 *(be worded)* **to r. well/badly** *(of text)* être bien/mal écrit; **his text reads like a translation** son texte sent la traduction; **the telegram reads as follows** le télégramme est libellé comme suit; **Arabic reads from right to left** l'arabe se lit de droite à gauche; **her life story reads like a fairytale** sa vie ressemble à un conte de fées

▸**read in** VT SEP *Comput (data)* emmagasiner, lire et stocker en mémoire

▸**read into** VT SEP **to r. sth into sth** voir qch dans qch; **don't r. too much into what she says** ne donne pas à ce qu'elle dit plus de signification que ça n'en a; **you're reading far too much into it** tu interprètes beaucoup trop

▸**read off** VT SEP *(names etc)* énumérer (**from** sur)

▸**read on** VI *(continue to read)* **now r. on** lisez

la suite; **to r. on from ...** lire à partir de ...

▸ **read out** VT SEP *(names, list, passage etc)* lire (à haute voix); *Comput (data)* sortir, extraire de la mémoire

▸ **read over** VT SEP *(quickly)* parcourir; *(with special care)* examiner; *esp Am (read again)* relire

▸ **read through** VT SEP *(skim)* parcourir; *(examine closely)* lire en détail, examiner; *Theat* **to r. through a play** faire la lecture d'une pièce

▸ **read up** VT SEP *(subject)* étudier

▸ **read up on** VT INSEP = **read up**

readability [riːdəˈbɪlɪtɪ] N *(of book, handwriting)* lisibilité *f*

readable [ˈriːdəb(ə)l] ADJ **1** *(book, style etc)* lisible; **highly** *or* **very r.** d'une lecture très agréable **2** *(legible) (handwriting, disk)* lisible; **not r.** illisible

readdress [riːəˈdres] VT *(forward) (letter)* faire suivre

reader [ˈriːdər] N **1** *(of books, newspapers etc)* lecteur, -trice; *Am (company librarian)* documentaliste *mf*; **she is a great** *or* **an avid r.** c'est une grande liseuse, elle lit beaucoup; **he's not much of a r.** il n'aime pas beaucoup la lecture, il ne lit pas beaucoup; **(proof) r.** correcteur, -trice d'épreuves; **publisher's r.** lecteur, -trice dans une maison d'édition **2** *Univ Br* ≃ maître *m* de recherches; *Am* ≃ assistant, -ante, *Can* ≃ chargé, -e de cours **3** *(book) (for teaching reading)* livre *m* de lecture; *(textbook)* livre, manuel *m*; *(anthology)* recueil *m*; **French/geography r.** recueil de français/géographie; **a Melville r.** un recueil d'extraits de Melville **4** *(machine)* lecteur *m*

readership [ˈriːdəʃɪp] N **1** *(of magazine, author etc)* lecteurs *mpl*; *(esp of paper)* lectorat *m*; **what is the paper's r.?** combien de personnes lisent le journal? **2** *Br Univ* **she holds a r. in mathematics** elle est maître de recherches en mathématiques

▸▸ **r. survey** étude *f* du lectorat

readies [ˈrediz] NPL *Br Fam (cash)* fric *m*; **£500 in r.** 500 livres en liquide; **I want the r. first** je veux le fric d'abord

readily [ˈredɪlɪ] ADV *(willingly)* de bonne grâce, volontiers; *(easily)* facilement

readiness [ˈredɪnɪs] N **1** *(willingness)* empressement *m* (**to do** à faire) **2** *(agility) (of speech, tongue)* facilité *f* d'expression; *(of mind, wit)* vivacité *f* d'esprit **3** *(preparedness)* **to be in r.** être prêt (**for** pour); **to have everything in r.** avoir tout prêt

reading [ˈriːdɪŋ] N **1** *(action, pastime)* lecture *f*; **r. is not his favourite activity** la lecture n'est pas son passe-temps favori; **I have a lot of r. to catch up on** j'ai beaucoup de retard à rattraper dans mes lectures; **I like a bit of light r.** j'aime un livre facile à lire de temps en temps; **his thesis makes (for) boring r.** sa thèse est ennuyeuse à lire; **a young woman of wide r.** une jeune femme très cultivée *ou* érudite *ou* lettrée; *Comput* **r. to disk** lecture *f* sur disque

2 *(saying aloud) (of play, poetry, will)* lecture *f*; *Parl* **first/second/third r.** *(of bill)* première/seconde/troisième lecture **3** *(measurement) (of meter)* relevé *m*; *(by instrument)* indication *f*, **the fuel gauge is giving the wrong r.** la jauge d'essence n'est pas fiable; **to take a barometric/temperature r.** lire le baromètre/le thermomètre **4** *(interpretation) (of facts, situation, character)* interprétation *f*, **this is one of two possible readings of the poem/novel** c'est l'une des deux lectures possibles du poème/roman

ADJ **to have a r. age of ten** lire comme un enfant de dix ans; **she has a r. age well in advance of her years** elle est très en avance

sur son âge pour ce qui est de la lecture; **children of r. age** des enfants en âge de lire; **I have a r. knowledge of Arabic** je peux lire l'arabe; **take some r. material** *or* **matter** prends de la lecture *ou* de quoi lire; **the r. public** les lecteurs *mpl*

▸▸ **r. book** livre *m* de lecture; **r. glasses** *(spectacles)* lunettes *fpl* pour lire; *Comput* **r. head** tête *f* de lecture; **r. lamp** lampe *f* de bureau; *(by bed)* lampe de chevet; **r. light** liseuse *f*, **r. list** *(syllabus)* liste *f* des ouvrages au programme; *(for further reading)* liste des ouvrages recommandés; **r. room** salle *f* de lecture **r. speed** *(of child, computer)* vitesse *f* de lecture

readjust [riːəˈdʒʌst] VT *(correct) (prices, wages)* rajuster, réajuster; *(microscope, telescope)* remettre au point; **to r. one's clothing** se rajuster

VI *(of person)* se réadapter (**to** à)

readjustment [riːəˈdʒʌstmənt] N **1** *(of prices, wages)* rajustement *m*, réajustement *m*; **some r. of the telescope is necessary** il faut régler à *ou* de nouveau le télescope **2** *(of person)* réadaptation *f*

read-me ADJ

▸▸ *Comput* **r. document** fichier *m* lisez-moi, ouvrez-moi *m inv*; *Comput* **r. file** fichier lisez-moi, ouvrez-moi *m*

readmission [riːədˈmɪʃən] N *(to club, political party)* réintégration *f* (**to** dans); **to gain r. to a party** réintégrer un parti; **his r. to hospital was seen as a bad sign** le fait qu'il soit réadmis à l'hôpital a été interprété comme un mauvais signe

readmit [riːədˈmɪt] VT *(take in again) (person)* réintégrer (**to** dans); **he was readmitted (to hospital) last night** il a été réadmis à l'hôpital la nuit dernière

read-only ADJ *Comput* (à) lecture seule; **that file is r.** ce fichier est protégé en écriture; **to make a file r.** mettre un fichier en lecture seule

▸▸ **r. disk** *(hard)* disque *m* en lecture seule; *(floppy)* disquette *f* en lecture seule; **r. file** fichier *m* en lecture seule; **r. memory** mémoire *f* morte; **r. mode** mode *m* lecture seule

read-out N *Comput* lecture *f*, *(on screen)* affichage *m*; *(on paper)* sortie *f* papier ou sur imprimante, listing *m*

▸▸ **r. device** unité *f* d'affichage

read-through N *(of script)* lecture *f* du scénario; **to give sth a quick r.** parcourir qch rapidement

readvertise [riːˈædvətaiz] VT *(job)* repasser une annonce pour

VI **they're readvertising** ils ont repassé l'annonce

readvertisement [riːədˈvɜːtɪsmənt] N deuxième annonce *f*, **this is a r.** *(notice on jobs page)* deuxième annonce d'offre d'emploi

read-write ADJ *Comput*

▸▸ **r. head** tête *f* de lecture-écriture; **r. memory** mémoire *f* lecture-écriture; **r. protection notch** encoche *f* de protection lecture-écriture

ready [ˈredɪ] ADJ **1** *(prepared)* prêt (**to do** à faire; **for sth** pour qch); **to get r.** se préparer, s'apprêter (**to do** à faire; **for sth** à qch); *Old-fashioned* **to make r.** faire des préparations, se préparer (**for** pour); **to get sth r.** préparer qch; **dinner is r.** le dîner est servi, *Fam* à table; **I'm r. if you are, r. when you are** quand tu veux; *Sport* **r.! steady! go!** à vos marques! prêts! partez!; **to get r. for school** se préparer pour aller à l'école; **to get r. for bed** se préparer à aller se coucher; **to get a patient r. for an operation** préparer un malade pour une opération; **to get some food r.** préparer à manger; **to get a room r. for a guest** préparer une chambre pour un invité;

r. for delivery livrable; *Com* **r. for shipping** sous palan; **r. for use** prêt à l'usage; **she's r. for anything** elle est prête à tout; **r. to go to press** bon à tirer, BAT; **are you r. to order?** *(in restaurant)* avez-vous choisi *ou* fait votre choix?; **r. to serve** *(food)* prêt à servir, tout prêt; **I'm r. to drop** *(exhausted)* je tombe de fatigue; **r. to hand** sous la main, à portée de (la) main

2 *(willing)* prêt, disposé (**to do** à faire); **she's always r. to help** elle est toujours prête à rendre service

3 *(quick)* prompt, facile; **to have a r. wit** avoir l'esprit prompt *ou* d'à-propos *ou* de repartie; **to be always r. with an answer** avoir la réplique prompte; **you're always a bit too r. with advice** tu donnes toujours trop de conseils; **he's very r. with his fists** il est prompt à se battre; **don't be too r. to condemn him** ne le condamnez pas trop rapidement, ne soyez pas trop prompt à lui jeter la pierre; **a r. source of income** une source de revenu facile; **the story found r. acceptance** l'histoire a été acceptée sans difficulté

N **1** *Fam* **the r.** *(money)* argent *m* liquide; **have you enough of the r. on you?** est-ce que tu as assez de liquide?

2 **the reporter had her notebook at the r.** la journaliste avait son carnet tout prêt; **with camera at the r., she ...** son appareil photo tout prêt, elle ...; **with their guns at the r.** prêts à tirer

VT *(the house)* préparer; **to r. oneself for action** se préparer à l'action

▸▸ **r. meal** plat *m* cuisiné; **r. money** argent liquide; **to pay in r. money** payer en espèces ou en argent liquide; *Br* **r. reckoner** barème *m*

ready- [redɪ-] PREF **r.-cut** précoupé

ready-made ADJ *(clothes)* de prêt-à-porter; *(food)* précuit; *(curtains, excuse, argument, solution)* tout fait; **a r. cake** un gâteau tout fait; *Fig* **to have a r. family** avoir une famille déjà constituée

N *(garment)* vêtement *m* de prêt-à-porter

ready-mix ADJ *(buns, cake etc)* fait à partir d'une préparation; *(concrete)* prémalaxé

ready-to-wear ADJ

▸▸ **r. clothing** prêt-à-porter *m*, *pl* prêts-à-porter

reaffirm [riːəˈfɜːm] VT *(one's loyalty, a belief, one's intentions)* réaffirmer

reafforest [riːəˈfɒrɪst] VT = **reforest**

reafforestation [riːəfɒrɪˈsteɪʃən] N = **reforestation**

Reaganite [ˈreɪgənaɪt] N partisan *m* de Reagan; **R. budget/programme** budget *m*/programme *m* reaganien

Reaganomics [reɪgəˈnɒmɪks] NPL *(usu with sing verb)* reaganisme *m*

reagent [riːˈeɪdʒənt] N *Chem* réactif *m*

REAL [rɪəl] ADJ **1** *(authentic) (diamond, pearl, mother)* vrai; *(gold, leather)* véritable; *(silk, flowers)* naturel; **a r. friend/idiot** un véritable ami/idiot; **a r. disaster/shock** un véritable *ou* vrai désastre/choc; **he's made a r. effort** il a fait un véritable effort, il a fait un effort réel; **that's what I call a r. man!** ça, c'est ce que j'appelle un (vrai) homme; **the r. reason** la vraie raison (**for** pour); **she has no r. feeling for poetry** elle n'a pas le sens de la poésie; **what is his r. name?** quel est son vrai nom?; **he's a r. gentleman** c'est un vrai gentleman; *Fam* **it's the r. McCoy** *or* **thing** c'est du vrai de vrai; **this orange drink is not bad but it's poor stuff compared to the r. thing** cette boisson à l'orange n'est pas mauvaise, mais ça ne vaut pas le vrai jus d'orange; *Fam* **she swears it's the r. thing this time** *(true love)* elle jure que cette fois-ci c'est le grand

amour; *Fam* **this is not a drill, it's the r. thing or for r.** ce n'est pas un exercice, c'est pour de vrai; *Fam* **is that man for r.?** il est pas vrai, ce type!; *Fam* **is that for r.?** c'est vrai?; *Fam* **get r.!** tu délires!
2 *(actual) (cost, salary, world etc), Math, Phys* réel; **in r. life** dans la réalité *ou* la vie
ADV *Am Fam (very)* vraiment, très; **a r. fine day** une très belle journée; **that's r. nice of you** c'est vraiment *ou* très gentil de votre part; **I'll see you r. soon** à très bientôt
N *Phil* **the r.** le réel
▸▸ *Fin* **r. accounts** comptes *mpl* de valeur; *Br* **r. ale** bière *f* artisanale; *Fin* **r. assets** biens *mpl* immobiliers; **r. estate** *Br Law* biens fonciers; *Am* biens immobiliers; **she works in r. estate** elle travaille dans l'immobilier; *Econ* **r. GDP** PIB *m* réel; *Econ* **r. growth** croissance *f* réelle; *Econ* **r. income** revenu *m* réel; *Rel* **r. presence** présence *f* réelle; *Econ* **r. purchasing power** pouvoir *m* d'achat réel; *Mktg* **r. repositioning** repositionnement *m* réel; **r. salary** salaire *m* réel; **r. tennis** jeu *m* de paume; **to play r. tennis** jouer à la paume; *Fin* **r. terms** termes *mpl* réels; **what does that mean in r. terms?** qu'est-ce que ça signifie au bout du compte?; *Comput* **r. time** temps *m* réel; *Fin* **r. value** valeur *f* effective

real-estate **ADJ**
▸▸ **r. agency** agence *f* immobilière; **r. agent** agent *m* immobilier; **r. developer** promoteur *m* immobilier

realign [riːəˈlaɪn] **VT** aligner (de nouveau); *Fin (currencies)* réaligner; *Pol* regrouper **VI** s'aligner (de nouveau); *Pol* se regrouper

realignment [riːəˈlaɪnmənt] **N** (nouvel) alignement *m*; *Fin* réalignement *m*; *Pol* regroupement *m*
▸▸ *Fin* **r. of currencies** réalignement monétaire

realism [ˈrɪəlɪz(ə)m] **N** *Art, Phil etc* réalisme *m*

realist [ˈrɪəlɪst] **ADJ, N** *Art, Phil etc* réaliste *mf*

realistic [rɪəˈlɪstɪk] **ADJ** *(person, proposal)* réaliste; *(style)* plein de réalisme

realistically [rɪəˈlɪstɪklɪ] **ADV** *(to act, behave)* avec réalisme

reality [rɪˈælɪtɪ] **N** réalité *f*; **in r.** en réalité; **to bring sb back to r.** ramener qn à la réalité; **they refuse to face the r. of their situation** ils refusent de voir la situation telle qu'elle est; **to become a r.** *(of dream, hope etc)* se réaliser, devenir réalité; **to make a dream/project (a) r.** réaliser un rêve/projet; **the realities of everyday life** les réalités de la vie quotidienne; **it was a r. check for him** ça l'a ramené à la réalité
▸▸ *Am TV* **r. show** reality show *m*; **r. television** télé-vérité *f*

realizable [ˈrɪəlaɪzəb(ə)l] **ADJ** *(plan, project etc), Fin* réalisable
▸▸ **r. assets** actif *m* réalisable; **r. securities** valeurs *fpl* réalisables

realization [rɪəlaɪˈzeɪʃən] **N 1** *(of plan, project etc), Fin* réalisation *f* **2** *(awareness)* prise *f* de conscience; **there is a growing r. that ...** on commence à se rendre compte que ...; **the sudden r. that ... made her weep** elle s'est mise à pleurer quand tout d'un coup elle s'est rendu compte que ...

realize [ˈrɪəlaɪz] **VT 1** *Fin (asset, profit)* réaliser; **to r. a high price** *(of goods)* atteindre un prix élevé; *(of seller)* obtenir un prix élevé; **how much did they r. on the sale?** combien est-ce qu'ils ont gagné sur la vente?; **these shares cannot be realized** il n'y a pas de marché pour ces titres **2** *(make real)* **our worst fears have been realized** nos pires craintes se sont réalisées; **our hopes were realized** nos espoirs se sont réalisés *ou* concrétisés; **he hasn't yet realized his full potential** il n'a

pas encore atteint son maximum **3** *(know, be aware of)* se rendre compte de, réaliser; **I r. that, but ...** je sais bien, mais ... **4** *(become aware of)* se rendre compte de/que, prendre conscience de/que; **we realized that he was blind** nous nous sommes aperçus *ou* rendu compte qu'il était aveugle; **I realized it at the first glance** je m'en suis aperçu *ou* rendu compte au premier coup d'œil
VI I'm sorry, I didn't r. je suis désolé, je ne m'en étais pas rendu compte *ou Fam* je n'avais pas réalisé

really [ˈrɪəlɪ] **ADV 1** *(actually)* vraiment; **things that r. exist** choses qui existent réellement; **that is r. a matter for the manager** c'est là proprement l'affaire du gérant; **is it r. true?** est-ce bien vrai? **2** *(intensifier)* **he r. likes you** il t'aime beaucoup; **you r. must go to it** il faut absolument que vous y alliez; **I r. have or ought to be going** il faut vraiment que j'y aille **3** *(very)* vraiment; **she's r. nice** elle est vraiment sympa
INT r.? vraiment?; **r.!** *(indignation)* vraiment!

realm [relm] **N 1** *Fml (kingdom)* royaume *m* **2** *Fig (of dreams, fancy etc)* monde *m*; *(of politics, science etc)* domaine *m*; **within the realms of possibility** dans le domaine du possible; **health is no longer exclusively the r. of doctors** la santé n'est plus l'apanage du médecin

real-time **ADJ** *(processing, system, control)* en temps réel
▸▸ **r. clock** horloge *f* (en) temps réel; **r. graphics** graphiques *mpl* en temps réel; **r. management** gestion *f* en temps réel; **r. operating system** système *m* d'exploitation en temps réel; *St Exch* **r. trading** cotation *f* en temps réel

Realtor® [ˈrɪəltər] **N** *Am* agent *m* immobilier

realty [ˈrɪəltɪ] **N** *Law* biens *mpl* immobiliers, (biens) immeubles *mpl*

ream¹ [riːm] **N** *(of paper)* rame *f*, *Fam* **to write reams** écrire des pages et des pages; *Fam* **reams of statistics/information** des quantités *fpl* de statistiques/d'informations

ream² [riːm] **VT 1** *Tech (bore) (part)* aléser **2** *Am (squeeze) (lemon)* presser
▸ **ream out** **VT SEP** *Am Sl* **to r. sb out** *(scold)* passer un savon à qn, remonter les bretelles à qn

reamer [ˈriːmər] **N 1** *Tech* alésoir *m* **2** *Am (for lemon)* presse-citron *m inv*

reanimate [riːˈænɪmeɪt] **VT** *Med* r(é)animer

reap [riːp] **VT** *(corn, field)* moissonner; *Prov* **he who sows the wind shall r. the whirlwind** qui sème le vent récolte la tempête; *Fig* **to r. the rewards of one's labours** recueillir le fruit de ses travaux; *Fig* **I r. no benefit from it** je n'en retire aucun avantage **VI** moissonner, faire la moisson

reaper [ˈriːpər] **N** *(machine)* moissonneuse *f*, *(person)* moissonneur, -euse; *Fig* **the (Grim) R.** la Faucheuse
▸▸ **r. binder** moissonneuse-lieuse *f*, *pl* moissonneuses-lieuses

reaping [ˈriːpɪŋ] **N** *(of corn etc)* moisson *f*
▸▸ **r. hook** faucille *f*; **r. machine** moissonneuse *f*

reappear [riːəˈpɪər] **VI** réapparaître

reappearance [riːəˈpɪərəns] **N** réapparition *f*

reapply [riːəˈplaɪ] **VT** *(cream, lotion etc)* réappliquer
VI *(for grant, job, loan etc)* renouveler sa demande (**for** de)

reappoint [riːəˈpɔɪnt] **VT** *(person)* renommer

reappointment [riːəˈpɔɪntmənt] **N** **nobody opposed his r.** personne ne s'opposa à ce qu'il soit reconduit dans ses fonctions

reappraisal [riːəˈpreɪz(ə)l] **N 1** *Fin (of property)* réévaluation *f* **2** *(of policy)* réexamen *m*

reappraise [riːəˈpreɪz] **VT 1** *Fin (property)* réévaluer **2** *(policy)* réexaminer

rear¹ [rɪər] **N 1** *(back part) (of building, car, train)* arrière *m*; **in the r.** en arrière, à l'arrière; **in the r. of the train** en queue du train; **at** *or Am* **in the r. of** *(behind)* derrière; **from the r.** par derrière; *(to recognize)* de derrière; **to bring up the r.** *(of procession)* venir en queue; *(be in last place)* être à la queue, *Pej* être la lanterne rouge; **r. legs** *(of dog, cat etc)* pattes *fpl* de derrière; *(of horse)* jambes *fpl* de derrière; *Aut* **r.-view** *or Am* **r.-vision mirror** rétroviseur *m*, rétro *m* **2** *(of military column)* queue *f*; **to bring up the r.** *(come at end) (of military column)* fermer la marche; **to protect one's r.** *Mil* protéger ses arrières; *Fig* assurer ses arrières **3** *Fam (buttocks)* **r. (end)** derrière *m*, fesses *fpl*; **he needs a kick in the r.** il lui faut un coup de pied au derrière *ou* dans les fesses
ADJ *(door, wheel)* arrière *inv*; de derrière; *(engine)* arrière; *(carriages)* de queue; **is there a rear entrance?** est-ce qu'il y a une entrée par derrière?
▸▸ *Naut* **r. admiral** contre-amiral *m*, *pl* contre-amiraux; *Aut* **r. drive axle** pont *m* arrière; *Br Aut* **r. lamps** feux *mpl* arrière; *Br Aut* **r. lights** feux arrière; *Cin, TV* **r. projection** projection *f* en transparence; *Aut* **r. spoiler** aileron *m ou* spoiler *m* arrière; *Aut* **r. window** lunette *f* arrière

rear² **VT 1** *(nurture) (child, sheep)* élever; *(plants)* cultiver **2** *(lift) (one's head)* relever; *Fig* **to r. its ugly head** *(of racism, violence etc)* faire son apparition
VI **to r. (up)** *(on its hind legs) (of horse)* se cabrer; **cliffs r. (up) above the shore** des falaises se dressent au-dessus du rivage

rear-drive **ADJ** à traction arrière

rear-end **VT** *esp Am Aut* **to r. sb** *(collide with)* emboutir l'arrière de la voiture de qn

rear-engined [rɪərˈendʒɪnd] **ADJ** *(car etc)* avec le moteur à l'arrière, à moteur arrière

rearguard [ˈrɪəɡɑːd] **N** *Mil* arrière-garde *f*, *pl* arrière-gardes
▸▸ **r. action** combat *m* d'arrière-garde; *also Fig* **to fight** *or* **mount a r. action** mener un combat d'arrière-garde

rearing [ˈrɪərɪŋ] **N 1** *(of children)* éducation *f*, *(of animals)* élevage *m*; *(of plants)* culture *f* **2** **r. (up)** *(of horse)* cabrage *m*

rearm [riːˈɑːm] **VT & VI** réarmer

rearmament [riːˈɑːməmənt] **N** *(of country, soldiers etc)* réarmement *m*

rearmost [ˈrɪəməʊst] **ADJ** dernier; *(carriage, compartment on train)* dernier, de queue

rear-mounted **ADJ** *(engine, gun)* monté à l'arrière

rearrange [riːəˈreɪndʒ] **VT** *(books, furniture, flowers)* changer la disposition de; *(room, office)* aménager de façon différente; *(one's clothing)* réajuster; *(schedule)* modifier; *(appointment)* changer, reporter; **they've rearranged everything in here** tout a changé de place ici; **could we r. things?** est-ce qu'on peut s'organiser autrement?; *Fam* **to r. sb's face** casser la gueule à qn

rearrangement [riːəˈreɪndʒmənt] **N** *(of books, flowers, room etc)* réarrangement *m*; *(of schedule)* modification *f*, *(of appointment)* changement *m*

rearward [ˈrɪəwəd] **ADJ 1** *(at back) (compartment etc)* (situé à l')arrière **2** *(backward) (glance, movement)* vers l'arrière
ADV *esp Am* = **rearwards**

rearwards [ˈrɪəwədz] **ADV** *esp Br (be situated)* à l'arrière; *(to glance, move)* vers l'arrière

rear-wheel drive N *Aut* propulsion *f* arrière; **car with r.** voiture *f* à traction arrière

rear-wheel steering N *Aut* roues *fpl* arrière directrices

REASON ['ri:z(ə)n] N **1** *(cause)* raison *f* (**for** de); **there is a r. for his doing so** il y a une raison pour qu'il fasse ça; **to state one's reasons for a decision** motiver une décision; **for reasons of health** pour raisons de santé; **reasons of state** la raison d'État; *usu Iron* **for reasons best known to themselves** pour des raisons qu'eux seuls connaissent *ou* qu'ils sont les seuls à connaître; **for some** *or* **one r.** *or* **other** pour une raison ou pour une autre; **for no other r. than that I forgot** pour la simple raison que j'ai oublié; **for no particular r.** sans raison particulière; **for no r. at all** sans aucune raison; **that's no r. for refusing to help me!** ce n'est pas une raison pour refuser de m'aider!; **for that very r.** pour cette raison même; **for the very r. that he had been asked not to do it** précisément parce qu'on l'avait prié de ne pas le faire; **the r. why** la raison; **I don't know the r. why** je ne sais pas pourquoi; **the r. (why) he left** la raison pour laquelle il est parti; **the r. (why** *or* **for which) he came, his r. for coming** la raison pour laquelle il est venu; **what's the r. for it?** à quoi cela tient-il?, quelle en est la raison?; **what r. did you give for your absence?** comment as-tu expliqué ton absence?; **what r. could they give for such inhuman acts?** comment peuvent-ils justifier des actes d'une telle cruauté?; **to have every r. to believe ...** avoir tout lieu de croire ...; **I have (good) r. to believe that he's lying** j'ai de bonnes raisons de croire qu'il ment; **to have r. enough (to do sth)** avoir de bonnes raisons (de faire qch); **she complains and with (good) r.** elle se plaint et pour cause; **it's not without (good) r. that I detest him** ce n'est pas pour rien que je le déteste; **to give sb good r. for doing sth** donner de bonnes raisons à qn de faire qch; **give me one good r. why I should!** donne-moi une raison valable pour que je le fasse!; **all the more r. for going there** *or* **why I should go there** raison de plus pour y aller *ou* pour que j'y aille; *Fml* **by r. of his infirmity** en raison de son infirmité; **to be found not guilty by r. of insanity** être déclaré non-coupable pour cause de démence

2 *(sanity, common sense)* raison *f*; **he lost his r.** il a perdu la raison; **to listen to** *or* **hear** *or* **see r.** entendre raison; **it stands to r.** il va de soi *ou* sans dire (**that ...** que ... + *ind*); **that stands to r.** ça va de soi *ou* sans dire, c'est logique; **within r.** dans des limites raisonnables

VI raisonner (**about** sur); **to r. with sb** raisonner (avec) qn; **there's no reasoning with him** il n'y a pas moyen de lui faire entendre raison, on ne peut pas raisonner avec lui; *Hum* **ours is not to r. why** il ne faut pas chercher à comprendre; **to r. from past experience** raisonner en fonction de ses expériences passées

VT **to r. that ...** estimer que ... + *ind*; **to r. sb into/out of doing sth** convaincre qn de faire/de ne pas faire qch

► **reason out** VT SEP *(maths problem)* résoudre; *(one's differences)* résoudre en discutant; **to r. out that ...** déduire que ...

reasonable ['ri:z(ə)nəb(ə)l] ADJ *(person, price, demand)* raisonnable; *(offer)* acceptable, raisonnable; *(effort)* acceptable; **(do) be r.** soyez *ou* tâchez d'être raisonnable; **as is only r.** ce qui est parfaitement normal; **to believe sth beyond all r. doubt** croire qch en son âme et conscience; **r. suspicions** soupçons *mpl* fondés; **r. excuse** excuse *f* valable (**for** de); **with a r. amount of luck** avec un peu de chance; **the weather/meal/film**

was r. le temps/le repas/le film était passable

reasonableness ['ri:z(ə)nəb(ə)lnɪs] N *(of person, offer etc)* caractère *m* raisonnable; *(of effort)* caractère acceptable; *(of suspicion)* bien-fondé *m*, *pl* bien-fondés

reasonably ['ri:z(ə)nəblɪ] ADV **1** *(to behave, act)* raisonnablement, de façon raisonnable; **r. priced** d'un prix raisonnable **2** *(fairly, rather)* assez; **r. fit** en assez bonne forme; **if we are r. lucky** avec un peu de chance

reasoned ['ri:zənd] ADJ *(analysis, decision etc)* raisonné

reasoning ['ri:zənɪŋ] N raisonnement *m*; **power of r.** *(ability)* capacité *f* de raisonnement; **the r. behind the decision** les raisons de cette décision; **such r. is dangerous** un tel raisonnement est dangereux

ADJ *(creature etc)* doué de raison; *(ability, process etc)* de raisonnement

reassemble [ri:ə'semb(ə)l] VT **1** *(gather)* rassembler **2** *(put together)* *(machine)* remonter; *(frame)* rassembler

VI *(of troops)* s'assembler de nouveau; **Parliament will r. on ...** le Parlement rouvrira le ...

reassembly [ri:ə'semblɪ] N *(gathering together)* rassemblement *m*; *Pol* rentrée *f*, *(of machine, gun)* remontage *m*

reassert [ri:ə'sɜːt] VT *(conviction, belief)* réaffirmer; **her self-confidence reasserted itself** sa confiance est revenue

reassess [ri:ə'ses] VT **1** *(policy, situation)* reconsidérer, réexaminer **2** *Fin (damages)* réévaluer; **you have been reassessed** votre situation fiscale a été réexaminée

reassessment [ri:ə'sesmənt] N **1** *(of policy, situation)* réexamen *m* **2** *Fin (of damages)* réévaluation *f*

reassign [ri:ə'saɪn] VT *(transfer)* *(employee, police officer etc)* muter (**to** à); *(funds)* réaffecter; *(work, project etc)* confier (**to** à); **the work has been reassigned** le travail a été confié à quelqu'un d'autre

reassignment [ri:ə'saɪnmənt] N **1** *(transfer)* *(of employee, police officer etc)* mutation *f*, *(of funds)* réaffectation *f* **2** *(duties)* nouveau poste *m*, nouvelles fonctions *fpl*

reassume [ri:ə'sju:m] VT *(one's duties)* reprendre

reassurance [ri:ə'ʃʊərəns] N **1** *(comfort)* réconfort *m*; *(guarantee)* assurance *f*, **the boss gave (them) reassurances about their jobs** le patron les a rassurés quant à leur emploi **2** *Br Fin* réassurance *f*

reassure [ri:ə'ʃʊər] VT **1** *(person)* rassurer (**about** à propos de); **to r. sb of one's esteem** assurer qn de son estime; **to feel reassured** se sentir rassuré (**about** sur) **2** *Br Fin* réassurer

reassuring [ri:ə'ʃʊərɪŋ] ADJ *(person, news etc)* rassurant

reassuringly [ri:ə'ʃʊərɪŋlɪ] ADV *(to behave, act)* d'une manière rassurante

reawaken [ri:ə'weɪk(ə)n] VT *(sleeper)* réveiller; *(interest, feeling)* ranimer, faire renaître; *(hope)* faire renaître

VI *(of person)* se réveiller de nouveau; *(of affection, feelings, interest)* se ranimer

reawakening [ri:ə'weɪk(ə)nɪŋ] N *(of person, feeling etc)* réveil *m*; *(of interest)* regain *m*; *(of idea)* renaissance *f*

rebate ['ri:beɪt] N *Com etc* **1** *(refund)* remboursement *m* (partiel); *(of tax)* dégrèvement *m* **2** *(discount on purchase)* rabais *m*, ristourne *f*

rebel [1] ['reb(ə)l] N *(opponent)* *(of government)* rebelle *mf*; *(armed)* rebelle, insurgé, -ée; *(in society)* rebelle, révolté, -ée; *Hist* **the**

Rebels *(Confederates)* les confédérés

ADJ *(soldier)* rebelle; *(camp, territory)* des rebelles; *(attack)* de rebelles

► ► **r. forces** forces *fpl* rebelles; **r. leader** chef *m* des rebelles; **r. MP** parlementaire *mf* rebelle

rebel [2] [rɪ'bel] VI *(-ll-)* *(against government)* se rebeller, se soulever (**against** contre); *(against society)* se rebeller, se révolter (**against** contre); **to r. against one's fate** se révolter *ou* s'insurger contre son destin; **her stomach rebelled at the thought of more food** elle avait l'estomac qui se soulevait rien que de penser à la nourriture

rebellion [rɪ'beljən] N *(against government)* rébellion *f*, soulèvement *m* (**against** contre); *(against society)* rébellion, révolte *f* (**against** contre); **to be in r. against** être en rébellion contre; **to rise up in r.** se soulever (**against** contre)

rebellious [rɪ'beljəs] ADJ *(soldier, troops etc)* insubordonné; *(student, inhabitants)* révolté, en révolte; *(behaviour, child, hair)* rebelle; **r. act** acte *m* de révolte

rebelliously [rɪ'beljəslɪ] ADV *(to behave, act)* d'une façon rebelle

rebelliousness [rɪ'beljəsnɪs] N *(of troops)* insubordination *f*, *(of students etc)* esprit *m* de rébellion

rebirth [ri:'bɜːθ] N *(of country etc)* renaissance *f*

reboot [ri:'bu:t] *Comput* VT réamorcer

VI se réamorcer

rebore ['ri:bɔːr] *Aut* N réalésage *m*; **my car needs a r.** le cylindre de ma voiture a besoin d'être réalésé *ou* d'un réalésage

VT réaléser

reborn [ri:'bɔːn] ADJ USU PRED né à nouveau; **to be r.** renaître; **hope was r.** l'espoir est revenu; **to feel r.** *(physically)* se sentir revigoré; *(spiritually)* se sentir renaître

rebound [1] ['ri:baʊnd] N *(of ball)* rebond *m*; **to hit a ball on the r.** frapper une balle au rebond; **he headed in the r.** il a marqué un but de la tête en prenant la balle au rebond; *Fig* **she married him on the r.** elle l'a épousé à cause d'une déception amoureuse; *Fig* **he caught her on the r.** il a commencé à la fréquenter au moment où elle sortait d'une déception amoureuse

rebound [2] [rɪ'baʊnd] VI **1** *(of ball etc)* rebondir; *(of cry, noise)* faire écho (**from** contre); *Fig (of joke, lie etc)* se retourner (**on** contre); **the trick he played rebounded on him** son mauvais tour s'est retourné contre lui **2** *(recover)* *(of person)* se ressaisir (**from** après); *(of share prices, business)* reprendre, se redresser (**from** après)

rebrand [ri:'brænd] VT *Mktg (product)* changer la marque de

rebranding [ri:'brændɪŋ] N *Mktg (of product)* changement *m* de marque

rebuff [rɪ'bʌf] N *(of person)* rebuffade *f*, *(of suggestion etc)* refus *m*; **to meet with** *or* **suffer a r.** *(of person)* essuyer une rebuffade; *(of suggestion etc)* être repoussé

VT *(reject)* *(advances)* repousser; *(person)* repousser, rejeter; *(offer, suggestion)* rejeter; *(allegation)* démentir; **to feel rebuffed** se sentir repoussé *ou* rejeté

rebuild [ri:'bɪld] VT *(pt, pp* **rebuilt** [ri:'bɪlt]*)* *(house, company)* reconstruire; *(one's life)* reconstruire, refaire; *(machine, engine)* remettre à neuf, refaire

rebuilding [ri:'bɪldɪŋ] N *(of house, company)* reconstruction *f*, *(of machine, engine)* réfection *f*, remise *f* à neuf

rebuke [rɪ'bju:k] N réprimande *f*; **to administer** *or* **deliver a r. to sb** réprimander qn, faire une réprimande à qn

vt *(person)* réprimander (**for doing sth** pour avoir fait qch)

rebus ['ri:bəs] **N** rébus *m*

rebut [rɪ'bʌt] **vt** (**-tt-**) *Fml (accusation, hypothesis etc)* réfuter

rebuttal [rɪ'bʌt(ə)l] **N** *Fml* réfutation *f*

rebuy ['ri:baɪ] **N** *Mktg* réachat *m*
▸▸ **r. rate** taux *m* de réachat

rec [rek] **N** *Fam* **1** *Br (ground)* terrain *m* de jeux **2** *Am Sch (break)* récré *f*
▸▸ *Br* **r. ground** terrain de jeux; *Am* **r. room** *(in home)* salle *f* de jeux

recalcitrance [rɪ'kælsɪtrəns] **N** *Fml* récalcitrance *f*

recalcitrant [rɪ'kælsɪtrənt] **ADJ** *Fml (horse, person)* récalcitrant; *(disease)* rebelle

recall[1] ['ri:kɔ:l] **N 1** *(remembering)* **she has remarkable powers of r.** elle a une mémoire remarquable; **to have instant r.** avoir une excellente mémoire; **to have total r.** (être capable de) se souvenir de tous les détails de quelque chose **2** *(calling back) (of troops, library book, defective goods etc)* rappel *m*; *(of Parliament)* reconvocation *f*, *Mil* **to sound the r.** battre le rappel; **lost beyond r.** perdu irrévocablement
▸▸ *Mktg* **r. rate** taux *m* de mémorisation; *Mktg* **r. score** score *m* de mémorisation; **slip** *(for library book)* fiche *f* de rappel; *Mktg* **r. test** test *m* de rappel *ou* de mémorisation

recall[2] [rɪ'kɔ:l] **vt 1** *(remember)* se souvenir de, se rappeler; **r. doing sth** se rappeler avoir fait qch; **to r. sth to sb** rappeler qch à qn; **legends that r. the past** légendes évocatrices du passé *ou* qui évoquent le passé; **how vividly I r. the scene!** avec quelle netteté je revois ce spectacle! **2** *(call back) (troops, defective goods etc)* rappeler; *(library book)* demander le retour de; **the sound of the telephone recalled her to the present** la sonnerie du téléphone la ramena à la réalité
vi as I r. si je me rappelle bien; **as you may r.** comme vous vous en souvenez *ou* le rappelez peut-être; **as you will r.** comme vous vous en souvenez sans doute

recant [rɪ'kænt] **vt** *(opinion)* rétracter, revenir sur; *(doctrinal error)* abjurer; *(doctrine)* désavouer
vi se rétracter

recantation [ri:kæn'teɪʃən] **N** *(of faith, statement)* abjuration *f* (**of** de)

recap ['ri:kæp] **N 1** *Fam (summary)* récapitulation *f*, **let's do a r.** faisons le point **2** *Am Aut* pneu *m* rechapé
vt (**-pp-**) *Fam* = **recapitulate vt 1**
2 *Am Aut (tyre)* rechaper
vi *Fam* récapituler

recapitalization [ri:kæpɪtəlaɪ'zeɪʃən] **N** recapitalisation *f*

recapitalize [ri:'kæpɪtəlaɪz] **vt** changer la structure financière de

recapitulate [ri:kə'pɪtjʊleɪt] **vt 1** *(summarize) (discussion etc)* récapituler; **let us r. the facts** faisons le point **2** *Mus (theme)* reprendre
vi récapituler

recapitulation [ri:kəpɪtjʊ'leɪʃən] **N 1** *(of discussion etc)* récapitulation *f* **2** *Mus* reprise *f*

recapture [ri:'kæptʃər] **N** *(of town)* reprise *f*, *(of prisoner)* capture *f*
vt 1 *(take again) (prisoner, town)* reprendre **2** *(recreate) (era, age, atmosphere)* faire revivre, recréer; *(one's youth)* retrouver

recarpet [ri:'kɑːpɪt] **vt** changer la moquette de, remoquetter

recast [ri:'kɑːst] **vt** *(pt, pp* **recast)** **1** *(reshape) (sentence, piece of writing)* remanier **2** *Theat (find new cast for) (play)* changer la distribu-

tion de; *(find new part for) (actor)* donner un nouveau rôle à; **the part has been r.** le rôle a été donné à quelqu'un d'autre

recce ['rekɪ] **N** *Fam (exploration)* reconnaissance *f*, **to make a quick r.** faire une reconnaissance rapide (**of** de)

recede [rɪ'si:d] **vi 1** *(of tide, sea)* se retirer, descendre; *(of coastline, person, thing)* s'éloigner, reculer; **as memories of the past r.** à mesure que les souvenirs du passé s'effacent **2** *(slope backwards)* **to have a receding chin/forehead** avoir le menton/front fuyant *ou* qui fuit; **his hair(line)** *or* **he is receding** son front se dégarnit **3** *(lose value)* perdre de la valeur; **the company's shares have receded five points** les actions de la société ont reculé de *ou* perdu cinq points

receipt [rɪ'si:t] **N 1** *(receiving) (of letter, parcel etc)* réception *f*, **on r. of this letter** dès réception de cette lettre; **on r. of the news** à la nouvelle (**about** de); **within one week of r.** dans un délai d'une semaine après réception; **to pay on r.** payer à (la) réception; **to acknowledge r.** accuser réception (**of** de); **we are in r. of** ... nous avons reçu ...; *Com* **r. at domicile** prise *f* à domicile; *Fin* **r. of a dividend** perception *f* de dividende **2** *(for payment)* reçu *m* (**for** de); *(in supermarket, bar)* ticket *m* de caisse; *(for letter, parcel)* récépissé *m*, accusé *m* de réception; **to give a r.** *(for meal, taxi fare etc)* donner un reçu; *(for rent)* donner une quittance **3 receipts** *(takings)* recettes *fpl*, rentrées *fpl*; **receipts and expenditure** recettes et dépenses *fpl*
vt *Com* acquitter, quittancer; **to r. a bill** *(in writing)* acquitter une facture; *(with stamp)* apposer le tampon 'pour acquit' sur une facture
▸▸ *Fin* **r. book** carnet *m* de quittances; *Com* **r. stamp** timbre-quittance *m*, *pl* timbres-quittances

receivable [rɪ'si:vəb(ə)l] *Com* **ADJ** *(account, bill etc)* à recevoir
N compte *m* ou effet *m* à recevoir

receive [rɪ'si:v] **vt 1** *(take delivery of) (gift, news, letter)* recevoir; *(money etc)* recevoir, toucher; *(salary etc)* toucher; **I have received your letter** j'ai reçu votre lettre, votre lettre m'est parvenue; **received with thanks** *(on bill)* pour acquit; *Radio, TV* **to r. a broadcast** recevoir une émission; *St Exch* **to r. a premium** encaisser un premium; **to r. a station** capter un poste; **are you receiving me?** *(on radio)* est-ce que vous me recevez?; **to r. (the) service** *(of tennis or badminton player)* recevoir le service; *Law* **to r. stolen goods** receler des objets volés
2 *(be given) (greeting, blow, communion etc)* recevoir; *(refusal)* essuyer; *(criticism)* faire l'objet de; *(commission, unemployment benefit, interest)* percevoir; *Law* **to r. thirty days** être condamné à un mois de prison; **I received the distinct impression that ...** j'ai eu la nette impression que ...; *Prov* **it is better** *or* **more blessed to give than to r.** il y a plus de joie à donner qu'à recevoir; **we don't want them to r. a bad impression of us** nous ne voulons pas leur faire mauvaise impression; *St Exch* **to r. a premium** encaisser un premium
3 *(welcome) (guests)* recevoir; **to be cordially received** *(of visitor etc)* trouver un accueil chaleureux, être bien reçu; **the proposal was well/badly received** la proposition reçut un accueil favorable/défavorable *ou* a été bien/mal reçue; **the film was well received by the critics** le film a été bien accueilli par la critique; **to r. sb into the Church** admettre qn dans l'Église; **to r. sb into one's family** admettre *ou* recevoir qn dans sa famille
vi *(of tennis or badminton player)* recevoir le service

received [rɪ'si:vd] **ADJ** *(idea)* reçu; *(opinion)* admis; **the r. view is that ...** il est communément admis *ou* accepté que ..., on admet communément que ...
▸▸ *Br* **R. Pronunciation** prononciation *f* standard (de l'anglais); *Com* **r. stamp** cachet *m* d'arrivée; **r. wisdom** sagesse *f* populaire

receiver [rɪ'si:vər] **N 1** *(of stolen goods)* receleur, -euse **2** *Tel* récepteur *m*; **to lift** *or* **pick up the r.** décrocher; **to replace the r.** raccrocher **3** *Radio, TV* récepteur *m* **4** *Law, Fin* **r. in bankruptcy, official r.** administrateur, -trice judiciaire, syndic *m* de faillite; **to be in the hands of the r.** être en règlement judiciaire
▸▸ *Radio, TV* **r. aerial** antenne *f* de réception; *Am* **r. general** receveur *m* des impôts; **r. rest** *(for telephone)* berceau *m* (du combiné)

receivership [rɪ'si:vəʃɪp] **N** *Law, Fin* liquidation *f* judiciaire; **to go into r.** être placé sous administration judiciaire

receiving [rɪ'si:vɪŋ] **N** *(of stolen goods)* recel *m*
ADJ *Fam* **to be at** *or* **on the r. end** écoper; **to be on the r. end of sb's temper** faire les frais du mauvais caractère qn; *Fam* **I've been on the r. end of customers' complaints all day** c'est moi qui me suis occupé des réclamations des clients toute la journée; *Fam* **it's different when you're on the r. end** c'est tout autre chose quand c'est à toi que ça arrive
▸▸ *Radio, TV* **r. aerial** antenne *f* de réception; *Am* **r. blanket** petite couverture *f* légère pour bébé; *Com* **r. depot** dépôt *m* de réception; *Radio, TV* **r. set** poste *m* récepteur; *Radio, TV* **r. station** station *f* réceptrice

recent ['ri:sənt] **ADJ** *(development, event, past)* récent; *(acquaintance)* nouveau, *f* nouvelle; **event of r. date** événement *m* récent; **all that is quite r.** tout cela est très récent; **in r. months** au cours des derniers mois; **r. news** nouvelles *fpl* récentes *ou* fraîches; **in r. times** récemment; **the most r. edition** *(of book etc)* la dernière édition; **her most r. novel** son dernier roman

recently ['ri:səntlɪ] **ADV** récemment; **as r. as yesterday** pas plus tard qu'hier; **until quite r.** jusqu'à récemment *ou* ces derniers temps; **I saw her quite r.** je l'ai vue tout dernièrement

receptacle [rɪ'septək(ə)l] **N 1** *(for litter, paper, water etc)* récipient *m* **2** *Am Elec* prise *f* de courant (femelle)

reception [rɪ'sepʃən] **N 1** *(welcome)* accueil *m*; **to give sb a chilly/warm r.** réserver à qn un accueil glacial/chaleureux; **what kind of r. did you get?** quel accueil est-ce qu'ils t'ont réservé?, comment est-ce qu'ils t'ont reçu?; **the play has had a favourable r.** la pièce a été accueillie favorablement *ou* bien reçue **2** *(party)* réception *f*, *(in the evening)* réception, soirée *f*; **wedding r.** réception de mariage **3** *(in hotel)* réception *f*, *(in office, hospital)* accueil *m*; **at** *or* **to r.** à la réception/à l'accueil **4** *Radio, TV* réception *f*
▸▸ *Br* **r. centre** centre *m* d'accueil; *Br Sch* **r. class** première année *f* de maternelle; *Am* **r. clerk** réceptionniste *mf*, *also Fig Hum* **r. committee** comité *m* d'accueil; **r. desk** *(in hotel)* réception; *(in office, hospital)* accueil; **r. room** *(in hotel)* salle *f* de réception; *Br (in house)* salon *m*

receptionist [rɪ'sepʃənɪst] **N** réceptionniste *mf*, *(at trade fair)* hôtesse *f* d'accueil

receptive [rɪ'septɪv] **ADJ** *(audience, listener)* réceptif (**to an idea** à une idée); **r. to sb** compréhensif envers qn

receptiveness [rɪ'septɪvnɪs], **receptivity** [rɪsep'tɪvɪtɪ] **N** *(of audience, listener)* réceptivité *f* (**to** à)

receptor [rɪ'septər] **N 1** *(for antibody, drug)*

récepteur *m* **2** *(for radio signals)* récepteur *m*

▸▸ *Physiol* **r. site** (site *m*) récepteur

recess [rɪˈses, *Am* ˈriːses] **N 1** *Br (holidays) (of law courts, Parliament)* vacances *fpl*; **while Parliament is in r.** pendant les vacances parlementaires **2** *Am Sch (break)* récréation *f* **3** *Am Law (break)* suspension *f* d'audience; **the court is now in r.** l'audience est maintenant suspendue; **we will take a ten minute r.** nous allons suspendre l'audience pendant dix minutes **4** *(nook)* recoin *m*; *(for bed etc)* renfoncement *m*; *(for statue)* niche *f*, **dining r.** coin *m* repas, coin salle à manger; **in the innermost recesses of the soul** dans les replis *ou* recoins les plus secrets de l'âme

VT *(place in a recess) (lighting, switch etc)* encastrer

VI 1 *Br* **Parliament will r. next week** les vacances parlementaires commenceront la semaine prochaine **2** *Am (of assembly)* suspendre la séance; *(of court)* suspendre l'audience

recession [rɪˈseʃən] **N** *Econ* récession *f*, **in (a) r.** en récession

recessionary [rɪˈseʃənərɪ] **ADJ** *Econ (conditions, policy etc)* de récession; **to have a r. effect** entraîner une récession

▸▸ **r. gap** écart *m* déflationniste

recessive [rɪˈsesɪv] **ADJ** *Biol (gene)* récessif

recharge [riːˈtʃɑːdʒ] **VT** *(battery)* recharger; *Fig* **to r. one's batteries** recharger ses batteries, reprendre du poil de la bête

VI *(of battery)* se recharger

rechargeable [riːˈtʃɑːdʒəb(ə)l] **ADJ** *(battery)* rechargeable

recharger [riːˈtʃɑːdʒər] **N** *(for battery)* chargeur *m*

recherché [rəˈʃeəʃeɪ] **ADJ** *(film, topic)* recherché

recidivism [rɪˈsɪdɪvɪz(ə)m] **N** *Law* récidivisme *m*

recidivist [rɪˈsɪdɪvɪst] **ADJ, N** *Law* récidiviste *mf*

recidivistic [rɪsɪdɪˈvɪstɪk] **ADJ** *Law (tendency etc)* à récidiver

recipe [ˈresɪpɪ] **N** *Culin, Fig* recette *f*; *Pharm* formule *f*, recette *f*; **r. for a happy life** recette pour vivre heureux; **a r. for failure** le meilleur moyen pour échouer; **those two working together would be a r. for disaster** si ces deux-là travaillaient ensemble ce serait l'échec *ou* la catastrophe assuré(e)

▸▸ **r. book** livre *m* de recettes; **r. card** fiche-recette *f*, *pl* fiches-recettes, fiche-cuisine *f*, *pl* fiches-cuisines

recipient [rɪˈsɪpɪənt] **N** *(of gift, letter etc)* destinataire *mf*, *(of cheque, money)* bénéficiaire *mf*, *(of award, honour)* récipiendaire *mf*, *Med (of organ transplant)* receveur, -euse

Note that the French word **récipient** is a false friend and is never a translation for the English word **recipient**. It means **container**.

reciprocal [rɪˈsɪprək(ə)l] **ADJ 1** *(mutual)* mutuel, réciproque; *(bilateral)* réciproque, bilatéral, -aux; **he dislikes me and it's r.** il ne m'aime pas et c'est réciproque *ou* je le lui rends bien **2** *Gram* réciproque **3** *Math* réciproque, inverse

N *Math* réciproque *f*, inverse *f*

▸▸ **r. agreement** accord *m* réciproque; **r. marketing** marketing *m* bilatéral; *Mktg* **r. relationships model** modèle *m* de relations réciproques; **r. trading** commerce *m* réciproque

reciprocally [rɪˈsɪprəklɪ] **ADV** *(to trade)* réciproquement

reciprocate [rɪˈsɪprəkeɪt] **VT** *(return) (compliment)* retourner; **to r. sb's kindness** payer la gentillesse de qn de retour; **he had great admiration for her but his feelings were never reciprocated** il avait beaucoup d'admiration pour elle mais ce n'était pas réciproque

VI 1 *(do the same)* en faire autant; *(counter-attack)* riposter **2** *Tech (of piston etc)* avoir un mouvement alternatif *ou* de va-et-vient

reciprocating [rɪˈsɪprəkeɪtɪŋ] **ADJ** *Tech (movement)* alternatif; *(machine)* à mouvement alternatif *ou* de va-et-vient

▸▸ **r. engine** moteur *m* alternatif

reciprocation [rɪsɪprəˈkeɪʃən] **N 1** *(of feeling)* réciprocité *f*; **I think some r. of her compliment is called for** je pense qu'il faudrait lui retourner le compliment; **these feelings met with no r.** ces sentiments n'ont pas été payés de retour; **in r. for …** en retour de … **2** *Tech* mouvement *m* alternatif, va-et-vient *m inv*

reciprocity [resɪˈprɒsɪtɪ] **N** réciprocité *f*

recirculated air [riːˈsɜːkjʊleɪtɪd] **N** *Aut* air *m* recyclé

recital [rɪˈsaɪt(ə)l] **N 1** *(of poetry)* récitation *f* **2** *Mus* récital *m*; **to give a r.** donner un récital; **Bach r.** récital Bach **3** *(of events etc)* récit *m*, narration *f*, *(of complaints, details etc)* énumération *f*

recitation [resɪˈteɪʃən] **N** *(of poem etc)* récitation *f*, **to give a r.** réciter; **to give a r. from Burns** réciter du Burns

recitative [resɪtəˈtiːv] **N** *Mus* récitatif *m*

recite [rɪˈsaɪt] **VT 1** *(poem etc)* réciter **2** *(complaints, details etc)* énumérer

VI réciter; **will you r. to us?** voulez-vous nous réciter quelque chose?

reckless [ˈreklɪs] **ADJ** *(foolhardy) (person)* inconscient, téméraire; *(attempt, action, decision etc)* téméraire; *(driving, gambler)* imprudent; **to be a r. spender** dépenser sans compter; **to be r. with one's money** dépenser son argent inconsidérément

▸▸ *Admin, Law* **r. driver** conducteur, -trice imprudent(e); *Fam* chauffard *m*; **r. driving** conduite *f* imprudente

recklessly [ˈreklɪslɪ] **ADV** *(to attempt)* témérairement; *(to drive, gamble)* imprudemment; *(to spend)* sans compter

recklessness [ˈreklɪsnɪs] **N** *(of attempt, person)* témérité *f*, *(of driving, gambling)* imprudence *f*

reckon [ˈrekən] **VT 1** *(consider) (person)* considérer **(as** comme**)**; **to r. sb among the greatest writers** mettre qn au rang *ou* au nombre des plus grands écrivains; **he is reckoned to be one of the richest men in England** il paraît *ou* ce serait l'un des hommes les plus riches d'Angleterre **2** *(calculate, count) (amount etc)* calculer, compter; **the cost has been reckoned at £100** le coût a été estimé à 100 livres **3** *Fam (think)* penser; **I r. he's forty** je lui donne quarante ans; **I r. he'll consent** à mon avis, il consentira; **maybe we should go, what do you r.?** nous devrions peut-être y aller, qu'est-ce que tu en penses?; **the Government obviously reckons it has a good chance of winning an early election** le gouvernement a bon espoir de gagner une élection anticipée **4** *Fam (regard favourably)* **I don't r. her chances** je ne donne pas cher de sa réussite

VI 1 *(calculate)* compter, calculer; **reckoning from today** à partir *ou* à compter d'aujourd'hui **2** *(expect, plan)* compter **(to go** partir**); you should r. to be there by 6 o'clock at the latest** il faut que tu prévoies d'arriver à six heures au plus tard

▸ **reckon in VT SEP** compter

▸ **reckon on VT INSEP** ▸ **r. on sth** compter sur

qch; **they had not reckoned on finding me here** ils ne comptaient pas me trouver ici

▸ **reckon up VT SEP** *(column of figures)* additionner; *(change, coins)* compter; **to r. up the cost of sth** calculer le coût de qch; **to r. up a bill** faire une facture

VI *(prepare bill)* faire la note

▸ **reckon with VT INSEP** compter avec; **to have sb to r. with** avoir affaire à qn; **she's a force to be reckoned with** c'est une femme avec laquelle il faut compter; **he hadn't reckoned with this response** il ne s'attendait pas à cette réaction

▸ **reckon without VT INSEP** compter sans; **he had reckoned without his rivals** il n'avait pas tenu compte de ses rivaux

reckoner [ˈrekənər] **N** **ready r.** barème *m*

reckoning [ˈrekənɪŋ] **N** *(of bill, interest etc)* calcul *m*; **by my r.** d'après mes calculs; **to be out in one's r.** s'être trompé dans ses calculs; **you're a long way out in your r.** vous êtes loin du compte; **to the best of my r.** autant je puisse en juger; **day of r.** *Rel* jour *m* du Jugement dernier; *Fig* instant *m* de vérité

reclaim¹ [rɪˈkleɪm] **VT 1** *(land)* mettre en valeur; *(from undergrowth)* défricher; *(marsh)* assécher; **to r. land from the sea/the desert** conquérir du terrain sur la mer/le désert **2** *(lost property, suitcase etc)* récupérer; *(tax, expenses)* se faire rembourser; **to r. VAT** récupérer la TVA **3** *Ind (rubber etc)* régénérer; *(by-product)* récupérer

Note that the French verb **réclamer** is a false friend and is never a translation for the English verb **to reclaim**. It means **to claim, to demand**.

reclaim² [ˈriːkleɪm] **N** luggage *or* baggage **r.** *(in airport)* retrait *m* des bagages

reclamation [rekləˈmeɪʃən] **N 1** *(of land)* mise *f* en valeur; *(from undergrowth)* défrichement *m*; *(of marsh)* assèchement *m* **2** *(of tax, expenses)* remboursement *m* **3** *Ind (of rubber etc)* régénération *f*, *(of by-product)* récupération *f*

reclassify [riːˈklæsɪfaɪ] **VT** *(plant etc)* reclasser; *(document etc)* reclassifier

recline [rɪˈklaɪn] **VT** *(one's head)* appuyer **(against** contre; **on** sur**);** *(seat)* incliner le dossier de

VI *(of person) (be lying)* être allongé *ou* étendu **(on** sur**);** *(lie down)* s'allonger, s'étendre; *(of head)* être appuyé **(on** sur**);** *(of seat)* avoir un dossier inclinable *ou* réglable

recliner [rɪˈklaɪnər] **N** *(for sunbathing)* chaise *f* longue; *(armchair)* fauteuil *m* à dossier inclinable, fauteuil relax

reclining [rɪˈklaɪnɪŋ] **ADJ** *(seat)* inclinable, à dossier inclinable; **to be in a r. position** *(of person)* être en position allongée *ou* couchée; *(of seat)* être incliné

▸▸ **r. chair** chaise *f* longue

recluse [rɪˈkluːs] **N** reclus, -use; **to live** *or* **lead the life of a r.** vivre en reclus *ou* ermite; **she has become a bit of a r.** elle est devenue assez solitaire

recognition [rekəgˈnɪʃən] **N 1** *(identification) (of person, style etc)* reconnaissance *f*, **she gave no sign of r.** elle n'a pas eu l'air de me/le/*etc* reconnaître; **to change beyond** *or* **out of all r.** devenir méconnaissable; *Mktg* **brand r.** identification *f* de la marque **2** *(acknowledgement) (of fact, government, speaker etc)* reconnaissance *f*, **to win r.** *(of artist etc)* s'imposer **(from** aux yeux de**); her work has won her international r.** son œuvre lui a permis de s'imposer sur le plan international; **to withhold r. from** *(government)* refuser de reconnaître; **in r. of his courage** en reconnaissance de son courage; **she re-**

ceived no r. on ne lui accordait aucune considération

►► *Mktg* **r. score** score *m* de reconnaissance; *Mktg* **r. test** test *m* de reconnaissance

recognizable [rekəg'naɪzəb(ə)l] **ADJ** *(person, style etc)* reconnaissable; **he's so changed as to be no longer r.** il est devenu méconnaissable

recognizably [rekəg'naɪzəblɪ] **ADV she is r. your daughter** on voit bien que c'est votre fille

recognizance [rɪ'kɒgnɪzəns] **N** *Law (promise)* engagement *m*; *(money paid)* caution *f* personnelle; **to enter into recognizances** donner caution; **to enter into recognizances for sb** se porter garant *ou* caution pour qn, cautionner qn; **to be released on one's own recognizances** être remis en liberté sur engagement personnel

recognize ['rekəgnaɪz] **VT 1** *(know again) (person, town etc)* reconnaître (**by** à); **to r. the truth when one sees it** être capable de savoir si quelque chose est vrai ou non, savoir discerner le vrai du faux; **he can certainly r. a good business opportunity** il sait repérer les bonnes affaires **2** *(acknowledge) (government, fact etc)* reconnaître; *Sport (record)* homologuer; **to r. sb as king** reconnaître qn comme *ou* en tant que roi; **to r. defeat** accepter *ou* admettre sa défaite; **to be the first to r. a fact** être le premier à reconnaître un fait **3** *Am* **to r. a member** *(of chairman of a meeting etc)* donner la parole à un membre; *Am* **to be recognized** *(of speaker)* avoir la parole

recognized ['rekəgnaɪzd] **ADJ** *(government etc)* reconnu; *(truth)* admis, accepté; *(method etc)* classique; **it is a r. fact that ...** c'est un fait avéré *ou* reconnu que ...; **the r. term** le terme consacré (**for** pour); **to be a r. authority** être une autorité reconnue (par tous) (**on** en)

►► *Com* **r. agent** agent *m* accrédité (**for** pour); *Fin* **r. investment exchange** marché *m* d'investissement agréé

recoil¹ ['riːkɔɪl] **N** *(of gun, rifle)* recul *m*; *(of spring)* détente *f*; *(of person)* mouvement *m* de recul

recoil² [rɪ'kɔɪl] **VI** *(of gun, rifle)* reculer; *(of spring)* se détendre; *(of person)* reculer (**from doing sth** à l'idée de faire qch); *Fig (of joke etc)* se retourner (**on** contre); **to r. (in horror/disgust)** avoir un mouvement de recul

recoilless [rɪ'kɔɪllɪs] **ADJ** *(rifle etc)* sans recul

recollect [rekə'lekt] **VT** se rappeler, se souvenir de; **she was unable to r. what had happened** elle était incapable de se souvenir de ce qui s'était passé

VI as far as I r. autant que je m'en souvienne

recollection [rekə'lekʃən] **N** souvenir *m*; **my earliest recollections** mes premiers souvenirs; **her r. differs from mine** nos souvenirs ne concordent pas, ses souvenirs et les miens ne concordent pas; **I have some r. of it** j'en ai un vague souvenir; **I have no r. of it** je n'en ai *ou* je n'en garde aucun souvenir; **I have no r. of doing it** je ne me souviens pas de *ou* je ne me rappelle pas l'avoir fait; **to the best of my r.** pour autant que je me souvienne

recombinant [riː'kɒmbɪnənt] **ADJ** *Biol*

►► **r. DNA** ADN *m* recombinant; **r. technology** recombinaison *f* génétique

recommend [rekə'mend] **VT 1** *(praise) (book, restaurant, doctor)* recommander (**to** à; **for** pour); **the hotel is to be recommended for its cooking** on recommande cet hôtel pour sa cuisine; **the film has little to r. it** on

ne peut pas dire grand-chose en faveur de ce film (**apart from, except** en dehors de); **the place has little to r. it apart from the weather** cet endroit n'a pas grand intérêt à part qu'il y fait beau; **the proposal has a lot to r. it** la proposition a beaucoup d'avantages *ou* d'attrait; **the hotel comes recommended** on dit beaucoup de bien de cet hôtel **2** *(advise) (caution)* conseiller; **to r. sb to do sth** recommander *ou* conseiller à qn de faire qch; **I r. going** *or* **that you go via Leeds** je vous recommande *ou* conseille de passer par Leeds; **this is not to be recommended** ce n'est pas recommandé; **recommended (retail) price** prix *m* (public) conseillé **3** *Old-fashioned (entrust)* **to r. sth to the care of sb** *or* **to sb's care** recommander qch aux soins de qn; **to r. one's soul to God** recommander son âme à Dieu

recommendable [rekə'mendəb(ə)l] **ADJ** *(book, person etc)* recommandable; **highly r.** très recommandable

recommendation [rekəmen'deɪʃən] **N 1** *(advice)* recommandation *f*; **I have come on the r. of one of your customers** je viens sur la recommandation d'un de vos clients; **through personal r.** par recommandation personnelle; **one can only join the club through personal r.** on ne peut devenir membre du club qu'en étant recommandé personnellement; **my r. is that ...** ce que je recommande *ou* conseille c'est que ...; **to follow/ignore sb's recommendations** suivre/ne pas suivre les recommandations de qn; **the report's recommendations** les recommandations contenues dans le rapport **2** *(commendation)* recommandation *f*; **the hotel's sole r. is its location** l'emplacement de l'hôtel est son seul intérêt

recompense ['rekəmpens] **N 1** *(reward)* récompense *f* (**for** de); **in r. for ...** en récompense de ... **2** *Law (for damage, loss)* dédommagement *m* (**for** de, pour); **as r.** en dédommagement

VT 1 *(reward)* récompenser (**for** de) **2** *Law (compensate)* dédommager (**for sth** de qch)

reconcilable [rekən'saɪləb(ə)l] **ADJ** *(ideas, opinions)* compatible, conciliable (**with** avec); **not r.** irréconciliable

reconcile ['rekənsaɪl] **VT 1** *(person)* réconcilier (**with** avec); **to be reconciled with sb** se réconcilier avec qn; **to r. sb to sth** faire accepter qch à *ou* par qn; **to r. oneself** *or* **become reconciled to sth** se résigner à quelque chose **2** *(settle) (quarrel)* régler, mettre fin à; **let us r. our differences** essayons de nous entendre **3** *(make agree) (opinions, facts)* concilier; *Fin (figures, bank statement)* rapprocher; *Acct (accounts, entries)* faire cadrer, faire accorder; **evidence which cannot be reconciled with the known facts** témoignage qui ne cadre pas avec les faits connus

> When translating the English verb **to reconcile**, note that the French verbs **concilier** and **réconcilier** are not interchangeable.

reconciliation [rekənsɪlɪ'eɪʃən] **N 1** *(of people)* réconciliation *f* (**between** entre; **with** avec) **2** *(of differences, of opinions)* conciliation *f* **3** *Fin (of figures, bank statements)* rapprochement *m*; *Acct (of accounts, entries)* ajustement *m*

►► *Fin* **r. account** compte *m* collectif; *Acct* **r. statement** état *m* de rapprochement

recondite [rɪ'kɒndaɪt, 'rekəndaɪt] **ADJ** *Fml (subject, knowledge)* abscons

recondition [riːkən'dɪʃən] **VT** *(engine etc)* refaire, remettre à neuf

reconditioned [riːkən'dɪʃənd] **ADJ** *(engine etc)* remis en état, refait

reconditioning [riːkən'dɪʃənɪŋ] **N** *(of engine etc)* remise *f* à neuf

reconfiguration [riːkənfɪgə'reɪʃən] **N** *Comput (of keyboard, system etc)* reconfiguration *f*

reconfigure [riːkən'fɪgər] **VT** *Comput (keyboard, system)* reconfigurer

reconnaissance [rɪ'kɒnɪsəns] **N** *Mil, Fig* reconnaissance *f*; **to make a r.** faire une reconnaissance; **to be on r.** être en reconnaissance; **r. flight/mission/satellite** vol *m*/mission *f*/satellite *m* de reconnaissance

reconnect [riːkə'nekt] **VT** *(telephone, cable etc)* rebrancher; *(pipe)* raccorder; **to r. the water supply** rétablir l'alimentation en eau; *Tel* **to r. sb** *(of operator)* rétablir la communication; *(of telephone company)* rebrancher le téléphone

VI se reconnecter

reconnection [riːkə'nekʃən] **N** *(of cable, telephone etc)* rebranchement *m*; *(of pipe)* raccordement *m*; *(of water supply, telephone call)* rétablissement *m*

►► *Tel* **r. charge** frais *mpl* de rebranchement

reconnoitre, *Am* **reconnoiter** [rekə'nɔɪtər] **VT** *Mil, Fig* reconnaître

VI faire une reconnaissance

reconquer [riː'kɒŋkər] **VT** *(country etc)* reconquérir

reconquest [riː'kɒŋkwest] **N** *(of country etc)* reconquête *f*

reconsider [riːkən'sɪdər] **VT** *(question)* reconsidérer, repenser; *(decision)* reconsidérer, réexaminer

VI reconsidérer la question; **I advise you to r.** je vous conseille de revoir votre position

reconsideration [riːkənsɪdə'reɪʃən] **N** *(of question)* reconsidération *f*; *(of decision)* reconsidération, réexamen *m*

reconstitute [riː'kɒnstɪtuːt] **VT** reconstituer

reconstitution [riːkɒnstɪ'tjuːʃən] **N** reconstitution *f*

reconstruct [riːkən'strʌkt] **VT** *(house etc)* reconstruire, rebâtir; *(company, corrupt computer file etc), Fig (facts, crime)* reconstituer; *(one's life, a country)* reconstruire

reconstruction [riːkən'strʌkʃən] **N** *(of house, country, life etc)* reconstruction *f*; *(of file, company etc), Fig (of crime)* reconstitution *f*; **economic and financial r.** restauration *f* économique et financière

reconstructive [riːkən'strʌktɪv] **ADJ**

►► **r. surgery** chirurgie *f* réparatrice

reconvene [riːkən'viːn] **VT** convoquer de nouveau

VI se réunir à nouveau

RECORD¹ ['rekɔːd]

> **N** registre **1, 2** ▪ procès-verbal **1** ▪ dossier **2** ▪ antécédents **4** ▪ disque **5** ▪ record **6**
> **ADJ ATTRIB** record

N 1 *(of attendance)* registre *m*; *(of proceedings)* procès-verbal *m*, *pl* procès-verbaux; *(of verdict, fact)* enregistrement *m*; **to keep a r. of sth** garder une trace de qch; **I can find no r. of it** je n'en trouve aucune mention; **to be on r.** *(of verdict, fact)* être enregistré; *Law* **to strike sth from the r.** rayer qch du procès-verbal; **to be on r. as saying sth** avoir déclaré qch publiquement; **to go on r. as a pacifist** se déclarer pacifiste; **to put sth on r.** noter qch, consigner qch; **it is on r.** *or* **a matter of r.** c'est un fait établi (**that** que); **this is the coldest winter on r.** c'est l'hiver le plus froid que l'on ait jamais enregistré; **to say sth off the r.** dire qch en confidence; **this is strictly off the r.** ceci est strictement confidentiel, ceci doit rester entre nous; **(just) for the r.,**

to keep the r. straight pour que les choses soient claires; **is this for the r.?** est-ce que cela est officiel?; **to put** *or* **set the r. straight** mettre les choses au clair, dissiper tout malentendu; **to leave few records** *(of ancient civilization)* laisser peu de témoignages écrits; **the Etruscans left little r. of their religious beliefs** les Étrusques n'ont laissé que peu de traces de leurs croyances

2 *(file)* dossier *m*; *Hist, Law* archive *f*; *Admin* registre *m*; **our records do not go back that far** nos registres *ou* nos archives ne remontent pas aussi loin; *Admin* **records management** gestion *f* des dossiers

3 *Comput (in database)* article *m*, enregistrement *m*

4 *(personal history)* antécédents *mpl*; *(of criminal)* casier *m* judiciaire; *(achievements)* résultats *mpl*; **to have a good/bad safety r.** *(of company etc)* avoir une bonne/mauvaise réputation en ce qui concerne la sécurité; *Mil, Fig* **he has a good r.** ses états de service sont bons; **his past r.** *(behaviour)* ses antécédents; *(achievements)* ses résultats antérieurs; **given your r. as a late payer** vu vos antécédents de mauvais payeur; *Law* **to have a clean r.** avoir un casier judiciaire vierge; *Law* **he has a r.** il a déjà été condamné, il a des condamnations antérieures; *Med* **case r.** fiche *f* de patient *ou* d'observation

5 *Mus (recording)* disque *m*; **to make a r.** faire *ou* enregistrer un disque; **to play** *or* **put on a r.** mettre *ou* passer un disque; **to change a r.** changer un disque; *Fig Hum* **change the r., will you?** change de disque!

6 *(best performance)* record *m*; **to set a r.** établir un record; **to hold the r.** détenir le record **(for** de); **to break** *or* **beat the r.** battre le record **(for, by** de); **to break all records** battre tous les records

ADJ ATTRIB record *inv*; **in r. time** en un temps record; **unemployment is at a r. high/low** le chômage a atteint son chiffre le plus haut/bas

▸▸**r. buff** discophile *mf*, collectionneur, -euse de disques; **r. card** fiche; **r. company** maison *f* de disques; **r. deck** platine *f* (tourne-disque); **r. form** *(for keeping records)* bordereau *m* de saisie; **r. label** label *m*; **r. library** discothèque *f (de prêt)*; **r. office** bureau *m* des archives; *Law* **r. player** tourne-disque *m*, *pl* tourne-disques, platine (disques); **r. producer** producteur *m* de disques; **r. shop** magasin *m* de disques; **r. token** chèque-disque *m*, *pl* chèques-disques

RECORD² [rɪˈkɔːd]

VT	noter **1** ▪ enregistrer **1–3** ▪ rapporter **1**
VI	enregistrer

VT 1 *(write down) (fact)* noter (par écrit), consigner, enregistrer; *(give account of) (events)* rapporter, relater; *(thoughts, ideas etc)* noter (par écrit), consigner, mettre sur papier; *(temperature, rainfall, hours of sunshine etc)* relever; *(of policeman)* consigner; *Law (judgment)* minuter; *Parl* **to r. a vote** voter; **throughout recorded history** aussi loin que les archives remontent; *Br* **to send a letter (by) recorded delivery** envoyer une lettre en recommandé; **to r. one's opposition** indiquer par écrit son opposition; *(in speech)* faire part de son opposition

2 *(tape) (song, programme)* enregistrer; **recorded** *(not live) (programme)* différé; **this is a recorded message** *(on telephone)* ceci est un message enregistré; **recorded highlights** extraits *mpl* pré-enregistrés

3 *(register) (earthquake, drop in sales, increase in accidents etc)* enregistrer; **the ther-** **mometer records ten degrees** le thermomètre marque dix degrés

4 *(be evidence of) (battle etc)* rappeler, commémorer

VI *(of machine, performer)* enregistrer; *(of sound)* s'enregistrer; **his voice doesn't r. well** sa voix ne se prête pas bien à l'enregistrement; **r./replay head** tête *f* de lecture/enregistrement

record-breaker N *(person)* personne qui a battu un/des record(s); *(sporting etc performance)* **it was a splendid run but I don't think it's a r.** c'était une belle prestation mais je ne pense pas que le record soit battu

record-breaking ADJ *(jump, success etc)* qui bat tous les records

recorder [rɪˈkɔːdər] N **1** *(machine)* (appareil *m)* enregistreur *m*; **(tape)** magnétophone *m*; **radio-cassette r.** radiocassette *m* **2** *Mus* flûte *f* à bec **3** *Eng Law* = avocat *m* nommé pour remplir certaines fonctions de juge

record-holder N détenteur, -trice du/d'un record

recording [rɪˈkɔːdɪŋ] N **1** *(on tape etc)* enregistrement *m*; **to play a r.** passer un enregistrement **2** *(writing down)* relation *f* par écrit; *(giving account)* consignation *f*

▸▸**r. artist** musicien, -ienne *(qui enregistre des disques)*; **r. contract** contrat *m* avec une maison de disques; **r. deck** magnétoscope *m* d'enregistrement; **r. engineer** ingénieur *m* du son; **r. head** tête *f* d'enregistrement; **r. instrument** appareil *m* enregistreur; **r. session** séance *f* d'enregistrement; **r. studio** studio *m* d'enregistrement; **r. tape** ruban *m* *ou* bande *f* d'enregistrement

recount [rɪˈkaʊnt] VT *(relate)* raconter **(to** à)

re-count¹ [ˈriːkaʊnt] N *(of people, money, votes etc)* recomptage *m*, nouveau comptage *m*; **to do a r.** *(of money, people, votes etc)* recompter; **to call for** *or* **demand a r.** exiger un nouveau compte des voix

re-count² [riːˈkaʊnt] VT *(money etc)* recompter; *(votes)* compter de nouveau

recoup [rɪˈkuːp] VT *(money, loss)* récupérer; *Law* défalquer, faire le décompte de; **to r. one's investment** rentrer dans ses fonds

recourse [rɪˈkɔːs] N **1** recours *m*; **to have r. to sth/sb** avoir recours *ou* recourir à qch/qn; **my only r. is …** mon seul recours est … (**to do** de faire); **she cannot remember without r. to her notes** elle ne peut pas se souvenir sans avoir recours à ses notes; **right of r.** droit *m* de recours **2** *Fin* recours *m*; **endorsement without r.** endossement *m* à forfait

recover [rɪˈkʌvər] VT **1** *(get back, find again)* retrouver, *Lit* recouvrer; *(one's appetite, voice)* retrouver; *Comput (file, data)* récupérer; **to r. one's breath/courage** reprendre haleine/courage; **to r. consciousness** reprendre connaissance, revenir à soi; **I am recovering my strength** mes forces me reviennent; **to r. one's money** *(lent to sb)* récupérer son argent; *(invested in project etc)* rentrer dans ses fonds; **to r. sth from sb** reprendre qch à qn; **to r. one's health** guérir, se rétablir, recouvrer la santé; **to r. oneself** *or* **one's composure** se ressaisir; **to r. one's balance** retrouver son équilibre **2** *(obtain, collect) (bodies)*, *Ind (by-product)* récupérer; *(from sea) (body, space ship)* repêcher

VI *(of person) (from shock etc)* se remettre (**from** de); *(from illness)* guérir, se remettre, se rétablir (**from** de); *(in competition, race etc)* se ressaisir; *(of export market, business)* reprendre; *(of stock market, economy, country)* se redresser; *(of currency)* remonter; **to be quite recovered** *(of patient)* être tout à fait remis *ou* guéri *ou* rétabli

re-cover VT *(chair etc)* recouvrir

recoverable [rɪˈkʌvərəb(ə)l] ADJ *(something lost)* récupérable; *(money)* recouvrable; *(by-product, computer file etc)* récupérable

▸▸*Com* **r. packaging** emballage *m* récupérable; *Petr* **r. resources** ressources *fpl* exploitables

recovery [rɪˈkʌvərɪ] N **1** *(of something lost)* récupération *f*; *(of money, deposit)* recouvrement *m*; *Comput (of file, data)* récupération *f*; **beyond** *or* **past r.** irrécupérable; *Law* **action for r. of property** (action *f* en) revendication *f*; **r. of damages** obtention *f* de dommages-intérêts

2 *(from illness)* guérison *f*; **to be on the way** *or* **road to r.** être en voie de guérison; **the patient is making a good r.** le malade fait des progrès rapides; **she made a quick r.** elle s'est vite rétablie; **he is past** *or* **beyond r.** *(patient)* on ne peut plus rien faire pour lui, il est dans un état désespéré; **I wish you a speedy r.** je vous souhaite un prompt rétablissement

3 *(of economy)* redressement *m*; *(of export market, business)* reprise *f*; *(of currency)* remontée *f*; **the textile industry has declined beyond r.** l'industrie textile connaît un déclin irrémédiable; **to make a r.** *(in competition, race etc)* se ressaisir

▸▸*Med* **r. position** position *f* latérale de sécurité; *Med* **r. room** salle *f* de réanimation; *Br Aut* **r. service** service *m* de dépannage; **r. ship** navire *m* de récupération; *Br* **r. vehicle** dépanneuse *f*, **r. vessel** navire de récupération

re-create VT *(in film, play etc) (age, era etc)* reconstituer, recréer

recreation [rekrɪˈeɪʃən] N loisirs *mpl*; *Sch (break)* récréation *f*; *Sch* **during (the) r.** pendant la récréation; **I only write poetry for r.** j'écris des poèmes uniquement pour le plaisir

▸▸**r. centre** centre *m* de loisirs; *Br* **r. ground** terrain *m* de jeux; **r. room** *(in school, hospital)* salle *f* de récréation; *(in hotel)* salle de jeux; *Am (at home)* salle de jeux

re-creation N *Cin, Theat etc (of era etc)* reconstitution *f*, recréation *f*

recreational [rekrɪˈeɪʃən(ə)l] ADJ *(activities, facilities)* de loisirs

▸▸**r. area** aire *f* de jeux; **r. centre** centre *m* de loisirs; **r. drug** drogue *f* à usage récréatif; **r. therapy** thérapie *f* par le jeu; *Am* **r. vehicle** camping-car *m*, *pl* camping-cars

recriminate [rɪˈkrɪmɪneɪt] VI récriminer

recrimination [rɪkrɪmɪˈneɪʃən] N récrimination *f* (**against** contre)

recriminatory [rɪˈkrɪmɪnət(ə)rɪ] ADJ *(remark etc)* de récrimination

recrudescence [riːkruːˈdesəns] N *Fml* recrudescence *f*

recrudescent [riːkruːˈdesənt] ADJ *Fml* recrudescent

recruit [rɪˈkruːt] N *Mil (in organization, company etc)* recrue *f*

VT *(army)* recruter; *(employee)* embaucher (**as** pour le poste de); **to r. sb to do sth** embaucher *ou* recruter qn pour faire qch

VI *Mil* recruter; *(of company)* recruter, embaucher (**for** pour)

recruiting [rɪˈkruːtɪŋ] N *(of soldier)* recrutement *m*; *(of employee)* recrutement, embauche *f*

▸▸**r. agent** agent *m* de recrutement; **r. office** bureau *m* de recrutement; **r. officer** *Mil* recruteur, -euse; *Hist* racoleur *m*; *Mil* **r. sergeant** sergent *m* recruteur

recruitment [rɪˈkruːtmənt] N *(of soldier, employee etc)* recrutement *m*

▸▸**r. agency** cabinet *m* de recrutement; **r. campaign** campagne *f* de recrutement; **r. consultant** conseil *m* en recrutement; **r. of-**

ficer recruteur, -euse; **r. scheme** programme *m* de recrutement

rectal ['rekt(ə)l] **ADJ** *Med, Anat* rectal, -aux
▸▸ **r. cancer** cancer *m* du rectum; **r. examination** examen *m* rectal *ou* du rectum

rectangle ['rektæŋg(ə)l] **N** rectangle *m*

rectangular [rek'tæŋgjʊlər] **ADJ** rectangulaire; **to be r. in shape** être rectangulaire

rectification [rektɪfɪ'keɪʃən] **N** *(of calculation, situation etc)* rectification *f*; *(of oversight)* réparation *f*; *Elec* redressement *m*; *Acct (of entry)* modification *f*, rectification

rectifier ['rektɪfaɪər] **N** *Chem* rectificateur *m*; *Elec* redresseur *m*

rectify ['rektɪfaɪ] **VT** *(calculation)* rectifier, corriger; *(mistake, situation)*, *Chem, Math* rectifier; *(oversight)* réparer; *Elec* redresser; *Acct (entry)* modifier, rectifier

rectilineal [rektɪ'lɪnɪəl], **rectilinear** [rektɪ'lɪnɪər] **ADJ** rectiligne
▸▸ *TV* **r. scanning** analyse *f* par lignes

rectitude ['rektɪtjuːd] **N** rectitude *f*

recto ['rektəʊ] **N** *Typ* recto *m*

rector ['rektər] **N 1** *(in Church of England)* pasteur *m* anglican; *(in Catholic church)* *(of seminary)* supérieur *m* **2** *Univ* président *m*; *Scot Sch* proviseur *m*; *Scot Univ* = personne *f* élue par les étudiants pour les représenter

rectorial [rek'tɔːrɪəl] **ADJ** *(decision, duties)* rectoral, -aux; *Scot Univ* **r. election** = élection *f* d'une personnalité dont le rôle est de représenter les étudiants

rectory ['rektərɪ] **N** *Rel (residence)* presbytère *m*

rectoscope ['rektəskəʊp] **N** *Med* rectoscope *m*

rectum, *pl* **rectums, recta** ['rektəm, -əmz, -ə] **N** *Anat* rectum *m*

recumbent [rɪ'kʌmbənt] **ADJ** *Lit* couché, étendu; **to be r.** être couché (**on** sur)
▸▸ *Art* **r. figure** figure *f* couchée, gisant *m*

recuperate [rɪ'kuːpəreɪt, -'kjuː-] **VT** *(one's strength, money, heat)* récupérer
VI *(of person)* se remettre, se rétablir, récupérer (**from** de); **he had gone to the South of France to r.** il était allé en convalescence dans le Midi; **she is still recuperating** elle est encore en convalescence

recuperation [rɪkuːpə'reɪʃən, -'kjuː-] **N 1** *(of strength, money, heat)* récupération *f* **2** *(from illness)* rétablissement *m*; **powers of r.** capacités *fpl* de rétablissement

recuperative [rɪ'kuːpərətɪv, -'kjuː-] **ADJ** *(powers)* de rétablissement

recur [rɪ'kɜːr] **VI** (**-rr-**) *(of theme)* revenir, être répété; *(of event)*, *Math (of figures)* se reproduire; *(of illness)* réapparaître; **to r. to the mind** revenir à la mémoire; **a festival that recurs every ten years** une fête qui a lieu tous les dix ans

recurrence [rɪ'kʌrəns] **N** *(of illness)* réapparition *f*, *(of infectious disease)* récurrence *f*, récidive *f*, *(of theme)* répétition *f*, réapparition; *(of event)* répétition *f*; **has there been any r. of the symptoms?** les symptômes se sont-ils manifestés à nouveau?

recurrent [rɪ'kʌrənt] **ADJ 1** *(event)* périodique, qui revient *ou* se répète périodiquement; *(fever, symptom, theme)* récurrent; *(dream, nightmare)* qui revient souvent **2** *Med, Anat* récurrent
▸▸ **r. expenses** dépenses *fpl* courantes; *Com* frais *mpl* généraux; *Math* **r. series** série *f* récurrente

recurring [rɪ'kɜːrɪŋ] **ADJ** *(event)* périodique; *(theme)* qui se répète, qui réapparaît; *(dream, nightmare)* qui revient souvent; **33. 33 r.** 33, 33 à l'infini
▸▸ **r. decimal** fraction *f* périodique

recusant ['rekjʊzənt] **ADJ** *Rel* réfractaire

recyclable [riː'saɪkləbəl] **ADJ** *(container etc)* recyclable

recycle [riː'saɪk(ə)l] **VT** *(waste, water, paper etc)* recycler; **recycled paper/glass/plastic** papier *m*/verre *m*/plastique *m* recyclé; *Fin* **to r. funds** remettre des fonds en circulation
▸▸ *Comput* **r. bin** corbeille *f*

recycling [riː'saɪklɪŋ] **N** *(of paper etc)* recyclage *m*; *(of funds)* remise *f* en circulation
▸▸ **r. facility** installation *f* de recyclage; **r. plant** usine *f* de recyclage

red [red] **ADJ** *(comp* **redder,** *superl* **reddest)* **1** *(dress, wine, lips etc)* rouge; *(beard, hair)* roux, *f* rousse; **r.(-rimmed) eyes** yeux *mpl* rouges; **to turn** *or* **go r.** *(of person, litmus paper)* rougir, devenir rouge; *(of leaves etc)* roussir; *(of sky)* rougeoyer; **wait till the lights turn r.** attend que le feu passe au rouge; **to be r. in the face** *or* **have a r. face** *(permanent state)* être rougeaud; **to be r. (in the face) with anger/embarrassment** être rouge de colère/gêne; **was my face r.!** ce que j'étais gêné!; **there will be some r. faces on the Opposition benches** cela va causer de l'embarras dans les rangs de l'Opposition; **to be as r. as a beetroot** *(with embarrassment)* être rouge comme une tomate; **to be as r. as a lobster** *(with sunburn)* être rouge comme une écrevisse; *Am Fam* **it isn't worth a r. cent** ça ne vaut pas un centime; **the mere mention of his name was like a r. rag to a bull (to him)** le simple fait d'entendre son nom le mettait dans une colère noire; **Little R. Riding Hood** Le Petit Chaperon rouge
2 *Fam (communist)* rouge
N 1 *(colour)* rouge *m*; **r. is my favourite colour** le rouge est ma couleur préférée; **dressed in r.** habillé de *ou* en rouge; *Fam* **to see r.** *(be angry)* voir rouge
2 *Fin Fam* **to be in the r.** *(of company, person)* avoir un découvert, être dans le rouge; *(of account)* avoir un solde déficitaire; **to go into the r.** passer dans le rouge; **at last I'm out of the r.** enfin je ne suis plus à découvert
3 *Pol Fam* rouge *mf*; **to see reds under the bed** avoir la phobie des communistes; **the reds-under-the-bed syndrome** la phobie anti-communiste
4 *(in billiards)* bille *f* rouge; *(on roulette table)* rouge *m*
5 *(red wine)* rouge *m*
▸▸ *Mil, Fig* **r. alert** alerte *f* rouge; **to be on r. alert** être en état d'alerte maximale; **R. Army** Armée *f* rouge; **r. card** *(in football, rugby)* carton *m* rouge, *Belg* carte *f* rouge; *Fig* **to put** *or* **roll out the r. carpet for sb** recevoir quelqu'un en grande pompe, dérouler le tapis rouge pour recevoir quelqu'un; **I got the r.-carpet treatment wherever I went** on m'a reçu en grande pompe partout où je suis allé; **r. channel** *(at airport etc)* = file *f* pour les passagers qui ont des objets à déclarer à la douane; *Fam* **R. China** la Chine communiste *ou* populaire; **the R. Crescent** le Croissant-Rouge; **R. Cross** Croix-Rouge *f*, *Astron* **r. dwarf** naine *f* rouge; *Br Naut* **R. Ensign** = pavillon *m* de la marine marchande britannique; **the R. Flag** = hymne *f* du parti travailliste britannique; **r. flag** drapeau *m* rouge; *Astron* **r. giant** géante *f* rouge; **R. Guard** *(in China)* garde *m* rouge; **r. herring** *(fish)* hareng *m* saur; *Fig* diversion *f*, **it's just a red herring** ce n'est qu'un truc pour nous dépister ou pour brouiller les pistes; **R. Indian** Peau-Rouge *mf*, *pl* Peaux-Rouges; *Am Fin Fam* **r. ink** déficit *m*; **to go into r. ink** *(of person)* se mettre à découvert; *(of company)* être en déficit; *Aut* **r. light** feu *m* rouge; **to go through a r. light** brûler le feu rouge; *Fig* **to get** *or* **be given the r. light** être rejeté; **r.-light district** quartier *m* des prostituées,

quartier chaud; **r. meat** viande *f* rouge; **r. pepper** *(spice)* *(poivre m* de) cayenne *m*; *(vegetable)* poivron *m* rouge; **the R. Sea** la mer Rouge; **r. setter** setter *m* irlandais; *Hist* **R. Shirts** Chemises *fpl* rouges; **r. snapper** vivanneau *m*; **R. Square** la place Rouge; *Zool* **r. squirrel** écureuil *m* roux; **r. tape** *(bureaucracy)* paperasserie *f*

red-blooded **ADJ** *(person)* vigoureux, robuste; *(policy, response etc)* musclé; **the average r. male** n'importe quel homme digne de ce nom

redbreast ['redbrest] **N** *(bird)* **(robin)** r. rouge-gorge *m*, *pl* rouges-gorges

redbrick ['redbrɪk] **ADJ** *(house, building)* en brique rouge
▸▸ *Br Fig* **r. university** = université *f* de province (par opposition à Oxford et Cambridge) construite à la fin du XIXe siècle

redcap ['redkæp] **N 1** *Br Mil Fam* soldat *m* de la police militaire **2** *Am Rail* porteur *m*

redcoat ['redkəʊt] **N** *Br* **1** *Hist* soldat *m* anglais (du dix-huitième siècle) **2** *(at holiday camp)* animateur, -trice

redcurrant ['redkʌrənt] **N** groseille *f* (rouge)
▸▸ **r. bush** groseillier *m* rouge; **r. jelly** gelée *f* de groseille

redden ['red(ə)n] **VT** rougir, rendre rouge
VI *(of sky)* rougeoyer; *(of leaves)* roussir; *(of person)* rougir

reddish ['redɪʃ] **ADJ** *(light, colour)* rougeâtre; *(hair)* rougeâtre, qui tire sur le roux

redecorate [riː'dekəreɪt] **VT** *(flat etc)* refaire
VI refaire la peinture et les papiers

redecoration [riːdekə'reɪʃən] **N** *(of house etc)* remise *f* à neuf de la peinture et des papiers

redeem [rɪ'diːm] **VT 1** *(recover)* *(pawned item)* dégager; **to r. one's good name** sauver son honneur **2** *Fin (pay off)* *(mortgaged property)* racheter, dégager; *(debt)* amortir, se libérer de; *(bill)* honorer; *(loan)* rembourser, amortir; *Fig Fml (obligations)* s'acquitter de; **to r. a mortgage** *(of mortgagor)* éteindre une hypothèque; *(of mortgagee)* purger une hypothèque; *Fml* **to r. one's promise** tenir sa promesse (**to do sth** de faire qch) **3** *(convert)* *(bond)* obtenir le remboursement de; *(gift token)* échanger; *(coupon)* rembourser; **to r. a bond** racheter une obligation **4** *(compensate for)* *(fault)* racheter, rattraper; **to r. oneself** se racheter; **it's his sole redeeming feature** c'est sa seule qualité **5** *Fml (free)* *(slave, prisoner)* libérer, racheter; *Rel (of Christ)* *(mankind)* racheter

redeemable [rɪ'diːməb(ə)l] **ADJ 1** *Fin (loan, mortgage)* remboursable; *(voucher)* encaissable; *(share)* réalisable, rachetable; *(debt)* remboursable, amortissable; *Fig (manuscript)* qui peut être sauvé; **coupons are r. for cash** les coupons sont remboursables en espèces **2** *(mistake)* réparable; *(sin, crime)* expiable; *(sinner)* rachetable

redeemer [rɪ'diːmər] **N** *Rel* **the R.** le Rédempteur

redefine [riːdɪ'faɪn] **VT** redéfinir

redefinition [riːdefɪ'nɪʃən] **N** redéfinition *f*

redemption [rɪ'dem(p)ʃən] **N 1** *(of item pawned)* dégagement *m* **2** *(of property)* rachat *m*; *Fin (of mortgage) (by mortgagor)* extinction *f*, *(by mortgagee)* purge *f*, *(of loan)* amortissement *m* **3** *(of gift token)* échange *m*; *Fin (of coupon)* remboursement *m* **4** *(of fault)* rachat *m*; **to be beyond** *or* **past r.** être irrécupérable; *(of smashed car, broken toy etc)* être irréparable **5** *(of slave, prisoner)* rachat *m*; *Rel* rédemption *f*, *Fig* **this setback proved his r.** ce revers de fortune fut son salut
▸▸ *Fin* **r. date** date *f* d'échéance; *Fin* **r. fee** prime *f* de remboursement; *Fin* **r. premium**

prime de remboursement; *Fin* **r. price** prix *m* de rachat; *Fin* **r. value** valeur *f* de remboursement *ou* de rachat; *Fin* **r. yield** rendement *m* à l'échéance

redemptive [rɪ'demtɪv] ADJ *esp Rel* rédempteur, -trice

redeploy [ri:dɪ'plɔɪ] VT *Mil (troops etc)* redéployer; *Admin (employees)* réaffecter

redeployment [ri:dɪ'plɔɪmənt] N *(of troops etc)* redéploiement *m*; *(of staff)* réaffectation *f*

redesign [ri:dɪ'zaɪn] VT reconcevoir

redevelop [ri:dɪ'veləp] VT *(poor district)* réaménager, revaloriser; **the docks are being redeveloped** les docks sont en cours de réaménagement

redevelopment [ri:dɪ'veləpmənt] N *(of town, street etc)* réaménagement *m*, remise *f* en valeur; **scheduled for r.** dont le réaménagement est prévu
▸▸ **r. area** zone *f* de réaménagement

red-eye N **1** *Am Fam* whisky *m* bon marché **2** *Aviat Fam (night flight)* vol *m* de nuit **3** *Phot* = phénomène *m* provoquant l'apparition de taches rouges dans les yeux des personnes photographiées au flash; **to avoid the r. effect** … pour éviter que le sujet n'apparaisse avec les yeux rouges …
▸▸ *Aviat Fam* **r. flight** vol de nuit

red-eyed ADJ aux yeux rouges; **to be r.** avoir les yeux rouges (**with, from** de); **she's r. from crying/staying up all night** elle a les yeux rouges d'avoir pleuré/d'avoir passé une nuit blanche

red-faced ['red'feɪst] ADJ *(naturally)* rougeaud, rubicond; *(with anger, embarrassment)* rouge, rougissant (**with** de); **a r. admission** un aveu confus

red-haired ADJ aux cheveux roux; **a r. man** un roux; **a r. girl** une rousse

red-handed [-'hændɪd] ADJ **to be caught r.** être pris en flagrant délit *ou Fam* la main dans le sac

redhead ['redhed] N **1** *(person)* roux *m*, rousse *f* **2** *TV, Cin (lighting)* mandarine *f*

red-headed ADJ **1** *(person)* = **red-haired 2** *(bird, animal)* à tête rouge

red-hot ADJ *(very hot)* brûlant; *(metal)* chauffé au rouge; *Fig (supporter, revolutionary etc)* ardent; *(enthusiasm)* débordant; *Fam (news, information)* de dernière minute; *Fam (very good)* excellent, sensass *inv*; **to make sth r.** *(by heating)* porter qch au rouge; **Rangers are the r. favourites to win the cup** Rangers sont les grandissimes favoris de la coupe
▸▸ *Bot* **r. poker** tritoma *m*

redial[1] [ri:'daɪəl] (*-ll-, Am -l-*) *Tel* VT **to r. a number** refaire un numéro
VI refaire le numéro

redial[2] ['ri:daɪəl] N *Tel* rappel *m* du dernier numéro; **the latest model has automatic r.** le dernier modèle est muni du système de rappel du dernier numéro
▸▸ **r. feature** rappel du dernier numéro

redirect [ri:dɪ'rekt, -daɪ-] VT **1** *(letter etc)* faire suivre; *(telephone call etc)* réacheminer **2** *(plane etc)* dérouter **3** *Fig* **to r. one's energies (into sth)** réorienter son énergie (dans qch)

redirection [ri:dɪ'rekʃən, -daɪ-] N **1** *(of letter etc)* réacheminement *m*, réexpédition *f* **2** *(of plane)* déroutement *m* **3** *Fig* **the situation demands the r. of some of our attention to …** la situation exige que l'on réoriente nos efforts vers …

rediscount [ri:'dɪskaʊnt] N réescompte *m*
VT *Am Com* réescompter

rediscover [ri:dɪ'skʌvər] VT redécouvrir

redistribute [ri:dɪ'strɪbjuːt] VT *(wealth,*

tasks) redistribuer; *Pol* **to r. seats** redécouper les circonscriptions électorales

redistribution [ri:dɪstrɪ'bjuːʃən] N *(of wealth, labour)* redistribution *f*; *Pol* **r. of seats** nouveau découpage *m* des circonscriptions

red-letter ADJ
▸▸ **r. day** jour *m* à marquer d'une pierre blanche; **this has been a r. day for everyone** ceci a été un jour mémorable pour tout le monde

redneck ['rednek] N *Am Fam Pej* plouc *mf*, bouseux, -euse *(du Sud des États-Unis)*; **a r. politician** un homme politique tout ce qu'il y a de plus réactionnaire; **a r. attitude** une attitude réactionnaire

redness ['rednɪs] N *(of face, sky etc)* rouge *m*; *(of hair)* rousseur *f*

redo [ri:'duː] VT *(pt* **redid** [ri:'dɪd]; *pp* **redone** [ri:'dʌn]) *(task, flat)* refaire; *Comput* rétablir, refaire

redolent ['redələnt] ADJ *Lit (sweet-smelling)* odoriférant, parfumé; *(strong-smelling)* qui a une odeur forte (**of** de); *Fig (reminiscent)* évocateur, -trice, suggestif; **r. of spring** qui exhale une odeur de printemps; **a house r. of the past** une maison qui évoque le passé

redouble [ri:'dʌb(ə)l] VT *(one's cries, entreaties)* redoubler; **to r. one's efforts** redoubler d'efforts *ou* de zèle; *Cards* **to r. spades** surcontrer pique
VI *(of noise, efforts, criticism etc)* redoubler; *Cards* surcontrer

redoubt [rɪ'daʊt] N *Mil* redoute *f*, *Fig* bastion *m*

redoubtable [rɪ'daʊtəb(ə)l] ADJ *(fearsome)* formidable; *(opponent)* redoutable

redound [rɪ'daʊnd] VI *Fml (of deeds)* se retourner (**upon, on** contre); **to r. to sb's credit** être à l'honneur de qn; **to r. to sb's advantage** tourner à l'avantage de qn

red-pencil VT *(-ll-, Am -l-)* *(text)* corriger, réviser

redraft[1] ['ri:drɑːft] N **1** *(action) (of proposal, submission)* refonte *f* **2** *(resulting text)* texte *m* revu; **this is the third r.** c'est la troisième version

redraft[2] [ri:'drɑːft] VT *(proposal, submission)* rédiger à nouveau

redress [rɪ'dres] N *(of grievance)* réparation *f*; **to seek r.** demander réparation (**for** de); **there is no r.** il n'y a pas de recours
VT *(rectify) (a wrong)* réparer; **to r. the balance** rétablir l'équilibre

re-dress VT **to r. a wound** refaire le pansement d'une blessure

redshank ['redʃæŋk] N *(bird)* chevalier *m* gambette

redskin ['redskɪn] N *Pol Old-fashioned Pej* Peau-Rouge *mf*, *pl* Peaux-Rouges

redstart ['redstɑːt] N *(bird)* rouge-queue *m* à front blanc, *pl* rouges-queues à front blanc

redtop ['redtɒp] N *Br Journ Fam* tabloïde *m*, journal *m* à sensation *(dont le titre est imprimé en rouge)*

reduce [rɪ'djuːs] VT **1** *(lessen) (price)* baisser, diminuer, réduire; *(drawing, photograph)* réduire; *(tax)* baisser, alléger; *(spending)* diminuer, réduire; *(temperature)* faire baisser; *Culin (sauce)* faire réduire; **oranges have been reduced** les oranges ont baissé *ou* diminué; *Com* **reduced to £10 from £15** soldé de 15 à 10 livres; **are these shoes reduced?** est-ce que ces chaussures sont soldées *ou* en solde?; **to buy sth at a reduced price** acheter qch à prix réduit; *Ind* **to r. output** ralentir la production; **to r. the risk** réduire le risque (**of sth** de qch); **to r. speed** diminuer *ou* réduire la vitesse, ralentir; **to r. stocks** dé-

stocker des marchandises; **to r. a prison sentence** accorder *ou* consentir une remise de peine; **his prison sentence was reduced to two years** sa peine de prison a été ramenée à deux ans
2 *(bring to a certain state)* **to r. sth to ashes/dust** réduire qch en cendres/poussière; **to r. sb to despair/silence** réduire qn au désespoir/silence; **his words reduced her to tears** ses paroles l'ont fait fondre en larmes; **to r. sb to helpless laughter** faire mourir qn de rire; **to r. sb to the ranks/the rank of …** rétrograder *ou* casser qn/descendre qn au rang de …; **to be reduced to doing sth** en être réduit à faire qch; **is this what I've been reduced to?** j'en suis donc réduit à cela?
3 *(simplify) (problem, question)* ramener (**to** à); *(fraction, equation)* réduire; **to r. sth to a percentage** exprimer qch en pourcentage; **to r. a fraction to its lowest terms** simplifier une fraction, ramener une fraction à sa plus simple expression; **to r. two fractions to the same denominator** réduire deux fractions au même dénominateur
VI *(slim)* maigrir; *Culin (of sauce)* se réduire

reduced [rɪ'djuːst] ADJ *(smaller)* réduit; **on a r. scale** à une échelle réduite; **at r. prices** au rabais, en solde; **at greatly r. prices** à prix très réduits; **at (a) r. rate** *(bus or theatre ticket etc)* à tarif réduit; **r. rate loan** prêt *m* à taux réduit; **everything r. by ten per cent** remise de dix pour cent sur tous nos articles; **r. to clear** *(sign)* (soldes) coup de balai; **to be/live in r. circumstances** être/vivre dans la gêne

reducer [rɪ'djuːsər] N *Elec* réducteur *m*; *Phot* affaiblisseur *m*

reducible [rɪ'djuːsɪb(ə)l] ADJ réductible (**to** à)

reduction [rɪ'dʌkʃən] N **1** *(of prices)* baisse *f*, diminution *f*, réduction *f*; *(of taxes)* allègement *m*; *(of costs, speed, spending)* diminution, réduction; *(of drawing, photograph, scale)* réduction; *(of temperature, voltage)* baisse; **I'll give you a r.** *(on purchase)* je vous fais un prix; **big reductions** *(sale notice)* rabais, soldes; *Law* **r. of sentence** remise *f* de peine; *Fin* **r. in borrowings** désendettement *m*; **r. in staff** compression *f* de personnel; **r. in stocks** déstockage *m*; **r. of capital** réduction de capital **2** *(of equation)* réduction *f* **3** *Med (of fracture)* réduction *f*
▸▸ *Tech* **r. gear** (engrenage *m*) démultiplicateur *m*

reductionism [rɪ'dʌkʃənɪz(ə)m] N *Phil* réductionnisme *m*

reductionist [rɪ'dʌkʃənɪst] N, ADJ *Phil* réductionniste *mf*

redundancy [rɪ'dʌndənsɪ] N **1** *Br Ind (dismissal)* licenciement *m*; **redundancies have been heavy** il y a eu beaucoup de licenciements; **the strike caused over three hundred redundancies** la grève a causé le licenciement de plus de trois cents personnes; **voluntary r.** départ *m* volontaire **2** *(of details, factory etc)* inutilité *f*, *Comput, Ling etc* redondance *f*
▸▸ *Br* **r. notice** préavis *m* de licenciement; *Br* **r. payment** indemnité *f* de licenciement

redundant [rɪ'dʌndənt] ADJ **1** *Br (worker)* licencié; **to make sb r.** *(of employer)* licencier qn, mettre qn au chômage; *(of technology etc)* entraîner le licenciement de qn; **to be made r.** être licencié, être mis au chômage **2** *(details, factory etc)* superflu; *(information, knowledge)* inutile; *Comput, Ling (file, information)* redondant; **I just feel r. round here now** j'ai l'impression de ne plus servir à rien ici

redwood ['redwʊd] N *(tree)* séquoia *m*

re-echo VT *(repeat) (sound)* répercuter, renvoyer; *Fig* répéter
VI *(of noise, voice etc)* retentir, résonner; **the**

hall echoed and re-echoed to the sound of applause la salle retentissait d'acclamations

reed [ri:d] **N 1** *(plant)* roseau *m*; *Fig* **broken r.** personne *f* sur laquelle on ne peut (pas) compter **2** *Mus (of instrument)* anche *f*
▸▸ **r. bed** roselière *f*; *Orn* **r. bunting** bruant *m* des roseaux; **r. pipe** pipeau *m*, chalumeau *m*; **r. stop** jeu d'anches; *Orn* **r. warbler** fauvette *f* des roseaux, rousserolle *f* effarvatte

re-edit **VT** *(text)* rédiger à nouveau; *Comput* rééditer

re-educate **VT** *(criminal etc), Med (limb)* rééduquer

re-education **N** *(of criminal etc), Med (of limb)* rééducation *f*

reedy ['ri:dɪ] **ADJ 1** *(covered in reeds)* plein *ou* couvert de roseaux **2** *(shrill) (instrument)* aigu, *f* aiguë; *(voice)* flûté, grêle

reef¹ [ri:f] **N** *(rocks)* écueil *m*, récif *m*; *Fig* écueil; **to hit a r.** *(of ship)* faire naufrage sur un récif; *Fig* **his plans had hit a r.** ses projets s'étaient heurté à un écueil

reef² *Naut* **N** *(of sail)* ris *m*
VT *(sail)* prendre un *ou* des ris à; **to r. the sails** prendre les ris
▸▸ **r. knot** nœud *m* plat

reefer ['ri:fər] **N 1** *(jacket)* caban *m*, vareuse *f* **2** *Old-fashioned Fam (marijuana cigarette)* joint *m* **3** *Am (for transporting goods)* camion *m*/navire *m*/wagon *m* frigorifique; *(refrigerator)* chambre *f* frigorifique
ADJ *(truck etc)* réfrigéré

reek [ri:k] **N** *(bad smell)* puanteur *f*
VI puer; *also Fig* **to r. of sth** puer qch; **this room reeks** ça pue ici; *Fig* **the whole affair reeks of corruption** toute cette affaire sent la corruption à plein nez

reel [ri:l] **N 1** *Br (for film, paper, thread)* bobine *f*, *(film itself)* pellicule *f*, *(for fishing line)* moulinet *m*; *(for cable, hose etc)* dévidoir *m*; **r. to r. tape** bande *f* en bobine; **r. to r. (tape recorder)** magnétophone *m* à bobines; *Am Fam* **(right) off the r.** *(continuously)* d'une seule traite, d'affilée; *(immediately)* sans hésiter, sur-le-champ **2** *(dance, music)* reel *m*, quadrille *m* écossais
VI *(sway)* chanceler; *(not walk straight)* tituber; **to go reeling down the street** descendre la rue en titubant; *Fig* **to make sb's senses r.** donner le vertige à qn; *Fig* **my head is reeling** la tête me tourne; *Fig* **I'm still reeling** *(after news)* je n'en suis toujours pas revenu; *Fig* **she was still reeling from shock at what had happened** elle était encore toute retournée par ce qui venait de se passer; **to send sb reeling** *(of punch)* envoyer valser qn; *Fig (of news, scene etc)* abasourdir qn; *Fig* **his mind or brain reeled at the thought** cette pensée lui donnait le vertige; *Fig* **the whole room was reeling** toute la salle tournoyait autour de moi/lui/*etc*
▸ **reel in** **VT SEP** **to r. a fish in** remonter un poisson (avec le moulinet)
▸ **reel off** **VT SEP** *(speech etc)* débiter

re-elect **VT** *(MP etc)* réélire; **she is sure to be re-elected** sa réélection est assurée; **he was re-elected (as) president** on l'a réélu président

re-election **N** réélection *f*; **to stand** *or Am* **run for r.** se représenter

reeling ['ri:lɪŋ] **ADJ** *(gait)* titubant

re-embark **VT** *(passengers)* rembarquer
VI rembarquer; *Fig* **to r. on sth** recommencer qch

re-embarkation **N** rembarquement *m*

re-emerge **VI** *(of person)* ressortir; *(of sun)* reparaître; **when the country re-emerges into prosperity** quand le pays connaîtra à nouveau la prospérité

re-employ **VT** *(former employee)* réembaucher

re-employment **N** *(of former employee)* réembauchage *m*

re-enact **VT 1** *(enforce) (law)* remettre en vigueur **2** *(depict) (accident, crime, battle)* reconstituer; *(scene, mistakes)* reproduire

re-enactment **N 1** *(of law)* remise *f* en vigueur **2** *(of accident, crime, battle)* reconstitution *f*; *(of scene, mistakes)* reproduction *f*

re-engage **VT 1** *(former employee)* réembaucher **2** *Tech (cogwheel)* rengrener; *Aut* **to r. the clutch** rembrayer

re-engagement **N 1** *(of former employee)* réembauchage *m* **2** *Tech (of cogwheel)* rengrènement *m*; *Aut (of clutch)* rembrayage *m*

re-enlist **VI** *Mil* se rengager

re-enter **VI** *(of person, spacecraft)* rentrer; *(of musical instrument)* faire une *ou* sa rentrée; **to r. for an examination** se présenter de nouveau à un examen; *Theat* **r. Macbeth** Macbeth rentre
VT 1 *(a room etc)* rentrer dans; **he never re-entered that house** il n'a jamais remis les pieds dans cette maison; **to r. the job market** se remettre à chercher du travail; **the spacecraft re-entered the atmosphere** le vaisseau spatial est rentré dans l'atmosphère **2** *(date, name)* réinscrire, inscrire de nouveau

re-entrant **ADJ** *(angle etc)* rentrant
N angle *m* rentrant

re-entry **N** *(of person, spacecraft)* rentrée *f*; **to make its r.** *(of spacecraft)* rentrer dans l'atmosphère

re-establish **VT** *(communications, diplomatic relations etc)* rétablir

re-establishment **N** *(of communications, relations etc)* rétablissement *m*

reeve [ri:v] **VT** *(pt* rove [rəʊv], **reeved**; *pp* **reeved, rove)** *Naut (rope)* passer (**through a block** dans une poulie)

re-examination **N 1** *(of file, question etc)* réexamen *m* **2** *Law (of witness)* nouvel interrogatoire *m*

re-examine **VT 1** *(review) (file, question etc)* réexaminer **2** *Law (witness)* interroger de nouveau

re-export¹ [ri:'ekspɔ:t] **N** *(of goods)* réexportation *f*

re-export² ['ri:ekspɔ:t] **VT** *(goods)* réexporter

re-exportation **N** réexportation *f*

ref **N** [ref] **1** *Br Sport Fam (abbr referee)* arbitre *m* **2** *Com (abbr reference) (at head of letter)* réf; **your r.** v/réf; **our r.** n/réf

re-face **VT** *(building)* ravaler les façades de; *(wall)* refaire

refashion [ri:'fæʃən] **VT** remodeler

refectory [rɪ'fekt(ə)rɪ] **N** réfectoire *m*
▸▸ **r. table** = table *f* longue et étroite *(souvent en chêne massif)*

REFER [rɪ'fɜ:r] **VT** (**-rr-**) *(direct) (matter, proposal etc)* soumettre (**to** à); **to r. a cheque to drawer** *(of bank)* retourner un chèque au tireur; **r. to drawer** *(notice on cheque)* voir le tireur; **he referred me to an article on the subject** il m'a renvoyé à un article sur la question; **to r. a matter to sb** soumettre une question à qn; **to r. a question to sb for (a) decision** soumettre une question à la décision de qn; **to r. a matter to a tribunal** soumettre une affaire à un tribunal; **the reader is referred to …** *(in book)* se reporter à …; **to r. a patient to a specialist** envoyer un malade chez un spécialiste; *Med* **she's going to r. me** elle va m'envoyer chez un spécialiste; **to r. a customer to another department** renvoyer un client à un autre service; **he just referred me back to you** il m'a renvoyé à vous; *Med* **referred pain** douleur *f* irradiée
▸ **refer to** **VT INSEP 1** *(consult)* se référer *ou* se

reporter à; **to r. (back) to an expert** consulter un expert
2 *(allude to)* faire allusion à; *(speak of)* parler de; **who are you referring to?** de qui parlez-vous?; **it's you I'm referring to** c'est de toi que je parle; **referred to as …** désigné sous le nom de …; **he never refers to it** il n'en parle jamais; **we won't r. to it again** nous n'en reparlons plus; *Com* **referring to …** nous référant à …; **referring to your letter** suite à votre lettre
3 *(apply to)* s'appliquer à; **these measures r. to large enterprises only** ces mesures ne concernent que les grandes entreprises; **this remark refers to you** *(is aimed at)* cette remarque s'adresse à vous; *(is about)* cette remarque vous concerne

referee [refə'ri:] **N 1** *Sport, Fig* arbitre *m* **2** *(for job etc)* **please give at least two referees** veuillez fournir aux moins deux références; **will you act as my r.?** voulez-vous me fournir des références? **3** *Fin* **r. in case of need** *(on bill of exchange)* adresse *f* au besoin
VT & VI *(pt, pp* **refereed)** *Sport, Fig* arbitrer

reference ['ref(ə)rəns] **N 1** *(to higher authority)* renvoi *m*; **without r. to the Board** sans consulter le conseil d'administration; **I'll have to make r. to my superior** il faudra que j'en réfère à mon supérieur; **terms of r.** *(of person, investigating body)* compétence *f*; *(of law)* étendue *f*; **outside the committee's terms of r.** hors de la compétence du comité **2** *(consultation)* consultation *f*; *(source)* référence *f*; **for r. only** *(on library book)* consultation sur place; *(on document etc in circulation)* pour information seulement; **to keep sth for future r.** garder qch à titre d'information; **for future r., please note …** pour votre information à l'avenir, veuillez noter …
3 *(allusion)* allusion *f* (**to** à); *(mention)* mention *f* (**to** de); *(connection)* rapport *m* (**to** avec); *(in book) (allusion)* référence *f*; *(cross-reference)* renvoi *m*; *(on map)* coordonnées *fpl*; **to make r. to a fact** faire mention d'un fait; **if any r. is made to me** si on parle de moi; **with r. to what was said …** en référence à ce qui a été dit …; **a talk on the environment with particular r. to …** un exposé sur l'environnement abordant tout particulièrement …; **with r. to my letter of the 20th March** me référant *ou* suite à ma lettre du 20 mars; **in r.** *or* **with r. to your letter** en ce qui concerne votre lettre; **with r. to what was said at the meeting** à propos de *ou* en ce qui concerne ce qui a été dit au cours de la réunion; **r. AB** *(at head of letter)* référence AB; **our/your r.** *(on letter)* notre/votre référence
4 *(testimonial) (from bank etc)* référence *f*; *(from employer)* référence, lettre *f* de recommandation, certificat *m* de travail; **to give sb a r.** donner son avis sur qn; **to have good references** avoir de bonnes références; **he got a very bad r. from his previous employer** son ancien employeur ne l'a pas du tout recommandé; **to take up references** prendre contact avec *ou* contacter les personnes dont un candidat se recommande; **to give sb as a r.** se recommander de qn; **you may use my name as (a) r.** vous pouvez donner mon nom comme référence, vous pouvez vous recommander de moi
VT 1 *(refer to)* faire référence à **2** *(thesis)* établir la liste des citations dans; *(quotation)* donner la référence de **3** *Comput* référencer
▸▸ **r. book** ouvrage *m* de référence; *Mktg* **r. customer** client, -ente de référence; *Mktg* **r. group** groupe *m* de référence; **r. library** bibliothèque *f* d'ouvrages de référence; **r. number** numéro *m* de référence; *Banking* **r. period** période *f* de référence; **r. point** point *m* de repère; *Mktg* **r. price** prix *m* de réfé-

rence; *Fin* **r. rate** taux *m* de référence; **r. room** (*in public library*) salle *f* de lecture; (*in university*) salle de consultation; *Mktg* **r. sale** vente *f* de référence; **r. work** ouvrage *m* de référence

referendum [refə'rendəm] N *Pol* référendum *m*, referendum *m*; **to hold a r.** organiser un référendum; **decided in a** *or* **by r.** décidé par référendum

referral [rɪ'fɜːrəl] N **1** (*forwarding*) renvoi *m* **2** (*consultation*) consultation *f* **3** *Univ* (*of thesis*) renvoi *m* pour révision **4** (*person*) patient *m* (*envoyé par son médecin chez un spécialiste*)

refill¹ ['riːfɪl] N (*for lighter, pen*) recharge *f*, cartouche *f*, (*for propelling pencil*) mine *f* de rechange; (*for notebook*) feuilles *fpl* de rechange; (*of drink*) autre verre *m*; **I'll have a r.** tu me remets la même chose?; **would you like a r.?** je vous ressers?; **she handed me her glass for a r.** elle m'a tendu son verre pour que je la reserve

refill² [riː'fɪl] VT (*glass etc*) remplir (à nouveau) (**with** de); (*lighter, pen etc*) recharger; (*shelves*) regarnir (**with** de)

refillable [riː'fɪləb(ə)l] ADJ (*lighter, pen*) rechargeable

refinance [riː'faɪnæns] *Fin* VT (*loan*) refinancer
▪ VI (*of company*) se refinancer (**on the money market** auprès du marché monétaire)

refinancing [riː'faɪnænsɪŋ] N *Fin* refinancement *m*; **to get r. from a bank** se refinancer auprès d'une banque

refine [rɪ'faɪn] VT **1** (*process, purify*) (*sugar, petroleum*) raffiner; (*metal*) affiner **2** (*develop*) (*technique, machine*) perfectionner
▸ **refine on, refine upon** VT INSEP (*improve*) parfaire

refined [rɪ'faɪnd] ADJ (*petroleum, sugar*) raffiné; (*metal*) affiné; *Fig* (*person, taste*) raffiné, *Pej* maniéré

refinement [rɪ'faɪnmənt] N **1** (*of manners, taste, person*) raffinement *m*; **of great r.** (*person*) très raffiné; **lack of r.** vulgarité *f* **2** (*of technique*) perfectionnement *m*; **machine with all the latest refinements** machine dotée des derniers perfectionnements; **to make refinements to** (*machine*) perfectionner; (*plan, tactics etc*) parfaire **3** (*of metal etc*) = **refining**

refiner [rɪ'faɪnər] N (*of petroleum, sugar*) raffineur *m*; (*of metal*) affineur *m*

refinery [rɪ'faɪnərɪ] N (*for petroleum, sugar*) raffinerie *f*, (*for metal*) affinerie *f*

refining [rɪ'faɪnɪŋ] N (*of petroleum, sugar*) raffinage *m*; (*of metal*) affinage *m*

refit¹ ['riːfɪt] N (*of ship*) réparation *f*, remise *f* en état; (*of factory*) réaménagement *m*; **the yacht is under r.** le yacht est en cours de réparation

refit² [riː'fɪt] (**-tt-**) VT (*ship*) remettre en état; (*factory*) réaménager
▪ VI (*of ship*) être en cours de réparation; (*of factory*) être en cours de réaménagement; **while we're refitting** (*the ship*) pendant les réparations; (*the factory*) pendant le réaménagement

reflate [riː'fleɪt] VT **to r. the economy** relancer l'économie
▪ VI relancer l'économie

reflation [riː'fleɪʃən] N relance *f*

reflationary [riː'fleɪʃənərɪ] ADJ *Econ* de relance; **r. pressure** pression *f* de relance

reflect [rɪ'flekt] VT **1** (*image*) réfléchir, refléter, renvoyer; (*light*) réfléchir, renvoyer; (*heat*) renvoyer; **to be reflected** se réfléchir (**in** sur); *TV etc* **reflected light** lumière *f* réfléchie; *Fig* **to bask** *or* **bathe in reflected glory** se parer des plumes du paon; **they basked**

or **bathed in the reflected glory of their famous daughter** ils se glorifiaient de la célébrité de leur fille; *Fig* **her personal problems are reflected in her poor performance at school** elle a des problèmes personnels et ses résultats scolaires s'en ressentent **2** (*think*) **to r. that ...** penser *ou* se dire que ... + *ind*
▪ VI (*think*) réfléchir (**on** à, sur)
▸ **reflect on** VT INSEP **to r. well on sb** (*of action etc*) faire honneur à qn; **to r. badly on sb** (*of action etc*) faire du tort à qn, nuire à (la réputation de) qn; **how is that going to r. on the company?** quelles en seront les conséquences *ou* répercussions pour la société?

reflecting [rɪ'flektɪŋ] ADJ (*surface etc*) réfléchissant

reflection [rɪ'flekʃən] N **1** (*image*) (*in mirror*) reflet *m*, image *f* (réfléchie); *Fig* reflet (**of** de); **to see one's r. in a mirror** voir son image dans un miroir; *Fig* **the final score was a fair r. of the Italians' superiority** le score final reflétait bien la supériorité des Italiens; **this report is not an accurate r. of the situation** ce rapport ne donne pas un aperçu exact de la situation **2** (*action*) (*of light, sound, image*) réflexion *f* **3** *Fig* (*on honesty, character etc*) (*negative*) blâme *m*, critique *f* (**on** de); **their conduct is a (bad) r. on all of us** leur conduite nous fait du tort à tous; **it's a good r. on the school** c'est bon pour la réputation de l'école; **it's a r. on your popularity** ça veut dire beaucoup quant à ta popularité; **it's no r. on your performance** il ne s'agit pas d'une remise en cause de votre performance, cela ne remet pas votre performance en cause **4** (*thought*) réflexion *f* (**on** sur); **on r.** à la réflexion, en y réfléchissant, tout bien réfléchi; **to do sth without due r.** faire qch sans avoir suffisamment réfléchi; **reflections** réflexions, pensées *fpl*; **reflections on the history of ...** considérations *fpl* sur l'histoire de ...

reflective [rɪ'flektɪv] ADJ **1** (*thoughtful*) (*person*) réfléchi **2** (*surface*) réfléchissant, réflecteur; (*power, angle*) réflecteur; (*light*) réfléchi

reflectively [rɪ'flektɪvlɪ] ADV (*to look at*) d'un air pensif; (*to say*) d'un ton pensif

reflector [rɪ'flektər] N (*on bicycle, vehicle*) réflecteur *m*, cataphote® *m*, catadioptre *m*; (*on sign, of heat*) réflecteur
▸ **r. board** panneau *m* réflecteur

reflex ['riːfleks] N (*reaction*) réflexe *m*; **to have good reflexes** avoir de bons réflexes; **to test sb's reflexes** tester les réflexes de qn; **your reflexes aren't what they should be** vos réflexes sont défaillants
ADJ **1** réflexe **2** *Math* (*angle*) rentrant
▸ *Physiol* **r. action** réflexe *m*; *Phot* **r. camera** (*appareil m*) reflex *m*

reflexion [rɪ'flekʃən] N = **reflection**

reflexive [rɪ'fleksɪv] VOIR GRAMMAIRE A29–30; B28–9 *Gram* ADJ (*pronoun, verb*) réfléchi
N (*verb*) verbe *m* réfléchi; (*pronoun*) pronom *m* (personnel) réfléchi

reflexively [rɪ'fleksɪvlɪ] ADV *Gram* au sens réfléchi

reflexology [riːflek'splədʒɪ] N réflexologie *f*

refloat [riː'fləʊt] VT **1** (*ship*) renflouer, (re)mettre à flot **2** *Fin* (*loan*) émettre de nouveau; (*company*) renflouer, remettre à flot; *Fig* (*proposals*) présenter à nouveau

reflux ['riːflʌks] N reflux *m*

refocus [riː'fəʊkəs] (**-s-**) VT *Cin, TV* (*camera*) refaire la mise au point de

reforest [riː'fɒrɪst] VT (*region, land*) reboiser

reforestation [riːfɒrɪ'steɪʃən] N reboisement *m*

reform [rɪ'fɔːm] N (*of law, institution etc*) réforme *f*, (*of person*) retour *m* à la vertu *ou* à une conduite meilleure; (*of alcoholics, criminals, delinquents*) réinsertion *f*; **to introduce reforms** introduire *ou* apporter des réformes; **to make reforms** faire des réformes; **to be beyond r.** être irrécupérable
VT (*improve*) (*institution, law etc*) réformer; (*system*) réformer, améliorer; (*person*) corriger, ramener à la vertu; **he's a reformed character** il s'est assagi, il a changé en bien; **a reformed alcoholic** un ancien alcoolique
VI (*of person*) se corriger, s'amender
▸▸ **Reformed Church** Église *f* réformée; *Am* **r. school** ≃ centre *m* d'éducation surveillée

re-form VT (*battalion, group etc*) reformer
VI (*of group, troops etc*) se reformer

reformat [riː'fɔːmæt] (**-tt-**) *Comput, Typ* VT (*text, disk, page etc*) reformater
VI reformater

reformation [refə'meɪʃən] N **1** (*of calendar, society etc*) réforme *f*, *Rel, Hist* **the R.** la Réforme **2** (*of person*) retour *m* à la vertu *ou* à une conduite meilleure

reformatory [rɪ'fɔːmət(ə)rɪ] ADJ (*measures etc*) réformateur, -trice
N *Am* ≃ centre *m* d'éducation surveillée; *Br Formerly* maison *f* de correction *ou* de redressement

reformatting [riː'fɔːmætɪŋ] N *Comput, Typ* (*of text, disk, page etc*) reformatage *m*

reformer [rɪ'fɔːmər] N (*of religion, society*) réformateur, -trice

reformism [rɪ'fɔːmɪz(ə)m] N réformisme *m*

reformist [rɪ'fɔːmɪst] ADJ, N réformiste *mf*

refract [rɪ'frækt] VT (*light*) réfracter; **to be refracted** être réfracté

refracting [rɪ'fræktɪŋ] ADJ (*material, prism*) réfringent; (*angle*) de réfraction
▸▸ **r. telescope** réfracteur *m*, lunette *f* astronomique

refraction [rɪ'frækʃən] N *Phys, Opt* réfraction *f*, **double r.** biréfringence *f*

refractive [rɪ'fræktɪv] ADJ *Phys* réfringent
▸▸ **r. index** indice *m* de réfraction

refractivity [riːfræk'tɪvɪtɪ] N *Phys* réfringence *f*

refractor [rɪ'fræktər] N **1** *Phys* (*material*) milieu *m* réfringent; (*object*) dispositif *m* réfringent **2** (*telescope*) réfracteur *m*, lunette *f* astronomique

refractory [rɪ'frækt(ə)rɪ] ADJ *Fml* (*person*) réfractaire, récalcitrant; (*animal*) récalcitrant; (*illness*) rebelle
N réfractaire *m*

refrain¹ [rɪ'freɪn] N *Mus, Fig* refrain *m*

refrain² VI se retenir, s'abstenir (**from doing** de faire); **to r. from comment** s'abstenir de tout commentaire; **he couldn't r. from smiling** il n'a pu s'empêcher de sourire; **kindly r. from smoking/talking** (*on notice*) prière de ne pas fumer/parler

refrangible [rɪ'frændʒɪb(ə)l] ADJ *Phys, Opt* réfrangible

re-freeze VT (*food*) recongeler

refresh¹ [rɪ'freʃ] N *Comput* actualisation *f*, rafraîchissement *m*
▸▸ **r. rate** taux *m* d'actualisation *ou* de rafraîchissement

refresh² VT (*person*) (*of bath, drink*) rafraîchir, *Fam* requinquer; (*of rest, amusement*) reposer, délasser; *Comput* rafraîchir, actualiser; **to r. oneself** (*with food*) se restaurer; (*with drink*) se rafraîchir; (*by taking bath*) se délasser; **to awake refreshed** s'éveiller frais et dispos *ou* bien reposé; *Hum* **to r. the inner man** se restaurer; **to r. one's memory** se rafraîchir la mémoire; *Fam* **let me r. your memory!** je vais vous rafraîchir la mémoire!;

can I r. your drink for you? voulez-vous que je vous resserve?

refresher [rɪ'freʃər] N
▸▸**r. course** stage m ou cours m de recyclage

refreshing [rɪ'freʃɪŋ] ADJ *(breeze, drink)* rafraîchissant; *(sleep)* réparateur, -trice, reposant; *(bath, shower, cup of tea)* revigorant, ravigotant; **it is r.** ou **a r. change to encounter such honesty** cela change agréablement de ou il est réconfortant de rencontrer une telle honnêteté; **his honesty is r.** son honnêteté est comme une bouffée d'air frais ou est réconfortante

refreshingly [rɪ'freʃɪŋlɪ] ADV d'une manière qui repose ou fait du bien; **r. honest** d'une honnêteté réconfortante; **a r. original style** un style dont l'originalité est comme une bouffée d'air frais

refreshments [rɪ'freʃmənts] NPL *(drinks)* rafraîchissements mpl; *(snacks)* collation f; **to order some r.** commander à manger/à boire; **r. will be served** une collation sera servie

refrigerant [rɪ'frɪdʒərənt] N (mélange m) réfrigérant m

refrigerate [rɪ'frɪdʒəreɪt] VT *(food etc)* réfrigérer; **r. after opening** *(notice on packet)* conserver au réfrigérateur après ouverture; **keep refrigerated** *(notice on packet)* conserver au réfrigérateur; **refrigerated lorry** camion m frigorifique; **refrigerated meat** viande f frigorifiée; **refrigerated ship** navire m frigorifique

refrigeration [rɪfrɪdʒə'reɪʃən] N *(of food etc)* réfrigération f
▸▸**r. plant** installation f frigorifique

refrigerator [rɪ'frɪdʒəreɪtər] N *(domestic)* réfrigérateur m, frigidaire® m; *(industrial)* réfrigérateur, chambre f ou appareil m frigorifique

refuel [ri:'fjʊəl] *(-ll-, Am -l-)* VT *(ship, aircraft, racing car)* ravitailler en carburant; *Fig* **to r. speculation** alimenter les conjectures
VI *(of ship, aircraft, racing car)* se ravitailler en carburant; **to r. in flight** se ravitailler en vol

refuelling, *Am* **refueling** [ri:'fjʊəlɪŋ] N *(of ship, aircraft, racing car)* ravitaillement m en carburant
▸▸**r. stop** *(of aircraft, ship)* escale f pour se ravitailler en carburant; *(of racing car)* arrêt m pour se ravitailler en carburant

refuge ['refju:dʒ] N *(from danger)* refuge m, asile m; *(from weather)* abri m (**from** contre); *(for battered women)* foyer m; *Br (island in road)* refuge; **place of r.** lieu m de refuge ou d'asile; **to seek r.** chercher refuge ou asile; **to take r.** *(from danger)* se réfugier (**with** chez); **to take r. from the storm** s'abriter de l'orage; *Fig* **to take r. in lying/drugs/religion** se réfugier dans le mensonge/la drogue/la religion; *Fig* **to seek r. in lying/drugs/religion** chercher refuge dans le mensonge/la drogue/la religion; **he has been accused of taking r. in evasive language** on l'a accusé de pratiquer la langue de bois; *Lit* **God is my r.** Dieu est mon refuge

refugee [refjʊ'dʒi:] N réfugié, -ée; **economic r.** migrant, -ante économique
▸▸**r. camp** camp m de réfugiés; **r. status** statut m de réfugié

refund¹ ['ri:fʌnd] N *(for ticket, tax etc)* remboursement m; **to obtain a r. for sth** se faire rembourser qch; **I'm due a r.** je dois être remboursé

refund² [ri:'fʌnd, rɪ-] VT *(money, payment etc)* rembourser; **to r. sb** rembourser qn (**sth** de qch)

refundable [ri:'fʌndəbl] ADJ **to charge a r. deposit on sth** consigner qch

refunding [ri:'fʌndɪŋ] N remboursement m
▸▸*Fin* **r. clause** clause f de remboursement; *Fin* **r. loan** prêt m de remboursement

refurbish [ri:'fɜ:bɪʃ] VT *(flat, restaurant etc)* remettre à neuf

refurbishment [ri:'fɜ:bɪʃmənt] N remise f à neuf

refusal [rɪ'fju:z(ə)l] N *(of offer, invitation etc)* refus m (**to do** de faire); *(of cheque)* rejet m; **to give a flat r.** refuser (tout) net; **to meet with a r.** *(of person)* se heurter à ou essuyer un refus; *(of offer, invitation etc)* se heurter à un refus; **she shook her head in r.** elle a fait non de la tête; **that's his third r.** *(of show-jumper)* c'est la troisième fois qu'il refuse l'obstacle; **to have first r.** avoir la priorité (**on sth** sur qch); **to give sb first r.** donner la priorité à qn; **you promised me first r. on the car** tu m'as promis que je serais le premier à qui tu proposerais (d'acheter) la voiture
▸▸*Mktg* **r. rate** taux m de refus

refuse¹ ['refju:s] N *(rubbish)* ordures fpl, détritus m; **household r.** ordures ménagères
▸▸**r. bag** sac m à ordures; *Br* **r. bin** poubelle f, *Br* **r. chute** vide-ordures m inv; *Br* **r. collection** ramassage m d'ordures; *Br* **r. collector** éboueur m; *Br* **r. disposal** traitement m des ordures; *Br* **r. disposal unit** broyeur m d'ordures; *Br* **r. dump** *(public)* décharge f (publique), dépotoir m; **r. material** détritus m

> Note that the French word **refus** is a false friend and is never a translation for the English word **refuse**. It means **refusal**.

refuse² [rɪ'fju:z] VT *(invitation, offer), Horseriding (fence etc)* refuser; *(request)* rejeter, repousser; **to r. to do sth** refuser de ou *Fml* se refuser à faire qch; **I r. to believe that** je ne peux pas le croire; **to r. to comment** se refuser à tout commentaire; **to r. to fight** refuser le combat; **the car refuses to start** la voiture ne veut pas démarrer; **to r. sb sth** refuser qch à qn; **to r. sb admittance** refuser (de laisser entrer) qn; **they were refused admittance** on ne les a pas laissés entrer; **to be refused** essuyer un refus; **I don't see how we can r. them** je ne vois pas comment on peut leur refuser; **she made me an offer I couldn't r.** elle m'a fait une proposition que je ne pouvais pas refuser; **she refused him** *(would not marry him)* elle l'a rejeté
VI *(of person)* refuser; *(of horse)* refuser l'obstacle

refus(e)nik [rɪ'fju:znɪk] N *Pol* refuznik mf

refutation [refjʊ'teɪʃən] N *(disproving)* réfutation f

refute [rɪ'fju:t] VT **1** *(disprove) (argument, theory etc)* réfuter; **to r. a statement** démontrer la fausseté d'une déclaration **2** *(deny)* **to r. an allegation** nier une allégation

regain [rɪ'geɪn] VT **1** *(get back) (person's confidence)* regagner; *(strength, money)* récupérer; *(strength, health, sight, balance, freedom)* retrouver, recouvrer; **to r. possession of sth** rentrer en ou reprendre possession de qch; **to r. consciousness** reprendre connaissance, revenir à soi; **to r. (lost) ground** regagner du terrain **2** *(reach) (a place, one's seat)* regagner

regal ['ri:g(ə)l] ADJ *(offer, salary, splendour etc)* royal, -aux; *(air, person)* majestueux, royal

regale [rɪ'geɪl] VT *(person)* régaler (**with** de)

regalia [rɪ'geɪlɪə] NPL *(of monarch)* insignes mpl royaux; *(of Freemason etc)* insignes; **the mayor came first in all his r.** le maire est venu en premier avec tous les insignes de ses fonctions; *Hum* **here comes Mrs Smith in full r.** voilà Mme Smith dans ses plus beaux atours

regally ['ri:g(ə)lɪ] ADV *(to entertain)* royalement; *(to behave, act)* majestueusement

regard [rɪ'gɑ:d] N **1** *(admiration, respect) (for person)* respect m, estime f; *(for skill, talent etc)* respect; **to have great r. for sb** avoir beaucoup d'estime pour qn; **I have great r. for him but I don't particularly like him** j'ai beaucoup de respect pour lui mais je ne l'apprécie pas particulièrement; **to hold sb in great or high r.** tenir qn en grande ou haute estime; **out of r. for sb** par respect pour qn
2 *(consideration)* égard m, considération f (**for** pour); **out of r. for** par égard pour; **without or with no r.** to sans égard pour; **without r. to race or colour** sans distinction de race ni de couleur; **to pay r. to** avoir égard à, faire attention à; **to pay no r. to** ne faire aucune attention à; **to have no r. for human life** faire peu de cas de la vie humaine
3 *(connection)* **in this or that r.** à cet égard; **in all regards** à tous (les) égards; **with r. to** en ce qui concerne, quant à; **with r. to your letter of ...** relativement à votre lettre du ...; **having r. to** si l'on tient compte de, eu égard à
4 *(in message etc)* **to give or send one's regards** transmettre son bon souvenir, *Fml* faire ses hommages; **(please give) my kindest or best regards to the family** (présentez) mon meilleur souvenir ou mes sincères amitiés à toute la famille; **kind or best regards** *(at end of letter)* cordialement
VT **1** *(admire, respect)* avoir de l'estime pour; **to r. sb highly** avoir beaucoup d'estime pour qn; **to be highly regarded** être tenu en haute estime
2 *(consider)* considérer (**as** comme), tenir (**as** pour)
3 *(concern)* regarder, concerner; **as regards ...** en ce qui concerne ..., pour ce qui est de ..., quant à ...; **she is very strict as regards discipline** elle est très sévère pour ce qui est de ou sur le chapitre de la discipline

> Note that the French word **regard** is a false friend and is never a translation for the English word **regard**. It means **look, gaze**.

> Note that the French verb **regarder** is a false friend and is never a translation for the English verb **to regard**. It means **to look at, to watch**.

regardful [rɪ'gɑ:dfʊl] ADJ **to be r. of** se soucier de

regarding [rɪ'gɑ:dɪŋ] PREP *(about)* en ce qui concerne, pour ce qui est de; *Fam* **what's it r.?** de quoi s'agit-il?

regardless [rɪ'gɑ:dlɪs] ADV **1 r. of** *(consequences, danger, noise etc)* sans se soucier de; **to be r. of the danger of infection** ne pas se soucier du risque d'infection; **r. of expense** sans regarder à la dépense **2** *(despite everything)* quand même; **press on r.!** allez-y quand même!, continuez!

regatta [rɪ'gætə] N régate f

regency ['ri:dʒənsɪ] N régence f; *Hist* **the R.** la Régence; **R. armchair/furniture** fauteuil m/meubles mpl Régence

regenerate [rɪ'dʒenəreɪt] VT régénérer; **to r. an industry/a political party** régénérer une industrie/un parti politique; **to r. interest in sth** raviver l'intérêt pour qch; *Fig* **to feel regenerated** se sentir régénéré
VI *(of industry, party etc)* se régénérer; *(of tail, organ etc)* repousser

regenerating [rɪ'dʒenəreɪtɪŋ] ADJ régénérateur, -trice

regeneration [rɪdʒenə'reɪʃən] N régénération f

regenerative [rɪ'dʒenərətɪv] **ADJ** régénérateur, -trice; *Med* régénératif
▸▸ *Aut* **r. braking** freinage *m* à régénération

regent ['ri:dʒənt] **ADJ** *Hist* régent
N 1 *Hist* régent, -ente; **prince r.** prince *m* régent **2** *Am* = membre *m* du conseil d'administration d'une université

reggae ['regeɪ] **N** *Mus* reggae *m*

regicide ['redʒɪsaɪd] **N** (*crime*) régicide *m*; (*person*) régicide *mf*

regime, régime [reɪ'ʒiːm] **N** *Pol* régime *m*; **the old r.** l'ancien régime

regimen ['redʒɪmen] **N** *Med* régime *m*

regiment ['redʒɪmənt] **N** *Mil*, *Fig* régiment *m*; **there's enough to feed a r.** il y a de quoi nourrir un régiment
VT (*people*) enrégimenter, embrigader; (*education system, organization*) réglementer

regimental [redʒɪ'ment(ə)l] *Mil* **ADJ** (*badge, flag etc*) régimentaire, du régiment
NPL regimentals (*uniform*) uniforme *m* (militaire), tenue *f* militaire; **in full regimentals** en grande tenue d'apparat
▸▸ **r. band** fanfare *f* du régiment; **r. sergeant major** ≃ adjudant-chef *m*, *pl* adjudants-chefs

regimentation [redʒɪmen'teɪʃən] **N** *Pej* discipline *f* excessive

regimented ['redʒɪmentɪd] **ADJ** strict; **it's a very r. organization** c'est une organisation très rigide

region ['ri:dʒ(ə)n] **N** (*of country, body etc*) région *f*; *Fig* **in the r. of** environ; **somewhere in the r. of £500** dans les 500 livres

regional ['ri:dʒən(ə)l] **ADJ** régional, -aux
▸▸ *Br* **r. development** (*building, land development*) aménagement *m* du territoire; (*for jobs*) action *f* régionale; *Br* **r. development corporation** = organisme *m* pour l'aménagement du territoire

regionalism ['ri:dʒənəlɪz(ə)m] **N** *Ling* (*word, expression*) régionalisme *m*

regionalization [ri:dʒən(ə)laɪ'zeɪʃən] **N** régionalisation *f*

REGISTER ['redʒɪstər]

N registre **1–4, 6** ▪ liste **1** ▪ caisse **5**
VT inscrire **1** ▪ immatriculer **1** ▪ déclarer **1** ▪ indiquer **2** ▪ manifester **2**
VI s'inscrire **1**

N 1 (*book*) registre *m*; (*list*) liste *f*; *Sch* cahier *m* d'appel; **to enter sth in a r.** inscrire qch sur *ou* dans un registre; **to keep a r.** tenir un registre; *Sch* **to take the r.** faire l'appel; **r. of births, marriages and deaths** registre de l'état civil; **electoral r., r. of voters** liste électorale; **r. of shareholders** livre *m* des actionnaires
2 (*range*) (*of instrument*) registre *m*; (*of voice*) registre, tessiture *f*
3 (*style*) (*of speaking, writing*) registre *m*
4 *Comput* registre *m*
5 (*cash*) **r.** caisse *f* enregistreuse
6 *Typ* registre *m*; **to be in/out of r.** être/ne pas être en registre
VT 1 (*enter in records*) (*member, student*) inscrire; (*vehicle, ship, goods*) immatriculer; (*company*) faire enregistrer; (*birth, marriage, death*) déclarer; (*trademark*) déposer; **to r. a complaint** se plaindre (**with sb** auprès de qn); **to r. a protest** protester; **to r. a letter** recommander une lettre; **I want to send it registered** je voudrais l'envoyer en recommandé; **is the car registered in your name?** est-ce que la voiture est à votre nom?; **she is not registered at this hotel** elle n'est pas descendue à cet hôtel
2 (*indicate, make known*) (*of thermometer*

etc) (*temperature etc*) indiquer; (*of person*) (*astonishment, displeasure*) manifester, exprimer; **his face registered disappointment/disapproval** son visage exprimait *ou* reflétait la déception/la désapprobation; **the earthquake registered seven on the Richter scale** le séisme a atteint sept sur l'échelle de Richter; **winds registering a hundred miles an hour** des vents atteignant 160 kilomètres/heure
3 (*realize*) se rendre compte de, prendre la mesure de; **she hadn't registered the danger she was in** elle ne s'était pas rendue compte du danger qu'elle courait
4 (*achieve*) (*progress, victory*) réaliser
VI 1 (*for course etc*) s'inscrire (**for** à); (*at hotel*) signer le registre; (*of voter*) se faire inscrire sur la liste électorale; **to r. with the police** se faire inscrire à la police
2 (*of gauge, machine*) marcher, fonctionner; (*of amount, measurement*) être indiqué, apparaître; **the quake was so small it barely even registered** la secousse a été à peine perceptible
3 *Fam* (*of fact, joke etc*) être compris; **he explained it to me yesterday but it didn't r.** il me l'a expliqué hier, mais je n'ai pas fait attention; **I don't think the bad news has registered (with him/her) yet** on lui a annoncé la mauvaise nouvelle mais je ne crois pas qu'il/elle ait bien réalisé; **I've been so busy his absence has barely registered** je suis tellement occupé que je me suis à peine aperçu de son absence; **I did give them the address but I don't think it registered** je leur ai bien donné l'adresse mais je ne crois pas qu'ils l'aient retenue
▸▸ *Admin* **r. office** bureau *m* de l'état civil

registered ['redʒɪstəd] **ADJ** (*member, voter*) inscrit; (*vehicle*) immatriculé; **to send sth by r. mail** envoyer qch en recommandé; **the r. unemployed** les personnes inscrites au chômage; *Br* **to be r. disabled** avoir une carte d'invalidité
▸▸ *Com* **r. agent** agent *m* agréé; *Fin* **r. bond** obligation *f* nominative; *Fin* **r. capital** capital *m* déclaré; **r. charity** organisme *m* de bienfaisance reconnu par l'État; **r. childminder** nourrice *f* agréée; **r. company** société *f* inscrite au registre du commerce; *Fin* **r. debenture** obligation nominative; *Mktg* **r. design** modèle *m* déposé; **r. letter** lettre *f* recommandée; **r. name** nom *m* déposé; *Br* **r. nurse** infirmière *f* diplômée (d'État); *Br* **r. office** siège *m* social; *Can Fin* **r. retirement savings plan** régime *m* enregistré d'épargne-retraite; *Fin* **r. securities** titres *mpl* nominatifs, valeurs *fpl* nominatives; *St Exch* **r. share** action *f* nominative; *Fin* **r. share certificate** certificat *m* nominatif d'action(s); *St Exch* **r. stock** titres nominatifs, valeurs nominatives; **r. trademark** marque *f* déposée; *Comput* **r. user** = utilisateur, -trice disposant d'une licence

registrar ['redʒɪstrɑːr] **N 1** *Br* (*in registry office*) officier *m* de l'état civil; **r.'s office** bureau *m* de l'état civil **2** *Am Univ* chef *m* du service *ou* du bureau des inscriptions; *Br Univ* secrétaire *m* général **3** *Com* **r. of companies** directeur *m* du registre des sociétés **4** *Br Med* chef *m* de clinique
▸▸ **the R. General** le Conservateur des actes de l'état civil

registration [redʒɪs'treɪʃən] **N** (*of student for course etc*) inscription *f*; (*of voter*) inscription sur la liste électorale; (*of vehicle*) immatriculation *f*; (*of birth, death, marriage*) déclaration *f*; (*of trademark*) dépôt *m*; **when does r. start?** (*for university, evening classes*) quand les inscriptions commencent-elles?
▸▸ *St Exch* **r. body** chambre *f* d'enregistrement; **r. card** (*for enrolling on course etc*) fiche *f* d'inscription; (*for foreign guests*) fiche

voyageur; (*for non-EU guests*) fiche de police; *Comput* licence *f*; **r. certificate** matricule *f*; *Br Aut* **r. document** ≃ carte *f* grise; **r. fees** droits *mpl* d'inscription; **r. form** bulletin *m* d'inscription; **r. number** (*of car*) numéro *m* minéralogique *ou* d'immatriculation; (*of student*) (*numéro*) matricule *m*; **r. and transfer fees** droits d'inscription et de transfert

registry ['redʒɪstrɪ] **N 1** (*office*) bureau *m* d'enregistrement **2** *Naut* **a ship of Canadian r.** un navire immatriculé au Canada; **port of r.** port *m* d'attache
▸▸ *Br Admin* **r. office** bureau *m* de l'état civil; **to be married at a** *or* **the r. office** se marier civilement, ≃ se marier à la mairie

regrade [ri:'greɪd] **VT 1** (*nurse, employee, officer etc*) reclasser **2** *Am Sch* (*homework*) renoter

regrading [ri:'greɪdɪŋ] **N** (*of nurse, employee, officer etc*) reclassement *m*

regress [rɪ'gres] **VI** régresser

regression [rɪ'greʃən] **N** régression *f*

regressive [rɪ'gresɪv] **ADJ** *Biol, Fin* régressif
▸▸ *Econ* **r. taxation** imposition *f* régressive

regret [rɪ'gret] **N** regret *m* (**for** de); **to feel r.** éprouver du regret (**at, about** à; **about doing** d'avoir fait); **to express one's r.** exprimer ses regrets; **to have** *or* **feel a pang of r.** éprouver une pointe de regret; **to have no regrets** n'avoir aucun regret, ne rien regretter (**about** au sujet de, quant à); **my only r. is that I didn't resign earlier** je n'ai qu'un regret, c'est de ne pas avoir donné ma démission plus tôt; **(much) to my r.** à mon grand regret; **it is with deep r. that we inform you that …** c'est à grand regret que nous vous informons que …; **she sends (you/us) her regrets** (*is unable to come*) elle vous/nous prie de l'excuser
VT (**-tt-**) (*be sorry for*) regretter; **to r. doing** *or* **having done sth** regretter d'avoir fait qch; **we r. any inconvenience to passengers** nous prions les voyageurs de bien vouloir nous excuser pour ce désagrément; **you'll r. this!** tu le regretteras!; **I r. to (have to) inform you that …** j'ai le regret *ou* je regrette de (devoir) vous annoncer que …; **then, I r. to say, she …** puis, malheureusement, elle …; **he bitterly regretted having spoken** il a amèrement regretté d'avoir parlé; **I r. to hear that …** je suis désolé d'apprendre que …; **it is to be regretted that …** il est regrettable *ou* à regretter que … + *sub*

regretful [rɪ'gretfʊl] **ADJ** (*glance, expression*) plein de regrets; (*feeling*) de regret; **to be r.** (*of person*) avoir des regrets (**about** au sujet de, quant à)

regretfully [rɪ'gretfəlɪ] **ADV** (*to say*) avec regret; **r., I cannot** je regrette, je ne peux pas

regrettable [rɪ'gretəb(ə)l] **ADJ** (*sad*) regrettable; (*inconvenient*) fâcheux; **it is r. that …** il est regrettable *ou* à regretter *ou* fâcheux que … + *sub*

regrettably [rɪ'gretəblɪ] **ADV** malheureusement; **r. few people were present** il est regrettable que si peu de personnes soient venues; **a joke in r. poor taste** une plaisanterie dont le mauvais goût est à déplorer; **that's r. short-sighted of him** c'est, de sa part, un manque de perspicacité regrettable

regroup [ri:'gruːp] **VT** regrouper
VI se regrouper, se rassembler

regrouping [ri:'gruːpɪŋ] **N** regroupement *m*

REGULAR ['regjʊlər]

ADJ régulier **1–3** ▪ uni **1** ▪ habituel **2** ▪ fidèle **2** ▪ permanent **2** ▪ normal **2, 5**
N habitué **1**

ADJ 1 *(steady, even) (features, pulse, service etc)* régulier; *(surface)* régulier, uni; **on a r. basis** régulièrement; **to have r. bowel movements** aller régulièrement à la selle; **bran will keep you r.** le son vous fera aller régulièrement à la selle; **to be as r. as clockwork** être réglé comme du papier à musique; **to do sth as r. as clockwork** faire qch avec une régularité infaillible; **he's there every Tuesday, (as) r. as clockwork** il est là tous les mardis, il est réglé comme du papier à musique; **to keep r. hours** *(have strict timetable)* avoir un emploi du temps précis, avoir des horaires réguliers; *(go to bed and rise at reasonable time)* se lever et se coucher à heures régulières; **you should keep more r. hours** *(go to bed earlier)* vous devriez vous coucher plus tôt; **he was a man of r. habits** il avait ses habitudes

2 *(usual) (doctor etc)* habituel; *(verb)* régulier; *(price, size)* normal, -aux, *Can* régulier; *(reader, listener)* fidèle; *(staff)* permanent; *Am Aut (gas)* ordinaire; **my r. bedtime** l'heure à laquelle je me couche habituellement; **you can stay up past your r. bedtime** tu peux te coucher plus tard que d'habitude; **a r. visitor to the house** un/une des habitué(e)s de la maison; *Ind* **r. model** modèle *m* courant; **r. supplier** fournisseur *m* habituel

3 *(professional) (army, soldier)* régulier
4 *Fam (real, thorough) (fool, slave etc)* vrai, véritable; **a r. hero** un vrai héros; *esp Am* **a r. guy** un type réglo *ou* sympa
5 *(normal) (procedure, behaviour etc)* normal, -aux

N 1 *(in bar, restaurant etc)* habitué, -ée
2 *Am Aut (gas)* ordinaire *m*
3 *Mil (professional)* régulier *m*
▸▸ *Journ* **r. column** chronique *f*; **r. customer** client, -ente habitué(e); **r. price** prix *m* de règle

regularity [regjʊˈlærɪtɪ] **N** *(of features, pulse etc)* régularité *f*; **to do sth with unfailing r.** faire qch avec une régularité infaillible

regularize [ˈregjʊləraɪz] **VT** *(situation)* régulariser

regularly [ˈregjʊlɪ] **ADV** *(to attend, visit etc)* régulièrement; *Am* **the coat is r. priced at …** le manteau coûte normalement …

regulate [ˈregjʊleɪt] **VT 1** *(adjust) (working of a machine, watch, flow of water etc)* régler; *(of valve)* contrôler **2** *(control) (people)* contrôler; **he leads a well-regulated life** il mène une vie très réglée; **rules regulating the use of additives** les réglementations qui régissent l'emploi des additifs

regulating [ˈregjʊleɪtɪŋ] **ADJ** *(knob, switch, valve)* de réglage; *(hormone, mechanism)* régulateur, -trice; **self-r.** à réglage automatique
▸▸ **r. body** autorité *f* de régulation

regulation [regjʊˈleɪʃən] **N 1** *(action)* *(of machine, watch etc)* réglage *m*; *(of voltage)* régulation *f*, *(of food additives etc)* réglementation *f*, *(of information)* contrôle *m* **2** *(rule)* règlement *m*; **r. dress/speed/uniform** tenue *f*/vitesse *f*/uniforme *m* réglementaire; **black shoes are r. wear** le port de chaussures noires est réglementaire; **regulations** règlement(s); **contrary to** *or* **against (the) regulations** contraire au règlement; **in accordance with the regulations** selon le règlement; **it's not in accordance with the regulations** ce n'est pas réglementaire; **under the regulations** en vertu du règlement; **EU regulations** règlements de l'UE; **safety regulations** règles *fpl* de sécurité

regulator [ˈregjʊleɪtər] **N 1** *(person)* régulateur, -trice **2** *(apparatus)* régulateur *m*
▸▸ **r. valve** régulateur

regulatory [ˈregjʊlətərɪ, regjʊˈleɪtərɪ] **ADJ**

(framework) réglementaire; *(authority)* de contrôle
▸▸ **r. body** instance *f* de contrôle

Regulo® [ˈregjʊləʊ] **N** *Br Culin* thermostat *m*

regurgitate [rɪˈgɜːdʒɪteɪt] **VT** *(food)* régurgiter; *Fig Pej* **to r. one's lecture notes** régurgiter ses cours

regurgitation [rɪgɜːdʒɪˈteɪʃən] **N** *(of food)*, *Fig Pej (of lecture notes)* régurgitation *f*

rehab [ˈriːhæb] **N** *Fam* désintoxication *f*; **to be in r.** être en cure de désintoxication
▸▸ **r. unit** centre *m* de désintoxication

rehabilitate [riːəˈbɪlɪteɪt, riːh-] **VT 1** *(criminal, drug addict, alcoholic)* réinsérer; *Med (stroke victim etc)* rééduquer **2** *(restore reputation of) (politician)* réhabiliter **3** *(restore) (building, area)* réhabiliter, remettre en état, rénover

rehabilitation [riːəbɪlɪˈteɪʃən, riːh-] **N 1** *(of criminal, drug addict, alcoholic)* réinsertion *f*, *Med (of stroke victim etc)* rééducation *f* **2** *(restoring of reputation) (of politician)* réhabilitation *f* **3** *(restoring) (of building, area)* réhabilitation *f*, remise *f* en état, rénovation *f*
▸▸ **r. centre** *(for work training)* centre *m* de réadaptation; *(for drug addicts)* centre de désintoxication

rehash¹ [ˈriːhæʃ] **N** *Fam (of book, script etc)* resucée *f*; **it was a r. of her first novel** c'était une resucée de son premier roman; **it's just a r.** c'est du réchauffé

rehash² [riːˈhæʃ] **VT** *Fam (rework) (old story etc)* remanier; *(old arguments etc)* ressasser, rabâcher

rehearsal [rɪˈhɜːs(ə)l] **N** *(of play, speech etc)* répétition *f*, **to have** *or* **hold a r.** faire une répétition; **to put a play into r.** commencer les répétitions d'une pièce; **we go into r. next week** nous commençons les répétitions la semaine prochaine; *Fig* **the naval exercises were just a r. for the real thing** les exercices navals n'étaient qu'un entraînement; *Theat* **dress r.** *(répétition)* générale *f*
▸▸ **r. room** salle *f* de répétition; **r. script** scénario *m* de répétition

rehearse [rɪˈhɜːs] **VT 1** *(play, part, piece of music, ballet)* répéter; *(actor, orchestra)* faire répéter; **I rehearsed what I was going to say** j'ai préparé ce que j'allais dire; **her indignation struck me as rather rehearsed** son indignation me sembla forcée; **the cast were well rehearsed** les acteurs connaissaient bien leur rôle; **she had been carefully rehearsed by her advisers** ses conseillers lui avaient soigneusement fait répéter ce qu'elle devait dire **2** *(list) (complaints, arguments etc)* répéter, rabâcher
VI *(of actor, musician etc)* répéter

reheat [riːˈhiːt] **VT & VI** réchauffer

rehouse [riːˈhaʊz] **VT** reloger

rehousing [riːˈhaʊzɪŋ] **N** relogement *m*

rehydration [riːhaɪˈdreɪʃən] **N** *Med* réhydratation *f*

reign [reɪn] **N** *(of monarch, champion etc)* règne *m*; **in** *or* **during the r. of …** sous le règne de …; **r. of terror** règne de la terreur; **their r. of terror/violence is at an end** la terreur/violence qu'ils faisaient régner a pris fin
VI *(of monarch, champion, silence etc)* régner; **to r. supreme** *(of monarch)* régner en maître absolu; *(of champion)* être inégalé *ou* sans rival; **to r. for ten years** régner (pendant) dix ans; **silence reigned** le silence régnait; **it's the usual situation in the office: chaos reigns** c'est comme d'habitude au bureau: il y règne le plus grand chaos
▸ **reign over VT INSEP** *(of monarch, silence etc)* régner sur

reigning [ˈreɪnɪŋ] **ADJ** *(monarch)* régnant; *(champion)* en titre

(framework) réglementaire; *(authority)* de contrôle

reimburse [riːɪmˈbɜːs] **VT** *(money)* rembourser; **to r. sb (for) sth** rembourser qn de qch

reimbursement [riːɪmˈbɜːsmənt] **N** *(of money, person)* remboursement *m*

reimport [riːɪmˈpɔːt] **VT** réimporter

reimportation [riːimpɔːˈteɪʃən] **N** réimportation *f*

reimpose [riːɪmˈpəʊz] **VT** réimposer

rein [reɪn] **N** *(for rider, on child)* rêne *f*, *(for coachman)* guide *f*; **to pull at** *or* **on the reins** *(of horse, rider)* tirer sur les rênes; **the reins of power** les rênes du pouvoir; *Fig* **to assume** *or* **take over/hold the reins of government** prendre/tenir les rênes du gouvernement; *Fig* **to hand over the reins** *(of politician, businessman etc)* passer les rênes du pouvoir (**to** à); **to give a horse the reins** *or* **free r.** lâcher les rênes *ou* la bride à un cheval; *Fig* **to give sb a free r.** donner carte blanche à qn (**to do sth** pour faire qch); *Fig* **to give free r. to one's imagination** donner libre cours à son imagination; *Fig* **to keep a tight r.** *on* or **over sb** tenir la bride haute à qn; *Fig* **to keep a tight r. on one's spending** surveiller étroitement ses dépenses; *Fig* **to keep a tight r. on one's emotions** ne pas se laisser aller à ses émotions, maîtriser ses émotions; *Fig* **to keep a tight r. on one's imagination** ne pas se laisser emporter par son imagination
▸ **rein back VT SEP** *(horse)* faire arrêter
VI *(of rider)* faire arrêter son cheval
▸ **rein in VT SEP** *(horse)* serrer la bride *ou* les rênes à; *Fig (enthusiasm, emotions, feelings)* modérer; *Fig* **to r. sb in** *(of person in authority)* serrer la bride *ou* la vis à qn; *(of colleague, friend)* faire se modérer; **to r. in one's spending** mettre un frein à *ou* modérer ses dépenses
VI *(of rider)* ramener son cheval au pas

reincarnate¹ [riːɪnˈkɑːnɪt, -eɪt] **ADJ** réincarné

reincarnate² [riːɪnkɑːˈneɪt] **VT** **to be reincarnated** se réincarner (**as** sous les traits de, sous la forme de)

reincarnation [riːɪnkɑːˈneɪʃən] **N** réincarnation *f*

reindeer [ˈreɪndɪər] **N** renne *m*; **r. moss** *or* **lichen** cladonie *f*

reinforce [riːɪnˈfɔːs] **VT** *(army, wall, fabric)* renforcer; *(foundations)* consolider; *(concrete, glass)* armer; *Fig (argument)* étayer (**with** avec); *(prejudices)* renforcer; *(request)* appuyer (**with** avec); **that just reinforces what I've been saying** ça ne fait que renforcer ce que j'ai dit

reinforcement [riːɪnˈfɔːsmənt] **N 1** *(action)* *(of army, wall, fabric)* renforcement *m*; *(of foundations)* consolidation *f*, *(of concrete, glass)* armature *f* **2** *(troops etc)* **reinforcements** renforts *mpl*; **to await reinforcements** attendre un renfort *ou* des renforts; **to call up reinforcements** demander des renforts

reinitialize [riːɪˈnɪʃəlaɪz] **VT** *Comput* réinitialiser

reinsert [riːɪnˈsɜːt] **VT** *(advert, coin, clause)* réinsérer

reinstall [riːɪnˈstɔːl] **VT** *Comput* réinstaller

reinstallation [riːɪnstəˈleɪʃən] **N** *Comput* réinstallation *f*

reinstate [riːɪnˈsteɪt] **VT** *(person)* réintégrer, rétablir (dans ses fonctions); *(clause etc)* réintroduire

reinstatement [riːɪnˈsteɪtmənt] **N** *(of person)* réintégration *f*, rétablissement *m* (**as** en tant que, au poste de); *(of clause etc)* réintroduction *f*

reinstitute [riːˈɪnstɪtjuːt] **VT** réintroduire

reinstitution [riːɪnstɪˈtjuːʃən] N réintroduction f

reinsurance [riːɪnˈʃʊərəns, -ˈʃɔːr-] N réassurance f

reinsure [riːɪnˈʃʊər, -ˈʃɔːr] VT réassurer

reinsurer [riːɪnˈʃʊərər, -ˈʃɔːr-] N réassureur m

reintegrate [riːˈɪntɪɡreɪt] VT (into society etc) réinsérer

reintegration [riːɪntɪˈɡreɪʃən] N réinsertion f

reinterpret [riːɪnˈtɜːprɪt] VT réinterpréter

reinterpretation [riːɪntɜːprɪˈteɪʃən] N réinterprétation f

reintroduce [riːɪntrəˈdjuːs] VT réintroduire

reintroduction [riːɪntrəˈdʌkʃən] N réintroduction f

reinvent [riːɪnˈvent] VT Fig to r. the wheel refaire ce qui a déjà été fait

reinvest [riːɪnˈvest] VT réinvestir

reinvestment [riːɪnˈvestmənt] N Fin nouveau placement m, réinvestissement m

reinvigorate [riːɪnˈvɪɡəreɪt] VT (usu passive) revigorer

reissue [riːˈɪʃuː] N (of book, recording) réédition f; (of banknotes, shares, stamps) nouvelle émission f
▶ VT (book, recording) rééditer; (banknotes, shares, stamps) émettre de nouveau

reiterate [riːˈɪtəreɪt] VT (request, promise etc) réitérer

reiteration [riːɪtəˈreɪʃən] N réitération f

reiterative [riːˈɪtərətɪv] ADJ réitératif

reject¹ [ˈriːdʒekt] N Com (in factory) article m de rebut, rebut m; (in shop) (article de) second choix m; Fig (person) personne f marginalisée; Fig (for job) candidat m refusé ou qui a échoué; Fam he's a bit of a (social) r.! il n'est pas sortable!; Fig I'm not going out with one of your rejects! (former boyfriend or girlfriend) ne crois pas que je vais sortir avec un/une de tes ex!; export rejects marchandises fpl impropres à l'exportation
▶ r. shop magasin m d'articles de second choix

reject² [rɪˈdʒekt] VT (refuse) (advice, offer, proposal) rejeter, repousser; (doctrine) réprouver; (goods, manuscript, applicant) refuser; (suitor) éconduire; (of animal, parent) (young, child) rejeter; to feel rejected se sentir rejeté; to r. one's food (not want) refuser la nourriture; Med (vomit) rendre la nourriture; Ind to r. a part mettre une pièce au rebut; Med to r. a transplant rejeter un greffon; the machine keeps rejecting this coin pas moyen que la machine accepte cette ou ma pièce

rejection [rɪˈdʒekʃən] N 1 (of advances, demands) rejet m; (of offer, manuscript) refus m; to meet with r. (of applicant etc) essuyer un refus; (of offer, suggestion) être rejeté; letter of r. lettre f de refus 2 Med (of transplant) rejet m; (of food) régurgitation f
▶ r. letter lettre de refus; r. slip lettre de refus

rejig [riːˈdʒɪɡ] VT (-gg-) 1 Fam (rearrange) (text etc) remanier 2 (re-equip) (factory) réaménager

rejoice [rɪˈdʒɔɪs] VI se réjouir (at, over de; in doing de faire); to r. in one's freedom/independence jouir de sa liberté/son indépendance; we r. to hear that you are safe nous sommes ravis d'apprendre que vous êtes sain et sauf; Hum Iron he rejoiced in the name of Winterbottom il répondait au nom délicieux de Winterbottom

rejoicing [rɪˈdʒɔɪsɪŋ] N 1 (joy) réjouissance f, allégresse f (at, over à); there was much r. at the announcement la nouvelle a suscité une très grande joie; it was an occasion for general r. ce fut la grande liesse ou la liesse générale 2 rejoicings (festivities) réjouissances fpl, festivités fpl; there were great rejoicings on the day of the Coronation il y a eu de grandes réjouissances le jour du couronnement

rejoin¹ [rɪˈdʒɔɪn] VT & VI (retort) répliquer

rejoin² [riːˈdʒɔɪn] VT 1 (attach) rejoindre, réunir (to à) 2 (return to) (person) rejoindre, retrouver; Mil (unit, regiment) rallier, rejoindre; to r. one's ship rallier le bord; to r. a political party se réinscrire à un parti politique ▶ VI (of roads, lines etc) se rejoindre

rejoinder [rɪˈdʒɔɪndər] N (retort) réplique f, sharp r. riposte f

rejuvenate [rɪˈdʒuːvɪneɪt] VT (person) rajeunir; I feel rejuvenated after a week off je me sens rajeuni ou revigoré ou Fam requinqué après une semaine de vacances; Fig to r. the economy donner un coup de fouet à l'économie

rejuvenating [rɪˈdʒuːvɪneɪtɪŋ] ADJ rajeunissant

rejuvenation [rɪdʒuːvɪˈneɪʃən] N rajeunissement m

rekey [riːˈkiː] VT Comput refrapper

rekeying [riːˈkiːɪŋ] N Comput refrappe f

rekindle [riːˈkɪnd(ə)l] VT (fire) rallumer; Fig (enthusiasm, hope) ranimer, raviver; (hatred) ranimer, raviver, rallumer; Fig a romantic dinner to r. the flame or spark un dîner en amoureux pour ranimer la flamme ▶ VI se rallumer

relapse [rɪˈlæps] Med N rechute f, to have or suffer a r. avoir ou faire une rechute, rechuter; his r. into alcoholism came as no surprise le fait qu'il soit retombé dans l'alcoolisme n'a surpris personne
▶ VI avoir ou faire une rechute, rechuter; to r. into unconsciousness reperdre connaissance; Fig to r. into alcoholism retomber dans l'alcoolisme

relate [rɪˈleɪt] VT 1 (narrate) (story etc) raconter, Fml conter; (one's adventures) faire le récit de; strange to r. ... chose étonnante à dire ... 2 (connect) (two facts) établir un rapport entre; to r. sth to sth (link) rattacher qch à qch
▶ VI 1 (of question etc) se rapporter, avoir rapport, avoir trait (to à); agreement relating to ... convention ayant trait à ... 2 (of person) he finds it difficult to r., he can't r. (to others) il lui est difficile de communiquer avec les autres; I can't r. to modern music je n'arrive pas à apprécier la musique moderne; I don't r. to my home town any more je ne me sens plus d'attaches avec ma ville natale

related [rɪˈleɪtɪd] ADJ 1 (languages, styles) apparenté; the cost of the project is directly r. to ... le coût du projet est directement lié à ...; questions r. to a subject questions relatives à un sujet; the two events are r. les deux événements sont liés; closely r. species espèces fpl voisines; r. activity activité f annexe; r. ideas idées fpl connexes 2 (people) apparenté (to à); (by blood) parent (to de); (by marriage) parent par alliance (to à); are you two r.? êtes-vous apparentés ou parents ou de la même famille?; we are not really r., I just call her 'aunt' nous ne sommes pas parents ou de la même famille, je l'appelle juste Tatie comme ça; we're r. by marriage nous sommes parents par alliance; he is closely/distantly r. to me nous sommes proches parents/parents éloignés

-related [rɪˈleɪtɪd] SUFF space-/industry-r. lié à l'espace/l'industrie

relating [rɪˈleɪtɪŋ] ADJ r. to (about) relatif à, qui se rapporte à; Admin, Law afférent à

relation [rɪˈleɪʃən] N 1 (relative) parent,

-ente; r. by marriage parent, -ente par alliance; what r. is he to you? quel est son lien de parenté avec vous?; are you any r. to ...? avez-vous un lien de parenté avec ...?; he's no r. to me or of mine il n'est pas de ma famille; she is my closest living r. c'est la plus proche parente qui me reste; I have relations in Montreal j'ai de la famille à Montréal; we've invited all the relations nous avons invité toute la famille
2 (connection, relationship) relation f, rapport m (between entre; with avec); in or with r. to relativement à, par rapport à; to bear no r. to n'avoir aucun rapport avec; to bear little r. to avoir peu de rapport avec; relations between us are rather strained nos relations sont plutôt tendues; to have or enjoy friendly relations entretenir des relations amicales ou des rapports amicaux (with avec); how are relations between you? comment est-ce que vous vous entendez?; to enter into relations with sb entrer ou se mettre en rapport ou en relations avec qn; to break off all relations with sb rompre toute relation ou cesser tout rapport avec qn; Fml to have (sexual) relations avoir des rapports sexuels (with avec)
3 (telling) (of adventures, story etc) relation f, récit m

relational [rɪˈleɪʃ(ə)l] ADJ relationnel
▶ Comput r. database base f de données relationnelle; Comput r. operator opérateur m relationnel

relationship [rɪˈleɪʃənʃɪp] N 1 (relations) rapports mpl; (sexual) liaison f; to have a love-hate r. with sb/sth avoir avec qn/qch des relations ou des rapports dans laquel(elle)s se mêlent l'amour et la haine; she has a good r. with her mother-in-law elle s'entend bien avec sa belle-mère; she's been trying to get out of the r. for months elle essaye de rompre depuis des mois; our r. is going nowhere notre relation ne nous mène nulle part; patient-doctor r. rapports patient-médecin ou entre le patient et le médecin; to have a r. (affair) avoir une liaison (with avec); I'm already in a r. j'ai déjà quelqu'un, je suis déjà avec quelqu'un; he finds it difficult to have relationships with people ça lui est difficile d'avoir des relations ou des rapports avec les autres; our r. is purely professional nos rapports ou relations sont purement professionnel(elle)s; what exactly is your r. with her? quelle est la nature de ou quels sont vos rapports ou relations avec elle?
2 (kinship) (between people of same family) lien(s) m(pl) de parenté; (by marriage) parenté f par alliance; (between languages, styles etc) parenté f; family r. lien de parenté; blood r. parenté, (degré m de) consanguinité f; what was your r. to the deceased? quel était votre lien de parenté avec le défunt?
3 (connection) (between things) rapport m, relation f (between ... and entre ... et); in r. to relativement à
▶ r. marketing marketing m relationnel

relative [ˈrelətɪv] ADJ relatif; r. to (compared to) relativement à, comparé à; (in terms of) en fonction de, par rapport à
▶ N 1 (person) parent, -ente; r. by marriage parent, -ente par alliance; he's no r. of mine il n'est pas de ma famille; she is my closest living r. c'est la plus proche parente qui me reste; I have relatives in Montreal j'ai de la famille à Montréal; we've invited all the relatives nous avons invité toute la famille 2 Phil the r. le relatif
▶ Gram r. clause (proposition f) relative f, Mktg r. market share part f de marché relative; Gram r. pronoun pronom m relatif VOIR
GRAMMAIRE A32–3; B22–3

Note that the French word **relatif** is never used to refer to members of one's family.

relatively ['relətɪvlɪ] ADV *(fairly)* relativement, assez; **r. few people were there** il y avait assez *ou* relativement peu de gens; **r. speaking** relativement parlant

relativism ['relətɪvɪz(ə)m] N *Phil* relativisme *m*

relativistic [relətɪ'vɪstɪk] ADJ relativiste

relativity [relə'tɪvɪtɪ] N relativité *f*; **r. theory, theory of r.** théorie *f* de la relativité

relaunch[1] ['ri:lɔ:ntʃ] N *Mktg* relancement *m*

relaunch[2] [ri'lɔ:ntʃ] VT *Mktg* relancer

relax [rɪ'læks] VT **1** *(person) (of bath, meditation etc) (physically)* détendre, délasser, relaxer; *(mentally)* détendre, relaxer **2** *(loosen) (muscles)* relâcher, décontracter, relaxer; *(discipline)* relâcher; *(policy, law)* assouplir; **to r. one's hold** *or* **grip** desserrer son étreinte; *Fig* **to r. one's grip on** relâcher son emprise sur; **to r. one's efforts** relâcher ses efforts

▶ VI **1** *(of person) (physically)* se détendre, se délasser, se relaxer; *(mentally)* se détendre, se relaxer; **r.!** *(calm down)* du calme!; **r.!, I'm not going to hurt you** détends-toi, je ne vais pas te faire mal **2** *(of muscles)* se relâcher, se détendre

relaxant [rɪ'læksənt] N *(drug, drink etc)* relaxant *m*; *Med* **muscle r.** myorelaxant *m*, décontracturant *m*

relaxation [ri:læk'seɪʃən] N **1** *(of person) (physical)* détente *f*, délassement *m*, relaxation *f*; *(mental)* détente, relaxation; **fishing is his only r.** la pêche est sa seule détente; **she finds r. in reading** elle se détend en lisant; **reading is one of my favourite forms of r.** lire est une de mes façons préférées de me détendre **2** *(of muscles)* décontraction *f*, relaxation *f*; *(of discipline)* relâchement *m*; *(of policy, law)* assouplissement *m*
▶▶ **r. therapy** relaxation

relaxed [rɪ'lækst] ADJ *(atmosphere, person)* décontracté, détendu; *Fam* **relax** *inv*; **she takes a very r. approach to** *or* **is very r. in her approach to bringing up her children** elle élève ses enfants de façon très décontractée

relaxing [rɪ'læksɪŋ] ADJ *(climate, medication)* relaxant; **a very r. day** une vraie journée de détente; **a r. place for a holiday** un endroit tranquille pour passer ses vacances

relay[1] ['ri:leɪ] N **1** *(of people, horses)* relais *m*; *(of workers)* relève *f*; **to work in relays** travailler par relais, se relayer; **they worked in r. all night to put out the fire** ils se sont relayés toute la nuit pour éteindre l'incendie; **they were organized into relays** ils étaient répartis en équipes et ils se relayaient **2** *Sport (race)* (course *f* de) relais *m*; **the 4 x 100 m relay** le relais 4 x 100 m **3** *Elec, Electron, Tel* relais *m*; *Radio, TV (transmitter)* relais, réémetteur *m*; *(broadcast)* émission *f* relayée
▶▶ *Sport* **r. race** (course de) relais; *Radio, TV* **r. station** relais; *Radio, TV* **r. transmitter** réémetteur

relay[2] [rɪ'leɪ, ri:-] VT *(pt, pp relayed)* *Elec, Tel, Radio etc (telephone message, broadcast etc)* relayer; **to r. information to sb** transmettre des informations à qn

re-lay VT *(carpet, tiles etc)* reposer

RELEASE [rɪ'li:s] N **1** *(of hostage, prisoner)* libération *f*; *(from care, worry)* délivrance *f*, libération (**from** de); *(from obligation, responsibility)* décharge *f*, libération (**from** de); **it was a merciful r.** *(when he or she died)* ça a été une véritable délivrance; *Law* **order of r.** (ordre *m* de) levée *f* d'écrou; *Law* **r. on bail** mise *f* en liberté sous caution; *Br* **day r.**

= jour *m* de liberté accordé aux employés d'une entreprise pour faire un stage de formation **2** *(of bomb)* largage *m*; *(of balloons, pigeons)* lâcher *m*; *(of gas etc)* dégagement *m*; *(of steam)* échappement *m*; *(of pressure)* relâchement *m*; *Phys (of energy)* libération *f*; *(of spring)* détente *f*; *(of mechanism)* déclenchement *m*; *(of clutch)* débrayage *m*; *(on typewriter)* levier *m* de dégagement du chariot; *Phot* **(shutter) r.** *(action)* déclenchement; *(mechanism)* déclencheur *m* **3** *(of book, record etc)* sortie *f*, mise *f* en vente; *(of film)* sortie; *(of document)* diffusion *f*; *(of computer software)* version *f*; **(press) r.** communiqué *m* de presse; **is the film on general r.?** est-ce que le film passe dans les salles?; **it's a new r.** ça vient de sortir; **latest r.** *(record)* dernier disque *m*; *(film)* dernier film *m* **4** *Fin (of credits, funds)* déblocage *m*, dégagement *m*

▶ VT **1** *(liberate) (hostage, prisoner)* libérer; *(patient) (from hospital)* laisser sortir (**from** de); *(from work)* libérer; **to r. a debtor** libérer un débiteur; **to r. sb from his** *or* **her promise** dispenser qn de sa promesse; **to r. sb from a duty** dispenser qn d'une corvée; *Law* **released on bail** remis en liberté sous caution **2** *(let go) (balloon, carrier pigeon)* lâcher; *(bomb)* lâcher, larguer; **to r. sb's hand** lâcher la main de qn; **to r. one's hold** desserrer son étreinte, lâcher prise; **playing squash is a good way of releasing tension** le squash est un bon moyen de se détendre **3** *(emit) (gas)* dégager, laisser échapper; *(fumes etc)* émettre; **to be released** *(of energy etc)* se libérer **4** *(unblock) (jammed part etc)* dégager; *(spring)* détendre; *(brake)* desserrer; *Phot (shutter)* déclencher; **to r. the safety catch** *(on gun)* libérer le cran de sûreté; *Aut* **to r. the clutch** débrayer **5** *(make available) (book, record etc)* sortir, mettre en vente; *(film)* sortir; *(news)* rendre public; *(document)* diffuser **6** *Fin (funds)* débloquer, dégager
▶▶ *Tech* **r. lever** *(on clutch)* levier de débrayage; *(on typewriter)* levier de dégagement du chariot; *Cin* **r. print** copie *f* d'exploitation

relegate ['relɪgeɪt] VT *(downgrade)* reléguer (**to** à); *Ftbl* **to r. a team (to the next division)** reléguer une équipe en division inférieure; *Fig* **we relegated the old bed to the spare room** on a relégué le vieux lit dans la chambre d'amis

relegation [relɪ'geɪʃən] N *(of person etc)* relégation *f* (**to** à); *(of soccer club)* relégation en division inférieure; **the r. struggle** la lutte pour rester dans la division supérieure

relent [rɪ'lent] VI *(of person)* s'adoucir, se radoucir; *(as result of argument, persuasion)* fléchir, se laisser amadouer; *(of storm, wind, rain)* diminuer de violence, se calmer

relentless [rɪ'lentlɪs] ADJ *(person)* implacable, inflexible, intransigeant; *(hatred)* implacable; *(persecution, pain etc)* sans rémission; *(criticism)* incessant, constant; **to be r. in doing sth** mettre de l'acharnement à faire qch

relentlessly [rɪ'lentlɪslɪ] ADV *(to beat etc)* implacablement; *(to continue, persecute etc)* sans rémission, avec acharnement; *(to argue)* continuellement, sans arrêt; *(to blow, rain)* sans interruption, continuellement

relet [ri:'let] VT *(house etc)* relouer

relevance ['reləvəns], **relevancy** ['reləvənsɪ] N **1** *(aptness) (of facts, remarks etc)* pertinence *f*, **to have** *or* **bear some r.** avoir un rapport (**to** avec); **I don't see what r. his re-**

marks have to the situation je ne vois en rien le rapport entre ses remarques et la situation; **what r. does that have to anything?** quel rapport est-ce que ça a? **2** *(significance)* intérêt *m*; **Latin no longer has any r. in the school curriculum** le latin ne sert plus à rien dans les programmes scolaires; **Shakespeare's plays are still full of r.** les pièces de Shakespeare sont toujours d'actualité; **whether I happen to agree or not is of no r.** *(makes no difference)* mon avis n'a aucune importance

relevant ['reləvənt] ADJ **1** *(apt) (fact, detail etc)* pertinent; **r. to** qui a un rapport avec; **to be r.** avoir un rapport (**to sth** avec qch); **that's not r.** ça n'a rien à voir (**to** avec); **opinions are not r.** ce n'est pas une question d'opinions; **that's hardly r.** ça n'a pas grand intérêt; **that's hardly r. to the discussion** ça n'a pas grand-chose à voir avec la discussion **2** *(appropriate, proper)* approprié; **you should report the matter to the r. department** vous devriez en référer au service compétent; **the r. documents** les documents qui se rapportent à l'affaire; *Law* les pièces justificatives; **to refer sb to the r. chapter of a book** renvoyer qn au chapitre correspondant; **she did not have the r. experience for the job** elle n'avait pas l'expérience requise pour le poste **3** *(significant)* important; *(useful)* utile; **is a knowledge of Latin r. to employers?** est-ce que la connaissance du latin a encore un intérêt quelconque pour les chefs d'entreprise?; **all r. information** tous renseignements utiles; **to be highly r.** *(of experience, qualifications)* être très utile (**for** pour); **to be/remain r.** *(of book, play, idea, ideology etc)* être/rester d'actualité
▶▶ *Acct* **r. costs** coûts *mpl* attribuables; **r. range** fourchette *f* pertinente d'activité

reliability [rɪlaɪə'bɪlɪtɪ] N *(of person, firm etc)* sérieux *m*; *(of information)* sérieux, sûreté *f*; *(of source, testimony)* sûreté; *(of device, machine, car)* fiabilité *f*; **I'm not altogether sure about the r. of our witnesses** je ne suis pas vraiment sûr qu'on puisse faire confiance à nos témoins

reliable [rɪ'laɪəb(ə)l] ADJ *(firm)* sérieux; *(information)* sérieux, sûr; *(person)* fiable, sur qui on peut compter; *(source, testimony)* sûr; *(car, machine etc)* fiable; **to have sth from a r. source** *or* **on r. evidence** tenir qch de source sûre; **my memory isn't r.** je n'ai pas bonne mémoire; **the weather is not very r.** on ne peut pas se fier au temps

reliably [rɪ'laɪəblɪ] ADV *(to operate, perform etc)* de façon fiable; **to be r. informed that ...** savoir de source sûre que ... + *ind*

reliance [rɪ'laɪəns] N **1** *(dependence)* dépendance *f* (**on** vis à vis de); **r. on alcohol** dépendance à l'alcool; **because of the country's r. on the arms industry** parce que l'économie du pays dépend de l'industrie de l'armement **2** *(trust)* confiance *f*; **to place r. in** *or* **on sb/sth** se fier à qn/qch

reliant [rɪ'laɪənt] ADJ **to be r. on** *(dependent on)* dépendre de (**for** pour)

relic ['relɪk] N **1** *(reminder of past, remnant)* vestige *m*; **the last surviving r. of** les derniers vestiges de; **relics of the past** vestiges du passé; *Hum* **their old r. of a car** leur vieille bagnole toute pourrie; *Lit* **relics** *(corpse)* dépouille *f* mortelle **2** *Rel* relique *f*

relief [rɪ'li:f] N **1** *(from pain, anxiety, poverty etc)* soulagement *m* (**from** de); **to bring r. to sb** apporter du soulagement à qn; **that's** *or* **what a r.!** quel soulagement!; **for the r. of pain** *(of pills etc)* pour soulager la douleur; **to my great r., much to my r.** à mon grand soulagement; **to feel r.** se sentir soulagé,

ressentir du soulagement (**at** à; **about, over** à propos de); **his feelings of r. were short-lived** son soulagement a été de courte durée; **you can imagine my r.** *or* **the r. that I felt** tu peux imaginer mon soulagement; **to provide light** *or* **comic r.** détendre l'atmosphère, introduire une note comique; **by way of light r.** pour se détendre un peu
2 (*help*) secours *m*, assistance *f*, aide *f*; *Am* **to be on r.** recevoir une aide sociale; **disaster/famine r.** secours *ou* assistance *ou* aide aux victimes d'un désastre/d'une famine; **tax r.** dégrèvement *m* fiscal
3 (*replacement*) personne *f* qui assure la relève, remplaçant, -ante; **my r. didn't show up** mon remplaçant/ma remplaçante ne s'est pas présenté(e)
4 (*liberation*) (*of city etc*) libération *f*
5 *Art* relief *m*, modelé *m*; **printed in r.** imprimé en relief; **to stand out in r.** ressortir, se détacher (**against** sur); **to stand out in bold** *or* **sharp r.** ressortir *ou* se détacher nettement; **to bring** *or* **throw sth into r.** faire ressortir qch; *Art* **high/low r.** haut/bas-relief
6 *Geog* relief *m* (terrestre); **an area of low r.** une zone au relief peu élevé
▸▸ **r. agency** organisme *m* d'aide humanitaire; **r. driver** chauffeur *m* qui assure la relève; **r. fund** caisse *f* de secours; **r. map** carte *f* en relief; **r. official** responsable *mf* d'un organisme d'aide humanitaire; **r. road** itinéraire *m* bis, route *f* de délestage; **r. staff** (*cover staff*) personnel *m* extra; **r. train** train *m* supplémentaire; **r. troops** la relève; **r. valve** soupape *f* de sûreté, clapet *m* de décharge; **r. work** coopération *f*; **r. worker** = membre *m* d'une organisation humanitaire qui travaille sur le terrain

> Note that the French word **relief** never means **assistance**.

relieve [rɪˈliːv] *vt* **1** (*alleviate*) (*pain, anxiety, poverty*) soulager; (*boredom*) tromper; (*the situation*) remédier à; (*pressure*) réduire; **to do sth to r. the boredom** faire qch pour tromper l'ennui; **to r. oneself** (*urinate*) se soulager; **black dress relieved by** *or* **with white lace** robe noire agrémentée de dentelle blanche; **to r. the monotony we went for a walk** pour nous changer les idées nous sommes allés nous promener; *Aut, Med* **to r. congestion in sth** décongestionner qch **2** (*replace*) (*person*) remplacer, relayer; *Mil, Naut* (*the guard, watch*) relever **3** (*liberate*) *Mil* (*city*) libérer; (*person*) (*from obligation*) dégager, affranchir (**from** de); **to r. sb of a burden** soulager qn d'un fardeau; **to r. sb of their coat** débarrasser qn de son manteau; **to r. sb of their duties** relever qn de ses fonctions; *Fam Hum* **to r. sb of sth** (*steal*) soulager qn de qch

relieved [rɪˈliːvd] *adj* soulagé; **I'm very r. to hear it** je suis très soulagé de l'apprendre, c'est un grand soulagement pour moi de l'apprendre; **to feel r.** se sentir relevé; **to be r. at the news** être soulagé en apprenant la nouvelle

religion [rɪˈlɪdʒən] *n* religion *f*, (*Catholic, Protestant*) religion, culte *m*; (*heading on form*) confession *f*, *Fam Pej* **to get r.** attraper le virus de la religion; **it's against my r. to work on Sundays** c'est contraire à ma religion de travailler le dimanche; *Hum* **it's against his r. to do the washing-up!** c'est contraire à sa religion de faire la vaisselle!; *Fig* **to make a r. of (doing) sth** se faire une obligation de (faire) qch; *Fig* **football is a r. with some people** le football est une religion pour certains

religiosity [rɪlɪdʒɪˈɒsɪtɪ] *n Pej* religiosité *f*

religious [rɪˈlɪdʒəs] *adj* (*person*) pieux, croyant; (*fanatic, order, service, leader, life*) religieux; (*war, book*) de religion; *Fig* (*care*) méticuleux; *Fig* **his r. attendance at every football match** sa fréquentation scrupuleuse de tous les matches de football; *Fig* **to be r. about doing sth** faire qch avec un soin méticuleux
n inv *Rel* religieux, -ieuse
▸▸ **r. beliefs** croyances *fpl* religieuses; **r. education** instruction *f* religieuse; **r. instruction** instruction religieuse; **r. persuasion** confession *f*; **r. programme** programme *m* à caractère religieux

religiously [rɪˈlɪdʒəslɪ] *adv* (*to behave, act*) religieusement, pieusement; *Fig* (*to attend, obey*) religieusement, scrupuleusement

religiousness [rɪˈlɪdʒəsnɪs] *n* (*of person*) piété *f*, dévotion *f*; (*of music, art*) caractère *m* religieux; *Fig* (*of attendance, obedience*) caractère scrupuleux; (*in carrying out task*) extrême méticulosité *f*

reline [riːˈlaɪn] *vt* (*coat*) remettre une doublure à; *Aut* **to r. the brakes** changer les garnitures de freins

relinquish [rɪˈlɪŋkwɪʃ] *vt* (*give up*) (*habit, hope*) abandonner; (*plan, right, inheritance*) renoncer à; **to r. all thoughts of doing sth** abandonner toute pensée de faire qch; **to r. (one's hold on) sth** (*let go*) lâcher qch, renoncer à qch; **to r. one's hold on one's children** laisser partir ses enfants; **her mind was beginning to r. its hold on reality** elle commençait à perdre le sens de la réalité

relinquishment [rɪˈlɪŋkwɪʃmənt] *n Fml* (*of hope etc*) abandon *m* (**of** de); (*of right etc*) renonciation *f* (**of** à)

reliquary [ˈrelɪkwərɪ] *n Rel* reliquaire *m*

relish [ˈrelɪʃ] *n* **1** (*liking, taste*) goût *m* (**for** pour); **to eat sth with r.** manger qch de bon appétit, savourer qch **2** (*pleasure*) plaisir *m*; **danger gives r. to an adventure** le danger donne du piquant à une aventure; **he used to tell the story with great r.** il se délectait à raconter cette histoire; **..., she said with great r.** ... dit-elle avec délectation **3** *Culin* (*pickle*) condiment *m*, *Can* achar *m*
vt (*enjoy*) apprécier; (*dish*) goûter, savourer; *Fig* (*victory, moment*) savourer; **to r. doing sth** trouver du plaisir à *ou* aimer faire qch; **I didn't r. the prospect** cette perspective ne me disait rien; **I didn't r. the prospect/thought/idea of telling her** j'appréhendais de le lui dire; **we didn't r. the idea** l'idée ne nous souriait pas

relive [riːˈlɪv] *vt* (*one's life, the past*) revivre

rellies [ˈrelɪz] *npl Br Fam* (*relatives*) famille *f*; **are you seeing your r. at Christmas?** tu vas voir ta famille à Noël?

reload [riːˈləʊd] *vt* (*ship, camera, rifle, software etc*) recharger
vi (*of ship, photographer etc*) recharger; (*of gun, software*) se recharger

relocate [riːləʊˈkeɪt] *vt* (*move*) (*factory, company*) réimplanter, déménager
vi (*of person, shop*) déménager; (*of company*) se réimplanter, déménager; **the firm is relocating out of Glasgow** la société se réimplante hors de Glasgow

relocation [riːləʊˈkeɪʃən] *n* (*of person, shop*) déménagement *m*; (*of company*) réimplantation *f*
▸▸ **r. allowance** (*for employee*) indemnité *f* de déménagement; **r. assistance** (*from employer*) contribution *f* aux frais de déménagement; **r. expenses** (*for employee*) frais *mpl* de déménagement

reluctance [rɪˈlʌktəns] *n* (*unwillingness*) réticence *f*, (*strong*) répugnance *f*, **to do sth with a show of r.** faire qch avec une réticence feinte; **to show (some) r. to do sth** se montrer peu disposé *ou* empressé à faire

qch; **to do sth with r.** faire qch à regret *ou* à contrecœur

reluctant [rɪˈlʌktənt] *adj* (*consent, greeting, promise etc*) accordé à contrecœur; **to be r. to do sth** hésiter *ou* être peu disposé *ou* peu empressé à faire qch; **to feel r.** hésiter, éprouver de la répugnance (**to do** à faire); **a r. teacher** un professeur malgré lui; **I was a r. witness of their quarrel** j'étais le témoin involontaire de leur querelle

reluctantly [rɪˈlʌktəntlɪ] *adv* (*to consent, greet, promise etc*) avec répugnance, à contrecœur; **I say it r.** il m'en coûte de le dire

▸ **rely on, rely upon** [rɪˈlaɪ] *vt insep* **1** (*count on*) (*person's help, discretion*) compter sur; (*have confidence in*) (*person, judgment etc*) avoir confiance en; **I'm relying on it** j'y compte (bien); **it's a car you can r. on** c'est une voiture fiable; **he's a lawyer you can r. on** c'est un avocat sur lequel on peut compter; **we can't r. on the weather** on ne peut jamais savoir quel temps il va faire; *Iron* **you can always rely on him to be late** tu peux compter sur lui pour arriver en retard à chaque fois **2** (*be dependent on*) (*person*) dépendre de (**for sth** pour qch)

REM [ɑːriːˈem] (*abbr* **rapid eye movement**) sommeil *m* paradoxal, phase *f* de mouvements oculaires

remailer [riːˈmeɪlər] *n Comput* service *m* de courrier électronique anonyme

remain [rɪˈmeɪn] *vi* **1** (*stay behind*) rester **2** (*continue to be*) (*of doubts*) rester, subsister; **to r. silent** garder le silence; **to r. faithful to sb/sth** rester fidèle à qn/qch; **please r. in your seats** veuillez rester assis; **let it r. as it is** laissez-le comme cela; **one thing remains certain** une chose demeure certaine; **to r. a problem** demeurer un problème; **to r. the same** demeurer inchangé; **the crime remains unsolved** le crime n'a toujours pas été élucidé; **the fact remains that ...** il n'en est pas moins vrai que ..., toujours est-il que ...; *Br Old-fashioned* **I r., Sir, yours truly** (*at end of letter*) veuillez agréer, Monsieur, l'expression de mes sentiments distingués **3** (*be left*) rester, subsister; **all that remains of ...** tout ce qui reste *ou* subsiste de ...; **much yet remains to be done** il reste encore beaucoup à faire; **it (only) remains for me to ...** il ne me reste qu'à ..., je n'ai plus qu'à ...; **it remains to be seen whether ...** reste à savoir si ...; **that remains to be seen** c'est ce que nous verrons, *Fam* ça reste à voir

remainder [rɪˈmeɪndər] *n* **1** (*of time, wine etc*) reste *m*; (*of salary, specific quantity*) restant *m*, reste; (*of amount due*) reliquat *m*; **the r. of his life** le reste *ou* le restant de sa vie; **the r.** (*remaining people*) les autres *mfpl* **2** *Math* reste *m*; **division with no r.** division *f* sans reste; **the r. is one** il reste un **3** (*book*) invendu *m* soldé
vt (*book*) solder

remaindered [rɪˈmeɪndəd] *adj* (*book*) soldé

remaining [rɪˈmeɪnɪŋ] *adj* (*food, money, wine etc*) qui reste, restant; **the r. travellers** le reste des voyageurs, les autres voyageurs; **our only r. hope** le seul espoir qui nous reste

remains [rɪˈmeɪnz] *npl* (*of fortune, meal*) restes *mpl*, (*of old building*) ruines *fpl*, vestiges *mpl*, *Fig* **the last r. of his self-respect** les derniers vestiges de son amour-propre; (**human**) **r. restes humains;** *Old-fashioned* (**literary**) **r. œuvres** *fpl* posthumes

remake[1] [ˈriːmeɪk] *n* (*of film, TV series*) remake *m*, nouvelle version *f*, **to do a r. of** faire un remake de

remake[2] [riːˈmeɪk] *vt* (*pt, pp* **remade** [riː-

'meɪd]) *(film)* refaire, faire un remake de; *(bed)* refaire

remand [rɪ'mɑːnd] *Law* **N to be on r.** *(in custody)* être en détention préventive; *(on bail)* être en liberté provisoire (sous caution)
VT to r. (in custody) placer en détention préventive; **to r. on bail** mettre en liberté provisoire sous caution
▸▸ **r. centre, r. home** maison *f* de détention préventive

remark [rɪ'mɑːk] **N 1** *(comment)* remarque *f*, commentaire *m*; **to make** *or* **pass a r.** faire une remarque *ou* une observation *ou* un commentaire *(about* sur*)*; **to let sth pass without r.** laisser passer qch sans commentaire; **to venture** *or* **hazard a r.** se permettre *ou* risquer une remarque *ou* une observation *ou* un commentaire; **no remarks, please!** pas de commentaires, s'il vous plaît! **2** *Fml (notice)* attention *f*, **worthy of r.** digne d'attention; **it could not escape r. that ...** on ne pouvait pas ne pas remarquer que ..., le fait que ... ne pouvait pas passer inaperçu; **her reaction could not escape r.** sa réaction n'a pu passer inaperçue
VT 1 *(comment)* faire remarquer **(that ... que ...** *+ ind)* **2** *Fml (note) (somebody)* remarquer; *(something)* remarquer, noter; **it may be remarked that ...** constatons que ...
VI to r. on sth *(on weather, food etc)* parler de qch; **I remarked on it to my mother** j'en ai fait la remarque à ma mère; **I remarked to her father on how well she was looking** j'ai fait remarquer à son père qu'elle avait l'air très en forme

> Note that the French verb **remarquer** is a false friend and is never a translation for the English verb **to remark**. Its most common meaning is **to notice**.

remarkable [rɪ'mɑːkəb(ə)l] **ADJ** *(change, coincidence, progress etc)* remarquable **(for** par*)*

remarkably [rɪ'mɑːkəblɪ] **ADV** *(to change, progress etc)* remarquablement, notablement; *(good, intelligent)* remarquablement; *(bad, stupid)* incroyablement

remarket [riː'mɑːkɪt] **VT** recommercialiser

remarketing [riː'mɑːkɪtɪŋ] **N** marketing *m* de relance

remarriage [riː'mærɪdʒ] **N** remariage *m*

remarry [riː'mærɪ] **VT 1** *(first spouse)* se remarier avec, épouser de nouveau **2** *(of registrar etc) (divorced couple)* remarier
VI se remarier

remaster [riː'mɑːstər] **VT** *(album)* remasteriser

rematch ['riːmætʃ] **N** *Sport* match *m* retour

remediable [rɪ'miːdɪəb(ə)l] **ADJ** *Fml (situation)* remédiable; *(illness)* curable; **an easily r. fault** un défaut auquel on peut facilement remédier

remedial [rɪ'miːdɪəl] **ADJ 1** *(measures, action)* de redressement; **to take r. action** prendre des mesures de redressement; **the public is demanding for r. action to halt the destruction of the environment** le public demande que des mesures soient prises pour stopper la destruction de l'environnement **2** *Br Sch (classes)* de rattrapage, de soutien; *(education)* spécialisé; *(pupil, student)* qui n'a pas le niveau; **she teaches r. maths** elle donne des cours de rattrapage *ou* de soutien en maths **3** *(treatment)* curatif, correctif
▸▸ *Br Sch* **r. class** classe *f* de rattrapage; *Br Sch* **r. education** éducation *f* spécialisée; *Med* **r. exercises** gymnastique *f* corrective; *Br Sch* **r. teacher** enseignant, -ante chargé(e) d'une classe de rattrapage; *Br Sch* **r. teaching** rattrapage *m* scolaire

remedy ['remɪdɪ] **N** *(for illness),* *Fig* remède *m* **(for** pour, contre*)*; **it's past** *or* **beyond r.** c'est irrémédiable *ou* sans remède
VT *(situation)* remédier à; **the situation hasn't been remedied yet** on n'a pas encore remédié à la situation

remember [rɪ'membər] **VT 1** *(recall) (somebody)* se souvenir de; *(something)* se souvenir de, se rappeler; **I r. him as being very generous** je me souviens de lui comme de quelqu'un de très généreux; **they r. me as a child** ils se souviennent de moi lorsque j'étais enfant; **she will long be remembered for her achievements** on se souviendra longtemps d'elle pour ses exploits; **he will be remembered as the man who ...** on se souviendra de lui comme de l'homme qui ...; **do you r. turning off the lights?** est-ce que tu te souviens (d')avoir éteint les lumières?; **do you r. me turning off the lights?** tu te souviens si j'ai éteint la lumière?; **to r. that ...** se souvenir *ou* se rappeler que ... *+ ind*; **the chairman, you will r., cannot vote** le président, ne l'oubliez pas, ne peut pas voter; **I can't r. his name for the moment** son nom m'échappe pour l'instant; **I'll r. his name in a minute** son nom me reviendra dans une minute; **it will be something to r. you by** ce sera un souvenir de vous; **I'll give him something to r. (me by)!** il se souviendra de moi! VOIR GRAMMAIRE A43-4
2 *(not forget) (lesson)* retenir, ne pas oublier; **it was a night/a holiday to r.** c'était une nuit/des vacances mémorable(s); **I'll r. to do it** je n'oublierai pas de le faire; **that's worth remembering** c'est à noter; **r.** *or* **you must r. (that) he's only ten years old** n'oubliez pas qu'il n'a que dix ans; **did you r. to turn off the lights?** est-ce que tu as pensé à éteindre les lumières?; **r. that we're going to the theatre next week** n'oublie pas que nous allons au théâtre la semaine prochaine; **r. where we are!** reprends-toi!; **I remembered myself just in time** je me suis ressaisi juste à temps VOIR GRAMMAIRE A43-4
3 *(give gift to)* ne pas oublier; **she always remembers the children at Christmas** elle n'oublie jamais les enfants à Noël; **he remembered me in his will** il ne m'a pas oublié dans son testament
4 *(speak of)* **let us r. them in our prayers** prions pour eux; **r. me (kindly) to them** rappelez-moi à leur bon souvenir, dites-leur bien des choses de ma part; *esp Fml* **he asked to be remembered to you** il me prie de le rappeler à votre bon souvenir
5 *(of service, monument etc) (the dead)* rendre hommage à
VI se souvenir, se rappeler; **as I r.** d'après mes souvenirs; **as far as I (can) r.** pour autant que je me souvienne; **if I r. rightly** si je m'en souviens bien, si j'ai bonne mémoire; **for as long as I can r.** aussi loin que remontent mes souvenirs

remembrance [rɪ'membrəns] **N 1** *(memory)* souvenir *m*; **in r. of sb/sth** en souvenir de qn/qch; **garden of r.** jardin *m* commémoratif **2** *Old-fashioned (keepsake)* souvenir *m* **3** *Old-fashioned (greeting)* **give my kind remembrances to him** rappelez-moi à son bon souvenir
▸▸ **R. Day,** *Br* **R. Sunday** (commémoration *f* de l')Armistice *m* (le dimanche avant ou après le 11 novembre)

REMIC [ɑːriːemaɪ'siː] **N** *Am Fin (abbr* **real estate mortgage investment conduit**) obligation *f* garantie par hypothèque

remind [rɪ'maɪnd] **VT** *(person)* rappeler à **(that ...** que ... *+ ind)*; **to r. sb of sth** rappeler qch à qn; **he reminds me of my brother** il me fait penser à *ou* me rappelle mon frère; **that reminds me of my childhood** cela me rappelle mon enfance; **to r. sb to do sth** faire

penser à qn à faire qch; **he reminded them of their duty to ...** il leur rappela qu'il était de leur devoir de ...; **r. me about it tomorrow** rappelle-le-moi demain; **that** *or* **which reminds me!** à propos!; **I would r. you that ...** permettez-moi de vous rappeler que ...

reminder [rɪ'maɪndər] **N** *(letter, of event)* rappel *m*; *(to jog memory)* pense-bête *m*, *pl* pense-bêtes; **to send/give sb a r. about sth** envoyer un rappel à qn à propos de qch; **the exhibition is a stark r. of the horrors of war** l'exposition rappelle la guerre dans toute son horreur; **such events are a r. that ...** de tels événements nous rappellent que ...; **it's a r. to myself to ...** c'est pour me rappeler de ...; *Fin* **r. of account due** rappel *m* d'échéance
▸▸ *Acct* **r. entry** poste *m* de mémoire

reminisce [remɪ'nɪs] **VI** évoquer *ou* raconter ses souvenirs **(about** de*)*; *(in thoughts)* évoquer le passé, repenser au passé; **to r. about the good old days** évoquer le bon vieux temps; **to r. about sb** parler de qn (en se souvenant)

reminiscence [remɪ'nɪsəns] **N** *(of past)* souvenir *m* **(about, of** de*)*; **to write one's reminiscences** écrire ses souvenirs

reminiscent [remɪ'nɪsənt] **ADJ 1** *(nostalgic)* nostalgique; **to be in a r. mood** être enclin à *ou* d'humeur à évoquer des souvenirs **2** *(suggestive)* **r. of** qui fait penser à *ou* rappelle **in a voice reminiscent of that of her mother** *or* **of her mother's** d'une voix qui fait penser à *ou* qui rappelle celle de sa mère

reminiscently [remɪ'nɪsəntlɪ] **ADV** **to smile r.** sourire en pensant à qch; **to talk r. of sth** évoquer des souvenirs de qch

remiss [rɪ'mɪs] **ADJ** *(negligent)* négligent **(in doing** de faire*)*; **that was very r. of her** c'était de la négligence de sa part

remission [rɪ'mɪʃən] **N 1** *Law* remise *f* de peine **2** *Med* rémission *f*, **to go into r.** *(of disease, patient)* entrer en rémission **3** *Rel* rémission *f*, **to pray for the r. of sins** prier pour la rémission des péchés **4** *(of debt)* remise *f*, *(of duty, fee, payment)* dispense *f*, *(of tax)* dispense, exemption *f*

remit¹ [rɪ'mɪt] **(-tt-) VT 1** *(send back)* renvoyer; *Law (case)* renvoyer à un autre tribunal; *Fin* **to r. a sum to sb** remettre une somme à qn **2** *(lessen), Law (sentence)* remettre; *Fig Fml (efforts)* relâcher **3** *(forgive) (sin)* pardonner, absoudre **4** *(cancel) (debt)* remettre, faire remise de; **to r. sb's fees** dispenser qn de ses frais; **to r. sb's income tax** dispenser *ou* exempter qn de l'impôt sur le revenu **5** *Fml (postpone) (matter)* remettre, différer
VI 1 *(of debtor)* régler, payer; **please r. by cheque** veuillez régler *ou* payer par chèque **2** *Fml (abate) (of efforts, zeal etc)* diminuer; *(of pain, storm)* se calmer

remit² ['riːmɪt] **N** *(area of authority)* attributions *fpl*; **to exceed one's r.** aller au-delà de ses attributions; **it is outside** *or* **not part of our r.** ceci ne relève pas de nos attributions

remittance [rɪ'mɪtəns] **N** *Com (payment)* versement *m*; *(settlement)* paiement *m*, règlement *m*; **return the form with your r.** renvoyez le formulaire avec votre règlement *ou* paiement
▸▸ *Fin* **r. advice** avis *m* de remise; *Fin* **r. date** date *f* de remise; *Fin* **r. of funds** remise *f* de fonds

remix¹ ['riːmɪks] **N** *Mus (record)* remix *m*

remix² [riː'mɪks] **VT** *Mus* remixer, refaire le mixage de

remnant ['remnənt] **N 1** *(of food)* reste *m*; *Fig (of imperialism, former glory)* vestige *m*; *Fig* **the remnants of one's dignity/an army** ce qui subsiste *ou* reste de sa dignité/d'une armée **2** *(of fabric)* coupon *m*; *(of carpet)* chute *f*; **remnants** *(of fabric)* coupons, fins *fpl* de série; **r. sale** *(of fabric)* soldes *mpl* de fins de série

remodel [ri:'mɒd(ə)l] **VT** (-ll-, *Am* -l-) *(bill, draft)* remanier; *(structure)*, *Fig (legislation)* modifier; **to have one's nose/chin remodelled** se faire refaire le nez/le menton

remonstrate ['remənstreıt] **VI** **to r. with sb** faire des remontrances à qn (**about** au sujet de); **there's no point in trying to r. with her about it** ça ne sert à rien d'en discuter avec elle; **to r. against sth** protester contre qch **VT to r. that** ... protester en disant que ...

remorse [ri'mɔːs] **N** remords *m* (**for, about** de); **without r.** *(not sorry)* sans remords; *(to do sth)* sans scrupules; **to feel r.** éprouver *ou* avoir du *ou* des remords (**for having done** d'avoir fait); **a feeling/twinge of r.** un sentiment/une pointe de remords; **in a fit of r.** dans un accès de remords; **to show r.** manifester des remords

remorseful [ri'mɔːsfʊl] **ADJ** plein de remords

remorsefully [ri'mɔːsfəlı] **ADV** *(to say)* d'un ton plein de remords

remorseless [ri'mɔːslıs] **ADJ** *(person, wind)* impitoyable; *(cruelty, persecution)* incessant; *Fig (ambition, logic, self-interest etc)* implacable; **he was r. in the demands that he made on his employees** il ne laissait aucun répit à ses employés; **she was r. with herself** elle était très dure avec elle-même; **he was r. in his pursuit of the criminal** il n'avait de cesse qu'il n'arrête le criminel

remorselessly [ri'mɔːslıslı] **ADV** *(to hit, pursue etc)* impitoyablement; *(ambitious, logical etc)* implacablement

remorselessness [ri'mɔːslısnıs] **N** *(of person, criticisms, attack)* acharnement *m*

remortgage [ri:'mɔːgıdʒ] **VT** *(house, property)* hypothéquer de nouveau, prendre une nouvelle hypothèque sur

remote [ri'məʊt] **ADJ 1** *(far-off) (house, village etc)* reculé; *(ancestor)* lointain; *(cousin)* éloigné, lointain; **r. from** loin *ou* éloigné de; **in the remotest part of Asia** au fin fond de l'Asie; **in the r. future/past** dans un avenir/un passé lointain

2 *(removed, not connected)* éloigné (**from** de); **his plays are r. from everyday life** ses pièces sont éloignées de la vie quotidienne **3** *Comput (terminal)* distant; *(user)* à distance

4 *(aloof)* distant, réservé; *(with mind elsewhere)* absent; **she had a rather r. look on her face** *(looked aloof)* elle avait une expression plutôt distante; *(was thinking of other things)* elle avait un air absent

5 *(slight) (chance, connection, possibility, resemblance)* vague; *(prospect)* peu probable; **I haven't the remotest idea of what he meant** je n'ai pas la moindre idée de ce qu'il voulait dire; **there is a r. possibility that ...** il y a une vague possibilité que ... + *sub*; **in the r. event of a water shortage** dans l'hypothèse improbable d'une pénurie d'eau; **he hasn't the remotest chance of winning** il n'a pas la moindre chance de gagner

N *Fam (remote control)* télécommande *f*
▶▶ *Comput* **r. access** accès *m* à distance; **r. antiquity** la haute antiquité; **r. control** télécommande, commande *f* à distance; *Comput* **r. data entry** entrée *f* de données à distance; *Comput* **r. data processing** télétraitement *m*; *Comput* **r. help** téléassistance *f*; *Comput* **r. interrogation** interrogation *f* à distance; *Comput* **r. job entry** télésoumission *f* de travaux; *Comput* **r. loading** téléchargement *m*; *Comput* **r. management** télégestion *f*; *Comput* **r. processing** télétraitement *m*; *Comput* **r. reading** lecture *f* à distance; *Comput* **r.**

sensing télédétection *f*; *Comput* **r. satellite** satellite *m* de télédétection; *TV etc* **r. station** téléstation *f*; *Comput* **r. terminal** terminal *m* distant; *Comput* **r. troubleshooting** télédépannage *m*; *TV etc* **r. van** voiture *f* de reportage

remote-controlled **ADJ** *(model aircraft, door, television etc)* télécommandé; *(bomb)* commandé à distance

remotely [ri'məʊtlı] **ADV 1** *(distantly) (situated)* loin, au loin; *(related)* de loin **2** *(absent-mindedly) (to answer etc)* d'un ton absent **3** *(slightly) (possible)* vaguement; **it's only r. connected with the subject** cela n'a qu'un faible rapport avec le sujet; **it isn't even r. connected with the subject** cela n'a même pas le moindre rapport avec le sujet; **I'm not r. interested in science fiction** la science-fiction ne m'intéresse pas le moins du monde; **not r. aware** nullement conscient; **it isn't even r. possible** c'est rigoureusement impossible

remoteness [ri'məʊtnıs] **N 1** *(distance) (of house, past etc)* éloignement *m*; *(isolation)* isolement *m* **2** *(aloofness)* distance *f*; **her air of r.** *(aloofness)* son air distant; *(absent-mindedness)* son air absent; **the r. of her manner** son côté distant **3** *(of resemblance)* faible degré *m*; **the r. of her chances of success** l'improbabilité *f* de sa réussite

remould[1] ['ri:məʊld] **N** *Br Aut* pneu *m* rechapé

remould[2] [ri:'məʊld] **VT** *Br* **1** *Aut (tyre)* rechaper **2** *(clay figure)*, *Fig (image, character etc)* remodeler

remount [ri:'maʊnt] **VT 1** *(get on again)* **to r. one's horse/bicycle** remonter à cheval/bicyclette, remonter sur son cheval/sa bicyclette **2** *(go up again) (stairs)* remonter **3** *(place on new support) (picture)* rentoiler; *(jewel)* remonter
VI remonter à cheval/à bicyclette

removable [ri'mu:vəb(ə)l] **ADJ 1** *(component, lid, lining etc)* amovible **2** *(mark, spot, stain etc)* qui peut partir; **the stain's not r.** la tache est indélébile
▶▶ *Comput* **r. disk** disque *m* amovible *ou* extractible

removal [ri'mu:v(ə)l] **N 1** *(taking away) (of rubbish, plate)* enlèvement *m*; *(of stain etc)* nettoyage *m*; *(of appendix, kidney, tumour etc)* ablation *f*; *(of doubt, fear)* dissipation *f*; *(of burden, worry, obstacle, threat, word)* suppression *f*, **r. of customs barriers** suppression des barrières douanières; **the r. of stains from a jacket** le détachage d'une veste; **for stain r.**, **for the r. of stains** pour enlever les taches, pour détacher **2** *(taking off) (of coat, glove etc)* enlèvement *m*; *(of tyre)* démontage *m*; *(of seal)* levée *f*, **after r. of the bandages** une fois les bandages enlevés; **after the r. of her make-up** une fois démaquillée **3** *(dismissal)* révocation *f*, renvoi *m*; *(of civil servant, judge etc)* destitution *f* **4** *(moving house)* déménagement *m*
▶▶ **r. company** entreprise *f* de déménagement; **r. expenses** frais *mpl* de déménagement; *Br* **r. man** déménageur *m*; **r. van** camion *m* de déménagement

remove [ri'mu:v] **VT 1** *(take away) (rubbish, plate)* enlever; *(stain)* enlever, faire partir (**from** de); *(source of infection)* éliminer; *(appendix, kidney, tumour)* procéder à l'ablation de, enlever; *(person)* emmener (**to** à); *Fig (doubt, fear)* dissiper; *(worry, obstacle, threat, word)* supprimer, éliminer; **to have a mole/wart removed** se faire enlever un grain de beauté/une verrue; **to r. sb's name from a list** rayer qn d'une liste; **she's having the plaster removed tomorrow** on lui enlève son plâtre demain; **to r. a burden from sb** soulager qn d'un fardeau; **to r. a child from**

school retirer un enfant de l'école; **police removed the demonstrators** la police a fait partir les manifestants; **the judge ordered her to be removed from the court room** le juge a ordonné qu'on la fasse sortir de la salle d'audience; **he has been removed to hospital** il a été transporté à l'hôpital; **death has removed him from our midst** la mort nous l'a enlevé

2 *(take off) (coat, gloves, hat)* enlever, retirer (**from sb** à qn); *(tyre)* démonter; *(seal)* lever; **to r. one's make-up** se démaquiller; **to r. the hair from one's legs** s'épiler les jambes

3 *(dismiss) (executive, director)* révoquer, renvoyer; *(civil servant, magistrate)* destituer; **to r. sb from his *or* her position** démettre qn de ses fonctions (**as** de)

4 *(of furniture movers) (furniture etc)* déménager

5 *Euph (kill) (person)* supprimer

VI *Old-fashioned (of people, company)* déménager (**to** à)

N *(degree of difference)* distance *f*, **at a certain r.** à une certaine distance; **at one r.** de façon interposée; **it is but *or* only one r. from ...** cela est tout près de ...; **her account is several removes from the truth** son récit est assez loin de la vérité

removed [ri'mu:vd] **ADJ** *(distant)* **his feeling was not far r. from love** son sentiment n'était pas très éloigné de l'amour; **her explanation is far r. from the truth** son explication est très éloignée de la vérité; **first cousin once r.** cousin, -ine issu(e) de germain

remover [ri'mu:vər] **N 1** *(company, person)* déménageur *m*; **a company of furniture removers** une entreprise de déménagement **2** *(substance)* **paint r.** décapant *m*; **stain r.** détachant *m*; **hair r.** (d)épilatoire *m*; **nail varnish r.** dissolvant *m*; **make-up r.** démaquillant *m*

removing [ri'mu:vıŋ] **ADJ**
▶▶ **r. cream** *(for hair)* crème *f* (d)épilatoire; *(for make-up)* crème démaquillante; *(for wrinkles)* crème antirides

remunerate [ri'mju:nəreıt] **VT** *Fml (person)* rémunérer (**for** de); *(service)* rémunérer

remuneration [rimju:nə'reıʃən] **N** *Fml (for service etc)* rémunération *f* (**for** de)
▶▶ **r. package** = salaire *m* et avantages *mpl* complémentaires

remunerative [ri'mju:nərətıv] **ADJ** *Fml* rémunérateur, -trice

Renaissance [ri'neısəns] **N** renaissance *f*, *Art, Hist* **the R.** la Renaissance; **R. art/literature** art *m*/littérature *f* de la Renaissance
▶▶ **R. man** esprit *m* universel

renaissance [ri'neısəns] **N** *(of industry etc)* renaissance *f*

renal ['ri:n(ə)l] **ADJ** *Anat (artery etc)* rénal, -aux
▶▶ **r. failure** insuffisance *f* rénale

rename [ri:'neım] **VT** *(person, street)* rebaptiser; *Comput (file)* changer le nom de, renommer

renascence [ri'næsəns, -'neı-] **N** *Lit (of nationalism)* renaissance *f*, *(of interest)* regain *m*

renascent [ri'næsənt, -'neı-] **ADJ** *Lit (interest, nationalism etc)* renaissant

renationalization [ri:næʃənəlaı'zeıʃən] **N** renationalisation *f*

renationalize [ri:'næʃənəlaız] **VT** renationaliser

rend [rend] **VT** *(pt, pp* **rent** [rent]*)* **1** *(pierce) (the silence)* déchirer; **the air was rent with her screams** l'air était déchiré par ses hurlements **2** *Lit (tear)* déchirer; **to r. sth asunder *or* apart** *(in two parts)* déchirer *ou* fendre qch en deux; *(in several parts) (car, ship etc)* déchiqueter qch; **he was rent from my arms** il fut arraché à mes bras; **a country rent by civil war** un pays déchiré par la guerre civile

render ['rendər] **VT 1** *Fml (give) (homage, service)* rendre; *(description)* faire; *(explanation)* donner; **to r. thanks to God** rendre grâce à Dieu; *Bible* **r. unto Caesar the things which are Caesar's** rendez à César ce qui appartient à César; **to r. an account of sth** *(describe)* faire le récit de qch; *Fin* **to r. an account to sb** remettre un compte à qn; *Fin* **as per account rendered** suivant compte remis; **to r. assistance to sb** prêter secours à qn; **to r. (up) a fortress** rendre une forteresse; *Lit* **to r. up one's soul** *(die)* rendre l'âme **2** *(make, cause to be)* rendre; **the blow rendered her unconscious** le coup lui a fait perdre connaissance; **the news rendered her speechless** la nouvelle l'a laissée sans voix **3** *(depict) (light)* rendre; *(perform) (piece of music)* interpréter **4** *(translate)* rendre, traduire **(in, into** en) **5** *(plaster) (wall etc)* plâtrer, enduire de plâtre **6** *Culin* **to r. (down) fat** faire fondre de la graisse

rendering ['rendərɪŋ] **N 1** *Fin (of account)* reddition *f* **2** *(of expression, features in painting)* rendu *m*; *(of music)* interprétation *f*; **his r. of what happened** sa version des faits **3** *(translating) (of phrase)* traduction *f* **4** *(of wall)* enduit *m* **5** *(of fat)* fonte *f*
　▸▸ **r. plant** usine *f* d'équarrissage

rendezvous ['rɒndɪvuː, *pl* -vuːz] **N** *(meeting, meeting-place)* rendez-vous *m inv* **(for** de); **to make a r. with sb** prendre rendez-vous avec qn; **to keep a r.** se rendre à un rendez-vous
　VI *(pt, pp* **rendezvoused** [-vuːd]; *prp* **rendezvousing** [-vuːɪŋ]) se réunir, se retrouver; **to r. with sb** retrouver qn

rendition [ren'dɪʃən] **N** *(of role etc)* interprétation *f*, *(translation) (of phrase)* traduction *f*; **to give a r. of** *(role etc)* interpréter; **they finished with a r. of the Marseillaise** ils ont terminé en chantant/jouant la Marseillaise

renegade ['renɪgeɪd] **N 1** *(traitor)* renégat, -ate **2** *(outlaw)* hors-la-loi *m inv*
　▸▸ **r. priest** prêtre *m* parjure

renege, renegue [rɪ'neɪg] **VI 1** manquer à *ou* revenir sur sa promesse **(on doing sth** de faire qch); **she has reneged (on her promise)** elle a manqué à sa promesse; **she has reneged (on our deal)** elle est revenue sur notre marché **2** *Cards* faire une fausse renonce

renegotiate [riːnɪ'gəʊʃɪeɪt] **VT** renégocier

renegotiation [riːnɪgəʊʃɪ'eɪʃən] **N** renégociation *f*

renew [rɪ'njuː] **VT 1** *(resume) (conversation)* reprendre; **to r. one's acquaintance with sb** renouer connaissance avec qn; **to r. pressure on sb** recommencer à faire pression sur qn **(to do** pour qu'il fasse); *Mil* **to r. an attack** attaquer de nouveau; *Fig* **to r. one's attack** revenir à la charge *ou* à l'attaque **(on** concernant) **2** *(restate) (request, promise)* renouveler **3** *(extend) (lease, passport, bill of exchange)* renouveler; **to r. a lease** reconduire un bail; **to r. one's subscription** se réabonner, renouveler son abonnement **(to** à); **to r. a library book** faire renouveler *ou* prolonger le prêt d'un livre de bibliothèque; **to r. one's wardrobe** renouveler sa garde-robe **4** *(revive) (hope, enthusiasm etc)* raviver

renewable [rɪ'njuːəb(ə)l] **ADJ** *(passport etc)* renouvelable; *(lease, contract)* reconductible, renouvelable; **your subscription is r. at the end of the year** *(must be renewed)* votre abonnement doit être renouvelé à la fin de l'année; *(may be renewed)* votre abonnement peut être renouvelé à la fin de l'année
　▸▸ **r. energy** énergie *f* renouvelable; **r. resources** ressources *fpl* renouvelables

renewal [rɪ'njuːəl] **N 1** *(of acquaintance)* renouement *m*; *(of hostilities, violence, bombing)* reprise *f*; *(of hopes, enthusiasm)* regain *m*; **r. of activity** reprise *ou* regain d'activité **2** *(of promise, request)* renouvellement *m* **3** *(of lease, passport etc)* renouvellement *m*; *(of library book)* renouvellement de prêt; **r. of subscription** réabonnement *m*, renouvellement d'abonnement **(to** à)
　▸▸ **r. clause** clause *f* de reconduction; **r. notice** avis *m* de renouvellement; **r. premium** prime *f* de renouvellement

renewed [rɪ'njuːd] **ADJ** *(effort, enthusiasm, vigour)* renouvelé; *(attempt, hope)* nouveau; *(activity, efforts)* redoublé; **r. bombing/outbreaks of violence** reprise *f* des bombardements/de la violence; **doctors are expressing r. concern about her condition** son état inspire de nouvelles inquiétudes aux médecins; **there is r. interest in ...** il y a un regain d'intérêt pour ...; **there has been r. military activity in the region** il y a eu un regain d'activité militaire dans la région

rennet ['renɪt] **N** présure *f*

re-nose **VT** *Journ (story)* réorienter

renounce [rɪ'naʊns] **VT 1** *(abandon, give up) (right, title, alcohol, violence etc)* renoncer à; *Law (nationality, inheritance)* répudier; **to r. all thought of doing sth** renoncer à toute idée de faire qch; *Lit* **to r. the world** renoncer au monde **2** *(disown) (treaty)* répudier, dénoncer; *(friend)* renier, désavouer; *(one's principles)* renier; **to r. one's faith** renoncer à sa foi, apostasier; **to r. Satan and all his works** renoncer à Satan, à ses pompes et à ses œuvres

renouncement [rɪ'naʊnsmənt] **N** = **renunciation**

renovate ['renəveɪt] **VT** *(house etc)* rénover

renovation [renə'veɪʃən] **N** *(of house etc)* rénovation *f*, **closed for r.** *(notice in shop window)* fermé pour cause de travaux de rénovation; **to be under r.** être en cours de rénovation; **to undergo renovations** subir des rénovations, être en rénovation; **r. project/work** projet *m*/travaux *mpl* de rénovation

renovator ['renəveɪtər] **N** rénovateur, -trice

renown [rɪ'naʊn] **N** renommée *f*, renom *m*; **woman of great or high r.** femme *f* de grand renom; **to win r.** acquérir une renommée, se faire une renommée **(as** en tant que; **for** pour)

renowned [rɪ'naʊnd] **ADJ** *(town, person)* renommé, célèbre **(for** pour; **as** comme); *(wine)* fameux; *(artist, writer)* célèbre, illustre; **Dr Hector Smith, the r. psychiatrist** le Dr Hector Smith, le célèbre psychiatre; **he is r. for being late** il est réputé pour être toujours en retard

rent¹ [rent] **N** *(on flat, house etc)* loyer *m*; **for r.** à louer; **how much do you pay in r.?, how much r. do you pay?** combien est-ce que tu paies de loyer?; **to live somewhere free of r.** habiter quelque part sans payer de loyer; **to be behind with the r.** être en retard pour *(payer)* le loyer; **Friday is r. day, it's r. day on Friday** on doit payer le loyer vendredi
　VT *(flat, video, car)* louer **(from, to** à); **to r. (out) rooms** louer des chambres **(from, to** à); **she lives in a rented house** elle habite dans une maison qu'elle loue; **rented accommodation** logement *m* en location, location *f*; **to r.** à louer
　VI **it rents at** *or* **for ...** cela se loue à ...
　▸▸ **r. book** carnet *m* de quittances de loyer; *Fam* **r. boy** jeune prostitué *m* homosexuel; **r. collector** receveur, -euse des loyers; **r. strike** grève *f* des loyers
　▸ **rent out VT INSEP** = **rent¹ VT**

rent² **N** *(in clothing)* déchirure *f*, accroc *m*; *(in clouds)* déchirure, trouée *f*; *(in relations)* rupture *f*

rent³ **PT, PP** *see* **rend**

rental ['rent(ə)l] **N 1** *(hire) (of car, flat, house etc)* location *f* **2** *(money paid) (for flat, house)* loyer *m*; *(for car, equipment, television, holiday flat)* (prix *m* de) location *f*; *(for telephone)* abonnement *m*; *Tel* **fixed r.** redevance *f* d'abonnement
　▸▸ **r. car** voiture *f* de location; **r. company** société *f* de location; **r. charge** *(for telephone)* abonnement; *(for TV, car)* prix *m* de location; **r. expenses** charges *fpl* locatives; **r. income** revenus *mpl* locatifs; **r. office** *(for car)* bureau *m* de location; **r. property** propriété *f* à louer

rent-a-mob **N** *Fam* agitateurs *mpl*

rent-free **ADJ** *(accommodation, flat etc)* exempt de loyer; **to live somewhere r.** habiter quelque part sans payer de loyer; **a house is available r.** il y a une maison où l'on peut habiter gratuitement *ou* sans payer de loyer

rents [rents] **NPL** *Am Fam (parents)* vieux *mpl*, renps *mpl*

renunciation [rɪnʌnsɪ'eɪʃən] **N 1** *(of right, title, alcohol, violence etc)* renonciation *f* **(of** à); *Law (of nationality, inheritance)* répudiation *f* **2** *(of treaty)* répudiation *f*, dénonciation *f*; *(of beliefs)* reniement *m*; *(of friend)* reniement, désaveu *m*; *(of world)* renoncement *m* **(of** à)

reoccupy [riː'ɒkjʊpaɪ] **VT** *(territory)* réoccuper; *(house)* habiter à nouveau; **the house is reoccupied** la maison est réhabitée

reopen [riː'əʊp(ə)n] **VT 1** *(book, frontier, investigation etc)* rouvrir; *Fig* **to r. an old wound** rouvrir une plaie **2** *(resume) (hostilities)* recommencer, reprendre; *(talks)* reprendre
　VI *(of wound)* se rouvrir; *(of shop, theatre etc)* rouvrir; *(law court)* rentrer; *(of schools, talks)* reprendre; **the border has reopened** la frontière a été rouverte

reopening [riː'əʊp(ə)nɪŋ] **N** *(of shop, theatre, border, investigation etc)* réouverture *f*; *(of hostilities, talks)* reprise *f*, *Fig* **this will merely lead to the r. of old wounds** ça ne fera que rouvrir d'anciennes blessures

reorder [riː'ɔːdər] **N** *(to obtain more supplies)* nouvelle commande *f*, *(reminder to supplier)* commande renouvelée; **to send** *or* **put a r. in** envoyer *ou* passer une nouvelle commande **(for** de); **r. form/procedure** formulaire *m*/procédure *f* de renouvellement de commande
　VT *(order more)* faire une nouvelle commande de; *(order again)* renouveler la commande de
　▸▸ *Com* **r. level** seuil *m* de réapprovisionnement

reorganization [riːɔːgənaɪ'zeɪʃən] **N** *(of company, system, files etc)* réorganisation *f*

reorganize [riː'ɔːgənaɪz] **VT** *(company, system, files etc)* réorganiser
　VI *(of company etc)* se réorganiser

Rep [rep] *Am Pol* **1** *abbr* **Representative 2** *abbr* **Republican**

rep¹ [rep] *Fam* **N** *(abbr* **representative)** *(door to door)* représentant, -ante; *(for large company)* représentant, -ante, VRP *m* **(for** chez); **sales r.** représentant, -ante de commerce, VRP
　VI travailler comme représentant, -ante **(for** chez)

rep² **N** *Br Theat Fam (abbr* **repertory)** *(theatre)* théâtre *m*; **what's on at the local r.?** qu'est-ce qu'on joue au théâtre municipal?; **to work in r.** faire du théâtre

repackage [riː'pækɪdʒ] **VT** *Mktg* reconditionner, repenser l'emballage de

repaginate [riː'pædʒɪneɪt] **VT** remettre en pages; *(renumber)* repaginer

repaint [riː'peɪnt] **VT** repeindre

repair [rɪ'peər] **N1** (of shoes, watch etc) réparation f; (of building, road) réparation, réfection f; (of machine) réparation, remise f en état; (of clothing) réparation, raccommodage m; **to be in need of r.** avoir besoin d'être réparé; **to be in for r.** (of car etc) être en réparation; **to be (damaged) beyond r.** être irréparable; **road under r.** (road sign) travaux; **(shoe) repairs while you wait** (notice in shop) cordonnerie minute; **to make repairs to sth** (machine, car, bike) faire des réparations sur qch; (shoes, garment) réparer; **to carry out repairs** effectuer des réparations; **he does all his own repairs** il fait toutes ses réparations lui-même; **to undergo repairs** or **be under r.** être en réparation **2** (condition) **to be in good/bad r.** être en bon/mauvais état, être bien/mal entretenu; **to keep a road/car/property in (good) r.** entretenir une route/voiture/propriété
VT (mend) (shoes, watch, building, road) réparer; (machine) réparer, remettre en état
▸▸**r. kit** trousse f à outils; **r. shop** atelier m de réparations

repairer [rɪ'peərər] **N** (of shoes) cordonnier, -ière; (of watch, machine etc) réparateur, -trice

repairman, pl **repairmen** [rɪ'peəmæn, -men] **N** (of televisions, washing machines etc) réparateur m; **a computer/TV/washing machine r.** un réparateur d'ordinateurs/de télévisions/de machines à laver

repaper [riː'peɪpər] **VT** (room) retapisser

reparation [repə'reɪʃən] **N** Fml (of wrong, omission) réparation f; **in r. of …** en réparation de …; **to make reparation for sth** réparer qch; **(war) reparations, r. payments** réparations

repartee [repɑː'tiː] **N** repartie f; **to be good** or **quick at r.** avoir la repartie facile, avoir de la repartie; **to engage in r.** faire de l'esprit

repast [rɪ'pɑːst] **N** Lit repas m

repatriate¹ [riː'pætrɪeɪt] **VT** (prisoner of war, capital etc) rapatrier (**to** vers)

repatriate² [riː'pætrɪət] **N** rapatrié, -ée

repatriation [riːpætrɪ'eɪʃən] **N** (of prisoner of war, capital etc) rapatriement m

repay [riː'peɪ, rɪ-] **VT** (pt, pp **repaid** [riː'peɪd, rɪ-]) **1** (pay back) (money) rendre, rembourser; (loan, person) rembourser **2** (reward) (person) récompenser (**for** de); (give same in return for) (favour) rendre; **is this how you r. me?** c'est comme ça que tu me récompenses ou remercies?; **to r. sb with ingratitude** payer qn d'ingratitude; **to r. a kindness** payer une gentillesse de retour; **I can never r. you for all you've done** je ne pourrai jamais vous remercier assez pour tout ce que vous avez fait; **how can I ever r. you?** pourrais-je jamais vous remercier?

repayable [riː'peɪəb(ə)l, rɪ-] **ADJ** (loan) remboursable

repayment [riː'peɪmənt, rɪ-] **N1** (of loan, mortgage etc) remboursement m; **the repayments are spread over five years** les remboursements sont échelonnés sur cinq ans **2** (of kindness) récompense f; **in r. of your helpfulness/support** pour te remercier de ton aide/soutien
▸▸Br **r. mortgage** prêt-logement m, pl prêts-logement (aux remboursements échelonnés); **r. plan** calendrier m des paiements

repeal [rɪ'piːl] **N** (of law) abrogation f; (of decree) révocation f
VT (law) abroger; (decree) révoquer

repeat [rɪ'piːt] **VT1** (do again) (action, motif) répéter; (one's efforts, prescription, attempt) renouveler; (as encore) (song, piece of music) bisser; Radio, TV (programme) rediffuser; Sch **to r. a year** redoubler; **history repeats itself** l'histoire se répète **2** (say again)

(question) répéter; (threat, order, promise) réitérer; **it can't be repeated too often** on ne saurait trop le répéter; Mus **r.** (after a line of a song etc) bis; **to r. oneself** se répéter; **am I repeating myself?** est-ce que je me répète?, Fam est-ce que je radote?; **I don't want to have to r. myself** je ne veux pas avoir à le répéter; **r. after me …** répétez après moi … **3** (say to others) (secret) répéter; **don't r. this, but …** ne le répète pas, mais …
VI1 (of decimal figure) se répéter **2** (of food) donner des renvois; **it's repeating on me** ça me donne des renvois
N (of event, motif, attempt) répétition f; Mus (passage) reprise f; Mus (mark) barre f de reprise, renvoi m; Radio, TV rediffusion f; **there's nothing on (television) but repeats** il n'y a que des rediffusions; **a r. of the attempt to assassinate him** une nouvelle tentative d'assassinat sur sa personne; **we get a lot of r. business** beaucoup de nos clients reviennent; **it will be a r. of last year's final** ça sera comme la finale de l'année dernière
▸▸Tel **r. dial** recomposition f, renumérotation f; Comput **r. function** fonction f de répétition; Law **r. offender** récidiviste mf; Com **r. order** commande f renouvelée; Theat **r. performance** deuxième représentation f; Fig **we don't want a r. performance of last year's chaos** nous ne voulons pas que le désordre de l'année dernière se reproduise; **r. prescription** ordonnance f (de renouvellement d'un médicament); Mktg **r. purchase** achats mpl répétés; **r. run** (of adverts etc) passage m répété; Mktg **r. sale** ventes fpl répétées

repeat-action key N Comput touche f de répétition

repeated [rɪ'piːtɪd] **ADJ** (action etc) répété; (question etc) réitéré; (effort) renouvelé; **after r. failures/warnings** après des échecs/des avertissements répétés

repeatedly [rɪ'piːtɪdlɪ] **ADV** à maintes reprises

repeater [rɪ'piːtər] **N** (rifle) fusil m à répétition

repeating [rɪ'piːtɪŋ] **ADJ1** (rifle) à répétition **2** (decimal) périodique
N (of word, action) répétition f

repel [rɪ'pel] **VT** (-ll-) **1** (repulse) (assailant) repousser; **r. moisture** empêcher l'infiltration de l'humidité; **like poles r. (each other)** les pôles semblables se repoussent; **a spray that repels greenfly** un aérosol qui éloigne les pucerons **2** (disgust) répugner à, dégoûter; **she was repelled by the sight** elle a été dégoûtée par ce qu'elle a vu

repellent [rɪ'pelənt] **ADJ** (person, sight etc) repoussant, répugnant; **he finds her/the idea quite r.** elle/l'idée lui répugne; **r. (to water)** imperméable
N (for insects) insecticide m

-repellent [rɪ'pelənt] **SUFF** moth/rust-r. antimites/antirouille

repent [rɪ'pent] **VI** se repentir (**of** de)
VT se repentir de

repentance [rɪ'pentəns] **N** repentir m (**for** pour); **to show r.** manifester du repentir; Rel venir à résipiscence, se repentir; **to show no sign of r.** ne manifester aucun signe de repentir

repentant [rɪ'pentənt] **ADJ** (sinner etc) repentant (**of** de)

repentantly [rɪ'pentəntlɪ] **ADV** (to say, look at) d'un ton/d'un air repentant

repercussion [riːpə'kʌʃən] **N1** (indirect effect) répercussion f; (of scandal) retentissement m; (consequence) contrecoup m; **to have repercussions** avoir des répercussions (**for, on** sur); **the repercussions are still be-**

ing felt on en ressent encore les répercussions **2** (from impact, of sound) répercussion f

repertoire ['repətwɑːr] **N** (of jokes, songs etc), Theat répertoire m; **to have a wide/limited r.** avoir un vaste répertoire/un répertoire restreint; Theat **the two plays will be performed in r.** les deux pièces seront jouées en alternance

repertory ['repət(ə)rɪ] **N1** Theat **to work in r.** faire du théâtre de répertoire; (theatre) théâtre m de répertoire; **what's on at the local r.?** qu'est-ce qu'on joue au théâtre municipal? **2** (repertoire) répertoire m
▸▸**r. company** compagnie f ou troupe f de répertoire; Theat **r. theatre** théâtre m de répertoire

répétiteur [repeti'tɜːr] **N** Theat (of opera singer etc) maître m de musique

repetition [repɪ'tɪʃən] **N** (of word, action etc) répétition f; (of effort) renouvellement m; Mus reprise f, Sport **it was an exact r. of last year's final** c'était exactement comme la finale de l'année dernière; **I don't want any r. of your behaviour!** que cela ne se reproduise pas!

repetitious [repɪ'tɪʃəs] **ADJ** (book, speech etc) plein de répétitions

repetitive [rɪ'petɪtɪv] **ADJ** (person) rabâcheur; (job) répétitif
▸▸Med **r. strain injury, r. stress injury** = douleur f due à la répétition d'un même mouvement lors d'une activité telle que taper à la machine, jouer du violon etc

rephrase [riː'freɪz] **VT** (question) formuler à nouveau, reformuler; **perhaps I should r. that …** peut-être devrais-je m'exprimer autrement …

repine [rɪ'paɪn] **VI** Lit être mécontent (**at** de)

replace [rɪ'pleɪs] **VT1** (put back) (object) replacer, remettre (en place); **I replaced the book on the shelf** j'ai replacé ou remis le livre sur l'étagère; **r. the book when you've finished with it** remets le livre à sa place quand tu n'en auras plus besoin; Tel **to r. the receiver** raccrocher (le combiné) **2** (substitute for) (person, object) remplacer (**as en tant que; with** par); **to be replaced by** or **with** être remplacé par; **it can be replaced** (of broken cup etc) on peut retrouver le/la même; Comput **r. all** tout remplacer

When translating the English verb **to replace**, note that the French verbs **replacer** and **remplacer** are not interchangeable. **Replacer** means to put back and **remplacer** means to take the place of.

replaceable [rɪ'pleɪsɪb(ə)l] **ADJ** (broken cup etc) remplaçable

replacement [rɪ'pleɪsmənt] **N1** (putting back) (of object) remise f en place **2** (substitution) (of person, object) remplacement m (**of** … **by** de … par) **3** (substitute) (for person) remplaçant, -ante; (for component) pièce f de rechange; **we are looking for a r. for our secretary** nous cherchons quelqu'un pour remplacer notre secrétaire
▸▸**r. cost** coût m de remplacement; Med **r. hip joint** prothèse f de (la) hanche; Med **r. knee joint** prothèse f de (la) rotule; Mktg **r. sale** vente f de remplacement; **r. teacher** professeur m suppléant, suppléant, -ante, remplaçant, -ante; **r. value** valeur f de remplacement

replant [riː'plɑːnt] **VT** (shrub, garden) replanter

replay¹ ['riːpleɪ] **N** Sport second match m, nouvelle rencontre f; TV instant or Br action **r.** répétition f immédiate d'une séquence; TV **(slow-motion) r.** répétition au ralenti; TV **to give** or **show a r.** repasser une séquence; *(in slow motion)* repasser une séquence au ralenti; **the r. clearly shows the foul** on voit bien la faute au ralenti

replay² [riː'pleɪ] **VT 1** *Sport (match)* rejouer; *Tennis* **to r. a point** rejouer un point **2** *(recording)* repasser

replenish [rɪ'plenɪʃ] **VT** *(cup etc)* remplir de nouveau (**with** de); **to r. one's supplies** se réapprovisionner (**with** de); *Banking* **to r. an account** approvisionner un compte; **she kept his glass replenished** elle veillait à ce que son verre fût toujours plein; **do you need replenishing?** est-ce que je remplis ton verre?

replenishment [rɪ'plenɪʃmənt] **N** *(of cup etc)* remplissage *m*; **r. of supplies** réapprovisionnement *m*

replete [rɪ'pliːt] **ADJ** *Fml* **1** *(full up)* rassasié; **r. with** gorgé de **2** *(well-supplied)* rempli, plein (**with** de)

repletion [rɪ'pliːʃən] **N** *Fml* satiété *f*; **to eat to r.** manger à satiété *ou* jusqu'à être rassasié

replica ['replɪkə] **N** *(of statue, painting, building)* réplique *f*; *(of document)* copie *f*; *Fig (of person)* portrait *m*; *(of match, dispute etc)* répétition *f*; **she is a r. of her grandmother** c'est (tout) le portrait de sa grandmère

replicate ['replɪkeɪt] **VT** *(document)* copier; *(experiment, cell, gene)* reproduire; *Comput (in spreadsheet)* recopier à l'identique; **the gene can r. itself** le gène peut se reproduire

reply [rɪ'plaɪ] **N** *(to letter, query etc)* réponse *f*; **I made no r.** je n'ai rien répondu; **his r. to that was …** *(in speech)* il a répondu à cela que …; **his r. to that was to march out of the room** il a réagi à cela en sortant d'un air furieux de la pièce; **what did you say in r.?** qu'est-ce que tu as répondu?; **what did you do in r.?** comment est-ce que tu as réagi?; **there was no r.** *(to telephone call)* on n'a pas répondu, ça ne répondait pas; *(to knock on door)* on n'a pas ouvert; **in r. to your letter** en réponse à votre lettre; **r. paid** réponse payée **VT & VI** répondre (**to** à); *(retort)* répliquer (**to** à); **yes, madam, he replied** oui, madame, a-t-il répondu

▸▸ *Mktg* **r. card** carte-réponse *f*, *pl* cartes-réponses; *Mktg* **r. coupon** coupon-réponse *m*, *pl* coupons-réponses; **r. slip** talon *m* à retourner

reply-paid **N** *Br* avec réponse payée

▸▸ *Mktg* **r. card** carte *f* T; **r. envelope** enveloppe *f* T, enveloppe-retour *f*, *pl* enveloppes-retour; **r. letter** lettre *f* avec réponse payée

repo ['riːpəʊ] **N 1** *Am Fam (abbr repossession)* saisie *f* **2** *(abbr repurchase)* rachat *m*; *St Exch, Banking* réméré *m*

▸▸ *St Exch, Banking* **r. agreement** opération *f* de réméré *ou* de prise en pension, opération repo; *Am Fam* **r. man** ≃ huissier *m* *(chargé par une société de saisir des meubles etc non payés)*; *St Exch, Banking* **r. operation** opération de réméré *ou* de prise en pension, opération repo; *St Exch, Banking* **r. rate** taux *m* de réméré *ou* de prise en pension

---

REPORT [rɪ'pɔːt]

N rapport **1** ▪ compte rendu **1** ▪ procès-verbal **1** ▪ reportage **1** ▪ bulletin **1**
VT rendre compte de **1** ▪ faire un reportage sur **1** ▪ signaler **2, 3** ▪ annoncer **2**
VI se présenter **1** ▪ faire un rapport **2**

N 1 *(account)*, *Com* rapport *m* (**on** sur); *(of meetings)* compte rendu *m*; *(in writing)* procès-verbal *m*, *pl* procès-verbaux; *(in newspaper)* *(short)* compte rendu; *(long)* reportage *m*; *(on radio, television)* repor-

---

tage; *(by eyewitness)* témoignage *m*; *Comput* état *m*; **there was a short r. of the incident in the newspaper** l'incident a fait l'objet d'un petit article *ou* d'un entrefilet dans le journal; **according to reports in the newspapers** selon les journaux/les services de renseignements; **to draw up** *or* **make a r. on sth** faire *ou* rédiger un rapport sur qch; *(of police officer)* dresser procès-verbal de qch; **r. of the board of directors** *(in annual account)* rapport de gestion; *Sch* **book r.** compte rendu de lecture; *Sch* **end-of-term r.** bulletin *m* (trimestriel); **progress r.** rapport périodique *ou* d'avancement (des travaux); *Sch* **school r.** bulletin scolaire; *Mil* **sick r.** rôle *m* des malades

2 *(rumour)* bruit *m* (qui court), rumeur *f*

3 *(sound)* *(of shot)* détonation *f*, coup *m* de fusil/de canon; *(of explosion)* bruit *m* d'explosion, détonation

4 *Old-fashioned (reputation)* renom *m*; **man of good r.** homme *m* de bonne réputation **VT 1** *(give account of)* rendre compte de; *(fact, incident)* rapporter; *(speech etc)* faire le compte rendu de; *Journ* faire un reportage sur; **to r. one's findings** rendre compte des résultats de ses recherches (**to sb** à qn); **the newspapers r. heavy casualties** les journaux font état de nombreuses victimes; **little progress has been reported so far** jusqu'à présent on n'a obtenu que peu de résultats; **the president was reported by the newspapers to have …** les journaux ont rapporté *ou* raconté que le président avait …; **her resignation is reported in several papers** sa démission est annoncée dans plusieurs journaux; **she is reported to be dead** elle serait morte, on dit qu'elle est morte, on la dit morte; **it is reported that …** on dit que … + *ind*; **the version reported in the press** la version parue dans la presse; **they are reported to be in France** ils seraient en France

2 *(make known)* *(accident, theft)* signaler (**to** à); *(announce)* *(change, developments, profits, loss etc)* annoncer; *Mil* **to r. sb sick/missing** porter qn malade/absent; **to r. sb missing** *(to police)* signaler la disparition de qn; **she has been reported missing** on a signalé sa disparition; **she was reported missing five years ago** elle a été portée disparue il y a cinq ans; **nothing to r.** rien à signaler; *(on form)* néant, RAS

3 *(denounce)* **I'm going to r. you** *(to authorities)* je vais te signaler; **to r. sb to the police** dénoncer qn à la police; **to r. a pupil to the headmaster** *(of teacher)* signaler la mauvaise conduite d'un élève au directeur; **to r. a pupil for smoking** signaler le nom d'un élève surpris en train de fumer; **I'm going to r. you for smoking** je dirai au directeur que je t'ai surpris en train de fumer

VI 1 *(present oneself)* se présenter (**to sb** à *ou* devant qn; **to a place** à un endroit); **please r. to reception** veuillez vous présenter à la réception; **you've to r. to the headmaster** tu dois aller chez le directeur; *Mil* **to r. sick** se faire porter malade; *Mil* **to r. fit** reprendre son service (après une maladie); *Mil* **to r. to one's unit** rallier son unité; **to r. for duty** prendre son service; **you will r. for duty on Monday** vous vous présenterez à votre poste lundi; **to r. back from leave** reprendre son service après un congé

2 *(give account)* faire un rapport (**on** sur); *(of journalist)* faire un reportage (**on** sur); **to r. (for a newspaper)** faire des reportages (pour un journal); *Parl* **to r. on a bill** rapporter un projet de loi; *TV, Radio* **reporting from Geneva is our foreign affairs correspondent …** de Genève, notre correspondant pour les affaires étrangères …; **this is Mary Smith reporting for ITN news** Mary Smith pour le journal d'ITN

▸▸ *Sch* **r. card** bulletin *ou* carnet *m* scolaire; *Comput* **r. form** rapport (d'édition), fiche *f* d'état; *Comput* **r. form generator** générateur *m* d'états; *Br Parl* **r. stage** = examen *m* d'un projet de loi avant la troisième lecture; **the bill has reached the r. stage** le projet de loi a été présenté au Parlement

▸ **report back VI 1** *(announce return)* se présenter **2** *(announce findings)* rendre compte (**on sth** de qch); **to r. back to a committee** faire son rapport à un comité; **they r. back to head office once a week** ils font un rapport pour le siège une fois par semaine

▸ **report to VT INSEP 1** *(be accountable to)* *(person)* rendre compte à; **who do you r. to?** qui est votre supérieur?; **you'll be reporting to Mr Jones** vous travaillerez sous la direction de M. Jones; **I r. directly to the board** je n'ai pas de supérieur hiérarchique à part le conseil d'administration **2** *(inform of developments)* **to r. to sb** faire son rapport à qn (**on** sur), rendre compte à qn (**on** de)

Note that the French word **report** is a false friend and is never a translation for the English word **report**. Its most common meaning is **postponement**.

Note that the French verb **reporter** is a false friend and is never a translation for the English verb **to report**. Its most common meaning is **to postpone**.

---

reportage [repɔː'taːʒ] **N** *Journ etc* reportage *m*

reported [rɪ'pɔːtɪd] **ADJ ATTRIB their last r. position was south of the river** *(given by themselves)* la dernière fois qu'ils ont donné leur position, ils étaient au sud de la rivière; *(given by third party)* ils ont été vus pour la dernière fois au sud de la rivière; **her r. lack of interest in her children** son soi-disant manque d'intérêt pour ses enfants

▸▸ *Gram* **r. speech** style *m* *ou* discours *m* indirect

reportedly [rɪ'pɔːtɪdlɪ] **ADV** à ce qu'on dit; **the President r. said that …** le Président aurait dit que …; **she is r. unharmed** elle serait indemne; **he is r. resident in Paris** il résiderait à Paris

reporter [rɪ'pɔːtər] **N** reporter *mf*, journaliste *mf*; *(correspondent)* envoyé, -ée, reporter; *Radio, TV* reporter

reporting [rɪ'pɔːtɪŋ] **N** *(of news)* reportage *m*; **his r. of the facts is always accurate** il rapporte toujours fidèlement les faits; **she is noted for her objective r.** elle est connue pour l'objectivité de ses reportages

▸▸ *St Exch* **r. limit** seuil *m* d'annonce obligatoire; **r. restrictions** restrictions *fpl* journalistiques; *esp Jur* **r. restrictions have been imposed** on a imposé des restrictions quant aux reportages; **r. structure** *(within company)* structure *f* hiérarchique

repose [rɪ'pəʊz] **VT** *Fml* **1** **to r. trust in sb** placer *ou* mettre sa confiance en qn **2** *(rest)* *(one's head)* reposer

VI 1 *(of argument, plan)* reposer (**on** sur) **2** *Fml (rest)* reposer

N *Fml, Lit (rest)* repos *m*; *(sleep)* sommeil *m*; **her face is beautiful in r.** son visage est très beau lorsqu'elle est détendue; **to pray for the r. of sb's soul** prier pour le repos de l'âme de qn

reposition [riːpə'zɪʃən] **VT 1** *(move)* **she repositioned herself nearer the door** elle a changé de place pour aller se placer près de la porte **2** *Com (product, party)* repositionner

repositioning [riːpə'zɪʃənɪŋ] **N** *Com (of product, party)* repositionnement *m*

repository [rɪ'pɒzɪt(ə)rɪ] **N** *(for books, fur-*

niture etc) dépôt m, entrepôt m; Fig Lit (of knowledge etc) mine f

repossess [riːpəˈzes] VT (for non-payment) (furniture, car etc) saisir

repossession [riːpəˈzeʃən] N (of furniture etc) saisie f

repot [riːˈpɒt] VT (plant) rempoter

reprehend [reprɪˈhend] VT Fml réprimander

reprehensible [reprɪˈhensɪb(ə)l] ADJ (behaviour, act) répréhensible; **that was most r. of you** c'était très répréhensible de votre part

reprehensibly [reprɪˈhensɪblɪ] ADV (to behave, act) de façon répréhensible

represent [reprɪˈzent] VT 1 (depict, portray) (person, object) représenter 2 (act as agent for) (person, company etc), Law, Pol représenter; **the Queen will be represented by …** la Reine sera représentée par … 3 (constitute) représenter, constituer; **this represents a great improvement** cela constitue un grand progrès 4 (symbolize, embody) (nation, love etc) symboliser 5 (typify) représenter; **the government's policy does not r. my opinions** la politique du gouvernement n'est pas représentative de mes opinions 6 (describe) (person, object) présenter (**to be, as** comme); **he represents himself as a model of virtue** il se présente comme ou il se donne pour un modèle de vertu 7 Fml (state, express) faire remarquer, signaler (**to** à); **I will r. your grievances to management** je ferai part de vos griefs à la direction

re-present VT (bill etc) présenter à ou de nouveau; **to r. a cheque** représenter un chèque à l'acceptation

representation [reprɪzenˈteɪʃən] N 1 Pol représentation f, **they have increased their r. to six** le nombre de leurs délégués est passé à six; **they still lacked r. in Parliament** ils n'étaient toujours pas représentés au Parlement 2 (in painting) représentation f 3 (of facts) exposé m des faits; **this is a fair r. of their point of view** cela représente bien leur point de vue 4 representations (complaints) protestations fpl; Fml **to make representations** faire des démarches (**about** concernant; **to** auprès de)

representational [reprɪzenˈteɪʃən(ə)l] ADJ (art) figuratif

representative [reprɪˈzentətɪv] N 1 (of group, company, organization etc) représentant, -ante; (for mail-order firm) délégué, -ée; (sales) r. représentante, -ante, VRP m; **to send a r. to a conference** envoyer un(e) représentant, -ante ou se faire représenter à une conférence; **sole representatives of a firm** représentants ou agents exclusifs d'une maison 2 Am Pol député m
  ADJ 1 (typical) représentatif, typique; **a r. cross-section of the population** un échantillon représentatif de la population 2 Pol (government) représentatif
  ▸▸ **r. sample** échantillon m type

repress [rɪˈpres] VT 1 (desire, passions, uprising) réprimer; (tears) retenir 2 Psy (unconsciously) refouler; (consciously) réprimer

repressed [rɪˈprest] ADJ (person, feelings) refoulé; (laughter) étouffé; **he is very r.** il est très refoulé ou Fam coincé; **she had a very r. adolescence** elle a été refoulée à l'adolescence

repression [rɪˈpreʃən] N 1 (of desire, uprising etc) répression f 2 Psy (unconscious) refoulement m; (conscious) répression f

repressive [rɪˈpresɪv] ADJ (government, law) répressif; (measures) répressif, de répression

reprieve [rɪˈpriːv] Law N (for condemned prisoner) (definitive) commutation f de la peine capitale; (temporary), Fig sursis m; Law **to grant a r.** accorder une commuta-

tion de peine/un sursis; Fig **this is a r. for the government** cela constitue un sursis pour le gouvernement; **we've got a r.** (for project etc) on nous a donné un peu plus de temps
  VT (prisoner) accorder une commutation de la peine capitale à; (temporary) accorder un sursis à; Fig **the shipyard has been reprieved** le chantier naval bénéficie d'un sursis

reprimand [ˈreprɪmɑːnd] N (of child) réprimande f, (of employee, accused person) blâme m; **to be given a r.** (of child) recevoir une réprimande; (of employee etc) recevoir un blâme; **she was let off with a r.** elle s'en est tirée avec une réprimande/un blâme
  VT (child) réprimander (**for** pour); (employee, accused person) blâmer (**for** pour)

reprint[1] [ˈriːprɪnt] N (of book) réimpression f, (of article) nouvelle parution f, nouvelle publication f, **the book is going into its fourth r.** le livre va être réimprimé pour la quatrième fois; **separate r.** (of article from journal) tirage m à part

reprint[2] [riːˈprɪnt] VT (book) réimprimer; (article) faire paraître ou publier à nouveau; **article reprinted from The Times** article reproduit du Times
  VI (of book) être en réimpression

reprisal [rɪˈpraɪz(ə)l] N représailles fpl; **to carry out** or **take reprisals** exercer des représailles, user de représailles (**against** contre); **to threaten reprisals** menacer de représailles; **there have been threats of r.** il y a eu des menaces de représailles; **as a** or **in r. for …** en ou par représailles pour …; **r. attack/raid** attaque f/raid m de représailles

reprise [rɪˈpriːz] N Mus reprise f

repro [ˈriːprəʊ] N Fam (abbr **reproduction, reprography**) repro f
  ▸▸ **r. head** tête f de lecture

reproach [rɪˈprəʊtʃ] N 1 (blame) reproche m; **she heaped reproaches on him** elle l'a accablé de reproches; **a look of r.** un regard plein de reproche; **there was a note of r. in his voice** il y avait une pointe ou une nuance de reproche dans sa voix; **a letter of r.** une lettre de reproches; **beyond** or **above r.** irréprochable 2 (shame) honte f, **to be a r. to …** être la honte de…; **it is a r. to the government that …** c'est une honte pour le gouvernement que …; **things that have brought r. upon him** choses qui ont jeté le discrédit sur lui
  VT reprocher (**sb for** or **with sth** qch à qn); **to r. oneself** s'en vouloir; **I have nothing to r. myself with** or **for** je n'ai rien à me reprocher; **she reproached him for not keeping his promise** elle lui a reproché de n'avoir pas tenu sa promesse

reproachful [rɪˈprəʊtʃfʊl] ADJ (tone) de reproche; (look) plein de reproche

reproachfully [rɪˈprəʊtʃfəlɪ] ADV (to say, look at) d'un ton/d'un air de reproche ou plein de reproche

reprobate [ˈreprəbeɪt] N Fml réprouvé, -ée, Old-fashioned Hum vaurien, -ienne

reprocess [riːˈprəʊses] VT Ind etc (waste etc) retraiter

reprocessing [riːˈprəʊsesɪŋ] N (of waste) retraitement m; **nuclear r.** retraitement des déchets nucléaires
  ▸▸ **r. plant** usine f de retraitement

reproduce [riːprəˈdjuːs] VT (copy) (painting) reproduire; (document) copier
  VI Biol, Bot se reproduire; (of photocopier) reproduire; **this print will r. well** cette estampe se prêtera bien à la reproduction

reproduction [riːprəˈdʌkʃən] N (of document, picture etc), Biol, Bot reproduction f, **thousands of reproductions have been made of this picture** ce tableau a été reproduit à des milliers d'exemplaires

▸▸ **r. furniture** reproduction ou copie f de meubles d'époque; **r. rights** droits mpl de reproduction

reproductive [riːprəˈdʌktɪv] ADJ Biol reproducteur, -trice
  ▸▸ **r. organs** organes mpl reproducteurs; **r. system** appareil m reproducteur

reprogram [riːˈprəʊgræm] VT Comput reprogrammer; **to r. a computer to do sth** reprogrammer un ordinateur pour qu'il fasse qch

reprogrammable [ˈriːprəʊˈgræməbəl] ADJ Comput (key) reprogrammable

reprographic [reprəˈgræfɪk] ADJ reprographique

reprography [reˈprɒgrəfɪ] N reprographie f

reproof[1] [rɪˈpruːf] N esp Fml réprobation f, (in speech, writing) blâme m; **he looked at her with r.** il l'a regardée avec réprobation; **word/look of r.** mot m/regard m de réprobation

reproof[2] [riːˈpruːf] VT (raincoat) réimperméabiliser

reprove [rɪˈpruːv] VT esp Fml (child) réprimander, reprendre; (person) réprimander (**for** pour); (action) condamner

reproving [rɪˈpruːvɪŋ] ADJ esp Fml (look, tone) réprobateur, -trice

reprovingly [rɪˈpruːvɪŋlɪ] ADV (to say, look at) d'un ton/d'un air réprobateur

reptile [ˈreptaɪl] N reptile m
  ▸▸ **r. house** vivarium m

reptilian [repˈtɪlɪən] ADJ (animal) reptilien; Pej (features) de reptile
  N reptile m

republic [rɪˈpʌblɪk] N république f

Republican [rɪˈpʌblɪkən] ADJ, N Pol républicain, -aine

> **Republican**
> Aux États-Unis, un "Republican" est un partisan du Parti républicain. En Irlande, le terme "Republican" désigne une personne qui souhaite le rattachement de l'Irlande du Nord à la république d'Irlande. Au Royaume-Uni et en Australie, le terme désigne les personnes favorables à l'abolition de la monarchie et à l'établissement d'une république.

republican [rɪˈpʌblɪkən] ADJ, N républicain, -aine

republicanism [rɪˈpʌblɪkənɪz(ə)m] N républicanisme m

republication [riːpʌblɪˈkeɪʃən] N réédition f

republish [riːˈpʌblɪʃ] VT rééditer

repudiate [rɪˈpjuːdɪeɪt] VT Fml (spouse, idea, treaty etc) répudier; (friend, opinion) désavouer; (offer) repousser; (debt, accusation) nier; **to r. the authorship of a book** désavouer la paternité d'un livre

repudiation [rɪpjuːdɪˈeɪʃən] N (of spouse, idea etc) répudiation f, (of friend, opinion) désaveu m; (of offer) refus m; (of debt, accusation) reniement m

repugnance [rɪˈpʌgnəns] N (abhorrence) répugnance f (**for** pour); **to have a r. for sth/for doing sth** avoir de la répugnance pour qch/à faire qch

repugnant [rɪˈpʌgnənt] ADJ (deed, person etc) répugnant (**to** à); **to be r. to sb** répugner à qn

repulse [rɪˈpʌls] N (of assistance, offer etc) refus m; Mil échec m; **to meet with a r.** (of person, offer) essuyer un refus
  VT (person, request), Mil repousser; Mil (enemy) repousser, refouler; **to be repulsed by sth** (disgusted) être révolté par qch

repulsion [rɪ'pʌlʃən] N **1** (of person) répulsion f (**for** à l'égard de); **to feel r. for sth/sb** éprouver de la répulsion à l'égard de qch/qn **2** Phys répulsion f

repulsive [rɪ'pʌlsɪv] ADJ **1** (person, sight, smell, habit, idea etc) repoussant, répugnant **2** Phys répulsif

repulsively [rɪ'pʌlsɪvlɪ] ADV (to behave, say etc) de façon répugnante; **r. ugly** d'une laideur repoussante

repulsiveness [rɪ'pʌlsɪvnɪs] N **1** (of person, sight, habit etc) caractère m repoussant ou répugnant **2** Phys force f répulsive

repurchase [riː'pɜːtʃɪs] N rachat m; **sale with option of r.** vente f avec faculté de rachat; St Exch **r. at a profit** rachat gagnant **VT** racheter
▸▸ St Exch, Banking **r. agreement** pension f livrée, opération f de réméré ou de prise en pension; Mktg **r. market** marché m de renouvellement; **r. period** délai m de réachat; **r. rate** taux m de réachat; St Exch, Banking taux de réméré ou de prise en pension; **r. right** droit m de rachat

reputable ['repjʊtəb(ə)l] ADJ (person, job) honorable; (shop, company) de bonne réputation; (source of information) sûr

reputation [repjʊ'teɪʃən, repjʊ-] N (of person, shop etc) réputation f; **to make a r. (for oneself)** se faire une réputation; **to have a good/bad r.** avoir (une) bonne/mauvaise réputation (**as** en tant que); Old-fashioned **to ruin a girl's r.** entacher l'honneur d'une demoiselle; **to have a r. for frankness** avoir la réputation d'être franc; **to know sb by r.** connaître qn de réputation; **his r. had gone before him** sa réputation l'avait précédé; **to live off one's r.** vivre sur sa réputation; Pol Old-fashioned Pej **he has a bit of a r.** il n'a pas très bonne réputation; **to live up to one's r.** (of person) se montrer à la hauteur de sa réputation; (of book, restaurant etc) être à la hauteur de sa réputation

repute [rɪ'pjuːt] N esp Fml réputation f, renom m; **to know sb by r.** connaître qn de réputation; **to be held in high r.** être estimé; **of r.** (doctor etc) réputé, de grand renom; Euph **house of ill r.** maison f de passe
VT (usu passive) **to be reputed wealthy** avoir la réputation d'être riche; **he is reputed to be a good doctor** il a la réputation d'être (un) bon médecin; **she is reputed to be a genius by her colleagues** c'est un véritable génie si l'on en croit ses collègues

reputed [rɪ'pjuːtɪd] ADJ ATTRIB putatif; **his r. father** son père putatif

reputedly [rɪ'pjuːtɪdlɪ] ADV (supposedly) à ce qu'on dit; **she is r. the best heart specialist** elle a la réputation d'être la meilleure cardiologue

request [rɪ'kwest] N demande f, requête f; **r. for money** demande d'argent; **at the r. of sb**, **at sb's r.** à la demande de qn; **samples sent on r.** échantillons sur demande; **to make a r.** faire ou formuler une demande (**for** de); **to grant sb's r.** répondre à la demande de qn; **by (popular) r.** à la demande générale; Radio **to play a r.** passer un disque demandé par un auditeur; Radio **to send in a r.** envoyer une demande
VT to r. sth from or **of sb** demander qch à qn, Fml solliciter qch de qn; **to r. sb to do sth** demander à qn de faire qch; (as a matter of urgency) prier qn de faire qch; **passengers are requested not to smoke** les passagers sont priés de ne pas fumer; **as requested** (on compliments slip etc) conformément à votre demande
▸▸ Radio **r. programme**, **r. show** programme m des auditeurs, émission f de disques à la demande; Br **r. stop** arrêt m facultatif

requiem ['rekwɪəm] N Mus requiem m; Rel (mass) messe f de requiem, messe des morts
▸▸ Rel **r. mass** messe de requiem, messe des morts; **to have a r. mass for sb** faire dire une messe de requiem pour qn

require [rɪ'kwaɪər] VT (necessitate) (work, patience, care etc) demander, exiger; (need) (of person) avoir besoin de; **to r. sth of sb** (demand) exiger qch de qn; **the parts don't r. any gluing** les pièces n'ont pas besoin d'être collées; **to r. sb to do sth** exiger de qn qu'il fasse qch; **you are required under the regulations to ...** en vertu du règlement vous êtes tenu de ...; **he had done all that was required by law** il s'était conformé à toutes les exigences de la loi; **my services are no longer required** on n'a plus besoin de mes services; Euph (I've been dismissed) j'ai été remercié; **this plant requires plenty of water** cette plante demande beaucoup d'eau; **have you everything you r.?** avez-vous tout ce qu'il vous faut ou tout ce dont vous avez besoin?; **I shall do whatever is required** je ferai tout ce qu'il faudra; **the qualifications required for this job** les qualités requises pour ce poste; **if required** s'il le faut, si besoin est; **when required** quand il le faut; **staff required** (notice in shop) on recherche du personnel

required [rɪ'kwaɪəd] ADJ ATTRIB (conditions, qualifications, standard) requis, exigé; **in the r. time** en temps voulu, dans le délai prescrit; **to reach the r. standard** atteindre le niveau requis
▸▸ Sch, Univ **r. reading** lectures fpl à faire

requirement [rɪ'kwaɪəmənt] N (need) exigence f, (condition) condition f (requise); Univ **requirements for the course**, **course requirements** conditions préalables d'admission; **a qualification in Greek is no longer a r.** un diplôme de grec n'est plus nécessaire; **to meet** or **satisfy sb's requirements** (wishes) correspondre aux besoins de qn; (demands) satisfaire les ou aux exigences de qn; **to meet the government's safety requirements** répondre aux normes de sécurités mises en place par le gouvernement

requisite ['rekwɪzɪt] ADJ (money, papers etc) requis (**for** pour), nécessaire (**for** à)
N 1 (for travel etc) article m; **toilet requisites** articles ou nécessaire m de toilette **2** (condition) condition f (requise); **a qualification in Greek is no longer a r.** un diplôme de grec n'est plus nécessaire

requisition [rekwɪ'zɪʃən] N demande f, Mil réquisition f, Com etc **to put in a r. for supplies** passer une commande de fournitures
VT Mil (supplies etc) réquisitionner (**from** de); Com (supplies) commander, faire la demande de; Fig (person) réquisitionner (**to do** pour faire); (person's services) recourir à, avoir recours à
▸▸ **r. number** numéro m de référence

requisitioning [rekwɪ'zɪʃənɪŋ] N
▸▸ Mil **r. officer** officier m chargé des réquisitions

requital [rɪ'kwaɪt(ə)l] N Fml (for service) récompense f, (of love) retour m; **in r. of** or **for her services** en récompense de ses services

requite [rɪ'kwaɪt] VT (service) récompenser; **to r. sb for sth** récompenser qn de qch; **her love had never been requited** son amour n'avait jamais été payé de retour

reread [riː'riːd] VT relire

reredos ['rɪədɒs] N (in church) retable m

rerelease [1] ['riːrɪliːs] N (film, recording) reprise f

rerelease [2] [riːrɪ'liːs] VT (film, recording) ressortir

reroute [riː'ruːt] VT (plane, train etc) dérouter (**through** via)

rerouting [riː'ruːtɪŋ] N (of flight etc) déroutement m; (of goods) déroutage m

rerun [1] ['riːrʌn] N (repeat) (of film) reprise f, Radio, TV rediffusion f, Fig répétition f

rerun [2] [riː'rʌn] VT (film, cassette) repasser; Radio, TV (programme) rediffuser

resale [riː'seɪl] N revente f, **not for r.** ne peut être vendu
▸▸ Mktg **r. price maintenance** prix m de vente imposé; Am **r. shop** vente f de charité; **r. value** valeur f à la revente

resaleable [riː'seɪləbəl] ADJ revendable

reschedule [riː'ʃedjuːl] VT (appointment, flight, departure) modifier l'heure/la date de; Fin (debt) rééchelonner

rescheduling [riː'ʃedjuːlɪŋ] N (of appointment, flight, departure) modification f d'heure/de date; Fin (of debt) rééchelonnement m

rescind [rɪ'sɪnd] VT (law) rescinder, abroger; (contract) annuler, résilier

rescue ['reskjuː] N (saving) sauvetage m; (help, troops etc) secours mpl, (setting free) délivrance f, **to the r.** à la rescousse; **to come/go to sb's r.** venir/aller au secours de qn; (financial) **r. package** plan m de sauvetage (financier)
VT (from death, difficult or embarrassing situation) sauver, secourir; (set free) délivrer (**from** de); **to r. sb from danger** arracher qn à un danger, sauver qn d'un danger; **to r. sb from drowning** sauver qn qui se noie; **to r. a company from bankruptcy** sauver une société de la faillite; **the rescued** (used as pl) les rescapés mpl
▸▸ **r. operation** opération f de sauvetage; **r. party** équipe f de sauveteurs; **r. services** services mpl de secours; **r. worker** sauveteur m

rescuer ['reskjuːər] N (from shipwreck, fire etc) secouriste mf, sauveteur m; (from embarrassing situation) sauveur m; (from captivity) libérateur, -trice

research [rɪ'sɜːtʃ] N recherche(s) f(pl) (**into**, **on** sur); some **r.** de la recherche; **a piece of r.** un travail de recherche; **to do** or **be engaged in r.** faire des recherches (**on**, **into** sur); **when I finish my degree I'd like to do r.** quand j'aurai mon diplôme, j'aimerais faire de la recherche ou devenir chercheur
VT (subject) faire des recherches sur; (book, thesis) faire des recherches pour; **a well-researched book** un livre bien documenté
VI faire des recherches (**on**, **into** sur)
▸▸ **r. assistant** assistant, -ante de recherche; **r. budget** budget m consacré à la recherche; **r. department** service m de recherche; **r. and development** recherche f et développement m, recherche-développement f, pl recherches-développements; **r. fellow** chercheur, -euse (qui a reçu une bourse); **r. finding** découverte f effectuée à l'occasion de recherches; **r. firm** société f d'études; **r. manager** chef m des études; Petr **r. octane number** indice m d'octane recherche; **r. programme** programme m de recherche; **r. scientist** chercheur, -euse; **r. student** étudiant, -ante qui fait de la recherche (après la licence); **r. team** équipe f de recherche; **r. technique** technique f de recherche; **r. tool** outil m de recherche; **r. work** recherches, travaux mpl de recherche; **r. worker** (scientific) chercheur, -euse; Am (literary) documentaliste mf

researcher [rɪ'sɜːtʃər] N chercheur, -euse

reseat [riː'siːt] VT **1 to r. the guests** (put in different positions) refaire les tables; **when they were all reseated** (had sat down again) lorsqu'ils se sont rassis **2** (pair of trousers, chair) remettre un fond à **3** Tech (valve) roder

resection [riː'sekʃən] N Surg résection f

reselection [riːsɪ'lekʃən] N Pol (of candi-

date) = fait d'être à nouveau choisi par son parti en tant que candidat pour des élections

resell [riːˈsel] **vt** (*pt, pp* **resold** [riːˈsəʊld]) revendre

reseller [riːˈselər] **n** *Com* revendeur, -euse

resemblance [rɪˈzembləns] **n** ressemblance *f* (**to** à, avec; **between** entre); **to bear a r. to sb/sth** ressembler à qn/qch; **there is a strong family r.** il y a un air de famille très prononcé; **his testimony bears no r. to the facts** il n'y a aucune ressemblance entre son témoignage et les faits

resemble [rɪˈzemb(ə)l] **vt** ressembler à; **to r. one another** se ressembler

resend [riːˈsend] **vt** (*e-mail, text message*) renvoyer, envoyer de nouveau

resent [rɪˈzent] **vt 1** (*object to*) ne pas aimer du tout; **I r. your remarks** je n'aime pas du tout vos remarques; **I r. that!** je n'aime pas ça du tout! **2** (*feel bitter about*) éprouver de l'amertume à l'égard de; **you r. my being here** ma présence vous déplaît; **your children r. me** tes enfants m'en veulent; **he resents having to take orders from a woman** il accepte mal d'avoir une femme comme supérieur

Note that the French verb **ressentir** is a false friend. It means **to feel, to experience**.

resentful [rɪˈzentfʊl] **adj** (*remark, look*) plein de ressentiment *ou* d'amertume, amer; **to be** *or* **feel r.** éprouver de l'amertume *ou* du ressentiment (**about** à propos de, concernant)

resentfully [rɪˈzentfəlɪ] **adv** (*to behave, act*) avec ressentiment *ou* amertume; (*to speak*) d'un ton plein de ressentiment *ou* d'amertume, d'un ton rancunier; (*to look at*) avec ressentiment *ou* amertume, d'un air rancunier

resentment [rɪˈzentmənt] **n** amertume *f*, ressentiment *m* (**at** à; **over** concernant; **of** à l'égard de); **to feel r. against sb** avoir de la rancune contre qn; **there is a lot of r. about her appointment** sa nomination suscite beaucoup d'amertume

reservation [rezəˈveɪʃən] **n 1** (*booking*) (*in restaurant etc*) réservation *f*; **to make a r.** réserver; **to make a r. for nine o'clock** (*in restaurant*) réserver une table pour neuf heures; **do you have a r.?** (*in restaurant, hotel*) est-ce que vous avez réservé?; (*in train*) est-ce que vous avez une réservation?; **for reservations, call …** pour réserver appeler …; **reservations book** agenda *m ou* livre *m* de réservation; **reservations system** système *m* de réservation

2 (*doubt*) (*about idea, plan etc*) réserve *f*; **without r.** sans réserve; **not without** *or* **with some r.** non sans réserves; **with this r.** à cette restriction près; **to have reservations about sth** avoir des doutes à propos de qch; **to have no reservations in doing sth** n'avoir aucune hésitation à faire qch

3 *Am* (*land*) terrain *m* réservé; **(Indian) r.** réserve *f* indienne; *Br Aut* **central r.** terre-plein *m* central, *pl* terres-pleins centraux

► ► **r. agent** agent *m* de réservation; *Am* **r. clerk** préposé, -ée aux réservations; **r. desk** bureau *m* des réservations; **r. sheet** feuille *f* de réservation, bordereau *m* de réservations; **r. ticket** coupon *m* de réservation

reserve [rɪˈzɜːv] **vt 1** (*book*) (*table*), *Rail* (*seat*) réserver; *Theat etc* (*seat*) louer; **reserved seat** (*on train*) place *f* réservée; (*at theatre, concert etc*) place louée

2 (*keep*) réserver, mettre en réserve; **to r. a seat for sb** réserver *ou* retenir une place à qn; **to r. the right to do sth** se réserver le

droit de faire qch; **to r. one's strength** ménager ses forces; **all rights reserved** tous droits de reproduction réservés

3 (*withhold*) **to r. judgement on sth/sb** réserver son jugement sur qch/qn

n 1 (*stock*) (*of money etc*) réserve *f*; **to have great reserves of energy** avoir beaucoup d'énergie en réserve; *Pol* **he still has a r. of support in the country** il bénéficie encore d'un certain soutien parmi les électeurs; **to draw on one's reserves** (*of courage, money, skill*) puiser dans ses réserves; *Petr* **known reserves** réserves prouvées; **to keep sth in r.** garder qch en réserve (**for** pour); **in r.** en réserve; **r. power/energy** réserve de puissance/énergie

2 *Mil etc* **the reserves** (*soldiers*) la réserve, les réservistes *mpl*; (*unit*) la réserve

3 *Sport* (*substitute*) remplaçant, -ante; **to play for the reserves** jouer dans l'équipe de réserve

4 (*for birds, game*) réserve *f*; **nature r.** réserve naturelle; *Can* **Indian r.** réserve indienne

5 (*limitation*) **without r.** sans réserve

6 *Br* (*at auction*) (*price*) prix *m* minimum; **to put a r. on sth** fixer un prix minimum à qch; **the item did not reach its r.** l'article n'a pas atteint le prix minimum fixé

7 (*reticence*) réserve *f*; **with typical English r.** avec une réserve toute britannique

► ► *Fin* **r. account** compte *m* de réserve; *Fin* **r. capital** capital *m* de réserve; *Fin* **r. currency** monnaie *f* de réserve; *Acct* **r. funds** fonds *mpl* de réserve; *Mil* **r. officer** officier *m* de réserve; *Br* **r. price** (*at auction*) prix minimum; *Fin* **r. ratio** taux *m* de mise en réserve; *Aut* **r. tank** réservoir *m* de secours

reserved [rɪˈzɜːvd] **adj** (*shy*) réservé; **to be r. with sb** être réservé *ou* se tenir sur la réserve avec qn

reservedly [rɪˈzɜːvɪdlɪ] **adv** avec réserve, de manière réservée

reservist [rɪˈzɜːvɪst] **n** *Mil etc* réserviste *m*

reservoir [ˈrezəvwɑːr] **n** (*for water*) réservoir *m*, bassin *m* de retenue; (*for oil*) réservoir; *Fig* **reservoirs of strength/courage** réserve *f* d'énergie/de courage

reset [riːˈset] (*pt, pp* **reset**; *prp* **resetting**) **vt 1** (*watch*) remettre à l'heure; (*stopwatch, counter*) remettre à zéro; (*computer*) réinitialiser; **to r. an alarm clock** régler la sonnerie d'un réveil; *Comput* **r. button** *or* **switch** bouton *m* de remise à zéro, bouton de réinitialisation **2** (*precious stone etc*) remonter; *Surg* (*fracture*) réduire; (*dislocation*) remettre, remboîter **3** *Typ* (*text*) recomposer

resettle [riːˈset(ə)l] **vt** (*refugees*) réinstaller; (*area*) repeupler

vi se réinstaller (**in** dans)

resettlement [riːˈset(ə)lmənt] **n** (*of refugees*) implantation *f*; (*of area*) repeuplement *m*

reshape [riːˈʃeɪp] **vt** (*industry etc*) réorganiser

reshuffle [riːˈʃʌf(ə)l] **n** (*of Cabinet, jobs etc*) remaniement *m*

vt 1 (*staff etc*) remanier **2** (*cards*) battre de nouveau

reside [rɪˈzaɪd] **vi 1** *Fml* (*of person*) résider (**at, in** à, dans) **2** *Fig* (*of power, quality*) résider (**in** dans)

residence [ˈrezɪdəns] **n 1** (*stay*) séjour *m*; **to take up r. in a country** se fixer *ou* s'établir dans un pays; **whenever the Queen is in r.** quand la reine est là; **in r.** (*doctor, poet*) sur place; **place of r.** lieu *m* de résidence; **six months' r. in the country is required** il faut avoir résidé dans le pays pendant six mois **2** *Fml* (*home*) demeure *f*, maison *f*, desirable **r. for sale** belle propriété à vendre; **official r.** résidence *f* officielle **3** *Br Univ* (**hall of) r.** ré-

sidence *f* universitaire; **to stay in residences** vivre en résidence universitaire

► ► *Am Univ* **r. hall** résidence (universitaire); **r. permit** ≃ permis *m* de séjour; *Am* **r. tax** taxe *f* de séjour

residency [ˈrezɪdənsɪ] **n 1** *Am Med* internat *m*; **to do one's r.** faire son internat **2** (*house*) (*of governor etc*) résidence *f* officielle **3** *Mus, Theat* (*engagement*) contrat *m* (à long terme)

resident [ˈrezɪdənt] **adj** résident; (*population*) fixe; *Journ* (*correspondent*) permanent; **to be r. in London** résider à Londres

n 1 (*of country, street*) habitant, -ante; (*of hotel*) pensionnaire *mf*; (*foreigner*) résident, -ente; **to be a permanent r.** être résident permanent (**of** de); **residents' association** association *f* de riverains; **residents' parking bay** *or* **place** emplacement *m* réservé aux riverains **2** *Am Med* interne *mf*

► ► **r. manager** directeur, -trice qui habite sur place; *Comput* **r. program** programme *m* résident; **r. teacher** professeur *m* à demeure, professeur résident

residential [rezɪˈdenʃəl] **adj 1** (*area, neighbourhood etc*) résidentiel; **the building is reverting to r. use** l'édifice va être à nouveau utilisé comme habitation **2** (*course*) à temps complet; **r. seminar** séminaire *m* résidentiel **3** (*staff*) à demeure

► ► **r. care** = mode *m* d'hébergement supervisé pour handicapés, délinquants etc

residual [rɪˈzɪdjʊəl] **adj 1** (*unrest, resentment etc*) qui subsiste **2** *Chem* résiduel

n 1 *Cin, TV* **residuals** (*repeat fees*) droits *mpl* de seconde diffusion **2** *Chem* résidu *m*

► ► *Fin* **r. income** revenu *m* résiduel

residuary [rɪˈzɪdjʊərɪ] **adj**

► ► *Law* **r. legatee** légataire *mf* universel(elle)

residue [ˈrezɪdjuː] **n 1** (*of army, fortune etc*) reste(s) *m(pl)*; *Law* (*of estate*) reliquat *m* **2** *Chem, Ind etc* résidu *m*

residuum, *pl* **residua** [rɪˈzɪdjʊəm, -ə] **n** *Chem* résidu *m*

resign [rɪˈzaɪn] **vi** démissionner, donner sa démission (**from** de); **he has resigned as Prime Minister** il a démissionné de son poste de Premier ministre; *Parl* **r.!, r.!** démission! démission!

vt (*position*) résigner; **to r. one's job** démissionner de son poste; **to r. sth to sb** abandonner *ou* céder qch à qn; **to r. oneself to sth/to doing sth** se résigner à qch/à faire qch

resignation [rezɪgˈneɪʃən] **n 1** (*from job*) démission *f*; **to give (in)** *or* **send in** *or* *Fml* **tender one's r.** donner sa démission **2** (*attitude*) résignation *f*; **to accept one's fate with r.** accepter son sort avec résignation

Note that the French word **résignation** never means **giving up one's job**.

resigned [rɪˈzaɪnd] **adj** résigné; **to be r. to sth** être résigné à qch; **to be r. to one's fate** s'être résigné

resignedly [rɪˈzaɪnɪdlɪ] **adv** (*to say, look at*) avec résignation, d'un ton/d'un air résigné

resilience [rɪˈzɪlɪəns] **n** (*of material, metal etc*) élasticité *f*; *Fig* (*of person*) (*physical*) résistance *f*; (*mental*) ressort *m*; (*of economy etc*) faculté *f* de reprise; **to have r.** (*of person*) avoir du ressort

resilient [rɪˈzɪlɪənt] **adj** (*material, metal*) élastique; *Fig* **to be r.** (*of person*) (*physically*) être résistant; (*mentally*) avoir du ressort; **children are more r. than adults** les enfants se remettent plus vite que les adultes; **the economy is proving remarkably r.** l'économie fait preuve d'une remarquable capacité de reprise

resin ['rezɪn] N résine f; **to tap trees for r.** gemmer des arbres

resinated ['rezɪneɪtɪd] ADJ (wine) résiné

resinous ['rezɪnəs] ADJ résineux

resist [rɪ'zɪst] VT (person, attack, corrosion, temptation etc) résister à; (influence, attempt) s'opposer à, résister à; (change) s'opposer à, ne pas aimer; (suggestion) repousser; Law **to r. arrest** opposer une résistance aux forces de l'ordre lors d'une arrestation; **I couldn't r. telling him** je n'ai pas pu m'empêcher ou me retenir de le lui dire; **I can't r. chocolates** je ne peux pas résister devant des chocolats
VI résister

resistance [rɪ'zɪstəns] N 1 (to attack, corrosion, temptation, influence, change etc) résistance f (**to** à); **to put up (a)** or **offer r.** résister, offrir une résistance (**to** à); **to make** or **offer no r.** n'offrir ou n'opposer aucune résistance; **to offer no r. to a suggestion** ne pas s'opposer à une proposition; **to meet with no r.** ne rencontrer aucune résistance; **to have no r. left** (to illness etc) ne plus avoir de résistance; Fig **to take the line of least r.** aller au plus facile, suivre la loi du moindre effort; **the (French) R.** la Résistance 2 Elec, Phys etc résistance f
▸ ▸ Elec, Phys **r. coupling** couplage m par résistance; **r. fighter** résistant, -ante; **r. movement** résistance f; Elec, Phys **r. thermometer** thermomètre m à résistance; Elec, Phys **r. welding** soudure f électrique par résistance

resistant [rɪ'zɪstənt] ADJ résistant (**to** à); **to be r. to change** (of person) s'opposer à ou ne pas aimer les changements; Med **r. to** rebelle à

-resistant [rɪ'zɪstənt] SUFF **corrosion/heat-r.** résistant à la corrosion/la chaleur

resistor [rɪ'zɪstər] N Elec résistance f

resit[1] ['riːsɪt] N Br Univ Fam (exam) **the resits are scheduled for August** la session de rattrapage est prévue pour le mois d'août; **how many resits do you have?** combien d'examens est-ce que tu as à repasser?; **the French r. is on Monday** la deuxième session de l'examen de français est lundi

resit[2] [riː'sɪt] VT Br (pt, pp **resat** [riː'sæt]; prp **resitting**) (exam, driving test) repasser

resizable [riː'saɪzəb(ə)l] ADJ Comput (window) redimensionnable

resize [riː'saɪz] VT Comput (window) redimensionner
▸ ▸ **r. box** case f de redimensionnement

resole [riː'səʊl] VT ressemeler

resolute ['rezəluːt] ADJ (person) résolu, déterminé; (answer, voice) résolu, ferme; (refusal, opposition) ferme

resolutely ['rezəluːtlɪ] ADV (to say) résolument; (to refuse, oppose sth) fermement

resoluteness ['rezəluːtnɪs] N résolution f, fermeté f

resolution [rezə'luːʃən] N 1 (decision) (of individual) résolution f; **to make a r. to do sth** prendre la résolution de faire qch; **have you made any New Year resolutions?** est-ce que tu as pris de bonnes résolutions pour le Nouvel An?; **to keep/break a New Year r.** tenir/ne pas tenir une résolution prise à l'occasion du Nouvel An
2 (decision) (of committee, meeting etc) résolution f; **to put a r. to the meeting** soumettre ou proposer une résolution à l'assemblée; **to pass** or **carry** or **adopt a r.** adopter une résolution; **the committee passed a r. that he should be expelled** or **to expel him** le comité a adopté la résolution de l'expulser; **the r. was rejected** la résolution a été refusée
3 (firmness) résolution f, fermeté f; **her r. was strengthened by their refusal** sa réso-

lution s'est trouvée renforcée par leur refus; **there was a note of r. in his voice** il parla d'un ton résolu
4 (solving) (of difficulty, problem etc) résolution f
5 Med (of tumour) résolution f
6 TV, Comput (of screen, image etc) résolution f; **high r. screen** écran m à haute résolution ou définition

resolve [rɪ'zɒlv] VT 1 (decide) **to r. to do sth** (of individual) se décider ou se résoudre à faire qch, décider ou résoudre de faire qch; (of committee) adopter la résolution de faire qch, décider ou résoudre de faire qch; **the committee has resolved that ...** le comité a décidé que ... 2 (solve) (problem, difficulty) résoudre; (crisis, situation) apporter une solution à 3 Chem (substance) résoudre en ses éléments; **to r. itself** (of substance) se résoudre
VI 1 (of person) **to r. (up)on/against doing** décider ou résoudre de faire/ne pas faire 2 Chem (of chemical etc) se résoudre (**into** en) 3 Med (of tumour) se résoudre, se résorber
N 1 (decision) résolution f; **to make a firm r. to do sth** prendre la résolution de faire qch 2 = **resolution 3**

resolved [rɪ'zɒlvd] ADJ résolu; **to be r. to do sth** être résolu ou décidé à faire qch

resolving [rɪ'zɒlvɪŋ] N
▸ ▸ Opt **r. power** (of lens) pouvoir m de résolution

resonance ['rez(ə)nəns] N (of instrument), Electron résonance f; (of voice) sonorité f
▸ ▸ Aut **r. chamber** (in silencer) pot m de résonance; Electron **r. curve** courbe f de résonance

resonant ['rezənənt] ADJ (sound), Electron résonnant; (voice, room) qui résonne, sonore; **to be r. with** résonner de; **his voice was r. with emotion** sa voix vibrait d'émotion
▸ ▸ Mus, Phys **r. frequency** fréquence f de résonance

resonate ['rezəneɪt] VI retentir (**with** de); **his voice resonated with emotion** sa voix vibrait d'émotion

resonator ['rezəneɪtər] N Electron etc résonateur m

resort [rɪ'zɔːt] N 1 (recourse) recours m (**to** à); (person resorted to) recours, ressource f; **to have r. to sth** avoir recours à qch; **without r. to** sans avoir recours à, sans recourir à; **in the** or **as a last r.** en dernier recours ou ressort, en désespoir de cause; **she would be my last r.** je ne m'adresserais à elle qu'en dernier recours 2 (holiday) **r.** lieu m de vacances; **health r.** station f climatique ou thermale; **seaside r.** station balnéaire; **ski r.** station de ski 3 (haunt) lieu m de rendez-vous (**of** pour), Pej repaire m (**of** de)
VI **to r.** avoir recours à, recourir à; **to r. to doing sth** en venir à faire qch; **to r. to drink** se rabattre sur la boisson; **to r. to sb (for help)** avoir recours ou faire appel ou recourir à qn; **to r. to force** avoir recours à la force
▸ ▸ **r. hotel** hôtel m de tourisme; **r. tax** taxe f sur l'hôtellerie

resound [rɪ'zaʊnd] VI (of place) résonner, retentir (**with** de); (of voice) résonner; Fig (of event) avoir du retentissement

resounding [rɪ'zaʊndɪŋ] ADJ (applause, defeat, failure) retentissant; (laugh) sonore; (success, victory) éclatant, retentissant; **her first novel was a r. success/failure** son premier roman a connu un succès/échec retentissant

resoundingly [rɪ'zaʊndɪŋlɪ] ADV d'une manière retentissante; **to be r. successful** (of author, play etc) connaître un succès retentissant

resource [rɪ'sɔːs, -'zɔːs] N 1 (wealth) resources ressources fpl; **human resources** ressources humaines 2 (expedient, recourse) ressource f; **inner resources** ressource; **to be at the end of one's resources** être au bout de ses ou à bout de ressources; **he was left to his own resources** il a dû se débrouiller tout seul 3 (ingenuity) ressource f; **person of great r.** personne f (pleine) de ressource(s)
VT (project) financer, encadrer financièrement, humainement et matériellement
▸ ▸ **r. allocation** allocation f des ressources; **r. management** gestion f des ressources; **r. market** marché m de ressources; **r. person** (in career centre) conseiller, -ère d'orientation; (in library) bibliothécaire mf (chargé d'orienter les usagers et d'entreprendre certaines recherches bibliographiques)

resource-based ADJ (tourist attraction) = faisant usage de ressources naturelles ou monument déjà sur place

resourceful [rɪ'sɔːsfʊl, -'zɔːs-] ADJ (person) habile, ingénieux, (plein) de ressources, Fam débrouillard; (solution etc) habile, ingénieux; **that was very r. of you** tu as fait preuve de beaucoup de débrouillardise; **he's a r. sort of person** il a de la ressource

resourcefully [rɪ'sɔːsfəlɪ, -'zɔːs-] ADV habilement, ingénieusement

resourcefulness [rɪ'sɔːsfʊlnɪs, -'zɔːs-] N (of person, solution) ingéniosité f, habileté f, Fam débrouillardise f

resourcing [rɪ'sɔːsɪŋ, -'zɔːs-] N financement m
▸ ▸ **r. officer** agent m de financement

respect [rɪ'spekt] N 1 (admiration) respect m (**for** pour); **to earn** or **gain** or **win sb's r.** gagner le respect de qn; **to have great r. for sb, to hold sb in great r.** avoir beaucoup de respect pour qn; **he knows how to command r.** il sait se faire respecter; **her achievements command r.** ses réussites suscitent le respect
2 (consideration) respect m (**for** pour); **to have r. for sb** avoir du respect pour qn; **she has little r. for the truth/other people's property** elle fait peu de cas de la vérité/du bien d'autrui, elle a peu de respect pour la vérité/le bien d'autrui; **to do sth as a mark of r.** faire qch par respect; **he took his hat off as a mark of r.** il a ôté son chapeau en signe de respect; **there was a new note of r. in his voice** il y avait maintenant une note de respect dans sa voix; **he shows little r. for his parents** il ne se montre guère respectueux avec ou envers ses parents; **show your father a little more r.!** sois un peu plus respectueux avec ou envers ton père!; **out of r. for ...** par respect ou égard ou considération pour ...; **out of r. for her feelings** pour ménager sa sensibilité; **treat those plates with r.** (they are fragile) fais attention à ces assiettes; **treat matches with r.** (they are dangerous) utilisez les allumettes avec prudence; **treat mountains with r.** (be careful) soyez prudent en montagne; **with all due r. (to you)** sauf votre respect, sauf le respect que je vous dois, sans vouloir vous vexer ou offenser; **with the greatest r. to my colleague, I feel that ...** sans vouloir critiquer ma collègue, je pense que ...; **with the greatest r., sir, I cannot agree** sans vouloir vous offenser, Monsieur, je ne suis pas d'accord
3 **respects** respects mpl, hommages mpl; **(give** or **send) my respects to your mother** (présentez ou envoyez) mes hommages à votre mère; **to pay one's respects to sb** présenter ses respects ou ses hommages à qn; **to pay one's last respects** (at funeral) rendre les derniers hommages (**to** à)
4 (aspect) égard m; **in some** or **certain respects** à certains égards; **in at least two res-**

pects à au moins deux égards; **in all respects** or **every r.** à tous (les) égards, sous tous les rapports; **in this r.** à cet égard; **in other respects** à d'autres égards; **with r. to, in r. of** en ce qui concerne

VT 1 *(admire)* respecter, avoir du respect pour; **he was greatly respected** il était très respecté (**for** pour); **to be universally respected** être respecté de tous **2** *(show consideration for) (person's wish, opinion etc)* respecter; **I r. myself too much to do that** je me respecte trop pour faire cela **3** *(comply with) (the law, speed limit etc)* respecter

respectability [rɪspektəˈbɪlɪtɪ] **N** respectabilité *f*

respectable [rɪˈspektəb(ə)l] **ADJ 1** *(honourable, decent) (family, person etc)* respectable, digne de respect; *(upbringing etc)* comme il faut; *(behaviour, clothes)* convenable, comme il faut; **he always looked so r.** il avait toujours l'air tellement comme il faut; **to be r.** *(dressed)* être présentable; **I'm not r., you answer the door** va ouvrir, je ne suis pas présentable **2** *(fairly good or large etc)* respectable; *(salary, mark, result)* honorable; **a r. number of people** un bon nombre de gens; **a r. sum** une somme respectable *ou* rondelette

respectably [rɪˈspektəblɪ] **ADV 1** de manière respectable; *(to behave, dress)* convenablement; *(brought up)* comme il faut; **to live r.** mener une existence respectable **2** *(rather well)* plutôt bien

respecter [rɪˈspektər] **N to be no r. of the law** ne pas respecter la loi; **to be no r. of persons** *(of death, taxes etc)* ne faire acception de personne; *(of person)* ne s'en laisser imposer par personne

respectful [rɪˈspektfʊl] **ADJ** respectueux (**to, towards** envers; **of** de); **to stand at a r. distance** se tenir à distance respectueuse

respectfully [rɪˈspektfəlɪ] **ADV** *(to listen, say etc)* respectueusement, avec respect; *Old-fashioned* **(I remain) yours r.** *(at end of letter)* veuillez agréer l'expression de mes sentiments respectueux

respectfulness [rɪˈspektfəlnɪs] **N** *(of person)* respect *m*; **the r. of his answer** le respect avec lequel il a répondu

respecting [rɪˈspektɪŋ] **PREP** *Fml* concernant, relatif à; **r. your article** à propos de votre article

respective [rɪˈspektɪv] **ADJ** respectif

respectively [rɪˈspektɪvlɪ] **ADV** respectivement

respiration [respɪˈreɪʃən] **N** respiration *f*

respirator [ˈrespɪreɪtər] **N** *Med* respirateur *m*; *(gas mask)* masque *m* à gaz; **to be on a r.** être sous respirateur

respiratory [rɪˈspɪrɪt(ə)rɪ] **ADJ** *(disease, organ)* respiratoire
▸▸ **r. failure** insuffisance *f* respiratoire; **r. system** système *m* respiratoire

respire [rɪˈspaɪər] **VT & VI** respirer

respite [ˈrespaɪt] **N 1** *(from worry etc)* répit *m*; **to work without r.** travailler sans relâche; **the weekend was a welcome r.** le weekend a constitué un répit bienvenu **2** *(from obligation)* sursis *m*, délai *m*; **to get/grant a r.** obtenir/accorder un délai

resplendence [rɪˈsplendəns] **N** *Fml* splendeur *f*, resplendissement *m*

resplendent [rɪˈsplendənt] **ADJ** *Fml* resplendissant, éblouissant

resplendently [rɪˈsplendəntlɪ] **ADV** de manière resplendissante *ou* éblouissante; *(decorated, dressed)* somptueusement

respond [rɪˈspɒnd] **VI 1** *(answer)* répondre (**to** à); *Rel* réciter *ou* chanter les répons; **he responded with a smile** il a répondu par un

sourire **2** *(react) (to affection, kindness etc)* répondre, être sensible (**to** à); *(to order)* répondre, réagir (**to** à); **to fail to r. to sb's advances** ne pas répondre aux avances de qn; **to r. generously to an appeal** répondre généreusement à un appel; *Fig* **r. to pressure** céder aux pressions; *Med* **to r. to treatment** *(of patient)* réagir positivement au traitement; *Med* **she is not responding** elle ne réagit pas; **the tumour/illness is not responding to treatment** le traitement n'a pas d'effet *ou* n'agit pas sur la tumeur/la maladie; *Aviat, Aut* **to r. well** bien répondre; **children r. well to responsibility** les enfants aiment bien qu'on leur donne des responsabilités; *Aut, Aviat* **to r. to the controls** obéir aux commandes

respondent [rɪˈspɒndənt] **N 1** *Law (esp in divorce case)* défendeur, -eresse; *(in appeal case)* intimé, -ée **2** *(to questionnaire)* sondé, -ée; *(in opinion poll)* personne *f* interrogée *ou* sondée, répondant, -ante; **the respondents** les sondés

response [rɪˈspɒns] **N 1** *(answer)* réponse *f*, *Rel* répons *m*; **he made no r.** il n'a pas répondu, il n'a pas donné de réponse; *Rel* **to make the responses at Mass** répondre la messe; **what was her r.?** *(answer)* quelle a été sa réponse?; **he smiled in r.** il a souri en guise de réponse; **in r. to your question** en réponse à votre question, pour répondre à votre question; **in r. to your letter** suite à votre lettre **2** *(reaction)* *Med* réaction *f*, *Physiol* réponse *f*, réaction; **what was the Government's r.?** comment le gouvernement a-t-il réagi?; **the appeal met with a generous r.** les gens ont répondu généreusement à l'appel; **the decision was taken in r. to …** la décision a été prise en réaction à …; *Mil* **flexible r.** réponse graduée
▸▸ *Mktg* **r. rate** *(to questionnaire)* taux *m* de réponse; **r. time** *Comput* temps *m* de réponse; *Med, Psy* temps de réaction

responsibility [rɪspɒnsɪˈbɪlɪtɪ] **N 1** *(authority)* responsabilité *f*; **to have r. for sth** avoir la responsabilité de qch; **a position of r.** un poste de *ou* à responsabilité; **to have a lot of r. at an early age** avoir beaucoup de responsabilités très jeune; **to do sth on one's own r.** prendre la responsabilité de faire qch **2** *(blame)* responsabilité *f*; **to take** *or* **accept full r. for sth** prendre *ou* accepter la responsabilité de qch; **we accept no r. for lost or stolen items** *(notice in restaurant etc)* nous déclinons toute responsabilité pour les objets perdus ou volés; **to refuse to accept any r. for the accident** décliner toute responsabilité pour *ou* quant à l'accident; **no-one has yet claimed r. for the attack** personne n'a encore revendiqué l'attaque; **the r. is mine** c'est moi qui suis responsable **3** *(obligation)* responsabilité *f*; **sense of r.** sens *m* des responsabilités; **you have a r. to your family** vous avez la responsabilité de votre famille **4** *(task, duty)* responsabilité *f*; **it's my r.** c'est ma responsabilité (**to do** de faire); **answering the phone is your r., not mine** c'est à toi de répondre au téléphone, pas à moi; **his new responsibilities give him no time for leisure** ses nouvelles fonctions *ou* responsabilités ne lui laissent aucune place pour ses loisirs; **bringing up children is quite a r.** élever des enfants est une grande responsabilité
▸▸ *Acct* **r. accounting** comptabilité *f* par centres de responsabilité

responsible [rɪˈspɒnsɪb(ə)l] **ADJ 1** *(trustworthy) (attitude, person)* responsable; **r. job** poste *m* à responsabilités; **no r. parent would have left the children alone** un parent responsable n'aurait pas laissé les en-

fants tout seuls; **try to be a bit more r. in future** essaye d'être un peu plus responsable à l'avenir **2** *(for accident, mistake etc)* responsable (**for** de); **to hold sb r.** tenir qn (pour) responsable (**for** de); *Law* **to be (legally) r. for sb's actions** être solidaire des actes de qn; **he is not r. for his actions** il n'est pas responsable de ses actes **3** *(accountable)* responsable (**for** de; **to sb** devant qn); **to be r. for sb/sth** avoir la responsabilité de qn/qch; **to make sb r. for sth** donner à qn la responsabilité de qch; **I will be r. for his safety** je me porte garant de sa sécurité; **you and she will be jointly r. for the project** vous et elle partagerez la responsabilité du projet; **she had been r. for the party's successful election campaign** c'est grâce à elle que la campagne électorale fut un succès
▸▸ **r. tourism** tourisme *m* vert

responsibly [rɪˈspɒnsɪblɪ] **ADV** *(to behave, act)* de façon responsable

responsive [rɪˈspɒnsɪv] **ADJ** *(reacting)* qui réagit; *(alert)* éveillé; *Med (illness, rash etc)* qui réagit bien (**to** à); *Aut (brakes, steering etc)* qui répond bien; *(engine)* nerveux; **r. to** *(to kindness)* sensible à; *(to idea, suggestion)* réceptif à; **he is very r. to my needs** il est très attentif à mes besoins; **you're not being very r.** *(not reacting verbally)* tu ne dis rien; *(not reacting physically)* il n'y a pas de réaction de ta part, tu ne réagis pas; **people become more r. if …** les gens sont plus réceptifs si …; **they're not very r. tonight** *(of audience)* ils ne réagissent pas beaucoup *ou* ils sont plutôt amorphes ce soir; **most allergies are r. to this treatment** on peut guérir la plupart des allergies avec ce traitement

responsiveness [rɪˈspɒnsɪvnɪs] **N** *(of person) (to kindness)* sensibilité *f* (**to** à); *(to idea etc)* réceptivité *f* (**to** à); **we were pleased by their r. to the plan** la façon dont ils ont réagi au projet nous a plu

respray[1] [ˈriːspreɪ] **N the car's had a r.** la voiture a été repeinte

respray[2] [riːˈspreɪ] **VT** repeindre au pistolet

REST[1] [rest]

N	repos **1** ▪ paix **1** ▪ support **2**
	▪ silence **3**	
VI	(se) reposer **1, 2**	
VT	(se) reposer **1, 2** ▪ appuyer **2**
	▪ fonder **2, 3**	

N 1 *(repose)* repos *m*; **to have** *or* **take a r.** se reposer (**from** de); **to have a good night's r.** passer une bonne nuit; **I need a r.** j'ai besoin de me reposer, j'ai besoin de repos; **my arms need a r.** j'ai besoin de me reposer les bras; **we've earned a r.** nous avons mérité un peu de repos; **to stop for a r.** faire une pause; **to put** *or* **set sb's mind at r.** dissiper les craintes *ou* inquiétudes de qn, rassurer qn; **to give sb a r. from sth** permettre à qn de se reposer de qch; *Fam* **give it a r., will you!** *(stop doing sth, talking etc)* arrête cinq minutes, tu veux bien!; *Fam* **give that music a r.!** arrête un peu cette musique!; **give studying a r. for a day or two** arrête de travailler pendant un ou deux jours; **she's giving tennis a r. this year** elle a arrêté le tennis cette année; **those children give her no r.** ces enfants ne lui laissent aucun repos; **his conscience gave him no r.** sa conscience ne lui laissait pas de répit; **you must get some more r.** vous devez vous reposer davantage; **a day of r., a day's r.** un jour de repos; **the day of r.** le jour dominical; **to come to r.** *(of ball, vehicle etc)* s'arrêter, s'immobiliser; *(of bird, eyes)* se poser (**on** sur); *Am Mil* **r. and recreation** permission *f*; *Am Mil* **two days' r. and recreation** deux jours de permission; *Euph* to be at r. *(be dead)* reposer en paix; *Euph* to be laid to r. *(buried)* être enterré; *Euph* to be or lie at r. *(dead)* reposer en paix; *Euph* to lay sb to r. porter qn en terre, enterrer qn; *Fig* to lay *or* put a plan to r. *(not carry any further)* renoncer *ou* abandonner un projet; **to lay *or* put allegations/doubts/suspicions to r.** dissiper des allégations/des doutes/des suspicions; **perhaps we could lay the matter to r.** *(not discuss any further)* peut-être qu'on pourrait arrêter de parler de cette affaire une bonne fois pour toutes; **the matter should be laid to r. as quickly as possible** *(resolved)* cette affaire doit être résolue au plus vite

2 *(support)* support *m*; *(for billiard cue)* chevalet *m*; *Tel (for receiver)* étrier *m*

3 *Mus (silence)* silence *m*

VI 1 *(relax)* se reposer, prendre du repos; **you need to r. (up)** il vous faut le repos complet; **to r. from one's work** se reposer de son travail; **to r. easy** se détendre; **to be resting** *(of actor)* = se trouver sans engagement; **she is resting comfortably** *(after operation etc)* son état est satisfaisant; **I won't r. until …** je n'aurai de cesse que … + *subj*; **to r. on** *(of roof etc)* reposer sur; **he was resting on his shovel** il s'appuyait sur sa pelle; **his head was resting on her shoulder** il avait la tête appuyée contre son épaule; *Fig* **to r. on one's oars** se reposer, *Fam* souffler; *Fig* **to r. on one's laurels** se reposer *ou* s'endormir sur ses lauriers

2 *(be buried)* être enterré, reposer; **may they r. in peace!** qu'ils reposent en paix!; **r. in peace** *(inscription on gravestone)* qu'il(s)/qu'elle(s) repose(nt) en paix

3 *(remain)* **there the matter rests** l'affaire en reste *ou* en est là; **I won't let it r. at that** cela ne se passera pas ainsi; **let it r.!** *(stop talking about it)* n'en parlons plus!; *(stop pursuing the matter)* ça suffit; **can't we let it r.?** *(stop talking about it)* restons-en là, je vous en prie; **r. assured** soyez certain *ou* assuré; (that que); **a heavy responsibility rests (up)on them** une lourde responsabilité pèse sur eux; **to r. with** *(of decision, responsibility etc)* incomber à; **it rests with you to …** il vous incombe de …; **it doesn't r. with me to decide** ce n'est pas à moi qu'il incombe de décider

4 *(be based)* **to r. on** *(of argument, fame)* reposer sur

5 *Law* **the defence/prosecution rests** = plaise au tribunal d'adopter mes conclusions

VT 1 *(repose)* **to r. oneself** se reposer; **to r. one's men/horses** laisser ses hommes/chevaux se reposer; **the coach wanted to r. his players** l'entraîneur voulait que son équipe se repose; **to r. one's eyes/legs** se reposer les yeux/les jambes; *Agr* **to r. a field** mettre un champ en jachère; **(God) r. his soul!** que Dieu ait son âme!, qu'il repose en paix!

2 *(lean)* *(one's elbows)* appuyer (on sur); *(one's head)* reposer (on sur); *(one's hopes, confidence etc)* fonder (on sur)

3 *(base)* *(argument, theory)* fonder (on sur)

4 *esp Am Law* **to r. one's case** conclure son plaidoyer; *Fig* **I r. my case** j'ai dit ce que j'avais à dire

▸▸ *Aut* **r. area** aire *f* de repos; *Am* **r. room** toilettes *fpl*; *Am Aut* **r. stop** aire de stationnement *ou* de repos

rest² **N the r.** *(remainder)* le reste (**of** de); *(others)* les autres *mfpl*; **where's the r. (of it)?** *(of money, food etc)* où est le reste?; **the r. of the men/cups** les autres hommes/tasses; **I'm keeping the r. of it for tomorrow** je garde le reste *ou* le restant pour demain; **do you want to watch the r. of the news?** est-ce que tu veux regarder le reste des actualités?; **(as) for the r.** quant au reste, pour le

reste; **and (all) the r. of it** et tout le reste; **the r. of us** nous autres, le reste (d'entre nous); **it's just another day like all the r.** c'est un jour comme un autre

restart [riːˈstɑːt] **VT** *(work etc)* recommencer, reprendre; *(machine)* (re)mettre en marche; *(engine)* remettre en marche, relancer; *(computer)* réamorcer

VI *(of job etc)* recommencer, reprendre; *(of machine, engine)* se remettre en marche; *(of computer)* se réamorcer

restate [riːˈsteɪt] **VT 1** *(repeat)* *(theory, viewpoint)* exposer de nouveau; *Mus (theme)* reprendre; **she restated her concern about the child's safety** elle a réitéré ses inquiétudes à propos de la sécurité de l'enfant **2** *(rephrase)* *(question)* reformuler, formuler de nouveau

restatement [riːˈsteɪtmənt] **N 1** *(repetition)* *(of theory, viewpoint)* nouvel exposé *m*; **it's a point that bears r.** c'est une chose qui mérite d'être répétée **2** *(rephrasing)* *(of question)* nouvelle formulation *f*

restaurant [ˈrestrɒnt] **N** restaurant *m*

▸▸ *Br* **r. car** wagon-restaurant *m*, *pl* wagons-restaurants, voiture-restaurant *f*, *pl* voitures-restaurants; **r. chain** chaîne *f* de restaurants; **r. manager** gérant, -ante de restaurant

restaurateur [restərəˈtɜː(r)] **N** restaurateur, -trice

rest-cure **N** cure *f* de repos; *Fig* **this job is no r.** ce travail n'est pas une sinécure

rest-day **N** *(of cricketer, tennis player etc)* jour *m* de repos; *(of shift worker)* jour *m* de congé

rested [ˈrestɪd] **ADJ** reposé; **to feel r.** se sentir (bien) reposé *ou* frais et dispos

restful [ˈrestfʊl] **ADJ** *(holiday, weekend, place etc)* reposant; **r. to the eyes** *(colour, lighting)* qui repose les yeux, reposant pour la vue

restfully [ˈrestfəlɪ] **ADV** *(to spend time)* paisiblement, tranquillement

rest-home **N 1** *(for convalescents)* maison *f* de repos **2** *(for elderly)* maison *f* de retraite; **to go into/to put sb in a r.** aller en/mettre qn en maison de retraite

resting [ˈrestɪŋ] **N**

▸▸ **r. place** lieu *m* de repos; *Fig Literary (grave)* dernière demeure *f*; **last r. place** dernière demeure

restitution [restɪˈtjuːʃən] **N** *Fml (of stolen property)* restitution *f*; *(compensation)* réparation *f*; **to make r. of sth** *(give back)* restituer qch; **to make r. for sth** *(make up for)* réparer qch; *(by providing monetary compensation)* verser des dommages-intérêts pour qch; **he should make full r.** il devrait verser une compensation intégrale

restive [ˈrestɪv] **ADJ** *(nervous)* *(person, crowd)* agité; *(apt to rebel)* *(person, child)* récalcitrant, indocile, rétif; *(horse)* rétif

restively [ˈrestɪvlɪ] **ADV** nerveusement

restiveness [ˈrestɪvnɪs] **N** *(of population, because of individual's nervousness)* agitation *f*, *(because of boredom)* *(of audience)* impatience *f*, *(of child)* nature *f* turbulente; *(of horse)* nature rétive

restless [ˈrestlɪs] **ADJ** *(person)* nerveux, agité; *(child)* agité, remuant; *(sea)* agité; *(wind)* incessant; **to be r. in one's sleep** *or* a **r. sleeper** avoir un *ou* le sommeil agité; **I've had *or* spent a r. night** j'ai passé une nuit agitée; **r. mind** esprit *m* agité; **she's feeling a bit r.** *(in present job, situation etc)* elle a envie de voir *ou* de faire autre chose; **the audience was getting r.** l'auditoire s'impatientait

restlessly [ˈrestlɪslɪ] **ADV** *(to move) (of*

person)* avec agitation; *Lit (of wind)* sans cesse

restlessness [ˈrestlɪsnɪs] **N** *(of person, sea)* agitation *f*, *(of mind)* nervosité *f*, état *m* fiévreux; *(of audience)* impatience *f*

restock [riːˈstɒk] **VT** *(shelves, shop)* réapprovisionner (**with** en); *(freezer)* refaire le plein de; **to r. a river (with fish)** rempoissonner une rivière

VI *(of shop)* se réapprovisionner

restocking [riːˈstɒkɪŋ] **N** réapprovisionnement *m*

restoration [restəˈreɪʃən] **N 1** *(of monument, building, furniture etc)* restauration *f* **2** *(of communications, law and order)* rétablissement *m* **3** *(of lost property, fortune)* restitution *f*, *(of dynasty)* restauration *f*, rétablissement *m* sur le trône; *Hist* **the R.** la Restauration

▸▸ *Br* **R. comedy** *(genre)* théâtre *m* de la Restauration anglaise *(caractérisé par la satire des mœurs du temps)*; *(play)* comédie *f* de l'époque de la Restauration anglaise *(caractérisée par la satire des mœurs du temps)*; *Fin* **r. fund** caisse *f* de restauration; **r. project** projet *m* de restauration; **r. work** travail *m* de restauration

restorative [rɪˈstɒrətɪv, -ˈstɔr-] **N** *(medicine)* cordial *m*

ADJ **the r. powers of sleep** les pouvoirs reconstituants du sommeil

restore [rɪˈstɔː(r)] **VT 1** *(monument, building, furniture etc)* restaurer; **to r. sth to its former glory** redonner son éclat d'antan à qch; **to be restored to its former glory** retrouver son éclat d'antan **2** *Comput (files)* restaurer **3** *(bring back)* *(law and order, calm)* rétablir; *(peace)* rétablir, restaurer; *(confidence)* faire renaître; *(discipline, dynasty)* restaurer; **order is being restored** l'ordre est en train d'être rétabli; **to r. sb to health** rétablir la santé de qn; **to r. sb to power** remettre quelqu'un au pouvoir; **to r. a company to profitability** permettre à une entreprise de redevenir bénéficiaire; **I feel quite restored** je me sens revigoré; **to r. sb to life** ramener qn à la vie; **to r. sb's strength** redonner des forces à qn; **to r. sb's sight/hearing** rendre la vue/l'ouïe à qn; **to r. the circulation** réactiver la circulation **4** *(give back)* restituer, rendre (**to sb** à qn); **to r. sth to its place/former condition** remettre qch à sa place *ou* en place/en état

N *Comput* **to do a r.** faire une restauration

restorer [rɪˈstɔːrə(r)] **N 1** *(of building, picture etc)* restaurateur, -trice **2** *(for hair)* régénérateur *m* capillaire

restrain [rɪˈstreɪn] **VT** *(person, dog, one's curiosity)* retenir; *(passions)* refréner; *(crowd, tears)* retenir, contenir; *(anger)* contenir, refouler; **to r. oneself** se maîtriser, se contenir; **I had to r. an impulse to laugh out loud/to hit him** il a fallu que je me retienne pour ne pas rire tout haut/pour ne pas le frapper; **to r. sb from doing sth** empêcher qn de faire qch; **he had to be forcibly restrained** il a fallu le retenir de force; **to r. sb's activities** mettre un frein aux activités de qn

restrained [rɪˈstreɪnd] **ADJ** *(feelings)* contenu; *(tone, terms)* mesuré; *(style)* sobre; *(silence)* prudent; *(response)* mitigé; **her manner was very r.** son attitude était très réservée

restraining [rɪˈstreɪnɪŋ] **ADJ** *(influence)* modérateur; *Law* qui retient, restrictif

▸▸ *Law* **r. order** injonction *f*

restraint [rɪˈstreɪnt] **N 1** *(moderation)* *(of person)* modération *f*, mesure *f*; *(of style)* sobriété *f*; **to throw aside all r.** abandonner toute mesure; **to show *or* exercise great r.** faire preuve de beaucoup de modération;

to urge r. demander instamment qu'on fasse preuve de modération (**in doing** en faisant) **2** (*restriction*) restriction *f*; (*of powers, wages*) limitation *f*; **to put a r. on sb** contraindre qn; **to break free of all r.** se déchaîner; **to be under no r.** avoir ses coudées franches; **without r.** (*to laugh, cry, speak etc*) sans se retenir; **to impose restraints** imposer des restrictions (**on** sur); **r. of trade** restrictions commerciales; **to put sb under r.** (*mental patient*) mettre la camisole de force à qn; (*prisoner*) mettre les menottes à qn

restrict [rɪ'strɪkt] *vt* (*speed etc*) limiter, restreindre (**to** à); **to r. oneself to ...** se limiter à ..., se restreindre à ...; **he is restricted to one glass of wine a day** il n'a droit qu'à un verre de vin par jour; **fog is restricting visibility** le brouillard limite la visibilité; **membership is restricted to the over-20s** la qualité de membre est réservée aux personnes âgées de plus de 20 ans; *Banking* **to r. the supply of a currency** raréfier une monnaie

restricted [rɪ'strɪktɪd] *adj* (*sense, space, use*) restreint, limité; (*sale*) contrôlé; (*speed*) limité; **to be on a r. diet** suivre un régime sévère *ou* strict; **she feels less r. wearing trousers** elle se sent plus libre (de ses mouvements) lorsqu'elle porte un pantalon; **r. access** (*sign*) accès réservé; *Comput* **r.-access system** système *m* à accès restreint; **r. area** (*out of bounds*) zone *f* interdite; *Br Aut* (*with parking restrictions*) zone à stationnement réglementé; (*with speed limit*) zone à vitesse limitée; **r. document** document *m* secret; *Theat* **seats with a r. view** (*of the stage*) des places depuis lesquelles on ne voit pas toute la scène

▸▸ *Comput* **r. users group** = nombre *m* restreint d'utilisateurs ayant accès à des informations confidentielles

restriction [rɪ'strɪkʃən] *n* restriction *f*; (*of speed etc*) limitation *f*; **to place** *or* **set on** *or* **impose restrictions on sth** apporter des restrictions à qch

restrictive [rɪ'strɪktɪv] *adj* **1** (*clause, measure*) restrictif **2** *Ling* (*clause*) déterminatif

▸▸ **r. clause** clause *f* restrictive; **r. practice** (*by union*) pratique *f* restrictive; (*by traders*) atteinte *f* à la libre concurrence

restring [riː'strɪŋ] *vt* (*pt, pp* **restrung** [riː'strʌŋ]) (*pearls*) enfiler de nouveau; (*violin*) remonter; (*guitar*) remplacer les cordes de; (*racket*) recorder

restructure [riː'strʌktʃər] *vt* (*company, industry, economy*) restructurer

restructuring [riː'strʌktʃərɪŋ] *n* restructuration *f*

restyle [riː'staɪl] *vt* (*car*) changer le style de; (*hair*) changer la coupe de

result [rɪ'zʌlt] *n* **1** (*of action, behaviour etc*), *Math, Sport etc* résultat *m* (**of** de); **the r. is that ...** il en résulte que ...; **as a r. of ...** à la suite de ...; **without r.** sans résultat; **results** (*of exam etc*) résultats; **I tried making some jam with disastrous results** j'ai essayé de faire des confitures mais ça a été un désastre; **if they get a good r. in this match** s'ils font un bon match; *Br Fam* **to get a r.** (*in sport*) gagner, l'emporter; **this paint gives excellent results** cette peinture donne d'excellents résultats; **to be a** *or* **the r. of sth** résulter *ou* être le résultat de qch; **as a r.** en conséquence; **to have little or no r.** avoir peu ou pas de résultats; *Comput* **results page** page *f* de résultats

2 (*good outcome*) **to yield** *or* **show results** donner des résultats; **she knows how to get results** elle sait comment s'y prendre pour arriver à quelque chose *ou* pour avoir des résultats; *Br Fam* **we need a r.** il faut qu'on fasse un résultat; *Br Fam* **a 20% pay**

rise? what a r.! 20% d'augmentation? tu as fait fort!

vi résulter (**from** de); **it results from this that ...** il s'ensuit que ...; **consequences resulting from ...** conséquences de ...; **to r. in** (*unpleasantness, increase, decrease*) entraîner, engendrer; (*loss of life*) entraîner, provoquer; **the summit talks resulted in a treaty** le sommet a abouti à la signature d'un traité

resultant [rɪ'zʌltənt] *adj attrib* qui en résulte, résultant

n Math résultante *f*

resume [rɪ'zjuːm] *vt* (*relations*) reprendre, renouer; (*after short break*) (*speech, negotiations, discussions, trip*) continuer, poursuivre; **to r. one's seat** reprendre sa place, se rasseoir; **to r. doing sth** se remettre à faire qch; **to r. work** se remettre au travail; **to r. one's duties** reprendre son service *ou* ses fonctions; **she resumed her maiden name** elle a repris son nom de jeune fille

vi (*of music, speaker etc*) continuer, reprendre; **we/the meeting will r. after lunch** nous reprendrons/la réunion reprendra après le déjeuner; *Cr* **play resumed at four** le match a repris à quatre heures

> Note that the French verb **résumer** is a false friend and is never a translation for the English verb **to resume**. It means **to summarize**.

résumé ['reɪzjʊmeɪ, -uːmeɪ] *n* **1** (*summary*) résumé *m*, abrégé *m*; **to give a r. of sth** faire un résumé de qch **2** *Am* (*curriculum vitae*) curriculum vitae *m inv*

resumption [rɪ'zʌmpʃən] *n* (*of relationship, negotiations etc*) reprise *f*

resurface [riː'sɜːfɪs] *vt* (*road*) refaire le revêtement de

vi (*of submarine*) faire surface, revenir à la surface; *esp Hum* **when did he eventually r.?** (*return*) quand est-ce qu'il a fini par refaire surface?

resurgence [rɪ'sɜːdʒəns] *n* (*of nationalism, trend, idea, ideology*) résurgence *f*, réapparition *f*; (*of disease*) réapparition *f*; (*of company etc*) reprise *f*

resurgent [rɪ'sɜːdʒənt] *adj usu attrib* (*idea, nationalism etc*) renaissant; (*company etc*) qui connaît une reprise

resurrect [rezə'rekt] *vt* (*the dead*), *Fig* (*fashion*) ressusciter; (*era*) faire revivre; (*quarrel, argument*) réveiller; (*hopes, fears*) ranimer

resurrection [rezə'rekʃən] *n* (*of the dead*), *Fig* résurrection *f*; **the R.** la résurrection du Christ; **this resulted in the r. of their old argument** cela a relancé leur querelle

resuscitate [rɪ'sʌsɪteɪt] *vt Med* (*person*) ranimer; *Fig* (*plan*) ressortir; (*ailing company*) faire repartir

> Note that the French verb **ressusciter** is a false friend and is never a translation for the English verb **to resuscitate**. It means **to resurrect** or **to revive**.

resuscitation [rɪsʌsɪ'teɪʃən] *n Med* réanimation *f*, ranimation *f*; **all attempts at r. failed** toutes les tentatives de réanimation *ou* de ranimation ont échoué; *Fig* **there was a r. of interest** il y a eu un regain d'intérêt

resuscitator [rɪ'sʌsɪteɪtər] *n* (*machine*) appareil *m* de réanimation

retail ['riːteɪl] *n Com* (*vente f au*) détail *m*; **to buy/sell goods r.** *or Am* **at r.** acheter/vendre des marchandises au détail; **wholesale and r. business** commerce *m* de gros et de détail

vt **1** (*goods*) vendre au détail **2** (*spread*) (*gossip*) colporter

vi (*of goods*) se vendre au détail (**at, for** à)

▸▸ **r. audit** audit *m* des détaillants; **r. audi-**

tor audit *m* des détaillants, auditeur, -trice des détaillants; **r. bank** banque *f* de détail; **r. banking** banque de détail; **r. chain** chaîne *f* de vente au détail, chaîne de détail; **r. customer** client, -ente qui achète au détail; **r. dealer** détaillant, -ante; **r. goods** marchandises *fpl* vendues au détail, marchandises au détail; **r. outlet** magasin *m* de (vente au) détail, point *m* de (vente au) détail; **r. panel** panel *m* de détaillants; *Br* **r. park** zone *f* commerciale; **r. price** prix *m* de *ou* au détail; *Br Fin* **R. Price Index** indice *m* des prix de détail; **r. price maintenance** prix imposé; **r. sales** ventes *fpl* de détail; **r. selling** vente au détail; **r. shipment** expédition *f* de détail; **r. shop** magasin de (vente au) détail; *Fam* **r. therapy** = le shopping envisagé comme remède à la dépression; **r. trade** commerce (de détail); **r. wholesale** demi-gros *m inv*

retailer ['riːteɪlər] *n* détaillant, -ante; **retailers' group** groupement *m* de détaillants

▸▸ **r. brand** marque *f* de revendeur *ou* de détaillant *ou* de distributeur; **r. margin** marge *f* du détaillant

retailing ['riːteɪlɪŋ] *n* vente *f* au détail

▸▸ *Com, Mktg* **r. mix** marchéage *m* de distribution

retain [rɪ'teɪn] *vt* **1** (*keep*) (*property, control etc*) conserver, garder; (*custom, heat etc*) conserver; **to r. the right to do sth** se réserver le droit de faire qch **2 to r. sb's services** s'assurer les services de qn; *Br Law* **to r. a barrister** *or* **counsel** retenir un avocat (à l'avance); *Law* **retaining fee** avance *f*, provision *f* **3** (*hold in place*) (*object*) retenir, maintenir; *Constr* **retaining wall** mur *m* de soutènement *ou* de retenue **4** (*remember*) garder en mémoire, mémoriser

retained [rɪ'teɪnd] *adj Acct*

▸▸ **r. earnings** revenu *m* non distribué; **r. profit** bénéfices *mpl* non distribués

retainer [rɪ'teɪnər] *n* **1** (*fee*) avance *f*, provision *f*; **to pay sb a r.** verser une avance *ou* provision à qn **2** *Old-fashioned* (*servant*) serviteur *m*

retake [1] ['riːteɪk] *n* **1** *Cin, TV* nouvelle prise *f*; **it took several retakes** il a fallu plusieurs prises **2** *esp Univ* (*exam*) examen *m* à repasser; (*candidate*) candidat, -ate qui repasse un examen; **how many retakes did you have to do?** combien d'examens est-ce que tu as dû repasser?; **the r. of the history exam** *or* **the history r. will be held on ...** l'examen d'histoire de la session de rattrapage aura lieu le ...

retake [2] [riː'teɪk] *vt* (*pt* **retook** [riː'tʊk]; *pp* **retaken** [riː'teɪk(ə)n]) **1** *Cin, TV* (*shot*) refaire, filmer à nouveau; (*scene*) refaire une prise (de vues) **2** *esp Univ* (*exam*) repasser **3** (*stronghold etc*) reprendre

retaliate [rɪ'tælɪeɪt] *vi* riposter, rendre la pareille; (*in speech*) riposter; *esp Mil* user de représailles (**with** par); **to r. for an attack** riposter à une attaque (**by doing** en faisant)

retaliation [rɪtælɪ'eɪʃən] *n* riposte *f*, représailles *fpl* (**against** contre); **r. for the attack** représailles contre l'attaque; **in r.** par mesure de représailles; **in r. for** en représailles de

retaliatory [rɪ'tælɪət(ə)rɪ] *adj attrib* de représailles, de rétorsion; **to take r. measures** exercer des représailles, riposter

▸▸ **r. attack** riposte *f*; **r. bombing** des représailles *fpl* sous forme de bombardements

retard [1] ['riːtɑːd] *n Fam Pej* (*retarded person*) demeuré, -ée

retard [2] [rɪ'tɑːd] *vt* (*delay growth or development of*) retarder, retarder la croissance *ou* le développement de; **to be severely (mentally) retarded** être très attardé *ou* arriéré; **mentally retarded person** (personne *f*) attardé(e) *ou* arriéré(e); **the retarded** (*used as pl*) les attardés *mpl*, les arriérés *mpl*

-retardant [rɪ'tɑːdənt] **suff** heat/flame-r. qui ralentit la propagation de la chaleur/des flammes

retardation [riːtɑː'deɪʃən] **N** (*of growth*) retard *m*; (*of mechanism*) retardement *m*; (**mental**) r. arriération *f* mentale

retch [retʃ] **vi** avoir des haut-le-cœur; *Fig* **to make sb r.** soulever le cœur à qn

retching ['retʃɪŋ] **N** haut-le-cœur *mpl*; r. **noises were coming from the bathroom** on entendait quelqu'un vomir dans la salle de bain

retd (*abbr* **retired**) retraité, à la retraite

retell [riː'tel] **vt** (*pt, pp* **retold** [riː'təʊld]) (*story*) raconter de nouveau

retelling [riː'telɪŋ] **N** the number of his assailants grew with each r. chaque fois qu'il racontait l'histoire le nombre de ses attaquants augmentait

retention [rɪ'tenʃən] **N** (*of custom*) conservation *f*, (*of authority, provisions, restrictions*) maintien *m*; (*of fact, impression etc*) mémoire *f*, *Med* (*of urine etc*) rétention *f*; **to have limited powers of r.** (*memory*) avoir peu de mémoire; **to have great powers of r.** (*memory*) avoir une excellente mémoire; *Com* r. of title réserve *f* de propriété

retentive [rɪ'tentɪv] **adj** (*memory*) fidèle; (*person*) qui a une bonne mémoire

retentiveness [rɪ'tentɪvnɪs] **N** (*of memory*) fidélité *f*

rethink[1] ['riːθɪŋk] **N to have a r. (about sth)** réfléchir à nouveau (à qch); **we need a complete r. of our strategy** il nous faut revoir entièrement notre stratégie; **the plan needs a complete r.** le projet doit être complètement repensé

rethink[2] [riː'θɪŋk] **vt** (*pt, pp* **rethought** [riː'θɔːt]) (*matter, plan*) repenser, reconsidérer

reticence ['retɪsəns] **N** (*on one occasion*) réticence *f*, (*character trait*) réserve *f*; **the r. of his manner** sa réticence/réserve; **without any r.** sans réticence(s); **this r. isn't like her** elle n'est pas aussi réservée d'habitude

reticent ['retɪsənt] **adj** peu communicatif, réservé; **to be r. about sth** ne pas vouloir parler de qch, faire mystère de qch

> Note that the French word **réticent** is a false friend and is never a translation for the English word **reticent**. It means **hesitant**.

reticently ['retɪsəntlɪ] **adv** avec réticence *ou* réserve

reticular [rɪ'tɪkjʊlər], **reticulate, reticulated** [rɪ'tɪkjʊlət, -leɪtɪd] **adj** *esp Biol* réticulé

reticulation [rɪtɪkjʊ'leɪʃən] **N** *esp Biol* réticulation *f*

reticule ['retɪkjuːl] **N 1** *Opt* réticule *m* **2** *Hist* (*bag*) réticule *m*

retina, *pl* **retinas, retinae** ['retɪnə, -əz, -iː] **N** (*of eye*) rétine *f*

retinal ['retɪnəl] **adj** rétinien
> *Med* r. **detachment** décollement *m* de la rétine

retinitis [retɪ'naɪtəs] **N** rétinite *f*

retinue ['retɪnjuː] **N** (*of prince etc*), *Hum* suite *f*

retire [rɪ'taɪər] **vi 1** (*of employee*) prendre sa retraite; **to r. from a company** prendre sa retraite d'une société; **to r. from teaching** prendre sa retraite de l'enseignement; **when I r.** quand je prendrai ma retraite; **to r. early** prendre une retraite anticipée; **to have retired** être à la retraite **2** (*withdraw*) se retirer (**to** dans, à; **from** de); (*of troops*)

reculer, se replier (**to** vers); (*from match, competition etc*) se retirer, abandonner; **to r. from boxing/the race** abandonner la boxe/la course; **to r. into oneself** se replier sur soi-même; *Fml* **to r. from the room** quitter la pièce; *Fml* **to r. (to bed/for the night)** (aller) se coucher

  vt 1 (*person*) (*from work*) mettre à la retraite **2** (*withdraw*), *Mil* (*troops*) retirer **3** *Fin* (*coins, bill, bonds, shares*) retirer

retired [rɪ'taɪəd] **adj 1** (*police officer, doctor etc*) retraité, à la retraite; **to be r.** être à la retraite; *Mil* **to put** *or* **place sb on the r. list** mettre qn à la retraite; **Admiral John Smith, r.** Amiral John Smith, retraité **2** (*secluded*) (*life*) retiré; (*place etc*) retiré, isolé **3** *Fin* (*coins, bill, bonds, shares*) retiré

retiree [rɪtaɪə'riː] **N** *Am* retraité, -ée

retirement [rɪ'taɪəmənt] **N 1** (*from work, army etc*) retraite *f*; **on my r.** (*when I retire*) quand je serai à la retraite; (*when I retired*) quand j'ai pris ma retraite; **to take early r.** prendre une retraite anticipée; **she's been offered early r.** on lui a proposé de prendre ou de faire valoir ses droits à une retraite anticipée; **to come out of r.** reprendre sa carrière; **to live in r.** (*no longer employed*) être à la retraite; (*in seclusion*) vivre retiré du monde; **compulsory r.** retraite d'office **2** (*withdrawal*) (*of troops*) repli *m*; (*from match, competition etc*) abandon *m* **3** *Fin* (*of coins, bill, bonds, shares*) retrait *m*

> ▸ r. **age** âge *m* de la retraite; *Br* r. **flat** appartement *m* pour retraités; r. **pension** (pension *f* de) retraite; *Am* r. **plan** régime *m* de retraite; r. **present** cadeau *m* de départ en *ou* à la retraite; *Fin* r. **savings plan** plan *m* d'épargne retraite

retiring [rɪ'taɪərɪŋ] **adj 1** (*reserved*) réservé; **to have** *or* **be of a r. nature** avoir un *ou* être d'un naturel réservé **2** (*employee*) qui prend sa retraite; (*elected official*) sortant; **to reach r. age** atteindre l'âge de la retraite

retool [riː'tuːl] **vt** *Ind* (*factory*) rééquiper; *Am Fam* (*company*) réorganiser
  vi *Ind* (*of factory*) se rééquiper; *Am Fam* (*of company*) se réorganiser

retort[1] [rɪ'tɔːt] **N** (*answer*) réplique *f* (**to** à), riposte *f*; **to make a r.** lancer une réplique
  vt & vi répliquer, rétorquer

retort[2] **N** *Chem, Ind* cornue *f*

retouch[1] ['riːtʌtʃ] **N** (*of photograph*) retouche *f*

retouch[2] [riː'tʌtʃ] **vt** (*photograph*) retoucher

retouching [riː'tʌtʃɪŋ] **N** (*of photograph etc*) retouche *f*

retrace [rɪ'treɪs] **vt** (*events*) reconstituer; **to r. one's steps** revenir sur ses pas, rebrousser chemin; **to r. sb's movements** (*of police etc*) reconstituer les faits et gestes de qn

retract [rɪ'trækt] **vt 1** (*what one said*) rétracter; (*statement, offer etc*) revenir sur; (*opinion etc*) désavouer, rétracter **2** (*of animal*) (*claws*) rentrer; *Aviat* **to r. the undercarriage** escamoter *ou* rentrer le train d'atterrissage
  vi 1 (*of person*) se rétracter **2** (*of cat's claws*) rentrer; *Aviat* (*of undercarriage*) s'escamoter, rentrer; (*of blade*) s'escamoter

retractable [rɪ'træktəb(ə)l] **adj** *Aviat* (*undercarriage*) rentrant, escamotable; (*handle etc*) escamotable; (*ballpoint pen*) à pointe rétractable

retraction [rɪ'trækʃən] **N 1** (*of statement*) rétractation *f*, (*of opinion*) désaveu *m*, reniement *m*; **to publish a r.** (*of newspaper*) publier un désaveu **2** (*of claws etc*) rétraction *f*

retrain [riː'treɪn] **vt** (*employee*) recycler; *Med* (*muscle*) rééduquer
  vi (*of employee*) se recycler

retraining [riː'treɪnɪŋ] **N** (*of person*) recyclage *m*; *Med* (*of muscle*) rééducation *f*

retread[1] ['riːtred] **vt** *Aut* (*pneu*) rechapé *m*

retread[2] [riː'tred] **vt** *Aut* (*tyre*) rechaper

retreat [rɪ'triːt] **N 1** *Mil, Fig* retraite *f*; *Mil* **to sound/beat the r.** sonner/battre la retraite; *Fig* **to beat a (hasty) r.** battre en retraite **2** (*of flood waters*) retrait *m*, recul *m* **3** *Rel* (*seclusion*) retraite *f*; **to go into** *or* **on r.** faire une retraite **4** (*place*) abri *m*, retraite *f*, refuge *m*; **a holiday/weekend r.** une maison paisible pour les vacances/le week-end; **a country r.** une maison paisible à la campagne
  vi 1 *Mil* battre en retraite, reculer; (*of crowd, spectators etc*) battre en retraite, reculer (**from** de); **to r. a few hundred yards** reculer de quelques centaines de mètres; **to r. into a world of one's own** s'isoler dans son petit monde (à soi); **to r. from the public eye** se retirer du monde **2** (*of flood waters, glacier*) reculer

retrench [rɪ'trentʃ] **vt** *Fin* (*expenditure*) restreindre; *Liter* (*literary work*) faire des coupures dans
  vi *Fin* restreindre ses dépenses, faire des économies

retrenchment [rɪ'trentʃmənt] **N** *Fin* (*of expenditure*) réduction *f*, **policy of r.** politique *f* d'économies

retrial [riː'traɪ(ə)l] **N** *Law* nouveau procès *m*

retribution [retrɪ'bjuːʃən] **N** châtiment *m*; **in r. for sth** comme châtiment pour qch; **to exact r.** se venger; **the Day of R.** le Jugement dernier; **just r. of** *or* **for a crime** juste châtiment pour un crime

> Note that the French word **rétribution** is a false friend and is never a translation for the English word **retribution**. It means **remuneration** or **reward**.

retributive [rɪ'trɪbjʊtɪv] **adj** (*measure etc*) punitif

retrievable [rɪ'triːvəb(ə)l] **adj** (*loss, error*) réparable; *Comput* accessible; *Fin* (*amount*) recouvrable

retrieval [rɪ'triːv(ə)l] **N** (*recovery*) (*of lost object*) récupération *f*, (*of error, loss*) réparation *f*, (*of fortune*) rétablissement *m*, *Fin* recouvrement *m*; *Comput* (*of data*) recherche *f*, (*of lost data*) récupération *f*; **information r. system** système *m* de recherche documentaire; (*computer system*) système de recherche d'information; **beyond** *or* **past r.** irréparable
> ▸ *Comput* r. **system** système de recherche

retrieve [rɪ'triːv] **vt** (*property*) récupérer; (*freedom*) retrouver; (*loss, error etc*) réparer; (*honour, fortune*) rétablir; (*of dog*) (*ball, game bird etc*) rapporter; *Fin* (*assets*) recouvrer; *Comput* (*file*) retrouver, extraire; **to r. one's losses** se refaire; **to r. the situation** sauver la situation
  vi (*in hunting*) (*of dog*) rapporter

retriever [rɪ'triːvər] **N** (*dog*) retriever *m*

retro ['retrəʊ] **adj** (*fashion etc*) rétro *inv*

retro- ['retrəʊ-] **pref** rétro-

retroactive [retrəʊ'æktɪv] **adj** (*increase, measure etc*) rétroactif; **the increase is r. to last January** l'augmentation a un effet rétroactif à compter de janvier dernier

retroactively [retrəʊ'æktɪvlɪ] **adv** (*to increase, come into effect etc*) rétroactivement

retrofit ['retrəʊfɪt] **vt** *Aviat* (*aircraft, machine*) moderniser (**with** en y intégrant)

retroflex ['retrəʊfleks] **adj** *Ling* rétroflexe

retroflexion [retrəʊ'flekʃən] **N** *Med* rétroflexion *f*

retrograde ['retrəgreɪd] **adj** (*movement, step etc*) rétrograde

retrogress [retrə'gres] **vi** rétrograder

retrogression [retrə'greʃən] N rétrogradation f, rétrogression f; Biol régression f

retrogressive [retrə'gresɪv] ADJ rétrograde; Biol régressif

retrorocket ['retrəʊrɒkɪt] N Astronaut rétrofusée f

retrospect ['retrəspekt] N in r. rétrospectivement, après coup; when I consider these events in r. quand je pense à ces événements rétrospectivement ou après coup

retrospective [retrə'spektɪv] ADJ (review) rétrospectif; (measure) à effet rétroactif
N (of film director's, artist's etc work) rétrospective f

retrospectively [retrə'spektɪvlɪ] ADV (to consider etc) rétrospectivement, après coup; (to take effect) rétroactivement

retroussé [rə'truːseɪ] ADJ (nose) retroussé

retrovirus ['retrəʊvaɪrəs] N Biol rétrovirus m

retry [riː'traɪ] VT Law juger à ou de nouveau
VI esp Comput réessayer

retsina [ret'siːnə] N retsina m

retune¹ ['riːtjuːn] N Aut (of engine) réglage m; the engine needs a r. il faut faire régler le moteur

retune² [riː'tjuːn] VT Aut (engine) régler; Mus (instrument) accorder; Radio régler
VI Radio to r. to medium wave régler son poste sur ondes moyennes

---

RETURN [rɪ'tɜːn]

| N retour **1** ▪ aller et retour **2** |
| ▪ renvoi **3** ▪ rapport **4** |
| VI revenir ▪ retourner ▪ rentrer |
| VT rendre **1** ▪ renvoyer **1** |
| ▪ remettre **1** ▪ rapporter **1, 2** |

N **1** (of person, peace, spring etc) retour m; **on my r.** dès ou à mon retour; **on his r. to France** à son retour en France; **by r.** (of post) par retour (du courrier); **the r. to school** la rentrée (des classes); **many happy returns (of the day)!** bon anniversaire!

2 Br (ticket) aller (et) retour; Br **day r.** = aller (et) retour valable pour la journée seulement; Br **cheap day r.** billet m d'aller (et) retour à tarif réduit valable pour la journée seulement; **I've lost the r. half of my ticket** j'ai perdu mon billet ou coupon de retour; **how much is the r. fare?** combien coûte l'aller (et) retour?; Br **r. air fare** tarif m aérien aller-retour; **point of no r.** point m de non-retour

3 (of goods to supplier) renvoi m; (of stolen property) restitution f; (of overpayment) remboursement m; Tennis (of service) renvoi (de la balle); (library book) livre m (de bibliothèque) que l'on rapporte; (election) (of politician) élection f; Comput (on keyboard) touche f (de) retour; (carriage) r. (on typewriter, keyboard) retour m (de chariot); Tennis **to make a good r. (of service)** bien renvoyer le service; **r. to office** (of politician) reprise f de fonctions; **on his r. to office** quand il a été réélu; Com **on sale or r.** (goods) vendu avec possibilité de retour; **no deposit, no r.** (on bottle) ni retour, ni consigne; Theat **returns may be available on the day of the performance** des places peuvent se libérer le jour de la représentation; **are there any returns?** est-ce que des places se sont libérées?; Com **returns** rendus mpl, (of books, newspapers) invendus mpl, bouillons mpl; Pol Fam **to announce the returns of the election** annoncer les résultats du scrutin; **early returns indicate a win for the incumbent** les premiers résultats laissent prévoir une victoire du candidat sortant

4 Fin (yield) rapport m (**on** de); **how much r. do you get on your investment?** combien est-ce que ton investissement te rapporte?; **returns** (profit) bénéfices mpl; Acct **returns ledger** journal m des rendus; **quick returns** bénéfices réalisés rapidement; **small profits and quick returns** bénéfices et ventes rapides; **to bring (in) a fair r.** rapporter un bénéfice raisonnable; **r. on capital** retour m sur capital; Acct **r. on capital employed** rendement m sur capital immobilisé; **r. on investment** retour sur investissement; **r. on sales** retour sur ventes

5 (form) rapport m officiel; (for tax) déclaration f

6 to give sth in r. donner qch en échange; (for favour, service) donner qch en guise de récompense ou de remerciement; **in r. for which ...** moyennant quoi ...; **if you will do sth in r.** si vous voulez bien faire qch en retour; **in r. for this service ...** en récompense de ce service ...; **you must expect the same treatment in r.** il faut vous attendre à la pareille; **it's a small r. for all your kindness** c'est une modeste récompense pour votre bonté
VI (come back) revenir; (go back) retourner; (of anxiety, fear) revenir, reprendre; **to r. home** rentrer (chez soi); **I was returning from a journey** je rentrais de voyage; **he/spring has returned** il/le printemps est revenu ou est de retour; **to r. from the dead** ressusciter d'entre les morts; **her colour returned** elle a repris des couleurs; **to r. to office** (be re-elected) être réélu; Naut **to r. to port** rentrer au port; **to r. to a task** reprendre une tâche; **to r. to a subject** revenir à un sujet; **to r. to one's old habits** reprendre ses vieilles habitudes; **to r. to work** reprendre le travail; **r. to sender** (on undelivered letter) retour à l'envoyeur
VT **1** (give or send back) (book, compliment, verdict etc) rendre; (something stolen etc) restituer; (gift, ball etc) renvoyer; (loan) rembourser; (elect) (MP) élire; **a returned letter** une lettre renvoyée à l'expéditeur; **returned cheque** chèque m retourné; **to r. a book to its place** remettre un livre à sa place; **to r. a purchase to a shop** rendre ou rapporter un article à un magasin; Tennis **to r. (the) service** renvoyer le service; Law **the jury returned a verdict of guilty/not guilty** le jury a déclaré l'accusé coupable/non coupable; **to r. an animal to the wild** remettre un animal en liberté; Mil **to r. fire** riposter (au feu adverse); **to r. the favour** rendre la pareille; **to r. sb's greeting** rendre un salut à qn; **to r. good for evil** rendre le bien pour le mal; **to r. sb's love** aimer qn en retour; Tel **to r. a call** rappeler; Pol **to r. the result of the poll** annoncer les résultats du scrutin

2 Com, Fin (produce) (profit) rapporter, dégager

3 Old-fashioned (answer) répondre, répliquer
▸▸ **r. address** adresse f de l'expéditeur; **r. flight** vol m de retour; **r. journey** (voyage m du) retour; Comput **r. key** touche f (de) retour; Sport **r. match** match m retour, revanche f; **I'll give you a r. match next week** on disputera le match retour ou la revanche la semaine prochaine; Br **r. ticket** (billet d')aller m (et) retour

returnable [rɪ'tɜːnəb(ə)l] ADJ Com (purchase, ticket etc) qui peut être rendu; (bottle) consigné; **sale items are not r.** (notice in shop) les articles en solde ne sont ni échangés ni repris; **empties are not r.** on ne reprend pas les bouteilles, les bouteilles ne sont pas consignées
▸▸ Com **r. packaging** emballage m consigné

returning [rɪ'tɜːnɪŋ] N
▸▸ Pol **r. officer** président, -ente du bureau de vote

reunification [riːjuːnɪfɪ'keɪʃən] N (of country) réunification f

reunify [riː'juːnɪfaɪ] VT (country) réunifier

reunion [riː'juːnɪən] N retrouvailles fpl, réunion f; Am **class r.** réunion d'anciens élèves de la même classe ou promotion; **to have or hold a r.** organiser une réunion ou des retrouvailles; **r. celebration** célébration f de retrouvailles; **r. dinner** dîner m de retrouvailles

reunite [riːjʊ'naɪt] VT (after quarrel) (family etc) réconcilier; **the freed hostage was reunited with his wife** l'otage libéré a retrouvé sa femme; **the dog was reunited with its owner** le chien a retrouvé son maître; **he reunited the band for one last gig** il a reformé le groupe pour un ultime concert
VI (of band) se reformer

reupholster [riːʌp'həʊlstər] VT (chair etc) rembourrer et recouvrir

reusable [re'juːzəb(ə)l] ADJ (paper, bottle etc) réutilisable; (battery) rechargeable

reuse¹ [riː'juːs] N (of paper, bottle etc) réutilisation f

reuse² [riː'juːz] VT (paper, bottle etc) réutiliser

Rev N Rel (abbr **Reverend**) révérend

rev [rev] Aut Fam N (abbr **revolution**) tour m (à la minute ou minute); **to do three thousand revs** faire trois mille tours (à la) minute
VT (-vv-) (engine) emballer; **he revs the engine too hard** il fait tourner le moteur trop vite
VI (of engine) s'emballer; (of driver) emballer le moteur
▸▸ **r. counter** compte-tours m inv; **r. limiter** limiteur m de régime
▸ **rev up** VT SEP, VI = rev VT, VI

revalidate [rɪ'vælɪdeɪt] VT revalider
▸▸ **r. sticker** autocollant m de revalidation

revaluation [riːvæljʊ'eɪʃən] N Econ, Fin (of currency, property etc) réévaluation f

revalue [riː'væljuː] VT Econ, Fin (currency, property) réévaluer

revamp¹ ['riːvæmp] N Fam (of method, play etc) remaniement m; (of policy) modification f, remaniement m; (of company) réorganisation f, restructuration f; (of house etc) retapage m, remise f en état

revamp² [riː'væmp] VT Fam (method, play etc) remanier; (policy) modifier, remanier; (company) réorganiser, restructurer; (house etc) retaper, remettre en état

revanchisme [rɪ'vænfɪz(ə)m] N revanchisme m

revanchiste [rɪ'vænfɪst] N, ADJ revanchiste mf, revanchard, -arde

Revd Rel (abbr **Reverend**) révérend

reveal [rɪ'viːl] VT (something hidden, secret, one's sources, name) révéler; (fact) révéler, faire connaître; (quality etc) laisser voir; **to r. one's identity** révéler son identité, dire ou donner son nom, se faire connaître; **the police do not want to r. the identity of the victim** la police ne veut pas révéler l'identité de la victime; **a medical examination revealed two cracked ribs** un examen médical a permis de découvrir deux côtes fêlées; **it was revealed that ...** on a révélé que ...

revealing [rɪ'viːlɪŋ] ADJ (sign, comment etc) révélateur, -trice; (dress) (low-cut) décolleté; (skirt, dress) (short) très court, qui ne cache pas grand-chose; (blouse) (transparent) transparent; **that was very r. about his intentions** cela en disait long sur ses intentions

revealingly [rɪ'viːlɪŋlɪ] ADV (to say) d'un ton révélateur; **a r. low dress** une robe très décolletée

reveille [rɪ'vælɪ] N Mil réveil m; **to sound (the) r.** sonner ou battre le réveil

revel ['rev(ə)l] VI (-ll-, Am -l-) se réjouir, se divertir, *Fam* faire la noce; **to r. in sth/in doing sth** se délecter à qch/à faire qch; **to r. in one's freedom** savourer pleinement sa liberté; **enjoy it?, he positively revels in it** s'il aime ça?, tu veux dire qu'il adore ça!

N *Old-fashioned (often pl)* divertissement(s) *m(pl)*, réjouissances *fpl*

revelation [revə'leɪʃən] **N** révélation *f*; **it was a r. to me** cela a été une révélation pour moi; *Bible* **the Book of R., Revelations** l'Apocalypse *f*

reveller, *Am* **reveler** ['rev(ə)lər] **N** joyeux, -euse convive, *Fam* noceur, -euse, fêtard, -arde; **there were no taxis left for the late-night revellers** il n'y avait plus de taxis pour les oiseaux de nuit

revelling ['rev(ə)lɪŋ], **revelry** ['revəlrɪ] **N** festivités *fpl*

revenge [rɪ'vendʒ] **N 1** vengeance *f*; **r. is sweet** la vengeance est douce; **to take** *or* **get** *or* **have (one's) r.** se venger (**for** de; **on** sur); **to want one's r.** vouloir se venger (**for** de); **in r.** pour se venger (**for** de); **to do sth out of r.** faire qch par esprit de vengeance **2** *Fig (esp in games)* revanche *f*; **to give sb his/her r.** laisser qn prendre sa revanche; **Liverpool got their r. for last week's defeat** Liverpool a pris la revanche de sa défaite de la semaine dernière

VT *(insult)* venger; **to r. oneself** *or* **be revenged** se venger (**on** sur; **for** de)

revengeful [rɪ'vendʒfʊl] **ADJ** *(attitude, person etc)* vindicatif; *(act)* vengeur, -eresse, de vengeance

revengefully [rɪ'vendʒfʊlɪ] **ADV** *(to do)* par esprit de vengeance, de façon vindicative; *(to say)* d'un ton vengeur

revenger [rɪ'vendʒər] **N** vengeur, -eresse (**of** de)

revenue ['revənju:] **N** *Fin, Com* revenu *m*; *(from land, property)* revenu, rentes *fpl*; *(from sales)* recettes *fpl*; **advertising r.** recettes de publicité; **oil r.** revenu pétrolier; **the** *Br* **Inland** *or* **Am** **Internal R.** le fisc; **tax r.** recettes fiscales

▸▸ *Fin* **r. account** *(from land, property)* compte *m* de recettes; *(profit and loss account)* compte d'exploitation; *Am Fin* **r. bond** obligation *f* à intérêt conditionnel; *Fin* **r. centre** centre *m* de revenus *ou* de profit; *Fin* **r. expenditure** dépenses *fpl* de fonctionnement; *Fin* **r. man** agent *m* du fisc; *Am* **r. passenger mile** revenu passager-kilomètre; *Fin* **r. sharing** partage *m* des recettes fiscales; *Fin* **r. stamp** timbre *m* fiscal; *Fin* **r. tariff** tarif *m* douanier fiscal

reverberate [rɪ'vɜ:bəreɪt] **VI** *(of sound)* retentir, résonner (**off** contre); *(of light, heat)* se réverbérer (**off** contre); **the room reverberated with the children's shouts** la pièce résonnait des cris des enfants; *Fig* **the news reverberated round the world** la nouvelle a fait du bruit partout dans le monde; *(had an effect)* la nouvelle a eu des répercussions partout dans le monde

reverberation [rɪvɜ:bə'reɪʃən] **N** *(of sound)* réverbération *f*; *Fig* **the announcement is still causing reverberations** la nouvelle continue à avoir des répercussions

revere [rɪ'vɪər] **VT** révérer

reverence ['revərəns] **N** révérence *f*; *(for artist, doctor etc)* vénération *f*; *Rel* respect *m* religieux; **to hold sb in r.** révérer *ou* vénérer qn; *Rel* **Your** *or* **His R.** monsieur l'abbé

VT *Fml* révérer

reverend ['rev(ə)rənd] **ADJ** *Rel* révérend; **the R. Father Martin** *(in Church of England)* le révérend père Martin; *(in Catholic Church)* l'abbé *m* ou le père Martin; **the R. Mother Superior** la révérende mère supérieure; **Right R.** *(bishop)* très révérend; **Very R.** *(dean)* très

révérend; **Most R.** *(archbishop)* révérendissime

N révérend *m*; *(in Church of England)* pasteur *m*; *(in Catholic Church)* abbé *m*; *Cathol* **Your R.** (mon) père

reverent ['revərənt] **ADJ** *(gesture, tone)* respectueux, plein de révérence, *Lit* révérencieux; **to be very r. towards sb** être très respectueux à l'égard de *ou* envers qn

reverential [revə'renʃəl] **ADJ** *(act)* révérenciel; *(tone, gesture etc)* révérencieux

reverently ['revərəntlɪ] **ADV** *(to treat)* avec révérence; *(to act, speak etc)* avec grand respect *ou* vénération, très respectueusement

reverie ['revərɪ] **N** rêverie *f*; **to be in a r.** être rêveur; **to be lost in r.** être perdu dans ses rêveries; **to fall into a r.** se mettre à rêver (**about** à, de)

revers [rɪ'vɪəz] **NPL** *(on jacket)* revers *mpl*

reversal [rɪ'vɜ:s(ə)l] **N 1** *(of opinion, policy, situation)* revirement *m*; *(of roles)* renversement *m*, inversion *f*; *(of fortune)* revers *m*; **to suffer a r.** *(of person)* essuyer un revers de fortune **2** *Law (annulment)* annulation *f* **3** *Phot* inversion *f*

▸▸ *Phot* **r. film** film *m* inversible

REVERSE [rɪ'vɜ:s] **ADJ** *(order, image)* inverse; **in r. order** à l'envers; **the r. side** *(of coin etc)* le revers; *(of fabric)* l'envers *m*; *(of paper)* le verso

N 1 *(opposite)* contraire *m*; **to be (quite) the r. of sth** être (tout) le contraire *ou* l'opposé de qch; **she was the r. of calm** elle était tout sauf calme; **quite the r.!** bien au contraire!; **printed in r.** imprimé à l'envers

2 *(back)* *(of coin)* revers *m*; *(of fabric)* envers *m*; *(of paper)* verso *m*

3 *(defeat)* *(of enemy, misfortune)* revers *m*; **to suffer a r.** essuyer un revers de fortune; *(be defeated)* essuyer un échec

4 *Aut (gear)* marche *f* arrière; **in r.** en marche arrière; **to put a car into r.** mettre une voiture en marche arrière; **to do a r.** faire une marche arrière

VT 1 *(turn in opposite direction) (coat, picture)* retourner; *Br Tel* **to r. the charge(s)** appeler *ou* téléphoner *ou* faire un appel en PCV, *Can* faire un appel à frais virés; *Mil* **to r. arms** renverser les fusils; *Tech* **to r. steam** renverser la vapeur

2 *(alter) (order, policy)* inverser, changer du tout au tout; *(situation)* renverser; *(decision)* annuler; **to r. a trend** renverser une tendance; **the roles are reversed** les rôles sont intervertis; *Aut* **to r. one's car** faire marche arrière; **to r. the car out of the garage** sortir du garage en marche arrière

VI *Aut* faire marche arrière; **to r. into a lamppost** rentrer dans un réverbère en faisant une marche arrière; **to r. out (of the garage)** sortir (du garage) en marche arrière

▸▸ *TV, Cin* **r. angle shot** contrechamp *m*; *TV, Cin* **r. cut** contrechamp; **r. discrimination** = discrimination *f* à l'encontre d'un groupe normalement privilégié; **r. engineering** ingénierie *f* inverse; *Acct* **r. entry** écriture *f* inverse; *Aut* **r. gear** marche arrière; *Comput* **r. mode** inversion *f* vidéo; *Comput* **r. slash** barre *f* oblique inversée; *Comput* **r. sort** tri *m* en ordre décroissant; *Aviat* **r. thrust** poussée *f* inversée; *Aut* **r. turn** virage *m* en marche arrière; *Aut* **to do** *or* **make a r. turn** faire un virage en marche arrière; **r. video** vidéo *f* inverse

▸ **reverse out VT SEP** *Typ* inverser

reverse-charge call N *Br Tel* communication *f* en PCV, *Can* appel *m* à frais virés

reversible [rɪ'vɜ:sɪb(ə)l] **ADJ** *(clothing) (fabric, jacket etc)* réversible, à double face; *Phot (film)* inversible; *(decree, judgment, sentence)* révocable; **the decision is not r.** la décision est irrévocable

reversing [rɪ'vɜ:sɪŋ] **N** *Aut* marche *f* arrière

▸▸ **r. beeper** avertisseur *m* de marche arrière; **r. lights** feux *mpl* de recul

reversion [rɪ'vɜ:ʃən] **N 1** *(to previous condition)* retour *m* (**to** à); *Biol* retour à l'état antérieur, régression *f*; *Biol* **r. to type** retour au type primitif; *Fig* **this was a not unexpected r. to type** comme on s'y attendait, le naturel a repris le dessus **2** *Law (of property)* retour *m*, réversion *f*; **right of r.** réversion; **estate in r.** bien *m* grevé d'une réversion

reversionary [rɪ'vɜ:ʃənərɪ] **ADJ 1** *Biol (characteristic, organ)* atavique **2** *Law (right)* de réversion, réversible

▸▸ *Fin* **r. bonus** prime *f* d'intéressement; *Fin* **r. owner** nu-propriétaire *m*, *pl* nus-propriétaires, nue-propriétaire *f*, *pl* nues-propriétaires; *Fin* **r. ownership** nue-propriété *f*, *pl* nues-propriétés

revert [rɪ'vɜ:t] **VI 1** *(of conversation, thoughts)* revenir (**to** à); *Biol* retourner à l'état sauvage; **to r. to type** *Biol* revenir *ou* retourner au type primitif; *Fig* laisser le naturel reprendre le dessus; **we shall r. to this matter** nous reviendrons sur cette question; **reverting to your question** pour (en) revenir à votre question; **the garden has reverted to a wilderness** le jardin s'est retourné à l'état sauvage; **to r. to one's maiden name** *(of divorced woman)* reprendre son nom de jeune fille **2** *Law (of property)* revenir, retourner (**to** à) **3** *Comput (undo)* défaire; **to r. to the previous settings** rétablir les paramètres précédents

revetment [rɪ'vetmənt] **N** *Constr* revêtement *m*

▸▸ **r. wall** mur *m* de revêtement, épaulement *m*

review [rɪ'vju:] **N 1** *(of past etc)* examen *m*; *(of policy, salary etc)* révision *f*, examen; *(of situation)* bilan *m*; **to come up for r.** *(of salary, contract etc)* devoir être réexaminé; **to be under r.** *(of policy, salary etc)* faire l'objet d'une révision, être en cours de révision; **they are keeping the question of student grants under r.** la question des allocations d'études fait l'objet de réexamens perpétuels; **to keep a question under r.** continuer d'étudier une question; **prices are subject to r.** les prix peuvent faire l'objet d'une révision; **a r. of the year** une rétrospective des événements de l'année

2 *(of book, play, film etc)* compte rendu *m*, critique *f*; **he gave it a good r.** il en a fait une bonne critique; **her last novel got very bad reviews** son dernier roman a eu de très mauvaises critiques

3 *(publication)* revue *f*

4 *Theat (show)* revue *f*

5 *Mil* revue *f*; **to hold a r.** passer une revue; **to pass troops in r.** passer des troupes en revue

6 *Law (of trial)* révision *f*

VT 1 *(the past)* revoir, examiner; *(policy, salary)* réviser, examiner; *(facts)* passer en revue; *(situation)* faire le bilan *ou* le point de; **your progress will be reviewed every six weeks** on fera le point sur *ou* le bilan de vos progrès toutes les six semaines

2 *(book, film etc)* faire la critique *ou* le compte rendu de

3 *Mil (troops)* passer en revue; **to be reviewed** *(of troops)* être passé en revue

4 *esp Am Sch (revise) (lessons)* revoir, réviser

5 *Law (trial)* revoir, réviser

VI 1 **he reviews for the Sunday Times** il rédige des critiques pour le Sunday Times

2 *esp Am Sch* réviser, faire des révisions

▸▸ **r. copy** exemplaire *m* de service de presse; *TV* **r. screen** écran *m* de vision

Attention: ne pas confondre avec le mot anglais **revue**, qui signifie uniquement **spectacle de cabaret**.

reviewer [rɪ'vjuːər] N (of book, play etc) critique m

revile [rɪ'vaɪl] VT injurier (**for** pour)

revise [rɪ'vaɪz] VT **1** (amend) (text) revoir, réviser; (proofs) corriger, réviser; (law, constitution) réviser; (decision) revenir sur; **to r. one's opinion of sb** changer d'opinion à l'égard de qn; **to r. figures upwards/downwards** corriger des chiffres ou des calculs à la hausse/à la baisse **2** Br (study) (lesson) réviser, revoir, repasser
VI Br (for exam) réviser, faire des révisions (**for** pour)
N Typ épreuve f de révision, seconde f; **second** or **final r.** troisième épreuve, tierce f

revised [rɪ'vaɪzd] ADJ (edition) revu et corrigé; (figures, estimate) révisé
▸▸ **R. Standard Version** = traduction f américaine de la Bible établie en 1952; **R. Version** = traduction de la Bible de 1884

reviser [rɪ'vaɪzər] N réviseur, -euse; Typ (of proof) correcteur, -trice

revision [rɪ'vɪʒən] N révision f; **for r.** à revoir; Br Sch **to do some r.** faire des révisions

revisionism [rɪ'vɪʒənɪz(ə)m] N Pol révisionnisme m

revisionist [rɪ'vɪʒənɪst] ADJ, N Pol révisionniste mf

revisit [riː'vɪzɪt] VT (place) visiter de nouveau, revisiter; (person) aller voir de nouveau, retourner voir; **nuclear power revisited** (title of article etc) un nouveau regard ou une nouvelle perspective sur la question de l'énergie nucléaire

revitalize [riː'vaɪtəlaɪz] VT (person) revigorer; (economy) relancer; (industry, the arts, trade unionism etc) donner un nouvel essor à

revival [rɪ'vaɪv(ə)l] N **1** (of person) réanimation f; **all attempts at r. failed** toutes les tentatives de réanimation ont échoué **2** (of arts, industry, hope) renaissance f; (of custom, fashion) réapparition f, renouveau m; (of interest) réveil m, renouveau; Law (of law) remise f en vigueur; (of economy) reprise f; **the r. of trade** la reprise des affaires **3** (of play etc) reprise f **4** Rel (of faith) réveil m, renouveau m; **religious r.** retour m à la religion
▸▸ Rel **r. meeting** = réunion f visant à ranimer la foi (dans une ville)

revivalism [rɪ'vaɪvəlɪz(ə)m] N Rel = mouvement m visant à ranimer la foi

revivalist [rɪ'vaɪvəlɪst] N Rel = personne f qui essaie de ranimer la foi
▸▸ Rel **r. meeting** = réunion f visant à ranimer la foi

revive [rɪ'vaɪv] VT **1** (sb who has fainted) ranimer; (dying person) réanimer; **that will r. you** voilà qui vous remontera **2** (memory, conversation) ranimer; (hope, interest) raviver, faire renaître; (custom) faire renaître; (fashion) relancer; **to r. sb's spirits** remonter le moral à qn; **this role could r. his flagging career** ce rôle pourrait faire redémarrer sa carrière sur le déclin **3** Theat (play) remonter
VI **1** (of unconscious person) reprendre connaissance; (of dying person) revenir à la vie **2** (of hope, arts) renaître; (of custom) revenir (à la mode), reprendre; (of fashion) revenir; (of business, commerce) reprendre; **his spirits revived** il a repris courage; **hopes have revived of finding the miners alive** l'espoir renaît de trouver les mineurs vivants

revivify [riː'vɪvɪfaɪ] VT Lit revivifier

revocable [rɪ'vəʊkəb(ə)l] ADJ Law (contract, law, will etc) révocable; (decision) sur la-

quelle on peut revenir; (order) que l'on peut annuler
▸▸ **r. letter of credit** crédit m documentaire révocable

revocation [revə'keɪʃən] N (of will) révocation f; (of decision, order, contract) annulation f; (of law) abrogation f

re-voice VT TV etc doubler

re-voiced ADJ TV etc doublé

revoke [rɪ'vəʊk] VT Law (will) révoquer; (order, contract) annuler; (law) abroger; (decision, promise) revenir sur; (driving licence) retirer

revolt [rɪ'vəʊlt] N révolte f; **to rise in r.** se soulever, se révolter (**against** contre); **to be in r.** être en révolte (**against** contre)
VI (of troops) se révolter, se soulever, s'insurger (**against** contre)
VT (disgust) révolter; **to be revolted by sth** être en révolté par qch

revolting [rɪ'vəʊltɪŋ] ADJ (disgusting) (action) révoltant; **it smells r.** ça a une odeur infecte; **it tastes r.** ça a un goût infâme; **that sounds r.** (what has just been described) ça semble répugnant

revoltingly [rɪ'vəʊltɪŋlɪ] ADV d'une façon révoltante; **a r. bad smell** une odeur infecte

revolution [revə'luːʃən] N **1** Pol, Fig révolution f; Hist **the French/Russian R.** la Révolution française/russe; **the Industrial R.** la Révolution industrielle; **this process has brought about a r. in the industry** ce procédé a révolutionné ou complètement transformé l'industrie **2** (of wheel) tour m, révolution f; (of record, turntable, propeller) tour; (of planet) révolution; **revolutions per minute** tours à la minute
▸▸ Aut, Tech **r. counter** compte-tours m inv

revolutionary [revə'luːʃən(ə)rɪ] ADJ, N Pol, Fig révolutionnaire mf

revolutionize [revə'luːʃənaɪz] VT (industry) révolutionner, transformer complètement

revolve [rɪ'vɒlv] VT (wheel etc) faire tourner; Fig **to r. a problem in one's mind** retourner un problème dans son esprit
VI (of wheel etc) tourner; **to r. around sth/sb** tourner autour de qch/qn; **all my thoughts r. around you** je ne pense qu'à toi; **her life revolves around her husband** son mari est le centre de son existence; **the play revolves around …** la pièce est centrée sur …

revolver [rɪ'vɒlvər] N (firearm) revolver m
▸▸ Fin **r. credit** crédit m renouvelable, crédit revolving

revolving [rɪ'vɒlvɪŋ] ADJ **1** (planet etc) en rotation, qui accomplit sa révolution **2** (chair etc) pivotant; (stage) tournant
▸▸ Fin **r. credit** crédit m renouvelable, crédit revolving; **r. door** tambour m (porte); Am Fig = le va-et-vient de fonctionnaires haut-placés entre les services publics et le secteur privé; Fin **r. fund** fonds m de roulement; Fin **r. letter of credit** crédit documentaire renouvelable, crédit revolving; **r. stand** (to display goods) tourniquet m

revue [rɪ'vjuː] N Theat revue f

Attention: ne pas confondre avec **review**.

revulsion [rɪ'vʌlʃən] N (disgust) dégoût m, répugnance f; **to draw back in r.** reculer dans un mouvement de dégoût; **to be filled with r.** être rempli de dégoût; **to fill sb with r.** (of scene, cruelty etc) remplir qn de dégoût

reward [rɪ'wɔːd] N récompense f; **to offer a r.** offrir une récompense (**for** pour); **as a** or **in r. for …** en récompense de ou pour …; **to get a fair r. for** or **from one's labour** tirer de son travail une récompense légitime
VT (person) récompenser, rémunérer (**for** de; **with** par); (financially) récompenser;

that's how he rewards me for my loyalty voilà comment il me récompense de mon dévouement; **their patience was finally rewarded** ils furent finalement récompensés de leur patience

rewarding [rɪ'wɔːdɪŋ] ADJ qui (en) vaut la peine; (satisfying) qui apporte des satisfactions; (financially) qui (en) vaut la peine financièrement, rémunérateur, -trice

rewind [riː'waɪnd] VT (pt, pp rewound [riː'waʊnd]) (film, tape) rembobiner

rewind [riː'waɪnd] N rembobinage m; (automatic) r. rembobinage (automatique)
▸▸ **r. button** (on tape deck) bouton m de rembobinage

rewire [riː'waɪər] VT (house, flat) refaire l'installation électrique de; (plug) recâbler

reword [riː'wɜːd] VT (paragraph etc) recomposer, rédiger à nouveau; **let me r. that** je vais essayer de m'exprimer autrement

rework [riː'wɜːk] VT (idea, theme) retravailler (sur); (text, thesis etc) retravailler; **to r. a letter** remanier une lettre

rewrite [riː'raɪt] N (of article, film script etc) nouvelle version f; **it needs a r.** cela demande à être réécrit
▸▸ Journ etc **r. man** rewriter m; Journ etc **r. sub** réviseur, -euse

rewrite [riː'raɪt] VT (pt rewrote [riː'rəʊt]; pp rewritten [riː'rɪt(ə)n]) (letter, article, film script etc) récrire, réécrire; Fig **to r. history** réécrire l'histoire

rewriteable [riː'raɪtəb(ə)l] ADJ Comput réinscriptible

rewriter [riː'raɪtər] N Journ etc réviseur, -euse, rewriter m; (of filmscript) rewriter

rewriting [riː'raɪtɪŋ] N Journ etc récriture f, rewriting m; (of filmscript) réécriture f

Reykjavik ['rekjəvɪk] N Reykjavik

Reynaud's disease ['reɪnəʊdz] N Med maladie f de Reynaud

RFL [ɑːref'el] N Br Sport (abbr **Rugby Football League**) = fédération f britannique de rugby à treize

RFU [ɑːref'juː] N Br Sport (abbr **Rugby Football Union**) = fédération f britannique de rugby

RGB [ɑːdʒiː'biː] N Comput (abbr **red, green and blue**) RVB m

Rgt (abbr **regiment**) rég

rhapsodic(al) [ræp'sɒdɪk, -ɪk(ə)l] ADJ (description etc) excessivement élogieux, dithyrambique; Mus r(h)apsodique

rhapsodize ['ræpsədaɪz] VI (of person) s'extasier (**over** sur)

rhapsody ['ræpsədɪ] N Mus r(h)apsodie f; Fig (feeling) transports mpl; (in words) dithyrambe m; Fig **to go into/be in rhapsodies** s'extasier (**over** sur); **to send sb into rhapsodies** rendre qn extatique

rhea ['riːə] N (bird) nandou m

Rhenish ['renɪʃ] ADJ Geog rhénan, du Rhin
N (wine) vin m du Rhin
▸▸ **R. wine** vin du Rhin

rheo ['riːəʊ], **rheostat** ['riːəʊstæt] N Elec rhéostat m

rhesus ['riːsəs] N Zool (monkey) rhésus m; **r. positive/negative** rhésus positif/négatif; **I'm r. negative** je suis rhésus négatif
▸▸ **r. baby** = enfant mf rhésus positif souffrant d'incompatibilité avec le rhésus négatif de la mère; Physiol **r. factor** (facteur m) rhésus; Zool **r. monkey** (macaque m) rhésus

rhetoric ['retərɪk] N **1** Pej (bombast) emphase f, rhétorique f; **his speech contained nothing but r.** son discours ne consistait qu'en de belles phrases vides de sens; **it's just empty r.** ce ne sont que des mots **2** (art of speaking) rhétorique f

rhetorical [rɪ'tɒrɪk(ə)l] ADJ **1** *(style)* emphatique, ampoulé **2** *(term etc)* de rhétorique; **his question was purely r.** sa question était purement rhétorique
▸▸**r. question** question *f* posée pour la forme

rhetorically [rɪ'tɒrɪklɪ] ADV **1** *(to speak)* avec emphase **2** *(to ask)* pour la forme

rhetorician [retɒ'rɪʃən] N *(expert in speaking)* rhétoricien, -ienne

rheumatic [ruː'mætɪk, rʊ-] Med ADJ *(pain etc)* rhumatismal, -aux; *(person)* rhumatisant; *(finger, joint)* atteint de rhumatisme; **he suffered from a r. condition** il souffrait de rhumatismes
N rhumatisant, -ante
▸▸**r. fever** rhumatisme *m* articulaire aigu

rheumaticky [ruː'mætɪkɪ, rʊ-] ADJ *Fam* = **rheumatic** ADJ

rheumatics [ruː'mætɪks, rʊ-], **rheumatism** ['ruːmətɪz(ə)m, rʊ-] N Med rhumatisme *m*; **to have** *or* **suffer from r.** avoir des *ou* souffrir de rhumatismes

rheumatoid ['ruːmətɔɪd, 'rʊ-] ADJ Med rhumatoïde
▸▸**r. arthritis** polyarthrite *f* rhumatoïde

rheumatologist [ruːmə'tɒlədʒɪst, rʊ-] N Med rhumatologue *mf*

rheumatology [ruːmə'tɒlədʒɪ, rʊ-] N Med rhumatologie *f*

rheumy ['ruːmɪ] ADJ chassieux

Rhine [raɪn] N **the (River) R.** le Rhin
▸▸**R. wine** vin *m* du Rhin

Rhineland (the) [ðə'raɪnlænd] N la Rhénanie

rhinestone ['raɪnstəʊn] N faux diamant *m*; **r. earring** boucle *f* d'oreille en strass

rhino ['raɪnəʊ] N *(animal)* rhino(céros) *m*

rhinoceros [raɪ'nɒsərəs] N *(animal)* rhinocéros *m*; *Fig* **to have a hide** *or* **skin like a r.** manquer totalement de *ou* être complètement dépourvu de sensibilité

rhizome ['raɪzəʊm] N Bot rhizome *m*

Rhode Island [rəʊd] N Rhode Island *m*
▸▸**R. Red** poule *f* Rhode-Island

Rhodes[1] [rəʊdz] N Rhodes *f*

Rhodes[2] N
▸▸**R. scholar** = titulaire *mf* d'une 'Rhodes Scholarship'; **R. Scholarship** = bourse *f* permettant à certains étudiants étrangers d'étudier à l'université d'Oxford

Rhodesia [rəʊ'diːʒə, -zɪə] N Formerly Rhodésie *f*

Rhodesian [rəʊ'diːʒən, -zɪən] Formerly ADJ rhodésien
N Rhodésien, -ienne

rhododendron, *pl* **rhododendrons, rhododendra** [rəʊdə'dendrən, -ənz, -ə] N rhododendron *m*
▸▸**r. bush** rhododendron

rhomb [rɒm] N Geom losange *m*, rhombe *m*

rhombic ['rɒmbɪk] ADJ rhombique

rhomboid ['rɒmbɔɪd] ADJ, N Geom rhomboïde *m*

rhombus, *pl* **rhombuses, rhombi** ['rɒmbəs, -əsɪz, -aɪ] N Geom = **rhomb**

Rhone (the) [ðə'rəʊn] N le Rhône; **the R. valley** la vallée du Rhône

rhubarb ['ruːbɑːb] N Bot, Culin rhubarbe *f*; **r. jam** confiture *f* de rhubarbe; *Theat* **r., r.** = mots *mpl* répétés par les acteurs lorsqu'ils doivent avoir l'air de parler entre eux sur scène

rhyme [raɪm] N **1** *(sound)* rime *f*; **can you think of a r. for …?** est-ce que tu peux trouver une rime pour …?; *Fig* **without r. or reason** sans rime ni raison; **there's neither r. nor reason to it** cela ne rime à rien *ou* n'a ni rime ni raison **2** *(poem)* vers *mpl*; **children's**

rhymes comptines *fpl*; **to make up a r.** faire *ou* composer des vers (**about** sur); **to speak in r.** faire des vers
VI *(of words)* rimer (**with** avec); **rhyming couplet** distique *m*; **rhyming dictionary** dictionnaire *m* de rimes
VT **to r. a word with another** faire rimer un mot avec un autre
▸▸**r. scheme** combinaison *f* de rimes

rhymed [raɪmd] ADJ rimé

rhymester ['raɪmstər] N Pej rimailleur, -euse

rhyming slang ['raɪmɪŋ] N = argot *m* rimé des Cockneys

Rhyming slang
Il s'agit d'un procédé complexe consistant à remplacer un mot par une expression dont le dernier terme rime avec le mot en question; bien souvent n'est prononcé que le premier terme de l'expression, à savoir celui qui ne rime pas avec le mot remplacé. Exemple: kids = dustbin lids = dustbins; head = loaf of bread = loaf. À l'origine ce type d'argot était pratiqué par les Cockneys (habitants de l'est de Londres) mais certains termes sont maintenant passés dans la langue courante et sont connus de la plupart des Britanniques.

rhythm ['rɪð(ə)m] N Mus etc rythme *m*; *(pace)* rythme, cadence *f*; **to have a sense of r.** avoir le sens du rythme; **he's got r.** il a le sens du rythme; **to keep up a steady r.** maintenir un rythme régulier; *(of worker)* travailler à un rythme régulier; **r. of work** rythme *ou* cadence de travail
▸▸**r. and blues** rhythm and blues *m inv*; **r. method** *(of contraception)* méthode *f* des températures; **r. section** section *f* rythmique

rhythmic(al) ['rɪðmɪk, -ɪk(ə)l] ADJ rythmé, cadencé; *(beat)* rythmique; **to be r.** *(of person)* avoir le sens du rythme
▸▸**r. breathing** respiration *f* cadencée; **r. dancing** danse *f* rythmique; **r. gymnastics** gymnastique *f* rythmique, GRS *f*

rhythmically ['rɪðmɪklɪ] ADV *(to breathe, dance etc)* avec rythme, de façon rythmée *ou* cadencée

rib [rɪb] N **1** *(of person, animal)* côte *f*; **his ribs stick out** on lui voit les côtes; **r.-tickling joke/ story** une plaisanterie/histoire à mourir de rire; *Fig Fam* **this soup will stick to your ribs!** *(is very thick)* cette soupe vous tiendra bien au corps!; *Culin* **spare ribs** travers *m* de porc **2** *(of aeroplane, ceiling, leaf)* nervure *f*; *(of umbrella)* baleine *f* **3** *(in knitting)* côte *f*; **knit two inches in r.** tricoter environ cinq centimètres (au point) de côtes
VT **(-bb-)** *Fam (person)* taquiner (**about** à propos de, au sujet de)
VI *Knitting* **r. for two inches** tricoter environ cinq centimètres (au point) de côtes
▸▸*Culin* **r. roast** côte de bœuf

ribald ['rɪbəld, 'raɪ-] ADJ *(joke, person, song)* grivois, paillard; *(laughter)* gras

ribaldry ['rɪbəldrɪ, 'raɪ-] N grivoiserie *f*, paillardise *f*; **enough of this r.!** assez de paillardises!

ribbed [rɪbd] ADJ *(ceiling, vault)* à nervures, nervuré; *(fabric)* côtelé, à côtes; *Knitting* au point de côtes

ribbing ['rɪbɪŋ] N **1** *Fam (teasing)* taquinerie *f*; **to take a r.** se faire mettre en boîte **2** *(on ceiling)* nervures *fpl*; *(of fabric, knitting)* côtes *fpl*

ribbon ['rɪbən] N **1** *(for hair, package, typewriter)* ruban *m*; **tied with r.** attaché avec du ruban; *Horseriding* **ribbons** *(reins)* guides

fpl; **to hang in ribbons** *(of clothes, curtains etc)* pendre en lambeaux; **to tear to ribbons** *(clothes etc)* mettre en lambeaux, déchiqueter, lacérer; *Fam (film, performance etc)* éreinter **2** *(on medal)* ruban *m*; *(of order)* cordon *m* **3** *Fig (of land, road etc)* bande *f* étroite, *Lit* ruban *m*; *(of smoke)* filet *m* **4** *Comput (under menu bar)* ruban *m*, barre *f* d'outils
▸▸**r. cartridge** ruban encreur; **r. cassette** cassette *f* de ruban; *Br* **r. development** croissance *f* urbaine linéaire *(le long des grands axes routiers)*; **r. guide** *(on printer)* guide-ruban *m*, *pl* guides-rubans; **r. microphone** microphone *m* à ruban

ribcage ['rɪbkeɪdʒ] N Anat cage *f* thoracique

riboflavin(e) [raɪbəʊ'fleɪvɪn] N Chem riboflavine *f*

ribonucleic [raɪbəʊnjuː'kliːɪk] ADJ
▸▸*Chem* **r. acid** acide *m* ribonucléique

rice [raɪs] N riz *m*; **long/short grain r.** riz à grains longs/courts; **brown r.** riz complet; **to grow r.** cultiver du riz; **r.-growing** *(country, region)* rizicole
VT Am Culin *(vegetables)* passer au presse-purée
▸▸**r. bowl** *(dish)* bol *m* à riz; *Fig (region)* région *f* productrice de riz; *Fig* **the country was once the r. bowl of Asia** le pays a fourni autrefois tout son riz à l'Asie; **r. field** rizière *f*; **r. grower** riziculteur, -trice; **r. growing** riziculture *f*; **r. paddy** rizière *f*; **r. paper** papier *m* de riz; **r. pudding** riz au lait; **r. water** eau *f* de riz; **r. wine** alcool *m* de riz, saké *m*

ricer ['raɪsər] N Am Culin presse-purée *m inv*

rich [rɪtʃ] ADJ *(person, country, food)* riche; *(profit)* gros; *(banquet)* somptueux; *(soil)* riche, fertile; *(vegetation)* luxuriant; *(harvest, supply)* abondant; *(costume, dress)* riche, somptueux; *(furnishings)* luxueux; *(colour)* intense; *(voice)* chaud, étoffé, ample; **extremely r.** *(person)* richissime; **r. people** les riches *mpl*; **to get** *or* **grow r.** s'enrichir; **a get-r.-quick scheme** un système pour s'enrichir rapidement; **I'm richer by a hundred pounds** *or* **a hundred pounds richer** j'ai une centaine de livres de plus; **to strike it r.** faire fortune, *Fam* décrocher le gros lot; **r. in …** riche *ou* abondant en …; *Fam Iron* **that's r. coming from you** venant de toi, c'est un peu fort
N **1** riches *(of country, seabed etc)* richesse(s) *f(pl)* **2** **the r.** *(pl)* les riches *mpl*
▸▸*Aut, Tech* **r. mixture** *(in engine)* mélange *m* riche

-rich [rɪtʃ] SUFF cotton/protein-**r.** riche en coton/protéines; **iron-r.** riche *ou* à haute teneur en fer

Richard ['rɪtʃəd] N **R. the Lionheart** Richard *m* Cœur de Lion

richly ['rɪtʃlɪ] ADV *(to dress)* richement, somptueusement; *(to decorate)* richement, magnifiquement; **r. deserved** bien mérité

richness ['rɪtʃnɪs] N *(of person, country, food, fuel mix, style)* richesse *f*, abondance *f*, *(of banquet)* somptuosité *f*, *(of soil)* richesse, fertilité *f*, *(of voice)* chaleur *f*, ampleur *f*, *(of colour)* intensité *f*

Richter ['rɪktər] N
▸▸**R. scale** échelle *f* de Richter; **to measure five on the R. scale** atteindre cinq sur l'échelle de Richter

rick[1] [rɪk] N *(of hay, straw etc)* meule *f*
VT *(hay etc)* mettre en meule(s)

rick[2] VT *(ankle)* se tordre; **to r. one's neck** attraper un torticolis; **to r. one's back** se donner un tour de reins

rickets ['rɪkɪts] NPL Med rachitisme *m*; **to have r.** être rachitique VOIR GRAMMAIRE A7

rickety ['rɪkɪtɪ] ADJ **1** *Fam (furniture)* bancal, -als; branlant; *(staircase)* branlant, délabré; *(bridge)* branlant; *Fig (explanation, alliance)* bancal, boiteux **2** *Med* rachitique

rickshaw ['rɪkʃɔː] N *(pulled)* pousse-pousse *m inv*; *(cycled)* cyclo-pousse *m inv*

ricochet ['rɪkəʃeɪ, -ʃet] N *(of ball, bullet etc)* ricochet *m*

VI *(pt, pp* **ricochetted** ['rɪkəʃeɪd]; *prp* **ricochetting** ['rɪkəʃeɪɪŋ]) *(of ball, bullet etc)* ricocher (**off** sur)

rictus, *pl* **rictus, rictusses** ['rɪktəs, -əsɪz] N rictus *m*

rid [rɪd] VT *(pt* **ridded, rid**; *pp* **rid**; *prp* **ridding**) *(person)* débarrasser, délivrer (**of** de); *(place)* débarrasser (**of** de); **to r. the world of poverty** délivrer le monde de la pauvreté; **to r. oneself of one's illusions** se défaire de ses illusions; **to r. sb of his enemies** délivrer qn de ses ennemis; **the kidneys r. the body of waste** les reins débarrassent le corps des déchets; **to get r. of** *(dismiss)* renvoyer; *(government, politician etc)* se débarrasser de; *(murder)* supprimer, éliminer; **to get r. or to r. oneself of sth** se débarrasser *ou* se défaire de qch; **I thought we were never going to get r. of them** *(guests)* j'ai cru que nous n'allions jamais arriver à nous en débarrasser *ou* à nous débarrasser d'eux; **to get r. of a cold** se débarrasser d'un rhume; **I'll get r. of it for you** je vais t'en débarrasser; **I've got r. of my car** je me suis débarrassé de ma voiture; **we can't get r. of the house** nous n'arrivons pas à vendre la maison; *Cards* **to get r. of a card** se défausser d'une carte; **to be well r. of sth/sb** être bien débarrassé de qch/qn; **you're well r. of him!** tu en es bien débarrassé!

riddance ['rɪd(ə)ns] N **good r.!** bon débarras!; *Fam* **good r. to bad rubbish!** bon débarras, on ne perd pas grand-chose!

ridden ['rɪd(ə)n] PP *see* **ride** VI, VT
ADJ **to be r. with** *or* **by guilt** être bourrelé de remords *ou* accablé par le remords

-ridden ['rɪd(ə)n] SUFF **debt-r.** criblé *ou* accablé de dettes; **disease-r.** rongé par la maladie; **guilt-r.** bourrelé de remords, accablé par le remords

riddle¹ ['rɪd(ə)l] N *(puzzle)* devinette *f*; *Fig (person, event)* énigme *f*; **to speak** *or* **talk in riddles** parler par énigmes; **to ask sb a r.** poser une devinette à qn

riddle² N *(for earth, gravel etc)* crible *m*
VT **1** *(gravel)* cribler **2 to r. sb with bullets** cribler qn de balles; **riddled with** *(holes)* criblé de; *(spelling mistakes)* cousu de; *(corruption)* en proie à; *(cancer)* rongé par

RIDE [raɪd]

N tour 1	▪ promenade 1	▪ trajet 2
VI faire du cheval 1	▪ aller 1	▪ faire 1
VT monter 1	▪ monter à 1	▪ prendre 2

N **1** *(journey)* *(on bicycle, motorbike, car)* tour *m*, promenade *f*; *(in taxi)* course *f*; *(on horse)* promenade; *(in train)* voyage *m*; *(on merry-go-round)* tour (de manège); *(in boat, helicopter, plane)* tour; **to go for a r. in a car** *or* **a car r.** aller se promener *ou* aller faire un tour en voiture; **we went for a r. in my car** nous sommes allés faire un tour dans ma voiture; **to go for** *or* **take a r.** *(on bicycle, motorbike)* aller se promener *ou* aller faire un tour à bicyclette/à moto; *(on horse)* faire une promenade à cheval; **to have a r. on** *(bicycle)* monter sur; *(horse)* monter à; **to give a child a r. on one's back** porter un enfant sur son dos; **the car gives a very smooth r.** la voiture a de bonnes qualités routières; *Fig* **he did not have an easy r.** *(at interview, press conference etc)* on ne l'a pas épargné; *Fig* **to give sb a rough r.** en faire baver *ou* voir à qn;

we're in for a bumpy r. *(in plane, car etc)* ça va secouer; *Fig* nous sommes bien partis pour en baver; *Fig* **to be** *or* **come along for the r.** venir juste pour voir; **he has three rides today** *(of jockey)* il a trois montes aujourd'hui; **to take sb for a r.** emmener qn faire une promenade (**on a horse** à cheval; **in one's car** en voiture); *Fig Fam (cheat)* faire marcher qn, mener qn en bateau; *Am Fig Fam (in order to kill)* emmener qn en voiture pour lui faire la peau; *Fig Fam* **he's been taken for a r.** *(cheated)* il s'est fait avoir **2** *(distance)* trajet *m*; *Br* **it's a 70p r. on the bus** il y en a pour 70p en autobus; **it's only a short r. away by car** il n'y en a pas pour longtemps en voiture; **it's a quarter of an hour's r. on a bicycle** il y en a pour un quart d'heure à bicyclette **3** *Am (lift)* **can I give you a r.?** est-ce que je peux vous emmener *ou* conduire quelque part?; **could you give me a r. into town?** est-ce que tu peux m'emmener *ou* me conduire en ville?; **does everyone have a r. to the church?** est-ce que tout le monde a un véhicule pour aller à l'église?; **do you have a r. to the airport?** est-ce que quelqu'un vous emmène *ou* conduit à l'aéroport? **4** *(path in forest)* allée *f* cavalière **5** *(attraction at funfair)* attraction *f* **6** *(passenger in taxi)* client, -ente **7** *Am Fam (car)* bagnole *f*, caisse *f* **8** *Vulg (sexual partner)* **a good r.** un bon coup

VI *(pt* **rode** [rəʊd]; *pp* **ridden** ['rɪd(ə)n]) **1** *(on horse)* faire du cheval, monter à cheval; *(on bicycle)* faire de la bicyclette; *(on motorbike)* faire de la moto; **he was riding when I saw him** il était à cheval/bicyclette/moto quand je l'ai vu; **can you r.?** *(on horse)* est-ce que vous savez monter à cheval?; **she doesn't r. much** *(on horse)* elle ne monte pas souvent à cheval; **I'm going riding this morning** *(on horse)* je vais faire du cheval ce matin; **he rides well** *(on horse)* il monte bien (à cheval), il est bon cavalier; **he rode into town on his horse/bicycle** il est allé en ville à cheval/bicyclette; **to r. to hounds** faire de la chasse à courre; **to r. on an elephant** aller à dos d'éléphant; **it's the first time I've ridden in a Porsche** c'est la première fois que je roule en *ou* que je monte dans une Porsche; **to r. on sb's knee** *(of child)* être à califourchon sur le genou de qn; **to r. to a place** *ou* **to r. to work on the bus** aller *ou* se rendre en bus à son travail; **he prefers to r. at the back of the bus** il préfère s'asseoir au fond du bus; **I don't mind riding in the back** *or Am* **in back** je veux bien m'asseoir à l'arrière; *Fig* **to be riding for a fall** courir à sa perte; **to be riding high** connaître une période de succès; **to r. up/down** *(in lift)* monter/descendre; *Horseracing* **he's riding in the 3.30** il dispute la course de 3h30 **2** *Fig* **to let sth r.** laisser courir qch **3** *Aut* **this car rides very smoothly** cette voiture a de bonnes qualités routières **4** *(of ship)* **to r. at anchor** être au mouillage

VT **1 she rode her horse across the fields** elle a fait traverser le champ à son cheval; **she rode her horse at the fence** elle a dirigé son cheval sur la barrière; **he's a very easy horse to r.** c'est un cheval très facile à monter; **to r. an ass/elephant** être monté à dos d'âne/d'éléphant; *Horseracing* **Comet ridden by Martin** Comet monté par Martin; **to r. a good/bad race** *(of horse)* bien/mal courir; *(of jockey)* bien/mal monter; **witches r. broomsticks** les sorcières chevauchent des balais *ou* des manches à balai; **to know how to r. a bike** savoir faire du vélo ou de la bicyclette; **can I r. your bike?** est-ce que je peux monter sur ta bicyclette?; **to r. 50 kilometres** aller *ou* faire 50 kilomètres (à cheval

ou en voiture *etc*); **to r. the waves** *Naut (of ship)* voguer sur les flots; *Sport (of surfer)* chevaucher les vagues; **to r. the storm** *Naut* soutenir le choc de la tempête; *Fig* attendre que l'orage passe; *Boxing* **to r. a punch** *(of boxer)* encaisser un coup; *Am* **to r. sb up/down** *(in elevator)* faire monter/descendre qn; **to r. sb down** *(on horse)* *(trample)* piétiner qn; **to r. a horse into the ground** monter un cheval jusqu'à l'épuisement

2 *Am (travel in)* *(bus, train)* prendre (**to** jusqu'à)

3 *esp Am Fam (harass)* **to r. sb** être (toujours) sur le dos de qn; **stop riding me!** fiche-moi la paix!

4 *Vulg (have sex with)* *(of man)* baiser, tringler, troncher, sauter; *(of woman)* baiser avec, s'envoyer

▸ **ride on** VT INSEP *Fig (depend on)* **there's a lot riding on this election** l'enjeu de cette élection est important; **what's riding on it?** quelle conséquence est-ce que ça peut avoir?

▸ **ride out** VT SEP **to r. out the storm** *Naut* étaler la tempête; *Fig* surmonter la crise; *Fig* **to r. out a problem/crisis** survivre à un problème/une crise; *Am* **to r. sb out of town** faire quitter la ville à qn

VI **we rode out to meet them** nous sommes partis à leur rencontre en vélo/à cheval

▸ **ride up** VI *(of skirt etc)* remonter

rider ['raɪdər] N **1** *(on horse)* cavalier, -ière; *(on racehorse)* jockey *m*; *(in circus)* écuyer, -ère; *(on bicycle)* cycliste *mf*; *(on motorcycle)* motocycliste *mf*; **to be a good r.** *(on horse)* bien monter à cheval, être bon cavalier; *(on motorcycle)* bien savoir faire de la moto; *Sport* être un bon/une bonne motocycliste **2** *(to bill)* clause *f* additionnelle (**to** à); *(document)* annexe *f* (**to** à); *(to contract)* avenant *m* (**to** à); **to add a r. (recommending) that …** ajouter une clause recommandant que …

riderless ['raɪdəlɪs] ADJ *(horse)* sans cavalier

ridership ['raɪdəʃɪp] N *Am* = nombre *m* total d'utilisateurs des transports en commun

ridesharing ['raɪdʃeərɪŋ] N *Am* = partage *m* d'un véhicule pour se rendre sur son lieu de travail

ridge [rɪdʒ] N **1** *(of roof, mountain)* arête *f*, crête *f* **2** *(chain of hills, mountains)* chaîne *f*, *Met* **r. of high pressure** dorsale *f* barométrique **3** *(on surface)* strie *f*; *(on sand)* ride *f*; *(in ploughed field)* crête *f* de labour
VT **1** *(roof)* enfaîter **2** *(surface)* strier, sillonner; *(sand)* rider, strier
▸ ▸ **r. roof** toit *m* en dos d'âne; **r. tile** *(tuile f)* faîtière *f*

ridged [rɪdʒd] ADJ *(surface)* strié, ridé

ridgepole ['rɪdʒpəʊl] N *(of roof)* panne *f* faîtière; *(of tent)* mât *m* de faîte

ridgetree ['rɪdʒtriː] N *(of roof)* panne *f* faîtière

ridgeway ['rɪdʒweɪ] N *Br* route *f* des crêtes

ridicule ['rɪdɪkjuːl] N ridicule *m*; **to hold sb/sth up to r.** tourner qn/qch en ridicule *ou* en dérision; **to lay oneself open to r.** s'exposer au ridicule; **object of r.** objet *m* de risée
VT ridiculiser, tourner en ridicule (**for** à cause de)

ridiculous [rɪ'dɪkjʊləs] ADJ *(behaviour, person etc)* ridicule; **to make sb/sth look r.** rendre qn/qch ridicule, ridiculiser qn/qch; **to make oneself look r.** se rendre ridicule, se ridiculiser; **it's r. that …** il est ridicule que … + *subj*; **to pay a r. price for sth** *(pay little)* payer qch un prix ridicule *ou* dérisoire; *(pay a lot)* payer qch beaucoup trop cher; *Fam* **don't be r.** ne sois pas ridicule
N **the r.** le ridicule *m*; **to verge on the r.** friser

le ridicule; **from the sublime to the r.** du sublime au ridicule

ridiculously [rɪˈdɪkjʊləslɪ] **ADV** *(to act, dress etc)* d'une façon ridicule, ridiculement; *(easy, expensive, low etc)* ridiculement

ridiculousness [rɪˈdɪkjʊləsnɪs] **N** *(of appearance, behaviour, situation etc)* ridicule *m*

riding [ˈraɪdɪŋ] **N 1** *(of horse)* équitation *f*; *(skill)* monte *f*; **r. is her favourite hobby** l'équitation est son passe-temps favori **2** *Aut* **smooth r.** suspension *f* douce **3** *(in Canada, New Zealand)* circonscription *f* électorale; *(in Yorkshire)* division *f* administrative
▸▸**r. boots** bottes *fpl* de cheval; **r. breeches** culotte *f* de cheval; **r. cap** bombe *f*; **r. crop** cravache *f*; **r. habit** tenue *f* d'amazone; **r. instructor** professeur *m* d'équitation; **r. kit** tenue de cheval; **r. lesson** leçon *f* d'équitation; **r. school** école *f* d'équitation; **r. whip** cravache

RIE [ɑːraɪˈiː] **N** *Fin* (*abbr* **recognized investment exchange**) marché *m* d'investissement agréé

rife [raɪf] **ADJ** *(widespread)* répandu; **to be r.** *(of corruption, crime, disease etc)* régner, sévir; *(of rumours)* aller bon train; **the city was r. with disease** la ville était en proie à la maladie, la maladie régnait dans la ville; **the city was r. with rumour** les rumeurs allaient bon train dans la ville; **the police force is r. with corruption** la corruption règne dans la police

riff [rɪf] **N** *Mus* riff *m*

riffle [ˈrɪf(ə)l] **N** *Am* *(ripple)* rides *fpl* sur l'eau, ondulations *fpl* de l'eau; *(shoal)* banc *m*
VT *(cards)* battre; *(pages)* feuilleter
▸ **riffle through VT INSEP** feuilleter

riffraff [ˈrɪfræf] **N** *Pej* racaille *f*; **he's just r.** c'est un vaurien

rifle¹ [ˈraɪf(ə)l] **VT** *(flat, office etc)* mettre sens dessus dessous; *(person's pockets, filing cabinet, drawer)* fouiller; *(tomb)* violer

rifle² **N** fusil *m*; *(for hunting)* fusil (de chasse); **within r. shot** à portée de fusil
▸▸**r. club** société *f* de tir; *Mil* **R. Corps** corps *m* des fusiliers *ou* des chasseurs à pied; *TV, Radio* **r. mike** micro *m* canon; **r. practice** (exercice *m* de) tir *m* au fusil; **r. shot** coup *m* de fusil

rifleman, *pl* **riflemen** [ˈraɪf(ə)lmən] **N** *Mil* fusilier *m*, fantassin *m*

rifling [ˈraɪflɪŋ] **N** *(on gun barrel)* *(grooves)* rayures *fpl*

rift [rɪft] **N** *(in earth, rock etc)* fissure *f*, crevasse *f*; *(in clouds etc)* éclaircie *f*, *Fig* *(in relationship)* rupture *f*, *Pol* *(in party)* scission *f*, *Fig* **to heal the r. between two people** réconcilier deux personnes; **to heal the r. in a party** réconcilier les adversaires au sein d'un parti
▸▸**r. valley** fossé *m* d'effondrement

rig [rɪg] **N 1** *(of ship)* gréement *m* **2** *(oil)* **r.** derrick *m*; *(at sea)* plate-forme *f* pétrolière, *pl* plates-formes pétrolières **3** *Am* *(truck)* semi-remorque *m*, *pl* semi-remorques **4** *Fam* *(outfit)* = **rigout 5** *St Exch* *Fam* *(rise)* hausse *f* factice; *(fall)* baisse *f* factice
VT (-gg-) **1** *Naut* *(ship)* gréer **2** *Fam* *(manipulate dishonestly)* *(election etc)* truquer; **to r. the market** *Com* manipuler le marché; *St Exch* manipuler la Bourse; **to r. prices** fixer illégalement les prix; **to r. a game** truquer un jeu
▸ **rig out VT SEP** *(dress)* *(person)* attifer, accoutrer (**as** en); **to r. oneself out** s'accoutrer (**in** dans, avec)
▸ **rig up VT SEP** *(aerial, shelter)* monter, installer; *Fam* **to r. something up** faire une installation de fortune

rigamarole [ˈrɪgəmərəʊl] **N** *Fam* = **rigmarole**

rigger [ˈrɪgər] **N 1** *(of ship)* gréeur *m*; **square r.** *(ship)* navire *m* gréé en carré **2** *(of plane)* monteur-régleur *m*, *pl* monteurs-régleurs

rigging [ˈrɪgɪŋ] **N 1** *(on ship)* gréement *m*; *(of ship)* gréage *m* **2** *Fam* *(of election)* truquage *m*; *St Exch* *(of market)* hausse *f* *ou* baisse *f* factice; *(of prices)* fixation *f* illégale

---

RIGHT [raɪt]

ADJ	bon **1, 3** ▪ juste **1, 2** ▪ bien **2, 4** ▪ vrai **5** ▪ droit **6**
N	droit **1, 2, 5** ▪ bien **1** ▪ droite **4, 6**
ADV	droit **1** ▪ juste **3, 4** ▪ bien **4, 5** ▪ à droite **6**
VT	redresser **1**

ADJ 1 *(correct, accurate)* *(answer etc)* bon, *f* bonne, exact, juste; *(word)* exact, juste; **that can't be r.** ça ne peut pas être ça, ça ne peut pas être juste; **have you got the r. amount?** avez-vous le compte exact?; **is this the r. house?** est-ce la bonne maison?, est-ce bien la maison?; **what's the r. time?** quelle heure est-il (exactement)?, quelle est l'heure juste *ou* exacte?; **my watch is r.** ma montre est à l'heure; **to be r.** *(of person)* avoir raison (**to do** de faire); **you're quite r.!** vous avez bien raison!; **to be r. about sth** avoir raison à propos de qch; **you were r. about him being a crook** vous aviez raison de dire que c'est une canaille; **you were quite r. to call the police** vous avez bien fait d'appeler la police; **it doesn't look r.** *(of answer, dress etc)* ça ne va pas; **the r. side of the material** l'endroit *m* du tissu; **r. side** *or* **way up** à l'endroit; **we're on the r. road** nous sommes sur le bon chemin *ou* la bonne route; *Fig* **to be on the r. lines** être dans la bonne direction; **that's r.!** parfaitement!, c'est ça!; **r. (you are)!** entendu!, d'accord!; *Fam* **r.?** d'accord?; **r. on!**, *Br, Austr* **too r.!** exactement!, bien parlé!; **he's on the r. side of forty** il n'a pas encore quarante ans; **to get on the r. side of sb** s'insinuer dans les bonnes grâces de qn; **to keep on the r. side of the law** respecter la loi **2** *(morally good)* bien; *(fair)* juste; **it's not r. to steal** ce n'est pas bien de voler; **it's not r. that ...** ce n'est pas juste que ... + *subj*; **I can't accept the money – it wouldn't look r.** je ne peux pas accepter l'argent, ça ferait mauvais effet; **it's only r.** ce n'est que justice; **I thought it r. to attend** j'ai jugé bon *ou* à propos d'y aller; **to do the r. thing** se conduire honnêtement *ou* honorablement; *Br Old-fashioned* **I hope he's going to do the r. thing by you** *(marry you)* j'espère qu'il va agir honorablement à ton égard (et demander ta main) **3** *(most appropriate)* **the r. thing to do** la meilleure chose à faire; **in the r. place** à la bonne place; **to be in the r. place at the r. time** être là où il faut quand il le faut; **the r. man/woman in the r. place** l'homme/la femme qu'il faut pour la tâche; **you came at the r. time** vous êtes venu au bon moment; **now is not the r. time to mention it** ce n'est pas le moment d'en parler; **to wait for the r. moment** attendre le bon moment *ou* le moment opportun; **to know the r. people** connaître les gens qu'il faut **4** *(mentally, physically well)* bien; **to be in one's r. mind** avoir toute sa raison, être en possession de toutes ses facultés; **no one in their r. mind would do such a thing** aucune personne sensée ne ferait une chose pareille; *Fam* **he's not quite r. in the head** il n'a pas toute sa tête; **I'm not feeling quite r.** je ne me sens pas très bien, *Fam* je ne me sens pas dans mon assiette; *Fam* **as r. as** *Br* **rain** *or Am* **a trivet** en parfaite santé **5** *Br Fam (as intensifier)* vrai; **I felt a r. fool** je

me suis senti vraiment stupide; **he's all r.** c'est un brave type; *SI* **she's a bit of all r.!** voilà une jolie pépée!

6 *(righthand)* droit; **on the r. side** à *ou* sur la droite; **r. hand** main *f* droite; **on my r. hand** sur *ou* à ma droite; **he's my r. hand** c'est mon bras droit; **r. justified** justifié à droite

N 1 *(morality)* droit *m*, bien *m*; **r. and wrong** le bien et le mal; **to know r. from wrong** faire la différence entre le bien et le mal; **to teach sb r. from wrong** apprendre à qn la différence entre le bien et le mal; **to be in the r.** avoir raison; **by rights** en toute justice **2** *(entitlement)* droit *m* (**to** à; **to do** de faire); **by what r.?** de quel droit?, à quel titre?; **what r. have you to do that?** de quel droit faites-vous cela?; **to exercise a r.** exercer un droit; **r. to know** droit de savoir; **r. to vote** droit de vote; *Law* **r. of abode** *(of refugee etc)* droit de séjour; **r. of reply** droit de réponse *ou* de rectification; **to hold the film/translation rights to a book** détenir les droits d'adaptation cinématographique/de traduction d'un livre; **all rights reserved** tous droits réservés; **it belongs to him by r.** cela lui appartient de droit; **to possess sth in one's own r.** avoir qch en propre; **she is famous in her own r.** c'est elle-même une célébrité; **the rights of man** les droits de l'homme; **human/animal rights** les droits de l'homme/l'animal; **women's rights** les droits de la femme; **to be within one's rights** être dans son droit (**in doing** en faisant); **to know one's rights** connaître ses droits; *St Exch* **rights issue** émission *f* de nouvelles actions à taux préférentiel, émission de droits

3 *(order)* **to put** *or* **set sth to rights** arranger qch, mettre qch en ordre; **I'll soon have this kitchen set to rights** j'aurai vite fait de remettre de l'ordre dans la cuisine; **to put** *or* **set the world to rights** refaire le monde; **to put** *or* **set things to rights** remettre de l'ordre

4 *(right-hand side)* droite *f*, côté *m* droit; **on the r.** à droite; **on your r.** sur *ou* à votre droite; **to drive on the r.** rouler *ou* conduire à droite; **to keep to the r.** tenir sa droite **5** *Boxing etc (blow)* droit *m*; **with a r. to the jaw** d'un droit à la mâchoire **6** *Pol* **the r.** la droite; **a government of the r.** un gouvernement de droite; **to be to** *or* **on the r.** être à droite; **to be to the r. of sb** *(more right-wing than)* être plus à droite que qn

ADV 1 *(straight)* (tout) droit; **he went r. at him** il est allé droit vers lui; **to put a mistake r.** corriger *ou* rectifier une erreur; **to put things r.** arranger les choses; **to put one's watch r.** mettre sa montre à l'heure; **to put sb r.** *(give directions)* aider qn; *(open eyes)* détromper qn, désabuser qn (**about** au sujet de); **drink this, it'll soon put you r.** bois ça, ça te remettra d'aplomb; **to do sth r. away** *or* **off** *(immediately)* faire qch sur-le-champ *ou* immédiatement; *(at the first attempt)* faire qch du premier coup; **I'll be r. back** je reviens tout de suite; *(at the moment)* en ce moment; **r. now** *(immediately)* tout de suite; **he was here r. now** il était là il y a une minute

2 *(completely)* **r. to the end of the peninsula** jusqu'au bout de la presqu'île; **a wall r. round the house** un mur tout autour de la maison; **he turned r. round** il a fait un tour complet; **r. at the top** tout en haut; *Fig* **you have to go r. to the top if you want to get anything done** il faut aller tout en haut de la hiérarchie pour arriver à quelque chose; **r. at the back** tout au fond; **to go r. through sth** traverser qch de part en part; **somebody had cut r. through the cable** quelqu'un avait sectionné le câble; **she walked r. up to me** elle se dirigea tout droit vers moi; **the water came r. up to her shoulders** l'eau lui arrivait jusqu'aux épaules; **r. up until the last mo-**

ment jusqu'à la dernière minute; **the dress came r. down to her ankles** la robe lui arrivait jusqu'aux chevilles

3 *(exactly)* exactement; **r. in the middle** au beau *ou* en plein milieu; **r. behind** juste derrière; **r. in the middle of the harvest** en pleine moisson; **the wind was r. behind us** nous avions le vent en plein dans le dos; **to be r. behind sb** *(in support)* soutenir qn à fond; **he parked r. in front of the gate** il s'est garé en plein devant le portail; **I'll be waiting r. here** j'attends ici, je ne bouge pas; **it was r. here on the table** il était là sur la table
4 *(correctly) (to answer)* correctement; *(to guess)* juste; **if I remember r.** si je me souviens bien; **did I hear r.?** est-ce que j'ai bien entendu?; **you did r.** tu avais vous avez bien fait d'attendre; **to act r.** bien agir
5 *(well)* bien; **nothing goes r. with me** rien ne me réussit; **I'm sure it'll all come r. for you** je suis sûr que tout s'arrangera pour vous; **I got your letter all r.** j'ai bien reçu votre lettre; **to see sb r.** *(financially)* veiller à ce que qn ne soit pas à court d'argent; **r. enough, she could have been more tactful** *(I agree with you)* c'est vrai elle aurait pu être plus délicate; **it was a mistake r. enough** c'était bien une erreur; **he's to blame r. enough** c'est bien de sa faute (à lui)
6 *(to the right-hand side) (to look, turn)* à droite; *Fam* **r., left and centre** *(everywhere)* de tous les côtés; *Fam* **he owes money r., left and centre** il doit de l'argent à droite et à gauche; *Fam* **he cheated us r., left and centre** il nous a eus sur tous les tableaux
7 *Br Dial Fam (very)* très; **I was r. glad to hear it** j'étais très heureux de l'apprendre
VT 1 *(put upright) (boat, car etc)* redresser; **to r. itself** *(of boat)* se redresser
2 *(correct) (a wrong)* réparer; *(mistake)* corriger, rectifier; **to r. itself** *(of situation)* s'arranger; *(of problem)* se résoudre
▸▸ **r. angle** angle *m* droit; *Comput* **r. arrow** flèche *f* vers la droite; *Comput* **r. arrow key** touche *f* de déplacement vers la droite; **r. bank** *(of river)* rive *f* droite; *Typ* **r. justification** justification *f* à droite; *Br* **R. Honourable** titre *m* utilisé pour s'adresser à certains hauts fonctionnaires ou à quelqu'un ayant un titre de noblesse; *TV, Cin* **r. pan** panoramique *m* horizontal GD; **r. of recourse** droit de recours; *Br* **r. to roam** = droit d'emprunter des sentiers sur des terres appartenant à de grands propriétaires terriens; *Am Geom* **r. triangle** triangle *m* rectangle; **r. of way** *Aut* priorité *f*, *(right to cross land)* droit de passage; *(path, road)* chemin *m*; *Am (for power line, railroad etc)* voie *f*; **there is no r. of way across this land** il n'y a pas de droit de passage sur cette terre; **to have r. of way** *(on road)* avoir (la) priorité; *Zool* **r. whale** baleine *f* franche; **r. wing** *Pol* droite *f*; *Sport (position)* aile *f* droite; *(player)* ailier *m* droit

right-angled ADJ à angle droit; *(triangle etc)* rectangle

right-click *Comput* VT cliquer avec le bouton droit de la souris sur
▸ VI cliquer avec le bouton droit de la souris (**on** sur); **r. on the icon to start the program** cliquez sur l'icône avec le bouton droit de la souris pour faire démarrer le programme

righteous ['raɪtʃəs] ADJ **1** *(person)* droit, vertueux; *Bible* juste; *(anger, indignation)* juste, justifié; *Pej* **in a r. tone of voice** d'un ton satisfait **2** *Am Fam (genuine)* authentique; *(excellent)* génial, -aux, super
▸ NPL **the r.** les bons *mpl*, les justes *mpl*

righteously ['raɪtʃəslɪ] ADV *(to live, behave)* vertueusement; *(to deny, protest)* de manière offensée; *Pej (to say)* d'un ton satisfait; **he became r. indignant** il s'indigna

righteousness ['raɪtʃəsnɪs] N *(of person)*

droiture *f*, vertu *f*; *Bible* **those who hunger and thirst after r.** ceux qui ont soif de justice

rightful ['raɪtfʊl] ADJ *(heir, king, claim, owner)* légitime; *(inheritance)* auquel on a droit; **to have one's r. share** avoir sa juste part; **she insisted on being given her r. share** elle insista pour qu'on lui donne la part à laquelle elle avait droit

rightfully ['raɪtfəlɪ] ADV légitimement; *(inherited)* à juste titre; **it is r. mine** cela m'appartient légitimement

right-hand ADJ *(glove etc)* de la main droite; *(bend, drawer etc)* de droite; **on the r. side** sur le côté droit
▸▸ *Aut* **r. drive** conduite *f* à droite; **to have r. drive** avoir la conduite à droite, avoir le volant à droite; **r. man** bras *m* droit

right-handed [-'hændɪd] ADJ *(person)* droitier; *(punch)* du droit; *(tool, scissors etc)* pour droitiers; **r. screw** vis *f* dont le pas est à droite
▸ ADV *(to play, hit etc)* de la main droite

right-hander [-'hændər] N **1** *(person)* droitier, -ière **2** *(blow)* coup *m* du droit, droit *m*

righting ['raɪtɪŋ] N *(of boat, wrong)* redressement *m*

rightism ['raɪtɪz(ə)m] N *Pol* idées *fpl* de droite; *(extreme right)* extrême droite *f*

rightist ['raɪtɪst] N *(person)* homme *m*/ femme *f* de droite
▸ ADJ *(ideas, politics etc)* de droite; *(extremely right-wing)* d'extrême droite

rightly ['raɪtlɪ] ADV *(correctly) (to act, judge, guess)* bien; *(to choose)* avec raison; *(justifiably) (to believe, be annoyed, concerned)* à juste titre, avec raison; **r. or wrongly** à tort ou à raison; **I can't r. say** je ne saurais dire au juste; **I don't r. know** je ne sais pas exactement *ou* au juste; **and r. so** et à juste titre, et avec raison

right-minded ADJ sensé

rightness ['raɪtnɪs] N *(of decision, cause)* légitimité *f*; *(of answer)* justesse *f*, exactitude *f*

righto [raɪ'təʊ] INT *Br Fam* OK!, d'accord!

right-of-centre ADJ *Pol* de centre-droite; **her political beliefs are r.** politiquement, elle se situe au centre-droit

right-on ADJ *Fam* politiquement correct

rightsize ['raɪtsaɪz] VT dégraisser

rightsizing ['raɪtsaɪzɪŋ] N dégraissage *m*

right-thinking ADJ sensé

right-to-lifer N *Am* personne *f* qui est contre l'avortement

right-wing ADJ *Pol (attitude, government, policy etc)* de droite; **he is very r.** il est très à droite

right-winger N *Pol* personne *f* de droite

righty-ho [raɪtɪ'həʊ] INT *Br Fam* OK!, d'accord!

rigid ['rɪdʒɪd] ADJ *(metal, plastic etc)* rigide; *Fig (discipline, principles, rules etc)* rigide, strict, inflexible; *(etiquette)* rigide; **she's very r. in her ideas** elle a des idées très rigides *ou* inflexibles; **r. with fear** pétrifié; *Br Fam* **to be bored r.** s'ennuyer ferme; *Br Fam* **it shook me r.** *(shocked me)* ça m'a fichu un sacré coup

rigidity [rɪ'dʒɪdɪtɪ] N *(of metal, plastic)* rigidité *f*, raideur *f*; *Fig (of discipline, principles, rules etc)* rigidité, inflexibilité *f*; *(of etiquette)* rigidité

rigidly ['rɪdʒɪdlɪ] ADV rigidement; *(censored, controlled)* sévèrement, strictement; **r. opposed to ...** rigoureusement opposé à ...

rigmarole ['rɪgmərəʊl] N *Fam* **1** *(process)* procédure *f* compliquée; **to go through a whole r.** faire tout un tas de démarches **2** *(speech)* galimatias *m*

rigor ['rɪgər] N *Am* = **rigour**

▸▸ **r. mortis** ['mɔːtɪs] rigidité *f* cadavérique

rigorous ['rɪgərəs] ADJ *(discipline, training, climate, analysis etc)* rigoureux

rigorously ['rɪgərəslɪ] ADV rigoureusement

rigorousness ['rɪgərəsnɪs] N rigueur *f*

rigour, *Am* **rigor** ['rɪgər] N rigueur *f*; **the r. of the law** la sévérité de la loi; **the rigours of prison life/the Scottish climate** les rigueurs de la vie en prison/du climat écossais

rigout ['rɪgaʊt] N *Fam (outfit)* tenue *f*, *Pej* accoutrement *m*; **to be in full r.** être en grande tenue

rile [raɪl] VT *Fam (person)* agacer, exaspérer; **to r. sb (up) about sth** faire (en)rager qn à propos de qch; **don't get riled!** ne t'énerve pas!

Riley ['raɪlɪ] N *Fam* **to lead** *or* **live the life of R.** mener la grande vie

rill [rɪl] N *Lit* ruisselet *m*, petit ruisseau *m*

rim [rɪm] N *(of cup, glass, crater etc)* bord *m*; *(of wheel)* jante *f*, *(of dirt, soap etc)* dépôt *m*, trace *f*; **spectacle rims** monture *f* de lunettes; **countries on the Pacific R.** pays *mpl* de la ceinture pacifique; **Pacific R. economy** économie *f* des pays de la ceinture pacifique
▸ VT *(-mm-) (wheel)* janter; *(of hills etc) (valley)* border; **nails rimmed with dirt** des ongles ourlés de crasse
▸▸ *TV, Cin* **r. light** éclairage *m* rasant

rime¹ [raɪm] N *Lit (frost)* givre *m*, gelée *f* blanche

rime² N, VT & VI *Arch* = **rhyme**

rimless ['rɪmlɪs] ADJ *(spectacles)* sans monture

-rimmed ['rɪmd] SUFF **horn/steel-r.** *(spectacles)* avec une monture en écaille/en acier

rimming ['rɪmɪŋ] N *TV, Cin* éclairage *m* frisant

rind [raɪnd] N *(of fruit)* écorce *f*, *(of cheese)* croûte *f*, *(of bacon)* couenne *f*, **a piece of orange/lemon r.** un zeste *ou* un morceau d'écorce de citron/d'orange

RING¹ [rɪŋ]

> N anneau **1** ▪ bague **1** ▪ cercle **2, 4** ▪ arène **3**
> VT entourer **2**

N **1** *(band) (for finger)* anneau *m*; *(with stone, for marking birds)* bague *f*, *(for keys)* porte-clés *m inv*, *(for napkin)* rond *m* de serviette; *Gym* **the rings** les anneaux *mpl*; *Tech* **retaining r.** plaquette *f* de fixation
2 *(circle) (of people, chairs etc)* cercle *m*; *(in water, of smoke)* rond *m*; *(burner on stove)* feu *m*, brûleur *m*; *(around planet)* anneau *m*; *(around sun, moon)* halo *m*; *(of tree)* anneau *ou* cercle annuel; *(stain)* marque *f*, trace *f*; **the cup will leave a r.** la tasse va faire une marque; **sitting in a r.** assis en cercle *ou* en rond; *Geol* **R. of Fire** ceinture *f* de feu; **to have rings round one's eyes** avoir des cernes sous les yeux *ou* les yeux cernés; **they formed a r. round her** ils ont formé un cercle autour d'elle; **to draw** *or* **put a r. round sth** entourer qch d'un cercle; *Fig* **to make** *or* **run rings round sb** *(at chess, tennis etc)* complètement dominer qn; *(in quiz game, general knowledge test etc)* être bien meilleur que qn; **(swimming) r.** bouée *f*
3 *(enclosure) (at circus)* arène *f*, piste *f*, *(for boxing, wrestling)* ring *m*; *(for bullfight)* arène; *(for showjumping)* enceinte *f*, **the r.** *(boxing as sport)* la boxe *f*, *Boxing* **to retire from the r.** abandonner la boxe; *St Exch* **R.** le Parquet; *Fig* **to throw** *or* **toss one's hat into the r.** faire connaître son intention de participer
4 *(organization) (of people)* groupe *m*, cer-

cle *m*; *(gang)* bande *f*, *Com* cartel *m*; *(of spies, drug traffickers)* réseau *m*
VT 1 *(bird)* baguer
2 *(of police, troops etc) (building etc)* encercler; *(item on list etc)* entourer d'un trait de crayon; **to r. sb/sth round** *or* **about** *or* **in** *(surround)* encercler *ou* entourer qn/qch (**with** de)
▶▶ **r. binder** classeur *m* (à anneaux); *Mus* **The R. Cycle** La Tétralogie; **r. finger** annulaire *m*; *Comput* **r. network** réseau en anneau; **r. road** périphérique *m*; *Br* **r. spanner** clé *f* polygonale; *Comput* **r. structure** structure *f* en anneau

---

RING²

| **N** sonnerie **1** ▪ tintement **1** ▪ coup de fil **2** |
| **VI** sonner **1** ▪ tinter **1** ▪ téléphoner **2** ▪ résonner **3** |
| **VT** sonner **1** ▪ téléphoner à **2** |

N 1 *(sound)* *(of bells, telephone)* sonnerie *f*, *(of small bell, coins)* tintement *m*; *(of voice)* timbre *m*; **there was a r. at the door** on a sonné; **a r. of bells** *(set of bells)* un carillon; *Tel* **I hung up on the sixth r.** j'ai raccroché à la sixième sonnerie; *Fig* **the name has a familiar r. to it** ce nom me dit quelque chose; **the r. of truth** l'accent *m* de la vérité; *Fig* **it has a hollow r.** cela sonne creux
2 *Br Tel Fam (communication)* coup *m* de fil; **to give sb a r.** passer un coup de fil à qn
VI *(pt* rang [ræŋ]; *pp* rung [rʌŋ]*)* **1** *(of bell, telephone, person)* sonner; *(of small bell)* tinter; *(of alarm)* retentir; **this will cause the alarm to r.** cela déclenchera l'alarme; **to r. at the door** sonner à la porte; **the bell is ringing for dinner** on sonne pour le dîner; **to r. for sb** sonner qn; **to r. for some coffee** *(by pushing bell)* sonner pour demander du café; *(by telephoning)* téléphoner pour demander du café; **to r. for room service** sonner pour appeler le service en chambre
2 *esp Br Tel* téléphoner; **to r. round** passer une série de coups de fil
3 *(resonate) (of street etc)* résonner, retentir (**with** de); *(of ears)* bourdonner; **her words still r. in my ears** ses paroles résonnent encore à mes oreilles
4 *Fig* **to r. true** être convaincant; **to r. false** sonner faux; *Fig* **his answer did not r. true** sa réponse sonnait faux
VT 1 *(bell)* (faire) sonner; *(alarm)* déclencher; **to r. the doorbell** sonner à la porte; *Fig* **does that r. a bell?** est-ce que cela vous rappelle *ou* vous dit quelque chose?; *Fig* **the name rings a bell** ce nom me dit quelque chose; *Fig* **to r. the changes** introduire des changements
2 *esp Br Tel* téléphoner à, appeler, passer un coup de fil à
▶ **ring back** *esp Br Tel* **VI** rappeler
VT SEP *(person)* rappeler
▶ **ring down VT SEP** *Theat* **to r. down the curtain** sonner pour faire baisser le rideau; *Fig* **to r. down the curtain on sth** marquer la fin de qch
▶ **ring in VI** *esp Br Tel* **to r. in sick** appeler pour dire qu'on est malade; **the boss wants her to r. in every hour** le patron veut qu'elle appelle toutes les heures
VT SEP **to r. in the New Year** marquer la nouvelle année par une volée de cloches
▶ **ring off VI** *esp Br Tel* raccrocher
▶ **ring out VI** *(of bell, telephone)* sonner; *(of voice, shot)* retentir
VT SEP **to r. out the Old Year** marquer la fin de l'année en sonnant les cloches
▶ **ring up** *esp Br* **VI** *Tel* téléphoner
VT SEP 1 *Tel (person)* téléphoner à, appeler, passer un coup de fil à
2 *Theat* **to r. up the curtain** sonner pour

faire lever le rideau; *Fig* **to r. up the curtain on sth** marquer le début de qch
3 to r. an amount up *(on cash register)* enregistrer une somme; **to r. up a profit** réaliser un bénéfice

ring-bound ADJ *(notebook, file)* à anneaux
ringed [rɪŋd] **ADJ 1** *(wearing ring)* *(bird)* bagué **2** *(with marking)* *(plover etc)* à collier
ringer ['rɪŋər] **N 1** *(of bell)* sonneur, -euse, carillonneur, -euse **2** *Am Horseracing* cheval *m* substitué à un autre **3** *Fam* **to be a dead r. for sb** être le sosie de qn **4** *Sl (stolen car with altered plates)* voiture *f* maquillée
ringing ['rɪŋɪŋ] **ADJ** *(bell)* qui tinte *ou* sonne; *(voice, laughter etc)* sonore, retentissant; **I still have a r. sound in my ears** j'ai encore les oreilles qui sifflent; **in r. tones** d'une voix vibrante
N *(of large bell, telephone)* sonnerie *f*, *(of small bell)* tintement *m*; *(in ears)* bourdonnement *m*
▶▶ *Br Tel* **r. tone** sonnerie, signal *m* d'appel
ringleader ['rɪŋliːdər] **N** *Pej (of gang)* chef *m* de bande; *(of rebellion, in mischief etc)* meneur, -euse
ringlet ['rɪŋlɪt] **N** *(curl)* anglaise *f*, boucle *f* (de cheveux); **to wear one's hair in ringlets** porter les cheveux en boucles, porter des anglaises
ringmaster ['rɪŋmɑːstər] **N** *(of circus)* ≃ Monsieur Loyal
ring-necked [-nekt] **ADJ** *(bird, snake)* à collier
▶▶ **r. dove** pigeon *m* ramier, palombe *f*
ring-pull N anneau *m*, bague *f* *(sur une boîte de conserve, de boisson etc)*
▶▶ **r. can** cannette *f*, boîte *f* *(qu'on ouvre en tirant sur une bague)*
ringside ['rɪŋsaɪd] **N** premier rang *m*; **at the r.** au premier rang; **to have a r. seat** *(at circus, boxing match)* avoir une place au premier rang; *Fig* être aux premières loges; **to have a r. view of sth** être bien placé pour voir qch
ring-tailed ADJ à queue zébrée
▶▶ **r. lemur** maki *m*
ringtone ['rɪŋtəʊn] **N** *Tel* tonalité *f* de sonnerie
ringworm ['rɪŋwɜːm] **N** *Med* teigne *f*
rink [rɪŋk] **N** *(for ice-skating)* patinoire *f*, *(for roller-skating)* piste *f*
rinkydink ['rɪŋkɪdɪŋk] **ADJ** *Am Fam (poor quality)* à la gomme
rinse [rɪns] **N 1** *(of bottle, hands etc)* rinçage *m*; **to give sth a r.** rincer qch **2** *(hair colouring)* rinçage *m* (colorant); **to have a r.** se faire faire un rinçage (colorant)
VT 1 *(washing, cup etc)* rincer; **to r. soap out of a sponge/clothes** rincer une éponge/des vêtements pour enlever le savon; **to r. one's hands** se passer les mains à l'eau; *(remove soap)* se rincer les mains; **to r. one's mouth** se rincer la bouche **2** *(with hair colouring)* **to r. one's hair** se faire un rinçage (colorant); **to r. sb's hair** faire un rinçage (colorant) à qn
▶▶ **r. cycle** *(in washing machine)* cycle *m* de rinçage, rinçage
▶ **rinse down VT SEP** *(meal, pill)* **can I have some water to r. the pill down with?** puis-je avoir de l'eau pour avaler mon cachet?; **a little glass of something to r. it down?** un petit verre de quelque chose pour le faire passer?
▶ **rinse out VT SEP** *(cup, bucket etc)* rincer; **to r. out the dirt/soap** rincer pour enlever la saleté/le savon; *Fig* **go and r. your mouth out!** va te laver la bouche!
VI *(of stain, dye)* partir à l'eau
riot ['raɪət] **N** *(uprising)* émeute *f*; *Fig* **there will be a r.** *(when people find out)* ça va faire

scandale; *Fig* **a r. of colour** une explosion de couleurs; **to run r.** *(of person)* se déchaîner; *(of plants, inflation)* devenir incontrôlable; **my imagination was running r.** j'ai commencé à imaginer toutes sortes de choses; *Fam* **he's/it's a r.** *(amusing)* il est/c'est tordant
VI *(-t-)* faire une émeute; *(of football supporters, demonstrators) (to fight)* se battre; *(to destroy things)* se livrer à de violentes manifestations; *(of prisoners)* se mutiner
▶▶ *Hist* **R. Act** loi *f* antiémeutes, loi contre les rassemblements séditieux; *Fig* **to read sb the r. act** souffler dans les bronches à qn, passer un savon à qn; **r. gear** matériel *m* antiémeutes; **r. police** police *f* *ou* forces *fpl* antiémeutes
rioter ['raɪətər] **N** émeutier, -ière; *(football fans, demonstrators)* vandale *mf*, casseur, -euse; *(prisoners)* mutin *m*
rioting ['raɪətɪŋ] **ADJ** **r. football hooligans** des hooligans qui cassent tout sur leur passage; **r. mob** bande *f* d'émeutiers; *(of football fans)* bande des vandales *ou* des casseurs
N émeutes *fpl*; *(fighting)* bagarres *fpl*; **r. broke out when …** des *ou* les bagarres ont éclaté quand …
riotous ['raɪətəs] **ADJ 1** *(crowd etc)* violent; *Law* **to charge sb with r. behaviour** accuser qn d'avoir eu un comportement séditieux; **r. living** vie *f* déréglée **2** *Fam (amusing) (party, occasion)* très gai et très bruyant; *(laughter)* exubérant; **we had a r. time** on a bien rigolé; **a r. success** un franc succès, un succès retentissant
riotously ['raɪətəslɪ] **ADV** violemment; *Fam* **to be r. funny** être à se tordre de rire; **a r. funny film** un film extrêmement drôle
RIP [ɑːraɪ'piː] *(abbr* **Rest In Peace***)* Repose en paix
rip [rɪp] **N** *(in fabric)* déchirure *f*; **there's a r. in your jacket** il y a une déchirure à ta veste
VT *(-pp-)* *(fabric etc)* déchirer; **to r. to pieces** *or* **shreds** *(garment)* déchirer en lambeaux; *(letter)* déchirer en mille morceaux; *Fig (play, film, director etc)* éreinter; *(argument)* mettre en pièces; **it's ripped to pieces** *or* **shreds** *(garment, carpet)* il est en lambeaux
VI 1 *(of fabric etc)* se déchirer
2 *Fam* **to r. along** aller *ou* avancer à toute vitesse *ou* à fond de train; **the explosion ripped through the building** le choc de l'explosion s'est propagé dans tout le bâtiment; **let her** *or* **it r.!** *(of car, motorboat etc)* mets les gaz!, fonce!
3 *Fam (be angry)* **to let r.** laisser éclater sa colère (**about** au sujet de); **to let r. (with) a stream of abuse** lancer une bordée d'injures; **to let r. at sb** s'en prendre à qn (**about** au sujet de); **to let r. against the government** s'en prendre *ou* s'attaquer au gouvernement (**for** au sujet de); **she really let r.** *(spoke her mind, let hair down etc)* elle s'est déchaînée
▶ **rip apart VT SEP** déchirer; *Fig* éreinter, mettre en pièces
VI se déchirer
▶ **rip away VT SEP** arracher
▶ **rip into VT INSEP** *Fam (person)* attaquer violemment
▶ **rip off VT SEP 1** *(by tearing, remove quickly)* arracher; *(one's jacket)* enlever en toute hâte; **they ripped off their clothes** ils se sont déshabillés en toute hâte **2** *Fam (steal)* piquer; *Fam* **to r. sb off** *(cheat)* arnaquer qn; *Fam* **you were ripped off** tu t'es fait arnaquer
▶ **rip open VT SEP** *(person)* éventrer; *(cheek)* déchirer; *(garment) (open quickly)* ouvrir d'un mouvement; **the bayonet ripped open his stomach** la baïonnette l'a éventré; **to r. open a letter** décacheter une lettre en la déchirant; **to r. open a package** ouvrir un pa-

quet en le déchirant; **jeans ripped open at the knee** un jean déchiré au genou **VI** se déchirer

▸ **rip out VT SEP** (remove) (fireplace, light fittings etc) enlever; (page from book) arracher

▸ **rip up VT SEP 1** (tear) (letter) déchirer **2** (remove) (floorboards) arracher; (pavement) creuser

riparian [raɪˈpɛərɪən] **ADJ, N** Fml riverain, -aine; (wildlife) des rivières

ripcord [ˈrɪpkɔːd] **N** (on parachute) corde f d'ouverture, cordelette f de déclenchement; (on hot-air balloon) corde de déchirure

ripe [raɪp] **ADJ** (fruit, grain) mûr; (cheese) bien fait, bien à point; (vulgar) grossier; **to live to a r. old age** vivre vieux, vivre jusqu'à un âge avancé; Hum **the r. old age of sixteen** l'âge avancé de seize ans; **the time is r. for speaking the truth** le temps est venu de dire la vérité; **the time is not yet r.** le temps n'est pas encore venu; **r. for change/revolution** mûr ou prêt pour le changement/la révolution; **the company is r. for takeover** la société est prête pour être rachetée; **a site r. for development** un site bon à exploiter; **to smell r.** (of fruit) avoir un parfum de fruit mûr; Pej (of person) sentir mauvais

ripen [ˈraɪp(ə)n] **VT** (fruit, grain) (faire) mûrir; (cheese) affiner

VI (of fruit), Fig (of plan etc) mûrir; (of cheese) se faire; Fig **to r. into manhood** atteindre l'âge d'homme

ripeness [ˈraɪpnɪs] **N** (of fruit, grain etc) maturité f, Fig (of comments, language) grossièreté f

ripening [ˈraɪp(ə)nɪŋ] **ADJ** Lit (sun) qui fait mûrir **2** (fruit, grain) mûrissant, qui mûrit; (cheese) qui se fait

N (of fruit, grain) maturation f, mûrissage m, mûrissement m; (of cheese) affinage m

rip-off [ˈrɪpɒf] **N** Fam **1** (swindle) escroquerie f, arnaque f, **that restaurant's a r.** ce restaurant est une arnaque; **what a r.!** quelle arnaque!; **r. prices** des prix astronomiques; **r. merchant** arnaqueur, -euse **2** (theft) vol m, fauche f, **it's a r. from an Osborne play** ils ont pompé l'idée dans une pièce d'Osborne

riposte [rɪˈpɒst] **N** Fencing riposte f, **to make a r.** riposter

VI (in argument etc), Fencing riposter

ripped [rɪpt] **ADJ** Fam (drunk) bourré, pété; (on drugs) raide, défoncé; Br Sl **r. to the tits** (drunk) bourré comme un coing, plein comme une barrique; (on drugs) complètement raide ou défoncé

ripper[1] [ˈrɪpər] **N** (killer) éventreur m

ripper[2] Austr Fam **N** (excellent person, thing) he's a r. c'est quelqu'un de super; **it's a r.** c'est super ou génial; **you little r.!** super!, génial! **ADJ** (excellent) super, génial, -aux

ripping [ˈrɪpɪŋ] **ADJ** Old-fashioned Br Fam épatant, formidable; **a r. yarn** une histoire épatante

ripple [ˈrɪp(ə)l] **N 1** (wave) (on water) ride f, (in corn, hair) ondoiement m, ondulation f, Fig **a r. of excitement ran through the crowd** un frémissement d'excitation a parcouru la foule **2** (noise) (of stream) murmure m, gazouillement m; (of conversation, voices) murmure(s); (of laughter, applause) vague f **3** (ice-cream) raspberry/strawberry r. = glace f vanille panachée à la framboise/ fraise

VI 1 (form ripples) (of water) se rider; (of corn, hair) onduler, ondoyer; (of muscles) saillir **2** (make sound) (of stream) murmurer, gazouiller; **laughter/applause rippled through the audience** des vagues de rires/ d'applaudissements ont traversé le public

VT (of wind) (water, sand) rider; **he rippled his muscles** il a fait saillir ses muscles

▸▸ TV, Cin **r. dissolve** fondu m par ondulation; **r. effect** répercussions fpl

rip-roaring **ADJ** Fam (party) tumultueux; **a r. success** un succès retentissant

ripsaw [ˈrɪpsɔː] **N** scie f à refendre

riptide [ˈrɪptaɪd] **N** courant m de retour

RISC [rɪsk] **N** Comput (abbr reduced instruction set chip/computer) RISC

RISE [raɪz]

N lever **1, 2**	• ascension **2**
• éminence **2**	• montée **3** • hausse **3**
VI se lever **1–4**	• se relever **1** • monter **3, 4** • s'élever **3, 4** • augmenter **4**

N 1 (appearance) (of sun, moon) lever m, Fig **to give r. to sth** donner lieu à qch

2 (ascent) (of theatre curtain) lever m; (of leader, party) ascension f, (to power) accession f, (in rank) avancement m, promotion f, (of industry, technology) essor m; (in ground) éminence f, **her r. to fame came overnight** elle est devenue célèbre du jour au lendemain; Fam **to take** or **get a r. out of sb** (tease) faire enrager qn

3 (increase) (in pressure etc) hausse f (in de); (in level of river) crue f, (of temperature) augmentation f, élévation f, (of tide) montée f, (of price) hausse, augmentation; Br **(pay) r.** augmentation (de salaire); Br **to get a r.** (in salary) être augmenté; **the r. and fall** (of empire, politician etc) la grandeur et la décadence; **the book charts his r. and fall** le livre retrace son ascension et sa chute; **the r. and fall of the tide** le flux et le reflux; **food prices are on the r.** le prix des denrées est en hausse; **a big r. in house prices is on the way** une hausse ou augmentation importante des prix de l'immobilier se prépare

VI (pt rose [rəʊz], pp risen [ˈrɪz(ə)n]) **1** (get up) Fml (from bed, chair) se lever; (from knees, after fall) se relever; (from the dead) ressusciter; (of Parliament, court) (at end of day) lever ou clore la séance; (at end of session) entrer en vacances; (on entry of judge) se lever; **all r.!** (in courtroom) levez-vous s'il vous plaît!; **to r. from the table** se lever de table; **to r. on its hind legs** (of horse) se cabrer; **to r. early/late** (from bed) se lever tôt/ tard; Fam **r. and shine!** debout!; **Christ is risen** le Christ est ressuscité

2 (appear, emerge) (of sun, star, moon) se lever; **a picture rose in my mind** une image s'est présentée à mon esprit; **a feeling of panic rose in me** un sentiment de panique s'est emparé de moi; **to r. from the ashes of sth** renaître des cendres de qch; **new buildings are rising all the time** on n'arrête pas de construire

3 (ascend) (of theatre curtain) se lever; (of road, ground, sap etc) monter; (of smoke, balloon) monter, s'élever (**from** de); Fig (in society) s'élever; Theat **the curtain rose at 7. 30** le lever de rideau a eu lieu à 19h30; **to r. off the ground** (of plane) quitter le sol, décoller; **to r. in the saddle** faire du trot enlevé; **to r. to the surface** (of fish), Fig (of anger) faire surface; (of doubts, conflict) se faire jour; **to r. to the bait** mordre à l'hameçon; **a murmur rose from the crowd** une rumeur s'est élevée parmi la foule; **the boat rose and fell on the water** le bateau se balançait sur l'eau; **trees rising a hundred feet above the plain** arbres qui s'élèvent à trente mètres au-dessus de la plaine; **his voice rose above the noise of the crowd** sa voix s'élevait au-dessus du bruit de la foule; **this book never rises above the level of potboiler** ce livre n'est pas de la littérature alimentaire; Fig **to r. above events/one's difficulties** ne pas se laisser abattre par les événements/ses problèmes; **she seems to r. above that kind of petty jealousy** elle semble être au-dessus

de ce genre de jalousie mesquine; **try to r. above it** tâche de rester au-dessus de la mêlée; **to r. to the occasion/challenge/task** se montrer à la hauteur de la situation/du défi/de la tâche; **to r. to fame** devenir célèbre; **to r. to power** accéder au pouvoir; **to r. in the world** faire son chemin; **he rose from nothing** il est parti de rien; **to r. to the rank of colonel** monter jusqu'au grade de colonel; **to r. through the ranks** monter les échelons un à un; **to r. in sb's esteem** monter dans l'estime de qn

4 (increase in amount, intensity) (of temperature) monter, augmenter; (of wind) se lever; (of voice) s'élever; (of hope) grandir; (of tide, pressure, river, water level) monter; (of dough) lever; (of prices) monter, augmenter; **prices are rising** les prix montent ou sont à la ou en hausse; **everything has risen in price** tout a augmenté, tous les prix ont augmenté; **the river has risen by two metres** la rivière est montée de deux mètres; **the wind has risen to gale force** le vent se mit à souffler en tempête; **my spirits rose at the sight of the mountains** j'ai repris courage à la vue des montagnes; **her colour rose** ses joues s'empourprèrent

5 (become erect) (of hair) se hérisser; **the dog's hackles rose** le chien s'est hérissé de colère; **the hair on the back of her neck rose** ses poils se sont hérissés

6 (revolt) se soulever, se révolter (**against** contre); **to r. in arms** prendre les armes; **to r. in protest against sth** se soulever ou se révolter contre qch

7 (originate) (of river) prendre sa source (**at** à; **in** dans); (of difficulty, quarrel) provenir, naître (**from** de)

▸▸ Comput **r. time** temps m de montée

▸ **rise up VI** (revolt) = **rise VI 6**

Attention: ne pas confondre avec le verbe **to raise**, qui est toujours accompagné d'un complément d'objet.

---

riser [ˈraɪzər] **N 1** early r. lève-tôt mf inv; **late r.** lève-tard mf inv **2** (on staircase) contremarche f **3** (pipe) tuyau m de montée

risibility [rɪzɪˈbɪlɪtɪ] **N** Lit (of situation etc) caractère m risible ou ridicule; (of offer) caractère dérisoire

risible [ˈrɪzɪb(ə)l] **ADJ** Lit (idea, plan etc) risible, ridicule; (offer) dérisoire

rising [ˈraɪzɪŋ] **ADJ 1** (sun) levant **2** (road, artist, politician etc) qui monte; **the r. generation** la nouvelle ou la jeune génération; **r. ground** élévation f du terrain, éminence f **3** (pressure, temperature) en hausse; (tide) montant; (stock market) orienté à la hausse; **r. prices** la hausse des prix

N 1 (of Parliament) levée f, clôture f, **I don't like early r.** je n'aime pas me lever tôt **2** (of sun, moon) lever m; (of star) lever, ascension f **3** (of theatre curtain) lever m; (of sap) montée f **4** (of river) montée f **5** (revolt) insurrection f, révolte f, soulèvement m

PREP he's r. sixty il va sur (ses) soixante ans

▸▸ **r. damp** humidité f ascensionnelle ou par capillarité; **r. star** Astron étoile f montante; Mktg (product) produit m d'avenir; Horseriding **r. trot** trot m enlevé ou à l'anglaise

risk [rɪsk] **N** (danger) risque m (**of doing** de faire); (in insurance) risque; **at r.** (life, person, child) en danger; Med (person, population) à risque; (job) menacé; **to place** or **put sth at r.** risquer qch; **to place** or **put sb at r.** faire courir un danger à qn; **is there any r. of that happening?** est-ce qu'il y a un risque que cela se produise?; **there's no r. of that happening** pas de danger que ça se passe, ça ne risque pas d'arriver; **to be full of risks** comporter beaucoup de risques; **to run**

risks courir des risques; **to run the r. of losing everything** courir le risque *ou* risquer de tout perdre; **to take risks** prendre des risques; **I'm not taking any risks** je ne veux prendre aucun risque, je ne veux rien risquer; **I'll take that r.** j'en prends le risque; **with no r. of infection** sans risque d'infection; **at the r. of his life** au péril de sa vie; **at the r. of sounding conceited** au risque de paraître prétentieux; **at considerable r. to herself** en courant (elle-même) un risque considérable; **at one's own r.** à ses risques et périls; **it's too much of a r.** c'est un trop grand risque; *Law* **risks and perils at sea** fortune *f* de mer; **the investment is a good/bad r.** c'est un bon/mauvais investissement; **he is a good/bad r.** *(for insurance purposes)* on peut l'assurer sans crainte/il serait trop risqué de l'assurer; *Fig* **he is a bad** *or* **not a good r.** *(as potential husband, employee etc)* ce n'est pas quelqu'un en qui on peut avoir confiance; **to underwrite a r.** *(in insurance)* souscrire un risque; **to be a fire/health/security r.** constituer un risque d'incendie/pour la santé/pour la sécurité

VT 1 *(endanger)* *(life, reputation etc)* risquer; **to r. one's neck** *or* **skin** risquer sa peau **2** *(take the chance of)* *(defeat, failure)* courir le risque de; **I'll r. it** je vais risquer le coup; **to r. sb's anger** s'exposer à la colère de qn; **she won't r. leaving** elle ne se risquera pas à partir; **to r. breaking one's leg** risquer de *ou* courir le risque de se casser une jambe

▸▸ **r. analysis** analyse *f* des risques; *Am St Exch* **r. arbitrage** arbitrage *m* risque; **r. assessment** évaluation *f* des risques; *Acct* **r. asset ratio** coefficient *m* de solvabilité; *Br Fin* **r. capital** capital *m* à risque; **r. factor** facteur *m* de risque; **r. management** gestion *f* des risques; **r. management tool** instrument *m* de maîtrise du risque; **r. monitoring** suivi *m ou* surveillance *f* des risques; *St Exch* **r. premium** prime *f* de risque de marché; *St Exch* **r.-reward ratio** ratio *m* risque-rentabilité; **r. spreading** répartition *f* des risques; *St Exch* **r. warning** = avertissement *m* donné aux personnes désirant investir dans les produits dérivés, les renseignant sur les risques inhérents à ce genre d'investissement

riskiness ['rɪskɪnɪs] **N** *(of venture etc)* risques *mpl*

risk-taker **N** preneur *m* de risque

risky ['rɪskɪ] **ADJ** *(job, venture etc)* risqué

risotto [rɪ'zɒtəʊ] **N** *Culin* risotto *m*

risqué ['rɪskeɪ, 'riː-] **ADJ** *(story etc)* osé

rissole ['rɪsəʊl] **N** *Culin* croquette *f*

rite [raɪt] **N** *Rel* rite *m*; *Rel* **the last rites** les derniers sacrements *or* *mpl*; **r. of passage** rite de passage; *Mus* **The R. of Spring** le Sacre du printemps

ritual ['rɪtjʊəl] **ADJ** *(dance, killing)* rituel; *Fig* **there was r. condemnation of him in the press** la presse l'a condamné pour la forme

▸ **N** *Rel, Fig* rituel *m*; *Fig* **to make a r. of sth** (se) faire un rituel de qch; **it's become a bit of a r.** c'est devenu comme un rituel; **he went through his nightly r. of locking the doors** il a verrouillé les portes selon son rituel de tous les soirs

ritualism ['rɪtjʊəlɪz(ə)m] **N** *Pej* ritualisme *m*

ritualist ['rɪtjʊəlɪst] **ADJ, N** *Pej* ritualiste *mf*

ritualistic [rɪtjʊə'lɪstɪk] **ADJ** *Pej* ritualiste

ritually ['rɪtjʊəlɪ] **ADV** *(killed)* rituellement, selon les rites

ritz [rɪts] **N** *Am Fam* tape-à-l'œil *m inv*; **to put on the r.** se mettre sur son trente et un, *Pej* faire du tape-à-l'œil

ritzy ['rɪtsɪ] **ADJ** *Fam* *(glamorous)* *(party, occasion etc)* chic

rival ['raɪv(ə)l] **ADJ** *(company, faction etc)* rival, -aux; *(forces, claim etc)* opposé

N rival, -ale, concurrent, -ente; **to be rivals for sth** être en compétition pour qch; **to be rivals in business/love** être rivaux en affaires/amour; **to be without** *or* **have no r.** ne pas avoir d'égal, être inégalé

VT (-ll-, *Am* -l-) **1** *(compete with)* rivaliser avec (**in** de) **2** *(equal)* égaler (**for, in** en); **it rivals anything to be seen in Paris** ça vaut largement tout ce que l'on peut voir à Paris; **New York cannot r. London for historic interest** New York ne vaut pas Londres du point de vue de l'intérêt historique; **her rudeness is rivalled only by her dishonesty** chez elle, l'impolitesse n'a d'égale que la malhonnêteté; **elegance/effrontery that could scarcely be rivalled** élégance/effronterie sans égale

rivalry ['raɪvəlrɪ] **N** rivalité *f* (**between** entre); **the party is torn by personal rivalries** le parti est divisé par des rivalités d'ordre personnel; **in r. with sb** en concurrence *ou* rivalité avec qn (**for** pour)

riven ['rɪv(ə)n] **ADJ PRED** *Lit* **a country r. by war** un pays déchiré par la guerre

river ['rɪvər] **N** *(small)* rivière *f*, *(flowing into sea)* fleuve *m*; *Fig* *(of lava)* coulée *f*, *(of blood)* flot *m*; *Fam* **to sell sb down the r.** trahir qn, vendre qn; *Am Fam* **he's up (the) r.** *(in prison)* il est en taule; *Br* **the R. Thames**, *Am* **the Thames R.** la Tamise

▸▸ **r. bank** rive *f*, berge *f*; **r. basin** bassin *m* fluvial; *Med* **r. blindness** cécité *f* des rivières; **r. mouth** *(of tributary)* embouchure *f* de la rivière *ou* du fleuve; **r. police** police *f* fluviale; **r. port** port *m* fluvial; **r. traffic** trafic *m* fluvial

riverbed ['rɪvəbed] **N** lit *m* de la rivière

riverside ['rɪvəsaɪd] **N** bord *m* de l'eau, rive *f*, **to walk along the r.** marcher le long de la rive

▸ **ADJ** au bord d'une rivière *ou* d'un fleuve; **a r. park** un parc situé au bord de l'eau *ou* d'une rivière; **r. properties** propriétés *fpl* riveraines

rivet ['rɪvɪt] **N** rivet *m*

VT *Tech* river, riveter; *Fig (eyes)* fixer (**on** sur); *Fig* **all eyes were riveted on her** tout le monde avait les yeux rivés sur elle; *Fig* **to be riveted to the spot** être rivé *ou* cloué sur place; **I was riveted to the television** j'étais cloué devant la télévision; **to be absolutely riveted** être absolument fasciné (**by** par); *Tech* **riveted joint** rivure *f*

▸▸ **r. gun** pistolet *m* à river; **r. head** tête *f* de rivet; **r. hole** trou *m* de rivet

riveter ['rɪvɪtər] **N** *(person)* riveur, -euse; *(machine)* riveteuse *f*, riveuse *f*

riveting ['rɪvɪtɪŋ] **N** rivetage *m*

▸ **ADJ** *Fig (story etc)* fascinant

▸▸ **r. machine** riveteuse *f*

Riviera (the) [ðərɪvɪ'eərə] **N the (French) R.** la Côte d'Azur

rivulet ['rɪvjʊlɪt] **N** ruisselet *m*; *Fig (of sweat etc)* filet *m*

Riyadh ['riːjæd] **N** R(i)yad, Riad

riyal [rɪ'jæl] **N** *(coin)* rial *m*

RN [ɑː'ren] **1** *Br Mil abbr* **Royal Navy 2** *Med abbr* **registered nurse**

RNA [ɑːre'neɪ] **N** *(abbr ribonucleic acid)* ARN *m*

RNLI [ɑːrene'laɪ] **N** *Br (abbr Royal National Lifeboat Institution)* = société *f* nationale de sauvetage en mer

roach [rəʊtʃ] **N 1** *(fish)* gardon *m* **2** *Am Fam (cockroach)* cafard *m*, blatte *f* **3** *Sl (of marijuana cigarette)* mégot *m* de joint

▸▸ *Am Fam* **r. motel** piège *m* à cafards; *Am Fam* **r. powder** poudre *f* pour tuer les cafards

road [rəʊd] **N 1** route *f* (**to** de); *(small and narrow)* chemin *m*; *(in town)* rue *f*, *(roadway)* chaussée *f*, *Fig (path)* voie *f*, chemin (**to** de); **the London/Paris r.** la route de Londres/Pa-

ris; **the r. into town** la route qui mène en ville; **across** *or* **over the r.** *(building etc)* en face; **the woman from across the r.** la dame d'en face; **by r.** par la route; **to send sth by r.** envoyer qch par route; *Fam* **get out of the r.!** ne gène *ou* bloque pas le passage!; *Fig* **it was getting in the r. of solving the problem** cela empêchait de résoudre le problème; *Fam* **sorry, am I in your r.?** pardon, je vous bloque le passage?; **to be off the r.** *(of car)* être en panne; *(banned)* s'être fait retirer son permis de conduire; **to step into the r.** descendre du trottoir; **the r. is up** la route est en travaux; *esp Am* **to burn up the r.** *(of driver)* brûler de la gomme; **down/up the r.** *(to live, work)* un peu plus loin dans cette rue; **I ran down the r.** j'ai dévalé la rue, j'ai descendu la rue en courant; *Fig* **no-one can see what is down the r.** personne ne peut savoir ce que l'avenir réserve; **a few years down the r.** dans quelques années; **yes, when I'm seventy, but that's a long way down the r. (yet)** oui, quand j'aurai soixante-dix ans, mais ce n'est pas pour tout de suite; *Fam* **one for the r.** un petit verre avant de partir; *Prov* **all roads lead to Rome** tous les chemins mènent à Rome; *Prov* **the r. to hell is paved with good intentions** l'enfer est pavé de bonnes intentions; **approach r.** route d'accès; **the price on the r.** *(of car)* le prix clé en main; **after three hours on the r.** après trois heures de route; **to be on the r.** *(travelling)* être en route ou en voyage; *(of salesman, theatre company, pop group etc)* être en tournée; *(work as salesman)* être représentant; **that car shouldn't be on the r.** cette voiture ne devrait pas rouler; *Fig* **to be on the r. to recovery/success** être sur le chemin de la guérison/du succès; **to be on the right r.** *Aut* être sur la bonne route; *Fig* être sur la bonne voie; *Fig* **we'd like to go a little further down this r.** nous aimerions aller un peu plus loin dans ce sens *ou* cette direction; *Fig* **we don't want to go down the r. of military intervention** nous ne voulons pas nous engager dans la voie d'une intervention armée; **somewhere along the r.** en chemin; *Fig* **to come to the end of the r.** *(of relationship etc)* toucher à sa fin; *Fig Fam* **let's get this show on the r.** allez, c'est parti, on y va!; *Fam* **let's hit the r.!** en route!; **hit the r.!** fiche le camp!; **he's got no r. sense** il n'a pas conscience des dangers de la circulation **2** *Naut* **road(s)** rade *f* **3** *Am Rail* chemin *m* de fer

▸▸ **r. accident** accident *m* de la route; *Am Fam* **r. apple** *(dung)* crottin *m*; *Am Theat* **r. company** troupe *f* itinérante; **r. conditions** état *m* des routes; **r. feel** *(of car)* sensation *f* au volant; **r. haulage** camionnage *m*, transports *mpl* routiers; **r. haulage company** entreprise *f* de transports routiers; **r. haulage forwarding agent** groupeur *m* routier; **r. haulier** transporteur *m* routier, affréteur *m* routier; *Fam* **r. hog** chauffard *m*; **r. junction** carrefour *m*; **r. manager** responsable *mf* de tournée *(d'un chanteur ou d'un groupe pop)*; **r. map** carte *f* routière; *(in process)* feuille *f* de route; **r. marking** marquage *m* au sol; **r. metal** *(for road)* empierrement *m*; *Rail* terre-plein *m*, *pl* terre-pleins, ballast *m*; **r. movie** road-movie *m*, *pl* road-movies; **r. noise** *(when driving)* bruit *m* de roulement; **r. race** *(in cycling)* course *f* cycliste sur route; **r. racer** *(bicycle)* bicyclette *f* de compétition; *(cyclist)* routier, -ière; **r. rage** = accès *m* de colère provoqué par la conduite des autres automobilistes; **r. safety** sécurité *f* routière; **r. sign** panneau *m* de signalisation; *Br* **r. tax** taxe *f* sur les automobiles; *Br* **tax disc** ≃ vignette *f* (automobile); **r. test** essai *m* sur route; **r. testing** essai routier; **R. Traffic Act** loi *f* de la circulation routière; **r. train** train *m ou* convoi *m* routier; **r. transport** transports routiers; **r. transport company** entreprise de transport routier; **r. user** usager m de la route; *Fam* **r. warrior** nomade m; *Aut* **r. wheel** roue f; **r. works** travaux mpl de voirie

roadbed ['rəʊdbed] N *(for road)* empierrement m; *Rail* terre-plein m, pl terre-pleins

roadblock ['rəʊdblɒk] N barrage m routier

roadbuilding ['rəʊdbɪldɪŋ] N construction f de routes
▸▸ **r. programme** programme m pour construire des routes

road-fund ADJ
▸▸ *Br* **r. licence** ≃ vignette f; *Br* **r. tax** taxe f routière

roadholding ['rəʊdhəʊldɪŋ] N tenue f de route

roadhouse ['rəʊdhaʊs] N **1** *Old-fashioned* hôtellerie f en bord de route **2** *Am* café m/ restaurant m pour les automobilistes/ camionneurs

roadie ['rəʊdɪ] N *Fam* roadie m

roadroller ['rəʊdrəʊlər] N rouleau m compresseur

roadshow ['rəʊdʃəʊ] N tournée f, spectacle m itinérant; *(radio show)* = animation f en direct proposée par une station de radio en tournée; *Mktg* tournée de présentation

roadside ['rəʊdsaɪd] N bord m de (la) route
▸▸ **r. advertising** affichage m routier; *Aut* **r. assistance** assistance f technique aux véhicules, assistance dépannage; **r. cafe** café m situé au bord de la route; **r. camera** caméra f en bord de route; **r. inn** auberge f située au bord de la route; **r. repairs** *(by driver)* réparations fpl de fortune; *(by mechanic)* dépannage m

roadstead ['rəʊdsted] N *Naut* rade f

roadster ['rəʊdstər] N *Aut Old-fashioned* torpédo m

roadsweeper ['rəʊdswiːpər] N balayeur, -euse; *(vehicle)* balayeuse f

road-test VT *(car)* essayer sur route; *Fig* tester

roadtrip ['rəʊdtrɪp] N *Am (short)* promenade f en voiture; *(longer)* voyage m en voiture

roadway ['rəʊdweɪ] N chaussée f

roadwork ['rəʊdwɜːk] N *(by boxer, athlete etc)* entraînement m consistant à courir le long de la route; **to do r.** courir le long de la route

roadworthiness ['rəʊdwɜːðɪnɪs] N *(of vehicle)* état m de marche

roadworthy ['rəʊdwɜːðɪ] ADJ *(vehicle)* en état de marche *ou* de rouler

roam [rəʊm] VI **1** errer; **to r. about the streets** *(of child etc)* traîner dans les rues; **to r. about the world** courir le monde **2** *Tel (of mobile phone user)* itinérer
VT *(the streets)* parcourir; *(the seas)* sillonner; *(the world)* courir

roamer ['rəʊmər] N vagabond, -onde

roaming ['rəʊmɪŋ] ADJ errant, vagabond
N **1** vagabondage m, errance f **2** *Tel (of mobile phone)* roaming m, itinérance f

roan [rəʊn] ADJ *(horse, cow)* rouan
N *(horse)* cheval m) rouan m; *(cow)* vache f rouanne

roar [rɔːr] N *(of person)* hurlement m; *(of anger)* vocifération f; *(of lion, wind, engine)* rugissement m; *(of thunder)* grondement m; *(of sea)* mugissement m; *(of crowd, spectators etc)* clameurs fpl; *(of furnace)* ronflement m; *(of applause)* tonnerre m; *(of traffic)* vrombissement m; **to give a r.** *(of person)* hurler; *(of lion)* rugir; **the crowd gave a r. of approval** la foule a poussé un hurlement d'approbation; **roars of laughter** grands éclats mpl de rire

VI *(of person)* hurler; *(in anger)* vociférer; *(of crowd)* hurler; *(of lion, wind, engine)* rugir; *(of thunder)* gronder; *(of sea)* mugir; *(of furnace)* ronfler; **to r. with laughter** hurler de rire

VT *(order)* hurler, vociférer; **to r. one's approval** manifester son approbation par des hurlements
▸ **roar by** VI *(of car etc)* passer dans un bruit de tonnerre
▸ **roar on** VT SEP **they roared their team on** *(encouraged)* ils ont crié de toutes leurs forces pour encourager leur équipe
▸ **roar out** VT SEP = **roar** VT
▸ **roar past** VI = **roar by**

roaring ['rɔːrɪŋ] ADJ **1** *(person)* hurlant; *(lion, wind, engine)* rugissant; *(thunder)* grondant; **a r. fire** une belle flambée; *Fam* **to be r. drunk** être complètement bourré *ou* rond **2** *Fig (excellent)* **a r. success** un succès fou; **to do a r. trade** faire un gros commerce, vendre beaucoup (**in** de)
N = **roar** N
▸▸ *Naut* **R. Forties** quarantièmes mpl rugissants; **R. Twenties** Années fpl folles

roast [rəʊst] N **1** *Culin* rôti m; **a pork r.**, **a r. of pork** un rôti de porc; **pot r.** rôti à la cocotte **2** *Am Fam (of celebrity etc)* = soirée f ou émission f en l'honneur d'une vedette, et au cours de laquelle cette dernière fait l'objet de taquineries et de flatteries
ADJ *Culin (pork, lamb etc)* rôti
VT **1** *Culin (meat)* (faire) rôtir; *(chestnuts)* rôtir; *(almonds)* (faire) griller; *(coffee)* torréfier, griller; **to r. oneself in front of the fire** se (faire) rôtir *ou* se (faire) griller devant le feu **2** *Fam (criticize) (book, film etc)* éreinter **3** *Am Fam (tease) (person)* railler, mettre en boîte
VI *(of meat etc)* rôtir; *(of coffee)* se torréfier; *Fam* **I was roasting in the sun** je grillais au soleil
▸▸ **r. beef** rôti de bœuf, rosbif m; **r. chestnuts** marrons mpl chauds; **r. chicken** poulet m rôti; **r. pork** rôti de porc; **r. potatoes** pommes fpl de terre rôties au four

roaster ['rəʊstər] N **1** *Br Culin (chicken)* volaille f à rôtir; *(pan) (with lid)* cocotte f **2** *(for coffee)* brûloir m, torréfacteur m

roasting ['rəʊstɪŋ] ADJ *Fam* **(-hot)** brûlant; **it's r. in here** il fait une chaleur à crever ici; **we're r. here** on cuit ici
N **1** *(of meat)* rôtissage m; *(of coffee)* torréfaction f **2** *Fam (reprimand)* semonce f; **to give sb a r.** *(reprimand)* passer un savon à qn; *(criticize)* éreinter qn
▸▸ **r. chef** rôtisseur, -euse; **r. jack** tournebroche m; **r. pan** plat m à rôtir; **r. spit** tournebroche; **r. tin** plat à rôtir

rob [rɒb] VT **(-bb-)** *(person)* voler; *(bank, house)* dévaliser; **to r. sb of sth** voler qch à qn; *(deprive)* priver qn de qch; *Fig* **the illness robbed him of his health for years to come** la maladie lui a rendu la santé fragile pour de longues années; **the illness had robbed him of his good looks** la maladie lui avait fait perdre sa beauté; **to r. the till** voler la caisse; *Prov* **to r. Peter to pay Paul** déshabiller Pierre pour habiller Paul; *Sport* **he was robbed of victory** il a été privé de sa victoire; *esp Ftbl Fam* **we were robbed!** nous aurions dû gagner!
N *Br Fam* **to go on the r.** aller faucher des trucs

robber ['rɒbər] N voleur, -euse

robbery ['rɒbərɪ] N vol m; **armed r.** vol à main armée; **highway r.** vol de grand chemin, brigandage m; *Fig* **it's highway** *or* **daylight r.!** c'est du vol (organisé)!; *Fig* **it's nothing short of r.!** c'est du vol!

robe [rəʊb] N **1** *(of priest, judge etc)* robe f;

magistrate in his robes magistrat m en robe **2** *(dressing gown) (heavy)* robe f de chambre; *(light, for women)* peignoir m; *(bathrobe)* sortie f de bain, peignoir (de bain) **3** *Am (blanket)* couverture f
VT *(judge, priest)* revêtir d'une robe
VI *(of judge etc)* revêtir sa robe

> Note that the most common meaning of the French word **robe** is **dress**.

robin ['rɒbɪn] N *Orn* **1** *(European)* rougegorge m, pl rouges-gorges **2** *(American)* merle m américain; *Am* **r.'s-egg blue** *(colour)* bleu vert m inv pâle
▸▸ **R. Hood** Robin des bois; *Orn* **r. redbreast** rouge-gorge

robing ['rəʊbɪŋ] N
▸▸ **r. room** *(for judge etc)* vestiaire m

robot ['rəʊbɒt] N robot m; *Fig* robot, automate m

robotics [rəʊ'bɒtɪks] N *(usu with sing verb)* robotique f VOIR GRAMMAIRE A10

robotize ['rəʊbətaɪz] VT *esp Am (assembly line)* robotiser

robust [rəʊ'bʌst] ADJ *(person, faith, appetite)* robuste, solide; *(machine, suitcase etc)* solide; *(coffee, wine)* corsé; *(defence, speech, statement)* vigoureux, musclé

robustness [rəʊ'bʌstnɪs] N *(of person)* robustesse f; *(of machine, suitcase, appetite, faith)* solidité f, robustesse; *(of coffee, wine)* goût m corsé; *(of defence, speech etc)* vigueur f

roc [rɒk] N *Myth (bird)* rock m

ROCE [ɑːrəʊsiː'iː] N *Fin (abbr* **return on capital employed**) retour m sur capital immobilisé

rock¹ [rɒk] N **1** *(substance)* roche f; **cut in(to) the r.** creusé dans le roc; **a layer of r.** une couche rocheuse
2 *(at seaside, boulder, rock face)* rocher m; *Am (stone)* pierre f, *Fig* roc m; *Geog Fam* **the R.** *(Gibraltar)* le Rocher de Gibraltar; *Fig* **she was an absolute r. during the crisis** elle nous a été d'un grand secours pendant cette épreuve; **you're a r.!** tu es formidable!; *Naut* **to run onto the rocks** s'échouer sur des rochers; *Fig* **on the rocks** *(marriage, relationship)* en pleine débâcle; *(company)* en faillite; *(whisky)* avec des glaçons, *Can* sur glace; **fall of rocks** chute f de pierres, éboulis m rocheux; **to be as solid as a r.** être solide comme le roc; *Am Prov* **to be between a r. and a hard place** être confronté à un choix impossible; *Am Fam* **to have rocks in one's head** être bête comme ses pieds; *Fig* **to reach** *or* **hit r. bottom** *(of prices)* être au plus bas; *(of person, morale)* toucher le fond; *Fig* **r. solid** *(support, morale etc)* solide comme le roc
3 *Sl (diamond)* diamant m
4 *Br (sweet)* = sorte de sucre d'orge, parfumé à la menthe; **a stick of r.** un sucre d'orge
5 *Sl* **rocks** *(testicles)* couilles fpl; **to get one's rocks off** *(have sex)* baiser; **to get one's rocks off doing sth** s'éclater *ou* prendre son pied en faisant qch
▸▸ *Culin* **r. bun** rocher; *Culin* **r. cake** rocher; **r. climber** varappeur, -euse; **r. climbing** escalade f *(de rochers)*, varappe f; **r. crystal** cristal m de roche; **r. face** paroi f rocheuse; **r. garden** *(jardin m de)* rocaille f; *Geog* **R. of Gibraltar** Rocher de Gibraltar; *Am Fam* **r. hound** *(professional)* géologue mf; *(amateur)* collectionneur, -euse de pierres; *Zool* **r. lobster** langouste f; *Am, Austr* **r. melon** cantaloup m; **r. painting** peinture f rupestre; *Bot* **r. plant** plante f de rocaille; **r. pool** flaque f dans les rochers; **r. salmon** roussette f, **r. salt** sel m gemme

When translating the English word **rock**, note that the French words **rocher** and **roche** are not interchangeable. **Rocher** describes an individual piece of rock whereas with **roche** the emphasis is on the matter or the type of rock.

rock² vt (baby) bercer; (boat, cradle) balancer; (violently) (building), Fig (person) secouer, ébranler; **to r. a baby to sleep** bercer un enfant pour qu'il s'endorme; Fig **to r. the boat** faire des vagues; Fig **don't r. the boat** ne fais pas d'histoires; Fig **the Government has been rocked by the latest sex scandal** le gouvernement a été secoué par la dernière histoire de mœurs
vi **1** (sway) se balancer; (of building, ground) trembler; **to r. (backwards and forwards) in one's chair** se balancer sur sa chaise; **to r. with laughter** être secoué par le fou rire **2** (dance) danser le rock **3** Fam (be excellent) **his new girlfriend really rocks!** sa nouvelle copine est vraiment géniale!; **the party was really rocking** (animated) il y avait une ambiance d'enfer à la soirée
N **1** (rocking motion) **to give the cradle a r.** balancer un peu le berceau **2** Mus rock m; **r. and roll, r. 'n' roll** rock-and-roll m inv
▶▶ Fam **r. chick** mordue f de hard rock; **r. music** rock; **r. star** rock star f

rock-and-roll facility N TV, Cin (for dubbing) dispositif m de marche avant-arrière synchronisé

rock-bottom ADJ (prices) les plus bas, très bas

rock-bound ADJ (bay etc) encerclé de rochers

rock-climb vi faire de la varappe

rocker ['rɒkər] N **1** (on cradle, rocking chair etc) bascule f; Fam **to be off one's r.** être timbré ou givré; **to go off one's r.** devenir givré **2** Aut, Tech culbuteur m **3** Am Fam (rocking chair) fauteuil m à bascule, rocking-chair m, pl rocking-chairs, Can berceuse f **4** Mus (person) rocker m **5** Br Hist (as opposed to mod) rocker m
▶▶ Aut, Tech **r. arm** culbuteur m; Aut, Tech **r. arms** culbuteurs, culbuterie f

rockery ['rɒkərɪ] N (in garden) rocaille f

rocket¹ ['rɒkɪt] N (firework, missile) fusée f; **to fire** or **launch a r.** lancer une fusée; Fig **to give sb a r.** engueuler qn (**about** au sujet de); Fig **he's just had a r. from the boss** il vient de se faire engueuler par le patron
vi (of prices) monter en flèche; **to r. to fame** devenir célèbre très rapidement; **to r. away/past** (of car etc) filer/passer à toute allure
▶▶ Mil **r. attack** attaque f à la roquette; **r. base** base f de lancement de fusées; **r. fuel** Aviat, Astron propergol m; Fig (strong drink) dynamite f; **r. launcher** Aviat, Astron lance-fusées m inv; Mil lance-roquettes m inv; **r. science** fuséologie m; Fam Fig **it's not exactly r. science** ce n'est pas sorcier; **r. scientist** spécialiste mf de fuséologie; St Exch Fam = personne f qui spécule sur le cours des monnaies; Fam Fig **she's no r. scientist** elle n'a pas inventé la poudre

rocket² N Br Bot, Culin roquette f

rocketry ['rɒkɪtrɪ] N (science) étude f ou technologie f ou technique f des fusées; (weaponry) arsenal m de fusées

rockfall ['rɒkfɔːl] N éboulement m; **beware of rockfalls** chute de pierres

rock-hard ADJ (soil etc) dur comme (de) la pierre

rockhouse ['rɒkhaʊs] N Am Sl = lieu m où l'on achète, vend et consomme du crack

Rockies (the) [ðə'rɒkɪz] NPL les (montagnes) Rocheuses fpl

rocking ['rɒkɪŋ] ADJ (movement) oscillant;

(building) branlant; **a r. movement** des oscillations
N (of baby) bercement m; (of boat, cradle) balancement m; (of chair) balancement, oscillation f
▶▶ **r. chair** fauteuil m à bascule, rocking-chair m, pl rocking-chairs, Can berçante f; **r. horse** cheval m à bascule

rockslide ['rɒkslaɪd] N (action) éboulement m de rochers; (result) éboulis m

rockumentary [rɒkjʊ'mentə(r)ɪ] N Cin Fam rockumentaire m (documentaire sur un groupe de rock)

rocky ['rɒkɪ] ADJ **1** (path) rocailleux; (soil) rocailleux, pierreux; (shoreline, terrain) rocheux; **r. outcrop** affleurement m rocheux **2** Fig (unstable) difficile; (marriage, relationship) instable, branlant; **his business is in a r. condition** ses affaires vont mal; **I feel a bit r.** (unwell) je ne suis pas dans mon assiette; **it's been a r. year for the oil industry** ça a été une année difficile pour l'industrie pétrolière; **to have a r. road ahead** avoir des problèmes en perspective; **to go through a r. patch** traverser une période difficile **3** Br Sl (cannabis) marocain m
▶▶ **the R. Mountains** les montagnes fpl Rocheuses

rococo [rə'kəʊkəʊ] ADJ, N Art etc rococo m

rod [rɒd] N **1** (stick) (wooden) baguette f; (metal) tige f; (of curtain) tringle f; (for fishing) canne f à pêche; Old-fashioned (for administering punishment) verge f; **to fish with r. and line** pêcher à la ligne; **r. fishing** pêche f à la ligne; **fuel r.** barreau m de combustible; Fig **to make a r. for one's own back** se préparer des ennuis; Prov **spare the r. and spoil the child** qui aime bien châtie bien; Fig **a r. to beat oneself with** des verges pour se faire battre; **that would be giving them a r. to beat us with** ce serait leur donner des bâtons pour nous faire battre; **to rule sb with a r. of iron** gouverner qn avec une main de fer **2** (symbol of office) verge f **3** Old-fashioned (measure) ≃ perche f **4** Am Sl (gun) flingue m, pétard m **5** Sl (penis) bite f

rode PP see **ride** VI, VT

rodent ['rəʊdənt] N rongeur m
ADJ rongeur, -euse; **r. characteristics/habitat** caractéristiques fpl/habitat m des rongeurs
▶▶ **r. control** dératisation f; Br Admin **r. operative** spécialiste mf de la dératisation

rodent-like ADJ qui fait penser à un rongeur

rodeo ['rəʊdɪəʊ, rəʊ'deɪəʊ] N rodéo m
▶▶ **r. rider** cavalier, -ière pratiquant le rodéo

rodomontade [rɒdəmɒn'teɪd, -'tɑːd] N Lit rodomontade f

roe¹ [rəʊ] N (deer) chevreuil m
▶▶ **r. deer** chevreuil

roe² N (of fish) œufs mpl (de poisson); **soft r.** laite f, laitance f

roebuck ['rəʊbʌk] N chevreuil m (mâle)

roentgen ['rɜːntgən] N Phys Röntgen m, Roentgen m
▶▶ **r. equivalent man** = unité f employée pour évaluer l'effet biologique d'un rayonnement radioactif; **measurements are given in r. equivalent man** les mesures sont données en Röntgen Equivalent Man; **r. rays** rayons mpl X

rogation [rəʊ'geɪʃən] N Rel rogations fpl
▶▶ **R. Days** rogations; **R. Sunday** dimanche m des rogations; **R. Week** la semaine des rogations

Roger ['rɒdʒər] INT **R.!** (in radio message) bien reçu!

roger ['rɒdʒər] VT Br Sl baiser

rogue [rəʊg] N (dishonest) filou m, crapule f; (mischievous) coquin, -ine, fripon, -onne; (maverick) franc-tireur, pl francs-tireurs
ADJ (animal) solitaire; **a r. elephant** un éléphant solitaire
▶▶ **rogues' gallery** collection f de portraits de criminels; Fig Hum bande f de personnes à la mine patibulaire; Biol **r. gene** gène m aberrant; **r. policeman** policier m corrompu; **r. state** État m voyou, État paria; St Exch **r. trader** opérateur, -trice peu scrupuleux (euse)

roguery ['rəʊgərɪ] N (dishonesty) crapulerie f, malhonnêteté f; (mischievousness) côté m farceur; (of child) espièglerie f

roguish ['rəʊgɪʃ] ADJ (smile, look etc) espiègle, coquin, fripon

roguishly ['rəʊgɪʃlɪ] ADV (to smile, wink) avec espièglerie, d'un air coquin ou fripon

roguishness ['rəʊgɪʃnɪs] N = **roguery**

ROI [ɑːrəʊ'aɪ] N (abbr return on investment) retour m sur investissement

roisterer ['rɔɪstərər] N Lit fêtard, -arde

role, rôle [rəʊl] N Theat, Fig rôle m; Fig **to play an important/a leading r.** jouer un rôle important/prépondérant
▶▶ **r. model** modèle m; **children need a r. model** les enfants ont besoin de quelqu'un à qui s'identifier; **r. play** jeu m de rôles; (in psychotherapy) psychodrame m; **r. reversal** inversion f des rôles

role-play, rôle-play VT jouer
N = **role-playing**

role-playing, rôle-playing N jeu m de rôle; (in psychotherapy) psychodrame m

rolf [rɒlf] VI Am Sl vomir

ROLL [rəʊl]

N	rouleau **1** ▪ petit pain **2**
	▪ roulement **3, 4** ▪ liste **5**
VT	rouler **1, 2**
VI	rouler **1** ▪ gronder **2** ▪ tourner **4**

N **1** (of paper) rouleau m; (of fat, flesh) bourrelet m; esp Am (of paper money) liasse f; **a r. of film** une pellicule (photo)
2 (bread) petit pain m; **ham/cheese r.** ≃ sandwich m au jambon/fromage; Br **jam r.** (gâteau m) roulé m à la confiture; **spring r.** rouleau m de printemps; **ham/cheese r.** ≃ sandwich m au jambon/fromage
3 (noise) (of drum, thunder) roulement m
4 (movement) (of ball, dice etc) roulement m; (of ship, vehicle) roulis m; (of sea) houle f; (of aircraft) (vol m en) tonneau m; (in canoe) esquimautage m; **to walk with a r.** se balancer ou se dandiner en marchant; **to have a r. on the ground** (of horse etc) se rouler par terre; **to do a r.** (in high jump) sauter en rouleau; Fig Fam **to have a r. in the hay** faire des galipettes dans le foin; Fam **to be on a r.** (of gambler, football team) avoir la chance de son côté; Fig (have good momentum going) être bien parti; **western r.** (high jump) rouleau m costal
5 (list) liste f, Mil Br **r. of honour**, Am **honor r.** = liste de ceux qui sont morts pour la patrie; Law **to strike sb off** or **from the rolls** rayer qn du tableau; **to call the r.** faire l'appel
VT **1** (cigarette, paper, carpet etc) rouler; (marble, ball, car) faire rouler; Cin (camera) faire tourner; **to r. sth along the ground** faire rouler qch sur le sol; **to r. string into a ball** rouler de la ficelle en pelote; **to r. one's own** (cigarettes) rouler ses cigarettes; **to r. a snowball** faire une boule de neige; Cin Fam **r. 'em!** ça tourne!; **to r. one's eyes** rouler les yeux; **to r. one's r's** rouler les r; Culin **loin of mutton boned and rolled** carré de mouton roulé; **to r. an umbrella** plier un parapluie; **to r. itself into a ball** (of animal) se mettre en boule; **he is a chauffeur and gardener**

rolled into one il est à la fois chauffeur et jardinier; **this room is a bedroom and study rolled into one** cette pièce sert à la fois de chambre et de bureau

2 *(flatten) (lawn)* rouler, passer au rouleau; *(road)* cylindrer; *(metal)* laminer; *(gold)* planer

3 *Am Fam* **to r. a drunk** *(rob)* dévaliser un ivrogne

VI 1 *(of ball, ship etc)* rouler; *(of aircraft)* faire un tonneau *ou* des tonneaux; **to r. on the ground/in the grass** *(of person, animal)* se rouler par terre/dans l'herbe; **the car rolled to a stop** la voiture s'est progressivement arrêtée; *Fig* **heads will r.** il va y avoir des têtes qui vont tomber; *Fig* **someone's head will r. for this** quelqu'un va payer pour cela; *Fam* **to be rolling in money** *or* **it** rouler sur l'or; *Fam* **to r. with laughter** se tordre (de rire), se tenir les côtes; *Fam* **he/the film had them rolling in the aisles** il/ce film les faisait se tordre de rire; *Fig Fam* **to get sth rolling** *(started)* mettre qch en route; *(conversation, discussion)* lancer qch; *Fig* **to get the ball rolling** mettre les choses en train; **to r. with the punches** *(of boxer)* encaisser les coups de l'adversaire; *Fig* encaisser

2 *(of thunder)* gronder; **to hear the drums rolling** entendre le roulement des tambours

3 *(of hills, prairie)* onduler; **the hills rolled away into the distance** il y avait des collines à perte de vue

4 *(of camera, machine etc)* tourner; *TV, Cin* **r.!** moteur!; **the cameras were rolling** les caméras tournaient; *Cin* **the credits started to r.** le générique commença à défiler; **it's too late, the presses are rolling** c'est trop tard, c'est déjà sous presse; **to get the presses rolling** mettre les rotatives en route

▸▸*Aut* **r. cage** cage *f* de roulement; **r. call** appel *m*; **to take (the) r. call** faire l'appel; **r. film** pellicule *f* en bobine

▸ **roll about** **VI** *(of marble, ball etc)* rouler çà et là; *(of person, animal)* se rouler; *(of ship)* rouler; **to r. about on the floor** *or* **ground** *(of person)* se rouler par terre; *(of object)* rouler par terre; **to r. about in pain/laughing** se tordre de douleur/de rire

VT SEP **to r. sth about** faire rouler qch

▸ **roll along** **VI 1** *(of ball, car etc)* rouler

2 *Fam (arrive)* arriver, se pointer

▸ **roll around** **VI** = **roll about** **VI**, **roll round** **VT SEP** = **roll about** **VT SEP**

▸ **roll away** **VI** *(of marble, ball etc)* rouler au loin; *(of clouds)* s'éloigner; *(of mist)* se retirer

VT SEP **to r. sth away** rouler qch

▸ **roll back** **VI** *(of car)* reculer, rouler en arrière; **her eyes rolled back in her head** ses yeux se révulsèrent

VT SEP *Mil* **to r. back the enemy** faire reculer l'ennemi; **to r. back a carpet** rouler un tapis (pour faire de la place); **to r. back reforms** faire marche arrière; **to r. back the frontiers of science/the state** faire reculer les frontières de la science/de l'état; **to r. back the years** revivre le passé; *Com* **to r. back prices** baisser les prix

▸ **roll by** **VI** *(of car)* passer (en roulant); *(of time)* s'écouler

▸ **roll down** **VI** *(of tears)* couler; **to r. down a hill** *(of car, children)* débouler une pente; **the tears rolled down his cheeks** les larmes coulaient le long de ses joues

VT SEP **to r. sth down** descendre qch (en le faisant rouler); **to r. down a blind/car window** baisser un store/la vitre d'une voiture; **she rolled down the car window** elle a baissé la vitre; **to r. down one's sleeves** se retourner les manches

▸ **roll in** **VI 1** *(of waves)* déferler; *(of mist, clouds, train)* arriver; *Fam (of orders, spectators etc)* affluer; *Fam (of person)* rappliquer, s'amener; *Fam* **she rolled in to work three**

hours late elle s'est amenée au travail avec trois heures de retard

2 *(at hockey)* remettre la balle en jeu

VT SEP **to r. sth in** faire entrer qch en le faisant rouler; **to r. the ball in** *(in hockey)* remettre la balle en jeu

▸ **roll off** **VI** tomber (en roulant); **to r. off the shelf/the table** rouler de l'étagère/de la table; **sweat was rolling off his back** la sueur lui coulait dans le dos; **cars are rolling off the production line** les voitures sortent de la chaîne de production

▸ **roll on** **VI** *(of time)* s'écouler; *Fam* **r. on tonight/the holidays!** vivement ce soir/les vacances!

VT SEP **to r. one's stockings/a condom on** mettre ses bas/un préservatif; **to r. paint on** étendre de la peinture au rouleau

▸ **roll out** **VI** *(of ball etc)* rouler (à l'extérieur); **to r. out of bed** *(of person)* se sortir du lit; *Fam* **we rolled out of the pub at midnight** nous sommes sortis du pub à minuit; **the train rolled out of the station** le train quitta la gare

VT SEP 1 **to r. sth out** *(through door etc)* faire sortir qch en le faisant rouler; **to r. a carpet out** dérouler un tapis; **to r. out any bumps** *(in lawn)* faire disparaître des inégalités au rouleau; **to r. out the dough** étendre la pâte au rouleau

2 *(launch) (product)* lancer; *(extend) (new scheme)* étendre; *(production)* accroître; **the new scheme will be rolled out nationwide** le nouveau système s'étendra à tout le pays

▸ **roll over** **VI** *(of person) (once)* se retourner; *(many times)* se rouler; *(of car) (once)* capoter; *(several times)* faire des tonneaux; **to r. over on the ground** rouler sur le sol; **to r. over (and over) on the bed/the ground** se rouler sur le lit/par terre; **the car rolled over and over and then fell into the ravine** la voiture a déboulé dans le ravin; *Fig* **he'll soon r. over** *(give in)* il se ravisera bientôt

VT SEP 1 *(person, stone)* retourner

2 *Fin (renew)* renouveler; *(extend)* prolonger

▸ **roll round** **VI** *(of season etc)* arriver

▸ **roll up** **VI** *(of blind)* remonter; *Fam (arrive) (of guests)* rappliquer, se pointer, s'amener; *(of customers, spectators)* rappliquer en foule; **to r. up into a ball** *(of animal)* se mettre *ou* se rouler en boule; **r. up!, r. up!** venez nombreux!

VT SEP *(map etc)* rouler; *(trousers)* relever, retrousser; *(blind, car window)* remonter; **to r. sth up in sth** *(for protection)* envelopper qch (in de); **to r. up one's sleeves** retrousser ses manches; **to r. oneself up in a blanket** s'enrouler dans une couverture

rollaway ['rəʊləweɪ] *esp Am* **N** *(bed)* lit *m* pliant sur roulettes

ADJ à roulettes

▸▸ **r. bed** lit pliant sur roulettes; **r. table** table *f* pliante sur roulettes

rollback ['rəʊlbæk] **N** *(of prices, inflation)* baisse *f*, réduction *f*

rollbar ['rəʊlbɑːr] **N** *(on vehicle)* arceau *m* de sécurité

rolled [rəʊld] **ADJ 1** *(paper etc)* en rouleau, roulé; **r. in a blanket** roulé dans une couverture **2** *(lawn)* passé au rouleau, roulé; *(metal etc)* laminé; *(umbrella)* plié

▸▸ **r. gold** plaqué *m* or; **a r. gold watch** une montre en plaqué or; **r. oats** flocons *mpl* d'avoine

rolled-up **ADJ** *(sleeves, trousers)* retroussé, relevé; *(paper etc)* enroulé; *(carpet)* roulé

Roller ['rəʊlə(r)] **N** *Br Fam* (*abbr* **Rolls Royce®**) Rolls Royce® *f*

roller ['rəʊlər] **N 1** *(for paint, garden etc)* rouleau *m*; *(for metal)* laminoir *m*; *Comput (in*

printer) rouleau; *Comput (in mouse)* galet *m*; *(for hair)* rouleau, bigoudi *m*; **to put rollers in (one's hair), to put one's hair in rollers** se mettre des rouleaux *ou* des bigoudis; **my hair's in rollers** j'ai des rouleaux *ou* des bigoudis sur la tête; **road r.** rouleau compresseur **2** *(on chair etc)* roulette *f* **3** *(wave)* rouleau *m* **4** *Am Fam* **high r.** *(gambler)* gros parieur *m*

▸▸ **r. bandage** bandage *m* enroulé; **r. bearing** roulement *m* à rouleaux; **r. blind** store *m* à enrouleur; *TV* **r. caption** déroulant *m*; **r. coaster** *(at funfair)* montagnes *fpl* russes; **the r. coaster fortunes of a company/a party** les hauts et les bas que connaît une société/un parti; **r. conveyor** transporteur *m* à rouleaux; **r. disco** = discothèque *f* où l'on tourne en patins à roulettes sur une piste; **r. map** carte *f* sur rouleau; *TV* **r. prompter** prompteur *m* déroulant; **r. skate** patin *m* à roulettes

Rollerblade® ['rəʊləbleɪd] **N** patin *m* en ligne, rollerblade *m*, roller *m*

rollerblading ['rəʊləbleɪdɪŋ] **N** roller *m*; **to go r.** faire du roller

roller-coaster **VI** *esp Am (of road)* faire des montagnes russes; *(of economy)* connaître des hauts et des bas prononcés

roller-skate **VI** faire du patin à roulettes

roller-skating **N** patin *m* à roulettes; **to go r.** aller faire du patin à roulettes

▸▸ **r. rink** piste *f* de patin à roulettes

rollick ['rɒlɪk] *Fam* **VT** *Br* engueuler, remonter les bretelles à

VI *(romp)* s'ébattre; *(celebrate)* faire la noce

▸ **rollick about** **VI** *Br Fam (romp)* s'ébattre

rollicking ['rɒlɪkɪŋ] **ADV** **to get r. drunk** se saoûler; **it's a r. good read!** *(of book)* c'est un livre excellent!; **to have a r. good time** bien se marrer

ADJ *(joyful)* joyeux; *(noisy)* bruyant; **to lead a r. life** mener une vie de patachon; **we had a r. (good) time** on s'est amusés comme des fous

N *Br Fam* **to give sb a r.** *(tell off)* engueuler qn; **to get a r.** se faire engueuler

rollie ['rəʊlɪ] **N** *Br Fam* cigarette *f* roulée à la main

rolling ['rəʊlɪŋ] **ADJ 1** *(ball etc)* roulant, qui roule; *(mist)* qui avance; *(boat)* qui roule, qui a du roulis; *Fig (subject to review) (programme)* réexaminé à intervalles réguliers; *Fam* **to be r. drunk** être ivre mort **2** *(thunder)* qui gronde **3** *(hills, prairie, ground)* ondulant, onduleux; *(gait)* chaloupé; *(sea)* gros, houleux; **to have a r. gait** avoir une démarche chaloupée; **r. countryside** paysage *m* vallonné

N 1 *(of ship, vehicle)* roulis *m* **2** *(of road, lawn)* cylindrage *m*; *(of metal)* laminage *m*

▸▸ *Acct* **r. budget** budget *m* glissant; *Cin, TV* **r. credits** générique *m* déroulant; **r. mill** *(factory)* usine *f* de laminage; *(equipment)* laminoir *m*; **r. pin** rouleau *m* à pâtisserie; *Acct* **r. plan** plan *m* glissant; *Aut* **r. resistance** résistance *f* au roulement; *Rail* **r. stock** matériel *m* roulant; **r. stone** *(person)* vadrouilleur, -euse; *Fig* **he's a r. stone** il ne reste jamais très longtemps au même endroit; *Prov* **a r. stone gathers no moss** pierre qui roule n'amasse pas mousse; **r. strikes** grèves *fpl* tournantes; *Cin, TV* **r. titles** générique déroulant

rollmop ['rəʊlmɒp] **N** *Culin* rollmops *m*

rollneck ['rəʊlnek] **ADJ** *(sweater)* à col roulé **N** *(sweater)* (pull *m* à) col *m* roulé

roll-on **N 1** *(deodorant)* déodorant *m* à bille **2** *Old-fashioned (corset)* gaine *f* (élastique)

▸▸ **r. deodorant** déodorant à bille

roll-on/roll-off **ADJ** *(ferry, traffic etc)* de type roll on-roll off, roulier; *(port)* à roulage direct; *(cargo)* à manutention horizontale *ou* de type roll on-roll off

rollout marketing ['rəʊlaʊt] N marketing *m* expansionniste

rollover ['rəʊləʊvər] N **1** *Br (in national lottery)* = à la loterie nationale, situation où, personne n'ayant gagné le gros lot, celui-ci est ajouté à l'enjeu du tirage suivant **2** *Fin (in taxation)* (disposition f de) roulement *m*; *(of loan)* reconduction f
ADJ *Am (renewable)* renouvelable; *(renegotiable)* renégociable; *(credit, loan)* à taux révisable
▸▸*Br* **r. jackpot** *(in national lottery)* = gros lot *m* composé de l'enjeu de plusieurs semaines successives

Rolls [rəʊlz] N *Br Fam (abbr* **Rolls Royce®)** Rolls Royce® f

roll-top N bureau *m* à cylindre
▸▸**r. desk** bureau à cylindre

roll-up, roll-your-own N *Br Fam (cigarette)* cigarette f roulée

roly-poly ['rəʊlɪ'pəʊlɪ] N **1** *Fam (plump person)* **he's a bit of a r.** il est plutôt grassouillet **2** *Culin* gâteau *m* roulé à la confiture
ADJ *Fam (person)* boulot, grassouillet
▸▸*Br Culin* **r. pudding** gâteau roulé à la confiture

ROM [rɒm] N *Comput (abbr* **read only memory)** mémoire f morte, (mémoire) ROM f

romaine [rəʊ'meɪn] N *Am (lettuce)* romaine f
▸▸**r. lettuce** (laitue f) romaine

Roman ['rəʊmən] **ADJ** *(law, numeral etc)* romain; **the Holy R. Empire** le Saint Empire romain (germanique)
N Romain, -aine; *Bible* **Epistle to the Romans** Épître f aux Romains
▸▸**R. candle** chandelle f romaine; *Rel* **R. Catholic** catholique *mf*; *Rel* **R. Catholicism** catholicisme *m*; **R. nose** nez *m* busqué *ou* aquilin

Note that the French adjective **roman** is a false friend and is never a translation for the English word **Roman**. It means **Romanesque**.

roman ['rəʊmən] N, **ADJ** *Typ* romain *m*; **in r.** *(word, abbreviation)* en romain

Romance [rə'mæns, 'rəʊ-] N *Ling* le roman; **R. languages** langues *fpl* roman(e)s; **student of R. languages** romaniste *mf*

romance [rə'mæns, 'rəʊ-] N **1** *(book)* histoire *f* ou roman *m* d'amour; *(film)* histoire d'amour; *Liter, Hist* roman de chevalerie *ou* d'aventures; **the age of r.** l'époque des chevaliers **2** *(between people)* idylle *f*, *(affair)* aventure *f* (amoureuse); *(love)* amour *m*; **a holiday r.** un amour *ou* une idylle de vacances; **r. is in the air** il y a de l'amour dans l'air **3** *(charm) (of place, situation)* poésie *f* **4** *Mus* romance *f*
VI *Old-fashioned* exagérer, inventer à plaisir
VT *esp Am (person)* faire la cour à

romancing [rə'mænsɪŋ, 'rəʊ-] N *(exaggeration)* exagération *f*, invention *f*

Romanesque [rəʊmə'nesk] **ADJ** *Archit* roman

Romania [rə'meɪnɪə] N Roumanie *f*

Romanian [rə'meɪnɪən] **ADJ** roumain
N **1** Roumain, -aine **2** *Ling* roumain *m*

romanize ['rəʊmənaɪz] VT *Typ (text)* transcrire en caractères romains

Romans(c)h [rəʊ'mænʃ] **ADJ, N** *Ling* romanche *m*

romantic [rə'mæntɪk, rəʊ-] **ADJ 1** *(love, landscape, spot etc)* romantique; *Pej (impractical) (scheme, notion)* romanesque; **he's very r.** il est très romantique; **a r. dinner for two** un dîner en tête à tête; **a r. young**

woman une jeune fille sentimentale *ou* romantique; **to play the r. lead** *(in film, play)* être le jeune premier/la jeune première **2** *Art, Liter, Mus* romantique
N *(person)* romantique *mf*
▸▸**r. adventure** aventure f romanesque; **r. comedy** comédie f romantique; **r. novelist** auteur *m* de romans d'amour; **r. play** pièce f romantique

When translating the English adjective **romantic**, note that the French words **romantique** and **romanesque** are not interchangeable. **Romantique** has to do with sentiment and romance, whereas **romanesque** is used to describe people or situations that one could expect to find in a novel.

romantically [rə'mæntɪklɪ, rəʊ-] **ADV** *(to behave)* de façon romantique; **to be r. involved with sb** avoir des relations amoureuses avec qn

romanticism [rə'mæntɪsɪz(ə)m, rəʊ-] N **1** *Art, Liter, Mus* romantisme *m* **2** *(of person)* idées *fpl* romanesques

romanticist [rə'mæntɪsɪst, rəʊ-] N romantique *mf*

romanticize [rə'mæntɪsaɪz, rəʊ-] VT *(idea, incident etc)* romancer; **to r. war** glorifier la guerre
VI donner dans le romanesque

Romany ['rəʊmənɪ] **ADJ** *(custom, life, language etc)* tzigane
N **1** tzigane *mf* **2** *Ling* tzigane *m*

rom-com ['rɒm'kɒm] N *Cin* comédie f romantique

Rome [rəʊm] N **1** Rome *m ou f*; *Prov* **R. wasn't built in a day** = Paris ne s'est pas fait en un jour; *Prov* **when in R.(, do as the Romans do)** il faut adopter les usages de l'endroit où l'on se trouve **2** *Rel* **(the Church of) R.** l'Église f de Rome; **to go over to R.** passer au catholicisme

Romeo ['rəʊmi:əʊ] N Roméo *m*; *Hum* **he's a bit of a R.** c'est un Roméo

romp [rɒmp] N **the book is a r. through two centuries of French history** le livre nous promène à travers deux siècles d'histoire de France; **the film/play is an enjoyable r.** ce film/cette pièce constitue un divertissement agréable; **sex romps** ébats *mpl* amoureux
VI **to r. (about** *or* **around)** *(of child, animal etc)* s'ébattre (bruyamment), gambader; **to r. away with a race** gagner une course haut la main; **to r. home** *(of candidate, horse, runner)* arriver dans un fauteuil; **to r. through an examination** passer un examen sans effort *ou Fam* faire les doigts dans le nez; **to r. through one's work** faire son travail sans effort; **the book romps through two centuries of French history** ce livre traverse deux siècles d'histoire de France

romper ['rɒmpər] N **r. suit, rompers** *(for baby)* barboteuse f

rondo ['rɒndəʊ] N *Mus* rondeau *m*

Roneo® ['rəʊnɪəʊ] N document *m*/etc ronéotypé *ou* ronéoté
VT *(document)* ronéotyper, ronéoter

roo [ru:] N *Austr Fam* kangourou *m*
▸▸**r. bar** pare-buffles *m inv*

rood [ru:d] N **1** *Rel* crucifix *m* **2** *Arch (measurement)* rood *m*, quart *m* d'arpent
▸▸**r. arch** arche f du jubé; **r. loft** (galerie f du) jubé *m*; **r. screen** jubé

roof [ru:f] N *(of building, vehicle)* toit *m*; *(of tunnel, cave, mine)* plafond *m*; **to be without** *or* **not have a r. over one's head** se trouver sans logement; **at least you have a r. over your head** au moins, tu as un endroit pour vivre; **to live under one** *or* **the same r.** habi-

ter sous le même toit *ou* dans le même bâtiment; **shops and sports facilities under one** *or* **the same r.** des boutiques et des aménagements sportifs dans un même endroit; **not under** <u>my</u> **r.** pas chez moi; *Fam* **to go through** *or* **hit the r.** *(get angry)* sortir de ses gonds; *Fam* **to go through the r.** *(of inflation, prices)* connaître une flambée; *Lit* **the r. of heaven** la voûte des cieux; **the r. of the mouth** la voûte du palais; *Fig* **the r. of the world** le toit du monde
VT *Constr (house etc)* couvrir (**with** de); **to r. sth in** *or* **over** recouvrir qch d'un toit; **a house roofed with slate/thatch** une maison à toit d'ardoises/de chaume
▸▸**r. garden** jardin *m* sur le toit; **r. light** *(of vehicle)* plafonnier *m*; *(window)* lucarne *f*; *Aut* **r. pillar** montant *m* de toit; **r. rack** *(on car)* galerie *f*; **r. timbering** combles *mpl*; **r. timbers** combles

-roofed [-ru:ft] **SUFF** slate-r. à toit d'ardoises

roofer ['ru:fər] N *Constr (of building etc)* couvreur *m*

roofie ['ru:fɪ] N *Sl (abbr* **Rohypnol®)** Rohypnol® *m*

roofing ['ru:fɪŋ] N *(operation)* pose f de la toiture; *(material)* toiture f
▸▸**r. felt** feutre *m* de couverture; **r. material** matériaux *mpl* de couverture; **r. tiles** tuiles *fpl* de couverture

roofless ['ru:flɪs] **ADJ** *(building)* sans toit, à ciel ouvert

rooftop ['ru:ftɒp] N toit *m*; *Fig* **to shout** *or* **proclaim sth from the rooftops** crier qch sur les toits

rooftree ['ru:ftri:] N poutre f de faîte, faîtage *m*

rook [rʊk] N **1** *(bird)* freux *m* **2** *(in chess)* tour *f*
VT *Old-fashioned Fam (cheat) (person)* rouler (**out of** de)

rookery ['rʊkərɪ] N *(of rooks, seals)* colonie *f*, *(of penguins)* rookerie *f*

rookie ['rʊkɪ] N *Am Fam (in army)* recrue *f*, bleu *m*; *(in sport)* novice *mf*; *(addition to a team)* nouveau membre *m*; *Am* **r. cop** flic *m* débutant, bleu

room [ru:m] N **1** *(in house etc)* pièce *f*, *(in hotel)* chambre *f*, *(bedroom)* chambre; *(large, public)* salle *f*, **one's rooms** ses appartements *mpl*; **to live in rooms** vivre dans un meublé; **(furnished) rooms to let** chambres (meublées) à louer; **r. and board** chambre et pension; **double/single r.** chambre pour deux personnes/une personne; **r. with twin beds** chambre à deux lits; **r. 22 wants some coffee** *(in hotel)* du café pour la chambre 22; *Euph Fam* **the smallest r. in the house** *(toilet)* le petit coin; *Am* **men's/ladies r.** toilettes *fpl*; **the r. fell silent** le silence s'est fait dans la pièce *ou* dans la salle; **the whole r. burst out laughing** toute la salle a éclaté de rire; **serve at r. temperature** *(of wine)* servir chambré; **to keep sth at r. temperature** garder qch à la température ambiante *ou* de la pièce
2 *(space)* place *f* (**for** pour); **(some) r.** de la place; **there's no r. to breathe in here** on étouffe ici; **to give sb r.** donner à qn plus d'espace *ou* de place pour bouger; **to take up a lot of r.** prendre beaucoup de place; **there's no r. to move in his flat** on n'a pas la place de bouger dans son appartement; *Fam* **there isn't (enough) r. to swing a cat in here** c'est vraiment exigu ici; **to have r. for manoeuvre** avoir une marge de manœuvre; **there is r. for negotiation** il existe une marge de négociation; **to make r. for sb** faire de la *ou* une place à qn; *Fig* laisser le champ libre à qn; **to make r. for sth** faire de la place pour qch; **to leave (sb) some r.** laisser de la place (à qn) (**for sth** pour qch);

is there r. for one more? *(person)* est-ce qu'il y a encore de la place pour une personne?; **r. for one more inside!** *(on bus)* il y a encore de la place pour une personne; *Fig* **there's r. for doubt** le doute est permis; **there is no r. for doubt** aucun doute n'est possible; **there is r. for improvement** cela laisse à désirer, on peut/il peut/vous pouvez/*etc* faire mieux; **there's no r. for slackers in this company** les fainéants n'ont pas leur place dans cette société

VI *Old-fashioned* vivre en meublé; *Am* **to r. with sb** partager un logement avec qn; **to r. together** vivre ensemble dans le même logement

▸▸**r. attendant** *(in hotel)* femme *f* de chambre; **r. card** fiche *f* de la chambre; **r. change** *(in hotel)* délogement *m*; *Am* **r. clerk** réceptionniste *mf*; **r. divider** cloison *f*, écran *m*; **r. key** clé *f* de la chambre; **your r. key** la clé de votre chambre; **r. night** *(in hotel)* nuitée *f*; **r. number** *(in hotel)* numéro *m* de chambre; **r. occupancy** *(in hotels)* occupation *f* des chambres, taux *m* d'occupation; **r. rack** *(in hotel)* room-rack *m*, *pl* room-racks, tableau *m* (de l'état) des chambres; **r. rack card** *(in hotel)* fiche client, fiche d'occupation; **r. sale** vente *f* de chambre; **r. service** service *m* dans les chambres; **to provide r. service** servir dans les chambres; **to call r. service** appeler le service en chambre *ou* le garçon d'étage

-roomed [ruːmd] **SUFF two/three-r.** *(house etc)* de deux/trois pièces

roomer ['ruːmər] **N** *Am* locataire *mf* en meublé

roomette [ruːˈmet] **N** *Am Rail* compartiment *m* avec couchette

roomful ['ruːmfʊl] **N** *(of people, objects etc)* salle *f* pleine; *(of soldiers)* chambrée *f*; **a r. of students** une salle pleine d'étudiants

roomie ['ruːmɪ] **N** *Am Fam* colocataire *mf*

roominess ['ruːmɪnɪs] **N** *(of house etc)* dimensions *fpl* spacieuses *ou* généreuses; *(of clothing)* coupe *f* confortable *ou* ample; *(of car)* dimensions spacieuses

rooming ['ruːmɪŋ] **N**
▸▸*Am* **r. house** maison *f* de rapport

roommate ['ruːmmeɪt] **N** *Br (sharing room)* camarade *mf* de chambre; *Am (sharing apartment or house)* colocataire *mf*

roomy ['ruːmɪ] **ADJ** *(house)* spacieux, où l'on a de la place; *(clothes)* ample; *(car)* spacieux; *(suitcase)* grand

roost [ruːst] **N** perchoir *m*; *(for domestic fowl)* juchoir *m*; *Fig (for person)* logement *m*, gîte *m*; **to go to r.** se percher; *Fig* **to come home to r.** *(of crime, mistake etc)* se retourner contre son auteur; *Fig* **your chickens have come home to r.** ça s'est retourné contre toi, ça a fait boomerang
VI se percher

rooster ['ruːstər] **N** coq *m*

root [ruːt] **N 1** *(of plant, tooth)*, *Math*, *Ling* racine *f*; **to pull up a plant by the roots** déraciner une plante; **to pull sb's hair out by the roots** arracher les cheveux de qn; **to touch up one's roots** *(of person with dyed hair)* refaire ses racines; **to take r.** *(of plant)*, *Fig* prendre racine *ou* pied; *Fig* **to destroy sth r. and branch** extirper qch; **a r. and branch reform** une réforme complète
2 *(cause)* *(of problem etc)* cause *f*, origine *f*, **to have its roots in sth** *(of crisis etc)* avoir ses origines dans qch; *Prov* **money is the r. of all evil** l'argent est la source de tous les maux; **to get to the r. of things** aller au fond des choses; **to strike at the r. of the problem** aller à la source du problème; **r. cause** cause première
3 *(ethnic, class, cultural origins)* *Fig* **my roots**

are in Canada mes racines sont au Canada; **I don't have any roots** je n'ai pas de racines; *Fig* **to put down roots** s'intégrer; **to get back to one's roots** retrouver ses racines

▸▸*Am* **r. beer** = boisson *f* gazeuse à base d'extraits végétaux; *Anat* **r. canal** canal *m* dentaire; **r. canal treatment, r. canal work** traitement *m* canalaire; *Am* **r. cellar** cave *f* potagère; **r. crop** racine *f* alimentaire; *Comput* **r. directory** racine, répertoire *m* principal; **r. vegetable** légume *m* à racine comestible

root[2] **VT** *(cuttings)* enraciner (**in** dans); *Fig* **rooted to the spot** *or* **ground** cloué *ou* figé sur place; **her behaviour is rooted in her political convictions** son comportement trouve ses origines dans ses convictions politiques
VI *(of cuttings)* s'enraciner, prendre racine

root[3] **VI** *(of pig)* fouiller avec le groin
VT *(of pig)* *(earth)* fouiller

▸**root about, root around** **VI** fouiller; **to r. about** *or* **around for one's keys/a pen** fouiller pour trouver ses clés/un stylo; **to r. around in a drawer** fouiller dans un tiroir

▸**root for** **VT INSEP** *Fam (cheer, support)* encourager; **to r. for a candidate** appuyer un candidat; **we'll be rooting for you** nous sommes de votre côté

▸**root out** **VT SEP 1** *(remove)* *(plant)* déraciner; *Fig* **to r. out abuse** supprimer *ou* extirper des abus **2** *Fam (find)* trouver, dénicher; **see if you can r. him out of the pub** essayez de le faire décoller du pub

▸**root through** **VT INSEP** fouiller dans

▸**root up** **VT SEP** *(plant)* déraciner; *(carrots, potatoes)* arracher

rooted ['ruːtɪd] **ADJ** *(plant)* enraciné; *(cutting)* qui a des racines; *Fig (prejudice)* enraciné; **deeply r.** bien ancré *ou* enraciné (**in** dans)

rooting ['ruːtɪŋ] **N** enracinement *m*
▸▸**r. compost** compost *m* spécial pour boutures; **r. out** *(of abuse, malpractice)* extirpation *f*, éradication *f*

rootless ['ruːtlɪs] **ADJ** *(plant, person)* sans racines

rootstock ['ruːtstɒk] **N** *(of plant)* souche *f*

rope [rəʊp] **N** corde *f*; *Naut* cordage *m*; *(of pearls)* sautoir *m*; *Boxing etc* **the ropes** les cordes; **to be on the ropes** *(of boxer)* se retrouver dans les cordes; *Fig (of company, economy etc)* battre de l'aile; **to be on the ropes financially** être sur la corde raide; **to have sb on the ropes** *Boxing* mettre qn dans les cordes; *Fig* acculer qn, mettre qn dans une position difficile; *Br Fam* **it's money for old r.** c'est grassement payé pour pas grand-chose; **wire r.** câble *m* métallique; **a piece of r.** une corde; **bell r.** *(in house)* cordon *m* de sonnette; *(in belltower)* corde de cloche; **to put on the r.** *(of climbers)* s'encorder; **(climbers on the) r.** (alpinistes *mpl* en) cordée *f*; *Fam* **to know the ropes** connaître les ficelles; *Fam* **to learn the ropes** apprendre les ficelles; *Fam* **to show** *or* **teach sb the ropes** mettre qn au courant, former qn; **the r.** *(death by hanging)* la pendaison; **to bring back the r.** remettre la pendaison en vigueur; *Fig* **to give sb enough r. (to hang himself/herself)** donner à qn la corde pour se pendre; *Fig* **to give sb lots** *or* **plenty of r.** donner du mou à qn
VT 1 *(person, object)* lier (avec une corde) (**to** à); **to r. climbers (together)** encorder les alpinistes; **climbers roped together** (alpinistes *mpl* en) cordée *f* **2** *Am (animal)* prendre au lasso
▸▸**r. bridge** pont *m* de corde; **r. ladder** échelle *f* de corde; **r. maker** cordier, -ière

▸**rope in** **VT SEP** *Fam* **to r. sb in** *(to help etc)* recruter qn (**to do** pour faire); **don't let yourself get roped in** ne te laisse pas embringuer là-dedans

▸**rope off** **VT SEP** séparer (par une corde); **part of the field has been roped off** une partie du champ a été fermée par des cordes

▸**rope up** **VI** *(of climbers)* s'encorder
VT SEP attacher avec de la corde

rope-soled [-səʊld] **ADJ** *(sandals etc)* à semelles de corde

rop(e)y ['rəʊpɪ] **ADJ** *Br Fam (unreliable)* *(translation etc)* minable; *(ill)* *(person)* patraque; **to feel a bit r.** se sentir patraque, ne pas être dans son assiette

ro-ro ['rəʊrəʊ] **ADJ** = roll-on/roll-off

Rorschach ['rɔːʃɑːk] **N**
▸▸*Psy* **R. test** test *m* de Rorschach

ROS [ɑːrəʊ'es] **N** *Fin (abbr* **return on sales**) retour *m* sur ventes

rosary ['rəʊzərɪ] **N** *Rel* rosaire *m*, chapelet *m*; **to say the** *or* **one's r.** dire *ou* réciter son rosaire *ou* son chapelet

rose[1] [rəʊz] **N 1** *(flower)* rose *f*, *(bush)* rosier *m*; *(on hat etc)* rosette *f*, *(on watering can)* pomme *f*, **(ceiling) r.** rosace *f*, *Fig* **life is not a bed of roses, life is not all roses** tout n'est pas rose dans la vie; *Fig* **her life wasn't a bed of roses** tout n'était pas rose dans sa vie; *Prov* **there is no r. without a thorn** il n'y a pas de rose sans épine; *Fig* **to come up always smelling of roses** s'en sortir toujours très bien; *Fig* **to come up roses** marcher parfaitement; *Fig* **to put the roses back in sb's cheeks** *(of holiday, sea air etc)* redonner des couleurs à qn; *Hist* **the Wars of the Roses** la guerre des Deux-Roses **2** *(colour)* rose *m*
ADJ *(colour)* rose
▸▸**r. bed** parterre *m* de rosiers; **r. bush** rosier; **r. garden** roseraie *f*, **r. grower** rosiériste *mf*; **r. petal** pétale *m* de rose; **r. pink** rose; *Miner* **r. quartz** quartz *m* rose; **r. red** vermillon *m*; *Archit* **r. window** rosace *f*

rose *PT see* **rise** **VI**

rosé ['rəʊzeɪ] **N** *(vin m)* rosé *m*

roseate ['rəʊzɪeɪt] **ADJ** *Lit* rose

rosebay ['rəʊzbeɪ] **N** *Bot* laurier-rose *m*, *pl* lauriers-roses

rosebud ['rəʊzbʌd] **N** bouton *m* de rose
▸▸**r. mouth** bouche *f* en cerise

rose-coloured, *Am* **rose-colored** **ADJ** rose, rosé; **to see things** *or* **the world through r. glasses** *or* **spectacles** voir tout en rose, voir la vie en rose

rose-cut **ADJ** *(diamond etc)* taillé en rose

rosehip ['rəʊzhɪp] **N** *Bot* gratte-cul *m inv*; *Spec* cynorhodon *m*
▸▸**r. jelly** gelée *f* d'églantine; **r. syrup** sirop *m* d'églantine

rosemary ['rəʊzmərɪ] **N** *Bot, Culin* romarin *m*
▸▸**r. bush** buisson *m* de romarin

rose-pink **ADJ** *(dress etc)* (couleur de) rose

rose-red **ADJ** *(complexion etc)* vermeil

rose-tinted [-tɪntɪd] **ADJ** rose, rosé; **to see things** *or* **the world through r. glasses** *or* **spectacles** voir tout en rose, voir la vie en rose

rosetree ['rəʊztriː] **N** rosier *m* sur tige

rosette [rəʊ'zet] **N 1** *(badge)* rosette *f*, *Sport etc (prize)* cocarde *f* **2** *Archit (carving)* rosette *f*, *(window)* rosace *f*

rosewater ['rəʊzwɔːtər] **N** eau *f* de rose

rosewood ['rəʊzwʊd] **N** bois *m* de rose; **r. desk/table** bureau *m*/table *f* en bois de rose

rosie ['rəʊzɪ] **N** *Br Sl (tea)* thé *m*
▸▸**r. lee** thé

rosin ['rɒzɪn] **N** colophane *f*
VT *Mus (bow)* traiter à la colophane

rosiness ['rəʊzɪnɪs] **N** couleur *f* rose, rose *m*; **the r. of her cheeks** le rose de ses joues

ROSPA ['rɒspə] **N** *Br (abbr* **Royal Society for the Prevention of Accidents**) ≃ société *f* pour la prévention des accidents

roster [ˈrɒstər] N *Mil etc* **(duty) r.** liste *f* (de service)
VT *esp Am* (*person*) mettre sur une liste (de service)

rostrum, *pl* **rostra, rostrums** [ˈrɒstrəm, -ə, -əmz] N (*for speaker*) estrade *f*, tribune *f*; (*for prizewinner*) podium *m*; (*for conductor*) estrade
▸▸ *Cin, TV* **r. camera** banc-titre *m*, *pl* bancs-titres; *Cin, TV* **r. cameraman** opérateur *m* banc-titre

rosy [ˈrəʊzɪ] ADJ (*pink*) rose, rosé; *Fig* (*future*) prometteur, -euse, tout rose; **her r. complexion** son teint de rose; **to have r. cheeks** avoir les joues roses; *Fig* **to paint everything in r. colours** peindre tout sous un jour favorable *ou* en rose; *Fig* **to paint a r. picture of sth** dépeindre qch sous un jour optimiste; *Fig* **a r. prospect** une perspective attrayante; *Fig* **to take a r. view of things** voir les choses sous un jour optimiste *ou* la vie en rose

rot [rɒt] N **1** (*in plant, wood etc*) pourriture *f*; (*of food*) putréfaction *f*; *Fig* **the r. has set in** (*among employees, players etc*) les choses ont commencé à aller mal; *Fig* **to stop the r.** empêcher les choses de se dégrader, remonter la pente; *Fig* **we have stopped the r.** on remonte la pente **2** *esp Old-fashioned Fam* (*nonsense*) bêtises *fpl*, inepties *fpl*; **to talk (utter** *or* **absolute) r.** dire des bêtises *ou* des inepties *ou* des imbécillités; **(what) r.!** n'importe quoi!
VI (**-tt-**) (*of leaves, wood, material etc*) pourrir; (*of food*) se décomposer, se putréfier; (*of manure*) se décomposer; *Fig* **they let him r. in prison** ils l'ont laissé croupir en prison
VT (*faire*) pourrir, décomposer; **oil rots rubber** l'huile désagrège le caoutchouc; **sugar rots your teeth** le sucre gâte les dents *ou* donne des caries
▸ **rot away** VI, VT SEP = **rot** VI, VT
▸ **rot down** VI (*of compost material*) se décomposer

rota [ˈrəʊtə] N *esp Br* liste *f* de service; **we have a r. for the housework** nous faisons le ménage (chacun) à tour de rôle; **according to a r.** (chacun) à tour de rôle

Rotarian [rəʊˈteərɪən] N, ADJ rotarien *m*

Rotary [ˈrəʊtərɪ] N
▸▸ **the R. Club** le Rotary Club

rotary [ˈrəʊtərɪ] ADJ (*movement, pump, engine*) rotatif; (*switch*) tournant
N *Am Aut* (*roundabout*) sens *m* giratoire
▸▸ **r. dryer** séchoir *m* rotatif; *Typ* **r. press** rotative *f*; *Typ* **r. printer** (*person*) rotativiste *mf*

rotate [rəʊˈteɪt] VI **1** (*of earth etc*) tourner; (*on pivot*) pivoter **2** (*in job*) remplir des fonctions à tour de rôle; **the presidency rotates every two years among members** les membres assument la présidence à tour de rôle tous les deux ans
VT 1 (*knob, dial*) (faire) tourner; (*on pivot*) faire pivoter **2** (*duties*) remplir à tour de rôle; (*housework*) faire à tour de rôle; *Agr* (*crops*) alterner

rotating [rəʊˈteɪtɪŋ] ADJ (*which can move*) tournant, rotatif; (*which is moving*) en rotation
N rotation *f*; (*of crops*) alternance *f*

rotation [rəʊˈteɪʃən] N **1** (*of planet*) rotation *f*; (*of machine*) rotation, tour *m*; **rotations per minute** tours-minute *mpl* **2** (*in job*) roulement *m*; **by** *or* **in r.** par roulement, à tour de rôle; *Agr* **r. of crops** alternance *f* des cultures, assolement *m*

rotator [rəʊˈteɪtər] N (*device*) appareil *m* rotateur

rotatory [rəʊˈteɪtərɪ] ADJ rotatoire

rote [rəʊt] N routine *f*; **to learn sth by r.** apprendre qch par cœur
▸▸ **r. learning** apprentissage *m* par cœur

rotgut [ˈrɒtgʌt] N *Br Fam Pej* (*wine, spirits*) tord-boyaux *m inv*

rotisserie [rəʊˈtiːsərɪ, -ˈtɪs-] N (*spit*) rôtissoire *f*

rotogravure [ˈrəʊtəʊgrəˈvjʊər] N rotogravure *f*

rotor [ˈrəʊtər] N (*of turbine, helicopter*) rotor *m*
▸▸ **r. arm** (*of helicopter*) rotor; (*of engine*) rotor, balai *m*; **r. blade** pale *f* de rotor

Rotovator® [ˈrəʊtəveɪtər] N *Br* motoculteur *m*

rotten [ˈrɒt(ə)n] ADJ **1** (*leaves, wood, egg, fruit etc*) pourri; **to smell r.** sentir le pourri; **to go r.** pourrir **2** *Fam* (*bad, of poor quality*) (*book, film etc*) nul, pourri; (*actor, golfer etc*) nul; (*job, day etc*) sale; **to feel r.** (*ill*) être mal fichu; **I feel r. about this but … (sorry)** ça me rend malade mais …; **I felt r. about it** (*sorry*) j'en étais malade; **to look r.** avoir l'air mal fichu; **he played a r. game** il a joué affreusement mal, il a été lamentable; **what r. luck!** quelle guigne!; **to have r. luck** avoir la guigne; **r. weather** temps *m* pourri, temps de chien; **the weather was r.** il a fait un temps de chien; **it's been a r. summer** (*with bad weather*) ça a été un été pourri; **she's been having a r. time of it lately** elle vient de traverser une sale période **3** *Fam* (*unpleasant*) **a r. trick** un sale tour, un tour vache *ou* de cochon; **you r. bastard!** espèce de pourriture!; **what a r. bastard he is** quelle pourriture; **don't be r.!** ne sois pas vache!; **that was a r. thing to do** c'était un sale tour; **she's r. to the core** elle est pourrie jusqu'à la moelle
▸▸ *Hist* **r. borough** = circonscription *f* électorale britannique dont les électeurs, bien que peu nombreux, pouvaient élire un député (avant 1832)

rottenly [ˈrɒt(ə)nlɪ] ADV (*to behave*) affreusement mal, de façon abominable *ou* épouvantable

rottenness [ˈrɒt(ə)nnɪs] N **1** (*of leaves, wood, fruit etc*) pourriture *f* **2** *Fam* (*of performance etc*) caractère *m* lamentable, nullité *f*

rotter [ˈrɒtər] N *Old-fashioned Br Fam* sale type *m*, propre *m* à rien

rotting [ˈrɒtɪŋ] ADJ qui pourrit, en putréfaction

rottweiler [ˈrɒtvaɪlər] N rottweiler *m* (*race de chiens réputés dangereux*)

rotund [rəʊˈtʌnd] ADJ (*large and round*) rond; (*plump*) rond, rondelet; (*speech, style*) grandiloquent; **his r. figure** ses formes arrondies

rotunda [rəʊˈtʌndə] N *Archit* rotonde *f*

rotundity [rəʊˈtʌndɪtɪ] N (*of person*) rotondité *f*, embonpoint *m*; (*of speech, style*) grandiloquence *f*

rouble, *Am* **ruble** [ˈruːb(ə)l] N (*currency*) rouble *m*

roué [ˈruːeɪ] N *Old-fashioned* roué *m*, débauché *m*

rouge [ruːʒ] N (*make-up*) rouge *m* (à joues)
VT to r. one's cheeks se mettre du rouge aux joues, se farder

ROUGH [rʌf]

ADJ rugueux **1** ▪ rêche **1** ▪ fruste **2** ▪ rude **2, 5** ▪ brutal **4** ▪ approximatif **6**
ADV rudement
N brouillon **4**

ADJ 1 (*uneven, not smooth*) (*material*) rude, rugueux; (*surface*) rugueux; (*skin*) rêche; (*road*) défoncé; (*terrain etc*) accidenté; (*ground*) inégal, -aux, raboteux; (*uncultivated*) (*land, pasture*) en friche; *Fam* **to give sb the r. edge of one's tongue** parler brutalement à qn

2 (*unrefined, unpolished*) (*manners*) grossier, fruste; (*speech*) bourru, rude; (*style*) fruste; **in a** *or* **its r. state** à l'état brut; **to knock the r. edges off sb/sth** dégrossir qn/qch

3 *Fam* (*ill, not working properly*) **to feel/look r.** se sentir/avoir l'air patraque; **the engine sounds a bit r.** le moteur ne semble pas tourner très rond

4 (*violent*) (*person, behaviour, treatment*) brutal, -aux; (*wind*) violent; **to suffer r. treatment** (*people*) être maltraité; (*objects*) souffrir; **to be r. with sb** brutaliser qn, rudoyer qn; **she's terribly r. with the children** elle est très brutale avec les enfants; **you were too r.** tu as été trop brutal; **don't be so r. with her** sois moins brutal avec elle; **to come in for some r. treatment** se faire maltraiter; **this is a r. neighbourhood** c'est un quartier dur; *Fam* **r. customer** violent *m*; **a r. crossing** (*on ferry etc*) une traversée agitée; **r. sea(s)** mer *f* grosse *ou* houleuse; **due to r. handling** parce qu'on l'a malmené

5 (*harsh, hard*) (*voice, wine*) rude, âpre; *Fam* **to give sb/sth a r. time** *or* **ride** vache avec qn/esquinter qch; **don't give me a r. time** ne me rends pas la vie difficile; *Fam* **he's had a r. time of it** il en a bavé, il a bouffé de la vache enragée; *Fam* **he's had a r. deal** ça a été très dur pour lui; **he received some r. handling from the press** la presse l'a présenté de façon défavorable; **to make it** *or* **things r. for sb** rendre la vie difficile à qn; *Fam* **it was r. on him** ç'a été dur pour elle; **it's r. on the skin** c'est mauvais pour la peau; **divorce is r. on children** le divorce est dur pour les enfants; **you were too r. on them** tu as été trop sévère avec eux; **it's r. having to work on Saturdays** c'est dur de devoir travailler le samedi; **they've had a lot of r. luck recently** ils n'ont pas eu beaucoup de chance dernièrement

6 (*approximate*) (*calculation, estimate etc*) approximatif; **r. guess** approximation *f*; **at a r. guess** *or* **estimate** approximativement; **as a r. guide, one metre equals three feet** un mètre équivaut approximativement à trois pieds; **could you give me a r. idea of how long it will take?** pourriez-vous me donner une idée approximative du temps que ça va prendre?, pourriez-vous me dire en gros combien de temps cela va prendre?; **I have a r. idea of what it's about** j'ai une petite idée de ce dont il s'agit

ADV rudement, grossièrement; **to play r.** jouer brutalement; (*in business, relationship*) ne pas faire de cadeaux; *Fam* **to sleep r.** coucher à la dure; *Fam* **to live r.** vivre à la dure

N **1** (*ground*) terrain *m* accidenté; *Golf* **to be in the r.** être dans l'herbe longue; *Fig* **to take the r. with the smooth** prendre le bon avec le mauvais

2 *Fam* (*hooligan*) voyou *m*

3 *Fam* (*in sexual sense*) **she likes a bit of r.** elle aime s'envoyer un prolo de temps en temps

4 (*draft*) brouillon *m*; (*of drawing etc*) ébauche *f*; (*sketch of layout etc*) crayonné *m*; **to do sth in r.** faire qch au brouillon
VT *Fam* **to r. it** vivre à la dure; **we'll just have to r. it** il faudra qu'on fasse avec les moyens du bord
▸▸ **r. book** brouillard *m*; **r. copy** brouillon *m*; *TV, Cin* **r. cut** premier montage *m*; **r. diamond** diamant *m* brut; **r. draft** brouillon *m*; *TV, Cin* **r. edit** montage bout à bout; *TV, Cin* **r. focus** première mise *f* au point; **r. justice** justice *f* sommaire; **r. layout** (*of page etc*) prémaquette *f*, esquisse *f*, squelette *f*; **r. paper** papier *m* brouillon; **r. sketch** croquis *m*, ébauche *f*; *Fam* **r. stuff** brutalités *fpl*; *Fam* **r. trade** (*male prostitute*) = jeune prostitué *m* homosexuel à tendances violentes; (*work-*

ing-class male homosexual) homosexuel *m* prolo; **r. work** brouillon

▸ **rough out** VT SEP *(drawing etc)* ébaucher; *(plan, project, play, novel)* ébaucher, concevoir dans ses grandes lignes

▸ **rough up** VT SEP **1** *(person's hair)* ébouriffer **2** *Fam* **to r. sb up** tabasser qn

roughage [ˈrʌfɪdʒ] N *(in food)* fibres *fpl* (alimentaires)

rough-and-ready ADJ *(meal)* vite préparé; *(accommodation, construction)* sommaire; *(person)* rustre; *(conditions, solution)* grossier

rough-and-tumble N bousculade *f*, mêlée *f*; **the children were having a bit of a r.** les enfants chahutaient; *Fig* **the r. of politics** la jungle de la politique; *Fig* **the r. world of publishing** la jungle de l'édition

roughcast [ˈrʌfkɑːst] *Constr* N crépi *m* VT (*pt, pp* **roughcast**) *(wall etc)* crépir

roughen [ˈrʌf(ə)n] VT *(surface)* rendre rugueux

VI **1** *(of surface)* devenir rugueux **2** *(of sea)* grossir, devenir houleux

rough-hewn ADJ *(lumber, statue etc)* dégrossi

roughhouse [ˈrʌfhaʊs] N *Fam* **there was a bit of a r. in the pub last night** il y a eu de la bagarre au pub hier soir

roughly [ˈrʌflɪ] ADV **1** *(crudely) (to build)* grossièrement; **a r. made table** une table de conception grossière; **to sketch sth r.** faire un croquis sommaire de qch **2** *(harshly) (to behave, answer)* rudement **3** *(violently)* brutalement; **to treat sb r.** maltraiter *ou* malmener *ou* rudoyer qn **4** *(approximately)* **r. (speaking)** approximativement, en gros, grosso modo; **to estimate sth r.** estimer qch approximativement; **they live in r. the same area** ils habitent approximativement dans le même quartier

roughneck [ˈrʌfnek] N **1** *Am Fam (hooligan)* voyou *m* **2** *(on oil rig)* = personne *f* travaillant sur une plate-forme pétrolière

roughness [ˈrʌfnɪs] N **1** *(of surface)* caractère *m* rugueux; *(of skin)* caractère rêche; *(of ground)* inégalité *f*; *(of road)* mauvais état *m* **2** *(of sea)* agitation *f*; *(of wind)* violence *f* **3** *(of voice)* âpreté *f*, rudesse *f*

roughrider [ˈrʌfraɪdər] N dresseur *m* de chevaux

roughshod [ˈrʌfʃɒd] ADJ **to ride r. over** *(person)* traiter cavalièrement, fouler aux pieds; *(objections)* fouler aux pieds

rough-spoken ADJ au langage grossier

roulette [ruːˈlet] N *(game)* roulette *f*; **to play r.** jouer à la roulette

▸▸ **r. table** table *f* de roulette; **r. wheel** roulette *f*

Roumania [ruːˈmeɪnɪə, rʊ-] N = **Romania**

Roumanian [ruːˈmeɪnɪən, rʊ-] N, ADJ = **Romanian**

ROUND [raʊnd]

ADJ	rond **1**, **2**
N	rond **1** ▪ tour **3** ▪ partie **3** ▪ série **4** ▪ tournée **4**, **5**
ADV	autour
PREP	autour de **1**, **2** ▪ environ **3**

ADJ 1 *(in shape)* rond, circulaire; *(cheeks, stomach, earth)* rond; **to become r.** s'arrondir; **to have r. shoulders** avoir le dos rond; *Mus* **a good r. top C** un mi du haut parfait; **r. hand(writing)** écriture *f* ronde

2 *(number)* rond; **in r. figures** en chiffres ronds; **a r. dozen** une douzaine exactement; **r. sum** compte *m* rond

N **1** *(circle)* rond *m*, cercle *m*

2 *(shape) (of bread)* tranche *f*; **a r. of sand-**

wiches = un sandwich au pain de mie coupé en deux ou en quatre; *Art* **sculpture in the r.** ronde-bosse *f*, *pl* rondes-bosses; **theatre in the r.** théâtre *m* en rond

3 *(stage of match, tournament, election etc)* manche *f*, tour *m*; *Boxing* round *m*; *(of golf)* partie *f*; **to play a r. of golf** faire une partie de golf; **he only went three rounds** *(of boxer)* il n'a fait que trois rounds; **in the first r., in r. 1** *(of boxing match)* au cours du premier round; **to have a r. of cards** faire une partie de cartes; *Horseriding* **clear r.** sans-faute *m inv*; **to have** *or* **get a clear r.** faire un sans-faute; **to be/get through to the next r.** se qualifier/s'être qualifié pour la manche suivante; **he came out on top in the first r. of voting** il est arrivé en tête du premier tour des élections

4 *(series) (of talks, visits)* série *f*; *(of drinks)* tournée *f*; **to pay for** *or* **buy** *or* **stand a r.** *(of drinks)* payer une tournée (générale); **whose r. is it?** qui paye cette tournée?; **it's my r.** c'est moi qui paye cette tournée, c'est ma tournée

5 *(route)* **rounds** *(of milkman etc)* tournée *f*, *(of doctor)* visites *fpl*, *(of policeman)* ronde *f*; **delivery r.** livraisons *fpl*, tournée; *Fig* **the daily r.** la routine de tous les jours; **the daily r. of cooking and cleaning** les travaux quotidiens de cuisine et de ménage; **one continual r. of pleasure** une succession perpétuelle de plaisirs; **to go** *or* **do the rounds** *(of story, rumour etc)* circuler; *(of virus, cold etc)* circuler, se propager; **the story went** *or* **did the rounds (of the village)** l'histoire a fait le tour (du village); **to be on** *or* **make** *or* **do one's rounds** *(of doctor)* faire ses visites; *(of policeman)* faire sa ronde; *(of milkman etc)* faire sa tournée; **to do a hospital r.** faire sa visite à l'hôpital, visiter ses malades; **to do a paper r.** distribuer un/le journal *ou* des/les journaux; **to do** *or* **go the rounds of the travel agencies/***etc* faire le tour des agences de voyages/*etc*

6 *Mil (bullet)* balle *f*, *(cartridge)* cartouche *f*; *Mil* **r. of ten shots** salve *f* de dix coups; **to fire a r.** tirer un coup

7 *Mus* canon *m*

ADV autour; **a garden with a wall right** *or* **all r.** un jardin avec un mur tout autour; **taking it all r.** *(on the whole)* dans l'ensemble, en général; **all r., it was a good result** dans l'ensemble, c'était un bon résultat; **the villages/people r. about** les villages/gens des alentours; **r. here** par ici; **all (the) year r.** toute l'année; **the long way r.** le chemin le plus long; **to have one's hat/jumper on the wrong way r.** avoir son chapeau/son pull à l'envers; **to do sth the wrong way r.** *(in the wrong order)* faire qch à l'envers; **it's the other way r.** *(quite the opposite)* c'est (tout) le contraire; **try the key the other way r.** essaie la clef dans l'autre sens; **to go r. (to sb's)** passer (chez qn); **to order the car** r. demander qu'on amène la voiture; **to ask sb r.** inviter qn (chez soi); **he brought his friend r. (with him)** il a amené son ami (avec lui); **he'll be r.** il passera

PREP **1** *(position)* autour de; **sitting r. the table** assis autour de la table; **he's 95 cm r. the chest** il fait 95 cm de tour de poitrine; **shells were exploding r. (about) him** des obus éclataient autour de lui; *Br* **he's r. the pub** il est au pub; *Br* **he's r. his brother's** il est chez son frère

2 *(motion)* autour de; **to look r. the room** parcourir une pièce du regard; **to travel r. the world** parcourir le monde; **she walked r. the town centre** elle s'est promenée dans le centre-ville; **to go r. (and round) sth** *(in circle)* tourner autour de qch; **to go r. an obstacle** contourner un obstacle; **to go r. the corner** *(of person)* tourner le coin; *(of vehicle)* prendre le virage; **the grocer r. the cor-**

ner l'épicier du coin; **if you are r. this way next week** si vous passez par ici la semaine prochaine

3 *(approximately)* **r. about** environ; **r. (about) midday** vers midi; **she's r. about forty** elle a la quarantaine

VT **1** *(shape) (object)*, *Ling (vowel)* arrondir

2 *Naut (headland)* doubler, franchir; *(island)* contourner; **to r. a corner** *(of car)* prendre un virage; *(of person)* tourner un coin

▸▸ **r. of applause** des applaudissements *mpl*; **let's have a big r. of applause for her** on l'applaudit bien fort!; *Culin* **r. of beef** gîte *m* à la noix; *Typ* **r. brackets** parenthèses *fpl*; **r. dance** ronde *f*; **r. robin** *(letter)* pétition *f* *(où les signatures sont disposées en rond)*; *esp Am (contest)* poule *f*; **the R. Table** la Table ronde; **r. table** table *f* ronde; **r. table conference** table ronde; **r. trip** *(voyage m)* aller et retour *m*

▸ **round down** VT SEP *(figure etc)* arrondir (**to** à) *(à un chiffre inférieur)*

▸ **round off** VT SEP **1** *(sentence etc)* conclure; *(negotiations etc)* conclure, achever; **to r. off one's speech** achever son discours; **to r. things off …** pour finir …; **we rounded the meal off with a bottle of brandy** nous avons fini le repas avec une bouteille de cognac **2** *(figures)* arrondir

▸ **round on** VT INSEP s'en prendre à; **she rounded on him for no reason** elle lui est tombée dessus sans aucune raison

▸ **round up** VT SEP **1** *(gather) (cattle)* rassembler; *(local criminals)* faire une rafle de; **r. up the usual suspects** rassemblez les suspects habituels; **to r. everyone up for a meeting** rassembler tout le monde pour une réunion **2** *(number etc)* arrondir (**to** à) *(à un chiffre supérieur)*; **to r. an amount up** arrondir une somme (**to** à)

roundabout [ˈraʊndəbaʊt] N *Br* **1** *(at fairground, in playground)* manège *m*; *Fam* **what you gain on the swings you lose on the roundabouts** ce que tu gagnes d'un côté, tu le perds de l'autre **2** *Aut* rond-point *m*, *pl* ronds-points, *Spec* sens *m* giratoire

ADJ *(method, statement, approach, route etc)* détourné, indirect; **to take a r. way** faire un détour; **to hear of sth in a r. way** apprendre qch indirectement; **to lead up to a question in a r. way** aborder une question de biais

rounded [ˈraʊndɪd] ADJ arrondi; *(breasts)* plein

roundel [ˈraʊnd(ə)l] N *(on wood, stone)* œil-de-bœuf *m*, *pl* œils-de-bœuf; *(on aircraft)* cocarde *f*

rounders [ˈraʊndəz] NPL *Br Sport* = jeu *m* similaire au baseball

round-eyed ADJ aux yeux ronds; **to listen in r. amazement** écouter les yeux ronds

Roundhead [ˈraʊndhed] N *Hist* **the Roundheads** les Têtes rondes *(partisans du Parlement pendant la guerre civile anglaise, de 1642 à 1646)*

▸▸ **R. army** armée *f* des Têtes rondes; **R. victory** victoire *f* des Têtes rondes

roundhouse [ˈraʊndhaʊs] N *Rail* rotonde *f*

roundly [ˈraʊndlɪ] ADV *(to praise, criticize etc)* franchement, carrément; **r. beaten** battu à plate(s) couture(s)

roundness [ˈraʊndnɪs] N rondeur *f*

round-shouldered [-ˈʃəʊldəd] ADJ *(person)* voûté; **to be r.** être voûté, avoir le dos voûté

roundsman, *pl* **roundsmen** [ˈraʊndzmən] N *Br Com* livreur *m*

round-the-clock ADJ *(activity etc)* de jour et de nuit; **police are keeping a r. vigil on them** la police les surveille de jour comme de nuit

ADV *(to work, study)* vingt-quatre heures sur

vingt-quatre; **open r.** ouvert vingt-quatre heures sur vingt-quatre

round-trip ADJ *Am (ticket etc)* aller (et) retour

roundup ['raʊndʌp] N *(of cattle)* rassemblement *m*; *(of criminals)* rafle *f*, **here is a r. of the news** voici un résumé des informations *ou* des actualités

roundworm ['raʊndwɜ:m] N ascaride *m*

rouse [raʊz] VT 1 *(awaken) (person) (from sleep)* (r)éveiller; *(make more active)* secouer, *Fam* remuer; **to r. sb from a daydream** tirer qn de sa rêverie; **I was suddenly roused by a loud cry** soudain, un cri m'a fait sortir de ma torpeur; **to r. oneself** se secouer; **to r. oneself to do sth** s'efforcer de faire qch; **to r. sb to action** pousser qn à agir; **to r. sb from his apathy** faire sortir qn de son apathie; **to r. the camp** donner l'alerte au camp 2 *(cause) (indignation etc)* soulever; *(admiration)* susciter; *Lit* **to r. the passions** éveiller les passions; **to r. sb to anger** susciter la colère de qn

roused [raʊzd] ADJ *(angry)* en colère

rousing ['raʊzɪŋ] ADJ *(speech)* stimulant; *(applause, welcome)* enthousiaste; *(music)* qui fait vibrer les cœurs

roust [raʊst] VT *Am Fam (harass)* harceler; *(arrest)* agrafer, alpaguer

roustabout ['raʊstəbaʊt] N *Fam Am* débardeur *m*; *Austr* homme *m* à tout faire, manœuvre *m*

rout [raʊt] N *Mil* déroute *f*; **to put troops to r.** mettre des troupes en déroute; *Fig* **the election was a r. for the government** l'élection a été une débâcle pour le gouvernement
VT *Mil, Fig* mettre en déroute
▸ **rout out** VT SEP 1 *(get rid of)* évincer (**from, of** de) 2 *(find) (information)* dénicher

route [ru:t, *Am* ru:t, raʊt] N 1 *(of traveller)* itinéraire *m*; *(of plane, ship)* route *f*, voie *f*, *(of parade)* parcours *m*; *(on mountain)* course *f*, *Am (of mailman etc)* tournée *f*; *Fig (to failure, success etc)* voie (**to** de); **to be en r.** être en route (**for a town** pour une ville); *Fig* **he's en r. for success** il est sur la voie du succès; **to map out a r.** établir un itinéraire; **sea r.** route maritime; **bus r.** *(service)* ligne *f* d'autobus; *(direction taken)* itinéraire *ou* parcours d'un autobus; **are you on a bus r.?** est-ce qu'un autobus passe près de chez vous?; **all routes** *(road sign)* toutes directions 2 *Am (highway)* ≃ route *f* nationale; **R. 66** ≃ la (route) nationale 66
VT *(parcel etc)* router, acheminer (**through, via** par); *(bus, train, flight etc)* faire passer (**via** par; **through** par, à travers); **the flight was routed via Turkey** notre itinéraire passait par la Turquie
▸▸ *Comput* **r. finder software** logiciel *m* cartographique de recherche d'itinéraires; **r. map** *(for roads)* carte *f* routière; *(for buses)* plan *m* du réseau; *(for trains)* carte du réseau; *Mil* **r. march** marche *f* d'entraînement

Note that the French word **route** also means **road**.

router ['ru:tə(r)] N *Comput* routeur *m*

routine [ru:'ti:n] N 1 *(habit)* routine *f*, **to establish a working r.** organiser son travail, s'organiser; **to do sth as a matter of r.** faire qch de façon systématique; **the daily r.** le train-train quotidien 2 *Theat (of dancer)* enchaînement *m* (de pas de danse); *(of comic)* numéro *m*; **to go through one's r.** *(of dancer)* faire son enchaînement; *(of comic)* faire son numéro; **to practise one's r.** répéter son enchaînement/son numéro; *Fig Fam* **don't give me that r.** arrête ton numéro 3 *Comput* sous-programme *m*, *pl* sous-programmes
ADJ 1 *(normal)* de routine; *(procedures)*

d'usage; **it's just r.** *(said by official)* c'est une simple formalité; **r. enquiries** *(of police)* constatations *fpl* d'usage; **it's just a r. enquiry** c'est simplement pour les constatations d'usage; **r. examination** examen *m* de routine; **it was a r. flight** c'était un vol sans aucun problème 2 *(boring, uninspired) (work, tasks)* routinier; **r. performance** une représentation qui n'a rien de particulier

routinely [ru:'ti:nlɪ] ADV *(systematically) (to check, proceed etc)* systématiquement

routing ['ru:tɪŋ] N *(action)* routage *m*; *(route)* itinéraire *m*; *(of parcel, goods)* acheminement *m*
▸▸ *TV etc* **r. switcher** grille *f* de régie

rove [raʊv] VI *(of person)* rôder, vagabonder; **his eyes roved from one to the other** son regard allait de l'un à l'autre
VT *(the countryside, country)* parcourir; *(the seas) (of pirate etc)* écumer

rover ['raʊvər] N vagabond, -onde; *(scout)* routier *m*

roving ['raʊvɪŋ] ADJ vagabond; *(ambassador)* itinérant; **to have a r. commission** avoir une grande liberté de manœuvre; *Fam* **he has a r. eye** c'est un dragueur; **r. life** vie *f* de nomade; **to lead a r. life** mener une vie de nomade
N vagabondage *m*
▸▸ **r. reporter** reporter *m* (*qui va sur le terrain*)

row[1] [raʊ] N *(of chairs, knitting)* rang *m*; *(of trees)* rangée *f*, *(of houses)* ligne *f*, rangée; *(in street names)* rue *f*, *(of people) (one beside the other)* rang *m*, rangée; *(one behind the other)* file *f*, *(of cars) (one beside the other)* rangée; *(one behind the other)* file; *Comput (in spreadsheet)* ligne; **in a r.** en rang *ou* ligne; **to put things in a r.** mettre des objets en rang, aligner des objets; **two Sundays in a r.** deux dimanches de suite *ou* d'affilée; **in rows** par rangs; **in two rows** sur deux rangs; **in the front/third r.** *(seat etc)* au premier/troisième rang; **r. of figures** ligne de chiffres; **r. of medals** rangée *ou Fam* brochette *f* de décorations
▸▸ *Am* **r. house** = maison *f* attenante aux maisons voisines *(qui fait partie d'une rangée de maisons attenantes)*; **r. houses** rangée de maisons attenantes

row[2] VI *(in boat)* ramer; *Sport* faire de l'aviron; **to r. hard** ramer de toutes ses forces, *Spec* faire force de rames
VT *(boat)* faire aller à la rame; *(person)* transporter en canot
N *(in boat)* promenade *f* en canot; **to go for a r.** canoter

row[3] [raʊ] N 1 *(noise)* chahut *m*, tapage *m*, vacarme *m*; **I can't concentrate with all this r. going on** je ne peux pas me concentrer avec tout ce chahut *ou* tapage *ou* vacarme; **make less r.!** faites moins de chahut *ou* de tapage *ou* de vacarme!; **to make** *or* **kick up a r.** *(be noisy)* faire du chahut *ou* tapage *ou* du vacarme; *(protest)* faire toute une histoire (**about** au sujet de) 2 *(quarrel)* dispute *f*, querelle *f*, *Fam* scène *f*, **family r.** querelle de famille; **to have a r.** se disputer, se quereller (**with** avec); *Fam* **to get into a r. with sb** *(into quarrel)* se disputer avec qn; *Fam* **I got into a r. with the bus driver** je me suis disputé avec le chauffeur du bus; *Scot* **the boss gave me a r. for being late** le patron m'a enguirlandé parce que j'étais en retard; **the r. in Parliament over defence policy** la controverse au Parlement au sujet de la politique de défense
VI *(quarrel)* se disputer, se quereller (**with** avec; **about** à propos de)

rowan ['raʊən, 'rəʊ-] N *(tree)* sorbier *m* (domestique), cormier *m*; *(berry)* sorbe *f*, corme *f*

rowboat ['rəʊbəʊt] N *Am* bateau *m* à rames

rowdiness ['raʊdɪnɪs] N tapage *m*, chahut *m*

rowdy ['raʊdɪ] ADJ tapageur, -euse, chahuteur, -euse; **to be r.** chahuter
N *(person)* voyou *m*

rowdyism ['raʊdɪɪz(ə)m] N tapage *m*, chahut *m*

rowel ['raʊəl] N *(on spur)* molette *f*

rower ['rəʊər] N *(of boat)* rameur, -euse

rowing[1] ['rəʊɪŋ] N *(in boat)* canotage *m*; *Sport* aviron *m*; **to go r.** faire du canotage/de l'aviron
▸▸ *Br* **r. boat** bateau *m* à rames; **r. club** club *m* d'aviron; **r. machine** rameur *m*

rowing[2] ['raʊɪŋ] N *(quarrelling)* disputes *fpl*, querelles *fpl*

rowlock ['rɒlək] N *Br* tolet *m*

royal ['rɔɪəl] ADJ 1 *(visit, family etc)* royal, -aux; *Fig (splendid)* royal, princier; **the r. we** le 'nous' de majesté 2 *Fig Formal (splendid)* royal, -aux, princier; **they gave us a (right) r. welcome** ils nous ont accueillis comme des rois; **to be in r. spirits** être d'excellente humeur 3 *Fam (for emphasis)* sombre, de première; *Iron* **that guy is a right r. pain in the arse** ce type est un véritable emmerdeur; **her whining gives me a r. pain** elle me fait vraiment chier avec ses jérémiades; **he's a r. idiot** c'est un sombre crétin *ou* un crétin de première
N *Fam* membre *m* de la famille royale; **the Royals** la famille royale
▸▸ **the R. Academy of Dramatic Art** = Conservatoire *m* national d'art dramatique, à Londres; **the R. Academy of Music** = Conservatoire national de musique, à Londres; **the R. Air Force** armée *f* de l'air britannique; **r. assent** = signature *f* royale qui officialise une loi; **R. Automobile Club** ≃ Touring Club *m* de France; **r. blue** bleu *m* roi; **the R. Canadian Mounted Police** la Gendarmerie royale du Canada; **r. charter** acte *m* du souverain; **the R. Commission** = commission *f* nommée par le monarque sur recommandation du premier ministre; **the R. Engineers** le génie militaire britannique; *Cards* **r. flush** quinte *f* royale; *(in poker)* flush *m* royal, **Your R. Highness** Votre Altesse Royale; **His R. Highness, the Prince of Wales** Son Altesse Royale, le prince de Galles; **Their R. Highnesses** Leurs Altesses Royales; *Br Culin* **r. icing** = glaçage *m* à base de sucre glace et de blancs d'œufs (utilisé pour les cakes); **r. jelly** gelée *f* royale; **the R. Mail** = la Poste britannique; **the R. Marines** les Marines *mpl* (britanniques); **R. National Lifeboat Institution** = société *f* nationale de sauvetage en mer; **the R. Navy** la marine *f* nationale britannique; **the R. School of Music** École *f* royale de musique; **the R. Society for the Prevention of Cruelty to Animals** = société britannique protectrice des animaux, ≃ SPA *f*, **the R. Society for the Protection of Birds** = ligue *f* britannique pour la protection des oiseaux; **the R. Ulster Constabulary** = corps *m* de police d'Irlande du Nord; **r. warrant** brevet *m* de fournisseur du souverain

royalism ['rɔɪəlɪz(ə)m] N royalisme *m*

royalist ['rɔɪəlɪst] ADJ, N royaliste *mf*

royally ['rɔɪəlɪ] ADV 1 *(to entertain, welcome etc)* royalement 2 *Fam (for emphasis)* dans les grandes largeurs; **they messed up r.** ils se sont plantés dans les grandes largeurs, ils se sont plantés, et pas qu'un peu

royalty ['rɔɪəltɪ] N 1 *(rank, position)* royauté *f*, hôtel patronized by r. hôtel fréquenté par les membres de la famille royale; **is he r.?** est-ce qu'il fait partie de la famille royale?; **we were treated like r.** nous avons été traités comme des princes **2** *Com (for invention etc)* redevance *f*, **royalties** *(for author, singer, musician)* droits *mpl* d'auteur; *Petr* royalties *fpl*; **to do sth on a r. basis** être rémunéré en droits d'auteur

rozzer ['rɒzər] N *Old-fashioned Br Sl (policeman)* flic *m*

RP [ɑː'piː] N *(abbr* **received pronunciation)** = prononciation *f* de l'anglais considérée comme la norme

RPI [ɑːpiː'aɪ] N *(abbr* **retail price index)** indice *m* des prix de détail

rpm [ɑːpiː'em] N *Aut etc (abbr* **revolutions per minute)** tours/minute *mpl*

R & R [ɑːrən'dɑːr] N *Am Mil (abbr* **rest and recreation)** permission *f*, *Fam Fig* **to get some R.** se reposer un peu

RRP [ɑːrɑː'piː] N *Br (abbr* **recommended retail price)** prix *m* public conseillé

RS [ɑː'res] N *Br (abbr* **Royal Society)** Académie *f* des sciences

RSA [ɑːres'eɪ] N *(abbr* **Republic of South Africa)** Afrique *f* du Sud

RSC [ɑːres'siː] N *Br Theat abbr* **Royal Shakespeare Company**

RSI [ɑːre'saɪ] N *Med abbr* **repetitive strain** *or* **stress injury**

RSM [ɑːre'sem] N **1** *Br Mil (abbr* **regimental sergeant-major)** adjudant-chef *m*, *pl* adjutants-chefs **2** *Br abbr* **Royal School of Music**

RSPB [ɑːrespi'biː] N *Br abbr* **Royal Society for the Protection of Birds**

RSPCA [ɑːrespisiː'eɪ] N *Br (abbr* **Royal Society for the Prevention of Cruelty to Animals)** ≃ SPA *f*

RSPCC [ɑːrespisiː'siː] N *Br Formerly (abbr* **Royal Society for the Prevention of Cruelty to Children)** ≃ fondation *f* pour l'enfance

RSVP [ɑːresviː'piː] N *(abbr* **répondez s'il vous plaît)** *(on invitation)* RSVP

RT [ɑː'tiː] N *(abbr* **return ticket)** AR *m*

RTGS [ɑːtiːdʒiː'es] N *Fin (abbr* **Real-Time Gross Settlement)** RTGS *m*
▸▸ **R. system** système *m* RTGS

Rt Hon *Br Pol (abbr* **Right Honourable)** très honorable

RTM [ɑːtiː'em] N *(abbr* **Registered Trademark)** marque *f* déposée

RTW [ɑːtiː'dʌb(ə)ljuː] *(abbr* **round the world)** tour du monde

rub [rʌb] N frottement *m*; *(massage)* friction *f*, **to give sth a r.** frotter qch; *(massage)* frictionner qch; *(to dry it)* donner un coup de torchon à qch; *(to polish it)* astiquer qch; *Fig* **there's the r.!** c'est là toute la difficulté!, *Fam* c'est là le hic!

VT **(-bb-)** frotter; *(massage)* frictionner; *(polish)* astiquer; **to r. one's eyes/chin** se frotter les yeux/le menton; **to r. one's leg with liniment** se frictionner la jambe avec un onguent; **to r. itself against sth** *(of cat etc)* se frotter contre qch; **to r. one's hands (together) (in** *or* **with satisfaction)** se frotter les mains *(de satisfaction)*; **to r. sb's hands** frictionner les mains à qn; **to r. sth dry** sécher qch en le frottant; **to r. sth through a sieve** passer qch au tamis; *Fig* **to r. shoulders with** côtoyer, coudoyer; *Fig* **I don't have two pennies to r. together** je n'ai pas un sou; *Fam* **he hasn't got two brain cells to r. together** il n'a pas deux sous de jugeote

VI *(of straps, shoes etc)* frotter; *(of person, animal)* se frotter **(against** contre); **these shoes r.** ces chaussures me font mal

▸ **rub against** VT INSEP *(thing)* frotter contre; *(person, animal)* se frotter contre

▸ **rub along** VI *Fam* **1** *(manage)* se débrouiller **2** *(get on)* **we r. along (together) very well** nous nous entendons très bien

▸ **rub away** VT SEP = **rub off** VT SEP

▸ **rub down** VT SEP **1** *(prepare for decorating) (wall)* regratter; *(paintwork)* poncer **2** *(dry etc)* **to r. a horse down** bouchonner un cheval; **to r. sb down** frictionner qn; **to r. oneself down** *(dry oneself)* se frictionner

▸ **rub in** VT SEP *(lotion, polish etc)* **r. the ointment in** faites bien pénétrer la pommade; **put some polish on the cloth and r. it in** mettez un peu de cirage sur le chiffon et frottez bien; **to r. a hole in sth** faire un trou dans qch à force de frotter; *Fig* **there's no need to r. it in!** ce n'est pas la peine d'insister; *Fig Fam* **to r. sb's nose in it** mettre le nez de qn dans son caca; *Fig* **to r. salt in(to) the wound** remuer le couteau dans la plaie

▸ **rub into** VT SEP **r. the ointment into the skin** faites bien pénétrer la pommade dans la peau; *Culin* **to r. the butter into the flour** ajouter le beurre à la farine en malaxant le mélange

▸ **rub off** VT SEP enlever en frottant
VI **this paint rubs off easily** cette peinture s'enlève facilement; *Fig* **to r. off on sb** *(of manners, enthusiasm etc)* déteindre sur qn; *Fig* **some of it is bound to r. off** il y aura forcément des influences

▸ **rub out** VT SEP *(word etc)* effacer, gommer; *Sl* **to r. sb out** *(murder)* descendre *ou* but(t)er qn

▸ **rub up** VT SEP **to r. oneself up against sb/sth** se frotter contre qn/qch; *Fig* **to r. sb up the wrong way** prendre qn à rebrousse-poil
VI **to r. up against sb/sth** se frotter contre qn/qch

rubber[1] ['rʌbər] N **1** *Br (eraser)* gomme *f*, *(for blackboards)* chiffon *m* **2** *(substance)* caoutchouc *m*; *Fig* **my legs feel like r.** j'ai les jambes en coton; *Am* **rubbers** caoutchoucs **3** *Am Sl (condom)* préservatif *m*, capote *f*
ADJ *(ball, gloves, hose)* en *ou* de caoutchouc; *(bullet)* en caoutchouc
▸▸ **r. band** élastique *m*; *Am* **r. boots** bottes *fpl* en caoutchouc; *Fam* **r. cheque** chèque *m* en bois; *Am Pol Fam* **r. chicken circuit** = série *f* de visites dans de petites villes au cours d'une campagne électorale; **r. dinghy** canot *m* pneumatique; *Bot* **r. plant** caoutchouc, ficus *m*; **r. plantation** plantation *f* d'hévéas; **r. planter** planteur, -euse d'hévéas; **r. ring** bouée *f* (de natation); *Aut* **r. sleeve** manchon *m* en caoutchouc; **r. stamp** tampon *m ou* timbre *m* en caoutchouc; *Fam* **r. stamp parliament** = parlement *m* qui ne fait qu'entériner les lois; *Bot* **r. tree** hévéa *m*

rubber[2] N *Cards* rob(re) *m*; **to play a r.** faire un robre

rubberize ['rʌbəraɪz] VT *(fabric)* caoutchouter

rubberneck ['rʌbənek] *Fam* N **1** *(at scene of accident etc)* badaud, -aude, curieux, -ieuse **2** *(tourist)* touriste *mf*
VI **1** *(at scene of accident etc)* faire le badaud **2** *(of tourist)* faire le touriste

rubber-stamp VT *(document etc)* apposer un cachet sur, estampiller; *Fig (decision)* approuver sans discussion

rubbery ['rʌbərɪ] ADJ caoutchouteux

rubbing ['rʌbɪŋ] N frottement *m*, frottage *m*; *Med etc* friction *f*, *Art (of brass etc)* frottis *m*; *Art* **to take a r. of an inscription** faire un frottis d'une inscription
▸▸ **r. alcohol** alcool *m* à 90 (degrés); **r. down**

rubbish ['rʌbɪʃ] N **1** *Br (refuse)* détritus *mpl*, *(household products)* ordures *fpl* **2** *(junk)* *Fam* saleté(s) *f(pl)*; **the house was full of r.** *(trashy items)* la maison était pleine de petites cochonneries; **shall I keep this stuff? – no, it's just r.** je garde ces trucs? – non, c'est bon à jeter; **it's amazing how much r. one accumulates** c'est incroyable toutes les cochonneries qu'on peut accumuler **3** *Fig*

(nonsense) bêtises *fpl*; **to talk r.** dire des bêtises; **(what) r.!**, **what a load of (old) r.!** quelles foutaises!; **her latest book is a load of r.** son dernier livre est vraiment nul; **the play is absolute r.** la pièce est nulle
VT *Fam (book, plan etc)* éreinter, descendre en flammes
▸▸ *Br* **r. bin** poubelle *f*, *Br* **r. chute** *(in building)* vide-ordures *m inv*, *(at building site)* gaine *f* d'évacuation des gravats; *Br* **r. collection** ramassage *m* des ordures; *Br* **r. dump** décharge *f* (publique), dépotoir *m*; *Br* **r. heap** *(household)* tas *m* d'ordures; *(garden)* tas de détritus; *(public)* décharge, dépotoir; *Br* **r. tip** décharge (publique), dépotoir

rubbishy ['rʌbɪʃɪ] ADJ *Br (worthless)* sans valeur; *(poor quality)* de mauvaise qualité; *(book, play)* nul

rubble ['rʌb(ə)l] N décombres *mpl*; **to reduce a town to r.** réduire une ville à des décombres; **from the r. of his marriage** des ruines de son mariage

rubdown ['rʌbdaʊn] N *(of person)* friction *f*, *(of horse)* bouchonnement *m*, bouchonnage *m*; *(of wood, paintwork)* frottement *m*; **to give sb a good r.** bien frictionner qn

rube [ruːb] N *Am Fam* paysan *m*, péquenaud *m*

Rube Goldberg ['ruːb'gəʊldbɜːg] ADJ *Am (device)* de bric et de broc; *(plan, idea)* tarabiscoté

rubella [ruː'belə] N *Med* rubéole *f*
▸▸ **r. injection** piqûre *f* contre la rubéole; **r. vaccine** vaccin *m* contre la rubéole

Rubicon ['ruːbɪkən] N Rubicon *m*; *Fig* **to cross the R.** franchir le Rubicon

rubicund ['ruːbɪkənd] ADJ *Lit* rubicond, rougeaud

ruble ['ruːb(ə)l] N *Am* = **rouble**

rub-out N *Am Fam* assassinat *m*

rubric ['ruːbrɪk] N rubrique *f*

ruby ['ruːbɪ] N **1** *(gem)* rubis *m* **2** *(colour)* couleur *f* (de) rubis, couleur vermeille
ADJ **1** *(in colour)* vermeil, rubis *inv*; **r. lips** lèvres *fpl* vermeilles **2** *(made of rubies)* de rubis; **r. earrings/necklace** boucles *fpl* d'oreille/collier *m* en rubis
▸▸ **r. port** porto *m* rouge; **r. red** rouge *m* rubis; **r. wedding** noces *fpl* de vermeil

RUC [ɑːjuː'siː] N *Br Formerly (abbr* **Royal Ulster Constabulary)** = corps *m* de police d'Irlande du Nord

ruche [ruːʃ] N *(on sleeves etc)* ruché *m*
VT *(sleeve etc)* garnir d'un ruché

ruck[1] [rʌk] N **1** *(in rugby)* mêlée *f* ouverte; *Fig* **the (common) r.** le commun; **to rise above the r.** se distinguer de la masse **2** *Fam (fight)* bagarre *f*, **there was a bit of a r. last night** il y a eu de la bagarre hier soir
VI *(in rugby)* former une mêlée ouverte

ruck[2] N *(in cloth)* faux pli *m*
VT *(sheet)* froisser
VI *(of sheet)* se froisser

rucksack ['rʌksæk] N *Br* sac *m* à dos

ruckus ['rʌkəs] N *esp Am Fam (argument, controversy)* bagarre *f*, *(noise)* chahut *m*, vacarme *m*; **to make a r.** faire du chahut *ou* du vacarme; *(complain noisily)* faire un scandale; **to cause a r.** *(of news etc)* faire du foin

rucola [ruː'kəʊlə] N *Am Bot, Culin* roquette *f*

ruction ['rʌkʃən] N *Fam* dispute *f*, **there'll be ructions** il va y avoir du grabuge *ou* de la casse

rudder ['rʌdər] N *(on boat)* gouvernail *m*; *(on plane)* gouverne *f*, *Aviat* **rudders** empennage *m*

rudderless ['rʌdələs] ADJ *(ship)* sans gouvernail; *Fig (country etc)* qui va à la dérive

ruddiness ['rʌdɪnɪs] N *(of complexion)* teint *m* coloré

ruddy ['rʌdɪ] ADJ **1** *(complexion)* rougeaud, haut en couleur; *(sky)* rougeâtre; **r. glow** *(of fire)* lueur *f* rouge **2** *Br Sl (for emphasis)* fichu; **you r. fool!** espèce d'imbécile!; **r. hell!** nom de dieu!; **he's eaten the r. lot!** il a tout mangé, ce sale goinfre!
ADV *Br Sl* **it's r. cold** il fait rudement froid; **r. fast/slow** bigrement rapide/lent

rude [ru:d] ADJ **1** *(impolite)* impoli, mal élevé (**to** envers) **2** *(indecent) (word, joke etc)* indécent, obscène; **he made a r. gesture** il a fait un geste obscène **3** *Lit (primitive) (tool)* grossier, rudimentaire; *(drawing)* primitif **4** *Fig (violent) (shock, surprise etc)* violent; *Fig* **to receive a r. awakening** recevoir un choc; *Fig* **it was a bit of a r. awakening** le réveil a été brutal **5** *(vigorous)* **to be in r. health** jouir d'une santé robuste

> Note that the French word **rude** is a false friend and is never a translation for the English word **rude**. It means **harsh, rough**.

rudely ['ru:dlɪ] ADV **1** *(impolitely) (to speak, interrupt)* impoliment, grossièrement **2** *Lit (primitively) (made, drawn)* primitivement, grossièrement **3** *Fig (violently)* violemment; **to be r. awakened** être réveillé brusquement; *Fig* sortir brusquement de sa torpeur; **they were r. awakened to the difficulties which such an operation entails** ils se rendirent soudain compte des difficultés qu'une telle opération implique

rudeness ['ru:dnɪs] N **1** *(impoliteness)* impolitesse *f*, grossièreté *f* **2** *(indecency) (of joke, story)* obscénité *f* **3** *Lit (primitiveness) (of tool)* caractère *m* rudimentaire *ou* grossier

rudiment ['ru:dɪmənt] N *Anat* rudiment *m*; **rudiments** *(of grammar etc)* rudiments, notions *fpl* élémentaires

rudimentary [ru:dɪ'ment(ə)rɪ] ADJ *(tail, knowledge etc)* rudimentaire; *(equipment, tool etc) (primitive)* rudimentaire; *(essential)* de base; **to have a r. grasp of sth** comprendre les rudiments de qch; **I speak r. Chinese** j'ai des rudiments de chinois

rue[1] [ru:] VT *Fml (action)* regretter amèrement; **to r. the day when …** regretter le jour où …; **you'll r. the day** *(that you did this)* tu vas le regretter

rue[2] N *Bot, Culin* rue *f*

rueful ['ru:fʊl] ADJ *(glance, smile)* désabusé

ruefully ['ru:fʊlɪ] ADV *(to laugh, say)* d'un air désabusé

ruefulness ['ru:fʊlnɪs] N *(of glance, smile)* caractère *m* désabusé

RUF [ɑ:ju:'ef] N *Fin (abbr* **revolving underwriting facility***)* facilité *f* renouvelable de prise ferme

ruff[1] [rʌf] N *(on costume)* collerette *f*; *Hist* fraise *f*, *(on bird, animal)* collier *m*, cravate *f*

ruff[2] VT *Cards* couper (avec un atout)

ruffian ['rʌfɪən] N brute *f*, **young ruffians** petits voyous *mpl*

ruffle ['rʌf(ə)l] N **1** *(clothing) (at wrist)* manchette *f* (en dentelle); *(at throat)* jabot *m* plissé **2** *(of bird)* collier *m*, cravate *f*
VT *(of wind) (surface of water)* troubler, rider; *(grass)* agiter; *(sb's hair)* ébouriffer; **to r. its feathers** *(of bird)* hérisser ses plumes; **to r. sb's feelings** *or* **sb's feathers** froisser qn; **to r. sb's composure** faire perdre contenance à qn

ruffled ['rʌfəld] ADJ **1** *(hair, feathers etc)* ébouriffé; *(clothes, sheets)* en désordre; *Fig* **to smooth sb's r. feathers** apaiser qn **2** *Fig* **to be r.** *(disconcerted)* être déconcerté; *(annoyed, irritated)* être irrité; **to get r.** perdre contenance; *(get annoyed)* s'irriter

rug [rʌg] N **1** *(blanket)* couverture *f*, **travelling r.** couverture de voyage, plaid *m* **2** *(car-*

pet) (petit) tapis *m*, carpette *f*, *Fig* **to pull the r. (out) from under sb's feet** faire capoter les projets de qn **3** *Fam (toupee)* postiche *m*

rugby ['rʌgbɪ] N rugby *m*
▸▸**r. ball** ballon *m* de rugby; **r. football** rugby; **r. league** rugby *ou* jeu *m* à treize; **r. player** joueur, -euse de rugby, rugbyman *m*; **r. tackle** plaquage *m*; **r. union** rugby à quinze

rugged ['rʌgɪd] ADJ **1** *(ground, country)* accidenté; *(rock, hill)* découpé; **r. features** traits *mpl* rudes *ou* irréguliers; **a man with r. good looks** un homme à la beauté brute **2** *(equipment, vehicle etc)* robuste **3** *(manners)* bourru, rude; **r. independence** indépendance *f* farouche; **r. individualist** individualiste *mf* farouche *ou* forcené(e); **r. life** vie *f* rude *ou* dure

ruggedness ['rʌgɪdnɪs] N **1** *(of ground, country)* aspect *m* accidenté; *(of rock)* aspect découpé; **the r. of his features** ses traits taillés au couteau **2** *(of vehicle etc)* robustesse *f*

rugger ['rʌgər] N *Br Fam* rugby *m*
▸▸*Pej* **r. bugger** amateur *m* de rugby

rugrat ['rʌgræt] N *Fam* môme *mf*, chiard *m*

ruin ['ru:ɪn] N *(of building etc)*, *Fig* ruine *f*, **the castle is a r.** le château est en ruine(s); **to fall into/lie in ruin(s)** tomber/être en ruine(s); **to be in ruins** *(of building, economy)* être en ruine(s); *(of career)* être fini; *(of hopes)* être anéanti; **the r. of my career/hopes** la fin de ma carrière/mes espoirs; **to go to r.** *(of building, economy, country)* tomber en ruine(s); *(of person)* sombrer; **he's on the road to r.** il va *ou* court à la ruine *ou* à sa perte; **to be the r. of sb** être la perte de qn; **it will be the r. of him** ça le perdra; **gambling has led to his r.** le jeu l'a perdu *ou* l'a mené à sa perte; **r. is staring us in the face** la ruine nous pend au nez
VT *(harvest, dress)* abîmer; *(person)* ruiner; *(person's life, future, holiday, day)* gâcher; **to r. one's eyesight** s'user la vue *ou* les yeux; **to r. one's health** se ruiner la santé; **being a miner had ruined his lungs** il s'était esquinté les poumons à la mine; **ruined castle** château *m* en ruine(s); **the meal's ruined** le repas est gâché *ou Fam* fichu; **to r. sb's plans** faire échouer les projets de qn; **he ruined my chances of playing in the World Cup** il a rendu impossible ma participation à la Coupe du monde; **we're ruined** *(financially)* nous sommes ruinés; **tourists are ruining the town** les touristes massacrent la ville; **the small villages along the coast have been ruined by mass tourism** les petits villages de la côte ont perdu tout leur charme à cause du tourisme de masse; **they're ruining that child** ils pourrissent cet enfant

ruination [ru:ɪ'neɪʃən] N ruine *f*, perte *f*, **to be the r. of sb** être la perte de qn

ruinous ['ru:ɪnəs] ADJ *(expense etc)* ruineux; **in a r. condition** *(of building, economy)* en ruine; **tobacco and alcohol are r. to the health** le tabac et l'alcool ruinent la santé

ruinously ['ru:ɪnəslɪ] ADV de façon ruineuse; **r. expensive** ruineux

RULE [ru:l] N **1** *(principle)* règle *f*, *(regulation)* règlement *m*; *(custom)* coutume *f*, **according to the rules** *(of game etc)* d'après la règle; *(regulation)* d'après le règlement; **it's a r. that …** c'est un fait établi que…, il est évident que…; **I'm sorry, but that's the r.** *or* **those are the rules** je suis désolé mais c'est le règlement; **to lay** *or* **set sth down as a r.** poser qch comme règle générale; **as a (general) r.** en règle générale; **the exception proves the r.** l'exception confirme la règle; **snow is the r. rather than the exception in winter** en hiver, il neige, il est normal; **to make it a r. to do sth** se faire un principe de faire qch; **we must make it a r. that**

everyone contributes equally nous devons poser comme principe que chacun contribue à part égale; **there are too many rules and regulations** la réglementation est trop lourde; *Ind* **work(ing) to r.** grève *f* du zèle; **to work to r.** faire la grève du zèle; **to play according to** *or* **to observe the rules (of the game)** jouer selon les règles (du jeu); **it's against the rules** c'est contre les règles; **to bend** *or* **stretch the rules** contourner *ou* oublier le règlement; **rules of conduct** règles de conduite; **the r. of the road** *(for cars)* le code de la route; *(for ships)* les règles de route; *Math* **r. of three** règle de trois; **as a r. of thumb, allow one pound of meat for four people** en règle générale, compter une livre de viande pour quatre personnes; **ground r.** règle de base; **Queensberry rules** *(in boxing)* règles du marquis de Queensberry
2 *(authority)* autorité *f*, *Pol* gouvernement *m*; **under British r.** sous l'autorité britannique; **the r. of law** l'autorité de la loi; **majority r., the r. of the majority** règle *f* majoritaire
3 *(for measuring)* règle *f*, **pocket r.** règle *ou* mètre *m* de poche; **folding r.** mètre pliant
4 *Typ* filet *m*
5 *(of religious order)* règle *f*
VT **1** *(country, people)* gouverner; *(one's passions, emotions)* maîtriser, dominer; **to r. a nation** régner sur une nation; **to r. sb** *(dominate)* dominer qn; **don't let him r. your life** ne le laisse pas mener ta vie; **don't let your heart r. your head** ne laisse pas tes émotions l'emporter sur la raison; *Lit* **to r. the waves** tenir la mer, être maître *ou* maîtresse des mers; *Fig* **to r. the roost** régner, faire la loi
2 *(decide)* décider (**that …** que … + *ind*); **the chairperson ruled her** *or* **her remark out of order** le président a déclaré que sa remarque n'était pas valable
3 *(paper)* rayer; **ruled paper** papier *m* rayé *ou* réglé
VI **1** *(of monarch)* régner (**over** sur); **Arsenal r. OK!** *(in graffiti)* vive Arsenal!
2 *(of judge)* statuer (**on** sur qch); **to r. in favour of/against sb** *(of judge, umpire etc)* décider en faveur de/contre qn
▸▸**r. book** *(of club etc)* règlement; *Fig* **to throw away the r. book** faire fi des règles
▸ **rule off** VT SEP tracer *ou* tracer un trait; **she ruled off a 2cm margin** elle a tracé une marge de 2cm
▸ **rule out** VT SEP **to r. sth out** exclure qch; **a possibility that can't be ruled out** une possibilité que l'on ne saurait exclure *ou* écarter *ou* éliminer; **the police have ruled out murder** la police exclut la possibilité d'un meurtre; **the presence of hostages ruled out an attack** la présence d'otages rendait toute attaque impossible

rule-governed [-gʌvənd] ADJ qui suit des règles

ruler ['ru:lər] N **1** *(of country)* dirigeant, -ante; *(sovereign)* souverain, -aine (**of, over** de) **2** *(for measuring)* règle *f*, *Comput (in word processor, in DTP)* règle
▸▸*Comput* **r. line** règle

ruling ['ru:lɪŋ] ADJ *(passion)* dominant; *(concern, consideration)* premier; *Pol (party)* au pouvoir; *(class)* dirigeant
N *(of judge, umpire etc)* décision *f*, **to give** *or* **hand down a r. in favour of sb** décider en faveur de qn

rum[1] [rʌm] N rhum *m*

rum[2] ADJ *(comp* **rummer**, *superl* **rummest***) Old-fashioned Br Fam (story etc)* drôle, bizarre; **a r. character** un drôle de type *ou* de numéro; **it was a bit of a r. do** c'était un peu louche

Rumania [ruːˈmeɪnɪə, rʊ-] N = **Romania**

Rumanian [ruːˈmeɪnɪən, rʊ-] ADJ, N = **Romanian**

rumba [ˈrʌmbə] N *(dance, music)* rumba *f*; **to do the r.** faire la rumba; **to play a r.** jouer une rumba

rumble [ˈrʌmb(ə)l] N **1** *(of thunder, gunfire)* grondement *m*; *(of voices)* bruit *m* confus; *(of cart)* roulement *m*; *Aut* ronflement *m*; *(of stomach)* gargouillement *m*; **my stomach gave a r.** mon estomac a gargouillé; **rumbles of discontent in the hall** des murmures de protestation dans la salle; **this caused rumbles of discontent in the press/party** cela a soulevé des vagues dans la presse/au sein du parti **2** *Sl (fight)* baston *m ou f* **VI 1** *(of thunder, gunfire etc)* gronder; *(of stomach)* gargouiller; **a cart rumbled along the street** une charrette qui passait remplit la rue de son fracas **2** *Am (fight)* se bagarrer, se friter
VT *Br Fam (see through) (scheme, plot etc)* deviner, découvrir; *(person)* deviner le jeu de; **we've been rumbled** on a deviné notre jeu
► ► *Aut* **r. strip** bande *f* rugueuse
► **rumble on** VI *(drone on) (of person)* ne pas cesser de parler (**about** de); *(carry on) (of dispute)* traîner

rumbling [ˈrʌmblɪŋ] N **1** *(of thunder)* grondement *m*; *(of tanks, underground train)* roulement *m*; *(of stomach)* gargouillements *mpl*, borborygmes *mpl* **2** *Fig (of discontent etc)* grognement *m*; **there have been rumblings about the proposal** la proposition a été accueillie avec des grognements
ADJ **a r. noise** un grondement

rumbustious [rʌmˈbʌstjəs] ADJ *Fam (person, behaviour)* exubérant; *(child)* exubérant, turbulent; *Theat (farce)* joyeux

rum-dum [-dʌm] N *Am Fam* **1** *(idiot)* abruti, -ie, crétin, -ine **2** *(drunken tramp)* **he's a r.** c'est un clodo et un poivrot

ruminant [ˈruːmɪnənt] ADJ, N *Zool* ruminant *m*

ruminate [ˈruːmɪneɪt] VI **1** *Fml (of person)* ruminer; **to r. over** or **about** or **on sth** retourner qch dans sa tête **2** *(of animal)* ruminer

rumination [ruːmɪˈneɪʃən] N **1** *Fml (of person)* rumination *f* **2** *(of animal)* rumination *f*

ruminative [ˈruːmɪnətɪv] ADJ *Fml (look, voice)* plein de questionnement

ruminatively [ˈruːmɪnətɪvlɪ] ADV *Fml (to say)* d'un ton méditatif; *(to gaze)* d'un air méditatif

rummage [ˈrʌmɪdʒ] N *(search)* **to have a r. (around/about)** fouiller, fourrager (**in** dans); **I had a quick r. in my/his suitcase** j'ai rapidement fouillé ma/sa valise
► ► *Am* **r. sale** vente *f* de charité
► **rummage about, rummage around** VI fouiller, fourrager (**among** dans); **what are you rummaging around here for?** qu'est-ce que tu farfouilles?
► **rummage in, rummage through** VT IN-SEP *(pockets, drawer etc)* fouiller dans, fourrager dans

rummy [ˈrʌmɪ] N *Cards* rami *m*; **to play r.** jouer au rami

rumour, *Am* **rumor** [ˈruːmər] N rumeur *f*, bruit *m* (qui court); **r. has it** or **there's a r. going round that …** le bruit court que …, on raconte que …; **rumours have been circulating** des rumeurs ont circulé (**that** selon lesquelles; **about** au sujet de); **so r. has it** c'est ce qu'on dit; **to hear a r. that …** entendre dire que …; **there are rumours of a takeover** on parle de ou d'un rachat; **have you heard any rumours about what's going to happen?** est-ce que vous avez entendu parler de ce qui va se passer?; **it's only a r.**

ce n'est qu'une rumeur ou qu'un bruit qui court ou qu'un on-dit
VT *(always passive)* **it is rumoured that …** le bruit court que …; **he is rumoured to be …** le bruit court ou on dit qu'il est…; **he was rumoured to be in hiding** le bruit courait qu'il se cachait; **so it was rumoured** c'est ce qu'on a dit
► ► **r. monger** colporteur, -euse de rumeurs

rumoured, *Am* **rumored** [ˈruːməd] ADJ **the r. takeover of the company/cancellation of the project** la rumeur selon laquelle l'entreprise serait rachetée/le projet serait annulé; **the table was sold for a r. £2m** selon la rumeur, la table aurait été vendue 2 millions de livres

rump [rʌmp] N **1** *(of animal)* croupe *f*, *(of bird)* croupion *m*; *Fam (of person)* postérieur *m* **2** *Fam (of army, political party etc)* restant *m*; **the organization was reduced to a r.** il ne restait pas grand-chose de l'organisation
► ► *Hist* **R. Parliament** le Parlement croupion *(nom du Parlement anglais pendant la période du Protectorat de Cromwell, de 1649 à 1660)*; **r. state** état *m* croupion; **the r. state of Yugoslavia** ce qui reste de la Yougoslavie; **r. steak** romsteck *m*, rumsteck *m*

rumple [ˈrʌmp(ə)l] VT *(dress etc)* chiffonner, friper, froisser; *(sheets)* froisser; *(person's hair)* ébouriffer

rumpled [ˈrʌmpəld] ADJ *(dress etc)* chiffonné, fripé, froissé; *(sheets)* froissé; *(hair)* ébouriffé; **to look r.** *(of person)* avoir l'air ébouriffé

rumpus [ˈrʌmpəs] N *Fam (noise)* chahut *m*, vacarme *m*; *(argument, protest)* bagarre *f*; **to kick up** or **make** or **raise** or **cause a r.** *(be noisy)* faire un chahut à tout casser; *(protest)* faire du raffut (**about** au sujet de); **there's been a bit of a r. about her appointment** il y a eu toute une histoire à propos de sa nomination
► ► *Am* **r. room** salle *f* de jeu *(souvent située au sous-sol et également utilisée pour des fêtes)*

rumpy-pumpy [rʌmpɪˈpʌmpɪ] N *Hum Fam (sex)* partie *f* de jambes en l'air

RUN [rʌn]

N course **1** ▪ balade **2** ▪ trajet **3** ▪ série **4, 5** ▪ ruée **6** ▪ piste **10**
VI courir **1, 3** ▪ se sauver **2** ▪ couler **4, 10** ▪ se présenter **3** ▪ circuler **6** ▪ marcher **7** ▪ passer **8**
VT courir **1** ▪ conduire **2** ▪ faire marcher **4** ▪ diriger **5** ▪ présenter **6** ▪ faire passer **7**

N 1 *(on foot)* course *f*; **he took a short r. and cleared the gate** après un court élan il a franchi la barrière; **at a r.** en courant; **to break into a r.** se mettre à courir; **to go for a r.** *(jog)* aller courir; **to take the dog for a r.** aller faire courir le chien; **we've got them on the r.** nous les avons mis en déroute; **to be on the r.** *(from police)* être en fuite ou *Fam* en cavale; *(of soldiers, rebels etc)* être en fuite ou en déroute; *(be busy)* courir; *Fam* **to make a r. for it** *(escape)* se tirer; *(to get out of rain, catch train etc)* se grouiller; *Fam* **to have a (good) r. for one's money** en avoir pour son argent; *Fam* **to give sb a (good) r. for their money** en donner pour son argent à qn; *Fig* **she's making a r. for the Presidency** *(bid)* elle se lance dans la course des présidentielles; **to make ten runs** *(in cricket match)* marquer dix points; *Fam* **to have the runs** *(diarrhoea)* avoir la courante

2 *(for pleasure) (in car etc)* balade *f*; **to go for a r.** *(in the car)* aller se balader en voiture; **he gave me a r. home** il m'a raccompagné en voiture

3 *(journey)* trajet *m*; **our town is a two-hour r. (by train/by car) from London** notre ville est à deux heures (de train/de voiture) de Londres; **he used to do the London (to) Glasgow r.** *(of pilot, bus or train driver)* il faisait la ligne Londres–Glasgow

4 *(of book)* tirage *m*; *(of product)* série *f*

5 *(sequence, series)* série *f*, suite *f*; **the recent r. of events** la récente série d'événements; **a r. of bad luck** une série ou suite de malheurs; **we had a r. of good luck last week** la semaine dernière la chance nous a souri; *Cards* **r. of three** suite de trois cartes; **the r. of the cards was against me** la suite de cartes n'était pas en ma faveur; **in the long r.** en fin de compte; **in the short r.** à court terme; **to have a long r.** *(of fashion, person in power)* tenir longtemps; *(of play)* tenir longtemps l'affiche; *Theat* **after its record r. in London** après être resté à l'affiche à Londres pendant un temps record; *Theat* **during its six-month r.** pendant les six mois où elle a tenu l'affiche; *Theat* **it will soon finish its r.** cela ne sera bientôt plus à l'affiche

6 *(rush) (on Stock Exchange)* ruée *f*; **a r. on the banks** un retrait massif des dépôts bancaires; **r. on the red** *(in roulette etc)* série *f* à la rouge; **a r. on the dollar** une ruée sur le dollar; **there's been a big r. on tickets** les gens se sont rués sur les billets

7 *(type)* **the ordinary r. of mankind** le commun des mortels; **in the ordinary r. of things** en temps normal; **out of the common r.** hors du commun

8 *(freedom)* **to give sb the r. of one's house** mettre sa maison à la disposition de qn; **to have the r. of the house** être libre d'aller partout dans la maison; **the children were allowed the r. of the fields behind the house** les enfants ont eu le droit d'aller jouer dans les champs derrière la maison

9 *(in stocking)* maille *f* qui file, échelle *f*

10 *(for skier)* piste *f*

11 *(of salmon)* remontée *f*

12 *(enclosure)* **(chicken) r.** enclos *m* des poulets

13 *Mus* roulade *f*

VI *(pt* **ran** [ræn]; *pp* **run**; *prp* **running**) **1** courir (**towards** à, vers); **to come running towards sb** accourir vers qn; **to r. up/down the street** monter/descendre la rue en courant; **r. up to your grandmother's** cours chez ta grand-mère; **I'll just r. across** or **round** or **over to the shop** je fais un saut à l'épicerie; **r. along!** allez-vous-en!; **the tram runs on special tracks** le tramway roule sur des rails spéciaux; **to r. to fetch** or **get help** courir chercher de l'aide; **she ran for the police** elle a couru chercher la police; **don't come running to me for help** ne viens pas me chercher quand tu auras besoin d'aide; *Fig* **she went running to the press with the story** elle a couru répéter l'histoire à la presse; *Fig* **he's running scared** il a la frousse

2 *(flee)* fuir, s'enfuir, se sauver; **r. for it!** sauve qui peut!; **to r. for one's life** s'enfuir pour sauver sa peau

3 *(compete in race) (of athlete, horse)* courir; **to r. for Parliament** se présenter aux élections législatives; **to r. for office** se porter candidat; **to r. for President** or **the Presidency** se porter candidat ou se présenter aux élections présidentielles

4 *(flow)* couler; **the river runs into a lake** la rivière débouche ou se jette dans un lac; **the floor was running with water** le sol ruisselait; **the streets were running with blood** le sang coulait dans les rues; **my nose is running** j'ai le nez qui coule; **the tears were running down her cheeks** les larmes coulaient le long de son visage; **the ice-cream is beginning to r.** la glace commence à fondre; **the water had r. cold** l'eau qui coulait était froide; **the water for my bath had just**

started to r. cold j'ai eu juste assez d'eau chaude pour mon bain; *Fig* **my blood ran cold** mon sang se glaça

5 *(of ship)* **to r. before the wind** courir vent arrière; **to r. aground** *(of ship)* échouer; *Fig (of project etc)* capoter

6 *(go)* **I must r. (along)** il faut que je file; **the lease has only a year to r.** il ne reste qu'un an de bail, le bail expire dans un an; *Theat* **the play has been running for a year** la pièce est à l'affiche depuis un an; **this soap opera has been running for 20 years** ça fait 20 ans que ce feuilleton est diffusé; **the film is currently running in Hull** le film est actuellement sur les écrans à Hull; **the conversation ran something like this** voilà en gros ce qui s'est dit; **few buses are running because of the strike** à cause de la grève, il y a peu de bus qui circulent; **this train is not running today** ce train ne circule pas aujourd'hui; **the buses stop running at midnight** après minuit il n'y a plus de bus; **trains running to Paris** trains à destination de Paris; **trains running between London and Manchester** trains qui circulent entre Londres et Manchester; **to be running late** *(of person, bus, train etc)* avoir du retard; **the train is running approximately twenty minutes late** le train aura environ vingt minutes de retard; **our programmes are running ten minutes late** il y a un retard de dix minutes dans nos programmes; **it runs in the family** c'est de famille

7 *(operate) (of machine)* fonctionner, marcher; **the hotel runs like clockwork** l'hôtel marche sans problème; **the engine's running** le moteur marche *ou* tourne *ou* est en marche; **the engine is running smoothly** le moteur tourne rond; **the car runs on unleaded petrol** la voiture roule à l'essence sans plomb; *Comput* **the software runs on this machine** le logiciel peut être utilisé sur cette machine; *Elec* **this machine runs off the mains** cet appareil se branche sur (le) secteur

8 *(pass) (of road, railway etc)* passer; **the line runs from ... to ...** la ligne va de ... jusqu'à ...; **the road runs alongside the river** la route suit *ou* longe la rivière; **to r. north and south** être orienté nord-sud; **the road runs quite close to the village** la route passe tout près du village; **the tunnel runs right through the Alps** le tunnel traverse les Alpes; **a tunnel running beneath the Channel** un tunnel qui passe sous la Manche; **to r. to seed** *(of plant)* monter en graine; **to r. to fat** *(of person)* prendre de l'embonpoint

9 to r. high *(of sea)* être grosse *ou* houleuse; **feelings** *or* **tempers are running high** les esprits sont échauffés; **his funds are running low** ses fonds baissent; **our stores are running low** nos provisions s'épuisent *ou* tirent à leur fin; **the river had r. dry** la rivière s'est asséchée

10 *(of colour in fabric)* déteindre; *(of ink)* couler; **colour that runs in the wash** couleur qui déteint au lavage

11 *(of stocking)* filer, se démailler

12 *(of salmon)* remonter les rivières

VT 1 to r. a race courir *ou* disputer une course; **to r. a kilometre** courir un kilomètre; **to r. an errand** faire une course; **to r. the blockade** forcer le blocus; **things must r. their course** il faut que les choses suivent leur cours; **to allow things to r. their course** laisser faire les choses; **the illness/crisis/recession had r. its course** la maladie/crise/récession était terminée; **to r. a fox to earth** chasser un renard jusqu'à son terrier; **to r. sb hard** *or* **close** talonner qn; *Fam* **I'm r. off my feet** je suis débordé

2 *(drive)* **to r. the car into the garage** rentrer la voiture dans le garage; **to r. one's car into a wall/tree** mettre la voiture dans un mur/

arbre; **to r. sb (in)to town/back home** conduire qn en ville/reconduire qn chez lui

3 *(smuggle) (drugs, arms)* faire la contrebande de

4 *(operate) (machine)* faire fonctionner, faire marcher; **I can't afford to r. a car** je n'ai pas les moyens d'entretenir une voiture; **the house is too expensive to r.** la maison coûte trop cher à entretenir; **this computer runs most software** on peut utiliser la plupart des logiciels sur cet ordinateur; *Comput* **to r. a program** exécuter *ou* faire tourner un programme; *Comput* **this software runs on DOS** ce logiciel tourne sous DOS; **to r. trains between Glasgow and Inverness** assurer un service de trains entre Glasgow et Inverness; **they are running an extra train** ils ont mis un train supplémentaire; *Aviat* **to r. the engines** *(for checking)* faire le point fixe; **to r. tests** effectuer des essais

5 *(manage) (business, theatre)* diriger; *(shop, hotel)* tenir; *(farm)* exploiter; *(newspaper, magazine)* rédiger; **stop trying to r. my life for me!** cesse de vouloir diriger ma vie!

6 *(enter in competition) (horse)* faire courir; *Pol* **to r. a candidate** présenter un candidat

7 *(pass)* faire passer; **to r. the vacuum cleaner over the carpet** passer l'aspirateur sur la moquette; **to r. pipes through a wall** faire passer des tuyaux à travers un mur; **to r. one's fingers over sth** promener ses doigts sur qch; *Mus* **to r. one's fingers over the keys** passer les doigts sur les touches; **she ran her eye over the page** ses yeux parcoururent la page; **he ran his eye over the room** il parcourut la pièce du regard; **to r. a comb/brush through one's hair** se donner un coup de peigne/de brosse; **he ran his hand through his hair** il a passé sa main dans ses cheveux

8 *(make flow) (water etc)* faire couler (**into sth** dans qch); **to r. a bath** faire couler un bain

9 *(have, carry)* **to r. a (high) temperature** faire de la température, avoir de la fièvre; **to r. a deficit** avoir un déficit; **to r. a story/an article** *(of newspaper etc)* publier un article

▸ **run about** VI courir çà et là (**in** dans); **I've been running about all day** *(been busy)* j'ai couru toute la journée

VT INSEP *(shops)* courir; **there were people running about the streets in their pyjamas** il y avait des gens en pyjama qui couraient dans les rues; **to r. about the streets** *(of children)* courir les rues

▸ **run across** VT INSEP *(person)* rencontrer par hasard; *(information, book, photo album etc)* tomber sur

▸ **run after** VT INSEP *(chase, also sexually)* courir après; **to r. after sb** *(chase)* courir après qn; *(coddle)* dorloter qn; *Fig* **to r. after men/women** courir les garçons/filles; **she spends half her life running after her kids** elle passe son temps à être derrière les enfants; **he's got all these assistants running after him the whole time** il a tout un tas d'assistants qui passent sans arrêt derrière ce qu'il fait

▸ **run around** VI, VT INSEP = **run about; he was sure his wife was running around** il était sûr que sa femme le trompait

▸ **run around with** VT INSEP *Fam (be friendly with)* fréquenter; *(have affair with)* sortir avec

▸ **run away** VI *(of person)* s'enfuir, se sauver; *(from home etc) (of child, teenager etc)* faire une fugue; *(of horse)* s'emballer; **they have r. away to get married** ils se sont enfuis pour se marier; **to r. away from home** faire une fugue; *Fig* **to r. away from the facts** se refuser à l'évidence; **to r. away from one's responsibilities** fuir ses responsabilités; **to r. away with sb** partir avec qn; **to r. away with**

sth emporter qch, partir avec qch; **the favourite ran away with the race** le favori a gagné la course haut la main; **don't r. away with the idea that I'm rich** ne va pas t'imaginer que je suis riche; **his imagination runs away with him** il a une imagination galopante; **she lets her enthusiasm r. away with her** elle se laisse emporter par son enthousiasme

▸ **run back** VI *(of person)* revenir en courant; *Fam* **to come running back** *(of errant husband etc)* revenir

VT SEP *(take back by car)* ramener

▸ **run by** VI, VT SEP = **run past**

▸ **run down** VI **1** *(of person)* descendre en courant

2 *(of clockwork, clock)* s'arrêter (faute d'être remonté); *(of battery)* se décharger

VT SEP **1** *(in car etc)* renverser; **to r. sb down in one's car** renverser qn avec sa voiture; **she was almost r. down by a bus** elle a failli se faire renverser par un bus

2 *(find) (person, object)* découvrir, dénicher

3 *(criticize)* dénigrer; **he's always running himself down** il se diminue tout le temps

4 *(reduce) (number of employees)* diminuer; *(stocks)* laisser s'épuiser; *(production)* réduire progressivement; *(industry, factory)* fermer progressivement; **you've r. the battery down** vous avez déchargé la pile; *(of car)* vous avez vidé *ou* déchargé la batterie, vous avez mis la batterie à plat

▸ **run in** VI entrer en courant

VT SEP **1** *Fam (arrest)* arrêter; **to be** *or* **get r. in** se faire pincer (**for** pour)

2 *Aut (engine)* roder

▸ **run into** VT INSEP *(in vehicle) (tree, car)* rentrer dans, entrer en collision avec; *(on foot) (person)* foncer dans; **you should be more careful, you nearly ran into me!** tu devrais faire attention, tu as failli me rentrer dedans!; *Fig (meet)* rencontrer par hasard; **to r. into debt** faire des dettes, s'endetter; **to r. into difficulties** rencontrer des difficultés; **takings r. into five figures** la recette atteint le cinq chiffres; **the cost will r. into millions** le coût va s'élever à des millions

▸ **run off** VI **1** fuir, s'enfuir, se sauver; **to r. off with the cash** partir en emportant l'argent; **to r. off with sb** *(elope with)* s'enfuir avec qn

2 *(of liquid)* s'écouler; *Am Sl* **to r. off at the mouth** parler sans arrêt

VT SEP **1** *(make copies of)* copier, reproduire; *Typ* **machine that runs off ten copies a minute** machine qui imprime dix feuilles par minute

2 *(write quickly) (article)* pondre

3 *(liquid)* faire écouler

4 *(lose by running)* **you'll soon r. off those few extra pounds** vous n'aurez pas de mal à perdre ces quelques kilos en trop si vous courez régulièrement

▸ **run on** VI **1** *(keep running) (of person)* continuer à courir

2 *(of verse)* enjamber; *Typ (of words)* se rejoindre, être liés; *(of text)* suivre sans alinéa; *Typ* **r. on** *(instruction)* alinéa *m* à supprimer; **how much longer is this going to r. on for?** *(of meeting, film etc)* ça va durer encore combien de temps?; *Fam* **he does r. on, doesn't he!** *(talks a lot)* quand il est parti celui-là, il ne s'arrête plus; **he can r. on for hours if you let him** si tu le laisses faire il peut tenir le crachoir pendant des heures

VT SEP *Typ* **to r. on the text** faire suivre le texte sans alinéa

▸ **run out** VI **1** *(from house etc)* sortir en courant; *Fig* **to r. out on sb** abandonner qn

2 *(of lease)* expirer; *(money, supplies etc)* s'épuiser; **time is running out** il ne reste plus beaucoup de temps

VT SEP **1** *Cr (batsman)* mettre hors jeu pendant sa course

2 to r. sb out of town faire quitter la ville à qn
▸ **run out of** VT INSEP *(money, food, cigarettes, wine, ideas etc)* ne plus avoir de; **to r. out of provisions** épuiser ses provisions; **we're running out of sugar** nous allons nous trouver à court de sucre; **we're/you're running out of time** il nous/vous reste peu de temps; **I've r. out of cigarettes** je n'ai plus de cigarettes; **I'm running out of patience** ma patience est à bout, je perds patience (**with** avec)
▸ **run over** VT INSEP **1** *(document)* parcourir; *Theat* **to r. over one's lines** revoir son texte
2 *(exceed)* **to r. over the allotted time** excéder le temps imparti
VT SEP *(person) (in car)* renverser; **he's been r. over** *(injured)* il s'est fait renverser; *(killed)* il s'est fait écraser; **the car ran over his legs** la voiture lui est passée sur les jambes
VI **1** *(of vessel or contents, bath, cup etc)* déborder; **to r. over with energy/enthusiasm** déborder d'énergie/d'enthousiasme
2 *(continue for too long) (of speech, TV programme etc)* déborder; **the programme ran over by 20 minutes** l'émission a dépassé son temps d'antenne de 20 minutes
▸ **run past** VI *(of person)* **to r. past sb/sth** passer devant qn/qch en courant
VT SEP *Fam* **can I r. something past you?** puis-je vous demander vos impressions?; **to r. an idea/proposal past sb** demander à qn ce qu'il pense d'une idée/proposition; **r. that one past me again** dis-moi ça encore une fois
▸ **run through** VI *(of person)* traverser *ou* passer en courant
VT INSEP **1** *(go over, rehearse etc) (text etc)* revoir; **let's just r. through the procedure one more time** reprenons une dernière fois la marche à suivre; *Theat* **to r. through one's part** répéter son rôle; **I'll r. through your speech with you** je vous ferai répéter votre discours
2 *(pass through)* **a murmur ran through the crowd** un murmure a parcouru la foule; **that song keeps running through my head** j'ai cette chanson dans la tête; **money runs through his fingers like water** l'argent lui brûle les doigts
3 *(use up) (money etc)* dépenser; *(case of wine, coffee)* consommer; **he runs through a dozen shirts a week** il lui faut une douzaine de chemises par semaine
VT SEP *(stab)* transpercer (**with a sword** d'une épée)
▸ **run to** VT INSEP *(of amount, number)* monter à, s'élever à; **I don't think our budget will r. to that** je ne crois pas que notre budget nous permette cela; **today's newspaper runs to 32 pages** le journal d'aujourd'hui a 32 pages; **I can't** *or* **my money won't r. to a car** je ne peux pas me permettre financièrement d'avoir une voiture
▸ **run up** VI *(to the flat etc above)* monter en courant; **to r. up to sb** courir vers qn; **people came running up** *(to me etc)* des gens sont arrivés en courant
VT INSEP **to r. up the stairs** monter l'escalier en courant
VT SEP **1** *(overdraft)* laisser grossir; *(debts)* laisser accumuler; **he ran up a huge phone bill** *(his own)* il s'est ruiné en téléphone; *(sb else's)* il m'a/nous a/les a/*etc* ruiné(s) en téléphone
2 *(raise) (flag)* hisser
3 *(sew quickly) (dress etc)* confectionner à la hâte
▸ **run up against** VT INSEP *(difficulties)* se heurter à

runabout ['rʌnəbaʊt] N *Aut* petite voiture f

runaround ['rʌnəraʊnd] N *Fam* **to give sb the r.** *(give contradictory instructions etc)*

faire tourner qn en bourrique; *(by telling lies etc)* faire marcher qn

runaway ['rʌnəweɪ] N *(person)* fuyard, -arde, fugitif, -ive; *(child, teenager)* fugueur, -euse; *(horse)* cheval m emballé *ou* échappé
ADJ **1** *(prisoner, slave)* en fuite, *Fam* en cavale; *(child, teenager)* fugueur, -euse; *(horse)* emballé, échappé **2** *(victory)* remporté haut la main; **r. lorry/train** camion m/train m fou; **the play has been a r. success** la pièce a connu un immense succès **3** *(inflation)* galopant

rundown ['rʌndaʊn] N **1** *(summary)* résumé m détaillé; **give me a r. on what's been happening** racontez-moi en détail ce qui s'est passé **2** *(reduction) (of staff, production)* diminution f, réduction f
▸▸ *TV, Cin* **r. sheet** feuille f d'ordre de passage à l'antenne

run-down ADJ **1** *(battery)* à plat **2** *(building)* délabré; *(person)* fatigué

rune [ruːn] N rune f

run-flat ADJ *(tyre)* anti-crevaison

rung [rʌŋ] N *(on ladder)* échelon m, barreau m; *(on chair)* barreau, bâton m; *Fig* **on the bottom** *or* **lowest r. of the ladder** *(in organization etc)* tout en bas de l'échelle

runic ['ruːnɪk] ADJ *(letters, verse)* runique

run-in N *Fam (quarrel)* prise f de bec; **to have a r. with the law** avoir des démêlés avec la justice (**about** au sujet de)

runnel ['rʌn(ə)l] N *Lit* ruisseau m; *(in street)* caniveau m

runner ['rʌnər] N **1** *(in race)* coureur, -euse; *Horseracing* partant m; **she's a very fast r.** elle court très vite **2** *(messenger)* messager, -ère, coursier, -ière; *(for film crew)* stagiaire mf, grouillot m; *esp Am* **bank r.** garçon m de recette **3** *(of guns, drugs etc)* contrebandier, -ière **4** *(on plant)* stolon m; *(on strawberry)* marcotte f **5** *(on sleigh)* patin m; *(on skate)* lame f de patin; *(on drawer)* coulisseau m; *Aut (for seats)* glissière f **6** *(carpet)* chemin m **7** *(for bed)* rallonge f **8** *Fam* **to do a r.** prendre la tangente
▸▸ *Br* **r. bean** haricot m d'Espagne

runner-up N *(in race, competition etc)* second, -onde (**to** après); **fifteen runners-up will also receive prizes** les quinze suivants recevront également des prix

running ['rʌnɪŋ] ADJ *(pattern etc)* continu; *(battle, feud etc)* incessant; **they have a r. battle about housework** ils se bagarrent continuellement à propos des travaux ménagers; **r. water** *(in house etc)* eau f courante; *(stream etc)* eau qui coule; **to rinse sth in r. water** rincer qch à l'eau courante; **a r. sore** *Med* une plaie suppurante; *Fig* une source de problèmes
N **1** *(on foot)* course f à pied; **to make the r.** *(in race), Fig* mener la course; *Fig* **to make all the r.** *(in relationship)* toujours prendre les devants; **to be in the r.** avoir des chances; **she's in the r. for the nomination** elle a des chances d'être nommée; **to be out of the r.** n'avoir aucune chance
2 *(working, operation) (of machine)* marche f, fonctionnement m; *(of train)* marche, circulation f; **we apologize for the late r. of this train** nous vous prions d'excuser le retard de ce train; **in r. order** en bon état (de marche)
3 *(management) (of hotel, restaurant etc)* direction f; *(of railway)* exploitation f
4 *(smuggling) (of arms, drugs)* introduction f en contrebande
5 *(of water)* écoulement m, ruissellement m
6 *Comput (of program)* exécution f
ADV de suite; **three years r.** trois ans de suite; **we talked for two hours r.** nous avons parlé pendant deux heures d'affilée *ou* de suite
▸▸ **r. board** marchepied m; **r. commentary**

commentaire m en direct; *Fig* **she gave us a r. commentary on what the neighbours were doing** elle nous a expliqué en détail ce que les voisins étaient en train de faire; **r. costs** frais mpl d'exploitation; *(of car)* frais d'entretien; **r. down** *(criticism of person, play)* dénigrement m; *(reduction of staff)* réduction f, diminution f; *(of industry, factory)* réduction *ou* diminution de la production; *Mil* **r. fire** feu m roulant; **r. hand** écriture f cursive; *Typ* **r. head** titre m courant; **r. in** *(of engine)* rodage m; **r. jump** saut m avec élan; *Fam* **go (and) take a r. jump** va te faire voir (ailleurs)!, va te faire cuire un œuf!; *Naut* **r. lights** feux mpl de position; *Am Pol* **r. mate** candidat, -ate à la vice-présidence; *TV* **r. order** ordre m de passage; **r. repairs** réparations fpl courantes; **r. shoe** chaussure f de course; *TV, Cin* **r. speed** *(of tape, film)* vitesse f de déroulement *ou* de défilement; *Sewing* **r. stitch** point m droit; *Journ* **r. story** actualité f en pleine évolution; **r. time** durée f; *Typ* **r. title** titre courant; **r. total** total m cumulé; **to keep a r. total of sth** calculer qch au fur et à mesure; **r. track** piste f

running-on N *(of engine)* autoallumage m

runny ['rʌnɪ] ADJ *(mixture)* liquide, *Pej* trop liquide; *(nose)* qui coule

run-off N **1** *Sport (final)* finale f, *(after tie)* belle f, *Pol* = élection f pour départager deux candidats **2** *(water) (from field etc)* eaux fpl de ruissellement **3** *Am (for desk)* rallonge f
▸▸ *Pol* **r. election** = élection pour départager deux candidats

run-of-the-mill ADJ *(film, play etc)* ordinaire, sans rien de particulier

run-on N *Typ* texte m continu sans alinéa

run-out N **1** *Ski* zone f d'arrivée **2** *(of film, tape)* amorce f de fin de bobine

run-proof, run-resist ADJ *(stocking etc)* indémaillable

runt [rʌnt] N *(of litter)* le plus faible *(d'une portée)*; *Pej (of man)* avorton m

run-through N *(of text etc)* lecture f, *Theat* répétition f; *Theat* **to have a r.** répéter

runtime system ['rʌntaɪm] N *Comput* système m en phase d'exécution

run-up N **1** *Sport (of high-jumper, pole-vaulter, bowler)* élan m; *Aviat* **the pilot was making his r. to the target** le pilote fonçait sur l'objectif **2** *(period)* période f préparatoire; **in the r. to the exams/election** dans la période qui précède/a précédé/*etc* les examens/les élections

runway ['rʌnweɪ] N **1** *Aviat* piste f **2** *(catwalk)* passerelle f *(de défilé de mode)*
▸▸ *Aviat* **r. lights** feux mpl de piste

rupee [ruː'piː] N *(currency)* roupie f

rupture ['rʌptʃər] N *(in negotiations, marriage, of container, pipeline etc)* rupture f; *Med (of artery)* éclatement m, rupture; *Med (hernia)* hernie f
VT *(relations)* rompre; *(container, pipeline etc)* percer, crever; *Med (blood vessel, appendix etc)* se rompre; *(spleen)* se faire éclater; **to r. oneself** se faire une hernie
VI *(of container, pipeline etc)* éclater, se rompre; *(of blood vessel, appendix)* se rompre; *(of spleen)* éclater

ruptured ['rʌptʃəd] ADJ *(relations, container, pipeline)* rompu; *Med (organ)* hernié; *(blood vessel, appendix)* rompu; *(spleen)* éclaté

rural ['rʊər(ə)l] ADJ *(life, custom etc)* rural, -aux

ruse [ruːz] N ruse f, stratagème m, subterfuge m

rush¹ [rʌʃ] N **1** *(plant)* jonc m **2** *(material)* jonc m, paille f; **made from rushes** fait de joncs
▸▸ **r. bed** jonchaie f, **r. mat** natte f (de jonc); **matting** tapis m de jonc

RUSH²

> **N** ruée **1, 4** ■ hâte **2**
> **VI** se précipiter ■ se dépêcher
> **VT** faire trop vite **1** ■ bousculer **2**
> ■ transporter d'urgence **3** ■ attaquer **4**

N 1 *(dash)* course *f* précipitée, ruée *f*; **to make a r. at sb** s'élancer *ou* se jeter *ou* se précipiter sur qn; **to make a r. for the exit/the phones** se précipiter vers la sortie/les téléphones; **to get lost in the r.** se perdre dans la bousculade; **let's leave before the r. starts** partons avant la bousculade; **there was a r. for the papers** on s'arrachait les journaux

2 *(hurry)* hâte *f*, empressement *m*; **in a r.** en (toute) hâte; **there's no r. (for it)** ce n'est pas pressé; **life is too much of a r. in London** à Londres, la vie va trop vite; **to be in a (bit of a) r.** être (un peu) pressé; **in the r. to finish the article, he forgot to check the spelling** dans sa hâte de terminer l'article, il a oublié de vérifier l'orthographe; **we left in such a r. that …** nous sommes partis avec une telle précipitation que …; **what's all the r. for?** qu'est-ce qui presse tant?; **there's a bit of a r. on** il y a quelque chose d'assez pressé; **a r. job** *(urgent)* un travail urgent; *(hurried)* un travail bâclé; **to have a r. job on** avoir un travail urgent à faire

3 *(surge)* **a r. of cold air** une bouffée d'air froid; **a r. of water** une arrivée soudaine d'eau; *Fig* **a r. of blood to the head** un coup de sang; **we had a r. (of customers) in the afternoon** les clients sont arrivés en masse l'après-midi

4 *(demand)* ruée *f* (**on** sur)

5 *Cin* **rushes** épreuves *fpl*, production *f* journalière, rushes *mpl*; **to see the rushes** voir les épreuves

VI *(move fast)* se précipiter, se ruer (**at** sur; **towards** vers); *(hurry)* se dépêcher (**to do** de faire); *(of blood)* affluer (**to** à); *(of vehicle)* foncer; **I must r.** il faut que je me dépêche; **there's no point in rushing** ça ne sert à rien de se dépêcher *ou* de se précipiter; **he came rushing down the stairs** il a dégringolé l'escalier; **a stream that rushes down the mountain side** un ruisseau qui dévale le flanc de la montagne; *Prov* **fools r. in (where angels fear to tread)** = agir sans réfléchir peut avoir des conséquences fâcheuses; **to r. to conclusions** conclure trop hâtivement; **the blood rushed to his cheeks/head** le sang lui est monté au visage/à la tête; **to r. upstairs** monter l'escalier à toute vitesse *ou* à la hâte; **to r. forward** se précipiter (en avant)

VT 1 *(hurry)* *(task)* faire trop vite; **they had obviously rushed the work** à l'évidence, ils avaient travaillé trop vite; *Pej* **a rushed job** un travail fait à la hâte *ou* *Fam* à la va-vite; **a horse that rushes its fences** un cheval qui se précipite sur les obstacles avec trop d'impétuosité; *Fig* **don't r. your fences!** réfléchissez donc!

2 *(hurry)* *(person)* bousculer; **don't r. me** laissez-moi le temps de souffler, ne me bousculez pas; **I won't be rushed** je ne veux pas qu'on me bouscule; **let's not r. things** ne nous précipitons pas; **to be rushed off one's feet** courir à droite et à gauche; **I've been rushed off my feet all day** j'ai passé ma journée à courir à droite et à gauche

3 *(transport quickly)* transporter d'urgence; **he was rushed to hospital** on l'a transporté d'urgence à l'hôpital; **please r. me your latest catalogue** *(notice on advertising material)* envoyez-moi d'urgence votre dernier catalogue

4 *(attack)* *(position)* prendre d'assaut; **to r. sb** attaquer qn; **the audience rushed the platform** le public a envahi l'estrade

5 *Br Fam (charge a lot)* **how much did they r. you for that?** combien est-ce qu'ils t'ont fait cracher pour ça?

> ► **r. hour** heure *f* de pointe *ou* d'affluence; **r. order** commande *f* urgente
> ► **rush about, rush around** VI courir çà et là
> ► **rush away** VI partir précipitamment; **do you have to r. away?** est-ce qu'il faut vraiment que vous partiez aussi vite?
> VT SEP *(person)* emmener d'urgence
> ► **rush back** VI revenir en toute hâte *ou* *Fam* revenir en vitesse
> ► **rush into** VT INSEP **to r. into a room** entrer précipitamment *ou* faire irruption dans une pièce; *Fig* **to r. into things** agir sans réfléchir; **to r. into marriage/divorce** se marier/divorcer trop vite
> VT SEP **to r. sb into sth** forcer qn à faire qch trop vite; **to be rushed into doing sth** être obligé *ou* contraint à faire qch précipitamment; **to be rushed into a decision/answer** être contraint à *ou* obligé de prendre une décision/donner une réponse à la hâte; **don't let yourself be rushed into anything** ne te sens pas obligé de faire quoi que ce soit à la hâte
> ► **rush off** VI, VT SEP = **rush away**
> ► **rush out** VI sortir précipitamment (**of** de)
> VT SEP *(product)* sortir à la hâte; *(troops)* envoyer d'urgence
> ► **rush through** VT INSEP **the wind was rushing through the tunnel** le vent s'engouffrait dans le tunnel; **to r. through one's work** faire son travail à la hâte *ou* *Fam* en vitesse
> VT SEP **to r. a bill through (the House)** faire passer un projet de loi à la hâte; **to r. an order/application through** traiter une commande/une demande en urgence
> ► **rush up** VI *(go upstairs etc)* monter à toute vitesse; **to r. up to sb** *(to say hello etc)* se précipiter sur qn
> VT SEP *Mil* **to r. up reinforcements** amener *ou* envoyer des renforts en toute hâte

rushfull ['rʌʃʊl] **N** *Journ* premier reportage *m*

rushing ['rʌʃɪŋ] **ADJ** *(wind, river)* déchaîné, *Lit* impétueux

rusk [rʌsk] **N** ≃ biscotte *f*; *(for baby)* gros biscuit *m*

russet ['rʌsɪt] **N 1** *(colour)* brun *m* roux **2** *(apple)* reinette *f* grise
ADJ *(colour)* brun roux *inv*

Russia ['rʌʃə] **N** Russie *f*

Russian ['rʌʃən] **ADJ** russe; *(history)* de la Russie; *(teacher, lesson, dictionary)* de russe; **R. language student** étudiant, -ante de russe
N 1 *(person)* Russe *mf* **2** *Ling* russe *m*
> ► **R. roulette** roulette *f* russe; *Culin* **R. salad** salade *f* russe; **R. service** *(from silver salver onto plate)* service *m* à la russe

Russianization [rʌʃənaɪ'zeɪʃən] **N** *(of population, republic etc)* russification *f*

Russianize ['rʌʃənaɪz] **VT** russifier

Russify ['rʌsɪfaɪ] **VT** = **Russianize**

Russky ['rʌskɪ] **N** *Fam* ruskof *m*

rust [rʌst] **N** *(on metal, wheat etc)* rouille *f*; *Br Fam* **r. bucket, r. heap** *(car)* bagnole *f* toute rouillée; **r. inhibitor, r. preventer** antirouille *m inv*
ADJ r. (coloured), r. red rouille *inv*
VI *(of metal)* se rouiller
VT *(metal, wheat etc)* rouiller; **badly rusted** très rouillé
> ► **rust away** VI *(of metal etc)* être rongé *ou* mangé par la rouille
> ► **rust through** VI être rongé *ou* mangé par la rouille

rustic ['rʌstɪk] **ADJ** *(bench, charm etc)* rustique
N paysan, -anne, campagnard, -arde, *Pej* rustaud, -aude

rusticate ['rʌstɪkeɪt] **VT** *Br Univ Fml (student)* renvoyer temporairement

rustication [rʌstɪ'keɪʃən] **N** *Br Univ Fml (of student)* renvoi *m* temporaire

rusticity [rʌ'stɪsɪtɪ] **N** rusticité *f*

rustiness ['rʌstɪnɪs] **N** *(of metal)* rouillure *f*, rouille *f*; **because of the r. of my French** parce que mon français est un peu rouillé

rustle¹ ['rʌs(ə)l] **N** *(of leaves)* bruissement *m*, frémissement *m*; *(of silk, dress)* frou-frou *m*, *pl* frous-frous; *(of paper)* froissement *m*
VI *(of leaves)* bruire, frémir; *(of silk, dress)* faire frou-frou, froufrouter; *(of paper)* froisser; **to hear papers rustling** entendre des froissements de papier
VT *(leaves)* faire bruire, faire frémir; *(silk, dress)* faire froufrouter; *(paper)* froisser

rustle² **VT** *(cattle etc)* voler
> ► **rustle up** VT SEP *Fam (meal, snack)* (se débrouiller pour) faire; **she can always r. up a good meal** elle se débrouille toujours pour servir un bon repas; **to r. up some coffee** faire du café; **to r. up support** rassembler des partisans

rustler ['rʌslər] **N** *(of cattle)* voleur, -euse (de bétail); *(of horses)* voleur, -euse (de chevaux)

rustling ['rʌslɪŋ] **N 1** = **rustle¹** **2** *(of cattle)* vol *m*

rustproof ['rʌstpruːf] **ADJ** *(paint, treatment etc)* antirouille *inv*; *(metal)* résistant à la rouille, inoxydable
VT *(metal)* protéger contre la rouille

rustproofing ['rʌstpruːfɪŋ] **N** *(substance)* produit *m* antirouille; *(process)* application *f* d'un produit antirouille (**of** sur)

rust-resistant **ADJ** *(metal)* résistant à la rouille

rusty ['rʌstɪ] **ADJ 1** *(iron etc)* rouillé; **to get r.** se rouiller; *Fig* **my French is getting r.** mon français est un peu rouillé; **my playing is very/a bit r.** je suis très/un peu rouillé; **the pianist sounded/the batsman looked a bit r.** le pianiste était/le batteur semblait un peu rouillé **2** *(colour)* rouille *inv*; **a r. red** un marron rouille

rut¹ [rʌt] **N** *(groove)* ornière *f*, *Fig* **to get into a r.** s'encroûter; *Fig* **to be (stuck) in a r.** être prisonnier d'une routine; *Fig* **to get out of the r.** sortir de l'ornière
VT *(-tt-)* *(path)* sillonner d'ornières; **deeply rutted** *(path etc)* coupé par les ornières

rut² **N** *(of stag etc)* rut *m*
VI *(-tt-)* *(of stag etc)* être en rut

rutabaga [ruːtə'beɪgə] **N** *Am* rutabaga *m*

ruthless ['ruːθlɪs] **ADJ** *(person)* impitoyable, sans pitié; *(act)* brutal, -aux; *(determination, schedule, pace)* impitoyable; **to be r. in enforcing the law** être impitoyable dans l'application de la loi; **he was r. in shortening the text** il n'a pas fait de sentiments quand il s'est agi d'abréger le texte; **I'm going to have to be r.** il faut que j'y aille carrément

ruthlessly ['ruːθlɪslɪ] **ADV** *(to act, say)* impitoyablement

ruthlessness ['ruːθlɪsnɪs] **N** *(of person, act)* nature *f* impitoyable

rutted ['rʌtɪd] **ADJ** *(road etc)* plein d'ornières

rutting ['rʌtɪŋ] **N** *(of stag etc)* rut *m*
> ► **r. season** saison *f* du rut

RV [ɑːˈviː] **N 1** *Am Aut (abbr recreational vehicle)* camping-car *m*, *pl* camping-cars **2** *(abbr Revised Version)* = traduction *f* de la Bible de 1884

Rwanda [rʊˈændə] **N** Rwanda *m*, Ruanda *m*

Rwandan [rʊˈændən] **ADJ** rwandais, ruandais
N Rwandais, -aise, Ruandais, -aise

rye [raɪ] **N 1** *(plant)* seigle *m* **2** *(bread)* pain *m* de seigle **3** *(drink)* whisky *m* (de seigle)
> ► **r. bread** pain de seigle; *Am* **r. whiskey** whisky (de seigle)

rye-grass **N** ivraie *f* vivace

S

S, s [es] **1** (letter) S, s m; **two s's** deux s **2** (abbr **south**) S **3** (abbr **small**) (on clothes label) S **4** Hist (abbr **shilling(s)**) shilling(s) m(pl)

's [s, z] CONTR **1** (shortened form of **is, has, us**) **it's raining** il pleut; **he's found a knife** il a trouvé un couteau; **let's go!** partons! **2** (genitive case) **the pupil's books** les livres de l'élève; **the pupils' books** les livres des élèves; **in an hour's time** dans une heure VOIR GRAMMAIRE A15–16 **3** (forming pl) **the Thomas's** les Thomas, la famille Thomas; **a series of o's** une série d'o

SA [es'eɪ] N **1** (abbr **Salvation Army**) Armée f du salut **2** (abbr **South Africa**) Afrique f du Sud

Saar [sɑːr] N **the S.** la Sarre

Sabbath ['sæbəθ] N **1** Rel (Jewish) (jour m du) sabbat m; (Christian) dimanche m; **S. day observance** observance f du sabbat/dimanche; **to keep/break the S.** observer/violer le sabbat/dimanche **2** **witches' S.** sabbat m (de sorcières)

sabbatical [sə'bætɪk(ə)l] N Univ année f/trimestre m sabbatique, congé m sabbatique (accordé(e) à un professeur etc pour faire des recherches etc); **to be on s.** (of teacher etc) être en année/en cours de trimestre sabbatique ◇ ADJ Univ **s. year/term** année f/trimestre m sabbatique (accordé(e) à un professeur etc pour faire des recherches etc)

sable [¹ ['seɪb(ə)l] N **1** (animal) zibeline f **2 s. (fur)** zibeline f, **s. coat** manteau de zibeline

sable [² N Arch, Lit (colour) sable m ◇ ADJ Lit noir; Her sable

sabot ['sæbəʊ] N (clog) sabot m

sabotage ['sæbətɑːʒ] N sabotage m ◇ VT (project, bridge etc) saboter

saboteur [sæbə'tɜːr] N saboteur, -euse

sabre, Am **saber** ['seɪbər] N (sword) sabre m; **s. cut** (blow) coup m de sabre; (scar) balafre f
▸▸ Fig **s. rattling** (words, talk) propos mpl agressifs; (action) actes mpl agressifs

SAC [sæk] N EU (abbr **Special Area of Conservation**) zone f spéciale de conservation

sac [sæk] N Biol sac m; **yolk s.** membrane f vitelline; **ink s.** (of squid, sepia etc) poche f d'encre

saccharin ['sækərɪn] N Chem etc saccharine f

saccharine ['sækəriːn] ADJ Chem saccharin; Fig, Pej (smile etc) mielleux; (story, film etc) édulcoré

sacerdotal [sæsə'dəʊt(ə)l] ADJ sacerdotal, -aux

sachet ['sæʃeɪ] N sachet m

sack [¹ [sæk] N **1** (bag) (grand) sac m; **s. of coal/flour** sac de charbon/farine **2** Br Fam **to give sb the s.** virer qn, mettre qn à la porte; **to get the s.** être viré, être mis à la porte **3** Fam (bed) pieu m, plumard m; **to hit the s.** se pieuter; **to be good/no good in the s.** être/ne pas être une affaire au pieu ◇ VT **1** Br Fam (dismiss from job) virer, mettre à la porte **2** (put in sacks) (coal etc) ensacher, mettre en sac
▸▸ **s. race** course f en sac

sack [² VT (plunder) (town etc) mettre à sac ◇ N Mil etc (plundering) sac m, pillage m

sack [³ N Arch (wine) = vin m blanc sec d'Espagne

sackcloth ['sækklɒθ] N **1** Tex toile f à sacs, grosse toile **2** Bible etc **s. and ashes** le sac et la cendre; Fig **he wasn't exactly wearing s. and ashes** il n'avait pas tellement l'air désolé ou contrit; **I'm not going to go around in s. and ashes just because I forgot our anniversary** je ne vais quand même pas porter le deuil parce que j'ai oublié notre anniversaire de mariage

sackful ['sækfʊl] N (of flour etc) plein sac m

sacking [¹ ['sækɪŋ] N **1** Fam (dismissal from job) (of employee) renvoi m **2** = **sackcloth 1**

sacking [² N (plundering) (of town etc) sac m, mise f à sac

sackload ['sækləʊd] N = **sackful**

sacrament ['sækrəmənt] N Rel sacrement m; **to take** or **receive the sacraments** communier; **the (Most) Holy S., the Blessed S.** le saint sacrement

sacramental [sækrə'ment(ə)l] ADJ sacramentel
◇ NPL Rel **the sacramentals** les sacramentaux mpl

sacred ['seɪkrɪd] ADJ **1** (held in awe) (place etc) sacré; **s. to the memory of …** à la mémoire de … **2** Rel sacré; (music) sacré, religieux; **s. place** lieu m saint; **s. books** livres mpl d'Église, livres saints **3** (serious) (promise) sacré, inviolable; (duty) sacré; **nothing was s. to him** il ne respectait rien; **is nothing s. any more?** on ne respecte vraiment plus rien!
▸▸ Fig **s. cow** vache f sacrée; (institution) institution f intouchable; (idea) idée f sacrée ou sacro-sainte; **the S. Heart** le Sacré-Cœur

sacredness ['seɪkrɪdnɪs] N **1** (of place etc) caractère m sacré **2** (of oath) caractère m sacré, inviolabilité f, (of duty) caractère sacré

sacrifice ['sækrɪfaɪs] N **1** (act of sacrificing) sacrifice m (of de); **to make great sacrifices** faire de grands sacrifices; **to make the supreme s.** faire le sacrifice suprême; **he succeeded at the s. of his health** il a réussi au prix de sa santé ou en sacrifiant sa santé; **it was a real s.** (selling sth) on y a perdu énormément **2** (person, animal) victime f sacrifiée; **to offer (up) sb/sth as a s.** offrir qn/qch en sacrifice (to à) ◇ VT sacrifier; **to s. oneself** se sacrifier (for pour); **to s. one's career/independence** sacrifier sa carrière/son indépendance; Fig **the Prime Minister sacrificed one of his Ministers to appease the press** le Premier ministre a sacrifié un de ses ministres pour calmer la presse ◇ VI **to s. to idols** sacrifier aux idoles

sacrificial [sækrɪ'fɪʃəl] ADJ (rites, dagger, lamb) du/de sacrifice; Fig **s. lamb** or **victim** victime f à sacrifier

sacrilege ['sækrɪlɪdʒ] N Rel, Fig sacrilège m

sacrilegious [sækrɪ'lɪdʒəs] ADJ Rel, Fig sacrilège

sacristan ['sækrɪstən] N Rel sacristain m

sacristy ['sækrɪstɪ] N Rel sacristie f

sacrosanct ['sækrəʊsæŋkt] ADJ usu Iron sacro-saint; pl sacro-saint(e)s

sacrum ['seɪkrəm, 'sæk-] N Anat sacrum m

SAD [ese'diː] N (abbr **Seasonal Affective Disorder**) dépression f saisonnière

sad [sæd] ADJ (comp **sadder**, superl **saddest**) **1** (unhappy) triste; **a s. old bicycle** une pauvre vieille bicyclette; **a s.-looking lettuce** une salade toute flétrie; **to become s.** s'attrister; **to look s.** avoir l'air triste; **to make sb s.** attrister qn, affliger qn; **we were very s. to hear of our friend's death** nous avons été désolés d'apprendre la mort de notre ami; **to be s. at heart** avoir le cœur gros ou serré **2** (depressing) (news, place, memories etc) triste; **that's very s. news** c'est bien triste; **a s. reflection** or **comment on our society** cela en dit long sur notre société; **it's s. that no one seems to care about the elderly** il est triste que personne ne semble se soucier des personnes âgées; **he came to a s. end** il a eu une triste fin; **s. to say** malheureusement **3** Fam (pathetic) (person) minable; **to be a s. case** être minable; **he's still living with his parents, how s. can you get?** il habite toujours chez ses parents, il est grave ou il craint!; **they've got really s. taste in music** ils écoutent de la musique vraiment craignos
▸▸ Am Fam **s. sack** (person) raté, -ée

sadden ['sæd(ə)n] VT (person) attrister, affliger

saddle ['sæd(ə)l] N **1** (on horse, bicycle) selle f, **hunting s.** selle anglaise; **in the s.** en selle, monté; Fig **to be in the s.** (in control) tenir les rênes (du pouvoir); **to rise in the s.** faire du trot enlevé **2** Culin (of mutton, venison) selle f **3** Geol (of mountain) col m ◇ VT **1** (horse) seller **2** Fam **to s. sb with sth** mettre qch sur les bras de qn, charger ou encombrer qn de qch; **I've been saddled with this project** on m'a mis ce projet sur les bras; **she's saddled with five children** elle a cinq enfants sur les bras; **saddled with debts** grevé de dettes
▸▸ **s. horse** cheval m de selle; **s. room** sellerie f, **s. soap** cirage m pour selles; **s. sore** (on rider) = meurtrissure f provoquée par de

longues heures en selle; *(on horse)* écorchure *f ou* excoriation *f* sous la selle
▸ **saddle up** VI *(of rider)* seller
VT SEP *(horse)* seller

saddleback ['sæd(ə)lbæk] N **1** *Archit* toit *m* en bâtière **2** *(of hill)* ensellement *m* **3** *(pig)* cochon *m* noir avec une ceinture blanche

saddlebag ['sæd(ə)lbæg] N *Horseriding, Cycling etc* sacoche *f* de selle

saddlecloth ['sæd(ə)lklɒθ] N couverture *f ou* tapis *m* de selle

saddler ['sædlər] N sellier *m*

saddlery ['sædlərɪ] N *(trade, articles)* sellerie *f*, bourrellerie *f*

saddle-sore ADJ to be s. *Horseriding* avoir mal aux fesses (d'avoir été en selle); *Cycling* avoir mal aux fesses (d'avoir fait du vélo)

saddling ['sædlɪŋ] N *(of horse)* sellage *m*

saddo ['sædəʊ] N *Br Fam* nul *m*, nulle *f*

Sadducee ['sædjʊsiː] N Saducéen, -enne

sadism ['seɪdɪz(ə)m] N sadisme *m*

sadist ['seɪdɪst] N sadique *mf*

sadistic [sə'dɪstɪk] ADJ sadique

sadistically [sə'dɪstɪklɪ] ADV sadiquement, avec sadisme

sadly ['sædlɪ] ADV **1** *(in an unhappy way)* *(to reply, smile)* tristement, d'un air triste **2** *(deplorably)* malheureusement; **s., this is so** c'est, hélas *ou* malheureusement, le cas **3** *(greatly)* vraiment; **you're s. mistaken** tu te trompes lourdement; **he is s. missed** il nous/leur manque beaucoup; **compassion is s. lacking in our society** la compassion fait tristement défaut dans notre société

sadness ['sædnɪs] N tristesse *f*, mélancolie *f*

sadomasochism [seɪdəʊ'mæsəkɪz(ə)m] N sadomasochisme *m*

sadomasochist [seɪdəʊ'mæsəkɪst] N sadomasochiste *mf*

sadomasochistic [seɪdəʊmæsə'kɪstɪk] ADJ sadomasochiste

s.a.e. [eseɪ'iː] N *Com etc (abbr* **stamped addressed envelope)** enveloppe *f* timbrée avec son adresse

safari [sə'fɑːrɪ] N safari *m*; **on s.** en safari; **to go on s.** faire un safari, aller en safari
▸ **s. holiday** safari; **s. jacket** saharienne *f*, **s. park** réserve *f* d'animaux sauvages; **s. suit** ensemble *m* avec saharienne

SAFE [seɪf]

ADJ en sécurité **1** ▪ sûr **2–4**
▪ sans danger **2** ▪ solide **2**
N coffre-fort

ADJ **1** *(not in danger)* en sécurité; **s. from sth** à l'abri de qch; **to be s. from recognition** ne pas risquer d'être reconnu; **at last we are s.** enfin nous voilà en sécurité *ou* saufs *ou* hors de danger; **I'm glad to hear you're s.** je suis content d'apprendre qu'il ne t'est rien arrivé; **your daughter's not s. with him** votre fille court un risque en le fréquentant; **to come home s.** rentrer sain et sauf; **s. and sound** sain et sauf

2 *(not dangerous)* *(street, town)* sûr; *(chemical, water etc)* sans danger; *(building, bridge etc)* solide; **she assured me the water was perfectly s. for drinking** elle m'a assuré qu'on pouvait boire l'eau sans danger; **not s. dangerous; is it s. to leave him alone?** est-ce qu'il n'y a pas de danger à le laisser seul?; **is the meat/water s. (to eat/drink)?** est-ce qu'on peut manger la viande/boire l'eau sans risque?; **to make a bomb s.** désamorcer une bombe; **it's as s. as houses** *(not dangerous)* cela ne présente pas le moindre risque; **a s. beach for children** une plage où les enfants peuvent se baigner en (toute) sécurité; **at a s. distance** à distance

respectueuse; *Med* **s. dose** dose *f* inoffensive; **s. driver** conducteur, -trice prudent(ente)

3 *(not entailing risk)* *(conversation, novel etc)* sûr; **it's a s. guess that ...** on ne prend pas beaucoup de risques en disant que ...; **it is s. to say that ...** on peut dire à coup sûr que ...; **(in order) to be on the s. side** pour plus de sûreté, pour être plus sûr; **s. investment** placement sûr *ou* de tout repos; **it's as s. as houses** *or Br* **as the Bank of England** *(of investment)* c'est de l'or en barres; *Prov* **better s. than sorry** deux précautions valent mieux qu'une; **it's a pretty s. assumption** *or* **bet that ...** il y a fort à parier que ...; **to wish sb a s. journey** souhaiter bon voyage à qn; **to have a s. journey** faire bon voyage

4 *(secure)* *(place etc)* sûr; **in s. keeping** en lieu sûr, en sûreté; **to give sth to sb for s. keeping** confier qch à qn; **it's in his s. keeping** c'est sous sa garde; **in s. hands** entre (de) bonnes mains; **he's a s. pair of hands** *(of goalkeeper)* il a les mains très sûres; *(of manager, minister etc)* il est très fiable; **to put sb/sth in a s. place** mettre qn/qch en lieu sûr; **a s. retreat** un asile assuré *ou* sûr

5 *Br Sl (good)* chouette, cool; **are we still on for tonight? – yeah, s.** ça marche toujours pour ce soir? – ouais, pas de problème

ADV **to play (it) s.** ne rien risquer

N **1** *(strongbox)* coffre-fort *m*, *pl* coffres-forts; *Banking* **night** *or* **deposit s.** coffre *m* de nuit

2 *(meat)* **s.** garde-manger *m inv*
▸ **s. area** zone *f* de sécurité; *Fin* **s. custody** garde *f* en dépôt de titres; **s. deposit** dépôt *m* en coffre-fort; **s. haven** refuge *m*; *Mil* zone de sécurité; **s. house** refuge; **s. load** *(for lorry)* charge *f* admissible; *(for lift)* charge maximum; *Elec* charge de sécurité; *Br Pol* **s. seat** = siège *m* de député qui traditionnellement va toujours au même parti; **s. sex** rapports *mpl* sexuels protégés; **to practise s. sex** se protéger *(contre les maladies sexuellement transmissibles)*; **a s. sex campaign** une campagne visant à promouvoir l'utilisation du préservatif

safe-blower N perceur, -euse de coffres-forts à l'explosif

safe-breaker N perceur, -euse de coffres-forts

safe-conduct N sauf-conduit *m*, *pl* sauf-conduits

safe-cracker N = safe-breaker

safeguard ['seɪfgɑːd] N garantie *f* (**against** contre)
VT *(sb's interests, rights)* sauvegarder, protéger
VI **to s. against sth** se protéger contre qch
▸ **s. clause** clause *f* de sauvegarde

safekeeping [seɪf'kiːpɪŋ] N **in s.** en lieu sûr, en sûreté; **to give sth to sb for s.** confier qch à qn; **it's in his s.** c'est sous sa garde

safelight ['seɪflaɪt] N *Phot* lampe *f* inactinique

safely ['seɪflɪ] ADV **1** *(to work, play, use a tool etc)* en toute sécurité; *(to drive, ride)* sans danger; **to arrive s.** *(of person)* bien arriver; *(after dangerous journey)* arriver sain et sauf; *(of parcel etc)* arriver sans dommage; *(of ship etc)* arriver à bon port; **to land s.** atterrir sans problème; **to put sth s. away** mettre qch en lieu sûr *ou* en sûreté; **the bomb has been s. defused** la bombe a été désamorcée et ne présente plus aucun danger; **the kids are s. tucked up in bed** les enfants sont bien sagement au lit **2** *(with certainty)* avec certitude; **I can s. say that ...** je puis dire avec certitude *ou* à coup sûr que ...; **you can s. expect her to remember** vous pouvez être sûr qu'elle s'en souviendra

safeness ['seɪfnɪs] N **1 a feeling of s.** un

sentiment de sécurité *ou* de sûreté **2** *(of bridge)* solidité *f*; *(of nuclear power, electrical appliances)* sûreté *f* **3** *(certainty)* *(of deal, investment, choice etc)* sûreté *f*; *(cautiousness)* *(of style, writing)* assurance *f*

safety ['seɪftɪ] N *(of person)* sécurité *f*, *(of thing)* sûreté *f*, **to seek s. in flight** chercher son salut dans la fuite; **to guarantee sb's s.** *(of police etc)* assurer la protection de qn; *Prov* **there's s. in numbers** plus on est nombreux, moins on court de risques; **for s.'s sake** pour plus de sûreté; **in a place of s.** en lieu sûr; **road s.** sécurité routière; **she's very s. conscious** elle se préoccupe beaucoup de la sécurité; **s. first!** ne prenez pas de risques!
▸▸ **s. belt** ceinture *f* de sécurité; *Aut* **s. cage** habitacle *m* de sécurité; **s. catch** *(on gun)* cran *m* de sécurité; *(on window, door)* cran de sûreté; *(on bonnet)* crochet *m* de sécurité; *Aut* **s. cell** cellule *f* de sécurité; **s. chain** *(on door)* chaîne *f* de sûreté; *(on bracelet)* chaînette *f* de sûreté; **s. deposit box** coffre(-fort) *m*, *pl* coffres(-forts); **s. device** dispositif *m* de sécurité; **s. drill** exercice *m* d'évacuation; **s. feature** *(device)* dispositif de sécurité; *(characteristic)* caractéristique *f* pour assurer la sécurité; **s. features** *(on car)* aménagements *mpl ou* dispositifs de sécurité; **s. glass** verre *m* de sécurité; **s. lamp** lampe *f* de mineur; **s. lock** verrouillage *m* de sécurité; **s. margin** marge *f* de sécurité; **s. matches** allumettes *fpl* de sûreté; **s. measures** consignes *fpl* de sécurité; **s. mechanism** mécanisme *m* de sécurité; **s. net** filet *m*; *Fig* filet de sécurité); **s. pin** *(fastener)* épingle *f* de nourrice *ou* de sûreté; *(of grenade, bomb)* goupille *f* de sûreté; **s. regulations** consignes de sécurité; **s. standards** normes *fpl* de sécurité; *Com* **s. stock** stock *m* de sécurité; **s. valve** *Tech* soupape *f* de sûreté; *Fig* soupape

safety-first ADJ *(campaign, measures)* de sécurité

saffron ['sæfrən] N **1** *Bot, Culin, Pharm* safran *m*; **wild** *or* **meadow s.** safran des prés **2** *(colour)* safran *m inv*
ADJ safran *inv*
▸▸ **s. crocus** safran; **s. yellow** jaune *m* safran

sag [sæg] N **1** *(of roof etc)* affaissement *m*, fléchissement *m*; *(in line, rope etc)* flèche *f*, ventre *m* **2** *(drop)* *(in prices, support etc)* baisse *f*
VI (**-gg-**) *(of platform, roof etc)* s'affaisser, fléchir; *(of cheek, breast etc)* pendre; *(of cable, rope)* *(state)* être détendu, pendre; *(action)* se détendre; *(of curtain)* pendre au milieu; *(of prices, support etc)* baisser, fléchir; **the gate was sagging on its hinges** le portail était branlant; **he's beginning to s. a little** il faiblit un peu

saga ['sɑːgə] N *Liter* saga *f*, *Fam* **the continuing s. of our washing machine** le feuilleton de notre machine à laver

sagacious [sə'geɪʃəs] ADJ *Fml (person, mind, remark etc)* sagace, avisé; *(action)* plein de sagesse

sagaciously [sə'geɪʃəslɪ] ADV *Fml* avec sagacité

sagacity [sə'gæsɪtɪ] N *Fml (of person, remark)* sagacité *f*, perspicacité *f*

sage[1] [seɪdʒ] *Lit* ADJ *(person, conduct etc)* sage, prudent
N *(wise man)* philosophe *m*, sage *m*

sage[2] N **1** *Bot, Culin* sauge *f* **2** *(colour)* vert *m* cendré
▸▸ **s. green** vert cendré *inv*; **s. tea** tisane *f* de sauge

sagely ['seɪdʒlɪ] ADV *Lit* sagement, prudemment

sagging ['sægɪŋ] ADJ *(roof etc)* affaissé;

(gate etc) penché d'un côté; *(breast, cheek etc)* pendant; *(line etc)* courbe; *(rope)* lâche; *(prices, market, support etc)* en baisse; *(enthusiasm, demand)* fléchissant, faiblissant

Sagittarius [sædʒɪˈteərɪəs] N *Astron* Sagittaire *m*; **to be (a) S.** être (du) Sagittaire

sago [ˈseɪgəʊ] N *Culin* sagou *m*
▸▸ *Bot* **s. palm** sagoutier *m*; *Culin* **s. pudding** sagou au lait

Sahara [səˈhɑːrə] N **the S. (Desert)** le Sahara

sahib [ˈsɑːɪb] N sahib *m*

said PT, PP *see* **say** VT, VI

sail [seɪl] N **1** *(on boat)* voile *f*; **square s.** voile carrée; **to hoist/lower a s.** hisser/amener une voile; **to make s.** *(set sail)* prendre la mer; *(spread sails)* hisser les voiles; **under s.** *(of ship)* sous voile(s), à la voile; **under full s.** toutes voiles dehors; **to set s.** prendre la mer; **to set s. for ...** partir pour ...; **s. ho!** voilier en vue!; **a fleet of twenty s.** une flotte de vingt voiles *ou* de vingt voiliers
2 *(journey)* traversée *f*; **it will be a three hours' s.** la traversée durera trois heures; **to go for a s.** faire de la voile
3 *(of windmill)* aile *f*, volant *m*, toile *f*
VI **1** *(of sailing ship)* faire voile; *(of any ship)* naviguer, faire route; *Sport* **do you s.?** est-ce que vous faites de la voile?; *Fig* **to s. (a bit) close to the wind** prendre des risques
2 *(start voyage)* prendre la mer; **we s. at noon** nous partons à midi
3 *(travel by sea)* voyager par mer; **to s. over the seas** parcourir les mers; **they sailed around the Mediterranean** ils ont fait le tour de la Méditerranée; **to s. round a cape** contourner un promontoire
4 *(of glider)* planer; **there were clouds sailing by** des nuages voguaient dans le ciel; **the ball/stone sailed through the air** le ballon/caillou vola; **his toupee went sailing out of the open window** son postiche s'est envolé par la fenêtre ouverte
5 to s. into a room entrer majestueusement dans une pièce; *Fam* **to s. through an examination** réussir un examen sans problèmes *ou Fam* les doigts dans le nez
VT *(sailing boat)* manœuvrer; *(ship)* piloter, commander; **to s. a toy boat on a pond** faire naviguer un petit bateau sur un bassin; **to s. the seas** parcourir les mers

sailboard [ˈseɪlbɔːd] *Sport* N planche *f* à voile
VI faire de la planche à voile *ou* du véliplanche

sailboarder [ˈseɪlbɔːdər] N *Sport* (véli)planchiste *mf*

sailboarding [ˈseɪlbɔːdɪŋ] N *Sport* planche *f* à voile, véliplanchisme *m*

sailboat [ˈseɪlbəʊt] N *Am* voilier *m*, bateau *m* à voile

sailcloth [ˈseɪlklɒθ] N *Tex (for sails)* toile *f* à voile(s); *(for clothes)* toile *f*

sailing [ˈseɪlɪŋ] N **1** *(activity)* *(in sailing ship, sailing boat)* navigation *f* à voile; *(in any ship)* navigation; *Sport* voile *f*; **to go s.** faire de la voile; *Fig* **it's (all) plain s.** cela va tout seul **2** *(departure)* départ *m*, appareillage *m*; **the 12 o'clock s.** le bateau de midi
▸▸ **s. boat** voilier *m*, bateau *m* (à voiles); **s. card** liste *f* des navires en partance; **s. orders** ordre *m* d'appareiller, instructions *fpl* pour l'appareillage; **s. schedule** horaires *mpl* de départ; **s. ship** (grand) voilier, navire *m* à voile *ou* à voiles

sailmaker [ˈseɪlmeɪkər] N voilier *m*

sailor [ˈseɪlər] N marin *m*; **to be a good s.** avoir le pied marin; **to be a bad s.** être sujet au mal de mer
▸▸ **s. hat** *(for boys)* béret *m* de marin; *(for women)* canotier *m*; **s. suit** costume *m* marin

sainfoin [ˈsænfɔɪn] N *(plant)* sainfoin *m*

saint [seɪnt] N **1** saint *m*, sainte *f*; **s.'s day** fête *f* de saint, fête patronale; **All Saints' (Day)** la Toussaint; *Fig* **I'm no s.** je ne suis pas un saint; *Fam* **to try the patience of a s.** lasser la patience d'un saint **2 the Communion of Saints** la Communion des Saints
▸▸ **S. Andrew's Day** La Saint-André *(fête nationale de l'Écosse, le 30 novembre)*; **S. Bernard** *(dog)* saint-bernard *m inv*; **S. David's Day** la Saint-David *(fête nationale du pays de Galles, le 1 mars)*; **S. George's Day** la Saint-Georges *(fête nationale de l'Angleterre, le 23 avril)*; **S. Helena** *(island)* Sainte-Hélène *f*; **S. John the Baptist** saint Jean-Baptiste; **the S. Lawrence (River)** le (fleuve) Saint-Laurent; **S. Patrick's Day** la Saint-Patrick *(fête nationale d'Irlande, le 17 mars)*; **S. Pierre and Miquelon** Saint-Pierre-et-Miquelon; **S. Sylvester** Saint Sylvestre

---

Saint Patrick's Day

Patrick, le saint patron de l'Irlande, est célébré le 17 mars, qui est le jour de sa mort, en l'an 461. Saint Patrick convertit les Irlandais au christianisme et établit monastères, églises et écoles dans tout le pays. Selon la légende, il aurait également réussi à chasser tous les serpents d'Irlande. Chômée en Irlande, la St Patrick est également fêtée dans certaines villes américaines comptant une forte proportion de personnes d'origine irlandaise.

---

sainted [ˈseɪntɪd] ADJ *Old-fashioned Fam* **my s. aunt!** mes aïeux!

sainthood [ˈseɪnthʊd] N sainteté *f*

saintliness [ˈseɪntlɪnɪs] N sainteté *f*

saintly [ˈseɪntlɪ] ADJ *(life, action etc)* de saint; *Iron* **to put on a s. air** prendre un air de petit saint

sake¹ [seɪk] N **1 to do sth for the s. of sb** *or* **for sb's s.** faire qch pour qn *ou* par égard pour qn; **I forgive you for her s.** je vous pardonne par égard pour elle; **do it for the s. of your family** faites-le pour (l'amour de) votre famille; **they stayed together for the s. of the children** *or* **for the children's s.** ils sont restés ensemble à cause des enfants; **for all our sakes, tell no one** ne le dis à personne dans notre intérêt à tous; **do it for my s.** *(do it to please me)* faites-le pour me faire plaisir; **for God's s., for goodness' s., for heaven's s., for Pete's s., for pity's s.** pour l'amour de Dieu *ou* du ciel; **all for the s. of a few pence!** tout ça pour quelques malheureux pence!; **for the s. of peace** dans l'intérêt de la paix; **for old times' s.** en souvenir du passé; **for economy's s.** par économie; **art for art's s.** l'art pour l'art; **this is talking for talking's s.** *or* **for the s. of talking** c'est parler pour parler; **let's say, for the s. of argument** *or* **for argument's s. ...** admettons que ...; **you're just saying that for the s. of an argument** *or* **of arguing!** tu dis cela uniquement par provocation!
2 *Am Fam* **sakes alive!, sakes!** grand Dieu!, par exemple!

sake² [ˈsɑːkɪ] N *(drink)* saké *m*

sal [sæl] N
▸▸ **s. ammoniac** sel *m* ammoniac; **s. volatile** sel volatile, sels (anglais)

salaam [səˈlɑːm] *Fam* N salutation *f* (chez les musulmans)
VT & VI saluer

salacious [səˈleɪʃəs] ADJ *(story, person)* salace

salaciousness [səˈleɪʃəsnɪs] N *(of story, person)* salacité *f*

salad [ˈsæləd] N salade *f*; **cheese/ham s.** salade au fromage/jambon; **green s.** salade

(verte); **fruit s.** macédoine *f ou* salade de fruits
▸▸ **s. bar** *(restaurant)* = restaurant *m* où l'on mange des salades; *(area)* salad bar *m*; **s. bowl** saladier *m*; *Br* **s. cream** = sorte *f* de mayonnaise (vendue en bouteille); **s. days** années *fpl* de jeunesse; **s. dressing** sauce *f* *(pour salade)*; *(French dressing)* vinaigrette *f*, **s. oil** huile *f* pour assaisonnement; **s. spinner** essoreuse *f* à salade

salamander [ˈsæləmændər] N salamandre *f*

salami [səˈlɑːmɪ] N salami *m*

salaried [ˈsælərɪd] ADJ *Ind, Com* **1** *(personnel)* salarié **2** *(employment)* rémunéré
▸▸ **s. employee** salarié, -ée; **s. staff** salariés *mpl*

salary [ˈsælərɪ] N salaire *m*; *(of civil servant)* traitement *m*; **s. plus commission** salaire fixe plus commission
▸▸ **s. earner** salarié, -ée; **s. level** niveau *m* de rémunération *ou* de salaires; **s. scale** échelle *f* de salaires

salaryman, *pl* **salarymen** [ˈsælərɪmæn, -men] N employé *m* de bureau japonais

sale [seɪl] N **1** *(act, event)* vente *f*, **sales** *(turnover)* chiffre *m* d'affaires; **house for s.** maison à vendre; **business for s.** fonds à céder; **to put sth up for s.** mettre qch en vente; **on s.** *Br (available to buy)* en vente; *Am (at reduced price)* en solde; *Com* **s. at arrival/departure** vente à l'arrivée/au départ; **s. by private agreement** vente à l'amiable; **s. of stock** écoulement *m* de stocks; **s. or return basis** vente avec faculté de retour; **bill of s.** acte *m* de vente; **s. by auction, auction s.** vente aux enchères; *Law* **compulsory s.** adjudication *f* forcée
2 *Com* **(clearance) s.** *or* **sales** soldes *mpl*; **in the s.,** *Am* **on s.** *(article)* en solde; **I got it in a s.** je l'ai acheté en solde; **I got it in the sale(s)** je l'ai acheté pendant les soldes
▸▸ **sales acumen** sens *m* du commerce; **sales agent** agent *m* commercial; **s. agreement** compromis *m* de vente; **sales analysis** analyse *f* des ventes; **sales area** *(in store)* surface *f* de vente; *(district)* région *f* desservie; *Br* **sales assistant** vendeur, -euse; **sales audit** audit *m* de vente; **sales campaign** campagne *f* de vente; **sales commission** commission *f* de vente; **sales consultant** conseiller, -ère commercial(e); **sales contract** contrat *m* de vente; **sales counter** comptoir *m* de vente; **sales department** service *m* commercial, service des ventes; **sales director** directeur, -trice des ventes; **sales drive** campagne de vente; **sales engineer** ingénieur *m* technico-commercial, ingénieur commercial, ingénieur des ventes; **sales figures** chiffre de vente; **sales floor** surface de vente; **sales force** force *f ou* équipe *f* de vente; **sales forecast** prévision *f* des ventes; **sales goal** objectif *m* de vente; **sales invoice** facture *f* de vente; *Acct* **sales ledger** grand livre *m* des ventes, journal *m* des ventes; **sales letter** lettre *f* de vente; **sales licence** licence *f* de vente; **sales literature** prospectus *mpl*, **sales manager** directeur, -trice commercial(e), responsable *mf* des ventes; **sales and marketing** vente-marketing *f*, **sales and marketing department** service vente-marketing; **sales and marketing director** directeur, -trice des ventes et du marketing; **sales meeting** réunion *f* de représentants; **sales monopoly** monopole *m* de vente; **sales network** réseau *m* de vente; **sales objective** objectif de vente; **sales outlet** point *m* de vente; **sales pitch** arguments *mpl* de vente; *(verbal)* boniment *m*, argumentation *f*, **s. price** *(selling price)* prix *m* de vente; *(reduced price)* prix soldé; **sales promoter** promoteur, -trice de ventes; **sales promotion** promotion *f* des ventes, animation *f* des ventes; **sales quota** quota *m* de ventes; **sales rally** rallye *m* de sti-

mulation; **sales representative,** *Fam* **sales rep** représentant, -ante commercial(ale), agent commercial; *Am* **sales slip** ticket *m* de caisse; **sales target** objectif de vente; **sales tax** taxe *f* sur le chiffre d'affaires, TCA *f*, **sales team** équipe de vente; **sales technician** agent technico-commercial; **sales technique** technique *f* de vente; **sales tool** instrument *m* de vente; **sales volume** volume *m* des ventes; *Mktg* **sales wave** vague *f* de vente; **s. of work** vente de charité

saleability [seɪlə'bɪlɪtɪ] **N** *Com* facilité *f* d'écoulement

saleable ['seɪləb(ə)l] **ADJ** *(goods etc)* vendable

saleroom ['seɪruːm] **N** salle *f* de(s) vente(s)

salesclerk ['seɪlzklɑːk] **N** *Am* vendeur, -euse

salesgirl ['seɪlzɡɜːl] **N** vendeuse *f*

salesman, *pl* **salesmen** ['seɪlzmən] **N** vendeur *m*; *(sales representative)* représentant *m* (de commerce)

salesmanship ['seɪlzmənʃɪp] **N** technique *f* de vente

salesperson, *pl* **salespeople** ['seɪlzpɜːsən, -piːp(ə)l] **N 1** *(for company)* représentant, -ante (de commerce) **2** *(in shop)* vendeur, -euse

saleswoman, *pl* **saleswomen** ['seɪlzwʊmən, -wɪmɪn] **N 1** *(for company)* représentante *f* (de commerce) **2** *(in shop)* vendeuse *f*

Salic law ['seɪlɪk] **N** *Hist* loi *f* salique

salient ['seɪlɪənt] **ADJ 1** *(angle etc)* saillant **2** *(characteristic)* saillant, frappant; **the s. points of an argument** les points forts d'une argumentation
N *(in trench warfare etc)* saillant *m*

saline ['seɪlaɪn] **ADJ** *(spring, water)* salin, salé
N *Med (salt solution)* sérum *m* physiologique
▸▸ *Med* **s. drip** perfusion *f* saline; **s. solution** solution *f* saline

salinity [sə'lɪnɪtɪ] **N** salinité *f*

saliva [sə'laɪvə] **N** salive *f*

salivary [sə'laɪvərɪ] **ADJ** *(glands etc)* salivaire

salivate ['sælɪveɪt] **VI** *also Fig* saliver

salivation [sælɪ'veɪʃən] **N** salivation *f*

sallow[1] ['sæləʊ] **N** *(willow)* saule *m*

sallow[2] **ADJ** *(complexion)* jaunâtre

sallowness ['sæləʊnɪs] **N** *(of complexion)* ton *m* jaunâtre

Sally ['sælɪ] **N** *Br Fam* **the S. Army** l'Armée *f* du salut

sally ['sælɪ] **N 1** *Mil* sortie *f*, *(excursion)* excursion *f*, sortie; **his first s. into travel writing** sa première tentative de récit de voyage **2** *Old-fashioned* **(of wit)** boutade *f*, trait *m* d'esprit
▸ **sally forth, sally out** **VI 1** *(go out)* sortir; *Hum (go for walk)* partir en promenade **2** *Mil* faire une sortie **3** *Lit (go out)* sortir; **young students who are now about to s. forth into the world** de jeunes étudiants sur le point de se lancer dans le monde

salmon ['sæmən] **N** *(usu inv in pl) (fish)* saumon *m*; **young s.** tacon *m*, saumoneau *m*
ADJ *(colour)* (rose *m*) saumon *m inv*
▸▸ **s. ladder, s. leap, s. pass** échelle *f* à saumon(s); **s. pink** (rose) saumon; **s. steak** darne *f* de saumon; **s. trout** truite *f* saumonée

salmonella [sælmə'nelə] **N** salmonelle *f*; **to have s. (poisoning)** avoir une salmonellose

salon ['sælɒn] **N 1** *(of fashion designer, hairdresser etc)* salon *m*; *Art* **the S.** le Salon; **(beauty) s.** institut *m ou* salon de beauté; **hairdressing s.** salon de coiffure **2** *Liter* salon *m* **3** *(drawing room)* salon *m*

saloon [sə'luːn] **N 1** *Am (bar)* saloon *m*, bar *m*; **billiard s.** salle *f* de billard **2** *Naut (of steamship)* salon *m*; *(on yacht)* cabine *f* **3** *Br Aut (car)* berline *f*, **two-door s.** coach *m*; **four-door s.** berline
▸▸ *Br* **s. bar** salle de pub *(plus confortable que le bar principal)*; *Br Aut* **s. car** berline *f*; *Am* **s. keeper** patron, -onne de saloon *ou* de bar

salopettes [sælə'pets] **NPL** *Ski (garment)* combinaison *f*

salsa ['sælsə] **N 1** *(sauce)* salsa *f* méxicaine **2** *(music, dance)* salsa *f*

salsify ['sælsɪfɪ] **N** *(plant)* salsifis *m*

SALT [sɔːlt] **N** *Mil (abbr* Strategic Arms Limitation Talks*)* SALT *m*
▸▸ **S. talks** négociations *fpl* SALT

salt [sɔːlt] **N 1** *(on roads)* Culin, Chem sel *m*; **kitchen s.** gros sel; **rock s.** sel gemme; **sea s.** sel marin, sel de mer; **table s.** sel de table; **(bath) salts** sels de bain; *Old-fashioned* **(liver) salts** sels; **to take a story with a pinch or grain of s.** ne pas prendre une histoire au pied de la lettre; **he's not worth his s.** il ne vaut rien; **any athlete worth his/her s.** n'importe quel(elle) athlète digne de ce nom, n'importe quel athlète qui se respecte; *Old-fashioned* **to sit (at table) above/below the s.** être assis au haut bout/au bas bout de la table; *Fig* **to rub s. in the wound** remuer le couteau dans la plaie; *Fig* **the s. of the earth** le sel de la terre
2 *(interest)* **to add s. to sth** mettre un peu de sel à qch, mettre du piment à qch
3 *Naut Fam* **old s.** vieux loup *m* de mer
ADJ 1 *(food)* salé; **too s.** trop salé **2** *(rocks, ground)* salifère
VT 1 *(food)* saler **2 = salt down**
▸▸ **s. beef** bœuf *m* salé; **s. cod** morue *f* salée; **s. flats** marais *m* salant; **s. lake** lac *m* salé; **s. lick** *(stone)* pierre *f* salée; **s. marsh** marais salant; **s. mine** mine *f* de sel; **s. pan** marais salant, salin *m*; **s. spoon** cuiller *f* à sel; *Hist* **s. tax** gabelle *f*; **s. water** eau *f* salée
▸ **salt away** **VT SEP** *(save) (money etc)* économiser, mettre en lieu sûr
▸ **salt down** **VT SEP** *(preserve with salt) (meat, fish etc)* saler

saltbox ['sɔːltbɒks] **N** boîte *f* à sel; *Am (house)* = maison *f* à toit penchant *(avec deux étages à l'avant et un étage à l'arrière)*

saltcellar ['sɔːltselər] **N** *(for salt)* salière *f*

salted ['sɔːltɪd] **ADJ** *(butter, herring etc)* salé

salt-free **ADJ** *(diet etc)* sans sel

saltine [sɔːl'tiːn] **N** *Am Culin* biscuit *m* salé

saltiness ['sɔːltɪnɪs] **N** *(of water etc)* salinité *f*, *(of food etc)* salure *f*

salting ['sɔːltɪŋ] **N** *(of meat etc) (for preserving)* salaison *f*, *(for flavouring)* salage *m*

saltmill ['sɔːltmɪl] **N** moulin *m* à sel

saltpetre, *Am* **saltpeter** [sɔːlt'piːtər] **N** salpêtre *m*

saltwater ['sɔːltwɔːtər] **ADJ ATTRIB** **s. fish** poisson *m* de mer

saltworks ['sɔːltwɜːks] **N** *(for sea salt)* salin *m*; *(for rock salt)* saline *f*, *(salt refinery)* raffinerie *f* de sel

saltwort ['sɔːltwɜːt] **N** *Bot* **1** soude *f*, **prickly s.** kali *m* **2** *(salicornia)* salicorne *f*

salty ['sɔːltɪ] **ADJ 1** *(taste, sauce, water etc)* salé **2** *Fam (anecdote, book)* piquant; *(licentious)* salé, corsé

salubrious [sə'luːbrɪəs] **N** *Fml* salubre, sain; *Fig* **one of his less than s. friends** un de ses amis pas très fréquentables

salubriousness [sə'luːbrɪəsnɪs] **N** *Fml* salubrité *f*

saluki [sə'luːkɪ] **N** *(dog)* sloughi *m*

salutary ['sæljʊt(ə)rɪ] **ADJ** salutaire; **to have a s. effect on sb** faire du bien à qn

salutation [sæljʊ'teɪʃən] **N** *Fml* salutation *f*, *(in letter)* titre *m* de civilité; **in s.** en guise de salut

salute [sə'luːt] **N** *Mil, Naut etc (gesture)* salut *m*; **to return sb's s.** rendre son salut à qn; **to take the s.** *(at march past)* passer les troupes en revue; **to fire a s.** tirer une salve; **to fire a ten-gun s.** saluer de dix coups
VT *(person)* saluer; *Lit* **to s. sb's achievements** saluer les exploits de qn; **I s. you** je te tire mon chapeau
VI *Mil, Naut* saluer, faire le salut militaire

salvage ['sælvɪdʒ] **N 1** *(salvaging) (of ship etc)* sauvetage *m*; *(of waste material)* récupération *f* **2** *(objects salvaged)* objets *mpl* sauvés *(après une catastrophe)* **3** *(money)* indemnité *f ou* prime *f* de sauvetage; *(paid to salvage tug)* indemnité de remorquage
VT *(ship etc)* sauver; *(items from fire etc)* sauver, récupérer; *(car etc)* récupérer; *Fam (dish, essay etc)* rattraper; **to s. something from the ruins of one's career** sauver quelque chose de la faillite qu'a été sa carrière; **salvaged goods** matériel *m* récupéré
▸▸ **s. company** = compagnie *f* spécialisée dans le remorquage et le renflouage de navires; **s. tug** remorqueur *m (pour les sauvetages)*; **s. vessel** navire *m* de relevage

salvation [sæl'veɪʃən] **N** salut *m*; **to work out one's own s.** travailler à son (propre) salut; **you've been my s.** vous m'avez sauvé; **beyond s.** irrécupérable
▸▸ **the S. Army** l'Armée *f* du salut

salvationist [sæl'veɪʃənɪst] **N** salutiste *mf*

salve [sælv, sɑːv] **N** *Pharm* baume *m*, onguent *m*; *Fig* baume
VT *Fml* adoucir, apaiser; *(conscience)* soulager

salver ['sælvər] **N** *(tray)* plateau *m (en argent etc)*

salvia ['sælvɪə] **N** *(plant)* sauge *f (ornementale)*

salvo ['sælvəʊ] **N** *Mil, Naut, Fig* salve *f*, **to fire a s.** tirer une salve; **s. of applause** salve d'applaudissements

SAM [sæm] **N** *Mil (abbr* surface-to-air missile*)* missile *m* sol-air

Samaritan [sə'mærɪt(ə)n] **ADJ** samaritain
N Samaritain, -aine; *Bible* **the Good S.** le bon Samaritain; **to be a good S.** se conduire en bon Samaritain; **the Samaritans** *(telephone service)* ≃ SOS *m* Amitié

samba ['sæmbə] **N** *(dance)* samba *f*
VI danser la samba

sambo ['sæmbəʊ] **N** *Offensive, Sl* bougnoul *m*

SAME [seɪm] **ADJ** même; **at the s. time that ... au moment même où ...;** **he's the s. age as me** il est du même âge que moi; **in the s. way** de la même façon; **we are going the s. way** nous allons dans la même direction; **do you still feel the s. way?** est-ce que vos sentiments sont toujours les mêmes?; **she's still the s. (old) Sarah** c'est toujours notre bonne vieille Sarah; **one and the s. thing** une seule et même chose; **the very s. thing** tout à fait *ou* exactement la même chose; **the *or* that very s. day** le jour même; **the very s. situation** la même situation exactement; **it is always/it is no longer the s. thing** c'est toujours/ce n'est plus la même chose; **it all amounts *or* comes to the s. thing** tout cela revient au même; *Fam* **it's the s. difference** c'est bonnet blanc et blanc bonnet; **at the s. time** en même temps; *(at once)* à la fois, du même coup; **that s. man is now a millionaire** ce même homme est maintenant millionnaire
PRON **the s.** le même, la même, *pl* les mêmes; *Fml (that one)* celui-là même, celle-là même, *pl* ceux-là mêmes, celles-là mêmes;

it's the s. everywhere c'est la même chose ou c'est pareil ou *Fml* il en est de même partout; it's all the s., it's just the s. c'est exactement la même chose, *Fam* c'est tout comme; if it's all the s. to you si cela ne vous fait rien, si ça vous est égal; it's much the s. c'est à peu près la même chose; low-alcohol lager just isn't the s. la bière à faible teneur en alcool, ça n'est tout simplement pareil ou pas la même chose; the house isn't the s. without her la maison n'est pas pareille sans elle; he had an accident and he's never been the s. since il a eu un accident et il n'est plus le même depuis; *Fam* (the) s. again? *(whisky etc)* encore un?; *Fam* (the) s. again! remettez ça!; *Fam* s. here! et moi aussi!, et moi de même!; a Happy New Year to you! – (the) s. to you! je vous souhaite une bonne année! – vous de même!; *Fam* (the) s. to you, you bastard! toi pareil, espèce de salaud!; I would have done the s. j'aurais fait la même chose ou de même, j'aurais agi de la même façon

ADV the s. de la même façon; to think/feel/act the s. penser/sentir/agir de même; they taste all the s. ils ont tous le même goût; all these houses look the s. to me je trouve que ces maisons se ressemblent toutes; all her songs sound the s. toutes ses chansons se ressemblent; all the s. *(nevertheless)* quand même, tout de même; when I am away, things go on just the s. quand je suis absent, tout continue à marcher comme d'habitude

same-day delivery N *Com* livraison *f* le jour même

same-day value N *Banking* valeur *f* jour

sameness ['seɪmnɪs] N 1 *(being identical)* identité *f*, similitude *f* 2 *(monotony)* monotonie *f*

samey ['seɪmɪ] ADJ *Fam* monotone

Samoa [sə'məʊə] N Samoa *m*

Samoan [sə'məʊən] N 1 *(person)* Samoan, -ane 2 *(language)* samoan *m*
ADJ samoan

samosa [sə'məʊsə] N samosa *m*

samovar ['sæməvɑːr] N samovar *m*

sampan ['sæmpæn] N *(boat)* sampan(g) *m*

sample ['sɑːmp(ə)l] N 1 *Com etc (of cloth etc)* échantillon *m*; *(of ore, blood, urine)* prélèvement *m*; a s. of one's work un échantillon de son travail; *Com* up to s. pareil ou conforme à l'échantillon; *Com* not up to s. non conforme à l'échantillon; to take a s. faire un prélèvement; to take a blood s. faire une prise de sang 2 *Mus* sample *m*
VT 1 *(wine, dish)* goûter à, déguster; *(experience)* essayer 2 *Mktg (public opinion)* sonder 3 *Mus* échantillonner, sampler
VI *Mus* échantillonner, sampler
▸▸ s. book catalogue *m* d'échantillons; s. card carte *f* d'échantillons; *Mktg* s. survey enquête *f* par sondage

sampler ['sɑːmplər] N 1 *Sewing* = modèle *m* de broderie 2 *Mus (equipment)* échantillonneur *m*

sampling ['sɑːmplɪŋ] N 1 prélèvement *m* ou prise *f* d'échantillons, échantillonnage *m*; *(of food, wine etc)* dégustation *f*; *Com, Ind* random s. prélèvement d'échantillons au hasard 2 *Mus* sampling *m*
▸▸ s. error erreur *f* d'échantillonnage

samurai ['sæmʊraɪ] N INV samouraï *m*

San Andreas Fault [sænæn'dreɪəs-] N the S. la faille de San Andreas *(faille géologique à l'origine de nombreux tremblements de terre en Californie)*

sanatorium, *pl* sanatoriums, sanatoria [sænə'tɔːrɪəm, -ɪəmz, -ɪə] N sanatorium *m*

sanctification [sæŋ(k)tɪfɪ'keɪʃən] N sanctification *f*

sanctified ['sæŋ(k)tɪfaɪd] ADJ *(person)* sanctifié; *(thing)* consacré

sanctify ['sæŋ(k)tɪfaɪ] VT 1 *(person, thing)* sanctifier; *(day, land etc)* consacrer 2 sanctified by time consacré par le temps

sanctimonious [sæŋ(k)tɪ'məʊnɪəs] ADJ d'une piété suffisante; *(air)* de petit saint; don't be so s. ne sois pas si moralisateur

sanctimoniously [sæŋ(k)tɪ'məʊnɪəslɪ] ADV d'un air de petit saint

sanction ['sæŋ(k)ʃən] N 1 *Law* (punitive) s. sanction *f* (pénale); *Pol* to impose (economic) sanctions on a country prendre des sanctions économiques contre un pays; accused of sanctions busting accusé de ne pas respecter des sanctions *(contre un pays, une organisation etc)* 2 *Fml* (consent) sanction *f*, autorisation *f*; without their s. sans leur consentement
VT 1 *Law (ratify) (law etc)* ratifier 2 *(authorize)* sanctionner, autoriser; sanctioned by usage consacré par l'usage

sanctity ['sæŋ(k)tɪtɪ] N 1 *Rel (of person, life etc)* sainteté *f* 2 *(of land, oath etc)* caractère *m* sacré; *(of private life etc)* inviolabilité *f*

sanctuary ['sæŋ(k)tjʊ(ə)rɪ] N 1 *Rel (place)* sanctuaire *m* 2 *(refuge)* refuge *m*, asile *m*; to take s. trouver asile 3 *(for birds)* refuge *m*; wildlife s. réserve *f* zoologique

sanctum ['sæŋ(k)təm] N *Rel, Fig (room etc)* sanctuaire *m*

Sanctus ['sæŋ(k)təs] N *Rel, Mus* sanctus *m*

sand [sænd] N sable *m*; the coast offers mile after mile of shining sands la côte vous offre des kilomètres de sable doré; *Constr, Fig* to build on s. bâtir sur le sable; on the sand(s) *(on the beach)* sur la plage; *(on sandbank)* sur un banc de sable; *Prov* the sands of time are running out for us nous n'aurons bientôt plus le temps, le temps qui nous est imparti sera bientôt écoulé
VT 1 *(with sandpaper) (make smoother)* poncer; *(remove paint, varnish from)* décaper au papier de verre 2 *(cover with sand) (pathway etc)* sabler; *(floor)* répandre du sable sur
▸▸ s. bar ensablement *m*; s. castle château *m* de sable; s. dune dune *f*, *Zool* s. eel lançon *m*, équille *f*, *Zool* s. flea *(sandhopper)* puce *f* de mer, talitre *m*; *(chigoe)* chique *f*, s. hopper *(crustacean)* puce de mer; *Br Orn* s. martin hirondelle *f* de rivage; *Am Golf* s. trap bunker *m* (de sable)

▸ **sand down** VT SEP = sand VT 1

sandal ['sænd(ə)l] N sandale *f*

sandalwood ['sænd(ə)lwʊd] N (bois *m* de) santal *m*

sandbag ['sændbæg] N *Mil etc* sac *m* de sable
VT (-gg-) 1 *Mil (building)* protéger avec des sacs de sable 2 *(hit)* assommer *(d'un coup de gourdin sur la nuque)*

sandbank ['sændbæŋk] N banc *m* de sable

sandblast ['sændblɑːst] VT décaper au jet de sable, sabler

sandblasting ['sændblɑːstɪŋ] N *(of surface)* décapage *m* ou décapement *m* au (jet de) sable

sandboy ['sændbɔɪ] N as happy as a s. gai comme un pinson, heureux comme un poisson dans l'eau

sander ['sændər] N *(tool)* ponceuse *f*

sandglass ['sændglɑːs] N sablier *m*

Sandhurst ['sændhɜːst] N *Br Mil* ≃ Saint-Cyr

sanding ['sændɪŋ] N 1 *(with sandpaper) (smoothing)* ponçage *m*; *(removal of paint, varnish)* décapage *m* au papier de verre 2 *(spreading of sand)* sablage *m*
▸▸ s. disc disque *m* en papier de verre; s. down *(smoothing)* ponçage; *(removal of paint, varnish)* décapage au papier de verre

sandman ['sændmæn] N *Fig* marchand *m* de sable

sandpail ['sændpeɪl] N *Am* seau *m* *(pour faire des châteaux de sable)*

sandpaper ['sændpeɪpər] N papier *m* de verre
VT frotter ou poncer au papier de verre

sandpiper ['sændpaɪpər] N *(bird)* bécasseau *m*

sandpit ['sændpɪt] N sablière *f*, sablonnière *f*, carrière *f* de sable; *(for children)* bac *m* à sable

sandshoes ['sændʃuːz] NPL *Br* rythmiques *fpl*

sandstone ['sændstəʊn] N grès *m*; s. buildings bâtiments *mpl* en grès

sandstorm ['sændstɔːm] N tempête *f* de sable

sandwich ['sændwɪtʃ] N sandwich *m*, *pl* sandwichs, sandwiches; *Culin (cake)* génoise *f* fourrée; ham/cheese s. sandwich au jambon/fromage; open s. canapé *m*; *Am* hero or submarine s. gros sandwich coupé dans une baguette; *Br Fam Hum* to be one s. short of a picnic ne pas être net
VT intercaler *(between* entre), *Fam* coincer *(between* entre); to be sandwiched between two people être coincé entre ou *Fam* pris en sandwich entre deux personnes
▸▸ *Br* s. bar ≃ snack *m* *(où on vend des sandwichs)*; s. board panneau *m* publicitaire *(porté par un homme-sandwich)*; *Culin* s. cake génoise fourrée; *Br* s. course ≃ stage *m* de formation professionnelle en alternance; s. filling garniture *f*, S. Islands îles *fpl* Sandwich; s. loaf ≃ pain *m* de mie; s. man homme-sandwich *m*, *pl* hommes-sandwichs; s. toaster appareil *m* à croque-monsieur

sandy ['sændɪ] ADJ 1 *(earth etc)* sableux, sablonneux; *(path)* sablonneux, de sable; *(beach)* de sable; are the beaches s.? est-ce que ce sont des plages de sable?; s. bottom *(of river, sea)* fond de sable; my hair is all s. *(full of sand)* mes cheveux sont pleins de sable 2 *(in colour) (hair etc)* roux pâle *inv*, blond roux *inv*

sane [seɪn] ADJ *(person)* sain d'esprit; *(views, speech etc)* raisonnable, sensé; to be s. *(of person)* avoir toute sa raison

sanely ['seɪnlɪ] ADV raisonnablement; he spoke quite s. il a dit des choses très sensées

sang PT *see* sing

sang-froid [sɒŋ'frwɑː] N sang-froid *m inv*

sanguinary ['sæŋgwɪnərɪ] ADJ *Lit (battle)* sanglant; *(tyrant)* sanguinaire

sanguine ['sæŋgwɪn] ADJ *Lit* 1 *(complexion etc)* d'un rouge sanguin, rubicond 2 *(person, disposition etc)* confiant, optimiste *(about* quant à); to be of a s. disposition être porté à l'optimisme

Note that the French adjective **sanguin** is a false friend and is never a translation for the English adjective **sanguine**.

sanguinely ['sæŋgwɪnlɪ] ADV avec confiance, avec optimisme

sanitarium [sænɪ'teərɪəm] N *Am* = sanatorium

sanitary ['sænɪt(ə)rɪ] ADJ hygiénique, sanitaire
▸▸ s. disposal bag sachet *m* pour garniture périodique; s. engineer technicien *m*, -ienne *f* du service sanitaire; s. inspector inspecteur, -trice de la santé publique; *Am* s. napkin, s. pad, *Br* s. towel serviette *f* hygiénique; s. ware appareils *mpl* sanitaires

sanitation [sænɪ'teɪʃən] N *(system)* système *m* sanitaire; the s. here is appalling les conditions sanitaires ici sont affreuses; there's no s. in the camps il n'y a pas d'installations sanitaires dans les camps

sanitize ['sænɪtaɪz] **vt** *esp Am (clean)* aseptiser; *(sterilize)* stériliser; *Fig (document, novel etc)* expurger

sanity ['sænɪtɪ] **N 1** *(of person)* santé *f* mentale; **there are doubts about his s.** on se demande s'il est sain d'esprit **2** *(of plan, policy etc)* bon sens *m*

sanserif [sæn'serɪf] *Typ* **N** caractères *mpl* sans empattement
  ADJ sans empattement

Sanskrit ['sænskrɪt] **ADJ, N** *Ling* sanscrit *m*, sanskrit *m*

Santa, Santa Claus ['sæntə(klɔːz)] **N** le père Noël

sap[1] [sæp] **N 1** *(of plant)* sève *f*; **the s. is rising** la sève monte; *Fig* **to feel the s. rising** être tout ragaillardi **2** *Fam (gullible person)* poire *f*, *(idiot)* andouille *f*

sap[2] **N** *Mil etc (trench)* sape *f*
  vt (-pp-) *Mil, Fig* saper, miner; **the fever has sapped (him of) his strength** la fièvre l'a miné

sap[3] **N** *Am (cosh)* gourdin *m*

saphead ['sæphed] **N** *Am Fam* andouille *f*

sapless ['sæplɪs] **ADJ** *(plant, wood)* sans sève, desséché

sapling ['sæplɪŋ] **N** *(young tree)* jeune arbre *m*

sapper ['sæpər] **N** *Mil* sapeur *m*; *(in charge of laying mines)* mineur *m*; *Fam* **the sappers** le génie

sapphic ['sæfɪk] **ADJ** *(in prosody)* saphique; *Lit (lesbian)* saphique
  ▸ ▸ *Old-fashioned* **s. vice** saphisme *m*

sapphire ['sæfaɪər] **N 1** *(precious stone)* saphir *m* **2** *(colour)* (couleur *f* de) saphir *m*
  ADJ *(in colour)* (couleur de) saphir *inv*

sappiness ['sæpɪnɪs] **N** *(of tree etc)* abondance *f* de sève, teneur *f* en sève

sappy ['sæpɪ] **ADJ 1** *(tree etc)* plein de sève; *(timber)* vert **2** *Old-fashioned Fam (stupid)* bête, stupide

saraband ['særəbænd] **N** *(dance, music)* sarabande *f*

Saracen ['særəs(ə)n] *Hist* **ADJ** sarrasin
  N Sarrasin, -ine

sarcasm ['sɑːkæz(ə)m] **N** *(characteristic, remark)* sarcasme *m*; **his constant s.** ses sarcasmes continuels

sarcastic [sɑː'kæstɪk] **ADJ** sarcastique; **a s. remark** un sarcasme, une remarque sarcastique

sarcastically [sɑː'kæstɪklɪ] **ADV** d'une manière sarcastique

sarcoma [sɑː'kəʊmə] **N** *Med* sarcome *m*

sarcophagus, *pl* **sarcophagi** [sɑː'kɒfəgəs, -fədʒaɪ] **N** sarcophage *m*

sardine [sɑː'diːn] **N** *(fish)* sardine *f*; **the passengers were packed in like sardines** les passagers étaient serrés comme des sardines
  ▸ ▸ **s. boat** sardinier *m*

Sardinia [sɑː'dɪnɪə] **N** Sardaigne *f*

Sardinian [sɑː'dɪnɪən] **ADJ** sarde
  N 1 Sarde *mf* **2** *Ling* sarde *m*

sardonic [sɑː'dɒnɪk] **ADJ** *(expression, laugh)* sardonique

sardonically [sɑː'dɒnɪklɪ] **ADV** d'une manière sardonique, sardoniquement

sarge [sɑːdʒ] **N** *Mil Fam* sergent *m*

sari ['sɑːrɪ] **N** *(garment)* sari *m*

Sark [sɑːk] **N** (île *f* de) Sercq *m*

sarky ['sɑːkɪ] **ADJ** *Fam* sarcastique

sarnie ['sɑːnɪ] **N** *Br Fam* casse-croûte *m inv,* casse-dalle *m inv*

sarong [sə'rɒŋ] **N** *(garment)* sarong *m*

SARS [sɑːz] **N** *Med* SRAS *m*

sarsaparilla [sɑːsəpə'rɪlə] **N** *(plant)* salsepareille *f*, *(drink)* boisson *f* à la salsepareille

sartorial [sɑː'tɔːrɪəl] **ADJ** *Fml (matters, taste)* vestimentaire; *(trade)* de tailleur; **s. elegance** élégance *f* vestimentaire; *Fam* **he is a s. disaster area** il n'a aucun sens de l'élégance vestimentaire

SAS [eseɪ'es] **N** *Br Mil (abbr* **special air service**) ≃ GIGN *m*

SASE [eseɪes'iː] **N** *Am (abbr* **self-addressed stamped envelope**) enveloppe *f* timbrée libellée à ses nom et adresse

sash[1] [sæʃ] **N** *(on dress)* large ceinture *f* à nœud bouffant; *(worn by officer)* écharpe *f*

sash[2] **N** *Constr (of window)* châssis *m* à guillotine
  ▸ ▸ **s. window** fenêtre *f* à guillotine

sashay ['sæʃeɪ] **vi** *Am Fam* **he sashayed across to the bar** *(walked affectedly)* il s'est approché du bar avec une nonchalance affectée; **I'll just s. down to Joe's place** *(go)* je vais juste faire un tour chez Joe

sashcord ['sæʃkɔːd] **N** corde *f* de fenêtre

sashimi [sæ'ʃɪmɪ] **N** sashimi *m*

Sask *abbr* **Saskatchewan**

sasquatch ['sæskwætʃ] **N** = géant *m* des légendes du Nord-Ouest des États-Unis et du Sud-Ouest du Canada

sass [sæs] **vt** *Am Fam (be insolent to)* répondre à

Sassenach ['sæsənæk] *Scot Hum or Pej* **N** Anglais, -aise
  ADJ anglais

sassy ['sæsɪ] **ADJ** *Am Fam* effronté, insolent

Sat *abbr* **Saturday**

sat **PT, PP** *see* **sit**

Satan ['seɪt(ə)n] **N** Satan *m*

satanic [sə'tænɪk] **ADJ** satanique, diabolique

satanically [sə'tænɪklɪ] **ADV** sataniquement, diaboliquement

satanism ['seɪtənɪz(ə)m] **N** satanisme *m*

satanist ['seɪtənɪst] **N** sataniste *mf*

satay ['sæteɪ] **N** *Culin* satay *m*
  ▸ ▸ **s. sauce** sauce *f* satay

satchel ['sætʃəl] **N** sacoche *f*, *Sch* cartable *m*

sate [seɪt] **vt 1** *Fml (hunger)* rassasier, assouvir; *(desire etc)* assouvir; *(person)* rassasier **2** = **satiate**

sateen [sə'tiːn] **N** *Tex* satinette *f*, satin *m* de coton

satellite ['sætəlaɪt] **N 1** *(natural, man-made)* satellite *m*; **artificial s.** satellite artificiel; **manned/unmanned s.** satellite habité/non habité; **(tele)communications s.** satellite de télécommunications; **meteorological** *or* **weather s.** satellite météorologique; **to watch sth on s.** regarder qch sur satellite **2** *(town)* ville *f* satellite; *(state)* (État *m*) satellite *m*
  ▸ ▸ **s. antenna** antenne *f* satellite; **s. broadcast** émission *f* retransmise par satellite; **s. broadcasting** retransmission *f* par satellite; **s. channel** chaîne *f* par satellite; **s. communication system** système *m* de communication par satellite; **s. dish** antenne parabolique; **s. link** liaison *f* par satellite; **s. network** réseau *m* satellite; **s. photo** photo *f* satellite; **s. picture** photo satellite; *Met* animation *f* satellite; **s. speaker** enceinte *f* satellite; **s. state** (État) satellite; **s. station** station *f* satellite; **s. television** télévision *f* par satellite; **s. town** ville satellite; **s. transmission** transmission *f* par satellite; **s. transponder** transpondeur *m* satellite; **s. uplink** liaison *f* par satellite

satiate ['seɪʃɪeɪt] **vt** *Fml* rassasier (**with** de)

satiated ['seɪʃɪeɪtɪd] **ADJ** *Fml (with food)* rassasié; *(with pleasure)* comblé

satiation [seɪʃɪ'eɪʃən] **N** *Fml* **1** *(process)* assouvissement *m* **2** *(state)* satiété *f*; **to reach (a point of) s.** *(when eating, drinking)* être rassasié; **to eat until one has reached (a point of) s.** manger à satiété

satiety [sə'taɪɪtɪ] **N** = **satiation 2**

satin ['sætɪn] **N** *Tex* satin *m*; **s. paper** papier *m* satiné
  ▸ ▸ **s. finish** *(of paper etc)* apprêt *m* satiné; **s. flower** stellaire *f*

satinette [sætɪ'net] **N** *Tex* satinette *f*

satire ['sætaɪər] **N** satire *f*; **a s. on sth** une satire de qch

satirical [sə'tɪrɪk(ə)l] **ADJ** satirique

satirically [sə'tɪrɪklɪ] **ADV** satiriquement

satirist ['sætɪrɪst] **N** *(writer)* satiriste *mf*, *(comedian)* chansonnier, -ière, comédien, -ienne satirique

satirize ['sætɪraɪz] **vt** faire la satire de; *(in literature)* satiriser

satisfaction [sætɪs'fækʃən] **N 1** *(pleasure)* satisfaction *f*, contentement *m* (**at, with** de); **to have the s. of doing sth** avoir la satisfaction de faire qch; **it gives me great s. to know that ...** je suis très satisfait d'apprendre que ...; **to one's complete s.** à sa satisfaction totale; *Com* **s. or your money back** remboursement garanti; *Com* **s. guaranteed** satisfaction garantie **2** *(act) (of creditor)* désintéressement *m*; *(of condition)* accomplissement *m*; *(of hunger, desire)* assouvissement *m*; **to demand s.** *(in duel)* demander réparation

satisfactorily [sætɪs'fækt(ə)rɪlɪ] **ADV** de manière *ou* de façon satisfaisante

satisfactory [sætɪs'fækt(ə)rɪ] **ADJ** satisfaisant; *(pupil)* qui donne satisfaction; **the result is not very s.** le résultat n'est pas très satisfaisant *ou* laisse à désirer; **to bring negotiations to a s. conclusion** mener à bien des négociations; *Med* **the patient is s.** *or* **in a s. condition** l'état du malade est satisfaisant

> Attention: ne pas confondre avec **satisfying**.

satisfied ['sætɪsfaɪd] **ADJ** *(customer etc)* content, satisfait (**with** de); *Iron* **not s. with that, she then broke the other chair** comme ça ne lui suffisait pas, elle a cassé l'autre chaise

satisfy ['sætɪsfaɪ] **vt 1** *(make happy)* satisfaire, contenter; *Sch* **to s. the examiners** *(of examinee)* être reçu à l'examen; **(in order) to s. your curiosity** pour satisfaire votre curiosité **2** *(convince)* convaincre, assurer; **I am satisfied that he was telling the truth** je suis convaincu *ou* persuadé *ou* sûr qu'il disait la vérité **3** *(creditors)* désintéresser; *(condition)* remplir; *Math (equation)* satisfaire à; *(sb's honour)* faire réparation à, satisfaire à; **to s. demand** satisfaire à la demande

satisfying ['sætɪsfaɪɪŋ] **ADJ** *(job, outcome, evening)* satisfaisant; *(meal)* substantiel

> Attention: ne pas confondre avec **satisfactory**.

satsuma [sæt'suːmə] **N** satsuma *f*

saturate ['sætʃəreɪt] **vt 1** *(soak)* imprégner, saturer (**with** de) **2** *Chem, Phys (solution)* saturer; *Com* **to s. the market** saturer le marché

saturated ['sætʃəreɪtɪd] **ADJ 1** *(ground, clothing etc)* détrempé, saturé d'eau; **to become s. with sth** s'imprégner de qch; *Fig* être saturé de qch; *Com* **the market is s.** le marché est saturé **2** *Chem, Phys (solution, compound etc)* saturé, intense **3** *(colour)* saturé, intense
  ▸ ▸ **s. fat** graisse *f* saturée

saturation [sætʃəˈreɪʃən] N imprégnation f, saturation f, *Chem, Phys* saturation; **the media's s. coverage of the affair** la couverture médiatique outrancière de l'affaire
▸▸ **s. bombing** bombardement m intensif; **s. point** point m de saturation; **the market has reached s. point** le marché est saturé, le marché est arrivé à saturation

Saturday [ˈsætədɪ] N samedi m; **S. 14 June** samedi 14 juin; **S. morning/evening** samedi matin/soir; **it's S. today** nous sommes samedi aujourd'hui; **he comes on Saturdays** il vient le samedi; **he's coming on S.** il vient samedi; **every S.** tous les samedis VOIR GRAMMAIRE A81–2; B61–2

Saturn [ˈsætɜːn] N *Astron* Saturne f, *Myth* Saturne m

saturnalia [sætəˈneɪlɪə] N saturnales fpl

saturnine [ˈsætənaɪn] ADJ *Lit (gloomy)* taciturne, sombre

saturnism [ˈsætənɪz(ə)m] N *Med* saturnisme m

satyr [ˈsætər] N *Myth etc* satyre m

sauce [sɔːs] N **1** *Culin* sauce f, **tomato s.** sauce tomate; **white s.** sauce blanche ou béchamel; **caper s.** sauce aux câpres; *Prov* **what's s. for the goose is s. for the gander** ce qui est bon pour l'un est aussi bon pour l'autre **2** *Old-fashioned Fam (impudence)* culot m, toupet m **3** *Fam (alcohol)* alcool m, bibine f, **to hit the s.** se mettre à picoler; **to be on the s.** s'être remis à picoler; **to be off the s.** être au régime sec
▸▸ **s. boat** saucière f

sauced [sɔːst] ADJ *Fam (drunk)* bourré, pété

saucepan [ˈsɔːspən] N casserole f, **double s.** bain-marie m, pl bains-marie
▸▸ **s. lid** couvercle m de casserole

saucer [ˈsɔːsər] N soucoupe f, **flying s.** soucoupe volante; *Fam* **eyes like saucers** yeux comme des soucoupes

saucily [ˈsɔːsɪlɪ] ADV *Fam (in risqué manner)* d'un air coquin

sauciness [ˈsɔːsɪnɪs] N *Fam* **1** *(impertinence)* impertinence f **2** *(risqué quality) (of joke, nightdress etc)* côté m coquin

saucy [ˈsɔːsɪ] ADJ *Fam* **1** *(impertinent)* impertinent, effronté **2** *(risqué) (person, joke, nightdress etc)* coquin; *Old-fashioned* **s. little hat** petit chapeau coquet

Saudi [ˈsaʊdɪ] ADJ saoudien
N *Fam* **1** *(person)* Saoudien, -ienne **2** *(country)* Arabie f séoudite ou saoudite

Saudi Arabia N Arabie f saoudite

Saudi Arabian N Saoudien, -ienne
ADJ saoudien

sauerkraut [ˈsaʊəkraʊt] N choucroute f

sauna [ˈsɔːnə] N sauna m

saunter [ˈsɔːntər] N balade f, **to go for a s. in the park** aller se balader dans le parc; **at a s.** *(to arrive)* tranquillement
VI **to s. (along)** se balader; **to s. along** or **down the street** descendre la rue en flânant; **to s. up to sb** s'approcher de qn tranquillement; **she sauntered in, half an hour late** elle est arrivée tranquillement, une demi-heure en retard; **she sauntered past as if nothing had happened** elle est passée d'un pas tranquille comme si de rien ne s'était rien passé

saurian [ˈsɔːrɪən] ADJ, N *(reptile)* saurien m

sausage [ˈsɒsɪdʒ] N *Culin (fresh)* saucisse f, *(preserved, hard, dry)* saucisson m; *Br Fig Fam* **not a s.** que dalle; **I was left without a s.** il ne me restait que dalle; *Fam Hum* **you silly s.!** que tu es bête ou nigaud!
▸▸ *Br Fam* **s. dog** saucisse f à pattes, teckel m; **s. roll** = sorte f de friand à la saucisse; **s. skin** boyau m

sausagemeat [ˈsɒsɪdʒmiːt] N chair f à saucisse

sauté [ˈsəʊteɪ] ADJ sauté
N sauté m
VT (faire) sauter
▸▸ **s. potatoes** pommes fpl de terre sautées

sautéed [ˈsəʊteɪd] ADJ sauté

savage [ˈsævɪdʒ] ADJ **1** *(fierce) (animal, criticism)* féroce; *(blow)* brutal, -aux, féroce; *(person)* enragé; **to make a s. attack on sb** attaquer sauvagement qn **2** *(primitive) (people, custom etc)* sauvage, barbare
N sauvage mf
VT **1** *(attack physically) (of animal)* attaquer sauvagement **2** *(criticize) (person, play)* éreinter; *(proposal, plan)* critiquer violemment

savagely [ˈsævɪdʒlɪ] ADV *(to beat, attack)* sauvagement, férocement; *(to criticize)* violemment

savageness [ˈsævɪdʒnɪs], **savagery** [ˈsævɪdʒ(ə)rɪ] N *(fierceness) (of animal, blow, attack, criticism)* férocité f

savanna(h) [səˈvænə] N savane f

SAVE [seɪv]

VT	sauver **1** ▪ garder **2** ▪ mettre de côté **2** ▪ économiser **2, 3** ▪ sauvegarder **5**
VI	économiser, épargner
N	arrêt
PREP	sauf, à l'exception de

VT **1** *(rescue) (person, animal)* sauver; **to s. sb's life** sauver la vie à ou de qn; *Fig* **she can't run to s. her life** elle est incapable de courir; *Fig* **to s. one's (own) neck** or **skin** sauver sa peau; **the doctors could not s. him** les médecins n'ont pas pu le sauver; **to s. sb from falling** empêcher qn de tomber; **this saved us from financial disaster** ça nous a sauvé d'une catastrophe financière; *Ftbl etc* **to s. a goal** arrêter le ballon; *Sport* **to s. the game** sauver le match; **to s. the situation** sauver la situation; *Rel* **to s. one's soul** sauver son âme; **to s. sth from a fire** récupérer qch des décombres d'un incendie; **God s. the King/the Queen!** vive le Roi/la Reine!
2 *(keep for future) (old jars, old wrapping paper etc)* garder, mettre de côté; *(money)* économiser, épargner, mettre de côté; *(collect) (stamps, cigarette coupons, petrol vouchers etc)* collectionner; **I s. £100 a month in a special account** j'économise 100 livres par mois sur un compte spécial; **how much money have you got saved?** combien d'argent avez-vous mis de côté?; **I'm saving this one for later** je garde celui-ci pour plus tard; **to s. oneself for sth** se réserver pour qch; **s. a dance for me** réservez-moi une danse
3 *(not waste) (money, work etc)* économiser; *(expenditure, effort)* éviter; *(space)* gagner; **to s. time** gagner du temps, économiser du temps; **I am saving my strength** je me ménage, je ménage mes forces; **I might as well have saved my breath** j'aurais mieux fait d'économiser ma salive; **I saved £10 by buying it there** j'ai économisé dix livres en l'achetant là; **s. pounds on washing machines** faites des économies sur l'achat d'une machine à laver
4 *(spare)* **to s. sb sth** éviter ou épargner qch à qn; **this has saved him a great deal of expense/trouble** cela lui a évité ou épargné beaucoup de dépense/peine; **this will s. us having to do it again** ça nous évitera de devoir le refaire; **to s. sb the trouble of doing sth** éviter ou épargner à qn la peine de faire qch; **to s. sb from sth** épargner à qn; **to s. sb from doing sth** épargner à qn la peine de faire qch
5 *Comput* sauvegarder; **to s. sth to disk** sauvegarder qch sur disquette
VI *(save money)* économiser, épargner; **I've never been able to s.** je n'ai jamais pu éco-

nomiser ou épargner; **they are saving for their holiday/a new car** ils économisent pour leurs vacances/pour acheter une voiture neuve; **s. on heating costs by insulating your house** économisez sur vos frais de chauffage en isolant votre maison
N *Ftbl* arrêt m; **to make a s.** arrêter la balle
PREP *Arch, Lit* sauf, excepté, à l'exception de
CONJ *Arch, Lit* **s. that ...** sauf que ..., excepté que ...
▸▸ *Comput* **s. command** commande f de sauvegarde
▸ **save up** VI *(save money)* économiser, faire des économies **(for** pour**); we're saving up to go to Canada/buy a fridge** nous économisons pour aller au Canada/pour acheter un réfrigérateur
VT SEP *(keep for future) (money etc)* économiser, mettre de côté; *(collect) (stamps, petrol vouchers etc)* collectionner

save-as-you-earn ADJ
▸▸ *Br Fin* **s. scheme** = plan m d'épargne à contributions mensuelles produisant des intérêts exonérés d'impôts

saveloy [ˈsævəlɔɪ] N *Culin* cervelas m

saver [ˈseɪvər] N *(person who saves money)* épargnant, -ante

saving [ˈseɪvɪŋ] ADJ *(redeeming)* **her/its s. grace** ce qui la/le rachète
N **1** *(rescue) (of lives etc)* sauvetage m; *(of person, souls)* salut m; **this was the s. of him** cela a été son salut **2** *(act of saving money)* économie f, épargne f, **we made a s. of £500 on the usual price** nous avons fait une économie de 500 livres sur le prix habituel; **savings** économies; *Econ* dépôts mpl d'épargne; **to live on one's savings** vivre de ses économies; **to make savings** faire des économies **3** *Comput* sauvegarde f
CONJ *Arch, Lit* = **save** CONJ
PREP *Arch, Lit* sauf; **s. your presence** sauf votre respect
▸▸ **savings account** compte m d'épargne; **Savings Bank** ≃ Caisse f (nationale) d'épargne; **savings certificate** ≃ bon m d'épargne; **savings club** club m d'épargne; *Am* **savings and loan association** caisse d'épargne-logement; **savings plan** plan m d'épargne; *Econ* **savings ratio** taux m d'épargne; *Fin* **savings scheme** plan d'épargne

saviour, *Am* **savior** [ˈseɪvjər] N sauveur m; *Rel* **Our S.** Notre Sauveur

savory [ˈseɪvərɪ] N *Bot, Culin* sarriette f

savour, *Am* **savor** [ˈseɪvər] N saveur f, goût m
VT *(success, moment etc)* savourer
VI *(of thing)* **to s. of sth** sentir qch; **the whole affair savours of corruption** tout cela sent la corruption

savoury, *Am* **savory** [ˈseɪvərɪ] ADJ **1** *(appetizing) (taste, dish)* savoureux, appétissant; **he looked even less s. than the other tramps** il avait l'air encore plus repoussant que les autres clochards; **he doesn't have a very s. reputation** il a une sale réputation **2** *Culin (not sweet)* salé
N *Culin (hors d'œuvre)* hors-d'œuvre m inv (chaud ou froid); *(course)* entremets m salé

Savoy [səˈvɔɪ] N **1** *Geog* Savoie f **2** *(cabbage)* chou m frisé de Milan
▸▸ **s. cabbage** chou frisé de Milan

savvy [ˈsævɪ] *Sl* N *(common sense)* jugeote f
VT piger; **s.?** tu piges?

saw [sɔː] **1** *(tool)* scie f, **metal s.** scie à métaux; **circular s.** scie circulaire
VT *(pt* **sawed** [sɔːd]; *pp* **sawn** [sɔːn], **sawed)** scier
▸▸ **s. blade** lame f de scie; **s. tooth** dent f de scie
▸ **saw off** VT SEP couper ou enlever à la scie
▸ **saw up** VT SEP *(wood)* débiter

saw² N *Lit (saying)* adage *m*, dicton *m*

saw³ PT*see* see¹

sawbones ['sɔːbəʊnz] N *Old-fashioned Fam* chirurgien *m*

sawbuck ['sɔːbʌk] N *Am* **1** = **sawhorse 2** *Fam (ten-dollar bill)* billet *m* de dix dollars

sawdust ['sɔːdʌst] N sciure *f* (de bois)

sawfish ['sɔːfɪʃ] N poisson-scie *m*, *pl* poissons-scies

sawhorse ['sɔːhɔːs] N *Carp* chevalet *m* de sciage, chèvre *f*

sawing ['sɔːɪŋ] N *(of wood)* sciage *m*
▸▸ **s. up** *(of wood)* débitage *m*

sawmill ['sɔːmɪl] N scierie *f*

sawn-off shotgun N carabine *f* à canon scié

sawyer ['sɔːjər] N scieur *m* (de long)

sax [sæks] N *Mus Fam* saxo *m*
▸▸ **s. player** saxophoniste *mf*

saxifrage ['sæksɪfreɪdʒ] N *(plant)* saxifrage *f*

Saxon ['sæks(ə)n] ADJ saxon
N **1** Saxon, -onne **2** *Ling* saxon *m*

Saxony ['sæksənɪ] N Saxe *f*

saxophone ['sæksəfəʊn] N *Mus* saxophone *m*

saxophonist [sæk'sɒfənɪst] N *Mus* saxophoniste *mf*

SAY [seɪ]

VT dire **1**, **2** ▪ indiquer **1** ▪ penser **1**
VI dire

VT *(pt, pp* said [sed]; *3rd sing pr* says [sez]) **1** *(utter)* dire; **to s. sth to sb** dire qch à qn; **to s. sth again** répéter qch, redire qch; **to s. hello/goodbye (to sb)** dire bonjour/au revoir (à qn); **s. hello to her from me** dis-lui bonjour de ma part; **to s. goodbye to one's chances of winning** dire adieu à ses chances de gagner; **to s. yes/no to an offer** accepter/refuser une offre; *Fam* **I wouldn't s. no to a glass of beer** je boirais bien *ou* volontiers un verre de bière; **to s. a word** dire un mot; **you have only to s. the word** vous n'avez qu'un mot à dire; **I didn't s. a word** je n'ai pas dit un mot; **it's for him/not for him to s.** c'est/ce n'est pas à lui de décider; *Tel* **who shall I s. is calling?** c'est de la part de qui?; **why he did it I can't** *ou* **couldn't s.** *(I have no idea)* je ne sais pas pourquoi il l'a fait; **I can't s.** *(I'm not allowed to tell you)* je ne peux pas le dire; **there's no saying what might happen if …** on ne sait pas ce qui pourrait se passer si …; **it goes without saying that …** il va de soi *ou* cela va sans dire que …; **what did you s.?** *(repeat what you said)* pardon?, qu'avez-vous dit?; **whatever he may s.** quoi qu'il en dise; **what do you s. to a drink?** ça te dit de prendre un verre?; **'good morning',** **she said** 'bonjour', dit-elle; **he said that you were here** il a dit que vous étiez ici; **as I said in my letter** comme je l'ai dit dans ma lettre; **the Bible says** *or* **it says in the Bible that …** comme il est écrit dans la Bible …; **it says in the newspaper that …** on dit dans le journal que …; **the church clock says ten** le cadran de l'église marque dix heures; **what does your watch s.?** quelle heure est-il à ta montre?; **the sign said ten more kilometres** la pancarte indiquait qu'il restait dix kilomètres; **let it be said** soit dit en passant; **you don't mean to s. he's 86** vous n'allez pas me dire qu'il a 86 ans; **one might as well s. …** autant dire …; **I must s. that …** j'avoue que …, je dois dire que …; **it has to** *or* **must be said** il faut le dire; **that is to s.** c'est-à-dire; **have you said anything about it to him?** est-ce que vous lui en avez parlé?; **the less said the better** moins nous parlerons, mieux cela vaudra; **to s. nothing of …** et je

ne parle pas de …; **getting there will be difficult enough, to s. nothing of getting home again** se rendre là-bas va déjà être assez difficile, alors je ne parle pas de revenir ici; **he has very little to s. for himself** il est peu communicatif; **what have you got to s. for yourself?** eh bien, expliquez-vous!; **there's a lot to be said for it** c'est une bonne idée; **there is little/much to be said for beginning now** on n'a pas/on a intérêt à commencer dès maintenant; **you're honest, I'll s. that for you** je dirais en votre faveur que vous êtes honnête; **the way you dress says something about you as a person** la manière dont les gens s'habillent est révélatrice de leur personnalité; **his response says a lot about …** sa réponse en dit long sur …; **don't s. you've forgotten already!** ne (me) dis pas que tu as déjà oublié!; *Fam* **you don't s. (so)!** pas possible!, ça alors!; **you can s. that again!**, vous l'avez dit!, comme vous dites!; **need I s. more?** est-il besoin d'en dire davantage?; **they s. that …, it is said that …** on dit que …, on prétend que …; **I've heard it said that …** j'ai entendu dire que …; **he is said to be rich, they s. he is rich** on le dit riche, on dit qu'il est riche; **what do you s., Amanda, should we go?** qu'en penses-tu Amanda, on y va?; **what do you s. to that?** qu'en dites-vous *ou* pensez-vous?; **is he stupid? – I wouldn't s. that** est-ce qu'il est bête? – je n'irais pas jusque-là; **on the whole, I should s. not** dans l'ensemble, je ne crois pas *ou* je crois que non; **it is difficult to s. (when/where/which)** il est difficile de dire (quand/où/quel); **didn't I s. so!** je vous l'avais bien dit!; **I should s. so!** et comment donc!; **what did I s.?** *(I was right)* qu'est-ce que j'avais dit?; **let us** *or* **shall we** *or* **shall I s. disons;** **if I had, s., £100,000 to spend** si j'avais, mettons *ou* disons, £100,000 livres à dépenser; **other countries such as Germany, s., or France** d'autres pays comme, par exemple, l'Allemagne ou la France; **she didn't accept their offer – I should s. not!** elle n'a pas accepté leur offre – il ne manquerait plus que ça! ~~VOIR GRAMMAIRE A78~~

2 *(recite) (prayer etc)* dire; **to s. one's prayers** dire *ou* faire ses prières; **to s. Mass** dire la messe

VI I'm not saying je ne dis rien; *Fam* **says you!** que tu dis!; **I mean to s.!** tout de même!, quand même!; **as they s., as people s.** comme on dit; **as one might s.** comme qui dirait; *Fam* **s., I've got an idea** dites donc, j'ai une idée; *Br Old-fashioned* **I s.!**, *Am* **s.!** *(exclamatory)* dites donc!; *Br Old-fashioned* **I s.!** *(expressing surprise)* pas possible!, fichtre!; **I'll s.!** et comment donc!

N **to have one's s.** dire ce qu'on a à dire; **to have a s. in a discussion** avoir son mot à dire dans un débat; **let me have my s.** laissez-moi parler; **I have no s. in the matter** je n'ai pas voix au chapitre

SAYE [eseɪwaɪˈiː] N *Br Fin (abbr* **save as you earn**) = plan *m* d'épargne à contributions mensuelles produisant des intérêts exonérés d'impôts

saying ['seɪɪŋ] N proverbe *m*, dicton *m*; **as the s. goes** *(according to the proverb)* comme dit le proverbe

say-so N *Fam (permission)* permission *f*; **I can't do it without her s.** je ne peux pas le faire sans sa permission; **on sb's s.** avec la permission de qn

S-bend N *Br* double virage *m*, virage en S

SBU [esbiːˈjuː] N *(abbr* **strategic business unit**) DAS *m*

SC [esˈsiː] *(abbr* **South Carolina**) Caroline *f* du Sud

scab [skæb] N **1** *(on wound)* croûte *f* **2** *Vet (disease)* gale *f* **3** *Ind Sl (person)* jaune *mf*, bri-

seur, -euse de grève; **s. miner** mineur *m* qui ne fait pas grève

VI *(-bb-)* **1** *(of wound)* former une croûte **2** *Ind Sl (replace strikers)* remplacer les grévistes; *(betray workmates)* trahir ses camarades
▸▸ **s. labour** des briseurs de grève
▸ **scab over** VI = **scab** VI **1**

scabbard ['skæbəd] N *(for sword)* fourreau *m*; *(for dagger)* gaine *f*

scabby ['skæbɪ] ADJ **1** *Vet (sheep etc)* galeux **2** *(sore etc)* croûteux, scabieux **3** *Fam (contemptible) (behaviour etc)* dégoûtant **4** *Fam (grotty) (coat, room etc)* pouilleux **5** *Br Fam (worthless)* merdique; **you can keep your s. car!** tu peux te la garder, ta caisse de merde!

scabies ['skeɪbiːz] N *Med* gale *f*

scabious ['skeɪbɪəs] N *(plant)* scabieuse *f*

scabrous ['skeɪbrəs] ADJ **1** *(surface etc)* rugueux, raboteux **2** *(topic, tale etc)* scabreux, risqué

scads [skædz] NPL *Am Fam* des tas (**of** de)

scaffold ['skæf(ə)ld] N **1** *(for execution)* échafaud *m*; **to go to the s.** monter à *ou* sur l'échafaud **2** *Constr* échafaudage *m*

scaffolding ['skæfəldɪŋ] N échafaudage *m*

scag [skæg] N *Sl* **1** *(heroin)* héro *f*, blanche *f* **2** *Am (ugly woman)* boudin *m*, cageot *m*

scalable font ['skeɪləb(ə)l] N *Typ* police *f* de taille variable

scalawag ['skæləwæg] N *esp Am Fam* = **scallywag**

scald [skɔːld] VT **1** *(burn) (hand etc)* ébouillanter; **to s. oneself** s'ébouillanter **2** *Culin (fruit, vegetables)* échauder, ébouillanter; *(milk etc)* faire chauffer sans bouillir; *(pot, container)* échauder, ébouillanter
N *(on hand etc)* brûlure *f*

scalding ['skɔːldɪŋ] ADJ **a s. hot day** une journée torride; *Lit* **s. tears** larmes brûlantes; **s. (hot)** *(liquid)* brûlant
N *(burning)* brûlure *f*; **the boiling water caused s. on her arms and face** elle s'est ébouillanté les bras et le visage

scale¹ [skeɪl] N **1** *(on fish, reptile etc)* écaille *f*; *Med (on skin)* squame *f* **2** *Metal* **scale(s)** écailles *fpl* de fer **3** *(incrustation) (in pipes, kettle etc)* tartre *m*, incrustation *f*; *(on teeth)* tartre; **boiler s.** tartre
VT *(fish)* écailler; *(teeth)* détartrer; *(boiler, pipe)* désincruster, détartrer
VI *(of skin)* (se) desquamer; *(of paint etc)* s'écailler
▸▸ **s. remover** *(for teeth)* détartrant *m*

scale² N *(for weighing)* balance *f*; *(for letters)* pèse-lettres *m inv*; *(in bathroom etc)* pèse-personne *m*, *pl* pèse-personnes; *(for baby)* pèse-bébé *m*, *pl* pèse-bébés; *(pan)* plateau *m* (de balance); *(deep)* bassin *m*; **pair of scales** balance à plateaux; **to tip the scales at 100 kilos** peser 100 kilos; *Fig* **to tip the scales** faire pencher la balance; **platform scales** bascule *f*; **letter scales** pèse-lettres; **bathroom scales** pèse-personne; **baby scales** pèse-bébé
▸▸ **s. pan** plateau (de balance); *(deep)* bassin

scale³ N **1** *(grading system)* échelle *f*; *(of thermometer)* échelle (graduée), graduations *fpl*; **sliding s.** *(of salaries, prices)* échelle mobile; **sliding s. tariff** tarif *m* dégressif; **at the top of the (social) s.** en haut *ou* au sommet de l'échelle (sociale); **to judge sth on a s. of one to ten** noter qch sur dix **2** *(size) (of map, drawing etc)* échelle *f*; **small-/large-scale map** carte *f* à petite/à grande échelle; **to draw sth to s.** dessiner qch à l'échelle; **to be in/out of s.** être/ne pas être à l'échelle; **on a national s.** à l'échelle nationale; **the s. of a problem/crisis/disaster/project** l'ampleur *ou* l'importance d'un problème/d'une crise/d'un sinistre/d'un projet

3 *Mus* gamme *f*; **major/minor s.** gamme majeure/mineure; **to practise one's scales** faire des gammes

VT 1 *(climb) (wall etc)* escalader; *(mountain, cliff)* escalader, faire l'ascension de **2** *Typ (font)* ajuster la taille de

▸▸ **s. drawing** dessin *m* à l'échelle; **s. model** *(of car, plane)* modèle *m* réduit; *(of building, town centre)* maquette *f*

▸ **scale down VT SEP 1** *(draw to smaller scale)* réduire l'échelle de; *Typ (font)* réduire (la taille de) **2** *(prices, demands etc)* réduire; *(expectations)* calmer; **to s. down production** ralentir la production

▸ **scale up VT SEP** *(prices, demands etc)* augmenter; *Typ (font)* agrandir

scales [skeɪlz] **NPL** *see* **scale²**

scaling¹ [ˈskeɪlɪŋ] **N 1** *(action) (of teeth)* détartrage *m*; *(of boiler, pipes)* détartrage, désincrustation *f* **2** *(deposit inside pipe, boiler, kettle etc)* tartre *m*, calcaire *m*; *(process of incrustation)* formation *f* du tartre, entartrage *m*

scaling² **N 1** *(climbing)* escalade *f* **2** *(grading) (of prices, salaries etc)* graduation *f*; *Typ (of font)* ajustement *m* de la taille

▸▸ **s. down** réduction *f*, diminution *f*; *(proportionately)* réduction proportionnelle; **s. up** augmentation *f*

scallion [ˈskæljən] **N** *Bot* échalote *f*

scallop [ˈskɒləp, ˈskæl-] **N 1** *(mollusc)*, *Culin* coquille *f* Saint-Jacques; *Culin (of veal etc)* escalope *f* **2** *Sewing etc* feston *m*
VT 1 *Culin (fish etc)* faire cuire en coquille(s) **2** *Sewing* festonner; **a scalloped handkerchief** un mouchoir festonné

scally [ˈskælɪ] **N** *Br Fam* arnaqueur, -euse

scallywag [ˈskælɪwæg] **N 1** *Fam* chenapan *m*; **little s.** *(child)* petit(e) coquin, -ine **2** *Hist* = partisan *m* des républicains après la guerre de Sécession

scalp [skælp] **N** *Anat* cuir *m* chevelu; *(war trophy)* scalp *m*
VT 1 *(in war)* scalper; *Hum (of hairdresser)* ratiboiser **2** *esp Am Fam (tickets)* revendre au noir

scalpel [ˈskælp(ə)l] **N** *Surg* scalpel *m*

scalper [ˈskælpər] **N 1** *St Exch Sl* spéculateur, -trice sur variation minimale **2** *esp Am Fam (ticket tout)* = revendeur, -euse de billets au marché noir

scaly [ˈskeɪlɪ] **ADJ** *(fish)* écailleux; *(skin)* squameux

scam [skæm] *Fam* **N** arnaque *f*
VT arnaquer

scammer [ˈskæmər] **N** *Fam* arnaqueur, -euse

scamp [skæmp] **N** fripouille *f*; *Fam* **little s.** *(child)* petit(e) coquin, -ine

scamper [ˈskæmpər] **VI** *(run playfully)* gambader; **it scampered up the tree** il a grimpé à l'arbre en un clin d'œil; **they all scampered across the bridge** ils ont traversé le pont à toute vitesse; *Fig* **the programme scampered through the 18th century in ten minutes** l'émission a survolé le XVIIIe siècle en dix minutes
N *(playful run)* course *f* folâtre *ou* allègre; *(quick run)* course rapide

▸ **scamper away, scamper off VI** *(of mice)* filer; *(of animals)* détaler; *(of person)* décamper

scampi [ˈskæmpɪ] **N** *Culin* scampi *mpl*

scan [skæn] **N 1** *(look)* regard *m* appuyé; **after a quick s. around the room, they left** ils examinèrent rapidement la pièce et s'en allèrent **2** *Electron, Radio etc* balayage *m*; *Comput* lecture *f* au scanne(u)r **3** *Med* examen *m* au scanne(u)r; *(in pregnancy)* écho-

graphie *f*; **to have a s.** se faire faire un examen au scanne(u)r; *(in pregnancy)* se faire faire une échographie
VT **(-nn-) 1** *(in prosody) (verse)* scander **2** *(examine closely)* scruter, examiner minutieusement; *(the horizon)* scruter **3** *(glance at, over)* jeter un coup d'œil sur; *(book etc)* feuilleter, parcourir **4** *Electron, Radio etc (image, soundtrack)* balayer; *Med* examiner au scanne(u)r; *(in pregnancy)* faire une échographie à; *Comput (text, graphics)* passer *ou* lire au scanne(u)r, scanner; **scanned input** entrée *f* (à partir du) scanne(u)r
VI *(in prosody)* **this line doesn't s.** ce vers est faux

▸ **scan in VT SEP** *Comput (graphics)* insérer par scanne(u)r, capturer au scanne(u)r

scandal [ˈskænd(ə)l] **N 1** *(outrage)* scandale *m*; **it's a s.** c'est un scandale; **to create** *or* **cause a s.** causer un scandale **2** *(gossip)* médisance *f*

▸▸ *Fam* **s. sheet** journal *m* à scandale

scandalize [ˈskændəlaɪz] **VT** scandaliser, choquer

scandalmonger [ˈskænd(ə)lmʌŋgər] **N** colporteur, -euse d'histoires scandaleuses

scandalmongering [ˈskænd(ə)lmʌŋgərɪŋ] **N** **it's just s.** c'est fait exprès pour faire du scandale; **to put a stop to this s.** mettre un terme à tous ces racontars
ADJ *(journalist etc)* qui cherche le scandale

scandalous [ˈskændələs] **ADJ** *(conduct, event, prices etc)* scandaleux

scandalously [ˈskændələslɪ] **ADV** scandaleusement

Scandinavia [skændɪˈneɪvɪə] **N** Scandinavie *f*

Scandinavian [skændɪˈneɪvɪən] **ADJ** scandinave
N Scandinave *mf*

scanner [ˈskænər] **N** *Med, Comput* scanne(u)r *m*; **radar s.** explorateur *m ou* balayeur *m* radar; *(radar aerial)* antenne *f* (de) radar

scanning [ˈskænɪŋ] **N 1** *(in prosody) (of verse)* scansion *f* **2** *(close examination)* examen *m* minutieux; *Electron, Radio etc (of image, soundtrack)* balayage *m*; *Comput* passage *m* au scanne(u)r, scannérisation *f*; **radar s.** exploration *f ou* balayage radar

scansion [ˈskænʃən] **N** *(in prosody)* scansion *f*

scant [skænt] **ADJ ATTRIB** insuffisant, peu abondant; **they paid s. regard to what he said** ils ont à peine fait attention à ce qu'il disait

scantily [ˈskæntɪlɪ] **ADV** peu abondamment; *(insufficiently)* insuffisamment; **s. dressed** *or* **clad** très peu vêtu; **she came to the party rather s. clad** elle est venue à la soirée dans une tenue des plus légères

scantiness [ˈskæntɪnɪs] **N** *(of supplies etc)* insuffisance *f*; *(of vegetation)* rareté *f*, pauvreté *f*

scants [skænts] **NPL** *Br Fam (men's)* calcif *m*; *(women's)* petite culotte *f*

scanty [ˈskæntɪ] **ADJ** *(supply etc)* peu abondant; *(insufficient)* insuffisant, à peine suffisant; **a s. meal** un maigre repas; **a s. little dress** une robe qui ne cache pas grand-chose

scapegoat [ˈskeɪpgəʊt] **N** *(who takes the blame)* bouc *m* émissaire; *(on whom frustrations are taken out)* souffre-douleur *m inv*

scapegrace [ˈskeɪpgreɪs] **N** *Old-fashioned (good-for-nothing)* vaurien, -ienne, bon *m*/ bonne *f* à rien

scapula, *pl* **scapulae** [ˈskæpjʊlə, -iː] **N** *Anat* omoplate *f*

scapular [ˈskæpjʊlər] **ADJ** *Anat etc* scapulaire

scar¹ [skɑːr] **N** *(mark of wound)* cicatrice *f*; *(on face, caused by knife etc)* balafre *f*; **the scars that the old mine workings have left on the hills** les cicatrices laissées sur les collines par les anciennes mines; **he carried the (mental) scars for the rest of his life** il est resté marqué à vie
VT **(-rr-)** *(leg, face etc)* marquer d'une cicatrice; *(face) (with knife etc)* balafrer; **to be scarred** porter *ou* avoir des cicatrices; *Fig* **to be scarred for life** *(by experience etc)* être marqué à vie; **war-scarred** *(of country etc)* dévasté par la guerre
VI *(of wound)* faire une cicatrice

▸▸ **s. tissue** tissu *m* cicatriciel

▸ **scar over VI** cicatriser

scar² **N** *(in mountain range etc)* rocher *m* escarpé

scarab [ˈskærəb] **N** *(precious stone)*, *Entom* scarabée *m*

scarce [skeəs] **ADJ** *(animal, water, edition, substance, news etc)* rare; *(commodities)* rare, peu abondant; *Fam* **to make oneself s.** s'éclipser, s'esquiver
ADV *Arch, Lit* = **scarcely**

scarcely [ˈskeəslɪ] **ADV** à peine, *Fml* guère; **I have s. any left** il ne m'en reste presque plus, *Fml* il ne m'en reste guère; **she could s. speak** c'est à peine si elle pouvait parler, elle pouvait à peine parler; **s. ever** presque jamais; **he had s. come in** *or* **s. had he come in when the telephone rang** à peine était-il rentré que le téléphone sonna; **she was s. 21 years old** elle avait à peine 21 ans; **it is s. likely that ...** il est peu vraisemblable que ...; **they would s. destroy their own home, would they?** ils n'iraient pas jusqu'à détruire leur propre maison! VOIR GRAMMAIRE A78

scarcity [ˈskeəsɪtɪ], **scarceness** [ˈskeəsnɪs] **N** *(rarity)* rareté *f*; *(lack)* manque *m*, disette *f*; **to have s. value** être précieux parce que rare; **because of their s. value** parce qu'ils sont rares

scare [skeər] **N** panique *f*; *Fam* **you gave me an awful s.** vous m'avez fait une drôle de peur; **a bomb s.** une alerte à la bombe; **a s. over poisoned food** une panique à propos de nourriture empoisonnée
VT *(alarm)* effrayer, alarmer; *(frighten)* faire peur à, effrayer; **they scared him into leaving** *(intentionally)* ils lui ont fait peur jusqu'à ce qu'il parte; *(unintentionally)* ils lui ont fait peur au point qu'il est parti; **the high costs scared them off the idea** les coûts élevés leur en ont fait abandonner l'idée; *Fam* **to s. the pants off sb** faire une peur bleue à qn
VI s'effrayer, s'alarmer; **I don't s. easily** je ne m'effraie pas facilement *ou* pour rien

▸ **scare away, scare off VT SEP** *(frighten) (person)* faire fuir; *(birds, deer etc)* effaroucher; *(discourage, put off)* faire fuir, effrayer

scarecrow [ˈskeəkrəʊ] **N** *Agr, Fig* épouvantail *m*; **to be dressed like a s.** être habillé à faire peur

scared [skeəd] **ADJ** *(look)* apeuré, effrayé; **to be s. of sb/sth** avoir peur de qn/qch; **I'm not s. of you** tu ne me fais pas peur, je n'ai pas peur de toi; **he's s. of his own shadow** il a peur de son ombre; **to be s. to death** *or* **out of one's wits**, *Fam* **to be s. stiff** avoir une peur bleue (**of** de)

scaredy-cat [ˈskeədɪ-] **N** *Fam (in children's language)* froussard, -arde

scaremonger [ˈskeəmʌŋgər] **N** alarmiste *mf*

scaremongering [ˈskeəmʌŋgərɪŋ] **N** alarmisme *m*

scarf, *pl* **scarfs, scarves** [skɑːf(s), skɑːvz] **N** écharpe *f*; *(of silk)* foulard *m*; **football s.** écharpe aux couleurs d'une équipe de football

VT 1 *Constr (join)* joindre par enture; *(cut)* entailler **2** *Am Fam (eat)* bouffer, boulotter

scarface ['skɑ:feɪs] N balafré, -ée

scarification [skærɪfɪ'keɪʃən] N *Agr, Med* scarification *f*

scarify ['skærɪfaɪ] VT **1** *(skin, ground)* scarifier **2** *Fam* = **scare VT**

scarily ['skeərɪlɪ] ADV à faire peur; **we came s. close to being killed** on est passé à deux doigts de la mort

scarlatina [skɑ:lə'ti:nə] N *Med* scarlatine *f*

scarlet ['skɑ:lɪt] ADJ écarlate; **to blush** *or* **go** *or* **turn s.** devenir cramoisi *ou* écarlate N écarlate *m*
▸▸ *Med* **s. fever** scarlatine *f*; *Cathol* **s. hat** chapeau *m* de cardinal; *Bot* **s. pimpernel** mouron *m* rouge; *Br Bot* **s. runner** haricot *m* (à rames); *Br Hum* **s. woman** femme *f* de mauvaise vie

scarp [skɑ:p] N **1** *Geog (of hill)* escarpement *m* **2** *Mil (in fortifications)* escarpe *f*

scarper ['skɑ:pər] VI *Br Fam* se tirer, déguerpir

SCART [skɑ:t] N *(abbr* **Syndicat des Constructeurs d'Appareils Radiorécepteurs et Téléviseurs)**
▸▸ **S. cable** câble *m* péritel®; **S. plug** prise *f* péritel®

scary ['skeərɪ] ADJ *Fam (frightening)* effrayant, qui fait peur; **it's s. here** ça fiche la frousse ici

scat [skæt] INT *Fam* filez!, fichez le camp!

scathing ['skeɪðɪŋ] ADJ *(remark, sarcasm etc)* acerbe, mordant, cinglant; **she was s. about security arrangements** elle a fait des remarques acerbes au sujet des mesures de sécurité

scathingly ['skeɪðɪŋlɪ] ADV d'une manière acerbe; *(to remark)* d'un ton cinglant *ou* acerbe

scatological [skætə'lɒdʒɪk(ə)l] ADJ *(joke etc)* scatologique

scatology [skə'tɒlədʒɪ] N scatologie *f*

scatter ['skætər] VT *(army etc)* disperser; *(clouds etc)* dissiper; *(birds)* faire envoler; *(leaves, papers etc)* éparpiller; *(sow) (corn, seed)* semer à la volée; *Phys (of surface) (light)* diffuser
VI *(of crowd etc)* se disperser; *(of birds etc)* s'égailler; *(of army)* se débander; *(of clouds etc)* se dissiper; *(of shot)* s'éparpiller
N *(of shot etc)* éparpillement *m*, dispersion *f*, écartement *m*
▸▸ **s. cushion** petit coussin *m*; **s. rug** petit tapis *m*, carpette *f*; *(by bed)* descente *f* de lit

scatterbrain ['skætəbreɪn] N *Fam* étourdi, -ie, tête *f* de linotte

scatterbrained ['skætəbreɪnd] ADJ *Fam* étourdi, écervelé

scattered ['skætəd] ADJ dispersé, éparpillé, épars; *(light)* diffus; **s. over the floor** éparpillé sur le sol; **houses s. here and there on the plain** des maisons çà et là dans la plaine
▸▸ *Met* **s. showers** averses *fpl* éparses

scattering ['skætərɪŋ] N *(small number)* petit nombre *m*; *(small quantity)* petite quantité *f*; **there was a s. of snow on the mountains** il y avait de la neige çà et là sur les montagnes; **he only has a s. of followers** il n'a qu'un petit nombre de disciples

scattiness ['skætɪnɪs] N *Br Fam (absentmindedness)* étourderie *f*, *(craziness)* loufoquerie *f*

scatty ['skætɪ] ADJ *Br Fam (absent-minded)* étourdi, écervelé; *(crazy)* barjo, barge

scavenge ['skævɪndʒ] VI *(hunt)* fouiller; **to s. in the dustbins** fouiller *ou* faire les poubelles; **to s. for information/news** être à l'affût des informations/nouvelles

VT récupérer; *(in engine) (burnt gas)* balayer, refouler

scavenger ['skævɪndʒər] N **1** *(person, animal)* fouilleur, -euse d'ordures; *(animal living off dead prey)* animal *m* nécrophage; **he's a real s.** *(gets things from other people's rubbish)* c'est le roi de la récupération **2** *Arch (street cleaner)* éboueur *m*

scenario [sɪ'nɑ:rɪəʊ] N *Cin, Theat, Fig* scénario *m*

scene [si:n] N **1** *Theat, Cin (place of action)* scène *f*; *Fig (of event)* théâtre *m*, lieu *m*; *Theat* **change of s.** changement de décor *ou* de scène; *Fig* **a change of s. would do him good** un changement d'air *ou* de décor lui ferait du bien; *Theat* **the s. is set in London** l'action se passe à Londres; **to set the s.** planter le décor; *Fig* **her success set the s. for more women to enter music** son succès a permis à un plus grand nombre de femmes d'avoir une carrière musicale; **the political/sporting s.** la scène politique/sportive; **the modern poetry s. in Paris** la poésie moderne à Paris; **this athlete is a newcomer to the international s.** cet athlète est nouveau sur la scène sportive internationale; **to arrive** *or* **come on the s.** faire son apparition; *(of police)* arriver sur les lieux (du crime/de l'accident/*etc*); **to be first on the s.** être le premier sur les lieux; **the s. of the crime/accident** les lieux du crime/de l'accident; *Fam* **it's not my s.** ce n'est pas mon genre
2 *Theat (subdivision of play)* scène *f*, **s. two** scène deux
3 *Theat (scenery)* décor *m*; **scenes painted by ...** décors par ...; *also Fig* **behind the scenes** dans la *ou* les coulisse(s)
4 *Fig (episode)* scène *f*, spectacle *m*; **it was a touching s.** c'était une scène émouvante *ou* un spectacle émouvant; **I can just picture the s.** je vois d'ici la scène
5 *(sight)* vue *f*; **the s. from the window** la vue de la fenêtre; **a s. of devastation** un spectacle de désolation
6 *Fam (fuss)* **now don't make a s.!** ne fais pas une scène!
▸▸ *Theat* **s. change** changement de décor *ou* de scène; *Theat* **s. dock** case *f* à décor *ou* décors; *Theat* **s. painter** décorateur, -trice de théâtre

scene-of-crime officer N = agent *m* responsable de l'enquête sur le lieu du crime

scenery ['si:nərɪ] N **1** *Theat* décor(s) *m(pl)*; *Fig Fam* **you need a change of s.** vous avez besoin de changer d'air *ou* de décor **2** *(countryside)* paysage *m*; *(view)* vue *f*

scene-set N *TV etc* mise *f* en place

sceneshifter ['si:nʃɪftər] N *Theat* machiniste *mf*

scenic ['si:nɪk] ADJ **1** *(countryside)* pittoresque; *(route etc)* panoramique; **an area of great s.** une région qui offre de très beaux panoramas **2** *Theat* scénique
▸▸ *Theat* **s. cloth** rideau *m* de fond scénique; *Theat* **s. designer** décorateur, -trice de théâtre, scénographe *mf*; **s. railway** *(for tourists)* petit train *m* (touristique); *(in fairground)* montagnes *fpl* russes; **s. route** *(for tourists)* route *f* touristique, itinéraire *m* panoramique; *TV etc* **s. treatment** scénographie *f*; *Theat* **s. workshop** atelier *m* de décors

scent [sent] N **1** *(smell)* parfum *m*; *(of flowers)* odeur *f*, *Lit* senteur *f*
2 *(liquid)* parfum *m*
3 *(in hunting)* fumet *m*, vent *m*; **s. gland** *or* **organ** glande *f* à sécrétion odoriférante; **to pick up the s.** *(of hounds)* trouver la piste; **to be on the s.** être sur la piste (**of** de); **to lose** *or* **be thrown off the s.** perdre la trace *ou* la piste; **to throw the police off the s.** mettre la police en déroute, semer la police
4 *(sense of smell) (of dog)* odorat *m*, flair *m*

VT 1 *(of hounds etc)* **to s. game** flairer *ou* sentir le gibier; *Fig* **to s. dishonesty**/*etc* flairer la malhonnêteté/*etc*; **a keen-scented dog** un chien au nez *ou* à l'odorat fin **2** *(of flower etc) (the air)* parfumer, embaumer; **to s. sth with sth** *(with perfume etc)* parfumer *ou* imprégner qch de qch

scented ['sentɪd] ADJ *(soap etc)* parfumé

scentless ['sentlɪs] ADJ *(flower)* inodore, sans odeur

sceptic, *Am* **skeptic** ['skeptɪk] N sceptique *mf*

sceptical, *Am* **skeptical** ['skeptɪk(ə)l] ADJ sceptique

sceptically, *Am* **skeptically** ['skeptɪklɪ] ADV sceptiquement, avec incrédulité

scepticism, *Am* **skepticism** ['skeptɪsɪz(ə)m] N scepticisme *m*

sceptre, *Am* **scepter** ['septər] N sceptre *m*

schedule ['ʃedju:l, *Am* 'skedju:l] N **1** *(plan)* programme *m*; *(for work)* plan *m* (de travail), planning *m*; *Rail etc (timetable)* horaire *m*; **to be behind/ahead of s.** être en retard/en avance sur les prévisions; **we're on s. (for March)** nous sommes dans les délais (pour mars); **everything went off according to s.** tout a marché comme prévu; **I work to a very tight s.** mon emploi du temps est très chargé; **on s.** *(train, bus etc)* à l'heure
2 *Com (list) (of items)* nomenclature *f*, *(of machines)* inventaire *m*; *(of prices)* barème *m*; *Admin (of taxes)* cédule *f*
3 *Law (to law, articles of association etc)* annexe *f*
VT 1 *(make plan for)* programmer, inscrire au programme, faire le programme de; *(put in timetable) (train etc)* inscrire à l'horaire; **the mayor is scheduled to make a speech** le maire doit prononcer un discours; **it's scheduled for three o'clock** c'est prévu pour quinze heures
2 *Br (class)* **to s. as an ancient monument** classer (comme) monument historique
3 *Com (list) (item)* inscrire sur une liste
4 *Law (add as appendix)* ajouter en annexe

scheduled ['ʃedju:ld, *Am* 'skedju:ld] ADJ *(flight, services etc)* régulier; **to arrive at the s. time** arriver à l'heure prévue *ou* annoncée *ou* indiquée; *TV* **a change to our s. programme** un changement dans notre grille des programmes
▸▸ *Fin* **s. territories** zone *f* sterling

scheduler ['ʃedju:lər, *Am* 'skedju:lər] N *Comput (package)* logiciel *m* de planification (de projets)

scheduling ['ʃedju:lɪŋ, *Am* 'skedju:lɪŋ] N ordonnancement *m*; *TV, Radio* programmation *f*
▸▸ *TV, Radio* **s. director** directeur, -trice des programmes

schema, *pl* **schemata** ['ski:mə, -ətə] N *Fml* schéma *m*

schematic [skɪ'mætɪk] ADJ schématique

scheme [ski:m] N **1** *(arrangement)* arrangement *m*, combinaison *f*, *(system)* système *m*; **colour s.** combinaison de(s) couleurs; **I like the colour s. on this carpet** j'aime le mélange de couleurs de ce tapis; **where does mankind fit into the s. of things?** quelle est la place de l'humanité dans l'univers?; **where does it come in your s. of things?** quelle place cela a-t-il dans votre conception des choses?
2 *(plan)* plan *m*, projet *m*
3 *Pej (intrigue)* intrigue *f*, *Fam* magouille *f*; **the best laid schemes** les combinaisons *fpl* *ou Fam* les combines *fpl* les mieux étudiées
4 *esp Br* pension **s.** caisse *f* de retraite; **(housing) s.** cité *f*
VI intriguer, *Fam* magouiller
VT *(plot)* machiner, combiner; **to s. sb's downfall** comploter pour renverser qn

schemer ['ski:mər] N *Pej* intrigant, -ante

scheming ['ski:mɪŋ] ADJ intrigant
N intrigues *fpl*, machinations *fpl*

scherzo ['skeətsəʊ] N *Mus* scherzo *m*

schilling ['ʃɪlɪŋ] N *Formerly (Austrian currency)* schilling *m*

schism ['s(k)ɪz(ə)m] N schisme *m*

schismatic [s(k)ɪz'mætɪk] ADJ, N schismatique *mf*

schist [ʃɪst] N *Miner* schiste *m*; **mica s.** micaschiste *m*

schizo ['skɪtsəʊ] ADJ, N *Fam* schizo(phrène) *mf*

schizoid ['skɪtsɔɪd] ADJ, N *Psy* schizoïde *mf*

schizophrenia [skɪtsəʊ'fri:nɪə] N *Psy* schizophrénie *f*

schizophrenic [skɪtsəʊ'frenɪk] ADJ, N schizophrène *mf*, schizophrénique *mf*

schlemiel [ʃlə'mi:l] N *Am Fam* minable *mf*

schlep(p) [ʃlep] *esp Am Fam* N **1** *(person)* lourdaud, -aude **2** *(journey)* trotte *f*; **it's a bit of a s. to the supermarket** ça fait une trotte jusqu'au supermarché
VT *(carry, drag)* trimballer, transbahuter; **I've got to s. all this stuff over to the office** il faut que je trimballe *ou* transbahute tous ces trucs au bureau
VI faire un tour, traîner; **to s. home** rentrer chez soi à pinces; **I had to s. to the grocery store** il a fallu que je crapahute jusqu'à l'épicerie

schlock [ʃlɒk] N *Am Fam* **1** *(junk)* camelote *f*, saloperies *fpl* **2** *(lazy person)* flemmard, -arde
ADJ *(worthless)* qui ne vaut pas un clou, nul; **s. jewelry** bijoux *mpl* en toc

schlong [ʃlɒŋ] N *Am Sl (penis)* zob *m*

schlub [ʃlʌb] N *Am Fam* crétin, -ine, andouille *f*

schmal(t)z [ʃmɔ:lts] N *Fam* guimauve *f*

schmaltzy ['ʃmɔ:ltsɪ] ADJ *Fam (film, novel, music etc)* à l'eau de rose, à la guimauve

schmo [ʃməʊ] N *Am Fam (unlucky person)* guignard, -arde; *(stupid person)* nul *m*, *f* nulle

schmooze [ʃmu:z] VI *Fam (at party, function etc)* faire des mondanités

schmuck [ʃmʌk] N *Am Sl (fool)* andouille *f*

schnapps [ʃnæps] N schnaps *m*

schnitzel ['ʃnɪts(ə)l] N côtelette *f* de veau

schnook [ʃnʊk] N *Am Fam* poire *f*, pigeon *m*

schnozzle ['ʃnɒz(ə)l] N *Sl (nose)* naze *m*

scholar ['skɒlər] N **1** *(learned person)* savant, -ante, érudit, -ite; **I'm not much of a s.** je ne suis pas très savant; **Latin s.** latiniste *mf* **2** *Sch, Univ (winner of scholarship)* boursier, -ière **3** *Arch (pupil)* élève *mf*, écolier, -ière

scholarly ['skɒləlɪ] ADJ savant, érudit

scholarship ['skɒləʃɪp] N **1** *(learning)* savoir *m*, érudition *f* **2** *Sch, Univ (sum of money)* bourse *f* (d'études)

scholastic [skə'læstɪk] ADJ *(philosophy, theology)* scolastique; *Sch Fml (work, success etc)* scolaire
N *Phil, Rel* scolastique *m*

school¹ [sku:l] N **1** *(for children)* école *f*; *Admin* établissement *m* scolaire; *(from 11 to 15)* collège *m*; *(from 15 to 18)* lycée *m*; **to go to s.** aller en classe *ou* à l'école/au collège/au lycée; **which s. do you go to?** à quelle école/à quel collège/à quel lycée est-ce que tu vas?; **I went to** *or* **was at s. with her** je suis allé à l'école/au collège/au lycée avec elle; **I'm still at s.** je vais encore à l'école; **at s.** à l'école *ou* en classe/au collège/au lycée; **there is no s. tomorrow** il n'y a pas d'école *ou* il n'y a pas classe demain; **when does s.**

start? *(primary)* à quelle heure est-ce que la classe commence?; *(secondary)* à quelle heure est-ce que les cours commencent?; **nursery s.** (école) maternelle *f*; *Br* **primary** *or Am* **elementary s.** école primaire; *Admin* établissement d'enseignement primaire; *Br* **comprehensive s.** établissement d'enseignement secondaire polyvalent; **grammar s.** *Br* ≃ lycée, *Am* ≃ école primaire; **high s.** *(from 11 to 15)* collège; *(from 15 to 18)* lycée; **independent** *or* **private s.** école *ou* collège libre; **public s.** *Br* école privée, *Am* école publique; **state s.** école publique *ou* d'Etat, établissement public; *Br Formerly* **approved s.** centre *m* d'éducation surveillée; **Sunday s.** catéchisme *m*; **the whole s. knew it** toute l'école le savait; **the upper/lower s.** *(the pupils)* les grandes/petites classes; **of s. age** d'âge scolaire VOIR GRAMMAIRE A6–7

2 *(part of university)* département *m*, institut *m*; *Am (college, university)* faculté *f*, université *f*; *Am* **to be at s.** être à l'université; **s. of art, art s.** école *f* des beaux-arts; **s. of dancing** académie *f ou* école de danse; **fencing s.** académie *ou* salle d'escrime; *Br* **driving s., s. of motoring** auto-école *f*, *pl* auto-écoles; **summer s.** cours *m* de vacances, université d'été VOIR GRAMMAIRE A6–7

3 *Art, Phil etc (group)* école *f*, *(following a master)* disciples *mpl*; **the Flemish s.** l'école flamande; **the Platonic s.** l'école de Platon; *Fam* **to be brought up in the s. of hard knocks** être élevé à la dure; **she is one of the old s.** elle est de la vieille école
VT **1** *(educate) (person)* instruire, faire l'éducation de **2** *(train) (child, sb's mind)* former; *(horse)* dresser; **to s. oneself** se discipliner
▸▸ **s. attendance** *(going to school)* scolarisation *f*, *(not being absent)* présence *f* à l'école; **s. board** conseil *m* d'établissement; **s. book** livre *m* de classe, livre scolaire; **schools broadcasting** émissions *fpl* scolaires; **s. building** bâtiment *m* scolaire; **s. day** journée *f* scolaire *ou* d'école; **s. friend** camarade *mf* de classe *ou* d'école; **s. hours** heures *fpl* de classe *ou* d'école; **s. leaver** jeune *mf* qui a terminé ses études secondaires; **s. magazine** journal *m* de l'école; **schools programmes** programmes *mpl* éducatifs; **schools radio** radio *f* scolaire; **s. report** bulletin *m* scolaire; *Br* **s. run** conduites *fpl* (scolaires); **s. of thought** école *f* de pensée; **s. trip** voyage *m* scolaire; *Fig* théorie *f*; **s. uniform** uniforme *m* scolaire; **s. year** année *f* scolaire

school² N *(of fish)* banc *m*; *(of porpoises)* bande *f*

schoolboy ['sku:lbɔɪ] N écolier *m*; *(11 to 15)* collégien *m*; *(15 to 18)* lycéen *m*
▸▸ **s. slang** argot *m* scolaire

schoolchild, *pl* **schoolchildren** ['sku:ltʃaɪld, -tʃɪldrən] N écolier, -ière

schooldays ['sku:ldeɪz] N *(period of life)* vie *f* scolaire; **in my s.** quand j'étais à l'école

schoolfellow ['sku:lfeləʊ] N *Old-fashioned* camarade *mf* de classe *ou* d'école

schoolgirl ['sku:lgɜ:l] N écolière *f*; *(11 to 15)* collégienne *f*; *(15 to 18)* lycéenne *f*

schoolhouse ['sku:lhaʊs] N **1** *(school building)* école *f* **2** *(head's residence)* maison *f* du directeur/de la directrice *(faisant corps avec l'école)*

schooling ['sku:lɪŋ] N **1** *(education)* instruction *f*, éducation *f*, *(sending up to school)* scolarisation *f*; **he paid for his nephew's s.** il a subvenu aux frais d'études de son neveu; **compulsory s.** scolarisation obligatoire **2** *(of horse)* dressage *m*

schoolkid ['sku:lkɪd] N *Fam* écolier, -ière

school-leaving age N âge *m* de fin de scolarité

schoolma'am, **schoolmarm** ['sku:lmɑ:m]

N *Old-fashioned Fam* institutrice *f*; *still current in Fig* **she's a real s.** elle est tellement pédante

schoolmaster ['sku:lmɑ:stər] N *Old-fashioned (in primary school)* instituteur *m*, maître *m* (d'école); *(in secondary school)* professeur *m*

schoolmate ['sku:lmeɪt] N camarade *mf* de classe

schoolmistress ['sku:lmɪstrɪs] N *Old-fashioned (in primary school)* institutrice *f*, maîtresse *f* (d'école); *(in secondary school)* professeur *m*

schoolroom ['sku:lru:m] N salle *f* de classe

schoolteacher ['sku:lti:tʃər] N *(in primary school)* instituteur, -trice, maître *m*/maîtresse *f* (d'école); *(in secondary school)* professeur *m*

schoolteaching ['sku:lti:tʃɪŋ] N enseignement *m*

schooner¹ ['sku:nər] N *Naut* schooner *m*, goélette *f*

schooner² N *(sherry glass)* grand verre *m* à xérès; *Am (beer glass)* grand verre à bière

schtuk [ʃtʊk] N *Br Fam* **to be in s.** être dans le pétrin, être dans la panade

sciatic [saɪ'ætɪk] ADJ *Anat (nerve)* sciatique

sciatica [saɪ'ætɪkə] N *Med* sciatique *f*

science ['saɪəns] N science *f*; **pure/applied s.** science pure/sciences appliquées; **natural s.** sciences naturelles; **social s.** sciences sociales; **s. teacher** professeur *m* de sciences
▸▸ **s. fiction** science-fiction *f*, *pl* sciences-fictions; **s. park** parc *m* scientifique

scientific [saɪən'tɪfɪk] ADJ scientifique; **let's be s. about this** faisons preuve d'esprit scientifique; **s. research** recherche *f* scientifique

scientifically [saɪən'tɪfɪklɪ] ADV scientifiquement

scientist ['saɪəntɪst] N scientifique *mf*, savant, -ante

scientistic [saɪən'tɪstɪk] ADJ *Pej* prétendument scientifique

sci-fi ['saɪfaɪ] *Fam* N SF *f*
ADJ de SF

Scilly ['sɪlɪ] N **the S. Isles, the Scillies** les Sorlingues *fpl*

scimitar ['sɪmɪtər] N cimeterre *m*

scintillate ['sɪntɪleɪt] VI scintiller; **scintillating with wit** pétillant d'esprit

scintillating ['sɪntɪleɪtɪŋ] ADJ *(wit, conversation etc)* étincelant, pétillant; *(book, match etc)* brillant; *Iron* **it wasn't exactly s.** ce n'était pas particulièrement brillant

scintillation [sɪntɪ'leɪʃən] N *(of wit etc)* éclat *m*

scion ['saɪən] N **1** *(of plant)* scion *m*, greffon *m* **2** *Lit (of noble family etc) (descendant)* descendant *m*, rejeton *m*

scissor ['sɪzər] VT (dé)couper avec des ciseaux
▸▸ *Orn* **s. bill** bec-en-ciseaux *m*, *pl* becs-en-ciseaux

scissors ['sɪzəz] N **(pair of) s.** ciseaux *mpl*; **s.** *(in wrestling)*, *Gym etc* ciseaux; *(in high jump)* saut *m* en ciseaux; *Fig* **it's a s.-and-paste job** *(of book etc)* c'est du réchauffé VOIR GRAMMAIRE A11
▸▸ *Sport* **s. kick** ciseau *m*

sclerosis, *pl* **scleroses** [sklɪə'rəʊsɪs, -əʊsi:z] N *Med* sclérose *f*

scoff¹ [skɒf] VI *(mock)* se moquer; **to s. at** *(somebody)* railler, se moquer de; *(something)* se moquer de; **don't s.!** ne te moque pas!; **to s. at danger** faire fi du danger
N *(mocking)* **we had a good s. at his expense** nous nous sommes bien moqués de lui

scoff² *esp Br Fam* **vt** *(eat)* bouffer; **he scoffed the whole packet** il s'est enfilé tout le paquet
N *(food)* boustifaille *f*, bouffe *f*

scoffing ['skɒfɪŋ] **ADJ** *(mocking)* moqueur, -euse, railleur, -euse
N moquerie(s) *f(pl)*, raillerie(s) *f(pl)*

scold [skəʊld] **vi** gronder, criailler
vt gronder, réprimander; **to s. sb for doing sth** gronder qn d'avoir fait qch; **she scolded him for being late** elle l'a grondé à cause de son retard
N *Old-fashioned (woman)* mégère *f*

scolding ['skəʊldɪŋ] **ADJ** *(tone)* de réprimande
N *(reprimand)* gronderie(s) *f(pl)*, réprimande *f*, semonce *f*; **to give sb a good s.** sermonner qn, *Fam* remonter les bretelles à qn; **constant s.** des réprimandes continuelles

scoliosis [skɒlɪ'əʊsɪs] **N** *Med* scoliose *f*

scollop ['skɒləp] **N, vt** = **scallop**

sconce [skɒns] **N 1** *(with handle)* bougeoir *m*
2 *(on wall)* applique *f*

scone [skɒn, skəʊn] **N** *Culin* = sorte *f* de petit pain sucré que l'on consomme avec ou sans beurre

scooby ['sku:bɪ] **N** *Br Fam* **he hasn't got a s.** *(is incompetent)* il est vraiment nul; *(doesn't suspect)* il se doute de rien; *(doesn't know)* il en a pas la moindre idée

scoop [sku:p] **N 1** *(device) (for flour, rice etc)* pelle *f*, *(for ice-cream)* cuiller *f* à glace, portionneuse *f*, *(for mashed potato)* cuiller à faire des boules de purée; *Naut (bailer)* épuisette *f*, écope *f*, *(of dredger)* godet *m* **2** *(portion)* cuillerée *f*, **a s. of ice-cream/mashed potato**/*etc* une boule de glace/purée/*etc* **3** *Journ* scoop *m*, exclusivité *f*; **to make a s.** faire un scoop
vt 1 *(shovel) (water from a boat)* écoper; *(earth)* enlever; **to s. sth into sth** évider qch dans qch; **to s. ice-cream into a cone** mettre de la glace dans un cornet **2** *Journ* **to s. a story** avoir un scoop; **to s. the other papers** publier avant les autres journaux
▸▸ **s. neck** décolleté *m* rond; *Fishing* **s. net** drague *f*
▸ **scoop out vt sep** *(wood, tomato etc)* évider; **to s. the water out of a boat** écoper un bateau
▸ **scoop up vt sep** *(sand, coal, flour etc) (with hands)* prendre à pleines mains; *(with scoop) (sand, mud etc)* ramasser; *(water)* puiser; *(ice-cream, mashed potato)* faire des boules de; **she scooped up the last of her soup** elle finit son assiette d'un coup de cuillère; **he scooped up the book from the floor** il ramassa le livre qui était par terre; **the helicopter scooped him up** l'hélicoptère le repêcha; **she scooped the baby up (in her arms)** elle a saisi le bébé (dans ses bras)

scoot [sku:t] **vi** *Fam* **to s. (off** or **away)** filer, déguerpir; **he came scooting up to me** il se précipita sur moi; **it's time to s.!** allez, on se casse!

scooter ['sku:tər] **N** *(for child)* trottinette *f*, patinette *f*, **(motor) s.** scooter *m*

scope [skəʊp] **N** *(of action, law etc)* portée *f*, étendue *f*, *(of science etc)* domaine *m*; *(of undertaking)* envergure *f*, *(for sb's movements etc)* espace *m*, place *f*, **s. of cover** *(in insurance)* objet *m* de garantie; **the guidelines leave a lot of s. for interpretation** les instructions laissent une grande place à l'interprétation; **it's beyond** or **outside my s.** cela n'est pas de mon ressort, cela n'est pas de ou ne rentre pas dans ma compétence; **it is beyond the s. of my comprehension how ...** je ne comprends absolument pas comment ...; **to have no/a lot of s. for manoeuvre** n'avoir aucune/avoir une grande marge de

manœuvre; **it's outside the s. of this enquiry** cela n'entre pas dans les limites de cette enquête; **to give full** or **free s. to sb** laisser le champ libre à qn; **to give full** or **free s. to one's imagination** laisser libre cours à son imagination; **there's little s. for people with your qualifications** il y a peu de possibilités pour des gens avec des qualifications telles que les vôtres
vt *Am Fam (look at)* mater, reluquer; *(see)* voir; **he's at the beach scoping the babes** il est à la plage en train de mater les nanas; **did you s. that ring he was wearing?** t'as vu un peu la bague qu'il avait au doigt?

scorch [skɔ:tʃ] **vt** *(of fire etc) (clothes etc)* (légèrement) brûler; *(of sun) (grass etc)* brûler, dessécher; *Culin (meat etc)* laisser brûler
vi 1 *(of material etc)* brûler **2** *Br Fam (move quickly)* **he scorched after her** il courut après elle; **to s. down the road** *(of person, car)* descendre la rue à toute vitesse; **she scorched past the other competitors** elle a dépassé les autres concurrents à toute vitesse; **she went scorching past us in her new car** elle passa devant nous comme une fusée dans sa nouvelle voiture
N trace *f* de brûlure
▸▸ *Mil* **scorched earth policy** tactique *f* ou politique *f* de la terre brûlée; **s. mark** trace de brûlure
▸ **scorch along vi** *Br Fam (of car, runner)* passer à toute allure

scorcher ['skɔ:tʃər] **N** *Fam (hot day)* journée *f* torride; **today's been a s.** il en a fait un plat aujourd'hui

scorching ['skɔ:tʃɪŋ] **ADJ** *(sun)* brûlant, ardent; *(wind)* brûlant; *(heat, day)* torride
ADV *(day)* torride; **s. hot** *(water, drink, saucepan etc)* brûlant; *Fam* **it's s. hot here** il fait une chaleur à crever ici

---

SCORE [skɔ:r]

N score **1**	▪ marque **1**	▪ rayure **1**
▪ rainure **2**	▪ entaille **2**	▪ strie **2**
▪ critère **4**	▪ partition **5**	▪ vingt **6**
VT marquer **1**	▪ rayer **2**	▪ composer la musique de **3**
▪ acheter **4**		
VI marquer **1**	▪ compter les points **2**	
▪ découper **4**	▪ faire une touche **5**	

N 1 *Sport etc* score *m*, marque *f*, *(in quiz)* score; **after 20 minutes, there was still no s.** après 20 minutes, le score était toujours zéro à zéro; **what's the s.?** quel est le score ou la marque?; *Fig Fam* on en est où?, qu'est-ce qui se passe?; **to keep the s.** marquer ou compter les points; *Cards* tenir la marque; **what was your s.?** combien tu as fait ou marqué?; *Fig Fam* **to know the s.** savoir ce qu'il en est
2 *(line made by cutting)* rayure *f*, rainure *f*, *(deeper)* entaille *f*, *(on rock etc)* strie *f*
3 *old s.* or *scores (dispute)* vieille(s) rancœur(s) *f(pl)*; **to have an old s. to settle with sb** avoir un vieux compte à régler avec qn; **to pay off** or **settle old scores** régler de vieux comptes
4 *(reason, grounds)* critère *m*; **on what s. was her application rejected?** sur quels critères sa candidature a-t-elle été rejetée?; **don't worry on that s.** n'ayez aucune crainte sur ce point ou à ce sujet
5 *Mus* partition *f*, **full s.** partition d'orchestre
6 *(pl* **score***) (twenty)* **a s.** vingt, une vingtaine; *Arch* **three** or **four s. people** entre soixante et quatre-vingts personnes; *Fam* **you can find them by the s.** on les trouve à la pelle; *Fam* **scores** *(a large number)* un grand nombre; *Fam* **scores of people** une foule de gens VOIR GRAMMAIRE A12–13; B59
vt 1 *Sport (goal, try, points)* marquer; **to s. a hit** *(with song)* faire un tube; *Fig (of idea etc)* faire un tabac; *(of person)* faire des ravages;

Fig **to s. a success** remporter un succès; *Fig Fam* **to s. points off sb** river son clou à qn; *Fig Fam* **to s. an own goal** se faire du tort à soi-même
2 *(cut line in) (cylinder, ground, paper, wood etc)* rayer; *(leather etc)* inciser; *(rock etc)* strier; **she scored her name on the bench** elle grava son nom sur le banc; **s. the meat/fish with a sharp knife** faites des petites entailles dans la viande/le poisson avec un couteau bien aiguisé; **a mountainside scored by torrents** un flanc de montagne creusé ou raviné par les torrents; **water had scored grooves into the rock** l'eau avait creusé des rainures dans le rocher
3 *Mus (film, play etc)* composer la musique de; **scored for piano, violin and flute** pour piano, violon et flûte
4 *Sl (drugs)* acheter
vi 1 *Sport (of football player, team)* marquer; *(in rugby)* marquer un essai; *(in basketball)* marquer un panier
2 *(keep the score)* compter ou marquer les points
3 *Fig* **that's where he scores** *(that's where he has the advantage)* c'est là qu'il est le plus fort; **this is where the new Renault really scores** c'est là que la nouvelle Renault est vraiment super; **he scores on looks but not much else** il est mignon mais ça s'arrête là
4 *(with knife, scissors)* découper; **s. along the dotted line** découper le long des pointillés
5 *Sl (find sexual partner)* faire une touche
6 *Sl (buy drugs)* acheter de la dope
▸ **score off vt insep** *Fam (win point in argument etc)* **to s. off sb** river son clou à qn
vt sep *(delete)* rayer; **s. his name off the list** rayez son nom de la liste
▸ **score out vt sep** *(delete)* rayer

---

scoreboard ['skɔ:bɔ:d] **N** tableau *m* d'affichage

scorecard ['skɔ:ka:d] **N** *Sport* carte *f* ou fiche *f* de score; *Golf* carte du parcours; *(at shooting range)* carton *m*

scorer ['skɔ:rər] **N** *Sport* **1** *(person who keeps score)* personne *f* qui marque les points **2** *Ftbl etc (person who scores goal, point etc)* buteur, -euse; **the team's top (goal) s.** le meilleur buteur de l'équipe

scoring ['skɔ:rɪŋ] **N 1** *Sport* **to open the s.** ouvrir la marque; **there was no s. until ...** aucun point ou *Ftbl etc* but n'avait été marqué jusqu'à ce que ... **2** *(grooves etc) (on surface)* rayure *f*, *(on rock)* stries *fpl*, striation *f*, *(on cylinder etc)* rayures **3** *Mus (of piece of music)* orchestration *f*, arrangement *m*

scorn [skɔ:n] **vt 1** dédaigner, mépriser; **she scorned their help** elle a dédaigné leur aide **2** **to s. to do sth** dédaigner de faire qch
N dédain *m*, mépris *m*; **to pour s. on sth** rejeter qch avec mépris

scornful ['skɔ:nfʊl] **ADJ** *(person, smile etc)* dédaigneux, méprisant; **to be s. of sb/sth** dédaigner ou mépriser qn/qch, traiter qn/qch avec mépris ou dédain

scornfully ['skɔ:nfʊlɪ] **ADV** dédaigneusement, avec mépris

Scorpio ['skɔ:pɪəʊ] **N** *Astrol* Scorpion *m*; **to be (a) S.** être (du) Scorpion

scorpion ['skɔ:pɪən] **N** *(animal)* scorpion *m*

Scot [skɒt] **N** Écossais, -aise VOIR GRAMMAIRE A19

Scotch [skɒtʃ] VOIR GRAMMAIRE A19 **ADJ** *(not used in Scotland)* écossais
N 1 *(whisky)* scotch *m* **2** *(not used in Scotland)* **the S.** les Écossais *mpl*
▸▸ *Culin* **S. broth** = soupe *f* écossaise à base de légumes et d'orge perlée; *Culin* **S. egg** = œuf *m* dur entouré de chair à saucisse et en-

robé de chapelure; **S. fir** pin *m* d'Écosse; **S. mist** bruine *f*; *Fam* **what do think that is, then, S. mist?** si tu allais à la mer, tu n'y trouverais pas d'eau; **S. pine** pin d'Écosse; *Am* **S. tape**® Scotch® *m*; **S. terrier** scottish-terrier *m*, *pl* scottish-terriers, Scotch-terrier *m*, *pl* Scotch-terriers; **S. whisky** scotch, whisky *m* écossais

scotch [skɒtʃ] **vt** *(project etc)* mettre fin à, faire échouer; *(rumour)* mettre fin à, mettre un terme à

scot-free ['skɒt-] **adj** *Fam* **to get off s.** *(unpunished)* s'en tirer à bon compte

Scotland ['skɒtlənd] **n** Écosse *f*
▸▸ **S. Office** = ministère *m* des affaires écossaises; **S. Secretary** =ministre des affaires écossaises à Westminster; **S. Yard** = ancien nom *m* du siège de la police à Londres (aujourd'hui "New Scotland Yard"), ≃ Quai *m* des Orfèvres

Scots [skɒts] VOIR GRAMMAIRE A19 **adj** écossais
n *Ling* écossais *m*
▸▸ **S. fir** pin *m* d'Écosse; **the S. Guards** la Garde écossaise; **S. pine** pin d'Écosse

Scotsman, *pl* **Scotsmen** ['skɒtsmən] **n** Écossais *m* VOIR GRAMMAIRE A19

Scotswoman, *pl* **Scotswomen** ['skɒtswʊmən, -wɪmɪn] **n** Écossaise *f* VOIR GRAMMAIRE A19

Scott [skɒt] **int** *Old-fashioned* **Great S.!** Grand Dieu!

Scotticism ['skɒtɪsɪz(ə)m] **n** expression *f* écossaise

Scottie (dog) ['skɒtɪ] **n** *Fam* scottish-terrier *m*, *pl* scottish-terriers

Scottish ['skɒtɪʃ] **adj** écossais VOIR GRAMMAIRE A19
▸▸ **S. Executive** = gouvernement *m* semi-autonome de l'Écosse; **S. Office** = ministère *m* des affaires écossaises; **S. Parliament** parlement *m* écossais; **S. terrier** scottish-terrier *m*, *pl* scottish-terriers, Scotch-terrier *m*, *pl* Scotch-terriers

---

Scottish Parliament

Le Parlement écossais fut établi dans le cadre du projet de décentralisation ("devolution") du gouvernement travailliste et fut inauguré à Édimbourg en mai 1999. Les 129 membres du Parlement écossais (MSP) siègent sous la houlette du "First Minister". Le Parlement est pourvu d'une grande autonomie en matière de fiscalité mais ses pouvoirs législatifs sont néanmoins limités.

---

scoundrel ['skaʊndr(ə)l] **n** scélérat *m*, vaurien *m*; *Fam (child, puppy etc)* chenapan *m*

scour¹ ['skaʊər] **vt** *(saucepan etc)* récurer; *(floor etc)* frotter; *(in metalwork) (metal surface)* décaper; **the stream had scoured a channel in the hillside** le cours d'eau avait creusé un passage dans la colline
n to give a saucepan/the bath a good s. bien récurer une casserole/la baignoire

scour² **vi** = **scour about**
vt *(search) (countryside)* parcourir, battre; *(woods, house)* fouiller; **to s. the country for sb** battre la campagne à la recherche de qn
▸ **scour about** **vi** *(search widely)* battre la campagne

scourer ['skaʊərər] **n** *(pan or pot)* **s.** *(metal)* tampon *m* à récurer; *(sponge)* éponge *f* à récurer

scourge [skɜːdʒ] **n 1** *(affliction)* fléau *m* **2** *Arch, Lit (whip)* fouet *m*; *Rel (for self-flagellation)* discipline *f*; *Fig* **he was the s. of ...** il était la terreur de ...

vt 1 *Arch, Lit (whip)* fouetter, flageller; *Rel* **to s. oneself** se donner la discipline **2** *Lit (afflict) (of war, famine, drought)* dévaster; *(of corruption)* accabler

scouring ['skaʊərɪŋ] **n, adj** *(scrubbing)* récurage *m*, frottage *m*; *(in metalwork)* décapage *m*
▸▸ **s. pad** *(metal)* tampon *m* à récurer; *(sponge)* éponge *f* à récurer; **s. powder** poudre *f* à récurer

Scouse [skaʊs] **n** *Br Fam* **adj** de Liverpool
n *Ling* dialecte *m* de Liverpool

Scouser ['skaʊsər] **n** *Fam* personne *f* originaire de Liverpool

scout [skaʊt] **n 1** *(person)*, *Mil* éclaireur *m*; *Br Aut Old-fashioned* dépanneur *m* *(employé par les organismes d'assistance automobile)*; **(boy) s.** *(Catholic)* scout *m*; *(non-Catholic)* éclaireur *m*; *Am* **(Girl) S.** guide *f*, éclaireuse *f*, *Cin, Sport etc (talent)* **s.** dénicheur, -euse de talents; *Am Fam* **a good s.** *(fellow)* un bon gars
2 *(aircraft)* avion *m* de reconnaissance
3 *Fam (search)* tour *m* de reconnaissance; **to have a s. around for sth** chercher qch; **I had a good s. around** j'ai bien cherché
4 *Univ (servant)* garçon *m* de service *(spécialement à Oxford)*
vi *Mil etc* aller en reconnaissance; *Cin, Sport etc* **to s. for talent** être à la recherche de futurs talents
▸▸ **s. camp** camp *m* scout
▸ **scout about, scout around** **vi** *(search)* chercher *(**for sth** qch)*

scouting ['skaʊtɪŋ] **n** scoutisme *m*
▸▸ **the S. Movement** le mouvement scout

scoutmaster ['skaʊtmɑːstər] **n** chef *m* de troupe

scow [skaʊ] **n** *Naut* chaland *m*

scowl [skaʊl] **n** air *m* renfrogné; **to look at sb with a s.** regarder qn d'un air renfrogné
vi se renfrogner; **to s. at sb** menacer qn du regard, regarder qn d'un air menaçant

scowling ['skaʊlɪŋ] **adj** renfrogné

Scrabble® ['skræb(ə)l] **n** Scrabble® *m*

scrabble ['skræb(ə)l] **vi** **to s. (about** *or* **around)** *(scrape)* gratter; *(grope)* tâtonner; **I was scrabbling about in the dark, trying to find my key** je tâtonnais dans le noir pour trouver ma clef; **beggars were scrabbling about in the dirt for coins** des mendiants grattaient dans la saleté pour trouver des pièces; **to s. about for work** chercher du travail désespérément

scrag [skræg] **n** **the s. of the neck** la nuque; *Culin* **s. (end) of mutton** collet *m* de mouton
vt **(-gg-)** *Old-fashioned Fam (tease, rag)* tourmenter

scraggy ['skrægɪ] **adj** *(person etc)* maigre, maigrichon, maigrelet; *(piece of meat)* maigrichon, maigrelet

scram [skræm] **vi** **(-mm-)** *Fam* filer, ficher le camp; **s.!** file!, fiche le camp!

scramble ['skræmb(ə)l] **n 1** *(rush, struggle)* bousculade *f*, *Hist* **the s. for Africa** la lutte des puissances coloniales pour se répartir l'Afrique; **a s. for jobs** une bataille pour l'emploi; **a s. for profits** une course effrénée aux profits; **there was a s. for the door** il y a eu une ruée vers la porte
2 *(climb)* ascension *f* difficile
3 *Aviat Fam (takeoff)* décollage *m* d'urgence
4 *Br Sport* **(motorcycle) s.** motocross *m inv*
vi 1 **to s. for sth** *(struggle)* se battre *ou* se bousculer pour avoir qch
2 *(move, often with difficulty)* **to s. up/down/in/out** monter/descendre/entrer/sortir péniblement; **we scrambled over the rocks** nous avons grimpé par-dessus les rochers; **to s. up a hill** grimper une colline à quatre pattes

3 *(move with speed)* **to s. up a ladder/tree** monter à une échelle/un arbre à toute vitesse; **he scrambled into his trousers** il a enfilé son pantalon à toute vitesse
4 *Aviat Fam (take off)* décoller d'urgence
5 *Sport* faire du motocross
vt 1 *Culin (eggs)* brouiller; **scrambled eggs** œufs *mpl* brouillés **2** *Tel, Electron etc (message)* brouiller; **scrambled** *(encoded)* brouillé, codé, crypté **3** *Aviat Fam (aircraft)* faire décoller d'urgence

scrambler ['skræmblər] **n 1** *Tel etc (device)* brouilleur *m* **2** *Br Sport (on motorbike)* motard *m* de motocross

scrambling ['skræmblɪŋ] **n 1** *Tel, Electron etc (of message)* brouillage *m* **2** *Br Sport* **(motorcycle) s.** motocross *m*

scramjet ['skræmdʒet] **n** statoréacteur *m* à combustion supersonique

scran [skræn] **n** *Br Fam (food)* bouffe *f*, graille *f*

scrap¹ [skræp] **n 1** *(piece) (of paper)* morceau *m*, bout *m*; *(of land etc)* parcelle *f*, *(of ribbon, information, evidence)* bout *m*; *(of bread etc)* petit morceau; *(for scrapbook)* image *f*, *(cutting from newspaper)* coupure *f*; **to fight over the scraps** se disputer les restes; **to tear sth into scraps** déchirer qch en morceaux; **scraps** *(of food)* restes *mpl*; *(of cloth)* bouts *mpl*; **not a s. of evidence** pas la moindre preuve; **there isn't a s. of truth in what she says** il n'y a pas une parcelle de vérité dans ce qu'elle dit; **to catch scraps of a conversation** saisir des bouts *ou* des bribes de conversation **2** **to sell sth for s.** vendre qch à la casse
vt **(-pp-) 1** *(discard) (part etc)* mettre au rebut; *(machine)* mettre hors service; *(nuclear missiles etc)* abandonner la construction de; *(project)* laisser tomber, abandonner **2** *(send for scrap) (car, lorry etc)* mettre à la ferraille *ou* à la casse
▸▸ **s. dealer** ferrailleur *m*; **s. iron** ferraille *f*, *Br* **s. merchant** ferrailleur; **s. metal** ferraille; **s. paper** *(papier m)* brouillon *m*

scrap² **n** *Fam (fight)* bagarre *f*, *(quarrel)* dispute *f*; **to have a s.** *(fight)* se bagarrer; *(quarrel)* se disputer; **to get into a s.** *(fight)* se bagarrer; *(quarrel)* se disputer *(**with sb** avec qn)*
vi **(-pp-)** *Fam (fight)* se bagarrer; *(quarrel)* se disputer

scrapbook ['skræpbʊk] **n** album *m* *(de découpages)*

scrape [skreɪp] **vt 1** *(scratch) (skin, polished surface etc)* érafler; **to s. one's shins** s'érafler les tibias; **to s. the bottom** *(of ship)* sillonner *ou* talonner le fond
2 *(clean) (dirt, burnt part)* racler *(**off** de)*; *(paint, wallpaper, surface)* gratter *(**off** de)*; *(wall)* ravaler; *Culin (carrots etc)* gratter; *(in tanning) (skin)* racler, dépiler; **to s. one's shoes** racler *ou* décrotter ses chaussures; **to s. one's plate clean** racler son assiette; *Naut* **to s. a ship's bottom** nettoyer la carène d'un navire; *Fig* **to s. (the bottom of the) barrel** *(with money)* racler les fonds de tiroir; *(be reduced to extremes)* être tombé bien bas
3 **with her hair scraped back** les cheveux tirés
4 *(achieve laboriously)* **to s. a living** gagner tout juste sa vie *ou Fam* sa croûte; **to s. a win** arracher une victoire; **to s. a pass** *(in exam)* réussir de justesse
vi 1 *(scratch)* gratter; *(make sound) (of wheel, pen, violin etc)* grincer; **branches that s. against the shutters** branches qui frottent contre les volets
2 **to s.** *or* **s. away (on the fiddle)** gratter du violon
3 *Fam (succeed with difficulty)* **to s. home** *(win game, race)* gagner de justesse; **to s. in-**

to college réussir de justesse à rentrer à l'université

N 1 *(action with scraper)* coup *m* de grattoir *ou* de racloir; *(wound on skin)* éraflure *f*, *(thin layer) (of butter etc)* mince couche *f*, *(sound) (of violin etc)* grincement *m*; **to give sth a s. with one's nail** gratter qch avec son ongle; **she had given the car a nasty s. on the side** elle avait fait une belle éraflure sur le côté de la voiture

2 *Fam (difficulty)* embarras *m*; **to get into a s.** se mettre dans l'embarras *ou Fam* le pétrin; **to get out of a s.** se tirer d'affaire *ou* d'embarras

▸ **scrape along** VI *(just manage financially etc)* vivoter, s'en tirer péniblement

▸ **scrape by** VI **1** = scrape along

2 *(just succeed) (in an exam)* réussir de justesse

▸ **scrape in** VI *(just succeed) (in entering university etc)* entrer de justesse; *(in winning election)* gagner de justesse; *Sport (in qualifying)* se qualifier de justesse

▸ **scrape off** VT SEP *(remove) (paint etc)* racler, gratter

▸ **scrape out** VT SEP *(saucepan)* récurer; *(pipes)* nettoyer

▸ **scrape through** VI = scrape by **2**
VT INSEP **to s. through an examination** être reçu de justesse à un examen; **the bill only just scraped through its first reading** le projet de loi a été adopté de justesse en première lecture

▸ **scrape together** VT SEP *(save with difficulty) (sum of money)* rassembler

▸ **scrape up** VT SEP **1** = scrape together

2 *Hum* he scraped himself up off the floor il a fini par se relever; **we had to s. him up off the ground** il a fallu le ramasser à la petite cuillère

scraper ['skreɪpər] N racloir *m*, grattoir *m*; *Aut etc (ice)* **s.** raclette *f*, grattoir *(pour pare-brise)*; **door** *or* **shoe s.** décrottoir *m*, grattoir

scrapheap ['skræphi:p] N tas *m* de ferraille; **to throw sth on the s.** mettre qch à la ferraille *ou* au rebut; *Fig* **to throw sb on the s.** laisser tomber qn comme une vieille savate; **he ended up on the s.** *(through redundancy etc)* on l'a mis au rebut; **to consign ideas/projects to the s.** mettre des idées/projets au rebut; **lots of companies are on the s.** beaucoup d'entreprises sont hors de combat

scrapie ['skreɪpɪ] N *Vet* tremblante *f*

scraping ['skreɪpɪŋ] N **1** *(sound) (of pen, saw, violin etc)* grattement *m*; *Fig* **bowing and s.** salamalecs *mpl* **2** *(thin layer) (of butter etc)* mince couche *f*

scrapman, *pl* **scrapmen** ['skræpmən] N ferrailleur *m*, casseur *m*

scrapple ['skræp(ə)l] N *Am Culin* = (genre de) friand *m* fait de farine de maïs et de morceaux de porc que l'on fait frire à la poêle

scrappy ['skræpɪ] ADJ *(collection etc)* hétérogène, hétéroclite; *(speech, film, novel)* décousu; *(work, performance)* inégal, -aux; *Sport* **a s. second half** une seconde mi-temps inégale; **s. knowledge** connaissances *fpl* fragmentaires

scratch [skrætʃ] N **1** *(mark, cut)* égratignure *f*, éraflure *f*, *(made by claw)* griffure *f*, *(on polished surface, record etc)* rayure *f*, **it's nothing, just a s.** ce n'est rien, juste une égratignure; **he came out of it without a s.** il s'en est sorti indemne, il s'en est sorti sans la moindre égratignure

2 *(blow) (with fingernail)* coup *m* d'ongle; *(with claw)* coup de griffe

3 *(repeated action) (of pen)* grincement *m*; **could you give my back a s.?** tu peux me gratter le dos?; **to give one's head a s.** se gratter la tête

4 *Fig Fam* **to start from s.** partir de rien; *(restart)* repartir à zéro; **to build a house from s.** construire une maison de bout en bout; **to write a dictionary from s.** écrire un dictionnaire totalement nouveau; **she built the business up from s.** elle a monté l'affaire à partir de rien; **to come up to s.** être à la hauteur, faire le poids; **to bring sb up to s.** mettre qn à niveau; *(prepare for exam)* préparer qn; **to bring sth up to s.** mettre qch à niveau; **he's not up to s.** il ne fait pas le poids, il n'est pas à la hauteur; **the work was not up to s.** le travail n'était pas à la hauteur

5 *Am Fam (money)* fric *m*, pognon *m*
ADJ *(meal etc)* improvisé, sommaire
VT **1** *(of cat, person etc)* griffer; *(of thorn etc) (skin)* égratigner, érafler; *(glass, record etc)* rayer; **he was badly scratched** il était tout écorché; **to s. oneself** s'égratigner, s'érafler; *(with nails)* se griffer; **to s. one's name on a bench** graver son nom sur un banc; *Fig* **she quickly scratched a few notes on her pad** elle griffonna rapidement quelques notes sur son calepin; *Fig* **to s. the surface (of the problem)** ne faire qu'effleurer le problème; *Fig* **s. a cynic and you'll often find an idealist** si l'on gratte un peu, on trouve souvent un idéaliste derrière un cynique

2 *(rub) (metal, itchy skin)* gratter; **to s. one's head** se gratter la tête; *Fig* **you s. my back and I'll s. yours** rends-moi service et je te renverrai l'ascenseur

3 *(of bird, animal) (ground)* gratter

4 *(delete)* **to s. sb off** *or* **from a list** rayer *ou* biffer qn d'une liste; **to s. sb from a team** exclure qn d'une équipe; *Horseracing* **to s. a horse** déclarer forfait pour un cheval; *(of stewards)* scratcher un cheval
VI **1** *(of person, animal) (to relieve itch)* se gratter; *(of bird, animal) (in the ground)* gratter; *(of thorns, branches etc)* piquer; *(of wool, new clothes)* gratter; **don't s.!** *(yourself)* arrête de te gratter!; *(stop scratching me)* arrête de me griffer!; **a cat that scratches** un chat qui griffe; **to s. at the door** gratter à la porte

2 *(of pen etc)* grincer, gratter

3 *Sport (of entrant)* déclarer forfait

▸▸ **s. card** carte *f* à gratter; *Golf* **s. golfer** *(in tournament)* joueur, -euse classé(e) zéro; *Am* **s. paper** *(papier m)* brouillon *m*; *Sport* **s. team** équipe *f* improvisée

▸ **scratch about, scratch around** VI **to s. about** *or* **around for sth** essayer de dénicher qch

▸ **scratch out** VT SEP **1** *(remove by scratching)* **to s. sb's eyes out** arracher les yeux à qn

2 *(delete) (word)* rayer, biffer, raturer; *(with penknife)* gratter, effacer

▸ **scratch together** VT SEP = scrape together

scratching ['skrætʃɪŋ] N **1** *(with fingernail)* coups *mpl* d'ongle; *(damaging) (action)* rayage *m*; *(on surface)* rayures *fpl* **2** *(to relieve itch)* grattement *m* **3** *(sound)* grattement *m*; *(of pen nib)* grincement *m*; *(of record)* craquement(s) *m(pl)*

scratchpad ['skrætʃpæd] N *Am Comput* bloc-notes *m*, *pl* blocs-notes

▸▸ **s. memory** mémoire *f* bloc-notes

scratchy ['skrætʃɪ] ADJ **1** *(drawing)* peu assuré; **s. writing** pattes *fpl* de mouche **2** *(pen etc) (messy)* qui gratte; *(noisy)* qui grince *(sur le papier)*; *(material etc) (coarse)* rugueux, grossier; *(that irritates skin)* qui gratte (la peau); *(record)* qui craque

scrawl [skrɔːl] *Pej* N *(writing)* griffonnage *m*, gribouillage *m*; **this s. is supposed to be your answer?** est-ce que c'est votre réponse, ces gribouillages-là?
VT *(letter etc)* griffonner, gribouiller
VI écrire comme un chat

scrawny ['skrɔːnɪ] ADJ *(neck)* maigre, décharné; *(piece of meat)* maigrichon

scream [skriːm] N **1** *(cry)* cri *m* perçant *ou* aigu, hurlement *m*; **a s. of pain** un cri *ou* un hurlement de douleur; **screams of laughter** de grands éclats *mpl* de rire **2** *Fam (amusing thing, person)* **it was a s.** c'était à se tordre (de rire); **he's a s.** il est tordant
VI *(once)* pousser un cri perçant *ou* aigu, hurler; *(repeatedly)* pousser des cris aigus, hurler; *(of rabbit, hare)* couiner; *(of jet, missile)* faire un bruit perçant; **jets screamed overhead** des jets sont passés au-dessus de nos têtes dans un bruit assourdissant; **to s. with pain** crier *ou* hurler de douleur; **to s. with laughter** rire à gorge déployée *ou* aux éclats; **everyone's screaming about high prices** tout le monde pousse les hauts cris à propos des prix élevés; **the poster screams at you** l'affiche vous saute à la figure
VT **to s. abuse** hurler des injures; **to s. oneself hoarse** crier à en avoir la voix rauque; **the headlines screamed 'guilty'** le mot 'coupable' s'étalait en grosses lettres sur les premières pages des journaux

screaming ['skriːmɪŋ] ADJ *(person)* criard; *(headlines)* tape-à-l'œil *inv*; *(missile, jet)* qui fait un bruit perçant
N *(of terror etc)* cris *mpl*, hurlements *mpl*, *(of birds etc)* cris perçants

screamingly ['skriːmɪŋlɪ] ADV *Fam* **s. funny** tordant, à se tordre (de rire)

scree [skriː] N *Geol* éboulis *m*

screech [skriːtʃ] N *(cry)* cri *m* perçant *ou* aigu; *(of tyres, brakes etc)* crissement *m*; **a s. of laughter** un éclat de rire perçant
VI *(of person, parrot etc)* pousser des cris perçants *ou* aigus; *(of tyres)* crisser; **the car screeched to a halt** la voiture s'est arrêtée dans un crissement de pneus; **she does tend to s. on the high notes** elle a tendance à hurler les notes aiguës
VT *(orders, insults)* hurler

▸▸ *Orn* **s. owl** chat-huant *m*, *pl* chats-huants, hulotte *f*

screeching ['skriːtʃɪŋ] ADJ *(laugh)* perçant, aigu; *(tyres)* qui crissent
N *(cries)* cris *mpl* perçants *ou* aigus; *(of tyres)* crissement *m*

screed [skriːd] N *usu Pej (long book)* pavé *m*; *(long article)* article *m* à rallonge; **to write screeds** en écrire des tartines; **she wrote me a s.** *(long letter)* elle m'a écrit une lettre qui fait des kilomètres

screen [skriːn] N **1** *(in front of fire)* écran *m*; *(against draught)* paravent *m*; *(partition)* cloison *f*, *(wrought iron etc)* grille *f*; **choir s.** *(in church)* grille de chœur; **rood s.** jubé *m*; **s. of trees** rideau *m* d'arbres; **to act as a s. for a criminal** couvrir un criminel; **the shop was just a s. for her criminal activities** le magasin n'était qu'une couverture pour ses activités criminelles; **protective/safety s.** écran de protection/de sécurité; **fire s.** écran ignifuge

2 *Cin, TV etc* écran *m*; **the s.** *(cinema)* l'écran *m*; **television s.** écran de télévision; **the big s.** *(cinema)* le grand écran; **the small s.** *(television)* le petit écran; **the multiplex has twelve screens** le multiplexe a douze salles; **stars of stage and s.** des vedettes de théâtre et de cinéma; **a picture/a face appeared on the s.** une image/un visage est apparu(e) sur l'écran

3 *Comput* écran *m*; **on s.** sur (l')écran; **to bring up the next s.** amener l'écran suivant; **this takes you back/forwards a s.** *or* **s. by s.** ceci vous fait reculer/avancer écran par écran; **s.-oriented** orienté écran

4 *Elec, Electron* écran *m*; **fluorescent s.** écran fluorescent

5 *Constr, Min (sieve)* crible *m*, tamis *m*, sas *m*; *Am (ventilation grill in door)* grille *f* de ventilation

VT 1 (conceal) (something) masquer, dissimuler, cacher; (behind a screen) cacher derrière un écran ou un paravent; (protect) abriter, protéger; (from harmful influences etc) mettre à l'abri (**from** de); **to s. sth from view** cacher ou masquer ou dérober qch aux regards ou à la vue

2 Cin (film) projeter, passer; (show on television) passer à l'écran

3 (personnel) trier, sélectionner; (job applicants) examiner; (immigrants etc) filtrer; (news etc) filtrer, passer au crible; Med (person) faire passer un test de dépistage à; **to s. sb for security** contrôler qn pour des raisons de sécurité

4 (sieve etc) (gravel, coal, ore, grain etc) cribler, passer au crible

▸▸ Cin **s. actor** acteur m de cinéma; Cin **s. actress** actrice f de cinéma; Cin, TV **s. adaptation** adaptation f à l'écran; Comput **s. capture** capture f d'écran; Comput **s. controller** contrôleur m d'écran; Comput **s. display** affichage m; Am **s. door** porte f avec moustiquaire; Comput **s. down command** commande f d'écran vers le bas, commande écran suivant; Comput **s. dump** capture d'écran; Comput **s. font** fonte f écran; Comput **s. generation** génération f d'écrans; Cin, TV **s. image** image f à l'écran; Psy **s. memory** souvenir-écran m, pl souvenirs-écrans; Comput **s. painting** modification f du papier peint; Comput **s. refresh** actualisation f ou régénération f de l'écran; Cin **s. rights** droits mpl d'adaptation à l'écran; Comput **s. saver** économiseur m d'écran; Comput **s. shot** capture d'écran; Cin **s. test** bout m d'essai; Comput **s. up command** commande écran vers le haut, commande écran précédent; Aut **s. wash** lave-glace m, pl lave-glaces; Cin, TV **s. writing** écriture f de scénarios

▸ **screen off** VT SEP (part of room) séparer par un paravent/une cloison/un rideau/etc; **their house is screened off (from ours) by a row of trees** nous ne pouvons voir leur maison de la nôtre à cause de la rangée d'arbres qui les sépare; **the nurses screened off the dying man** les infirmières ont tiré les rideaux/ont mis des paravents autour du lit du mourant

▸ **screen out** VT SEP éliminer, écarter

screening ['skriːnɪŋ] N **1** Cin (of film) projection f, passage m à l'écran; (show on television) passage à l'écran; **when the film had its first s.** quand le film est passé pour la première fois à l'écran **2** (of personnel) triage m, sélection f; (of immigrants, news etc) filtrage m; (of job applicants) examen m sélectif; Med (of contagious patients) dépistage m; **s. for a disease** dépistage d'une maladie; Med **to have a s.** se faire faire un test de dépistage **3** (sieving) (of gravel, coal etc) criblage m; (of grain) sassement m

▸▸ Cin **s. room** salle f de projection

screenplay ['skriːnpleɪ] N Cin scénario m

screenporch ['skriːnpɔːtʃ] N Am véranda f (entourée d'une moustiquaire)

screenwriter ['skriːnraɪtər] N Cin scénariste mf

screw [skruː] N **1** (for fixing) vis f; Tech Archimedes' or Archimedean **s.** vis d'Archimède; Fam **to have a s. loose** avoir une case de vide ou une araignée au plafond; Fam **to put the screws on sb, to tighten the s. on sb** mettre la pression sur qn

2 Aviat, Naut hélice f; **twin-s.** hélice double

3 (turn of screw) tour m de vis; (turn of screwdriver) coup m de tournevis; **give it another s.** serrez-le encore un peu

4 Old-fashioned (twist) (of tobacco) papillote f; (of paper) tortillon m

5 Billiards effet m; **to put (a** or **some) s. on the ball** donner de l'effet à la balle

6 Br Sl (prison officer) maton, -onne

7 Vulg (sexual intercourse) baise f; **what she needs is a good s.** c'est une mal-baisée; **to have a good s.** baiser un bon coup; **she's a good s.** c'est un bon coup

8 Br Old-fashioned Fam (salary) salaire m, paye f; **to be on a good s.** avoir un bon salaire

VT 1 (fix) visser; **to s. sth (on) to sth** visser qch à ou sur qch; **screwed together** vissés l'un(e) à l'autre; **to s. one's head round to see sth** se tordre le cou pour voir qch; **to s. one's face into a smile** or **grin** se forcer à sourire, faire une grimace plutôt qu'un sourire

2 Fam (cheat) (person) avoir, rouler; **we've been screwed!** on s'est fait avoir!; **to s. money from** or **out of sb** extorquer de l'argent à qn; **they're out to s. you for every penny you've got** ils essayent de vous extorquer tout l'argent que vous avez

3 Billiards (ball) donner de l'effet à

4 Vulg (have sexual intercourse with) s'envoyer, sauter, baiser; Fig **s. you!** va te faire foutre!; **s. him!** qu'il aille se faire foutre!; **s. the expense!** et merde, je peux bien m'offrir ça!

5 Am Fam **to s. the pooch** (blunder) faire une gaffe ou une boulette

VI 1 (of tap etc) tourner; **the knobs s. into the drawer** les boutons se vissent sur le tiroir **2** Billiards (of ball) rebondir de travers, dévier **3** Vulg (have sexual intercourse) baiser, s'envoyer en l'air

▸▸ **s. cap** (of bottle) bouchon m à vis; (of jar) couvercle m à vis; Aviat, Naut **s. propeller** hélice; **s. thread** pas m ou filet m de vis; **s. top** (of bottle) bouchon m à vis; (of jar) couvercle à vis

▸ **screw around** VT SEP Fam **to s. sb around** (treat badly) se foutre de la gueule de qn; (waste time of) faire perdre son temps à qn

VI 1 Fam (mess around) glander **2** Vulg (be promiscuous) baiser ou coucher avec tout le monde

▸ **screw back** VI Billiards (of player) faire de l'effet rétrograde, faire un rétro; (of ball) revenir en arrière

▸ **screw down** VT SEP (secure) fixer ou tenir avec une/des vis

▸ **screw off** VT SEP (lid) dévisser

VI se dévisser

▸ **screw on** VT SEP (attach) visser; Fam **he's got his head screwed on, his head's screwed on the right way** il a la tête solide ou la tête sur les épaules

VI se visser

▸ **screw up** VT SEP **1** (tighten by screwing) visser; (nut) serrer; **to s. sth up tight** visser qch à bloc; **to s. up a piece of paper** froisser une feuille de papier; **to s. up one's eyes** plisser les yeux; **to s. up one's face** grimacer; **to s. up one's courage** prendre son courage à deux mains **2** Sl (spoil) (job) bousiller, foutre en l'air; **this has screwed up my plans** ça m'a foutu mes plans en l'air; **he screwed up the interview** il a complètement merdé à l'entretien **3** Sl (make neurotic) **to s. sb up** foutre qn en l'air; **her parents' divorce has really screwed her up** le divorce de ses parents l'a vraiment foutue en l'air

VI 1 (of lid, nut etc) se visser **2** **her face screwed up in distaste** or **disgust** elle fit une grimace de dégoût **3** Sl (make a mess of sth) merder

screwball ['skruːbɔːl] ADJ, N esp Am Fam dingue mf

screwdriver ['skruːdraɪvər] N **1** (tool) tournevis m; **crossheaded s.** tournevis cruciforme **2** (cocktail) vodka-orange f, pl vodkas-orange

▸▸ **s. blade** lame f de tournevis; **s. handle** poignée f de tournevis

screwed [skruːd] ADJ Fam **1** (in trouble) **to be s.** être foutu **2** Br (drunk) bourré, rond

screw-loose ADJ Am Fam loufoque, loufedingue

screw-on ADJ (earrings) à vis; Phot (lens) détachable, mobile

screwy ['skruːɪ] ADJ Fam dingue, loufoque

scribble ['skrɪb(ə)l] VT (a few words, notes) griffonner, gribouiller

VI gribouiller; (write quickly, in notebook etc) griffonner; **don't s. on the walls** ne gribouille pas sur les murs; **I used to s. a bit** j'écrivais un peu, quoi, autrefois

N 1 (act of scribbling) griffonnage m, gribouillage m **2** (bad handwriting) écriture f illisible, pattes fpl de mouche; **that's not drawing, it's just (a) s.** ce n'est pas du dessin, c'est du gribouillage

▸ **scribble down** VT SEP (write) = scribble VT

scribbler ['skrɪblər] N **1** (person who scribbles) griffonneur, -euse, gribouilleur, -euse **2** Fam (inferior writer) écrivailleur, -euse

scribbling ['skrɪblɪŋ] N (bad handwriting) griffonnage m, gribouillage m; Fam **scribblings** (inferior writings) écrits mpl de deuxième zone

▸▸ **s. pad** bloc-notes m, pl blocs-notes; **s. paper** (papier m) brouillon m

scribe [skraɪb] N Hist (person) scribe m

scrim [skrɪm] N Cin diffuseur m

scrimmage ['skrɪmɪdʒ] N **1** (struggle) mêlée f, bagarre f, bousculade f **2** Am Ftbl mêlée f

VI se bousculer

VT Am Ftbl (ball) mettre en mêlée

scrimp [skrɪmp] VI **to s. (and save)** faire des économies de bouts de chandelle

scrip [skrɪp] N Fin (share) titre m provisoire

▸▸ **s. certificate** certificat m d'actions provisoire; **s. issue** émission f d'actions gratuites

script [skrɪpt] N **1** (manuscript) manuscrit m; Sch (in exam) copie f; Theat texte m; Cin scénario m, script m; **to read from a s.** (of newsreader, politician etc) lire son texte; also Fig **that's not in the s.** ce n'est pas prévu au programme **2** (as opposed to print) écriture f script; **Gothic s.** écriture gothique

VT écrire le script pour

▸▸ Cin, TV **s. department** équipe f des scénaristes; Cin, TV **s. development** développement m du scénario; Cin, TV **s. editor** scénariste mf (de réécriture); Cin, TV **s. girl** scripte f, script girl f; Typ **s. type** cursive f

scripted ['skrɪptɪd] ADJ (remark etc) préparé à l'avance

scriptural ['skrɪptʃər(ə)l] ADJ Rel scripturaire

scripture ['skrɪptʃər] N **1** (Holy) S., the Scriptures l'Écriture f sainte, les (saintes) Écritures **2** Sch instruction f religieuse

▸▸ Sch **s. lesson** cours m d'histoire sainte

scriptwriter ['skrɪptraɪtər] N Cin etc scénariste mf

scriptwriting ['skrɪptraɪtɪŋ] N écriture f de scénarios

scrofula ['skrɒfjʊlə] N Med scrofule f

scrofulous ['skrɒfjʊləs] ADJ **1** Med scrofuleux **2** (corrupt) dépravé

scroll [skrəʊl] N **1** (roll of paper, parchment) rouleau m; **the Dead Sea Scrolls** les manuscrits mpl de la mer Morte **2** (decoration), Archit etc spirale f; (of Ionic capital) volute f; (in writing) enjolivement m, arabesque f; (in engraving etc) cartouche m (encadrant un titre); (of violin) crosse f **3** Comput défilement m

VI Comput défiler

VT Comput faire défiler

▸▸ Comput **s. arrow** flèche f de défilement; Comput **s. bar** barre f de défilement; Comput **s. box** ascenseur m; Comput **s. button** bouton m de défilement; Comput **s. lock (key)** touche f d'arrêt de défilement; Comput **s. wheel** (on mouse) roue f de défilement

▶**scroll down** *Comput* **VI** *(of operator)* faire défiler de haut en bas; *(of text)* défiler de haut en bas
  VT INSEP to s. down a page passer à la page suivante

▶**scroll through** **VT INSEP** *Comput (text)* parcourir

▶**scroll up** *Comput* **VI** *(of operator)* faire défiler de bas en haut; *(of text)* défiler de bas en haut
  VT INSEP to s. up a page passer à la page précédente

scrolling ['skrəʊlɪŋ] **N** *Comput* défilement *m*

Scrooge [skru:dʒ] **N** *Fam* grippe-sou *m*, *pl* grippe-sous

scrotal ['skrəʊtəl] **ADJ** *Anat* scrotal, -aux

scrotum ['skrəʊtəm] **N** *Anat* scrotum *m*

scrounge [skraʊndʒ] *Fam* **VT** *(meal, cigarette)* se faire offrir; **to s. money** taper les gens; **to s. sth from** *or* **off sb** se faire offrir qch par qn; **to s. money from sb** taper qn; **can I s. a cigarette off you?** tu m'offres une cigarette?; **could I s. a lift from someone?** est-ce que quelqu'un peut m'emmener?; **she managed to s. together the money** elle a réussi à trouver l'argent en tapant les gens **VI to s. round for sth** essayer de se faire offrir *ou* payer qch; **to s. off sb** vivre aux crochets de qn, profiter de qn
  N he's on the s. il cherche quelqu'un à taper; **he's always on the s.** c'est un tapeur

scrounger ['skraʊndʒər] **N** *Fam* tapeur, -euse; *(living off state etc)* profiteur, -euse; *(getting invitations to meals)* pique-assiette *mf inv*

scrub[1] [skrʌb] **N** *(bushes)* broussailles *fpl*; *(land)* brousse *f*; *(in Mediterranean country)* garrigue *f*

scrub[2] **VT** (-bb-) **1** *(clean)* *(pot)* récurer; *(floor)* frotter (avec une brosse *ou* à la brosse); *Naut (deck etc)* briquer; **to s. one's hands** bien se laver *ou* se frotter les mains **2** *Fam (cancel)* annuler; *(tape)* effacer; **she's been scrubbed from the team** on l'a virée de l'équipe
  N give your hands a good s. frottez-vous bien les mains; **to give the table a good s.** frotter la table (à la brosse)
  ▸▸*Am* **s. brush** brosse *f* à récurer; *Am* **s. team** équipe *f* de deuxième ordre

▶**scrub down** **VT SEP** *(walls etc)* lessiver; **go and s. yourself down** va te décrasser

▶**scrub off** **VT SEP** enlever, frotter (pour faire partir)
  VI s'enlever

▶**scrub out** **VT SEP** *(stain, mud, dirt etc)* faire partir; *(writing)* effacer

▶**scrub up** **VI** *Med (wash)* *(of surgeon)* se brosser les mains *(avant d'opérer)*

scrubber ['skrʌbər] **N 1** *(implement)* **(pan)** s. tampon *m* à récurer **2** *Br Fam (promiscuous woman)* pute *f*, putain *f*, marie-couche-toi-là *f inv*

scrubbing ['skrʌbɪŋ] **N 1** *(cleaning)* *(of pot)* récurage *m*; *(with brush)* nettoyage *m* avec une brosse dure **2** = **scrub**[2] **N**
  ▸▸*Br* **s. brush** brosse *f* à récurer

scrubland ['skrʌblænd] **N** brousse *f*

scruff [skrʌf] **N 1** *(part of neck)* nuque *f*; *(skin)* peau *f* du cou; **to take sb by the s. of the neck** saisir qn par la peau du cou **2** *Fam (scruffy person)* **he's a real s.!** il est vraiment peu soigné!, il fait vraiment négligé!; **a s. like you** quelqu'un d'aussi peu soigné que toi

scruffily ['skrʌfɪlɪ] **ADV** *Fam* dépenaillé; **s. dressed** débraillé

scruffiness ['skrʌfɪnɪs] **N** *(in dress, appearance)* négligence *f*; *(of district)* état *m* de délabrement

scruffy ['skrʌfɪ] **ADJ** *(person)* *(badly* *dressed)* peu soigné, débraillé, *Fam* dépenaillé; *(clothes etc)* sale, en piteux état; *(hotel)* minable; *(district)* délabré; **this jacket's getting a bit s.** cette veste commence à s'user; **a s. old van** un vieux camion tout pourri *ou* déglingué

scrum [skrʌm] **N** *Rugby* mêlée *f*; *Fam (pushing, shoving)* mêlée, bousculade *f*
  ▸▸**s. cap** protège-oreilles *m inv*; **s. half** demi *m* de mêlée

scrummage ['skrʌmɪdʒ] **N** = **scrum**

scrummy ['skrʌmɪ] **ADJ** *Br Fam (delicious)* délicieux, super bon

scrump [skrʌmp] **VI** *Br Fam* chiper des fruits *(dans un verger etc)*

scrumptious ['skrʌm(p)ʃəs] **ADJ** *Fam* épatant, fameux

scrumpy ['skrʌmpɪ] **N** *Br* cidre *m* fermier

scrunch [skrʌntʃ] **VT** *(with teeth)* croquer avec les dents; **to s. a cigarette into the ground** écrabouiller une cigarette sur le sol; **to s. a piece of paper into a ball** faire une boule avec une feuille de papier
  VI *(make scrunching sound)* craquer; *(of snow)* crisser
  N *(of boots on snow etc)* crissement *m*

▶**scrunch up** **VT SEP** *(paper)* écraser; **to s. one's face up in disgust** faire une grimace de dégoût

scrunchy[1] ['skrʌntʃɪ] **ADJ** *(cereal etc)* qui craque sous la dent

scrunchy[2] **N** *(for hair)* chouchou *m*

scruple ['skru:p(ə)l] **N** scrupule *m*; **to have scruples about sth** avoir des scrupules à propos de qch; **to have scruples about doing sth** avoir des scrupules à faire qch; **he has no scruples about lying to them** il n'a aucun scrupule à leur mentir
  VI *Fml* **not to s. to do sth** ne pas avoir de scrupules à faire qch

scrupulous ['skru:pjʊləs] **ADJ 1** *(person, conscience etc)* scrupuleux; **the newspaper was s. about checking its sources** le journal vérifiait très soigneusement ses sources **2** *(care, work)* scrupuleux, minutieux

scrupulously ['skru:pjʊləslɪ] **ADV 1** *(with moral correctness)* scrupuleusement **2** *(carefully)* scrupuleusement, minutieusement; **s. clean** d'une propreté rigoureuse

scrupulousness ['skru:pjʊləsnɪs] **N** *(quality)* esprit *m* scrupuleux; **his s. in noting down all his expenses** les scrupules qu'il avait à relever toutes les dépenses

scrutineer [skru:tɪ'nɪər] **N** *(of votes)* scrutateur, -trice

scrutinize ['skru:tɪnaɪz] **VT** scruter, sonder; *(examine in depth)* examiner soigneusement; *(votes)* vérifier

scrutiny ['skru:tɪnɪ] **N** *(examination)* examen *m* minutieux *ou* attentif; **to come under s.** faire l'objet d'un examen

SCSI ['skʌzɪ] **N** *Comput (abbr small computer systems interface)* SCSI *f*
  ▸▸**s. address** adresse *f* SCSI; **s. card** carte *f* SCSI; **s. chain** chaîne *f* SCSI

scuba ['sku:bə] **N** scaphandre *m* autonome
  ▸▸**s. diver** plongeur, -euse sous-marin(e); **s. diving** plongée *f* sous-marine

scud [skʌd] **VI** (-dd-) filer comme le vent; **the clouds were scudding across the sky** les nuages filaient à travers le ciel

scuff [skʌf] **VT** frotter, racler *(avec les pieds)*; *(leather, shoes etc)* érafler
  VI marcher en traînant les pieds; **to s. through the autumn leaves** marcher dans les feuilles mortes
  N *(mark)* éraflure *f*; *(on floor)* rayure *f*
  ▸▸**s. mark** éraflure *f*; *(on floor)* rayure *f*

▶**scuff up** **VT SEP** *(raise into the air)* *(snow, dust)* soulever *(en traînant les pieds)*

scuffed [skʌft] **ADJ** *(shoe)* éraflé; *(floor)* rayé

scuffing ['skʌfɪŋ] **N** *(on piston)* rayures *fpl* (d'usure)

scuffle ['skʌf(ə)l] **N** échauffourée *f*, bagarre *f*
  VI se battre, se bagarrer

scull [skʌl] **N** *(oar)* *(one of a pair)* aviron *m* de couple; *(used at stern)* godille *f*; *(boat)* scull *m*
  VI *(row in pair)* ramer *ou* nager en couple; *(at stern)* godiller
  VT *(row in pair)* faire avancer en couple; *(at stern)* faire avancer à la godille

scullery ['skʌlərɪ] **N** *Br* arrière-cuisine *f*, *pl* arrière-cuisines
  ▸▸*Br* **s. maid** fille *f* de cuisine

sculling ['skʌlɪŋ] **N** *(rowing)* *(in pair)* nage *f* à couple; *(at stern)* nage à la godille

sculpt [skʌlpt] *Art* **VT** *(statue)* sculpter
  VI faire de la sculpture

sculptor ['skʌlptər] **N** *Art* sculpteur *m*

sculptress ['skʌlptrɪs] **N** *Art* femme *f* sculpteur, sculptrice *f*

sculptural ['skʌlptʃər(ə)l] **ADJ** *(art)* sculptural, -aux

sculpture ['skʌlptʃər] **N** *(art or object)* sculpture *f*
  VT *(carve)* *(statue, stone etc)* sculpter; **she has finely sculptured features** elle a le visage très fin
  VI faire de la sculpture

scum [skʌm] **N 1** *(film of dirt)* pellicule *f* de crasse; *(froth)* écume *f*, mousse *f*; **to take the s. off sth** *(off boiled food)* écumer qch, enlever l'écume de qch; *(off bath etc)* enlever la crasse de qch **2** *Pej (people)* **the s. of society** le rebut de la société; **the s. of the earth** la lie de la société; **he's/they're s.** c'est une ordure/ce sont des ordures; **she treats him like s.** elle le traite comme de la merde

scumbag ['skʌmbæg] **N** *Fam (person)* salaud *m*, ordure *f*

scunner ['skʌnər] **N** *Scot* dégoût *m*; **to take a s. to sb/sth** prendre qn/qch en dégoût

scunnered ['skʌnəd] **ADJ** *Scot* **to be s. (with)** en avoir marre (de)

scupper ['skʌpər] **N** *Naut* dalot *m*
  VT *Fam (ship, project etc)* couler, saborder; **we're scuppered!** on est fichus!

scurf [skɜ:f] **N** *(on head)* pellicules *fpl*; *(on skin)* désquamation *f*

scurfy ['skɜ:fɪ] **ADJ** *(head etc)* pelliculeux; *(skin)* squameux

scurrility [skə'rɪlɪtɪ] **N** *(of language, person)* grossièreté *f*; *(of attack)* ignominie *f*

scurrilous ['skʌrɪləs] **ADJ** *(language etc)* grossier, injurieux; *(person)* grossier; *(attack)* ignoble

scurrilously ['skʌrɪləslɪ] **ADV** *(coarsely)* grossièrement; *(insultingly)* injurieusement

scurrilousness ['skʌrɪləsnɪs] **N** = **scurrility**

scurry ['skʌrɪ] **N** *(dash)* course *f* précipitée, débandade *f*
  VI *(dash)* aller à pas précipités, *Fam* filer

▶**scurry away, scurry off** **VI** *(of mice)* filer; *(of people)* décamper; *(of animals)* détaler

S-curve **N** *Am* double virage *m*, virage en S

scurvy ['skɜ:vɪ] **N** *Med* scorbut *m*; **to get s.** attraper le scorbut

scutcheon ['skʌtʃən] **N** *Her* écu *m*, écusson *m*

scuttle[1] ['skʌt(ə)l] **N** *(container)* **(coal)** s. seau *m* à charbon

scuttle[2] **N** *Naut (hatch)* écoutille *f*; *Am (in ceiling)* trappe *f*
  VT *Naut (ship)* saborder

scuttle[3] **VI** *(run)* courir

▶**scuttle away, scuttle off** **VI** *(of crab, insect etc)* déguerpir; *(of person)* décamper

scuttling ['skʌtlɪŋ] N *(of ship)* sabordage *m*

scuzzy ['skʌzɪ] ADJ *Fam* crade, cradingue

Scylla ['sɪlə] N *Lit* **to be between S. and Charybdis** être tiraillé entre deux maux

scythe [saɪð] N *Agr* faux *f*
 VT *(corn etc)* faucher
► **scythe through** VT INSEP *(with a weapon)* faucher; **her stick scythed through the air** son bâton fendit l'air

SDI [esdiːˈaɪ] N *Mil (abbr* **strategic defence initiative)** initiative *f* de défense stratégique

SDLP [esdiːelˈpiː] N *(abbr* **Social Democratic and Labour Party)** = parti *m* politique d'Irlande du Nord

SDP [esdiːˈpiː] N *(abbr* **Social Democratic Party)** Parti *m* social démocrate

SDRAM [esdiːˈræm] N *Comput (abbr* **synchronous dynamic random access memory)** SDRAM *f*

SE *(abbr* **south east)** SE

SEA [esiːˈeɪ] N *(abbr* **Single European Act)** AUE *m*

sea [siː] N **1** mer *f*, **at the bottom of the s.** au fond de la mer; **by the s.** au bord de la mer; **by s.** par *(voie de)* mer; **beyond** *or* **over the sea(s)** au delà des mers; **to go to s.** *(become sailor)* devenir marin; *(set sail) (of person, ship)* prendre la mer; **to put (out) to s.** *(of ship)* prendre la mer *ou* le large; **the open s., the high seas** le large, la haute mer; **on the high seas, out at s.** en haute mer, en pleine mer, au grand large; *Fig* **to be all at s.** *(perplexed)* être complètement perdu; **heavy** *or* **strong s.** grosse mer, mer grosse *ou* houleuse; **there's a heavy s.** il y a de la mer; *Naut* **to run before the s.** avoir la mer de l'arrière; *Fam* **old s. dog** vieux loup *m* de mer; **to find** *or* **get one's s. legs** s'habituer à la mer; **he hasn't found his s. legs** il n'a pas encore le pied marin; **a room with a s. view** une chambre avec vue sur la mer
 2 *Fig (of faces)* mer *f*, *(of blood)* bain *m*; *Lit (of troubles)* multitude *f*
 ►►**s. air** air *m* marin *ou* de la mer; *Zool* **s. anemone** anémone *f* de mer; **s. bass** bar *m*, loup *m*; **s. bathing** bains *mpl* de mer; **s. battle** bataille *f* navale; **s. breeze** *(wind)* brise *f* marine; *(cocktail)* sea breeze *m*; *Zool* **s. calf** veau *m* marin, phoque *m*; **s. captain** capitaine *m* de la marine marchande; **s. change** changement *m* radical, profond changement; **s. chest** coffre *m* de marin *ou* de bord; **s. coast** côte *f*; *Zool* **s. cow** vache *f* marine, sirénien *m*; **s. crossing** traversée *f*; **s. cucumber** concombre *m* de mer, holothurie *f*; *Orn* **s. eagle** aigle *m* des mers; *Zool* **s. elephant** éléphant *m* de mer; **s. fight** combat *m* naval; **s. fish** poisson *m* de mer; **s. fishery** pêche *f* maritime; **s. fishing** pêche maritime; **s. floor** fond *m* de la mer; **s. fog** brouillard *m (en mer)*; **s. freight** fret *m* maritime; **s. freight services** messageries *fpl* maritimes; **s. god** dieu *m* marin *ou* de la mer; **s. kayak** kayak *m* de mer; **s. kayaking** kayak de mer; **to go s. kayaking** faire du kayak de mer; **s. lane** couloir *m* de navigation; **s. level** niveau *m* de la mer; *Zool* **s. lion** otarie *f*; *Scot* **s. loch** bras *m* de mer; *Br Mil* **S. Lord** lord *m* de l'Amirauté; **s. mile** mille *m* marin; **s. mist** brume *f* de mer; **s. monster** monstre *m* marin; *Zool* **s. otter** loutre *f* de mer; **s. power** puissance *f* navale; **s. salt** sel *m* marin *ou* de mer; **s. scout** scout *m* marin; *Zool* **s. serpent** serpent *m* de mer; **s. shanty** chanson *f* de marins; *Zool* **s. snake** serpent *m* de mer; **s. travel** voyages *mpl* en mer; **s. trout** truite *f* de mer; *Zool* **s. urchin** oursin *m*; **s. voyage** voyage *m* en mer; **s. wall** digue *f*

seabed ['siːbed] N fond *m* de la mer

seabird ['siːbɜːd] N oiseau *m* de mer

seaboard ['siːbɔːd] N *(coastline)* littoral *m*;

(coastal region) bord *m* de la mer, région *f* côtière

seaboots ['siːbuːts] NPL bottes *fpl* de marin *ou* de mer

seaborne ['siːbɔːn] ADJ *(trade)* maritime; *(goods)* transporté par mer

seafarer ['siːfeərər] N *(sailor)* marin *m*

seafaring ['siːfeərɪŋ] ADJ **a s. people** un peuple de navigateurs

seafood ['siːfuːd] N *(no pl)* fruits *mpl* de mer; **s. restaurant** restaurant *m* de fruits de mer

seafront ['siːfrʌnt] N *(area facing sea)* bord *m* de (la) mer; *(promenade)* esplanade *f*, front *m* de mer; **house on the s.** maison sur le front de mer

seagoing ['siːgəʊɪŋ] ADJ *(ship)* de mer; *(nation)* de navigateurs

sea-green N, ADJ bleu-vert *m inv*

seagull ['siːgʌl] N *(bird)* mouette *f*, goéland *m*

seahorse ['siːhɔːs] N hippocampe *m*

seal[1] [siːl] N **1** *(animal)* phoque *m*; **elephant s.** éléphant *m* de mer; **grey s.** phoque gris; **fur s.** otarie *f* à fourrure; **s. cull** abattage *m* de phoques **2** *(skin)* (peau *f* de) phoque *m*
 VI *(hunt seals)* chasser le phoque; **to go sealing** aller à la chasse au phoque

seal[2] N **1** *(on deed etc)* sceau *m*; *(on letter, bottle of wine etc)* cachet *m*; *(on door etc)* scellés *mpl*; *Com (on goods for export)* plomb *m*; *Law* **given under my hand and s.** signé et scellé par moi; **under the s. of silence/secrecy** sous le sceau du silence/du secret; **to give one's s. of approval to sth** donner son approbation à qch; **to set one's s. to sth** *(to mark with one's seal)* mettre son sceau sur qch; *(to authorize)* autoriser qch, confirmer qch; *(to give approval to)* donner son approbation à qch; **to set the s. on sth** *(on alliance, friendship)* sceller qch; *(on fate, defeat)* décider de qch; **this event set the s. on their fate** cet événement allait décider de leur sort; **under s.** sous scellés; *Rel* **under the s. of confession** dans le secret de la confession; *Law* **official s.** *(affixed to property etc)* scellé *m*
 2 *(instrument)* sceau *m*; *Admin* **the Great S.** le grand sceau *(employé pour les actes publics)*
 3 *Tech (device for making airtight)* joint *m* d'étanchéité; *(airtight join)* joint étanche; **in order to get a good s.** pour obtenir une bonne étanchéité
 VT **1** *(put seal on) (deed etc)* sceller; *(letter, bottle)* cacheter; *(at customs) (goods)* (faire) plomber; *Law (door etc)* apposer les scellés sur; **to s. sb's fate** *(of event etc)* décider du sort de qn; **his fate is sealed** son sort est décidé
 2 *(close) (letter etc)* cacheter; *(block) (mineshaft, pipe)* obturer, boucher; *(jar)* fermer hermétiquement; *(box)* sceller; *(make airtight)* rendre étanche, étancher; *(of joint etc)* assurer l'étanchéité de; *Culin (meat)* saisir; **sealed with a kiss** *(of letter)* fermé avec un baiser; **the frontier has been sealed** la frontière est fermée; **my lips are sealed** *(I am not allowed to say)* il m'est défendu de parler; *(I shall not say)* je ne dirai pas un mot
► **seal in** VT SEP *(contain)* enfermer; **fry the meat at a high temperature to s. in the flavour** faites revenir la viande à feu vif afin de lui conserver toute sa saveur
► **seal off** VT SEP *(isolate)* isoler; **the area was sealed off by the police** le quartier a été bouclé par la police
► **seal up** VT SEP = seal[2] VT 2

sealant ['siːlənt] N produit *m* d'étanchéité

sealed [siːld] ADJ *(envelope)* cacheté; *(train)* plombé; *(box, door)* scellé; **in a s. jar** dans un bocal fermé hermétiquement

►►*Com* **s. bid** soumission *f* cachetée; *Com* **s.-bid pricing** fixation *f* d'un prix de soumission; *Aut* **s. cooling system** circuit *m* de refroidissement pressurisé; **s. envelope** pli *m* cacheté; *Mil, Naut* **s. orders** ordres *mpl* cachetés

sealer ['siːlər] N **1** *(ship)* bateau *m* pour la chasse aux phoques **2** *(seal hunter)* chasseur *m* de phoques

sealing[1] ['siːlɪŋ] N *(seal hunting)* chasse *f* au phoque

sealing[2] N **1** *(putting on seal) (on deed etc)* scellage *m*; *(of letter etc)* cachetage *m*; *(at customs) (of goods)* plombage *m* **2** *(closing) (of letter)* cachetage *m*; *(of pipe etc)* obturation *f*
 ►►**s. compound** lut *m*, mastic *m*; *Aut (for radiator)* anti-fuite *m inv*; **s. wax** cire *f* à cacheter

sealskin ['siːlskɪn] N *(peau f de)* phoque *m*; **s. coat** manteau *m* en (peau de) phoque

seam [siːm] N **1** *Sewing* couture *f*, *(in metal pipe, between boards etc)* joint *m*; *(weld)* soudure *f*, **flat s.** couture rabattue *ou* plate; **French s.** couture double *ou* anglaise; **a ship's seams** les coutures d'un navire; *Fig* **bursting at the seams** *(of room, building etc)* plein à craquer; **to be coming apart at the seams** *(of garment)* craquer de partout; *Fig (of economy, system etc)* aller à vau-l'eau **2** *(wrinkle) (on face etc)* ride *f* **3** *Min etc (of coal etc)* veine *f*
 VT **1** *Sewing (garment)* faire une couture à; **a face seamed with scars** un visage couvert de cicatrices
 ►►**s. bowler** *(in cricket)* = lanceur *m* qui utilise les coutures de la balle pour la faire dévier

seaman, *pl* **seamen** ['siːmən] N marin *m*; *(ordinary sailor)* matelot *m*, marin; *Br* **ordinary s.** matelot de troisième classe *ou* de pont; *Br* **able(-bodied) s.** matelot de deuxième classe; *Br* **leading s.** matelot (breveté) de première classe, quartier-maître *m*, *pl* quartiers-maîtres

seamanship ['siːmənʃɪp] N qualités *fpl* de navigateur; **thanks to his s.** grâce à ses qualités de navigateur

seamless ['siːmlɪs] ADJ **1** *(stocking)* sans couture; *(in metalworking) (tube etc)* sans soudure **2** *Fig (changeover, whole)* continu; **a s. transition** un passage très progressif

seamlessly ['siːmlɪslɪ] ADV *Fig* très progressivement

seamstress ['semstrɪs] N couturière *f*

seamy ['siːmɪ] ADJ sordide; **one of the city's seamier districts** l'un des quartiers les plus sordides de la ville; **the s. side of life/politics** le côté sordide de l'existence/la politique

seance ['seɪɒns] N *(of spiritualists)* séance *f* de spiritisme

seaplane ['siːpleɪn] N *Aviat* hydravion *m*

seaport ['siːpɔːt] N port *m* maritime *ou* de mer

SEAQ [esiːeɪˈkjuː] N *(abbr* **Stock Exchange Automated Quotations System)** système *m* de cotation automatisé

sear [sɪər] VT **1** *(to burn)* brûler; *(a wound)* cautériser; *Fig* **the image would forever be seared on his memory** l'image resterait à tout jamais gravée dans sa mémoire **2** *Culin (meat etc)* saisir **3** *Fig Lit (harden) (conscience etc)* endurcir; *(heart)* durcir, dessécher
 ADJ *Lit (withered)* flétri, desséché

search [sɜːtʃ] N recherche(s) *f(pl)*; *(in a drawer etc)* fouille *f*, *Law* perquisition *f*, *(at customs)* visite *f*; **to have a s. for sth** chercher qch; **her s. for her son/the truth** la recherche de son fils/la vérité; **in s. of sth** à la recherche de qch; **to be in s. of sth** être en quête de qch, être à la recherche de qch;

Comput **to do a s.** faire une recherche; *Comput* **s. and replace** recherche *f* et remplacement *m*; *Comput* **s. and replace command** commande *f* de recherche et remplacement; *Comput* **s. and replace function** fonction *f* recherche et remplacement; **to make a s.** faire des recherches; **right of s.** droit *m* de visite; *(at sea)* droit *m* de recherche

VT *(place, house, drawer, box, suspect, sb's pockets, one's memory)* fouiller; *(face)* scruter; *(at customs)* *(ship, sb's bags)* visiter; *Comput* *(file, directory)* rechercher dans; *Comput* **to s. and replace sth** rechercher et remplacer qch; *Law* **to s. a house** faire une perquisition *ou* une visite domiciliaire; *Law* **to s. the scene of a crime** fouiller le lieu d'un crime; *Fam* **s. me!** je n'ai pas la moindre idée!

VI faire des recherches; *Comput* effectuer une recherche; **to s. after the truth** rechercher la vérité; **to s. for sb/sth** (re)chercher qn/qch

▸▸ *Comput* **s. command** commande de recherche; *Comput* **s. direction** direction *f* de la recherche; *Comput* **s. engine** moteur *m* de recherche; **s. party** équipe *f* de secours; *Comput* **s. time** temps *m* de recherche; **s. warrant** mandat *m* de perquisition

▸ **search out** VT SEP chercher
▸ **search through** VT INSEP fouiller

searchable ['sɜːtʃəb(ə)l] ADJ *Comput* **s. by name/price/date** sur lequel/laquelle on peut effectuer une recherche par nom/prix/date

searcher ['sɜːtʃər] N *(member of search party)* sauveteur *m*; **he was a s. after truth** c'était un homme qui recherchait la vérité

searching ['sɜːtʃɪŋ] ADJ *(examination)* minutieux; *(look)* scrutateur, -trice; **s. questions** questions *fpl* de fond

N *(of suspect, house, ship etc)* fouille *f*; *(at customs)* visite *f*; *Law* perquisition *f*

searchlight ['sɜːtʃlaɪt] N projecteur *m*; *(beam)* faisceau *m* d'un/du projecteur; **to turn a s. on sth** braquer un projecteur sur qch

searing ['sɪərɪŋ] ADJ *(pain)* fulgurant; *(criticism, indictment etc)* virulent

seascape ['siːskeɪp] N 1 *(view)* vue *f* sur la mer 2 *(picture)* marine *f*

seashell ['siːʃel] N coquille *f* de mer, coquillage *m*

seashore ['siːʃɔːr] N bord *m* de (la) mer; *(beach)* plage *f*

seasick ['siːsɪk] ADJ **to be s.** avoir le mal de mer; **to be a little/very s.** avoir un léger/fort mal de mer

seasickness ['siːsɪknɪs] N mal *m* de mer, *Spec* naupathie *f*

seaside ['siːsaɪd] N bord *m* de (la) mer; **at the s.** au bord de la mer; **a s. village/boarding house** un village/une pension au bord de la mer
▸▸ **s. resort** station *f* balnéaire

season ['siːz(ə)n] N VOIR GRAMMAIRE A7; A81–2; B4; B61-2 1 *(period of year)* saison *f*; **the four seasons** les quatre saisons; **the rainy s.** la saison des pluies; **hunting s.** saison de la chasse; **close/open s.** *(in hunting)* chasse fermée/ouverte; *Fishing* pêche *f* fermée/ouverte; **the tourist s.** la saison touristique; **S.'s Greetings** meilleurs vœux de fin d'année 2 *(for fruit, vegetables etc)* saison *f*; **oysters are in/out of s.** c'est/ce n'est pas la saison des huîtres; **strawberries are in s.** c'est la saison des fraises; **in s.** *(of animal)* en rut; *(of female animal)* en chaleur; *Com* **the high s.** la haute saison; *Com* **the slack s., the off s.** la morte-saison, *pl* mortes-saisons 3 *Fam (season ticket)* abonnement *m* 4 *Theat* saison *f*; *TV, Cin* cycle *m*; **a s. of**

French films un cycle de films français 5 *Sport* saison *f*; **the football/cricket/etc s.** la saison de football/cricket/*etc*

VT *(dish)* assaisonner; *(wood)* dessécher; *(barrel)* aviner; *(wine)* mûrir

VI *(of wood)* se sécher; *(of wine etc)* mûrir, se sécher

▸▸ **s. ticket** (carte *f* d')abonnement; **s. ticket holder** abonné, -ée

seasonable ['siːzənəb(ə)l] ADJ 1 **s. weather** un temps de saison 2 *Lit (help, advice)* opportun, à propos

seasonal ['siːzən(ə)l] ADJ *(changes etc)* des saisons; *(trade, occupation)* saisonnier; ▸▸ *Econ* **s. adjustment** ajustement *m* saisonnier; *Med* **s. affective disorder** dépression *f* saisonnière; **s. employment** emploi *m* saisonnier; **s. fluctuation** fluctuation *f* saisonnière; **s. worker** saisonnier, -ière

seasonally ['siːzən(ə)lɪ] ADV selon la saison; **s. adjusted unemployment figures** chiffres *mpl* du chômage en données corrigées des variations saisonnières

seasoned ['siːzənd] ADJ 1 *Culin (dish)* assaisonné; **highly s.** dish plat *m* relevé *ou* épicé 2 *(wood, cigar etc)* sec, *f* sèche; *(wine)* mûr, fait 3 *Fig (soldier)* aguerri; **a s. political campaigner** un militant politique chevronné; **s. traveller** voyageur, -euse expérimenté(e)

seasoning ['siːzənɪŋ] N 1 *(act) Culin (of dish)* assaisonnement *m*; *(of wood)* séchage *m*; *(of wine)* maturation *f*; *(of troops)* aguerrissement *m* 2 *Culin (condiment)* assaisonnement *m*, condiment *m*

seat [siːt] N 1 *(chair) (in Parliament, on bus, train etc)* siège *m*; *(in theatre)* place *f*; *(of toilet)* lunette *f*, siège; *(bench) (in park etc)* banc *m*; *Aut* **car s.** siège de voiture; *Aviat* **ejection or ejector s.** siège éjectable; *Aut, Theat etc* **flap or folding s.** strapontin *m*; *Fam* **to be in the hot s.** être sur la sellette; **to book a s.** *(on train, in theatre)* réserver une place 2 *(somewhere to sit)* place *f*; **there were no seats left** il n'y avait plus de places; **to take a s.** s'asseoir; **to keep one's s.** rester assis; **keep a s. for me** gardez-moi une place; *Pol* **to have a s. in the House** avoir un siège à l'Assemblée; **to have a s. on the Council** être conseiller (municipal); **to have a s. on the board** avoir un siège au conseil d'administration 3 *(part) (of chair)* siège *m*, fond *m*; *Fam (of person)* derrière *m*, fesses *fpl*; *(of trousers)* fond 4 *(centre) (of government)* siège *m*; *(of disease)* foyer *m*; *Med (of pain etc)* siège; **s. of learning** haut lieu *m* du savoir; **the s. of the emotions** le siège des émotions; **country s.** château *m* 5 *Horseriding (way of sitting)* assiette *f*; **to have a good s.** avoir une bonne assiette 6 *Tech (of valve)* siège *m*

VT 1 *(cause to sit)* *(child etc)* (faire) asseoir; *(guests) (decide where to place)* placer; *(show to seat)* faire asseoir; **you will be seated in five minutes, madam** votre table sera prête dans cinq minutes, madame; **to remain seated** rester assis; *Fml* **please be seated** veuillez vous asseoir, je vous prie de vous asseoir 2 *(accommodate)* **bus which seats thirty** autobus à trente places (assises); **this table seats twelve** on tient à douze à cette table; **the hall seats two hundred** deux cents personnes peuvent tenir dans la salle 3 *Tech (valve)* assurer *ou* ajuster l'assise de

▸▸ **s. number** numéro *m* de place (assise); *Aviat* **s. pitch** espacement *m* des sièges

seatback ['siːtbæk] N dossier *m*

seatbelt ['siːtbelt] N *Aut, Aviat* ceinture *f* de sécurité

-seater ['siːtər] SUFF a **two/single/***etc* **-s.** *Aut* une voiture à deux places/une place/*etc*;

Aviat un avion biplace *ou* à deux places/à une place/*etc*

seating ['siːtɪŋ] N *(allocation of seats)* allocation *f* des sièges *ou* des places; *(positioning)* placement *m*; *(seats) (in hall etc)* sièges *mpl*; *Tech (of valve)* siège *m*; **there is more s. upstairs** il y a encore des places en haut
▸▸ **s. arrangements** le placement *ou* la disposition des gens; **s. capacity** nombre *m* de places assises; *(of stadium etc)* capacité *f* d'accueil; **s. plan** *(in theatre)* plan *m* de la disposition des places; *(at table)* plan *m* de table

SEATO ['siːtəʊ] N *Mil (abbr* **Southeast Asia Treaty Organization)** OTASE *f*

seat-of-the-pants ADJ *Fam* **the project has been a bit of a s. operation** le projet a été mené au pif

seaward ['siːwəd] ADV *(also* **seawards)** vers la mer, du côté du large
ADJ de (la) mer
N **to s.** du côté du large, vers le large
▸▸ **s. breeze** brise *f* de mer

seawater ['siːwɔːtər] N eau *f* de mer
▸▸ **s. therapy** thalassothérapie *f*

seaway ['siːweɪ] N *Naut* route *f*, **the St Lawrence S.** la voie maritime du Saint-Laurent

seaweed ['siːwiːd] N algue *f*

seaworthiness ['siːwɜːðɪnɪs] N (état *m* de) navigabilité *f*

seaworthy ['siːwɜːðɪ] ADJ *(of ship)* en (bon) état de navigabilité

sebaceous [sɪ'beɪʃəs] ADJ *(gland, cyst)* sébacé

sebum ['siːbəm] N *Physiol* sébum *m*

SEC [esiː'siː] N *(abbr* **Securities and Exchange Commission)** = commission *f* américaine des opérations de Bourse, ≃ COB *f*

sec [sek] N *Fam* = **second** N 1; **half a s.!, just a s.!** une seconde!, deux secondes!

secant ['siːkənt] *Math* ADJ sécant
N sécante *f*

secateurs [sekə'tɜːz] NPL *Br* sécateur *m*

secede [sɪ'siːd] VI faire sécession; *(from party)* se séparer, faire scission (**from** de)

secession [sɪ'seʃən] N sécession *f*; *(from party)* scission *f*; *Hist* **the War of S.** la guerre de Sécession

secessionist [sɪ'seʃənɪst] ADJ, N scissionniste *mf*; *Hist* sécessionniste *mf*

seclude [sɪ'kluːd] VT tenir retiré *ou* éloigné *ou* écarté (**from** de)

secluded [sɪ'kluːdɪd] ADJ *(place)* écarté, retiré; **s. life** vie *f* retirée *ou* de reclus; **to live a s. life** vivre une vie retirée *ou* de reclus

seclusion [sɪ'kluːʒən] N solitude *f*; *(of village, farm)* isolement *m*; **in s.** retiré du monde; **to live in s.** vivre dans la solitude, vivre en reclus

---

SECOND[1] ['sekənd]

N	seconde **1–3** ▪ second **3**	
	▪ deuxième **3** ▪ témoin **6**	
ADJ	second **1** ▪ deuxième **1**	
	▪ deuxièmement **1**	
VT	seconder **1** ▪ appuyer **1**	

N 1 *(of time)* seconde *f*; **in a split s.** en une fraction de seconde; **for a s.** pendant une seconde; **wait a s.!** attendez une seconde *ou* un instant!; **I won't be a s.** je reviens tout de suite, j'en ai pour deux secondes 2 *Math, Astron* seconde *f* 3 *(in order)* second *m*, seconde *f*, deuxième *mf*; *Sport etc* **to come in a good s.** arriver second en très bonne position derrière le vainqueur; *Mil etc* **s. in command** commandant *m* en second; *Br Univ* **to get a s.** être reçu à la licence avec mention assez bien; *Br Univ* **upper/lower s.** *(degree)* mention *f* bien/assez bien; *Aut* **to start in s.** démarrer en seconde; *Fam* **anyone for seconds?** *(at meal)* qui veut se resservir?, *Fam* qui veut du rabiot *ou* du rab?

4 *Mus* **major/minor s.** seconde *f* majeure/mineure

5 *Com* **seconds** articles *mpl* de deuxième choix, produits *mpl* de second choix

6 *(in duel)* témoin *m*; *Boxing* soigneur *m*

ADJ 1 second, deuxième; **the s. of March** le deux mars; **twenty-/thirty-s.** vingt-/trente-deuxième; **Charles the S.** Charles Deux *ou* II; **our roads are s. to none** nos routes sont les meilleures du monde; **to be s. in line for the throne** être deuxième prétendant au trône; **I'm s. in line for promotion** je suis deuxième sur la liste des gens à promouvoir; **to be s. in command** commander en second; **to marry a s. time** *or* **for the s. time** se marier pour la deuxième *ou* seconde fois; **Spain's s. city** la deuxième ville d'Espagne; **the s. largest city in the world/in Portugal** la deuxième ville du monde/du Portugal; **to take a s. helping** *(at meal)* se resservir; **he's the s. oldest player in the team** après le doyen de l'équipe, c'est lui le plus vieux; **she knew she would never be more than s. best** *(in person's affection)* elle savait qu'elle ne serait jamais plus qu'un second choix; *(of athlete)* elle savait qu'elle serait toujours deuxième; **we're not happy with s. best** nous ne nous contenterons pas d'un pis-aller; **in a fight with him, you'll come off s. best** si tu t'affrontes à lui, tu n'en sortiras pas vainqueur; **to take a s. holiday** reprendre des vacances; **it has become s. nature to her** elle le fait presque par instinct; **in s. place** deuxièmement, en second lieu; **to take s. place** passer second; **on s.** *Br* **thoughts** *or* *Am* **thought** tout bien réfléchi; **to have s. thoughts** avoir des hésitations (**about sth** au sujet de qch); **are you having s. thoughts?** est-ce que vous hésitez?; **I've had s. thoughts** j'ai bien réfléchi, j'ai changé d'avis; **to get one's s. wind** *(in race etc)* trouver un second souffle; *Fig (after feeling tired)* trouver un second souffle, se remettre

2 *(another)* **a s.** Camus/Churchill un nouveau Camus/Churchill

VT *(support) (person)* seconder; *(in debate etc) (motion)* appuyer

▸▸ **s. ballot** deuxième tour *m*; *Pol* **s. chamber** deuxième chambre *f*, *(in UK)* Chambre *f* des lords; *(in US)* Sénat *m*; **s. chance** deuxième chance *f*, **s. childhood** gâtisme *m*, seconde enfance *f*; *Rail* **s. class** seconde (classe *f*); **the S. Coming** le second avènement; **s. cousin** cousin, -ine issu(e) de germains; *Cin* **s. feature** deuxième film *m* *(d'un programme où figurent deux longs métrages)*; **s. floor** *(in UK)* deuxième étage *m*; *(in US)* premier étage; *Sch* **s. form** ≃ *(classe de)* cinquième *f*; *Aut* **s. gear** seconde *f*, **s. hand** *(of watch, clock)* aiguille *f* des secondes, trotteuse *f*; **s. home** résidence *f* secondaire; **my s. home** *(country)* mon deuxième pays; *(family)* ma deuxième famille; **s. language** deuxième langue *f*, *Journ* **s. lead** gros titre *m* de deuxième ordre; **s. name** nom *m* de famille; **s. nature** seconde nature *f*, **s. opinion** deuxième avis *m*; *Gram* **s. person** deuxième personne *f*, *Parl* **s. reading** deuxième lecture *f*, **s. sight** seconde *ou* double vue *f*, *Mus* **s. violin** deuxième violon *m*

---

second ² [sɪ'kɒnd] **VT** *Br (detach) Mil (officer)* mettre en disponibilité *ou* hors cadre *(pour fonctions spéciales etc)*; *(employee)* détacher, envoyer en détachement; **she's been seconded to head office** elle a été détachée au siège social

secondary ['sekənd(ə)rɪ] **ADJ** secondaire; *(evidence)* indirect; *(rôle etc)* peu important, accessoire; **the s. meaning of a word** le sens

dérivé d'un mot; **of s. importance** d'importance secondaire

▸▸ *Med* **s. cancer** métastase *f*, **s. education** enseignement *m* secondaire *ou* du second degré; *Med* **s. infection** surinfection *f*, **s. legislation** législation *f* secondaire; *Br Formerly* **s. modern** = collège *m* offrant un enseignement semi-professionnel; **s. road** route *f* secondaire *ou* départementale; **s. school** = établissement *m* secondaire, *Can, Suisse* école *f* secondaire; *Econ* **s. sector** secteur *m* secondaire

second-class **ADJ** *(ticket, carriage)* de seconde (classe)

▸▸ **s. citizen** citoyen, -enne de seconde zone; *Br Univ* **s. degree** = licence *f* avec mention assez bien; **s. mail** courrier *m* (à tarif) non urgent

second-degree burns **NPL** *Med* brûlures *fpl* au deuxième degré

seconder ['sekəndər] **N** personne *f* qui soutient une proposition; **I need a s.** il me faut quelqu'un qui soutienne ma proposition

second-generation **ADJ** *(immigrant etc)* de la deuxième génération; *(computer, mobile phone etc)* de deuxième génération

second-guess **VT to s. sb** anticiper ce que qn va dire/faire

second-hand **ADV** *(to buy)* d'occasion; **to hear news s.** recevoir des nouvelles de seconde main *ou* d'un tiers

ADJ *(car, book, furniture etc)* d'occasion; *(news etc)* de seconde main; **s. bookshop** librairie *f* d'occasion; **s. clothes shop** boutique *f* de vêtements d'occasion; **the s. market** le marché de l'occasion

▸▸ **s. dealer** marchand, -ande d'articles d'occasion; *(in clothes)* fripier, -ière; *(in books)* bouquiniste *mf*, **s. shop** magasin *m* d'articles d'occasion

secondly ['sekəndlɪ] **ADV** deuxièmement, en second lieu

secondment [sɪ'kɒndmənt] **N** *Br Mil etc* détachement *m* (**to** à; **from** de); **to be on s. to another department** être détaché auprès d'un autre service

second-rate **ADJ** *(goods, equipment)* de qualité inférieure; *(movie, book)* médiocre; *(politician, player)* médiocre, de second ordre

second-row forward **N** *Rugby* avant *m* de deuxième ligne

secrecy ['si:krɪsɪ] **N** secret *m*; **in s.** en secret; **why all the s.?** pourquoi tous ces secrets?; **there's no s. about it** ça n'a rien de secret; **business conducted in complete s.** affaires menées dans le plus grand secret; **to swear sb to s.** faire jurer le silence à qn

secret ['si:krɪt] **ADJ** secret, -ète; *(place)* secret, caché; **to keep sth s.** tenir *ou* garder qch secret, cacher qch, taire qch; **he'd kept it s. from me for years** il me l'avait caché pendant des années; **a desk with a s. compartment** un bureau à secret

N secret *m*; **in s.** en secret; **can you keep a s.?** est-ce que tu peux garder un secret?; **it can be our little s.** ça sera notre petit secret à nous; **I make no s. of it** je n'en fais pas mystère, je ne le cache pas; **to let sb into the s.** mettre qn dans le secret; **the s. is not to press too hard** l'astuce consiste à ne pas appuyer trop fort; **it's no s.** ce n'est pas un secret; **an open s.** un secret de Polichinelle

▸▸ **s. admirer** admirateur, -trice secret(ète); **s. agent** agent *m* secret; **s. ballot** vote *m* à bulletin secret; **s. door** porte *f* cachée *ou* dérobée; **s. meeting** réunion *f* secrète; **s. police** police *f* secrète; **the S. Service** = service *m* de protection des hauts fonctionnaires américains et de leurs familles; *Mil, Fig* **s. weapon** arme *f* secrète

secretarial [sekrə'teərɪəl] **ADJ** *(work)* de secrétariat

▸▸ **s. college** école *f* de secrétariat; **s. course** cours *m* de secrétariat; **s. post** poste *m* de secrétaire; **s. service** service *m* de secrétariat; **s. skills** notions *fpl* de secrétariat; **the s. staff** le secrétariat

secretariat [sekrə'teərɪət] **N** secrétariat *m*

secretary ['sekrət(ə)rɪ] **N 1** secrétaire *mf*; **private s.** secrétaire particulier(-ière); *Br* **company s.** secrétaire *mf* général(e); **(1st/2nd/3rd) s.** *(to ambassador)* ≃ secrétaire d'ambassade **2** *(bird)* serpentaire *m*, secrétaire *m*

▸▸ **s. bird** serpentaire, secrétaire; **S. of State** *Br* ≃ ministre *m*, *Am* ≃ ministre des Affaires étrangères

secretary-general **N** secrétaire *mf* général(e)

secrete [sɪ'kri:t] **VT 1** *(of gland etc)* sécréter **2** *(hide)* cacher

secretion [sɪ'kri:ʃən] **N** *Physiol* sécrétion *f*

secretive ['si:krɪtɪv] **ADJ** *(person)* secret, -ète; *(in negative sense)* cachottier; *(behaviour)* fermé; **why are you being so s. about it?** pourquoi fais-tu tant de cachotteries là-dessus?

secretively ['si:krɪtɪvlɪ] **ADV** avec dissimulation

secretiveness ['si:krɪtɪvnɪs] **N** caractère *m* secret; *(on particular occasion)* cachotterie *f*

secretly ['si:krɪtlɪ] **ADV** en secret; *(to think etc)* secrètement

sect [sekt] **N** secte *f*

sectarian [sek'teərɪən] **ADJ** *(attitude, cult)* sectaire

N sectaire *mf*

▸▸ **s. killing** = meurtre *m* motivé par le sectarisme religieux

> Note that, unlike the word **sectarian** in British English, the French word **sectaire** does not specifically refer to tensions between Catholics and Protestants.

sectarianism [sek'teərɪənɪz(ə)m] **N** sectarisme *m* religieux; *(attitude)* esprit *m* sectaire

> Note that, unlike the word **sectarianism** in British English, the French word **sectarisme** does not specifically refer to tensions between Catholics and Protestants.

section ['sekʃən] **N 1** *(part)* section *f*, portion *f*, *(of structure, company)* division *f*, partie *f*, *(of tube, railway etc)* tronçon *m*; *Com (of store)* rayon *m*; *(in shop)* secteur *m*; *Am Rail (of sleeping car)* compartiment *m*; *(component, prefabricated part)* élément *m*; *(of document, text etc)* partie; *(of law etc)* article *m*; *Mus (in orchestra)* section; *Mil (fighting unit) (of infantry section)* groupe *m* de combat; *(of fusiliers, grenadiers)* équipe *f*, *Am (area)* lotissement *m*; *Aviat* **nose s.** partie avant, nez *m*; **tail s.** partie arrière, queue *f*; **the bookcase comes in sections** la bibliothèque est démontable; *Journ* **sports/travel/financial/TV s.** rubrique *f* sport/voyage/finances/télé; **all sections of the population** toutes les couches de la population, toutes les catégories sociales

2 *(cut)* *Geom* section *f*, *Archit, Constr etc* coupe *f*, profil *m*, section; *(in metalwork)*, *Constr* profilé *m*; *(thin slice)* tranche *f*, lamelle *f*, **microscopic s.** mince lame *f*, plaque *f* *(pour examen au microscope)*; **conic/plane s.** section conique/plane; **horizontal s.** coupe *ou* section horizontale

VT 1 *(cut)* sectionner **2** *(send to psychiatric hospital)* faire interner

▸▸ **s. manager** chef *m* de section

sectional ['sekʃən(ə)l] **ADJ 1** *(interests)* particulier; *(rivalries)* interne **2** *(drawing etc)* en coupe, en profil; *(area)* de section **3** *(furniture)* modulaire

sectionalism ['sekʃənəlɪz(ə)m] N *Am* régionalisme *m*, esprit *m* de clocher

sector ['sektər] N **1** *Geom, Astron, Mil, Comput* secteur *m*; *Admin* **public/private s.** secteur public/privé; **public s. spending** dépenses *fpl* publiques **2** *Geom (instrument)* compas *m* de proportion

secular ['sekjʊlər] ADJ *Rel (history, art etc)* laïque, séculier; *(music)* profane; **s. priest** (prêtre *m*) séculier *m*

secularism ['sekjʊlərɪz(ə)m] N **1** laïcisme *m* **2** *Phil* laïcité *f*

secularization [sekjʊləraɪ'zeɪʃən] N *(of church property etc)* sécularisation *f*; *(of school)* laïcisation *f*

secularize ['sekjʊləraɪz] VT *(property, priest)* séculariser; *(school)* laïciser

secure [sɪ'kjʊər] ADJ **1** *(free from anxiety) (person)* tranquille, en paix; *Psy* sûr de soi; *(future, nomination)* assuré; **you make me feel s.** tu me donnes confiance; **to feel s. of victory** être assuré *ou* certain de la victoire; *Fml* **s. in the knowledge that …** sachant avec certitude que … **2** *(safe) (valuables)* en sûreté; *(investment, place, job)* sûr; **s. communications** communications *fpl* inviolables; **s. from attack** à l'abri d'une attaque; **the prisoner is s.** le prisonnier est en lieu sûr **3** *(door, plank, foundations, lock etc)* solide; *(foothold, grasp)* ferme, sûr; **that rope doesn't look very s.** cette corde n'a pas l'air très solide; **to make the boat s.** bien amarrer le bateau
▸ VT **1** *(keep out of danger)* mettre en sûreté; *(prisoner)* mettre en lieu sûr; **to s. a pass** *(in mountains)* garder un défilé **2** *(immobilize) (sth which is loose)* bien fixer; *(flapping shutter etc)* attacher, fixer; *(cargo)* arrimer; **doors and windows should be properly secured** les portes et les fenêtres doivent être bien fermées **3** *Law, Com (borrower)* garantir; **to s. a debt by mortgage** hypothéquer une créance; *Fin* **to s. a loan** garantir un emprunt, nantir un prêt; *Fin* **to s. by warrant** warranter **4** *(obtain)* obtenir; *(objective)* atteindre; **to s. sth for sb** *(future, victory, holiday etc)* assurer qch pour qn; **he secured his future with the company by …** il a assuré son avenir dans l'entreprise en …
▸ ▸ *Comput* **s. electronic transaction** protocole *m* SET; *Comput* **s. HTTP** protocole HTTP sécurisé; *Comput* **s. server** serveur *m* sécurisé; *Comput* **s. sockets layer** protocole SSL; **s. unit** *(in psychiatric hospital)* quartier *m* de haute sécurité; *(in children's home)* section *f* surveillée; *Comput* **s. Web site** site *m* sécurisé

secured [sɪ'kjʊəd] ADJ *Fin (loan)* garanti; *(bond)* cautionné

securely [sɪ'kjʊəlɪ] ADV **1** *(safely)* en sécurité; **to be s. protected** être parfaitement protégé; **he is s. behind bars** il est hors d'état de nuire **2** *(firmly)* solidement; **s. tightened** bien serré; **make sure your seat belt is s. fastened** assurez-vous que vous avez bien attaché votre ceinture de sécurité

securitization [sɪkjʊərɪtaɪ'zeɪʃən] N *St Exch* titrisation *f*

securitize [sɪ'kjʊərɪtaɪz] VT *St Exch* titriser

security [sɪ'kjʊərɪtɪ] N **1** *(of lock, person etc)* sécurité *f*, sûreté *f*; **to live in s.** vivre en sécurité; **s. of tenure** *(in job)* sécurité *f* de l'emploi; *(as tenant)* jouissance *f* d'une location; **(job) s.** sécurité de l'emploi
2 *(at military base, during state visit etc)* sécurité *f*; **a s. cordon has been thrown around**

the airport un déploiement de forces de l'ordre a été organisé autour de l'aéroport; **the (United Nations) S. Council** le Conseil de sécurité (des Nations unies); **he's/it's a s. risk** il/cela constitue un danger *ou* un risque pour la sécurité; **(maximum) s. wing** quartier *m* de haute sécurité
3 *(safeguard)* sécurité *f*; **there's a further s. against theft** il y a un dispositif de sécurité antivol supplémentaire
4 *Com, Law (financial guarantee)* garantie *f*; *(for payment of debt)* caution *f*, cautionnement *m*; *(collateral)* nantissement *m*; *(person)* garant, -ante; **s. for a debt** *(money etc)* garantie d'une créance; **to stand s. for sb** se porter garant *ou* caution pour qn; **to give sth as (a) s.** donner qch en cautionnement; **to lend money on s./without s.** prêter de l'argent sur nantissement/sur gage à découvert
5 *St Exch* **securities** titres *mpl*, papiers *mpl* valeurs, valeurs *fpl* (mobilières); **government securities** fonds *mpl* d'État; **securities lodged as collateral** titres déposés en nantissement; **securities issued** valeurs émises
6 (social) s. sécurité *f* sociale; **to live on s.** vivre des allocations
▸ ▸ **s. alert** alerte *f* au danger; **s. blanket** doudou *m*; *Psy* objet *m* transitionnel; *Comput* **s. certificate** certificat *m* de sécurité; *Admin, Mil* **s. clearance** habilitation *f*, *(document)* laissez-passer *m inv*; **s. code** code *m* confidentiel; *Fin* **s. deposit** dépôt *m* de garantie; **s. device** sécurité *f*; *Am St Exch* **Securities and Exchange Commission** = commission *f* américaine des opérations de Bourse; ≃ COB *f*; **s. firm** société *f* de gardiennage; **s. forces** forces *fpl* de sécurité; **s. guard** garde *m* (chargé de la sécurité); *(for armoured van)* convoyeur, -euse de fonds; *St Exch* **securities house** société *f* de Bourse; *Comput* **s. level** niveau *m* de sécurité; *St Exch* **securities market** marché *m* des valeurs, marché des titres; **s. measures** mesures *fpl* de sécurité; **s. officer** *(on ship)* officier *m* chargé de la sécurité; *(in firm)* employé, -ée chargé(e) de la sécurité; *(inspector)* inspecteur, -trice de la sécurité; *Comput* **s. password** mot *m* de passe sécuritaire; **s. patrol** patrouille *f* de sûreté *ou* de protection; **s. personnel** personnel *m* de sécurité

security-coded ADJ *(radio)* codé, à code de sécurité
▸ ▸ *Aut* **s. immobilizer** antidémarrage *m* codé

sedan [sɪ'dæn] N *Am Aut* voiture *f* de tourisme; **four-door s.** berline *f*
▸ ▸ *Hist* **s. chair** chaise *f* à porteurs

sedate [sɪ'deɪt] ADJ *(person)* posé, pondéré, réfléchi; *(lifestyle)* calme; *(deportment)* composé, calme
▸ VT *Med* donner un sédatif à

sedately [sɪ'deɪtlɪ] ADV posément

sedation [sɪ'deɪʃən] N *Med* sédation *f*; **to be under s.** être sous sédatifs *ou* sous calmants

sedative ['sedətɪv] ADJ, N *Med* sédatif *m*, calmant *m*

sedentary ['sedəntrɪ] ADJ *(posture)* assis; *(job, life)* sédentaire

sedge [sedʒ] N *(plant)* joncs *mpl*, roseaux *mpl*
▸ ▸ *Orn* **s. warbler** phragmite *m* des joncs

sediment ['sedɪmənt] N sédiment *m*; *(in bottle)* dépôt *m*; *(in wine)* lie *f*; *Chem* résidu *m*

sedimentary [sedɪ'ment(ə)rɪ] ADJ *Geol (layer, rock)* sédimentaire

sedimentation [sedɪmen'teɪʃən] N sédimentation *f*

sedition [sɪ'dɪʃən] N sédition *f*

seditious [sɪ'dɪʃəs] ADJ séditieux

seduce [sɪ'djuːs] VT séduire; **they seduced**

him away from the company with … ils ont réussi à le convaincre de quitter l'entreprise en lui faisant miroiter …; **to s. sb into doing sth** convaincre qn de faire qch

> Note that the most common meaning of the French verb **séduire** is **to charm** or **to appeal to**, depending on the context.

seducer [sɪ'djuːsər] N séducteur, -trice

seduction [sɪ'dʌkʃən] N **1** *(sexual)* séduction *f* **2** *(attractiveness) (usu pl)* attrait *m*, charme *m*; **the seductions of such a lifestyle** les attraits *ou* charmes d'un tel style de vie

seductive [sɪ'dʌktɪv] ADJ *(look, charm)* séducteur, -trice; *(music, argument, speech)* charmeur, -euse; *(smile)* aguichant; *(offer)* séduisant, attrayant, alléchant

seductively [sɪ'dʌktɪvlɪ] ADV avec séduction; **s. attractive** très attirant

seductiveness [sɪ'dʌktɪvnɪs] N *(of offer etc)* caractère *m* séduisant *ou* attrayant *ou* alléchant; *(of woman)* séduction *f*, charme *m*; *(of style)* charme

sedulous ['sedjʊləs] ADJ *Fml* assidu, scrupuleux

sedulously ['sedjʊləslɪ] ADV *Fml* scrupuleusement

SEE¹ [siː] VOIR GRAMMAIRE A41; B35 *(pt saw* [sɔː]; *pp seen* [siːn])

VT voir **1, 4, 5, 9, 10** ▪ comprendre **2** ▪ reconnaître **2** ▪ percevoir **4** ▪ s'assurer que **8** ▪ recevoir **9** ▪ consulter **9** ▪ reconduire **11** ▪ accompagner **11**
VI voir **1–6**

VT 1 *(with eyes)* voir; **I saw it with my own eyes** je l'ai vu de mes propres yeux, je l'ai de mes yeux vu; **the cathedral can be seen from a long way off** on voit la cathédrale de très loin; **to s. the sights of the town** visiter les monuments de la ville; **there's nothing to s.** il n'y a rien à voir; **I can't s. anything** je ne vois rien; **the moment I saw him** dès que je l'ai aperçu ou vu; **did you s. that programme last night?** tu as vu cette émission hier soir?; **now s. what you've done!** regarde ce que tu as fait!; **s. page 50** voir page 50; **s. above** se reporter plus haut; **s. (on) the back** voir au verso; **I'm not fit to be seen** je ne suis pas présentable; **to s. things** *(hallucinate)* avoir des hallucinations *ou* des visions; **it has to be seen to be believed** il faut le voir pour le croire; **the squalor in which they live has to be seen to be believed** ils vivent dans une misère, il faut le voir pour le croire; **to s. sb do** *or* **doing sth** voir qn faire qch; **I saw him fall** je l'ai vu tomber; **to s. sb coming** voir venir qn; *Fig* **they saw you coming a mile off** ils t'ont vu arriver de loin; **to s. one's way** voir où l'on va; **I can't s. a way out of this problem** je ne vois pas d'issue à ce problème; **could you s. your way to lending me your car?** est-ce que, par hasard, tu pourrais me prêter ta voiture?; **to s. the back of sb** se débarrasser de qn; **to s. sense** *or* **reason** entendre raison; **I'll s. him in hell first!** qu'il aille au diable!, qu'il aille se faire pendre!; **he has seen a great deal of the world** *(he has travelled a great deal)* il a beaucoup voyagé; *(he has a great deal of experience)* il a une vaste expérience; **the city hasn't seen such crowds in decades** la ville n'a pas connu une foule pareille depuis des dizaines d'années; **the country saw many changes** le pays a connu de grands changements; *Mil* **the first time he saw action** quand il a reçu le baptême du feu; *Mil* **he saw action in the desert** il a combattu dans le désert
2 *(understand)* comprendre, saisir; *(the er-*

ror of one's ways etc) reconnaître; **I don't s. how/why/where ...** je ne vois pas comment/pourquoi/où ...; **I don't s. the need** or **necessity for ...** je ne vois pas l'intérêt de ...; **they cannot s. the truth** la vérité leur échappe; **I can't s. the difference** je ne vois pas la différence; **I don't s. the point** je ne vois pas l'intérêt; **he can't s. a joke** il ne comprend pas la plaisanterie; **I s. what you mean** je vois ce que vous voulez dire; **I don't s. that at all!** (I don't agree) je ne suis pas du tout d'accord;

3 (observe) **to s. oneself in one's children** se reconnaître dans ses enfants; **I don't know what you s. in her** je ne vois pas ce que tu lui trouves; **it remains to be seen whether ...** (il) reste à savoir si ...; **whether this is true remains to be seen** (il) reste à savoir si ceci est vrai; **I can't s. any sense** or **the sense in continuing this discussion** je ne vois pas l'intérêt de continuer cette discussion; **I s.** or **saw in the paper that ...** j'ai vu dans le journal que ...; **he never lived to s. the project finished** il est mort avant que le projet ne soit achevé; **I s. (that) you're a sports fan** je vois que vous êtes un fan de sport

4 (perceive sth in a certain way) voir, percevoir; **I s. things differently now** aujourd'hui, je vois les choses autrement; **this is how I s. it** voici comme je perçois la chose

5 (envisage) voir; **what do you s. happening next?** d'après vous, qu'est-ce qui va se passer ensuite?; **how do you s. the situation in a year's time?** comment pensez-vous que la situation aura évolué dans un an?; **I don't s. myself still doing this in a year's time** je ne me vois ou m'imagine pas faire encore cela dans un an; **how do you s. things developing?** comment est-ce que vous envisagez l'avenir?; **I can't s. them accepting this** je ne peux pas croire qu'ils vont accepter cela; **they say this will be more efficient, but I don't s. it** ils disent que cela sera plus efficace, mais je n'y crois pas; **I don't s. any chance of that** à mon avis, c'est peu probable; **I can't s. you as a boxer** je ne te vois pas en boxeur; **I can't s. myself doing this** je ne me vois ou m'imagine pas en train de faire cela

6 (examine) examiner; **let me s. that letter again** repassez-moi cette lettre (pour que je la relise)

7 (investigate, enquire, discover) **I'll s. what I can do** je vais voir ce que je peux faire; **let's s. what happens if ...** voyons ce qu'il se passe si ...

8 (make sure) **to s. (to it) that everything is in order** s'assurer que tout est en ordre; **I shall s. (to it) that he comes** je me charge de le faire venir; **s. (to it) that you don't miss the train!** faites attention de ne pas manquer le train!; Fam **he'll s. you (all) right** il s'occupera de toi

9 (meet) (person) voir; (visitor) recevoir; (doctor, solicitor etc) consulter, voir; **he sees a great deal of the Longs** il fréquente ou voit beaucoup les Long; **we don't s. much of each other** nous ne nous voyons pas souvent; **when shall I s. you again?** quand est-ce que je vais vous revoir?; **are you seeing another woman?** est-ce que tu as ou vois une autre femme?; **s. you soon!, (I'll) be seeing you!** à bientôt!; **(I'll) s. you Thursday!** à jeudi!; Fam **s. you!** salut!, à plus! [aplys]; **to go to** or **and s. sb** aller voir qn; **I can't s. him today** (visitor) je ne peux pas le recevoir aujourd'hui

10 (speak to) **I want to s. the manager** je veux voir le directeur; **can I s. you for a minute in my office?** je peux vous voir un instant dans mon bureau?; **I'd like to s. you on business** je voudrais vous parler affaires

11 (escort, accompany) **to s. sb home** reconduire qn ou accompagner qn jusque chez

lui/elle; **I saw him to the station** je l'ai accompagné jusqu'à la gare; **I'll s. you to the door** je vous accompagne jusqu'à la porte

12 (at cards) **I'll s. you** je demande à voir; **I'll s. your hundred** je vous suis à cent

VI 1 voir; **she can't s. very well** (her sight is poor) elle ne voit pas très bien, sa vue n'est pas très bonne; (on specific occasions) elle ne voit pas très bien; **cats can s. in the dark** les chats voient clair la nuit; **as far as the eye can s.** à perte de vue; **to s. into the future** voir l'avenir; **to s. into sb's heart** lire dans le cœur de qn; Old-fashioned Fam **s. here!** (annoyance) dites donc!, voyons!

2 (understand) voir; **as far as I can s.** autant que je puisse en juger; **I s.** je vois, je comprends; **ah, I s.!** ah, je vois!; **do you see?**, Fam **s.?** tu vois?; **you s., I never liked them** voyez-vous, je ne les ai jamais aimés

3 (observe) voir; **s. for yourself** voyez par vous-même; **seeing is believing** on ne peut nier ce qu'on voit de ses propres yeux; **we shall s.** nous verrons (bien); **we'll soon s.** on le saura vite; **we'll soon s. if ...** on saura vite si ...; **I'll be a good musician one day, you'll s.** je serai un bon musicien un jour, vous verrez; **s.! I told you he wouldn't let us down** tu vois! je t'avais dit qu'il ne nous laisserait pas tomber

4 (examine) voir; **can I s.?** je peux voir?; **let me s.!, let's s.!** fais voir!; **have you got a free room? – let me s.** est-ce que vous avez une chambre libre? – voyons (voir); **it was, let me s., in 1998** c'était, voyons (voir), en 1998

5 (consider) voir; **can we go to the beach, Mummy? – we'll** or **I'll s.** est-ce qu'on peut aller à la plage, maman? – on verra

6 (find out) (aller) voir

▸ **see about VT INSEP 1** (attend to) s'occuper de; **I'll have to s. about that old door** il faudra que je m'occupe de cette vieille porte

2 (consider) voir; **I'll s. about it** je verrai ça; Iron **we'll (soon) s. about that!** c'est ce qu'on va voir!

▸ **see across VT SEP** (escort to other side of) **to s. sb across the road** aider qn à traverser la rue

▸ **see in VI** (look in) voir à l'intérieur; **the curtains were drawn, so we couldn't s. in** les rideaux étaient tirés, nous ne pouvions rien voir à l'intérieur

VT SEP (escort in) (person) faire entrer; **to s. the new year in** faire le réveillon du nouvel an

▸ **see into VT INSEP to s. into sth** (investigate) se renseigner sur qch, examiner qch

▸ **see off**

VT SEP 1 to s. sb off at the station accompagner qn (jusqu')à la gare; **we'll come to s. you off** nous viendrons vous dire au revoir

2 to s. sb off (the premises) (escort) accompagner qn jusqu'à la sortie; (make sure they go) s'assurer du départ de qn

3 (in fight etc) **she saw off two bigger girls** elle a battu deux filles plus grandes qu'elle; **the dogs saw them off** les chiens les ont fait fuir

▸ **see out VT SEP 1** (escort to door) accompagner jusqu'à la porte; **I'll s. myself out** je connais le chemin, ce n'est pas la peine de me raccompagner

2 (stay until end of) voir la fin de; (undertaking) mener à bonne fin; **I'll s. another year out here, then go home** je vais passer une autre année ici, puis je rentrerai; **I don't think these boots will s. the winter out** je ne crois pas que ces bottes feront l'hiver; **he isn't expected to s. out the week** il y a peu de chances qu'il survive jusqu'à la fin de la semaine; **he'll s. us all out!** (will survive us) il nous enterrera tous!

▸ **see over, see round VT INSEP** (tour) (house etc) visiter, voir

▸ **see through VT INSEP** (not be deceived by)

(person) deviner les intentions de; **I saw through him** j'ai deviné ses intentions, je l'ai percé à jour; **I saw through their little game** j'ai vite compris leur petit jeu

VT SEP 1 (stay until end of) **to s. a show/film through** assister à un spectacle/regarder un film jusqu'au bout; **to s. a matter through** mener une affaire à bonne fin ou jusqu'au bout; **I'll s. it through** je tiendrai jusqu'au bout

2 (help to cope) aider; **£20 should s. me through (to Monday)** 20 livres devraient me suffire (jusqu'à lundi); **friends and relatives are seeing her through this bad time** ses amis et sa famille l'aident à traverser cette période difficile; **200 gallons should s. us through the winter** 200 gallons devraient nous suffire pour l'hiver

▸ **see to VT INSEP** (deal with) s'occuper de; **I'll have to get it seen to** il faut que je m'en occupe; **I'll s. to it** je vais m'en occuper, je m'en charge; **I'll s. to it that you're not disturbed** je ferai en sorte que vous ne soyez pas dérangé

▸ **see up VT SEP** (accompany) **to s. sb up** faire monter qn

see² N Rel (of bishop) siège m épiscopal, évêché m; (of archbishop) archevêché m; **the Holy S.** le Saint-Siège

seed [siːd] **N 1** graine f; (of apple, pear, grapes etc) pépin m; **mustard s.** graine de moutarde; **seed(s)** (in gardening, agriculture) semence(s) f(pl), graine(s); **to go** or **run to s.** (of plant) monter en graine; (of land) tomber en friche; (of person) se laisser aller; Fig **the seeds of discord** les germes mpl de la discorde; **to sow (the) seeds of discord/doubt** semer la discorde/le doute

2 Arch, Lit = semen

3 Bible Lit (descendants) descendance f, lignée f; **the s. of Abraham** la descendance d'Abraham

4 Tennis tête f de série

VI (of plant) monter en graine; (of cereals) venir à graine

VT 1 (sow with seeds) (field etc) semer; Met **to s. clouds** provoquer la pluie **2** (remove seeds from) (melons, grapes etc) épépiner **3** Tennis **to s. the players** classer les joueurs; **seeded players** têtes fpl de série; **she was seeded tenth** elle était classée dixième

▸▸ **s. bed** (couche f de) semis m, germoir m; **s. box** boîte f à semis; Fin **s. capital** capital m initial ou de départ, mise f de fonds initiale; **s. corn** grain m de semence; Br **s. merchant** grainetier, -ière; Fin **s. money** capital initial ou de départ, mise de fonds initiale; **s. pearls** semence de perles; **s. potatoes** pommes fpl de terre de semence; **s. tray** terrine f à semis; Bot **s. vessel** péricarpe m

seedcake ['siːdkeɪk] N Culin gâteau m parfumé au carvi

seediness ['siːdɪnɪs] **N 1** (of clothes) état m miteux; (of building) état minable; **the s. of the area surprised him** il fut surpris de voir à quel point l'endroit était minable **2** Fam (feeling of being unwell) indisposition f

seedless ['siːdlɪs] ADJ (grapes etc) sans pépins

seedling ['siːdlɪŋ] N (plant grown from seed) (jeune) plant m; **seedlings** semis m

seedsman, pl **seedsmen** ['siːdzmən] N grainetier m

seedy ['siːdɪ] ADJ **1** (shabby) (person) miteux; (hotel etc) minable, miteux **2** Fam (unwell) mal fichu, patraque; **to feel s.** se sentir patraque, être mal fichu, ne pas être dans son assiette **3** (full of seeds) plein de pépins

seeing ['siːɪŋ] CONJ **s. (that** or Fam **as how) ...** vu que ... + ind, étant donné que ... + ind; **s. as how it's all so simple, why don't you do**

it yourself? pourquoi ne le fais-tu pas toi-même puisque c'est si simple?
▪ **N s. is believing** voir c'est croire
▸▸ *Am* **s. eye dog** chien *m* d'aveugle

seeing-to N *Br Sl* **to give sb a good s.** *(beat up)* tabasser qn; *(have sex with)* faire passer qn à la casserole

seek [si:k] *(pt, pp* **sought** [sɔ:t]*)* VT **1** *(look for) (sth lost, job etc)* chercher; *(sb's friendship, promotion etc)* rechercher; *(somebody)* chercher; **to be actively seeking employment** être en recherche effective d'emploi; **to s. one's fortune** chercher fortune; **to s. shelter** chercher un abri; **they sought shelter under a tree** ils se sont réfugiés sous un arbre **2** *(request)* **to s. sth from** *or* **of sb** demander qch à qn; **to s. sb's help** rechercher *ou* demander l'aide de qn; **to s. advice** demander conseil **3** **to s. to do sth** essayer *ou* tenter de faire qch; **she sought in vain to convince them of her innocence** elle tenta en vain de les convaincre de son innocence
▪ VI **s.!** *(to dog)* cherche!; *Prov* **s. and you** *or Arch* **ye shall find** quand on cherche, on trouve
▸▸ *Comput* **s. time** temps *m* d'accès
▸ **seek after** VT INSEP *(look for) (truth)* chercher; **to be much sought after** être très recherché *ou* demandé
▸ **seek out** VT SEP *(find) (person)* trouver

seeker ['si:kər] N chercheur, -euse; **a s. after truth** un chercheur/une chercheuse de vérité; **pleasure seekers** gens *mpl* en quête de plaisirs

[si:m] VI sembler, paraître, avoir l'air; **to s. tired** paraître *ou* sembler *ou* avoir l'air fatigué; **how did she s. to you?** comment l'as-tu trouvée?; **do whatever seems best (to you)** fais au mieux; **how does it s. to you?** qu'en penses-tu?; **it seems like a dream** on croit rêver; **it all seems a long time ago now** ça me paraît loin maintenant; **it doesn't s. right, them getting away with it** ça ne semble pas juste qu'ils s'en tirent à bon compte; **she seems to be** *or* **she seems (like) a nice person** elle a l'air bien; **I s. to have heard his name somewhere** il me semble avoir entendu son nom quelque part; **I seemed to be floating on a cloud** j'avais l'impression de flotter sur un nuage; **I s. to have dropped your vase** je crois (bien) que j'ai laissé tomber votre vase; **I can't s. to get it right** je n'y arrive pas; **she seemed to be trying to say something** elle semblait essayer de dire quelque chose
▪ V IMPERS **it seems (that) …, it would s. that … il** paraît que … + *ind,* il semble que … + *ind ou sub*; **it seemed best to …** il semblait préférable de …; **it seems like only yesterday** c'est comme si c'était hier; **it seems likely that this will happen soon** cela risque d'arriver bientôt; **it seems to me that …** il me semble que …; **it seemed to me (that) I was dreaming** il me semblait *ou* j'avais l'impression que je rêvais; **it seemed as though** *or* **as if …** il semblait que … + *sub,* on aurait dit que … + *ind*; **it seems so, it would s. so** à ce qu'il paraît; **it seems not, it wouldn't s. so** il paraît que non; **it seems to be raining** on dirait qu'il pleut; **there doesn't s. to be any butter left** j'ai l'impression qu'il n'y a plus de beurre

seeming ['si:mɪŋ] ADJ apparent
seemingly ['si:mɪŋlɪ] ADV apparemment
seemliness ['si:mlɪnɪs] N *Fml* bienséance *f*
seemly ['si:mlɪ] ADJ *Fml* convenable, bienséant
seen [si:n] PP *see* **see¹**
▪ ADJ ATTRIB *Sch* **a s. translation** une traduction préparée

seep [si:p] VI suinter; *(into sth)* s'infiltrer; **the water was seeping into the earth** l'eau s'infiltrait dans la terre; **information was seeping out** des renseignements filtraient

seepage ['si:pɪdʒ] N **1** *(act)* suintement *m*; *Fig (of workers)* fuite *f* **2** *(lost liquid)* fuite *f,* déperdition *f*

seer [sɪər] N *Lit* prophète *m,* prophétesse *f*

seersucker ['sɪəsʌkər] N *Tex* coton *m* gaufré

seesaw ['si:sɔ:] N bascule *f,* tapecul *m*
▪ ADJ *(movement)* de bascule, de va-et-vient
▪ VI **1** *(play on a seesaw)* jouer à la bascule, faire du tapecul **2** *(of machine part etc)* basculer; *Fig (oscillate)* osciller
▸▸ *Fin* **s. effect** effet *m* balançoire

seethe [si:ð] VI *(of liquid)* bouillonner; *(of crowd etc)* s'agiter; **the street is seething with people** la rue grouille de monde; **to be seething (with anger)** bouillir de colère; **he's absolutely seething** il est fou de rage; **the country was seething with discontent** le mécontentement agitait tout le pays

seething ['si:ðɪŋ] ADJ *(liquid)* bouillonnant; **a s. mass of worms** une masse grouillante de vers

see-through ADJ transparent

segment¹ ['segmənt] N **1** *(of sphere, circle, worm)* segment *m*; *(of orange)* quartier *m*; *(of population, public opinion)* partie *f,* **s. of a line** segment linéaire **2** *Mktg (of market, population)* segment *m*

segment² [seg'ment] VT **1** *(divide)* couper en segments, segmenter **2** *Mktg (market, population)* segmenter
▪ VI *(of worm)* se segmenter

segmentation [segmən'teɪʃən] N *Biol, Mktg* segmentation *f*

segregate ['segrɪgeɪt] VT *(something)* isoler, mettre à part; *(somebody)* séparer **(from** de); *(races)* soumettre à la ségrégation

segregation [segrɪ'geɪʃən] N séparation *f,* isolement *m*; *Pol* ségrégation *f,* **policy of s.** ségrégationnisme *m*

segregationist [segrɪ'geɪʃənɪst] ADJ, N *Pol* ségrégationniste *mf*

segue ['segweɪ] N *TV etc* transition *f* musicale
▪ VI enchaîner; **to s. into** enchaîner sur

sei whale [seɪ] N *Zool* rorqual *m* boréal

seismic ['saɪzmɪk] ADJ sismique; *Fig (shock waves, changes)* gigantesque

seismograph ['saɪzməgrɑːf] N sismographe *m*

seismologist [saɪz'mɒlədʒɪst] N sismologue *mf*

seismology [saɪz'mɒlədʒɪ] N sismologie *f*

seize [si:z] VT **1** *(grab)* saisir; **to s. hold of sb/sth** saisir *ou* empoigner qn/qch; **to s. hold of an idea** se jeter sur une idée; **to s. sb by the throat** saisir qn à la gorge; **to s. the opportunity of doing sth** sauter sur *ou* saisir l'occasion de faire qch; **to be seized with fright/panic/doubt** être saisi de peur/panique/doute **2** *(take for oneself)* s'emparer de; *(fortress)* prendre; *(enemy ship)* capturer; *Law (drugs, stolen goods etc)* saisir; *(person)* arrêter **3** *(understand) (meaning, implication etc)* saisir; **to s. the meaning of sth** prendre *ou* saisir le sens de qch
▸ **seize on** VT INSEP *(grasp) (idea)* saisir; **to s. on a pretext for leaving** saisir *ou* sauter sur un prétexte pour partir
▸ **seize up** VI *Tech etc (become stuck) (of part, machine etc)* se gripper, coincer; *(of engine)* caler; **my knee's seized up** *(completely)* mon genou est coincé; *(partially)* mon genou est ankylosé
▸ **seize upon** VT INSEP = **seize on**

seizing ['si:zɪŋ] N *Mil (of fortress)* prise *f,* *(of enemy ship)* capture *f,* *Law (of property, goods)* saisie *f*

seizure ['si:ʒər] N **1** *(of fortress)* prise *f,* *(of enemy ship)* capture *f,* *Law (of property, goods)* saisie *f* **2** *Med* crise *f,* attaque *f*; **(apoplectic) s.** attaque d'apoplexie; *Fam* **he just about had a s. when he found out!** il a failli faire une crise quand il a su!

seldom ['seldəm] ADV rarement; **he is s. seen** on le voit rarement; **such things are s. seen now** de telles choses se font rares de nos jours; **s. have I heard such nonsense** j'ai rarement entendu de bêtises pareilles VOIR GRAMMAIRE A78

select [sɪ'lekt] VT choisir, sélectionner; *Comput, Sport* sélectionner; **to s. from …** choisir parmi …; *Comput* **s. 'enter'** tapez 'entrée'; *Comput* **to s. an option** activer une option
▪ ADJ *(exclusive)* de (premier) choix, d'élite; *(club)* très fermé, sélect; *(audience)* choisi
▸▸ *Pol* **s. committee** commission *f* d'enquête parlementaire

selectable [sɪ'lektəb(ə)l] ADJ *Comput* qui peut être sélectionné

selected [sɪ'lektɪd] ADJ choisi; *Com* de choix; *Liter* **s. passages** morceaux *mpl* choisis

selection [sɪ'lekʃən] N **1** *(act of choosing)* choix *m,* sélection *f*; *(for team)* sélection; **to make a s.** faire un choix; *Biol* **natural s.** sélection naturelle **2** *(range)* choix *m*; **a wide s.** un grand choix; **a narrow s.** un choix limité; **a good s. of wines** un bon choix de vins; **they don't have a very good s.** ils n'ont pas beaucoup de choix **3** *(thing(s) chosen)* **selections from Byron** morceaux *mpl* choisis de Byron; *Horseracing* **our selections** nos pronostics
▸▸ **s. box** *(of chocolate bars)* assortiment *m* de barres chocolatées; *Mktg* **s. method** méthode *f* de sélection; **s. procedure** procédure *f* de sélection; *(for staff)* démarche *f* de sélection

selective [sɪ'lektɪv] ADJ sélectif; **to be s.** *(of person)* savoir choisir, choisir avec discernement; **he's very s. about what he eats** il est très difficile sur la nourriture; **you should be more s. about your friends** tu devrais mieux choisir tes amis; **to be s. in the application of a law** appliquer la loi en fonction de ses intérêts
▸▸ **s. breeding** élevage *m* sélectif; *Sch* **s. entry** sélection *f*

selectively [sɪ'lektɪvlɪ] ADV de manière sélective

selectivity [sɪlek'tɪvɪtɪ] N sélectivité *f*

selectman, *pl* **selectmen** [sɪ'lektmən] N *Am (in New England)* = conseiller *m* municipal

selector [sɪ'lektər] N **1** *Sport* sélectionneur, -euse **2** *Tel, Aut* sélecteur *m*
▸▸ *Aut* **s. lever** *(in automatic gearbox)* levier *m* de sélection

selenium [sɪ'li:nɪəm] N sélénium *m*

self, *pl* **selves** [self, selvz] N **1** **that wasn't his real s.** il n'était pas lui-même; **he's quite his old** *or* **former s. again** *(he has recovered)* il est complètement rétabli; *(his character has returned to normal)* il est tout à fait comme auparavant; **she is a shadow of her former s.** elle n'est plus que l'ombre d'elle-même; **she was her usual cheerful/tactless s.** comme à son habitude, elle était gaie/blessante; **preoccupation with s.** préoccupation *f* de sa propre personne; *Old-fashioned* **your good selves** vous-mêmes, vous **2** *Psy* **the s.** *(personality)* la personnalité; *(ego)* le moi; **two selves in one body** deux personnalités dans une seule personne; **the notion of the s.** la notion du moi **3** *(flower)* fleur *f* de couleur uniforme

PRON *(on cheque)* **pay s.** payez à moi-même

self- [self] PREF **1** *(of and by oneself)* auto-; **s.-analysis** autoanalyse f **2** *(in oneself)* de soi-même; **s.-belief** confiance f en soi **3** *(automatic)* automatique; **s.-closing** à fermeture automatique

self-abasement N rabaissement m de soi-même

self-abnegation N = self-denial

self-absorbed [-əb'zɔːbd] ADJ égocentrique

self-abuse N *Old-fashioned* masturbation f

self-acting ADJ automatique

self-addressed [ə'drest] ADJ
▶▶ **s. envelope** enveloppe f à son propre nom

self-adhesive ADJ autocollant
▶▶ **s. label** étiquette f autocollante

self-adjusting ADJ à autoréglage, à réglage automatique
▶▶ **s. tappet** poussoir m autorégleur

self-advertisement N publicité f qu'on se fait à soi-même; **to indulge in s.** aimer se faire de la publicité

self-advocacy N *esp Am Admin (of mentally handicapped person)* affirmation f de soi

self-aggrandizement N autoglorification f

self-analysis N autoanalyse f

self-apparent ADJ évident

self-appointed ADJ **a s. critic of the régime** une personne qui s'érige en critique du régime; **a s. spokesperson** un porte-parole qui s'est lui-même désigné; **s. moral guardians** des moralisateurs qui s'érigent en censeurs

self-appraisal N auto-évaluation f, pl auto-évaluations
▶▶ **s. scheme** système m d'auto-évaluation

self-assembly ADJ *(furniture etc)* à monter soi-même
N **flat-packed for s.** en pièces détachées à monter soi-même

self-assertive ADJ décidé; **be more s.** vous devriez vous affirmer davantage

self-assertiveness N affirmation f de soi

self-assessment N **1** auto-évaluation f, pl auto-évaluations **2** *Br (for tax purposes)* = système m de déclaration des revenus pour le paiement des impôts, par opposition au prélèvement à la source

self-assurance N assurance f

self-assured ADJ sûr de soi, plein d'assurance

self-aware ADJ conscient de soi-même

self-awareness N conscience f de soi

self-belief N confiance f en soi; **to have s.** croire en soi-même

self-betterment N *(material)* amélioration f de sa condition; *(spiritual)* progrès mpl spirituels

self-catering ADJ *(holiday)* en appartement meublé; *(flat)* meublé avec cuisine équipée
ADV **to go s.** louer un meublé pour ses vacances
▶▶ **s. accommodation** meublé m de tourisme; **s. apartment** meublé, location f de vacances, appartement m en location; **s. holiday** vacances fpl en location; **to be on a s. holiday** être en location

self-censorship N autocensure f; **to practise s.** s'autocensurer

self-centred, *Am* **self-centered** [-'sentəd] ADJ égocentrique

self-centredness, *Am* **self-centeredness** [-'sentədnɪs] N égocentrisme m

self-certification N = système m dans lequel les employés n'ont pas besoin de certificat médical pour justifier d'une absence

self-check routine N *Comput* routine f d'autotest

self-cleaning ADJ *(oven)* autonettoyant

self-coloured, *Am* **self-colored** ADJ uni

self-composed ADJ posé, calme

self-composure N calme m

self-concept N *(self-image)* image f de soi

self-confessed [-kən'fest] ADJ **as a s. pervert, I …** tout perverti que je suis, je …; **he is a s. workaholic** de son propre aveu, c'est un bourreau de travail

self-confidence N confiance f en soi, assurance f

self-confident ADJ sûr de soi, plein d'assurance

self-congratulation N autosatisfaction f

self-congratulatory ADJ *(person)* qui fait de l'autosatisfaction; *(remarks, tone)* d'autosatisfaction, dénotant l'autosatisfaction

self-conscious ADJ **1** *(person)* embarrassé, gêné, contraint; **he's very s. about his large nose** il est très complexé par son gros nez **2** *(affected) (writing style etc)* affecté **3** *Phil* conscient, qui a conscience de soi

self-consciously ADV avec gêne *ou* embarras

self-consciousness N **1** *(embarrassment)* contrainte f, embarras m, gêne f **2** *(affectedness) (of writing style etc)* affectation f **3** *Phil* conscience f de soi

self-contained [-kən'teɪnd] ADJ **1** *(person)* réservé; *(uncommunicative)* peu communicatif; *(independent)* indépendant **2** *(apartment)* indépendant, avec entrée particulière

self-contempt N mépris m de soi-même; **to be full of s.** se mépriser

self-contradictory ADJ contradictoire

self-control N maîtrise f de soi; **to exercise s.** faire un effort sur soi-même; **to have no s.** ne pas savoir se maîtriser; **to lose one's s.** perdre tout empire sur soi-même, ne plus se maîtriser *ou* se contrôler; **to regain one's s.** se ressaisir

self-controlled ADJ **to be s.** *(of person)* avoir du sang-froid

self-correcting [-kə'rektɪŋ] ADJ à correction automatique, autocorrecteur, -trice

self-critical ADJ **to be s.** être critique à l'égard de soi-même; **you're too s.** tu es trop sévère avec toi-même

self-criticism N autocritique f

self-deception N aveuglement m; **it's pure s. on his part** il se fait des illusions

self-defeating [-dɪ'fiːtɪŋ] ADJ **that would be s.** cela irait à l'encontre du but recherché

self-defence, *Am* **self-defense** N *Law* légitime défense f; **to kill sb in s.** tuer qn en *(état de)* légitime défense; **a course in s.** un cours d'autodéfense *ou* de self-défense

self-delusion N illusion f; **it is nothing but s. on her part** elle se fait des illusions

self-denial N abnégation f

self-denying [-dɪ'naɪɪŋ] ADJ qui fait preuve d'abnégation; **a s. life** une vie de sacrifice

self-deprecation [-deprɪ'keɪʃən] N dénigrement m de soi-même

self-deprecatory ADJ *(person)* qui se dénigre; *(remarks)* critique envers soi-même

self-destruct VI s'autodétruire

self-destruction N autodestruction f

self-destructive ADJ *(behaviour, character)* suicidaire

self-determination N *Pol* autodétermination f

self-discipline N autodiscipline f

self-doubt N manque m de confiance en soi

self-drive ADJ *(car)* sans chauffeur

self-educated ADJ autodidacte

self-effacing [-ɪ'feɪsɪŋ] ADJ effacé

self-employed ADJ qui travaille à son (propre) compte, indépendant
NPL **the s.** les travailleurs mpl indépendants

self-employment N travail m à son propre compte, travail en indépendant

self-esteem N estime f *ou* respect m de soi, amour-propre m; **to suffer from low s.** avoir peu d'estime de soi

self-evident ADJ évident en soi, qui saute aux yeux

self-evidently ADV à l'évidence

self-examination N *(of conscience)* examen m de conscience; *(of breast)* autopalpation f

self-explanatory ADJ qui s'explique de soi-même

self-expression N libre expression f

self-fertilization N *Biol* autofécondation f

self-fertilizing [-'fɜːtɪlaɪzɪŋ] ADJ *Biol* autofécondant

self-financing ADJ *(entreprise)* qui s'autofinance
N autofinancement m

self-fulfilling ADJ
▶▶ **s. prophecy** = prophétie f défaitiste qui se réalise

self-fulfilment N accomplissement m de soi, épanouissement m

self-funding ADJ qui s'autofinance

self-governing ADJ autonome

self-government N autonomie f

self-hatred N haine f de soi

self-help N efforts mpl personnels
▶▶ **s. book** = manuel m prodiguant des conseils au lecteur pour améliorer un aspect particulier de sa vie; **s. group** groupe m d'entraide

self-hypnosis N autohypnose f

self-ignition N *Aut* auto-allumage m

self-image N image f qu'on a de soi-même, image de soi

self-importance N suffisance f, présomption f

self-important ADJ suffisant, présomptueux

self-imposed [-ɪm'pəʊzd] ADJ *(task etc)* dont on a pris de soi-même la responsabilité; *(exile)* volontaire

self-improvement N amélioration f personnelle; *(material)* amélioration de sa condition

self-induction N *Elec* self-induction f, auto-induction f
▶▶ **s. coil** bobine f de self-induction, *Fam* self f

self-indulgence N sybaritisme m, habitude f de ne rien se refuser; **a typical example of the author's stylistic s.** un exemple typique de la complaisance stylistique de l'auteur envers lui-même

self-indulgent ADJ sybarite, qui ne se refuse rien; *(writer, artist etc)* complaisant envers soi-même; *(novel, film etc)* complaisant

self-inflicted [-ɪn'flɪktɪd] ADJ *(damage etc)* que l'on s'inflige à soi-même; **s. wound** mutilation f volontaire

self-interest N intérêt m (personnel); **to act from** *or* **out of s.** agir dans un but intéressé

self-interested ADJ intéressé

selfish ['selfɪʃ] ADJ égoïste

selfishly ['selfɪʃlɪ] ADV égoïstement; **to act s.** agir en égoïste

selfishness ['selfɪʃnɪs] N égoïsme m

self-justification N justification f (de ses propres actes); **his attempts at s.** ses tentatives pour se justifier

self-knowledge N connaissance f de soi

selfless ['selflɪs] ADJ désintéressé, altruiste

selflessness ['selflɪsnɪs] N désintéressement m, altruisme m

self-loading ADJ (gun) automatique

self-loathing N dégoût m de soi-même

self-locking ADJ (door etc) à verrouillage ou fermeture automatique; Tech à blocage automatique, auto-bloqueur, -euse; (nut) indesserrable

self-love N narcissisme m

self-made ADJ
▸▸ **s. man** self-made-man m, pl self-made-men

self-mockery N moquerie f à l'égard de soi-même

self-mocking ADJ (tone, remarks) empreint d'ironie à l'égard de soi-même

self-motivated ADJ capable de prendre des initiatives

self-motivation N motivation f

self-obsessed [əb'sest] ADJ obsédé par soi-même

self-opinionated ADJ entêté; **he's very s.** il veut toujours avoir raison

self-op studio N (in broadcasting) studio m de reportage

self-parking ADJ Aut (wipers) à retour automatique

self-perpetuating [-pə'petjʊeɪtɪŋ] ADJ qui se reproduit indéfiniment

self-pity N attendrissement m sur soi-même; **full of s.** attendri sur soi-même; **to wallow in s.** s'apitoyer sur son sort

self-pitying ADJ qui s'apitoie sur son sort

self-pollination N Bot autopollinisation f

self-portrait N autoportrait m

self-possessed [-pə'zest] ADJ maître de soi, qui a beaucoup de sang-froid

self-possession N sang-froid m, maîtrise f de soi

self-praise N éloge m de soi-même; **I'm not saying that in s.** ce n'est pas laudatif à mon égard

self-preservation N (instinct for) s. instinct m de conservation

self-proclaimed [-prə'kleɪmd] ADJ autoproclamé

self-propelled, self-propelling [-prə'peld] ADJ (vehicle) automoteur, -trice, autopropulsé

self-publicist N he is an accomplished s. il sait soigner sa publicité

self-raising, Am **self-rising** ADJ (flour) contenant de la levure chimique

self-regard N = self-esteem

self-regulating ADJ Tech autorégulateur, -trice, à autoréglage; (economy) qui se régule d'elle-même

self-regulation N autorégulation f

self-reliance N indépendance f

self-reliant ADJ indépendant

self-repairing bumper [-rɪ'peərɪŋ] N Aut pare-chocs m inv auto-réparable

self-replicate VI s'autoreproduire

self-replicating [-'replɪkeɪtɪŋ] ADJ autoreproducteur, -trice

self-replication [-replɪ'keɪʃən] N autoreproduction f

self-respect N respect m de soi, amour-propre m; **have you no s.?** tu n'as pas d'amour-propre?; **to lose all s.** perdre toute dignité

self-respecting ADJ qui se respecte; **no s. journalist/doctor** aucun journaliste/médecin qui se respecte

self-restraint N retenue f; **to exercise s.** se contenir, se retenir

self-righteous ADJ pharisaïque, content de soi; **stop being so s.!** cesse d'être aussi content de toi!

self-righteousness N pharisaïsme m, satisfaction f de soi

self-righting ADJ (lifeboat etc) à redressement automatique

self-rule N Pol autonomie f

self-sacrifice N abnégation f

selfsame ['selfseɪm] ADJ même; **the s. thing** exactement la même chose

self-satisfaction N contentement m de soi, fatuité f, suffisance f

self-satisfied ADJ (person) content de soi, suffisant; (look) suffisant; **to look s.** avoir l'air content de soi-même

self-sealing ADJ (envelope) autocollant

self-seeking [-'siːkɪŋ] ADJ (person) égoïste

self-service N Com libre-service m, pl libres-services; **s. petrol station** station f libre-service
▸▸ **s. restaurant** self-service m, pl self-services

self-serving ADJ égoïste, intéressé

self-starter N 1 Aut Old-fashioned démarreur m (automatique) 2 (person) personne f très motivée et capable d'initiatives

self-styled [-staɪld] ADJ soi-disant inv, prétendu

self-sufficiency N indépendance f, Econ national s. autarcie f

self-sufficient ADJ (independent) indépendant, autosuffisant; **the country is s. in foodstuffs** le pays pourvoit à ses propres besoins en denrées alimentaires

self-supporting ADJ indépendant; (person) qui pourvoit à ses besoins; (business) qui couvre ses frais; Archit (vault) autoportant

self-tapping ADJ
▸▸ **s. screw** vis f autotaraudeuse

self-taught ADJ 1 (person) autodidacte 2 (skills) que l'on a acquis tout seul

self-test N Comput autotest m; **the printer does a s.** l'imprimante procède à une vérification de ses fonctions
VI s'autotester
▸▸ **s. button** bouton m d'autotest; **s. program** programme m d'autotest

self-timer N Phot retardateur m

self-willed [-wɪld] ADJ obstiné, volontaire

self-winding [-waɪndɪŋ] ADJ (watch) à remontage automatique

SELL [sel]

VT vendre 1 ▪ faire vendre 2, 4	
VI se vendre 1 ▪ faire vendre 2	

VT (pt, pp **sold** [səʊld]) **1** vendre; (goods) vendre, placer; **to s. sb sth, to s. sth to sb** vendre qch à qn; **he sold it to me for £10** il me l'a vendu (pour) 10 livres; **to s. sth for cash** vendre qch au comptant; **to s. sth on credit** vendre qch à crédit; **to s. sth privately** vendre qch de gré à gré; **a shop that sells clothes/furniture** un magasin de vêtements/meubles; **the album/book sold nearly a million copies** l'album/le livre s'est vendu à près d'un million d'exemplaires; **the Guardian**

sells roughly 400,000 copies a day le Guardian tourne à environ 400 000 exemplaires par jour; **to s. sb into slavery/prostitution** vendre qn comme esclave/prostituée; **to s. sth at a loss** vendre qch à perte; **to s. sth at a profit** faire un bénéfice en vendant qch; Lit **to s. one's life dearly** vendre chèrement sa vie; **to s. one's soul** vendre son âme

2 (cause to be sold) faire vendre; **scandal sells newspapers** ce sont les scandales qui font vendre les journaux; **you need at least one major star to s. the film** il faut au moins une star pour que le film fasse recette

3 to s. oneself (in interview etc) se faire valoir, Fam se vendre; **to s. oneself short** ne pas se montrer à sa juste valeur; **you have to s. yourself more to the electorate** il faudrait vous vendre mieux auprès des électeurs; **to s. an idea to the electorate** faire passer une idée auprès des électeurs; **to s. a party to the electorate** vendre les idées d'un parti auprès des électeurs; **they had difficulty selling the changes to the workforce** ils ont eu des difficultés à faire accepter les changements aux ouvriers; **I couldn't s. my father the idea** je n'ai pas pu faire accepter l'idée à mon père; Fam **to be sold on an idea** être emballé par une idée

4 (betray) (secret, one's country etc) vendre; **to s. oneself** se vendre; **to s. sb down the river** (betray) trahir qn

VI 1 (of product etc) se vendre; **to s. well/badly** se vendre bien/mal; **to s. like hot cakes** se vendre comme des petits pains; **shares in the company are selling at 109 pence** les actions de cette compagnie s'échangent à 109 pence

2 (helps sales) faire vendre; **sex sells** le sexe fait vendre

3 (work in sales) être dans la vente; **to be good at selling** être (un) bon vendeur; **I'm not selling** (my car etc) je ne ne suis pas vendeur

N **1 hard s.** vente f par des méthodes agressives; **soft s.** vente par des méthodes de suggestion ou de persuasion

2 Old-fashioned Fam (trick) attrape-nigaud m, pl attrape-nigauds

3 St Exch **s. order** injonction f à la vente

▸ **sell forward** VT SEP, VI Fin vendre à terme

▸ **sell off** VT SEP (dispose of at low price) (of shop) solder; (stock) liquider; (of person) vendre; **to s. off goods** écouler ou liquider des marchandises

▸ **sell out** VT SEP **1 the concert is sold out** il n'y a plus de billets pour le concert; **the tickets are sold out** tous les billets ont été vendus; **the edition is sold out** l'édition est épuisée; **I'm sold out** j'ai tout vendu; **the supermarket was sold out of butter** le supermarché était à court de beurre

2 St Exch (portfolio of shares) réaliser

3 (betray) (person, principles etc) vendre, trahir

VI 1 (sell all stocks) **to s. out (of sth)** se trouver à court (de qch); **have you got any bread? – no, I'm afraid we've sold out** est-ce que vous avez du pain? – non, nous n'en avons plus

2 (sell business) liquider; (sell shares) retirer sa participation d'une/de la société; **to s. out to sb** vendre sa participation à qn

3 (betray cause) trahir sa cause

▸ **sell up** VT SEP **to s. up a business/property** vendre (complètement) une affaire/propriété

VI (sell property) vendre ses effets; (sell business) vendre son fonds; **he sold up and went to Canada** il a tout vendu et est parti au Canada

sell-by date N Com date f limite de vente; Fig Fam **to be past one's s.** avoir fait son temps

seller ['selər] N **1** *(person)* vendeur, -euse; *(stockist)* marchand, -ande (**of** de); *Fin (of stocks)* réalisateur m; **s.'s market** marché m à la hausse **2** *(item)* **good/bad s.** article m qui se vend bien/mal; **it's one of our biggest sellers** c'est un de nos articles qui se vend le mieux

selling ['selɪŋ] N *(of goods etc)* vente f, écoulement m; **buying and s.** la vente et l'achat; **the job doesn't involve much s.** le travail ne fait pas intervenir beaucoup de vente
▸▸ **s. off** *(of stock)* liquidation f; **s. point** point m fort; **s. price** prix m de vente; **s. rate** *(of currency)* taux m de vente

sell-off N *(of state-owned company)* vente f

Sellotape® ['seləteɪp] N ruban m adhésif, Scotch® m

sellotape VT **to s. sth to sth** scotcher qch à qch

sellout ['selaʊt] N **1 this play's a s.** on joue à guichets fermés; **this line has been a s.** cet article s'est vendu à merveille (et il ne nous en reste plus) **2** *(act of betrayal)* trahison f

selvage, selvedge ['selvɪdʒ] N *(of fabric)* lisière f

semantic [sɪ'mæntɪk] ADJ *Ling* sémantique; **a purely s. distinction** une distinction purement sémantique

semantically [sɪ'mæntɪklɪ] ADV sémantiquement, du point de vue sémantique

semantics [sɪ'mæntɪks] NPL *(usu with sing verb)* sémantique f; **it's just s.** ce ne sont que des discours VOIR GRAMMAIRE A10

semaphore ['seməfɔːr] N sémaphore m VT *(message)* transmettre par sémaphore
▸▸ *Rail etc* **s. signal** signal m à bras

semblance ['sembləns] N *(appearance)* apparence f, semblant m; **to re-establish a s./ some s. of order** rétablir un semblant d'ordre; **a (mere) s. of friendship** un semblant d'amitié

semen ['siːmen] N *Physiol* sperme m

semester [sɪ'mestər] N *Am* semestre m

semi ['semɪ] N *Br Fam (house)* maison f jumelée

semi- ['semɪ] PREF semi-, demi-

semiautomatic ['semɪɔːtə'mætɪk] ADJ semi-automatique, *pl* semi-automatiques N arme f semi-automatique

semibreve ['semɪbriːv] N *Br Mus* ronde f

semicircle ['semɪsɜːk(ə)l] N demi-cercle m, *pl* demi-cercles

semicircular ['semɪ'sɜːkjʊlər] ADJ demi-circulaire, *pl* demi-circulaires, semi-circulaire, *pl* semi-circulaires

semicolon ['semɪ'kəʊlən] N point-virgule m, *pl* points-virgules

semiconductor ['semɪkən'dʌktər] N *Elec* semi-conducteur m, *pl* semi-conducteurs

semiconscious ['semɪ'kɒnʃəs] ADJ à demi conscient

semiconsciousness ['semɪ'kɒnʃəsnɪs] N demi-inconscience f

semidarkness ['semɪ'dɑːknɪs] N demi-jour m, pénombre f

semidetached ['semɪdɪ'tætʃt] ADJ *(house)* jumelé, jumeau, f jumelle; *Fig* **a s. member of the Government** = un membre du gouvernement en qui le Premier ministre ne peut pas totalement avoir confiance N maison f jumelée

semi-documentary N film m semi-documentaire

semifinal ['semɪ'faɪn(ə)l] N *Sport* demi-finale f, *pl* demi-finales; **to reach the semifinals** atteindre les demi-finales

semifinalist ['semɪ'faɪnəlɪst] N *Sport* demi-finaliste mf, *pl* demi-finalistes

semi-finished goods NPL produits *mpl* semi-finis

semi-graphics N *Comput* semi-graphisme m VOIR GRAMMAIRE A10

semi-invalid N **he's a s.** il ne peut presque plus se déplacer

semiliterate ['semɪ'lɪtərɪt] ADJ quasi illettré

semi-manufactured product [mænjʊ'fæktʃəd] N demi-produit m, *pl* demi-produits

semimonthly ['semɪ'mʌnθlɪ] ADJ *Am (publication)* bimensuel

seminal ['semɪnəl] ADJ **1** *Anat, Bot* séminal, -aux **2** *(event, work)* fructueux
▸▸ *Anat, Bot* **s. fluid** liquide m séminal

seminar ['semɪnɑːr] N *Univ* séminaire m

seminarist ['semɪnərɪst] N *Cathol* séminariste m

seminary ['semɪnərɪ] N *Cathol* séminaire m

semi-obscurity N *(darkness)* pénombre f, *Fig* quasi-obscurité f

semi-official ADJ semi-officiel, *pl* semi-officiels

semiological [semɪə'lɒdʒɪk(ə)l] ADJ sémiologique

semiology [semɪ'ɒlədʒɪ] N sém(é)iologie f

semiotic [semɪ'ɒtɪk] ADJ sémiotique

semiotician [semɪə'tɪʃən] N sémioticien, -ienne

semiotics [semɪ'ɒtɪks] NPL *(usu with sing verb)* sémiotique f VOIR GRAMMAIRE A10

semi-precious ADJ semi-précieux, fin

semiquaver ['semɪkweɪvər] N *Br Mus* double croche f

semi-retired ADJ **he is s.** il est en retraite partielle

semi-retirement N retraite f partielle

semi-skilled ADJ *(worker)* spécialisé

semi-skimmed ['skɪmd] ADJ
▸▸ **s. milk** lait m demi-écrémé

Semite ['semaɪt] N Sémite mf

Semitic [sɪ'mɪtɪk] ADJ sémitique

semitone ['semɪtəʊn] N *Br Mus* demi-ton m, *pl* demi-tons

semitropical ['semɪ'trɒpɪkəl] ADJ = **subtropical**

semivowel ['semɪ'vaʊəl] N semi-voyelle f, *pl* semi-voyelles

semolina [semə'liːnə] N semoule f

SEN [esɪ'en] N *Br Med (abbr* **State Enrolled Nurse)** infirmier, -ière diplômé(e) d'État

Sen 1 *(abbr* **senator)** sénateur m **2** *(abbr* **senior)** aîné, père

senate ['senɪt] N **1** *Pol* Sénat m **2** *Univ* conseil m d'université
▸▸ **s. house** Sénat

Senate
Le Sénat constitue, avec la Chambre des représentants, l'organe législatif américain; composé de 100 membres (deux par État), il détient l'exclusivité du droit d'impeachment.

senator ['senətər] N *Pol* sénateur m

senatorial [senə'tɔːrɪəl] ADJ sénatorial, -aux

SEND [send] VT *(pt, pp* **sent** [sent]) **1** *(dispatch) (something)* envoyer; *(in business letters, administration etc)* faire parvenir; *(by post) (letter etc)* envoyer, expédier; *(money)* remettre; *(person)* envoyer; **to s. word to sb** avertir qn; **to s. one's love to sb** envoyer ou faire ses amitiés à qn; **to s. clothes to the laundry** donner du linge à blanchir; **to s. a child to school** envoyer un enfant à l'école; **to s. sb to prison** envoyer qn en prison; **to s. sb on an errand** envoyer qn faire une cour-

se; **to s. sb for sth** envoyer qn chercher qch; *Comput* **s. to the printer** envoyer à ou vers ou sur l'imprimante
2 *(cause to move, change etc)* **force that sends sth in a certain direction** force qui fait marcher ou qui pousse qch dans une certaine direction; **it sends a current down the wire** cela fait passer un courant dans le fil; **it sent a shiver down my spine** cela m'a fait un frisson dans le dos; **the blow sent him sprawling** le coup l'a renversé; **that sent him into fits of laughter** cela l'a fait éclater de rire; **you'll s. me mad** vous allez me rendre fou; **the rain sent us scurrying for shelter** nous avons couru nous abriter dès que la pluie a commencé; **to s. sb into a panic/a fit of depression/a rage** paniquer/déprimer/faire enrager qn; **to s. sb's profits tumbling** faire chuter les bénéfices de qn; *Fam* **to s. sb packing, to s. sb about his/her business** envoyer promener qn
3 *Lit (grant) (something)* accorder, envoyer; **s. him/her victorious** que Dieu lui donne ou lui accorde la victoire; **what fortune sends us** ce que la fortune nous envoie
4 *Old-fashioned Fam (thrill)* **it sends me** ça me transporte
▸ **send along** VT SEP envoyer; **s. him along** *(send him to see me)* envoyez-le-moi; *(tell him to see me)* dites-lui de venir me voir
▸ **send away** VT SEP **1** *(send to another place)* envoyer; **to be sent away to school** être envoyé à l'école
2 *(dismiss)* renvoyer, congédier
VI *(write to obtain something)* écrire
▸ **send away for** VT INSEP *(write to obtain)* demander par courrier; **s. away for your free copy now** demandez dès maintenant votre exemplaire gratuit
▸ **send back** VT SEP *(return) (somebody, something)* renvoyer; *(food in restaurant)* renvoyer à la cuisine
▸ **send down** VT SEP **1** *(send to lower place)* faire descendre
2 *(cause to fall) (prices, temperature etc)* faire descendre
3 *Br Univ (expel)* renvoyer, expulser
4 *Br Fam (send to prison)* envoyer en prison, coffrer
▸ **send for** VT INSEP **1** *(summon) (somebody, something)* envoyer chercher; **we sent for a couple of pizzas** nous nous sommes fait livrer deux pizzas; **we sent for the doctor** nous avons appelé le médecin, nous avons envoyé chercher le médecin
2 = **send away for**
▸ **send in** VT SEP *(send to a place) (invoice, bill)* soumettre; *(request etc)* remettre; *(dinner)* (faire) servir; **he has sent in his bill (to us/them)** il nous/leur a envoyé sa note; **many viewers sent in comments on the programme** de nombreux spectateurs ont envoyé leurs commentaires sur l'émission; **s. Mrs Jones in** faites entrer Mme Jones; **to s. the army in** envoyer l'armée
VI *(write to obtain sth)* faire une demande écrite (**for sth** de qch)
▸ **send off** VT SEP *(by post)* envoyer, expédier; *Ftbl etc (player)* renvoyer ou expulser du terrain
VI = **send away 2**
▸ **send on** VT SEP *(forward) (letter)* faire suivre; *(order)* transmettre; *(luggage)* expédier à l'avance; *Ftbl etc (player)* envoyer sur le terrain
▸ **send on ahead** VT SEP *(luggage etc)* envoyer à l'avance; *(person)* envoyer en reconnaissance
▸ **send out** VT SEP **1** *(person)* envoyer dehors; *(pupil)* mettre à la porte; **to s. sb out for more food/wine** envoyer qn chercher de la nourriture/du vin
2 *(leaflets)* lancer, expédier; *(invitations)* envoyer

3 *(signals, heat etc)* émettre; **the chimney/engine sent out billows of smoke** la cheminée/le moteur crachait des tourbillons de fumée

VI *(for food, wine)* envoyer chercher

▶**send up** **VT SEP 1** *(send to higher place)* *(person, object)* faire monter; *(rocket)* lancer **2** *(prices, temperature etc)* faire monter *ou Fam* grimper **3** *Br Fam (parody)* se moquer de, parodier; *(play, part)* faire une parodie de; **he sent her up as an eccentric duchess** il l'avait caricaturée sous les traits d'une duchesse excentrique **4** *Am Fam (send to prison)* envoyer en taule, coffrer

sender ['sendər] **N** *(of letter, fax, goods)* expéditeur, -trice; *(of radio message)* transmetteur *m*

sending ['sendɪŋ] **N** envoi *m*; **s. by rail** expédition *f* par chemin de fer
▶▶**s. depot** dépôt *m* d'expédition

send-off N *Fam* **we went to the station to give her a good s.** nous sommes allés à la gare pour marquer son départ; **to give sb a good s.** *(funeral)* faire à qn de belles funérailles; **to give sb a big s.** venir nombreux pour dire au revoir à qn

send-up N *Br Fam* satire *f*, parodie *f*; **is this a s.?** est-ce qu'on se moque de moi?

Senegal [senɪ'gɔːl] **N** Sénégal *m*

Senegalese [senɪgə'liːz] **ADJ** sénégalais **N** Sénégalais, -aise

senescence [sɪ'nesəns] **N** *Med* sénescence *f*

senile ['siːnaɪl] **ADJ** sénile
▶▶**s. dementia** démence *f* sénile

senility [sɪ'nɪlɪtɪ] **N** sénilité *f*

senior ['siːnjər] **ADJ** *(in age)* aîné; *(in rank, position etc)* plus haut placé; *(longer-serving)* plus ancien; *Mil etc (officer)* supérieur; **Bernard Long s.** Bernard Long père; **he's two years s. to me** il est mon aîné de deux ans; **s. in rank** de grade supérieur; **the s. boys/girls of a school** les garçons/filles des grandes classes

N 1 *(in age)* aîné, -ée; **she is his s. by three years, she is three years his s.** elle est son aînée de trois ans; **to be sb's s.** *(in age)* être l'aîné de qn; *(in rank)* être d'un rang plus élevé que qn; **the seniors** *(pupils)* les grand(e)s **2** *Am Sch* étudiant, -ante de quatrième *ou* dernière année

▶▶**s. citizen** personne *f* âgée *ou* du troisième âge; **s. executive** cadre *m* supérieur; **s. management** la direction; **s. officer** l'officier *m* commandant; **I'll report you to your s. officer** je vais vous signaler à votre supérieur; **s. official** haut fonctionnaire *m*; **s. partner** associé, -ée principal(e); **s. reporter** grand reporter *m*; *Br* **the S. Service** la marine

seniority [siːnɪ'ɒrɪtɪ] **N 1** *(in age)* priorité *f* d'âge, supériorité *f* d'âge; **he was chairman by virtue of s.** il était président en raison de son âge **2** *(in rank)* ancienneté *f* (de grade); **to be promoted by s.** avancer (de grade) *ou* être promu à l'ancienneté; **to have s. over sb** avoir plus d'ancienneté que qn

senna ['senə] **N** *Bot* séné *m*
▶▶*Pharm* **s. pods** follicules *mpl* de séné

sensation [sen'seɪʃən] **N 1** *(power of feeling)* sensibilité *f*; *(feeling) (of wellbeing, discomfort, heat, cold etc)* sensation *f*; **I had the s. of falling** j'avais la sensation de tomber **2** *(excitement)* **to create** *or* **make** *or* **cause a s.** *(of event etc)* faire sensation; **the film was the s. of the year** le film a été l'événement de l'année; **s.-hungry readers** des lecteurs avides de sensationnel

sensational [sen'seɪʃən(ə)l] **ADJ 1** *(film, novel, press etc)* à sensation **2** *Fam (excellent)* sensationnel, fantastique

sensationalism [sen'seɪʃənəlɪz(ə)m] **N 1** recherche *f* du sensationnel **2** *Phil* sensualisme *m*, sensationnisme *m*

sensationalist [sen'seɪʃənəlɪst] **N** *(with news)* colporteur *m* de nouvelles à sensation; *(who overdramatizes)* personne *f* ayant tendance à dramatiser; *(writer)* auteur *m* à sensation; *(journalist)* journaliste *mf* qui fait du sensationnel

ADJ *(article, style, journalism)* à sensation; **to be s.** *(of tabloids, reporting)* faire du sensationnel

sensationalize [sen'seɪʃənəlaɪz] **VT** *(event etc)* faire du sensationnel sur; **it's been so sensationalized that ...** on a fait tant de battage là-dessus que ...

sensationally [sen'seɪʃ(ə)nəlɪ] **ADV 1** **the murder was treated s. in the tabloids** les tabloïdes ont fait du meurtre une histoire à sensations **2** *Fam (successful, good)* d'une manière sensationnelle *ou* fantastique; **they did s. well in the first round** ils ont été fantastiques dans les premières épreuves

SENSE [sens]

N sens **1, 3, 5** • sensation **3**
• sentiment **3** • conscience **3** • bon sens **4** • signification **5**
VT sentir **1** • avoir l'impression que **1**

N 1 *(faculty)* sens *m*; **the five senses** les cinq sens; **to have a keen s. of smell/hearing** avoir l'odorat fin/l'ouïe fine; **she seemed to have a sixth s.** elle semblait posséder un sixième sens; **to be in possession of all one's senses** jouir de toutes ses facultés; **pleasures of the senses** plaisirs sensuels *ou* des sens

2 **have you taken leave of your senses?** avez-vous perdu l'esprit *ou* la raison?; **to come to one's senses** *(be sensible again)* revenir à la raison; *(regain consciousness)* revenir à soi; **to bring sb to his senses** ramener qn à la raison

3 *(feeling)* sensation *f*, sens *m*; *(awareness)* sentiment *m*, conscience *f*; **she has a s. for what is likely to sell** elle a du flair pour deviner ce qui va se vendre; **a s. of achievement** un sentiment d'accomplissement; **to have a s. of belonging** avoir le sentiment d'être intégré; **s. of colour/beauty** sens des couleurs/de la beauté; **s. of injustice** sentiment d'injustice; **a s. of pleasure/warmth** une sensation de plaisir/chaleur; **to lose all s. of reality/time** perdre la notion de la réalité/du temps

4 *(rationality)* bon sens *m*; **common s.** sens *m* commun; **good s.** bon sens; **to talk s.** parler raison; **there's no s. in that, that doesn't make s.** cela n'a pas de sens, cela ne rime à rien; **it would make more s. if ...** cela serait plus intelligent si ...; **there's a lot of s. in what she says** ce qu'elle dit est très sensé; **it doesn't make s. to do that** cela n'a pas de sens de faire une chose pareille; **it makes good political/business s. to ...** il est bon sur le plan politique/commercial de ...; **it makes more s. to do this first** c'est plus logique de commencer par cela; **that makes good s.** c'est logique, c'est une bonne idée; **where's the s. in that?** à quoi ça sert?; **there's no s. in doing that** ça ne sert à rien; **to have the (good) s. to do sth** avoir l'intelligence *ou* le bon sens de faire qch; **to have more s. than to do sth** avoir assez de bon sens pour ne pas faire qch

5 *(meaning) (of word etc)* sens *m*, signification *f*; **these words don't make s.** ces mots n'ont pas de sens *ou* sont incompréhensibles; **now the sentence makes more s.** maintenant la phrase a plus de sens; **does this sentence make s.?** cette phrase veut-elle dire quelque chose?; **you're not making s.**

vous êtes illogique; **make s.!** sois logique!; **I can't make s. of it** je n'arrive pas à le comprendre; **in the literal/figurative s.** au sens propre/figuré; **in every s. of the word, in more senses than one** dans tous les sens du terme; **in a s.** d'une certaine façon, dans un *(certain)* sens; **in the s. that ...** en ce sens que ..., au sens où ...; **in the normal s. (of the word)** à proprement parler; **in no s., not in any s.** en aucun cas; **this is not in any real s. a change of policy** ça ne représente pas du tout un changement de politique; **in a very real s.** véritablement

VT 1 *(know intuitively)* sentir; *(have premonition)* pressentir; **I sensed no difference in his mood from last time** je n'ai décelé chez lui aucun changement d'humeur par rapport à la dernière fois; **I sensed that she was hiding something** j'avais l'impression qu'elle cachait quelque chose **2** *Phil* percevoir par le sens **3** *Electron etc* détecter
▶▶**s. impression** sensation *f*, **s. organ** organe *m* des sens *ou* sensoriel

senseless ['senslɪs] **ADJ 1** *(unconscious)* sans connaissance, inanimé; **to fall s.** tomber sans connaissance; **to knock/beat sb s.** assommer qn **2** *(pointless) (action)* insensé, stupide, absurde; **a s. killing** un meurtre gratuit; **a s. remark** une remarque stupide; **what a s. waste (of human life)** *(one person)* voilà une vie humaine absurdement gâchée; *(more than one person)* que de vies humaines gâchées

senselessly ['senslɪslɪ] **ADV** absurdement

senselessness ['senslɪsnɪs] **N** *(stupidity)* absurdité *f*

sensibility [sensɪ'bɪlɪtɪ] **N 1** *(of person)* sensibilité *f*, émotivité *f*; **I do not want to offend anyone's sensibilities** je ne veux pas heurter la susceptibilité de qui que ce soit **2** *(of organ etc)* sensibilité *f*

sensible ['sensɪb(ə)l] **ADJ 1** *(rational) (person, decision)* sensé, raisonnable; *(choice)* judicieux; **it would be more s. to ...** il serait plus raisonnable de ...; **be s.** soyez raisonnable **2** **s. clothes** vêtements commodes *ou* pratiques; **s. shoes** chaussures confortables et pratiques **3** *Arch, Lit (aware)* conscient (**of** de); **to be s. of the fact that ...** être sensible au *ou* apprécier le fait que ... **4** *Fml (perceptible) (quantity, difference etc)* sensible, appréciable

> Note that the French word **sensible** is a false friend and is almost never a translation for the English word **sensible**. It means **sensitive**.

sensibly ['sensɪblɪ] **ADV 1** *(rationally) (to behave, discuss)* raisonnablement; *(to decide, divide)* judicieusement; **to be s. dressed** porter des vêtements pratiques **2** *(perceptibly)* sensiblement, perceptiblement

sensitive ['sensɪtɪv] **ADJ 1** *(person, skin)* sensible; *(portrayal, interpretation)* plein de sensibilité; **he's very s. about his accent** il est très susceptible sur son accent; **to be s. to noise** être sensible au bruit; **to be s. to the cold** *(of person)* être frileux **2** *Fin (market)* sensible; *Phot (plate)* impressionnable, sensible à la lumière; *(paper)* sensible, sensibilisé; **s. to sth** sensible à qch **3** *(question, issue etc)* délicat, sensible; *(document, information)* confidentiel
▶▶*Phot etc* **s. layer** couche *f* sensible

sensitively ['sensɪtɪvlɪ] **ADV** sensiblement, d'une manière sensible; *(to write etc)* avec sensibilité

sensitiveness ['sensɪtɪvnɪs], **sensitivity** [sensɪ'tɪvɪtɪ] **N** *(of person, skin, machine, instrument etc)* sensibilité *f*; *Phot* impressionnabilité *f*, rapidité *f*, *(of question etc)* caractère *m* délicat; *(of document, information etc)* caractère confidentiel

sensitization [sensɪtaɪ'zeɪʃən] **N** *Med, Phot* sensibilisation *f*

sensitize ['sensɪtaɪz] **VT** sensibiliser; *Phot* **sensitized paper** papier *m* sensible *ou* sensibilisé

sensitizer ['sensɪtaɪzər] **N** *Phot* sensibilisateur *m*

sensor ['sensər] **N** *Electron* détecteur *m*, capteur *m*

sensory ['sensərɪ] **ADJ** *(nerve etc)* sensoriel
▸▸ **s. organs** organes *mpl* des sens

sensual ['sensjʊəl] **ADJ 1** sensuel; *(instinct)* animal, -aux; **s. pleasures** plaisirs *mpl* des sens **2** *(person, art)* sensuel, voluptueux

> Attention: ne pas confondre avec **sensuous**.

sensualism ['sensjʊəlɪz(ə)m] **N 1** sensualité *f* **2** *Phil* sensualisme *m*

sensualist ['sensjʊəlɪst] **N 1** sensualiste *mf*, voluptueux, -euse **2** *Phil* sensualiste *mf*

sensuality [sensjʊ'ælɪtɪ] **N** sensualité *f*

sensuous ['sensjʊəs] **ADJ** *(pleasure, life, charm etc)* sensuel, voluptueux

> Attention: ne pas confondre avec **sensual**.

sensuously ['sensjʊəslɪ] **ADV** voluptueusement, avec volupté

sensuousness ['sensjʊəsnɪs] **N** volupté *f*

sent **PT, PP** *see* send

sentence ['sentəns] **N 1** *Gram* phrase *f* VOIR GRAMMAIRE A78–9; B62–4 **2** *Law* (conviction) condamnation *f*, sentence *f*, *(period in prison)* peine *f*; **life s.** condamnation à perpétuité; **s. of death, death s.** condamnation à mort, arrêt *m* de mort; **under s. of death** condamné à mort; **to pass (a) s.** prononcer une condamnation *ou* une sentence; **while he was serving his s.** pendant qu'il purgeait sa peine
VT *Law* condamner; **to s. sb to a month's imprisonment/to death** condamner qn à un mois de prison/à mort
▸▸ *Mktg* **s. completion** *(in market research)* phrases *fpl* à compléter

sententious [sen'tenʃəs] **ADJ** *Fml (person, speech etc)* sentencieux

sententiousness [sen'tenʃəsnɪs] **N** *Fml (of person)* caractère *m* sentencieux; *(of writing etc)* ton *m* sentencieux

sentient ['sentɪənt] **ADJ** *Fml* sensible

sentiment ['sentɪmənt] **N 1** *(opinion)* sentiment *m*, opinion *f*, avis *m*; **these are my sentiments** voilà mon sentiment *ou* mon opinion; **my sentiments exactly** je partage entièrement votre avis; **noble sentiments** sentiments nobles **2** *(sentimentality)* sentimentalité *f*, *(mawkish)* sensiblerie *f* **3** *Arch, Lit (emotion)* sentimentalité *f*

sentimental [sentɪ'ment(ə)l] **ADJ** sentimental, -aux; **don't be so s.!** ne sois pas si sentimental!
▸▸ **s. value** valeur *f* sentimentale

sentimentalism [sentɪ'mentəlɪz(ə)m] **N** sentimentalisme *m*; *(mawkishness)* sensiblerie *f*

sentimentalist [sentɪ'mentəlɪst] **N** personne *f* sentimentale; **he's/she's a s.** c'est un sentimental/une sentimentale

sentimentality [sentɪmen'tælɪtɪ] **N** sentimentalité *f*, *(mawkishness)* sensiblerie *f*

sentimentalize [sentɪ'mentəlaɪz] **VI** faire du sentiment
VT *(novel, work, situation etc)* romancer

sentimentally [sentɪ'ment(ə)lɪ] **ADV** sentimentalement; *(mawkishly)* avec sensiblerie

sentinel ['sentɪn(ə)l] **N** *Mil* factionnaire *m*, sentinelle *f*; *Fig* **the s. of democracy** le garant *ou* gardien de la démocratie; **to stand s. over sth** être de garde à qch; *Fig* protéger qch

sentry ['sentrɪ] **N** *Mil* factionnaire *m*, sentinelle *f*; **to be on** *or* **to do s. duty, to stand s.** être en sentinelle *ou* de faction; **to relieve a s.** relever une sentinelle
▸▸ **s. box** guérite *f*

Seoul [səʊl] **N** Séoul

sepal ['sep(ə)l] **N** *Bot* sépale *m*

separable ['sep(ə)rəb(ə)l] **ADJ** séparable

separate¹ ['sep(ə)rət] **ADJ** *(parts, box, booklet etc)* séparé, détaché (**from** de); *(distinct)* distinct; *(independent)* indépendant; *(times, days)* différent; **the two issues are quite s.** les deux problèmes sont distincts; **to keep sth s. (from sth else)** séparer qch (de qch d'autre); **to sleep in s. rooms/beds** *(of married couple)* faire chambre/lit à part; **use a s. piece of paper** utilisez une feuille séparée; **it's now become a s. company** c'est maintenant une société indépendante; **they went their/we went our s. ways** ils sont partis chacun de leur côté/nous sommes partis chacun de notre côté
N 1 *(print)* tiré *m* à part **2** *Com (items of dress)* **separates** coordonnés *mpl*

separate² ['sepəreɪt] **VT** séparer (**from** de); *(milk)* écrémer; *(members of a family etc)* désunir; *(sb from his family etc)* détacher; **to s. eggs** séparer les blancs des jaunes; **s. two eggs** prenez deux œufs, séparez les blancs des jaunes; **murder cases can be separated under four headings** on distingue quatre types de meurtres; **to s. two boxers** séparer deux boxeurs; **he is separated (from his wife)** il est séparé (de sa femme); **the Channel separates England from France** la Manche sépare la France et l'Angleterre; **the gulf that separates him from his colleagues** l'abîme entre lui et ses collègues, l'abîme qui le sépare de ses collègues; **what separates their language from other African languages is …** ce qui distingue leur langue des autres langues africaines, c'est …; **to s. the men from the boys** faire un tri
VI *(of group of people, man and wife)* se séparer; **when we separated for the night** quand nous nous sommes quittés pour la nuit; **to s. from sb** se séparer de qn, rompre avec qn
▸ **separate off** **VT SEP** séparer
▸ **separate out** **VI** se séparer
VT SEP séparer (**from** de)

separately ['sep(ə)rətlɪ] **ADV** séparément; **are you paying s.?** *(in shop, restaurant etc)* est-ce que vous payez séparément?; **not to be sold s.** *(on multiple pack, promotional item etc)* ne peut être vendu séparément; **wash s.** *(on garment label etc)* laver séparément; **keep this s.** gardez ceci à part

separation [sepə'reɪʃən] **N** séparation *f* (**from sb** d'avec qn); **(judicial) s.** séparation (judiciaire)
▸▸ **s. allowance** *Mil* allocation *f* mensuelle *(versée par l'armée à la femme d'un soldat)*; *(alimony)* pension *f* alimentaire; *Psy* **s. anxiety** peur *f* de l'abandon; *Pol* **s. of powers** séparation *f* des pouvoirs

separatism ['sepərətɪz(ə)m] **N** séparatisme *m*

separatist ['sepərətɪst] **ADJ, N** séparatiste *mf*

separator ['sepəreɪtər] **N** *Tech, Comput* séparateur *m*

sepia ['siːpɪə] **N** *Art* sépia *f*
▸▸ **s. drawing** dessin *m* à la sépia

sepoy ['siːpɔɪ] **N** *Mil* cipaye *m*

sepsis ['sepsɪs] **N** *Med* septicité *f*

Sept *abbr* **September**

September [sep'tembər] **N** septembre *m*; **in**

s. au mois de septembre, en septembre; (on) the first/the seventh of S. le premier/le sept septembre VOIR GRAMMAIRE A81–2; B60–2

septet [sep'tet] **N** *Mus* septuor *m*

septic ['septɪk] **ADJ** *Med* septique; *(wound)* infecté; **to become** *or* **go s.** s'infecter; **I have a s. finger** j'ai un doigt infecté
▸▸ **s. poisoning** septicémie *f*; **s. tank** fosse *f* septique

septicaemia, *Am* **septicemia** [septɪ'siːmɪə] **N** *Med* septicémie *f*

septuagenarian [septjʊədʒɪ'neərɪən] **N, ADJ** septuagénaire *mf*

Septuagesima [septjʊə'dʒesɪmə] **N** *Rel* septuagésime *f*
▸▸ **S. Sunday** le dimanche de la Septuagésime

Septuagint ['septjʊədʒɪnt] **N** version *f* (de la Bible) des Septante, Septante *f*

septum, *pl* **septa** [septəm, -ə] **N** *Anat* septum *m*; *Bot* cloison *f*

sepulchral [sɪ'pʌlkrəl] **ADJ** *Lit* sépulcral, -aux

sepulchre, *Am* **sepulcher** ['sepəlkər] **N** sépulcre *m*; **the Holy S.** le Saint Sépulcre

sequel ['siːkwəl] **N** *(to novel etc)* suite *f*; **as a s. to these events** comme suite à ces événements; **action that had an unfortunate s.** acte qui a entraîné des suites malheureuses

sequelize ['siːkwəlaɪz] **VT** *esp Am (movie)* donner une suite à

sequence ['siːkwəns] **N 1** *(order)* ordre *m*; *(in time)* ordre, succession *f*, **what's the s. of events going to be?** quelle est l'ordre du programme?; **in some sort of s.** dans un ordre quelconque; **in s.** l'un après l'autre; **out of s.** *(one item)* mal rangé; *(set of pictures, items)* dans le désordre; **the films were deliberately shown out of s.** les films ont été présentés dans le désordre exprès; **logical s.** enchaînement *m* logique **2** *(series) (of events, disasters etc)* suite *f*, série *f* **3** *Cards, Mus, Cin, Comput* séquence *f*, *Mus* **a chord s.** une suite d'accords
▸▸ *Comput* **s. check** contrôle *m* de séquence; *Comput* **s. checking** contrôle de séquence; *Gram* **s. of tenses** concordance *f* des temps

sequencer ['siːkwənsər] **N** *Comput* coordonnateur *m*, séquenceur *m*

sequencing ['siːkwənsɪŋ] **N** *Comput* mise en séquence

sequential [sɪ'kwenʃəl] **ADJ 1** *Comput* séquentiel **2** *Fml (following)* séquentiel
▸▸ *Comput* **s. file** fichier *m* séquentiel; *Comput* **s. processing** traitement *m* séquentiel; *Cin, TV* **s. shooting** tourné-monté *m*, *pl* tournés-montés

sequentially [sɪ'kwenʃəlɪ] **ADV** séquentiellement

sequester [sɪ'kwestər] **VT 1** *Fml (confiscate)* confisquer; *Law (property of debtor)* séquestrer, mettre sous séquestre **2** *Lit* **to s. oneself (from the world)** se retirer (du monde); **to lead a sequestered life** vivre une vie de reclus; **a sequestered corner of the property** un coin isolé de la propriété

sequestrate [sɪ'kwestreɪt] **VT** confisquer; *Law (property of debtor)* séquestrer, mettre sous séquestre

sequestration [siːkwe'streɪʃən] **N** confiscation *f*, *Law* séquestration *f*, mise *f* sous séquestre

sequin ['siːkwɪn] **N** *(on dress etc)* paillette *f*

sequined ['siːkwɪnd] **ADJ** à paillettes

sequoia [sɪ'kwɔɪə] **N** *(tree)* séquoia *m*

seraglio [se'rɑːlɪəʊ] **N** sérail *m*, *pl* -ails

seraph, *pl* **seraphs, seraphim** ['serəf, -əfs, -əfɪm] **N** séraphin *m*

seraphic [sɪˈræfɪk] ADJ séraphique

Serb [sɜːb] ADJ serbe
N Serbe *mf*

Serbia [ˈsɜːbɪə] N Serbie *f*

Serbian [ˈsɜːbɪən] ADJ serbe
N 1 Serbe *mf* 2 *Ling* serbe *m*

Serbo-Croat [sɜːbəʊˈkrəʊæt], **Serbo-Croatian** [-krəʊˈeɪʃən] ADJ serbo-croate, *pl* serbo-croates
N 1 Serbo-croate *mf*, *pl* Serbo-croates 2 *Ling* serbo-croate *m*

sere [sɪər] ADJ *Lit (vegetation)* desséché; *(lake)* asséché

serenade [serəˈneɪd] N sérénade *f*
VT donner une sérénade à

serendipitous [serənˈdɪpɪtəs] ADJ *Lit* génial et fortuit

serendipity [serənˈdɪpɪtɪ] N *Lit* don *m* de faire des trouvailles

serene [sɪˈriːn] ADJ 1 *(sky, sea, person)* serein, calme, tranquille; *(sky)* clair; **her face wore a s. look** son visage exprimait le calme *ou* la sérénité 2 *(in title)* sérénissime; **His S. Highness** son Altesse sérénissime

serenely [sɪˈriːnlɪ] ADV calmement, avec sérénité

serenity [sɪˈrenɪtɪ] N sérénité *f*, calme *m*

serf [sɜːf] N serf *m*, serve *f*

serfdom [ˈsɜːfdəm] N servage *m*

serge [sɜːdʒ] N *Tex* serge *f*; **cotton s.** sergé *m*
▸▸ **s. suit** costume *m* en sergé

sergeant [ˈsɑːdʒənt] N *(in infantry, air force)* sergent *m*; *(in artillery, armoured corps, cavalry)* maréchal *m* des logis; **(police) s.** brigadier *m*; **quartermaster s., staff s.** *(in infantry, air force)* sergent fourrier *ou* comptable; *(in artillery, armoured corps, cavalry)* maréchal des logis fourrier *ou* comptable; *Law* **s. at arms** huissier *m*

sergeant-major N *Mil* adjudant *m*; **regimental s.** adjudant-chef *m*, *pl* adjudants-chefs

serial [ˈsɪərɪəl] ADJ 1 *Mus (belonging to series)* sériel 2 *(arranged in series)* en série; *(from series)* d'une série; *(forming series)* formant série 3 *Comput (processing, transmission, data)* série *inv*; **s. to parallel convertor** convertisseur *m* série-parallèle
N *(story published in parts) (in magazine)* feuilleton *m*, roman-feuilleton *m*, *pl* romans-feuilletons; *Radio* feuilleton (radiophonique); *TV* feuilleton (télévisé); **it was first published in s. form** cela a d'abord été publié sous forme de feuilleton
▸▸ *Comput* **s. access** accès *m* séquentiel; *Comput* **s. cable** câble *m* série; **s. data** données *fpl* série; **s. device** périphérique *m* série; **s. drama** feuilleton *m*; **s. input** entrée *f* série; *Comput* **s. interface** interface *f* série; **s. killer** tueur, -euse en série; **s. monogamist** = personne *f* qui a une succession de relations monogamiques; **s. monogamy** = succession *f* de relations monogamiques; **s. number** *(of product, publication)* numéro *m* de série; *(of cheque, voucher)* numéro; *(of soldier)* (numéro) matricule *m*; **s. output** sortie *f* série; *Comput* **s. port** port *m* série; *Comput* **s. printer** imprimante *f* série; *Comput* **s. printer port** port d'imprimante série **s. rights** droits *mpl* de reproduction en feuilleton; **s. writer** feuilletoniste *mf*

serialization [sɪərɪəlaɪˈzeɪʃən] N mise *f* en feuilleton, publication *f* en feuilleton; *TV, Radio* adaptation *f* en feuilleton
▸▸ **s. rights** droits *mpl* de reproduction en feuilleton

serialize [ˈsɪərɪəlaɪz] VT *(novel etc)* publier en feuilleton, adapter en feuilleton; *TV, Radio* diffuser en feuilleton; **serialized in six parts** *(novel etc)* publié en six épisodes; *TV,*

Radio diffusé en six parties; **it's being serialized in the Observer** ça sort en feuilleton dans l'Observer

serially [ˈsɪərɪəlɪ] ADV 1 en *ou* par série 2 *Journ* en feuilleton

seriatim [sɪərɪˈeɪtɪm] ADV *Fml* point par point

sericulture [ˈserɪkʌltʃər] N sériciculture *f*

series [ˈsɪəriːz] N 1 série *f*; *(of colours)* échelle *f*, gamme *f*; *(of books)*, TV, Radio série; *(in magazine, newspaper)* série d'articles; **a s. of terrorist attacks** une série d'attaques terroristes; **in s.** en série, en succession 2 *Elec* série *f*; **connection in s.** montage *m* en série
▸▸ *Elec* **s. connection** montage en série; *TV* **s. producer** producteur *m* de série télévisée; *Elec* **s. winding** enroulement *m* en série

series-connected ADJ *Comput* connecté en série

series-wound ADJ *Elec* à enroulements série
▸▸ **s. motor** moteur *m* à enroulements série

serif [ˈserɪf] N *Typ* empattement *m*

seriocomic [sɪərɪəʊˈkɒmɪk] ADJ moitié sérieux moitié comique

serious [ˈsɪərɪəs] ADJ 1 *(grave, critical)* sérieux, grave; **things are becoming s.** cela devient sérieux; **s. injury** blessure grave; **s. mistake** grosse faute
2 *(in earnest, thoughtful) (person, decision, newspaper etc)* sérieux; **she's not really a s. novelist** *(not considered a real novelist)* ce n'est pas un écrivain majeur; **to be s. about sth** parler sérieusement à propos de qch; **is he s. about emigrating?** est-ce qu'il envisage sérieusement d'émigrer?; **I have never seen him so s. about a girl** je ne l'ai jamais vu aussi sérieux avec une fille; **I'm s.** je ne plaisante pas; **are you s.?** tu parles sérieusement?; **surely you're not s.?** vous n'êtes pas sérieux?, vous plaisantez?; **I was being s. when I said …** je ne plaisantais pas quand j'ai dit …; **I have never given the subject s. thought** je n'y ai jamais pensé sérieusement; *Fam* **an evening of s. drinking** une soirée bien arrosée; *Fam* **they go in for some really s. drinking at the weekends** le week-end, qu'est-ce qu'ils descendent!; *Fam* **that is one s. computer!** c'est pas de la gnognotte, cet ordinateur!; *Fam* **s. money** beaucoup de fric; **the s. press** la presse sérieuse
▸▸ *Br* **s. crime squad** brigade *f* criminelle; *Br* **S. Fraud Office** ≃ Service *m* de la répression des fraudes

seriously [ˈsɪərɪəslɪ] ADV 1 *(gravely, critically)* sérieusement, gravement; **s. ill** gravement malade; **s. wounded** grièvement blessé; *Mil* **the s. wounded** les grands blessés; **the project is s. late** le projet est vraiment en retard; **he got it s. wrong** il s'est complètement trompé; *Fam* **her boyfriend is s. gorgeous** son petit ami est super beau
2 *(in earnest) (to talk)* sérieusement; **to take sth s.** prendre qch au sérieux; **to take oneself s.** se prendre au sérieux; **she takes everything far too s.** elle prend tout bien trop au sérieux; **if we are to be taken s. as a world-class football team** pour qu'on nous prenne au sérieux en tant qu'équipe de football de niveau international; **you can't s. expect them to believe that** vous ne pouvez pas penser sérieusement qu'ils vont croire ça; **but s., what will you do?** plaisanterie à part, qu'allez-vous faire?

serious-minded ADJ *(person)* réfléchi, sérieux

seriousness [ˈsɪərɪəsnɪs] N 1 *(gravity) (of situation, illness etc)* gravité *f* 2 *(of tone, personality etc)* sérieux *m*; **in all s.** sérieusement

serjeant [ˈsɑːdʒənt] N S. at Arms *Parl*

commandant *m* militaire du Parlement; *Hist (attendant)* huissier *m* d'armes

sermon [ˈsɜːmən] N 1 *Rel* sermon *m*; *(in Protestant church)* prêche *m*; **to deliver a s.** faire un sermon; **collection of sermons** sermonnaire *m*; *Bible* **the S. on the Mount** le Sermon sur la Montagne 2 *Fig* sermon *m*; **to give sb a s.** sermonner qn; **the editor does tend to go in for sermons** le rédacteur en chef a tendance à faire des sermons

sermonize [ˈsɜːmənaɪz] VI *Pej* sermonner, prêcher

sermonizing [ˈsɜːmənaɪzɪŋ] N *Pej* prêchi-prêcha *m inv*

seroconversion [sɪərəʊkənˈvɜːʃən] N *Med* séroconversion *f*

seronegative [sɪərəʊˈnegətɪv] ADJ séronégatif

seronegativity [sɪərəʊnegəˈtɪvɪtɪ] N séronégativité *f*

seropositive [sɪərəʊˈpɒzɪtɪv] ADJ séropositif

seropositivity [sɪərəʊpɒzɪˈtɪvɪtɪ] N séropositivité *f*

serotonin [serəˈtəʊnɪn] N sérotonine *f*

serous [ˈsɪərəs] ADJ *Anat etc (fluid etc)* séreux
▸▸ **s. membrane** séreuse *f*

serpent [ˈsɜːpənt] N serpent *m*

serpentine [ˈsɜːpəntaɪn] ADJ *Lit* serpentin, *(path)* sinueux, tortueux

SERPS [sɜːps] N *Br (abbr* state earnings-related pension scheme*)* = pension *f* de retraite versée par l'État et calculée en fonction des salaires

serrated [seˈreɪtɪd] ADJ *(edge)* en dents de scie, dentelé; *(knife, scissors, instrument)* cranté, en dents de scie

serration [seˈreɪʃən] N denture *f*

serried [ˈserɪd] ADJ *Lit* serré; **in s. ranks** en rangs serrés

serum, *pl* **serums, sera** [ˈsɪərəm, -əms, -ə] N *Physiol* sérum *m*; **blood s.** sérum sanguin

servant [ˈsɜːvənt] N 1 *(of God, the community etc)* serviteur *m*, servante *f*; **public servants** employés *mpl* d'un service public, employés de la fonction publique; *Arch Fml* **your most humble and obedient s.** votre très humble serviteur
2 *(in household)* domestique *mf*; *(female)* bonne *f*; *(in 19th century and before) (male)* serviteur *m*; *(female)* servante *f*; **the servants** les domestiques; *(19th century and before)* les serviteurs; **a large staff of servants** une nombreuse domesticité; **servants' quarters** logement des domestiques

serve [sɜːv] VT 1 *(master, cause etc)* servir; **to s. God/one's country** servir Dieu/sa patrie; **to have served one's country well** avoir bien servi sa patrie, *Lit* bien mériter de la patrie; **he has served the company faithfully** il a rendu de grands services à la société; **to s. one's own interests** servir ses propres intérêts; *Old-fashioned* **he served me very badly** *(treated)* il a très mal agi envers moi
2 *(of thing)* être utile à; **to s. the purpose** faire l'affaire; **that old computer does not really s. my purpose** ce vieil ordinateur ne convient pas à mes besoins; **tool that serves several purposes** outil qui sert à plusieurs usages; **this dictionary should s. the purposes of most users** ce dictionnaire devrait rendre service à la majorité des utilisateurs; **it has served its purpose and has been discarded** il a bien servi et on s'en est débarrassé; **I think this one's served its purpose** *(is useless)* je crois qu'il a fait son temps, celui-ci; **if my memory serves me right** si j'ai bonne mémoire
3 *(complete) (prison sentence)* purger; *(apprenticeship)* faire; **to s. one's sentence** or

one's time purger sa peine; **he served a sentence of five years' imprisonment** il a fait cinq ans de prison; **to have served ten years** *(in army)* avoir dix ans de service; *(in prison)* avoir fait dix ans de prison; *Pol* **to s. a term of office** exercer un mandat (présidentiel/ de député *etc*)

4 *(of bus, rail service, TV station etc) (region, population etc)* desservir

5 *(in shop)* **to s. a customer** servir un client; **are you being served?** est-ce qu'on s'occupe de vous?; **I'm being served, thank you** on s'occupe de moi, merci; **we don't s. (alcohol to) people under eighteen** *(in bar)* nous ne servons pas d'alcool aux moins de dix-huit ans

6 *(at table etc)* **to s. sb with soup/vegetables** servir du potage/des légumes à qn; **to s. a dish** servir un plat; **dinner is served, madam** Madame est servie; **s. chilled** servir très frais; *Rel* **to s. Mass** servir la messe; **serves four** *(on packet, in recipe)* pour quatre personnes; **beef served in a mushroom sauce** bœuf servi avec une sauce aux champignons

7 *Tennis* **to s. the ball** servir; **he served the ball into ...** il a envoyé la balle de service dans ...; **to s. an ace** faire un ace

8 *Law* **to s. a writ/a summons on sb, to s. sb with a writ/a summons** délivrer *ou* signifier *ou* notifier une assignation/une citation à qn

9 it serves you right! c'est bien fait pour toi!, tu n'as que ce que tu mérites!; **it serves him right for not listening to me** il ne m'a pas écouté, c'est bien fait pour lui; **it would have served you right** tu l'aurais bien mérité

10 *(of male animal) (female)* couvrir

VI 1 *(carry out duty etc)* **to s. in the army** servir dans l'armée; **to s. in the war with sb** faire la guerre avec qn; **she served under three presidents** elle a servi sous trois présidents; **to s. in a government** servir dans un gouvernement

2 *(meet requirements) (of tool, plan etc)* **the boxes s. as tables** les boîtes tiennent lieu de tables; **to s. as a pretext/as an example** servir de prétexte/d'exemple; **it serves to remind us how vulnerable we all are** il est bon de nous rappeler à quel point nous sommes vulnérables; **events in Bosnia s. to demonstrate just how fragile peace is** les événements de Bosnie démontrent à quel point la paix est fragile

3 *(in shop)* être vendeur, -euse

4 **to s. (at table)** servir à table

5 *Rel* **to s. (at Mass)** servir la messe

6 *Tennis* servir

N *Tennis* service *m*; **(it's) your s.!** à vous de servir!

▸ **serve out VT SEP 1** *(food)* servir **2** *(prison sentence)* purger; *(term of office)* finir, aller jusqu'au bout de; **before she had served out her term of office** avant la fin de son mandat; **to s. out one's time** *(in post etc)* aller jusqu'au bout de son mandat; *Mil* finir son temps de service; *Pej* **the Chairman was just serving out his time** le Président se contentait d'attendre sa retraite

▸ **serve up VT SEP** *(dinner etc)* servir; *Fig (programme, excuse etc)* sortir, pondre; *(performance)* servir

VI servir

server ['sɜːvər] **N 1** *(at table)* serveur, -euse **2** *Tennis* serveur, -euse **3** *Rel (at Mass)* servant *m* d'autel **4** *(tray)* plateau *m* (de service) **5** *(utensil)* couvert *m* de service; **(set of) salad/fish servers** service *m* à salade/à poisson **6** *Comput* **(file) s.** serveur *m*

▸▸ *Comput* **s. administrator** administrateur *m* de serveur; *Comput* **s. engine** processeur-serveur *m*, *pl* processeurs-serveurs

SERVICE ['sɜːvɪs] **N 1** service *m*; **in the s. of God/of one's country** au service de Dieu/de son pays; **to die in the King's/Queen's s.** mourir au service du roi/de la reine; **I am**

(entirely) at your s. je suis à votre (entière) disposition; **to do sb a s.** rendre (un) service à qn; **to be of some s.** se rendre utile; **to be of s. to sb** être utile à qn; **can I be of any s. to you?** puis-je vous être utile *ou* vous aider en aucune manière?; **to bring** *or* **put into s.** *(piece of machinery, vehicle etc)* mettre en service; **this pen has given me good s.** ce stylo m'a bien servi; **to offer one's services** offrir ses services; **his services to education** les services qu'il a rendus à l'enseignement; **services rendered** services rendus; *Econ* **goods and services** biens *mpl* et services

2 *Old-fashioned* **to be in/go into s.** *(of servant)* être/devenir domestique; **to go into s. with sb** entrer au service de qn

3 *(with army, firm etc)* service *m*; *Com* **promotion according to length of s.** avancement à l'ancienneté; *Com* **to give many years of loyal s. to a company** faire de nombreuses années de bons et loyaux services dans une société; *Mil* **fit/unfit for s.** apte/inapte au service; *Mil* **to see s.** faire la guerre; *Naut* **s. afloat/ashore** service à bord/à terre; **military** *or Br Formerly* **national s.** service militaire; **when I was doing my military s.** quand j'étais au régiment; **active s.** service actif; **the civil s.** l'administration *f*, la fonction publique; **to be in the civil s.** être fonctionnaire; **the Foreign** *or* **Diplomatic S.** le service diplomatique, la diplomatie, *Fam* la carrière; **the Secret S.** = le Deuxième Bureau

4 *(in shop, restaurant etc)* service *m*; **the s. there is good/slow** *(in restaurant)* le service y est de qualité/lent; **s. is included** le service est compris; **s. not included** service non-compris; **24-hour s.** *(open 24 hours)* ouvert 24 heures sur 24; *(service carried out within 24 hours)* travail effectué dans les 24 heures

5 *(system) (rail, air, postal etc)* service *m*; *(for water, gas, electricity)* distribution *f*; **bus s.** service d'autobus/de cars; **we have a good bus/train s.** notre ville est bien desservie par les autobus/par le chemin de fer; **goods** *or* **freight s.** service de marchandises; **passenger s.** service de voyageurs; **public services** services publics; **postal/telephone services** services postaux/téléphoniques; **social/medical services** services sociaux/médicaux; **it provides a s. to the community** cela offre un service aux gens

6 *Mil* **the s.** *(army)* l'armée *f*, *(navy)* la marine; *(air force)* l'armée de l'air; **Joint Services Staff College** ≃ École *f* d'État-major inter-armes

7 *(maintenance)* entretien *m*; *Aut* révision *f*; *Mil (of gun)* service *m*; **my car needs a complete s.** ma voiture a besoin d'une révision complète; **after-sales s.** service après-vente; **s. manual** *or* **handbook** manuel *m* d'entretien

8 *Rel* office *m*, culte *m*; **to attend s.** assister à l'office *ou* au culte; **the marriage s.** la cérémonie du mariage

9 *Law (of deed, writ)* délivrance *f*, signification *f*

10 *(crockery)* service *m*; **tea/dinner s.** service à thé/de table

11 *Tennis* service *m*

VT 1 *(do maintenance work on)* entretenir; *(car)* faire la révision de; *(domestic appliance)* assurer l'entretien de

2 *(in breeding) (of bull, stallion) (female)* couvrir

3 *(provide services to)* pourvoir aux besoins de; *Fin (loan, debt)* rembourser

▸▸ **s. accommodation** hébergement *m* avec restauration; **s. agreement** contrat *m* de service; **s. area** *Aut (on motorway)* aire *f* de service; *TV, Radio* zone *f* desservie *ou* de réception; *Aut* **s. bay** *(in garage)* zone de travail; **s. bell** *(in hotel)* sonnette *f (pour appeler un employé de l'hôtel)*; *Comput* **s. bureau** so-

ciété *f* de traitement à façon; *Austr, NZ* **s. bus** autocar *m*; *Austr, NZ* **s. car** autocar; *Aviat* **s. ceiling** plafond *m* de fonctionnement normal; *Am Aut* **s. center** aire de services *(au bord d'une autoroute)*; **s. charge** service *m*; *Journ* **s. column** rubrique *f* services; **s. company** entreprise *f* prestataire de services; **s. contract** contrat d'entretien; **s. court** *(in tennis)* rectangle *m* de service; **s. engineer** technicien, -enne de maintenance; **s. fault** *(in tennis)* faute *f* de service; *Br* **s. flat** = appartement *m* avec services ménagers et de restauration; **s. hatch** passe-plat *m*, *pl* passe-plats; *Aut* **s. history** historique *m* d'entretien; **s. industry** industrie *f* de services; **s. life** durée *f* de vie; *Br* **s. lift** monte-charge *m*, *pl* monte-charge(s); **s. line** *(in tennis)* ligne *f* de service; *Mil* **s. personnel** personnel *m* militaire; **s. provider** *(person, company)* prestataire *m* de service(s); *Comput (for Internet)* fournisseur *m* d'accès; *Mil* **s. rifle** fusil *m* réglementaire *ou* de l'armée; **s. road** *(behind shops, factory)* = voie *f* d'accès réservée aux livreurs; *(on motorway)* = voie d'accès réservée à l'entretien et aux services d'urgence; *Com, Econ* **s. sector** secteur *m* tertiaire, tertiaire *m*; **s. station** station-service *f*, *pl* stations-service; **s. supplier** prestataire *m* de service(s); *Bot* **s. tree** alisier *m*, sorbier *m*; *Mil* **s. vehicle** véhicule *m* militaire *ou* de l'armée

serviceable ['sɜːvɪsəb(ə)l] **ADJ** *(in functioning state)* en état de fonctionner; *(usable)* utilisable; *(useful)* pratique

serviced ['sɜːvɪst] **ADJ** *(apartment etc)* avec service d'entretien
▸▸ **s. accommodation** résidence *f* hôtelière; **s. apartment** appartement *m* dans une résidence hôtelière

serviceman, *pl* **servicemen** ['sɜːvɪsmən] **N** militaire *m*; *Hist* **national s.** appelé *m*

services ['sɜːvɪs] **NPL 1** *(on motorway)* services *mpl*; *(place)* aire *f* de services; **s. 10 km** *(on sign)* aire de services, 10 km **2 the (armed) s.** les forces *fpl* armées

servicewoman, *pl* **servicewomen** ['sɜːvɪswʊmən, -wɪmɪn] **N** femme *f* soldat, *Fam* soldate *f*

servicing ['sɜːvɪsɪŋ] **N** entretien *m*
▸▸ **s. manual** manuel *m* d'entretien

serviette [sɜːvɪ'et] **N** *Br* serviette *f* de table

servile ['sɜːvaɪl] **ADJ** *(person, behaviour)* servile

servility [sɜː'vɪlɪtɪ] **N** servilité *f*

serving ['sɜːvɪŋ] **ADJ** *(member, chairman)* actuel, en exercice; **the longest-s. official** la personnalité officielle ayant le plus d'ancienneté
N 1 *(of drinks, meal)* service *m* **2** *(helping)* portion *f*, part *f*
▸▸ **s. dish** plat *m*, assiette *f* de service; **s. hatch** passe-plat *m*, *pl* passe-plats

servitude ['sɜːvɪtjuːd] **N** *(slavery)* servitude *f*, esclavage *m*; **to be sold into s.** être vendu comme esclave; *Law* **penal s. for life** *(imprisonment)* travaux forcés à perpétuité

servo ['sɜːvəʊ] **N** *Fam* = **servomechanism**
ADJ
▸▸ *Aut* **s. brake** servofrein *m*

servo-assistance **N** *Tech* servo-assistance *f*

servocontrol [sɜːvəʊkən'trəʊl] **N** *Tech* servocommande *f*

servomechanism [sɜːvəʊ'mekənɪz(ə)m] **N** *Tech* servomécanisme *m*

servomotor [sɜːvəʊ'məʊtər] **N** *Tech* servomoteur *m*

servo-unit **N** *Tech* servocommande *m*

sesame ['sesəmɪ] **N 1** *(plant)* sésame *m* **2 open s.!** *(magic formula)* sésame, ouvre-toi!

▸▸ *Culin* **s. oil** huile *f* de sésame; *Culin* **s. seeds** graines *fpl* de sésame

sesh [seʃ] **N** *Br Fam (session)* **to have a drinking s.** se pinter; **we had a bit of a s. last night** on s'en est donné hier soir

session ['seʃən] **N 1** *(period of activity)* séance *f*; **morning/evening s.** *(at swimming pool etc)* séance du matin/soir; **skiing tuition at £75 per 3-hour s.** cours de ski à 75 livres par séance de 3 heures; **training s.** séance d'entraînement; **we had a long s. on the phone** nous sommes restés très longtemps au téléphone; **I've just had a long s. with the lawyers** je viens d'avoir un long entretien avec les avocats; *Fam* **she has a complaining s. every morning** tous les matins, il faut qu'elle se plaigne **2** *(meeting)* session *f*; *Parl* **the autumn s.** la session d'automne; **the House is now in s.** la Chambre siège actuellement **3** *Am, Scot Univ (term)* trimestre *m* (universitaire); *(year)* année *f* (universitaire); *Am* **school is in s.** on est en période scolaire

▸▸ *Mus* **s. artist** *mf* de studio; **s. musician** musicien, -enne de studio

SET® **N** *Comput* *(abbr* **secure electronic transaction)** SET *f*

SET [set]

| **N** jeu **1** ▪ série **1** ▪ service **1** |
| ▪ collection **1** ▪ groupe **2** ▪ poste **6** |
| ▪ décor **8** ▪ plateau **8** ▪ manche **11** |
| ▪ set **11** |
| **ADJ** fixe **1** ▪ prêt **2** ▪ résolu **3** |
| ▪ prédéterminé **4** |
| **VT** poser **1** ▪ situer **2** ▪ régler **3** |
| ▪ monter **4** ▪ tendre **5** ▪ fixer **6** |
| ▪ établir **6** ▪ composer **10** |
| **VI** se coucher **1** ▪ prendre **2** |

N 1 *(group) (of keys, boxes, chesspieces etc)* jeu *m*; *(of problems, rules, symptoms, pans etc)* série *f*; *(of glasses, china)* service *m*; *(of tyres, wheels)* train *m*; *(of turbines)* batterie *f*; *(of stamps, butterflies etc) (collection)* collection *f*; *(series)* série *f*; *(of sb's works)* œuvres *fpl* complètes; *(of lingerie)* parure *f*; *Comput (of characters, instructions)* jeu, ensemble *m*; *Math* ensemble *m*; **s. of bills of exchange** jeu de lettres de change; **s. of data** ensemble de données; **s. of teeth** denture *f*, dentition *f*, *(artificial)* dentier *m*; **s. of golf clubs** jeu de crosses; **s. of bells** sonnerie *f* *(d'église etc)*; **Old-fashioned toilet s.**, **dressing-table s.** garniture *f* de toilette; **construction s.** jeu de construction; **a s. of cooking utensils** une batterie de cuisine; **a s. of sheets** une parure de lit; **a s. of screwdrivers** une série de tournevis; **a s. of tests** une batterie de tests; **to collect the (whole) s.** rassembler toute la collection, faire la collection; **chairs, the s. of six, £200** chaises, 200 livres les six **2** *(of people)* groupe *m*; *Pej* **literary/political s.** coterie *f* littéraire/politique; **he got in with the literary/political s.** il s'est mêlé au groupe de ceux qui s'intéressaient à la littérature/politique; **the smart s.** les élégants; **I'm not one of their s.** je ne suis pas de leur monde **3** *Br Sch* **top/bottom s.** classe *f* des forts/des plus faibles **4** *(position) (of public opinion)* tendances *fpl*; **his anxiety was betrayed in the s. of his shoulders** la position de ses épaules trahissait son anxiété; **I could tell she was angry by the s. of her jaw** je voyais sa colère à ses mâchoires serrées **5** *(in hairdressing)* mise *f* en plis **6** *(apparatus)* **(radio) s.** poste *m* de radio; **(television) s.** téléviseur *m*, poste de télévision **7** *Constr* **(paving) s.** pavé *m* d'échantillon

8 *Theat (scenery)* décor *m*; *TV, Cin* plateau *m* *(de tournage)*; **on s.** *Theat* sur scène; *TV, Cin* sur le plateau; **rehearsal on the s.** *Theat* répétition *f* sur scène; *Cin* répétition sur le plateau **9** *Mus etc (performance)* set *m*; **the band played two sets** le groupe a joué deux sets **10** *(tool)* **nail s.** chasse-clou *m*, *pl* chasse-clous; **saw s.** tourne-à-gauche *m inv* **11** *Tennis* manche *f*, set *m* **12** *(of badger)* terrier *m*

ADJ 1 *(face)* immobile, aux traits rigides; *(look)* fixe; *(smile)* figé; **(hard) s.** ferme, figé; *(cement)* bien pris **2** *(prepared)* **to be (all) s. to do sth** être prêt à faire qch; **to be all s.** *(ready to begin)* être prêt à commencer; *Sport* **(get) s.!** en position, attention!; *Journ* **sterling s. to fall** la livre sterling sur le point de chuter **3** *(determined)* **to be (dead) s. on sth** être résolu *ou* déterminé à qch; **to be (dead) s. on doing sth** être résolu *ou* déterminé à faire qch; **to be dead s. against sb/sth** être résolument contre qn/qch **4** *(fixed) (ideas, opinions etc)* arrêté; *(time, price)* fixé; *(way)* prédéterminé; **he has a s. way of doing it** il a sa méthode pour le faire; **to be s. in one's ways** avoir ses habitudes, être coincé dans ses habitudes; **at s. hours** à heures fixes; **with no s. purpose** sans but précis; **s. forms of behaviour** comportements fixés par l'usage; **s. form of prayer** prière liturgique

VT *(pt, pp* **set**; *prp* **setting)** **1** *(place) (sth on or against sth, sth before sb)* mettre, poser; **to s. one's glass on the table** poser son verre sur la table; **to s. sth before sb** présenter qch à qn; **to s. a dish in front of sb** servir un plat à qn; **to s. a stake in the ground** enfoncer *ou* planter un pieu dans la terre; **to s. one's hand/seal to a document** apposer sa signature/son sceau à un acte; **to s. sb on his feet again** remettre qn sur pied; **her eyes are s. too close together** elle a les yeux trop rapprochés; **the house is s. in the heart of the woods** la maison est située au milieu des bois; **to s. a match to sth** mettre le feu à qch; **to s. a value on sth** décider de la valeur de qch; **to s. a proposal before the board** présenter un projet au conseil d'administration; **to s. one's heart on sth** avoir qch à cœur, vouloir absolument qch; **to s. the table** mettre le couvert *ou* la table; **to s. the table for two** mettre deux couverts; **to s. a trap (for sb)** tendre un piège (à qn) **2** *(story, film)* situer; **where is the story/film s.?** où est-ce que l'histoire/le film se passe?; *Theat* **to s. a scene** monter un décor; **the second act is s. in a street** le second acte se passe dans une rue **3** *(adjust) (mechanism, watch etc)* régler; **to s. one's watch by the town clock** régler sa montre sur l'horloge de la ville; **to s. the alarm clock for** *or* **at five o'clock** mettre le réveil à cinq heures; **to s. the milometer to zero** ramener *ou* remettre le compteur à zéro; **to s. one's hat straight** remettre son chapeau droit; **to have one's hair s.** se faire faire une mise en plis **4** *(mount) (stone)* monter, sertir; **s. with diamonds** orné *ou* incrusté de diamants; **(with) all sails s.** toutes voiles dehors **5** *(prepare) (trap), also Fig* dresser, tendre **6** *(fix) (date, day)* fixer, arrêter; **to s. a date for a meeting** fixer une date de réunion; **to s. a price** fixer *ou* établir un prix; **to s. the rate of sth** tarifer qch; **to s. limits to sth** fixer des limites à qch; **to s. prices high/low** fixer les prix hauts/bas; **to s. an age limit at …** fixer une limite d'âge à …; **to s. oneself a target** se fixer un but; **to s. a fashion/trend** lancer une mode/tendance; **to s. a record** établir un record; **to s. oneself a task** s'imposer une tâche; **to s. sb a problem** poser un

problème à qn; *Sch* **to s. an essay** donner un sujet de dissertation; *Sch* **to s. a book** mettre un livre au programme; **to s. an exam(ination) paper** choisir les questions d'une épreuve écrite; **to s. the page margins** marger la page **7** *(cause to start)* **to s. sb to do sth** faire faire qch à qn; **to s. a man to work** mettre un homme au travail; **that s. me thinking** cela m'a fait réfléchir *ou* m'a donné à réfléchir; **to s. the dog barking** faire aboyer le chien; **to s. people talking** *(provoke comment)* faire parler les gens; **to s. sth going** mettre qch en train; **to s. a mechanism going** mettre un mécanisme en marche; **to s. sb free** libérer qn, rendre sa liberté à qn **8** *Mus* **to s. a melody half a tone higher/lower** transcrire un air un demi-ton plus haut/bas; **to s. words to music** mettre des paroles en musique **9** *Surg (bone, limb)* remettre; *(fracture)* réduire **10** *Typ* composer; **to s. type** composer; **to s. a page** composer une page **11** *(of plant) (fruit)* donner, porter

VI 1 *(of sun, moon)* se coucher; **we saw the sun setting** nous avons vu le coucher du soleil **2** *(become firm) (of jelly)* prendre; *(of broken bone)* se recoller; *(of cement)* prendre, durcir; **her features had s. in an expression of determination** ses traits s'étaient durcis en une expression de très forte détermination; *Fig* **public opinion was beginning to s. against the proposal** l'opinion publique commençait à se durcir contre la proposition **3** *(in hunting) (of dog)* tomber en arrêt

▸▸ *Sch* **s. books** ouvrages *mpl* au programme; **one of our s. books is 'Oliver Twist'** un des ouvrages au programme est 'Oliver Twist'; *Theat, Cin, TV* **s. designer** décorateur, -trice; **s. dressing** agencement *m* des éléments du décor; *Gram* **s. expression** expression *f* figée; *Gram* **s. menu** menu *m* fixe; *Gram* **s. phrase** expression figée; *Sport* **s. piece** combinaison *f* préparée; *Tennis* **s. point** balle *f* de set; **s. price** prix *m* fixe; **s. task** tâche *f* assignée; **to give sb a s. task to do** assigner à qn une tâche bien précise; *Math* **s. theory** théorie *f* des ensembles

▸ **set about** **VT INSEP 1** *(start)* **to s. about a piece of work** se mettre à *ou* entreprendre un travail; **to s. about doing sth** se mettre à faire qch; **I don't know how to s. about it** je ne sais pas comment m'y prendre **2** *(attack)* **to s. about sb** attaquer qn

▸ **set against** **VT SEP 1** *(cause to oppose)* **to s. sb against sb** dresser qn contre qn, *Fam* monter (la tête à) qn contre qn; **it had s. members of the family one against the other** cela avait dressé les membres de la famille les uns contre les autres; **something's s. him against the idea** quelque chose lui en a fait détester l'idée; **to s. oneself** *or* **one's face against sth** s'opposer résolument à qch **2** *(weigh against)* **to s. sth against sth** contrebalancer qch par qch; **to s. the benefits against the costs** évaluer les bénéfices par rapport aux coûts **3** *Fin (offset)* **to s. expenses against taxes** déduire les dépenses des impôts **4** *(compare)* **to s. sth against sth** comparer qch à qch; **we must s. the government's promises against its achievements** nous devons examiner les promesses du gouvernement à la lumière de ses actions

▸ **set apart** **VT SEP 1** *(distinguish)* distinguer (**from** de); **what sets them apart from other companies is …** ce qui les distingue des autres sociétés, c'est … **2** *(isolate) (person)* isoler; **they s. themselves apart** ils faisaient bande à part

▸ **set aside** **VT SEP 1** *(abandon temporarily)*

(*job, task*) mettre de côté; **could you s. aside what you're working on for a while?** pouvez-vous laisser ce que vous êtes en train de faire un moment?

2 (*not consider*) ne pas prendre en ligne de compte, laisser de côté; **setting that aspect aside** sans prendre cet aspect en ligne de compte, si on laisse de côté cet aspect; **to s. aside one's personal feelings** mettre de côté tout sentiment personnel

3 (*save*) (*money*) mettre de côté *ou* en réserve; (*hours, weekend etc*) réserver; **to s. aside some money every week** mettre de l'argent de côté chaque semaine

4 *Law* (*judgement, verdict etc*) casser, infirmer; (*claim*) rejeter; (*will*) annuler

▸ **set back** VT SEP **1** *Constr etc* **house s. back (from the road)** maison en retrait (de la route)

2 (*delay*) retarder le progrès de; **the news may s. him** *or* **his recovery back** la nouvelle risque de retarder sa guérison; **this decision will s. the economy back ten years** cette décision va faire revenir l'économie dix ans en arrière

3 *Fam* (*cost*) **it s. me back £5,000** ça m'a coûté 5 000 livres; **that new car must have s. her back a bit** cette nouvelle voiture a dû lui coûter un fric fou

▸ **set by** VT SEP = **set aside 3**

▸ **set down** VT SEP **1** (*put down*) poser, déposer; **the train stops to s. down passengers only** ce train ne prend pas de voyageurs

2 to s. sth down in writing coucher qch par écrit; **condition s. down in the contract** condition énoncée dans le contrat; **permissible levels of pollution are s. down in the regulations** les taux de pollution tolérés sont fixés dans les réglementations

▸ **set forth** VI *Arch, Lit* (*leave*) se mettre en route, partir

VT SEP (*present*) (*case etc*) présenter, mettre en avant; **the document sets forth a detailed description of …** le document présente une description détaillée de …

▸ **set in** VI (*take hold*) (*of gangrene, fog, winter, cynicism*) s'installer; **night was setting in** la nuit tombait; **the rain had s. in** la pluie ne s'arrêtait plus

VT SEP *Sewing* (*sleeve*) monter

▸ **set off** VT SEP **1** (*ignite*) (*rocket*) faire partir; (*bomb*) faire exploser

2 (*cause*) (*explosion, alarm, argument, chain of events*) déclencher

3 (*cause to do sth*) **this answer s. them off (laughing)** cette réponse a déclenché les rires; **one look at his face s. me off again** en le voyant, mon fou rire a repris de plus belle; **if you say anything, it'll only s. him off (crying) again** si tu dis quoi que ce soit, il va se remettre à pleurer; **the smallest amount of pollen will s. her off** la moindre dose de pollen lui déclenche une réaction allergique; **don't mention Maradona or you'll s. him off again** surtout ne prononce pas le nom de Maradona, sinon il va recommencer; **someone mentioned the war and, of course, that s. Uncle Arthur off** quelqu'un mentionna le mot guerre et, évidemment, oncle Arthur embraya aussitôt sur le sujet

4 (*enhance*) mettre en relief *ou* en valeur; (*colour, person's best points*) faire ressortir, faire valoir, rehausser; **those curtains really s. the room off** ces rideaux mettent vraiment la pièce en valeur

5 *Fin* (*debt*) compenser; **to s. off a gain against a loss** compenser une perte par un gain; **can I s. these expenses off against my tax liability?** est-ce que je peux déduire ces frais de mes impôts?

6 *Comput* (*num lock, insert, etc*) désactiver

VI (*depart*) se mettre en route, partir; **to s. off on a journey** partir; **to s. off again** se mettre en route; **to s. off running** partir en courant

▸ **set on** VT INSEP (*attack*) attaquer

VT SEP **1** *Comput* (*num lock, insert etc*) activer

2 (*cause to follow*) **to s. the police on the tracks of a thief** mettre la police aux trousses d'un voleur; **to s. sb (off) on the wrong track** mettre qn sur une fausse piste; **to s. sb on his way** mettre qn sur les rails

3 (*cause to attack*) **to s. a dog on sb** lâcher un chien sur qn

▸ **set out** VT SEP **1** (*arrange*) disposer; (*goods*) étaler; (*one's ideas*) exposer; **his work is well s. out** son travail est bien présenté

VI **1** (*depart on journey*) se mettre en route, partir; **just as he was setting out** au moment de son départ; **to s. out for school** partir pour l'école; **to s. out again** repartir; **to s. out in pursuit/in search of sb** se mettre à la poursuite/à la recherche de qn

2 (*start job etc*) **I didn't realize when I s. out how difficult it would be** je n'avais pas réalisé combien ce serait difficile lorsque j'ai commencé; **I didn't s. out with any preconceptions** au départ, je n'avais aucune idée préconçue

3 (*intend*) **I didn't s. out to attack the government** je n'avais aucune intention d'attaquer le gouvernement; **they deliberately s. out to cause trouble** ils avaient l'intention de créer des problèmes; **his theory sets out to prove that …** sa théorie a pour objet de prouver que …

▸ **set to** VI **1** (*start working*) se mettre au travail *ou* à l'œuvre

2 *Fam* (*of two people*) (*start arguing*) avoir une prise de bec; (*start fighting*) en venir aux mains

VT INSEP (*start doing*) **to s. to work** se mettre au travail *ou* à l'œuvre

▸ **set up** VT SEP **1** (*erect*) (*mast*) dresser; (*statue*) ériger; (*computer system, stereo system, model train set*) installer; (*machine, tent, tripod etc*) monter; (*barrier*) élever; **to s. sth up again** (*because it has fallen*) relever qch; *Fig* **to s. up a barrier between people** mettre une barrière entre les gens

2 (*arrange*) (*dinner, meeting, appointment*) organiser; (*system, link*) établir; **I've s. things up (so that …)** j'ai organisé les choses (de telle manière que …); **will you s. things up for the meeting?** veux-tu t'occuper d'organiser la réunion?

3 (*establish*) (*committee, tribunal*) instituer, constituer; (*business*) créer, fonder; (*programme*) monter; (*distinction, connection*) établir; **to s. up an account** ouvrir un compte; **to s. up house or home** s'installer dans une maison; **to s. sb up in business** aider qn à monter une affaire; **to s. oneself up as a lawyer** monter un cabinet d'avocat

4 *Med etc* (*cause*) (*infection, irritation*) provoquer, causer

5 *Fam* (*fabricate evidence against sb*) (*usu passive*) **I've been s. up** on m'a monté le coup, on m'a bien eu

6 (*invigorate*) (*person*) revivifier; **a fortnight in the country will s. you up** une quinzaine à la campagne va vous remettre d'aplomb

7 *Typ* (*text*) composer

VI **1** (*establish oneself*) **to s. up in business** se mettre à son compte; **to s. up as a chemist** s'établir pharmacien(ne); **he has s. up for himself** il s'est établi à son compte; **to s. up overseas** s'implanter à l'étranger

2 (*claim to be*) **to s. up as a critic** se poser en critique

▸ **set upon** VT INSEP attaquer; **to be s. upon by sb** être attaqué par qn

set-aside N *EU* gel *m* des terres

setback ['setbæk] N **1** (*reversal, stroke of bad luck*) mésaventure *f*, *Fin, St Exch* tassement *m*, repli *m*; *Med* rechute *f*; **they encountered a number of setbacks** ils ont eu de nom-

breux déboires; **to suffer a s.** (*of patient*) rechuter; **the dollar suffered a s. today** le dollar a connu un repli aujourd'hui; **to suffer a s. in one's plans** voir ses plans compromis; **this will prove a s. in his career** cela va compromettre sa carrière **2** *Archit* décrochement *m*

set-in ADJ
▸▸ *Sewing* **s. sleeve** manche *f* rapportée

setmeter ['setmiːtər] N *TV etc* audimètre *m*

set-square N équerre *f* (à dessin)

sett [set] N **1** *Constr* (*paving*) **s.** pavé *m* d'échantillon **2** (*of badger*) terrier *m*

settee [se'tiː] N canapé *m*; **bed s.** canapé-lit *m*, *pl* canapés-lits

setter ['setər] N **1** (*person*) (*of diamonds etc*) sertisseur *m*; *Typ* (*type*) **s.** compositeur, -trice **2** (*dog*) setter *m*; **Irish s.** setter irlandais

setting ['setɪŋ] ADJ **1** (*sun, star*) couchant **2** **slow-/quick-s. cement** ciment *m* à prise lente/rapide

N **1** (*act of adjusting*) réglage *m* **2** (*act of mounting*) (*of specimen, jewel*) montage *m*; (*result*) monture *f* **3** *Typ* composition *f* **4** (*act of fixing, arranging*) (*of date etc*) désignation *f*; **s. up of an account** ouverture *f* d'un compte; **s. up of a business** création *f* ou fondation *f* d'une entreprise **5** (*of sun etc*) coucher *m* **6** *Surg* (*of broken bone*) recollement *m*; (*of fracture*) réduction *f* **7** (*hardening*) (*of cement*) affermissement *m*, prise *f* **8** (*location*) (*of story, festival etc*) cadre *m*; *Theat* mise *f* en scène; **a novel in an 18th century s.** un roman dans un décor XVIIIᵉ siècle **9** (*arrangement*) **s. for violin** arrangement *m* pour violon; (*place*) **s.** (*at table*) couvert *m*; **the s. to music of …** la mise en musique de … **10** (*on washing machine, iron etc*) réglage *m*; **try a higher s.** (*of oven, iron, microwave etc*) augmentez la température; **what s. was it on?** sur quoi était-elle réglée? **11** *Comput* (*of tabs etc*) (*action*) pose *f*, (*position*) positionnement *m*; **printer settings** paramètres *mpl* de l'imprimante
▸▸ **s. lotion** lotion *f* pour mise en plis; *Typ* **s. width** largeur *f* de composition

---

SETTLE ['set(ə)l]

VT	régler **1, 4** ▪ mettre en place **1**
	▪ coloniser **1** ▪ calmer **2** ▪ fixer **3**
	▪ résoudre **4** ▪ payer **4**
VI	s'établir **1** ▪ se poser **1** ▪ se déposer
	2 ▪ reposer **2** ▪ se calmer **4**

VT **1** (*make stable*) (*put carefully in place*) mettre bien en place; (*of person, population etc*) (*country*) coloniser, peupler; (*one's affairs*) régler, mettre de l'ordre dans; **to s. one's feet in the stirrups** bien installer ses pieds dans les étriers; **she had settled herself in an armchair** elle s'était installée dans un fauteuil; **to s. an invalid for the night** installer un malade pour la nuit; **to s. the children for the night** mettre les enfants au lit

2 (*calm*) (*person, nerves etc*) apaiser, calmer; **give me something to s. my stomach** donnez-moi quelque chose pour l'estomac; **to s. sb's doubts** dissiper les doutes de qn

3 (*fix*) (*day, venue etc*) fixer, déterminer; **it's as good as settled** c'est comme si c'était fait; **everything is settled, it's settled** l'affaire est conclue; **that's settled, then** c'est entendu *ou* convenu

4 (*resolve*) (*question*) résoudre, décider; (*quarrel, dispute, account*) régler; (*debt*) payer; **to s. a matter** régler une question; **to s. accounts or old scores or an old score with sb** régler des comptes avec qn; **to s. one's differences (with sb)** se mettre d'accord (avec qn); **questions not yet settled** questions en suspens; **that settles it!** voilà qui est réglé!; **s. it among yourselves** arrangez cela entre vous; **to s. a matter out of court** régler une question à l'amiable; **to s. one's bills** payer ses factures; *Fam* **that settled him** *or* **his hash** *(that put a stop to him)* ça lui a réglé son compte; *(that put a stop to his boasting)* ça lui a rabattu le caquet

5 *(bestow)* **to s. an annuity on sb** constituer une rente à qn; **to s. all one's property on one's wife** mettre tous ses biens au nom de sa femme

VI 1 *(of person, people)* s'établir, se fixer (**in a place** dans un lieu); *(of bird, insect etc)* se poser; **to s. in an armchair** s'installer dans un fauteuil; **she had settled in a corner** elle s'était installée dans un coin; **they settled along the Ohio** ils se sont installés au bord de l'Ohio; **she lived here a few years, but didn't s.** elle a vécu ici quelques années, mais ne s'est pas installée définitivement; *(never felt at home)* elle a vécu ici quelques années, mais ne s'est jamais habituée; **the snow is settling** la neige tient; **to s. to work/to do sth** se mettre sérieusement au travail/à faire qch; **he can't s. to anything** il n'arrive pas à se concentrer sur quoi que ce soit; **I couldn't s.** *(in bed)* je n'arrivais pas à m'endormir; *Fig* **a look of despair/contentment had settled on his face** le désespoir/la satisfaction se lisait sur son visage

2 *(of liquid, beer)* reposer; *(of sediment)* se déposer; *(of dust)* retomber; **to let s.** *(dregs etc)* laisser déposer; *(wine)* laisser se rasseoir; *(solution)* laisser reposer; **allow the mixture to s.** laissez reposer le mélange

3 *(of ground, pillar etc)* prendre son assiette, s'asseoir; *(of foundation etc)* s'affaisser; **let your food s. before you go swimming** attendez d'avoir digéré avant d'aller nager

4 *(of excitement)* s'apaiser, se calmer; **the weather is settling** le temps se calme

5 *Law* **to s.** *(out of court)* régler l'affaire (à l'amiable)

N *(seat)* = banquette *f* en bois avec un dossier

▸ **settle down** VI **1** *(make oneself comfortable)* s'installer; **they settled down by the fire/to watch TV** ils s'installèrent près de la cheminée/pour regarder la télévision; **to s. down to sleep** s'apprêter à dormir; **it took the children some time to s. down to sleep** les enfants ont mis du temps à se décider à dormir; **to s. down with a book** s'installer avec un livre

2 *(give serious attention to sth)* **to s. down to work** se mettre sérieusement au travail; **to s. down to a job** s'attaquer *ou* se mettre à une tâche

3 *(adopt regular life)* se ranger, s'assagir; *(of situation)* s'arranger, redevenir normal; *(of excitement)* se calmer; **it's time you settled down and got married** il est temps que tu te ranges et que tu te maries; **he's not someone you could imagine settling down with** ce n'est pas le genre de personne avec qui on peut imaginer se marier; **s. down, children!** calmez-vous, les enfants!, du calme, les enfants!; **he's beginning to s. down at school** il commence à s'habituer à l'école; **things are settling down** *(becoming more definite)* les choses commencent à prendre tournure; *(calming down)* les choses sont en train de se calmer; **as soon as the market settles down** aussitôt que le marché se sera stabilisé

VT SEP 1 *(make comfortable)* **to s. the baby down for the night** installer le bébé pour la nuit

2 *(make calm)* **to s. a class down** calmer une classe

▸ **settle for** VT INSEP *(accept)* accepter; **I settled for £100** j'ai accepté 100 livres; **I insist on the best quality, I never s. for (anything) less** j'exige ce qu'il y a de mieux, je n'accepte

jamais rien en dessous; **we haven't got any brandy, will you s. for Scotch?** nous n'avons pas de cognac, est-ce qu'un whisky fera l'affaire?

▸ **settle in** VI *(become established)* s'installer, s'établir; **to s. in a new school** s'habituer à une nouvelle école; **to s. in at a job** s'habituer à un emploi; **to s. in at a company** s'intégrer à une société

VT SEP *(help become established)* *(new employee, person in new home)* aider à s'installer

▸ **settle on** VT INSEP *(decide on)* décider de; **have you settled on a name for the baby/a date for the wedding?** avez-vous décidé d'un prénom pour le bébé/d'une date pour le mariage?; **they couldn't s. on a price** ils n'ont pas réussi à se mettre d'accord sur un prix

▸ **settle up** VI **1** *(pay bill)* payer

2 *(pay debt)* s'acquitter; **I'll s. up with you tomorrow** je vous réglerai demain

▸ **settle with** VT INSEP **to s. with sb** *(pay debt)* régler ses comptes avec qn

settled ['set(ə)ld] ADJ **1** *(stable, calm)* *(life)* stable; *(idea, habit)* fixe, enraciné; *(intention)* bien arrêté; *(person, character)* posé, réfléchi; *(bearing etc)* tranquille, calme; **I am a man of s. habits** je suis un homme d'habitudes; **she is s. in her job** elle est habituée à son emploi **2** *(established in home)* *(person)* installé, établi; **to get s.** s'installer **3** *(colonized)* colonisé **4** *Met* *(calm)* beau, *f* belle; **the weather will remain s.** le temps demeurera au beau fixe

settlement ['set(ə)lmənt] N **1** *(action)* *(of people in a country)* établissement *m*, installation *f*; *(of country)* colonisation *f* **2** *(of ground)* tassement *m*, affaissement *m* **3** *(of matter)* règlement *m*; *(of difference)* arrangement *m*; *(of question)* résolution *f*, décision *f*; *(of treaty etc)* conclusion *f*; *Com (of account)* règlement, paiement *m*; *St Exch* liquidation *f*; *Com* **in (full) s.** pour solde de tout compte **4** *(agreement)* accord *m*; **they have reached a s.** ils sont arrivés à un accord; *Law* **s. of an annuity** constitution *f* de rente (**on** en faveur de); **marriage s.** contrat *m* de mariage **5** *(colony)* colonie *f*, **penal s.** colonie pénitentiaire **6** *Am (small community)* village *m*

▸▸ *St Exch* **s. day** jour *m* de (la) liquidation; *Com* **s. discount** remise *f* pour règlement rapide; *Com* **s. period** délai *m* de règlement; *St Exch* **s. price** cours *m* de résiliation; *St Exch* **s. value** valeur *f* liquidative

settler ['setlər] N *(colonist)* colon *m*

settling ['setlɪŋ] N **1** = **settlement 1 2** *(of liquid)* clarification *f* **3** *(of ground)* affaissement *m* **4** = **settlement 3**

set-to N *Fam (fight)* bagarre *f*; *(argument)* prise *f* de bec

set-top box N boîtier *m* décodeur, décodeur *m*

setup ['setʌp] N **1** *Fam (organization)* fonctionnement *m*; **it's an odd s.** *(company)* c'est une drôle de boîte; *(marriage, relationship)* c'est un drôle de ménage; *(collection of people)* c'est une drôle d'équipe; **you've got a nice s. here** vous êtes bien installé ici **2** *esp Am Fam (something rigged)* machination *f*, coup *m* monté **3** *Cin, TV* = installation *f* du matériel technique pour le tournage d'une scène

seven ['sev(ə)n] N sept *m*; **two sevens are fourteen** deux fois sept font quatorze; **it's s. o'clock** il est sept heures; *Cards* **the s. of hearts** le sept de cœur; **to be s.** *(in age)* avoir sept ans

PRON sept; **s. is not enough** sept, ce n'est pas assez

NUM ADJ sept; **the s. deadly sins** les sept péchés capitaux; **s.-league boots** bottes *fpl* de

sept lieues; *Fam* **the s.-year itch** le cap difficile des sept ans de mariage; *Fam* **to have the s.-year itch** arriver au cap difficile des sept ans de mariage

▸▸ **s. seas** toutes les mers *fpl* (du monde); *Lit* **to sail the s. seas** parcourir les océans

seven-bit character N *Comput* caractère *m* à sept bits

seven-bit data N *Comput* données *fpl* à sept bits

sevenfold ['sev(ə)nfəʊld] ADJ septuple

ADV sept fois autant; **to increase s.** septupler

seventeen [sev(ə)n'ti:n] NUM ADJ, N dix-sept *m*; **she's s.** elle a dix-sept ans

seventeenth [sev(ə)n'ti:nθ] ADJ dix-septième

N 1 *(of month)* dix-sept *m*; **(on) the s. of May** le dix-sept mai **2** *(person, thing)* dix-septième *mf* **3** *(fraction)* dix-septième *m*

seventh ['sev(ə)nθ] ADJ septième; **to be in s. heaven** être aux anges *ou* au septième ciel; **Edward the S.** Édouard Sept; *Rel* **S.-day Adventist** adventiste *mf* du septième jour

N 1 *(of month)* sept *m*; **(on) the s. (of May)** le sept (mai) **2** *(person, thing)* septième *mf*; **you're the s. this morning to ask me that** tu es la septième personne qui me demande *ou* à me demander ça ce matin **3** *(fraction)* septième *m* **4** *Mus (interval)* septième *f*

seventieth ['sev(ə)ntɪɪθ] ADJ soixante-dixième, *Belg, Suisse* septantième

N 1 *(person, thing)* soixante-dixième *mf* **2** *(fraction)* soixante-dixième *m*

seventy ['sev(ə)ntɪ] NUM ADJ, N soixante-dix *m*, *Belg, Suisse* septante *m*; **s.-one** soixante et onze; **s.-five** soixante-quinze; **s.-nine** soixante-dix-neuf; **to be in one's seventies** être septuagénaire

sever ['sevər] VT *(cut off)* *(arm, finger, leg)* sectionner (**at** au niveau de); *(friendship, link, relationship)* rompre; *(communications)* interrompre; **to s. one's connections with sb** couper les liens avec qn; **to s. sth from sth** séparer qch de qch; **a severed head** une tête coupée

VI *(of rope etc)* (se) rompre

several ['sev(ə)r(ə)l] ADJ **1** *(a number of)* plusieurs; **I've been there s. times** j'y suis allé plusieurs fois; **he and s. others** lui et plusieurs autres SEE GRAMMAR B15 **2** *Lit (respective)* respectif; **they have their s. reasons for wanting …** ils avaient chacun leurs raisons de vouloir …; **they went their s. ways** ils s'en allèrent, chacun de son côté; **we've decided to go our s. ways** nous avons décidé de suivre chacun notre chemin

PRON plusieurs *mfpl*; **s. of us/of them** *etc* plusieurs d'entre nous/d'entre eux *etc*; **s. of our party heard it** plusieurs membres de notre groupe l'ont entendu

severally ['sevrəlɪ] ADV *Fml* séparément, individuellement

severance ['sevərəns] N séparation *f* (**from** de); *(of relations etc)* rupture *f*, cessation *f*; *(of communications, contact)* interruption *f*, rupture *f*

▸▸ **s. pay** indemnité *f* *ou* indemnités *fpl* de licenciement

severe [sɪ'vɪər] ADJ **1** *(person, measures)* sévère, strict (**with** envers); **a s. reprimand** une verte réprimande **2** *(winter, weather)* rigoureux, rude; *(illness, wound)* grave; **a s. blow** un coup dur; **to suffer s. hardship** connaître de grosses difficultés; **s. loss** grosse *ou* forte perte *f*; **s. pain** douleur *f* violente *ou* vive; **she was in s. pain** elle a énormément souffert **3** *(style etc)* sévère, austère

severely [sɪ'vɪəlɪ] ADV **1** *(punished, dealt with etc)* sévèrement, avec sévérité **2** *(wounded)* grièvement; *(ill)* gravement; **her**

patience was s. tried by his behaviour sa patience a été durement éprouvée par son comportement **3** *(to frown, dress etc)* sévèrement, de façon austère

severity [sɪ'verɪtɪ] N **1** *(of person, punishment, criticism)* sévérité *f; (of conditions)* dureté *f* **2** *(of weather, climate etc)* rigueur *f,* rudesse *f; (of illness, loss, injury)* gravité *f, (of pain)* violence *f* **3** *(of style)* sévérité *f,* austérité *f*

Seville [sə'vɪl] N Séville *f*
▸▸ **S. orange** orange *f* amère, bigarade *f*

sew [səʊ] *(pt* **sewed** [səʊd]; *pp* **sewn** [səʊn], *occ* **sewed)** VI coudre
VT coudre; *Typ* brocher; **hand/machine sewn** cousu (à la) main/à la machine
▸ **sew on** VT SEP *(button) (put on)* coudre; *(put back on)* recoudre
▸ **sew up** VT SEP **1** *(close by sewing), Surg (wound, cut etc)* recoudre **2** *Fam* **it's all sewn up** tout est arrangé; **we've got it all sewn up** l'affaire est dans le sac; **to have the elections/the match sewn up** avoir gagné les élections/le match d'avance

sewage ['suːɪdʒ] N eau(x) *f(pl)* d'égout(s)
▸▸ **s. disposal** évacuation *f* des eaux usées; **s. farm** champs *mpl* d'épandage; **s. system** égouts *mpl;* **s. works** champs d'épandage

sewer¹ ['səʊər] N *(person who sews)* couseur, -euse; **to be a good/bad s.** être bon/mauvais couturier

sewer² ['suːər] N *(pipe)* égout *m;* **main s.** égout collecteur; *Fig* **s. of vice** cloaque *m* de vice; **he's got a mind like a s.** il a l'esprit mal placé; *(he interprets everything sordidly)* c'est un véritable obsédé sexuel
▸▸ **s. rat** rat *m* d'égout

sewerage ['suːərɪdʒ] N **1** *(system of sewers)* système *m* d'égouts **2** = **sewage**

sewermouth ['suːəmaʊθ] N *Am Fam* **to be a s.** jurer comme un charretier

sewing ['səʊɪŋ] N **1** *(activity)* couture *f* **2** *(work)* ouvrage *m* (à l'aiguille); **the s. on this shirt is terrible** cette chemise est très mal cousue
▸▸ **s. basket** boîte *f* à couture; **s. cotton** fil *m* à coudre; **s. kit** nécessaire *m* de couture; **s. machine** machine *f* à coudre; **s. needle** aiguille *f* à coudre; **s. thread** fil à coudre

sewn PP *see* **sew**

sex [seks] N sexe *m;* **to have s. with sb** *(on ongoing basis)* avoir des rapports sexuels avec qn; *(on one occasion)* coucher avec qn; **how many times have you had s. with him?** combien de fois est-ce que vous avez eu des rapports avec lui?; **he's got s. on the brain** il a l'esprit dans la culotte; **a novel full of s.** un roman plein de passages érotiques; **the fair(er)** *or* **weaker s.** le beau sexe; **the s. act** l'acte *m* sexuel; **to have a low/high s. drive** avoir un appétit sexuel faible/élevé; *Fam* **s. mad** qui ne pense qu'au sexe; **to be s. mad** ne penser qu'au sexe; **sex-starved** en manque (de sexe); *Psy* **the s. urge** le désir sexuel
VT *(person, animal)* déterminer le sexe de
▸▸ **s. addict** dépendant, -ante sexuel(elle); **s. addiction** dépendance *f* sexuelle; **s. aid** gadget *m* érotique; **s. appeal** sex-appeal *m;* **s. change** opération *f* de changement de sexe; **to have a s. change** *(operation)* changer de sexe; **s. change operation** opération de changement de sexe; **s. crime** crime *m* sexuel; *Biol* **s. determination** détermination *f* du sexe; **s. discrimination** discrimination *f* sexuelle; **s. education** éducation *f* sexuelle; **s. fiend** maniaque *mf* sexuel(elle); **the s. industry** l'industrie *f* du sexe; *Fam* **s. kitten** bombe *f* sexuelle; **s. life** vie *f* sexuelle; *Hum* **how's your s. life?** et ta vie amoureuse, comment ça va?; **s. maniac** obsédé, -e sexuel(elle); **s. object** objet *m* sexuel; **s. offen-**

der auteur *m* d'un délit sexuel; **s. organs** organes *mpl* sexuels; *Fam* **s. pest** obsédé *m (qui harcèle les femmes);* **s. scandal** affaire *f* de mœurs, scandale *m* sexuel; **s. shop** sex-shop *m, pl* sex-shops; **s. symbol** sex-symbol *m, pl* sex-symbols; **s. therapist** sexologue *mf;* **s. tourism** tourisme *m* sexuel; **s. toy** gadget érotique

sexagenarian [seksədʒɪ'neərɪən] ADJ, N sexagénaire *mf*

sexed [sekst] ADJ **1** *Biol* sexué **2** *Psy* **highly s.** qui a une forte libido

sexiness ['seksɪnɪs] N caractère *m* sexy; **the s. of her appearance** son air sexy; **they are all agreed on his s.** elles sont toutes d'accord pour dire qu'il est sexy; **the s. of the way she walks** sa démarche sexy

sexism ['seksɪz(ə)m] N sexisme *m*

sexist ['seksɪst] ADJ sexiste
N sexiste *mf*

sexless ['sekslɪs] ADJ **1** *Biol (neuter)* asexué **2** *(person)* asexué; *(marriage etc)* où il n'y a pas/plus de relations sexuelles

sexologist [sek'sɒlədʒɪst] N sexologue *mf*

sexology [sek'sɒlədʒɪ] N sexologie *f*

sexploitation [seksplɔɪ'teɪʃən] N *Fam* exploitation *f* commerciale de la sexualité; **a s. movie** un film dont le propos se résume au sexe

sexploits ['seksplɔɪts] NPL *Fam Hum* aventures *fpl* sexuelles

sexpot ['sekspɒt] N *Fam* femme *f*/homme *m* très sexy

sextant ['sekstənt] N *Geom, Naut* sextant *m*

sextet [seks'tet] N *Mus* sextuor *m; (jazz band)* sextet *m*

sexton ['sekst(ə)n] N *Rel* sacristain *m (qui fait également office de sonneur de cloches et de fossoyeur)*

sextuple ['sekstjʊp(ə)l] ADJ, N sextuple *m*

sextuplet ['sekstjʊplɪt] N **1** *(child)* sextuplé, -ée **2** *Mus* sextolet *m*

sexual ['seksjʊəl] ADJ sexuel; **the s. organs** les organes *mpl* sexuels
▸▸ **s. assault** agression *f* sexuelle; **s. attraction** attirance *f* sexuelle; **s. discrimination** discrimination *f* sexuelle, sexisme *m;* **s. harassment** harcèlement *m* sexuel; **s. intercourse** rapports *mpl* sexuels; **s. reproduction** reproduction *f* sexuelle

sexuality [seksjʊ'ælɪtɪ] N sexualité *f*

sexually ['seksjʊəlɪ] ADV sexuellement; **to be s. active** avoir des rapports sexuels; **to be s. attracted to sb** éprouver une attirance sexuelle pour qn
▸▸ *Med* **s. transmitted disease** maladie *f* sexuellement transmissible, *Can* maladie transmise sexuellement

sex-worker N *(prostitute)* prostitué, -ée

sexy ['seksɪ] ADJ *Fam (person, clothes)* sexy; *(book, film)* érotique; *Mktg (product)* branché; *Fig* **skiing has become very s.** le ski est devenu très chic; **hi there, s.!** *(man)* salut, beau gosse!; *(woman)* salut, ma beauté!

Seychelles [seɪ'ʃelz] NPL **the S.** les Seychelles *fpl*

sez [sez] INT *Sl* **s. you!** *(that's what you think)* tu parles!; *(you're not telling the truth)* et ta sœur!

SF [es'ef] N *(abbr* **Science Fiction)** S.F. *f,* anticipation *f*

SFA [esef'eɪ] N *Sport (abbr* **Scottish Football Association)** Fédération *f* écossaise de football

SFO [esef'əʊ] N *Br (abbr* **Serious Fraud Office)** ≃ Service *m* de la répression des fraudes

sfx [ese'feks] NPL *Cin, TV (abbr* **special effects)** effets *mpl* spéciaux

SGML [esdʒiːe'mel] N *Comput (abbr* **Standard Generated Markup Language)** SGML *m*

Sgt *Mil (abbr* **Sergeant)** Sgt

sh [ʃ] INT chut!

shabbily ['ʃæbɪlɪ] ADV **1** *(furnished, dressed etc)* pauvrement **2** *(to treat, behave)* mesquinement

shabbiness ['ʃæbɪnɪs] N **1** *(of clothing etc)* aspect *m* râpé *ou* usé; *(of furniture etc)* piètre état *m; (of person)* apparence *f* pauvre *ou* miteuse **2** *(of conduct etc)* mesquinerie *f,* petitesse *f*

shabby ['ʃæbɪ] ADJ **1** *(clothing etc)* râpé, usé; *(furniture, room, house etc)* pauvre, minable; **to become s.** *(of material)* s'élimer; **to look s.** *(of person)* avoir l'air minable *ou* miteux; **s. genteel** pauvre mais digne **2** *(conduct)* mesquin, petit; **a s. excuse** un prétexte mesquin; **s. trick** mesquinerie *f*

shack [ʃæk] N *(hut)* cabane *f,* hutte *f, Pej (house)* baraquement *m; Fam Hum* **nice little s. you have here** c'est une belle petite baraque que vous avez
▸ **shack up** VI *Sl (cohabit)* **to s. up (together)** se mettre à la colle; **to s. up with sb** *(start to live with)* se mettre à la colle avec qn; **are they still shacking up together?** est-ce qu'ils vivent toujours ensemble?

shackle ['ʃæk(ə)l] VT *(prisoner)* enchaîner, mettre les fers à; *Fig* **shackled by convention** entravé par les conventions

shackles ['ʃæk(ə)lz] NPL *(on prisoner etc)* fers *mpl; Fig* **the s. of convention** le carcan des conventions sociales; **to throw off the s. of convention** rejeter le carcan des conventions sociales

shacktown ['ʃæktaʊn] N *Am Fam* bidonville *m*

shade [ʃeɪd] N **1** *(darkness), Art* ombre *f;* **in the s. of a tree** à l'ombre d'un arbre; **a tree provided some s.** un arbre donnait de l'ombre; **temperature in the s.** température à l'ombre; *Fig* **to put sb in the s.** éclipser qn; *Myth Lit* **the Shades** *(the underworld)* les Enfers *mpl*
2 *(nuance) (of colour, opinion)* nuance *f,* **different shades of blue** différentes nuances de bleu; *Comput* **shades of grey** niveaux *mpl ou* tons *mpl* de gris; **a s. too big** un tantinet trop grand; **he is a s. better** il va un tout petit peu mieux; **a s. (too) sweet** un petit peu (trop) sucré; **a s. of irony** une nuance d'ironie; **just a s.** un petit peu
3 *Lit (ghost)* ombre *f,* fantôme *m; Fig* **shades of 1995** ça rappelle 1995
4 *(device)* **(eye) s.** visière *f,* **(lamp) s.** abat-jour *m inv; Am* **(window) s.** store *m* (de fenêtre); *Fam* **shades** *(sunglasses)* lunettes *fpl* de soleil
VT **1** *(put in darkness)* ombrager, donner de l'ombre à; *(of hat) (face)* obscurcir; **to s. sth from the sun** protéger qch du soleil; **to s. one's eyes with one's hand** s'abriter les yeux de la main; **to s. a light** voiler *ou* masquer une lumière
2 *Art (drawing)* ombrer, mettre des ombres à
VI **blue that shades into green** bleu qui se fond en vert; **these categories s. into one another** ces catégories se confondent
▸ **shade away, shade off** VT SEP *(change by degrees) (colours)* dégrader
VI **red shading off into pink** du rouge qui se fond en rose

shadeband ['ʃeɪdbænd] N *Aut* bande *f* pare-soleil

shaded ['ʃeɪdɪd] ADJ **1** *(path etc)* ombragé; *(lamp etc)* à abat-jour **2** *Art (drawing)* ombré; *(area on diagram, map)* hachuré

shadeless ['ʃeɪdlɪs] ADJ sans ombre

shadiness ['ʃeɪdɪnɪs] N **1** *(of path etc)* ombre *f,* ombrage *m* **2** *Fam (suspiciousness) (of* *affair etc)* aspect *m* louche; *(of person)* réputation *f* suspecte

shading ['ʃeɪdɪŋ] N **1** *Art (on drawing)* ombres *fpl*; *(on map etc)* hachures *fpl* **2 subtle shadings of meaning** *(nuances)* nuances *fpl* de sens subtiles

shadow ['ʃædəʊ] N **1** ombre *f*; *(dark area)* obscurité *f*; *(on picture, photograph)* noir *m*; **in the s.** *(in the shade)* à *ou* dans l'ombre; *(in dark place)* dans l'obscurité; **to cast a s.** jeter une ombre; *Fig* **this cast a s. over the festivities** cela a jeté une ombre sur la fête; *Fig* **coming events cast their shadows** les événements à venir se font pressentir; *Fig* **to catch at shadows, to run after a s.** se bercer d'illusions; **town nestling in the s. of a mountain** ville nichée à l'ombre d'une montagne; **a figure (standing) in the shadows** une silhouette (se tenant) dans l'ombre; *Fig* **to be afraid of one's own s.** avoir peur de son ombre; **not the s. of a doubt** pas l'ombre d'un doute; **to be a (mere) s. of one's/its former self** *(of person, country)* n'être que l'ombre de soi-même; **the s. of death/war** l'ombre de la mort/guerre; **under the s. of a terrible accusation** sous le coup d'une accusation terrible; *Med* **a s. on the right lung** un voile au poumon droit; **to have (dark) shadows round** *or* **under one's eyes** avoir les yeux cernés; **eye s.** *(make-up)* ombre à paupières **2** *(person) (constant companion)* compagnon *m*/compagne *f* inséparable; *(person following someone)* = personne *f* qui prend qn en filature; **the dog was her s.** le chien la suivait comme son ombre; **to put a s. on sb** faire suivre qn **ADJ** *Br Pol* fantôme; **the S. Home Secretary** le Ministre de l'Intérieur du cabinet fantôme **VT 1** *(cast shadows over)* ombrager **2** *(follow) (person)* filer, pister, prendre en filature ▸▸ **s. boxing** *Sport* shadow-boxing *m*, boxe *f* dans le vide; *Fig* attaque *f* rituelle *ou* de pure forme; *Br Pol* **s. cabinet** cabinet *m* fantôme; **s. economy** économie *f* parallèle; *Comput* **s. printing** impression *f* ombrée; **s. puppet** = silhouette *f* découpée utilisée dans les spectacles d'ombres chinoises

---

Shadow cabinet

En Grande-Bretagne, le "shadow cabinet" est composé de parlementaires de l'opposition qui deviendraient ministres si l'opposition accédait au pouvoir. Chaque ministre du gouvernement dispose de son homologue "fantôme" dans l'opposition (on parle de "shadow minister"), qui étudie les mêmes dossiers et se spécialise ainsi dans un domaine donné. Les ministres fantômes occupent les "frontbenches" de l'opposition à la Chambre des communes.

---

shadowing ['ʃædəʊɪŋ] N *(of suspect etc)* filature *f*

shadowy ['ʃædəʊɪ] ADJ **1** *(path etc)* ombragé, ombreux **2** *(vague) (project)* indécis, vague; **a s. form** une silhouette vague

shady ['ʃeɪdɪ] ADJ **1** *(tree etc)* qui donne de l'ombre; *(place, lane etc)* ombragé **2** *Fam (suspicious) (person, transaction, business etc)* louche; *(financier, affair)* véreux; **the s. side of politics** les dessous *mpl* de la politique

shaft [ʃɑːft] N **1** *(of spear etc)* hampe *f*, bois *m*; *(of golf club, tool)* manche *m* **2** *esp Lit (arrow)* flèche *f*, trait *m*; *Fig* **shafts of wit** des traits d'esprit **3** *(beam) (of light)* rayon *m*; *(of lightning)* éclair *m* **4** *(of column)* fût *m*; *(of feather)* tige *f* **5** *Min* puits *m*; **air** *or* **ventilation s.** puits d'aérage, conduit *m* d'air; **to sink a s.**

creuser *ou Tech* foncer un puits **6** *Br* **lift** *or Am* **elevator s.** cage *f* (d'ascenseur) **7** *Tech* arbre *m*; *(stationary)* axe *m*; **driving s.** arbre moteur; **transmission s.** arbre de transmission; **propeller s.** arbre porte-hélice, arbre d'hélice **8** *(on horse-drawn vehicle)* brancard *m* **9** *Vulg (penis)* chibre *m*, queue *f* **VT 1** *Sl (have sexual intercourse with)* tringler **2** *Sl Fig (cheat)* entuber; **to get shafted** se faire entuber ▸▸ *Aut* **s. pin** fusée *f*

shafted ['ʃɑːftɪd] ADJ *Br Sl (drunk)* beurré, bourré

shag [ʃæg] N **1** *(of carpet)* long poil *m*; **s. pile (carpet)** moquette *f* très moelleuse **2** *(tobacco)* tabac *m* fort *(coupé fin)* **3** *(bird)* cormoran *m* huppé **4** *Br Vulg (sex act)* baise *f*; **to have a s.** tirer un coup; **to be a good s.** *(of person)* être un bon coup **5** *Br Vulg (boring task)* plaie *f*; **it's a real s. having to get up so early every morning** c'est vraiment chiant de devoir se lever si tôt tous les matins **VT & VI** *Br Vulg (have sexual intercourse (with))* baiser ▸ **shag out** VT SEP *Br Sl (exhaust)* crever; **I'm shagged out** je suis crevé

shagged [ʃægd] ADJ *Br Sl (exhausted)* crevé, claqué

shagger ['ʃægər] N *Br Vulg* baiseur *m*

shaggy ['ʃægɪ] ADJ *(hairy)* poilu; *(pony etc)* à longs poils; *(hair)* hirsute, ébouriffé; *(beard)* hirsute, touffu; *(eyebrows)* en broussailles; *(carpet)* poilu, à long poil; **s. dog story** = histoire *f* farfelue

shah [ʃɑː] N shah *m ou* chah *m* (d'Iran)

SHAKE [ʃeɪk] VT *(pt* **shook** [ʃʊk]; *pp* **shaken** ['ʃeɪk(ə)n]) **1** secouer; *(liquid, bottle etc)* agiter; *(building etc)* ébranler, secouer; *Fig (opinion, sb's faith)* ébranler; **s. well (before use)** *(on carton etc)* bien agiter avant l'emploi; **to s. one's head** *(in disbelief etc)* secouer *ou'* hocher la tête; *(to indicate 'no')* faire non de la tête; **to s. one's fist at sb** menacer qn du poing; **to s. hands with sb** serrer la main à *ou* de qn; **to s. sb's hand, to s. sb by the hand** donner une poignée de main à qn; **the French s. hands more often** les Français se serrent la main plus souvent; **they shook hands on it** ils ont topé; **to s. oneself free (from sth)** se dégager (de qch) d'une secousse; *Fig* se dégager (de qch); **to s. sb out of his/her complacency/apathy** faire sortir qn de sa suffisance/son apathie; **to s. the snow from one's head** secouer sa tête pour se débarrasser de la neige; **that has shaken my faith in him** cela a ébranlé la confiance que j'avais en lui; **event that shook the country** événement qui a bouleversé le pays; **she was badly shaken by the accident** elle a été terriblement bouleversée par l'accident; **to feel shaken after a fall** se ressentir d'une chute; *Fam* **that'll s. him!** ça va le choquer!; *Br Fam* **he's won more awards than you can s. a stick at** on lui a décerné une floppée de prix **2** *Austr Sl (rob)* voler **VI 1** trembler; *(of voice)* trembloter, chevroter; **her hand was shaking** sa main tremblait; **the whole building shook** *(after explosion etc)* tout le bâtiment a tremblé; **the door shakes whenever a bus passes** à chaque fois qu'un bus passe, ça fait trembler la porte; **the ground shook** le sol a tremblé; **to s. with fright/rage** trembler *ou* frémir de crainte/colère; **in a voice shaking with emotion** d'une voix émue *ou* tremblotante; *Fam* **to s. in one's shoes** trembler *ou* greloter de peur, *Fam* trembler dans ses baskets **2** *Fam* **to s. on it** *(shake hands)* toper **N 1** *(act of shaking)* secousse *f*; *(trembling) (of hand, voice etc)* tremblement *m*; *Am (earthquake)* tremblement de terre; **to give**

sth a good s. bien secouer *ou* agiter qch; **to give oneself a s.** se secouer; **a s. of the head** un hochement de tête; *Fam* **to be all of a s.** trembler de tous ses membres; *Fam* **to have the shakes** *(to be trembling) (with fear)* avoir les chocottes; *(with illness, from alcohol)* avoir la tremblote; **with a s. in his voice** d'une voix tremblotante; *Fig* **in two shakes (of a lamb's tail)** en un rien de temps, *Fam* en moins de deux **2** *Culin* **milk s.** milk-shake *m*, *pl* milk-shakes **3** *Fam* **to be no great shakes** ne pas casser des briques, ne pas casser trois pattes à un canard; *Fam* **he is no great shakes as a writer/at German** comme écrivain/en allemand, il ne casse pas des briques ▸ **shake down** VT SEP **1** *(cause to fall)* **to s. down apples** *etc* faire tomber des pommes *etc* en secouant l'arbre **2** *Am Fam (extort money from)* **to s. sb down for ten dollars** faire cracher dix dollars à qn **3** *Am Fam (search) (person, apartment etc)* fouiller **VI 1** *(fall) (of fruits etc)* tomber **2** *(settle down) (get used to routine, job)* s'habituer; *Fam* **to s. down (for the night)** se mettre au pieu, se pieuter ▸ **shake off** VT SEP **1** *(remove by shaking)* **to s. the dust off sth** secouer la poussière de qch **2** *(get rid of) (illness, cold, depression etc)* se débarrasser de **3** *Fam (escape from) (person)* se débarrasser de; *(other runner)* semer; **I can't s. him off** il ne me lâche pas d'une semelle; **she's always phoning me up, I can't s. her off** elle me téléphone sans cesse, je n'arrive pas à m'en débarrasser ▸ **shake out** VT SEP **1** *(remove dust from) (rug, tablecloth etc)* secouer; *(empty) (bag)* vider en le secouant **2** *(remove by shaking) (dirt, sand etc)* faire sortir en secouant; **he picked up his shoes and shook the sand out** il a ramassé ses chaussures et en a secoué le sable **3** *(unfurl) (sail, flag)* déferler ▸ **shake up** VT SEP **1** *(mix by shaking) (liquid, container etc)* secouer; **don't s. the lemonade up** ne secoue pas la limonade **2** *(plump up) (pillow etc)* secouer **3** *(upset) (person)* secouer; **she looks pretty shaken up** elle a l'air assez secouée; **he was badly shaken up after the accident** l'accident lui a fait un coup **4** *(arouse from indifference etc)* secouer; **he needs shaking up** il a besoin qu'on le secoue

shakedown ['ʃeɪkdaʊn] N **1** *Am Fam (extortion)* chantage *m*, extorsion *f* **2** *Am Fam (search)* fouille *f* **3** *Fam (improvised bed)* lit *m* de fortune

Shaker ['ʃeɪkər] N *Rel* = membre *m* d'une secte protestante du XVIIIe siècle, aujourd'hui presque disparue, qui prêchait le célibat

shaker ['ʃeɪkər] N **sugar s.** saupoudreuse *f (pour le sucre)*; **salad s.** panier *m* à salade; **cocktail s.** shaker *m*

Shakespearian, Shakespearean [ʃeɪks-'pɪərɪən] ADJ shakespearien

shake-up N *Fam (of staff)* remaniement *m*

shakily ['ʃeɪkɪlɪ] ADV *(to walk)* à pas chancelants; *(to write)* d'une main tremblante; *(to speak)* d'une voix chevrotante

shakiness ['ʃeɪkɪnɪs] N *(of building, chair etc)* manque *m* de stabilité *ou* de solidité; *(of person, health, knowledge)* faiblesse *f*; *(of hand)* tremblement *m*; *(of position)* précarité *f*

shaking ['ʃeɪkɪŋ] N *Med* tremblement *m*

shako ['ʃækəʊ] N *Mil (headgear)* s(c)hako *m*

shaky ['ʃeɪkɪ] ADJ *(furniture etc)* branlant, peu solide; *(health)* faible, chancelant; *(position)* précaire; *(hand)* tremblant, vacillant;

(writing) tremblé; *(voice)* mal assuré; *(knowledge)* pas très sûr; **to be s. on one's legs** *ou Fam* **one's pins** ne pas tenir sur ses jambes *ou Fam* quilles; **I feel very s.** *(I am trembling)* je suis tout tremblant; *(I feel unsteady on my feet)* je ne me sens pas bien solide sur mes jambes; *(I feel rather unwell)* je suis patraque *ou* tout chose; **his English is s.** il est faible en anglais

shale [ʃeɪl] N *Geol* schiste *m* argileux *ou* ardoisier, argile *f* schisteuse
▸▸ **s. oil** huile *f* de schiste

shall VOIR GRAMMAIRE A58; B39 *(stressed* [ʃæl], *unstressed* [ʃəl]*)* MODAL AUX V *(pr* shall; *pt,* cond **should** stressed [ʃʊd], *unstressed* [ʃəd]; *Arch* **shouldst** [ʃʊdst]; *no other parts;* shall not *and* should not *are often contracted into* shan't [ʃɑːnt], shouldn't [ʃʊd(ə)nt]*)* **1** *(with full meaning, denotes duty or command) Fml* **he s. do it if I order it** il sera obligé de le faire si je le lui ordonne; **he s. not do it** je lui interdis de le faire; **he says he won't do it** – s'il dit qu'il ne le fera pas – je l'ordonne!; **you shall do it!** vous le ferez, je le veux!; *Law* **ships s. carry three lights** les navires sont tenus de porter trois feux
2 *(making suggestion, asking permission)* **s. I open the window?** voulez-vous que j'ouvre la fenêtre?; **I'll make some coffee, s. I?** je vais faire du café, d'accord?; **let's go in, s. we?** rentrons, voulez-vous?
3 *(future)* **you shan't have any!** tu n'en auras pas!; **you s. pay for this!** vous me le payerez!; **tomorrow I s. go and he will arrive** demain, moi je partirai et lui il arrivera; **will you be there?** – **I s.** y serez-vous? – oui(, j'y serai); **will you be there?** – **no, I s. not** *or* **I shan't** y serez-vous? – non(, je n'y serai pas); **I s. explain the situation to you and you will listen** je vais vous expliquer la situation et vous allez m'écouter; **as we s. see** comme nous le verrons, comme nous allons le voir VOIR GRAMMAIRE A50–1; A78

shallot [ʃə'lɒt] N échalote *f*

shallow ['ʃæləʊ] ADJ **1** *(water, dish etc)* peu profond; *(soil)* superficiel; **s.-rooted** *(tree)* à enracinement superficiel; **s. breathing** respiration *f* faible; **the s. end** *(of swimming pool)* le petit bain **2** *Fig (superficial) (person, mind etc)* superficiel; *(friendship)* de surface
▸▸ *Cin, TV* **s. focus** faible profondeur *f* de champ

shallowness ['ʃæləʊnɪs] N **1** *(of water, dish etc)* peu *m* de profondeur **2** *Fig (of person, mind)* caractère *m* superficiel, superficialité *f*

shallows ['ʃæləʊz] NPL *(in sea etc)* bas-fond *m, pl* bas-fonds, haut-fond *m, pl* hauts-fonds

shalt [ʃælt] 2ND PERS SING MODAL AUX V *Bible, Arch* **thou s. not kill** tu ne tueras point

shaly ['ʃeɪlɪ] ADJ schisteux

sham [ʃæm] ADJ faux, *f* fausse, truqué; *(illness etc)* simulé, feint; *(piety)* apparent; **s. peace** paix *f* de pacotille
N feinte *f*, trompe-l'œil *m inv*; *Fam* chiqué *m*; **it was nothing but a s.** c'était du chiqué; **that's all s.** *Fam* tout ça, c'est de la frime; **he's a s.** c'est un imposteur; **you big s., you're not sad at all!** espèce de comédien, tu n'es pas triste du tout!; **the elections were a s.** les élections n'étaient qu'une imposture
VT *(-mm-)* feindre, simuler; **to s. sickness** faire semblant d'être malade
VI **he's only shamming** c'est une comédie qu'il nous joue, il fait semblant

shaman ['ʃæmən] N chaman *m*

shamanism ['ʃæmənɪz(ə)m] N chamanisme *m*

shamanistic [ʃæmə'nɪstɪk] ADJ relatif au chamanisme

shamateur ['ʃæmətɜːr] N *Sport Fam* = ath-

lète *etc* prétendument amateur mais qui, en réalité, perçoit de l'argent

shamble ['ʃæmb(ə)l] VI **to s. (along)** aller à pas traînants; **to s. up to sb** approcher qn d'un pas traînant

shambles ['ʃæmb(ə)lz] NPL *(usu with sing verb) (disorder)* désordre *m*, fouillis *m*; *(department, company, accounts)* foutoir *m*; *(reception)* désastre *m*; **what a s.!** quelle pagaille!; **it's a bloody s.!** quel foutoir!; **the match was a s.** le match était totalement nul; **the cupboard was in a s.** le placard était rangé n'importe comment

shambolic [ʃæm'bɒlɪk] ADJ *Fam* bordélique

shame [ʃeɪm] N **1** *(disgrace, guilt etc)* honte *f*, **hooligans are the s. of our country** les hooligans sont la honte de notre pays; **to bring s. on one's family/country** faire honte à sa famille/son pays; *also Fig* **to put sb to s.** faire honte à qn; **to my s.** à ma grande honte; **s. (up)on you!** quelle honte!; **for s.!** vous n'avez pas honte!; **he hid his face in s.** il s'est caché la face de honte; **to blush for** *or* **with s.** rougir de honte; **without s.** effronté, éhonté; **she is utterly without s.** elle n'a aucune pudeur; **to be past all s., to be lost to all s.** avoir perdu toute honte; **to have no s.** *(no scruples)* n'avoir aucune honte; **have you no s.?** tu n'as pas honte?; **six cakes! have you no s.?** six gâteaux! tu n'as pas honte?
2 *(pity)* dommage *m*; **it would be a s. to … il** serait dommage de …; **it's a s. you can't come** c'est dommage que vous ne puissiez pas venir; **what a s.!** quel dommage!; *Parl* **s.!** = cri *m* des députés anglais à la Chambre des communes pour manifester leur désapprobation ou leur indignation
VT *(cause to feel ashamed)* faire honte à; *(bring shame on)* couvrir de honte; **to be shamed into doing sth** faire qch par amour-propre; **they tried to s. her into donating more** ils ont essayé de lui faire honte pour qu'elle donne davantage

shamefaced ['ʃeɪmfeɪst] ADJ *(ashamed)* (à l'air) honteux; *(embarrassed)* embarrassé, décontenancé

shamefacedly [ʃeɪm'feɪsɪdlɪ] ADV d'un air honteux; *(with embarrassment)* d'un air embarrassé

shameful ['ʃeɪmfʊl] ADJ honteux, scandaleux

shamefully ['ʃeɪmfəlɪ] ADV honteusement, scandaleusement; **they've been s. neglected** ils ont été honteusement négligés; **he was s. ignorant about the issue** son ignorance sur la question était honteuse

shamefulness ['ʃeɪmfʊlnɪs] N honte *f*, infamie *f*

shameless ['ʃeɪmlɪs] ADJ **1** *(without shame) (person, conduct)* éhonté, effronté; **he was quite s. about it all** il ne montrait aucun scrupule; *usu Hum* **a s. (little) hussy** une diablesse **2** *(immodest) (person)* sans pudeur, dévergondé; *(conduct)* impudique

shamelessly ['ʃeɪmlɪslɪ] ADV **1** *(without shame)* effrontément **2** *(immodestly) (to carry on, have affair etc)* avec impudeur

shamelessness ['ʃeɪmlɪsnɪs] N **1** *(lack of shame)* effronterie *f* **2** *(sexual immodesty)* impudeur *f*, *(of conduct)* impudicité *f*

shaming ['ʃeɪmɪŋ] ADJ humiliant

shammy ['ʃæmɪ] N *(leather)* peau *f* de chamois
▸▸ **s. leather** peau de chamois

shampoo [ʃæm'puː] N shampo(o)ing *m*; **liquid/dry s.** shampo(o)ing liquide/sec; **carpet s.** shampo(o)ing pour moquette; **to give sb a s.** faire un shampo(o)ing à qn; **s. and set** shampo(o)ing et mise en plis
VT **to s. one's hair** se faire un shampo(o)ing; **to s. sb** *or* **sb's hair** faire un shampo(o)ing à

qn; **to s. a carpet** shampouiner une moquette

shamrock ['ʃæmrɒk] N *(plant)* trèfle *m*; **the land of the s.** = l'Irlande *f*

shamus ['ʃeɪməs] N *Am Fam (détective m)* privé *m*

shandy ['ʃændɪ], *Am* **shandygaff** ['ʃændɪgæf] N panaché *m*; **a lager s.** un panaché à la bière blonde

Shanghai [ʃæŋ'haɪ] N Shanghai *m*, Changhai *m*

shanghai [ʃæŋ'haɪ] VT *Naut Fam* **to s. sb** embarquer qn de force sur un navire à court d'équipage; *Fig* **to s. sb into doing sth** *(force)* forcer qn à faire qch

Shangri-La [ʃæŋgrɪ'lɑː] N paradis *m* terrestre

shank [ʃæŋk] N **1** *Culin (of beef)* jarret *m*; *(of horse's leg)* canon *m* **2** *(of key, rivet)* tige *f*; *Typ (of letter)* corps *m*, tige; *Naut (of anchor)* verge *f* **3** *Am Fam (knife)* surin *m*, lame *f*

Shanks [ʃæŋks] N *Fam* **to go** *or* **ride on S.'s pony** y aller à pinces

shan't CONTR = shall not, *see* shall

shantung [ʃæn'tʌŋ] N *Tex* shant(o)ung *m*

shanty¹ ['ʃæntɪ] N *(hut)* bicoque *f*, cabane *f*
▸▸ **s. town** bidonville *m*

shanty² N *Naut (sea)* **s.** chanson *f* de marin

SHAPE [ʃeɪp] N *Mil (abbr* Supreme Headquarters Allied Powers, Europe*)* quartier *m* général des forces alliées de l'OTAN en Europe

SHAPE [ʃeɪp] N **1** *(form)* forme *f*, **what s. is it?** de quelle forme est-ce?; **they were the same s.** ils étaient de la même forme, ils avaient la même forme; **a cake in the s. of a …** un gâteau en forme de …; **oblong/triangular in s.** de forme oblongue/triangulaire; **spherical in s., of spherical s.** de forme sphérique; **trees of all shapes** des arbres de toutes les formes; **my hat was knocked out of s.** mon chapeau a été déformé; **to get out of s., to lose (its) s.** se déformer; **to mould sth into s.** donner forme à qch; *Journ etc Fam* **to knock an article into s.** mettre un article au point; *Fam* **to knock** *or* **lick a team into s.** faire quelque chose d'une équipe; **to give s. to a plan** donner corps à un projet; **to take s.** prendre forme *ou* tournure; **this is the s. of things to come** c'est ça l'avenir, *esp Pej* voilà ce qui nous attend; **progress, in the s. of motorways/supermarkets** le progrès que représentent les autoroutes/les supermarchés; **wealth in the s. of a large house** la richesse symbolisée par la possession d'une grande maison; **no communication in any s. or form** aucune communication de quelque forme que ce soit; **something in the s. of …** une espèce *ou* une sorte de …; **help arrived in the s. of …** l'aide est arrivée sous la forme de …
2 *(condition)* **to keep in/get back into s.** *(physically)* garder/retrouver la forme; **to be in good/poor s.** *(of person etc)* être en bonne/petite forme; *Fam* **she was in pretty bad s.** *(very ill, badly injured)* elle était mal en point *ou* dans un sale état; **what sort of s. is he in?** *(after accident, ordeal)* dans quel état est-il?; **he's in no s. to be doing this kind of work!** il n'est pas en état de faire ce genre de travail!
3 *(figure, human figure)* forme *f*, **two shapes loomed up in the darkness** deux formes surgirent dans l'obscurité
VT *(clay etc)* façonner, modeler; *(block of stone etc)* tailler; *Fig (plan)* former; **to s. sth out of sth** façonner qch avec qch; **to s. the clay into an urn** donner à l'argile la forme d'une urne; **to s. sb's character** façonner le caractère de qn; **to s. the destiny of man** diriger *ou* régler la destinée de l'homme; **to**

s. the course of public opinion manipuler l'opinion publique; **the war shaped her perception of the army** la guerre a influencé sa perception de l'armée

vi = **shape up 1**

▸ **shape up** vi **1** (turn out) to s. up well promettre; (of affair) prendre bonne tournure; **let's see how he shapes up in his new job** voyons comment il va s'en tirer dans son nouvel emploi; **the new player is shaping up well** le nouveau joueur promet beaucoup; esp Am Fam **s. up or ship out!** secouez-vous, sinon c'est la porte!

2 (prepare to tackle) to s. up to a problem/ situation s'attaquer à un problème/faire face à une situation

shaped [ʃeɪpt] ADJ **1** façonné, taillé; (in metalwork) (piece) profilé, embouti **2 well-/badly s.** bien/mal formé; **an awkwardly s. room** une pièce de forme bizarre; **s. like an egg** en forme d'œuf

-shaped [ʃeɪpt] SUFF **egg/heart/**etc **-s.** en forme d'œuf/de cœur/etc

shapeless [ˈʃeɪplɪs] ADJ informe

shapelessness [ˈʃeɪplɪsnɪs] N manque m de forme

shapeliness [ˈʃeɪplɪnɪs] N (of woman) beauté f de forme, belles proportions fpl; (of legs) galbe m

shapely [ˈʃeɪplɪ] ADJ bien fait; **a s. leg** une jambe bien galbée; **to be s.** (of woman) être bien faite ou Fam bien roulée

shaper [ˈʃeɪpər] N (who creates projects etc) personne f qui lance des projets

shaping [ˈʃeɪpɪŋ] N (of block of stone etc) façonnement m, façonnage m; **the s. of his character** le développement ou la formation de son caractère; **the s. of a policy** la conception d'une politique

shard [ʃɑːd] N (of pottery) tesson m

SHARE [ʃeər] N **1** (part) part f; **in equal shares** en parts égales; **to have a s. in sth** participer à qch; **to have a s. in the profits** participer aux bénéfices; **you had a s. in this** (you are partly responsible) vous y êtes pour quelque chose; (you contributed) votre participation a été importante; **I had no s. in this decision** je n'ai aucune responsabilité dans cette décision; **to come in for a s. of the blame** être reconnu responsable; **to take a s. of the profits** prendre sa part des bénéfices; **to take a s. of the blame** reconnaître sa part de responsabilité; **the lion's s.** la part du lion; **s. in profits** (participation) participation f aux bénéfices; (amount) tantième m; **to give sb a s. of the profits** donner à qn une part des bénéfices; Fam **to go shares** partager (with avec); Fam **I went half shares with him** (in buying sth) on l'a acheté à deux; **(fair) s.** part équitable; **I'm entitled to a fair s. of the profits** j'ai droit à ma part des bénéfices; **I've had my s. of worries** j'ai eu mon lot de soucis; **she's had more than her (fair) s. of problems** elle a eu largement son lot de problèmes; Fam **we've had more than our fair s. of rain and then some** question pluie, nous avons été servis; Law **legal s.** (of inheritance) réserve f légale; **to pay one's s.** payer sa (quote-)part; **to do one's s., to take** ou **bear one's s. of the burden** participer; **he doesn't do his s.** il ne fait pas sa part; **to have a s. in an undertaking** avoir un intérêt ou être intéressé dans une entreprise

2 Fin action f, titre m; **to hold** or **have shares** détenir des actions, être actionnaire; **to have shares in a company** détenir des actions dans une société; **to own 51% of the shares** détenir 51% du capital

3 Agr (of plough) soc m (de charrue)

VT partager; **to s. sth with sb** partager qch

avec qn; **to s. a bathroom** (of tenants) partager une salle de bain; **a shared bathroom** une salle de bain commune; **to s. sb's opinion** partager l'avis de qn; **to s. one's ideas/impressions with sb** partager des idées/impressions avec qn; Iron **thank you very much for sharing that with me!** c'est vachement intéressant ce que tu dis!; **he shares all his secrets with me** il me fait part de tous ses secrets; **they s. an interest in music** ils s'intéressent tous les deux à la musique

VI partager; **to s. and s. alike** partager équitablement; **to s. in sth** (in blame, praise etc) partager qch; **to s. in the profits** participer aux ou avoir part aux bénéfices; **to s. in sb's grief/happiness** partager la douleur/le bonheur de qn

▸▸Fin **s. account** compte-titres m, pl comptes-titres; Fin **s. capital** capital-actions m, pl capitaux-actions; Fin **s. certificate** certificat m ou titre d'actions; St Exch **s. dealing** opérations fpl de Bourse, négoce m de titres; St Exch **s. index** indice m boursier; **s. issue** émission f d'actions; **s. market** marché m des valeurs mobilières; **s. option** possibilité f d'acheter des actions; Fin **s. option scheme** plan m de participation par achat d'actions; **s. owner** détenteur, -trice d'actions; **s. ownership** actionnariat m; **s. point** point m de part de marché; St Exch **s. price index** indice des cours d'actions

▸ **share out** VT SEP (loot etc) partager, distribuer, répartir; (work) répartir, distribuer

sharecropper [ˈʃeəkrɒpər] N Agr métayer, -ère

sharecropping [ˈʃeəkrɒpɪŋ] N Agr métayage m

shareholder [ˈʃeəhəʊldər] N Fin actionnaire mf; **the shareholders** l'actionnariat m, les actionnaires; **minority/majority s.** actionnaire minoritaire/majoritaire; **small s.** petit porteur m; **shareholders' funds** capitaux mpl propres, haut m de bilan; **shareholders' meeting** réunion f ou assemblée f des actionnaires

shareholding [ˈʃeəhəʊldɪŋ] N Fin (shares) participation f, (share ownership) actionnariat m

share-out N partage m, répartition f

shareware [ˈʃeəweər] N Comput shareware m, logiciel m en libre essai, logiciel contributif

▸▸ **s. programs** sharewares mpl

sharing [ˈʃeərɪŋ] N **1** (of loot, property etc) distribution f, partage m **2** (participation) participation f, partage m; **profit s.** participation aux bénéfices

shark [ʃɑːk] N **1** (fish) requin m **2** Fam (ruthless person) requin m **3** Am Fam (talented person) as m; **to be a s. at math** être calé en maths, être une bête en maths

sharkskin [ˈʃɑːkskɪn] N peau f de requin

sharp [ʃɑːp] ADJ **1** (knife, edge) tranchant, affilé; (spear, tooth, point) aigu, f aiguë, pointu

2 (features etc) anguleux, tiré; (peak etc) pointu; (angle) saillant, aigu, f aiguë; (curve) prononcé; (ascent, descent) raide; (roof) pointu, en pointe; (turning) brusque; (outline, focus) Phot (image) net, f nette; Fig **to be at the s. end** être en première ligne; **s. rise/drop in prices** forte ou nette hausse/baisse des prix; **s. contrast** contraste marqué ou net; **this accident brings into s. relief the need for extra precautions** cet accident démontre à quel point il est nécessaire de prendre des précautions supplémentaires

3 (sight) perçant; (hearing) fin; (cunning, shrewd) rusé, malin; (unscrupulous) peu scrupuleux; **to have a s. mind** avoir l'esprit

vif; **he's as s. as a needle** (quick to understand) il a l'esprit vif; (cunning) il est malin comme un singe; **s. practice(s)** procédés indélicats ou peu honnêtes

4 (wind) vif, f vive, perçant; (cold) pénétrant, piquant; **it's a bit s. this morning** il fait frisquet ce matin; **a s. frost** une forte gelée; **s. pain** douleur aiguë

5 (fast) rapide; (trot) vif, f vive

6 (harsh) (voice, words) cinglant; (person) brusque; **to make a s. retort** (to reply in a sharp tone) répondre d'une voix cassante; (to make a cutting reply) répondre de façon cinglante; **a s. reproof** une verte réprimande; **in a s. tone** d'un ton brusque; **a s. tongue** une langue acérée ou caustique

7 (taste) âpre, piquant; (sauce) piquant; (apple etc) acide; (wine) vert

8 (sound) perçant, aigu, f aiguë

9 Mus (note) dièse; **you're s.** (to singer) vous chantez trop aigu; (to violinist) vous jouez trop aigu; **a semitone s.** un demi-ton trop haut

10 Fam (in dress) classe inv; **to be a s. dresser** s'habiller classe

N Mus dièse m; **double s.** double dièse m

ADV **1 s. pointed pencil** crayon taillé fin; **s. edged** (knife etc) tranchant, affilé **2** (to turn) brusquement, court; **turn s. right** prenez à angle droit; **the road turns s. right** la route fait un virage serré à droite **3** (punctually) **at four o'clock s.** à quatre heures sonnantes ou précises ou Fam tapantes **4** Fam **look s.!** dépêchez-vous!, remuez-vous! **5** Mus (to sing, play) trop aigu

sharpen [ˈʃɑːp(ə)n] VT **1** (knife, tool etc) affiler, aiguiser; (stick etc) tailler en pointe, aiguiser; (pencil) tailler; (angle) rendre plus saillant; (feature, contrast) accentuer; **to s. its claws** (of cat etc) faire ses griffes **2** to s. sb's wits éveiller l'esprit de qn, Fam dégourdir qn **3** (pain, animosity) aviver; (passion, desire) exciter; (of walk etc) (appetite) aiguiser, ouvrir **4** to s. one's voice prendre un ton plus acerbe ou âpre **5** Culin (sauce) donner du piquant à **6** Mus (note) diéser

VI **1** (of faculties etc) s'aiguiser **2** (of tone) devenir plus acerbe ou âpre **3** (of sound) devenir plus perçant ou aigu, f aiguë

sharpener [ˈʃɑːp(ə)nər] N (device) aiguisoir m; (knife) s. aiguisoir m (pour couteaux); (pencil) s. taille-crayon m, pl taille-crayon(s)

sharpening [ˈʃɑːp(ə)nɪŋ] N (of tool etc) affilage m, aiguisage m

sharper [ˈʃɑːpər] N escroc m; Cards tricheur, -euse

sharp-eyed ADJ (good at finding things) à qui rien n'échappe; (keen-sighted) à la vue perçante

sharply [ˈʃɑːplɪ] ADV **1 s. pointed** très pointu **2 this contrasts s. with …** ceci contraste nettement avec …; **s. in focus** très net; **to bring sth s. home, to bring sth s. into focus** faire apparaître qch de façon évidente **3** (to drop, descend, brake) brusquement; (to turn) brusquement, court; **he looked up s. when I mentioned her name** il a brusquement levé les yeux lorsque j'ai mentionné son nom **4** (to reprimand) sévèrement; (to reply) d'un ton brusque; **he looked s. at her** (angrily, warning etc) il l'a regardée sévèrement; (trying to understand) il l'a regardée d'un œil pénétrant

sharpness [ˈʃɑːpnɪs] N **1** (of knife edge etc) tranchant m; (of contours, photograph) netteté f; (of contrast) caractère m marqué; **s. of focus** (of photo) netteté f; (of analysis etc) précision f; Aut etc **s. of the turn** raideur f du virage **2** (of mind, hearing) finesse f, (of child) intelligence f, **s. of sight** acuité f visuelle **3** (of pain) violence f; **there's a s. in**

the air il fait frisquet **4** *(of tone, reprimand)* sévérité *f*, âpreté *f*; *(of tone)* brusquerie *f*; *(of character, voice)* aspérité *f* **5** *(taste) (of sauce)* piquant *m*; *(of apple etc)* acidité *f* **6** *(of sound)* acuité *f*, qualité *f* perçante

sharpshooter [ˈʃɑːpʃuːtər] **N** *Mil* tireur, -euse d'élite

sharp-sighted **ADJ** *(keen-sighted)* à la vue perçante; *(observant)* observateur, -trice

sharp-tongued [ʃɑːpˈtʌŋd] **ADJ** caustique

sharp-witted **ADJ** vif, *f* vive

shatter [ˈʃætər] **VT 1** *(smash)* fracasser, briser en éclats; *(bone)* briser en plusieurs morceaux **2** *(hopes)* briser, renverser; *(silence)* rompre **3** *(health, nerves)* détraquer; *Fam* **I was absolutely shattered!** *(stunned)* j'ai été scié!; *(exhausted)* j'étais complètement crevé!

VI se briser (en éclats), se fracasser; **the windscreen shattered** le pare-brise a volé en éclats

shattering [ˈʃætərɪŋ] **ADJ** *(blow)* écrasant; **s. news** des nouvelles renversantes

shatterproof [ˈʃætəpruːf] **ADJ** *(glass, windscreen)* feuilleté

shave [ʃeɪv] **VT 1** *(face, legs etc)* raser; *(remove hair from face of) (person)* faire la barbe à; **to s. sb's head** raser la tête à qn; **to s. one's legs** s'épiler les jambes **2** *(wood)* planer; *(corner)* rogner; **to s. prices** rogner les prix **3** *(brush against)* effleurer

VI se raser; **to start shaving** *(of boy)* commencer à se raser

N 1 *(of face, legs etc)* rasage *m*; **to have a s.** se raser; *(be shaved)* se faire raser; **this razor gives you a really close s.** avec ce rasoir, vous pouvez vraiment vous raser de près; *Fam* **that was a close s.!** vous l'avez/il l'a *etc* échappé belle!, il était moins une! **2** *(tool)* plane *f*, racloir *m*

▸ **shave off** **VT SEP** **to s. off one's moustache** se raser la moustache; **to s. off a piece of cheese/sausage** couper une mince tranche de fromage/saucisson; **you'll need to s. a bit more off the drawer** il faut raboter un peu plus le tiroir; **this has shaved a few points off the government's lead in the polls** cela a légèrement rogné l'avance du gouvernement dans les sondages

shaven [ˈʃeɪv(ə)n] **ADJ** *(monk)* tonsuré; *(head, chin)* rasé; **clean s.** *(man)* sans barbe ni moustache; *(face)* glabre

shaver [ˈʃeɪvər] **N 1** **(electric) s.** rasoir *m* électrique **2** *Old-fashioned Fam* **(young) s.** *(lad)* gosse *m*, gamin *m*

▸▸ **s. socket** prise *f* pour rasoir électrique

Shavian [ˈʃeɪvɪən] **N** admirateur, -trice de George Bernard Shaw

ADJ *(of Shaw)* de George Bernard Shaw; *(like Shaw)* à la George Bernard Shaw

shaving [ˈʃeɪvɪŋ] **N 1** *(act)* rasage *f* **2** *(small piece shaved off) (of wood, metal)* copeau *m*

▸▸ **s. brush** blaireau *m*; **s. cream** crème *f* à raser; **s. foam** mousse *f* à raser; **s. mirror** miroir *m* à raser; **s. soap** savon *m* à barbe; **s. stick** *(bâton m de)* savon à barbe

shawl [ʃɔːl] **N** châle *m*

she [ʃiː] **PERS PRON** VOIR GRAMMAIRE A27–8 **1** elle; *(of ship)* il; **s. was running** elle courait; **what's s. doing?** qu'est-ce qu'elle fait?; **here s. comes!** la voici (qui vient)!; **s. sails at ten o'clock** *(of ship)* il part à dix heures; **s.'s had it, this old car** elle est bonne pour la casse, cette vieille voiture **2** *(stressed)* elle; **s. and I** elle et moi; she **knows nothing about it** elle n'en sait rien, elle; *esp Lit* **s. of whom you speak** celle dont vous parlez

N *Fam* femelle; **it's a s.** *(of newborn child)* c'est une petite fille; *(of animal)* c'est une femelle

she- [ʃiː] **PREF** **s.-ass** ânesse *f*; **s.-bear** ours *m*

femelle, ourse *f*; **s.-cat** chatte *f*; **s.-devil** diablesse *f*

sheaf, *pl* **sheaves** [ʃiːf, ʃiːvz] **N** *(of corn etc)* gerbe *f*; *(of papers)* liasse *f*; **I had a whole s. of letters this morning** j'ai reçu toute une pile de lettres ce matin

shear [ʃɪər] *(pt* **sheared**; *pp* **shorn** [ʃɔːn], **sheared)** **VT 1** *(sheep etc)* tondre; *Fig* **to be shorn of sth** être dépouillé *ou* privé de qch **2** *(cut) (branch etc)* couper; **to s. through sth** trancher qch **3** *Phys etc* cisailler

VI *(of material)* se fendre

▸ **shear off** **VI** se détacher

shearer [ˈʃɪərər] **N 1** *(person) (of sheep)* tondeur, -euse **2** *(machine) (for sheep)* tondeuse *f*

shearing [ˈʃɪərɪŋ] **N 1** *(of sheep)* tonte *f* **2** **shearings** *(of wool)* tontes *fpl*

shears [ʃɪəz] **N (pair of) s.** *(large scissors)* cisaille(s) *f(pl)*; *(for sheep, at hairdresser)* tondeuse *f*; *(garden)* sécateur *m*; *Sewing etc* **pinking s.** ciseaux *mpl* à denteler VOIR GRAMMAIRE A10

sheath [ʃiːθ] **N** *(pl* **sheaths** [ʃiːðz, ʃiːθs]*)* *(protective sleeve)* manchon *m* protecteur; *(for sword, umbrella etc)* fourreau *m*; *(for scissors)* étui *m*; *(for knife, electric cable)* gaine *f*, *Anat* *(of organ)* enveloppe *f*, *(of muscle)* gaine; *Bot* gaine; **(contraceptive) s.** préservatif *m*

▸▸ **s. dress** *(robe f)* fourreau *m*; **s. knife** couteau *m* à gaine

sheathe [ʃiːð] **VT 1** *(sword etc)* (re)mettre au fourreau, rengainer; *(knife etc)* engainer; **sheathed in** gainé de **2** *Elec* *(cable)* gainer

sheathing [ˈʃiːðɪŋ] **N** *Elec* *(sheath) (of cable)* gaine *f*

sheave [ʃiːv] **VT** *(corn etc)* mettre en gerbes

Sheba [ˈʃiːbə] **N** **the Queen of S.** la reine de Saba

shebang [ʃɪˈbæŋ] **N** *Sl* **the whole s.** tout le bazar

shebeen [ʃɪˈbiːn] **N** *Dial Irish* débit *m* de boissons clandestin

shed¹ [ʃed] **N** *(larger)* hangar *m*; *(smaller)* remise *f*, **lean-to s.** appentis *m*; **(garden) s.** cabane *f* de jardin; *Rail* **(engine) s.** remise de locomotives; **tool s.** cabane à outils; **bicycle s.** *(small)* remise à vélo; *(big)* hangar à vélo; **cattle s.** étable *f*

shed² *(pt, pp* **shed**; *prp* **shedding)** **VT 1** *(drop, get rid of) (leaves, teeth, skin, horns etc)* perdre; *(of lorry etc) (load)* renverser; **snakes s. their skin** les serpents muent; **its feathers s. water** l'eau lui glisse sur les plumes; **to s. its leaves** *(of plant)* s'effeuiller; **to s. jobs** supprimer des emplois; **to s. labour** licencier de la main-d'œuvre; *Elec* **to s. the load** délester; **he s. 20 pounds in a month** il a perdu neuf kilos en un mois; **to s. one's clothes** se dépouiller de ses vêtements **2** *(spill) (tears, blood)* répandre, verser; *(light)* diffuser; **before more blood is s.** avant que davantage de sang ne soit versé; *Fig* **to s. light on sth** jeter la lumière sur qch

VI *(of cat)* perdre ses poils

she'd [ʃiːd] **CONTR 1** = **she had**, *see* **have²** **2** = **she would**, *see* **will³**

shedding [ˈʃedɪŋ] **N 1** *(of leaves, teeth etc)* perte *f*, chute *f*; *Elec* **load s.** délestage *m* **2** *(of blood)* effusion *f*

shedload [ˈʃedləʊd] **N** *Br Fam* **a s. of**, **shedloads of** une tapée de; **she earns a s.** *or* **shedloads of dosh** elle se fait un fric fou

sheen [ʃiːn] **N** reflet *m*; **hair with a golden s.** cheveux aux reflets d'or; *Fig* **to take the s. off sb's reputation/image** ternir la réputation/l'image de qn

sheep [ʃiːp] **N** *(inv in pl)* mouton *m*; *Fig* **the black s. (of the family** *etc***)** la brebis galeuse; *Fig* **lost** *or* **stray s.** brebis perdue *ou* égarée;

they follow one another like s. ce sont des moutons de Panurge; *Fig* **to separate the s. from the goats** *or* **the s. and the goats** séparer les brebis d'avec les boucs; **to make s.'s eyes at sb** faire les yeux doux à qn

▸▸ **s. farmer** éleveur, -euse de moutons; **s. farming** élevage *m* de moutons; **s. pen** parc *m* à moutons; **s. shearer** *(person)* tondeur, -euse; *(machine)* tondeuse *f* mécanique; **s. shearing** tonte *f*

sheep-dip **N 1** *(place)* enclos *m* *(avec bain désinfectant)* **2** *(disinfectant)* bain *m* désinfectant *(pour les moutons)*

sheepdog [ˈʃiːpdɒg] **N** *(chien m de)* berger *m*; **Old English s.** berger *m* anglais sans queue

▸▸ **s. trials** concours *m* de chiens de berger

sheepfold [ˈʃiːpfəʊld] **N** parc *m* à moutons

sheepish [ˈʃiːpɪʃ] **ADJ** *(embarrassed)* penaud; **to look s.** avoir l'air penaud

sheepishly [ˈʃiːpɪʃlɪ] **ADV** d'un air penaud

sheepishness [ˈʃiːpɪʃnɪs] **N** *(embarrassment)* air *m* penaud

sheepskin [ˈʃiːpskɪn] **N 1** *(skin)* peau *f* de mouton; *(jacket)* canadienne *f*, veste *f* en peau lainée **2** *esp Am* *(diploma)* diplôme *m*

▸▸ **s. jacket** canadienne *f*, veste en peau lainée

sheer **ADJ 1** *(pure)* pur, véritable; **this accident was caused by s. carelessness** c'est la négligence de l'accident et elle seule qui est à l'origine de l'accident; **that's s. carelessness!** c'est de la négligence pure et simple!; **it's s. madness** *or* **lunacy** *or* **folly** c'est de la folie pure (et simple), c'est de la pure folie; **with a look of s. disbelief** avec un air d'incrédulité absolue; **a s. waste of time** une pure perte de temps; **out of s. malice** par pure méchanceté; **it was s. stupidity** c'était franchement stupide; **in s. desperation, she wrote to him** en désespoir de cause, elle lui écrivit; **by s. chance** tout à fait par hasard; **by s. necessity** par pure nécessité

2 *(perpendicular) (cliff, path etc)* perpendiculaire, à pic, abrupt, escarpé

3 *Tex* fin, transparent; **s. silk stockings** bas *mpl* de soie extra-fins

ADV 1 *(completely) (crazy)* complètement; **this goes s. against everything I've ever been taught** ceci va complètement à l'encontre de tout ce qu'on m'a toujours appris; **the tree was torn s. out by the roots** l'arbre a été littéralement déraciné

2 *(to drop etc)* perpendiculairement, à pic, à plomb

VI *Naut* embarder, faire une embardée

▸ **sheer away** **VI** *(move away) (of vehicle, boat)* faire une embardée; *Fam* **to s. away from a subject** éviter un sujet

sheesh [ʃiːʃ] **INT** *Fam* *(in surprise)* tiens!; *(in exasperation)* allez!

sheet [ʃiːt] **N 1** *(on bed)* drap *m*; **fitted s.** drap-housse *m*, *pl* draps-housses; *Fam* **to get between the sheets** se mettre au lit, *Fam* se pieuter; *Fam* **what's he like between the sheets?** comment est-il au lit? **2** *(of paper)* feuille *f*, feuillet *m*; **a s. of newspaper** une feuille de journal; **loose s., fly s.** feuille volante; *Com* **order s.** bulletin *m* de commande; *Ind* **time** *or* **work** *or* **job s.** feuille de présence; *Typ* **the book is still in sheets** le livre n'a pas encore été relié **3** *(of glass)* feuille *f*; *(of metal)* feuille, tôle *f*, plaque *f*; *Culin* **baking s.** plaque à pâtisserie **4** *(of water, foam)* nappe *f*; *(of flame)* rideau *m*; *(of ice)* couche *f*; **the rain was coming down in sheets** la pluie tombait à verse **5** *Br Sl* **sheets** livres *fpl* sterling; **his DVD player cost him 500 sheets** son lecteur de DVD lui a coûté 500 livres **6** *Naut* *(rope)* écoute *f*; *Old-fashioned Fam* **to be three sheets to the wind** *(drunk)* avoir du vent dans les voiles

▸▸*Naut* **s. bend** nœud *m* d'écoute; *Comput* **s. feeder** bac *m* d'alimentation papier; **s. glass** verre *m* à vitres; **s. lightning** éclair *m* en nappe *ou* en nappes; **s. metal** tôle; **s. mill** laminoir *m* à tôles, tôlerie *f*; **s. music** partitions *fpl*

▸ **sheet down** *vi* *(of rain)* tomber à verse; **it was sheeting down** il pleuvait à verse

sheet-fed ADJ *Comput* à alimentation feuille par feuille

▸▸ **s. printer** imprimante *f* feuille à feuille

sheetfeed [ˈʃiːtfiːd] N *Comput* alimentation *f* feuille par feuille, feuille à feuille *m*; *(device)* dispositif *m* d'alimentation papier

sheeting [ˈʃiːtɪŋ] N *(fabric)* toile *f* pour draps; **(plastic) s.** bâche(s) *f(pl)* (en plastique)

sheik(h) [ʃeɪk, ʃiːk] N cheik(h) *m*, scheik *m* **sheik(h)dom** [ˈʃeɪkdəm, ˈʃiːk-] N territoire *m* d'un/du cheik(h)

sheila [ˈʃiːlə] N *Austr Sl (girl)* nana *f*

shekel [ˈʃek(ə)l] N **1** *Hist (coin, weight)* sicle *m* **2** *Fam* **shekels** *(money)* fric *m*, flouse *m*

shelf, *pl* **shelves** [ʃelf, ʃelvz] N **1** *(in shelving unit)* tablette *f*, *(in cupboard)* planche *f*, rayon *m*; *(in bookcase)* rayon; *(of sideboard)* étagère *f*; *(in oven)* plateau *m*; **(set of) shelves** étagère *f*; **these machines can be bought off the s.** ces machines sont disponibles en stock; **to stay on the shelves** *(of goods)* *(not get sold)* ne pas se vendre; *(not sell well)* être difficile à vendre; *Fam* **to be on the s.** *(abandoned)* être laissé pour compte; *(of unmarried woman)* être en passe de devenir vieille fille; *Aut* **(window) s.** plage *f* arrière; *(at front)* vide-poche *m*, *pl* vide-poches

2 *(of cliff, rock face)* rebord *m*, saillie *f*; *(in oceanography), Geog* terrasse *f*, plate-forme *f*, *pl* plates-formes; *(of rock, sand)* banc *m*; **continental s.** plate-forme continentale

▸▸*Mktg* **s. facing** facing *m*, frontale *f*, **s. filler** *(person in supermarket)* réassortisseur, -euse; **s. life** durée *f* de conservation avant vente; **the s. life is six months** la durée de conservation avant vente est de six mois; *Fig* **to have a short s. life** *(of ideas, pop groups etc)* avoir une durée de vie courte; *Com* **s. space** linéaire *m*, rayonnage *m*; **s. stacker** *(person in supermarket)* réassortisseur, -euse

shell [ʃel] N **1** *(of mollusc, oyster, mussel, snail, egg, nut)* coquille *f*; *(of lobster, turtle)* carapace *f*; *(of pea etc)* cosse *f*; *(of chrysalis)* enveloppe *f*; **shells** *(on beach etc)* coquillages *mpl*; *Fig* **to come out of/withdraw into one's s.** sortir de/rentrer dans sa coquille; **I'm just an empty s.** je me sens tout vide **2** *Naut (of ship etc)* carcasse *f*, squelette *m*, coque *f*; *Constr (of building)* charpente *f*; *(damaged)* carcasse; **the burnt-out s. of a car/house** la carcasse brûlée d'une voiture/maison **3** *(bomb)* obus *m*

vt **1** *(nuts etc)* écaler, décortiquer; *(peas)* écosser; *(oysters, mussels)* écailler; *(prawns)* éplucher **2** *Mil* bombarder

vi **nuts that s. easily** noix faciles à décortiquer; **peas that s. easily** pois faciles à écosser

▸▸ **s. pink** *(colour)* rose *m* pâle; *Comput* **s. program** logiciel *m* shell; **s. shock** syndrome *m* commotionnel; **s. suit** survêtement *m* (en polyamide froissé et doublé)

> When translating the English word **shell**, note that the French words **coquillage** and **coquille** are not interchangeable. **Coquillage** applies mostly to seashells, whereas **coquille** refers to the more general sense of a shell as the outer layer of something.

▸ **shell out** *Fam* *vt sep* cracher, casquer; **I was**

shelling out £100 a week on petrol je casquais 100 livres d'essence par semaine *vi* casquer, banquer

she'll [ʃiːl] CONTR = she will, *see* will³

shellac [ʃəˈlæk] N gomme-laque *f*, *pl* gommes-laques; *Chem* shellac *m*

vt (**shellacked**) **1** traiter à la gomme-laque **2** *Am Sport Sl (defeat)* battre à plate(s) couture(s)

shellacking [ʃəˈlækɪŋ] N *Am Sport Sl* **to get a s.** se faire battre à plate(s) couture(s)

shelled [ʃeld] ADJ *(nuts etc)* écalé; *(peas)* écossé

shellfire [ˈʃelfaɪər] N tir *m* d'obus; **to be under s.** subir des tirs d'obus; **we came under heavy s.** nous avons subi un pilonnage intensif

shellfish [ˈʃelfɪʃ] N **1** *(mollusc)* mollusque *m* (comestible), coquillage *m*; *(crustacean)* crustacé *m* **2** *(collectively)* mollusques *mpl* et crustacés *mpl*; *Culin* fruits *mpl* de mer

shelling [ˈʃelɪŋ] N *Mil* bombardement *m*

shell-shaped ADJ en forme de coquillage, conchoïde

shellshocked [ˈʃelʃɒkt] ADJ *Med, Mil* commotionné; *Fig* **to feel s.** être en état de choc

shelter [ˈʃeltər] N **1** *(place)* refuge *m*; *(from rain, bombs, at bus stop etc)* abri *m*; *(bus stop)* Abribus® *m*; *(for the homeless etc)* asile *m*, refuge; *(for guards)* abrivent *m*; *Mil* **air raid s.** abri contre les attaques aériennes, abri de défense passive **2** *(protection)* **under s.** à l'abri, à couvert; **to take s. under/from sth** s'abriter *ou* se mettre à l'abri sous/de qch; **to seek s. under a tree** chercher à s'abriter sous un arbre; **to find s.** trouver un abri; *(of refugee etc)* trouver asile *ou* refuge; **to give s. to sb** abriter qn; *(give asylum etc)* offrir un asile *ou* un refuge à qn

vt abriter; *(lost person etc)* donner asile à, recueillir; **to s. sb/sth from the rain** abriter qn/qch de la pluie

vi s'abriter, se mettre à l'abri *ou* à couvert (**from** de); **to s. under a tree** s'abriter sous un arbre; **to s. from the wind** s'abriter du vent; **to s. from the rain** s'abriter de la pluie

sheltered [ˈʃeltəd] ADJ abrité, protégé (**against, from** de); **to have had** *or* **led a s. life** avoir eu une vie protégée, à l'écart des réalités de l'existence; **you've led a s. life!** tu n'as rien vu!

▸▸ **s. housing** foyers *mpl (pour personnes handicapées, personnes âgées, femmes battues etc)*; *Am* **s. workshop** = atelier *f* pour personnes handicapées

shelve [ʃelv] *vt* **1** *(fit with shelves) (cupboard etc)* munir *ou* garnir de rayons **2** *(put on shelves) (books etc)* mettre sur les rayons **3** *(postpone) (question etc)* ajourner; *(project)* mettre en veilleuse; **the project has been shelved for 6 months** le projet a été mis de côté pendant 6 mois

vi *(slope downwards)* **the land shelves down to the sea** le terrain descend en pente douce jusqu'à la mer

shelving [ˈʃelvɪŋ] N **1** *(no pl) (shelves)* rayons *mpl*, rayonnage *m*; **adjustable s.** rayons amovibles **2** *(postponing) (of question etc)* ajournement *m*

shemozzle [ʃɪˈmɒz(ə)l] N *Am Fam (fight)* bagarre *f*

shenanigans [ʃɪˈnænɪgənz] NPL *Fam* manigances *fpl*; **he's having s. with my wife** il a une aventure avec ma femme

shepherd [ˈʃepəd] N berger *m*, *Lit* pâtre *m*; *Rel* **the Good S.** le bon Pasteur; *Bible* **the Lord is my S.** l'Éternel est mon berger; **German s. (dog)** berger allemand

vt *(sheep)* garder; *Fig (of priest) (his flock)* guider; *(tourists etc)* conduire, piloter; **we**

were shepherded into the next room nous avons été conduits dans la pièce suivante

▸▸ **s. dog** (chien *m* de) berger; **s.'s pie** ≃ hachis *m* Parmentier; *Bot* **s.'s purse** capselle *f*, bourse-à-pasteur *f*, *pl* bourses-à-pasteur

shepherdess [ʃepəˈdes] N bergère *f*

sherbet [ˈʃɜːbət] N **1** *(powder) (sweet)* poudre *f* acidulée; *(for drink)* = poudre servant à préparer une boisson gazeuse **2** *Am (water ice)* sorbet *m* **3** *Br Fam (alcoholic drink)* verre *m*; **fancy going for a couple of sherbets?** ça te dirait de sortir prendre un verre?

▸▸ **s. powder** poudre acidulée

sheriff [ˈʃerɪf] N **1** *Br Admin* shérif *m* *(représentant de la Couronne dans un comté)* **2** *Scot Law* juge *m* de première instance **3** *Am* chef *m* de la police *(d'un comté)*, shérif *m*; **deputy s.** = citoyen *m* assermenté faisant fonction d'agent de police

sherry [ˈʃerɪ] N vin *m* de Xérès, xérès *m*

▸▸ **s. glass** verre *m* à madère

she's [ʃiːz] CONTR **1** = she is, *see* be **2** = she has, *see* have²

Shetland [ˈʃetlənd] N **1** **the Shetlands** les îles *fpl* Shetland **2** *Tex* shetland *m*

▸▸ **the S. Islands** les îles Shetland; **S. pony** poney *m* des Shetland; **S. wool** laine *f* d'Écosse *ou* de Shetland

shew [ʃəʊ] *(pt* **shewed** [ʃəʊd]; *pp* **shewn** [ʃəʊn]) *Arch, Lit* = show²

Shia [ˈʃiːə] N **1** *(religion)* chiisme *m* **2** *(person)* chiite *mf*

shiatsu, shiatzu [ʃɪˈætsuː] N shiatsu *m*

shibboleth [ˈʃɪbəleθ] N *Bible* schibboleth *m*; *Fig (of party etc)* mot *m* d'ordre; **outworn shibboleths** *(doctrines)* doctrines vieux jeu *ou* désuètes

shield [ʃiːld] N **1** *(worn on arm)* bouclier *m*; *Her* écu *m*, écusson *m*; **he used his body as a s. to protect the president** il a fait un bouclier de son corps pour protéger le président; *Fig* **a s. against sth** une protection contre qch **2** *(around nuclear reactor)* bouclier *m*; *(on cable)* blindage *m*; *Astron* **heat s.** bouclier thermique; *Aut* **sun s.** pare-soleil *m inv* **3** *(in spray painting)* masque *m*, cache *m* **4** *(police badge)* plaque *f* de policier **5** *Sport (trophy)* plaque *f*

vt **1** protéger (**from, against** contre); **to s. sb from criticism** protéger qn des critiques; **to s. sb from punishment** soustraire qn à une punition; **to s. sb from danger** protéger qn contre le danger; **to s. sb with one's (own) body** faire un bouclier de son corps à qn; **to s. one's eyes** se protéger les yeux **2** *(in spray painting) (surfaces)* masquer **3** *Elec, Radio* blinder; **shielded cable** câble *m* blindé

▸▸ **s. bearer** écuyer *m*

SHIFT [ʃɪft]

N	changement **1** ▪ poste **2** ▪ équipe **2**
VT	déplacer **1** ▪ vendre **2**
VI	bouger **1** ▪ se magner **2** ▪ se débrouiller **3** ▪ se vendre **4**

N **1** *(of position etc)* changement *m*; *(of tide, current)* renverse *f*; *(of wind)* saute *f*; **s. in meaning** glissement *m* de sens; **there has been a s. in public opinion** il y a eu un glissement de l'opinion publique; **a s. to the right/left** un glissement à droite/gauche; *Aut* **(gear) s.** levier *m* de vitesses; *Ling* **consonant/vowel s.** mutation *f* consonantique/vocalique; *Astron* **red s.** décalage *m* vers le rouge

2 *Ind etc (work period)* poste *m*; *(group of workers)* équipe *f*, brigade *f* *(d'ouvriers)*; **day/night s.** *(period)* poste de jour/nuit; *(workers)* équipe de jour/nuit; **to work in shifts** travailler par équipes, se relayer; **she**

works long shifts elle fait de longues journées; **to work eight-hour shifts** travailler par poste(s) de huit heures, faire les trois-huit; **we each did three-hour shifts** nous nous sommes relayés toutes les trois heures **3** (dress) robe f fourreau; Arch (undergarment) chemise f (de femme) **4** Comput (on typewriter, computer) touche f majuscule; **press s.** appuyer sur la touche majuscule; **an asterisk is s. 8** pour un astérisque, il faut appuyer simultanément sur la touche majuscule et la touche 8 **5** Old-fashioned **to make s.** s'arranger **VT 1** (move) changer de place; (with difficulty) bouger, déplacer; **could you s. your car?** pouvez-vous déplacer votre voiture?; **the drawer's stuck, I can't s. it** le tiroir est coincé, je ne peux le faire bouger; **they've shifted offices again** ils ont déménagé de nouveau; **he keeps getting shifted to a different job** on n'arrête pas de le muter; **he's shifted his position** (in negotiations) il a changé de position; **once she's decided on something, it's impossible to s.** her une fois qu'elle a pris sa décision, il est impossible de lui faire changer d'avis; **to s. a stain** (of washing powder etc) enlever une tache; **to s. the blame onto sb** rejeter la responsabilité sur qn; Theat **to s. the scenery** changer le décor; Aut **to s. the gears** changer de vitesse **2** Fam (sell) vendre; **we've been shifting these at 50 a day** (selling them) on en vend 50 par jour **VI 1** (move) (of person, object) bouger, se déplacer; (change places) changer de place; Naut (of cargo) se désarrimer, se déplacer; **it won't s.!** (of object etc) ça ne veut pas bouger!; **this stain won't s.** cette tache ne veut pas partir; Theat **the scene shifts** la scène change; **the wind has shifted (round)** le vent a tourné ou viré; **could you s.?** (out of the way) pouvez-vous dégager?; **could you possibly s. a little?** pourriez-vous vous déplacer un peu?; **the building is shifting** l'immeuble bouge; **he wouldn't s.** (in negotiations etc) il est resté ferme sur ses positions; **he shifted nervously from foot to foot** il oscillait d'un pied sur l'autre avec nervosité **2** Fam (move quickly) se magner (le train); **I didn't know she could s. so fast** je ne savais pas qu'elle pouvait aller aussi vite; **this car can really s.!** cette voiture est un vrai bolide!; **that's really shifting** ça, c'est de la vitesse **3** Fam **to s. for oneself** (manage) se débrouiller; **she can or knows how to s. for herself** elle est débrouillarde **4** Fam (sell) se vendre; **those TVs just aren't shifting at all** ces télés ne se vendent pas du tout ▸▸ Comput **s. key** touche majuscule; Comput **s. lock** touche de blocage des majuscules; Am Aut **s. stick** levier m de (changement de) vitesse; **s. work** travail m en équipe; **she does s. work** elle fait les trois-huit; **s. worker** = personne f qui fait les trois-huit ▸ **shift about, shift around VT SEP** (object) changer de place; **we've shifted the office around** nous avons changé la disposition du bureau; **he's always being shifted around** (in job) il est tout le temps muté; (in location in office etc) on le change tout le temps de place; (from town to town etc) on le fait tout le temps déménager **VI 1** (fidget) bouger **2** (move around) changer de place; (change jobs) changer d'emploi ▸ **shift along VI** (move on seat etc) se décaler; **s. along a bit** pousse-toi ▸ **shift over VI s. over!** pousse-toi! ▸ **shift up VI 1 = shift along 2** Am Aut passer à la vitesse supérieure

shift-click Comput **N** majuscule-clic m, pl majuscules-clics **VI** faire un majuscule-clic

shift-drag N Comput majuscule-glisser m

shiftily ['ʃɪftɪlɪ] **ADV** sournoisement

shiftiness ['ʃɪftɪnɪs] **N** sournoiserie f, fausseté f

shifting ['ʃɪftɪŋ] **ADJ** qui se déplace; (relationship, scene etc) changeant; (wind etc) inégal, -aux; Fig **the s. sands of public opinion** l'opinion publique toujours versatile **N** (moving) (of an object by somebody) déplacement m; (movement) (of something) mouvement m, déplacement m; (of cargo) désarrimage m; (change) (of position, direction etc) changement m; Theat **scene s.** changement de décors; Aut **(gear) s.** changement de vitesse

shiftless ['ʃɪftlɪs] **ADJ 1** (lazy) paresseux **2** (lacking resourcefulness) peu débrouillard, qui manque d'initiative ou de ressource

shiftlessness ['ʃɪftlɪsnɪs] **N 1** (laziness) paresse f **2** (lack of resourcefulness) manque m de ressource ou d'initiative

shiftwork ['ʃɪftwɜːk] **N** Ind travail m par équipes ou par roulement

shiftworker ['ʃɪftwɜːkər] **N** Ind ouvrier, -ière qui fait les trois-huit

shifty ['ʃɪftɪ] **ADJ** (person) louche; (look) sournois; (behaviour) ambigu, -uë; **s. eyes** regard m fuyant; **there is something s. about him** il y a quelque chose de louche chez lui

Shiism ['ʃiːɪz(ə)m] **N** chiisme m

Shiite ['ʃiːaɪt] **N** chiite mf **ADJ** chiite

shill [ʃɪl] Am Fam **N** baron m **VT 1** (lure into swindle) arnaquer; **they shilled him into handing over his life savings** ils ont réussi à lui soutirer toutes ses économies **2** (hype) faire de la pub pour; **they've got a quarterback shilling their new frozen yoghurt** il y a un joueur de football américain qui fait la pub pour leur nouveau yaourt glacé

shillelagh [ʃɪ'leɪlə] **N** gourdin m irlandais

shilling ['ʃɪlɪŋ] **N** shilling m; Fig **to cut sb off without a s.** déshériter qn; Hist **to take the king's/queen's s.** = s'engager dans l'armée

shillyshally ['ʃɪlɪʃælɪ] **VI** Fam hésiter, tergiverser

shillyshallying ['ʃɪlɪʃælɪɪŋ] **N** Fam hésitation f, tergiversation f

shimmer ['ʃɪmər] **N** lueur f, (of sea, silk etc) miroitement m; (in heat) reflets mpl; (of TV picture) scintillement m; **a s. of light** une lueur; **the s. of the moon on the lake** les reflets de la lune sur le lac **VI** (of sea) miroiter; (of silk) chatoyer

shimmering ['ʃɪmərɪŋ] **ADJ** (sea) miroitant; (silk) chatoyant

shimmy ['ʃɪmɪ] **N 1** Am Aut (movement of front wheels) flottement m des roues avant **2** (dance) shimmy m **VI 1** Aut (of wheels) osciller **2** (dance) danser le shimmy

shin [ʃɪn] **N** tibia m; Culin jarret m (de bœuf), gîte m de devant; **to kick sb in the shins** donner un coup de pied dans les tibias à qn; Sport **s. guard** or **pad** jambière f ▸ **shin up** (-nn-) **VT INSEP** (climb) **to s. up a tree** grimper à un arbre **VI** (climb) grimper

shinbone ['ʃɪnbəʊn] **N** Anat tibia m

shindig ['ʃɪndɪg] **N** Fam **1** (party) fête f **2 = shindy 1**

shindy ['ʃɪndɪ] **N** Fam **1** (din) raffut m, ramdam m; **to kick up a s.** (make a din) faire du raffut ou du ramdam; **to kick up a s. about**

sth (protest loudly) faire du raffut pour protester contre qch **2** Am **= shindig 1**

shine [ʃaɪn] **VI** (pt, pp shone [ʃɒn]) (of sun etc) briller; (of polished article) (re)luire; Fig (excel) briller; **the moon/the sun is shining** il y a un clair de lune/il fait soleil; **the sun was shining straight into my eyes** j'avais le soleil dans les yeux; **the light from the torch shone on a piece of paper** la lumière de la lampe de poche éclaira un morceau de papier; **her face was shining with joy** son visage rayonnait de joie; **her eyes shone with enthusiasm** ses yeux brillaient d'enthousiasme; Fig **s. at maths/Latin** être brillant en maths/latin; Fig **he doesn't s. in company** il ne brille pas en société; Sl **stick it where the sun don't s.!** tu peux te le mettre où je pense! **VT 1** **to s. a light on sth** (illuminate) éclairer qch (avec une lampe etc); (direct at) braquer une lampe sur qch **2** (pt, pp shined [ʃaɪnd]) (polish) (shoes etc) polir, cirer; (brass) astiquer **N 1** (brightness) éclat m; (on shoes etc) brillant m; (on textiles etc) luisant m; **to take the s. off sth** délustrer qch, ternir qch; Fig ternir qch, entacher qch **2** (action) **to give one's shoes a s.** cirer ses chaussures; **to give the brass a s.** astiquer les cuivres **3** Fam **to take a s. to sb** s'enticher de qn **4** Offensive Sl (black man) nègre m, bamboula m; (black woman) négresse f

shiner ['ʃaɪnər] **N** Fam (black eye) œil m poché, Fam œil au beurre noir

shingle[1] ['ʃɪŋg(ə)l] **N 1** Constr (wooden tile) bardeau m, aisseau m **2** Am (sign) (of doctor, lawyer etc) plaque f (de cuivre); **to put one's s. up** (to open business) s'installer **3** (hairstyle) coupe f à la garçonne **VT 1** Constr (roof) couvrir de bardeaux **2** **to s. sb** or **sb's hair** couper les cheveux de qn à la garçonne ▸▸ **s. roof** toit m en bardeaux

shingle[2] ['ʃɪŋg(ə)l] **N** (no pl) (on beach) galets mpl ▸▸ **s. beach** plage f de galets

shingles ['ʃɪŋg(ə)lz] **N** Med zona m VOIR GRAMMAIRE A10

shingly ['ʃɪŋglɪ] **ADJ** (covered in pebbles) couvert de galets; (beach) de galets

shininess ['ʃaɪnɪnɪs] **N** éclat m, brillance f, (due to wear) lustrage m

shining ['ʃaɪnɪŋ] **ADJ** brillant, (re)luisant; (face) rayonnant; **a s. example** un parfait exemple (**of sth** de qch)

▸ **shinny up** ['ʃɪnɪ] **VT INSEP, VI** Am Fam **= shin up**

Shintoism ['ʃɪntəʊɪz(ə)m] **N** shintoïsme m, shinto m

shiny ['ʃaɪnɪ] **ADJ** brillant, luisant; **clothes made s. by long wear** vêtements lustrés par l'usage

ship [ʃɪp] **N 1** navire m; (smaller) bateau m; (esp warship) bâtiment m; **to go by s.** aller en bateau; **to send sth by s.** envoyer qch par bateau; **is there a doctor/swimming pool on the s.?** y a-t-il un docteur/une piscine à bord?; **sailing s.** voilier m, navire à voiles; **passenger s.** paquebot m; **merchant s.** navire marchand, cargo m; **container s.** navire porte-conteneurs; **depot** or **supply s.** ravitailleur m; **training s.** navire-école m, pl navires-écoles; Fig **the s. of State** le char de l'État; **the s. of the desert** (camel) le vaisseau du désert; Fig **when my s. comes home** or **in** dès que j'aurai fait fortune; Fig **to be like ships that pass in the night** (of lovers) être des amants de passage; **s.'s biscuit** biscuit m de mer; **s.'s boat** embarcation f de bord; **s.'s boy** mousse m; **s.'s carpenter** charpentier m de bord; **s.'s chandler** shipchandler m, fournisseur m de navires; **the s.'s company**

l'équipage *m*; **s.'s manifest** manifeste *m* **2** *(spaceship)* vaisseau *m*; *Fam (aeroplane)* avion *m*

vt (-pp-) **1** *Com (to send by sea, rail etc)* envoyer, expédier **2** *(to take on board) (cargo etc)* embarquer; **to s. water** *(of ship)* embarquer de l'eau; **to s. oars** rentrer *ou* border les avirons

vi 1 *(of passenger)* s'embarquer; *(of sailor)* armer sur un navire **2** *(be delivered)* sortir des usines

▸ **ship off vt sep** *Fam (send) (thing, person)* expédier; **his mother shipped him off to boarding school** sa mère l'a expédié dans un pensionnat

▸ **ship out vt sep** *(send) (goods)* expédier; *(troops etc)* envoyer

vi *esp Am Fam (leave)* mettre les voiles; *see* **shape up**

shipboard ['ʃɪpbɔːd] **adj attrib** à bord d'un/du navire

ship-broker n courtier *m* maritime

shipbuilder ['ʃɪpbɪldər] **n** constructeur *m* de navires

shipbuilding ['ʃɪpbɪldɪŋ] **n** construction *f* navale; **a s. firm** une entreprise de construction navale; **the s. industry** l'industrie *f* de la construction navale

shipload ['ʃɪpləʊd] **n** chargement *m*, cargaison *f*; *Fig* **by the s., in shiploads** en masse

shipmate ['ʃɪpmeɪt] **n** compagnon *m ou* camarade *m* de bord

shipment ['ʃɪpmənt] **n** *(sending)* expédition *f*, envoi *m*; *(goods sent)* envoi; **the containers awaiting s.** les conteneurs prêts pour l'expédition; **three shipments of …** trois cargaisons *ou* chargements de …

shipowner ['ʃɪpəʊnər] **n** armateur *m*, propriétaire *m* de navires, fréteur *m*

shipped bill [ʃɪpt] **n** *Com* connaissement *m* embarqué

shipped weight n *Com* poids *m* embarqué

shipper ['ʃɪpər] **n** expéditeur, -trice

shipping ['ʃɪpɪŋ] **n** *(ships)* navires *mpl* (d'un pays, d'un port etc); *(sending)* expédition *f*, envoi *m*; **dangerous to** *or* **for s.** dangereux pour la navigation

▸ ▸ **s. address** adresse *f* de livraison; **s. agent** agent *m* maritime; **s. bill** connaissement *m*; **s. company** entreprise *f* de transport routier; **s. costs** frais *mpl* d'expédition; *(by ship)* frais d'embarquement; **s. department** service *m* expédition, expéditions; **s. documents** documents *mpl* d'expédition, documents maritimes; **s. exchange** bourse *f* de fret; **s. instructions** instructions *fpl* pour l'expédition; **s. intelligence** nouvelles *fpl* maritimes; **s. lanes** routes *fpl* de navigation; **s. line** ligne *f ou* compagnie maritime; **s. marks** marques *fpl* d'expédition; **s. note** permis *m* d'embarquement; **s. office** bureau *m* d'expédition; **s. routes** routes de navigation

shipshape ['ʃɪpʃeɪp] **adj** *(très)* bien rangé; *(documents etc)* en bon ordre; **everything's s.** tout est à sa place; **to get a room s.** ranger une pièce, mettre de l'ordre dans une pièce; *Old-fashioned* **s. and Bristol fashion!** impeccable!

shipwreck ['ʃɪprek] **n** naufrage *m*; **to suffer s.** *(of ship)* faire naufrage; *Fig* **the s. of one's hopes** le naufrage de ses espoirs

vt *(usu in passive)* **to be shipwrecked** faire naufrage

shipwrecked ['ʃɪprekt] **adj** naufragé

shipwright ['ʃɪpraɪt] **n** constructeur *m* de navires; *(on board ship)* charpentier *m* du bord

shipyard ['ʃɪpjɑːd] **n** chantier *m* naval, chantier de constructions navales; **hundreds of s. workers were sacked** des centai-

nes d'ouvriers des chantiers navals ont été licenciés

shire [ʃaɪər] **n** *Br* **1** comté *m* **2** *(horse)* shire *m*
▸ ▸ **s. horse** shire

Shires [ʃaɪəz] **npl** = comtés *mpl* ruraux du centre de l'Angleterre

shirk [ʃɜːk] **vt** *(obligation etc)* manquer à, se soustraire à; *(task)* renâcler à; *(a duty)* esquiver; *(one's duty)* négliger; **to s. doing sth** se défiler (pour ne pas faire qch); **to s. the question** esquiver *ou* éluder la question
vi *(avoid work)* tirer au flanc; **stop shirking!** arrête de tirer au flanc *ou* de te défiler devant le travail!

shirker ['ʃɜːkər] **n** *Fam* tire-au-flanc *m inv*; **she's no s.** elle n'a rien d'un tire-au-flanc

shirr [ʃɜːr] **vt** *Sewing* bouillonner

shirring ['ʃɜːrɪŋ] **n** *Sewing* bouillonné *m*

shirt [ʃɜːt] **n** chemise *f*; *(with short sleeves)* chemisette *f*; *Sport* maillot *m*; **sports** *or* **casual s.** chemise sport; *Fam* **he's a stuffed s.** il est guindé; **to change one's s., to put on a clean s.** changer de chemise; *Fam* **to put one's s. on a horse** parier sa chemise sur un cheval; *Fam* **to take the s. off sb's back** faire cracher jusqu'à son dernier centime à qn; *Fam* **he'd have the s. off your back** il te mangerait la laine sur le dos; *Fam* **he'd give you the s. off his back** il donnerait sa chemise; *Fam* **to lose one's s.** *(lose everything)* y laisser sa chemise; *Am* *(lose one's temper)* s'emporter, prendre la mouche; *Fam* **keep your s. on!** ne vous emballez pas!, calmez-vous!; *Hist* **Red/Black/Brown Shirts** Chemises rouges/noires/brunes
▸ ▸ **s. collar** col *m* de chemise; **s. cuff** poignet *m* de chemise; **s. front** plastron *m ou* devant *m* de chemise

shirting ['ʃɜːtɪŋ] **n** shirting *m*

shirtlifter ['ʃɜːtlɪftər] **n** *Offensive Sl* tantouze *f*, tapette *f*

shirtmaker ['ʃɜːtmeɪkər] **n** chemisier, -ière

shirtsleeve ['ʃɜːtsliːv] **n** manche *f* de chemise; **to be in one's shirtsleeves** être en bras *ou* en manches de chemise

shirt-tail n pan *m* de chemise

shirtwaister, *Am* **shirtwaist** ['ʃɜːtweɪst(ər)] **n** *(dress)* robe *f* chemisier

shirty ['ʃɜːtɪ] **adj** *Br Fam* irritable; **to get s.** se fâcher

shit [ʃɪt] **n** *Vulg (excrement)*, *Fig (rubbish)* merde *f*; *(nonsense)* conneries *fpl*; **to have a s.** chier; **to have the shits** *(to have diarrhoea)* avoir la chiasse; *(to be frightened)* faire dans son froc; **bird/dog s.** merde d'oiseau/de chien; *Fig* **the s. will really hit the fan** ça va chier; **tough s.!** pas de bol!; **this is a s. book** c'est un livre de merde; **he doesn't give a s.** il s'en fout, *Vulg* il n'en a rien à branler; **to beat the s. out of sb** démolir qn; **to scare the s. out of sb** foutre une trouille bleue à qn; **to bore the s. out of sb** faire crever qn d'ennui; **I'm not taking any more of his s.** je ne le laisserai plus m'emmerder; **to be in the s.** être dans la merde; **to be up s. creek (without a paddle)** être dans la merde jusqu'au cou; *Am* **no s.!** arrête tes conneries!

2 *Vulg (person)* salaud *m*, salope *f*

3 *Sl (heroin)* came *f*, *(marijuana)* shit *m*

int merde!

vi *(pt, pp* **shat** [ʃæt], **shitted** ['ʃɪtɪd]) *Vulg* chier; **they'll s. on us from a great height** ils vont bien se foutre de nous

vt *Vulg* chier; **I was shitting myself** je chiais dans mon froc; **he'll s. a brick** il va chier dans son froc
▸ ▸ **s. stirrer** fouille-merde *mf inv*

shitake mushroom [ʃɪ'tæk] **n** champignon *m* shitake

shite [ʃaɪt] **n, vt & vi** *Vulg* = **shit etc**

shit(e)house ['ʃɪthaʊs, 'ʃaɪt-] **n** *Vulg (toilet)* chiottes *fpl*, gogues *mpl*

shitface ['ʃɪtfeɪs] **n** *Vulg* gueule *f* de con

shit-faced adj *Sl (drunk)* bourré, pété, beurré; *(on drugs)* défoncé, raide

shithead ['ʃɪthed] **n** *Sl* enfoiré, -ée

shithole ['ʃɪthəʊl] **n** *Sl (dirty place)* porcherie *f*, taudis *m*; **this town's a complete s.** *(boring, ugly)* cette ville est un vrai trou

shit-hot adj *Sl* vachement bien

shitless ['ʃɪtlɪs] **adj** *Sl* **to be scared s.** chier dans son froc; **to be bored s.** s'emmerder profondément

shitload ['ʃɪtləʊd] **n** *Sl* **a (whole) s. (of)** une chiée (de)

shit-scared adj *Sl* **to be/look s.** avoir/avoir l'air d'avoir une trouille bleue

shitstorm ['ʃɪtstɔːm] **n** *Am Sl* foin *m*; **the announcement caused a helluva s.** la déclaration a fait un sacré foin

shitty ['ʃɪtɪ] **adj** *Sl (nappies, trousers)* plein de merde; *(weather, job)* merdique, de merde; **I feel s.** je me sens vasouillard; *(feel guilty etc)* je me trouve dégueulasse; **that was a s. thing to say/do to someone** c'était dégueulasse de dire/faire ça à quelqu'un; **he was really s. to her** il a été vraiment dégueulasse avec elle

shitweasel ['ʃɪtwiːzəl] **n** *Am Sl* ordure *f*, raclure *f*

shiv [ʃɪv] *Sl* **n** *(knife)* surin *m*, lame *f*
vt *(stab)* planter

shiver¹ ['ʃɪvər] **vi 1** frissonner, trembler (**with cold/fear** de froid/peur); **to s. like a leaf** *or* **a jelly** trembler comme une feuille **2** *(of sail)* faseyer, ralinguer
n *(from cold, fear)* frisson *m*; **it sent cold shivers down my back** cela m'a fait froid dans le dos; **to feel a s.** avoir un frisson; **to have the shivers** avoir la tremblote; *Fam* **it gives me the shivers to think of it** ça me donne des frissons quand j'y pense

shiver² **vt** *(break)* casser en morceaux; *Arch, Hum* **s. me timbers!** tonnerre de Dieu!
vi *(break)* se casser en morceaux
n *(fragment)* éclat *m*, fragment *m*; **to break sth into shivers** casser qch en mille morceaux

shivering ['ʃɪvərɪŋ] **adj** frissonnant; *(with cold)* grelottant
n frissonnement *m*; **to have a s. fit** être pris de frissons

shivery ['ʃɪvərɪ] **adj** = **shivering 1**; **to feel s.** avoir des frissons; *(feverish)* se sentir fiévreux; **it gives you a s. feeling** cela donne le frisson

shoal¹ [ʃəʊl] **n** *(shallow)* haut-fond *m*, *pl* hauts-fonds; *(sandbank)* banc *m* de sable

shoal² **n** *(of fish)* banc *m*; *Fam (of people)* foule *f*, multitude *f*; *(of letters, applications etc)* grande quantité *f*, tas *m*

shock [ʃɒk] **n 1** *(impact)* choc *m*; *(of collision etc)* impact *m*; *(jolt)*, *Geol* secousse *f*; **to stand the s.** résister au choc; **slight (earthquake) shocks were felt** on a senti de petites secousses; *Fig* **the news sent s. waves through the financial world** la nouvelle a provoqué des ondes de choc dans le monde de la finance

2 *(emotional blow)* coup *m*; *(caused by bad news etc)*, *Med* choc *m*; **it was a s. to find out I'd got no money left/I'd won** ça m'a fait un choc de découvrir que je n'avais plus d'argent/que j'avais gagné; **the news of his death came as a terrible s. to all of us** la nouvelle de sa mort nous a tous énormément choqués; **the s. killed him, he died of the s.** le choc l'a tué; **be prepared for a s.** prépare-toi à un choc; *Med* **post-operative s.** choc post-opératoire; **to be in s.** être en état de

choc; **to go into s.** entrer en état de choc; **in a state of s.** en état de choc; *Fam Hum* **s. horror story** histoire *f* abominable; *Fam Hum* **s. horror!** l'horreur!
3 *(electric)* **s.** décharge *f*; **to get a(n electric) s.** recevoir une décharge; **electric s. treatment** traitement *m* par électrochocs
4 *(mass)* **s. of hair** tignasse *f*
vt *(person) (scandalize)* choquer; **to s. the eye/ear** choquer la vue/l'oreille; **a book that shocked the public** un livre qui a fait scandale; **easily shocked** qui se choque facilement; **to be shocked at** *or* **by sth** *(scandalized)* être choqué de *ou* scandalisé par qch; **she wanted to s. them into action** elle voulait les choquer pour les faire réagir; **to s. sb out of doing sth** dissuader qn de faire qch en lui faisant peur; **I was shocked to hear that …** j'ai été choqué d'apprendre que …; **millions were shocked by pictures of the famine** des millions de personnes ont été choquées *ou* bouleversées par les images de la famine
▸▸ **s. absorber** amortisseur *m*; *Am Fam* **s. jock** = animateur ou animatrice de radio au ton irrévérencieux et provocateur; **s. tactics** tactique *f* *ou* action *f* de choc; **s. therapy** (traitement par) électrochoc *m*; *Fig* traitement de choc; *Mil* **s. troops** troupes *fpl* de choc; **s. wave** onde *f* de choc

shockable ['ʃɒkəb(ə)l] **ADJ he's easily/not easily s.** il se choque facilement/ne se choque pas facilement

shocked [ʃɒkt] **ADJ** *(person, voice etc) (scandalized)* choqué; *(stunned)* atterré; **there was a s. silence when …** il y eut un silence atterré lorsque …

shocker ['ʃɒkər] **N** *Fam* **1** *(shocking news)* **that was a real s.** ça a été un rude coup **2** *(bad mistake)* faute *f* énorme; *(in behaviour)* grosse bourde *f* **3** *(novel)* roman *m* à sensations; *(film)* film *m* à sensations **4** *(person)* **he really is a s.!** il est vraiment impossible!

shocking ['ʃɒkɪŋ] **ADJ** *(sight etc) (scandalizing)* choquant; *(revolting)* abominable, affreux; *(news)* atterrant, bouleversant; *(weather)* abominable, exécrable; *(pain)* atroce; **to be in a s. state** être dans un état lamentable; **s. behaviour** *(scandalizing)* comportement scandaleux; *(unworthy)* conduite indigne; **how s.!** quelle horreur!; **the s. truth about conditions in our prisons** la terrible vérité sur les conditions de vie dans nos prisons; **their s. ignorance** leur scandaleuse ignorance
ADV *Fam* **he carried on something s.!** il nous a fait une scène abominable!
▸▸ **s. pink** rose *m* bonbon

shockingly ['ʃɒkɪŋlɪ] **ADV** *(to behave)* scandaleusement; *(to treat)* abominablement; *Fam (extremely)* affreusement; **they did s. in the exam** leurs résultats à l'examen ont été lamentables; **s. deprived** dans une misère atroce; **s. immoral** d'une immoralité scandaleuse; **a s. low-cut dress** une robe outrageusement décolletée; **in s. bad taste** du dernier mauvais goût

shockproof ['ʃɒkpruːf] **ADJ 1** *(scientific instrument etc)* antichoc **2** *Fam (person)* qui ne se choque pas facilement

shod **PT, PP** *see* **shoe VT**

shoddily ['ʃɒdɪlɪ] **ADV s. made** mal fait; **to treat sb s.** traiter qn peu honorablement; **to behave s. (towards sb)** se conduire mesquinement (envers qn)

shoddiness ['ʃɒdɪnɪs] **N** *(of material, workmanship)* mauvaise qualité *f*, **the s. of their treatment of him** leur mesquinerie envers lui

shoddy ['ʃɒdɪ] **ADJ** *(goods etc)* de camelote, de pacotille; *(conduct)* mesquin; *(workmanship)* médiocre; **s. goods** camelote *f*

N *Tex (cloth)* drap *m* de laine d'effilochage, laine *f* *ou* tissu *m* de récupération

shoe [ʃuː] **N 1** *(for foot)* chaussure *f*, soulier *m*; **a pair of shoes** une paire de chaussures; **lace-up shoes** richelieus *m*; **high-heeled shoes** chaussures à talons hauts; **to put on/take off one's shoes** se chausser/se déchausser, mettre/enlever ses chaussures; **to shake** *or* **quake in one's shoes** être dans ses petits souliers; *Fig* **to step into sb's shoes** prendre la place de qn, succéder à qn; *Fig* **I wouldn't like to be in his shoes** je ne voudrais pas être à sa place; **put yourself in my shoes** mets-toi à ma place; *Fig* **to be waiting for dead men's shoes** attendre la mort de qn *(pour le remplacer)*
2 *(horseshoe)* fer *m* à cheval; **to cast** *or* **throw a s.** *(of horse)* perdre un fer, se déferrer
3 *Aut (of brake)* mâchoire *f*
4 *(of sledge etc)* patin *m*
vt *(pt, pp shod* [ʃɒd]*; prp shoeing)* **1** *(provide with shoes)* chausser; **to be well shod** être bien chaussé **2** *(pt, pp also shoed)* *(horse)* ferrer
▸▸ **s. box** boîte *f* à chaussures; **s. cream** cirage *m* en crème; *Aut* **s. expander** écarteur *m* de mâchoire; **s. leather** cuir *m* pour chaussures; **I've worn out a lot of s. leather** j'ai marché des kilomètres; *Fig* **you might as well save your s. leather** c'est inutile que vous y alliez; **s. polish** cirage; **s. rack** porte-chaussures *m inv*; **s. repairs** cordonnerie *f*, **s. scraper** gratte-pieds *m inv*; **s. shop** magasin *m* de chaussures; **s. size** pointure *f*, **s. tree** embauchoir *m*

shoeblack ['ʃuːblæk] **N** cireur *m*

shoebrush ['ʃuːbrʌʃ] **N** brosse *f* à chaussures

shoehorn ['ʃuːhɔːn] **N** chausse-pied *m*, *pl* chausse-pieds
vt *Fig* **we can s. a few more in** on peut en faire tenir encore quelques-uns

shoeing ['ʃuːɪŋ] **N** *(of horse)* ferrage *m*, ferrure *f*

shoelace ['ʃuːleɪs] **N** lacet *m* (de chaussure); *Fig* **he's not fit to tie your shoelaces** il n'est pas digne de cirer vos chaussures

shoemaker ['ʃuːmeɪkər] **N** *(who makes shoes)* fabricant *m* de chaussures; *(who makes and sells shoes)* chausseur *m*; *(shoe repairer)* cordonnier *m*; *Prov* **let the s. stick to his last** cordonnier, mêlez-vous de votre pantoufle!

shoemender ['ʃuːmendər] **N** cordonnier *m*

shoe-polishing machine N machine *f* à cirer les chaussures

shoeshine ['ʃuːʃaɪn] **N** *Am* **1** *(action)* cirage *m* de chaussures **2** *(person)* cireur *m* de chaussures
▸▸ **s. boy** (petit) cireur (de chaussures)

shoeshop ['ʃuːʃɒp] **N** magasin *m* de chaussures

shoestring ['ʃuːstrɪŋ] **N** lacet *m* de chaussure; *Fig Fam* **on a s.** à peu de frais; *Fam* **they're doing it on a s.** ils tirent sur la corde; *Fam* **a film made on a s. (budget)** un film réalisé à peu de frais

shone **PT, PP** *see* **shine VI, VT**

shoo [ʃuː] **INT** *(to animal, children)* allez!, ouste!
▸ **shoo away, shoo off** **VT SEP** *(scare away)* *(chickens etc)* chasser

shoo-in **N** *Fam* **it's a s.** c'est couru d'avance; **they're a s. to win the next election** ils vont gagner les prochaines élections, c'est couru d'avance

shook **PT** *see* **shake VT, VI**

SHOOT [ʃuːt]

> **N** pousse **1** ▪ tournage **2** ▪ séance photo **2** ▪ concours de tir **4**
> **VI** se précipiter **1** ▪ tirer **4** ▪ chasser **4** ▪ tourner **5** ▪ shooter **6**
> **VT** franchir **1** ▪ lancer **3** ▪ tirer **3** ▪ tuer par balle(s) **4** ▪ tirer sur **4** ▪ tourner **5** ▪ filmer **5** ▪ photographier **5**

N 1 *Bot (plant)* pousse *f*, *(on a plant)* rejet *m*; *scion m*; *(of vine)* sarment *m*, pampre *m*; **young** *or* **tender s.** tendrille *f*, tendron *m*
2 *Cin, TV* tournage *m*; *Phot* séance *f* photo, prise *f* de vues; **he has a s. all afternoon** il a une prise de vue tout l'après-midi
3 = **chute**
4 *(shooting contest)* concours *m* de tir; *esp Br (hunting party)* partie *f* de chasse; *(land)* chasse *f* gardée
5 *Fam* **the whole (bang) s.** *(everything)* tout le bazar
6 *Fam Euph* **oh s.!** miel!
VI *(pt, pp shot* [ʃɒt]*)* **1** *(move rapidly)* se précipiter; *(of star)* filer; **he shot into the room** il est entré dans la pièce en éclair *ou* en trombe; **to s. forward** foncer *ou* s'élancer à toute allure; **to s. ahead** prendre la tête; **he's always shooting across to New York** il va sans arrêt à New York; **the cat shot out of his arms** le chat bondit de ses bras
2 *(of pain)* élancer; **I've got pains shooting through my shoulder** j'ai des élancements dans l'épaule
3 *(of tree, bud etc)* pousser, bourgeonner; *(of plant)* germer
4 *(fire gun)* tirer; *(hunt)* chasser; **don't s.!** ne tirez pas!; **to s. straight** bien viser; **to s. at sb/sth** tirer *ou* faire feu sur qn/qch; **to be shot at** se faire tirer dessus; *Fig* **to s. from the hip** parler sans réfléchir
5 *Cin* tourner; *Phot (take photo)* prendre la/une photo; *Cin* **s.!** moteur!, on tourne!
6 *Ftbl, Hockey* shooter
7 *esp Am Fam* **s.!** *(say what you want to)* allez-y!
VT 1 *(pass rapidly) (rapids)* franchir; *Aut* **to s. the (traffic) lights** griller *ou* brûler le feu rouge
2 *(move rapidly) (bolt)* pousser; *Fishing (net)* jeter; *Fig* **he had shot his bolt** il avait brûlé ses dernières cartouches; **we were shot out of the car** nous avons été éjectés de la voiture; *Am Fam* **to s. the breeze** *(chat)* bavarder; *(exaggerate)* en rajouter; *Fam* **to s. a line** *(boast)* faire du baratin; **he's just shooting a line** ce qu'il raconte, c'est du baratin
3 *(unleash) (arrow)* décocher; *(projectile)* lancer; *(bullet)* tirer; *Ftbl* **he shot the ball into the net** il a envoyé le ballon dans le filet, il a marqué un but; **to s. a glance at sb** lancer *ou* décocher un regard à qn; **the chimney shot a shower of sparks into the air** la cheminée envoya un jet d'étincelles dans l'air; *Fam* **to s. heroin** se shooter à l'héroïne; *Sl* **to s. one's load** *or* **wad** *(ejaculate)* décharger
4 *(person) (hit with bullet)* atteindre d'un coup de feu; *(kill)* tuer d'un coup de feu; *(wound)* blesser d'un coup de feu; *(spy)* abattre; *(partridge, woodsnipe etc)* tirer; *(hunt) (game)* chasser; **I've been shot** j'ai reçu une balle; **a man was shot (and killed) yesterday** un homme a été tué par balle hier; **everybody remembers the day Kennedy was shot** tout le monde se souvient du jour où Kennedy a été assassiné; **to be shot in the arm** être atteint au bras; **the robbers tried to s. their way out** les voleurs tentèrent de se sauver en tirant des coups de feu; **to s. sb dead** tuer qn par balle; **to s. sb through the head** tirer une balle dans la tête de qn; **she was shot through the heart** elle a été tuée d'une balle

en plein cœur; **to s. oneself in the foot** se tirer dans le pied; *Fig (spoil one's chances)* se faire du tort à soi-même; **to s. holes in sb's argument/case** démonter les arguments/la théorie de qn; **to s. sb/sth to pieces** mettre qn/qch en pièces; *Mil* **to be (court-martialled and) shot** être passé par les armes, être fusillé; *Fig Fam* **I'll be shot** je suis foutu; *Fig Fam* **you'll get me shot** tu vas me faire avoir des ennuis

5 *Cin (film)* tourner; *(scene, actor)* filmer; *Phot* photographier; **the photos were all shot on location in Paris** les photos ont toutes été prises à Paris; *TV, Cin* **to s. sound** effectuer une prise de son

6 to s. dice lancer les dés; **to s. pool** faire une partie de billard; **to s. a goal** marquer un but; **to s. a basket** marquer un panier; *Golf* **to s. a 64** faire le parcours en 64 coups

▸ **shoot back** vi **1** *(fire back)* riposter

2 *(into its shell, into office)* disparaître

vt sep *(return quickly)* envoyer; **the candidate shot back his answers** le candidat répondait du tac au tac

▸ **shoot down** vt sep **1** *(cause to fall by gunfire etc) (person)* abattre (par balle); *(plane)* abattre, descendre

2 *(show to be wrong or unacceptable) (person, argument, proposal etc)* descendre; **she was shot down in flames when …** elle a été descendue en flammes lorsque …

▸ **shoot off** vi **1** *(leave quickly)* partir comme une flèche; **I've got to s. off now** il faut que je me sauve

2 *Sl (ejaculate)* décharger

vt sep **1** *(remove by bullet or shell)* emporter par une balle/par un obus; **he had a foot shot off** il a eu un pied fauché par un obus

2 *(fire)* **she shot off a few rounds into the darkness** elle a tiré plusieurs fois dans le noir; **he shot off an entire magazine** il a vidé son chargeur; *Fig* **to s. off a letter/memo to sb** envoyer une lettre/un mémo à qn; *Sl* **to s. one's mouth off** *(be indiscreet)* ouvrir sa grande gueule (**about sth** à propos de qch)

▸ **shoot out** vi *(emerge quickly) (of water, flames)* jaillir; **to s. out of a side street** déboucher brusquement d'une rue latérale

vt sep **1** *(extend quickly) (sparks etc)* lancer; **the snake shot out its tongue** le serpent a dardé sa langue

2 *(extinguish, destroy etc with gunshots) (light, window)* tirer dans; **his right eye had been shot out** il avait perdu l'œil droit dans une fusillade

3 *Fam* **to s. it out** régler ses comptes à coups de feu

▸ **shoot through** vi *Br (leave suddenly)* se tirer, mettre les bouts

▸ **shoot up** vt sep **they shot the bar up** ils ont mitraillé le bar; **he was badly shot up in the war** il a été sérieusement blessé à la guerre; **he's been shot up** il a reçu des balles (dans la peau)

vi **1** *(of plants, children)* pousser; *(of rocket)* s'élever; *(of prices)* monter en flèche; *(of fountain etc)* jaillir; **he's really shot up!** *(he's grown)* qu'est-ce qu'il a poussé!; **new tower blocks are shooting up all over the city** de nouvelles tours poussent dans toute la ville

2 *Sl (with drugs)* se shooter

shoot-'em-up [ˈʃuːtəmʌp] n *Fam* = film *m* ou jeu vidéo ultra-violent

shooter [ˈʃuːtər] n **1** *Sl (gun)* flingue *m*, feu *m* **2** *(drink)* cocktail *m* servi dans un petit verre

shooting [ˈʃuːtɪŋ] adj *(pain)* lancinant

n **1** *(gunfire)* coups *mpl* de feu; *(killing)* fusillade *f*; *(of spies, revolutionaries etc)* mise à mort; *(hunting)* chasse *f*; **there was no s.** *(in robbery etc)* aucun coup de feu n'a été tiré; **there was a s.** il y a eu une fusillade; **anyone who witnessed the s. is asked to contact the police** tout témoin de la fusillade est prié de

prendre contact avec la police; **pigeon s.** tir *m* aux pigeons; **the s. season** la saison de la chasse **2** *Cin (of film)* tournage *m*; **s. starts next week on her new film** le tournage de son nouveau film commence la semaine prochaine

▸▸ **s. angle** angle *m* de prise de vue; *Br Aut* **s. brake** break *m*; **s. gallery** *(at fairground)* (stand *m* de) tir; *Sl (for buying drugs)* = lieu *m* où l'on achète, vend et consomme de la drogue; **s. match** concours *m* de tir; *Hunt* **s. party** partie *f* de chasse; **s. plan** plan *m* de travail; **s. range** champ *m* de tir; **s. schedule** plan *m* de tournage; *Cin* **s. script** découpage *m*; **s. star** étoile *f* filante; **s. stick** canne-siège *f*, *pl* cannes-sièges

shoot-out n *Fam* échange *m* de coups de feu, fusillade *f*; **they settled it with a s.** ils ont réglé leurs comptes à coups de feu

shop [ʃɒp] n **1** *Com (building)* magasin *m*; *(small)* boutique *f*; **I'm just going down to the shops** je sors faire des courses; **the ones you buy in shops** ceux que l'on achète en magasin; **you can't get these in the shops** on ne les trouve pas en magasin; **the new book should reach the shops in July** le nouveau livre devrait être en vente en juillet; **grocer's s.** épicerie *f*; **baker's s.** boulangerie *f*; **shoe s.** magasin de chaussures; **duty-free s.** boutique hors taxes; **mobile s.** boutique ambulante; *Old-fashioned* **s.!** il y a quelqu'un?; **to set up s.** *(to open a shop)* ouvrir un magasin; *(to set up as shopkeeper)* s'établir comme commerçant, -ante; **to set up s. as a hairdresser** ouvrir un salon de coiffure; **to set up s. on one's own** se mettre à son compte; **to keep (a) s.** tenir un magasin; **to mind the s.** garder le magasin; *Fig* assurer la permanence; *also Fig* **to shut up s.** fermer boutique; *(at the end of the day)* fermer le magasin; *Fig Fam* **you've come to the wrong s.** vous vous trompez de porte; *Fam* **he was staggering about all over the s.** il titubait fortement; **they're all over the s. on defence policy** leur politique de défense n'est absolument pas cohérente; **my notes are all over the s.** c'est la pagaille dans mes notes; **the defence was all over the s.** c'était la pagaille dans la défense; *Mktg* **s.'s own brand** marque *f* de magasin *ou* de détail(lant)

2 *Fam (act of shopping)* courses *fpl*, shopping *m*; **I do my big s. on a Friday** je fais mes grosses courses le vendredi

3 *Ind etc (workshop)* atelier *m*; **assembly s.** atelier de montage; **pattern s.** atelier de modelage; **repair s.** atelier de réparations; **carpenter's s.** atelier de menuiserie; **closed s.** = entreprise *f* qui n'admet que du personnel appartenant à un certain syndicat

4 *Fam* **to talk s.** parler boutique

vi **(-pp-)** **to s., to go shopping** *(aller)* faire ses courses; *(for food)* aller aux provisions; *(at market)* aller faire son marché; **to go shopping for clothes** aller acheter des vêtements, *Can* magasiner

vt *Br Sl (betray) (person)* dénoncer

▸▸ *Br* **s. assistant** vendeur, -euse (de magasin), employé, -ée de magasin; **s. floor** atelier *m*; **the s. floor** *(workforce)* les ouvriers *mpl*; **s. foreman** chef *m* d'atelier; *Br* **s. front** devanture *f*, façade *f*; **s. steward** porte-parole *mf inv* des ouvriers, délégué, -e syndical(e); **s. window** vitrine *f* (de magasin); *(display)* étalage *m*; **in the s. window** dans la *ou* en vitrine; *Fig* **a s. window for British exports** une vitrine pour les exportations britanniques

▸ **shop around** vi comparer les prix; **I shopped around before opening a bank account** j'ai comparé plusieurs banques avant d'ouvrir un compte; **our company is shopping around for new premises** notre société est à la recherche de nouveaux locaux

shopaholic [ʃɒpəˈhɒlɪk] n **he's a real s.** il adore faire les boutiques

shopfitter [ˈʃɒpfɪtər] n installateur *m ou* agenceur *m* de magasins

shopgirl [ˈʃɒpɡɜːl] n *Old-fashioned* vendeuse *f*, employée *f* de magasin

shop-in-shop n *Com* boutiquage *m*, magasin *m* à l'intérieur d'une grande surface

shopkeeper [ˈʃɒpkiːpər] n commerçant, -ante

shoplifter [ˈʃɒplɪftər] n voleur, -euse à l'étalage

shoplifting [ˈʃɒplɪftɪŋ] n vol *m* à l'étalage

shopman, *pl* **shopmen** [ˈʃɒpmən] n *Am* mécanicien *m (dans un atelier de réparations)*

shopper [ˈʃɒpər] n **1** *(person)* **streets crowded with shoppers** des rues pleines de gens qui font leurs courses; **for the convenience of shoppers** *(sign in shop)* pour mieux servir nos clients **2** *Fam (bag)* sac *m* à provisions

shopping [ˈʃɒpɪŋ] n courses *fpl*; **to do one's/the s.** faire ses/les courses; *(for food)* aller aux provisions; *(at market)* faire son marché; **I hate s.** *(for food etc)* je déteste faire les courses; *(for clothes, wandering round shops)* je déteste faire du shopping; **to do one's Christmas s.** faire ses achats de Noël; **I had a lot of heavy s.** j'étais lourdement chargé d'achats; **I haven't got much s. to do** je n'ai pas beaucoup de courses à faire; **Saturday is my main s. day** le samedi est le jour où je fais mes grosses courses; **only three s. days to Christmas** il ne reste plus que trois jours pour faire les courses avant Noël; **my weekly s. trip** mes courses hebdomadaires; **for my next s. trip** la prochaine fois que j'irai faire les courses

▸▸ **s. arcade** galerie *f* marchande; **s. bag** sac *m ou* filet *m* à provisions, cabas *m*; **s. basket** panier *m* (à provisions); *Econ* panier de la ménagère; *Comput (for Internet shopping)* caddie *m*; *Am* **s. cart** chariot *m*, Caddie® *m*; *Comput (for Internet shopping)* caddie *m*; **s. centre** centre *m* commercial; *TV* **s. channel** chaîne *f* de télé-achat; **s. list** liste *f* des courses; *Am* **s. mall** galerie marchande; **s. plaza,** *Br* **s. precinct** centre commercial; **s. street** rue *f* commerçante; *Br* **s. trolley** chariot, Caddie®

shopsoiled [ˈʃɒpsɔɪld] adj *Br (article)* défraîchi; *(display goods)* qui a fait l'étalage

shoptalk [ˈʃɒptɔːk] n *Fam* **no s., OK?** on ne parle pas métier *ou* affaires *ou Fam* boutique, d'accord?

shopwalker [ˈʃɒpwɔːkər] n *Br* chef *m* de rayon

shopworn [ˈʃɒpwɔːn] adj *Am* = **shopsoiled**

shore¹ [ʃɔːr] n *(coast)* côte *f*, *(shoreline)* rivage *m*; *(of sea, lake, river)* bord *m*; **on the s.** sur le rivage; *(on beach)* sur la plage; *(by sea)* au bord de la mer; *Naut* **on s.** à terre; **to go on s.** se rendre à terre; *(disembark)* débarquer; *Lit* **distant shores** de lointains rivages; **she rarely visits our shores** elle visite rarement nos contrées; **to keep rabies from our shores** empêcher la rage d'atteindre nos côtes

▸▸ **s. excursion** excursion *f (lors d'une escale)*; **s. leave** permission *f* à terre

shore² n *Constr etc* étai *m*, étançon *m*

vt = **shore up**

▸ **shore up** vt sep *(support) (house, wall)* étayer, étançonner; *Fig (government)* étayer, consolider

shoreline [ˈʃɔːlaɪn] n rivage *m*; *(by sea)* côte *f*

shoreward(s) [ˈʃɔːwəd(z)] adv vers la terre

shorn [ʃɔːn] adj **1** *(head)* rasé **2** *(sheep)* tondu

pp *see* **shear**

SHORT [ʃɔːt]

ADJ court **1**, **2** ■ petit **1** ■ bref **2** ■ brusque **3** ■ insuffisant **4**
N court-métrage **1** ■ court-circuit **3**

ADJ 1 *(physically)* court; *(person)* petit, de petite taille; **to be s. in the arm/leg** avoir les bras courts/les jambes courtes; *(of garment)* être court au niveau des bras/des jambes; **(at) a s. distance from the station** à peu de distance de la gare; **to have s. hair** avoir les cheveux courts; **to go by the shortest road, to go the shortest way** aller par le chemin le plus court; **a s. history of France** un précis d'histoire de France; **s. back and sides** *(haircut)* coupe f dégagée autour des oreilles; **at s. range** à courte portée;

2 *(in time)* court, bref, f brève; **to take quick s. breaths** respirer à petits coups rapides; **the days are getting shorter** les jours raccourcissent; **s. and sweet** court mais bon; **that was s. and sweet!** c'était court mais c'était bien!; **in s.** *(to sum up)* bref, en résumé, en somme; **Bill is s. for William** Bill est le diminutif de William; **the s. answer is 'no'** en deux mots, la réponse est non; **a s. drink** un petit verre; **we've just got time for a s. game** nous avons juste le temps de faire une petite partie; **at s. intervals** à intervalles rapprochés; **to have a s. memory** avoir la mémoire courte; **to have a s. temper** s'emporter facilement; **for a s. time** pour un petit moment; **a s. time ago** il y a peu de temps; *Ind* **to be on s. time** être en chômage partiel; **to make s. work of sth** *(problem, difficulty)* résoudre qch en un clin d'œil; **he made s. work of his meal** il a avalé son repas en une minute; **you sure made s. work of that!** tu n'y es pas allé par quatre chemins!; **he made s. work of his opponent** il s'est débarrassé de son adversaire en un rien de temps

3 *(abrupt)* **to be s. with sb** être cassant avec qn; **he was very s. with me** il a été très brusque avec moi

4 *(insufficient, lacking)* *(weight, measure etc)* insuffisant; **to give sb s. measure** donner à qn moins que la quantité que l'on fait payer; **money is very s.** *or* **is in s. supply** on est à court d'argent; **water is in s. supply** l'eau se fait rare; **it is two euros s.** il manque deux euros; **I am twenty euros s.** il me manque vingt euros; **50 s. of the thousand** mille moins 50; **to be s. of sth** *(of person)* être à court de qch, manquer de qch; **I'm a bit s. of cash** je suis un peu à court d'argent; **the country is s. of engineers** le pays manque d'ingénieurs; *Fam Hum* **he's one sandwich s. of a picnic** il a une case vide; **he's a bit s. on common sense** il manque un peu de bon sens

5 *(less than)* **little** *or* **not far s. of it** peu s'en faut; **he is not far s. of thirty** il frise la trentaine; **it is little s. of folly** c'est de la folie (pure); **it was nothing s. of a masterpiece** ce n'était rien moins qu'un chef-d'œuvre; **nothing s. of violence would compel him** il n'y a que la violence qui l'y obligerait

6 *St Exch* court, en position courte; *Fin* **bills at s. date** billets *mpl ou* traites *fpl* à courte échéance

N 1 *Cin (short film)* court métrage *m*, court *m*
2 *(drink)* alcool *m* fort
3 *Elec Fam (short circuit)* court-circuit *m*, *pl* courts-circuits
4 *(in prosody) (syllable)* brève f, *Ling (vowel)* voyelle f brève

ADV 1 **hair cut s.** cheveux coupés court

2 **to stop s.** s'arrêter (tout) net, *Fam* s'arrêter pile; **to stop s. of doing sth** se retenir de faire qch; **it just stops s. of being criminal** c'est à la limite de la criminalité; **she stopped s. of actually calling him a liar** pour un peu, elle aurait traité de menteur; **to cut sb s.** couper la pa-

role à qn; *Fam* **to be caught s.** *(need to relieve oneself)* être pris d'un besoin pressant; *(not have enough money)* être à court d'argent

3 to go s. se priver; **to go s. of sth** se priver de qch; **we're running s. of …** *(supplies etc)* on est presqu'à court de …; **we are running s. of provisions, our provisions are running s.** nos vivres vont bientôt s'épuiser; **to fall s.** *(of arrow, bomb etc)* ne pas arriver jusqu'à la cible; **to fall s. of sb's expectations** décevoir qn; **to fall s. of one's duty** manquer à son devoir; **it falls far s. of what we need** c'est loin de suffire à nos besoins; **s. of a miracle, we are ruined** à moins d'un miracle, nous sommes perdus; **there's not much we can do, s. of selling the house** il n'y a pas grand-chose à faire, à part vendre la maison

4 *Fig* **to sell sb s.** *(betray)* trahir qn; *(trick)* rouler qn; **to sell oneself s.** ne pas se montrer à sa juste valeur

5 *St Exch* **to buy s.** acheter à court terme; **to sell s.** vendre à découvert

VT & VI *Elec Fam* = **short-circuit**

▸▸ *Fin* **s. bills** billets *ou* traites à courte échéance; **s. break** *(holiday)* mini-séjour *m*, *pl* mini-séjours; *Elec* **s. circuit** court-circuit; *pl* courts-circuits; *Horseracing etc* **s. odds** *or* **price** faible cote f; **s. order cook** = cuisinier *m* qui prépare les plats au fur et à mesure des commandes; *Culin* **s. pastry** pâte f brisée; *Fin* **s. payment** moins-perçu *m*, *pl* moins-perçus; *Fin, St Exch* **s. position** position f vendeur, position à découvert; *Horseracing etc* **s. price** faible cote; **s. sale** vente f à découvert; *Liter* **s. story** nouvelle f; *Ling* **s. syllable** syllabe f brève; **s. trousers** culottes *fpl* courtes; *Ling* **s. vowel** voyelle brève; *Radio* **s. wave** onde f courte

shortage [ˈʃɔːtɪdʒ] **N** *(of money, food etc)* manque *m*, pénurie f; **the paper s.** la crise du papier; **we have constant staff shortages** nous manquons constamment de personnel; **there is no s. of applicants** on ne manque pas de candidats

short-arse N *Br Sl* nabot, -ote; **he/she is a little s.** il/elle est un peu court(e) sur pattes, *Pej* il/elle a le cul un peu bas

shortbread, shortcake [ˈʃɔːtbred, -keɪk] **N** *Culin* = sablé *m*

short-change VT *(intentionally)* voler (en rendant la monnaie); *(accidentally)* ne pas rendre assez de monnaie à; *Fig (cheat)* posséder

short-circuit N *Elec* court-circuit *m*, *pl* courts-circuits
VT *Elec, Fig* court-circuiter
VI *Elec* se mettre en court-circuit

shortcode [ˈʃɔːtkəʊd] **N** *Tel* code *m* abrégé
▸▸ **s. dialling** numérotation f abrégée

shortcoming [ˈʃɔːtkʌmɪŋ] **N** *(flaw) (usu pl)* **shortcomings** défauts *mpl*, imperfections *fpl*

shortcrust [ˈʃɔːtkrʌst] **ADJ**
▸▸ *Culin* **s. pastry** pâte f brisée

shortcut [ˈʃɔːtkʌt] **N** raccourci *m*; *Fig* **don't try to take shortcuts** n'essayez pas d'aller trop vite; **there are no shortcuts** on ne peut pas aller plus vite que la musique; **useful shortcuts** des trucs
▸▸ *Comput* **s. key** touche f de raccourci

short-dated ADJ *Fin (bill)* à courte échéance; *(paper)* court

shorten [ˈʃɔːt(ə)n] **VT** *(skirt etc)* raccourcir; *(text, task)* abréger; *(stay)* écourter; **Albert is often shortened to Bert** on utilise souvent le diminutif Bert à la place d'Albert; *Culin* **to s. pastry** travailler la pâte avec une matière grasse
VI *(of days etc)* raccourcir

shortening [ˈʃɔːtnɪŋ] **N 1** *(of days)* raccour-

cissement *m* **2** *(of text)* raccourcissement *m*, abrègement *m* **3** *Culin* matière f grasse

shortfall [ˈʃɔːtfɔːl] **N** manque *m*; *(financial)* déficit *m*; **there's a s. of $100** il manque 100 dollars

short-focus lens N *Phot* objectif *m* à courte focale

shorthaired [ˈʃɔːtheəd] **ADJ** *(person)* aux cheveux courts; *(animal)* à poil ras

shorthand [ˈʃɔːthænd] **N** *(writing system)* sténo(graphie) f; **to take a speech down in s.** sténographier un discours, prendre un discours en sténo; *Fig* **this is s. for …** c'est l'abréviation de …, en bref, ça signifie …
▸▸ **s. reporter** sténographe *mf*; **s. typing** sténodactylographie f; **s. typist** sténodactylo *mf*; **s. writer** sténographe *mf*; **s. writing** écriture f sténographique

shorthanded [ʃɔːtˈhændɪd] **ADJ** **to be s.** manquer de personnel

short-haul ADJ *(flight, route)* court-courrier, *pl* court-courriers
▸▸ **s. aircraft** court-courrier *m*, *pl* court-courriers

shorthorn [ˈʃɔːthɔːn] **N** shorthorn *m*

shortish [ˈʃɔːtɪʃ] **ADJ** assez *ou* plutôt court; *(person)* courtaud

short-legged ADJ aux jambes courtes

shortlist [ˈʃɔːtlɪst] **VT** *Br* sélectionner, retenir la candidature de; **to s. a candidate** retenir une candidature *(en vue d'une sélection ultérieure)*; **you've been shortlisted** on a retenu votre candidature
N liste f des candidats retenus

short-lived ADJ *(joy, triumph etc)* bref, f brève, éphémère, de courte durée

shortly [ˈʃɔːtlɪ] **ADV 1** *(soon)* bientôt, prochainement; *(in a couple of minutes)* sous peu; **s. after(wards)** *(soon afterwards)* peu (de temps) après; **President Smith, who was s. to be** *or* **would s. be re-elected** le président Smith, qui allait bientôt être réélu **2** *(abruptly) (to answer etc)* brusquement, sèchement

Attention: ne pas confondre avec **briefly**.

shortness [ˈʃɔːtnɪs] **N 1** *(physical) (of arm, skirt)* peu *m* de longueur; *(of person)* petite taille f **2** *(in time) (of life)* brièveté f, courte durée f; **s. of memory** manque *m* de mémoire **3** *(abruptness)* brusquerie f **4** *(lack) (of supplies etc)* manque *m*, insuffisance f

short-range ADJ *Mil* à courte portée; *(forecast)* à court terme

shorts [ʃɔːts] **NPL** *(short trousers)* short *m*; *Am (underwear)* caleçon *m*; **a pair of s.** un short VOIR GRAMMAIRE A10

shortsheet [ˈʃɔːtʃiːt] **VT** *Am (bed)* mettre en portefeuille

shortsighted [ʃɔːtˈsaɪtɪd] **ADJ 1** *Opt* myope **2** *Fig (approach etc)* imprévoyant; **that was very s. of you/him** *etc* ça n'était pas faire preuve de beaucoup de prévoyance

shortsightedness [ʃɔːtˈsaɪtɪdnɪs] **N 1** *Opt* myopie f **2** *Fig (of approach etc)* imprévoyance f

short-staffed [-stɑːft] **ADJ** à court de personnel; **to be s.** manquer de personnel

short-stay car park N parking *m* courte durée

short-tempered ADJ vif, f vive, d'un caractère emporté

short-term ADJ *(prisoner)* qui purge une peine de prison de courte durée; *(contract)* de courte durée; *(solution, memory)*, *Fin* à court terme
▸▸ **s. borrowings** emprunts *mpl* à court terme; **s. loan** prêt *m* à court terme

short-termism [-'tɜːmɪz(ə)m] N politique f du court terme

short-time N to be on s. être en chômage partiel

ADJ to be on s. working être en chômage partiel

▸▸ s. worker chômeur, -euse partiel(elle); s. working chômage m partiel

short-wave ADJ (radio) à ondes courtes

short-winded ADJ au souffle court; to be s. manquer de souffle

shorty ['ʃɔːtɪ] N Fam petit m, petite f; come on, s.! allez, le petit!

shot [ʃɒt] N1 (act of firing, sound) coup m (de feu); **pistol s.** coup de pistolet; **warning s.** coup d'avertissement; Naut coup de semonce; **to fire a s.** tirer un coup de feu; **without firing a s.** sans tirer un (seul) coup de feu; **parting s.** (remark) remarque f ou réplique f qu'on lance en partant, dernière remarque; **he's a good s.** c'est un bon tireur; Fam **a big s.** un type important, un grand manitou, Sl une grosse légume; **a s. across the bows** un tir d'avertissement; Fig un avertissement; **to fire a s. across the bows** tirer un coup en guise d'avertissement; Fig donner un avertissement

2 (inv in pl) (projectiles) (from shotgun) plomb m; **bird s.** cendrée f; Fig **like a s.** (speedily) comme une flèche; (with no hesitation) d'emblée, sans hésitation; Am Fam **the whole s.** tout le tremblement; Metal **lead s.** grenaille f de plomb

3 Sport (of shot putter) poids m; **to put the s.** lancer le poids

4 Sport (in tennis, golf etc) coup m; (in football, hockey) shoot m; **good s.!** bien joué!; Tennis etc **drop s.** amortie f, **passing s.** passing-shot m, pl passing-shots; **to make a long s.** (aim from a distance) viser de loin; Fig (guess wildly) deviner au hasard; (take a risk) prendre un (gros) risque; **not by a long s.** il s'en faut de beaucoup; Fig **to take a s. in the dark** (make a wild guess) donner une réponse complètement au hasard, Fam y aller au pifomètre; **I'm going to take a s. in the dark and say 1,000** je vais donner un chiffre au hasard, disons 1 000; Fig **to call the shots** prendre les décisions; Fig **they call the shots** c'est eux qui décident

5 Phot photo f, Cin, TV plan m, prise f de vue; **you can get a good s. of the castle from here** d'ici vous prendrez bien le château; **the opening shots of the movie** les premières images du film; **in s.** dans le champ; **out of s.** hors champ; **to go out of s.** sortir du champ; **high angle s.** plongée f

6 Fam (injection) piqûre f, Fam (drink) (of brandy etc) petit verre m; **a s. in the arm** (injection) une piqûre au bras; Fig (stimulation) un coup de fouet; **to give sb a s.** faire une piqûre à qn

7 Fig (attempt) **I'll have a s. at it/at doing it** je vais essayer ou tenter le coup; **I had a s. at learning Swahili** j'ai essayé d'apprendre le swahili; **it's worth having a s. at** ça vaut le coup; **her second s. at the presidency** sa deuxième tentative pour obtenir la présidence; **she made** or **had a good s. at it** elle a fait tout ce qu'elle pouvait; esp Am Fam **give it your best s.** fais de ton mieux

8 Fam (turn) tour m; **it's your s.** (in game) à vous de jouer; **to have a s. of sth** essayer qch; **it's my s. next** c'est mon tour; **you've had two shots already** tu as déjà essayé deux fois

ADJ 1 to get s. of sb/sth se débarrasser de qn/qch; **to be s. of sb/sth** être débarrassé de qn/qch; **I can't wait to be s. of this house** j'ai hâte de me débarrasser de cette maison

2 esp Am Fam (exhausted) épuisé, crevé; (broken, spoilt) fichu, bousillé; **my nerves are s.** je suis à bout de nerfs; **that's another**

day s.! une autre journée de foutue (en l'air)!

▸▸ s. glass petit verre; Cin, TV s. list liste f des prises (de vue); Sport s. put lancer m du poids; Sport s. putter lanceur, -euse de poids; Sport s. putting (lancer du) poids; Tex s. silk soie f changeante

shotgun ['ʃɒtɡʌn] N fusil m de chasse

▸▸ TV, Cin s. mike micro m canon; s. wedding mariage m forcé (lorsque la future mariée est enceinte)

SHOULD [ʃʊd] MODAL AUX V VOIR GRAMMAIRE A58 **1** (duty or command) **you s. do it at once** vous devriez le faire tout de suite; **you s. have come earlier** vous auriez dû arriver plus tôt; **you/he etc s. not have gone** il ne fallait pas y aller; **a present? oh you shouldn't have!** un cadeau? vous n'auriez pas dû!; **it was an accident that s. have been foreseen** c'était un accident à prévoir; **you s. have seen her!** il fallait la voir!, si vous l'aviez vue!; **you shouldn't laugh at him** vous avez tort de vous moquer de lui; **I shouldn't do that if I were you** je ne ferais pas ça si j'étais toi; **I don't remember – well, you s.** je ne m'en souviens pas – eh bien, tu devrais

2 (expression of opinion) **she s. have arrived by this time** elle devrait être arrivée à l'heure qu'il est; **that s. suit you!** voilà qui fera sans doute votre affaire!; **this weather s. be ideal for anglers** ce temps devrait être idéal pour les pêcheurs; **what s. I have said?** qu'est-ce que j'aurais dû dire?; Iron **you s. worry!** (I don't worry about it) ce n'est pas mon affaire!; Iron **you s. worry about getting fat!** tu ne risques pas de grossir!; Iron **you s. complain!** tu n'as aucune raison de te plaindre!

3 (exclamatory, in rhetorical questions) **why s. you suspect me?** pourquoi me soupçonner?; **how s. I not be happy?** comment ne serais-je pas heureux?; **who s. I meet but Martin!** (et) voilà que je rencontre Martin!

4 (in subordinate clauses) **he ordered that they s. be released** il ordonna qu'on les relâchât; **she insisted that he s. wear his hair short** elle a exigé qu'il porte les cheveux courts; **I didn't want to, but he told me I s.** je ne voulais pas, mais il m'a dit que je devais le faire VOIR GRAMMAIRE A53-4

5 (in conditional clauses) **if he s. come** or Fml **s. he come, let me know** s'il vient, faites-le-moi savoir; **s. the occasion arise, s. it (so) happen** le cas échéant; **in case she s. not be there** au cas où elle ne serait pas là VOIR GRAMMAIRE A52

6 **my holiday was over, the next day I s. be far away** mes vacances étaient finies, le lendemain je serais bien loin

7 (in the main clause of conditional sentences) **we s. come if we were invited** nous viendrions si on nous invitait; **had you written to me I s. have answered you** si vous m'aviez écrit, je vous aurais répondu VOIR GRAMMAIRE A52-3

8 (in softened affirmation) **I s. like a drink** je prendrais bien quelque chose; **I s. have thought that you would have known better** j'aurais pensé que vous auriez été plus avisé; **I shouldn't be surprised (if...)** cela ne me surprendrait pas (que ... + pr sub)

shoulder ['ʃəʊldər] N (of person), Culin épaule f, (of hill etc) épaulement m; (of mountain) contrefort m; **round shoulders** dos m rond ou voûté; **he's got broad shoulders** il est large d'épaules; Fig il a bon dos; **too tight across the shoulders** (of coat etc) trop étroit de carrure; **off-the-s. dress** robe f dégageant les épaules; **slung across** or **over the s.** (bag, rifle etc) en bandoulière; **to look over one's s.** vérifier si on est suivi; **to tell sb sth straight from the s.** dire qch carrément ou brutalement à qn; **to have a good head on one's shoulders** avoir la tête sur les épau-

les; **to rub shoulders with millionaires/film stars** côtoyer des millionnaires/stars du cinéma; **to lay the blame on sb's shoulders** rejeter la faute sur qn, Fam mettre la faute sur le dos de qn; Fig **to put one's s. to the wheel** se mettre à l'œuvre avec énergie; **to stand head and shoulders above the rest** (be far taller) dépasser les autres d'une tête; Fig (be far better) surpasser tous les autres; **s. high** à la hauteur des épaules; **to carry sb s. high** porter qn en triomphe; **s. to s.** (side by side) côte à côte, épaule contre épaule; **hard s.** (on road) bas-côté m, pl bas-côtés; **soft s.** (on road) accotement m non stabilisé

vt 1 (push) pousser avec l'épaule; **to s. one's way through the crowd** se frayer un passage à travers la foule à coups d'épaule; **to s. sb out of the way** or **aside** écarter ou repousser qn d'un coup d'épaule; **she shouldered the door open** elle ouvrit la porte d'un coup d'épaule **2** (put on shoulder) (object) mettre sur l'épaule; Fig **to s. the responsibility** endosser la responsabilité; Mil **to s. arms** se mettre au port d'armes; **s. arms!** portez armes!

▸▸ s. bag sac m à bandoulière; s. belt ceinture f épaulière; s. blade omoplate f, (of horse etc) paleron m; Mil s. braid fourragère f, s. harness Aviat bretelles fpl; TV, Cin harnais m caméra; s. knot aiguillette f, Am Mil s. loop patte f d'épaule, épaulette f, s. pad (in garment) épaulette (coussinet de rembourrage); Sport protège-épaule m, pl protège-épaules; TV, Cin s. pod crosse f d'épaule; s. rate (in tourism) tarif m moyenne saison; s. season (in tourism) moyenne saison f, s. strap (on dress, bra, accordion) bretelle f, (on bag) bandoulière f, Mil patte d'épaule, épaulette

shout [ʃaʊt] N (of joy, pain etc) cri m; **shouts of laughter** éclats mpl de rire; **there was a s. of 'no more taxes!'** on cria 'plus d'impôts!'; Br, Austr Fam **it's my s.** (my round) c'est ma tournée

vi crier, pousser un cri/des cris; **there's no need to s.** inutile de crier; **to s. at sb** crier contre qn, Fam crier après qn; **don't s. at me!** baisse le ton!, Fam ne me crie pas après!; **to s. for sb** appeler qn de toutes ses forces; **to s. for help** crier ou appeler au secours; **to s. to sb to do sth** crier à qn de faire qch; Fig **it's nothing to s. about** (to boast about) il n'y a pas de quoi se vanter; Fig **to have something to s. about** avoir quelque raison de se réjouir

vt crier; (insults etc) vociférer; **to s. oneself hoarse** s'enrouer à force de crier; **'look out!', he shouted** 'attention!', cria-t-il

▸ **shout down** VT SEP (person) huer, conspuer; (proposal) conspuer; **the speaker was shouted down** l'orateur n'a pas réussi à se faire entendre

▸ **shout out** VI **I shouted out in pain** je hurlais de douleur

VT SEP crier

shouting ['ʃaʊtɪŋ] N cris mpl, (uproar) clameur f, **there was a lot of s.** on criait beaucoup; Fig **it's all over bar the s.** c'est dans le sac, c'est du tout cuit

shove [ʃʌv] N poussée f, (with shoulder etc) coup m; **to give sb/sth a s.** pousser qn/qch, donner une poussée à qn/à qch; Fig **he's lazy, he just needs a little s.** il est paresseux, il a juste besoin qu'on le pousse un peu

vt (person, object) pousser; **to s. sb/sth along** or **forward** pousser qn/qch en avant, faire avancer qn/qch; **to s. sth into a drawer** fourrer qch dans un tiroir

vi pousser; **stop shoving!** arrêtez de pousser!; **she shoved past me** elle m'a bousculé en passant

▸ **shove around** VT SEP **1** (push) bousculer **2**

Fam (bully) malmener; **I don't like being shoved around** je n'aime pas passer pour quantité négligeable

▶ **shove aside, shove away** VT SEP *(push away) (person, object)* écarter d'une poussée

▶ **shove off** VI *Fam (leave)* décamper; **s. off!** fiche le camp!
VT SEP *(launch) (boat)* pousser au large

▶ **shove over** VI *Fam (move over)* se pousser

shove-halfpenny, shove-ha'penny [ˈʃʌvheɪpnɪ] N *Br* = (jeu m du) galet m

shovel [ˈʃʌv(ə)l] N pelle f, *Constr etc* **power/steam s.** pelle mécanique/à vapeur
VT *(-ll-) (coal etc)* pelleter, prendre *ou* jeter à la pelle; *Fam* **to s. food into one's mouth** s'empiffrer

▶ **shovel away** VT SEP *(snow etc)* déblayer

▶ **shovel up** VT SEP *(grain etc)* ramasser *ou* entasser à la pelle

shoveler [ˈʃʌvələr] N *(duck)* souchet m

shovelful [ˈʃʌvəlfʊl] N *(of sand etc)* pelletée f

SHOW [ʃəʊ]

| N exposition **1** ▪ foire **1** ▪ spectacle **2** ▪ émission **2** ▪ apparence **3** ▪ ostentation **3** ▪ démonstration **3** |
| VT montrer **1** ▪ présenter **1** ▪ témoigner **1** ▪ manifester **1** ▪ indiquer **2** ▪ prouver **3** ▪ démontrer **3** ▪ passer **4** ▪ diffuser **4** |
| VI se voir **1** ▪ venir **2** |

N 1 *(exhibition)* exposition f, *(agricultural etc)* concours m, comice m; *(of animals)* foire f, **to be on s.** être exposé; **motor/air s.** salon m de l'automobile/de l'aviation; **fashion s.** présentation f de collections; **dog s.** exposition canine

2 *(play etc)* spectacle m; *(on television, radio)* émission f; **to go to a s.** aller au spectacle; *Theat* **to stop the s.** *(be a success)* faire un tabac; **the s. must go on** *Theat* le spectacle continue; *Fig* il faut continuer *(malgré le décès de qn etc)*; *Theat* **to steal the s.** (r)emporter la vedette; *Fig* **let's get this s. on the road!** allez, c'est parti, on y va!; *Fig* **to run the s.** être à la tête de *ou* diriger l'affaire; *Fig* **to make a s. of oneself** se donner en spectacle; **film s.** séance f de cinéma; *Radio, TV* **talk** *or* **chat s.** talk-show m, *pl* talk-shows; **one-man s.** solo m; **travelling s.** *(at a fair)* spectacle forain

3 *(act of showing) (appearance)* apparence f, *(pretence)* semblant m, simulacre m; *(ostentation)* parade f, ostentation f, **to vote by s. of hands** voter à mains levées; **it's all a s.** *(not genuine)* ce n'est qu'une façade; **to do sth for s.** *(to impress)* faire qch pour la forme; *(show off skills etc)* faire qch pour épater la galerie; **to be fond of s.** aimer l'éclat *ou* la parade; **s. of generosity** affectation f de générosité; **s. of strength** démonstration f de force; **to make a s. of resistance** faire semblant *ou* mine de résister; **to make a s. of being angry** faire semblant *ou* faire mine d'être fâché; **to make a great s. of friendship** faire de grandes démonstrations d'amitié; **to make of learning** étaler sa culture

4 to put up a good s. *(of athlete, competitor etc)* bien se défendre; **the party put up a good s.** le parti s'est bien débrouillé; *Old-fashioned Fam* **good s.!** très bien!, bravo!; *Fam* **it was a poor** *or* **bad s.** c'était plutôt manqué; **it's a pretty poor s.** c'est vraiment lamentable

VT *(pt* **showed** [ʃəʊd]; *pp* **shown** [ʃəʊn]*)* **1** *(display) (thing, quality etc)* montrer; *(allow to be seen)* faire voir, laisser voir; *(passport)* présenter; *(gratitude etc)* témoigner; *(one's feelings)* manifester, laisser voir, laisser pa-

raître; *(courage, enthusiasm)* montrer, faire montre de; **to s. sth to sb, to s. sb sth** montrer *ou* faire voir qch à qn; **to s. sb how to do sth** montrer à qn comment faire qch; **to s. one's wares** étaler ses marchandises; **to s. one's cards** *or* **one's hand** *Cards* découvrir son jeu; *Fig (make one's intentions known)* jouer cartes sur table; **the picture shows three figures** le tableau représente trois personnes; **to have sth to s. for one's money** en avoir pour son argent; *Fam* **that dress shows everything she's got** cette robe ne cache pas grand-chose; **he won't s. his face here again** il ne se montrera plus ici; **a colour that doesn't s. the dirt** une couleur qui n'est pas salissante; **to s. oneself** se montrer, se faire voir; *(at a reception etc)* faire acte de présence; **to s. itself** se montrer; *(of emotion, tendency)* se manifester; **to s. a profit** faire ressortir un bénéfice, dégager des profits; **to s. a loss** accuser *ou* faire ressortir une perte; **to s. great improvement** faire apparaître une grande amélioration; **to s. a taste for sth** témoigner d'un goût pour qch; **his face showed his delight** la joie se voyait sur son visage; **she showed no sign of having heard anything** *(didn't reveal she had)* elle n'a pas montré qu'elle avait entendu; *(didn't seem to have)* elle n'a pas montré si elle avait entendu; **to s. one's age** faire son âge; **to s. oneself (to be) a coward** se montrer lâche; **she showed herself to be a hard worker** elle s'est révélée *ou* avérée dure à la tâche; **he showed me no mercy** il n'a fait preuve d'aucune pitié envers moi; **to s. willing** faire preuve de bonne volonté

2 *(indicate)* indiquer; **a diagram shows how the system works** un diagramme indique le fonctionnement du système; **place shown on a map** lieu indiqué sur une carte; **to s. the time/the temperature** *(of watch, thermometer etc)* indiquer l'heure/la température

3 *(prove, demonstrate)* prouver, démontrer; **these remarks s. how worried the government is** ces remarques témoignent de l'inquiétude du gouvernement; **a mere glance will s. that ...** il suffit d'un coup d'œil pour se rendre compte que ...; **which only** *or* **all goes to s. that ...** ce qui prouve que ...; **it just shows you how lucky we are** ça vous montre la chance que nous avons; *Fam* **I'll s. you!** je vais vous apprendre!; *Law* **to s. cause** *or* **reason** *(set out one's reasons)* exposer ses raisons; *(offer valid reasons)* offrir des raisons valables

4 *(film)* passer, projeter; *(TV programme)* diffuser; *TV* **this programme will be shown tomorrow** cette émission passera (à l'écran) demain

5 *(escort, lead)* **to s. sb the way** indiquer *ou* montrer le chemin à qn; **to s. sb to his/her room** conduire qn à sa chambre; **to s. sb round the town** faire visiter *ou* faire voir la ville à qn; **we were shown over the house** on nous a fait visiter la maison; **to s. sb into a room** introduire *ou* faire entrer qn dans une pièce

VI **1** *(be or become visible)* se montrer, paraître, se voir; *(of buds)* sortir; **your slip's showing** votre jupon dépasse; **she lets her feelings s. too much** elle laisse trop voir ses sentiments; **it shows in your face** cela se voit *ou* se lit sur votre visage; **has she started to s. yet?** *(of pregnant woman)* est-ce que ça se voit qu'elle est enceinte?; **she's used to getting what she wants – it shows!** elle a l'habitude d'obtenir ce qu'elle veut – ça se voit!; **it doesn't s.** ça ne se voit pas, on ne dirait pas; **ah well, it just** *or* **all goes to s.!** eh oui, c'est la vie!

2 *Fam (arrive)* se pointer; **he didn't s.** il n'est pas venu

▶ ▶ **s. animal** animal m de concours; **s. apartment** appartement m témoin; *TV etc* **s. copy** copie f antenne *ou* exploitation; **s. format** format m de présentation; **s. girl** girl f; **s. house** maison f témoin; **s. jumper** *(rider)* cavalier, -ère *(participant à des concours de saut d'obstacle); (horse)* sauteur m; **s. jumping** jumping m, concours m de saut d'obstacles; *TV* **s. print** copie antenne *ou* exploitation; *Cin* **s. reel** film m *ou* cassette f de démonstration; *Theat Fam* **s. stopper** numéro m qui fait un tabac; *Law* **s. trial** procès m à grand spectacle; **s. window** vitrine f *(de magasin); (display)* étalage m

▶ **show in** VT SEP *(escort inside)* faire entrer

▶ **show off** VT SEP *(flaunt)* faire montre *ou* étalage de; *(show to advantage)* faire valoir, mettre en valeur; **they like to s. off their culture** ils aiment bien faire étalage de leur culture; **he likes to s. off his muscles/knowledge** il aime bien exhiber ses muscles/connaissances; **she was showing off her new car** elle exhibait sa nouvelle voiture; **she came in to s. off her new baby** elle est venue faire admirer son nouveau-né; **coat that shows off the figure well** manteau qui marque *ou* dessine bien la taille; **wearing white shows off a tan** porter du blanc met le bronzage en valeur
VI *(try to impress)* se donner des airs, *Fam* faire de l'épate; *(with clothes, possessions etc)* parader, se pavaner; **to s. off in front of sb** chercher à épater qn; **stop showing off!** arrête de faire l'important *ou* de te donner des airs!; **you don't have to drive that fast, you're just showing off** ce n'est pas la peine de conduire aussi vite, tu cherches juste à nous épater

▶ **show out** VT SEP *(escort out)* reconduire, accompagner jusqu'à la porte; **it's okay, I'll s. myself out** inutile de vous déranger, je saurai retrouver le chemin (tout seul)

▶ **show through** VI se voir au travers; **her knickers showed through under her dress** on voyait sa culotte au travers de sa robe

▶ **show up** VT SEP **1** *(reveal) (impostor etc)* démasquer, dénoncer; *(flaw etc)* révéler; **he's been shown up** il est grillé

2 *(shame)* faire honte à, embarrasser; *(deliberately humiliate)* humilier, vexer; **you're always showing me up in front of other people!** *(embarrassing me)* tu me mets toujours dans l'embarras devant les gens!

3 *(escort upstairs)* accompagner en haut
VI **1** *(be evident) (against a background)* se dessiner, se détacher, ressortir; **the dirt really shows up on a white carpet** la saleté ressort vraiment sur une moquette blanche

2 *Fam (arrive)* venir; **to fail to s. up** ne pas se présenter; **they'll s. up at twelve** ils s'amèneront à midi; **you're the boss, you really ought to s. up** tu es le patron, tu devrais vraiment y aller *ou* te montrer

---

showbiz [ˈʃəʊbɪz] N *Fam* industrie f *ou* monde m du spectacle, showbiz m
▶ ▶ **s. personality** personnalité f du showbiz *ou* du monde du spectacle

showboat [ˈʃəʊbəʊt] N *Am* bateau-théâtre m, *pl* bateaux-théâtres

showbusiness [ˈʃəʊbɪznɪs] N industrie f *ou* monde m du spectacle; **that's s.!** c'est ça, la vie d'artiste!
▶ ▶ **s. personality** personnalité f du monde du spectacle

showcase [ˈʃəʊkeɪs] N *Com* vitrine f, *Fig* **the exhibition will be a s. for Italy's best furniture designers** l'exposition sera la vitrine de tous les meilleurs créateurs de mobilier d'Italie

showdown [ˈʃəʊdaʊn] N *Fam (confrontation)* confrontation f

shower [ˈʃaʊər] N **1** *(of rain)* averse f, *(of*

blows, stones) volée f, (of sparks) gerbe f, (of insults) avalanche f; **heavy s.** (of rain) ondée f, grosse averse **2** (for washing) (act, device) douche f; **to have** or **take a s.** prendre une douche, se doucher; **he was in the s. for half an hour** il est resté une demi-heure sous la douche **3** Astron meteor **s.** essaim m de météores **4** Am Fam (party) réception f où chacun apporte un cadeau **5** Br Fam Pej (group) **what a s.!** quelle bande ou quel tas de crétins!; **you lazy s!** bande de flemmards!

VT verser; (water) faire gicler (**onto** sur); **to s. blows on sb** faire pleuvoir des coups sur qn; **to s. gifts/honours on sb** combler qn de cadeaux/d'honneurs; **I've been showered with invitations** je suis submergé d'invitations; **to s. compliments on sb** inonder qn de compliments

VI (take a shower) prendre une douche, se doucher

▸▸ Old-fashioned **s. bath** bain-douche m, pl bains-douches; **s. cabinet** cabine f de douche; **s. cap** bonnet m de douche; **s. curtain** rideau m de douche; **s. gel** gel m de douche; **s. head** pomme f de douche; **s. room** salle f de douches ou d'eau; **s. unit** bloc-douche m, pl blocs-douches

▸ **shower down** **VI** (of rocks) tomber; Fig (of compliments, insults) pleuvoir; **rocks showered down on us** des pierres s'abattirent sur nous

showerproof ['ʃaʊəpruːf] **ADJ** Tex imperméable

showery ['ʃaʊərɪ] **ADJ** (weather) pluvieux; **it's s. (weather)** le temps est à l'averse

showground ['ʃəʊɡraʊnd] **N** (fairground) champ m de foire; (for equestrian event etc) terrain m de concours hippique etc

showily ['ʃəʊɪlɪ] **ADV** de façon voyante ou ostentatoire; **s. dressed** habillé de façon voyante

showiness ['ʃəʊɪnɪs] **N** faste m, ostentation f; (of jewellery) clinquant m; (of dress, decoration) luxe m criard ou tapageur

showing ['ʃəʊɪŋ] **N 1** (exhibition) exposition f **2** (of film) projection f, TV, Cin présentation f; **the first s. will be at ...** la première projection aura lieu à ... **3** (performance) performance f; **a poor s. by our team** une déplorable performance de la part de notre équipe; **on this s. we don't stand a chance in the championship** vu cette performance, on n'a pas une chance de gagner le championnat **4** esp Fml **on your own s.** (admission) comme vous le dites vous-même

▸▸ **s. off** vantardise f

showman, pl **showmen** ['ʃəʊmən] **N** (at fair) forain m; Fig **he's a real s.** il a le sens du spectacle

showmanship ['ʃəʊmənʃɪp] **N** (of person) sens m du spectacle; **the s. of his act** son numéro spectaculaire; Fig Pej **it's just s.** c'est du cinéma

shown **PP** see **show** **VT, VI**

show-off **N** Fam (person) m'as-tu-vu mf inv, Fam frimeur, -euse; **John's a terrible s.** John est un sacré prétentieux; **don't be a s.** (with clothes, possessions, skills) arrête de faire de l'épate ou Fam de frimer

showpiece ['ʃəʊpiːs] **N** (in exhibition etc) œuvre f, Fig **the locals regarded the new theatre as something of a s.** les gens du quartier considéraient le nouveau théâtre comme leur joyau

showplace ['ʃəʊpleɪs] **N** (scenic place) endroit m pittoresque

showring ['ʃəʊrɪŋ] **N** (at auction) (for horses, cattle etc) arène f de vente; (at equestrian event) arène f de concours hippique

showroom ['ʃəʊruːm] **N** (for purchasing) magasin m; (display only) salle f ou salon m d'exposition; (for cars etc) salle d'exposition, showroom m; **electricity s.** magasin d'électroménager (où l'on peut aussi payer ses factures d'électricité); **in s. condition** à l'état neuf

show-stopping **ADJ** sensationnel

showy ['ʃəʊɪ] **ADJ** (appearance, dress) voyant, Pej tapageur, -euse, tape-à-l'œil inv; (jewellery) clinquant; (decoration, wallpaper) criard, tape-à-l'œil; **he's a bit s. in the way he dresses** la façon dont il s'habille est un peu voyante; **he's a bit s. in the way he acts** il se fait un peu trop remarquer

shrapnel ['ʃræpn(ə)l] **N 1** Mil (fragments) éclats mpl d'obus; (shell) shrapnel m; **a piece of s.** un éclat d'obus **2** Fam (loose change) mitraille f

▸▸ **s. wound** blessure f provoquée par des éclats d'obus

shred [ʃred] **N** (of fabric, paper etc) lambeau m; (of meat etc) morceau m; **to tear sth (in)to shreds** (into small pieces) déchiqueter qch; (into strips) mettre qch en lambeaux; **to tear sb's reputation to shreds** démolir la réputation de qn; **to tear sb to shreds** démolir qn; **to tear sb's argument/a play to shreds** démolir l'argument de qn/une pièce; **his reputation was in shreds** sa réputation était ruinée; **his argument was in shreds** son argument était réduit à néant; **her dress was all in shreds** sa robe était tout en lambeaux; **there isn't a s. of evidence** il n'y a pas la moindre preuve; **anyone with a s. of decency would have refused** n'importe qui ayant un minimum de décence aurait refusé; **not a s. of truth** pas un grain de vérité; **without a s. of clothing** on nu comme un ver

VT (**-dd-**) (something) déchirer en lambeaux; (confidential documents) déchiqueter, broyer, détruire; Culin (grate) couper en lamelles

shredded ['ʃredɪd] **ADJ** Am Fam (drunk) bourré, pété

shredder ['ʃredər] **N** (device) (for confidential documents) destructeur m de documents

shreddies ['ʃredɪz] **NPL** Fam (underwear) calbute m, calcif m

shredding ['ʃredɪŋ] **N** (of fabric, paper) déchiquetage m, broyage m; (confidential documents) destruction f

▸▸ **s. machine** déchiqueteuse f, broyeuse f

shrew [ʃruː] **N 1** Zool (animal) musaraigne f **2** Pej (woman) mégère f

shrewd [ʃruːd] **ADJ** (person etc) sagace; (businessman) astucieux; **he's a s. man** c'est une fine mouche; **s. answer** réponse f adroite; **that was a s. move** c'était bien joué; **I've got a s. idea that ...** je suis porté à croire que ...; **to make a s. guess** deviner juste; **I could make a pretty s. guess** ce n'est pas difficile à deviner

shrewdly ['ʃruːdlɪ] **ADV** astucieusement

shrewdness ['ʃruːdnɪs] **N** sagacité f, finesse f

shrewish ['ʃruːɪʃ] **ADJ** Pej (woman) acariâtre

shriek [ʃriːk] **N** (of person, animal) cri m aigu ou perçant; **shrieks of joy** cris joyeux; **shrieks of laughter** grands éclats mpl de rire; **to give a s.** pousser un cri perçant

VI (of person) pousser un cri aigu ou perçant; (of wind) hurler; **to s. with laughter/pain** hurler de rire/douleur

VT to s. (out) a warning pousser un cri d'avertissement

shrieking ['ʃriːkɪŋ] **N** cris mpl aigus ou perçants

shrift [ʃrɪft] **N** Fam **to give sb short s.** expédier qn, envoyer promener qn; **I got short s. from him** il m'a envoyé promener, Iron il m'a bien reçu

shrike [ʃraɪk] **N** (bird) pie-grièche f, pl pies-grièches

shrill [ʃrɪl] **ADJ** (voice, sound etc) aigu, f aiguë, perçant; (complaint etc) véhément; **in a s. voice** d'une voix perçante; **a s. whistle** (sound) un coup de sifflet strident

VI Lit pousser un son aigu ou strident; **a whistle shrilled** un coup de sifflet déchira l'air

shrillness ['ʃrɪlnɪs] **N** (of sound) acuité f, stridence f

shrilly ['ʃrɪlɪ] **ADV** (to say) d'un ton aigu; (to protest) de façon virulente

shrimp [ʃrɪmp] **N** (crustacean) crevette f (grise); Fam Pej (short person) nabot, -ote

VI to go shrimping, to s. pêcher la crevette, aller à la pêche à la crevette

▸▸ **s. boat** crevettier m; **s. net** haveneau m

shrimping net ['ʃrɪmpɪŋ] **N** crevettier m (filet)

shrine [ʃraɪn] **N 1** (saint's tomb) tombeau m de saint(e) **2** (reliquary) châsse f, reliquaire m **3** (place of pilgrimage) lieu m de pèlerinage

shrink [ʃrɪŋk] **VI** (pt **shrank** [ʃræŋk]; pp **shrunk** [ʃrʌŋk], as adj **shrunken** ['ʃrʌŋk(ə)n]) **1** (become smaller) (se) rétrécir, rapetisser; (of income, budget) diminuer; (of material etc) rétrécir; (of person) (out of shyness etc) se faire tout petit; **tropical rainforests are shrinking in size** la surface des forêts tropicales humides est en train de diminuer; **he is beginning to s. (with age)** il commence à se tasser; **to s. in the wash** rétrécir au lavage; Fig **to s. into oneself** rentrer en soi-même **2** (move away) reculer; **to s. from sth** reculer devant ou se dérober à qch; **to s. in horror** reculer d'horreur; **to s. from doing sth** reculer ou répugner à faire qch

VT (fabric) (deliberately) faire rétrécir; **I've shrunk my pullover** (accidentally) mon pull a rétréci; **fully shrunk material** tissu irrétrécissable

N Fam (psychiatrist) psy mf

▸ **shrink back** **VI** (move away) avoir un mouvement de recul; **to s. back in horror** reculer d'horreur

shrinkage ['ʃrɪŋkɪdʒ] **N 1** (of wood) retrait m; Tex etc rétrécissement m **2** Com (through pilferage) coulage m; (through damage) casse f

shrinking ['ʃrɪŋkɪŋ] **N 1** (act of becoming smaller) = **shrinkage 1 2** (act of moving back) **s. from sth** recul m devant qch; **she's no s. violet** elle n'est pas timide; **stop acting like a s. violet** arrête de faire ton/ta timide

shrink-wrap **VT** emballer sous film plastique

shrink-wrapped **ADJ** sous film plastique

shrink-wrapping **N 1** (process) emballage m sous film plastique **2** (material) film m plastique

shrive [ʃraɪv] **VT** (pt **shrove** [ʃrəʊv]; pp **shriven** ['ʃrɪv(ə)n]) Arch (a penitent) confesser, absoudre

shrivel ['ʃrɪv(ə)l] (**-ll-**, Am **-l-**) **VT** (skin) rider; (apple) rider, ratatiner; (of sun) (plants) dessécher

VI (of plant, apple) se rider, se ratatiner

▸ **shrivel up** **VI** (of plant, skin) se ratatiner; Fig **I shrivelled up with embarrassment** je serais rentré dans un trou de souris, tellement j'étais gêné

VT SEP (apple, skin) ratatiner; (plants, leaves) complètement dessécher

shrivelled ['ʃrɪv(ə)ld] **ADJ** ratatiné

shroud [ʃraʊd] **N 1** (for dead body) linceul m, suaire m; Fig **in a s. of mystery** enveloppé de mystère; Lit **under a s. of darkness** sous les voiles de la nuit **2** (rope, cord) (for aerial, mast) hauban m; (of parachute) suspente f

VT *(body)* ensevelir; *Fig (something)* envelopper, voiler (**in** de); **shrouded in mist/mystery** enveloppé de brume/mystère; **shrouded in gloom** *(meeting, person)* plongé dans la tristesse

▸▸**s. line** *(of parachute)* suspente

Shrove [ʃrəʊv] **ADJ**
▸▸**S. Tuesday** Mardi *m* gras

Shrovetide ['ʃrəʊvtaɪd] **N** *Rel* les jours *mpl* gras

shrub [ʃrʌb] **N** *(plant)* arbrisseau *m*, arbuste *m*

shrubbery ['ʃrʌbərɪ] **N** massif *m* d'arbustes; **the ball disappeared into the s.** la balle disparut dans les massifs (d'arbustes)

shrug [ʃrʌg] **N s.** (of the shoulders) haussement *m* d'épaules; **with a s.** (of his shoulders) en haussant les épaules; **he gave a s. of contempt** il haussa les épaules en signe de mépris

VT (-gg-) **to s. one's shoulders** hausser les épaules

VI hausser les épaules

▸**shrug off** **VT SEP** *(treat as unimportant)* *(problem, other people's feelings etc)* ignorer; *(danger)* mépriser

shrunken ['ʃrʌŋk(ə)n] **ADJ** *(garment, fabric)* rétréci; *(person, body)* ratatiné; *(head)* réduit; **s. with age** *(person)* tassé par l'âge

shtick [ʃtɪk] **N** *Am Fam* numéro *m*

shuck [ʃʌk] *Am* **N1** *(of peas, beans)* cosse *f*, gousse *f*, *(of sweetcorn)* spathe *f*, *(of nut)* écale *f*, *(of oyster, clam)* coquille *f* **2** *Fam (trick)* arnaque *f*

INT *Fam* **shucks!** mince (alors)!, flûte (alors)!

VT 1 *(peas, beans)* écosser; *(sweetcorn)* éplucher; *(nuts)* écaler; *(oysters, clams)* écailler **2** *Fam (garment)* ôter; **to s. one's clothes** se déshabiller **3** *Fam (tease)* faire marcher, mener en bateau; *(trick)* arnaquer **4 = shuck off**

▸**shuck off** **VT SEP** *Am (discard)* se débarrasser de; *(rid oneself of) (bad habit)* se défaire de

shudder ['ʃʌdər] **N** *(of person)* frisson *m*, frémissement *m*; *(of engine)* vibration *f*; *Fam* **it gives me the shudders** j'en ai des frissons

VI frissonner (**with** de); *(of machine, vehicle, ship etc)* vibrer; **I s. to think of it or at the thought of it** j'ai des frissons rien que d'y penser; **I s. to think what went into this soup** je frémis à l'idée de ce qu'il peut y avoir dans cette soupe; **I s. to think** je n'ose y penser; **the bus shuddered to a halt** le bus s'immobilisa en vibrant

shuffle ['ʃʌf(ə)l] **N 1** *(in walking)* traînement *m* de pieds, pas *m* traînant; *(in dancing)* frottement *m* de pieds; **soft shoe s.** = danse *f* de music-hall *(exécutée en chaussons)* **2** *Cards* mélange *m*; **to give the cards a s.** battre *ou* mélanger les cartes

VT *(mix) (papers etc)* brasser; *Cards* battre, mélanger; **to s. one's feet** *(in walking)* traîner les pieds; **he stood there shuffling his feet** il était là debout dansant d'un pied sur l'autre

VI 1 *(drag one's feet)* traîner les pieds; **she shuffled into the room** elle entra dans la pièce en traînant les pieds; **the children were shuffling in their seats** les enfants s'agitaient sur leur chaise **2** *Cards* mélanger

▸**shuffle along** **VI** *(walk dragging one's feet)* avancer en traînant les pieds

▸**shuffle off** **VI** *(walk away dragging one's feet)* s'en aller en traînant les pieds; **the badger shuffled off into the bushes** le blaireau disparut dans les buissons en trottinant

VT SEP *(set aside) (responsibility)* rejeter (**onto sb** sur qn); **to s. a job off onto sb** refiler un boulot à qn; *Hum* **to s. off this mortal coil** mourir

shuffleboard ['ʃʌf(ə)lbɔːd] **N** (jeu *m* de) palet *m*

shuffling ['ʃʌflɪŋ] **ADJ** *(gait)* traînant

shufti, shufty ['ʃʊftɪ] **N** *Br Fam* coup *m* d'œil; **have a s. at this** jettes-y un coup d'œil; **can I have a s.?** je peux jeter un coup d'œil?

shun¹ [ʃʌn] **INT** *Mil etc Fam (attention!)* garde-à-vous!

shun² **VT** (-nn-) *(somebody, something)* fuir, éviter; *(publicity)* fuir; **to s. society** fuir le monde; **to s. everybody** éviter tout le monde

shunt [ʃʌnt] **VT 1** *Rail (train, carriages)* manœuvrer; **to s. a train onto a siding** aiguiller un train sur une voie de garage; *Fam* **we were shunted into another room** on nous a parqués dans une autre pièce; *Fam* **the responsibility was shunted back and forth between departments** la responsabilité a été renvoyée de service en service **2** *Elec (circuit etc)* shunter, dériver; *(condenser)* monter en dérivation **3** *Fam (to push)* pousser; **he just shunted me out of his way** il m'a poussé hors de son chemin; **s. that box of files over here, will you?** passe-moi ce carton de dossiers, tu veux!

VI *Fam* **I spent the day shunting back and forth between the two offices** j'ai passé ma journée à faire la navette entre les deux bureaux

N *Elec* shunt *m*, dérivation *f*

shunter ['ʃʌntər] **N** *Rail (train)* locomotive *f* de manœuvre

shunting ['ʃʌntɪŋ] **N 1** *Rail* manœuvre *f* **2** *Elec* dérivation *f*, shuntage *m*

▸▸*Rail* **s. engine** locomotive *f ou* machine *f* de manœuvre; *Rail* **s. operations** manœuvres *fpl* de triage; *Rail* **s. yard** gare *f* de triage

shush [ʃʌʃ] **INT** chut!

VT *(person)* faire taire

shut [ʃʌt] **VT** *(pt, pp* **shut***; prp* **shutting***)* *(door, shop, box, book etc)* fermer; **to s. the door on sb** *or* **in sb's face** fermer la porte au nez de qn; **to s. one's eyes** fermer les yeux; **to s. one's ears to sth** refuser d'entendre qch; **to s. one's mind to the possibility that …** se refuser à l'éventualité que …; **s. your mind to it!** ne pense pas à ça!; **to s. one's finger in the door** se pincer le doigt dans la porte; *Fam* **to s. sb's mouth (for him)** faire taire qn; *Sl* **s. your mouth** *or* **face!** la ferme!, ta gueule!

VI *(of door, lid etc)* (se) fermer; *(of shop, museum etc)* fermer; **the door won't s.** la porte ne ferme pas; **the door s. to** la porte s'est fermée (toute seule)

ADJ fermé; **to find the door s.** trouver la porte fermée, trouver porte close; *Fam* **to keep one's mouth s.** avoir la bouche cousue; **keep your mouth s.!** ferme-la!; **they always keep the door s.** ils gardent toujours la porte fermée; **keep the door s.!** ferme la porte!

▸**shut away** **VT SEP** **to s. oneself away** s'enfermer; **to s. oneself away from the world** s'isoler du monde; **these objects have been s. away for centuries** ces objets sont restés enfermés pendant des siècles

▸**shut down** **VT SEP** *(factory, airport etc)* fermer; *(production)* arrêter; *Tech (steam, power)* couper; *Aviat (engine)* couper, arrêter; *Comput (system)* arrêter; *(computer)* éteindre

VI *(of factory etc) (through lack of work)* fermer temporairement; *(for holiday)* fermer; *(permanently)* fermer ses portes; *(of TV station etc for the night)* arrêter ses programmes; *Comput (of system)* s'arrêter

▸**shut in** **VT SEP** *(confine) (person, object)* enfermer; **to s. oneself in** s'enfermer; **to feel s. in** avoir un sentiment d'étouffement; **we're s. in by hills** nous sommes entourés de collines

▸**shut off** **VT SEP 1** *(stop) (electricity, water)* couper; *Aut (engine)* couper, arrêter; **to s. off funds** couper des crédits **2** *(block) (road)* couper; *(pipe, exit)* boucher **3** *(isolate)* isoler (**from** de); **she s. herself off from other people** elle s'isolait du reste des gens; **to be s. off from society** être exclu du monde; **you shouldn't s. yourself off so** tu ne devrais pas t'isoler comme ça

▸**shut out** **VT SEP 1** *(exclude) (person)* exclure; *(air, light, competition)* bloquer; *(memory etc)* chasser; **the trees s. out the view** les arbres bouchent la vue; **to s. sb out from** *or* **of sth** exclure qn de qch; **I've s. her out of my life** je l'ai rayée de ma vie **2** *(keep outside)* **to s. sb out (of doors)** fermer la porte à qn; **I've s. myself out (of my house)** je me suis enfermé dehors; **he's taken the keys and has s. me out** il a pris les clefs et du coup je suis enfermé dehors **3** *Am Sl (prevent from scoring)* empêcher de marquer

▸**shut up** **VT SEP 1** *(confine) (person, object)* enfermer; **to s. oneself up** s'enfermer chez soi; **to s. sb up (in prison)** emprisonner qn **2** *(close) (room)* fermer; **to s. up shop** *(close shop at end of day)* fermer le magasin; *(close shop permanently)* fermer boutique; *(of theatre etc)* fermer ses portes **3** *(close completely) (west wing etc)* condamner; *(opening etc)* obstruer, boucher; **to s. up a house** *(when going away)* boucler une maison **4** *Fam (make quiet) (person)* faire taire; *(using threats or violence)* réduire au silence; **s. those kids up!** faites taire ces gamins!; **that ought to s. him up** *(stop him boasting)* ça devrait lui rabattre son caquet; *(stop him complaining)* ça devrait le calmer

VI *Fam* **s. up!** tais-toi!; *(aggressive) Sl* la ferme!, ta gueule!; **he never knows when to s. up** il ne sait pas se taire *ou* la fermer quand il faut; **to s. up about sth** la fermer à propos de qch

shutdown ['ʃʌtdaʊn] **N** *(of factory) (temporary)* fermeture *f* temporaire; *(permanent)* fermeture; *(of machine, computer)* fermeture, arrêt *m* de fin de session

shut-eye **N** *Fam* roupillon *m*; **to have** *or* **get a bit of s.** roupiller, coincer la bulle

shut-in **ADJ** **to have a s. feeling** *(in room etc)* se sentir enfermé; *(in relationship)* se sentir prisonnier, -ière

N *Am* invalide *mf* confiné chez lui/elle

shut-off **N 1** *(device)* **the automatic s. didn't work** le dispositif d'arrêt automatique n'a pas fonctionné **2** *(action)* arrêt *m*

shut-out **N 1** *Ind* lock-out *m inv* **2** *Am Sl (win)* éclatante victoire *f*

▸▸*Cards* **s. bid** ouverture *f* préventive

shutter ['ʃʌtər] **N 1** *(on window)* volet *m*; *(slatted)* **shutters** persiennes *fpl*, *(folding)* **shutters** volets pliants; **to open/close the shutters** ouvrir/fermer les volets; **to put up the shutters** *(of shop)* fermer la/les devanture(s), mettre les volets; *Fig (close shop permanently)* fermer boutique **2** *Phot* obturateur *m*; **to release the s.** actionner l'obturateur

▸▸**s. release** déclencheur *m* d'obturateur; **s. speed** vitesse *f* d'obturation

shuttered ['ʃʌtəd] **ADJ** *(window) (with shutters)* à volets; *(with shutters closed)* à volets fermés; **the house has s. windows** la maison a des volets

shuttering ['ʃʌtərɪŋ] **N** *(for concrete)* coffrage *m*

shutting ['ʃʌtɪŋ] **N** fermeture *f*
▸▸**s. down** *(of factory)* fermeture; *(of machine, computer)* arrêt *m* de fin de session

shuttle ['ʃʌt(ə)l] **N 1** *Tex, Sewing etc* navette *f* **2** *(vehicle, service)* navette *f*, *Astronaut* **space s.** navette spatiale **3 = shuttlecock**

VI faire la navette (**between** entre)

VT to s. sb back and forth or **to and fro** (of shuttle bus etc) transporter qn d'un endroit à un autre; Pej (from office to office etc) envoyer qn à droite et à gauche, Fam balader qn; **to s. back and forth** (tape) faire avancer et reculer rapidement pour repérer un point précis; **to s. a document to and fro** transbahuter un document d'un endroit à un autre

▸ ▸ **s. diplomacy** navette diplomatique; **s. service** service m de navettes, navette

shuttlecock [ˈʃʌt(ə)lkɒk] N Sport volant m

shy [ʃaɪ] N **1** (throw) (of stone etc) jet m, lancement m; **to take a s. at sth with a stone** tirer sur qch avec un caillou; **5p a s.** (at fairs) 5 pence le coup **2** Old-fashioned Fam (attempt) (to achieve sth) essai m, tentative f; **to have a s. at doing sth** s'essayer à faire qch **VT** (pt, pp **shied**; prp **shying**) (throw) (stone etc) lancer, jeter (**at sb** à qn)

shy [ʃaɪ] ADJ (comp **shyer**, superl **shyest**) **1** (person, child) timide; (bird) sauvage, farouche; **to make sb s.** intimider qn; **to be s. of people** être gêné ou mal à l'aise en société; **to be s. of doing sth** hésiter à faire qch; **he fought s. of admitting his interest** il a fait tout ce qu'il a pu pour ne pas avoir à admettre qu'il était intéressé **2** esp Am **to be s. of** (lack) (something) manquer de; **we're still 500 dollars s.** il nous manque encore 500 dollars

shy [ʃaɪ] VI (pt, pp **shied**; prp **shying**) (of horse) s'effaroucher; **to s. at sth** (of horse) s'effaroucher devant qch; Fig (of person) renâcler devant qch

▸ **shy away** VI (retreat in fear, nervousness) **to s. away from sth/doing sth** éviter qch/de faire qch; **to s. away from an idea** se méfier d'une idée; **he has shied away from driving since the accident** il évite de conduire depuis l'accident

Shylock [ˈʃaɪlɒk] N Fam Pej usurier, -ière

shyly [ˈʃaɪlɪ] ADV (to smile, suggest, look on etc) timidement; (to blush) de timidité

shyness [ˈʃaɪnɪs] N (of person, child) timidité f, (of animal) caractère m farouche; **to lose one's s.** s'enhardir

shyster [ˈʃaɪstər] N esp Am Pej Fam (lawyer) avocat m marron; (businessman) escroc m

SI [ɛsˈaɪ] N Tech (abbr **Système International**) SI m; **SI units** unités fpl de SI

si [siː] N Mus si m

Siam [saɪˈæm] N Hist Siam m

Siamese [saɪəˈmiːz] ADJ Hist siamois **N 1** Hist (person) Siamois, -oise **2** Ling, Hist siamois m **3** (cat) siamois m
▸ ▸ **S. cat** chat m siamois; **S. twins** (male) frères mpl siamois; (female) sœurs fpl siamoises; Fam Fig **they're like S. twins, those two!** c'est des vrais siamois, ces deux-là!

siamesed [saɪəˈmiːzd] ADJ Aut (joined together) siamois

Siberia [saɪˈbɪərɪə] N Sibérie f

Siberian [saɪˈbɪərɪən] ADJ sibérien **N** Sibérien, -ienne

sibilance [ˈsɪbɪləns] N TV, Radio sifflante f

sibilant [ˈsɪbɪlənt] ADJ sifflant **N** Ling sifflante f

sibling [ˈsɪblɪŋ] N (brother) frère m; (sister) sœur f
▸ ▸ **s. rivalry** rivalité f entre frères et sœurs

sibyl [ˈsɪbɪl] N sibylle f

sibylline [ˈsɪbɪlaɪn] ADJ (book etc) sibyllin

sic [sɪk] ADV sic, ainsi

siccative [ˈsɪkətɪv] ADJ, N siccatif m

Sicilian [sɪˈsɪlɪən] ADJ sicilien **N** Sicilien, -ienne

Sicily [ˈsɪsɪlɪ] N Sicile f

sick [sɪk] ADJ **1** (ill) malade; (humour) noir; (joke) macabre; **to be s.** (ill) être malade; **to**

---

report s. se faire porter malade; **to be s. in the head** (mad) être malade de la tête; Fig **you have to be pretty s. to desecrate somebody's grave** il faut être vraiment malade pour profaner la tombe de quelqu'un; Fig **he has a s. mind** c'est quelqu'un de malsain **2 to be s.** (vomit) rendre; **to feel s.** avoir mal au cœur; **to make oneself s.** (on purpose) se faire vomir; (by eating too much chocolate etc) se rendre malade; **he was as s. as a dog** il a été malade comme un chien; Fig il en a fait une maladie; **to be s. to one's stomach** avoir mal au cœur; Fig en être malade, en faire une maladie; Fig **it makes me s.** cela m'écœure!; Fig **you make me s.!** tu m'écœures!; Fig **he was very s. at** or **about failing his exam** son échec à l'examen l'a complètement bouleversé; **I'm s. about having to cancel my holiday** je suis malade de devoir annuler mes vacances; Fig **she looked pretty s. when she didn't get the prize** elle avait l'air plutôt écœurée quand elle n'a pas reçu le prix; Fig **to be s. with jealousy** être malade de jalousie; Lit **to be s. at heart** être navré; **s. feeling** malaise m **3 to be s. of sth** être las de qch; **to grow s. of sth** se dégoûter de qch; **I'm s. of spaghetti every night/your constant complaining** j'en ai assez de manger des spaghetti tous les soirs/que vous vous plaignez sans cesse; **I'm s. and tired** or **I'm s. to death of it** j'en ai assez, j'en ai marre
▸ N **1 the s.** (pl) les malades mpl **2** Br Fam (vomit) vomi m
▸ ▸ **s. bag** = sachet m mis à la disposition des passagers souffrant du mal des transports; **s. bay** infirmerie f, Naut poste m des malades; **s. bed** lit m de malade; **s. benefit** prestations fpl de l'assurance maladie; **s. building syndrome** syndrome m des bâtiments malsains, = syndrome comprenant des maux de tête, qu'on retrouve chez des personnes résidant ou travaillant dans des bâtiments équipés de la climatisation; Br **s. headache** migraine f, **s. leave** congé m (de) maladie; **s. list** liste f des malades; **to be on the s. list** être porté malade; Br **s. note** mot m d'absence (pour cause de maladie); Br Mil **s. parade** (soldiers) = ensemble m des soldats se rendant à la consultation; (time) = heure f à laquelle les soldats se rendent à la consultation; **to go on s. parade** se faire porter malade; **s. pay** indemnité f de maladie (versée par l'employeur)
▸ **sick up** VT SEP Br Fam (vomit) vomir, rendre

sicken [ˈsɪk(ə)n] VI (become ill) tomber malade; (of plants) languir, dépérir; **to be sickening for an illness/for something** couver une maladie/quelque chose; Fig Lit **to s. of sth** se lasser ou se dégoûter de qch
▸ VT (make nauseous) donner mal au cœur à, donner envie de vomir à; Fig (disgust) dégoûter, donner la nausée à; Fig **his business methods s. me** ses procédés en affaires me révoltent ou me rendent malade

sickening [ˈsɪk   nɪŋ] ADJ (disgusting) écœurant, dégoûtant; (smell) nauséabond; (sight) révoltant; Fam **how perfectly s.!** (annoying) c'est vraiment écœurant!; Fam **she's so good at maths – I know, it's s.** elle est tellement bonne en maths – je sais, c'est écœurant; **there was a s. crunch as the boats collided** il y a eu un craquement sinistre lorsque les bateaux sont entrés en collision

sickeningly [ˈsɪknɪŋlɪ] ADV (de façon) à vous soulever le cœur ou à vous écœurer

sickie [ˈsɪkɪ] N Br, Austr Fam **to take a s.** se faire porter pâle (lorsqu'on est bien portant)

sickle [ˈsɪk(ə)l] N faucille f, Med **s. cell anaemia** drépanocytose f

sickliness [ˈsɪklɪnɪs] N **1** (of person) état m maladif; (of complexion) pâleur f **2** (of cake) goût m écœurant

---

sickly [ˈsɪklɪ] ADJ **1** (person) maladif, souffreteux; (plant) étiolé, rabougri; (colour, light) faible, pâle; (complexion) pâle; (pallor) maladif; (sun) blafard; (smile) pâle **2** Old-fashioned (climate) malsain, insalubre **3** (taste) écœurant; Fig (sentiment) qui écœure, qui dégoûte; (story, tune) plein de sensiblerie, à la guimauve; **s. sweet** douceâtre

sickness [ˈsɪknɪs] N (illness) maladie f, (nausea) mal m de cœur; **you agreed to stay with him in s. and in health** vous aviez accepté de rester avec lui qu'il soit malade ou en bonne santé; (bouts of) **s.** (nausea) nausée(s) f(pl); **sleeping s.** maladie du sommeil; **altitude** or **mountain s.** mal des montagnes; **morning s.** nausées matinales
▸ ▸ Br **s. benefit** prestations fpl de l'assurance maladie

sicko [ˈsɪkəʊ] Fam ADJ dérangé, malade **N** malade mf, tordu, -ue

sickroom [ˈsɪkruːm] N chambre f de malade; (in school etc) infirmerie f

SIDE [saɪd]

N côté **1–6** ▪ flanc **1, 2** ▪ versant **2** ▪ paroi **2** ▪ face **3** ▪ aspect **4** ▪ équipe **5**		
VI prendre le parti de (to side with)		

N 1 (of person, animal) côté m, flanc m; **to be lying on one's s.** être couché sur le côté; **right/left s.** côté droit/gauche; **by sb's s.** à côté de qn; **by** or **at my s.** à côté de moi, à mes côtés; **they were standing s. by s.** ils se tenaient l'un à côté de l'autre; Fig **they worked s. by s. with their former enemies** ils ont travaillé en étroite collaboration avec leurs anciens ennemis; Fam **to split** or **burst one's sides (laughing)** se tenir les côtes (de rire), se tordre (de rire); **s. of bacon** flèche f de lard; **s. of beef** demi-carcasse f de bœuf **2** (part) (of house, box, triangle etc) côté m; (of mountain) flanc m, versant m; (of ditch, vase) paroi f, (of ship) bord m, côté; Math (of equation) membre m; **to put two boxes s. by s.** mettre deux boîtes l'une à côté de l'autre **3** (surface) côté m; (of record) face f, **the right/wrong s. of a fabric** l'endroit m/l'envers m d'un tissu; **the under/upper s. of sth** le dessous/le dessus de qch; **printed on one s. only** imprimé d'un seul côté; **on the other s. of the paper** (when looking at the front) au verso; (when looking at the back) au recto; **buttered s. up** (of slice of bread) le côté beurré vers le haut; Fig **the other s. of the picture** le revers de la médaille; **the right/wrong s. (of sth)** le bon/mauvais côté (de qch); Com **this s. up** haut!; **on this s. (of)** de ce côté(-ci) (de); **on that s. (of)** de ce côté-là (de); **on the other s. (of sth)** de l'autre côté (de qch); **with a dog on either s.** flanqué de deux chiens; **on both sides** des deux côtés, de part et d'autre; **on all sides, on every s.** de tous les côtés; (everywhere) partout; **on the left-/right-hand s.** à (main) gauche/droite; **on the south s.** du côté sud; **the tower leans on** or **to one s.** la tour penche d'un côté; **to put sth on** or **to one s.** mettre qch de côté; **to take sb on** or **to one s.** prendre qn à part ou en particulier; **to stand on** or **to one s.** se tenir à l'écart ou à part; **from all sides, from every s.** de tous (les) côtés, de toutes parts; **from s. to s.** d'un côté à l'autre; Fig **to get on the right s. of sb** gagner les faveurs de qn; **to be on the right s. of sb** être dans les petits papiers de qn; Fig **to get on the wrong s. of sb** prendre qn à rebrousse-poil; **to be on the right s. of the law** avoir la loi pour soi; **to be on the wrong s. of the law** aller contre la loi; **to be on the right s. of forty** avoir moins de quarante ans; **to be on the wrong s. of forty** avoir quarante ans bien sonnés; **it costs the**

wrong s. of £1,000 ça coûte plus de 1 000 livres; **it's a bit on the expensive/long/hot s.** c'est plutôt cher/long/chaud

4 *(aspect) (of situation, argument etc)* aspect *m*, côté *m*; *(of personality)* côté; **I could see the funny s. of the situation** je voyais le côté drôle de la situation; **I can't see the funny s. of that** je ne vois pas ce qu'il y a de drôle làdedans; **his good s.** ses bons côtés; **to have a jealous/thoughtful s.** avoir un côté jaloux/méditatif; **there are many sides to her character** elle a bien des facettes à son caractère; **I had never seen that s. of him before** je n'avais jamais vu cet aspect de sa personnalité; **the good/bad s. of the business** le bon/mauvais côté de l'affaire; **to look on the bright s. (of things)** voir les choses du bon côté, prendre les choses du bon côté; **he always looks on the gloomy s. of things** il voit tout en noir; **to hear/look at both sides of the question** *(consider both aspects)* considérer les deux aspects de la question; *(consider arguments for and against)* envisager le pour et le contre; **you haven't heard my s. of the story!** vous n'avez pas entendu ma version de l'histoire!

5 *(in dispute)* côté *m*; *Sport* équipe *f*, camp *m*; **the two sides to the dispute will meet on Monday** les deux partis se rencontreront lundi; **to be on the right/wrong s.** être du bon/mauvais côté; **to take sides** choisir son camp, prendre parti; **to refuse to take sides** refuser de prendre parti; **to take sides with sb, to take the s. of sb** se ranger avec *ou* du côté de qn; **he's on our s.** il est avec nous *ou* de notre côté; **whose s. are you on?** de quel côté êtes-vous?; **to change sides** changer de camp, virer de bord; *Pol etc* faire volte-face; **they fought on our s.** ils se sont battus à nos côtés; **they were on the other s.** *(in war etc)* ils étaient de l'autre côté; **time is on our s.** le temps travaille pour nous; *Ftbl* **a club/national s.** une équipe locale/nationale; **to pick sides** faire les équipes; **to let the s. down** trahir *ou* décevoir ses amis *etc*

6 *(lineage)* côté *m*; **on his mother's s.** du côté maternel *ou* de sa mère

7 *Old-fashioned Br Fam (affectation)* **to put on s.** se donner des airs; **there's no s. to her at all** c'est quelqu'un de très simple

8 *Fig* **he does a bit of gardening on the s.** il a un petit boulot: il fait du jardinage; *Fam* **to make something** *or* **a bit on the s.** se faire des extras; *Fam* **profits on the s.** de la gratte; *Fam* **to have a bit on the s.** *(have lover) (of man)* avoir une petite amie *ou* une maîtresse; *(of woman)* avoir un petit ami *ou* un amant; **he has his bit on the s. every Tuesday** il a son cinq à sept tous les mardis

9 *Billiards* **to put s. on a ball** donner de l'effet à une balle

VI to s. with sb *(support)* prendre le parti de qn; **to s. against sb** prendre parti contre qn

▸▸ **s. aisle** *(in church)* bas-côté *m*, *pl* bas-côtés; *Theat* allée *f* latérale; **s. chair** chaise *f* (de salle à manger *etc*); **s. chapel** chapelle *f* latérale; **s. dish** plat *m* d'accompagnement; *(vegetables)* garniture *f*; **it is served with a s. dish of potatoes** nous le servons avec des pommes de terre en accompagnement; **s. door** porte *f* latérale; *Fig* **to enter a profession by the s. door** entrer dans une profession par la petite porte; **s. drum** tambour *m*; **s. effect** effet *m* secondaire; **s. entrance** entrée *f* sur le côté; **s. face** profil *m*; **s. glance** regard *m* oblique ou de côté; *Fig (allusion)* allusion *f*; **s. issue** question *f* secondaire; **the s. issues of a question** les à-côtés *mpl* d'une question; **s. panel** *(of vehicle)* ridelle *f*; **s. pocket** poche *f* extérieure; **s. rail** *(on bridge)* garde-fou *m*, *pl* garde-fous; *Naut* rambarde *f*; **s. road** *(minor road in country)* route *f* secondaire; *(in town)* petite rue *f*, *(road at right angles)* rue *f* transversale; **s. sa-**

lad salade *f* *(pour accompagner un plat)*; **s. street** *(minor street)* petite rue; *(at right angles)* rue transversale; **s. table** petite table *f*, *(for dishes)* desserte *f*, *(beside bed)* table *f* de chevet; **s. view** vue *f* de côté; **s. wall** *(of tyre)* flanc *m*; **s. whiskers** favoris *mpl*; **s. window** *(of car)* vitre *f* latérale

sideboard [ˈsaɪdbɔːd] N **1** *(piece of furniture)* buffet *m* **2** *Br* **sideboards** *(whiskers)* favoris *mpl*

sideburns [ˈsaɪdbɜːnz] NPL *(whiskers)* favoris *mpl*

sidecar [ˈsaɪdkɑːr] N **1** *(of motorbike)* sidecar *m*, *pl* side-cars **2** *esp Am (cocktail)* = cocktail *m* composé de Cointreau®, de cognac et de jus de citron

-sided [-ˈsaɪdɪd] SUFF **a four-s. figure** une figure à quatre côtés; **a many-s. debate** *(with many facets)* un débat qui touche à bien des problèmes; *(with many participants)* un débat auquel se confronte des opinions très diverses; **three-s. contract** contrat à trois parties *ou* tripartite

side-impact bar N *Aut* renfort *m* anti-impact latéral

sidekick [ˈsaɪdkɪk] N *Fam* acolyte *mf*; *Hum* **can I bring along a couple of sidekicks?** est-ce que je peux emmener quelques copains?

sidelight [ˈsaɪdlaɪt] N **1** *Phot etc* lumière *f* de côté; *Fig* **to throw a s. on a subject** donner un aperçu sur un sujet **2** *Constr (window)* fenêtre *f* latérale **3** **sidelights** *Br Aut* feux *mpl* de position; *Naut* feux de côté

sideline [ˈsaɪdlaɪn] N **1** *Ftbl etc* ligne *f* de touche; *Fig* **to be on the sidelines** *(excluded)* rester sur la touche; **I prefer to stay on the sidelines** je préfère ne pas m'en mêler; **all his life, he has stayed on the sidelines** toute sa vie, il est resté à l'écart; **to watch from the sidelines** *Sport* regarder de la ligne de touche; *Fig* être là en spectateur **2** *(secondary job)* petit boulot *m*; **it's just a s.** *(which earns money)* c'est un petit à-côté; **we sell guide books as a s.** en plus de nos activités principales, nous vendons des guides

VT *(usu passive)* **to be sidelined** être mis sur *ou* rester sur la touche; *Fig* **to be feeling sidelined** avoir l'impression d'avoir été laissé sur la touche

sidelong [ˈsaɪdlɒŋ] ADV *(to fall)* à l'oblique, obliquement, de côté; *(to look at sb)* de côté, du coin de l'œil

ADJ *(glance)* oblique, de côté; **to give sb a s. glance** regarder qn de côté *ou* du coin de l'œil

sidereal [saɪˈdɪərɪəl] ADJ *Astron* sidéral, -aux

side-saddle N selle *f* de dame *ou* de femme

ADV to ride s. monter en amazone

sideshow [ˈsaɪdʃəʊ] N *(at fair) (stall)* stand *m* de foire; *(show)* spectacle *m* de foire; *Fig (secondary matter)* affaire *f* d'importance secondaire

sideslip [ˈsaɪdslɪp] N **1** *Aut, Cycling, Ski* dérapage *m* **2** *Aviat* glissade *f* (sur l'aile), glissement *m* latéral

VI 1 *Aut, Cycling, Ski* déraper **2** *Aviat* glisser sur l'aile

sidesman, *pl* **sidesmen** [ˈsaɪdzmən] N *Br Rel* = marguillier *m* adjoint

sidesplitting [ˈsaɪdsplɪtɪŋ] ADJ *Fam (joke)* tordant

sidesplittingly [ˈsaɪdsplɪtɪŋlɪ] ADV *Fam* **s. funny** drôle à se tordre de rire

sidestep [ˈsaɪdstep] VI faire un pas de côté; *Boxing etc* esquiver

VT *(tackle)* éviter; *(player)* passer; *Fig (question)* éviter

sidestroke [ˈsaɪdstrəʊk] N *Swimming* nage *f* indienne

sideswipe [ˈsaɪdswaɪp] N *(blow)* coup *m* sur le côté; *Fig* **to take a s. at sb** frapper qn sur le côté; *Fig* faire une remarque désagréable sur qn en passant; *Fig* **that was a s. at the Prime Minister** c'était une allusion malveillante à propos du Premier ministre

VT *Am (car etc)* donner un coup dans *ou* cogner le côté de

sidetrack [ˈsaɪdtræk] N *Am Rail* voie *f* secondaire

VT *Fig (divert from aim)* distraire; *(divert from subject)* faire dévier (**from** de); **they tried to s. him onto something else** ils ont essayé de le faire dévier sur un autre sujet; **he's easily sidetracked** il se laisse facilement distraire; **to be** *or* **get sidetracked** *(be diverted from one's aim)* se détourner de son but; *(digress)* s'écarter de son sujet

sidewalk [ˈsaɪdwɔːk] N *Am* trottoir *m*

▸▸ *Am* **s. café** café *m* avec terrasse

sideways [ˈsaɪdweɪz] ADV latéralement; *(to look)* en biais; *(to turn sth)* en travers, de biais; **to lean/fall s.** se pencher/tomber sur le côté; **to slide s.** *(of door etc)* coulisser latéralement; **to walk s.** marcher en crabe; **to put sth s. on to sth** mettre qch à angle droit avec qch

ADJ de côté; **s. motion** mouvement *m* latéral

sidewinder [ˈsaɪdwaɪndər] N **1** *(snake)* serpent *m* à sonnettes cornu **2** *Am (blow)* coup *m* sur le côté

siding [ˈsaɪdɪŋ] N *Rail* voie *f* de garage; *Br (secondary line)* embranchement *m*; *(of factory)* voie de raccordement; **goods s.** voie de chargement

sidle [ˈsaɪd(ə)l] VI **to s. up to sb** se glisser auprès de qn; **to s. out of the room** se glisser hors de la salle; **to s. along** s'avancer de côté *ou Fam* de guingois

SIDS [sɪdz] N *Med (abbr* **sudden infant death syndrome***)* mort *f* subite du nourrisson

siege [siːdʒ] N *Mil, Fig* siège *m*; **to lay s. to a town** assiéger une ville; **to raise the s.** lever le siège; **to declare a state of s.** déclarer l'état de siège; **to be under s.** être assiégé; **they have a s. mentality** ils se sentent persécutés

▸▸ **s. gun** *(in military history)* pièce *f* de siège

Siena [sɪˈenə] N Sienne

sienna [sɪˈenə] N **1** *(earth)* terre *f* de Sienne; **raw/burnt s.** terre de Sienne naturelle/brûlée **2** *(colour)* ocre *m* brun

ADJ ocre brun *inv*

sierra [sɪˈerə] N *Geog* sierra *f*

▸▸ **S. Leone** Sierra Leone *f*

siesta [sɪˈestə] N sieste *f*; **to take a s.** faire la sieste

sieve [sɪv] N *(with coarse mesh)* crible *m*; *(with fine mesh)* tamis *m*; *(for powders and liquids)* sas *m*; *(for liquids)* passoire *f*; **to pass sth through a s.** passer qch au tamis/au crible; *Fam* **he's got a memory like a s.** il a la tête comme une passoire; **this bucket leaks like a s.** ce seau est une vraie passoire

VT = **sift 1 1**

sift [sɪft] VT **1** *(flour)* tamiser, passer au tamis; *(sand etc)* cribler, passer au crible; **to s. sugar over a cake** saupoudrer un gâteau de sucre **2** *Fig (examine) (evidence)* examiner minutieusement, passer au crible; **to s. the facts** passer les faits au crible

VI *(of dust etc)* filtrer (**through** à travers); **the sand sifted through his fingers** le sable lui coulait entre les doigts

▸ **sift out** VT SEP *(remove by sifting) (impurities)* ôter en tamisant; *Fig (unsuitable candidates etc)* éliminer

▸ **sift through** VT INSEP *(facts, evidence)* parcourir

sifter [ˈsɪftər] N **1** *(sieve)* tamis *m*, crible *m* **2** *(for sugar)* saupoudroir *m*

sifting ['sɪftɪŋ] N tamisage m, criblage m; *Fig (examination) (of evidence etc)* examen m minutieux

sigh [saɪ] N soupir m; **heavy/deep/long(-drawn) s.** gros/profond/long soupir; **he breathed** *or* **heaved a s. of relief** il a poussé un soupir de soulagement; **with a s.** en soupirant, avec un soupir

VI soupirer, pousser un soupir; *Lit (of wind)* gémir; **to s. with relief** pousser un soupir de soulagement; *Old-fashioned* **to s. for sb/sth** soupirer pour *ou* après qn/qch

sighing ['saɪɪŋ] N soupirs mpl; *Lit (of wind)* plainte f

SIGHT [saɪt]

N vue **1–3** ▪ viseur **4** ▪ spectacle **5** ▪ site pittoresque **5** **VT** apercevoir **1** ▪ observer **1** ▪ viser **2**

N 1 *(faculty)* vue f; **to have good/bad s.** avoir une bonne/mauvaise vue; **to have long s.** avoir la vue longue, être presbyte; **short s.** myopie f; **to lose one's s.** perdre la vue

2 *(act of seeing)* **to catch s.** *or* **get a s. of sb/sth** apercevoir *ou* entrevoir qn/qch; **to lose s. of sb/sth** perdre qn/qch de vue; **to lose s. of the fact that ...** perdre de vue (le fait) que ...; **I can't bear the s. of him, I hate the very s. of him** je ne peux pas le sentir *ou* le voir; **I can't stand the s. of blood** je ne supporte pas la vue du sang; **to shoot sb at** *or* **on s.** faire feu *ou* tirer sur qn à vue; *Mus* **to play at s.** déchiffrer; *Com, Fin* **bill payable at s.** effet payable à vue; *Com* **we need to have s. of it first** il faut le voir d'abord; **to buy goods s. unseen** acheter des marchandises sans les avoir vues; **at first s.** à première vue, au premier abord; **at first s., everything seemed normal** à première vue, tout semblait normal; **to fall in love at first s.** avoir le coup de foudre (**with** pour); **it was (a case of) love at first s.** ce fut le coup de foudre; **to know sb by s.** connaître qn de vue; **to find favour in sb's s.** trouver grâce aux yeux de qn; *Med* **to have a s. test** faire vérifier sa vue

3 *(range of vision)* **to come into s.** (ap)paraître; **to be within s.** être à portée de vue, être en vue; **to be (with)in s. of land** avoir la terre en vue; **it sank within s. of land** il a coulé près des côtes; **land in s.!** terre!; **keep him in s.** ne le perdez pas de vue; **out of s.** caché aux regards; *Old-fashioned Sl (excellent)* sensas *inv*; **to vanish out of s.** disparaître; **to put sth out of s.** faire disparaître qch, cacher qch; **keep it out of s. of the kids** fais attention à ce que les gamins ne le voient pas; **to keep out of s.** se cacher, se dérober; **out of my s.!** hors de ma vue!, hors d'ici!; *Prov* **out of s. out of mind** loin des yeux, loin du cœur

4 *(aiming device) (of firearm)* viseur m; **front s.** guidon m; **back s.** cran m de mire; *(circular)* œilleton m; *(of sextant)* lumière f; **angle of s.** angle m de visée *ou* de site, site m; **line of s.** *(of optical instrument)* ligne f de visée; *(of firearm)* ligne de mire *ou* de tir; **to take a s. on sth** viser qch, mirer qch; *Mil* **telescopic s.** hausse f télescopique, hausse à lunette; **to adjust sights** prendre *ou* régler la hausse; **to have sb/sth in one's sights** avoir qn/qch en ligne de mire; *Fig* avoir qn/qch en vue; *Fig* **to have** *or* **set one's sights on sb/sth** avoir des vues sur qn/qch; **to set one's sights on becoming rich** avoir la ferme intention de devenir riche; *Fig* **to lower one's sights** viser moins haut

5 *(spectacle)* spectacle m; **sad s.** spectacle navrant; **it's a s. to see** cela vaut la peine d'être vu; **it was a s. for sore eyes** cela faisait plaisir à voir; **you're a s. for sore eyes!** c'est un plaisir de te voir!; **what a s. you are!, you**

look a s.! *(wet, dirty)* te voilà dans un drôle d'état!; *(ridiculous)* de quoi tu as l'air comme ça!; **the sights** *(scenic places)* les sites mpl pittoresques; *(of a city etc)* les monuments mpl, les curiosités fpl; **we're going to see the sights** nous allons visiter la ville/la région/etc

6 *Fig Fam* **not by a long s.** loin de là; *Fam* **a damn s. longer/harder/more expensive** vachement plus long/difficile/cher

7 *(for inspection purposes)* regard m

VT 1 *(see) (person, object, land)* apercevoir; *(star, planet etc)* observer; **a golden eagle has been sighted here twice** on a aperçu un aigle royal ici à deux reprises

2 **to s. a gun** *(aim)* viser; *(adjust sights of)* régler la lunette d'un fusil

▸▸ *Fin* **s. bill** effet m à vue; *Tech* **s. check** contrôle m à vue, contrôle visuel; *Fin* **s. deposit** dépôt m à vue; *Fin* **s. draft** traite f à vue; *Aut* **s. glass** hublot m de contrôle; **s. hole** *(for inspection purposes)* regard m; *Fin* **s. letter of credit** crédit m utilisable à vue

sighted ['saɪtɪd] ADJ qui voit

NPL **the s.** les voyants mpl

sighting ['saɪtɪŋ] N **several sightings of teal have been reported** on a vu des sarcelles à plusieurs reprises; **this is the first s. this year** c'est la première fois qu'on le/la/les voit cette année

sightless ['saɪtlɪs] ADJ aveugle; *Fig (eyes)* éteint

sightlessness ['saɪtlɪsnɪs] N cécité f

sightly ['saɪtlɪ] ADJ **not very s.** pas très beau à voir

sight-read VT & VI *Mus* déchiffrer

sight-reading N *Mus* déchiffrage m

sightsee ['saɪtsiː] VI visiter des monuments

sightseeing ['saɪtsiːɪŋ] N **I don't really enjoy s.** je n'aime pas tellement faire le touriste; **we spent the day s.** nous avons passé la journée à visiter le pays/les monuments; **to go s.** visiter la ville/la région/etc; **a s. tour of Paris** un tour de Paris

▸▸ **s. tour** visite f guidée

sightseer ['saɪtsiːər] N touriste mf

SIGN [saɪn]

N signe **1** ▪ indice **2** ▪ indication **2** ▪ enseigne **3** ▪ panneau **3** ▪ symbole **4** **VT** signer **1** ▪ embaucher **4** **VI** signer **1**

N 1 *(gesture)* signe m; **to make a s./signs to sb** faire (un) signe/des signes à qn; **s. of the cross** signe de la croix; **to make the s. of the cross** se signer; **s. of recognition** signe de reconnaissance; *Tel* **call s.** indicatif m d'appel

2 *(indication)* indice m, indication f; **a sure s.** un signe qui ne trompe pas; **it's a sure s. that ...** à n'en pas douter, c'est le signe que ...; **it's a good/bad s.** c'est bon/mauvais signe; **s. of the times** signe des temps; **as a s. of ...** en signe de ...; **no s. of ...** *(no trace of)* nulle *ou* aucune trace de ...; **there is no s. of an end to the recession** il n'y a aucun élément qui indiquerait la fin de la récession; **he gave no s. of having heard anything** il n'a manifesté en aucune façon avoir entendu quoi que ce soit; **to show no s. of life** ne donner aucun signe de vie, ne pas donner signe de vie; **there was no s. of her** elle n'y était pas; **is there any s. of him yet?** il ne serait pas arrivé, par hasard?; **is there any s. of the missing child?** est-ce qu'il y a une trace de l'enfant disparu?; **there is little s. of progress in the negotiations** les négociations ne semblent pas avancer; **if there's the slightest s. of unrest** s'il y a le moindre signe

d'agitation; **all the signs are that ...** tout porte à croire que ...; **the room showed signs of having been recently occupied** il était clair que la pièce avait récemment été occupée

3 *(of pub, inn etc)* enseigne f; *(notice)* panneau m; **(shop) s.** enseigne, écriteau m; **a 'for sale' s.** un écriteau 'à vendre'; **neon s.** enseigne *ou* réclame f au néon; **(road) s.** panneau de signalisation (routière); **road signs** *(collectively)* signalisation f routière; **follow the signs for Manchester** suivre les panneaux indiquant Manchester; **traffic s.** panneau de signalisation (routière)

4 *(symbol)* symbole m; **plus/minus s.** signe m plus/moins; **s. of the zodiac** signe du zodiaque; **lucky s.** signe de chance

VT 1 *(one's name, a document, cheque etc)* signer; *(bill of exchange)* accepter; *(contract)* signer, passer; *Fin* **to s. a bill** viser un effet; **to s. a deal** passer un marché; **the letter was signed by the president** la lettre portait la signature du président *ou* était signée de la main du président; *Law* **signed, sealed and delivered in the presence of ...** fait et signé en présence de ...

2 *(say in sign language)* **to s. sth** dire qch dans le langage des sourds-muets

3 *Old-fashioned (indicate by gesture)* **to s. assent** faire signe que oui; **to s. sb to do sth** faire signe à qn de faire qch

4 *Ftbl etc (player)* embaucher, engager; **he was signed to United for £1,000,000** il a été embauché par United pour 1 000 000 livres, il a signé un contrat de 1 000 000 livres avec United

VI 1 *(write signature)* signer; **to s. by proxy, to s. per pro** signer par procuration; **s. here** signez là; *Ftbl etc* **he signed for United** il a signé avec United

2 *(know sign language)* connaître le langage des sourds-muets; *(use sign language)* communiquer dans le langage des sourds-muets

3 *(indicate by gesture)* **to s. to sb to do sth** faire signe à qn de faire qch

▸▸ **s. language** langue f des signes; **s. painter** *(of lettering)* peintre m en lettres; *(of pub signs etc)* peintre d'enseignes **s. writer** *(of lettering)* peintre m en lettres; *(of pub signs etc)* peintre d'enseignes

▸ **sign away** VT SEP *(concede by signing) (right etc)* renoncer à *(par écrit)*; **to s. sth away to sb** céder qch par écrit à qn; **you're signing your life away** c'est comme si tu signais ton arrêt de mort; **to s. one's freedom away** renoncer à sa liberté *(en signant un contrat etc)*

▸ **sign for** VT INSEP *(acknowledge receipt of) (delivery, registered letter etc)* signer pour accuser réception de, émarger

▸ **sign in** VI *(sign when entering) (of employee)* pointer; *(of hotel guest)* signer à l'entrée; **all visitors must s. in** tous les visiteurs doivent signer en entrant

VT SEP *(gain entrance for)* signer pour faire entrer; **I'm a member, so I can s. you in** je suis membre, donc je peux vous faire entrer

▸ **sign off** VI 1 *Radio, TV* terminer l'émission *(en jouant l'indicatif)*; **it's time to s. off for today** il est l'heure de nous quitter pour aujourd'hui

2 *(close letter)* finir une lettre; **I'll s. off now and go to bed** je vais finir cette lettre maintenant et aller au lit

▸ **sign on** VT SEP *Mil (person)* engager; *(hire) (worker)* embaucher

VI 1 *(of worker)* être engagé, se faire embaucher; *(of soldier)* s'engager

2 *Br Fam (register for unemployment benefit)* s'inscrire au chômage; **Tuesday is my day for signing on** je pointe le mardi

3 *Comput* ouvrir une session

▸ **sign out** VI *(sign when leaving) (of employee)* pointer; *(of hotel guest)* signer à la sortie;

visitors must s. out les visiteurs doivent signer en sortant

VT SEP *(indicate departure of)* **could you s. me out?** est-ce que vous pouvez noter que je suis parti?

▸ **sign over VT SEP to s. sth over to sb** céder qch à qn (par écrit)

▸ **sign up VI 1** *(register)* s'inscrire (**for a course** *etc* à un cours*etc*)

2 *(enlist) (of soldier)* s'engager

VT SEP *Sport, Theat etc (player, actor etc)* *(hire)* donner un contrat à, engager; **can I s. you up as a driver?** est-ce que je peux vous inscrire comme chauffeur?

signal ['sɪgn(ə)l] **N 1** signal *m*, -aux; *Fig* signe *m*; **warning s.** signal avertisseur *ou* d'avertissement; **alarm s.** signal d'alarme *ou* d'alerte; **all clear s.** signal de fin d'alerte; **time s.** signal horaire; *Sport etc* **starting s.** signal de du départ; *Tel* **call** *or Am* **line s.** indicatif *m* d'appel; *Am* **busy s.** tonalité *f* de ligne occupée; **to give/send/receive a s.** faire/envoyer/recevoir un signal; **when I give the s.** quand je donne/donnerai le signal; *Fig* **he's putting out a lot of confusing signals** son attitude n'est pas claire; *Fig* **we don't want to send the wrong signals** nous ne voulons pas induire les gens en erreur (par notre comportement); **you're sending all the wrong signals if you want her to realize you're attracted to her** si tu veux qu'elle comprenne que tu es attiré par elle, il faut que ton attitude le montre; **his statement sent all the right signals** sa déclaration a clairement laissé voir ses intentions; **the demonstration is a clear s. to the government to change its policy** la manifestation signifie clairement que le gouvernement doit changer de politique; **traffic signals** feux *mpl* de circulation; **light s.** signal lumineux; *Mil* **arm** *or* **hand s.** signal à bras; **semaphore s.** signal sémaphorique; *Naut* **signal à bras; flag s.** *Mil* signal par fanion(s); *Naut* signal à pavillon; *Rail* signal par drapeau; **Morse signals** signaux Morse; **stop s.** signal d'arrêt immédiat; *Br Mil* **Signals** transmissions; *Br Mil* **Signals officer** officier *m* des transmissions

2 *Electron, Radio etc* signal *m*, -aux; **input/output s.** signal *m* d'entrée/de sortie; **I can't get a s.** *(on mobile phone)* je n'ai pas de réception

ADJ ATTRIB *Lit (success)* éclatant, remarquable; *(failure)* notoire; *(service)* insigne; *(importance)* capital, -aux; **a s. lack of sth** un manque flagrant de qch

VI **(-ll-**, *Am* **-l-)** faire un signal/des signaux (**to** à); **I signalled to him (to stop)** je lui ai fait signe (de s'arrêter); **she signalled for the bill** elle a fait signe qu'on lui apporte l'addition; *Aut etc* **to s. before stopping** *(with hand)* prévenir *ou* avertir avant de s'arrêter; *Aut* **he didn't s. before he turned** *(with light)* il n'a pas mis son clignotant avant de tourner; *(with hand)* il n'a pas fait signe avant de tourner

VT *(order)* transmettre; *(train, ship)* faire signe à; *Aut* **to s. that one is turning** *(with hand)* signaler un changement de direction; *(with light)* mettre son clignotant avant de tourner; **the train was signalled to stop** le train a reçu le signal de s'arrêter; **this signals the start of the rainy season** cela indique le début *ou* c'est le signe du début de la saison des pluies; **her resignation signalled the beginning of the end** sa démission a marqué le début de la fin; **he signalled the car on** il a fait signe à la voiture d'avancer

▸▸ *Naut* **s. book** code *m* international des signaux; *Rail* **s. box** poste *m* de signalisation; **s. communications** télécommunications *fpl*, transmissions *fpl*; **s. flag** *Mil* fanion *m* de signalisation; *Naut* pavillon *m* pour signaux; **s. flare** *(rocket)* fusée *f* éclai-

rante; *(stationary)* feu *m* de Bengale; **s. frequency** fréquence *f* du signal; **s. lamp** *(for making signals)* lampe *f ou* projecteur *m* de signalisation; *(serving as a signal)* (lampe) témoin *m*; **s. light** *Naut* fanal *m*, -aux; *Mil* voyant *m* (lumineux); *Am* **s. red** vermillon *m* chinois; **s. rocket** fusée de signalisation; **s. strength** intensité *f* du signal

signalize ['sɪgnəlaɪz] **VT** *(victory, success)* marquer

signaller ['sɪgnələr] **N** signaleur *m*

signalling, *Am* **signaling** ['sɪgnəlɪŋ] **N 1** *(act)* signalisation *f*, *(sending signals)* transmission *f* de signaux; *Naut* pavillon *m* pour signaux; *Rail* drapeau *m* **2** *(signals)* signaux *mpl*

▸▸ **s. flag** *Naut* pavillon de signalisation; *Mil* drapeau de signalisation

signally ['sɪgnəlɪ] **ADV** *Lit* remarquablement, d'une façon éclatante; **... which he had s. failed to do** ... ce qu'il avait totalement manqué de faire; **the performance was s. lacking in enthusiasm** l'interprétation manquait singulièrement d'enthousiasme

signalman, *pl* **signalmen** ['sɪgnəlmən] **N** signaleur *m*; *(using semaphore)* sémaphoriste *m*; *Rail* bloqueur *m*

signatory ['sɪgnət(ə)rɪ] **N** signataire *mf* (**to a treaty** d'un traité)

ADJ *(nation)* signataire

signature ['sɪgnətʃər] **N 1** signature *f*, *Admin* visa *m*; **to put one's s. to a letter** apposer sa signature au bas d'une lettre; **his s. was on the letter** la lettre portait sa signature; *Com etc* **for s.** pour signature; **s. by proxy** signature par procuration **2** *Typ (mark)* signature *f*, *(pages)* cahier *m* d'imprimerie **3** *Mus* **(key) s.** armature *f*

▸▸ **s. book** parapheur *m*; **s. file** fichier *m* signature, signature; **s. line** fichier signature, signature; **s. stamp** griffe *f*; *Br Radio, TV* **s. tune** indicatif *m* (musical)

signboard ['saɪnbɔːd] **N** *(of pub, shop etc)* enseigne *f*

signet ['sɪgnɪt] **N** sceau *m*, cachet *m*

▸▸ **s. ring** chevalière *f*; *Hist (for sealing)* anneau *m* sigillaire

significance [sɪg'nɪfɪkəns] **N 1** *(importance)* importance *f*, portée *f*, **event of no/of great s.** événement sans importance/de la plus haute importance **2** *(meaning) (of word, gesture etc)* signification *f*, **what is the s. of this ceremony?** que signifie cette cérémonie?; **she gave him a look of deep s.** elle lui glissa un regard très significatif **3** *(in statistics)* signification *f*

significant [sɪg'nɪfɪkənt] **ADJ 1** *(event, difference, improvement etc)* important, significatif; *(amount of money)* important; **do you think this is s.?** pensez-vous que cela a de l'importance?; **what's s. about it is that ...** ce qu'il y a d'important là-dedans, c'est que ... **2** *(word, gesture)* significatif; *(look)* lourd de sens **3** *(in statistics)* significatif

▸▸ **s. figures** chiffres *mpl* significatifs; **s. other** partenaire *mf (dans une relation affective)*; *Psy* = personne *f* dont on se sent très proche

significantly [sɪg'nɪfɪkəntlɪ] **ADV 1** *(appreciably) (to differ)* sensiblement; **s. cheaper** sensiblement moins cher; **it's not s. different** ça ne fait pas une grosse différence; **there have been s. fewer problems** on a nettement moins de problèmes **2** *(in a meaningful way) (to look at etc)* d'une manière significative; **she paused s. at this point** à ce moment-là, elle s'est interrompue et son silence était lourd de sens; **s., no one mentioned it** personne n'a mentionné ce point, ce qui, en soi, était très significatif

signification [sɪgnɪfɪ'keɪʃən] **N** *Fml (of word, event)* signification *f*, sens *m*

significative [sɪg'nɪfɪkətɪv] **ADJ** révélateur, -trice (**of** de)

signify ['sɪgnɪfaɪ] **VT 1** *(indicate)* signifier, indiquer; **a broad forehead signifies intelligence** un front large est (un) signe d'intelligence **2** *(mean)* signifier, vouloir dire; *(make known) (one's intentions etc)* signifier, faire connaître

VI importer; **it doesn't s.** cela n'a aucune importance, peu importe

signing ['saɪnɪŋ] **N 1** *(of document etc)* signature *f*, *(of deed)* passation *f*, *Com (of bill)* acceptation *f*; **s. for the post** émargement *m* du courrier; **a manager with s. authority** un fondé de pouvoir **2** *(sign language)* langage *m* des sourds-muets; **her s. is excellent** elle connaît très bien le langage des sourds-muets **3** *Ftbl etc* transfert *m*

signing-in **N** *(of employees)* pointage *m*

sign-off **N** *TV* annonce *f* de la fin des émissions

signpost ['saɪnpəʊst] **N** poteau *m* indicateur; *Fig* jalon *m*, point *m* de repère

VT *(road etc)* signaliser, marquer de poteaux indicateurs; *Fig (thesis, meaning, references etc)* signaler; **well-/badly signposted road** route qui est bien/mal signalisée; **signposted footpath** sentier *m* balisé

signposting ['saɪnpəʊstɪŋ] **N** signalisation *f* routière; *Fig* **despite obvious s. from the author, some readers failed to spot that ...** bien que l'auteur ait placé des indices très clairs ici et là, certains lecteurs n'ont pas vu que ...

Sikh [siːk] **ADJ, N** *Rel* sikh

silage ['saɪlɪdʒ] **N** *Agr* ensilage *m*

silence ['saɪləns] **N** silence *m*; **s.!** silence!; *(notice in library etc)* défense de parler; **there was a sudden s.** soudain, il y a eu un silence; **to break the s.** rompre le silence; **a shot broke the s.** un coup de feu déchira le silence; **to reduce sb to s.** réduire qn au silence, faire taire qn; **there's been complete s. from head office** le siège est resté totalement silencieux; **a deafening s.** un silence éloquent; **to suffer in s.** souffrir en silence; **to buy sb's s.** acheter le silence de qn; **to write to sb after five years' s.** écrire à qn après un silence de cinq ans; **to pass over sth in s.** passer qch sous silence; **the s. of the night** le silence de la nuit; *Prov* **s. is golden** le silence est d'or

VT *(person)* réduire au silence, faire taire; *(the opposition)* réduire au silence; *(pupils etc)* imposer le silence à; *(one's conscience, criticism)* faire taire; *(complaints)* étouffer; *Mil (enemy fire)* faire cesser, faire taire; *(muffle) (noise)* amortir, étouffer; **that really silenced him!** *(made speechless)* ça l'a laissé sans voix!

silencer ['saɪlənsər] **N 1** *Br Aut (on exhaust)* silencieux *m* **2** *(on gun)* silencieux *m*

silent ['saɪlənt] **ADJ 1** *(person, place etc)* silencieux; *(taciturn)* silencieux, taciturne, peu loquace; **to fall s.** devenir silencieux; **he's trying to come across as the strong, s. type** il veut qu'on le prenne pour un mec viril; *Hum* **he's the strong, s. type** c'est un viril; **to keep s.** observer le silence; *(not reveal information)* garder le silence, se taire (**about** sur); **to remain s.** rester muet, -ette; **be s.!** taisez-vous!; **they stood a minute in s. memory of ...** ils ont observé une minute de silence à la mémoire de ...; **to give sb the s. treatment** ne pas adresser la parole à qn; **as the grave** muet comme une tombe; **the document is s. on this point** le document ne dit rien sur ce point; **stars of the s. screen** vedettes du cinéma muet

2 *Ling (letter)* muet, -ette; **the k is s.** le k ne se prononce pas, le k est muet

N *Cin* film *m* muet; **the silents** le (cinéma) muet

▸▸**s. actor** acteur de film(s) muet(s); **s. actress** actrice de film(s) muet(s); **s. camera** caméra *f* muette; **s. film** film muet; **s. majority** majorité *f* silencieuse; **s. movie** film muet; *Rel* **s. order** ordre *m* silencieux; *Am Com* **s. partner** (associé *m*) commanditaire *m*, bailleur *m* de fonds; **s. protest** manifestation *f* silencieuse

silently ['saɪləntlɪ] ADV *(to walk, move, do sth)* sans faire de bruit, silencieusement; *(to nod, sit)* en silence; *(to change sth)* discrètement

silex ['saɪleks] N *Miner* silex *m*

silhouette [sɪlu:'et] N silhouette *f*; **in s.** en silhouette
▸VT silhouetter, projeter en silhouette; **to be silhouetted against a light background** se détacher (en silhouette) sur un fond clair; **a tree silhouetted against the sky** un arbre qui se détachait *ou* qui se découpait sur le ciel
▸▸*TV, Cin* **s. lighting** éclairage *m* en contre-jour

silica ['sɪlɪkə] N *Chem* silice *f*; **s. gel desiccant crystals** cristaux *mpl* dessiccatifs de Silica gel®

silicate ['sɪlɪkət] N *Chem* silicate *m*

siliceous [sɪ'lɪʃəs] ADJ *Chem* siliceux

silicon ['sɪlɪkən] N *Chem* silicium *m*
▸▸**s. chip** puce *f*; **S. Glen** = appellation *f*, formée sur le modèle de Silicon Valley ("glen" signifie "vallée" en écossais), d'une région du centre de l'Écosse où sont concentrées un grand nombre de sociétés informatiques; **s. technology** technologie *f* du silicium; **S. Valley** Silicon Valley *f* (centre de l'industrie électronique américaine, situé en Californie); **s. wafer** tranche *f* de silicium

silicone ['sɪlɪkəʊn] N *Chem* silicone *f*
▸▸**s. implant** implant *m* mammaire en silicone; **s. rubber** caoutchouc *m* silicone

silicosis [sɪlɪ'kəʊsɪs] N *Med* silicose *f*

silk [sɪlk] N **1** *(fabric, fibre)* soie *f*; *(thread)* fil *m* de soie; **raw s.** soie grège *ou* écrue; **artificial s.** rayonne *f*, **a black s. dress** une robe de soie noire; **fine ladies in their silks and satins** de belles dames dans leurs plus beaux atours **2** *Horseracing* **silks** *(of jockey)* casaque *f* **3** *Br Law Fam* (King's, Queen's Counsel) conseiller *m* du roi/de la reine; *(collectively)* conseillers du roi/de la reine; **to take s.** être nommé conseiller du roi/de la reine
▸▸**s. screen printing** sérigraphie *f*; **s. finish** similisage *m*; **the S. Road** la route de la soie; **s. stockings** bas *mpl* de soie

silken ['sɪlk(ə)n] ADJ *Lit* **1** *Tex* de soie; *Fig (curls)* soyeux, de soie **2** *(voice, words)* doux, *f* douce, *Pej* doucereux, mielleux

silkiness ['sɪlkɪnɪs] N **1** *(of fabric)* nature *f* soyeuse **2** *(of voice, words)* moelleux *m*, *Pej* mielleux *m*

silkworm ['sɪlkwɜ:m] N ver *m* à soie
▸▸**s. breeder** sériciculteur, -trice; **s. breeding** sériciculture *f*; **s. farm** magnanerie *f*, **s. moth** bombyx *m* du mûrier; **s. nursery** magnanerie

silky ['sɪlkɪ] ADJ **1** *(like silk) (fabric, hair, cheek)* soyeux **2** *(suave) (tone, manner)* doux, *f* douce **3** *(made of silk)* en soie

sill [sɪl] N *Constr etc (of door)* seuil *m*; *(of window)* rebord *m*, appui *m*; *(of frame)* sole *f*, semelle *f*, *Aut* bas *m* de marche

sillabub ['sɪləbʌb] N *Culin* = entremets *m* sucré semblable au sabayon

silliness ['sɪlɪnɪs] N sottise *f*, bêtise *f*, **that's enough s. for one morning** assez de bêtises pour ce matin

silly ['sɪlɪ] ADJ *(person)* sot, *f* sotte, stupide; *(question, answer)* stupide; **don't be so s.!** ne sois pas si bête!; **I'll pay – don't be s.!** je vais payer – il n'en est pas question!; **(you) s. fool** *or* **ass!** imbécile!, espèce d'idiot!; **it would make me look s.** j'aurais l'air bête *ou* ridicule; **that was a s. thing to do!** ça *ou* ce n'était pas très intelligent!; **to say something s.** dire une bêtise; **but that's s., she was here half an hour ago** mais c'est ridicule, elle était ici il y a une demi-heure; **there was a new manager every week, it was** *or* **things were getting s.** il y avait un nouveau gérant chaque semaine, ça en devenait ridicule; **it was s. of me to ask** c'était idiot de ma part de demander ça; **he's forgotten his umbrella, (the) s. man** il a oublié son parapluie, cet idiot; *Journ Fam* **the s. season** = la période creuse des mois d'été; **to laugh oneself s.** mourir de rire; **to worry sb s.** rendre qn malade d'inquiétude; **she's been worrying herself s.** elle est morte d'inquiétude; **she'll worry herself s.** elle se rendra malade d'inquiétude (**about** à cause de); **to knock sb s.** étourdir *ou* assommer qn
▸N *Fam* idiot, -ote; **don't be such a s.!** que tu es bête!

sillybilly ['sɪlɪbɪlɪ] N *Fam (to child)* gros bêta *m*, grosse bêtasse *f*, **don't be such a s.!** ne sois pas si bête!; **oh, I am a s.!** oh, que je suis bête!

silo ['saɪləʊ] N *Agr, Mil* silo *m*

silt [sɪlt] N boue *f*, *(in waterway)* dépôt *m*, vase *f*, limon *m*
▸VT = silt up
▸**silt up** VI *(of harbour etc)* s'envaser
▸VT SEP *(fill with silt) (port, canal)* envaser

silting up N *(of port, canal etc)* envasement *m*

silty ['sɪltɪ] ADJ limoneux

silver ['sɪlvər] N **1** *(metal)* argent *m* **2** *Br (coins)* pièces *fpl* en argent; **a pound in s.** une livre en argent, une livre en pièces *ou* en monnaie d'argent **3** *(silverware)* argenterie *f* **4** *Sport (medal)* médaille *f* d'argent; **to get a s. in the shot put** remporter une médaille d'argent au lancer du poids **5** *(colour)* (couleur *f*) argent *m*
▸ADJ **1** *(made of silver)* en argent, d'argent; **is that spoon s.?** est-ce que cette cuiller est en argent?; *Prov* **he was born with a s. spoon in his mouth** il est né coiffé **2** *(in colour)* argenté, argent *inv*; **s. hair** des cheveux argentés; *Prov* **every cloud has a s. lining** à quelque chose malheur est bon; **to look for the s. lining** regarder le bon côté des choses **3** *(sound)* argentin; **she has a s. tongue** elle sait parler
▸VT *(mirror)* étamer; *(cutlery etc)* argenter; *Lit (waves etc)* argenter
▸▸**s. birch** bouleau *m* blanc; **s. bromide** bromure *m* d'argent; **s. fox** renard *m* argenté; **s. gilt** vermeil *m*, argent recouvert d'or; **s. grey** gris *m* argenté; *Sport etc* **s. medal** médaille d'argent; **s. paper** papier *m* d'argent; **s. plate** *(layer of silver)* plaqué *m* argent; *(tableware)* argenterie *f*, **s. plating** argentage *m*; *(layer)* argenture *f*; **s. service** *(in restaurant)* service *m* de grande classe; **s. service waiter** serveur *m* pour service au guéridon; **s. service waitress** serveuse *f* pour service au guéridon; **the s. screen** le grand écran; *Comput Fam* **s. surfer** internaute *mf* âgé(e); **s. wedding** noces *fpl* d'argent

silverfish ['sɪlvəfɪʃ] N **1** *(fish)* argentine *f* **2** *(insect)* lépisme *m*, petit poisson *m* d'argent

silver-haired ['sɪlvəheəd] ADJ aux cheveux argentés

silver-plate VT argenter

silver-plated ADJ argenté

silverside ['sɪlvəsaɪd] N *Br Culin* gîte *m* à la noix

silversmith ['sɪlvəsmɪθ] N orfèvre *m*

silverware ['sɪlvəweər] N argenterie *f*

silverwork ['sɪlvəwɜ:k] N orfèvrerie *f*

silvery ['sɪlvərɪ] ADJ *Lit (cloud, water)* argenté; *(scales etc)* d'argent; *(laugh)* argentin

SIM [sɪm] N *Tel (abbr* **subscriber identity module)**
▸▸**S. card** *(in mobile phone)* carte *f* SIM

simian ['sɪmɪən] ADJ *Zool* simien; *Fig (gait, appearance etc)* simiesque
▸N *Zool* simien *m*

similar ['sɪmɪlər] ADJ semblable (**to** à), pareil (**to** à), similaire; *Math (triangles)* semblable; **your case is s. to mine** votre cas est semblable au mien; **they are s. in appearance** d'apparence, ils sont semblables; **the two women are s.** les deux femmes se ressemblent; **there was a s. mistake on page 1** il y avait une erreur semblable à la page 1; **something s. happened to me** il m'est arrivé quelque chose de semblable

similarity [sɪmɪ'lærɪtɪ] N ressemblance *f*, *Math (of triangles)* similitude *f*, **there the s. ends** c'est là que s'arrête la comparaison

similarly ['sɪmɪləlɪ] ADV pareillement; **they were s. dressed** ils/elles étaient habillé(e)s de la même façon; **s., ...** de même ...

simile ['sɪmɪlɪ] N comparaison *f*

similitude [sɪ'mɪlɪtju:d] N *Fml (resemblance)* ressemblance *f*, similitude *f*, *(comparison)* comparaison *f*

SIMM [sɪm] N *Comput (abbr* **single in-line memory module)** SIMM *m*

simmer ['sɪmər] N *Culin* **to keep sth at a s.** *or* **on the s.** (faire) mijoter qch, faire cuire qch à petit feu *ou* à feu doux
▸VI **1** *Culin etc (of liquid)* frémir; *(of food in pot)* mijoter, cuire à petit feu *ou* à feu doux **2** *Fig (of revolt, discontent etc)* fermenter; **he was simmering with rage** il bouillonnait de rage
▸VT *Culin (stew etc)* mijoter, mitonner
▸**simmer down** VI *(of person)* se calmer

simnel ['sɪmn(ə)l] N
▸▸*Br* **s. cake** gâteau *m* de Pâques *ou* de la mi-carême

simoleon [sɪ'məʊlɪən] N *Am Fam (dollar)* dollar *m*

Simon ['saɪmən] N Simon *m*
▸▸**S. says** *(game)* Jacques a dit *m*

simon crane ['saɪmən] N *TV, Cin* grue *f* hydraulique

simony ['saɪmənɪ] N *Rel* simonie *f*

simp [sɪmp] N *Am Fam* andouille *f*, crétin, -ine

simper ['sɪmpər] N minauderies *fpl*, **..., he said with a s.** ..., dit-il en minaudant; **she puts on when ...** la façon dont elle minaude quand ...
▸VI minauder, mignarder; *(smile affectedly)* sourire avec affectation; **I could hear him simpering down the phone to her** je l'entendais lui dire des minauderies au téléphone

simpering ['sɪmpərɪŋ] ADJ mignard, affecté
▸N minauderie *f*, **I've had enough of her s.** j'en ai assez de ses minauderies

simple ['sɪmp(ə)l] ADJ *(method etc)* simple, élémentaire; *(character)* simple, naturel; *(naive)* simple, naïf, -ïve, crédule; **he's a bit s.** il est un peu simplet; **for the s. reason that ...** pour la simple raison que ...; **I'm not so s. as to believe that** je n'ai pas la naïveté de croire cela; **to become simpler** se simplifier; **the simplest thing to do is to ...** le plus simple est de ...; **a meal that is s. to prepare** un repas qui est simple à préparer; **he won't understand, keep it s.** il ne va rien comprendre, reste simple; **let's keep it s.** restons simples; **it's as s. as that** c'est aussi simple que ça; **in s. terms** avec des mots simples; **reduced to its simplest terms** réduit à sa plus simple expression; **to have s. tastes** avoir des goûts simples; **that's the s. truth** c'est la vérité pure et simple

▸ ▸ *Med* **s. fracture** fracture *f* simple; *Fin* **s. interest** intérêts *mpl* simples; *St Exch* **s. position** position *f* élémentaire; *Gram* **s. sentence** proposition *f* indépendante

simple-hearted ['hɑːtɪd] ADJ simple, ingénu, candide

simple-minded ADJ simple (d'esprit), simplet, -ète; *(naive)* naïf, -ïve, candide

simple-mindedness [-'maɪndɪdnɪs] N simplicité *f*, *(naiveness)* naïveté *f*, candeur *f*

simpleness ['sɪmp(ə)lnɪs] N = **simplicity**

simple-rank order N *Mktg* classement *m* simple

simpleton ['sɪmp(ə)ltən] N nigaud, -aude, niais, -aise

simplex ['sɪmpleks] N *Ling (of word)* forme *f* de base

simplicity [sɪm'plɪsɪtɪ] N **1** *(candour) (of child etc)* candeur *f*, simplicité *f*; *(foolishness)* bêtise *f*, sottise *f* **2** *(of problem, dress etc)* simplicité *f*; **it's s. itself** c'est simple comme bonjour

simplification [sɪmplɪfɪ'keɪʃən] N simplification *f*

simplify ['sɪmplɪfaɪ] VT simplifier

simplistic [sɪm'plɪstɪk] ADJ simpliste; **am I being too s.?** est-ce que je simplifie trop?

simply ['sɪmplɪ] ADV **1** *(in simple manner) (to speak, act)* simplement; *(dressed)* avec simplicité **2** *(absolutely)* absolument; **it's s. impossible** c'est tout bonnement impossible; **I s. won't do it** je refuse absolument de le faire; **I was s. amazed by it** j'en étais tout à fait abasourdi **3** *(just)* tout simplement; **purely and s.** purement et simplement; **it's s. a matter** *or* **question of time** c'est une simple question de temps, c'est tout simplement une question de temps

simulacrum, *pl* **simulacra** [sɪmjʊ'leɪkrəm, -ə] N *Fml* simulacre *m*

simulate ['sɪmjʊleɪt] VT **1** *(imitate) (illness etc)* simuler, feindre; *(enthusiasm etc)* affecter; **simulated leather** similicuir *m*; **simulated fur** fausse fourrure *f*, **simulated marble** marbre *m* artificiel; *(painted)* faux marbre **2** *Tech* simuler; **simulated test marketing** marché-test *m* simulé

simulation [sɪmjʊ'leɪʃən] N simulation *f*

simulator ['sɪmjʊleɪtər] N *Tech (device)* simulateur *m*; **flight s.** simulateur de vol

simulcast ['saɪməlkɑːst] ADJ radiotélévisé N émission *f* radiotélévisée VT diffuser simultanément sur différents médias

simultaneity [sɪməltə'neɪɪtɪ] N simultanéité *f*

simultaneous [sɪməl'teɪnɪəs] ADJ simultané; **s. with ...** qui a lieu en même temps que ...

▸ ▸ **s. broadcast** émission *f* diffusée simultanément, retransmission *f* simultanée; *Math* **s. equations** système *m* d'équations simultanées; **s. interpreting** interprétation *f* simultanée

simultaneously [sɪməl'teɪnɪəslɪ] ADV simultanément, en même temps

sin [sɪn] N péché *m*; *Fam (against taste etc)* offense *f*; **sins of omission/commission** péchés par omission/action; **original s.** péché originel; **the seven deadly sins** les sept péchés capitaux; **the forgiveness of sins** le pardon des offenses; *Old-fashioned* **Hum to live in s.** vivre dans le péché; *Fam Hum* **for my sins, I was appointed ...** pour mes péchés, j'ai été nommé ...; *Fam* **if it's not a s. to ask ...** s'il est permis de poser la question ...; *Fam* **it would be a s. to stay indoors on a**

day like this c'est un crime de rester à l'intérieur par une si belle journée VI **(-nn-)** pécher, commettre un péché/des péchés; **to s. against** *(the proprieties)* pécher contre, blesser; *(a rule etc)* manquer à; **more sinned against than sinning** plus à plaindre qu'à blâmer

▸ ▸ *Sport* **s. bin** banc *m* des pénalités; prison *f*, *Hum* **s. tax** = appellation *f* humoristique de la taxe sur l'alcool et le tabac

Sinai ['saɪnaɪ] N Sinaï *m*; **Mount S.** le mont Sinaï

▸ ▸ **the S. Peninsula** la presqu'île de Sinaï

since [sɪns] ADV **1** depuis; **I've not seen him s.** je ne l'ai pas revu depuis; **he's been in perfect health ever s.** depuis (lors), il est en parfaite santé **2** *(ago)* **she had long s. given up hope of promotion** elle avait, depuis longtemps, abandonné tout espoir de promotion; **long s.** *(for a long time)* depuis longtemps; *(a long time ago)* il y a longtemps; **not long s.** il n'y a pas très longtemps; *Old-fashioned* **many years s.** il y a bien des années

PREP depuis; **s. his death** depuis sa mort; **s. early June** dès les premiers jours de juin; **I've been here (ever) s. lunch** je suis là depuis le déjeuner; **she has lived here s. 1998** elle vit ici depuis 1998; **she had lived there s. 1996** elle vivait là depuis 1996; **I haven't seen her s. Christmas** je ne l'ai pas vue depuis Noël; **s. then, s. that time** depuis ce temps-là, depuis lors; **s. when?** depuis quand?; *Fam* **s. when do you come into a room without knocking?** depuis quand est-ce qu'on entre sans frapper?; **s. seeing you** depuis que je vous ai vu SEE GRAMMAR B31

CONJ **1** *(in time)* depuis que; **s. I've been here** depuis que je suis ici; **it's a long time s. I saw her** il y a longtemps que je ne l'ai vue, ça fait longtemps que je ne l'ai pas vue; **(ever) s. I have lived in London** depuis que j'habite (à) Londres; **s. he had been there** depuis qu'il était là SEE GRAMMAR B31 **2** *(because)* puisque; **I'll do it s. it's you that's asking** je le ferai puisque c'est vous qui me le demandez

sincere [sɪn'sɪər] ADJ sincère; **he is completely s.** il est de bonne foi

sincerely [sɪn'sɪəlɪ] ADV sincèrement; **it is my s. held conviction that ...** je suis sincèrement convaincu que ...; *Br* **Yours s.,** *Am* **S. yours** *(letter ending)* veuillez agréer, Monsieur *etc*, l'expression de mes sentiments distingués *ou* les meilleurs

sincerity [sɪn'serɪtɪ] N *(of person)* sincérité *f*, bonne foi *f*; *(of emotion)* sincérité; **in all s.** de la meilleure foi du monde, en toute sincérité

sine [saɪn] N *Math (of angle)* sinus *m*

▸ ▸ *Law* **s. die** sine die; *Law* **s. qua non** condition *f* sine qua non

sinecure ['saɪnɪkjʊər] N sinécure *f*

sinew ['sɪnjuː] N *Anat* tendon *m*

sinewy ['sɪnjuːɪ] ADJ **1** *(meat)* tendineux **2** *(arm etc)* musclé, nerveux

sinful ['sɪnfʊl] ADJ *(deed, urge, thought)* coupable, honteux; *(world)* plein de péchés, souillé par le péché; **his s. ways** sa vie de pécheur; **s. man** pécheur *m*; **s. woman** pécheresse *f*, **how could such pleasure be s.?** comment un tel plaisir pourrait-il être coupable?; **she thought alcohol was s.** pour elle, boire de l'alcool était un péché; **it's downright s.!** c'est un vrai scandale!

sinfully ['sɪnfʊlɪ] ADV *(to act)* d'une façon coupable; **it is s. wasteful to ...** c'est un gaspillage honteux de ...

sinfulness ['sɪnfʊlnɪs] N *(of behaviour, act)* caractère *m* scandaleux; **his/her s.** son état de pécheur/pécheresse; **a life of s.** une vie de péché

sing [sɪŋ] *(pt* **sang** [sæŋ]; *pp* **sung** [sʌŋ]) VI **1** *(of person, bird)* chanter; **I can't s.** je ne sais pas chanter **2** *(of the wind etc)* siffler; *(of the ears)* tinter, bourdonner; **the kettle is singing** la bouilloire chante *ou* siffle **3** *Sl (inform)* moucharder, balancer

VT *(song)* chanter; **s. me a song** chante-moi une chanson; **Sinatra sings the Beatles** Sinatra chante les Beatles; *Fig* **to s. another** *or* **a different tune** changer de ton; **to s. sb to sleep** chanter quelque chose pour endormir qn; **to s. sb's praises** chanter les louanges de qn

▸ **sing along** VI **s. along if you like** chantez avec moi/nous *etc* si vous voulez

▸ **sing of** VT INSEP *Lit* chanter

▸ **sing out** VI *(sing loudly)* chanter (plus) fort; *Fam* **s. out if you need me** *(call)* appelle-moi si vous avez/tu as besoin de moi

VT SEP *(note)* chanter clairement

▸ **sing up** VI *(sing louder)* chanter plus fort

singable ['sɪŋəb(ə)l] ADJ chantable

Singapore [sɪŋə'pɔːr] N Singapour *m*

Singaporean [sɪŋə'pɔːrɪən] ADJ singapourien

N Singapourien, -ienne

singe [sɪndʒ] VT *(accidentally)* brûler légèrement; *(clothes, hair)* roussir; *(deliberately) (poultry, hair)* flamber

N *(burn)* brûlure *f* (légère); *(mark)* marque *f* de brûlure

singer ['sɪŋər] N **1** *(artiste)* chanteur, -euse; **s. songwriter** auteur-compositeur-interprète *mf* **2** *Br Sl (informer)* indic *mf*

Singhalese [sɪŋgə'liːz] ADJ, N = **Sinhalese**

singing ['sɪŋɪŋ] ADJ *(bird)* qui chante; **to have a fine s. voice** chanter admirablement N *(of person, bird)* chant *m*; **his s. is awful** il chante atrocement

▸ ▸ **s. lesson** leçon *f* de chant; **s. telegram** = vœux *mpl* présentés sous forme chantée, généralement à l'occasion d'un anniversaire

SINGLE ['sɪŋg(ə)l]

N 45 tours **1** ▪ single **1** ▪ aller simple **1** ▪ célibataire **2**
ADJ seul **1** ▪ unique **1** ▪ pour une personne **2** ▪ célibataire **3**

N **1** *(record)* 45 tours *m*; *(CD or cassette)* single *m*; *(ticket)* aller *m* simple; *(banknote) (one pound)* billet *m* d'une livre; *(one dollar)* billet d'un dollar

2 *(unmarried person)* célibataire *mf*; **a package holiday for singles** des vacances organisées pour célibataires

3 *Tennis etc* **singles** simple *m*; **men's/women's singles** simple messieurs/dames

ADJ **1** *(just one)* seul; **one s. case of ...** un cas unique de ...; **every s. day** tous les jours; **to do sth in a s. movement** faire qch d'un seul geste; **not a s. one** pas un seul, pas un; **I haven't seen a s. soul** je n'ai pas vu âme qui vive; **in a s. moment** en une fois; **don't say a s. word** ne dites pas un (seul) mot

2 *(for one person, not double etc) (bed)* à une place, pour une personne; *(room)* à un lit, pour une personne; *Naut (cabin)* individuel; **in s. rank** sur un rang

3 *(not married)* célibataire, non-marié; **a s. man/woman** un/une célibataire; **he remained s.** il est resté célibataire

▸ ▸ *Phot* **s. camera** monocaméra *f*, **s. combat** combat *m* singulier; **s. currency** monnaie *f* unique; **S. European Market** Marché *m* unique européen; *Bot* **s. flower** fleur *f* simple; **s. market** marché unique; **s. occupancy** *(of hotel room)* occupation *f* par une seule personne; **s. parent** père *m*/mère *f* célibataire; *Admin* parent *m* isolé; **s. price** prix *m* unique; **s. quotes** guillemets *mpl*; **s. (room) supplement** supplément *m* chambre individuelle; **s. seater** *(vehicle)* monoplace *f; Comput* **s. sheet feed** alimentation *f* feuille à feuille; *Typ* **s. spacing** interlignage *m* simple; *Comput* **s. user licence** licence *f* individuelle d'utilisation; **s. yellow line** = ligne *f* jaune indiquant que le stationnement est autorisé à certaines heures

▶ **single out** VT SEP *(choose from many)* isoler, choisir; **she was singled out for praise** elle a fait l'objet de félicitations particulières; **why s. him out (for blame)?** pourquoi le blâmer en particulier?

single-breasted [-'brestɪd] ADJ *(jacket, coat)* droit

single-chamber ADJ *Pol* monocaméral, -aux

single-column ADJ *Typ* à une colonne

single-cylinder ADJ monocylindrique
▶▶ *Aut* **s. engine** moteur *m* monocylindrique

single-decker [dekər] N *Br* autobus *m* sans impériale

single-density ADJ *Comput (disk)* à simple densité

single-drive ADJ *(computer)* à un seul lecteur de disquettes

single-engined [-'endʒɪnd] ADJ monomoteur
▶▶ **s. aircraft** (avion *m*) monomoteur *m*

single-handed [-'hændɪd] ADV **I did it s.** je l'ai fait tout seul; **to sail s.** naviguer seul
ADJ **thanks to his s. efforts** grâce aux efforts qu'il a fournis seul

single-handedly [-'hændɪdlɪ] ADV seul, tout seul

single-income ADJ *(family, couple)* à salaire unique

single-lane ADJ *(traffic)* à voie unique

single-lens ADJ
▶▶ *Phot* **s. camera** appareil *m* photo monoculaire; *Phot* **s. reflex** reflex *m* (mono-objectif)

single-line ADJ *Aut* **s. traffic only** circulation *f* à une (seule) voie

single-minded ADJ *(in pursuit of a goal) (person)* constant; *(determination, pursuit of power)* farouche; *(convictions)* absolu; *(determined) (attitude, deeds)* résolu; **he was s. in his pursuit of power** sa soif de pouvoir était sans bornes

single-mindedly [-'maɪndɪdlɪ] ADV résolument

single-mindedness [-'maɪndɪdnɪs] N *(constancy)* constance *f*, *(determination)* résolution *f*

single-mode ADJ *Tel* single-mode

singleness ['sɪŋg(ə)lnɪs] N **with s. of purpose** avec un seul but en vue; **his s. of purpose** sa détermination

single-parent family N famille *f* monoparentale

single-phase ADJ *Elec (current)* monophasé
▶▶ **s. current** courant *m* monophasé

singles bar N bar *m* pour célibataires

single-sex ADJ non mixte
▶▶ **s. school** école *f* non-mixte

single-sided ADJ *Comput (disk)* à une seule face

single-spaced [-'speɪst] ADJ *Typ* à interligne simple

single-spoke ADJ *(steering wheel)* monobranche

singlet ['sɪŋglɪt] N *Br* maillot *m* de corps, *(of cotton, flannel)* gilet *m*; *Sport* maillot

single-tasking [-'tæskɪŋ] *Comput* N monotâche *m*
ADJ monotâche

singleton ['sɪŋg(ə)ltən] N *Cards, Math* singleton *m*

single-track ADJ
▶▶ **s. railway** chemin *m* de fer à voie unique; **s. road** route *f* à une seule voie

singly ['sɪŋglɪ] ADV *(one by one)* séparément, un à un; *Com* **articles sold s.** articles qui se vendent séparément *ou* à la pièce; **people entered s. or in pairs** les gens sont entrés seuls ou par deux

singsong ['sɪŋsɒŋ] ADJ *(tone)* chantant; **in a s. voice** d'un ton chantant
N *Fam (singing session)* concert *m* improvisé; **to have a s.** pousser la chansonnette

singular ['sɪŋgjʊlər] ADJ **1** *Gram (number)* singulier, -ière **2** *(remarkable)* rare, remarquable; *(strange)* singulier, -ière, bizarre
N *Gram* singulier *m*; **in the s.** au singulier
VOIR GRAMMAIRE A14–15

singularity [sɪŋgjʊˈlærɪtɪ] N *(remarkableness)* particularité *f*, *(strangeness)* bizarrerie *f*

singularize ['sɪŋgjʊləraɪz] VT singulariser

singularly ['sɪŋgjʊləlɪ] ADV *(remarkably)* singulièrement, remarquablement; **I was s. unimpressed** cela ne m'a vraiment pas impressionné

Sinhalese [sɪn(h)əˈliːz] ADJ cing(h)alais
N **1** *(person)* Cing(h)alais, -aise **2** *Ling* cing(h)alais *m*

sinister ['sɪnɪstər] ADJ **1** *(event, smile, atmosphere, appearance)* sinistre; *(air)* menaçant **2** *Her* senestre, sénestre

sink [sɪŋk] N **1** *(basin) (in kitchen)* évier *m*; **to pour sth down the s.** jeter qch dans l'évier; *Fig Lit* **s. of iniquity** lieu *m* de perdition *ou* de tous les vices
2 *Geol etc* bétoire *f*
VI *(pt* **sank** [sæŋk]; *pp* **sunk** [sʌŋk]; *Arch & as adj* **sunken** ['sʌŋkən]) **1** *(in water)* disparaître dans l'eau; *(of ship)* sombrer, couler; **to s. like a stone** *(of person)* couler à pic; *Fig* **here goes! s. or swim!** allons-y! il faut risquer le tout pour le tout!; **to s. into the mud/the snow** s'enfoncer dans la boue/la neige; **to s. into quicksand** s'enliser dans des sables mouvants
2 **to s. into one's memory** *(of facts etc)* se graver dans la mémoire; **to s. into oblivion** tomber dans l'oubli; **to s. into poverty/a life of crime/depression** s'enfoncer dans la pauvreté/le crime/la dépression; **to s. into a deep sleep** s'endormir profondément; **to s. into a coma** sombrer dans le coma; **sunk in thought** plongé dans ses pensées
3 *(subside)* **to s. (down)** *(of ground)* s'affaisser; *(of wall, building etc)* s'affaisser, se tasser; **to s. (down) into an armchair** *(of person)* se laisser tomber *ou* s'effondrer dans un fauteuil; **to s. to the ground** (se laisser) tomber à terre; **her heart sank at the news** à cette nouvelle, son cœur s'est serré; **his spirits sank** il perdit tout courage; **the sun is sinking** le soleil baisse
4 *(decrease) (of prices etc)* baisser; **the pound has sunk** la livre a chuté *ou* baissé; **they've sunk to the bottom of the league table** ils sont tombés tout en bas du classement; **the patient is sinking fast** le malade baisse *ou* décline rapidement; **her voice sank to a whisper** sa voix s'est réduite à un murmure; **he has sunk in my estimation** il a baissé *ou* diminué dans mon estime; **how could anyone s. so low?** comment peut-on tomber aussi bas?
VT **1** *(ship)* couler, faire sombrer, envoyer au fond; *Fam* **we're sunk** nous sommes fichus
2 *(well)* creuser, forer; *(stake etc)* enfoncer; **stone sunk into the wall** pierre encastrée dans le mur; **to s. one's teeth into sth** enfoncer ses dents dans qch; **they sank their differences** ils ont fait abstraction de leurs différences

3 *Fam (to drink)* s'envoyer; **to s. a pint** s'envoyer une pinte de bière
4 *Fin (debt)* amortir
5 **to s. money in a project** *(invest)* investir des capitaux dans un projet
6 **to s. the ball** *Billiards* mettre la bille dans la blouse; *Golf* envoyer la balle dans le trou
▶▶ **s. unit** bloc-évier *m*, *pl* blocs-éviers

▶ **sink in** VI **1** *(be absorbed) (of liquid)* pénétrer **2** *(be understood)* **her remark didn't s. in until later** ce n'est que plus tard que j'ai/il a *etc* compris le sens de sa remarque; **the lesson hasn't sunk in** la leçon n'a pas été retenue; **it was beginning to s. in that things had changed** je commençais/il commençait *etc* à comprendre que les choses avaient changé

sinker ['sɪŋkər] N *(of fishing rod)* plomb *m*

sinkhole ['sɪŋkhəʊl] N *Geol* entonnoir *m*

sinking ['sɪŋkɪŋ] ADJ *(ground)* qui s'enfonce, qui s'affaisse; *(wall etc)* qui se tasse; *(ship)* qui fait naufrage; **with a s. heart** avec un serrement de cœur; **I'm getting that s. feeling that something has happened** j'ai le pressentiment qu'il s'est passé quelque chose; **I get that s. feeling every time I think about what happened** à chaque fois que je pense à ce qui s'est passé, j'ai l'estomac qui se serre
N **1** *(of ship)* engloutissement *m*; *(intentional, in war etc)* torpillage *m* **2** *(subsiding) (of ground etc)* affaissement *m*; *(of building etc)* tassement *m* **3** *(of well)* creusage *m*, forage *m* **4** *Fin (of debt)* amortissement *m*
▶▶ *Fin* **s. fund** caisse *f* *ou* fonds *mpl* d'amortissement

sinless ['sɪnlɪs] ADJ sans péché; *(pure)* innocent, pur

sinner ['sɪnər] N pécheur *m*, pécheresse *f*

sinning ['sɪnɪŋ] N péché *m*

Sinologist [saɪˈnɒlədʒɪst, sɪ-] N sinologue *mf*

Sinology [saɪˈnɒlədʒɪ, sɪ-] N sinologie *f*

sinuosity [sɪnjʊˈɒsɪtɪ] N sinuosité *f*

sinuous ['sɪnjʊəs] ADJ **1** *(movement, river etc)* sinueux, tortueux **2** *(supple) (person)* souple, agile

sinus ['saɪnəs] N *Anat* sinus *m*; **I've got a bit of s. trouble** j'ai un problème de sinus

sinusitis [saɪnəˈsaɪtɪs] N *Med* sinusite *f*

Sioux [suː] ADJ sioux *inv*
N **1** Sioux *mf inv* **2** *Ling* sioux *m*

sip [sɪp] N petite gorgée *f*; **to drink sth in sips** siroter qch, boire qch à petits coups; **have a s. and see if you like it** goûte pour voir si tu aimes
VT (-pp-) *(tea, wine etc)* boire à petites gorgées *ou* à petits coups, siroter
VI **to s. at sth** boire qch à petites gorgées

siphon ['saɪf(ə)n] N siphon *m*
VT *(liquid)* siphonner

▶ **siphon off** VT SEP **1** *(liquid)* siphonner **2** *Fin (money, supplies etc)* détourner; *(staff)* prendre; **they siphoned off all the profits** ils ont détourné *ou Fam* pompé tous les bénéfices

sir [sɜːr, sər] N **1** *(as form of address to a superior, esp to an equal in US)* monsieur *m*; **yes, s.** oui, monsieur; *Mil etc (to superior officer)* oui, mon capitaine/mon colonel *etc*; *Naut* oui, commandant/amiral *etc*; **dinner is served, s.** monsieur est servi; **Dear S.** *(in letter)* Monsieur; *(less formal)* Cher Monsieur; **Dear Sirs** Messieurs; *Sch Fam* **s. told me** le maître me l'a dit **2** *(title)* sir (= titre d'un 'baronet' et d'un 'knight', ne s'emploie jamais sans le prénom, ainsi Sir Walter Scott, Sir Walter)

sire ['saɪər] N **1** *(in breeding)* père *m*; *(stallion)* étalon *m* **2** *Arch, Lit (father)* père *m*; *Arch (address to sovereign)* sire *m*
VT *(of stallion, man)* engendrer

siren ['saɪərən] N **1** *Myth*, sirène *f*; *Fig (temptress)* sirène, femme *f* fatale **2** *(device)* sirène *f*; **ambulance/police s.** sirène d'ambulance/de voiture de police
▸▸**s. song** chant de sirène

sirloin ['sɜːlɔɪn] N *Culin* aloyau *m (de bœuf)*; **a s. steak** un steak d'aloyau

sirocco [sɪ'rɒkəʊ] N *Met* siroc(c)o *m*

sirup ['sɪrəp] N *Am* = **syrup**

sis [sɪs] N *Fam (sister)* sœurette *f*, *Fam* frangine *f*

sisal ['saɪs(ə)l] N *(plant, fibre)* sisal *m*

sissy ['sɪsɪ] *Pej* N *(cowardly child etc)* poule *f* mouillée; *(effeminate man, boy)* garçon *m* efféminé; **that's a game for sissies!** c'est un jeu de filles!
ADJ *(cowardly)* lâche, peureux; *(effeminate)* efféminé; **he thinks it's s. to …** il pense que ça fait efféminé de …

sister ['sɪstər] N **1** *(in family)* sœur *f*; **sisters unite!** *(to female workers, feminists)* sœurs, unissez-vous! **2** *Am Fam (black woman)* = nom *m* donné par les Noirs américains à une femme noire; **you don't treat your sisters like that!** c'est pas des façons de traiter d'autre Noires! **3** *Rel* religieuse *f*, *(bonne)* sœur *f*; **S. of Mercy** sœur de la Charité; **come in, S.** entrez, ma sœur **4** *(nurse)* infirmière *f* chef; **thank you, s.** merci madame/mademoiselle
ADJ *(publication, hotel)* qui appartient au même groupe; **s. state/party** pays *m*/parti *m* frère; **s. company** société *f* sœur
▸▸**s. cities** villes *fpl* jumelées; **to be a s. city with** être jumelé avec; **s. ship** *(belonging to same company)* navire *m* de la même ligne; *(identical)* navire-jumeau *m*, *pl* navires-jumeaux, sister-ship *m*, *pl* sister-ships

sisterhood ['sɪstəhʊd] N **1** *Rel* communauté *f* religieuse *(de sœurs)* **2** *(solidarity)* solidarité *f* féminine; **the s.** *(women)* la communauté des femmes

sister-in-law, *pl* **sisters-in-law** N belle-sœur *f*, *pl* belles-sœurs

sisterly ['sɪstəlɪ] **ADJ** de sœur; **in a s. fashion** en sœur

Sistine ['sɪstiːn, -taɪn] **ADJ** **the S. chapel** la chapelle Sixtine

Sisyphus ['sɪsɪfəs] N Sisyphe *m*

SIT *(pt, pp* **sat** [sæt]; *prp* **sitting)**

| **VI** s'asseoir **1** ▪ être assis **1** ▪ siéger **3** ▪ se trouver, être posé **4** ▪ être perché **5** ▪ couver **5**
| **VT** asseoir **1** ▪ passer **2** |

VI 1 *(of person)* s'asseoir; **to be sitting** *(in armchair, on ground etc)* être assis; **s.!** *(to dog)* assis!; **we usually s. in the living room** nous sommes d'ordinaire dans le salon; **where would you like me to s.?, where shall I s.?** où est-ce que je me mets?; **she was sitting reading** elle était assise à lire *ou* en train de lire; **I'm fed up with sitting at home** j'en ai assez de rester enfermé à la maison; **don't just s. there, say something!** mais enfin, dis quelque chose!; **don't just s. there, do something!** eh bien, allez, remue-toi!; **to s. at (the) table** s'asseoir *ou* se mettre à (la) table, s'attabler; **they were sitting at (the) table** ils étaient à table, ils étaient attablés; **we were sitting at lunch/dinner** nous étions en train de déjeuner/dîner; **he sits for hours over his books** il passe des heures penché sur ses livres; *Fam* **to s. tight** *(not move)* ne pas bouger de sa place; *(not give in)* ne pas céder
2 to s. in Parliament = être député
3 *(of assemblies)* siéger, être en séance; **the court is sitting** la séance est ouverte
4 *Fam (of object)* **the diskette was sitting on**

the radiator la disquette était *ou* se trouvait sur le radiateur; **I found it sitting on the fridge** je l'ai trouvé sur le frigo; **the car was sitting in the drive** la voiture était stationnée dans l'allée
5 *(of bird)* être perché; **to s. (on eggs)** *(of hen)* couver
6 *(of responsibility)* **to s. heavy on sb** peser sur qn
7 to s. well/badly *(of jacket etc)* tomber bien/mal; **the jacket sits well/badly on him** la veste lui va bien/ne lui va pas
VT 1 to s. a child on the table asseoir un enfant sur la table
2 *Br Sch etc (exam)* passer

▸ **sit about, sit around** VI *(hang around)* traîner; *(do nothing)* ne rien faire

▸ **sit back** VI **1** *(lean back)* **to s. back in one's chair** s'appuyer contre le dossier de sa chaise/son fauteuil
2 *Fam (relax)* se relaxer; **to s. back and let the others do the work** *(not intervene)* regarder les autres travailler; **the authorities just sat back and did nothing** les autorités n'ont pas daigné faire quoi que ce soit; **we can't just s. back and do nothing** nous ne pouvons pas rester comme ça sans rien faire

▸ **sit down** VI s'asseoir; **to be sitting down** être assis; **please s. down** asseyez-vous, *Fml* veuillez vous asseoir; **to s. down again** se rasseoir; *(at table)* se remettre à (la) table; **to s. down at (the) table** se mettre à table, s'attabler; **to s. down to a meal** se mettre à table pour un repas; **to s. down to a game of bridge** s'installer pour faire une partie de bridge; **I think we should s. down and talk about it** je crois qu'il faut qu'on en discute *ou* parle
VT SEP *(child etc)* asseoir; *Fam* **s. yourself down!** asseyez-vous donc!

▸ **sit for** VT INSEP **1** *Br (be candidate in) (exam)* passer
2 *(pose for)* **to s. for one's portrait** se faire faire son portrait

▸ **sit in** VI **1** *(at meeting etc)* assister sans participer; **do you mind if I s. in for a while?** cela vous ennuie-t-il si je reste à écouter un moment?
2 to s. in for sb *(replace)* remplacer qn
3 *(occupy building, office etc)* faire grève avec occupation des locaux

▸ **sit in on** VT INSEP *(attend as observer)* **to s. in on a rehearsal/a meeting** assister à une répétition/une réunion (sans y participer)

▸ **sit on** VT INSEP *Fam* **1** *(not deal with) (proposal, suggestion etc)* ne pas s'occuper de; *(deliberately)* faire traîner; **they sat on it for two months** ils ne s'en sont pas occupés pendant deux mois
2 *(repress)* rembarrer

▸ **sit out** VI *(sit down outside)* s'asseoir dehors; *(be seated outside)* être assis dehors
VT SEP 1 *(not participate in) (game etc)* ne pas prendre part à; **I'll s. this one out** *(dance)* je ne veux pas danser celle-ci; **I'll s. out this round** *(of card game etc)* je passe mon tour
2 *(wait until end of) (conference etc)* rester (patiemment) jusqu'à la fin de; **he sat out the war in Switzerland** il est resté en Suisse en attendant la fin de la guerre

▸ **sit through** VT INSEP *(wait until end of)* rester pendant toute la durée de; **he sat through the whole play** il est resté jusqu'à la fin de la pièce; **to s. through dinner** rester à table jusqu'à la fin du repas; **we had to s. through two hours of Wagner** nous avons dû nous payer deux heures de Wagner

▸ **sit up** VI *(straighten one's back)* se tenir droit *(sur sa chaise, son lit etc)*, se redresser; *(from lying position)* se dresser *ou* se mettre sur son séant; **s. up straight!** tiens-toi droit!; *Fig* **to make sb s. up** étonner qn, épater qn; *Fig* **her competitors are beginning to s. up**

and take notice ses concurrents commencent à prendre conscience de son existence; **to s. up (and beg)** *(of dog)* faire le beau; **to s. up (late)** veiller; **to s. up for sb** *(wait up for)* (rester debout à) attendre qn, veiller en attendant le retour de qn; **to s. up with a sick man** garder *ou* veiller un malade; **to s. up to (the) table** *(sit closer)* approcher sa chaise de la table; *(come to table)* venir à table
VT SEP **to s. sb up** soulever qn pour l'asseoir; **to s. sb up against a wall** adosser qn contre un mur

sitar ['sɪtɑːr, sɪ'tɑːr] N sitar *m*

sitcom ['sɪtkɒm] N *TV, Radio* sitcom *m ou f*

sit-down N *(act)* **come and have a s.** venez vous asseoir
ADJ **there are too many guests for a s. meal** il y a trop d'invités pour que tout le monde puisse s'asseoir à table
▸▸**s. meal** dîner *m* pris à table; *Br* **s. strike** grève *f* sur le tas

site [saɪt] N **1** *(position) (of building etc)* emplacement *m*, situation *f*; *(archaeological etc)* site *m*; *Med (of pain etc)* siège *m*; **the s. of a battle/a historic meeting** le site d'une bataille/d'une réunion historique; **(camp) s.** (terrain *m* de) camping *m* **2** **(building) s.** chantier *m* (de construction); **on s.** sur place; **to be on s.** être à pied d'œuvre **3** *Comput* site *m*
VT *(building, stadium)* placer; *(factory)* implanter; **to be sited** être situé
▸▸**s. manager** chef *m* de chantier; *Comput* **s. map** plan *m* de navigation; **S. of Special Scientific Interest** = site protégé présentant un intérêt particulier du point de vue de la faune, de la flore ou de la géologie

sit-in N sit-in *m inv*; *(strike)* occupation *f* des locaux

siting ['saɪtɪŋ] N emplacement *m*

sitter ['sɪtər] N **1** *Art* modèle *m* **2** *Fam (childminder)* gardien, -ienne d'enfants **3** *(hen)* couveuse *f* **4** *Sport Fam* **to miss a s.** rater un but/une balle *etc* facile; **you gave him a s.** tu lui as fait une excellente passe

sitting ['sɪtɪŋ] **ADJ** *(seated)* assis; *(hare)* au gîte; *Art* **a s. figure** une figure assise; **a s. hen** une poule en train de couver; *Parl* **our s. member** le député qui nous représente actuellement
N *(for meal)* service *m*; *(for portrait etc)* pose *f*; *(of committee, court etc)* séance *f*; **s. and standing room** places assises et places debout; **to paint a portrait in three sittings** faire un portrait en trois séances; **first/second s.** *(for meals)* premier/deuxième service; **to serve 500 people in or at one s.** servir 500 personnes à la fois; **to write two chapters at one s.** écrire deux chapitres d'un trait *ou* d'un (seul) jet
▸▸**s. duck** *(target)* cible *m* facile; *(victim)* proie *f* facile, pigeon *m*; **old people are s. ducks for all sorts of confidence tricksters** les personnes âgées sont des proies faciles pour les escrocs en tous genres; *Br* **s. room** salon *m*, salle *f* de séjour; *Br* **s. tenant** locataire *mf* en place

situate ['sɪtjʊeɪt] **VT** *(house etc)* situer; **from where we were situated …** d'où nous nous trouvions …; **pleasantly situated house** maison bien située; **awkwardly situated** *(person)* dans une situation *ou* une position embarrassante; **he's well situated to know what's going on** il est bien placé pour savoir ce qui se passe

situation [sɪtjʊ'eɪʃən] N **1** *(of building, town)* situation *f*, emplacement *m*
2 *(state of affairs)* situation *f*; **to explain the s.** exposer la situation; **to find oneself in an unfortunate s.** se trouver dans une situation

déplorable; *Fam* **what's** *or* **how's the coffee s.?** combien nous reste-t-il de café?; *Fam* **we're in a staff shortage s.** nous n'avons pas assez de personnel; **what to do in an emergency s.** que faire en cas d'urgence

3 *Old-fashioned (employment)* emploi *m*, position *f*; **to look for/find a s.** chercher/ trouver un emploi; **situations vacant/wanted** *(in advertisements)* offres *fpl*/demandes *fpl* d'emploi

▸▸ *TV, Radio* **s. comedy** sitcom *m*

sit-up N **to do sit-ups** faire des abdominaux

sit-upon N *Old-fashioned Fam* derrière *m*, postérieur *m*

six [sɪks] N **1** six *m*; **number s.** (le) numéro six; **twenty-s.** vingt-six; **s. fours** *or* **four sixes are twenty-four** six fois quatre *ou* quatre fois six font vingt-quatre; **s. and a half** six et demi; **it's s. o'clock** il est six heures; **at s. thirty** à six heures et demie; **to be s.** *(in age)* avoir six ans; **double s.** *(at dominoes etc)* double-six *m, pl* doubles-six; *Cards* **the s. of hearts** le six de cœur; *Fam* **it's s. of one and half a dozen of the other** c'est blanc bonnet et bonnet blanc, c'est kif-kif; **we're all** *or* **everything's at sixes and sevens** tout est sens dessus dessous

2 *Cr* six points *mpl* (marqués par le batteur); **he scored five sixes** il a marqué cinq fois six points; *Fam* **to knock for s.** *(person) (knock down)* étendre; *(flabbergast)* abasourdir; *(enemy etc)* battre à plate(s) couture(s), écraser; *(project etc)* ficher en l'air; **that's knocked everything for s.** ça a tout fichu en l'air

PRON six; **I need s. (of them)** il m'en faut six, j'en ai besoin de six

NUM ADJ six; *Fam* **to be s. feet under** être six pieds sous terre; **a s.-cylinder car** une six cylindres; **s.-seater (car)** voiture à six places

▸▸ **the S. Counties** = l'Irlande *f* du Nord; *Hist* **the S. Day War** la guerre des six jours; *Sport* **the S. Nations (tournament)** le tournoi des six nations

sixfold ['sɪksfəʊld] ADJ sextuple

ADV au sextuple; **to increase s.** sextupler

six-foot ADJ *(beam)* de six pieds; **a s. bodyguard** un garde du corps très baraqué

six-footer N homme *m*/femme *f* mesurant six pieds, *Fam* armoire *f* à glace; **he's obviously going to be a s.** on voit bien qu'il sera grand

six-pack N **1** *(of bottles, cans)* pack *m* de six **2** *Hum (stomach muscles)* abdos *mpl*; **he's got a great s.** il a des super abdos

sixpence ['sɪkspəns] N **1** *(sum)* six pence *mpl* **2** *Formerly (coin)* pièce *f* de six pence

sixpenny ['sɪkspənɪ] ADJ *Old-fashioned (costing six pence)* qui coûte six pence; *(stamp)* de six pence

▸▸ **s. piece** pièce *f* de six pence

sixpennyworth ['sɪks'penɪwəθ] N *Old-fashioned* **to buy s. of chocolate** acheter pour six pence de chocolat

six-shooter N six-coups *m inv*

six-sided ADJ qui a six côtés, hexagonal, -aux

sixteen [sɪks'tiːn] NUM ADJ, N seize *m*; **she is s.** elle a seize ans

sixteenth [sɪks'tiːnθ] ADJ seizième; **Louis the S.** Louis XVI

N **1** *(in series)* seizième *mf* **2** *(fraction)* seizième *m* **3** *(of month)* seize *m inv*

▸▸ *Am Mus* **s. note** double croche *f*

sixth [sɪksθ] ADJ sixième; **Henry the S.** Henri VI

N **1** *(person, thing)* sixième *mf* **2** *(fraction)* sixième *m* **3** *Mus* sixte *f* **4** *(of month)* six *m inv*

▸▸ *Br Sch* **s. form** ≃ = classe *f* terminale de l'enseignement secondaire en Angleterre et au Pays de Galles, préparant aux A-levels,

≃ classes de première et de terminale; *Br Sch* **s. form college** = établissement *m* préparant aux "A-levels"; *Br Sch* **s. former** = élève *mf* de première ou de terminale; *Am Sch* **s. grade** = classe du primaire pour les 10-11 ans; **s. sense** sixième sens *m*; **some s. sense told me she wouldn't come** j'avais l'intuition qu'elle ne viendrait pas

sixthly ['sɪksθlɪ] ADV sixièmement

sixtieth ['sɪkstɪɪθ] ADJ, N soixantième *mf*

sixty ['sɪkstɪ] NUM ADJ, N soixante *m*; **s.-third** soixante-troisième; **about** *or* **some s. books** une soixantaine de livres; **she's in her sixties** elle a la soixantaine, elle a plus de soixante ans; **in the sixties** dans les années soixante

sixty-four NUM ADJ, N soixante-quatre *m*; *Fam* **the s. (thousand) dollar question** la question cruciale

sixty-nine N *(sexual position)* soixante-neuf *m*

sizable ['saɪzəb(ə)l] ADJ = sizeable

size¹ [saɪz] N **1** *(of building, room)* grandeur *f*, *(of town, country, island)* superficie *f*, *(of carpet, machine, car)* dimensions *fpl*, taille *f*; *(of apple, cake, print)* grosseur *f*, taille; *(of problem, undertaking)* importance *f*, ampleur *f*, *Comput (of file etc)* taille; **of equal** *or* **the same s., of a s.** de (la) même grandeur/ taille *etc*; **I was surprised by the s. of the bill** j'ai été étonné par le montant de la note; **bicycles/people come in all shapes and sizes** il y a des bicyclettes/des gens de toutes les formes et de toutes les tailles; **books arranged according to s.** livres disposés par ordre de taille; **it's the s. of an egg** c'est gros comme un œuf; **to grow/decrease in s.** augmenter/diminuer de taille; **actual** *or* **full s.** grandeur nature; **a town of that s.** une ville de cette importance; *Fam* **that's about the s. of it** c'est un peu ça; **to cut a piece to s.** tailler une pièce à la dimension *ou* à la cote; *Fam* **to cut sb down to s.** rabattre le caquet à qn, remettre qn à sa place

2 *(of person)* taille *f*, *Com (of clothes)* taille; *(of shirt)* encolure *f*, *(of shoes, gloves, hat)* pointure *f*, *(of book, paper)* format *m*; **a boy half/twice his s.** un garçon deux fois moins/ plus grand que lui; **a s. larger/smaller** *(shoes)* une pointure au-dessus/en-dessous; *(dresses etc)* une taille au-dessus/en-dessous; **what s. do you take?, what's your s.?, what s. are you?** *(in shoes)* quelle pointure chaussez-vous?; *(in dresses, shirts etc)* quelle est votre taille?; **s. ten shoes** ≃ chaussures *fpl* de pointure 44; **I've nothing in your s.** je n'ai rien à votre taille/à votre pointure; **to try sth for s.** essayer qch *(pour voir si la taille va)*; *Fam* **try this one for s.** prends ça

VT *(classify according to size) (objects)* classer par grosseur *ou* par dimension; *(adjust size of)* adapter les dimensions de; *Comput* dimensionner

▸▸ *Comput* **s. box** case *f* de dimensionnement

▸ **size up** VT SEP **to s. sb up** évaluer qn, jauger qn; **they soon sized him up** ils ont eu vite fait de le jauger

size² *Tech* N apprêt *m*; *(glue)* colle *f*, encollage *m*

VT *(wallpaper)* apprêter, encoller

sizeable ['saɪzəb(ə)l] ADJ assez grand, plutôt grand; *(difference)* assez important; *(fine, sum)* assez élevé

sized [saɪzd] ADJ **fair s.** *(quite large)* assez grand; **medium s.** de grandeur *ou* de taille moyenne; **large/small s.** de grande/petite taille; *(book, paper etc)* de grand/petit format

sizing ['saɪzɪŋ] N *Tech* **1** *(process)* apprêtage *m*; *(of wallpaper)* collage *m*, encollage *m* **2** *(substance)* colle *f*, *(in painting)* apprêt *m*

sizzle ['sɪz(ə)l] N *(of something frying)* grésillement *m*

VI *(of frying pan, sausages etc)* grésiller

sizzler ['sɪz(ə)lər] N *Fam* journée *f* de canicule; **it was a real s. (of a day)** on se serait cru dans un four, on crevait de chaleur

sizzling ['sɪzlɪŋ] ADJ *(heat, temperature)* torride; *(food)* grésillant

ADV *Fam (day)* torride

N grésillement *m*

skank [skæŋk] N *Am Fam (ugly woman)* cageot *m*, boudin *m*

skanky ['skæŋkɪ] ADJ *Am Fam (ugly)* hyper moche

skate¹ [skeɪt] N *(fish)* raie *f*

skate² N *(ice/roller)* s. patin *m* (à glace/à roulettes); *Fig Fam* **to get one's skates on** se dépêcher

VI *(on ice)* patiner, faire du patin; *(on roller skates)* faire du patin à roulettes; **he skated across the lake** il a traversé le lac en patins à glace; *Fig Fam* **to s. round sth** tourner autour du pot

▸ **skate over** VT INSEP **1** *(skate across surface of)* parcourir en patin **2** *(discuss superficially) (subject)* ne faire qu'effleurer; *(difficulties)* passer rapidement sur

skateboard ['skeɪtbɔːd] N *Sport* planche *f* à roulettes, *Fam* skate-board *m, pl* skateboards, skate *m, Can* rouli-roulant® *m, pl* rouli-roulants

VI *Sport* faire de la planche à roulettes *ou Fam* du skate *ou Can* du rouli-roulant®

skateboarder ['skeɪtbɔːdər] N *Sport* personne *f* pratiquant le skate (-board); **a champion s.** un champion du skate-board

skateboarding ['skeɪtbɔːdɪŋ] N skate(-board) *m*; **to go s.** aller faire du skate-board

skater ['skeɪtər] N patineur, -euse

skating ['skeɪtɪŋ] N *(on ice)* patinage *m*; *(on roller skates)* patin *m* à roulettes

▸▸ **s. rink** *(for ice-skating)* patinoire *f*, *(for roller-skating)* piste *f* pour patin à roulettes

skean-dhu [skiːən'duː] N *Scot* = dague *f* décorative que l'on porte dans la chaussette

skedaddle [skɪ'dæd(ə)l] VI *Fam (run off)* déguerpir, prendre ses jambes à son cou

skeet [skiːt] N *Sport* skeet *m*

▸▸ **s. shooting** *(tir m)* skeet *m*

skeezer ['skiːzər] N *Am Sl Pej (ugly woman)* cageot *m*, boudin *m*; *(promiscuous woman)* pouffiasse *f*, traînée *f*

skein [skeɪn, skiːn] N **1** *(of silk, wool)* écheveau *m* **2** *(of wild geese)* vol *m*

skeletal ['skelɪt(ə)l] ADJ squelettique; *Fig (presentation etc)* sommaire

skeleton ['skelɪt(ə)n] N **1** *(of human being, animal etc)* squelette *m*; *Fig* **s. in the cupboard** *or Am* **in the closet** secret *m* honteux (de la famille); **to have a s. in the cupboard** *or Am* **in the closet** avoir un squelette dans le placard; **s. at the feast** rabat-joie *m inv*, trouble-fête *m inv*; **he's a living s.** c'est un vrai squelette **2** *Fig (of building etc)* charpente *f*, squelette *m*; *(of novel, essay)* canevas *m*, esquisse *f*

▸▸ **s. crew** personnel *m* réduit; **s. key** passe-partout *m inv*; passe *m*; **s. staff** équipage *m* réduit

skeptic, skeptical *etc Am* = **sceptic, sceptical** *etc*

sketch [sketʃ] N **1** *Art, Liter* croquis *m*, esquisse *f*; **the map is only a s.** la carte n'est qu'un croquis; **character s.** portrait *m* littéraire; **to make a s. of sth** faire le croquis de qch; **preliminary s.** premier jet *m*; **(parliamentary) s. writer** = journaliste *mf* spécialiste de l'actualité parlementaire qu'il/ qu'elle présente de façon humoristique **2** *Fig (of project)* exposé *m*, ébauche *f*, **she**

drew a brief **s. of the situation** elle a fait un bref résumé de la situation **3** *Theat, TV* sketch *m*, saynète *f*

VT 1 *Art (landscape, building etc)* esquisser, croquer; *(person, thing)* faire un *ou* le croquis de **2 = sketch out**
▸▸ **s. pad** bloc *m* à croquis
▸ **sketch in VT SEP** *(draw roughly)* dessiner sommairement, esquisser; *Fig (details)* esquisser
▸ **sketch out VT SEP** *(draw up outline of)* *(novel)* faire le canevas *ou* l'ébauche de; *(provide outline of) (project etc)* esquisser, ébaucher

sketchbook ['sketʃbʊk] **N** cahier *m* de croquis

sketchily ['sketʃɪlɪ] **ADV** sans les détails, *Pej* d'une manière incomplète *ou* vague; *(to remember)* vaguement

sketching ['sketʃɪŋ] **N to do some s.** faire des croquis; **to go s.** aller faire des croquis; **s. block** *or* **pad** bloc *m* à croquis

sketchy ['sketʃɪ] **ADJ** *(work)* qui manque de fini; *(drawing)* qui manque de détails; *(knowledge)* superficiel, sommaire; *(ideas)* plutôt vague; **I'm a bit s. on this** mes connaissances sont un peu sommaires

skew [skjuː] **VI** *(of truck etc)* biaiser, obliquer
VT *(distort) (results)* biaiser
ADJ en biais, oblique
ADV de *ou* en biais
N on the s. de *ou* en biais, en oblique

skewbald ['skjuːbɔːld] **ADJ** *(horse)* pie *inv*

skewer ['skjuːər] *Culin* **N** *(for pieces of meat, vegetables etc)* brochette *f*, *(larger, for whole pig etc)* broche *f*
VT *(pieces of meat, vegetables etc)* mettre sur une brochette; *(whole pig etc)* embrocher; **his hand had been skewered to the table** il s'est fait clouer la main à la table

skew-whiff **ADJ** *Br Fam* de travers, *Fam* de traviole

ski, *pl* **skis** [skiː, skiːz] **N** ski *m*
VI *(pt, pp* **skied)** skier, faire du ski; *(move)* aller à *ou* en skis; **he skis well** il skie bien; **to learn to s.** apprendre à skier *ou* à faire du ski; **to s. down the slope** descendre la piste à *ou* en skis; **we skied back** nous sommes rentrés à *ou* en skis
▸▸ **s. binding** fixation *f*; **s. boots** chaussures *fpl* de ski; *Aut* **s. box** coffre *m* porte-skis; *Aut* **s. carrier** porte-skis *m inv*; **s. centre** station *f* de ski; **s. club** club *m* de ski; *Aut* **s. flap** trappe *f* à skis; **s. instructor** moniteur, -trice de ski; **s. jump** *(ramp)* tremplin *m* de ski; **s. jumper** sauteur *m*; **s. jumping** saut *m* à skis; **s. lift** remontée *f* mécanique; *(chair lift)* télésiège *m*; **s. pants** fuseau *m*, pantalon *m* de ski; **s. pass** forfait *m* de remonte-pente; **s. pole** bâton *m* de ski; *Aut* **s. rack** porte-skis; **s. resort** station de ski; **s. run** piste *f* de ski; **s. slope** piste de ski; **s. stick** bâton de ski; **s. suit** combinaison *f* de ski; **s. tow** téléski *m*; **s. wax** fart *m* (pour skis)

skid [skɪd] **N 1** *Aut (action)* dérapage *m*; **to go into a s.** déraper, faire un dérapage; **to correct a s.** redresser **2** *(device) Com* palette *f* sur patins; *Aviat (for landing etc)* patin *m*; *Fig Fam* **to put the skids under sb** *(hurry)* faire se magner qn; *(bring about ruin of)* glisser des peaux de bananes à qn; *Fig Fam* **to be on the skids** *(of economy, company, marriage etc)* battre de l'aile; **he's on the skids** il va mal finir
VI *(-dd-) (of car, tyre etc)* déraper; *(of wheel)* patiner; **his glasses went skidding across the table** ses lunettes ont glissé jusqu'à l'autre bout de la table
VT *(car)* faire faire un dérapage à
▸▸ *Am Fam* **s. row** bas-fonds *mpl*, quartier *m* mal famé

skidlid ['skɪdlɪd] **N** *Aut Sl* casque *m* de moto

skidmark ['skɪdmɑːk] **N** *(on road)* trace *f* de dérapage; *Fig Fam Hum (on underpants, nappy etc)* trace

skidpan ['skɪdpæn] **N** *Aut* terrain *m* de dérapages

skier ['skiːər] **N** skieur, -euse

skiff [skɪf] **N** esquif *m*, yole *f*, *(in rowing)* skiff *m*

skiffle ['skɪf(ə)l] **N** *Mus* skiffle *m*
▸▸ **s. group** skiffle-group *m inv*

ski-flying **N** *Ski* vol *m* à ski

skiing ['skiːɪŋ] **N** ski *m*; **to go s.** faire du ski; **we went on a s. holiday** nous sommes allés aux sports d'hiver
▸▸ **s. instructor** moniteur, -trice de ski

skilful, *Am* **skillful** ['skɪlfʊl] **ADJ** adroit, habile; **to be s. at** *or* **in (doing) sth** être habile à *(faire)* qch; **to be s. with one's hands** être habile *ou* adroit de ses mains

skilfully, *Am* **skillfully** ['skɪlfʊlɪ] **ADV** habilement, adroitement

skilfulness, *Am* **skillfulness** ['skɪlfʊlnɪs] **N** habileté *f*, adresse *f*

skill [skɪl] **N 1** *(ability)* habileté *f*, adresse *f*, *(manual)* dextérité *f*, *(as translator, negotiator, footballer, driver)* talent *m*; *(on basis of learning)* connaissances *fpl*; **s. in doing sth** talent *ou* habileté pour faire qch; **a game involving no s.** un sport/un jeu n'exigeant aucune aptitude particulière; **repairing pianos requires great s.** réparer les pianos demande une grande compétence; **language skills** connaissances en langues; **I don't have the necessary skills** je n'ai pas les connaissances nécessaires; **an archaeologist requires many skills** un archéologue doit posséder de nombreuses aptitudes; **they have very different skills** ils ont des aptitudes très différentes; *Iron* **it's one of my special skills** je suis expert en la matière **2** *(trade)* métier *m*; *(learned technique)* technique *f*, **learn new skills** apprenez un nouveau métier

skilled [skɪld] **ADJ** habile; *(work)* de spécialiste; **to be s. in doing sth** être habile à faire qch; **highly s. staff** personnel très qualifié; **s. labour** main-d'œuvre *f* qualifiée; **s. manual worker** ouvrier *m* spécialisé, OS *m*; **s. worker** ouvrier qualifié

skillet ['skɪlɪt] **N** *Am* poêle *f* (à frire)

skillful, skillfully *etc Am* **= skilful, skilfully** *etc*

skim [skɪm] **N just give it a quick s.** *(read through quickly)* jetez-y un coup d'œil rapide
VT *(-mm-)* **1** *(stock, gravy etc)* écumer; *(milk)* écrémer; *Mktg* écrémer; **skim(med) milk** lait *m* écrémé **2** *(pass lightly over) (surface)* effleurer, raser; **to s. stones on water** faire des ricochets; *Fig* **the book just skims the surface (of the problem)** le livre se contente de survoler le problème
VI to s. along *or* **over the ground** *(fly just above)* voler au ras du sol; *(move on surface)* raser le sol; **to s. over the water** *(fly just above)* voler à fleur d'eau; *(move on surface)* raser l'eau; *Fig* **the author skims over the real problems** l'auteur survole les vrais problèmes
▸ **skim off VT SEP** *(remove by skimming) (cream, fat etc)* enlever, prélever; *Fig* **to s. the cream off sth** prendre la meilleure partie de qch; **the accounts department skims off the best recruits** la comptabilité récupère les meilleures recrues
▸ **skim through VT INSEP** *(read superficially) (novel, document etc)* lire en diagonale

skimmer ['skɪmər] **N** *(for milk)* écrémeuse *f*

skimp [skɪmp] **VT** *(food, fabric of dress)* lésiner sur; *Fam (one's work)* bâcler
VI lésiner sur tout; *(live parsimoniously)* vi-

vre chichement; **they skimped on the cost of the new road** ils lésinaient sur le coût de la nouvelle route

skimpily ['skɪmpɪlɪ] **ADV** *(furnished etc)* parcimonieusement; **s. dressed** légèrement vêtu; **s. made** *(garment)* étriqué

skimpiness ['skɪmpɪnɪs] **N** insuffisance *f*, *(of garment)* aspect *m* étriqué

skimpy ['skɪmpɪ] **ADJ** insuffisant; **s. meal** maigre repas; **s. skirt** jupe étriquée; **to be s. with sth** *(be mean)* lésiner sur qch

skin [skɪn] **N 1** peau *f*, *Fig* **to have a thin/thick s.** être/ne pas être susceptible; **to cast** *or* **throw its s.** *(of snake etc)* muer; **I always wear cotton next to my s.** je porte toujours du coton sur la peau; **to strip to the s.** se mettre tout nu; **she was soaked to the s.** elle était trempée jusqu'aux os; *Fam* **she's nothing but** *or* **she's all s. and bone** elle n'a que la peau et les os; **I nearly jumped out of my s.** cela m'a fait sursauter; **to escape by the s. of one's teeth** l'échapper belle; **to save one's (own) s.** sauver sa peau; *(escape criticism, scandal etc)* se tirer d'affaire; *Fam* **to get under sb's s.** *(annoy)* ennuyer qn; *(get on sb's nerves)* taper sur les nerfs de qn; *Fam* **I've got her under my s.** je l'ai dans la peau; *Fam* **it's no s. off my nose** ça n'a aucune conséquence pour moi; **s. deep** *(emotions)* à fleur de peau; *(wound)* superficiel; **beauty is only s. deep** la beauté n'est pas tout
2 *(of dead animal)* peau *f*
3 *(of fruit, sausage)* peau *f*, *(of onion)* pelure *f*, *Culin* **potatoes (cooked) in their skins** pommes *fpl* de terre en robe de chambre *ou* en robe des champs
4 *Naut (of canoe)* bordé *m* extérieur; *(of ship)* bordé extérieur, enveloppe *f*, coque *f*, *Aviat (of fuselage)* revêtement *m*
5 *(on milk, sauce, custard etc)* peau *f*, pellicule *f*
6 *Sl (skinhead)* skin *mf*
7 *Sl (cigarette paper)* papier *m* à cigarette
VT *(-nn-)* *(rabbit, cat etc)* écorcher, dépouiller; *(tomato etc)* peler, éplucher; **to s. one's knees** s'écorcher les genoux; *Prov* **there's more than one way to s. a cat** il y a plus d'une façon d'arriver à ses fins; *Fam* **to s. sb alive** écorcher qn, estamper qn; *Am Fam* **s. me!** tape-moi dans la main!
▸▸ **s. cancer** cancer *m* de la peau; **s. care** soins *mpl* de la peau; **s. complaint** maladie *f* de peau; **s. cream** crème *f* pour la peau; **s. disease** maladie de peau; **s. diver** plongeur, -euse; **s. diving** plongée *f* sous-marine; *Fam* **s. flick** film *m* porno; *Fam* **s. game** arnaque *f*, **s. graft** greffe *f* de la peau; *Fam* **s. mag(azine)** magazine *m* porno; *Med* **s. patch** timbre *m* transdermique; *Med* **s. test** cuti-réaction *f*, *pl* cuti-réactions
▸ **skin up VI** *Br Sl* rouler un joint

skinflint ['skɪnflɪnt] **N** *Fam* pingre *mf*, grippe-sou *m*, *pl* grippe-sous

skinful ['skɪnfʊl] **N** *Fam* **he's had a s.** *(of alcohol)* il a pris une (bonne) cuite

skinhead ['skɪnhed] **N** skinhead *mf*

skinless ['skɪnlɪs] **ADJ** *(sausage etc)* sans peau

skinned [skɪnd] **ADJ** *(rabbit)* à qui on a enlevé la peau; **to keep one's eyes s.** ouvrir l'œil; **keep your eyes s.** ouvre l'œil (et le bon); **to keep one's eyes s. for sb/sth** guetter qn/qch; **I'll keep my eyes s. for one** j'ouvrirai l'œil pour voir si j'en trouve un

-skinned [-skɪnd] **SUFF** **dark/fair-s.** à la peau mate/claire

skinniness ['skɪnɪnɪs] **N** maigreur *f*, *(no negative overtones)* minceur *f*

skinny ['skɪnɪ] **ADJ** maigre; *(without negative overtones)* mince; *(sweater, pullover etc)* collant

N *Am Fam (inside information)* renseignements *mpl*; **what's the s. on the situation?** est-ce qu'il y a du nouveau?

skinny-dip *Fam* **N** baignade *f* tout nu *ou* à poil
VI nager *ou* se baigner tout nu *ou* à poil

skinny-malinky [-mə'lɪŋkɪ] **N** *Scot Fam* asperge *f*, grande perche *f*

skin-pop *Sl* **VT** *(drugs)* se piquer *ou* se shooter à
VI *(inject drugs)* se piquer, se shooter

skint [skɪnt] **ADJ** *Br Fam* **to be s.** être sans le sou, être fauché

skintight ['skɪntaɪt] **ADJ** *(garment)* collant, moulant

skip[1] [skɪp] **VI** (-pp-) **1** *(of lambs, children)* sautiller, gambader; *(with rope)* sauter à la corde; **they came skipping out of school** ils sont sortis de l'école en gambadant; **to s. from one subject to another** sauter d'un sujet à un autre; **to read without skipping** lire sans rien sauter
2 *Fam* **I skipped across to Paris** j'ai fait un saut à Paris; **he's just skipped out to the shops** il vient d'aller faire des courses; **if you s. through the work too fast …** si vous travaillez à la va-vite …
3 *Fam (leave without paying)* filer à l'anglaise
VT 1 *(meal, year at school, stage in process)* sauter; *(in planning trip etc) (not go to)* ne pas aller à; *(word, line etc) (intentionally)* omettre; *(accidentally)* sauter (par-dessus), passer; *Comput (command)* sauter; *Sch* **to s. a class** *(play truant)* sécher un cours; *(move up)* sauter une classe; **my heart skipped a beat** mon cœur a fait un bond; *Fam* **to s. bail** se dérober à la justice *(alors qu'on jouit de la liberté provisoire)*; *Fam* **they've skipped the country** ils ont quitté le pays; *Fam* **s. it!** *(that's enough)* ça suffit!; *(forget it)* passons!, laisse courir!
2 *Am* **to s. rope** sauter à la corde
N *(jump)* (petit) saut *m*, gambade *f*
▸▸ *Am* **s. rope** corde *f* à sauter
▸ **skip off** **VI** *Br Fam (leave)* filer, décamper
▸ **skip over** **VT INSEP** *(omit) (word, line etc) (intentionally)* omettre; *(accidentally)* sauter (par-dessus), passer

skip[2] **N** *Constr, Min etc* benne *f*

skip[3] **N** *Fam (skipper)* cap'taine *m*

skipper ['skɪpər] **N 1** *Naut* capitaine *m*, patron *m*; *Aviat* commandant *m* de bord; *Sport Fam* capitaine, chef *m* **2** *Fam (who leaves without paying bill)* client *m* qui part sans payer *ou* qui file à l'anglaise
VT *Fam (ship)* être le commandant de; *(plane)* être le commandant à bord de; *(sports team)* être le chef de

skipping ['skɪpɪŋ] **N** *(with rope)* saut *m* à la corde
▸▸ **s. rope** corde *f* à sauter

skirl [skɜ:l, *Scot* skɪrl] **N** *Scot (of bagpipes)* son *m* aigu

skirmish ['skɜ:mɪʃ] **N** *Mil* escarmouche *f*, échauffourée *f*; *Fig* altercation *f*
VI *Mil* se livrer à une guerre d'escarmouches; **they are still skirmishing in the hills** il y a encore des escarmouches dans les collines; *Fig* **they've been skirmishing for months** il y a des accrochages depuis des mois entre eux

skirmisher ['skɜ:mɪʃər] **N** *Mil* tirailleur *m*

skirt [skɜ:t] **N 1** *(garment)* jupe *f*; *(of overcoat, uniform etc)* pan *m*, basque *f* **2** *Br Offensive Sl (women)* nanas *fpl*, gonzesses *fpl*; **they've gone out looking for s.** ils sont allés draguer; **a bit of s.** une nana, une gonzesse **3** *Culin* **s. of beef** = flanchet *m* de bœuf **4** **(saddle) s.** petit quartier *m* (de la selle) **5** *(of hovercraft)* jupe *f* **6** *(in engine) (of piston)* jupe *f*

VT *(village, hill, problem)* contourner; *(of person) (wall)* longer, serrer; **the path skirts the wood** le sentier côtoie *ou* contourne le bois
▸▸ **s. clearance** jeu *m* à la jupe
▸ **skirt around** **VT INSEP** = **skirt**

skirting ['skɜ:tɪŋ] **N** *Br Constr* plinthe *f*
▸▸ **s. board** plinthe

skit [skɪt] **N** *Liter, Mus, Theat* pièce *f* satirique, satire *f*; **a s. on the current crisis** une satire sur la crise actuelle

skitter ['skɪtər] **VI** *(move quickly)* **to s. away** *or* **off** *(of spider etc)* s'enfuir; **the pencil skittered across the floor** le crayon glissa sur le sol

skittish ['skɪtɪʃ] **ADJ 1** *(horse)* ombrageux **2** *(person) (playful)* espiègle; *(frivolous)* frivole

skittishly ['skɪtɪʃlɪ] **ADV** *(playfully)* avec espièglerie; *(frivolously)* frivolement

skittishness ['skɪtɪʃnɪs] **N 1** *(of horse)* caractère *m* ombrageux **2** *(of person) (playfulness)* espièglerie *f*; *(frivolousness)* frivolité *f*

skittle ['skɪt(ə)l] **N** quille *f*; **(game of) skittles** (jeu *m* de) quilles *fpl*; **to play skittles** jouer aux quilles
▸▸ **s. alley** piste *f* de jeu de quilles; **s. pin** quille

skive [skaɪv] *Br Fam* **N** *(easy job)* planque *f*; **she's taking PE because it's such a s.** elle a choisi éducation physique parce que c'est pépère
VI tirer au flanc
▸ **skive off** **VI** *Br Fam (leave work etc)* s'esquiver

skiver ['skaɪvər] **N** *Br Fam* tire-au-flanc *m inv*

skiving ['skaɪvɪŋ] **N** *Br Fam* manque *m* de travail; **there's too much s. round here** on tire trop au flanc ici

skivvy ['skɪvɪ] **N 1** *Br Pej* bonniche *f*, bonne *f* à tout faire; *Fig* **I'm not your s.!** je ne suis pas ta bonne!
VI *Br* faire la bonne (à tout faire); *Fig* **I'm not skivvying for you** je ne suis pas ta bonne

skua ['skju:ə] **N** *(bird)* stercoraire *m*

skulduggery [skʌl'dʌgərɪ] **N** *Fam* magouille *f*; **political/financial s.** magouille politique/financière

skulk [skʌlk] **VI 1** *(hide)* se cacher **2** *(move furtively)* rôder; **to s. in/out** entrer/sortir furtivement

skull [skʌl] **N** crâne *m*; **he's got a thick s.** il a la tête dure; *Fam* **can't you get that into your thick s.?** est-ce que tu ne peux pas te rentrer ça dans le crâne?; *Fam* **I was bored out of my s.** je crevais d'ennui; *Sl* **to be out of one's s.** *(drunk)* être bourré; **to get out of one's s.** se bourrer la gueule
▸▸ **s. and crossbones** *(motif)* tête *f* de mort; *(flag)* pavillon *m* à tête de mort

skullcap ['skʌlkæp] **N** *(of priest etc)* calotte *f*

skunk [skʌŋk] **N** *(animal)* mouffette *f*, *(fur)* scons(e) *m*, skons *m*, skun(k)s *m*; *Fam Pej (person)* mufle *m*, salaud *m*

sky [skaɪ] **N** ciel *m*, *pl* cieux, *(in art)* ciels; **under the open s.** *(to picnic, wander)* au grand air; **to sleep under the open s.** dormir à la belle étoile; *Fig* **the s.'s the limit** il n'y a pas de limite; **to praise sb to the skies** porter qn aux nues; *Prov* **red s. at night, shepherd's delight** rouge le soir, l'espoir; *Prov* **red s. in the morning, shepherd's warning** ≃ araignée du matin, chagrin; **the bridge was blown s. high** le pont a volé en éclats; **his project was blown s. high** son projet a été anéanti; **prices were s. high** les prix sont astronomiques
VT *(pt, pp* **skied)** *Cr, Tennis etc (ball)* envoyer en chandelle

▸▸ **s. blue** bleu ciel *m*; *TV* **s. cloth** rideau *m* de fond; **s. marshal** = garde *m* armé embarqué sur un avion de ligne en cas d'attentat

sky-blue **ADJ** bleu ciel *inv*; bleu azur *inv*

skydiver ['skaɪdaɪvər] **N** *Aviat, Sport* parachutiste *mf* qui pratique la chute libre

skydiving ['skaɪdaɪvɪŋ] **N** *Aviat, Sport* parachutisme *m* en chute libre

Skye [skaɪ] **N** (l'île *f* de) Skye *f*
▸▸ **S. terrier** skye-terrier *m*, *pl* skye-terriers

skyjack ['skaɪdʒæk] **VT** *Fam (plane)* détourner

skyjacker ['skaɪdʒækər] **N** *Fam* pirate *m* de l'air

skyjacking ['skaɪdʒækɪŋ] **N** *Fam* piraterie *f* aérienne

skylark ['skaɪlɑ:k] **N** *(bird)* alouette *f* des champs
VI *Fam (play about)* rigoler, batifoler

skylarking ['skaɪlɑ:kɪŋ] **N** *Fam* rigolade *f*

skylight ['skaɪlaɪt] **N** *(in roof, ceiling)* jour *m*; *(in attic)* lucarne *f*; *(skylight f, (hinged)* *(châssis m ou* fenêtre *f ou* lucarne à) tabatière *f*

skyline ['skaɪlaɪn] **N** *(horizon)* (ligne f d')horizon *m*; *(of city)* silhouette *f*; **it radically alters the s.** ça change radicalement le profil de la ville

skypilot ['skaɪpaɪlət] **N** *Mil Old-fashioned Sl (padre)* aumônier *m* militaire

skyrocket ['skaɪrɒkɪt] **N** fusée *f*
VI *Fam (of prices etc)* monter en flèche

skyscape ['skaɪskeɪp] **N** *Art* paysage *m* céleste

skyscraper ['skaɪskreɪpər] **N** gratte-ciel *m inv*

skyward(s) ['skaɪwəd(z)] **ADV** *(to fly)* dans le ciel; *(to look)* vers le ciel

skyway ['skaɪweɪ] **N** *Am* **1** *Aviat* couloir *m* aérien **2** *(flyover)* saut-de-mouton *m*, *pl* sauts-de-mouton; *(raised road)* route *f* surélevée

sky(-)writing **N** publicité *f* aérienne

S & L [esə'nel] **N** *Am (abbr* **savings and loan association)** société *f* immobilière

slab [slæb] **N 1** *(of stone, marble etc)* plaque *f*, dalle *f*, *(of timber)* plaque; *(in mortuary)* table *f*; *(paving)* **s.** dalle; **butcher's s.** étal *m* de boucher **2** *(of cake)* (grosse) tranche *f*, *(of chocolate)* plaque *f*, tablette *f*, *(of meat)* pavé *m*

slack[1] [slæk] **N 1** *(in cable, belt)* mou *m*; *Tech* jeu *m* (nuisible); **to take up the s. in a cable** mettre un câble au raide; *Fig* **to take up the s.** relancer le marché **2** *Naut (sea)* mer *f* étale **3** *(trousers)* **slacks** pantalon *m*
ADJ 1 *(rope etc)* mou, *f* molle, lâche; *(screw)* desserré; *(handshake, grip)* mou; **to be or hang s.** *(of rope)* avoir du mou; *Fig* **to have a s. rein on sth** diriger qch sans fermeté *ou* mollement **2** *(careless) (person, attitude, work)* négligent; *(lazy)* paresseux, *Fam* flemmard; *(analysis)* flou; **things are getting far too s. around here** il y a beaucoup trop de relâchement ici; **to get** *or* **become s.** *(of person)* se laisser aller, se relâcher; **to be s. in** *or* **about doing sth** être négligent en faisant qch; **security at the base is very s.** les mesures de sécurité à la base militaire ne sont pas du tout strictes **3** *(not busy) (market, economy)* peu actif, -ive; *(business)* stagnant; **business is** les affaires ne marchent pas fort; **we're s. this afternoon** *(in business etc)* nous ne sommes pas très occupés cet après-midi; **when things are a bit slacker** quand les choses se calmeront; **s. periods** moments de creux, périodes calmes; **the s. season** la morte-saison, la saison creuse; **s. time** période d'accalmie
VI *Fam (of person) (become negligent)* se

laisser aller; *(in one's work, efforts)* se relâcher; **dear me, I must be slacking!** mon Dieu, je vieillis!
▸ **slack off** VI *(diminish) (of pressure, demand, rain etc)* se calmer
VT SEP *Tech (diminish) (pressure)* relâcher

slack² N *(coal)* menu charbon *m*, poussier *m*

slacken ['slæk(ə)n] VT *(pace, speed)* ralentir; *(rope)* détendre, relâcher, donner du mou à; *(sail)* donner du mou à; **to s. speed** diminuer la vitesse, ralentir (la marche); **to s. the reins** lâcher la bride *ou* les rênes
VI *(of person)* se relâcher, devenir négligent; *(of rope)* prendre du mou; *(of speed)* ralentir; *(of storm)* se calmer; *(of energy, enthusiasm)* retomber; **business is slackening** les affaires stagnent
▸ **slacken off** VI, VT SEP = **slack off**

slackening ['slæk(ə)nɪŋ] N *(of zeal)* ralentissement *m*, diminution *f*; *(of strength, speed)* diminution; *(of rope, efforts)* relâchement *m*; **s. of speed** ralentissement

slacker ['slækər] N *Fam* paresseux, -euse, *Fam* flemmard, -arde

slackly ['slæklɪ] ADV **1** *(to hang)* mollement **2** *(carelessly)* négligemment

slackness ['slæknɪs] N **1** *(negligence)* négligence *f*, *(laziness)* paresse *f*, *Fam* flemme *f*, *(laxity)* mollesse *f*, *(of discipline)* laxisme *m* **2** *(of muscles etc)* relâchement *m*; *(of rope)* mou *m* **3** *Com (of business)* stagnation *f*

slag [slæg] N **1** *Metal (of metal)* scorie(s) *f(pl)*; *(of blast furnace)* crasse *f*, laitier(s) *m(pl)*; *Min* déchets *mpl* miniers; *Geol* **volcanic s.** scories volcaniques; **s. heap** *Metal* crassier *m*; *Min* terril *m* **2** *Pej Sl (woman)* salope *f*
VT *Br Sl* **1** *(criticize)* débiner, éreinter, descendre en flammes **2** *(make fun of)* se foutre de
▸ **slag off** VT SEP *Br Sl* **1** *(criticize)* débiner, éreinter, descendre en flammes **2** *(make fun of)* se foutre de

slagging ['slægɪŋ] N *Br Sl* **to give sb a s.** débiner qn

slaggy ['slægɪ] ADJ *Br Sl* qui fait pute; **she looks really s. in all that make-up** elle fait vraiment pute avec tout son maquillage

slain [sleɪn] ADJ *Lit* mort
NPL *Lit* **the s.** les morts *mpl*
PP *see* **slay**

slake [sleɪk] VT **1** *Lit* **to s. one's thirst** étancher *ou* apaiser sa soif, se désaltérer **2** *Chem (lime)* éteindre; **slaked lime** chaux *f* éteinte

slalom ['slɑːləm] N *Ski* slalom *m*

slam² [slæm] VT *(-mm-)* **1** *(door)* (faire) claquer; **to s. the door in sb's face** claquer la porte au nez de qn; **she slammed the book (down) on the table** elle a flanqué le livre sur la table; **he slammed the phone down** il raccrocha d'un geste furieux; *Ftbl* **he slammed the ball into the back of the net** il a logé le ballon au fond des filets; **she slammed her fist into his face** elle lui a flanqué son poing dans la figure; **he slammed the money down on the counter** il jeta rageusement l'argent sur le comptoir **2** *Fam (criticize severely)* critiquer; *(person)* éreinter; **he was slammed in the press** il a été éreinté par la presse **3** *Fam (drink quickly)* descendre, écluser; **let's go s. some beers** allons écluser quelques bières
VI *(of door etc)* claquer; **to s. out of the house** sortir de la maison en claquant la porte
N *(of door etc)* claquement *m*; **he shut the door after him with a s.** il claqua la porte derrière lui

slam² N *Cards (at bridge)* chelem *m*, schelem *m*; *Cards, Sport* **grand s.** grand chelem; **to make a s.** faire (le) chelem
▸ **slam on** VT SEP *Fam* **to s. on the brakes** freiner à fond

slammer ['slæmər] N *Sl (prison)* taule *f*

slander ['slɑːndər] N calomnie *f*, *Law* diffamation *f* verbale
VT calomnier; *Law* diffamer

slanderer ['slɑːndərər] N détracteur, -trice; *Law* diffamateur, -trice

slanderous ['slɑːndərəs] ADJ *(words, article)* calomnieux; *Law* diffamatoire

slanderously ['slɑːndərəslɪ] ADV calomnieusement; *Law* de façon diffamatoire

slang [slæŋ] N *(in general, of specific group)* argot *m*; **prisoners'/schoolboy s.** argot des prisonniers/écoliers; **s. phrase** *or* **expression** expression *f* argotique
VT *Br (person) (abuse)* injurier; *(reprimand)* engueuler

slangily ['slæŋɪlɪ] ADV *(to express oneself)* en argot

slanging match ['slæŋɪŋ] N *Fam* prise *f* de bec, engueulade *f*; **they were having a s.** ils se sont engueulés

slangy ['slæŋɪ] ADJ *(style, language, term)* argotique

slant [slɑːnt] N **1** *(oblique angle)* biais *m*, biseau *m*; **on the** *or* **at a s.** de biais, obliquement **2** *(emphasis)* perspective *f*; **to put a different s. on things** apporter une perspective différente sur les choses; **to put a left-/right-wing s. on events** interpréter les événements dans une perspective de gauche/de droite; **these historians put a different s. on events** ces historiens ont envisagé les événements sous un angle différent; **report with a s. to it** reportage tendancieux **3** *Offensive Sl (Oriental)* bridé, -ée
VI *(slope)* être en pente, être incliné; *(of handwriting)* pencher **(to** à)
VT **1** *(angle)* incliner **2** *Fig (bias)* fausser; **the article was slanted** l'article était orienté; **slanted news** informations tendancieuses *ou* faussées

slant-eyed ADJ aux yeux bridés; **to be s.** avoir les yeux bridés

slanting ['slɑːntɪŋ] ADJ *(roof)* en pente, incliné; *(writing)* couché, penché

slantwise, slantways ['slɑːntwaɪz, -weɪz] ADV en *ou* de biais

slap [slæp] N **1** *(with hand)* claque *f*, tape *f*, *(of waves)* clapotis *m*; **s. in the face** gifle *f*, *Fig (rebuff)* gifle, affront *m*, soufflet *m*; **s. on the back** tape dans le dos; *Fig* félicitations *fpl*; **to get a s. on the back for one's efforts** être félicité pour les efforts que l'on a fournis; *Br Hum Fam* **they were having a bit of s. and tickle on the sofa** ils se faisaient un câlin sur le divan **2** *Br Fam (make-up)* maquillage *m*
ADV *Fam* **s. (bang) in the middle** en plein milieu; **the car went s. bang into the wall** la voiture est rentrée dans le mur de plein fouet; **they ran s. bang into each other** ils se sont rentrés en plein dedans
VT *(-pp-)* [slæpt] **1** *(person) (with open hand)* donner une claque *ou* une tape à; **to s. sb's face, to s. sb in the face** gifler qn; **to s. sb on the back** donner une tape sur le dos à qn; *Fig (congratulate)* féliciter qn **2** *(put brusquely)* **she slapped the money on the table** elle a jeté *ou* flanqué l'argent sur la table
▸ **slap around** VT SEP battre, *Fam* cogner
▸ **slap down** VT SEP **1** *(put down brusquely)* jeter; *Fam* flanquer, balancer **2** *Fam (repress) (person)* rembarrer; *(put in his place)* remettre à sa place; *(suggestion)* rejeter
▸ **slap on** VT SEP **he slapped on some aftershave** il s'est aspergé de lotion après-rasage; *Fam* **they slapped on another £50** ils ont augmenté le prix de 50 livres; **the paint had been just slapped on** la peinture avait été appliquée n'importe comment

slapdash ['slæpdæʃ] ADJ sans soin(s); *(work)*

à la six-quatre-deux; *(person)* expéditif; **to do sth in a s. manner** faire qch à la va-vite *ou* à la six-quatre-deux
ADV sans soin(s), à la va-vite, à la six-quatre-deux

slap-happy ADJ *Fam (careless)* insouciant; **this work's a bit s.** ce travail a été fait à la va-vite

slaphead ['slæp(h)ed] N *Sl (bald person)* crâne *m* d'œuf

slapper ['slæpər] N *Br Sl* **1** *(promiscuous woman)* pouffiasse *f*, traînée *f*, salope *f* **2** *Pej (any woman)* gonzesse *f*, grognasse *f*

slapping ['slæpɪŋ] N *(blows)* claques *fpl*, gifles *fpl*

slapstick ['slæpstɪk] N grosse farce *f*, bouffonerie *f*
ADJ *(humour)* bouffon
▸▸ **s. comedy** comédie *f* bouffonne, farce *f*

slap-up ADJ *Br Fam* **a s. meal** un repas de derrière les fagots; **he invited me out for a s. lunch** il m'a invité à déjeuner dans un restaurant chic

slash [slæʃ] N **1** *(cut)* entaille *f*, *(on the face)* estafilade *f*, balafre *f* **2** *Sewing (in sleeve)* crevé *m* **3** *Typ* barre *f* oblique **4** *Br Sl* **to have a s.** *(urinate)* pisser un coup
VT *(cut) (flesh)* taillader; *(face)* balafrer; *(rope etc)* couper *ou* trancher net; *Fig (shorten) (text etc)* couper radicalement; *(criticize) (novel etc)* éreinter, *Fam* casser; *(reduce) (prices, interest rates)* casser; *(unemployment, spending)* réduire de façon radicale; **he slashed the sack open** il a fendu le sac d'un coup de couteau; **prices slashed** prix sacrifiés; *Sewing* **slashed sleeve** manche *f* à crevés
VI **to s. at sb with a knife** donner des coups de couteau à qn; **to s. about with a knife** donner des coups de couteau dans tous les sens; **they slashed through the undergrowth** ils se sont taillés un chemin dans les sous-bois

slasher film ['slæʃər] N *Fam* = film *m* d'horreur particulièrement sanglant

slashing ['slæʃɪŋ] ADJ *(criticism)* mordant, cinglant

slat [slæt] N *(of shutter etc)* lame *f*, lamelle *f*, planchette *f*, *(of bed)* traverse *f*

slate¹ [sleɪt] N **1** *Geol* ardoise *f*; *Constr (feuille f d')*ardoise; *Br Fam* **to have a s. loose** avoir une case de vide, avoir une araignée au plafond **2** *(writing)* ardoise *f*; *Br Fam* **put it on my s.** *(as debt)* mettez-le-moi sur mon ardoise; *Fig* **to wipe the s. clean** faire table rase (du passé); **I have a clean s.** *(have no debts)* je n'ai pas de dettes; *(have committed no offence)* mon casier judiciaire est vierge; **to start again with a clean s.** repartir sur de nouvelles bases **3** *TV etc* clap *m*
VT **1** *Constr (roof)* couvrir d'ardoises *ou* en ardoise; **slated roof** toit d'ardoises **2** *Am Pol (candidate)* inscrire sur la liste; **to be slated to do sth** être susceptible de faire qch; **he was slated for promotion but …** il aurait dû être promu mais …
▸▸ **s. blue** bleu ardoise *m inv*; **s. pencil** crayon *m* d'ardoise; **s. quarry** ardoisière *f*, **s. roof** toit *m* d'ardoises

slate² VT *Br Fam (criticize severely) (person, book, decision, government)* critiquer, éreinter, *Fam* casser

slate-blue ADJ bleu ardoise *inv*

slate-coloured ADJ ardoise *inv*

slate-grey ADJ gris ardoise *inv*

slater ['sleɪtər] N **1** *(person)* couvreur *m* (en ardoises) **2** *Dial (woodlouse)* cloporte *m*

slating ['sleɪtɪŋ] N *Br Fam* **1** *(reprimand)* savon *m*; **he got a s. from the PM** il s'est fait passer un savon par le Premier ministre **2** *(severe criticism)* critique *f* acerbe; **the play**

got a **s. in the press** la pièce a été éreintée *ou Fam* cassée par la presse

slatted ['slætɪd] ADJ *(shutters etc)* à lames, à planchettes

slattern ['slætən] N femme *f* mal soignée, souillon *f*

slatternly ['slætənlɪ] ADJ *(woman)* mal soigné; *(habit, dress)* négligé

slaty ['sleɪtɪ] ADJ *Geol* ardoisier; *(colour)* ardoisé

slaughter ['slɔːtər] N **1** *(of cattle, sheep etc)* abattage *m* **2** *(of people)* tuerie *f*, carnage *m*, massacre *m*; **the senseless s. of innocent civilians** le massacre insensé de civils innocents
▪ VT **1** *(cattle, sheep)* abattre **2** *(kill) (people)* tuer, massacrer; *Fam (defeat heavily) (opponent)* battre à plate(s) couture(s), massacrer

slaughtered ['slɔːtəd] ADJ *Br Fam (drunk)* bourré, beurré, pété

slaughterer ['slɔːtərər] N **1** *(of cattle, sheep)* abatteur *m*, tueur *m* **2** *(of people)* tueur, -euse

slaughterhouse ['slɔːtəhaʊs] N abattoir *m*

slaughtering ['slɔːtərɪŋ] N **1** *(of cattle, sheep)* abattage *m* **2** *(of people)* tuerie *f*, carnage *m*, massacre *m*

Slav [slɑːv] ADJ slave
▪ N Slave *mf*

slave [sleɪv] N esclave *mf*; **to be sb's s.** être l'esclave de qn; **to be the s. of** *or* **a s. to one's passion** être esclave de sa passion; **to be a s. to duty** ne connaître que son devoir; **to be a s. to convention** être esclave des conventions; **to be a s. to one's work** être esclave de son travail; *Fam Hum* **what did your last s. die of?** je ne suis pas ta bonne!
▪▪ **s. camera** caméra *f* asservie *ou* esclave; **s. cylinder** cylindre *m* récepteur; **s. driver** meneur *m* d'esclaves; *Fig* négrier *m*; **s. labour** *(work)* travail *m* fait par des esclaves; *Fig* travail de forçat; *(workers)* = personnes *fpl* que l'on utilise comme esclaves; **s. trade** commerce *m* des esclaves; *(of Africans)* traite *f* des Noirs; **s. trader** marchand *m* d'esclaves, négrier

slave VI travailler comme un nègre (**over** à); **to s. over a hot stove** trimer à ses fourneaux
▪ **slave away** VI *(work hard)* trimer (**over, at** sur)

slaver [sleɪvər] N **1** *(ship)* bâtiment *m* négrier **2** *(person)* marchand *m* d'esclaves; *(of Blacks)* négrier *m*; **White s.** personne *f* pratiquant la traite des Blanches

slaver ['slævər] N *(saliva)* bave *f*, salive *f*
▪ VI *(dribble)* baver (**over** sur)

slavery ['sleɪvərɪ] N esclavage *m*; **to sell sb into s.** vendre qn comme esclave; **to reduce to s.** *(person)* réduire en esclavage; *(a people)* asservir; **White s.** traite *f* des Blanches; **this work is sheer s.** ce travail est un véritable esclavage

Slavic ['slɑːvɪk] ADJ, N slave *m*

slavish ['sleɪvɪʃ] ADJ *(submission)* d'esclave; *(imitation)* servile

slavishly ['sleɪvɪʃlɪ] ADV *(to imitate)* servilement

slavishness ['sleɪvɪʃnɪs] N servilité *f*

Slavonic [slə'vɒnɪk] ADJ slave; **student of S. languages** slavisant, -ante
▪ N *Ling* slave *m*; **Church S., Old S.** slavon *m*

slaw [slɔː] N *esp Am Culin* salade *f* de chou cru

slay [sleɪ] VT *(pt* slew [sluː]; *pp* slain [sleɪn]) *Lit* tuer; *esp Am Journ* assassiner; **the slain** *(npl)* les morts *mpl*; *Fam* **this one will really s. you** *(of joke etc)* celle-là va vous faire mourir de rire

slayer ['sleɪər] N *Lit (killer)* tueur, -euse; *esp Am Journ (murderer)* assassin *m* (**of** de)

slaying ['sleɪɪŋ] N *Lit (killing) (of dragon)* destruction *f*; *(of person)* meurtre *m*; *esp Am Journ (murder)* assassinat *m*, meurtre *m*

sleaze [sliːz] N *Fam* corruption *f*, *(gossip in newspapers, on TV)* ragots *mpl* sordides; *(dirt, immorality)* perversité *f*; **the s. factor will affect his chances in the election** tous les ragots sordides qui ont circulé à son sujet risquent de compromettre son succès aux élections; **the s. factor in politics** la corruption de la vie politique

sleazebag ['sliːzbæg], *Am* **sleazeball** ['sliːzbɔːl] N *Sl* ordure *f*, raclure *f*

sleaziness ['sliːzɪnɪs] N *Fam (of place etc)* sordide *m*

sleazo ['sliːzəʊ] N *Fam* personne *f* louche; **he's a s.** c'est un type louche

sleazy ['sliːzɪ] ADJ *Fam* sordide, glauque

sled [sled] N, VI *Am* = **sledge**[1,2]

sledge[1] [sledʒ] N *(means of transport)* traîneau *m*; *(toy)* luge *f*
▪ VI *(travel)* aller en traîneau; *(play)* faire de la luge; **to go sledging** se promener en traîneau, faire une promenade en traîneau; *(of children)* aller faire de la luge

sledge[2] N = **sledgehammer**

sledgehammer ['sledʒhæmər] N *(tool)* masse *f*; **to have (all) the subtlety of a s.** manquer totalement de subtilité; **a s. blow** *(punch)* un coup de massue; *Fig (to industry etc)* un coup fatal; **to use a s. to crack a walnut** employer les grands moyens (pour régler un problème mineur)
▪▪ *Fam* **s. arguments** arguments massue(s)

sleek [sliːk] ADJ **1** *(smooth) (hair, fur etc)* lisse et brillant; *(person) (well-groomed)* trop pomponné; **a s. black limousine** une limousine d'un noir brillant; **the car's s. lines** la ligne aérodynamique de la voiture **2** *(unctuous) (manner)* mielleux, onctueux
▪ VT *(hair, horse's coat)* lisser
▪ **sleek down** VT SEP **to s. down one's hair** se lisser les cheveux; *(with oil)* se brillantiner les cheveux

sleekly ['sliːklɪ] ADV **1 to glisten s.** luire **2** *(unctuously) (to talk, act)* mielleusement, onctueusement

sleekness ['sliːknɪs] N **1** *(of skin, satin)* luisant *m* **2** *(of manners)* onctuosité *f*

SLEEP [sliːp] N sommeil *m*; *Fam (substance in eye)* chassie *f*; **short s.** somme *m*; **deep** *or* **sound s.** sommeil profond; **beauty s.** sommeil avant minuit *(considéré comme le plus réparateur)*; **to go to** *or* **drop off to s.** s'endormir, s'assoupir; **to go to** *or* **drop off to s. again** se rendormir; **to send sb to s.** endormir qn; *Med* **to put sb to s.** endormir qn; *Vet* **to put an animal to s.** piquer un animal; **to read oneself to s.** lire pour s'endormir; **to rouse sb from his/her s.** réveiller qn, arracher qn au sommeil; **to have a good (night's) s.** bien dormir; **I need my s.** j'ai besoin de beaucoup de sommeil; **to get two hours' s.** dormir deux heures; **I didn't get a wink of s. all night** je n'ai pas fermé l'œil de la nuit; *(stayed up working etc)* j'ai passé une nuit blanche; **a night without s.** une nuit blanche; **to rub the s. out of one's eyes** se frotter les yeux pour se réveiller; **I won't lose any s. over it** cela ne m'empêchera pas de dormir; **in my s.** *(to cry, talk, call out)* en dormant; **to walk in one's s.** être somnambule; **my foot's gone to s.** j'ai des fourmis dans le pied, j'ai le pied engourdi
▪ VI *(pt, pp* slept [slept]) **1** *(not be awake)* dormir; **to s. like a log** dormir à poings fermés, dormir comme une souche *ou* comme un loir; **to s. soundly** dormir profondément; **to s. the night through** dormir toute la nuit; **to s. through a noise** ne pas être réveillé par un bruit; **I slept right through the alarm** je n'ai

pas entendu le réveil; **I haven't slept a wink all night** je n'ai pas fermé l'œil de (toute) la nuit; **to s. (for) six hours** dormir six heures; **to try to s.** chercher le sommeil; **he can't s. for thinking about it** il n'en dort pas; **to s. late** faire la grasse matinée; **I'll s. on it** je déciderai demain, la nuit porte conseil; **s. on it** la nuit porte conseil
2 *(spend a night)* coucher; **to s. rough** coucher à la dure; **to s. on the floor/in a bed** coucher par terre/dans un lit; **the bed had not been slept in** le lit n'avait pas été défait
▪ VT **1 a house that sleeps ten people** une maison où l'on peut coucher à dix; **this room sleeps four** on peut coucher à quatre dans cette chambre
2 *Lit* **to s. the sleep of the just** dormir du sommeil du juste
▪▪ *Comput* **s. mode** veille *f*
▪ **sleep around** VI *Fam (be promiscuous)* coucher avec n'importe qui
▪ **sleep away** VT SEP **to s. the day/the hours away** passer la journée/les heures à dormir
▪ **sleep in** VI **1** *(have a lie-in)* faire la grasse matinée; *(wake up too late)* ne pas se réveiller à l'heure
2 *(of servant)* coucher à la maison
▪ **sleep off** VT SEP *Fam (remove by sleeping) (headache)* faire passer en dormant; **to s. off one's hangover, to s. it off** cuver son vin/sa bière *etc*
▪ **sleep out** VI *(not sleep at home)* découcher; *(in open air)* coucher à la belle (étoile); *(of servant)* coucher à domicile, venir en journée
▪ **sleep together** VI coucher ensemble
▪ **sleep with** VT INSEP **to s. with sb** coucher avec qn

sleeper ['sliːpər] N **1** *(person)* dormeur, -euse; **a late s.** un couche-tard; **to be a light/heavy s.** avoir le sommeil léger/profond; **to be a good s.** *(of baby)* bien dormir **2** *Br Rail (on track)* traverse *f* **3** *Rail (carriage)* wagon-lit *m*, *pl* wagons-lits; *(train)* train-couchettes *m inv* **4** *Am (pajamas)* sleeper(s) pyjama *m* d'enfant **5** *(spy)* espion *m* en sommeil **6** *(earring)* dormeuse *f* **7** *Fam (unexpected success)* = film *m*, livre *m*, chanson *f* etc qui rencontre un succès inattendu et tardif
▪▪ **s. cell** cellule *f* terroriste dormante *ou* en sommeil

sleepily ['sliːpɪlɪ] ADV d'un air endormi; **a village nestled s. in the hills** un village blotti tranquillement contre les collines

sleepiness ['sliːpɪnɪs] N **1** *(desire to sleep)* envie *f* de dormir, somnolence *f* **2** *(of town)* calme *m*, *Pej* apathie *f*

sleeping ['sliːpɪŋ] ADJ dormant, endormi; *Prov* **let s. dogs lie** ne réveillez pas le chat qui dort
▪ N sommeil *m*; **the house has s. accommodation for ten** c'est une maison où dix personnes peuvent dormir; **there's no s. accommodation here** il n'y a rien pour dormir; **this is the s. accommodation here** c'est ici qu'on dort; **what are the s. arrangements?** et pour dormir, comment on fait?; **she was a bit vague about the s. arrangements** elle est restée vague concernant les lits
▪▪ **s. bag** sac *m* de couchage; *Rail* **s. car** wagon-lit *m*, *pl* wagons-lits; *Br* **s. draught** soporifique *m*; *Br Com* **s. partner** (associé *m*) commanditaire *m*, bailleur de fonds; **s. pill** somnifère *m*; *Br* **s. policeman** casse-vitesse *m inu*, ralentisseur *m*; **s. quarters** chambres *fpl* à coucher; *Mil* chambrées *fpl*; *Sch* dortoir *m*; **s. sickness** maladie *f* du sommeil; *Am* **s. suit** grenouillère *f*; **s. tablet** somnifère

sleepless ['sliːplɪs] ADJ sans sommeil; *(night)* d'insomnie; **to have a s. night** ne pas fermer l'œil de la nuit, passer une nuit blanche; *Lit* **s. vigilance** vigilance sans faille

sleeplessly ['sli:plɪslɪ] ADV sans dormir

sleeplessness ['sli:plɪsnɪs] N insomnie f

sleepsuit ['sli:psju:t] = **sleeping suit**

sleepwalk ['sli:pwɔ:k] VI (be a sleepwalker) être somnambule; **he's sleepwalking** il marche en dormant; **I was sleepwalking last night** j'ai eu une crise de somnambulisme la nuit dernière; Fig **we are sleepwalking into disaster** nous allons tout droit à la catastrophe sans nous en rendre compte

sleepwalker ['sli:pwɔ:kər] N somnambule mf

sleepwalking ['sli:pwɔ:kɪŋ] N somnambulisme m

sleepy ['sli:pɪ] ADJ 1 somnolent; **to be** or **feel s.** avoir envie de dormir, avoir sommeil; **to make sb (feel) s.** endormir qn; **s. look** air endormi 2 **s. little town** petite ville endormie

sleepyhead ['sli:pɪhed] N Fam endormi, -ie; **wake up, s.!** debout, paresseux/paresseuse!

sleet [sli:t] N 1 (icy rain) pluie f mêlée de neige 2 Am (ice) verglas m
▸ V IMPERS **it's sleeting** il tombe de la neige fondue

sleeve [sli:v] N 1 (of garment) manche f; **short s.** manche courte; Fig Fam **he's got something up his s.** il a une idée derrière la tête; **he's got a surprise up his s.** il nous/leur etc réserve une surprise; **to have more than one trick up one's s.** avoir plus d'un tour dans son sac 2 Tech chemise f, fourreau m, gaine f (souple); (tubular casing) douille f 3 (of record) pochette f
▸▸ **s. board** jeannette f; **s. hole** (in clothing) emmanchure f; Br **s. notes** = texte m figurant au dos des pochettes de disques

sleeved [sli:vd] ADJ (garment) à manches

-sleeved [-sli:vd] SUFF **long/short-s.** à manches longues/courtes

sleeveless ['sli:vlɪs] ADJ (dress, pullover etc) sans manches

sleigh [sleɪ] N traîneau m
▸▸ **s. bell** grelot m (de traîneau); **s. ride** promenade f en traîneau

sleight [slaɪt] N (conjuring trick) tour m de passe-passe; **it's done by s. of hand** c'est de la prestidigitation; **by s. of hand** par un tour de passe-passe

slender ['slendər] ADJ 1 mince; (figure) svelte, fluet, -ette; **s. waist** taille fine 2 (hope) ténu; (income) modique, maigre, modeste; **the slenderest of margins** une marge des plus étroites; **there is a very s. chance that ...** il y a une chance très faible que ...; **s. means** de maigres ressources; **of s. means** qui a de petits moyens

slenderize ['slendəraɪz] VT Am amincir

slenderly ['slendəlɪ] ADV **s. built** mince, svelte

slenderness ['slendənɪs] N 1 minceur f, (of person, waist) sveltesse f 2 (of fortune) modicité f, (of resources) maigreur f

slept PT, PP see **sleep** VI, VT

sleuth [slu:θ] N Fam usu Hum limier m, détective m; **a good bit of s. work** un travail de fin limier
▸ VI Fam faire le détective

sleuthhound ['slu:θhaʊnd] N (dog) limier m; Fam (detective) limier, détective m

slew¹ [slu:] N (turn) virage m; Aut (180-degree turn) tête-à-queue m inv
▸ VT faire pivoter
▸ VI pivoter; (of car) (turn right round) faire un tête-à-queue; **the car slewed off the track** la voiture a dérapé hors de la piste
▸ **slew around, slew round** VT SEP (rotate) faire pivoter; **she slewed the car round** elle a fait pivoter la voiture; (180-degree turn) elle a fait un tête-à-queue

VI (rotate) pivoter; (of car) (through 180 degrees) faire un tête-à-queue

slew² N Fam (large number) tas m

slew³ PT see **slay**

slice [slaɪs] N 1 (of bread, cake, meat etc) tranche f, (of pizza) part f, (of apple) quartier m; **(round) s.** (of lemon, sausage etc) rondelle f, **s. of bread and butter** tartine f beurrée; **apple s.** tartelette f aux pommes; **to take a large s. of the credit for sth** s'attribuer une large part du mérite de qch; **a. s. of the profits** une part des bénéfices; **a s. of life** une tranche de vie 2 (utensil) **fish s.** pelle f (à poisson); **cake s.** pelle f à tarte 3 Sport coup m qui fait dévier la balle; Tennis balle coupée
▸ VT 1 couper ou découper en tranches; **to s. thinly** (meat) couper en tranches fines; (onions etc) émincer; **to s. sth in two** or **in half** couper qch en deux; Am **no matter how thin you s. it, it's still baloney** par quelque bout que tu le prennes, c'est un bobard 2 (ball) Tennis couper; Golf, Rugby faire dévier
▸ VI **this meat slices easily** cette viande est facile à couper
▸ **slice into** VT INSEP (cut easily) couper facilement; **the knife sliced into the flesh** le couteau a pénétré dans la chair
▸ **slice off** VT SEP (remove by slicing) (piece) trancher, couper, détacher; **to s. off the tip of one's finger** se trancher le bout du doigt
▸ **slice through** VT INSEP (cut easily) couper sans effort; **the knife sliced through the rope** le couteau a tranché la corde; Fig **the river slices through the city** la rivière coupe la ville en deux; **to s. through the enemy lines** transpercer les lignes adverses; **he sliced through the red tape** il a éliminé toute la paperasserie d'un seul coup
▸ **slice up** VT SEP (cut into slices) couper ou découper en tranches

slice-and-dice movie N Fam = film m d'horreur particulièrement sanglant

sliced [slaɪst] ADJ (bread, ham etc) en tranches; Fam **he thinks it's the best thing since s. bread** il pense que c'est ce qu'on a fait de mieux depuis l'invention du fil à couper le beurre

slicer ['slaɪsər] N Culin (device) couteau m à découper; (electric) couteau électrique; (bacon) s. coupe-jambon m inv

slick [slɪk] ADJ Fam (skilful, deft) habile, adroit; (catch, changeover) adroit; (movie) bien fait, Pej malin, -igne; **s. talker** beau parleur m
▸ N (oil) s. nappe f de pétrole; (on beach and sea) marée f noire
▸ **slick back** VT SEP (comb back with oil etc) **to s. back one's hair** se lisser les cheveux en arrière
▸ **slick down** VT SEP (comb down with oil etc) **to s. one's hair down** se lisser les cheveux
▸ **slick up** VI Fam (make oneself attractive) se faire beau

slicker ['slɪkər] N Am 1 (raincoat) imperméable m; (oilskin) ciré m 2 (person) (city) s. homme m de finance habile, Pej requin m

slickly ['slɪklɪ] ADV usu Pej (skilfully) habilement; (cunningly) habilement, adroitement

slickness ['slɪknɪs] N usu Pej (skill, deftness) habileté f, adresse f, (cunning) ruse f

slide [slaɪd] N 1 (action) glissade f, glissement m; (of land) glissement de terrain; **to have a s.** (of person) faire une glissade; **the alarming s. of the economy** le dérapage alarmant de l'économie; **a s. in prices/popularity** une chute des prix/de la popularité; **a mud s.** une coulée de boue; **a rock s.** un éboulement 2 (place) (on snow or ice) glissoire f, (in playground) toboggan m; Aviat (escape) s. toboggan d'évacuation 3 Mus (or-

nament) coulé m; (in violin playing etc) glissade f, (part of trombone etc) coulisse f 4 Tech (sliding part) pièce f qui glisse ou qui coulisse; (of slide rule) coulisseau m, réglette f, (in rowing) glissière f 5 (of microscope) (object) s. (plaque f ou lame f) porte-objet m, pl porte-objet(s); (what is on the slide) préparation f 6 Phot (colour) s. diapositive f (en couleur), Fam diapo f (en couleur); **lecture illustrated with slides** conférence f avec projections 7 Br (hair) s. barrette f
▸ VI (pt, pp slid [slɪd]) 1 (slip) (of mechanism between runners etc) coulisser; (of person) glisser; **to s. (on ice)** (of person) glisser (sur la glace), faire une glissade/des glissades; **she slid on the floor** elle a glissé sur le parquet; **the dish slid off the table/onto the floor** le plat a glissé de la table/sur le sol; Fig **to let things** or **everything s.** laisser tout aller à la dérive; (lose interest in everything) se désintéresser de tout; **the country was sliding into anarchy** le pays glissait vers l'anarchie; **prices/profits had begun to s.** les prix/profits avaient commencé à chuter 2 (move quietly) (into room, behind curtain etc) se glisser; **the snake slid through the grass** le serpent s'est glissé entre les herbes; **the pilot slid into the cockpit** le pilote s'est glissé dans le cockpit; **to s. over a delicate subject** glisser sur un sujet délicat
▸ VT (faire) glisser; **to s. sth into one's pocket** glisser qch dans sa poche
▸▸ Am **s. fastener** fermeture f à glissière, fermeture Éclair®; **s. guitar** slide guitar f, TV etc **s. matter** cache m latéral; **s. projector** projecteur m de diapositives; **s. show** diaporama m; Comput diaporama, projection f de diapositives
▸ **slide down** VI (go down by sliding) descendre en glissant; (of prices) chuter
▸ VT INSEP (go down by sliding) descendre en glissant; **to s. down a rope** se laisser couler ou glisser le long d'une corde; **to s. down the banisters** glisser le long de la rampe; **it's sliding down the charts** il perd des places au hit-parade
▸ **slide off** VI 1 (be removed by sliding) **the lid slides off** pour enlever le couvercle, il faut le faire glisser ou coulisser; **it keeps sliding off** ça n'arrête pas de glisser 2 Fam (sneak away) filer en douce
▸ VT SEP (lid etc) faire glisser
▸ **slide out** VI 1 (come out by sliding) sortir en glissant 2 Fam (sneak outside) se glisser dehors
▸ VT SEP (drawers, battery) enlever en faisant glisser
▸ **slide out of** VT INSEP (evade) se sortir de; **to s. out of doing the housework** échapper aux tâches ménagères; **I'd like to see him s. out of that one** j'aimerais bien voir comment il va se tirer d'affaire

sliding ['slaɪdɪŋ] ADJ (part) qui glisse; (movement) glissant; (panel) mobile; (door) coulissant
▸▸ **s. roof** toit m ouvrant; **s. scale** (for salaries) échelle f mobile; (for prices) barème m des prix; (for tax) barème des impôts; **s. seat** (in rowing boat) banc m à coulisses ou à glissières; (in car) siège m réglable ou mobile; **s. sunroof** toit ouvrant coulissant

slight [slaɪt] ADJ 1 (small) (pain, mistake etc) léger, -ère, petit; (intelligence, difference etc) faible; (damage) peu important; (wound) sans gravité; **a s. accident** un petit incident; **a s. improvement** un léger mieux; **not the slightest danger/interest** etc pas le moindre danger/intérêt etc; **to take offence at the slightest thing** se vexer pour un rien; **I haven't the slightest (idea)** je n'en ai pas la moindre idée; **not in the slightest** pas du tout, pas le moins du monde; **they weren't**

(in) the slightest bit interested, they weren't interested in the slightest ils n'étaient pas le moins du monde intéressés; there's a s. chance of some sunshine tomorrow il y a une petite chance qu'il fasse beau demain **2** (thin) ténu; (person) menu; (figure) frêle **N** (affront) m

VT (person) (affront) faire un affront à; (treat without consideration) traiter sans considération, manquer d'égards pour ou à; **to feel slighted** se sentir vexé ou froissé

slighting ['slaɪtɪŋ] **ADJ** (tone) de mépris, de dédain; (remark) plein de mépris

slightingly ['slaɪtɪŋlɪ] **ADV** avec dédain, dédaigneusement

slightly ['slaɪtlɪ] **ADV 1** (to a small degree) légèrement, un peu; **s. better** un (petit) peu mieux; **I know him s.** je le connais un peu **2** (thinly) s. built menu

slightness ['slaɪtnɪs] **N 1** (small extent) (of mistake etc) légèreté f, (of difference) petitesse f, (of damage) insignifiance f **2** (thinness) **the s. of her arms** ses bras menus; **her s.** son corps menu

slim [slɪm] **ADJ** (comp **slimmer**, superl **slimmest**) (person) svelte; (fingers etc) fuselé, menu; (book etc) mince; (chance, hope etc) petit; **tall and s.** élancé; **his first s. volume** son premier petit opuscule

VT (-mm-) amincir

VI maigrir; **to be slimming** être au régime, suivre un régime amaigrissant; **dress that is slimming** robe qui mincit

► **slim down VT SEP** (reduce) (labour force) réduire; **the company is slimming down its electronics operation** la société réduit ses activités dans le domaine de l'électronique

VI 1 (lose weight) maigrir **2** (become smaller in size) (of company, army etc) diminuer de taille

slime [slaɪm] **N 1** (mud) vase f **2** (on fish etc) humeur f visqueuse; (of slug) bave f, **what's this horrible s.?** qu'est-ce que c'est ce truc dégueulasse? **3** Fam (person) ordure f

slimebag ['slaɪmbæg], **slimeball** ['slaɪmbɔːl] **N** Fam (despicable person) ordure f, raclure f, (repulsive man) gros dégueulasse m

sliminess ['slaɪmɪnɪs] **N 1** état m vaseux; (of fish etc) viscosité f **2** Fam (servility) servilité f, obséquiosité f

slimly ['slɪmlɪ] **ADV** s. built svelte

slimmer ['slɪmər] **N** personne f qui suit un régime amaigrissant; **ideal for slimmers** l'idéal pour maigrir

slimming ['slɪmɪŋ] **N** amincissement m; s. can be bad for you les régimes peuvent parfois nuire à la santé

► ► **s. club** centre m d'amaigrissement; **s. course** cure f d'amaigrissement; **s. diet** régime m amaigrissant; **s. pill** pilule f amaigrissante

slimness ['slɪmnɪs] **N** (of person) minceur f, sveltesse f, (of book etc) minceur f

slimy ['slaɪmɪ] **ADJ 1** (consistency) vaseux; (mud) gras, f grasse; (paste etc) visqueux, gluant; **the frog felt all s.** la grenouille était toute visqueuse **2** (tracks of slug) visqueux; (covered in slime) couvert de vase; (fish) couvert d'une sécrétion visqueuse; (slug etc) couvert de bave; **it was a horrible s. mess** c'était parfaitement dégueulasse **3** Fam (person) servile, obséquieux; **he's a real s. creep** c'est un vrai lèche-bottes

sling [slɪŋ] **N 1** Med écharpe f, (of rifle etc) bretelle f, (for hoisting), Naut etc élingue f, (for hoisting people) agui m; **to have one's arm in a s.** avoir le bras en écharpe **2** (weapon) fronde f

VT (pt, pp **slung** [slʌŋ]) **1** (hang) suspendre; **to s. sth over one's shoulder** jeter qch sur l'épaule; **to s. sth across one's chest** mettre

qch en bandoulière; Fam **to s. one's hook** mettre les bouts **2** (throw) lancer, jeter; **s. that paper over, will you?** lance-moi le journal, s'il te plaît; **they were slinging insults at each other** ils se lançaient des insultes

► **sling off VT SEP** Fam **to s. sb off a course** virer qn d'un cours

► **sling out VT SEP** Fam **1** (dismiss) (person) flanquer dehors; **he was slung out of the army** il s'est fait jeter de l'armée **2** (throw away) jeter, balancer

► **sling up VT SEP** (hoist) hisser (avec une grue)

slingback ['slɪŋbæk] **N** chaussure f à talon ouvert, sandale f

ADJ (shoe) à talon ouvert

slingshot ['slɪŋʃɒt] **N** esp Am fronde f

slink [slɪŋk] **VI** (pt, pp **slunk** [slʌŋk]) **to s. off** or **away** partir en catimini, s'éclipser; **to s. in/out** entrer/sortir furtivement; **she was slinking about in a velvet dress** elle ondulait dans sa robe en velours

slinkily ['slɪŋkɪlɪ] **ADV** Fam (to move) avec des ondulations; **s. cut dress** robe qui épouse bien les courbes du corps; **she sidled s. up to him** elle s'est dirigée vers lui en roulant des hanches

slinking ['slɪŋkɪŋ] **ADJ** furtif

slinky ['slɪŋkɪ] **ADJ** Fam (figure) svelte, mince; (clothing) collant, ajusté; (walk) ondulant

SLIP [slɪp] **N** Comput (abbr **serial line Internet protocol**) protocole m SLIP

SLIP¹ [slɪp]

N chute **1, 5**	▪ faute d'inattention **2**
▪ lapsus **2**	▪ glissement **4, 5**
▪ éboulement **4**	▪ baisse **5**
▪ combinaison **6**	
VI glisser **1**	▪ chuter **1** ▪ baisser **1**
▪ patiner **1**	▪ se glisser **2**
VT échapper à **1**	▪ glisser **2**

N 1 (fall) **he had a s. on the ice** il a fait une chute sur la glace; **he had a nasty s.** il est mal tombé, il a fait une mauvaise chute

2 (error) faute f d'inattention ou d'étourderie; (in speaking) lapsus m; **to make a s.** faire une erreur; (in speaking) faire un lapsus; **s. of the pen** petite erreur f d'orthographe; **she made a s. of the tongue** sa langue a fourché; **it was a s., I meant to say …** ma langue a fourché, je voulais dire …; Prov **there's many a s. 'twixt cup and lip** il y a loin de la coupe aux lèvres

3 to give sb the s. fausser compagnie à qn **4** Geol (of land) glissement m; (of rocks) éboulement m

5 (by thing) glissement m; (in share values etc) chute f, (in standards) baisse f, Aut (of clutch) patinage m

6 (garment) combinaison f (de femme); **half** or **waist s.** jupon m; **your s.'s showing** votre jupon dépasse; **(pillow) s.** taie f d'oreiller

7 (of ferry) cale f de chargement; **the ship is still on the slips** le navire est toujours sur cale(s) ou en construction

8 Theat **the slips** les coulisses fpl

9 Cr (player) chasseur m posté à droite du garde-guichet; **the slips** (position) la station à droite du garde-guichet

10 (in pottery) (for decoration) engobe m

VI (-pp-) **1** (slide) glisser; (of knot) couler, courir; (of earth etc) s'ébouler; (of prices) chuter; Tech etc (of clutch, belt etc) patiner, glisser; TV **the picture keeps slipping** l'image descend; **his foot slipped** son pied a glissé; **I slipped on a banana skin** j'ai glissé sur une peau de banane; **to s. from sb's hands** or **grasp** (of vase, book etc) glisser des mains ou des doigts de qn; **to s. through sb's fingers** filer entre les doigts de qn; **to s.**

into bad habits prendre de mauvaises habitudes; **an error that has slipped into the text** une faute qui s'est glissée dans le texte; **the patient slipped into a coma** le malade est tombé dans le coma; **money just slips through his fingers** l'argent lui file entre les doigts; **they let the terrorists s. through their fingers** ils ont laissé filer les terroristes; **he let his guard s.** il a baissé sa garde; **don't let your concentration s.** ne relâche pas ta concentration; **the record has slipped to number 22** le disque est descendu en 22ème position; **the quality is slipping** la qualité baisse

2 (move quickly, smoothly etc) **to s. into bed** se glisser ou se couler dans son lit; **to s. into one's dressing gown** passer ou Fam enfiler sa robe de chambre; **she slipped into the next room** elle s'est glissée dans la pièce voisine; **just s. round** or **over to the post office** fais un saut jusqu'au bureau de poste

3 (make mistake) faire une (faute d')étourderie; **you're slipping!** (performing below one's usual standard) tu baisses!; **he slipped and said 'twenty' by mistake** sa langue a fourché et il a dit 'vingt' par erreur

4 to let s. (opportunity, word, secret) laisser échapper; **she let s. a few swearwords** elle a laissé échapper quelques jurons; **to let (it) s. that …** laisser échapper que …

VT 1 Aut **to s. the clutch** laisser patiner l'embrayage; **to s. its chain** or **leash** or **lead** (of animal) se détacher; **the dog has slipped its collar** le chien s'est dégagé de son collier; **his name has slipped my mind** son nom m'échappe; **to s. sb's attention** échapper à qn

2 (put) (sth into sb's hand, a letter into the postbox) glisser; **he slipped it into his pocket** il l'a glissé dans sa poche; **to s. sth into the conversation** glisser qch dans la conversation; **to s. the bolt (home)** pousser le verrou à fond; **I slipped my arm round her waist** j'ai glissé mon bras autour de sa taille; Fam **to s. something** or **one over on sb** rouler qn

3 Naut **to s. a cable** larguer ou filer une amarre par le bout; **to s. one's moorings** filer le corps-mort

4 Knitting (stitch) glisser

5 Med **to s. a disc** se faire une hernie discale

► ► Br **s. road** bretelle f d'accès; Sewing **s. stitch** point m perdu

► **slip away VI 1** (of person) (get away) filer; (leave work early) s'éclipser; (of lead in elections etc) s'effriter; **the patient was slipping away** le malade s'éteignait doucement; **control of the party was slipping away from her** elle perdait peu à peu son emprise sur le parti; **my life seemed to be slipping away from me** ma vie m'échappait; **you're slipping away from me** (in relationship) tu t'éloignes de moi

► **slip back VI 1** (return) revenir (into dans) **2** (get worse) (of work) se dégrader

VT SEP (put back) remettre

► **slip by VI 1** (of time, years etc) passer; (fast) fuir

2 (pass unnoticed) (of person) passer sans se faire remarquer

VT INSEP to s. by sb (of errors, escapee) échapper à qn

► **slip down VI** (slide down) descendre en glissant; (of socks) descendre; **this whisky slips down very nicely** ce whisky descend tout seul

VT INSEP to s. down a pole glisser le long d'un poteau; **they've slipped down the league** ils sont descendus au classement

► **slip in VI** (enter quickly, inconspicuously) entrer sans se faire remarquer; **a few mistakes slipped in** (in text) quelques erreurs se sont glissées dans le texte

VT (insert inconspicuously) glisser; **she slipped in several references to …** elle a placé plusieurs allusions à …

▸ **slip off** VT SEP *(jacket, shoes)* enlever
VI *(of person)* s'éclipser
▸ **slip on** VT SEP *(put on quickly) (garment)*
passer, *Fam* enfiler
▸ **slip out** VI **1** *(escape)* s'échapper; **the soap
slipped out of my hands** le savon m'a glissé
des mains; **to let sth s. out** laisser échapper
qch; **the secret has slipped out** le secret a
transpiré; **it slipped out that …** le bruit s'est
répandu selon lequel …
2 *(leave quickly, inconspicuously) (to avoid
somebody or something)* filer (à l'anglaise);
I'm just slipping out for a few minutes je
m'éclipse quelques minutes, je reviens dans
une minute; **could you s. out and buy me
some chocolate?** tu pourrais faire un saut à
l'épicerie*etc* pour m'acheter du chocolat?
▸ **slip past** VI passer
VT INSEP **to s. past sb/sth** se glisser devant
qn/qch
VT SEP *Fam* **to s. one past sb** rouler qn
▸ **slip through** VI *(of errors etc)* échapper à
l'attention; **too many mistakes are slipping
through** il y a trop d'erreurs qui nous/leur*etc*
échappent
▸ **slip up** VI *(make mistake)* se tromper; *(socially etc)* faire une gaffe, gaffer

---

Note that the French word **slip** is a false
friend and is never a translation for the
English word **slip**. It means **underpants**
or **briefs**.

---

slip² N **1** *(piece) (of paper)* bout *m*; *(coupon)*
bon *m*; *(docket)* fiche *f*, *(of land etc)* bande *f*
étroite; **pay s.** bulletin *m* de paie; **sales s.** récépissé *m*
2 *Old-fashioned Fam* **s. of a girl** jeune fille
fluette; *(young)* fillette *f*
3 *(in horticulture)* bouture *f*, *(for grafting)*
scion *m*
▸▸ *Journ* **s. page** page *f* volante; *Typ* **s. sheet**
feuille *f* intercalaire
slipcase ['slɪpkeɪs] N *(for books)* étui *m*
slipcover ['slɪpkʌvər] N *esp Am* **1** *(for furniture)* housse *f* **2** *(book cover)* jaquette *f*
slipknot ['slɪpnɒt] N nœud *m* coulant
slip-on N *Fam* **1** slip-ons *(shoes)* mocassins
mpl **2** *Am (sweater)* pull-over *m*, *pl* pull-
overs, pull *m*
ADJ *(shoe)* sans lacets
▸▸ **s. shoes** mocassins
slipover ['slɪpəʊvər] N débardeur *m*
slippage ['slɪpɪdʒ] N *(in production)* retard
m; **there's too much s.** *(loss of time)* on perd
de plus en plus de temps; **s. in prices** dérapage *m* des prix
slipped disc [slɪpt] N *Med* hernie *f* discale
slipper ['slɪpər] N **1** *(footwear) (backless)*
mule *f*, *(with back)* chausson *m*, pantoufle *f*
2 *Tech (of brake)* patin *m*
▸▸ *Old-fashioned* **s. baths** bains *mpl* publics
slipperiness ['slɪpərɪnɪs] N **1** *(of surface)*
nature *f* glissante **2** *(of person)* caractère *m*
rusé
slippery ['slɪpərɪ] ADJ **1** *(pavement, fish etc)*
glissant; *(difficult) (subject, concept)* délicat;
it's s. (underfoot) ça glisse; *Fig* **it's a
s. slope** nous sommes/il est*etc* sur une
pente glissante; **this was the start of the s.
slope that led to (his) alcoholism** ce fut le
début de la déchéance qui l'a mené à l'alcoolisme **2** *(devious) (person)* retors; **he's as
s. as an eel** il glisse comme une *ou* est aussi
insaisissable qu'une anguille
slippy ['slɪpɪ] ADJ *Fam* **1** *(slippery)* glissant **2**
Old-fashioned Br Fam (quick) **you'll have to
be pretty s. about it** il va falloir que tu fasses
ficelle; **look s.!** grouille-toi!
slipshod ['slɪpʃɒd] ADJ *(negligent) (person,
attitude)* négligent; *(work)* négligé, bâclé;

book written in a s. manner livre écrit sans
soin
slipstream ['slɪpstriːm] N *(of car, boat etc)*
sillage *m*, remous *mpl*; *Aviat* souffle *m ou*
vent *m* de l'hélice; *Fig* **to be dragged along
in sb's s.** se laisser entraîner par qn
VT *(car)* se mettre dans le sillage de
slip-up N *Fam* gaffe *f*; **there's been a s.** il y a
eu une gaffe de faite; **to make a s.** faire une
gaffe
slipway ['slɪpweɪ] N *Naut (for building, repairing)* cale *f ou* chantier *m* de construction; *(for launching)* slip *m*
slit [slɪt] N fente *f*, *(between curtains etc)* entrebâillement *m*; *(for shooting through)*
meurtrière *f*
ADJ *(skirt)* fendu; *(eyes)* bridé
VT *(pt, pp* **slit**; *prp* **slitting)** *(make slit in)* fendre; *(envelope)* ouvrir; *Surg (flesh)* inciser;
the knife had s. his leg open le couteau lui
avait ouvert la cuisse; **the blow s. his cheek**
le coup lui a déchiré la joue; **to s. sb's throat**
couper la gorge à qn; **to s. open a sack** éventrer un sac
▸▸ **s. pocket** poche *f* fendue; *Mil* **s. trench**
tranchée *f* étroite
slither ['slɪðər] N glissement *m*
VI glisser; *(of snake, worm)* ramper; **the dog
was slithering about on the ice** le chien dé-
rapait sur la glace; **to s. down a hill** déraper
dans une pente
sliver ['slɪvər] N *(thin slice)* petite tranche *f*,
(of wood) éclat *m*
Sloane, Sloane Ranger [sləʊn('reɪndʒər)] N
Br Fam jeune fille *f* BCBG
Sloaney ['sləʊnɪ] ADJ *Br Fam* BCBG
slob [slɒb] N *Fam (untidy, rude)* rustaud,
-aude; *(lazy)* flemmard, -arde; **big fat s.** gros
lard *m*
slobber ['slɒbər] N *(saliva)* bave *f*, salive *f*
VI *(salivate)* baver; **stop slobbering on me**
arrête de me baver dessus
▸ **slobber over** VT INSEP *(of dog, baby) (person, shoulder)* baver; *(kiss etc) (person)* faire
des bises baveuses à; **he doesn't like them
slobbering all over him** il n'aime pas qu'ils
lui bavent dessus
sloe [sləʊ] N **1** *(fruit)* prunelle *f* **2** *(tree)* prunellier *m*
▸▸ **s. gin** gin *m* à la prunelle
slog [slɒg] *Fam* N **1** *(blow)* coup *m* (violent);
to give the ball a real s. frapper dans la balle
un bon coup **2** *(hard work)* boulot *m* pénible; **it was a bit of a s.** on en a bavé; **a hard
s.** *(great effort, reading book)* un gros effort;
(walk, ride) un trajet pénible; **it's a long s. to
the top** *(of hill, in organization)* on en bave
pour arriver en haut
VT *(-gg-)* *(hit) (person, object)* cogner, battre;
Cr (ball) frapper fort sur; **he slogged his way
through the text** il a déchiffré le texte avec
grande difficulté
VI *(work hard)* turbiner, trimer; **they
slogged for miles** *(walking)* ils marchèrent
à grand-peine pendant des kilomètres
▸ **slog along** VI *Fam (keep walking)* marcher
d'un pas lourd *ou* péniblement
▸ **slog away** VI *Fam (keep working, trying)*
trimer
▸ **slog away at** VT INSEP *Fam* **1** *(work hard at)*
travailler avec acharnement à **2** *(keep hitting)* continuer à frapper
▸ **slog on** VI *Fam* **1** = slog along **2** *(keep
working)* continuer à trimer; **I think I'll s. on
a little longer** je pense que je vais continuer
à bosser encore un peu
slogan ['sləʊgən] N *Pol, Com* slogan *m*; **elec-
tion/advertising s.** slogan électoral/
publicitaire
slogger ['slɒgər] N *Fam* **1** *Boxing, Cr* cogneur *m* **2** *(hard worker)* bûcheur, -euse

slo-mo ['sləʊməʊ] N, ADJ *Fam abbr* slow-
motion
sloop [sluːp] N *Naut* sloop *m*
slop [slɒp] VT *(-pp-)* *(spill) (liquid)* renverser
(**over the table** sur la table)
VI *(of liquids)* déborder
N **1** slops *(pig food)* soupe *f* à cochons; *Pej
(food)* brouet *m*; *(spilt drinks) (on table etc)*
boissons *fpl* renversées **2** *Fam (sentimentality)* bêtises *fpl* à l'eau de rose
▸▸ *Br* **s. basin** vide-tasses *m inv*; **s. bucket**
seau *m* (à ordures); *(in prison)* seau hygiénique; *(for pigs)* seau à pâtée
▸ **slop about, slop around** VI **1** *Fam (walk
in water, mud etc)* patauger, barboter **2** *(of liquid)* clapoter **3** *Fig Fam* **he just slops around
the house all day** il passe toute la journée à
traîner *ou Fam* à glandouiller chez lui
▸ **slop out** VI *(in prison)* vider les seaux hygiéniques
▸ **slop over** VI = slop
slope [sləʊp] N **1** *(incline)* pente *f*, inclinaison *f*, *(in road, railway)* rampe *f*, **steep/
gentle s.** pente raide/douce; *Mil* **with rifle
at the s.** l'arme sur l'épaule **2** *(hill)* pente *f*,
(of mountain) versant *m*; *Ski* piste *f*; **on the
slopes of the Himalayas** sur les pentes de
l'Himalaya; **on the northern s.** sur le versant
nord; **halfway down/up the s.** à mi-pente
VI *(of ground etc)* être en pente; *(not be
straight) (of picture etc)* pencher; **to s. forward** *or* **to the right/backward** *or* **to the left**
(of writing) pencher à droite/à gauche; **the
garden slopes down to the river** le jardin
descend (en pente) vers la rivière; **the
ground slopes up to the house** le terrain
monte en pente vers la maison
VT incliner; *Mil* **to s. arms** mettre l'arme sur
l'épaule; **s. arms!** arme sur l'épaule!
▸ **slope away, slope off** VI *Fam (leave furtively)* décamper, filer
sloping ['sləʊpɪŋ] ADJ *(table, roof)* en pente;
(writing) penché; *(shoulders)* tombant
sloppily ['slɒpɪlɪ] ADV **1** *(carelessly)* sans
soin **2** *Fam (sentimentally)* avec sensiblerie
sloppiness ['slɒpɪnɪs] N **1** *(carelessness) (in
work)* manque *m* de soin, négligence *f*, *(of
style)* négligence **2** *Fam (sentimentality)* sentimentalité *f* excessive
slopping out ['slɒpɪŋ] N *(in prison)* vidange *f* des seaux hygiéniques
sloppy ['slɒpɪ] ADJ **1** *(careless) (work, person)* négligé; *(worker)* négligent; *(organization, approach)* nul, *f* nulle; *(language,
spelling)* relâché **2** *Fam (sentimental) (novel)*
guimauve; *(person)* fleur bleue
▸▸ *Br Fam* **s. joe** *(sweater)* pull-over *m* très
ample, *pl* pull-overs très amples; *Am (hamburger)* steak *m* haché servi en sandwich
slosh [slɒʃ] VI *(of liquid) (move around)* clapoter
VT **1** *(spill) (water etc)* renverser **2** *Fam (apply liberally) (paint on wall etc)* flanquer **3**
Br Sl (hit) (person) flanquer un coup à, tabasser
▸ **slosh about, slosh around** VI **1** *Fam (walk
in water, mud etc)* patauger, barboter **2** *(of liquid)* clapoter
sloshed [slɒʃt] ADJ *Br Sl (drunk)* bourré, rond
slot [slɒt] N **1** *(groove) (in vending machine,
head of screw etc)* fente *f*, *Comput* emplacement *m*; **to put a coin in the s.** *(of vending
machine etc)* introduire une pièce de monnaie dans la fente; *Comput* **expansion s.** emplacement pour carte d'extension **2** *(in
broadcasting schedule, waiting list etc)* créneau *m* horaire; *(for aircraft in flight control)*
créneau; **we could put the new series in the
7:30 s.** on pourrait caser *ou* placer le nouveau feuilleton dans le créneau de 19 heures
30; **we've missed our s.** nous avons raté notre créneau; **there's a s. for somebody with**

editorial skills il y a un créneau pour quelqu'un ayant une formation de rédacteur; **to fill a s.** boucher un trou; *Radio, TV* **prime time s.** heure *f* de grande écoute

VT (**-tt-**) **to s. sth into sth** insérer *ou* mettre qch dans qch; **to s. sb into a job** caser qn dans un travail; **where can we s. him in?** comment est-ce qu'on peut l'intégrer?

VI s'introduire, se glisser (**into sth** dans qch); **it slots well into our programme** cela s'insère bien dans notre programme; **she slotted into the department well** elle s'est bien intégrée au service

▸▸ **s. machine** (*for vending*) distributeur *m* (automatique); (*for gambling*) machine *f* à sous; *Br* **s. meter** compteur *m* à pièces

▸ **slot in VT SEP** (*fit in*) (*patient, customer etc*) prendre; **to s. a book in a space on a shelf** glisser un livre dans un espace sur une étagère

VI (*fit in*) **the book will s. in here** le livre rentrera là-dedans

▸ **slot together VT SEP** (*pieces*) encastrer l'un dans l'autre/les uns dans les autres

VI s'encastrer l'un dans l'autre/les uns dans les autres

sloth [sləʊθ] **N 1** (*laziness*) paresse *f* **2** (*animal*) paresseux *m*

▸▸ **s. bear** ours *m* lippu; **s. monkey** loris *m* lent

slothful ['sləʊθfʊl] **ADJ** paresseux, -euse

slothfully ['sləʊθfəlɪ] **ADV** paresseusement

slothfulness ['sləʊθfʊlnɪs] **N** paresse *f*

slot-in card N *Comput* carte *f* enfichable

slouch [slaʊtʃ] **N 1** (*way of walking*) démarche *f* mollasse; (*deportment*) allure *f* avachie *ou* molle; **s. of the shoulders** épaules tombantes **2** *Fam* **he's no s.** il n'est pas empoté

VI (*hold oneself badly*) être avachi; (*walk badly*) avoir une démarche mollasse; **don't s.!** tenez-vous droit!

▸▸ **s. hat** chapeau *m* à larges bords

▸ **slouch about, slouch around VI** (*in town*) traîner; (*at home, in front of television*) traînasser

slough¹ [slaʊ] **N** (*bog*) bourbier *m*, fondrière *f*; *Lit* **to be in a s. of despair/gloom** sombrer dans le désespoir/la tristesse

slough² [slʌf] **N** (*of reptile, insect*) mue *f*, **to cast its s.** muer

VI (*of reptile etc*) muer

VT to s. its skin (*of reptile, insect*) muer; *Lit* **to s. a bad habit** se débarrasser d'une mauvaise habitude

▸ **slough away VI** = **slough off**

▸ **slough off VT SEP** = **slough²**

VI (*become detached*) (*of scab etc*) se détacher, tomber

Slovak ['sləʊvæk] **ADJ** slovaque

N 1 (*person*) Slovaque *mf* **2** *Ling* slovaque *m*

Slovakia [sləʊ'vækɪə] **N** Slovaquie *f*

Slovakian [sləʊ'vækɪən] **ADJ, N** = **Slovak**

sloven ['slʌv(ə)n] **N 1** (*untidy person*) mal soigné, -ée; (*woman*) souillon *f* **2** *Old-fashioned* (*careless worker*) saboteur, -euse

Slovene ['sləʊviːn] **ADJ, N** = **Slovenian**

Slovenia [sləʊ'viːnɪə] **N** Slovénie *f*

Slovenian [sləʊ'viːnɪən] **ADJ** slovène

N 1 (*person*) Slovène *mf* **2** *Ling* slovène *m*

slovenliness ['slʌv(ə)nlɪnɪs] **N** (*of work, appearance*) négligence *f*

slovenly ['slʌv(ə)nlɪ] **ADJ 1** (*untidy*) (*person*) mal soigné; (*dress*) débraillé **2** (*negligent*) (*person*) négligent; (*work*) négligé, bousillé; (*style*) débraillé; **done in a s. way** fait sans soin

SLOW [sləʊ] **ADJ 1** (*not fast*) lent; (*boring*) (*film, show etc*) ennuyeux; (*stupid*) (*person*) simple; **I'm being a bit s. this morning** je suis un peu lent ce matin; **to be s. over doing sth**

mettre longtemps à faire qch; **business is s.** les affaires languissent *ou* ne vont pas fort; **to be s. to do sth** (*of person*) être lent à faire qch; **s. to act** *or* **to take action** lent à agir; **progress has been s.** les progrès ont été lents; **this method is s. but sure** cette méthode est lente mais sûre; **he wasn't s. to respond** *or* **in responding** il n'a pas été long à réagir; **he's been s. to get it done** il a mis du temps à le faire; **sorry I was s. getting back to you** désolé d'avoir mis du temps à vous rappeler; **you're very s. today** tu es très lent aujourd'hui; *Fam* **to be as s. as treacle** *or Am* **molasses** (*in winter*) être lent comme un escargot *ou* une tortue; **to be s. off the mark** (*in race*) démarrer en douceur; (*to start sth*) prendre son temps pour faire qch; (*to understand*) être lent à la détente; **a s. child** un enfant attardé; **to cook sth in a s. oven** faire cuire qch à four doux; *Am Sl* **to s. a burn** avoir la moutarde qui vous monte au nez; **it's s. work** ça ne va pas vite; **she's a s. worker** elle travaille lentement

2 (*clock, watch*) en retard; **my watch is five minutes s.** ma montre retarde de cinq minutes

ADV lentement; **to go s.** aller lentement; (*as industrial action*) faire la grève perlée; **to run s.** (*of engine*) tourner au ralenti; (*of clock*) retarder; **s.!** (*on road sign*) ralentir!; *Naut* **s. ahead/astern!** en avant/en arrière doucement!; **s. spoken** qui parle lentement; **s. moving** (*traffic*) au ralenti; (*queue, crowd, river, film, etc*) lent; **s. burning** à combustion lente; (*in explosives*) (*powder*) lent

VT & VI = **slow down, slow up**

▸▸ *Culin* **s. burner** feu *m* doux; **s. cooker** mijoteuse *f*; **the s. lane** (*when driving on left*) la file de gauche; (*when driving on right*) la file de droite; *Cin, TV* **s. motion** ralenti *m*; **in s. motion** au ralenti; *Tech* **s. running** ralenti; **s. train** omnibus *m*

▸ **slow down, slow up VI** (*go more slowly*) ralentir; *Aut* (*of engine*) prendre le ralenti; **to s. down** *or* **up** (**to a stop**) s'arrêter; *Fig* **s. down a bit!** doucement!; **as he got older, he slowed down** à mesure qu'il prenait de l'âge, il a ralenti son rythme

VT SEP ralentir; **I'll only s. you down** je vais vous retarder

slowcoach ['sləʊkəʊtʃ] **N** *Br Fam* lambin, -ine, traînard, -arde

slow-cook VT mijoter, faire cuire à feu doux

slowdown ['sləʊdaʊn] **N** (*slowing*) (*in business etc*) ralentissement *m*; *Am* (*industrial action*) travail *m* au ralenti

slowing ['sləʊɪŋ] **N s.** (**down** *or* **up**) ralentissement *m*

slowly ['sləʊlɪ] **ADV** lentement; **the time/ morning has gone very s.** le temps/la matinée a passé très lentement; **to run s.** (*engine*) tourner au ralenti; **he's s. realizing that ...** il se rend compte peu à peu que ...; **s. but surely** lentement mais sûrement; **to cook sth s.** faire cuire qch à feu doux

slow-motion replay N ralenti *m*

slowness ['sləʊnɪs] **N** (*lack of speed*) lenteur *f*, (*of mind*) lourdeur *f*, lenteur *f*; (*of film, show etc*) lenteur *f*; (*of clock etc*) retard *m*

slowpoke ['sləʊpəʊk] **N** *Am Fam* lambin, -ine, traînard, -arde

slow-release ADJ *Med* (*medicine*) retard *inv*

slow-running jet N *Aut* gicleur *m* de ralenti

slow-witted ADJ à l'esprit lent

slow-worm N orvet *m*, serpent *m* de verre

SLR [esel'ɑ:r] **N** *Phot* (*abbr* **single-lens reflex**) reflex *m* monoculaire

sludge [slʌdʒ] **N** (*mud*) vase *f*, fange *f*; *Ind*

boue *f*, (*in engine*) cambouis *m*; **sewage s.** vidanges *fpl*

sludgy ['slʌdʒɪ] **ADJ** (*muddy*) vaseux; *Ind* boueux

slug¹ [slʌg] **N** *Zool* limace *f*

▸▸ **s. pellet** pastille *f* anti-limace

slug² **N 1** (*bullet*) balle *f*, plomb *m* **2** *Fam* (*of brandy etc*) goutte *f*, coup *m*

slug³ *esp Am Fam* **N** (*blow*) coup *m* violent

VT (*hit*) (*person, ball*) frapper; **he slugged me with a piece of wood** il m'a frappé avec un bâton

▸ **slug out VT SEP** *Fam, also Fig* **to s. it out** (*of two people*) se rentrer dedans; **he slugged it out with him** il s'est battu avec lui

slugfest ['slʌgfest] **N** *Am Fam* **1** *Boxing* combat *m* **2** (*fight*) baston *m ou f*, castagne *f*

sluggard ['slʌgəd] **ADJ, N** *Lit* paresseux, -euse, fainéant, -ante

sluggish ['slʌgɪʃ] **ADJ** (*person, day*) (*lazy*) paresseux, *Fam* flemmard; (*not energetic*) léthargique; (*mind*) lent, engourdi; (*response, attempt, engine*) mou, *f* molle; (*river, pulse etc*) lent, paresseux; (*market*) stagnant; (*sales*) médiocre; (*organization, bureaucracy*) lourd; **the economy is s.** l'économie tourne au ralenti; **at a s. pace** au ralenti

sluggishly ['slʌgɪʃlɪ] **ADV 1** (*lazily*) paresseusement **2** (*slowly*) lentement

sluggishness ['slʌgɪʃnɪs] **N 1** (*of person*) paresse *f*, *Fam* flemme *f*; (*of mind*) lenteur *f* **2** (*of river etc*) lenteur *f*, *Aut* (*of engine*) mollesse *f*, (*of organization, bureaucracy*) lourdeur *f*

sluice [sluːs] **N 1** (*structure*) écluse *f* **2** = **sluicegate 3** (*action*) *Fam* **to give sth a s. down** laver qch à grande eau

VT (*wash*) laver à grande eau

▸ **sluice down VT SEP** (*wash down*) laver à grande eau; **to s. oneself down with cold water** s'asperger d'eau fraîche

▸ **sluice out VT SEP 1** *Tech* (*release*) (*water from reservoir*) laisser échapper (*par les vannes*) **2** (*rinse*) (*cup, pot etc*) rincer

VI (*of water etc*) (*flow out in great quantity*) couler à flots

sluicegate ['sluːsgeɪt] **N** porte *f* d'écluse, vanne *f*

sluiceway ['sluːsweɪ] **N** canal *m*, -aux à vannes

slum [slʌm] **N** (*district*) bas quartiers *mpl*, quartier *m* pauvre; *also Fig* (*house*) taudis *m*

VT (**-mm-**) *Fam* **to s. it** s'encanailler; *Fig Hum* **I'm slumming it tonight** j'ai décidé d'aller m'encanailler ce soir

▸▸ *Br* **s. clearance** rénovation *f ou* aménagement *m* des quartiers insalubres; **s. landlord** marchand *m* de sommeil

slumber ['slʌmbər] **N** *Lit* sommeil *m*; **her s. was** *or* **her slumbers were interrupted by ...** son sommeil a été interrompu par ...; *Fig* **the country had finally awoken from its slumbers** le pays était enfin sorti de sa torpeur; *Fig Lit* **he awoke from his intellectual slumbers** il est sorti de ses hibernations intellectuelles

VI sommeiller, dormir (paisiblement)

▸▸ *Am* **s. party** soirée *f* entre copines (*au cours de laquelle on regarde des films, on discute et on dort dans la même pièce*); **s. wear** vêtements *mpl* de nuit

slumlord ['slʌmlɔːd] **N** *esp Am Fam* marchand *m* de sommeil

slummy ['slʌmɪ] **ADJ** sordide; **the s. area of town** les bas quartiers

slump [slʌmp] **N** *Econ* (*of prices etc*) effondrement *m*; **s. in prices** dégringolade *f* des prix; **the s. in oil prices** l'effondrement des prix du pétrole; **there's been a s. in the**

pound la livre a chuté; *Econ* **the s.** la crise *ou* dépression économique

VI 1 *(of person)* s'effondrer, s'affaisser (**into a chair** dans un fauteuil); **the editor was slumped unconscious over his desk** le rédacteur était effondré sans connaissance sur son bureau **2** *Econ (of prices, pound) (fall suddenly)* s'effondrer, *Fam* dégringoler; *(of economy, demand)* chuter

slumpflation [slʌmpˈfleɪʃən] **N** *Econ* = forte récession *f* accompagnée d'une inflation des prix et des salaires

slung PT, PP *see* **sling** VT

slunk PT, PP *see* **slink**

slur [slɜ:r] **N 1** *(insult)* insulte *f*, *(on reputation)* tache *f*; **a racial s.** une réflexion raciste; **to cast a s. on sb's reputation** porter atteinte à *ou* ternir la réputation de qn **2** *Mus (sign)* liaison *f*, *(passage)* coulé *m* **3** *(in speech)* mauvaise articulation *f*, **in a drunken s.** de la voix traînante d'un ivrogne; **to speak with a s.** mal articuler; *(as result of stroke etc)* parler d'une voix traînante

VT (-rr-) **1** *(words)* mal articuler; **his speech was slurred** il articulait mal; *(because of stroke etc)* il parlait d'une voix traînante **2** *Mus (two notes)* lier; *(passage)* couler; **slurred notes** notes liées coulant

VI *(speak indistinctly)* mal articuler ses mots, manger la moitié de ses mots

▸ **slur over** VT INSEP *(not deal with fully)* **to s. over a fact** passer *ou* glisser sur un fait

slurp [slɜ:p] **VT** *(soup etc)* faire du bruit en mangeant; *(tea)* faire du bruit en buvant

VI *(eating)* faire du bruit en mangeant; *(drinking)* faire du bruit en buvant

▸ **slurp up** VT SEP *(soup)* avaler en faisant du bruit

slush [slʌʃ] **N 1** *(snow)* neige *f* fondue **2** *Fam (sentimentality)* sensiblerie *f*

▸▸ **s. fund** caisse *f* noire *(servant généralement au paiement des pots-de-vin)*; *Fam* **s. money** dessous-de-table *mpl*

slushy [ˈslʌʃɪ] **ADJ 1** *(from snow)* détrempé par la neige **2** *Fam (novel, film etc)* guimauve; *(person)* fleur bleue *inv*

slut [slʌt] **N 1** *(dirty woman)* souillon *f* **2** *(promiscuous woman)* salope *f*

sluttish [ˈslʌtɪʃ] **ADJ 1** *(dirty)* sale; **to lead a s. existence** vivre salement **2** *(morals)* dépravé; *(behaviour)* débauché, dépravé; **a s. woman** une salope

sluttishness [ˈslʌtɪʃnɪs] **N 1** *(dirtiness)* saleté *f* **2** *(promiscuity)* conduite *f* immorale

slutty [ˈslʌtɪ] **ADJ** *Fam (promiscuous)* coucheuse; *(clothes, behaviour, make-up)* qui fait pute

sly [slaɪ] **ADJ** *(comp* **slyer,** *superl* **slyest) 1** *(cunning)* rusé; **he's a s. dog** c'est un fin matois **2** *(dishonest)* sournois **3** *(mischievous)* malin, *f*-igne, espiègle; **s. grin** sourire espiègle

N on the s. à la dérobée, en cachette

slyboots [ˈslaɪbu:ts] **N** *Fam* petit malin *m*, petite maligne *f*

slyly [ˈslaɪlɪ] **ADV 1** *(cunningly)* avec ruse **2** *(dishonestly)* sournoisement **3** *(mischievously)* d'une manière espiègle, avec espièglerie

slyness [ˈslaɪnɪs] **N 1** *(cunning)* ruse *f* **2** *(dishonesty)* sournoiserie *f* **3** *(mischievousness)* espièglerie *f*

smack¹ [smæk] **N 1** *(blow)* claque *f*, **s. in the face** gifle *f*, *Fig Fam* **s. (in the eye)** affront *m*, rebuffade *f*; **to give a child a s. on the bottom** donner une fessée à un enfant **2** *(sound)* claquement *m*; **with a s. of his lips** avec un claquement de langue; **the s. of the waves** le fouettement des vagues **3** *Fam (loud kiss)* gros baiser *m* retentissant, grosse bise *f*

ADV to go s. *(make sound)* faire clac; *Fam* **to bump s. into a tree** rentrer en plein dans un arbre; **to bump s. into a lamppost** se prendre un lampadaire; **s. in the middle** en plein milieu, au beau milieu; **he caught him s. on the chin** il l'a frappé en plein sur le menton

VT *(hit)* frapper, taper *(avec le plat de la main)*; *(person)* donner une claque à; **to s. sb's face** donner une gifle à qn, gifler qn; **to s. a child's bottom** donner une fessée à un enfant

smack² **N** *Naut* **(fishing) s.** bateau *m* de pêche

smack³ **N** *Sl (heroin)* héro *f*

smack⁴ **N** *(slight taste) (of garlic etc)* léger goût *m*

▸ **smack of** VT INSEP *(have slight taste of)* avoir un léger goût de; *Fig* **to s. of heresy** sentir l'hérésie *ou* le brûlé *ou* le fagot

smacker [ˈsmækər] **N 1** *Fam (big kiss)* grosse bise *f*, gros baiser *m* **2** *Sl (pound)* livre *f*, *(dollar)* dollar *m*; **fifty smackers** cinquante livres/dollars

smacking [ˈsmækɪŋ] **N** *(spanking)* fessée *f*, **to give sb a s.** donner une fessée à qn

small [smɔ:l] **ADJ 1** *(not large)* petit; *(dose etc)* petit, faible; **to make sth smaller** rapetisser qch; **to make oneself s.** se faire tout petit; **s. child** *(young)* enfant en bas âge, petit enfant; *(small in size)* enfant de petite taille; **a s. coffee** une petite tasse (de café); **a s. white coffee please!** un petit crème, s'il vous plaît!; **s. details** menus détails; **the smallest details** les moindres détails; **of s. dimensions** de petites dimensions; **he's a s. eater** il a un petit appétit; **a s. hotel** un hôtel modeste; **s. income** revenu modique *ou* modeste; **in s. numbers** en petit nombre; **the smallest number of people possible** le moins de gens possible; **s. voice** voix fluette, petite voix

2 *(not important)* peu important; *Br Fam* **to be s. beer** être insignifiant; **this was s. beer** c'était de la petite bière; **of no s. consequence** très important, qui porte à conséquence; **she took no s. pride in ...** elle n'était pas peu fière de ...; **it makes not the smallest difference** ça ne fait pas la moindre différence; **it was no s. surprise to me** cela m'a beaucoup surpris; **it's s. wonder that ...** ce n'est guère étonnant que ... + *sub*; **a s. matter** une bagatelle; **I do some acting, in a s. way** je fais un peu de théâtre; **he's a farmer in a s. way** il tient une petite exploitation agricole; **in her own s. way, she had ...** dans la limite de ses moyens, elle avait ...

3 *(petty)* mesquin; **I felt very s.** *(ashamed)* je n'étais pas fier, *(humiliated)* je me suis senti très humilié; **to make sb look** *or* **feel s.** humilier qn, rabaisser qn; **s. mind** esprit mesquin

N 1 s. of the back creux *m ou* chute *f* des reins **2** *Fam* **smalls** lingerie *f*, sous-vêtements *mpl*; **to wash one's smalls** faire sa petite lessive **3** *(small size) (in T-shirt etc)* petite taille *f*, **this T-shirt is a s.** ce T-shirt est une petite taille

ADV 1 *(to chop etc)* menu, fin **2** *(to write)* petit; **to think s.** voir petit

▸▸ **s. ad** petite annonce *f*, **s. arms** armes *fpl* portatives; **s. business** *(firm)* petite entreprise *f*, PME *f*, *(shop)* petit commerce *m*; **s. businessman** petit entrepreneur *m ou* patron *m*, *Typ* **s. capitals** petites capitales *fpl*, *Typ Fam* **s. caps** petites capitales; **s. change** petite monnaie *f*, *Aut* **s. end** *(of connecting rod)* pied *m*; **s. fry** menu fretin *m*; **s. hours** petit matin *m*; **in the s. hours** au petit matin; *Anat* **s. intestine** intestin *m* grêle; *Fin* **s. investor** petit porteur *m*; *Typ* **s. letters** minuscules *fpl*; **s. print** petits caractères *mpl*; **s. scale** petite échelle *f*; **s. screen** petit écran *m*; **s. shopkeeper** petit commerçant *m*; **s. talk** banalités *fpl*; *Typ* **s. type** petits corps *mpl*

smallholder [ˈsmɔːlhəʊldər] **N** *Agr* petit cultivateur *m*

smallholding [ˈsmɔːlhəʊldɪŋ] **N** *Agr* petite ferme *f*

smallish [ˈsmɔːlɪʃ] **ADJ** assez *ou* plutôt petit

small-minded **ADJ** à l'esprit mesquin *ou* étroit

smallness [ˈsmɔːlnɪs] **N 1** *(of income)* petitesse *f*, modicité *f*, *(of sum)* faible montant *m* **2** *(pettiness)* **the s. of his mind** sa mesquinerie

smallpox [ˈsmɔːlpɒks] **N** *Med* petite vérole *f*, variole *f*, **s. case** un cas de variole

small-scale **ADJ 1** *(model)* réduit; *(map)* à petite échelle **2** *(business)* peu important, de peu d'importance

▸▸ *Comput* **s. integration** intégration *f* à petite échelle

small-time **ADJ** *Fam* insignifiant, médiocre; **s. crook** petit escroc *m*

small-town **ADJ** *Fam* provincial, -aux, de province; **a s. attitude** une mentalité provinciale

▸ **smarm down** VT SEP **to s. down one's hair** se brillantiner les cheveux

▸ **smarm up to** VT INSEP *Fam Pej* lécher les bottes à

smarminess [ˈsmɑːmɪnɪs] **N** *Fam Pej* caractère *m* doucereux; **his s. gets on my nerves** ses flagorneries me tapent sur les nerfs

smarmy [ˈsmɑːmɪ] **ADJ** *Fam Pej* doucereux, flagorneur; **a s. git** un lèche-bottes *inv*

smart [smɑːt] **ADJ 1** *(clever)* habile, intelligent; *(shrewd)* malin, *f*-igne, rusé; *(quick-thinking)* à l'esprit vif; *(resourceful)* qui a des idées, *Fam* dégourdi, débrouillard; *Comput* intelligent; **it isn't s. to break the law** ce n'est pas malin d'enfreindre la loi; **to be too s. for sb** être trop intelligent pour qn; **trying to be s., eh?** tu essaies de faire le malin, hein?; **don't try to be s. with me** n'essaie pas de faire le malin avec moi; **that wasn't very s., was it?** ce n'était pas très malin, tu ne trouves pas?; **s. lad wanted** on recherche un jeune garçon intelligent; **s. businesswoman** femme d'affaires habile; **s. answer** réponse habile; **the s. money is on JJ for chairman** les gens au parfum prédisent JJ comme PDG; **a s. move** une sage décision; *Fam* **he's a s. one** c'est un malin

2 *(dress, person, building etc) (elegant)* élégant, chic *inv*; *(attractive)* coquet, pimpant; **to make oneself s.** se faire beau/belle; *(for interview etc)* bien s'habiller; **you do look s.!** comme tu es beau/belle!; **the s. set** la haute; **to be a s. dresser** bien s'habiller

3 *(quick)* vif, *f* vive, rapide; *(prompt)* prompt; **s. pace** allure vive; **that's s. work** vous avez vite fait; **a s. box on the ear** une bonne gifle; **s. reprimand** réprimande assez sèche

ADV look s. (about it)! dépêchez-vous!, remuez-vous!

N *(pain)* douleur *f* cuisante

VI 1 *(of wound, graze etc)* brûler; **my eyes are smarting** les yeux me brûlent **2** *(of person)* souffrir; **to s. under an insult** souffrir sous le coup d'une insulte

▸▸ *Fam* **s. Alec, s. Aleck** petit malin *m*; **s. bomb** bombe *f* intelligente; **s. card** carte *f* à puce; **s. card reader** lecteur *m* de cartes à puce *ou* de cartes à mémoire; **s. drug** psychotrope *m*; **s. missile** engin *m* intelligent

smartarse, *Am* **smartass** [ˈsmɑːtɑːs, -æs] *Fam* **N** petit malin *m*, petite maligne *f*, **don't be such a s.!** arrête de faire le malin!

ADJ *(answer)* malin, *f*-igne

smarten [ˈsmɑːt(ə)n] **VT to s. (the appearance of) sth** arranger qch; **to s. one's pace** accélérer, activer

▸ **smarten up** VT SEP **1** *(make more elegant)*

(something) donner du chic à; (make more presentable) arranger; **to s. oneself up** se faire beau **2** Fam (improve) **you'd better s. up your ideas** or **your act!** tu ferais bien de te reprendre!; (to lazy person) tu ferais bien de te secouer!

VI 1 (make oneself elegant) se faire beau **2** Fam (improve performance) se reprendre

smarting ['smɑːtɪŋ] ADJ (pain, eyes) brûlant N douleur f cuisante

smartish ['smɑːtɪʃ] ADV Br Fam vite fait, en vitesse; **you'd better get ready pretty s.** tu ferais mieux de te préparer vite fait

smartness ['smɑːtnɪs] N **1** (cleverness) habileté f, intelligence f; (shrewdness) ruse f; (quickness of thought) vivacité f (d'esprit); (resourcefulness) débrouillardise f **2** (elegance) élégance f, chic m **3** (speed) rapidité f

smarts [smɑːts] NPL Am Fam (intelligence) intelligence f, **to have s.** en avoir dans le ciboulot; **he's pretty low on s.** c'est pas une lumière

smarty-pants ['smɑːtɪ] N Fam petit malin m, petite maligne f

smash [smæʃ] N **1** (heavy blow) coup m violent; (loud noise) fracas m; Tennis smash m **2** (collision) collision f, (accident) accident m; (pile-up) télescopage m **3** (failure) (in business) débâcle f, (bankruptcy) faillite f **4** Fam (success) succès m bœuf; **it was a s.** ça a fait un tabac

ADV **to go s.** (of firm, bank) faire faillite

VT **1 to s. sth on** or **against sth** heurter ou lancer qch contre qch avec violence; **to s. sth open** ouvrir qch d'un coup violent; **she smashed him over the head with a chair** elle lui a cassé une chaise sur la tête; **she smashed her fist into his face** elle lui a fichu son poing dans la figure; **he smashed the ball into the back of the net** d'un tir terrible, il a envoyé le ballon au fond des filets; Tennis **to s. the ball** faire un smash, smasher **2 to s. sth (to pieces)** briser qch (en mille morceaux); (shatter) fracasser qch; **to s. the door open** enfoncer la porte **3** (destroy) (object, person) anéantir; (army etc) écraser; Sport (record) pulvériser; **to s. a drugs ring** démanteler un réseau de trafiquants de drogue

VI **1** (strike) se heurter violemment (**into sth** contre qch); **the car smashed into the wall** la voiture est allée s'écraser contre le mur **2 to s. (in pieces)** éclater (en mille morceaux) **3** (of firm etc) faire faillite

▸▸ **s. hit** (song, record) gros succès m
▸ **smash down** VT SEP (door etc) défoncer
▸ **smash in** VT SEP **1** (break open) (door etc) enfoncer, défoncer; (safe) forcer **2** Fam **to s. sb's face in** casser la figure ou Fam la gueule à qn; **I'll s. your face in** je vais te casser la gueule
▸ **smash open** VT SEP **1 = smash in 1 2** (box etc) ouvrir en cassant d'un coup de marteau etc; **he smashed his head open on a rock** il s'est ouvert la tête en heurtant un rocher
▸ **smash up** VT SEP (something) briser en morceaux; (car etc) démolir; **they smashed the place up in revenge** ils ont tout démoli pour se venger

smash-and-grab ADJ pillage m de vitrine
▸▸ **s. raid** pillage de vitrine

smashed [smæʃt] ADJ Sl (drunk) bourré, rond; (on drugs) camé; **to get s.** (drunk) se bourrer; (on drugs) se camer

smasher ['smæʃər] N Br Fam **what a s.!** (attractive person) il/elle est vachement bien!; **that's a s.!** (car etc) il est génial(e)!

smashing ['smæʃɪŋ] ADJ **1** (blow) violent **2** Br Fam (excellent) super, génial, -aux; **we had a s. time** c'était vachement bien

smash-up N Aut, Rail etc Fam (collision) télescopage m

smattering ['smæt(ə)rɪŋ] N (of French, maths etc) connaissances fpl sommaires; **to have a s. of English** savoir un peu d'anglais; **to have a s. of chemistry** avoir quelques notions de chimie

smear [smɪər] N **1** (stain) tache f, souillure f; (defamation) diffamation f, (spoken) calomnie f; **they resorted to s. tactics** ils eurent recours à la diffamation/la calomnie **2** Med frottis m

VT **1** (stain) barbouiller, salir (**with** avec); (non-pejorative sense, cover) enduire (**with** de); **their faces were smeared with coaldust** ils avaient le visage tout barbouillé de charbon; **to s. sth with grease, to s. grease on sth** étaler de la graisse sur qch; **the walls were smeared with blood** les murs étaient tout maculés de sang; **to s. oneself with grease, to s. grease on oneself** s'enduire de graisse **2** (page of writing etc) maculer, barbouiller; **don't s. the paint!** ne salis pas la peinture!; **the colours had been smeared into one another** les couleurs s'étaient mélangées; **to get smeared** (of outline) s'estomper; **the rain has smeared the address** la pluie a en partie effacé l'adresse **3** (defame) diffamer; (verbally) calomnier; (person's reputation) salir

VI (of paint etc) couler; (of ink) baver
▸▸ **s. campaign** campagne f de diffamation ou dénigrement; Med **s. test** frottis (vaginal), Can test m de Papanicolaou

smeary ['smɪərɪ] ADJ (stained) taché, barbouillé; (with blurred outlines) aux contours estompés; (windows etc) sale

smell [smel] N **1** (sense of) s. odorat m; (of animals) flair m; **to have a keen sense of s.** avoir l'odorat très développé; (of dog etc) avoir beaucoup de flair **2** (odour) (of flowers) odeur f, parfum m, senteur f; **(bad) s.** mauvaise odeur; **there's a bad s.** ça sent mauvais; **what's that s.?** quelle est cette odeur?; **stale s.** (of beer etc) relent m; **it has no s.** ça n'a pas d'odeur; **(pleasant) s.** of cooking bonne odeur de cuisine; **the s. was unbearable** l'odeur était intolérable; **to take a s. at sth** sentir qch, renifler qch; Fig **a s. of death** une odeur de mort; Fig **I don't like the s. of this at all** ça ne me plaît pas du tout, c'est louche

VT (pt, pp smelt [smelt], occ smelled) (inhale smell of) (something) sentir; (flowers) respirer l'odeur de; (of dog) (something) flairer, renifler; (perceive smell of) (something) sentir l'odeur de; (odour) sentir; Fig (danger etc) sentir, flairer; **I can s. something burning** je sens quelque chose qui brûle; **I can s. gas** ça sent le gaz; **I can s. cooking/chocolate** je sens une odeur de cuisine/chocolat; Fig **I s. a rat** il y a quelque chose de louche

VI **1** (of flower etc) sentir; **to s. good/bad/strong(ly)** sentir bon/mauvais/fort; **to s. of violets** sentir la violette; **it smells like lemon** ça sent le citron, on dirait du citron; **to s. of gas** sentir le gaz; **these flowers don't s.** ces fleurs n'ont pas d'odeur, ces fleurs ne sentent rien **2** (have bad smell) sentir (mauvais); **it smells (awful)!** ça pue!; **his breath smells** il a mauvaise haleine **3** (have sense of smell) **he can't s.** il n'a pas d'odorat
▸ **smell out** VT SEP **1** (discover by smelling) (of dog) flairer; Fig (of person) (secret) découvrir **2 his cigarettes are smelling the office out** ses cigarettes empestent ou empuantissent le bureau

smelliness ['smelɪnɪs] N mauvaise odeur f, puanteur f

smelling ['smelɪŋ] ADJ
▸▸ **s. salts** sels mpl

smelly ['smelɪ] ADJ **1** malodorant, puant; **it's**

s. in here ça sent mauvais ici; **to be s.** sentir mauvais; **he's got s. feet** il sent des pieds; **am I still s.?** je sens encore (mauvais)? **2** Fam (objectionable, unpleasant) dégueulasse

smelt[1] [smelt] N (fish) éperlan m

smelt[2] VT (ore) fondre; (metal) extraire par fusion

smelter ['smeltər] N haut-fourneau m, pl hauts-fourneaux

smelting ['smeltɪŋ] N (of ore) fonte f, fusion f, (of metal) extraction f par fusion
▸▸ **s. works** fonderie f

smidgen ['smɪdʒən] N Fam **a s. of sth** un tout petit peu de qch

smile [smaɪl] N sourire m; **with a s.** en souriant, avec un sourire; **with a s. on his lips** le sourire aux lèvres; **to give sb a s.** adresser un sourire à qn, sourire à qn; **she was all smiles** elle était toute souriante ou tout sourire; (pretence) elle était tout sucre tout miel; **that'll take** or **wipe s. off his face!** cela va lui faire passer l'envie de sourire!

VI sourire; **to s. at sb** sourire à qn, adresser un sourire à qn; **fortune smiles on him** la fortune lui sourit; **to keep smiling** Lit **to s. in the face of adversity** garder le sourire; **he always comes up smiling** il garde toujours le sourire; Phot **s.!** souriez!; **she smiled back (at him)** elle lui rendit son sourire

VT **to s. a bitter s.** sourire amèrement, avoir un sourire amer; **to s. a welcome to sb** accueillir qn avec ou par un sourire; **to s. one's gratitude** exprimer sa gratitude par un sourire

smiley ['smaɪlɪ] N Comput souriant m, émoticon m

smiling ['smaɪlɪŋ] ADJ souriant

smilingly ['smaɪlɪŋlɪ] ADV en souriant, avec un sourire

smirch [smɜːtʃ] N tache f, salissure f, souillure f
VT salir, souiller

smirk [smɜːk] N (affected smile) sourire m affecté; (mocking) petit sourire supérieur; (gloating) petit sourire narquois
VI (affectedly) sourire d'un air affecté; (mockingly) sourire d'un air supérieur; (gloatingly) sourire d'un air narquois

smite [smaɪt] VT (pt smote [sməʊt]; pp smitten ['smɪt(ə)n]) **1** Arch, Lit (strike) (the enemy) frapper, battre **2 to be smitten with blindness** être frappé de cécité; **to be smitten with remorse** être pris de remords; **to be smitten with a desire to do sth** être pris d'un ou du désir de faire qch; Fam **to be smitten with a girl** être amoureux fou d'une jeune fille; **he's totally smitten** il est sous le charme
▸ **smite down** VT SEP Arch, Lit abattre

smith [smɪθ] N forgeron m; (who shoes horses) maréchal-ferrant m, pl maréchaux-ferrants

smithereens [smɪðə'riːnz] NPL **the ship was blown to s.** l'explosion a réduit le navire en miettes; **he was blown to s. in the explosion** il a été déchiqueté dans l'explosion; **to smash sth to s.** briser qch en mille morceaux

Smithsonian Institution [smɪθ'səʊnɪən] N = complexe m culturel à Washington

smithy ['smɪðɪ] N forge f; (for shoeing horses) (atelier m de) maréchalerie f

smitten PP see smite

smock [smɒk] N (garment) blouse f, sarrau m
VT Sewing (dress etc) orner de smocks

smocking ['smɒkɪŋ] N smocks mpl

smog [smɒg] N smog m

smoke [sməʊk] N **1** (substance) fumée f, **tobacco s.** fumée de tabac; Fig Fam **to go up in s.** (of building, papers etc) partir en fumée;

Fam he had s. coming out of his ears *(was angry)* ses yeux lançaient des éclairs; *Prov* **(there's) no s. without fire** il n'y a pas de fumée sans feu
2 *(act of smoking)* **let's have a s.** si on fumait (une cigarette/une pipe/un cigare)?; **I always have a s.** at about 10 je me fume toujours ma petite cigarette aux alentours de dix heures
3 *Fam (cigarette)* cigarette *f*, *(cigar)* cigare *m*
4 *(cannabis cigarette)* joint *m*; *(cannabis)* chichon *m*, shit *m*
5 *Br Sl* **the (Big) S.** Londres *m*
VI 1 *(smoke tobacco)* fumer; **do you s.?** (est-ce que) vous fumez?; **do you mind if I s.?** est-ce que ça vous dérange si je fume?; *Fam* **to s. like a chimney** *(of person)* fumer comme un pompier *ou* un sapeur
2 *(emit smoke, vapour)* fumer; *(of lamp)* fumer; **the horses' flanks were smoking** les chevaux étaient tout fumants
VT 1 *(tobacco)* fumer; **to s. a pipe/cigarettes** fumer la pipe/des cigarettes; **to s. twenty a day** fumer vingt cigarettes par jour
2 *Culin (ham, meat, fish)* fumer
▸▸ **s. alarm** détecteur *m* de fumée; **s. bomb** bombe *f* fumigène; **s. detector** détecteur de fumée; **s. screen** *Mil* rideau *m* ou écran *m* de fumée; *Fig (comments, action etc)* tentative *f* de dissimulation; **s. signal** signal *m* de fumée
▸ **smoke out VT SEP 1** *(flush out with smoke) (insects)* enfumer pour les chasser; *Fig* faire sortir; *(bandits, snipers)* débusquer **2** *(fill with smoke)* enfumer **3 my pipe is smoked out** j'ai fini ma pipe

smoked [sməʊkt] **ADJ** *Culin* fumé
▸▸ **s. glass** verre *m* fumé; **s. salmon** saumon *m* fumé

smoke-filled [-fɪld] **ADJ** plein de fumée, enfumé

smokeless ['sməʊklɪs] **ADJ** *(fuel)* sans fumée
▸▸ **s. zone** = zone *f* où il est interdit de brûler du charbon afin de limiter la pollution atmosphérique

smoker ['sməʊkər] **N 1** *(of tobacco)* fumeur, -euse; **cigarette/pipe s.** fumeur de cigarettes/pipe; **heavy s.** gros fumeur; **s.'s cough** toux *f* de fumeur **2** *Rail etc Fam (compartment)* compartiment *m* fumeurs

smokestack ['sməʊkstæk] **N** cheminée *f*
▸▸ *esp Am* **s. industry** industrie *f* lourde

smoking ['sməʊkɪŋ] **ADJ** fumant, qui fume
N 1 *(of tobacco) (habit)* tabagisme *m*; **the effects of s. on the foetus** les effets du tabagisme sur le fœtus; **s. can damage your health** fumer nuit à votre santé; **no s. (allowed)** défense de fumer **2** *Culin (of ham etc)* fumage *m*
▸▸ **s. area** zone *f* fumeurs; **s. carriage** voiture *f* fumeurs; **s. compartment** compartiment *m* fumeurs; *Fig* **s. gun** *(clue)* indice *m* flagrant; **s. jacket** veste *f* d'intérieur; **s. room** fumoir *m* *(pour fumeurs)*

smoky ['sməʊkɪ] **ADJ 1** *(atmosphere, room, town)* enfumé **2** *(ceiling etc)* noirci par la fumée **3** *(fire, lamp)* qui fume **4** *(taste)* qui a un goût de fumée
▸▸ **s. blue** gris bleu *m inv*; **s. grey** gris fumée *m inv*; *Geol* **s. quartz** quartz *m* fumé

smolder, smoldering *Am* = **smoulder, smouldering**

smooch [smu:tʃ] *Fam* **VI 1** *(kiss)* se bécoter; *(cuddle)* se peloter **2** *(dance)* danser un slow
N to have a s. *(kiss)* se bécoter; *(cuddle)* se peloter; *(dance)* danser un slow

smoochy ['smu:tʃɪ] **ADJ** *Fam (music)* doux, *f* douce, et romantique

smooth [smu:ð] **ADJ 1** *(surface, paper)* lisse; *(skin)* doux, *f* douce; *(road etc)* uni, égal, -aux; *(forehead)* sans rides; *(mixture, sauce*

etc) onctueux; **to make s.** *(jagged edges)* lisser; *(hair)* défriser; *(road, surface)* aplanir; **the steps were worn s.** les marches étaient devenues lisses; *Br Fam* **as s. as a baby's bottom** *(skin, face etc)* doux comme une peau de bébé; **as s. as a millpond** *(sea)* d'un calme plat; **s. chin** *(without a beard)* menton glabre; *(close-shaven)* menton rasé de près; **a s. shave** un rasage parfait
2 *(gentle)* doux, *f* douce; *(trip, flight etc) (comfortable)* confortable; *(without problems)* sans anicroches; *(wine)* moelleux; *(style)* coulant; *(person)* doucereux, mielleux; **the conference got off to a s. start** la conférence a commencé très bien; **to ensure a s. passage for a bill** s'assurer qu'un projet de loi sera adopté sans difficulté; **to make things s. for sb** faciliter les choses pour qn; **he's a s. operator** il sait s'y prendre; *TV etc* **s. cut** montage *m* régulier; **s. ride** conduite aisée; *Fig* **the bill had a s. ride** le projet de loi est passé sans problème; **s. running** *(of machine)* fonctionnement doux *ou* régulier; *(of project)* déroulement sans anicroches; **the s. running of the department** le bon fonctionnement du service; **s. talker** beau parleur *m*; **to have a s. tongue** être doucereux; *Fam* **s. character** personne mielleuse
N to give one's hair a s. (down) lisser ses cheveux, se lisser les cheveux; **to give sth a s. down with sandpaper** égaliser qch avec du papier de verre; **you have to take the rough with the s.** il faut prendre le bon avec le moins bon
VT *(feathers, hair etc)* lisser; *(plank)* aplanir; *(ground)* égaliser; *(garment)* défroisser; **to s. one's brow** dérider son front; **to s. the way for sb/sth** faciliter les choses pour qn/qch
▸ **smooth away VT SEP** *(problems, fears etc)* faire oublier
▸ **smooth back VT SEP to s. back one's hair** mettre ses cheveux en arrière
▸ **smooth down VT SEP** *(make smooth) (feathers, hair etc)* lisser; *(wood)* égaliser
▸ **smooth off VT SEP** *(make smooth) (angle)* adoucir
▸ **smooth out VT SEP 1** *(map, sheets)* défroisser; *(remove by smoothing) (crease)* faire disparaître **2** = **smooth over**
▸ **smooth over VT SEP** *(make easier)* **to s. over difficulties** aplanir des difficultés; **to s. things over** arrondir les angles

smoothbore ['smu:ðbɔ:r] **ADJ** à canon lisse

smoothie ['smu:ðɪ] **N 1** *Fam (smooth talker)* baratineur, -euse **2** *(drink)* smoothie *m*, = jus *m* de fruit épais avec sa pulpe

smoothly ['smu:ðlɪ] **ADV** *(to work, function)* sans heurts, sans problèmes; *(of car, engine etc)* en douceur; **to run s.** *(of car)* rouler en douceur; *(of meeting, project)* se dérouler sans heurts; **everything's going s.** tout va bien, *Fam* tout marche comme sur des roulettes, tout baigne; **the journey went s.** le voyage s'est déroulé sans problèmes; **the interview went quite s. until I …** l'entretien s'est bien passé jusqu'à ce que je …

smoothness ['smu:ðnɪs] **N 1** *(of surface)* égalité *f*; *(of skin, fur)* douceur *f*, satiné *m*; *(of sea)* calme *m* **2** *(of operation of machine)* douceur *f*, régularité *f*; *(of machine, administration etc)* bon fonctionnement *m*; *(of style)* fluidité *f* **3** *(suavity) (of person)* air *m* doucereux

smooth-running ADJ *(machine etc)* qui marche bien; *(project)* qui se déroule sans anicroches

smooth-spoken ADJ doucereux, mielleux

smooth-talk VT to s. sb prendre qn par les sentiments, *Fam* embobiner qn; **to s. sb into doing sth** embobiner qn pour qu'il fasse

qch; **let's see if he can s. his way out of this one** voyons si cette fois-ci il réussit à s'en sortir à force de baratin

smooth-talking ADJ doucereux, mielleux

smooth-tongued [-'tʌŋd] **ADJ** doucereux, mielleux

smoothy ['smu:ðɪ] **N** *Fam* = **smoothie**

smote PT *see* **smite**

smother ['smʌðər] **VT 1** *(stifle) (person)* étouffer, suffoquer; *(fire)* étouffer; *(sound)* éteindre, étouffer; *(cry)* étouffer, retenir; *(oath, groan, yawn)* réprimer; *Fig (person, criticism, call for inquiry, scandal)* étouffer; *(one's feelings)* cacher; **to s. sb with kisses** étouffer qn de baisers **2** *(cover)* couvrir; **strawberries smothered in or with cream** fraises recouvertes de crème; **to be smothered in furs** être emmitouflé dans des fourrures
VI suffoquer, étouffer

smothered ['smʌðəd] **ADJ** *(cry)* sourd, étouffé; *(sound)* étouffé

smother-love N *Fam* amour *m* étouffant d'une mère

smoulder, Am smolder ['sməʊldər] **VI** *(of coal etc)* brûler lentement *ou* sans flamme; *(of fire, rebellion etc)* couver (sous la cendre); **to s. with anger/passion** se consumer de colère/passion

smouldering, Am smoldering ['sməʊldərɪŋ] **ADJ** *(coal etc)* qui brûle sans flamme; *(fire, dissent, passion, jealousy etc)* qui couve (sous la cendre)

SMS [ese'mes] **N** *Tel (abbr* **short message service)** *(service)* texte *m*; *(message)* message *m* texte

SMTP [esemti:'pi:] **N** *Comput (abbr* **Simple Mail Transfer Protocol)** protocole *m* SMTP

smudge [smʌdʒ] **N** tache *f*, salissure *f*, *(slip with pen)* bavure *f* de stylo; **you've got a s. on your nose** tu as une tache sur le nez; **the house was just a white s. in the distance** la maison n'était qu'une tache blanche dans le lointain
VT *(ink)* étaler; *(drawing, paint)* salir; *(eye make-up)* faire couler; **don't kiss me or you'll s. my lipstick** ne m'embrasse pas, sinon mon rouge à lèvres va s'en aller
VI *(of ink, writing)* s'étaler; *(of paint)* couler

smudgy ['smʌdʒɪ] **ADJ** *(face etc)* sali; *(text)* taché; *(handwriting, drawing)* sale; **the heat had made her make-up s.** la chaleur avait fait couler son maquillage

smug [smʌg] **ADJ** *(tone, look)* suffisant, satisfait de soi-même; **he has a s. look** il a un air suffisant, il a l'air content de lui; **stop looking so s.** arrête de te croire supérieur; **he was s. about his success** sa réussite le rendait plein de suffisance

smuggle ['smʌg(ə)l] **VT** *(arms, drugs etc)* faire de la contrebande de; *(when coming through customs)* faire passer en fraude; **to s. sth into/out of the country** (faire) entrer/sortir qch en contrebande; **to s. sb into/out of a country** faire entrer qn clandestinement dans un pays/sortir qn clandestinement d'un pays; **they are being smuggled into France by boat** on les fait entrer clandestinement en France par bateau; **to s. sth into a room** apporter qch subrepticement dans une pièce
VI *(of arms or drugs smuggler)* faire de la contrebande; *(when coming through customs)* frauder
▸ **smuggle in VT SEP** *(into country) (arms, drugs etc)* introduire en contrebande; *(when coming through customs)* faire passer en fraude; *(into prison etc)* introduire illégalement
▸ **smuggle out VT SEP** *(from country) (arms,*

drugs etc) faire sortir en contrebande; *(when coming through customs)* faire sortir en fraude; *(from prison etc)* faire sortir illégalement

smuggler ['smʌglər] N *(of drugs, arms etc)* contrebandier, -ière; *(when coming through customs)* fraudeur, -euse

smuggling ['smʌglɪŋ] N *(of drugs, arms etc)* trafic *m*, contrebande *f*; *(when coming through customs)* fraude *f*; **drug s.** trafic *m* de stupéfiant; **s. operation** opération *f* de contrebande

smugly ['smʌglɪ] ADV *(to look at)* d'un air suffisant; *(to say)* d'un ton suffisant; **he's so s. self-righteous** il est tellement suffisant

smugness ['smʌgnɪs] N suffisance *f*

smut [smʌt] N **1** *(soot)* parcelle *f* de suie; *(soot mark)* tache *f* de suie (**on the face** au *ou* sur le visage) **2** *(obscenity)* cochonneries *fpl*, grivoiseries *fpl*; **to talk s.** dire des cochonneries; **that book's/film's just s.** il n'y a que des cochonneries dans ce livre/film **3** *Agr (on grain crops)* charbon *m*

smuttiness ['smʌtɪnɪs] N *(lewdness) (of remark etc)* grivoiserie *f*, grossièreté *f*

smutty ['smʌtɪ] ADJ **1** *(remark, conversation etc)* grossier, grivois **2** *(dirty)* noirci, noir, sali *(de suie)*

snack [snæk] N casse-croûte *m inv*, collation *f*; **if you eat too many snacks between meals …** si vous grignotez (trop) entre les repas …; **to have a s.** casser la croûte, manger un morceau sur le pouce

▸ VI manger entre les repas; **I've been snacking on chocolates all day** aujourd'hui je ne suis nourri de chocolat

▸ ▸ **s. bar** snack *m*, snack-bar *m*, *pl* snack-bars; **s. food** amuse-gueules *mpl*

snaffle ['snæf(ə)l] N *Horseriding* mors *m* brisé, bridon *m*

▸ VT *Br Fam (take, steal)* piquer; **who's snaffled my pen?** qui est-ce qui m'a piqué mon stylo?

▸ ▸ *Horseriding* **s. bit** mors brisé, bridon

▸ **snaffle up** VT SEP *Br Fam (bargains, cakes etc)* rafler

snafu [snæˈfuː] *Sl* ADJ en (grand) désordre, chaotique

▸ N grosse gaffe *f*

snag [snæg] N **1** *(protrusion) (of tree)* aspérité *f*; *Fig (problem)* accroc *m*; *Fig* **to strike a** *or* **hit a** *or* **come across a s.** se heurter à un obstacle *ou* à une anicroche; **that's the s.!** voilà le hic!; **the s. is that it's too expensive** le hic, c'est que c'est trop cher **3** *(tear) (in garment)* accroc *m* **4** *Austr Fam (sausage)* saucisse *f*

▸ VT (-gg-) *(dress etc)* faire un accroc à; *(stocking etc)* accrocher

▸ VI *(of clothes)* s'accrocher

snail [sneɪl] N escargot *m*; **at a s.'s pace** à pas d'escargot

▸ ▸ *Aut* **s. cam** came *f* en colimaçon; *Fam* **s. mail** courrier *m* escargot, = courrier postal

snake [sneɪk] N **1** *(reptile)* serpent *m*; *Fig (person)* faux jeton *m*; **common s., grass s.** couleuvre *f* à collier; *Fig* **a s. in the grass** un faux jeton; **snakes and ladders** *(game)* ≃ le jeu de l'oie; *Am Fam* **snakes alive!** grand Dieu! **2** *Fin* serpent *m* monétaire

▸ VI *(of road etc)* serpenter

▸ ▸ **s. charmer** charmeur, -euse de serpent; **s. oil** remède *m* de charlatan; *Am Fig* **s. pit** fosse *f* aux serpents, nid *m* de vipères

snakebite ['sneɪkbaɪt] N **1** *(wound)* morsure *f* de serpent **2** *Fam (drink)* = boisson *f* comprenant une mesure de bière et une mesure de cidre

snakeskin ['sneɪkskɪn] N peau *f* de serpent

SNAP [snæp]

▸ N coup de dents **1** ▪ claquement **2** ▪ crac **2** ▪ photo **5**
▸ ADJ instantané
▸ VI essayer de mordre **1** ▪ faire un bruit sec **2** ▪ se casser net **3** ▪ parler sèchement **4** ▪ prendre des photos **5**
▸ VT faire claquer **1** ▪ casser **2** ▪ prendre (en photo) **3** ▪ dire sur un ton sec **4**

N **1** *(action) (of teeth)* coup *m* de dents; **to have a s. at sth** *(of dog etc)* essayer de happer qch; **with a s. of the fingers** claquant ses doigts

2 *(sound) (of teeth, whip etc)* coup *m* sec, claquement *m*; *(of sth breaking)* crac *m*; **I heard a s.** j'ai entendu un crac

3 *(cold weather)* **cold s.** courte période *f* de temps froid, coup *m* de froid

4 *Culin* **ginger s.** biscuit *m* sec au gingembre

5 *Phot Fam* instantané *m*; **holiday snaps** photos *fpl* de vacances

6 *Cards* ≃ *(jeu m de)* bataille *f*

▸ ADJ instantané, imprévu; **s. decision** décision *f* immédiate; **to call a s. election** procéder à une élection surprise

▸ ADV **to go s.** *(make sound)* faire clac; *(break cleanly)* (se) casser net; **s. went my stick!** et crac! ma canne s'est cassée!

▸ INT **1** *Cards* **s.!** ≃ bataille!

2 *Fam (in identical situation)* **I'm going to Paris – s.!** je vais à Paris – ça par exemple! moi aussi!; **do you like my new tie? – yes, but look, s.!** tu aimes ma nouvelle cravate? – oui, mais regarde, j'ai la même!

▸ VI (-pp-) **1** *(of dog etc)* **to s. at sb/sth** essayer de mordre qn/qch

2 *(of teeth, whip etc)* claquer, faire un bruit sec; **to s. (shut)** *(of fastener, door etc)* se fermer avec un bruit sec; **he snapped to attention** il se mit au garde-à-vous en un quart de seconde

3 *(of stick, rope etc)* **to s. (in two)** *(break cleanly)* (se) casser net; *(break with sound)* se rompre avec un bruit sec

4 *(speak abruptly)* parler sèchement; **to s. at sb** s'adresser à qn d'un ton sec *ou* cassant; **there's no need to s.** ce n'est pas la peine de me parler sur ce ton

5 *Phot* **tourists snapping away with their cameras** des touristes qui n'arrêtent pas de prendre des photos

▸ VT **1** *(whip etc)* faire claquer; **to s. one's fingers** (faire) claquer ses doigts; **to s. one's fingers at sb** narguer qn, faire la nique à qn

2 *(break) (stick etc)* casser, rompre; **to s. sth in two** casser qch en deux

3 *Phot Fam (take photo of)* prendre; *(facial expression etc)* saisir; **she snapped him eating a cake** elle l'a pris en photo en train de manger un gâteau

4 *(say sharply)* **to s. an order at sb** lancer un ordre à qn d'un ton sec; **'mind your own business!', he snapped (at me)** 'occupe-toi de ce qui te regarde', dit-il d'un ton cassant

▸ ▸ **s. fastener** *(press stud)* bouton-pression *m*, *pl* boutons-pression, pression *f*; *(clasp on handbag, necklace)* fermoir *m* (à pression); **s. lock** serrure *f* à ressort

▸ **snap back** VI *(of trigger etc)* revenir brusquement

▸ **snap off** VT SEP *(break off) (with hands etc)* arracher; *(with teeth)* enlever d'un coup de dents; *(accidentally) (end of stick etc)* casser; *Fig Fam* **to s. sb's head off** rembarrer qn vivement

▸ VI *(break off)* se casser

▸ **snap out** VT SEP *(say sharply) (order)* donner d'un ton sec

▸ VI *Fam (return to normal mood)* **s. out of it!** fais pas la tête *ou* la gueule; **I'm sure she'll s.**

out of it soon je suis sûr qu'elle va finir par se dérider

▸ **snap to** VI *(close with snap) (of lid, door etc)* se (re)fermer avec un bruit sec

▸ VT SEP (re)fermer (avec un bruit sec)

▸ **snap up** VT SEP **1** *(seize in jaws)* saisir, happer

2 *(buy, take quickly etc)* rafler; **to s. up a bargain** sauter sur *ou* saisir une occasion; **the tickets are being snapped up like hot cakes** les billets s'arrachent comme des petits pains

snapdragon ['snæpdræg(ə)n] N *(flower)* muflier *m*, gueule-de-loup *f*, *pl* gueules-de-loup

snapper ['snæpər] N **1** *(fish)* vivaneau *m* **2** *Ir Fam* môme *mf*, gosse *mf*

snappily ['snæpɪlɪ] ADV *(to reply)* d'un ton hargneux

snappish ['snæpɪʃ] ADJ *(person, dog)* hargneux

snappishly ['snæpɪʃlɪ] ADV *(to reply)* d'un ton hargneux

snappishness ['snæpɪʃnɪs] N hargne *f*

snappy ['snæpɪ] ADJ **1** *(person, tone, reply, dog)* hargneux **2** *(style, prose etc)* vif, *f* vive, plein d'allant; *(organization)* dynamique; *(slogan, campaign)* plein de punch; *Fam* **make it s.!** grouille-toi!, magne-toi!; **he's a s. dresser** il s'habille chic *ou Fam* classe

snapshot ['snæpʃɒt] N *Phot, Fig Fam* instantané *m*; *Comput (of screen)* instantané *m*, impression *f* immédiate

snare [sneər] N *(in hunting)* lacet *m*, collet *m*; *Fig* piège *m*; **to lay** *or* **set a s.** *(for animal)* poser un collet; *(for opponent)* tendre un piège; **to be caught in a s.** *(of animal)* être pris au lacet; *Fig (of person)* être pris au piège

▸ VT *(bird)* prendre au filet; *(rabbit)* prendre au collet *ou* au lacet; *Fig (person)* prendre au piège

▸ ▸ *Mus* **s. drum** caisse *f* claire

snarl¹ [snɑːl] N *(sound) (of dog, person)* grondement *m*, grognement *m*; *(of tiger)* feulement *m*

▸ VI *(show teeth)* montrer les dents; *(make sound) (of person, dog)* grogner, gronder; *(of tiger)* feuler; **to s. at sb** *(of person, dog)* grogner *ou* gronder contre qn; **'go away!', he snarled** 'va-t'en', gronda-t-il

snarl² N *(entanglement) (of ropes, wires etc)* enchevêtrement *m*; *(of traffic)* embouteillage *m*

▸ VI *(become entangled)* s'emmêler, s'enchevêtrer

▸ VT *(entangle)* emmêler, enchevêtrer

▸ **snarl up** VT SEP **to s. up the traffic** provoquer des embouteillages; **to s. up a system** paralyser un système; **the traffic gets snarled up at the traffic lights** la circulation bouchonne aux feux; **I got snarled up on the ringroad** je suis resté coincé dans un bouchon sur le périphérique

▸ VI *(of traffic)* bouchonner; *(of system, country etc)* être paralysé

snarling ['snɑːlɪŋ] ADJ grondant, grognant

▸ N *(sound)* grondement *m*, grognement *m*

snarl-up N *(of traffic)* embouteillage *m*, bouchon *m*; *(in system etc)* paralysie *f*; **there's a s. in the switchboard** le standard est saturé

snatch [snætʃ] N **1** *(grab)* mouvement *m* vif *(pour saisir qch)*; *Fam (kidnapping)* kidnapping *m*, enlèvement *m*; *Fam (robbery)* vol *m*; *Sport (in weightlifting)* arraché *m*; **to make a s. at** *or* **for sth** chercher à saisir qch; **to carry out a wages/jewellery s.** *(theft)* voler la paye/les bijoux

2 *(short period)* courte période *f*; *(small piece)* fragment *m*; **s. of sleep** petit somme *m*; **in** *or* **by snatches** *(to sleep)* par intervalles; *(to work)* de façon intermittente, à bâtons

rompus; **to overhear snatches of conversation** surprendre des bouts *ou* des bribes de conversation; **I could hear a s. of music** quelques notes de musique me parvenaient
3 *Sl (female genitals)* chatte *f*
VT *(object)* saisir, empoigner; *(kidnap) (baby)* kidnapper; *(steal)* voler; *Sport (in weightlifting) (weight)* arracher; **to s. sth from sb** arracher qch à qn; **to s. sth out of sb's hands** arracher qch des mains de qn; **to s. an opportunity** saisir une occasion; **to s. something to eat** manger sur le pouce; **to s. a bit of sleep** faire un petit somme; **I snatched three hours' sleep** j'ai fait un petit somme de trois heures
VI saisir brusquement *ou* arracher les objets; **don't s.!** on n'arrache pas les choses des mains des gens!
▸▸ *Br* **s. squad** = groupe *m* de policiers chargé d'arrêter les meneurs (lors d'une manifestation)
▸ **snatch at** **VT INSEP** *(try to grab)* tâcher de saisir; **to s. at an opportunity** saisir une occasion (au vol)
▸ **snatch away** **VT SEP** *(grab)* arracher, enlever (**from** de); **he snatched away the book I was reading** il m'a arraché des mains le livre que je lisais; **he snatched it away from me/ George** il me l'a arraché des mains/il l'a arraché des mains de George
▸ **snatch up** **VT SEP** *(pick up quickly)* ramasser vivement; **she snatched up the baby** elle s'est emparée vivement du bébé

snazzy ['snæzɪ] **ADJ** *Fam (shirt, tie, car)* classe *inv*; **he's a s. dresser** il s'habille classe

sneak [sniːk] **N 1** *esp Br Fam (telltale)* cafard, -arde, mouchard, -arde **2** *Fam (devious person)* faux jeton *m*
VI 1 *esp Br Fam (tell tales)* moucharder, cafarder **2** *(move furtively)* **to s. past the guard** passer devant la garde sans se faire voir; **to s. into the cinema without paying** entrer au cinéma sans payer
VT *(remove surreptitiously) (from desk, room etc)* subtiliser; *(deliver surreptitiously) (cigarettes, whisky etc)* donner en cachette; *(letter)* glisser; **to s. a glance at sb** glisser un œil vers qn; **they sneaked him past the guards** ils le firent passer sans que les gardes le voient; **someone must have sneaked it into my suitcase** quelqu'un a dû le glisser dans ma valise; **she sneaked her boyfriend into her bedroom** elle fit subrepticement entrer son petit ami dans sa chambre
▸▸ **s. preview** avant-première *f* privée, *pl* avant-premières privées; **to have a s. preview of sth** *(of exhibition, film etc)* voir qch en avant-première; *(of book, product etc)* avoir la primeur de qch; *Br* **s. thief** chapardeur, -euse
▸ **sneak about, sneak around** **VI** *(move furtively)* rôder
▸ **sneak away** **VI** = **sneak off**
▸ **sneak in** **VI** *(enter furtively)* entrer sans se faire repérer; **to s. in without paying** entrer sans payer
VT SEP *(bring in furtively) (object)* introduire furtivement *ou* subrepticement; **I'll s. you in after dark** je te ferai entrer discrètement à la nuit tombée
▸ **sneak off** **VI** *(leave furtively)* filer; **he sneaked off and joined another team** il a filé en douce et a rejoint une autre équipe
▸ **sneak on** **VT INSEP** *esp Br Fam (tell tales on)* moucharder
▸ **sneak out** **VI** *(leave furtively)* filer; **to s. out of a room** sortir d'une pièce sans se faire voir
VT SEP *(take out furtively) (object)* emporter subrepticement; *(person)* faire sortir subrepticement

sneakers ['sniːkəz] **NPL** *esp Am* tennis *fpl*

sneaking ['sniːkɪŋ] **ADJ** **I have a s. respect**

for him j'avoue que j'ai un certain respect pour lui; **to have a s. feeling** *or* **suspicion that …** avoir comme une vague impression que …

sneaky ['sniːkɪ] **ADJ** sournois

sneer [snɪər] **N** *(smile)* sourire *m* de mépris; *(laugh)* ricanement *m*; *(remark)* sarcasme *m*
VI *(smile)* sourire d'un air moqueur; *(laugh)* ricaner; **to s. at sb** se moquer de qn; *(address scornful remarks to)* lancer des sarcasmes à qn
VT 'you couldn't do that', he sneered 'tu n'en serais pas capable', a-t-il lancé en ricanant

sneerer ['snɪərər] **N** moqueur, -euse, ricaneur, -euse

sneering ['snɪərɪŋ] **ADJ** *(face, look)* ricaneur; *(remark, laughter)* sarcastique
N *(laughing)* ricanement *m*; *(remarks)* sarcasmes *mpl*

sneeringly ['snɪərɪŋlɪ] **ADV** *(contemptuously)* avec mépris; *(sarcastically)* d'un air sarcastique; *(laughing scornfully)* en ricanant

sneeze [sniːz] **N** éternuement *m*
VI éternuer; **she sneezed all over her plate** elle a éternué sur son assiette
▸ **sneeze at** **VT INSEP** *Fam* **that's not to be sneezed at** il ne faut pas cracher dessus

sneezing ['sniːzɪŋ] **N** éternuement *m*; **his s. irritates me** ses éternuements m'agacent
▸▸ **s. fit** crise *f* d'éternuements; **s. powder** poudre *f* à éternuer

snick [snɪk] **N** *(notch)* entaille *f*, encoche *f*
VT 1 *(wood etc)* entailler, faire une entaille dans; *(fabric)* faire une fente dans **2** *Cr (ball)* couper légèrement

snicker ['snɪkər] **N, VI** = **snigger** etc

snide [snaɪd] **ADJ** *Fam (scornful)* méprisant; *(sarcastic)* sarcastique; **she was very s. about it** elle s'est montrée très méprisante/ très sarcastique à ce sujet

sniff [snɪf] **N** reniflement *m*; **to take a s. at sth** renifler qch; **with a s. of disgust** avec un reniflement de dégoût; **I caught a s. of his aftershave** j'ai senti son after-shave; **there's still a s. of gas** ça sent toujours le gaz; **to have a little s.** *(smell)* renifler un petit coup; *Fam (have a slight cold)* avoir un léger rhume
VI renifler; **he sniffed with disdain** il a reniflé avec dédain
VT 1 *(investigate by smelling)* flairer, renifler; *(detect) (good meal, danger etc)* flairer; **the dog sniffed my hand** le chien m'a flairé la main **2** *(inhale) (snuff etc)* humer, renifler; *(cocaine, glue)* sniffer
▸ **sniff at** **VT INSEP 1** *Fam (disdain)* **the offer is not to be sniffed at** il ne faut pas cracher sur une proposition comme celle-ci **2** *(smell)* flairer, renifler; **the dog sniffed at my hand** le chien m'a flairé la main
▸ **sniff out** **VT SEP** *(discover by smelling) (of dog) (person, object)* détecter, flairer; *Fig (scandal etc)* déterrer

sniffer dog ['snɪfər] **N** chien *m* renifleur

sniffle ['snɪf(ə)l] **N** *(slight cold)* petit rhume *m* (de cerveau); **to have a s.** *or* **the sniffles** avoir un petit rhume
VI 1 *(sniff repeatedly)* renifler **2** *(cry)* pleurnicher

sniffy ['snɪfɪ] **ADJ** *Fam* **1** *(disdainful)* dédaigneux; **to be s. about sth** *(take exception to sth)* voir qch d'un mauvais œil; *(regard with contempt)* considérer qch avec mépris **2** *(bad-smelling)* **it's a bit s. in here** ça pue un peu ici **3** *(with cold)* **I'm still a bit s.** je renifle encore

snifter ['snɪftər] **N 1** *Old-fashioned Fam (drink)* goutte *f*, petit verre *m* **2** *Am (glass)* verre *m* à cognac

snigger ['snɪgər] **N** *(stifled laughter)* ricane-

ment *m*; *(at dirty story etc)* petit rire *m* grivois
VI *(stifle laughter)* ricaner (**at** à propos de)

sniggering ['snɪgərɪŋ] **N** *(stifled laughter)* ricanement *m*; **her s. irritates me** ses ricanements m'agacent

snip [snɪp] **N 1** *(cut)* petite entaille *f*; *(act of cutting with scissors)* coup *m* de ciseaux **2** *(piece cut off) (of paper, fabric)* morceau *m* coupé, bout *m* **3** *Br Fam (bargain)* affaire *f* (avantageuse), occasion *f*; **to get a s.** faire une affaire; **at £25 it's a s.** à 25 livres c'est une affaire
VT *(-pp-)* couper *(en donnant de petits coups de ciseaux)*
▸ **snip off** **VT SEP** couper

snipe [snaɪp] **N INV** *(bird)* bécassine *f*
VI *Mil* tirer; *Fig (criticize)* critiquer; **to s. at sb** *Mil* tirer sur qn *(d'une position embusquée)*; *Fig* critiquer qn sournoisement; **to s. at the enemy** canarder l'ennemi; **to be sniped at** se faire canarder

sniper ['snaɪpər] **N** *Mil* tireur *m* embusqué; **to be killed by a s.'s bullet** être tué par un tireur embusqué
▸▸ **s. fire** tir *m* d'embuscade

sniping ['snaɪpɪŋ] **N** *Mil* tir *m* d'embuscade; *Fig* critique *f* sournoise (**at sb** de qn)
ADJ *(criticism, remarks etc)* sournois

snippet ['snɪpɪt] **N** *(small piece)* bout *m*, morceau *m* (coupé); *(of book etc)* court extrait *m*; *(of conversation)* bribes *fpl*

snit [snɪt] **N** *Am* **to be in a s.** faire la gueule

snitch [snɪtʃ] *Sl* **N 1** *(informer)* balance *f* **2** *(nose)* pif *m*
VI *(inform)* moucharder; **to s. on sb** balancer qn
VT *(steal)* chaparder

snivel ['snɪv(ə)l] **N** *(whine)* pleurnichement *m*; **to say sth with a s.** dire qch en pleurnichant
VI *(-ll-, Am -l-)* *(whine)* pleurnicher

sniveller, *Am* **sniveler** ['snɪv(ə)lər] **N** pleurnicheur, -euse

snivelling, *Am* **sniveling** ['snɪv(ə)lɪŋ] **ADJ** *(person) (whining)* pleurnicheur, -euse; **you s. little idiot!** espèce de pleurnicheur!
N *(whining)* pleurnicherie *f*

snob [snɒb] **N** snob *mf*; **she's a bit of a s.** c'est une snobinarde; **a music s.** un snob en matière de musique

snobbery ['snɒbərɪ] **N** snobisme *m*; **inverted s.** snobisme à rebours; **intellectual s.** snobisme intellectuel

snobbish ['snɒbɪʃ] **ADJ** snob *inv*

snobbishness ['snɒbɪʃnɪs] **N** snobisme *m*

snockered ['snɒkəd] **ADJ** *Am Fam (drunk)* bourré, pété

snog [snɒg] *Br Fam* **VI** se bécoter
VT bécoter
N **to have a s.** se bécoter

snogging ['snɒgɪŋ] **N** *Br Fam* bécotage *m*

snood [snuːd] **N** *(hairnet)* résille *f*

snook [snuːk] **N** *Fam* **to cock a s. at sb** *(make gesture at)* faire un pied de nez à qn; *Fig (defy)* faire la nique à qn

snooker ['snuːkər] **N** *(game)* billard *m* snooker; *(shot)* snooker *m*
VT **to s. sb** *(in game)* empêcher qn de frapper la boule directement; *Fig Fam* mettre qn dans une impasse; *Fig Fam* **now I've snookered myself** je suis coincé maintenant; **to be snookered** *(in game)* se trouver dans l'impossibilité de frapper la boule directement; *Fig* être coincé, être dans une impasse

snoop [snuːp] *Fam* **N 1** = **snooper 2** **I'll have a s. around** je vais jeter un petit coup d'œil
VI fourrer son nez partout, fouiner; **he was snooping behind the lab** il fouinait derrière le labo
▸ **snoop around** **VI** *Fam* fourrer son nez par-

tout; **to s. around in sb's papers/desk** fouiller dans les papiers/le bureau de qn

▶ **snoop on** VT INSEP *Fam (spy on) (person)* espionner

snooper ['snu:pər] N *Fam* **1** *(official investigator)* fouine *f* **2 he's a terrible s.** il fourre son nez partout

snoot [snu:t] N *Fam (nose)* blaire *m*, tarin *m*

snooty ['snu:tɪ] ADJ *Fam* arrogant, hautain

snooze [snu:z] *Fam* N **1** petit somme *m*; **to have a s.** faire un petit somme **2** *(on alarm clock)* (position *f)* sommeil *m*

VI sommeiller, faire un petit somme; *(be not quite asleep)* somnoler

▶▶ **s. button** bouton *m* de veille; **s. position** *(on alarm clock)* (position) sommeil

snore [snɔ:r] N ronflement *m*
VI ronfler

snorer ['snɔ:rər] N ronfleur, -euse

snoring ['snɔ:rɪŋ] N ronflement *m*; **the sound of his s.** le bruit de ses ronflements; **his s. could be heard halfway down the corridor** on l'entendait ronfler du milieu du couloir

snorkel ['snɔ:k(ə)l] N *Swimming* tuba *m*; *(of submarine)* schnorchel *m*, schnorkel *m*
VI **to s., to go snorkelling** faire de la plongée avec un tuba

snort [snɔ:t] N **1** *(exhalation)* reniflement *m*; *(of horse etc)* ébrouement *m* **2** *(expressing impatience, disgust)* grognement *m* d'impatience/de dégoût; *(of anger)* grommellement *m*; **s. of laughter** court éclat *m* de rire; **she gave a s. of disbelief** elle a reniflé *ou* pouffé en signe d'incrédulité **3** *Sl (of drink)* petit coup *m*; *(of cocaine)* prise *f*; **he had a quick s. of whisky** il s'est jeté un petit whisky derrière la cravate

VI *(exhale)* renifler bruyamment; *(of horse)* s'ébrouer; **to s. with laughter** pouffer de rire; **to s. in disbelief** pouffer en signe d'incrédulité; **to s. with anger** s'étrangler de colère; *Fig Fam* **to s. at sth** dédaigner qch

VT **1** *(answer)* grogner; **'that's preposterous!', she snorted** 'c'est absurde!', a-t-elle jeté **2** *Sl (cocaine)* sniffer

snorter ['snɔ:tər] N *Sl* **1** *Br (strong letter)* lettre *f* carabinée; **that's a real s. (of a problem)** ça va nous/vous/*etc* donner du fil à retordre **2** *(short drink) (of alcohol)* goutte *f*, petit verre *m*

snot [snɒt] N *Fam (from nose)* morve *f*, **a bit of s.** de la morve

▶▶ **s. rag** tire-jus *m inv*, tire-moelle *m inv*

snotty ['snɒtɪ] ADJ *Fam* **1** *(handkerchief)* sale, dégoûtant; *(nose)* couvert de morve; **s.(-nosed)** cradingue, crade; **some s.(-nosed) little brat** un petit morveux **2** *(arrogant)* arrogant; **one of those incredibly s. officials** un de ces officiels qui pètent plus haut que leur cul

snout [snaʊt] N **1** *(of animal)* museau *m*; *(of pig, hedgehog)* groin *m*; *(of boar)* boutoir *m*; *(of gun)* bout *m* (du canon); *Fam (nose)* naze *m*, tarin *m*, pif *m* **2** *Br Sl (tobacco)* tabac *m* **3** *Br Sl (police informer)* indic *m*

snow [snaʊ] N **1** neige *f*, **the roads are covered with s.** les routes sont enneigées; **to be s. blind** souffrir de cécité des neiges **2** *TV, Radio* neige *f* **3** *Sl (cocaine)* neige *f*, *(heroin crystals)* cristaux *mpl* d'héroïne

V IMPERS neiger; **it's snowing** il neige

▶▶ **s. blindness** cécité *f* des neiges; **s. chains** chaînes *fpl* (à neige); **s. fence** pare-neige *m inv*; **s. goggles** lunettes *fpl* de ski; *Orn* **s. goose** oie *f* des neiges; **s. hole** *(in mountaineering)* trou *m* de neige; *Am Fam* **s. job** baratin *m*; **to give sb a s. job** baratiner qn, rouler qn dans la farine; **s. leopard** léopard *m* des neiges, once *f*, **s. tyre** pneu *m* neige

▶ **snow in** VT SEP *(usu passive)* **to be snowed in** être bloqué par la neige

▶ **snow off** VT SEP *(usu passive)* **the match was snowed off** le match a été annulé à cause de la neige

▶ **snow under** VT SEP *(usu passive)* **snowed under with work** débordé de travail

▶ **snow up** VT SEP *(usu passive)* **to be snowed up** être bloqué par la neige

snowball ['snaʊbɔ:l] N **1** boule *f* de neige; *Can* balle *f* de neige; *Fam* **he hasn't a s.'s chance (in hell)** il n'a pas l'ombre d'une chance **2** *(drink)* snowball *m*

VI **1** *(of story, debts etc)* faire boule de neige **2** *(fight with snowballs)* se battre à coups de boules de neige

▶▶ **s. effect** effet *m* boule de neige; **s. fight** bataille *f* de boules de neige

snowbank ['snaʊbæŋk] N congère *f*

snowbike ['snaʊbaɪk] N motoski *m*

snowboarding ['snaʊbɔ:dɪŋ] N snowboard *m*; **to go s.** faire du snowboard

snowboot ['snaʊbu:t] N après-ski *m*, *pl* après-skis

snowbound ['snaʊbaʊnd] ADJ *(person, airport)* bloqué par la neige

snowcapped ['snaʊkæpt] ADJ couronné de neige

snowdrift ['snaʊdrɪft] N congère *f*

snowdrop ['snaʊdrɒp] N *(flower)* perce-neige *m ou f inv*

snowfall ['snaʊfɔ:l] N chute *f* de neige

snowfield ['snaʊfi:ld] N champ *m* de neige

snowflake ['snaʊfleɪk] N flocon *m* de neige

snowline ['snaʊlaɪn] N limite *f* des neiges éternelles

snowman, *pl* **snowmen** ['snaʊmæn, -men] N bonhomme *m* de neige; **they built** *or* **made a s.** ils ont fait un bonhomme de neige; **the abominable s.** l'abominable homme des neiges

snowmobile ['snaʊməbi:l] N *Am (open)* motoneige *f*, *(enclosed)* autoneige *f*

snowplough, *Am* **snowplow** ['snaʊplaʊ] N *Rail, Ski etc* chasse-neige *m inv*

snowshoe ['snaʊʃu:] N raquette *f* *(pour la neige)*

snowstorm ['snaʊstɔ:m] N tempête *f* de neige

snowsuit ['snaʊsu:t] N combinaison *f* de ski

snow-white ADJ **1** *(in colour)* blanc comme neige **2** *Fig* pur, innocent

snowy ['snaʊɪ] ADJ neigeux; *(day etc)* de neige; *(field etc)* enneigé; *(season)* des neiges; **s. (white) hair** cheveux blancs (comme la neige)

SNP [esen'pi:] N *Pol (abbr* **Scottish National Party)** parti *m* nationaliste écossais

snub [snʌb] N *(refusal)* rebuffade *f*, *(insult)* affront *m*; **to meet with a s.** être rejeté d'une rebuffade

VT *(-bb-)* *(person)* faire un affront à; **I said hello but he just snubbed me** je lui ai dit bonjour mais il m'a ignoré *ou* m'a snobé

ADJ *(nose)* (plat et) retroussé

snub-nosed ['snʌbnəʊzd] ADJ au nez retroussé

▶▶ **s. revolver** revolver *m* au canon court

snuff [snʌf] N tabac *m* à priser; **to take s.** priser; **a pinch of s.** une prise

VT **1** *(extinguish) (candle)* moucher; *(hope, enthusiasm etc)* éteindre **2** *Br Sl* **to s. it** *(die)* clamecer, clamser, passer l'arme à gauche **3** *(sniff) (air)* humer

▶▶ *Fam* **s. movie** = film *m* pornographique au cours duquel un participant est réellement assassiné

▶ **snuff out** VT SEP *(life)* mettre un terme à; *(opposition)* étouffer; *Fam (person)* éliminer

snuffbox ['snʌfbɒks] N tabatière *f*

snuffer ['snʌfər] N *(for candle)* mouchette *f*

snuffle ['snʌf(ə)l] N **1** *(sniff)* reniflement *m*; *Fam* **snuffles** *(cold)* rhume *m* **2** *(nasal tone)* voix *f* nasillarde

VI **1** *(sniff)* renifler; *(have a cold)* avoir un rhume **2** *(speak in nasal tone)* nasiller, parler en nasillant

snug [snʌg] ADJ *(house etc)* confortable, où l'on est bien; *(person) (sheltered)* bien à l'abri; *(warm)* bien au chaud; *(bed)* douillet, -ette; *(jacket)* bien chaud; **to make oneself s.** se mettre à son aise; **to lie s. in bed** être bien au chaud dans son lit; *Fam* **as s. as a bug in a rug** tranquille comme Baptiste; **it's a s. fit** *(of machine part etc)* ça s'emboîte parfaitement; *(of clothing)* c'est bien ajusté; **it's a bit of a s. fit, it's a bit too s.** *(of clothing)* c'est un peu trop serré

N *Br* petite arrière-salle *f* *(dans un pub)*, *pl* petites arrière-salles

snuggery ['snʌgərɪ] N petite pièce *f* intime (et confortable); *Br (in pub)* petite arrière-salle *f*, *pl* petites arrière-salles

snuggle ['snʌg(ə)l] VI **to s. under the covers** se pelotonner sous les couvertures; **village snuggling in the valley** village niché dans la vallée

VT **to s. a child close to one** serrer un enfant dans ses bras

▶ **snuggle down** VI *(make oneself comfortable)* **to s. down in bed** se blottir (bien au chaud) dans son lit

▶ **snuggle up** VI *(come close)* se pelotonner, se blottir (**to sb** contre qn); **to s. up with a good book** s'installer bien confortablement avec un bon livre

snugly ['snʌglɪ] ADV confortablement; *(warmly)* bien au chaud; **s. wrapped** *(in blanket etc)* douillettement enveloppé; **garment that fits s.** vêtement bien ajusté; **this piece should fit s. into …** cette pièce devrait s'emboîter parfaitement *ou* exactement dans …

So. **1** *(abbr* **South)** S. **2** *(abbr* **Southern)** S.

SO [səʊ]

| ADV si **1** ▪ tellement **1** ▪ ainsi **2** ▪ environ *(or so)* **2** ▪ pour que *(so that)* **3** ▪ de sorte que *(so that)* **4** ▪ comme si comme ça *(so so)* **5** |
| CONJ donc **1, 2** |

ADV **1** *(to such an extent)* si, tellement; **it's so easy** c'est si *ou* tellement facile; **I was so disappointed** j'étais tellement déçu; **we're so pleased you could come** nous sommes tellement *ou* si contents que vous ayez pu venir; **she isn't so very old** elle n'est pas tellement *ou* si vieille; **the young and the not so young** les jeunes et les moins jeunes; **I'm not so sure of that** je n'en suis pas si sûr; **so serious a wound** une blessure aussi grave; **what's so important about this case?** qu'est-ce que cette affaire a de si important?; **he's not so clever as she is** il n'est pas aussi intelligent qu'elle; **she wouldn't be so stupid as to do that** elle ne serait pas bête au point de faire cela, elle ne serait pas assez bête pour faire cela; **would you be so kind as to …?** voudriez-vous avoir la gentillesse de …?; **I was so hungry I could have eaten it all** j'avais si faim que j'aurais pu tout manger; **he's so rich that he doesn't know what he's worth** il est riche au point d'ignorer le montant de sa fortune; **I loved her so (much)** je l'aimais tant; **we enjoyed ourselves so much** nous nous sommes tellement amusés; **it's not so much that I dislike them, more that I don't** like **them** ce n'est pas tant qu'ils me déplaisent, ça serait plutôt qu'ils ne me plaisent pas; **you do exaggerate so!** tu exagères tellement! **VOIR GRAMMAIRE A5**

2 *(in this way)* ainsi, de cette façon, de cette manière; **stand just so** tenez-vous ainsi *ou* comme ça; **while he was so occupied ...** pendant qu'il était ainsi occupé ...; **as X is to Y, so Y is to Z** X est à Y ce que Y est à Z; **she so arranged things that ...** elle a fait en sorte que ... + *subj*; **I have been so informed** c'est ce que l'on m'a dit; **so I believe** c'est ce que je crois; **it so happened that I was there** le hasard a voulu que je fusse là, il s'est trouvé que j'étais là; **and so on, and so forth** et ainsi de suite; **so to speak** *or* **say** pour ainsi dire; **has the train gone? – I think so** est-ce que le train est parti? – je crois *ou* je pense que oui; **he's clever – do you think so?** il est intelligent – vous trouvez?; **I suppose so, I expect so** je (le) suppose; **I hope so** je l'espère bien, j'espère bien; **I'm afraid so** j'en ai bien peur, je le crains; **I didn't say so** moi, je n'ai pas dit cela; **is she really ill? – so it seems** elle est donc vraiment malade? – à ce qu'il paraît; **so I told him** c'est ce que je lui ai dit; **there is a train at six, or so I was told** il y a un train à six heures, ou du moins c'est ce qu'on m'a dit; **I'm not very organized – so I see!** je ne suis pas très organisé – c'est ce que je vois!; **I told you so!** je vous l'avais bien dit!; **so much so that ...** à tel point que ..., tellement que ...; **(much) more so** (bien) plus encore; **that's so** c'est bien vrai; **is that so?** vraiment?; **that being so** *(as this is the case)* puisqu'il en est ainsi; *(should this prove the case)* dans ces conditions; **so be it!** soit!, qu'il en soit ainsi!; **if so** s'il en est ainsi; **why so?** pourquoi cela?; **how so?** comment cela?; **perhaps so** cela se peut; **quite so** parfaitement, absolument; **a hundred pounds or so** une centaine de livres; **a week or so** une huitaine de jours; **a little girl so high** une petite fille grande comme ça; **she's right and so are you** elle a raison et vous aussi; **and so am I/are we** et moi/et nous aussi; **he thinks he can do it – so he can** il pense qu'il peut le faire – en effet il le peut; **you're late! – so I am!** vous êtes en retard! – c'est vrai!; **it was Mr Smith – so it was!** c'était Monsieur Smith – en effet!; *Fam* **they aren't French – they are so!** ils ne sont pas français – si! **VOIR GRAMMAIRE A29**

3 *(purpose)* **so that, so as to** afin que + *sub*, pour que + *sub*, afin de + *inf*, pour + *inf*; **she stood up so as to or so that she could see better** elle s'est levée afin de *ou* pour mieux voir; **she sat down so that I could see better** elle s'est assise afin que *ou* pour que je puisse mieux voir; **we hurried so as not to be late, we hurried so that we shouldn't be late** nous nous sommes dépêchés pour ne pas être *ou* afin de ne pas être en retard **VOIR GRAMMAIRE A75; B58**

4 *(consequence)* **so that** de sorte que; **the flight was cancelled so that we had to stay at home** le vol a été annulé de sorte que *ou* si bien que nous avons dû rester à la maison; **the crates had fallen over so that we couldn't get past** comme les caisses étaient tombées, nous n'avons pas pu passer **VOIR GRAMMAIRE A75; B58**

5 *Fam* **so so** *(not too bad)* comme ci comme ça; **the cooking is only so so** la cuisine n'est pas terrible

CONJ 1 *(therefore)* donc, c'est pourquoi; **she has a bad temper, so be careful** elle a un mauvais caractère, donc faites attention; **he wasn't there, so I came back again** il n'était pas là, donc je suis revenu; **so what?** et alors?; **it's very expensive – so? what am I supposed to do about it?** c'est très cher – et alors? que voulez-vous que j'y fasse?; **so, we're a bit late, what difference does that make?** et alors, nous sommes un peu en retard, quelle différence cela fait-il?

2 so there you are! vous voilà donc!; **so**

that's what it is! ah! c'est comme ça!; **so you're not coming?** vous ne venez donc pas?; **so, what do we do?** eh bien, qu'est-ce qu'on fait?

soak [səʊk] **VT 1** *(of liquid, person)* tremper (**in** sth dans qch); *(beans etc)* faire tremper; **the rain soaked me to the skin** la pluie m'a trempé jusqu'aux os; **soaked with blood/sweat** plein de sang/trempé de transpiration; **I got soaked** je me suis tout trempé; *(by rain)* je me suis fait tremper **2** *Fam (customer)* écorcher; **to s. the rich** faire payer les riches

VI baigner, tremper (**in** sth dans qch); *(of liquid)* s'infiltrer, s'imbiber (**into** sth dans qch); **to leave a saucepan to s.** laisser une casserole tremper

N 1 give them a good s. mets-les bien à tremper; **to have a good s. (in the bath)** prendre un bon bain **2** *Fam (drunkard)* poivrot, -ote

▸ **soak in** VI *(of liquid)* pénétrer, être absorbé; *Fig* **has it soaked in yet?** est-ce qu'il a/est-ce que tu as/*etc* pigé?

VT SEP *(absorb)* **to s. in water** s'imprégner d'eau, absorber l'eau; **she went to the main square to s. in the atmosphere** elle est allée sur la place principale pour s'imprégner de son atmosphère

▸ **soak through** VI **1** *(seep through to other side)* s'infiltrer à travers **2** *(be absorbed)* pénétrer, s'infiltrer

▸ **soak up** VT SEP *(liquid)* absorber, boire; **to s. up water** s'imprégner d'eau, absorber l'eau; *Fig* **to s. up the sun** se rôtir au soleil; **to s. up the atmosphere** s'imprégner de l'atmosphère

soaked [səʊkt] **ADJ** trempé; *(ground)* détrempé; **s. to the skin, s. through** trempé jusqu'aux os

soaking [ˈsəʊkɪŋ] **N** trempage *m*; **give the beans a good s.** faites tremper les haricots pendant plusieurs heures; **give the clothes a good s.** mettez le linge à tremper pendant un bon moment; **to get a s.** se faire tremper **ADJ** *(wet)* trempé; **you're absolutely s.!** vous êtes tout trempé!

ADV s. wet trempé; **to get s. wet** se tremper; *(in rain)* se faire tremper

so-and-so **N** *Fam* **1** *(unspecified person)* Untel *m*, Unetelle *f*; **Mr S.** Monsieur Untel; **Mrs S.** Madame Unetelle **2** *Pej (unpleasant person)* type *m*; **a crafty s.** une fine mouche, un malin; **you old s.!** *(reproving)* espèce de vilain!; **the old s.!** *(angry)* le salaud!; *(admiring, surprised)* le bougre!; **you greedy old s.** espèce de gourmand!; **don't cry, you silly old s.!** faut pas pleurer, espèce d'idiot!

soap [səʊp] **N** savon *m*; **a bar** *or* **cake of s.** un savon; *(small)* une savonnette; **shaving s.** savon à barbe; **to wash sth with s.** savonner qch **2** *Fam (flattery)* flagornerie *f*, flatterie *f* **3** *Radio, TV Fam* feuilleton *m* (populaire), soap opera *m* **4** *Am Sl* **no s.!** des clous!, des nèfles!

VT *(clothes etc)* savonner

▸ ▸ **s. bubble** bulle *f* de savon; *Radio, TV* **s. opera** feuilleton (populaire), soap opera; **s. powder** lessive *f* (en poudre), poudre *f* à laver; *Radio, TV* **s. star** vedette *f* de feuilleton

▸ **soap down** VT SEP savonner

Soap opera

Le soap opera est un genre radiophonique et télévisé très populaire dans les pays anglophones. Il s'agit de feuilletons diffusés à raison de trois ou quatre épisodes par semaine sur une très longue période. Les soap operas sont ainsi nommés car les premiers d'entre eux étaient financés par des marques de détergents, aux États-Unis. Il n'est pas rare que les soap operas alimen-

tent les conversations de tous les jours, ou soient le sujet d'articles de journaux. Les soap operas britanniques ('Eastenders' et 'Coronation Street' par exemple) ont souvent pour cadre le milieu ouvrier et diffèrent en cela de leurs équivalents américains et australiens dont le ton est beaucoup moins réaliste et dont l'action se déroule le plus souvent dans des milieux privilégiés.

soapbox [ˈsəʊpbɒks] **N 1** *(container)* caisse *f* à savon; *Fig (for speaker)* tribune *f* improvisée *ou* de fortune; **to get up on a s.** faire un discours improvisé, haranguer les foules; **get off your s.!** ne monte pas sur tes grands chevaux! **2** *(go-kart)* chariot *m*, ≃ kart *m* *(sans moteur)*

▸ ▸ **s. orator** personne *f* qui harangue les foules

soapdish [ˈsəʊpdɪʃ] **N** porte-savon *m*, *pl* porte-savons

soap-dodger **N** *Br Fam Hum (man)* mec *m* cradingue; *(woman)* bonne femme *f* cradingue

soapflakes [ˈsəʊpfleɪks] **NPL** savon *m* en paillettes

soapiness [ˈsəʊpɪnɪs] **N** *(of something)* caractère *m* savonneux

soapstone [ˈsəʊpstəʊn] **N** stéatite *f*

soapsuds [ˈsəʊpsʌdz] **NPL** *(lather)* mousse *f* de savon; *(water)* eau *f* savonneuse

soapy [ˈsəʊpɪ] **ADJ** *(water)* savonneux; *(body)* couvert de savon; *(taste)* de savon; **this beer tastes s.** cette bière a un goût de savon **2** *Fam (flattering) (person, voice)* doucereux, onctueux

soar [sɔːr] **VI** *esp Lit (fly up)* prendre son essor, s'élever; *(glide)* planer; *(of spirits)* remonter en flèche; **rents have soared** les loyers ont augmenté de façon vertigineuse

soaring [ˈsɔːrɪŋ] **ADJ** *(bird, arrow)* qui monte *ou* s'élève dans les airs; *(steeple)* élancé; *(price, popularity etc)* qui monte en flèche; **the s. flight of the eagle** le vol majestueux de l'aigle

N *(rising) (of bird)* essor *m*; *(of prices)* hausse *f*

sob [sɒb] **N** sanglot *m*; **with a s. in her voice** la voix étouffée par un sanglot

VI (**-bb-**) sangloter

VT *(say)* dire en sanglotant; **she sobbed herself to sleep** elle s'est endormie en sanglotant

▸ ▸ *Am Fam* **s. sister** journaliste *f* qui fait le courrier du cœur; *Fam Pej* **s. story** histoire *f* larmoyante, histoire à vous fendre le cœur; *Fam* **to tell sb a s. story** raconter une histoire pour apitoyer qn; *Fam Pej* **s. stuff** sensiblerie *f*, mélo *m*

▸ **sob out** VT SEP **1** *(say)* dire en sanglotant **2 to s. one's heart out** pleurer à chaudes larmes

s.o.b. [esəʊˈbiː] **N** *esp Am Sl (abbr* **son of a bitch**) fils *m* de pute, salaud *m*

sobbing [ˈsɒbɪŋ] **ADJ in a s. voice** d'une voix brisée par les sanglots

N sanglots *mpl*

sober [ˈsəʊbər] **ADJ 1** *(not drunk)* sobre; **as s. as a judge** *(temperate)* sobre comme un chameau; *(serious)* sérieux comme un pape; **when he's s. (again)** quand il sera dessoûlé **2** *(moderate)* sobre, modéré; *(calm)* calme, posé; *(face)* grave; *(colours, dress)* sobre; **s. opinion** opinion *f* réfléchie; **the s. truth** la simple vérité

VT dessoûler; **this news sobered him** cette nouvelle l'a dégrisé

▸ **sober down** VI *(become calmer)* s'assagir **VT SEP** dégriser

▸**sober up** VI (become less drunk) se dégriser; **s. up!** reprends-toi!

VT SEP dessoûler; (of news etc) dégriser

sobering ['səʊbərɪŋ] ADJ qui dégrise; **it's had a s. effect on him** ça l'a dégrisé; **it's a s. thought** ça vous fait réfléchir

sober-minded ADJ (serious) sérieux, réfléchi

soberness ['səʊbənɪs] N **1** (not drinking) sobriété f **2** (of style, dress, character) sobriété f, (seriousness) sérieux m

sobersides ['səʊbəsaɪdz] N Old-fashioned Fam (solemn person) bonnet m de nuit

sobriety [səʊ'braɪətɪ] N also Fig sobriété f

Soc 1 abbr **society** 2 abbr **Socialist**

so-called [-'kɔːld] ADJ **1** (so named) appelé ainsi, ainsi nommé; **the s. temperate zone** la zone dite tempérée **2** (supposed) **a s. doctor** un soi-disant ou un prétendu docteur; **s. progress** de prétendus progrès

soccer ['sɒkər] N football m, foot m
▸▸**s. match** match m de football ou de foot; Am **s. mom** = femme f de milieu bourgeois qui accompagne et encourage ses enfants lors de leurs séances d'entraînement de foot; **s. pitch** terrain m de football; **s. player** footballeur, -euse

sociability [səʊʃə'bɪlɪtɪ] N sociabilité f

sociable ['səʊʃəb(ə)l] ADJ sociable; **I had a drink with them to be s.** j'ai pris un verre avec eux pour me montrer sociable; **to become more s.** (of person) (become less shy) s'apprivoiser; (become more friendly) devenir plus sociable; **I'm not feeling very s. at the moment** je n'ai pas envie de voir du monde en ce moment; **I'm not in a s. mood** je ne suis pas d'humeur à voir du monde

sociably ['səʊʃəblɪ] ADV sociablement; **she's not very s. inclined** elle n'est pas très mondaine

social ['səʊʃəl] ADJ **1** social, -aux; **to have a busy s. life** (see a lot of people) voir beaucoup de monde; (go out a lot) sortir beaucoup; **work is getting in the way of my s. life** j'ai trop de travail pour pouvoir sortir; **since he's been married, he's had to give up his s. life** depuis son mariage, il ne voit presque plus personne; **to be sb's s. equal** être l'égal de qn sur le plan social; **the s. ladder** l'échelle f sociale; **to take sth into s. ownership** nationaliser qch

2 Zool social, -aux; **man is a s. animal** l'homme est un animal grégaire

N (party) soirée f
▸▸**s. benefits** prestations fpl sociales; EU **the S. Chapter** le volet social (du traité de Maastricht); **s. class** classe f sociale; **s. climber** arriviste mf; **s. climbing** arrivisme m; **s. democrat** social-démocrate m, pl sociaux-démocrates, sociale-démocrate f, pl sociales-démocrates; **s. disease** = maladie f provoquée par des facteurs socio-économiques; Euph (venereal) maladie vénérienne; **s. drinker** = personne f qui ne boit d'alcool qu'en société; **s. drinking** = consommation f d'alcool lors de réunions entre amis; **s. engineering** manipulation f des structures sociales; **s. evening** (party) soirée f, (gathering) réunion f; **s. fund** = caisse f d'aide sociale; **s. group** catégorie f socio-professionnelle, CSP f; **s. marketing** marketing m social; **s. movement** mouvement m social; **s. order** ordre m social; **s. outcast** paria m; **s. position** rang m dans la société; **s. reformer** réformateur, -trice de la société; **s. sciences** sciences fpl humaines; **s. security** prestations sociales; **to be on** or **get s. security** toucher une aide sociale; Am **s. security number** numéro m de Sécurité sociale; **s. services** services mpl sociaux; **s. work** assistance f sociale, travail m

social; **s. worker** assistant, -ante social(e), travailleur, -euse social(e)

socialism ['səʊʃəlɪz(ə)m] N socialisme m

socialist ['səʊʃəlɪst] ADJ, N socialiste mf

socialite ['səʊʃəlaɪt] N membre m de la haute société, homme m/femme f du monde

socialize ['səʊʃəlaɪz] VI **to s. with sb** fréquenter qn; (chat) bavarder avec qn; **he won't s.** il n'accepte jamais une invitation; **they do a lot of socializing** ils voient beaucoup de gens

VT Econ (property) nationaliser
▸▸Am **socialized medicine** médecine f d'État

socially ['səʊʃəlɪ] ADV socialement; **to be s. active** (go out a lot) sortir beaucoup; (see a lot of people) voir beaucoup de monde; **we don't do much s.** nous sortons peu, nous fréquentons peu de gens; **I saw her s. for a while, but nothing beyond that** je l'ai vaguement fréquentée pendant un temps, mais rien de plus; **I don't know him s. at all, just at work** en dehors du travail, je ne le connais pas du tout; **s. mobile** mobile sur le plan social; **s. disadvantaged** défavorisé

society [sə'saɪətɪ] N **1** (social community, company) société f, **he's a danger** or **menace to s.** c'est un danger pour la société; **to avoid the s. of one's colleagues** éviter la compagnie de ses collègues; **this word isn't used in polite s.** on n'utilise pas ce mot chez les gens bien élevés; **consumer s.** société de consommation

2 (nation, group) société f, **primitive/industrial societies** des sociétés primitives/industrielles

3 (fashionable circles) **(high) s.** la haute société, le (beau ou grand) monde; **s. people** gens mpl du monde; **a s. wedding** un mariage dans le grand monde

4 (body) société f, (association) association f, **charitable s.** œuvre f de bienfaisance ou de charité; Br **National S. for the Prevention of Cruelty to Children** organisation f de protection de l'enfance
▸▸Journ **s. column** chronique f mondaine; Rel **the S. of Friends** la Société des Amis, les Quakers mpl; **the S. of Jesus** la Compagnie de Jésus; **S. for the Protection of the Unborn Child** = ligue f contre l'avortement

---

Note that the French word **société** is also used as a translation for the English words **company** and **firm**.

---

sociocultural [səʊsɪəʊ'kʌltʃər(ə)l] ADJ socioculturel

socioeconomic [səʊsɪəʊiːkə'nɒmɪk] ADJ socio-économique
▸▸**s. grouping** classification f socio-économique

sociolinguistic [səʊsɪəʊlɪŋ'gwɪstɪk] ADJ sociolinguistique

sociolinguistics [səʊsɪəʊlɪŋ'gwɪstɪks] N sociolinguistique f VOIR GRAMMAIRE A10

sociological [səʊsɪə'lɒdʒɪk(ə)l] ADJ sociologique

sociologist [səʊsɪ'ɒlədʒɪst] N sociologue mf

sociology [səʊsɪ'ɒlədʒɪ] N sociologie f

sociometry [səʊsɪ'ɒmɪtrɪ] N sociométrie f

sociopath ['səʊsɪəpæθ] N inadapté, -ée

socioprofessional [səʊsɪəʊprə'feʃən(ə)l] ADJ socioprofessionnel
▸▸**s. group** catégorie f socioprofessionnelle, CSP f

sock 1 [sɒk] N (Am pl also **sox**) (garment) chaussette f, (ankle) socks socquettes fpl; Br Fig Fam **to pull one's socks up** se secouer; Br Fam **put a s. in it, will you!** ferme-la!

sock 2 Fam N (blow) gnon m, beigne f, (in the

eye) cocard m; **to give sb a s. on the jaw** flanquer une beigne à qn

VT (hit) (person) flanquer une beigne à; **s. it to me!** (show me what you can do) montre-moi ce que tu sais faire!

socket ['sɒkɪt] N Anat (of eye) orbite f, (of tooth) alvéole f, (of bone) cavité f articulaire, glène f, (of pipe) (in plumbing) emboîtement m, manchon m; esp Br (for electric plug) prise f (de courant); (of lightbulb) douille f, Comput (slot) prise (femelle); (on Internet) socket f, port m; (tool) douille f, embout m; **ball and s. joint** Anat énarthrose f, Tech articulation f, **microphone s.** prise microphone
▸▸**s. set** coffret m de douilles

Socrates ['sɒkrətiːz] N Socrate

Socratic [sɒ'krætɪk] ADJ socratique

sod 1 [sɒd] N (piece of turf) motte f de gazon; **to cut** or **turn the first s.** donner le premier coup de bêche; **under the s.** (buried) enterré

sod 2 esp Br Sl N (obnoxious person or thing) **he's a real s.** c'est un vrai salaud; **you silly s.!** espèce d'imbécile!; **you stupid s.!** andouille!; **poor s.!** pauvre bougre!; **he's a rude s.!** quel ours!; **the kid's being an absolute little s.!** ce gosse est une vraie peste!; **this problem/screw is a real s.!** ce putain de problème/cette putain de vis!; **odds and sods** petits bouts mpl, bribes fpl et morceaux mpl

VT (to damn) **s. you!** va te faire foutre!; **s. them!** ils peuvent toujours aller se faire voir!; **s. the party, I'm tired** la soirée, je m'en fous, je suis fatigué; **s. it!** merde, alors!

▸**sod off** VI (go away) foutre le camp; **s. off!** fous-moi le camp!; **I told him to s. off** je lui ai dit d'aller se faire voir

soda ['səʊdə] N **1** Chem etc soude f, **caustic s.** soude caustique; **washing s.** carbonate m de soude; **bicarbonate of s., baking s.** bicarbonate m de soude **2** (fizzy water) eau f de Seltz **3** Am (soft drink) soda m
▸▸**s. bread** pain m à la levure chimique; Am **s. cracker** = biscuit m sec à la levure chimique; Am **s. fountain** (café) ≃ café m; (device) siphon m (d'eau de Seltz); **s. water** eau de Seltz

sod-all esp Br Sl N (nothing) que dalle; **that's got s. to do with it!** ça n'a foutrement rien à voir avec ça!; **they do s. all day** ils n'en fichent pas une rame de la journée

ADJ ATTRIB **I have s. money** je n'ai pas un putain de rond; **they've got s. hope of winning** ils n'ont pas une putain de chance de gagner

sodden ['sɒd(ə)n] ADJ (field) (dé)trempé; (clothes etc) trempé; **s. with drink** imbibé d'alcool

sodding ['sɒdɪŋ] esp Br Sl ADJ (as intensifier) **this s. weather/government/car** ce putain de temps/de gouvernement/cette putain de voiture; **he's a s. nuisance!** c'est un sacré emmerdeur!

ADV vachement; **you can s. well do it yourself!** démerde-toi tout seul pour le faire!; **don't be so s. lazy!** ce que tu peux être flemmard!

sodium ['səʊdɪəm] N Chem sodium m
▸▸**s. chloride** chlorure m de sodium

Sodom ['sɒdəm] N Sodome f

sodomite ['sɒdəmaɪt] N sodomite m

sodomize ['sɒdəmaɪz] VT sodomiser

sodomy ['sɒdəmɪ] N sodomie f

Sod's law [sɒdz] N loi f de l'emmerdement maximum

sofa ['səʊfə] N canapé m
▸▸**s. bed** canapé-lit m, pl canapés-lits

SOFT [sɒft]

ADJ mou **1** ▪ doux **1, 2** ▪ tendre **1, 2** ▪ souple **1** ▪ indulgent **3** ▪ tranquille **3** ▪ stupide **4**

ADJ 1 *(substance, ground, cheese etc)* mou, *f* molle; *(pillow, carpet, fabric, toilet paper etc)* doux, *f* douce, moelleux; *(rock, pencil etc)* tendre; *(hat)* mou; *(leather)* souple; **a nice s. bed** un lit moelleux; **this bed is too s.** ce lit est trop mou; **as s. as silk** doux comme de la soie; **to the touch** doux au toucher; **s. skin** peau douce *ou* veloutée; **to become** *or* **get s.** s'amollir
  2 *(gentle) (voice, music, rain, wind etc)* doux, *f* douce; *(shade, blue etc)* tendre; **s. step** pas feutré *ou* de loup; **s. words** mots doux *ou* tendres
  3 *(person) (not strict)* indulgent, coulant; *(easy) (job, life etc)* tranquille; *Fam* **to be s. on sb** *(fond of)* être amoureux *ou* entiché de qn; *(lenient towards)* être coulant avec qn; **you mustn't be so s. with** *or* **on them** il faut les traiter plus sévèrement; **to have a s. spot for sb** avoir un faible pour qn; *Fam* **to be a s. touch** *(easy to get money from)* être facile à taper; *(easy to take advantage of)* être bonne poire; **to have a s. heart** avoir le cœur tendre
  4 *Fam (stupid)* stupide, bête; **don't be s.!** ne sois pas bête!; **he's gone s. in the head!** il a perdu la boule!
  ADV *Fam* **don't talk s.!** ne dis pas de bêtises! ▸▸ *Ling* **s. consonant** consonne *f* douce; *Comput* **s. copy** visualisation *f* sur écran; *Fin* **s. currency** devise *f* faible; **s. drinks** boissons *fpl* non alcoolisées; *Phot* **s. focus** flou *m* artistique, point *m* diffus; **s. fruit** ≃ fruits *mpl* rouges; *Br* **s. furnishings** tissus *mpl* d'ameublement; *Comput* **s. hyphen** césure *f* automatique, tiret *m* conditionnel; *Comput* **s. key** touche *f* programmable; *Aviat, Astronaut, Econ* **s. landing** atterrissage *m* en douceur; **s. lighting** éclairage *m* diffus; *Econ, Fin* **s. loan** prêt *m* avantageux *ou* à des conditions avantageuses; **s. option** solution *f* de facilité; **s. outline** contour *m* flou; **s. page break** changement *m* conditionnel de page; **s. porn** pornographie *f* peu explicite, *Fam* soft *m*; *Comput* **s. reset** simple réinitialisation *f*; *Comput* **s. return** saut *m* de ligne automatique; *Comput* **s. sectoring** formatage *m* logiciel; *Com* **s. sell** = méthodes *fpl* de vente non agressives; **s. shoulder** *(on road)* accotement *m* non stabilisé; **s. space** espace *m* ressort; *Anat* **s. tissue** parties *fpl* charnues; **s. verge** *(on road)* accotement *m* non stabilisé; **s. water** eau *f* douce *ou* non calcaire

softback ['sɒftbæk] **N** (livre *m* de) poche *m* ▸▸ **s. version** version *f* poche

softball ['sɒftbɔːl] **N** *Am Sl* = variante *f* du baseball qui se joue avec une balle plus grande et plus molle

soft-boiled **ADJ** *(egg)* mollet

soft-centre, *Am* **soft-center** **N** *(chocolate)* chocolat *m* fourré

soft-centred, *Am* **soft-centered** **ADJ** *(chocolate, sweet)* fourré

soft-core **ADJ** *(pornography)* soft *inv*

soft-cover **N** *esp Am* (livre *m* de) poche *m*

soften ['sɒf(ə)n] **VT** *(wax etc)* ramollir; *(skin)* adoucir; *(leather)* assouplir; *(person) (physically)* ramollir; *(emotionally)* attendrir; *(colour)* adoucir, atténuer; *(voice, personality, water etc)* adoucir; *(light, contrast etc)* atténuer; *(one's tone)* radoucir; *(person's anger)* calmer, atténuer; **troops softened by idleness** troupes amollies par l'oisiveté; **the government has softened its stance in its talks with the unions** le gouvernement a adouci sa position lors des négociations avec les syndicats; *Fig* **to s. the blow** amortir le choc
  VI *(of wax etc)* se ramollir; *(of skin etc)* s'adoucir; *(of meat)* s'attendrir; *(of person)* se radoucir; *(of anger)* se calmer; **the union's stance has softened** le syndicat a adouci sa position

▸ **soften up** **VT SEP 1** *(make softer)* adoucir **2** *Mil etc (prisoner, suspect etc)* réduire la résistance de **3** *(hard-hearted person)* amadouer
  VI = **soften VI**

softener ['sɒf(ə)nər] **N** **water s.** adoucisseur *m* d'eau; **fabric s.** adoucissant *m*

softening ['sɒf(ə)nɪŋ] **N** *(of wax etc)* ramollissement *m*; *(of leather)* assouplissement *m*; *(of character, attitudes, water)* adoucissement *m*; *(of light, contrast, outlines)* atténuation *f*; *Hum* **he has suffered from a s. of the brain** son cerveau s'est ramolli; **there has been a s. of attitudes** il y a eu un adoucissement *ou* un fléchissement des attitudes

soft-faced hammer [-feɪst] **N** maillet *m*

soft-focus **ADJ** ▸▸ **s. lens** objectif *m* pour créer des effets de flou

softheaded [sɒft'hedɪd] **ADJ** *Fam* bête, niais

softhearted [sɒft'hɑːtɪd] **ADJ** au cœur tendre, sensible; **he's too s.** il a trop de cœur

softie ['sɒftɪ] **N** *Fam* = **softy**

softly ['sɒftlɪ] **ADV** *(to talk, whisper, tap etc)* doucement; *(to walk)* sans bruit; *(tenderly)* tendrement; *(to land)* en douceur; **the room is s. lit** l'éclairage de la pièce est doux; **the prisoners are treated too s.** les prisonniers ne sont pas traités assez sévèrement

softly-softly **ADJ** *(approach etc)* doux, *f* douce

softness ['sɒftnɪs] **N 1** *(of skin, fabric, climate etc)* douceur *f*; *(of character)* mollesse *f*; *(of outlines)* flou *m* **3** *Fam (foolishness)* niaiserie *f*

soft-pedal **VI 1** *Mus* mettre la pédale douce **2** *Fam (not emphasize strongly)* y aller doucement, ne pas trop insister
  VT *Fig* atténuer, amoindrir

soft-sectored [-sektəd] **ADJ** *Comput (disk)* formaté par programme, à secteurs logiciels

soft-soap **VT** *Fam* flatter, passer la pommade à

soft-spoken **ADJ** **to be very s.** avoir la voix très douce

soft-top **N** *Aut* décapotable *f*

software ['sɒftweər] **N** *Comput* logiciel *m*, software *m*; **all the s. written for …** tous les logiciels réalisés pour …; **a piece of s.** un logiciel ▸▸ **s. company** éditeur *m* de logiciels; **s. developer** développeur, -euse; **s. engineer** ingénieur *m* logiciels; **s. error** erreur *f* de logiciel; **s. house** éditeur *m* de logiciel; **s. package** logiciel; **s. piracy** piratage *m* de logiciels; **s. platform** plate-forme *f* logicielle, *pl* plates-formes logicielles; **s. problem** problème *m* de logiciel; **s. tool** outil *m* logiciel; **s. writer** concepteur *m* de logiciel

software-compatible **ADJ** compatible du point de vue logiciel

softwood ['sɒftwʊd] **N** *Carp etc* bois *m* tendre

softy ['sɒftɪ] **N** *Fam (gentle person)* cœur *m* sensible; *(coward)* couard, -arde; **to be a terrible s.** *(sentimental)* être sentimental à l'excès; **you know I'm a big s.** *(can't say no)* tu sais que je suis trop gentil

SOGAT ['sɔʊgæt] **N** *Br abbr* **Society of Graphical and Allied Trades**

soggy ['sɒgɪ] **ADJ** *(ground)* détrempé, imbibé; *(clothes, carpet, shoes, bread)* trempé; *(cake)* imbibé

soh [sɔʊ] **N** *Mus* sol *m inv*

soil [sɔɪl] **N 1** *(earth)* terre *f*, **to cultivate the s.** cultiver la terre; **alluvial s.** terrain *m* d'alluvion(s); *Lit* **one's native s.** sa terre natale **2** *Old-fashioned* **night s.** *(excrement)* excréments *mpl* humains

VT *(clothes, sheet, underwear)* souiller, salir; **they had soiled the carpet with mud** ils avaient maculé la moquette de boue; *Fig* **to s. one's hands** se salir les mains; *Fig* **to s. sb's reputation** salir la réputation de qn
  VI **fabric that soils easily** tissu salissant *ou* qui se salit facilement

soiled [sɔɪld] **ADJ** *(dressings)* usagé; *(bedlinen)* souillé; *(goods)* défraîchi; *Fig (reputation)* entaché; **if it's s., the shop won't exchange it** si c'est sale, la boutique ne fera pas l'échange; **some slightly s. items at reduced prices** des articles légèrement salis à prix réduits

soirée ['swɑːreɪ] **N** soirée *f*

soixante-neuf [swæsɑːnt'nɜːf] **N** soixante-neuf *m*

sojourn ['sɒdʒɜːn] *Lit* **N** séjour *m*
  VI séjourner

sol [sɒl] **N** *Mus* sol *m inv*

solace ['sɒləs] *Lit* **N** consolation *f*, soulagement *m*; **to find s. in sth** trouver une consolation dans qch
  VT *(person)* consoler; **I solaced myself with this thought** cette pensée m'a consolé

sola of exchange ['sɔʊlə] **N** *Fin* seule *f* de change

solar ['sɔʊlər] **ADJ** *(system, energy etc)* solaire ▸▸ **s. battery** batterie *f* solaire; **s. cell** pile *f* solaire, photopile *f*; **s. eclipse** éclipse *f* solaire; **s. panel** panneau *m* solaire; *Anat* **s. plexus** plexus *m* solaire; **s. power** énergie *f* solaire

solarium, *pl* **solaria** [sɔʊ'leərɪəm, -ɪə] **N** solarium *m*

solar-powered **ADJ** à énergie solaire

sold **PT, PP** *see* **sell**

solder ['sɒldər, 'sɔʊldər] **N** soudure *f*
  VT souder

soldering ['sɒldərɪŋ, 'sɔʊldərɪŋ] **N** soudure *f* ▸▸ **s. iron** fer *m* à souder

soldier ['sɔʊldʒər] **N** soldat *m*, militaire *m*; **private s.** simple soldat, (soldat de) deuxième classe *m*; **to become a s.** se faire soldat, entrer dans l'armée; **an old s.** un ancien soldat, un vétéran; **tin s.** soldat de plomb
  VI *(be a soldier)* faire le métier de soldat ▸▸ **s. ant** *(fourmi f)* soldat; **s. of fortune** soldat de fortune

▸ **soldier on** **VI** *Br (persevere)* persévérer; **we soldiered on through the blizzard** nous avons progressé à grand-peine dans le blizzard; **I'll s. on with this for another half hour** je vais encore m'escrimer là-dessus pendant une demi-heure

soldiering ['sɔʊldʒərɪŋ] **N** la carrière militaire *ou* des armes; **he was tired of s.** il en avait assez du métier de soldat; **to go s.** se faire soldat

soldierlike, soldierly ['sɔʊldʒəlaɪk, -lɪ] **ADJ** de soldat

soldiery ['sɔʊldʒərɪ] **N** *(no pl) Old-fashioned (soldiers)* soldats *mpl*, militaires *mpl*

sole¹ [sɔʊl] **N** *(of foot)* plante *f*, *(of shoe)* semelle *f*
  VT *(shoe) (fit with sole)* mettre une semelle à; *(resole)* ressemeler

sole² **N** *(fish)* sole *f*, **Dover s.** (vraie) sole

sole³ **ADJ 1** *(only)* seul, unique; **his s. reason** son unique raison **2** *(exclusive)* exclusif; **to have s. responsibility for sth** être entièrement responsable de qch ▸▸ **s. agency** représentation *f* exclusive; **s. agency contract** contrat *m* de représentation exclusive; **s. agent** agent *m* exclusif; **s. contract** contrat exclusif; **s. right** droit *m* exclusif; *Br Com* **s. trader** entreprise *f* individuelle *ou* unipersonnelle

solecism ['sɒlɪsɪz(ə)m] **N** *Ling* solécisme *m*; *Fml (social error)* bévue *f*

solely ['səʊlɪ] ADVseulement, uniquement; **I went there s. to see it** j'y suis allé dans le seul but de le voir

solemn ['sɒləm] ADJ **1** (oath etc) solennel; (duty) sacré; (question) grave; Law **s. agreement** contrat m solennel; **s. warning** avertissement m formel **2** (person) grave, sérieux; (tone, atmosphere) solennel; **to look s.** avoir l'air solennel

solemness ['sɒləmnɪs] N = **solemnity 1**

solemnity [sə'lemnɪtɪ] N **1** (of occasion, ceremony) solennité f; (of expression, attitude) gravité f, sérieux m; **with all s.** en toute solennité **2** Lit **the solemnities** (religious festival) les fêtes fpl solennelles, les solennités fpl

solemnization [sɒləmnaɪ'zeɪʃən] N (of marriage) célébration f

solemnize ['sɒləmnaɪz] VT (religious festival) solenniser, célébrer; (marriage) célébrer

solemnly ['sɒləmlɪ] ADV **1** (to promise etc) solennellement **2** (seriously) gravement; (to speak) avec solennité

solenoid ['sɒlənɔɪd] N Elec solénoïde m
▸▸**s. switch** contacteur m à solénoïde

solfa ['sɒlfɑː] N Mus tonic **s.** solfège m

solicit [sə'lɪsɪt] VT **1** solliciter (**from sb** de qn); (votes) solliciter, briguer **2** (of prostitute) (customers) racoler
VI (of prostitute) racoler

solicitation [səlɪsɪ'teɪʃən] N sollicitation f

soliciting [sə'lɪsɪtɪŋ] N Law (of prostitute) racolage m

solicitor [sə'lɪsɪtər] N **1** Br Law (for drawing up documents, conveyancing) ≃ notaire m; (for court work, divorce cases) avocate, -ate **2** (seeking trade etc) solliciteur, -euse
▸▸ Br **S. General** conseiller m juridique de la Couronne

solicitous [sə'lɪsɪtəs] ADJ Lit (eager) soucieux, désireux (**of sth** de qch); (concerned) préoccupé; (caring) plein de sollicitude; **s. attention to detail** soin méticuleux des détails

solicitously [sə'lɪsɪtəslɪ] ADVavec sollicitude

solicitousness [sə'lɪsɪtəsnɪs], **solicitude** [sə'lɪsɪtjuːd] N sollicitude f, préoccupation f

solid ['sɒlɪd] ADJ **1** (brick, stone, business), Fig (business) solide; (mass, line) compact; (gold, silver) massif; (tyre) plein; (wall) plein, sans ouvertures; (in a single piece) en une seule pièce, d'un seul tenant; Fig **a s. wall of demonstrators** un mur compact de manifestants; **frozen s.** (water, pond) gelé jusqu'au fond; Fig **there is s. support for the proposal** il y a une majorité de gens en faveur de la proposition; Pol etc **the union was s. behind him** le syndicat était tout entier derrière lui; **the town was s. for Labour** la ville a massivement voté Travailliste; **the workers were s. behind the strike** les employés étaient tous pour la grève; **to become s.** (of fluid) se solidifier; **s. as a rock** (ice, mud) dur comme de la pierre; Fig **solide comme le roc**; **to build on s. foundations** bâtir sur des fondations solides; Fig construire sur des bases solides; **on s. ground** sur un terrain ferme; **man of s. build** homme bien charpenté; **s. common sense** solide bon sens; **to have s. reasons for believing sth** avoir de bonnes raisons de croire qch; **a good s. meal** un repas consistant; **some good s. research** des recherches bien concrètes; **to sleep/work for nine s. hours** dormir/travailler neuf heures d'affilée; **three days' s. rain** trois jours de pluie continue; **s. vote** vote m massif

2 Am Fam (excellent) génial, -aux, super
N solide m; **solids** (food) aliments mpl solides; **is the baby on solids yet?** le bébé mange-t-il déjà des aliments solides?
ADV **1 to sleep/work for nine hours s.** dormir/travailler neuf heures d'affilée **2** Am Fam (absolutely) absolument; **I s. gotta do it!** il faut absolument que je le fasse!
▸▸ Math **s. angle** angle m solide; **s. food** nourriture f solide; **s. fuel** combustible m solide

solidarity [sɒlɪ'dærɪtɪ] N solidarité f; **to show s. with sb** faire preuve de solidarité envers qn

solidification [səlɪdɪfɪ'keɪʃən] N solidification f; (of oil) congélation f

solidify [sə'lɪdɪfaɪ] VT **1** solidifier; (oil) congeler **2** Fig (union, fact) consolider
VI **1** se solidifier; (of oil) se congeler **2** Fig (of opinions etc) se consolider

solidity [sə'lɪdɪtɪ] N solidité f

solidly ['sɒlɪdlɪ] ADV **1** solidement; (without interruption) sans interruption, sans s'arrêter; **s. held** tenu fermement ou solidement; **s. built man** homme bien charpenté **2** (to vote) massivement; **we're s. behind you** nous vous soutenons à fond

solid-state ADJ (physics) des solides; (electronics, circuit, device) à semi-conducteurs
▸▸**s. electronics** semi-conducteurs mpl

solidus ['sɒlɪdəs], pl **solidi** [-daɪ] N Typ barre f oblique

soliloquize [sə'lɪləkwaɪz] VI faire un monologue, soliloquer

soliloquy [sə'lɪləkwɪ] N soliloque m, monologue m

solitaire [sɒlɪ'teər] N **1** (game with pegs etc) solitaire m; Am Cards (jeu m de) patience f, réussite f **2** (gem) solitaire m

solitary ['sɒlɪt(ə)rɪ] ADJ solitaire; (on one's, its own) seul, solitaire; (isolated) isolé; **not a s. one** pas un seul
N Fam régime m (d'isolement) cellulaire; **he got three months' s.** il a pris trois mois de cachot
▸▸**s. confinement** isolement m cellulaire; **to be kept in s. confinement** être détenu en régime (d'isolement) cellulaire

solitude ['sɒlɪtjuːd] N solitude f; **to live in s.** vivre dans la solitude

solo ['səʊləʊ] N **1** Mus solo m; **violin s.** solo de violon **2** (flight) vol m solo **3** Cards solo m (variante du whist)
ADV **1** Mus solo; **to play/to sing s.** jouer/chanter en solo **2** (unaided) seul, en solitaire, en solo; **to fly s.** voler en solo **to go s.** Cards jouer solo; (of business partner, member of rock group etc) faire une carrière en solo
ADJ **1** Mus solo; **she plays s. violin** elle est soliste de violon, elle est violon solo **2** (unaided) en solitaire; **a s. act** un one-man-show
▸▸**s. album** album m solo; **s. flight** vol m solo; **her first s. flight** son premier vol en solo; Cards **s. whist** solo (variante du whist)

soloist ['səʊləʊɪst] N Mus soliste mf

Solomon Islands ['sɒləmən] NPL îles fpl Salomon

solstice ['sɒlstɪs] N solstice m; **the winter/ summer s.** le solstice d'hiver/d'été

solubility [sɒljʊ'bɪlɪtɪ] N (of a salt etc) solubilité f

soluble ['sɒljʊb(ə)l] ADJ **1** soluble (**in water** dans l'eau) **2** (problem) soluble

solution [sə'luːʃən] N **1** (act of solving) (of difficulty, equation) résolution f, solution f **2** (answer) (to problem) solution f; **there is no real s. to this** il n'y a aucune solution dans ce cas **3** (fluid) solution f; **salt in s.** sel m en solution

solvable ['sɒlvəb(ə)l] ADJ (problem) soluble

Note that the French adjective **solvable** is a false friend and is never a translation for the English adjective **solvable**. It means financially solvent.

solve [sɒlv] VT (problem, equation, riddle) résoudre; (mystery) éclaircir

solvency ['sɒlvənsɪ] N Com, Law solvabilité f

solvent ['sɒlvənt] ADJ **1** Com, Law solvable **2** (liquid) dissolvant, solvant
N dissolvant m, solvant m
▸▸**s. abuse** usage m de solvants hallucinogènes; **s. abuser** toxicomane mf utilisant des solvants hallucinogènes

Som abbr Somerset

Somali [sə'mɑːlɪ] ADJ somali, somalien
N **1** Somali, -ie; **the S.** (pl) les Somalis mpl **2** Ling somali m

Somalia [sə'mɑːlɪə] N Somalie f

Somaliland [sə'mɑːlɪlænd] N Hist Somalie f

somatic [sə'mætɪk] ADJ Biol somatique

sombre, Am somber ['sɒmbər] ADJ (colour etc) sombre; (person, look) sombre; (mood) maussade; **to be in a s. mood** être d'humeur maussade

sombrely, Am somberly ['sɒmbəlɪ] ADV (to look at sb etc) d'un air sombre; **s. dressed** habillé de couleurs sombres

sombrero [sɒm'breərəʊ] N sombrero m

SOME [sʌm] VOIR GRAMMAIRE A34–5; B14–15

ADJ	quelconque **1** ▪ certains **1** ▪ de, du, de la, des **2** ▪ intensive **3**
PRON	certains **1** ▪ quelques-uns **1, 2** ▪ un peu **2**
ADV	environ **1**

ADJ 1 (not specified) **s.** (sort of an) **excuse** une excuse quelconque; **he'll come s. day** il arrivera un de ces jours; **s. days she is better** certains jours elle va mieux; **s. books are difficult to read** certains livres sont difficiles à lire, il y a des livres qui sont difficiles à lire; **s. people say ...** certaines personnes disent ..., il y en a qui disent ...; **s. fool left the door open** un imbécile a laissé la porte ouverte; **s. bureaucrat decided the road would be here** un bureaucrate quelconque a décidé que la route passerait ici; **s. book or other** un livre quelconque

2 (certain quantity, number) de; **to drink s. water** boire de l'eau; **I ate s. fruit** j'ai mangé des fruits; **s. strange people appeared** d'étranges personnes ou des personnes étranges ont fait leur apparition; **s. people** des personnes; (a few) quelques personnes; **s. people think ...** il y a des gens qui pensent ...; **I felt s. uneasiness** je ressentais quelque inquiétude; **that would be s. help** cela faciliterait un peu les choses; **in s. measure, to s. degree** jusqu'à un certain point, dans une certaine mesure; **s. distance away** à quelque distance, à une certaine distance; **s. days ago** il y a quelques jours; **for s. time** pendant quelque temps ou un certain temps; **he has been waiting for s. time** il attend depuis quelque temps ou depuis un certain temps; **it will be s. time** or **s. little while before it's finished** ça va prendre un certain temps ou un moment avant que ça soit fini; **at s. length** assez longuement SEE GRAMMAR B5

3 Fam (intensive) (that was) **s. storm!** quelle tempête!; **she's s. girl!** c'est une fille formidable!; **that was s. meal!** ce que nous avons bien mangé!, Fam ce qu'on s'est mis!; **s. people!** il y a des gens, vraiment! Iron **s. father you are!** quel père tu fais!; **s. hope!** tu peux toujours rêver!

PRON 1 (people) certain(e)s, quelques-uns,

quelques-unes; **s. or all of them** tous ou seulement certains d'entre eux; **s. believe that …** certains croient que …, il y en a qui croient que …; **they went off, s. one way, s. another** ils se sont dispersés, les uns d'un côté, les autres de l'autre ou *Lit* qui d'un côté, qui de l'autre; **s. of my friends** certains de mes amis

2 *(things, quantity) (referring to countable nouns)* quelques-uns, quelques-unes; *(referring to uncountable nouns)* un peu; **s. of the guests had already left** quelques invités étaient déjà partis; **s. of the money has been recovered** on a retrouvé une partie de l'argent; **I have s.** j'en ai; **give me s.** donnez-m'en; **I've s. more** *(I have some left)* j'en ai encore; *(I have some others)* j'en ai d'autres; **s. of the time** une partie du temps; **Norway has s. of the most beautiful scenery in the world** les paysages de la Norvège sont parmi les plus beaux du monde; **at least there's some left** *(not nothing)* il en reste quand même un peu

ADV 1 *(approximately)* environ, quelque *inv*; **s. thirty pounds** une trentaine de livres, quelque trente livres; **s. fifteen minutes** un bon quart d'heure; **s. few minutes ago** il y a quelques minutes

2 *Am Fam (intensive)* **to go it s.** y aller en plein; **it annoyed him s.** ça l'a plutôt énervé

somebody ['sʌmbədɪ] **PRON** *(some person)* quelqu'un; **s. told me so** quelqu'un *ou* on me l'a dit; **s. I know told me** quelqu'un que je connais me l'a dit; **he's not s. you can trust** ce n'est pas quelqu'un en qui on peut avoir confiance; **s. is knocking** on frappe; **s. is missing** il manque quelqu'un; **s. (or other) has told him** quelqu'un lui a dit; **is this s.'s wallet?** est-ce que ce portefeuille est à quelqu'un?; **s. important** quelqu'un d'important; **we need a. bit taller/who speaks Russian** il nous faut quelqu'un d'un peu plus grand/ qui parle russe; *Fam* **Mr S. (or other)** quelqu'un; **there was a Mr S. (or other) to see you** il y a un M. Machin (Truc) qui voulait te voir; **s. else** quelqu'un d'autre; **he went and s. else came along** il est parti et un autre est venu VOIR GRAMMAIRE A34; B16

PRON, N *(pl* **somebodies** ['sʌmbədɪz]*) (important person)* **he's (a) s.** c'est un personnage, ce n'est pas le premier venu; **she thinks she's s.** elle se croit quelqu'un, elle ne se prend pas pour n'importe qui; **I want to be s.** je veux être quelqu'un

someday ['sʌmdeɪ] **ADV** un jour

somehow ['sʌmhaʊ] **ADV 1** *(in some way or other)* d'une façon ou d'une autre, d'une manière ou d'une autre; **we'll manage it s. (or other)** nous y parviendrons tant bien que mal; **s. we got there on time** nous nous sommes débrouillés pour arriver à l'heure

2 *(for some reason or other)* **I never liked her s.** pour une raison ou pour une autre, elle ne m'a jamais été sympathique; **s. (or other) it's different** il y a pourtant une différence; **s. it doesn't seem right** je ne sais pas pourquoi mais j'ai l'impression que c'est faux

someone ['sʌmwʌn] **PRON** = **somebody**

someplace ['sʌmpleɪs] **ADV** *Am* = **somewhere**

somersault ['sʌməsɔːlt] **N** *(on ground or accidental)* culbute *f*, *(in air)* saut *m* périlleux; **to turn** *ou* **do a s.** *(on ground or accidentally)* faire une culbute; *(in air)* faire un saut périlleux; *(of car)* faire un tonneau

VI *(of person) (on ground or accidentally)* faire la/des culbute(s); *(in air)* faire un/des saut(s) périlleux; *(of car)* faire un/des tonneau(x); **the car somersaulted twice** la voiture a fait deux tonneaux; **he's good at somersaulting** il est doué pour les culbutes/les sauts périlleux

SOMETHING ['sʌmθɪŋ] VOIR GRAMMAIRE A34; B16 **N, PRON 1** quelque chose *m*; **I've brought you a little s.** je vous ai apporté un petit quelque chose *ou* une bricole; **say s.** dites quelque chose; **s. or other** une chose ou une autre; **s. or other was bothering her** quelque chose l'ennuyait; **Anne s. (or other)** Anne je ne sais plus quoi; **there's s. about him I don't like** il y a en lui quelque chose qui me déplaît; **s. tells me she'll come** quelque chose me dit qu'elle viendra; **s. has happened** il est arrivé quelque chose; **was it s.? I said** est-ce que j'ai dit quelque chose (qu'il ne fallait pas)?; **s. to drink/eat/read** quelque chose à boire/ manger/lire; **to ask for s. to drink** demander (quelque chose) à boire; **can I get you s.?** est-ce que je peux vous offrir quelque chose (à manger/à boire)?; **let's have s. to eat** mangeons quelque chose; **it must have been s.** he ate that made him ill ça doit être quelque chose qu'il a mangé qui l'a rendu malade; **s. to live for** une raison de vivre; **to have s. to cry/be annoyed about** avoir une bonne raison de pleurer/se fâcher; **to have s. to hang on to** avoir quelque chose à quoi se raccrocher; **s. new** quelque chose de nouveau *ou* de neuf; **I've s. else to do** j'ai autre chose à faire; **he's s. in a bank** il travaille dans une banque; **in the year eleven hundred and s.** en l'an onze cent et quelque chose; **she's eighty s.** elle a quatre-vingts ans et quelques, *Fam* elle a quatre-vingts ans et des poussières; **a certain (indefinable) s.** je-ne-sais-quoi; **he has seen s. of the world** *(is mature, experienced)* il connaît la vie; *(has travelled)* il a pas mal voyagé; **her plan has s. in it, there's s. in her plan** son projet mérite considération; **there's s. in what you say** il y a du vrai dans ce que vous dites; **she has s. to do with it** elle y est pour quelque chose; **it's s. to do with the way he speaks** ça a un rapport avec la façon dont il parle; **well, that's s.!** c'est déjà quelque chose!; **that was quite s.!** c'était vraiment quelque chose!; *Fam* **that meal was s. else!** c'était quelque chose, ce repas; *Fam* **he really is s. else!** il est pas possible!; **she's an accountant or s.** elle est comptable ou quelque chose comme ça; **is it broken or s.?** c'est cassé ou quoi?; **she's off work with a cold or s.** elle n'est pas venue travailler à cause d'un rhume, je crois; **he bought it from a man in a bar or s.** je crois qu'il l'a acheté à un type dans un bar

2 there's s. of an improvement il y a une certaine amélioration; **she's s. of a miser** elle est un peu *ou* quelque peu avare

ADV 1 **it looks s. like a guinea pig** ça ressemble à un cochon d'Inde; **s. like 500** 500 environ, quelque chose comme 500; **is this s. like him?** est-ce que ça lui ressemble un peu?; **s. like that** quelque chose comme ça

2 *Fam (intensifying)* **he treated me s. awful** il m'a traité d'une façon abominable; **he fancies her s. rotten** il en est amoureux comme pas possible

sometime ['sʌmtaɪm] **ADV** *(often written as two words)* **s. (or other)** un jour ou l'autre; **you'll have to make your mind up s.** tôt ou tard, il faudra que tu prennes une décision; **the last time I saw him was s. in August** la dernière fois que je l'ai vu, c'était en août; **we'll talk about it s. before/after Christmas** on en reparlera à un moment ou à un autre avant/après Noël; **I'll do it s.** je vais le faire; **I hope to go there s.** j'espère y aller un jour; **s. before 7 o'clock** avant 7 heures; **s. in August** au cours de l'année dernière; **s. before last Tuesday** avant mardi dernier; **s. between 1997 and 2001** entre 1997 et 2001; **s. soon** bientôt; *Fam* **see you s.!** à bientôt!

ADJ ATTRIB *Lit* **Mr Martin, my s. tutor** M. Martin, autrefois mon professeur

Attention: ne pas confondre avec **sometimes**.

sometimes ['sʌmtaɪmz] **ADV** quelquefois, parfois; **s. one, s. the other** tantôt l'un, tantôt l'autre

Attention: ne pas confondre avec **sometime**.

somewhat ['sʌmwɒt] **ADV** un peu, quelque peu; **it's s. difficult** c'est assez difficile

N **he was s. of a coward** il était plutôt poltron; **this was s. of a relief** ce fut, en quelque sorte, un soulagement

somewhere ['sʌmweər] **ADV 1** *(in or to some place)* quelque part; **it's s. in the Bible** cela se trouve quelque part dans la Bible; **s. near us** pas bien loin de nous; **s. along the way** sur le chemin, quelque part en chemin; **now we're getting s.!** voilà un premier résultat!, enfin nous avançons!; **I need s. quiet to work** j'ai besoin d'un endroit calme pour travailler; **s. in the world** quelque part (dans le monde); **s. in France** quelque part en France; **s. else** ailleurs, autre part; **s. or other** je ne sais où; **he lives s. near Oxford** il habite dans les environs d'Oxford

2 *(approximately)* **he is s. around fifty** il a à peu près cinquante ans; **it costs s. in the region of £500** cela coûte environ 500 livres; **there were s. around 50 kilobytes left** il restait environ 50 kilo-octets

sommelier ['sɒməljeɪ] **N** sommelier *m*

somnambulism [sɒmˈnæmbjʊlɪz(ə)m] **N** somnambulisme *m*

somnambulist [sɒmˈnæmbjʊlɪst] **N** somnambule *mf*

somniferous [sɒmˈnɪfərəs] **ADJ** somnifère, soporifique; *Fig* soporifique

somnolence ['sɒmnələns] **N** *Fml* somnolence *f*

somnolent ['sɒmnələnt] **ADJ** *Fml* somnolent

son [sʌn] **N 1** *(family member)* fils *m*; **she's got two sons** elle a deux fils ou garçons; *Fig* **a s. of the people** un fils du peuple; *Am Sl* **s. of a bitch** *(obnoxious person)* fils *m* de pute, salaud *m*; *Am Fam* **s. of a gun** coquin *m*; *Rel* **the S. of God** le fils de Dieu; *Rel* **the S. of Man** le fils de l'homme

2 *Fam (term of address)* fiston *m*; **OK, s.?** *(lad)* OK, mon petit gars?

sonar ['səʊnɑːr] **N** *Naut* sonar *m*

sonata [səˈnɑːtə] **N** *Mus* sonate *f*

sonatina [sɒnəˈtiːnə] **N** *Mus* sonatine *f*

sonde [sɒnd] **N** *Met etc* sonde *f*

son et lumière ['sɒneɪ ˈluːmjeə(r)] **ADJ** spectacle *m* son et lumière, son et lumière *m*

song [sɒŋ] **N 1** chanson *f*, *Lit* chant *m*; *Rel* cantique *m*; **marching s.** chanson de route; **give us a s.** chantez-nous quelque chose; *Fam* **to buy sth for a s.** acheter qch pour rien *ou* pour une bouchée de pain; *Fam* **it went for a s.** cela s'est vendu pour une bouchée de pain; *Fam* **he made a great s. and dance about it** il en a fait tout un plat; *Lit* **s. of victory** chant de victoire; **s. of praise** *Lit* louanges *fpl*; *Rel* cantique *m*; *Lit* **with a s. in one's heart** la joie au cœur, le cœur léger; *Bible* **the S. of Songs, the S. of Solomon** le Cantique des Cantiques; **a festival of French s.** un festival de la chanson française; *Fam* **to be on s.** *(of engine)* tourner rond; *(of team)* être en bonne forme

2 *(singing)* chant *m*; **to burst** *or* **break into s.** se mettre à chanter; **the s. of the birds** le chant *ou* le ramage des oiseaux

▸▸ **s. book** recueil *m* de chansons, chansonnier *m*

songbird ['sɒŋbɜːd] N oiseau m chanteur

songster ['sɒŋstər] N **1** (singer) chanteur m **2** (poet) poète m, chantre m **3** = songbird

songstress ['sɒŋstrɪs] N (singer) chanteuse f

songwriter ['sɒŋraɪtər] N Mus (writes the music) compositeur, -trice (de chansons); (writes the words) parolier, -ière; (writes both) auteur-compositeur m, pl auteurs-compositeurs

sonic ['sɒnɪk] ADJ Phys acoustique, audible; Aviat (speed) sonique
▸▸ **s. boom** bang m

son-in-law, pl **sons-in-law** N gendre m, beau-fils m, pl beaux-fils

sonnet ['sɒnɪt] N (in poetry) sonnet m

sonny ['sʌnɪ] N Fam mon petit gars m, fiston m; **look here, s. Jim** or **boy** attention, mon petit gars

sonority [sə'nɒrɪtɪ] N sonorité f

sonorous ['sɒnərəs] ADJ **1** (resonant) sonore **2** (grandiloquent) grandiloquent

> Note that the French adjective **sonore** only applies to sounds.

sonorously ['sɒnərəslɪ] ADV (to speak) d'une voix sonore; **the organ boomed s.** l'orgue résonnait

sonorousness ['sɒnərəsnɪs] N sonorité f

soon [suːn] ADV VOIR GRAMMAIRE A21 **1** (within a short time) bientôt; **how s. can you get here?** combien de temps vous faut-il pour y aller?; **s. after** peu après; **s. after four** (un) peu après quatre heures; **it will s. be three years since …** voici bientôt trois ans que …, cela fera bientôt trois ans que …; **he'll be here very s.** il sera ici sous peu, il sera ici très bientôt; **must you leave so s.?** vous faut-il partir si tôt?; **too s.** trop tôt, avant l'heure; **an hour too s.** (to arrive etc) avec une heure d'avance; **they were s. making friends** ils se sont bien vite fait des amis; **it ended all too s.** cela a fini bien trop tôt; **none too s.** juste à temps
2 as s. as aussitôt que, dès que; **I'll see him as s. as he comes** je le verrai aussitôt ou dès qu'il arrivera; **as s. as I arrived in London** dès mon arrivée à Londres; **as s. as he saw them** dès qu'il les a vus; **as s. as possible** le plus tôt possible, aussitôt que possible, dès que possible SEE GRAMMAR B31–2
3 sooner (earlier) plus tôt; **we would have got there sooner if …** nous serions arrivés plus tôt si …; **the sooner you begin, the sooner you will have finished** plus tôt vous commencerez, plus vite vous aurez fini; **the problem should be dealt with sooner rather than later** il faut faire face au problème le plus tôt possible; **the sooner the better** le plus tôt sera le mieux; **sooner or later** tôt ou tard; **no sooner said than done** (aus)sitôt dit, (aus)sitôt fait; **no sooner had he finished than he was arrested** à peine eut-il fini qu'il fut arrêté
4 (preference) **I would just as s. stay** j'aime autant rester; **I would die sooner than give in** je mourrais plutôt que de céder; **I would sooner die** j'aimerais mieux mourir; **someone will have to do it – sooner you than me!** quelqu'un devra le faire – il vaudrait mieux que ce soit vous, plutôt que moi!
5 soonest (to do sth) aussitôt que possible; **it will be next week at the soonest** ce sera la semaine prochaine au plus tôt; Prov **least said soonest mended** moins on en dit, mieux ça vaut

soot [sʊt] N suie f

sooth [suːθ] N Arch **in s.** en vérité

soothe [suːð] VT (pain, burn etc) calmer, apaiser; (the mind) tranquilliser; (person) apaiser; **to s. sb's anger** apaiser la colère de qn

▸ **soothe down** VT SEP (make less angry, worried) (person) calmer

soothing ['suːðɪŋ] ADJ calmant, apaisant; Med lénitif; **in a s. voice** d'une voix apaisante

soothingly ['suːðɪŋlɪ] ADV (to say) d'un ton apaisant

soothsayer ['suːθseɪər] N Arch devin m, devineresse f

soothsaying ['suːθseɪɪŋ] N Arch divination f

sooty ['sʊtɪ] ADJ **1** (covered in soot) couvert de suie; (black) noir de suie **2** (deposit) de suie; (resembling soot) fuligineux

sop [sɒp] N **1** (bread) morceau m de pain trempé **2** Lit (concession) concession f, **as a s. to his conscience** pour soulager sa conscience; **he just said that as a s. to her feelings** il a dit ça seulement pour lui plaire ou (if she is angry etc) pour l'amadouer; **a concession that was not much more than a s. to the unions** une concession qui n'avait pour but que d'amadouer les syndicats
VT (-pp-) (bread) (faire) tremper

▸ **sop up** VT SEP (mop up) (liquid) éponger; **the paper towel sopped up the water** l'essuie-tout a absorbé toute l'eau

soph [sɒf] N Am Fam (sophomore) étudiant, -ante de deuxième année

sophism ['sɒfɪz(ə)m] N sophisme m

sophist ['sɒfɪst] N sophiste mf

sophistical [sə'fɪstɪk(ə)l] ADJ sophistique, captieux

sophisticate [sə'fɪstɪkɪt] N personne f sophistiquée

sophisticated [sə'fɪstɪkeɪtɪd] ADJ (person) sophistiqué; (in matters of food, wine, conversation, tastes etc) raffiné; (style) recherché, sophistiqué; (plan) subtil; (machinery) (très) perfectionné; (technology) sophistiqué; **for the s. look this winter …** si vous voulez être élégante cet hiver …; **our more s. readers** nos lecteurs les plus cultivés; **teenagers think it's very s. to …** les adolescents pensent que ça fait très bien de …

sophistication [səfɪstɪ'keɪʃən] N (of person) (appearance) raffinement m, sophistication f, (tastes) goûts mpl raffinés; (of style, dress) recherche f, (of machinery) (degré m de) perfectionnement m

sophistry ['sɒfɪstrɪ] N **1** (reasoning) sophistique f, **to indulge in s.** se laisser aller à la sophistique **2** (example) sophisme m

Sophocles ['sɒfəkliːz] N Sophocle m

sophomore ['sɒfəmɔːr] N Am Univ étudiant, -ante de seconde année; **I'm a s.** je suis en deuxième année (de fac)

soporific [sɒpə'rɪfɪk] ADJ somnifère, soporifique
N somnifère m

soppiness ['sɒpɪnɪs] N Br Fam (sentimentality) sentimentalisme m, sensiblerie f

sopping ['sɒpɪŋ] ADJ **s. (wet)** (person) trempé jusqu'aux os; (shirt, cloth) détrempé

soppy ['sɒpɪ] ADJ Br Fam **1** (sentimental) (person) gnangnan inv; (sentiment) fadasse; (story, film etc) à l'eau de rose **2** (silly) stupide, bête; **don't be s.!** ne sois pas si bête!

soprano, pl **sopranos, soprani** [sə'prɑːnəʊ, -əʊz, -iː] N Mus (singer) soprano mf, (voice, part, instrument) soprano m; **to sing s.** avoir une voix de soprano
ADJ (voice, part) de soprano; (music) pour soprano
▸▸ **s. saxophone** saxophone m soprano; **s. voice** voix f de soprano

sorb [sɔːb] N **1** (fruit) sorbe f **2** (tree) sorbier m

sorbet ['sɔːbeɪ] N Culin (water ice) sorbet m

sorbitol ['sɔːbɪtɒl] N sorbitol m

sorcerer ['sɔːs(ə)rər] N sorcier m

sorceress ['sɔːs(ə)rɪs] N sorcière f

sorcery ['sɔːs(ə)rɪ] N sorcellerie f

sordid ['sɔːdɪd] ADJ sordide; (place etc) sale, crasseux; (business, motives) bas, f basse, vil

sordidly ['sɔːdɪdlɪ] ADV sordidement

sordidness ['sɔːdɪdnɪs] N sordidité f, (of place etc) saleté f, (of business, motives) bassesse f

sore [sɔːr] ADJ **1** (painful) douloureux, endolori; (eyes, throat, gums) irrité; **s. to the touch** douloureux au toucher; **s. throat** mal m de gorge; **I've (got) a s. throat** j'ai mal à la gorge, j'ai la gorge irritée; **to have a s. finger** avoir mal au doigt; **it's still s.** ça fait toujours mal; Fig **it's a s. point** or **subject with him** il est très sensible sur ce point
2 esp Am Fam (annoyed) embêté (about au sujet de); (upset) chagriné (about par); **Mom's s. because I forgot her birthday** Maman a de la peine parce que j'ai oublié son anniversaire
3 Am Fam (angry) en rogne; **to be** or **get s.** se ficher en rogne
4 Lit **to be in s. need of sth** avoir grandement besoin de qch
N Med plaie f, Fig **to (re)open an old s.** raviver une plaie ancienne; (running) **s.** ulcère m

sorehead ['sɔːhed] N esp Am Fam ronchon, -onne

sorely ['sɔːlɪ] ADV **1** Lit (painfully) **s. wounded** gravement ou grièvement blessé **2** (greatly) gravement, grandement; **s. distressed** dans une grande ou profonde détresse; **s. needed** dont on a grandement besoin; **s. tempted** fortement tenté; **s. tried** cruellement éprouvé

soreness ['sɔːnɪs] N Med douleur f

sorghum ['sɔːgəm] N (plant) sorgho m

sorrel[1] ['sɒrəl] N (plant) oseille f

sorrel[2] ADJ (horse) alezan
N (colour, horse) alezan m

sorrow ['sɒrəʊ] N douleur f, chagrin m; **to my s.** à mon (grand) regret; **more in s. than in anger** avec plus de tristesse que de colère; Bible **the Man of Sorrows** l'Homme m de douleur
VI esp Lit s'affliger, être affligé (over or at or about sth de qch); **to s. for** or **after sb/sth** pleurer qn/qch

sorrowful ['sɒrəfʊl] ADJ (person) triste, affligé, chagriné; (look, smile) affligé; (news, situation) triste, attristant

sorrowfully ['sɒrəfəlɪ] ADV tristement

sorrowing ['sɒrəʊɪŋ] ADJ affligé

SORRY ['sɒrɪ]

> désolé **1** ▪ pardon **1** ▪ regretter (to be sorry) **1** ▪ piteux **2**

ADJ **1** (regretful) fâché, chagriné, désolé (about de qch); **she's s. she did it** or **for having done it** elle regrette de l'avoir fait; **to be s. not to have done sth** regretter ou avoir du regret de ne pas avoir fait qch; **I'm only s. we couldn't have stayed longer** je regrette que nous n'ayons pas pu rester plus longtemps; Fam **you'll be s.!** il vous en cuira!, vous vous en repentirez!; **you'll be s. you ever came here!** vous allez regretter d'être venu ici!; **I'll make him s.** je le lui ferai regretter; **I'll make him s. (that) he ever came here** je lui ferai regretter d'être venu ici; **I'm s. I ever let him in the house** je regrette de l'avoir laissé entrer dans la maison; **I'm (very) s. to hear that …** je regrette (infiniment) que …, je suis désolé d'apprendre que …; **you won't be s. you bought a …** vous ne regretterez pas d'avoir acheté un …; **I'm s. to say that …** je regrette d'avoir à vous dire que …; **I'm so s. to keep you waiting** excusez-moi de vous faire attendre; (I'm) s.! pardon!, excusez-moi!; s.? *(what?)* pardon?; s., did you really mean what you said earlier? à propos, parliez-vous sérieusement tout à l'heure?; I'm s., but that's crap! je suis désolé, mais c'est de la merde!; so s.! vraiment désolé!; s., I can't help désolé, je ne peux rien pour vous; to feel s. for sb *(take pity on)* avoir pitié de qn; *(feel sympathy for)* plaindre qn; I'm s. for him *(I feel pity for him)* il me fait pitié; *(I sympathize with him)* je le plains; to look s. for oneself faire grise mine; he's just feeling s. for himself il s'apitoie sur son sort; once you've stopped feeling s. for yourself une fois que tu auras fini de te plaindre; I'm just feeling a bit s. for myself je suis un peu déprimé; I don't usually feel this s. for myself d'habitude, je ne me laisse pas aller comme ça; to say one is s. (for sth) demander pardon (pour qch); say s. to the lady *(to child)* demande pardon à la dame

2 *(pitiful)* misérable, piteux; to be in a s. plight être dans une mauvaise passe; to be in a s. state être dans un piteux état; to cut a s. figure faire piètre figure; it was/they were a s. sight c'était/ils offraient un spectacle navrant; the whole s. tale toute cette malheureuse affaire

---

sorry-ass, **sorry-assed** ADJ *Am Sl (inferior, contemptible)* à la con; that s. son-of-a-bitch stole my woman! cet enfoiré m'a piqué ma gonzesse!

SORT [sɔːt]

| N sorte **1** ▪ genre **1** ▪ espèce **1** ▪ un peu *(sort of)* **2** ▪ tri **4** |
| VT trier, classer |
| VI trier |

N **1** *(kind)* sorte *f*, genre *m*, espèce *f*; all sorts of people des gens de toutes sortes; it takes all sorts (to make a world) il faut de tout (pour faire un monde); what s. of tree is it? quelle sorte d'arbre est-ce?; what s. of day did you have? comment s'est passée ta journée?; what s. of a man is he? quelle sorte d'homme est-ce?; she's not the s. to give in easily elle n'est pas du genre à abandonner facilement; I know your s.! je connais les gens comme toi!; *Fam* she's a good s. c'est une fille sympa; we don't want your s. here nous ne voulons pas de gens comme vous ici; these s. of people ces gens-là; you get all sorts at these parties on rencontre toutes sortes de gens dans ces soirées; I've heard all sorts of things about him j'en ai entendu de toutes les couleurs sur son compte; I can't stand that s. of thing je ne peux pas souffrir ce genre de chose; something of the s. or of that s. quelque chose de pareil *ou* de semblable *ou* dans ce genre-là; nothing of the s.! *(not in the least)* pas du tout!; he's a liar – he's nothing of the s.! c'est un menteur – pas du tout!; I've a s. of feeling that … j'ai comme l'impression que …; the trees formed a s. of arch les arbres formaient comme une arche; that's my s. of holiday voilà des vacances comme je les aime; *Pej* coffee of a s. du soi-disant café; a peace of sorts une paix, si l'on peut dire; he is some s. of writer il est écrivain mais je ne sais pas quel genre de livres il écrit; *Pej* a writer of sorts un écrivaillon; to make some s. of (a) reply répondre d'une façon quelconque *ou* tant bien que mal; to be out of sorts *(a little unwell)* être mal fichu, ne pas être dans son assiette; *(in a bad mood)* être de mauvaise humeur VOIR GRAMMAIRE A13

2 *Fam (used adverbially)* s. of *(a bit)* plutôt, un peu; *(in a way)* d'une certaine façon; it's s. of heavy c'est un peu lourd, c'est plutôt lourd; I s. of feel that … j'ai dans l'idée que

…, j'ai comme l'impression que …; I s. of expected it je m'en doutais un peu; it's getting s. of late il se fait tard, quoi; did he say sorry? – s. of il s'est excusé? – en quelque sorte; he s. of apologized d'une certaine façon, il s'est excusé

3 *Old-fashioned (manner)* in this s. de cette manière *ou* façon; in some s. en quelque sorte, d'une certaine manière

4 *(order)*, *Comput* tri *m*; to have a quick s. through the mail faire un tri rapide du courrier, trier rapidement le courrier; to do a s. trier

VT *(make selection from) (something)* trier, faire le tri de; *(put together)* assortir; *(papers etc)* classer; *Comput* trier; to s. sth in ascending/descending order trier qch par ordre croissant/décroissant; to s. the letters *(in post office)* trier les lettres; to s. things into categories classer des choses par catégories; s. these documents into piles triez ces documents et faites-en des piles; it's the kind of drink that sorts the men from the boys c'est une boisson d'hommes; situations like this s. the men from the boys des situations comme celle-ci vous permettent de voir qui est un homme

VI *Comput (arrange in list)* trier; *(of file, data)* se trier; s. on this field to a new file trier à partir de ce champ et sauvegarder les données réordonnées dans un nouveau fichier
  ▸▸ *Banking* s. code code *m* guichet; *Comput* s. routine routine *f* de tri
▸ **sort out** VT SEP **1** *(eliminate by sorting)* trier, sélectionner; to s. out the foreign stamps from the British ones séparer les timbres étrangers des timbres britanniques
  2 *(organize) (papers, desk etc)* mettre de l'ordre dans; it's time she sorted herself out il est temps qu'elle se reprenne; give me a few minutes to get (myself) sorted out *or* to s. myself out *(on arrival in office, at home etc)* donnez-moi quelques minutes pour souffler; *(arrange papers for meeting etc)* donnez-moi quelques minutes pour m'organiser; to s. out who's sleeping where décider qui dort où; to s. out a room/some clothes for sb *(allocate)* préparer une chambre/des vêtements pour qn; I'll go and s. the tickets out *(make arrangements for, obtain)* je vais m'occuper des billets; I've sorted out the tickets j'ai tout arrangé en ce qui concerne les billets
  3 *(establish, clarify)* we never sorted out what really happened nous n'avons jamais compris ce qui s'était vraiment passé; let's s. out how much we owe you voyons combien nous vous devons; to s. out the details mettre au clair les détails; you've got to s. out your priorities il faut que tu définisses ce qui prime pour toi
  4 *Fam (deal with) (problem)* régler; *(difficult person)* régler son compte à; everything's sorted out now tout est arrangé *ou* réglé maintenant; two aspirins ought to s. out that headache deux aspirines devraient avoir raison de ce mal de tête
▸ **sort through** VT INSEP *(search among) (old clothes, papers etc)* faire un *ou* le tri dans; to s. through the mail dépouiller le courrier

---

sorta [ˈsɔːtə] CONTR *Fam* = sort of

sorted [ˈsɔːtɪd] *Br Fam* ADJ to be s. *(psychologically)* être bien dans ses baskets; *(have everything one needs)* être paré; to be s. for sth disposer de qch; are you s. for whizz? t'as ce qu'il te faut comme speed?; if I get that pay rise, I'll be s. si j'obtiens cette augmentation j'aurai plus à m'en faire
  INT super!, génial!

sorter [ˈsɔːtər] N **1** *(person)* trieur, -euse; *(who classifies)* classeur, -euse **2** *(device)* machine *f* trieuse; **(letter)** s. trieur *m* de lettres

sortie [ˈsɔːtɪ] N *Mil, Aviat etc* sortie *f*; I make the occasional s. to the shops de temps en temps, je vais faire un tour dans les magasins

sorting [ˈsɔːtɪŋ] N triage *m*, tri *m*; *(classifying)* classement *m*; *Comput* tri
  ▸▸ *Comput* s. algorithm algorithme *m* de tri; s. office centre *m* de tri

SOS [esəʊˈes] N SOS *m*; to send (out) an S. envoyer un SOS; *Fig* relief organizations are sending out an S. for food and clothing les organisations d'aide demandent d'urgence de la nourriture et des vêtements
  ▸▸ S. call appel *m* de détresse

sot [sɒt] N ivrogne *m*

> Note that the French word **sot** is a false friend and is never a translation for the English word **sot**. It means **fool**.

sottish [ˈsɒtɪʃ] ADJ *(person)* abruti par l'alcool; *(behaviour)* d'ivrogne

sotto voce [sɒtəʊˈvəʊtʃɪ] ADV *(to speak)* tout bas

soufflé [ˈsuːfleɪ] N *Culin* soufflé *m*; cheese/spinach s. soufflé au fromage/aux épinards
  ▸▸ s. dish moule *m* à soufflé

sough [saʊ] *Lit* N *(of wind)* murmure *m*
  VI *(of wind)* murmurer

sought PT, PP see **seek**

sought-after ADJ *(job, car etc)* recherché; much s. très recherché

soul [səʊl] N **1** *(spirit)* âme *f*; to throw oneself body and s. into sth se donner corps et âme à qch; *Old-fashioned* upon my s.! sur mon âme!; he's the s. of discretion il est la discrétion même; departed souls les âmes des trépassés *ou* des disparus; to pray for sb's s. prier pour l'âme de qn; to sell one's s. vendre son âme; *Fig* this music's/drama's got no s. cette musique/ce théâtre n'a pas d'âme; God rest her s.! que Dieu ait son âme!; All Souls' Day la Fête des Morts
  2 *(person)* âme *f*; population of two thousand souls population de deux mille âmes; without meeting a (living) s. sans rencontrer âme qui vive; there wasn't a s. in the street il n'y avait pas un chat dans la rue; I promise I won't tell a s. je promets que je ne le dirai à personne; he's a good s. c'est une bonne âme; she's a happy s. elle a un tempérament heureux *ou* optimiste; poor s.! le/la pauvre!; poor little s.! pauvre petit(e)!
  3 *(music)* soul *f*, soul music *f*
  ▸▸ s. brother = nom *m* que les Noirs américains donnent aux hommes noirs; *Fam* s. food cuisine *f* afroaméricaine; s. music soul, soul music; s. singer chanteur, -euse de soul; s. sister = nom que les Noirs américains donnent aux femmes noires

soul-destroying [-dɪstrɔɪɪŋ] ADJ *(job etc)* abrutissant, d'une monotonie mortelle

soulful [ˈsəʊlfʊl] ADJ *(with deep feeling)* tendre; *(music)* qui touche l'âme

soulfully [ˈsəʊlfəlɪ] ADV *(to sing)* tendrement; *Pej (sentimentally)* avec sensiblerie

soulless [ˈsəʊllɪs] ADJ **1** *(person)* sans âme **2** *(job)* abrutissant

soullessly [ˈsəʊllɪslɪ] ADV sans émotion; the house had been s. renovated on a rénové la maison sans aucune sensibilité

soullessness [ˈsəʊllɪsnɪs] N *(of person)* manque *m* de sensibilité; *(of building)* côté *m* inhumain; the s. of my surroundings le décor inhumain qui est le mien

soulmate [ˈsəʊlmeɪt] N âme *f* sœur

soul-searching N examen *m* de conscience; after a lot of s. après un profond examen de conscience

soul-stirring ADJ émouvant

SOUND¹ [saʊnd]

N son ▪ bruit ▪ sonorité
VI résonner **1** ▪ retentir **1** ▪ sembler **2** ▪ avoir l'air **2** ▪ sonner **2**
VT sonner **1** ▪ prononcer **2** ▪ ausculter **3**

N *Phys, Mus etc* son *m*; *(of door, car engine, wind etc)* bruit *m*; **the device recognizes the s. of your voice** l'appareil reconnaît le son de votre voix; **the s. of one's own voice** le son de sa (propre) voix; **he likes (listening to) the s. of his own voice** il aime s'écouter parler; **there was not a s. to be heard** on n'entendait pas le moindre bruit; **no s. escaped his lips** pas un son ne sortait de ses lèvres; **not a s. could be heard** le silence était total; **the s. of a dog barking/a door closing** le bruit d'un chien qui aboie/d'une porte qui se ferme; **every violin has its own s.** chaque violon a sa propre sonorité; **within (the) s. of ...** à portée du son de ...; **TV etc to turn up/turn down the s.** augmenter/diminuer le volume; **I don't like the s. of it** cela ne me dit rien qui vaille; **he's angry by the s. of it** on dirait bien qu'il est fâché; *Fam* **today's sounds** *(music)* les sons d'aujourd'hui; **it has a sixties s. to it** ça ressemble à la musique des années soixante

VI 1 *(make sound)* sonner, résonner; *(resound)* retentir; **the trumpet sounded** la trompette retentit *ou* sonna

2 *(seem)* paraître, sembler, avoir l'air; **name that sounds French** nom qui sonne français; **she sounds French** elle a l'air d'être française; **the translation still sounds a bit French** la traduction sonne toujours un peu français; **that sounds like trouble!** voilà les ennuis!; **he sounds like my kind of guy** c'est le genre de type avec qui je m'entendrais; **you s. like the kind of person we're looking for** je crois que vous êtes la personne qu'il nous faut; **it still sounds a bit wrong** *(of words, music)* ça sonne encore un peu faux; **that sounds odd!** cela paraît bizarre!; **what about an omelette? – that sounds good!** que dirais-tu d'une omelette? – bonne idée!; **'attractive four-bedroomed house', how does that s.?** 'belle maison avec quatre chambres à coucher', qu'est-ce que tu en penses?; **their suggestion sounds interesting** leur suggestion semble intéressante; **how does that s. to you?** *(referring to suggestion)* qu'est-ce que tu en dis?; **she sounded interested/happy** elle semblait intéressée/heureuse; **the noise sounded a long way off** le bruit semblait venir de loin; **it sounds like Mozart** on dirait du Mozart; **he doesn't s. like a man to ...** d'après ce que vous dites, il ne serait pas homme à ...

VT 1 *(trumpet, retreat)* sonner; *(the alert, the alarm)* donner; *Aut* **to s. one's horn** klaxonner; *Lit* **to s. sb's praises** chanter les louanges de qn

2 *(pronounce) (letter)* prononcer; **the h is not sounded** l'h ne se prononce pas *ou* est muet

3 *Med (person, person's chest)* ausculter; **he sounded my chest** il m'a ausculté

▸ ▸ **s. archives** phonothèque *f*; **s. barrier** mur *m* du son; **s. board** *(of piano)* table *f* d'harmonie; *(of organ)* tamis *m*; *Mus* **s. box** caisse *f* de résonance; *Comput* **s. card** carte *f* son; **s. check** soundcheck *m*; **s. effects** bruitage *m*; **s. engineer** ingénieur *m* du son; **s. camera** caméra *f* sonore; *Cin, TV, Radio* **s. crew** équipe *f* du son; **s. designer** concepteur *m* sonore; **s. detector** *(of missile)* détecteur *m* par le son; **s. editing** montage *m* sonore; **s. editor** monteur *m* son; **s. film** film *m* sonore; **s. generator** générateur *m* de son; **s. hole** *(of violin, viola etc)* ouïe *f*, esse *f*; *(of guitar, lute etc)* rosace *f*, rose *f*; **s. level** niveau *m* sonore;

s. logo logo *m* sonore; **s. man** preneur *m* de son, opérateur *m* du son; **s. mixer** table *f* *ou* console *f* de mixage; **s. mixing** mixage *m* sonore; **s. plot** = liste *f* des sons et bruitages nécessaires pour la production d'une pièce de théâtre ou radiophonique; **s. quality** qualité *f* du son, qualité sonore; **s. recording** enregistrement *m* du son, enregistrement sonore; **s. recordist** preneur de son; **s. reel** bande *f* son; **s. stage** studio *m* insonorisé; **s. studio** auditorium *m* *ou* studio d'enregistrement; **s. system** *(hi-fi)* chaîne *f* hifi; *(PA system)* sonorisation *f*; **s. wave** onde *f* sonore

▸ **sound off** **VI** *Fam (express opinions forcefully, complain)* **to s. off about sth** faire de grands laïus sur qch; **to s. off at sb** engueuler qn; **she's always sounding off about rude shop assistants** elle est toujours en train de se plaindre des vendeuses peu aimables

sound² **N** *Med (probe)* sonde *f*
VT 1 *Naut, Med* sonder **2 to s. public opinion** sonder l'opinion publique
VI *(of whale)* plonger au fond
▸ **sound out** **VT SEP** *(ascertain opinion, allegiance of) (person)* sonder

sound³ **N** *(channel)* détroit *m*, bras *m* de mer

sound⁴ **ADJ 1** *(lungs, foundations)* sain; *(wood)* sans tare; *(bridge, engine) (in good condition)* en bon état; *(not damaged)* non endommagé; **s. in body and mind** sain de corps et d'esprit; **of s. mind** sain d'esprit; *Fam* **to be s. in wind and limb** *(of person)* avoir bon pied bon œil; **I'm as s. as a bell** je suis en parfaite santé

2 *(argument, knowledge, basis)* solide; *(reason, reasoning)* valable; *(policy etc)* sage; *(investment)* sûr, solide, fiable; *(goalkeeper, manager, musician, lawyer etc)* bon, *f* bonne, fiable; **ecologically s. legislation** législation juste du point de vue écologique; **s. doctrine** doctrine saine; *Rel (orthodox)* doctrine orthodoxe; **a s. piece of advice** un bon conseil; **s. financial position** situation financière saine; **s. business** entreprise saine *ou* solide; **he's pretty s. on his grammar** il a de bonnes bases en grammaire; **it makes good s. sense** c'est tout à fait raisonnable

3 a s. sleep un sommeil profond; **I'm a s. sleeper** je dors bien; **to give sb a s. thrashing** administrer une bonne correction à qn
ADV to be s. asleep être profondément endormi, dormir à poings fermés

soundbite ['saʊndbaɪt] **N** petite phrase *f*
sounder ['saʊndər] **N** *Naut* sondeur *m*
sounding¹ ['saʊndɪŋ] **N** *Mil* **s. of the retreat** le signal de la retraite

sounding² **N 1** *Naut (act)* sondage *m*; **echo s.** sondage par ultra-sons **2** *Naut* **soundings** *(measurements)* sondages *mpl*; *(bottom)* fonds *mpl*; **to take soundings** sonder, prendre le fond; *Fig* sonder
▸ ▸ **s. board** *(of pulpit etc)* abat-voix *m inv*; *(of piano)* table *f* d'harmonie; *(of organ)* tamis *m*; *Fig* **to use sb as a s. board** tester ses idées sur qn; **s. lead** *(plomb *m* de)* sonde *f*, **s. line** sonde

soundless ['saʊndlɪs] **ADJ** muet, -ette, silencieux
soundlessly ['saʊndlɪslɪ] **ADV** silencieusement, sans bruit
soundly ['saʊndlɪ] **ADV 1** *(solidly)* solidement **2** *(to reason)* sainement; *(wisely)* judicieusement; **to invest s.** investir dans des valeurs sûres; **he argued s.** son argumentation était solide **3** *(to sleep)* profondément; **to thrash sb s.** *(with stick etc)* administrer une bonne correction à qn; *Sport* **we were s. beaten** nous avons été battus à plate(s) couture(s)
soundness ['saʊndnɪs] **N 1** *(of merchandise, mind etc)* bon état *m*; *(of company)* solidité *f*,

(solvency) solvabilité *f* **2** *(of argument, reasoning, decision etc)* validité *f*; *(of judgment)* justesse *f*; *(of advice, policy)* sagesse *f*; *(of doctrine)* orthodoxie *f*

soundproof ['saʊndpruːf] **ADJ** *(room etc)* insonorisé; *(material)* insonore
VT *(room etc)* insonoriser
▸ ▸ **s. hood** capot *m* antibruit
soundproofing ['saʊndpruːfɪŋ] **N** *(material)* matériau *m* isolant *ou* insonore; *(act)* insonorisation *f*
soundtrack ['saʊndtræk] **N** *Cin* bande *f* sonore; **s. (album)** bande originale

soup [suːp] **N** soupe *f*, *(thin)* potage *m*; **onion/fish s.** soupe à l'oignon/de poisson; *Fig Fam* **to be in the s.** être dans le pétrin; *Fig Fam* **to land sb in the s.** mettre qn dans le pétrin
▸ ▸ **s. kitchen** soupe populaire; **s. ladle** louche *f*, **s. plate** assiette *f* creuse *ou* à soupe; **s. spoon** cuillère *f* *ou* cuiller *f* à soupe; *Am Fam Hum* **s. strainer** *(large moustache)* grosses bacchantes *fpl*; **s. tureen** soupière *f*
▸ **soup up** **VT SEP** *Fam (car, engine)* gonfler

soupçon ['suːpsɒn] **N** *(of garlic, sarcasm)* soupçon *m*, pointe *f*
souped-up ['suːpt-] **ADJ** *Fam* gonflé; **a s. job** *(car, motorcycle)* une bagnole/une moto au moteur gonflé

sour ['saʊər] **ADJ 1** *(fruit etc)* aigre, acide; *(milk, cream, bread etc)* aigre; *(wine)* suret, -ette, verjuté; *(soil)* acide; **to turn s.** *(of food)* (s')aigrir, surir; *Fig (of situation, relationship)* tourner à l'aigre, *Fam* tourner au vinaigre; **to turn sth s.** (faire) aigrir qch; **to smell s.** sentir l'aigre; *Fig* **the plan went s. on him** *(went wrong)* le projet a mal tourné pour lui
2 *(person)* revêche, aigre; **he's s. about being left out** il est amer parce qu'on l'a laissé à l'écart
VI surir, (s')aigrir; **her temper has soured** son caractère s'est aigri
VT *(milk, character etc)* aigrir; *Culin* **soured cream** crème *f* aigre; **soured by disappointment** *(person)* aigri par une déception; **these events have soured their relationship** ces événements ont aigri leur relation
▸ ▸ **s. cream** crème aigre; **s. grapes** dépit *m*; **it was just s. grapes that made her say that** elle a simplement dit ça par rancœur

source [sɔːs] **N** *(of river, misfortune, light etc)* source *f*; *(of heat, infection etc)* foyer *m*; **the Rhone has its s. in the Alps** le Rhône prend sa source dans les Alpes; **a good s. of vitamin C** une bonne source de vitamine C; **this book is a good s. of information about ...** ce livre est une bonne source d'informations sur ...; **I have it from a good s.** je le sais *ou* tiens de source sûre; **a historian's/reporter's sources** les sources d'un historien/reporter
▸ ▸ *Comput* **s. disk** disque *m* source; *(floppy)* disquette *f* source; *Comput* **s. document** document *m* de base, document source; *Comput* **s. drive** unité *f* source *ou* d'origine; *Comput* **s. file** fichier *m* source; **s. language** *(in translation, interpreting)* langue *f* de départ; *Comput* langage *m* source; **s. materials** *(of book)* sources *fpl*; *Comput* **s. program** programme *m* source; **s. text** texte *m* de départ

sourdough ['saʊədəʊ] **N**
▸ ▸ **s. bread** pain *m* au levain
sourface ['saʊəfeɪs] **N** *Fam* = **sourpuss**
sourfaced ['saʊəfeɪst] **ADJ** *(person)* au visage rébarbatif; *(look)* revêche; *(reply)* aigre
sourly ['saʊəlɪ] **ADV** *(to answer)* aigrement; *(to look at sb)* d'un air revêche
sourness ['saʊənɪs] **N 1** *(of fruit etc)* aigreur *f*, acidité *f*; *(of milk)* aigreur *f* **2** *(of person)* aigreur *f*

sourpuss ['saʊəpʊs] N *Fam* grincheux, -euse; *(kill-joy)* rabat-joie *m inv*

sousaphone ['su:zəfəʊn] N *Mus* sousaphone *m*

sous chef ['su:ʃef] N second *m*, assistant *m* du chef de cuisine

souse [saʊs] N *Culin* saumure *f*, marinade *f*
▸ VT plonger, immerger (**in** dans); *Culin (herring)* faire mariner; **to s. sth with water** arroser qch d'eau

soused [saʊst] ADJ **1** *Culin* mariné **2** *Sl (drunk)* bourré, pété; **to get s.** se soûler
▸▸ *Culin* **s. herrings** harengs *mpl* marinés

south [saʊθ] N sud *m*, midi *m*; **the house faces the s.** la maison est exposée au sud *ou* au midi; **to the s.** au sud (**of** de); **the s.** *(region of a country)* le sud, le midi; **the S. of France** le sud *ou* le Midi (de la France); *Hist* **the S.** *(of United States)* le Sud, les États *mpl* du sud
▸ ADV au sud; **to travel s.** voyager vers le sud; **it's s. of here** c'est au sud d'ici; **I'm going down s.** *(to southern part of country)* je vais dans le sud; **s. by east** sud-quart-sud-est; **s. by west** sud-quart-sud-ouest
▸ ADJ sud *inv*; *(wind)* du sud; *(wall, window)* exposé au sud; **s. side** côté *m* sud; **on the s. side** du côté sud; **the s. coast** la côte sud
▸▸ **S. Africa** l'Afrique *f* du Sud; **S. African** sud-africain, -aine; **S. America** l'Amérique *f* du Sud; **S. American** sud-américain, -aine; **S. Korea** la Corée du Sud; **S. Pacific** Pacifique *m* sud; **S. Pole** le pôle Sud; **S. Sea Islands** l'Océanie *f*; **S. Seas** mers *fpl* du sud; **S. Vietnam** le Viêt Nam du Sud; **S. Yemen** le Yémen du Sud

southbound ['saʊθbaʊnd] ADJ *(traffic)* en direction du sud; *(lane, carriageway)* du sud; *(road)* vers le sud; **s. traffic is subject to delays** la circulation est ralentie dans le sens sud; **there's a jam on the s. carriageway** il y a un bouchon en direction du sud

southeast [saʊθ'i:st] N sud-est *m*; *Naut* suet *m*
▸ ADJ **1** *Geog* sud-est *inv*, du sud-est; **in s. England** dans le sud-est de l'Angleterre **2** *(wind)* de sud-est, du sud-est
▸ ADV au sud-est; *(to travel)* vers le sud-est; **it's 50 miles s. of Liverpool** c'est à 80 kilomètres au sud-est de Liverpool
▸▸ **S. Asia** Asie *f* du Sud-Est; **the S. Asian Treaty Organization** l'Organisation *f* du traité de l'Asie du Sud-Est

southeaster ['saʊθ'i:stə(r)] N *(wind)* vent *m* de *ou* du sud-est; *Naut* suet *m*

southeasterly [saʊθ'i:stəlɪ] ADJ **1** *Geog* sud-est *inv*, du sud-est; **to travel in a s. direction** aller vers le sud-est; *Naut* **to steer a s. course** faire route vers le sud-est; *(when setting out)* mettre le cap au sud-est **2** *(wind)* de sud-est, du sud-est
▸ ADV vers le sud-est
▸ N vent *m* de *ou* du sud-est; *Naut* suet *m*

southeastern [saʊθ'i:stən] ADJ sud-est *inv*, du sud-est, *(wind)* du sud-est; **the s. suburbs** la banlieue sud-est

southerly ['sʌðəlɪ] ADJ **1** *Geog* sud *inv*, du sud; **to travel in a s. direction** voyager vers le sud; **s. point** point situé au sud *ou* vers le sud; **the most s. point of the United States** le point situé le plus au sud des États-Unis; **a room with a s. aspect** une pièce exposée au sud *ou* au midi; *Naut* **to steer a s. course** faire route vers le sud; *(change course)* mettre le cap au sud **2** *(wind)* de sud, du sud
▸ ADV vers le sud

southern ['sʌðən] ADJ **1** *Geog* sud *inv*, du sud, méridional, -aux; **he has a s. accent** il a un accent du sud; *(in France)* il a l'accent méridional; **the s. wing of the castle** l'aile sud

du château; **in s. India** dans le sud de l'Inde; **the s. hemisphere** l'hémisphère *m* sud *ou* austral **2** *(wind)* de sud, du sud **3** *Hist (in American Civil War)* sudiste
▸▸ **s. Africa** l'Afrique *f* australe; *Astron* **the S. Cross** la Croix du Sud; **s. Europe** l'Europe *f* méridionale; **S. Ireland** l'Irlande *f* du Sud; **s. lights** aurore *f* australe

southerner ['sʌðənər] N **1** habitant, -ante du sud; *(in continental Europe)* méridional, -ale; **she's a s.** elle vient du sud **2** *Hist (of United States)* sudiste *mf*

south-facing ADJ *(house, wall)* (exposé) au sud *ou* au midi

southpaw ['saʊθpɔ:] N *Boxing etc* gaucher, -ère

south-south-east, *Naut* **sou'sou'east** [saʊ(θ)saʊ(θ)'i:st] N sud-sud-est *m inv*
▸ ADJ **1** *Geog* sud-sud-est *inv*, du sud-sud-est **2** *(wind)* de *ou* du sud-sud-est
▸ ADV au sud-sud-est; *(to travel)* vers le sud-sud-est

south-south-west, *Naut* **sou'sou'west** [saʊ(θ)saʊ(θ)'west] N sud-sud-ouest *m*; *Naut* susuroît *m*
▸ ADJ **1** *Geog* sud-sud-ouest *inv*, du sud-sud-ouest **2** *(wind)* de *ou* du sud-sud-est
▸ ADV au sud-sud-ouest; *(to travel)* vers le sud-sud-ouest

southward ['saʊθwəd] ADJ vers le sud, en direction du sud
▸ ADV vers le sud, en direction du sud
▸ N sud *m*

southwards ['saʊθwədz] ADV vers le sud

southwest, *Naut* **sou'west** [saʊ(θ)'west] N sud-ouest *m*; *Naut* suroît *m*
▸ ADV au sud-ouest; *(to travel)* vers le sud-ouest; **s. by west** sud-ouest-quart-ouest; **s. by south** sud-ouest-quart-sud
▸ ADJ **1** *Geog* sud-ouest *inv*, du sud-ouest; **in s. Scotland** dans le sud-ouest de l'Écosse **2** *(wind)* de *ou* du sud-ouest

southwester, *Naut* **sou'wester** ['saʊ(θ)-'westər] N *(wind)* vent *m* de *ou* du sud-ouest; *Naut* suroît *m*

southwesterly, *Naut* **sou'westerly** [saʊ(θ)-'westəlɪ] ADJ **1** *Geog* sud-ouest *inv*, du sud-ouest; **in a s. direction** vers le sud-ouest; *Naut* **to steer a s. course** faire route vers le sud-ouest; *(when setting out)* mettre le cap au sud-ouest **2** *(wind)* de *ou* du sud-ouest
▸ ADV vers le sud-ouest
▸ N = **southwester**

southwestern [saʊθ'westən] ADJ sud-ouest *inv*, du sud-ouest; **to travel in a s. direction** voyager vers le sud-ouest

souvenir [su:və'nɪər] N souvenir *m*
▸▸ **s. shop** boutique *f* de souvenirs

> Note that the French word **souvenir** also means **memory**.

sovereign ['sɒvrɪn] ADJ souverain, suprême; **the s. good** le bien souverain; **s. rights** droits *mpl* de souveraineté
▸ N **1** *(monarch)* souverain, -aine, monarque *m* **2** *Hist (coin)* souverain *m* *(pièce d'or de la valeur d'une livre)*

sovereignty ['sɒvrəntɪ] N souveraineté *f*

Soviet ['saʊvɪət] N **1** *(council)* soviet *m*; **Supreme S.** Soviet suprême **2 the Soviets** *(people)* les Soviétiques *mpl*
▸ ADJ soviétique; *Formerly* **the Union of S. Socialist Republics** l'Union *f* des Républiques socialistes soviétiques
▸▸ *Formerly* **S. Union** Union *f* soviétique

sovietization [saʊvɪətaɪ'zeɪʃən] N soviétisation *f*

sow [saʊ] *(pt* sowed [saʊd]; *pp* sown [saʊn], sowed) VT *(seeds, field)* semer; **to s. a field with wheat** ensemencer un champ de blé;

Fig **to s. (the seeds of) discord/doubt** semer la discorde/le doute
▸ VI semer

sow [saʊ] N *(female pig)* truie *f*, *(wild)* laie *f*

sower ['saʊər] N *(person)* semeur, -euse; *(device)* semoir *m*

sowing ['saʊɪŋ] N *(task)* ensemencement *m*; **s. time** *or* **season** (saison *f* des) semailles *fpl*

sown PP *see* **sow**[1]

sox [sɒks] NPL *Am* = **socks,** *see* **sock**[1]

soya ['sɔɪə] N soja *m*
▸▸ *Br* **s. bean** graine *f* de soja; **s. flour** farine *f* de soja; **s. milk** lait *m* de soja; **s. sauce** sauce *f* de *ou* au soja

soybean ['sɔɪbi:n] N *Am* graine *f* de soja

soy sauce [sɔɪ] N sauce *f* de *ou* au soja

sozzled ['sɒz(ə)ld] ADJ *Br Sl (drunk)* pété, bourré; **to get s.** se soûler

SP [es'pi:] N *Horseracing (abbr* **starting price**) dernière cote *f* avant le départ; *Br Fam* **to give sb the SP** mettre qn au parfum (**on** à propos de *ou* concernant)

spa [spa:] N *(spring)* source *f* thermale; *(in sports centre, health farm etc)* Jacuzzi® *m*
▸▸ **s. bath** bain *m* bouillonnant; **s. hotel** hôtel *m* médicalisé; **s. resort** station *f* hydrominérale; **s. town** ville *f* d'eau, station thermale

space [speɪs] N **1** *(gap)* espace *m*; *(room)* place *f*; **he sat staring into s.** il était assis le regard perdu dans le vide; **open spaces** *(green)* espaces verts; *(not built on)* étendues *fpl* non bâties; **wide open spaces** grands espaces; **living s.** espace vital; **in a confined s.** dans un espace restreint; *Com* **to sell s.** **(in a newspaper)** vendre de l'espace (dans un journal); **to take up a lot of s.** prendre *ou* occuper beaucoup de place; **there's no s. left** il n'y a plus de place; **this cupboard is a great s. saver** avec ce placard, on gagne beaucoup de place

2 *Astron* espace *m*; **the conquest of s.** la conquête de l'espace; **outer s.** espace extra-atmosphérique

3 *(free area, place)* espace *m* libre; *(interval)* espacement *m*, intervalle *m*; *(on form etc)* blanc *m*, espace; **a s. in the timetable** un créneau dans l'emploi du temps; **a (parking) s.** une place de parking

4 *(between lines of writing etc)* interligne *m*; *Typ* espace *m* blanc; **blank s.** *(between letters)* intervalle *m* entre les lettres

5 *(period)* espace *m*, intervalle *m*; **in the s. of a year** dans *ou* en l'espace d'un an; **after a short s. of time** après un court intervalle
▸ VT *(trees, words, visits)* espacer; *(troops, payments)* échelonner; **evenly spaced** régulièrement espacés; **the posts are spaced ten feet apart** les poteaux sont plantés à dix pieds d'intervalle
▸▸ **s. age** ère *f* de l'exploration spatiale; **s. bar** *(on keyboard)* barre *f* d'espacement; **s. blanket** couverture *f* de survie; *Fam* **s. cadet** allumé, -ée; *Fam* **s. cake** gâteau *m* au cannabis, space cake *m*; **s. flight** vol *m* *ou* voyage *m* spatial; **s. heater** radiateur *m*; **S. Invaders®** Space Invaders® *m*; **s. mission** mission *f* spatiale; **s. probe** sonde *f* spatiale; **s. rocket** fusée *f* spatiale *ou* interplanétaire; *Typ* **s. rule** filet *m* maigre; **s. shot** lancement *m* spatial; **s. shuttle** navette *f* spatiale; **s. station** station *f* spatiale *ou* orbitale; **s. suit** scaphandre *m* *ou* combinaison *f* de cosmonaute; **s. travel** voyages *mpl* dans l'espace, *Spec* astronautique *f*
▸ **space out** VT SEP **1** *(arrange at intervals)* = **space** VT **2** *Sl* **to be** *or* **feel spaced out** *(dazed)* être dans le coaltar; *(after taking drugs)* être raide, planer

spaceage ['speɪseɪdʒ] ADJ *(technology etc)* futuriste

spacebar ['speɪsbɑːr] N *Typ* barre f d'espacement

spacecraft ['speɪskrɑːft] N véhicule m ou vaisseau m spatial, astronef m

spacelab ['speɪslæb] N laboratoire m spatial

spaceman, pl **spacemen** ['speɪsmæn, -men] N astronaute m

spacer ['speɪsər] N *Tech* pièce f d'écartement

space-saving ADJ qui permet de gagner de la place; (furniture etc) compact; **if you're looking for some s. ideas** si vous cherchez des idées pour gagner de la place

spaceship ['speɪsʃɪp] N véhicule m ou vaisseau m spatial, astronef m

space-time N *Phys* espace-temps m inv

spacewalk ['speɪswɔːk] N *Astronaut* marche f dans l'espace

spacewoman, pl **spacewomen** ['speɪswʊmən, -wɪmɪn] N astronaute f

spacing ['speɪsɪŋ] N (of trees etc) espacement m, écartement m; *Typ* (of letters, lines) espacement m; **in single/double s.** (with typewriter) à simple/double interligne

spacious ['speɪʃəs] ADJ (kitchen, house, car boot) spacieux, vaste; (clothes) ample

spaciousness ['speɪʃəsnɪs] N (of kitchen, house, car boot) dimensions fpl spacieuses

spade¹ [speɪd] N (tool) bêche f, (child's) pelle f, **to call a s. a s.** appeler les choses par leur nom, appeler un chat un chat
▶ VT (earth etc) bêcher

spade² N **1** *Cards* pique m; **ace of spades** as m de pique; **to play a s., to play spades** jouer pique **2** *Offensive Sl* (black person) nègre m, négresse f

spadeful ['speɪdfʊl] N pelletée f

spadework ['speɪdwɜːk] N (with spade) travaux mpl à la bêche; *Fig* travaux préliminaires

spag bol [spæɡˈbɒl] N *Br Fam* (spaghetti bolognese) spaghettis mpl (à la) bolognaise

spaghetti [spəˈɡetɪ] N *Culin* spaghetti mpl; *Elec Fam* (cables, wires) souplisseau m VOIR GRAMMAIRE A14
▶ ▶ **S. Junction** = surnom d'un échangeur sur l'autoroute M6 au nord de Birmingham; *Fig* **it's like S. Junction around here!** tous ces échangeurs, c'est compliqué!; **s. western** western-spaghetti m, pl westerns-spaghetti

Spain [speɪn] N Espagne f

spam [spæm] *Comput* N messages mpl publicitaires, pourriels mpl; **a s. e-mail** un message publicitaire, un pourriel
▶ VT envoyer des messages publicitaires ou des pourriels à
▶ VI spammer

spammer ['spæmər] N *Comput* = personne f qui envoie des messages publicitaires en masse

spamming ['spæmɪŋ] N *Comput* spamming m

span¹ [spæn] N **1** (of hand) empan m; **wing s.** (of bird, aircraft) envergure f
2 (between two points of support) portée f, (of arch) largeur f, (of bridge) travée f, **single s. bridge** pont m à travée unique
3 (duration, period of time) durée f, **the party's twenty-year s. in power is coming to an end** les vingt années de pouvoir du parti arrivent à leur fin
4 (extent) (of knowledge, interests, activity etc) étendue f
▶ VT (-nn-) **1** (of bridge etc) (river etc) enjamber; **once the river had been spanned** une fois qu'on a eu construit un pont pour traverser la rivière
2 (include) couvrir; **her knowledge spans a wide range of subjects** ses connaissances couvrent une grande variété de sujets; **his**

life spans nearly the whole century sa vie embrasse presque tout le siècle; *Mus* **to s. an octave** couvrir une octave

span² N (pair) (of horses, oxen) paire f, couple m

spangle ['spæŋɡ(ə)l] N *Tex etc* paillette f, (large) paillon m
▶ VT pailleter (**with** de); **spangled with silver** pailleté d'argent

Spaniard ['spænjəd] N Espagnol, -ole VOIR GRAMMAIRE A19

spaniel ['spænjəl] N épagneul m; **cocker/springer s.** épagneul cocker/springer

Spanish ['spænɪʃ] VOIR GRAMMAIRE A19 ADJ espagnol
▶ N **1** *Ling* espagnol m **2 the S.** (pl) les Espagnols mpl
▶ ▶ **S. America** Amérique f hispanophone; **S. fly** mouche f d'Espagne, cantharide f, **S. guitar** guitare f classique; **the S. Inquisition** l'Inquisition f espagnole; **S. moss** tillandsia m; **S. omelette** omelette f à l'espagnole; **S. onion** oignon m d'Espagne

Spanish-American ADJ hispano-américain
▶ ▶ *Hist* **the S. war** la guerre hispano-américaine

Spanish-speaking ADJ hispanophone

spank [spæŋk] N fessée f
▶ VT (child) fesser, donner une fessée à
▶ **spank along** VI (go fast) aller bon train

spanking ['spæŋkɪŋ] N fessée f, **to give a child a s.** donner une fessée à un enfant
▶ ADJ *Old-fashioned Fam* **1** (excellent) épatant **2 to go at a s. pace** aller bon train
▶ ADV *Fam* **s. new** flambant neuf; **a s. good time was had** on s'est diablement bien amusé

spanner ['spænər] N *Br* clef f, **adjustable s.** clef à molette; **box s.** clef à douille ou à tire-fonds; *Fig* **to throw a s. in the works** causer des problèmes; **that's really thrown a s. in the works!** cela nous/leur/etc a vraiment mis des bâtons dans les roues!; **so that's the s. in the works** alors, c'est ça le hic

spar¹ [spɑːr] N *Naut* espar m; *Aviat* **wing s.** longeron m d'aile

spar² N *Miner* spath m

spar³ VI (-rr-) **to s. with sb** *Boxing* s'entraîner avec qn; *Fig* (argue) jouter avec qn

SPARE ['speər]

ADJ en plus **1** ▪ disponible **1** ▪ libre **1** ▪ frugal **2** ▪ dépouillé **2** ▪ sec **3**	
N pièce de rechange ▪ roue de secours	
VT se passer de **2** ▪ ménager **3** ▪ faire grâce à **3**	

ADJ 1 (surplus) (copy, trousers) en plus; (free) disponible; **have you got a s. plastic bag?** est-ce que tu as un sac en plastique qui ne te sert pas?; **with the s. cash, they bought a table** avec l'argent qui leur restait, ils ont acheté une table; **that left a few hours s.** ça a laissé quelques heures libres; **is this bed s.?** est-ce que ce lit est libre?; **we have a s. bed** (can put you/him up for the night) nous avons un lit qui ne sert pas; *Fam* **is this cake going s.?** si vous ne savez pas quoi faire de ce gâteau, je le prends; *Fam* **if you have any tickets going s.** si vous avez des tickets en trop; *Fam* **if you hear of any flats going s.** si vous entendez parler d'appartements qui se libèrent
2 (frugal) (meal etc) frugal, -aux; (style, room) dépouillé
3 (thin) (person) sec, f sèche; **he was tall and s.** il était grand et mince
4 *Br Fam* (mad) **to drive sb s.** rendre qn dingue; **he'll go s. if he finds out** il va être fou s'il apprend ça

N (spare part) pièce f de rechange, pièce détachée; (tyre) roue f de secours; **I've lost my pencil, have you got a s.?** j'ai perdu mon crayon, en as-tu un à me prêter?
▶ VT **1** (in negative constructions) (be grudging of) **to s. no expense** ne pas regarder à la dépense; **to s. no pains** se donner beaucoup de mal; **to s. no effort** ne pas ménager ses efforts
2 (go without) se passer de; **can you s. that much money?** pouvez-vous vous en passer?; **can you s. the time?** avez-vous le temps?; **we can't s. him** il nous est indispensable, nous ne pouvons pas nous passer de lui; **to have nothing to s.** n'avoir que le strict nécessaire, ne rien avoir de superflu; **to have enough and to s. (of sth)** avoir plus qu'il n'en faut (de qch); **there is room to s.** la place ne manque pas; **I cannot s. the time to finish it** je n'ai pas le temps de le finir; **to have no time to s.** ne pas avoir le temps; **to have no time to s. for sb/sth** ne pas avoir de temps à consacrer à qn/qch; **when I have time to s.** quand j'ai des loisirs, quand j'ai du temps libre; **whenever I have a minute to s.** dès que j'ai une minute; **I have a minute to s., so send her in** j'ai une minute à lui consacrer, faites-la donc entrer; **to catch a train with five minutes to s.** prendre un train avec cinq minutes de battement; **we caught the plane with absolutely no time to s.** nous avons attrapé l'avion vraiment de justesse; **we'll have at least half an hour to s.** nous aurons au minimum une demi-heure de battement; **to s. sb some sugar/ten pounds** donner à qn du sucre/dix livres; **are you sure you can s. it?** tu es sûr que ça ne te dérange pas?; *Iron* tu es sûr que ça ne va pas te manquer?; **can you s. a couple of people this afternoon?** est-ce que vous pourriez vous passer de quelques personnes cet après-midi?; **can you s. me a few moments?** pouvez-vous m'accorder quelques minutes?; **to s. a thought for sb** penser à qn
3 (show mercy towards) (person, horse) ménager; (person condemned to die) faire grâce à; **to s. sb's life** épargner la vie de qn; **s. me!** (do not kill me) de grâce!, épargnez-moi!; *Fig* (don't expose me here) par pitié, pas çà!; **if she is spared** (lives) si elle vit; **death spares no one** la mort n'épargne personne; **the flood spared nothing** l'inondation n'a rien épargné; **to s. sb's feelings** ménager qn, épargner qn; **tell me, don't s. my feelings** dis-moi, n'essaye pas de me ménager; **the report spared no one** le rapport ne ménageait personne; **s. my blushes!** ne me faites pas rougir!; **he doesn't s. himself** il ne se ménage pas; **to s. sb the trouble of doing sth** éviter à qn la peine de faire qch; **you could have spared yourself/us the trouble** vous auriez pu vous/nous éviter cette peine; **s. me the details!** (don't tell me) épargne-moi les détails!; **I'll s. you the rest** je vous fais grâce du reste
▶ ▶ **s. parts** pièces fpl de rechange, pièces détachées; **s. room** chambre f d'amis; **s. time** temps m libre; **in my s. time** à mes heures perdues; **I don't get much s. time** je n'ai pas beaucoup de temps libre; *Am* **s. tire**, *Br* **s. tyre** pneu m de rechange; *Fam* (around waist) bourrelet de graisse, pneu; *Br* **s. wheel** roue f de secours

sparing ['speərɪŋ] ADJ (economical) économe; **to be s. with the butter** ménager le beurre; **she is very s. with her money** elle fait très attention à son argent; **he is s. with his praise** il est avare de louanges

sparingly ['speərɪŋlɪ] ADV (to eat) sobrement; (moderately) avec modération; **to use sth s.** utiliser qch avec modération; **apply the cream s. to the affected area** appliquer la crème en couche fine sur la région touchée

spark [spɑːk] **N 1** *(glowing particle)* étincelle *f*, *(from fire)* flammèche *f*; **the s. of life** l'étincelle de la vie; *Fig* **sparks flew** ça a fait des étincelles; **he hasn't a s. of imagination** il manque totalement d'imagination; **he hasn't a s. of generosity in him** il n'est pas généreux pour deux sous; **a bright s.** *(intelligent person)* une tête; *Fam Iron* **you're a bright s.!** tu es un rapide, toi!; **who's the bright s. who ...?** qui est le petit malin qui ...?

2 *Elec etc* étincelle *f*, *(in engine)* éclateur *m*, pont *m* d'allumage

3 *Fam* **sparks** *(radio operator)* radio *m*; *(electrician)* électricien *m*

vi jeter des étincelles; *(of dynamo etc)* cracher; **to s. across the terminals** *(of current)* jaillir entre les bornes

▸▸ *Aut* **s. advance** correcteur *m* d'avance; *Aut* **s. gap** écartement *m* des électrodes; *Aut* **s. plug** bougie *f*; *Aut* **s. plug spanner** clé *f* à bougie

▸ **spark off** **vt sep** *(initiate)* *(revolution, reaction etc)* déclencher, provoquer; *(idea etc)* donner naissance à; **this remark sparked off a discussion about ...** cette remarque a déclenché *ou* donné lieu à une discussion au sujet de ...

sparkle ['spɑːk(ə)l] **N 1** *(spot of light)* étincelle *f*, *(lasting only short time)* brève lueur *f* **2** *(act, state of sparkling)* scintillement *m*; *(of eyes)* éclat *m*, pétillement *m*; *(of diamond)* feux *mpl*; **wine that has lost its s.** vin qui ne pétille plus; *Fig* **if the s. has gone out of your marriage ...** si la magie a disparu de votre mariage ...; **he's got no s. about him** il est plutôt terne; **he's lost his s.** il a perdu sa joie de vivre

vi *(of jewel, tinsel, metal, snow etc)* étinceler, scintiller; *(of surface of lake)* miroiter; *(of wine)* pétiller, mousser; **her eyes sparkled (with joy)** ses yeux pétillaient (de joie); **sparkling with wit** *(book)* plein d'esprit

sparkler ['spɑːklər] **N 1** *(firework)* cierge *m* magique **2** *Fam (diamond)* diam *m*

sparkling ['spɑːklɪŋ] **ADJ** étincelant, brillant; *(conversation)* brillant; *(wine)* mousseux, pétillant; *(lemonade)* gazeux; **he was a s. conversationalist** sa conversation était des plus brillantes

ADV **s. clean** étincelant de propreté, d'une propreté étincelante

sparring ['spɑːrɪŋ] **N** *Boxing* entraînement *m*; *(arguing)* échanges *mpl* verbaux; **it was just a little good-natured s.** *(verbal)* ce n'était qu'une petite bagarre amicale

▸▸ **s. match** *(in boxing)* match *m* d'entraînement; *Fig (argument)* discussion *f* animée; **I could hear them having a s. match in the corridor** je les entendais se disputer dans le couloir; **s. partner** *(in boxing)* partenaire *m* d'entraînement, sparring-partner *m*, *pl* sparring-partners; *Fig* adversaire *m*

sparrow ['spærəʊ] **N** *(bird)* moineau *m*; **hedge s.** fauvette *f* d'hiver

sparrowhawk ['spærəʊhɔːk] **N** *(bird)* épervier *m*

sparse [spɑːs] **ADJ** *(trees, population)* clairsemé, épars; **s. hair** cheveux rares *ou* clairsemés

sparsely ['spɑːslɪ] **ADV** peu abondamment; **s. covered with trees** aux arbres clairsemés; **s. furnished** à peine meublé; **s. populated** peu peuplé

sparseness ['spɑːsnɪs] **N** *(of population)* faible densité *f*; *(of vegetation)* manque *m*

Sparta ['spɑːtə] **N** Sparte

Spartan ['spɑːtən] **ADJ** *Hist, Fig* spartiate; *Fig* **to lead a s. life** vivre une vie spartiate, mener une vie de spartiate

N *Hist* Spartiate *mf*

spasm ['spæz(ə)m] **N** *Med* spasme *m*; *Fig (of coughing, jealousy)* accès *m*; *Med* **to go into spasms** avoir des spasmes; **to work in spasms** travailler par à-coups; **after a sudden s. of feverish activity** après un accès soudain d'activité fébrile

spasmodic [spæz'mɒdɪk] **ADJ** *Med* spasmodique; *Fig (irregular)* irrégulier, -ère; *(intermittent)* intermittent; **s. work** travail fait par à-coups

spasmodically [spæz'mɒdɪklɪ] **ADV** *Med* spasmodiquement; *Fig (irregularly)* irrégulièrement; *(intermittently)* de façon intermittente; *(to work)* par à-coups

spastic ['spæstɪk] **ADJ** *Med* spastique; *(paralysis etc)* spasmodique; *Offensive Sl (performance, attempt etc)* minable, nul, *f* nulle

N *Med* handicapé, -ée moteur; *Offensive Sl (clumsy person)* gol *mf*, gogol *mf*

spat¹ [spæt] **N** *(of oysters etc)* naissain *m*

spat² **N** *(item of clothing)* demi-guêtre *f*, *pl* demi-guêtres

spat³ *Fam* **N** *(quarrel)* querelle *f*
▸▸ **s.** **vi** **(-tt-)** *(quarrel)* se quereller

spat⁴ **PT, PP** *see* **spit²** **vi, vt**

spate [speɪt] **N** *(of river)* crue *f*, *Fig (of letters etc)* avalanche *f*, *(of abuse)* torrent *m*; **river in (full) s.** rivière en crue; *Fig* **to be in full s.** être en plein dans son sujet; **a s. of burglaries** une série de cambriolages; **there's been a sudden s. of orders** il y a eu une soudaine avalanche *ou* un soudain déluge de commandes

spatial ['speɪʃəl] **ADJ** *Math, Phys etc* spatial, -aux
▸▸ **s. awareness** perception *f* de l'espace

spatiotemporal [speɪʃɪəʊ'tempərəl] **ADJ** spatio-temporel, *pl* spatio-temporels

spatter ['spætər] **N** *(of liquid)* éclaboussure *f*, *Ind (of solder)* projection *f*

vt éclabousser (**with** de); **the wall was spattered with grease** le mur était couvert d'éclaboussures *ou* tout éclaboussé de graisse

vi *(of liquid)* jaillir, gicler; **the rain spattering down on the pavement** la pluie qui rebondit sur le trottoir

-spattered [-spætəd] **suff** blood-/mud-/oil-spattered couvert d'éclaboussures de sang/de boue/d'huile

spatula ['spætjʊlə] **N** *Pharm, Surg, Culin etc* spatule *f*

spavin ['spævɪn] **N** *Vet* éparvin *m*

spawn [spɔːn] **N 1** *(of frog, fish etc)* frai *m*, œufs *mpl*, *Lit, Pej (offspring)* progéniture *f* **2** *(mushroom)* **s.** blancs *mpl* de champignon, mycélium *m*

vi *(of fish etc)* frayer; *Fam (of people)* se multiplier

vt *(of fish, frog etc)* *(eggs)* déposer; *Fig* engendrer, donner naissance à; **the organization/movement spawned various offshoots** l'organisation/le mouvement a donné naissance à plusieurs ramifications

spawning ['spɔːnɪŋ] **N** *Zool* frai *m*
▸▸ **s. ground** frayère *f*, **s. season** frai

spay [speɪ] **vt** *Vet* châtrer

spaz [spæz] **N** *Fam* gol *mf*, gogol *mf*
▸ **spaz out** **vt sep** *Fam* faire le con

SPEAK [spiːk] *(pt* **spoke** [spəʊk]; *pp* **spoken** ['spəʊk(ə)n])

vi	parler **1** ▪ se parler **1** ▪ faire un discours **2**
vt	dire **1** ▪ parler **2** ▪ indiquer **3**

vi 1 *(talk)* *(of person)* parler; **can he s.?** est-ce qu'il parle?, est-ce qu'il sait parler?; **without speaking** sans parler, sans rien dire; **to s. to sb** parler à qn (**about sth** de qch); **he spoke slowly/hesitatingly/too quickly** il s'est ex-

primé *ou* il a parlé lentement/avec hésitation/trop rapidement; **she hasn't spoken to me since** elle ne m'a pas adressé la parole depuis; **I can't give you a rise, you'll have to s. to the boss** je ne peux pas vous donner une augmentation, il va falloir que vous vous adressiez au patron; **they're not speaking (to each other)** ils ne s'adressent pas *ou* plus la parole; **I hate it when Mum and Dad aren't speaking** j'ai horreur des fois où Papa et Maman refusent de se parler; **isn't it about time you two started speaking again?** est-ce que vous ne devriez pas faire la paix?; **I'll s. to him about it** je lui en toucherai un mot, je lui en parlerai; **I know her/him to s. to** on se dit bonjour; **roughly speaking** approximativement; **legally/morally speaking** légalement/moralement parlant; **so to s.** pour ainsi dire; *Tel* **who's speaking?** qui est à l'appareil?; *(before transferring call)* c'est de la part de qui?; **Mr Thomas? – yes, speaking** M. Thomas? – lui-même

2 *(give a speech)* faire un discours; **he spoke on the subject of ...** il a parlé *ou* traité de ...; **to have the right to s.** avoir le droit de se faire entendre, avoir droit à la parole

vt 1 *(a word, the truth)* dire; **she has never spoken a word to me** elle ne m'a jamais adressé la parole, elle ne m'a jamais dit un mot; **he didn't s. a word about it** il n'en a pas soufflé mot; **to s. one's mind** dire ce qu'on pense; **to s. one's lines** *(in play)* dire son rôle

2 *(language)* parler; **do you s. French?** parlez-vous français?; **English is spoken everywhere** l'anglais est parlé partout; **English spoken** *(on sign)* on parle anglais; *also Fig* **to s. the same language** parler le même langage

3 *Lit (show)* *(feeling, emotion)* indiquer, témoigner de; **eyes that s. affection** yeux qui témoignent de l'amitié

▸ **speak against** **vt insep** *(motion, bill, proposal)* se prononcer contre; **she spoke passionately against the practice** elle a condamné cette pratique avec virulence

▸ **speak for** **vt insep 1** *(person)* *(speak on behalf of)* parler pour; *(speak in support of)* plaider pour; **I'm sure I s. for everyone when I say ...** je suis sûr que j'exprime la pensée générale lorsque je dis ...; **speaking for myself** pour ma part, en ce qui me concerne; **I'll tell him when to leave, I can s. for myself!** c'est moi qui lui dirai de partir, je suis parfaitement capable de le faire moi-même!; **he is old enough to s. for himself** *(ask for something)* il est assez grand pour le demander tout seul; *(say something)* il est assez grand pour le dire lui-même; *Fam usu Hum* **s. for yourself!** parle pour toi!; **the facts s. for themselves** ces faits se passent de commentaires *ou* parlent d'eux-mêmes; **it doesn't s. very well for her chances of winning** ça ne laisse présager rien de bon quant à ses chances de victoire

2 to be spoken for *(to be reserved)* être réservé; *(of man, woman)* *(at dance etc)* être accompagné; *(have girlfriend, boyfriend)* avoir un(e) petit(e) ami(e); *(have wife, husband)* être marié(e)

▸ **speak of** **vt insep 1** *(talk about)* parler de; **speaking of ...** à propos de ..., en parlant de ...; **it's nothing to s. of** ce n'est rien, n'en parlons plus; **there's nothing on television/in the town, or nothing to s. of anyway** il n'y a rien de spécial à la télévision/en ville; **to s. well/highly of sb/sth** dire du bien/beaucoup de bien de qn/qch; **he is well spoken of** il a une bonne réputation, on dit du bien de lui; **to s. ill of sb** dire du mal de qn, médire de qn

2 *(indicate)* être significatif de; **this speaks of large-scale corruption** c'est le signe d'une corruption à grande échelle

▸**speak out** VI **1** *(speak with courage)* oser parler, oser prendre la parole; **to s. out against injustice** oser dénoncer l'injustice **2** *(speak loudly)* parler (plus) fort
▸**speak up** VI **1** *(speak louder)* parler plus fort *ou* plus haut
2 *(take active part in discussion etc)* prendre la parole, participer à la discussion; **she speaks up in class/meetings** elle prend la parole en classe/lors de réunions
3 = **speak out 1**
▸**speak up for** VT INSEP *(person)* parler en faveur de; **why don't you s. up for yourself?** pourquoi est-ce que tu ne te défends pas?; **you've got to learn to s. up for yourself** il faut que tu apprennes à défendre tes intérêts

speakeasy ['spiːkiːzɪ] N *Am* débit *m ou* bar *m* clandestin

speaker ['spiːkər] N **1** *(in dialogue)* interlocuteur, -trice; **as a s. of Italian** *or* **an Italian s. myself …** moi qui parle italien …; **there are very few surviving speakers of the language** il reste très peu de personnes qui parlent cette langue; **there were three speakers on the tape** il y avait trois personnes (qui parlaient) sur la bande; **I'm a plain s.** j'appelle les choses par leur nom, je dis ce que je pense, je dis les choses comme elles sont **2** *(at meeting, in discussion programme)* intervenant, -ante; *(at conference)* conférencier, -ière; *(political, orator)* orateur, -trice; *Am TV (announcer)* speaker *m*, speakerine *f*; **we have three speakers this evening** nous avons trois intervenants ce soir; **the next s. will be …** la parole est maintenant à …; **to be a good s.** s'exprimer très bien **3** *Parl* **the S.** *Br, Can* = le Président (des Communes); *Am* = le Président du Congrès; **Mr/Madam S.** Monsieur/Madame le Président **4** *(loudspeaker)* haut-parleur *m*, *pl* haut-parleurs, enceinte *f*

speaking ['spiːkɪŋ] ADJ *(involving speech)* **do you have a s. part in the play** est-ce que vous avez du texte?; **she has a good s. voice** elle a une belle voix **2** *(which speaks) (doll, robot etc)* parlant
N **plain s.** franchise *f*, franc-parler *m*; **public s. art** *m* oratoire; **unaccustomed as I am to public s.** bien que je n'aie pas l'habitude de parler en public; **s. a foreign language is easier than writing it** parler une langue étrangère, c'est plus facile que de l'écrire; **he finds s. very difficult** il a du mal à parler; **we're no longer on s. terms** on ne s'adresse plus la parole
▸▸*Br* **s. clock** horloge *f* parlante; **s. tube** tuyau *m* acoustique

-speaking [-'spiːkɪŋ] SUFF **Chinese-/Russian-s.** *(as mother tongue)* de langue maternelle chinoise/russe; *(as learnt language)* qui parle chinois/russe; **slow-s.** qui s'exprime lentement; **plain-s.** qui appelle les choses par leur nom

spear [spɪər] N **1** *Mil* lance *f*, *(in hunting)* épieu *m*; *(for throwing)* javelot *m*; **to be a s.-carrier** *Theat* être figurant; *Fig* avoir un rôle mineur **2** *Fishing* harpon *m* **3** *(of grass)* brin *m*; **spears of asparagus, asparagus spears** pointes *fpl* d'asperges
VT **1** *(pierce) (person)* transpercer *ou (kill)* tuer d'un coup de lance; *(olive, piece of food etc)* piquer *(avec une fourchette etc)* **2** *Fishing (fish)* harponner
▸▸**s. fishing** pêche *f ou* chasse *f* (sous-marine) au harpon; *Bot* **s. grass** pâturin *m*

spearhead ['spɪəhed] N *(of spear)* fer *m* de lance; *Mil (of attack)* pointe *f*, *Fig (of organization etc)* fer de lance
VT *Mil* **they spearheaded the crossing of the river** ils ont forcé les premiers le passage du

fleuve; *Fig* **to s. a movement** être le fer de lance d'un mouvement

spearmint ['spɪəmɪnt] N *(plant, flavour)* menthe *f* verte; *(sweet)* bonbon *m* à la menthe

spec [spek] N *Fam* **we've got it on s. for a week** on l'a à l'essai pour une semaine; **to buy sth on s.** acheter qch à tout hasard

speccy ['spekɪ] *Br Fam* N binoclard, -arde
ADJ binoclard

special ['speʃəl] ADJ spécial, -aux, particulier, -ère **(to** à); *(friend)* intime; **nothing s.** rien de particulier; **the food was OK but nothing s.** la nourriture était assez bonne mais elle n'avait rien d'exceptionnel; **are you doing anything s. for your birthday?** tu fais quelque chose de spécial pour ton anniversaire?; **what's so s. about the 19th of November?** qu'est-ce que le 19 novembre a de si spécial?; **to pay s. attention** faire particulièrement attention **(to sth** à qch); **for someone s.** *(on card)* pour quelqu'un qui m'est cher; **for s. occasions** pour les jours de fête, pour les occasions spéciales; **to get s. treatment** bénéficier d'un traitement de faveur; **s. case** cas *m* particulier; **s. characteristic** particularité *f*, **s. feature** particularité *f*
N *(train)* train *m* spécial; *(newspaper)* édition *f* spéciale; *(programme)* émission *f* spéciale; **today's s.** *(in restaurant)* plat *m* du jour
▸▸**s. agent** *(spy etc)* agent *m* secret; **S. Air Service** = commando *m* d'intervention spéciale de l'armée britannique; *EU* **S. Area of Conservation** zone *f* spéciale de conservation; **S. Branch** = service *m* de police britannique chargé des crimes contre la sûreté de l'État, ≃ Renseignements *mpl* généraux; *Typ* **s. character** caractère *m* spécial; **s. clause** clause *f* particulière; *Br* **s. constable** auxiliaire *mf* de police; *Journ* **s. correspondent** envoyé, -ée spécial(e); **s. delivery** = service postal britannique garantissant la distribution du courrier sous 24 heures; **to mail sth s. delivery** envoyer qch en exprès; *Fin* **s. drawing rights** droits *mpl* de tirage spéciaux; **s. edition** édition spéciale, hors *m* série; *Cin, TV* **s. effects** effets *mpl* spéciaux; **s. indications** *(on ticket)* indications *fpl* spéciales; *Comput* **s. interest group** groupe *m* d'intérêt; **s. interest holidays** vacances *fpl* à thème; *Journ etc* **s. issue** numéro *m* spécial; *Br* **s. licence** dispense *f* de bans; *Br* **they were married by s. licence** ils se sont mariés avec dispense de bans; **s. offer** promotion *f*, **s. pleading** argument *m* spécieux; *Law* plaidoyer *m* partial; *Pol* **s. powers** pouvoirs *mpl* extraordinaires; *Com* **s. price** prix *m* spécial; **s. rate** tarif *m* préférentiel *ou* spécial; *Br* **s. school** établissement *m* d'enseignement spécialisé *(pour enfants handicapés ou inadaptés)*

Note that the French adjective **spécial** also means **peculiar, odd**.

specialist ['speʃəlɪst] N spécialiste *mf*; **to become a s. in electronics** *or* **an electronics s.** se spécialiser dans l'électronique; *Med* **heart/lung/cancer s.** cardiologue *mf*/pneumologue *mf*/cancérologue *mf*
ADJ *(skills, vocabulary, knowledge)* spécialisé, de spécialiste; *(writing, publication)* pour spécialistes; *(bookshop, TV channel, dictionary)* spécialisé; **what are your s. subjects?** dans quels sujets vous spécialisez-vous?; **it requires s. skills** ça demande les compétences d'un spécialiste; **if you don't have the s. knowledge** si vous n'avez pas les connaissances d'un spécialiste
▸▸*Com* **s. retailer** détaillant, -ante spécialisé(e); **s. teacher** professeur *m* spécialisé

speciality [speʃɪˈælɪtɪ], *Am* **specialty** ['speʃəltɪ] N **1** *(of store, restaurant, region etc)*

spécialité *f*, *(area of study) (of student)* matière *f* principale; *(of researcher)* sujet *m* de recherches; **his s. is Vietnamese art** il se spécialise dans l'art du Vietnam; *also Iron* **that's my s.** c'est ma spécialité, je suis spécialiste; **skiing holidays our s.** *(in advertisement)* les sports d'hiver sont notre spécialité; **s. goods** produits *mpl* de spécialité, produits spécialisés; **s. restaurant** restaurant *m* de spécialités; **s. shop** magasin *m* spécialisé **2** *Law* = **specialty 1**

specialization [speʃəlaɪˈzeɪʃən] N spécialisation *f* **(in** dans)

specialize ['speʃəlaɪz] VI *(of shop, researcher etc)* se spécialiser **(in** dans); *Iron* **she specializes in that sort of blunder** elle est spécialiste de ce genre de gaffes

specialized ['speʃəlaɪzd] ADJ *(work, subject)* spécialisé

specially ['speʃəlɪ] ADV *(in particular)* spécialement, particulièrement; **I'm s. interested in antique furniture** je m'intéresse plus particulièrement *ou* surtout aux antiquités; **I went there s. to see them** j'y suis allé dans le seul but de les voir, j'y suis allé exprès pour les voir; **I waited up s.** je suis resté debout exprès; **s. designed to …** spécialement conçu pour …; **I s. asked you not to …** je t'avais bien demandé de ne pas …; **it's not s. good** ce n'est pas particulièrement bon; **s. at night** surtout le soir; **they had a cake s. made** ils ont fait faire un gâteau spécialement

Attention: ne pas confondre avec **especially**.

specialty ['speʃəltɪ] N **1** *Law* contrat *m* par acte scellé **2** *Am* = **speciality 1**

specie ['spiːʃiː] N *(no pl) Fin* espèces *fpl* (monnayées)

species ['spiːʃiːz] N INV **1** *Biol* espèce *f*; **the human s.** l'espèce humaine; **the origin of s.** l'origine *f* des espèces **2** *(type)* espèce *f*, sorte *f*

specific [spɪˈsɪfɪk] ADJ *(particular)* spécifique; *(clear) (statement, example, rule, aim)* précis; *(command)* explicite; **or, to be s., …** ou, pour être précis …; **in this s. case** dans ce cas précis *ou* particulier; **to be s.** *(of person)* être explicite; **she was pretty s. about her intentions** elle a été très précise quant à ses intentions; **could you be a bit more s.?** pourriez-vous être plus précis?, pourriez-vous préciser?
N *Med* spécifique *m* **(for** contre); *Am Ind* **specifics** *(precise description)* description *f* précise; *(characteristics)* caractéristiques *fpl*; *Fam* **to get down to specifics** en venir aux faits précis
▸▸*Phys* **s. gravity** densité *f*

specifically [spɪˈsɪfɪk(ə)lɪ] ADV spécifiquement; *(precisely)* précisément; **your name was mentioned s.** votre nom a été bien précisément mentionné; **you must state quite s. what the requirements are** vous devez bien spécifier les conditions requises; **I s. told you not to …** je t'ai dit très précisément de ne pas …; **I s. asked for a small portion** j'ai bien demandé une petite portion; **we were s. forbidden to …** il nous était expressément défendu de …; **it is s. designed for use in …** c'est (tout) spécialement conçu pour une utilisation dans …; **a book which is s. written for people who …** un livre écrit tout particulièrement pour les gens qui …

specification [spesɪfɪˈkeɪʃən] N **1** *(act) (of details etc)* spécification *f* **2** *(description) (of car)* caractéristiques *fpl*; *(of work to be done)* prescriptions *fpl*; *Constr, Ind* **specifications** *(of contract)* cahier *m* des charges **3** *(condition, stipulation)* spécification *f*; **there's no**

s. about the number of times you can enter on ne précise pas combien de fois on peut participer; **their only s. was that the press should not be told** la seule condition qu'ils avaient posée était que la presse ne devait pas être informée

▸▸ *Com* **s. buying** achats *mpl* spécifiés

specificity [spesɪˈfɪsɪtɪ] N spécificité *f*

specify [ˈspesɪfaɪ] VT *(conditions etc)* spécifier, préciser; **I specified blue** j'ai spécifié la couleur bleue; **specified load** charge prévue *ou* prescrite; **unless otherwise specified** sauf indication contraire

specimen [ˈspesɪmɪn] N spécimen *m*; *(sample)* spécimen, échantillon *m*; **the finest specimens in his collection** les plus belles pièces de sa collection; **that's a magnificent s.** *(butterfly etc)* c'est un très beau spécimen; **a s. of sb's handwriting** un échantillon *ou* exemple de l'écriture de qn; *Med* **to take a s. of sb's blood, to take a blood s. from sb** faire une prise de sang à qn; *Fam* **s.** *(of urine)* un prélèvement d'urine; *Fam* **an odd s.** *(person)* un drôle de type; *Fam* **you're a pretty pathetic s., aren't you!** tu es vraiment lamentable!

▸▸ **s. bottle** flacon-échantillon *m*, *pl* flacons-échantillons; **s. copy** spécimen *m* *(livre, magazine)*; **s. page** page *f* spécimen, page type; **s. signature** spécimen de signature

specious [ˈspiːʃəs] ADJ *(appearance)* spécieux, trompeur; *(argument, promises)* captieux, spécieux

speciousness [ˈspiːʃəsnɪs] N *(of argument, promises)* caractère *m* spécieux

speck [spek] N **1** *(mark)* petite tache *f*, *(of colour, ink)* point *m*; *(on fruit)* tavelure *f*; *Med* **specks (in front of the eyes)** mouches *fpl*, taches *fpl* *(devant les yeux)* **2** *(small piece)* *(of dust)* grain *m*, atome *m*; **the ship was only a s. on the horizon** le navire n'était qu'un point à l'horizon

speckle [ˈspek(ə)l] N petite tache *f*, *(of colour)* point *m*; *(on animal, egg)* moucheture *f*, tacheture *f*

VT tacheter, moucheter

speckled [ˈspek(ə)ld] ADJ tacheté, moucheté; *(plumage)* grivelé; *(hen)* tacheté; **bird s. with white** oiseau tacheté de blanc

specs [speks] NPL *Fam* **1** *(spectacles)* carreaux *mpl* **2** *Ind* *(specifications)* spécifications *fpl*

spectacle [ˈspektək(ə)l] N **1** *(show, sight)* spectacle *m*; **to make a s. of oneself** se donner en spectacle **2** **(pair of) spectacles** (paire *f* de) lunettes *fpl*; **to put on one's spectacles** mettre *ou* chausser ses lunettes VOIR GRAMMAIRE A10

spectacled [ˈspektək(ə)ld] ADJ à lunettes

spectacular [spekˈtækjʊlər] ADJ spectaculaire N *Theat, Cin* superproduction *f*; **an ice-skating s.** une revue de patinage artistique

spectacularly [spekˈtækjʊləlɪ] ADV *(to improve, collapse etc)* de façon spectaculaire

spectate [spekˈteɪt] VI *esp Sp* **to s. at** *(match etc)* assister à; **I prefer to s.** je préfère être spectateur/spectatrice

spectator [spekˈteɪtər] N spectateur, -trice; **the spectators** les spectateurs; **we don't want any spectators** nous ne voulons pas qu'on nous regarde

▸▸ **s. sport** sport *m* grand public; **swimming is not a very good s. sport** la natation n'est pas un sport très intéressant à regarder; *Fig* **television has turned war into a s. sport** la télévision a transformé la guerre en spectacle

specter [ˈspektər] N *Am* = **spectre**

spectral [ˈspektr(ə)l] ADJ **1** *Phys (analysis, band, density)* spectral, -aux **2** *(ghostly)* spectral, -aux

▸▸ *Phys* **s. colours** couleurs *fpl* spectrales; *Phys* **s. range** domaine *m* spectral

spectre [ˈspektər] N spectre *m*, fantôme *m*; *Fig* **the s. of war/famine** *(threat)* le spectre de la guerre/famine

spectrogram [ˈspektrəʊɡræm] N spectrogramme *m*

spectrograph [ˈspektrəʊɡræf] N spectrographe *m*

spectrometer [spekˈtrɒmɪtər] N spectromètre *m*

spectroscope [ˈspektrəskəʊp] N spectroscope *m*

spectroscopy [spekˈtrɒskəpɪ] N spectroscopie *f*

spectrum, *pl* **spectra** [ˈspektrəm, -trə] N **1** *Phys etc* spectre *m*; **the colours of the s.** les couleurs spectrales *ou* du spectre **2** *(of opinions)* éventail *m*; **a wide s. of opinions** un large éventail d'opinions; **the whole s. of political opinion** tout l'éventail des opinions politiques; **across the political s.** dans l'ensemble des tendances politiques

▸▸ **s. analysis** analyse *f* spectrale

speculate [ˈspekjʊleɪt] VI **1 to s. on** *or* **about sth** *(wonder)* spéculer *ou* méditer sur qch; *(conjecture)* faire des conjectures sur qch **2** *Fin* spéculer; **to s. on the Stock Exchange** spéculer en Bourse

speculating [ˈspekjʊleɪtɪŋ] N *Fin* spéculation *f*

speculation [spekjʊˈleɪʃən] N **1** *(wondering)* spéculation *f*, méditation *f*, *(conjecture)* conjecture *f* (**on, about** sur); **it was pure s. on his part** c'était (une) pure conjecture de sa part **2** *Fin* spéculation *f*; **to buy sth on s.** acheter qch à titre de spéculation

speculative [ˈspekjʊlətɪv] ADJ spéculatif; **these are merely s. assumptions** ce sont là de pures hypothèses *ou* de pures conjectures

▸▸ *St Exch* **s. securities, s. shares** valeurs *fpl* spéculatives

speculatively [ˈspekjʊlətɪvlɪ] ADV *(to suggest, argue)* à titre d'hypothèse; *(to invest)* spéculativement

speculator [ˈspekjʊleɪtər] N spéculateur, -trice; *St Exch* joueur, -euse en Bourse, spéculateur, -trice

speculum, *pl* **speculums, specula** [ˈspekjʊləm, -əmz, -ə] N *Med* spéculum *m*

sped PT, PP *see* **speed** VI, VT

speech [spiːtʃ] N **1** *(faculty)* la parole; **to lose the power of s.** perdre la parole; **her s. was slow and deliberate** elle parlait lentement en pesant ses mots; **to be slow of s.** parler lentement; **to be abrupt in one's s.** parler d'une manière brusque

2 *(language)* *(of a people)* langue *f*, *(of a region etc)* parler *m*; **things which people say in everyday s.** des choses que les gens disent dans la langue de tous les jours

3 *(address)* discours *m*, allocution *f*; **to give** *or* **make a s.** faire *ou* prononcer un discours *ou* une allocution; **s.! s.!** un discours! un discours!

4 *Gram* **part of s.** partie *f* du discours; **direct/indirect s.** discours *m ou* style *m* direct/indirect; **figure of s.** figure *f* de rhétorique VOIR GRAMMAIRE A63; A78

▸▸ *Comput* **s. chip** puce *f* de traitement de la parole; *Ling* **s. community** communauté *f* linguistique; *Br Sch* **s. day** distribution *f* des prix; **s. defect** défaut *m* de prononciation, *Spec* trouble *f* du langage; **s. impediment** défaut d'élocution *ou* de prononciation; *Comput* **s. recognition** reconnaissance *f* de la parole; *Radio* **s. station** station *f* de radio à vocation culturelle; **s. synthesizer** synthétiseur *m* de parole; **s. therapist** orthophoniste *mf*, *Belg, Suisse* logopède *mf*; **s. therapy** orthophonie *f*

speechify [ˈspiːtʃɪfaɪ] VI *Pej* discourir, pérorer

speechifying [ˈspiːtʃɪfaɪɪŋ] N *Pej* beaux discours *mpl*, laïus *m*

speechless [ˈspiːtʃlɪs] ADJ **1** *(struck dumb)* interdit, interloqué, muet, -ette; **to be s. with anger/fear/rage** être muet de colère/peur/rage; **emotion left him s.** l'émotion l'a laissé muet; **I was s.** *(with anger, surprise etc)* j'étais sans voix; **I'm s.!** je ne sais pas quoi dire! **2** *(for physiological reasons)* incapable de parler

speechlessly [ˈspiːtʃlɪslɪ] ADV sans voix

speechwriter [ˈspiːtʃraɪtər] N rédacteur, -trice de discours

speed [spiːd] N **1** vitesse *f*, rapidité *f*, *(of engine, machine)* vitesse, régime *m*; *Phot (of film, shutter)* vitesse; *(of lens)* rapidité *f*; **the s. of light/sound** la vitesse de la lumière/du son; *Lit* **to make all s.** faire diligence, se hâter; **with all possible s.** aussi rapidement *ou* aussi vite que possible; **the s. with which she learnt/the building was completed** la vitesse à laquelle elle a appris/le bâtiment a été terminé; *Aut etc* **at s.** *(to travel)* à grande vitesse; **at top** *or* **full s.** à toute vitesse; *(of runners)* à toutes jambes; **to drive at top s.** rouler à toute vitesse *ou* à toute allure; *Naut* **full s. ahead/astern!** en avant/en arrière toute!; **car with a maximum s. of 150 km an hour** voiture qui plafonne à 150 km à l'heure; **cruising s.** vitesse *ou* régime de croisière; *Aviat* **take-off s.** vitesse de décollage; **to gather/lose s.** prendre/perdre de la vitesse; **to reduce s.** ralentir; **to pick up s.** *(of train, car)* prendre de la vitesse; *Fam* **to be up to s. on sth** être au courant de qch; *Fam* **to bring sb up to s. on sth** mettre qn au courant de qch

2 *(gear)* vitesse *f*, **five-s. gearbox** boîte *f* à cinq vitesses

3 *Comput* vitesse *f*, **32 s. CD-ROM** lecteur *m* de CD-ROM 32 x

4 *Arch* **to wish sb good s.** souhaiter bonne chance à qn

5 *Fam (amphetamines)* amphets *fpl*, amphés *fpl*, speed *m*

VI **1** *(pt, pp* **sped** [sped] *or* **speeded**) *(hasten)* se hâter, se presser; *(go fast)* aller vite; *Aut etc (go fast)* faire de la vitesse; **the car was speeding towards us** la voiture arrivait sur nous à toute vitesse; **we are speeding towards a crisis** nous allons à grands pas vers une crise

2 *(pt, pp* **speeded**) *Aut (exceed speed limit)* faire un excès de vitesse; **I was caught speeding** j'ai eu une contravention pour excès de vitesse

3 *Fam* **to be speeding** *(be under effect of amphetamines)* être sous amphés, speeder

VT *(pt, pp* **sped** *or* **speeded**) *Arch, Lit* **to s. sb on his/her way** *(wish a good journey)* souhaiter bon voyage à qn; *esp Hum (encourage to leave)* encourager *ou* presser qn à partir plus vite; *Arch* **God s. (you)!** bon voyage!

▸▸ **s. bump** casse-vitesse *m inv*, ralentisseur *m*; **s. camera** radar *m*; *Am Fam* **s. cop** motard *m* (de la police); **s. dating** speed dating *m*, = soirées *fpl* de rencontre dont chaque participant dispose d'un temps limité pour s'entretenir avec tous les autres; *Tel* **s. dial** numérotation *f* abrégée; **s. limit** limitation *f* de vitesse; *Br, Austr Fam* **s. merchant** mordu, -ue de vitesse; *Aut* **s. sensor** capteur *m* de vitesse; **s. trap** contrôle *m* de vitesse

▸ **speed along** VI *(in car, on bike)* rouler vite, *Fam* foncer; *(on foot)* marcher *ou* courir vite; **the work is speeding along** le travail avance à bonne allure

VT SEP *(work)* faire avancer *ou* progresser en vitesse

▸ **speed back** VI *(of person, driver)* rentrer à toute vitesse; **she sped back to Edinburgh** elle est retournée à Édimbourg à toute vitesse

VT SEP *(person)* ramener à toute vitesse

▸ **speed off** VI *(on foot, in car)* partir à toute allure

VT SEP **they sped him off to hospital** ils l'ont transporté à l'hôpital à toute vitesse

▸ **speed up** VI *(of driver, runner etc)* accélérer; *(of work, pace)* s'accélérer; *(work faster)* travailler plus rapidement

VT SEP *(staff, project)* activer; *(job)* activer, accélérer; **to s. things up** accélérer *ou* activer les choses

speedball ['spi:dbɔ:l] N *Sl* speedball *m (mélange d'héroïne et de cocaïne)*

speedboat ['spi:dbəʊt] N vedette *f;* *(with outboard motor)* hors-bord *m inv*

speedfreak ['spi:dfri:k] N *Sl* **to be a s.** consommer beaucoup d'amphets

speedily ['spi:dɪlɪ] ADV rapidement

speediness ['spi:dɪnɪs] N rapidité *f*

speeding ['spi:dɪŋ] N *Aut (exceeding speed limit)* excès *m* de vitesse

▸▸ **s. fine** contravention *f* pour excès de vitesse; **s. ticket** P-V *m inv* pour excès de vitesse; **s. up** accélération *f*

speedo ['spi:dəʊ] N *Fam* = **speedometer**

speedometer [spi:'dɒmɪtər] N *Aut etc* compteur *m* (de vitesse)

speedster ['spi:dstər] N *(car)* bolide *m;* *(driver)* fou *m* du volant, *Pej* chauffard *m*

speed-up N accélération *f*

speedway ['spi:dweɪ] N **1** *Sport (motorcycle racing)* speedway *m;* *(track)* circuit *m* de speedway; *Am (for cars)* circuit automobile **2** *Am (fast road)* autoroute *f*

▸▸ **s. rider** pilote *m* de speedway

speedwell ['spi:dwel] N *(plant)* véronique *f*

Speedwriting® ['spi:draɪtɪŋ] N écriture *f* abrégée

speedy ['spi:dɪ] ADJ *(person, work, response etc)* rapide, prompt; *(car)* rapide

speleologist [spi:lɪ'ɒlədʒɪst] N spéléologue *mf*

speleology [spi:lɪ'ɒlədʒɪ] N spéléologie *f*

spell¹ [spel] N *(magic words)* formule *f* magique, charme *m;* *(enchanted state)* sort *m*, maléfice *m*, charme; **to cast a (magic) s. over sb, to put a (magic) s. on sb** jeter un sort à qn, ensorceler qn; **to break the s.** rompre le charme; **under a s.** sous un charme, ensorcelé

spell² *(pt, pp* **spelt, spelled** [spelt, speld]*)* VT **1** *(out loud)* épeler; *(in writing)* orthographier; **how is it spelt?, how do you s. it?** comment ça s'épelle *ou* s'écrit?; **how do you s. 'Mississippi'?** comment écrit-on 'Mississippi'?; **can you s. that for me?** *(on telephone etc)* pouvez-vous me l'épeler?; **it's spelt** *or* **you s. it with an 'o'** ça s'écrit avec un 'o' **2 what do these letters s.?** quel mot forment ces lettres? **3** *(signify)* signifier; **to s. disaster** être un désastre; **this spells disaster** on est perdu; **it would s. disaster** cela serait un désastre

VI orthographier *ou* écrire correctement; **he can't s.** il est nul en orthographe; **she can't s. very well** elle n'est pas très bonne en orthographe

▸ **spell out** VT SEP *(address, name etc) (pro-* nounce individual letters of) épeler; *(have difficulty in reading)* déchiffrer péniblement; *Fig (explain explicitly)* expliquer bien clairement; **… even though I spelled my name out for him** … bien que je lui aie épelé mon nom; *Fig* **do I have to s. it out for you?** faut-il que je te fasse un dessin?; *Fig* **I'll s. it out for you** je vais te le dire clairement

spell³ N **1** *(period)* période *f, Austr (rest period)* repos *m;* **to rest for a (short) s.** se reposer pendant quelque temps; **a long s. of cold weather** une longue période de froid; **during the cold s.** pendant le coup de froid; **we're in for a s. of wet weather** le temps se met à la pluie; **to suffer from dizzy spells** être sujet à des vertiges; **it's his second s. in prison** c'est son deuxième séjour en prison; **the end of the party's long s. in power is in sight** le parti est en train de vivre ses derniers moments au pouvoir

2 *(turn) (of duty)* tour *m;* **to do a s. of duty** faire un tour de service; **to take spells at the pumps** se relayer aux pompes; **do you want to take a s. at the wheel?** tu veux me relayer au volant?

VT **1** *Am Fam (relieve) (person)* relayer, relever *(dans son travail)* **2** *Austr (allow to rest) (horse)* laisser reposer

spellbinder ['spelbaɪndər] N *(speaker)* orateur, -trice captivant(e)

spellbinding ['spelbaɪndɪŋ] ADJ envoûtant

spellbound ['spelbaʊnd] ADJ *(fascinated)* envoûté, fasciné; **to hold sb s.** envoûter qn, fasciner qn

spellcheck ['speltʃek] *Comput* N correction *f* orthographique; **to do** *or* **run a s. on a document** effectuer une correction orthographique sur un document

VT faire la vérification orthographique de

spellchecker ['speltʃekər] N *Comput* correcteur *m* orthographique *ou* d'orthographe

spellchecking ['speltʃekɪŋ] N *Comput* correction *f* orthographique *ou* d'orthographe

speller ['spelər] N **1** *(person)* **to be a good/a bad s.** être fort/faible en orthographe **2** *(book)* alphabet *m*

spelling ['spelɪŋ] N orthographe *f;* **his s. is atrocious** son orthographe est déplorable
VOIR GRAMMAIRE A79–80

▸▸ **s. mistake** faute *f* d'orthographe; **s. test** test *m* d'orthographe

spelt PT, PP *see* **spell²**

spend [spend] VT *(pt, pp* **spent** [spent]*)* **1** *(money)* dépenser; **to s. one's money on cigarettes** dépenser son argent en cigarettes; **her father has spent a great deal on her education** son père a dépensé beaucoup pour ses études; **to s. money on sb** dépenser son argent pour qn; **she spends money like water** l'argent lui fond *ou* glisse entre les mains; *Br Fam* **to s. a penny** *(urinate)* faire pipi

2 *(pass) (time)* passer; **to s. the night** passer la nuit; **to s. Sunday in the country** passer le dimanche à la campagne; **haven't you got any better ways of spending your time?** c'est tout ce que tu trouves à faire pour t'occuper?; **could you please s. a little time talking to her about it?** pourrais-tu prendre un peu de temps pour lui en parler?; **how do you s. your weekends?** qu'est-ce que tu fais le week-end?

3 *(expend) (time, energy)* consacrer; **to s. time on (doing) sth** consacrer *ou* employer du temps à (faire) qch; **to s. a lot of effort on a job** se donner beaucoup de mal pour un travail; **if you spent a bit more care on …** si tu apportais *ou* mettais un peu plus de soin à …

4 *(usu passive) (use up) (one's strength, ammunition)* épuiser; **her strength/energy was** all but spent elle n'avait presque plus de forces/d'énergie

VI dépenser

N *esp Com* dépenses *fpl*

spendable ['spendəb(ə)l] ADJ

▸▸ **s. income** revenu *m* dépensable

spender ['spendər] N **to be a big s.** être très dépensier; **they are the biggest arms s.** ce sont eux qui dépensent le plus en armement

spending ['spendɪŋ] N dépense *f,* **public s.** dépenses *fpl* publiques

▸▸ **s. cuts** réductions *fpl* des dépenses; **s. money** argent *m* de poche; **s. power** pouvoir *m* d'achat; **s. spree** vague *f* de dépenses; **to go on a s. spree** faire des folies

spendthrift ['spendθrɪft] N dépensier, -ière; **s. habits** habitudes *fpl* dépensières

spent [spent] ADJ **1** *(tired)* épuisé **2** *(used up)* épuisé; **s. bullet** balle *f* morte; **s. match** allumette *f* usagée

PT, PP *see* **spend**

sperm [spɜ:m] N **1** *Physiol* sperme *m* **2** *(cell)* spermatozoïde *m*

▸▸ **s. bank** banque *f* de sperme; **s. cell** spermatozoïde; **s. donor** donneur *m* de sperme; **s. oil** blanc *m* de baleine, spermaceti *m; Zool* **s. whale** cachalot *m*

spermaceti [spɜ:mə'setɪ] N spermaceti *m*, blanc *m* de baleine

spermatozoon, *pl* **spermatozooa** [spɜ:-mətəʊ'zəʊɒn, -əʊə] N spermatozoïde *m*

spermicidal [spɜ:mɪ'saɪd(ə)l] ADJ spermicide

spermicide ['spɜ:mɪsaɪd] N spermicide *m*

spew [spju:] *Br Fam* VT & VI *(vomit)* dégueuler; **it makes you want to s.!** ça fait gerber! N *(vomit)* dégueulis *m*

▸ **spew forth, spew out** VI *(of lava, flames etc)* jaillir, fuser **(from, of** de); *Fig (of propaganda, lies, etc)* fuser

VT SEP *(lava, propaganda), Fig (propaganda)* déverser

▸ **spew up** VI, VT SEP *Br Fam (vomit)* dégueuler

spewing ['spju:ɪŋ] ADJ *Br Fam (angry)* fumasse, furax

sphagnum, *pl* **sphagna** ['sfægnəm, -ə] N *Bot* sphaigne *f*

▸▸ **s. moss** sphaigne

sphere [sfɪər] N **1** *Astron, Geom* sphère *f,* **the celestial s.** la sphère céleste **2** *(field)* domaine *m*, sphère *f,* *(social circle)* milieu *m*, sphère; **to extend one's s. of activity** étendre sa sphère d'activité; **that is not within my s.** cela n'est pas de mon domaine *ou* de mon ressort; **in the political s.** sur le plan politique; **in political/academic spheres** dans les milieux politiques/universitaires; **s. of influence** sphère *ou* zone *f* d'influence

spherical ['sferɪk(ə)l] ADJ sphérique

spheroid ['sfɪərɔɪd] N sphéroïde *m*

sphincter ['sfɪŋktər] N sphincter *m*

sphinx, *pl* **sphinxes** [sfɪŋks, 'sfɪŋksɪz] N *Myth* sphinx *m*

sphinx-like ADJ de sphinx; *(smile)* énigmatique

spic [spɪk] N *Am Offensive Sl* métèque *mf (d'origine latino-américaine)*

spice [spaɪs] N **1** *Culin* épice *f,* **mixed spice(s)** épices mélangées **2** *Fig* sel *m*, piquant *m;* **to give s. to a story** pimenter un récit; **the s. of life** le sel *ou* le piquant de la vie; **the s. of adventure** le piment de l'aventure

VT **1** *(cake, drink etc)* épicer **2** *Fig (story etc)* pimenter, relever

▸▸ **s. rack** étagère *f ou* présentoir *m* à épices

spiciness ['spaɪsɪnɪs] N **1** *(of food)* caractère *m* épicé **2** *Fig (of story)* piquant *m*, sel *m*

spick [spɪk] ADJ s. and span reluisant de propreté, propre comme un sou neuf; *(person)* tiré à quatre épingles

N *Am Offensive Sl (Spanish-American)* latino *mf*

spicy ['spaɪsɪ] ADJ **1** *Culin (spiced)* épicé; *(taste)* relevé **2** *Fig (story, conversation etc)* piquant, croustillant; *(risqué)* salé, épicé, poivré; **to tell s. stories** en dire de vertes

spider ['spaɪdər] N **1** araignée *f* **2** *Br (for luggage)* araignée (à bagages) **3** *Am Culin* poêle *f* (à trépied) **4** *Comput* araignée

▸▸ **s. crab** araignée (de mer); **s. monkey** singe *m* araignée; **s. plant** chlorophytum *m*; *Br* **s.'s web, s. web** toile d'araignée

spiderman, *pl* **spidermen** ['spaɪdəmæn, -men] N *Br* = ouvrier *m* qui travaille au sommet des édifices

spidery ['spaɪdərɪ] ADJ *(resembling a spider)* qui ressemble à une araignée; **s. handwriting** pattes *fpl* de mouches

spiel [ʃpiːl, spiːl] N *Fam* baratin *m*, speech *m*; *(of salesman)* boniment *m*; **he gave me some s. about having been held up at the airport** il m'a servi tout un baratin comme quoi il avait été bloqué à l'aéroport

▸ **spiel off** VT SEP *Am Fam (recite)* débiter

spiffing ['spɪfɪŋ] ADJ *Old-fashioned Br Fam* épatant

spigot ['spɪgət] N **1** *(stopper) (of barrel)* fausset *m* **2** *Am (faucet for water etc)* robinet *m* **3** *(handle of tap)* clef *f* (de robinet)

spike [spaɪk] N **1** *(of railing, helmet)* pointe *f*, *(of barbed wire etc)* piquant *m*; **impaled on the spikes of the railings** empalé sur la grille; *Sport* **spikes** *(running shoes)* chaussures *fpl* à pointes

2 *Bot* épi *m*

3 *Elec* pointe *f ou* crête *f* de tension

4 *Journ* pique *f*, **on the s.** rejeté

5 *Sl (hypodermic needle)* shooteuse *f*, pompe *f*

6 *(nail)* gros clou *m*

VT **1** *(fit with spikes)* armer de pointes; **spiked gate** grille *f* à pointes *ou* garnie de pointes; *Sport* **spiked shoes** chaussures *fpl* à pointes

2 *(thwart) (affair)* faire avorter, *(plan)* contrecarrer, entraver; *Fig* **to s. sb's guns** priver qn de ses moyens d'action, mettre qn hors d'action

3 *(add alcohol to) (drink)* corser

4 *Journ (story, article)* rejeter, *Fam* balancer

▸▸ **s. heel** *(on woman's shoes)* talon *m* aiguille; **s. lavender** lavande *f* aspic *m*, spic *m*; **s. nail** gros clou

spiked [spaɪkt] ADJ *Journ* rejeté

spikenard ['spaɪknɑːd] N *Lit (ointment)* nard *m* (indien)

spiky ['spaɪkɪ] ADJ **1** *(with sharp points)* piquant; **s. hair** *(short)* cheveux *mpl* en brosse; *(of punk etc)* cheveux hérissés **2** *Fam (touchy, irritable)* susceptible, chatouilleux

spill¹ [spɪl] VT *(pt, pp* spilt, spilled [spɪlt, spɪld]) *(liquid, salt)* renverser; *(blood)* verser; **without spilling a drop** sans laisser tomber une goutte; *Fig Fam* **to s. the beans** révéler un secret; *(under interrogation)* cracher *ou* lâcher le morceau

VI **1** *(of liquid)* se répandre, couler; **some wine had spilled on the carpet** du vin s'était répandu sur le tapis **2** *Fig Fam (reveal information)* vendre la mèche; *(under interrogation)* cracher *ou* lâcher le morceau; **come on, s.!** allez, accouche!

N *(fall)* **to have** *or* **take a s.** culbuter; *(from bicycle, horse)* tomber, faire une chute, *Fam* ramasser *ou* se prendre une pelle

▸ **spill out** VI *(of liquid etc)* déborder; *Fig (of words)* sortir; **the crowd started spilling out of the stadium** la foule commença à se déverser hors du stade

VT SEP *(liquid)* renverser; *Fig (story)* répandre

▸ **spill over** VI *(of liquid)* déborder, se déverser; *Fig (of scandal, conflict)* se répandre (**into** dans); **the population has spilled over into the surrounding areas** la population s'est déversée sur les zones avoisinantes; **the conflict could s. over into neighbouring countries** le conflit risquerait de s'étendre aux pays voisins

spill² N *(for lighting fire etc)* allume-feu *m, pl* allume-feux

▸▸ *TV* **s. light** lumière *f* parasite, mouche *f*

spillage ['spɪlɪdʒ] N *(action)* déversement *m* accidentel; *(liquid)* liquide *m* déversé; **there's been a diesel s. on the M25** un chargement de gasoil s'est renversé sur la M25

spillover ['spɪləʊvər] N *(excess population)* surpopulation *f*

spillway ['spɪlweɪ] N *Tech* déversoir *m*

spilt PT, PP *see* spill¹ VT, VI

SPIN [spɪn]

N tournoiement **1** ■ essorage **1**	
■ promenade **2** ■ manipulation **3**	
VT filer ■ faire tourner	
VI tourner **1** ■ tournoyer **1** ■ patiner **2** ■ manipuler l'information **3**	

N **1** *(turning movement)* tournoiement *m*; *(of ball etc)* mouvement *m* de) rotation *f*, *(of washing machine)* essorage *m*; *Aviat* vrille *f*, **to give sth a s.** *(in spin-dryer)* essorer qch; **give the washing a quick s.** donne un petit coup d'essorage au linge; *Sport* **to put s. on a ball** donner de l'effet à une balle; **there was a lot of s. on that ball** il y avait beaucoup d'effet dans cette balle; **to go into a s.** *Aut* faire un tête-à-queue; *Fig* perdre la tête; *Fig* **the news sent him into a s.** la nouvelle l'a complètement paniqué; *Fam* **to have the spins** avoir le tournis *(généralement après avoir trop bu)*; *Aviat* **flat s.** vrille à plat, tonneau *m*; *Fig Fam* **to be in a flat s.** ne pas savoir où donner de la tête; *Br Fam* **on the s.** *(in a row)* de suite; *Br Fam* **they've won seven games on the s.** ils ont gagné sept matchs de suite

2 *Fam (short journey) (in car etc)* tour *m*, promenade *f*, **to go for a s.** aller faire un tour

3 *Fam (on information)* **to put the right s. on a story** présenter une affaire sous un angle favorable; **the government put its own s. on the situation** le gouvernement a présenté la situation sous un angle qui lui convenait; **the government has been criticized for indulging in too much s.** on a reproché au gouvernement de trop manipuler les informations fournies au public

4 *Austr Fam (luck)* coup *m* de chance; *(bad luck)* malchance *f*

VT *(pt, pp* spun [spʌn]; *prp* spinning) **1** *(wool, cotton etc)* filer; **to s. its web** *(of spider)* tisser sa toile; **to s. a top** lancer *ou* faire tourner une toupie; **to s. a coin** jouer à pile ou face

2 = spin-dry

VI **1** *(of top etc)* tourner; *(of suspended object)* tournoyer; *(of compass)* être affolé, s'affoler; **my head's spinning** la tête me tourne; **the room's spinning** *(because I'm dizzy, drunk etc)* la pièce tourne (autour de moi); **the blow sent him spinning** le coup l'a envoyé rouler

2 *(of wheel)* patiner *(sur place)*; *Fishing* pêcher à la cuillère; **to s. for fish** pêcher, lancer

3 *Fam (of spin doctor)* manipuler l'information, présenter les choses sous un angle favorable

▸▸ *Sport* **s. bowler** = lanceur *m* qui donne de l'effet à la balle; *Pol Fam Pej* **s. doctor** = chargé *m* des relations publiques d'un parti politique

▸ **spin out** VT SEP *(prolong) (speech)* délayer;

(discussion) faire durer, prolonger; *(affair, story)* faire traîner en longueur; **to s. out one's money** économiser; **to s. out one's drink** faire durer sa boisson

▸ **spin round** VI *(turn) (of car)* faire un tête-à-queue; *(of person)* pivoter, virevolter; *(turn around sharply)* se retourner vivement, faire volte-face; **she spun round in her chair** elle pivota sur sa chaise; **to s. round and round** tournoyer, tourbillonner

VT SEP *(turn fast) (wheel, person etc)* faire tourner; *(several times) (person)* faire tournoyer

spina bifida [spaɪnə'bɪfɪdə] N *Med* spinabifida *m*

spinach ['spɪnɪtʃ] N *(plant)* épinard *m*; *Culin* épinards *mpl*

spinal ['spaɪn(ə)l] ADJ spinal, -aux, vertébral, -aux

▸▸ **s. column** colonne *f* vertébrale; *Spec* rachis *m*; **s. cord** moelle *f* épinière; **s. curvature** déviation *f* de la colonne vertébrale; **s. injury** lésion *f* de la colonne vertébrale

spindle ['spɪnd(ə)l] N **1** *Tex* fuseau *m*; **s.-shaped** fusiforme, fuselé **2** *Tech etc* arbre *m*, axe *m*, mandrin *m*; *(of potter's wheel etc)* pivot *m*; *(of axle, shaft)* fusée *f*

spindleshanks ['spɪnd(ə)lʃæŋks] N *Old-fashioned Fam (person)* grand échalas *m*

spindly ['spɪndlɪ] ADJ *(person)* maigrelet; *(legs)* grêle; *(furniture etc)* peu solide, peu robuste

spindrift ['spɪndrɪft] N embrun(s) *m(pl)*, poudrin *m*

spin-dry VT *(clothes)* (faire) essorer

spin-dryer N essoreuse *f* (centrifuge)

spin-drying N essorage *m*

spine [spaɪn] N **1** *Anat* épine *f* dorsale, colonne *f* vertébrale, *Spec* rachis *m* **2** *Geog* arête *f* **3** *(of book)* dos *m* **4** *(spike) (of plant, fish, hedgehog etc)* piquant *m*, épine *f*

spine-chiller N *(story)* histoire *f* à vous glacer le sang; *(novel, film)* roman *m*/film *m* d'épouvante

spine-chilling ADJ à vous glacer le sang

spineless ['spaɪnlɪs] ADJ **1** *(person) (lacking character)* mou, *f* molle, sans caractère; *(lacking courage)* poltron, lâche **2** *(without spines) (plant, fish etc)* sans épines, sans piquants

spinelessness ['spaɪnlɪsnɪs] N lâcheté *f*

spinet [spɪ'net] N *Mus* épinette *f*

spinnaker ['spɪnəkər] N *Naut* spinnaker *m*, spi *m*

spinner ['spɪnər] N **1** *Tex* fileur, -euse; *Fig* **s. of tales** *or* **yarns** conteur, -euse **2** *Fishing* cuillère *f* **3** *Cr (bowler)* lanceur *m* qui donne de l'effet à la balle; *(ball)* balle *f* avec de l'effet

spinneret ['spɪnəret] N *(of spider etc)* filière *f*

spinney ['spɪnɪ] N *Br* petit bois *m*, bosquet *m*

spinning ['spɪnɪŋ] ADJ tournant, tournoyant; **my s. head** ma tête qui tourne/tournait

N **1** *Tex (of wool, cotton etc)* filage *m*; *Ind* filature *f* **2** *(in fishng)* pêche *f* à la cuiller *ou* cuillère

▸▸ **s. factory** filature; **s. jenny** jenny *f*, **s. mill** filature; **s. top** toupie *f*, **s. wheel** rouet *m*

spin-off N *(advantage)* retombée *f*, avantage *m ou* bénéfice *m* supplémentaire; *(by-product)* sous-produit *m, pl* sous-produits, *(produit m)* dérivé *m*; **the film is a s. from a TV series** le film est tiré d'une série télévisée; **a s. of the Olympics was meant to be the creation of permanent jobs** on estimait qu'une des retombées des Jeux olympiques serait la création d'emplois permanents

spinster ['spɪnstər] N célibataire *f*, femme *f*/fille *f* non mariée, *Pej* vieille fille

spinsterhood ['spɪnstəhʊd] N état m de vieille fille

spiny ['spaɪnɪ] ADJ Biol, Zool épineux; (covered in spines) épineux, couvert d'épines ou de piquants
▸▸Zool s. anteater échidné m; Zool s. lobster langouste f

spiracle ['spaɪərək(ə)l] N (of whale etc) évent m; (of insect) stigmate m

spiral ['spaɪər(ə)l] N spirale f; (single curve) spire f, tour m; in a s. en spirale; wage-price or inflationary s. course f ou spirale des prix et des salaires
ADJ (motif, shell, curve) en (forme de) spirale; (descent, spring) en spirale; the plane went into a s. descent l'avion amorça une descente en vrille
VI (-ll-, Am -l-) (form a spiral) former une spirale; (turn) tourner en spirale; (rise) (of steam, smoke) s'élever en spirale; spiralling prices dérapage m des prix
▸▸s. binding reliure f à spirale; s. staircase escalier m en colimaçon
▸ spiral down VI (of plane) descendre en spirale ou en vrille; (of steps) descendre en spirale ou en colimaçon
▸ spiral up VI (of rocket etc) s'élever ou monter en spirale; (of smoke) s'élever en spirale; (of steps) monter en spirale ou en colimaçon; (of prices) monter en vrille

spirally ['spaɪərəlɪ] ADV en spirale

spire ['spaɪər] N Archit (of church) aiguille f, flèche f

SPIRIT ['spɪrɪt] N 1 (soul) esprit m, âme f; I'll be with you in s. je serai avec vous en pensée; Bible the poor in s. les pauvres d'esprit; Rel, Prov the s. is willing but the flesh is weak l'esprit est prompt, mais la chair est faible
2 (incorporeal being) esprit m; the (Holy) S. le Saint-Esprit, l'Esprit saint; evil s. esprit malin, mauvais génie m; to raise a s. évoquer un esprit; to believe in spirits croire aux esprits ou aux revenants
3 (person) esprit m; the leading s. (in undertaking) l'âme f, le chef; (of revolt) le meneur, la meneuse
4 (mood, attitude) esprit m, disposition f; the s. of the age l'esprit du siècle; the s. of liberty l'esprit de liberté; that was not the s. of the agreement ce n'était pas l'esprit de cet accord; to have the party s. avoir envie de s'amuser; to enter into the s. of sth entrer dans l'esprit de qch; to enter into the s. of the thing entrer de bon cœur dans la partie; to take sth in the right/wrong s. prendre qch bien/mal; he took it in the s. in which it was intended il l'a pris comme il fallait; Fam that's the s.! à la bonne heure!
5 (courage) caractère m, courage m; (ardour) ardeur f, entrain m; man of unbending s. homme au caractère inflexible; woman of s. (having strong character) femme de caractère; (brave) femme courageuse; to show s. montrer du caractère ou du courage; to have s. avoir de l'allant; the pianist played with more s. than skill le pianiste jouait avec plus d'ardeur que de talent; his s. was broken quelque chose s'était brisé en lui; to be in good spirits (cheerful) être gai; (in a good mood) être de bonne humeur; to be in high spirits être en train ou en verve; to be in low spirits (depressed) être abattu; (feel sad) se sentir tout triste; to keep up one's spirits ne pas perdre courage; to raise or revive sb's spirits remonter le moral à qn; their spirits rose ils reprirent courage; with s. (to say sth, react) énergiquement; ... she replied with s. ... répondit-elle avec beaucoup de verve
6 spirits (drinks) spiritueux mpl; wines and spirits vins mpl et spiritueux; methylated

spirits alcool m dénaturé ou à brûler; surgical s. alcool à 90°
VT they spirited him out of the back door ils l'ont fait sortir discrètement par la porte de derrière; to s. weapons into a building introduire des armes dans un bâtiment; the film spirits us back to 18th century France le film nous transporte dans la France du XVIIIᵉ siècle
▸▸s. gum colle f gomme; s. lamp lampe f à alcool; s. level niveau m à bulle; s. stove réchaud m à alcool; s. writing = écrits mpl dictés au médium par les esprits
▸ spirit away, spirit off VT SEP (remove secretly, quickly) (person) faire disparaître ou enlever comme par enchantement; (object) subtiliser, escamoter

spirited ['spɪrɪtɪd] ADJ 1 (person) (lively) vif, f vive, animé; (passionate) plein de fougue ou de verve; (intrepid) intrépide; (horse) fougueux 2 (style, reply etc) plein de verve; s. attack attaque pleine de fougue; s. discussion discussion vive ou animée; Mus to give a s. performance jouer avec brio ou avec verve

spiritless ['spɪrɪtlɪs] ADJ 1 (style) sans vie; (conversation etc) qui manque d'entrain 2 (person) (lacking courage, character) sans courage, sans caractère; (cowardly) lâche; (lacking vigour, passion) sans vigueur, sans ardeur; (weak) mou, f molle

spiritual ['spɪrɪtjʊəl] ADJ Rel spirituel; (not material, physical) spirituel, immatériel; s. father père m spirituel; France is my s. home la France est ma terre spirituelle; Cambridge is his s. home Cambridge, c'est la ville où il se sent chez lui; his s. home is probably 18th century Holland c'est probablement dans la Hollande du XVIIIᵉ siècle qu'il se sentirait le plus à l'aise
N Mus (negro) s. negro spiritual m, pl negro spirituals
▸▸s. life vie f spirituelle

spiritualism ['spɪrɪtjʊəlɪz(ə)m] N 1 (belief in spirits) spiritisme m 2 Phil spiritualisme m

spiritualist ['spɪrɪtjʊəlɪst] N, ADJ 1 (believing in spirits) spirite mf 2 Phil spiritualiste mf

spirituality [spɪrɪtjʊˈælɪtɪ] N (of soul, person) spiritualité f

spiritually ['spɪrɪtjʊəlɪ] ADV spirituellement

spirituous ['spɪrɪtjʊəs] ADJ Fml spiritueux, alcoolique
▸▸s. liquor alcool m fort, spiritueux m

spirt [spɜːt] N, VT & VI = spurt

spit¹ [spɪt] N 1 Culin broche f 2 Geog s. (of land) pointe f (de terre), langue f (de terre)
VT (-tt-) Culin (put on a spit) (meat etc) embrocher, mettre à la broche

spit² N 1 (saliva) salive f, (act of spitting) crachement m; he wiped the s. from his face il essuya le crachat de son visage; a gob of s. un crachat; Fam he's the s. of his father c'est son père tout craché; Fam s. and polish astiquage m, fourbissage m; a s. and sawdust bar un bar tout simple 2 (of rain) crachin m
VI (pt, pp spat [spæt]; prp spitting) (of person, cat, pen) cracher; (of fire) crépiter; (of hot fat) grésiller; to s. in sb's face, to s. at sb cracher au visage à qn; I wouldn't trust him further than I could s. je n'ai pas la moindre confiance en lui; it's spitting (with rain) il crachine, il fait du crachin
VT (saliva, blood, insults) cracher
▸ spit back VI (of engine) avoir des retours de flamme (au carburateur)
▸ spit out VT SEP (expel from mouth) cracher; (something bad) recracher; 'you're fired!', he spat out 'vous êtes viré!', lança-t-il; Fam s. it out! (say what you want to) accouche!, vide ton sac!
▸ spit up VT SEP (blood) cracher

spit³ N (depth of spade) profondeur f de fer de bêche; to dig the ground two spits deep labourer la terre à deux fers de bêche

spite [spaɪt] N 1 (malice) rancune f, (ill will) malveillance f, (pique) dépit m; from or out of s. (out of maliciousness) par pure malice ou méchanceté; he broke her toy out of pure or sheer s. il a cassé son jouet par pure méchanceté envers elle; she went to a different university out of s. (to annoy sb) elle est allée dans une autre université pour ennuyer son monde
2 in s. of ... en dépit de ..., malgré ...; in s. of everything malgré tout; in s. of the fact that I had warned her, in s. of my having warned her en dépit du fait que je l'avais prévenue, bien que je l'aie prévenue
VT (person) vexer, contrarier; he does it to s. me il le fait pour me tracasser ou m'ennuyer

spiteful ['spaɪtfʊl] ADJ méchant, malveillant; (because of a grudge) rancunier, vindicatif; s. remark observation f méchante; s. tongue langue f de vipère

spitefully ['spaɪtfəlɪ] ADV par malveillance, méchamment, par dépit ou rancune; 'that's a stupid idea', he said s. 'c'est une idée stupide', dit-il méchamment

spitefulness ['spaɪtfʊlnɪs] N méchanceté f, malveillance f, (because of grudge) rancœur f

spitfire ['spɪtfaɪər] N (person) furie f

spitroast ['spɪtrəʊst] VT Culin cuire à la broche; s. lamb agneau m à la broche

spitting ['spɪtɪŋ] N crachement m; no s. (on sign) défense de cracher; Fam within s. distance of the front door à deux pas de la porte d'entrée; Fam he's the s. image of his father c'est son père tout craché

spittle ['spɪt(ə)l] N (saliva) salive f, (of animal) bave f, she was covered in s. elle était couverte de crachats

spittoon [spɪˈtuːn] N crachoir m

spitz [spɪts] N (dog) loulou m

spiv [spɪv] N Br Fam filou m; (on black market) profiteur m ou trafiquant m du marché noir

spivvy ['spɪvɪ] ADJ Br Fam (appearance, clothes) tape-à-l'œil inv, tapageur; do I look a bit s. in this? n'ai-je pas l'air un peu filou avec ça?

splash [splæʃ] N 1 (action) (of water, molten metal) éclaboussement m; (of waves) clapotement m, clapotis m; to fall into the water with a s. tomber dans l'eau en faisant floc ou flac; Fig Fam to make a (big) s. faire sensation 2 (mark, amount) (of mud, ink etc) éclaboussure f, (of colour, light) tache f, Fam a whisky and s. un whisky soda; just a s., please (of water etc) très peu ou juste un soupçon, s'il vous plaît
INT floc!, flac!, ploc!
VT éclabousser (with water d'eau); Journ étaler; to s. water at one another se jeter de l'eau; Journ a photo was splashed across the front page une photo s'étalait en première page; to s. one's way across a river traverser une rivière en pataugeant; to s. oneself (with water etc) s'éclabousser; (with paint etc) se tacher; to s. oneself/one's face with water s'asperger/s'asperger la figure d'eau; he really splashes the aftershave on il s'asperge de lotion après-rasage
VI (of liquid) faire des éclaboussures; (of waves) clapoter; (of tap) cracher; (of person, animal) barboter, patauger
▸▸s. back (for sink etc) panneau m protecteur; s. headline manchette f, Comput s. page page f de garde; Comput s. screen splash screen m; Journ s. story sujet m à sensation
▸ splash about, splash around VT SEP

(spread by splashing) (water) faire jaillir, faire gicler; *Fam* **to s. one's money about** claquer son argent

VI *(of person, animal)* barboter, patauger

▸ **splash down** **VI** *Astronaut (land in sea)* amerrir

▸ **splash out** *Br Fam* **VI** *(spend more money than usual)* claquer des ronds; **I've splashed out on a new car** je me suis offert une nouvelle voiture; **you have been splashing out, haven't you!** tu as fait des frais *ou* des folies, dis-moi!

VT SEP **we splashed out £500 on a new camera** nous avons dépensé *ou Fam* claqué 500 livres dans un nouvel appareil-photo

▸ **splash up** **VI** *(be thrown up) (of liquid, mud etc)* gicler

VT SEP *(liquid, mud etc)* faire gicler

splashdown ['splæʃdaʊn] **N** *(of spacecraft)* amerrissage *m*

splat [splæt] **INT** floc!; **the fruit landed s. on the ground** le fruit tomba sur le sol en faisant floc

splatter ['splætər] **N** éclaboussure *f*

VT **to s. sb with mud, to s. mud over sb** éclabousser qn de boue; **blood was splattered everywhere** tout était éclaboussé de sang

VI *(of liquid)* jaillir, gicler; **the tomato splattered against the wall** la tomate a giclé sur le mur

▸▸ *Fam* **s. movie** = film *m* violent et sanglant

splay [spleɪ] **VT** *(one's fingers)* écarter; *Archit etc* **to s. the sides of a window** ébraser *ou* évaser une fenêtre; **to walk with splayed feet** marcher en canard; **splayed opening** ouverture ébrasée *ou* évasée

ADJ *(knees etc)* tourné en dehors

▸ **splay out** **VT SEP** *(spread) (one's fingers)* écarter

VI *Archit etc* s'évaser

splayfooted [spleɪ'fʊtɪd] **ADJ** *(person)* **to be s.** marcher en canard

spleen [spliːn] **N 1** *Anat* rate *f* **2** *Fml (anger)* bile *f*; **in a fit of s. ...** dans un accès de mauvaise humeur ...; **to vent one's s. on sb** décharger sa mauvaise humeur sur qn **3** *Arch, Lit (melancholy)* spleen *m*

splendid ['splendɪd] **ADJ** *(gown, occasion, view)* splendide, superbe, magnifique; *(meal)* magnifique; *(opportunity)* splendide; **we had a s. time** c'était formidable; **a policy of s. isolation** une politique isolationniste; *Fig* **he sat in s. isolation** il était assis, superbe dans sa solitude; **that's s., thanks very much!** c'est formidable, merci beaucoup!

splendidly ['splendɪdlɪ] **ADV** splendidement, magnifiquement; **s. dressed** superbement vêtu; **they got along s.** ils s'entendirent magnifiquement bien

splendiferous [splen'dɪfərəs] **ADJ** *Fam usu Hum* magnifique, rutilant

splendour, *Am* **splendor** ['splendər] **N** splendeur *f*, magnificence *f*; **the mountains in all their s.** les montagnes dans toute leur splendeur

splice [splaɪs] **N** *(in rope, cable etc)* épissure *f*, *Carp* enture *f*, *Cin (in film)* (point *m* de) collage *m*; *(in magnetic tape)* raccord *m*

VT *Naut etc (rope, cable)* épisser; *Carp (two pieces of wood)* enter; *Cin (film)* coller; *(tape)* raccorder, faire un raccord à; *Old-fashioned Fam* **to s. the mainbrace** boire un coup; *Fam* **to get spliced** *(marry)* se caser

splicer ['splaɪsər] **N** *(for tape, film)* colleuse *f*

splicing ['splaɪsɪŋ] **N** *Naut (of rope, cable)* épissage *m*; *Carp (of two pieces of wood)* enture *f*, *(of film)* collage *m*; *(of tape)* raccordement *m*

▸▸ **s. table** table *f* de montage (de films); **s. unit** presse *f* à coller

spliff [splɪf] **N** *Sl* joint *m*

splint [splɪnt] *Med* **N** attelle *f*, éclisse *f*; **to put a limb in splints** éclisser un membre

VT *(broken limb)* éclisser

splinter ['splɪntər] **N** *(of wood, glass, shrapnel)* éclat *m*; *(in finger etc)* écharde *f*, *Surg (of fractured bone)* esquille *f*; **I've got a s. in my finger** j'ai une écharde dans le doigt

VT *(something)* briser en mille morceaux; *(violently)* faire voler en éclats; *(oar, mast)* craquer

VI *(shatter)* éclater; *(violently)* voler en éclats; *(of oar, mast etc)* craquer, éclater; *(of bone)* se briser; *Fig (of political party)* éclater

▸▸ **s. group** groupe *m* dissident *ou* scissionniste

splinterproof ['splɪntəpruːf] **ADJ** *(glass)* se brisant sans éclats

SPLIT [splɪt] **N 1** *(in floorboard etc)* fente *f*, *(small)* fissure *f*, *(in rock etc)* crevasse *f*, *(in dress, robe etc)* déchirure *f*, *(in skin)* gerçure *f*

2 *(division) (in group)* division *f*, scission *f*, *(in personality)* dédoublement *m*; *(of screen)* éclatement *m*; **a three-/four-way s. (in the voting)** division en trois/quatre (de l'électorat); **there was a s. in the party over ...** il y avait une division *ou* une scission dans le parti à propos de ...; **to heal the s.** effacer les divisions

3 *(share in profits, loot etc)* part *f*, **they suggested a fifty-fifty s. of the profits** ils ont proposé de partager les bénéfices fifty-fifty

4 banana s. banana split *m inv*

5 *Gym* **to do the splits** faire le grand écart

6 *(in meaning of word etc)* distinction *f*

ADJ *(lip, skirt)* fendu; **in a s. second** en une fraction de seconde; **it only took a s. second** cela n'a demandé qu'une fraction de seconde; **to work a s. shift** avoir une journée de travail discontinue

VT *(pt, pp split; prp splitting)* **1** *(wood etc)* fendre; *(slate)* (re)fendre; *(rock etc)* cliver; *(tear)* déchirer; *Comput (file, image)* découper; **to s. one's head** s'ouvrir la tête (**on sth** sur qch); *Fam* **to s. one's sides laughing** *or* **with laughter** se tenir les côtes; *Fig* **to s. hairs** ergoter, couper les cheveux en quatre

2 *(divide) (amount of money, people into groups etc)* diviser (**into equal shares** en parts égales); **to s. sth in two** *or* **in half** *or* **down the middle** couper qch en deux; *Nucl* **to s. the atom** fissionner l'atome; **to s. a company** scinder une société; *Pol* **to s. the party** provoquer une scission dans le parti; **this s. the party three ways** ceci a divisé *ou* scindé le parti en trois; **to s. the vote** disperser les voix; **the Labour Party paid the price of a s. vote** le parti travailliste a fait les frais de la division; **to s. one's vote,** *esp Am* **to s. the ticket** partager ses votes entre plusieurs candidats; **to s. shares** fractionner des actions; **to s. a bottle** *(share)* partager une bouteille; **to s. the difference** partager la différence; *Fam* **can you s. a fiver for me?** pouvez-vous me faire la monnaie de cinq livres?

VI 1 *(of wood etc)* se fendre; *(of rock)* se cliver; *(of skin etc)* se gercer; *(of dress etc)* se déchirer; *(of seam in dress)* craquer; *Fig (of political party etc)* se scinder; *Fam* **my head's splitting** j'ai un mal de tête fou

2 *Sl (leave)* mettre les bouts

▸▸ **s. end** fourches *f* pl; **I tend to get s. ends** j'ai des cheveux qui ont tendance à fourcher; *Gram* **s. infinitive** = infinitif *m* où un adverbe ou une expression adverbiale est intercalé entre "to" et le verbe; **s. peas** pois *m* pl cassés; *Psy* **s. personality** double personalité *f*, dédoublement *m* de personalité; **he has a s. personality** il souffre d'un dédoublement de personalité; *Br* **s. pin** goupille *f* fendue; *Cin, Comput* **s. screen** écran *m* divisé; **s. second** fraction *f* de seconde

▸ **split away** **VI** = **split off** **VI**

▸ **split off** **VI** *(become detached)* se séparer, se détacher *(par clivage)*; *Fig (leave group)* se séparer

VT SEP *(break off)* détacher *(par clivage)*

▸ **split on** **VT INSEP** *Br Sl (inform on) (person)* dénoncer; *(accomplice, friend)* donner

▸ **split open** **VI** *(burst open)* se fendre, s'ouvrir

VT SEP *(break open)* ouvrir; **to s. one's head open** s'ouvrir la tête

▸ **split up** **VT SEP** **1** *(divide) (money, work, loot)* répartir, partager; *(couple, people fighting)* séparer; *(organization, party)* diviser, scinder; *(break up into several parts) (party etc)* fragmenter; **we s. the work up amongst ourselves** nous nous sommes réparti le travail; **I don't want to s. you and Joyce up** je ne veux pas te séparer de Joyce; **the police tried to s. the crowd up** la police a essayé de disperser la foule

2 *(break down, analyse) (meaning of a word)* analyser, décomposer; **it should be s. up into paragraphs** il faudrait le décomposer *ou* diviser en paragraphes; *Chem* **to s. up a compound into its elements** dédoubler un composé en ses éléments

VI *(divide)* **the compound had s. up into its elements** le composé s'était divisé en ses éléments; **the party s. up (into three groups)** le parti s'est divisé (en trois groupes); **Paul and Anne have s. up** Paul et Anne se sont séparés *ou* ont rompu; **the rock group s. up in 1992** le groupe de rock s'est séparé en 1992

split-level **ADJ** *Archit (building, room etc)* à deux niveaux

▸▸ **s. cooker** cuisinière *f* à éléments de cuisson séparés

split-second **ADJ** **with s. timing** avec un minutage réglé au dixième de seconde; **trapeze work requires s. timing** le trapèze requiert une synchronisation réglée au dixième de seconde

splitter, splitter box ['splɪtər] **N** *Aut* doubleur *m* de gamme

splitting ['splɪtɪŋ] **ADJ** *Fam* **to have a s. headache** avoir un mal de tête fou

N 1 *Nucl* **s. of the atom** fission *f* de l'atome **2** = **splitting up**

▸▸ **s. up** *(of wood)* fendage *m*; *(division)* division *f*, *(of two people)* séparation *f*, *(of political party)* scission *f*

split-up **N** *(in political party)* division *f*, scission *f*, *(of couple)* séparation *f*, rupture *f*, *(of friends)* séparation

split-view mirror **N** *Aut* rétroviseur *m* à double miroir

splodge [splɒdʒ] *Fam* **N** *(stain) (of colour, ink)* pâté *m*; *(piece) (of ice cream, ketchup etc)* plâtrée *f*

VT *(stain)* tacher, barbouiller (**with** de); **he splodged a great lump of cream on top** il balança une grosse cuillerée de chantilly par-dessus

splotch [splɒtʃ] *Fam* **N** *(of colour, ink)* pâté *m*

VT tacher, barbouiller (**with** de)

splurge [splɜːdʒ] *Fam* **N 1** *(ostentation)* esbroufe *f*, épate *f* **2** *(extravagant spending)* folles dépenses *f* pl; **I have a bit of a s. from time to time** je m'autorise quelques folies de temps en temps; **let's have a s. and give the biggest party ever** et si on claquait du fric et qu'on organisait la plus grande fête qu'on ait jamais vue

VI = **splurge out**

▸ **splurge out** **VI** *Fam (spend extravagantly)* faire des dépenses extravagantes; **to s. out on sth** faire des folies pour qch

splutter ['splʌtər] **N 1** *(speech)* bredouillement *m* **2** *(of engine)* bafouillage *m*; **the engine gave a s. and died** le moteur a toussé, puis est mort

VT *(excuse, threat)* bredouiller

VI *(of person) (because of surprise, emotion)* bafouiller; *(because of anger)* s'étrangler; *(of engine)* bafouiller; **the engine finally spluttered into life** finalement, le moteur a toussé, puis a démarré

▸ **splutter out VT SEP = splutter VT**

VI *(of fire, firework etc)* s'éteindre avec un crépitement

spoil [spɔɪl] **VT** *(pt, pp* **spoiled, spoilt** [spɔɪld, spɔɪlt]*)* **1** *(ruin) (evening, holiday, view)* gâcher; *(goods, decorations etc)* abîmer; **her hat was spoilt by the rain** son chapeau a été abîmé par la pluie; **the picnic was spoilt by the rain** le pique-nique a été gâché par la pluie; **to get spoilt** *or* **spoiled** *(of object)* s'abîmer; **to s. sb's fun** gâter *ou* gâcher le plaisir de qn; **it spoils (the beauty of) the view** ça gâche la vue; **to s. sb's appetite** couper l'appétit *ou* la faim à qn; **to s. the market** gâter le marché; **to s. the surprise** tout gâcher *(en dévoilant une surprise)*; **don't s. the surprise for me** ne me gâche pas tout; **to s. the ending of a film/book (for sb)** gâcher un film/livre (à qn) en lui révélant la fin; **spoiled goods** marchandises *fpl* avariées; *Pol* **spoilt paper** bulletin *m* nul **2** *(indulge) (person)* gâter; **a spoilt child** un enfant gâté; **we're spoilt here, not many cities have 20 theatres** nous sommes gâtés ici, peu de villes comptent 20 théâtres; **to be spoilt for choice** avoir l'embarras du choix

VI 1 *(of fruit, fish etc)* s'abîmer **2 to be spoiling for a fight** avoir envie de se battre, *Fam* chercher la bagarre

N *(usu pl)* butin *m*; *Fig* **to claim one's share of the spoil(s)** demander sa part du gâteau; **one of the spoils of war** une prise de guerre

spoilage [ˈspɔɪlɪdʒ] **N** *Typ* déchets *mpl* de tirage

spoiler [ˈspɔɪlər] **N 1** *Aviat* déporteur *m*; *Aut* béquet *m*, becquet *m*, spoiler *m* **2** *Pol etc (candidate)* = candidat *m* qui se présente dans le seul but de compromettre les chances d'un autre candidat **3** *Journ* = tactique *f* utilisée pour s'approprier le scoop d'un journal rival

spoilsport [ˈspɔɪlspɔːt] **N** *Fam* trouble-fête *mf inv*, rabat-joie *mf inv*; **don't be a s.!** ne joue pas les trouble-fête *ou* les rabat-joie!

spoke[1] [spəʊk] **N 1** *(of wheel)* rayon *m* **2** *(airport)* aéroport *m* d'apport **3** *Br Fig* **to put a s. in sb's wheel** mettre des bâtons dans les roues à qn

▸▸ **s. wheel** roue *f* à rayons

spoke[2] **PT** *see* **speak**

spoken [ˈspəʊk(ə)n] **PP** *see* **speak**

ADJ *(dialogue)* parlé, oral, -aux; **the s. word** la parole; **s. language** langue *f* parlée; **my s. French is quite good** en français, je suis assez bon à l'oral

spoken-voice ADJ *(record)* parlé

spokeshave [ˈspəʊkʃeɪv] **N** *Carp (tool)* vastringue *f*

spokesman, *pl* **spokesmen** [ˈspəʊksmən] *(of party etc)* porte-parole *m inv*; **to act as s. for sb** être le porte-parole de qn; *(on one occasion)* prendre la parole au nom de qn

spokesperson [ˈspəʊkspɜːsən] **N** porteparole *mf inv*

spokeswoman, *pl* **spokeswomen** [ˈspəʊkswʊmən, -wɪmɪn] **N** *(femme f)* porte-parole *f inv*

spoliation [spəʊlɪˈeɪʃən] **N** *Fml (despoiling)* spoliation *f*

spondaic [spɒnˈdeɪɪk] **ADJ** *(in prosody)* spondaïque

spondee [ˈspɒndiː] **N** *(in prosody)* spondée *m*

spondulicks, spondulix [spɒnˈdjuːlɪks] **NPL** *Fam* fric *m*

sponge [spʌndʒ] **N 1** *(for washing etc)*, *Zool*

éponge *f*; **to throw in the s.** *Boxing* jeter l'éponge; *Fig* s'avouer vaincu, abandonner la partie **2** *(action)* coup *m* d'éponge; **to give sth a s.** passer l'éponge sur *ou* donner un coup d'éponge à qch **3** *(cake)* gâteau *m* de Savoie

VT 1 éponger, passer l'éponge sur **2** *Fam (cadge) (meal etc)* écornifler, grappiller; **to s. sth off** *or* **from sb** chiper *ou* taper qch à qn **VI** *Fam (be parasite)* faire le parasite

▸▸ *Br* **s. bag** trousse *f ou* sac *m* de toilette; **s. bath** toilette *f* à l'éponge; **s. biscuit** ≃ madeleine *f*, **s. cake** gâteau de Savoie, génoise *f*, *Tex* **s. cloth** tissu *m* éponge; **s. fisher** pêcheur, -euse d'éponge

▸ **sponge down VT SEP** *(wash) (person)* doucher avec une éponge; *(horse)* éponger; *(car)* nettoyer à l'éponge

▸ **sponge off VT SEP** *(stain)* enlever à l'éponge

VT INSEP *Fam (parents, friends etc)* vivre aux crochets *ou* aux dépens de; **they're just sponging off the state!** ce ne sont que des parasites de l'État!

▸ **sponge on VT INSEP** *Fam* = **sponge off VT INSEP**

▸ **sponge out VT SEP** *(blood etc)* enlever à l'éponge; *(wound)* nettoyer à l'éponge

▸ **sponge up VT SEP** *(liquid)* éponger

sponger [ˈspʌndʒər] **N** *Fam* parasite *m*

sponginess [ˈspʌndʒɪnɪs] **N** spongiosité *f*, *(of cake, pastry)* moelleux *m*; *(of road surface)* caractère *m* mou; *(of soles)* souplesse *f*

spongy [ˈspʌndʒɪ] **ADJ** spongieux; *(cake, pastry)* moelleux; *(road surface)* mou, *f* molle; *(soles)* souple

sponsor [ˈspɒnsər] **N** *(for athlete, team, festival, programme, giving money)* sponsor *m*; *(introducing new member to club, for student)* parrain *m*; *(at baptism)* parrain, marraine *f*; *Law* garant *m*, répondant *m*, caution *f (* **for sb** de qn); **to stand s. to a child** *(at baptism)* tenir un enfant sur les fonts (baptismaux)

VT 1 *(athlete, team, charity walker, festival etc)* sponsoriser; *(student, candidate)* parrainer; *Radio, TV (programme)* sponsoriser, parrainer; **sponsored walk** marche *f* sponsorisée *(pour aider une œuvre de charité)* **2** *Law (act as guarantor for)* être le garant de, répondre de, se porter caution pour **3** *Rel (act as godparent to)* parrainer

Sponsored event

La Grande-Bretagne compte de très nombreuses organisations caritatives ("charities"). L'un des moyens employés pour rassembler des fonds est de s'engager auprès d'autres gens (généralement des amis, voisins et collègues de travail) à accomplir une épreuve en échange d'une somme d'argent déterminée. Il peut s'agir d'épreuves physiques ("sponsored walk", "sponsored swim") ou de défis saugrenus, tels que se rendre au bureau en pyjama ou bien encore garder le silence pendant toute une journée ("sponsored silence"). Des "sponsored events" sont également organisés par des écoles et des clubs sportifs afin d'obtenir de l'argent pour acheter du matériel.

sponsoring [ˈspɒnsərɪŋ] **N** *Mktg* parrainage *m*, mécénat *m*

sponsorship [ˈspɒnsəʃɪp] **N 1** *(of athlete, team, festival etc)*, *Radio, TV (of programme)* parrainage *m*, sponsorat *m*; *(of student, candidate)* parrainage; *Mktg* **under the s. of** sous le patronage de **2** *Law* garantie *f*, caution *f* **3** *Rel (by godparent)* parrainage *m*

▸▸ **s. agreement, s. deal** contrat *m* de sponsoring

spontaneity [spɒntəˈniːɪtɪ, -ˈneɪ-] **N** spontanéité *f*

spontaneous [spɒnˈteɪnɪəs] **ADJ** *(person, gesture)* spontané; *(act, confession)* volontaire

▸▸ **s. combustion** combustion *f* spontanée

spontaneously [spɒnˈteɪnɪəslɪ] **ADV** spontanément; **she s. offered to help** elle a spontanément proposé son aide

spoof [spuːf] *Fam* **N 1** *(play, film etc)* satire *f* *(* **on** de); **s. thriller** satire de film à sensations **2** *(trick)* blague *f*, **they erected some s. factories to fool the enemy** ils ont installé des usines factices pour tromper l'ennemi; **he sent round a s. memo about redundancies** il a fait passer une fausse circulaire *ou Fam* une circulaire bidon parlant de licenciements

VT *(parody, satirize)* parodier, caricaturer

spook [spuːk] *Fam* **N 1** *(ghost)* fantôme *m* **2** *esp Am Fam (spy)* espion, -ionne **3** *Am Offensive Sl (black man)* nègre *m*, bamboula *m*; *(black woman)* négresse *f*

VT *(startle)* foutre la trouille à; *(frighten, disturb)* donner la chair de poule à

spooky [ˈspuːkɪ] **ADJ** *Fam (story etc)* qui fait peur; *(place)* sinistre; *(strange)* dingue; **it's s. here at night** c'est sinistre ici le soir; **he's a s. sort of person** il est du genre sinistre

spool [spuːl] **N 1** *Tex* bobine *f*, can(n)ette *f*; *(of sewing machine)* can(n)ette; **s. of thread** bobine de coton (à coudre) **2** *Fishing* tambour *m* (de moulinet) **3** *Elec* (corps *m* de) bobine *f*, *Phot, Cin* bobine (de film); **take-up s.** bobine enrouleuse; **(ribbon) s.** *(for typewriter)* bobine du ruban

VT *Tex* bobiner; *Comput* spouler, mettre en (file d')attente

spooler [ˈspuːlər] **N** *Comput (for printing)* spouleur *m*, pilote *m* de mise en file d'attente

spoon [spuːn] **N 1** *(utensil)* cuillère *f*, cuiller *f*, **serving s.** cuillère de service *ou* à service **2** *Golf* bois m numéro 3, spoon *m*; *Fishing* **s. (bait), trolling s.** cuillère *f*

VT 1 *(liquid)* prendre *ou* verser à l'aide d'une cuillère; **to s. syrup/gravy onto sth** verser un sirop/une sauce sur qch à l'aide d'une cuillère; **he spooned soup into his mouth** il enfournait de grandes cuillerées de soupe **2** *Fishing* pêcher à la cuillère

VI *Old-fashioned Fam (of couple)* se faire des mamours

▸ **spoon out VT SEP** *(serve) (sauce etc)* servir (avec une cuillère)

▸ **spoon up VT SEP** *(eat)* manger à la cuillère

spoonbill [ˈspuːnbɪl] **N** *(bird)* spatule *f* (blanche)

spoonerism [ˈspuːnərɪz(ə)m] **N** contrepèterie *f*

spoon-feed VT *(pt, pp* **spoon-fed** [-fed]*)* nourrir à la cuillère; *Fig (student etc)* mâcher le travail à

spoonful [ˈspuːnfʊl] **N** cuillerée *f*

spoor [spʊər] **N** *(in hunting)* foulées *fpl*, piste *f*

sporadic [spəˈrædɪk] **ADJ** sporadique; *(showers)* épars, isolé; *(work)*, *Mil (firing)* intermittent

sporadically [spəˈrædɪk(ə)lɪ] **ADV** sporadiquement; *(to fire, work)* par intervalles, à intermittence

spore [spɔːr] **N** *Biol* spore *f*

sporran [ˈspɒrən] **N** *Scot* = aumônière *f* en cuir parfois agrémentée de fourrure, portée sur le devant du kilt

sport [spɔːt] **N 1** sport *m*; **aquatic/winter sports** sports nautiques/d'hiver **2** *Fam* **he's a (good** *or* **real) s.** *(good loser)* c'est un beau joueur; *(generous, fair, lively person)* c'est une personne sympa; **you're a real s.** tu es vraiment sympa; **a bad s.** *(bad loser)* un mauvais perdant, une mauvaise perdante; **come on, be a s.!** allez, sois sympa!; *esp Austr* **hello, (old) s.!** salut, mon vieux!

3 *Old-fashioned (amusement)* jeu *m*, divertissement *m*, amusement *m*; **in s.** pour rire, par plaisanterie; **to make s. of sth** s'amuser ou se moquer de qch; **to have good s.** *(in hunting)* faire bonne chasse; *(in fishing)* faire bonne pêche *ou* bonne prise

4 *Bot, Biol* variété *f* anormale, type *m* anormal

VT *(wear) (red waistcoat, carnation etc)* arborer

VI 1 *Old-fashioned (amuse oneself)* se divertir, s'amuser **2** *Biol, Bot (of plants, animals)* produire une variété anormale

▸▸ **sports car** voiture *f* de sport; **sports coat,** *Am* **s. coat** veste *f* sport; **sports commentator** commentateur *m* sportif; **sports correspondent** journaliste *m* sportif, journaliste *f* sportive; **sports centre** complexe *m ou* centre *m* sportif; **sports club** club *m* de sport; **sports day** = réunion *f* sportive annuelle où les parents sont invités; **sports editor** rédacteur *m* en chef sportif; **sports facilities** installations *fpl* sportives; **sports ground** terrain *m* de sport *ou* de jeux; **sports jacket,** *Am* **s. jacket** veste sport; **sports journalist** journaliste *m* sportif, journaliste *f* sportive; *Journ* **sports page** rubrique *f* sportive, page *f* des sports; **sports paper** journal *m* sportif; **sports press** presse *f* sportive; **sports programme** émission *f* sportive; **sports reporter** reporter *m* sportif; *TV etc* **sports results** résultats *mpl* sportifs; *Aut* **sports saloon** berline *f* sport; **sports shoes** trainings *mpl*; **sports shop** magasin *m* de sport

sporting ['spɔːtɪŋ] ADJ **1** *(to do with sport)* sportif **2** *(fair, reasonable)* **it's very s. of him** c'est très chic de sa part; **you've got a s. chance** tu as tes chances; **to give sb a s. chance** donner sa chance à qn; **I'll make you a s. offer** je vais vous faire une offre honnête; **in a s. spirit** avec un esprit sportif **3** *Old-fashioned (fond of hunting or fishing)* amateur de chasse/de pêche

▸▸ **s. event** manifestation *f* sportive; **s. man, s. woman** *(horseracing enthusiast)* turfiste *mf*

sportingly ['spɔːtɪŋlɪ] ADV sportivement

sportive ['spɔːtɪv] ADJ *Old-fashioned (joking)* badin; *(playful)* folâtre

sportscast ['spɔːtskɑːst] N *Am Radio, TV* émission *f* sportive

sportscaster ['spɔːtskɑːstər] N *Am Radio, TV* journaliste *m* sportif, journaliste *f* sportive

sportsman, *pl* **sportsmen** ['spɔːtsmən] N **1** *(player)* sportif *m*; *(hunter)* chasseur *m*; *(angler)* pêcheur *m* **2** **he's a real s.** *(fair-minded person)* il a l'esprit sportif; *(good loser)* il est beau joueur

sportsmanlike ['spɔːtsmənlaɪk] ADJ sportif; **in a s. way** sportivement

sportsmanship ['spɔːtsmənʃɪp] N **1** *(skill)* habileté *f ou* qualités *fpl* de sportif **2** *(fairmindedness)* esprit *m* sportif, sportivité *f*

sportsperson ['spɔːtspɜːsən] N *(player)* sportif, -ive

sportswear ['spɔːtsweər] N vêtements *mpl* de sport

sportswoman, *pl* **sportswomen** ['spɔːtswʊmən, -wɪmɪn] N *(player)* sportive *f*

sporty ['spɔːtɪ] ADJ *Fam* **1** *(fond of sport)* sportif **2** *(jacket etc)* gai; *(car)* sportif; **it's a bit too s.** c'est un peu trop sport

---

SPOT [spɒt]

N endroit **1**	▪ lieu **1**	▪ tache **2**
▪ bouton **3**	▪ pois **4**	▪ point **4**
▪ goutte **5**	▪ projecteur **6**	▪ numéro **7**
▪ créneau **7**		
VT tacher **1**	▪ repérer **2**	
VI pleuvioter		

N 1 *(place)* endroit *m*, lieu *m*; **a remote s.** un endroit écarté *ou* isolé; **beauty s.** site *m* touristique; *Aut* **a black s.** *(on road)* un point noir; **an unemployment black s.** une zone particulièrement touchée par le chômage; **X marks the s.** *(of crime etc)* la croix indique le lieu; **the police are on the s.** la police est sur les lieux; **to have sb on the s.** *(reporter, representative, agent etc)* avoir qn sur place; **our reporter on the s., Mary Smith** notre correspondant sur place, Mary Smith; *Fam* **to put sb on the s.** *(put in difficult position)* mettre qn dans une situation difficile; *(force to answer difficult question)* embarrasser qn par des questions; **to be fined on the s.** recevoir une amende sur-le-champ; **to do sth on the s.** *(straightaway)* faire qch sur place *ou* sur-le-champ; **to be killed on the s.** être tué sur le coup, être tué net; *Fam* **her performance failed to hit the high spots** sa représentation n'a pas été brillante; *Fam* **to be in a (tight) s.** *(in predicament)* être dans le pétrin; *Fam* **to get into a bit of a s.** se ficher dans le pétrin; **night s.** boîte *f* de nuit; **weak s.** point faible; **to find sb's weak s.** trouver le défaut dans la cuirasse de qn, trouver le point faible de qn; **blind s.** *Anat* point aveugle; *Aut* angle *m* mort; *(in road)* endroit *m* sans visibilité; *Fam* **that's your blind s.** c'est là où vous refusez de voir clair; **I have a blind s. about maths** je ne comprends rien aux mathématiques

2 *(stain)* tache *f*, macule *f*; *(on fruit etc)* tavelure *f*

3 *(pimple)* bouton *m*; **to come out in spots** se couvrir de boutons; **it makes me come out in spots** ça me donne des boutons

4 *(dot) (of colour) (on shirt, tie etc)* pois *m*; *(on playing card, domino)* point *m*; *Billiards* mouche *f*; **blue tie with red spots** cravate bleue à pois rouges; **a leopard's spots** la tacheture *ou* la moucheture du léopard; *Fam* **to knock spots off sb** *(beat)* battre qn à plate(s) couture(s); **she knocks spots off him** *(is much better than)* il ne lui arrive pas à la cheville; **the new Peugeot knocks spots off the ...** face à la nouvelle Peugeot, le ... ne fait pas le poids; *Med* **a s. on the lung** un voile au poumon

5 *Br Fam (small amount) (of rain, wine)* goutte *f*, **a s. of whisky** une larme de whisky; **what about a s. of lunch?** si nous déjeunions?; **to do a s. of work** faire un peu de travail; **a s. of bother** *or* **trouble** un petit ennui; **to get into a s. of bother** s'attirer des ennuis

6 *(spotlight), Theat* projecteur *m*; *(in home, on exhibition stand)* spot *m*

7 *TV, Radio (for artist, interviewee)* numéro *m*; *(time reserved for adverts, specific commentator)* créneau *m*; **he got a s. on the Margie Warner show** *(as singer, comedian)* il a fait un numéro dans le show de Margie Warner; *(interview)* il s'est fait interviewer *ou* il est passé dans le show de Margie Warner

VT (**-tt-**) **1** *(mark with spots)* tacher, moucheter; *(stain, mark)* tacher, souiller; *Billiards (ball)* mettre sur la mouche

2 *(notice) (person, object)* repérer, apercevoir; *Horseracing etc (winner)* prédire, repérer; *Mil (enemy positions etc)* repérer, observer; *(trains etc)* repérer; *(talent)* dénicher; **to s. sb doing sth** apercevoir qn en train de faire qch; **I spotted her in the crowd** je l'ai repérée au milieu de la foule; **to s. a**

mistake détecter une erreur; **to s. an opportunity** repérer une occasion; **well spotted!** *(when noticing mistake)* bien vu!; *(when finding sb in crowd)* quel œil!; **I'd never have spotted it** je ne l'aurais jamais remarqué; **she was last spotted in the pub** la dernière fois qu'on l'a vue, elle était au pub; **I spotted him as a potential troublemaker** j'ai très vite repéré qu'il était un agitateur

VI it's spotting (with rain) il pleuviote

▸▸ *Fin* **s. buying** achat *m* au comptant; *Br* **s. cash** argent *m* liquide; **s. check** *(investigation)* contrôle *m* surprise; *(for quality)* contrôle par sondage; *(by customs)* fouille *f* au hasard; *Fin* **s. deal** opération *f ou* transaction *f* au comptant; *Geog* **s. height** altitude *f*; *Fin* **s. market** marché *m* au comptant; **s. news** brève *f*; *Fin* **s. price** cours *m* spot; *Fin* **s. rate** cours à vue, cours spot; *Fin* **s. trading** négociations *fpl* au comptant; *Fin* **s. transaction** opération *ou* transaction *f* au comptant

spot-check VT *(randomly)* contrôler par sondage(s); *(at random intervals)* contrôler à intervalles irréguliers; *(without notice)* faire des contrôles surprises; **athletes are regularly spot-checked for anabolic steroids** on effectue souvent des contrôles surprises sur les athlètes pour détecter les anabolisants

spotless ['spɒtlɪs] ADJ *(shirt, reputation)* sans tache, immaculé; *(house, kitchen)* impeccable

spotlessly ['spɒtlɪslɪ] ADV **s. clean** impeccable; **s. white** d'une blancheur immaculée *ou* parfaite

spotlessness ['spɒtlɪsnɪs] N propreté *f*

spotlight ['spɒtlaɪt] N *Theat, Cin (beam)* lumière *f* de projecteur; *(device)* spot *m*, projecteur *m* (à faisceau concentré); *(in home, on exhibition stand etc)* spot; *Aut* projecteur auxiliaire orientable; **to hold the s.** *Theat* occuper le centre de la scène *(dans la lumière du projecteur)*; *Fig* avoir *ou* tenir la vedette; *Fig* **she has always been in** *or* **has never been out of the s.** elle n'a pas cessé de tenir la vedette *ou* d'être sur la sellette

VT *(person, object), Theat* diriger les projecteurs sur; *Fig* mettre en vedette

spotlighting ['spɒtlaɪtɪŋ] N *(in home), Theat, Cin* éclairage *m* à effet

spot-on *Fam* ADJ exact, au point; **that's s.** c'est exact; **his answer was s.** sa réponse était parfaitement exacte *ou* correcte; **the missiles were s.** les missiles ont atterri en plein dans le mille

ADV *(guess)* en plein dans le mille; **he timed it s.** il a calculé son coup à la seconde près

INT *(excellent)* super!, génial!

spotter ['spɒtər] N *Mil, Aviat* observateur *m*; **train s.** = personne *f* qui regarde passer des trains *(pour repérer les différents modèles)*; **talent s.** dénicheur, -euse de talent

▸▸ **s. plane** avion *m* d'observation

spotting ['spɒtɪŋ] N **train/plane s.** repérage *m* de trains/d'avions

spotty ['spɒtɪ] ADJ **1** *(marked with spots)* moucheté, tacheté; *(covered with stains)* plein de taches **2** *(pimply) (face, person)* couvert de boutons, boutonneux; **a s. adolescent** un adolescent boutonneux

N *Fam* **hi there, s.!** salut, le boutonneux/la boutonneuse!

spot-weld VT souder par points

N soudure *f* par points

spot-welding N soudure *f* par points

spouse [spaʊz, spaʊs] N *Admin, Law* conjoint, -ointe; *Arch, Lit* époux *m*, épouse *f*

spout [spaʊt] N **1** *(of teapot, kettle etc)* bec *m*; *(of watering can)* canon *m*, goulot *m*; *(of whale)* évent *m*; *Constr* **rainwater s.** *(of gutter)* tuyau *m* de décharge, gargouille *f*, chan-

tepleure *f*; *Sl* **to be up the s.** *(ruined)* être fichu *ou* foutu; *(pregnant)* être en cloque; **our plans are up the s.** nos projets sont tombés à l'eau; **now we're really up the s.** maintenant nous sommes vraiment dans de beaux draps *ou* dans le pétrin **2** *(jet of liquid)* jet *m*; **a s. of water shot up** un jet d'eau partit **vi 1** *(of liquid)* jaillir, rejaillir; *(more forcefully)* gicler; *(of whale)* lancer un jet d'eau/d'air, souffler **2** *Fig Fam (of person)* parler à jet continu, dégoiser; **what's he spouting on about now?** qu'est-ce qu'il est en train de débiter maintenant?
vt 1 *(of person) (water etc)* faire jaillir, lancer; **the pipe spouted water everywhere** de l'eau jaillissait du tuyau **2** *Fig Fam (speech, nonsense)* dégoiser *ou* débiter à jet continu
▸▸**s. hole** *(of whale)* évent
▸ **spout out vi** *(of water, lava etc)* jaillir, sortir en giclant; **the liquid was spouting out of the barrel** le liquide sortait du tonneau en giclant, le liquide jaillissait du tonneau
vt sep 1 *(lava)* cracher; **the pipe spouted out water** de l'eau jaillissait du tuyau et éclaboussait partout **2** *Fig Fam (utter) (statistics etc)* débiter

sprain [spreɪn] **n** *Med* entorse *f*, *(less serious)* foulure *f*
vt *(ankle, wrist)* se fouler; *(more seriously)* se faire une entorse à; **sprained ankle** foulure *f* à la cheville; *(more serious)* entorse *f* à la cheville

sprang **pt** *see* **spring vi, vt**

sprat [spræt] **n** *(fish)* sprat *m*, harenguet *m*

sprawl [sprɔːl] **n 1** *(position)* position *f* affalée **2** *(of houses etc)* étendue *f*; **an urban s.** une agglomération
vi 1 *(of person)* s'affaler, s'étaler; **he was lying sprawled (out) on the sofa** il était affalé sur le divan; **to send sb sprawling** faire tomber qn de tout son long; **to go sprawling** s'étaler par terre **2** *(of town etc)* s'étendre de tous les côtés; *(of plant)* s'étendre, se déployer

sprawling [ˈsprɔːlɪŋ] **adj 1** *(person)* affalé **2** *(suburbs, plants)* tentaculaire; **s. handwriting** écriture *f* irrégulière et étalée

spray¹ [spreɪ] **n** *(of plant)* brin *m*, ramille *f*; **s. of flowers** branche *f* de fleurs, rameau *m* fleuri; *Archit, Sewing etc* chute *f* de fleurs; **s. of diamonds** aigrette *f* de diamants

spray² **n 1** *(liquid) (of seawater)* embrun *m*, poudrin *m*; *(water in particles)* poussière *f* d'eau, eau *f* vaporisée; *(of perfume, fuel etc)* jet *m* atomisé *ou* pulvérisé; *(for hair)* spray *m* coiffant, laque *f*
2 *(act of spraying)* coup *m* de vaporisateur; *(of perfume, paint etc)* jet *m*; **to give sth a s.** *(fields, roses etc)* pulvériser qch; *(walls etc)* peindre qch au pistolet; *(hair)* mettre du spray *ou* de la laque sur qch
3 *(device) (for hair spray, paint etc)* bombe *f*, *(non-gas operated)* atomiseur *m*, vaporisateur *m*; **deodorant s.** désodorisant *m* atomiseur; **perfume s.** atomiseur à parfum; **fly s.** atomiseur *ou* bombe insecticide
vt 1 *(perfume, hair conditioner, deodorant)* atomiser, vaporiser; *(paint, chemicals)* pulvériser; **he sprayed water all over me** il m'a aspergé d'eau; **to s. a solution up one's nostrils** se vaporiser un liquide dans le nez; *Ind* **to s. dry** sécher par atomisation; **slogan sprayed on a wall** slogan écrit à la bombe sur un mur; **this liquid is sprayed on the oil slick** ce liquide est pulvérisé sur le pétrole; **three layers of paint are sprayed onto the metal** on passe trois couches de peinture au pistolet sur le métal
2 *(cover with spray)* asperger, arroser; *(plants etc)* bassiner; *(tree)* passer au vaporisateur; *(with paint-sprayer)* peindre au pistolet; **she sprays her hair in position** elle se

coiffe en se mettant du spray; **to s. the crops/the fields** pulvériser les récoltes/champs; **to s. sth with machine-gun fire** mitrailler qch
vi **water sprayed up in our faces** de l'eau éclaboussait nos visages
▸▸**s. can** *(for aerosol)* bombe, aérosol *m*; *(refillable)* vaporisateur; *Ind* **s. drying** *(of milk etc)* séchage *m* par atomisation; **s. gun** *(for paint)* pistolet *m* (à peinture); **s. nozzle** gicleur *m*; **s. paint** peinture *f* en bombe; **a can of s. paint** une bombe de peinture

sprayer [ˈspreɪər] **n 1** vaporisateur *m*, pulvérisateur *m*; *(for paint)* pistolet *m* **2** *(vehicle, plane)* arroseuse *f*

SPREAD [spred]

n étendue **1**	▪ diffusion **2**
▪ propagation **2**	▪ pâte à tartiner **5**
vt étendre **1, 3**	▪ tendre **1** ▪ déployer
1 ▪ répandre **2**	▪ propager **2** ▪ étaler
3 ▪ enduire **4**	
vi s'étendre **1, 2**	▪ se répandre **2** ▪ se
propager **2**	▪ s'étaler **3**

n 1 *(of land etc)* étendue *f*, *(of wings, sails etc)* envergure *f*, *Com (between two rates)* différence *f*, *(in interest rates)* différentiel *m* de taux d'intérêt; *St Exch* écart *m*; *Am (ranch)* ranch *m*; *St Exch* **s. of investments** diversification *f* des placements; **we have a good s. of products** *(range)* nous avons un bel éventail *ou* une belle gamme de produits
2 *(expansion) (of education)* diffusion *f*, *(of doctrine, disease)* propagation *f*, *(of ideas)* expansion *f*, dissémination *f*
3 *Fam (big meal)* festin *m*, repas *m* somptueux; **cold s.** repas froid
4 *Journ etc* double page *f*, *(advertisement)* double page publicitaire
5 *Culin* pâte *f* à tartiner; **cheese s.** fromage *m* à tartiner; **chocolate s.** chocolat *m* à tartiner
vt *(pt, pp spread)* **1** *(one's arms etc)* étendre; *(net)* tendre; *(sails)* déployer; *(one's fingers)* écarter; **a bird with its wings s.** un oiseau aux ailes étendues; **to s. one's wings** *(of bird)*, *Fig* déployer ses ailes
2 *(distribute) (sand, straw)* répandre; *(manure, fertilizer)* épandre; *(terror)* semer; *(news)* répandre, rapporter; *(lies etc)* colporter; *(disease)* propager; **to s. sb's fame (abroad)** faire connaître la réputation de qn; *Fig* **he's in danger of spreading himself too thin** il risque de faire trop de choses à la fois; **the payments are s. over several months** les paiements sont échelonnés *ou* étalés *ou* répartis sur plusieurs mois; **if we can s. the work over three months** si nous pouvons répartir le travail sur trois mois; **could you s. the word?** voulez-vous passer le mot?
3 *(apply)* **to s. butter on a slice of bread** étendre *ou* étaler du beurre sur une tranche de pain, tartiner une tranche de pain de beurre; **to s. ointment on a burn** appliquer *ou* mettre de la pommade sur une brûlure; **to s. the paint evenly** étendre *ou* étaler la peinture en couches égales
4 **to s. a surface with sth** recouvrir *ou* enduire une surface de qch; *Am Old-fashioned* **to s. the table** dresser *ou* mettre la table, mettre le couvert
vi 1 *(stretch) (of forest, city, suburbs)* s'étendre, s'étaler; *(of desert)* s'étendre
2 *(of rumour, news, ideas etc)* se répandre, se propager; *(of disease, fire, theory, epidemic etc)* se propager, s'étendre (**to** à, jusqu'à); *(of smell, smoke, sound)* se répandre (**throughout** dans); *(of fame)* s'étendre (**throughout** dans); *(of cancer)* se généraliser; *(of evil)* s'étendre, se généraliser; *(of group of people)* se disperser; **the fire is**

spreading l'incendie gagne; **her ideas are spreading** ses idées font tache d'huile
3 *(of butter, paste, cheese etc)* s'étaler; **it spreads easily** c'est facile à tartiner
▸▸**s. betting** = système *m* de paris portant sur le résultat d'un événement sportif ou autre, où les gains sont proportionnels à la justesse des prédictions, selon une fourchette de résultats préétablie; **s. eagle** *Her* aigle *f* éployée; *(in skating)* grand aigle *m*
▸ **spread about, spread around vt sep 1** *(rumour, disease etc)* répandre; **have you been spreading it around that I'm pregnant?** est-ce que tu as été raconter partout que je suis enceinte?
2 *Euph* **he spreads himself about a bit** *(is promiscuous)* il couche à droite et à gauche
▸ **spread out vt sep 1** *(open out) (map etc)* déployer, étaler; **the plain lay s. out in front of us** la plaine s'étalait *ou* se déployait devant nous; **a bird with its wings s. out** un oiseau aux ailes déployées; **to s. oneself out** *(on sofa etc)* s'étendre, s'allonger; **he s. his papers out on the desk** il étala ses papiers sur le bureau
2 *(space out in time) (deliveries, payments)* échelonner; **to s. out over several financial years** étaler sur plusieurs exercices
vi *(of person) (on sofa etc)* s'étendre, s'allonger; *(of troops, rescue party etc)* se disperser; **give yourself room to s. out** *(doing craft work etc)* accordez-vous de l'espace pour vous étaler

spread-eagled [-ˈiːg(ə)ld] **adj** étalé de tout son long

spreader [ˈspredər] **n 1** *(person) (of idea)* propagateur, -trice; *(of news)* rapporteur, -euse; *(of rumour)* colporteur, -euse, propagateur, -trice **2** *Agr, Constr* épandeur *m*, épandeuse *f*, *(for putty, plaster etc)* spatule *f*

spreading [ˈspredɪŋ] **adj** **under a s. chestnut tree** sous un châtaignier bien déployé
n *(act of spreading) (of lies)* colportage *m*; *(of disease, doctrine, rumours)* propagation *f*, *(of ideas)* dissémination *f*, *(of paint etc)* étendage *m*

spreadsheet [ˈspredʃiːt] **n** *Comput* feuille *f* de calcul; *(software)* tableur *m*

spree [spriː] **n** nouba *f*; **to have a s., to go (out) on a s.** faire la nouba; **to go on a shopping** *or* **spending s.** aller claquer son argent dans les magasins; **a s. of looting** des saccages

sprig [sprɪg] **n** brin *m*

sprightliness [ˈspraɪtlɪnɪs] **n** vivacité *f*

sprightly [ˈspraɪtlɪ] **adj** *(person, tune)* vif, *f* vive; *(old person)* alerte, fringant; **her s. commentary on current events** ses commentaires pétillants sur l'actualité; **he's very s. for 80** il est très fringant pour ses 80 ans

spring [sprɪŋ] **n 1** *(of water)* source *f*, *Fig Lit (of custom etc)* source, origine *f*, **hot** *or* **thermal s.** source thermale; **hot** *or* **thermal springs** eaux thermales; **mineral s.** source d'eau minérale
2 *(season)* printemps *m*; **in (the) s.** au printemps; **a lovely s. evening** une belle soirée de printemps; **to have s. fever** être amoureux, *Can* avoir la fièvre du printemps; **s. flowers** fleurs printanières VOIR GRAMMAIRE A7
3 *(leap)* saut *m*, bond *m*
4 *(elasticity)* élasticité *f*, **the s. of a bow** la force *ou* la souplesse d'un arc; **with a s. in his step** d'un pas léger; **the s. had gone out of her step** sa démarche avait perdu de sa souplesse; *Carp* **there's too much s. in this type of wood** ce type de bois est trop souple
5 *(device)* ressort *m*; **(watch) s.** ressort (de montre); **springs, s. suspension** *(of car etc)* suspension *f* à ressort(s)

VI (*pt* **sprang** [spræŋ]; *pp* **sprung** [sprʌŋ]) **1** (*jump*) bondir, sauter; **to s. to one's feet** se lever vivement *ou* d'un bond; **to s. into action** (*of person*) passer à l'action; **he sprang into life when I mentioned the subject** il a semblé revivre quand j'ai mentionné le sujet; **the engine sprang to life** le moteur partit d'un coup; **to s. to sb's defence** (*in words*) prendre vivement la défense de qn; (*in case of assault etc*) se précipiter pour porter secours à qn; **the lid sprang open** le couvercle a sauté; **the door sprang open** la porte s'est ouverte d'un coup; **the lever springs out** le levier sort tout d'un coup; **to s. into public view** être propulsé sur la scène publique; **he sprang to fame overnight** il est devenu célèbre du jour au lendemain; **they sprang to attention** d'un bond, ils se mirent au garde-à-vous; **one thing that immediately springs to mind is ...** une chose qui vient immédiatement à l'esprit est ...; *Lit* **a tear sprang to her eye** une larme surgit dans ses yeux; *Lit* **an oath sprang to his lips** un juron lui est monté aux lèvres

2 (*to originate, come into being*) **to s. from** venir de, provenir de; **hope springs eternal** l'espérance reste toujours vivace; **to s. into existence** surgir, apparaître soudain; *Fam* **where did you s. from?** d'où sortez-vous?

3 (*warp*) (*of wood*) gauchir, se déformer, se déjeter
VT **1 to s. a leak** faire une voie d'eau
2 (*partridge etc*) (faire) lever
3 (*trap*) faire jouer; (*mine*) faire sauter
4 (*car*) munir de ressorts; **sprung carriage** voiture suspendue
5 *Fam* (*help to escape from prison*) faire échapper de prison
▸▸ *Br* **s. balance** peson *m* à ressort; *Culin* **s. chicken** poussin *m*; *Fam Fig* **she's no s. chicken** elle n'est plus toute jeune; **s. lock** serrure *f* à fermeture automatique; **s. mattress** matelas *m* à ressorts; *Br* **s. onion** petit oignon *m*; **s. roll** rouleau *m* de printemps; **s. tide** grande marée *f*, (*at equinox*) marée d'équinoxe (de printemps); **s. vegetables** primeurs *fpl*; **s. water** eau *f* de source
▸ **spring back** VI (*move back suddenly*) (*of object*) se redresser, repartir en arrière; **the branch sprang back** la branche s'est redressée; **she sprang back in horror** elle recula d'un bond, horrifiée
▸ **spring forward** VI (*rush forward*) s'élancer *ou* se précipiter en avant
▸ **spring on** VT SEP (*confront with*) **to s. a question on sb** (*unexpectedly*) poser à qn une question inattendue; (*point-blank*) poser une question à brûle-pourpoint à qn; **to s. a surprise on sb** faire une surprise à qn; **I wish you wouldn't s. things on me like that** (*without warning*) j'aimerais bien que tu arrêtes de me prendre par surprise; **sorry to have to s. this on you** désolé de vous demander ça à la dernière minute
▸ **spring up** VI **1** (*jump to one's feet*) se lever vivement *ou* d'un bond **2** (*appear suddenly*) **a breeze sprang up** une brise s'est levée; **an intimacy sprang up between them** l'intimité naquit entre eux; **a doubt sprang up in his mind** un doute a germé dans son esprit; **the company sprang up almost overnight** la société s'est montée quasiment du jour au lendemain; **to (begin to) s. up** (*of plant etc*) (commencer à) pousser; **McDonalds are springing up all over the place** les McDonald poussent partout comme des champignons

springboard ['sprɪŋbɔːd] N *Gym, Swimming, Fig* tremplin *m*

springbok ['sprɪŋbɒk] N (*antelope*) springbok *m*

spring-clean N nettoyage *m* de prin-

temps; **to give a house a s.** faire le nettoyage de printemps dans une maison
VT (*house*) nettoyer à fond
VI faire le nettoyage de printemps, *Can* faire le grand ménage

spring-cleaning N grand nettoyage *m* de printemps

springe [sprɪndʒ] N (*snare*) lacet *m*, collet *m*

springer ['sprɪŋər] N (*dog*) springer *m*
▸▸ **s. spaniel** springer

springiness ['sprɪŋɪnɪs] N effet *m* de ressort; (*of hair*) gonflant *m*; (*of mattress*) élasticité *f*; (*of turf, ground*) souplesse *f*

springing ['sprɪŋɪŋ] N (*of car, bed*) suspension *f*

springless ['sprɪŋlɪs] ADJ *Tech* sans ressort(s)

springlike ['sprɪŋlaɪk] ADJ (*weather etc*) de printemps; (*dress*) printanier, -ère

spring-loaded ADJ à ressort

springtide ['sprɪŋtaɪd] N *Lit* = **springtime** N

springtime ['sprɪŋtaɪm] N printemps *m*; **in s.** au printemps
ADJ ATTRIB (*weather, feeling*) printanier, -ère

springy ['sprɪŋɪ] ADJ élastique, qui fait ressort; (*brake pedal*) flexible; (*carpet*) moelleux; (*wood*) élastique; (*hair*) qui ont du volume; **with a s. step** (*to walk*) d'un pas léger

sprinkle ['sprɪŋk(ə)l] VT (*cake, pie etc*) (*with sugar, salt etc*) saupoudrer (**with sth** de qch); (*with liquid*) arroser légèrement (**with sth** de qch); **to s. the floor with sand** répandre du sable par terre; **he should s. a few well-known names in the text** il devrait introduire quelques noms fameux par-ci par-là dans le texte; **a house or two was sprinkled here and there on the hillside** quelques maisons étaient éparpillées sur la colline
N (*of salt, sugar, nutmeg etc*) pincée *f*, **a s. of rain** quelques gouttes *fpl* de pluie

sprinkler ['sprɪŋklər] N **1** (*for lawns etc*) arroseur *m*; (**rotary**) **s.** arroseur (rotatif); (**fire**) **s.** (*extinguisher*) extincteur *m* (automatique) d'incendie **2** *Rel* goupillon *m*, aspersoir *m* **3** (*for sugar*) saupoudreuse *f*
▸▸ **s. head** (*of shower*) pommeau *m*; (*of watering can*) pomme *f*, (*buried in ground*) arroseur; **s. system** installation *f* d'extinction automatique d'incendie, installation sprinkler

sprinkling ['sprɪŋklɪŋ] N **1** (*action*) (*with sugar etc*) saupoudrage *m*; (*with water*) arrosage *m* léger; *Rel* **s. of holy water** aspergès *m*, aspersion *f* **2** (*quantity*) (*of nutmeg, sugar etc*) pincée *f*, **a s. of gravel** une légère couche de gravier; **a s. of knowledge** quelques connaissances; **with a liberal s. of literary references** avec moult références littéraires données ici et là; **with a larger than usual s. of mistakes** avec çà et là encore plus de fautes que d'habitude; **a s. of new faces in the congregation** quelques nouvelles têtes ici et là dans la congrégation; **there was now a s. of grey among the auburn hair** il y avait maintenant quelques fils d'argent dans la chevelure auburn
▸▸ *Am* **s. can** arrosoir *m*

sprint [sprɪnt] N *Sport* sprint *m*; (*acceleration, spurt*) pointe *f* de vitesse; *Sport, Fig Fam* **to put on a s.** (*run*) piquer un sprint; **you'll need to put on a bit of a s. if you're going to finish that translation in time** il va falloir que tu passes la seconde si tu veux finir cette traduction à temps; **there was a s. finish** il y a eu un sprint à l'arrivée; **he has a good s. finish** il est très rapide dans les sprints de fins de courses
VI *Sport* sprinter; **I was good at sprinting** j'étais bon dans les courses de vitesse; **to s. past sb** sprinter pour dépasser qn; **the little boy sprinted off** le petit garçon s'élança à

toutes jambes; **he sprinted upstairs** il est monté en courant; **he sprinted after her** il a couru derrière elle à toute vitesse; **I had to s. for the bus** j'ai dû courir *ou Fam* piquer un sprint pour attraper le bus

sprinter ['sprɪntər] N *Sport* sprinter *m*

sprite [spraɪt] N lutin *m*, esprit *m* (follet), farfadet *m*

sprocket ['sprɒkɪt] N *Tech* **1** (*cog*) dent *f* (de pignon) **2** (*wheel*) pignon *m*
▸▸ **s. hole** (*for film*) perforation *f*, **s. wheel** pignon

sprog [sprɒg] N *Sl* (*child*) môme *mf*, gosse *mf*

sprout [spraʊt] N *Bot* **1** (*shoot*) pousse *f* **2** (**Brussels**) **sprouts** choux *mpl* de Bruxelles
VI **1** (*of plant*) pousser; (*of branch, shrub*) bourgeonner; (*of seed*) germer **2** = **sprout up**
VT **1 to s. horns** (*of animal*) pousser des cornes; *Fam* **to s. a moustache** se laisser pousser la moustache **2** (*seeds*) faire germer
▸ **sprout up** VI (*of plants*), *Fam* (*of child*) pousser; *Fig* (*of new buildings, towns etc*) pousser comme un champignon/des champignons; (*of new community, sect*) surgir, naître

spruce[1] [spruːs] ADJ (*person*) (très) soigné, tiré à quatre épingles; (*house, room*) (très) soigné, bien entretenu
▸ **spruce up** VT SEP (*make neat*) (*house, room*) donner de l'éclat à; **to s. oneself up** se faire beau/belle; **all spruced up** sur son trente et un

spruce[2] N (*tree*) épicéa *m*; **Norway s.** sapin *m* de Norvège
▸▸ **s. fir** (*sapin*) épicéa

spruceness ['spruːsnɪs] N (*of person*) mise *f* soignée; (*of house, room etc*) propreté *f*

sprung [sprʌŋ] ADJ (*mattress etc*) à ressorts
PP *see* **spring** VI, VT

spry [spraɪ] ADJ (*comp* **spryer**, *superl* **spryest**) vif, *f* vive, actif, plein d'allant

spud [spʌd] N **1** *Fam* (*potato*) patate *f* **2** (*weeding hoe*) sarcloir *m*
▸▸ *Mil Sl* **s. bashing** corvée *f* de patates, (corvée de) pluches *fpl*

spume [spjuːm] N *Arch, Lit* (*of sea*) écume *f*

spun [spʌn] ADJ filé
PT, PP *see* **spin**[2] VT, VI
▸▸ **s. silk** schappe *f*, *Culin* **s. sugar** sucre *m* filé

spunk [spʌŋk] N **1** *Old-fashioned Fam* (*courage*) cran *m*; **to have plenty of s.** avoir du cran **2** *Br Vulg* (*semen*) foutre *m*

spunky ['spʌŋkɪ] ADJ *Fam* **1** *Old-fashioned* (*brave*) courageux, qui a du cran **2** *Br, Austr* (*attractive*) canon

spur [spɜːr] N **1** (*for riding*) éperon *m*; *Fig* **to win one's spurs** faire ses preuves **2** *Fig* (*stimulus*) stimulant *m*; **this hope was the s. that drove her on** cet espoir fut l'aiguillon qui la fit aller de l'avant; **to do sth on the s. of the moment** faire qch sous l'impulsion du moment *ou* sur un coup de tête; **it was a s.-of-the-moment decision** j'ai pris/il a pris/*etc* cette décision sur un coup de tête **3** (*of cock*) ergot *m*; (*of fighting cock*) éperon *m* **4** *Geog* éperon *m*, contrefort *m*; (*of railway line*) épi *m*; (*to motorway*) bretelle *f* d'accès, voie *f* d'accélération **5** *Bot* éperon *m*
VT (-**rr**-) (*horse*) éperonner, talonner; *Fig* **to s. sb into action** pousser qn à agir; **booted and spurred** botté et éperonné
▸ **spur on** VT SEP **1** (*horse*) éperonner, talonner **2** *Fig* (*motivate*) aiguillonner, stimuler; **spurred on by a desire to ...** stimulé *ou* aiguillonné par un désir de ...; **this spurred us on to redouble our efforts** ceci nous a stimulés et fait redoubler d'efforts

spurge [spɜːdʒ] N (*plant*) euphorbe *f*, épurge *f*

spurious ['spjʊərɪəs] ADJ *(false)* faux, *f* fausse; *(argument, objection)* non valable; *(distinction, reasoning)* douteux; *(writings)* apocryphe; *(edition)* de contrefaçon

spuriously ['spjʊərɪəslɪ] ADV faussement

spuriousness ['spjʊərɪəsnɪs] N fausseté *f* (**of** de); *(of distinction)* non-validité *f*; *(of text)* caractère *m* apocryphe

spurn [spɜːn] VT *(offer)* rejeter avec mépris; *(person, person's advances)* repousser avec mépris; **she's feeling spurned** *(by lover, boyfriend)* elle se sent rejetée

spurt [spɜːt] N **1** *(of liquid)* jaillissement *m*, jet *m*, giclée *f* **2** *(sudden effort)* effort *m* soudain; *(burst of energy)* poussée *f* d'énergie; *Sport (of speed)* effort de vitesse; *Cycling Fam* emballage *m*; **a s. of anger/jealousy** un bref moment de colère/jalousie; **a s. of energy** une poussée d'énergie; **to put on a s.** *(when running)* démarrer; *Cycling Fam* emballer; *(in work etc)* donner un coup de collier; **there's been a sudden s. of activity** il y a eu un regain d'activité; **she tends to work in spurts** elle a tendance à travailler par à-coups; *Sport* **final s.** pointe *f* finale, rush *m*
▮ VI **1** *(of liquid)* jaillir, gicler **2** *Sport* produire son effort; **she spurted past the other competitors** elle a produit son effort et a dépassé les autres concurrents; **he spurted into the lead** *Sport* il a produit son effort et s'est placé en tête de la course; *Fig* il est soudain venu se placer en tête
▮ VT *(of person)* *(liquid)* faire jaillir, faire gicler; *(of fountain pen)* gicler; **the pipe spurted water everywhere** de l'eau jaillissait du tuyau et éclaboussait partout; **the pen spurted ink onto the carpet** l'encre jaillit du stylo et tacha la moquette
▸ **spurt out** VI = **spurt** VI **1**
  VT SEP = **spurt** VT

sputnik ['spʊtnɪk] N *Astronaut* spoutnik *m*

sputter ['spʌtər] VT *(say while spitting saliva)* dire en lançant des postillons
▮ VI *(mumble)* bredouiller; *(talk while spitting saliva)* lancer des postillons en parlant; *Aut (of engine)* tousser; *(of pen)* fuir irrégulièrement; *(of kindling wood)* pétiller; *(of meat on grill, candle)* grésiller; *(of flame)* grésiller, crépiter; **the engine sputtered into life** le moteur toussa avant de démarrer
▸ **sputter out** VI *(stop burning)* **the candle sputtered out** la bougie s'est éteinte en grésillant

sputum, *pl* **sputa** ['spjuːtəm, -ə] N *Med* crachat *m*

spy, *pl* **spies** [spaɪ, spaɪz] N *Pol, Ind* espion, -ionne; *(for police, prison warden etc)* Fam mouchard, -arde; **another s. scandal would ruin us** la découverte d'un autre espion et le scandale qui en résulterait équivaudrait à notre perte
▮ VI espionner; **to s. on sb** épier *ou* espionner qn; **I had the feeling I was being spied on all the time** j'avais l'impression qu'on m'épiait tout le temps
▮ VT *(notice)* apercevoir, voir
▸▸ **s. network** réseau *m* d'espionnage; **s. plane** avion-espion *m*, *pl* avions-espions; **s. ring** réseau d'espionnage; **s. satellite** satellite *m* espion, *pl* satellites-espions
▸ **spy out** VT SEP **to s. out the land** explorer le terrain

spyglass ['spaɪɡlɑːs] N *Old-fashioned* lunette *f* d'approche, longue-vue *f*, *pl* longues-vues

spyhole ['spaɪhəʊl] N *(in wall, floor)* trou *m*; *(in door)* judas *m*

spying ['spaɪɪŋ] N espionnage *m*

spyware ['spaɪweər] N *Comput* logiciel *m* espion

Sq *(abbr* **Square)** place, square

---

sq *(abbr* **square)** carré

sq. ft. *(abbr* **square foot/feet)** pied(s) carré(s)

SQL [eskjuː'el] N *Comput abbr* **structured query language**

SQL engine N *Comput* processeur *m* SQL

Sqn. Ldr. *Br Mil, Aviat abbr* **Squadron Leader**

squab [skwɒb] N **1** *(young pigeon)* pigeonneau *m* sans plumes **2** *Br Aut* coussin *m*

squabble ['skwɒb(ə)l] N querelle *f*, chamaillerie *f*
▮ VI se quereller, se chamailler (**with** avec)

squabbler ['skwɒblər] N querelleur, -euse, chamailleur, -euse

squabbling ['skwɒblɪŋ] N querelles *fpl*, chamailleries *fpl*

squad [skwɒd] N **1** *(of workmen etc)* brigade *f*, équipe *f*; *Sport* équipe *f*; **rescue s.** équipe de secours **2** *Mil* escouade *f*; **firing s.** peloton *m* d'exécution
▸▸ **s. car** voiture *f* de patrouille de police

squaddie ['skwɒdɪ] N *Br Fam (private soldier)* bidasse *m*

squadron ['skwɒdrən] N **1** *Mil, Aviat* escadron *m*; **fighter/bomber s.** escadron de chasse/bombardiers **2** *Naut* escadre *f*
▸▸ *Br* **s. leader** *(in air force)* ≃ commandant *m*, *Belg, Can* ≃ major *m*

squalid ['skwɒlɪd] ADJ *(dirty)* sale; *(sordid)* sordide

squalidly ['skwɒlɪdlɪ] ADV de façon sordide

squalidness ['skwɒlɪdnɪs] N = **squalor**

squall [skwɔːl] N **1** *(cry)* cri *m* rauque *ou* discordant **2** *(gust)* bourrasque *f*, rafale *f*, *Naut* grain *m*
▮ VI *(cry)* crier, *Fam* brailler

squalling ['skwɔːlɪŋ] ADJ criard, *Fam* braillard
▮ N criaillerie *f*

squally ['skwɔːlɪ] ADJ *(weather)* à rafales; *Naut* à grains; **it's s. today** il y des bourrasques *ou Naut* des grains aujourd'hui

squalor ['skwɒlər] N *(dirtiness)* saleté *f*, *(poverty)* misère *f*; **to die in s.** mourir dans la misère

squander ['skwɒndər] VT *(money, time), Fig (talents)* gaspiller; *(fortune)* dissiper, dilapider, *Fam* claquer; *Fig (natural resources)* dilapider

squandering ['skwɒndərɪŋ] N *(of money, time)* gaspillage *m*; *(of fortune)* dissipation *f*

SQUARE [skweər]

N carré **1, 2** ▪ case **1** ▪ place **1** ▪ square **3** ▪ équerre **4**	
ADJ carré **1** ▪ catégorique **2** ▪ quitte **2** ▪ honnête **2** ▪ ringard **3**	
ADV à angle droit **1** ▪ honnêtement **2**	
VT régler **2** ▪ élever au carré **5** ▪ quadriller **6**	
VI s'accorder	

N 1 *(shape) (of chocolate etc), Geom* carré *m*; *(on chessboard etc)* case *f*; *(on map)* carreau-module *m*, *pl* carreaux-modules; **to divide a map into squares** quadriller une carte; **to fold sth into a s.** plier qch en carré; *Fig* **to be back at s. one** être revenu à son point de départ; *Fig* **let's start again from s. one** repartons du point de départ; *(in relationship)* repartons à zéro; **(silk) s.** carré *ou* foulard *m* (de soie)
2 *Math (of number)* carré *m*; **magic s.** carré magique
3 *(of town, village)* place *f*; *(with garden)* square *m*; *Mil* terrain *m* de manœuvre(s)
4 *(for drawing, measuring angles)* équerre *f*; **set s.** équerre à dessin; **to cut sth on the s.** couper qch à angles droits; **out of s.** qui n'est pas d'équerre
5 *Fam* ringard, -arde

ADJ 1 *(figure, shoulders, neckline), Naut (sail), Math (metre, centimetre etc)* carré; **nine metres s.** de neuf mètres sur neuf, de neuf mètres au carré; **nine s. metres** neuf mètres carrés; **a s. mile** = 2,5 kilomètres carrés; *Fig* **to be a s. peg in a round hole** ne pas être à sa place [VOIR GRAMMAIRE B59]
2 *Fig (refusal, denial)* net, *f* nette, catégorique; *(meal)* copieux; **what he needs is a good s. meal** tout ce dont il a besoin, c'est d'un vrai repas; **to get things s.** *(arrange)* arranger les choses; *(put in order)* mettre tout en ordre; **to make an account s.** régler un compte; **to be s. with sb** être quitte envers qn; **they are (all) s.** *(in competition)* ils sont à égalité; *(debts to each other have been paid)* ils sont quittes; **to get s. with sb** *(get even)* régler son compte à qn; *(settle bills etc)* être quitte envers qn; **to get things s. with sb** *(arrange matters)* arranger les choses avec qn; **a s. deal** une affaire honnête; **he always gives you a s. deal** il est toujours loyal en affaires
3 *Fam* ringard; **you're so s.** qu'est-ce que tu peux être ringard
ADV 1 *(at right angles)* à angle droit; *Tech* d'équerre (**to, with** avec); **set s. upon its base** d'aplomb sur sa base; **he hit him (fair and) s. on the jaw** il l'a frappé en plein sur le menton
2 *(to act)* honnêtement; **fair and s.** loyalement, carrément
VT 1 *(block of marble, wood)* carrer, équarrir
2 *(account)* régler; **to s. accounts with sb** *(pay money owed)* régler (ses comptes avec) qn; *(get revenge)* régler son compte à qn; **to s. matters** arranger les choses; **to s. one's practice with one's principles** accorder ses actions avec ses principes; **how do you s. it with your conscience?** comment arrangez-vous cela avec votre conscience?; **it's OK, I'll s. it with him** ça va, j'arrangerai ça avec lui
3 *Fam (bribe)* acheter, soudoyer, *Fam* graisser la patte à
4 *Geom, Fig* **to s. the circle** faire la quadrature du cercle; **it's like squaring the circle** c'est la quadrature du cercle
5 *Math (number, expression)* élever *ou* mettre au carré; **four squared** quatre au carré
6 *(divide into squares) (sheet of paper)* quadriller; **squared paper** papier quadrillé *ou* à carreaux
7 *Sport* **to s. the match** *(of team, player)* égaliser; **that goal squares the match** avec ce but, ils ont égalisé
VI 1 **the end and the side should s. with each other** le bout et le côté doivent se raccorder
2 *(coincide)* s'accorder (**with** avec); **the theory does not s. with the facts** la théorie ne correspond pas aux faits
▸▸ *Typ* **s. brackets** *(right-angled)* crochets *mpl*; **s. corner** coin *m* à angle droit; **s. dance** quadrille *m*, *Can* danse *f* carrée; *Fam* **s. eyes** *(person)* téléphage *m*; **s. measure** mesure *f* de surface *ou* de superficie; **the S. Mile** = City de Londres *(dont la superficie fait environ un mile carré)*; **s. number** carré *m*; *Naut* **s. rigger** navire *m* gréé en carré; **s. root** racine *f* carrée; **s. ruler** carrelet *m*, règle *f* quadrangulaire; *Am Fam* **s. shooter** personne *f* franche; *Electron* **s. wave** onde *f* carrée *ou* rectangulaire
▸ **square away** VT SEP *Am (tidy) (books)* ranger; *(room)* arranger
▸ **square off** VT SEP **1** *(divide into squares) (sheet of paper)* quadriller
2 *Carp etc (make square) (end of a plank)* mettre d'équerre, équarrir
▮ VI *esp Am (assume fighting position)* se mettre en position de combat
▸ **square up** VI **1** *(settle debts)* régler ses dettes *ou* comptes; **can we s. up later?** pouvons-nous nous arranger *ou* faire nos

comptes plus tard?; **to s. up with sb** (*pay money owed*) régler (ses comptes avec) qn; *Fig* (*get even with*) se venger de qn, régler son compte à qn

2 (*face up*) **to s. up to the difficulties/to sb** faire face aux difficultés/à qn

3 (*assume fighting position*) se mettre en position de combat

4 *Am Fam* (*of criminal*) raccrocher, se ranger des voitures; (*of drug addict*) décrocher

▸ **VT SEP** *Carp etc* (*make square*) (*end of plank*) mettre d'équerre, équarrir

─────

square-bashing N *Br Mil Sl* ≃ exercice *m*

square-built ADJ (*person*) aux épaules carrées; (*short and sturdy*) trapu; (*building*) carré

square-headed ADJ à tête carrée

squarely ['skweəlɪ] ADV **1** (*directly*) carrément; **look me s. in the eyes** regarde-moi bien dans les yeux; **stand it s. on its base** placez-le bien en équilibre sur son socle **2** (*honestly*) carrément, honnêtement; (*to act*) loyalement

squareness ['skweənɪs] N **1** (*shape*) forme *f* carrée **2** *Fam* (*of person, views*) conservatisme *m*

square-shouldered [-'ʃəʊldəd] ADJ aux épaules carrées

square-toed ADJ (*shoes*) à bout carré

squaring ['skweərɪŋ] N **1** (*of account*) règlement *m* **2 the s. of the circle** la quadrature du cercle

squash[1] [skwɒʃ] N **1** (*crush*) **there was a dreadful s. at the doors** la foule s'écrasait aux portes; **it was a s., but everyone got in the car** nous étions serrés comme des sardines mais tout le monde a tenu dans la voiture **2** (*crowd*) cohue *f* **3** *Br* **orange/lemon s.** (*concentrate, drink*) sirop *m* d'orange/de citron **4** *Sport* squash *m*

▸ **VT** écraser, aplatir; *Fig* (*revolt etc*) écraser, étouffer; *Fig* (*person*) remettre à sa place, rembarrer; *Fig* **she looked rather squashed** (*humiliated*) elle avait l'air plutôt dépité

▸ **VI** (*become squashed*) s'écraser, s'aplatir; **to s. into a room/car** se serrer dans une pièce/voiture

▸▸ *Sport* **s. court** court *m* de squash; *Old-fashioned* **s. hat** chapeau *m* mou; *Br Sport* **s. rackets** squash

▸ **squash up VI** (*sit, stand together closely*) se serrer

▸ **VT SEP** écraser

squash[2] N (*vegetable*) courge *f*

squashy ['skwɒʃɪ] ADJ (*fruit*) trop mûr; (*easily squashed*) qui s'écrase facilement; (*ground*) bourbeux, détrempé

squat [skwɒt] VI (-tt-) **1** (*crouch down*) s'accroupir; (*of animal*) se tapir; **she was squatting by the fire** elle était accroupie au coin du feu **2** (*occupy house illegally*) squatter; **to s. on a piece of land** occuper un terrain illégalement

▸ **VT** (*occupy illegally*) (*house*) squatter

▸ N **1** (*posture*) posture *f* accroupie **2** (*place*) squat *m*

▸ ADJ (*person*) ramassé, trapu; (*object, building etc*) écrasé; (*arc*) surbaissé

squatter ['skwɒtər] N squatter *m*

squaw [skwɔː] N squaw *f*

squawk [skwɔːk] N **1** (*of bird*), *Fam* (*of person*) cri *m* rauque; **a s. of protest** un tollé; **to give a s. of outrage** pousser un cri d'indignation **2** *Am Fam* (*complaint*) rouspétance *f*; **what's your s.?** c'est quoi ton problème?

▸ **VI 1** (*of bird*) pousser des cris rauques; *Fam* (*of person, baby*) brailler; **to s. with rage/in protest** pousser des cris de rage/en signe de protestation **2** *Fam* (*complain*) rouspéter **3** *Sl* (*inform*) moucharder

▸▸ *Am Fam* **s. box** (*loudspeaker*) haut-

parleur *m*, *pl* haut-parleurs; (*intercom*) interphone *m*; (*telephone*) bigophone *m*

squeak [skwiːk] N **1** (*noise*) (*of animal, person*) couinement *m*, cri *m* aigu; (*of unoiled door, wheel etc*) grincement *m*; **to let out a s.** pousser un couinement; *Fam* **I don't want to hear another s. out of you** je ne veux pas entendre le moindre murmure **2** *Fam* **that was a near** or **narrow s.!** nous l'avons/il l'a/etc échappé belle!

▸ **VI** (*of animal*) couiner; (*of person*) pousser des cris aigus, couiner; (*of machine part etc*) grincer; (*of shoes*) crisser

▸ **VT** crier d'une petite voix aiguë

squeaking ['skwiːkɪŋ] N (*of animal*) couinements *mpl*; (*of door etc*) grincement *m*

squeaky ['skwiːkɪ] ADJ (*floorboard, bed, hinge*) grinçant; (*voice*) aigu, -uë; *Fam* **s. clean** (*hands, hair*) extrêmement propre; (*image, reputation*) sans tache

squeal [skwiːl] N cri *m* aigu; (*of animal*) cri perçant; (*of brakes*) grincement *m*; (*of tyres*) crissement *m*

▸ **VI 1** (*scream*) pousser des cris aigus, couiner; (*of tyres*) crisser; (*of brakes*) grincer; **to s. like a stuck pig** crier comme un porc qu'on égorge **2** *Fam* (*complain*) protester, jeter les hauts cris **3** *Sl* (*inform*) moucharder; **to s. on sb** dénoncer qn

▸ **VT** crier d'une voix aiguë ou perçante

squealer ['skwiːlər] N *Sl* (*informer*) mouchard, -arde

squealing ['skwiːlɪŋ] N cris *mpl* aigus; (*of tyres*) crissement *m*; (*of brakes*) grincement *m*

squeamish ['skwiːmɪʃ] ADJ sensible, *Fam* chochotte; **to feel s.** avoir des nausées, avoir mal au cœur; **it makes me feel s.** ça me donne mal au cœur; **I'm s. about seeing blood** je ne supporte pas la vue du sang; **don't be so s.!** ne fais pas le dégoûté!, *Fam* ne fais pas ta chochotte!

▸ **NPL the s.** les petites natures *fpl*; **this programme/film is not for the s.** cette émission/ce film est réservé à ceux qui ont l'estomac bien accroché

squeamishness ['skwiːmɪʃnɪs] N sensibilité *f*

squeegee ['skwiːdʒiː] N **1** (*mop*) balai *m* en caoutchouc; (*for window cleaning*) racloir *m* (avec bordure de caoutchouc) **2** *Phot etc* raclette *f*; **roller s.** rouleau *m* en caoutchouc

SQUEEZE [skwiːz] N **1** (*pressure*) compression *f*, (*of hand*) serrement *m*; (*hug*) étreinte *f*, **a s. of lemon** quelques gouttes *fpl* de citron; **to give sth a s.** (*toothpaste*) serrer qch; (*cloth*) essorer qch; (*lemon*) presser qch; **to give sb's hand a s.** serrer la main à qn; **to give sb a s.** serrer qn dans ses bras; **credit s.** restriction *f* de crédit; *Fam* **to put the s. on sb** mettre la pression sur qn; **to put the s. on prices/wages** bloquer les prix/salaires; **it'll be a s. but I think we should all fit in** on sera serrés mais je crois que tout le monde tiendra; **it was a tight s.** (*but we fitted in*) on tenait tout juste; **it's something of a s. getting into these jeans** quelle gymnastique pour enfiler ce jean!; *Fam* **(main) s.** (*boyfriend*) mec *m*, Jules *m*; (*girlfriend*) nana *f*, gonzesse *f*

2 (*in bridge*) squeeze *m*

▸ **VT 1** (*sponge, lemon*) presser; (*hug*) (*person*) embrasser, étreindre; (*wring*) (*cloth*) essorer; **to s. sb's hand** serrer la main à qn; **to s. the life out of sb** (*of bear, person*) étouffer qn; **to s. liquid out of sth** faire sortir un liquide de qch; **to s. the water out of a sponge** essorer une éponge; **to s. the juice out of a lemon** extraire le jus d'un citron; **to s. sth into a box** faire entrer qch de force dans une boîte; **he squeezed his way under the fence** il s'est glissé ou faufilé sous le grillage; **to s.**

prices/wages bloquer les prix/salaires; **I think we can just s. you in** (*find time for in schedule etc*) je crois qu'on pourra vous trouver un petit moment; (*in class, car etc*) je crois qu'on pourra vous trouver une petite place; **to s. money out of sb** extorquer de l'argent à qn

2 *Fig* (*put pressure on*) pressurer; **we'll have to s. him a bit harder** il va falloir qu'on augmente encore la pression sur lui; **to s. the working class/rich** pressurer les classes ouvrières/les riches; **the British car industry has been squeezed by foreign competition** l'industrie automobile britannique subit la pression de la concurrence étrangère

▸ **VI to s. into a crowded train** entrer de force dans un train bondé; **to find a little parking space to s. into** trouver une petite place de parking où se faufiler; **any room for one more to s. in?** y a-t-il encore une toute petite place?; **we squeezed under the fence** nous nous sommes glissés ou faufilés sous le grillage

▸ **squeeze out VT SEP** (*juice etc*) extraire; **to s. out a tear** y aller de sa (petite) larme; *Fam* **they're trying to s. me out** (*off company board etc*) ils essaient de se débarrasser de moi

▸ **squeeze through VI** se faufiler, se glisser

▸ **VT INSEP to s. through a narrow window** se glisser par une fenêtre étroite

▸ **squeeze up VI** (*sit, stand together closely*) **to s. up (together)** se serrer (les uns contre les autres); **s. up a bit so Jane can sit down** serrez-vous un peu pour que Jane puisse s'asseoir

─────

squeezebox ['skwiːzbɒks] N *Fam* accordéon *m*, concertina *m*

squeezer ['skwiːzər] N presse *f*, **lemon s.** presse-citron *m inv*

squelch [skweltʃ] N (*of mud*) bruit *m* de succion; (*of wet shoes etc*) gargouillement *m*, gargouillis *m*

▸ **VI to s. through the mud** patauger dans la boue; **they squelched across the muddy farmyard** ils ont traversé la cour de la ferme en pataugeant; **the water squelched in his shoes** l'eau gargouillait dans ses chaussures

squib [skwɪb] N **1** (*firework*) pétard *m*, serpenteau *m*; *Fig* **to be a damp s.** faire l'effet d'un pétard mouillé **2** (*satire*) satire *f*, brocard *m*

squid [skwɪd] N calmar *m*, calamar *m*

squiffy ['skwɪfɪ] ADJ *Old-fashioned Br Fam* un peu ivre, gris, éméché

squiggle ['skwɪg(ə)l] N (*mark, line*) trait *m* ou ligne *f* en paraphe; (*writing*) gribouillis *m*

squiggly ['skwɪglɪ] ADJ tortueux, -euse, sinueux, -euse

squillion ['skwɪljən] N *Br Fam Hum* **squillions (of)** une foultitude (de), une ribambelle (de)

squint [skwɪnt] N **1** (*eye defect*) strabisme *m*; **he has a slight s.** il louche légèrement **2** (*sideways glance*) regard *m* de côté ou de travers; **I had a s. at his paper** j'ai jeté un coup d'œil oblique sur son journal; *Fam* **let's have a s. at it!** faites voir!

▸ ADJ **1** (*eyes*) louche **2** *Fam* (*crooked*) de travers, *Fam* de traviole

▸ **VI 1** (*have eye defect*) loucher **2** (*look through half-closed eyes*) plisser les yeux; **they're all squinting because of the sun** ils font tous la grimace à cause du soleil **3** (*look sideways*) **to s. at sb/sth** regarder qn/qch de côté ou de travers ou furtivement

squint-eyed ADJ au regard louche

squinting ['skwɪntɪŋ] N strabisme *m*

squire ['skwaɪər] N **1** *Br* (*local landowner*) châtelain *m* **2** *Hist* (*attendant to knight*) écuyer *m* **3** *Br Fam* **evening, s.** 'soir, patron

▸ **VT** (*lady*) servir de cavalier à, escorter

squirearchy ['skwaɪərɑːkɪ] **N** classe *f* des châtelains

squirm [skwɜːm] **VI** *(of worm etc)* se tordre, se tortiller; *(with embarrassment)* être très mal à l'aise; **he was squirming with embarrassment** il se tordait d'embarras; **to s. with delight** se tortiller de joie; **to s. out of a situation** se sortir d'une situation; **to s. out of one's commitments** se défiler de ses obligations; **his over-politeness makes me s.** sa politesse excessive me met extrêmement mal à l'aise; **the sight of all that blood made me s.** tout ce sang m'a donné la nausée
VT to s. one's way out of a situation se sortir d'une situation; **to s. one's way out of one's commitments** se défiler de ses obligations
N *(of pain etc)* tortillement *m*

squirrel ['skwɪr(ə)l] **N 1** *(animal)* écureuil *m* **2** *Fig (hoarder)* **she's a real s.** c'est une vraie fourmi
▸ **squirrel away VT SEP** mettre de côté

squirrelly ['skwɪr(ə)lɪ] **ADJ** *Am Fam (eccentric)* loufedingue

squirt [skwɜːt] **N 1** *(of liquid)* jet *m*, giclée *f*; **to add a s. of soda** ajouter une giclée d'eau de Seltz; **to give sb a s. with a water pistol** arroser qn avec un pistolet à eau **2** *Fam (insignificant person)* morveux, -euse, péteux, -euse
VT *(liquid etc)* faire gicler; **to s. soda water into a glass** mettre une giclée d'eau de Seltz dans un verre; **he squirted a little deodorant under each arm** il se vaporisa du déodorant sur chaque aisselle
VI *(of liquid etc)* gicler, jaillir; **water was squirting out everywhere** l'eau giclait de partout

squish [skwɪʃ] *Fam* **N** *(sound)* bruit *m* d'écrabouillement; **the s. of mud underfoot** le gargouillement de la boue sous les pieds
VT *(squash)* écraser
VI **the mud squished beneath his feet** la boue gargouillait sous ses pieds

squishy ['skwɪʃɪ] **ADJ** *Fam (ground)* détrempé; *(fruit etc)* mou, *f* molle; **the ground's s. underfoot** le sol gargouille sous les pas

squits [skwɪts] **NPL** *Br Fam* **the s.** la courante

Sr *(abbr* **Senior***)* Sr

SRAM ['esræm] **N** *Comput (abbr* **static random access memory***)* mémoire *f* vive statique

Sri Lanka [sriː'læŋkə] **N** Sri Lanka *m*

Sri Lankan [sriː'læŋkən] **ADJ** srilankais
N Sri Lankais, -aise

SRN [esɑːr'en] **N** *Br Med abbr* **State Registered Nurse**

SS [es'es] **N** *Naut (abbr* **steamship***)* = initiales précédant le nom des navires de la marine marchande; **the SS Normandie** le Normandie

S-shaped **ADJ** en S; **S. hook** crochet *m* en S

SSL [eses'el] **N** *Comput (abbr* **secure sockets layer***)* protocole *m* SSL

SSN **N** *abbr* **social security number**

SSSI ['eses'es'aɪ, 'trɪpələs'aɪ] **N** *(abbr* **Site of Special Scientific Interest***)* = en Grande-Bretagne, site *m* déclaré d'intérêt scientifique

St 1 *(abbr* **Street***)* rue **2** *(abbr* **Saint***)* S(t), *f* Ste

st *(abbr* **stone***)* = 6,35 kg

stab [stæb] **N 1** *(with dagger)* coup *m* de poignard; *(with knife)* coup de couteau; *Fig* **s. in the back** coup de Jarnac, attaque *f* déloyale; **s. of pain** élancement *m*; **a s. of remorse/envy** une pointe de remords/de jalousie; *(with knife)* coup(s) de couteau; **he had severe s. wounds in the chest** il était dans un état grave, ayant reçu des coups de couteau dans la poitrine
2 *Fam (attempt)* **to have a s. at sth** essayer

de faire qch; **I'll have a s.** je vais essayer
VT *(-bb-) (person) (with dagger)* poignarder; *(with knife)* donner un coup/des coups de couteau à; **to s. sb with a fork/pair of scissors** donner un coup/des coups de fourchette/ciseaux à qn; **to s. sb to death** tuer qn à coups de couteau, poignarder qn; **to s. sb in the back** poignarder qn dans le dos; *Fig* tirer dans le dos de qn; **he's been stabbed** il a été poignardé; **he stabbed his knife into the tabletop** il planta son couteau dans la table; **she stabbed a piece of sausage with her fork** elle piqua un morceau de saucisse avec sa fourchette
VI to s. at sb *(with knife)* porter un coup de couteau à qn; *(with dagger)* porter un coup de poignard à qn; **he stabbed at the map with his finger** il a indiqué un point sur la carte avec son doigt; **to s. at sb with one's finger** menacer qn du doigt

stabbing ['stæbɪŋ] **ADJ** *(pain)* lancinant
N *(act) (with dagger)* coups *mpl* de poignard; *(with knife)* coups de couteau; *(murder)* meurtre *m* à coups de couteau; *(attack)* coup(s) de couteau; **there was a s. in the pub last night** quelqu'un s'est fait poignarder au pub hier soir; **to die in a s.** mourir poignardé; **the number of stabbings has increased** le nombre d'attaques à l'arme blanche est en hausse

stability [stə'bɪlɪtɪ] **N** *(of building)* stabilité *f*, solidité *f*; *(economic, of aircraft, chemical compound etc)* stabilité; **mental s.** équilibre *m* mental

stabilization [steɪbɪlaɪ'zeɪʃən] **N** *(of economy, aircraft)*, *Phys, Elec* stabilisation
▸▸ *Econ* **s. fund** fonds *m* de stabilisation

stabilize ['steɪbɪlaɪz] **VT** *(economy, ship, exchange rate)* stabiliser
VI se stabiliser

stabilizer ['steɪbɪlaɪzər] **N 1** *Naut* stabilisateur *m*; *Aviat* stabilisateur, empennage *m* **2** *(on bicycle)* stabilisateur **m 3** *(in foodstuffs, explosives etc)* stabilisant *m*
▸▸ *Aut* **s. bar** barre *f* stabilisatrice

stabilizing ['steɪbɪlaɪzɪŋ] **ADJ** stabilisateur, -trice; **to have** *or* **exert a s. effect on prices** exercer une action stabilisatrice sur les prix; **her new job had a s. effect on her** son nouvel emploi a eu un effet stabilisateur *ou* équilibrant sur elle
▸▸ **s. agent** *(in foodstuffs)* agent *m* stabilisant

stable¹ ['steɪb(ə)l] **N 1** *(building)* écurie *f*; *Fig* **to lock the s. door after the horse has bolted** fermer la cage quand les oiseaux se sont envolés **2** *(horses)* chevaux *mpl* *(d'une certaine écurie)*; *Horseracing, Aut etc* écurie *f*; *Fig (of boxers, film stars)* équipe *f*; *(of publications, newspapers)* empire *m*; **racing s.** écurie de courses; **s. companion** *or* **mate** *(horse)* cheval *m* de la même écurie; *Fig (person) (in sport, film)* membre *m* de la même équipe; **they are political s. mates** ils partagent les mêmes idées politiques
VT *(horse)* loger dans une écurie; **we can s. three horses** nous avons de la place pour trois chevaux

Note that the French word **étable** is a false friend and is never a translation for the English word **stable**. It means **cowshed**.

stable² **ADJ 1** *(steady) (marriage, job, surface, economy, political situation)*, *Chem, Phys* stable; *(ground, stairs, stepladders)* solide; **s. currency** monnaie stable; **the government is becoming more s.** le gouvernement se stabilise; **to be in a s. condition** *(of patient)* être dans un état stationnaire; **s. state** état stable, état de stabilité **2** *(well-balanced) (person)* équilibré; **he's perfectly s.** il est parfaitement équilibré; **he's not s.** il n'est pas équilibré, il est instable

stableboy ['steɪblbɔɪ] **N** garçon *m* d'écurie
stablelad ['steɪblæd] **N** lad *m*

stabling ['steɪblɪŋ] **N 1** *(of horses)* logement *m* dans une écurie **2** *(space in stables)* **we have plenty of s.** nous ne manquons pas de place aux écuries

staccato [stə'kɑːtəʊ] *Mus* **ADJ** *(note)* staccato; *Fig (style, dialogue of play)* haché; *(voice)* saccadé
ADV staccato
N staccato *m*; **she replied in a rapid s.** elle répondit d'un ton rapide et saccadé

stache [stæʃ] **N** *Am Fam (moustache)* bacchantes *fpl*, moustagache *f*

stack [stæk] **N 1** *(of hay etc)* meule *f*, *(of wood, coal, plates etc)* pile *f*, tas *m*; *(of weapons)* faisceau *m*; **stacks** *(in library)* rayonnages *mpl*
2 *Fam* **stacks of ...** *(a lot of)* des tas de ..., beaucoup de ...; **I've stacks of work to do** j'ai plein de boulot; **I've got stacks of things to read** j'ai une tonne de choses à lire; **we've got stacks of time** on a largement le temps; **to make stacks of money** ramasser l'argent à la pelle; **stacks** *or* **a s. of letters/complaints** des tonnes de courrier/plaintes
3 *(of chimney)* souche *f*, corps *m*; *(of locomotive etc)* cheminée *f*
4 *Geog (rock formation)* haut rocher *m* *(au large d'une côte)*
5 *Aviat (aircraft waiting to land)* = avions *mpl* dans le ciel en attente d'un créneau d'atterrissage
6 *Comput* pile *f*
VT1 *(put in stacks) (hay)* mettre en meule(s); *(wood, coal, plates etc)* empiler, entasser; *(weapons)* mettre en faisceaux; **the odds were stacked against them** tout était contre eux; *Sl* **a woman stacked the way she is** une femme roulée comme elle
2 *Am* **to s. the cards** tricher aux cartes; **the jury was stacked against him** le jury avait un parti pris contre lui
3 *Aviat (aircraft waiting to land)* mettre en attente d'atterrissage
4 *(fill) (shelf, room)* bourrer
▸▸ **s. room** *(in library)* réserve *f*
▸ **stack up VT SEP** *(objects, books etc)* empiler

stacker ['stækər] **N** *(on printer)* dispositif *m* d'alimentation feuille à feuille; *(for output)* récepteur *m* (de sortie d'imprimante)

stacking chairs ['stækɪŋ] **NPL** chaises *fpl* superposables

stadium, *pl* **stadiums, stadia** ['steɪdɪəm, -ɪəmz, -ɪə] **N** *Sport etc* stade *m*

staff [stɑːf] **N 1** *(stick)* bâton *m*; *(of banner, lance)* hampe *f*; *(of bishop)* crosse *f*; *Naut (of flag)* mât *m*; *(in surveying)* mire *f*; *Am* **at half s.** *(of flag)* en berne; *Lit* **the s. of life** *(bread)* le pain
2 *(personnel, employees)* personnel *m*; **when he joined the s.** quand il est entré dans le personnel; **how many people are there on the s.?** combien de personnes y a-t-il en tout?; **s. cutbacks** réduction *f* de personnel; **domestic s.** domestiques *mfpl*; *Journ* **editorial s.** rédaction *f*; **teaching s.** personnel enseignant; **nursing s.** infirmiers *mpl*, infirmières *fpl*; **office s.** personnel de bureau; **sales-support s.** personnel de soutien commercial; **senior** *or* **managerial s.** cadres *mpl* supérieurs; **s.-student ratio** rapport *m* entre le nombre de professeurs et le nombre d'étudiants VOIR GRAMMAIRE A11
3 *Mil (officers)* état-major *m*, *pl* états-majors; **general s.** état-major général; **chief of s.** chef *m* d'état-major; **joint chiefs of s.** état-major interarmées
4 *Mus (pl* **staves** [steɪvz]*)* portée *f*
VT *(office etc)* pourvoir en personnel; **the office is almost entirely staffed by women** le personnel du bureau est presque entière-

ment composé de femmes; **the office is only staffed between the hours of 2 and 4** il y a quelqu'un au bureau de 14 h à 16 h seulement

▸▸**s. association** ≃ comité *m* d'entreprise; *Mil* **s. college** école *f* supérieure de guerre; *Journ* **s. correspondent** envoyé *m* de la rédaction, correspondant *m* permanent; *Br* **s. nurse** infirmier, -ière diplômé(e); *Mil* **s. officer** officier *m* d'état-major; *Sch* **s. room** salle *f* des professeurs; **s. turnover** roulement *m* du personnel

staffer ['stɑːfər] N *Fam* membre *m* du personnel; *Journ* journaliste *mf* permanent(e)

staffing ['stɑːfɪŋ] N *(finding staff)* recrutement *m* de personnel; **the delay is due to s.difficulties** le retard est dû à des problèmes de recrutement

▸▸**s. arrangements** organisation *f* du personnel; **s. levels** effectifs *mpl*; **s. policy** politique *f* de recrutement du personnel

Staffs *abbr* **Staffordshire**

stag [stæg] N **1** *(animal)* cerf *m* **2** *Br St Exch ·Fam (premium hunter)* loup *m*

▸▸*Entom* **s. beetle** cerf-volant *m*, *pl* cerfs-volants, *Spec* lucane *m*; **s. night** *(before wedding)* enterrement *m* de la vie de garçon

STAGE [steɪdʒ]

| **N** scène **1** ▪ plateau **1** ▪ estrade **2** ▪ échafaudage **2** ▪ stade **3** ▪ étape **3, 4** ▪ diligence **5** |
| **VT** mettre en scène **1** ▪ organiser **1** ▪ monter **1** |

N **1** *Theat (place)* scène *f*, *TV*, *Cin* plateau *m*; **the s.** *(theatre)* le théâtre; **to go on the s.** *(take up acting)* devenir acteur/actrice; **front of the s.** avant-scène *f*; **to come on (the) s.** entrer en scène; **to set the s.** monter les décors; *Fig* préparer le terrain; *Fig* **now the s. was set for …** maintenant tout était prêt pour …; **s. left/right** côté cour/jardin **2** *(platform)* estrade *f*, *(for workmen)* échafaudage *m*, *(of microscope)* platine *f* **3** *(phase)* stade *m*, étape *f*; **to be at a particular s.** *(in one's development etc)* en être à un certain stade; **to go through a particular s.** *(in one's development etc)* traverser un certain stade; **at this s.** à ce point, à ce moment; **in the larval s.** à l'état de larve, au stade larvaire; **to do sth in (successive) stages** faire qch par étapes (successives); **at what s. in its development?** à quel moment *ou* stade de son développement?; **at this s. in the project** à ce stade du projet; **at a later s. in his life** à un stade plus avancé de sa vie; **to pay in easy stages** payer en petits versements; **to do sth one s. at a time** faire qch étape par étape; **s. of production** phase *f* de production **4** *(part of journey)* étape *f*; *Hist (for stage-coach etc)* relais *m*; **s. by s.** d'étape en étape; **we did the journey in easy stages** nous avons fait le voyage en petites étapes; *Br* **fare s.** *(changement m de)* section *f* *(de l'itinéraire d'un autobus)* **5** *(stagecoach)* diligence *f* **6** *Astronaut (of rocket)* étage *m*

VT 1 *Theat etc* mettre en scène; *(play)* monter, porter à la scène; *(demonstration etc)* organiser, faire; *(coup)* monter; **to s. a comeback** faire un come-back; **the whole incident had been staged** l'incident avait été monté de toutes pièces **2** *(phase)* **staged payments** paiements *mpl* échelonnés; **carefully staged reduction of nuclear weapons** réduction soigneusement planifiée des armes nucléaires

▸▸**s. direction** indication *f* scénique; **s. diving** = fait de se jeter dans la foule depuis la scène; **s. door** entrée *f* des artistes; **s. effects** effets *mpl* scéniques; **s. fright** trac *m*;

s. lighting éclairage *m* de plateau; **s. manager** régisseur *m*; **s. name** nom *m* de scène; **s. school** école *f* d'art dramatique; **s. whisper** aparté *m*; **'it's midnight'**, **he announced in a loud s. whisper** 'il est minuit', chuchota-t-il, suffisamment fort pour que tout le monde l'entende

> Note that the French word **stage** is a false friend and is never a translation for the English word **stage**. It means **training course**.

stagecoach ['steɪdʒkrəʊtʃ] N diligence *f*

stagecraft ['steɪdʒkrɑːft] N *Theat* technique *f* de la scène

stagehand ['steɪdʒhænd] N *Theat* machiniste *mf*, *TV* machiniste de plateau

stage-manage VT *Theat* mettre en scène; *Fig Pej (demonstration etc)* organiser depuis les coulisses

stager ['steɪdʒər] N **old s.** vieux routier *m*

stage-struck ADJ épris *ou* féru de théâtre

stagey ['steɪdʒɪ] ADJ *Pej* = **stagy**

stagflation [stæg'fleɪʃən] N *Econ* stagflation *f*

stagger ['stægər] VI chanceler, tituber; **she staggered beneath the weight** elle chancela sous le poids; **to s. along** marcher en chancelant *ou* en titubant; **to s. to one's feet** se relever en chancelant

VT **1** *(overwhelm) (person)* stupéfier; **to be staggered** tomber à la renverse; **I'm staggered!** je n'arrive pas à le croire! **2** *(hours of work, holidays etc)* échelonner

N **1** pas *m* chancelant **2** *Vet* **staggers** vertigo *m*

staggered ['stægəd] ADJ *Fam (amazed)* estomaqué

▸▸**s. junction** carrefour *m* décalé; **s. payments** paiements *mpl* échelonnés

staggering ['stægərɪŋ] ADJ *(news)* renversant, atterrant; *(price)* incroyable; **s. blow** coup *m* de massue; **s. increase in prices** hausse vertigineuse des prix; **it cost a s. £4,000** ça a coûté la somme incroyable de 4000 livres

N *(of hours of work, holidays)* échelonnement *m*

staghorn ['stæghɔːn] N bois *mpl* de cerf

staghunt(ing) ['stæghʌnt(ɪŋ)] N chasse *f* au cerf

staging ['steɪdʒɪŋ] N **1** *Theat (of play)* mise *f* à la scène **2** *(scaffolding)* échafaudage *m*; *(shelving)* rayonnage *f* **3** *Astron* largage *m* *(d'un étage de fusée)*

▸▸*Mil* **s. area, s. point** lieu *m* de rassemblement; *Br* **s. post** lieu *ou* point *m* de ravitaillement; *Aviat* escale *f* aérienne; *Hist (for coaches)* relais *m* *(de diligences)*

stagnant ['stægnənt] ADJ *(water)* stagnant; *(trade, business)* en stagnation, dans le marasme

stagnate [stæg'neɪt] VI *(of water, trade, business)*, *Fig (of person)* stagner

stagnation [stæg'neɪʃən] N *(of water)* stagnation *f*, *(of trade)* stagnation, marasme *m*

stagy ['steɪdʒɪ] ADJ *Pej* théâtral, -aux

staid [steɪd] ADJ sérieux

staidness ['steɪdnɪs] N sérieux *m*

stain [steɪn] N **1** *(mark)* tache *f*; **to remove a s.** enlever une tache *(from* de); *Fig* **without a s. on his character** sans atteinte à sa réputation; **to leave a s. on sb's reputation** entacher la réputation de qn; **a grease/blood s.** une tache de graisse/sang **2** *(dye)* colorant *m*; **(wood) s.** teinture *f* *(pour bois)*

VT **1** *(mark)* tacher *(with* de); *Fig (person's reputation)* entacher, souiller, ternir; **hands stained with blood** mains tachées *ou* souillées de sang; *Fig* **hands stained with the**

blood of innocent people mains tachées du sang d'innocents **2** *(dye) (wood)* teindre, teinter; *(glass)* peindre

VI **material that stains easily** tissu qui se tache facilement

▸▸**s. remover** détachant *m*

stained glass [steɪnd] N *(material)* verre *m* coloré; *(windows)* vitraux *mpl*

stained-glass window N vitrail *m*, *pl* -aux

staining ['steɪnɪŋ] N *(of wood)* teinture *f*

stainless ['steɪnlɪs] ADJ **1** *(rust-resistant)* inoxydable **2** *Fig (reputation)* sans tache

▸▸**s. steel** acier *m* inoxydable

stair ['steər] N **1** stair(s) *(flight of stairs)* escalier *m*; **she took the stairs** elle prit l'escalier; **I met him on the stairs** je l'ai rencontré dans l'escalier; **back stairs** escalier de service **2** *(step)* marche *f*, degré *m*

▸▸**s. carpet** tapis *m* d'escalier

staircase ['steəkeɪs] N *(stairs)* escalier *m*; *(structure)* cage *f* d'escalier; **secret s.** escalier dérobé

stairway ['steəweɪ] N = **staircase**

stairwell ['steəwel] N cage *f* d'escalier

stake [steɪk] N **1** *(piece of wood, metal)* pieu *m*; *(for marking land)* jalon *m*, fiche *f*; *(for tethering animal)* piquet *m*; *(in horticulture)* tuteur *m*; *(for vine)* échalas *m*; *(in surveying)* jalon; *Fam* **to pull up stakes** *(leave)* partir; *(leave one's home)* déménager **2** *(for execution)* **to die** *or* **be burned at the s.** mourir sur le bûcher; **she went to the s. for her beliefs** on l'a brûlée pour ses croyances; *Fig* **but I'm not going to go to the s. for it** mais je n'ai aucune intention de mourir pour ça **3** *(in gambling)*, *Fig* mise *f*, enjeu *m*; **the stakes are down** les jeux sont faits; **to play for high stakes** jouer gros jeu; **our honour is at s.** il y va de notre honneur, notre honneur est en jeu; **there's a lot at s.** de lourds intérêts sont en jeu; **to have large sums at s. in an enterprise** avoir de fortes sommes engagées dans une entreprise; **to have a s. in sth** avoir des intérêts dans qch; *Horseracing* **stakes** *(prize)* prix *m*

VT **1** *(mark out) (piece of land)* jalonner, piqueter; *(in surveying) (line, road etc)* jalonner; **to s. a claim** *Min* jalonner une concession; *Fig* faire valoir ses droits **2** *(support with stakes) (object)* soutenir avec des pieux; *(vine etc)* échalasser; *(tomatoes)* tuteurer **3** *(in gambling) (amount of money)* mettre en jeu, jouer; *Fig (reputation, job etc)* risquer; **to s. twenty euros** miser *ou* jouer vingt euros; **to s. everything** *or* **one's all** jouer son va-tout, mettre tout en jeu; **I'd s. my life on it** j'en mettrais ma tête à couper **4** *Am Fam (person) (provide with money)* financer; *(provide needs of)* subvenir aux besoins de

▸▸**s. boat** bateau *m* de ligne de départ

▸ **stake off** VT SEP = **stake** VT **1**

▸ **stake out** VT SEP **1** = **stake** VT **1** **2** *(keep under observation) (building etc)* surveiller

stakeholder ['steɪkhəʊldər] N personne *f* participant à une affaire, partie *f* prenante

▸▸**s. pension** = système *m* de retraite accessible aux salariés (notamment ceux qui ont de faibles revenus) ne bénéficiant pas d'une retraite complémentaire; **s. society** = terme popularisé par Tony Blair, qui désigne un type de société où chaque citoyen a un rôle à jouer car il y va de son propre intérêt

stakeout ['steɪkaʊt] N surveillance *f*; **to be on s.** faire le guet; **he was caught in a s.** la police faisait le guet et on l'a arrêté

staking ['steɪkɪŋ] N **1** (marking off) (of piece of land etc) jalonnement m, piquetage m **2** (support) (of vine) échalassage m; (of tomatoes) tuteurage m

stalactite ['stæləktaɪt, Am also stə'læktaɪt] N Geol stalactite f

stalagmite ['stæləgmaɪt, Am also stə'lægmaɪt] N Geol stalagmite f

stale [steɪl] ADJ **1** (not fresh) qui n'est pas frais, f fraîche; (bread, cake) rassis; (air) vicié; **s. breath** mauvaise haleine f, **s. smell** odeur f de renfermé; (of beer, perfume etc) relent m

2 Fig (old) (excuse, cliché, argument etc) vieux, f vieille; **s. joke** plaisanterie éculée; **s. news** nouvelle plus très fraîche; **it soon becomes s. and boring** on s'en lasse rapidement et ça devient ennuyeux

3 (person) qui a perdu sa fraîcheur; **to go s.** (of athlete etc) se surentraîner; (of actor, musician etc) perdre son inspiration; **I'm s.** (of athlete, executive) je suis vidé; (of actor, writer, musician) je n'ai plus d'inspiration; **I'm feeling a bit s.** j'ai un peu perdu de ma fraîcheur; Fam **it's gone s. on me** ça ne m'intéresse plus, j'ai perdu mon enthousiasme; **her marriage had gone s.** son mariage avait perdu de sa passion

4 Fin (market) lourd, plat

VI (of news etc) perdre de son intérêt; **pleasure that never stales** plaisir toujours nouveau

▸▸ Fin **s. cheque** chèque m prescrit

stalemate ['steɪlmeɪt] N Chess pat m; Fig **negotiations have reached a s.** les négociations sont dans l'impasse; Fig **it's s. between them** ils sont dans une impasse; Fig **it's s.** c'est l'impasse

VT Chess **Black is stalemated** les Noirs sont pat; Fig **this has stalemated the talks** cela a mis les négociations dans l'impasse; **stalemated industry** industrie f dans l'impasse

staleness ['steɪlnɪs] N **1** (of bread) état m rassis; (of beer etc) évent m; (stale smell) odeur f de renfermé; (of beer, perfume etc) relent m **2** (of news) manque m de fraîcheur

Stalinism ['stɑːlɪnɪz(ə)m] N stalinisme m

Stalinist ['stɑːlɪnɪst] ADJ, N stalinien, -ienne

stalk¹ [stɔːk] VI (walk haughtily) marcher ou s'avancer l'air hautain; **to s. out of a room** sortir d'une pièce l'air hautain

VT **1** (of animal) (prey) être sur les traces de; (of hunter) (game) traquer; (deer) chasser à l'approche; Fig (person) suivre furtivement; (of private detective) filer; (of murderer) traquer **2** (prowl about in) (corridor, street) rôder dans

N (way of walking) (imposing) démarche f majestueuse; (disdainful) démarche hautaine

stalk² N **1** (of plant) tige f; (of fruit) queue f; (of wheat, corn) chaume m; (of bunch of grapes) rafle f, râpe f; (of cabbage) trognon m; Zool pédoncule m, pédicule m; **s.-eyed** aux yeux pédonculés; **her eyes came out/were (out) on stalks** les yeux lui sont sortis/sortaient de la tête **2** (of wineglass) pied m **3** Aut (for controls) tige f, manette f

stalker ['stɔːkər] N (hunter) chasseur m à l'approche; (criminal) = criminel m suivant sa victime à la trace; (obsessive fan) = admirateur m obsessionnel qui harcèle une célébrité ou une de ses connaissances

stalking ['stɔːkɪŋ] N **1** (in hunting) chasse f à l'approche **2** (form of harassment) = forme de harcèlement qui consiste à suivre quelqu'un en permanence

▸▸ **s. horse** (in hunting) cheval m d'abri; Fig (pretext) prétexte m; Pol **we'll use him as a s. horse** on va s'en servir comme d'un candidat bidon

stall [stɔːl] N **1** (in stable) stalle f; (in byre) case f **2** (for selling etc) étalage m (en plein vent), éventaire m; (at exhibition etc) stand m; **(market) s.** place f ou emplacement m (au marché); **newspaper s.** kiosque m à journaux; **I bought it at a fruit s.** je l'ai acheté chez le petit marchand de fruits; also Fig **to set out one's s.** déballer sa marchandise

3 choir s. stalle f; Theat (orchestra) stalls fauteuils mpl d'orchestre; **a seat in the stalls** un fauteuil d'orchestre

4 Med (for finger) doigtier m

5 (act of stalling) Aut (of engine) calage m; **I thought his story was just a s. to gain time** j'ai pensé qu'il ne cherchait qu'à gagner du temps avec son histoire

6 Horseracing (starting) stalls stalle f (de départ)

VT **1** Aut (engine) caler **2** (put in stalls) (cattle) mettre à l'étable **3** (hold off) (enemy) **s. them for half an hour** essaie de les retenir une demi-heure; **I think he's deliberately stalling us** je crois qu'il nous fait attendre délibérément; **they tried to s. us with some nonsense** ils ont tenté de nous retarder avec des bêtises

VI **1** (of engine) caler; Aviat, Fig (of campaign) être en perte de vitesse **2 to s. (for time)** chercher à gagner du temps; **stop stalling!** arrête de tergiverser!; **we'll have to s. on this for another week or so** il faudra que nous gagnions environ une semaine de plus pour ça

stall-feed VT (pt, pp **stall-fed** [-fed]) (cattle) engraisser à l'étable

stallholder ['stɔːlhəʊldər] N étalagiste mf, marchand, -ande en plein vent; **I've agreed to be a s. at the fête** j'ai accepté de tenir un stand à la fête

stalling ['stɔːlɪŋ] N Aut **to prevent s.** pour empêcher que le moteur ne cale

stallion ['stæljən] N étalon m

stalwart ['stɔːlwət] ADJ (strong) robuste, vigoureux; (brave) vaillant; Fig (defender) résolu; (supporter) fidèle; (refusal) inébranlable; **they put up a s. defence** ils se sont défendus d'arrache-pied

N Pol **a party s.** un pilier du parti

stamen ['steɪmən] N Bot étamine f

stamina ['stæmɪnə] N résistance f

stammer ['stæmər] N (permanent) bégaiement m; (out of nervousness etc) bégaiement, balbutiement m; **man with a s.** homme qui bégaie, bègue m

VI (normally) bégayer; (out of nervousness etc) bégayer, balbutier

VT = **stammer out**

▸ **stammer out** VT SEP (excuse etc) bégayer, balbutier

stammerer ['stæmərər] N bègue mf

stammering ['stæmərɪŋ] N bégaiement m; (through nervousness etc) bégaiement, balbutiement m

STAMP [stæmp] N **1** (postage) s. timbre(-poste) m, pl timbres(-poste); Br **(National Insurance) s.** = mois m de cotisation à l'assurance chômage

2 (device for marking) tampon m; (esp for metal) estampe f, étampe f; (esp for gold etc) poinçon m; **signature s.** griffe f, **date s.** (timbre m) dateur m; **rubber s.** tampon ou timbre de caoutchouc

3 (mark) marque f (apposée); Ind estampille f ou marque de contrôle; Fig **it needs his s. of approval** il faut son approbation; **to bear the s. of genius** porter l'empreinte du génie; **to leave one's s. on sth** marquer qch de son empreinte; **there are few politicians of her s.** (calibre) il y a peu de politiciens de sa trempe, Pej il y a peu de politiciens de son espèce

4 (in metalwork) étampeuse f, estampeuse f

5 (of foot) battement m de pied (d'impatience, de colère); **with a s. of the foot** en frappant du pied; **the ceaseless s. of feet past my window** le bruit continuel des pas devant ma fenêtre

VT **1 to s. one's foot** taper du pied; **he stamped the toy to pieces** il a écrabouillé le jouet à coups de talon; **he stamped the snow/mud off his boots** il tapait du pied pour faire tomber la neige/boue; **he stamped the earth down** il a tassé la terre avec le pied

2 (imprint mark on) (object) imprimer sur; (gold, silver) poinçonner; (coins etc) frapper, estamper; (leather) frapper, estamper, gaufrer; **each article is stamped with the manufacturer's mark** chaque article porte la marque du fabricant; **a design is stamped on the butter** un dessin est imprimé dans le beurre; Fig **he was determined to s. his mark on the party** il était déterminé à marquer le parti de son empreinte

3 (mark with ink) (document) timbrer, estampiller; (passport) viser; (letter) timbrer, affranchir; (goods) estampiller; Fin **to s. a bill** viser un effet; **they s. the details on your cheque** ils tamponnent les détails sur votre chèque; **a machine that stamps the date on ...** une machine qui marque ou tamponne la date sur ...

4 (put postage stamp on) (letter, parcel) timbrer, affranchir

5 (in metalwork) (metal objects) étamper, estamper

6 Fig **to s. sb/sth (as) ...** donner à qn/qch le caractère de ...; **this stamped him (as) a rebel** à partir de là, on lui a collé l'étiquette de rebelle

VI **to s. upstairs/outside** monter l'escalier/sortir d'un pas bruyant

▸▸ **s. album** album m de timbres-poste; **s. collecting** philatélie f; **s. collector** collectionneur, -euse de timbres ou de timbres-poste, philatéliste mf; Law **s. duty** droit m de timbre, timbre fiscal; **s. hinge** charnière f; **s. machine** distributeur m automatique de timbres-poste; **s. pad** tampon (encreur)

▸ **stamp about, stamp around** VI (stamp feet) trépigner, piétiner; (for warmth) battre la semelle

▸ **stamp on** VT INSEP **1** (step on) (cockroach, worm) écraser (avec le talon)

2 Fig (repress) (person) écraser, bafouer; (suggestions) fouler aux pieds

VT SEP (date etc) tamponner, marquer

▸ **stamp out** VT SEP **1** (eradicate) (rebellion) écraser; (abuse, resistance, independence etc) éradiquer; (epidemic, inflation) enrayer

2 (extinguish by stamping) (fire) éteindre en piétinant

3 (in metalwork) (sheet metal) découper à la presse ou à l'emporte-pièce

stamped [stæmpt] ADJ (with seal) estampillé

▸▸ **s. addressed envelope** enveloppe f timbrée

stampede [stæm'piːd] N (rush, flight) (of troops, horses etc) fuite f précipitée, débandade f; **several people were injured in the s.** plusieurs personnes ont été blessées dans la panique; **there was a s. for the door** tout le monde s'est précipité vers la porte

VI (rush) se ruer, se précipiter (**for, towards** vers, sur); (flee) fuir en désordre ou à la débandade; (of cattle etc) partir à la débandade

VT (cattle, people) semer la panique parmi; **to s. a nation into war** précipiter un peuple dans la guerre; **to s. sb into doing sth** pousser qn à faire qch, bousculer qn pour qu'il fasse qch; **I don't want to s. you into (making) a decision** je ne veux pas te presser ou te bousculer dans ta décision

stamping ['stæmpɪŋ] N **1** (with feet) piétinement m, trépignement m **2** (in metalwork) estampage m, étampage m; (item) pièce festampée **3** (of letters, parcels) affranchissement m, timbrage m

▸▸ Fam **s. ground** lieu m favori; **this was one of my old s. grounds** j'y allais tout le temps; **s. out** (of disease, crime, corruption, abuse) éradication f, (of strike, movement, rebellion) répression f, (of dissent, protest) étouffement m; **s. press** estampeuse f

stance [stæns] N (posture) position f, Fig position, attitude f; Golf, Cr etc (of player) posture f, **she took up her usual s. at the window** elle s'est mise à la fenêtre comme à son habitude; **the government's s. on this** la position ou l'attitude du gouvernement làdessus

stanch [stɑːntʃ] VT = **staunch²**

stanchion ['stɑːnʃən] N étançon m, étai m

STAND [stænd]

N position 1 ▪ représentation 2
▪ station 3 ▪ support 4 ▪ béquille 4
▪ étalage 5 ▪ stand 5 ▪ tribune 6
▪ barre des témoins 8
VI être debout 1 ▪ se lever 1 ▪ se
trouver 2, 5 ▪ être 2, 5 ▪ être valable
4 ▪ tenir 4 ▪ reposer 6
VT mettre 1 ▪ placer 1 ▪ supporter 3
▪ subir 3 ▪ offrir 4

N 1 (position) position f (on concernant); **to take up a s. near the door** se poster ou prendre position près de la porte; **to take a s.** prendre position et s'y tenir; **to take a firm s.** ne pas transiger; **you should take a firmer s. with them** tu devrais adopter une attitude plus ferme envers eux; **to make a s. against an abuse** s'opposer résolument à un abus; **to make a s. (against the enemy)** (of troops) faire face (à l'ennemi)

2 Theat représentation f, (by band) concert m

3 (for taxis) station f

4 (support) (of lamp etc) support m, pied m; (for motorbike etc) béquille f, **(revolving) s.** (for books, postcards etc) tourniquet m

5 (stall) (in open air) étalage m, étal m; (at exhibition etc) stand m

6 (at sports ground, for watching procession) tribune f, **the stands** les tribunes

7 Agr (crop) récolte f sur pied; (of trees) peuplement m

8 Law (witness box) barre f des témoins; **to take the s.** venir à la barre

VI (pt, pp **stood** [stʊd]) **1** (have upright position) être debout, se tenir debout; (maintain upright position) rester debout; (assume upright position) se lever; **she stood with her back to me** elle se tenait debout en me tournant le dos; **to be/keep standing** être/rester debout; **I was too weak to s.** j'étais trop faible pour me tenir debout; **I could hardly s.** je pouvais à peine me tenir debout; Fig **to s. on one's own two feet** se débrouiller tout seul; Fam **he hasn't/you haven't/etc a leg to s. on** ça ne tient pas; **I've lost everything but what I s. up in** j'ai tout perdu sauf ce que j'ai sur le dos; **to s. six feet high** (of object) avoir six pieds de haut, mesurer six pieds; (of person) mesurer six pieds; **the house is still standing** la maison tient toujours debout; **not a stone (of the building) was left standing** le bâtiment avait été complètement détruit; Sch **s.!** levez-vous!; Mil **to s. to attention** se mettre au garde-à-vous

2 (be situated, be) se trouver, être; **a chapel stands at the top of the hill** une chapelle se dresse au sommet de la colline; **a car was standing at the door** il y avait une voiture à la porte; **the monument stands as a memorial to his life's work** le monument a été

érigé pour célébrer l'œuvre de sa vie; **I found the door standing open** j'ai trouvé la porte ouverte; **nothing stands between you and success** rien ne s'oppose à votre succès; **a man stood in the doorway** un homme se tenait à la porte; **I'll s. at or by the window** je me mettrai à la fenêtre; **I didn't know where to s.** je ne savais où me mettre; **I stood and looked at him, I stood looking at him** je suis resté à le regarder; **I was standing a few feet away from him** je me tenais à quelques pas de lui; **to s. talking/watching** rester à parler/regarder; **don't just s. there! do something!** ne reste pas là les bras ballants! fais quelque chose!; **don't s. in the passage!** ne reste pas là, tu gênes le passage!; **if you insist on leaving school at 16, I won't s. in your way** si tu veux vraiment arrêter tes études à 16 ans, je ne m'y opposerai pas; **to leave sb standing (there)** laisser qn planté (là); Sport etc **to be left standing** être laissé sur place; **to leave the competition standing** Sport griller la concurrence; Fig laisser les autres très loin derrière; **s. and deliver!** la bourse ou la vie!; **we're standing right behind you** nous sommes avec vous; **with the union standing behind him/her/etc** avec le soutien du syndicat

3 (maintain position) **to s. fast** or **firm** (not retreat) tenir, tenir bon; **to s. still** se tenir immobile; **time seemed to s. still** le temps semblait s'être arrêté; **we s. or fall together** nous sommes solidaires (les uns des autres); **I shall s. or fall by the issue** mon sort dépend du résultat; **to s. alone** faire face ou tenir tête seul; **to s. on ceremony** faire des manières; **she's standing on her dignity** elle exige le respect qui lui est dû; **she doesn't s. on her dignity at these occasions** elle ne fait pas la fière dans de telles circonstances

4 (remain valid) tenir, se maintenir; **the passage must s.** le passage doit rester comme il est ou sans modification; **the bet stands** le pari tient; **the objection stands** cette objection est toujours valable; **what you said last week, does that still s.?** et ce que tu as dit la semaine dernière, ça tient toujours?

5 (be in certain state) être, se trouver; **to s. convicted of ...** avoir été déclaré coupable de ..., être convaincu de ...; **to s. in need of ...** avoir besoin de ...; **you s. in danger of getting killed** vous risquez de vous faire tuer; **to s. to lose £5,000** risquer de perdre 5 000 livres; **to s. to win a lot of money** avoir des chances de gagner beaucoup d'argent; **no one stands to gain from a quarrel like this** personne n'a rien à gagner d'une telle querelle; **to s. as security for a debt** assurer une créance; **to s. guarantor or surety for sb** se porter garant envers qn, cautionner qn; **the thermometer stood at 30°** le thermomètre marquait 30°; **the debt now stands at $3.5 billion** la dette s'élève à présent à $3,5 milliards; **the balance stands at £50** le reliquat de compte est de cinquante livres; **the amount standing to your credit** votre solde créditeur; **how do we s.?** (in work etc) où en sommes-nous?; (financially) où en sont nos comptes?; **as matters s., as it stands** au point où en sont les choses, dans l'état actuel des choses; **to know how things s.** être au fait de la situation; **I don't know where I s.** j'ignore quelle est ma situation ou ma position; **how do you s. with him?** quelle est votre position vis-à-vis de lui?; **you never know how or where you s. with her** on ne sait jamais sur quel pied danser avec elle; **I s. corrected** je reconnais mon erreur

6 (remain motionless) **to allow a liquid to s.** laisser reposer ou laisser déposer un liquide

VT 1 (place upright) mettre, poser, placer; **to s. sth on the table** mettre ou poser qch sur la

table; **to s. sth against the wall** dresser qch contre le mur; **to s. sth upright** mettre qch debout

2 to s. one's ground tenir bon ou ferme; **s. your ground!** (don't retreat) ne reculez pas d'une semelle!; (don't give up opposition) tenez ferme!, ne lâchez pas prise!

3 (endure) supporter, soutenir, subir; **to s. the cold** supporter le froid; **to s. a shock** résister à ou supporter un choc; **his argument does not s. investigation** son argument ne tient pas; **to s. comparison with sb/sth** soutenir la comparaison avec qn/qch; **he can't s. her** il ne peut pas la souffrir ou la sentir; **I won't s. such behaviour** je ne supporterai pas une pareille conduite; **I can't s. it any longer** (heat, cold, discomfort etc) je ne tiens plus; (emotional tension, cruelty etc) je n'en peux plus

4 Fam (pay for) payer, offrir; **to s. sb a drink** payer à boire à qn; **to s. sb a dinner** payer un dîner à qn; **I'll s. you** c'est moi qui paie

5 to s. a chance (of doing sth) avoir de bonnes chances (de faire qch); **if this initiative is to s. a chance ...** si vous voulez que cette initiative ait la moindre chance de succès ...

▸▸ TV etc **s. lamp** lumière f sur pied; TV etc **s. microphone** microphone m sur pied

▸ **stand about, stand around** VI (be standing, doing nothing) se tenir là; **there were a lot of people standing around talking** il y avait beaucoup de monde qui se tenait là à parler; **I can't afford to pay people to s. around all day doing nothing** je n'ai pas les moyens de payer les gens à ne rien faire

▸ **stand aside** VI **1** (be standing apart) se tenir à l'écart

2 (move aside) s'écarter; **to s. aside to let sb pass** s'effacer pour laisser passer qn; Fig **to s. aside in favour of sb** se désister en faveur de qn

▸ **stand away** VI (move away) s'éloigner (**from** de)

▸ **stand back** VI **1** (of person) (move away) (se) reculer; (keep in background) se tenir en arrière; **s. well back, please!** reculez(vous), s'il vous plaît

2 (of building etc) être situé en retrait; **a house standing back from the road** une maison située en retrait (de la route)

▸ **stand by** VI **1** (be ready) se tenir prêt; Naut se tenir paré; Mil **the troops are standing by** les troupes sont en état d'alerte; Naut **s. by!** paré!, attention!; Radio **s. by to receive** prenez l'écoute

2 (wait) attendre, patienter; **viewers were told to s. by for further developments** on demanda aux téléspectateurs de patienter et d'attendre la suite des événements

3 (not get involved) se tenir là (sans intervenir); **people just stood by and watched him being beaten up** les gens restèrent là à le regarder se faire cogner

VT INSEP 1 (stand next, near to) (of person) se tenir près de ou à côté de

2 (person) (support, defend) soutenir, défendre; (take side of) se ranger du côté de; **she stood by her friend throughout the trial** elle a soutenu son amie tout au long du procès

3 (keep, honour) (promise) rester fidèle à; **I s. by what I said** je m'en tiens à ce que j'ai dit

▸ **stand down** VI (retire) (from team, position etc) se retirer; (of candidate) retirer sa candidature (**in favour of** en faveur de); Mil quitter son service; Law (of witness) quitter la barre

▸ **stand for** VT INSEP **1** esp Br (present oneself as candidate for) se présenter à; **to s. for parliament** se présenter aux élections parlementaires; **to s. for the chairmanship** se présenter à la présidence; **to s. for election** se présenter aux élections; **half the committee are standing for re-election** la moitié des membres du comité se représente

2 *(mean, represent) (something)* signifier, vouloir dire; **'tsp' stands for 'teaspoonful'** 'tsp' signifie 'teaspoonful'; **the letters AA s. for 'Alcoholics Anonymous'** les lettres AA veulent dire 'Alcooliques anonymes'; **our party stands for freedom and democracy** notre parti est celui de la liberté et de la démocratie

3 *(tolerate) (something)* supporter, tolérer; **I won't s. for it** je ne supporterai pas cela

▸ **stand in** VI *(act as replacement)* assurer le remplacement

▸ **stand in for** VT INSEP *(act as replacement for) (person)* remplacer; *Cin (actor)* doubler; **sparkling wine will have to s. in for champagne** le vin mousseux tiendra lieu de champagne

▸ **stand off** VI *(remain at a distance)* se tenir éloigné *ou* à l'écart
VT INSEP *Naut* **to s. off the coast** être au large

▸ **stand out** VI **1** *(be noticeable) (of objects)* ressortir; *Pej* détonner; *(protrude)* faire saillie; **to s. out in sharp relief** ressortir, se détacher; *Fig* se distinguer; **to s. out against sth** faire contraste avec qch; **mountains that s. out against the horizon** montagnes qui se dessinent à *ou* sur l'horizon; **the qualities that s. out in his work** les qualités marquantes de son œuvre; **she stands out in a crowd** on la remarque dans la foule; *Fig* **characteristics that make him s. out in the crowd** traits qui le caractérisent; *Fam* **that stands out a mile!** *(is very obvious)* ça se voit comme le nez au milieu de la figure!; **it really stands out that he's not a local** ça se voit *ou* se remarque vraiment qu'il n'est pas d'ici
2 *(adopt firm position)* résister (**against** à), tenir bon *ou* ferme (**against** contre)

▸ **stand out for** VT INSEP *(something)* insister sur

▸ **stand over** VI *(be postponed)* rester en suspens; **to let a question s. over, to allow a question to s. over** remettre une question à plus tard, laisser une question en suspens
VT INSEP **to s. over sb** *(lean over)* se pencher sur qn; *(watch)* surveiller qn de près; **if I don't s. over him, he does nothing** si je ne suis pas toujours sur son dos, il ne fait rien

▸ **stand to** VI être prêt, être en état d'alerte; **s. to!** aux armes!
VT SEP *Mil etc* mettre en état d'alerte

▸ **stand together** VI **1** *(form a group)* être en groupe; **they were standing together in a line** ils formaient une colonne
2 *Fig (show solidarity)* être *ou* rester solidaire

▸ **stand up** VI **1** *(rise to one's feet)* se lever, se mettre debout; *(to be standing up)* se tenir debout; **this lamp won't s. up straight** cette lampe ne tient pas droite; **s. up!** levez-vous!, debout!; **we must s. up and be counted!** il ne faut pas nous laisser faire!
2 *(be valid)* se tenir, être valide; **there isn't enough evidence for the charge to s. up in court** il n'y a pas suffisamment de preuves pour que l'accusation tienne au tribunal
VT SEP **1** *Fam (fail to meet)* poser un lapin à
2 *(put in upright position) (object)* mettre debout; **to s. a child up (again)** (re)mettre un enfant sur ses pieds

▸ **stand up for** VT INSEP *(defend) (person)* soutenir, défendre; **only Chris stood up for her** seul Chris l'a soutenue *ou* s'est mis de son côté; **s. up for what you believe in** défendez ce en quoi vous croyez

▸ **stand up to** VT INSEP *(resist, oppose) (person)* tenir tête à; *(endure) (of object)* résister à; **it won't s. up to that sort of treatment** ça ne résistera pas à ce genre de traitement; **it doesn't s. up to close analysis** ça ne résiste pas à une analyse poussée

stand-alone *Comput* N poste *m* autonome, monoposte *m*

ADJ *(system)* autonome
▸▸ **s. computer** ordinateur *m* autonome; **s. workstation** station *f* de travail autonome

STANDARD ['stændəd] N **1** *(flag etc)* bannière *f*, *Mil* étendard *m*; *Naut* pavillon *m*
2 *(accepted length, quantity etc)* étalon *m*, référence *f*, **to use sth as a s.** prendre qch comme référence; *Fin* **gold/silver s.** étalon (d')or/d'argent; **s. model** *(of car)* voiture *f* de série; *(of machine)* modèle *m* standard *ou* de série
3 *(set requirement)* norme *f*; **to meet government standards** être conforme aux normes établies par le gouvernement; **to make a product comply with standards** adapter un produit aux normes; **standards and practices** normes et usages; **standards catalogue** catalogue *m* de normes
4 *(level, quality)* niveau *m*; **to have high/low standards** *(of person)* être exigeant/ne pas être exigeant; *(of school)* exiger un bon niveau/ne pas exiger un bon niveau; **they have no standards** ils ne sont pas exigeants du tout; **s. of living** niveau de vie; **everyone has his own standards** chacun voit midi à sa porte; **to raise the standards of behaviour** améliorer la discipline; **a high s. of playing/academic achievement** un niveau de jeu/de réussite académique élevé; **he sets very high standards for his students** il exige de ses étudiants un niveau très élevé; **not to come up to s.** ne pas atteindre le niveau exigé; **my cooking isn't up to your s.** ma cuisine n'est pas à la hauteur de la vôtre
5 *(in horticulture)* **s. rose (tree)** rosier *m* sur tige
ADJ **1** *(length, width etc)* standard *inv*, normalisé; **s. thickness** *(of iron etc)* épaisseur *f* type *ou* courante; **s. weight** poids *m* normal; **British S. Time** heure *f* légale anglaise
2 *(usual) (criticism, problem, behaviour, approach)* classique; *(price)* normal, -aux; **headrests are s. or are fitted as s.** les appuis-têtes sont montés en série; **s. spelling/pronunciation** orthographe *f*/prononciation *f* correcte; **a s. French dictionary** un dictionnaire général de la langue française; **one of his s. jokes** une de ses plaisanteries habituelles; **to come in s. sizes** *(of clothes)* exister dans les tailles standards; **the cooking is fairly s.** la cuisine n'a rien de sensationnel; **that's s.** c'est normal; **s. closure** *(for letter)* formule *f* de politesse pour terminer une lettre; **s. cost** coût *m* standard *ou* préétabli; **s. opening** *(for letter)* formule de politesse pour commencer une lettre; **s. service** service *m* standard
▸▸ **s. bearer** *(of cause)* porte-drapeau *m, pl* porte-drapeau(x); *(of political party)* chef *m* de file; *(of flag)* porte-étendard *m, pl* porte-étendard(s); **s. class** deuxième classe *f*; **standards committee** organisme *m* de normalisation; **standards conversion** *(in broadcasting)* transcodage *m*; **standards converter** *(in broadcasting)* transcodeur *m*; **s. deviation** *(in statistics)* écart-type *m, pl* écarts-types; **s. document** document *m* type; **s. edition** *(of an author)* édition *f* courante; **s. English** l'anglais *m* standard; *Rail* **s. gauge** voie *f* normale, écartement *m* normal; *Br* **s. lamp** lampadaire *m* (de salon); **s. measure** mesure *f* étalon; *Comput* **s. memory** mémoire *f* standard; **s. practice** pratique *f* courante; **s. rate** *(of tax)* taux *m* standard

standardization [stændədaɪ'zeɪʃən] N standardisation *f*, *(of weights etc)* étalonnage *m*, étalonnement *m*; *(of methods etc)* uniformisation *f*

standardize ['stændədaɪz] VT normaliser, standardiser; *(weights etc)* étalonner; *(methods, conditions)* uniformiser
VI **to s. on sth** adopter qch comme standard

stand-by N **1** *(substitute person)* **to act as a s.** remplacer qn
2 *(sth held in reserve)* réserve *f*, **to have a sum in reserve as a s.** avoir une somme en réserve en cas de besoin; **a fruitcake can be a useful s. for unexpected guests** il est toujours bon d'avoir un cake en réserve pour les invités surprises
3 *Mil etc (state of readiness)* (état *m* d')alerte *f*, **to be on s.** *(of troops, firemen etc)* être en état d'alerte
4 *Aviat (passenger)* passager, -ère (en) stand-by; *(ticket)* stand-by *m inv*, **to be on s.** être en stand-by
ADV **to fly s.** voler en stand-by
▸▸ **s. mode** *(of printer etc)* veille *f*, **in s. mode** en veille; *Aviat* **s. passenger** passager, -ère (en) stand-by; *Aviat* **s. ticket** stand-by; **s. time** *(of mobile phone)* autonomie *f* en veille

standee [stæn'di:] N *esp Am (in bus)* voyageur, -euse debout; *Theat* spectateur, -trice debout

stand-in N *(person)* remplaçant, -ante; *(actor)* doublure *f* ; *(stunt person)* cascadeur, -euse
ADJ remplaçant; **a s. teacher/speaker/etc** un remplaçant

standing ['stændɪŋ] ADJ **1** *(in upright position)* debout **2** *(permanent) (price)* fixe; *(on bill)* frais *mpl* d'abonnement; **I have a s. invitation** je peux aller chez lui/elle/eux quand je veux; **you have a s. invitation** tu peux venir chez moi/nous quand tu veux
N **1** *(upright position)* station *f* debout; **no s.!** *(in bus etc)* défense de voyager debout **2 of long s.** *(friends)* de longue date; **friend of twenty years' s.** ami de vingt ans **3** *(position) (of country, firm)* rang *m*, position *f*, *(of party, person)* popularité *f*, **financial s.** situation *f* financière; **social s.** position sociale
▸▸ *Mil* **s. army** armée *f* de métier; **s. charges** *(on bill)* frais *mpl* d'abonnement; **s. committee** comité *m* permanent; **s. crop** récolte *f* sur pied; *Com* **s. expenses** frais *mpl* généraux; **s. joke** grosse plaisanterie *f*, **he's become a s. joke** il est devenu un objet de risée; *Sport* **s. jump** saut *m* à pieds joints; *Br Banking* **s. order** virement *m* automatique; *Br Pol* **s. orders** règlement *m* intérieur *(d'une assemblée délibérative)*; **s. ovation** ovation *f*, **s. places, s. room** places *fpl* debout; **it was s. room only on the train** il n'y avait plus de places assises dans le train; **s. rule** règle *f* fixe; **s. start** *Sport* départ *m* debout; *Aut* départ arrêté; **s. stone** pierre *f* levée; **s. water** eau *f* stagnante *ou* dormante

stand-off N *(between opponents)* impasse *f*

stand-off, stand-off half N *Rugby* demi *m* d'ouverture

stand-offish [-'ɒfɪʃ] ADJ *(person)* peu accessible, distant, réservé; **to be s.** se mettre *ou* se tenir sur son quant-à-soi

stand-offishness [-'ɒfɪʃnɪs] N raideur *f*, réserve *f*

standout ['stændaʊt] N *Am* **his article was a real s.** son article sortait vraiment du lot

standpipe ['stændpaɪp] N *(in street)* colonne *f* d'alimentation

standpoint ['stændpɔɪnt] N point *m* de vue; **from the s. of ...** du point de vue de ...; **from a late 20th century s.** dans une perspective de fin de XXe siècle

standstill ['stændstɪl] N arrêt *m*, immobilisation *f*, **traffic has come to a s.** la circulation est immobilisée; **to bring to a s.** arrêter; *(railways, production etc)* paralyser; **many factories are at a s.** beaucoup d'usines chôment; **the railways are at a s.** les chemins de fer sont paralysés

stand-up ADJ **1** *(collar)* droit, montant **2** *(meal)* pris debout **3 a s. fight** *(physical)* une bagarre en règle; *(verbal)* une discussion violente

N *(comedy)* spectacle *m* comique; **to do s.** faire des spectacles comiques

▶▶ **s. comedian** comique *mf* (de scène); **s. comedy** spectacles *mpl* comiques; **s. comic** comique (de scène); *Boxing* **s. fight** combat *m* en règle

stank **PP** *see* stink

Stanley knife® ['stænlɪ] **N** cutter *m*

stannic ['stænɪk] **ADJ** *Chem* stannique

stanza, *pl* **stanzas** ['stænzə, -əz] **N** *(in poetry)* strophe *f*

staphylococcus, *pl* **staphylococci** [stæfɪ-ləʊ'kɒkəs, -'kɒksaɪ] **N** staphylocoque *m*

staple[1] ['steɪp(ə)l] **N** *(for papers)* agrafe *f*, *(for cable etc)* crampon *m*; **wire s.** (clou *m*) cavalier *m*

VT *(piece of paper, cheque etc)* agrafer (**to** à); *Constr etc* fixer avec un crampon, agrafer; **to s. two pieces of paper together** agrafer deux morceaux de papier

▶▶ **s. gun** agrafeuse *f* (professionnelle); **s. remover** arrache-agrafes *m inv*

staple[2] **N** *(basic foodstuff)* aliment *m* de base; *Com, Econ* *(item)* article *m* de base; *(raw material)* matière *f* première; **staples** *(goods)* biens *mpl* de première nécessité; **sex scandals are a s. of the tabloid press** la presse à sensation se nourrit des scandales sexuels; **such accusations are a s. of the annual conference** ces accusations reviennent régulièrement à chaque conférence annuelle; **s. convenience goods** produits *mpl* de première nécessité; *Fig* pain *m* quotidien; **I grew up on a s. diet of television and violence** j'ai grandi nourri de télévision et de violence

▶▶ **s. crop** culture *f* de base; **s. diet** alimentation *f* de base

stapler ['steɪplər] **N** *(device)* agrafeuse *f*

stapling ['steɪplɪŋ] **N** *(of papers)* fixation *f* à l'aide d'agrafes, agrafage *m*; *(of cables etc)* fixation à l'aide de crochets *ou* crampons

star [stɑ:r] **N 1** *Astron* étoile *f*; **shooting s.** étoile filante; **the morning s.** l'étoile du matin; **the pole s.** l'étoile polaire, la polaire; **he was born under a lucky s.** il est né sous une bonne étoile; *Fig* **to reach for the stars** essayer d'atteindre les sommets; *Fig Fam* **to see stars** voir les étoiles en plein midi, voir trente-six chandelles; **the Stars and Stripes** *(American flag)* la bannière étoilée

2 *(insignia) (of order)* plaque *f*; *Mil (on shoulder of uniform)* étoile *f*; **S. of David** étoile de David; **three s. brandy** cognac *m* trois étoiles; **three s. hotel** hôtel *m* trois étoiles

3 *(shape) (on horse's forehead)* étoile *f*; *Typ* astérisque *m*; *Comput* **in a s. configuration** connecté en étoile

4 *Cin etc (person)* étoile *f*, vedette *f*, star *f*, *Mktg* vedette, star; **film** *or* **movie s.** étoile *ou* star *ou* vedette du cinéma; **rock s.** star du rock; **s. presenter** animateur, -trice vedette; **the s. attraction of tonight's show** la principale attraction du spectacle de ce soir; **to get s. billing** tenir le haut de l'affiche; *Fam (of performance, conference, evening)* clou *m*

VT (-rr-) **1** *(mark with asterisk) (word etc)* marquer d'un astérisque

2 *Cin, Theat, TV etc (of film, play etc) (actor)* mettre en scène dans le rôle principal, avoir pour vedette; **the film/play stars Katharine Hepburn (as** *or* **in the role of)** le film/la pièce met en scène Katharine Hepburn dans le rôle principal (de); **'The Last Metro', starring Catherine Deneuve and Gérard Depardieu** 'le Dernier Métro', avec Catherine Deneuve et Gérard Depardieu dans les rôles principaux

VI *Cin, Theat, TV etc (of actor, actress)* être en vedette; **who starred with Redford in 'The Sting'?** qui jouait avec Redford dans 'l'Arnaque'?; **'Othello', with Laurence Olivier starring in the title role** 'Othello', avec Laurence Olivier dans le rôle principal; **he's starring in a new TV serial** il est la vedette d'un nouveau feuilleton télévisé; **he starred as a gangster** il avait un rôle de gangster; **to have a starring role** avoir un des premiers rôles

▶▶ **s. part** rôle *m* de vedette; *Sport* **s. player** joueur, -euse vedette; **s. rating** *(of hotel)* classement *m* par étoiles *Comput* **s. structure** structure *f* en étoile; *Cin, Theat* **s. system** star-system *m*, *pl* star-systems; **s. turn** numéro *m* de premier ordre; *Fam (of performance, conference, evening)* clou *m*

starboard ['stɑːbəd] **N** *Naut* tribord *m*; **on the s. side,** to s. à tribord; **on the s. bow** par tribord devant; **hard a-s.!** tribord toute!

starch [stɑːtʃ] **N** *(for collar, tablecloth etc)* amidon *m*, empois *m*; *Culin (from potatoes)* fécule *f*, *(from rice, corn, wheat etc)* amidon *m*

VT *(collar, tablecloth etc)* empeser, amidonner

starched [stɑːtʃt] **ADJ** *Literary* maudit par le sort empesé, amidonné

starchy ['stɑːtʃɪ] **ADJ 1** *(diet)* riche en féculents; *(taste)* farineux; **s. foods** féculents *mpl* **2** *Fam (person, manner)* guindé

star-crossed ADJ
▶▶ **s. lovers** amants *mpl* maudits

stardom ['stɑːdəm] **N** *Cin, Theat etc (state)* célébrité *f*, vedettariat *m*; **to rise to s.** devenir une vedette, atteindre la célébrité; **dreams of s.** rêves *mpl* de célébrité

stardust ['stɑːdʌst] **N 1** *Astron* amas *m* stellaire **2** *(magic dust)* poudre *f* magique; **to have s. in one's eyes** être plein d'illusions

stare [steər] **N** regard *m* fixe; **glassy/stony s.** regard terne/dur; **vacant s.** regard vague; **to have a long s. at sb/sth** fixer longuement qn/qch

VI regarder fixement; *(with astonishment)* ouvrir de grands yeux; **to s. into the distance** regarder au loin; **don't s.!** ne regarde pas comme ça!; **it's rude to s.** ce n'est pas poli de dévisager les gens; **to s. at sb/sth** *(look at hard)* regarder qn/qch fixement, fixer qn/qch; *(begin to look at)* porter son regard sur qn/qch; *(be stupefied by)* regarder qn/qch d'un air hébété; **to s. at sb** *(look at insolently)* regarder qn effrontément, dévisager qn; **what are you staring at?** que regardez-vous comme ça?

VT to s. sb in the face dévisager qn; **it's staring you in the face** *(it's obvious)* ça vous saute aux yeux; **the answer was staring me in the face all the time** la réponse était sous mon nez depuis le début

▶ **stare out** **VT SEP to s. sb out** fixer qn jusqu'à ce qu'il/elle détourne les yeux

starfish ['stɑːfɪʃ] **N** étoile *f* de mer, astérie *f*

stargaze ['stɑːgeɪz] **VI 1** *Fam (look at stars)* regarder les étoiles **2** *(daydream)* rêvasser, bayer aux corneilles

stargazer ['stɑːgeɪzər] **N 1** *(astrologist)* astrologue *m*, *Fam (astronomer)* passionné, -ée d'astronomie **2** *(daydreamer)* rêveur, -euse, rêvasseur, -euse

stargazing ['stɑːgeɪzɪŋ] **N 1** *(astrology)* astrologie *f*, *Fam (looking at stars)* étude *f* des étoiles **2** *(daydreaming)* rêvasserie(s) *f(pl)*

staring ['steərɪŋ] **ADJ** *(bystanders)* curieux; **with s. eyes** *(fixedly)* aux yeux fixes; *(wide-open)* aux yeux écarquillés; *(blank)* aux yeux vides

stark [stɑːk] **ADJ** *(contrast)* absolu, fort; *(light)* cru; *(furnishing, black and white)* austère, sobre; *(truth, facts)* brut; *(landscape)*

nu; **this stands in s. contrast to** ... ceci se démarque nettement de ...; **s. realism** *(of novel, painting)* réalisme *m* brut; **a very s. flat** un appartement très nu *ou* sobre; **the s. simplicity of** ... la sobre *ou* l'austère simplicité de ...; **the s. desolation of the region** l'absolue désolation de la région; **s. madness** folie *f* pure; **the s. towns of the North** les mornes villes du Nord

ADV s. staring mad complètement fou; **s. naked** tout nu

starkers ['stɑːkəz] **ADJ, ADV** *Br Fam* à poil

starkness ['stɑːknɪs] **N** *(of furnishing etc)* austérité *f*, sobriété *f*, *(of landscape)* nudité *f*; **the s. of the contrast between** ... le contraste violent entre ...

starless ['stɑːlɪs] **ADJ** sans étoiles

starlet ['stɑːlɪt] **N** *Cin etc* starlette *f*, starlet *f*

starlight ['stɑːlaɪt] **N** lumière *f* des étoiles; **in the** *or* **by s.** à la lumière des étoiles

starling ['stɑːlɪŋ] **N** *(bird)* étourneau *m*

starlit ['stɑːlɪt] **ADJ** *(sky)* étoilé; **a s. night** une nuit étoilée

star-of-Bethlehem N *(plant)* ornithogale *m* (à ombelle), *Fam* dame *f* d'onze heures

starred [stɑːd] **ADJ** *Typ (asterisked)* marqué d'un astérisque

starry ['stɑːrɪ] **ADJ** *(sky)* étoilé, *(par)semé* d'étoiles
▶▶ **s. night** nuit *f* étoilée

starry-eyed **ADJ** *(person)* naïf, *f* naïve; **the children stood s. in front of the Christmas tree** les enfants étaient debout devant le sapin de Noël, émerveillés; **a s. scheme** un projet utopique; **she was all s. about him until** ... elle était tout émerveillée par lui jusqu'à ce que ...

starshell ['stɑːʃel] **N** *Mil* obus *m* éclairant *ou* à étoiles

star-spangled [-spæŋg(ə)ld] **ADJ** étoilé
▶▶ **the S. Banner** *(flag)* la bannière étoilée; *(national anthem)* l'hymne *m* national des États-Unis

START [stɑːt]

| **N** commencement **1** ▪ début **1** |
| ▪ départ **1, 2** ▪ démarrage **1** ▪ sursaut **3** |
| **VI** commencer **1** ▪ débuter **1** |
| ▪ sursauter **2** ▪ se mettre en route **3** |
| ▪ partir **3, 4** ▪ démarrer **4** |
| **VT** commencer **1** ▪ entamer **1** |
| ▪ lancer **1, 3, 4** ▪ fonder **3** ▪ mettre en marche **4** ▪ démarrer **4** |

N 1 *(beginning)* commencement *m*, début *m*; *(of journey, race)* départ *m*; *Aut* démarrage *m*; *Aviat* envol *m*; **for a s.** pour commencer; **at the s.** au début; **at the very s.** au tout début; **from the s.** dès le début; **there were problems from the s.** il y a eu des problèmes dès le début; **I never liked him, right from the s.** il m'a toujours déplu, dès le début; **from s. to finish** du début (jusqu')à la fin; **£5 isn't much, but it's a s.** 5 livres ce n'est pas grand-chose, mais c'est un début; **I've cleaned the kitchen – well, it's a s.** j'ai nettoyé la cuisine – eh bien, c'est déjà ça; **she had a good s. in life** elle a bien débuté dans la vie; **to make a s.** *(begin work)* commencer; *(begin journey)* se mettre en route; **to make a s. on sth** commencer qch; **to make a fresh s. in one's life** refaire sa vie; **to make a good s.** bien commencer; **to make a fresh s.** recommencer; *Sport* **false s.** faux départ; **to give sb a s.** *(in business etc)* lancer qn; *Sport* laisser qn partir le premier, donner un peu d'avance à qn; **to give sb a 60 metre(s) s.** donner à qn 60 mètres d'avance; **to have a s. on sb** être en avance sur qn

2 *(starting place)* départ *m*; **the runners**

lined up at the s. les coureurs se rangèrent sur la ligne de départ

3 *(sudden movement) (with fear, surprise)* tressaillement *m*, sursaut *m*, soubresaut *m*; **to wake with a s.** se réveiller en sursaut; **he gave a s.** il a tressailli, il a sursauté; **to give sb a s.** faire sursauter qn; **you gave me such a s.!** tu m'as fait peur!

VI 1 *(begin)* commencer; *(in career)* débuter; **to s. again** recommencer; **the story starts with a murder** l'histoire commence par un meurtre; **well, to s. at the beginning …** bon, commençons par le commencement …; **you'd better s. by telling me your name** vous devriez commencer par me dire votre nom; **let's s. with the cost** commençons par le coût; **to s. the way one means to go on** donner la mesure dès le début; **starting Monday** à partir de lundi; **she had started as a doctor** elle avait débuté *ou* commencé en tant que médecin; **to s. in business** se mettre *ou* se lancer dans les affaires; **to s. with** *(in the first place)* au début; **there were only six members to s. with** il n'y avait que six membres au début; **to s. on a job** commencer un travail; **she started on $500 a week** elle a débuté à 500 dollars par semaine; *Fam* **now don't you s.!** tu ne vas pas t'y mettre aussi!

2 *(move suddenly) (with surprise, fear etc)* sursauter, tressaillir, tressauter; **he started at the sound of my voice** il a tressailli au son de ma voix; **she started with surprise** surprise, elle sursauta; **to s. out of one's sleep** se réveiller en sursaut

3 *(begin journey)* partir, se mettre en route; **to s. again** repartir, se remettre en route; **to s. on a journey** commencer un voyage; **we s. tomorrow** nous partons demain

4 *(begin to move) (of car)* démarrer; *(of train)* partir, s'ébranler; *(of engine)* partir, démarrer; **the engine won't s.** le moteur refuse de partir *ou* de démarrer

VT 1 *(work, campaign etc)* commencer; *(conversation, talks etc)* entamer; *(a fashion, rumour etc)* lancer; **to s. a job** démarrer un travail; **to s. a meeting** débuter une séance; **to s. legal proceedings** engager une action en justice; **to s. a fire** provoquer un incendie; **you started it** c'est toi qui as commencé; **to s. doing sth, to s. to do sth** commencer *ou* se mettre à faire qch; **to s. crying again** se remettre à pleurer; **it's just started raining** il se met à pleuvoir; **now you've started something!** en voilà une affaire!; **if you s. him on this subject, he will never stop** si vous le lancez sur ce sujet, il ne tarira pas; **we started him in the sales department** nous l'avons fait débuter au service des ventes; **to get started** *(of person) (on task)* commencer, s'y mettre; *(on journey)* partir, se mettre en route; *(in career etc)* débuter, démarrer; **to help sb get started in life** aider qn à démarrer dans la vie; **when does he s. school?** quand est-ce qu'il commence l'école?

2 *Sport (runners etc)* donner le signal du départ à; *(in hunting) (stag, hare)* lever; *Horseriding* **to s. a horse at a gallop** faire partir un cheval au galop

3 *(set up) (company, newspaper)* lancer; *(business)* fonder; **to s. sb in business** lancer qn dans les affaires

4 *(cause to function) (machine)* mettre en marche, lancer; *(car)* démarrer; *(engine)* mettre en marche; *(computer, pump)* amorcer

▸▸*Comput* **s. bit** bit *m* de départ; *Comput* **s. button** *(in Windows)* bouton *m* Démarrer; *Comput* **s. code** code *m* de départ; *Comput* **s. menu** *(in Windows)* menu *m* Démarrer

▸**start in** *on* VT INSEP *esp Am (attack)* s'attaquer à

▸**start off** VI **1** *(begin journey)* = **start** VI **4**

2 *(begin)* commencer; **you s. off** *(in discussion etc)* commencez; **she started off by talking about …** elle commença en parlant de …

VT SEP **1** *(begin)* commencer; **s. your talk off with a reference to …** commencez votre discours en mentionnant …; **he lent us a couple of thousand pounds to s. us off** *(in business etc)* il nous a prêté quelques milliers de livres pour nous aider à démarrer; **here are three specimens to s. you off** *(with your collection)* voici trois spécimens pour commencer; **the pianist played a few bars to s. them off** *(in singing etc)* le pianiste a joué quelques mesures d'introduction; **what started the whole thing off?** comment tout a-t-il commencé?

2 to s. sb off *(on a subject)* lancer qn sur un sujet; **don't s. him off on that!** *(get him talking about it)* ne le lance pas sur ce sujet!; **the baby's crying again, what started him off this time?** le bébé s'est remis à pleurer, qu'est-ce qu'il a cette fois?; **dad's finally calmed down, don't you s. him off again** papa s'est enfin calmé, ne va pas l'énerver

▸**start on** VT INSEP *(begin quarrelling with, shouting at etc)* s'en prendre à

▸**start out** VI *(begin)* commencer, débuter; *(begin journey)* se mettre en route (**for** pour); **she started out as a postwoman/driving a van** elle a commencé *ou* débuté comme factrice/conductrice de camion; **he started out to write a novel** au départ, il voulait écrire un roman

▸**start over** VI *Am (start again)* recommencer

▸**start up** VI **1** *(start functioning) (of engine)* démarrer, se mettre en marche; *(of machine)* se mettre en marche; *(of computer, program)* se mettre en route

2 *(in business)* s'installer; **to s. up in business** monter sa propre affaire; **he decided to s. up by himself** il a décidé de se mettre à son compte

VT SEP **1** *(cause to function) (engine, car)* mettre en marche, démarrer; *(machine)* mettre en marche; *(computer, program)* mettre en route

2 *(company, newspaper)* lancer; *(business)* fonder; *(restaurant, school)* ouvrir

starter ['stɑːtər] N **1** *Sport (runner, horse)* partant *m*; **to be an early s.** *(start work early)* commencer son travail de bonne heure; **to be a slow s.** être lent à démarrer **2** *Sport etc (official)* starter *m*; **to be under s.'s orders** attendre le signal du starter **3** *(device), Aut* démarreur *m*; *Tech* dispositif *m* de mise en marche; *Elec* (rhéostat *m*) démarreur, rhéostat de démarrage **4** *esp Br Culin* entrée *f*, hors-d'œuvre *m inv*; **would you like a s.?** désirez-vous une entrée?; *Fig Fam* **for starters** *(for a start)* pour commencer, (tout) d'abord

▸▸*Br* **s. flat** = appartement *m* convenant à ceux qui achètent pour la première fois; **s. motor** démarreur *m*; *Tech* **s. solenoid** électrovalve *f* de starter

Note that the most common meaning of the French word **starter** is **choke** (in an engine).

starting ['stɑːtɪŋ] N **1** *(beginning)* commencement *m*, début *m*; *(causing to start) (of war, fight etc)* instigation *f* **2** *(of business etc)* mise *f* en route *ou* en train **3** *(of engine etc)* mise *f* en marche, démarrage *m*; *(of machine)* lancement *m*

▸▸**s. block** *(in athletics)* starting-block *m, pl* starting-blocks; *(for swimmers)* plot *m* de départ; *Br Aut* **s. handle** manivelle *f*; *Sport* **s. line** ligne *f* de départ; *Tech* **s. motor** moteur *m* de démarrage; **s. pistol** pistolet *m* du starter; **s. place, s. point** point *m* de départ; *Sport*

s. post ligne de départ; **s. price** prix *m* initial; *Horseracing* cote *f* au départ; *(at auction)* mise *f* à prix, prix d'appel; **s. salary** salaire *m* d'embauche; **s. signal** signal *m* de *ou* du départ; **s. up** *(of business etc)* mise en route *ou* en train; *(of engine)* mise en marche, démarrage; *(of machine)* lancement *m*

startle ['stɑːt(ə)l] VT *(alarm)* effrayer, alarmer; *(cause to jump)* faire sursauter; **she was startled to see him so pale** sa pâleur l'alarma

startled ['stɑːt(ə)ld] ADJ effrayé; **to give a s. cry** crier d'effroi

startling ['stɑːtlɪŋ] ADJ étonnant, surprenant; *(contrast, resemblance)* saisissant; **s. green eyes** des yeux d'un vert saisissant

start-up N **1** *(of machine)* démarrage *m* **2** *(of new business)* ouverture *f*, lancement *m*; **there have been 500 start-ups this year** il y a eu 500 créations d'entreprises cette année

▸▸*Fin* **s. capital** capital *m* initial, capital de départ; *Fin* **s. costs** frais *mpl* d'établissement; *Comput* **s. disk** disquette *f* de démarrage; *Comput* **s. screen** écran *m* d'accueil

starvation [stɑːˈveɪʃən] N privation *f ou* manque *m* de nourriture, inanition *f*, **millions are threatened with s. if …** des millions de gens vont peut-être mourir de faim si …; **to die of s.** mourir de faim; **prisoners were kept on a s. diet** les prisonniers étaient presque entièrement privés de nourriture; **a s. diet of rice and a few vegetables** une alimentation très pauvre à base de riz et de quelques légumes; **I'm on a s. diet** *(to slim)* je suis un régime draconien

▸▸**s. wages** salaire *m* de famine *ou* de misère

starve [stɑːv] VI *(lack food)* manquer de nourriture; *(endure hunger)* souffrir de la faim; **to s. (to death)** mourir de faim; *Fam* **I'm starving** *(hungry)* je meurs *ou* je crève de faim

VT *(deprive of food) (person)* priver de nourriture; **to s. sb (to death)** faire mourir qn de faim; **they were prepared to s. themselves to death rather than give in** ils étaient prêts à se laisser mourir de faim plutôt que de capituler; **to s. a city into surrender** affamer une ville pour l'amener à se rendre; *Fig* **to s. sb/sth of sth** priver qn/qch de qch

▸**starve out** VT SEP *Mil etc (town, garrison)* affamer *(pour le/la/etc faire sortir)*

starved [stɑːvd] ADJ affamé; **she looks half s.** elle a l'air famélique; **s. of affection** privé d'affection; **I'm feeling s. of affection** je suis en manque d'affection; *Fam* **I'm s.** *(hungry)* je crève de faim

starving ['stɑːvɪŋ] ADJ affamé; **the s. millions** tous ceux qui souffrent de la faim

Star Wars NPL *Mil* guerre *f* des étoiles

stash [stæʃ] *Fam* N **1** *(of arms)* cache *f*, *(of biscuits etc)* réserve *f* (secrète); **a s. of drugs was discovered** de la drogue a été découverte; **I hid my s.** *(of drugs)* j'ai caché ma part de drogue **2** *(place)* planque *f*

VT *(object) (hide)* cacher, planquer; *(put)* ficher

▸**stash away** VT SEP = **stash** VT

stasis ['steɪsɪs] N stase *f*

STATE [steɪt]		
N état **1** ▪ condition **1** ▪ situation **1** ▪ rang **2** ▪ État **3, 4**		
VT déclarer **1** ▪ formuler **1**		

N **1** *(condition)* état *m*, condition *f*, *(situation)* situation *f*; **to be in a good s. of repair** être en bon état; *Iron* **here's a nice s. of affairs!** nous voilà bien!, c'est du joli *ou* du propre!; **a body in a s. of rest/motion** un corps au repos/en mouvement; **to declare a s. of war/ emergency** déclarer l'état de guerre/d'urgence; **s. of consciousness** état de conscience; **s. of health** état de santé; **what's the current s. of play?** où en sont-ils?; **what's the current s. of play on our project?** où en est notre projet?; **I am not in a fit s. to travel** je ne suis pas en état de voyager; **he was in a s. of panic** il a été pris de panique; **she was in a s. of terror** elle était terrifiée; **the married s.** le mariage; **the single s.** le célibat; **in a solid/liquid s.** à l'état solide/liquide; **nitrogen is more easily transportable in its liquid s.** l'azote est plus facilement transportable à l'état liquide; **to be in a terrible s.** (emotionally) être dans tous ses états; (of room, papers etc) être dans un état désastreux; **this represents the s. of the art in ...** c'est la pointe de la technologie en matière de ...

2 (rank) rang m; (ceremony) pompe f, apparat m; **she lived in a style befitting her s.** elle avait un train de vie digne de son rang; **to live in s.** mener grand train; **to travel in s.** voyager en grand apparat; **to dine in s.** dîner en grande pompe; **to lie in s.** (of body) être exposé; **lying in s.** (of body) exposition f; **he was in his robes of s.** il était en costume d'apparat

3 Pol (country, nation) État m; **the S.** l'État; **Church and S.** l'Église et l'État; **Secretary of S.** Br secrétaire m d'État, Am ≃ ministre m des Affaires étrangères; **affairs of S.** affaires fpl d'État; **s.-run** public

4 (administrative region in some countries) État m; **the United States of America,** Fam **the States** les États-Unis (d'Amérique)

VT **1** (declare) déclarer; (conditions, demands, reasons, objections) énoncer; (claim etc) exposer, formuler; Math, Fig (problem) poser, énoncer; **this condition was expressly stated** cette condition était clairement énoncée; **the receipt should s. the source of payment** le reçu doit stipuler l'origine du paiement; **please s. below ...** veuillez noter en bas ...; **I have stated my opinion** j'ai donné mon opinion; **they stated their opposition to that measure** ils ont clairement fait savoir leur opposition à cette mesure; **I can s. with certainty that ...** je peux affirmer avec certitude que ...; Law **to s. the case** faire l'exposé des faits; **please s. your name and address (and qualifications)** veuillez décliner vos nom et adresse (et qualités)

2 (fix) (time, date) at the stated times aux heures indiquées; **on the stated dates** aux jours indiqués; **at stated intervals** à intervalles fixes

▸▸ **s.-aided industry** industrie f subventionnée par l'État; **s. apartments** appartements mpl de parade; **s. ball** grand bal m officiel; **s. capitalism** capitalisme m d'État; **s. carriage** voiture f d'apparat; **s. church** église f d'État; **s. coach** voiture d'apparat; **s. control** contrôle m étatique; (doctrine) étatisme m; **to bring an industry under s. control** étatiser une industrie; Am **S. Department** ≃ ministère m des Affaires étrangères; **s. documents** documents mpl officiels; **the s. education system** l'enseignement m public; Br **S. Enrolled Nurse** aide-soignant, -ante diplômé(e), pl aides-soignant(e)s diplômé(e)s; **s. funeral** funérailles fpl nationales; Hist **the States General** les États généraux; **s. government** gouvernement m d'État; **s. intervention** intervention f de l'État; **s. of mind** état d'esprit; **s. monopoly** monopole m d'État; **the S. Opening of Parliament** = l'ouverture f officielle du Parlement britannique en présence du souverain; **s.-owned company** entreprise f publique; **s.-owned industry** industrie du secteur public; **s. paper** imprimé m officiel; **s. pension** pension f de l'État; **s. planning** planification f nationale; **s. police** police f de l'État; Br Formerly **S. Registered Nurse** infirmier, -ière diplômé(e)

(remplacé en 1992 par 'Registered Nurse'); Br **s. school** école f publique; **s. secret** secret m d'État; Br **s. sector** secteur m public; **s. subsidy** subvention f d'État; Law **S. Supreme Court** = instance f judiciaire suprême dans chaque État américain; **the s. system** (education) le public, l'enseignement public; Am **s. trooper** ≃ gendarme m; **S. of the Union address** discours m sur l'état de l'Union; Am **S. university** = université f subventionnée et contrôlée par un État; Pol **s. visit** visite f officielle

---

State of the Union
Ce discours radiotélévisé, dans lequel le président des États-Unis dresse le bilan de son programme et en définit les orientations, est prononcé devant le Congrès. L'allocution présidentielle a lieu tous les ans en janvier.

statecraft ['steɪtkrɑːft] N savoir m d'un homme d'État

Statehouse ['steɪthaʊs] N Am = bâtiment m où siège le corps législatif d'un État

stateless ['steɪtlɪs] ADJ apatride
▸▸ **s. person** apatride mf; **s. society** société f sans État

statelessness ['steɪtlɪsnɪs] N apatridie f

stateliness ['steɪtlɪnɪs] N **1** (grandeur) majesté f, grandeur f **2** (dignity) dignité f

stately ['steɪtlɪ] ADJ **1** (imposing) majestueux, imposant **2** (dignified) plein de dignité; (noble) noble, élevé; **s. bearing** allure pleine de majesté
▸▸ **s. home** = château m ou manoir m à la campagne, généralement ouvert au public

statement ['steɪtmənt] N **1** déclaration f, (of facts) exposé m, énoncé m; (official, to Press, House of Commons) communiqué m; Law (made by witness etc) déposition f, **she made the following s.:** ... elle a déclaré ce qui suit; **I have no further statement(s) to make** je n'ai plus rien à ajouter; Fig **the film is making a s.** il y a un message dans ce film; Fig **someone who wears jeans to a wedding reception is making a s.** quelqu'un qui va à un mariage en jeans veut faire comprendre quelque chose; **a s. appeared in the press to the effect that ...** il fut affirmé dans la presse que ...; **a bare s. of the facts** un simple énoncé des faits; Law **to take sb's s.** prendre la déposition de qn; **to volunteer a s.** faire une déposition de son propre gré; **to call him a thief is nothing more than a s. of fact** le traiter de voleur, c'est une constatation

2 (received from bank, credit card company) (of account) relevé m de compte; **monthly s.** fin f de mois
▸▸ **s. of account** relevé m de compte; **s. of affairs** (in bankruptcy) bilan m de liquidation

state-of-play report N état m de situation

state-of-the-art ADJ (technology, design etc) de pointe, très avancé; **it's very s.** c'est le nec plus ultra, c'est très moderne

stateroom ['steɪtruːm] N **1** Naut cabine f, Am Rail Old-fashioned (compartiment m de) wagon-lit m, pl wagons-lits **2** esp Br (in palace etc) chambre f d'apparat, grand appartement m

stateside ['steɪtsaɪd] ADV aux États-Unis
ADJ des États-Unis, américain

statesman, pl **statesmen** ['steɪtsmən] N homme m d'État

statesmanlike ['steɪtsmənlaɪk] ADJ (attitude etc) d'homme d'État; Fig stratégique

statesmanship ['steɪtsmənʃɪp] N art m de gouverner; **a decision which shows considerable s.** une décision qui prouve des qualités d'homme d'État

statewide ['steɪtwaɪd] ADJ, ADV partout dans un/l'État

static ['stætɪk] N **1** électricité f statique; (on telephone line, radio) parasites mpl **2** Am Fam (insolence) insolence f; (hassle, interference) embêtements mpl; **I'm not taking that s. from you!** arrête de faire l'insolent! **you can expect plenty of s. from mom** tu vas avoir Maman sur le dos
ADJ **1** (electricity) statique **2** (not moving) statique; (unchangeable) immuable; Pej (relationship etc) qui stagne; **the situation remains s.** la situation reste inchangée
▸▸ Aut **s. lap belt** ceinture f ventrale statique; Comput **s. RAM, s. random access memory** mémoire f vive statique; TV, Cin **s. shot** plan m fixe

statics ['stætɪks] NPL Phys (usu with sing verb) statique f VOIR GRAMMAIRE A10

station ['steɪʃən] N **1** (railway) s. gare f, underground or Am subway s. station f de métro; **bus** or Br **coach s.** gare routière; Rail **passenger/goods s.** gare de voyageurs/de marchandises

2 (place) position f, place f, (post) poste m; **to take up one's s.** (take one's place) prendre sa place; (go to one's post) se rendre à son poste; Rel **the stations of the Cross** le chemin de la Croix; Mil etc **action stations** postes de combat; Mil, Fig **action stations!** à vos postes!; **naval s.** station f navale; (port) port m de guerre; **military s.** poste militaire; (garrison) garnison f, Naut **lifeboat s.** station de sauvetage; Met **weather s.** station météo(rologique); **(police) s.** commissariat m (de police), poste (de police); **fire s.** poste ou caserne f de pompiers; **power s.** centrale f électrique; **atomic power s.** centrale atomique; Aut **filling s., petrol s.,** Am **gas s.** poste d'essence, station-service f, pl stations-service

3 (radio) s. station f (de radio); (television) s. chaîne f (de télévision)

4 Austr (farm) = ferme f (et ses dépendances); **sheep s.** élevage m de moutons

5 (social condition) position f, condition f, (rank) rang m; **s. in life** situation f sociale; Old-fashioned **to marry below or beneath one's s.** faire une mésalliance, se mésallier
VT (person in a place) placer, mettre; (soldier) désigner son poste à; (troops) poster; **to be stationed at ...** Mil être stationné ou être en garnison à ...; Naut être en station à ...; **he stationed himself behind a door** il s'est posté derrière une porte
▸▸ TV, Radio **s. ident, s. identification** indicatif m de chaîne; Rail **s. manager** chef m de gare; Rail **s. master** chef de gare; **s. presetting** Radio programmation f des stations; TV programmation des chaînes; Am Aut **s. wagon** break m; **s. waiter** chef de rang

stationary ['steɪʃ(ə)rɪ] ADJ **1** (not moving) immobile; (car) (parked) en stationnement; (not moving) à l'arrêt; **to remain s.** rester immobile **2** (fixed) fixe; (permanent) à demeure
▸▸ Mil **s. target** cible f fixe

Attention: ne pas confondre avec **stationery.**

---

stationer ['steɪʃənər] N papetier m; **s.'s (shop)** papeterie f

stationery ['steɪʃ(ə)rɪ] N papeterie f, (writing paper) papier m à lettres; **office/school s.** fournitures fpl de bureau/scolaires; **hotel s.** = papier à lettres à en-tête d'un hôtel; **headed s.** papier à en-tête
▸▸ Br Admin **the S. Office** = maison f d'édition britannique publiant les documents approuvés par le Parlement, les ministères et autres organismes officiels, ≃ l'Imprimerie f nationale

Attention: ne pas confondre avec **stationary**.

statism ['steɪtɪz(ə)m] N étatisme m

statist ['steɪtɪst] ADJ étatiste

statistic [stə'tɪstɪk] N *(statistical item)* élément m d'un/du tableau statistique; **statistics** statistiques fpl; **a worrying s.** un chiffre inquiétant; **to become just another s.** *(unimportant person)* n'être plus qu'un numéro; **he became just another s.** *(was killed)* il est juste venu s'ajouter aux statistiques (des morts); **vital statistics** statistiques démographiques; *Fam (of woman)* mensurations fpl

statistical [stə'tɪstɪk(ə)l] ADJ statistique
▸▸ **s. data** données fpl statistiques; **s. tables** statistiques fpl

statistically [stə'tɪstɪk(ə)lɪ] ADV statistiquement

statistician [stætɪs'tɪʃən] N statisticien, -ienne

statistics [stə'tɪstɪks] NPL *(usu with sing verb) (science)* statistique f VOIR GRAMMAIRE A10

stator ['steɪtər] N *Tech, Elec (of turbine)* stator m

statuary ['stætjʊərɪ] ADJ *(art, marble etc)* statuaire
N **1** *(art)* statuaire f, art m statuaire **2** *(statues)* statues fpl

statue ['stætjuː] N statue f; **don't stand there like a s.!** ne reste pas là comme une souche!

statuesque [stætjʊ'esk] ADJ sculptural, -aux

statuette [stætjʊ'et] N statuette f

stature ['stætʃər] N stature f, taille f; **to be short of s.** être de petite taille; **it will increase her s.** *(of author etc)* sa réputation y gagnera; **he grew in s. as he …** *(in reputation)* il acquit une certaine réputation à mesure qu'il …; **a writer of some international s.** un écrivain ayant une certaine renommée internationale; **a politician of his s.** un homme politique de son envergure

status ['steɪtəs] N *(position)* statut m; *(marital)* situation f de famille; *(prestige, standing)* prestige m, standing m; **(personal) s.** statut (personnel); *Admin* **civil s.** état m civil; **social s.** rang m social; **with no official s.** sans titre officiel; **he's only interested in the job because of the s. that's attached to it** cet emploi ne l'intéresse qu'en raison du prestige qui y est attaché
▸▸ *Comput* **s. bar** barre f d'état; *Comput* **s. box** zone f d'état; **s. enquiry** *(about creditworthiness)* prise f de renseignements sur la solvabilité; **s. enquiry department** service m des renseignements commerciaux; *Comput* **s. line** ligne f d'état; **s. meeting** réunion f de bilan; *Comput* **s. printout** *(of printer)* impression f des paramètres de l'imprimante; **s. quo** statu quo m; **to maintain the s. quo** maintenir le statu quo; *Comput* **s. report** état m du projet; **s. symbol** marque f de prestige

status-conscious ADJ attaché à son standing

statute ['stætjuːt] N *Law* loi f, ordonnance f; *Br Pol (act)* acte m du Parlement; **statutes** *(of company)* statuts mpl, règlements mpl
▸▸ *Br* **s. book** code m (des lois), recueil m de lois; **to put sth in the s. book** faire passer qch en loi; *(of trade union etc)* faire passer qch dans le règlement; **s. law** droit m écrit; **s. of limitations** loi de prescription, prescription f légale; **the s. of limitations in this country is ten years** dans ce pays, il y a prescription de dix ans

statutory ['stætjʊt(ə)rɪ] ADJ **1** *(established by law)* établi par la loi; *(by regulations)* réglementaire; *(offence)* prévu par la loi; **there**
is no **s. obligation to …** il n'y a aucune obligation légale de … **2** *(according to law)* statutaire, conforme aux statuts
▸▸ **s. duty** devoir m défini par la loi; **s. holiday** jour m férié, fête f légale; *Am* **s. rape** détournement m de mineur; **s. regulations** règlements mpl statutaires; **s. reserve** réserve f statutaire; **s. rights** droits mpl statutaires; **s. sick pay** = indemnité f de maladie versée par l'employeur

staunch[1] [stɔːntʃ] ADJ *(person)* sûr, dévoué; *(supporter)* dévoué, loyal; **a s. Catholic** un(e) catholique à tout crin; **a s. socialist** un(e) socialiste convaincu(e)

staunch[2] VT *(blood)* étancher; **to s. a wound** étancher le sang d'une blessure

staunchly ['stɔːntʃlɪ] ADV avec fermeté; *(with resolve)* avec résolution; **s. Catholic/ republican area** région résolument catholique/républicaine

staunchness ['stɔːntʃnɪs] N *(of person)* fermeté f, *(loyalty)* dévouement m

stave [steɪv] N **1** *(wooden stick)* bâton m; **staves** *(of barrel)* douves fpl **2** *(in prosody) (of poem)* stance f, strophe f **3** *Mus* portée f
▸ **stave in** VT SEP *(pt, pp staved, stove* [stəʊv]*) (break) (barrel, ship's sides)* défoncer, enfoncer
▸ **stave off** VT SEP *(keep away) (problem etc)* détourner, écarter; *(danger)* prévenir, parer à; *(disaster)* conjurer; **to s. off a cold** éviter un rhume; **to s. off hunger** tromper la faim

STAY[1] [steɪ]

VI		
rester **1**	séjourner **2**	loger **2**
s'arrêter **4**	habiter **5**	
VT arrêter **1**	enrayer **1**	ajourner **2**
tenir **3**		
N séjour	visite	

VI **1** *(not move, remain)* rester; **s. there!** tenez-vous là!; **s. where you are!** restez où vous êtes!; *Fam* **to s. put** ne pas bouger; *(refuse to move)* refuser de bouger; *Fam* **I'll s. put, I'm staying put** j'y suis, j'y reste; **to s. still** rester tranquille; **to s. at home** rester à la maison *ou* chez soi; **to s. in bed** rester au lit; *(when ill)* garder le lit; **to s. to** *or* **for dinner** rester (à *ou* pour) dîner; **computers are here to s.** les ordinateurs sont entrés dans les mœurs; **this word is here to s.** ce mot est entré dans la langue; **these changes are here to s.** ces changements sont passés dans les mœurs; **the weather stayed fine/ wet all week** le temps est resté au beau/à la pluie toute la semaine; **it stays dark until after eight in winter** il fait nuit jusqu'à plus de huit heures en hiver; **if the weather stays like this** si le temps se maintient; **s.!** *(to dog)* pas bouger!; **it won't s. in position** impossible de le/la faire tenir en place

2 *(reside) (for short time)* séjourner; **I stayed five years in the States** j'ai passé *ou* habité cinq ans aux États-Unis; **where are you staying?** où loges-tu?; **he has come to s.** *(for a visit)* il est venu passer quelques jours chez nous; *(for good)* il est venu habiter chez nous; **to s. at a hotel** être à l'hôtel; **I'm staying at a hotel** je suis descendu à l'hôtel; **to s. with sb** loger chez qn; *(for holiday)* passer quelque temps chez qn; **we're staying with relations** nous sommes chez des parents

3 *Sport (endure)* **a horse that can s.** un cheval qui a du fond; **to s. with sth** s'atteler à qch; **it won't be finished unless you s. with it** ce ne sera jamais fini à moins que tu ne t'y tiennes

4 *Arch (stop)* s'arrêter

5 *Scot (live)* habiter, demeurer

VT **1** *esp Lit (stop) (person's progress)* arrêter; *(epidemic)* enrayer; **to s. sb's arm** *or* **hand** retenir le bras de qn; **to s. one's hand** se retenir
2 *Law etc* remettre; *(decision etc)* ajourner; **to s. judgement** surseoir à un/au jugement
3 *(endure)* **she can s. five kilometres** elle peut tenir cinq kilomètres; **to s. the course** tenir le rythme; *Sport* **will he s. the distance?** tiendra-t-il la distance?

N *(in a town etc)* séjour m; *(at friend's house)* visite f; *(fortnight's* **s.** séjour de quinze jours
▸▸ **s. of execution** *Law* ordonnance f à surseoir (à un jugement), sursis m; *Fig* sursis; *Law* **s. of proceedings** suspension f d'instances

▸ **stay away** VI *(not approach)* ne pas s'approcher (**from** de); *(not attend)* ne pas assister (**from** à); **to s. away from school** ne pas aller à l'école; **to s. away from danger** se tenir à l'écart du danger; **you can play outside, but s. away from the road** tu peux jouer dehors, mais ne va pas sur la route

▸ **stay behind** VI rester en arrière; *(after school, work)* rester plus tard

▸ **stay down** VI **1** *Sch (repeat year)* redoubler
2 *(of hair, lid etc)* tenir en place; **I've tried to eat but nothing will s. down** j'ai essayé de manger mais je ne garde rien
3 *(under water)* **the turtle/diver can s. down for …** la tortue/le plongeur peut rester sous l'eau pendant …

▸ **stay in** VI **1** *(not go out)* ne pas sortir; *(stay in house)* rester à la maison
2 *(of screw, fitting etc)* rester en place

▸ **stay off** VI **1** *(not go to work, school)* rester à la maison
2 *(hold off) (of bad weather)* ne pas arriver; **we're hoping the rain will s. off a little longer** nous espérons que la pluie attendra encore un peu
VT INSEP **1** *(keep away from) (main roads, private property etc)* éviter, ne pas passer par; *(alcohol, drugs, sweets etc)* ne pas prendre, éviter; **s. off the whisky!** pas de whisky!
2 *(not attend) (school, work etc)* ne pas aller à

▸ **stay on** VI **1** *(remain longer)* rester plus longtemps
2 *(remain in place) (of hat, wig etc)* tenir *ou* rester en place; *(of sticker etc)* tenir

▸ **stay out** VI **1** *(stay outside)* rester dehors; *(not come home)* ne pas rentrer; **to s. out all night** découcher; **to s. out late** rentrer tard; **to s. out until all hours of the night** rester dehors jusque très tard dans la nuit
2 *Ind (continue strike)* poursuivre *ou* continuer la grève
3 *(not interfere)* **to s. out of sth** ne pas se mêler de qch; **s. out of this!** ne t'en mêle pas!

▸ **stay over** VI prolonger son séjour, rester plus longtemps; **you can s. over if you like** *(spend the night)* tu peux dormir ici si tu veux

▸ **stay up** VI **1** *(not go to bed)* ne pas se coucher, veiller; **to s. up late** se coucher *ou* veiller tard; **we stayed up all night talking** nous sommes restés à parler toute la nuit; **my parents always s. up until I get home** mes parents attendent toujours jusqu'à ce que je sois rentré pour aller se coucher; **don't s. up for me** ne m'attends pas pour aller dormir
2 *(remain in place) (of picture, shelf, tent, trousers)* tenir; **the decorations stayed up until February** les décorations sont restées en place jusqu'en février
3 *Br (at university)* **he used to s. up over the vacations** il restait (travailler) à l'université pendant les vacances

stay[2] N **1** *(support)* soutien m; *Constr, Tech etc* étai m, étançon m; *Naut (for mast)* étai m; *Aut (for bonnet)* béquille f
2 **stays** *(corset)* corset m

stay-at-home ADJ, N casanier, -ière

stayer ['steɪər] N **1** *Sport (runner)* coureur m de fond; *(cyclist)* stayer m; *(horse)* stayer, cheval m qui a du fond **2** *(person who perseveres)* personne f persévérante; **she's a real**

s. elle va jusqu'au bout de ce qu'elle entreprend; **gifted but not a s.** doué mais manque de suivi *ou* de persévérance

staying ['steɪɪŋ] N
▸▸**s. power** résistance *f,* endurance *f;* **to have good s. power** *(of horse)* avoir du fond

stay-over N *(reused hotel room)* chambre *f* en recouche, recouche *f*

stays list N *(at hotel)* liste *f* des clients en recouche

STD [estiː'diː] N **1** *Br Tel* (*abbr* **subscriber trunk dialling**) automatique *m* (interurbain) **2** *Med* (*abbr* **sexually transmitted disease**) MST *f*
▸▸*Br Tel* **S. code** indicatif *m* de zone

stead [sted] N **1** **to stand sb in good s.** être fort utile à qn **2** *esp Lit* **in sb's s.** à la place *ou* au lieu de qn

steadfast ['stedfɑːst] ADJ ferme, stable; **s. in love/in adversity** constant en amour/dans l'adversité; **they were s. in their refusal to compromise** ils se sont montrés très déterminés dans leur refus du compromis
ADV *(to hold, stand)* sans fléchir

steadfastly ['stedfɑːstlɪ] ADV *(to refuse)* fermement; *(to love, serve etc)* avec constance; **she has s. refused to identify her sources** elle a toujours refusé de désigner ses sources

steadfastness ['stedfɑːstnɪs] N *(determination)* fermeté *f,* *(constancy)* constance *f*

Steadicam® ['stedɪkæm] N *TV, Cin* Steadicam® *f*
▸▸**S. operator** opérateur *m* Steadicam®

steadily ['stedɪlɪ] ADV **1** *(solidly)* fermement **2** *(at regular rate)* régulièrement; *(without stopping)* sans arrêt; *(without jolting)* sans à-coups; *(constantly)* continuellement; *(to work)* assidûment; **to walk s.** *(not stagger)* bien tenir sur ses jambes; **s. increasing output** rendement augmentant de façon régulière; **his health grows s. worse** sa santé empire régulièrement; **to work s. at sth** travailler assidûment à qch; **they were s. gaining on us** inexorablement, ils nous rattrapaient **3** *(calmly)* d'une manière posée; **she looked at him s.** elle l'a fixé du regard, elle l'a regardé fixement

steadiness ['stedɪnɪs] N **1** *(of table, hand etc)* fermeté *f;* **s. of hand** sûreté *f* des gestes; **s. of hand is vital for surgeons** il est vital que les chirurgiens aient la main sûre **2** *(regularity)* *(of movement, action)* régularité *f;* *(perseverance)* assiduité *f,* persévérance *f;* *(stability)* stabilité *f;* **s. of purpose** constance *f* (avec laquelle l'on poursuit ses objectifs); *St Exch* **s. of prices** bonne tenue *f* des prix **3** *(calm)* *(of person)* calme *m;* *(non-volatility)* régularité *f*

steady ['stedɪ] ADJ **1** *(stable, solid)* *(table, ladder etc)* stable; **to make a bookshelf s.** rendre une étagère stable; **to hold sth s.** bien tenir qch; **to keep s.** ne pas bouger; **to be s. on one's feet** *or* **legs** être d'aplomb sur ses jambes; **to have a s. hand** avoir la main sûre; **with a s. hand** d'une main sûre *ou* ferme

2 *(regular)* *(rate, increase, growth)* continu, soutenu; *(income)* fixe, régulier; *(pulse)* égal; *Com (market)* soutenu; *(person)* *(in work, lifestyle etc)* régulier; **s. breeze** brise *f* étale; *Com* **s. demand** demande suivie (**for** pour); *Sport* **to play a s. game** avoir un jeu régulier; **beneath her s. gaze** sous son regard soutenu; **s. increase** augmentation *f* régulière; **s. pace** allure *f* régulière; **to drive at a s. 90** rouler constamment à 90; **s. prices** prix *mpl* stables; **s. progress** progrès *mpl* constants; **s. rain** pluie *f* persistante; **s. worker** travailleur *m* régulier *(concernant la productivité)*; **to be s. in one's affections** être constant dans ses affections; **he hasn't been**

in s. work for years il n'a pas (eu) de travail stable depuis des années

3 *(calm)* posé; **s. horse** cheval *m* calme; **in a s. voice** d'une voix posée

4 **he has a s. girlfriend** il a la même copine depuis longtemps; **I don't have a s. boyfriend** je n'ai pas vraiment de petit ami
ADV *Fam* **they are going s. now** ça devient sérieux entre eux deux; **they've been going s. for two years now** ça fait deux ans qu'ils sortent ensemble
INT **s.!** *(don't move)* ne bougez pas!; *(watch out you don't fall)* attention (de ne pas tomber)!; *Fam* **s. (on)!** *(gently)* doucement!
N *Fam* **my s.** *(boyfriend)* mon petit ami; *(girlfriend)* ma petite amie
VT raffermir, affermir; **to s. one's hand** s'assurer que sa main ne tremble pas; **to s. oneself** retrouver son équilibre; **to s. oneself against sth** s'appuyer contre qch; **to s. one's nerves** sans nerfs; **marriage has steadied him** le mariage lui a donné un certain équilibre
VI *(of boat etc)* retrouver son équilibre; **prices are steadying** les prix se raffermissent
▸ **steady down** VI *(become a calmer person)* se calmer

steak [steɪk] N *Culin (beef)* bifteck *m,* steak *m;* *(cut from the ribs)* entrecôte *f,* *(of meat, fish)* tranche *f;* *(of salmon)* darne *f;* **fillet s.** *(beef)* tournedos *m;* **s. and chips** steak frites
▸▸**s. and kidney pie** tourte *f* à la viande et aux rognons de bœuf; **s. and kidney pudding** pudding *m* à la viande et aux rognons de bœuf; **s. knife** couteau *m* à steak *ou* à viande; **s. tartare** steak *m* tartare

steakhouse ['steɪkhaʊs] N grill *m*

steal [stiːl] VT *(pt* **stole** [stəʊl]; *pp* **stolen** ['stəʊl(ə)n]) *(property, person's idea, husband)* voler (**from sb** à qn); **I've had my purse stolen** on m'a volé mon portemonnaie; **to s. money from the till** *(of employee)* prendre de l'argent *ou* se servir dans la caisse; **to s. sb's heart** prendre le cœur de qn; **to s. a kiss** voler un baiser; **to s. a few hours from one's studies** laisser ses études de côté pendant quelques heures; **to s. a glance at sb** jeter un coup d'œil furtif à qn; **to s. a march on sb** devancer qn; *Theat* **to s. the show** ravir la vedette; **to s. sb's thunder** couper l'herbe sous le pied de qn
VI **1** voler (**from sb** qn); *Bible* **thou shalt not s.** tu ne voleras point **2** *(move quietly)* **to s. away/in/out** s'en aller/entrer/sortir sans bruit; **she stole into the room** elle s'est faufilée *ou* glissée dans la pièce; **to s. up on sb** se glisser vers qn; *Fig (of old age etc)* prendre qn par surprise
N *Fam (bargain)* affaire *f;* **at $35, it's a s.!** à 35 dollars, c'est une affaire!

stealing ['stiːlɪŋ] N vol *m;* **s. is wrong** c'est mal de voler

stealth [stelθ] N ruse *f;* **by s.** par la ruse; *(furtively)* à la dérobée, furtivement; **to do good by s.** faire le bien en restant dans l'ombre
▸▸*Mil* **s. bomber** avion *m* furtif; **s. tax** = mesure *f* visant à augmenter les recettes du gouvernement par un moyen détourné, afin d'éviter une hausse directe et visible des impôts qui mécontenterait les citoyens

stealthily ['stelθɪlɪ] ADV furtivement, à la dérobée

stealthiness ['stelθɪnɪs] N *(of action etc)* caractère *m* furtif; *(of person)* manières *fpl* furtives; **his s. in defaming his rivals** la ruse avec laquelle il parvenait à diffamer ses rivaux

stealthy ['stelθɪ] ADJ furtif; *(look)* dérobé, à la dérobée; **with a s. step** à pas furtifs *ou* feutrés *ou* de loup

steam [stiːm] N vapeur *f* (d'eau); *(condensa-*

tion) buée *f;* *Tech etc* **to get up** *or* **to raise s.** mettre la chaudière sous pression; **to get up s.** *(of person)* rassembler toutes ses forces *ou* toute son énergie; **at full s.** à toute vapeur; *Naut* **full s. ahead!** en avant toute!; **to run out of s.** *(of engine etc)* ne plus être sous pression; *Fam (of project, campaign etc)* s'essouffler; *Fam (of person)* manquer de souffle; *Fam* **I'm running out of s.** je commence à peiner; *Fig* **to let off s.** se défouler; **to proceed under its own s.** *(of damaged ship etc)* parvenir à naviguer sans être remorqué; *Fig* **I'll get there under my own s.** j'irai par mes propres moyens
VT passer à la vapeur, étuver; *Culin (vegetables etc)* cuire à la vapeur *ou* à l'étuvée; **to s. open an envelope** décacheter une lettre à la vapeur
VI **1** *(give off steam)* fumer; **horses steaming with sweat** chevaux fumants (de sueur) **2** *(cook in steam)* *(of vegetables etc)* cuire à la vapeur **3** **to s. ahead** *(of ship, locomotive)* avancer (à la vapeur); *Fig (make rapid progress)* avancer à toute vapeur; **the train steamed out of the station** le train quitta la gare dans un nuage de fumée; **the ferry steamed into port** le ferry entra dans le port; *Fig Fam* **he came steaming into the room** *(fast)* il est entré dans la pièce à toute pompe; *(angry)* il est entré dans la pièce en fulminant
▸▸**s. bath** bain *m* de vapeur; **s. cooking** cuisson *f* à la vapeur; **s. engine** *Tech* moteur *m* à vapeur; *Rail* locomotive *f* à vapeur; **s. iron** fer *m* (à repasser) à vapeur; **s. power** vapeur *f;* *Old-fashioned Br Fam* **s. radio** *(broadcasting)* ≃ la bonne vieille radio *(par opposition à la télévision); (set)* poste *m* de radio antédiluvien; **in the days of s. radio** aux débuts de la radio; **s. room** hammam *m;* *Am* **s. shovel** bulldozer *m*
▸ **steam off** VT SEP *(stamp)* décoller à la vapeur
VI *(of ship)* s'éloigner (en fumant)
▸ **steam up** VI *(become covered in condensation)* *(of window, windscreen, glasses etc)* s'embuer
VT SEP *(usu passive)* **to get all steamed up** *(of windows, glasses etc)* se couvrir de buée, s'embuer; *Fig Fam (lose one's composure)* s'énerver

steamboat ['stiːmbəʊt] N (bateau *m* à) vapeur *m*

steamboats ['stiːmbəʊts] ADJ *Br Fam (drunk)* rond comme une queue de pelle, pété à mort

steamed [stiːmd] ADJ *(vegetables etc)* à la vapeur

steamer ['stiːmər] N **1** *(ship)* (bateau *m* à) vapeur *m* **2** *Culin (saucepan)* cuiseur *m* à vapeur; *(insert for saucepan)* panier *m* de cuisson à la vapeur

steaming ['stiːmɪŋ] ADJ **1** *(emitting steam)* fumant **2** *Fig Fam (angry)* fumant de colère; *Br (drunk)* bourré, pété
ADV **s. hot** bien chaud; *Br Fam* **s. drunk** bourré, pété
N **1** *Culin* cuisson *f* à la vapeur *ou* à l'étuvée **2** *Sl (street robbery by gangs)* = vol *m* de sacs à main pratiqué en bande

steamroller ['stiːmrəʊlər] N *Constr* rouleau *m* compresseur; *Fig* force *f* écrasante
VT *Constr (road)* passer au rouleau compresseur; *Fig (the opposition etc)* écraser; **to s. a bill through Parliament** imposer un projet de loi au Parlement; **he steamrollered his plans through the committee** il a imposé ses projets au comité

steamship ['stiːmʃɪp] N bateau *m* à vapeur

steamy ['stiːmɪ] ADJ *(full of steam)* plein de vapeur; *(covered in steam)* couvert de buée; *Fig Fam (novel, movie, scene)* torride

steed [stiːd] N *Lit* coursier *m,* destrier *m*

steel [sti:l] N 1 *(metal)* acier *m*; **rolled s.** acier laminé; **a grip/a will of s.** une poigne/une volonté de fer; **nerves of s.** nerfs *mpl* d'acier; **s. knife/ladder** couteau *m*/échelle *f* en acier; **s. plate** plaque *f* d'acier 2 *Arch, Lit (sword)* fer *m*, épée *f*; *(blade)* lame *f* 3 *(for sharpening knives)* affiloir *m*, fusil *m*
VT **to s. oneself** *or* **one's heart to do sth** s'armer de courage pour faire qch; **to s. oneself against sth** se blinder contre qch
▸▸ *Mus* **s. band** steel band *m*; **the s. industry** la sidérurgie; **s. mill** aciérie *f*; **s. wool** paille *f* de fer

steelclad ['sti:lklæd] ADJ couvert *ou* revêtu d'acier; *(knight)* bardé de fer

steel-plated ADJ cuirassé

steelwork ['sti:lwɜ:k] N 1 *Tech* tôleries *fpl*; **constructional s.** profilés *mpl* pour constructions 2 *(usu with sing verb)* **steelworks** *(factory)* aciérie *f*

steelworker ['sti:lwɜ:kər] N ouvrier *m* de l'industrie sidérurgique

steely ['sti:lɪ] ADJ 1 *(of steel)* d'acier; **s. blue** bleu *m* acier 2 *(hard)* dur; *(gaze etc)* d'acier; *(determination)* inflexible

steelyard ['sti:ljɑ:d, 'stɪljəd] N (balance *f*) romaine *f*

steep¹ [sti:p] ADJ 1 *(path, hill, street)* escarpé, raide; *(slope)* raide; *(cliff)* à pic; **s. climb** *(hill)* pente *f* raide; **the plane went into a s. climb/dive** l'avion monta à la verticale/descendit en piqué; **s. gradient** forte pente, pente raide *ou* rapide; **s. rise in prices** hausse *f* considérable des prix 2 *Fam (excessive) (price etc)* excessif; **that's pretty s.!** *(of price)* c'est un peu raide!; **that's a bit s.!** *(unreasonable)* c'est un peu fort!

steep² VT *(clothes, food)* faire tremper; *(hides)* tremper; **terrace steeped in sunshine** terrasse baignée de soleil; **steeped in prejudice** imbibé de préjugés; **steeped in history** imprégné d'histoire; **to s. oneself in the atmosphere of the Middle Ages** se tremper *ou* se plonger dans l'atmosphère du Moyen Âge
VI tremper; *Culin* macérer, mariner

steepen ['sti:p(ə)n] VI *(of slope etc)* devenir plus raide; *(of prices)* augmenter

steeple ['sti:p(ə)l] N *(bell tower)* clocher *m*; *(spire)* flèche *f* (de clocher)

steeplechase ['sti:p(ə)ltʃeɪs] N *Sport, Horseracing* steeple-chase *m*, *pl* steeple-chases, steeple *m*

steeplechaser ['sti:p(ə)ltʃeɪsər] N *Sport, Horseracing (rider)* cavalier *m* qui monte en steeple-chases; *(horse, athlete)* steeplechaser *m*, *pl* steeple-chasers

steeplechasing ['sti:p(ə)ltʃeɪsɪŋ] N *Sport, Horseracing* steeple-chases *mpl*

steeplejack ['sti:p(ə)ldʒæk] N réparateur *m* de clochers et de cheminées d'usines

steeply ['sti:plɪ] ADV *(to drop)* en pente raide, à pic; *(to climb)* à pic; **road that climbs s.** route à forte pente; **to rise s.** *(of path)* monter à pic; *Fig (of prices)* monter en flèche

steepness ['sti:pnɪs] N *(of slope)* escarpement *m*

steer [stɪər] VT *(car)* conduire, diriger; *(ship)* gouverner; *(yacht)* barrer; *(person)* diriger (**towards** vers); **to s. sb out of trouble** sortir qn du pétrin; **to s. a northerly course, to s. north** faire route vers le nord; *(turn north)* mettre le cap sur le nord; *Fig* **to s. a middle course** trouver un compromis; **he tried to s. the conversation away from the subject** il a essayé de détourner la conversation; **to s. the conversation round to another subject** aiguiller la conversation sur un autre sujet; **to s. a country out of a crisis** faire sortir un pays de la crise
VI *(of person)* conduire; *(of ship)* gouverner;

to s. for sth se diriger vers qch; **to s. clear of sb/sth** éviter qn/qch
N *(bull)* bœuf *m*

steerage ['stɪərɪdʒ] N *Naut Old-fashioned (third-class accommodation)* entrepont *m*; **to travel s.** voyager dans l'entrepont

steerageway ['stɪərɪdʒweɪ] N *Naut* vitesse *f* nécessaire pour gouverner

steering ['stɪərɪŋ] N *(act) (of car)* direction *f*; *(mechanism) (of car)* timonerie *f*, (boîte *f* de) direction; *(of ship)* appareil *m* à gouverner; *(of plane)* direction
▸▸ *Aut* **s. arm** bras *m* de direction; *Aut* **s. box** boîtier *m* de direction; **s. column** colonne *f* de direction; **s. column lock** antivol *m* de direction; *Br* **s. committee** comité *m* directeur; *Aut* **s. geometry** géométrie *f* du train avant; *Aut* **s. lock** *(turning circle)* rayon *m* de braquage; *(antitheft device)* antivol *m* de direction; **s. play** jeu *m* à la direction; **s. rod** bielle *f* de direction; **s. wheel** *Aut* volant *m*; *Naut* roue *f* du gouvernail, barre *f*

steersman, *pl* **steersmen** ['stɪəzmən] N *Naut* homme *m* de barre, timonier *m*

stellar ['stelər] ADJ stellaire

stem¹ [stem] N 1 *Bot (of plant)* tige *f*, *Spec* pédoncule *m*; *(of leaf)* queue *f*, *Spec* pétiole *m*; *Am Fam* **stems** *(legs)* quilles *fpl*, gambettes *fpl* 2 *(of glass)* pied *m*; *(of tobacco pipe)* tuyau *m*; *(of valve)* tige *f*, *Mus (of note)* queue *f*, *Typ (of letter)* hampe *f* 3 *Ling (of word)* radical *m* 4 *(of ship)* étrave *f*; **from s. to stern** de l'avant à l'arrière; *Fig* **the party is split from s. to stern on this issue** le parti est totalement divisé sur cette question
VI (-mm-) **to s. from sth** *(of problems, errors, theories etc)* provenir de qch; *(of models, versions, designs etc)* être issu de qch; **much harm stemmed from this** il en est résulté beaucoup de mal
▸▸ *Biol* **s. cell** cellule *f* souche; **s. glass** verre *m* à pied

stem² VT *(hold back) (flow of liquid etc)* arrêter, contenir; *Fig* **to s. an epidemic** enrayer une épidémie; *Fig* **to s. the tide of …** arrêter le flot de …; *Fig* **to s. the rise in unemployment/crime** enrayer la montée du chômage/de la criminalité; *Fig* **to s. the advance of fascism/an army** bloquer l'avancée du fascisme/d'une armée
VI *Ski* faire un stem
N *Ski (virage en)* stem *m*
▸▸ *Ski* **s. Christie** stem christie; **s. parallel** stem parallèle

stemmed [stemd] ADJ *(glass)* à pied

stemware ['stemweər] N *Am (glasses)* verres *mpl*

stench [stentʃ] N odeur *f* nauséabonde, puanteur *f*; *Fig* **the s. of corruption** l'odeur nauséabonde de la corruption

stencil ['stens(ə)l] N 1 *(device)* pochoir *m*; **coloured by s.** colorié au pochoir 2 *(work)* peinture *f* au pochoir 3 *(typewritten copy etc)* stencil *m*
VT (-ll-, *Am* -l-) *(leaf, flower etc)* peindre au pochoir; *Ind, Com (packing case)* marquer; *(letter etc)* polycopier, tirer au stencil
VI peindre au pochoir
▸▸ **s. paper** papier *m* stencil; **s. plate** pochoir

sten gun [sten] N mitraillette *f*

stenographer, *Am* **stenographist** [stə-'nɒgrəfər, -ɪst] N sténographe *mf*, *Fam* sténo *mf*

stenography [stə'nɒgrəfɪ] N sténographie *f*

stenotyper ['stenətaɪpər] N sténotype *m*

stenotypist ['stenətaɪpɪst] N sténotypiste *mf*

stenotypy ['stenətaɪpɪ] N sténotypie *f*

stentorian [sten'tɔ:rɪən] ADJ *(voice)* de stentor

N pas 1, 2 ▪ démarche 3 ▪ mesure 3
▪ marche 4 ▪ échelon 4 ▪ étape 5
VI faire un pas ▪ marcher

N 1 *(movement, sound)* pas *m*; **with quick steps** d'un pas rapide; **to take a s.** faire un pas (**back** en arrière; **forward** en avant); **one s. forward, two steps back** un pas en avant et deux pas en arrière; *esp Lit* **to turn one's steps towards a place** diriger ses pas *ou* se diriger vers un lieu; **a child's first steps** les premiers pas d'un enfant; **at every s.** à chaque pas; **s. by s.** pas à pas; *(little by little)* petit à petit, graduellement, progressivement; **within a few steps of the house** à quelques pas de la maison; **it's quite a s.** *(quite a long way)* ce n'est pas tout près; *(quite a big change)* c'est une décision importante; **that's a great s. forward** c'est déjà un grand pas de fait, c'est déjà un grand progrès; **a s. in the right direction** un pas dans la bonne voie; **you'll have to watch your s.** il va falloir que tu fasses attention où tu mets les pieds; *Fig* fais attention à ce que tu fais; *Fig* **they fought us every s. of the way** ils nous ont combattu sans répit *ou* sur chaque point; *Fig* **we're behind you every s. of the way** nous sommes avec vous sur toute la ligne 2 *(in walking, dancing)* pas *m*; **marching s.** pas ordinaire; **to be in s.** marcher au pas, être au pas; **to fall into s.** se mettre au pas; **to keep (in) s.** rester au pas; **to break s.** rompre le pas; *Fig* **to be out of s. with sb** être à contre-courant de qn; *Fig* **supply has got out of s. with demand** l'offre ne correspond plus à la demande
3 *(action, measure)* démarche *f*, mesure *f*; **to take the necessary steps** faire *ou* entreprendre les démarches nécessaires; **to take steps to do sth** prendre des mesures pour faire qch; **the first s. will be to …** la première chose à faire, ce sera de …
4 *(of staircase)* marche *f*, degré *m*; *(of ladder)* échelon *m*; *(of stepladders)* marche; **flight of steps** escalier *m*, volée *f* de marches; *(outside building)* perron *m*; **mind the s.** attention à la marche; **to go up a s.** *(be promoted)* monter en grade; **it's a s. up from the old house** c'est un peu mieux que la vieille maison; **this new job is a s. up for me** ce nouveau travail va me permettre de progresser dans ma carrière; **to cut steps** *(in mountaineering)* tailler
5 *(stage)* étape *f*, **it is a simple two-s. procedure** c'est une procédure simple en deux étapes; **the next s. is to …** l'étape suivante consiste à …
6 *(ladder)* **(pair of) steps** escabeau *m*, échelle *f* double; *Aviat* **steps** passerelle *f*
7 *(type of exercise)* step *m*; **I go to s. twice a week** je vais à un cours de step deux fois par semaine
VI **(stepped** [stept]) *(take a step, steps)* faire un pas/des pas; *(walk)* marcher, aller; **to s. on sb's foot** marcher sur le pied de qn; **s. this way** venez par ici; **s. inside for a moment** entrez pour un moment; **he stepped carefully over the cat** il enjamba soigneusement le chat; **to s. off a ladder** descendre d'une échelle; *Fam Hum* **he stepped under a bus** il est passé sous un bus

▸ **step aside** VI s'écarter; **to s. aside to let sb pass** s'écarter pour laisser passer qn; **it's time the chairman stepped aside** il est temps que le président se retire et laisse la place à quelqu'un d'autre

▸ **step back** VI faire un pas en arrière; *Fig* **if we could s. back into the last century** si nous pouvions revenir au siècle passé; **sometimes it helps to s. back and look at things** il est parfois bon de prendre du recul

▸ **step down** VT SEP *(decrease) Elec (current)* dévolter; *Tech* **to s. down the gear** démultiplier la transmission
VI **1** *(resign)* démissionner; **he stepped down in favour of the other candidate** *(withdrew)* il s'est retiré en faveur de l'autre candidat
2 *(descend)* descendre (**from** de)
▸ **step forward** VI faire un pas en avant; *Fig (of volunteer etc)* se désigner, se porter volontaire
▸ **step in** VI entrer (**to** dans); *(intervene)* intervenir, s'interposer
▸ **step on** VT INSEP *(tread on)* marcher sur; *Fam* **to s. on the gas, to s. on it** *Aut* appuyer sur l'accélérateur *ou Fam* sur le champignon; *(hurry)* se dépêcher, *Fam* se grouiller; **to s. on the brakes** donner un coup de frein brusque
▸ **step out** VI **1** *(go outside house etc)* sortir
2 *(walk faster)* allonger *ou* forcer le pas; **to s. out briskly** marcher rapidement
3 *Old-fashioned* **to be stepping out with sb** *(courting)* sortir avec qn
▸ **step up** VI **to s. up to sb/sth** s'approcher de qn/qch; **s. up! s. up! come and see ...** approchez! approchez! venez voir ...; **he stepped up onto the platform** il est monté sur le podium
VT SEP *(increase, intensify)* accroître, augmenter

stepbrother ['stepbrʌðər] N demi-frère *m*, *pl* demi-frères *(fils du beau-père ou de la belle-mère)*
stepchild, *pl* **stepchildren** ['steptʃaɪld, -tʃɪldrən] N beau-fils *m*, belle-fille *f*, *pl* beaux-fils, belles-filles
stepdaughter ['stepdɔːtər] N belle-fille *f*, *pl* belles-filles
stepfather ['stepfɑːðər] N beau-père *m*, *pl* beaux-pères
stepladder ['steplædər] N escabeau *m*
stepless transmission ['steplɪs] N *Aut* transmission *f* à variation continue
stepmother ['stepmʌðər] N belle-mère *f*, *pl* belles-mères
steppe [step] N *Geog* steppe *f*
stepper ['stepər] N
▸▸ *Elec* **s. motor** moteur *m* pas-à-pas
stepping stone ['stepɪŋ] N pierre *f* (pour passer une rivière/etc à gué); *Fig* tremplin *m*
stepping up N *(of production etc)* augmentation *f*, *(of campaign etc)* intensification *f*
stepsister ['stepsɪstər] N demi-sœur *f*, *pl* demi-sœurs *(fille du beau-père ou de la belle-mère)*
stepson ['stepsʌn] N beau-fils *m*, *pl* beaux-fils
stereo, *pl* **stereos** ['sterɪəʊ, -əʊz, 'stɪə-] N **1** *(equipment)* chaîne *f* stéréo **2** *(sound)* stéréo *f*; **to listen to sth in s.** écouter qch en stéréo **3** *Typ* = **stereotype** N **2**
ADJ *(equipment, record, cassette)* stéréo *inv*, *(recording, broadcast)* en stéréo
▸▸ **s. signal** signal *m* stéréo; **s. system** chaîne *f* stéréo; **s. transmitter** émetteur *m* stéréo
stereophonic [sterɪə'fɒnɪk, stɪə-] ADJ stéréophonique
stereoscope ['sterɪəskəʊp, 'stɪər-] N *Opt* stéréoscope *m*
stereoscopic [sterɪəʊ'skɒpɪk, stɪə-] ADJ stéréoscopique
stereotype ['sterɪətaɪp, 'stɪə-] N **1** *Fig* stéréotype *m* **2** *Typ* cliché *m*
VT **1** *Fig* stéréotyper **2** *Typ* clicher
stereotyped ['sterɪətaɪpt, 'stɪə-] ADJ *Typ, Fig* stéréotypé; **the s. idea of a farmer** le stéréotype de l'agriculteur

stereotypical [sterɪə'tɪpɪkəl, stɪə-] ADJ stéréotypé; **the s. image of an American tourist** le stéréotype du touriste américain
stereotyping ['sterɪətaɪpɪŋ, 'stɪə-] N **1** *Fig* fabrication *f* de stéréotypes; **the s. of women** les stéréotypes que l'on colle aux femmes **2** *Typ* clichage *m*
sterile ['steraɪl] ADJ stérile
sterility [ste'rɪlɪtɪ] N stérilité *f*
sterilization [sterɪlaɪ'zeɪʃən] N stérilisation *f*
sterilize ['sterɪlaɪz] VT stériliser; **sterilized milk** lait *m* stérilisé
sterilizer ['sterɪlaɪzər] N *(device)* stérilisateur *m*
sterilizing ['sterɪlaɪzɪŋ] N stérilisation *f*
sterling ['stɜːlɪŋ] ADJ *(silver)* de bon aloi, fin; *Fig* vrai, solide; **a s. fighter** un combattant inlassable; **s. qualities** qualités *fpl* solides; **pound s.** livre *f* sterling
N *(currency)* (livre *f*) sterling *m*; **to pay in s.** payer en livres sterling
▸▸ **s. area** zone *f* sterling
stern[1] [stɜːn] ADJ sévère; **we are made of sterner stuff** nous, nous sommes d'une autre trempe
stern[2] N *Naut* arrière *m*
sternly ['stɜːnlɪ] ADV sévèrement
sternness ['stɜːnnɪs] N sévérité *f*
sternum, *pl* **sterna, sternums** ['stɜːnəm, -ə, -əmz] N *Anat* sternum *m*
steroid ['stɪərɔɪd, 'ste-] N *Biol, Chem* stéroïde *m*
stertorous ['stɜːtərəs] ADJ *Med, Lit* stertoreux, ronflant
stet [stet] *Typ* N bon *m*
VT (**-tt-**) *(text)* maintenir
stethoscope ['steθəskəʊp] N *Med* stéthoscope *m*
Stetson® ['stets(ə)n] N chapeau *m* mou à larges bords
stevedore ['stiːvɪ(ə)dɔːr] N docker *m*, arrimeur *m*
stew [stjuː] N **1** *Culin* ragoût *m*; **Irish s.** ragoût de mouton à l'irlandaise; *Fam* **to be in a s.** *(of person)* être dans tous ses états **2** *Arch (brothel)* bordel *m*
VT *Culin (meat etc)* faire cuire en ragoût; **to s. apples** faire une compote de pommes
VI **1** *Culin (of meat)* mijoter; *Fam* **to let sb s. in his/her own juice** laisser qn cuire dans son jus, laisser mariner qn **2** *Br Fam (of person)* **to be stewing** crever de chaleur; **it's stewing in here** il fait une chaleur à crever ici
steward ['stjʊəd] N **1** *(of estate)* régisseur *m*, intendant *m*; *Naut (manager of provisions)* distributeur *m*, commis *m ou* agent *m* aux vivres; *Naut, Aviat (attendant)* steward *m*; *Naut* **s.'s mate** cambusier *m* **2** *(at sporting event)* commissaire *m*; *(at demonstration etc)* membre *m* du service d'ordre; *(at dance)* organisateur, -trice; *Ind* **shop s.** délégué *m* d'atelier *ou* d'usine *ou* du personnel
▸▸ *Horseracing* **s.'s inquiry** enquête *f* des commissaires
stewardess [stjʊə'des] N *Naut* hôtesse *f*; *Aviat* **air s.** hôtesse de l'air
stewardship ['stjʊədʃɪp] N économat *m*, intendance *f*; *Fig* **under his s., the situation improved markedly** quand il était responsable, les choses s'étaient nettement améliorées
stewed [stjuːd] ADJ **1 this tea is s.** ce thé a trop infusé **2** *Fam (drunk)* **s. (to the gills)** rond comme une queue de pelle
▸▸ **s. beef** ragoût *m* de bœuf, bœuf *m* (à la) mode; **s. fruit** compote *f* de fruits
stewing ['stjuːɪŋ] N
▸▸ **s. beef** bœuf *m* à braiser; **s. pears** poires *fpl* à cuire

stewpan ['stjuːpæn] N (grande) casserole *f*
stewpot ['stjuːpɒt] N cocotte *f*, fait-tout *m inv*
St. Ex. *Fin (abbr* **Stock Exchange)** Bourse *f*

STICK [stɪk]

N	bâton **1, 3** ▪ morceau de bois **1** ▪ canne **1** ▪ bâtonnet **1** ▪ branche **4** ▪ critiques **6**
VT	piquer **1** ▪ planter **1** ▪ mettre **2** ▪ coller **3** ▪ supporter **4**
VI	coller **2** ▪ tenir **2** ▪ rester **2** ▪ (se) coincer **3**

N 1 *(piece of wood)* bâton *m*; *(small piece of wood)* morceau *m* de bois; *Fig* **the big s.** la manière forte, (la politique de) la force; *Fig* **you're giving him a s. to beat you with** vous lui donnez des verges pour vous faire fouetter *ou* le bâton pour vous faire battre; **(walking) s.** canne *f*; **to gather sticks** ramasser du bois sec *ou* du petit bois; **cocktail s.** cure-dents *m inv* (utilisé *à l'apéritif*); *(swizzle)* **s.** *(for cocktails etc)* agitateur *m*; **not a s. was left standing** tout était rasé; **my few sticks of furniture** mes quelques meubles; *Prov* **sticks and stones may break my bones (but words will never hurt me)** = les chiens aboient, la caravane passe; *Fam* **he lives out in the sticks** il habite un trou perdu, il vit dans la brousse; *Sl* **to be up the s.** *(pregnant)* être en cloque
2 *Old-fashioned Fam (person)* **he's/she's a funny old s.** c'est un drôle de personnage; **he's/she's a good old s.** c'est un type/une fille bien; **a dry old s.** un pince-sans-rire; **Jeremy, old s.!** Jeremy, vieille branche!
3 *(of barley sugar, chewing gum, glue etc)* bâton *m*; *(of deodorant)* applicateur *m*; *(of dynamite)* bâtonnet *m*
4 *Culin* **s. of celery** branche *f* de céleri; **s. of rhubarb** tige *f* de rhubarbe
5 *Mil, Aviat* **s. of bombs** chapelet *m* de bombes
6 *Fam (criticism)* critiques; **to take a lot of s.** *(to be criticized)* se faire taper sur les doigts; *(to be mocked)* se faire mettre en boîte; *Fam* **to give sb s.** *(criticize)* taper sur les doigts de qn (**for sth** à cause de qch); *(laugh at)* se payer la tête de qn (**for sth** à cause de qch); *Fam* **to give it some s.** *(exert oneself)* s'y mettre
VT *(pt, pp* **stuck** [stʌk]*)* **1** *(insert)* piquer, enfoncer (**sth into sth** qch dans qch), planter, fixer (**sth on a spike** qch sur une pointe); **to s. a pin into sth** enfoncer une épingle dans qch; **she stuck the spade into the ground** elle a planté la bêche dans le sol; **to s. pigs** chasser le sanglier à l'épieu
2 *Fam (put)* mettre; **to s. one's hat on one's head** mettre *ou* planter son chapeau sur sa tête; **s. it in your pocket** fourrez-le dans votre poche; **s. it in the corner** collez ça dans le coin; **s. it on the table** mettez ça sur la table
3 *(attach with glue, sticky tape)* coller; **to s. sth on(to) sth** coller qch à *ou* sur qch; **their trunk was stuck all over with labels** leur malle était couverte d'étiquettes
4 *Br Fam (endure)* supporter, endurer; **to s. it** tenir le coup, tenir bon; **I can't s. it any longer** je n'en peux plus; **I can't s. him** je ne peux pas le sentir
5 *(in horticulture) (peas etc)* ramer; *(plants)* mettre des tuteurs à
6 to be stuck *(unable to move)* être coincé; *(in mud etc)* être embourbé; *(mentally, in a problem etc)* être bloqué *ou* en panne; **to get stuck in a bog** s'embourber dans un marécage; **he got his head stuck** sa tête est restée coincée; **I got stuck on the last question** j'ai séché sur la dernière question; **there's something stuck in the pipe** il y a quelque chose de coincé dans le tuyau; **here I am**

stuck in hospital for six weeks me voilà cloué à l'hôpital pour six semaines; **I was stuck at Heathrow for six hours** j'ai été bloqué six heures à Heathrow; **to be stuck in a job** être coincé dans un emploi; **the book's finished but I'm stuck for a title** le livre est fini mais je ne trouve pas de titre; **stuck for money** à court d'argent; *Fam* **I'm stuck with it/him** *(can't get rid of)* je ne peux pas m'en débarrasser; *Fam* **we're stuck with it** *(decision etc)* il faut s'y résigner

7 *Fam* **you can s. your job** ton boulot tu peux te le mettre où je pense; **he can s. his money!** son fric, il peut se le mettre où je pense!; **s. it!** va te faire voir!

VI 1 the point was sticking through the lining la pointe avait percé la doublure; **don't leave the spade sticking in the ground** ne laisse pas la pelle plantée dans le sol

2 *(adhere)* (se) coller, s'attacher, tenir (**to** à); *Culin (of rice etc)* attacher; **the stamp won't s.** le timbre ne colle pas; **the name stuck** ce nom leur/lui/*etc* est resté

3 *(of key, drawer, mechanism)* (se) coincer; *(in sand, bog etc)* s'enfoncer; *Aut (of valve, cut-out)* rester collé; **Fig the words stuck in his throat** les mots lui restèrent dans la gorge; **it sticks in my throat** *(of situation, sb's arrogance etc)* c'est dur à digérer; **to s. fast** *(of boat)* s'enliser; **the lift has stuck** l'ascenseur est coincé

▸▸ **s. deodorant** déodorant *m* en stick; **s. figure** personnage *m* stylisé; **s. insect** phasme *m*; *TV* **s. mike** micro *m* tenu à la main

▸ **stick around VI** *Fam (wait)* attendre; *(stay)* rester

▸ **stick at VT INSEP 1** *(persevere with)* s'acharner à (faire); **s. at it!** persévérez!

2 *(stop in face of)* **to s. at nothing** ne reculer devant rien

▸ **stick by VT INSEP 1** *(remain loyal to)* **to s. by a friend** ne pas abandonner un ami

2 *(continue to affirm)* maintenir; **I s. by what I said** je maintiens ce que j'ai dit

▸ **stick down VT SEP 1** *Fam (put down)* **s. it down anywhere** mettez-le *ou* collez-le n'importe où; **to s. sth down in a notebook** inscrire qch sur un carnet

2 *(with glue)* *(envelope)* coller

▸ **stick in VT SEP 1** *(with glue)* coller

2 *Fam (put in)* mettre, *Fam* coller; *(knife etc)* enfoncer

3 *Fam* **to get stuck in** *(start working)* s'y mettre; *(start eating)* se mettre à manger; **to get stuck into sth** *(work etc)* se mettre à qch; *(food)* se mettre à manger qch; **let's get stuck in!** allons, on s'y met!

VI 1 *(of knife etc)* s'enfoncer; **she threw the knife at the wall and it stuck in** elle a lancé le couteau contre le mur et il s'y est planté

2 *Fam (persevere)* **just s. in there!** tenez bon!

▸ **stick on VT SEP** *(stamp etc)* coller, fixer; *Sl* **to s. one on sb** *(hit)* coller *ou* ficher un marron à qn; *Fam* **to be stuck on sb** être fou de qn; *Fam* **he is stuck on the idea** il s'enthousiasme pour cette idée

VI *(adhere)* adhérer; *(to stay stuck on)* rester collé

▸ **stick out VT SEP 1** *(cause to protrude)* faire dépasser, sortir; **to s. out one's tongue** tirer la langue; **to s. out one's hand** tendre la main; **to s. out one's chest** bomber la poitrine; **he stuck his head out (of the window)** il sortit la tête (par la fenêtre); *Fam* **to s. one's neck out** prendre des risques (**for sb** pour qn)

2 *Fam* **to s. it out** *(persevere)* persévérer

VI 1 *(protrude)* faire saillie, ressortir; **to s. out** dépasser (**beyond sth** de qch); **his ears s. out** il a les oreilles décollées; **her teeth s. out** elle a les dents qui avancent

2 *Fam (be noticeable)* se voir, se remarquer; **the way she dresses makes her s. out** la manière dont elle s'habille fait qu'elle ne passe

pas inaperçue; **it sticks out a mile** c'est clair comme le jour; **it sticks out like a sore thumb** ça détonne, ça jure

▸ **stick out for VT INSEP** *Fam (insist on)* **to s. out for sth** s'obstiner à demander qch

▸ **stick to VT INSEP 1** *(adhere to)* coller à; **the rice had stuck to the pan** le riz avait collé *ou* attaché à la casserole; **her shirt stuck to her back** elle avait la chemise collée au dos; **the name stuck to him** ce nom lui est resté; **to s. to sb like a limpet** *or* **like a leech** *or* **like glue** se cramponner *ou* s'accrocher à qn, *Fam* coller qn

2 *(remain true to)* **to s. to one's promise** tenir sa promesse; **s. to it!** *(don't give in)* persévérez!; *Fam* **to s. to one's guns** ne pas en démordre; **to s. to an opinion** maintenir une opinion, ne pas démordre d'une opinion

3 *(restrict oneself to)* **to s. to the facts** s'en tenir aux faits; **to s. to the point** ne pas s'écarter de la question; **to s. to the text** serrer le texte de près

4 *(continue to affirm)* **I s. to what I said** je maintiens ce que j'ai dit; **she's sticking to her version of what happened** elle maintient sa version des faits; **that's my story and I'm sticking to it** c'est ma version et je m'y tiens

5 *(keep)* **s. to what you've got!** contente-toi de ce que tu as!

6 *(not leave)* **to s. to one's post** rester à son poste; **he sticks to his room** il ne sort pas de sa chambre

▸ **stick together VI 1** *(with glue etc)* être collé

2 *(of friends etc)* **it's amazing they've stuck together** c'est incroyable qu'ils soient restés ensemble; **they always s. together** ils sont inséparables; *(show solidarity)* ils sont toujours solidaires

VT SEP coller (ensemble)

▸ **stick up VT SEP 1** *Fam (erect)* *(fence)* ériger; *(signpost)* mettre, planter

2 *Sl (raise)* **s. 'em up!** haut les mains!

3 *Fam (attach to wall etc)* *(notice, poster etc)* afficher

4 *Fam* **to s. up a bank** attaquer une banque à main armée

VI *(point upwards)* se dresser; **his hair's sticking up** il est ébouriffé; **an overturned table with its legs sticking up in the air** une table à l'envers avec les pieds en l'air

▸ **stick up for VT INSEP** *(defend)* prendre la défense de, soutenir; **to s. up for one's rights** défendre ses droits; **she can s. up for herself** elle peut se défendre toute seule

▸ **stick with VT INSEP 1** *(remain loyal to)* rester fidèle à

2 *(stay near)* rester avec; **the other runners couldn't s. with him** les autres coureurs ne pouvaient pas le suivre

3 *(persevere with)* *(English, tennis etc)* continuer; **to s. with doing sth** continuer à faire qch; **I'm sticking with my old car for now** je garde ma vieille voiture pour le moment

sticker ['stɪkər] **N 1** *(label)* étiquette *f* gommée; *Am Fam (poster)* affiche *f*; *Am Fam (election poster)* affiche électorale **2** *Fam (determined person)* personne *f* persévérante; **she's a s.** elle ne manque pas de persévérance

stickiness ['stɪkɪnɪs] **N** *(of substance, hands etc)* moiteur *f*; *(of product)* nature *f* gluante *ou* collante

sticking ['stɪkɪŋ] **ADJ**

▸▸ *Br* **s. plaster** pansement *m* adhésif, sparadrap *m*; *Fig* **s. point** point *m* de désaccord, point de friction

stick-in-the-mud *Fam* **N** **he's an old s.** *(killjoy)* c'est un rabat-joie; *(fogey)* c'est un vieux réac

ADJ *(attitude, person etc)* *(killjoy)* rabat-joie *inv*; *(fogey)* réac

stickleback ['stɪklbæk] **N** *(fish)* épinoche *f*

stickler ['stɪklər] **N to be a s. for discipline** être à cheval sur la discipline

stick-on ADJ *(label)* adhésif

▸▸ **s. soles** semelles *fpl* autocollantes

stick-up N *Fam* attaque *f* à main armée, braquage *m*; **this is a s.!** ceci est un hold-up!

stickweed ['stɪkwiːd] **N** *Bot* jacobée *f*

sticky ['stɪkɪ] **ADJ 1** *(substance, hands)* poisseux, gluant; *(paper etc)* collant, adhésif; *(climate)* moite; **to have s. fingers** avoir les doigts poisseux; *Fam (be a thief)* être voleur; **s. weather** temps *m* lourd; *Br Fig Fam* **to be on a s. wicket** être dans une situation difficile **2** *Fam (awkward)* *(problem, situation)* difficile; **is he being s. about it?** est-ce qu'il fait des histoires (à ce sujet)?; **he'll come to a s. end** il finira mal

▸▸ *Fam* **s. bun** petit pain *m* sucré; *Comput* **s. key** touche *f* à auto-maintien; **s. label** étiquette *f* autocollante, étiquette gommée; **s. tape** ruban *m* adhésif; **s. toffee pudding** = pudding *m* au caramel cuit à la vapeur

stickybeak ['stɪkɪbiːk] *Austr Fam* **N** fouineur, -euse, fouinard, -arde

VI fouiner

stiff [stɪf] **ADJ 1** *(rigid, hard)* raide, rigide, dur; *(brush)* dur; *(person, manner)* raide, guindé; *(stubborn)* inflexible, obstiné; *(style)* guindé, empesé; *Fin (market, commodity)* ferme; **s. joint** articulation *f* ankylosée; **to grow s.** *(of joint)* s'ankyloser; **to be quite s.** *(with sitting still)* être engourdi; *(after exercise)* être tout courbaturé; *(through lack of exercise)* être raide, manquer de souplesse; **he is very s.** *(formal)* il est d'un abord difficile; *Fam* **exams scare me s.** j'ai une peur bleue des examens; **I was bored s.** je m'ennuyais à mourir; **I was frozen s.** j'étais frigorifié; **a s. smile** un sourire forcé; **book bound in s. covers** livre relié en carton; **s. neck** torticolis *m*; **to offer s. resistance** *(of person)* résister opiniâtrement, tenir bon; *(of thing)* tenir bon

2 *(door-handle, hinge etc)* qui fonctionne mal; *(paste, batter)* ferme; *(soil, clay)* dur; **the handle is s.** la poignée est dure; *Naut* **s. breeze** forte brise *f*

3 *(exam)* difficile; **I sent them a s. letter** je leur ai envoyé une lettre bien sentie; **s. price** prix *m* élevé; **s. sentence** peine *f* sévère; **you need a s. drink** tu as besoin d'un remontant; **a s. whisky** un whisky bien tassé; **that's a bit s.!** *(going too far)* c'est un peu fort!

4 *Br Fam (full)* plein (à craquer); **the place was s. with men in suits** l'endroit était plein de messieurs en costume

5 *Am Fam (drunk)* bourré, rond

N 1 *Sl (corpse)* macchabée *m* **2** *Am Fam (tramp)* clodo *mf*; *(stupid person)* nul *m*, nulle *f*; *(ordinary working man)* prolo *m*

VT *Sl (kill)* buter

stiffen ['stɪf(ə)n] **VT 1** *(wall, beam, plate etc)* renforcer; *(with starch) (collar etc)* empeser; **age has stiffened his joints** l'âge lui a raidi les articulations; **this action stiffened their resolve** cette action a raffermi leur résolution **2** *(paste)* rendre ferme, donner de la consistance à; *(drink)* corser **3** *(exam, test)* rendre plus difficile

VI 1 *(become rigid)* (se) raidir, devenir raide; *(of person)* se raidir; **opposition is stiffening** l'opposition se durcit **2** *(of paste etc)* devenir ferme, prendre de la consistance; *Naut (of wind)* fraîchir

stiffener ['stɪf(ə)nər] **N 1** *(in shoe)* contrefort *m*; *(in collar)* baleine *f* (de col) **2** *Fam (drink)* remontant *m*

stiffening ['stɪf(ə)nɪŋ] **N 1** *(action)* raidissement *m*, renforcement *m*; *(of resistance)* durcissement *m*; **s. of the joints** ankylose *f* **2** *(for cloth)* amidon *m*

stiffly ['stɪflɪ] ADV *(to bow)* avec raideur; *(to answer, greet etc)* avec froideur; *(to resist)* obstinément

stiff-necked [-nekt] ADJ *(stubborn)* obstiné, entêté

stiffness ['stɪfnɪs] N **1** *(of limbs, beam etc)* raideur *f*, rigidité *f*; *(of spring etc)* dureté *f*; *Fin (of market)* fermeté *f*; **s. of the legs** *(after exercise)* courbatures *fpl* dans les jambes; *(through lack of exercise)* raideur, manque *m* de souplesse; *(after sitting)* engourdissement *m* des jambes; **s. of manner** raideur, air *m* guindé **2** *(of paste)* fermeté *f*, consistance *f*; *(of soil)* dureté *f*, fermeté **3** *(of price)* montant *m* élevé; *(of exam)* difficulté *f*

stiffy ['stɪfɪ] N *Sl* **to have a s.** *(erection)* triquer, avoir la trique

stifle ['staɪf(ə)l] VT *(person)* étouffer, suffoquer; *(shouts, cries, yawn, laugh)* étouffer; *(rebellion)* réprimer; *(cry)* retenir
VI suffoquer, étouffer

stifled ['staɪf(ə)ld] ADJ *(cry etc)* étouffé; **with a s. voice** d'une voix éteinte

stifling ['staɪflɪŋ] ADJ étouffant, suffocant; *(sensation)* d'étouffement; **it's s. here!** on étouffe ici!

stigma, *pl* **stigmas, stigmata** ['stɪgmə, -əz, 'stɪgmətə, stɪg'mɑːtə] N **1** *(pl usu* **stigmas***) (social disgrace)* honte *f*; **there is no longer any s. in being a single mother** il n'y a plus de honte à être mère célibataire **2** **stigmata** *(of saint)* stigmates *mpl* **3** *(pl* **stigmata***) Biol (of insect etc)* stigmate *m* **4** *(pl* **stigmas***) Bot (of pistil)* stigmate *m*

stigmatic [stɪg'mætɪk] N *Rel* stigmatisé, -ée

stigmatize ['stɪgmətaɪz] VT stigmatiser; **stigmatized as a coward** marqué comme lâche; **stigmatized as illegitimate** entaché de bâtardise

stile[1] [staɪl] N **1** *(in fence, hedge etc)* échalier *m* **2** *(turnstile)* tourniquet *m*

stile[2] N *Constr (of door etc)* montant *m*

stiletto, *pl* **stilettos, stilettoes** [stɪ'letəʊ, -əʊz] N **1** *(dagger)* stylet *m* **2** **s. heels, stilettos** talons *mpl* aiguille **3** *Sewing etc* poinçon *m*

still[1] [stɪl] ADJ *(motionless)* immobile; *(calm)* calme; *(silent)* silencieux; *(wine)* non mousseux; *(orange juice, mineral water)* non gazeux; **s. water** eau *f* dormante; *Prov* **s. waters run deep** il faut se méfier de l'eau qui dort
ADV **to keep s.** ne pas bouger, se tenir *ou* rester tranquille; **sit s.!** restez *ou* tenez-vous tranquille!; **to stand s.** *(not move)* ne pas bouger, se tenir immobile; *(of science etc)* ne pas faire de progrès; **her heart stood s.** son cœur cessa de battre
N **1** **in the s. of the night** dans le calme de la nuit **2** *Cin* photo *f (tirée du film)*
VT *(person)* tranquilliser, calmer, apaiser; **to s. sb's fears** calmer les craintes de qn
▸▸ *TV, Cin* **s. frame** image *f* fixe; **s. life** nature *f* morte

still[2] ADV **1** *(up to now)* encore; **he is s. here** il est encore *ou* toujours ici; **he's s. not here** il n'est toujours pas là; **it's stuck – s.?** c'est coincé – encore?; **I s. have 500 euros** il me reste 500 euros, j'ai encore 500 euros; **I have s. to thank you** il me reste à vous remercier; **it s. remains to be seen** ça reste à voir; **I s. can't see what was wrong with my suggestion** je ne vois toujours pas en quoi ma suggestion était mauvaise; **in spite of his faults, I love him s.** malgré ses défauts, je l'aime toujours
2 *(even)* encore; **s. more/less** encore plus/moins; **s. more worrying ...** plus inquiétant encore ...; **if you can reduce the price s. further** si vous pouvez réduire encore le prix
3 *(nonetheless, all the same)* pourtant; **he's s. the boss** c'est pourtant lui le patron; **but**

that s. doesn't justify ... mais cela ne justifie pourtant pas ...; **OK, but I s. think we ought to do it** d'accord, mais je pense qu'on devrait quand même le faire; **it s. won't make me change my mind** je ne vais pas changer d'avis pour autant; **but s., if she** **did** **accept, wouldn't it be marvellous!** peut-être, mais si elle acceptait, ce serait formidable!
CONJ cependant, pourtant, néanmoins, toutefois; **s. the fact remains that ...** toujours est-il que ..., il n'en reste pas moins vrai que ...; **s., what else could I have done?** qu'aurais-je pu faire d'autre, enfin?

still[3] N *(for distilling)* alambic *m*

stillbirth ['stɪlbɜːθ] N enfant *m* mort-né; **the number of stillbirths** la mortinatalité

stillborn ['stɪlbɔːn] ADJ mort-né, -ée, *pl* mort-nés, -ées; *Fig (project etc)* avorté, mort-né

stillness ['stɪlnɪs] N tranquillité *f*, *(of person)* calme *m*, repos *m*; *(of place, atmosphere)* tranquillité, paix *f*

stilt [stɪlt] N **1** *(for walking)* échasse *f*; **to walk on stilts** marcher sur des échasses **2** *Constr* pilotis *m*

stilted ['stɪltɪd] ADJ *(style, manner etc)* guindé, raide

Stilton® ['stɪlt(ə)n] N fromage *m* de Stilton, stilton *m*

stimulant ['stɪmjʊlənt] N *(tea, coffee etc)* excitant *m*; *Med* stimulant *m*; *(for heart)* tonicardiaque *m*
ADJ ATTRIB **it has a s. effect** ça a un effet stimulant

stimulate ['stɪmjʊleɪt] VT **1** *(person, enthusiasm)* stimuler; *(mind, appetite)* aiguiser; *Ind (production)* encourager, activer **2** *Med (liver etc)* stimuler

stimulating ['stɪmjʊleɪtɪŋ] ADJ *(competition, work)* stimulant; *(music)* entraînant; *(book)* stimulant, qui donne à penser; **it's s. to work with talented people** c'est stimulant de travailler avec des gens qui ont du talent

stimulation [stɪmjʊ'leɪʃən] N stimulation *f*; **to need s.** avoir besoin d'être stimulé
▸▸ **s. marketing** marketing *m* de stimulation

stimulative ['stɪmjʊlətɪv] ADJ stimulant
N stimulant *m*

stimulus, *pl* **stimuli** ['stɪmjʊləs, -aɪ] N **1** *(incentive)* encouragement *m*; **to give a s. to trade** donner un coup de fouet au commerce **2** *Physiol* stimulus *m*; **to apply a s. to a muscle** exciter un muscle
▸▸ *Physiol* **s. response** réponse *f* stimulée

sting [stɪŋ] N **1** *(of bee)* dard *m*, aiguillon *m*; *(of scorpion)* aiguillon *m*; *(of nettle)* poil *m* piquant
2 *(injury) (from bee etc)* piqûre *f*, *Fig (of joke)* pointe *f*, *(of wound)* douleur *f* cuisante; *(of attack)* vigueur *f*, mordant *m*; **with the s. of the wind in our faces** le visage fouetté par le vent; **joke with a s. in it** plaisanterie qui comporte une pointe; **to have a s. in the tail** *(of story etc)* avoir une fin inattendue; *Lit* **the s. of remorse** l'aiguillon du remords; *Fig* **to take the s. out of sth** affaiblir qch
3 *esp Am Sl (con trick)* arnaque *f*, *(by police)* coup *m* monté
VT *(pt, pp* **stung** [stʌŋ]*)* **1** *(of bees, nettles etc)* piquer; **a bee stung her finger** *or* **stung her on the finger** une abeille lui a piqué le doigt; **that reply stung her (to the quick)** cette réponse l'a piquée (au vif); **smoke that stings the eyes** fumée qui picote les yeux; **this stung him into action** cela l'a incité à agir
2 *Fam (cheat)* **to s. sb for £50** rouler qn en lui faisant payer 50 livres, dépouiller qn de 50 livres; **to get stung** essuyer le coup de fusil; **could I s. you for a tenner?** *(borrow)* est-

ce que je peux te taper dix livres?
VI *(of parts of the body)* cuire; *(of cut, graze)* picoter, brûler; *(of bees, nettles etc)* piquer; **my eyes were stinging** les yeux me brûlaient; **this is going to s. a bit** ça va faire un peu mal; *Fig* **that stung!** *(of remark etc)* c'est blessant!

stingily ['stɪndʒɪlɪ] ADV mesquinement, chichement

stinginess ['stɪndʒɪnɪs] N *(of person)* pingrerie *f*, *(of portion etc)* insuffisance *f*

stinging ['stɪŋɪŋ] ADJ *(pain etc)* cuisant; *(blow, answer)* cinglant; **s. remark** remarque *f* blessante
▸▸ **s. nettle** ortie *f*

stingray ['stɪŋreɪ] N *(fish)* pastenague *f*

stingy ['stɪndʒɪ] ADJ *(person)* chiche, pingre; **a s. portion** une portion peu généreuse; **to be s. with one's money** être avare (avec son argent); **to be s. with the cream** lésiner sur la crème

stink [stɪŋk] N **1** *(smell)* puanteur *f* **2** *Fam (trouble)* grabuge *m*; **to raise** *or* **kick up a s.** faire un esclandre *ou* du grabuge; **there'll be a s.!** il va y avoir du grabuge!
VI *(pt* **stank** [stæŋk]*,* **stunk** [stʌŋk]*; pp* **stunk***) (of place, person etc)* puer, empester; **it stinks in here** ça pue ici; **to s. of garlic** puer *ou* empester l'ail; *Fam* **to s. of money** puer le fric; *Fam* **this film/book stinks!** ce film/livre est nul!; **the whole business stinks of corruption** tout ça sent la corruption à plein nez
▸ **stink out** VT SEP *(fill with bad smell) (room etc)* empester

stinkbomb ['stɪŋkbɒm] N boule *f* puante

stinker ['stɪŋkər] N *Fam* **1** **to be a s.** *(unpleasant, difficult thing)* être vachement dur, être coton; *(worthless thing)* être nul, être merdique; **the algebra paper was a s.** on a eu une composition d'algèbre carabinée; **I had a s. of a cold** j'avais un rhume carabiné **2** *(person)* individu *m* méprisable, salaud *m*

stinkhorn ['stɪŋkhɔːn] N *Bot* phallus *m* impudique

stinking ['stɪŋkɪŋ] ADJ **1** *(smelly)* puant **2** *Fam (disgusting)* dégueulasse; *(worthless)* nul, merdique; **a s. cold** un rhume carabiné
ADV *Fam* **to be s. rich** puer le fric

stinko ['stɪŋkəʊ] ADJ *Am Fam (drunk)* pété, bourré

stinkpot ['stɪŋkpɒt] N *Old-fashioned Fam (unpleasant person)* salaud *m*; **what a s.!** *(smelly)* qu'est-ce qu'il pue!

stint [stɪnt] N **1** *(period)* temps *m*, période *f*, *(amount of work)* besogne *f* assignée; **to do one's daily s.** accomplir sa tâche quotidienne; **if you do a regular s. (with the weights/your clarinet)** si tu travailles régulièrement (tes haltères/ta clarinette); **do you want a s. at the wheel?** est-ce que tu veux prendre un peu le volant?; **I did the last s.** c'est moi qui ai pris le dernier tour; **after a long s. at the keyboard** après être resté longtemps au clavier; **she had a two-year s. in the army** elle a fait deux ans dans l'armée **2** *(restriction)* restriction *f*, **without s.** sans limite; *(to spend money)* sans compter
VT *(money, effort)* épargner; **don't s. the cream/whisky** ne lésine pas sur la crème/le whisky; **to s. oneself** se sacrifier; **to s. sb of sth** priver qn de qch, refuser qch à qn; **to give without stinting** donner sans compter; **he doesn't s. his praise** il n'est pas avare de compliments
▸ **stint on** VT INSEP lésiner sur

stipend ['staɪpend] N traitement *m*, appointements *mpl (d'un ecclésiastique, d'un magistrat)*

stipendiary [staɪ'pendjərɪ] ADJ qui reçoit des appointements fixes

N *Br* juge *m* d'un tribunal d'instance *(à Londres et dans les grandes villes)* ▸▸*Br* **s. magistrate** juge *m* d'un tribunal d'instance *(à Londres et dans les grandes villes)*

stipple ['stɪp(ə)l] *Art* VT *(drawing)* faire en pointillé
VI pointiller

stipulate ['stɪpjʊleɪt] VT *(date, condition etc)* stipuler; **to s. (in writing) that …** stipuler (par écrit) que …; **within the period stipulated** dans le délai prescrit; **to s. the terms of a contract** fixer les conditions d'un contrat

stipulation [stɪpjʊ'leɪʃən] N condition *f, Law* stipulation *f*; **the only s. I make is that …** la seule condition que je pose, c'est que …; **on the s. that …** à condition que …

stir¹ [stɜːr] N **1** *(act of stirring liquid etc)* **to give sth a s.** remuer *ou* tourner qch **2** *(agitation)* agitation *f*, émoi *m*; **there was a great s.** il y eut un grand remue-ménage; **to make or cause a s.** faire du bruit, faire sensation; **the news caused a s. in the town** la nouvelle a mis la ville en émoi
VT **(-rr-)** *(set in motion)* (leaves, water) remuer, faire bouger; *(tea etc)* remuer, tourner; *(move emotionally) (person)* émouvoir, remuer; *(emotions)* agiter; *(curiosity, interest)* éveiller; *Culin (sauce, cream etc)* tourner; *(mixture)* agiter; *(fire)* activer, attiser; **not a breath stirs the leaves** pas un souffle ne remue *ou* ne fait trembler les feuilles; **to s. sb to pity** provoquer la compassion de qn; **events that s. the soul** événements qui remuent l'âme; **these words stirred her to action** ces mots l'ont fait agir; *Fam* **s. yourself or your stumps!** remue-toi!; *Br Fam* **to s. it** *(make trouble)* fomenter la discorde
VI **1** *(move)* bouger, remuer; **don't s. from here** ne bougez pas d'ici; **he didn't s. out of the house** il n'est pas sorti de la maison; **he hasn't stirred yet** *(is still in bed)* il n'est pas encore levé; **to s. in one's sleep** remuer dans son sommeil; **the audience were stirring in their seats** les spectateurs s'agitaient dans leur fauteuil
2 *Br Fam (set people against each other)* semer la zizanie
▸ **stir up** VT SEP **1** *(of wind)* remuer, faire bouger; *(fire)* ranimer, activer **2** *(rebellion, dissent)* fomenter **3** *(workers, crowd etc)* inciter à la révolte; **to s. up hatred** attiser les haines; **to s. up trouble** fomenter la discorde; **to s. things up** faire bouger les choses

stir² N *Sl (prison)* taule *f*; **in s.** en taule

stir-crazy ADJ *esp Am Sl* fou, *f* folle, détraqué *(à cause d'une longue période de détention)*

stir-fry *Culin* N sauté *m*
VT faire sauter *ou* frire rapidement; **stir-fried vegetables** légumes *mpl* sautés

stirrer ['stɜːrər] N **1** *Br Fam (person who provokes trouble)* personne *f* qui sème la zizanie **2** *Chem, Phot (device)* agitateur *m*

stirring ['stɜːrɪŋ] ADJ *(moving)* émouvant; **s. times** une époque passionnante; **it's s. stuff** c'est passionnant
N **1** *Br Fam (troublemaking)* **s. is her speciality** semer la zizanie, c'est sa spécialité **2** *stirrings (beginnings)* frémissement *m*; **the first stirrings of passion** les premiers frémissements de la passion; **the first stirrings of revolt/resistance** les premiers signes de la révolte/de la résistance

stirrup ['stɪrəp] N **1** *Horseriding* étrier *m*; **to put one's feet in the stirrups** chausser les étriers **2** *Med* stirrups étriers *mpl*
▸▸**s. cup** coup *m* de l'étrier; **s. leather** étrivière *f*; **s. pump** seau-pompe *m*, *pl* seaux-pompes; **s. strap** étrivière

stitch [stɪtʃ] N **1** *Sewing* point *m*; *(in knitting, crochet)* maille *f*, *Surg* (point de) suture *f*;

(machine) **s.** piqûre *f* (à la machine); **to put a few stitches in a garment** faire un point à un vêtement; *Fam* **he hasn't got a dry s. on him** il est trempé jusqu'aux os; *Fam* **without a s. on** nu comme un ver; **to drop a s.** *(in knitting, crochet)* sauter une maille; **dropped s.** *(in knitting, crochet)* maille coulée; **to make a s.** *(in knitting, crochet)* faire une maille; **to put stitches in a wound** suturer à *ou* suturer une plaie, recoudre une plaie; **she had to have ten stitches** ils ont dû lui faire dix points de suture; **when are you having the stitches out?** quand allez-vous vous faire retirer vos points de suture?; *Prov* **a s. in time saves nine** un point à temps en épargne cent, un point fait à temps en vaut mille
2 *(pain)* point *m* de côté; **I've got a s.** j'ai un point de côté
3 *Fam* **we were in stitches** *(laughing)* on se tordait de rire; **his story/the film had us in stitches** son histoire était tordante/le film était tordant *ou* à se tordre de rire; **he had us in stitches** il nous a fait (nous) tordre de rire
4 *Am Fam (amusing person, thing)* **to be a s.** être tordant *ou* crevant
VT **1** *(clothing)* coudre; *(leather)* piquer; *(machine)* **s.** piquer (à la machine); **to s. sth onto sth** coudre qch sur qch **2** *Surg (wound)* suturer **3** *(in bookbinding) (book)* brocher
▸ **stitch down** VT SEP coudre; *(repair)* recoudre
▸ **stitch up** VT SEP **1** *(repair by sewing) (bag etc)* recoudre **2** *(of surgeon) (person, wound)* recoudre; **we'll soon have you stitched up** on va vous faire quelques points de suture et ce sera fini **3** *Sl (falsely incriminate)* faire porter le chapeau à; **I've been stitched up** on m'a fait porter le chapeau

stitching ['stɪtʃɪŋ] N **1** *(act) Sewing* couture *f*, *(in leather)* piqûre *f*, *(ornamental)* broderie *f*, *Surg* suture *f*, *(in bookbinding)* brochage *m*, brochure *f* **2** *Sewing (stitches)* points *mpl*, piqûres *fpl*; **the s.'s coming undone** les piqûres se sont défaites

St John's wort [wɜːt] N millepertuis *m*

stoat [stəʊt] N hermine *f*

stoater ['stəʊtər] N *Scot Fam* **1** *(excellent thing)* **what a s. of a goal!** quel but d'enfer!; **we had a s. of an idea** on a eu une idée géniale **2** *(beautiful person)* canon *m*; **his new girlfriend's a s.!** sa nouvelle copine est canon!

stochastic [stə'kæstɪk] ADJ stochastique

stock [stɒk] N **1** *(supply)* provision *f*, approvisionnement *m*, stock *m*; *(in forestry)* peuplement *m*; *Com* marchandises *fpl* (en magasin), stock; *Ind* stock; **to lay in a s. of food** faire provision de vivres, s'approvisionner en vivres; **old s.** fonds *mpl* de boutique; **surplus s.** surplus *mpl*; **stocks are low** il y a peu de marchandises en stock; **while stocks last** jusqu'à épuisement des stocks; **to take s.** *Com* faire *ou* dresser l'inventaire; *Fig* faire le bilan; *Fig* **to take s. of sb** évaluer qn; *(by looking at)* toiser qn; **to take s. of the situation** faire le bilan de la situation, faire le point de la situation; **in s.** en magasin, en stock; **to be out of s.** *(of goods)* manquer en magasin; *(of book)* être épuisé; **we're out of s.** nous ne sommes en rupture de stock; *Rail* **locomotive s.** effectif *m ou* dotation *f* en locomotives; *Cin* **(film) s.** film *m* vierge, films *ou* bandes *fpl* vierges
2 *(livestock)* bétail *m*; **grazing s.** bétail, animaux *mpl* sur pied; **fat s.** bétail de boucherie
3 *Fin* fonds *mpl*, valeurs *fpl*, actions *fpl*; **government s.** fonds d'État, fonds *ou* effets *mpl* publics, rentes *fpl* (sur l'État); **stocks and shares** valeurs mobilières, valeurs de Bourse, titres *mpl*; *Fig* **her s. is going up/down** sa cote est en hausse/en baisse

4 *(of tree) (trunk)* tronc *m*; *(stump)* bloc *m*; *(in horticulture)* sujet *m*, ente *f*, porte-greffe *m*, *pl* porte-greffe(s); *Fig (lineage)* souche *f*; **he's of German s.** il est d'origine allemande
5 *(of rifle)* fût *m*, bois *m*, monture *f*, *(of whip)* manche *m*; *(of plough)* macheron *m*; *Naut (of anchor)* jas *m*
6 *Naut* stocks cales *fpl*; **to be on the stocks** être sur cales, être en construction; *Fig (of new novel etc)* être en chantier
7 stocks *(for punishment)* pilori *m*
8 *Ind (raw materials)* matières *fpl* premières
9 *Culin* bouillon *m*; **beef/chicken/vegetable s.** bouillon *m* de bœuf/poulet/légumes
10 *(plant)* matthiole *f*, giroflée *f* des jardins
11 *(neckwear)* col-cravate *m* *(d'équitation)*, *pl* cols-cravates; *(of English clergy)* plastron *m* en soie noire
ADJ *(conventional)* habituel; **he has three s. speeches** il a, en tout et pour tout, trois discours qu'il ressort périodiquement; **s. answer** réponse *f* classique; **s. phrase** expression *f* toute faite, expression consacrée
VT **1** *(supply) (shop)* approvisionner (**with** de, en); *(farm)* monter en bétail; *(house)* approvisionner (**with** de); *(pond)* empoissonner; *(forest)* peupler (**with** de); **this shop is well stocked** ce magasin est bien approvisionné; **to have a well-stocked cellar** avoir une cave bien remplie
2 *(have, keep in stock) (goods)* avoir *ou* tenir *ou* garder en magasin *ou* en dépôt, stocker; **I don't s. this article** je ne vends pas cet article; **we s. all leading makes of furniture** nous faisons toutes les grandes marques de meubles
▸▸**s. availability** disponibilité *f* en stock; **s. book** livre *m* des inventaires; **s. breeder** éleveur *m*; **s. breeding** élevage *m*; *Fin* **s. check** contrôle *m* des stocks; *Theat* **s. company** troupe *f* à demeure *(dans une ville)*; **s. control** contrôle *m* des stocks; **s. control system** système *m* de contrôle de stocks; *Culin* **s. cube** bouillon *m* Kub®; **S. Exchange** Bourse *(de Londres)*; **s. exchange** Bourse; **s. farm** élevage (de bétail); **s. farmer** éleveur; **s. farming** élevage de bétail *(activité)*, *Cin, TV* **s. footage** séquences *fpl* d'archives; **s. index** indice *m* de la Bourse; **s. in hand** marchandises en stock, marchandises en magasin; *Com* **s. in trade** marchandises (en magasin), stock; *Fig* **the double entendre was her s. in trade** l'ambiguïté, c'était sa spécialité; *Com* **s. issued docket** bon *m* de sortie; *Com* **s. keeper** magasinier *m*; *Com* **s. keeping** tenue *f* des stocks; **s. level** niveau *m* de stock; **s. list** *St Exch* cours *mpl* de la Bourse; **s. market** Bourse (des valeurs), marché *m* financier; **s. market gamble** spéculation *f* boursière; **s. market crash** krach *m* boursier; **s. market value** valeur *f* en Bourse; **s. outage** rupture *f* de stock; *Theat* **s. piece**, **s. play** pièce *f* de ou du répertoire; *Com* **s. received docket** bon d'entrée; **s. replacement** renouvellement *m* des stocks; *Austr* **s. rider** cow-boy *m*, *pl* cow-boys; **s. sheet** fiche *f* de stock; *TV* **s. shot** image *f* ou document *m* d'archives; **s. shrinkage** coulage *m* de stock; *Com* **s. take** inventaire des stocks; **s. turnaround**, **s. turnover** rotation *f* des stocks
▸ **stock up** VI *(build up a stock)* faire des provisions *ou* des réserves; **to s. up with sth** bien s'approvisionner en *ou* de qch
VT SEP *(larder, cellar)* approvisionner

stockade [stɒ'keɪd] N **1** *(fort)* palissade *f*, palanque *f* **2** *Am Mil (prison)* bloc *m*; **to be in the s.** être au bloc
VT palissader, palanquer

stockboy ['stɒkbɔɪ] N magasinier *m*

stockbroker ['stɒkbrəʊkər] N agent *m* de change
▸▸*Br Fam* **the s. belt** la banlieue aisée

stockbroking ['stɒkbrəʊkɪŋ] N commerce *m* des valeurs en Bourse

stock-car N *Sport* stock-car *m*
▸▸ **s. racing** course *f* de stock-cars

stockfish ['stɒkfɪʃ] N stockfisch *m*, merluche *f*

stockgirl ['stɒkgɜːl] N magasinière *f*

stockholder ['stɒkhəʊldər] N *Fin* actionnaire *mf*, porteur *m* ou détenteur *m* de titres

stockily ['stɒkɪlɪ] ADV s. built trapu

stockiness ['stɒkɪnɪs] N stature *f* trapue

stockinet(te) [stɒkɪ'net] N *Tex* wool/cotton s. jersey *m* de laine/coton

stocking ['stɒkɪŋ] N *(garment)* bas *m*; *Old-fashioned (knee-length sock)* chaussette *f*; *Med* **elastic** *or* **support s.** bas à varices; **body s.** combinaison *f* (une pièce)
▸▸ **s. filler** = petit cadeau *m* destiné à remplir le 'Christmas stocking' à Noël; **s. mask** bas *(utilisé par un bandit masqué)*; *Knitting* **s. stitch** point *m* de jersey

stockist ['stɒkɪst] N *Com* revendeur *m*; *(agent)* stockiste *m*

stockjobber ['stɒkdʒɒbər] N *Br St Exch Formerly* = avant 1986, intermédiaire *mf* en Bourse qui traitait directement avec les agents de change et non avec le public

stockman, *pl* **stockmen** ['stɒkmən] N **1** *(man who works with livestock)* gardien *m* de bestiaux; *(owner)* bouvier *m* **2** *Am (warehouseman)* magasinier *m*

stockpile ['stɒkpaɪl] N *(of sugar, ammunition etc)* stocks *mpl* de réserve *ou* de sécurité; **nuclear s.** réserve(s) *f(pl)* d'armements nucléaires ▸ VT *(goods)* stocker; *(arms)* entasser, accumuler

stockpiling ['stɒkpaɪlɪŋ] N stockage *m*, constitution *f* de réserves; *(of nuclear weapons)* accumulation *f*

stockpot ['stɒkpɒt] N *Culin* marmite *f*

stockroom ['stɒkruːm] N *Com* magasin *m*, réserve *f*, resserre *f*

stock-still ADV **to stand s.** rester (complètement) immobile; **he suddenly stood s.** soudain, il s'immobilisa

stocktaking ['stɒkteɪkɪŋ] N *Com, Ind* (établissement *m ou* levée *f* d')inventaire *m*, inventaire des stocks; **s. is in February** on fait l'inventaire en février

stocky ['stɒkɪ] ADJ trapu; *(horse)* ragot

stockyard ['stɒkjɑːd] N parc *m* à bétail *ou* à bestiaux

stodge [stɒdʒ] N *Fam (food)* aliment *m* bourratif, étouffe-chrétien *m inv*; **the s. we get in the canteen** les trucs bourratifs qu'on nous sert à la cantine

stodgy ['stɒdʒɪ] ADJ **1** *(meal, food)* bourratif **2** *(book)* indigeste; *(style)* lourd; *(person)* ennuyeux à force de sérieux, assommant

stogie ['stəʊgɪ] N *Am* cigare *m* bon marché

stoic ['stəʊɪk] ADJ, N stoïque *mf*; *Antiq* **S.** stoïcien, -ienne

stoical ['stəʊɪk(ə)l] ADJ stoïque

stoically ['stəʊɪklɪ] ADV stoïquement

stoicism ['stəʊɪsɪz(ə)m] N stoïcisme *m*

stoke [stəʊk] VT *(fire)* entretenir; *(furnace)* alimenter, entretenir le feu de; *(steam engine)* chauffer le foyer de; *Fig Fam* **the way he stokes his food in** la façon dont il engouffre sa nourriture
▸ **stoke up** VT SEP = stoke
▸ VI **1** *Naut* pousser les feux; *Rail* alimenter le feu **2** *Fam (eat heavily)* bouffer (comme quatre), bâfrer
▸ **stoke up on** VT INSEP *Fam (eat a lot of)* se bourrer de

stoker ['stəʊkər] N *Rail* chauffeur *m*; *Naut* mécanicien *m*; *(of blast furnace)* chargeur *m*

STOL [stɒl] N *Mil, Aviat (abbr* **short takeoff and landing) 1** *(system)* décollage *m* et atterrissage *m* courts **2** *(aircraft)* ADAC *m*

stole¹ [stəʊl] N **1** *Rel* étole *f* **2** *(garment)* étole *f (de vison etc)*

stole² PT *see* steal VT, VI

stolen ['stəʊlən] ADJ *(car, property etc)* volé ▸ PP *see* steal VT, VI
▸▸ **s. goods** objets *mpl* volés; **he was charged with receiving s. goods** on l'a inculpé de recel (de marchandises volées)

stolid ['stɒlɪd] ADJ flegmatique, impassible; **his s. exterior concealed …** sous des dehors impassibles, il cachait …

stolidity [stɒ'lɪdɪtɪ] N flegme *m*

stolidly ['stɒlɪdlɪ] ADV flegmatiquement

stolidness ['stɒlɪdnɪs] N flegme *m*

stoma, *pl* **stomata** ['stəʊmə, -ətə] N stomate *m*

stomach ['stʌmək] N *(organ)* estomac *m*; *(front of abdomen)* ventre *m*; **pain in the s.** mal *m* d'estomac; **upset s.** troubles *mpl* de la digestion; *Pharm* **to be taken on an empty s.** à prendre à jeun; **to drink on an empty s.** boire lorsqu'on a l'estomac vide, boire à jeun; **to turn sb's s.** soulever le cœur à qn, écœurer qn; **to have a cast iron s.** avoir un estomac à toute épreuve *ou* d'autruche; **an army marches on its s.** une armée ne se bat pas le ventre vide; **first s.** *(of ruminants)* panse *f*, **to have a large s.** *(be fat)* avoir un gros ventre; *Fig* **to have no s. for sth** *(not feel like)* ne pas se sentir d'humeur à qch; *Fig* **he had no s. for a fight** il n'avait pas le cœur à se battre ▸ VT *(support) (something)* supporter, endurer; *(person)* supporter; **I can't s. it any longer** j'en ai plein le dos, j'en ai ras le bol; **I can't s. oysters** je ne peux pas avaler les huîtres; **I can't s.the way he looks at me** il a une façon de me regarder qui me débecte
▸▸ **s. ache** douleurs *fpl* d'estomac, *Fam* mal *m* de ventre; **to have s. ache** avoir mal au ventre; **s. pump** pompe *f* stomacale; **s. upset** troubles *mpl* de la digestion

stomp [stɒmp] VI frapper du pied; **to s. out of the room** quitter la pièce en martelant des pieds; **I wish you wouldn't s. around like that** j'aimerais que tu arrêtes de marteler des pieds comme ça; **he was stomping up and down the room** il arpentait la pièce d'un pas lourd; **she stomped off** elle est partie en tapant des pieds
▸ VT *Am Fam (defeat)* flanquer une peignée *ou* une déculottée à

stomping ground ['stɒmpɪŋ ground] = **stamping ground**

stone [stəʊn] N **1** *(piece of rock)* pierre *f*, *(pebble)* caillou *m*, -oux; *Constr* mœllon *m*, pierre de taille; *(gravestone)* pierre tombale; **not to leave a s. standing** tout raser *ou* démolir; **to throw stones at sb** lancer des pierres sur *ou* à qn; *Fig* **who's going to cast the first s. (at him)?** qui lui jettera la (première) pierre?; *Fig* **to leave no s. unturned** mettre tout en œuvre, remuer ciel et terre (**to do sth** pour accomplir qch); **a s.'s throw from here** à deux pas d'ici
2 *(precious stone)* pierre *f*, **precious stones** *(in raw state)* pierres précieuses; *(cut)* pierreries *fpl*, pierres précieuses
3 *(material)* pierre *f* (à bâtir); **s. coloured** beige; **s. floor** sol *m* dallé; **s. jug** cruche *f* de grès
4 *Med* calcul *m*
5 *(of fruit)* noyau *m*
6 *Br (unit of weight)* = 6,348 kg ▸ ADJ *Am Fam (absolute, real)* véritable, total; **she is a s. babe!** c'est une supernana!; **this is turning into a s. drag!** ça devient vraiment galère! ▸ VT **1** *(fruit)* dénoyauter
2 *(person)* attaquer *ou* assaillir à coups de pierres, lapider; *(as punishment)* lapider; *(car etc)* lancer des pierres contre; **to s. sb to death** lapider qn *(jusqu'à ce que mort s'ensuive)*; *Br Sl* **s. the crows!, s. me!** ça alors!
▸▸ **the S. Age** l'âge *m* de (la) pierre; **s. axe** hache *f* de pierre; **s. cutter** *(person who cuts blocks)* tailleur *m ou* équarrisseur *m* de pierres; *Zool* **s. marten** fouine *f*, **s. saw** scie *f* à pierre *ou* de carrier; *Journ* **s. sub** correcteur *m* de mise en page

stone-blind ADJ complètement aveugle

stonechat ['stəʊntʃæt] N *(bird)* traquet *m* pâtre

stone-cold ADJ froid comme le marbre; **the tea is s.** ce thé est complètement froid *ou* glacé ▸ ADV **s. sober** complètement sobre

stonecrop ['stəʊnkrɒp] N *(plant)* orpin *m*

stoned [stəʊnd] ADJ **1** *Sl* **to be s.** *(on drugs)* être pété *ou* défoncé; *Old-fashioned (drunk)* être bourré **2** *(fruit)* dénoyauté

stone-dead ADJ raide mort ▸ ADV raide mort; **the blow killed him s.** le coup l'a tué instantanément; *Fig* **to kill a proposal s.** sonner le glas d'une proposition; **the teacher killed French s. for her** le professeur l'a complètement dégoûtée du français

stone-deaf ADJ complètement sourd, sourd comme un pot

stoneground ['stəʊngraʊnd] ADJ *(flour)* à l'ancienne

stonemason ['stəʊnmeɪs(ə)n] N maçon *m*

stoner ['stəʊnər] N *Sl* adepte *mf* de la fumette

stonewall [stəʊn'wɔːl] VI **1** *Sport* = pratiquer un jeu défensif pour tenir jusqu'à la fin **2** *Parl, Fig* faire de l'obstruction

stonewalling [stəʊn'wɔːlɪŋ] N **1** *Sport* jeu *m* défensif **2** *Parl, Fig* obstructionnisme *m*

stoneware ['stəʊnweər] N poterie *f* de grès

stonewashed ['stəʊnwɒʃt] ADJ *(jeans etc)* délavé

stonework ['stəʊnwɜːk] N maçonnerie *f*

stonily ['stəʊnɪlɪ] ADV froidement; *(to look at sb)* d'un air glacial; *(to reply)* d'un ton glacial

stoniness ['stəʊnɪnɪs] N **1** *(of soil)* nature *f* pierreuse **2** *(of heart)* dureté *f*, *(of look)* froideur *f*

stoning ['stəʊnɪŋ] N *(of person)* lapidation *f*

stonker ['stɒŋkər] N *Br Fam* **1** *(impressive thing)* **what a s. of a goal!** quel but d'enfer!; **their latest album's a complete s.** ! leur dernier album est absolument génial! **2** *(large thing)* mastodonte *m*; **that new skyscraper is a s. !** ce nouveau gratte-ciel est un vrai mastodonte

stonking ['stɒŋkɪŋ] ADJ *Br Fam* super, génial, -aux; **he scored a s. goal** il a marqué un but d'enfer

stony ['stəʊnɪ] ADJ **1** *(full of, covered in stones)* pierreux, rocailleux **2** *(hard like stone)* dur comme la pierre **3** *(lacking in emotion)* dur; *(reception)* froid; *(look, stare, silence)* glacial, -als *ou* -aux; **s. heart** cœur *m* de glace *ou* de marbre **4** *Br Fam* **s. broke** sans le sou, dans la dèche; **I'm s. broke** je n'ai pas un sou, je suis fauché (comme les blés)

stony-hearted [-'hɑːtɪd] ADJ au cœur de pierre; **to be** *or* **remain s.** être *ou* rester de glace *ou* marbre; **he's s.** il a un cœur de pierre

stood PT, PP *see* stand² VI, VT

stooge [stuːdʒ] N **1** *Theat* faire-valoir *m inv (d'un comique)* **2** *Fig, Fam (lackey)* larbin *m*; *(dupe)* pigeon *m*, poire *f*, *(idiot)* andouille *f*, crétin, -ine ▸ VI *Theat* **to s. for a comedian** servir de faire-valoir à un comique

stook [stu:k] *Agr* **N** tas *m* de gerbes, moyette *f*
VT mettre en moyettes

stool [stu:l] **N 1** *(seat)* tabouret *m*; *(with steps)* escabeau *m*; **folding s.** pliant *m*; **piano s.** tabouret de piano; *Fig* **to fall between two stools** être assis entre deux chaises; **prayer s.** prie-Dieu *m inv* **2** *Med* selles *f* **3** *(in horticulture)*, *Agr* pied *m* mère, plante *f* mère
►► *Fam* **s. pigeon** indic *mf*, mouchard, -arde

stoop [stu:p] **VI** *(bend down)* se pencher, se baisser; *(have bent back)* avoir le dos rond, être voûté; *Fig (abase oneself)* s'abaisser, s'avilir (**to do sth** à *ou* jusqu'à faire qch); *(deign)* daigner (**to do sth** faire qch); *Lit* **to s. to conquer** s'abaisser pour triompher; **she stooped to pick up the pin** elle s'est baissée pour ramasser l'épingle; **he was beginning to s.** il commençait à se voûter; *Fig* **he would s. to anything** c'est un homme prêt à toutes les bassesses; *Fig* **I never thought they'd s. so low as to …** je ne pensais pas qu'ils s'abaisseraient jusqu'à …
VT *(head)* pencher, incliner; *(back)* courber, arrondir
N 1 *(posture)* dos *m* rond, épaules *fpl* voûtées; **to have a s.** avoir le dos rond ou les épaules voûtées; **to walk with a s.** marcher les épaules voûtées, marcher voûté **2** *Am (porch)* porche *m* *(avec perron)*; *(platform)* terrasse *f* surélevée *(devant une maison)*

stooping ['stu:pɪŋ] **ADJ** penché (en avant); *(permanently)* voûté

STOP [stɒp]

N arrêt **1** • halte **1** • pause **1** • escale **1** • arrêt d'autobus **1** • point **2**
VT arrêter **1, 2** • interrompre **1** • cesser **2** • boucher **3** • obstruer **3**
VI s'arrêter **1, 2** • stopper **1** • cesser **2** • rester **3**

N 1 *(halt)* arrêt *m*; *(pause)* arrêt, halte *f*, pause *f*, *Aviat (in flight)* escale *f*; **to put a s. to sth** arrêter *ou* faire cesser qch, mettre fin à qch; **ten minutes' s.** dix minutes d'arrêt; **to come to a s.** s'arrêter; *(of car)* stopper; **to make a s.** faire (une) halte; *(for short period)* faire une pause; **we made four stops along the way** nous nous sommes arrêtés *ou* nous avons fait halte quatre fois en chemin; **the bus/train makes a s. at …** le bus/le train s'arrête à …; **to bring sth to a s.** arrêter qch; **let's have a s. for lunch** faisons une pause pour le déjeuner; **we travelled without a s.** nous avons voyagé sans escale; **we had a s. at the castle on the way back** nous nous sommes arrêtés au château sur le chemin du retour; **(bus) s.** arrêt (d'autobus); **request s.** arrêt facultatif **2** *(full stop)* point *m*; *(in telegram)* stop *m* **3** *Mus (on organ)* jeu *m*, registre *m*; **to pull out a s.** tirer un registre; *Fig Fam* **to pull out all the stops** faire un effort surhumain (**to do sth** pour faire qch) **4** *Carp, Tech etc* dispositif *m* de blocage, arrêt *m*, taquet *m*, butée *f*; *(for door)* heurtoir *m*; *Tech (for end of travel)* butoir *m* **5** *Opt, Phot (of lens)* diaphragme *m* **6** *Ling* occlusive *f*
VT *(-pp-)* **1** *(halt)* arrêter; *(traffic)* arrêter, interrompre; *(clock)* arrêter; *(machine)* arrêter, stopper; *Boxing (blow)* parer; *(fight)* interrompre; *(abuse, evil practice, rumours)* mettre fin à, faire cesser; *(strike)* briser, enrayer; **s. thief!** au voleur!; **to s. an opponent** *Ftbl* arrêter un adversaire; *Boxing* mettre un adversaire K.O.; **this bullet will s. a man at 200 metres** cette balle arrêtera un homme à 200 mètres; *Mil Sl* **to s. a bullet** prendre une balle; **the curtains s. the light** les rideaux cachent la lumière; **to s. sb's**

doing sth *or* **sb (from) doing sth** empêcher qn de faire qch; **I couldn't s. myself** je n'ai pas pu m'en empêcher; **to s. sth being done** empêcher que qch (ne) se fasse; **nothing will s. her** rien ne l'arrêtera; **what's stopping you?** qu'est-ce qui vous retient?, qu'est-ce qui vous en empêche?; **to s. the bleeding** arrêter l'hémorragie; **dumping nuclear waste should be stopped** il faut qu'on arrête de jeter n'importe où les déchets nucléaires; **it ought to be stopped** *(put an end to)* il faut que cela cesse
2 *(cease) (efforts, visits, work)* cesser; *Com* **to s. payment** cesser les paiements; **to s. doing sth** arrêter *ou* cesser de faire qch; **to s. smoking/drinking** s'arrêter *ou* cesser de fumer/boire; **he never stops talking** il n'arrête pas de parler, il parle sans cesse; **s. that noise!** arrête ce bruit!; **s. it!** *(to naughty child)* ça suffit!, assez!; *(you're hurting me)* arrête!; **it has stopped raining** il a cessé de pleuvoir, la pluie a cessé
3 *(block) (hole)* boucher, fermer; *(pipe)* obstruer, obturer; *Br (tooth)* plomber; **to s. one's ears** se boucher les oreilles; **to s. a gap** *(around door etc)* boucher un espace; *Fig* combler une lacune; *Com* **to s. (payment of) a cheque** faire opposition à un chèque; **to s. sb's wages** retenir le salaire de qn; **to s. £100 out of sb's wages** faire une retenue de 100 livres sur le salaire de qn; **to s. sb's pension** supprimer la pension de qn; *Mil* **all leave is stopped** toutes les troupes sont consignées, toutes les permissions sont suspendues
4 *(in horticulture) (plant)* pincer
5 *Mus* **to s. a string** presser une corde; **to s. a flute** boucher les trous d'une flûte
VI 1 *(halt)* s'arrêter; *(of ship, car)* s'arrêter, stopper; **to s. short** *or* **dead** s'arrêter net *ou Fam* pile; **to s. and talk to sb** s'arrêter pour parler à qn; **to do a hundred kilometres without stopping** faire cent kilomètres sans s'arrêter *ou* sans arrêt *ou* (tout) d'une traite; **we stopped in Caen** nous nous sommes arrêtés à Caen; **to go through a station without stopping** passer dans une gare sans s'y arrêter; *Naut* **to s. at a port** faire escale à *ou* dans un port
2 *(cease) (of rain, pain, headache, person doing sth)* s'arrêter, cesser; **my watch has stopped** ma montre s'est arrêtée; **to work fifteen hours without stopping** travailler pendant quinze heures d'affilée *ou* de suite; **to s. for lunch** faire une pause pour déjeuner; **he never stops** *(working, talking etc)* il ne s'arrête jamais; **she stopped in the middle of a sentence** elle s'arrêta au milieu d'une phrase; **he never stops to think** il ne prend jamais le temps de réfléchir; **she doesn't know when to s.** elle ne sait pas s'arrêter; **she didn't s. at that** elle ne s'en tint pas là; **he'll s. at nothing** rien ne l'arrêtera; **s. a moment!** arrêtez un instant!; **the matter will not s. there** l'affaire n'en demeurera pas là; **the rain has stopped** la pluie a cessé
3 *Br Fam (stay)* rester; **to s. at home** rester à la maison; **she's stopping with us for a few days** elle est venue passer quelques jours chez nous; **we decided to s. at a hotel** nous avons décidé de descendre à l'hôtel; **we stopped at a hotel for two weeks** nous avons passé deux semaines à l'hôtel
►► *Phot* **s. bath** bain *m* d'arrêt; *Comput* **s. bit** bit *m* d'arrêt; *Comput* **s. button** bouton *m* arrêt; *Comput* **s. code** code *m* d'arrêt; *Cin* **s. frame** arrêt *m* sur image; *Br* **s. sign** *(signal m de)* stop; *Am* **s. street** = rue *f* non prioritaire
► **stop away** **VI** *Br Fam (not come)* ne pas venir; *(not go)* ne pas y aller
► **stop by** **VI** *(visit briefly)* faire une petite visite; **s. by any time** tu peux passer quand tu veux; **I'll s. by at the post office on my way home** je passerai à la poste en rentrant à la

maison; **we'll s. by and see you next week** nous passerons te voir la semaine prochaine
► **stop down** *Phot* **VT SEP** diaphragmer
VI réduire l'ouverture
► **stop in** **VI** *Fam* **1** *(visit)* **to s. in to see sb** passer voir qn
2 *Br (stay at home)* rester chez soi
► **stop off** **VI** *(stay briefly)* faire (une) halte; **they're stopping off at Bali for a couple of days on their way home** ils font étape à Bali pour quelques jours en rentrant
► **stop out** **VI** *Br Fam (not come home)* **to s. out all night** découcher, ne pas rentrer de toute la nuit; **to s. out (till) late** rentrer tard
► **stop over** **VI** *(stay briefly)* faire escale, faire halte; **we stopped over at Manchester on the flight to Toronto** nous avons fait escale à Manchester en route pour Toronto
► **stop up** **VT SEP** *(block) (hole)* boucher; *(pipe)* obstruer, obturer
VI 1 *Br Fam (not go to bed)* **to s. up late** veiller tard; **to s. up all night** veiller toute la nuit
2 *Phot* augmenter l'ouverture

stop-go, stop-and-go **ADJ**
►► *Br Econ* **s. policy** politique *f* économique en dents de scie *(alternant arrêt de la croissance et mesures de relance)*, politique du stop-and-go

stopcock ['stɒpkɒk] **N** robinet *m* d'arrêt

stopgap ['stɒpgæp] **N** bouche-trou *m*, *pl* bouche-trous; **s. measure** pis-aller *m inv*

stoplight ['stɒplaɪt] **N 1** *(in street)* feu *m* rouge **2** *(on car)* stop *m*

stop-limit order **N** *St Exch* ordre *m* stop à cours limité

stop-list **N** *Banking (for lost cheques)* liste *f* de chèques volés ou perdus

stop-motion photography **N** prise *f* de vues image par image

stop-off **N** escale *f*

stopover ['stɒpəʊvər] **N** *(break in journey)* escale *f*, *Rail (option of breaking journey)* faculté *f* d'arrêt
►► **s. ticket** billet *m* avec (faculté d')arrêt

stoppage ['stɒpɪdʒ] **N 1** *(of traffic)* arrêt *m*, interruption *f*; *Mil etc (of pay, leave)* suspension *f*; *(of work)* arrêt, interruption; *(by discontented employees)* débrayage *m*; *(longer)* grève *f* **2** *(obstruction) (of pipe)* obstruction *f*, engorgement *m*; *Med* occlusion *f* **3** *(of salary)* retenue *f*

stopper ['stɒpər] **N** *(of bottle etc)* bouchon *m*; *(of pipe)* obturateur *m*
VT *(carafe, flask etc)* boucher

stopping ['stɒpɪŋ] **N 1** *(act of ending)* cessation *f*, *(of service)* suppression *f*, **s. of payment** suspension *f* de paiement **2** *Br (in tooth)* plombage *m*
►► **s. place** *(point m d')* arrêt *m*, halte *f*, *Br* **s. train** omnibus *m*

stop-press **N** *Br Journ (news)* informations *fpl* de dernière heure
►► **s. news** informations de dernière heure

stopwatch ['stɒpwɒtʃ] **N** chronomètre *m*; **they used a s. to time them** ils les ont chronométrés

storage ['stɔːrɪdʒ] **N 1** *(act of storing)*, *Com*, *Elec* emmagasinage *m*, emmagasinement *m*; *(of heat)* accumulation *f*, *Comput* stockage *m*; **to put sth into s.** mettre qch en dépôt **2** *(available space) (in store, for storing)* espace *m* disponible; *(of business)* entrepôts *mpl*, magasins *mpl*; **the kitchen has plenty of s. space** la cuisine a beaucoup d'espace de rangement; **there is additional s. for luggage in the rack above your head** vous pouvez également déposer vos bagages dans les casiers au-dessus de vos têtes **3** *(cost)* frais *mpl* d'entrepôt, magasinage *m*
►► *Comput* **s. capacity** capacité *f* de sto-

ckage; *Elec* **s. cell** accumulateur *m*, batterie *f* secondaire; *Com* **s. costs** frais *mpl* d'entreposage; *Comput* **s. device** dispositif *m* de stockage; **s. heater** radiateur *m* à accumulation; *Comput* **s. medium** support *m* de stockage; **s. room** *(small)* cagibi *m*; *(larger)* débarras *m*; **s. tank** *(for fuel)* réservoir *m* (de stockage); *(for rainwater)* citerne *f*; **s. tray** *(in car)* videpoche *m inv*; **s. unit** meuble *m* de rangement

store [stɔːr] **N 1** *(supply)* provision *f*, approvisionnement *m*; **to have a good s. of wine** avoir une bonne cave; **a s. of jokes** un stock d'histoires drôles; **his vast s. of knowledge** ses vastes connaissances, sa culture impressionnante; **to lay in a s. of sth** faire une provision de qch, s'approvisionner en qch; **to lay in stores** s'approvisionner; **to hold** *ou* **keep sth in s.** tenir *ou* garder qch en réserve; **what the future holds in s. for us** ce que l'avenir nous réserve; **I have a surprise in s. for her** je lui ménage *ou* réserve une surprise; **to set great/little s. by sth** faire grand/peu de cas de qch

2 stores *(supplies)* provisions *fpl*, approvisionnement *m*; *(food and drink)* provisions, vivres *mpl*

3 *Com, Ind (warehouse etc)* entrepôt *m*, magasin *m*; *(for furniture)* garde-meuble *m*, *pl* garde-meubles; *Mil, Naut (in barracks)* magasin

4 *(large shop)* grand magasin *m*; *Am (shop)* magasin; **general s.** épicerie *f*; **the village s.** l'épicerie du village; **toy/book s.** magasin de jouets/librairie *f*; **(department) s.** grand magasin

5 *Comput* mémoire *f*

VT 1 *(put in a store)* *(hay, corn)* emmagasiner; *(beetroot etc)* mettre en silo; *(take into store)* *(furniture)* prendre en dépôt; *(put in store)* *(furniture)* mettre en dépôt; **squirrels s. food for the winter** les écureuils font des provisions pour l'hiver

2 *(accumulate)* amasser, accumuler; *(put in reserve)* mettre en réserve; *(electricity, heat)* emmagasiner; **s. in a cool place** conserver au frais

3 *Comput* stocker

4 *(supply)* approvisionner (**with** en); **he stored the larder with enough tinned goods to last the winter** il a rempli le placard avec assez de boîtes de conserve pour passer l'hiver

VI goods that don't s. well marchandises qui ne se conservent *ou* ne se gardent pas bien

▸▸ **s. audit** contrôle *m* des points de vente; **s. brand** marque *f* de magasin; **s. card** carte *f* de crédit *(d'un grand magasin)*; **s. detective** vigile *m* *(dans un magasin)*; **s. manager** chef *m* de magasin

▸ **store away VT SEP** *(put away for future)* emmagasiner; *Fig* **he's storing it all away** il enregistre tout

▸ **store up VT SEP** = **store VT 2**; **to s. up problems for oneself** se garantir des problèmes pour l'avenir; **feelings of resentment that have been stored up over the years** des sentiments d'amertume qui se sont accumulés au fil des ans

store-bought ADJ de commerce; *(clothes)* de confection; **a s. cake** un gâteau de pâtisserie

storefront ['stɔːfrʌnt] **N** *Am* devanture *f* de magasin

storehouse ['stɔːhaʊs] **N** magasin *m*, entrepôt *m*, dépôt *m*; *Fig* **a s. of information** une mine de renseignements

storekeeper ['stɔːkiːpər] **N** magasinier *m*; *(in hospital)* dépensier, -ière *f*; *Am (shopkeeper)* commerçant, -ante

storeroom ['stɔːruːm] **N** *(for food)* office *m*; *(for old furniture etc)* débarras *m*; *(in school, offices etc)* réserve *f*; *Ind* halle *f* de dépôt;

Naut soute *f* aux vivres *ou* à provisions, magasin *m*, cambuse *f*

store(s)man, *pl* **store(s)men** ['stɔː(z)mən] **N** manutentionnaire *m*, magasinier *m*

storey, *Am* **story** ['stɔːrɪ] **N** *(of building)* étage *m*; *Br* **on the third s.,** *Am* **on the fourth s.** au troisième étage; **single** *or* **one s. house** maison sans étage *ou* de plain-pied

> Attention: ne pas confondre avec **story**.

-storeyed, *Am* **-storied** ['stɔːrɪd] **SUFF two-s. house** maison à un étage; **one-s.** *or* **single-s. house** maison sans étage *ou* de plain-pied

storing ['stɔːrɪŋ] **N** *Com* magasinage *m*

stork [stɔːk] **N** *(bird)* cigogne *f*

storm [stɔːm] **N 1** *Met* orage *m*; *(wind)* tempête *f*; **rain s.** tempête de pluie; **there's a s. coming** le temps est à l'orage; *Fig* **a s. in a teacup** une tempête dans un verre d'eau; *Fig* **political s.** ouragan *m* *ou* tourmente *f* politique; *Fig* **to bring a s. about one's ears** déclencher un tollé général; *Fig* **to cause a s.** faire l'effet d'une bombe; **to go down a s.** *(be very successful)* faire un tabac, faire un malheur

2 *(of insults)* bordée *f*; *(of applause, protest)* tempête *f*; **to raise a s. of laughter** déchaîner l'hilarité générale

3 *Mil* assaut *m*; **to take a stronghold by s.** prendre d'assaut une place forte; *Fig* **to take the audience by s.** soulever l'auditoire; **the play took Broadway by s.** la pièce a connu un succès foudroyant à Broadway; *Fig* **to take sb by s.** *(emotionally)* bouleverser qn

VI *(of person)* tempêter, pester; **to s. at sb** s'emporter contre qn; **to s. into/out of the room** entrer dans/quitter la pièce comme un ouragan; **she was storming about the place like a madwoman** elle se démenait dans la pièce comme une folle; **she went storming into the lead** elle est venue prendre la tête comme un ouragan

VT 1 *Mil (attack)* donner l'assaut à; *(capture)* prendre d'assaut, emporter d'assaut, enlever **2** *(say angrily)* fulminer

▸▸ **s. cloud** *Met* nuage *m* d'orage; *Fig* nuage menaçant; **s. cone** cône *m* de tempête; **s. damage** dommages *mpl ou* dégâts *mpl* causés par l'orage *ou* la tempête; *Am* **s. door** porte *f* extérieure *(qui double la porte de la maison pour éviter les courants d'air)*; **s. drain** égout *m* pluvial; **s. lantern** lampe *f* tempête; **s. sewer** égout pluvial; **s. troops** troupes *fpl* d'assaut; **s. warning** avis *m* de tempête

stormbound ['stɔːmbaʊnd] **ADJ** bloqué par une tempête

storming ['stɔːmɪŋ] **N** *Mil* prise *f* d'assaut (**of** de); **the s. of the Bastille** la prise de la Bastille

stormy ['stɔːmɪ] **ADJ** *(weather, sky)* orageux; *(sea)* démonté; **the weather is s.** le temps est orageux *ou* à l'orage; *Fig* **s. discussion** discussion *f* orageuse; **s. life** vie *f* tumultueuse; **s. marriage** mariage *m* orageux; **s. meeting** réunion *f* houleuse

▸▸ *Orn* **s. petrel** pétrel-tempête *m*, *pl* pétrels-tempête

story[^1] ['stɔːrɪ] **N 1** *(tale, account)* histoire *f*; **to tell a s.** raconter *ou* conter une histoire; **there is a s. that ...** on raconte que ...; **as the s. goes** à ce que l'on raconte; *Fig* **that is quite another s.** ça, c'est une autre histoire; *Fam* **it's the (same) old s.** *or* **the old, old s.** c'est toujours la même histoire; *Fam* **it's the s. of my life** c'est le genre de chose qui m'arrive tout le temps; **it's a long s.** c'est toute une histoire, c'est une longue histoire; **these bruises tell their own s.** ces meurtrissures en disent long; **each photo tells its** *or* **a s.** toutes les photos racontent une histoire; **she can tell a good s.** elle en connaît de bonnes; **so, to cut a long s. short ...** bref, pour résumer ...

2 short s. nouvelle *f*, conte *m*; **short s. writer** nouvelliste *mf*

3 *(plot)* *(of novel, play etc)* intrigue *f*

4 *Journ* *Fam* affaire *f*, information *f*; **who have we got on the s.?** qui est sur l'affaire?; **they decided to publish the s.** ils ont décidé de publier l'information; **all the papers ran** *or* **carried the s.** tous les journaux en ont parlé; **the s. broke just after the morning papers had gone to press** on a appris la nouvelle juste après la mise sous presse des journaux du matin

5 *Fam (lie)* histoire *f*, conte *m*; **to tell stories** raconter des histoires

▸▸ *Mktg* **s. completion** histoire *f ou* scénario *m* à compléter

> Attention: ne pas confondre avec **storey**.

story[^2] **N** *Am (of building)* = **storey**

storyboard ['stɔːrɪbɔːd] **N** story-board *m*, *pl* story-boards, scénarimage *m*

storybook ['stɔːrɪbʊk] **N** livre *m* de contes, livre d'histoires; **it looks like a s. castle** cela ressemble à un château de conte de fées; **it had a s. ending** ça s'est terminé comme un conte de fées

storyline ['stɔːrɪlaɪn] **N** intrigue *f*, **it was quite hard to follow the s.** j'ai/il a/*etc* eu du mal à suivre le fil de l'histoire

storyteller ['stɔːrɪtelər] **N 1** conteur, -euse; **to be a good/bad s.** être bon/mauvais conteur **2** *Fam (liar)* menteur, -euse; **you big s.!** gros menteur!, grosse menteuse!

storytelling ['stɔːrɪtelɪŋ] **N 1** art *m* de conter; **to be good at s.** avoir l'art de raconter des histoires **2** *Fam (telling lies)* mensonges *mpl*

stoup [stuːp] **N** *Rel* bénitier *m*

stout [staʊt] **ADJ 1** *(fat)* corpulent, fort; **to grow s.** prendre de l'embonpoint **2** *(solid)* *(door, shoes, beam)* solide; *(cloth)* renforcé **3** *(strong)* *(shoulders, legs, arms etc)* fort, vigoureux; *(brave)* brave, vaillant; *(resolute)* ferme, résolu; *Old-fashioned* **s. fellow** *(brave)* homme vaillant *ou* courageux; *(sturdy)* costaud *m*; **s. heart** cœur *m* vaillant; **to put up a s. resistance** se défendre vaillamment

N *(beer)* stout *m*, bière *f* brune forte

stouthearted [staʊt'hɑːtɪd] **ADJ** *Lit* courageux, intrépide

stoutly ['staʊtlɪ] **ADV 1** *(vigorously)* fortement, vigoureusement; *(to deny sth)* catégoriquement; **she s. maintained that ...** elle affirmait énergiquement que ... **2** *(sturdily)* *(built)* solidement

stoutness ['staʊtnɪs] **N 1** *(fatness)* embonpoint *m* **2** *(solidity)* solidité *f* **3** *(vigorousness)* *(of resistance etc)* fermeté *f*, vigueur *f*

stove [staʊv] **N 1** *(cooker)* cuisinière *f*, *(oven)* fourneau *m*; *(small, portable)* réchaud *m*; **electric/gas s.** cuisinière électrique/à gaz; **oil s.** poêle *m* à pétrole; *(heater)* calorifère *m* à mazout **2** *Chem, Ind* étuve *f*, four *m*

stovepipe ['staʊvpaɪp] **N** tuyau *m* de poêle

▸▸ **s. hat** chapeau *m* tuyau de poêle

stow [staʊ] **VT 1** *(put away)* ranger, mettre; *Sl* **s. it!** *(shut up)* la ferme!; *(that's enough)* ça suffit! **2** *Naut (cargo)* arrimer; *(anchor, ship's boats)* saisir **3 to s. sth full of sth** remplir qch de qch

▸ **stow away VT SEP** = **stow**; *Fam* **to s. away a huge meal** s'envoyer un repas énorme; *Fam* **he can certainly s. it away** il a un bon coup de fourchette

VI *(hide)* s'embarquer clandestinement

stowage ['staʊɪdʒ] **N** *Naut (of goods)* arrimage *m*; *(space)* espace *m* utile; *(cost)* frais *mpl* d'arrimage

▸▸ *Aut* **s. bin** vide-poches *m inv*, bac *m* de rangement

stowaway ['stǝʊǝweɪ] N *Naut, Aviat* passager *m ou* voyageur *m* clandestin

strabismus [strǝ'bɪzmǝs] N *Med* strabisme *m*

straddle ['stræd(ǝ)l] VT **1** *(be on both sides of) (horse)* enfourcher; *(chair)* se mettre à califourchon sur; *(wall)* se mettre à califourchon *ou* à cheval sur; **their empire straddled the Mediterranean** leur empire couvrait la Méditerranée; **to s. a river** *(of bridge)* enjamber une rivière; **the village straddles the border** le village est à cheval sur la frontière; **her life straddled two centuries** sa vie est à cheval sur deux siècles; **a company that straddles two continents** une entreprise qui a des intérêts dans deux continents **2** *Am Pol etc (question)* refuser de se compromettre sur; **to s. the fence** ne pas prendre parti, ne pas s'engager

N **1** *Sport (in high jump)* rouleau *m* ventral **2** *St Exch* stellage *m*

strafe [streɪf] VT *Mil* mitrailler en rasemottes

straggle ['stræg(ǝ)l] VI **1** *(walk in disorderly fashion)* marcher sans ordre; *(not keep up)* rester en arrière, traîner; **other climbers straggled behind and got lost** d'autres grimpeurs sont restés à la traîne et se sont perdus; **his hair straggled over his jacket collar** les mèches de sa nuque pendouillaient sur le col de son veston **2** *(of plants)* pousser en désordre; **the roses are straggling everywhere** les roses poussent dans tous les sens

straggler ['stræglǝr] N *(person)* traînard, -arde; *Naut (ship, sailor)* retardataire *m*, lanterne *f* rouge

straggling ['stræglɪŋ] ADJ **a few s. houses** quelques maisons *fpl* éparpillées; **s. hairs** mèches *fpl* rebelles

straggly ['stræglɪ] ADJ *(branches, hair)* épars; *(beard)* rare; **a s. line of refugees** une file étirée de réfugiés

---

STRAIGHT [streɪt]

ADJ droit **1, 7** ▪ rectiligne **1** ▪ raide **1**	
▪ honnête **2** ▪ franc **2** ▪ hétéro **4**	
▪ pur **5**	
N ligne droite **2** ▪ hétéro **3**	
▪ personne sérieuse **4**	
ADV droit **1** ▪ directement **2, 3**	
▪ honnêtement **4** ▪ clair **5**	

ADJ **1** *(not curved) (back, leg, line etc)* droit; *(trajectory)* rectiligne; *(movement)* en ligne droite; *Tennis* **to win in three s. sets** gagner en trois sets; *Am* **she got s. As in the exam** *(all As)* elle n'a obtenu que des mentions très bien à l'examen; **a s. A student** un étudiant brillant; *Fig* **to play with** *or* **keep a s. bat** se conduire honorablement; **to have a s. back** avoir le dos bien droit, se tenir bien droit; **s. hair** cheveux *mpl* raides; **he's a s. arrow** *(person of integrity)* on peut compter sur lui; *(too conventional)* il est un peu coincé

2 *(honest)* honnête, loyal; *(frank)* franc, *f* franche; *(answer)* sans équivoque, franc; **s. as a die** d'une droiture absolue; **to be s. with sb** agir loyalement avec qn *ou* envers qn; **be s. with me, is he ...?** sois franc avec moi, est-il ...?; **I want a s. answer!** je veux une réponse franche!; **to play a s. game** jouer franc jeu; **s. talking** conversation très franche; **it's time for some s. talking** il est temps que nous ayons une conversation très franche

3 *(serious, conventional)* **to keep a s. face** garder son sérieux; **I couldn't keep a s. face** je n'ai pas pu m'empêcher de rire

4 *Fam (heterosexual)* hétéro(sexuel)

5 *(neat)* pur; **s. whisky** whisky *m* sec; **to drink one's whisky s.** boire son whisky sec

6 *Fam (not on drugs)* **to be s.** ne pas avoir pris de drogue; *Am* **to get s.** = prendre une dose d'héroïne (ou d'une drogue comparable) de façon à éviter l'effet de manque

7 *(aligned)* droit; **your tie isn't s.** votre cravate n'est pas droite *ou* est de travers; **your skirt isn't s.** ta jupe est de travers; **to put a picture s.** redresser un tableau; **to put the room s.** remettre de l'ordre dans la pièce; *Fig* **to put things** *or* **matters s.** arranger les choses; *(sort problem out)* débrouiller l'affaire; **to put sb s.** révéler son erreur à qn; **you ought to put her s. about what he's (really) like** tu devrais lui dire la personne qu'il est vraiment; **let's try to get things s.** essayons d'y voir clair; **let's get this s., he left at two o'clock?** mettons les choses au clair, il est parti à deux heures?; *Fam* **get this s.!** comprends-moi bien!; *Fam* **I need five hundred pounds to get me s.** il me faut cinq cents livres pour me remettre d'aplomb *ou* me refaire

N **1** **to be out of (the) s.** n'être pas d'aplomb, être de travers; **to cut a material on the s.** couper une étoffe de droit fil; **the s. and narrow** le droit chemin; **to keep on** *or* **stick to the s. and narrow** rester dans le droit chemin

2 *Sport* **the s.** *(on race track)* la ligne droite; **the back s.** la ligne opposée *ou* d'en face; **the home s.** la (dernière) ligne droite; *Fig* **we're on the home s. now** nous sommes dans la dernière ligne droite

3 *Sl (heterosexual)* hétéro *mf*

4 *Sl (conventional person)* personne *f* conventionnelle *ou* sérieuse; **don't be such a s.!** sois pas si sérieux!

ADV **1** *(in straight line)* droit; **to fly s. as an arrow** voler droit comme une flèche; **to shoot s.** tirer juste; **to go s.** aller droit; *Fam (of criminal)* se ranger des voitures; **keep** *or* **go s. on** continuez tout droit; **to read a book s. through** *(from beginning to end)* lire un livre d'un bout à l'autre; *(without stopping)* lire un livre d'une traite

2 *(without delay)* directement; **it comes s. from Paris** ça vient directement *ou* tout droit de Paris; **I'll be s. back** je reviens directement; **to come/go** *or* **get s. to the point** venir/aller droit au fait; **to get s. on with one's work** se mettre directement au travail; **to walk s. in** entrer sans frapper; **s. away** immédiatement, aussitôt, tout de suite; *Fam* **s. off** sur-le-champ, tout de suite; *Fam* **I can't tell you s. off** je ne peux pas vous le dire tout de suite

3 *(directly)* directement; **to drink s. from the bottle** boire au (même) la bouteille; **it is s. across the road** c'est juste en face; **s. above sth** juste au-dessus de qch; **to look sb s. in the face** regarder qn bien en face; **he looked s. through me** il m'a regardé sans me voir; **we drove s. through Nantes** nous avons traversé Nantes sans nous arrêter; *Fam* **to let sb have it s.** dire son fait à qn; **I told him s. (out) what I thought of it** je lui ai dit carrément *ou* tout net ce que j'en pensais; **to come s. out with sth** dire qch tout net; **to tell** *or* **give sb sth s. from the shoulder** dire qch carrément à qn; *Theat* **to play a part s.** jouer un rôle de façon classique

4 *(honestly)* honnêtement; **to deal s. with people** être loyal en affaires; **to play s.** jouer franc jeu; *Br Sl* **s. up!** sans blague!

5 *(clearly)* **I can't see s.** je ne vois pas clair; **I can't think s.** mon cerveau refuse de fonctionner

▸▸ *Theat* **s. actor** acteur, -trice sérieux(euse); **s. edge** *(tool)* règle *f* (à araser); **s. fight** campagne *f* électorale à deux candidats; *Cards* **s. flush** quinte *f* flush; *Boxing* **s. left** direct *m* du gauche; **s. line** (ligne *f*) droite *f*, *Theat* **s. man** *(of comedian)* fairevaloir *m inv*; *Theat* **s. part** rôle *m* sérieux;

Am **s. razor** rasoir *m* à main; *Boxing* **s. right** direct du droit; *Am Pol* **s. ticket** liste *f* non panachée; *Horseracing, Fin* **s. tip** tuyau *m* sûr *ou* de source sûre

straightaway ['streɪtǝweɪ] ADV immédiatement, tout de suite

ADJ *Am* en ligne droite

straight-edged ADJ *(knife, blade)* à tranchant droit

straighten ['streɪt(ǝ)n] VT *(make straight)* rendre droit; *(nail, rod etc)* redresser; *(bar)* défausser; *(put in order)* ranger, mettre en ordre; **to s. one's back** se redresser; **to s. one's hair** se recoiffer; *(take curls out)* se défriser les cheveux; **to s. one's tie** arranger sa cravate; **to s. one's affairs** mettre de l'ordre dans ses affaires

VI *(of person)* se redresser; *(of thing, road etc)* devenir droit

▸ **straighten out** VT SEP **1** *(make straight)* redresser; *(bar)* défausser; **he straightened out the crumpled bedclothes** il a remis les draps en place **2** *(put right) (one's affairs)* arranger, mettre en ordre; **I will try to s. things out** je vais essayer d'arranger les choses

VI *(become straight) (of river, road etc)* redevenir droit

▸ **straighten up** VT SEP **1** *(put straight) (picture etc)* redresser **2** *(put in order) (room etc)* mettre de l'ordre dans

VI *(straighten one's back)* se redresser

straight-faced [-'feɪst] ADJ impassible

straightforward [streɪt'fɔːwǝd] ADJ **1** *(person, conduct)* franc, *f* franche; **to give a s. answer to a question** répondre sans détours à une question; **to be quite s. about it** y aller franc jeu **2** *(simple)* simple; **it's a very s. cooker to use** c'est une cuisinière très simple à utiliser **3** *(clear)* manifeste; **a case of s. racism** un exemple de racisme manifeste

straightforwardly [streɪt'fɔːwǝdlɪ] ADV **1** *(to act)* avec droiture, loyalement; *(to speak)* franchement, d'une manière franche, sans détours **2** *(simply)* facilement; **it can be assembled s. enough** le montage est assez facile; **you then quite s. remove the lid** puis vous ôtez le couvercle tout simplement *ou* très facilement **3** *(clearly)* manifestement; **to be s. wrong** *(of person)* avoir manifestement tort

straightforwardness [streɪt'fɔːwǝdnɪs] N *(of person)* franchise *f*; *(of matter, question)* simplicité *f*

straightline depreciation ['streɪtlaɪn] N *Acct* amortissement *m* linéaire

straightness ['streɪtnɪs] N **1** *(of line)* rectitude *f* **2** *(of conduct)* droiture *f*, rectitude *f*

straight-to-video ADJ *(movie)* sorti directement sur cassette vidéo

STRAIN¹ [streɪn] N **1** *(tension)* tension *f*, *Phys (ratio)* rapport *m* de la déformation, allongement *m* unitaire; **the s. on the rope was too great** la corde était soumise à une trop grande tension; **to relieve the s. on** *or* **take the s. off a beam** soulager une poutre; *Tech* **breaking s.** force *f ou* contrainte *f* à la rupture, effort *m* de rupture; **to take the s.** *(of beam) (be subjected to)* être soumis à la tension; *(to support)* supporter la tension; *(of person)* supporter la tension nerveuse; **it would be** *or* **put too great a s. on my finances** ce serait trop lourd pour ma bourse; **the long hours put a s. on her marriage** ses horaires impossibles ont occasionné des tensions dans son mariage; **the s. of modern life** la tension de la vie moderne; **the s. of business life** la fatigue propre au monde des affaires; **all this driving's getting a bit of a s.** tous ces déplacements en voiture commencent à me fatiguer; **I find it a s.** je trouve cela fatigant; **the s. was beginning to tell**

(on them/*etc***)** la tension devenait visible; **mental s.** surmenage *m* (intellectuel); **eye s.** fatigue *f* des yeux

2 *Med* entorse *f*; *(less serious)* foulure *f*; **s. in the back** tour *m* de reins

VT 1 *(cable)* tendre, surtendre; **to s. one's ears** tendre l'oreille; **to s. one's eyes** *(overuse)* se fatiguer *ou* s'abîmer les yeux *ou* la vue (**doing sth** à faire qch); *(make effort)* s'efforcer (**to see sth** pour voir qch); **to s. one's voice** *(overuse)* se fatiguer la voix; *(make effort)* forcer sa voix; **to s. every nerve to do sth** mettre toute sa force à faire qch; **to s. relations** tendre les rapports (**between** entre); **to s. one's resources** grever ses ressources jusqu'à la limite

2 *Tech (part)* déformer; **I've strained my wrist/ankle** je me suis foulé le poignet/la cheville; *(more seriously)* je me suis fait une entorse au poignet/à la cheville; **to s. one's back** se faire mal au dos; **to s. one's heart** se fatiguer le cœur; **to s. a muscle** se froisser un muscle; **to s. oneself** *(overexert oneself)* se surmener, s'éreinter (**doing sth** à faire qch); *Iron* **he doesn't (exactly) s. himself** on ne peut pas dire qu'il se foule (la rate); *Iron* **don't s. yourself, will you!** surtout ne te foule pas!

3 *(liquid)* filtrer, passer; *(stock)* tamiser, passer; *(vegetables)* faire égoutter

VI 1 *(make great effort)* peiner; **to s. at a door** essayer d'ouvrir une porte; **to s. at a rope/at the oars** tirer sur une corde/sur les rames; **to s. at the leash** *(of dog)* tirer sur la laisse; *Fig (be restless)* ne pas tenir en place; *(be rebellious)* se rebeller

2 *(of beam)* fatiguer, travailler; *(of rope)* être trop tendu

3 *Tech (of piece of metal)* gauchir, se fausser
4 *Lit* **s. at sth** *(be unwilling)* se faire un scrupule de qch; **to s. at doing sth** avoir des scrupules à faire qch

5 *(of liquid)* filtrer (**through** à travers)

strain² **N 1** *Biol (of virus)* souche *f*, *(of grain, plant)* variété *f*, *(of animal)* race *f*, lignée *f*
2 a s. of weakness un fond de faiblesse; **he said much more in the same s.** il s'est étendu longuement dans ce sens; **other stories/films in the same s.** d'autres histoires/films dans la même veine

3 *esp Lit* **strains** *(sounds, music)* accents *mpl*; **sweet strains** doux accords *mpl*

strained [streɪnd] **ADJ 1** *(rope, conversation, atmosphere etc)* tendu; **s. nerves** nerfs *mpl* tendus; **s. relations** rapports *mpl* tendus **2** *Med* **s. ankle** cheville *f* foulée **3** *(forced)* *(laughter)* forcé, contraint; *(language, interpretation)* forcé, exagéré **4** *(liquid)* filtré; *(stock)* tamisé; *(vegetables)* égoutté

strainer [ˈstreɪnər] **N** *Culin* passoire *f*, **tea s.** passe-thé *m inv*, passette *f* à thé; **milk s.** passoire

strait [streɪt] **N 1** détroit *m* **2 to be in dire** *or* **desperate straits** être dans une situation désespérée; *(financially)* avoir de gros problèmes financiers

▸▸**the Straits of Dover** le Pas de Calais; **the Straits of Gibraltar** le détroit de Gibraltar

straitened [ˈstreɪtənd] **ADJ in s. circumstances** dans une situation (financière) difficile

straitjacket [ˈstreɪtdʒækɪt] **N** camisole *f* de force; *Fig* carcan *m*; *Fig* **a financial s.** un carcan financier

VT *Fig* gêner, entraver; **to be straitjacketed by a lack of investment/by censorship** être bloqué par le manque d'investissement/par la censure

straitlaced [ˈstreɪtˈleɪst] **ADJ** collet monté *inv*

strand¹ [strænd] **N** *Lit (shore)* rive *f*, grève *f*
VT *(ship)* échouer; **tourists stranded by the**

air controllers' strike touristes bloqués à cause de la grève des aiguilleurs du ciel

strand² **N 1** *(piece) (of rope)* brin *m*, toron *m*; *Sewing (of cotton)* brin; *(of cloth)* fil *m*, *(of hair)* mèche *f* **2** *Fig (of plot)* fil *m*; **to unravel the strands of a complicated affair** démêler les fils d'une affaire compliquée

stranded [ˈstrændɪd] **ADJ 1** *(ship)* échoué; **s. whale** baleine échouée (sur la plage) **2** *(person)* **to leave sb s.** laisser qn en rade; **to be s.** rester en rade; **s. tourists** touristes bloqués

strange [streɪndʒ] **ADJ 1** *(unusual)* étrange, bizarre; **they didn't write – (that's) s.** ils n'ont pas écrit – (c'est) bizarre; **s. beasts** bêtes *fpl* fantastiques; **she wears the strangest clothes** elle porte les vêtements les plus bizarres; **she's a s. girl** c'est une fille bizarre; **it's a s. thing** c'est (une chose) étrange; **s. to say, I've never met him** bien que cela paraisse bizarre, je ne l'ai jamais rencontré; **it's s. that you haven't heard of it** c'est bizarre que tu n'en aies pas entendu parler; **it was s. to see her in a dress** ça faisait bizarre *ou* drôle de la voir en robe; **s. how some faces stick in your mind** c'est bizarre *ou* drôle comme certains visages restent gravés dans la mémoire; **they've got a s. way of saying thank you** ils ont une drôle de façon de dire merci; **it felt s. to be back in Scotland again** cela m'a fait bizarre de revenir en Écosse

2 *(unfamiliar)* **s. faces** des visages *mpl* nouveaux *ou* inconnus; **a s. place/house** un endroit/une maison qu'on ne connaît pas; **I can't work with s. tools** je ne peux pas travailler avec des outils qui ne sont pas les miens; **don't talk to s. men** ne parle pas aux étrangers

3 *Arch (foreign)* étranger; **in a s. land** dans un pays étranger

strangely [ˈstreɪndʒlɪ] **ADV** bizarrement; **it all seemed s. familiar** tout avait un étrange goût de déjà-vu; **he's behaving very s.** il se conduit de manière très étrange; **s. enough, he felt nothing** ce qui est bizarre c'est qu'il n'a rien senti

strangeness [ˈstreɪndʒnɪs] **N 1** *(unusual quality)* bizarrerie *f* **2** *(unfamiliarity) (of surroundings etc)* étrangeté *f*

stranger [ˈstreɪndʒər] **N** *(from somewhere else)* étranger, -ère; *(someone not known)* inconnu, -ue; **don't talk to strangers** ne parle pas aux inconnus; **I'm a s. here** je ne suis pas d'ici; **they're strangers (to us)** nous ne les connaissons pas; **you're quite a s. these days!** vous vous faites rare!; *Fam* **hello, s.!** salut toi! on ne te voit plus!; *(to unknown person)* bonjour, l'étranger!; **to become a s. to sb** devenir étranger à qn; **they had become complete strangers to one another** ils étaient devenus des étrangers l'un pour l'autre; **to become a s. to sth** perdre l'habitude de qch; **he's a s./no s. to fear** il ne connaît pas/il connaît bien la peur; **she's no s. to controversy/success** elle a l'habitude de la polémique/du succès

Attention: ne pas confondre avec **foreigner.**

strangle [ˈstræŋɡ(ə)l] **VT** *(person)*, *Fig* étrangler; *(laugh)* étouffer

strangled [ˈstræŋɡ(ə)ld] **ADJ** *(person)* étranglé; *(voice, laughter)* étouffé

stranglehold [ˈstræŋɡ(ə)lhəʊld] **N 1** *(in wrestling)* étranglement *m* **2** *Fig* **to have a s. on sb** tenir qn à la gorge; **to have a s. on sth** avoir la mainmise sur qch; **economic s.** mainmise *f* économique; **to break the s. on a country's economy** mettre fin à la mainmise sur l'économie d'un pays

strangler [ˈstræŋɡlər] **N** *(person)* étrangleur, -euse

strangling [ˈstræŋɡlɪŋ] **N** étranglement *m*

strangulate [ˈstræŋɡjʊleɪt] **VT 1** *Med (intestine)* étrangler; **strangulated hernia** hernie *f* étranglée **2** = **strangle**

strangulation [stræŋɡjʊˈleɪʃən] **N** strangulation *f*; *Fig* **economic s.** asphyxie *f* économique

strap [stræp] **N** *(of leather, canvas)* sangle *f*, lanière *f*, courroie *f*; *(on bra etc)* bretelle *f*, *(on shoe)* lanière *f*, patte *f*, *(for watch)* bracelet *m*; *(on underground train, bus)* poignée *f*, **watch s.** bracelet de montre; **(trouser) s.** *(under foot)* sous-pied *m*, *pl* sous-pieds; **to give sb the s.** *(punishment)* fouetter qn (avec une sangle)

VT (**-pp-** [stræpt]) **1** *(attach) (object)* attacher avec une sangle, sangler; *(trunk)* boucler; **to s. sth to sth** sangler qch à qch **2** *(punish)* **to s. a child** frapper un enfant avec une sangle **3** *Med (broken limb etc)* bander

▸ **strap down VT SEP** *(containers etc)* arrimer; *(prisoner, patient)* attacher

▸ **strap in VT SEP** *(passenger)* attacher; **to s. oneself in** s'attacher, attacher sa ceinture

▸ **strap up VT SEP 1** *(suitcase)* sangler **2** *Med* = **strap VT 3**

straphang [ˈstræphæŋ] **VI** voyager debout *(en se tenant à la courroie ou à la poignée)*

straphanger [ˈstræphæŋər] **N** *(in underground etc)* voyageur, *-euse* debout; **after 15 years of being a s.** *(commuting)* après être allé au travail pendant 15 ans en métro

strapless [ˈstræplɪs] **ADJ** *(dress, bra etc)* sans bretelles; **s. top** bustier *m*

strapline [ˈstræplaɪn] **N** *Journ* surtitre *m*

strapped [stræpt] **ADJ** *Fam* **1 to be s. (for cash)** être à court d'argent, être fauché **2** *Am (armed)* armé, chargé

strapping [ˈstræpɪŋ] **ADJ** solide, robuste; **s. fellow** grand gaillard; **tall s. girl** fille grande et costaude

strata [ˈstrɑːtə] **NPL** *see* **stratum**

stratagem [ˈstrætədʒəm] **N** stratagème *m*

strategic [strəˈtiːdʒɪk] **ADJ** stratégique
▸▸**s. business area** domaine *m* d'activité stratégique; **s. business plan** plan *m* stratégique d'entreprise; **s. business unit** domaine d'activité stratégique; **s. management** gestion *f* stratégique; **s. marketing** marketing *m* stratégique; **s. planning** planification *f* stratégique; *Br* **S. Rail Authority** = organisme *m* chargé de résoudre les problèmes posés par le système de transport ferroviaire

strategically [strəˈtiːdʒɪk(ə)lɪ] **ADV** stratégiquement; **s. placed** placé à un endroit/aux endroits stratégique(s)

strategist [ˈstrætədʒɪst] **N** stratège *m*

strategy [ˈstrætɪdʒɪ] **N** stratégie *f*

stratification [strætɪfɪˈkeɪʃən] **N** stratification *f*

stratified [ˈstrætɪfaɪd] **ADJ** *(formation, society)* stratifié

stratify [ˈstrætɪfaɪ] **VT** stratifier
VI se stratifier

stratosphere [ˈstrætəsfɪər] **N** stratosphère *f*

stratum, *pl* **strata** [ˈstrɑːtəm, -ə] **N** *Geol* strate *f*, couche *f*; *Fig* couche *f*; **the various strata of society** les différentes couches sociales VOIR GRAMMAIRE A13

straw [strɔː] **N 1** paille *f*; **it's not worth a s.** cela ne vaut pas un clou *ou* un pet de lapin; *Fig* **to clutch** *or* **grasp at straws** se raccrocher à de faux espoirs; *Prov* **a drowning man will clutch at a s.** = quand on se noie, on est prêt à se raccrocher à n'importe quoi; *Fig* **straws in the wind** un signe, un indice; *Prov* **it's the last s. that breaks the camel's back** c'est la goutte d'eau qui fait déborder le vase; **it's the last s.!** ça c'est le comble *ou* le bouquet!; *Fig* **man of s.** homme *m* de paille **2** *(for drinking)* paille *f*; **to drink lemonade through a s.** boire de la limonade avec une paille **3** *(colour)* jaune *m* paille

▸▸ **s. hat** chapeau *m* de paille; *Am Fig* **s. man** homme de paille; **s. mat** paillasson *m*; **s. mattress** paillasse *f*; **s. poll** sondage *m* d'opinion

strawberry ['strɔːb(ə)rɪ] **N** *(fruit, flavour)* fraise *f*; **s. (plant)** fraisier *m*; **wild s.**, *Am* **field s.** fraise des bois; **s. ice cream** glace *f* à la fraise; **s. jam** confiture *f* de fraises

▸▸ **s. bed** planche *f* ou plant *m* de fraisiers; **s. blonde** blonde *f* qui tire sur le roux; **s. field** fraiseraie *f*; **s. mark** tache *f* de vin, envie *f*

Strawberries and cream

En Grande-Bretagne, les fraises à la crème sont traditionnellement consommées lors de certaines manifestations en plein air, notamment au tournoi de tennis de Wimbledon.

---

strawberry-blonde **ADJ** blond vénitien *inv*

straw-coloured **ADJ** jaune paille *inv*

stray [streɪ] **N 1** *(animal)* animal *m* égaré; *(dog)* chien *m* errant; *Law* animal sans maître **2 waifs and strays** *(children)* enfants *mpl* abandonnés **3** *Radio* strays parasites *mpl*, friture *f*

ADJ 1 *(animal)* égaré, perdu; *Law* sans maître **2** *Fig (example, specimen)* isolé; **s. bullet** balle *f* perdue; **here are a few s. thoughts on the project** voilà quelques idées en vrac concernant le projet; **any s. thoughts you might have …** si vous avez des idées …

VI *(of person, animal)* s'égarer, errer; *(of sheep)* s'écarter du troupeau; **the plane had strayed off course** l'avion s'était écarté de sa route; **the sheep will s. onto the road** les moutons vont se sauver sur la route; *Fig* **to s. from the right path** s'écarter du droit chemin; **to let one's thoughts s.** laisser vagabonder *ou* vaguer ses pensées; **to s. from the point** s'écarter du sujet

streak [striːk] **N 1** *(stripe)* raie *f*, rayure *f*; *(of mist, vapour, dirt)* traînée *f*; *(of light)* rai *m*, trait *m*; **a s. of sunlight** un rayon de soleil; **the first streaks of dawn** les premières lueurs de l'aube; **like a s. of lightning** comme un éclair; **streaks of grey hair** mèches *fpl* de cheveux gris; **I've had a s. of luck** je tiens le filon; **winning/losing s.** *(in sport)* suite *f* de victoires/défaites; **to be on a winning s.**, **to hit a winning s.** être en veine; **there's a s. of Irish blood in her** elle a un peu de sang irlandais; *Br Sl* **he's a long s. of piss** *(tall and thin)* c'est une grande perche; *(insipid in character)* c'est une lavette **2** *Fig (tendency)* tendance *f*; **to have a jealous/mean/cruel s.** être d'une nature jalouse/avare/cruelle; **there was a s. of cowardice in him** il avait un côté lâche **3** *Fam (act of running naked)* **to do a s.** courir nu (en public)

VT rayer, strier (**with** de); **fur streaked with black** pelage rayé de noir; **streaked with tears** strié de larmes; **her face was streaked with dirt/blood** elle avait des traces de saleté/sang sur le visage; **wall streaked with damp** mur plein de traces d'humidité; **white marble streaked with red** marbre blanc veiné de rouge; **his hair was streaked with silver** ses cheveux étaient parsemés de fils d'argent; **to have one's hair streaked** se faire faire des mèches

VI 1 *(run, move etc fast)* **to s. along/past** aller/passer comme un éclair; **to s. off** partir à toute allure; **the Ferrari streaked past him** la Ferrari le dépassa en trombe; **the rocket streaked up into the sky** la fusée partit comme un éclair dans le ciel **2** *Fam (run naked)* courir nu (en public)

streaker ['striːkər] **N** *Fam* = personne *f* qui court nu(e) (en public)

streaking ['striːkɪŋ] **N** *(streaks)* raies *fpl*, rayures *fpl*, bandes *fpl*; *(in hairdressing)* effet *m* de mèches

streaky ['striːkɪ] **ADJ** *(paint)* irrégulier; *(pattern)* strié; *(mirror, plates etc)* couvert de traces; *(cloud)* effiloché; **her make-up had gone s.** son maquillage avait dégouliné

▸▸ *Br Culin* **s. bacon** bacon *m* entrelardé

stream [striːm] **N 1** *(brook)* ruisseau *m*; **mountain s.** torrent *m*

2 *(flow)* *(of light, blood, water)* flot(s) *m(pl)*, jet *m*; *(of lava)* coulée *f*; *(of tears, words, congratulations, insults)* flot, torrent *m*; *(of people, cars)* flot; **in one continuous s.** à jet continu

3 *(current)* courant *m*; **with the s.** dans le sens du courant, au fil de l'eau; **against the s.** contre le courant, à contre-courant; *Fig* **to go with the s.** suivre le mouvement; *Fig* **to go against the s.** aller à contre-courant; **the main s. of public opinion** le courant de l'opinion publique

4 to come on s. *(of oil)* commencer à couler; *(of new power station etc)* entrer en production; **to go off s.** *(of oil)* cesser de couler; *(of power station etc)* cesser de produire

5 *Br Sch* groupe *m* de niveau

VI 1 *(of liquid)* couler à flots, ruisseler; **people were streaming over the bridge** un flot continu de gens traversait le pont; **people streamed out of the stadium** des flots de gens sortaient du stade; **the sunlight streams in(to the room)** le soleil entre à flots (dans la chambre)

2 *(of surface)* ruisseler (**with** de); **his eyes were streaming** *(he was crying)* il était ruisselant de larmes; *(his eyes were watering)* il avait les yeux qui pleuraient

3 *(of hair, garment, banner)* flotter (au vent)

VT 1 to s. blood ruisseler de sang **2** *Br Sch* **to s. pupils** répartir les élèves selon leur niveau d'aptitude **3** *(audio, video)* transmettre en continu *(sur l'Internet)*

▸▸ **s. feed** *(on photocopier)* alimentation *f* automatique; *Liter* **s. of consciousness** monologue *m* intérieur

streamer ['striːmər] **N 1** *(flag)* banderole *f*; **(paper)** streamers serpentins *mpl* (de carnaval) **2** *Journ (headline)* titre *m* flamboyant, bandeau *m*, cinq colonnes *fpl* à la une **3** *Comput* streamer *m*, dévideur *m*

streaming ['striːmɪŋ] **ADJ** *(liquid)* qui coule; *Fam* **to have a s. cold** avoir un gros rhume

N 1 *Br Sch* répartition *f* par niveaux **2** *(of audio, video)* streaming *m*, transmission *f* en continu *(sur l'Internet)*

streamline ['striːmlaɪn] **VT 1** *(car etc)* caréner **2** *Fig (method, economy)* rationaliser; *(department, company, army etc)* dégraisser

streamlined ['striːmlaɪnd] **ADJ 1** *Aut, Aviat* caréné; *(fuselage)* aérodynamique; *(ship)* hydrodynamique **2** *Fig (system, economy)* rationalisé; *(department, organization, army etc)* dégraissé

streamlining ['striːmlaɪnɪŋ] **N 1** *(of bodywork)* carénage *m*, profilage *m* **2** *Fig (of system, economy)* rationalisation *f*; *(of department, organization, army etc)* dégraissage *m*

street [striːt] **N** rue *f*; **back s.** petite rue écartée; *Pej* rue pauvre; *(dangerous)* rue mal fréquentée; **the High S.** la Grand-rue; **to turn or throw sb (out) into the s.** jeter qn à la rue; **to walk the streets** courir les rues, battre le pavé; *(of prostitute)* faire le trottoir; **on the s.** dans la rue; **to be on the street(s)** *(of prostitute)* faire le trottoir; *(of homeless person)* être à la rue; **the whole s. heard the row** toute la rue a entendu la dispute; **the man in the s.** Monsieur Tout-le-Monde, l'homme de la rue; *Fam* **she's streets ahead of the rest of the class** elle est largement en tête de la classe; *Fig* **that's right up my s.** c'est tout à fait mon rayon

▸▸ *Br Old-fashioned* **s. Arab** gamin, -ine *ou* gosse *mf* des rues; **s. art** peintures *fpl* murales *(dans la rue)*; **s. cred** image *f* de marque; **to have a lot of s. cred** être très branché; **it gives him a lot of s. cred** ça lui donne une bonne image de marque; **they're gaining s. cred** leur image de marque s'améliore; **this won't do much for my s. cred** ça va craindre pour mon image de marque; **s. furniture** mobilier *m* urbain; **s. guide** plan *m* de la ville; *Am Sport* **s. hockey** hockey *m* sur roulettes; **s. interview** micro-trottoir *m*, pl micros-trottoirs; **s. lamp** réverbère *m*; **s. level** rez-de-chaussée *m inv*; **below s. level** au sous-sol; **s. life** *(activity)* animation *f* (des rues); **s. light** réverbère *m*; **s. lighting** éclairage *m* public; **s. map** plan de la ville; **s. market** marché *m* en plein air *ou* à ciel ouvert; *St Exch* marché hors Bourse; **s. musician** musicien, -ienne des rues; **s. party** = fête *f* de rue organisée pour célébrer un événement; **s. person** SDF *mf*; **s. photographer** photostoppeur, -euse; **s. plan** plan de la ville; **s. sweeper** *(person)* balayeur, -euse; *(machine)* balayeuse *f*; **s. theatre** théâtre *m* de rue *ou* de foire; **s. trader** marchand, -ande ambulant(e); *Old-fashioned* **s. urchin** gamin, -ine *ou* gosse des rues; **s. value** *(of drugs)* valeur *f* marchande

streetcar ['striːtkɑːr] **N** *Am* tramway *m*

streetwalker ['striːtwɔːkər] **N** racoleuse *f*

streetwise ['striːtwaɪz] **ADJ** averti, malin

strength [streŋθ] **N 1** *(of person, acid, player, team)* force *f*, *Chem (of solution)* titre *m*; *Elec (of current)* intensité *f*, *(of beam, rope)* solidité *f*, *(of emotion)* force, intensité; *(of market)* fermeté *f*, **solution at full s.**, **full-s. solution** solution *f* concentrée; **s. of character** force de caractère; **s. of purpose** détermination *f*, **s. of will** résolution *f*, volonté *f*, **by sheer (physical) s.** uniquement grâce à la force physique; **to recover** *ou* **regain one's s.** reprendre des forces; **you must keep up your s.** il faut garder vos forces; **she doesn't know her own s.** elle ne connaît pas sa force; **to build up one's s. again** reprendre des forces; **to lose s.** s'affaiblir; *Fig* **to do sth on the s. of what one has been told** faire qch en se fiant à *ou* en s'appuyant sur ce qu'on vous a dit; **convicted on the s. of eyewitness evidence** condamné sur la foi des déclarations des témoins oculaires; **he got a good job on the s. of his qualifications** il a obtenu un bon emploi grâce à ses diplômes; **s. of a friendship** solidité d'une amitié; **s. of materials** résistance *f* des matériaux; **to go from s. to s.** *(of person's health)* aller de mieux en mieux; *(of project etc)* avancer à pas de géant; *(of company, new writer etc)* connaître une réussite de plus en plus remarquable; **we went from s. to s.** *(in business or political relationship)* nous avons progressé à pas de géant; *(in personal relationship)* nous nous entendions de mieux en mieux; *Mktg* **strengths and weaknesses** forces et faiblesses *fpl*; *Fam* **give me s.!** pitié!

2 *(numbers)* **to be present in great s.** être présents en grand nombre; **they were there in full s.** il y avait un grand complet

3 *Mil (of army)*, *Fig* effectif(s) *m(pl)*; **wartime/peacetime s.** effectif de guerre/de paix; **to be under s.** avoir un effectif insuffisant; **to bring a battalion/department up to s.** compléter l'effectif d'un bataillon/service; **there are 30 of us when we're at full s.** nous sommes 30 quand nous sommes au complet

strengthen ['streŋθ(ə)n] **VT** *(wall, house, position, friendship)* consolider; *(beam, ma-*

terial, law, pound sterling) renforcer; *(person, body)* fortifier; *(sb's authority)* (r)affermir; *Chem (solution)* augmenter la concentration de; *Typ (colour)* charger; **it would s. my hand** *or* **position** cela renforcerait ma position; **this merely strengthened their resolve** ça n'a fait que renforcer leur détermination

VI *(of resolve, position etc)* se renforcer, s'affermir; *(of sterling etc)* se raffermir; *(of patient, industry, country etc)* prendre *ou* reprendre des forces

strengthening ['streŋθ(ə)nɪŋ] **ADJ** *(tonic)* fortifiant

N *(of material)* renforcement *m*; *(of wall, building)* consolidation *f*; *(of sb's authority)* (r)affermissement *m*; **there was a s. of opposition** l'opposition s'est renforcée; **there was a slight s. of the pound on foreign markets** il y a eu un léger renforcement de la livre sur les marchés étrangers

strenuous ['strenjʊəs] **ADJ** *(work, match, day at the office)* fatigant; *(campaigner)* zélé; *(effort, opposition)* acharné; *(denial)* formel, énergique; **to make s. efforts to get sth done** faire des efforts acharnés pour accomplir qch; **a s. advocate of sth** un défenseur passionné de qch; **s. opponent of sth** un adversaire acharné de qch; **s. life** vie *f* harassante

strenuously ['strenjʊəslɪ] **ADV** vigoureusement; *(to work, oppose)* avec acharnement; *(to deny)* formellement, énergiquement

strenuousness ['strenjʊəsnɪs] **N** *(of work)* dureté *f* (de l'effort physique exigé); *(of opposition)* acharnement *m*

strep throat [strep] **N** *Am* **to have a s.** avoir mal à la gorge

streptococcal [streptəʊ'kɒk(ə)l] **ADJ** *Med* streptococcique

streptococcus, *pl* **streptococci** [streptəʊ-'kɒkəs, -'kɒk(s)aɪ] **N** *Med* streptocoque *m*

streptomycin [streptəʊ'maɪsɪn] **N** *Med* streptomycine *f*

stress [stres] **N1** *(mental)* stress *m*, tension *f*; **to be under a lot of s.** être en proie au stress, être très tendu; **how does he react under s.?** comment réagit-il sous le stress *ou* sous la pression?; **I work better under s.** je travaille mieux sous la pression; **this puts our relationship under s.** ça crée des tensions dans nos relations; **how to cope with s.** comment vivre avec le stress; **some people thrive on s.** certaines personnes travaillent mieux sous la pression; **a major s. factor** un important facteur de stress *ou* de tension; **the stresses and strains of modern life** les tensions et les pressions de la vie moderne

2 *Tech etc (tension)* tension *f*, travail *m*; *Tech (in components)* sollicitation *f*; **to be in s.** *(of beam)* travailler

3 *(emphasis)* insistance *f*; *Ling* accent *m* tonique; *(in prosody)* accentuation *f*; **to put s. on sth** insister sur qch; **to lay s. on** *(fact)* insister sur, faire ressortir; *(word)* insister sur; *(syllable)* accentuer, appuyer sur; **the s. falls on the last syllable** l'accent tonique tombe sur la dernière syllabe; **there was too much s. on memorization of facts** on demandait d'apprendre trop de faits par cœur

VT1 *(emphasize)* insister sur; *(fact)* faire ressortir; *(word)* souligner, insister sur; **she stressed that no decision had been taken** elle a insisté sur *ou* souligné le fait qu'aucune décision n'avait été prise

2 *Ling (syllable)* accentuer, appuyer sur; **stressed syllable** syllabe *f* accentuée

3 *Tech (beam)* charger, fatiguer, faire travailler; **to be stressed** *(of beam)* travailler

▸ ▸ *Med* **s. fracture** fracture *f* de surmenage; *Tech etc* **s. limit** limite *f* de travail *ou* de fatigue; *Ling* **s. mark** marque *f* d'accent

stressed [strest] **ADJ** *Tech* sollicité; *(beam etc)* sous tension; *(person)* stressé, sous tension, tendu; *(syllable)* accentué; **to let oneself get s.** se laisser gagner par le stress

stressed-out **ADJ** *(complètement)* stressé

stressful ['stresfʊl] **ADJ** *(situation, job)* stressant

stress-related **ADJ** dû au stress
▸ ▸ **s. illness** maladie *f* due au stress

STRETCH [stretʃ] **N 1** *(act of stretching)* étirement *m*; **with a yawn and a s.** en bâillant et en s'étirant; **to have a s.** s'étirer; **at full s.** au maximum de ses capacités; **by no s. of the imagination could it be called a democracy** même avec beaucoup d'imagination *ou* même en faisant un gros effort d'imagination, on ne pourrait pas dire qu'il s'agit d'une démocratie; **it's not ready yet, not by a long s.** ce n'est pas encore prêt, et il s'en faut de beaucoup; *Mus* **s. of the fingers** *(at the piano)* écart *m* des doigts

2 *(elasticity)* élasticité *f*; **with two-way s.** *(of elastic fabric)* extensible dans les deux sens **3** *(of country, water)* étendue *f*; *(of land)* bande *f*; *(of road)* section *f*; *(of time, silence etc)* période *f*; **for a long s. of time** *(pendant)* longtemps, pendant une longue période de temps; **at a s., at one s.** (tout) d'un trait, d'affilée; **she's been working for hours at a s.** voilà des heures qu'elle travaille sans désemparer; *Fam* **to do a five-year s.** *(in prison)* faire cinq ans de taule

VT 1 *(extend)* *(elastic, belt, cable, spring)* tendre; *(shoes, gloves)* détendre, élargir; *(sb's patience)* éprouver, exercer; *(meaning of a word)* forcer; *(arm)* allonger; *(hand)* tendre, avancer; *(leg)* étirer; **to s. oneself** s'étirer; **to s. one's neck to see sth** tendre le cou pour voir qch; **to s. one's legs** *(take short walk etc)* se dégourdir les jambes; **to s. its wings** *(of bird)* déployer ses ailes; *Fig* **to s. one's wings** voler de ses propres ailes; **he stretched his arm through the broken window** il allongea le bras à travers le carreau cassé; **to s. the truth** exagérer; **to s. a point** faire une exception (**for sb** en faveur de qn); *Fam* **that's stretching it a bit!** vous y allez/il y va/etc un peu fort!; *Art* **to s. the canvas on the frame** tendre la toile sur le châssis; **to s. a rope across a room** tendre une corde à travers une pièce; **to s. an awning over the deck** tendre une tente sur le pont

2 *(put demands on)* demander un effort maximum à; *(resources)* grever jusqu'à la limite; **to be fully stretched** *(of person)* être à son rendement maximum; *(of resources, services)* être sollicité à fond; **she needs a job that will s. her** elle a besoin d'un travail qui la pousse à donner le maximum

3 *(make last)* *(income, supplies etc)* tirer au maximum sur; **we should be able to s. the food until the weekend** nous devrions pouvoir faire durer les provisions jusqu'au week-end; **our money could be stretched to last until Christmas** nous pourrions faire durer notre argent jusqu'à Noël

VI 1 *(become longer)* s'allonger; *(of person, rope)* s'étirer; *(of elastic)* se détendre; *(of gloves etc)* se détendre, s'élargir; **the rope stretched across the ravine** la corde allait d'un côté à l'autre du ravin; **it's rude to s.!** *(with arm)* il est impoli d'allonger le bras comme ça!; **she stretched across the table** elle allongea le bras *ou* tout le corps en travers de la table; **he stretched down under the table to pick up …** il allongea le bras *ou* le corps sous la table pour ramasser …; **I have to s. up to reach the top shelf** il faut que je m'étire pour atteindre l'étagère du haut

2 *(of terrain, road etc)* s'étendre; **the road stretches away into the distance** la route s'étire dans le lointain

3 my resources won't s. to that mes moyens (pécuniaires) ne vont pas jusque-là; **the dish will s. to six helpings** on pourra faire six portions; **there is enough material here to s. to two books** il y a assez de matière pour en faire deux livres
▸ ▸ **s. fabric** Stretch ® *m*; **s. mark** vergeture *f*

▸ **stretch out** **VI 1** *(extend limbs)* s'étirer; *(of horse when racing)* aller ventre à terre

2 *(extend)* *(of road, valley etc)* s'étendre; **a barren future stretched out ahead of her** un avenir sombre se profilait devant elle

VT SEP *(extend)* *(arm)* allonger; *(hand)* tendre, avancer; **to lie stretched out on the ground** être étendu par terre; **we could s. the meat out till Sunday** nous pourrions faire durer la viande jusqu'à dimanche

stretcher ['stretʃər] **N 1** *(for casualty)* brancard *m*, civière *f*; **he was carried** *or* **taken off on a s.** on l'a emmené sur une civière *ou* un brancard; **he's a s. case** *Med* il faut l'emporter sur une civière; *Fig Fam (having been beaten up etc)* il est bon pour l'hôpital **2** *Art (canvas)* **s.** châssis *m*
▸ ▸ **s. bearer** brancardier *m*; **s. party** détachement *m* de brancardiers

▸ **stretcher off** **VT SEP** *(remove on stretcher)* emmener sur une civière

stretching ['stretʃɪŋ] **N 1** *Sport (warm-up)* étirement *m* (musculaire) **2 s. of the rules** entorse *f* au règlement

stretchy ['stretʃɪ] **ADJ** élastique, extensible

strew [struː] **VT** *(pp* **strewed** [struːd] *or* **strewn** [struːn]) **s. sth over the floor** *(on purpose)* jeter *ou* répandre qch sur le plancher, (re)couvrir le plancher de qch; *(accidentally)* répandre qch sur le plancher; **the ground was strewn with rushes** une jonchée de roseaux recouvrait le sol, le sol était jonché de roseaux; **the bomb exploded, strewing the crowd with pieces of broken glass** la bombe explosa, couvrant la foule de débris de verre; **his clothes were strewn everywhere in the house** ses vêtements étaient éparpillés partout dans la maison; **toys were strewn over** *or* **around** *or* **on the floor** des jouets jonchaient le plancher; **references to classical literature are strewn throughout his work** son œuvre est émaillée de références à la littérature classique

strewth [struːθ] **INT** *Br Sl* ça alors!

striated [straɪ'eɪtɪd] **ADJ** strié

stricken ['strɪk(ə)n] **ADJ** *esp Lit (person, voice, look)* affligé; **he looked s.** il avait l'air affligé; **s. with grief** accablé de douleur; **s. with guilt** accablé par les remords; **s. by** *or* **with polio** atteint de polio; **s. by** *or* **with blindness** frappé de cécité; **the s. city** la ville sinistrée; **the s. vessel** le vaisseau en détresse *ou* naufragé; **the s. animal hid in the bushes** l'animal blessé se cacha dans les fourrés
PP *see* **strike** **VT, VI**

strict [strɪkt] **ADJ 1** *(teacher, boss, parent etc)* strict, sévère; **to be s. with sb** être sévère *ou* strict avec *ou* envers qn **2** *(ruling, etiquette)* strict, péremptoire; *(discipline, regime)* sévère, strict; *(fast)* strict, austère; **s. deadline** délai *m* de rigueur; **s. morals** morale *f* rigide, mœurs *fpl* sévères; **s. Muslim** musulman de stricte obédience; **she gave s. orders not to be woken** elle a donné l'ordre formel *ou* strict qu'on ne la réveille pas **3** *(exact)* exact, strict; **the s. minimum** le strict minimum; **in the s. sense of the word** au sens strict du mot; **to observe s. neutrality** observer la neutralité la plus stricte; **in strictest confidence** à titre tout à fait *ou* strictement confidentiel

strictly ['strɪktlɪ] **ADV 1** *(sternly)* strictement, sévèrement; *(treated, brought up)* avec rigueur **2** *(totally)* strictement; **s. confi-**

dential strictement confidentiel; **smoking (is) s. prohibited** il est strictement ou formellement interdit de fumer; **it is s. forbidden** c'est strictement défendu, c'est formellement interdit **3** *(exactly)* exactement, rigoureusement; **s. (speaking)** à proprement parler; **this rule was s. observed** cette règle a été rigoureusement ou strictement observée

strictness ['strɪktnɪs] N **1** *(of discipline)* sévérité *f* **2** *(of rules)* rigueur *f*; **their s. in applying the rules** la rigueur avec laquelle ils appliquaient le règlement **3** *(of interpretation)* exactitude *f*

stricture ['strɪktʃər] N *Fml* **1** *(usu pl)* **strictures** *(criticism)* critiques *fpl*; **to pass strictures (up)on sb/sth** diriger ses critiques contre qn/qch **2** *(restriction)* restriction *f*, limitation *f* **3** *Med (of ureter)* rétrécissement *m*; *(of intestine)* étranglement *m*

stride [straɪd] N **1** *(grand)* pas *m*, enjambée *f*; *(when running)* foulée *f*; **to shorten/lengthen one's s.** ralentir/allonger le pas; *Fig* **to make great strides** faire de grands progrès *ou* des progrès rapides; *Fig* **to take sth in one's s.** *or Am* **in s.** *(do easily)* faire qch sans le moindre effort; *(not be disconcerted by)* ne pas se laisser troubler par qch; **she left him after 6 months, but he took it all in his s.** après 6 mois, elle l'a quitté brusquement, mais il ne s'est pas laissé troubler pour autant; **these things happen, you just have to learn to take them in your s.** ce sont des choses qui arrivent, il faut savoir les accepter; **eventually you come to take it all in your s.** on finit par s'y faire; **to get into** *or Fam* **to hit one's s.** *(in walking)* prendre son allure normale; *Sport (of runner)* trouver son rythme; *(in working)* prendre la cadence; *Fig* **to put sb off his/her s.** faire perdre la cadence à qn **2** *esp Austr Fam* **strides** *(trousers)* fute *m*, futal *m*

VI *(pt* **strode** [strəʊd] *pp* **stridden** ['strɪd(ə)n]*)* marcher à grands pas *ou* à grandes enjambées; **she strode into the room** elle est entrée dans la pièce à grandes enjambées; **to s. along/away** avancer/s'éloigner à grands pas; **science is striding further ahead each year** chaque année, la science avance *ou* progresse à pas de géant; **she just strode straight up to him and said ...** elle se dirigea droit vers lui et dit ...; **Bonaparte strode impatiently up and down the room** Bonaparte arpentait impatiemment la pièce; **to s. over sth** enjamber qch

VT *Lit* **he strode the deck/the streets** il arpentait le pont/les rues

stridency ['straɪdənsɪ] N stridence *f*; *(of protests)* véhémence *f*

strident ['straɪdənt] ADJ strident; *(colour)* criard; *(protest)* véhément

stridently ['straɪdəntlɪ] ADV *(to talk)* d'une voix stridente; *(to laugh, shout)* de façon stridente; *(to protest)* avec véhémence

strife [straɪf] N contestation *f*, **domestic s.** querelles *fpl* de ménage; **political/sectarian s.** des luttes *fpl* politiques/sectaires; **after years of industrial s.** après des années de conflits sociaux

STRIKE [straɪk]

N grève	**1**	■ rencontre	**2**	■ coup	**3**
■ sonnerie	**3**
VT frapper	**1, 3, 12**	■ heurter	**2**
■ frotter	**4**	■ impressionner	**5**
■ découvrir	**6**	■ démonter	**7**
■ supprimer	**9**
VI attaquer	**1**	■ frapper	**1**	■ survenir	**1**
■ sonner	**2**	■ se mettre en grève	**3**

N **1** *Ind* grève *f*; **teachers'/miners' s.** grève des professeurs/mineurs; **postal s.** grève des postiers; **power s.** = grève dans le secteur de l'électricité; **an unofficial s.** = grève qui n'est pas soutenue par les syndicats; **lightning s.** grève surprise; **sit-down s.** grève sur le tas; **sympathy s.** grève de solidarité; **to be on s.** être en grève, faire grève; **to go on** *or* **come out on s.** se mettre en grève; **to bring people out on s.** amener des gens à faire grève; **to go on hunger s.** *(of prisoner)* faire la grève de la faim; **there have been calls for s. action** on a appelé à la grève; **the dispute could easily lead to s. action** le conflit pouvait très facilement amener une grève **2** *Min (of ore, oil)* rencontre *f*; *(of bed)* découverte *f*; **there has been a major oil s.** il y a eu une découverte d'un important gisement de pétrole; *Fig Fam* **lucky s.** coup *m* de veine **3** *(blow)* coup *m*; *(of clock)* sonnerie *f*, *Mil* raid *m* (on sur); *Fishing (by angler)* ferrage *m*; *(by fish)* mordage *m*; *(in baseball)* balle *f* manquée *(par le batteur)*; *(in tenpin bowling)* honneur *m* double; *Mil* **first s. weapon** arme *f* de première frappe; *Mil, Aviat* **air s.** raid, intervention *f* aérienne

VT *(pt* **struck** [strʌk]; *pp* **struck**, *Arch, Lit* **stricken** ['strɪk(ə)n]*)* **1** *(hit) (person, piano key)* frapper; **to s. sb in the face** frapper qn à la figure; **to be struck by a stone** être frappé par une pierre; **to s. sb a blow** porter ou assener un coup à qn; **they got what they wanted without striking a blow** ils ont obtenu ce qu'ils voulaient sans coup férir; **to be struck by a huge wave** essuyer un coup de mer; **ready to s. a blow for freedom of speech** prêt à se battre pour défendre la liberté de parole; **who struck the first blow?** qui a frappé le premier?; *Fig* **in his speech, he struck a blow for freedom/those who ...** par son discours, il a fait avancer la cause de liberté/de ceux qui ...; *Fig* **to s. a blow at sth** taper sur qch; *Mus* **to s. a chord** plaquer un accord; *Fig* **that strikes a chord (with me)** je me retrouve là-dedans; *Fig* **that strikes a familiar note** cela fait l'effet du déjà vu/du déjà entendu, ça me rappelle des choses; **to s. the right/wrong note** sonner juste/faux; **the clock strikes the hour and half hour** l'horloge sonne l'heure et la demi-heure; **the clock struck the hour** l'horloge sonna l'heure juste; **as the clock struck ten** lorsque l'horloge sonna dix heures **2** *(collide with)* frapper contre, heurter; **his head struck the pavement** sa tête a heurté le trottoir; **to s. (the) bottom** *(of ship)* toucher (le fond), talonner; **struck by lightning** *(house)* frappé par la foudre; *(tree, person)* foudroyé; **lightning had struck the house** la foudre était tombée sur la maison; **to s. a mine** *(of ship)* heurter une mine; **to s. a pedestrian** *(of car)* heurter un piéton; **a sound struck my ear** un bruit attira mon attention **3 to s. terror into sb** frapper qn de terreur; **it struck fear into their hearts** ils furent glacés d'effroi; **to s. sb with surprise** frapper qn d'étonnement; **struck with panic/terror** pris de panique/terrorisé; **to be struck dumb/blind** être frappé de mutisme/cécité; **he was struck dead by a heart attack** il a été emporté par une crise cardiaque; **the bullet hit her in the head, striking her dead** la balle l'a frappée en pleine tête, la tuant sur le coup; *Lit* **he struck his opponent dead** il a tué son adversaire d'un coup **4** *(match)* allumer, frotter; *(sparks)* faire jaillir; *Old-fashioned Br Sl* **s. a light!** nom de Dieu! **5** *(impress)* impressionner; *(the eye, imagination)* frapper; **how does she s. you?** quelle impression vous fait-elle?; **he strikes me as (being) sincere** il me paraît sincère; **the place struck her as familiar** l'endroit lui a paru familier; **that is how it struck me** voilà l'effet que cela m'a fait; **did it never s. you that you weren't wanted there?** ne vous est-il jamais venu à l'esprit que vous étiez de trop?; **what struck me was his brazen impudence** ce qui m'a frappé, c'est son impudence sans nom; **the thought struck me that ...** l'idée m'est venue *ou* il m'est venu à l'idée que ...; **it strikes me that we'd do better to say no** j'ai la nette impression que nous ferions mieux de dire non **6** *(discover) (path)* tomber sur, découvrir; *(gold)* découvrir; **to s. oil** atteindre une nappe de pétrole, rencontrer *ou* toucher du pétrole; *Fig* trouver un filon; *Fam* **she has struck it rich** elle a fait fortune **7** *(lower) (tent)* démonter; *Naut (sail)* amener, caler; *Theat* **to s. the set** démonter le décor; **to s. camp** lever le camp; **to s. one's flag** *or* **one's colours** *Naut* amener *ou* rentrer son pavillon, mettre pavillon bas; *Fig (surrender)* se rendre **8 to s. an attitude** poser **9 to s. a bargain** faire *ou* conclure un marché; **to s. a balance between X and Y** trouver un équilibre entre X et Y; **to s. an agreement/deal** conclure un accord/un marché (**with sb** avec qn) **10** *(delete)* enlever, supprimer; **that remark must be struck** *or Am* **stricken from the record** cette remarque doit être retirée du procès-verbal **11** *(of plant)* **to s. root** prendre racine **12** *(coin, medal)* frapper

VI **1** *(attack) (of enemy)* attaquer; *(of assassin, burglar etc)* frapper; *(of disaster, earthquake etc)* survenir; *(with dagger, club etc)* frapper; *(of serpent)* foncer; *Fig* **to s. at sth** menacer qch; **these reforms s. deep at the heart of our traditional way of life** ces réformes mettent en péril notre mode de vie traditionnel; **to s. home** faire mouche; *Prov* **s. while the iron is hot** il faut battre le fer tant qu'il est chaud; **the terrorists struck twice** les terroristes ont frappé deux fois; **where the missile struck** là où le missile a frappé **2** *(of clock)* sonner **3** *Ind* se mettre en grève; **to s. for better conditions** se mettre en grève pour de meilleures conditions de travail; **striking workers** ouvriers en grève **4** *(travel, head)* prendre *(une certaine direction)*; **to s. across country** prendre à travers champs; **they then struck west** ils sont ensuite partis vers l'ouest **5** *(of cutting)* prendre *(racine)*

▸▸ **s. aircraft** avion(s) *m(pl)* d'assaut; **s. ballot** = vote *m* avant que les syndicats ne décident d'une grève; **s. force** *(nuclear capacity)* force *f* de frappe; *(of police, soldiers, squad)* détachement *m ou* brigade *f* d'intervention; *(larger force)* force d'intervention; **s. fund** = caisse *f* de prévoyance permettant d'aider les grévistes; **s. notice** préavis *m* de grève; **s. pay** salaire *m* de gréviste *(versé par le syndicat ou par un fonds de solidarité)*; *Fin* **s. price** *(for share)* prix *m* d'exercice

▸ **strike back** VT SEP *(hit with return blow)* **to s. sb back** rendre son coup à qn; **if anyone strikes me, I s. him back** si quelqu'un me frappe, je rends le coup

VI *(hit return blow)* rendre le coup; *Fig (retaliate)* effectuer des représailles; **to s. back at the enemy** répliquer à l'ennemi, contre-attaquer; **the government struck back at its critics** le gouvernement a répondu à ceux qui le critiquaient

▸ **strike down** VT SEP *(knock down)* renverser; *(kill)* abattre; *Fig* **struck down by disease** terrassé par la maladie

▸ **strike off** VT SEP **1** *(remove by hitting)* enlever d'un coup; *(sb's head)* trancher

2 *(delete)* **to s. off a name from a list, to s. a name off a list** biffer *ou* rayer un nom d'une liste; **to be struck off** *(of doctor, solicitor)* être radié

3 *Com (deduct)* **to s. off £5** faire une réduction de *ou* déduire 5 livres
4 *Typ (number of copies)* tirer
VI *(travel, head)* **to s. off to the left** *(of person)* prendre à gauche; *(of road)* tourner à gauche; **we left the path and struck off into the depths of the forest** nous avons quitté le sentier et nous nous sommes enfoncés dans la forêt
▸ **strike on VT INSEP** *(discover)* tomber sur
▸ **strike out VT SEP** *(delete)* *(word)* rayer, biffer, barrer; **s. out whichever does not apply** rayer la mention inutile
VI 1 *(hit out)* **to s. out at sb** allonger *ou* porter un coup à qn; *Fig (criticize, attack)* attaquer qn; **to s. out right and left** frapper à droite et à gauche
2 *(travel, head)* **I struck out for the shore** *(swimming)* j'ai commencé à nager dans la direction du rivage; *(rowing)* j'ai commencé à ramer dans la direction du rivage; *Fig* **to s. out in a new direction** *(in life, thinking etc)* prendre une direction nouvelle
3 *(become independent)* **to s. out for oneself, to s. out on one's own** voler de ses propres ailes
4 *(in baseball)* sortir (du jeu)
▸ **strike up VT SEP** *(song)* entonner; *(piece of music)* commencer de *ou* à jouer; **to s. up a friendship with sb** se lier d'amitié avec qn, se prendre d'amitié pour qn; **to s. up an acquaintance with sb** lier connaissance avec qn; **to s. up a conversation with sb** entrer en conversation avec qn; **they immediately struck up a conversation** ils sont immédiatement entrés en conversation
VI on his arrival the band struck up à son arrivée, la fanfare attaqua un morceau

strikebound ['straɪkbaʊnd] **ADJ** paralysé par une/la grève; *(commuters)* coincé par une/la grève
strikebreaker ['straɪkbreɪkər] **N** *Ind* briseur, -euse de grève
strike-out mode N *Comput* mode *m* barré
striker ['straɪkər] **N 1** *Ind* gréviste *mf* **2** *Ftbl* buteur *m*; *Cr* = batteur *m* qui reçoit; *(in baseball)* batteur **3** *(device)* frappeur *m*; *(of clock)* marteau *m*; *(of firearm)* percuteur *m*
▸ *Aut* **s. plate** gâche *f* de porte
strike-thru mode N *Comput* mode *m* barré
striking ['straɪkɪŋ] **ADJ 1** *(sight, similarity, difference, appearance)* frappant, saisissant; *(feature)* saillant; *(situation)* dramatique; **he was a s. figure** c'était un personnage impressionnant; **of s. beauty** d'une beauté frappante **2** *(workers)* en grève
N 1 *(of coins)* frappe *f* **2 within s. distance** à quelques kilomètres; **we were within s. distance of the summit** nous étions tout près du sommet; **we haven't finished, but we're within s. distance** nous n'avons pas encore fini, mais on en est tout près **3** *(of clock)* sonnerie *f*
▸ ▸ **s. clock** pendule *f* à sonnerie; **s. mechanism** sonnerie *f* (des heures); **s. off** *(of name)* suppression *f*; *(of lawyer, doctor)* radiation *f*; **s. surface** *(for match)* frottoir *m*
strikingly ['straɪkɪŋlɪ] **ADV** d'une manière frappante *ou* saisissante; **s. beautiful** d'une beauté frappante
Strine [straɪn] **N** *Fam Hum* anglais *m* australien
string [strɪŋ] **N 1** *(cord)* ficelle *f*; *(piece of string)* bout *m* de ficelle; *(of puppet)* fil *m*; **ball of s.** pelote *f* de ficelle; *Fig* **to have sb on a s.** mener qn par le bout du nez; *Fig* **to keep sb on a s.** *(in uncertainty)* laisser qn dans l'incertitude; *(keep control over)* tenir qn en laisse; *Fig* **(with) no strings (attached)** sans conditions, sans condition aucune; **with strings attached** avec des conditions;

Fig **to pull the strings** tirer les ficelles; *Fig* **to pull strings** faire jouer ses relations *ou Fam* le piston; *Fig* **somebody pulled strings to get him the job** il a eu le poste par piston
2 *(of violin, piano, bow)* corde *f*; *Tennis* **strings** *(of racket)* cordes, cordage *m*; **the strings of a violin** la monture d'un violon; **guitar/violin s.** corde de guitare/de violon; **the strings** *(in orchestra)* *(instruments, players)* les cordes; **a s. of horses** un groupe de chevaux; **our first s.** *(athlete, horse etc)* le meilleur; **our second s.** *(athlete, horse)* nos athlètes/notre cheval numéro deux; *Fig* **to have more than one s. to one's bow** avoir plus d'une corde à son arc
3 *(of onions, islands)* chapelet *m*; *(of medals)* brochette *f*; *(of vehicles)* file *f*; *(of barges)* train *m*; *(of words, shops, defeats)* série *f*; **s. of beads** collier *m*; *Rel* chapelet *m*; **s. of pearls** collier de perles; **a whole s. of children/names** toute une kyrielle d'enfants/de noms
4 *Comput* suite *f*, chaîne *f*; **s. of characters** suite de caractères
VT *(pp, pt strung* [strʌŋ]*)* **1** *(fit with strings)* *(tennis racket)* corder; *(violin)* mettre les cordes à, monter; *(bow)* bander; **to be highly strung** *(of person, horse etc)* être nerveux; *(likely to suffer for emotional reasons)* être émotif
2 *(pearls)* enfiler; **to s. fairy lights across a garden** accrocher des guirlandes de lampions dans un jardin; *Fig* **to s. sentences together** enfiler des phrases; **he can't s. two sentences together** il est incapable d'aligner trois mots
3 *Culin* **to s. beans** ôter les fils des haricots
▸ ▸ **s. bag** filet *m* à provisions; **s. band** orchestre *m* à cordes; **s. bass** contrebasse *f*; **s. bean** haricot *m* vert; **s. orchestra** orchestre à cordes; **s. quartet** quatuor *m* à cordes; *Comput* **s. variable** variable *f* alphanumérique; **s. vest** tricot *m* de corps à grosses mailles
▸ **string along VT SEP** *Fam (deceitfully encourage)* duper, tromper; **they're just stringing you along** ils se moquent de toi; **let's s. them along a bit longer** et si on les faisait marcher encore un peu
▸ **string along with VT INSEP** *Fam (accompany)* accompagner, faire route avec
▸ **string out VI** *(form long line)* s'espacer; *Sport* **the field strung out behind** le peloton des coureurs s'effilochait
VT SEP 1 *(in time)* **to s. sth out** faire durer qch; **the TV series was strung out over six weeks** le feuilleton (de) télé a traîné pendant six semaines **2** *(in space)* **the troops were strung out over 200 kilometres** les troupes s'échelonnaient sur 200 kilomètres; **you're all too strung out, get closer together** vous êtes trop clairsemés, rapprochez-vous les uns des autres
▸ **string up VT SEP** *Fam (hang)* pendre haut et court
stringboard ['strɪŋbɔːd] **N** *Constr* limon *m* (d'escalier)
stringed [strɪŋd] **ADJ** *Mus (instrument)* à cordes
stringency ['strɪndʒənsɪ] **N** *(of rules)* rigueur *f*, sévérité *f*; *Fin (of market)* resserrement *m*
stringent ['strɪndʒənt] **ADJ** *(rules)* rigoureux, -euse, strict; *Fin (market)* tendu, serré
stringently ['strɪndʒəntlɪ] **ADV** rigoureusement, strictement
stringer ['strɪŋər] **N** *(journalist)* reporter *m* local, stringer *m*, stringman *m*
stringing ['strɪŋɪŋ] **N** *(act)* *(of violin)* montage *m*; *(of racket)* cordage *m*; *(of bow)* bandage *m*
stringpiece ['strɪŋpiːs] **N** *Constr* longrine *f*
string-puller [-pʊlər] **N** *Fam* **he could be a**

useful s. il peut nous/leur/*etc* être utile s'il fait jouer ses relations
stringy ['strɪŋɪ] **ADJ 1** *(vegetables)* fibreux, -euse, filandreux, -euse; **s. meat** viande *f* filandreuse **2** *(person)* élancé

STRIP [strɪp] **N 1** *(of cloth, paper)* bande *f*, *(of metal)* lame *f*, lamelle *f*; *(of ground)* bande, langue *f*, **narrow s.** bandelette *f*; *Fig* **to tear sb off a s.** donner *ou* passer un savon à qn, laver la tête à qn; *Med* **dressing s.** bande à pansement; *Aviat* **(landing) s.** piste *f* (d'atterrissage); **comic s.** bande dessinée, BD *f*
2 *Sport (clothes)* *(of football team)* tenue *f*
3 to do a s. *(undress)* se déshabiller, se dévêtir; *(for show)* faire un strip-tease
VT *(-pp-)* **1** *(undress)* déshabiller, dévêtir; **to s. sb to the skin, to s. sb naked** mettre qn à poil; **stripped to the waist** nu jusqu'à la ceinture, torse nu
2 *(deprive)* **to s. sb of sth** dépouiller *ou* déposséder qn de qch; **to s. sb of his/her clothes** dépouiller qn de ses vêtements; **trees stripped of their leaves** arbres dépouillés de leurs feuilles; **stripped of all his worldly goods** dépouillé de tous ses biens; **to be stripped of one's title/rank/office** être dépouillé de son titre/rang/poste
3 *(bed)* défaire; *Elec (cable)* dénuder; *Phot (plate)* pelliculer; **to s. a tree** *(of leaves)* effeuiller un arbre; *(of bark)* écorcer un arbre; *(of branches)* ébrancher un arbre; *(of fruit)* *(of person)* cueillir les fruits sur un arbre; *(of bird)* manger tous les fruits d'un arbre; **to s. a wall** *(remove wallpaper)* arracher le papier d'un mur; *(remove paint)* enlever *ou* gratter la peinture d'un mur; **thieves have stripped the house** les cambrioleurs ont complètement vidé la maison; *Mil Fam* **to s. an NCO** dégrader un sous-officier; **to s. an engine/a gun** démonter un moteur/un fusil; *Aut* **stripped chassis** châssis *m* nu
4 *(remove)* **to s. sth from sth** enlever *ou* ôter qch de qch
VI *(undress)* se déshabiller, se dévêtir; **to s. to the waist** se mettre nu jusqu'à la ceinture
▸ ▸ **s. cartoon** bande dessinée, BD; **s. club** boîte *f* de strip-tease; **s. light** néon *m*, tube *m* (au) néon; *Br* **s. lighting** éclairage *m* fluorescent *ou* au néon; *esp Am* **s. mining** exploitation *f* à ciel ouvert; **s. poker** strip-poker *m*; **s. show** *(spectacle m de)* strip-tease *m, pl* strip-teases
▸ **strip down VT SEP** *(dismantle)* *(engine, gun)* démonter; *(remove non-essential parts from)* *(bike etc)* enlever les parties non essentielles de; *Fig* **to s. a theory down to (its) essentials** simplifier une théorie pour n'en garder que l'essentiel
VI *(undress)* se déshabiller; **to s. down to one's underwear** se mettre en sous-vêtements
▸ **strip off VI 1** *(undress)* se déshabiller, *Fam* se dépoiler
2 *(of wallpaper etc)* se décoller, s'enlever
VT SEP *(remove)* *(paint)* gratter; *(wallpaper)* décoller; **to s. the paint off a wall** enlever *ou* gratter la peinture d'un mur

stripe [straɪp] **N 1** *(on cloth)* rayure *f*, raie *f*; *(on animal's coat)* rayure, zébrure *f*; *Mil* galon *m*; *(magnetic)* piste *f*; **black with a red s.** noir à raie rouge; **to mark sth with stripes** rayer *ou* zébrer qch; *Mil* **long service s.** chevron *m*; *Mil* **to get/lose a s.** être promu/dégradé **2** *Am* **a man of that s.** un homme de ce genre
striped [straɪpt] **ADJ** *(socks, material etc)* à raies, à rayures; *(animal's coat)* rayé, zébré; **red and blue s. jacket** veston rayé rouge et bleu
stripling ['strɪplɪŋ] **N** tout jeune homme *m*
strippagram ['strɪpəgræm] **N** = message *m* d'adieu ou d'anniversaire etc délivré par une

jeune fille ou un jeune homme qui fait un strip-tease

stripped-down [strɪpt-] **ADJ s. version** version *f* simplifiée

stripper ['strɪpər] **N 1** *(striptease artist)* strip-teaseuse *f, pl* strip-teaseuses; **(male) s.** strip-teaseur *m, pl* strip-teaseurs **2 (paint) s.** décapant *m*; **wallpaper s.** produit *m* pour décoller le papier peint

strip-search N fouille *f* d'une personne dévêtue; **to undergo a s.** devoir se déshabiller afin d'être fouillé
VT to s. sb faire déshabiller qn pour le/la fouiller

striptease ['strɪptiːz] **N** (spectacle *m* de) strip-tease *m, pl* strip-teases; **to do a s.** faire un strip-tease
▸▸ **s. artist** strip-teaseur *m, pl* strip-teaseurs, strip-teaseuse *f, pl* strip-teaseuses

stripy ['straɪpɪ] **ADJ** = **striped**

strive [straɪv] **VI** (*pt* strove [strəʊv]; *pp* striven ['strɪv(ə)n]) **to s. to do sth** s'efforcer de faire qch, faire des efforts pour faire qch; **to s. for** *or* **after sth** essayer d'obtenir qch; **to s. after effect** chercher à faire de l'effet; **s. as we might** malgré tous nos efforts; **to s. against sb** lutter contre qn

strobe [strəʊb] **N** *Phys etc* stroboscope *m*
▸▸ **s. lighting** lumière *f* stroboscopique

stroboscope ['strəʊbəskəʊp] **N** stroboscope *m*

strode PT see stride VI, VT

stroke[1] [strəʊk] **N 1** *(blow)* coup *m*; **to receive twenty strokes** *(with whip, cane etc)* recevoir vingt coups; *Fig* **at a s.** d'un coup; **to abolish a practice at a s.** abolir un usage d'un seul coup; **s. of lightning** coup de foudre
2 *(movement) (of wing, oar)* coup *m*; *Tech (of piston etc)* mouvement *m*, course *f*; *Cr, Tennis etc* coup; *Swimming (style)* nage *f*, *(arm movement)* mouvement des bras; *(in breast stroke)* brasse *f*, **she was only a few strokes from the bank** elle était à quelques mètres seulement de la rive; **to lengthen the s.** *(in rowing)* allonger la nage; **to keep s.** *(in rowing)* nager ensemble, garder la cadence; *Fig* **to be off one's s.** n'être pas au mieux de sa forme; *Fig* **to put sb off his/her s.** déconcerter qn; **not to do a s. of work** ne rien faire; **s. of (good) luck** coup de chance, aubaine *f*, **s. of wit/of genius** trait *m* d'esprit/de génie; **bold s.** coup hardi
3 *(of clock)* coup *m*; **on the s. of nine** sur le coup de neuf heures, à neuf heures sonnantes *ou* tapantes; **to arrive on the s.** arriver à l'heure juste
4 *Med* attaque *f*, **to have a s.** avoir une attaque
5 *(mark)* trait *m*; *Typ* barre *f* oblique; *(of pencil, brush)* coup *m* de crayon/de pinceau; *(of pen)* trait de plume; **at the s. of a pen** d'un coup de crayon; **with a few bold strokes of the brush** de trois coups de pinceau; *Fig* **to put the finishing strokes to one's work** apporter les dernières touches *ou* mettre la dernière main à son travail
6 *(oarsman)* chef *m* de nage; **to row s.** donner la nage, être chef de nage
VT *(in rowing)* être chef de nage de
VI *(in rowing)* être chef de nage, donner la nage
▸▸ **s. oar** *(oar)* aviron *m* du chef de nage; *(person)* chef de nage; *Golf* **s. play** partie *f* par coups

stroke[2] **N 1** *(caress)* caresse *f*, **to give sb/sth a s.** caresser qn/qch **2** *esp Am (remark)* **(positive) s.** encouragement *m*; **to give sb a s.** encourager
VT *(caress) (fur, sb's hair)* caresser; **to s. one's chin** se caresser le menton; **to s. one's hair down** *or* **into place** lisser ses cheveux; **s.**

the ointment evenly over the ... passer la pommade en couche régulière sur le ...; **he just stroked the ball into the net** il fit glisser le ballon dans les buts
▸▸ *Am SI* **s. magazine** magazine *m* de cul

-stroke [-strəʊk] **SUFF two/four-s. engine** moteur *m* à deux/à quatre temps

stroll [strəʊl] **N** tour *m*, *Fam* balade *f*, **to take** *or* **go for a s.** aller faire un tour
VI flâner, *Fam* se balader; **to s. around town** flâner en ville; **she strolled in an hour late and didn't even say sorry** elle est arrivée tranquillement avec une heure de retard et ne s'est même pas excusée; **he strolled across to me** il s'avança tranquillement vers moi

stroller ['strəʊlər] **N 1** *(person)* flâneur, -euse, promeneur, -euse **2** *Am (pushchair)* poussette *f* (d'enfant)

strolling ['strəʊlɪŋ] **ADJ**
▸▸ *Theat* **s. player** comédien, -ienne ambulant(e); **s. players** troupe *f* ambulante

STRONG [strɒŋ]

ADJ	fort **1, 2**	▪ robuste **1**	▪ solide **2**
▪ puissant **2**	▪ ferme **2**	▪ vigoureux **2**
▪ énergique **2**	▪ résistant **3**	

ADJ *(comp* stronger ['strɒŋgər]; *superl* strongest ['strɒŋgɪst]) **1** *(physically powerful) (person, horse etc)* fort; **he's not very s.** *(not muscular)* il n'est pas très fort; *(not healthy)* il n'est pas très robuste; **to be s. in the arm** avoir beaucoup de force dans le bras; **she's as s. as a horse** *or* **an ox** elle est forte comme un cheval *ou* un bœuf; **to be getting stronger** *(after illness)* reprendre ses forces; **his eyesight is not as s. as it was** sa vue a baissé, sa vue n'est pas aussi bonne qu'elle était
2 *(belief, will, currency, feelings, food, tastes, drink)* fort; *(wind, voice, light)* fort, puissant; *(character)* fort, ferme; *(nerves, constitution)* solide; *(country)* puissant; *(colour)* vif; *(protest, plea)* puissant, énergique; *Com (market)* ferme; *Elec (current)* fort, intense; *(supporter)* ardent, vigoureux; **there's s. evidence that he committed suicide/the economy is recovering** tout porte à croire qu'il s'est suicidé/qu'il va y avoir une reprise de l'économie; **she's a s. character** elle a une forte personnalité; **he's a s. candidate for the post** il a le profil idéal pour le poste; **this is a s. possibility** il y a de fortes chances; **to have s. reasons for doing sth** avoir de bonnes raisons de faire qch; **if you have s. feelings about it** si cela vous tient très à cœur; **he comes from a s. Catholic family** il vient d'une famille très catholique; **the religion which is strongest in Scandinavia** la religion qui prédomine en Scandinavie; **the pound is getting stronger** la livre sterling se raffermit; **to be in a s. position** *(politically, financially, militarily)* être dans une position de force; **s. conviction** ferme conviction *f*, **you've got to be s. and say 'no'** il faut être ferme et dire 'non'; **be s.** *(be brave)* sois courageux *ou* fort; **company two hundred s.** société forte de deux cents personnes; **the wind is growing stronger** le vent forcit; **to give s. support to sb/a measure** appuyer fortement qn/une mesure; **to be s. on sth** *(good at)* être fort en qch; *Mus* **s. beat** temps *m* fort; **a s. chance** une forte chance; **a s. accent** un fort accent; **s. verb** verbe *m* fort; **s. syllable** syllabe *f* accentuée; **s. likeness** grande *ou* forte ressemblance *f*, **s. measures** mesures *fpl* draconiennes; *Fig* **I found the book rather s. meat** j'ai trouvé ce livre plutôt salé; **s. point** point fort; **politeness is not her s. point** la politesse n'est pas son fort; **to have a s. smell** sentir fort; *Chem* **s. solution** solution forte *ou* concentrée; *Cards* **s. suit** (couleur *f*) longue *f*, *Fig* **languages are not**

my **s. suit** les langues ne sont pas mon fort; **s. wind** grand vent
3 *(resistant) (rope, cloth, shoes)* solide, résistant
4 s. language *(forceful)* langage *m* énergique *ou* vigoureux; *(swearwords)* grossiè-retés *fpl*; **to write in s. terms to sb** écrire une lettre énergique à qn; **to put sth in the strongest possible terms** exprimer qch dans des termes les plus énergiques possible
NPL the s. les forts *mpl*, les puissants *mpl*
ADV *Fam* **to be still going s.** *(be in good condition etc) (of athlete)* avoir encore un bon rythme; *(of old person, party, company etc)* se porter toujours bien; **how's grandfather? – still going s.** comment va le grand-père? – toujours solide; **you're pitching it a bit s.** vous y allez un peu fort

strong-arm ADJ to use s. methods *or* **tactics** utiliser la manière forte; **by s. methods** à la méthode forte
VT 1 *Am Fam (beat)* rouer de coups **2** *(use forceful methods on)* Labour **strong-armed the union leaders into calling off the strike** le parti travailliste a forcé la main aux dirigeants syndicaux pour qu'ils mettent fin à la grève

strong-box N coffre-fort *m, pl* coffres-forts

stronghold ['strɒŋhəʊld] **N** *(fortress)* forteresse *f*, *Fig* bastion *m*; **s. of trade unionism** bastion du syndicalisme

strongly ['strɒŋlɪ] **ADV 1** *(solidly)* solidement **2** *(forcefully) (to believe)* fortement; *(to support, oppose, endorse)* vigoureusement, énergiquement; **the sun shone s.** le soleil brillait fort; **he argued s. in favour of/against ...** il s'est montré très partisan de/opposé à ...; **to be s. in favour of sth** être fortement en faveur *ou* très partisan de qch; **s. worded letter** lettre dans laquelle on ne mâche pas ses mots; **I don't feel s. about it** je n'y attache pas une grande importance; **I feel very s. that they should be punished** je suis convaincu qu'ils devraient être punis

strongman ['strɒŋmæn] **N 1** *(powerful man)* homme *m* à poigne **2** *(in circus)* Monsieur Muscle *m*; **could you do your s. act with this coffee jar?** viens nous faire admirer ta force, on a besoin d'ouvrir un pot de café

strong-minded ADJ to be s. *(of person)* avoir de la volonté; **s. person** forte tête *f*

strong-mindedness [-'maɪndɪdnɪs] **N** force *f* de caractère

strongroom ['strɒŋruːm] **N** chambre *f* forte

strong-willed [-'wɪld] **ADJ** = **strong-minded**

strontium ['strɒntɪəm] **N** *Chem* strontium *m*

strop [strɒp] **N 1** *(razor)* **s.** cuir *m* (à repasser *ou* à rasoir), affiloir *m* **2** *Br Fam* **to be in a s.** être mal luné, être de mauvais poil
VT (-pp-) *(razor)* affiler *ou* repasser sur le cuir

strophe ['strəʊfɪ] **N** *(in poetry)* strophe *f*

stroppiness ['strɒpɪnɪs] **N** *Br Fam (insolence)* insolence *f*, *(awkwardness)* mauvais caractère *m*; *(aggressiveness)* agressivité *f*

stroppy ['strɒpɪ] **ADJ** *Br Fam (insolent)* insolent; *(not cooperative)* contrariant; *(aggressive)* agressif, hargneux; **she got a bit s. when I asked her if ...** elle est montée sur ses grands chevaux quand je lui ai demandé si ...; **don't get s. with me!** ce n'est pas la peine de monter sur tes grands chevaux!

strove PT see strive

struck PT, PP see strike VT, VI

structural ['strʌktʃər(ə)l] **ADJ 1** *Phil, Geol etc* structural, -aux; *(relating to structure)* structurel **2** *Constr* de construction
▸▸ *Econ* **s. adjustment** ajustement *m* struc-

turel; **s. damage** dégâts *mpl* de structure; **s. engineer** ingénieur *m* civil; **s. fault** défaut *m* de construction; **s. iron** fer *m* de construction; **s. linguistics** linguistique *f* structurale; **s. steel** acier *m* de construction

structuralism ['strʌktʃər(ə)lɪz(ə)m] N *Psy, Ling* structuralisme *m*

structurally ['strʌktʃər(ə)lɪ] ADV **1** *(to think, analyse)* structurellement; **s., the novel is …** du point de vue de la structure, le roman est … **2 the building is sound s.** la structure du bâtiment est saine

structure ['strʌktʃər] N **1** *(composition, framework) (of building, society, language etc)* structure *f*; *Mil etc* **command s.** structure *f* de commandement; *Econ* **price s.** structure des prix **2** *(building, monument)* construction *f*, édifice *m*, bâtiment *m*; *Fig* **the social s.** l'édifice social
VT *(organization)* structurer; *(novel etc)* structurer, architecturer

structured ['strʌktʃəd] ADJ structuré; **highly s.** très structuré
▸▸**s. interview** entretien *m* structuré *ou* centré; *Comput* **s. query language** langage *m* d'interrogation structuré; **s. questionnaire** questionnaire *m* structuré

struggle ['strʌg(ə)l] N lutte *f* (**for** pour; **against** contre); **fierce/desperate s.** lutte acharnée/désespérée; **he gave in without a s.** il n'a opposé aucune résistance; **the class s.** la lutte des classes; **s. for freedom** lutte pour la liberté; **life is a s.** la vie est un combat; **the s. for life/for existence** la lutte pour la vie/pour l'existence; **it's a s. getting the kids to wash properly** il faut se battre pour que les enfants se lavent correctement; **it'll be a s. but I think we'll make it** ce sera difficile *ou* dur, mais je crois que nous y arriverons; **I finished the book but it was a real s.** j'ai terminé le livre mais ça a été très dur; **I had a s. getting him to change his mind** j'ai eu du mal à le faire changer d'avis; **he's not worried about the s. that many people have just to make ends meet** il se fiche que des tas de gens doivent se battre pour arriver à joindre les deux bouts
VI lutter (**with** avec; **against** contre; **for** pour); *(move violently)* se débattre, se démener; **to s. to do sth** avoir du mal à faire qch; **she struggled to control her temper** elle a eu du mal à ne pas s'emporter; **the child struggled and kicked** l'enfant se débattait des pieds et des mains; **she was struggling with her umbrella** elle se débattait avec son parapluie; **he struggled to his feet** il s'est levé avec difficulté; **to s. along** *(walking etc)* marcher *ou* avancer péniblement; **we're struggling along** *(in life, with work etc)* nous nous débrouillons tant bien que mal; **he struggled through the hole in the wall** il réussit à passer par le trou du mur; **the more he struggled, the deeper he sank in the mud** plus il se débattait, plus il s'enfonçait dans la boue; **let's s. on for another month/couple of kilometres or so** essayons de tenir encore un mois/kilomètre ou deux; **the climbers struggled back to camp** les grimpeurs sont rentrés au camp tant bien que mal; **we had to struggle through the crowd to get to the bar** il a fallu que l'on se fraie un chemin à travers la foule pour accéder au bar; *Fig* **we struggled through** nous avons surmonté tous les obstacles; **to be struggling (badly)** *(in one's job, university course etc)* avoir du mal; **the team is struggling** *(in match, to retain position in league etc)* l'équipe a des difficultés; **to s. against circumstances** lutter contre les événements; **to s. with death** lutter contre la mort; **to s. with one's conscience/homework** être aux prises avec sa conscience/ ses devoirs; **we have to s. to make ends**

meet nous avons du mal à joindre les deux bouts; **many companies are struggling** *(financially)* beaucoup d'entreprises ont du mal *ou* sont en difficulté; **I had to s. to make myself understood** j'ai eu de la peine *ou* du mal à me faire comprendre; **he was obviously struggling for** *or* **to find the right word** il avait visiblement de la peine à trouver le mot juste

struggling ['strʌglɪŋ] ADJ *(artist etc)* qui vit péniblement; *(masses)* laborieux; **when I was a s. young actor** quand je débutais comme acteur

strum [strʌm] N **the s. of a guitar** le son d'une guitare
VT **(-mm-)** *(guitar)* pincer les cordes de; **to s. (out) a tune** *(on guitar)* jouer un air
VI *(on a guitar)* pincer les cordes

strumming ['strʌmɪŋ] N **a gentle s. from the guitar** les doux accords de la guitare; *Pej* **his s. gets on my nerves** les raclements de sa guitare me tapent sur les nerfs

strumpet ['strʌmpɪt] N *Arch, Lit* prostituée *f*

strung PT, PP *see* **string** VT

strung-out ADJ *Sl (on heroin)* en manque

strung-up ADJ *(person)* tendu

strut¹ [strʌt] N *Constr (support)* étai *m*; *(crosspiece)* traverse *f*, *(in roofing)* jambe *f* de force; *(of roof truss)* contrefiche *f*, *Aviat* pilier *m*, mât *m*

strut² N *(walk)* démarche *f* affectée
VI **(-tt-)** se pavaner; *(after victory, compliment etc)* se rengorger; **to s. in/out** entrer/ sortir en se pavanant
VT *esp Am Fam* **to s. one's stuff** frimer
▸ **strut about, strut around** VI *(parade oneself)* se pavaner; *(walk around self-importantly)* parader

struth [struːθ] INT *Br Sl* = **strewth**

strychnine ['strɪkniːn] N strychnine *f*

stub [stʌb] N **1** *(of pencil)* bout *m*; *(of cigarette, cigar)* mégot *m*; *(of dog's tail)* bout de queue **2** *(of cheque)* talon *m*, souche *f*
VT **(-bb-) to s. one's toe (on** *or* **against sth)** se heurter *ou* se cogner le pied (contre qch)
▸▸**s. axle** essieu *m* à chapes fermées
▸ **stub out** VT SEP *(cigarette)* écraser

stubble ['stʌb(ə)l] N **1** *Agr* chaume *m*, éteule *f*, **to clear a field of s.** chaumer un champ; **to burn the s.** brûler les chaumes **2** *(on face)* barbe *f* piquante *(de plusieurs jours)*
▸▸*Agr* **s. field** chaume

stubbly ['stʌblɪ] ADJ **1** *Agr (field)* couvert de chaume *ou* d'éteule **2 s. beard** barbe *f* piquante *(de plusieurs jours)*; **s. chin** menton *m* qui pique

stubborn ['stʌbən] ADJ **1** *(person)* entêté, têtu, obstiné; *(determination, resistance)* farouche; **their s. refusal to surrender** leur refus obstiné de se rendre; **as s. as a mule** têtu comme un mulet *ou* une mule **2** *(stain, infection)* rebelle

stubbornly ['stʌbənlɪ] ADV obstinément, avec entêtement; **she s. refused to give up hope** elle a refusé obstinément d'abandonner espoir

stubbornness ['stʌbənnɪs] N *(of person)* entêtement *m*, obstination *f*, opiniâtreté *f*, *(of determination, resistance)* inflexibilité *f*

stubby ['stʌbɪ] ADJ *(person)* trapu; *(finger)* boudiné
N *Br, Austr Fam (bottle of beer)* canette *f*

stucco ['stʌkəʊ] N stuc *m*
VT *(pt, pp* **stuccoed;** *prp* **stuccoing)** stuquer; **stuccoed decorations** des décorations en stuc
▸▸**s. work** *(act, process)* stucage *m*; *(result)* stuc *m*

stuck PT, PP *see* **stick²** VT, VI

stuck-up ADJ *Fam Pej* snob; *(conceited)* prétentieux

stud¹ [stʌd] N **1** *(nail)* clou *m* à grosse tête; *(as ornament)* clou doré; *(of pedestrian crossing)* clou; **studs** *(on football boots)* crampons *mpl* **2** *(of dress shirt)* bouton *m* (double); **(collar)** bouton de col **3** *Tech (short pin)* goujon *m*, tourillon *m*; *(bolt)* goujon **4** *Constr* poteau *m*, montant *m* **5** *(earring)* clou *m* (d'oreille)
VT **(-dd-) 1** *(fit with studs)* garnir de clous, clouter; **studded door** porte garnie de clous *ou* cloutée; **studded tyre** pneu *m* clouté; *Fig* **studded with stars** *(sky)* parsemé d'étoiles; **her dress was studded with jewels** sa robe était constellée de pierreries **2** *Constr (partition)* établir la charpente de
▸▸**s. bolt** goujon *m*; **s. earring** clou *m* (d'oreille); **s. fastener** pression *f* *(bouton)*; *Constr* **s. wall** mur *m* de séparation

stud² N **1 to be at s.** *(of horse)* être à la monte; *(of dog)* faire des saillies; **to put a horse to s.** utiliser un cheval comme étalon **2** *(stallion)*, *Fig Sl (man)* étalon *m*; **he's a real s.** *(promiscuous)* c'est un vrai tombeur **3** *Cards* poker *m*
▸▸**s. farm** haras *m*; **s. mare** *(jument f)* poulinière *f*, *Am Fam* **s. muffin** super beau mec *m*; *Cards* **s. poker** poker

studbook ['stʌdbʊk] N stud-book *m*, *pl* stud-books

student ['stjuːdənt] N **1** *Univ* étudiant, -ante; *Sch* élève *mf*, **law/medical/arts s.** étudiant en droit/en médecine/en lettres **2** *(observer etc) (of human nature etc)* observateur, -trice *(* **of** de); **students of Middle East politics will know that …** ceux qui étudient la politique du Moyen-Orient savent que …
▸▸**the s. body** les étudiants *mpl*, *Am* **s. driver** apprenti, -ie conducteur(trice); **s. flat** appartement *m* d'étudiants; **s. grant** bourse *f* (d'études); **s. house** maison *f* d'étudiants; **s. life** vie *f* d'étudiant; **s. loan** = prêt *m* bancaire pour étudiants; **s. nurse** élève *mf* infirmier(ière); **s. radio** radio *f* universitaire; **s. rate** *(for travel etc)* tarif *m* étudiant; **s. riots** émeutes *fpl* étudiantes; **s. teacher** *(in primary school)* instituteur, -trice stagiaire; *(in secondary school)* professeur *m* stagiaire; **students' union** syndicat *m* étudiant; *(premises)* ≃ foyer *m* des étudiants

Students' union

Dans les universités britanniques et américaines, on appelle "students' union" à la fois le syndicat et les locaux où il se trouve. Le syndicat est chargé de défendre les intérêts des étudiants, sert de centre d'information et de conseil en matière de logement, de santé et de financement, et organise des événements culturels et des activités.

studhorse ['stʌdhɔːs] N étalon *m*

studied ['stʌdɪd] ADJ *(style, attitude, posture)* étudié, recherché; *(move, act)* prémédité, calculé; *(negligence)* voulu; **s. elegance** élégance *f* recherchée

studio ['stjuːdɪəʊ] N *(of artist, photographer)* atelier *m*, studio *m*; **(film/television) s.** studio de cinéma/de télévision; **recording s.** studio d'enregistrement; *Radio* auditorium *m*
▸▸*Am* **s. apartment** studio; **s. audience** public *m* *(présent lors de la diffusion ou de l'enregistrement d'une émission)*; **s. bed** canapé-lit *m*, *pl* canapés-lits; **s. broadcast camera**, **s. camera** caméra *f* en studio; **s. couch** canapé-lit, canapé *m* convertible; *Br* **s. flat** studio; **s. manager** directeur *m* de studio; **s. monitor** écran *m* de contrôle studio; **s. rehearsal** répétition *f* en studio; **s. supervisor** chef *m* de studio; *Cin* **the s. system** l'hégémonie *f* des

grands studios (hollywoodiens); **s. talkback** interphone *m* de studio

studious ['stju:dɪəs] ADJ **1** *(person, atmosphere)* studieux; **person of s. habits** personne studieuse **2** *(careful)* **with s. attention** avec une attention soutenue; **because of his s. avoidance of the topic** parce qu'il évitait soigneusement le sujet

studiously ['stju:dɪəslɪ] ADV **1** *(listen to teacher)* studieusement **2** *(carefully)* attentivement; **she s. avoided me** elle s'ingéniait à m'éviter; **he was s. polite** il était d'une politesse étudiée

studiousness ['stju:dɪəsnɪs] N **1** *(eagerness to study)* amour *m* de l'étude **2** *(carefulness)* empressement *m*, zèle *m* (**in doing sth** à faire qch)

study ['stʌdɪ] N **1** *(investigation)* étude *f* (**of** de); *(report)* étude, rapport *m*; **to make a s. of sth** étudier qch; **I've made a special s. of ...** je me suis spécialisé dans ...; *Sch, Univ* **studies** études; **Department of Classical Studies** Section des lettres classiques **2** *(room)* cabinet *m* de travail, bureau *m*; *Sch* salle *f* d'étude **3** *Old-fashioned* **brown s.** *(reverie)* rêverie *f*, **to be (lost) in a brown s.** être plongé *ou* absorbé dans ses réflexions *ou* dans de vagues rêveries **4** *Art, Mus* étude *f*; *Fam* **her face was a s.!** il fallait voir sa tête!

VT *(language, music, part)* étudier; *(terrain, stars)* observer; *Scol, Univ (French, law)* faire des études de; *(plans)* examiner, étudier; *(question)* mettre à l'étude; **she studied history at Yale** elle a étudié l'histoire à Yale; **he studied her face for signs of emotion** il examina son visage pour y détecter des signes d'émotion

VI étudier; **you ought to s. harder** tu devrais étudier davantage; **he's studying** il étudie; *(he's at college etc)* il fait ses études; **she's studying to be a doctor** elle fait des études de médecine; **to s. for an examination** se préparer pour un examen, préparer un examen; **he studied under Professor Green** il a étudié avec le Professeur Green, il a été l'élève du Professeur Green

▶▶ **s. group** groupe *m* de travail *ou* d'étude; *Am* **s. hall** *(place)* salle d'étude; *(period)* heure *f* d'étude; **s. period** heure de permanence *ou* d'étude; **s. tour** voyage *m* d'étude; **s. trip** voyage d'études

STUFF [stʌf]

N matière **1** ▪ substance **1** ▪ truc **1, 2** ▪ affaires **2** ▪ étoffe **4**	
VT bourrer **1** ▪ rembourrer **1** ▪ farcir **1** ▪ empailler **1**	

N **1** *(substance)* matière(s) *f(pl)*, substance *f*, *Fam* truc *m*; **here's some s. to put on that burn** voilà de quoi soigner cette brûlure; **there's some sticky s. in the sink** il y a quelque chose qui colle dans l'évier; **he is of the s. that heroes are made of** il est du bois dont on fait les héros; *Fam* **she writes good s.** elle écrit de bons trucs; *Fam* **there was some s. about unions on the news** ils ont dit un truc sur les syndicats aux informations; **dangerous s., acid** c'est dangereux, l'acide; *Fam* **this wine is good s.** ce vin, c'est du bon; **I don't like that s. you gave me** je n'aime pas ce que vous m'avez donné là **2** *(objects)* truc *m*; *(possessions)* affaires *fpl* **3** *(more vaguely)* **come on, do your s.!** allons, montre-nous ce que tu sais faire!; **he knows his s.** il s'y connaît; **that's the s.!** voilà ce qu'il faut!; **good s.!** *(well done etc)* bien!; **old s.** vieilleries *fpl*, **silly s.** sottises *fpl*, balivernes *fpl*, *Old-fashioned* **s. and nonsense!** ça, c'est de la bêtise!; *Sl* **she's a nice bit of s., she's hot s.** elle est vraiment bien balan-

cée, elle est canon; *Sl* **he was there with his bit of s.** il était là avec sa petite copine **4** *Tex* **(woollen) s.** étoffe *f* de laine **5** *Sl (drug)* came *f*

VT **1** *(fill)* bourrer (**with** de); *(chair, cushion)* rembourrer (**with** de); *Culin (chicken etc)* farcir; *(zoological specimen)* empailler, naturaliser; *Vulg (have sex with)* se faire; **her pockets are stuffed with sweets** elle a des bonbons plein les poches; *Fam* **to s. oneself, to s. one's face** s'empiffrer; **his head was stuffed with romantic ideas** il avait la tête bourrée *ou* farcie d'idées romanesques; *Br Vulg* **get stuffed!** va te faire foutre!; *Br Vulg* **he can get stuffed** il peut aller se faire foutre; *Pol* **to s. the ballot box** *(fill with false ballot papers)* remplir les urnes de faux bulletins de vote; *(rig election)* truquer les élections; **the only way he'll win is if they s. the ballot box** sa seule chance de gagner, c'est la fraude électorale **2** *(shove)* **to s. sth into sth** fourrer qch dans qch; **to s. one's fingers in one's ears** se boucher les oreilles (avec les doigts); *Br Vulg* **you can s. it (up your arse)!** tu peux te le mettre où je pense!; *Br Vulg* **s. your job!** ton boulot, tu peux te le mettre où je pense!; *Br Vulg* **s. this, I'm going home!** et puis merde, je rentre!

▶ **stuff up** VT SEP *(hole etc)* boucher; **I'm all stuffed up with a cold** j'ai le nez complètement bouché avec ce rhume; **I'm or my nose is stuffed up** j'ai le nez bouché

stuffed [stʌft] ADJ **1** *(olives, peppers etc)* farci; *(owl, fox, rabbit etc)* empaillé **2** *Br, Austr Fam (in trouble)* cuit, fichu; **if that cheque doesn't arrive soon, we're s.** si ce chèque n'arrive pas bientôt, on est cuits

▶▶ **s. shirt** prétentieux, -ieuse

stuffing ['stʌfɪŋ] N *(filling for meat, poultry etc)* farce *f*, *(for upholstery)* bourre *f*, rembourrage *m*; **horsehair s.** matelassure *f* de crin; *Fam* **to knock the s. out of sb** *(defeat heavily)* mettre la pâtée à qn; *(of blow, attacker, illness)* mettre qn K.O.

stuffy ['stʌfɪ] ADJ **1** *(room etc)* mal ventilé, mal aéré; **to smell s.** sentir le renfermé; **it's a bit s. in here** on manque d'air ici **2** *(standoffish)* collet monté; *(over-conventional)* vieux jeu *inv*, **don't be so s.** *(don't be offended)* il n'y a pas de quoi se scandaliser **3** **to feel s.** *(have blocked nose)* avoir le nez bouché

stultify ['stʌltɪfaɪ] VT *(make stupid)* *(of work)* abrutir, assommer

stultifying ['stʌltɪfaɪɪŋ] ADJ *(work)* abrutissant

stumble ['stʌmb(ə)l] VI **1** *(when walking)* trébucher; *(of horse)* faire un faux pas, broncher; **to s. off** partir en trébuchant; **she stumbled over my briefcase** elle a trébuché sur ma serviette **2** **to s. when one speaks** *(hesitate)* hésiter en parlant; *(confuse words etc)* s'embrouiller en parlant; **she stumbled through her speech** elle s'est embrouillée tout au long de son discours

N *(when walking)* trébuchement *m*; *(of horse)* faux pas *m*

▶ **stumble across** VT INSEP *(find)* tomber sur par hasard

▶ **stumble along** VI avancer en trébuchant

▶ **stumble on, stumble upon** VT INSEP = **stumble across**

stumblebum ['stʌmbəlbʌm] N *Am Fam (drunken vagrant)* clodo *mf* alcolo; *(clumsy, incompetent person)* manche *m*

stumbling ['stʌmblɪŋ] ADJ *(speech)* hésitant; **she took her first s. steps** elle a fait ses premiers pas

▶▶ **s. block** pierre *f* d'achoppement

stump [stʌmp] N **1** *(of tree)* souche *f*, chicot *m*; *(of tooth)* reste *m* d'une dent cassée, *Fam*

chicot; *(of arm, leg)* moignon *m*; *(of pencil)* bout *m*; *(of cigar)* bout, *Fam* mégot *m*; *(of tail, column, mast)* tronçon *m*; *(of cabbage)* trognon *m* **2** *Fam* **stumps** *(legs)* pattes *fpl*, quilles *fpl*, **stir your stumps!** remuez-vous!, grouillez-vous! **3** *Pol Fam* **to be on the s.** faire campagne **4** *Cr* piquet *m*; **to draw stumps** enlever les piquets, cesser le match

VT **1** *(baffle)* coller; **to be stumped for an answer** ne savoir que répondre, sécher; **it stumped me** ça m'a désarçonné; **this one has got me stumped** alors là, je sèche **2** *Cr* mettre hors jeu *(un batteur qui est sorti de son camp)* **3** *esp Am Pol Fam* **she stumped the country from one end to the other** elle a parcouru le pays d'un bout à l'autre pour sa campagne électorale

VI *esp Am Pol Fam* faire campagne

▶▶ *esp Am Pol Fam* **s. orator, s. speaker** orateur *m*

▶ **stump along** VI *(walk heavily)* marcher *ou* avancer d'un pas lourd; *(limping)* marcher *ou* avancer en clopinant

▶ **stump off** VI *(annoyed)* partir d'un pas lourd

▶ **stump up** *Br Fam* VT SEP *(pay)* cracher

VI casquer

stumpy ['stʌmpɪ] ADJ *(person, thing)* trapu; *(figure)* ramassé; **s. pencil** petit bout *m* de crayon

stun [stʌn] VT (-nn-) **1** *(make unconscious)* étourdir, assommer **2** *Fig (shock)* abasourdir; **the news stunned us** cette nouvelle nous a fait l'effet d'un coup de massue *ou* nous ont abasourdis; **we were stunned to hear of your accident** nous avons été consternés d'apprendre que vous aviez eu un accident; **to be stunned** être stupéfait; **stunned with surprise** stupéfié, frappé de stupeur

▶▶ **s. grenade** grenade *f* incapacitante; **s. gun** fusil *m* hypodermique

stung PT, PP *see* **sting** VT, VI

stunner ['stʌnər] N *Fam* **1** **he's/she's a s.** il/elle est vachement beau/belle, il/elle est canon **2** *(excellent thing)* chose *f* extraordinaire, *Fam* truc *m* super

stunning ['stʌnɪŋ] ADJ **1** *(blow)* étourdissant, abrutissant; *(misfortune)* accablant, bouleversant **2** *(shocking)* renversant; *(amazing, excellent)* formidable, épatant; **she's really s.** *(beautiful)* elle est éblouissante; **his/her s. good looks** sa beauté éblouissante

stunningly ['stʌnɪŋlɪ] ADV **s. beautiful** d'une beauté éblouissante; **s. dressed** magnifiquement vêtu

stunt[1] [stʌnt] VT *(person, thing)* arrêter dans sa croissance; *(growth)* ralentir très fortement; **the economy had been stunted by the lack of investment** l'économie avait été freinée dans son développement par la faiblesse de l'investissement

stunt[2] N **1** *(skilful act)* tour *m* de force; *Cin* cascade *f*, **to do one's own stunts** *(of actor, actress)* ne pas se faire doubler dans les scènes dangereuses; *Aviat* **to perform stunts** faire des acrobaties **2** *(sth done to gain attention, for publicity)* coup *m* de pub; *usu Pej* **to pull a s.** faire un coup de pub

▶▶ **s. double** doublure *f* pour les cascades; **s. driver** conducteur, -trice cascadeur(euse); *Aviat* **s. flying** vol *m* acrobatique; **s. man** cascadeur *m*; **s. pilot** pilote *m* de voltige aérienne, voltigeur *m*; **s. woman** cascadeuse *f*

stunted ['stʌntɪd] ADJ *(tree, person)* rabougri; *(intellect, development)* atrophié; **to become s.** *(of tree, person)* se rabougrir

stupe [stjuːp] N *Am Fam* andouille *f*, crétin, -ine

stupefaction [stjuːpɪˈfækʃən] N stupeur *f*, stupéfaction *f*

stupefy [ˈstjuːpɪfaɪ] VT 1 *(astound)* abasourdir, stupéfier; **I'm absolutely stupefied (by what has happened)** je n'en reviens pas, j'en suis stupéfait 2 *(make insensitive)* abrutir; *Med* engourdir

stupefying [ˈstjuːpɪfaɪɪŋ] ADJ stupéfiant

stupendous [stjuːˈpendəs] ADJ prodigieux, *Fam* formidable

stupendously [stjuːˈpendəslɪ] ADV prodigieusement

stupid [ˈstjuːpɪd] ADJ bête, idiot; **I did a s. thing** j'ai fait une bêtise; **don't be s.!** ne faites pas l'idiot!; **how s. of me!** que je suis bête!; **I'm not s., you know!** je ne suis pas idiot quand même!; **what a s. place to put it!** c'est idiot de l'avoir mis là!; **a s. film** un film idiot; **I don't want your s. book!** je ne veux pas de ton livre idiot!; *Fam* **to drink oneself s.** s'abrutir d'alcool
▪ N *Fam (term of address)* **of course not, s.!** bien sûr que non, gros bêta/grosse bêtasse!

stupidity [stjuːˈpɪdɪtɪ] N stupidité *f*, bêtise *f*

stupidly [ˈstjuːpɪdlɪ] ADV stupidement, bêtement; **rather s., I agreed** bêtement, j'ai accepté

stupor [ˈstjuːpər] N stupeur *f*; **in a drunken s.** abruti par la boisson

sturdily [ˈstɜːdɪlɪ] ADV 1 *(constructed)* fortement; **s. built** solide 2 *(to refuse, defend etc)* résolument

sturdiness [ˈstɜːdɪnɪs] N 1 *(of person, plant etc)* vigueur *f*, robustesse *f*; *(of table, piece of equipment)* solidité *f* 2 *(of resolve, opposition)* résolution *f*, fermeté *f*

sturdy [ˈstɜːdɪ] ADJ 1 *(person)* vigoureux, robuste; *(table, furniture)* solide; **a s. fellow** un gaillard robuste 2 *(opposition, resistance)* résolu, ferme

sturgeon [ˈstɜːdʒ(ə)n] N *(fish)* esturgeon *m*

stutter [ˈstʌtər] N bégaiement *m*; **he has a s.** il est bègue, il bégaie
▪ VI bégayer; **the engine stuttered into life** le moteur toussa avant de démarrer
▪ VT bégayer

stutterer [ˈstʌtərər] N bègue *mf*

stuttering [ˈstʌtərɪŋ] ADJ bègue; **s. machine-gun fire** le crépitement des mitrailleuses
▪ N bégaiement *m*

sty [staɪ] (*pl* **sties** [staɪ, staɪz]) N *Agr, Fig* porcherie *f*

sty [staɪ], **stye**, (*pl* **sties, styes**) N *Med* orgelet *m*

Stygian [ˈstɪdʒɪən] ADJ *Lit* d'une noirceur impénétrable
▪ ▸ **S. gloom** ténèbres *fpl* impénétrables *ou* insondables

style [staɪl] N 1 *(manner)* style *m*, manière *f*; *(of car etc)* type *m*, modèle *f*; *(of clothes)* mode *f*; *(of hair)* coiffure *f*; **s. of living** style *ou* train *m* de vie; **Gothic/Byzantine s.** style gothique/byzantin; **building in the classical s.** bâtiment *m* de style classique; **that's not my s.** ce n'est pas mon genre *ou* style; **that's the s.!** c'est cela!, bravo!; **you've got to admire his s.!** on ne peut admirer la façon dont il s'y prend!; **something in that s.** quelque chose de ce genre *ou* style; **in the latest s.** à la (dernière) mode, *Fam* dernier cri
2 *(in writing, speaking)* style *m*; *(way of writing)* manière *f* d'écrire; **written in a humorous s.** écrit dans un style humoristique; **written in the s. of a 1940s thriller** écrit dans le style du roman policier des années 1940; **this writer lacks s.** *(good style)* cet écrivain manque de style
3 *(distinction, sophistication)* chic *m*, classe *f*; **she has s.** elle a de l'allure *ou* de la classe;

to live in (grand *or* **great) s.** mener grand train, vivre sur un grand pied; **they arrived in s.** ils ont fait leur entrée en grande pompe; **let's do things in s.** faisons bien les choses; **let's travel in s.** voyageons en grand style
4 *(of calendar)* **old/new s.** vieux/nouveau style *m*
5 *(tool in engraving)* burin *m*
6 *Bot* style *m*
▪ VT 1 *(design)* créer; **dress styled by X** robe créée par X; **hair styled by X** coiffé(e) par X 2 *(designate)* *(person)* dénommer; *(thing)* appeler; **to s. oneself doctor** se faire appeler docteur
▪ ▸ *Comput* **s. bar** barre *f* de style; **s. book** manuel *m* *ou* protocole *m* de style; *Comput* **s. sheet** feuille *f* de style

stylechecker [ˈstaɪltʃekər] N *Comput* correcteur *m* de style

styling [ˈstaɪlɪŋ] N façon *f*, *(of car)* ligne *f*; **hair s.** coiffure *f*
▪ ▸ **s. gel** gel *m* coiffant; **s. mousse** mousse *f* coiffante

stylish [ˈstaɪlɪʃ] ADJ qui a de la classe; *(clothes)* élégant, chic *inv*; *(camerawork, design)* artistique; **a s. writer** un écrivain qui a du style

stylishly [ˈstaɪlɪʃlɪ] ADV élégamment, avec chic, avec classe

stylishness [ˈstaɪlɪʃnɪs] N élégance *f*, chic *m*, classe *f*; *(of prose)* élégance

stylist [ˈstaɪlɪst] N styliste *mf*; **hair s.** coiffeur, -euse (d'art)

stylistic [staɪˈlɪstɪk] ADJ stylistique, du *ou* de style

stylistically [staɪˈlɪstɪk(ə)lɪ] ADV du point de vue de la stylistique

stylistics [staɪˈlɪstɪks] NPL *(usu with sing verb)* stylistique *f* VOIR GRAMMAIRE A10

stylization [staɪlaɪˈzeɪʃən] N stylisation *f*

stylize [ˈstaɪlaɪz] VT *Art* styliser; **stylized flowers** fleurs stylisées

stylus, *pl* styli, styluses [ˈstaɪləs, -aɪ, -əsɪz] N *(in engraving etc)* style *m*; *(on record player)* pointe *f* de lecture; *(made of sapphire)* saphir *m*; *(made of diamond)* diamant *m*

stymie [ˈstaɪmɪ] VT *Fam* **this question stymied me** cette question m'a coincé; **to be stymied** être dans une impasse

styptic [ˈstɪptɪk] *Med* ADJ styptique, astringent
▪ N styptique *m*, astringent *m*
▪ ▸ **s. pencil** crayon *m* hémostatique

suasion [ˈsweɪʒ(ə)n] N *Arch, Lit* persuasion *f*; **to subject sb to moral s.** agir sur la conscience de qn

suave [swɑːv] ADJ affable, courtois, *Lit* urbain, *Pej* doucereux, mielleux

> Note that the French word **suave** is a false friend and is almost never a translation for the English word **suave**. It is used to describe something that appeals to the senses in a pleasant way.

suavely [ˈswɑːvlɪ] ADV avec affabilité, affablement, *Pej* de façon doucereuse, doucereusement

suaveness [ˈswɑːvnɪs], **suavity** [ˈswɑːvɪtɪ] N affabilité *f*, courtoisie *f*, *Lit* urbanité *f*, *Pej* manières *fpl* doucereuses, airs *mpl* mielleux

sub [sʌb] *Fam* N 1 *(subscription)* *(to club, union etc)* cotisation *f*; **to pay one's subs** payer sa cotisation 2 *Sport (substitute)* remplaçant *m* 3 *Naut (submarine)* sous-marin *m*, *pl* sous-marins 4 *Journ (subeditor)* secrétaire *mf* de rédaction 5 *Br (small loan)* prêt *m*; **to give sb a s.** dépanner qn; **to get a s.** se faire dépanner
▪ VI (-bb-) 1 *(substitute)* **to s. for sb** remplacer

qn 2 *Journ (subedit)* mettre un article au point, travailler comme secrétaire de rédaction
▪ VT 1 *Br (lend)* **to s. sb sth** dépanner qn de qch; **can you s. me a fiver?** tu peux me dépanner de cinq livres? 2 *Journ (article)* mettre au point, corriger

sub-account N *Acct* sous-compte *m*, *pl* sous-comptes

subagent [sʌbˈeɪdʒənt] N sous-agent *m*, *pl* sous-agents

subalpine [sʌbˈælpaɪn] ADJ subalpin

subaltern [ˈsʌbəltən] N *Mil* (officier *m*) subalterne *m*

subaqua [sʌbˈækwə] ADJ sous-marin, sub-aquatique
▪ ▸ **s. club** club *m* de plongée sous-marine; **s. diving** plongée *f* sous-marine

subatomic [sʌbəˈtɒmɪk] ADJ subatomique

subbed [sʌbd] ADJ *Journ* corrigé

subclass [ˈsʌbklɑːs] N sous-classe *f*, *pl* sous-classes

subclause [ˈsʌbklɔːz] N *esp Jur (of contract)* paragraphe *m*

subcommittee [ˈsʌbkəmɪtɪ] N sous-comité *m*, *pl* sous-comités; *(in larger organizations)* sous-commission *f*, *pl* sous-commissions

subconscious [sʌbˈkɒnʃəs] ADJ, N *Psy* subconscient *m*

subconsciously [sʌbˈkɒnʃəslɪ] ADV subconsciemment

subcontinent [sʌbˈkɒntɪnənt] N sous-continent *m*, *pl* sous-continents; **the Indian s.** le sous-continent indien

subcontract [sʌbˈkɒntrækt] N (contrat *m* de) sous-traitance *f*, *pl* sous-traitances

subcontract [sʌbkənˈtrækt] VT *(work, order)* sous-traiter; **to s. a job (out) to sb** sous-traiter un travail avec qn

subcontracting [ˈsʌbkəntræktɪŋ] N sous-traitance *f*
▪ ADJ sous-traitant, *pl* sous-traitants; **the s. firm** le sous-traitant

subcontractor [ˈsʌbkəntræktər] N sous-traitant *m*, *pl* sous-traitants

subculture [ˈsʌbkʌltʃər] N 1 *(in sociology)* groupe *m* *ou* phénomène *m* culturel secondaire; **youth s.** phénomène *m* culturel propre à la jeunesse 2 *(in bacteriology)* repiquage *m*, culture *f* secondaire

subcutaneous [sʌbkjʊˈteɪnɪəs] ADJ sous-cutané, *pl* sous-cutanés

subdeacon [sʌbˈdiːkən] N *Rel* sous-diacre *m*, *pl* sous-diacres

subdirectory [ˈsʌbdɪrektərɪ] N *Comput* sous-répertoire *m*, *pl* sous-répertoires

subdivide [sʌbdɪˈvaɪd] VT subdiviser, sous-diviser
▪ VI se subdiviser

subdivision [sʌbdɪˈvɪʒən] N subdivision *f*

subdominant [sʌbˈdɒmɪnənt] N *Mus* sous-dominante *f*, *pl* sous-dominantes

subdue [səbˈdjuː] VT 1 *(tribe, enemy etc)* subjuguer, soumettre, assujettir; *(fire)* maîtriser; *(angry impulse)* dompter, réprimer; *(emotions)* maîtriser, dominer 2 *(light, heat, voice)* adoucir; *(light, pain)* atténuer

subdued [səbˈdjuːd] ADJ *(person)* *(quieter than usual)* inhabituellement calme; *(sad)* triste; *(heat, sound)* adouci; **s. colours** couleurs *fpl* sobres; **s. conversation** conversation *f* à voix basse; **s. light** demi-jour *m*, lumière *f* tamisée; **in a s. tone** *or* **voice** à voix basse, à mi-voix

subedit [sʌbˈedɪt] *Journ* VI mettre un article au point, travailler comme secrétaire de rédaction
▪ VT *(article)* mettre au point, corriger

subediting [sʌb'edɪtɪŋ] N mise f au point, correction f

subeditor [sʌb'edɪtər] N *Journ* secrétaire mf de rédaction; *(in publishing)* rédacteur, -trice; *Journ* **assistant s.** secrétaire mf adjoint(e)

subfamily ['sʌbfæmɪlɪ] N *Biol* sous-famille f, pl sous-familles

subfolder ['sʌbfəʊldər] N *Comput* sous-dossier m, pl sous-dossiers

sub-frame N *Aut* faux-châssis m inv, sous-châssis m inv

subfusc [sʌb'fʌsk] ADJ *(clothing)* sombre

subgenre ['sʌbʒɑ̃nrə] N sous-genre m

subgenus, pl **subgenera** ['sʌbdʒiːnəs, -dʒenərə] N *Biol* sous-genre m, pl sous-genres

subgroup ['sʌbgruːp] N sous-groupe m, pl sous-groupes

subhead, subheading ['sʌbhed(ɪŋ)] N sous-titre m, pl sous-titres

subhuman [sʌb'hjuːmən] ADJ sous-humain, pl sous-humains; *(intelligence, behaviour)* inférieur à celui/celle des humains N sous-homme m, pl sous-hommes

subject¹ ['sʌbdʒɪkt] N **1** *(of conversation, book, fugue)* sujet m; *(of legal case)* objet m; *Sch, Univ* matière f; **this will be the s. of my next lecture** ma prochaine conférence portera sur ce sujet; **to wander from the s.** s'écarter du sujet, faire une digression; **while we are on the s.** à ce propos, pendant que nous sommes sur ce sujet; **on the s. of** à propos de; **to change the s.** parler d'autre chose, changer de sujet; **to change the s., has anyone seen Andy?** pour changer de sujet, est-ce que quelqu'un a vu Andy?; **don't try to change the s.!** n'essaie pas de changer de sujet ou de détourner la conversation!; *Sch, Univ* **science subjects** matières fpl scientifiques

2 *Biol, Med etc* sujet m; **to be the s. of an experiment** servir de sujet d'expérience

3 *Gram (of verb)* sujet m VOIR GRAMMAIRE A78; B18

4 *Art, Phot* sujet m

5 *(of monarch)* sujet, -ette; **British s.** sujet britannique

ADJ **1** *(state, country)* assujetti, soumis; **s. to military laws** justiciable des tribunaux militaires

2 *(liable)* **s. to** *(rheumatism, hayfever etc)* sujet à; **to be s. to violent mood swings/fits of jealousy** avoir tendance à avoir des sautes d'humeur/des crises de jalousie; **prices s. to 5% discount** prix bénéficiant d'une remise de 5%; **s. to stamp duty** soumis au timbre; **all trains will be s. to delay** des retards sont à prévoir sur toutes les lignes; **we're all s. to taxation** nous sommes tous assujettis à l'impôt; **an area that is s. to avalanches** une zone d'avalanches; **I'm very s. to colds** j'attrape des rhumes facilement; **s. to variation** variable

3 *(conditional)* **s. to ...** sous réserve de ...; **s. to payment** moyennant paiement; **s. to your consent** sous réserve de votre consentement; **it's all s. to her approval** tout dépend de ou est subordonné à son approbation

▸▸ **s. matter** *(topic)* sujet, thème m; *(substance)* substance f, contenu m

subject² [səb'dʒekt] VT **1** *(subjugate) (people, nation)* soumettre, assujettir, subjuguer **2** *(force to undergo)* soumettre, exposer (**sb/sth to sth** qn/qch à qch); **to s. sb to torture** mettre qn à la torture, torturer qn; **to s. sb/sth to an examination** faire subir un examen à qn/qch, soumettre qn/qch à un examen; **to be subjected to much criticism** être en butte à de nombreuses critiques; **metal subjected to great heat** métal exposé à une forte chaleur; **to s. oneself to sth** se soumettre à qch; **to s. sth to tax** soumettre qch à l'impôt

subjection [səb'dʒekʃən] N soumission f, assujettissement m (**to** à); **in a state of s.** dans la sujétion

subjective [səb'dʒektɪv] ADJ subjectif

subjectively [səb'dʒektɪvlɪ] ADV subjectivement

subjectivism [səb'dʒektɪvɪz(ə)m] N subjectivisme m

subjectivity [sʌbdʒek'tɪvɪtɪ] N subjectivité f

subjoin [sʌb'dʒɔɪn] VT *(list)* ajouter, adjoindre

sub judice ['sʌb'dʒuːdɪsɪ] ADJ *Law* **the case is s.** l'affaire n'est pas encore jugée

subjugate ['sʌbdʒʊgeɪt] VT *(people, nation)* assujettir, subjuguer

subjugation [sʌbdʒʊ'geɪʃən] N assujettissement m, subjugation f

subjunctive [səb'dʒʌŋktɪv] VOIR GRAMMAIRE A53–4; B32–3 *Gram* ADJ subjonctif N subjonctif m; **in the s. (mood)** au (mode) subjonctif

sublease¹ ['sʌbliːs] N **1** *(document, type of contract)* sous-bail m, pl sous-baux; *(of farm)* sous-ferme f, pl sous-fermes **2** *(act)* sous-location f, pl sous-locations

sublease² [sʌb'liːs] VT *(apartment)* sous-louer; *(land)* sous-affermer

sub-lessee N sous-locataire mf, pl sous-locataires

sub-lessor N sous-bailleur, -eresse, pl sous-bailleurs, -eresses

sublet [sʌb'let] VT *(pt, pp* sublet; *prp* subletting) *(apartment)* sous-louer; *(land)* sous-affermer

sub-letting N sous-location f

sub-lieutenant N *Naut* enseigne m *(de vaisseau)* de première classe

sublimate ['sʌblɪmeɪt] N *Chem* sublimé m VT **1** *(feeling, instinct)* sublimer **2** *Chem (solid)* sublimer

sublimation [sʌblɪ'meɪʃən] N sublimation f

sublime [sə'blaɪm] ADJ *(noble, inspiring), Fam (very good)* sublime; **s. indifference** suprême indifférence N **the s.** le sublime; **to go from the s. to the ridiculous** passer du sublime au ridicule VT *Chem (solid)* sublimer VI *Chem (of solid)* se sublimer

sublimely [sə'blaɪmlɪ] ADV **1 s. beautiful** d'une beauté sublime **2** *(indifferent)* suprêmement; **he remained s. unaware of what was going on** il n'a jamais rien su de ce qui se passait

subliminal [sʌb'lɪmɪn(ə)l] ADJ *Psy* subliminal, -aux subliminaire ▸▸ **s. advertising** publicité f subliminale ou invisible; **s. message** message m subliminal

sublimity [sʌb'lɪmɪtɪ] N sublimité f

sub-machine-gun N mitraillette f

submarine [sʌbmə'riːn] ADJ *(cable, volcano)* sous-marin, pl sous-marins N **1** *Naut* sous-marin m, pl sous-marins; **midget or pocket s.** sous-marin de poche **2** *Am (sandwich)* gros sandwich m

submariner [sʌb'mærɪnər] N sous-marinier m, pl sous-mariniers

sub-market N sous-marché m, pl sous-marchés

submediant [sʌb'miːdɪənt] N *Mus* sous-dominante f, pl sous-dominantes

submenu ['sʌbmenjuː] N *Comput* sous-menu m, pl sous-menus

submerge [səb'mɜːdʒ] VT **1** *(put in liquid)* immerger (**in** dans) **2** *(cover) (field etc)* submerger, inonder; **submerged in details** perdu dans les détails VI plonger; *(of submarine)* effectuer sa plongée

submerged [səb'mɜːdʒd] ADJ *(field etc)* submergé, inondé; *(submarine)* en plongée; *(reef)* sous-marin; *Fig* **s. in work** submergé de travail, qui croule sous le travail

submergence [səb'mɜːdʒəns] N submersion f

submersible [səb'mɜːsɪb(ə)l] *Naut* ADJ submersible N *(bateau m)* submersible m, sous-marin m, pl sous-marins

submersion [səb'mɜːʃən] N submersion f

submission [səb'mɪʃən] N **1** *(to person's will, authority)* soumission f; *(to defeat)* résignation f; *(in wrestling)* abandon m; **to starve/beat sb into s.** réduire qn par la famine/violence **2** *(of matter to arbitration)* soumission f; *(of proof of identity)* présentation f **3** *Law* plaidoirie f; **in my s. ...** selon ma thèse ...; **it's my s. that ...** j'ai la conviction que ...

submissive [səb'mɪsɪv] ADJ *(tone, look)* soumis; *(person)* docile; **to be sexually s.** être soumis sur le plan sexuel

submissively [səb'mɪsɪvlɪ] ADV avec soumission, docilement

submissiveness [səb'mɪsɪvnɪs] N soumission f, docilité f

submit [səb'mɪt] (-tt-) VI *(to sb, sb's will, superior power)* se soumettre; *(to necessity)* se plier; *(to discipline)* s'astreindre; *(to misfortune)* se résigner; *(in wrestling)* abandonner; **to s. to authority** se soumettre à l'autorité VT soumettre; **to s. sth for sb's approval/for sb's inspection** soumettre ou présenter qch à l'approbation/à l'inspection de qn; **to s. proof of identity** présenter des pièces d'identité; **to s. that ...** représenter ou alléguer que ...; *Law* **I s. that there is no case against my client** je plaide le non-lieu; **I s. that you are not in fact ...** j'affirme que vous n'êtes pas en fait ...; **the author submits that ...** l'auteur affirme que ...

subnormal [sʌb'nɔːməl] ADJ *(person, behaviour)* arriéré; *(temperature)* au-dessous de la normale; **educationally s.** arriéré

suborder ['sʌbɔːdər] N *Biol* sous-ordre m, pl sous-ordres

subordinate¹ [sə'bɔːdɪnət] ADJ *(rank)* inférieur, subalterne; *(role)* accessoire; **s. to** subordonné à N subordonné, -ée ▸▸ *Gram* **s. clause** *(proposition f)* subordonnée f

subordinate² [sə'bɔːdɪneɪt] VT subordonner (**to** à); **everything is subordinated to religion** tout est subordonné à la religion

subordination [səbɔːdɪ'neɪʃən] N subordination f (**to** à)

suborn [sə'bɔːn] VT *Law (witness)* suborner

suborning [sə'bɔːnɪŋ] N *Law* subornation f

subplot ['sʌbplɒt] N *(of film, play etc)* intrigue f secondaire

subpoena [sə'piːnə] *Law* N *(of witness)* citation f, assignation f VT *(pt, pp* subpoenaed) **to s. sb (to appear)** assigner qn à comparaître, citer qn; **to s. sb as witness** citer qn à comparaître; **to s. a witness** assigner un témoin à comparaître; **he has been subpoenaed** il a été cité à comparaître

sub-postmaster N *Br* receveur m d'un bureau de poste *(dans un village)*

sub-postmistress N *Br* receveuse f d'un bureau de poste *(dans un village)*

sub-post office N *Br* petit bureau *m* de poste

sub-prefect N *Admin* sous-préfet *m, pl* sous-préfets

subprogram ['sʌbprəʊɡræm] N *Comput* sous-programme *m, pl* sous-programmes

subroutine ['sʌbruːtiːn] N *Comput* sous-programme *m, pl* sous-programmes

subscribe [səb'skraɪb] VI **1** *(contribute, give money)* souscrire (**to** à); **to s. to a newspaper** *(become a subscriber)* s'abonner à un journal; *(be a subscriber)* être abonné à un journal; *Com* **to s. to a service** s'abonner à un service; **to s. to the Internet** s'abonner à l'Internet; *Fin* **to s. to a loan** souscrire un prêt; *St Exch* **to s. to a share issue** souscrire à une émission d'actions

2 to s. to an opinion souscrire à une opinion; **I don't s. to that theory** je ne souscris pas à cette théorie; **I cannot s. to that** je ne suis pas d'accord avec cela

VT **1** *(money)* verser; **to s. ten pounds** verser dix livres; *St Exch* **to s. shares** souscrire des actions; **subscribed capital** capital *m* souscrit, souscription *f* **2** *Fml* (one's name) souscrire; **to s. one's name to a document** apposer sa signature à un document

subscriber [səb'skraɪbər] N **1** *(to newspaper, Internet)* abonné, -ée; **telephone s.** abonné du *ou* au téléphone **2** *(to charity)* souscripteur *m* **3** *Fml (of document)* signataire *mf*, souscripteur *m*; **the s.** le/la soussigné, -ée
▸▸ *Br* **s. trunk dialling** automatique *m*

subscript ['sʌbskrɪpt] N *Typ* indice *m*; **s. 3** 3 en indice

subscription [sʌb'skrɪpʃən] N **1** *(to newspaper, Internet)* abonnement *m*; **to take out a s. to a paper** s'abonner à un journal, prendre un abonnement à un journal; **s. to a club** cotisation *f* à un club **2 s. to a charity** souscription *f* à une œuvre de bienfaisance; **to get up a s.** se cotiser; **monument erected by public s.** monument élevé par souscription publique; *Fin* **s. to a loan** souscription à un emprunt **3** *(to an opinion)* adhésion *f* (**to** à); *(to an act, a decision etc)* approbation *f* (**to** de)
▸▸ *TV* **s. channel** chaîne *f* payante, chaîne à péage; **s. charges** tarifs *mpl* d'abonnement; **s. fee** frais *mpl* d'inscription; *(for share purchase)* droit *m* de souscription; **s. list** liste *f* de souscription *ou* des souscripteurs; **s. renewal** réabonnement *m*; **s. television, s. TV** télévision *f* par abonnement

subsection ['sʌbsekʃən] N subdivision *f*, *(in text)* paragraphe *m*

subsequent ['sʌbsɪkwənt] ADJ suivant, ultérieur, *Law Fml* subséquent; **at a s. meeting** au cours d'une séance ultérieure; **any s. corrections** toutes corrections ultérieures; **the investigation and all the s. recriminations** l'enquête et toutes les plaintes qui s'en sont suivies; **s. events proved us right** la suite des événements a prouvé *ou* les événements ultérieurs ont prouvé que nous avions raison; **s. to this** à la suite de ceci, par la suite

subsequently ['sʌbsɪkwəntlɪ] ADV plus tard, par la suite; **s. to sth** postérieurement à qch

subservience [səb'sɜːvɪəns] N soumission *f*, servilité *f*, *(to fashion)* assujettissement *m*

subservient [səb'sɜːvɪənt] ADJ **1** *(servile)* obséquieux, servile; **s. to sb** soumis à qn **2** *(subordinate)* subordonné; **to make sth s. to sth** subordonner qch à qch

subset ['sʌbset] N *Math* sous-ensemble *m, pl* sous-ensembles

subside [səb'saɪd] VI **1** *(of ground, building)* s'affaisser, se tasser; *Fam* **to s. into an armchair** s'affaler dans un fauteuil **2** *(of water)* baisser, diminuer; *(of blister, bump)* dégonfler; **the flood is subsiding** la crue diminue

3 *(of storm, excitement, fever)* s'apaiser, se calmer

subsidence ['sʌbsɪdəns, səb'saɪdəns] N **1** *(of building, road)* affaissement *m*; *(of land, foundations)* tassement *m* **2** *(of river)* décrue *f*, baisse *f*; *Med (of tumour)* délitescence *f*, *(of fever)* apaisement *m* **3** *Geol* subsidence *f*

subsidiarity [səbsɪdɪ'ærɪtɪ] N subsidiarité *f*

subsidiary [səb'sɪdɪərɪ] ADJ subsidiaire, auxiliaire
 N *Fin (company)* filiale *f*
▸▸ **s. account** sous-compte *m, pl* sous-comptes; **s. company** filiale

subsidize ['sʌbsɪdaɪz] VT *(project, industry, person)* subventionner; **to be subsidized by the State** *or* **the government** recevoir une subvention de *ou* être subventionné par l'État; **why should I carry on subsidizing you?** je ne vois pas pourquoi je continuerais à te donner de l'argent!; **subsidized industry** industrie *f* subventionnée

subsidy ['sʌbsɪdɪ] N subvention *f*, **export/building s.** prime *f ou* subvention à l'exportation/à la construction

subsist [səb'sɪst] VI *(stay alive)* tirer sa subsistance, vivre (**on** de); *(remain in existence)* subsister; **custom that still subsists** coutume qui existe *ou* subsiste encore (de nos jours)

subsistence [səb'sɪstəns] N subsistance *f*, *(allowance)* frais *mpl* de subsistance; **means of s.** moyens *m* de subsistance; **to live at s. level** avoir tout juste de quoi vivre; **a bare s. wage** un salaire à peine suffisant pour vivre
▸▸ **s. allowance** frais de subsistance; **s. economy** économie *f* de subsistance; **s. farming** agriculture *f* de subsistance

subsoil ['sʌbsɔɪl] N sous-sol *m*

subsonic [sʌb'sɒnɪk] ADJ *Aviat* subsonique

subspecies ['sʌbspiːʃiːz] N *Biol* sous-espèce *f, pl* sous-espèces

substance ['sʌbstəns] N **1** *(matter)* substance *f*, matière *f*, *Rel (spiritual, bodily)* substance **2** *(essential element)* *(of article, argument)* fond *m*, substance *f*, essentiel *m*; **I agree in s.** je suis d'accord sur le fond **3** *(strength, solidity)* solidité *f*; **the candidate was long on image but short on s.** le candidat faisait bonne impression mais manquait d'épaisseur; **book of s.** livre solide; **his argument has little s.** son argument n'a rien de solide; **he's a man of s.** *(financially)* il a du bien; *(intellectually etc)* c'est un homme d'envergure
▸▸ **s. abuse** abus *m* de stupéfiants

substandard [sʌb'stændəd] ADJ de qualité inférieure; **it's s. English/French** ce n'est pas du bon anglais/français

substantial [səb'stænʃəl] ADJ **1** *(significant)* *(point, progress, reduction)* important; *(progress, difference)* grand; *(reason, evidence)* valable; **s. proof** preuve *f* concluante *ou* valable; **a s. number of ...** un nombre important de ... **2** *(meal)* substantiel, copieux; *(structure, book)* solide; *(cloth)* résistant **3** *(company)* solide, bien assis; *(sum of money)* gros; *(profit, loss)* important

┌─────────────────────────────────────┐
│ Attention: ne pas confondre avec   │
│ **substantive**.   │
└─────────────────────────────────────┘

substantially [səb'stænʃəlɪ] ADV **1** *(considerably)* considérablement; **it's now s. improved** cela s'est maintenant considérablement amélioré; **this contributed s. to our success** cela a largement contribué à notre succès **2** *(for the most part)* **they are s. the same** dans l'ensemble *ou* pour l'essentiel, ils sont pareils; **the text is s. unaltered** le texte est dans l'ensemble *ou* pour

l'essentiel resté inchangé **3** *(solidly)* *(built)* solidement

substantiate [səb'stænʃɪeɪt] VT *(statement)* prouver, justifier; *(corroborate)* corroborer; *(claim, accusation etc)* prouver *ou* établir le bien-fondé de

substantiation [səbstænʃɪ'eɪʃən] N *(of statement)* justification *f*, *(corroboration)* confirmation *f*, *(of accusation, charge)* preuves *fpl*

substantival [sʌbstən'taɪv(ə)l] ADJ *Gram* substantivé

substantive ['sʌbstəntɪv] ADJ **1** *(measures, issue)* important **2** *Gram* substantif
 N *Gram* substantif *m*
▸▸ *Law* **s. law** droit *m* positif

┌─────────────────────────────────────┐
│ Attention: ne pas confondre avec   │
│ **substantial**.   │
└─────────────────────────────────────┘

substantively ['sʌbstəntɪvlɪ] ADV **1** *Gram* substantivement **2** *(considerably)* considérablement

substation ['sʌbsteɪʃən] N *Elec etc* sous-station *f, pl* sous-stations

substitute ['sʌbstɪtjuːt] N **1** *(foodstuff, drug)* succédané *m*; **as a s. for ...** comme succédané de ...; **coffee s.** ersatz *m* de café; **there's no s. for parental love** rien ne remplace l'amour parental; **low-alcohol lager is a poor s. for the real thing** la bière à faible teneur en alcool n'a rien de comparable avec la vraie bière

2 *(person)* remplaçant, -ante, suppléant, -ante; *Sport* remplaçant; *Law Rel* substitut *m*; **as a s. for ...** en remplacement de ..., pour remplacer ...; **to act as a s. for sb/sth** remplacer qn/qch, se substituer à qn/à qch

VT substituer; *Sport* remplacer; **to s. margarine for butter** remplacer le beurre par la margarine

VI **to s. for sb** remplacer *ou* suppléer qn
▸▸ *Mktg* **s. product** produit *m* de substitution

substitution [sʌbstɪ'tjuːʃən] N substitution *f*, remplacement *m*; *Sport* remplacement; *Sport* **to make a s.** faire un remplacement
▸▸ *Mktg* **s. market** marché *m* de substitution, marché environnant

substitutional market [sʌbstɪtjuːʃən(ə)l] N *Mktg* marché *m* de substitution, marché environnant

substratum, *pl* **substrata, substratums** [sʌb'strɑːtəm, -ə, -əmz] N couche *f* inférieure; *Geol, Phil* substrat *m*

substring ['sʌbstrɪŋ] N *Comput* sous-chaîne *f, pl* sous-chaînes

substructure ['sʌbstrʌktʃər] N *(of building)* fondement *m*; *(of road)* infrastructure *f*

subsume [səb'sjuːm] VT subsumer; **to s. X under Y** incorporer X à Y

subsystem ['sʌbsɪstəm] N sous-système *m, pl* sous-systèmes

subtenancy ['sʌbtenənsɪ] N sous-location *f, pl* sous-locations

subtenant ['sʌbtenənt] N sous-locataire *mf, pl* sous-locataires

subtend [səb'tend] VT sous-tendre

subterfuge ['sʌbtəfjuːdʒ] N subterfuge *m*; **to resort to s.** user de subterfuge; **this was a s. to ...** c'était un subterfuge pour ...

subterranean [sʌbtə'reɪnɪən] ADJ souterrain

subtext ['sʌbtekst] N message *m* sous-jacent

subtitle ['sʌbtaɪt(ə)l] N *Cin, TV, Typ* N sous-titre *m, pl* sous-titres; **film with English subtitles** film sous-titré en anglais
 VT sous-titrer

subtitled ['sʌbtaɪt(ə)ld] **ADJ** *Cin, TV* sous-titré, *pl* sous-titrés

subtitler ['sʌbtaɪtlər] **N** *Cin, TV* sous-titreur, -euse

subtitling ['sʌbtaɪtlɪŋ] **N** *Cin, TV* sous-titrage *m*

subtle ['sʌt(ə)l] **ADJ** *(person, mind, reasoning, perfume, charm)* subtil; *(cunning)* rusé, astucieux; **s. distinction** distinction *f* ténue *ou* subtile; **you are being too s.** vous finassez; **s. irony** fine ironie *f*; **s. remark** observation *f* subtile

subtlety ['sʌt(ə)ltɪ] **N 1** *(of distinction, mind, reasoning)* subtilité *f*; *(of policy)* subtilité, raffinement *m*, finesse *f* **2** *(subtle thing)* subtilité *f*

subtly ['sʌt(ə)lɪ] **ADV** subtilement, avec finesse; *(to argue etc)* avec subtilité; **s. different** légèrement différent

subtonic [sʌb'tɒnɪk] **N** *Mus* note *f* sensible, sensible *f*

subtotal ['sʌbtəʊt(ə)l] **N** sous-total *m*, *pl* sous-totaux, total *m* partiel

subtract [səb'trækt] **VT** soustraire, retrancher (**from** de)

subtraction [səb'trækʃən] **N** soustraction *f* (**from** de) VOIR GRAMMAIRE A77; B59

subtropical [sʌb'trɒpɪk(ə)l] **ADJ** subtropical, -aux

subtype ['sʌbtaɪp] **N** sous-type *m*, *pl* sous-types

suburb ['sʌbɜːb] **N** banlieue *f*, *(nearer city)* faubourg *m*; **the suburbs** la banlieue; **in the suburbs** en banlieue; **in the suburbs of Paris** dans la banlieue de Paris; **garden s.** cité-jardin *f*, *pl* cités-jardins

suburban [sə'bɜːbən] **ADJ** suburbain; *(house, station, train)* de banlieue; *Pej (narrow-minded) (person)* à l'esprit étroit; *(life)* étriqué; **even the city centre's s.** même le centre-ville sent la banlieue

suburbanite [sə'bɜːbənaɪt] **N** banlieusard, -arde

suburbia [sə'bɜːbɪə] **N** la banlieue

subvention [səb'venʃən] **N** subvention *f*

subversion [səb'vɜːʃən] **N** *Pol etc* subversion *f*

subversive [səb'vɜːsɪv] **ADJ** subversif (**of** de) **N** individu *m* subversif; **a group of subversives** un groupe de subversifs

subvert [səb'vɜːt] **VT** renverser, subvertir

subway ['sʌbweɪ] **N 1** *Br (walkway under road etc)* passage *m* souterrain, souterrain *m* **2** *esp Am Rail* métro *m*

subwoofer [sʌb'wuːfər] **N** caisson *m* de graves, subwoofer *m*

sub-zero **ADJ** au-dessous de zéro
▸▸ **s. temperatures** températures *fpl* en-dessous de zéro

succeed [sək'siːd] **VI 1** *(be successful)* réussir; **hard workers always s.** les grands travailleurs arrivent *ou* réussissent toujours; **how to s. in business** comment réussir dans les affaires; **young man who will s.** jeune homme qui ira loin; **to s. in doing sth** réussir *ou* arriver à faire qch; **she always succeeds** tout lui réussit; **I/the plan only succeeded in making things worse** je n'ai/le projet n'a réussi qu'à aggraver la situation; **to s. in one's attempt to ...** réussir à ...; *Prov* **if at first you don't s., try, try again** pour réussir il faut persévérer; *Prov* **nothing succeeds like success** la réussite appelle la réussite
2 *(to the throne or the Crown)* succéder à la couronne; **to s. to an office/estate** hériter d'une fonction/d'une propriété; *Law* **right to s.** droits *mpl* de succession
VT *(person, thing)* succéder à; **George III was succeeded by George IV** George IV succéda à *ou* fut le successeur de George III

succeeding [sək'siːdɪŋ] **ADJ 1** *(following)* suivant; *(in future)* futur, à venir **2** *(successive)* successif; **with each s. year** d'année en année

success [sək'ses] **N** succès *m*, réussite *f*; **we wish you s.** bonne chance!; **to meet with** *or* **to achieve s.** avoir *ou* remporter du succès; **the film was a great s. in Italy** le film a eu énormément de succès en Italie; **without s.** sans succès, en vain; **to score a s.** remporter un succès; **to be a s.** *(go well, work out well etc)* réussir, être réussi, être un succès; *(be popular)* *(of film, book etc)* être un succès; *(of party, cake)* être une réussite, être réussi; **the cake was a big s.** *(everyone liked it)* le gâteau a eu beaucoup de succès; **to be a s. with sb** *(be popular etc)* avoir un *ou* du succès auprès de qn; **it was a huge** *or* **great s.** cela a eu un succès fou; **the company has been one of the few successes of recent years** l'entreprise fait partie des quelques exemples de réussite de ces dernières années; **the film has been his biggest s. to date** ce film a été son plus grand succès à ce jour; **to make a s. of sth** réussir qch; **he made a big s. of it** il a très bien réussi; **a second attempt met with no better s.** une seconde tentative n'a pas eu plus de succès
▸▸ **s. fee** prime *f* de rendement; **s. rate** *(of operation, treatment etc)* taux *m* de succès; **s. story** réussite *f*

successful [sək'sesfʊl] **ADJ** *(project)* couronné de succès; *(outcome)* heureux; *(play)* qui a du succès; **to be s. in doing sth** réussir à faire qch; *(after an effort)* arriver *ou* parvenir à faire qch; **were you s.?** avez-vous réussi?, *Fam* est-ce que ça a marché?; **he is s. in everything** tout lui réussit, il réussit dans tout ce qu'il entreprend; **a s. businesswoman** une femme d'affaires qui a réussi; **to be s. at the polls** sortir victorieux du scrutin; **s. candidates** *Pol* candidats *mpl* élus; *Sch* candidats reçus; **to bring an operation to a s. conclusion** mener à bien une opération; **a s. evocation of a bygone age** une évocation fort réussie d'une époque révolue; *Com* **s. tenderer** adjudicataire *mf*

successfully [sək'sesfəlɪ] **ADV** avec succès; **when we've s. completed this stage of the operation** quand nous aurons mené à bien cette partie de l'opération

succession [sək'seʃən] **N 1** *(series)* *(of victories, visitors etc)* succession *f*, série *f*, suite *f*; **an endless s. of ...** une suite ininterrompue de ...; **in s.** successivement; **for two years in s.** pendant deux années consécutives *ou* de suite; **in close s.** se succédant de près; **in rapid s.** coup sur coup; **a rapid s. of governments** une succession rapide de gouvernements; **a long s. of kings** une longue suite de rois **2** *(to throne)*, *Law* succession *f*, *(descendants)* lignée *f*; **he was third in s. to the throne** c'était le troisième dans l'ordre de succession au trône; **to settle the s.** régler la succession; **at the time of his s. to the throne** au moment de son avènement; **law of s.** droit *m* des successions; **right of s.** droits de succession

successive [sək'sesɪv] **ADJ** successif; **on five s. Sundays** cinq dimanches consécutifs *ou* de suite; **s. generations** les générations *fpl* successives

successively [sək'sesɪvlɪ] **ADV** successivement

successor [sək'sesər] **N** successeur *m* (**to** à); **the s. to the throne** l'héritier *m* du trône; **my first car and its successors** ma première voiture et celles qui lui ont succédé *ou* qui sont venues ensuite

succinct [sʌk'sɪŋkt] **ADJ** *(account, writer)* succinct

succinctly [sʌk'sɪŋktlɪ] **ADV** succinctement

succinctness [sʌk'sɪŋktnɪs] **N** concision *f*

succour, *Am* **succor** ['sʌkər] *Lit* **N** secours *m*, aide *f*; **to give s.** porter secours *ou* assistance
VT venir en aide à, venir à l'aide de; *(the poor)* secourir

succulence ['sʌkjʊləns] **N** succulence *f*

succulent ['sʌkjʊlənt] **ADJ 1** *(food)* succulent **2** *Bot* **s. leaf** feuille *f* charnue
N *Bot* plante *f* grasse

succumb [sə'kʌm] **VI** succomber (**to** à), céder (**to** à); **to s. to one's injuries** succomber à *ou* mourir de ses blessures; **we have all succumbed to her charm** son charme nous a tous conquis, nous avons succombé à son charme; **I eventually succumbed** j'ai fini par céder

SUCH [sʌtʃ] **ADJ 1** *(of that kind)* tel, pareil; **animals s. as the lion or the tiger** des animaux tels que le lion ou le tigre; **s. a man** un tel homme; **on s. an occasion** en semblable occasion, en une telle occasion, en une occasion pareille; **why do you ask s. a question?** pourquoi demander une chose pareille?, pourquoi poser une question pareille?; **did you ever see s. a thing!** a-t-on jamais vu pareille chose!; **you wouldn't have s. a thing as a corkscrew, would you?** vous n'auriez pas un tire-bouchon, par hasard?; **s. is not my intention** ce n'est pas là mon intention; **if s. were the case** s'il en était ainsi, si tel était le cas; **the village boasts a bus, s. as it is** le village a un autobus, si l'on peut dire; **s. books as these are always useful** les livres de ce genre sont toujours utiles; **in s. cases** en pareils cas; **in s. weather** par un temps pareil; **how can you tell s. lies?** comment pouvez-vous mentir de la sorte?, comment pouvez-vous dire des mensonges pareils?; **she has s. ideas!** elle a de ces idées!; **s. courage** tant de courage, un tel courage; **some s. plan was in my mind** j'avais dans l'esprit un projet de ce genre; **there is no s. thing** cela n'existe pas; **if there were no s. thing as money** si l'argent n'existait pas; **I said no s. thing** je n'ai rien dit de semblable *ou* de pareil; **no s. thing!** pas du tout!; *Law* **persons guilty of s. offences** personnes coupables des délits susmentionnés
2 **on s. (and such) a day in s. (and such) a place** tel jour en tel endroit; **your letter of s. and s. a date** votre lettre du tant; **s. a one** un tel, une telle
3 **she arranges things in s. a way that she is free on Saturdays** elle s'arrange de manière à être libre le samedi; **his kindness was s. as to make us feel ashamed** sa bonté était telle que nous en étions confus; *Fml* **to take s. steps as shall be considered necessary** prendre toutes les mesures qui paraîtront nécessaires; *Fml* **until s. time as is convenient to me** jusqu'à ce que cela me convienne
ADV **s. large houses** de si grandes maisons; **I had never heard s. good music** je n'avais jamais entendu d'aussi bonne musique; **he's not s. a good player as you** ce n'est pas un aussi bon joueur que vous; **s. a clever woman** une femme si intelligente; **it was s. a long time ago** il y a si longtemps de cela; **he is s. a liar** il est tellement menteur, c'est un tel menteur; **s. an enjoyable day** une journée si *ou* tellement agréable; **we had s. a good time** on s'est tellement *ou* si bien amusé(s), on s'est tant amusé(s); **don't be in s. a hurry** ne soyez pas si pressé; **you gave me s. a fright!** vous m'avez fait une (telle) peur! VOIR GRAMMAIRE A5
PRON 1 **he enjoys cakes, ice creams and s.** il mange avec plaisir des gâteaux, des glaces et autres choses de ce genre
2 **that's not for s. as you** cela n'est pas pour quelqu'un comme toi; **s. as have the money can afford it** ceux qui ont de l'argent peu-

vent se l'offrir; **I haven't many, but I will send you s. as I have** je n'en ai pas beaucoup, mais je vous enverrai ce que j'ai; **s. is life!** c'est la vie!

3 she was a very brave woman and well known as s. c'était une femme très courageuse, et elle était bien connue en tant que telle; **history as s. is too often neglected** l'histoire en tant que telle est trop souvent négligée; **the text as s. is fine but …** le texte en soi est bien mais …; **I wasn't scared as s.** je n'avais pas vraiment peur

suchlike ['sʌtʃlaɪk] *Fam* **ADJ** semblable, pareil

PRON **beggars, tramps and s.** mendiants, vagabonds et autres gens de la sorte; **concerts, theatres and s.** concerts, théâtres, et autres choses de ce genre

suck [sʌk] **VT** sucer; *(mother's milk)* téter; *(drink, sweets)* sucer, suçoter; *(handkerchief)* mordiller; *(pipe)* tirer sur; *(not smoking)* sucer; *Tech (liquid, air)* aspirer; **to s. sth through a straw** aspirer qch avec une paille; **to s. one's fingers** se sucer les doigts; **to s. one's thumb** sucer son pouce; **to s. poison out of a wound** extraire le poison d'une blessure en la suçant; *Fig* **to s. sb dry** sucer qn jusqu'à la moelle; **the dust is sucked into the bag** la poussière est aspirée dans le sac; *Fig* **to get sucked into a conspiracy** être entraîné dans une conspiration; *Am Fam* **to s. face** *(kiss)* se rouler des pelles *ou* des patins

VI 1 *(with mouth)* téter (le lait); *(of pump)* aspirer; **to s. at a sweet** sucer *ou* suçoter un bonbon; **to s. on one's pipe** tirer sur sa pipe; *(not smoking)* sucer sa pipe; **to s. on a straw** tirer sur *ou* aspirer avec une paille **2** *Sl (be very bad, unpleasant etc)* être merdique; **this city sucks** cette ville est merdique; **I've got to work all weekend – that sucks!** il faut que je travaille tout le week-end – ça craint!

N 1 to give sth a s. sucer qch; **to have** *or* **take a s. at a sweet** sucer un bonbon **2 to give a child s.** donner à téter *ou* la tétée à un enfant

▸ **suck down VT SEP** *(of whirlpool etc)* engloutir, entraîner vers le fond

▸ **suck in VT SEP** *(with mouth)* sucer; *(draw in by vacuum)* aspirer; *(of air pump)* aspirer; *(in vortex)* engloutir; *(cheeks)* creuser; *(knowledge)* absorber; **to get sucked in** *(to conspiracy, plot etc)* se laisser entraîner (**to** dans)

▸ **suck off VT SEP** *Vulg (fellate)* sucer, faire une pipe à

▸ **suck out VT SEP** *(with mouth) (juice)* sucer; **to s. out the poison from a wound** aspirer *ou* sucer le poison d'une blessure

▸ **suck up VT SEP** *Tech (liquid, air)* sucer, aspirer, pomper; **these gases get sucked up into the upper atmosphere** ces gaz sont aspirés dans les couches supérieures de l'atmosphère

▸ **suck up to VT INSEP** *Fam Pej (ingratiate oneself with)* faire de la lèche à, lécher les bottes à

sucker ['sʌkər] **N 1** *Fam (gullible person)* niais, -aise, nigaud, -aude; **to be a s. for a pretty/handsome face** ne pas savoir résister à un joli visage **2** *(of octopus etc)* suçoir *m*; *(of bloodsucker, on machine)* ventouse *f* **3** *(of plant)* rejeton *m*, rejet *m*; *(of tree)* drageon *m*, surgeon *m*; **to throw out suckers** *(of tree)* drageonner, surgeonner **4** *Am Fam (object)* truc *m*, machin *m*; **what's this s. for?** à quoi ça sert, ce truc?

VT *esp Am Fam (dupe)* pigeonner; **he suckered them out of a million dollars** il les a eus d'un million de dollars

VI *(of tree)* drageonner

sucking ['sʌkɪŋ] **N** *(of baby)* succion *f*, *(of pump)* aspiration *f*

▸▸ **s. pig** cochon *m* de lait

suckle ['sʌk(ə)l] **VT** *(child, young)* allaiter; *(baby)* donner le sein *ou* donner à téter à

VI *(of baby, animal)* téter

suckling ['sʌklɪŋ] **N 1** *(act)* allaitement *m* **2** *Arch (child)* nourrisson, -onne, enfant *mf* au sein; *(animal)* jeune animal *m* qui tète encore

▸▸ **s. pig** cochon *m* de lait

sucrose ['suːkrəʊs] **N** *Chem* saccharose *m*

suction ['sʌkʃən] **N** succion *f*, *(of water in pump)* aspiration *f*, *(of air)* aspiration, appel *m*; **to adhere by s.** faire ventouse

▸▸ **s. cup, s. pad** ventouse *f*, **s. pump** pompe *f* aspirante; **s. stroke** temps *m* de l'aspiration

Sudan [ðəsuːˈdæn] **N (the) S.** le Soudan

Sudanese [suːdəˈniːz] **ADJ** soudanais, soudanien

N Soudanais, -aise, Soudanien, -ienne

sudden ['sʌd(ə)n] **ADJ 1** soudain, subit; *(movement, bend)* brusque; **this is rather s.** c'est plutôt inattendu; **it was a very s. decision** j'ai/il a/etc pris cette décision très vite; **it's all so s.** tout est arrivé si vite; **their marriage was rather s.** leur mariage s'est fait assez soudainement *ou* brusquement; **s. rise** hausse *f* subite; **s. shower** averse *f* subite **2 all of a s.** soudain, tout à coup, tout d'un coup

▸▸ **s. death** mort *f* subite; *(in games), Sport* = jeu *m* pour partager les ex aequo (où le premier point perdu, le premier but concédé etc, entraîne l'élimination immédiate); *Ftbl* **s. death play-off** épreuve *f* des penalties; **s. infant death syndrome** mort *f* subite du nourrisson

suddenly ['sʌd(ə)nlɪ] **ADV** soudain, tout à coup, tout d'un coup; *(to move)* brusquement; **she died s.** elle est morte subitement; **it happened so s.** c'est arrivé si vite; **then s. he was gone** et puis soudain, il avait disparu; **she very s. changed her mind** elle a changé d'avis très soudainement

suddenness ['sʌd(ə)nnɪs] **N** soudaineté *f*, *(of movement)* brusquerie *f*

suds [sʌdz] **NPL (soap) s. (foam)** mousse *f* de savon; *(soapy water)* eau *f* savonneuse

sue [suː] **VT** *Law* **to s. sb (at law)** intenter un procès à qn, poursuivre qn en justice; **to s. sb for damages** poursuivre qn en dommages-intérêts; **to s. sb for libel** poursuivre qn pour diffamation

VI 1 *Law* **to s. for a separation** plaider en séparation; **to s. for libel** attaquer en diffamation; **to s. for a divorce** entamer une procédure de divorce; **if you print that story, I'll s.** si vous publiez cette histoire, je vous fais un procès **2 to s. for peace** demander la paix

suede [sweɪd] **N** daim *m*, *Spec* suède *m*; **s. gloves/shoes** gants/chaussures en daim

▸▸ *Sl* **s. head** crâne *m* rasé

suet ['suːɪt] **N** *Culin* graisse *f* de rognon

▸▸ **s. dumpling** boulette *f* de graisse de bœuf; **s. pudding** = sorte de pudding sucré *ou* salé à base de farine et de graisse de bœuf

Suez ['suːɪz, 'sʊɪz] **N** Suez

▸▸ **the S. Canal** le canal de Suez; **the S. crisis** la crise de Suez

suffer ['sʌfər] **VT** *(undergo) (loss, indignity, consequence)* subir; *(pain)* endurer; *(sorrow)* subir, éprouver; *(tolerate, endure)* supporter, tolérer; **to s. defeat** essuyer *ou* subir une défaite; **to s. hunger** souffrir de la faim; **she doesn't s. fools gladly** elle ne peut pas supporter *ou* souffrir les imbéciles

VI *(of person, business, marriage, relations, health etc)* souffrir; *(of economy)* être perturbé; *(of profits)* subir une perte; **to s. from rheumatism** souffrir de rhumatismes; **to s. for one's misdeeds** supporter les consé-

quences de ses méfaits; **you'll s. for it** il vous en cuira, vous allez le payer; **I'll make (sure) you s. for this!** tu me le paieras!; **to be made to s. for what others have done** payer pour les actions d'autrui; **to s. from neglect** pâtir d'un manque de soins; **the country suffers from labour troubles** le pays est en proie à l'agitation ouvrière; **his good name has suffered** sa réputation a souffert; **she started drinking and her work suffered** elle a commencé à boire et son travail en a pâti; **the vines have suffered from the frost** les vignes ont souffert de la gelée

sufferance ['sʌf(ə)rəns] **N** tolérance *f* (**of** de); **children are admitted on s.** l'entrée des enfants est tolérée; **I get the feeling I'm just here on s.** j'ai l'impression de n'être ici que parce qu'on m'y tolère

sufferer ['sʌf(ə)rər] **N** **to be a s. from ill health** avoir une mauvaise santé; **sufferers from asthma/arthritis** asthma/arthritis sufferers personnes sujettes à l'asthme/l'arthrite

suffering ['sʌf(ə)rɪŋ] **ADJ** souffrant, qui souffre

N souffrance *f*; **the depression caused great s.** la dépression a causé de grandes souffrances; **cheerful in spite of his s.** gai malgré ses souffrances

suffice [səˈfaɪs] *Fml* **VI** suffire; **that will s. (for me)** cela (me) suffira

VT *(person)* suffire à, être suffisant pour; **s. (it) to say that I got nothing out of it** il suffit de dire que je n'en ai rien obtenu

sufficiency [səˈfɪʃənsɪ] **N** *Fml* quantité *f* suffisante, *Arch* suffisance *f*; **to have a s. of sth** avoir assez de qch; **to have no more than a bare s.** avoir tout juste assez; *(of food, money)* avoir tout juste de quoi manger/vivre

sufficient [səˈfɪʃənt] **ADJ** *(reason, explanation)* suffisant; **s. care/attention** suffisamment de *ou* assez de soins/d'attention; **lack of s. food/funds** insuffisance *f* de nourriture/de moyens; **this is s. to feed them** cela suffit pour les nourrir; **a hundred euros will be s.** cent euros (me) suffiront; **one light will be s.** une lampe suffira; **this work is not s.** ce travail n'est pas suffisant; **an apology is no longer s.** une excuse ne suffit plus; **it was s. to give her the address and she would find her way there** il suffisait de lui donner l'adresse et elle trouvait son chemin; **this news was s. to make him worry** cette nouvelle suffit à l'inquiéter; **they didn't have s. warning** on ne les a pas prévenus suffisamment à l'avance; **is that s. time for you?** cela vous donne-t-il suffisamment de temps?; **let me know in s. time so that I can …** prévenez-moi suffisamment à l'avance pour que je puisse …; **with s. supplies** avec des réserves suffisantes, avec suffisamment de réserves; **there was nowhere near s. heating in the building** l'immeuble était loin d'être suffisamment chauffé

N assez; **have you had s. (to eat)?** avez-vous assez mangé?; **they don't have s. to live on** ils n'ont pas assez pour vivre

sufficiently [səˈfɪʃəntlɪ] **ADV** suffisamment, assez; **to be s. tactful to …** avoir suffisamment de tact pour …

suffix¹ ['sʌfɪks] **N** *Gram, Comput* suffixe *m*

suffix² ['sʌfɪks, sʌˈfɪks] **VT** *Gram, Comput* suffixer

suffocate ['sʌfəkeɪt] **VT** *(kill)* étouffer; *(of smell)* suffoquer; *Fig* **all initiative was suffocated** la moindre initiative était étouffée; *Fig* **the secret police suffocated any dissent** la police secrète étouffa toutes les dissensions

VI étouffer, suffoquer (**with rage** de colère); **they were suffocating for lack of oxygen** ils étouffaient à cause du manque d'oxygène;

the stowaways suffocated (to death) les passagers clandestins périrent étouffés

suffocating ['sʌfəkeɪtɪŋ] ADJ suffocant, étouffant; **it's s. (in) here** on étouffe ici

suffocation [sʌfə'keɪʃən] N suffocation f, étouffement m; **to die of s.** mourir étouffé ou par asphyxie

suffragan ['sʌfrəgən] ADJ, N Rel bishop s., s. (bishop) (évêque m) suffragant m

suffrage ['sʌfrɪdʒ] N Pol (right to vote) droit m de vote; **universal s.** suffrage m universel; **women's s.** droit de vote pour les femmes

suffragette [sʌfrə'dʒet] N Pol, Hist suffragette f

suffuse [sə'fjuːz] VT esp Lit se répandre sur; **a blush suffused her cheeks** ses joues s'empourprèrent; **eyes suffused with tears** yeux baignés de larmes; **suffused with light** inondé de lumière

sugar ['ʃʊɡər] N 1 sucre m; **granulated s.** sucre cristallisé; **lump s.** sucre en morceaux; **lump or cube of s.** morceau m ou carré m de sucre; Br **caster s.** sucre en poudre; **icing s.** sucre glace; **brown s.** sucre roux; **help yourself to s.** prenez donc du sucre; **milk, no s., please** avec du lait, sans sucre, s'il vous plaît; **he takes two spoonfuls of s. or two sugars** il prend deux sucres
2 milk s. sucre m de lait, lactose f; Physiol **blood s.** glucose m sanguin; **blood s. level** taux m de sucre dans le sang
3 Fam (term of address) (mon) trésor m
4 Fam **she's found herself a s. daddy** elle s'est trouvé un vieux friqué qui l'entretient; **I've no intention of being your s. daddy** je n'ai pas l'intention de t'entretenir
5 Euph **oh s.!** oh mercredi!
VT (coffee etc) sucrer; (pill) dragéifier, recouvrir de sucre; **sugared almond** dragée f; Fig **to s. the pill** dorer la pilule
▸▸ **s. almond** dragée f; **s. basin** sucrier m; **s. beet** betterave f sucrière ou à sucre; **s. bowl** sucrier m; **s. cane** canne f à sucre; **s. maple** érable m à sucre; **s. mouse** souris f en sucre; **s. pea** mange-tout m inv; **s. refinery** raffinerie f (de sucre), sucrerie f; **s. shaker** saupoudreuse f (à sucre); **s. tongs** pince f à sucre

sugar-coat VT recouvrir de sucre; Fig (unpleasant measure) faire passer

sugar-coated ADJ recouvert de sucre; (almond) lissé
▸▸ **s. pill** comprimé m dragéifié

sugar-free ADJ sans sucre

sugaring ['ʃʊɡərɪŋ] N épilation f au sucre

sugarloaf ['ʃʊɡələʊf] N pain m de sucre
▸▸ **s. mountain** montagne f en pain de sucre

sugarplum ['ʃʊɡəplʌm] N bonbon m; **yes, my s.** oui, mon petit chou

sugary ['ʃʊɡərɪ] ADJ 1 (containing sugar) sucré; (sprinkled with sugar) saupoudré de sucre; **to go s.** (of jam) se cristalliser; **s. taste** goût m sucré 2 (smile, tone) mielleux, sucré; (tone) doucereux

suggest [sə'dʒest] VT 1 (propose) (something) suggérer, proposer (**to sb** à qn); Law **I s. that ...** n'est-il pas vrai que ...?; **she suggested going for a walk** elle a suggéré ou proposé de faire une promenade; **what do you s. I do?** que suggérez-vous que je fasse?; **I shall do as you s.** je ferai comme vous le suggérez; **a solution suggested itself to me** une solution m'est venue à l'esprit; **or was it a conspiracy, as some have suggested?** ou s'agissait-il d'une conspiration, comme on l'avait suggéré auparavant?; Com **suggested retail price** prix m conseillé
2 (inspire, recommend) (idea) inspirer, faire naître; **common sense would s. we give up** le bon sens nous dirait ou conseillerait d'abandonner

3 (insinuate, imply) insinuer; **are you suggesting that I am lying?** est-ce que vous insinuez que je mens?; **which suggests that it was an accident** ce qui semblerait indiquer qu'il s'agissait d'un accident; **are eggs as scarce as the price would s.?** les œufs sont-ils aussi rares que le prix le laisse supposer?; **the marks in the sand s. a person of about ...** les traces sur le sable indiquent la présence d'une personne d'environ ...
4 (evoke) évoquer; **what do these abstract forms s. to you?** que vous suggèrent ou évoquent ces formes abstraites?

suggestible [sə'dʒestɪb(ə)l] ADJ 1 Psy suggestible 2 (easily influenced) influençable

suggestion [sə'dʒestʃən] N 1 (proposal) suggestion f, proposition f; **to be open to suggestions** être prêt à accueillir des suggestions; **at her s., I stayed at home** suivant son conseil, je suis resté chez moi; **to make a s.** faire une suggestion ou proposition; **practical s.** conseil m pratique; **suggestions for improvement** propositions en vue d'une amélioration; **to be full of suggestions** être fécond en idées ou en conseils; **it was only a s.** ce n'était qu'une suggestion VOIR GRAMMAIRE A59–60
2 Law **my s. is that you were not there at the time** n'est-il pas vrai que vous étiez absent à ce moment-là?
3 Psy etc suggestion f; **hypnotic s.** suggestion hypnotique; **adverts work by s.** les publicités fonctionnent à la suggestion
4 (insinuation) indication f; **there is no s. that he might be guilty** rien/personne ne suggère ou dit qu'il est coupable
5 (hint) to speak with just a s. of a foreign accent** parler avec une pointe d'accent étranger; **s. of regret** nuance f ou pointe f de regret
▸▸ **suggestions box** boîte f à idées

suggestive [sə'dʒestɪv] ADJ 1 (reminiscent, thought-provoking) suggestif; **s. of sth** évocateur de qch 2 (indecent, erotic) (lyrics, dance etc) suggestif; **s. joke** plaisanterie f grivoise

suggestively [sə'dʒestɪvlɪ] ADV d'une façon suggestive

suggestiveness [sə'dʒestɪvnɪs] N (of picture etc) caractère m suggestif

suicidal [suːɪ'saɪd(ə)l] ADJ suicidaire; **it would be s. (to do it)** ce serait du suicide ou ce serait suicidaire (d'agir de la sorte); Fig **as far as your career is concerned, it would be s.** sur le plan professionnel, ça serait du suicide; **s. tendencies** tendances fpl au suicide ou suicidaires; **to be feeling s.** se sentir suicidaire, avoir des idées de suicide; **an absolutely s. bit of driving** une conduite complètement suicidaire

suicide ['suːɪsaɪd] N 1 (act) suicide m; **to commit s.** se suicider; **attempted s.** tentative f de suicide; Fig **to commit political/economic/financial s.** se suicider politiquement/économiquement/financièrement; Fig **it would be s. to go there** ce serait du suicide d'y aller; **mass s.** suicide collectif 2 (person) suicidé, -ée; **there was an attempted s. in the next bed** il y avait quelqu'un qui avait tenté de se suicider dans le lit d'à côté
▸▸ **s. attempt** tentative f de suicide; Mil **s. mission** mission f suicide; **s. note** lettre f (que l'on laisse quand on se suicide); **s. pact** = accord m de suicide collectif entre deux ou plusieurs personnes; **s. squad** équipe f (en mission) suicide

suit [s(j)uːt] N 1 (clothing) ensemble m; (man's) costume m, complet m; (woman's) tailleur m; **two-piece/three-piece s.** costume deux/trois pièces; **s. of armour** armure f complète; Aviat **flying or flight s.** combinaison f de vol; **pressure s.** combinai-

son pressurisée; **space s.** combinaison spatiale
2 Cards couleur f; Fig **politeness is not his strong or long s.** la politesse n'est pas son fort; **to follow s.** fournir à la couleur (demandée); Fig en faire autant, faire de même
3 Law **s. (at law)** (lawsuit) procès m (civil); (act of suing) poursuites fpl judiciaires; **to bring a s. against sb** intenter un procès à qn, poursuivre qn en justice; **criminal s.** action f ou procès criminel(le); **to be a party in a s.** être en cause
4 Old-fashioned, Lit (request) prière f, demande f; **to press one's s. with a girl** (when courting) faire une cour assidue à une jeune fille
5 Fam Pej (person) employé, -ée de bureau (en costume ou tailleur)
VT 1 (of clothes, colours etc) aller à; (of arrangement, time, job etc) convenir à; **to be suited to or for sth** être fait pour qch; **blue suits you** le bleu te va bien; **this climate/this food does not s. me** ce climat/cette nourriture ne me convient pas; **this hat suits you** ce chapeau vous va (bien); **clothes not suited to the climate** vêtements non convenant pas au climat; **the premises are not suited for display purposes** les locaux ne se prêtent pas à la présentation des marchandises; **he is not suited to be a doctor** il n'est pas fait pour être médecin; **they are suited to or s. each other** ils sont faits l'un pour l'autre; **a small job in the country would s. me very well** un petit emploi en province m'irait ou me conviendrait très bien; **she found a house that suited her** elle a trouvé une maison à son gré; **marriage suits you** le mariage vous réussit; **that suits me best** c'est ce qui m'arrange le mieux; **that suits me (just) fine** or Fam **down to the ground** ça me va à merveille, ça me convient parfaitement; **I shall do it when it suits me** je le ferai quand cela me conviendra; **you can't just come and go when(ever) it suits you** tu ne peux pas aller et venir à ta guise; **(would) two o'clock s. you?** est-ce que deux heures vous conviendrait?; **s. yourself** faites comme vous voudrez; **we have something to s. every taste/pocket** nous en avons pour tous les goûts/toutes les bourses
2 Am (dress in suit) vêtir d'un costume; **his followers were suited in black** ses disciples étaient vêtus d'un costume noir
3 (adapt) adapter (**sth to sth** qch à qch); esp Fml **to s. the action to the word** joindre les gestes à la parole
VI **that date does not s.** cette date ne convient pas; **would tomorrow s.?** demain conviendrait-il?

suitability [s(j)uːtə'bɪlɪtɪ] N (of date, arrangement, character) convenance f; (of comment, translation) à-propos m; (of decision, action etc) bien-fondé m; (of a person for a job) capacité f; **they doubted his s. as a husband for her** ils n'étaient pas sûrs qu'il était le mari qu'il lui fallait; **we've got doubts about the s. of this film/book for young children** nous ne sommes pas sûrs que ce film/livre convienne aux jeunes enfants; **s. of a candidate for a post** aptitude f d'un candidat pour un poste

suitable ['s(j)uːtəb(ə)l] ADJ (subject, work) convenable, qui convient; (candidate) valable; (date, title, clothes, example) adéquat; **we have found nothing s.** nous n'avons rien trouvé qui convienne; **wherever you think s.** où bon vous semblera; **the most s. date** la date qui conviendra le mieux; **is tomorrow s.?** demain te convient-il?; **s. expression** expression f pertinente ou appropriée; **s. marriage** union f bien assortie; **I've nothing s. to wear** je n'ai rien de convenable à me mettre; **with a s. note of sarcasm** avec une touche de sarcasme appropriée; **s. to** *or* **for sth** bon *ou* propre *ou* approprié à qch; **he's not s. for our Christine** ce n'est pas l'homme qu'il faut à notre Christine; **is it a book s. for children?** est-ce un livre pour les enfants?, est-ce que ce livre convient aux enfants?; **s. for children of seven years and under** pour les enfants de sept ans ou moins; **to make sth s. for sth** adapter qch à qch

suitably ['s(j)u:təblɪ] ADV convenablement; *(to say)* à propos; **s. impressed/embarrassed** très impressionné/gêné; **s. matched** bien assortis; *Iron* **I hope you're s. impressed!** j'espère que tu es content maintenant!

suitcase ['s(j)u:tkeɪs] N valise *f*; **I'm still living out of a s.** je ne suis pas encore installé; **I've been travelling around, living out of a s.** j'ai voyagé un peu partout sans jamais vraiment m'installer

suite [swi:t] N **1 s. (of rooms)** suite *f*, appartement *m* **2** *(furniture)* **(three piece) s.** canapé *m* avec deux fauteuils assortis, salon *m* trois pièces; **bathroom s.** (meubles *mpl* de) salle *f* de bains; **bedroom s.** (meubles de) chambre *f* à coucher **3** *Mus* suite *f*, **orchestral s.** suite d'orchestre **4** *Comput (of software)* suite *f* logicielle, ensemble *m* logiciel **5** *(of prince)* suite *f*

suiting ['s(j)u:tɪŋ] N *Com (cloth)* tissu *m* de confection; **men's suitings** tissus pour complets

suitor ['s(j)u:tər] N **1** *Arch, Hum* soupirant *m* **2** *Law* plaideur, -euse

sulfa, sulfate etc *Am* = **sulpha, sulphate** etc

sulk [sʌlk] N bouderie *f*, **to be in a s.** bouder; **to have (a fit of) the sulks** bouder, faire la tête

  VI bouder, faire la tête

sulkily ['sʌlkɪlɪ] ADV *(to reply)* d'un ton bouder; *(to look at sb)* d'un air bouder; **he retreated s. to his room** il partit dans sa chambre en boudant

sulkiness ['sʌlkɪnɪs] N bouderie *f*

sulking ['sʌlkɪŋ] N bouderie *f*

sulky ['sʌlkɪ] ADJ bouder; **to be s.** bouder; **to look s.** avoir un air bouder, faire la tête; *(of model)* prendre un air bouder

sullen ['sʌlən] ADJ *(person)* maussade, renfrogné, morose; *(silence)* obstiné, buté; *Lit (sky, clouds)* maussade

sullenly ['sʌlənlɪ] ADV d'un air maussade *ou* renfrogné; *(to obey)* de mauvaise grâce

sullenness ['sʌlənnɪs] N maussaderie *f*, air *m* renfrogné

sullied ['sʌlɪd] ADJ souillé, terni

sully ['sʌlɪ] VT **1** *Lit (make dirty)* souiller, ternir **2** *Fig (reputation)* entacher, salir; **to s. one's hands** se salir les mains

sulpha, *Am* **sulfa** ['sʌlfə] N
  ▸▸**s. drug** sulfamide *m*

sulphate, *Am* **sulfate** ['sʌlfeɪt] N sulfate *m*; **copper s.** sulfate de cuivre

sulphide, *Am* **sulfide** ['sʌlfaɪd] N sulfure *m*; **hydrogen s.** sulfure d'hydrogène, hydrogène *m* sulfuré

sulphonamide, *Am* **sulfonamide** [sʌl'fɒnəmaɪd] N sulfamide *m*

sulphur, *Am* **sulfur** ['sʌlfər] N soufre *m*
  ▸▸**s. dioxide** dioxyde *m* de soufre, anhydride *m* sulfureux; **s. mine** soufrière *f*, *Geol* **s. spring** source *f* sulfureuse

sulphureous, *Am* **sulfureous** [sʌl'fjʊərɪəs] ADJ sulfureux; *(coloured)* couleur de soufre *inv*, soufré

sulphuric, *Am* **sulfuric** [sʌl'fjʊərɪk] ADJ *(acid)* sulfurique

sulphurous, *Am* **sulfurous** ['sʌlfərəs, -fjʊər-] ADJ **1** = **sulphureous 2** *Chem (acid)* sulfureux

sultan ['sʌltən] N sultan *m*

sultana [sʌl'tɑ:nə] N **1** *Culin (fruit)* raisin *m* de Smyrne **2** *(female sultan)* sultane *f*

sultanate ['sʌltəneɪt] N sultanat *m*

sultriness ['sʌltrɪnɪs] N **1** *(of climate etc)* chaleur *f* étouffante; *(of atmosphere)* lourdeur *f*, **the s. of the weather** le temps lourd **2** *Fig (sensuality)* sensualité *f*, volupté *f*

sultry ['sʌltrɪ] ADJ **1** *(heat)* étouffant, suffocant; *(weather)* lourd, orageux; **it's s.** il fait très lourd **2** *(voice, look)* sensuel, voluptueux

sum [sʌm] N **1** *(amount) (of money etc)* somme *f*, *(total)* somme, total *m*; *(of account)* montant *m*; **in s.** en somme, somme toute; **a nice little s.** une jolie petite somme, une somme rondelette; **the s. of sb's efforts** la somme des efforts de qn; **the whole is greater than the s. of its parts** l'ensemble est encore meilleur que la somme des éléments qui le compose **2** *Math (problem)* problème *m*, exercice *m* (d'arithmétique); *Sch* **sums** *(arithmetic)* calcul *m*; **to do a s. in one's head** faire un calcul de tête; **to do sums** faire du calcul ou de l'arithmétique

  VT (**-mm-**) *(numbers)* additionner; *Math (series)* sommer
  ▸▸*Fin* **s. payable** charge *f* à payer; **s. total** totalité *f*, somme totale; *Fig (of sb's efforts etc)* totalité; **is that the s. total of what you've done today?** c'est tout ce que vous avez fait aujourd'hui?

▸ **sum up** VT SEP **1** *(summarize)* résumer, faire un résumé de; **to s. up what one has said before** se résumer, résumer les faits; *Law* **to s. up the case** *or* **the evidence** *(of judge)* résumer les débats; **to s. up a situation in a word** résumer une situation en un mot **2** *(assess quickly)* **to s. up the situation at a glance** évaluer la situation d'un coup d'œil; **to s. sb up** juger *ou* évaluer qn **3** *(add) (numbers)* faire la somme de, totaliser
  VI *(summarize)* résumer; **to s. up, I will say that ...** en résumé, je dirai que ...; **in summing up, the judge said ...** dans son résumé, le juge a dit ...

sumac(h) ['s(j)u:mæk, 'ʃu:-] N sumac *m*

summarily ['sʌmərɪlɪ] ADV sommairement

summarize ['sʌməraɪz] VT *(book etc)* résumer sommairement; *(debate etc)* récapituler

summary ['sʌmərɪ] ADJ *(brief)* sommaire; **he was dealt rather s. justice** on lui a rendu une justice plutôt sommaire

  N sommaire *m*, résumé *m*, aperçu *m*; *(of book)* argument *m*; *(of commercial operations)* récapitulation *f*, relevé *m*; *TV, Radio* **s. of the news, news s.** rappel *m* des titres
  ▸▸**s. account** *(providing summary)* résumé; *Law* référé *m*; *Acct* **s. balance sheet** bilan *m* condensé; **s. dismissal** renvoi *m* sommaire; *Law* **s. offences** = délits *mpl* qui peuvent être jugés en procédure sommaire; **s. proceedings** affaire *f* sommaire; **s. report** rapport *m* récapitulatif

summation [sʌ'meɪʃən] N **1** *(addition)* sommation *f*, addition *f* **2** *(total)* somme *f*, total *m* **3** *(summary)* résumé *m*; **the exhibition was a s. of his life's work** l'exposition résumait parfaitement son œuvre **4** *Am Law* résumé *m* des débats *(par le juge)*

summer ['sʌmər] N été *m*; **in s.** en été; **in the s.** pendant l'été; **in the s. of 1995** pendant l'été 1995; **a summer('s) day** un jour d'été; **winter and s. alike, I live in the country** été comme hiver, j'habite la campagne; **next s.** l'été prochain; **Indian s.** été de la Saint-Martin, été indien; *Lit* **many summers ago** il y a bien longtemps; *Lit* **a girl of 12 summers** une fille de 12 printemps

  VI *(by the sea etc)* passer l'été; *(of cattle)* estiver
  VT *(cattle)* estiver

  ▸▸**s. break** petites vacances *fpl* d'été; **s. clothes** habits *mpl* ou vêtements *mpl* d'été; **the s. holidays** les vacances ou congés *mpl* d'été; *Scol* **les grandes vacances; s. resort** station *f* estivale; **s. school** université *f* d'été; **s. season** saison *f* d'été, période *f* estivale; *Admin* **s. time** *(by clock)* heure *f* d'été; **s. visitor** estivant, -ante

summerhouse ['sʌməhaʊs] N *(in garden)* pavillon *m*

summertime ['sʌmətaɪm] N *(season)* (saison *f* d')été *m*

summery ['sʌmərɪ] ADJ d'été, estival, -aux; **you look very s. in that** ça te donne un petit air estival

summing-up ['sʌmɪŋ-] N *Law* résumé *m* des débats *(par le juge)*; **in her s. up, the judge said ...** dans son résumé (des débats), le juge a dit ...

summit ['sʌmɪt] N **1** *(of mountain)* sommet *m*, cime *f*, *Fig* **the s. of greatness** le faîte *ou* sommet des grandeurs; **to be at the s. of one's power/fame** être au sommet *ou* à l'apogée du pouvoir/de sa gloire **2** *Pol* sommet *m*; **talks will be held at s. level** des négociations auront lieu au sommet
  ▸▸**s. conference** (conférence *f* au) sommet

summiteer [sʌmɪ'tɪər] N *Pol* participant, -ante à un sommet

summon ['sʌmən] VT **1** *(call) (servant, help, police, doctor)* appeler, faire venir; *(assembly, person to meeting, employee)* convoquer; *Law* citer à comparaître; **business summoned him back to London** les affaires l'ont rappelé à Londres; **to s. a defendant/a witness to appear** citer *ou* assigner un défendeur/un témoin; **s. the next witness!** faites entrer le témoin suivant! **2** = **summon up**

▸ **summon up** VT SEP **1** *(courage, help, support etc)* faire appel à; **to s. up all one's strength** rassembler toutes ses forces; **summoning up all her courage ...** prenant son courage à deux mains ...; *(more serious)* rassemblant tout son courage ... **2** *(memory)* faire resurgir; *(spirits)* invoquer

summons, *pl* **summonses** ['sʌmənz, -zɪz] N **1** *(order to attend etc)* convocation *f* **2** *Law* citation *f* (à comparaître), assignation *f* (à comparaître); **to issue a s.** lancer une assignation; **to serve a s. on sb** citer qn à comparaître; **to take out a s. against sb** faire assigner qn
  VT *Law* citer à comparaître, assigner, appeler en justice

sump [sʌmp] N **1** *(oil)* **s.** carter *m* à huile; **to drain the s.** faire la vidange **2** *Min etc* puisard *m* **3** *(cesspool)* fosse *f* d'aisance
  ▸▸**s. guard** protection *f* de carter; **s. pan** carter d'huile

sumptuous ['sʌm(p)tjʊəs] ADJ somptueux

sumptuously ['sʌm(p)tjʊəslɪ] ADV somptueusement

sumptuousness ['sʌm(p)tjʊəsnɪs] N somptuosité *f*

Sun *abbr* **Sunday**

sun [sʌn] N soleil *m*; **the s. is shining** il fait (du) soleil, le soleil brille; **the s. rises/sets** le soleil se lève/se couche; **rising/setting s.** soleil levant/couchant; **against the s.** face au soleil; **to have the s. in one's eyes** avoir le soleil dans les yeux; **let's get out of the s.** mettons-nous à l'abri du soleil; **too much s. can be harmful** de trop longues expositions au soleil peuvent être dangereuses; **to take the s.** prendre le soleil; **to catch the s.** *(of person) (get suntanned)* bronzer; *(get sunburnt)* prendre des coups de soleil; *(of garden etc)* voir le soleil; **to get a touch of**

the s. prendre *ou* attraper un coup de soleil; **every species/subject under the s.** toutes les espèces existantes/tous les sujets possibles; **there's nothing new under the s.** (il n'y a) rien de nouveau sous le soleil; **to try everything under the s.** essayer tout ce qu'il est possible d'imaginer; **to call sb every name** *or* **everything under the s.** traiter qn de tous les noms; **nothing under the s. was going to stop her now** rien ni personne n'allait l'arrêter maintenant; *Fig* **to have a place in the s.** avoir une place au soleil; *Br Sl* **she thinks the s. shines out of his arse** elle n'a rien vu d'aussi beau que lui

vT **(-nn-)** exposer au soleil; **to s. oneself** prendre le soleil, *Fam* faire le lézard

▸▸ **s. awning** store *m*; **s. deck** *(of house)* véranda *f*, terrasse *f*; *Naut* pont *m* supérieur, pont-promenade *m*, *pl* ponts-promenades; *Aut* **s. gear** planétaire *m*; **s. helmet** casque *m* (colonial); *Hist* **the S. King** le Roi Soleil; **s. lamp** lampe *f* à bronzer; **s. lotion** lotion *f* solaire; *Br* **s. lounge** solarium *m*; **s. oil** huile *f* solaire; *Am* **s. parlor** solarium *m*; **s. porch** solarium; *Aut* **s. shield** pare-soleil *m inv*; **s. terrace** terrasse *f*; **s. visor** *(on cap, for eyes)* visière *f*; *Aut* **s. wheel** roue *f* solaire

sunbaked ['sʌnbeɪkt] **ADJ** *(earth)* brûlé par le soleil

sunbathe ['sʌnbeɪð] **vI** prendre un bain de soleil, se faire bronzer

sunbather ['sʌnbeɪðər] **N** personne *f* qui prend un bain/des bains de soleil; **suddenly the park was full of sunbathers** soudain le parc s'est rempli de gens venus prendre un bain de soleil

sunbathing ['sʌnbeɪðɪŋ] **N** bains *mpl* de soleil

sunbeam ['sʌnbiːm] **N** rayon *m* de soleil

sunbed ['sʌnbed] **N** *(for tanning)* lit *m* à ultraviolets; *(in garden etc)* (fauteuil *m*) relax *m*

sunblind ['sʌnblaɪnd] **N** store *m*

sunblock ['sʌnblɒk] **N** écran *m* total

sunburn ['sʌnbɜːn] **N** coup *m* de soleil; **suffering from s.** souffrant de coups de soleil

sunburnt, sunburned ['sʌnbɜːnt, -bɜːnd] **ADJ** brûlé par le soleil; **to get s.** attraper *ou* prendre un coup de soleil

sunburst ['sʌnbɜːst] **N** *Met* éclaircie *f*; *(brooch)* broche *f* (en forme de) soleil

sundae ['sʌndeɪ] **N** *Culin* = glace *f* aux fruits recouverte d'un coulis, de noix, de crème Chantilly etc

Sunday ['sʌndɪ] **N** dimanche *m*; **S. 26 July** dimanche 26 juillet; **S. morning/evening** dimanche matin/soir; **it's S. today** nous sommes dimanche aujourd'hui; **he comes on Sundays** il vient le dimanche; **they're coming on S.** ils viennent dimanche; **every S.** tous les dimanches; **to put on one's S. best** s'habiller en dimanche, s'endimancher; **in one's S. best** dans ses habits du dimanche; *Fam* **the Sundays** *(newspapers)* les journaux du dimanche VOIR GRAMMAIRE A81–2; B61–2

▸▸ *Br* **S. lunch** déjeuner *m* du dimanche; **S. newspaper** journal *m* du dimanche; **S. opening** = ouverture *f* des magasins le dimanche; **S. paper** journal du dimanche; **S. school** catéchisme *m*; **S. school teacher** catéchiste *mf*, personne *f* qui fait le catéchisme; **S. supplement** = supplément *m* joint à un journal du dimanche; **S. trading** = ouverture des magasins le dimanche; **S. trading laws** = lois *fpl* réglementant l'ouverture des magasins le dimanche

---

Sunday papers

La lecture des journaux du dimanche constitue une sorte de rituel pour de nombreux Britanniques. Les journaux du dimanche sont très volumineux; ils comprennent de nombreux suppléments sur des sujets tels que le sport, la mode, les voyages et les arts, et sont souvent accompagnés d'un magazine en couleurs. Ils coûtent plus cher que les journaux vendus en semaine. Certains journaux du dimanche sont des éditions dominicales de quotidiens paraissant en semaine (c'est le cas de 'The Sunday Times' et de 'The Independent on Sunday' par exemple) tandis que d'autres, comme 'The Observer', paraissent uniquement le dimanche.

---

sunder ['sʌndər] *Lit* **vT** détruire

vI *(of ship's hull)* se rompre; *(of bridge, empire)* s'écrouler

sundial ['sʌndaɪəl] **N** cadran *m* solaire, gnomon *m*

sundown ['sʌndaʊn] **N** coucher *m* du soleil; **at s.** au coucher du soleil

sundowner ['sʌndaʊnər] **N** *Fam* **1** *Br (drink)* = boisson *f* alcoolisée prise le soir **2** *Austr (tramp)* clochard *m*

sun-drenched [-dren(t)ʃt] **ADJ** *(beach etc)* baigné *ou* arrosé de soleil

sun-dried **ADJ** séché au soleil

sundry ['sʌndrɪ] **ADJ** divers; **on s. occasions** à diverses reprises

N 1 all and s. tout le monde; **this is not for all and s. to hear** je ne veux pas que tout le monde entende ça **2 sundries** *(items)* articles *mpl* divers; *(costs)* frais *mpl* divers

▸▸ *Acct* **s. expenses** frais divers

sunfish ['sʌnfɪʃ] **N** môle *f*, poisson-lune *m*, *pl* poissons-lunes

sunflower ['sʌnflaʊər] **N** *(plant)* tournesol *m*, soleil *m*, hélianthe *m*

▸▸ **s. oil** huile *f* de tournesol; **s. seeds** graines *fpl* de tournesol

sung **PP** *see* **sing**

sunglasses ['sʌnglɑːsɪz] **NPL** lunettes *fpl* de soleil

sun-god **N** dieu *m* soleil

sungun ['sʌngʌn] **N** *TV, Cin* sun-gun *m*, *pl* sun-guns, éclairage *m* sur batterie

sunhat ['sʌnhæt] **N** chapeau *m* de soleil

sunk **PT** *see* **sink**

sunken ['sʌŋk(ə)n] **ADJ** *(rock)* immergé; *(wreck)* englouti; *(cheeks)* creux; *(garden etc)* encaissé, en contrebas; **s. eyes** yeux *mpl* creux *ou* enfoncés; **s. chest** poitrine *f* creuse

PP *see* **sink**

sunless ['sʌnlɪs] **ADJ** sans soleil

sunlight ['sʌnlaɪt] **N** *(lumière f* du) soleil *m*; **in the s.** au soleil, en plein soleil; **to keep out of the s.** éviter la lumière du soleil; **keep it out of the s.** protégez-le du soleil, évitez-lui le soleil

sunlit ['sʌnlɪt] **ADJ** éclairé par le soleil; *(full of sunlight)* ensoleillé

sunniness ['sʌnɪnɪs] **N** *(of place)* ensoleillement *m*; *Fig* **the s. of her disposition** ses bonnes dispositions

sunny ['sʌnɪ] **ADJ 1** *(day, place)* ensoleillé; *(building)* éclairé par le soleil; *(side)* exposé au soleil; **it's s.** il fait (du) soleil; *esp Am* **s. side up** *(fried egg)* sur le plat **2** *Fig (face)* radieux, rayonnant; *(person)* joyeux; **to have a s. disposition** être d'une nature joyeuse; *Fig* **to look on the s. side of things** voir le bon côté des choses; *Fam* **to be on the s.**

side of forty ne pas avoir encore atteint la quarantaine

sunray ['sʌnreɪ] **N** rayon *m* de soleil, rayon solaire

▸▸ *Br* **s. lamp** *Med* lampe *f* à rayons ultraviolets; *(for tanning)* lampe à bronzer; *Med* **s. treatment** héliothérapie *f*

sunrise ['sʌnraɪz] **N** lever *m* du soleil; **at s.** au soleil levant, au lever du soleil

▸▸ **s. industry** industrie *f* de pointe

sunroof ['sʌnruːf] **N** *Aut* toit *m* ouvrant; *(of hotel etc)* toiture-terrasse *f*, *pl* toitures-terrasses, solarium *m*

sunset ['sʌnset] **N** coucher *m* du soleil; **at s.** au soleil couchant, au coucher du soleil

▸▸ **s. industry** industrie *f* déclinante

sunshade ['sʌnʃeɪd] **N** *(parasol)* ombrelle *f*; *(for table etc)* parasol *m*; *(in car)* pare-soleil *m inv*

sunshine ['sʌnʃaɪn] **N 1** *(light)* (clarté *f ou* lumière *f* du) soleil *m*; **in the s.** au soleil; **in the bright** *or* **brilliant s.** en plein soleil; **they need more s.** il leur faut davantage de soleil; **period of s.** période d'ensoleillement **2** *Fam* **hello s.!** *(to girl, woman)* bonjour ma jolie!; *(to boy, man)* salut mon vieux!; *Fam Iron* **where d'you think you're going, s.?** eh, tu vas où comme ça, mon coco?

▸▸ **s. roof** toit *m* ouvrant; **the S. State** = la Floride

sun-soaked **ADJ** *(beach etc)* baigné de soleil

sunspot ['sʌnspɒt] **N 1** *(on the sun)* tache *f* solaire, tache du soleil **2** *(holiday resort etc)* *(for summer holiday)* station *f* estivale; **it's our favourite winter s.** c'est là que nous préférons aller prendre du soleil pendant nos vacances d'hiver

sunstroke ['sʌnstrəʊk] **N** *Med* insolation *f*; **to get s.** attraper une insolation

suntan ['sʌntæn] **N** bronzage *m*, hâle *m*; **to get a s.** (se faire) bronzer; **she's got a tremendous s.** elle a un bronzage magnifique

▸▸ **s. lotion** lotion *f* solaire; **s. oil** huile *f* solaire

suntanned ['sʌntænd] **ADJ** bronzé, hâlé

suntrap ['sʌntræp] **N** coin *m* très ensoleillé

sun-up **N** *Am* lever *m* du soleil; **at s.** au lever du soleil

sun-worship **N** *Rel* culte *m* du soleil

sun-worshipper **N** *Rel* adorateur, -trice du soleil; *Fig (on beach etc)* amateur, -trice de soleil

sup [sʌp] **N** *esp North Eng* petite gorgée *f*; **to take a s. of soup** prendre une goutte de bouillon

vT **(-pp-** [sʌpt]) *esp North Eng* boire à petites gorgées

vI *Old-fashioned (have supper)* souper (**off**, **on** de)

▸ **sup up** *esp North Eng* **vT SEP** *(drink up)* finir

vI finir son verre

super ['suːpər] **ADJ** *Fam (excellent)* super *inv*, formidable, génial, -aux

N 1 *Am Fam (in apartment block)* concierge *mf*, gardien *m* (d'immeuble) **2** *Fam* = **supervisor 3** *Aut (petrol)* super *m*

▸▸ **S. League** *(in rugby league)* = ligue *f* de rugby composée des meilleures équipes britanniques

superable ['suːpərəb(ə)l] **ADJ** surmontable

superabundance [suːpərə'bʌndəns] **N** surabondance *f* (**of** de)

superabundant [suːpərə'bʌndənt] **ADJ** surabondant

superabundantly [suːpərə'bʌndəntlɪ] **ADV** surabondamment

superannuate [suːpər'ænjʊeɪt] **vT** *(person)* mettre à la retraite; *Fig (thing)* mettre au rancart, remiser

superannuated [su:pər'ænjʊeɪtɪd] ADJ (person) (mis) en ou à la retraite, retraité; (ideas) suranné; (system, equipment) démodé

superannuation [su:pərænjʊ'eɪʃən] N retraite f
▸▸ s. fund caisse f de retraite

superb [su:'pɜ:b] ADJ superbe

superbly [su:'pɜ:blɪ] ADV superbement

supercargo ['su:pəka:gəʊ] N Naut subrécargue m

supercharge ['su:pətʃɑ:dʒ] VT Aut, Aviat etc (engine) suralimenter, surcomprimer; **supercharged engine** moteur m suralimenté ou surcomprimé ou à compresseur

supercharger ['su:pətʃɑ:dʒər] N Aut, Aviat etc compresseur m, surpresseur m

supercilious [su:pə'sɪlɪəs] ADJ hautain, dédaigneux

superciliously [su:pə'sɪlɪəslɪ] ADV avec hauteur, dédaigneusement

superciliousness [su:pə'sɪlɪəsnɪs] N hauteur f

superconductor [su:pəkən'dʌktər] N Phys, Elec supraconducteur m

supercooling [su:pə'ku:lɪŋ] N sous-refroidissement m

supercritical [su:pə'krɪtɪk(ə)l] ADJ Nucl supercritique, surcritique

super-duper [-'du:pər] ADJ Fam super, superchouette

superego ['su:pərɪgəʊ] N Psy surmoi m

superelevation [su:pərelɪ'veɪʃən] N (of road) dévers m

supererogation [su:pərerə'geɪʃən] N Fml surérogation f

superficial [su:pə'fɪʃəl] ADJ 1 superficiel; he has a s. charm il a un charme superficiel; to have a s. knowledge of sth avoir des connaissances superficielles de qch; s. learning vernis m de connaissances 2 Med s. wound blessure f superficielle

superficiality [su:pəfɪʃɪ'ælɪtɪ] N superficialité f

superficially [su:pə'fɪʃəlɪ] ADV superficiellement

superfine ['su:pəfaɪn] ADJ 1 Com etc surfin, superfin 2 (mind etc) raffiné

superfluity [su:pə'flu:ɪtɪ] N superfluité f; s. of good things surabondance f de biens; s. of words surabondance de paroles

superfluous [su:'pɜ:flʊəs] ADJ superflu, Lit superfétatoire; it would be s. to mention ... il serait superflu de mentionner ...; Fam I'm starting to feel a bit s. je commence à me sentir un peu de trop ici; s. weight excédent m de poids

superfluously [su:'pɜ:flʊəslɪ] ADV d'une manière superflue

superfluousness [su:'pɜ:flʊəsnɪs] N superfluité f

Superglue® ['su:pəglu:] N super-glu® f

superglue ['su:pəglu:] VT coller à la super-glu®

supergrass ['su:pəgrɑ:s] N Br Sl indic m de choc

superhighway ['su:pəhaɪweɪ] N Comput autoroute f

superhuman [su:pə'hju:mən] ADJ surhumain

superimpose [su:pərɪm'pəʊz] VT superposer, surimposer; Phot, Cin faire une surimpression de, surimprimer; **superimposed photos** des photos en surimpression; Fig a Western culture superimposed on an indigenous one une culture occidentale venue se superposer à une culture indigène

superimposition [su:pərɪmpə'zɪʃən] N superposition f, Phot, Cin surimpression f

superintend [su:pərɪn'tend] VT diriger, surveiller; to s. the election présider au scrutin

superintendence [su:pərɪn'tendəns] N direction f, surveillance f

superintendent [su:pərɪn'tendənt] N 1 (director) directeur, -trice; (of works etc) surveillant, -ante, chef m; Am Fam sidewalk s. passant, -ante qui regarde les travaux de construction 2 (police officer) commissaire m (de police) 3 Am (of apartment block) concierge mf, gardien m (d'immeuble)

superior [su:'pɪərɪər] ADJ 1 (position, officer, quality) supérieur (to à); Geog Lake S. le lac Supérieur; to be s. in numbers to the enemy être supérieur en nombre à l'ennemi, avoir la supériorité du nombre sur l'ennemi; they were overcome by s. numbers ils ont succombé sous le nombre, ils ont été vaincus par le nombre; she felt s. to her colleagues elle se sentait supérieure à ses collègues 2 (arrogant) (person) orgueilleux; (air) de supériorité; with a s. smile avec un sourire condescendant
N supérieur, -ieure; he is your s. il est votre supérieur; to be sb's s. in courage être plus courageux que qn; Father S. père m supérieur; Mother S. mère f supérieure
▸▸ Typ s. letter lettre f supérieure; Typ s. number chiffre m supérieur

superiority [su:pɪərɪ'ɒrɪtɪ] N supériorité f, s. in men and materials supériorité en hommes et en matériel; Mil, Aviat air s. supériorité aérienne
▸▸ Psy s. complex complexe m de supériorité

superlative [su:'pɜ:lətɪv] ADJ 1 (excellent) excellent 2 Gram superlatif
N Gram superlatif m; in the s. au superlatif; Fig to speak in superlatives s'exprimer par superlatifs VOIR GRAMMAIRE A24–6; B11; B13–14

superlatively [su:'pɜ:lətɪvlɪ] ADV extrêmement, au plus haut degré; s. fit dans une forme excellente

superman, pl **supermen** ['su:pəmæn, -men] N Phil surhomme m; Fam superman m

supermarket ['su:pəmɑ:kɪt] N supermarché m
▸▸ s. prices prix mpl dans les supermarchés

supermarketing ['su:pəmɑ:kɪtɪŋ] N supermarketing m

supermini ['su:pəmɪnɪ] N Aut citadine f

supermodel ['su:pəmɒd(ə)l] N supermodel m

supernatural [su:pə'nætʃərəl] ADJ surnaturel
N surnaturel m

supernaturally [su:pə'nætʃərəlɪ] ADV de manière surnaturelle

supernova [su:pə'nəʊvə] N Astron supernova f, pl supernovæ

supernumerary [su:pə'nju:m(ə)rərɪ] ADJ surnuméraire; (staff) en surnombre
N surnuméraire m; Theat, Cin figurant, -ante

superphosphate [su:pə'fɒsfeɪt] N superphosphate m

superpose [su:pə'pəʊz] VT superposer (upon, on à); (planks etc) étager

superpower ['su:pəpaʊər] N Pol superpuissance f
▸▸ s. talks négociations fpl entre les superpuissances

superscript ['su:pəskrɪpt] Typ ADJ (number) en exposant; s. 3 3 en exposant
N (number) exposant m

superscription [su:pə'skrɪpʃən] N (on coin) inscription f

supersede [su:pə'si:d] VT (person) (get rid of) supplanter; (replace) remplacer; (object) remplacer; this catalogue supersedes pre-

vious issues ce catalogue annule les précédents; method now superseded méthode périmée; the RWQ20 has long been superseded by smaller models la RWQ20 a depuis longtemps été supplantée par des modèles plus petits

supersensitive [su:pə'sensɪtɪv] ADJ hypersensible

supersonic [su:pə'sɒnɪk] ADJ (plane, speed) supersonique
▸▸ s. bang, s. boom bang m

superstar ['su:pəstɑ:r] N Cin, Sport superstar f

superstition [su:pə'stɪʃən] N superstition f

superstitious [su:pə'stɪʃəs] ADJ superstitieux

superstitiously [su:pə'stɪʃəslɪ] ADV superstitieusement

superstore ['su:pəstɔ:r] N hypermarché m

superstructure ['su:pəstrʌktʃər] N superstructure f

supertanker ['su:pətæŋkər] N Naut superpétrolier m, supertanker m

supertax ['su:pətæks] N surimposition f, surtaxe f

supertonic [su:pə'tɒnɪk] N Mus sus-tonique f, pl sus-toniques

superuser ['su:pəju:zər] N Comput gros utilisateur m

supervene [su:pə'vi:n] VI esp Fml survenir; if no complications s. s'il ne survient pas de complications

supervention [su:pə'venʃən] N Fml survenue f

super-VGA [-vi:dʒi:'eɪ] N Comput Super-VGA m

supervise ['su:pəvaɪz] VT 1 (keep watch on) (children, prisoners) surveiller 2 (department, thesis) diriger

supervision [su:pə'vɪʒən] N 1 (keeping watch on) surveillance f, children are under the s. of trained instructors at all times les enfants se trouvent toujours sous la surveillance de moniteurs diplômés 2 (control) (of department, thesis) direction f

supervisor ['su:pəvaɪzər] N 1 (in factory etc) surveillant, -ante 2 (manager) directeur, -trice 3 Univ (of thesis) directeur, -trice de thèse(s)

supervisory [su:pə'vaɪz(ə)rɪ] ADJ (committee etc) de surveillance; a s. function une fonction de surveillance; a s. role un rôle de surveillant
▸▸ s. board conseil m de surveillance

superwoman, pl **superwomen** ['su:pəwʊmən, -wɪmɪn] N Fam superwoman f

supine ['su:paɪn] N Gram supin m
ADJ 1 (lying on back) couché ou étendu sur le dos 2 (inactive) mou, f molle, indolent

supper ['sʌpər] N VOIR GRAMMAIRE A7 (early evening meal) dîner m; (snack before going to bed) souper m; to have s. dîner; (before bed) souper; Fig you'll have to sing for your s. c'est un prêté pour un rendu, c'est donnant, donnant; the Last S. la Cène, le dernier repas (du Seigneur); Rel the Lord's S. la communion, la cène, l'eucharistie f

suppertime ['sʌpətaɪm] N l'heure f du dîner; (before bed) l'heure du souper; (it's) s.! à table!

supplant [sə'plɑ:nt] VT (person) supplanter, prendre la place de, évincer

supple ['sʌp(ə)l] ADJ (limb, object, material) souple, flexible; (person) souple; to become s. s'assouplir; s.-limbed aux membres souples

supplement¹ ['sʌplɪmənt] N (of newspaper, for travel, of angle) supplément m

supplement² ['sʌplɪment] VT (book) ajouter un supplément à; **to s. one's income by writing articles** augmenter ses revenus en écrivant des articles

supplementary [sʌplɪ'ment(ə)rɪ] ADJ supplémentaire (**to** de)
▸▸ *Math* **s. angle** angle *m* supplémentaire; *Br Formerly* **s. benefit** = allocation *f* versée par l'État à ceux qui ont les plus faibles revenus; **s. cover** garanties *fpl* complémentaires; **s. income** revenus *mpl* annexes

suppleness ['sʌp(ə)lnɪs] N souplesse *f*

suppliant ['sʌplɪənt] ADJ *(attitude, gesture)* suppliant, de supplication
N suppliant, -ante

supplicant ['sʌplɪkənt] N suppliant, -ante

supplicate ['sʌplɪkeɪt] *Fml, Lit* VT *(person)* supplier (**to do sth** de faire qch); *(sb's protection)* solliciter humblement
VI supplier

supplicating ['sʌplɪkeɪtɪŋ] ADJ suppliant, de supplication

supplication [sʌplɪ'keɪʃən] N **1** *(act)* supplication *f* **2** *(request)* supplique *f*

supplier [sə'plaɪər] N *Com* fournisseur, -euse
▸▸ **s. code** code *m* fournisseur; *Acct* **s. credit** crédit-fournisseur *m*

supply [sə'plaɪ] N **1** *(act of supplying)* approvisionnement *m*, fourniture *f*; **electricity s.** alimentation *f* en électricité; *Econ* **s. and demand** l'offre *f* et la demande
2 *(stock)* provision *f*; **to get (in) a fresh s. of sth** se réapprovisionner en qch; **money/information is in short s.** on manque d'argent/d'informations; **supplies** *(for office, photography)* fournitures *fpl*; **supplies of money** fonds *mpl*, ressources *fpl*; **food supplies** vivres *mpl*; **to cut off** *or* **stop the enemy's supplies** couper l'ennemi de ses approvisionnements; **supplies and services** fournitures et services *mpl*
3 **to do s. teaching** faire des remplacements
VT **1** fournir, approvisionner (**sb with sth** en qch); *(market)* alimenter; *(goods)* fournir, procurer; *(information)* fournir; *(services)* assurer; *(water, gas etc)* amener; **to s. oneself with sth** s'approvisionner en qch; **the tradesmen who s. us** nos fournisseurs; *Elec* **to s. a factory with current** alimenter une usine en courant; **the arteries that s. the brain** les artères qui amènent le sang au cerveau; **to s. proof** fournir des preuves
2 *(omission)* réparer; *(need)* répondre à; **to s. sb's needs** pourvoir *ou* subvenir aux besoins de qn
VI **to s. for sb** *(of teacher etc)* assurer l'intérim *ou* la suppléance de qn
▸▸ *Mil* **s. lines** lignes *fpl* de ravitaillement; **s. pipe** *(for fuel)* conduite *f* d'arrivée du combustible; **s. price** prix *m* d'offre; **s. ship** ravitailleur *m*; **s.-side economics** théorie *f* économique de l'offre; *Br* **s. teacher** remplaçant, -ante

> Note that the French verb **supplier** is a false friend and is never a translation for the English verb **to supply**. It means **to implore, to beg**.

SUPPORT [sə'pɔːt]

▪ N appui **1, 2** ▪ soutien **2** ▪ support **2**
▪ VT supporter **1** ▪ soutenir **1, 2**
▪ appuyer **2** ▪ sponsoriser **2**
▪ entretenir **3** ▪ pourvoir aux besoins de **3** ▪ permettre l'utilisation de **4**

N **1** *(act of supporting)* appui *m*, soutien *m*; *(of arch, vault)* soutènement *m*; **moral s.** appui *ou* soutien moral; **to give s. to a proposal** appuyer une proposition; **this discovery lends s. to those who have argued ...** cette découverte va dans le sens de ceux qui soutiennent que ...; **the rebels have little s.** les

rebelles bénéficient d'un soutien limité; **there is widespread s. for the government** le gouvernement bénéficie d'un très large soutien; **can I expect your s.?** est-ce que je peux compter sur votre soutien?; **to produce documents in s. of an allegation** produire des pièces à l'appui d'une allégation *ou* pour appuyer une allégation; *Law* fournir les pièces au soutien; **to argue in s. of a measure** défendre une mesure; **in s. of this theory** à l'appui de cette théorie; *Mil* **air s.** appui *ou* soutien aérien; **with (financial) s. from the council** avec l'appui (financier) du conseil; **insufficient air for the s. of life** air en quantité insuffisante pour permettre la vie; **their son was their only means of s.** leur fils était leur seul soutien; **to be without means of s.** être sans ressources
2 *(person, thing supporting)* soutien *m*; *(of arch, vault)* appui *m*, support *m*, soutien; *(in horticulture)* tuteur *m*; *Cin (supporting actor)* second rôle *m*; **she is the s. of the family** c'est elle qui fait vivre la famille; *Sport* **(athletic) s.** suspensoir *m*; *Am* **price supports** subventions *fpl*
3 *Mus* groupe *m* en première partie
VT **1** *(hold up) (vault, arch)* supporter, soutenir; *Tech (load)* supporter, résister à; *(prices)* soutenir; **I supported him with my arm** je lui ai donné le bras; **he supported himself on a stick/my arm** il s'appuyait sur un bâton/mon bras
2 *(encourage, aid) (person, claims)* appuyer; *(theory)* soutenir; *(government, project)* apporter son soutien à; *(charitable event)* sponsoriser; *(charitable organization)* faire une donation à; *Sport (team)* supporter; *Mil (troops)* soutenir; *(of new discoveries etc) (theory)* renforcer; **proof that supports a case** preuves à l'appui d'une cause; **his theory is supported by facts** sa théorie est corroborée par les faits; *Parl* **to s. the motion** soutenir la motion; **to be supported by sb** *(in a proposal)* être soutenu par qn; **environmentalists s. the bill** les écologistes soutiennent le projet de loi; **the mayor, supported by the clergy** le maire, avec le soutien du clergé; **supported by a superb cast** avec une distribution superbe; **his parents supported him in his attempt to become an actor** ses parents l'ont soutenu lorsqu'il a essayé de devenir acteur
3 *(help to exist) (life)* entretenir; *(person)* soutenir financièrement, pourvoir aux besoins de; **to have a wife and three children to s.** avoir une femme et trois enfants à charge; **it was impossible to s. his family on his meagre salary** il lui était impossible de subvenir aux besoins de sa famille avec son maigre salaire; **hospital supported by voluntary contributions** hôpital financé par les souscriptions volontaires; **to s. oneself** se suffire (à soi-même), gagner sa vie
4 *Comput* permettre l'utilisation de, supporter; **this package, which is supported by all ABC workstations ...** ce progiciel, qui peut être utilisé sur tous les postes de travail ABC ...; **56K supported** gère l'accès en 56 kbit/s
▸▸ **s. band** groupe *m* en première partie; **who was the s. band?** qui est-ce qu'il y avait en première partie?; *Comput* **s. line** assistance *f* technique téléphonique; **s. market** marché *m* support *ou* d'appui; **s. price** prix *m* de soutien; *Admin* **s. services** services *mpl* d'assistance technique; **s. staff** personnel *m* de soutien *ou* des services généraux; **s. stockings** bas *mpl* à varices; *Mil* **s. unit** unité *f* de soutien

> Note that the English verb **to support** only translates **supporter** when it means **to hold up**. The most common meaning of the French verb **supporter** is **to bear, to withstand**.

supportable [sə'pɔːtəb(ə)l] ADJ **1** *(bearable)* supportable, tolérable **2** *(theory etc)* soutenable

supporter [sə'pɔːtər] N **1** *(person) (of opinion)* défenseur *m*, tenant *m*; *(of party)* partisan *m*, sympathisant, -ante; *(of politician)* partisan *m*; *Sport (of team)* supporter *m*; **supporters' club** club *m* des supporters **2** *(device)* soutien *m*, support *m*

supporting [sə'pɔːtɪŋ] ADJ *Cin (film, programme)* supplémentaire; *(actor)* qui a un rôle secondaire *ou* de second plan; *Theat* **the s. cast** les seconds *ou* deuxièmes rôles *mpl*; **there is an excellent s. cast** les seconds rôles sont excellents
▸▸ *Theat, Mus* **s. act** première partie *f*; **in the days when the Beatles were one of the s. acts** quand les Beatles se produisaient en première partie; *Theat, Cin* **s. part**, **s. role** second rôle *m*; **s. wall** mur *m* d'appui *ou* de soutènement

supportive [sə'pɔːtɪv] ADJ *(parent, friend, ally etc)* qui soutient; **to be s.** prêter son appui; **she's been very s.** elle l'a/nous a/etc bien soutenu(s); **she's usually so s.** d'habitude, elle fait tout ce qu'elle peut pour les/nous/etc aider; **I was trying to be as s. as I could** je faisais de mon mieux pour les/etc aider; **you could be more s.!** vous pourriez me/nous/etc soutenir un peu plus!; **to be s. of sb's efforts** soutenir qn dans ses efforts

supportiveness [sə'pɔːtɪvnɪs] N soutien *m*, appui *m*

suppose [sə'pəʊz] VT **1** *(assume)* supposer; *(imagine)* imaginer; *(think)* croire, penser; **you mustn't s. that ...** il ne faut pas vous imaginer que ...; **what makes you s. that I trust you?** qu'est-ce qui vous fait croire que j'ai confiance en vous?; **I don't s. he'll do it** je ne crois pas qu'il le fera; **will you go? – I s. so** irez-vous? – probablement; **please can I stay up late? – oh, I s. so** s'il te plaît, est-ce que je peux veiller tard? – bon, si tu veux; **I don't think he'll come – no, I s. not** *or* **I don't s. so** je ne crois pas qu'il viendra – non, sans doute *ou* probablement pas; **I don't s. you remember me** vous ne vous souvenez sans doute pas de moi; **I s. you can't remember that either!** tu ne te souviens probablement pas de ça non plus!; **supposing** *or* **(let us) s. (that) you're right** supposons *ou* en supposant *ou* mettons que vous ayez raison; **s.** *or* **supposing you were ill** supposez que vous soyez malade; **s. we do stay another year, what then?** suppose qu'en effet, nous restions une année de plus, et après?; **supposing** *or* **s. he came back** si, par supposition, il revenait, supposons qu'il revienne; **s. I was talking to him, what of it?** et si j'étais en train de lui parler, qu'est-ce que ça peut faire?; **yes, but s. I were to die** oui, mais si je venais à mourir; *Fam* **s. we change the subject** et si nous changions de sujet; **just supposing it did happen** supposons que ça se produise; **the plan supposes we can keep inflation under 1.5%** le projet part du principe que nous arriverons à maintenir l'inflation au-dessous de 1,5%; **that supposes rather more enthusiasm than I think will be forthcoming** cela suppose un enthousiasme qui ne viendra pas, à mon avis VOIR GRAMMAIRE A47–8
2 **to be supposed to do sth** être censé faire qch; **she's supposed to be in London** *(they say she is, she should be)* elle est censée être à Londres; **the film's supposed to be very good** à ce qu'il paraît, c'est un très bon film; **it's supposed to have been discovered by ...** on dit que cela a été découvert par ...; **there's supposed to be a well in the garden** on dit qu'il y a un puits dans le jardin; **I'm not supposed to do it** je ne suis pas censé le faire; **you're not supposed to know that** *(so*

keep quiet about it) vous n'êtes pas censé le savoir; *(so I won't tell you)* je n'ai pas à vous le dire; **you're not supposed to park here** vous n'avez pas le droit de vous garer ici; **don't ask me! – you're supposed to be in charge!** ne me demande pas ça! – je croyais pourtant bien que c'était toi le responsable!; **you're supposed to be my friend!** je te croyais mon ami!; **could you lend me the key? – well, I'm not supposed to, but …** pourriez-vous me prêter la clef? – eh bien, je ne devrais pas, mais …; **the computer's not supposed to make a noise like that** l'ordinateur ne devrait pas faire un tel bruit; **how am I supposed to work in conditions like these?** comment veut-on que je travaille dans de telles conditions?; **how is anybody supposed to make sense of that?** comment est-on censé s'y retrouver?

supposed [sə'pəʊzɪd] **ADJ** **ATTRIB** *(presumed, alleged)* présumé

supposedly [sə'pəʊzɪdlɪ] **ADV** soi-disant

supposition [sʌpə'zɪʃən] **N** supposition *f*, hypothèse *f*; **unfounded s.** supposition gratuite; **on the s. that …** à supposer que … + *sub*, dans l'hypothèse où … + *cond*; **on the s. that she had caught the train** dans l'hypothèse où elle aurait pris le train VOIR GRAM-MAIRE A57

suppositious [sʌpə'zɪʃəs] **ADJ** *Fml* supposé

supposititious [səppɒzɪ'tɪʃəs] **ADJ** *Fml (false)* faux, *f* fausse

suppository [sə'pɒzɪtrɪ] **N** *Pharm* suppositoire *m*

suppress [sə'pres] **VT 1** *(uprising)* réprimer, étouffer; *(newspaper, association)* interdire; *(malpractice)* faire disparaître **2** *(scandal)* étouffer; *(sob)* étouffer, ravaler; *(feelings, emotions)* réprimer, refouler; *(emotion)* dominer; **to s. one's feelings** se contenir, faire taire ses sentiments; **to s. a cough** réprimer son envie de tousser **3** *(hide)* cacher, dissimuler; *(keep silent about)* passer sous silence; *(fact)* ne pas révéler; *Law* faire disparaître; *(name)* taire, ne pas donner **4** *Radio, Elec* déparasiter

Note that the French verb **supprimer** is a false friend and is almost never a translation for the English verb **to suppress**. Its most common meaning is **to cancel, to abolish**.

suppressed [sə'prest] **ADJ** *(feeling etc)* étouffé, réprimé; **s. anger** colère *f* refoulée; **s. excitement** agitation *f* contenue

suppression [sə'preʃən] **N 1** *(of uprising, malpractice)* répression *f*; *(of book, newspaper)* interdiction *f* **2** *(of emotions)* refoulement *m*; *Med (of sweat, urine)* suppression *f* **3** *(of truth, fact, evidence)* dissimulation *f*; **she could not tolerate this s. of the truth** elle ne pouvait tolérer que l'on dissimule la vérité de cette manière; **the minister demanded the s. of the story** le ministre a exigé que l'on étouffe l'affaire **4** *Radio* antiparasitage *m*

suppressor [sə'presər] **N 1** *(person)* **the s. of the uprising** celui qui dirige/dirigeait/*etc* la répression **2** *Radio (device)* (dispositif *m* ou appareil *m*) antiparasite *m*
▸▸ *Radio* **s. grid** grille *f* d'arrêt

suppurate ['sʌpjʊreɪt] **VI** *(of wound, sore)* suppurer

suppurating ['sʌpjʊreɪtɪŋ] **ADJ** *(of wound, sore)* purulent, suppurant

suppuration [sʌpjʊ'reɪʃən] **N** *(of wound, sore)* suppuration *f*

supranational [su:prə'næʃən(ə)l] **ADJ** supranational, -aux

suprarenal gland [su:prə'ri:n(ə)l] **N** *Anat* glande *f* surrénale

supremacist [sʊ'premPsɪst] **N =** personne *f* croyant en la supériorité d'un groupe, racial ou autre

supremacy [sʊ'preməsɪ] **N** suprématie *f*; **white s.** la suprématie de la race blanche

supreme [sʊ'pri:m] **ADJ** suprême; **to reign s.** *(of monarch)* régner en souverain absolu; *Fig (of champion etc)* régner; **to make the s. sacrifice** *(die)* se sacrifier
▸▸ *Rel* **the S. Being** l'Être *m* suprême; **S. Commander** commandant *m* en chef; *Am Law* **the S. Court** la Cour suprême *(des États-Unis)*

supremely [sʊ'pri:mlɪ] **ADV** suprêmement; **we are s. happy** nous jouissons d'un bonheur suprême, nous sommes suprêmement heureux

supremo, *pl* **supremos** [sʊ'pri:məʊ, -məʊz] **N** *Br* grand chef *m*, *Fam* big boss *m*

Supt *abbr* **superintendent**

surcharge ['sɜ:tʃɑ:dʒ] **N** *(additional charge)* supplément *m*; *(as penalty)* majoration *f* d'impôt; **s. on a letter** surtaxe *f* d'une lettre; **there's a s. for late bookings** il y a un supplément à payer pour les réservations de dernière minute
VT *(letter etc)* surtaxer; **if motorists were surcharged for …** si on surtaxait les automobilistes pour …

surd [sɜ:d] **N 1** *Math* quantité *f* irrationnelle **2** *Ling (consonant)* sourde *f*

SURE [ʃʊər] **ADJ** *(convinced, definite)* sûr, certain; *(judgement, shot)* sûr; *(remedy, cure)* infaillible; *(profit, success)* sûr, assuré; **to be s. of** *or* **about sth** être sûr *ou* certain de qch; **I'm s. of it** j'en suis sûr *ou* certain; **I'm not so s. of** *or* **about that** je n'en suis pas bien sûr *ou* certain; *(implying permission won't be given)* ça, ça m'étonnerait; **I can't be s., but I think it was two o'clock** je n'en suis pas tout à fait sûr, mais je pense qu'il était deux heures; **I'm s. you're mistaken** je suis sûr que vous vous trompez; **are you quite s. he hasn't left yet?** êtes-vous bien sûr qu'il n'est pas encore parti?; **I'm s. you must be** *or* **you're very tired** je suis sûr que vous êtes très fatigué; **to be s. of oneself** être sûr de soi; **I don't know, I'm s.** ma foi, je ne sais pas; **we're all very grateful, I'm s., but …** nous vous/leur/*etc* en sommes certainement très reconnaissants, mais …; **to make s. of sth** s'assurer de qch; **make s. (that) the door is shut** assurez-vous que la porte est fermée, vérifiez que la porte est fermée; **I'll just go and make s.** je vais vérifier; **to make s. of a seat** s'assurer une place; **don't be too** *or* **so s.!** vous êtes bien sûr de vous!; **what makes you so s.?** comment pouvez-vous en être si sûr?; **with a s. hand** d'une main assurée; **there is only one s. way of doing it** il n'y a qu'un moyen sûr de le faire; *Iron* **that's a s. way of failing the interview** c'est un moyen sûr d'échouer à l'entretien; **it's a s. thing** c'est une certitude *ou* une chose certaine; *esp Am Fam* **s. thing!** pour sûr!; **I don't know for s.** je n'en suis pas bien sûr; **tomorrow for s.** demain sans faute; **she won't come, that's for s.** elle ne viendra pas, c'est certain; **it's s. to be fine** il fera sûrement beau; **he's s. to come** il viendra sûrement *ou* à coup sûr; **be s. to come early** ne manquez pas d'arriver de bonne heure; **be s. and ask him what time he's coming** assure-toi de l'heure à laquelle il arrivera; **be s. not to lose it, be s. that you don't lose it** prenez garde de ne pas le perdre

ADV 1 *esp Am Fam (really)* vraiment; **it s. is cold** il fait vraiment froid; **it s. was difficult** c'était vraiment *ou* bien difficile; **you s. do know your history!** vous vous y connaissez vraiment *ou Fam* drôlement bien en histoire! **2 as s. as fate, as s. as eggs are** *or Fam* **is**

eggs aussi vrai qu'il fait jour, aussi sûr que deux et deux font quatre; **s. enough, he was there** il était bien là; **she'll come, s. enough** elle viendra, tu peux compter là-dessus; **no, it's whisky s. enough** non, c'est bien du whisky; *Fam* **for s.!,** *esp Am* **s.!** mais oui!, bien sûr!

surefooted [ʃʊə'fʊtɪd] **ADJ** au pied sûr; **to be s.** avoir le pied sûr; *Fig* **the Prime Minister gave a s. performance in the debate** le Premier ministre a très bien intervenu lors du débat

surely ['ʃʊəlɪ] **ADV 1** *(in a sure manner)* sûrement; **slowly but s.** lentement mais sûrement **2** *(certainly)* assurément, sans doute; **s. he will come** il viendra sûrement; **s. you don't believe that!** vous ne croyez quand même pas cela!; **s. you're not going to leave us?** vous n'allez quand même pas nous quitter?; *esp Am* **will you help me? – s.!** voulez-vous m'aider? – bien sûr!; **it's all gone – s. not!** il n'y en a plus – c'est pas vrai!

sureness ['ʃʊənɪs] **N** *(of hand, judgement etc)* sûreté *f*; *(of remedy)* efficacité *f*; *(certainty)* certitude *f*; **the s. of his aim** la précision de son tir

surety ['ʃʊərətɪ] **N** *Law (person)* caution *f*, garant, -ante; *Com* donneur *m* d'aval; **to stand s. for sb** se porter caution pour qn, se rendre *ou* se porter garant de qn; **s. for a debt** garant d'une dette; **s. for a loan** sûreté *f* en garantie d'un crédit; **in his own s. of £5,000** sous sa propre caution de 5000 livres

surf [sɜ:f] **N** ressac *m*, vagues *fpl* déferlantes
VI *(on surfboard)* faire du surf
VT **to s. the Internet** naviguer *ou* surfer sur l'Internet

surface ['sɜ:fɪs] **N 1** *(exterior, face)* surface *f*; **the earth's s.** la surface de la terre; **to rise to the s. of the water** remonter *ou* revenir à la surface de l'eau; **to rise** *or* **come to the s.** *(of submarine)* revenir en surface *ou* à la surface; **to break s.** faire surface; **smooth/even s.** surface lisse/unie; **his politeness is only on the s.** sa politesse est toute de surface; **on the s. she is very calm** en surface, elle est très calme; **meaning that lies below the s.** signification *f* cachée; **we're still very much on the s. of the problem** nous n'avons pas encore attaqué le fond du problème; **to send a letter by s. mail** envoyer une lettre par voie de terre/de mer

2 *(area)* aire *f*, étendue *f*, superficie *f*; *Geom* **s. of revolution** surface *f* de révolution *ou* de rotation; **working s.** plan *m* de travail; *(in office)* surface utile; *Aviat* **lifting s.** surface portante *ou* de sustentation

3 *(of road)* revêtement *m*; **temporary s.** chaussée *f* provisoire

VT *(treat surface of)* apprêter la surface de; *(in papermaking)* calandrer; *Constr (road)* revêtir (**with** de); **they surfaced the back yard with concrete** ils ont recouvert la surface de la cour d'une couche de béton

VI 1 *(of submarine, whale etc)* faire surface; *(return to surface)* revenir en surface, remonter à la surface

2 *Fam (of person) (reappear, regain consciousness)* refaire surface
▸▸ *Ling* **s. grammar** grammaire *f* de surface; **s. noise** bruit *m* de surface; **s. speed** *(of submarine)* vitesse *f* en surface; **s. structure** structure *f* superficielle *ou* de surface; **s. tension** tension *f* superficielle; **s. transport** transport *m* terrestre et/ou maritime; **by s. transport** par voie de terre et/ou de mer; **s. water** eau *f* superficielle, eaux de surface; *Min* **s. work** travail *m* au jour; *Min* **s. worker** ouvrier *m* du jour

surface-mounted **ADJ** *Comput (chips)* monté en surface

surface-to-air ADJ
▸▸ *Mil* **s. missile** missile *m* sol-air

surface-to-surface ADJ
▸▸ *Mil* **s. missile** missile *m* sol-sol

surfacing ['sɜːfɪsɪŋ] N *Constr (of/on road etc)* revêtement *m*

surfboard ['sɜːfbɔːd] N planche *f* de surf, surf *m*

surfboarder, surfboarding ['sɜːfbɔːdər, -ɪŋ] = **surfer, surfing**

surfeit ['sɜːfɪt] N *(excess)* surabondance *f*; **to have a s. of oysters/of music** être rassasié d'huîtres/de musique
VT gorger, rassasier (**with** de); **to s. oneself with sth** se gorger de qch jusqu'à s'en dégoûter; **surfeited with pleasure** blasé *ou* écœuré par les plaisirs

surfer ['sɜːfər] N surfeur, -euse; **(Internet) s.** internaute *mf*, navigateur, -trice *ou* surfeur, -euse de l'Internet

surfie ['sɜːfɪ] N *Austr Fam* surfeur, -euse

surfing ['sɜːfɪŋ] N surf *m*

surfrider, surfriding ['sɜːfraɪdər, -ɪŋ] = **surfer, surfing**

surge [sɜːdʒ] N *(of sea)* houle *f*, *Elec (of electricity)* surtension *f*, *Fig (of activity)* poussée *f*, *(of enthusiasm)* accès *m*; *Fig* **the s. of the crowd** les remous *mpl* de la foule; **a s. of anger** un flot *ou* une vague de colère; **there has been a s. of public interest in …** il y a eu un mouvement *ou* une poussée de l'intérêt public pour …; **she felt a s. of fury** elle sentit la fureur monter en elle; **these seasonal surges in production/sales** ces poussées saisonnières de la production/des ventes
VI *(of sea)* être houleux; *(of waters)* se soulever; *Elec (of power)* être en surtension; *Fig* **the crowd surged along the street/onto the pitch** la foule s'est répandue en flots dans la rue/sur le terrain; **the crowd surged back** la foule a reflué
▸ **surge up** VI *(well up)* monter d'un seul coup; **anger surged up within her** un flot de colère est monté en elle; **a figure surged up out of the darkness** une silhouette surgit de l'ombre

surgeon ['sɜːdʒ(ə)n] N chirurgien *m*
▸▸ **s. general** *Mil* médecin-général *m*, *pl* médecins-généraux; *Am Admin* chef *m* des services de santé

surgery ['sɜːdʒərɪ] N **1** *(technique etc)* chirurgie *f*, *(operation)* intervention *f* chirurgicale; **major/minor s.** grande/petite chirurgie; **he'll need s.** il faudra l'opérer; **heart s.** chirurgie du cœur; **he's had heart s.** il a eu une opération du cœur; **the s. was successful** l'opération a réussi; **a clever piece of s.** une opération habile **2** *Br (place) (of doctor)* cabinet *m* (de consultation); *(of dentist)* cabinet *m*; **s. (hours)** heures *fpl* de consultation **3** *Br Pol (of MP etc)* permanence *f* publique; **our MP holds a weekly s.** notre député tient une permanence hebdomadaire

> Note that the French word **chirurgie** only has a medical sense.

surgical ['sɜːdʒɪk(ə)l] ADJ chirurgical, -aux; *Fig* **with s. precision** avec une précision mathématique
▸▸ **s. boot** chaussure *f* orthopédique; **s. collar** minerve *f*, **s. instruments** instruments *mpl* de chirurgie; *Br* **s. spirit** alcool *m* à 90°; *Mil* **s. strike** frappe *f* chirurgicale

surging ['sɜːdʒɪŋ] ADJ **a s. sea** une mer houleuse; **a s. mass of people** un flot pressé de gens

surliness ['sɜːlɪnɪs] N *(mood)* humeur *f* maussade; *(of expression)* air *m* bourru; *(of remark)* ton *m* bourru

surly ['sɜːlɪ] ADJ *(person)* revêche; *(tone, look, remark)* bourru

surmise[1] ['sɜːmaɪz] N conjecture *f*

surmise[2] [sɜːˈmaɪz] VT conjecturer; **as you may well have surmised** comme vous l'avez peut-être deviné, comme vous le soupçonnez peut-être

surmount [sɜːˈmaʊnt] VT **1** *(be on top of)* surmonter; **column surmounted by a cross** colonne surmontée d'une croix **2** *(overcome) (obstacle, difficulty)* surmonter; *(emotion)* maîtriser

surmountable [sɜːˈmaʊntəb(ə)l] ADJ surmontable

surname ['sɜːneɪm] N nom *m* de famille; **s. and Christian** *or* **first names** nom et prénoms *mpl* VOIR GRAMMAIRE B8

> Note that the French word **surnom** is a false friend and is never a translation for the English word **surname**. It means **nickname**.

surpass [sɜːˈpɑːs] VT **1** *(be superior to) (person)* surpasser; *(rivals)* devancer; **to s. sb in kindness** renchérir sur la bonté de qn; **he has surpassed himself** il s'est surpassé; *Iron* **you've surpassed yourself this time** vous vous êtes surpassé cette fois **2** *(exceed)* dépasser, excéder; **the result surpassed my hopes** le résultat a dépassé mes espérances; **this surpasses all previous records** ceci surpasse tous les records précédents

surpassing [sɜːˈpɑːsɪŋ] ADJ sans égal, sans pareil; **of s. beauty** d'une beauté incomparable *ou* sans pareille

surplice ['sɜːplɪs] N *Rel* surplis *m*

surplus ['sɜːpləs] N surplus *m*, excédent *m*; **to have a s. of sth** avoir qch en excès; *EU* **grain surpluses** excédents de céréales de l'UE; **government s.** surplus *mpl* du gouvernement
ADJ *(items)* en trop, en surplus, excédentaire; **s. food/wine/oil** excédent *m* alimentaire/de vin/d'huile; **s. to requirements** en trop; **s. population/products** population *f*/produits *mpl* excédentaire(s)
▸▸ *Com* **s. stock** stocks *mpl* excédentaires, surplus

surprise [səˈpraɪz] N surprise *f*, **to take sb by s.** surprendre qn, prendre qn au dépourvu; **to give sb a s.** faire une surprise à qn; **it was a s. to see her there** ce fut une surprise de la voir là; **what a s. to see you here!** je ne m'attendais pas à vous rencontrer ici!; **what a pleasant s.!** quelle bonne surprise!; **the party was meant to be a s.** la fête était censée être une surprise; **to spoil the s.** gâcher la surprise; **it was no s. to learn that he had a criminal record** il n'y avait rien d'étonnant à ce qu'il ait un casier judiciaire; **he's in for a bit of a s.!** s'il savait ce qu'on lui prépare!; **s., s.! it's us!** surprise! c'est nous!; **to my great s., much to my s.** à ma grande surprise, à mon grand étonnement; **imagine my s. when …** imaginez comme j'ai été surpris quand …, imaginez quelle a été ma surprise *ou* quel a été mon étonnement quand …
ADJ surprise; **the President's s. announcement** l'annonce surprise du président
VT **1** *(astonish)* surprendre, étonner; **nothing surprises him** rien ne l'étonne; **you could s. yourself** tu pourrais t'étonner toi-même; **to be surprised at sth** être surpris *ou* étonné de qch; **I am surprised to see you** *or* **at seeing you** je m'étonne de vous voir, je suis surpris de vous voir; **I should be surprised if he came back** cela m'étonnerait qu'il revienne; **there can't be many people who don't have a phone – you'd be surprised** il ne doit pas y avoir beaucoup de gens qui n'ont pas le téléphone – ne crois pas ça; **I wouldn't** *or*

shouldn't be surprised if they knew already cela ne me surprendrait pas qu'ils le sachent déjà; **it doesn't s. me in the least** ça ne m'étonne pas du tout; **I was agreeably surprised** j'ai été agréablement surpris; **I'm surprised at you!** tu m'étonnes! **2** *(catch unawares)* surprendre; **to s. sb in the act** surprendre qn en flagrant délit, prendre qn sur le fait
▸▸ **s. party** = fête *f* organisée pour quelqu'un sans qu'il ou elle le sache; **s. visit** visite *f* surprise; **to pay sb a s. visit** aller chez qn sans le prévenir

surprised [səˈpraɪzd] ADJ *(look)* étonné, surpris; *(expression)* de surprise; **don't look so s.** ne prends pas un air aussi étonné

surprising [səˈpraɪzɪŋ] ADJ surprenant, étonnant; **well, it's not s., is it?** ça n'a vraiment rien de surprenant; **it wouldn't be s. if he was in the plot** ça n'aurait rien de surprenant s'il était du complot; **that's s. coming from him** (venant) de sa part, c'est surprenant

surprisingly [səˈpraɪzɪŋlɪ] ADV étonnamment; **I found him s. young** je lui ai trouvé l'air étonnamment jeune; **s. enough, he agreed** cela peut paraître surprenant, mais il a accepté; **not s., she changed her mind** comme on pouvait s'y attendre *ou* évidemment, elle a changé d'avis

surreal [səˈrɪəl] ADJ surréaliste
N surréalisme *m*

surrealism [səˈrɪəlɪz(ə)m] N surréalisme *m*

surrealist [səˈrɪəlɪst] ADJ, N surréaliste *mf*

surrealistic [sərɪəˈlɪstɪk] ADJ surréaliste

surrealistically [sərɪəˈlɪstɪk(ə)lɪ] ADV d'une manière *ou* dans un style surréaliste

surrender [səˈrendər] N **1** *(act of surrendering) (of army, fortress)* reddition *f*, **no s.!** nous ne nous rendrons pas! **2** *Law (of possessions, rights)* abandon *m*, cession *f*, *(of right to property)* restitution *f*, *(of rights, authority)* abdication *f*, **to make a s. of principle** transiger avec ses principes **3** *(in insurance) (of policy)* rachat *m*
VI se rendre; *Mil* faire (sa) soumission, rendre les armes; **to s. to the police** se constituer prisonnier, se livrer à la police; *Fig* **all right! I s.!** ça va! je me rends!; **to s. to temptation** céder à la tentation
VT **1** *(fortress)* rendre, livrer **2** *(right, possessions)* abandonner, céder; *(right)* abdiquer; **she was instructed to s. her children to the care of the social services** on l'a obligé à laisser la garde de ses enfants à l'autorité des services sociaux; **to s. all hope of sth** abandonner *ou* renoncer à tout espoir de qch; **to s. an advantage** laisser un avantage; **to s. control of sth** abandonner la direction de qch **3** *(in insurance) (policy)* racheter
▸▸ **s. value** *(in insurance)* valeur *f* de rachat

surreptitious [sʌrəpˈtɪʃəs] ADJ subreptice, clandestin

surreptitiously [sʌrəpˈtɪʃəslɪ] ADV subrepticement, clandestinement

surreptitiousness [sʌrəpˈtɪʃəsnɪs] N caractère *m* subreptice

surrogacy ['sʌrəgəsɪ] N maternité *f* de substitution

surrogate ['sʌrəgɪt] N *(person)* suppléant, -ante, substitut *m*; *Rel, Law* subrogé, -ée; *(thing)* succédané *m* (**for** *or* **of sth** de qch)
▸▸ **s. mother** *Psy* substitut *m* maternel; *Med* mère *f* porteuse; **s. motherhood** maternité *f* de substitution

surround [səˈraʊnd] N encadrement *m*, bordure *f*
VT entourer; *Mil (enemy)* entourer, cerner; *(town)* investir; **the crowd surrounded the car** la foule a assiégé la voiture; **surrounded by** *or* **with dangers** cerné de dangers; **he li-**

kes to be surrounded by ... il aime être entouré de ...; **give up! you're surrounded!** rendez-vous! vous êtes cernés!; **the decision has been surrounded by controversy** la décision n'a pas cessé d'être controversée ▸▸ *TV, Comput* **s. sound** son *m* 3D

surrounding [sə'raʊndɪŋ] **ADJ** entourant, environnant; **the s. country** le pays alentour *ou* environnant

surroundings [sə'raʊndɪŋz] **NPL 1** *(environment)* environnement *m*, milieu *m*; **in its natural s.** dans son milieu naturel; **to be in familiar s.** être en pays de connaissance **2** *(surrounding area) (of city etc)* environs *mpl*, alentours *mpl*

surtax ['sɜːtæks] **N** surtaxe *f*, *(on income)* = surtaxe progressive sur le revenu
VT surtaxer

surtitle ['sɜːtaɪtəl] **N** surtitre *m*

surveillance [sɜː'veɪləns] **N** surveillance *f*, contrôle *m*; **to keep sb under s.** surveiller qn; **to be under s.** être sous surveillance

survey[1] ['sɜːveɪ] **N 1** *(study) (of subject, situation)* étude *f*, *(of opinions, voting intentions)* sondage *m*; *(for market research)* enquête *f* **2** *(inspection)* inspection *f*, visite *f*; *Br (of house, flat)* expertise *f* **3** *(in surveying) (action)* levé *m*; **aerial s.** levé aérophotogrammétrique; **to make a s. of an estate** relever un domaine; **quantity s.** métrage *m*, métré *m*, toisé *m*
▸▸ *Mktg* **s. research** recherche *f* par sondage

survey[2] [sɜː'veɪ] **VT 1** *(look at) (countryside etc)* regarder, scruter; *(question)* étudier, mettre à l'étude **2** *(in market research) (population)* enquêter; **to s. the scale of the damage** contempler l'ampleur du désastre; **to s. the situation** examiner la situation **3** *(inspect) (ship, building)* inspecter, faire l'expertise de l'état de; *Br* **to have a house surveyed** faire expertiser une maison **4** *(in surveying) (city, property)* relever, lever le(s) plan(s) de; *(coast)* hydrographier, faire l'hydrographie de

> Note that the French verb **surveiller** is a false friend and is never a translation for the English verb **to survey**. Its most common meaning is **to supervise, to keep an eye on**.

surveying [sɜː'veɪɪŋ] **N 1** *Constr* expertise *f*, *(for mapmaking)* topographie *f*, **quantity s.** métrage *m*, métré *m*, toisé *m* **2** *(inspection)* inspection *f*, visite *f*
▸▸ **s. instruments** instruments *mpl* topographiques

surveyor [sə'veɪər] **N** *(of land)* géomètre *mf* expert; **naval s.** (ingénieur *m*) hydrographe *m*; **s.'s table** planchette *f*, *Admin* **land s. and valuer, district s.** cadastreur *m*; **(quantity) s.** métreur *m* vérificateur; *Naut* **marine s.** visiteur *m ou* inspecteur *m* de navires; *Br* **(property) s.** (architecte *mf*) expert *m*

> Note that the French word **surveillant** is a false friend and is never a translation for the English word **surveyor**. Its most common meaning is **supervisor**.

survivable [sə'vaɪvəb(ə)l] **ADJ** **a s. attack** une attaque à laquelle on peut survivre; **the conditions were not s.** il était impossible de survivre dans de telles conditions

survival [sə'vaɪv(ə)l] **N 1** *(continued existence) (of tradition)* survivance *f*, *(of injured person etc)* survie *f*; **her s. as party leader** sa survie en tant que tête du parti; **it's a question of s.** c'est une question de survie; *Biol, Fig* **the s. of the fittest** la survie du plus apte **2** *(remaining part) (of ancient custom)* vestige *m*; **a s. of times past** un vestige du passé

▸▸ **s. bag** sac *m* de couchage de survie; **s. kit** équipement *m* de survie

survivalism [sə'vaɪvəlɪz(ə)m] **N** = préparation *f* à une catastrophe nucléaire ou autre

survivalist [sə'vaɪv(ə)lɪst] **N** = personne *f* qui se prépare à une catastrophe nucléaire ou autre

survive [sə'vaɪv] **VI** survivre; *(of custom)* survivre, subsister; **enough to s. on** de quoi survivre; **those who survived** les survivants *mpl*; **those toys wouldn't s. two minutes with our kids** ces jouets ne survivraient pas plus de deux minutes avec nos gamins; *Fam* **it's not serious, you'll s.** ce n'est pas grave, tu t'en remettras; *Fam* **it'll be awful, I don't know how I'll s.!** ça va être horrible, je ne sais pas comment je vais m'en sortir!; *Fam* **how's things? – I'm surviving** comment ça va? – pas trop mal
VT *(of person)* survivre à; *(of house, clothes)* supporter; **he will s. us all** il nous enterrera tous; **he is survived by a family of four** il laisse derrière lui une famille de quatre personnes; **to s. an injury** survivre à une blessure; **to s. an illness** réchapper d'une maladie; **I couldn't s. another meeting with him** je ne supporterais pas une autre réunion avec lui; **to s. a recession** *(of company)* survivre à une récession

surviving [sə'vaɪvɪŋ] **ADJ** *(person)* survivant; *(remains, copy)* qui reste; **the only s. member of ...** le seul survivant de ...; **there is one s. sister** une des sœurs est encore en vie, il y a une sœur encore en vie

survivor [sə'vaɪvər] **N** survivant, -ante; **he is the sole s. of his family** il est le seul qui reste de sa famille; **the survivors of the disaster** les rescapés *mpl*; **earthquake/flood s.** rescapé, -ée d'un tremblement de terre/d'une inondation; **she's a s.** *(in politics, business etc)* c'est une battante; *Pej* c'est une miraculée

susceptibility [səsɛptɪ'bɪlɪtɪ] **N 1** *(liability to be affected)* susceptibilité *f*, **s. to a disease** prédisposition *f* à une maladie; **s. to pain** sensibilité *f* à la douleur **2** *Fml (sensitivity)* sensibilité *f*, susceptibilité *f*, **to avoid wounding any susceptibilities** éviter de blesser la susceptibilité de qui que ce soit

susceptible [sə'sɛptɪb(ə)l] **ADJ** *(liable to be affected)* sensible (**to** à); *(touchy)* susceptible, qui se froisse facilement; **s. to media influences** sensible à l'influence des médias; **s. to a disease** prédisposé à une maladie; **this will make you less s. to colds** ceci vous rendra plus résistant au rhume; **s. to cold** frileux; *Fml* **s. of proof** qui peut être prouvé, démontrable

suspect[1] ['sʌspɛkt] **ADJ** suspect
N 1 suspect, -ecte **2** *Mktg* client *m* potentiel, suspect *m*
▸▸ *Mktg* **s. pool** clients *mpl* potentiels

suspect[2] [sə'spɛkt] **VT 1** *(person) (of crime etc)* soupçonner; **to s. sb of sth/of having done sth** soupçonner qn de qch/d'avoir fait qch **2** *(have intuition of) (reason, truth)* soupçonner; *(danger)* flairer, subodorer; **he suspects nothing** il ne se doute de rien; **does your husband s. anything?** est-ce que ton mari se doute de quelque chose?; **I never suspected it for a moment** je n'avais pas le moindre soupçon, je ne m'en suis jamais douté **3** *(doubt) (authenticity of a work etc)* avoir des doutes sur; **to s. sb's motives** mettre en doute les raisons de qn **4** *(consider likely)* croire, penser; **I suspected as much** je m'en doutais; **I s. that what she really means is ...** je pense que ce qu'elle veut vraiment dire, c'est ...; **I s. you're right** je crois bien que tu as raison

suspected [sə'spɛktɪd] **ADJ** présumé; **a s. terrorist** un terroriste présumé; *Med* **a s.**

case of typhoid un cas présumé de typhoïde; **he has a s. fracture** on craint qu'il (n')ait une fracture

suspend [sə'spɛnd] **VT 1** *(hang)* suspendre, pendre; **to s. sth from the ceiling** suspendre *ou* pendre qch au plafond **2** *(stop) (bus service, work)* suspendre; *Law* **to s. judgment** surseoir au jugement; *Law* **to s. proceedings** suspendre les poursuites; *Com* **to s. payment** suspendre ses paiements **3** *(exclude temporarily) (officer, footballer etc)* suspendre; *(jockey)* mettre à pied; *(newspaper)* suspendre; **to s. sb from his/her office** suspendre qn de ses fonctions; **to s. a pupil (from school)** renvoyer un élève (provisoirement); **suspended on full pay** *Admin* suspendu sans suppression de traitement; *Mil* suspendu sans suppression de solde

suspended [sə'spɛndɪd] **ADJ** suspendu; *(particles)* en suspension; *Law* en suspens, suspendu; **she was given a s. prison sentence of six months** elle a été condamnée à six mois de prison avec sursis; **to be in a state of s. animation** *(of person, animal)*, *Fig* être en hibernation; **the scheme is in a state of s. animation** le projet est en suspens

suspender [sə'spɛndər] **N 1** *Br (for stocking)* jarretelle *f*, *(for sock)* fixe-chaussette *m*, *pl* fixe-chaussettes **2** *Am* **(pair of) suspenders (braces)** (paire *f* de) bretelles *fpl*
▸▸ *Br* **s. belt** porte-jarretelles *m inv*

suspense [sə'spɛns] **N 1** *(uncertainty)* suspense *m*, incertitude *f*, *Liter, Cin etc* suspense; **to keep** *or* **hold sb in s.** tenir *ou* garder qn en haleine; **the s. is killing me!** ce suspense me rend fou!; *Iron* quel suspense! **2** *Law* **the question remains in s.** la question reste posée *ou* en suspens
▸▸ *Fin* **s. account** compte *m* d'ordre

suspension [sə'spɛnʃən] **N 1** *(of car etc)* suspension *f* **2** *(of hostilities, supplies etc)* suspension *f*, *Law (of judgement)* surséance *f*; *Com* **s. of payments** suspension de paiements **3** *(of official, officer etc)* suspension *f*, *(of jockey)* mise *f* à pied **4** *Chem* **(substance in) s.** (substance *f* en) suspension *f*
▸▸ **s. bridge** pont *m* suspendu; *Aut* **s. bush** bague *f* de suspension; **s. cable** câble *m* porteur; *Tech* **s. chain** chaîne *f* de suspension; **s. file** hamac *m*, dossier *m* suspendu; *Aut* **s. geometry** géométrie *f* de la suspension; *Typ, Gram* **s. points** points *mpl* de suspension

suspensory [sə'spɛnsərɪ] **ADJ** *Anat (ligament)* suspenseur
▸▸ *Med* **s. bandage** suspensoir *m*

suspicion [sə'spɪʃən] **N 1** *(belief of guilt)* soupçon *m*; *Law* suspicion *f*, **not the shadow** *or* **ghost of a s.** pas l'ombre d'un soupçon; **to be under s.** être soupçonné; **to have (one's) suspicions about sb** avoir des doutes sur qn, soupçonner qn; **to arouse s.** éveiller *ou* faire naître les soupçons; **to arouse** *or* **awaken sb's suspicions** éveiller les soupçons de qn; **above s.** au-dessus de tout soupçon; **praise free from any s. of flattery** louanges aucunement suspectes de flatterie; **to be right in one's suspicions** soupçonner juste; *Law* **to arrest/detain sb on s.** arrêter/détenir qn préventivement; **on s. of arson** sous la présomption d'incendie volontaire; **detention on s.** détention *f* préventive; **I had my suspicions about it** je m'en doutais, j'avais mes soupçons là-dessus; **I had no s. of it** je n'avais pas le moindre soupçon **2** *(characteristic, quality)* défiance *f*, suspicion *f*, **to look at sb with s.** regarder qn avec défiance; **the s. in her eyes/voice** la défiance dans ses yeux/sa voix **3** *(hint)* petite dose *f*, soupçon *m* (**of** de); *(of irony, malice)* pointe *f*

suspicious [sə'spɪʃəs] ADJ **1** *(arousing suspicions)* suspect, louche; **it looks s.** cela me paraît louche *ou* suspect; **a s. character** un individu louche *ou* suspect; **he died in s. circumstances** il est mort dans des circonstances suspectes **2** *(having suspicions)* méfiant, soupçonneux; **she has a very s. mind** elle est très soupçonneuse *ou* méfiante; **to be** or **feel s. about** or of sb/sth avoir des soupçons à l'endroit *ou* à l'égard de qn/sur qch; **her behaviour made me s.** sa conduite a éveillé mes soupçons

suspiciously [sə'spɪʃəslɪ] ADV **1** *(to act)* d'une manière suspecte *ou* louche; **he was s. eager to leave** l'empressement qu'il avait de partir était suspect; **it sounded s. as though she had lost it** on aurait dit qu'elle l'avait perdu; **it looks s. like the one I lost** il ressemble étrangement à celui que j'ai perdu; **two texts that are s. similar** deux textes qui sont étrangement similaires; **it looks s. like measles (to me)** cela m'a tout l'air d'une rougeole **2** *(to watch, ask)* d'un air méfiant, avec méfiance; *(to think)* avec méfiance

suspiciousness [sə'spɪʃəsnɪs] N **1** *(causing suspicion) (of behaviour, parcel etc)* caractère *m* suspect *ou* louche **2** *(feeling suspicion) (of person, in voice etc)* caractère *m* soupçonneux, méfiance *f*

suss [sʌs] VT *Br Fam* = **suss out**
► **suss out** VT SEP *Br Fam (work out) (person)* classer; *(system, technique)* piger; **I finally sussed out what she was doing** j'ai fini par piger ce qu'elle faisait; **to have sth sussed out** avoir pigé qch; **I've got him sussed out** j'ai pigé quel genre de type c'est

sussed [sʌst] ADJ *Sl* **to be s.** *(well-informed)* être au jus

sustain [sə'steɪn] VT **1** *(support) (person, weight, growth, pace, level)* soutenir, supporter; **enough oxygen to s. life** suffisamment d'oxygène pour que la vie soit possible; **to s. the body** sustenter le corps; **evidence to s. an assertion** témoignages pour appuyer une affirmation; *Mus* **to s. a note** tenir *ou* prolonger une note **2** *(suffer, receive) (loss)* éprouver, essuyer, subir; *(attack)* soutenir; **to s. an injury** recevoir une blessure, être blessé **3** *Law* **to s. an objection** *(of court)* admettre une objection; **objection sustained** objection admise

sustainable [sə'steɪnəb(ə)l] ADJ **1** *(rate, lifestyle)* que l'on peut maintenir **2** *Ecol (forest)* viable; *(energy, resources)* renouvelable; **s. growth** croissance *f* durable

sustained [sə'steɪnd] ADJ soutenu; **s. applause** applaudissements *mpl* prolongés
► ► *Mil* **s. fire** feu *m* soutenu *ou* nourri; *Mus* **s. note** tenue *f*

sustaining [sə'steɪnɪŋ] ADJ *(food, meal)* nourrissant; **the s. power of faith** le soutien que constitue la foi

sustenance ['sʌstənəns] N **1** *(act)* subsistance *f*, **necessary for the s. of our bodies** nécessaire à notre subsistance; **means of s.** moyens *mpl* de subsistance **2** *(food)* aliments *mpl*, nourriture *f*

suttee [sʌ'tiː] N *Rel (practice)* satī *m*; *(widow)* satī *f*

suture ['suːtʃər] N **1** *Anat, Bot* suture *f* **2** *Surg (action)* suture *f*; *(stitch)* point *m* de suture; *(thread)* fil *m* pour sutures
VT *Surg (wound)* suturer

SUV [esjuː'viː] N *(abbr* **sport utility vehicle)** SUV *m*

suzerain ['suːzəreɪn] N suzerain, -aine

suzerainty ['suːzərəntɪ] N suzeraineté *f*

svelte [svelt] ADJ svelte

Svengali [sven'gælɪ] N manipulateur, -trice

SVGA [esviːdʒiː'eɪ] N *Comput (abbr* **super video graphics array)** SVGA *m*
► ► **S. monitor** moniteur *m* SVGA

SW [es'dʌb(ə)ljuː] N *Radio (abbr* **short wave)** OC

swab [swɒb] N **1** *(floorcloth)* serpillière *f*, *Naut* vadrouille *f*, *Mil* écouvillon *m* **2** *Med (material)* tampon *m*; *(specimen)* prélèvement *m*; *(smear)* frottis *m*; **s. of cotton wool** tampon d'ouate; **to take a s. of sb's throat** faire un prélèvement dans la gorge de qn
VT (-bb-) **1** *(clean with floorcloth)* nettoyer, essuyer; **to s. the decks** laver le pont **2** = swab down **3** = swab out
► **swab down** VT SEP *(clean) (courtyard)* laver à grande eau; *Naut (deck)* laver
► **swab out** VT SEP *(clean out) Mil (firearm)* écouvillonner; *Med (wound)* nettoyer avec un tampon

swacked [swækt] ADJ *Am Fam (drunk)* bourré

swaddle ['swɒd(ə)l] VT emmailloter **(with, in** de)

swaddling ['swɒdlɪŋ] N
► ► *Arch* **s. clothes** maillots *mpl*, langes *mpl*

swag [swæg] N *Fam (of thief)* butin *m*; *Austr (of tramp)* baluchon *m*

swagger ['swægər] N *(in walk)* démarche *f* balancée et crâneuse; *(carefree manner)* air *m* cavalier *ou* désinvolte; **to walk with a s.** se pavaner
VI **1** *(strut)* when he walks, he swaggers il marche en se pavanant; **to s. (about)** se pavaner; **to s. in/out** entrer/sortir en se pavanant **2** *(boast)* fanfaronner, faire le faraud; **to s. about sth** se vanter de qch
► ► *Mil* **s. cane, s. stick** badine *f*

swaggering ['swægərɪŋ] ADJ *(air)* crâneur
N **1** = swagger **2** *(boasting)* fanfaronnades *fpl*, rodomontades *fpl*

swagman, pl swagmen ['swægmæn, -mən] N *Austr Fam* chemineau *m* *(qui porte son baluchon)*

Swahili [swɑ'hiːlɪ] ADJ souahéli, swahéli, swahili
N **1** *(pl* **Swahili(s))** Souahéli, -ie, Swahéli, -ie, Swahili, -ie, *pl* -i(es) **2** *Ling* souahéli *m*, swahéli *m*, swahili *m*

swain [sweɪn] N **1** *Lit, Arch (rustic)* jeune berger *m* **2** *Old-fashioned, Hum (suitor)* soupirant *m*

SWALK [swɔːlk] N *(abbr* **sealed with a loving kiss)** *(written on envelope)* = scellée d'un tendre baiser

swallow¹ ['swɒləʊ] VT **1** *(food, drink)* avaler; **to s. sth whole** avaler qch tout rond; **to s. one's words** *(speak indistinctly)* avaler ses mots **2** *(believe) (story)* gober, avaler; **to s. the bait** *(of person)* se laisser prendre à l'appât; **I told her a lie and she swallowed it** je lui ai raconté un mensonge et elle l'a gobé *ou* avalé; **her story is hard to s.** son histoire est difficile à avaler **3** *(accept without protest) (insult)* avaler; *(one's anger, pride)* ravaler
VI avaler; **to s. hard** *(when nervous, afraid)* avaler sa salive
N *(act of swallowing)* déglutition *f*, *(mouthful) (of water)* gorgée *f*, **at one s.** d'un seul coup *ou* trait
► **swallow down** VT SEP *(drink, pill)* avaler
► **swallow up** VT SEP *(engulf)* engloutir, engouffrer; *Fig* **they were soon swallowed up by** or **in the mist** ils ont vite été engloutis par le brouillard; **the small country/company was swallowed up** le petit pays/la petite société a été englouti(e)

swallow² N *(bird)* hirondelle *f*, *Prov* **one s. doesn't make a summer** une hirondelle ne fait pas le printemps
► ► *Br Swimming* **s. dive** saut *m* de l'ange

---

swallow-dive VI *Br Swimming* faire le saut de l'ange

swallowtail ['swɒləʊteɪl] N **1** *(forked tail)* queue *f* fourchue **2** *Old-fashioned Fam (coat)* queue-de-morue *f*, *pl* queues-de-morue **3** *(butterfly)* machaon *m*, grand porte-queue *m*, *pl* grands porte-queue(s)
► ► **s. butterfly** machaon, grand porte-queue

swallow-tailed ADJ *(bird)* à queue fourchue
► ► **s. coat** = swallowtail 2

swam PT *see* swim VI, VT

swamp [swɒmp] N marais *m*, marécage *m*
VT *(flood)* inonder; *(field)* submerger; *(boat)* remplir d'eau; *Fam* **to be swamped with sth** *(work, orders, requests)* être submergé *ou* débordé de qch; *(letters, offers of help)* être submergé de qch
► ► *Am* **s. fever** *(malaria)* paludisme *m*, malaria *f*

swampy ['swɒmpɪ] ADJ *(terrain)* marécageux

swan [swɒn] N cygne *m*; **mute s.** cygne commun *ou* muet; **black s.** cygne noir
VI (-nn-) *Fam* **to s. around** se balader, musarder; **he just sort of swans around the office all day** il ne fait que musarder dans le bureau toute la journée; **she came swanning in at a quarter to ten** elle est arrivée les mains dans les poches à dix heures moins le quart; **where's he swanning off to now?** où est-ce qu'il va encore traîner?; **don't think you can come swanning back just when you feel like it** ne crois pas que tu pourras revenir les mains dans les poches quand tu en auras envie
► ► *Am Swimming* **s. dive** saut *m* de l'ange; *Fig* **s. song** chant *m* du cygne

swank [swæŋk] *Fam* N **1** *(ostentation)* épate *f*, **I've had enough of all this s.** j'en ai assez de toute cette esbroufe **2** *(ostentatious person)* frimeur, -euse; *(boastful person)* crâneur, -euse
ADJ *esp Am* = swanky
VI se donner des airs, faire de l'épate

swanky ['swæŋkɪ] ADJ *Fam (person)* prétentieux, poseur; *(restaurant, dinner, hotel)* hyperchic; *(car)* tapageur

swan-necked [-nekt] ADJ *(person)* au cou de cygne

swannery ['swɒnərɪ] N réserve *f* de cygnes

swansdown ['swɒnzdaʊn] N *Tex (cotton fabric)* molleton *m*

swap [swɒp] N *(exchange)* troc *m*, échange *m*; *(object, article)* objet *m* ou article *m* à échanger/qu'on a échangé; *St Exch* swap *m*, échange financier; **to do a s.** faire un troc ou un échange; **it wasn't a very good s.** ce n'était pas un échange très équitable; **it's a good s.** c'est un échange avantageux; **she took my old car as a s. for this one** elle a pris ma vieille voiture en échange de celle-ci; **swaps** *(in stamp collecting etc)* doubles *mpl*
VT (-pp-) **1** **to s. sth for sth** échanger *ou* troquer qch contre *ou* pour qch; **I'll s. you mine for yours** je t'échange le mien contre le tien; *Fam* **(I'll) s. you!** je te l'échange!; **to s. places with sb** changer de place avec qn; **to s. insults/ideas** échanger des insultes/idées; **to s. stories** échanger ses impressions **2** *St Exch* swaper
VI faire du troc; **shall we s.?** si nous faisions un échange?

SWAPO ['swaːpəʊ] N *Pol (abbr* **South-West Africa People's Organization)** SWAPO *f*

sward [swɔːd] N *Lit* gazon *m*, pelouse *f*

swarm [swɔːm] N *(of bees, people, children)* essaim *m*; *(of locusts)* vol *m*; *(of gnats, people)* nuée *f*, *(of small boats)* fourmillement *m*; **there were swarms of tourists** il y avait des nuées de touristes

vI 1 *(of bees)* essaimer; *(of people)* accourir en masse, se presser (**round** autour de; **in** dans); **the crowd swarmed over the pitch** la foule a fait irruption sur *ou* a envahi le terrain **2** *(of place)* fourmiller, grouiller (**with** de)

vT = swarm up

▸ **swarm up vT INSEP** *(climb) (tree, mast)* grimper à; **they all swarmed up the side of the ship** ils grimpèrent comme un seul homme sur les flancs du navire

swarming ['swɔːmɪŋ] **N** *(in beekeeping)* essaimage *m*

swarthiness ['swɔːðɪnɪs] **N** teint *m* basané *ou* bistré

swarthy ['swɔːðɪ] **ADJ** *(complexion)* basané, bistré, *Pej* noiraud

swash [swɒʃ] **N** *(of waves, water)* clapotis *m* **vI** *(of waves, water)* clapoter

swashbuckler ['swɒʃbʌklər] **N** bravache *m*

swashbuckling ['swɒʃbʌklɪŋ] **ADJ** fanfaron; **s. film** *(with musketeers)* film *m* de cape et d'épée; *(with pirates)* film de corsaires; **s. tale** fanfaronnade *f*; **s. hero** héros *m* superbe **N** fanfaronnades *fpl*, rodomontades *fpl*

swashplate ['swɒʃpleɪt] **N** *Aut* plateau *m* oscillant

swastika ['swɒstɪkə] **N** *Antiq* svastika *m*; *(Nazi)* croix *f* gammée

swat [swɒt] **N** *(blow)* tape *f*; **to take a s. at** *(person, dog etc)* donner une tape à; *(insect)* donner un coup de tapette à; **fly s.** *(swatter)* tapette *f* tue-mouches
vT (**-tt-**) taper; *(insect)* écraser

swath [swɔːθ] **N** *Agr* = **swathe¹**

swathe¹ [sweɪð] **N** *Agr* andain *m*; *Fig* **the cannons had cut great swathes through the troops** les canons avaient décimé les troupes

swathe² **vT** emmailloter, envelopper; **head swathed in bandages** tête enveloppée de bandages; **swathed in mist** baigné de brume

sway [sweɪ] **N 1** *(movement)* balancement *m*, oscillation *f*, mouvement *m* de va-et-vient; *Rail (of trucks)* mouvement de lacet
2 *(control, power)* empire *m*, domination *f*; **under her s.** sous son empire, sous son influence; **to have** *ou* **hold s. over a people/country** avoir *ou* tenir un peuple/pays sous sa domination; **emotions that no longer hold any s. over me** des émotions qui n'ont plus aucun empire *ou* aucune emprise sur moi
vI se balancer, osciller; *(of drunkard)* vaciller; *(remain undecided)* rester indécis, hésiter; **to s. in the wind** *(of trees)* se balancer dans le vent; **he swayed back up to the bar** il revint au bar en vacillant; **public opinion is prone to s. this way and that** l'opinion publique oscille souvent d'un côté et de l'autre
vT 1 *(trees)* faire osciller, faire se balancer; **she sways her hips when she walks** elle balance *ou* roule les hanches en marchant
2 *(influence)* **considerations that s. our opinions** considérations qui influencent nos opinions; **to s. sb from his/her course** détourner qn de ses projets; **to refuse to be swayed** refuser de se laisser influencer; **what can we say or do to s. you?** *(convince)* que pouvons-nous dire ou faire pour vous convaincre?; *(make you change your mind)* que pouvons-nous dire ou faire pour vous faire changer d'avis?; **what finally swayed them was ...** ce qui les a finalement décidés a été ...; **it was close but one thing swayed it** *(in vote etc)* la lutte était serrée mais une chose a fait pencher la balance

swaying ['sweɪɪŋ] **ADJ** qui se balance de-ci de-là, qui oscille; **s. motion** balancement *m*, mouvement *m* de va-et-vient

N balancement *m*, oscillation *f*, mouvement *m* de va-et-vient; *(of boat, car)* roulis *m*

Swazi ['swɑːzɪ] **ADJ** souazi
N 1 Souazi, -ie **2** *Ling* le dialecte souazi

Swaziland ['swɑːzɪlænd] **N** Souaziland *m*

swear [sweər] *(pt* **swore** [swɔːr]; *pp* **sworn** [swɔːn]) **vT 1** jurer; *(on oath)* déclarer sous la foi du serment; **to s. an oath** faire un serment, jurer; **to s. sth on the Bible** jurer qch sur la Bible; **to s. to do sth** jurer de faire qch; **I could have sworn I heard a shout** j'aurais juré avoir entendu un cri; **it wasn't me, I s. (it)!** ce n'était pas moi, je le jure!; **to s. allegiance to sb/sth** prêter serment d'allégeance à qn/qch; **to s. revenge** jurer *ou* faire serment de se venger; **to s. sb to secrecy** faire jurer le secret à qn
2 *(utter swearwords)* **'bloody idiot!', she swore** 'espèce d'abruti!', proféra-t-elle
vI 1 *(use swearwords)* jurer, proférer *ou* lâcher un juron/des jurons; **to s. at sb** injurier qn; **to s. like a trooper** jurer comme un charretier
2 *(give one's word)* jurer

▸ **swear by vT INSEP 1** *(invoke)* jurer par; **to s. by one's honour** jurer sur l'honneur; **to s. by all that one holds sacred** jurer sur tout ce qu'on a de plus sacré **2** *(have confidence in)* se fier à; **she swears by him/those vitamin pills** elle ne jure que par lui/par ces vitamines; **it's marvellous stuff, we all s. by it!** c'est merveilleux, nous ne jurons plus que par ça!

▸ **swear in vT SEP** *(jury, witness)* faire prêter serment à

▸ **swear off vT INSEP** *(alcohol etc)* jurer de renoncer à

▸ **swear to vT INSEP** *(on oath)* attester *ou* certifier sous serment; **I s. to it** je l'atteste; **I would s. to it** j'en jurerais, *Fam* j'en mettrais ma main au feu, *Fam* j'en mettrais ma main à couper; **I couldn't** *ou* **wouldn't s. to it** je n'en mettrais pas ma main au feu, je n'en mettrais pas ma tête à couper

swearing ['sweərɪŋ] **N 1** *(use of swearwords)* jurons *mpl*, gros mots *mpl*; **there's too much s. on television** il y a trop de grossièretés à la télévision **2** *Law* **after the s. in of the jury** après que le jury eut prêté serment

swearword ['sweəwɜːd] **N** gros mot *m*, juron *m*

sweat [swet] **N 1** sueur *f*, transpiration *f*; **covered in s.** *(of people, clothes)* couvert *ou* trempé de sueur; **by the s. of one's brow** à la sueur de son front; **the s. was pouring off him** il dégoulinait de sueur; **to be in a s., to be all of a s.** suer, être en nage; *Fig (to be excited)* être tout excité; *Fig* **to be in a s. about sth** avoir des sueurs froides à cause de qch; *Fig* **to work oneself (up) into a s.** se faire du mauvais sang (**about sth** au sujet de qch); **to break into a s.** se mettre à transpirer; **to be in a cold s.** avoir des sueurs froides; *Fam* **it was a real s. getting this piano up the stairs** monter le piano par l'escalier, c'était vraiment tout; *Fam* **no s.** pas de problème; *Mil Old-fashioned* **old s.** vieux troupier *m* **2** *(on wall etc)* suintement *m*
vI suer, transpirer; *(of walls)* suinter; *(of cheese)* suer; *Fig Fam (work hard)* peiner; *Fam (worry)* se faire de la bile, se faire un sang d'encre; **to s. profusely** suer à grosses gouttes; **Johnny was sweating over his homework** Johnny potassait ses devoirs; **I've been sweating over this piece of work for the last three hours** ça fait trois heures que je m'escrime à faire ce travail
vT *(person, horse)* faire suer; *(workers)* exploiter; *Culin (onions)* faire revenir *ou* blondir; *Am Fig Fam (suspect)* cuisiner; *Fam* **to s. blood** suer sang et eau; *Fam* **to s. buckets** être en nage

▸▸ *Anat* **s. duct** conduit *m* sudorifère; **s. gland** glande *f* sudoripare

▸ **sweat off vT SEP** *(lose by exercise) (weight)* perdre en faisant de l'exercice; *(in sauna)* perdre en transpirant

▸ **sweat out vT SEP 1** *(cure) (cold)* chasser *ou* guérir en transpirant **2** *Fam* **to s. it out** *(endure)* prendre son mal en patience, tenir jusqu'au bout **3** *Sl* **to s. one's guts out** s'échiner

sweatband ['swetbænd] **N** *(of hat)* cuir *m* intérieur; *Sport* bandeau *m* en éponge

sweated ['swetɪd] **ADJ**
▸▸ **s. goods** articles *mpl* produits par des ouvriers exploités; **s. labour** *(staff)* main-d'œuvre *f* exploitée; *(work)* exploitation *f*

sweater ['swetər] **N** *(garment)* pullover *m*, pull *m*

sweatiness ['swetɪnɪs] **N** *(of body etc)* moiteur *f*

sweating ['swetɪŋ] **ADJ** *(person)* en sueur; *(hand, body)* moite; *(wall)* suintant
N transpiration *f*; *Med* sudation *f*; *(of wall)* suintement *m*
▸▸ **s. room** *(in Turkish bath)* étuve *f*, salle *f* de sudation

sweatpants ['swetpænts] **NPL** pantalon *m* de survêtement

sweatshirt ['swetʃɜːt] **N** *Sport* sweat-shirt *m*, *pl* sweat-shirts, sweat *m*

sweatshop ['swetʃɒp] **N** atelier *m* clandestin; *Fig Hum* **it's a real s. here** c'est le bagne ici

sweaty ['swetɪ] **ADJ** *(person)* en sueur; *(hands, palms)* moite; *(work)* qui fait transpirer; *(shirt etc)* imprégné de sueur *ou* de transpiration; *(smell)* de sueur, de transpiration; **to get s.** *(of person)* suer, transpirer; **s. afternoon** après-midi d'une chaleur humide; **s. socks** chaussettes puantes (de sueur)

Swede [swiːd] **N** *(person)* Suédois, -oise VOIR GRAMMAIRE A19

swede [swiːd] **N** *(plant)* rutabaga *m*

Sweden ['swiːd(ə)n] **N** Suède *f*

Swedish ['swiːdɪʃ] VOIR GRAMMAIRE A19 **ADJ** suédois
N *Ling* suédois *m*

SWEEP [swiːp] **N 1** *(single stroke of broom, paintbrush, scythe)* coup *m* de balai/de pinceau/de faux; *(cleaning)* balayage *m*; **at one s.** d'un seul coup; **to give a room a good s. (out)** balayer une chambre à fond; **this room could do with a s.** cette chambre a bien besoin d'un coup de balai; *Fig* **to make a clean s.** *(replace staff etc)* faire table rase; *(in gambling)* rafler le tout; **the thieves made a clean s.** les voleurs ont tout enlevé *ou* raflé
2 *(movement) (with arm)* mouvement *m* circulaire; *Mil, Aviat* balayage *m*; **with a wide s. of the arm** d'un geste large; **s. of the eye** regard *m* circulaire
3 *(area covered)* *Mil (of gun)* portée *f*; *(of lighthouse)* balayage *m*, portée; *(of wings)* envergure *f*; *(of knowledge)* étendue *f*
4 *Radio, Electron* **scan(ning) s.** balayage *m*
5 *(rapid flow) (of river)* course *f ou* flot *m* rapide
6 *(curve)* courbe *f*, courbure *f*; *(of river)* boucle *f*; *Archit (of arch)* courbure; **to make a wide s. to take a bend** prendre du champ pour effectuer un virage; **s. of a car's lines** galbe *f* d'une voiture; **a fine s. of grass/of country** une belle étendue de gazon/de pays
7 *(chimney)* **s.** *(person)* ramoneur *m*
8 *Fam (sweepstake)* sweepstake *m*
vT (*pt, pp* **swept** [swept]) balayer; *(room, streets, dust etc)* balayer; *(chimney)* ramoner; *Naut (channel) (for mines)* draguer; **her dress sweeps the ground** sa robe balaie le sol; **a storm swept the town** un orage ravagea la ville; **the deck was swept by a huge wave** une grosse vague balaya le pont; **to s. the**

horizon with a telescope parcourir *ou* balayer l'horizon avec un télescope; **to s. the seas** parcourir les mers; **to s. the board** *(in gambling)* rafler le tout; *Fig* avoir un succès fou; **the latest craze to s. the country** la dernière tocade à envahir le pays; **the most outlandish rumours swept the besieged city** les rumeurs les plus folles parcouraient la ville assiégée; *Fig* **to s. sth under the carpet** enterrer qch; **a wave swept him overboard** une lame s'a entraîné par-dessus bord; **she was swept to power on a wave of nationalism** elle a été propulsée au pouvoir par une vague de nationalisme; **the victorious army swept all before it** l'armée victorieuse a tout balayé sur son passage

vi 1 *(with broom)* balayer

2 *(move rapidly)* avancer avec un mouvement rapide et uni; **she swept into/out of the room** elle est entrée dans/sortie de la salle d'un air majestueux; **to s. round the corner** *(of car)* tourner le coin de la rue en décrivant un large virage; **the plague swept across Europe** la peste a ravagé toute l'Europe; **the beam swept across the sea** le faisceau lumineux balaya la mer; **the rolling prairies s. away into the distance** les prairies ondoyantes se perdent dans le lointain; **the road sweeps round the lake** la route décrit une courbe autour du lac

3 *Naut* **to s. for mines** draguer des mines

▸ ▸ **s. hand** trotteuse *f*

▸ **sweep along** **vi** *(move rapidly)* avancer rapidement

vt sep *(carry forward)* *(of current etc)* entraîner, emporter; **we were swept along by a tide of nationalism** nous avons été balayés par une vague nationaliste

▸ **sweep aside vt sep** *(move aside)* écarter d'un geste large; **to s. aside opposition** écarter l'opposition; **they were swept aside by the crowd** ils ont été repoussés par la foule

▸ **sweep away vt sep** *(snow, clouds)* balayer; *(malpractice, abuse)* supprimer; **the bridge was swept away by the torrent** le pont a été emporté par le torrent

▸ **sweep by vi** *(move past rapidly)* *(of car)* passer à toute vitesse; *(of person)* *(majestically)* passer majestueusement; *(disdainfully)* passer dédaigneusement

▸ **sweep down vt sep** **the current sweeps the logs down with it** le courant emporte *ou* entraîne le bois

vi 1 *(attack)* **the enemy swept down upon us** l'ennemi s'abattit *ou* fonça sur nous

2 *(curve downwards)* **hills sweeping down to the sea** des collines qui descendent vers la mer

▸ **sweep in vi** *(approach, enter rapidly)* **the wind sweeps in** le vent s'engouffre; **she swept in** elle a fait son entrée d'un air majestueux

▸ **sweep off vt sep** *(remove forcefully)* enlever *ou* emporter avec violence; **he swept her off to Paris for the weekend** il l'a emmenée en week-end à Paris; **to be swept off one's feet by sb** être emballé par qn; **to s. sb off his/her feet** enthousiasmer qn; *(in love affair)* faire perdre la tête à qn

▸ **sweep on vi** *(advance rapidly)* *(of flood)* avancer régulièrement; *(continue)* continuer d'avancer (irrésistiblement)

▸ **sweep out vt sep** *(clean)* *(room)* balayer (à fond)

vi *(leave majestically)* **she swept out** elle est sortie d'un air majestueux

▸ **sweep past vi** = **sweep by**

▸ **sweep up vt sep** *(collect by sweeping)* *(dust, leaves etc)* balayer, ramasser; *(sweep into a pile)* ramasser en tas; **with her hair swept up into a chignon** avec ses cheveux relevés en chignon; **she swept up her two babies and left** en toute hâte, elle prit ses

---

deux bébés dans ses bras et partit

vi 1 *(clean up)* balayer

2 *(arrive)* **the car swept up to the door** la voiture a roulé majestueusement jusqu'à la porte

sweepback ['swiːpbæk] **N** *Aviat* (angle *m* de) flèche *f*

sweeper ['swiːpər] **N 1** *(person)* balayeur, -euse; *Ftbl* arrière *m* volant **2** *(machine)* *(for industrial use)* balayeuse *f*; *(for domestic use)* balai *m* (mécanique)

sweeping ['swiːpɪŋ] **ADJ** *(gesture)* large; *(movement)* circulaire; **s. changes** changements *mpl* radicaux; **s. generalization** *or* **statement** généralisation *f* hâtive; *Art* **s. line** ligne *f* allongée *ou* élancée; **low s. lines** *(of car)* lignes basses et allongées; **s. plain** vaste plaine *f*; **s. reform** réforme *f* radicale

N sweepings *(refuse)* balayures *fpl*, ordures *fpl*; *Fig* *(of a country, society)* rebut *m*

▸ ▸ **s. up** balayage *m*, ramassage *m*

sweepingly ['swiːpɪŋlɪ] **ADV** *(too generally)* *(to describe things, criticize etc)* de façon trop générale *ou* hâtive

sweepstake ['swiːpsteɪk] **N** *Horseracing* sweepstake *m*

sweet [swiːt] **ADJ 1** *(in taste)* sucré; **as s. as honey** doux comme le miel; **to taste s.** avoir une saveur douce; **to have a s. tooth** aimer les sucreries

2 *(fragrant)* **to smell s.** avoir une odeur agréable, sentir bon; *(of rose)* embaumer; *Fig* **the s. smell of success** la douceur du succès; *Fig* **it hardly smells very s.** ça ne sent pas très bon

3 **s. breath** haleine *f* fraîche

4 *(sound)* doux, *f* douce, mélodieux; *(flattery)* doux à l'oreille

5 *(pleasant)* agréable; *(smile)* doux, *f* douce; **revenge is s.** douce est la vengeance; *Fam* **to keep sb s.** s'assurer les bonnes grâces de qn; **a s. old lady** une vieille dame charmante; **that's very s. of you** c'est bien gentil à vous; **a s. little dress** une gentille petite robe, une petite robe exquise; **a s. girl** une gentille petite fille; **what a s. kitten!** quel petit chat adorable!; **to say** *or* **whisper s. nothings to sb** *or* **in sb's ear** conter fleurette à qn, dire des mots doux à l'oreille de qn; **s. temper** caractère *m* doux *ou* aimable

6 *Old-fashioned Fam* **to be s. on sb** avoir un béguin pour qn

7 *(intensifier)* **she'll do it in her own s. time** elle le fera quand elle le jugera bon; **it's only going to be of benefit to his own s. self** c'est à sa petite pomme qu'ira tout le bénéfice; **he'll go his own s. way** il fera ce qui lui plaira; *Fam* **you bet your s. life I am!** je pense bien!

8 *(engine)* doux, *f* douce; **s. running** *(of machine)* fonctionnement régulier

N *esp Br* *(piece of confectionery)* bonbon *m*; *(dessert)* dessert *m*; **sweets** *(confectionery)* sucreries *fpl*, confiseries *fpl*, friandises *fpl*; **my s.!** mon chéri!, ma chérie!; **be a s.!** sois un amour!

INT *Br Fam* **s. (as a nut)!** cool!, génial!

▸ ▸ *Bot* **s. cherry** merisier *m*; *Bot* **s. pea** pois *m* de senteur; **s. potato** patate *f* douce; *Br* **s. shop** confiserie *f*; *Culin* **s. and sour sauce** sauce *f* aigre-douce; *Fam* **s. talk** flatteries *fpl*, paroles *fpl* mielleuses; *Bot* **s. violet** violette *f* odorante; *Bot* **s. william** œillet *m* de poète

sweetbread ['swiːtbred] **N** *Culin* veal/lamb **s.** ris *m* de veau/d'agneau

sweetcorn ['swiːtkɔːn] **N** *Culin* maïs *m* doux

sweeten ['swiːt(ə)n] **vt** *(food, drink)* sucrer; *(air)* désodoriser; *(breath)* purifier; *(task)* adoucir, rendre plus agréable; **to s. the pill** dorer la pilule; **to s. sb's temper** adoucir qn; **to s. sb** *(bribe etc)* graisser la patte à qn

---

sweetener ['swiːt(ə)nər] **N 1** *Culin* édulcorant *m*; **artificial s.** édulcorant de synthèse **2** *Fam* *(bribe)* pot-de-vin *m*, *pl* pots-de-vin; **to give sb a s.** graisser la patte à qn, verser un pot-de-vin à qn

sweetening ['swiːt(ə)nɪŋ] **N** *(substance)* édulcorant *m*; **what s. did you use?** avec quoi l'avez-vous sucré?

sweetheart ['swiːthɑːt] **N** amoureux, -euse; **(my) s.!** mon amour!, mon cœur!; **they've been sweethearts since childhood** ils s'aiment depuis leur enfance; **a childhood s.** un amour d'enfance

▸ ▸ *Ind* **s. agreement** = accord *m* entre un employeur et des dirigeants syndicaux dont les termes sont favorables aux deux parties mais pas aux travailleurs concernés

sweetie ['swiːtɪ] **N** *Fam* **1** *Br* *(confectionery)* bonbon *m* **2 s. (pie)** *(term of endearment)* mon (ma) mignon, -onne; **he's such a s.** il est croquignolet; **be a s. and …** sois mignon tu veux et …

sweetish ['swiːtɪʃ] **ADJ** sucré; *(unpleasantly)* douceâtre

sweetly ['swiːtlɪ] **ADV 1** *(to sing)* mélodieusement; **the engine's running s.** le moteur tourne bien; **he kicked the ball s. into the corner of the net** il a mis la balle dans le coin du filet comme à l'entraînement **2** *(pleasantly)* agréablement, gentiment; **to smile s.** sourire gentiment

sweetmeat ['swiːtmiːt] **N** *Old-fashioned, Lit* *(sweet)* bonbon *m*; **sweetmeats** sucreries *fpl*, douceurs *fpl*

sweetness ['swiːtnɪs] **N 1** *(of honey, victory, revenge etc)* douceur *f*; **I prefer the s. of this beer** je préfère cette bière parce qu'elle est plus douce **2** *(of person, gesture etc)* gentillesse *f*, charme *m*; **she's s. itself when you are there** c'est la douceur personnifiée quand tu es là; **now that he's got what he wanted he's all s. and light** maintenant qu'il a eu ce qu'il voulait il est tout miel

sweet-scented, sweet-smelling ADJ *(flower, plant)* odorant, odoriférant; *(room)* parfumé

sweet-talk vt *Fam* baratiner; **to s. sb into doing sth** baratiner qn pour lui faire faire qch; **you can't s. your way around me this time** cette fois, tu ne m'auras pas par la flatterie *ou* ce n'est pas la peine de me baratiner

sweet-tempered ADJ doux, *f* douce, agréable

swell [swel] **N 1** *Naut* houle *f* **2** *(of sound)* augmentation *f*; *Lit* **the majestic s. of the organ** les accents *mpl* majestueux de l'orgue **3** *Mus* *(of organ)* *(device)* soufflet *m* **4** *Old-fashioned Fam* *(well-dressed man)* élégant *m*

ADJ *Am Fam* *(excellent)* épatant; *Iron* **that's just s.!** ça, c'est la meilleure!; **a s. guy** un chic type

VT *(pt* **swelled***; pp* **swollen** ['swəʊl(ə)n], *occ* **swelled)** (r)enfler, gonfler; *Mus* *(note)* enfler; **the river was swollen by the rain** la pluie avait grossi la rivière; **eyes swollen with tears** yeux gonflés de larmes; **all this has helped to s. the ranks of the unemployed** tout cela est venu grossir le nombre de chômeurs; **to s. the number(s)** grossir les effectifs

vi enfler; *(of part of the body)* se tuméfier; *(of wood)* gonfler; *(of number, crowd)* augmenter, grossir; *(of sea)* se soulever; *(of music)* enfler; **her arm is swelling** son bras enfle; **his heart swelled with pride** son cœur se gonflait d'orgueil; **the problem had swollen to massive proportions** le problème avait pris des proportions énormes

▸ ▸ *Mus* **s. box** boîte *f* expressive

▸ **swell out vi** *(be swollen)* être bombé; *(expand)* bomber; **the sails s. out** les voiles se gonflent

▸**swell up** VI (of injured part of body etc) enfler; esp Lit **all swollen up with pride** tout bouffi d'orgueil

swellheaded [swel'hedɪd] ADJ Fam vaniteux, suffisant

swelling ['swelɪŋ] ADJ qui s'enfle ou se gonfle; (sail) gonflé; (numbers) croissant
   N **1** (of number) augmentation f; (of column) renflement m **2** Med (of face) tuméfaction f, gonflement m, enflure f; (on forehead) bosse f, enflure; (growth) tumescence f, tumeur f

swelter ['sweltər] VI étouffer ou être accablé de chaleur

sweltering ['sweltərɪŋ] ADJ (heat) étouffant, accablant; **s. (hot) day** journée f étouffante ou d'une chaleur accablante; **it's s. in here** on étouffe ici

swept PT, PP see **sweep** VT, VI

sweptwing ['sweptwɪŋ] ADJ Aviat (aircraft) à ailes en flèche

swerve [swɜːv] VI (of pedestrian, cyclist, footballer) faire un écart; (of horse) se dérober; (of car) faire un écart ou une embardée; (of ball) décrire une courbe; Fig (from truth etc) s'écarter; **the cyclist was swerving in and out of the traffic** le cycliste zigzaguait entre les voitures; **to s. to avoid sb/sth** (of car, driver) faire une embardée pour éviter qn/qch; Fig **she never swerves from her duty** elle ne s'écarte jamais de son devoir
   VT (ball) dévier; **to s. the car** faire un écart avec la voiture
   N écart m, déviation f; Aut embardée f; Sport **to put a** or **some s. on the ball** faire dévier une balle

swift [swɪft] ADJ **1** (fast) rapide; (reaction etc) prompt; **as s. as an arrow** vif ou rapide comme l'éclair; Lit **s. of foot** rapide à la course; Lit **s. to anger** toujours prêt à s'emporter, irascible **2** Am Fam (clever) malin, -igne; **that was a real s. move** c'était bien joué; **she's not real s.** c'est pas une lumière, elle est pas très maligne
   N (bird) martinet m

swift-flowing ADJ (river) au cours rapide

swift-footed [-'fʊtɪd] ADJ rapide à la course

swiftly ['swɪftlɪ] ADV (to run etc) vite, rapidement; (to react etc) promptement

swiftness ['swɪftnɪs] N (speed) rapidité f, vitesse f; (of reply etc) promptitude f

SWIFT transfer [swɪft] N Fin virement m SWIFT

swig [swɪg] Fam N lampée f; **to take a s. at the bottle** boire un coup à la bouteille; **he took a s. of whisky** il a bu une lampée ou gorgée de whisky; **fancy a s.?** (passing bottle etc) un petit coup?
   VT (-gg-) (beer, lemonade etc) boire à grands traits ou à grands coups
▸**swig down** VT SEP Fam (beer, lemonade etc) boire ou descendre d'un seul trait

swill [swɪl] N **1** (for pigs) pâtée f; Fig Pej **this horrible s.** (food, drink) cette saloperie **2** esp Br (act of rinsing) lavage m à grande eau; **to give sth a s. (out)** laver ou rincer qch à grande eau
   VT **1** Fam (drink) boire avidement **2** esp Br = **swill out**
▸**swill out** VT SEP esp Br (rinse) laver à grande eau; **to s. out a basin** rincer une cuvette à grande eau

swim [swɪm] N **1** (for leisure) baignade f; (for exercise) nage f; **to have** or **take a s.** se baigner; **to go for a s.** (for leisure) aller se baigner; (for exercise) aller nager; **coming for a s.?** (for leisure) tu t'es bien baigné?; **did you enjoy your s.?** (for leisure) tu t'es bien baigné?; (for exercise) tu as bien nagé?; **it was a long s. to the shore** il a fallu nager longtemps pour atteindre le rivage; **I have a big breakfast after my**

morning s. le matin je prends un gros petit-déjeuner après avoir nagé; **that's a long s.!** à la nage cela fait loin! **2** Fig Fam **to be in the s.** (of things) être dans le coup
   VI (pt swam [swæm]; pp swum [swʌm]; prp swimming) (of person, animal) nager; (of fat, scum) (float) surnager, flotter; (of eyes, vision) se brouiller; Sport **to s. for one's country** faire partie de l'équipe nationale de natation; **to s. like a fish** nager comme un poisson; **to s. to the shore** gagner le rivage à la nage; **to s. over** or **across a river** traverser une rivière à la nage; **they swam under the net** ils sont passés sous le filet (en nageant); **let's s. back** rentrons (à la nage); Fig **to s. with the tide** suivre le courant; **to go swimming** (for leisure) aller se baigner; (for exercise) aller nager; **the meat was swimming in gravy** la viande nageait dans la sauce; **eyes swimming with tears** yeux noyés ou baignés de larmes; **to make sb's head s.** faire tourner la tête à qn; **my head is swimming** la tête me tourne, j'ai la tête qui tourne; **everything swam before my eyes** tout semblait tourner autour de moi
   VT (river) traverser ou passer à la nage; **to s. the Channel** traverser la Manche à la nage; **to s. four lengths** nager ou faire quatre longueurs; **to s. the breast stroke** nager la brasse; **she swam one stroke and ...** elle fit une brasse et ...; **to s. a race** faire une course de natation (**with sb** contre qn)
▸▸**s. bladder** vessie f natatoire

swimmer ['swɪmər] N (person) nageur, -euse

swimming ['swɪmɪŋ] N nage f; esp Sp natation f
▸▸Br **s. costume** maillot m de bain; **s. instructor** maître-nageur m, pl maîtres-nageurs; **s. lesson** leçon f de natation; **s. match** concours m de natation; **s. pool** piscine f; **s. trunks** maillot ou slip m de bain

swimmingly ['swɪmɪŋlɪ] ADV Fam au mieux, à merveille; **everything is going s.** tout va comme sur des roulettes

swimsuit ['swɪms(j)uːt] N maillot m de bain

swimwear ['swɪmweər] N maillots mpl de bain

swindle ['swɪnd(ə)l] N escroquerie f, filouterie f, **it's a s.** c'est une escroquerie
   VT escroquer, filouter, Fam rouler; **to s. sb out of sth** escroquer qch à qn; **I'm afraid you've been swindled** j'ai bien peur que tu ne te sois fait rouler

swindler ['swɪndlər] N escroc m, filou m

swine [swaɪn] N (inv in pl) **1** Sl (man) salaud m; (woman) garce f; **(dirty** or **filthy) s.!** sale cochon!; **he's a lazy s.!** c'est une grosse feignasse! **2** Arch, Dial (pig) cochon m, porc m, Arch, Lit pourceau m
▸▸**s. fever** peste f porcine

swineherd ['swaɪnhɜːd] N Old-fashioned, Lit porcher m, gardeur m de cochons

SWING [swɪŋ] N **1** (movement) (of pendulum) oscillation f, balancement m, va-et-vient m inv; (of crank) tour m; Boxing, Golf swing m; Fig **the s. of the pendulum** le mouvement de balancier; **to give a child a s.** (on swing) pousser un enfant (sur une balançoire); Fam **to take a s. at sb** balancer un coup de poing à qn; Golf **he took a huge s. at the ball** il prit un grand élan pour frapper la balle; **s. of a door** ouverture f d'une porte; **to be in full s.** (of party etc) battre son plein; (of organization) être en pleine activité; **when the season is in full s.** quand la saison bat son plein; **he has dramatic mood swings** il a des sautes d'humeur incroyables; Fig **sudden s. of** or **in public opinion** revirement m inattendu de l'opinion publique; Pol **s. to the left** glissement m à gauche ou vers la gauche; Econ **seasonal swings** variations fpl saisonnières

2 (rhythmic movement) mouvement m rythmé; Mus (style of music) swing m; **to walk with a s.** marcher d'un pas rythmé ou d'un pas cadencé; **song that goes with a s.** chanson très rythmée; Fam **everything went with a s.** (of party) tout a baigné; Fam **to get into the s. of things** se mettre au courant ou dans le bain

3 (in playground, hanging from tree etc) balançoire f, Fig Fam **what you gain on the swings, you lose on the roundabouts, it's swings and roundabouts** ce qu'on gagne d'un côté, on le perd de l'autre; Fam **it's a swings and roundabouts situation** c'est une situation où l'on n'a rien à perdre ni à gagner
   VI (pt, pp swung [swʌŋ]) (on child's swing) se balancer; (change direction) changer de direction; Mus swinguer; Old-fashioned Fam (be up to date) être dans le vent; (be going well) (of party) battre son plein; **to s. (to and fro)** se balancer; (of bell) se balancer; (of pendulum) osciller; **shop sign that swings (to and fro) in the wind** enseigne de magasin qui ballotte au vent; Fam **to s. for a crime** être pendu pour un crime; **to s. (on** or **round an axis)** tourner ou pivoter sur un axe; **the door swings on its hinges** la porte tourne sur ses gonds; **to s. open** (of door) s'ouvrir; **to s. to** (of door) se refermer; **to s. (at anchor)** (of ship) éviter (sur l'ancre); Mil **the whole line swung to the left** toute la ligne fit une conversion vers la gauche; **to s. along** (walk) marcher d'un pas balancé; Fam **to s. for sb** (hit out at) essayer d'en coller une à qn; **to s. into the saddle** sauter à cheval ou en selle; **to s. from branch to branch** se balancer d'une branche à une autre; **to s. into action** passer à l'action; Sl **to s. both ways** (be bisexual) marcher à voile et à vapeur
   VT (to and fro) (faire) balancer; (pendulum) faire osciller; (turn) faire tourner; Aviat (propeller) lancer; (hammock) suspendre, pendre, accrocher; Mus (tune etc) interpréter en swing; **to s. one's arms** balancer les bras; **to s. one's hips (in walking)** balancer les hanches; Boxing **to s. a blow** balancer un coup; **to s. oneself into the saddle** sauter à cheval ou en selle; **to s. a child** faire balancer un enfant; Cr **to s. the ball** faire dévier la balle en l'air; **to s. the voting in favour of sb** faire pencher la balance en faveur de qn; Fam **to s. a deal** (bring it off) mener une affaire à bien; Fam **if we get their support I think we can s. it** si on arrive à obtenir leur soutien, je crois qu'on est bon; Fam **to s. it so that ...** (arrange things) arranger les choses de manière (à ce) que ...
▸▸**s. boat** balançoire f (en forme de bateau); **s. bridge** pont m tournant; **s. door** porte f battante; **s. glass, s. mirror** miroir m à bascule; (full length) psyché f; Mus **s. music** swing; Am Fam **s. shift** (work period) = poste m de 16 heures à minuit; (team) = équipe f qui travaille de 16 heures à minuit
▸**swing at** VT INSEP (aim blow at) **to s. at sb** balancer un coup de poing à qn; **he swung wildly at the ball** il a fait un grand mouvement du bras pour atteindre la balle
▸**swing back** VI (of door) se rabattre; (of pendulum, branch) revenir; **public opinion swung back** il y eut un revirement d'opinion
▸**swing out** VI (of car, driver) faire un écart; (from side road) déboucher
▸**swing round** VI (turn around) (of person) se retourner vivement; (of public opinion, person etc) faire volte-face; (of car) virer (brusquement), faire un brusque virage; **the car swung right round** la voiture a fait un tête-à-queue; **this part swings round on this pivot** cette pièce tourne autour de ce pivot; Fig **to s. round behind the party leadership** se rallier à la direction du parti
   VT SEP (turn round suddenly) (car) faire faire un brusque virage à; (dancer) faire tourner;

Fig **to s. sb round** convaincre qn; **to s. a car right round** faire faire un tête-à-queue à une auto

swingeing ['swindʒɪŋ] ADJ *(increase, reduction etc)* énorme; *(attack, criticism)* violent; **s. blow** coup *m* bien envoyé; **s. cuts** compressions *fpl* budgétaires démesurées; **s. damages** forts dommages-intérêts *mpl*; **s. majority** majorité *f* écrasante

swinger ['swɪŋər] N **1** *Old-fashioned Fam* **to be a s.** *(fashionable)* être dans le vent; *(sociable)* être un(e) fêtard, -arde **2** *(promiscuous person)* débauché, -ée; *(who swaps sexual partners)* échangiste *mf*

swinging ['swɪŋɪŋ] ADJ *(to and fro)* balançant; *(mirror)* à bascule; *Old-fashioned Fam (person)* dans le vent; **with s. arms** les bras ballants; **s. blow** coup *m* balancé; **s. door** porte *f* battante; *Old-fashioned Fam* **s. party** réception *f* endiablée; **s. stride** allure *f* rythmée *ou* cadencée *ou* dégagée; **s. tune** air *m* qui swingue
 N *(to and fro)* balancement *m*; *(of pendulum)* oscillation *f*; **s. motion** balancement
 ▸▸ **s. London** = le Londres branché des années soixante; **the s. sixties** les folles années *fpl* soixante

swingometer [swɪŋ'ɒmɪtər] N tableau *m* des estimations *(des résultats des élections)*

swing-wing ADJ *(aircraft)* à géométrie variable

swinish ['swaɪnɪʃ] ADJ *Fam (behaviour)* dégueulasse; **that s. brother of yours** ton dégueulasse de frère

swipe [swaɪp] N *(with fist or stick)* coup *m* de poing/de bâton; *Cr, Golf* coup à toute volée; **I gave myself a s. round the head with it** je me suis donné un coup sur la tête avec; **to take a s. at sb** *(aim blow at)* balancer un coup (de poing) à qn; *Fig (in satire etc)* taper sur qn
 VI **to s. at the ball** *(hit it)* frapper la balle de toutes ses forces; **he swiped at the ball but missed** il a voulu frapper la balle de toutes ses forces mais il a frappé dans le vide
 VT *Fam* **1** *(hit) (person) (with fist or stick)* donner un coup de poing/de bâton à; *Cr, Golf (ball)* frapper de toutes ses forces; **I managed to s. myself in the eye** j'ai réussi à me donner un coup dans l'œil **2** *(steal)* chiper **3** *(pass through credit card reader)* passer au pressographe
 ▸▸ **s. card** badge *m*

swirl [swɜːl] N *(of water)* remous *m*; *(of gases)* tourbillonnement *m*; *(of cream etc)* spirale *f*; **a s. of dust** un tourbillon de poussière; **a s. of skirts** un tournoiement de jupes
 VI tournoyer, tourbillonner
 VT faire tournoyer

swirling ['swɜːlɪŋ] ADJ tourbillonnant, tournoyant

swish¹ [swɪʃ] N **1** *(sound) (of water)* bruissement *m*; *(of dress)* froufrou *m*; *(of curtains being drawn)* frôlement *m*; *(of whip)* sifflement *m*; *(of scythe, tyres)* crissement *m* **2** *(blow with whip)* coup *m* de fouet; **the cow flicked away the flies with a s. of its tail** la vache chassait les mouches avec sa queue
 VI *(of water)* bruire; *(of silk)* froufrouter; *(of whip)* siffler
 VT *(stick, cane)* faire siffler; **to s. its tail** *(of animal)* battre l'air de sa queue

swish² ADJ *esp Br Fam (elegant) (person)* élégant, chic; *(flat, car)* super
 N *Am Offensive Sl (effeminate homosexual)* folle *f*

swishy ['swɪʃɪ] ADJ *Am Offensive Sl (effeminate)* chochotte

Swiss [swɪs] ADJ suisse; **the S. government** le gouvernement helvétique; **S. French**

suisse romand; **S. German** suisse alémanique
 N *(inv in pl)* Suisse *m*, Suissesse *f*
 ▸▸ **S. army knife** couteau *m* suisse; **S. cheese** emmental *m*; **S. cheese plant** monstera *m*; **S. roll** (gâteau *m*) roulé *m*

SWITCH [swɪtʃ]

| N interrupteur **1** • commutateur **1** • revirement **2** • changement **2** • baguette **4** • canne **4** |
| VT changer de **2** • donner un coup de baguette à **4** |
| VI changer |

N **1** interrupteur *m*, *Fam* bouton *m*; *(more than two positions)* commutateur *m*; **two-way s.** va-et-vient *m inv*
 2 *(change) (in policy, opinion)* revirement *m*; *(of resources, emphasis)* changement *m*; **to make a s.** effectuer un changement; **to make the s. from gas to electricity** passer du gaz à l'électricité
 3 *Am Rail (point)* aiguille *f*, *(siding)* voie *f* de raccordement *ou* de garage
 4 *(stick)* baguette *f*, badine *f*, *(for caning pupil)* canne *f*, **(riding) s.** petite cravache *f*
 VT **1** *Elec (current)* commuter
 2 *(change) (places etc)* changer de; *(lever)* changer la position de; *(exchange)* échanger; **to s. the conversation (to something else)** détourner la conversation; **to s. the conversation to money** faire passer la conversation sur le sujet de l'argent; **why do you always have to s. the conversation to ...?** pourquoi faut-il toujours que tu en reviennes à des questions de ...?; **can I s. it for another one?** puis-je l'échanger contre un autre?; **he's been switched to another department** il a été muté dans un autre service
 3 *Am Rail (train)* aiguiller; **to s. a train onto a branch line** aiguiller un train sur un embranchement
 4 *(hit with stick)* donner un coup de baguette à; **to s. its tail** *(of cow)* battre l'air de sa queue
 VI *(change)* **to s. (from gas) to electricity** passer (du gaz) à l'électricité; **I see no reason to s. to another brand** je ne vois vraiment pas pourquoi je changerais de marque; **they switched to another topic when I arrived** ils ont changé de conversation quand je suis arrivé; **she later switched to teaching** par la suite, elle s'est réorientée vers l'enseignement
 ▸▸ **S. card**® = carte *f* de paiement utilisée en Grande-Bretagne; ≃ Carte *f* bleue; **s. gear** appareillage *m* de commutation *ou* de distribution
 ▸ **switch back** VI *(revert to)* **to s. back (from electricity) to gas** repasser de l'électricité au gaz; **we switched back to gas** nous sommes revenus au gaz; **to s. back to BBC2** remettre sur BBC2
 ▸ **switch off** VT SEP *(radio, light, heating etc)* couper, éteindre; *(printer etc)* éteindre; **it switches itself off** ça s'éteint automatiquement; **they switched off the power** ils ont coupé le courant; **s. the light off when you go out!** éteignez la lampe *ou* n'oubliez pas d'éteindre quand vous sortirez!; *Aut* **to s. off the ignition** *or* **the engine** couper le moteur
 VI *(of person) (turn off lights etc)* éteindre; *(of appliance etc)* s'éteindre; **where does it s. off?** où est l'interrupteur?, où est-ce que cela s'éteint?; *Fam* **to s. off (completely)** *(stop listening)* décrocher
 ▸ **switch on** VT SEP *(radio, TV, heating etc)* mettre (en marche); *(light, current)* mettre; *(electricity, printer)* allumer; *Aut* **to s. on the ignition** *or* **the engine** mettre le contact; **to s. on the charm** faire du charme; **to be swit-**

ched on *Fam (be up to date)* être bien au courant de ce qui se passe; *Sl (be under influence of drugs)* être défoncé; *Fam* **they switched me on to new ideas** ils m'ont initié aux idées nouvelles
 VI *(of heating, light, computer, TV)* s'allumer
 ▸ **switch over** VI **1** *Radio, TV* **to s. over (to another station/channel)** changer de station/chaîne; **let's s. over to Channel 4** et si on mettait la 4?
 2 **to s. over to modern languages** *(of student)* réorienter ses études vers les langues vivantes; **we switched over to gas** nous sommes passés au gaz
 ▸ **switch round** VT SEP *(exchange one for the other)* échanger; **someone's switched these photos round** quelqu'un a échangé ces photos; **why don't we s. the desks round?** et si on changeait les bureaux de place?
 VI *(change places)* changer de place; *(in job)* *(alternate)* tourner

switchback ['swɪtʃbæk] N *(road)* route *f* en lacets; *(railway)* voie *f* ferrée en lacets; *(bend)* virage *m* en lacet; *Br (at fair)* montagnes *fpl* russes

switchblade ['swɪtʃbleɪd] N *Am* couteau *m* à cran d'arrêt

switchboard ['swɪtʃbɔːd] N **1** *Tel* central *m* (téléphonique); *(in office)* standard *m* **2** *Elec* tableau *m* (commutateur *ou* de distribution)
 ▸▸ **s. line** ligne *f* principale; **s. operator** standardiste *mf*

switched [swɪtʃt] ADJ
 ▸▸ **s. line** *(in datacomms)* ligne *f* commutée; *Comput* **s. network** réseau *m* commuté

switcher ['swɪtʃər] N *TV* console *f* vidéo, pupitre *m* de mélange vidéo

switchman, *pl* **switchmen** ['swɪtʃmən] N *Am Rail* aiguilleur *m*

Switzerland ['swɪtsələnd] N Suisse *f*, **German(-speaking) S.** la Suisse alémanique; **French(-speaking) S.** la Suisse romande; **Italian(-speaking) S.** la Suisse italienne

swivel ['swɪv(ə)l] N *(device)* pivot *m*
 VI (-ll-, *Am* -l-) pivoter, tourner
 VT faire pivoter
 ▸▸ **s. arm** bras *m* pivotant; **s. base** socle *m* pivotant; **s. chair** siège *m* tournant, chaise *f* pivotante; **s. joint** (joint *m* à) rotule *f*, *Aut* **s. pin** pivot central; **s. seat** siège tournant, chaise pivotante
 ▸ **swivel round** VI *(turn)* pivoter, tourner; **to s. round on one's heels** pivoter sur ses talons
 VT SEP faire pivoter

swivelling, *Am* **swiveling** ADJ *(screen, arm etc)* pivotant, mobile

swiz(z) [swɪz] N *Br Sl* arnaque *f*, **it's a s.!**, **what a s.!** c'est du vol!

swizzle ['swɪz(ə)l] N **1** *Am Fam (cocktail)* cocktail *m* **2** *Br Sl* = swiz(z)
 ▸▸ **s. stick** diablotin *m*

swollen ['swəʊl(ə)n] ADJ enflé, gonflé; *(face)* bouffi; *(stomach)* ballonné; **his arm was very s.** il avait le bras très enflé; **s. glands** ganglions *mpl*; **the river is s.** la rivière est en crue; *Fig Fam* **to suffer from** *or* **to have a s. head** avoir la grosse tête

swollen-headed ADJ *Fam* vaniteux, qui a la grosse tête

swoon [swuːn] *Old-fashioned* N évanouissement *m*, défaillance *f*; **to fall** *or* **go into a s.** s'évanouir, se pâmer
 VI **1** *(faint)* s'évanouir **2** *(in rapture)* se pâmer

swoop [swuːp] N *(of plane)* descente *f* en piqué (**upon** sur); *(of falcon on its prey)* descente; **police s.** *(on nightclub etc)* descente de police; **cocaine found in drugs s.** de la cocaïne découverte à la suite d'une descente de police; *Fam* **at one (fell) s.** d'un seul coup
 VI **the hawk swooped down on its prey** *(dived)* le faucon a plongé sur sa proie;

(caught it) le faucon a fondu sur sa proie; **the gunship swooped down over the village** l'hélicoptère de combat est descendu en piqué sur le village; **the swallows were swooping and whirling** les hirondelles tourbillonnaient; **the police swooped on the nightclub** la police a fait une descente dans la boîte de nuit

swoosh [swuːʃ] N *(of water)* bruissement *m*; *(of wind)* sifflement *m*

VI **the water swooshes round the toilet then ...** l'eau swooshes dans la cuvette des toilettes puis ...; **the waves swooshed over the deck** les vagues déferlaient sur le pont; **you could hear the liquid swooshing around in the tank** on entendait le liquide clapoter dans le réservoir; **the rocket/whip swooshes through the air** la fusée/le fouet siffle dans l'air

VT **he swooshed it down the loo** il l'a fait disparaître dans les toilettes; **she then swooshed it out with clean water** *(rinsed)* elle l'a ensuite rincé à grande eau; **s. the detergent all over the stain** répandre le détergent généreusement sur la tache

swop [swɒp] N, VT& VI = **swap**

sword [sɔːd] N épée *f*, *Arch, Lit* glaive *m*; *Mil, Naut* sabre *m*; **to draw one's s.** tirer son épée, dégainer; **to cross swords with sb** croiser l'épée *ou* le fer avec qn; *Fig (argue)* se disputer avec qn; *(in debate)* se mesurer avec qn; **to put the inhabitants to the s.** passer les habitants au fil de l'épée; *Prov* **those that live by the s. shall die by the s.** ceux qui ont vécu par le fer *ou* par l'épée périront par le fer *ou* par l'épée

▸▸ **s. arm** bras *m* droit; **s. cut** *(blow)* coup *m* de sabre; *(wound)* blessure *f* faite avec le sabre; *(on face)* balafre *f*; **the S. of Damocles** l'épée de Damoclès; **s. dance** danse *f* du sabre; *Lit* **the S. of Justice** le glaive de la Justice; *Cin Fam* **s. and sandals film, s. and sandals movie** péplum *m*

swordbearer [ˈsɔːdbeərər] N *(esp municipal)* officier *m* qui porte le glaive

swordbelt [ˈsɔːdbelt] N ceinturon *m*

swordfight [ˈsɔːdfaɪt] N combat *m* à l'épée

swordfish [ˈsɔːdfɪʃ] N espadon *m*

swordplay [ˈsɔːdpleɪ] N *(technique)* escrime *f* à l'épée; **the very realistic s. in the fight scenes** le réalisme des scènes de combat à l'épée; **verbal s.** joute *f* oratoire

swordsman, *pl* **swordsmen** [ˈsɔːdzmən] N épéiste *m*, tireur *m* d'épée; **good** *or* **fine s.** fine lame *f*, bonne épée *f*

swordsmanship [ˈsɔːdzmənʃɪp] N habileté *f* à l'épée, talents *mpl* d'escrimeur

swordstick [ˈsɔːdstɪk] N canne *f* à épée, canne-épée *f*, *pl* cannes-épées

sword-swallower [-swɒləʊər] N avaleur *m* de sabres

swore PT *see* **swear**

sworn [swɔːn] ADJ ATTRIB *(declaration)* sous serment; *(witness)* qui a prêté serment; **s. enemies** ennemis *mpl* jurés
PP *see* **swear**

SWOT [swɒt] N *Mktg (abbr* **strengths, weaknesses, opportunities, threats**) forces, faiblesses, opportunités et menaces *fpl*

▸▸ **S. analysis** analyse *f* des forces, faiblesses, opportunités et menaces

swot [swɒt] *Br Sch Fam* N *(person)* bûcheur, -euse, bosseur, -euse, *Pej* bachoteur, -euse

VI (**-tt-**) bûcher, bosser, *Pej* bachoter

▸ **swot up** *Br Sch Fam* VT SEP *(maths etc)* potasser, bûcher

VI = **swot** VI

▸ **swot up on** VT INSEP *Br Sch Fam (maths etc)* potasser, bûcher

swotting [ˈswɒtɪŋ] N *Br Sch Fam Pej* bacho-

tage *m*; **I'd better do some s.** je ferais mieux de bûcher

swum PP *see* **swim** VI, VT

swung PT, PP *see* **swing** VI, VT

▸▸ *Typ* **s. dash** tilde *m*

sybarite [ˈsɪbəraɪt] ADJ, N sybarite *mf*

sybaritic [sɪbəˈrɪtɪk] ADJ sybaritique, sybarite

sycamore [ˈsɪkəmɔːr] N *(maple)* sycomore *m*, faux platane *m*; *Am (plane tree)* platane *m*

sycophancy [ˈsɪkəfənsɪ] N *Fml* flagornerie *f*

sycophant [ˈsɪkəfənt] N *Fml* flagorneur, -euse

sycophantic [sɪkəˈfæntɪk] ADJ *Fml* flagorneur

syllabic [sɪˈlæbɪk] ADJ syllabique

syllabification [sɪlæbɪfɪˈkeɪʃən] N syllabation *f*

syllabify [sɪˈlæbɪfaɪ] VT *(word)* découper en syllabes

syllable [ˈsɪləb(ə)l] N syllabe *f*; **short s.** *(in prosody)* brève *f*; **long s.** *(in prosody)* longue *f*, *Fig* **to explain sth in words of one s.** expliquer qch en termes très simples

syllabub [ˈsɪləbʌb] N *Culin* sabayon *m*

syllabus, *pl* **syllabi, syllabuses** [ˈsɪləbəs, -aɪ, -əsɪz] N *Sch, Univ (of course)* programme *m*; **on the s.** au programme; **to take a subject off the s.** enlever une matière du programme

▸▸ **s. design** conception *f* de programme

syllogism [ˈsɪlədʒɪz(ə)m] N *(in logic)* syllogisme *m*

syllogistic [sɪləˈdʒɪstɪk] ADJ *(in logic)* syllogistique

sylph [sɪlf] N **1** *Myth* sylphe *m*, sylphide *f* **2** *Lit (slim woman)* sylphide *f*, *Fam* **she's no s.** elle n'a rien d'une sylphide

sylph-like ADJ *(waist etc)* de sylphide; *(woman)* à la taille de sylphide

sylvan [ˈsɪlvən] ADJ *Lit* sylvestre

symbiosis, *pl* **symbioses** [sɪmb(a)ɪˈəʊsɪs, -siːz] N *Biol, Fig* symbiose *f*

symbiotic [sɪmb(a)ɪˈɒtɪk] ADJ *Biol, Fig* symbiotique

symbol [ˈsɪmb(ə)l] N symbole *m* (**of, for** de); *Am* **road symbols** pictogrammes routiers

VT *Am* = **symbolize**

symbolic [sɪmˈbɒlɪk] ADJ symbolique

▸▸ **s. logic** logique *f* symbolique

symbolically [sɪmˈbɒlɪklɪ] ADV symboliquement

symbolism [ˈsɪmbəlɪz(ə)m] N symbolisme *m*

symbolist [ˈsɪmbəlɪst] ADJ, N symboliste *mf*

symbolization [sɪmbəlaɪˈzeɪʃən] N symbolisation *f*

symbolize [ˈsɪmbəlaɪz] VT symboliser

symmetrical [sɪˈmetrɪk(ə)l] ADJ symétrique

symmetrically [sɪˈmetrɪklɪ] ADV symétriquement

symmetry [ˈsɪmɪtrɪ] N symétrie *f*

sympathetic [sɪmpəˈθetɪk] ADJ **1** *(kind, understanding)* *(person)* compréhensif, -ive; *(stronger)* compatissant; *(letter)* de sympathie, qui marque la sympathie; *(look, smile)* de sympathie; **he's always very s.** il est toujours prêt à vous écouter; **I didn't find him very s. (about it)** je ne l'ai pas trouvé très compréhensif; **you could try to be more s. (towards her)** tu pourrais essayer de te montrer plus compréhensif (envers elle); **to be s. to a proposal** être bien disposé à l'égard d'une proposition; **s. audience** auditoire *m* bien disposé; **her novel got a very s. reception** son roman a été très bien accueil-

li **2** *(pain)* sympathique; *Phys (vibration)* due à la résonance

▸▸ *Mus* **s. string** corde *f* qui vibre par résonance

Note that the French word **sympathique** is a false friend and is never a translation for the English word **sympathetic**. It means **kind, friendly**.

sympathetically [sɪmpəˈθetɪklɪ] ADV **1** *(showing understanding)* avec bienveillance; *(showing pity)* avec compassion; **the new play was s. received** la nouvelle pièce a été bien accueillie **2** *Med* par sympathie; *Phys (to vibrate)* par résonance

sympathize [ˈsɪmpəθaɪz] VI **1** *(show sympathy)* compatir; *(have understanding)* comprendre; **I s. because I used to have similar problems** je compatis car j'ai connu des problèmes du même genre; **I s. with your point of view but ...** je comprends votre point de vue mais ...; **I do s.** *(feel pity etc)* je compatis; *(feel understanding)* je (vous) comprends très bien **2** *(agree)* **those who s. with Professor Smith in his view that ...** ceux qui s'associent au Professeur Smith pour dire que ...; **to s. with a cause** avoir des sympathies pour une cause

Note that the French verb **sympathiser avec** is a false friend and is almost never a translation for the English verb **to sympathize with**. It means **to be friendly with**.

sympathizer [ˈsɪmpəθaɪzər] N **1** *(person in agreement)* sympathisant, -ante (**with a cause** d'une cause); **a rebel/an IRA s.** un sympathisant des rebelles/de l'IRA **2** *(person who shows sympathy, understanding)* **to be a s. in sb's grief** compatir au chagrin de qn; **we have received many letters from sympathizers** nous avons reçu de nombreuses lettres de personnes qui voulaient nous témoigner leur sympathie

sympathy [ˈsɪmpəθɪ] N **1** *(compassion)* compassion *f*; **to have s. for sb** éprouver de la compassion pour qn; **to show s. to sb** faire preuve de compassion envers qn; **you have my deepest s.** *Fml (on bereavement etc)* je vous présente toutes mes condoléances; *Hum (on your new girlfriend etc)* je te souhaite bien du plaisir; **a letter of s.** une lettre de condoléances; **we'd all like to express our s. on this tragic loss** nous aimerions tous vous exprimer nos condoléances à la suite de cette perte tragique; **our sympathies are with the families of the dead** nous compatissons avec les familles des victimes; **I don't need s., I need help** ce n'est pas de compassion dont j'ai besoin, c'est d'une aide; **if you do catch a cold, don't expect any s. from me!** si tu attrapes un rhume, ne compte pas sur moi pour te plaindre!

2 *(understanding, support etc)* sympathie *f* (**for** pour); **popular sympathies are on his side** il a l'opinion pour lui; **to view a proposal with s.** regarder une proposition d'un bon œil; **to be in s. with sb's ideas** partager les idées de qn; **my s. is** *or* **my sympathies are with the opposition** ma sympathie va à l'opposition; **she was accused of having communist/federalist sympathies** on l'accusait d'avoir des sympathies pour les communistes/les fédéralistes; **to strike** *or* **come out (on strike) in s.** se mettre en grève de solidarité (**with** avec); **prices went up in s.** les prix sont montés par contrecoup; *Phys* **string that vibrates in s.** corde qui vibre par résonance; *Physiol* **the temperature of the other hand falls in s.** la température de l'autre main tombe par réaction

▸▸ **s. strike** grève *f* de solidarité

Note that the French word **sympathie** is a false friend and is rarely a translation for the English noun **sympathy**. It is usually used to convey the idea of liking somebody.

symphonic [sɪm'fɒnɪk] ADJ *Mus* symphonique

symphony ['sɪmfənɪ] N *Mus* **1** *(composition), Fig* symphonie f **2** *Am (orchestra)* orchestre m symphonique
▸▸ **s. concert** concert m symphonique; **s. orchestra** orchestre m symphonique

symposium, pl **symposia, symposiums** [sɪm'pəʊzɪəm, -ɪə, -ɪəmz] N symposium m; *(collection)* recueil m d'articles *(de spécialistes)*

symptom ['sɪm(p)təm] N *Med, Fig* symptôme m; **to show all the symptoms of …** présenter tous les symptômes de …

symptomatic [sɪm(p)tə'mætɪk] ADJ symptomatique (**of** de)

synagogue ['sɪnəgɒg] N synagogue f

synapse ['sɪnæps] N synapse f

sync [sɪŋk] N *(abbr* **synchronization)** **in s.** *(of film etc)* synchronisé; **out of s.** *(of film etc)* mal synchronisé; **the engine is a bit out of s.** le moteur ne tourne pas très rond; **to be in s. with the times** être en harmonie avec son temps; **to be out of s. with the times** être déphasé; **he's somehow out of s. with the others** *(not in tune, not thinking the same way etc)* il est un peu décalé *ou* déphasé par rapport aux autres; **her ideas are out of s. with …** ses idées sont en décalage par rapport à …; **the translation is out of s.** il y a un décalage dans cette traduction

synchromarketing [sɪŋkrəʊ'mɑːkɪtɪŋ] N synchromarketing m

synchromesh ['sɪŋkrəʊmeʃ] N *Aut* synchronisation f, synchronisateur m, synchro m; **s. on all gears** boîte de vitesses avec rapports synchronisés
▸▸ **s. gearbox** boîte f de vitesses à synchroniseur

synchronic [sɪŋ'krɒnɪk] ADJ *(synchronous)* synchrone; *Ling (descriptive)* synchronique

synchronism ['sɪŋkrənɪz(ə)m] N synchronisme m

synchronization [sɪŋkrənaɪ'zeɪʃən] N synchronisation f

synchronize ['sɪŋkrənaɪz] VT *(watches, actions, movements, events)* synchroniser (**sth with sth** qch avec qch); *Elec (generators)* coupler en phase
VI *(of events)* arriver *ou* avoir lieu simultanément; **we'll try to s. with you** nous essaierons de nous synchroniser avec vous

synchronized ['sɪŋkrənaɪzd] ADJ synchronisé
▸▸ **s. generators** générateurs mpl synchronisés *ou* en phase; **s. sound** son m synchrone; **s. swimming** natation f synchronisée

synchronizer ['sɪŋkrənaɪzər] N *Elec, Comput* synchronisateur m

synchronizing generator ['sɪŋkrənaɪzɪŋ] N *TV etc* générateur m de synchro

synchronous ['sɪŋkrənəs] ADJ synchrone (**with** de)

syncline ['sɪŋklaɪn] N *Geol* synclinal m

syncopate ['sɪŋkəpeɪt] VT syncoper; **syncopated music** musique f syncopée; **syncopated rhythm** rythme m syncopé

syncopation [sɪŋkə'peɪʃən] N *Mus* syncope f

syncope ['sɪŋkəpɪ] N *Med, Gram* syncope f

syncretic [sɪŋ'kretɪk] ADJ syncrétique

syncretism ['sɪŋkrətɪz(ə)m] N syncrétisme m

syndic ['sɪndɪk] N syndic m

syndicalism ['sɪndɪkəlɪz(ə)m] N syndicalisme m

syndicalist ['sɪndɪkəlɪst] N, ADJ syndicaliste mf

syndicate¹ ['sɪndɪkət] N **1** *Com, Fin* syndicat m; *Am (criminal organization)* association f de malfaiteurs; *Am (news agency)* agence f de presse; *Am (chain of newspapers)* chaîne f de journaux; **member of a s., s. member** syndicaliste mf **2** *(board of syndics)* conseil m de syndics

syndicate² ['sɪndɪkeɪt] VT *Journ (article)* publier simultanément dans plusieurs journaux; *Radio* vendre à plusieurs stations; *TV* vendre à plusieurs chaînes; **the photograph was syndicated in all the local newspapers** la photographie a été publiée dans toute la presse régionale; *Fin* **syndicated loan** prêt m en participation

syndication [sɪndɪ'keɪʃən] N *Journ (of article)* publication f simultanée dans plusieurs journaux; *Radio* diffusion f simultanée sur plusieurs stations; *TV* diffusion simultanée sur plusieurs chaînes
▸▸ **s. agency** agence f de presse

syndrome ['sɪndrəʊm] N *Med, Fig* syndrome m

synectics [sɪ'nektɪks] N synectique f VOIR GRAMMAIRE A10

synergism ['sɪnədʒɪz(ə)m] N synergisme m

synergy ['sɪnədʒɪ] N synergie f

synod ['sɪnəd] N **1** *Rel* synode m; **the General S.** = le conseil d'administration de l'Église anglicane **2** *(council)* assemblée f, convention f

synonym ['sɪnənɪm] N synonyme m

synonymous [sɪ'nɒnɪməs] ADJ synonyme (**with** de); **their name is s. with quality** leur nom est synonyme de qualité

synonymously [sɪ'nɒnɪməslɪ] ADV *(to use a word)* comme synonyme (**with** de); **these two words can be used s.** ces deux mots peuvent être employés comme synonymes

synonymy [sɪ'nɒnɪmɪ] N synonymie f

synopsis, pl **synopses** [sɪ'nɒpsɪs, -psiːz] N résumé m; *(of science, film)* synopsis m

synoptic [sɪ'nɒptɪk] ADJ synoptique

synovia [sɪ'nəʊvɪə, saɪ-] N *Physiol, Anat* synovie f

synovial [sɪ'nəʊvɪəl] ADJ
▸▸ *Med* **s. fluid** liquide m synovial; **s. membrane** membrane f synoviale

syntactic(al) [sɪn'tæktɪk, -ɪk(ə)l] ADJ *Gram, Comput* syntaxique, syntactique

syntax ['sɪntæks] N *Gram, Comput* syntaxe f
▸▸ *Comput* **s. error** erreur f de syntaxe

synthesis, pl **syntheses** ['sɪnθɪsɪs, -iːz] N synthèse f

synthesize ['sɪnθəsaɪz] VT *(elements)* synthétiser; *(product)* faire la synthèse de

synthesizer ['sɪnθəsaɪzər] N synthétiseur m

synthetic [sɪn'θetɪk] ADJ *(product, fibre etc)* synthétique; *Fam* **s. smile** sourire m artificiel *ou* factice
N **synthetics** matières fpl synthétiques
VOIR GRAMMAIRE A10

synthetically [sɪn'θetɪklɪ] ADV synthétiquement

syph [sɪf] N *Fam* = **syphilis**

syphilis ['sɪfɪlɪs] N *Med* syphilis f

syphilitic [sɪfɪ'lɪtɪk] ADJ, N *Med* syphilitique mf

syphon ['saɪf(ə)n] N, VT = **siphon**

Syria ['sɪrɪə] N Syrie f

Syrian ['sɪrɪən] ADJ syrien
N Syrien, -ienne

syringe ['sɪrɪndʒ, sɪ'rɪndʒ] N seringue f
VT *(wound etc)* seringuer; **to s. (out) the ears** laver les oreilles avec une seringue

syrup ['sɪrəp] N **1** *(sweet liquid)* sirop m; **rosehip/maple s.** sirop d'hibiscus/d'érable; *Pharm* **cough s.** sirop pectoral, sirop pour *ou* contre la toux **2** *(Br golden)* **s.** mélasse f raffinée **3** *(sentimentality)* douceur f affectée **4** *Br Fam (wig)* moumoute f

syrupy ['sɪrəpɪ] ADJ sirupeux; *Fig (tone)* mielleux, doucereux; **s. music/prose** musique/prose f à l'eau de rose

SYSADMIN [sɪs'ædmɪn] N *Comput (abbr* **Systems Administrator)** administrateur m du système

SYSOP ['sɪsɒp] N *Comput (abbr* **Systems Operator)** sysop m, opérateur m système

system ['sɪstəm] N **1** *(structure, organization)* système m; **the feudal s.** le régime féodal; **the s.** *(established order)* l'ordre m établi, le système; **you can't beat the s.** on ne peut rien contre le système; *Astron* **the solar s.** le système solaire; *Anat* **nervous/muscular s.** système nerveux/musculaire; **the digestive s.** l'appareil m digestif; **bad for the s.** mauvais pour l'organisme; **it's a bit of a shock to the s.** ça fait un choc; *Fam* **to get sth out of one's s.** se libérer de qch; *Fam* **to get sb out of one's s.** *(after romance)* se sortir qn de la tête
2 *(network) (railway, telephone etc)* réseau m; **road/river s.** réseau routier/fluvial; **s. of pulleys** système m de poulies; **central heating s.** installation f de chauffage central
3 *Comput* **the XYZ is an excellent s.** le XYZ est un excellent ordinateur; **operating s.** système m d'exploitation; **to return to s.** retourner *ou* revenir au système
4 *Comput* **systems analyse** f fonctionnelle
5 *(method)* système m; *(methodicalness)* méthode f, **to lack s.** manquer de méthode *ou* d'organisation
▸▸ *Comput* **systems analysis** analyse des systèmes; **systems analyst** analyste-programmeur m, pl analystes-programmeurs, analyste-programmeuse f, pl analystes-programmeuses; **systems board** carte f système; **s. bus** bus m système; **s. crash** panne f du système; **s. disk** disque f du système; **systems engineer** ingénieur m système; **s. error** erreur f système; **s. failure** panne du système; **s. file** fichier m système; **s. folder** dossier m système; **systems management** direction f systématisée; **s. manufacturer** fabricant m d'ordinateurs; **s. privilege** privilège m d'accès au système; **s. program** programme m système; **s. prompt** invite f du système, message m d'attente du système; **s. software** logiciel m d'exploitation, logiciel système; **s. unit** unité f système

systematic [sɪstə'mætɪk] ADJ systématique, méthodique; **the s. destruction of the forest** la destruction systématique de la forêt; **she's very s.** elle a de l'ordre *ou* de la méthode

systematically [sɪstə'mætɪklɪ] ADV systématiquement, avec méthode; *(to destroy etc)* systématiquement

systematization [sɪstəmətaɪ'zeɪʃən] N systématisation f

systematize ['sɪstəmətaɪz] VT systématiser

systemic [sɪs'tiːmɪk] ADJ *(insecticide), Ling* systémique

systemization [sɪstəmaɪ'zeɪʃən] N = **systematization**

systemize ['sɪstəmaɪz] VT = **systematize**

systole ['sɪstəlɪ] N *Med* systole f

T, t [tiː] N (letter) T, t m; **to cross one's t's** barrer ses t; **to a T** à la perfection; **she has the accent off to a T** (of actress etc) elle maîtrise l'accent à perfection, elle maîtrise parfaitement l'accent; **that's you to a T** c'est tout à fait toi; **my job suits me to a T** mon travail me convient à merveille

TA [tiː'eɪ] N **1** Br Mil (abbr **Territorial Army**) = force f armée constituée de réservistes volontaires **2** Am Univ (abbr **teaching assistant**) = étudiant, -ante de deuxième cycle qui assure quelques heures de cours en échange d'une bourse d'étude

ta [tɑː] N, INT Br Fam merci m

TAB [tæb] N Med (abbr **typhoid-paratyphoid A and B**) (vaccin m) TAB m; **he has had a T. injection** on lui a fait le TAB

tab [tæb] N **1** (on garment) (maker's name tab) griffe f, (owner's name tab) étiquette f, (on boot) tirant m; (on file) onglet m; (for file, removable) cavalier m; (on can) languette f; (on lace) ferret m; Fig **to keep tabs on sb/ sth** avoir qn/qch à l'œil, ne pas perdre qn/ qch de vue; **to keep tabs on expenses** contrôler les dépenses; **to keep tabs on sb's movements** surveiller les moindres mouvements de qn
2 (loop) (for hanging) attache f, patte f
3 esp Am (bill) (in restaurant) addition f, (in hotel) note f, Fam **to pick up the t.** (for meal, accommodation) régler l'addition ou la note; (for government programme, research etc) payer; (for damage done by others) casquer
4 (on typewriter, word processor etc) (position) colonne f, (in text, figures), Comput tabulation f, (key) tabulateur m, touche f de tabulation; **to set tabs** régler ou positionner les tabulateurs (at à)
5 Sl (of LSD) buvard m
6 Br Sl (cigarette) clope f
VT (text) mettre en colonnes (avec des tabulations); (figures) disposer en colonne(s)
▸▸ **t. key** tabulateur, touche de tabulation; **t. points** points mpl de tabulation; **t. setting** (act) pose f de tabulations; (result) tabulations fpl; **t. stop** taquet m de tabulation

tabard ['tæbəd] N (garment) tabar(d) m

Tabasco® [tə'bæskəʊ] N Tabasco® m

tabbing ['tæbɪŋ] N Comput (act) pose f de tabulations; (result) tabulations fpl

tabbouleh [tæ'buːleɪ] N taboulé m

tabby ['tæbɪ] N chat m tigré ou moucheté
▸▸ **t. cat** chat tigré ou moucheté

tab-delimited ADJ Comput délimité par des tabulations

tabernacle ['tæbənæk(ə)l] N Rel **1** (receptacle) tabernacle m **2** (place of worship) temple m

table ['teɪb(ə)l] N **1** (piece of furniture) table f; (small and round) guéridon m; **card** or **gaming t.** table de jeu; **changing/ironing t.** table à langer/repasser; **nest of tables** table

gigogne; **to set** or Br **lay the t.** mettre ou dresser la table ou le couvert; **to sit down to (the) t.** se mettre à table; **to be at (the) t.** être attablé ou à table; **to be (sitting) at the breakfast/dinner t.** être à table pour le petit déjeuner/(le) dîner; **to leave the t.** se lever ou sortir de table, quitter la table; **he has awful t. manners** il se tient très mal à table; **mind your t. manners!** tiens-toi bien à table!; Fam **to drink sb under the t.** mieux tenir l'alcool que qn; **he drank us under the t.** il était encore debout alors que nous roulions sous la table; **I could drink you under the t. any day!** je te parie que je peux boire plus que toi!; **two drinks and I'm under the t.** deux verres et je suis complètement paf!; Parl **to lay a bill on the t.** Br, Can (submit) déposer un projet de loi; Am (suspend) ajourner la discussion d'un projet de loi; Fig **to give sb money under the t.** donner un dessous de table ou un pot-de-vin à qn; Fig **to get back to the negotiating t.** reprendre les pourparlers; Fig **management has nothing new to put on the t.** la direction n'a rien de nouveau à proposer; Fig **the offer is still on the t.** la proposition tient toujours; Fig **to turn the tables on sb** retourner la situation, renverser les rôles; Fig **the tables have been turned** les rôles sont renversés; **high** or Fam **top t.** (at banquet etc) table d'honneur; Rel **the Lord's T., the communion t.** la sainte table
2 (group of diners) table f, tablée f, **she kept the entire t. amused** elle a distrait tout le monde à table; Am **to wait (on) t.** travailler comme serveur/serveuse; Am **I'm not going to wait t. all my life** je ne vais pas être serveur/serveuse toute ma vie
3 (food) table f, **she keeps a good t.** on mange bien chez elle; **the restaurant has a hot and cold t.** le restaurant propose des plats chauds et des plats froids
4 (list) (of facts, figures etc) table f, tableau m; (of fares) liste f; Math **twelve times t.** table de (multiplication par) douze; Sport (league) **t.** classement m; **where is the team in the (league) t.?** quel est le classement de l'équipe?; Chem **periodic t.** (of the elements) tableau de la classification périodique; Naut **tide t.** annuaire m ou indicateur m des marées
5 Geog (plateau) plateau m
6 (slab) (of stone) plaque f, tablette f; Rel **the Tables of the Law** les Tables fpl de la Loi
7 Mus (sounding board) table f d'harmonie
VT **1** Br, Can Parl (submit) (proposal, resolution) présenter; (bill) déposer; (amendment) proposer; **to t. a motion of confidence** poser la question de confiance **2** Am (suspend) (proposal, resolution, bill) ajourner la discussion de; (enquiry) ajourner
▸▸ Geog **T. Bay** la baie de la Table; **t. centre** décor m de table; **t. of contents** table des matières; **t. dancing** table dancing m, danse f aux tables; **t. d'hôte** ['tɑːbl'dəʊt] menu m; **t. d'hôte dinner** dîner m à prix fixe; **t. knife**

couteau m de table; **t. lamp** petite lampe f, **t. leg** pied m de table; **t. linen** linge m de table; Comput **t. look-up** consultation f de table; **t. mat** set m de table; Geog **T. Mountain** la montagne de la Table; **t. napkin** serviette f de table; **t. runner** chemin m de table; **t. salt** sel m de table, sel fin; **t. service** service m à table; **t. talk** menus propos mpl, propos légers; **t. tennis** tennis m de table, ping-pong m; **t.-tennis ball** balle f de ping-pong; **t.-tennis bat** raquette f de ping-pong; **t.-tennis player** joueur, -euse de ping-pong, pongiste mf; **t. top** dessus m de table; **t. wine** vin m de table

tableau, pl **tableaux, tableaus** ['tæbləʊ, -əʊz] N Theat tableau m
▸▸ **t. vivant** tableau vivant

tablecloth ['teɪb(ə)lklɒθ] N nappe f

table-hop VI = aller de table en table dans un restaurant ou une réception, pour montrer qu'on a des relations

tableland ['teɪb(ə)llænd] N Geog plateau m

table-rapping [-ræpɪŋ] N (in spiritualism) coups mpl frappés sur un guéridon

tablespoon ['teɪb(ə)lspuːn] N **1** (utensil) cuiller f ou cuillère f à soupe **2** (quantity) cuillerée f à soupe (of de)

tablespoonful ['teɪb(ə)lspuːnfʊl] N cuillerée f à soupe (of de)

tablet ['tæblɪt] N **1** (pill) (for swallowing) comprimé m, cachet m; (for sucking) pastille f (slab) (of clay, slate etc) tablette f, (inscribed stone) plaque f commémorative **3** (bar) (of soap) pain m **4** Scot (sweet) fondant m au caramel

tableware ['teɪb(ə)lweər] N vaisselle f

tabloid ['tæblɔɪd] N (format) tabloïd m; **the tabloids** les tabloïds; Pej (popular press) la presse populaire à scandales ou à sensation
ADJ **t., in t. form** (news etc) en condensé ou raccourci
▸▸ **t. format** format m tabloïd; **the t. press** la presse petit format; Pej (popular press) la presse populaire à scandales ou à sensation; **t. television, t. TV** émissions fpl à sensation

---

Tabloids
Dans les pays anglo-saxons, le format tabloïde est caractéristique des journaux populaires. En Grande-Bretagne, les plus connus sont le 'Sun', le 'Daily Mirror', le 'Daily Mail' et le 'Daily Express'. Ces journaux sont très influents en Grande-Bretagne – le 'Sun' affiche ainsi les plus grands tirages de la presse britannique. Les "tabloids" privilégient tout particulièrement les histoires à scandale et à sensation, ce qui a suscité un débat sur le code de conduite de la presse et sur la législation à mettre en place pour protéger la vie privée.

tabloidese [tæblɔɪ'diːz] **N** style *m* de la presse tabloïde

taboo, tabu [tə'buː] *Rel, Fig* **N** tabou *m*, *pl* -ous; **there is a t. on the subject/place** le sujet/l'endroit est tabou
  ADJ *(subject, place etc)* tabou *(often inv in pl)*; **to declare sth t.** déclarer qch tabou; **these subjects are t.** ces sujets sont tabou(s)
  VT *(something)* interdire, déclarer tabou; *(somebody)* déclarer tabou

tabular ['tæbjʊlər] **ADJ** *(information, statistics)* tabulaire, disposé en table(s) *ou* tableau(x); **in t. form** *(information, statistics etc)* sous forme de table(s) *ou* tableau(x)
  ▸▸t. ledger grand livre *m* (à colonnes)

tabulate ['tæbjʊleɪt] **VT** *(arrange in table) (figures, facts)* présenter sous forme de table(s) *ou* de tableau(x); *(on word processor etc) (figures etc)* mettre en colonnes; **to t. data** classer des données

tabulation [tæbjʊ'leɪʃən] **N** *(of figures etc)* présentation *f* sous forme de table(s) *ou* tableau(x); *(on typewriter)* mise *f* en colonnes

tabulator ['tæbjʊleɪtər] **N 1** *(on typewriter, word processor etc)* tabulateur *m* **2** *(machine)* tabulatrice *f*
  ▸▸t. key touche *f* de tabulation

tacheometer [tækɪ'ɒmɪtər] **N** tachéomètre *m*

tachistoscope [tə'kɪstəskəʊp] **N** tachistoscope *m*

tachograph ['tækəʊɡræf] **N** *Aut* tachygraphe *m*

tachometer [tæ'kɒmɪtər] **N** *Aut* tachymètre *m*, compte-tours *m inv*

tachycardia [tækɪ'kɑːdɪə] **N** *Med* tachycardie *f*

tachycardiac [tækɪ'kɑːdɪæk] **ADJ** *Med* tachycardique

tachymeter [tæ'kɪmɪtər] **N** tachéomètre *m*

tacit ['tæsɪt] **ADJ** *(admission, consent)* tacite

tacitly ['tæsɪtlɪ] **ADV** *(to admit, consent)* tacitement

taciturn ['tæsɪtɜːn] **ADJ** taciturne

taciturnity [tæsɪ'tɜːnɪtɪ] **N** taciturnité *f*

Tacitus ['tæsɪtəs] **N** *Hist* Tacite *m*

tack[1] [tæk] **N 1** *(fastener) (for carpet)* clou *m*; *(for upholstery)* broquette *f*, semence *f*, *(for poster, notice etc)* punaise *f*; **Fam to get down to brass tacks** en venir aux faits
  2 *Sewing (stitch)* point *m* de bâti; **to take out the tacks** retirer le bâti
  3 *(course)*, *Naut* bord *m*, bordée *f*, *Fig* voie *f*, *Naut* **to make a t.** faire *ou* courir *ou* tirer un bord *ou* une bordée; **to be/run/sail on the starboard/port t.** être/courir/faire route tribord amures/bâbord amures; *Fig* **to be on the right t.** être sur la bonne voie; *Fig* **to be on the wrong t.** être sur la mauvaise voie, faire fausse route; *Fig* **let's try another t.** essayons une autre tactique, changeons de tactique; *Fig* **to go off on a fresh t.** *(in career)* changer de voie; *(in conversation)* passer à un autre sujet
  VT 1 *(fasten)* **to t. (down)** clouer; *(poster)* punaiser (**to** à); *Fig* **to t. sth on** *(add)* rajouter qch (**to** à) **2** *Sewing* **to t. (down/in/on/together)** bâtir, faufiler; **to t. up a hem** faire le bâti d'un ourlet, faufiler un ourlet
  VI *(of ship)* louvoyer, faire *ou* courir *ou* tirer un bord *ou* une bordée; **to t. to port** virer (de bord) sur bâbord

tack[2] **N** *Horseriding (harness)* sellerie *f*
  ▸▸t. room sellerie *f*

tack[3] **N** *Naut (ship's biscuits)* biscuits *mpl* de marin

tackiness ['tækɪnɪs] **N 1** *(stickiness) (of paint, varnish)* adhésivité *f*, *(of glue)* viscosité *f* **2** *Fam (shabbiness) (of shop, neighbourhood etc)* apparence *f* minable; *(vulgarity)*

(of remark, joke etc) goût *m* douteux; *(of clothes, jewellery)* aspect *m* bon marché; *(of person)* vulgarité *f*

tacking ['tækɪŋ] **N 1** *(of carpet)* clouage *m* **2** *Sewing* bâti *m*, faufilage *m*; **to take out the t.** retirer le bâti (**from** de) **3** *(of ship)* louvoiement *m*
  ▸▸t. about *(of ship)* louvoiement; **t. stitch** point *m* de bâti; **t. thread** fil *m* à bâtir, faufil *m*

tackle ['tæk(ə)l] **N 1** *(equipment) (for hobby, sport)* attirail *m*, matériel *m*, équipement *m*; *Naut etc (for lifting)* appareil *m* de levage; **under ship's t.** sous palan; **fishing t.** articles *mpl* de pêche **2** *Ftbl, Hockey* tacle *m*; *Rugby* plaquage *m*, placage *m* **3** *Br Fam Hum (wedding)* **t.** *(man's genitals)* service *m* trois-pièces, bijoux *mpl* de famille
  VT 1 *(deal with) (problem, task)* s'attaquer à; *(pudding etc)* attaquer; *(subject)* aborder; *Sch (homework)* se mettre à; **to t. a thief** attraper un voleur; **I don't know how to t. it** je ne sais pas comment m'y prendre **2** *(speak to)* **to t. sb (about sth)** parler à qn (de qch), dire deux mots à qn (au sujet de qch) **3** *(in hockey), Ftbl* tacler; *Rugby* plaquer

tackler ['tæklər] **N** *Ftbl, Hockey* tacleur *m*; *Rugby* plaqueur *m*

tackling ['tæklɪŋ] **N** *Ftbl, Hockey* tacle *m*; *Rugby* plaquage *m*, placage *m*; **you need to work on your t.** il faut que vous amélioriez vos tacles/vos plaquages

tacky ['tækɪ] **ADJ 1** *(sticky) (paint, varnish)* collant, qui n'est pas sec, *f* sèche; *(glue)* qui commence à prendre; *(surface)* collant, poisseux **2** *Fam (shop, neighbourhood etc)* minable, moche; *(vulgar) (remark, joke etc)* d'un goût douteux; *(clothes, jewellery)* minable, à deux sous; *(person)* vulgaire; **a t. colour-scheme** une association de couleurs hideuse; **what a t. way to treat someone** quelle façon minable de traiter quelqu'un

taco ['tɑːkəʊ] **N** *Culin* crêpe *f* de maïs

tact [tækt] **N** *(of person)* tact *m*; *(in difficult situation)* délicatesse *f*; **a matter requiring t.** un problème qu'il faut aborder avec tact; **to show a lack of/great t.** faire preuve de peu/beaucoup de tact

tactful ['tæktfʊl] **ADJ** *(person)* plein de tact, diplomate; *(in difficult situation)* délicat; *(answer, remark)* plein de tact, diplomatique; *(question, reference)* délicat; **to be t.** *(of person)* avoir du tact; **that wasn't very t. of him** il a manqué de tact, ce n'était pas très délicat de sa part; **she was her usual t. self** elle a fait preuve de son tact habituel; **the t. thing would have been to say nothing** il aurait mieux valu ne rien dire; **that wasn't very t.** quel manque de tact, ce n'était pas très délicat

tactfully ['tæktfəlɪ] **ADV** *(to behave, act)* avec tact *ou* délicatesse *ou* diplomatie; **I t. refrained from asking him** par tact *ou* délicatesse, je me suis retenu de lui poser la question

tactfulness ['tæktfʊlnɪs] **N** = **tact**

tactic ['tæktɪk] **N** *Mil, Fig* tactique *f*, manœuvre *f*, **tactics** la tactique; **to use delaying tactics** utiliser une tactique pour gagner du temps

tactical ['tæktɪk(ə)l] **ADJ** *Mil, Fig* **1** *(move, weapon etc)* tactique; **t. mistake** erreur *f* tactique; **t. withdrawal** retrait *m* stratégique **2** *(person, conduct)* adroit
  ▸▸t. voter = personne *f* qui fait un vote utile; **t. voting** vote *m* utile

tactically ['tæktɪklɪ] **ADV** *(to behave, act)* adroitement; **t. (speaking)** *Mil* du point de vue de la tactique; *Fig* du point de vue tactique

tactician [tæk'tɪʃən] **N** *Mil, Fig* tacticien, -ienne

tactile ['tæktaɪl] **ADJ** *(organ, reflex etc)* tactile

tactless ['tæktlɪs] **ADJ** *(person)* qui manque de tact; *(answer, remark)* dépourvu de tact, qui manque de tact; *(question, reference)* indélicat; **that was a bit t. of you** tu as fait preuve d'un certain manque de tact, ce n'était pas très délicat de ta part

tactlessly ['tæktlɪslɪ] **ADV** *(to behave, act)* sans tact *ou* délicatesse; **she asked him, rather t., about his first wife** avec un manque de tact évident, elle lui a posé des questions sur sa première femme

tad [tæd] **N** *Fam* **1 a t.** *(of milk, sugar etc)* un peu; *(somewhat)* quelque peu, un tantinet; **it's a t. long** c'est un peu longuet; **it's a t. worrying** c'est un tantinet inquiétant; **I think you're exaggerating a t.** je crois que t'exagères un tantinet *ou* quelque peu **2** *(child)* gosse *mf*

tadger ['tædʒər] **N** *Br Sl (penis)* chipolata *f*

Tadjik ['tɑːdʒɪk, tɑː'dʒiːk] **N** = **Tadzhik**

tadpole ['tædpəʊl] **N** têtard *m*

Tadzhik ['tɑːdʒɪk, tɑː'dʒiːk] **N** Tadjik *mf*; **T. Soviet Socialist Republic** République *f* socialiste soviétique du Tadjikistan

Tadzhiki [tɑː'dʒiːkiː, -'dʒiːkiː] **N** *Ling* tadjik *m*
  ADJ tadjik

Tadzhikistan [tɑːdʒɪkɪ'stɑːn] **N** Tadjikistan *m*

taffeta ['tæfɪtə] **N** *(fabric)* taffetas *m*; **t. dress/skirt** robe/jupe en *ou* de taffetas

taffrail ['tæfreɪl] **N** *Naut (structure)* couronnement *m*; *(rail)* lisse *f* de couronnement

Taffy ['tæfɪ] **N** *Fam esp Pej (Welshman)* Gallois *m*; **hey, T.!** hé, toi le Gallois!

taffy ['tæfɪ] **N 1** *Am (sweet)* caramel *m* (dur), *Can* tire *f* **2** *Am Sl (flattery)* flagornerie *f*

tag [tæɡ] **N 1** *(for identification) (on garment)* marque *f*; *(label)* étiquette *f*, *(on animal)* agrafe *f*, *(on file)* onglet *m*
  2 *(end piece) (on cord, shoelace)* ferret *m*; *(of material etc)* bout *m*, *Gram (question)* question-tag *f*, *pl* question-tags **VOIR GRAMMAIRE** A47; B64
  3 *(epithet, nickname)* surnom *m*
  4 *(quotation)* citation *f*, *(trite saying)* lieu *m* commun, cliché *m*
  5 *Am (paper etc flag)* insigne *m*, cocarde *f*
  6 *(game)* jeu *m* de chat; *(with sanctuary)* jeu de chat perché; **to play** *or* **have a game of t.** jouer à chat; *(with sanctuary)* jouer à chat perché
  7 *Comput (code)* balise *f*
  VT **(-gg-) 1** *(clothing)* marquer; *(merchandise, software)* étiqueter; *(cattle)* mettre une agrafe à; *(file)* mettre un onglet à; *Comput (code)* baliser
  2 *(term) (person)* qualifier, traiter (**as** de); *(nickname)* surnommer
  3 *Am (for traffic offence) (vehicle)* coller une contravention *ou Fam* un papillon sur; *(person)* mettre une contravention à
  4 *(in game of tag)* toucher; *Baseball* **to t. sb (out)** mettre un coureur hors jeu
  5 *esp Am Fam (follow) (person)* suivre; *(of police etc)* filer
  VI **to t. after sb** suivre qn
  ▸▸ *Am* **t. day** = journée *f* de vente d'insignes pour une œuvre de bienfaisance; *Am* **t. end** *(oddment of cloth, thread)* bout *m*; *(of goods)* restes *mpl*, *(end of performance, day)* fin *f*, **t. line** *(in play)* mot *m* de la fin; *(in poem)* dernier vers *m*; *(of entertainer)* slogan *m*; *Journ* chute *f*; *Gram* **t. question** question-tag, *pl* question-tags

▸tag along VI *(follow)* suivre; **mind if I t. along?** est-ce que je peux venir avec vous?; **to t. along behind** *(lagging)* traîner derrière

▸ **tag on** vi to t. on to sb coller (aux talons de) qn

vt sep to t. sth on (add) rajouter (to à)

Tagalog [təˈgɑːlɒg] N 1 (person) Tagal m, Tagalog m 2 Ling tagal m, tagalog m

tagboard [ˈtægbɔːd] N Am carton m

tagliatelle [tæljəˈtelɪ] N Culin tagliatelles fpl

Tahiti [təˈhiːtɪ] N Tahiti m; in T. à Tahiti

Tahitian [təˈhiːʃən] ADJ tahitien N Tahitien, -ienne

tai chi [ˈtaɪtʃiː] N tai-chi m, tai-chi-chuan m

taiga [ˈtaɪgɑː] N Geog taïga f

tail [teɪl] N 1 (of animal, bird, fish, reptile) queue f; to spread its t. (of peacock) faire la roue; with his t. between his legs (of dog), Fig la queue entre les jambes; Fig to turn t. prendre ses jambes à son cou, montrer les talons; Fig to keep one's t. up ne pas se laisser abattre; Fig the t.'s wagging the dog c'est le monde à l'envers; the t. of the hostages is wagging the dog of foreign policy le problème des otages décide de la politique étrangère

2 (of shirt) pan m; (of coat) basque f, pan; tails (tail coat) habit m, queue-de-pie f, pl queues-de-pie; to see sb out of the t. of one's eye voir qn du coin de l'œil

3 (of comet, kite, plane) queue f; (of car, ski) arrière m; (of coin) pile f, revers m; story with a sting in the t. histoire qui se termine sur une pointe de méchanceté; Aut Fam to sit on sb's t. coller qn; tails! pile!

4 Fam (someone following) personne f en filature; to put a t. on sb filer qn; we've got a t. quelqu'un nous file, nous sommes suivis; to be on sb's t. suivre qn de près; (of detective) filer qn

5 Fam (buttocks) derrière m

6 Am Sl (woman in sexual terms) she's a great piece of t. elle est très baisable; he's looking for some t. il est en chasse

vt 1 Fam (follow) filer, prendre en filature 2 (lamb etc) couper la queue à

vi to t. after sb suivre qn de près; (of several persons one behind another) suivre qn à la queue leu leu

▸▸ Aviat t. assembly dérive f; t. coat habit m, queue-de-pie f; t. end (of storm, season, meeting, story) fin f; (of cloth) bout m; (of procession) queue f, fin; t. feather penne f; TV t. slate clap m de fin; Aviat t. unit empennage m

▸ **tail away** vi (of attendance, clientele etc) diminuer, décroître; (of voice) s'affaiblir; (of book etc) se terminer en queue de poisson; (of competitors in race etc) s'espacer, s'égrener; (of column on the march) s'allonger; (of interest, enthusiasm, support) diminuer

▸ **tail back** vi (of traffic) bouchonner; the traffic tailed back all the way to … les voitures étaient pare-chocs contre pare-chocs jusqu'à …

▸ **tail off** vi = tail away

tailback [ˈteɪlbæk] N Aut (queue) bouchon m, embouteillage m, point m noir

tailboard [ˈteɪlbɔːd] N (on lorry) porte f à rabattement arrière; (on car) hayon m (arrière)

-tailed [teɪld] SUFF short/long-t. à queue courte/longue

tailender [teɪlˈendər] N (in race) dernier, -ière

tailgate [ˈteɪlgeɪt] Aut N (on lorry) porte f à rabattement arrière; (on car) hayon m (arrière)

vt Fam to t. sb coller qn

vi Fam don't t.! ne roulez pas trop près!

tailhopping [ˈteɪlhɒpɪŋ] N Ski ruade f

tailings [ˈteɪlɪŋz] NPL (from mining) déchets mpl

taillamp [ˈteɪllæmp] N Am Aut feu m arrière

taillight [ˈteɪllaɪt] N Am Aut feu m arrière

tailor [ˈteɪlər] N (for men) tailleur m; (for women) couturière f

vt (suit) faire, façonner; Fig (speech) adapter (to, to suit à); (woman's) tailored suit tailleur m; the tailored look is back la mode des tailleurs ajustés est de retour; a tailored shirt une chemise cintrée; a tailored skirt une jupe de tailleur

▸▸ t.'s chalk craie f de tailleur; t.'s dummy mannequin m; Fig Pej he looks like a t.'s dummy il est tout endimanché

tailoring [ˈteɪlərɪŋ] N 1 (profession) métier m de tailleur 2 (work) ouvrage m de tailleur

tailor-made ADJ (suit etc) fait sur mesure; t. for (specially designed) conçu pour; (suited) fait pour; it's t. for me c'est du sur mesure, c'est juste ce qu'il me faut; the part's t. for her ce rôle lui va à merveille

tailpiece [ˈteɪlpiːs] N (to document, speech etc) appendice m; (to letter) post-scriptum m inv; Mus (on stringed instrument) cordier m; Typ cul-de-lampe m, pl culs-de-lampe

tailpipe [ˈteɪlpaɪp] N Aut tuyau m d'échappement

tailplane [ˈteɪlpleɪn] N Aviat stabilisateur m

tailrace [ˈteɪlreɪs] N (for mill) bief m d'aval

tailshaft [ˈteɪlʃɑːft] N Aut arbre m de sortie

tailskid [ˈteɪlskɪd] N Aviat béquille f de queue

tailspin [ˈteɪlspɪn] N Aviat (descente f en) vrille f; to go into a t. vriller; Fig (panic) s'affoler, paniquer (about de); (of economy, interest rates) s'effondrer; the news sent her into a t. la nouvelle l'a affolée ou paniquée

tailwind [ˈteɪlwɪnd] N Aviat vent m arrière

taint [teɪnt] N (of food) corruption f, décomposition f; (of air, water) contamination f, pollution f; (of reputation, corruption) souillure f, Fig (of madness) tare f; the t. of sin la tache ou souillure du péché; book with no t. of bias livre sans trace de préjugés

vt (contaminate) (food) gâter; (air, water) contaminer, polluer; (minds, morals) infecter, vicier, corrompre; (reputation) souiller, entacher

tainted [ˈteɪntɪd] ADJ (air, water) contaminé, pollué; (food) gâté; (meat) avarié; Fig (reputation) souillé, entaché; (money) sale

Taiwan [taɪˈwɑːn] N Taïwan

Taiwanese [taɪwəˈniːz] ADJ taïwanais N Taïwanais, -aise

Tajik [ˈtɑːdʒɪk, tɑːˈdʒiːk] N = Tadzhik

Tajikistan [tɑːdʒɪkɪˈstɑːn] N = Tadzhikistan

TAKE [teɪk]

N	prise de vue **1** ▪ enregistrement **1**
	▪ prise de son **1** ▪ prise **2** ▪ recette **3**
VT	prendre **1, 2, 7–19, 23** ▪ contenir **3**
	▪ supporter **4** ▪ emmener **5** ▪ amener
	5 ▪ conduire **5** ▪ apporter **6**
	▪ consommer **8** ▪ louer **10** ▪ faire **12**
	▪ s'emparer de **14** ▪ gagner **14**
	▪ passer **21** ▪ se présenter à **21**
	▪ emprunter **22** ▪ tirer **22**
VI	prendre

N 1 (recording) (of film, scene) prise f de vue(s); (of record) enregistrement m; Radio enregistrement, prise de son; we'll do that t. again on va refaire cette prise/cet enregistrement; they did the scene in one t. ils ont tourné la scène en une prise

2 (catch) (of fish, game) prise f

3 (money) (of restaurant, shop) recette f; our t. is up this week nos recettes sont en hausse cette semaine; Fam to be on the t. toucher des pots-de-vin

vt (pt took [tʊk], pp taken [ˈteɪk(ə)n]) 1 (grasp) (knife, somebody's hand) prendre; to

t. sth again reprendre qch; to t. sth in one's hand prendre qch dans la main; you're taking your life in your hands doing that c'est ta vie que tu risques en faisant cela; to t. sb's arm (lean on etc) prendre le bras de qn; to t. sb by the arm, to t. sb's arm (to prevent escape) attraper qn par le bras; to t. sb in one's arms prendre qn dans ses bras; to t. (hold of) sb saisir ou empoigner qn; to t. (hold of) sth se saisir ou s'emparer de qch; to t. sb by the throat/collar prendre qn à la gorge/au collet; to t. the opportunity to do or of doing sth profiter de l'occasion pour faire qch; t. your partners (at dance) invitez vos partenaires

2 (remove) (book, pen etc) prendre; to t. sth (away) from sb enlever ou prendre qch à qn; (steal) prendre ou voler qch à qn; to t. one number from another soustraire ou ôter un chiffre d'un autre; to t. sth from the table/out of a drawer prendre qch sur la table/dans un tiroir; to t. sth from one's pocket prendre qch dans sa poche; to t. a saucepan off the heat ôter ou retirer une casserole du feu; to t. sth out of sb's hands prendre qch des mains de qn; Fig to t. the food out of sb's mouth retirer le pain de la bouche de qn; to t. sth off the market retirer qch du marché

3 (hold) (of container, building etc) contenir, avoir une capacité de; this bus takes fifty passengers c'est un car de cinquante places

4 (tolerate) (heat, criticism, insolence, pressure) supporter; she can't t. a joke elle ne comprend pas la plaisanterie; I can't t. any more je n'en peux plus; I can't t. any more of him je ne peux plus le supporter; I can't t. much more of this je commence à en avoir assez, je ne vais pas supporter cela bien longtemps; he can't t. his drink il ne supporte pas l'alcool; esp Am I'm not taking any! je ne marche pas!; he can t. it il sait encaisser

5 (lead) (person) amener (to à); (away) emmener; (in car) conduire (to à); (of road) (person) mener (to à); to t. the dog for a walk aller promener le chien; to t. oneself to bed aller se coucher; Hum I can't t. you anywhere tu n'es pas sortable; to t. sb home (on foot, by car etc) raccompagner ou ramener qn; (to meet parents) amener qn chez ses parents ou à la maison; he's taking me (out) to dinner/the theatre il m'emmène au restaurant/au théâtre; to t. sb (along) with one emmener qn avec soi; to t. sb round a museum faire visiter un musée à qn; she took me round the exhibition elle m'a fait faire le tour de l'exposition; to t. sb round a house faire visiter une maison à qn; to t. sb across the road faire traverser la rue à qn; her job takes her all over the world son travail l'amène à voyager dans le monde entier; the scandal has taken her to the top of the best-seller list le scandale l'a propulsée en haut de la liste des best-sellers; whatever took him there? qu'allait-il faire là-bas?; to t. sb to court intenter un procès contre qn

6 (carry) (flowers, sweets etc) apporter (to à); (one's coat) prendre; will this train t. me to Cambridge? est-ce que ce train va à ou passe par Cambridge?; to t. sb to hospital transporter qn à l'hôpital; to t. sth along or over or round apporter qch (to sb à qn); to t. sth with one emporter qch; t. some food with you emportez des provisions; to t. sth down(stairs) descendre qch; Fam you can't t. it with you (money when you die) tu ne l'emporteras pas avec toi dans la tombe; to t. a problem/matter to sb soumettre un problème/une affaire à qn

7 (go by) (bus, shortcut, road) prendre; t. the turning on the left prenez à gauche

8 (require) (of journey, work etc) (time) prendre; (of engine, machine) (diesel, paraffin etc) consommer; it takes an army/courage il

faut une armée/du courage (**to do** pour faire); **it takes one to know one** il faut en être un/une pour savoir ce que c'est; **it took four of us to carry him** il a fallu s'y mettre *ou* nous avons dû nous y mettre à quatre pour le porter; **that will t. some explaining** voilà qui va demander des explications; **the work took some doing** le travail a été difficile; **it will t. him two hours** il en aura pour deux heures; **it took us longer than I expected** cela nous a pris plus de temps que je ne pensais; **how long does it t. to get there?** combien de temps faut-il pour y aller?; **how long does it t.?** *(for journey, job to be done etc)* combien de temps est-ce que cela prend?; **I took an hour to do it** *or* **over it** j'ai mis une heure à *ou* cela m'a pris une heure pour le faire; **it takes a clever man to do that** bien malin *ou* habile qui peut le faire; **she's got what it takes to be a leader** elle a l'étoffe d'un chef; **she's got what it takes** *(for job etc)* elle a les qualités requises; **he doesn't have what it takes to be a politician** il n'a pas l'étoffe d'un politicien; *Gram* **verb that takes a preposition** verbe qui réclame *ou* nécessite une préposition; **noun that takes an 's' in the plural** nom qui prend un 's' au pluriel

9 *(adopt)* *(precautions, measures)* prendre; **to t. legal advice** consulter un avocat; **to t. legal proceedings** entamer *ou* engager des poursuites judiciaires; **to t. the veil** prendre le voile; **to t. holy orders** entrer dans les ordres; **to t. a dislike to sb** prendre qn en aversion *ou* en grippe; **to t. a decision about sth** prendre une décision concernant qch; **to t. the view that ...** penser *ou* estimer *ou* considérer que ...

10 *(occupy)* *(flat, house)* louer; *(seat)* prendre; **all the seats are taken** toutes les places sont prises; **please t. a seat** asseyez-vous, *Fml* veuillez vous asseoir, **t. your seats!** prenez vos places!

11 *(consume)* *(tablet, sugar etc)* prendre; **to t. something to drink** prendre quelque chose à boire; **how do you t. your coffee?** qu'est-ce que tu prends dans ton café?; **to t. drugs** *(of addicts etc)* se droguer; *(in hospital etc)* prendre des médicaments; **to be taken twice a day** à prendre deux fois par jour; **not to be taken internally** à usage externe; **are you taking anything for that cold?** est-ce que tu soignes ce rhume?, est-ce que tu prends quelque chose pour ce rhume?

12 *(do, perform)* *(walk, trip)* faire; *(holiday)* prendre; **t. a look at this!** regarde-moi ça!; **t. your pick** faites votre choix; **to t. a bath** *(wash)* prendre un bain; *Am Fam (lose money)* perdre gros; *Ftbl* **to t. a penalty** tirer un penalty; **to t. a print from a negative** tirer une épreuve d'un négatif; **to t. a photograph of sb/sth** prendre qn/qch en photo; **to have one's photograph taken** se faire photographier *ou* prendre en photo; **to t. a good photo(graph)** *(be photogenic)* être photogénique; *Rel* **to t. a service** célébrer un office; *Sch* **he takes them for English** il leur enseigne l'anglais; **to t. the part of Hamlet** jouer (le rôle d')Hamlet

13 *(record)* *(temperature, letter, notes, name and address)* prendre

14 *(capture)* *(power, town)* s'emparer de; *(prize)* gagner, remporter; **to t. a woman** *(sexually)* prendre une femme; **t. him alive!** attrapez-le vivant!; **to t. sb prisoner** faire qn prisonnier; **to t. sb by surprise** prendre *ou* surprendre qn; *Chess etc* **to t. a piece** prendre une pièce; *Cards* **to t. a trick** faire une levée

15 *(experience, feel)* **to t. fright** prendre peur; **to be taken ill** tomber malade

16 *(assume)* **to t. sb/sth for sb/sth** prendre qn/qch pour qn/qch; **I took you for an Englishman** je vous ai pris pour un Anglais; **what do you t. me for?** pour qui tu me

prends?; **to t. the news as** *or* **to be true** tenir la nouvelle pour vraie; **how old do you t. her to be?** quel âge est-ce que tu lui donnes?; **I t. it that you agree** je présume que vous êtes d'accord; **she took your silence to mean refusal** elle a interprété votre silence comme *ou* a pris votre silence pour un refus

17 *(pass successfully)* *(bend)* prendre; *(obstacle)* sauter

18 *(consider)* *(case)* prendre; **t. (for example) the pensioners** prenez (par exemple) les *ou* le cas des retraités; **taking one thing with another** l'un dans l'autre

19 *(accept, receive)* *(client, guest)* prendre; *(cheque)* accepter; *Fam* **t. it or leave it!** c'est à prendre ou à laisser; *Fam* **t. five!** cinq minutes de pause!, reposez-vous cinq minutes!; **to t. sth well/badly** bien/mal prendre qch; **he took the news better than I thought he would** il a pris la nouvelle mieux que je ne l'aurais cru; **to t. sb/sth the wrong way** *(misunderstand)* mal comprendre qn/qch; **don't t. this the wrong way, but ...** *(be offended)* ne le prends pas mal, mais ...; **I wonder how she'll t. it** je me demande quelle tête elle fera *ou* comment elle va le prendre; **I'll t. it here** *(phone call)* je le prends ici; **I took a phone call for her yesterday** j'ai pris un coup de fil pour elle hier; *Old-fashioned* **to t. a wife** prendre femme; **do you t. this man to be your lawful wedded husband?** *(in wedding ceremony)* consentez-vous à prendre M. Lapoire pour époux?; **to t. a chance** *or* **risk** *or* **gamble** risquer le coup; *Com etc* **to t. so much a week** faire (une recette de) tant par semaine; **what** *or* **how much will you t. for it?** combien en voulez-vous?; **does this machine t. pound coins?** cette machine accepte-t-elle les pièces d'une livre?; **to t. the hook** *or* **bait** *(of fish)* mordre à l'hameçon; *Fig* tomber dans le panneau; **to t. a beating** *(be punched)* recevoir une rossée; *(be defeated)* essuyer une défaite; **to t. a bet** tenir un pari; **to t. all responsibility** assumer toute la responsabilité; **we must t. things as we find them** *or* **as they come** il faut prendre les choses comme elles sont *ou* comme elles viennent; **t. it from me!** croyez-moi!; **to t. sb seriously** prendre qn au sérieux; **nylon does not t. dyes well** le nylon ne prend pas bien la teinture; **to t. heavy loads** *(of crane, engine etc)* supporter de lourdes charges; **it won't t. your weight** ça ne supportera pas ton poids

20 *(newspaper, magazine etc)* **what paper do you t.?** *(buy at shop)* quel journal achetez-vous?; *(subscribe to)* à quel journal êtes-vous abonné?

21 *Scol (sit)* *(exam)* passer, se présenter à; *(study)* *(subject)* faire; *(course)* suivre; **I didn't t. Latin at school** je n'ai pas fait de latin au lycée; **she took her degree last year** elle a obtenu son diplôme l'an dernier

22 *(copy, quote)* *(passage from author)* emprunter (**from** à); *(quotation, figures)* *(from book, report etc)* tirer (**from** de); **the title is taken from the Bible** le titre vient de la Bible; **the word is taken from (the) Latin** ce mot vient du latin

23 *(use)* *(eggs, flour etc)* prendre; **t. the scissors to it** vas-y avec les ciseaux; **t. a hammer to it** prends un marteau; **I'll have to t. bleach to this stain** il faudra que je nettoie cette tache à l'eau de javel; **his father took a stick to him** son père lui a donné des coups de bâton

vi *(be successful)* *(of fire, graft, plant cutting, vaccine, dye etc)* prendre

▸▸ *TV, Cin* **t. sheet** liste *f* des prises

▸ **take aback** **vt sep** *(surprise)* décontenancer, interloquer (**with** par)

▸ **take after** **vt insep** *(be like)* *(one's father etc)* *(in looks)* ressembler à; *(in personality)* tenir de

▸ **take apart** **vt sep** *(dismantle)* *(machine etc)* démonter; *Fig (criticize)* *(project etc)* démolir; *Fig* **to t. sb apart** *(in fight)* démolir qn; *(scold)* passer un savon à qn

▸ **take away** **vt sep** **1** *(remove)* *(from person)* *(licence)* retirer (**from sb** à qn); *(furniture)* confisquer; *(from place)* *(person, thing)* enlever (**from** de); *Math (number)* soustraire, ôter (**from** de); **they took his books and files away from him** ils lui ont confisqué ses livres et ses dossiers; **to t. a child away from school** retirer un enfant de l'école; **it takes away the fun** ça gâche tout

2 *(lead)* *(person)* emmener; *(carry)* *(thing)* emporter; *(wounded person)* transporter; **what takes you away so soon?** qu'est-ce qui vous fait partir de si bonne heure?; **his work took him away from his family for long periods** son travail le tenait éloigné de sa famille pendant de longues périodes; *Br* **sandwiches to t. away** sandwich(e)s *mpl* à emporter; **not to be taken away** *(on book in library)* à consulter sur place

vi **to t. away from the pleasure/value of sth** diminuer le plaisir/la valeur de qch; **I don't want to t. away from his achievements in the past, but ...** je ne veux pas minimiser ses performances passées mais ...

▸ **take back** **vt sep** **1** *(lead)* *(person)* reconduire, ramener, raccompagner; **they took him back to hospital/his family** ils l'ont reconduit à l'hôpital/dans sa famille

2 *(return)* *(book etc)* rapporter (**to** à); **that takes me back to my childhood** cela me rappelle mon enfance; **it takes you back a bit, doesn't it?** ça ne nous rajeunit pas tout ça, hein?

3 *(accept)* *(former employee, unsold goods)* reprendre; **she's a fool to t. him back** *(husband etc)* elle est idiote d'accepter qu'il revienne

4 *(withdraw)* *(what one said)* retirer; *(one's word)* retirer, reprendre; *(gift)* reprendre; **I t. it (all) back** je retire tout ce que j'ai dit

5 *Typ* transférer à la ligne précédente

▸ **take down** **vt sep** **1** *(remove)* *(poster etc)* enlever; *(plate etc)* *(from cupboard, shelf etc)* descendre; *(coat, picture etc)* *(from hook)* décrocher

2 *(lower)* *(one's trousers, one's pants)* baisser

3 *(destroy)* *(wall etc)* démolir; *Fam* **to t. sb down a peg or two** remettre qn à sa place, rabattre son caquet à qn

4 *(dismantle)* *(scaffolding, circus tent)* démonter

5 *(record)* *(name, address, instructions etc)* noter; *(notes)* prendre; **they took down everything she said** ils ont noté tout ce qu'elle disait; **to t. down a letter in shorthand** prendre une lettre en sténo

▸ **take in** **vt sep** **1** *(lead)* *(person)* faire entrer; *(carry)* *(washing, harvest etc)* rentrer

2 *(admit, receive)* *(orphan)* recueillir; *(lodge)* *(person)* héberger, loger, recevoir; *(lodgers)* prendre; **to t. in sewing/washing** faire la couture/la lessive à domicile

3 *(reduce)* *(skirt, sleeve)* reprendre; *Naut* **to t. in sail** prendre un ris; **to t. in the slack** *(on rope)* reprendre du mou

4 *(cover)* *(several countries etc)* comprendre, englober; *(questions, possibilities)* embrasser; **the tour takes in all the important towns** l'excursion passe par toutes les villes importantes

5 *(understand)* *(intellectually)* comprendre, se rendre compte de; *(emotionally)* *(bad news)* réaliser, bien comprendre; **it took me a while to t. in the full implications of this news** il m'a fallu un certain temps pour mesurer entièrement la portée de cette nouvelle; **he took in the situation at a glance** en un clin d'œil il a compris ce qui se passait; **to t. it all** *or* **everything in** *(listen)* être tout oreilles

6 *(deceive)* tromper, rouler (**with** avec); **to be taken in** se faire avoir; **I've been taken in** on m'a eu, je me suis fait rouler; **to allow oneself to be taken in** se laisser avoir *ou* duper *ou* tromper; **to be taken in by appearances** se laisser tromper par les apparences **7** *Am (see, visit) (museum)* visiter; **to t. in the sights** visiter la ville; **to t. in a movie/show** aller au cinéma/théâtre

▸ **take off** VT SEP **1** *(remove) (glasses, hat, make-up, lid)* enlever; *(clothing)* enlever, retirer, ôter; *(leg)* amputer; **t. your feet off the table!** retire *ou* enlève tes pieds de la table!; **to t. sb's attention off sth** détourner l'attention de qn; **he never took his eyes off us** il ne nous quittait pas des yeux; **to t. a couple of pounds off** *(off price)* baisser le prix *ou* faire un rabais de quelques livres; *(by dieting etc)* perdre quelques kilos; **to t. sb off a list** rayer qn d'une liste; **to t. sth off sb's hands** débarrasser qn de qch; **I'll t. the baby off your hands for a few hours** je vais garder le bébé pendant quelques heures, ça te libérera; **to t. sth off the market** retirer qch du marché; **t. your hands off me!** bas les pattes!; **to t. a load off sb's mind** ôter un poids à qn *ou* de la poitrine de qn; **to t. years off sb** *(of clothes, diet etc)* rajeunir qn; **to t. the passengers off** *(from ship) (by boat)* débarquer les passagers; **the injured man was taken off the ship by helicopter** le blessé a été évacué du bateau par hélicoptère

2 *(lead) (person)* emmener (**to** à, chez, en); **to t. oneself off** s'en aller, *Fam* décamper **3** *(cancel) (train, bus etc)* supprimer; *(show, programme)* annuler **4** *(mimic)* imiter **5 to t. some time off** prendre un congé; **to t. three days off** prendre trois jours de congé; **I'm going to t. the day off tomorrow** demain je prends ma journée

VI **1** *(leave) (of plane)* décoller (**for** pour); *(of athlete)* prendre son appel (**from** de); *(of person)* partir (**for** pour); *(hurriedly)* s'en aller, *Fam* décamper, filer; **she's taken off for two weeks in the Caribbean** elle est partie passer deux semaines aux Caraïbes **2** *Fam (succeed) (of company etc)* prendre un grand essor, être en plein essor; *(of film, book etc)* faire un tabac; **the craze never took off in France** cette mode n'a jamais pris en France

▸ **take on** VT SEP **1** *(accept) (task)* entreprendre; *(responsibility)* assumer; **to t. sb on** *(accept challenge of)* se battre contre qn; **to t. sb on at tennis** défier qn au tennis; **to t. it on oneself to do sth** prendre sur soi de faire qch; **to t. on passengers** *(of train etc)* prendre *ou* embarquer des voyageurs **2** *(hire) (worker)* engager, embaucher **3** *(acquire) (colour, appearance)* prendre (**of** de); **the word takes on another meaning** le mot prend une autre signification **4** *(escort) (person)* **in the end, he took me on to the station** en fin de compte, il m'a emmené jusqu'à la gare

VI *Old-fashioned Br Fam (be upset)* s'en faire; **she does t. on so** elle s'en fait pour rien

▸ **take out** VT SEP **1** *(remove)* sortir (**of** de); *(tooth)* arracher; *(stain)* ôter, enlever; *Fig Fam* **it really takes it out of you!** *(is tiring)* c'est vraiment épuisant!; *Fig Fam* **to t. it out on sb/sth** passer sa colère sur qn/qch; *Fig* **to t. sb out of himself/herself** changer les idées à qn **2** *(carry) (chairs, washing etc)* sortir; *Am* **sandwiches to t. out** sandwich(e)s *mpl* à emporter **3** *(dog)* promener, sortir; **to t. sb out to the theatre/a restaurant** emmener qn au théâtre/restaurant; **why don't you t. me out more often?** pourquoi est-ce qu'on ne sort pas plus souvent tous les deux?; **he's taking**

me out to dinner tonight il m'invite au restaurant ce soir; **he's been taking her out for a couple of months** il sort avec elle depuis quelques mois **4** *(obtain) (permit, licence)* prendre, obtenir; *(insurance policy, subscription)* souscrire à; **to t. out insurance** contracter une assurance **5** *esp Am (destroy)* détruire; *(kill)* éliminer

▸ **take over** VT SEP **1** *(become responsible for) (restaurant, company etc)* prendre la direction de; **to t. over sb's job** remplacer qn; **he took over the family business** il a repris l'entreprise familiale

2 *(buy out) (company)* racheter **3** *(overrun) (country)* envahir; **she takes over** *(of bossy person etc)* elle est envahissante **4 to t. over the lead** *(in race, polls)* prendre la tête **5** *Typ* transférer à la ligne suivante

VI **1** *Mil, Pol (assume power)* prendre le pouvoir; *(succeed)* prendre la succession (**from** de); *(of new manager etc)* prendre la direction **2** *(relieve)* prendre la relève (**from** de)

▸ **take to** VT INSEP **1** *(go to)* **to t. to the road** prendre la route; **to t. to one's heels** *or* **to flight** prendre ses jambes à son cou; **to t. to one's bed** prendre le lit, s'aliter; **to t. to the hills** se réfugier dans les collines; **to t. to the boats** monter dans les canots de sauvetage **2** *(adopt) (bad habits)* prendre; **he's taken to going for early-morning runs** il a pris l'habitude d'aller courir tous les matins tôt; **to t. to drink** *or* **drinking** se mettre à boire **3** *(like) (person)* éprouver de la sympathie pour; **they took to each other instantly** ils se sont tout de suite plu; **I didn't t. to him/it** il/ça ne m'a pas plu; **to t. to a game** prendre goût à un jeu

▸ **take up** VT SEP **1** *(lead) (person)* faire monter; **there's a lift to t. you up** vous pouvez monter en ascenseur; **the lift took us up to the 25th floor** l'ascenseur nous a amenés au 25ᵉ étage

2 *(carry) (suitcase, shopping etc)* monter **3** *(lift) (carpet)* enlever, déclouer; *(paving stones, railway tracks)* enlever; *(street)* dépaver, défoncer; *Rail (passengers)* prendre; **to t. up a book from the table** prendre un livre sur la table **4** *(shorten) (skirt)* raccourcir; **to t. up the slack** *(in cable)* retendre le câble **5** *(accept) (challenge)* relever; *(offer)* accepter; *(suggestion)* retenir; *St Exch (shares)* souscrire à; **to t. up a bet** tenir un pari; **to t. sb up on an offer** accepter l'offre de qn; **can I t. you up on your offer?** est-ce que ton offre tient toujours?; **I'll t. you up on that one day** je te prendrai au mot un de ces jours **6** *(discuss) (subject, problem etc)* parler de, discuter (**with** à); **I'd like to t. you up on what you said about ...** si vous le permettez, j'aimerais revenir sur ce que vous avez dit à propos de ...; **I'll have to t. you up on that** je ne suis pas du tout d'accord là-dessus **7** *(absorb) (water)* absorber **8** *(adopt) (idea etc)* adopter; **to t. up an attitude on sth** prendre *ou* adopter une attitude à l'égard de qch **9** *(begin) (career)* embrasser; *(hobby, studies)* se mettre à; *(continue) (task, book etc)* reprendre, se remettre à; **to t. up one's duties** entrer en fonctions; **to t. up (the thread of) the conversation** reprendre le fil de la conversation **10** *(occupy) (space, time)* occuper, prendre; *(attention)* absorber, occuper; **he is entirely taken up with his business** il est complètement absorbé par ses affaires

VI **to t. up with sb** se lier avec qn

takeaway ['teɪkəweɪ] *Br* ADJ *(meal, sandwich etc)* à emporter

N **1** *(café, restaurant)* café *m*/restaurant *m* qui fait des plats à emporter **2** *(sandwich)* sandwich *m* à emporter; *(dish, meal)* plat *m* à emporter; **a Chinese t.** un plat chinois à emporter

take-home ADJ
▸▸ **t. pay** salaire *m* net

taken ['teɪkən] ADJ **1** *(seat, table)* occupé, pris **2** *(impressed)* impressionné (**with** par); **he was very much t. with the idea** l'idée l'enchantait; **I was not t. with her** elle ne m'a pas fait bonne impression

takeoff ['teɪkɒf] N **1** *(mimicry)* imitation *f*; **to do a t. of sb** imiter qn **2** *(departure) (of plane)* décollage *m*; *(of high-jumper, long-jumper etc)* appel *m* **3** *(success) (of country, industry etc)* essor *m*
▸▸ **t. slot** *(for plane)* créneau *m* horaire de décollage

takeout ['teɪkaʊt] ADJ, N *Am* = **takeaway**

takeover ['teɪkəʊvər] N **1** *(of company)* prise *f* de contrôle, rachat *m* **2** *Pol* prise *f* de pouvoir
▸▸ *Fin* **t. bid** offre *f* publique d'achat, OPA *f*; **to make** *or* **launch a t. bid (for)** faire *ou* lancer une OPA (sur); **to be the subject of a t. bid** être l'objet d'une OPA; **t. fever** opeamania *f*

taker ['teɪkər] N *(of lease)* preneur *m*; *(at auction etc)* acheteur *m*, preneur; **any takers?** *(to go to cinema etc)* est-ce qu'il y a des amateurs?; **I put it up for sale but there were no takers** je l'ai mis en vente mais il n'y a pas eu d'amateurs

take-up N *(of benefits)* réclamation *f*; **the level of t. has been low** peu de gens ont profité de l'offre; **there has been a 10% t. of the grants** 10% des subventions ont été attribuées
▸▸ **t. point** *(of clutch)* point *m* de prise; *Tech* **t. reel** bobine *f* enrouleuse; *Tech* **t. spool** bobine réceptrice

taking ['teɪkɪŋ] ADJ *Old-fashioned (person)* attirant, séduisant; *(smile, manners)* engageant

N **1** *(of city etc)* prise *f*; **the money/job is his for the t.** il n'a qu'à accepter l'argent/le poste **2** *Com* recette *f* **3** *Old-fashioned* **to be in a t.** être agité

talc [tælk] N *(toiletry, mineral)* talc *m*

talcum ['tælkəm] N *(toiletry, mineral)* talc *m*
▸▸ **t. powder** talc

tale [teɪl] N **1** *(story)* conte *m*; *(legend)* légende *f*, **thereby hangs a t.** il y a toute une histoire là-dessous; **his drawn face told the t. of his sufferings** ses traits tirés en disaient long sur ses souffrances; **she lived to tell the t.** elle a survécu **2** *(lie)* histoire *f*; **to tell tales** raconter des histoires **3** *(account, report)* récit *m*; **to tell tales** *(sneak)* rapporter, cafarder; *Fig* **to tell tales out of school** *(be indiscreet)* être indiscret, trop parler

talebearer ['teɪlbeərər] N *(sneak)* rapporteur, -euse, cafard *m*

talent ['tælənt] N **1** *(ability)* talent *m*, don *m*; **to have a t. for sth** être doué en *ou* pour qch, avoir du talent pour qch; **to have a t. for annoying everyone/getting into trouble** avoir le don d'agacer tout le monde/de s'attirer des ennuis; **he has no t. for business** il n'a pas le don des affaires; **a woman of** *or* **with t.** une femme talentueuse *ou* de talent **2** *(person with ability)* talent *m*; *TV Sl (actors, presenters etc)* artistes *mpl* **3** *Br Fam (people of the opposite sex) (women)* nanas *fpl*, belles minettes *fpl*; *(men)* beaux mecs *mpl*; **what's the local t. like?** comment sont les nénettes/les mecs par ici?; **where does the t. hang out?** où est-ce qu'on trouve de

belles nanas/de beaux mecs? **4** *Hist (coin)*
talent *m*
  ▸▸ **t. scout, t. spotter** *(for films)* dénicheur,
-euse de vedettes; *(for sport)* dénicheur,
-euse de futurs grands joueurs

talented ['tæləntɪd] ADJ talentueux, de talent; *(performance)* plein de talent

taletelling ['teɪltelɪŋ] N rapportage *m*, cafardage *m*

talisman, *pl* **talismans** ['tælɪzmən] N talisman *m*

TALK [tɔːk]

| N entretien **1** ▪ conversation **1** |
| ▪ pourparlers *(talks)* **2** ▪ racontars **3** |
| ▪ exposé **6** |
| VI parler **1, 2, 4, 5** ▪ bavarder **1** |
| ▪ jaser **3** ▪ faire un discours **5** |
| VT parler |

N **1** *(conversation)* entretien *m*, conversation
f, **to have a t. with sb** *(chat)* parler *ou* s'entretenir avec qn; **we had an interesting t.** nous
avons eu une conversation intéressante; **it's
time you and I had a little t.** il est temps que
nous ayons une petite conversation; **it's
time we had a t. about your behaviour** il
est temps que nous discutions *ou* parlions
de votre conduite; **that was just sales t.** tout
ça ce n'était que des boniments
  2 *(discussion)* **there is some t. of his returning** il est question qu'il revienne; **there has
been t. of** it on en a parlé, il en a été question; *Pol etc* **talks** dialogue *m*, pourparlers
mpl; **to start talks** engager le dialogue, entrer en pourparlers; **peace talks** pourparlers
de paix
  3 *(rumour)* **there is some t. of his returning**
le bruit court qu'il va revenir; **it's the t. of
the town** on ne parle que de cela; **she's the
t. of the town** elle défraie la chronique;
their behaviour is causing a lot of t. leur
conduite fait jaser; **it's just t.** ce ne sont que
des racontars
  4 *(words, speech)* langue *f*, langage *m*; **baby
t.** babil *m* enfantin; **double t.** *(unclear)* propos *mpl* ambigus; *(false)* propos insincères;
small t. banalités *fpl*, conversation *f* banale,
propos sans importance; **to make** *or* **indulge** *or* **engage in small t.** parler de choses
et d'autres, parler à bâtons rompus; **I'm no
good at small t.** je ne suis pas doué pour
faire la conversation
  5 *(bravado)* **to be all t.** *(of person)* être fort
en gueule; **he's all t. and no action** il parle
beaucoup, mais il ne fait pas grand-chose
  6 *(lecture)* exposé *m* (**on** sur); **to give a t. on**
or **about sth** faire un exposé sur qch
VI **1** *(converse)* parler; *(chat)* bavarder (**of,
about de; with** avec); **to t. to** *or* **with sb** parler à *ou* avec qn, s'entretenir avec qn; **to t. to
oneself** parler tout seul; **she didn't t. to me
the whole evening** elle ne m'a pas dit un mot
de la soirée; **who do you think you are talking to!** à qui croyez-vous donc parler?; **to t.
of** *or* **about doing sth** parler de faire qch; **to
t. and t.** parler sans arrêt; **don't all t. at once**
ne parlez pas tous en même temps; *Iron,
Hum* surtout, ne parlez pas tous en même
temps; **you're the only one I can t. to** tu es
le seul auquel je puisse parler *ou* me
confier; **that's no way to t.!** il ne faut pas
dire des choses pareilles!; *(referring to bad
language)* en voilà un langage!; **he likes to
hear himself t.** il s'écoute parler; **to t.
through one's hat** dire *ou* débiter des sottises; *Fam* **now you're/we're talking!** voilà
qui est mieux!; *Fam* **you can** *or* **can't t.!** tu
peux (bien) parler, toi!; **to make a prisoner
t.** faire parler un prisonnier; **his accomplices
are afraid he'll t.** ses complices ont peur
qu'il ne parle; *Fam* **he talks big** il fanfaronne;
money talks avec de l'argent on peut tout

faire; **what are you talking about?** *(asking
question)* de quoi parlez-vous?; *(expressing
disbelief)* qu'est-ce que vous racontez?; **I
don't know what you're talking about** *(in
answer to accusation)* je ne sais pas ce que
vous voulez dire; **she knows what she is
talking about** elle sait de quoi elle parle, elle
s'y connaît; **t. about luck/laugh** tu parles
d'une chance/d'un fou rire
  2 *(about problem, in reprimanding way)* **to
t. to sb** dire un mot *ou* deux mots à qn, parler à qn; **I'll t. to him!** je vais lui dire deux
mots!, je vais lui en toucher deux mots!
  3 *(gossip)* cancaner, jaser; **people will t.** on
va jaser; **you know how people t.** tu sais
comme les gens sont cancaniers *ou* comme
les langues vont bon train; **we don't want
people to t.** il ne faut pas faire jaser; **this will
give them something to t. about** voilà
quelque chose qui va les faire jaser; **the
whole town was talking about it** toute la
ville en parlait; **to get oneself talked about**
faire parler de soi
  4 *(speak)* parler; **to learn to t.** apprendre à
parler; **can he t.?** *(of bird)* est-ce qu'il parle?; **is
the baby talking yet?** est-ce que le bébé parle?
  5 *(lecture)* **to t. on the radio** faire un discours *ou* parler à la radio
  6 how much are we talking about? il faut
compter combien?, ça va chercher combien?,
combien?; **we're talking about at least
£10,000** il faut compter au moins 10 000 livres, ça va chercher au moins dans les 10
000 livres
VT *(speak) (French etc)* parler; **to t. nonsense** dire des bêtises; **to t. politics** parler
politique; **to t. (common) sense** tenir des
propos raisonnables; **do t. sense!** sois sérieux!; **to t. (some) sense into sb** faire entendre raison à qn; **to t. oneself hoarse**
s'enrouer à force de parler; **to t. oneself into
a job** *(by trying to impress)* obtenir un emploi grâce à son baratin; **you've just talked
yourself into a job** *(by saying that)* ce que
vous avez dit là m'a convaincu et vous avez
le poste; **to t. oneself out of trouble** se tirer
d'affaire grâce à son baratin; **t. yourself out
of that one!** va-t-y, essaie de t'en sortir cette
fois-ci!; **she can t. her way out of anything**
avec son bagou elle arrive toujours à se tirer
d'affaire; **to t. sb into/out of doing sth** per-
suader/dissuader qn de faire qch; **to t. sb into a better frame of mind** remonter le moral
à qn en lui parlant; **to t. sb out of a bad
mood** rendre à qn sa bonne humeur en lui
parlant
  ▸▸ **t. show** causerie *f* (radiodiffusée/télévi-
sée), talk-show *m*, *pl* talk-shows
▸ **talk away** VT SEP **to t. the night away** passer la nuit à parler; **to t. a child's fears away**
rassurer un enfant en lui parlant
  VI ne pas s'arrêter de parler
▸ **talk back** VI *(answer cheekily)* répondre
avec insolence (**to** à), répliquer; **don't t.
back to me!** je te défends de me répondre
▸ **talk down** VI **to t. down to sb** parler avec
condescendance *ou* comme à un inférieur à
qn
  VT SEP **1** *(silence)* réduire au silence en parlant
  2 *(plane, pilot)* donner des instructions d'atterrissage à; **the priest talked the man
down from the parapet** le prêtre a persuadé
l'homme de descendre du parapet
▸ **talk out** VT SEP **to t. things out** discuter la
chose à fond; *Parl* **to t. a bill out** prolonger
les débats de façon qu'un projet de loi ne
puisse être voté avant la clôture
▸ **talk over** VT SEP *(question)* discuter (de),
débattre; **let's t. it over** discutons-en
▸ **talk round** VT SEP *(somebody)* persuader,
faire changer d'avis à; **I talked them round
to my way of thinking** je les ai amenés à
partager mon avis

VT INSEP **to t. round the problem** *or* **issue**
tourner autour du pot
▸ **talk up** VT SEP *(film, book etc)* vanter; **to t.
up sb's chances** surestimer les chances de
qn; **the Chancellor is trying to t. up the economy** le Chancelier s'est montré optimiste
pour tenter de redynamiser l'économie
  VI *Am (speak openly, without hesitation)* parler franchement

talkathon ['tɔːkəθən] N *Am (in Congress, on
television etc)* débat-marathon *m*, *pl* débats-
marathon

talkative ['tɔːkətɪv] ADJ *(person) (chatty)*
causant, loquace; *(chatterbox)* bavard; **he's
very t.** il est très bavard, *Fam* il a la langue
bien pendue, il n'a pas la langue dans sa
poche

talkativeness ['tɔːkətɪvnɪs] N *(of person)*
loquacité *f*

talkback ['tɔːkbæk] N interphone *m*

talker ['tɔːkər] N *(conversationalist)* **to be a
good t.** avoir de la conversation; **to be a brilliant t.** briller dans la conversation; **my father was never much of a t.** mon père n'a
jamais été très bavard

talkie ['tɔːkɪ] N *Cin Old-fashioned Fam* film
m parlant

talking ['tɔːkɪŋ] ADJ parlant
  N **1** *(discussion, conversation)* **that's enough
t.** assez parlé; **to do all the t.** *(in conversation)* faire la conversation à soi tout seul;
let me do the t. laisse-moi parler **2** *(chatter)*
bavardage *m*; **no t., please!** pas de bavardage!
  ▸▸ **t. book** livre *m* enregistré; **t. doll** poupée
f qui parle; *Cin* **t. film** film *m* parlant; *TV* **t.
head** *(presenter)* présentateur, -trice de télévision *(dont on ne voit que la tête et les
épaules)*; *Hum, Pej (interviewee)* = expert *m*
qui s'exprime à la télévision; **t. point** sujet
m de conversation *ou* de discussion; *Br* **t.
shop** lieu *m* de palabres; **the United Nations
is accused of being a t. shop** on accuse les
Nations Unies de ne faire que la parlotte

talking-to N *Fam (scolding)* réprimande *f*,
semonce *f*; **to give sb a t.** passer un savon à
qn (**about** sur; **for** pour); **he needs a good t.**
il a besoin d'un bon savon

talktime ['tɔːktaɪm] N *Tel* autonomie *f*

talky ['tɔːkɪ] ADJ *Am (book, film etc)* saturé
de dialogues

tall [tɔːl] ADJ *(person)* grand; *(building etc)*
grand, haut, élevé; **how t. are you?** combien
mesurez-vous?; **she's taller than I am** elle
est plus grande que moi; **he was taller by a
head** *or* **stood a (whole) head taller than me**
il me dépassait d'une tête; **she's growing
taller** elle grandit; **he has grown t.** (qu'est-
ce qu')il a grandi; **how t. is that mast?**
quelle est la hauteur de ce mât?; **tree five
metres t.** arbre de cinq mètres de hauteur;
I'd love a t. glass of something cold je boirais
volontiers un grand verre de quelque chose
de bien frais; *Fig* **a t.** *Br* **story** *or* *Am* **tale** une
histoire invraisemblable *ou* à dormir de-
bout; *Fig* **that's a t. order** voilà qui va être
difficile *ou* compliqué
  ADV *Fig* **to walk** *or* **stand t.** marcher la tête
haute

tallboy ['tɔːlbɔɪ] N *Br* grande commode *f*

Tallin(n) ['tælɪn] N Tallinn

tallness ['tɔːlnɪs] N *(of person)* taille *f*, *(of
building etc)* hauteur *f*

tallow ['tæləʊ] N *(fat)* suif *m*
  ▸▸ **t. candle** chandelle *f*

tally ['tælɪ] N **1** *(record) (of merchandise)*
pointage *m*; **to keep a t. of goods/names**
pointer des marchandises/des noms **2** *(calculation)* compte *m*; **to keep (a) t. of one's
score** noter son score; **to keep (a) t. of one's**

spending tenir le compte de ses dépenses; **who's keeping t.?** qui fait les comptes *ou Sport* compte les points?
VT *(goods)* pointer
VI *(of figure, report etc)* correspondre (**with** à), concorder (**with** avec); **these accounts do not t.** ces comptes ne correspondent *ou* ne concordent pas

tally-ho **INT, N** *(in hunting)* taïaut *m*, tayaut *m*

Talmud ['tælmʊd] **N** *Rel* Talmud *m*

Talmudic [tæl'mʊdɪk] **ADJ** *(scholar etc)* talmudique

Talmudist ['tælmʊdɪst] **N** Talmudiste *m*

talon ['tælən] **N** *(of bird)* serre *f*, griffe *f*; *Fig (of person)* griffe

tamable ['teɪməb(ə)l] **ADJ** = **tameable**

tamarind ['tæmərɪnd] **N** *(fruit)* tamarin *m*; *(tree)* tamarinier *m*
▸▸ **t. tree** tamarinier

tamarisk ['tæmərɪsk] **N** *(plant)* tamaris *m*

tambour ['tæmbʊər] **N 1** *Sewing (frame)* tambour *m* à broder **2** *Archit, Mus* tambour *m*
▸▸ *Sewing* **t. frame** tambour à broder; **t. lace** dentelle *f* (brodée) sur tulle

tambourine [tæmbə'riːn] **N** *Mus* tambourin *m*

tame [teɪm] **ADJ 1** *(animal) (unafraid)* familier; *(domesticated)* apprivoisé; *Am (plant, land)* cultivé; **the squirrels are very t.** les écureuils sont très familiers *ou* ne sont pas farouches; **to grow** *or* **become t.** *(of animal)* s'apprivoiser **2** *(person)* soumis, docile; *(story, speech, film, show etc)* fade, banal, -als; **the story's ending was rather t.** l'histoire se terminait sur une note plutôt banale; *Hum* **we have a t. builder who does that sort of thing** on a un ouvrier très serviable qui fait ce genre de choses
VT *(animal)* apprivoiser; *(lion)* dompter; *Am (plant, wilderness)* cultiver; *(person, passion)* dominer; **to t. the elements** dominer les éléments

tameable ['teɪməb(ə)l] **ADJ** *(animal)* qu'on peut apprivoiser; *(lion etc)* domptable

tamely ['teɪmlɪ] **ADV** *(to submit)* sans résistance, docilement; **the story ends very t.** l'histoire se termine de façon très banale; **a t. worded letter of complaint** une lettre de réclamation timide

tamer ['teɪmər] **N** *(of lions etc)* dompteur, -euse

Tamil ['tæmɪl] **ADJ** tamoul, tamil *(no f)*
N 1 *(person)* Tamoul, -oule, Tamil *m* **2** *Ling* tamoul *m*, tamil *m*

taming ['teɪmɪŋ] **N** *(of animal)* apprivoisement *m*; *(of lion), Fig (of person)* domptage *m*; **theT. of the Shrew** la Mégère Apprivoisée

tammy ['tæmɪ] **N** *Fam (cap)* béret *m* écossais

tam-o'-shanter [tæmə'ʃæntər] **N** béret *m* écossais

tamp [tæmp] **VT** *Constr (earth)* damer; *(pipe, tobacco)* bourrer
▸ **tamp down VT SEP** = **tamp**

tampax® ['tæmpæks] **N** tampon *m*, tampax® *m*

tamper ['tæmpər] **N 1** *(person)* bourreur *m* **2** *(tool)* dame *f* à fouler **3** *Phys* réflecteur *m* de neutrons
▸ **tamper with VT INSEP** *(interfere with) (mechanism etc)* toucher à, *Fam* trifouiller; *(lock)* essayer d'ouvrir; *(rules)* truquer; *(register)* falsifier; *(accounts, document)* truquer, tripatouiller; **to t. with sb's mail** ouvrir le courrier de qn; *Horseracing* **to t. with a horse** doper un cheval; **to t. with a witness** suborner un témoin

tampon ['tæmpɒn] **N** *Surg (of cotton wool,*

gauze) tampon *m*; *(to absorb menstrual flow)* tampon (périodique)

tan [tæn] **N 1** *(on skin)* bronzage *m*, hâle *m*; **to get a (good) t.** bronzer; **to have a t.** être bronzé *ou* hâlé; **to lose one's t.** perdre son bronzage **2** *(colour)* marron *m* clair
ADJ *(colour, shoes)* marron clair *inv*; **t. gloves** des gants *mpl* en cuir marron clair
VT *(-nn-) (leather)* tanner; *(of sun) (skin)* hâler, donner un hâle à; *Fam* **to t. sb** *or* **sb's hide** tanner le cuir à qn
VI *(of complexion)* se hâler, bronzer; **I t. easily** je bronze facilement
▸▸ **t. line** marque *f* de bronzage

tanager ['tænədʒər] **N** tangara *m*

tandem ['tændəm] **N** *(bicycle)* tandem *m*; **to do sth in t.** faire qch ensemble; **the party and the unions must work in t.** le parti et les syndicats doivent travailler ensemble; **in t.** *(of horses, turbines etc)* en tandem

tang [tæŋ] **N 1** *(flavour)* saveur *f* piquante, piquant *m*; **a t. of irony** une pointe d'ironie; **the t. of the morning air** l'air *m* vif du matin **2** *(of knife)* soie *f*, *(of file)* queue *f*

tangent ['tændʒənt] **N** *Geom* tangente *f*; **at a t. to a curve** tangentiellement à une courbe; *Fig* **to go off at a t.** changer de sujet

tangential [tæn'dʒenʃəl] **ADJ** *Geom etc* tangentiel; *Fig* secondaire; **that is t. to the main issue** étant donné le sujet, ceci est secondaire

tangerine [tændʒə'riːn, 'tænd-] **N** mandarine *f*
ADJ *(colour)* mandarine *inv*

tangibility [tændʒɪ'bɪlɪtɪ] **N** tangibilité *f*

tangible ['tændʒɪb(ə)l] **ADJ 1** *(palpable)* tangible, palpable **2** *(real)* réel; **t. difference** différence *f* sensible
▸▸ *Fin* **t. assets** actif *m* corporel, valeurs *fpl* matérielles; *Fin* **t. fixed assets** immobilisations *fpl* corporelles

tangibles ['tændʒɪb(ə)lz] **NPL** *Acct* actif *m* corporel, valeurs *fpl* matérielles

tangibly ['tændʒɪblɪ] **ADV 1** *(palpably)* tangiblement **2** *(really)* sensiblement

Tangier(s) [tæn'dʒɪər, -'dʒɪəz] **N** Tanger *m*

tanginess ['tæŋɪnɪs] **N** saveur *f* piquante, piquant *m*

tangle ['tæŋg(ə)l] **N** *(bundle, confusion) (of undergrowth)* fouillis *m*; *(of branches, hair, threads, barbed wire, roads)* enchevêtrement *m*; **to be (all) in a t.** *(of string etc)* être (tout) embrouillé; *(of wool, hair)* être (tout) emmêlé; *Fig (of person)* ne savoir plus où on en est; **his finances are in such a t.** ses comptes sont tellement embrouillés; **her private life is in a terrible t.** sa vie privée est un véritable sac de nœuds; **to get into a t.** *(of string, business)* s'embrouiller; *(of wool, hair)* s'enchevêtrer; *(making speech, explaining sth)* s'embrouiller, s'emmêler; **to get into an emotional t.** se mettre dans une situation compliquée sur le plan affectif
VT = **tangle up**
VI *(of string etc)* s'embrouiller, s'emmêler, s'enchevêtrer
▸ **tangle up VT SEP 1** *(make confused) (threads, hair)* emmêler; *(question)* embrouiller; **to get tangled up** *(of threads, wires etc)* s'emmêler; **to get tangled up in sth** *(in rope, net) (of animal, person)* être enchevêtré dans qch; **she had got tangled up in some barbed wire** elle était prise dans des barbelés **2** *(involve)* **he got himself tangled up in the Smith case** il s'est retrouvé impliqué dans l'affaire Smith; **they got tangled up in something dishonest** ils ont été mêlés à une affaire malhonnête
▸ **tangle with VT INSEP** *Fam (quarrel, fight with)* s'en prendre à; **I wouldn't t. with him if I was you** à ta place je ne me frotterais

pas à lui; **to t. with the law** avoir des démêlés avec la justice

tangled ['tæŋg(ə)ld] **ADJ** *(hair, threads)* emmêlé; *(love life, story)* embrouillé

tango ['tæŋgəʊ] **N** *(dance)* tango *m*
VI danser le tango; *Fig* **it takes two to t.** *(sexual)* il faut être deux pour ces choseslà; *(share responsibility)* tu as ta/il a sa/*etc* part de responsabilité

tangy ['tæŋɪ] **ADJ** *(flavour)* qui a un goût piquant; **the t. sea air** l'air *m* vif de la mer

tank [tæŋk] **N 1** *(container) (for water, petrol etc)* réservoir *m*; **water t.** réservoir à eau *ou* d'eau; *Naut* caisse *f* à eau; *Rail* caisse à eau, soute *f* (à eau); *(alongside track)* château *m* d'eau; **storage t.** réservoir de stockage; **a full t. (of fuel)** un plein (réservoir de carburant); *Aut, Aviat* **fuel** *or Br* **petrol** *or Am* **gas(oline) t.** réservoir de carburant **2** *Ind (for processing etc)* cuve *f*, bac *m*; *Pol* **think t.** comité *m ou* groupe *m* d'experts; **(air/buoyancy) t.** caisson *m* (à air/de flottabilité) **3** *Mil* char *m*; *Fam* **to be built like a t.** être une armoire à glace; **the tanks** les blindés *mpl*
▸▸ *Am Rail* **t. car** wagon-citerne *m*, *pl* wagons-citernes; **t. commander** commandant *m* de char; **t. regiment** régiment *m* de chars (d'assaut); **t. top** débardeur *m*, pull *m* sans manches; **t. trap** piège *m* à chars; **t. truck** camion-citerne *m*, *pl* camions-citernes; *Rail* **t. wagon** wagon-citerne; **t. warfare** guerre *f* combattue à l'aide de chars
▸ **tank along VI** *Fam (go fast) (of driver, car etc)* foncer
▸ **tank up** *Br* **VI** *Aut (fill fuel tank)* faire le plein d'essence
VT SEP *(usu passive) Br Sl* **to get tanked up** *(drunk)* se prendre une biture; **to be tanked up** être bourré *ou* bituré

tankard ['tæŋkəd] **N** chope *f*, *Arch* **a t. of ale** un pot de bière

tanker ['tæŋkər] **N** *Naut* navire-citerne *m*, *pl* navires-citernes; *Rail* wagon-citerne *m*, *pl* wagons-citernes; *Aviat* avion-citerne *m*, *pl* avions-citernes; *(for refuelling)* avion *m* de ravitaillement; *Naut* **oil t.** (navire *m*) pétrolier *m*
▸▸ **t. aircraft** avion-citerne; *(for refuelling)* avion de ravitaillement; **t. lorry**, *Am* **t. truck** camion-citerne *m*, *pl* camions-citernes

tanned [tænd] **ADJ** *(leather)* tanné; *(face, complexion)* hâlé, bronzé; *(deeply, naturally)* basané

tanner[1] ['tænər] **N** *(person)* tanneur *m*

tanner[2] **N** *Hist Sl (coin)* (pièce *f* de) six pence *mpl*

tannery ['tænərɪ] **N** tannerie *f*

tannic ['tænɪk] **ADJ** *(acid)* tannique

tannin ['tænɪn] **N** tan(n)in *m*

tanning ['tænɪŋ] **N 1** *(act of tanning hides)* tannage *m*; **t. (trade)** tannerie *f* **2** *Fam (beating)* raclée *f*, **to give sb a good t.** flanquer une bonne raclée à qn
▸▸ **t. booth** cabine *f* de bronzage; **t. cream** *(self-tanning)* crème *f* autobronzante; *(for natural tan)* crème solaire

Tannoy® ['tænɔɪ] **N** système *m* de haut-parleurs; **an announcement came over the T.** il y a eu une annonce au haut-parleur

tansy ['tænzɪ] **N** *(plant)* tanaisie *f*

tantalize ['tæntəlaɪz] **VT** tourmenter, mettre au supplice

tantalizing ['tæntəlaɪzɪŋ] **ADJ** terriblement alléchant; **it's t.** c'est un vrai supplice de Tantale

tantalizingly ['tæntəlaɪzɪŋlɪ] **ADV** **the cool water was t. near** cette eau fraîche à proximité était un véritable supplice; **we came t. close to solving it** c'était exaspérant *ou* rageant de voir à quel point nous étions près de la solution

tantamount ['tæntəmaʊnt] ADJ équivalent (to à); **to be t. to sth** équivaloir à qch; **that's t. to saying I'm a liar** cela revient à dire que je mens

tantrum ['tæntrəm] N (of child) caprice m; (of adult) colère f; **to throw a t.** (of child) faire un caprice; (of adult) piquer une colère

Tanzania [tænzə'nɪə] N Tanzanie f

Tanzanian [tænzə'nɪən] ADJ tanzanien N Tanzanien, -ienne

Taoism ['taʊɪz(ə)m] N taoïsme m

Taoist ['taʊɪst] N taoïste mf

tap¹ [tæp] N **1** Br (for water) robinet m; (plug) bonde f; **to turn on/turn off the t.** ouvrir/ fermer le robinet; Fig **to turn on the t.** (cry) pleurer; Fig **to turn off the t.** fermer le robinet; **on t.** (of beer etc) à la pression; Fig **to be on t.** (of person, thing) être (toujours) disponible; **they've got cheap labour on t.** ils ont de la main-d'œuvre pas chère à volonté **2** esp Am Elec prise f (intermédiaire) **3** (action) (into pipe) branchement m; Tel (of telephone communication) écoute f; Tel **who authorized the t.?** qui a autorisé la mise sur écoute? **4** Fin valeur f du Trésor mise aux enchères; **long/medium/short t.** valeurs fpl émises à un prix déterminé par l'État à long/ moyen/court terme

VT (-pp-) **1** (barrel) percer, mettre en perce; (tree) inciser, entailler; (pine tree) gemmer; (wine) tirer; (natural resources etc) exploiter; (water course) capter; (gas or water pipe) faire un branchement sur; **we must t. all the resources we have** nous devons puiser dans toutes nos ressources; **to t. a telephone conversation** écouter une communication téléphonique à l'aide d'une table d'écoutes; **the phones are tapped** les téléphones sont sur écoute; Fam **to t. sb for fifty euros** taper qn de cinquante euros **2** Tech (nut, screw) tarauder, fileter

▶▶**t. water** eau f du robinet

tap² N **1** (light blow, sound) petit coup m; (with hand) tape f; **t. at the door** coup léger ou discret à la porte; **there was a t. on the window** on frappa à la fenêtre; **a t. on the shoulder** une tape sur l'épaule **2** Mil **to play taps** sonner l'extinction des feux

VT (-pp-) (strike lightly) (surface) taper légèrement, tapoter; (hit gently) (person) donner un petit coup à; **she tapped me on the shoulder** (to attract attention) elle m'a tapé sur l'épaule

VI **1 to t. at** or **on the door** frapper doucement à la porte **2 to t.** (dance) faire des claquettes

▶▶**t. dance** claquettes fpl (danse); **t. dancer** danseur, -euse de claquettes; **t. dancing** claquettes (danse); **to do t. dancing** faire des claquettes

▶ **tap out** VT SEP **1 to t. out the rhythm** marquer le rythme; **to t. out the rhythm on the table** taper le rythme sur la table; **to t. out a message** (in morse code) émettre un message; **to t. out a message on the central heating pipes** transmettre un message en tapant sur les tuyaux du chauffage central **2 to t. out one's pipe** débourrer sa pipe

tape [teɪp] N **1** (ribbon) (of cotton) ruban m; (of cloth, paper) bande f; Sport bande d'arrivée; (for measuring) mètre m (ruban); (dressmaker's for measuring) centimètre m; masking t. ruban-cache m; ((self-) adhesive or Fam sticky) t. ruban adhésif, scotch® m; Pharm adhesive t. sparadrap m; Elec insulating t. ruban isolant, chatterton m; Sport **to breast the t.** franchir la ligne d'arrivée ou arriver le premier; Horseracing (at start) les rubans **2** (in recording) (length of tape) bande f; (cassette) cassette f (audio); (recording) enregistrement m; **magnetic** or **recording t.** bande magnétique; **(video) t.**

cassette vidéo; **pre-recorded t.** bande enregistrée; **a classical t.** une cassette de musique classique; **to get** or **put sth on t.** enregistrer qch; **I've got it on t.** je l'ai en cassette

VT**1** (parcel) scotcher; (electric wire) guiper; **to t. sth to sth** scotcher qch à qch **2** Fig **I've got him taped** je sais comment il est ou ce qu'il vaut **3** (record) enregistrer; **she was taped talking to them** elle a été enregistrée en train de leur parler; **taped music** musique f enregistrée

▶▶Comput **t. backup** sauvegarde f sur bande; Comput **t. backup system** système m de sauvegarde sur bande; Comput **t. back-up unit** unité f de sauvegarde sur bande; **t. deck** platine f de magnétophone; **t. drive** dérouleur m de bande (magnétique), lecteur m de bande (magnétique); **t. head** tête f de lecture; **t. library** collection f de cassettes; **t. measure** mètre (ruban); (dressmaker's) centimètre; Comput **t. reader** lecteur de bande; **t. recorder** magnétophone m, lecteur de cassettes; **t. recording** enregistrement (sur bande magnétique); Comput **t. streamer** streamer m; **t. transport** mécanisme m d'entraînement (d'une bande magnétique); Comput **t. unit** unité f de bande

▶ **tape up** VT SEP (parcel, broken object) scotcher

taper¹ ['teɪpər] N **1** (candle) bougie f filée; Rel cierge m **2** (to light candle, fire etc) allume-feu m inv

taper² VT tailler en pointe ou en cône; (hair) effiler; Archit (column) fuseler, diminuer

VI s'effiler; **column that tapers upwards** colonne f taillée en pointe; **her hair tapers in to the neck** ses cheveux sont effilés sur son cou; **it tapers to a point** c'est taillé en pointe N Archit, Constr etc (shape) conicité f, cône m

▶ **taper off** VI (of line, long thin object) s'amincir, se rétrécir; (get smaller gradually) (of production, numbers etc) diminuer, se réduire

VT SEP (long thin object) effiler; (production etc) réduire, diminuer

tape-record VT enregistrer

tapered ['teɪpəd] ADJ (hair) effilé; (column, candle) en fuseau; **t. trousers** fuseau m

tapering ['teɪpərɪŋ] ADJ en pointe; (finger) effilé, fuselé; Archit (column) en fuseau; Fin **t. rate** tarif m dégressif

N (in hairdressing) effilage m

tapestry ['tæpɪstrɪ] N tapisserie f

▶▶**t. maker, t. weaver** tapissier, -ière

tapeworm ['teɪpwɜ:m] N ténia m, ver m solitaire

taping ['teɪpɪŋ] N (recording) enregistrement m

tapioca [tæpɪ'əʊkə] N tapioca m

tapir ['teɪpər] N (often inv in pl) (animal) tapir m

tapped out ['tæpt-] ADJ Am Fam crevé, lessivé

tappet ['tæpɪt] N Tech poussoir m

▶▶**t. clearance** jeu m aux culbuteurs

tapping¹ ['tæpɪŋ] N Tel (telephone) **t.** écoutes fpl (de communications téléphoniques)

tapping² N (knocking) petits coups mpl; (with hand) tapotement m

taproom ['tæpru:m] N bar m

taproot ['tæpru:t] N Bot racine f pivotante, pivot m

tar [ta:r] N **1** (for roads, in cigarettes) goudron m; Fig Fam **to spoil the ship for a ha'porth of t.** tout gâcher pour des économies de bouts de chandelle **2** Naut Old-fashioned Fam (Jack) t. (sailor) loup m de mer

VT (-rr-) (road, wood) goudronner; (pavement) bitumer; Naut (boat) goudronner, brayer; **to t. and feather sb** rouler qn dans le goudron et les plumes; Fig **we're all tarred with the same brush** on nous a tous mis dans le même panier ou sac

▶▶**t. paper** papier m goudronné

ta-ra [tə'ra:] INT Br Fam salut!, ciao!

taradiddle ['tærədɪd(ə)l] N Fam (lie) bobard m

tarantella [tærən'telə] N (dance), Mus tarentelle f

tarantula [tə'ræntjʊlə] N (spider) tarentule f

tardily ['ta:dɪlɪ] ADV Fml **1** (late) tardivement; (too late) en retard **2** (slowly) lentement

tardiness ['ta:dɪnɪs] N Fml **1** (lateness) retard m **2** (slowness) lenteur f (**in doing sth** à faire qch)

tardy ['ta:dɪ] ADJ Fml **1** (late) (payment, reaction) tardif **2** (slow) lent; (unhurried) peu empressé

tare¹ [teər] N Bible **tares** (weeds) ivraie f

tare² Com N tare f; (of lorry) poids m net; (of vehicle) poids à vide

VT (goods) tarer; (vehicle) peser à vide

target ['ta:gɪt] N Mil, Fig cible f, objectif m; (person) cible; **moving t.** objectif mobile ou mouvant; **to land on t.** (of bomb etc) atteindre son objectif; **sitting t.** cible facile; Fig **to be an easy t.** être une cible facile; Fig **we're on t.** (to meet the deadline) nous sommes dans les temps (pour ce qui est du respect des échéances); **to set oneself a t.** se fixer un but ou un objectif

VT**1** Mil, Fig (aim at) (place, building etc) viser, prendre pour cible; Com (market) cibler; **they targeted the magazine at 18-to-25-year-olds** le magazine a été conçu pour les 18-25 ans; **services should be better targeted** il faudrait qu'on cible mieux les services **2** (direct) (missiles, advertising campaign) diriger

▶▶Mil **t. area** zone f cible; Mktg **t. audience** audience f cible; Mktg **t. buyer** acheteur, -euse cible; **t. company** société f opéable; Mktg **t. consumer** consommateur, -trice cible; Mktg **t. cost** coût m cible; **t. date** (for delivery etc) date f ciblée ou visée; Comput **t. disk** (hard) disque m cible; (floppy) disquette f cible; Comput **t. drive** unité f de destination; **t. figure** objectif m; Comput **t. file** fichier m de destination; Mktg **t. group** groupe m cible; Mktg **T. Group Index** indice m des groupes cibles; **t. language** langue f cible, langue d'arrivée; Mktg **t. market** marché m cible; Mktg **t. marketing** marketing m ciblé; Mktg **t. population** population f cible; Mil **t. practice** exercices mpl de tir; Mktg **t. price** prix m d'équilibre; Mktg **t. pricing** fixation f du prix en fonction de l'objectif; **t. readership** lectorat m cible; Com **t.-return pricing** fixation du prix en fonction du taux de rentabilité souhaité; **t. sales figure** chiffre m de ventes ciblé; **t. setting** arrêt m des objectifs

targeted ['ta:gɪtɪd] ADJ visé, ciblé

targetting ['ta:gɪtɪŋ] N **1** (setting targets) détermination f d'objectifs; **because of unrealistic t.** en raison d'objectifs non réalistes **2** Mktg ciblage m **3** (of funds, resources etc) **we need better t. of resources** il nous faut mieux cibler les ressources

tariff ['tærɪf] N **1** (at customs) tarif m; **reduced t.** tarif réduit; **full t.** plein tarif **2** (price list) tarif m, tableau m des prix

ADJ tarifaire

▶▶**t. barrier, t. wall** barrière f douanière ou tarifaire

Tarmac® ['ta:mæk] N **1** Constr macadam m, goudron m **2** Aviat (runway) piste f

VT (*pt, pp* **tarmacked**) (*road etc*) goudronner, macadamiser

tarmacadam [tɑːməˈkædəm] **N** = **Tarmac 1**

tarn [tɑːn] **N** (*in mountains*) petit lac *m* de montagne

tarnish ['tɑːnɪʃ] **N** ternissure *f*
VT (*surface of metal, person's reputation*) ternir
VI (*of metal etc*) se ternir

tarnishing ['tɑːnɪʃɪŋ] **N** (*of metal*) ternissure *f*

tarot ['tærəʊ] **N** *Cards* tarot *m*
▶▶ **t. cards** tarots

tarp [tɑːp] **N** *Am Fam* = **tarpaulin**

tarpaulin [tɑːˈpɔːlɪn] **N** (*fabric*) toile *f* goudronnée; (*sheet*) bâche *f*, prélart *m*

tarragon ['tærəgən] **N** (*plant*), *Culin* estragon *m*
▶▶ **t. vinegar** vinaigre *m* à l'estragon

tarry[1] ['tɑːrɪ] **ADJ 1** (*made of tar*) goudronneux, bitumineux **2** (*covered, stained with tar*) couvert de goudron

tarry[2] ['tærɪ] **VI** *Lit* **1** (*stay*) rester, demeurer (**at** *or* **in a place** dans un endroit) **2** (*delay*) s'attarder (**over sth** sur qch)

tarsus, pl tarsi ['tɑːsəs, -aɪ] **N** *Anat* tarse *m*

tart[1] [tɑːt] **N 1** *esp Br Culin* tarte *f*, (*small*) tartelette *f* **2** *Fam* (*prostitute*) putain *f*, poule *f*, *Pej* (*promiscuous woman*) pute *f*, (*woman*) pépée *f*, *Pej* grognasse *f*, *Pej* **the silly t.** cette andouille

tart[2] **ADJ** (*in taste*) au goût âpre, aigrelet; (*tone*) acerbe, aigre
▶ **tart up VT SEP** *Fam usu Pej* (*room, car etc*) retaper; **to t. oneself up** se faire beau; **this car's just a tarted up version of the …** cette voiture n'est qu'une version améliorée du …

tartan ['tɑːt(ə)n] **N** *Tex* (*cloth or pattern*) tartan *m*, écossais *m*; **t. shirt** chemise *f* écossaise
▶▶ **T. Army** = surnom *m* donné aux supporters de l'équipe de football d'Écosse

Tartar ['tɑːtər] **ADJ** tatar
N 1 Tatar, *f* Tatare **2** *Fig Pej* (*man*) homme *m* intraitable; (*woman*) mégère *f*

tartar ['tɑːtər] **N** (*on teeth*), *Chem* tartre *m*

tartar(e) sauce ['tɑːtə] **N** sauce *f* tartare

tartaric [tɑːˈtærɪk] **ADJ** *Chem* (*acid etc*) tartrique

tartly ['tɑːtlɪ] **ADV** (*to say*) d'un ton acerbe

tartness ['tɑːtnɪs] **N** (*of fruit, wine, tone*) aigreur *f*

tarty ['tɑːtɪ] **ADJ** *Sl Pej* (*clothes etc*) vulgaire; **to look t.** avoir l'air d'une pute

tash [tæʃ] **N** *Br Fam* (*abbr* **moustache**) moustache *f*, bacchantes *fpl*

task [tɑːsk] **N 1** travail *m*, -aux, tâche *f*; **these are your tasks** voici votre travail; **their t. is to …** leur travail *ou* tâche consiste à …; **the unpleasant t. of informing the parents** la tâche désagréable d'informer les parents; **it's an endless t.** c'est un travail sans fin; **to set sb a t.** imposer une tâche à qn **2 to take sb to t. for (doing) sth** prendre qn à partie *ou* réprimander qn pour (avoir fait) qch
VT to t. sb with sth/doing sth charger qn de qch/faire qch

taskbar ['tɑːskbɑːr] **N** *Comput* barre *f* des tâches

taskforce ['tɑːskfɔːs] **N** *Mil* corps *m* expéditionnaire; *Fig* (*to investigate*) commission *f*, (*to do special job*) groupe *m* de travail

taskmaster, taskmistress ['tɑːskmɑːstər, -mɪstrɪs] **N he is a hard t.** il est terriblement exigeant; (*stronger*) c'est un véritable tyran

Tasmania [tæzˈmeɪnɪə] **N** Tasmanie *f*

Tasmanian [tæzˈmeɪnɪən] **ADJ** tasmanien
N Tasmanien, -ienne

TASS [tæs] **N** *Formerly* (*abbr* **telegraphic news agency of the Soviet Union**) TASS *f*

tassel ['tæs(ə)l] **N 1** (*on furniture, clothing etc*) gland *m* **2** *Bot* (*on corn*) barbe *f*

tasselled ['tæs(ə)ld] **ADJ** à glands, orné de glands

TASTE [teɪst]

N	goût **1, 2, 4, 5** ▪ saveur **1**
VT	sentir **1** ▪ percevoir la saveur de **1** ▪ goûter **2** ▪ déguster **2** ▪ goûter à **3**
VI	avoir le goût de (*to taste of*)

N 1 (*flavour*) goût *m*, saveur *f*; **it has a burnt t.** cela a un goût de brûlé; **this drink has no t.** cette boisson n'a pas de goût *ou* est insipide; *Fig* **the whole business left a nasty t. in my mouth** toute cette histoire m'a franchement dégoûté *ou* m'a laissé un méchant arrière-goût

2 (*sense of*) **t.** goût *m*

3 (*small amount*) **a t. of cheese** *etc* un petit peu de fromage *etc*; **a t. of wine** *etc* une petite gorgée de vin *etc*; **have a t. of this claret** goûtez-moi ce bordeaux; *Fig* **to give sb a t. of the whip** faire tâter du fouet à qn; **this was my first t. of freedom** c'était la première fois que je goûtais à la liberté; **she's already had a t. of prison** elle a déjà tâté de la prison; **is this a t. of things to come?** est-ce là un avant-goût de ce qui nous attend?; **to give sb a t. of their own medicine** rendre à qn la monnaie de sa pièce

4 (*liking*) goût *m* (**for** pour); **to have a t. for** (*music etc*) aimer, avoir le goût de; **to have expensive tastes** avoir des goûts de luxe; **to acquire** *or* **develop a t. for sth** prendre goût à qch; **to find sth to one's t.** trouver qch à son goût; *Culin* **add sugar to t.** on ajoute du sucre à volonté; **it's a matter of t.** c'est une question de goût; *Prov* **everyone to his t.** des goûts et des couleurs on ne discute pas, chacun ses goûts

5 (*judgement*) goût *m*; **she has excellent t. in dress** elle s'habille avec (beaucoup de) goût; **to be in perfect t.** être d'un goût parfait; **in bad t.** de mauvais goût; **it would be bad t. to wear that to a funeral** il serait de mauvais goût de porter cela à un enterrement
VT 1 (*distinguish taste of*) sentir, percevoir la saveur de; **I can't t. anything when I have a cold** les aliments n'ont plus aucun goût quand je suis enrhumé; **can't you t. the cinnamon?** tu ne sens pas la cannelle?; **I can t. something like cloves in it** ça sent un peu le clou de girofle

2 (*sample quality of*) (*dish*) goûter; (*wines, teas etc*) déguster

3 (*get a little taste of*) goûter de *ou* à; (*liquid*) boire une petite gorgée de; *Fig* (*whip, prison etc*) tâter de; **I haven't even tasted it** je n'y ai pas même goûté; **he had not tasted food for three days** il n'avait pas mangé depuis trois jours; **to t. happiness/success** goûter au bonheur/à la réussite

VI the cake tasted of lemon le gâteau avait un goût de citron; **it tastes like spinach** ça a un goût d'épinard; **to t. good/bad** être bon/mauvais, avoir un bon/mauvais goût; **it tastes fine to me** moi je trouve ça bon; **it tastes salty** c'est salé; **it tastes funny** ça a un drôle de goût; **it doesn't t. of anything to me** moi, je trouve que ça ne sent rien; *esp Lit* **to t. of despair/defeat** connaître le désespoir/la défaite
▶▶ **t. bud** papille *f* gustative

tasteful ['teɪstfʊl] **ADJ** (*remark, action*) de bon goût; (*decoration*) fait avec goût

tastefully ['teɪstfəlɪ] **ADV** avec goût

tastefulness ['teɪstfʊlnɪs] **N** bon goût *m*

tasteless ['teɪstlɪs] **ADJ 1** (*food etc*) sans

goût, fade, insipide; **the poison is t. and odourless** le poison est inodore et sans saveur **2** (*clothes, remarks etc*) de mauvais goût

tastelessly ['teɪstlɪslɪ] **ADV** (*to dress, furnish etc*) sans goût

tastelessness ['teɪstlɪsnɪs] **N 1** (*of food*) insipidité *f*, fadeur *f* **2** (*of person, clothes, remark etc*) manque *m* de goût

taster ['teɪstər] **N 1** (*person*) (*of wines, teas etc*) dégustateur, -trice **2** (*foretaste*) **this is just a t.** (*of what's to come*) ceci n'est qu'un avant-goût (de ce qui va suivre)

tastiness ['teɪstɪnɪs] **N** saveur *f ou* goût *m* agréable

tasting ['teɪstɪŋ] **N** (*of wines*) dégustation *f*

tasty ['teɪstɪ] **ADJ 1** (*dish, meal*) savoureux; **it's not very t.** ça n'a pas beaucoup de goût; **a t. morsel** un mets succulent **2** *Br Fam* (*good-looking*) bien foutu; **she's a t. piece** c'est un beau morceau

TAT [tiːeɪˈtiː] **N** *Mktg* (*abbr* **thematic apperception test**) TAT *m*

tat[1] [tæt] **N** *see* **tit**[2]

tat[2] **N** *Fam* (*junk*) camelote *f*

ta-ta [tæˈtɑː] **INT** *Br Fam* au revoir!

Tatar ['tɑːtər] **ADJ** tatar
N Tatar *m*, Tatare *f*
▶▶ **the T. Republic** la République de Tatarie

Tatary ['tɑːtərɪ] **N** Tatarie *f*

tater ['teɪtər] **N** *Br Sl* (*potato*) patate *f*

tatter ['tætər] **N** lambeau *m*, loque *f*; **in tatters** en lambeaux, en loques; *Fig* (*reputation, confidence*) anéanti; **to tear sb's reputation to tatters** ruiner la réputation de qn

tattered ['tætəd] **ADJ** (*clothes*) en loques, en lambeaux; (*person*) déguenillé, loqueteux

tattie ['tætɪ] **N** *esp Scot Fam* (*potato*) patate *f*

tattle ['tæt(ə)l] **N** (*gossip, rumour*) commérages *mpl*, potins *mpl*
VI (*gossip*) commérer, cancaner

tattler ['tætlər] **N** (*gossip, rumour-monger*) commère *f*, cancanier, -ière

tattle-tale N = **telltale**

tattoo[1] [təˈtuː] **N** *Mil* **1** (*drum signal*) retraite *f* (du soir); **to beat** *or* **sound the t.** battre *ou* sonner la retraite **2** (*parade*) parade *f* militaire

tattoo[2] **N** (*design*) tatouage *m*; **a t. of an anchor, an anchor t.** un tatouage représentant une ancre
VT tatouer
▶▶ **t. artist** tatoueur *m*

tattooing [təˈtuːɪŋ] **N** tatouage *m*

tattooist [təˈtuːɪst] **N** tatoueur *m*

tatty ['tætɪ] **ADJ** *Fam* (*in poor condition*) miteux; (*of poor quality*) minable

taught **PT, PP** *see* **teach**

taunt [tɔːnt] **N** (*words*) sarcasme *m*, raillerie *f*
VT accabler de sarcasmes; **to t. sb into action** pousser qn à agir en usant de sarcasmes; **to t. sb with sth** railler qn à propos de qch

taunting ['tɔːntɪŋ] **ADJ** sarcastique, railleur

tauntingly ['tɔːntɪŋlɪ] **ADV** d'un ton sarcastique *ou* railleur

Taurus ['tɔːrəs] **N** *Astrol* Taureau *m*; **to be (a) T.** être (du) Taureau

taut [tɔːt] **ADJ** (*rope*) tendu; (*muscle*) tendu, contracté; (*prose, style, sentence*) dépouillé; **she looked t.** elle avait l'air tendu; **t. situation** situation *f* tendue

tauten ['tɔːt(ə)n] **VT** (*cable etc*) tendre
VI se tendre

tautness ['tɔːtnɪs] **N** (*of cable etc*) raideur *f*; (*of muscles*) tension *f*, (*of piece of prose*) caractère *m* dépouillé

tautological [tɔːtəˈlɒdʒɪk(ə)l] **ADJ** tautologique

tautology [tɔː'tɒlədʒɪ] N tautologie f

tavern ['tæv(ə)n] N *(in proper names), Lit* taverne f, cabaret m

tawdriness ['tɔːdrɪnɪs] N *(of piece of jewellery)* clinquant m, faux éclat m; *(of decor)* clinquant; **there was a t. about everything in the hotel** tout dans l'hôtel était clinquant

tawdry ['tɔːdrɪ] ADJ **1** *(clothing, ornament)* tape-à-l'œil, tapageur; *(decor)* clinquant; **t. jewellery** clinquant m, toc m; **a t. hotel** un hôtel à la décoration tape-à-l'œil **2** *(conduct, motive etc)* lâche

tawny ['tɔːnɪ] ADJ fauve
▸▸ *Orn* **t. eagle** aigle m ravisseur; *Orn* **t. owl** chouette f hulotte; **t. port** = porto m qui a jauni dans le fût

tax [tæks] N **1** *Admin* impôt m, taxe f; **you pay out a small fortune in t.** on paye une petite fortune en impôts; **after t.** net, après impôt; **before t.** hors taxe, HT; *(income)* avant impôt; **direct/indirect t.** impôt direct/indirect; **income t.** impôt sur le revenu; **capital gains t.** impôt sur les plus-values; *Br* **value added t.**, *Am* **processing t.** taxe à la valeur ajoutée; **to levy a t. on sth** frapper qch d'un droit; **t. exempt** exempt d'impôts; **t. paid** net d'impôt **2** *(strain)* charge f
VT **1** *Admin (person)* imposer, frapper d'un impôt; *(luxury items etc)* taxer; **to t. income** imposer le revenu; **to be heavily taxed** être lourdement imposé; **small businesses are being taxed out of existence** accablées d'impôts, les petites entreprises disparaissent; **we're being taxed out of existence** on nous accable d'impôts; *Br Aut* **taxed** avec vignette
2 *(put under strain)* mettre à l'épreuve; **to t. sb's intellect/imagination** éprouver l'intelligence/l'imagination de qn; **to t. sb's patience to the limit** abuser sérieusement de la patience de qn
3 *esp Lit (accuse)* **to t. sb with sth** taxer qn de qch; **to t. sb with doing sth** accuser qn d'avoir fait qch
4 *Br Fam (steal)* taxer, piquer, chouraver
▸▸ **t. allowance** abattement m fiscal, déduction f fiscale; **t. assessment** avis m d'imposition, fixation f de l'impôt; **t. audit** vérification f fiscale; **t. authorities** administration f fiscale; **t. avoidance** optimisation f *ou* évasion f fiscale, *Can* évitement m fiscal; **t. band** tranche f d'imposition; **t. base** assiette f fiscale; **t. benefit** avantage m fiscal; **t. bite** proportion f du revenu pris par l'impôt; **t. bracket** tranche f d'imposition, fourchette f d'imposition; **t. break** réduction f d'impôt, allègement m fiscal; **t. burden** pression f fiscale, poids m de la fiscalité; **t. ceiling** plafond m fiscal, plafond de l'impôt; **t. centre** centre m des impôts, CDI m; **t. clearance** quitus m fiscal; **t. code** barème m fiscal; **t. collection** recouvrement m d'impôts, perception f d'impôts; **t. collector** percepteur m d'impôt, receveur m des contributions; **t. consultant** conseiller, -ère fiscal(e), conseil m fiscal; **t. credit** aide f fiscale, avoir m fiscal; **t. cut** baisse f *ou* réduction f des impôts; **t. deduction** prélèvement m fiscal, déduction f fiscale; **t. deduction at source** perception f à la source; *Br* **t. disc** vignette f *(automobile)*; *Am* **t. dollars** argent m du contribuable; **t. domicile** foyer m *ou* domicile m fiscal; **t. evasion** fraude f fiscale, évasion f fiscale; **t. exemption** exonération f d'impôt, exemption f d'impôt; **t. exile** = personne f qui réside à l'étranger pour minimiser sa responsabilité fiscale; **t. expenditure** dépenses fpl fiscales; **t. expert** fiscaliste mf; **t. form** feuille f *ou* déclaration f d'impôts; **t. fraud** fraude f fiscale; **t. harmonization** harmonisation f fiscale; **t. haven** paradis m fiscal; **t. holiday** période f de grâce *(accordée pour le paiement des impôts)*; **t. impact**

incidence f fiscale; **t. incentive** incitation f fiscale, avantage m fiscal; **t. inspection** contrôle m fiscal; **t. inspector** inspecteur, -trice des contributions directes *ou* des impôts; **t. law** droit m fiscal; **t. liability** *(of person)* assujettissement m à l'impôt; *(of goods, product)* exigibilité f de l'impôt; **t. loophole** échappatoire f fiscale; **t. loss** déficit m fiscal reportable; *Br Fam* **the t. man** le fisc; **t. office** centre m des impôts; **t. official** agent m du fisc; **t. point** date f de facturation; **t. provision** disposition f fiscale; **t. rate** taux m d'imposition; **t. rebate** dégrèvement m fiscal; **t. reduction** abattement m fiscal; **t. refund** *(of income tax)* restitution f d'impôts; *(on goods)* détaxe f; **t. relief** dégrèvement m fiscal; **t. return** déclaration f de revenu, feuille f d'impôts; **to make one's t. return** faire sa déclaration d'impôts; **t. revenue** recettes fpl *ou* rentrées fpl fiscales; **t. roll** rôle m d'impôt *ou* des contributions; **t. shelter** échappatoire f fiscale; **t. shield** protection f fiscale; **t. specialist** fiscaliste mf; **t. and spend** = financement m des grandes dépenses budgétaires par des taux d'imposition élevés; **t. stamp** timbre m fiscal; **t. system** régime m fiscal *ou* d'imposition; **t. threshold** minimum m imposable, seuil m d'imposition; **t. tolerance** tolérance f fiscale; **t. write-off** *(expense)* dépense f déductible des impôts; *(loss)* perte f déductible des impôts; **t. year** année f fiscale, année d'imposition *(qui commence en avril en Grande-Bretagne)*

taxable ['tæksəbl] ADJ **1** *(revenue, land etc)* imposable, taxable; **to make sth t.** imposer qch **2** *Law* **costs t. to sb** frais mpl à la charge de qn
▸▸ **t. base** base f d'imposition; **t. income** revenu m imposable, assiette f fiscale *ou* de l'impôt; **t. profit** bénéfice m fiscal *ou* imposable; **t. transaction** opération f imposable

taxation [tæk'seɪʃən] N *(imposing taxes)* imposition f, *(taxes)* charges fpl fiscales; *(tax revenue)* impôts mpl, taxes fpl; **t. at source** prélèvement m de l'impôt à la source, imposition f à la source

tax-deductible ADJ déductible des impôts

tax-free ADJ *(income)* exempt d'impôts; *(goods)* exonéré de taxes
▸▸ **t. shop** boutique f hors taxes; **t. shopping** achats mpl hors taxes

taxi ['tæksɪ] N taxi m; **to go by t.** aller en taxi
VI *(pt, pp* **taxied**; *prp* **taxiing**) *(of aircraft)* rouler; **the plane taxied back to the terminal** l'avion regagna le terminal
▸▸ **t. driver** chauffeur m de taxi; **t. fare** *(in general)* tarif m de taxi; *(cost of journey)* coût m du taxi, prix m de la course (en taxi); **t. rank**, *esp Am* **t. stand** station f de taxis

taxicab ['tæksɪkæb] N taxi m

taxidermist ['tæksɪdɜːmɪst] N taxidermiste mf

taxidermy ['tæksɪdɜːmɪ] N taxidermie f

taximeter ['tæksɪmiːtər] N taximètre m, compteur m (de taxi)

taxing ['tæksɪŋ] ADJ *(job, course)* ardu; **these long hours are very t.** ces longues journées sont complètement éreintantes

taxiplane ['tæksɪpleɪn] N avion-taxi m, pl avions-taxis

taxonomic [tæksə'nɒmɪk] ADJ taxonomique

taxonomy [tæk'sɒnəmɪ] N taxonomie f

taxpayer ['tækspeɪər] N contribuable mf

TB [tiː'biː] N *Med (abbr* **tuberculosis**) tuberculose f

T-bar N *Ski* téléski m, tire-fesses m inv

T-bone N
▸▸ *Culin* **T. steak** steak m d'aloyau

tbs, tbsp *Culin (abbr* **tablespoonful**) cuillerée f à soupe

T-card N fiche f en T

TCP® [tiːsiː'piː] N *(antiseptic)* ≃ Merchryl® m

TCP/IP [tiːsiːpiːaɪ'piː] N *Comput (abbr* **transmission control protocol/Internet protocol**) TCP-IP m

TD [tiː'diː] N *Pol abbr* = membre m de la chambre basse du Parlement irlandais

tea [tiː] N **1** *(leaves, drink)* thé m; *(herbal infusion)* tisane f, infusion f; **camomile t.** infusion de camomille *etc*; **to drink t.** boire *ou* prendre du thé; **a cup of t.** une tasse de thé; **t. and coffee making facilities** nécessaire m pour préparer le thé et le café; **China t.** thé de Chine; **black/green t.** thé noir/vert
2 *esp Br (meal)* **(afternoon) t.** thé m, = goûter m; **high t.** repas m du soir; *Scot, North Eng* **t.** *(dinner)* dîner m; **to ask sb to t.** inviter qn à (venir) prendre le thé; **to give a t. party** inviter des gens pour le thé; *(for children)* organiser un goûter
3 *(plant)* thé m
▸▸ **t. bag** sachet m de thé; **t. blend** mélange m de thés; *Br* **t. boy** = jeune employé m chargé de préparer le thé pour ses collègues; *Br* **t. break** pause f pour prendre le thé, pause-thé f, pl pauses-thé; **t. caddy** boîte f à thé; **t. chest** caisse f (à thé); *Br* **t. cloth** torchon m (à vaisselle); **t. cosy** cosy cvre-théière m, pl couvre-théières; *Br* **t. lady** = dame f qui prépare ou sert le thé pour les employés d'une entreprise; **t. leaf** feuille f de thé; *Br Sl (thief)* voleur, -euse; **(used) t. leaves** marc m de thé; **to read the t. leaves** ≃ lire dans le marc de café; **t. plant** arbre m à thé, théier m; **t. plantation** plantation f de thé; **t. planter** planteur m de thé; **t. rose** rose f thé; **t. service, t. set** service m à thé; **t. strainer** passoire f à thé, passe-thé m inv; **t. table** table f (mise) pour le thé, table à thé; *Br* **t. towel** torchon m (à vaisselle); **t. urn** fontaine f à thé

teacake ['tiːkeɪk] N *Br Culin* = sorte de petit pain

teach [tiːtʃ] VT *(pt, pp* **taught** [tɔːt]) *(subject)* enseigner; **to t. sb sth, to t. sth to sb** enseigner *ou* apprendre qch à qn; **to t. sb (how) to do sth** apprendre à qn à faire qch; **to t. oneself sth** apprendre qch tout seul; **your Japanese is very good, who taught you?** tu parles très bien japonais, qui t'a appris?; **I taught myself** j'ai appris tout seul; **who taught you to drive!** où as-tu appris à conduire!; **can you t. me the butterfly stroke?** est-ce que tu peux m'apprendre la nage papillon?; **he teaches the young pupils** il fait la classe *ou* l'école aux petits; **she teaches the piano** elle est professeur de piano; **he teaches French** il enseigne le français, il est professeur de français; *Am* **to t. school** enseigner; *(as profession)* être dans l'enseignement; **the way history is taught** la manière dont on enseigne l'histoire; *Prov* **you can't t. your grandmother to suck eggs** ce n'est pas au vieux singe qu'on apprend à faire la grimace; *Fam* **to t. sb a lesson** donner une leçon à qn; *Fam* **that'll t. him!** ça lui apprendra!; *Fam* **to t. sb a thing or two** dégourdir qn; *Fam* **I'll t. you to speak to me like that!** je vous apprendrai à me parler comme ça!
VI enseigner; *(as profession)* être dans l'enseignement; **she has taught abroad** elle a enseigné à l'étranger; **when you've been teaching for 25 years …** quand tu as passé 25 ans dans l'enseignement …
N *Fam (teacher)* prof mf

teachable ['tiːtʃəbl] ADJ **1** *(person)* qui apprend facilement **2** *(subject)* enseignable; **it's not t.** c'est impossible à enseigner; **it's not easily t.** cela n'est pas facile à enseigner

teacher ['ti:tʃər] N (at primary school) instituteur, -trice, maître, -esse d'école; (at secondary school) professeur m, enseignant, -ante; **history/French/maths t.** professeur d'histoire/de français/de maths; **to become a t.** devenir professeur
▸▸ **t.'s pet** chouchou mf du professeur; **t.-pupil ratio** taux m d'encadrement des élèves; Br **t. training** formation f pédagogique des enseignants; **to do one's t. training** suivre une formation pédagogique; **to get one's t. training certificate** obtenir son certificat d'aptitude pédagogique; Br **t. training college** centre m de formation pédagogique, ≃ école f normale

teach-in N séminaire m

teaching ['ti:tʃɪŋ] N **1** (profession, action) enseignement m; **a low/high standard of maths/language t.** un niveau bas/élevé dans l'enseignement des maths/des langues; **to go into t.** entrer dans l'enseignement **2** (classes) cours mpl; **most of the t. is done in the morning** la plupart des cours ont lieu le matin **3** (doctrine) doctrine f; **teachings** préceptes mpl
▸▸ **t. aids** matériel m ou équipement m pédagogique; **t. hospital** centre m hospitalo-universitaire, CHU m; **t. method** méthode f d'enseignement; Br **t. practice** stage m pédagogique (pour futurs enseignants); **the t. profession** (teachers) le corps enseignant; **the t. staff** (of primary school) les instituteurs mpl; (of secondary school) les professeurs mpl

teacup ['ti:kʌp] N tasse f à thé

teacupful ['ti:kʌpfʊl] N (measure) tasse f (**of** de)

teak [ti:k] N (wood, tree) teck m, tek m

teal [ti:l] N (pl usu **teal**) (duck) sarcelle f

team [ti:m] N (of players, workers etc) équipe f; (of horses, oxen) attelage m; **football t.** équipe de football; **he's one of the t.** il fait partie de l'équipe; **a t. effort** un travail d'équipe; **he's not much of a t. player** (at football), Fig il n'a pas l'esprit d'équipe VOIR GRAMMAIRE A11

VT & VI = **team up**
▸▸ **t. games** jeux mpl d'équipe; **t. member** membre m d'une équipe; Sport équipier m; **t. spirit** esprit m d'équipe; **t. sports** sports mpl d'équipe
▸ **team up** VI s'associer (**with sb** avec qn); **the two companies have teamed up to work on this project** les deux entreprises se sont associées pour travailler sur ce projet
VT SEP associer, mettre en collaboration (**with** avec)

team-mate N Sport coéquipier m

teamster ['ti:mstər] N **1** (of mules etc) conducteur m (d'attelage), charretier m **2** Am (trucker) camionneur m, routier m; **the Teamsters** (union) = syndicat m américain des camionneurs

teamwork ['ti:mwɜ:k] N (combined effort) travail m d'équipe; (ability to work together) collaboration f; Sport jeu m d'équipe; **success due to t.** réussite due à un travail d'équipe

teapot ['ti:pɒt] N théière f

tear¹ [tɪər] N (from eye) larme f; **in tears** en larmes; **on the verge of tears** au bord des larmes; **to burst into tears** fondre en larmes, éclater en sanglots; **to bring tears to sb's eyes** faire venir des larmes aux yeux de qn; **to shed bitter tears/tears of joy** verser des larmes amères/de joie; **crocodile tears** larmes de crocodile
▸▸ **t. duct** canal m lacrymal; **t. gas** gaz m lacrymogène; **t. gas bomb** bombe f lacrymogène

tear² [teər] N (rip) déchirure f; (in garment) accroc m

tear VT (pt **tore** [tɔ:r]; pp **torn** [tɔ:n]) (dress, letter etc) déchirer; **to t. a muscle** (of person) se déchirer un muscle; **torn tendon** tendon m déchiré; **to t. a hole in sth** faire un trou ou un accroc à qch; **to t. sth in two** or **in half** déchirer qch en deux; **to t. sth open** ouvrir qch en le déchirant; **to t. sth to pieces** (document, bank note etc) déchirer qch en mille morceaux; Fig (film, argument etc) mettre qch en pièces; **the fox was torn to pieces by the hounds** le renard a été déchiqueté ou mis en pièces par la meute; Fig **to t. sb to pieces** mettre qn en pièces; écharper qn; Fig **they'll t. you to pieces** ils vont vous mettre en pièces, vous allez vous faire écharper; Fig **to t. sb's character to shreds** or **pieces** démolir qn; **country torn by civil war** pays déchiré par la guerre civile; **torn between two feelings** tiraillé entre deux émotions; Fig **that's torn it** il ne manquait plus que ça; Fig **to t. one's hair** s'arracher les cheveux
VI **1** (of material, muscle etc) se déchirer **2 to t. at sth** déchirer qch
▸ **tear about, tear around** VI (rush around) courir partout; **I've been tearing around on my bike all day** j'ai pédalé comme un fou toute la journée; **he's always tearing around** il est toujours à se démener; **he tears about from auction to auction** il est toujours à courir d'une vente aux enchères à une autre
VT INSEP **he spends most of his time tearing around the country** il passe la plus grande partie de son temps à sillonner le pays; **to t. around the shops** faire des courses en vitesse; **to t. around a museum** parcourir un musée à toute vitesse
▸ **tear along** VI (go fast) aller à toute vitesse, Fam foncer; **to t. along at top speed** aller à toute vitesse; **to t. along at 100 mph** foncer à 100 à l'heure
VT INSEP (go fast on) **he was tearing along the road** (in vehicle, on bike) il dévalait la rue; (on foot) il descendait la rue à toute vitesse
▸ **tear away** VT SEP **1** (remove by tearing) arracher (**from** de) **2 to t. oneself away from** (leave reluctantly) (television, book etc) s'arracher de; **I couldn't t. myself away from the place** je n'arrivais pas à me décider à partir
VI (leave at high speed) partir à toute vitesse; (of car) démarrer en trombe
▸ **tear down** VT SEP (take down forcefully) (poster etc) arracher (**from** de); (wall, building etc) démolir; (statue) renverser
▸ **tear into** VT INSEP **1** (attack physically) attaquer, assaillir; **the lion's teeth tore into the antelope's flesh** le lion lacéra la chair de l'antilope ou avec ses crocs **2** (attack verbally) incendier, passer un savon à
▸ **tear off** VT SEP (detach by tearing) arracher (**from** de); **he had had one of his arms torn off by a machine** il avait eu le bras arraché par une machine; Fam **to t. sb off a strip, to t. a strip off sb** donner ou passer un savon à qn
VI = **tear away** VI
▸ **tear out** VT SEP (remove by tearing) arracher (**from** de); **to t. a page out of a book** arracher une page d'un livre; Fig **he was tearing his hair out** il s'arrachait les cheveux
VI (leave at high speed) partir en trombe; **she tore out of the house after them** elle sortit en trombe de la maison derrière eux
▸ **tear up** VT SEP **1** (tear into small pieces) (letter etc) déchirer; (ground, fields etc) (of tanks, car wheels etc) labourer; (deliberately) (of JCB) défoncer; (contract) déchirer; Fig oublier **2** (pull up) (plant, tree) déraciner; (railings, telegraph pole) arracher
VT INSEP (go up fast) **to t. up the stairs** monter l'escalier quatre à quatre

tearaway ['teərəweɪ] N Br casse-cou m inv

teardrop ['tɪədrɒp] N larme f

tearful ['tɪəfʊl] ADJ (person) en pleurs; (farewell) déchirant; **in a t. voice** avec des larmes dans la voix; **she gets all t.** les larmes lui montent aux yeux

tearfully ['tɪəfəlɪ] ADV (crying) en pleurant; (on verge of tears) les larmes aux yeux

tearing ['teərɪŋ] N (of fabric etc) déchirement m; **a t. sound** un bruit de déchirure; Fam **to be in a t. hurry** être terriblement pressé

tearjerker ['tɪədʒɜ:kər] N Fam (film, book) mélo m

tearless ['tɪəlɪs] ADJ **t. grief** chagrin m sans larmes

tear-off ADJ (label etc) perforé; (reply slip etc) détachable
▸▸ **t. calendar** calendrier m éphéméride; Comput **t. menu** menu m flottant

tearoom ['ti:ru:m] N salon m de thé

tearstained ['tɪəsteɪnd] ADJ (face) (dirty) barbouillé de larmes; (in tears) baigné de larmes

tease [ti:z] N **1** (person) taquin, -ine; **he's a t.** il est taquin **2** (sexual) (woman) allumeuse f; **don't be a t.** arrête de m'allumer
VT **1** (person) taquiner; (dog etc) embêter; (maliciously) tourmenter; **to t. sb about sth** taquiner qn à propos de qch **2** (sexually) allumer **3** Tex (comb out) (fabric etc) effiler, effilocher; (wool) démêler **4 he teased the wire through the slot** avec beaucoup de minutie, il a réussi à mettre le fil dans la fente; **he teased the engine into life** il a réussi à démarrer la voiture à force de la bichonner
VI **don't worry, he's just teasing** ne t'inquiète pas, il fait ça pour rire
▸ **tease out** VT SEP **1** Fig **she carefully teases out the important facts** elle prend soin de dégager les faits importants; **to t. information out of sb** faire donner des informations à qn **2** Tex = **tease** VT **3**

teasel ['ti:z(ə)l] N **1** (plant) cardère f **2** Tex carde f

teaser ['ti:zər] N **1** = **tease 2** Fam (problem) question f difficile, colle f; (advert) aguiche f
▸▸ Mktg **t. ad** aguiche f; Mktg **t. campaign** campagne f teasing

teashop ['ti:ʃɒp] N salon m de thé

teasing ['ti:zɪŋ] ADJ (tone etc) taquin
N (provoking) taquinerie f

teasingly ['ti:zɪŋlɪ] ADV (in a teasing tone) sur le ton de la taquinerie; (in order to tease) pour taquiner

teaspoon ['ti:spu:n] N cuillère f ou cuiller f à café

teaspoonful ['ti:spu:nfʊl] N cuillerée f à café

teat [ti:t] N (of woman) mamelon m, bout m de sein, téton m; (of cow etc) trayon m; (of feeding bottle) tétine f

teatime ['ti:taɪm] N l'heure f du thé

teazel, teazle ['ti:z(ə)l] N = **teasel**

tech [tek] N Br Fam (abbr **technical college**) ≃ IUT m

techie ['tekɪ] N Comput Fam = terme péjoratif ou humoristique désignant les informaticiens

technical ['teknɪk(ə)l] ADJ (term, dictionary, problem etc) technique; (difficulty) d'ordre technique; **don't get t.** n'emploie pas de termes trop techniques
▸▸ Comput **t. assistance** assistance f technique; **t. college** ≃ IUT m; St Exch **t. correction** correction f d'un cours en Bourse; **t. director** directeur m technique; **t. drawing** dessin m industriel; Br **t. hitch** incident m technique; Boxing **t. knockout** knock-out m

inv technique; **t. manager** directeur *m* technique; *Law* **t. offence** quasi-délit *m, pl* quasi-délits; *Cin, TV* **t. operator** preneur *m* de son, opérateur *m* du son; **t. specifications** spécifications *fpl* techniques; **t. standard** norme *f* technique; *Comput* **t. support** support *m* technique

technicality [teknɪˈkælɪtɪ] N **1** *(of term)* technicité *f* **2** *(detail)* détail *m* technique; *(technical term)* terme *m* technique; *Law* **she was acquitted on a t.** elle a été acquittée sur un point de droit

technically [ˈteknɪklɪ] ADV **1** techniquement; *(to express oneself)* en termes techniques; **t., it shouldn't be able to fly** d'un point de vue technique, il ne devrait pas pouvoir voler **2** *(strictly, in reality)* en réalité; **t. (speaking), you're not allowed to do that** théoriquement tu n'as pas le droit de faire ça

technician [tekˈnɪʃən] N technicien, -ienne

Technicolor® [ˈteknɪkʌlər] ADJ, N *Cin* Technicolor® *m*

technique [tekˈniːk] N technique *f*; **his t. is poor** il manque de technique

techno [ˈteknəʊ] N *Mus* techno *f*

technobabble [ˈteknəʊbæb(ə)l] N jargon *m* technique

technocracy [tekˈnɒkrəsɪ] N technocratie *f*

technocrat [ˈteknəkræt] N technocrate *mf*

technological [teknəˈlɒdʒɪk(ə)l] ADJ technologique

technologist [tekˈnɒlədʒɪst] N technologue *mf*, technologiste *mf*

technology [tekˈnɒlədʒɪ] N technologie *f*; **the lastest t.** la technologie de pointe *ou* la plus avancée
▶▶ **t. transfer** transfert *m* de technologie

technophobia [teknəʊˈfəʊbɪə] N technophobie *f*

techy [ˈtetʃɪ] ADJ = **tetchy**

tectonic [tekˈtɒnɪk] ADJ tectonique

tectonics [tekˈtɒnɪks] NPL tectonique *f* VOIR GRAMMAIRE A10

Ted [ted] N *Br Fam (teddy boy)* ≃ blouson *m* noir

tedder [ˈtedər] N *Agr (machine)* faneuse *f*

teddy [ˈtedɪ] N *(toy)* ours *m* en peluche
▶▶ **t. bear** ours en peluche; *Br* **t. boy** ≃ blouson *m* noir *(personne)*

tedious [ˈtiːdɪəs] ADJ *(job, speech etc)* ennuyeux, fastidieux; *(person, film)* ennuyeux; **how t. for you!** comme c'est ennuyeux!; **as he explained in t. detail** comme il l'a expliqué avec force détails fastidieux

tediously [ˈtiːdɪəslɪ] ADV d'une manière ennuyeuse *ou* fastidieuse

tediousness, tedium [ˈtiːdɪəsnɪs, -dɪəm] N *(of job, existence, film)* manque *m* d'intérêt

tee [tiː] *Golf* N *(support for ball)* tee *m*; *(piece of ground)* tertre *m ou* point *m* de départ
VT *(ball)* mettre sur un tee
▶ **tee off** VI *Golf* jouer le départ
▶ **tee up** VI *Golf* placer la balle sur le tee
VT SEP *Golf* **to t. up the ball** placer la balle sur le tee; *Fig* **to t. up a deal** préparer le terrain pour obtenir un contrat; **to t. up a job for sb** apporter un travail à qn sur un plateau

teem [tiːm] VI **1** grouiller, fourmiller (**with** de); *(with ideas)* regorger (**with** en) **2 the rain was teeming down** la pluie tombait à verse; **it's teeming with rain** il tombe des cordes

teeming [ˈtiːmɪŋ] ADJ **1** grouillant **2 in the t. rain** sous la pluie battante

teen [tiːn] ADJ *Fam* = **teenage**
▶▶ **t. idol** idole *f* des jeunes

teenage [ˈtiːneɪdʒ] ADJ *(boy, girl etc)* adoles-

cent, jeune; *(problems)* de l'adolescence; *(party, novels)* d'adolescents; **in her t. years** quand elle était adolescente; **t. magazine** magazine *m* pour adolescents

teenager [ˈtiːneɪdʒər] N adolescent, -ente

teenpic [ˈtiːnpɪk] N *Cin Fam* film *m* d'ados

teens [tiːnz] NPL **one's t.** l'adolescence *f*; **to be in one's t.** être adolescent(e); **to be hardly out of one's t.** avoir juste vingt ans

teeny-bopper [ˈtiːnɪbɒpər] N *Fam* petite minette *f*

teeny(-weeny) [ˈtiːnɪ(ˈwiːnɪ)], **teensy (weensy)** [ˈtiːnzɪ(ˈwiːnzɪ)] ADJ *Fam* minuscule, tout petit; **just a t. drop, please** juste une toute petite goutte, s'il vous plaît

teeshirt [ˈtiːʃɜːt] N tee-shirt *m*, T-shirt *m*

teeter [ˈtiːtər] VI *(be unsteady)* chanceler; *Fig* **to t. on the brink of ruin/war** être à deux doigts de la ruine/d'un conflit armé
N *esp Am (seesaw)* jeu *m* de bascule, tapecul *m*

teethe [tiːð] VI *(usu in progressive tenses)* faire ses (premières) dents, percer ses dents

teething [ˈtiːðɪŋ] N dentition *f*, poussée *f* dentaire
▶▶ **t. ring** anneau *m* de dentition; **t. troubles** douleurs *fpl* provoquées par la poussée des dents; *Fig* difficultés *fpl* initiales *ou* de départ

teetotal [tiːˈtəʊt(ə)l] ADJ qui ne boit jamais d'alcool

teetotalism [tiːˈtəʊtəlɪz(ə)m] N abstention *f* de toute boisson alcoolisée; **after two weeks of enforced t.** après une quinzaine de jours au régime sec

teetotaller, *Am* **teetotaler** [tiːˈtəʊt(ə)lər] N personne *f* qui ne boit jamais d'alcool

TEFL [ˈtef(ə)l] N *(abbr* **Teaching of English as a Foreign Language)** enseignement *m* de l'anglais langue étrangère
▶▶ **T. course** formation *f* en anglais langue étrangère

tegument [ˈtegjʊmənt] N tégument *m*

Teh(e)ran [teəˈrɑːn] N Téhéran

tel *(abbr* **telephone)** tél.

telebanking [ˈtelɪbæŋkɪŋ] N monétique *f*, *(home banking)* banque *f* à domicile

telecast [ˈtelɪkɑːst] N *TV* émission *f* de télévision
VT *(pt, pp* **telecast)** téléviser

telecaster [ˈtelɪkɑːstər] N *(broadcaster)* téléaste *mf*; *(broadcasting company)* société *f* de télédiffusion

telecine [ˈtelɪsɪnɪ] N télécinéma *m*

telecomms [ˈtelɪkɒmz] NPL télécommunications *fpl*

telecommunications [telɪkəmjuːnɪˈkeɪʃənz] N télécommunications *fpl*
▶▶ **t. engineer** technicien *m* des télécommunications; **t. industry** industrie *f* des télécommunications; **t. link** liaison *f* de télécommunications; **t. media** médias *mpl* de télécommunications; **t. network** réseau *m* de télécommunications; **t. satellite** satellite *m* de télécommunications

telecommute [ˈteləkəmjuːt] VI faire du télétravail, télétravailler

telecommuter [ˈteləkəmjuːtər] N télétravailleur, -euse

telecommuting [ˈteləkəmjuːtɪŋ] N télétravail *m*

teleconference [ˈtelɪkɒnf(ə)rəns] N téléconférence *f*

teleconferencing [ˈtelɪkɒnf(ə)rənsɪŋ] N téléconférences *fpl*

telefilm [ˈtelɪfɪlm] N téléfilm *m*, film *m* télévisé

telegenic [telɪˈdʒenɪk] ADJ télégénique

telegram [ˈtelɪgræm] N télégramme *m*; **greetings t.** télégramme de félicitations
▶▶ **t. form** formule *f* de télégramme

telegraph [ˈtelɪgrɑːf] N télégraphe *m*; *Fam* **bush t.** téléphone *m* arabe
VT *(news)* télégraphier; *(person)* télégraphier à; *Sport* **to t. a punch/pass/etc** téléphoner un coup/une passe/*etc*
VI télégraphier
▶▶ **t. pole** poteau *m* télégraphique; **t. wire** fil *m* télégraphique

telegrapher [tɪˈlegrəfər] N *Am* télégraphiste *mf*

telegraphese [telɪgrəˈfiːz] N langage *m ou* style *m* télégraphique

telegraphic [telɪˈgræfɪk] ADJ télégraphique
▶▶ **t. money order** mandat *m* télégraphique; **t. payment** paiement *m* télégraphique; **t. transfer** transfert *m* télégraphique

telegraphist [tɪˈlegrəfɪst] N télégraphiste *mf*

telegraphy [tɪˈlegrəfɪ] N télégraphie *f*

telejector [ˈtelɪdʒektər] N *TV* projecteur *m* de télévision

telekinesis [telɪkɪˈniːsɪs] N télékinésie *f*

telemarket [ˈtelɪmɑːkɪt] N télémarché *m*

telemarketing [ˈtelɪmɑːkɪtɪŋ] N télémarketing *m*

telematics [telɪˈmætɪks] N télématique *f* VOIR GRAMMAIRE A10

Telemessage® [ˈtelɪmesɪdʒ] N *Br* télégramme *m*

telemeter [ˈtelɪmiːtər] N *(in surveying)* appareil *m* de télémesure; *Mil etc* télémètre *m*

teleological [telɪəˈlɒdʒɪk(ə)l] ADJ *Phil* téléologique

teleology [telɪˈɒlədʒɪ] N *Phil* téléologie *f*

telepathic [telɪˈpæθɪk] ADJ télépathique; *(person)* télépathe; **you must be t.!** tu dois avoir des dons de télépathie!; **tell me, I'm not t.!** dis-le moi, je ne suis pas médium!

telepathically [telɪˈpæθɪklɪ] ADV *(to communicate)* par télépathie

telepathy [tɪˈlepəθɪ] N télépathie *f*

telepayment [ˈtelɪpeɪmənt] N télépaiement *m*

telephone [ˈtelɪfəʊn] N téléphone *m*; **to be on the t.** *(be subscriber)* avoir le téléphone, être abonné au téléphone; *(be speaking on it)* être au téléphone; **to speak to sb on the t.** avoir qn au téléphone; **come on, get off the t.!** allez, raccroche!; **you're wanted on the t.** on vous demande au téléphone; **to have a good t. manner** savoir bien parler au téléphone; *Mil* **field t.** téléphone de campagne; **public t.** téléphone public VOIR GRAMMAIRE A77
VI téléphoner (**to** à); **to t. for a taxi** appeler un taxi (par téléphone)
VT *(message)* téléphoner; *(person)* téléphoner à; **to t. a warning** envoyer un avertissement par téléphone; **to t. a bomb-warning to the police** prévenir la police par téléphone d'une alerte à la bombe
▶▶ **t. banking** opérations *fpl* bancaires par téléphone, banque *f* à domicile; **t. book** annuaire *m* (téléphonique); **t. booking** réservation *f* par téléphone; *Am* **t. booth** cabine *f* téléphonique; **t. box** cabine *f* téléphonique; **t. call** appel *m* téléphonique, coup *m* de téléphone; *Mktg* **t. canvassing** prospection *f* téléphonique, démarchage *m* à distance, télédémarchage *m*; **t. code area** circonscription *f* téléphonique; **t. conversation** conversation *f* téléphonique; **t. directory** annuaire *m* (téléphonique); **t. exchange** central *m* téléphonique; *Mktg* **t. follow-up** relance *f* téléphonique; **t. help desk** assis-

tance *f* téléphonique; **t. interview** entretien *m* téléphonique, entretien par téléphone; **t. interviewing** enquête *f* téléphonique, sondage *m* par téléphone; **t. jack** fiche *f* téléphonique; *Br* **t. kiosk** cabine *f* téléphonique; **t. line** ligne *f* téléphonique; **t. link** liaison *f* téléphonique; **t. marketing** marketing *m* téléphonique, télémarketing *m*; **t. memo** fiche *f* téléphonique; **t. message** message *m* téléphoné *ou* téléphonique; **t. message pad** bloc *m* télé-mémo; **t. network** réseau *m* téléphonique; **t. number** numéro *m* de téléphone; **t. operator** téléphoniste *mf*, standardiste *mf*; **t. order** commande *f* téléphonique *ou* par téléphone; *Mktg* **t. prospecting** télédémarchage *m*, démarchage *m* à distance; **t. reservation** réservation *f* par téléphone *ou* téléphonique; **t. sales** ventes *fpl* par téléphone, téléventes *fpl*; **t. salesman** télévendeur *m*, téléacteur *m*; **t. saleswoman** télévendeuse *f*, téléactrice *f*; **t. selling** vente *f* par téléphone, télévente *f*; **t. services** services *mpl* téléphoniques; **t. subscriber** abonné, -ée du téléphone; **t. survey** enquête *f* téléphonique, enquête par téléphone; **t. switchboard** standard *m* téléphonique

telephonic [telɪ'fɒnɪk] **ADJ** téléphonique

telephonist [tɪ'lefənɪst] **N** *Br* téléphoniste *mf*

telephony [tɪ'lefənɪ] **N** téléphonie *f*

telephotography [telɪfə'tɒɡrəfɪ] **N** téléphotographie *f*

telephoto lens [telɪ'fəʊtəʊ] **N** téléobjectif *m*

teleplay ['telɪpleɪ] **N** pièce *f* écrite pour la télévision

teleprinter ['telɪprɪntər] **N** téléimprimeur *m*

teleprocessing [telɪ'prəʊsesɪŋ] **N** *Comput* télégestion *f*

Teleprompter® ['telɪprɒm(p)tər] **N** *TV* téléprompteur *m*, télésouffleur *m*

telesales ['telɪseɪlz] **N** télévente(s) *f(pl)*, phoning *m*
► ► **t. person** télévendeur, -euse, téléacteur, -trice

telescope ['telɪskəʊp] **N** **(reflecting) t.** télescope *m* (à réflexion *ou* à miroir); **(refracting) t.** lunette *f* (d'approche), longue-vue *f*, *pl* longues-vues; *Astron* réfracteur *m*; **radio t.** radiotélescope *m*
VT *(train etc)* télescoper; *Fig (condense)* condenser (**into** en)
VI *(of train etc)* se télescoper; **parts made to t.** pièces qui s'emboîtent

telescopic [telɪs'kɒpɪk] **ADJ 1** télescopique *(visible with telescope)* visible au télescope **2** *(expanding)* télescopique; *(gangway etc)* coulissant; **t. tripod** trépied *m* télescopique; **t. umbrella** parapluie *m* télescopique
► ► **t. damper** amortisseur *m* télescopique; **t. lens** téléobjectif *m*; **t. sight** lunette *f*

teleselling ['telɪselɪŋ] **N** télévente *f*

teleshopping ['telɪʃɒpɪŋ] **N** télé-achat *m*

teletex ['telɪteks] **N** *Comput* télétex *m*

teletext ['telɪtekst] **N** *TV* télétexte *m*

telethon ['telɪθɒn] **N** *TV* téléthon *m*

Teletype® ['telɪtaɪp] **N** télétype *m*

teletyper ['telɪtaɪpər] **N** télétype *m*

teletypewriter [telɪ'taɪpraɪtər] **N** *Am* = **teleprinter**

televangelism [telɪ'vændʒəlɪz(ə)m] **N** = prêche *m* évangéliste à la télévision

televangelist [telɪ'vændʒəlɪst] **N** = évangéliste *mf* qui prêche à la télévision

televiewer ['telɪvjʊər] **N** téléspectateur, -trice

televise ['telɪvaɪz] **VT** téléviser

television [telɪ'vɪʒən] **N** télévision *f*, *(set)* téléviseur *m*, *(poste m de)* télévision; **closed-circuit t.** télévision à *ou* en circuit fermé; **colour t.** télévision (en) couleur; **colour t. (set)** téléviseur couleur; **pay t.** télévision payante; **what's on t.?** qu'est-ce qu'il y a à la télévision?; **I saw it on t.** je l'ai vu à la télévision; **have you been on t.?** êtes-vous passé à la télévision?; **to watch t.** regarder la télévision; **from a t. point of view** d'un point de vue télévisuel; **it makes/doesn't make good t.** ça a/n'a pas un bon impact télévisuel; **a film made for t.** un téléfilm
► ► **t. advertisement** publicité *f* télévisée; **t. advertising** publicité *f* télévisée; **t. archives** archives *fpl* télévisuelles; **t. audience** *(reached by advertising)* audience *f* télévisuelle; **t. broadcaster** télédiffuseur *m*; **t. broadcasting network** réseau *m* de télédistribution; **t. camera** caméra *f* de télévision; **it's my first time in front of the t. cameras** c'est la première fois que je suis devant les caméras; **t. campaign** campagne *f* télévisuelle; **t. channel** chaîne *f* de télévision; **t. commentary** téléreportage *m*; **t. commercial** spot *m* télévisé; **t. crew** équipe *f* de télévision; **t. on demand** télévision *f* à la demande; **t. drama** dramatique *f*; **t. engineer** réparateur *m* de télévisions; **t. guide** journal *m* de télévision; **t. interview** interview *f* télévisée *ou* à la télévision; **t. journalism** journalisme *m* de télévision; **t. journalist** journaliste *mf* de télévision; *Br* **t. licence** *(fee)* redevance *f*, *(document)* quittance *f* de télévision; **t. movie** téléfilm *m*, film *m* pour la télévision; **t. network** réseau *m* télévisuel; **t. news** journal *m* télévisé, JT *m*; **t. personality** vedette *f* de la télévision; **t. play** pièce *f* de théâtre pour la télévision; **t. programme** émission *f* de télévision; **t. receiver** récepteur *m* de télévision; **t. rights** droits *mpl* de télédiffusion; **t. room** salle *f* de télévision; **t. screen** écran *m* de télévision; **t. series** série *f* télévisée; **t. set** téléviseur *m*, *(poste m de)* télévision *f*; **t. show** spectacle *m* télévisé; **t. sponsoring** parrainage-télévision *m*; **t. station** studios *mpl* de télévision; **t. studio** studio *m* de télévision; **t. tie-in** *(arrangement)* partenariat *m* avec la télévision; **t. tube** tube *m* cathodique; **t. viewer** téléspectateur, -trice; *Mktg* **t. viewing panel** panel *m* de téléspectateurs

televisual [telɪ'vɪʒʊəl] **ADJ** télévisuel

teleworking ['telɪwɜːkɪŋ] **N** télétravail *m*

telewriting ['telɪraɪtɪŋ] **N** téléécriture *f*

telex ['teleks] **N** télex *m*; **to send sth by t.** télexer qch
VT *(message)* télexer; **I'll t. you** je vous enverrai un télex
► ► **t. operator** télexiste *mf*; **t. transfer** virement *m* par télex

TELL [tel] *(pt, pp* told [təʊld]*)*

VT dire **1** ▪ raconter **1** ▪ différencier **2** ▪ reconnaître **2** ▪ compter **4**
VI se faire sentir **3**

VT 1 *(say)* dire; *(story etc)* raconter; **to t. the truth** dire la vérité; **to t. a lie** dire un mensonge; **to t. sb sth** dire qch à qn; **I know – Dennis told me** je sais – Dennis me l'a dit; **she doesn't t. me anything** elle ne me dit *ou* raconte rien; **to t. sb a joke** raconter une blague à qn; **to t. sb a lie** dire *ou* raconter un mensonge à qn; **can you t. me the way to the station?** pouvez-vous m'indiquer le chemin de la gare?; **I can't t. you how pleased I am** je ne saurais vous dire combien je suis content; **we are told that ...** on nous dit que ...; **I told you no!** je t'ai dit non!; **it's just as I told you** c'est exactement ce que je t'avais dit; **I told you so!, didn't I t. you!, what did I t. you!** je te l'avais bien dit!;

you're telling me! à qui le dis-tu?, tu l'as dit!; **are you telling me (that) you spent £50 on that?** tu ne vas pas me dire que tu as payé 50 livres pour ça?; **t. me another!** à d'autres!; *esp Am Fam* **t. him goodbye (for me)!** dis-lui au revoir de ma part!; **I'll t. you what happened** je vais vous raconter ce qui est arrivé; *Fam* **(I) t. you what!** *(solving problem, making suggestion)* bon!; **t. me something about yourself** parlez-moi un peu de vous(-même); **to hear t. of ...** entendre parler de ...; **to hear t. that ...** entendre dire que ...; **that would be telling!** ça c'est mon secret!; *Fam* **to t. teacher** rapporter, cafarder; **to t. the time** *(of clock)* donner l'heure; **to t. sb the time** *(of person)* dire l'heure qu'il est *ou* donner l'heure à qn; **to t. sb about sb** parler de qn à qn; **she wrote to t. me of her father's death** elle m'a écrit pour m'annoncer la mort de son père; **t. me what you know about it** dites-moi ce que vous en savez; **let me t. you ...** permets-moi de te dire ...; **it's not so easy, let me t. you!** ce n'est pas si facile, je t'assure *ou* je te le dis!; **what does this t. us about his character?** qu'est-ce que cela nous apprend sur son caractère?; **this example tells us nothing about the meaning of the word** cet exemple ne nous renseigne absolument pas sur le sens du mot

2 *(discern)* **it's difficult to t. the difference between them** c'est difficile de les différencier; **to t. good from bad** *or* **right from wrong** discerner le bien du mal; **you can hardly t. him from his brother** c'est à peine si on peut le distinguer de son frère; **in the dark it was hard to t. friend from foe** dans l'obscurité il était difficile de distinguer ses amis de ses ennemis; **one can t. him by his voice** on le reconnaît à sa voix; **she can't t. the time** elle ne sait pas lire l'heure; **one** *or* **you can t. (that) she's lived abroad** on voit qu'elle a vécu à l'étranger; **I can t. it from the look in your eyes** ça se lit dans tes yeux; **I could t. they were lying** je voyais bien qu'ils mentaient; **we couldn't t. if he was angry or not** nous n'arrivions pas à savoir s'il était en colère ou non; **nobody can t. what the future has in store for us** on ne peut pas savoir ce que l'avenir nous réserve; **there's no telling what he might do!** je ne sais pas comment il va réagir!

3 *(order etc)* **to t. sb to do sth** dire à qn de faire qch; **you can't t. me what to do!** tu n'as pas à me dire ce que je dois faire!; **t. him to come** dis-lui de venir; **do as you are told!** fais ce qu'on te dit; **she'll do as she's told!** elle fera ce qu'on lui dira (de faire)!

4 *(count)* compter; *Rel* **to t. one's beads** égrener son chapelet; **all told** au total; **I made £100 out of it all told** en tout j'ai gagné 100 livres; **I had quite a good holiday all told** en fin de compte *ou* tout compte fait j'ai passé de bonnes vacances

VI 1 *(say)* **please don't t.** ne dis rien, s'il te plaît; **time will t.** qui vivra verra; **more than words can t.** plus qu'on ne saurait dire

2 *(discern)* **it's difficult** *or* **hard to t.** c'est difficile à dire; **it's too early to t.** il est trop tôt pour se prononcer; **who can t.?, there's no telling!** qui sait?; **you never can t.** on ne sait jamais; **it's a male – how can you t.?** c'est un mâle – comment le sais-tu?

3 *(have effect)* *(of drug etc)* produire son effet; *(of sleepless nights etc)* se faire sentir; **breeding will t.** bon sang ne saurait mentir; **it will t. against you** cela vous nuira

► **tell apart VT SEP** *(distinguish)* **I can't t. them apart** je n'arrive pas à les distinguer l'un de l'autre *ou* à les différencier

► **tell of VT INSEP 1** *(of story, poem etc)* raconter l'histoire de

2 *(indicate, reveal)* **faces which t. of ...** des visages dans lesquels se lit ...; **rings under her eyes told of sleepless nights** on voyait à ses yeux cernés qu'elle avait passé des nuits blanches

▸ **tell off** VT SEP **1** *Fam (scold)* gronder (**about sth** à propos de qch); **he told them off in no uncertain terms** il leur a dit leurs quatre vérités

2 *Mil etc (assign) (sb for duty)* désigner

▸ **tell on** VT INSEP **1** *(affect badly)* **the heat is telling on him** il commence à souffrir de la chaleur; **his age is beginning to t. on him** il commence à accuser son âge; **the effects of the embargo were beginning to t. on the country's economy** les effets de l'embargo commençaient à se faire sentir sur l'économie du pays

2 *Fam (inform on)* dénoncer; **I'll t. on you!** je le dirai!

teller ['telər] N **1** *(of story etc)* conteur, -euse **2** *(in bank etc)* guichetier, -ière; *Parl (of votes)* scrutateur m

telling ['telɪŋ] ADJ **1** **t. blow** coup m bien asséné *ou* qui porte; **what he said had a t. effect** ce qu'il a dit a porté; **a t. criticism/remark** une critique/remarque bien sentie; **a t. speech** un discours percutant **2** *(revealing)* révélateur, -trice; **her remarks were very t.** ses remarques étaient très révélatrices

N **the t. of tales plays an important part in their culture** les contes oraux jouent un rôle important dans leur culture; **it loses nothing in the t.** ça ne perd rien à être raconté

▸ ▸ **t. off** réprimande f, **to give sb a t. off** gronder qn

telltale ['telteɪl] N *(person)* rapporteur, -euse, cafard, -arde

ADJ **a t. sign** un signe révélateur; **a t. odour** une odeur qui ne trompe pas

tellurium [te'lʊərɪəm] N *Chem* tellure m

telly ['telɪ] N *esp Br Fam* télé f; **on the t.** à la télé

▸ ▸ **t. addict** accro mf de la télé

Telnet ['telnet] N *Comput* Telnet m

temerity [tɪ'merɪtɪ] N témérité f, audace f, **she had the t. to accuse me!** elle a eu l'audace de m'accuser!

temp[1] [temp] *Fam* N intérimaire mf, *(temporary secretary)* secrétaire mf intérimaire; **to do t. work** faire de l'intérim; *(as secretary)* être secrétaire intérimaire

VI faire de l'intérim; *(as secretary)* être secrétaire intérimaire

temp[2] *(abbr* **temperature**) température

temper ['tempər] N **1** *(anger)* colère f, *(bad mood)* mauvaise humeur f, **in an outburst of t.** dans un mouvement de colère; **to be in a t.** être en colère; **to be in a good/bad t.** être de bonne/mauvaise humeur; **to send sb into a t.** mettre qn en colère; *Fam* **t.(, t.)!** du calme!, on se calme!; **to keep one's t.** rester calme, garder son calme; **to lose one's t.** se mettre en colère, s'emporter; **to fly into a t.** piquer une colère **2** *(character)* caractère m, tempérament m; **fiery/even t.** caractère fougueux/égal; **she's got (quite) a t.** elle a un sacré caractère; **to have a quick t.** s'emporter facilement **3** *Metal (of steel)* coefficient m de dureté, trempe f

VT **1** *Tech (steel, blade)* donner la trempe à; *(metal)* recuire, adoucir **2** *(moderate) (action etc)* modérer, adoucir; *(one's grief etc)* maîtriser; *(one's enthusiasm etc)* tempérer, modérer; **to t. justice with mercy** faire preuve de clémence **3** *(piano)* accorder par tempérament

tempera ['tempərə] N *Art* **to paint in t.** peindre à tempera

▸ ▸ **t. painting** détrempe f

temperament ['temp(ə)rəmənt] N *(character)* caractère m, tempérament m; **an outburst** *or* **show of t.** un coup de colère

temperamental [temp(ə)rə'ment(ə)l] ADJ **1**

(difference etc) du tempérament; **he has a t. aversion to conflict/hard work** fondamentalement il déteste les conflits/le travail **2** *(person)* capricieux, fantasque; *(machine)* capricieux; **his knee has been a bit t. since his accident** son genou lui joue des tours depuis son accident

temperamentally [temp(ə)rə'ment(ə)lɪ] ADV *(by nature)* de nature; **t. different** d'un tempérament différent; **they were t. unsuited** *(of couple)* leurs caractères étaient incompatibles; **she's t. unsuited to this sort of work** elle n'est pas de nature à *ou* elle n'a pas le caractère pour faire ce genre de travail

temperance ['temp(ə)rəns] N **1** *(moderation) (in taking pleasure, eating, drinking etc)* tempérance f, modération f, retenue f **2** *(abstinence from alcohol)* tempérance f, sobriété f

▸ ▸ **t. hotel** = hôtel m où l'on ne sert pas de boissons alcoolisées; **t. movement** mouvement m antialcoolique; **t. society** ligue f antialcoolique

temperate ['temp(ə)rət] ADJ **1** *(climate, zone etc)* tempéré **2** *(language etc)* modéré, mesuré

temperature ['temp(ə)rətʃər] N température f, **fall in t.**, **t. drop** chute f de température; **room t.** température ambiante; **at room t.** *(of wine)* chambré; **the t. was in the thirties** il faisait plus de trente degrés; *Med* **to take sb's t.** prendre la température de qn; **to have a raised t.**, **to have** *or* **to run a t.** avoir de la température *ou* de la fièvre; **he's got a t. of forty** il a quarante de fièvre; *Fig* **to judge the t. of a meeting** prendre la température d'une réunion; **to raise/lower the t.** faire monter/faire baisser la température

▸ ▸ **t. chart** feuille f de température; **t. gauge** indicateur m de température; **t. sensor** capteur m de température

tempered ['tempəd] ADJ *(steel)* trempé, recuit; **t. safety glass** verre m de sécurité trempé

-tempered [-'tempəd] SUFF **to be good-/bad-t.** *(habitually)* avoir un bon/mauvais caractère; *(on one occasion)* être de bonne/mauvaise humeur; **to be quick-t.** s'emporter facilement

tempest ['tempɪst] N *Lit* tempête f, tourmente f

tempestuous [tem'pestjʊəs] ADJ **1** *(weather, wind etc)* de tempête **2** *(meeting etc)* orageux, tempétueux; *(person, mood, relationship etc)* turbulent, agité

tempestuously [tem'pestjʊəslɪ] ADV **1** *Lit* **the winds blew t. outside** un vent de tempête soufflait au dehors **2** *(violently) (to argue etc)* violemment

tempestuousness [tem'pestjʊəsnɪs] N **1** *(of weather)* violence f **2** *(of meeting)* caractère m orageux; *(of crowd)* turbulence f, agitation f

temping ['tempɪŋ] N intérim m

▸ ▸ **t. agency** société f d'intérim

Templar ['templər] N *Hist* **(Knight) T.** Templier m, chevalier m du Temple

template ['templɪt] N **1** *(in metalworking)*, *Carp etc* gabarit m, calibre m, patron m **2** *Comput (for keyboard)* réglette f, *(for program)* modèle m; *(for DTP document)* gabarit m

temple[1] ['temp(ə)l] N *Rel* temple m

temple[2] N *Anat* tempe f

tempo, pl tempi ['tempəʊ, -iː] N *Mus* tempo m; *Fig* **strikes that upset the t. of production** grèves qui perturbent le rythme de la production

temporal[1] ['tempər(ə)l] ADJ **1** *(power etc)* temporel **2** *Gram* temporel

temporal[2] ADJ *Anat (bone etc)* temporal, -aux

temporarily ['temp(ə)rərɪlɪ, tempə'reərɪlɪ] ADV temporairement; *(for the present time)* momentanément, temporairement; **we were t. delayed** nous avons été retardés quelques minutes

temporary ['temp(ə)rərɪ] ADJ *(office, entrance etc)* temporaire; *(hearing loss etc)* momentané, passager; *(work, employee)* intérimaire; **the improvement is only t.** l'amélioration n'est que passagère *ou* momentanée; **on a t. basis** temporairement; *(to work)* par intérim; **to exercise t. command** commander par intérim; **this will at least give you t. relief** cela vous soulagera pendant un moment; **t. appointment** poste m temporaire; *Admin* emploi m amovible; **t. job** emploi temporaire

▸ ▸ **t. contract** *(for employment)* contrat m de mission d'intérim, contrat temporaire; *Comput* **t. file** fichier m temporaire; *Law* **t. injunction** injonction f temporaire; **t. manager** directeur, -trice intérimaire; **t. replacement** suppléance f, *Am Law* **t. restraining order** injonction f du tribunal; **t. surface** *(of road)* revêtement m provisoire; **t. work** intérim m; **t. worker** intérimaire mf

temporize ['tempəraɪz] VI *Fml (seek to gain time)* temporiser, chercher à gagner du temps

tempt [tem(p)t] VT tenter; **to t. sb to do sth** inciter qn à faire qch; **to let oneself be tempted** se laisser tenter, céder à la tentation; **I'm tempted to try** je suis tenté *ou* j'ai envie d'essayer; **the fine weather tempted us to go out** le beau temps nous a donné envie de sortir; **to t. providence/fate** tenter la providence/le sort; **don't t. me!** ne me tente pas!

temptation [tem(p)'teɪʃən] N tentation f, **to throw** *or* **put t. in sb's way** exposer qn à la tentation; **to give in** *or* **yield to t.** succomber *ou* céder à la tentation; *Bible* **lead us not into t.** ne nous soumets pas à la tentation; **there's a great t. to say that …** on est très tenté de dire que …

tempter ['tem(p)tər] N tentateur m

tempting ['tem(p)tɪŋ] ADJ tentant, alléchant; *(meal)* appétissant

temptingly ['tem(p)tɪŋlɪ] ADV d'une manière tentante; **the grapes glistened t. in their bowl** les grappes dans le plat étaient brillantes et appétissantes; **the cool water beckoned t.** l'eau fraîche donnait envie de se baigner

temptress ['tem(p)trɪs] N *Lit, Hum* tentatrice f

ten [ten] N dix m; **number t.** le numéro dix; **some** *or* **about t. years ago** il y a une dizaine d'années; **three tens are thirty** trois fois dix font trente; **tens of thousands** des dizaines de milliers; **it's t. o'clock** il est dix heures; **to be t.** *(in age)* avoir dix ans; *Rugby* **t. metre line** ligne f des dix mètres; **they're t. a penny** il y en a à la pelle; **t. to one he'll mention it** je vous parie qu'il en parlera; **the top t.** *(in record charts)* palmarès m des dix meilleurs *ou* des dix meilleures ventes

PRON dix; **about ten** une dizaine; **I need t.** *(of them)* il m'en faut dix, j'en ai besoin de dix

ADJ dix; **t. people** dix personnes

▸ ▸ **the T. Commandments** les dix commandements mpl

tenable ['tenəb(ə)l] ADJ *(position, fortress etc)* tenable; *(theory)* soutenable; *Mktg* **t. firm** entreprise f défendable **2** **appointment t. for three years** poste auquel on est nommé pour trois ans

tenacious [te'neɪʃəs] ADJ tenace; **t. memory** excellente mémoire f

tenaciously [te'neɪʃəslɪ] ADV avec ténacité; (stubbornly) obstinément

tenacity, tenaciousness [te'næsɪtɪ, te-'neɪʃəsnɪs] N ténacité f; (of memory) sûreté f

tenancy ['tenənsɪ] N location f; **expiration of t.** expiration f de bail, échéance f de location; **during my t.** pendant la période de ma location

tenant ['tenənt] N locataire mf; **t. in possession, sitting t.** occupant, -ante
▸ VT (house etc) occuper comme locataire; **only half the farms were still tenanted** il n'y avait de locataires que dans la moitié des fermes
▸ ▸ **t. farmer** métayer, -ère; **t. farming** métayage m

tenantry ['tenəntrɪ] N, no pl (tenants) métayers mpl

tench [tenʃ] N (fish) tanche f

tend¹ [tend] VT (sick person etc) soigner; (machine etc) surveiller; (sheep etc) garder; (garden, fire) entretenir
▸ **tend to** VT INSEP (look after) s'occuper de

tend² VI 1 doctrine that tends towards socialism doctrine socialisante, doctrine qui penche vers le socialisme; **blue tending to green** bleu tirant sur le vert; **her tastes t. towards the exotic** elle a une attirance pour les choses exotiques; **I t. to(wards) the view that …** j'ai tendance à penser que …
2 **to t. to do sth** avoir tendance à faire qch; **to t. to skid** (of car) déraper facilement; **she tends to exaggerate** elle a tendance à exagérer; **we t. to think of man as being separate from nature** nous avons tendance à considérer que l'homme ne fait pas partie de la nature; **some people like that kind of film, but I t. not to** il y a des gens qui aiment ce genre de film, moi (je n'aime) pas trop

tendency ['tendənsɪ] N tendance f (to à); **t. to drink** penchant m pour la boisson; **he has artistic tendencies** il a des dons artistiques; **to have a t. to (do) sth** avoir (une) tendance à (faire) qch; **a growing t.** une tendance de plus en plus marquée

tendentious [ten'denʃəs] ADJ tendancieux

tendentiously [ten'denʃəslɪ] ADV tendancieusement

tendentiousness [ten'denʃəsnɪs] N caractère m tendancieux

tender¹ ['tendər] N Naut (boat) navire m annexe; (for supplies) ravitailleur m; Rail tender m

tender² ADJ 1 (meat) tendre; **to make meat t.** attendrir la viande 2 (sensitive) tendre, sensible; **t. conscience** conscience f délicate ou susceptible; **t. to the touch** sensible ou douloureux au toucher; **t. heart** cœur m tendre ou sensible; **to touch sb on a t. spot** toucher qn à un endroit sensible; Fig toucher le point sensible chez qn 3 (plant etc) délicat, fragile; esp Lit, Hum **a child of t. years** un(e) petit(e) enfant 4 (affectionate) (person, sentiment etc) tendre, affectueux; **they bade each other a t. farewell** ils se sont tendrement dit au revoir; Iron **I leave him to your t. mercies** je l'abandonne à vos soins

tender³ N Com soumission f, offre f; **to invite tenders for a job, to put a job out to t.** mettre un travail en adjudication; **to make or put in a t. for sth** soumissionner ou faire une soumission pour qch; **a call for t.** un appel d'offres; **by t.** par voie d'adjudication; Law, Com **legal t.** cours m légal, monnaie f libératoire; **to be legal t.** (of money) avoir cours, avoir force libératoire
▸ VT (one's services, money etc) offrir; **to t. one's resignation** présenter sa démission; **to t. one's apologies** faire ou présenter ses excuses; Law **to t. money in discharge of**

debt faire une offre réelle; **please t. exact fare** veuillez avoir la monnaie exacte
▸ VI Com **to t. for sth** soumissionner (pour) qch, faire une soumission pour qch; **to t. for a contract** soumissionner à une adjudication
▸ ▸ **t. documents** documents mpl d'appel d'offres; **t. form** formule f de soumission; **t. insurance** assurance f offre; **t. price** prix m d'offre

tenderer ['tendərər] N Com soumissionnaire mf; **successful t.** adjudicataire mf

tenderfoot, pl **tenderfoots, tenderfeet** ['tendəfʊt(s), -fiːt] N esp Am (in wild place) nouveau venu m

tenderhearted [tendə'hɑːtɪd] ADJ au cœur tendre ou sensible; **to be too t.** avoir trop de cœur

tenderheartedness [tendə'hɑːtɪdnɪs] N compassion f, sensibilité f

tenderize ['tendəraɪz] VT Culin (meat) attendrir

tenderizer ['tendəraɪzər] N Culin attendrisseur m

tenderloin ['tendəlɔɪn] N Culin (of beef etc) filet m

tenderly ['tendəlɪ] ADV 1 (to touch, hold sth) doucement, délicatement 2 (to look at, feel) tendrement, avec tendresse

tenderness ['tendənɪs] N 1 (of meat) tendreté f 2 (of plant) délicatesse f, fragilité f; (of conscience) délicatesse f 3 (affection) tendresse f, affection f (for pour)

tendinitis [tendɪ'naɪtəs] N tendinite f

tendon ['tendən] N Anat tendon m

tendril ['tendrɪl] N Bot vrille f, cirre m

tenement ['tenɪmənt] N (building) immeuble m d'habitation, Pej vieil immeuble d'habitation en mauvais état
▸ ▸ **t. building** immeuble m d'habitation, Pej vieil immeuble d'habitation en mauvais état; **t. flat** appartement m, Pej appartement dans un vieil immeuble

tenet ['tenɪt, 'tiː-] N (dogma) doctrine f, dogme m; (belief) croyance f

tenfold ['tenfəʊld] ADJ décuple
▸ ADV au décuple; **to increase t.** décupler

ten-gallon ADJ
▸ ▸ **t. hat** = chapeau m de cowboy haut et à larges bords

Tenn abbr Tennessee

tenner ['tenər] N Fam Br (ten-pound note) billet m de dix livres; (sum) dix livres fpl; Am (ten-dollar bill) billet de dix dollars; **it cost a t.** ça a coûté dix livres

tennis ['tenɪs] N Sport (lawn) **t.** tennis m; **to play t.** jouer au tennis; **table t.** tennis de table; **deck t.** deck-tennis m; **(real or royal or Am court) t.** (jeu m de) paume f
▸ ▸ **t. ball** balle f de tennis; **t. club** club m de tennis; **t. court** court m de tennis; (in real tennis) jeu de paume; **t. elbow** tennis-elbow m, synovite f du coude; **t. player** joueur, -euse de tennis; **t. racket, t. racquet** raquette f de tennis; **t. shoes** chaussures fpl de tennis, tennis fpl ou mpl

tenon ['tenən] N Carp tenon m
▸ ▸ **t. saw** tenonneuse f

tenor ['tenər] N 1 Mus (voice, singer) ténor m 2 (general sense) (of letter etc) contenu m, sens m général 3 Fin (of bill) (terme m d')échéance f
▸ ▸ **t. clef** clé f d'ut quatrième ligne; **t. sax(ophone)** saxo(phone) m ténor; **t. voice** voix f de ténor

tenpence ['tenpəns, -'pens] N Br (pièce f de) dix pence mpl

tenpenny ['tenpənɪ] ADJ Br de ou à dix pence; **t. stamp** timbre m de dix pence

tenpin ['tenpɪn] N quille f; Am **tenpins** (game) jeu m de quilles; (in bowling alley) bowling m
▸ ▸ Br **t. bowling** jeu de quilles; (in bowling alley) bowling

tense¹ [tens] N Gram temps m; **verb in the present/future t.** verbe au (temps) présent/futur VOIR GRAMMAIRE A39–40; B30–2

tense² ADJ 1 (nerves, situation, silence, moment etc) tendu; (muscle) contracté, noué; **t. voice** voix f étranglée (par l'émotion); **to be t.** (of person) être tendu 2 (cord etc) tendu, raide
▸ VT tendre; **he tensed himself as the door opened** il se raidit au moment où la porte s'ouvrit
▸ VI se raidir
▸ **tense up** VT SEP, VI = tense VT, VI

tensely ['tenslɪ] ADV **he waited t. for the judge's decision** l'air tendu, il attendait la décision du juge; **we watched t. as he approached the door** nous le regardâmes s'approcher de la porte avec appréhension; **she spoke t.** on sentait la tension dans sa voix

tenseness ['tensnɪs] N 1 (of nerves, situation etc) tension f 2 (of muscles etc) contraction f

tensile ['tensaɪl] ADJ (stretchable) extensible, élastique; (metal) ductile
▸ ▸ **t. load** charge f de traction; **t. strength** résistance f à la tension, limite f élastique à la tension; **t. stress** force f de tension

tension ['tenʃən] N 1 (of mind, nerves), Pol (in region etc) tension f 2 (of cord, muscular etc) tension f; Phys (of fluid) tension, force f élastique; Elec tension, voltage m; **to keep a cable under t.** garder un câble sous tension 3 Tech (stress) (force f de) traction f; (of spring) tension f; **to be in t.** être en traction
▸ ▸ **t. headache** mal m de tête dû à la tension nerveuse

tent [tent] N tente f; **bell t.** tente conique; **oxygen t.** tente à oxygène; **to pitch/strike tents** monter/démonter les tentes
▸ ▸ **t. peg** piquet m de tente; **t. pole** mât m de tente

tentacle ['tentək(ə)l] N Biol, Fig tentacule m

tentative ['tentətɪv] ADJ d'essai; (hesitant) hésitant; (conclusion) provisoire; **to make a t. move towards peace** faire un petit pas vers la paix; **t. offer** offre f préliminaire ou d'essai; **it was just a t. suggestion** ce n'était qu'une suggestion

tentatively ['tentətɪvlɪ] ADV à titre d'essai; (hesitantly) avec hésitation; (to conclude) provisoirement

tenterhooks ['tentəhʊks] N **to be on t.** être au supplice ou sur le gril ou sur des charbons ardents; **to keep sb on t.** faire languir qn, mettre qn sur des charbons ardents

tenth [tenθ] ADJ dixième
▸ N 1 (of month) dix m; **(on) the t. (of May)** le dix (mai) 2 (person, thing) dixième mf 3 (fraction) dixième m 4 Mus (intervalle m de) dixième f

tenting ['tentɪŋ] N toile f de tente

tenuous ['tenjʊəs] ADJ (argument, link etc) ténu, faible

tenuously ['tenjʊəslɪ] ADV de façon ténue

tenuousness ['tenjʊəsnɪs] N (of argument, link etc) fragilité f

tenure ['tenjər] N 1 Hist, Law (of property) tenure f; **system of land t.** régime m foncier 2 Law (period) (of office, property etc) (période f de) jouissance f ou (d')occupation f; (permanency of employment) titularisation f; **during his t. of office** pendant qu'il exerçait ses fonctions

tepee ['tiːpiː] N tipi m, wigwam m

tepid ['tepɪd] ADJ (water etc) tiède; (feeling, welcome etc) tiède, mitigé

tepidly ['tepɪdlɪ] **ADV** mollement, de façon mitigée

tepidness ['tepɪdnɪs] **N** tiédeur *f*

tequila [tɪ'kiːlə] **N** tequila *f*

terabyte ['terəbaɪt] **N** *Comput* téraoctet *m*

tercentenary [tɜːsen'tiːnərɪ], **tercentennial** [tɜːsen'tenɪəl] **ADJ**, **N** tricentenaire *m*

tercet ['tɜːsɪt] **N** *(in prosody)* tercet *m*

TERM [tɜːm]

N terme **1-6** ▪ conditions *(terms)* **4** ▪ clauses *(terms)* **4** ▪ période **5** ▪ durée **5** ▪ trimestre **5** ▪ fin **6** **VT** désigner ▪ qualifier

N 1 *(word, expression)* terme *m*; **technical/scientific t.** terme *ou* expression *f* technique/scientifique; **he spoke of him in the most flattering terms** il a parlé de lui en des termes les plus flatteurs; **I told her in no uncertain terms** je le lui ai dit carrément *ou* sans mâcher mes mots; **in terms of difficulty I'd say it was in the medium range** si on considère le degré de difficulté, je dirais que c'était moyennement difficile; **in terms of salary/pollution** du point de vue du salaire/de la pollution; **in terms of time, I think we're talking about twelve weeks** question temps, je pense qu'il faut compter douze semaines; **in layman's terms** pour parler clairement, en matière de finance; **I was thinking more in terms of a family car/something under £50** je voyais plus une voiture du genre voiture familiale/quelque chose de moins de 50 livres; **in personal/political terms it was a disaster** d'un point de vue personnel/politique ça a été une catastrophe

2 *(relations)* **to be on good/bad terms with sb** être en bons/mauvais termes avec qn; **to be on friendly terms with sb** être en bons termes avec qn; **we remained on friendly terms** nos relations sont restées amicales; **to be on the best of terms with sb** être au mieux avec qn, être dans les meilleurs termes avec qn; **we're not on those kind of terms** nous ne nous connaissons pas aussi bien; **to come to terms with sth** accepter qch, se faire à qch

3 *(in logic)*, *Math* terme *m*; **to express one quantity in terms of another** exprimer une quantité en fonction d'une autre

4 *Com etc* **terms** *(conditions)* conditions *fpl*; *(of contract)* clauses *fpl*, termes *mpl*; **terms and conditions of a contract** conditions d'un contrat; **on these terms I accept** à ces conditions j'accepte; **make** *or* **name your own terms** fixez vos conditions; **under the terms and conditions of the contract** selon les termes du contrat; **to dictate terms** imposer ses conditions; **to come to** *or* **make terms** s'arranger **(with sb** avec qn); **weekly terms** *(in hotel etc)* pension *f* par semaine; **on easy terms** avec facilités de paiement; **not on any terms** à aucun prix

5 *(period)* terme *m*, période *f*, durée *f*; *Sch*, *Univ* trimestre *m*; *(of court)* session *f*; **to serve a t. of five years (in prison)** faire cinq ans de prison; **during her t. of** *or* **in office** *(of president, mayor etc)* pendant son mandat; *Com* **long-/short-t. transaction** opération *f* à long/court terme; **a long-t. policy** une politique à longue échéance; **in the long t.** à la longue; **in the short t.** à court terme; *Sch*, *Univ* **in t. time, during t.** pendant le trimestre; *Sch, Univ* **half t. (holiday)** congé *m* de mi-trimestre

6 *(limit)* terme *m*, fin *f*; *Com (of bill of exchange)* (terme d')échéance *f*; **to have reached (full) t.** *(of pregnancy)* être à terme; **to set** *or* **put a t. to sth** mettre fin *ou* un terme à qch

VT désigner, appeler; **critics termed the play a total disaster** les critiques ont qualifié la pièce d'échec complet

▸▸ *Fin* **t. bill** effet *m* à terme; *Fin* **terms of credit** conditions de crédit; *Fin* **t. day** *(jour m* du) terme; *Fin* **t. deposit** dépôt *m* à terme; *Fin* **t. draft** traite *f* à terme; *Fin* **terms of exchange** termes d'échange; *Fin* **t. insurance cover** couverture *f* à terme; *Fin* **t. loan** *(money lent)* prêt *m* à terme (fixe); *(money borrowed)* emprunt *m* à terme (fixe); *Am Sch, Univ* **t. paper** dissertation *f* trimestrielle; **terms of payment** conditions *ou* termes de paiement; **terms of reference** *(of commission etc)* attributions *fpl*, mandat *m*; *Econ* **terms of trade** termes de l'échange

termagant ['tɜːməgənt] **N** *Lit* mégère *f*, virago *f*

terminal ['tɜːmɪn(ə)l] **ADJ** *(phase, stage)* terminal, -aux; *(illness)* incurable; *Med* **I'm afraid it's t.** je crains que vous ne soyez/qu'il ne soit/*etc* condamné; *Fam* **t. boredom** ennui *m* mortel

N 1 *Elec (of battery)* pôle *m* **2** *(rail, bus)* terminus *m*, gare *f* terminus; *(maritime)* gare maritime; *(for containers)* terminal *m*; *Aviat* **(air) t.** aérogare *f* **3** *Comput* (poste *m*) terminal *m*

▸▸ *Ins* **t. bonus** = bonus *m* versé au titulaire d'une assurance-vie, au terme de celle-ci; **t. building** *(at airport)* aérogare *f*; *Med* **t. case** malade *mf* en phase terminale; *Fin* **t. charges** charges *fpl* terminales; *Comput* **t. emulation** émulation *f* de terminal; *Comput* **t. emulator** émulateur *m* de terminal; *Acct* **t. loss** perte *f* finale; *St Exch* **t. market** marché *m* à terme; *Fin* **t. price** cours *m* du livrable; *Comput* **t. server** serveur *m* de terminaux; *Rail* **t. station** terminus *m*; *Elec* **t. voltage** tension *f* aux bornes

terminally ['tɜːmɪn(ə)lɪ] **ADV** *Med* **to be t. ill** être en phase terminale; **the t. ill** *(npl)* les malades *mpl* incurables *ou* condamnés

terminate ['tɜːmɪneɪt] **VT** *(employment, project, commitment)* mettre un terme à, mettre fin à; *(contract etc)* résilier; **the project was terminated in 1997** on a mis fin au projet en 1997; **to t. a pregnancy** *(of doctor)* interrompre une grossesse, pratiquer une IVG; *(of woman)* avoir une IVG; **to have one's pregnancy terminated** avoir une IVG

VI *(of word etc)* se terminer, finir **(in** en, par); *(of line etc)* se terminer, aboutir **(in, at** à); *(of train)* avoir son terminus **(at** à); **this train terminates here** terminus du train!

termination [tɜːmɪ'neɪʃən] **N 1** *(of trial etc)* fin *f*, conclusion *f*; *(of relations, dealings etc)* cessation *f*; *Law (of obligation etc)* résolution *f*, résiliation *f*; **t. of pregnancy** interruption *f* (volontaire) de grossesse, IVG *f* **2** *Gram* terminaison *f*, désinence *f*

▸▸ **t. clause** clause *f* de résiliation

terminator ['tɜːmɪneɪtər] **N** *Comput* terminateur *m*

▸▸ *Agr* **t. gene** gène *m* terminator *ou* terminateur

terminological [tɜːmɪnə'lɒdʒɪk(ə)l] **ADJ** terminologique

terminologist [tɜːmɪ'nɒlədʒɪst] **N** terminologue *mf*

terminology [tɜːmɪ'nɒlədʒɪ] **N** terminologie *f*

terminus, *pl* **termini, terminuses** ['tɜːmɪnəs, -aɪ, -əsɪz] **N** *Rail etc* (gare *f*) terminus *m*

▸▸ **t. hotel** *(at train station)* hôtel *m* de gare

termite ['tɜːmaɪt] **N** *(insect)* termite *m*

tern [tɜːn] **N** *(bird)* sterne *f*; **arctic t.** sterne arctique

ternary ['tɜːnərɪ] **ADJ** *Chem, Math etc* ternaire

terrace ['terɪs] **N 1** *Constr, Geol, Agr* terrasse *f*; *Ftbl etc* **the terraces** les gradins *mpl* **2** *Br* **t.**

(of houses) rangée *f* de maisons attenantes

VT *(garden etc)* disposer en terrasse(s); *(hillside etc)* terrasser

terraced ['terɪst] **ADJ** *(garden)* en terrasse; **t. hillsides** collines cultivées en terrasses

▸▸ *Br* **t. house** = maison *f* située dans une rangée de maisons attenantes et identiques; **t. houses** *(row)* rangée *f* de maisons attenantes

terracotta ['terə'kɒtə] **N** terre *f* cuite; *(colour)* ocre *m* foncé

terra firma ['terə'fɜːmə] **N** la terre ferme, *Fam* le plancher des vaches; **to be back on t. again** être de retour sur le plancher des vaches; *Fig (in known area etc)* se retrouver en terrain connu

terrain [tə'reɪn] **N** *Mil, Geog* terrain *m*

terrapin ['terəpɪn] **N** *(reptile)* tortue *f* d'eau douce

terrarium, *pl* **terraria, terrariums** [te-'reərɪəm, -ɪə, -ɪəmz] **N** terrarium *m*

terrestrial [tɪ'restrɪəl] **ADJ** *(globe, plant, life, TV programmes etc)* terrestre

N *(inhabitant of the Earth)* terrien, -ienne

▸▸ **t. broadcasting** diffusion *f* hertzienne *ou* terrestre; **t. channel** chaîne *f* hertzienne; **t. television** diffusion hertzienne *ou* terrestre; **the Cup Final will no longer be broadcast on t. television** la finale ne sera plus diffusée sur le réseau hertzien

terrible ['terɪb(ə)l] **ADJ** terrible; *(accident, crime, shock)* affreux, épouvantable; *(film, teacher etc)* nul; *(coffee, food etc)* infecte; *(injury)* très grave; **what a t. thing to say** c'est horrible de dire ça; **I'm t. at maths** je suis nul en math; **he's a t. talker** *(talks a lot)* c'est un sacré bavard; **going without a meal isn't so t.** ce n'est pas si terrible de sauter un repas

terribly ['terɪblɪ] **ADV 1** *(badly)* terriblement; *(to behave)* de manière atroce; **the economy has performed t.** les résultats économiques sont désastreux; **t. injured** très gravement blessé **2** *Fam (very)* très; **t. busy** très *ou* terriblement occupé; **t. worried** terriblement *ou* affreusement inquiet; **that's t. kind of you** vous êtes vraiment trop aimable; **he's t. keen to meet you** il a vraiment envie de te rencontrer; **not t. interesting** pas très intéressant; **are you interested? – not t.** ça vous intéresse? – pas vraiment

terrier ['terɪər] **N** *(dog)* (chien *m*) terrier *m*; *Fig* **he's a real t.** il n'abandonne jamais; **bull t.** bull-terrier *m*, *pl* bull-terriers

terrific [tə'rɪfɪk] **ADJ** *Fam (excellent)* génial, -aux; *(enormous)* énorme; **we had a t. time** c'était génial; **t.!** génial!; **a t. noise** un bruit énorme; **a t. pace** une allure vertigineuse

terrifically [tə'rɪfɪklɪ] **ADV** *Fam (very)* très; **it was t. hot** il faisait terriblement chaud

terrified ['terɪfaɪd] **ADJ** *(look, person)* terrifié; **to be t. of sb** avoir une peur bleue de qn; **they're t. of losing their jobs** ils tremblent à l'idée de perdre leur emploi; **to be t. (that)** être terrifié *ou* mort de peur (à l'idée que + *sub)*

terrify ['terɪfaɪ] **VT** terrifier, faire très peur à; **this remark terrified me** cette remarque m'a terrifié; **it terrifies me what he'll do next** je suis terrifié à la pensée de ce qu'il pourrait faire

terrifying ['terɪfaɪɪŋ] **ADJ** terrifiant, terrible, épouvantable

terrifyingly ['terɪfaɪɪŋlɪ] **ADV** *(difficult, dangerous)* épouvantablement; *(to scream)* d'une manière terrifiante; **to come t. close to death** passer à deux doigts de la mort, frôler la mort

terrine [te'riːn] **N** terrine *f*

territorial [terɪ'tɔːrɪəl] **ADJ 1** *(possessions,*

tax, claim etc) territorial, -aux **2 a t. animal** un animal qui a tendance à protéger son territoire; **gorillas are very t. creatures** les gorilles mettent toujours beaucoup d'acharnement à défendre leur territoire; **the sales director is highly t.** le directeur des ventes est prêt à tout pour défendre son territoire; **they're very t. about their part of the office** ils veulent que personne ne s'immisce dans leur partie du bureau
N *Br Mil* **T.** réserviste *m* volontaire
▸▸ *Br Mil* **T. Army** = armée *f* de réservistes volontaires; **t. waters** eaux *fpl* territoriales

territoriality [terɪtɔːrɪˈælɪtɪ] **N** territorialité *f*

territory [ˈterɪt(ə)rɪ] **N** *(of state, animal)* territoire *m*; *Fig* **I'm afraid this isn't my t.** désolé, ce n'est pas mon domaine; *Fig* **this will be familiar t. for his readers** le lecteur se retrouvera en terrain familier

terror [ˈterər] **N 1** *(fear)* terreur *f*, effroi *m*, épouvante *f*; **a look of t.** un regard épouvanté; **to be in (a state of) t.** être terrorisé; **to be in t. of one's life** craindre pour sa vie; **to go in t. of sb** avoir une peur bleue de qn; *Fam* **to have a holy t. of sth** craindre qch comme la peste; **a reign of t.** un régime de terreur; *Hist* **the T.** la Terreur; **t. campaign, campaign of t.** campagne *f* de terreur
2 *(person)* **he was the t. of the countryside** c'était la terreur du pays; *Fam* **she's a little** *or* **a holy t.** c'est un petit diable; *Fam* **he's a t. for being late** il est épouvantable avec sa manie d'être toujours en retard; *Fam* **he's a t. for the whisky/chocolate biscuits** c'est un fou de whisky/de petits gâteaux au chocolat

terrorism [ˈterərɪz(ə)m] **N** terrorisme *m*

terrorist [ˈterərɪst] **N** terroriste *mf*
ADJ terroriste
▸▸ **t. attack** attentat *m* (terroriste); **t. bombing** attentat à la bombe

terrorize [ˈterəraɪz] **VT** terroriser

terror-stricken, terror-struck **ADJ** *(expression, look)* de terreur; **to be t.** être saisi de terreur

terry [ˈterɪ] **N** *(fabric)* tissu *m* éponge
▸▸ **t. towel** serviette *f* éponge; **t. towelling** tissu éponge

terse [tɜːs] **ADJ** abrupt, brusque

tersely [ˈtɜːslɪ] **ADV** abruptement, brusquement

terseness [ˈtɜːsnɪs] **N** *(of reply etc)* brusquerie *f*, *(of style)* caractère *m* abrupt

tertiary [ˈtɜːʃɪərɪ] **ADJ, N** tertiaire *m*
▸▸ **t. education** enseignement *m* du troisième cycle; **t. sector** secteur *m* tertiaire

Terylene® [ˈterɪliːn] **N** *Br Tex* tergal® *m*; **T. skirt** jupe en tergal

TESL [ˈtes(ə)l] **N** *(abbr* **Teaching English as a Second Language)** enseignement *m* de l'anglais deuxième langue

TESOL [ˈtesɒl] **N** *(abbr* **Teaching English to Speakers of Other Languages)** enseignement *m* de l'anglais langue étrangère

TESSA [ˈtesə] **N** *Br (abbr* **tax exempt special savings account)** plan *m* d'épargne exonéré d'impôts

TEST [test]

N épreuve **1** ▪ test **1** ▪ essai **1**
▪ examen **2** ▪ interrogation **2** ▪ match international **3**
VT essayer ▪ tester ▪ vérifier ▪ analyser
VI expérimenter ▪ se révéler

N 1 *(trial, check etc)* épreuve *f*, *(scientific)* test *m*; **to put sth to the t.** mettre qch à l'épreuve *ou* à l'essai, éprouver qch; **to undergo a t.** subir une épreuve; **to pass** *or* **stand the t.** soutenir *ou* supporter l'épreuve; **method that has stood the t. of time** méthode *f*

éprouvée; **it was a t. of our friendship** ça a mis notre amitié à l'épreuve; **endurance t.** épreuve d'endurance; *Aut etc* **road t.** essai *m* sur route; **nuclear t.** essai nucléaire
2 *Sch, Med etc (examination)* examen *m*; **eye/blood t.** examen des yeux/du sang; *Sch* **French/maths t.** examen *ou* interrogation *f* de français/math; *Med etc* **blood t.** prise *f* de sang; *Aut* **driving t.** permis *m* de conduire; **hearing t.** examen de l'ouïe; *Cin etc* **screen t.** bout *m* d'essai
3 *Cr, Rugby (match)* match *m* international
VT *(try out) (car, computer system, product, method etc)* essayer, tester; *(weights and measures etc)* contrôler, vérifier; *(sb's sight)* examiner; *(procedure)* expérimenter; *(beam etc)* sonder; *(water etc)* analyser; **to t. sb's hearing** faire passer des tests auditifs à qn; **to t. sb's blood** faire une analyse de sang à qn; **to t. sb's fitness** tester l'endurance de qn; **to t. sb's knowledge** tester les connaissances de qn; *Sch* **to t. a class in algebra** faire faire un examen d'algèbre à une classe; *Med* **to t. sb for AIDS** faire subir le test de dépistage du SIDA à qn; **to t. an athlete for steroids** faire subir des tests à un athlète pour détecter l'usage de stéroïdes; **to t. a drug on sb/animals** expérimenter un médicament sur qn/des animaux
VI *(of scientist etc)* expérimenter; **to t. for AIDS/TB** procéder à un test de dépistage du SIDA/de la tuberculose; **she tested positive for AIDS** son test de dépistage du SIDA s'est révélé positif; *Sport* **he tested positive for banned substances** son contrôle antidopage s'est révélé positif; **to t. for alkaloids** faire la réaction des alcaloïdes; **one, two, testing** *(in soundcheck)* un, deux, essai
▸▸ **t. area** région *f* test; **t. ban** interdiction *f* des essais nucléaires; **t. ban treaty** traité *m* de prohibition des essais nucléaires; **t. bench** banc *m* d'essai; *Br TV* **t. card** mire *f*, *Law* **t. case** affaire *f* qui fait jurisprudence; *Aut* **t. centre** *(for repairs)* centre *m* d'essai; **t. certificate** certificat *m* d'essai; *TV* **t. chart** mire *f* (de réglage); *Mktg* **t. city** ville *f* test; **t. drive** essai *m* sur route; **to take a car for a t. drive** essayer une voiture; *Aviat* **t. flight** vol *m* d'essai; **t. market** marché-test *m, pl* marchés-tests, marché *m* témoin; *Cr, Rugby* **t. match** match *m* international; *Br Sch* **t. paper** *(questions)* sujets *mpl* d'examen; *(answers)* copie *f* d'examen; *Am TV* **t. pattern** mire *f* (de réglage); *Mus* **t. piece** morceau *m* imposé *ou* de concours; **t. pilot** pilote *m* d'essai; **t. run** essai *m*; **t. shot** lancement *m* d'essai; **t. site** site *m* témoin; *Aut* **t. track** piste *f* d'essai; **t. tube** éprouvette *f*
▸ **test out** **VT SEP** *(person, idea etc)* mettre à l'épreuve; **to t. out a scheme** essayer un projet; **to t. out an idea on sb** tester une idée sur qn

testament [ˈtestəmənt] **N 1** *(will)* testament *m*; **to make one's (last will and) t.** tester, faire son testament **2** *(tribute)* preuve *f*, témoignage *m*; **the victory was a t. to her bravery** cette victoire a été le témoignage de son courage **3** *Bible* **the Old/the New T.** l'Ancien/le Nouveau Testament *m*

testamentary [testəˈment(ə)rɪ] **ADJ** testamentaire

testate [ˈtesteɪt] **ADJ** *Law* **to die t.** mourir en laissant un testament valable

testator, *f* **testatrix,** *pl* **testatrices, testatrixes** [tesˈteɪtər, -ˈteɪtrɪks, -trɪsiːz, -trɪksɪz] **N** testateur, -trice

test-bed **N** banc *m* d'essai

test-drive **VT** *Aut* essayer

tester[1] [ˈtestər] **N 1** *(person)* contrôleur, -euse; *(device)* appareil *m* de contrôle **2** *(sample) (of cosmetic)* échantillon *m*

tester[2] **N** *(canopy over bed)* baldaquin *m*, ciel *m*

test-fly **VT** **to t. a plane** faire le vol d'essai d'un avion

testicle [ˈtestɪk(ə)l] **N** testicule *m*

testify [ˈtestɪfaɪ] **VI** *Law* témoigner; **to t. in sb's favour/against sb** témoigner en faveur de qn/contre qn; **to t. to a fact** *(of things)* témoigner d'un fait; *(of person)* attester *ou* affirmer un fait, témoigner d'un fait
VT 1 *(one's regret, faith etc)* témoigner **2** *Law* déclarer, affirmer sous serment

testily [ˈtestɪlɪ] **ADV** d'un ton irrité

testimonial [testɪˈməʊnɪəl] **N 1** *(character reference) (given by company, director)* références *fpl*, *(letter of recommendation)* lettre *f* de recommandation **2** *(tribute)* témoignage *m* d'estime; *Ftbl (match)* jubilé *m*
▸▸ *Mktg* **t. advertising** témoignage *m*, publicité *f* testimoniale; *Ftbl* **t. match** jubilé

testimony [ˈtestɪmənɪ] **N** *(of senses etc)* témoignage *m*; *Law* attestation *f*, *(of witness)* déposition *f*, **to bear t. to sth** témoigner de qch, rendre témoignage de qch; **in t. whereof** en foi de quoi

testing [ˈtestɪŋ] **ADJ** *(problem, time, experience etc)* difficile
N *(of machine, bridge etc)* essai *m*, épreuve *f*, *(of drug, cosmetic)* expérimentation *f*, **animal t.** expérimentation animale *ou* sur les animaux
▸▸ **t. laboratory** laboratoire *m* d'essai de produits

testis, *pl* **testes** [ˈtestɪs, ˈtestiːz] **N** testicule *m*

test-market **VT** tester sur le marché

testosterone [tesˈtɒstərəʊn] **N** testostérone *f*

test-tube baby **N** bébé-éprouvette *m, pl* bébés-éprouvette

testy [ˈtestɪ] **ADJ** irritable

tetanus [ˈtetənəs] **N** *Med* tétanos *m*
▸▸ **t. injection** piqûre *f* antitétanique

tetchily [ˈtetʃɪlɪ] **ADV** d'un ton irrité

tetchiness [ˈtetʃɪnɪs] **N** irritation *f*

tetchy [ˈtetʃɪ] **ADJ** irritable

tête-à-tête [teɪtɑːˈteɪt] **ADV** tête-à-tête
N *(pl* **tête-à-têtes)** tête-à-tête *m inv*

tether [ˈteðər] **N** *(for tying horse etc)* longe *f*, attache *f*, *Fig* **to be at the end of one's t.** être à bout
VT *(horse etc)* attacher

tetrachloride [tetrəˈklɔːraɪd] **N** tétrachlorure *m*

tetragon [ˈtetrəgən] **N** quadrilatère *m*

tetragonal [teˈtræg(ə)l] **ADJ** quadrilatère

tetrahedron [tetrəˈhiːdrən, -ˈhed-] **N** tétraèdre *m*

tetrameter [teˈtræmɪtər] **N** *(in poetry)* tétramètre *m*

Teutonic [tjuːˈtɒnɪk] **ADJ** teuton, teutonique; *Hist* **the T. Order (of Knights)** l'ordre *m* Teutonique

Tex *abbr* **Texas**

Texan [ˈteks(ə)n] **ADJ** texan
N Texan, -ane

Texas [ˈteksəs] **N** le Texas

Tex-Mex [teksˈmeks] **ADJ** tex-mex *inv*

text [tekst] **N 1** *(of manuscript, author, in computing)* texte *m*; *(passage from Bible)* citation *f* tirée des Saintes Écritures; *Sch* **set texts** textes au programme **2** *(text message)* texto *m* , SMS *m*
VT *(send text message to)* envoyer un texto *ou* SMS à
VI *(send text messages)* envoyer des textos *ou* SMS
▸▸ **t. area** zone *f* de texte; *Comput* **t. block** bloc *m* de texte; **t. box** fenêtre *f* de saisie;

Comput **t. buffer** mémoire *f* tampon de texte; **t. editing** édition *f* de texte, mise *f* en forme de texte; **t. editing feature** fonction *f* d'éditeur de texte, fonction d'édition; *Comput* **t. editor** éditeur *m* de texte; *Comput* **t. field** champ *m* de texte; *Comput* **t. file** fichier *m* texte; **t. input** entrée *f* ou introduction *f* de texte; *Comput* **t. layout** disposition *f* de texte; **t. message** *(on mobile phone, pager)* texto *m* , SMS *m*; **t. messaging** envoi *m* de textos *ou* de SMS; *Comput* **t. mode** mode *m* texte; *Comput* **t. processing** traitement *m* de texte; *Comput* **t. processing capabilities** potentiel *m* de traitement de texte; *Comput* **t. processor** (unité *f* de) traitement *m* de texte; *Typ, Comput* **t. wrap** texte *m* en habillage

textbook ['tekstbʊk] N *Sch etc* manuel *m*; **physics/algebra t.** manuel *ou* livre *m* de physique/d'algèbre; *Fig* **a t. example** un exemple parfait *ou* typique (**of** de); **this was a t. example of how not to impress your boss** c'était l'exemple parfait de ce qu'il ne faut pas faire devant son patron; **a t. landing** *(of plane)* un atterrissage parfait
  ▸ ▸ **t. definition** définition *f* classique

textile ['tekstaɪl] N *(fabric)* textile N *(fabric)* tissu *m*; *(raw material)* textile *m*; **the t. industries** l'industrie *f* textile

texting ['tekstɪŋ] N *(sending text messages)* envoi *m* de textos *ou* de SMS

text-message vt envoyer un texto *ou* SMS à
  vi envoyer des textos *ou* SMS

text-size ADJ *(newspaper)* plein format

textual ['tekstjʊəl] ADJ textuel
  ▸ ▸ **t. error** erreur *f* dans le texte

textually ['tekstjʊəlɪ] ADV textuellement

texture ['tekstʃər] N *(of fabric)* tissage *m*; *(of skin, wood etc)* texture *f*, grain *m*; *Fig (of prose)* texture *f*; *Tex* **close/loose t.** tissage serré/lâche; **it'll improve the t. of your life** ça améliorera la qualité de votre vie

TFT [tiːef'tiː] N *(abbr* **thin film transistor)** transistor *m* en couche mince
  ▸ ▸ **T. display** affichage *m* TFT; **T. screen** écran *m* TFT

TGWU [tiːdʒiːdʌbljuː'juː] N *Br (abbr* **Transport and General Workers' Union)** = syndicat *m* des transports et des travailleurs confédérés

Thai [taɪ] ADJ thaïlandais; *Ling* thaï
  N **1** Thaïlandais, -aise **2** *Ling* thaï *m*

Thailand ['taɪlænd] N Thaïlande *f*

thalassotherapy [θæləsəʊ'θerəpɪ] N thalassothérapie *f*

thalidomide [θə'lɪdəmaɪd] N thalidomide *f*
  ▸ ▸ **t. baby** = bébé *m* victime de la thalidomide

Thames [temz] N **the T.** la Tamise; *Fig* **he'll never set the T. on fire** il n'a pas inventé l'eau chaude

than [ðæn, *unstressed* ð(ə)n] CONJ *(in comparison of inequality)* que; *(with numbers)* de; **I have more/less t. you** j'en ai plus/moins que vous; **more t. twenty** plus de vingt; **more t. once** plus d'une fois; **he's taller t. me** *or* **t. I am** *or Fml* **t. I** il est plus grand que moi; **I know her better t. you** je la connais mieux que toi; **I feel better t. ever** je me sens mieux que jamais; **she would do anything rather t. let him suffer** elle ferait n'importe quoi plutôt que de le laisser souffrir; **no sooner had we entered t. the music began** nous étions à peine entrés que la musique a commencé; **any person other t. himself** tout autre que lui; **it was none other t. her old friend** ce n'était nul autre que son vieil ami

thane [θeɪn] N *Hist* ≃ baron *m*

thank [θæŋk] VT remercier; *(God)* rendre grâce(s) à; **to t. sb for sth** remercier qn de *ou* pour qch; **to t. sb for doing sth** remercier qn d'avoir fait qch; **t. God!, t. heaven(s)!, t. goodness!** Dieu merci!; **t. you** merci, je te/vous remercie; **will you have some tea? – no, t. you** veux-tu du thé? – non merci *ou* non je te remercie; **yes, t. you** oui, s'il te plaît; **are you comfortable? – yes, t. you** tu es bien installé? – oui, je te remercie *ou* merci; **t. you very much** merci beaucoup, merci bien; **t. you for coming** merci d'être venu; *Fam Iron* **t. you for nothing!** je te remercie!; *Iron* **I'll t. you to mind your own business!** je te prie de t'occuper de ce qui te regarde!; **you can t. your lucky stars you're not dead** tu peux remercier ta bonne étoile de ne pas être mort; **to have sb to t. for sth** devoir qch à qn; *Iron* **you have only yourself to t. for it** c'est à toi seul qu'il faut t'en prendre; **the curtains are torn – we've got the cat to t. for that** les rideaux sont déchirés – c'est le chat qui a fait ce beau travail
  ▸ ▸ **t. you** remerciement *m*; **a big t. you from all of us** un grand merci de nous tous; **say t. you** dis merci; **t. you letter** lettre *f* de remerciement; **t. you note** mot *m* de remerciement

thankful ['θæŋkfʊl] ADJ reconnaissant; **to be t. to sb for sth** être reconnaissant à qn de qch, *esp Fml* savoir gré à qn de qch; **to be t. that ...** être bien content que ...; **at least that's something to be t. for** voilà au moins quelque chose de positif; **you should be t. you weren't charged extra** vous pouvez vous estimer heureux *ou* vous devriez être content qu'on ne vous ait pas fait payer de supplément

thankfully ['θæŋkfəlɪ] ADV **1** *(gratefully)* avec reconnaissance, avec gratitude **2** *(fortunately)* heureusement; **t. no one was hurt** heureusement *ou* Dieu merci, personne n'a été blessé

thankfulness ['θæŋkfʊlnɪs] N reconnaissance *f*, gratitude *f*

thankless ['θæŋklɪs] ADJ *(task etc)* ingrat

thanks [θæŋks] NPL remerciements *mpl*; **give him my t.** remerciez-le de ma part; **to give t. to sb for sth** remercier qn de *ou* pour qch; **to offer** *or* **give t. to God** rendre grâce à Dieu; **to propose a vote of t. to sb** faire un discours de remerciements pour qn; **t. be to God!** (rendons) grâce à Dieu!; **that's all the t. I get!** voilà comment on me remercie!
  VOIR GRAMMAIRE A10
  INT *Fam* **t.!** merci!; **t. very much!, t. a lot!** merci beaucoup!, merci bien!; **many t. for ...** mille mercis pour ...; **t. for your letter** merci pour *ou* de ta lettre; **t. for coming** merci d'être venu; **no t.** non merci; *Fam Iron* **t. for nothing!** je te remercie!
  PREP **t. to him/to his help** grâce à lui/à son aide; **no t. to you/them** on ne peut pas dire que ce soit grâce à toi/eux

thanksgiving [θæŋks'gɪvɪŋ] N action *f* de grâce(s)
  ▸ ▸ **T. Day** *Am* = fête *f* célébrée le 4e jeudi de novembre; *Can* le jour de l'action de grâces *(fête célébrée le 2e lundi d'octobre)*

Thanksgiving

Aux États-Unis, "Thanksgiving" commémore, le quatrième jeudi de novembre, l'installation des premiers colons en Amérique. Le dîner en famille qui a généralement lieu à cette occasion est traditionnellement composé d'une dinde servie avec une sauce aux airelles accompagnée de patates douces, et se termine par une tarte au potiron.

THAT [ðæt, *unstressed* ðət] VOIR GRAMMAIRE A30-1; B14-15

DEM PRON	cela **1** ▪ ce **1** ▪ celui-là **2** ▪ celui **3**
DEM ADJ	ce ▪ ce... -là
DEM ADV	tellement **2** ▪ si **2**
REL PRON	qui **1** ▪ que **1** ▪ lequel **2** ▪ où **3** ▪ que **3**
CONJ	que **1** ▪ pour que *(so that)* **2**

DEM PRON *(pl* **those** [ðəʊz]) **1** cela, ça, ce; **give me t.** donnez-moi ça; **what's t.?** qu'est-ce (que c'est) que cela *ou* ça?; **who's t.?** qui est-ce?; **t.'s Mr Thomas** c'est M. Thomas; **is t. you, Anne?** est-ce toi *ou* c'est toi Anne?; **those are my things** ce sont mes affaires; **those are my orders** voilà mes ordres; **is t. all the luggage you're taking?** c'est tout ce que tu emportes comme bagages?; **t.'s where he lives** c'est là qu'il habite; **after/before t.** après/avant cela; **t. was two years ago** il y a deux ans de cela, c'était il y a deux ans; **with t. she took out her handkerchief** là-dessus, elle a sorti son mouchoir; **what do you mean by t.?** qu'entendez-vous par là?; **t. is** *or* **t.'s to say** c'est-à-dire; **so that's settled** bon, ça c'est réglé *ou* voilà qui est réglé; **it was a bad meal and an expensive one at t.** non seulement le repas n'était pas bon mais en plus il était cher; **t.'s right!, t.'s it!** c'est cela!, ça y est!; **t.'s all** c'est tout, voilà tout; **t.'s strange!** voilà qui est curieux!; *Fam* **good stuff, t.!** ah c'est bon ça!; **and t.'s t.!, so t.'s t.!** et puis voilà, voilà tout!; **t. will do** ça suffit, c'est bon; **t.'s enough of t.!** en voilà assez!

2 *(opposed to* **this, these)** celui-là, *f* celle-là, *pl* ceux-là, *f* celles-là; **this is new and t.'s old** celui-ci est neuf et celui-là est vieux

3 *(indefinite, as antecedent to a relative)* celui, *f* celle, *pl* ceux, *f* celles; **what's t. (t.) you're holding?** qu'est-ce que tu as dans la main?; **all those t. I saw** tous ceux que j'ai vus; **one of those who were present** (l')un de ceux qui étaient présents; **I'm not one of those who ...** je ne suis pas du genre à *ou* de ceux qui ...; **all those present at the wedding** tous ceux qui ont assisté au mariage

DEM ADJ *(pl* **those)** ce; *(before vowel or h mute)* cet, *f* cette, *pl* ces; *(for emphasis and in opposition to* **this, these)** ce ... -là, cet ... -là, cette ... -là, *pl* ces ... -là; **t. book** ce livre(-là); **those books** ces livres(-là); **compare t. edition with these two** comparez cette édition-là avec ces deux-ci; **t. one** celui-là, celle-là; **at t. time** à ce moment-là, à cette époque; **in those days** en ce temps-là, à cette époque; **everybody is agreed on t. point** tout le monde est d'accord là-dessus; **t. fool of a gardener** cet imbécile de jardinier; *Dial* **t. there table** cette table-là; *Dial* **how's t. there son of yours?** et ton fils, comment il va?; **well, how's t. leg of yours?** eh bien, et cette jambe *ou* comment va votre jambe?; **it's t. wife of his who's to blame** c'est la faute de sa femme; **all those flowers t. you have there** toutes ces fleurs que vous avez là; **what about t.** *or* **those five pounds you owe me?** et ces cinq livres que tu me dois?

DEM ADV **1** *(with adj or adv of quantity)* **t. high** aussi haut que ça; **it was about t. big** c'était grand comme ça; **can you swim t. far?** tu peux nager aussi loin?; **I don't go there t. often** *(not much)* je n'y vais pas très souvent; **I don't go there that often** je n'y vais pas aussi souvent que ça; **I don't have t. much confidence in him to believe all he says** je n'ai pas assez confiance en lui pour croire tout ce qu'il raconte

2 *(so)* tellement, si; **is she t. tall?** est-elle si grande (que ça)?; **he's t. stupid he ...** il est tellement stupide qu'il ...

REL PRON SING, PL *(sometimes omitted)* VOIR GRAMMAIRE A32–3 **1** *(for subject)* qui; *(for object)* que; **the letter t. came yesterday** la lettre qui est arrivée hier; **the letter t. I sent you** la lettre que je vous ai envoyée; **you're the only person t. can help me** vous êtes la seule personne qui puisse m'aider; **miser t. he was, he would not pay** avare comme il était, il n'a pas voulu payer

2 *(with preposition)* lequel, *f* laquelle, *pl* lesquels, *f* lesquelles; **the envelope t. I put it in** l'enveloppe dans laquelle je l'ai mis; **the woman t. we're talking about** la femme dont nous parlons; **the person t. I gave it to** la personne à laquelle *ou* à qui je l'ai donné; **not t. I know of** pas que je sache, pas à ma connaissance

3 *(after expression of time)* où, que; **the time t. I saw him** la fois *ou* le jour où je l'ai vu; **during the years t. she had spent in prison** pendant les années qu'elle avait passées en prison CONJ VOIR GRAMMAIRE A74; B22–3 **1** *(introducing subordinate clause; often omitted)* que; **she said t. she would come** elle a dit qu'elle viendrait; **I'll see to it t. everything is ready** je veillerai à ce que tout soit prêt; **he's so ill t. he can't work** il est tellement malade qu'il est incapable de travailler; **to wish/hope t.** souhaiter/espérer que + *sub or ind*; **I wish t. it had never happened** je voudrais que cela ne soit jamais arrivé; **I hope t. you'll come** j'espère que vous viendrez

2 so t., in order t. (afin) que, pour que + *sub*; *(same subject in both clauses)* afin de + *inf*, pour + *inf*; **they kept quiet so t. he could sleep** ils n'ont pas fait de bruit pour que *ou* afin qu'il puisse dormir; **come nearer so t. I can see you** approchez, que je vous voie; **put it there so t. it won't be forgotten** mettez-le là pour qu'on ne l'oublie pas; **I sold it so t. I would have the money** je l'ai vendu afin d'avoir *ou* pour avoir l'argent

3 *esp Lit (exclamatory)* **t. he should behave like this!** dire qu'il se conduit comme cela!; **oh t. it were possible!** oh, si c'était possible!

---

thatch [θætʃ] N *(roof)* chaume *m*; *Fam (hair)* crinière *f*; **under this great t. of hair** sous cette épaisse crinière, sous cette masse de cheveux
VT *(roof)* couvrir de *ou* en chaume; **thatched cottage** chaumière *f*; **thatched roof** toit *m* de chaume

thatcher ['θætʃər] N couvreur *m* en chaume

Thatcherism ['θætʃərɪz(ə)m] N thatchérisme *m*

Thatcherite ['θætʃəraɪt] ADJ, N thatchérien, -ienne

thaw [θɔː] N dégel *m*, fonte *f* des neiges; **the t. is setting in** c'est le dégel; *Fig* **a t. in relations** un dégel *ou* une détente des relations
VT *(snow etc)* dégeler; *(frozen food)* décongeler
VI *(of snow, ice)* fondre; *(of frozen food etc)* se décongeler; *(of lake etc)* dégeler; *Fig (of person) (relax)* se dégeler; **it's thawing** il dégèle
▸ **thaw out** VI *(of frozen food etc)* se décongeler; *(of lake etc)* dégeler; *(of person) (become warm)* se réchauffer; **come in and t. out** entrez et réchauffez-vous
VT SEP *(frozen food)* décongeler

thawing ['θɔːɪŋ] N *(of river etc)* dégel *m*; *(of snow)* fonte *f*; *(of frozen food)* décongélation *f*; **a t. in relations** un dégel *ou* une détente des relations

the [ðiː; *unstressed before consonant* ðə; *unstressed before vowel* ðɪ] DEF ART **1** le, *f* la, *(before vowel or h mute)* l', *pl* les; **at/to t. ...** au ..., à la ..., *pl* aux ...; **of/from t. ...** du ..., de la ..., *pl* des ...; **t. father and (t.) mother** le père et la mère; **I spoke to t. driver** j'ai parlé au conducteur; **t. roof of t. house** le toit de la maison; **t. arrival of t. guests** l'arrivée des invités; **at** *or* **on t. corner** au coin; **on t. other side** de l'autre côté; **on t. Monday he fell ill** le lundi il est tombé malade; **I'll see him in t. summer** je le verrai cet été; **in t. summer of 1996** pendant l'été 1996, en été 1996; **in t. year 1564** en l'an 1564; **t. Greeks** les Grecs; **t. Martins** *(family)* les Martin; **Edward t. Seventh** Édouard Sept; **t. England of today** l'Angleterre d'aujourd'hui; **he's t. best-looking man I know** c'est le plus bel homme que je connaisse; *Fam* **well, how's t. throat then?** eh bien, et cette gorge?; *Fam* **t. wife** *(my/your wife)* ma/ta femme; **Mrs Long, t. managing director of t. firm** Mme. Long, PDG de l'entreprise; **t. impudence/cheek of it!** quelle audace/quel culot!; **t. concept of t. beautiful/good** le concept du beau/bon; **words borrowed from t. French** mots empruntés au français; **t. poor** les pauvres; **Catherine t. Great** Catherine la Grande; **she's got t. measles/flu** elle a la rougeole/grippe; **t. golden eagle lives in mountainous regions** l'aigle royal vit dans les régions montagneuses; **who invented t. wheel?** qui a inventé la roue?; **to be paid by t. hour** être payé à l'heure; **eight apples to t. kilo** huit pommes au kilo; **thirty miles to t. gallon** = dix litres aux cent kilomètres; **to play t. trumpet/drums** jouer de la trompette/de la batterie; **I was absent at t. time** j'étais absent à cette époque *ou* à ce moment-là; **do leave t. child alone!** mais laissez-le donc, cet enfant!; **she's giving up her job – t. woman's mad!** elle quitte son emploi – elle est folle! VOIR GRAMMAIRE A5–8; B3–4

2 *(stressed)* [ðiː]: **her father is Professor Smith, the Professor Smith** son père est le professeur Smith, le fameux *ou* le célèbre professeur Smith; **Maurice's is the shop for furniture** pour les meubles, la maison Maurice est la meilleure qui soit
ADV **I am all t. more/t. less surprised that ...** j'en suis d'autant plus/d'autant moins surpris que ...; **he ran all t. faster** il a couru d'autant plus vite; **t. longer t. wait t. bigger t. disappointment** plus on attend plus on est déçu; **t. sooner t. better** le plus tôt sera le mieux; **t. less said about it t. better** moins on en parlera mieux cela vaudra; **t. more he drinks t. thirstier he gets** plus il boit, plus il a soif

theatre, *Am* **theater** ['θɪətər] N **1** *(building, drama)* théâtre *m*; **open air t.** théâtre en plein air; **to go to the t.** aller au théâtre *ou* au spectacle; **the English t.** le théâtre anglais **2** *(lecture)* **t.** amphithéâtre *m*; *Br Med (operating)* **t.** salle *f* d'opération; **in t.** en salle d'op **3** *(area)* **the t. of war** le théâtre de la guerre
▸▸ **t. bill** affiche *f* de théâtre; **t. company** troupe *f* de théâtre, compagnie *f* théâtrale; **t. critic** critique *mf* de théâtre; **t. nuclear weapon** arme *f* nucléaire tactique; **t. review** critique *f* théâtrale; *Med* **t. sister** infirmière *f* au bloc opératoire; **t. weapon** arme *f* tactique; **t. workshop** atelier *m* de théâtre

theatre-goer, *Am* **theater-goer** N amateur, -trice de théâtre

theatre-going, *Am* **theater-going** ADJ **the t. public** ceux qui vont au théâtre
N fréquentation *f* des théâtres

theatrical [θɪˈætrɪk(ə)l] ADJ **1** *Theat* théâtral, -aux **2** *Fig (attitude etc)* théâtral, -aux
▸▸ **t. company** compagnie *f* théâtrale

theatrically [θɪˈætrɪklɪ] ADV **1** *Theat* théâtralement **2** *Fig* théâtralement, avec affectation

theatricals [θɪˈætrɪkəlz] NPL *(amateur)* **t.** théâtre *m* d'amateurs; *Fig* **we don't need all the t.!** épargnez-nous toute cette mise en scène *ou* toute cette comédie!

thee [ðiː] PERS PRON OBJECTIVE CASE **1** *Arch, Dial, Lit (unstressed)* te; *(before a vowel or h mute)* t'; **we beseech t.** nous te supplions; **sit t. down** assieds-toi **2** *(stressed)* toi; **he thinks of t.** il pense à toi

theft [θeft] N vol *m*
▸▸ **t. cover** garantie *f* vol; *Aut* **t. deterrent faceplate** cache-radio *m inv*; **t. insurance** assurance *f* vol; **t. risk** risque *m* de vol

theftproof ['θeftpruːf] ADJ *(vehicle etc)* muni d'un dispositif antivol; *(lock etc)* antivol, de sécurité

their [ðeər] VOIR GRAMMAIRE A30; A43; B21–2 POSS ADJ **1** leur, *f* leur, *pl* leurs; **t. neighbour(s)** leur(s) voisin(s); **t. father and mother** leur père et leur mère, leurs père et mère; **t. eyes are blue** ils ont les yeux bleus; **they have a car of t. own** ils ont leur propre voiture; **they've lost t. hats** ils ont perdu leur chapeau; **T. Majesties** Leurs Majestés **2** *Fam (after indef pron or to replace his/her)* son, *f* sa, *pl* ses; **someone's left t. umbrella** quelqu'un a laissé son parapluie; **each candidate should bring t. ...** chaque candidat doit amener son ... VOIR GRAMMAIRE A28

theirs [ðeəz] POSS PRON VOIR GRAMMAIRE A30; B21–2 **1** le leur, la leur, *pl* les leurs; **this house is t.** cette maison est la leur *ou* est à eux/elles *ou* leur appartient; **a friend of t.** un ami à eux/elles, un de leurs amis; **that damn dog of t.!** leur sacré chien!; **I'm interested in them and (in) t.** *(their family)* je m'intéresse à eux et aux leurs; *Fml* **t. is not to reason why** ce n'est pas à eux de leur demander la raison **2** *Fam (indef or to replace his/hers)* le sien, la sienne VOIR GRAMMAIRE A28

theism ['θiːɪz(ə)m] N *Rel* théisme *m*

theist ['θiːɪst] N théiste *mf*

theistic [θiːˈɪstɪk] ADJ *Rel* théiste

them [ðem, ðəm] PERS PRON PL OBJECTIVE CASE VOIR GRAMMAIRE A27–9; A43; B18–21 **1** *(unstressed) (direct)* les *mf*; *(indirect)* leur *mf*; *(after prepositions)* eux, *f* elles; **I like t.** je les aime bien; **have you seen t.?** les avez-vous vu(e)s?; **give t. some** donnez-leur-en; **speak to t.** parlez-leur; **look at t.** regardez-les; **they took the keys away with t.** ils ont emporté les clefs avec eux

2 *(stressed)* eux, *f* elles; **I'm thinking of t.** c'est à eux/elles que je pense; **it's t.!** c'est eux/elles!, ce sont eux/elles!, les voilà!; **we're not as rich as t.** nous ne sommes pas aussi riches qu'eux

3 *(other prep combinations)* **every one of t. was killed** ils ont tous été tués; **there were three of t.** *(of people)* ils/elles étaient trois; *(of objects)* il y en avait trois; **it was nice/good of t. to come** c'est gentil de leur part d'être venus; **give me half of t.** donnez-m'en la moitié; **several/many/most of t.** plusieurs/beaucoup/la plupart d'entre eux; **neither of t.** ni l'un ni l'autre; **none of t.** aucun d'entre eux

4 *Fam (as indef pron)* **when anyone comes she says to t. ...** quand quelqu'un vient elle lui dit ... VOIR GRAMMAIRE A28
ADJ *Dial (those)* ces

thematic [θiːˈmætɪk] ADJ *Mus etc* thématique
▸▸ *Mktg* **t. apperception test** test *m* d'aperception thématique

theme [θiːm] N **1** *(of speech etc)* sujet *m*, thème *m* **2** *Sch, Am (essay)* dissertation *f* **3** *Art, Liter, Mus etc* thème *m*, motif *m*; *Mus* **t. with variations** thème et variations *fpl*
▸▸ **t. advertising** publicité *f* thématique; **t. bar** bar *m* à thème; **t. evening** soirée *f* à thème; **t. music** Radio, TV *(of programme)* générique *m*; *Cin (in film)* thème principal de la musique d'un/du film; **t. park** parc *m* à thème; **t. pub** pub *m* à thème; **t. restaurant** restaurant *m* à thème; **t. song** *(from film)*

chanson *f* (de film); *Am (signature tune)* indicatif *m*; **t. tune** *(from film)* musique *f* (de film); *Br (signature tune)* indicatif *m*; **t. weekend** week-end *m* à thème, *pl* week-ends

themed [θiːmd] ADJ thématique
▸▸ *TV* **t. channel** chaîne *f* thématique; **t. evening, t. night** soirée *f* thématique

themselves [ðəmˈselvz, *stressed* ðem-] PERS PRON PL 1 *(emphatic)* eux-mêmes, *f* elles-mêmes; **they did it t.** ils l'ont fait eux-mêmes; **they t. are resigned to it** eux-mêmes s'y sont résignés; **they were standing in a corner by t.** ils étaient tout seuls dans un coin; **they were whispering among t.** ils chuchotaient entre eux; **the houses t. were quite elegant, but …** les maisons elles-mêmes étaient assez belles, mais … **2** *(reflexive)* se; **they've hurt t.** ils se sont fait mal; **they don't see t. living here forever** ils ne se voient pas vivre ici toute leur vie VOIR GRAMMAIRE A29–30; B28–9 **3** *Fam (indef use)* **if anybody hurts t.** si quelqu'un se fait mal VOIR GRAMMAIRE A28

then [ðen] ADV **1** *(at that time)* alors, en ce temps-là, à cette époque; **what were you doing t.?** que faisiez-vous alors?; **the t. existing system** le système qui existait à cette époque *ou* en ce temps-là; **in the conditions t. prevailing, in the t. prevailing conditions** dans les conditions d'alors *ou* de l'époque; **t. and there** séance tenante, sur-le-champ **2** *(next)* puis, ensuite, alors; *(in space)* puis; **we'll have soup first (and) t. some fish** on prendra d'abord du potage (et) ensuite du poisson; **what t.?** et puis (quoi)?, et (puis) après?; **on the left the church, t. a few old houses** à gauche l'église, puis quelques vieilles maisons **3** *(in addition)* d'ailleurs, et aussi, et puis; **and t. there are the children to be considered** et puis *ou* et aussi il faut penser aux enfants **4** **but t.** mais; **she lost her temper, but t. that's hardly surprising** elle s'est énervée, mais à vrai dire ce n'est pas étonnant; **it's beautiful material, but t. it is expensive** c'est du beau tissu, mais c'est vrai qu'il coûte cher **5** **before t.** avant cela; **will you have finished by t.?** est-ce que vous aurez fini d'ici là?; **by t. it will be too late** à ce moment-là il sera trop tard; **between now and t.** d'ici là; **(every) now and t.** de temps en temps, de temps à autre; **(ever) since t., from t. on** dès lors, depuis ce temps-là; **until t.** *(referring to past time)* jusqu'alors; *(until future time)* jusque-là **6** *(in that case)* donc, alors; **if you want to go, t. go!** si tu veux y aller, (eh bien) vas-y!; **well t., you're coming?** alors tu viens?; **right t. …** bon …, bien …; **(but) t. you should have told him so** en ce cas vous auriez dû le lui dire; **you knew all the time t.?, t. you knew all the time?** donc tu le savais depuis le début?

ADJ *(in front of noun)* **the t. Foreign Secretary** le Ministre des Affaires Étrangères d'alors *ou* de l'époque; **his t. wife** son épouse d'alors

thence [ðens] ADV *Fml, Lit* **1** *(from there)* de là; **we went to Paris and (from) t. to Rome** nous sommes allés à Paris et de là à Rome **2** *(from that time)* = **thenceforth 3** *(as a result of that)* pour cette raison, par conséquent

thenceforth, thenceforward [ˈðensˈfɔːθ, -ˈfɔːwəd] ADV *Fml, Lit* **(from) t.** dès lors

theocracy [θiːˈɒkrəsɪ] N théocratie *f*

theocratic [θiːəˈkrætɪk] ADJ théocratique

theodolite [θiːˈɒdəlaɪt] N *(in surveying)* théodolite *m*

theologian [θiːəˈləʊdʒ(ɪ)ən] N théologien *m*

theological [θiːəˈlɒdʒɪk(ə)l] ADJ théologique
▸▸ **t. college** séminaire *m*

theologically [θiːəˈlɒdʒɪklɪ] ADV théologiquement; *(from a theological point of view)* d'un point de vue théologique

theology [θiːˈɒlədʒɪ] N théologie *f*

theorem [ˈθɪərəm] N *Math, Phys etc* théorème *m*

theoretical [θiːəˈretɪk(ə)l] ADJ *(reasoning etc)* théorique; *(doctrine)* théorétique; **it's only t.** ce n'est que de la théorie

theoretically [θiːəˈretɪklɪ] ADV théoriquement, du point de vue théorique; **t., individuals can travel where they like** théoriquement *ou* en théorie, les individus peuvent voyager où ils le désirent

theoretician [θiːərɪˈtɪʃən] N théoricien, -ienne

theorist [ˈθiːərɪst] N théoricien, -ienne

theorize [ˈθiːəraɪz] VI théoriser

theorizing [ˈθiːəraɪzɪŋ] N théorisation *f*

theory [ˈθiːərɪ] N théorie *f*; **in t.** en théorie; **I have a t. about that** j'ai mon idée là-dessus

theosophical [θiːəˈsɒfɪk(ə)l] ADJ théosophique

theosophist [θiːˈɒsəfɪst] N théosophe *mf*

theosophy [θiːˈɒsəfɪ] N théosophie *f*

therapeutic [θerəˈpjuːtɪk] ADJ *Med, Fig* thérapeutique

therapeutically [θerəˈpjuːtɪklɪ] ADV thérapeutiquement; *(from therapeutic point of view)* d'un point de vue thérapeutique

therapeutics [θerəˈpjuːtɪks] NPL *Med* thérapeutique *f* VOIR GRAMMAIRE A10

therapist [ˈθerəpɪst] N **1** *(psychological)* psychothérapeute *mf* **2** *(in general)* thérapeute *mf*

therapy [ˈθerəpɪ] N *Med* **1** *(psychological)* psychothérapie *f* **2** *(in general)* thérapie *f*, **speech t.** orthophonie *f*

THERE [ðeər, *unstressed* ðər] ADV **1** *(in that place)* là; **the keys aren't t.** les clefs ne sont pas là *ou* n'y sont pas; **put it t.** mets-le là; *(extending hand)* serre-moi la main; **she's still t.** elle est encore là, elle y est toujours; **does he work t.?** c'est là qu'il travaille?; **we're t.!** nous voilà arrivés!; **who's t.?** qui est là?; *Fam* **to be all t.** *(alert, shrewd)* être malin; *(in full possession of one's faculties)* avoir toute sa raison *ou* toute sa tête; *Fam* **she's not all t.** elle a un (petit) grain, elle est un peu marteau; **I'm going t.** j'y vais; **t. and back** aller et retour; **t. and then** séance tenante, sur-le-champ; *Fig* **I've been t.** je suis passé par là, j'ai connu ça; *Fam* **I'll always be t. for you** tu pourras toujours compter sur moi; **give me that book t.** donnez-moi ce livre-là; **that man t.** cet homme-là; **your friend t.** votre ami; **hey! you t.!** hé, vous là-bas!; **move along t., please!** circulez, s'il vous plaît; **they are!** les voilà!; **t. she comes!** la voilà (qui arrive)!; **we go to Paris and from t. to Rome** nous allons à Paris et de là à Rome; **somewhere round t. or near t.** quelque part par là; **put it over t.** mettez-le là-bas *ou* par là; **down t.** en bas; **up t.** là-haut; **in t.** là-dedans; **under t.** là-dessous; **t.'s a dear!** tu seras gentil!; **t. you are!** *(here's what you asked for)* (et) voilà!; **just press the button and t. you are!** *(it's done)* vous n'avez qu'à appuyer sur le bouton et ça y est! VOIR GRAMMAIRE A21

2 **t. is/are** il y a; **t. was/were** il y avait, il était; **t. will be** il y aura; **t. was once a king** il était *ou* il y avait une fois un roi; **t. was singing and dancing** on a chanté et dansé; **will t. be food?** est-ce qu'il y aura à manger?; **t.'s a page missing** il manque une page; **t. is only one** il n'y en a qu'un; **t.'s one slice left** il reste

une tranche; **t. are** *or Fam* **t.'s two slices left** il reste deux tranches; **t.'s nothing we can do to help them** on ne peut rien faire pour les aider; **t.'s no need to shout** c'est inutile de crier; **t. isn't any** il n'y en a pas; **t.'s someone at the door** il y a quelqu'un à la porte; **t. comes a time when …** il arrive un moment où …; **t.'s the bell ringing** voilà la cloche qui sonne

3 *(in that matter)* quant à cela, dans ce domaine, sur ce sujet; **t.'s or t. lies the difficulty** voilà le problème, c'est là *Fam* **t. you have me!, you've got me t.!** ça, ça me dépasse

4 *(at this point)* là; **we'll have to stop t. for today** nous nous arrêterons là pour aujourd'hui

INT voilà!; **t. now, that's done!** là! voilà qui est fait!; **t. now, that wasn't too painful, was it?** alors, ça n'a pas été trop douloureux, hein?; **t. (you are), I told you so là!** je te l'avais bien dit!; **t.!, t.! (now), don't worry!** allons, allons, ne t'inquiète pas!; **I'll do as I like, so t.!** je ferai comme il me plaira, et puis c'est tout!

thereabouts [ˈðeərəˈbaʊts] ADV **1** *(with place) (nearby)* près de là; *(in that area)* dans le voisinage; **in Brighton or t.** à Brighton ou quelque part par là **2** *(with number, quantity, distance etc) (approximately)* à peu près, environ; **the parcel weighs two kilos or t.** le colis pèse environ deux kilos

thereafter [ðeərˈɑːftər] ADV *Fml, Lit* après (cela), par la suite

thereby [ðeəˈbaɪ *when at the end of clause*, ˈðeəbaɪ *when preceding verb*] ADV *Fml* ainsi, de cette façon; *Prov* **t. hangs a tale!** c'est toute une histoire!

therefore [ˈðeəfɔːr] ADV donc, aussi; **I think, t. I am** je pense, donc je suis; **I should t. be grateful if you would …** je vous serais donc reconnaissant *ou* aussi vous serais-je reconnaissant de bien vouloir …; **they had t. decided to …** ils avaient donc décidé de …; **you are his friend and t. mine** vous êtes son ami et donc vous êtes aussi le mien

therefrom [ðeəˈfrɒm] ADV *Lit, Fml* de là; **it follows t. that …** cela signifie donc que …

therein [ðeərˈɪn] ADV *Lit, Fml* **1** *(in that matter)* en cela; **t. you are mistaken** en cela vous vous trompez **2** *(in that place)* (là-)dedans; **and all the furniture t.** *(in house)* et tous les meubles qu'elle contient

thereof [ðeərˈɒv] ADV *Lit, Fml* de cela, en; **in lieu t.** au lieu de cela; **he drank t.** il y but; **the building and the owner t.** l'immeuble et le propriétaire de celui-ci

there's [ðeəz] CONTR = **there is, there has**

thereto [ðeəˈtuː] ADV *Lit, Fml* à cela, y; **the house and the garden pertaining t.** la maison et le jardin qui va avec celle-ci

thereupon [ˈðeərəˈpɒn] ADV *Fml* **1** *(at which point)* sur ce, sur quoi, là-dessus; **t. he left** sur quoi il est parti **2** *Lit* **there is much to be said t.** il y aurait beaucoup à dire là-dessus *ou* à ce sujet

therewith [ðeəˈwɪð, -ˈwɪθ] ADV *Fml, Lit* **1** *(with that)* avec cela **2** = **thereupon 1**

therm [θɜːm] N *Br Phys etc* thermie *f*

thermal [ˈθɜːm(ə)l] ADJ **1** thermal **2** *Phys* thermal, -aux, thermique, calorifique

N **1** *Met, Aviat* thermique *m*, ascendance *f* thermique **2** *Fam* **thermals** *(underwear)* (sous-vêtements *mpl* en) thermolactyl® *m*
▸▸ **t. energy** énergie *f* thermique *ou* calorifique; **t. imaging** thermographie *f*, *Comput* **t. paper** papier *m* thermique *ou* thermosensible; *Comput* **t. printer** imprimante *f* thermique *ou* thermoélectrique; **t. reactor** réacteur *m* thermique; **t. springs** eaux *fpl* *ou* sources *fpl* thermales; *Comput* **t. transfer**

transfert *m* thermique; **t. underwear** sous-vêtements *mpl* en thermolactyl®; **t. unit** unité *f* thermique

thermic ['θɜːmɪk] ADJ *Phys etc* thermique, calorifique

thermionic [θɜːmɪ'ɒnɪk] ADJ *Electron* thermoélectronique, thermionique

thermistor [θɜː'mɪstər] N thermistor *m*

thermocouple ['θɜːməʊkʌp(ə)l] N *Elec* couple *m* thermoélectrique, thermocouple *m*

thermodynamic [θɜːməʊdaɪ'næmɪk] ADJ thermodynamique

thermoelectric [θɜːməʊɪ'lektrɪk] ADJ thermoélectrique

thermoluminescence [θɜːməʊluːmɪ-'nesəns] N thermoluminescence *f*

thermometer [θə'mɒmɪtər] N thermomètre *m*

thermonuclear [θɜːməʊ'njuːklɪər] ADJ *Nucl, Mil* thermonucléaire

thermopile ['θɜːməʊpaɪl] N *Elec* pile *f* thermoélectrique

thermoplastic [θɜːməʊ'plæstɪk] ADJ, N thermoplastique *m*

Thermos® ['θɜːməs] N (bouteille *f*) Thermos® *m or f inv*
  ▸▸ **T. flask** (bouteille) Thermos®

thermostat ['θɜːməstæt] N thermostat *m*, calorstat *m*

thermostatic [θɜːmə'stætɪk] ADJ thermostatique
  ▸▸ **t. control** réglage *m* (de la température) par thermostat; **t. switch** thermocontact *m*

thermostatically [θɜːmə'stætɪklɪ] ADV **t. controlled** réglé par thermostat

thesaurus, *pl* **thesauri** [θɪ'sɔːrəs, -aɪ] N dictionnaire *m* de synonymes

these *see* **this**

thesis, *pl* **theses** ['θiːsɪs, -iːz] N *(in logic)*, *Univ etc* thèse *f*; **to uphold/defend a t.** soutenir/défendre une thèse; **PhD** *or* **doctoral t.** thèse de doctorat

Thespian ['θespɪən] *Lit, Hum* ADJ tragique, dramatique
  N acteur, -trice (de théâtre)

they [ðeɪ] PERS PRON PL VOIR GRAMMAIRE A27–9; B18–19 *(unstressed)* ils, *f* elles; *(stressed)* eux, *f* elles; *(with dem force)* ceux, *f* celles; **t. are dancing** ils/elles dansent; **here t. come** les voici (qui arrivent); **t. alone can …** eux seuls/elles seules peuvent …; **we are as rich as t. are** nous sommes aussi riches que/qu'elles; *Lit* **t. who believe** ceux/celles qui croient
  INDEF PRON **1** *(people)* on; **t. say that …** on dit que … **2** *Fam (after indef pron or to replace he/she)* nobody ever admits **t.**'re wrong on ne veut jamais reconnaître qu'on a tort; **each candidate must be told that t. should …** chaque candidat doit être informé qu'il doit … VOIR GRAMMAIRE A28

they'd [ðeɪd] CONTR **1** = **they had**, *see* **have 2** = **they would**, *see* **will**²

they'll [ðeɪl] CONTR = **they will**, *see* **will**²

they're [ðeər] CONTR = **they are**, *see* **be**

they've [ðeɪv] CONTR = **they have**, *see* **have**

thiamine ['θaɪəmɪ(ə)n] N *Biol, Chem* thiamine *f*

thick [θɪk] ADJ **1** *(walls, material etc)* épais, *f* épaisse; *(book, thread etc)* gros, *f* grosse; *(lips)* épais, gros; **wall one metre t.** mur d'un mètre d'épaisseur; *Fam* **to give sb a t. ear** arranger le portrait à qn; **the t. end of a stick** le gros bout d'un bâton; *Fig* **to have a t. skin** avoir la peau dure; *Fam* **can't you get it into your t. skull** *or* **head that …?** tu ne peux pas faire entrer dans ta petite tête que …?
  2 *(dense)* *(forest, undergrowth)* épais, *f* épaisse, touffu; *(carpet)* épais; *(hair)* abon-

dant, épais; *(voice)* *(from alcohol)* aviné; *(from sleep)* ensommeillé; **t. eyebrows** sourcils *mpl* touffus *ou* épais; **the leaves were/snow was t. on the ground** il y avait une belle épaisseur de feuilles/neige sur le sol; *Fig* **Conservative voters aren't very t. on the ground in these parts** ici les gens qui votent conservateur ne sont pas légion
  3 *(liquid)* épais, *f* épaisse, visqueux; *(mist)* dense, épais; *(darkness)* profond; **t. mud** boue *f* grasse; **the air was t. with smoke** l'air était plein de fumée
  4 *Fam* **to be very t. with sb** être très copain avec qn; *Prov* **they're as t. as thieves** ils s'entendent comme larrons en foire
  5 *Fam (excessive)* **that's a bit t.!** ça c'est un peu raide *ou* un peu fort!; **it's a bit t. expecting us to take them to the airport!** ils exagèrent de compter sur nous pour les conduire à l'aéroport!
  6 *Fam (stupid)* abruti, bouché; **to be as t. as two short planks** *or* **a brick** être bête comme ses pieds
  N **in the t. of the forest** au beau milieu de la forêt; **in the t. of (the) battle** au cœur de la bataille; **when you are in the t. of it** *or* **of things** dans le feu de l'action; **we soon found ourselves in the t. of things** nous nous sommes vite retrouvés au cœur de l'action; **in the t. of the fight** au (plus) fort *ou* au vif de la mêlée; **to go through t. and thin for sb** faire n'importe quoi pour qn; **to follow sb** *or* **stick to sb through t. and thin** soutenir qn *ou* se rallier à qn quoi qu'il arrive
  ADV **1** *(in a thick layer)* en couche épaisse; **snow lay t. on the ground** une neige épaisse *ou* une épaisse couche de neige couvrait le sol; **to cut the bread t.** couper le pain en tranches épaisses; *Fam* **to lay it on a bit t.** exagérer
  2 **his blows fell t. and fast** il frappait à coups redoublés, les coups pleuvaient dru; **insults were flying t. and fast** les insultes pleuvaient dru; **letters were coming in t. and fast** les lettres pleuvaient *ou* affluaient

thicken ['θɪk(ə)n] VT *(wall etc)* épaissir; *(sauce)* épaissir, lier
  VI *(of tree trunk, figure, air etc)* (s')épaissir; *(of sauce)* épaissir; *esp Hum* **the plot thickens** … ça se corse …

thickener ['θɪk(ə)nər] N épaississant *m*

thickening ['θɪkənɪŋ] N épaississement *m*; **t. agent** agent *m* épaississant

thicket ['θɪkɪt] N fourré *m*

thickhead ['θɪkhed] N *Fam* abruti, -ie

thickheaded [θɪk'hedɪd] ADJ *Fam* bête

thickie ['θɪkɪ] N *Br Fam* idiot, -ote; **so that a t. like me can understand** de sorte qu'un lourdaud *ou* idiot comme moi puisse comprendre; **he's a complete t.** ce n'est pas une flèche; **I was a t. at maths** j'étais nul en maths

thick-lipped ADJ lippu

thickly ['θɪklɪ] ADV **1** *(in thick layer(s))* en couche(s) épaisse(s); *(cut sth)* en tranches épaisses; **to spread butter t.** étaler généreusement du beurre **2** *(densely)* dru; **the snow fell t.** la neige tombait dru; **t. wooded** très boisé **3** **to speak t.** *(with suppressed rage, lust)* parler d'une voix étouffée; *(when drunk)* avoir la voix avinée

thickness ['θɪknɪs] N **1** *(of wall etc)* épaisseur *f*, *(of lips etc)* grosseur *f*; **roll the pastry out to a t. of ⅛ of an inch** étalez la pâte jusqu'à ce qu'elle fasse environ 3 mm d'épaisseur **2** *(of forest etc)* épaisseur *f*, *(of hair, beard etc)* abondance *f* **3** *(of liquid)* consistance *f*, *(of fog)* épaisseur *f* **4** *(layer)* *(of paper etc)* couche *f*

thicko ['θɪkəʊ] N *Br Fam* = **thickie**

thickset ['θɪk'set] ADJ *(person)* trapu

thick-skinned ADJ *(animal, fruit)* à la peau épaisse; *Fig (person)* qui a la peau dure

thick-sliced ADJ *(bread)* coupé en tranches épaisses

thief, *pl* **thieves** [θiːf, θiːvz] N voleur, -euse; **horse t.** voleur *m* de chevaux; **stop t.!** au voleur!; *Prov* **set a t. to catch a t.** à fripon, fripon et demi; *Prov* **once a t. always a t.** qui a volé volera
  ▸▸ *Fam* **thieves' kitchen** repaire *m* de voleurs

thieve [θiːv] VI voler, commettre des vols
  VT voler

thieving ['θiːvɪŋ] ADJ voleur, -euse; **keep your t. hands off!** bas les pattes!
  N vol *m*

thigh [θaɪ] N cuisse *f*
  ▸▸ **t. boots** cuissardes *fpl*

thighbone ['θaɪbəʊn] N *Anat* fémur *m*

thigh-length ADJ *(dress, coat)* qui descend jusqu'à mi-cuisse
  ▸▸ **t. boots** cuissardes *fpl*

thimble ['θɪmb(ə)l] N *Sewing* dé *m* (à coudre); **hunt the t.** *(game)* ≃ cache-tampon *m inv*
  ▸▸ **t. printer** *Comput* imprimante *f* à tulipe

thimbleful ['θɪmb(ə)lfʊl] N *(of brandy etc)* doigt *m*

thin [θɪn] *(comp* **thinner,** *superl* **thinnest)* ADJ **1** *(paper etc)* mince, fin; *(thread etc)* ténu, fin; *(material)* fin, mince, léger; *(person)* maigre, mince; *(air)* raréfié; **to grow** *or* **become thinner** *(of person)* maigrir; **to get** *or* **become thinner** *(of air)* se raréfier; **as t. as a rake** maigre comme un clou, sec comme un coup de trique; *Fig* **this was only the t. end of the wedge** à partir de là, ce fut l'escalade
  2 *(sparse)* *(hair etc)* clairsemé, rare; *(population, audience)* clairsemé; **attendance has been rather t. recently** le taux de présence est très bas en ce moment; **his hair was getting t.** ses cheveux s'éclaircissaient; **t. on the ground** peu nombreux; **t. beard** barbe peu fournie
  3 *(liquid)* clair, peu consistant; *(blood)* appauvri; **t. soup** potage *m* clair; **t. voice** voix *f* fluette *ou* grêle
  4 *Fig* **my patience is wearing t.** ma patience a des limites; **my patience was wearing t.** je commençais à perdre patience; **his excuse was rather t.** son excuse était un peu légère; **to have a t. time (of it)** *(not enjoy oneself)* s'ennuyer, s'embêter; *(go through hard times)* manger de la vache enragée
  ADV **to spread sth t.** étaler qch en couche fine *ou* mince; **they cut the cheese as t. as possible** ils ont coupé le fromage aussi fin que possible
  N **to follow sb** *or* **stick to sb through thick and t.** soutenir qn *ou* se rallier à qn quoi qu'il arrive; **to go through thick and t. for sb** faire n'importe quoi pour qn
  VT *(-nn-)* *(paint)* diluer, délayer; *(sauce)* allonger, éclaircir
  VI *(of trees, crowd, hair etc)* s'éclaircir; *(of liquid)* devenir clair; **his hair is thinning** il perd ses cheveux
  ▸▸ *Electron* **t. film transistor** transistor *m* en couche mince; *Typ* **t. stroke** délié *m*
  ▸ **thin down** VT SEP *(dilute)* *(paint)* diluer, délayer; *(sauce)* allonger, éclaircir
  ▸ **thin out** VI *(become less dense)* *(of hair)* s'éclaircir; **he's thinning out on top** il se dégarnit sur le dessus du crâne
  VT SEP *(make less dense)* *(plants)* éclaircir; *(hair)* éclaircir, désépaissir

thine [ðaɪn] *Arch, Lit* POSS PRON le tien, *f* la tienne, *pl* les tiens, *f* les tiennes; **for thee and t.** pour toi et les tiens; **what is mine is t.** ce qui est à moi est à toi

POSS ADJ (*used instead of* **thy** *before a noun or adj beginning with a vowel or h mute*) ton, *f* ta, *pl* tes

THING [θɪŋ]

chose **1, 3** ▪ truc **1** ▪ affaires (*things*) **1**
▪ vêtements (*things*) **1** ▪ être **2**
▪ créature **2** ▪ idée **3** ▪ mode **4**

N 1 chose *f*, *Fam* truc *m*; **a t. of beauty** une belle chose; **the things of this world** les choses de ce monde; **chocolate, sweets, and things (like that)** le chocolat, les bonbons, et autres choses de ce style; *Fam* **what's that t.?** qu'est-ce que c'est que ce machin-là?; *Fam* **where's that scraper t.?** où est le machin pour gratter?; **my things** (*clothes etc*) mes vêtements *mpl*; (*belongings*) mes affaires *fpl*; **winter things** (*clothes*) vêtements d'hiver; **bring along your swimming things** apportez vos affaires de bain; **to pack (up) one's things** faire ses valises; **I didn't bring a lot of things** (*on holiday*) je n'ai pas pris beaucoup d'affaires
2 *Fam* (*person*) (*with adj expressing pity, contempt etc*) être *m*, créature *f*; **poor t.!** le/la pauvre!; **you silly t.!** sot/sotte tu es!; **poor little things!** pauvres petits!; **she's a dear old t.** c'est une petite vieille bien sympathique
3 (*action, remark, fact etc*) chose *f*; **that was a silly t. to do** ça, ce n'est pas très malin de ta/sa/*etc* part; **what a silly/nasty t. to say!** c'est vraiment stupide/méchant de dire ça *ou* une chose pareille; **the things you say!** les choses que tu peux dire parfois!; **how could you do such a t.?** comment avez-vous pu faire une chose pareille?; **how could you say such a t.!** comment avez-vous pu dire une chose pareille!; **did you ever hear of such a t.?** on n'a pas idée d'une chose pareille!; **you take things too seriously** vous prenez les choses trop au sérieux; **she gets things done** avec elle, le travail avance bien; **to think things over** réfléchir; **it's just one of those things** ce sont des choses qui arrivent; **it's a t. you need to give careful consideration to** c'est une chose à laquelle tu dois bien réfléchir; **to talk of one t. and another** parler de choses et d'autres; **it's been one t. after the other** (*problems*) on a eu des problèmes en cascade *ou* une cascade de problèmes; **what with one t. and another we haven't had time** on a été pris par plein de choses et on n'a pas eu le temps; **that's the very t.** c'est juste ce qu'il faut; **the t. is this** voici ce dont il s'agit; **the t. is, I haven't got any money** le problème, c'est que je n'ai pas d'argent; **the only t. left is to ...** il ne reste plus qu'à ...; **the important t. is that ...** l'important c'est que ...; **the t. to remember is that ...** ce dont il faut se souvenir est que ...; **that's quite another t.** ça, c'est tout autre chose; **neither one t. nor another** ni l'un(e) ni l'autre; **and another t.** en plus; *Fam* **he's on to a good t.** il est sur un bon filon *ou* un bon coup; **I don't know a t. about algebra** je n'y connais absolument rien en algèbre; **it doesn't mean a t. to me** (*I don't understand it at all*) je n'y comprends (absolument) rien; (*it isn't at all familiar to me*) ça ne me dit absolument rien; (*it doesn't concern me at all*) ça ne me concerne pas; **there isn't a t. we can do about it** il n'y a absolument rien que nous puissions y faire; **to know a t. or two** (*to know a few tricks etc*) avoir plus d'un tour dans son sac; (*to be well informed*) en savoir long; *Fam* **she's got a t. about French** (*loves it*) le français, c'est son truc; (*hates it*) le français, c'est pas son truc; *Fam* **he's got a t. about that, it's a t. with him** c'est son idée fixe; *Fam* **do your (own) t.!** fais comme il te plaira!; **things are going badly** ça va mal; **as things are** les choses étant comme elles

sont; *Fam* **how are things?, how's things?** comment ça va?
4 the latest t. in shoes la dernière mode en matière de chaussures; **it's the (very) latest t.** c'est tout ce qu'il y a de plus moderne; **he looks quite the t.** il est vraiment très chic; **the t. (to do)** (*etiquette*) l'usage *m*; **it's not the done t.** cela ne se fait pas
5 *Fam* (*penis*) machin *m*

thingummy, **thingamy**, **thingumajig**, **thingumabob**, **thingy** ['θɪŋəmɪ, -dʒɪg, -bɒb, 'θɪŋɪ] **N** *Fam* (*object*) truc *m*, machin *m*, bidule *m*; (*person*) machin *m*, machine *f*, trucmuche *mf*; **have you seen the t. for the food processor?** tu as vu le bitoniau du robot de cuisine?; **I saw t. who you used to work with last week** la semaine dernière, j'ai vu Machin-Chose avec qui tu travaillais dans le temps

THINK [θɪŋk]

N moment de réflexion
VI penser ▪ réfléchir
VT penser à **1** ▪ comprendre **1**
▪ s'imaginer **1** ▪ penser **2** ▪ croire **2**,
3 ▪ supposer **2** ▪ juger **3**
▪ considérer **3**

N moment *m* de réflexion; **to have a t.** réfléchir; **what do you say? – I'll have a t. about it** qu'en dis-tu? – je vais réfléchir; *Fam* **you've got another t. coming!** tu peux toujours courir!

VI (*pt, pp* **thought** [θɔːt]) penser, réfléchir; **to t. aloud** penser tout haut; **to t. (long and) hard** bien réfléchir, *Fam* se creuser la tête; *Fam* **to t. big** être ambitieux; **I did it without thinking** je l'ai fait sans réfléchir *ou* sans y penser; **I'm sorry, I wasn't thinking** désolé, je l'ai fait/dit sans réfléchir; **I was so pressed for time that I wasn't even thinking** (*during exam*) j'étais tellement pris par le temps que j'écrivais n'importe quoi; **you just don't t., do you!** (*are inconsiderate, careless etc*) jamais tu ne réfléchis, hein!; **t. before you speak** réfléchissez avant de parler; **just t. a minute!** réfléchissez un peu!; **give me time to t.** laissez-moi une minute que je réfléchisse; **you t. too much** tu réfléchis trop; **to t. again** se raviser; **you can (just) t. again!** tu peux toujours courir!; **it makes you t.** ça vous fait réfléchir; **I'd t. twice about that, if I were you** j'y réfléchirais à deux fois si j'étais toi; **to t. on one's feet** savoir prendre des décisions rapidement

VT 1 (*imagine, suppose*) **what are you thinking?** à quoi pensez-vous?; **I know what you're thinking** je sais ce que vous pensez *ou* ce que vous vous dites, je sais à quoi vous pensez; **I was just thinking 'I wonder where he is' when ...** j'étais justement en train de me demander où il était lorsque ...; **I (really) can't t. why/what/where ...** je me demande bien pourquoi/ce que/où ...; **I can't t. what you mean** je n'arrive pas à comprendre *ou* voir ce que vous voulez dire; **what will people t.?** que vont penser les gens?; **he thinks he knows everything** il s'imagine tout savoir; **one would have thought that ...** on aurait pu croire que ...; **anyone would t. she was asleep** on dirait qu'elle dort; **who'd have thought it!** qui l'eût cru?!; **just t.!** songez donc!; **to t. that he's only twenty!** et dire qu'il n'a que vingt ans!; **and to t. it used to cost just ...!** quand je pense qu'avant ça ne coûtait que ...; **t. what we could do with all that money!** pense *ou* songe à tout ce que nous pourrions faire avec tout cet argent!; **I have been thinking that ...** l'idée m'est venue que ...; *esp Lit* **I only thought to help you** ma seule pensée était de vous aider; **did you t. to bring any money?** avez-vous pensé *ou* songé à apporter de l'argent?; **to**

t. evil/kind thoughts avoir de sombres/douces pensées
2 (*believe, have as opinion*) **do you t. you could do it? – I t. I could** pensez-vous que cela vous serait possible? – je pense que oui; **it's better to get it over with, don't you t.?** il vaut mieux en finir, vous ne trouvez pas?; **I thought I heard her** j'ai cru l'entendre; **I thought it was all over** je croyais que tout était fini; **everyone asked him what he thought** chacun lui a demandé son avis; **what do you t., Jenny?** et toi, qu'en penses-tu, Jenny?; **well what do you t.? does it suit me?** alors, qu'est-ce que tu en penses, ça me va?; **I t. she's pretty/nice** je la trouve jolie/sympa; **everyone thought he was mad** on le tenait pour fou; **I rather t. it's going to rain** j'ai dans l'idée qu'il va pleuvoir; **it is thought that ...** on suppose que ... + *ind*; **I t. so** je pense que oui; **I don't t. so, I t. not** je pense que non; **that's what I t. (too)** c'est (aussi) mon impression; **so I thought, I thought so, I thought as much** c'est bien ce que je pensais; **I (should) hardly t. so** c'est peu probable; **I should t. so!** je crois bien!; **do you t. they'll agree? – I should t. so** croyez-vous qu'ils accepteront? – je pense que oui; **he's going to apologize – I should t. so (too)!** il va s'excuser – j'espère bien!; **he apologized – I should t. so (too)!** ce n'est pas trop tôt!; **I shouldn't t. so** je ne crois pas; *Fam* **that's what you t.!** c'est ce que tu crois!, tu te fais des idées! VOIR GRAMMAIRE A47–8
3 (*judge*) juger, considérer, croire; **if you t. it necessary to ...** si vous jugez nécessaire de ...; **I hardly t. it likely that ...** il me semble peu probable que ... + *subj*; **to t. fit** *or* **t. it proper to ...** juger bon *ou* convenable de ...; **you thought her (to be) a fool** vous l'avez prise pour une sotte; **they were thought to be rich** on les disait *ou* supposait riches; (*they passed for rich*) ils passaient pour (être) riches
4 (*expect*) **I little thought I would see him again** je ne m'attendais guère à le revoir
5 *Fam* **designers are thinking pink** le rose, c'est la couleur in chez les stylistes; **the company is thinking expansion** le maître mot dans la société, c'est expansion
▸ **think about VT INSEP 1** penser à; **what are you thinking about?** à quoi penses-tu?; **do you still t. about her?** pensez-vous encore à elle?; **he can't sleep for thinking about it** il perd le sommeil à force d'y penser, *Fam* il n'en dort plus; **that's worth thinking about** cela mérite réflexion; **quite cheap when you t. about it** plutôt bon marché quand on y pense
2 (*consider*) (*proposal etc*) réfléchir à; **what do you say? – I'll t. about it** qu'en dites-vous? – j'y songerai *ou* réfléchirai; **that will give them something to t. about** voilà qui va leur donner matière à réflexion; **to t. about doing sth** envisager de *ou* songer à faire qch
3 (*take into account*) penser à; **I've got my family/future to t. about** il faut que je pense à ma famille/mon avenir
4 (*have opinion about*) penser de; **what do you t. about him?** que pensez-vous de lui?; **what do you t. about it?** qu'en pensez-vous?
▸ **think back VI** repenser; **to t. back on past events** repenser à des événements passés; **when I t. back** quand j'y repense; **t. back to what you were doing in 1995** songez à *ou* rappelez-vous ce que vous faisiez en 1995; **thinking back, I suppose I never really liked him** réflexion faite, je crois que je ne l'ai jamais vraiment aimé
▸ **think of VT INSEP 1** (*be attentive to*) penser à, songer à; **to t. of others** penser aux autres; **I've got the children/the children's education to t. of** il faut que je songe aux enfants/à l'éducation des enfants; **I can't t. of everything!** je ne peux pas penser à tout!

2 *(reflect on)* penser à; **we're thinking of you** nous pensons à toi; **I was thinking of how much times have changed** je songeais combien les temps ont changé; **when I t. of what might have happened!** quand je pense à ce qui aurait pu arriver!; **it's rather silly, when you (come to) t. of it** c'est plutôt bête, quand on y pense; **come to t. of it, I did see her that night** maintenant que j'y pense, je l'ai vue cette nuit-là; **what am I thinking of?** où ai-je la tête?; **what were you thinking of, letting the child out on his own?** où avais-tu la tête, pour laisser cet enfant sortir seul?; **we wouldn't t. of letting our daughter travel alone** il ne nous viendrait pas à l'esprit de laisser notre fille voyager seule; **I couldn't t. of it!** c'est impossible!

3 *(recall, bring to mind) (name etc)* se rappeler (de); **I can't t. of their number at the moment** je n'arrive pas à me rappeler leur numéro là maintenant; **I can't t. of the right word** le mot juste m'échappe

4 *(imagine)* imaginer, se figurer; **just t. of it, a holiday in the Caribbean!** imagine, des vacances aux Caraïbes!; **and it weighs two tons, (just) t. of that!** et figure-toi que ça pèse deux tonnes!

5 *(have opinion about)* penser de; **what do you t. of him?** que penses-tu de lui?; **what do you t. of it?** qu'en pensez-vous?; **what do you t. of this picture?** que dites-vous de ce tableau?; **I don't t. much of the idea/her taste** je ne trouve pas que cette idée soit très bonne/qu'elle ait très bon goût; **to t. a lot of** or **highly of sb** avoir une haute opinion de qn; **to t. a great deal of oneself, to t. too much of oneself** avoir une haute idée de soi-même ou de sa personne; **to t. too much of sth** attacher trop d'importance à qch; **I told her what I thought of her** je lui ai dit son fait; **to t. well/badly of sb** avoir une bonne/mauvaise opinion de qn; **he is well thought of** il est bien vu ou considéré

6 to t. of doing sth envisager de ou songer à faire qch; **what were you thinking of giving her?** que pensais-tu lui donner?

7 *(have idea of)* imaginer, penser à, avoir l'idée de; *(solution)* imaginer; **the longest word I can t. of** le mot le plus long auquel je puisse penser; **I've thought of a way of persuading her** j'ai pensé à ou imaginé un moyen de la persuader; **try every method you can t. of** essayez toutes les méthodes que vous puissiez imaginer; **who thought of coming to this restaurant?** qui a eu l'idée de venir dans ce restaurant?; **why didn't you phone? – I didn't t. of it** pourquoi n'avez-vous pas téléphoné? – je n'y ai pas pensé; **who thought of the idea?** qui a eu cette idée?; **what a clever idea!, now why didn't I t. of that?** quelle idée géniale!, pourquoi n'y ai-je pas pensé ou songé?; **t. of a number** pensez à un chiffre; **I thought of him as being tall** je le voyais grand

▸ **think out** VT SEP *(plan, solution)* imaginer; **he likes to t. things out for himself** il aime juger des choses par lui-même; **see if you can t. something out** essaie d'imaginer ou de trouver une solution; **well thought out plan** projet bien étudié; **carefully thought out answer** réponse bien pesée

▸ **think over** VT SEP *(question etc)* réfléchir à; **I'll t. it over** j'y réfléchirai; **t. it over (carefully)** réfléchissez-y ou songez-y bien; **on thinking it over** réflexion faite, à la réflexion

▸ **think through** VT SEP *(plan etc)* bien considérer; **I thought it through all night** j'y ai réfléchi toute la nuit; **the scheme has not been properly thought through** le plan n'a pas été suffisamment considéré en détail

▸ **think up** VT SEP *(project, method)* imaginer; **who thought that idea up?** qui a eu cette idée?

thinkable ['θɪŋkəb(ə)l] ADJ concevable, imaginable; **is it t. that …?** peut-on imaginer que … + *sub*?; **it is scarcely** or **barely t. that …** il est difficilement concevable ou imaginable que … + *sub*

thinker ['θɪŋkər] N penseur, -euse

thinking ['θɪŋkɪŋ] ADJ pensant, qui pense; **the paper for t. people** le journal pour les gens qui réfléchissent; **the t. man's pin-up** la pin-up des intellectuels; **any t. person would agree that …** n'importe qui réfléchissant un tant soit peu serait d'accord pour dire que …

N **1** *(process of thought)* pensée(s) *f(pl)*, réflexion(s) *f(pl)*; **to do some t.** réfléchir un peu; **he did some hard t.** il a sérieusement réfléchi; **we'd better do a bit of quick t.** nous ferions bien de réfléchir en vitesse; **to put on one's t. cap** cogiter; **good t.!** bien vu! **2** *(opinion)* opinion *f*, avis *m*; **to my (way of) t.** à mon avis; **I hope to bring you round to my way of t.** j'espère vous amener à mon opinion ou à mon point du vue; **she influenced the t. of a generation** elle a influencé la façon de penser de toute une génération

▸▸ *Aut* **t. distance** temps *m* de réaction

think-tank N comité *m* ou groupe *m* d'experts

thin-lipped ADJ aux lèvres minces; **he was rather t.** *(displeased)* il avait les lèvres plutôt pincées

thinly ['θɪnlɪ] ADV *(in thin layers)* en couche(s) mince(s); *(in thin slices)* en tranches fines; **t. sown wheat** blé *m* clairsemé; **t. populated** peu peuplé; **t. clad** *(lightly)* légèrement vêtu; *(inadequately)* vêtu insuffisamment; **a t. veiled allusion** une allusion à peine voilée

thinner ['θɪnər] N *(for paint etc)* diluant *m*

thinness ['θɪnnɪs] N **1** *(of sheet of paper etc)* minceur *f*, *(of material etc)* légèreté *f*, *(of person)* minceur; *(excessive)* maigreur *f* **2** *(of liquid)* fluidité *f*, *(of air)* raréfaction *f*

thinning ['θɪnɪŋ] ADJ **his t. hair** ses cheveux qui commencent à se clairsemer

▸▸ **t. agent** diluant *m*

thin-skinned ADJ *Fig (person)* susceptible, trop sensible

thin-sliced ADJ *(bread)* coupé en tranches fines, finement coupé

third [θɜːd] NUM ADJ, N *(day, floor etc)* troisième *mf*, **Edward T.** Édouard III; **the t. of May** le trois mai; **on the t. of May** le trois mai; **every t. day** tous les trois jours; **we must find a t. way** il faut trouver une troisième voie

N **1** *(fraction)* tiers *m*; **to lose a t./two thirds of one's money** perdre le tiers/les deux tiers de son argent; **one t. full** plein au tiers **2** *Mus* tierce *f* **3** *Aut* **to go into t.** passer en troisième

▸▸ **the t. age** le troisième âge; *Fam* **t. degree** interrogatoire *m* serré; **to give sb the t. degree** faire subir un interrogatoire serré à qn; *(treat roughly)* cuisiner qn; *Hist* **the T. Estate** le Tiers État; *Aut* **t. gear** troisième vitesse *f*, *(gearwheel)* pignon *m* de troisième; **t. party** tierce personne *f*, tiers *m*; **t. party cover** assurance *f* au tiers; **t. party fire and theft insurance** assurance au tiers vol et incendie; **t. party holder** tiers détenteur *m*; **t. party owner** tiers possesseur *m*; *Gram* **t. person** troisième personne *f*; **to act through a t. person** *(in negotiation etc)* passer par une tierce personne; *Fin* **t. quarter** *(of financial year)* troisième trimestre *m*; *Hist* **the T. Reich** le Troisième Reich; **the T. World** le tiers-monde

third-class ADJ *Br Univ (degree)* obtenu avec la mention passable

third-degree burn N *Med* brûlure *f* du troisième degré

third-generation ADJ *Tel* de troisième génération

thirdly ['θɜːdlɪ] ADV troisièmement, en troisième lieu

third-rate ADJ médiocre, de troisième ordre

thirst [θɜːst] N soif *f*, *Fig esp Lit* **the t. for** or **after knowledge** la soif de connaissances; **to satisfy one's t. for adventure** satisfaire sa soif d'aventures

VI *Arch, Lit* être altéré ou avide **(for** de); *Lit* **to t. for blood/revenge** être assoiffé de sang/de vengeance

thirstily ['θɜːstɪlɪ] ADV avidement

thirsty ['θɜːstɪ] ADJ *(person)* qui a soif; *(stronger)* assoiffé; *(earth etc)* desséché; *Fam (car)* qui consomme énormément; **to be** or **feel t.** avoir soif; **I'm t.** j'ai soif; **to make sb t.** donner soif à qn; *Fam* **all this talking is t. work** de parler autant, cela donne soif ou cela vous sèche le gosier; *Fig Lit* **t. for blood/ for riches** assoiffé ou altéré ou avide de sang/de richesses

thirteen [θɜː'tiːn] NUM ADJ, N treize *m*; **she's t. (years old)** elle a treize ans; **at t. hundred hours** à treize heures

thirteenth [θɜː'tiːnθ] NUM ADJ, N treizième *mf*; **(on) the thirteenth (of May)** le treize (mai); **Friday the t.** vendredi treize N *(fraction)* treizième *m*

thirtieth ['θɜːtɪɪθ] NUM ADJ, N trentième *mf*; **(on) the t. (of June)** le trente (juin)

thirty ['θɜːtɪ] NUM ADJ, N trente *m*; **t.-three** trente-trois; **t.-first** trente et unième; **t.-second** trente-deuxième; **(on) the t.-first of May** le trente et un mai; **about t. guests** une trentaine d'invités; **to be t. (years old)** avoir trente ans; **the thirties** les années trente; **he leaves at two-t.** il part à deux heures trente

thirty-year rule N = loi *f* qui prescrit que, au bout de 30 ans, toute archive ou document secret tombe dans le domaine public

THIS [ðɪs] VOIR GRAMMAIRE A30-1; B14-15 DEM PRON *(pl* these [ðiːz]) **1** ceci, ce; **what's t.?, what are these?** qu'est-ce que c'est (que ceci ou *Fam* que ça)?; **who's t.?** qui est-ce?; *Tel* **who is t.?** qui est à l'appareil?; **you'll be sorry for t.** vous le regretterez; **at t.** sur ce, là-dessus; **it ought to have happened before t.** cela aurait dû être fait depuis longtemps; **after t.** après cela, ensuite; **t. is curious** c'est curieux, voilà qui est curieux; **t. is what she told me** voici ce qu'elle m'a dit; **t. is Mr. Ford** je vous présente M. Ford; **these are my children** voici mes enfants; **t. is where she lives** c'est ici qu'elle habite; **these are things we cannot do without** ce sont des choses dont on ne peut se passer; **listen to t.** écoutez bien ceci; **eat/drink some of t.** mangez-/buvez-en un peu; **what's t. (that) I hear?** qu'est-ce que j'apprends?; **do it like t.** comme ceci; **what's all t.?** *(these objects)* qu'est-ce que c'est que tout ça?; *(what's happening?)* qu'est-ce qu'il y a?, qu'est-ce qui se passe?

2 *(opposed to that)* **will you have t. or that?** voulez-vous ceci ou cela?; *Fam* **they were talking about t. and that** ils parlaient de choses et d'autres

3 *(referring to sth already mentioned)* celui-ci, *f* celle-ci, *pl* ceux-ci, *f* celles-ci; **I prefer these to those** je préfère ceux-ci à ceux-là DEM ADJ *(pl* these) ce, *(before vowel or h mute)* cet, *f* cette, *pl* ces; *(for emphasis and in opposition to* that, those) ce … -ci, cet … -ci, cette … -ci, *pl* ces … -ci; **t. book** ce livre(-ci); **these books** ces livres(-ci); **t. morning** ce matin; **t. afternoon** cet(te) après-midi; **t. week** cette semaine; **one of these days** un de ces jours; **(in) these days, in t. day and age** de nos jours; **by t. time** à l'heure qu'il est; **to run t. way and that** courir de-ci de-là; **he will tell you that in t. or that case you should …** il vous dira qu'en tel ou tel cas il faut …; **for t. reason …** voilà pourquoi …, pour cette raison …; *Fam* **t. here house** cette maison(-ci); *Fam* **I've known him these three years** je le connais depuis trois ans

DEM ADV aussi … que ceci; **t. high, as high as t.** aussi haut que ceci *ou* que cela *ou* que ça; **t. far** jusqu'ici, jusque-là; **can you eat t. much?** pourras-tu manger tout cela?; **t. much is certain …** ceci au moins est sûr …

thistle ['θɪs(ə)l] **N** chardon *m*

thistledown ['θɪs(ə)ldaʊn] **N** duvet *m* de chardon

thither ['ðɪðər] **ADV** *Arch, Lit* là; *Lit* **to run hither and t.** courir çà et là

tho' [ðəʊ] **CONJ, ADV** *Fam, Lit* = **though**

thole, tholepin ['θəʊl(pɪn)] **N** *Naut* tolet *m*

thong [θɒŋ] **N 1** lanière *f* de cuir; *(of whip)* lanière; *Am, Austr* **a pair of thongs** *(sandals)* des tongs *fpl* **2** *(G-string)* string *m*

thoracic [θɔː'ræsɪk] **ADJ** thoracique

thorax, *pl* **thoraces** ['θɔːræks, θɔː'reɪsiːz] **N** thorax *m*

thorn [θɔːn] **N 1** *Bot* épine *f*, *Fig* **to be a t. in sb's flesh** *or* **side** être un sujet continuel d'irritation pour qn **2** *(tree)* épine *f*

thornback ['θɔːnbæk] **N** *(fish)* raie *f* bouclée

thornbush ['θɔːnbʊʃ] **N** (arbrisseau *m*) épineux *m*

thornless ['θɔːnlɪs] **ADJ** sans épines

thorny ['θɔːnɪ] **ADJ** épineux; *Fig* **t. question** question *f* épineuse

thorough ['θʌrə] **ADJ** *(search etc)* minutieux; *(knowledge)* approfondi; *(understanding)* profond; *(job)* consciencieux; **to be t. in one's work** travailler consciencieusement; **to give a room a t. cleaning** nettoyer une pièce à fond; **it needs a t. revision** il/elle a besoin d'une révision en profondeur; **a t. scoundrel** un fieffé coquin; **to make a t. nuisance of oneself** se rendre complètement insupportable

thoroughbred ['θʌrəbred] **ADJ** *(cheval)* pur-sang *inv; (dog etc)* de race
N *(horse)* pur-sang *m inv; (animal)* animal *m*, -aux de race; **she's a real t.** *(person)* elle a de la classe

thoroughfare ['θʌrəfeər] **N** voie *f* de communication; **busy t.** *(street)* rue *f* très passante; *(road)* importante voie de communication; **one of the main thoroughfares of the town** une des rues principales *ou* une des artères de la ville; **no t.** *(on sign) (no through road)* rue barrée; *(no access)* passage interdit (au public)

thoroughgoing ['θʌrəgəʊɪŋ] **ADJ** *(search, inspection etc)* minutieux; *(knowledge, revision etc)* approfondi; *(changes)* profond; *(reform)* en profondeur; **such a t. rogue as him** un fieffé coquin de cette espèce

thoroughly ['θʌrəlɪ] **ADV** *(to know language etc)* parfaitement; *(to know sth, to clean sth)* à fond; *(stupid)* complètement; **to be t. bored** s'ennuyer mortellement; **t. honest** d'une honnêteté à toute épreuve; **t. untrustworthy** totalement indigne de confiance

thoroughness ['θʌrənɪs] **N** *(of work)* minutie *f*, **the t. of his knowledge** ses connaissances très complètes

those *see* **that**

thou¹ [ðaʊ] **PERS PRON** *Bible, Arch (unstressed)* tu; *(stressed)* toi; **t. seest** tu vois; **t. art** tu es; **hearest t.?** entends-tu?; **t. and I** toi et moi

thou² [θaʊ] **N** *Fam (abbr* **thousand)** mille *m inv*

---

though [ðəʊ] **CONJ 1** *(in spite of the fact that)* quoique, bien que + *subj*; **t. she is poor she is generous** quoiqu'elle soit pauvre, elle est généreuse; **I respect him t.** je le respecte, bien qu'il ne me soit pas sympathique; **t. I am a father** tout père que je suis; **t. not handsome, he was attractive** sans être beau, il avait du charme; **I think I did quite well, t. I say so** *or* **it myself** je ne m'en suis pas mal sorti, si je peux me permettre de le dire

2 *this statement*, **terrible t. it be** cette déclaration, pour terrible qu'elle soit; **strange t. it may seem** si étrange que cela puisse sembler; **even t. you'll laugh at me** même si vous vous moquez de moi

3 *as t.* comme si; **it looks as t. she's gone** il semble qu'elle soit partie; **as t. nothing had happened** comme si de rien n'était

ADV cependant, pourtant; **it's not what I want** ce n'est pas ce que je veux; **I didn't mean it t.** mais je ne disais pas ça sérieusement; **he had promised to go, he didn't t.** il avait promis d'y aller, cependant, il n'en a rien fait; **did she t.!** elle a dit/fait cela?

thought¹ [θɔːt] **N 1** *(thinking)* pensée *f*, **contemporary t.** la pensée contemporaine; **capable of t.** capable de penser

2 *(idea)* pensée *f*, idée *f*; **he hasn't a t. in his head** il n'a pas une idée dans la tête; **happy t.** heureuse idée; **what a nice/kind t.!** quelle agréable/douce pensée!; **dark** *or* **gloomy thoughts** de sombres pensées; **that's** *or* **there's a t.** *(good idea)* ça, c'est une idée; *(that's true)* ça, c'est vrai; **now there's a t., why don't we …?** j'ai une idée, et si nous …?; *(sb else's thought)* ça c'est une bonne idée, et si nous …?; **it's quite a t.!** *(pleasant)* le rêve!; *(unpleasant)* quelle horreur!; **to read sb's thoughts** lire dans les pensées de qn; **the mere t. of it** rien que d'y penser; **have you ever given it a single t.?** y avez-vous jamais pensé?; **I didn't give it another t.** je n'y ai pas repensé; **what are your thoughts on the matter?** quelle est votre opinion sur ce sujet?; **to collect one's thoughts** rassembler ses idées; **her thoughts were elsewhere** son esprit était ailleurs

3 *(reflection)* réflexion *f*, considération *f*, *(meditation)* pensées *fpl*, rêverie *f*, méditation *f*; **after much t.** après mûre réflexion; **to give a great deal of t. to sth** réfléchir beaucoup à qch; **on second thoughts** réflexion faite, à la réflexion; **to be deep** *or* **lost in t.** être perdu *ou* absorbé dans ses pensées, être plongé dans ses réflexions

4 *(intention)* intention *f*, dessein *m*; **I had no t. of offending you** je n'avais pas l'intention de vous offenser; **you must give up all thought(s) of seeing him** il faut renoncer à le voir, il ne faut plus penser à le voir; **his one t. is to get money** il ne pense qu'à l'argent

5 *Old-fashioned Fam* **a t. too sweet** un rien trop sucré

▸▸ **t. reader** liseur, -euse de pensées

thought² **PT, PP** *see* **think**

thoughtful ['θɔːtfʊl] **ADJ 1** *(pensive) (person, expression)* pensif, méditatif; **to look t.** avoir l'air pensif

2 *(considerate) (person)* attentionné; **he was t. enough to warn me** il a eu la prévenance de m'avertir; **it was very t. of her to …** c'était très attentionné de sa part de …; **that wasn't very t.** ce n'était pas très gentil de sa/ta/*etc* part; **how t. (of you)!** comme c'est gentil (de ta part)!; **it was a very t. gesture (on his part)** c'était une belle preuve d'attention (de sa part); *Fml* **he was always t. of others' needs** il a toujours été très attentif aux besoins des autres

---

3 *(to which thought has been given) (analysis, book)* profond; **he gave me his usual t. advice** comme d'habitude, il m'a aidé avec ses sages conseils

thoughtfully ['θɔːtfəlɪ] **ADV 1** *(pensively)* pensivement, d'un air pensif *ou* méditatif **2** *(considerately)* avec prévenance

thoughtfulness ['θɔːtfʊlnɪs] **N 1** *(pensiveness)* méditation *f* **2** *(consideration)* prévenance *f*

thoughtless ['θɔːtlɪs] **ADJ 1** *(ill-considered)* irréfléchi, étourdi; **t. action** acte *m* inconsidéré **2** *(inconsiderate)* **t. of others** qui manque d'égards *ou* de prévenance pour les autres; **that was t. of me** j'ai fait ça sans réfléchir; **it was very t. of you not to have phoned** ce n'était pas très gentil de ta part de ne pas téléphoner

thoughtlessly ['θɔːtlɪslɪ] **ADV 1** *(without thinking)* étourdiment, sans réfléchir **2** *(inconsiderately)* **to treat sb t.** manquer d'égards envers qn; **he very t. left it locked** il l'a laissé fermé sans se soucier des autres le moins du monde; **they t. took the whole lot** sans aucun égard, ils ont pris le tout

thoughtlessness ['θɔːtlɪsnɪs] **N 1** *(lack of forethought)* irréflexion *f*, étourderie *f* **2** *(lack of consideration)* manque *m* d'égards *ou* de prévenance

thought-out **ADJ** **well/poorly t. plan** projet bien/mal conçu; **carefully t. answer** réponse bien pesée; **this needs a carefully t. answer** il va falloir bien réfléchir avant de répondre

thought-provoking **ADJ** qui invite à la réflexion, qui donne à *ou* fait réfléchir

thousand ['θaʊz(ə)nd] VOIR GRAMMAIRE A12–13; B58–9 **NUM ADJ** mille *inv;* **a t. years** mille ans; **the year 4000 B.C.** l'an quatre mille av. J.-C.; *Law, Admin* **the year one t. nine hundred and thirty** l'an mil neuf cent trente; **about a t. men** un millier d'hommes; **three hundred t. people** trois cent mille personnes; *Fam* **I've got a t. and one things to ask you/to do** j'ai mille choses à vous demander/faire; **no, no, a t. times no!** non, non, et cent fois non!

N mille *m inv;* **a t.** mille; **a. t. and one** mille un; **how many people were there? – about a t.** combien de gens étaient là? – un millier; **thousands of people** des milliers de gens; **in thousands** par milliers; **in hundreds of thousands** par centaines de mille; **she's one in a t.** c'est la femme entre mille

▸▸ **T. Island dressing** = sauce *f* à base de mayonnaise, de ketchup et de cornichons hachés

thousandfold ['θaʊz(ə)n(d)fəʊld] **ADJ** multiplié par mille
ADV mille fois autant

thousandth ['θaʊz(ə)n(t)θ] **NUM ADJ, N** millième *mf*

thraldom ['θrɔːldəm] **N** *Lit* esclavage *m*, assujetissement *m*, servitude *f*

thrall [θrɔːl] **N** *Lit* **kept in t.** maintenu en esclavage *m*

thrash [θræʃ] **VT** *(beat) (person, animal)* battre, rosser, rouer de coups; *(defeat heavily in game etc)* battre à plate(s) couture(s); **to t. sb soundly** donner une bonne raclée à qn; **to t. the water** donner des coups dans l'eau; **to t. one's arms and legs in the air** se débattre des mains et des pieds
VI *(of water)* battre, clapoter *(against* contre); **the doctor was trying to avoid his thrashing limbs** le docteur essayait d'éviter ses coups de pieds et ses coups de poings
N 1 *Br Fam (party)* fiesta *f* **2** *(music)* thrash *m* (metal)

▸ **thrash about, thrash around** **VT SEP** **to t.**

one's arms and legs about se débattre des mains et des pieds

vi *(move furiously) (of person)* se débattre (des mains et des pieds); *(of fish)* remuer, se débattre; **the fish thrashed about in the net** le poisson se débattait dans le filet

▸ **thrash out vt sep 1** *(discuss thoroughly)* discuter à fond; **to t. it out with sb** en débattre avec qn **2** *(reach) (solution, truth etc)* arriver à

thrashing ['θræʃɪŋ] **n** *(beating)* volée *f* (de coups), *Fam* raclée *f, Sport etc* défaite *f*; **to give sb a t.** donner une raclée à qn; **they were given a t. at the elections** ils ont pris une raclée aux élections; **to give one's opponent a t.** battre son adversaire à plate(s) couture(s)

thread [θred] **n 1** *(of cotton, nylon, silk etc)* fil *m*; **(length of) t.** *(of cotton, silk etc)* brin *m*, bout *m*; **gold t.** fil d'or; **button t.** fil à boutons; *Fig* **his life hung by a t.** sa vie ne tenait qu'à un fil; **to lose the t. of the conversation** perdre le fil de la conversation; **to gather up the threads of a story** retrouver le fil d'une histoire **2** *Tech (of screw, bolt etc)* filet *m*, filetage *m* **3** *Fam* **threads** *(clothes)* fringues *fpl* **4** *Comput* fil *m* de discussion

vt 1 *(needle, beads)* enfiler (**through sth** dans qch); **to t. one's way between the cars** se faufiler entre les voitures **2** *Tech (screw etc)* fileter; *(pipe, nut etc)* tarauder

vi 1 we threaded through the crowd nous nous sommes faufilés à travers la foule **2 to t. into sth** *(of screw etc)* se visser dans qch; **the tape threads through these holes** la bande passe par ces trous

▸ ▸ **t. mark** filigrane *m (des billets de banque)*

threadbare ['θredbeər] **adj** *(clothes etc)* râpé, élimé, usé jusqu'à la corde; *Fig (subject, argument, joke etc)* rebattu

threadworm ['θredwɜːm] **n** oxyure *m*

threat [θret] **n** menace *f*; **to make threats** faire des menaces; **to utter a t.** proférer une menace; **to make idle threats** lancer des menaces en l'air; **it was no idle t.** ce n'était pas une menace en l'air; **there is a t. of rain** il y a un risque de pluie; **to see sb/sth as a t.** considérer qn/qch comme une menace; **is that a t. or a promise?** est-ce qu'il faut que je m'en/qu'il s'en/*etc* réjouisse ou pas; **if we exist under the t.** of nuclear war si nous vivons sous la menace d'une guerre nucléaire

threaten ['θret(ə)n] **vt** *(person)* menacer; *Law (person)* intimider; **to t. sb with sth** menacer qn de qch; **(to be) threatened with sth** (être) menacé de qch; **a species threatened with extinction** une espèce en voie de disparition; **the threatened strike didn't come off** cette menace de grève n'a pas abouti; **the sky threatened rain** la pluie menaçait, le ciel était menaçant; **to t. to do sth** menacer de faire qch; **this situation threatens to become dangerous** cette situation menace de devenir dangereuse

vi a storm is threatening l'orage menace

threatening ['θret(ə)nɪŋ] **adj** *(tone, appearance)* menaçant; *(letter)* de menaces; *Law* d'intimidation; **the weather looks t.** le temps est menaçant; **t. language** menaces *fpl* (verbales)

threateningly ['θret(ə)nɪŋlɪ] **adv** de manière menaçante

three [θriː] **n** trois *m*; **every t. months** tous les trois mois; **twenty-t.** vingt-trois; **t. and a half** trois et demi; **t. and t. are six** trois et trois font six; **to be t.** *(in age)* avoir trois ans; **it's t. o'clock** il est trois heures; **he leaves at t. thirty** *or* **at half past t.** il part à trois heures trente *ou* à trois heures et demie; **to come in t. by t.** *or* **in threes** entrer (trois) par

trois; *Hist* **the Big T.** les Trois Grands *mpl (Roosevelt, Churchill et Staline);* **t.-engine(d) aircraft** trimoteur *m*; **t.-pointed** à trois pointes; **t. sided** *or* **t. party conversations** conversations *fpl* tripartites; **t.-stranded rope** corde *f* à trois cordons

pron trois; **t. is not enough** trois, ce n'est pas assez

adj trois; **t. people** trois personnes

▸ ▸ *Theat* **t. act play** pièce *f* en trois actes; **t. seater** triplace *m*; **t. star brandy** cognac *m* trois-étoiles; **t. star hotel** hôtel *m* trois-étoiles

three-button mouse n *Comput* souris *f* à trois boutons

three-colour(ed), *Am* **three-color(ed) adj** tricolore; *Phot* trichrome

▸ ▸ **t. printing** impression *f* en trois couleurs *ou* en trichromie, trichromie *f*; **t. process** trichromie

three-cornered adj triangulaire; **a t. discussion** un débat à trois

▸ ▸ **t. hat** tricorne *m*

three-course adj *(meal)* à trois plats

three-D adj *Fam* = **three-dimensional**

n in t. en trois dimensions

three-dimensional adj tridimensionnel

threefold ['θriːfəʊld] **adj** triple; **a t. increase in the membership figures** une augmentation au triple du nombre d'adhérents

adv trois fois autant; **to increase t.** tripler

three-four adj

▸ ▸ *Mus* **t. time** trois-quatre *m inv*

3G [θriː'dʒiː] **adj** *Comput, Tel* 3G

three-handed adj *Cards etc* **t. game** partie *f* à trois

three-legged adj *(stool etc)* à trois pieds

▸ ▸ **t. race** = course *f* où les participants courent par deux, la jambe gauche de l'un attachée à la droite de l'autre

three-line whip n *Br Pol* = obligation *f* absolue faite aux députés de prendre part à un vote et de suivre les recommandations de leur parti

threepence ['θrep(ə)ns] **n** *Br* trois pence *mpl*

threepenny ['θrep(ə)nɪ] **adj** *Br* coûtant trois pence, à *ou* de trois pence

▸ ▸ *Hist* **t. bit** pièce *f* de trois pence

three-piece adj en trois pièces

▸ ▸ *Mus* **t. band** trio *m*; **t. suit** (costume *m*) trois-pièces *m inv*; *Br* **t. suite** salon *m* trois pièces *(canapé et deux fauteuils)*

three-pin adj

▸ ▸ **t. plug** prise *f* à trois fiches

three-ply adj *(wool etc)* à trois fils; *(rope)* à trois brins; *(tissues, toilet paper)* à trois épaisseurs

three-point adj

▸ ▸ *Aviat* **t. landing** atterrissage *m* trois points; *Aut* **t. seatbelt** ceinture *f* trois points; *Aut* **t. turn** demi-tour *m* en trois manœuvres, *pl* demi-tours

three-quarter n *Rugby* trois-quarts *m inv*

▸ ▸ *Rugby* **t. back** trois-quarts; **t. face portrait** portrait *m* de trois-quarts; **t. length coat** trois-quarts; *Rugby* **the t. line** la ligne des trois-quarts; *Aut* **t. vision** visibilité *f* de trois-quarts

three-ring adj

▸ ▸ *Am* **t. circus** = cirque *m* contenant trois arènes et montrant plusieurs numéros à la fois; *Fig* cirque, chantier *m*

threescore ['θriːskɔːr] **adj** *Arch, Lit* soixante; **t. (years) and ten** soixante-dix ans

threesome ['θriːsəm] **n** *(three people)* groupe *m* de trois personnes; *Golf* partie *f* à trois; **do you want to make up a t.?** *(in games)* veux-tu faire le troisième?; *(going out etc)* veux-tu te joindre à nous (deux)?;

we went as a t. nous y sommes allés à trois

three-speed adj à trois vitesses

▸ ▸ **t. gearbox** boîte *f* trois vitesses

three-storey(ed), *Am* **three-story, three-storied adj** *(house)* à trois étages

three-way adj *(division etc)* en trois; *(discussion etc)* à trois

▸ ▸ *Aut* **t. catalytic convertor** catalyseur *m* à trois voies; *Br Pol* **t. marginal** = circonscription *f* où trois candidats ont d'égales chances de succès

three-wheeled vehicle n trois-roues *m*

three-wheeler n *Aut* (petite) voiture *f* à trois roues; *(tricycle)* tricycle *m*

threnody ['θrenədɪ] **n** *Lit* thrène *m*, chant *m* funèbre

thresh [θreʃ] **vt** *(wheat)* battre; *Fig* **to t. the water** *(of ship's screw, of whale's tail etc)* battre l'eau

thresher ['θreʃər] **n** *(person)* batteur, -euse en grange; *(machine)* batteuse *f*

threshing ['θreʃɪŋ] **n** *(of wheat)* battage *m*

▸ ▸ **t. floor** aire *f* de battage; **t. machine** batteuse *f*

threshold ['θreʃəʊld] **n 1** *(of door etc)* seuil *m*, pas *m* de la porte; **on the t.** sur le seuil; *Fig* **on the t. of a great discovery** au seuil d'une grande découverte; **to cross the t.** franchir le seuil; *Fig* **to be on the t. of life** être au seuil de la vie **2** *Phys etc (of fission, reaction)* seuil *m*; **to have a low boredom t.** être prédisposé à l'ennui, s'ennuyer facilement; **to have a low/high pain t.** mal tolérer/bien tolérer la douleur

▸ ▸ *Br Econ* **t. agreement** accord *m* d'indexation des salaires sur les prix; *Physiol* **t. of audibility, t. of hearing** seuil d'audibilité; *Br Econ* **t. policy** politique *f* d'indexation des salaires sur les prix; *Fin* **t. price** prix *m* du seuil

threw pt *see* **throw vt**

thrice [θraɪs] **adv** *Lit* trois fois

thrift [θrɪft] **n** économie *f*, épargne *f*

▸ ▸ *Am* **t. institution** caisse *f* d'épargne; *Am* **t. shop** = magasin *m* vendant des articles d'occasion au profit d'œuvres charitables

thriftily ['θrɪftɪlɪ] **adv** avec économie; *(live)* frugalement

thriftiness ['θrɪftɪnɪs] **n** économie *f*, épargne *f*

thriftless ['θrɪftlɪs] **adj** *(spendthrift)* dépensier; *(improvident)* imprévoyant

thriftlessness ['θrɪftlɪsnɪs] **n** gaspillage *m*; *(improvidence)* imprévoyance *f*

thrifty ['θrɪftɪ] **adj** économe

thrill [θrɪl] **n** *(exciting feeling)* (vive) émotion *f*, *(trembling)* frisson *m*, tressaillement *m*; **t. of pleasure** frisson de plaisir; **the t. of riding a motorbike** le frisson que donne la moto; **to get a t. out of sth** se donner des sensations fortes avec qch; **it gave me quite a t.** ça m'a fait quelque chose; **all the thrills of the big wheel** tous les frissons que procure la grande roue; **all the thrills and spills of the circus** toutes les joies et tous les frissons que procure le cirque; *Fam* **go on, give us a t., let's see you dance!** allez, montre-nous ce que tu sais faire, danse!

vt *(of experience, thought, prospect)* exalter; *(of sb's touch)* faire frémir ou frissonner, donner des frissons à; *(of conjuror etc) (audience, children)* faire vibrer; **a novel/film that will t. you** un roman/film qui vous fera frémir; **he was absolutely thrilled with his present** son cadeau le transportait de joie *ou* le ravissait; **she's thrilled with her new car** elle est ravie de sa nouvelle voiture; **I'm thrilled for you** je suis très heureux pour vous; **to be thrilled at the sight of sth** être fou de joie à la vue de qch; *Fam* **to be thrilled to bits** être fou de joie; **we were absolutely thrilled** (*Fam* **to bits**) **to hear your news/to have won the holiday** nous avons été ravis d'apprendre la nouvelle/d'avoir gagné les vacances

vi *esp Lit* tressaillir, frissonner (de joie)

thriller ['θrɪlər] N (*play, film, novel*) pièce f/ film m/roman m à suspense, thriller m

thrilling ['θrɪlɪŋ] ADJ passionnant; (*sight*) saisissant; *Sport* **t. finish** arrivée f palpitante; *Iron* **how t. for you!** c'est passionnant, ce qui t'arrive!

thrive [θraɪv] vi (*pt, pp* **thrived** [θraɪvd]; *Arch, Am pt* **throve** [θrəʊv]; *pp* **thriven** ['θrɪvn]) (*grow well*) (*of child, plant*) (bien) se développer; (*of adult*) bien se porter; (*of business etc*) bien marcher, bien aller; (*prosper*) (*of person*) prospérer; (*develop potential*) s'épanouir; **children who t. on milk** enfants à qui le lait profite bien; **plant that thrives in all soils** plante qui s'accommode de tous les sols; **to t. on danger** se nourrir du danger; **to t. on other people's misfortunes** se réjouir des malheurs d'autrui; **some people t. on stress** certaines personnes s'épanouissent dans le stress; **do I like it? I t. on it!** si j'aime ça? mais, j'adore!

thriving ['θraɪvɪŋ] ADJ (*physically*) (*plant*) vigoureux; (*person*) vigoureux, bien portant; (*prosperous*) (*person, business*) prospère, florissant

thro' [θruː] PREP *Fam* = **through**

throat [θrəʊt] N *Anat* gorge f, (*gullet*) gorge, gosier m; **the back of the t.** le fond de la gorge, l'arrière-gorge f, pl arrière-gorges; **to cut sb's t.** couper la gorge à qn; *Fig* **he's cutting his own t.** il travaille à sa propre ruine; *Com, Fig* **they're cutting each other's throats** ils se font une concurrence désastreuse; **to grab sb by the t.** attraper *ou* saisir qn à la gorge; **to have a sore t.** avoir mal à la gorge; **to clear one's t.** s'éclaircir la voix *ou* la gorge, se racler la gorge; *Fig Fam* **she's always ramming** *or* **shoving** *or* **forcing it down my t.** elle m'en rebat toujours les oreilles; *Fam* **there's no need to jump down my t.!** inutile de me rabrouer!; *Fam* **they're always at each other's throats** ils se battent continuellement; *Fam* **if you pour enough alcohol down his t., he'll tell you anything** si tu le fais boire suffisamment, il te dira tout ce que tu veux savoir; *Fam Hum* **my stomach thinks my t.'s cut** je crève la dalle

▸▸ **t. microphone** laryngophone m; *Med* **t. spray** insufflateur m

throatiness ['θrəʊtɪnɪs] N (*of voice*) qualité f gutturale

throaty ['θrəʊtɪ] ADJ (*voice, laugh*) guttural, -aux

throb [θrɒb] N (*of pulse, heart etc*) pulsation f, (*of engine*) vrombissement m; **the t. of the tom-toms** les vibrations fpl des tam-tams; **she felt a sudden t. of pain in her arm** soudain, elle ressentit un élancement dans le bras

vi (**-bb-**) (*of heart, pulse etc*) battre fort; (*of engine*) vrombir; (*of tom-toms*) vibrer; **a city throbbing with activity** une ville palpitante d'activité; **my finger is throbbing** j'ai des élancements dans le doigt, *Fam* mon doigt me lance; **my head is throbbing** j'ai une douleur lancinante dans la tête

throbbing ['θrɒbɪŋ] ADJ (*heart, pulse etc*) qui bat fort; (*engine*) vrombissant; (*pain*) lancinant; **the t. rhythm of the drums** les tambours qui battent fort *ou* qui vibrent

N (*of heart, pulse etc*) battement m (fort), pulsations fpl; (*of engine*) vrombissement m; (*of wound, infection etc*) élancements mpl

throes [θrəʊz] NPL **the t. of death** *or* **death t.** les affres fpl de la mort; *Fig* **the death t. of**

the old regime l'agonie f de l'ancien régime; **the company is in its death t.** l'entreprise est à l'agonie; **a country in the t. of revolution** un pays en proie à la révolution *ou* dans la tourmente de la révolution; *Fam* **we're in the t. of moving house** nous sommes en plein déménagement; *Fam* **don't disturb him while he's in the t. of writing** ne le dérange pas en pleine inspiration; **in the t. of a divorce** dans la tourmente d'un divorce

thrombosis, *pl* **thromboses** [θrɒm'bəʊsɪs, -iːz] N *Med* thrombose f, **coronary t.** infarctus m du myocarde

throne [θrəʊn] N trône m; *Fam* (*lavatory*) **on the t.** sur le trône; **to come to** *or* **ascend** *or* *Lit* **mount the t.** monter sur le trône; **the heir to the t.** l'héritier m au trône; **the power behind the t.** (*of king etc*), *Fig* l'Éminence f grise

throneroom ['θrəʊnruːm] N salle f du trône; *Fam Hum* **in the t.** (*on the toilet*) sur le trône

throng [θrɒŋ] N foule f, **a t. of angels** une multitude d'anges

vi affluer; (*gather*) s'assembler en foule; **to t. to Paris/the main cities/the square** affluer à Paris/dans les grandes villes/sur la place; **to t. round sb** se presser autour de qn; **they thronged into the square** ils arrivèrent en foule sur la place

vt emplir; **the room was thronged with people** la pièce était bondée

thronging ['θrɒŋɪŋ] ADJ **a t. mass** une foule grouillante

throttle ['θrɒt(ə)l] N *Aut etc* étrangleur m, obturateur m, papillon m (des gaz); (*on motorbike*) poignée f d'accélération; (*in plane*) commande f des gaz; *Tech* (*in steam engine*) régulateur m, prise f de vapeur; *Aut* **to open/to close the t.** ouvrir/fermer les gaz; **at full t.** à pleins gaz

vt (*strangle*), *Fig* étrangler

▸▸ **t. cable** câble m d'accélération; **t. control, t. lever** (*on motorbike, speedboat, plane*) manette f des gaz

▸ **throttle back, throttle down** vi (*slow engine*) mettre le moteur au ralenti; (*cut, close off fuel*) couper *ou* fermer les gaz; **the pilot/rider gradually throttled back** le pilote/motard coupa les gaz progressivement

vt SEP (*engine*) mettre au ralenti

THROUGH [θruː]

PREP à travers **1, 2** ▪ par **1, 3** ▪ dans **1**
▪ pendant **2** ▪ par l'intermédiaire de **3**
ADV à travers **1** ▪ d'un bout à l'autre **2**
▪ jusqu'au bout **2**
ADJ direct

PREP **1** (*place*) à travers; **t. a hedge** au travers d'une haie; **to go t. sb's garden** passer par le jardin de qn; **I was wandering t. the garden/ trees** j'errais dans le jardin/parmi les arbres; **to go t. a tunnel** passer dans un tunnel; **the nail/arrow went t. the wood/wall** le clou/la flèche traversa le bois/le mur; **the path goes** *or* **leads t. the forest** le sentier traverse la forêt; **I'm on my way t. Paris** je traverse Paris; **let's have dinner when I'm on my way t. Paris** on pourrait dîner ensemble pendant mon passage à Paris; **to look t. the window/a telescope/a hole** regarder par la fenêtre/dans un télescope/par un trou; **she came in t. the window** elle est entrée par la fenêtre; **to go t. someone's pockets** fouiller les poches de qn; *Aut* **to go t. a red light** brûler un feu (rouge); *Fam* **he's been t. it** *or* **t. a lot** il en a bavé, il en a vu de dures; **to speak t. one's nose** parler du nez; **she got t. her exam** elle a été reçue à son examen; *Fam* **to put sb t. it** rendre la vie dure à qn; **I'm halfway t. this book** j'ai lu la moitié de ce livre

2 (*time*) **all t. his life** durant *ou* pendant

toute sa vie; **t. the ages** à travers les âges; *esp Am* **Monday t. Friday** de lundi à vendredi, du lundi au vendredi

3 (*by means of*) **t. sb** par qn, par l'entremise *ou* l'intermédiaire de qn; **t. sth** par le *ou* au moyen de qch; (*as a result of*) en conséquence de qch, par suite de qch, à cause de qch; **to send sth t. the post** envoyer qch par la poste; **t. ignorance** par ignorance; **absent t. illness** absent par suite *ou* pour cause de maladie; **to act t. fear** agir sous le coup de la peur; **it's (all) t. me that he missed his train** c'est à cause de moi qu'il a manqué son train; **t. failing to lock the door ...** pour n'avoir pas fermé la porte à clé ...

4 *esp Am* **to be t. doing sth** avoir fini de faire qch; **are you t. telling me what to do?** tu as fini de me dire ce que j'ai à faire?

ADV **1** (*place*) à travers; **the water poured t.** l'eau coulait à travers; **the nail has come t.** le clou est passé à travers; **to let sb t.** laisser passer qn; **her trousers are t. at the knees** son pantalon est déchiré aux genoux; **he's t. in the living-room** il est de l'autre côté, dans le salon; **will you be t. tomorrow?** (*are you coming here?*) est-ce que tu viens demain?; **England are t. to the semi-final** l'Angleterre s'est qualifiée pour *ou* jouera la demi-finale; *Sport* **France are not t.** la France n'est pas qualifiée; **to be soaked t.** (*of person*) être trempé jusqu'aux os; (*of jacket etc*) être complètement trempé

2 (*from one end to the other*) d'un bout à l'autre; (*to the end*) jusqu'au bout, jusqu'à la fin; **to read a book (right) t.** lire un livre d'un bout à l'autre; **to see** *or* **carry sth t.** mener qch à bien; **I slept all night t.** j'ai dormi d'une traite cette nuit; **we'll stay t. until Friday** nous resterons jusqu'à vendredi; **I was aware all t. that ...** j'étais conscient tout du long de ce que ...; **we must go t. with it** il faut aller jusqu'au bout; **to be t. with sth** (*to have finished sth*) avoir fini qch; (*with scissors etc*) avoir fini avec qch; (*to have had enough of*) avoir (eu) assez de qch; **are you t. with your work?** avez-vous fini votre travail?; **I'm t. with you** j'en ai fini avec toi; **we're t.** c'est fini entre nous; *esp Am* **to be t.** (*to have stopped talking etc*) avoir terminé *ou* fini; *Fam* (*to be done for*) être fichu

3 to book t. to Paris prendre un billet direct pour Paris; *Tel* **to get t. to sb** obtenir la communication avec qn; *Fam* **I can't get t. to him** (*make him understand*) je n'arrive pas à lui faire comprendre quoi que ce soit; *Tel* **I'll put you t. to the secretary** je vous passe la/le secrétaire; *Tel* **you're t.** vous avez la communication, vous êtes en ligne

4 to be good/bad t. and t. (*of person*) être foncièrement bon/mauvais; **to know sb t. and t.** connaître qn comme si on l'avait fait; **to know a district t. and t.** connaître un quartier comme sa poche

ADJ (*train, road, ticket*) direct; **no t. road** (*on sign*) voie f sans issue; **closed to t. traffic** (*on sign*) interdit aux non-résidents, riverains autorisés

▸▸ *Com* **t. bill** connaissement m direct; **t. carriage** transport m direct; **t. fare** tarif m direct; **t. freight** marchandises fpl en transit; **t. passenger** (*on same vehicle to final destination*) passager m 'direct'; **t. passenger to Paris** voyageur, -euse direct(e) pour Paris; **t. traffic** transit m; **t. train** train m direct

throughout [θruː'aʊt] PREP **t. the country** dans tout le pays; **t. the world** à travers le monde; **t. the year** pendant toute l'année; **t. her life** durant *ou* pendant toute sa vie

ADV (*place*) partout; (*time*) tout le temps; **the coat is lined t.** le manteau est entièrement doublé; **they remained loyal t.** ils sont restés loyaux du début à la fin

throughput ['θruːpʊt] N débit m

throughway [ˈθruːweɪ] N *Am* autoroute *f*

throve PT *see* **thrive**

THROW [θrəʊ]

| N jet **1** ▪ lancement **1** ▪ lancer **1**
▪ essai **1** ▪ tour **1** ▪ coup **1**
| VT lancer **1** ▪ jeter **1** ▪ couvrir **1**
▪ projeter **2** ▪ organiser **3**
▪ déconcerter **8**

N **1** *(action)* jet *m*, lancement *m*; *Sport (of javelin, discus etc)* lancer *m*; *(in wrestling) (of opponent)* mise *f* à terre; **his longest t. so far** son meilleur jet jusqu'à présent; **3 throws for 50p** *(at fair etc)* 3 essais *ou* tours pour 50 pence; **it's your t.** *(of javelin, dice etc)* à toi de lancer; **a t. of the dice** un coup de dés
2 *(of crankshaft)* maneton *m*, bras *m* de manivelle
3 *(cover)* jeté *m* de canapé/de fauteuil
VT *(pt* **threw** [θruː]; *pp* **thrown** [θrəʊn]*)* **1** *(ball etc)* lancer, jeter; *Sport (discus, javelin etc)* lancer; **to t. sth at sb/sth** lancer *ou* jeter qch à qn/qch; **to t. sth in sb's face** jeter qch à la figure de qn; *Fig* **don't t. that in my face** ne me faites pas de reproches à ce sujet; **to t. sb a kiss** envoyer un baiser à qn; **to t. the dice** jeter les dés; **to t. a five/a six** *(at dice)* avoir un cinq/six; **to t. a glance at sb** jeter un coup d'œil à *ou* sur qn; **to t. oneself forwards/backwards** se jeter en avant/arrière; **to t. oneself into sth** *(into river etc)* se jeter dans qch; *Fig (into undertaking)* se lancer à corps perdu dans qch; **to t. oneself on sb's mercy** s'en remettre à la merci de qn; *Fig* **she threw herself at him** *(in relationship)* elle s'est jetée à sa tête; **to t. temptation in sb's way** exposer qn à la tentation; **to t. the blame on sb** rejeter la faute sur qn; **to t. a sheet over sth** couvrir qch d'un drap; **to t. a shawl over one's shoulders** jeter un châle sur ses épaules; **to t. sb into prison** jeter *ou* mettre en prison; **to t. sb to the lions** jeter qn aux lions; **to t. into confusion** *(government, court, assembly)* semer la confusion au sein de; **to t. a switch** appuyer sur un interrupteur; **to t. open the door** ouvrir la porte toute grande; **to t. open one's house to sb** ouvrir sa maison à qn; **to t. sb out of work** mettre qn au chômage
2 *(image, shadow)* projeter (**on** sur); *Fig* **to t. light on the matter** éclairer la question
3 *Fam* **to t. a fit** piquer une crise; **to t. a party** organiser une soirée
4 *(opponent)* renverser; **to t. its rider** *(of horse)* désarçonner son cavalier; **to be thrown** *(of rider)* vider les arçons, être désarçonné
5 **to t. its skin** *(of reptile)* muer
6 *(of animals)* **to t. a litter** mettre bas
7 *Cer (pot)* tourner, façonner au tour
8 *Fam (disconcert)* déconcerter; **his question threw me for a moment** pendant un moment, je n'ai su que répondre (à sa question); **I was completely thrown** j'étais complètement déconcerté
9 *Sport Fam (deliberately lose) (match, race etc)* perdre délibérément
VI **she can t. a hundred metres** elle est capable de lancer à cent mètres; **I can't t. straight** je n'arrive pas à lancer droit
▸ **throw about, throw around** VT SEP jeter çà et là; *(scatter)* éparpiller, disséminer; **to t. a ball around** jouer à la balle; **to t. one's money about** *or* **around** gaspiller son argent; **to t. one's arms about** *or* **around** faire de grands gestes; **to t. oneself about** se démener; **to be thrown about** *(in vehicle etc)* être ballotté; **to like to t. one's weight around** aimer faire sentir sa force
▸ **throw aside** VT SEP *(throw to one side)* jeter sur le côté; *Fig (discard) (career, everything*

one's worked for etc)* renoncer à; *(person)* rejeter, écarter; *(prejudices, fears, hatred etc)* se débarrasser de
▸ **throw away** VT SEP **1** *(discard)* jeter
2 *(waste)* gaspiller; **to t. away a chance** laisser passer une occasion; **to t. away one's life** *(waste)* gâcher sa vie; *(sacrifice for nothing)* se sacrifier inutilement; **don't t. yourself away on a waster like him** ne gâche pas ta vie pour un bon à rien pareil; **you're just throwing money away buying that stuff** tu gaspilles vraiment ton argent en achetant ce truc; **to t. away a line** *(of actor)* énoncer une phrase avec une indifférence calculée
▸ **throw back** VT SEP **1** *(return by throwing) (fish into water etc)* rejeter; *(ball etc)* renvoyer, relancer; *Fig* **to t. sth back in sb's face** jeter qch à la figure de qn
2 *(reflect) (of mirror) (image etc)* refléter, réfléchir; *(light, heat)* réverbérer
3 *(open forcefully) (shutters etc)* repousser
4 **to t. one's head back** rejeter la tête en arrière
5 *Fig* **to be thrown back upon sb/sth** être forcé de se rabattre sur qn/qch
▸ **throw down** VT SEP *(throw from height)* jeter *(du haut de qch)*; *(throw to the ground)* jeter à *ou* par terre; *(cast aside quickly)* jeter; *Cards* abattre; **to t. oneself down** se jeter sur le sol; **to t. down one's arms** jeter ses armes; *Fig (surrender)* se rendre; *Fam* **it's throwing it down!** *(raining)* qu'est-ce qui tombe!
▸ **throw in** VT SEP **1** *(throw into a place)* jeter dedans; *Ftbl* **to t. in the ball** remettre la balle en jeu; **to t. in one's hand** *or* **one's cards** *(leave game)* abandonner *ou* quitter la partie; *Fig (admit defeat)* s'avouer vaincu; **to t. in the towel** *Boxing* jeter l'éponge; *Fig (admit defeat)* s'avouer vaincu, jeter l'éponge
2 *(add)* ajouter; *(give as extra)* donner en plus; **if you buy that table I'll t. in the bookcase** si vous achetez cette table, je vous donne la bibliothèque en supplément
3 *(remark, word)* placer
4 **to t. in one's lot with sb** partager le sort de qn
▸ **throw off** VT SEP **1** *(remove hastily) (one's clothes)* enlever *ou* ôter très rapidement; *(mask)* enlever d'un coup
2 *(get rid of) (cold etc)* guérir de; *(pursuer etc)* se débarrasser de; *(oppressive regime)* se libérer de; *(old image)* secouer, se débarrasser de
3 *(write hastily) (poem etc)* composer au pied levé
4 **to t. sb off his bicycle** faire tomber qn de sa bicyclette; **to t. off its rider** *(of horse)* désarçonner son cavalier
5 *(put off)* **to t. the dogs/the police off the scent** semer les chiens/la police
▸ **throw on** VT SEP *(put on hastily) (clothes)* mettre *ou* passer à la hâte; *(wood on fire)* jeter
▸ **throw out** VT SEP **1** *(eject)* jeter dehors; *(person) (from job, pub, nightclub)* mettre à la porte, mettre dehors; *(from school, private club, political party)* exclure
2 *(discard)* jeter *ou* mettre au rebut; *(reject) (bill etc)* rejeter, repousser; **the takeover will t. a lot of people out of work** le rachat va mettre beaucoup de monde au chômage
3 *(give out) (rays etc)* jeter, émettre; *(heat etc)* répandre; **to t. out roots** donner des racines
4 **to t. out one's chest** bomber la poitrine
5 *(challenge etc)* lancer; **to t. out a suggestion** émettre une proposition *(sans insister)*
6 *(disconcert) (speaker etc)* troubler, déconcerter; **to t. sb out in his calculations** tromper les calculs de qn
7 *Cr (batsman)* mettre hors jeu en lançant la balle sur le guichet

▸ **throw over** VT SEP *(friend etc)* abandonner; *(lover etc) Fam* lâcher, plaquer; **to t. sb over for sb else** laisser tomber qn pour qn d'autre
▸ **throw together** VT SEP **1** *Fam (make hurriedly) (meal)* préparer en vitesse
2 *(gather together hurriedly)* assembler à la hâte; **a few paintings/facts thrown together** quelques tableaux/faits assemblés à la hâte; **the film looks as if it's been thrown together** le film semble bâclé; **chance had thrown us together** le hasard nous avait réunis
▸ **throw up** VT SEP **1** *(throw upwards)* jeter en l'air; *(raise high) (hands etc)* lever haut, mettre haut; **to t. up one's hands in despair** lever les mains en l'air de désespoir
2 *Fam (vomit)* vomir, rendre
3 *(build hurriedly) (house etc)* construire à toute vitesse
4 *(abandon) (project etc)* renoncer à, abandonner; **to t. up one's job** quitter son emploi; **to feel like throwing everything up** avoir envie de tout plaquer
5 *(reveal)* révéler, indiquer; **recent events have thrown up anomalies in the law** les derniers événements ont révélé des anomalies dans la loi; **the discussion threw up some new ideas** la discussion a amené de nouvelles idées
VI *Fam (vomit)* vomir, rendre

---

throwaway [ˈθrəʊəweɪ] ADJ **1** *(disposable) (nappy, lighter)* à jeter, jetable **2** **it was just a t. line** *or* **remark** il/elle/*etc* a dit ça comme ça N *esp Am Fam (leaflet)* prospectus *m*

throwback [ˈθrəʊbæk] N **1** *Biol* régression *f*, **he's a t. to his great-grandfather** il a hérité (des caractéristiques) de son arrière-grand-père **2** *Fig* retour *m* (en arrière); **it's a t. to the 16th century** c'est un retour au 16ème siècle

thrower [ˈθrəʊər] N *(of javelin, ball etc)* lanceur, -euse; **discus t.** discobole *m*

throw-in N *Ftbl, Rugby* remise *f* en jeu, touche *f*

throwing [ˈθrəʊɪŋ] N *(of projectile etc)* jet *m*, lancement *m*; *Sport (of discus etc)* lancer *m*

throw-outs NPL *Com* rebuts *mpl*

thru [θruː] PREP, ADV, ADJ *Am Fam* = **through**

thrum [θrʌm] VI **1** *(drum) (with fingers)* tambouriner **2** *(vibrate)* vrombir

thrush[1] [θrʌʃ] N *(bird)* grive *f*

thrush[2] N *Med* muguet *m*

thrust [θrʌst] N **1** *(push)* poussée *f*; *Fencing* coup *m* d'estoc; *Mil, Com etc Fig* poussée; **a bayonet t.** un coup de baïonnette; **with a single t. of his knife** d'un seul coup de couteau; *Fencing* **t. and parry** la botte et la parade; **the cut and t. of political debate** le jeu d'attaques et de ripostes des débats politiques **2** *(of argument)* **the general** *or* **main t. of an argument** l'idée générale d'une argumentation; **the argument has two main thrusts** l'argumentation a deux aspects principaux **3** *Tech* poussée *f*, butée *f*
VT *(pt, pp* **thrust**) pousser (avec force); **to t. sth into sth** enfoncer *ou* fourrer qch dans qch; **to t. one's hands into one's pockets** fourrer *ou* plonger les mains dans ses poches; **to be t. into a position of responsibility** être parachuté à un poste à responsabilités; **to t. oneself** *or* **one's way through the crowd** se frayer un chemin à travers la foule
VI **to t. at sb** *(with end of stick etc)* porter un coup à qn; *Fencing* porter un coup d'estoc à qn
▸▸ **t. washer** rondelle *f* de butée
▸ **thrust aside, thrust away** VT SEP *(reject)* repousser *ou* écarter d'un geste brusque;

Lit **to t. temptation aside** repousser *ou* écarter la tentation
▸ **thrust forward** VT SEP *(push forward)* pousser en avant; *Fig* **to t. oneself forward** se mettre en avant
▸ **thrust on, thrust upon** VT SEP *(force on)* **to. t. sth on sb** forcer qn à accepter qch; **to t. an opinion on sb** imposer son opinion à qn; **the responsibility was t. upon me** on m'en a imposé la responsabilité; **and some have greatness t. upon them** et à certains la grandeur *ou* la noblesse s'impose; **to t. oneself (up)on sb** s'imposer à qn *ou* chez qn
▸ **thrust out** VT SEP *(one's arm, leg)* allonger brusquement; *(chest)* bomber; **he t. his head out of the car window** il passa brusquement la tête par la vitre de la voiture

thruster ['θrʌstər] N *Astronaut (rocket engine)* propulseur *m*

thrustful ['θrʌstfʊl] ADJ = **thrusting**

thrusting ['θrʌstɪŋ] ADJ *(dynamic)* entreprenant, dynamique

thruway ['θruːweɪ] N *Am* autoroute *f*

thud [θʌd] N bruit *m* sourd
VI (**-dd-**) tomber avec un bruit sourd; **his feet went thudding along the corridor** ses pas résonnaient sourdement dans le couloir; **my heart was thudding against my ribs** mon cœur cognait sourdement dans ma poitrine; **the missile thudded into its target** le projectile frappa sa cible avec un bruit sourd

thug [θʌg] N brute *f*

thumb [θʌm] N pouce *m*; *Fam* **he's all thumbs** il est maladroit; *Fig* **to be under sb's t.** être sous la domination de qn; **she's got him right under her t.** elle le mène à la baguette; *Fam* **to stick out like a sore t.** choquer la vue; *Fam* **thumbs up!** bravo!; *Fam* **to give the thumbs up/down to a proposal** accepter/rejeter une proposition
VT **1 to t. a book** feuilleter *ou* parcourir un livre; **well thumbed book** livre qui a beaucoup servi **2 to t. one's nose at sb** faire un pied de nez à qn **3** *Fam* **to t. a lift** *or* **ride** faire de l'auto-stop *ou* du stop; **I thumbed a lift with a Dutch motorist** un conducteur hollandais m'a pris en stop
VI **to t. through a book** feuilleter *ou* parcourir un livre
▸▸ **t. index** répertoire *m* à onglets

thumb-indexed ['θʌmˈɪndekst] ADJ *(edition etc)* à onglets

thumbmark ['θʌmmɑːk] N marque *f* de pouce

thumbnail ['θʌmneɪl] N **1** ongle *m* du pouce **2** *Comput* vignette *f*
▸▸ **t. sketch** *(of plan)* aperçu *m*, croquis *m* rapide; *(of personality)* bref portrait *m*

thumbprint ['θʌmprɪnt] N empreinte *f* de pouce

thumbscrew ['θʌmskruː] N *Tech* vis *f* à oreilles; *(for torture)* = instrument *m* de torture utilisé pour écraser les pouces des prisonniers

thumbstall ['θʌmstɔːl] N *Med* doigtier *m* pour pouce

thumbtack ['θʌmtæk] N *Am* punaise *f*

thump [θʌmp] N **1** *(sound)* bruit *m* sourd; **with a loud t.** avec un gros bruit sourd **2** *(blow with fist)* coup *m* de poing; **he's given himself a t. on the head** il s'est cogné la tête
VT *(person)* cogner; *(repeatedly)* bourrer de coups; *(table)* cogner sur; **don't t. it down like that, be careful!** *(put down heavily)* ne le cogne pas comme ça en le posant, fais attention!; **he thumped his fist on the table** il cogna du poing sur la table
VI *(on table etc)* cogner; **my heart was thumping** mon cœur battait la chamade;

the upstairs neighbours were thumping about les voisins d'en haut martelaient le sol; **stop thumping about!** vous voulez bien cesser ce boucan!
▸ **thump out** VT SEP *(play heavily)* **to t. out a tune** *(on piano)* marteler un air

thumping ['θʌmpɪŋ] ADJ *Fam* **a t. great ...** un/une énorme ...; **a t. headache** un mal de tête de tous les diables; **a t. big lie** un gros mensonge

thunder ['θʌndər] N tonnerre *m*; **clap of t.** coup *m* de tonnerre; **peal** *or* **roll of t.** roulement *m ou* grondement *m ou* coup de tonnerre; **there's t. in the air** le temps est à l'orage; **voice like t.** voix *f* tonnante *ou* tonitruante; **with a face like t.** le visage fulminant de colère; *Fig* **to steal sb's t.** couper ses effets à qn; *Old-fashioned* **what in t. do you think you're doing?** tonnerre de Dieu! mais qu'est-ce qui te prend?
VI **1** *Met* tonner; *(of guns, waves)* faire un bruit de tonnerre; **it's thundering** il tonne; **it's thundering and lightning** il y a du tonnerre et des éclairs **2** *(move noisily)* **the avalanche thundered down** l'avalanche dévala dans un bruit de tonnerre; **the train thundered past** le train passa dans un bruit de tonnerre; **lorries thundered through the village** des camions traversèrent le village dans un bruit de tonnerre **3** *(of speaker)* tonitruer, tonner; **to t. against sb/sth** tonner contre qn/qch; **he thundered about the need for greater vigilance** il tonnait *ou* tonitruait sur la nécessité d'une plus grande vigilance
VT *(order)* ordonner d'une voix tonitruante; **get out!, he thundered** dehors!, tonitrua-t-il *ou* dit-il d'une voix tonitruante

thunderbolt ['θʌndəbəʊlt] N coup *m* de foudre; *Fig (astounding event etc)* coup *m* d'éclat; *(piece of news)* nouvelle *f* foudroyante; **the news came like a t.** cette nouvelle m'a/l'a/*etc* stupéfait

thunderclap ['θʌndəklæp] N coup *m* de tonnerre

thundercloud ['θʌndəklaʊd] N nuage *m* orageux

thundering ['θʌnd(ə)rɪŋ] ADJ *(sound etc)* tonnant, tonitruant; **t. applause** tonnerre *m* d'applaudissements; **to be in a t. rage** être dans une colère noire; *Old-fashioned Fam* **what a t. nuisance!** que c'est embêtant!; *Old-fashioned Fam* **what a t. (great) lie!** quel mensonge énorme!

thunderous ['θʌnd(ə)rəs] ADJ *(voice etc)* tonnant, tonitruant; **t. applause** tonnerre *m* d'applaudissements, applaudissements *mpl* à tout rompre

thunderstorm ['θʌndəstɔːm] N orage *m*

thunderstruck ['θʌndəstrʌk] ADJ abasourdi; **I was t. by the news** cette nouvelle m'a stupéfait *ou* stupéfié

thunderthighs ['θʌndəθaɪz] N *Fam Hum* = femme *f* aux grosses cuisses

thundery ['θʌndərɪ] ADJ *(sky)* orageux; *(weather)* orageux, d'orage; **the weather's t.** le temps est orageux *ou* à l'orage
▸▸ **t. shower** averse *f* accompagnée de tonnerre

Thur *abbr* **Thursday**

thurible ['θjʊərɪb(ə)l] N *Rel* encensoir *m*

Thurs *abbr* **Thursday**

Thursday ['θɜːzdɪ] N jeudi *m*; **T. 5 May** jeudi 5 mai; **T. morning/evening** jeudi matin/soir; **it's T. today** nous sommes jeudi aujourd'hui; **he comes on Thursdays** il vient le jeudi; **he's coming on T.** il vient jeudi; **every T.** tous les jeudis; **Maundy T.** jeudi saint VOIR GRAMMAIRE A81–2; B61–2

thus [ðʌs] ADV **1** *esp Lit (in this way)* ainsi, de cette façon, de cette manière; **t. prepared** ainsi préparé, préparé de cette façon **2**

(therefore) ainsi, donc; **t., when he arrived** donc, lorsqu'il est arrivé **3 t. far** *(as far as this)* jusqu'ici; *(as far as that)* jusque-là; **t. much** autant que cela (et pas davantage)

thwack [θwæk] N *(blow)* coup *m*; *(with hand)* claque *f*, *Fam* taloche *f*; *(noise)* claquement *m*; **with a t.** avec un coup sec; **I gave myself a t. on the shin** je me suis donné un coup dans le tibia
VT *(hit hard) (ball, head)* frapper; *(slap)* gifler; **I thwacked my head on the beam** je me suis cogné la tête contre la poutre

thwart[1] ['θwɔːt, *Naut* θɔːt] N *(in rowing boat)* banc *m* de nage

thwart[2] VT *(person)* contrarier; *(plot, scheme)* déjouer; **to be thwarted** *(of person)* essuyer un échec

thy [ðaɪ] POSS ADJ *(before a vowel* **thine**) *Arch, Lit* ton, *f* ta, *pl* tes

thyme [taɪm] N *Bot, Culin* thym *m*; **wild t.** serpolet *m*

thymus ['θaɪməs] N *Anat* thymus *m*, glande *f* thymique

thyristor [θaɪˈrɪstər] N thyristor *m*

thyroid ['θaɪrɔɪd] ADJ, N thyroïde *f*

thyself [ðaɪˈself] PERS PRON *Arch, Lit* toi(-même); *(reflexive)* te

ti [tiː] N *Mus* si *m*

tiara [tɪˈɑːrə] N **1** diadème *m* **2** *Rel* tiare *f*

Tiber (the) [ðəˈtaɪbər] N le Tibre

Tiberius [taɪˈbɪərɪəs] N Tibère

Tibet [tɪˈbet] N Tibet *m*

Tibetan [tɪˈbet(ə)n] ADJ tibétain
N **1** Tibétain, -aine **2** *Ling* tibétain *m*

tibia ['tɪbɪə] N *Anat* tibia *m*

tic [tɪk] N *Med* tic *m*; **a nervous t.** un tic nerveux

tich [tɪtʃ] N *Br Fam* **a (little) t.** *(person)* un (petit) bout de chou

tichy ['tɪtʃɪ] ADJ *Br Fam* minuscule

tick[1] [tɪk] N **1** *(sound) (of clock)* tic-tac *m* **2** *Br Fam (moment)* instant *m*; **just a t.!, half a t.!** un instant!, une seconde!; **it'll only take me a couple of ticks** je vais faire ça en deux secondes **3** *(mark)* marque *f*, coche *f*; **to put a t. against a name** cocher un nom
VI **to t.** *(of clock)* faire tic-tac, tictaquer; **the minutes are ticking by** les minutes passent; *Fam* **I'd like to know what makes him t.** je voudrais bien savoir ce qui le motive
VT = **tick off 1**
▸▸ *St Exch* **t. size** échelon *m* de cotation
▸ **tick away** VI **time is ticking away** le temps passe
▸ **tick off** VT SEP **1** *(mark with tick) (article on list etc)* pointer; *(name)* cocher **2** *Br Fam (reprimand)* attraper, enguirlander; **to get ticked off** se faire rembarrer **3** *Am Fam (irritate)* **to t. sb off** embêter qn; **he's really ticked off** il est drôlement en rogne
▸ **tick over** VI *(of engine)* tourner au ralenti; **the engine is ticking over nicely** le moteur tourne bien; **my business is just ticking over** les affaires vont doucement; **business is ticking over nicely** les affaires tournent bien; **it keeps my brain ticking over** ça fait travailler ma cervelle

tick[2] N *(parasite) (on cattle etc)* tique *f*

tick[3] N *Br Fam (credit)* crédit *m*; **to buy** *or* **get sth on t.** acheter qch à crédit

tick[4] N *(mattress cover)* enveloppe *f*, housse *f (à matelas)*

ticker ['tɪkər] N **1** *Sl (watch)* montre *f*, *(clock)* pendule *f*; *(heart)* palpitant *m* **2** *St Exch* téléimprimeur *m*, téléscripteur *m*
▸▸ **t. tape** bande *f* de téléimprimeur; **to be given a t. tape welcome** être accueilli sous une pluie de serpentins

ticket ['tɪkɪt] N **1** *(railway, air, theatre, lottery*

etc) billet *m*; (*underground, bus, for cloak-room etc*) ticket *m*; *Theat etc* **complimentary t.** billet de faveur; *Rail etc* **single t.** billet simple, (billet d') aller *m*; **return t.** billet d'aller-retour, aller-retour *m inv*, **left-luggage t., cloakroom t.** bulletin *m ou* ticket de consigne; **platform t.** ticket de quai; **season t.** carte *f* d'abonnement; **season-t. holder** abonné, -ée; *Aut Fam* **(parking) t.** P.V. *m inv*; papillon *m*; **to get a (parking) t.** attraper un P.V.; **t. holders only** (*on sign*) réservé aux personnes munies de billets
2 *Com* **(price) t.** étiquette *f*; **this doesn't have a t. on it** il n'y a pas de prix sur cet article
3 *esp Am Pol* (*list of candidates*) liste *f* des candidats; *Fam* **the Democratic t.** (*policies*) le programme du parti démocrate
4 *Naut Fam* **to get one's (master's) t.** passer (son brevet de) capitaine
5 *Fam* **it was just the t.!** voilà juste ce qu'il me fallait
vt (**ticketed**) (*goods*) étiqueter
▸▸**t. agency** *Theat* agence *f* de spectacles; *Rail* agence de voyages; **t. barrier** portillon *m* automatique; *Rail* **t. collector** contrôleur, -euse, *Belg* accompagnateur, -trice de train; **t. desk** guichet *m*; *Br Rail* **t. inspector** contrôleur, -euse, *Belg* accompagnateur, -trice de train; **t. machine** distributeur *m* de tickets, billetterie *f* automatique; **t. office** bureau *m* de vente des billets, guichet *m*; **t. punch** (*of ticket inspector*) poinçon *m*; (*for use by passengers*) composteur *m*; *esp Am Pol* **t. splitting** panachage *m*; *Am* **t. taker** contrôleur, -euse; *Br* **t. tout** revendeur, -euse de billets (*au marché noir*); **t. window** guichet *m*

ticketing ['tɪkɪtɪŋ] **N** (*issuing of tickets*) billetterie *f*

ticketless ['tɪkɪtləs] **ADJ** (*travel etc*) sans billet

ticking¹ ['tɪkɪŋ] **N** (*of clock*) tic-tac *m*
▸▸ *Br Fam* **t. off** engueulade *f*; **to get a t. off** (se) prendre un savon; **to give sb a t. off** passer un savon à qn

ticking² **N** *Tex* toile *f ou* coutil *m* à matelas

tickle ['tɪk(ə)l] **N** chatouillement *m*; **he gave her a t.** il lui a fait des chatouilles; **to have a t. in one's throat** avoir un chatouillement dans la gorge
vt 1 (*person*) chatouiller; *Fam* (*amuse*) amuser; **to t. the palate** (*of food, wine*) chatouiller le palais; *Fam* **to t. sb's fancy** faire envie à qn; *Fam* **to be tickled to death** *or* **tickled pink at** *or* **by sth** (*be amused*) s'amuser beaucoup de qch; (*be delighted*) être enchanté *ou* ravi de qch **2** *Fishing* (*trout*) pêcher à la main **3** *Hum* **to t. the ivories** pianoter, tapoter
vi **hey, that tickles!** eh, ça chatouille!; **you're tickling!** tu me chatouilles!

tickler ['tɪklər] **N** *esp Br Fam* (*problem*) os *m*; (*delicate subject*) sujet *m* délicat

tickling ['tɪklɪŋ] **ADJ** qui chatouille
N chatouillement *m*

ticklish ['tɪklɪʃ] **ADJ 1** (*person*) chatouilleux **2** (*touchy*) chatouilleux; (*subject, task etc*) délicat; **to be in a t. situation** se trouver dans une situation délicate

tickly ['tɪklɪ] **ADJ** (*blanket, pullover*) qui grattouille; (*cough*) irritant, d'irritation; **a t. throat** une irritation dans la gorge

ticktack ['tɪktæk] **N** *Br Horseracing* = signaux *mpl* utilisés entre les bookmakers
▸▸**t. man** aide *m* de bookmaker (qui fait des signaux avec les bras)

tick-tack-toe **N** *Am* morpion *m*

tidal ['taɪd(ə)l] **ADJ 1** de la marée; (*energy etc*) marémoteur, -trice **2** (*river etc*) à marée
▸▸**t. basin** bassin *m* à flot; **t. harbour** port *m* à *ou* de marée; **t. wave** raz-de-marée *m inv*; *Fig* (*of sympathy, enthusiasm, emotion*) vague *f*

tidbit ['tɪdbɪt] **N** *Am* = **titbit**

tiddler ['tɪdlər] **N** *Br Fam* (*small fish*) petit poisson *m*; (*minnow*) épinoche *f*; (*child*) bambin *m*, mioche *mf*

tiddl(e)y ['tɪdlɪ] **ADJ** *Br Fam* **1** (*small*) minuscule **2** (*drunk*) éméché

tiddlywinks ['tɪdlɪwɪŋks] **N** jeu *m* de puce

tide [taɪd] **N 1** marée *f*; **ebb t.** marée descendante, jusant *m*; **high/low t.** marée haute/basse; **neap t.** marée de morte-eau; **spring t.** grande marée, marée de vive eau; *Naut* **to go out with the t.** partir à la marée; **rise/fall of the t.** montée *f*/baisse *f* de l'eau; *also Fig* **against the t.** à contre-courant; *Fig* **the rising t. of discontent** la vague croissante du mécontentement; *Fig* **the t. of events** le cours des événements; *Fig* **when the t. of the battle turned** quand le cours de la bataille changea; *Fig* **the t. has turned** le vent a tourné
2 *Arch* (*season*) temps *m*, saison *f*
▸▸**t. gate** porte *f* à flot; **t. race** courant *m* de marée rapide; **t. table** échelle *f ou* table *f* des marées, almanach *m* (des marées)
▸ **tide over** **vt sep** aider à surmonter une difficulté, *Fam* dépanner; **can you lend me five pounds to t. me over till Monday?** pourrais-tu me prêter cinq livres pour me dépanner jusqu'à lundi?

tidemark ['taɪdmɑːk] **N 1** (*mark left by tide*) laisse *f* de haute mer **2** *Br Fam* (*line of dirt*) (*in bath etc*) ligne *f* de crasse

tidewater ['taɪdwɔːtər] **N** eau *f* de marée; *Am* (*coastal land*) côte *f*

tideway ['taɪdweɪ] **N** lit *m* de la marée

tidily ['taɪdɪlɪ] **ADV** avec ordre; (*dressed etc*) avec soin, soigneusement; **he puts everything away t. in a drawer at night** il range tout bien en ordre *ou* soigneusement dans un tiroir le soir

tidiness ['taɪdɪnɪs] **N** (*of room, files etc*) ordre *m*; (*of person*) goût *m* de l'ordre; (*in appearance, dress, of handwriting*) soin *m*

tidings ['taɪdɪŋz] **NPL** *Lit* nouvelle(s) *f(pl)*

tidy ['taɪdɪ] **ADJ 1** (*desk, room*) bien rangé, en ordre; (*handwriting*) net, soigné; (*hair*) soigné; **to have a t. mind** être méthodique, avoir l'esprit clair; **a clean and t. room** une pièce propre et nette; **he's very t.** (*in habits*) il est très ordonné; (*in appearance*) il est très soigné **2** *Fam* (*considerable*) assez considérable; (*profit*) joli petit; **a t. sum** une somme rondelette
N vide-poches *m inv*; **sink t.** coin *m* d'évier
vt (*room*) ranger, mettre de l'ordre dans; **to t. one's hair** s'arranger les cheveux
▸ **tidy away** **vt sep** (*put away*) (*books etc*) ranger
▸ **tidy up** **vi** (*clear things away*) ranger
vt sep (*room*) ranger, mettre de l'ordre dans; (*file, essay*) faire le ménage dans; **to t. things up** ranger; **to t. oneself up** faire un bout de toilette

tidy-out **N** nettoyage *m* par le vide

tidy-up **N** **to give a room a t.** ranger une pièce

TIE [taɪ]

N lien **1, 2**	attache **1**	cordon **2**
cravate **3**	traverse **4**	match nul **6**
VT nouer **1**	faire **1**	attacher **1**
ligoter **1**		
VI être à égalité **1**	s'attacher **2**	

N 1 (*link*) lien *m*; **he has no ties to the place** il n'y a rien qui l'attache à cet endroit; **family ties** liens de famille; **ties of friendship** liens d'amitié
2 (*of rope, straw, wicker etc*) lien *m*; (*for plastic bag*) cordon *m*

3 (*neck tie*) cravate *f*; **bow t.** nœud *m* papillon; **black t.** (*on invitation*) = smoking *m*; **old school t.** = cravate *f* portée par les anciens élèves d'une école; **it's the old school t.** (*that's why he got the job etc*) ce sont les vieilles relations *ou* amitiés d'école
4 *Constr etc* crampon *m*; *Am Rail* traverse *f*
5 *Mus* liaison *f*
6 *Sport* (*match*) match *m* nul; (*competition*) = compétition *f* dont les gagnants sont ex æquo; **(cup) t.** (*match*) = match de coupe
vt (*pt, pp* **tied**, *prp* **tying**) **1** (*piece of string, neck tie etc*) nouer; (*knot*) faire; (*shoelace, hood strings*) attacher, nouer; (*dog to kennel etc*) attacher; (*sb to post*) attacher, ligoter; **to t. sth to sth** attacher qch à qch; **to t. two things together** lier deux choses entre elles, attacher deux choses l'une à l'autre; *also Fig* **to t. sb's hands** lier les mains à qn; **to be tied hand and foot** être ligoté; **to have one's hands tied (behind one's back)** avoir les mains liées (derrière le dos); *Fig* **to have one's hands tied** avoir les mains liées, être pieds et poings liés
2 (*restrict*) **he was tied to his desk** il est resté rivé à son bureau; **the children kept her tied to the house** elle était clouée chez elle à cause des enfants; **she felt tied by her sense of duty** elle se sentait contrainte par son sens du devoir
3 (*link*) **to be tied to** avoir un lien avec
4 *Mus* (*two notes*) lier
vi 1 *Sport etc* être *ou* arriver à égalité (**with** avec); (*of candidates*) obtenir un nombre égal de suffrages; *Sch* **to t. for first place** être premier ex æquo (**with** avec)
2 (*apron, shoelace*) s'attacher, se nouer; **the dress ties at the back** la robe s'attache par derrière
▸▸ *Constr* **t. beam** longrine *f*; **t. clip** fixe-cravate *m*, *pl* fixe-cravates; **t. microphone** micro-cravate *m*, *pl* micros-cravates; **t. rack** porte-cravates *m inv*
▸ **tie back** **vt sep** (*hair, curtains*) attacher (en arrière)
▸ **tie down** **vt sep 1** (*prevent from moving by tying*) **to t. sb down** immobiliser qn en l'attachant; **to t. sth down** assujettir qch
2 (*restrict to certain conditions*) assujettir à certaines conditions; **children t. you down** les enfants représentent une contrainte; **this ticket doesn't t. you down to specific dates** ce billet vous laisse libre de changer vos dates de départ; **to t. sb down to facts** obliger qn à ne pas s'écarter des faits; **tied down to one's job** accaparé par son travail
▸ **tie in** **vi** (*correspond*) (*of facts, story*) concorder, cadrer, *Fam* coller (**with** avec); **the two versions don't t. in** les deux versions ne concordent *ou Fam* ne collent pas
vt **to t. sth in with sth** faire concorder *ou Fam* coller qch avec qch; **this sequence has to be tied in with the rest of the film** il faut qu'on intègre cette séquence au reste du film
▸ **tie on** **vt sep 1** (*attach by tying*) (*label etc*) attacher avec une ficelle
2 *Am Fam* **to t. one on** (*get drunk*) prendre une cuite, se cuiter
▸ **tie up** **vt sep 1** (*tie together*) (*parcel etc*) attacher, ficeler; (*hair*) nouer, attacher; (*top of bag*) lier, ficeler; (*injured arm etc*) bander, panser; **her hair was tied up with a ribbon** ses cheveux étaient attachés par un ruban; **there were various strands of the plot to t. up in the last episode** il y avait, dans l'histoire, beaucoup de péripéties qui demandaient une conclusion au dernier épisode
2 (*prevent from moving*) (*animal*) attacher; (*person*) ligoter; (*boat*) amarrer
3 (*prevent from being spent*) (*capital*) immobiliser; **my capital is tied up in stocks and shares** mon capital est immobilisé sous forme d'actions *ou* en actions

4 *Fam* **to be tied up** *(busy)* être très occupé, avoir beaucoup à faire; **he's going to be tied up all afternoon** il va être pris tout l'après-midi; **to get oneself tied up** s'embrouiller; *Am* **the traffic was all tied up** il y avait un embouteillage

5 to be tied up with sth *(be connected)* être lié à qch; **it's tied up with the increase in the bank rate** c'est lié à l'augmentation des taux d'intérêt; **our firm is tied up with theirs** notre maison a des accords avec la leur; **he's much too tied up with his work** son travail l'accapare vraiment

VI 1 *(of boat)* jeter l'ancre

2 *(connect, make sense)* avoir des rapports

▸ **tie up with** VT INSEP *(fit in with)* concorder *ou* cadrer avec; coller avec

tie-break, tie-breaker N *Tennis* tie-break *m, pl* tie-breaks; *(in TV game etc)* question *f* visant à départager les candidats, question subsidiaire

tied [taɪd] ADJ
▸▸ *Fin* **t. agent** agent *m* lié; *Br* **t. cottage** = logement *m* attaché à une ferme et occupé par un employé agricole; **t. house** *(pub)* = pub *m* lié par contrat à une brasserie qui l'approvisionne; *(house)* logement *m* de fonction; *Fin* **t. loan** prêt *m* conditionnel *ou* à condition; *Mus* **t. notes** notes *fpl* liées; *Mktg* **t. outlet** concession *f* exclusive, magasin *m* sous franchise exclusive

tied up ADJ *(capital)* immobilisé

tie-dye VT = teindre qch en le nouant pour que la couleur soit irrégulière

tie-in N rapport *m*, association *f*, *(film from book)* film *m* tiré d'un livre; *(book from film, TV series)* livre *m* tiré d'un film/d'un feuilleton; **we've got a film t.** nous avons vendu les droits pour le cinéma
▸▸ **t. promotion** promotion *f* collective

tie-on ADJ
▸▸ **t. label** étiquette *f* à œillets

tiepin ['taɪpɪn] N épingle *f* de cravate

tier [tɪər] N étage *m*; *(of seats etc)* rangée *f*, **tiers of an amphitheatre** gradins *mpl* d'un amphithéâtre; **two-t. postal system** courrier *m* à deux vitesses; **to arrange sth in tiers** disposer qch par étages, étager qch; **to rise in tiers** s'étager

tiered ['tɪəd] ADJ **three-t. cake** pièce montée *f* à trois étages; **three-t. stand** *(for cakes etc)* étagère *f* à trois tablettes
▸▸ **t. seating** sièges *mpl* disposés en gradins

tie-rod N *Aut* barre *f* d'accouplement

Tierra del Fuego [tɪ'eərədel'fweɪgəʊ] N la Terre de Feu

tie-tack mike N micro *m* cravate

tie-up N **1** *Am* *Aut* *(traffic jam)* embouteillage *m*; *Am* *(of work)* suspension *f* forcée **2** *(connection) (between two things)* rapport *m* **3** *Com, Fin (merger)* (absorption-)fusion *f*, unification *f*

TIF [tiːaɪ'ef] *(abbr* **transport international ferroviaire)** TIF *m*

TIFF [tɪf] N *Comput (abbr* **Tagged Image File Format)** format *m* TIFF

tiff [tɪf] N petite querelle *f* *(souvent entre amoureux)*

tiffin ['tɪfɪn] N *(Anglo-Indian)* déjeuner *m*

tig [tɪg] N *(game)* (jeu *m* de) chat *m*

tiger ['taɪgər] N *(animal)*, *Fig* tigre *m*; *Fig* **we've got a t. by the tail** on va se faire bouffer
▸▸ **t. economy** = pays *m* à l'économie très performante; **the (Asian) t. economies** les dragons *mpl* *ou* les tigres asiatiques; **t. lily** lis *m* tigré; *Entom* **t. moth** écaille *f*

tiger's-eye [taɪgəz'aɪ] N *(stone)* œil *m* de tigre

tight [taɪt] ADJ **1** *(clothes)* serré; *(skintight)* collant, moulant; *(mortise etc)* bien ajusté; *(knot, screw)* serré; *(cord etc)* raide, tendu; **to draw a cord t.** serrer un cordon; **to keep a t. hold over sb** tenir la bride haute à qn; **too t.** *(clothes)* étriqué, trop serré, trop juste; **t. shoes** chaussures *fpl* trop petites *ou* trop étroites; **it's a bit t.** *(of clothes)* c'est un peu juste; **the key's a bit t. in the lock** la clé ne tourne pas bien dans la serrure, la serrure est dure; **to have a t. feeling across the chest** avoir une barre sur la poitrine; **it's going to be t. but we should just make it** ça va être juste, mais nous devrions y arriver; **there was just room to park, but it was a t. squeeze** il y avait tout juste la place pour se garer; *Fam* **to be in a t. corner** *or* **a t. spot** être dans une mauvaise passe, *Fam* être dans le pétrin; **to run a t. ship** mener tout le monde à la baguette; **t. rules** règles *fpl* (très) strictes

2 *(money)* rare; *Sport (race)* serré, chaudement disputé; *(schedule)* chargé; **it should be a t. finish** *(in race)* l'arrivée devrait être serrée; *Fam* **money's a bit t. at the moment** je suis/nous sommes/*etc* un peu à court (d'argent) en ce moment

3 *(mean with money)* pingre, radin; **she's a bit t. with money** elle est un peu pingre

4 *Fam (drunk)* pompette; **to get t.** prendre une cuite

5 *(joint)* hermétique

6 *(turn, corner)* serré; *Aut (lock)* faible, petit

ADV **1** *(firmly)* fortement; **to hold sth t.** serrer fort qch; **to hold sb t.** *(child, lover etc)* serrer qn fort (contre soi); *(person attempting to escape)* bien tenir qn; **hold t.!** tenez bon!, tenez ferme!; **to screw a nut up t.** serrer un écrou à fond *ou* à bloc; **to squeeze sth t.** serrer qch étroitement *ou* fort; **to sit t.** ne pas bouger **2** *(to seal, shut)* hermétiquement; *(properly)* bien; **shut t., t. shut** *(door, eyes)* bien fermé
▸▸ *Cin, TV* **t. shot** plan *m* serré

tight-arsed ['taɪtɑːst], *Am* **tight-assed** ['taɪtæst] ADJ *Sl* coincé

tighten ['taɪt(ə)n] VT *(screw, knot etc)* serrer, resserrer; *(nut)* bloquer; *(spring)* bander, tendre; *(blockade, restrictions)* renforcer; **to t. one's grip on sth** resserrer son emprise sur qch; **to t. one's belt** serrer sa ceinture; *Fig* se serrer la ceinture

VI *(of knot etc)* se (res)serrer; *(of spring, cable etc)* se tendre; **her lips tightened** elle serra les lèvres

▸ **tighten up** VT SEP **1** *(screw etc)* resserrer; *(shoelaces)* refaire **2** *(blockade, restrictions, regulations)* renforcer; **the company has tightened up (its) security** la société a renforcé ses mesures de sécurité

VI *(in discipline, security etc)* devenir plus ferme *ou* strict; **to t. up on sth** renforcer qch

tightening ['taɪt(ə)nɪŋ] N *(of blockade etc)* renforcement *m*; *Fin (of credit etc)* resserrement *m*

tight-fisted [taɪt'fɪstɪd] ADJ *Fam* radin

tight-fitting ADJ *(dress, trousers)* moulant; *(suit, joint etc)* bien ajusté; *(door, lid)* qui ferme bien

tightknit ['taɪt'nɪt] ADJ *(community)* uni, dont les membres sont étroitement liés

tight-lipped ADJ les lèvres serrées; *Fig* **to be t.** ne rien dire **(about sth** au sujet de qch); **they kept a t. silence** ils ont gardé le silence, *Fam* ils sont restés bouche cousue; **you're being very t. about this** tu es très peu loquace là-dessus

tightly ['taɪtlɪ] ADV **1** *(firmly)* fermement; **to hold on t. to sth** se cramponner à qch; **to squeeze sth t.** serrer qch étroitement *ou* fort; **to fit t.** être bien ajusté; **to fit too t.** être (trop) serré *ou* (trop) juste; **we were t.**

packed *Fam* nous étions serrés comme des sardines; **don't screw it on too t.** ne le serre pas trop fort **2** *(to seal, close)* hermétiquement; *(properly)* bien; **eyes t. shut** yeux *mpl* bien fermés

tightness ['taɪtnɪs] N **1** *Med (of chest)* oppression *f*, *(of link, clothing)* étroitesse *f*, *(of embrace)* force *f* **2** *(of joint)* étanchéité *f* **3** *(of regulations, security)* rigueur *f*

tightrope ['taɪtrəʊp] N corde *f* raide; **to walk a t.** marcher sur une corde raide; *Fig* être sur la corde raide; *Fig* **political t.** walking acrobatie *f* politique; **we're walking a diplomatic t.** au point de vue diplomatique nous sommes sur la corde raide
▸▸ **t. walker** funambule *mf*

tights [taɪts] NPL *(garment)* collant *m* VOIR GRAMMAIRE A10

tightwad ['taɪtwɒd] N *Am Fam* avare *m*, radin, -ine

tigress ['taɪgrɪs] NF *(animal)*, *Fig (fierce woman)* tigresse *f*

Tigris (the) [ðə'taɪgrɪs] N le Tigre

tike [taɪk] N *Fam* = **tyke**

'til [tɪl] PREP, CONJ *Lit* = **until**

tilde ['tɪldə] N *Gram* tilde *m*

tile [taɪl] N *(of roof etc)* tuile *f*, *(on ground, floor)* carreau *m*; *Fam* **to spend a night on the tiles** faire la bringue toute la nuit; **(floor) t.** carreau de pavage *ou* de revêtement de sol; **(wall) t.** carreau de revêtement mural
VT **1** *(roof)* couvrir de tuiles; *(floor)* carreler **2** *Comput (windows)* afficher en mosaïque
▸▸ **t. kiln** tuilerie *f*, **t. works** tuilerie

tiled [taɪld] ADJ *(roof)* de *ou* en tuiles; *(floor)* carrelé, en carrelage; *(wall)* carrelé, revêtu de carrelage

tiling ['taɪlɪŋ] N **1** *(activity) (on roof)* pose *f* des tuiles; *(on floor)* carrelage *m*, pose des carreaux **2** *(covering) (of roof)* (couverture *f* en) tuiles *fpl*, *(of floor)* carrelage *m*

till [tɪl] VT *Agr (field etc)* labourer, cultiver

till [tɪl] N *Com* tiroir-caisse *m*, *pl* tiroirs-caisses; **pay at the t.** payez à la caisse; *Fig Fam* **to be caught with one's hand in the t.** être surpris la main dans le sac
▸▸ **t. money** encaisse *f*, **t. receipt** ticket *m* de caisse

till [tɪl] PREP jusqu'à; **t. tomorrow** jusqu'à demain; **t. now** jusqu'ici, jusqu'à maintenant; **t. then** jusque-là, jusqu'alors; **from morning t. night** du matin (jusqu')au soir; **(goodbye) t. Thursday!** à jeudi!; **wait t. after the holidays** attendez jusqu'après les vacances; **not t. Monday** pas avant lundi; **he won't come t. after dinner** il ne viendra qu'après le dîner; **I'd never heard of it t. now** c'est la première fois que j'en entends parler
CONJ jusqu'à ce que + *subj*, **we won't go t. all the doors are shut** nous ne partirons pas tant que toutes les portes ne seront pas fermées; **I have to wait t. all the doors are shut** je dois attendre jusqu'à la fermeture de toutes les portes; **t. I met you ...** avant de te rencontrer ...; **to laugh t. one cries** rire aux larmes; **I'm not going t. I get my money** je ne sortirai d'ici que lorsque j'aurai mon argent

tillage ['tɪlɪdʒ] N **1** *Agr (activity)* labour *m*, labourage *m*, culture *f* **2** *(land)* terres *fpl* en labour

tiller ['tɪlər] N *Naut* barre *f* franche (de direction); **who was at the t.?** qui était à la barre?

tiller N *(ploughman)* laboureur *m*; *Lit* **a t. of the soil** un homme de la terre

tilt [tɪlt] N **1** *(angle)* inclinaison *f*, pente *f*, *(in dancing)* tilt *m*; **to give sth a t.** incliner qch **2** *Hist (lance blow)* coup *m* de lance; *Fig* **to have a t. at sb** lancer une pointe à qn; **(at) full t.** à toute vitesse, *Fam* à fond de train;

to run full t. into sth donner en plein contre qch, rentrer en plein dans qch

VI 1 *(incline) (state)* pencher; *(act)* incliner, pencher; *Fig* pencher (**towards pour**); **to t. backwards/forwards** incliner *ou* pencher vers l'arrière/vers l'avant **2** *Hist (joust)* jouter (**at contre**); **to t. at windmills** se battre contre des moulins à vent; *Fig* **to t. at sb** *(in debate etc)* lancer une pointe à qn

VT *(barrel, one's chair etc)* pencher, incliner; **to t. one's hat over one's eyes** rabattre son chapeau sur les yeux; **to t. one's chair back** se balancer sur sa chaise

▸▸ **t. cab** *(on truck)* cabine *f* basculante; *Cin, TV* **t. shot** panoramique *m* vertical; *Aut* **t. and slide sunroof** toit *m* ouvrant entre-bâillant et coulissant

▸ **tilt over VI** *(fall)* se renverser

tilted ['tɪltɪd] **ADJ** incliné, penché

tilth [tɪlθ] **N** *Agr* **1** *(ploughing)* labour *m* **2** *(soil turned up)* couche *f* arable; *(tilled land)* cultures *fpl*

tilting ['tɪltɪŋ] **ADJ 1** *(at an angle)* incliné, penché **2** *(able to be tilted)* inclinable **N** *Hist (jousting)* joute *f*

timber ['tɪmbər] **N 1** *(wood)* bois *m*; **building t.** bois de construction *ou* de charpente; **standing t.** bois sur pied, arbres *mpl*; **to fell t.** abattre *ou* couper des arbres; **to put an area under t.** boiser une région **2** *(beam)* poutre *f*, madrier *m*; *(of ship)* membre *m* **INT t.!** attention à l'arbre (qui tombe)!

VT *(mine shaft, tunnel etc)* boiser, cuveler

▸▸ *Naut* **t. hitch** nœud *m* de bois *ou* d'anguille; **t. line** limite *f* des arbres; *Br* **t. merchant** marchand *m* de bois; **t. raft** train *m* de bois *ou* de flottage; **t. trade** commerce *m* du bois; **t. yard** chantier *m* de bois (de charpente)

timbered ['tɪmbəd] **ADJ 1** *(house etc)* en bois; **half t.** à *ou* en colombage **2** *(land)* boisé

timbering ['tɪmbərɪŋ] **N 1** *(of region)* boisage *m*, boisement *m* **2** *(of mine shaft)* boisage *m*, cuvelage *m* **3** *Constr (wooden frame)* armature *f*, **half t.** colombage *m*

timberwork ['tɪmbəwɜːk] **N 1** *(activity)* charpenterie *f* **2** *(framework)* charpente *f*

timbre ['tæmbr] **N** *(of voice)* timbre *m*

Timbuktu [tɪmbʌk'tuː] **N** Tombouctou

TIME [taɪm]

N temps **1, 2** ▪ délai **2** ▪ durée **2**
▪ époque **3, 4** ▪ moment **4** ▪ parfois
(at times) **4** ▪ heure **4, 5** ▪ à l'heure *(on time)* **5** ▪ fois **8, 9** ▪ mesure **10**
▪ espace **11**
VT fixer l'heure de **1** ▪ calculer **1**
▪ chronométrer **2** ▪ minuter **2**

N 1 temps *m*; **in (the course of) t.** avec le temps, à la longue; **it's just a matter of t.** ce n'est qu'une question de temps; **a race against t.** une course contre la montre; *Prov* **t. is money** le temps c'est de l'argent; **t. will tell** *or* **show** qui vivra verra; **my t. is my own** je suis libre de mon temps; **when I have the t.** quand j'aurai le temps; **to have t. on one's hands** avoir du temps libre; **now that the children have grown up I have t. on my hands** maintenant que les enfants sont grands, j'ai du temps à moi; **to have no t. to do sth** ne pas avoir le temps de faire qch; **I've no t. for him** il m'embête; **I've got no t. for people like that!** les gens comme ça me cassent les pieds; **to gain t.** gagner du temps; **to play for t.** chercher à gagner du temps; **you've got plenty of t.** vous avez tout votre temps; **there's no t. to lose** il n'y a pas de temps à perdre; **to make up for lost t.** rattraper le temps perdu; **to lose no t. doing sth** s'empresser *ou* se hâter de faire qch; **to**

waste t. perdre du temps; **to make t. to do sth** trouver le temps de faire qch; **I can always make t. for you** pour vous, je suis toujours là; *Am Sl* **to make t. with sb** *(chat up)* draguer qn; *(have sex with)* se faire qn, s'envoyer qn; **it takes t.** cela prend du temps; **t.'s up!** c'est l'heure!; *Br* **t., gentlemen, please!** *(in pub)* on ferme!; *Ftbl etc* **to play extra t.** jouer les prolongations *fpl*; *Ftbl etc* **two minutes into extra t.** au bout de deux minutes de prolongations; *Fam* **to do t.** *(go to prison)* faire de la taule; **convict nearing the end of his t.** prisonnier qui a bientôt fait *ou* fini son temps; **if I had my t. over again** si j'avais à recommencer (ma vie); **she's seen a few things in her t.** elle a vu pas mal de choses dans sa vie

2 *(period)* **in a short t.** *(quickly)* en peu de temps; *(soon)* sous peu; **in three weeks' t.** dans trois semaines; **in a month's t.** dans un mois; **in no t. (at all)**, **in next to no t.** en un rien de temps, en moins de rien; **within the required t.** dans le délai prescrit; **to take a long t. over sth** mettre longtemps à faire qch; **to take t. over sth/to do sth properly** prendre le temps qu'il faut pour qch/pour faire qch; **take your t.!** prenez (tout) votre temps!; **you took your t.!** tu as pris ton temps!, tu en as mis un (de ces) temps!; **what a (long) t. he's taking!** il n'en finit pas!, il prend son temps!; **to take the t. and trouble to check the facts** ne ménager ni son temps ni sa peine pour vérifier les faits; **she took the t. to explain it to us** elle a pris le temps de nous l'expliquer; **we haven't seen him for a long t.** voilà longtemps que nous ne l'avons (pas) vu; **for some t. past** depuis quelque temps; **for some t. (to come)** pendant quelque temps; **a short t. after, after a short t.** peu (de temps) après; **after a t.** après quelque temps, au bout d'un certain temps; **after a long t.** longtemps après; **all this t.** pendant tout ce temps; **to take t. out** *(pause)* faire une pause; **I'm taking t. out from my job** j'ai pris un congé; **I think you need t. out from looking after the kids** je pense que tu as besoin de t'éloigner des gosses pendant quelque temps; **she does it all the t.** elle le fait toujours *ou* tout le temps; **you knew all the t., didn't you?** tu le savais pourtant, n'est-ce pas? *Cin* **running t.** *(of film)* durée *f* de projection; *Sport* **1 minute 34 seconds is her best/a good t.** 1 minute 34 secondes, c'est son meilleur temps/c'est un bon temps

3 *(age)* époque *f*, **sign of the times** signe *m* des temps; **in times past, in former times** autrefois, jadis, dans le temps; **the good old times** le bon vieux temps; **in happier times** en un *ou* des temps plus heureux; **in times to come** à l'avenir; **in our times** *or* **these times** de nos jours; **to be ahead of** *or* **in advance of one's t.** être en avance sur son temps; **it was a very popular car in its t.** c'était une voiture très populaire à l'époque (où elle est sortie); **she was probably a good singer in her t.** en son temps, c'était sûrement une bonne chanteuse; **that was before my t.** c'était avant que je sois né; **very advanced for his t.** très en avance sur son temps *ou* sur l'époque; **to move with the times** être à la page; **to be behind the times** retarder *ou* être en retard sur son siècle, *Fam* ne pas être à la page; **times are bad** les temps sont difficiles *ou* durs; **hard times** temps difficiles; **to have fallen on hard times** connaître des temps difficiles

4 *(moment)* moment *m*; **I didn't know it at the t.** *(at that moment)* je n'en savais rien à ce moment-là; *(at that period)* je n'en savais rien à cette époque; **at that t.** en ce temps-là; **at the present t.** à l'heure qu'il est, actuellement, à présent; **at one t. it was different** autrefois *ou* dans le temps, ce n'était

pas comme ça *ou* c'était différent; **at no t.** jamais, à aucun moment; **at no t. did I say that …** je n'ai jamais dit que …, à aucun moment je n'ai dit que …; **at times** parfois, quelquefois, par moments; **at all times** toujours; **(at) any t. (you like)** n'importe quand, quand vous voudrez; **if at any t. …** si à l'occasion …; **some t. or other** un jour ou l'autre; **some t. next month** dans le courant du mois prochain; **this t. next year** l'an prochain à pareille époque *ou* à la même date; **by the t. (that) I got there** lorsque je suis arrivé; **from t. to t.** de temps en temps, de temps à autre; **from that t. (onwards)** dès lors, à partir de ce moment-là; **at the proper t.** en temps utile; **we shall see when the t. comes** nous verrons (cela) quand le moment sera venu; **now is the t./our t./your t. to …** c'est le (bon) moment pour …; **to choose one's t.** choisir son heure *ou* le moment; **this is no t.** *or* **this is not the t. to …** ce n'est pas le moment de …; **in due t. and place** en temps et lieu; **all in good t.** chaque chose en son temps; **in her own good t.** à son heure; **t. of (the) year** époque *f* de l'année; **at my/her/their/etc t. of life** à mon/son/leur/etc âge; **it was holiday t.** c'était l'époque des vacances; **before one's/its t.** prématurément; **his t. had not yet come** son heure n'était pas encore venue; **to be nearing her t.** *(of pregnant woman)* approcher de son terme; **the t. for talking is past** ce n'est plus le moment de parler

5 *(time of day etc)* heure *f*, **Greenwich mean t.** heure de Greenwich; **standard t.** heure du fuseau; *Br* **summer t.**, *Am* **daylight saving t.** heure d'été, *Can* heure avancée; **what's the t.?** quelle heure est-il?; **do you have the t.?** vous avez l'heure?; **what t. do you make it?** quelle heure avez-vous?; **to look at the t.** regarder l'heure; *(look at one's watch)* regarder sa montre; **watch that keeps (good) t./that loses t./that gains t.** montre qui est toujours à l'heure/qui retarde/qui avance; **what are you doing here at this t. of day/ night?** qu'est-ce que tu fais ici à cette heure-ci?; **at any t. of the day or night** à n'importe quelle heure du jour ou de la nuit; **to pass the t. of day with sb** parler de la pluie et du beau temps avec qn; **this t. tomorrow** demain à la même heure; **at the t. of delivery** au moment de la livraison; **at a given t.** à un moment donné *ou* déterminé; **dinner t.** heure du dîner; **(dead) on t.** à l'heure (pile); **to run on t.** *(of trains etc)* être à l'heure; **to be ahead of/behind t.** être en avance/en retard; **I was just in t. to see it** je suis arrivé juste à temps pour le voir; **to start in good t.** s'y prendre (bien) à temps; *(on journey)* se mettre en route de bonne heure; **it is t. we left** il est temps de partir; **it's t. he understood** il est temps qu'il comprenne; *Fam* **it's high t.!, and about t. too!** ce n'est pas *ou* c'est pas trop tôt!; **VOIR GRAMMAIRE A80–1; B60**

6 *Ind etc* **to put in t.** faire des heures; **to be paid by t.** être payé à l'heure; **to work** *or* **to be on short t.** être en chômage partiel; **to be on t. and a half/double t.** être payé une fois et demie/deux fois le taux horaire; **t. off in lieu** repos *m* compensateur

7 **to have a good t. (of it)** bien s'amuser; *(lead a pleasant life)* mener une vie agréable; *Fam* **to have a high old t.** faire la noce; **to have the t. of one's life** s'amuser comme un fou; **to have a bad** *or* **hard** *or* **rough t. (of it)** *(long period)* manger de la vache enragée, en voir de dures; *(shorter period)* passer un mauvais quart d'heure; **to have an easy t. of it** se la couler douce; **to give sb a hard** *or* **rough** *or* **tough t.** en faire voir de dures à qn, en faire voir de toutes les couleurs à qn

8 *(occasion)* fois *f*, **five times** cinq fois; **this**

is the third t. c'est la troisième fois; **next t.** la prochaine fois; **another t.** une autre fois; **the first t. I saw her** la première fois que je l'ai vue; **to do sth several times over** faire qch plusieurs fois *ou* à plusieurs reprises; **four times running** quatre fois de suite, à quatre reprises; **t. and t. again, t. after t.** à maintes reprises, maintes et maintes fois; **he succeeds every t.** il réussit à chaque coup; **every t. that …** chaque fois que …; **to do two things at a t.** faire deux choses à la fois; **to run upstairs four at a t.** monter l'escalier quatre à quatre; **for weeks at a t.** des semaines durant *ou* d'affilée; **it costs me £6 a t. to have my hair cut** une coupe de cheveux me coûte six livres; **at the same t. we must not forget that …** en même temps, nous ne devons pas oublier que …; **at the same t. will you also check the names of …** par la même occasion, vous vérifierez aussi les noms de …; **to do two things at the same t.** faire deux choses à la fois *ou* en même temps; *Prov* **you can't be in two places at the same t.** on ne peut être à la fois au four et au moulin

9 *(in multiplication)* **four times two is eight** quatre fois deux font huit; **three times as big as the other** trois fois plus grand que l'autre; **six times as much** six fois autant

10 *Mus* mesure *f*, *(of note)* valeur *f*, **double/triple t.** mesure à deux/trois temps; **in strict t.** en mesure; **to keep t., to be in t.** être en mesure; **to get out of t.** perdre la mesure; *Gym etc* **in quick t.** au pas accéléré

11 *Radio, TV* espace *m*; **to buy/sell t. on television** acheter/vendre de l'espace publicitaire à la télévision

VT 1 *(set time of)* fixer l'heure de; *Phot (exposure)* calculer; **the meeting has been timed for 6 o'clock** l'heure de la réunion a été fixée à 6 heures; **to t. one's arrival to coincide with one's friend's** s'arranger pour arriver en même temps que son ami; **to t. a blow/a remark** choisir le moment de *ou* pour porter un coup/placer un mot; **well timed** *(remark etc)* opportun, à propos; **badly timed** *(remark etc)* inopportun, mal à propos **2** *(measure time of) (person, race)* chronométrer; *(runner)* prendre le temps de; *Mil etc (operation etc)* minuter; **to t. a journey** calculer la durée d'un voyage; **to t. how long it takes sb to do sth** mesurer le temps que qn met à faire qch; **t. yourself doing it** mesure le temps que tu mets à le faire **3** *Aut etc (ignition etc)* caler; **to t. the valves** caler la distribution

▸▸*Fin* **t. bargain** marché *m* à terme; **t. belt** fuseau *m* horaire; *Fin* **t. bill** traite *f* à terme; **t. bomb** bombe *f* à retardement; *Fig* **you're sitting on a t. bomb** vous êtes sur une poudrière; *Ind* **t. card** carte *f ou* fiche *f* de pointage; *Gram* **t. clause** proposition *f* temporelle; *Ind* **t. clock** pointeuse *f*; **t. and date signal** signal *m* horodateur; **t. and date stamp** horodateur *m*; **t. and date stamping** horodatage *m*; **t. difference** décalage *m* horaire; *Fin* **t. draft** traite à terme; *Phot* **t. exposure** *(of film)* (temps *m* de) pose *f*, *(photograph)* photo *f* prise en pose; **t. machine** machine *f* à voyager dans le temps; **t. and motion expert** spécialiste *mf* des temps et mouvements; **t. and motion studies** organisation *f* scientifique du travail, OST *f*; **t. and motion study** étude *f* des temps et mouvements; *Mktg* **t. pricing** fixation *f* des prix en fonction du moment; *Phot* **t. release** déclencheur *m* automatique; **t. sheet** feuille *f* de présence; *Radio* **t. signal** signal *m ou* top *m* horaire; *Mus* **t. signature** indication *f* de la mesure; **t. slot** créneau *m ou* tranche *f* horaire; **t. switch** *(for oven, heating)* minuteur *m*; *(for lighting)* minuterie *f*, **t. travel** voyage *m* dans le temps; *Sport* **t. trial** course *f* contre la montre, contre-la-montre *m inv*; *Tel* **t. unit**

unité *f*; **t. value** *Mus* valeur *f (d'une note)*; *Fin* valeur temporelle; **t. warp** *(in science fiction)* faille *f* spatio-temporelle; **it's like going into a t. warp** c'est comme être transporté dans le passé/le futur; **t. zone** fuseau horaire

time-consuming ADJ *(job etc)* qui prend beaucoup de temps

time-honoured [-ɒnəd] ADJ *(custom etc)* consacré (par l'usage), vénérable, séculaire

timekeeper ['taɪmkiːpər] N **1** *(official)* *Ind* contrôleur *m* (de présence); *Sport* chronométreur *m* **2 to be a good t.** *(of person, watch)* être toujours à l'heure; **to be a poor t.** *(of person)* être toujours en retard; *(of watch)* (be slow) retarder; *(be fast)* avancer

timekeeping ['taɪmkiːpɪŋ] N **1** *Ind (regulation)* contrôle *m ou* pointage *m* de présence; *Sport etc (calculation of time)* chronométrage *m* **2 good t.** *(punctuality) (of person)* ponctualité *f*, *(of watch)* exactitude *f*; **her t. was poor** elle ne respectait pas les horaires

time-lapse ADJ
▸▸**t. photography** accéléré *m*

timeless ['taɪmlɪs] ADJ *(scene, appeal, novel etc)* intemporel; *Phil* atemporel; *(eternal)* éternel

timeliness ['taɪmlɪnɪs] ADJ *(of remark etc)* opportunité *f*, à-propos *m*

timely ['taɪmlɪ] ADJ opportun, à propos; **I made a t. escape** je me suis échappé juste à temps

time-out N *esp Am Sport* temps *m* mort; **to take a t.** faire un temps mort

timepiece ['taɪmpiːs] N *(clock)* pendule *f*, *(watch)* montre *f*

timer ['taɪmər] N **1** *(person)* chronométreur *m* **2** *(device)* *Aut etc* commutateur *m* d'allumage, temporisation *f*; *(on electric appliance etc)* minuterie *f*; *Culin* compte-minutes *m inv*; **egg t.** sablier *m*

time-saving ADJ *(device, method)* qui permet de gagner du temps
N gain *m ou* économie *f* de temps

timescale ['taɪmskeɪl] N période *f* (de temps); **the overall t.** la durée totale; **what sort of t. were you thinking of?** *(for completing the job, being absent from work etc)* de combien de temps allez-vous avoir besoin?; **the t. of a novel** la période sur laquelle s'échelonne un roman

time-sensitive ADJ qui requiert un minutage très précis

time-served [-sɜːvd] ADJ *(toolmaker etc)* qui a fait son apprentissage

time-server N *Pej (opportunist)* opportuniste *mf* **2** *(lazy worker)* employé, -ée qui fait de la présence

time-serving [-sɜːvɪŋ] N *Pej* **1** *(opportunism)* opportunisme *m* **2** *(laziness)* paresse *f*

time-share ADJ *(flat, house)* en multi-propriété
N appartement *m*/maison *f* en multi-propriété

time-sharing system N *Comput* système *m* à temps partagé

timespan ['taɪmspæn] N intervalle *m* de temps

timetable ['taɪmteɪb(ə)l] N **1** *(of departures etc)* horaire *m*; *Rail* horaire, indicateur *m* **2** *Sch* emploi *m* du temps; *Ind* plan *m* de mise en exécution; *(for negotiations, meetings etc)* calendrier *m*; **to work to a t.** travailler selon un emploi du temps
VT établir un emploi du temps/un calendrier/un horaire pour; **it's been timetabled for 9 o'clock** cela a été prévu pour 21 heures; **to t. sth to coincide with sth else** prévoir qch pour que cela coïncide avec qch d'autre

VI établir un emploi du temps/un calendrier/un horaire

time-wasting N perte *f* de temps; *Sport* **the referee clamped down hard on t.** l'arbitre a sévèrement pénalisé ceux qui jouaient la montre

timework ['taɪmwɜːk] N travail *m* à l'heure; **to be on t.** travailler à *ou* être payé à l'heure

timeworn ['taɪmwɔːn] ADJ *(worn)* usé (par le temps)

timid ['tɪmɪd] ADJ timide, peureux

timidity [tɪ'mɪdɪtɪ] N timidité *f*

timidly ['tɪmɪdlɪ] ADV timidement

timing ['taɪmɪŋ] N **1** *Sport etc (of movement)* rythme *m*; **good/bad t.** *(of remark)* à-propos *m*/manque *m* d'à-propos; *(of action)* opportunité *f*/inopportunité *f*; **good t., we've just started dinner!** tu arrives juste à temps, nous venons à peine de commencer à dîner!; **the actors' t. was awful** la synchronisation entre les acteurs était très mauvaise; **a comedian with a perfect sense of t.** un comique qui a vraiment le sens du timing; **he has no sense of t.** *(of what is suitable)* il n'a aucun sens de l'à-propos; **we must get the t. right between us** il faut que nous nous synchronisions; **how's that for t.!, we've finished one day before the deadline** c'est bien calculé! nous avons terminé un jour avant la fin; **they're still discussing the t. of the election** ils sont encore en train de discuter de la date *ou Fam* du timing des élections; **the t. of the election to coincide with …** la date des élections choisie pour coïncider avec …; **the t. of the election is crucial** il ne faudra pas se tromper quand nous choisirons/ils choisiront/*etc* la date des élections; **the t. of the announcement was criticized** on a critiqué le manque d'à-propos de cette déclaration **2** *Phot (of exposure)* calcul *m* **3** *(measuring of time), Sport etc* chronométrage *m*; *Mil etc (of operation)* minutage *m* **4** *Aut etc* distribution *f*, *(of ignition)* réglage *m*; *(of valve)* calage *m*
▸▸*Aut* **t. case** carter *m* de distribution; *Aut* **t. gear** pignon *m* de distribution

timorous ['tɪmərəs] ADJ timoré, timide

timorously ['tɪmərəslɪ] ADV timidement

timpani ['tɪmpənɪ] NPL *Mus* timbales *fpl*

timpanist ['tɪmpənɪst] N *Mus* timbalier *m*

tin [tɪn] N **1** *(metal)* étain *m*; **t.-bearing** stannifère **2** *(tin plate)* fer-blanc *m*, *pl* fers-blancs **3** *(mould) (for cake)* moule *m*, *(for tart)* tourtière *f* **4** *esp Br (can)* boîte *f* en fer-blanc; *(containing food)* boîte de conserves; **t. of sardines** boîte de sardines
VT (-nn-) *esp Br (put in cans) (sardines etc)* mettre en boîtes
▸▸*esp Br* **t. can** boîte en fer-blanc; *(containing food)* boîte de conserves; **t. god** *(petty dictator)* petit chef *m*, chefaillon *m*; *(object of veneration)* idole *f* de pacotille; *Fam* **he's just a little t. god** ce n'est qu'un petit tyran *m* d'opérette; *Br* **t. hat** casque *m* (militaire); **t. mine** mine *f* d'étain; **t. mug** timbale *f*, **T. Pan Alley** = le monde de la musique populaire; **t. plate** *(metal)* fer-blanc; **t. roof** toit *m* en tôle; **t. soldier** soldat *m* de plomb; **t. whistle** flûtiau *m*, pipeau *m*

tincture ['tɪŋ(k)tjər] N **1** *(of iodine etc)* teinture *f* **2** *(colour)* teinte *f*, nuance *f*
VT teindre, colorer

tinder ['tɪndər] N amadou *m*

tinderbox ['tɪndəbɒks] N briquet *m* (à silex); *Fig* **the country is a t.** le pays est une poudrière

tine [taɪn] N *(of fork)* dent *f*, fourchon *m*; *(of antler)* andouiller *m*

tinfoil ['tɪnfɔɪl] N papier *m* (d')étain, papier (d')aluminium, *Fam* papier alu

ting [tɪŋ] N (of bell) tintement m
vi tinter
vt faire tinter

ting-a-ling N, ADV drelin drelin m; (electrical) dring dring m

tinge [tɪn(d)ʒ] N nuance f, soupçon m; **a t. of irony** une pointe ou une note d'ironie
vt teinter, colorer; **sky tinged with pink** ciel teinté de rose; **words tinged with malice** paroles teintées de malice; **memories tinged with sadness** souvenirs empreints de tristesse

tingle ['tɪŋg(ə)l] N (feeling) (of skin) picotement m, fourmillement m; **a t. of fear ran up her spine** un frisson de peur lui remonta le long du dos; **a t. of excitement ran up her spine** un frisson d'enthousiasme la parcourut; **she felt a t. of anticipation** elle tressaillit de plaisir à cette idée
vi (prickle) picoter; **my hand tingles** j'ai des picotements dans la main; **to t. with impatience** vibrer d'impatience; **her legs tingled with cold** le froid lui donnait des picotements dans les jambes; **breeze that makes the blood t.** brise qui fouette le sang; **champagne that makes your mouth t.** champagne qui vous chatouille la bouche

tingling ['tɪŋglɪŋ] ADJ (prickling) **t. sensation** picotement m
N = tingle

tingly ['tɪŋglɪ] ADJ **t. sensation** picotement m; **my arm has gone all t.** j'ai des picotements dans tout le bras, tout mon bras me picote; **the sauna made me (feel) t. all over** le sauna m'a ravigoté

tininess ['taɪnɪnɪs] N petitesse f (extrême)

tinker ['tɪŋkər] N esp Pej (who repairs pots and pans) rétameur m ambulant; (gypsy) bohémien m; Br Fam **you little t.!** espèce de petit coquin!; Fam **he doesn't give a t.'s cuss** il s'en moque ou s'en fiche comme de sa première chemise ou comme de l'an quarante
vi bricoler (**with** avec); **to t. with a text** trafiquer un texte; **to t. with the radio** passer du temps à rafistoler le poste de radio; **someone's been tinkering with the water heater** quelqu'un a trafiqué ou tripoté le chauffe-eau

tinkle ['tɪŋk(ə)l] N (of bells, glasses) tintement m; Br Fam **I'll give you a t.** (telephone) je vous passerai un coup de fil
vi tinter; **to t. on the piano** pianoter
vt (small bell) faire tinter; Fam usu Hum **to t. the ivories** (play the piano) pianoter

tinkling ['tɪŋklɪŋ] N (of bells, glasses) tintement m

tinned [tɪnd] ADJ Br (meat etc) en boîte; **to eat t. fruit** manger des fruits en conserve
▸▸ **t. foods** conserves fpl

tinnie ['tɪnɪ] N Austr Fam boîte f de bière

tinnitus [tɪn'aɪtəs] N Med acouphène m

tinny ['tɪnɪ] ADJ (sound) grêle; (loudspeaker, radio) qui rend un son grêle; **to sound t.** rendre un son métallique ou grêle, faire un bruit de casserole; Pej **a t. car** une voiture pas robuste pour un sou; **food with a t. taste** aliment m qui a un goût d'étain ou de boîte de conserve

tin-opener N esp Br ouvre-boîte(s) m, pl ouvre-boîtes

tinpot ['tɪnpɒt] ADJ Fam de rien du tout; **a t. dictator** un dictateur en carton-pâte

tinsel ['tɪns(ə)l] N (Christmas decoration) guirlandes fpl de Noël; Fig Pej clinquant m
ADJ Fig Pej clinquant
▸▸ Hum Pej **T. Town** = surnom donné à Hollywood

tinsmith ['tɪnsmɪθ] N (maker of tin objects) ferblantier m

tint [tɪnt] N (shade) teinte f, nuance f, (for hair) colorant m, couleur f; Typ hachure f, hachures fpl; **red with a blue t.** teinte rouge avec une nuance de bleu; **warm tints** tons mpl chauds; **half t.** demi-teinte f, pl demi-teintes
vt (colour) teinter, colorer; Opt **tinted glasses** verres mpl teintés; **to have one's hair tinted** se faire un rinçage; **tinted windows** vitres fpl teintées; Aut **tinted shadeband** pignon m de distribution

tintack ['tɪntæk] N broquette f, clou m de tapisserie

tinting ['tɪntɪŋ] N coloration f

tintinnabulation [tɪntɪnæbjʊ'leɪʃən] N tintinnabulement m

tiny ['taɪnɪ] ADJ minuscule; **a t. bit** un tout petit peu; **a t. little house** une toute petite maison; **in a t. voice** d'une toute petite voix

tip¹ [tɪp] N (end) bout m, extrémité f, (pointed) pointe f, (of walking stick etc) bout ferré, embout m; Billiards (of cue) procédé m; (of cigarette) bout (filtre); **steel t.** (of shoe) fer m; **on the tips of one's toes** sur la pointe des pieds; **to be a politician/musician to the tips of one's fingers** être politicien/musicien jusqu'au bout des doigts; **to have sth on the t. of one's tongue** avoir qch sur le bout de la langue; **from t. to toe** de la tête aux pieds; Fig **that's just the t. of the iceberg** (et) ce n'est que la partie émergée de l'iceberg; Culin **asparagus tips** pointes fpl d'asperge
vt (-pp-) (put tip on) (walking stick etc) emboutir; (shoe) mettre un bout à; **arrow tipped with poison** flèche à bout empoisonné

tip² N **1** (payment) pourboire m; **to give sb a t.** donner un pourboire à qn **2** Horseracing, St Exch etc (advice) tuyau m, -aux; **to give sb a t.** renseigner ou Fam tuyauter qn; **to take a t. from sb** suivre le conseil de qn; **a book full of useful tips on how to save energy** un livre plein de tuyaux utiles ou plein de bons trucs pour économiser l'énergie
vt (-pp-) **1** (give money to) donner un pourboire à **2** Horseracing, St Exch etc donner comme favori; **to t. a certain horse to win** pronostiquer qu'un certain cheval sera le gagnant; **she's widely tipped for the job** on estime qu'elle a toutes ses chances pour le poste, on la donne comme favorite pour le poste; **he is strongly tipped to become Home Secretary** il est pressenti pour le poste de ministre de l'Intérieur
vi (of customer) **she tips well** elle donne toujours de bons pourboires
▸ **tip off** vt SEP (police, journalist) informer, Fam tuyauter; **to be tipped off about sth** avoir des renseignements sur qch, Fam être tuyauté sur qch

tip³ N **1** (for rubbish) dépotoir m; Fam **this room's a t.!** cette pièce est un vrai dépotoir! **2** Constr etc chantier m de versage
vt 1 (pour) (stones, earth, rubbish) déverser; **to t. sth into sth** verser qch dans qch; **to t. sth on the ground** déverser qch par terre; **no tipping** (on sign) dépôt d'ordures interdit, décharge interdite **2** (cause to lean) faire pencher, faire incliner; **to t. one's hat over one's eyes** rabattre son chapeau sur ses yeux; **to t. one's hat to sb** tirer son chapeau à qn
▸ **tip in** vt SEP Typ monter en hors-texte
▸ **tip out** vt SEP déverser, décharger; **to t. sth out on the ground** déverser qch par terre
▸ **tip over** vt SEP (overturn) renverser; (boat) chavirer
vi (overturn) se renverser, basculer; (of boat etc) chavirer
▸ **tip up** vt SEP (tilt upwards) (seat) soulever; (cart) faire basculer
vi (tilt upwards) (of seat etc) se soulever, basculer

tip-off N renseignement m, Fam tuyau m, pl -aux; (warning) avertissement m; **to give sb a t.** renseigner ou Fam tuyauter qn; **the police received a t.** la police a été informée

tipped [tɪpt] ADJ (cigarettes) (à) bout filtre

-tipped [tɪpt] SUFF gold/silver-t. à bout doré/d'argent

tipper ['tɪpər] N **1** (truck) camion m à benne **2 to be a generous t.** (in restaurant etc) donner des pourboires généreux
▸▸ **t. truck**, Br **t. lorry** camion à benne

tippet ['tɪpɪt] N (fur) pèlerine f, collet m

Tipp-ex® ['tɪpeks] N correcteur m liquide, Fam blanco m, tippex® m
▸ **Tipp-ex**® **out** vt SEP effacer avec un correcteur liquide

tipping ['tɪpɪŋ] ADJ (wagon etc) basculant, à bascule
N (giving money) distribution f de pourboires; (system) (système m des) pourboires mpl; **is t. normal?** est-ce qu'il est normal de donner des pourboires?

tipple¹ ['tɪp(ə)l] Fam N (drink) **time for a quick t.?** on a le temps de prendre un petit verre?; **what's your t.?** qu'est-ce que vous prenez habituellement?; **gin was my t.** je buvais du gin à l'époque
vi picoler

tipple² N Am Min (apparatus) basculeur m de wagons; (place) décharge f

tippler ['tɪplər] N Fam picoleur, -euse

tippy-toe ['tɪpɪtəʊ] N, ADV, VI Am = tiptoe

tipsily ['tɪpsɪlɪ] ADV (to say) d'une voix qui accuse l'ivresse; (to walk) en titubant

tipsiness ['tɪpsɪnɪs] N (légère) ivresse f

tipstaff, pl **tipstaffs** ['tɪpstaːf, -staːfs] N Br Law huissier m

tipster ['tɪpstər] N Horseracing etc pronostiqueur m

tipsy ['tɪpsɪ] ADJ gris, Fam pompette; **slightly t.** un peu éméché; **to get t.** se griser, s'enivrer

tiptoe ['tɪptəʊ] N **on t.** sur la pointe des pieds
ADV sur la pointe des pieds
vi marcher sur la pointe des pieds; **to t. in/out** entrer/sortir sur la pointe des pieds

tiptop ['tɪptɒp] ADJ excellent; (hotel etc) de premier ordre; **I feel t.** je me sens en pleine forme

tip-up ADJ (barrow etc) à bascule
▸▸ **t. seat** (in cinema, theatre) siège m rabattable, strapontin m; (in metro) strapontin

TIR [tiːaːˈɑːr] (abbr transport international de marchandises per route) TIR m

tirade [taɪ'reɪd] N diatribe f (against contre); **t. of invective** bordée f d'injures

tire¹ ['taɪər] vt fatiguer; (to weary) lasser; **to t. oneself doing sth** se fatiguer à faire qch
vi se fatiguer; (to weary) se lasser (of sb/sth de qn/qch); **he never tires of telling me** il ne se lasse pas de me le dire; **they tired of his complaining** or **complaints** ils se sont fatigués ou lassés de ses plaintes
▸ **tire out** vt SEP (exhaust) épuiser ou briser de fatigue; **to t. oneself out** se fatiguer; **she was tired out** elle n'en pouvait plus (de fatigue)

tire² N Am = tyre

tired ['taɪəd] ADJ fatigué; (weary) las, f lasse; **to get t.** se fatiguer; Hum **it makes me t. just watching them/thinking about it** ça me fatigue rien que de les voir/d'y penser; Fam Hum **t. and emotional** (drunk) dans les vignes du Seigneur; **to be t. of sth** être las de qch, en avoir assez de qch; **to grow** or **get t. of sb/sth** se lasser ou se fatiguer de qn/qch; **my eyes get t. very easily** mes yeux se fatiguent très facilement; **to grow** or **get t. of doing sth** se lasser de faire qch; Fam **I'm t. of you** j'en ai assez de vous; **t. of arguing, he consented** de guerre lasse, il a donné son consentement; Fam **t. old carpet** vieux tapis m usé; **t. phrase** expression f usée; **in a t. voice** d'une voix lasse ou fatiguée

tiredly ['taɪədlɪ] ADV avec lassitude

tiredness ['taɪədnɪs] N fatigue f, Med asthénie f

tireless ['taɪəlɪs] ADJ (worker, campaigner etc) infatigable; (efforts) inlassable

tirelessly ['taɪəlɪslɪ] ADV infatigablement, inlassablement

tiresome ['taɪəsəm] ADJ (boring) assommant, ennuyeux; (irritating, annoying) fatigant, exaspérant; **how t.!** que c'est ennuyeux ou assommant!

> Attention: ne pas confondre avec **tiring**, qui se rapporte le plus souvent à la fatigue physique.

tiring ['taɪərɪŋ] ADJ (work, journey, day, person etc) fatigant

> Attention: ne pas confondre avec **tiresome**, qui signifie **ennuyeux**.

tiro, pl tiros, tiroes ['taɪrəʊ, -əʊz] N = **tyro**

'tis [tɪz] CONTR = **it is**, see **be**

tissue ['tɪʃuː] N 1 Biol tissu m 2 (paper handkerchief) mouchoir m en papier; (paper) papier m de soie; Fig **t. of lies** tissu de mensonges
▸▸ **t. paper** papier de soie

> Note that the French word **tissu** also means **fabric**.

tiswas ['tɪzwɒz] N Fam = **tizzy**

tit¹ [tɪt] N (bird) mésange f; **blue t.** mésange bleue; **coal t.** mésange noire; **great t.** (mésange) charbonnière f

tit² N **t. for tat** un prêté pour un rendu; **to give sb t. for tat** rendre la pareille à qn; (verbally) répondre du tac au tac

tit³ N Sl 1 (breast) nichon m, téton m, néné m; **to get on sb's tits** (annoy, irritate) porter sur le système à qn 2 (idiot) imbécile mf; **I felt a right t.** je me suis senti vraiment bête, j'ai eu l'impression d'être un parfait imbécile

Titan ['taɪt(ə)n] N Myth Titan m; Fig **t.** titan m

titanic [taɪ'tænɪk] ADJ titanesque

titanium [taɪ'teɪnɪəm] N Chem titane m

titbit ['tɪtbɪt] N (food) morceau m, pl -aux, de choix; (sweet) friandise f, (of gossip) potin m

titch, titchy [tɪtʃ, 'tɪtʃɪ] Br Fam = **tich, tichy**

titfer ['tɪtfər] N Old-fashioned Br Sl (hat) galurin m, bitos m

tit-for-tat ADJ (killing, expulsions etc) fait en représailles ou en riposte

tithe [taɪð] N dîme f
▸▸ **t. barn** = grange f où l'on mettait les recettes de la dîme

Titian ['tɪʃɪən] N le Titien
ADJ (hair) acajou inv

titillate ['tɪtɪleɪt] VT (readers, viewers) émoustiller; (senses) émoustiller, titiller; (palate) chatouiller
VI (of film, book etc) titiller les sens

titillating ['tɪtɪleɪtɪŋ] ADJ titillant, émoustillant

titillation [tɪtɪ'leɪʃən] N titillation f

titivate ['tɪtɪveɪt] VT Old-fashioned (person) faire beau, pomponner; (thing) pomponner, bichonner; **to t. oneself** se faire beau, se pomponner

title ['taɪtl] N 1 (of book, chapter) titre m; (of

article, act) titre, intitulé m; **the story that gives the collection its t.** l'histoire qui donne son titre à la collection; **the t. is taken from …** le titre est tiré de …; **to publish fifty titles a year** publier cinquante titres par an 2 (of person) titre m; **to give sb a t.** donner un titre à qn, titrer qn; **to have a t.** (of nobility) avoir un titre de noblesse, être titré 3 Sport titre m; **to hold the t.** détenir le titre (de champion) 4 Law (deed) titre m (constitutif) de propriété, acte m de propriété; **t. to property** titre de propriété 5 Cin, TV **titles** (credits) générique m
VT (book etc) intituler
▸▸ Comput **t. bar** barre f de titre; Law **t. deed** titre (constitutif) de propriété, acte de propriété; Boxing **t. fight** combat m comptant pour le titre; **non t. fight** combat m ne comptant pas pour le titre; Law **t. holder** propriétaire mf, **t. music** musique f de générique; **t. page** page f de titre; **t. piece** (of anthology) conte m/morceau m qui donne son titre au recueil; Theat **t. rôle** rôle m qui donne son titre à la pièce; Mus **t. track** morceau m qui donne son titre à l'album

titled ['taɪtld] ADJ (person) titré; **to be t.** avoir un titre (de noblesse)

titleholder ['taɪtlhəʊldər] N Sport tenant, -ante du titre

titler ['taɪtlər] N Cin titreur, -euse

titmouse, pl titmice ['tɪtmaʊs, -maɪs] N (bird) mésange f

titrate ['taɪtreɪt] VT Chem, Ind (solution) titrer

titter ['tɪtər] N (suppressed laughter) rire m étouffé; (nervous laughter) petit rire nerveux ou bête
VI (in suppressed way) avoir un petit rire étouffé; (laugh nervously) rire nerveusement ou bêtement

tittering ['tɪtərɪŋ] N petits rires mpl

tittie ['tɪtɪ] N Sl = **titty**

tittle ['tɪt(ə)l] N = **jot**

tittle-tattle N (gossip) potins mpl, Fam cancans mpl
VI (gossip) Fam cancaner

titty ['tɪtɪ] N Sl (breast) nichon m; Fig **that's tough t., that's his tough t.** (c'est) tant pis pour lui

titular ['tɪtjʊlər] ADJ titulaire; (function, office etc) nominal, -aux; **t. possessions** terres fpl attachées à un titre

tizzy ['tɪzɪ] N Fam **to be in a t.** ne (pas) savoir où donner de la tête; **to get into a t.** se mettre dans tous ses états

T-junction N bifurcation f en T

TLC [tiːel'siː] N (abbr tender loving care) affection f

TNT [tiːen'tiː] N (abbr trinitrotoluene) TNT m

TO [tuː, unstressed tə]

PREP	à 1, 2, 4–7, 9–11, 15	▪ en 1, 4
▪ vers 2	▪ jusqu'à 5	▪ sur 8	▪ de 9
▪ contre 11		
WITH THE INFINITIVE	pour 1	▪ à 2

PREP 1 à; **to go to church/to school** aller à l'église/à l'école; **what school do you go to?** à quelle école allez-vous?, Fam tu vas où à l'école?, tu es dans quelle école?; **I'm off to bed** je vais au lit ou me coucher; **I'm off to Paris** je pars pour Paris; **he went to France/to Japan** il est allé en France/au Japon; **she returned home to her family** elle est rentrée auprès de sa famille; **I am going to the grocer's** je vais chez l'épicier; **from town to town** de ville en ville; **flights to the Continent** vols à destination de l'Europe; **the road to London** la route de Londres; **a journey to Paris** un voyage à Paris; **the shortest way to the station** le plus court chemin pour aller à la gare

2 (towards) vers, à; **to the east** vers l'est; **to the trains** (on sign) accès aux quais; **to the right** à droite; **to the left** à gauche; **the rooms to the back** les chambres de derrière 3 (next to) **elbow to elbow** coude à coude; **I told him so to his face** je le lui ai dit en face; **to clasp sb to one's heart** serrer qn sur son cœur; **to fall to the ground** tomber à ou par terre

4 (of time) **from morning to night** du matin au soir; **from day to day** de jour en jour; **the day to day running of the school** l'administration de tous les jours de l'école; **ten minutes to six** six heures moins dix; **it's ten to** il est moins dix

5 (until) jusqu'à; **to this day** jusqu'à ce jour; **to count up to ten** compter jusqu'à dix; **moved to tears** ému (jusqu')aux larmes; **fight to the death** bataille ou combat à mort; **to a high degree** à un haut degré; **generous to a fault** généreux à l'excès; **accurate to a millimetre** exact au millimètre près; **a year to the day** un an jour pour jour; **to cut sth down to a minimum** réduire qch au minimum

6 (purpose) **to this end** à cet effet, dans ce but

7 (result) **to my despair** à mon grand désespoir; **to everyone's surprise** à la surprise de tous; **to put to flight** mettre en fuite; **to pull to pieces** mettre en pièces

8 **what tune is it sung to?** sur quel air cela se chante-t-il?

9 (of) **heir to sb/to an estate** héritier de qn/ d'une propriété; **ambassador to the King of Sweden** ambassadeur auprès du roi de Suède; **apprentice to a joiner** apprenti chez un menuisier; **the key to the door** la clef de la porte; **the answer to a question** la réponse à une question

10 (in comparisons) **superior to** supérieur à; **compared to this** comparé à ou en comparaison de celui-ci; **that's nothing to what I have seen** cela n'est rien à côté de ce que j'ai vu

11 (expressing a proportion) **three is to six as six is to twelve** trois est à six ce que six est à douze; **six votes to four** six voix contre quatre; **three goals to nil** trois buts à zéro; **to bet ten to one** parier dix contre un

12 **to all appearances** selon les apparences; **not to my taste** pas à mon goût; **to the best of my recollection** (pour) autant que je m'en souvienne

13 **to drink to sb** boire à la santé de qn

14 (concerning) **what did she say to my suggestion?** qu'est-ce qu'elle a dit de ma proposition?; **is that all there is to it?** c'est tout?; **there's nothing to it** (it's easy) c'est simple comme bonjour; **there's nothing** or **there isn't a lot to these cameras** ils ne sont pas bien compliqués, ces appareils-photos

15 (used to form the dative) à; **to give sth to sb** donner qch à qn; **he gave it to her** il le lui a donné; **who did you give it to?** à qui l'avez-vous donné?; **to speak to sb** parler à qn; Fml **to whom?** à qui?; **what's it to you?** qu'est-ce que ça peut te faire?; **to keep sth to oneself** garder qch pour soi; **he has been a father to me** il a été un père pour moi; **known to the ancients** connu des anciens

VOIR GRAMMAIRE A40–2; B35–7 (with the infinitive) 1 (purpose, result) pour; **he came to help me** il est venu (pour) m'aider; **we must eat (in order) to live** il faut manger pour vivre; **so to speak** pour ainsi dire; **born to rule** né pour régner; **happy to do it** heureux de le faire; **ready to listen** prêt à écouter; **old enough to go to school** en âge d'aller à l'école; **built to house 10 people** construit pour loger 10 personnes; **too hot to drink** trop chaud pour qu'on puisse le boire; **to hear her speak, you'd think she owned the place!** à l'entendre, on dirait que c'est elle le propriétaire des lieux!; **he left the house never to return to it again** il quitta la maison pour ne plus y revenir

2 I have a letter to write j'ai une lettre à écrire; **I have a lot to do** j'ai beaucoup à faire; **there was not a sound to be heard** on n'entendait pas le moindre bruit; **he isn't one to forget his friends** il n'est pas homme à oublier ses amis; **there's a tendency to forget that** on a tendance à l'oublier; **I have no desire to do that** je n'ai aucun désir de le faire

VOIR GRAMMAIRE A55

3 to lie is shameful, it is shameful to lie il est honteux de mentir; **to be or not to be** être ou ne pas être; **it is better to do nothing** il vaut mieux ne rien faire; **he learned to do it** il a appris à le faire; **I refuse to do it** je refuse de le faire

4 (infinitive clause) **I want him to know** je veux qu'il sache; **it seemed to grow** il/elle semblait grandir

5 (in headline) **a hundred employees to go** cent employés vont être mis au chômage; **Blair to meet Chirac** entretiens entre Messieurs Blair et Chirac

6 (with ellipsis of verb) **you ought to** vous devriez le faire; **I want to** j'ai envie de le faire; (I would like to) je voudrais bien; **take it, it would be absurd not to** prenez-le, ce serait absurde de ne pas le faire ou de ne manquer l'occasion; **we shall have to** il le faudra bien, nous serons bien obligés

ADV (stressed) **1 to pull the door to** fermer la porte; **to turn to** or **set to with a will** se mettre résolument à l'ouvrage; **to come to** (to one's senses) reprendre connaissance

2 to go to and fro aller et venir; (of shuttle bus etc) faire la navette

toad [təʊd] **N 1** (animal) crapaud m; Fam Pej, Hum (person) crapule f; **you lying t.!** espèce de salaud de menteur! **2** Br Culin **t. in the hole** = saucisses fpl cuites au four dans de la pâte à crêpes

toadstool ['təʊdstuːl] **N** champignon m vénéneux

toady ['təʊdɪ] **N** lèche-bottes mf inv
VI to t. to sb lécher les bottes à qn

to-and-fro ADJ t. movement mouvement m de va-et-vient

toast [təʊst] **N 1** (toasted bread) pain m grillé, toast m; **piece** or **slice of t.** toast, tartine f grillée, rôtie f; **as warm as t.** bien chaud

2 (tribute) toast m; **to give** or **propose a t.** porter un toast; **to drink a t. to sb** boire à la santé de qn; **the t. was the future** on a porté un toast à l'avenir; **to be the t. of the town** être la célébrité de la ville

3 Fam **to be t.** (in trouble) être foutu; (exhausted) être naze ou crevé; **if Mum finds out, you're t.** si Maman s'en rend compte, t'es mort ou foutu!; **I can't drink any more or I'll be t. tomorrow** il faut que j'arrête de boire, sinon demain je serai dans le coaltar

VT 1 (bread) griller, faire griller; Fam **to t. one's feet (in front of the fire)** se rôtir les pieds (devant le feu); **toasted cheese** toast m au fromage; **toasted sandwich** sandwich m grillé

2 to t. sb porter un toast à (la santé de) qn, boire à la santé de qn

VI (of bread) griller; **it toasts well** ça fait du bon pain grillé

▸▸**t. master** maître m de cérémonies, animateur m (de réception); Br **t. rack** portetoasts m inv

toaster ['təʊstər] **N** grille-pain m inv; **sandwich t.** grill m (électrique)

toastie ['təʊstɪ] **N** Fam sandwich m grillé

toasting fork ['təʊstɪŋ] **N** fourchette f à rôties

toasty ['təʊstɪ] **N** Fam = toastie

tobacco, pl **tobaccos** [tə'bækəʊ, -əʊz] **N 1** tabac m; **chewing t.** tabac à chiquer ou mâcher; **t.-coloured** tabac inv **2** (plant) tabac m
▸▸**t. plant** tabac; **t. pouch** blague f à tabac; **t. smoke** fumée f de tabac; **t. tin** boîte f à tabac, tabatière f

tobacconist [tə'bækənɪst] **N** Br (person) marchand, -ande de tabac, buraliste mf; **t.'s** (shop) (bureau m ou débit m de) tabac m
▸▸**t.'s shop** (bureau ou débit de) tabac

Tobin tax ['təʊbɪn] **N** Fin taxe f Tobin

toboggan [tə'bɒgən] **N** (for children), Sport luge f
VI (of child), Sport faire de la luge; **to t. down a slope** descendre une pente en luge
▸▸**t. run** piste f de luge

> Note that the French word **toboggan** is a false friend. Its most common meaning is **slide** (in a playground).

tobogganing [tə'bɒgənɪŋ] **N** luge f; **to go t.** faire de la luge

toby jug ['təʊbɪ] **N** = pot m à bière décoratif (en forme de gros bonhomme à tricorne)

tocsin ['tɒksɪn] **N** tocsin m

tod [tɒd] **N** Br Sl **on my/his/etc t.** tout seul

today [tə'deɪ] **ADV** aujourd'hui; **it's a week ago t.** ça fait une semaine aujourd'hui; **t. week** aujourd'hui en huit; Fam **he's the kind who'll be here t. and gone tomorrow** (in job, relationship etc) c'est le genre de type qui ne peut pas se fixer; **a here today and gone tomorrow fashion** une mode qui ne durera pas
N aujourd'hui m; **t.'s the day …!** c'est aujourd'hui que …!; **t.'s paper** le journal d'aujourd'hui ou du jour; **t.'s date/price** la date/ le prix du jour; **t.'s date is …** aujourd'hui, nous sommes le … ; **t.'s special** plat m du jour; **the young people of t.** les jeunes d'aujourd'hui

toddle ['tɒd(ə)l] **N** Fam (short walk) petite promenade f, balade f; **I'm going for a t.** je vais faire un tour, je vais me balader
VI 1 (of young child) marcher à petits pas chancelants; **she's just started toddling** elle commence à peine à marcher **2** Fam (of adult) trottiner; **I'd better be toddling (along)** (leaving) il faut que j'y aille; **I'm just going to t. into town** je vais juste faire un tour en ville
▸**toddle off VI** Fam (leave) partir, lever le camp

toddler ['tɒdlər] **N** enfant mf qui commence à marcher

toddy ['tɒdɪ] **N** grog m

todger ['tɒdʒər] **N** Br Sl (penis) chipolata f

to-die-for ADJ Fam de rêve

to-do N Fam remue-ménage m inv; **what a t.!** quelle histoire!; **there was a great t. about it** l'affaire a fait grand bruit

toe [təʊ] **N** Anat orteil m, doigt m de pied; **big/little t.** gros/petit orteil; **on the tips of one's toes** sur la pointe des pieds; **to tread** or **stand on sb's toes** marcher sur les pieds de qn; Fig **I hope I'm not treading on any toes** j'espère que je n'empiète sur les platesbandes de personne; Fig **to be on one's toes** être en alerte, être vigilant; Fig **to keep people on their toes** faire en sorte que les gens restent vigilants **2** (of shoe etc) bout m, pointe f
VT 1 Ftbl (ball) frapper de la pointe du pied **2** Sport **to t. the line** or **the mark** s'aligner; Fig **to t. the line** obéir, s'exécuter; Fig **to t. the party line** s'aligner sur la position officielle du parti

toecap ['təʊkæp] **N** bout m rapporté

-toed [-təʊd] **SUFF two/three/etc-t.** à deux/ trois/etc orteils; **square/pointed/etc-t.** (shoes) à bouts carrés/pointus/etc

toehold ['təʊhəʊld] **N** (in climbing) prise f de pied; Fig **to gain a t. in the market** mettre un pied sur le marché; **to maintain a t. on reality** garder un lien, si ténu soit-il, avec la réalité

toe-in N Aut pincement m des roues avant

toenail ['təʊneɪl] **N** ongle m d'orteil

toe-out N Aut ouverture f, pincement m négatif

toepiece ['təʊpiːs] **N** (on ski) butée f

toerag ['təʊræg] **N** Br Sl merdeux, -euse

toff [tɒf] **N** Old-fashioned Br Fam aristo mf; **the toffs** le gratin

toffee ['tɒfɪ] **N** caramel m au beurre; Fam **he can't sing for t.** il chante comme une casserole
▸▸**t. apple** pomme f d'amour (confiserie)

toffee-nosed [-nəʊzd] **ADJ** esp Br Fam snob, snobinard

tofu ['təʊfuː] **N** tofu m

▸**tog up, tog out** [tɒg] **VT SEP** Fam (dress smartly) fringuer; **to t. oneself up** bien se fringuer, se mettre sur trente et un; **to be (all) togged up** (dressed up) être sur son trente et un; (for tennis, football etc) être en tenue

toga ['təʊgə] **N** (garment) toge f

together [tə'geðər] **ADV** ensemble; **to go or belong t.** aller ensemble; **we stand or fall t.** nous sommes tous solidaires; **t. with** (as well as) ainsi que; (at the same time as) en même temps que; **the Swedes objected t. with the French** les Suédois émirent une objection, de même que les Français; **to gather** or **collect** or **bring t.** réunir, rassembler; **to gather t.** (come together) se réunir, se rassembler; **to add t.** additionner; **to act t.** agir de concert; **to be t. again** (of couple, partners) être de nouveau ensemble; **to get t. again** (of couple, partners) se remettre ensemble; **the family will all be t. at Christmas** la famille sera réunie à Noël; **all t.** (everybody gathered) tous ensemble; (at the same time) tous à la fois; **all t. now!** (sing) tous en chœur maintenant!; **all t. now! – push!** tous ensemble maintenant! – poussez!; **all t. it cost us £480** l'ensemble nous a coûté 480 livres; **for hours t.** des heures durant, pendant des heures et des heures; Fam **she's really got it t.** (in life) elle sait ce qu'elle fait; (in job etc) elle domine son sujet; **I never thought he would get it t.** je n'aurais jamais pensé qu'il y arriverait
ADJ Fam (person) équilibré; **the band weren't very t.** (didn't play in unison) le groupe ne jouait pas vraiment ensemble

togetherness [tə'geðənɪs] **N** (unity) unité f, harmonie f; **the earlier feeling of t. had gone out of their relationship** le sentiment de former un couple uni qu'ils avaient éprouvé auparavant avait disparu; **the feeling of t. generated by a family Christmas** ce sentiment de chaleureuse communion que l'on ressent lors des Noëls passés en famille; **we all had a feeling of t. at the party conference** nous avons tous éprouvé un sentiment de cohésion lors du congrès du parti

toggle ['tɒg(ə)l] **N** (on duffel coat etc) olive f, barrette f
VI Comput basculer; **to t. between two applications** alterner entre deux applications; **to t. sth on/off** sélectionner/désélectionner qch
▸▸Comput **t. key** touche f à bascule; **t. switch** Elec interrupteur m à bascule; Comput commande f à bascule

Togo ['təʊgəʊ] **N** Togo m

Togolese [təʊgə'liːz] **ADJ** togolais
N Togolais, -aise

togs [tɒgz] **NPL** Fam (clothes) fringues fpl, frusques fpl

toil [tɔɪl] N *Fml, Lit* dur labeur *m*, peine *f*; **a life of t. and trouble** une vie de douleur et de peine

vi (*work hard*) travailler dur (**at** à), peiner (**at** sur); **to be toiling** (*having difficulty in race, finishing meal etc*) peiner; **I'm toiling to finish this drink as it is** j'ai déjà assez de mal à finir ce verre; **to t. up a hill** gravir péniblement une colline; **to t. on** (*continue work*) continuer péniblement son travail; (*continue journey*) continuer péniblement sa route

vt he toiled his way through a mass of papers il a dû laborieusement lire tout un tas de documents

toiler ['tɔɪlər] N travailleur, -euse

toilet ['tɔɪlɪt] N **1** (*lavatory*) (*device*) cabinets *mpl*; (*room*) cabinet de toilette; **toilets** toilettes *fpl*; **to go to the t.** aller aux toilettes; **he's still in the t.** il est encore aux toilettes; **to throw sth down the t.** jeter qch dans les toilettes; *Fam* **to go down the t.** (*of plan, career, work*) être foutu en l'air; **that's our holidays down the t.!** on peut faire une croix sur nos vacances! **2** *Old-fashioned* (*washing and dressing*) toilette *f*; **to make** or **perform one's t.** faire sa toilette

► ► **t. block** bloc *m* sanitaire; **t. bowl** cuvette *f* (de W-C); **t. case** nécessaire *m* ou trousse *f* de toilette; **t. humour** humour *m* scatologique; **t. paper** papier *m* hygiénique; **t. roll** (*roll*) rouleau *m* de papier hygiénique; (*paper*) papier hygiénique; **t. seat** siège *m* des cabinets ou W-C ou toilettes; **t. soap** savon *m* de toilette; **t. table** (table *f* de) toilette, coiffeuse *f*; **t. tissue** papier hygiénique; **t. training** apprentissage *m* de la propreté (*pour un enfant*); **t. water** eau *f* de toilette

toiletries ['tɔɪlɪtrɪz] NPL articles *mpl* de toilette

toilet-trained ADJ propre

toils [tɔɪlz] NPL *Lit, Fig* (*net*) filets *mpl*

toilsome ['tɔɪlsəm] ADJ *Lit* pénible

toing and froing [tu:ɪŋən'frəʊɪŋ] N va-et-vient *m*

Tokay [tə'kaɪ] N (*wine*) tokai *m*, tokaï *m*, tokay *m*

toke [təʊk] *Sl* N (*of joint*) taffe *f*; **to take a t.** prendre une taffe

vi to t. on a joint prendre une taffe d'un joint

token ['təʊk(ə)n] N **1** (*indication*) (*of identity, respect etc*) marque *f*, témoignage *m*; **in t.** or **as a t. of sincerity** en signe ou en témoignage de bonne foi; **by the same t.** (*therefore*) donc; (*equally*) pareillement; **a t. black person/t. woman** un noir/une femme qui est là pour la forme; *Mil etc* **a t. force** une force symbolique **2** (*disc etc*) (*for vending machine etc*) jeton *m*; **gift t.** bon *m* d'achat; **book t.** chèque-livre *m*, *pl* chèques-livres; **record t.** chèque-disque *m*, *pl* chèques-disques **3** *Old-fashioned* (*symbol*) signe *m*; **love t.** gage *m* d'amour

► ► **t. payment** paiement *m* symbolique ou d'avertissement; *Comput* **t. ring network** réseau *m* en anneau à jeton; **t. strike** grève *f* symbolique ou d'avertissement

tokenism ['təʊkənɪz(ə)m] N = pratique *f* qui consiste à nommer une ou deux personnes des minorités (femme, noir etc) pour donner l'impression d'une libéralisation; **the appointment of a woman to the board was nothing but t.** ils ont nommé une femme au conseil d'administration uniquement pour la forme

Tokyo ['təʊkɪəʊ] N Tokyo

told PT, PP *see* **tell**

Toledo [tɒ'leɪdəʊ] N Tolède

tolerable ['tɒlərəb(ə)l] ADJ **1** (*pain etc*) tolérable, supportable **2** (*acceptable*) passable; (*quite good*) assez bon; **we're in t. health** nous nous portons assez bien

tolerably ['tɒlərəblɪ] ADV passablement; **I'm t. well** je me porte assez bien; **it was t. well done** c'était assez bien fait

tolerance ['tɒlərəns] N **1** (*religious etc*) tolérance *f*; **to show great t.** faire preuve de beaucoup de tolérance ou d'une grande indulgence **2** (*for drug, alcohol*) tolérance *f* (**of, for** à); **increasing t.** (*to drug*) accoutumance *f* **3** *Tech etc* tolérance *f*, écart *m* admissible

tolerant ['tɒlərənt] ADJ **1** tolérant; (*parent etc*) tolérant, indulgent **2** *Med* **t. of a drug** (*patient*) qui tolère une drogue

tolerantly ['tɒlərəntlɪ] ADV avec tolérance; **to be t. disposed toward sb/sth** se montrer tolérant envers qn/qch

tolerate ['tɒləreɪt] VT **1** (*pain, contradiction etc*) tolérer, supporter; (*person, behaviour*) supporter; **I will not t. this behaviour** je ne supporterai pas une telle conduite **2** *Med* (*drug*) tolérer

toleration [tɒlə'reɪʃən] N tolérance *f*

toll¹ [təʊl] N **1** (*charge*) péage *m*, droit *m* de passage; *Fig* **to take its t.** (*of disease etc*) faire beaucoup de victimes; (*have severe effect*) laisser des traces (**of sb** sur qn); **accident that takes a heavy t. of human life** accident qui cause beaucoup de morts; **the years had taken their t.** or **a heavy t. on her health** sa santé s'était affaiblie avec le temps **2** *Am* **to call t. free** appeler gratuitement

► ► **t. bar** barrière *f* (de péage); **t. booth** poste *f* de péage; **t. bridge** pont *m* à péage; *Am Tel* **t. call** communication *f* interurbaine; **t. gate** barrière (de péage); **t. house** péage; **t. road** route *f* à péage

toll² N (*of bell*) tintement *m*, son *m* (de cloche); (*for death*) glas *m*

vt (*bell*) sonner; **the church clock tolled midday** l'horloge de l'église a sonné midi; **to t. sb's death** sonner le glas pour la mort de qn

vi (*of bell*) tinter, sonner; (*for death*) sonner le glas; **to t. for the dead** sonner pour les morts

toll-free number N *Am* ≃ numéro *m* vert

tolling ['təʊlɪŋ] N (*of bell*) tintement *m*; (*for death*) glas *m*

tollway ['təʊlweɪ] N *Am* autoroute *f* à péage

Tom [tɒm] N Thomas, Tom; *Fam* **any T., Dick or Harry** n'importe qui, le premier venu

► ► **T. Thumb** le Petit Poucet

tom [tɒm] N (*cat*) matou *m*

► ► **t. cat** matou

tomahawk ['tɒməhɔ:k] N hache *f* de guerre, tomahawk *m*

tomato, *pl* **tomatoes** [tə'mɑ:təʊ, -əʊz, *Am* tə'meɪtəʊ] N tomate *f*

► ► **t. juice** jus *m* de tomates; **t. ketchup** ketchup *m*; **t. purée** concentré *m* ou purée *f* de tomates; **t. sauce** sauce *f* tomate; (*ketchup*) ketchup

tomb [tu:m] N tombe *f*, tombeau *m*

tombac ['tɒmbæk] N *Metal* tombac *m*

tombola [tɒm'bəʊlə] N *Br* tombola *f*

tomboy ['tɒmbɔɪ] N garçon *m* manqué

tomboyish ['tɒmbɔɪɪʃ] ADJ (*behaviour etc*) de garçon manqué

tombstone ['tu:mstəʊn] N pierre *f* tombale

tomcat ['tɒmkæt] N matou *m*

► **tomcat around** VI *Am Fam* courir les filles

tome [təʊm] N (*volume*) tome *m*; (*large book*) gros livre *m*; *Fam* (*book*) bouquin *m*

tomfool [tɒm'fu:l] ADJ *Fam* idiot; **t. scheme** projet *m* insensé

tomfoolery [tɒm'fu:lərɪ] N *Fam* âneries *fpl*, bêtises *fpl*

tommy ['tɒmɪ] N *Br* (*soldier*) simple soldat *m* (de l'armée britannique), *Fam* troufion *m*

► ► *Mil* **T. gun** mitraillette *f*

tommyrot ['tɒmɪrɒt] N *Old-fashioned Fam* bêtises *fpl*, inepties *fpl*; **that's all t.** tout ça, c'est de la blague

tomography [tə'mɒgrəfɪ] N *Med* tomographie *f*

tomorrow [tə'mɒrəʊ] ADV demain; **t. morning** demain matin; **t. night** demain soir; **t. week** demain en huit

N demain *m*; **the day after t.** après-demain; **t.'s breakfast** le petit déjeuner de demain; **who knows what t. holds?** qui sait ce que demain nous réserve?; **t. never comes** c'est maintenant ou jamais; *Prov* **never put off till t. what you can do today** il ne faut pas remettre au lendemain ce qu'on peut faire le jour même; *Fam* **she was eating like there was no t.** elle mangeait comme si son dernier jour était arrivé; *Fig* **what will the world be like t.?** à quoi ressemblera le monde demain?; **the cities of t., t.'s cities** les villes de demain

tomtit ['tɒmtɪt] N (*bird*) mésange *f* bleue

tom-tom N tam-tam *m*, *pl* tam-tams

ton [tʌn] N **1** (*weight*) tonne *f*; *Br* (**long**) **t.** tonne longue (= 1016 kg); *Am* (**short** or **net**) **t.** tonne courte (= 907 kg); **metric t.** tonne (métrique) (= 1 000 kg); *Fam* **this suitcase weighs a t.** cette valise est rudement lourde ou pèse une tonne **2** *Fam Fig* **tons of …** (*lots of*) des tonnes de …; **we've tons of time** nous avons tout notre temps; **there's tons of it** il y en a des tas **3** *esp Br Sl* (*100 mph*) vitesse *f* de cent soixante à l'heure; (*score of 100*) cent *m*; (£*100*) cent livres *fpl*; **to do a t.** (*of vehicle, driver etc*) faire du cent soixante à l'heure

tonal ['təʊn(ə)l] ADJ tonal, -als

tonality [təʊ'nælɪtɪ] N tonalité *f*

tone [təʊn] N **1** (*sound*) son *m*; (*quality*) sonorité *f*; (*of voice, musical instrument*) timbre *m*; *Tel* **ringing t.** tonalité *f* d'appel; **record your message after the t.** laissez votre message après le bip sonore

2 (*sound of voice*) ton *m*, timbre *m*; **I knew by the t. of his voice** j'ai compris au ton ou timbre de sa voix; **in an impatient t.** avec impatience; **in an angry t. of voice** sur le ton de la colère; **I don't like your t.** (*of voice*), **don't take that t. with me** je vous prierai de ne pas me parler sur ce ton; **in a low t.** à voix basse; **to give a serious t. to a discussion** donner un ton sérieux à une discussion; **it was the t. of the letter I didn't like** c'est le ton de cette lettre qui ne m'a pas plu

3 (*in acoustics*), *Mus* ton *m*; **whole t.** ton entier; **quarter t.** quart *m* de ton

4 *Art* (*of colour*) ton *m*, nuance *f*; *Phot* (*of print*) ton; **warm tones** tons chauds; *Art* **half t.** similigravure *f*, *Fam* simili *f*

5 *Ling* ton *m*, accent *m* tonique, accent de hauteur

6 *Med* (*of muscles etc*) tonicité *f*, tonus *m*

vt (*picture*) adoucir les tons de; *Phot* (*print*) virer; **toned paper** papier *m* teinté, papier crémé

► ► **t. arm** bras *m* de lecture; **t. control** bouton *m* de tonalité; *Ling* **t. language** langue *f* à tons; *Mus* **t. poem** poème *m* symphonique

► **tone down** VT SEP **1** (*make less bright*) (*colour etc*) adoucir, atténuer **2** (*moderate*) (*remarks etc*) modérer, adoucir; **the editor had to t. down the article** le rédacteur a dû atténuer les termes de l'article

► **tone in** VI (*of colour etc*) s'harmoniser (**with** avec)

► **tone up** VT SEP (*make stronger*) (*muscles*) tonifier

vi (*become stronger*) (*of muscles*) se tonifier

▸**tone with** VT INSEP *(match, nearly match) (of colour, wallpaper etc)* s'harmoniser avec

tone-deaf ADJ incapable de reconnaître les notes; *(not appreciating music)* qui n'a aucun sens musical

tone-deafness N incapacité f à reconnaître les notes; *(lack of musical appreciation)* manque m de sens musical

toneless ['təʊnlɪs] ADJ *(voice)* blanc, f blanche, atone

tonelessly ['təʊnlɪslɪ] ADV *(to say)* d'une voix blanche *ou* atone

toner ['təʊnər] N 1 *(cosmetic)* lotion f tonique 2 *(for photocopier, printer, fax)* toner m, encre f; **t. cartridge** *or* **cassette** cartouche f de toner; **t. low warning** signal m de baisse du toner

Tonga ['tɒŋgə] N Tonga fpl

Tongan ['tɒŋgən] ADJ tongan
N 1 Tonguien, -ienne 2 *Ling* tongan m

tongs [tɒŋz] NPL **(pair of) t.** pince(s) f(pl); *(in glassmaking)* morailles fpl; **fire t.** pincettes fpl; *Culin* **sugar t.** pince à sucre VOIR GRAMMAIRE A10

tongue [tʌŋ] N 1 *Anat, Culin* langue f; **to stick one's t. out** tirer la langue (**at sb** à qn); **the dog's t. was hanging out** le chien tirait la langue; **his t. was hanging out** *(from thirst)* il crevait de soif; *(in expectation)* il en bavait d'envie; **to have a ready** *or* **glib t.** avoir la langue déliée *ou* bien pendue; **hold your t.!** taisez-vous!; **to find one's t.** retrouver la parole *ou* sa langue; **have you lost your t.?** tu as perdu ta langue?; *Fig* **with one's t. in one's cheek** en plaisantant; **she was being t. in cheek** elle plaisantait; **it's hard to get your t. round these words** ces mots sont difficiles à prononcer 2 *esp Lit (language)* langue f, idiome m; **the German t.** la langue allemande; *esp Bible* **the gift of tongues** le don des langues 3 *(of land, flame)* langue f, *(of shoe)* patte f, languette f, *(of bell)* battant m; *Mus (of oboe)* anche f; *Carp* languette f
VT *Mus* **to t. a passage** *(on wind instrument)* détacher les notes d'un passage avec la langue
▸▸**t. twister** = mot m *ou* phrase f difficile à prononcer

tongue-and-groove *Carp* N *(joint, edge)* assemblage m à languette; *(wood)* lattes fpl à languette
VT *(boards, slats)* pratiquer des languettes et des rainures sur

tongue-in-cheek ADJ *(remark, article)* fait pour plaisanter, ironique

tongue-lash VT tancer vertement

tongue-lashing N **to give sb a t.** tancer qn vertement

tongue-tied ADJ *(with shyness etc)* muet; *(with surprise etc)* interdit; **it's not like her to be t.** ça ne lui ressemble pas de rester sans rien dire

tonguing ['tʌŋɪŋ] N *Mus (on wind instrument)* coup m de langue

tonic ['tɒnɪk] ADJ 1 *Med etc* tonique, fortifiant 2 *Gram (accent)* tonique; *Mus (note)* tonique
N 1 *Med* tonique m, remontant m, fortifiant m; *Fig* **to be a t. for sb** *(of news etc)* réconforter *ou* remonter qn; **he's a t.** il vous remonte le moral, il est stimulant 2 *(drink)* Schweppes® m, **gin and t.** gin-tonic m, pl gin-tonics 3 *Mus* tonique f
▸▸*Mus* **t. solfa** solfège m; **t. water** ≃ Schweppes®

tonicity [təʊ'nɪsɪtɪ] N *(of muscles etc)* tonicité f

tonight [tə'naɪt] ADV *(evening)* ce soir; *(night)* cette nuit
N *(evening)* ce soir m; *(night)* cette nuit; **t.'s main news** et voici les titres du journal *ou* de l'actualité

toning ['təʊnɪŋ] N *Phot (of prints)* virage m
▸▸**t. down** *(of colour, remarks)* atténuation f, adoucissement m; **t. lotion** lotion f tonifiante

tonnage ['tʌnɪdʒ] N *Naut* tonnage m; **register(ed) t.** tonnage net
▸▸**t. certificate** certificat m de jaugeage

tonne [tʌn] N tonne f (métrique)

tonneau cover ['tɒnəʊ] N *Aut* bâche f

tonsil ['tɒns(ə)l] N *Anat* amygdale f, **to have one's tonsils out** se faire opérer des amygdales; *Fam Hum* **to play t. hockey** se rouler des pelles *ou* des patins

tonsillectomy [tɒnsɪ'lektəmɪ] N amygdalectomie f

tonsillitis [tɒnsɪ'laɪtɪs] N *Med* angine f, *Spéc* amygdalite f; **to have t.** avoir une angine *ou* *Spéc* amygdalite

tonsure ['tɒnʃər] N tonsure f
VT *(monk)* tonsurer

tontine [tɒn'tiːn] N *(in insurance)* tontine f

ton-up ADJ
▸▸*Old-fashioned Br Fam* **t. boy** = fou m de moto

tonus ['təʊnəs] N *Med* tonicité f, tonus m

too [tuː] ADV 1 *(excessively)* trop; **it's t. difficult** c'est trop difficile; **t. difficult a job** un travail trop difficile; **t. many people** trop de gens; **t. far** trop loin; **to work t. much** *or* **t. hard** travailler trop, trop travailler; **50p t. much** 50p de trop; **this job's t. much for me** ce travail est au-dessus de mes forces; **I've listened to him t. long** je l'ai trop écouté; **I know her all** *or* **only t. well** je ne la connais que trop; **you're t. kind** vous êtes très *ou* trop gentil; **he's not t. well today** il ne va pas très bien aujourd'hui; *Br Fam* **t. right!** et comment!, vous l'avez dit! VOIR GRAMMAIRE A5

2 *(also)* aussi, également; **you're coming t.** vous venez aussi; **she t. is a painter** elle aussi est peintre

3 *(moreover)* en *ou* de plus; **30° in the shade and in September t.** 30° à l'ombre et en septembre en plus

toodle-oo, **toodle-pip** ['tuːd(ə)l'uː, -'pɪp] INT *Old-fashioned Br Fam (goodbye)* salut!

took PT *see* **take** VT, VI

tool [tuːl] N 1 *(implement)* outil m; **(set of) tools** outillage m; **garden** *or* **gardening tools** outils de jardinage; **power t.** outil à moteur; **you have to learn the tools of your trade** on ne peut pratiquer un métier sans apprentissage 2 *Fig (means, instrument)* instrument m; **to use sb as a t.** utiliser qn; **he was a mere t. in their hands** il n'était qu'un instrument entre leurs mains 3 *Sl (penis)* bite f
VT 1 *(leather, binding)* ciseler; *Tech (wrought iron)* usiner, travailler; **tooled leather** cuir m repoussé 2 = **tool up** VT SEP 1
▸▸**t. bag** sac m à outils; **t. holder** porte-outil m, pl porte-outil(s); **t. kit** trousse f à outils; **t. rack** râtelier m à outils; **t. set** jeu m d'outils, pl jeux d'outils; **t. shed** reserre f, remise f
▸**tool up** VT SEP 1 *(equip with tools) (factory etc)* outiller 2 *Br Sl* **to be tooled up** *(carrying a weapon)* être armé
VI *(become equipped with tools)* s'outiller

toolbar N *Comput* barre f d'outils

toolbox ['tuːlbɒks] N boîte f *ou* coffre m à outils; *Comput* boîte à outils

tooling ['tuːlɪŋ] N *(of leather, binding)* ciselage m; *Tech* usinage m

tool-maker N fabricant m d'outils, outilleur m

toon [tuːn] N *Am Fam (cartoon)* dessin m animé

toot [tuːt] N 1 *Naut* coup m de sirène; *Aut* coup de klaxon; *Aut* **to give sb a t.** donner un coup de klaxon à qn, klaxonner qn 2 *Sl (of cocaine)* prise f de coke 3 *Am Fam (drink-*

ing spree) **to go on the t.** prendre une cuite
VT 1 **to t. a horn/a trumpet** sonner du cor/ de la trompette; *Aut* **to t. the horn** klaxonner; *Aut Fam* **to t. sb** klaxonner qn 2 *Sl (cocaine)* sniffer
VI 1 *(of person)* sonner du cor; *(of instrument)* sonner; *Aut (of driver)* klaxonner 2 *Sl (sniff cocaine)* sniffer de la coke

tooth, pl **teeth** [tuːθ, tiːθ] N 1 dent f, **(set of) teeth** denture f, dentition f; **first** *or* **milk teeth** dents de lait; **buck teeth** dents proéminentes; **(set of) false teeth** dentier m, *Fam* râtelier m; **to have a fine set of teeth** avoir de belles dents; **to cut one's teeth** faire *ou* percer ses dents; *Fig* **to cut one's teeth on sth** se faire les dents pour qch; **to have a t. out** se faire arracher une dent; **to kick sb in the teeth** donner un coup de pied à qn dans les dents; *Fig* traiter qn avec mépris; **in the teeth of all opposition** malgré *ou* en dépit de toute opposition; **to show** *or* **bare one's teeth** montrer les dents; **armed to the teeth** armé jusqu'aux dents; **to give a law teeth** renforcer une loi; **to fight t. and nail** se battre bec et ongles; **a meal/book you can get your teeth into** un repas/livre consistant; *Fam* **a job you can get your teeth into** un boulot dans lequel on peut s'en donner à cœur joie; **I want to get my teeth into the problem** je veux m'attaquer à ce problème; **to grit one's teeth** serrer les dents; *Fam* **I'm fed up to the back teeth with it** j'en ai plein le dos de ce truc-là; *Fam* **she's a bit long in the t.** elle n'est plus toute jeune; *Fam* **I'm getting a bit long in the t. for that** je commence à me faire un peu trop vieux pour ça 2 *(of saw, comb, cog)* dent f; **teeth** *(of wheel)* denture f
▸▸**t. decay** carie f dentaire; **the t. fairy** ≃ la petite souris; **t. glass, t. mug** verre m à dents; **t. powder** poudre f dentifrice

toothache ['tuːθeɪk] N mal m *ou* rage f de dents; **to have t.** avoir mal aux dents

toothbrush ['tuːθbrʌʃ] N brosse f à dents

toothed [tuːθt] ADJ 1 *(animal)* denté; *(leaf etc)* dentelé 2 *Tech etc* **t. belt** courroie f crantée; **t. wheel** roue f dentée

toothless ['tuːθlɪs] ADJ sans dents, édenté; *Fig (law etc)* qu'on n'a pas les moyens de faire respecter; **the committee has been criticized for being t.** on a reproché son impuissance à la commission

toothpaste ['tuːθpeɪst] N pâte f dentifrice, dentifrice m

toothpick ['tuːθpɪk] N cure-dent(s) m, pl cure-dents

toothsome ['tuːθsəm] ADJ *(tasty)* savoureux

toothy ['tuːθɪ] ADJ aux dents fpl saillantes, *Pej* aux dents de cheval; **to give a big t. grin** sourire à pleines dents
▸▸**t. peg** *(in children's language)* dent f

tooting ['tuːtɪŋ] N *Aut* coups mpl de klaxon

tootle ['tuːt(ə)l] VI 1 *Aut (toot)* corner, klaxonner 2 *Br Fam (go) (in car)* rouler tranquillement; *(on foot)* se balader
▸**tootle along** VI *Br Fam (go)* aller tout tranquillement; **well, I'll t. along now** bon, je vais me mettre en route

toots [tʊts] N *Fam (term of address)* chéri, -ie

tootsy ['tʊtsɪ] N *Fam (in children's language) (foot)* peton m; *(toe)* doigt m de pied

TOP [tɒp]

N	haut **1, 3** ▪ sommet **1** ▪ cime **1** ▪ bout **1** ▪ surface **2** ▪ dessus **2, 3** ▪ couvercle **3** ▪ bouchon **3** ▪ capsule **3** ▪ corsage **3** ▪ toupie **8**
ADJ	du dessus **1** ▪ du haut **1** ▪ d'en haut **1** ▪ dernier **1** ▪ premier **2**
VT	surmonter **2** ▪ garnir **2** ▪ dépasser **3** ▪ être en tête de **5**

N 1 *(highest point) (of tree, mountain)* haut *m*, sommet *m*, cime *f*, faîte *m*; *(of tower, head)* sommet; *(of page, map)* haut; *(end) (of table)* bout *m*; **he always sat at the t. of the table** à table, c'était toujours lui qui présidait; **to make it to the t.** *(in profession, sport, music etc)* se faire une place parmi les grands; **at the t. of the stairs** en haut de l'escalier; **at the t. of the street** au bout de la rue; **at the t. of the tree** en haut de l'arbre; *Fig* au sommet de sa profession; **it went right to the t.** *(of complaint, request etc)* cela est remonté jusqu'au sommet; *Sch* **to be (at) the t. of the class** être le premier/la première de la classe; **to be (at) the t. of the bill** *(of actor, singer etc)* être en haut de l'affiche; **from t. to bottom** de haut en bas; *(to search a flat etc)* de fond en comble; **from t. to toe** de la tête aux pieds; **to shout/sing at the t. of one's voice** crier/chanter à tue-tête; **to be on** *or* **at the t. of one's form** être *ou* se sentir en pleine forme; *Ir Fam* **(the) t. of the morning (to you)** bien le bonjour!; *Mil* **to go over the t.** (sortir des tranchées pour) aller à l'assaut; *Fam* **over the t.** *(overdone)* excessif; **I find her a bit over the t.** je trouve qu'elle exagère un peu; **turnip/carrot tops** fanes *fpl* de navets/de carottes

2 *(surface) (of table etc)* surface *f*, dessus *m*; *(of bus)* impériale *f*; **t. of the milk** crème *f* du lait

3 *(part) (of shoe)* dessus *m*; *(of box, pan etc)* couvercle *m*; *(of bottle etc)* bouchon *m*, capsule *f*; *(of pen etc)* capuchon *m*; *(of dress)* haut *m*, corsage *m*; *(separate garment)* haut; *Fam* **to blow one's t.** sortir de ses gonds

4 on t. of *(on)* sur; **on t. (of the pile)** sur le dessus (de la pile); **to put sth on t. of sth** mettre qch sur qch; **to put sth right on the t. of sth** mettre qch tout en haut de qch; **just put it on t.** mets-le sur le dessus; **a cake with a cherry on t.** un gâteau avec une cerise dessus; **to be on t.** *(be in control)* avoir le dessus; **to be on t. of the situation** maîtriser la situation; **you mustn't let things get on t. of you** il ne faut pas te laisser dépasser par les événements; **to come out on t.** prendre le dessus; **it's just one thing on t. of another** ça n'arrête jamais; **on t. of it all** et pour comble (de malheur), et en plus de tout cela; **to be** *or* **to feel on t. of the world** être *ou* se sentir en pleine forme

5 *Fam* **the tops** la crème, le gratin; **he's (the) tops!** c'est un as!; *Fam* **he's tops with me** pour moi, c'est le meilleur

6 the Big T. *(in circus)* le chapiteau

7 *Aut (gear)* vitesse *f* supérieure; **in t.** au rapport supérieur

8 (spinning *or* **peg) t.** *(toy)* toupie *f*

ADJ 1 *(highest)* du dessus, du haut, d'en haut; *(floor, stair)* dernier; **the t. people** *(prominent people)* les gens *mpl* en vue; *(in an organization)* les gros bonnets *mpl*; **all the t. people in New York eat there** c'est un restaurant où se retrouve toute l'élite new-yorkaise; *Fam* **to pay t. dollar for sth** dépenser beaucoup d'argent pour qch; **to be/to feel on t. form** être/se sentir en pleine forme; **t. shelf** étagère *f* du dessus *ou* du haut

2 *(best, major)* premier; **she got the t. mark** *or* **came t. in history** elle a eu la meilleure note en histoire; **the country's t. ten companies** les dix premières sociétés du pays; **one of the world's t. ten players** un des dix meilleurs joueurs mondiaux

VT (-pp-) 1 *(remove top of) (tree, plant)* écimer; *(tree)* étêter; **to t. and tail carrots** retirer les fanes et couper les bouts des carottes

2 *(provide top for)* surmonter, couronner, coiffer (**with** de); *Culin (dessert etc)* garnir (**with** de); *Fig* **and to t. it all** et pour comble (de malheur), et en plus de tout cela

3 *(exceed)* excéder, dépasser; **the takings have topped a thousand pounds** les recettes dépassent mille livres; **to t. sb by a head** dépasser qn d'une tête

4 *(reach top of) (hill etc)* atteindre le sommet de

5 *(be at top of)* être en tête de; **to t. a list/a class** être à la tête d'une liste/de la classe; **topping the bill tonight we have ...** le clou de cette soirée est ...; **to t. the charts** *(of record, singer)* être à la première place *ou* en tête des hit-parades

6 *Golf (ball)* calotter

7 *Sl* **to t. oneself** *(commit suicide)* se foutre en l'air

▸▸ *Br* **t. boots** bottes *fpl* hautes; *Fam* **the t. brass** *(in army)* les officiers *mpl* supérieurs; *(in company etc)* les gros bonnets *mpl*; **t. coat** *(of paint)* dernière couche *f*; *Br* **t. copy** original *m*; *Fam* **t. dog** chef *m*; **to be t. dog** *(have the advantage)* avoir le dessus; *Br Aut* **t. gear** vitesse supérieure; **t. hat** *(chapeau m)* haut-de-forme *m*, *pl* hauts-de-forme; **t. pupil** premier, -ière de la classe; **t. rate** *(of tax)* taux *m* maximum; **t. security** sécurité *f* maximum; **he was given t. security** il a bénéficié du maximum de sécurité; **t. speed** vitesse maximum, vitesse de pointe; **to travel at t. speed** *(of plane, train etc)* aller à sa vitesse maximale; **car with a t. speed of 150 kph** voiture avec un plafond de 150 km/h; **t. table** *(at wedding)* table *f* d'honneur; **t. ten** = hit-parade *m* des dix meilleures ventes de disques pop et rock; **in the t. ten** au hit-parade; **t. twenty** = hit-parade des vingt meilleures ventes de disques pop et rock; **in the t. twenty** au hit-parade

▸ **top off** VT SEP *(complete) (evening)* couronner; **topped off with a cherry** garni d'une cerise

▸ **top out** *Br Constr* VT SEP *(building)* célébrer l'achèvement de la construction de

  VI célébrer l'achèvement de la construction d'un immeuble

▸ **top up** VT SEP *(add more to) (glass etc)* remplir; *(mobile phone)* recharger le compte de; **to t. up one's life assurance premium** augmenter les versements de son assurance-vie; *Fam* **let me t. you up** vous en reprendrez bien un peu?; *Aut* **to t. up the battery/the oil/the tank/etc** ajouter de l'eau/de l'huile/de l'essence/etc; **the government tops up the rest** *(pays the balance)* le gouvernement met l'argent qui manque *ou* rajoute la différence

  VI *Aut (with oil)* ajouter de l'huile; *(with petrol)* faire le plein; *(add credit to one's mobile phone)* recharger son compte

topaz ['təʊpæz] N *(gem)* topaze *f*

top-bracket ADJ de première catégorie

topcoat ['tɒpkəʊt] N pardessus *m*, manteau *m*

top-down ADJ *(management)* contrôlé par le haut

▸▸ *Mktg* **t. forecasting** prévisions *fpl* hiérarchisées

top-drawer ADJ **1** *Old-fashioned Fam (upper class)* de la haute **2** = **top-flight**

top-dress VT *Agr* fumer en surface

tope [təʊp] VI *Old-fashioned Fam* boire, picoler

topee ['təʊpiː] N casque *m* colonial

toper ['təʊpər] N *Old-fashioned Fam* picoleur, -euse

top-flight ADJ de premier ordre, excellent

top-heavy ADJ trop lourd du haut; *Naut (ship)* trop chargé dans les hauts; *Fig (organization)* dont les dirigeants sont trop nombreux

top-hole ADJ *Old-fashioned Br Fam* épatant, au poil

topi ['təʊpiː] N = **topee**

topic ['tɒpɪk] N *(of text, discussion)* matière *f*, *(of conversation)* sujet *m*, thème *m*

topical ['tɒpɪk(ə)l] ADJ **1** *(question)* d'actualité; **matters of t. interest** des questions d'actualité; **it's very t.** c'est tout à fait d'actualité; **a few t. references in the text** quelques références à l'actualité dans le texte **2** *(index)* (organisé) par matières

topicality [tɒpɪ'kælɪtɪ] N actualité *f*

topically ['tɒpɪklɪ] ADV *(to write etc)* sur des thèmes d'actualité

topknot ['tɒpnɒt] N *(of bird)* huppe *f*, *(hair)* petit chignon *m*

topless ['tɒplɪs] ADJ *(dancer)* aux seins nus; **to go t.** *(of woman)* ne pas porter de haut ▸▸ **t. beach** plage *f* seins nus

top-level ADJ *(talks etc)* au plus haut niveau

topline ['tɒplaɪn] VT *Cin* jouer le rôle principal de

top-loader N *(washing machine)* machine *f* à laver à chargement par le haut

topmast ['tɒpməst] N *Naut* mât *m* de hune

topmost ['tɒpməʊst] ADJ le plus haut, le plus élevé

topnotch ['tɒpnɒtʃ] ADJ *Old-fashioned Fam* de premier ordre

top-of-the-range ADJ haut de gamme

topographer [tə'pɒɡrəfər] N topographe *m*

topographic(al) [tɒpə'ɡræfɪk, -ɪk(ə)l] ADJ topographique

topographically [tɒpə'ɡræfɪklɪ] ADV topographiquement

topography [tɒ'pɒɡrəfɪ] N topographie *f*

topologic(al) [tɒpə'lɒdʒɪk, -ɪk(ə)l] ADJ topologique

topology [tə'pɒlədʒɪ] N topologie *f*

-topped [-tɒpt] SUFF *Lit* **cloud-t. peaks** sommets couronnés de nuages; **ivory-t. walking stick** canne à pommeau d'ivoire

topper ['tɒpər] N *Fam (top hat)* haut-de-forme *m*, *pl* hauts-de-forme

topping ['tɒpɪŋ] ADJ *Old-fashioned Br Fam* excellent, formidable

  N *Culin (for dessert, pizza etc)* garniture *f*, **ice-cream with raspberry t.** glace recouverte d'un coulis de framboises

topple ['tɒp(ə)l] VI *(fall)* tomber; *Fig (of government etc)* tomber; *(of share prices)* chuter; **he toppled into the pool/over the edge of the cliff** il a culbuté dans la piscine/par-dessus la falaise

  VT faire tomber; *(building etc)* faire s'écrouler; *(government etc)* renverser

▸ **topple down, topple over** VI, VT SEP = **topple**

top-quality ADJ de qualité supérieure

top-rank(ing) ADJ haut placé; **t. civil servant** haut fonctionnaire *m*

tops [tɒps] ADV *Fam (at the most)* maxi; **it'll cost a fiver t.** ça coûtera cinq livres maxi *ou* à tout casser

topsail ['tɒps(ə)l] N *Naut* hunier *m*

top-secret ADJ *(information etc)* top secret, -ète

top-security ADJ ▸▸ **t. prison** prison *f* de haute sécurité; **t. wing** aile *f ou* quartier *m* de haute sécurité

top-shelf ADJ ▸▸ *Br* **t. magazine** revue *f* érotique

topside ['tɒpsaɪd] N **1** *Culin (of beef)* tende *f* de tranche **2** *Naut* **topsides** *(of ship)* accastillage *m*

topsoil ['tɒpsɔɪl] N *Agr* couche *f* arable

topsy-turvy [tɒpsɪ'tɜːvɪ] ADJ sens dessus dessous; **everything's t.** *(of organization etc)* c'est la confusion totale

  ADV **the whole world's turned t.** c'est le monde à l'envers

top-up N *Aut* (remplissage *m* d')appoint *m*; *(for mobile phone)* rechargement *m*; **let me give you a t.** *(when serving drinks)* vous en reprendrez bien un peu?

▸▸ **t. card** *(for mobile phone)* recharge *f*; **t. fees** = frais *mpl* de scolarité complémentaires déterminés par chaque université, venant s'ajouter aux frais fixes payés par tous les étudiants britanniques; **t. finance** fonds *m* complémentaire; **t. loan** prêt *m* complémentaire

toque [təʊk] N *(hat)* toque *f*

tor [tɔːr] N *(hill)* pic *m*, butte *f* rocheuse

torch [tɔːtʃ] N **1** *(flame)* torche *f*, flambeau *m*; *Fig* **the t. of liberty** le flambeau de la liberté; *Fig* **to carry a t. for sb** avoir un faible pour qn; **to put sth to the t.** mettre le feu à qch **2** *(for welding)* chalumeau *m* **3** *Br* **(electric) t.** lampe *f* (électrique) (de poche), torche *f* électrique

▸▸ **t. song** chanson *f* d'amour triste

torchbearer ['tɔːtʃbeərər] N porte-flambeau *m inv*

torchlight ['tɔːtʃlaɪt] N lumière *f* de torche(s) *ou* de flambeau(x); *(of electric torch)* lumière d'une/de la torche (électrique); **by t.** à la lumière des torches *ou* des flambeaux/d'une torche électrique

▸▸ **t. procession** retraite *f* aux flambeaux

tore PT *see* **tear²**

toreador ['tɒrɪədɔːr] N toréador *m*, torero *m*

torment¹ ['tɔːment] N *esp Lit* tourment *m*, supplice *m*; **the torments of jealousy** les tourments de la jalousie; **he suffered torments** il souffrait le martyre; **to be in t.** être au supplice

torment² [tɔːˈment] VT *(cause suffering to)* *(person)* tourmenter, *(stronger)* torturer; *(pester)* *(person, animal etc)* harceler; **tormented with remorse** tourmenté par les remords, en proie aux remords; **tormented soul** âme *f* tourmentée

tormentor [tɔːˈmentər] N bourreau *m*

torn PP *see* **tear²**

tornado, *pl* **tornadoes** [tɔːˈneɪdəʊ, -əʊz] N tornade *f*

Toronto [təˈrɒntəʊ] N Toronto

torpedo, *pl* **torpedoes** [tɔːˈpiːdəʊ, -əʊz] N **1** *Naut etc* torpille *f* **2** *(fish)* (poisson *m*) torpille *f* VT *(ship)*, *Fig* *(peace)* torpiller

▸▸ **t. boat** torpilleur *m*, vedette *f* lance-torpilles; **t. fish** (poisson) torpille *f*; **t. tube** tube *m* lance-torpilles

torpid ['tɔːpɪd] ADJ engourdi, torpide; **t. state** *(of animal)* engourdissement *m*

torpor ['tɔːpər], **torpidity** [tɔːˈpɪdɪtɪ] N torpeur *f*, engourdissement *m*

torque [tɔːk] N *Tech, Phys etc* moment *m* de torsion *ou* de rotation; *Aut* couple *m*, torque *m*; **starting t.** couple de *ou* au démarrage

▸▸ **t. converter** convertisseur *m* de couple; **t. plate** plateau *m* absorbeur de couple; **t. wrench** clé *f* dynamométrique

torqued [tɔːkt] ADJ *Am Fam* **1** *(angry)* furibard, furax **2** *(drunk)* bourré, fait

torrent ['tɒrənt] N torrent *m*; **it's raining in torrents** il pleut à torrents *ou* à verse; **t. of abuse/of tears** torrent *ou* déluge *m* d'injures/de larmes

torrential [tɒˈrenʃəl] ADJ torrentiel; **t. rain** pluie *f* diluvienne *ou* torrentielle

torrid ['tɒrɪd] ADJ *(heat, region, love affair)* torride

torsion ['tɔːʃən] N torsion *f*

▸▸ **t. bar** barre *f* de torsion

torso, *pl* **torsos** ['tɔːsəʊ, -əʊz] N *Anat, Art* torse *m*

tort [tɔːt] N *Law* acte *m* dommageable, préjudice *m*, délit *m* civil

tortoise ['tɔːtəs] N tortue *f* (terrestre)

tortoiseshell ['tɔːtəsʃel] N écaille *f* (de tortue); **t. comb** peigne *m* en écaille

▸▸ **t. cat** chat *m* écaille de tortue

tortuous ['tɔːtjʊəs] ADJ *(path, means)* tortueux; **to have a t. mind** avoir l'esprit tordu

tortuously ['tɔːtjʊəslɪ] ADV tortueusement

tortuousness ['tɔːtjʊəsnɪs] N *(of path, thinking etc)* caractère *m* tortueux

torture ['tɔːtʃər] N **1** torture *f*, instruments of t. instruments *mpl* de torture **2** *Fig (physical, mental pain)* torture *f*, supplice *m*; **wearing these shoes is t.** c'est un vrai supplice de porter ces chaussures

VT *(somebody)* torturer; *Fig (by making sb wait etc)* mettre au supplice; *Fig (text etc)* torturer; **tortured by remorse** torturé *ou* tenaillé par le remords

▸▸ **t. chamber** chambre *f* de torture; **t. victim** victime *f* de torture

torturer ['tɔːtʃərər] N tortionnaire *m*; *Hist* bourreau *m*

Tory ['tɔːrɪ] *Br Pol* N *(party member)* tory *m*, *(voter, supporter)* = partisan *m* du parti conservateur

ADJ tory, conservateur, -trice

Toryism ['tɔːrɪɪz(ə)m] N *Br Pol* torysme *m*

tosh [tɒʃ] N *Old-fashioned Br Fam* bêtises *fpl*, blague(s) *f(pl)*

toss [tɒs] N **1** *(of ball etc)* lancer *m*, lancement *m*; **it was decided by the t. of a coin** on a décidé cela (en tirant) à pile ou face; **to win/lose the t.** gagner/perdre à pile ou face; **to argue the t.** discuter inutilement *ou* pour rien **2** **t. of the head** brusque mouvement *m* de tête **3** *(fall)* **to take a t.** *(from horse etc)* faire une chute **4** *Br Sl* **he doesn't give a t.** **(what happens/etc)** il n'en a rien à fiche (de ce qui arrivera/etc); **who gives a t.?** qu'est-ce que ça peut foutre?

VT *(ball etc)* lancer, jeter en l'air; *(of bull)* *(person)* projeter en l'air; *(of sea etc)* secouer, ballotter; **to t. sth to sb** jeter qch à qn; **to t. sb in a blanket** faire sauter qn en l'air sur une couverture; **to t. a salad** remuer *ou* tourner *ou Fam* fatiguer une salade; **to t. a pancake** faire sauter une crêpe; **to t. a coin** jouer à pile ou face; **who's going to pay? – I'll t. you for it** qui va payer? – décidons-le à pile ou face; **to t. one's head** relever la tête avec dédain

VI **1** **to t. for sth** jouer qch à pile ou face **2** **to t. and turn in bed** se tourner et se retourner dans son lit **3** *(of waves)* s'agiter; **to t. on the waves** être ballotté par les flots; **to pitch and t.** *(of ship)* tanguer

▸ **toss about, toss around** VT SEP *(ball)* lancer, taper dans; *Fig Fam (idea)* étudier; **the ship, tossed about by the waves, …** le bateau, agité *ou* secoué *ou* ballotté par les vagues, …; **let's t. the idea around for a while** creusons un peu pour voir

▸ **toss across** VT SEP envoyer; **t. the newspaper across, will you?** envoie-moi le journal, s'il te plaît

▸ **toss away** VT SEP *(get rid of)* jeter

▸ **toss back** VT SEP *(ball)*, *Fig (report, proposal etc)* renvoyer; *(one's hair)* rejeter en arrière

▸ **toss off** VT SEP **1** *(drink quickly) (drink)* avaler d'un trait **2** *(complete quickly) (task, essay, article)* expédier **3** *Br Vulg (masturbate)* branler

VI *Br Vulg (masturbate)* se branler

▸ **toss out** VT SEP jeter; *Fam (rubbish)* balancer; **to t. sb out of a club** *(physically, cancel membership)* mettre qn à la porte *ou Fam* jeter qn d'un club

▸ **toss over** VT SEP = **toss across**

▸ **toss up** VT SEP *(throw up)* lancer, envoyer; **t. that brush up, will you** lance-moi *ou* envoie-moi la brosse, s'il te plaît; **to t. sth up**

into the air lancer *ou* envoyer qch en l'air

VI *(with coin)* tirer à pile ou face; **let's t. for it** jouons-le *ou* décidons-le à pile ou face

tosser ['tɒsər] N *Br Sl* connard *m*

tossing ['tɒsɪŋ] N *(of boat etc)* ballottement *m*

toss-up N **1** *(with coin)* coup *m* de pile ou face; **in the event of a tie the winner will be decided by a t.** en cas d'égalité, on tirera à pile ou face pour désigner le gagnant **2** *Fam* in the end it was a t. between Majorca and Rhodes finalement, nous avons dû choisir entre Majorque et Rhodes; **it's a t. which is best** il est impossible de dire quel est le meilleur; **I don't know, it's a t.** je ne sais pas, c'est kif-kif

tot [tɒt] N **1** *(child)* **(tiny) t.** tout(e) petit(e) enfant *mf*; **books for tiny tots** livres pour les tout-petits **2** *(small quantity) (of whisky etc)* (petite) goutte *f*

▸ **tot up** VT SEP *(add)* additionner; *(total)* faire le total de; **she has totted up 2,500 hours' flying time** elle totalise 2 500 heures de vol

VI *(of expenses etc)* s'élever (**to** à)

total ['təʊt(ə)l] ADJ total, -aux, global, -aux; **marketing the product accounts for 20% of the t. costs** le coût de commercialisation du produit revient à 20% du coût total; **t. failure** échec *m* complet; **t. guarantee** garantie *f* totale; **they were in t. ignorance of it** ils l'ignoraient complètement; **the t. population** la population totale; **t. receipts** total *m* des recettes; **t. sales** ventes *fpl* totales, chiffre *m* d'affaires global

N total *m*; *(sum of money)* montant *m*; **grand t.** total global; **there are a t. of thirteen inspectors in the whole country** au total, il y a treize inspecteurs dans tout le pays; **sum t.** somme *f* totale; **the t. amounts to £100** la somme *ou* le montant s'élève à 100 livres; **the t. payable** le total à payer; **a t. of 102 hours/people** un total de 102 heures/personnes; **in t.** au total

VT *(pt, pp totalled, Am totaled)* **1** *(add up) (expenditure)* additionner, totaliser **2** *(amount to)* se chiffrer à; **to t. £100** s'élever à *ou* se monter à 100 livres **3** *Am Fam (write off) (car)* bousiller, déglinguer, fusiller

▸▸ **t. amount** somme *f* totale *ou* globale, montant total; *Fin* **t. annual expenses** consommations *fpl* de l'exercice; *Fin* **t. assets** total de l'actif; *Fin* **t. asset value** valeur *f* de bilan; *Fin* **t. constructive loss** perte *f* totale; *Astron* **t. eclipse** éclipse *f* totale; *Com* **t. fixed cost** coût *m* fixe total; *Fin* **t. gross income** revenu *m* brut global; *Fin* **t. insured value** valeur *f* totale assurée; *Fin* **t. liabilities** total du passif; *Fin* **t. loss** perte totale; *Fin* **t. loss settlement** règlement *m* en perte totale; *Fin* **t. net income** revenu *m* net global; *Fin* **t. quality control** contrôle *m* de la qualité totale; *Com* **t. quality management** qualité *f* totale; *Com* **t. unit cost** coût *m* complet unitaire; **t. war** guerre *f* totale

totalitarian [təʊtælɪˈteərɪən] ADJ *Pol* totalitaire

totalitarianism [təʊtælɪˈteərɪənɪz(ə)m] N *Pol* totalitarisme *m*

totality [təʊˈtælɪtɪ] N totalité *f*

totalizator ['təʊtəlaɪzeɪtər] N *Horseracing (for bets)* totalisateur *m*, totaliseur *m*

totalize ['təʊtəlaɪz] VT additionner, totaliser

totalling, *Am* **totaling** ['təʊtəlɪŋ] N chiffrage *m*

totally ['təʊtəlɪ] ADV totalement

tote¹ [təʊt] N *Horseracing Fam* = **totalizator**

tote² VT *esp Am (goods etc)* transporter; *(bag, gun)* porter

▸▸ **t. bag** grand sac *m*, fourre-tout *m inv*

totem ['təʊtəm] N totem *m*

▸▸ **t. pole** mât *m* totémique

totemic [təʊ'temik] ADJ totémique

totemism ['təʊtəmɪz(ə)m] N totémisme m

t'other, tother ['tʌðər] ADJ, PRON Dial, Fam = the other

totter ['tɒtər] VI 1 (of person) chanceler, tituber; **to t. in/out** entrer/sortir d'un pas mal assuré ou chancelant 2 (of building, government) chanceler

tottering ['tɒtərɪŋ] ADJ (person) chancelant, titubant; (building, regime) chancelant; **t. steps** pas mpl chancelants ou mal assurés

tottery ['tɒtərɪ] ADJ chancelant

totty ['tɒtɪ] N Br Fam (attractive women) belles nanas fpl, belles gonzesses fpl; **he's at the beach checking out the t.** il est en train de mater les nanas sur la plage

toucan ['tuːkæn] N (bird) toucan m

TOUCH [tʌtʃ]

> **N** toucher **1, 2, 4** ▪ contact **1, 3, 6**
> ▪ touche **4, 7** ▪ soupçon **5** ▪ pointe **5**
> **VT** toucher **1, 3–5** ▪ toucher à **1**
> ▪ rivaliser avec **2** ▪ émouvoir **4**
> **VI** se toucher

N 1 (act of touching) toucher m, contact m; **I felt a t. on my arm** j'ai senti qu'on me touchait le bras; **the engine starts at the first t. of the starter** le moteur démarre du premier coup

2 (sense) toucher m; **hard/soft to the t.** dur/mou au toucher

3 (feel) contact m; **the cold t. of marble** le contact froid du marbre

4 (light blow) léger coup m; (with paintbrush) touche f; (with pencil) coup de crayon; **t. of** or **with a stick** léger coup de baguette; **to give one's horse a t. of the spurs** toucher son cheval de l'éperon; **to add a few touches to a picture** faire quelques retouches à un tableau; **to put the finishing touch(es)** or **to add the final t. to sth** mettre la dernière main à qch; **sculptor with a bold/light t.** sculpteur au ciseau hardi/délicat; **to have a light t.** (on piano) avoir un toucher délicat; (in cooking) avoir des doigts de fée; (in writing) avoir un style raffiné; **delicate t. (with** or **of the brush)** coup de pinceau délicat; Fig **there were some nice touches in the film** il y avait quelques notes bien vues dans le film; **he's lost his t.** il a perdu la main; **this house needs a woman's t.** il faut qu'une femme s'occupe de cette maison

5 (hint) pointe f, soupçon m; **t. of garlic** pointe ou soupçon d'ail; **a t. of bitterness** une pointe d'amertume; **there's a t. of colour in her cheeks** ses joues ont pris un peu de couleur; **the first touches of autumn** les premières teintes de l'automne; **a t. of originality** une note d'originalité; **to have a t. of flu** être un peu grippé

6 (communication) contact m; **to be in t. with sb** être ou se tenir en contact avec qn, être en rapport avec qn; **they're still in t.** ils ont maintenu le contact ou sont toujours en contact; **to get in t. with sb** joindre ou contacter qn, prendre contact ou se mettre en contact avec qn; **to get in t. with the police** prendre contact avec la police; **I'll be in t.** je vous ferai signe; **to put sb in t. with sb** mettre qn en relations ou en rapport avec qn; **to keep** or **stay in t. with sb** rester en contact avec qn; **keep in t.!** on reste en contact!; **to keep sb in t. with sth** tenir qn au courant de qch; **to be out of t. with foreign affairs** ne plus être au courant des affaires étrangères; **to be out of t.** or **to have lost t. with sb** ne plus être en contact avec qn; **to lose t. with reality** perdre le contact avec la réalité; **the President has lost t. with**

the electorate le Président a perdu le contact avec son électorat

7 Sport touche f; **kick into t.** envoi m en touche; Fig Fam **to kick a proposal into t.** mettre une proposition au placard; **the ball has gone into t.** le ballon est sorti en touche

8 Sl (financially) **to make a t.** taper quelqu'un; **easy** or **soft t.** (person) pigeon m; **I'm no easy** or **soft t.** il n'y a pas écrit 'pigeon' sur mon front

VT 1 (be in contact with) toucher; (finger, handle) toucher à; Fencing (one's opponent) toucher; **to t. sth with one's finger** toucher qch du doigt; **to t. sb on the shoulder** toucher qn à l'épaule; **to t. sb on the arm** toucher le bras à qn; **I never touched him!** (didn't hit) je ne l'ai même pas touché; **he touched his hat to me** il m'a salué en touchant son chapeau; **t. wood!** je touche/touchons du bois!; Fam **I wouldn't t. it with a bargepole** or Am **a ten foot pole** je ne voudrais pas y toucher, même avec des pincettes; Fam **I wouldn't t. him with a bargepole** or Am **a ten foot pole** je ne veux rien avoir à faire avec lui; **nobody will t. him these days** personne ne veut plus rien avoir à faire avec lui; **to t. (the) bottom** (of ship) toucher le fond; **he touched the bell** (pushed button) il a appuyé sur (le bouton de) la sonnette; **the curtains t. the floor** les rideaux descendent jusqu'au plancher; **the law can't t. her** la loi ne peut rien contre elle; **I never t. wine** je ne bois jamais de vin; **you haven't touched your meat!** tu n'as pas touché à la viande!; **stains that other detergents won't t.** des taches contre lesquelles les autres détergents ne peuvent rien; **you haven't really touched the problem of … in your essay** vous n'avez pas vraiment abordé le problème de … dans votre essai; **if it's against the law, we won't t. it** si c'est illégal, nous ne nous en mêlerons pas

2 (rival) when it comes to reliability, no other car can t. it pour ce qui est de la fiabilité, aucune voiture ne peut l'égaler; **there's no one to t. him in comedy** il est sans égal dans les comédies; **there's only one other company that can t. them** il n'y a qu'une autre entreprise qui puisse rivaliser avec eux ou qui soit à leur niveau

3 (produce an effect on) (something) avoir un effet sur; **this quiet corner of the country was scarcely touched by the war** ce petit coin du pays n'a presque pas été touché par la guerre; **to t. sb on a raw** or **tender spot** toucher qn à un endroit sensible; **flowers touched by the frost** fleurs atteintes par la gelée

4 (move) (somebody) toucher, émouvoir; **to be touched by sb's kindness** être touché de ou par la bonté de qn

5 esp Fml (concern) (somebody) toucher, regarder; **the question touches you closely** la question vous touche de près

6 Fam **to t. sb for a fiver** taper qn de cinq livres

VI (of people, things) se toucher; **don't t.!** n'y touchez pas!; **please do not t.** (on notice) prière de ne pas toucher; **the two ships touched** les deux navires ont touché; Naut **to t. at a port** faire escale à un port

▸ ▸ Comput **t. pad** souris f tactile; **t. screen** écran m tactile; **t. screen computer** ordinateur m à écran tactile

▸ **touch down** VI 1 Rugby marquer un essai; Am Ftbl faire un touché-en-but, toucher dans les buts

2 Astronaut, Aviat (land) atterrir; (in midjourney) toucher

VT SEP (ball) Rugby plaquer au sol; Am Ftbl toucher dans les buts

▸ **touch off** VT SEP (detonate) (cannon etc) décharger; (mine) faire partir, faire exploser; (revolt, quarrel) déclencher

▸ **touch on** VT INSEP (make brief reference to) (subject) aborder; **her speech didn't even t. on this problem** elle n'a même pas abordé ou effleuré ce problème dans son discours

▸ **touch up** VT SEP 1 (add paint etc to) (painting) faire des retouches à; (colours of sth) aviver, rafraîchir; (story) enjoliver; (piece of work) retaper; **to t. up (the paint on) a window frame** etc donner un coup de pinceau à un châssis de fenêtre etc; **to t. up one's make-up** rafraîchir son maquillage; **to t. up a photograph** retoucher une photo

2 Br Sl (touch sexually) toucher, peloter

▸ **touch upon** VT INSEP = touch on

touch-and-go ADJ (affair) très risqué, hasardeux; **it's t. whether we'll have time** il n'est pas du tout sûr que nous ayons ou aurons le temps; **it's t. whether he'll live** il a une chance sur deux de s'en sortir; **right up to the minute they signed it was t.** jusqu'au moment où ils ont signé, rien n'était sûr

touchdown ['tʌtʃdaʊn] N 1 Rugby essai m; (in American football) touché-en-but m, pl touchés en-but, touché-à-terre m, pl touchés-à-terre 2 Astronaut, Aviat atterrissage m

touché ['tuːʃeɪ] INT touché!

touched [tʌtʃt] ADJ 1 (moved) touché, ému 2 Fam **t. (in the head)** toqué, timbré

touchiness ['tʌtʃɪnɪs] N susceptibilité f

touching ['tʌtʃɪŋ] ADJ (moving) touchant, émouvant

N t. is not allowed, no t.! il est défendu de toucher

PREP Fml concernant

touchingly ['tʌtʃɪŋlɪ] ADV d'une manière touchante ou émouvante

touch-judge N Rugby juge m de touche

touchline ['tʌtʃlaɪn] N Ftbl etc ligne f de touche

touch-sensitive ADJ Comput (screen etc) tactile; (key, switch) à effleurement

touchstone ['tʌtʃstəʊn] N pierre f de touche

touch-tone telephone N téléphone m à touches

touch-type VI taper au toucher

touch-typing N dactylographie f au toucher

touch-up N Phot retouche f

touchwood ['tʌtʃwʊd] N amadou m

touchy ['tʌtʃɪ] ADJ (person) susceptible (about sur); (subject) délicat; **to be t.** (of person) se froisser ou s'offusquer facilement; **she's very t. on that point** elle est très susceptible ou chatouilleuse là-dessus

touchy-feely [-'fiːlɪ] ADJ Pej qui affectionne les contacts physiques

tough [tʌf] ADJ 1 (meat etc) dur, coriace; (material, metal) dur, résistant

2 (resistant, strong) (person) fort, solide; **you have to be t. to …** il faut être solide ou résistant ou Fam costaud pour …; **to become t.** s'endurcir; Fam **a t. guy** un dur (à cuire); **as t. as old boots** coriace; (steak) dur comme de la semelle

3 (mentally) fort; (stubborn) opiniâtre; (strict) dur, sévère; **she's a t. customer** (not easy to deal with) elle n'est pas commode; (mentally resistant) c'est une dure (à cuire); **is he t. enough to be sales director?** a-t-il la force de caractère nécessaire à un directeur des ventes?; **we'll have to get t. with them** il faudra que nous nous montrions plus durs avec eux; Prov **when the going gets t., the t. get going** c'est dans les moments difficiles que les vrais hommes entrent en action

4 (difficult) (question, job, climb) dur, ardu; Hum **it's t. at the top** (in job etc) c'est dur au sommet; **it was a t. job** c'était une rude besogne; **to give sb a t. time** faire passer un mauvais quart d'heure à qn; **they had a t. time when their parents died** ils en ont connu de dures quand leurs parents sont morts

5 *Fam (unfortunate)* dur; **that's t. on the rest of them** c'est dur pour ceux qui restent; **it's t. for him, great for us** c'est dur pour lui, mais génial pour nous; **well, isn't that just t.!** quel dommage!; **t. luck!** pas de chance!; **that's your t. luck!** ce n'est pas de chance pour toi, c'est tant pis pour toi

N voyou *m*

ADV *(to talk, act)* comme un dur

▸ **tough out** VT SEP *Fam* **to t. it out** *(face up to sth)* faire front; *(endure sth)* tenir le coup

toughen ['tʌf(ə)n] VT durcir; *(person)* endurcir; **toughened glass** verre *m* trempé

VI durcir; *(of person)* s'endurcir

▸ **toughen up** VT & VI = **toughen**

toughie ['tʌfɪ] N *Fam* **1** *(person)* dur *m* **2** *(question, problem)* casse-tête *f inv*; **question 5 was a real t.** la question 5 était une horreur

toughly ['tʌflɪ] ADV **1** *(to fight)* vigoureusement **2** *(to argue, refuse)* avec opiniâtreté; **a t. worded reply** une réponse très dure

toughness ['tʌfnɪs] N **1** *(of wood etc)* dureté *f*, résistance *f* **2** *(of person)* *(physical strength)* force *f*, solidité *f*; *(resistance to fatigue)* résistance *f*, *(mentally)* force de caractère; *(inflexibility)* ténacité *f*, opiniâtreté *f* **3** *(of task)* difficulté *f*

toupee ['tuːpeɪ] N postiche *m*

tour [tʊər] N **1** *(journey to different places)* voyage *m*; *(excursion)* excursion *f*, **conducted** *or* **guided t.** voyage organisé; *(of museum, city, factory etc)* visite *f* (guidée); **to go on a t. of the Highlands** partir en voyage dans les Highlands; **to go on a bus t. of Paris** faire une visite guidée de Paris en bus; **the PM was taken on a t. of the factory/hospital** le Premier Ministre a fait la visite de l'usine/l'hôpital; **would you like a t. of the garden?** voulez-vous que je vous fasse visiter le jardin?; **would you like a t. of the new offices?** aimeriez-vous visiter nos nouveaux bureaux?; **package t., Am all-expense t.** voyage à forfait *ou* à prix forfaitaire; **cycle** *or* **cycling t.** excursion *ou* randonnée *f* à bicyclette; **walking t.** excursion *ou* randonnée à pied

2 *(by orchestra, theatre company etc)* tournée *f*; **during their European t.** *or* **t. of Europe** pendant leur tournée européenne *ou* en Europe; **concert t.** tournée de concerts; **to go on t.** partir en tournée; **to take a play on t.** jouer une pièce en tournée

VT **1** *(country)* voyager dans; *(hospital, factory etc)* visiter

2 *Mus, Theat* **to t. the provinces** *(of orchestra, company)* faire une tournée en province; *(of play)* passer en province

VI **1 we're just touring around** nous ne faisons que visiter la région; **we decided to t. through the Loire Valley** nous avons décidé de visiter la Vallée de la Loire

2 *(of orchestra, theatre company etc)* **we spend most of the year touring** nous passons la plus grande partie de l'année en tournée; **we go touring every summer** nous partons en tournée tous les étés

▸▸ **t. brochure** brochure *f ou* catalogue *m* de voyages; *Am* **t. conductor, t. director** *(courier)* accompagnateur, -trice; *Mil* **t. of duty** service *m*; **to do a t. of duty** servir; **t. de force** accompagnateur, -trice; **t. group** groupe *m* (de touristes); **t. guide** *(person)* guide *mf*; *(book)* guide *m* touristique; **t. of inspection** tournée d'inspection; *Am* **t. leader, t. manager** accompagnateur, -trice; **t. operator** *(travel agency)* tour-opérateur *m*, *pl* tour-opérateurs, voyagiste *m*; *(bus company)* compagnie *f* de cars *(qui organise des voyages)*; **t. package** forfait *m* voyage

tourer ['tʊərər] N *(car)* voiture *f* de tourisme; *(cycle)* vélo *m* de randonnée

touring ['tʊərɪŋ] N **to do some t.** faire un circuit

ADV **we had a t. holiday in the North of Italy** pour nos vacances nous avons visité le Nord de l'Italie

▸▸ **t. bike** vélo *m* de randonnée; **t. car** voiture *f* de tourisme; **t. caravan** caravane *f* de tourisme; *Theat* **t. company** *(permanently)* troupe *f* ambulante; *(temporarily)* troupe en tournée; **t. cycle** vélo *m* de tourisme; **t. site** *(caravan site)* terrain *m* de caravaning

tourism ['tʊərɪz(ə)m] N tourisme *m*

tourism-generated [-dʒenəreɪtɪd] ADJ généré par le tourisme

tourist ['tʊərɪst] N touriste *mf*; **t. restaurant/pub** restaurant *m*/pub *m* pour touristes

▸▸ **t. agency** agence *f ou* bureau *m* de tourisme; **t. area** zone *f* touristique; **t. attraction** attraction *f ou* site *m* touristique; **t. board** comité *m* du tourisme; **t. centre** centre *m* *ou* ville *f* touristique; *Br* **t. class** classe *f* touriste; **t. destination** destination *f* touristique; **t. enclave** enclave *f* touristique; **t. guide** *(book)* guide *m* touristique; *(person)* guide *mf* (touristique); **t. industry** industrie *f* touristique, industrie du tourisme; **t. information centre** syndicat *m* d'initiative, office *m* du tourisme; **t. night** nuitée *f*; **t. route** itinéraire *m* touristique; **t. season** saison *f* touristique; **t. trade** tourisme *m*; **t. traffic** flot *m* des touristes; **t. trail** sentier *m* touristique; **t. trap** attrape-touristes *m inv*

touristic [tʊəˈrɪstɪk] ADJ touristique

touristy ['tʊərɪstɪ] ADJ *Fam Pej* (trop) touristique

tournament ['tʊənəmənt] N *Sport, Hist* tournoi *m*

tourniquet ['tʊənɪkeɪ] N *Med* garrot *m*

tousle ['taʊz(ə)l] VT *(sb's hair)* ébouriffer; **tousled hair** cheveux *mpl* ébouriffés

tout [taʊt] N **1** *(for hotels)* rabatteur, -euse; *(for shows etc)* racoleur *m*; *(of tickets)* revendeur, -euse de billets (au marché noir) **2** *(racing)* **t.** *(who sells tips)* vendeur, -euse de tuyaux; **according to the touts** d'après les gens qui s'y connaissent

VI **to t. for custom** racoler des clients

VT *(one's services)* offrir; **she had touted her article around all the newspapers** elle avait fait le tour de tous les journaux pour essayer de placer son article; **to t. a product (around)** faire l'article d'un produit; **to t. one's wares** vendre sa marchandise

tow [taʊ] N *(act of towing)* **to give sb/sth a t.** remorquer qn/qch; **to take a car in t.** prendre une voiture en remorque; **to be taken in t.** se mettre en remorque; **to be on** *or* **in t.** être en remorque; *(of boat)* être à la traîne; *Fam* **he always has his family in t.** il trimbale toujours toute sa famille avec lui; *Fam* **with six assistants in t.** avec six assistants dans son sillage

VT *(boat, car)* remorquer; *(barge) (from towpath)* haler

▸▸ *Aut* **t. ball** rotule *f* d'attelage; **t. hook** croc *m* de remorque; **t. rope** câble *m* de remorquage; *Am* **t. truck** dépanneuse *f*; **t. weight** poids *m* remorqué

▸ **tow away** VT SEP remorquer, prendre en remorque; *(of police)* emmener à la fourrière; **you'll get towed away** tu vas te retrouver à la fourrière

tow² N *(fibres)* étoupe *f* (blanche), filasse *f*

towage ['taʊɪdʒ] N **1** *(act)* remorquage *m* **2** *(charge)* (frais *mpl* de) remorquage *m*

toward [təˈwɔːd, twɔːd] PREP *esp Am* = **towards**

towards [təˈwɔːdz, twɔːdz] PREP **1** *(of direction)* vers; **t. the town** vers la ville, du côté

de la ville; **he came t. me** il est venu vers moi; **it's out t. Versailles** c'est du côté de Versailles **2** *(of time)* vers; **t. evening** vers le soir; **t. the end of his life** vers *ou* sur la fin de sa vie **3** *(directed at) (of feelings, behaviour, attitude)* envers, à l'égard de; **her feelings t. me** ses sentiments envers *ou* pour moi, ses sentiments à mon égard; **they behaved strangely t. us** ils se sont conduits d'une manière étrange envers nous *ou* à notre égard **4** *(contributing to)* pour; **to save t. the children's education** économiser pour *ou* en vue de l'éducation des enfants; **to contribute (something) t. the cost of ...** participer à l'achat de ...; **would you like to give something t. it?** voulez-vous donner quelque chose?, voulez-vous participer?

towbar ['taʊbɑːr] N *Aut* timon *m* de remorque; *(of glider)* barre *f* de remorquage

towel ['taʊəl] N serviette *f* (de toilette); **hand t.** essuie-main(s) *m*, *pl* essuie-mains; *Fig* **to throw in the t.** jeter l'éponge; **roller t.** essuie-main(s) *(pour rouleau)*, serviette sans fin; **tea t., dish t.** torchon *m* (à vaisselle); **sanitary t.** serviette hygiénique *ou* périodique

VT (-ll-, *Am* -l-) essuyer *ou* frotter avec une serviette; **to t. oneself (dry)** *(after bath etc)* s'essuyer

▸▸ **t. rail** porte-serviettes *m inv*

towelhead ['taʊəlhed] N *Offensive Sl (Arab)* bougnoule *mf*

towelling, *Am* **toweling** ['taʊəlɪŋ] N *(fabric)* tissu-éponge *m*; **t. robe** peignoir *m* en tissu-éponge

tower ['taʊər] N **1** *Archit, Constr* tour *f*; **she's a t. of strength** c'est quelqu'un sur qui on peut compter en cas de problème, c'est quelqu'un de solide; **he is a t. of strength in the defence line** *(in football)* c'est le pilier de la défense; **church t.** clocher *m*; **clock t.** tour de l'horloge; *Tech* **water t.** château *m* d'eau; *Aviat* **control t.** tour de contrôle **2** *Comput* boîtier *m* vertical, tour *f* **3** *(for camera)* échafaudage *m* pour caméra

▸▸ **the T. of Babel** la tour de Babel; *Br* **t. block** tour d'habitation; **the T. of London** la Tour de Londres; *Comput* **t. system** système *m* à boîtier vertical, système à tour

▸ **tower above, tower over** VT INSEP *(be much higher than)* dominer, dépasser de beaucoup, être beaucoup plus grand que; *(in ability)* être bien meilleur que

towering ['taʊərɪŋ] ADJ *(building, cliff etc)* très haut, très grand; *(person)* très grand; *(ambitions)* sans bornes; **a t. great figure of a man** un géant; **in a t. rage** au paroxysme de la colère

towheaded ['taʊhedɪd] ADJ aux cheveux (blond) filasse

towing ['taʊɪŋ] N remorque *f*, remorquage *m*

▸▸ **t. rod** barre *f* de remorquage; **t. rope** câble *m* de remorquage; **t. weight** charge *f* remorquable

towline ['taʊlaɪn] N (câble *m* de) remorque *f*

town [taʊn] N **1** ville *f*; **fortified t.** place *f* forte; **the whole t. is talking about it** toute la ville en parle; **to go out on the t.** faire la bombe *ou* la noce **2** *(without article)* **to go into t.** aller *ou* se rendre à la *ou* en ville; **she's in t. shopping** elle est en train de faire ses courses en ville; **he's out of t.** il n'est pas en ville; **the best pizzas in t.** les meilleures pizzas de la ville; **man about t.** mondain *m*; *Fig Fam* **to go to t.** *(make great effort)* se mettre en quatre; *Fig Fam* **they really went to t.** *(on redecoration, doing a job etc)* ils ont vraiment mis le paquet; *(preparing a party etc)* ils ont vraiment fait les choses en grand; *Fig Fam* **I really went to t. on the third question** je me suis vraiment foulé pour la troisième question; *Fig Fam* **no need to go to t.**

on it ce n'est pas la peine de trop se fatiguer ►► **t. centre** centre-ville *m*, *pl* centres-villes; *Hist* **t. clerk** secrétaire *mf* de mairie; **t. council** conseil *m* municipal; **t. and gown** = expression désignant collectivement les habitants et les étudiants de certaines villes universitaires et soulignant les différences de culture entre les deux milieux; **t. hall** hôtel *m* de ville, mairie *f*; **t. house** maison *f* en ville; *(aristocratic mansion)* ≃ hôtel particulier; *Am (semi-detached house)* maison mitoyenne (en ville); **t. house hotel** grande maison en ville aménagée en hôtel; **t. life** vie *f* urbaine; **t. planner** urbaniste *mf*; **t. planning** urbanisme *m*

townee, townie ['taʊnɪ] N *Fam* habitant, -ante de la ville

townsfolk ['taʊnfəʊk] NPL habitants *mpl* ou gens *mpl* de la ville/des villes, citadins *mpl*

township ['taʊnʃɪp] N **1** *(small town)* commune *f*, bourg *m* **2** *Admin Am* municipalité *f*, *Can* canton *m*; *Am (in New England)* commune *f* **3** *(in S Africa)* banlieue *f* noire

townsman, *pl* **townsmen** ['taʊnzmən] N habitant *m* de la ville, citadin *m*

townspeople ['taʊnzpiːp(ə)l] NPL habitants *mpl* ou gens *mpl* de la ville/des villes, citadins *mpl*

townswoman, *pl* **townswomen** ['taʊnzwʊmən, -wɪmɪn] N habitante *f* de la ville, citadine *f*

towpath ['taʊpɑːθ] N chemin *m* de halage

towrope ['taʊrəʊp] N (câble *m* de) remorque *f*

tow-start N **to give sb a t.** démarrer qn en remorque
VT démarrer en remorque

toxaemia, *Am* **toxemia** [tɒk'siːmɪə] N *Med* toxémie *f*

toxic ['tɒksɪk] ADJ *(substance)* toxique ►► *Med* **t. shock syndrome** syndrome *m* du choc toxique; **t. waste** déchets *mpl* toxiques

toxicologic(al) [tɒksɪkə'lɒdʒɪk, -ɪk(ə)l] ADJ *Med* toxicologique

toxicologist [tɒksɪ'kɒlədʒɪst] N *Med* toxicologue *mf*

toxicology [tɒksɪ'kɒlədʒɪ] N *Med* toxicologie *f*

toxin ['tɒksɪn] N *Biol, Chem* toxine *f*

toy [tɔɪ] N jouet *m*; **he's like a child with a new t.** il est comme un enfant avec un nouveau jouet
►► *Br Fam* **t. boy** jeune amant *m*; **she's got herself a t. boy** elle s'est déniché un petit jeune *ou* un jeune amant; **t. dog** chien *m* nain; **t. poodle** caniche *m* nain; **t. shop** magasin *m* de jouets; **t. soldier** soldat *m* de plomb; **t. trumpet** trompette *f* d'enfant

► **toy with** VT INSEP *(play with)* jouer avec; **to t. with one's food** jouer avec sa nourriture; **to t. with an idea** caresser une idée; **to t. with sb** s'amuser avec qn; **to t. with sb's affections** jouer avec le cœur de qn

tpi *Comput (abbr* **tracks per inch**) pistes *fpl* par pouce

TQC [tiːkjuː'siː] N *(abbr* **total quality control**) QG *f*

TQM [tiːkjuː'em] N *(abbr* **total quality management**) gestion *f* de la QG

trace¹ [treɪs] N **1** *(vestige)* trace *f*, vestige *m*; **they could find no t. of him** ils n'ont retrouvé aucune trace de lui; **there's not a t. of it** *(there's nothing left of it)* il n'en reste pas trace; **there's not a t. of your wallet anywhere in the house** ton portefeuille n'est nulle part dans la maison; **he has disappeared without t.** il a disparu sans laisser de trace; **the last remaining traces of an ancient civi-**

lization les derniers vestiges d'une civilisation ancienne
2 *(small amount)* trace *f*, quantité *f* infime; *(of irony, sarcasm)* soupçon *m*; **traces of cyanide/poison** des traces de cyanure/poison; **he said with a t. of amusement** dit-il, l'air légèrement amusé; **there was the t. of a smile on her face** il y avait l'ombre d'un sourire sur son visage
VT **1** *(outline) (plan, scheme etc)* exposer
2 *(draw) (plan, diagram)* tracer, faire le tracé de; *(copy) (drawing)* calquer; **to t. sth in the sand/dirt with a stick** dessiner qch dans le sable/la poussière avec un bâton
3 *(follow tracks of) (person, animal)* suivre la trace *ou* la piste de; *(locate) (lost property)* recouvrer; *(influence etc)* retracer, retrouver; **they traced him as far as Paris** *or* **to Paris** on a suivi sa piste jusqu'à Paris; **to t. the evil to its source** remonter à la source du mal
►► **t. element** oligo-élément *m*, *pl* oligo-éléments
► **trace back** VT SEP *(uncover origins of)* **to t. sth back to its source** remonter jusqu'à l'origine de qch; **to t. one's family back to William the Conqueror** faire remonter son arbre généalogique jusqu'à Guillaume le Conquérant
► **trace out** VT SEP = **trace** VT **1**

trace² N *(part of harness)* trait *m*; **in the traces** attelé; *Fig* **to kick over the traces** *(of person) (rebel)* ruer dans les brancards; *(break free)* s'émanciper

tracer ['treɪsər] N *Mil*
►► **t. bullet** balle *f* traçante; **t. shell** traçant *m*

tracery ['treɪsərɪ] N **1** *Archit (of rose window)* réseau *m*, remplage *m* **2** *(of leaf etc)* nervures *fpl*

trachea, *pl* **tracheae** [trə'kiːə, -iːiː] N *Anat* trachée *f*

tracheal [trə'kiːəl] ADJ *Anat* trachéal, -aux

tracheostomy [trækɪ'ɒstəmɪ], **tracheotomy** [trækɪ'ɒtəmɪ] N *Surg* trachéotomie *f*

trachoma [trə'kəʊmə] N *Med* trachome *m*

tracing ['treɪsɪŋ] N *(copy)* calque *m*
►► **t. paper** papier-calque *m inv*, papier *m* à décalquer

track [træk] N **1** *(marks left) (of animal)* trace(s) *f(pl)*, piste *f*, foulées *fpl*; *(of person)* trace(s), piste; *(of wheel)* sillon *m*; **to follow in sb's tracks** suivre la voie tracée par qn; **to be on sb's t.** être sur la piste de qn; **to throw sb off the t.** dépister qn, *Fam* semer qn; *Fig Fam* **to be off the t.** divaguer; **to be on the right t.** être sur la (bonne) voie; *Fig* **to be on the wrong t.** *(in search, guess etc)* se fourvoyer, être sur la mauvaise piste; **to keep t. of sb/sth** suivre les progrès de qn/qch; **I've lost t. of her** je l'ai perdue de vue; **I've lost t. of all the times I've …** je ne compte plus les fois où j'ai …; *Fam* **to make tracks** *(leave)* partir, filer; **to stop in one's tracks** s'arrêter net; **to stop sb in his/her tracks** arrêter qn net
2 *(path)* piste *f*, chemin *m*, sentier *m*; *Rail* voie *f* (ferrée); **cycle t.** piste cyclable; *Sport* **(running) t.** piste; **the train left the t.** le train a déraillé; *Rail* **single-t./double-t. line** ligne *f* à une voie/à deux voies
3 *(in recording process, on disk)* piste *f*; *(song) (on record, CD etc)* morceau *m*; **sound t.** piste sonore; *Comput* **tracks per inch** pistes par pouce
4 *(of tracked vehicle)* chenille *f*
5 *(distance between wheels)* écartement *m* des roues, voie *f*
VT *(animal, thief etc)* suivre à la piste, pister; *(fugitive)* traquer; *(missile)* suivre la trajectoire de
VI *(of gear wheels etc)* être en alignement; *(of camera)* faire un travelling; **the band of**

rain that is tracking across the country le front de pluie qui se déplace à travers le pays
►► *Aut* **t. arm** bras *m* de direction; *Sport* **t. event** épreuve *f* sur piste; *Sport* **t. and field events** épreuves *fpl* d'athlétisme; *Sport* **t. racing** courses *fpl* sur piste; *Sport, Fig* **t. record** *(past record, career to date)* antécédents *mpl*; *(list of achievements)* palmarès *m*; **he doesn't have a very good t. record for punctuality** il n'est pas réputé pour sa ponctualité; **in view of his t. record of getting home late every Friday night …** vu l'habitude qu'il a de rentrer tard tous les vendredis soirs …; **a company with a good/poor t. record in winning export orders** une entreprise avec un bon/mauvais palmarès sur le plan des commandes à l'exportation; **no wonder the insurance is high with your t. record!** pas étonnant que l'assurance soit chère avec ton palmarès!; **given the government's t. record in the field of cutting benefits** vu les antécédents du gouvernement en matière de réduction des prestations sociales; *Br Aut* **t. rod** biellette *f* de connexion; *Sport* **t. shoes** chaussures *fpl* de course; **t. vehicle** véhicule *m* chenillé
► **track down** VT SEP *(discover) (criminal, prey etc)* dépister; *(information)* découvrir; *(missing object)* retrouver; **they tracked her down to her hideout** ils ont remonté sa trace *ou* sa piste jusqu'à sa cachette

trackball ['trækbɔːl] N *Comput* boule *f* de commande, trackball *m ou f*

tracked [trækt] ADJ *(vehicle)* chenillé

tracker ['trækər] N **1** *(of game)* traqueur *m* **2** *TV* machiniste *m* de travelling
►► **t. dog** chien *m* policier; *Fin* **t. fund** fonds *m* indiciel *ou* à gestion indicielle

tracking ['trækɪŋ] N
►► **t. down** *(of criminal, cause etc)* dépistage *m*; *Cin, TV* **t. shot** traveling *m*, travelling *m*; *Astron* **t. station** station *f* d'observation; **t. systems** systèmes *mpl* de repérage et poursuite

tracklayer ['trækleɪər] N *Rail (person)* poseur *m* de voie

tracklaying ['trækleɪɪŋ] N
►► **t. vehicle** véhicule *m* à chenilles

trackless ['træklɪs] ADJ *(place)* sans chemins, sans sentiers
►► *Am* **t. trolley** trolleybus *m*

trackpad ['trækpæd] N *Comput* tablette *f* tactile

tracksuit ['træks(j)uːt] N *Sport* survêtement *m*

tract¹ [trækt] N **1** *(of land)* étendue *f* **2** *Anat (respiratory, digestive)* appareil *m*

tract² N *(pamphlet)* brochure *f*, tract *m*

tractable ['træktəb(ə)l] ADJ *(person, character)* docile; *(material)* facile à ouvrer; **a t. problem** un problème que l'on peut résoudre

traction ['trækʃən] N **1** *Tech* traction *f*, tirage *m* **2** *Med* traction *f*; **in t.** en traction
►► **t. cable** câble *m* tracteur; *Aut* **t. control** contrôle *m* de traction; **t. engine** locomotive *f*, machine *f*; **t. wheels** roues *fpl* motrices

tractive ['træktɪv] ADJ tractif; *(force)* de traction

tractor ['træktər] N *(vehicle)* tracteur *m*; *(of lorry)* tracteur routier; **t.-drawn** tracté
►► **t. driver** conducteur, -trice de tracteur; *Comput* **t. feed** dispositif *m* d'entraînement à picots; **t. holes** *(on tractor wheel)* trous *mpl* à ergots; **t. pin** *(in tractor wheel)* ergot *m* de tracteur; **t. wheel** *(on printer etc)* roue *f* d'entraînement

trad [træd] N *Br Mus Fam* jazz *m* traditionnel

tradable ['treɪdəb(ə)l] ADJ négociable

trade [treɪd] **N 1** *(commerce)* commerce *m*, affaires *fpl*, négoce *m*, échanges *mpl* commerciaux; *Am (commercial transaction)* transaction *f* (commerciale); *(swap)* échange *m*; **to do a t.** faire un échange; **(illicit) t.** trafic *m*; **to be in t.** être dans le commerce; **wholesale/retail t.** commerce de gros/de détail; **balance of t.** balance *f* commerciale; **the tea t.** le commerce du thé; **the t. in animal skins** le commerce des peaux; **it's good for t.** cela fait marcher le commerce; **we don't get much t. nowadays** les affaires ne marchent pas très bien ces temps-ci; **she's doing a roaring t.** elle fait des affaires en or; **he's t.** *(not old money)* c'est un nouveau-riche

2 *(profession)* métier *m*; *(as a body)* *(corps m de)* métier; **to be in the t.** être du métier; **to follow** *or* **carry on a t.** exercer un métier; **to learn a t.** apprendre un métier; **he's a plumber by t.** il est plombier de son état *ou* métier; **everyone to his t.** chacun son métier; **it's what we in the t. call a ...** c'est ce que, dans le métier, on appelle un ...; **the building t.** le bâtiment; **the publishing t.** l'édition *f*; **the printing t.** l'imprimerie *f*

VI 1 faire du commerce, commercer, faire le commerce *ou* le négoce (**in sth** de qch; **with sb** avec qn); **the company trades under the name of ...** l'entreprise opère sous le nom de ...; **he trades from a small stall in the market** il tient un petit étal au marché

2 *Am (to shop)* se ravitailler (**at, with** chez)

3 *St Exch (of shares)* s'échanger (**at** à)

VT 1 to t. sth for sth échanger *ou* troquer qch contre qch; **to t. places with sb** changer de place avec qn; **to t. insults/blows** échanger des insultes/coups

2 *St Exch* négocier

▸▸**t. advertising** publicité *f* auprès des intermédiaires; **t. agreement** accord *m* commercial; **t. allowance** remise *f* entre professionnels; **t. association** association *f* professionnelle; **t. ban** interdiction *f* de commerce; **t. barriers** barrières *fpl* douanières; **t. bill** effet *m* de commerce; **t. bloc** union *f* douanière; **t. body** syndicat *m* professionnel; **t. centre** place *f* commerciale; *Acct* **t. credit** crédit *m* fournisseur *ou* commercial; *Acct* **t. creditor** créancier, -ière d'exploitation; **t. cycle** cycle *m* de commercialisation; *Acct* **t. debtor** compte *m ou* créance *f* client; **t. deficit** balance *f* commerciale déficitaire, déficit *m* extérieur *ou* commercial; *Br* **the T. Descriptions Act** = loi *f* qui empêche la publicité mensongère; **t. directory** annuaire *m* de commerce; **t. discount** *(to customer)* escompte *m* commercial, escompte d'usage; *(to retailer)* escompte professionnel, remise professionnelle; **t. embargo** embargo *m* commercial; **t. exhibition** foire-exposition *f*, *pl* foires-expositions, exposition *f* commerciale; *Br* **t. fair** foire *f* commerciale, salon *m*; **t. gap** déficit *m* commercial; **t. journal** journal *m* professionnel, revue *f* professionnelle; **t. mission** mission *f* commerciale; **t. name** *(of product)* nom *m* de marque; *(of firm)* raison *f* commerciale; *Br Aut* **t. plate** plaque *f* d'immatriculation provisoire; **t. policy** politique *f* commerciale; **t. press** presse *f* spécialisée, presse professionnelle; **t. price** *Com* prix *m* marchand; *St Exch* prix de négociation; **t. promotion** promotion *f* auprès des intermédiaires; **t. publication** revue *f* spécialisée *ou* professionnelle; **t. references** références *fpl* commerciales; **t. register** registre *m* du commerce; **t. route** route *f* commerciale; **t. secret** secret *m* de fabrication; **t. show** salon *m* (professionnel); **t. ticket** avis *m* d'opéré, avis d'opération sur titres; **t. tribunal** tribunal *m* de commerce; *Br* **t. union** syndicat *m* (ouvrier); **she's very active in the t. union** c'est une syndicaliste militante; *Br* **t. union**

council conseil *m* syndical; *Br* **t. unionism** syndicalisme *m*; *Br* **t. unionist** (ouvrier, -ière) syndiqué(e); *Br* **t. union member** syndiqué, -ée; **t. war** guerre *f* commerciale; **t. wind** alizé *m*

▸**trade down VI 1** *St Exch* acheter des valeurs basses **2** *(of car, home owner etc)* changer pour un modèle/un appartement/*etc* moins cher

▸**trade in VT SEP** *(give in part exchange) (car etc)* donner en reprise

▸**trade off VT SEP they have traded off quality against speed** ils ont fait primer la rapidité sur la qualité; **you can't ask me to t. off reputation against profit** vous ne pouvez pas me demander de choisir entre ma réputation et un profit; **you have to t. one thing off against another** il faut faire des choix

▸**trade on VT INSEP** *(exploit) (sb's ignorance)* exploiter, tirer profit de

▸**trade up VI 1** *St Exch* acheter des valeurs hautes **2** *(of car, home owner etc)* changer pour un modèle/un appartement/*etc* plus cher

tradeable ['treɪdəb(ə)l] **ADJ** négociable

traded option ['treɪdɪd] **N** *St Exch* option *f* négociable

trade-in N objet *m* donné en reprise; **will you take my old car as a t.?** est-ce que vous reprendrez ma vieille voiture?

▸▸**t. allowance** (valeur *f* de) reprise *f*, **t. facility** facilité *f* de reprise; **t. price** prix *m* à la reprise; **t. value** valeur *f* de reprise; **what's its t. value?** quelle est sa valeur de reprise?

trademark ['treɪdmɑːk] **N** marque *f* (de fabrique), marque de commerce; *Fig* **these close-up shots are her t.** ces gros-plans sont sa marque *ou* sa signature

▸▸**t. registration** dépôt *m* de marque

trade-off N 1 *(compromise)* compromis *m*; **you're going to have a t. between speed and quality** si l'on va plus vite, ce sera au détriment de la qualité; **we do not believe there is a t. between ... and ...** nous ne croyons pas qu'il y ait incompatibilité entre ... et ... **2** *esp Am (exchange)* échange *m*

▸▸*Mktg* **t. analysis** analyse *f* conjointe

trader ['treɪdər] **N 1** *(person)* négociant, -ante, commerçant, -ante, marchand, -ande; *St Exch* opérateur *m*, spéculateur *m* **2** *(ship)* navire *m* marchand

trades [treɪdz] **NPL** *(winds)* (vents *mpl*) alizés *mpl*

tradesman, *pl* **tradesmen** ['treɪdzmən] **N** marchand *m*, fournisseur *m*; **tradesmen's entrance** entrée *f* des fournisseurs

trade-weighted index N *Econ* indice *m* pondéré par le commerce extérieur

trading ['treɪdɪŋ] **N** commerce *m*, négoce *m*

▸▸*Acct* **t. account** compte *m* d'exploitation générale; **t. bank** banque *f* commerciale; **t. capital** capital *m* engagé *ou* de roulement; **t. company** société *f* commerciale; *St Exch* **t. day** jour *m* de Bourse; *Br* **t. estate** zone *f* artisanale et commerciale; *St Exch* **t. floor** corbeille *f*, parquet *m*; **t. hours** heures *fpl* d'ouverture; *St Exch* horaires *mpl* des criées; *St Exch* **t. instrument** outil *m* de spéculation; **t. licence** carte *f* de commerce; **t. loss** perte *f*, *St Exch* **t. member** intermédiaire *m* négociateur; *St Exch* **t. month** mois *m* d'échéance; *St Exch* **t. order** ordre *m* de négociation; **t. partners** partenaires *mpl* commerciaux; **France is our most important t. partner** la France est notre principal partenaire commercial; *Am* **t. post** *(store)* comptoir *m* commercial; *St Exch* **t. range** parquet *m*, corbeille *f*, *Com* **t. profit** bénéfice(s) *m(pl)* d'exploitation; *Acct* **t. and profit and loss account** compte de résultat; *St Exch* **t. range** écart *m* de prix, fourchette *f* de cotation; **prices are stuck in a t. range** les prix ne varient pas beaucoup; *St Exch* **t. rate**

cours *m*; **t. results** résultats *mpl* de l'exercice; *St Exch* **t. room** salle *f* des changes *ou* des marchés; *St Exch* **t. session** séance *f* boursière; **t. stamp** timbre-prime *m*, *pl* timbres-prime(s), vignette-épargne *f*, *pl* vignettes-épargne; **t. standards** normes *fpl* de conformité; **t. year** année *f* d'exploitation, exercice *m*

tradition [trə'dɪʃən] **N** tradition *f*; **t. has it that ...** selon la tradition ...; **it has become a t.** c'est passé dans la tradition; **the t. is to ...** la tradition veut que l'on ... + *sub*

traditional [trə'dɪʃənəl] **ADJ** traditionnel

traditionalism [trə'dɪʃənəlɪz(ə)m] **N** traditionalisme *m*

traditionalist [trə'dɪʃənəlɪst] **ADJ, N** traditionaliste *mf*

traditionally [trə'dɪʃənəlɪ] **ADV** traditionnellement

traduce [trə'djuːs] **VT** *Fml, Lit* calomnier, diffamer

traffic ['træfɪk] **N 1** circulation *f*, trafic *m*; **heavy t.** circulation intense; **ocean t.** navigation *f* au long cours; **road t.** circulation routière; **rail(way) t.** trafic ferroviaire; **through t.** circulation directe; **southbound t. should avoid ...** les conducteurs se dirigeant vers le sud ont intérêt à éviter ...; *Fam* **go play in the t.!** va voir ailleurs si j'y suis! **2** *(movement of people)* passage *m*; *(on telephone network)* volume *m* de communications; *(on website)* trafic *m* **3** *Pej (trade)* trafic *m*

VT & VI *(pt, pp* **trafficked** ['træfɪkt]*)* *Pej* trafiquer (**in** de); *Fig* **reporters who t. in human misery** journalistes qui exploitent la misère humaine

▸▸*Mktg* **t. builder** *(product)* article *m* d'appel; **t. calming** contrôle *m* de la circulation; *Am* **t. circle** rond-point *m*, *pl* ronds-points, sens *m* giratoire; **t. cone** cône *m* de signalisation (pour la circulation routière); **t. control** régulation *f* de la circulation; *Aviat, Naut, Rail* contrôle *m* du trafic; *Am Fam* **t. cop** agent *m* de la circulation; **t. island** refuge *m*; *Br* **t. jam** embouteillage *m*, bouchon *m*; **t. lights,** *Am* **t. light** feu *m* de signalisation; **at the next t. lights** au(x) prochain(s) feu(x); **t. news** = informations *fpl* sur l'état de la circulation routière; **t. offence** infraction *f* au code de la route; **t. patrol** patrouille *f* de la circulation (routière); **t. police** *(for speeding, safety)* police *f* de la route; *(on point duty)* agents *mpl* de la circulation; **t. policeman** agent *m* de police; *(on point duty)* agent de la circulation; **t. pollution** pollution *f* automobile; *Radio* **t. programme** informations *fpl* routières; **t. regulations** règlements *mpl* sur la circulation; **t. sign** panneau *m* de signalisation, poteau *m* indicateur; **t. signals** feu *m* de signalisation; *Br* **t. warden** contractuel, -elle

trafficator ['træfɪkeɪtər] **N** *Br Aut Old-fashioned* flèche *f* de direction

trafficker ['træfɪkər] **N** *Pej* trafiquant, -ante (**in** de, en); **drug t.** trafiquant de drogue

tragedian [trə'dʒiːdɪən] **N** *(dramatist)* auteur *m* tragique; *(actor)* tragédien *m*

tragedienne [trədʒiːdɪ'en] **N** *(actress)* tragédienne *f*

tragedy ['trædʒɪdɪ] **N** *(accident, disaster)*, *Theat* tragédie *f*, **to make a t. out of sth** prendre qch au tragique; **the t. of his death** sa mort tragique; **it will be a t. if ...** ce serait une tragédie *ou* un drame si ...; **the real t. was that ...** ce qu'il y avait de vraiment tragique, c'était que ...

tragic ['trædʒɪk] **ADJ** tragique; *Fam* **to put on a t. act** jouer la comédie pour se faire plaindre; **the t. side of the story is that ...** ce que cette histoire a de tragique c'est que ...; *Iron*

how t. for you! c'est bête ce qui t'arrive!; **t. dad in rescue bid** *(newspaper headline)* un père tente un sauvetage désespéré
▸▸ **t. actor** tragédien *m*; **t. actress** tragédienne *f*

tragically ['trædʒɪklɪ] ADV tragiquement; **he died at a t. early age** c'est tragique qu'il soit mort si jeune

tragicomedy [trædʒɪ'kɒmɪdɪ] N tragi-comédie *f*, *pl* tragi-comédies

tragicomic(al) [trædʒɪ'kɒmɪk, -ɪk(ə)l] ADJ tragi-comique

trail [treɪl] N **1** *(of blood)* traînée *f*; *(of smoke)* panache *m*; *(of meteor)* queue *f*; *Mil (of gun carriage)* flèche *f*, crosse *f*; **a t. of broken promises** une série de promesses non tenues **2** *(marks left) (of animal, person)* piste *f*, trace *f*; *(of snail)* trace; **to pick up the t.** *(of hounds)* retrouver la trace; **false t.** fausse piste; **to be on the t. of sb** être sur la piste de qn; **the criminals left with the police hot on their t.** les criminels sont partis avec la police sur leurs talons; **the t. was cold by then** la piste était déjà froide; **to leave a t. of destruction** tout détruire sur son passage **3** *(path)* sentier *m* (battu); *(in forest, cross-country skiing)* piste *f*
VT **1** *(pull) (something)* traîner après soi; *(of car etc) (caravan etc)* remorquer; *Fig* **to t. one's coat** se montrer délibérément provocateur **2** *(track) (animal, criminal)* traquer, pister, suivre à la piste; *(of crook) (victim)* suivre, filer **3** *Cin, TV* annoncer
VI **1** *(drag)* traîner; **your skirt is trailing (on the ground)** votre jupe traîne (par terre) **2** *(move slowly)* avancer lentement **3** *(of plant)* grimper, ramper **4** **to be trailing** *(be last)* être à la traîne; **our team is trailing at the bottom of the league** notre équipe se traîne en fin de classement
▸▸ **t. bike** moto *f* de cross; **t. mix** = mélange *m* de cacahuètes et de fruits secs; *Fishing* **t. net** traîne *f*, chalut *m*, traîneau *m*
▸ **trail away** VI **his voice trailed away in embarrassment** il se tut, gêné; **her voice trailed away in the distance** sa voix se perdit dans le lointain
▸ **trail behind** VI **1** *(linger)* traîner derrière (les autres), être à la traîne; *Fig (of team etc)* être en retard sur les autres **2** *(be towed)* se faire remorquer, être en remorque; **with a boat trailing behind** avec un bateau en remorque
▸ **trail off** VI *(of voice)* diminuer jusqu'à s'éteindre; **her voice trails off** sa voix diminue jusqu'à devenir inaudible; **his voice trailed off in mid-sentence** il s'interrompit au milieu de sa phrase

trailblazer ['treɪlbleɪzər] N pionnier, -ière

trailblazing ['treɪlbleɪzɪŋ] ADJ *(work)* de pionnier, *(discovery)* qui ouvre la voie

trailer ['treɪlər] N **1** *Aut etc (behind vehicle)* remorque *f*, *Am (towed)* caravane *f*, *(mobile home)* camping-car *m*, *pl* camping-cars **2** *Cin, TV* bande-annonce *f*, *pl* bandes-annonces (**for** de)
▸▸ *Am* **t. hitch** timon *m* de remorque; *Am* **t. park** = terrain *m* aménagé pour les camping-cars; *Am Fam Pej* **t. trash** prolos *mpl* *(qui vivent dans des camping-cars)*

trailer-truck N *Am* semi-remorque *f*, *pl* semi-remorques

trailing ['treɪlɪŋ] ADJ **1** *(skirt etc)* traînant **2** *(plant)* grimpant, rampant
▸▸ *Aut* **t. arm** bras *m* tiré; *Aut* **t. brake shoe** segment *m* de frein secondaire; *Aviat* **t. edge** *(of wing)* bord *m* de fuite; *Mktg* **t. firm** entreprise *f* à la traîne; *Aut* **t. shoe** segment *m* secondaire; *Comput* **t. spaces** espaces *mpl* à droite; *Comput* **t. zeroes** zéros *mpl* à droite

train¹ [treɪn] N **1** *Rail* train *m*; *(underground)* rame *f*, **passenger/goods t.** train de voyageurs/de marchandises; **express t.** train express; **slow** *or* **stopping t.** train omnibus; **relief t.** train supplémentaire; **the 5 o'clock t.** le train de 5 heures; **the Cardiff t., the t. to Cardiff** le train de Cardiff; **she wasn't on the t.** elle n'était pas dans le train; **by t.** *(to travel)* par *ou* en chemin de fer, en train; **to the trains** *(on sign)* accès aux quais
2 *(of carriages, barges)* train *m*, convoi *m*; *(of events, circumstances)* succession *f*, série *f*, enchaînement *m*; **Min** traînée *f* (de poudre); **t. of thought** enchaînement d'idées; **to set** *or* **put sth in t.** mettre qch en route
3 *Tech (system of gears)* système *m* d'engrenages
4 *(retinue) (of prince etc)* suite *f*, cortège *m*, équipage *m*; *Mil* équipage, train *m*; **the evils that follow in the t. of war** les maux que la guerre engendre
5 *(of dress)* traîne *f*, queue *f*; *(of peacock)* queue
▸▸ **t. bearer** demoiselle *f*/garçon *m* d'honneur; **t. journey** voyage *m* en *ou* par chemin de fer, voyage en train; **t. station** gare *f* *(de chemin de fer)*

train² VT **1** *(person)* former, instruire; *(animal)* dresser; *(character, mind)* former; *(ear)* exercer; *Sport (runner, racehorse etc)* entraîner; **he was trained at the Academy of Dramatic Art** il sort de l'Académie des Arts Dramatiques; **to t. sb for sth/to do sth** exercer qn à qch/à faire qch; **to t. sb in the use of a machine/weapon** apprendre à qn à se servir d'une machine/d'une arme; **to t. oneself to do sth** s'exercer à faire qch **2** *(in horticulture) (fruit tree, vine)* palisser, mettre en espalier **3** *(direct) (telescope, spotlight etc)* braquer, diriger (**on** sur); *Mil (gun)* pointer; *Naut (gun)* orienter, diriger
VI s'exercer; *Mil* faire l'exercice; *Sport* s'entraîner; **to t. for sth** s'exercer *ou* se préparer à qch; **to t. as a typist** suivre des cours de dactylographie; **she trained as a typist** elle est dactylographe de formation; **to t. as a ballet dancer** suivre une formation de danseur de ballet
▸ **train up** VT SEP *(employees)* donner une formation complémentaire à

trained [treɪnd] ADJ *(person, worker etc)* formé; *(chien etc)* dressé; *(eye)* exercé; *Sport* entraîné; **highly/poorly t.** très bien/peu entraîné; **t. nurse** infirmière *f* diplômée; *Hum* **her husband is very well t.** *(does as he's told)* son mari est très bien dressé

trainee [treɪ'ni:] N stagiaire *mf*; **t. manager, management** stagiaire de direction

traineeship [treɪ'ni:ʃɪp] N stage *m*

trainer ['treɪnər] N **1** *(person) (of animals)* dresseur *m*; *Sport, Horseracing (of athletes, football team, racehorses)* entraîneur *m*; *(for job)* formateur *m* **2** *(aircraft)* avion-école *f*, *pl* avions-écoles **3** **trainers** *(shoes)* chaussures *fpl* de sport
▸▸ **t. aircraft** avion-école

training ['treɪnɪŋ] N **1** *(of person)* formation *f*; *Sport* entraînement *m*; *(of animal)* dressage *m*; **physical t.** éducation *f* physique; **vocational t.** formation professionnelle; **I'm a historian by t.** je suis historien de formation; *Fig* **it's good t. for when you're a parent** ça vous prépare pour quand vous aurez des enfants; *Mil* **military t.** instruction *f* militaire; *Sport* **to go into t.** s'entraîner; **to be in t.** *(being trained)* être à l'entraînement; *(fit)* être bien entraîné; **to be out of t.** ne plus être en forme **2** *(in horticulture) (of plant, fruit tree)* palissage *m*; *Mil (of gun)* orientation *f*
▸▸ *Mil* **t. base** base *f* école; **t. centre** centre *m* de formation; **t. college** école *f* spécialisée *ou* professionnelle; **t. contract** contrat *m* d'apprentissage; **t. course** stage *m* (de formation); **t. manual** manuel *m* d'utilisation, manuel d'instruction; **t. period** stage (de formation); **t. programme** programme *m* de formation; **t. scheme** plan *m* de formation; **t. session** entraînement *m*; **t. ship** navire-école *m*, *pl* navires-écoles

trainload ['treɪnləʊd] N **t. of coal** train *m* chargé de houille; **t. of tourists** plein train de touristes; **they were arriving by the t.** ils arrivaient par trains entiers

trainspotter ['treɪnspɒtər] N = personne *f* dont le passe-temps est de noter les numéros des trains; *Fam* **he's a bit of a t.** il est vraiment ringard

trainspotting ['treɪnspɒtɪŋ] N = activité *f* consistant à repérer et répertorier les numéros des trains

traipse [treɪps] VI *Fam* **to t. through the streets** battre le pavé; **to t. around** traîner çà et là; **to t. around the shops** traîner dans les magasins; **we had to t. all the way back to …** il a fallu qu'on se retape tout le trajet jusqu'à …

trait [treɪt] N *(of character etc)* trait *m*

traitor ['treɪtər] N traître *m* (**to** à); **to turn t.** passer à l'ennemi, se vendre (à l'ennemi)

traitorous ['treɪtərəs] ADJ traître, *f* traîtresse, fourbe, perfide

traitorously ['treɪt(ə)rəslɪ] ADV traîtreusement

traitress ['treɪtrɪs] N *Old-fashioned* traîtresse *f*

trajectory [trə'dʒekt(ə)rɪ] N trajectoire *f*, *Fig (of company)* itinéraire *m*

TRAM [træm] N *(abbr* **transputer module**) module *m* de transputer

tram [træm] N *Br (vehicle)* tramway *m*; **to go by t.** aller en tramway
▸▸ **t. driver** conducteur, -trice de tramway

tramcar ['træmkɑ:r] N *Br Old-fashioned* tramway *m*

tramline ['træmlaɪn] N **1** *(route)* ligne *f* de tramways **2** **tramlines** *(track)* voie *f* de tramway; *Tennis* couloir *m*; *Sl (on arm)* traces *fpl* de piquouses

trammel ['træm(ə)l] *Lit* N *(hindrance)* **the trammels of routine** les entraves *fpl* de la routine
VT (**-ll-,** *Am* **-l-**) entraver, empêtrer; **trammelled by prejudices** entravé par les préjugés

tramp¹ [træmp] N **1** *(vagabond)* chemineau *m*, vagabond, -onde, clochard, -arde **2** *(sound)* bruit *m* de pas marqués; **I heard the (heavy) t. of the guard** j'ai entendu le pas lourd du gardien **3** *(walk)* promenade *f* à pied **4** *Fam Pej (promiscuous woman)* traînée *f*
VI **1** *(walk heavily)* marcher lourdement; **to t. on sth** piétiner *ou* écraser qch; **I wish you'd stop tramping on my foot!** j'aimerais bien que tu arrêtes de m'écraser le pied **2** *(travel on foot)* se promener *ou* voyager à pied; **to t. wearily along** suivre péniblement son chemin
VT **to t. the streets** battre le pavé; **to t. the country** parcourir le pays à pied
▸▸ *Naut* **t. steamer** tramp *m*

tramp² N *Aut (of wheels)* rebondissement *m*, martèlement *m*

trample ['træmp(ə)l] VI **to t. on sth/sb** piétiner *ou* écraser qch/qn; **to t. on sb's feelings** fouler aux pieds les susceptibilités de qn
VT *(ground)* piétiner; **to t. sb/sth underfoot** piétiner qn/qch, fouler qn/qch aux pieds; *Fig* fouler qn/qch aux pieds; **to t. down the grass** fouler l'herbe; **the child was trampled to death (by the crowd)** l'enfant est mort piétiné (par la foule)

trampoline ['træmpəli:n] N *Gym etc* trampoline *m*
VI faire du trampoline

tramway ['træmweɪ] N rails *mpl* de tramway; *(system)* réseau *m* de tramway

trance [trɑːns] N *Med (catalepsy)* catalepsie *f*, **(hypnotic) t.** transe *f*, hypnose *f*; **to send** *or* **put sb into a t.** hypnotiser qn, mettre qn en transe; **to go into a t. (state)** *(in spiritualism etc)* se mettre en transe; **he's been wandering around in a t. ever since ...** il erre en transe *ou* dans un état de transe depuis que ...

tranche [trɑ̃ʃ] N *Fin (of loan, payment, shares)* tranche *f*

trank [træŋk], **trankie** ['træŋkɪ] N *Fam* tranquillisant *m*

tranny ['trænɪ] N **1** *Old-fashioned esp Br Fam (transistor radio)* transistor *m* **2** *(transparency)* diapositive *f* **3** *Br Sl (transvestite)* travelo *m*

tranquil ['træŋkwɪl] ADJ tranquille, serein, calme

tranquillity, *Am* **tranquility** [træŋ'kwɪlɪtɪ] N tranquillité *f*, calme *m*, sérénité *f*

tranquillize, *Am* **tranquilize** ['træŋkwɪlaɪz] VT *(person, state of mind etc)* tranquilliser, calmer, apaiser; *(animal)* anesthésier

tranquillizer, *Am* **tranquilizer** ['træŋkwɪlaɪzər] N *Med etc* tranquillisant *m*, calmant *m*; **to be on tranquillizers** être sous calmants

transact [træn'zækt] VT **to t. business with sb** faire des affaires avec qn; **the business was successfully transacted** la transaction *ou* l'affaire a été conclue à notre/sa/*etc* satisfaction

transaction [træn'zækʃən] N **1** *(act of transacting)* **open for the t. of business from ...** ouvert au commerce à partir de ... **2** *(instance of transacting)* opération *f* (commerciale); *St Exch, Fin* transaction *f*, **cash t.** opération *ou* marché *m* au comptant; **business transactions** affaires *fpl*, commerce *m* **3 transactions** *(of learned society)* mémoires *mpl*, procès verbaux *mpl*, comptes *mpl* rendus des séances
▸▸ *St Exch* **t. costs** frais *mpl* de Bourse

transalpine [trænz'ælpaɪn] ADJ transalpin

transatlantic [trænzət'læntɪk] ADJ transatlantique
▸▸ **t. carrier** transporteur *m* transatlantique

transaxle ['trænzæks(ə)l] N *Aut* boîte-pont *f*, *pl* boîtes-ponts

transceiver [træn'siːvər] N *Radio* émetteur-récepteur *m*, *pl* émetteurs-récepteurs

transcend [træn'send] VT **1** *(go beyond)* transcender, aller au delà de **2** *(be superior to)* surpasser

transcendence, transcendency [træn'sendəns(ɪ)] N *Fml* transcendance *f*

transcendent [træn'sendənt] ADJ transcendant

transcendental [trænsen'dent(ə)l] ADJ *Phil* transcendental, -aux

transcendentalism [trænsen'dentəlɪz(ə)m] N *Phil* transcendentalisme *m*

transcoder [trænz'kəʊdər] N transcodeur *m*

transcontinental [trænzkɒntɪ'nent(ə)l] ADJ transcontinental, -aux

transcribe [træns'kraɪb] VT **1** *(write out)* copier, transcrire; *(shorthand)* traduire; *Acct* **to t. entries** transcrire des écritures **2** *Mus (piece of music for another instrument)* transcrire **3** *TV (record)* enregistrer; *(broadcast)* retransmettre en différé

transcript ['trænskrɪpt] N transcription *f*, copie *f*; *(of shorthand notes)* traduction *f*; *Am Scol, Univ* livret *m* scolaire

transcription [træns'krɪpʃən] N **1** *(written copy)* = **transcript 2** *Mus* transcription *f*

transdermal [træns'dɜːm(ə)l] ADJ transdermique
▸▸ **t. patch** timbre *m* autocollant transdermique

transducer [trænz'djuːsər] N transducteur *m*

transect [træn'sekt] VT couper transversalement

transept ['trænsept] N *(of church)* transept *m*; **(arm of the) t.** croisillon *m*

transfer¹ ['trænsfɜːr] N **1** *(act) (of person, object, department etc)* transfert *m*; *(of employee etc)* mutation *f*; *Law (of right etc)* transfert, transmission *f*; *(of property)* translation *f*, mutation; *Banking etc (of money from one account to another)* transfert, virement *m*; *Fin (of shares)* transfert; *(disposal) (of assets, shares etc)* cession *f*; *Comput (of data)* transfert; **t. of capital** transfert de capitaux; **t. of funds** virement de fonds, transfert de fonds; **t. of title** cession de titre; **t. to main airport** pré-acheminement *m*, *pl* pré-acheminements; **t. from main airport** post-acheminement *m*, *pl* post-acheminements; *Br Sport* **the new striker has asked for a t.** le nouveau buteur a demandé son transfert
2 *(document) St Exch* (feuille *f* de) transfert *m*; *Law* **(deed of) t.** acte *m* de cession
3 *Cer, Sewing etc (design)* décalque *m*
4 *Can (ticket)* correspondance *f*
▸▸ **t. advice** avis *m* de virement; *Aut* **t. box** boîte *f* de transfert; **t. bus** navette *f*; **t. cheque** chèque *m* de virement; **t. desk** *(at airport)* guichet *m* de transit; *Acct* **t. entry** article *m* de contre-passation; *Ftbl etc* **t. fee** *(of player)* prix *m* de transfert; *Aut* **t. gearbox** boîte *f* de transfert; *Br* **t. lounge** *(at airport)* salle *f* de transit; **t. order** ordre *m* *ou* mandat *m* de virement; **t. parameter** *(in datacomms)* paramètre *m* de transfert; *Aviat* **t. passengers** voyageurs *mpl* en transit; *Pol* **t. of power** passation *f* de pouvoir; *Comput* **t. rate** taux *m* de transfert; *St Exch* **t. register** registre *m* des transferts; *Comput* **t. speed** vitesse *f* de transfert; **t. tax** droits *mpl* de succession; *(between living persons)* droit de mutation; *Can* **t. ticket** correspondance *f*; **t. transport** transport *m* d'acheminement

transfer² [træns'fɜːr] (-rr-) VT **1** *(something, somebody, from one place to another)* transférer; *(employee, soldier etc)* muter; *Law (rights etc)* transmettre; *(privilege etc)* céder; *(attention)* déplacer (**to** sur); *Banking etc (sum of money)* virer; *(dispose of) (assets, shares etc)* céder; *Acct (debt)* transporter; *Acct (entry)* contre-passer; **to t. one's affections to another person** transférer son affection sur quelqu'un d'autre; **let's t. this desk into the blue room** mettons ce bureau dans la pièce bleue; **to t. a call** transférer un appel; *Br Tel* **transfer(red) charge call** communication *f* en PCV **2** *Typ, Sewing etc (drawing)* calquer, décalquer
VI **1** **to t. to a different department** *(of person)* être transféré dans un autre service; **to t. from one course to another** changer de cours; *Ftbl* **to t. to a different team** obtenir son transfert dans une autre équipe **2** *(to change trains etc)* changer; **to t. to a different plane** *etc* changer d'avion *etc*; **we then t. back to the train at ...** puis on reprend le train à ...

transferable [træns'fɜːrəb(ə)l] ADJ transmissible; *Law (right, property)* cessible, communicable, transférable; **non t.** *(on ticket etc)* non cessible; *Fin* **t. by endorsement** transmissible par endossement
▸▸ **t. credit** crédit *m* transférable; **t. document** document *m* transmissible; **t. letter of credit** crédit transférable; **t. securities** valeurs *fpl* négociables *ou* mobilières; **t. share** action *f* au porteur

transferee [trænsfə'riː] N cessionnaire *mf*

transference ['trænsfərəns] N transfert *m*; **(thought) t.** transmission *f* de pensée

transfiguration [trænsfɪɡjə'reɪʃən] N transfiguration *f*

transfigure [træns'fɪɡər] VT transfigurer; **her face was transfigured with happiness** la joie l'avait transfigurée

transfix [træns'fɪks] VT **1** *(with lance etc)* transpercer **2** *Fig* rendre immobile; **transfixed with fear** pétrifié *ou* cloué par la peur; **they were transfixed by the sight/her singing** *(impressed)* ils étaient hypnotisés par le spectacle/son chant

transform [træns'fɔːm] VT transformer (**into** en), métamorphoser; *Elec (current)* transformer

transformation [trænsfə'meɪʃən] N transformation *f* (**into** en); *(of person)* métamorphose *f* (**into** en)

transformational [trænsfə'meɪʃ(ə)nl] ADJ *Ling* transformationnel

transformer [træns'fɔːmər] N *Elec* transformateur *m*
▸▸ **t. station** station *f* de transformation

transfuse [træns'fjuːz] VT *Med (blood)* transfuser; *Fig Lit* **in a voice transfused with emotion** d'une voix emplie d'émotion

transfusion [træns'fjuːʒ(ə)n] N *Med* **(blood) t.** transfusion *f* de sang, transfusion sanguine; **to give sb a t.** faire une transfusion à qn

transgenic [trænz'dʒenɪk] ADJ transgénique

transgress [trænz'ɡres] *Fml* VT *(law etc)* transgresser, enfreindre
VI enfreindre la loi; *(sin)* pécher

transgression [trænz'ɡreʃən] N *Fml (of law etc)* transgression *f*, infraction *f* (**of** à); *(sin)* péché *m*

transgressor [trænz'ɡresər] N *Fml (of law etc)* transgresseur *m*; *(sinner)* pécheur *m*, pécheresse *f*

tranship [træn'ʃɪp] VT *(passengers, goods)* transborder
VI changer de bateau

transhipment [træn'ʃɪpmənt] N transbordement *m*; **t. bill of lading** connaissement *m* de transbordement

transience ['trænzɪəns] N *(of phenomenon etc)* nature *f* passagère *ou* transitoire

transient ['trænzɪənt] ADJ transitoire; *(happiness etc)* passager, -ère; *(beauty etc)* éphémère; *Am* **t. visitor** client, -ente de passage
N *Am* client, -ente de passage

transire [træn'saɪər] N *Com* passavant *m*, laissez-passer *m inv*

transistor [træn'zɪstər] N *Electron* transistor *m*; *(radio)* transistor, poste *m* à transistors
▸▸ **t. radio, t. set** transistor, poste à transistors

transistorize [træn'zɪstəraɪz] VT transistoriser

transit ['trænsɪt] N **1** *(of goods)* transit *m*; **goods in t.** marchandises *fpl* en transit; **goods lost in t.** marchandises perdues en cours de route **2** *(of people) (through country etc)* voyage *m* **3** *Astron (of planet over face of sun, heavenly body through meridian)* passage *m*
▸▸ *Com* **t. bill** passavant *m*; **t. camp** camp *m* de transit; *Astron* **t. circle** cercle *m* méridien; *Com* **t. declaration** déclaration *f* de transit; *Com* **t. duty** droit *m* de transit; **t. hotel** hôtel *m* de passage *ou* de transit; **t. lounge** salle *f* de transit; **t. passenger** passager, -ère en transit; **t. visa** visa *m* de transit

transition [træn'zɪʃ(ə)n] N transition *f*; **t. from day to night/from fear to hope** pas-

sage *m* du jour à la nuit/de la crainte à l'espoir
▸▸*Chem* t. **element** élément *m* de transition; t. **period** période *f* de transition, période transitoire

transitional [træn'zɪʃən(ə)l] ADJ transitionnel, de transition; *Archit, Art* t. **style** style *m* de transition

transitive ['trænzɪtɪv] *Gram* ADJ transitif
N *(verb)* transitif *m*; **in the t.** à la forme transitive, transitivement

transitively ['trænzɪtɪvlɪ] ADV *Gram* transitivement

transitory ['trænsɪt(ə)rɪ] ADJ transitoire, passager, -ère; *(happiness, desire etc)* passager; *(glory etc)* de courte durée

translatable [træns'leɪtəb(ə)l] ADJ traduisible

translate [træns'leɪt] VT **1** *(book etc)* traduire (**from** de; **into** en); **to t. words into action(s)** *or* **deeds** passer des paroles à l'acte; *Fam* **can you t. that (into plain English), please?** tu peux traduire (en langage de tous les jours), s'il te plaît; **we can now t. these figures into a graph** nous pouvons maintenant traduire ces chiffres en un graphe; **to t. a novel into film terms** adapter un roman à l'écran **2** *Rel (bishop)* transférer (**to** à); *Bible* **Enoch was translated (to heaven)** Énoch fut enlevé au ciel
VI *(of person)* faire de la traduction; *(of writing)* se traduire; **this expression translates literally as ...** la traduction littérale de cette expression est ...; **it doesn't really t. into film** cela se laisse difficilement adapter à l'écran; **how does that t. into economic reality?** comment est-ce que ça se traduit sur le plan économique?

translation [træns'leɪʃən] N **1** *(of book etc)* traduction *f*; *Sch (Latin, Russian etc)* version *f*; *(of novel into film etc)* adaptation *f*; **a lot of the beauty is lost in t.** le texte perd beaucoup de sa beauté à la traduction; **a t. problem** un problème de traduction; **simultaneous t.** traduction simultanée **2** *Rel (of bishop)* translation *f*; *Bible* **(to heaven)** enlèvement *m* (au ciel)
▸▸t. **agency** bureau *m* *ou* agence *f* de traduction; t. **company** cabinet *m* *ou* société *f* de traduction; *Comput* t. **table** table *f* de traduction

translator [træns'leɪtər] N traducteur, -trice

transliterate [trænz'lɪtəreɪt] VT *(in different or phonetic characters)* translit(t)érer, transcrire

transliteration [trænzlɪtə'reɪʃən] N *(in different or phonetic characters)* translit(t)ération *f*, transcription *f*

translucence [trænz'luːsəns] N translucidité *f*

translucent [trænz'luːsənt] ADJ translucide

transmigrate [trænzmaɪ'greɪt] VI *(of people)* migrer; *(of soul)* transmigrer

transmigration [trænzmaɪ'greɪʃən] N *(of people)* migration *f*; *(of soul)* transmigration *f*

transmissible [trænz'mɪsɪb(ə)l] ADJ transmissible

transmission [trænz'mɪʃən] N **1** *Radio, TV, Phys (action)* transmission *f* **2** *(programme)* TV programme *m* télévisé; *Radio* programme radiodiffusé **3** *Aut* transmission *f*
▸▸t. **brake** frein *m* sur transmission; t. **shaft** arbre *m* de transmission; t. **speed** vitesse *f* de transmission

transmit [trænz'mɪt] **(-tt-)** VT *(disease, radio waves)* transmettre; *Radio, TV (programme)* diffuser; *Tech* **to t. a motion to sth** communiquer un mouvement à qch
VI *Radio, TV* émettre, diffuser

transmitter [trænz'mɪtər] N *Tel etc* transmetteur *m*; *Radio, TV* (poste *m*) émetteur *m*, poste d'émission
▸▸*Tel, Radio* t. **receiver** émetteur-récepteur *m*, *pl* émetteurs-récepteurs; *TV, Radio* t. **van** car *m* de transmission

transmogrify [trænz'mɒgrɪfaɪ] VT *Hum* transformer, métamorphoser (**into** en)

transmutation [trænzmju:'teɪʃən] N *Fml* transmutation *f* (**into** en)

transmute [trænz'mju:t] VT transformer, changer (**into** en); *(in alchemy)* transmuer

transom ['trænsəm] N **1** *Archit (of window, door)* traverse *f*, linteau *m* **2** *Am (window over door)* imposte *f*

transparency [træns'pærənsɪ, -'peər-] N **1** *(quality)* transparence *f*; *(of water, excuse etc)* limpidité *f* **2** *(picture) Phot* diapositive *f*, *(for overhead projector)* transparent *m*; *Phot* **colour t.** diapositive en couleur

transparent [træns'pærənt, -'peər-] ADJ **1** *(glass etc)* transparent; *(eau, quartz etc)* limpide **2** *(obvious)* évident, clair, transparent

transparently [træns'pærəntlɪ, -'peər-] ADV *(obviously)* de toute évidence; **that's t. obvious** c'est clair comme de l'eau de roche

transpiration [trænspɪ'reɪʃən] N transpiration *f*

transpire [træns'paɪər] VI **1** *(turn out)* **it transpired that ...** il s'est avéré que ... **2** *(happen)* arriver, se passer **3** *Physiol, Bot* transpirer
VT *(of body, plant etc) (fluid)* exsuder; *(smell)* exhaler

Note that the French verb **transpirer** is a false friend. Its most common meaning is **to sweat**.

transplant[1] ['trænsplɑ:nt, 'trɑ:-] N **1** *Surg (act of transplanting) (of organ)* transplantation *f*, greffe *f*; *(of skin)* greffe; *(transplanted organ etc)* transplant *m*, greffon *m*; **heart/kidney/liver t.** greffe du cœur/rein/foie **2** *(in horticulture)* plant *m* repiqué

transplant[2] [træns'plɑ:nt, trɑ:-] VT **1** *Surg (organ)* transplanter, greffer **2** *(population etc)* transplanter, transporter **3** *(in horticulture) (trees etc)* transplanter; *(plants)* repiquer

transplantation [trænsplɑ:n'teɪʃən, trɑ:-] N transplantation *f*

transponder [træns'pɒndər] N transpondeur *m*

transport[1] ['trænspɔ:t] N **1** *(of goods, passengers, troops etc)* transport *m*; **public t.** transports en commun; **road/rail t.** transport routier/ferroviaire **2** *(means of transport)* moyen *m* de transport; *(aircraft)* (avion *m* de) transport *m*; *(for cargo)* avion cargo; *Naut* **(troop) t.** (bâtiment *m* de) transport; *Fam* **have you got t.?** *(car)* est-ce que vous avez un moyen de transport? **3** *Lit (emotion)* **t. of joy** transports *mpl* de joie; **to go into a t. of joy** être transporté de joie
▸▸t. **advertising** affichage *m* transport; t. **aircraft** (avion de) transport; *(for cargo)* avion cargo; t. **allowance** prime *f* de transport; *Br* t. **café** ≃ routier *m* *(restaurant)*; t. **company** entreprise *f* *ou* société *f* de transport; t. **costs** frais *mpl* de transport; t. **cover** garantie *f* transport; t. **document** titre *m* *ou* document *m* de transport; t. **facilities** moyens *mpl* de transport; t. **museum** musée *m* des transports; t. **plane** (avion de) transport; *(for cargo)* avion cargo; *Br* t. **police** = service *m* d'ordre des chemins de fer

transport[2] [træns'pɔ:t] VT **1** *(passengers, goods)* transporter; **to t. under armed guard** convoyer **2** *(usu passive) Lit* **to be transported with joy** être transporté de joie

transportable [træns'pɔ:təb(ə)l] ADJ transportable

transportation [trænspɔ:'teɪʃən] N **1** transport *m*; *(means of transport)* moyen *m* de transport **2** *Law, Hist (to colonies)* transportation *f*
▸▸*Am* t. **advertising** affichage *m* transport; t. **agreement** contrat *m* de transport; t. **company** société *f* de transport; *Am* t. **desk** *(in hotel)* bureau *m* de voyages; *Am* t. **insurance** assurance *f* transport

transporter [træns'pɔ:tər] N *(vehicle)* transporteur *m*, transporteuse *f*; *(person)* entrepreneur *m* de transports; **car t.** *(lorry)* camion *m* pour transport d'automobiles; *Rail* wagon *m* transporteur de voitures

transpose [træns'pəʊz] VT **1** *(words, terms of equation etc)* transposer **2** *Mus* transposer

transposition [trænspə'zɪʃən] N *(of letters etc), Mus* transposition *f*; *Typ* mastic *m*

transputer [træns'pju:tər] N *Comput* transputeur *m*

transsexual [træn(z)'seksjʊəl] ADJ, N transsexuel, -elle

transship [træn(z)'ʃɪp] = **tranship**

transshipment [træn(z)'ʃɪpmənt] = **transhipment**

Trans-Siberian [træns-] ADJ
▸▸**T. Railway** chemin *m* de fer transsibérien, Transsibérien *m*

transubstantiation [trænsəbstænʃɪ'eɪʃən] N *Rel* transsubstantiation *f*

Transvaal ['trɑ:nzvɑ:l] N **the T.** le Transvaal; **a T. farmer** un fermier transvaalien

transversal [trænz'vɜ:s(ə)l] ADJ transversal, -aux
N *Geom* transversale *f*

transversally [trænz'vɜ:səlɪ] ADV transversalement

transverse ['trænzvɜ:s] ADJ *(section, muscle)* transversal; *Anat (colon)* transverse
▸▸*Constr* t. **beam** traverse *f*; *Aut* t. **engine** moteur *m* transversal; *Geom* t. **line** transversale *f*

transversely ['trænzvɜ:slɪ] ADV *(mounted)* transversalement, en travers

transvestism [trænz'vestɪz(ə)m] N tra(ns)vestisme *m*

transvestite [trænz'vestaɪt] N travesti, -ie

trap [træp] N **1** *(in hunting etc)* piège *m*; *(pit)* trappe *f*; *Fig* piège, ruse *f*, attrape *f*; **to set a t.** *(for animal), Fig (for person)* dresser *ou* tendre un piège (**for** à); **to catch an animal in a t.** prendre une bête au piège; **she's fallen into her own t.** elle est prise à son propre piège; **he fell into the t.** il s'y laissa prendre, il tomba dans le piège; **to walk** *or* **fall straight into the t.** tomber en plein dans le piège; *Mil* **tank t.** (obstacle *m*) antichar *m*; **radar** *or* **speed t.** zone *f* de contrôle de vitesse
2 *(trap door)* trappe *f*
3 *Sl (mouth)* gueule *f*; **shut your t.!** ta gueule!, la ferme!; **you would have to go and open your big t.!** il a fallu que tu ouvres ta grande gueule!
4 *Sport (for clay pigeons)* (projecteur *m*) ball-trap *m*, *pl* ball-traps; *(for live pigeons)* boîte *f* de lancement; *(in dog racing)* box *m* (de départ)
5 *Tech (for water, oil etc)* collecteur *m*; *(in plumbing), Constr* siphon *m*
6 *(horse-drawn vehicle)* cabriolet *m*
7 *esp Am Mus* **traps** instruments *mpl* à percussion
VT **(-pp-)** **1** *(animal, person)* prendre au piège, piéger; **to t. sb into saying sth** faire dire qch à qn en usant de ruse; **to t. sb into making a false move** piéger qn pour qu'il fasse un faux pas; **she trapped him into mar-**

riage elle l'a obligé à se marier avec elle en usant de ruse; **to t. one's finger in the door** se coincer le doigt dans la porte; **I was trapped in the lift for two hours** je suis resté coincé dans l'ascenseur pendant deux heures; **the climbers were trapped by an avalanche** les alpinistes ont été bloqués par une avalanche; **trapped by the flames** cerné par les flammes; **to feel trapped** *(in a relationship)* se sentir prisonnier *ou Fam* coincé **2** *(in pipe) (gas etc)* arrêter **3** *Sport (stop) (ball)* bloquer
VI *(set traps)* tendre des pièges, *Can* trapper
▸▸**t. door** trappe

trapeze [trə'piːz] **N** trapèze *m*
▸▸**t. artist** trapéziste *mf*

trapezium, *pl* **trapeziums, trapezia** [trə'piːzɪəm, -əmz, -ə] **N** *Geom* trapèze *m*

trapezoid ['træpɪzɔɪd] **N** *Geom* trapézoïde *m*

trapper ['træpər] **N** *(hunter)* trappeur *m*

trappings ['træpɪŋz] **NPL 1** *(of power, success etc)* signes *mpl* extérieurs, apparat *m*; **the t. of authority** les signes extérieurs de l'autorité **2** *(for horses)* harnachement *m*, caparaçon *m*

Trappist ['træpɪst] **ADJ, N** *Rel* trappiste *m*

trapshooting ['træpʃuːtɪŋ] **N** *Sport* ball-trap *m*

trash [træʃ] **N** *(worthless objects)* camelote *f*; *Am (refuse)* détritus *mpl*, déchets *mpl*, ordures *fpl*; *(people)* vermine *f*, racaille *f*, *(nonsense)* sottise *f*, *(literature)* littérature *f* de bas étage; *Comput* poubelle *f*; **the food was t.** la nourriture était très mauvaise; **she's t.** elle ne vaut rien; **those people are t.** c'est de la racaille, ces gens-là; **to talk a lot of t.** dire des tas d'imbécilités
▸▸*Am* **t. can** poubelle *f*, boîte *f* à ordures; *Am Comput* **t. icon** icône *f* de la corbeille

trashed [træʃt] **ADJ** *Fam (drunk)* rond, fait, bourré; *(on drugs)* défoncé, raide

trashy ['træʃɪ] **ADJ** *(goods etc)* de pacotille; *(literature)* de bas étage

trauma, *pl* **traumas, traumata** ['trɔːmə, -əz, -ətə] **N** *Med, Psy* trauma *m*; *Med* traumatisme *m*

traumatic [trɔː'mætɪk] **ADJ** *Med* traumatique; *Fig (experience, journey, exam)* traumatisant

traumatism ['trɔːmətɪz(ə)m] **N** *Med* traumatisme *m*

traumatize ['trɔːmətaɪz] **VT** *Med, Fig* traumatiser

travail ['træveɪl] **N 1** *Lit (labour, hard work)* dur labeur *m* **2** *Arch, Lit (childbirth pains)* douleurs *fpl* de l'enfantement, travail *m*

travel ['træv(ə)l] **N 1** voyages *mpl*; **t. was slower in those days** on voyageait plus lentement à cette époque; **what do you spend on t. (to and from work)?** à combien vous reviennent vos déplacements (pour aller et revenir du travail)?; **when are you next off on your travels?** quand repartez-vous en voyage?; **I met him on my** *or* **in the course of my travels** j'ai fait sa connaissance au cours d'un de mes voyages **2** *Tech etc (of piston)* course *f*
VI *(-ll-, Am -l-)* **1** *(journey)* voyager; *(journey around)* faire des voyages; *(of news)* circuler, se répandre; **he has travelled a great deal** *or* **widely** il a beaucoup voyagé; **to t. round the world** faire le tour du monde; **to t. all over the world** voyager partout dans le monde, courir le monde; **to t. through a country** *(visit all parts of)* parcourir un pays; *(on way to another destination)* traverser un pays; **light travels faster than sound** la lumière va *ou* se propage plus vite que le son; **news travels fast round here** les nouvelles vont vite par ici; **the train was travelling at**

150 km an hour le train roulait à 150 km à l'heure; **that's travelling!** *(is fast)* ça c'est de la vitesse!; **we were really travelling** nous allions très vite; **this wine won't t.** ce vin voyage mal
2 *Com* **to t. (for a firm)** voyager (pour une maison), représenter une maison; **to t. on business** voyager pour affaires; **to t. in wine** être représentant en vins
3 *Tech (of part)* se mouvoir, se déplacer; *(of electric current)* se déplacer
VT *(country)* parcourir; **to t. the length and breadth of the country** parcourir le pays de long en large; **I t. this road every day** je prends cette route tous les jours
▸▸**t. agency** agence *f* de voyages; **t. agent** agent *m* de voyages; **t. agent's voucher** bon *m* d'agence *ou* d'échange, voucher *m*; **t. allowance** indemnité *f* de déplacement; **t. bag** sac *m* de voyage; **t. book** *(account)* récit *m* de voyages; *(guide)* guide *m* de voyage; **t. bureau** agence de voyages; **t. company** voyagiste *m*; **t. directory** guide *m* de voyages; **t. documents** documents *mpl* de voyage; **t. expenses** frais *mpl* de déplacement; **t. firm** voyagiste *m*; *Am* **t. group charter** achat *m* de bloc-sièges; **t. guide** guide touristique; **t. insurance** assurance-voyage *f*; **t. literature** documentation *f* touristique; **t. medical insurance** assurance *f* médicale de voyage; *TV* **t. programme** émission *f* sur les voyages; **t. rug** plaid *m*; **t. trade** industrie *f* du voyage; **t. writer** auteur *m* de récits de voyage

travelator ['trævəleɪtər] **N** trottoir *m ou* tapis *m* roulant

travelled, *Am* **traveled** ['træv(ə)ld] **ADJ** much *or* well t. *(person)* qui a beaucoup voyagé; **much t.** *(road)* très fréquenté

traveller, *Am* **traveler** ['træv(ə)lər] **N** voyageur, -euse; *(salesperson)* représentant, -ante; *Br (living in caravan etc)* nomade *mf*; **I'm not a good t.** je supporte mal les voyages; **frequent t.** personne *f* qui est souvent en voyage

traveller's cheque, *Am* **traveler's check** **N** chèque *m* de voyage

travelling, *Am* **traveling** ['træv(ə)lɪŋ] **ADJ** *(circus)* ambulant, forain; *(preacher)* itinérant; *Tech (walkway etc)* roulant; *(crane)* mobile
N voyages *mpl*; **to do a lot of t.** beaucoup voyager; **there isn't a lot of t. in this job** on ne voyage pas beaucoup dans ce travail
▸▸**t. clock** réveil *m* de voyage; **t. companion** compagnon *m* de voyage; **t. expenses** frais *mpl* de déplacement; **t. people** gens *mpl* du voyage; *Cin* **t. platform** travelling *m*; *Br* **t. rug** plaid *m*; **t. salesman** représentant *m ou* voyageur *m* de commerce; **t. scholarship** bourse *f* de voyage; *Cin* **t. shot** prise *f* de vue en travelling, plan *m* travelling; **t. show** *(at a fair)* spectacle *m* forain

travelogue, *Am* **travelog** ['trævəlɒg] **N** *(film)* documentaire *m* de voyage

travel-sick **ADJ** she always gets t. elle est toujours malade en voyage

travel-sickness **N** mal *m* des transports
▸▸**t. pill** cachet *m* contre le mal des transports

travel-size **ADJ** *(shampoo etc)* de voyage

travelstained ['træv(ə)lsteɪnd] **ADJ** sali par le voyage

travel-weary **ADJ** fatigué par le(s) voyage(s)

traverse ['trævəs] **N 1** *Tech, Constr etc (of chassis, frame etc)* traverse *f*, entretoise *f* **2** *Geom* (ligne *f*) transversale *f*, *(in surveying)* cheminement *m* **3** *(in mountaineering, skiing) (across face of escarpment)* traverse *f*, vire *f*
VT *Lit (region, bridge, sea)* traverser

VI *(in mountaineering, skiing)* traverser, prendre une traversée; *(of horse)* se traverser

travesty ['trævəstɪ] **N** *(of play etc)* travestissement *m*; **a t. of the truth** un travestissement de la vérité; **it was a t. of justice** c'était une parodie de justice
VT *(story, figure etc)* parodier, travestir

trawl [trɔːl] **N 1** *Fishing (line)* palangre *f*, *(net)* chalut *m*, traille *f* **2** *Fig (search)* ratissage *m*
VI *Fishing* pêcher au chalut *ou* à la traille; *Fig* **to t. for business** aller à la pêche au client
VT *Fishing (net)* traîner; *(fish)* prendre à la traille *ou* au chalut; *Fig* **she trawled the small-ads for bargains** elle épluchait les petites annonces à la recherche de bonnes affaires; *Fig* **he trawled the singles bars** il écumait les bars pour célibataires
▸▸*Fishing* **t. line** palangre; **t. net** chalut, traille

trawler ['trɔːlər] **N 1** *Fishing (ship)* chalutier *m* **2** *(man)* pêcheur *m* au chalut, chalutier *m*

trawlerman, *pl* **trawlermen** ['trɔːləmən] **N** *Fishing* = **trawler 2**

trawling ['trɔːlɪŋ] **N** *Fishing* pêche *f* au chalut, chalutage *m*

tray [treɪ] **N 1** *(for carrying)* plateau *m*; *(of trunk etc)* casier *m*, châssis *m*; *(in office etc)* corbeille *f* (à correspondance); *(of printer)* bac *m*; *(for selling ice-cream etc)* éventaire *m*; **tea t.** plateau à thé; **to bring/take sth in on a t.** apporter/prendre qch sur un plateau; **a t. of sandwiches** un plateau de sandwiches; **in-t.** *(in office etc)* corbeille de la correspondance reçue; **out-t.** *(in office etc)* corbeille du courrier à expédier/des documents à classer **2** *Phot etc* cuvette *f*

traycloth ['treɪklɒθ] **N** napperon *m* (de plateau)

treacherous ['tretʃərəs] **ADJ** *(person, character)* traître, *f* traîtresse, déloyal, -aux; *(action)* déloyal; *(roads, mountains, ice)* traître

treacherously ['tretʃərəslɪ] **ADV** *(act)* en traître, traîtreusement, perfidement; **we drove in t. bad conditions** nous avons conduit dans des conditions terriblement mauvaises; **it can get t. icy up there** il y a parfois un verglas traître par là-haut

treachery ['tretʃərɪ] **N** trahison *f*, perfidie *f*; **act of t.** trahison, perfidie

treacle ['triːk(ə)l] **N** mélasse *f*
▸▸**t. tart** tarte *f* à la mélasse

treacly ['triːklɪ] **ADJ** *also Fig* sirupeux

tread [tred] **N 1** *(footstep)* pas *m*; *(sound)* bruit *m* de pas; **I heard his familiar t. on the path** j'ai entendu son pas familier sur le chemin; **heavy t.** pas lourd; *esp Lit* **to walk with measured t.** marcher à pas mesurés
2 *(of shoe)* semelle *f*, *(of stepladder etc)* échelon *m*; *Rail (of track)* surface *f ou* table *f* de roulement
3 *Aut (of tyre) (outer layer)* bande *f* de roulement, chape *f*, *(pattern)* sculpture *f*; **there isn't much t. left** *(on tyre)* le pneu est presque lisse; **the t. marks of a heavy vehicle on the sand** les empreintes *fpl* de pneus d'un véhicule lourd sur le sable
VI *(pt* **trod** [trɒd], *pp* **trodden** ['trɒd(ə)n]) marcher; **to t. in/on sth** marcher dans/sur qch; **watch where you t.** regarde où tu mets les pieds; *Fig* **we shall have to t. carefully** *or* **warily** il va falloir marcher sur des œufs *ou* faire très attention
VT 1 *(ground)* marcher sur; **to think that he has trodden this very soil!** quand je pense qu'il a foulé ce sol; **to t. sth underfoot** écraser qch du pied, fouler qch aux pieds; *Fig* **to t. sb underfoot** écraser qn; **don't t. it into the carpet!** ne marche pas dessus, ça va s'incruster dans la moquette!; **to t. mud/dirt into the carpet** mettre de la boue/de la terre

sur le tapis (avec ses chaussures); **well-trodden path** chemin *m* battu; *(much used)* chemin (très) fréquenté; *Old-fashioned* **to t. a path** suivre un chemin; *Fig* **he trod the same path as his father before him** il a suivi la même voie que son père; **to t. grapes** fouler la vendange; **to t. water** *Swimming* flotter en remuant les jambes; *Fig* faire du surplace

2 *Orn (of male bird) (female bird)* couvrir, côcher

▸▸*Aut* **t. plate** repose-pied *m*, *pl* repose-pieds; *Aut* **t. wear indicator** indicateur d'usure

▸ **tread down** VT SEP *(grass etc)* piétiner

treading ['tredɪŋ] N *(of grapes)* foulage *m*

treadle ['tred(ə)l] N *(of sewing machine etc)* pédale *f*

▸▸**t. machine** machine *f* à pédale

treadmill ['tredmɪl] N *Hist (in prisons)* moulin *m* de discipline; *Fig (routine)* besogne *f* (quotidienne) ingrate; **the same old t.** le train-train quotidien

treason ['tri:z(ə)n] N trahison *f*; **high t.** haute trahison

treasonable ['tri:z(ə)nəb(ə)l] ADJ *(remarks etc)* traître, *f* traîtresse, perfide; *(act)* de trahison

treasure ['treʒər] N **1** trésor *m*; **art treasures** trésors *ou* richesses *fpl* artistiques **2** *Fig Fam (person)* trésor *m*; **my home help's a real t.** ma femme de ménage est une perle

VT *(person) (prize)* estimer; *(have affection for) (object, freedom)* tenir beaucoup à; *(advice)* faire beaucoup de cas de; *(memory)* chérir; **to t. sth in one's memory** garder précieusement le souvenir de qch

▸▸**t. hunt** chasse *f* au trésor

treasure-house N *Old-fashioned* trésor *m*

treasurer ['treʒərər] N trésorier, -ière

treasure-trove N *Law* trésor *m* (qu'on a découvert); *Fig* **the museum is a real t.** le musée est une véritable caverne d'Ali-Baba; *Fig* **the book was a t. of anecdotes** le livre était une mine d'anecdotes

treasury ['treʒərɪ] N *(funds)* trésor *m* (public); *(place)* trésorerie *f*, *(of cathedral etc)* trésor; **the T.** *(government department)* ≃ ministère *m* des Finances

▸▸*Fin* **t. bills, t. bonds** bons *mpl* du Trésor; *Com, Fin* **T. Department** Direction *f* du Trésor; *Br* **T. Minister** ≃ ministre *m* des Finances; *Fin* **T. note** billet *m* de trésorerie; *Am* **T. Secretary** ≃ ministre des Finances; *Fin* **t. swap** échange *m* cambiste; *Fin* **T. warrant** mandat *m* du Trésor

treat [tri:t] N *(pleasure)* plaisir *m*; **these chocolates are a real t.** ces chocolats sont un véritable délice *ou* un vrai régal; **to give sb a t.** gâter qn; **to give oneself a t.** se faire un petit extra, se faire plaisir; **it's my t.** *(I'm paying)* c'est moi qui paie; **it would be a great t. to go to the theatre** ce serait un véritable plaisir d'aller au théâtre; **it's a t. seeing you look so well!** c'est un plaisir de te voir aussi en forme!; **to have a t. in store for sb** avoir une surprise pour qn; **if you haven't seen the film yet you've got a t. in store** si tu n'as voir le film tu vas (l')adorer; *Fam* **to go down a t.** être très apprécié; **that whisky went down a t.!** ce whisky m'a fait du bien!; **it worked a t.** *(of plan)* ça a marché comme sur des roulettes; *(of machine, system)* ça a marché à merveille

VT **1** *(behave towards, use)* traiter; **to t. sb well** bien traiter qn; **to t. sb badly** mal traiter qn, ne pas bien traiter qn; **to t. sb/an animal roughly** malmener *ou* maltraiter qn/un animal; **my father still treats me like a child** mon père me traite encore comme un enfant; **he doesn't t. things seriously** il ne prend pas les choses au sérieux; **to t. sth as a joke** prendre qch comme une plaisan-

terie; **you t. this place like a hotel!** ce n'est pas un hôtel ici!

2 *(metal, paper etc)* traiter; *Med (patient, illness)* traiter; **to t. sb for rheumatism** soigner qn qui souffre de rhumatismes; **she was treated in hospital** elle a reçu des soins à l'hôpital; **to t. wood with creosote** traiter le bois à la créosote

3 *Liter, Mus etc (subject, theme)* traiter; **to t. a subject thoroughly/superficially** traiter un sujet à fond/de manière superficielle

4 **to t. sb to sth** offrir qch à qn; **to t. oneself to sth** s'offrir qch; **to t. sb to a night out at the theatre** inviter qn au théâtre; **I'll t. you to an ice-cream** je t'offre une glace; **to t. oneself to oysters** s'offrir des huîtres; **I'll t. you** *(pay for you)* je t'invite; *Iron* **he treated us to a fair old display of petulance** nous avons eu droit à une belle démonstration de mauvaise humeur

VI *Fml (negotiate)* **to t. with sb** traiter *ou* négocier avec qn; **to t. with the enemy** pactiser avec l'ennemi

▸ **treat of** VT INSEP *Fml (deal with)* traiter de

treatise ['tri:tɪz] N traité *m* (**on** de)

treatment ['tri:tmənt] N **1** *(of person)* traitement *m*; **to give special/preferential t. to sb** réserver un traitement spécial/un traitement de faveur à qn; **to receive good/bad t.** être bien/mal traité; *Fam* **to give sb the (full) t.** *(beat up)* rosser qn **2** *(of metal, paper etc)*, *Med* traitement *m* **3** *Liter, Mus etc (of subject, theme)* traitement *m*, façon *f* de traiter; **the subject is given fuller t. elsewhere** le sujet est traité à fond ailleurs **4** *Cin* traitement *m*

treaty ['tri:tɪ] N **1** *(international) (peace, trade)* traité *m*; **T. on European Union** traité sur l'Union européenne **2** *(between individuals)* accord *m*; *(contract)* contrat *m*; **to sell sth by private t.** vendre qch de gré à gré *ou* à l'amiable

treble ['treb(ə)l] ADJ *(triple)* triple

ADV trois fois plus; **t. the number** le triple; **the amount** trois fois plus

N **1** *Mus (person, voice)* soprano *m* **2** *Electron* aigus *mpl*; **we could do with a bit more t.** il faudrait un peu plus d'aigus

VT *(value, number)* tripler

VI tripler

▸▸*Mus* **t. clef** clef *f* de sol; **t. control** touche *f* de tonalité aiguë; *Aut* **t. seat** trois places *f*; *Mus* **t. voice** *(voix f de)* soprano

trebly ['treblɪ] ADV trois fois plus

tree [tri:] N **1** arbre *m*; **fruit t.** arbre fruitier; **timber t.** arbre de haute futaie; *Fig* **to be at the top of the t.** être au sommet; *Fig* **to get to the top of the t.** arriver au sommet de sa profession; *Fig Fam* **to be up a (gum) t.** être dans une impasse ou dans le pétrin; *Fam* **to be out of one's t.** *(crazy)* débloquer; *(drunk)* être rond *ou* bourré; *(on drugs)* être défoncé *ou* raide; *Fam* **money doesn't grow on trees!** l'argent ne pousse pas sur les arbres; *Fam* **good handymen don't grow on trees** les bons hommes à tout faire ne courent pas les rues; *Bible* **the t. of life** l'arbre de vie

2 **family t.** arbre *m* généalogique

3 *Comput (of folders)* arborescence *f*

4 *Hist* **gallows t.** gibet *m*, potence *f*

5 *(shoe)* **t.** embauchoir *m* (pour chaussures)

VT *(chase up a tree) (animal, prey)* obliger à se réfugier sur un arbre

▸▸**t. creeper** *(bird)* grimpereau *m* des bois; **t. diagram** organigramme *m*; **t. fern** fougère *f* arborescente; **t. frog** rainette *f*; *Pej* **t. hugger** écologiste *mf* fanatique; *Geog* **t. line** limite *f* des arbres; **above/below the t. line** au-dessus/en-dessous de la limite des arbres; **t. pipit** pipit *m* des arbres; *Comput* **t. structure** arborescence, structure *f* arborescente; **t. surgeon** arboriculteur, -trice *(qui*

s'occupe de soigner et d'élaguer les arbres)*; **t. trunk** tronc *m* d'arbre

treehouse ['tri:haʊs] N = cabane *f* construite dans un arbre

treeless ['tri:lɪs] ADJ sans arbres

treetop ['tri:tɒp] N cime *f* d'un/de l'arbre; *Aviat* **to skim the treetops** voler en rase-mottes

trefoil ['tri:fɔɪl, 'tref-] N *Bot, Her etc* trèfle *m*

trek [trek] N *(hike)* marche *f*, **a long t.** *(especially on foot)* un trajet long et pénible; **it's quite a t. to the shops** ça fait une trotte pour aller jusqu'aux boutiques; **it's a long t. back up from the beach** le chemin est long et pénible pour remonter de la plage; *Hist* **the Great T.** le Grand Trek

VI (-kk-) *(make long journey)* faire un trajet long et pénible *(à pied)*; *(as holiday activity)* faire du trekking; *Fam* **to t. to the shops** aller jusqu'aux boutiques à pied; *Fam* **and I had to t. all the way back to the shops** et il a fallu que je me retape tout le trajet à pied jusqu'aux boutiques; **he trekked all over the country** il a sillonné le pays

trekking ['trekɪŋ] N *(as holiday activity)* randonnée *f*, trekking *m*; **a t. holiday in Nepal** des vacances *fpl* de trekking au Népal

trellis ['trelɪs] N treillis *m*, treillage *m*

VT **1** *(window etc)* treillisser, treillager **2** *(vine)* échalasser

▸▸**t. window** fenêtre *f* treillissée

trelliswork ['trelɪswɜ:k] N treillis *m*, treillage *m*

tremble ['tremb(ə)l] N tremblement *m*; **to be all of a t.** être tout tremblant

VI *(vibrate)* trembler; *(shiver)* trembler, frissonner; *(with emotion)* frémir; *(of voice)* trembler; **to t. like a leaf** trembler comme une feuille; **to t. with fear** trembler de peur; **where are they? – I t. to think!** où sont-ils? – je n'ose y penser!

trembling ['tremblɪŋ] ADJ tremblant

N tremblement *m*; *(of leaf)* frémissement *m*; **in fear and t.** tout tremblant

tremendous [trɪ'mendəs] ADJ **1** *(enormous)* immense, énorme; **there was a t. crowd** il y avait un monde fou; **a t. difference** une énorme différence; **a. t. lot of sth** une quantité énorme de qch **2** *Fam (excellent)* formidable; **thanks, that's t.** merci, c'est formidable

tremendously [trɪ'mendəslɪ] ADV *(enormously)* extrêmement; **it was t. successful** ce fut un grand succès

tremolo ['treməlaʊ] N *Mus* trémolo *m*

tremor ['tremər] N **1** *(of emotion)* tremblement *m*, frémissement *m*; *(of fear)* frisson *m*; *Med* tremblement, trémulation *f* **2** *(of windows etc)* tremblement *m*; **earth t.** secousse *f* sismique

tremulous ['tremjʊləs] ADJ tremblotant, frémissant; *(smile)* timide, craintif; **to be t. with fear/emotion/joy** frémir de peur/émotion/joie; **t. voice** voix *f* tremblante *ou* chevrotante

tremulously ['tremjʊləslɪ] ADV en tremblant, en tremblotant; *(timidly)* timidement

trench [tren(t)ʃ] N **1** *Agr* tranchée *f*, fossé *m*; *(for draining)* rigole *f*; **water** *or* **irrigation t.** fossé d'irrigation **2** *Mil* tranchée *f*, **communication t.** boyau *m*, -aux

VT *(ground)* creuser un fossé *ou* une tranchée dans

VI creuser des fossés *ou* des tranchées

▸▸**t. coat** trench-coat *m*, *pl* trench-coats; **t. plough** rigoleuse *f*, **t. warfare** guerre *f* de tranchées

trenchant ['tren(t)ʃənt] ADJ *(style, tone)* tranchant, net, incisif; *(reply, epigram)* mordant, caustique

trencher ['tren(t)ʃər] N *Hist* tranchoir *m*, tailloir *m*

trencherman, *pl* **trenchermen** ['tren(t)ʃəmən] N *Old-fashioned* gros mangeur *m*

trend [trend] N *(of public opinion etc)* tendance *f, (fashion)* mode *f, (direction)* direction *f,* **upward/downward t.** tendance à la hausse/la baisse; **to set** *or* **start a t.** lancer une mode; **a t. towards ...** une tendance vers ...; **current trends** tendances actuelles; **the general t. of the market** les tendances du marché; **if present trends continue** si les tendances actuelles se poursuivent
VI se diriger, s'orienter (**to, towards** vers)
▸▸ *Mktg* **t. analysis** analyse *f* des tendances; *Mktg* **t. reversal** renversement *m* de tendance

trendiness ['trendɪnɪs] N *esp Br Fam* côté *m* branché *ou* à la mode; **the t. of his haircut/views** sa coupe/ses idées à la mode; **the t. of the decor** le décor branché

trendsetter ['trendsetər] N lanceur, -euse de modes *ou* de nouvelles tendances

trendsetting ['trendsetɪŋ] ADJ *(innovation, design etc)* qui lance une mode

trendspotter ['trendspɒtər] N = personne *f* employée par une société commerciale pour identifier les nouvelles tendances de la mode telles qu'elles apparaissent dans la rue, les bars, etc

trendy ['trendɪ] *esp Br Fam* ADJ *(clothes, person, views etc)* branché
N *Pej (person)* personne *f* branchée

trepan [trɪ'pæn] *Surg* N trépan *m*
VT (**-nn-**) trépaner

trepanning [trɪ'pænɪŋ] N *Surg* trépanation *f*

trepidation [trepɪ'deɪʃən] N *(anxiety)* agitation *f* nerveuse; **he stood there in t. before the headmaster** il se tenait tout tremblant devant le directeur de l'école; **he opened the letter with t.** il ouvrit la lettre en tremblant; **he picked up the phone and, not without t., dialled** il saisit l'écouteur et composa le numéro non sans nervosité

trespass ['trespəs] N **1** *Law (on property)* violation *f* de propriété **2** *Rel* offense *f,* péché *m*; **forgive us our trespasses** pardonne-nous nos offenses
VI **1** *Law* **to t. (on sb's property)** entrer sans autorisation dans la propriété de qn; **please leave, you're trespassing** veuillez quitter les lieux, vous n'êtes pas autorisés à être ici; **to t. (up)on sb's rights** violer *ou* enfreindre les droits de qn; **I don't wish to t. on your time** je ne veux pas abuser de votre temps; **I don't wish to t. on your area of responsibility** je ne veux pas empiéter sur vos attributions **2** *Rel* pécher (**against** contre); **as we forgive those that t. against us** comme nous pardonnons à ceux qui nous ont offensés

Note that the French verb **trépasser** is a false friend and is never a translation for the English verb **to trespass**. It means **to die**.

trespasser ['trespəsər] N *Law (on sb's land)* intrus, -use *(dans une propriété privée)*; **trespassers will be prosecuted** *(on sign)* défense d'entrer sous peine d'amende

trespassing ['trespəsɪŋ] N *(on sb's land)* violation *f* de propriété (foncière); **no t.** *(on sign)* défense d'entrer

tress [tres] N boucle *f, (plait)* tresse *f, Lit* **tresses** *(of woman)* chevelure *f,* cheveux *mpl*

trestle ['tres(ə)l] N tréteau *m,* chevalet *m*
▸▸ **t. bridge** pont *m* sur chevalets; **t. table** table *f* à tréteaux

trews [truːz] NPL *(trousers) Scot* pantalon *m* en tartan; *Br Fam* pantalon *m*

triad ['traɪæd] N **1** *(group of three)* triade *f* **2** *(Chinese secret society)* triade *f* **3** *Chem* élément *m* trivalent **4** *Mus* accord *m* parfait
▸▸ *Mktg* **t. markets** marchés *mpl* de la triade

trial ['traɪəl] N **1** *Law (proceedings)* procès *m*; **to bring sb to t.** faire passer qn en jugement; **to be on t. for a crime/for one's life** passer en jugement pour un crime/pour un crime passible de la peine de mort; **they were sent for t.** ils furent renvoyés en jugement; **t. by jury** jugement *m* par jury; *Hist* **t. by combat** combat *m* judiciaire; **famous trials** causes *fpl* célèbres
2 *(test)* épreuve *f, (of instrument, vehicle etc)* essai *m* (technique); *Sport* match *m* de sélection; **t. of strength** épreuve de force; **to give sth a t.** faire l'essai de qch; **on t.** à l'essai; **to proceed by t. and error** procéder par tâtonnements *ou* par approximations successives; **sheepdog trials** concours *m* de chiens de berger; **speed t.** essai de vitesse
3 *(ordeal)* épreuve *f* (douloureuse); **that child is a great t. to his parents** cet enfant met ses parents au martyre; **despite the trials and tribulations** en dépit des caprices de la fortune; **after all your trials and tribulations** après tout ce que vous avez dû souffrir
▸▸ *Acct* **t. balance** balance *f* d'inventaire; *Fig* **t. balloon** ballon *m* d'essai; *Aviat* **t. flight** vol *m* d'essai; *Sport* **t. game** match *m* de sélection; **t. judge** ≃ juge *m* d'instance; **t. offer** offre *f* d'essai; *Mktg* **t. order** commande *f* d'essai; **t. period** période *f* d'essai; **to be on a t. period** *(of employee)* faire une période d'essai; **t. run** essai *m*; **to give sth a t. run** essayer qch, faire un essai avec qch; **t. separation** séparation *f* à l'essai

triangle ['traɪæŋg(ə)l] N **1** *Geom etc* triangle *m*; *Fam* **the eternal t.** l'éternel triangle **2** *Mus* triangle *m*; *(drawing instrument)* équerre *f* (en triangle)
▸▸ *Phys* **t. of forces** triangle *m* des forces

triangular [traɪ'æŋgjʊlər] ADJ *(shape etc)* triangulaire, en triangle; *(contest, relationship etc)* triangulaire

triangulate [traɪ'æŋgjʊleɪt] VT *(in surveying)* trianguler

triangulation [traɪæŋgjʊ'leɪʃən] N *(in surveying)* triangulation *f*

triathlon [traɪ'æθlɒn] N triathlon *m*

tribal ['traɪb(ə)l] ADJ *(society, warfare, system)* tribal, -aux *ou* -als; *(leader)* de tribu; *(people etc)* qui vit en tribus

tribalism ['traɪbəlɪz(ə)m] N tribalisme *m*

tribalistic [traɪbə'lɪstɪk] ADJ tribal, -aux *ou* -als

tri-band ['traɪ-] ADJ *Tel* triple bande

tribe [traɪb] N **1** tribu *f, Fig Fam* tribu, smala *f*; **the twelve tribes of Israel** les douze tribus d'Israël **2** *Biol* tribu *f*

tribesman, *pl* **tribesmen** ['traɪbzmən] N membre *m* d'une/de la tribu; **Bedouin t.** membre *m* d'une/de la tribu bédouine

tribulation [trɪbjʊ'leɪʃən] N *Fml* tribulations *fpl*; **I had no wish to add to her tribulations** je ne voulais pas ajouter à ses tourments

tribunal [tr(a)ɪ'bjuːnəl] N tribunal *m,* -aux

tribune¹ ['trɪbjuːn] N *(platform), Fig* tribune *f*

tribune² N *(officer in ancient Rome etc)* tribun *m*

tributary ['trɪbjʊt(ə)rɪ] ADJ *(state)* tributaire; *(road)* secondaire
N **1** *Geog (of river)* affluent *m* **2** *(person, country)* tributaire *m*

tribute ['trɪbjuːt] N **1** *(homage)* tribut *m,* hommage *m*; **to pay (a) t. to sb** rendre hommage à qn; **it is a t. to her/his determina-** tion that the work was finished at all c'est grâce à elle/à sa détermination que le travail a été terminé; **to pay a last t. to sb** rendre à qn les derniers devoirs; **floral tributes** gerbes *fpl* et couronnes *fpl* (de fleurs) **2** *Hist (money)* tribut *m*
▸▸ *Hist* **t. money** tribut

trice [traɪs] N **in a t.** en un clin d'œil, en moins de rien

tricentenary, *esp Am* **tricentennial** [traɪsen'tiːnərɪ, -'tenɪəl] ADJ, N tricentenaire *m*

triceps ['traɪseps] N *Anat* triceps *m*
▸▸ **t. muscle** triceps

triceratops [traɪ'serətɒps] N tricératops *m*

trichinosis [trɪkɪ'nəʊsɪs] N *Med* trichinose *f*

trick [trɪk] N **1** *(ruse)* tour *m,* ruse *f, (dishonest)* supercherie *f, (practical joke)* farce *f,* tour; *(knack)* truc *m*; *(taught to animal, child etc)* tour d'adresse; *(of conjuror)* tour; **by a t.** *(to obtain sth)* par ruse; **to play a t. on sb** faire une farce *ou* une blague à qn; **my eyes must have been playing tricks on me** *or* **playing me tricks** mes yeux ont dû me jouer des tours, j'ai dû avoir la berlue; **t. of the light** effet *m* de lumière; **that was a nasty** *or* **mean** *or* **dirty t.** ça c'était un vilain tour!; **you've been up to your tricks again** vous avez encore fait des vôtres; **the car's up to its old tricks again** la voiture recommence à faire des siennes; **the tricks of the trade** les trucs *ou* les astuces *fpl* du métier; **that should do the t.** ça devrait faire l'affaire, ça devrait marcher; **he has the t. of always being in the right place at the right time** il a le chic pour être toujours au bon endroit au bon moment; **to teach a dog tricks** apprendre des tours à un chien; **card t.** tour de cartes; **conjuring t.** tour de prestidigitation *ou* de passe-passe; *Fam* **the whole bag of tricks** tout le bataclan, tout le tremblement; **she doesn't miss a t.** rien ne lui échappe; *Fam* **how's tricks?** *(how are you?)* comment vas-tu?; *(what's the news?)* quoi de neuf?
2 *Old-fashioned (mannerism)* manie *f, (habit)* habitude *f*; **he has a t. of repeating himself** il a la manie de se répéter
3 *Cards* pli *m*; **to take** *or* **make a t.** faire une levée *ou* un pli
4 *Sl (of prostitute)* passe *f,* **to turn a t.** faire une passe; **she's been turning tricks for years** ça fait des années qu'elle fait la pute
VT *(person)* attraper, duper; **I've been tricked** j'ai été refait, je me suis fait avoir; **to t. sb into doing sth** amener qn à faire qch en usant de ruse; **you won't t. me into doing that again!** tu ne m'y reprendras pas!; **to t. sb out of sth** *(of opportunity etc)* frustrer qn de qch; *(of money etc)* escroquer qch à qn
▸▸ **t. cyclist** *(in circus)* cycliste *mf* acrobate; *Br Fam (psychiatrist)* psy *mf*, **t. photography** trucages *mpl*; **t. question** question-piège *f,* *pl* questions-pièges; **t. riding** *(on horseback)* voltige *f*
▸ **trick out** VT SEP *esp Lit (dress)* attifer (**in, with** de)

trickery ['trɪkərɪ] N tricherie *f,* duperie *f,* **piece of t.** supercherie *f,* **by t.** par ruse

trickiness ['trɪkɪnɪs] N *(of mechanism, situation)* difficulté *f*

trickle ['trɪk(ə)l] N *(of water etc)* filet *m*; **sales were down to a t.** il n'y avait presque plus de ventes; **emigration is down to a t.** l'émigration ne se fait plus qu'au compte-goutte; **we've had a slow but steady t. of contributions** les contributions nous arrivent assez lentement mais de manière régulière
VI couler (goutte à goutte); **water was trickling down the wall** l'eau dégoulinait *ou* coulait le long du mur; **tears were trickling down her cheeks** les larmes coulaient le long de ses joues; **news is beginning to t.**

through *or* out from the devastated area on commence à recevoir peu à peu des nouvelles de la région sinistrée; **refugees are still trickling across the border** quelques rares réfugiés continuent à passer la frontière; **the ball just trickled into the hole** la balle a roulé tout doucement dans le trou; **the results began to t. in** les résultats commençaient à arriver lentement

VT *(liquid)* laisser goutter, laisser tomber goutte à goutte

▸▸ *Elec* **t. charger** chargeur *m* à régime lent; *Econ* **t.-down theory** = théorie *f* selon laquelle les richesses accumulées par un petit nombre bénéficieront à tous les membres de la société

trickster ['trɪkstər] **N** escroc *m*; **confidence t.** voleur, -euse à l'américaine

tricky ['trɪkɪ] **ADJ 1** *(difficult)* difficile; *(awkward)* compliqué, délicat **2** *(deceitful)* rusé; *Fam* **he's a t. customer** c'est un rusé *ou* un malin

tricolour, *Am* **tricolor** ['trɪkələr] **N** *(flag)* drapeau *m* tricolore *(principalement français ou irlandais)*

tricorn(e) ['traɪkɔːn] **ADJ** *(hat)* tricorne **N** tricorne *m*

tricuspid [traɪ'kʌspɪd] **ADJ** *Anat* tricuspide

tricycle ['traɪsɪk(ə)l] **N** tricycle *m*

trident ['traɪdənt] **N** trident *m*

tried [traɪd] **ADJ** well **t.** *(remedy)* éprouvé, qui a fait ses preuves; **t. and tested** *(formula)* éprouvé, qui a fait ses preuves; **t. and trusted** *(friend, employee)* sur qui l'on peut compter

triennial [traɪ'enɪəl] **ADJ** triennal, -aux; *(plant)* trisannuel

triennially [traɪ'enɪəlɪ] **ADV** tous les trois ans

trier ['traɪər] **N** to be a **t.** *(persevere)* faire des efforts, s'accrocher; **she might not be the best but she's a t.** ce n'est peut-être pas la meilleure mais elle est persévérante

trifle ['traɪf(ə)l] **N 1** *(insignificant thing)* broutille *f*, bagatelle *f*, vétille *f*; *(money)* petite somme *f* d'argent; *(object, gift)* bricole *f*; **to quarrel over a mere t.** se quereller pour un oui pour un non, se quereller sur des riens; **it was sold for a mere t.** on l'a vendu pour un rien **2** a **t.** *(a little)* un tout petit peu, (un) tant soit peu; a **t. too wide/too short** un tantinet trop large/trop court **3** *Br Culin* = dessert *m* où alternent une couche de génoise imbibée d'alcool et de fruits en gelée et une couche de crème anglaise, le tout recouvert de Chantilly

▸ **trifle away VT SEP** *(waste)* gaspiller; **to t. one's time away** gaspiller son temps

▸ **trifle with VT INSEP** *(affections etc)* jouer *ou* badiner avec; **she's not a woman to be trifled with** on ne joue pas *ou* ne plaisante pas avec elle; **to t. with one's food** manger du bout des dents, grignoter

trifling ['traɪflɪŋ] **ADJ** *(unimportant)* insignifiant, peu important; *(negligible)* négligeable; **t. incidents** menus incidents *mpl*; **that's a t. matter** ce n'est qu'une bagatelle; *Iron* **the t. sum of 10,000 euros** la bagatelle de 10 000 euros

triforium, *pl* **triforia** [traɪ'fɔːrɪəm, -ɪə] **N** triforium *m*

trigger ['trɪɡər] **N** *(on gun)* détente *f*, gâchette *f*; *(on movie camera), Tech* déclencheur *m*, poussoir *m* *(à ressort)*; *Fig* catalyseur *m*; **to be quick on the t.,** *Fam* **to be t. happy** ne pas hésiter à tirer, *Fam* avoir la gâchette facile

VT *also Fig* déclencher

▸▸ **t. action** déclenchement *m*; **t. finger** index *m* *(avec lequel on appuie sur la gâchette)*; **my t. finger's itching** j'ai à la gâchette qui me

démange; **t. mechanism** mécanisme *m* de déclenchement

▸ **trigger off VT SEP** *Fig* = **trigger VT**

trigonometric(al) [trɪɡənə'metrɪk, -ɪk(ə)l] **ADJ** trigonométrique

trigonometrically [trɪɡənə'metrɪklɪ] **ADV** trigonométriquement

trigonometry [trɪɡə'nɒmɪtrɪ] **N** trigonométrie *f*

trike [traɪk] **N** *(abbr* **tricycle)** tricycle *m*

trilateral [traɪ'læt(ə)rəl] **ADJ** trilatéral, -aux

trilby ['trɪlbɪ] **N** *Br* chapeau *m* mou, feutre *m*

▸▸ **t. hat** chapeau mou, feutre

trilingual [traɪ'lɪŋɡw(ə)l] **ADJ** trilingue

trill [trɪl] **N 1** *Mus* trille *m* **2** *(of birds)* chant *m* perlé, trille *m* **3** *Ling* consonne *f* roulée

VI *Mus etc* faire des trilles

VT *Mus etc (note)* triller; *Ling* **trilled consonant** consonne *f* roulée; **I'm up here, trilled Penelope** je suis en haut, dit Pénélope d'une voix flûtée

trillion ['trɪljən] VOIR GRAMMAIRE A76 **1** *Br* *(10^{18})* trillion *m* **2** *Am* *(10^{12})* billion *m*

trilogy ['trɪlədʒɪ] **N** trilogie *f*

trim [trɪm] **N 1** *(of hair etc)* coupe *f* d'entretien; **just a t.** *(said to hairdresser)* c'est simplement pour se rafraîchir

2 in (good) t. en bon ordre; *(of person)* *(in good health)* en bonne santé; *(fit)* en (bonne) forme; **in fighting t.** prêt pour le combat

3 *Naut (of sails)* orientation *f*, **in t.** équilibré; **out of t.** déséquilibré

4 *(on car)* habillage *m*; **interior t.** garniture *f* intérieure; **seat t.** garnissage *m* des sièges

5 *Sl (women)* nanas *fpl*, gonzesses *fpl*; **that's his new bit of t.** c'est sa nouvelle gonzesse

ADJ soigné; **a t. little yacht** un joli petit voilier; **to have a t. figure** *(of person)* avoir une silhouette svelte; **a t. little garden** un petit jardin coquet *ou* bien tenu

VT *(-mm-)* **1** *(cut)* *(hedge, tree)* tailler; *(edge of book)* ébarber, rogner; *(beard etc)* tailler; *(sb's hair)* couper, rafraîchir; *Comput (database)* supprimer les espaces blancs inutiles de; **to t. (the wick of) a lamp** moucher une lampe; **to t. the budget** réduire le budget; *Culin* **to t. meat** habiller *ou* parer la viande

2 *(ship, plane)* équilibrer; *(load)* arrimer; *Naut (sails)* orienter

3 *Sewing etc (dress etc)* orner, garnir (**with** de); *(hat)* garnir; *Am (Christmas tree)* décorer; **trimmed with lace** garni de dentelles

▸ **trim away VT SEP** *(excess growth, unnecessary details, verbiage)* élaguer

▸ **trim down VT SEP** *(text, size of company, expenditure etc)* réduire

VI *(spend less)* réduire ses dépenses; *(shed staff)* réduire ses effectifs

▸ **trim off VT SEP** *Culin etc (fat)* enlever; **to t. the fat off the meat** enlever le gras de la viande; *Fig* **they've trimmed £200 off the budget** ils ont réduit le budget de 200 livres; **I think we could t. a couple of hours off the journey** je pense que nous pourrions gagner environ deux heures sur le trajet

trimaran ['traɪməræn] **N** *Naut* trimaran *m*

trimester [tr(a)ɪ'mestər] **N** *esp Am* trimestre *m*

trimmer ['trɪmər] **N 1** *(machine)* *(for wood etc)* machine *f* à trancher; *(in papermaking, bookbinding etc)* massicot *m* **2** *Pej (opportunist)* opportuniste *mf*

trimming ['trɪmɪŋ] **N 1** *(cutting)* *(of hedges, trees)* taille *f*, *(of edges of book)* ébarbage *m*, rognage *m*; **trimmings** *(pieces)* *(of iron, wood, paper etc)* rognures *fpl*, ébarbures *fpl* **2** *(reduction)* *(of expenses etc)* réduction *f* **3** *(decoration)* *(of clothes, curtains etc)* garniture *f*, ornement *m*; **trimming(s)** *(on garment*

etc) passementerie *f*, *Br Culin* (usual) **trimmings** *(of dish)* accompagnements *mpl*, garniture *f*; **roast beef and all the trimmings** du rosbif et tout ce qui l'accompagne; *Fig* **with all the trimmings** avec tout le tralala

trimness ['trɪmnɪs] **N** *(of person, thing)* air *m* soigné; *(of figure)* sveltesse *f*

Trinidad ['trɪnɪdæd] **N** (l'île de) la Trinité; **T. and Tobago** la Trinité-et-Tobago

Trinity ['trɪnɪtɪ] **N** *Rel* **the (Holy) T.** la (sainte) Trinité

▸▸ **T. Sunday** (la fête de) la Trinité; *Univ* **T. term** troisième trimestre *m* (universitaire) *(à Oxford, Cambridge et au Trinity College de Dublin)*

trinket ['trɪŋkɪt] **N** *(jewellery)* petit bijou *m* en toc; *(worthless object)* babiole *f*

trinomial [traɪ'nəʊmɪəl] **ADJ, N** *Math* trinôme *m*

trio, *pl* **trios** ['triːəʊ, -əʊz] **N** *Mus etc* trio *m*

trip [trɪp] **N 1** *(journey)* voyage *m*; *(outing)* excursion *f*, **business/honeymoon t.** voyage d'affaires/de noces; **to go on a shopping t.** aller faire des courses; **the t. takes two hours** le trajet dure deux heures; **he's away on a t. to Italy** il est en voyage en Italie; **I'm afraid I'm going to have to make another t. to the loo** je crois que je vais devoir refaire un tour aux cabinets; **round t.** *(circular journey)* voyage circulaire; *Naut* croisière *f*, *(journey there and back)* voyage d'aller et retour; *Br Sch* **school t.** excursion scolaire; *(longer)* voyage scolaire; *Br Sch* **geography field t.** excursion d'études géographiques; *(longer)* voyage d'études géographiques

2 (drug) t. voyage *m*, trip *m*; **to be on a t.** faire un voyage *ou* un trip, être en plein trip **3** *Sl (quantity of LSD)* dose *f* de LSD

4 *(stumble)* faux pas *m*

5 *Fam (experience)* **to be on a guilt t.** culpabiliser; **to be on a power t.** être en plein trip mégalo; **to be on an ego t.** se faire mousser **6** *Sport (foul)* croc-en-jambe *m*, *pl* crocs-en-jambe, croche-pied *m*, *pl* croche-pieds; **that was a t.!** il lui a fait un croc-en-jambe!

VI *(-pp-)* **1** *(stumble)* trébucher, faire un faux pas; *(of horse)* broncher

2 *(step lightly)* aller d'un pas léger; **he tripped merrily into the room** il entra dans la pièce d'un pas léger

3 *Tech (of catch etc)* se déclencher; *(of part of mechanism)* basculer, culbuter

4 *Sl (on drugs)* faire un trip; **I was tripping at the time** j'étais en plein trip; **I don't know what she was tripping on** je ne sais pas ce qu'elle avait pris

5 to t. off the tongue *(of name, jingle etc)* bien couler; **her name doesn't exactly t. off the tongue** son nom n'est pas facile à prononcer

VT 1 = **trip up VT SEP 1 2** *Tech (part of machine)* déclencher; *(lever etc)* culbuter **3** *Hum* **to t. the light fantastic** *(dance)* danser

▸▸ **t. computer** ordinateur *m* de bord; *Aut* **t. recorder** compteur *m* journalier, totalisateur *m* partiel; **t. wire** fil *m* tendu *(pour déclencher un mécanisme, pour faire tomber quelqu'un ou pour avertir de son arrivée)*

▸ **trip over VI** trébucher et tomber

VT INSEP *(something)* trébucher sur, buter contre; *Fig* **you can't go anywhere here without tripping over celebrities** par ici on ne peut pas faire un pas sans tomber sur une célébrité; **to t. over one's (own) feet** s'emmêler les pieds

▸ **trip up VT SEP 1** *(cause to fall)* faire un croc-en-jambe *ou* un croche-pied à; *(of obstacle)* faire trébucher, faire tomber **2** *Fig (catch out)* démonter, désarçonner

VI 1 *(stumble)* trébucher, faire un faux pas; **to t. up over a word** trébucher sur un mot **2** *(make mistake)* faire une erreur; **the rob-**

bers/fugitives finally tripped up les voleurs/fugitifs ont fini par commettre une erreur; that's where we tripped up *(blundered)* c'est là que nous avons fait une gaffe

tripartite [traɪˈpɑːtaɪt] ADJ tripartite; *(divided into three)* divisé en trois, en trois parties

tripe [traɪp] N *Culin* tripes *fpl*; *Fam (nonsense)* bêtises *fpl*; *Fam* **that's all** *or* **a lot of t.** tout ça c'est des sottises

triphammer [ˈtrɪphæmər] N *Tech* marteau *m* à bascule *ou* à soulèvement

triphase [ˈtraɪfeɪz] ADJ *Elec (current)* triphasé

triphthong [ˈtrɪfθɒŋ] N triphtongue *f*

triplane [ˈtraɪpleɪn] N triplan *m*

triple [ˈtrɪp(ə)l] ADJ triple; *St Exch* **t. A rated** noté triple A
ADV **t. the number/amount** trois fois le nombre/la quantité
N triple *m*
VT & VI tripler
▸▸ *Hist* **the T. Alliance** *(1668)* la Triple Alliance; *(1882-1914)* la Triple-Alliance, la Triplice; *St Exch* **t.-A rating** notation *f* AAA; *Med* **t. combination therapy** trithérapie *f*; **t. glazing** triple vitrage *m*; *Sport* **t. jump** triple saut *m*; *Med* **t. therapy** trithérapie *f*; *Mus* **t. time** mesure *f* ternaire *ou* à trois temps

triple-band ADJ *Tel* triple bande

triplet [ˈtrɪplɪt] N *(child)* triplé, -ée; *Mus* triolet *m*; *(in poetry)* tercet *m*

triplex [ˈtrɪpleks] ADJ *(planche)* de trois épaisseurs

triplicate¹ [ˈtrɪplɪkət] ADJ **t. copies** trois exemplaires *mpl*
N triple *m*, triplicata *m*; **in t.** en triple *ou* trois exemplaire(s); **invoice in t.** facture en triplicata *ou* en trois exemplaires

triplicate² [ˈtrɪplɪkeɪt] VT *Com (document)* rédiger en trois exemplaires

triply [ˈtrɪplɪ] ADV triplement

tripod [ˈtraɪpɒd] N trépied *m*

Tripoli [ˈtrɪpəlɪ] N Tripoli

tripos [ˈtraɪpɒs] N *Univ (at Cambridge)* = épreuves *fpl* pour l'obtention de la licence ès lettres/ès sciences

tripper [ˈtrɪpər] N *esp Br (person)* excursionniste *mf*; **they're (just) day trippers** ils sont (juste) venus passer la journée

trippy [ˈtrɪpɪ] ADJ *Fam* psychédélique

triptych [ˈtrɪptɪk] N *Art* triptyque *m*

trireme [ˈtraɪriːm] N trirème *f*, trière *f*

trisect [traɪˈsekt] VT *Geom etc (line, angle)* diviser *ou* couper en trois

trisomy [ˈtraɪsəʊmɪ] N *Med* trisomie *f*

trisyllabic [traɪsɪˈlæbɪk] ADJ *(in prosody)* tris(s)yllabe, tris(s)yllabique

trisyllable [traɪˈsɪləb(ə)l] N *(in prosody)* tris(s)yllabe *m*

trite [traɪt] ADJ banal, -als; *(theme)* rebattu; **t. remarks** banalités *fpl*, lieux *mpl* communs

tritely [ˈtraɪtlɪ] ADV banalement

triteness [ˈtraɪtnɪs] N banalité *f*

tritium [ˈtrɪtɪəm] N *Chem* tritium *m*

triton [ˈtraɪt(ə)n] N *(mollusc), Myth* triton *m*

triturate [ˈtrɪtjəreɪt] VT *Tech* triturer, broyer

trituration [trɪtjəˈreɪʃən] N *Tech* trituration *f*

triumph [ˈtraɪəmf] N triomphe *m* (**over** sur); **to achieve great triumphs** remporter de grands succès; **she came home in t.** elle est rentrée triomphante chez elle; **a look of t.** un air triomphant; **the t. in his voice/eyes** le triomphe dans sa voix/ses yeux
VI triompher; **to t. over one's enemies** *(defeat)* triompher de ses ennemis

triumphal [traɪˈʌmf(ə)l] ADJ triomphal, -aux; **to get a t. reception** avoir une arrivée triomphale

triumphant [traɪˈʌmfənt] ADJ triomphant; *(success)* retentissant; **a t. expression** un air de triomphe; **to be t. over sb/sth** triompher de qn/qch

triumphantly [traɪˈʌmfəntlɪ] ADV *(to return etc)* en triomphe; *(to look at etc)* d'un air triomphant; *(to say)* d'un ton triomphant

triumvirate [traɪˈʌmvɪrɪt] N *Hist* triumvirat *m*; *Fig (of people)* trio *m*

triune [ˈtraɪjuːn] ADJ *Rel* d'une unité triple, en trois parties, trin

trivet [ˈtrɪvɪt] N *Culin* trépied *m*

trivia [ˈtrɪvɪə] NPL vétilles *fpl*, petits riens *mpl*; **to get bogged down in t.** s'embarrasser de futilités; **he has an amazing memory for t.** il a une mémoire remarquable pour les choses sans importance

trivial [ˈtrɪvɪəl] ADJ **1** *(unimportant)* insignifiant, sans importance; **t. matter** bagatelle *f*, **t. offence** peccadille *f* **2** *(person)* superficiel, frivole; **he's just being t.** il plaisante **3** *(banal)* banal, -als, dépourvu d'originalité

> [!NOTE]
> Note that the French word **trivial** is a false friend. It means **vulgar, coarse**.

triviality [trɪvɪˈælɪtɪ] N **1** *(of loss, offence etc)* caractère *m* insignifiant; *(of remark etc)* banalité *f*, futilité *f* **2** **to talk polite trivialities** dire des futilités *ou* des banalités pour être poli

trivialization [trɪvɪəlaɪˈzeɪʃən] N banalisation *f*

trivialize [ˈtrɪvɪəlaɪz] VT banaliser

trochaic [trəʊˈkeɪɪk] ADJ, N *(in prosody)* trochaïque *m*

trochee [ˈtrəʊkiː] N *(in prosody)* trochée *m*

trod PT, **trodden** PP *see* tread

trog [trɒg] N *Br Fam (ugly person)* mocheté *f*

trogloditic [trɒgləˈdɪtɪk] ADJ troglodytique

troglodyte [ˈtrɒglədaɪt] N troglodyte *m*

troika [ˈtrɔɪkə] N troïka *f*

troilism [ˈtrɔɪlɪz(ə)m] N amour *m ou* sexe *m* à trois

Trojan [ˈtrəʊdʒən] ADJ *Hist* troyen, de Troie
N *Hist* Troyen, -enne; **like a T.** *(to work)* sans relâche; *(to fight)* vaillamment
▸▸ *Hist, Fig* **T. Horse** cheval *m* de Troie; **the T. War** la guerre de Troie

troll¹ [trəʊl] *Fishing* N cuiller *f*, *(of fishing rod)* moulinet *m*
VI **to t. for pike** pêcher le brochet à la cuiller

troll² [trəʊl] N *Myth* troll *m*; *Br Fam (ugly person)* mocheté *f*

trollied [ˈtrɒlɪd] ADJ *Br Fam (drunk)* bourré, pété

trolley [ˈtrɒlɪ] N **1** *Br (cart)* chariot *m*; *(two wheeled)* diable *m*; *(for luggage)* chariot à bagages; *(shopping)* **t.** *(in supermarket etc)* chariot, caddie *m*; *(dinner or tea)* **t.** table *f* roulante **2** *(wheel)* (poulie *f* de) trolley *m*; *Fam* **he's off his t.** *(mad)* il débloque
▸▸ *Am* **t. car** tramway *m*; *Br Fam Pej* **t. dolly** *(air hostess)* hôtesse *f* de l'air; **t. jack** cric *m* rouleur; **t. wheel** (poulie de) trolley

trolleybus [ˈtrɒlɪbʌs] N trolleybus *m*

trolling [ˈtrəʊlɪŋ] N *Fishing* pêche *f* à la cuiller

trollop [ˈtrɒləp] N *Old-fashioned, Hum* **1** *(dirty woman)* souillon *f* **2** *(promiscuous woman)* catin *f*, gourgandine *f*

trombone [trɒmˈbəʊn] N *Mus* trombone *m*

trombonist [trɒmˈbəʊnɪst] N tromboniste *mf*

troop [truːp] N **1** *(of people)* groupe *m*, bande *f* **2** *Mil (unit) (of cavalry, tanks)* peloton *m*;

troops troupes *fpl*; **to raise troops** lever des troupes; **shock troops** troupes de choc **3** *(in scouting)* troupe *f*
VI **to t. in/off/past** entrer/partir/passer en groupe *ou* en bande
VT *esp Br Mil* **to t. the colour** faire le salut au drapeau
▸▸ **t. carrier** *(ship)* transport *m* de troupes; *(plane)* avion *m* de transport militaire; *(vehicle)* véhicule *m* de transport de troupes; **t. train** train *m* militaire

trooper [ˈtruːpər] N **1** *Mil (soldier)* cavalier *m*, soldat *m* de la cavalerie; *Am, Austr (mounted police officer)* membre *m* de la police montée; *(horse)* cheval *m* de cavalerie; *Am (state)* **t.** *(policeman)* = agent *m* de la police d'État; *Fam* **to swear like a t.** jurer comme un charretier **2** *Br* = **troopship**

trooping [ˈtruːpɪŋ] N *esp Br Mil* **t. (of) the colour** salut *m* au drapeau, présentation *f* du drapeau; *Br* **the T. of the Colour** = la parade militaire à l'occasion de l'anniversaire de la Reine

troopship [ˈtruːpʃɪp] N (navire *m* de) transport *m* de troupes

trophic [ˈtrəʊfɪk] ADJ *Med* trophique

trophy [ˈtrəʊfɪ] N *(in hunting), Sport, Fig* trophée *m*
▸▸ *Hum Pej* **t. wife** = épouse *f* considérée comme un signe extérieur de réussite sociale

tropic [ˈtrɒpɪk] N *Astron, Geog* tropique *m*; **the tropics** les tropiques

tropical [ˈtrɒpɪk(ə)l] ADJ *(climate, heat, fish etc)* tropical, -aux; *(illness etc)* des tropiques; **it's absolutely t. in here!** il fait une chaleur torride ici!
▸▸ **t. rain forest** forêt *f* tropicale humide

tropism [ˈtrəʊpɪz(ə)m] N *Biol* tropisme *m*

troposphere [ˈtrɒpəsfɪər] N *Met* troposphère *f*

Trot [trɒt] N *Pol Fam* trotskyste *mf*

trot [trɒt] N **1** *Horseriding etc* trot *m*; **at a brisk t.** au grand trot; **to set off at a t.** partir au trot; *Fam* **they've had 22 wins on the t.** ils ont gagné vingt-deux fois à la file *ou* de suite; *Fam* **for five days on the t.** pendant cinq jours de suite; *Fam* **to keep sb on the t.** ne laisser aucun repos à qn **2** *Sl* **to have the trots** *(diarrhoea)* avoir la chiasse *ou* la courante
VI *(-tt-)* *Horseriding* trotter, aller au trot; *(of person)* trotter; *(of child)* trottiner; *Fam* **I must be trotting (along)** il faut que je file; *Fam* **I'll just t. up/down/along to the post office** je vais juste faire un saut à la poste; *Fam* **I'll just t. round to the shops** je vais faire quelques courses en vitesse; *Fam* **he trotted off down the road** il s'éloigna en trottinant dans la rue
VT *(horse)* faire trotter
▸ **trot out** VT SEP *Fam (produce) (excuses)* débiter; *(one's knowledge etc)* faire étalage de, débiter; *(old grievances)* rabâcher; **he can always t. out excuses** il est toujours prêt à débiter des excuses

troth [trəʊθ] N *Arch, Lit* foi *f*; **by my t.!** sur ma foi!

Trotskyism [ˈtrɒtskɪɪzm] N trotskisme *m*

Trotskyite [ˈtrɒtskɪaɪt] ADJ, N trotskyste *mf*

trotter [ˈtrɒtər] N **1** *(horse)* cheval *m* de trot, trotteur, *-euse* **2** *Culin* **sheep's/pigs' trotters** pieds *mpl* de mouton/de porc **3** *Fam* **trotters** *(feet)* pieds *mpl*

trotting [ˈtrɒtɪŋ] N *Horseriding* trot *m*
▸▸ **t. race** course *f* de trot (attelé)

troubadour [ˈtruːbədʊər] N *Liter* troubadour *m*

TROUBLE [ˈtrʌb(ə)l]

> ☐ ennuis **1** ▪ difficultés **1**
> ▪ problème(s) **1, 3** ▪ désordre **2**
> ▪ troubles **3** ▪ soucis **3**
> ▪ dérangement **4** ▪ peine **4** ▪ mal **4**
> ☐ inquiéter **1** ▪ faire souffrir **1**
> ▪ déranger **2**
> ☐ se déranger

N 1 *(problem, difficulty)* ennui *m*, difficulté *f*, problème *m*; **he told me his troubles** il m'a raconté ses malheurs *ou* ses problèmes; **her troubles are over** ses malheurs *ou* ses ennuis sont finis; **in one's time of t.** quand on a des ennuis; **money troubles** problèmes *mpl* d'argent; **what's the t.?** qu'est-ce qu'il y a?, quel est le problème?; **we must get to the root of the t.** il faut chercher la source du mal; **the t. is that …** l'ennui *ou* le problème c'est que …; **the t. with you** *or* **your t. is you don't think** ton problème *ou* le problème chez toi c'est que tu ne réfléchis pas; **the t. with these machines is (that) they're too complicated** le problème avec ces machines c'est qu'elles sont trop compliquées; **you'll have t. with him** il va vous causer des difficultés *ou* des ennuis; **did you have any t. finding the place?** est-ce que tu as eu du mal à trouver?; **this new machine's/system's more t. than it's worth** cette nouvelle machine/ce nouveau système pose plus de problèmes qu'elle/qu'il n'en résoud; **this machine's been** *or* **given nothing but t.** cette machine ne m'a/ne nous a apporté que des problèmes; **to be in t.** avoir des ennuis *ou* des difficultés; **to get into t.** s'attirer des ennuis *ou* des désagréments; *Fam (become pregnant)* tomber enceinte; **to get into t. with the police** avoir affaire à la police; **to get sb into t., to make t. for sb** créer des ennuis à qn; *Fam* **to get a girl into t.** *(make her pregnant)* mettre une fille enceinte; **to get sb out of t.** tirer qn d'affaire; **to keep out of t.** éviter les ennuis; **to be looking** *or* **asking for t.** *(cause problems for the future)* se préparer des ennuis; **he was asking for t., the way he drank** il cherchait des ennuis, à boire autant; **are you looking for t.?** *(said aggressively)* tu cherches des ennuis?; **that's asking for t., not locking the door** ne pas verrouiller la porte, c'est tenter le diable; **to make** *or* **cause t.** semer la discorde; **to make t. for oneself** se créer des ennuis

2 *(disorder, unrest)* désordre *m*; **there was t. in the streets** il y a eu des violences dans la rue; **the Troubles** *(in Northern Ireland)* les troubles *mpl*; **there will be t.** il va y avoir du grabuge; **there'll be t. if he finds out** je vais/ tu vas/on va/*etc* avoir des ennuis s'il s'en rend compte; *Br Hum* **there's t. at mill** la révolte gronde

3 *(physical, medical, mechanical)* **eye t.** affection *f* de l'œil; *(sight disorder)* troubles *mpl* de vision; **stomach t.** troubles digestifs; **to have heart t.** être malade du cœur; **to locate** *or* **trace the t.** *(in machine, engine etc)* trouver la source de la panne; **my eyes have been giving me some t.** mes yeux me donnent quelques soucis; **the car/engine hasn't given me any t.** je n'ai eu aucun problème avec la voiture/le moteur; *Aut etc* **engine t.** panne *f* de moteur; *Fam* **he's got woman/ she's got man t.** ça ne va pas très bien pour lui/elle côté cœur

4 *(inconvenience)* dérangement *m*, peine *f*, mal *m*; **to take the t. to do sth, to go to the t. of doing sth** prendre *ou* se donner la peine de faire qch; **to go to** *or* **put oneself to** *or* **to take a great deal of t.** se donner beaucoup de mal *ou* de peine; **it's not worth the t.** cela n'en vaut pas la peine; **nothing's too much t. for him** il est toujours prêt à aider les autres; **(it's) no t.** (ça ne pose) aucun problème; **if**

it's no t. si ça ne vous dérange pas; **they've gone to all that t. for nothing** ils se sont donné du mal pour rien

VT 1 *(worry)* inquiéter; *Med* affliger; **my back's been troubling me for years** ça fait des années que mon dos me fait souffrir *ou* que j'ai des douleurs dans le dos; **I'm troubled about his future** son avenir me préoccupe *ou* m'inquiète; **don't let it t. you!** que cela ne vous inquiète pas!, ne vous tourmentez pas à ce sujet!; **how long has this cough been troubling you?** depuis combien de temps souffrez-vous de cette toux?; **her conscience was troubling her** elle avait des problèmes de conscience

2 *(disturb)* déranger; **I'm sorry to t. you** excusez-moi de vous déranger; **could I t. you a minute?** excusez-moi, vous auriez une minute?; **may I t. you to shut the door?** cela vous dérangerait-il de fermer la porte?

VI don't t.!, you needn't t.! ne vous dérangez pas!; **he didn't even t. to …** il n'a même pas pris la peine de …

▸▸ **t. spot** point *m* chaud *ou* de conflit

troubled [ˈtrʌb(ə)ld] **ADJ** *(worried) (look)* inquiet, -ète; **t. period** *(of history)* époque *f* troublée; **t. sleep** sommeil *m* agité; **he's got a t. conscience** il n'a pas la conscience tranquille

▸▸ *Fig* **t. waters** eaux *fpl* troubles

trouble-free **ADJ** sans problèmes; **a t. holiday** des vacances qui se déroulent/se sont déroulées sans incidents *ou* sans anicroches

troublemaker [ˈtrʌb(ə)lmeɪkər] **N** fauteur, -trice de troubles

troubleshooter [ˈtrʌb(ə)lʃuːtər] **N** *Pol, Ind etc* médiateur, -trice, conciliateur, -trice; *(for machinery etc)* dépanneur *m*

troubleshooting [ˈtrʌb(ə)lʃuːtɪŋ] **N** *Pol, Ind etc* médiation *f*, conciliation *f*; *Comput* dépannage *m*

▸▸ **t. section** *(in manual)* section *f* de dépannage

troublesome [ˈtrʌb(ə)lsəm] **ADJ** *(problem, workforce, child etc)* difficile; *(rival)* gênant; *(cough)* pénible

troubling [ˈtrʌblɪŋ] **ADJ** inquiétant

troublous [ˈtrʌbləs] **ADJ** *Arch, Lit* troublé, agité

trough [trɒf] **N 1** *(feeding)* **t.** auge *f*, mangeoire *f*; *(drinking)* **t.** abreuvoir *m*; *Fig Fam* **to have** *or* **get one's snout in the t.** avoir sa part du gâteau **2** *Chem, Phys (for mercury, water)* cuve *f*, cuvette *f* **3** *Geol* auge *f* **4** *Phys, Math, Econ (of wave, graph, cycle)* creux *m*; *Met (barometric)* dépression *f*, zone *f* dépressionnaire

trounce [traʊns] **VT** *Sport (defeat heavily)* écraser, battre à plate(s) couture(s)

trouncing [ˈtraʊnsɪŋ] **N** *Sport (heavy defeat)* défaite *f* écrasante; **Wales gave France a t.** le pays de Galles a battu la France à plate(s) couture(s)

troupe [truːp] **N** *(of actors etc)* troupe *f*

trouper [ˈtruːpər] **N** *Theat* membre *m* d'une/ de la troupe; *Fig* **he's an old t.** c'est un vieux de la vieille; *Fig* **she's a real t.** elle s'y connaît

trousered [ˈtraʊzəd] **ADJ** *Br Fam (very drunk)* rond comme une queue de pelle, fin plein

trouser [ˈtraʊzər] **N**

▸▸ **t. press** presse *f* à pantalons; **t. suit** tailleur-pantalon *m*, *pl* tailleurs-pantalons

trousers [ˈtraʊzəz] **NPL** *esp Br* **(pair of) t.** pantalon *m*; *Fam* **she's the one who wears the t.** c'est elle qui porte la culotte; *Fig Fam* **to be caught with one's t. down** être pris au dépourvu; **short t.** shorts *mpl*; **when I was still in short t.** quand j'étais encore en culottes courtes VOIR GRAMMAIRE A10

trousseau [ˈtruːsəʊ] **N** trousseau *m*

trout [traʊt] **N 1** *(inv in pl) (fish)* truite *f* **2** *Fam (woman)* **old t.** vieille bique *f*

▸▸ **t. fishing** la pêche à la truite

trove [trəʊv] **N = treasure-trove**

trowel [ˈtraʊəl] **N** *Constr* truelle *f*; *(in gardening)* déplantoir *m*; *Fig Fam* **to lay it on with a t.** en faire trop

Troy [trɔɪ] **N** Troie *f*

troy [trɔɪ] **N** *(weight for gold, money)* poids *m* troy

▸▸ **t. ounce** once *f* troy *(31,1g)*; **t. weight** poids troy

truancy [ˈtruːənsɪ] **N** *Sch* absentéisme *m* scolaire

truant [ˈtruːənt] **N** élève *mf* qui fait l'école buissonnière; **to play t.** faire l'école buissonnière

ADJ ATTRIB qui fait l'école buissonnière

> Note that the French word **truand** is a false friend. It means **crook**.

truce [truːs] **N** trêve *f*; **to call a t.** demander une trêve; **let's call it a t.!** faisons une trêve!

truck[1] [trʌk] **N 1** *(lorry)* camion *m*; *(big, HGV)* poids *m* lourd; *Min* berline *f*, benne *f*, bac *m*; **fork-lift t.** chariot *m* élévateur à fourche; *Am* **wrecking t.** camion de dépannage, dépanneuse *f* **2** *Rail (for freight)* wagon *m*; **cattle t.** fourgon *m* à bestiaux

VT *(goods)* camionner, acheminer par camion

VI *esp Am (drive a truck)* être conducteur de camion, être camionneur; *Fam* **keep on trucking!** bon courage!

truck[2] **N 1** *Fam (relations) (with sb)* rapports *mpl*, relations *fpl*; **I'll have no t. with him** je ne veux rien avoir à faire avec lui **2** *Am (vegetables)* produits *mpl* maraîchers

▸▸ *Am* **t. farmer** maraîcher, -ère; *Am* **t. garden** jardin *m* maraîcher; *Am* **t. gardener** maraîcher, -ère; *Am* **t. gardening** maraîchage *m*

truckdriver [ˈtrʌkdraɪvər], **trucker** [ˈtrʌkər] **N** *esp Am* camionneur *m*, routier *m*

trucking [ˈtrʌkɪŋ] **N** *Am* camionnage *m*

▸▸ **t. company** entreprise *f* de transports routiers

truckle [ˈtrʌk(ə)l] **N** *(of cheese)* = petit fromage *m* rond

VI *Lit* ramper, s'abaisser (**to** devant)

▸▸ **t. bed** lit *m* gigogne

truckstop [ˈtrʌkstɒp] **N** *esp Am* café *m* de routiers, routier *m*

truculence [ˈtrʌkjʊləns] **N** agressivité *f*

truculent [ˈtrʌkjʊlənt] **ADJ** agressif

> Note that the French word **truculent** is a false friend. It means **colourful** or **vivid**.

truculently [ˈtrʌkjʊləntlɪ] **ADV** agressivement

trudge [trʌdʒ] **N** marche *f* pénible; **a long t.** un trajet long et pénible

VT **they trudged the streets looking for a cheap hotel** ils se traînaient péniblement à travers les rues à la recherche d'un petit hôtel bon marché

VI marcher lourdement *ou* péniblement, se traîner; **we trudged across the sodden fields** nous avancions avec peine à travers les champs détrempés; **I've been trudging around the shops all day** je me suis traîné péniblement dans les magasins toute la journée

▸ **trudge along** **VI** *(walk heavily, with difficulty)* cheminer *ou* avancer péniblement, se traîner

true [truː] **ADJ 1** *(according with reality, not fictional)* vrai; *(accurate)* exact; **t. account** récit *m* fidèle *ou* exact; **t. adventures** aventures *fpl* vécues; **it is t. that** … il est vrai que …; **if it were t. that** … s'il était vrai que … + *subj*; **to come t.** *(of wish etc)* se réaliser; **this also holds t. for** … il en est de même pour …; **how t.!, how very t.!** c'est bien vrai!; **that's all too t., I'm afraid** ce n'est que trop vrai, malheureusement; **I can't believe it's t.** je n'arrive pas à le croire; **it's getting late – t.** il se fait tard – tu as raison

2 *(genuine)* véritable; *(real)* vrai, réel; **t. repentance** repentir *m* sincère *ou* véritable; **her t. nature** son véritable caractère; **he's a t. Irishman** *(conforms to stereotype)* c'est bien un Irlandais; *(by birth)* c'est un Irlandais, un vrai; **to get a t. idea of the situation** se faire une idée juste de la situation

3 *Tech, Carp* juste, droit, rectiligne; **to make a piece t.** ajuster une pièce; **his aim was t.** *(was a good shot)* il était bon tireur; *(hit target)* il a visé juste; **the table isn't t.** la table n'est pas d'aplomb

4 *(faithful)* fidèle, loyal, -aux; **to be t. to a friend** être loyal envers *ou* fidèle à un ami; **to be t. to oneself** être fidèle à soi-même; **to be** *or* **remain t. to one's principles** être fidèle à ses principes; **to be t. to a promise** rester fidèle à une promesse; **t. to life** qui correspond bien à la réalité; **t. to form, he** … fidèle à lui-même, il …; **she was an accountant, and t. to type she** … elle était comptable, et bien entendu elle …; **t. friend** ami, -ie loyal(e), vrai(e) ami, -ie; **a jury of twelve good men and t.** un jury de douze citoyens de bonne renommée

5 *(voice, instrument)* juste

ADV 1 *Fam (truthfully)* **tell me t.** dis-moi la vérité **2** *(to sing, aim)* juste; **to run t.** *(of wheel)* tourner rond *ou* sans balourd

N *Tech* **etc out of t.** *(of vertical post, member etc)* hors d'aplomb; *(of horizontal post, member etc)* dénivelé; *(of axle etc)* faussé, dévoyé; *(of timber)* déjeté; *(of wheel)* désaxé

VT *(thing)* mettre bien en place

▸▸ **t. copy** copie *f* conforme; *Fin* **t. discount** escompte *m* en dedans; *Acct* **t. and fair view** *(of accounts)* image *f* fidèle; **t. love** *(feeling, person)* grand amour *m*; **t. north** vrai nord *m*, nord géographique; *Mktg* **t. sample** échantillon *m* représentatif

true-blue N *Br (Conservative)* Conservateur, -trice pur(e) et dur(e)

ADJ loyal, -aux, convaincu

trueborn ['tru:bɔːn] **ADJ** *Old-fashioned* vrai, véritable; **a t. Englishman** un vrai Anglais d'Angleterre

true-false ADJ

▸▸ **t. questionnaire** questionnaire *m* auquel on répond par 'vrai' *ou* 'faux'

truffle ['trʌf(ə)l] **N** truffe *f*; *Br (rum)* **t.** *(sweet)* truffe au rhum

▸▸ **t. hound** chien *m* truffier

trug [trʌg] **N** *Br* panier *m* *ou* corbeille *f* de jardinier

truism ['tru:ɪz(ə)m] **N** truisme *m*, vérité *f* de La Palice, lapalissade *f*; **it is a t. that** … c'est un lieu commun de dire que …

truly ['tru:lɪ] **ADV 1** *(really, genuinely)* vraiment, véritablement; **a t. difficult situation** une situation vraiment difficile; **I am t. grateful to her** je lui suis sincèrement reconnaissant; **it's t. tragic** c'est vraiment tragique; **I t. believe that** … je crois vraiment *ou* sincèrement que …; **yours t.** *(letter ending)* ≃ je vous prie d'agréer *ou* de croire à mes sentiments distingués; *Fam* **yours t.** *(myself)* votre serviteur; *Fam* **meanwhile yours t. had left** entretemps mézigue *ou* votre serviteur était parti **2** *(in truth)* en vérité, à vrai dire; **(really and) t.?** vrai de vrai? **3** *(faithfully) (to serve sb)* fidèlement, loyalement

trump *Cards* **N** *Cards (card)* atout *m*; **spades are trumps** c'est atout pique; **to play trumps** jouer l'atout; **to call no trumps** jouer sans atout; *Fig Fam* **she turned up trumps** elle a fait des miracles

VT *(card)* couper avec l'atout

▸▸ **t. card** atout *m*; *Fig* **to play one's t. card** jouer son atout

▸ **trump up VT SEP** *(invent) (excuse)* inventer; **to t. up a charge against sb** fabriquer une accusation contre qn; **trumped-up story** histoire *f* inventée

trumpery ['trʌmpərɪ] **N** *(worthless objects)* camelote *f*; *(nonsense)* absurdités *mpl*

trumpet ['trʌmpɪt] **N** *Mus* trompette *f*; *Fig* **to blow one's own t.** chanter ses propres louanges

VI (-t-) trompeter, sonner de la trompette; *(of elephant)* barrir

VT *esp Lit (success)* claironner

▸▸ **t. blast, t. call** coup *m* *ou* sonnerie *f* de trompette; *Mil* **t. major** trompette-major *m*, *pl* trompettes-majors; **t. player** trompettiste *mf, (in band)* trompette

trumpeter ['trʌmpɪtər] **N** *Mil* trompette *m*; *Mus (by profession)* trompettiste *mf*

trumpeting ['trʌmpɪtɪŋ] **N** sonnerie *f* de trompette; *(of elephant)* barrissement *m*

truncate [trʌŋ'keɪt] **VT** *(body, text etc)* tronquer; *(meeting etc)* écourter

truncated [trʌŋ'keɪtɪd] **ADJ** *(body, text)* tronqué; *(meeting etc)* écourté

▸▸ *Geom* **t. cone** cône *m* tronqué

truncheon ['trʌn(t)ʃən] **N** matraque *f*, *(esp for directing traffic)* bâton *m*

VT matraquer

trundle ['trʌnd(ə)l] **VT** *(hoop etc)* faire rouler; *(wheelbarrow, hand cart)* pousser; **they trundled him in on his bed** ils l'ont fait entrer sur son lit à roulettes

VI *(of hoop etc)* rouler; *(of vehicle)* rouler péniblement; *(of cart)* rouler lourdement; **the project trundled on** le projet avançait péniblement

▸▸ **t. bed** lit *m* gigogne

▸ **trundle out VT SEP** *(old bicycle, theory etc)* ressortir

trunk [trʌŋk] **N 1** *(of tree, body, artery)* tronc *m*; *Archit (of column)* fût *m* **2** *(luggage)* malle *f* **3** *Am Aut* coffre *m* **4** *(of elephant)* trompe *f* **5** **trunks** *(for men, for swimming)* maillot *m* (de bain), slip *m* de bain

▸▸ *Br Tel Old-fashioned* **t. call** appel *m* interurbain; **t. line** *Rail* ligne *f* principale, grande ligne; *Tel* inter *m*; *Br* **t. road** (route *f*) nationale *f*

trunnion ['trʌnjən] **N** *Mil, Tech* tourillon *m*

truss [trʌs] **N 1** *Med* bandage *m* herniaire **2** *Constr (of beam etc)* armature *f, (for roof timbers, bridge)* ferme *f, (for vaulting)* cintre *m* **3** *(of flowers)* touffe *f, (of tomatoes)* grappe *f*

VT 1 *Constr, Tech (beam etc)* armer, renforcer **2** *Culin (fowl)* trousser, brider

▸ **truss up VT SEP** *(tie up) (person)* ligoter; **trussed up like a chicken** ficelé comme un poulet

trust [trʌst] **N 1** *(belief)* confiance *f* (in en); **to put one's t. in sb** mettre sa confiance en qn; **to put one's t. in sth** se reposer sur qch; **to betray sb's t.** trahir la confiance de qn; **I took what you said on t.** je t'ai cru sur parole, je t'ai fait confiance

2 *(responsibility)* responsabilité *f*; **to be in a position of t.** occuper un poste de confiance; **he placed his child in my t.** il m'a confié la garde de son enfant

3 *Law* fidéicommis *m*, fiducie *f*, **to hold in t.** *(property etc)* administrer par fidéicommis; *Br* **National T.** = société *f* pour la conservation des sites et monuments

4 *Ind etc (group)* trust *m*; **brains t.** brain-trust *m*, *pl* brain-trusts; *Fin* **(investment) t.** société *f* de placement(s); **unit t.** société d'investissement à capital variable

VT 1 *(believe in) (person)* faire confiance à, se fier à; *(something)* se fier à; **she's not to be trusted** on ne peut pas se fier à elle; **are the figures to be trusted?** est-ce que ces chiffres sont fiables?; **she's not to be trusted on the question of** … on ne peut pas lui faire confiance quand il s'agit de …; **I don't t. you with money** je ne te confierais pas mon argent; **you can't t. anyone nowadays** on ne peut faire confiance *ou* se fier à personne de nos jours; **I don't t. you with her!** je ne la laisserais pas seule avec toi!; **I couldn't t. myself not to say anything** je ne pourrais pas résister à l'envie de dire quelque chose; **to t. sb with sth** confier qch à qn; **to t. sb to do sth** laisser à qn le soin de faire qch; *Fam* **t. him to say that!** c'est bien de lui!; *Fam* **I've lost it – t. you!** je l'ai perdu – ça c'est tout toi! *ou* c'est typique de toi! *ou* ça ne m'étonne pas de toi!; **she won't t. him out of her sight** elle lui fait si peu confiance qu'elle ne le quitte pas des yeux; **to t. one's instincts** se fier à son instinct; **to t. sb's judgement** se fier au jugement de qn; *Fam* **I wouldn't t. her as far as I could throw her** je ne lui ferais pas confiance du tout; **there's no-one's judgement I t. as much as hers** je lui fais confiance comme à personne d'autre

2 *(entrust)* **to t. sth to sb** confier qch à qn

3 *esp Fml* **to t. (that)** … espérer que …; *(express wish that)* exprimer le vœu que … + *subj*; **I t. he is not ill** j'espère bien qu'il n'est pas malade

VI **to t. to luck** s'en remettre au hasard

▸▸ *Fin* **t. bank** banque *f* de gestion de patrimoine; *Fin* **t. company** société *f* fiduciaire; *Fin* **t. fund** fonds *m* en fidéicommis; *Pol* **t. territories** territoires *mpl* sous tutelle

▸ **trust in VT INSEP** *(put one's hopes in) (something)* mettre ses espérances *ou* son espoir en; **to t. in God** croire en Dieu; **I want someone I can t. in** *(have confidence in)* il me faut une personne de confiance

trustafarian [trʌstə'feərɪən] **N** *Br Fam* = jeune personne *f* de milieu relativement aisé et de race blanche qui cultive une image rasta

trustbusting ['trʌstbʌstɪŋ] *Am* **N** démantèlement *m* des trusts

ADJ ATTRIB qui a trait au démantèlement des trusts

trusted ['trʌstɪd] **ADJ** *(person)* de confiance; **tried and t.** *(remedy, method)* éprouvé; *(friend)* fidèle, éprouvé

▸▸ *Comput* **t. third party** *(for Internet transactions)* tierce partie *f* de confiance

trustee [trʌs'tiː] **N 1** *Law* fidéicommissaire *m*, fiduciaire *m*; *(with powers of attorney)* mandataire *m* **2** *(of museum, charity, company, life assurance policy)* administrateur *m*; **board of trustees** conseil *m* d'administration

trusteeship [trʌs'tiːʃɪp] **N 1** *Law* fidéicommis *m* **2** *(of museum, charity etc)* fonction *f* d'administrateur **3** *Pol (of territory)* tutelle *f*

trustful ['trʌstfʊl] **ADJ** plein de confiance, confiant

trustfully ['trʌstfəlɪ] **ADV** avec confiance

trustfulness ['trʌstfʊlnɪs] **N** confiance *f*

trusting ['trʌstɪŋ] **ADJ** confiant; *(look)* plein de confiance; **you're far too t.** tu fais trop confiance aux gens; **it's very t. of you to lend it to them** tu leur fais drôlement confiance pour le leur prêter

trustingly ['trʌstɪŋlɪ] **ADV** avec confiance

trustworthiness ['trʌstwɜːðɪnɪs] **N** *(person)* loyauté *f*, honnêteté *f*, *(of testimony, account etc)* crédibilité *f*, véracité *f*

trustworthy ['trʌstwɜːðɪ] ADJ (person) digne de confiance; (information) digne de foi; (testimony) irrécusable; (critic, guidebook etc) très fiable

trusty ['trʌstɪ] ADJ Arch, Lit fidèle, loyal, -aux; Hum my t. old typewriter ma bonne vieille machine à écrire

truth [truːθ, pl truːðz] N vérité f; in t. en vérité; the plain or honest t. la pure vérité, la vérité pure et simple; to speak or tell the t. dire la vérité; the t. (of the matter) is or to tell the t., I forgot it pour dire la vérité ou à dire vrai je l'ai oublié; … and that's the t. … et voilà la vérité; there's some t. in what you say il y a du vrai dans ce que vous dites; there's not a word of t. in it il n'y a pas un brin de vérité là-dedans; I told him a few home truths je lui ai dit son fait ou ses quatre vérités; Law the t., the whole t., and nothing but the t. la vérité, toute la vérité, rien que la vérité; Prov t. will out la vérité finit toujours par se faire jour; Prov t. is the first casualty of war toute guerre s'accompagne de son cortège de mensonges
▸▸ t. drug sérum m de vérité; t. function fonction f de vérité; t. table table f ou matrice f de vérité; t. value variable f 'vrai' ou 'faux'

truthful ['truːθfʊl] ADJ (person) sincère, honnête; (account etc) véridique; (description, portrait etc) fidèle; to be t. (of person) dire la vérité, être sincère ou honnête

truthfully ['truːθfəlɪ] ADV (to speak, answer, claim etc) en disant la vérité; (to portray etc) fidèlement

truthfulness ['truːθfʊlnɪs] N (of statement, claim etc) véracité f, (of portrait etc) fidélité f

TRY [traɪ]

| N essai 1, 2 ▪ tentative 2 |
| VT essayer 1–3 ▪ tenter 2 ▪ vérifier 4 ▪ juger 5 ▪ éprouver 6 ▪ mettre à l'épreuve 6 |
| VI essayer ▪ faire des efforts |

N 1 (attempt) essai m, tentative f; to have a t. at doing sth essayer de faire qch; to have a t. at sth s'essayer à qch; I had a t. at skin-diving je me suis essayé à la plongée sous-marine; let's have a t.! essayons toujours!; can I have a t.? (est-ce que) je peux essayer?; I think I'll have a t. for this job je crois que je vais me présenter pour ce travail; you've already had three tries vous avez déjà essayé trois fois; OK, you can have one more t. bon d'accord, tu peux encore essayer une fois ou tu as encore un essai; go on, give it a t. (activity) allez, essaie; (food) allez, goûte; at the first t. du premier coup; it won't be easy but it's worth a t. ça ne va pas être facile mais ça vaut la peine ou le coup d'essayer; worth a t.? ça vaut le coup d'essayer?
2 Rugby essai m; to score a t. marquer un essai; the t. scorer celui qui a marqué l'essai; France's leading t. scorer celui qui a marqué le plus d'essais pour la France
VT (pt, pp tried [traɪd]) 1 (sample) essayer; here, t. my pen tenez, essayez avec mon stylo; to t. a dish goûter (à) un mets; t. some (food) goûtes-y; I'll t. anything once il faut tout essayer dans la vie
2 (attempt to do) essayer, tenter; to t. an experiment tenter une expérience; to t. the door/the window essayer (d'ouvrir) la porte/la fenêtre; I'd like to see you t. it! je voudrais bien t'y voir!
3 (attempt) to t. to do sth essayer de faire qch; she tried to smile elle a essayé de sourire; he was trying hard to keep back the tears il s'efforçait de retenir ses larmes; it's worth trying cela vaut la peine d'essayer; Fam to t. and do sth tâcher ou essayer de faire qch; Fam t. and be nice to her tâche d'être gentil avec elle; to t. doing sth essayer de faire qch; t. (asking) Jane demande à Jane; have you tried the chemist's? tu es allé voir à la pharmacie?; I tried the number in the book but there was no reply j'ai essayé le numéro de l'annuaire mais ça ne répondait pas VOIR GRAMMAIRE A43–4
4 (check) (mechanism) vérifier
5 Law (case, person) juger; Am (of advocate) (case) plaider; to be tried for theft passer en correctionnelle pour vol
6 (test) (person) éprouver, mettre à l'épreuve; (sb's courage, sb's patience etc) mettre à l'épreuve; to t. one's strength against sb se mesurer avec ou à qn; a people sorely tried une nation fort ou durement éprouvée; to t. one's eyes (reading) se fatiguer les yeux (à lire)
VI faire un effort ou des efforts; to t. again essayer de nouveau; you must t. harder il faut faire de plus grands efforts; at least you tried au moins tu as/auras essayé; he didn't really t. il n'a pas vraiment essayé; you weren't really trying tu n'as pas vraiment essayé; go on then, t.! alors vas-y, essaie!; … and she wasn't even trying … et elle l'a fait sans le moindre effort; just you t.! essaie un peu pour voir!; I'd like to see you t.! (answer to threat, challenge) je voudrais bien t'y voir!
▸ try for VT INSEP (attempt to obtain) tâcher d'obtenir; to t. for a job poser sa candidature à un emploi; he's trying for (a place at) music school il essaie d'obtenir une place à l'école de musique; Sport etc she's trying for the record elle essaie de battre le record
▸ try on VT SEP 1 (clothes etc) essayer
2 Fam to t. it on tenter le coup (with sb avec qn); they're just trying it on ils bluffent, c'est du bluff; you're (just) trying it on! ça ne marche pas ou ne prend pas!; she tried it on with my husband (attempted to seduce) elle a essayé de séduire mon mari
▸ try out VT SEP (test) faire l'essai de; (new procedure) essayer, expérimenter; to t. sth out on sb essayer ou expérimenter qch sur qn; they're trying him out in goal ils l'essaient ou l'ont mis à l'essai comme gardien de but

trying ['traɪɪŋ] ADJ (time, experience) pénible, difficile; (person) pénible
N Law (of case, person) jugement m

try-on N Br Fam bluff m; it's just a t. c'est du bluff

try-out N (of machine etc) premier essai m, essai préliminaire; Am Theat audition f; Sport épreuve f de sélection; to give sb/sth a t. mettre qn à l'essai/essayer qch

tryst [trɪst] N Lit rendez-vous m amoureux

tsar [tsɑːr] N tsar m, czar m

tsarevitch ['tsɑːrəvɪtʃ] N tsarévitch m, czarévitch m

tsarina [tsɑːˈriːnə] N tsarine f, czarine f

tsarist ['tsɑːrɪst] ADJ, N tsariste mf

tsetse ['t(s)etsɪ] N (mouche f) tsé-tsé f inv
▸▸ t. fly (mouche) tsé-tsé

T-shirt N tee-shirt m

tsp Culin (abbr teaspoon, teaspoonful) cu. à c.; 2 t. sugar (in recipe) 2 cu. à c. de sucre

TSS [tiːesˈes] N (abbr toxic shock syndrome) SCT m

T-stop N Phot diaphragme m

TT [tiːˈtiː] N 1 Br Sport (abbr Tourist Trophy) = course f motocycliste sur l'île de Man 2 (abbr teetotal) I'mTT je ne bois pas d'alcool

TTL [tiːtiːˈel] ADJ Phot (abbr through the lens) TTL

TTP [tiːtiːˈpiː] N Comput (abbr trusted third party) (for Internet transactions) TPC f

tub [tʌb] N 1 (container) baquet m, bac m; (for flowers, shrubs) bac, caisse f, (for washing) baquet; (in washing machine) cuve f, (of ice-cream, cream etc) pot m; Br Fam a t. of lard (man) un gros lard, un gros plein de soupe; (woman) une grosse dondon, une grosse vache 2 (bathtub) baignoire f, a hot t. (bath) un bain chaud 3 Fam (boat) old t. vieux rafiot m
▸▸ t. chair (fauteuil m) crapaud m

tuba ['tjuːbə] N Mus tuba m

tubby ['tʌbɪ] ADJ Fam (person) dodu, boulot, -otte

tube [tjuːb] N 1 (of paint, toothpaste) tube m; (pipe) tuyau m; Med etc (for deep wound) drain m; Austr Fam (of beer) boîte f, Aut etc inner t. (of tyre) chambre f à air; Chem, Phys etc test t. éprouvette f, (Fallopian) tubes trompes fpl (de Fallope); (bronchial) tubes bronches fpl; Fam to have one's tubes tied (be sterilized) se faire ligaturer les trompes; Fam that's £500 down the tubes voilà 500 livres de foutues en l'air; Fam that's all our efforts (gone) down the tubes et voilà tous nos efforts réduits à néant; Fam he watched his marriage/life's work go down the tubes il a vu son mariage/le travail de toute une vie tourner en eau de boudin 2 Elec, Electron, TV etc (electronic, thermionic) tube m; cathode-ray t. tube cathodique ou à rayons cathodiques; esp Am Fam the t. (television) la télé 3 Br Fam the t. (London underground) ≃ le métro
▸▸ Br Fam t. station ≃ station f de métro

tube-feeding N Med gavage m

tubeless ['tjuːblɪs] ADJ (tyre) sans chambre (à air)

tuber ['tjuːbər] N (root) racine f tubéreuse; (on potato) tubercule m

tubercle ['tjuːbɜːk(ə)l] N Anat, Med, Bot tubercule m

tubercular [tjuːˈbɜːkjʊlər] ADJ Med, Bot tuberculeux

tuberculin [tjʊˈbɜːkjʊlɪn] N Med tuberculine f
▸▸ t. test épreuve f de la tuberculinisation, tuberculino-diagnostic m

tuberculin-tested [-ˈtestɪd] ADJ
▸▸ t. milk ≃ lait m certifié

tuberculosis [tjʊbɜːkjʊˈləʊsɪs] N Med tuberculose f

tuberculous [tjʊˈbɜːkjʊləs] ADJ Med tuberculeux

tubful ['tʌbfʊl] N cuvée f, plein baquet m (of de)

tubing ['tjuːbɪŋ] N (no pl) tubes mpl, (pipework) tuyauterie f, rubber t. tuyau(x) m(pl) en caoutchouc

tub-thumper [-θʌmpər] N Fam harangueur m

tubular ['tjuːbjʊlər] ADJ tubulaire
▸▸ Mus t. bells carillon m d'orchestre

TUC [tiːjuːˈsiː] N Br Ind (abbr Trades Union Congress) = confédération f des syndicats britanniques

tuck [tʌk] N 1 Sewing (petit) pli m, rempli m, plissé m 2 Br Sch Fam (cakes, sweets) gâteaux mpl, friandises fpl, sucreries fpl
VT 1 Sewing (garment) faire des plis à 2 (fold) replier 3 (put) mettre; to t. one's legs under one replier les jambes; she tucked her arm in(to) mine elle a passé son bras sous le mien; he tucked his briefcase under his arm il mit ou cala son porte-documents sous son bras; to t. one's trousers into one's socks mettre son pantalon dans ses chaussettes; to t. a rug round sb envelopper qn dans une couverture; the bird tucked its head under its wing l'oiseau a caché sa tête sous son aile; she tucked her hair under her

hat elle a glissé ses cheveux sous son chapeau
▸▸ *Br Sch* **t. box** gamelle *f (d'écolier)*; *Br Sch* **t. shop** = petite boutique *f* où les écoliers achètent bonbons, gâteaux etc
▸**tuck away** VT SEP *(put away)* ranger; *(hide)* cacher, mettre de côté; **he tucked it away in his bag** il l'a rangé dans son sac; **village tucked away in the valley** village blotti au fond de la vallée; **you are** *or* **your house is a bit tucked away** vous êtes *ou* votre maison est un peu à l'écart; **to have some money tucked away** avoir de l'argent de côté; *Fam* **she really can't. it away!** *(eat a lot)* qu'est-ce qu'elle peut bouffer!; *Ftbl Fam* **he tucked it away nicely** *(scored)* il l'envoya dans les filets
▸**tuck in** VT SEP *(put in, under)* rentrer; **to t. one's shirt in** rentrer sa chemise dans son pantalon; **to t. in the bedclothes** border le lit; **to t. sb in** border qn
VI *Fam (eat heartily)* manger à belles dents; **t. in!** allez-y!, mangez!
▸**tuck into** VT INSEP *Fam (eat heartily) (meal)* manger de bon appétit, avaler; **here, t. into this** allez, attaque!
▸**tuck up** VT SEP **1** *(one's skirt, sleeves)* relever, retrousser **2** *(somebody) (in bed)* border
tucker ['tʌkər] N **1** *Fam* **in one's best bib and t.** endimanché **2** *esp Austr Fam (food)* bouffe *f*
VT *esp Am Fam (tire out)* fatiguer; **tuckered (out)** épuisé, éreinté
tuck-in N *Fam* **to have a good t.** *(eating session)* s'envoyer un bon repas
Tudor ['tjuːdər] N **the Tudors** la maison des Tudors
ADJ des Tudors; *Archit* **T. house** maison *f* de style Tudor, maison élisabéthaine
▸▸ *Archit* **T. style** style *m* Tudor *ou* élisabéthain
Tue(s) *abbr* **Tuesday**
Tuesday ['tjuːzdɪ] N mardi *m*; **T. 30 April** mardi 30 avril; **T. morning/evening** mardi matin/soir; **it's T. today** nous sommes mardi aujourd'hui; **on Tuesdays** il vient le mardi; **she's coming on T.** elle vient mardi; **every T.** tous les mardis VOIR GRAMMAIRE A81–2; B61–2
tufa ['t(j)uːfə] N *Geol* tuf *m* calcaire
tuft [tʌft] N *(of grass, feathers, hair)* touffe *f*, *(small beard)* barbiche *f*; *(of bird)* huppe *f*, aigrette *f*; **t. of bristles** *(in brush)* loquet *m* de soies
tufted ['tʌftɪd] ADJ *(bird)* huppé
▸▸ **t. duck** *(fuligule f)* morillon *m*; **t. heron** héron *m* à aigrette, aigrette *f*
tug [tʌg] N **1** *(pull)* **to give sth a t.** tirer sur qch d'un coup sec; **to give a good t.** tirer fort; **he gave a t. at the bell** il a tiré (sur) la sonnette; **I felt a t. at my sleeve** j'ai senti qu'on me tirait par la manche; *Fig* **to feel a t. at one's heartstrings** avoir un serrement de cœur **2** *(boat)* remorqueur *m*
VI (-gg-) **to t. at** *(door, handle, sleeve, one's moustache)* tirer sur; *(sb's ear)* tirer
VT **1** *(door, handle, sleeve, one's moustache)* tirer sur; *(sb's ear)* tirer **2** *Naut (ship)* remorquer
▸▸ *Journ Fam* **t. of love** lutte *f* d'un couple pour la garde d'un/des enfant(s); **t. of war** *Sport* lutte *f* de traction à la corde; *Fig* lutte acharnée et prolongée
tugboat ['tʌgbəʊt] N remorqueur *m*
tuition [tjuː'ɪʃən] N instruction *f*, enseignement *m*; **maths t., t. in maths** enseignement en mathématiques; **private t.** leçons *fpl* particulières
tulip ['tjuːlɪp] N tulipe *f*
▸▸ **t. glass** *(verre m)* tulipe *f*; **t. tree** tulipier *m*
tulle [tjuːl] N *Tex* tulle *m*

tum [tʌm] N *(in children's language), Fam* ventre *m*
tumble ['tʌmb(ə)l] N *(fall)* chute *f*, *(head over heels)* culbute *f*; **to take a t.** tomber, faire la culbute; *(off horse, bike)* faire une chute; **she had a nasty t.** elle a fait une mauvaise chute; *Fig* **the party's popularity took a t.** le parti a beaucoup perdu de sa popularité; **prices have taken a bit of a t.** les prix ont chuté
VI *(fall)* tomber (par terre), faire une chute; *(head over heels)* culbuter, faire la culbute; *(of acrobat)* faire des culbutes; *Fig (of prices)* chuter; **to t. down the stairs** *(fall)* tomber dans les escaliers; *(rush)* descendre les escaliers quatre à quatre; **to t. into bed** se jeter dans son lit; **to t. out of bed** tomber du lit; **they were tumbling over one another** ils se bousculaient
VT **1** **they tumbled the snowball down the hill** ils ont fait débouler la boule de neige dans la pente **2** *(clothes) (in tumble dryer)* mettre dans le sèche-linge **3** *Fam (make love to)* culbuter **4** *Fam (get wise to) (person)* démasquer
▸**tumble about** VI *(of children, kittens)* gambader
▸**tumble down** VI *(of wall etc)* s'écrouler; **the wall came tumbling down** le mur s'est écroulé; **building that is tumbling down** édifice qui s'écroule *ou* qui tombe en ruine
▸**tumble out** VI **the suitcase came open and everything tumbled out** la valise s'est ouverte et tout est tombé par terre; **the van doors flew open and the children came tumbling out** les portes de la camionnette se sont ouvertes et les enfants se sont rués à l'extérieur
▸**tumble to** VT INSEP *Fam (understand)* piger; **eventually she tumbled to it** elle a fini par piger
tumbledown ['tʌmb(ə)ldaʊn] ADJ *(house)* qui tombe en ruine(s)
tumble-drier N sèche-linge *m inv*
tumble-dry VT *(clothes)* faire sécher au sèche-linge
tumbler ['tʌmblər] N **1** *(glass)* verre *m (sans pied)* **2** *(of lock)* gorge *f*, *Elec (of switch etc)* culbuteur *m* **3** *(pigeon)* (pigeon *m*) culbutant *m* **4** *(toy)* poussa(h) *m* **5** *(acrobat)* acrobate *mf* **6** *(tumble-drier)* sèche-linge *m inv*
▸▸ **t. lock** serrure *f* à gorge(s); **t. pigeon** (pigeon) culbutant
tumblerful ['tʌmbləfʊl] N plein verre *m* (of de)
tumbleweed ['tʌmb(ə)lwiːd] N herbes *fpl* roulées par le vent
tumbrel ['tʌmbrəl], **tumbril** ['tʌmbrɪl] N *Hist* charrette *f* (des condamnés)
tumefaction [tjuːmɪ'fækʃən] N tuméfaction *f*
tumefy ['tjuːmɪfaɪ] VT tuméfier
VI se tuméfier
tumescent [tjuː'mesənt] ADJ tumescent
tumid ['tjuːmɪd] ADJ **1** *Med* enflé, gonflé **2** *(style etc)* ronflant
tummy ['tʌmɪ] N *Fam* ventre *m*; **to have t. trouble** avoir l'estomac dérangé
▸▸ **t. ache** mal *m* de ventre; *Br* **t. button** nombril *m*
tumour, *Am* **tumor** ['tjuːmər] N *Med* tumeur *f*
tumult ['tjuːmʌlt] N tumulte *m*; *(of emotions)* trouble *m*, émoi *m*; **the t. of his emotions** son trouble; **to be in a t.** *(of person)* être en émoi; *(of country)* être agité; **her emotions were in a t.** elle était en émoi
tumultuous [tjuː'mʌltjʊəs] ADJ tumultueux; **t. meeting** réunion *f* orageuse; **t. session** séance *f* mouvementée
tumultuously [tjuː'mʌltjʊəslɪ] ADV tumultueusement

tumulus, *pl* **tumuli** ['tjuːmjʊləs, -aɪ] N tumulus *m*
tun [tʌn] N *(liquid measure)* tonneau *m*, fût *m*; *(vat) (in brewing)* cuve *f*
tuna ['tjuːnə] N *(fish)* thon *m*
tundra ['tʌndrə] N *Geog* toundra *f*
tune [tjuːn] N **1** *Mus (melody)* air *m*, mélodie *f*, *Fam* **give us a t.!** faites-nous un peu de musique!, jouez-nous un air!; **it's got no t.** il n'y a pas de mélodie; *Fig* **to call the t.** commander; **to the t. of the Marseillaise** sur l'air de la Marseillaise; *Fig* **to change one's t.** changer de discours; *Fig* **to be fined to the t. of £50** avoir une amende de 50 livres
2 **the piano is in/out of t.** le piano est accordé/désaccordé; **to get out of t.** se désaccorder; **to be out of t.** *(of singer, player)* chanter/jouer faux, détonner; **to sing in/out of t.** chanter juste/faux; **the trumpet isn't in t.** *or* **is out of t. with the other instruments** la trompette n'est pas en harmonie *ou* en accord avec les autres instruments; *Fig* **to be in t. with sb/with one's surroundings** être en harmonie avec qn/avec son milieu; *Fig* **the government's out of t. with public opinion** le gouvernement n'est pas en harmonie avec l'opinion publique; **perfectly in t.** *(of engine)* parfaitement réglé
VT **1** *Mus (instrument)* accorder; **to t. a string to …** accorder une corde sur …
2 *(radio)* régler; **to t. one's radio/TV to a station** régler son poste de radio/télévision sur une station/chaîne; *Radio, TV* **stay tuned (to this station/channel)** restez avec nous
3 *Aut etc (engine)* régler; **to be tuned** *(of engine)* être bien réglé
VI *Mus* **to t. to a note** s'accorder sur une note
▸**tune in** VI *esp Radio* **don't forget to t. in again tomorrow** n'oubliez pas de nous rejoindre ou de nous mettre à l'écoute demain; **to t. in to a station/programme** se brancher sur *ou* mettre une station *ou* TV une chaîne/ une émission
▸**tune up** VI *Mus (get in tune) (of orchestra)* s'accorder
VT SEP *Aut etc* = **tune** VT **3**
tuned-in [tjuːnd-] ADJ *Sl (aware)* branché; **she's very t. to other people's needs** elle est toujours consciente des besoins des gens
tuneful ['tjuːnfʊl] ADJ mélodieux, harmonieux
tunefully ['tjuːnfəlɪ] ADV mélodieusement
tunefulness ['tjuːnfʊlnɪs] N qualité *f* mélodieuse
tuneless ['tjuːnlɪs] ADJ *(unpleasant)* discordant; *(without melody)* sans mélodie
tuner ['tjuːnər] N **1** *Mus (person) (of pianos etc)* accordeur *m* **2** *Radio etc* tuner *m*, syntoniseur *m*
tune-up N *(of engine)* mise *f* au point
tungsten ['tʌŋstən] N *Chem* tungstène *m*
▸▸ **t. steel** acier *m* au tungstène
tungsten-halogen N tungstène-halogène *m*
▸▸ **t. lamp** lampe *f* tungstène-halogène, lampe au tungstène
tunic ['tjuːnɪk] N tunique *f*
tuning ['tjuːnɪŋ] N **1** *Mus* accord *m*; **fine t.** accord précis **2** *Aut etc* réglage *m*, (re)mise *f* au point **3** *Radio, TV* réglage *m*
▸▸ **t. fork** diapason *m*; **t. hammer** accordoir *m*, clef *f* d'accordeur
Tunisia [tjuː'nɪzɪə] N Tunisie *f*
Tunisian [tjuː'nɪzɪən] ADJ tunisien
N Tunisien, -ienne
tunnel ['tʌn(ə)l] N tunnel *m*; *(dug by mole etc)* galerie *f*; **to drive a t. through a mountain** percer un tunnel à travers *ou* sous une

montagne; *Fig* **at last we can see (some** *or* **the) light at the end of the t.** enfin on voit le bout du tunnel; **is there light at the end of the t.?** est-ce qu'un jour on verra le bout du tunnel?; *Tech etc* **wind t.** tunnel aérodynamique, soufflerie *f* (aérodynamique)

VI (*-ll-, Am -l-*) creuser *ou* percer un tunnel; **to t. through into a hill** percer un tunnel à travers *ou* dans *ou* sous une colline; **rats had tunnelled under the foundations** des rats avaient creusé des galeries sous les fondations

VT **to t. one's way out (of sth)** creuser un tunnel pour s'échapper (de qch)

▸ ▸ *Fishing* **t. net** verveux *m*; **t. vision** *Opt* rétrécissement *m* du champ visuel; *Fig* esprit *m* borné; *Fig* **to suffer from t. vision** avoir une vision limitée des choses, avoir des œillères

tunnelling, *Am* **tunneling** ['tʌn(ə)lɪŋ] **N** percement *m* d'un tunnel/de tunnels

▸ ▸ **t. equipment** équipement *m* pour le percement d'un tunnel

tunny ['tʌnɪ] **N** thon *m*

▸ ▸ **t. fish** thon

tuppence ['tʌp(ə)ns] **N** *Old-fashioned Br Fam* = **twopence**

tuppenny ['tʌp(ə)nɪ] **ADJ** *Old-fashioned Br Fam* = **twopenny**; **t. halfpenny** = **twopenny-halfpenny**

turban ['tɜːbən] **N** turban *m*

turbid ['tɜːbɪd] **ADJ 1** (*liquid*) trouble, bourbeux **2** *Fig Lit* (*thoughts*) embrouillé

turbidity [tɜː'bɪdɪtɪ] **N** turbidité *f*

turbine ['tɜːbaɪn] **N** turbine *f*, **gas/steam t.** turbine à gaz/à vapeur

▸ ▸ **t. engine** turbomoteur *m*

turbo ['tɜːbəʊ] **N** turbo *m*

▸ ▸ *Comput* **t. button** bouton *m* de turbo; *Aut* **t. diesel** turbodiesel *m*; **t. diesel engine** moteur *m* turbodiesel

turbocharged ['tɜːbəʊtʃɑːdʒd] **ADJ** turbocompressé

▸ ▸ **t. engine** moteur *m* turbocompressé

turbocharger ['tɜːbəʊtʃɑːdʒər] **N** turbocompresseur *m*, turbo *m*

turbocharging ['tɜːbəʊtʃɑːdʒɪŋ] **N** suralimentation *f* par turbocompresseur

turbo-electric **ADJ** turbo-électrique

turbofan ['tɜːbəʊfæn] **N** *Aviat* turboréacteur *m* à double flux

turbogenerator [tɜːbəʊ'dʒenəreɪtər] **N** *Elec* turbogénérateur *m*, turbogénératrice *f*

turbojet ['tɜːbəʊdʒet] **N** (*aircraft*) avion *m* à turbopropulseur; (*engine*) turboréacteur *m* (*à simple flux*)

▸ ▸ **t. aircraft** avion à turbopropulseur; **t. engine** turboréacteur (*à simple flux*)

turbomarketing ['tɜːbəʊ'mɑːkɪtɪŋ] **N** *Mktg* turbo-marketing *m*

turboprop ['tɜːbəʊprɒp] **N** (*aircraft*) avion *m* à turbopropulseur; (*engine*) turbopropulseur *m*

▸ ▸ **t. aircraft** avion à turbopropulseur; **t. engine** turbopropulseur

turbo-supercharger **N** turbocompresseur *m*

turbot ['tɜːbət] **N** (*fish*) turbot *m*

turbulence ['tɜːbjʊləns] **N** agitation *f*, *Met, Aviat* turbulences *fpl*

turbulent ['tɜːbjʊlənt] **ADJ** (*crowd*) agité; *Met, Aviat* turbulent

turbulently ['tɜːbjʊləntlɪ] **ADV** d'une manière turbulente

turd [tɜːd] **N** *Sl* **1** (*piece of excrement*) étron *m* **2** (*person*) con *m*, conne *f*

tureen [tjʊə'riːn] **N** soupière *f*

turf *pl* **turves, turfs** [tɜːf, tɜːvz, tɜːfs] **N** (*grass-covered earth*) gazon *m*; (*piece*) motte *f* de

gazon; *Sl* (*territory*) territoire *m*; *Sl* **that's not my t.** c'est pas mon rayon; *Horseracing* **the t.** le turf, les courses *fpl* de chevaux

VT 1 (*area*) gazonner **2** *Br Fam* (*throw*) balancer

▸ ▸ *Br Formal* **t. accountant** bookmaker *m*; **t. cutting** extraction *f* de la tourbe; **t. war** conflit *m* pour le contrôle d'un territoire

▸ **turf out** **VT SEP** *Br Fam* (*eject*) (*person*) virer; (*throw away*) (*thing*) foutre en l'air, bazarder; (*reject*) (*plan etc*) rejeter

▸ **turf over** **VT SEP** (*ground*) gazonner

turgid ['tɜːdʒɪd] **ADJ 1** (*swollen*) enflé, gonflé, *Lit* turgide **2** (*style etc*) boursouflé, ampoulé

turgidly ['tɜːdʒɪdlɪ] **ADV** (*written etc*) emphatiquement, pompeusement

Turin Shroud [tjʊə'rɪn] **N** **the T.** le Saint-suaire

Turk [tɜːk] **N** Turc *m*, Turque *f*; *esp Pol* **young T.** jeune turc

Turkey ['tɜːkɪ] **N** Turquie *f*

turkey ['tɜːkɪ] **N 1** (*bird*) dindon *m*, dinde *f*, *Culin* dinde, dindonneau *m*; **hen t.** dinde **2** *esp Am Fam* **to talk t.** parler franchement; *Sl* **cold t.** état de manque de drogue(s) **3** *esp Am Sl* (*failed play, film*) bide *m*, four *m*; (*ineffectual person*) abruti, -ie, crétin, -ine

▸ ▸ **t. buzzard** vautour *m* aura; **t. cock** dindon *m*; *Fam Fig* crâneur, -euse

Turkish ['tɜːkɪʃ] **ADJ** turc, *f* turque

N *Ling* turc *m*

▸ ▸ **T. bath** bain *m* turc; **T. delight** loukoum *m*; **T. towel** serviette *f* éponge

Turkmenistan [tɜːkmenɪ'stɑːn] **N** le Turkménistan

turmeric ['tɜːmərɪk] **N** curcuma *m*

turmoil ['tɜːmɔɪl] **N** trouble *m*, tumulte *m*, agitation *f*; (*of rushing water*) remous *m*; **to be in a t.** (*of country, house*) être en ébullition; (*of person*) être agité; **the whole town is in (a) t.** toute la ville est agitée *ou* est en ébullition; **my mind was in a t.** la confusion régnait dans mon esprit

---

TURN [tɜːn]

N tour **1, 2, 5, 7**	▪ changement de direction **2**	▪ virage **2** ▪ tournant **2** ▪ tournure **2, 9** ▪ choc **3** ▪ crise **4** ▪ numéro **6** ▪ service **7**
VT tourner **1–5, 8**	▪ retourner **2** ▪ diriger **4** ▪ changer **6** ▪ transformer **6** ▪ faire devenir **7**
VI tourner **1, 4**	▪ se retourner **2, 3** ▪ se diriger **4** ▪ devenir **6**

N 1 (*revolution*) (*of wheel*) tour *m*, révolution *f*; **with a t. of the wrist** avec un tour de poignet; **the meat is done to a t.** la viande est cuite à point

2 (*act of changing direction*) changement *m* de direction; *Ski* virage *m*; (*in path etc*) tournant *m*; (*of rope*) tour *m*; (*of spiral*) tour, spire *f*, *Aut* **the next t. on the left** la prochaine (rue/route) à gauche; *Aut* **no right/left t.** défense de tourner à droite/à gauche; **sharp t.** virage serré; **twists and turns** tours et détours *mpl*, (*of events*) tournure *f*, U **t.** demi-tour *m*, *pl* demi-tours; **three-point t.** demi-tour en trois manœuvres; *Fig* **at every t.** à tout bout de champ; **to take a tragic t.** (*of events*) tourner au tragique; **to take an unexpected t.** (*of events, conversation etc*) prendre une tournure que l'on n'aurait pas imaginée; **to take a t. for the better/worse** (*of situation etc*) s'améliorer/se détériorer; **the patient has taken a t. for the better/ the worse** l'état du malade s'est amélioré/a empiré; **the t. of the tide** le changement *ou* renversement de la marée; *Fig* le renversement de tendances; **the milk is on the t.** le lait est en train de commencer à tourner; **at**

the t. of the century au tournant du siècle

3 *Fam* (*surprise, shock*) choc *m*, coup *m*; **it gave me quite a t.** ça m'a fait un coup; **you gave me such a t.!** vous m'avez fait une belle peur!

4 *Med Fam* **she had one of her turns** elle a eu une de ses crises *ou* attaques

5 (*short walk*) tour *m*, petite promenade *f*, **to take a t. in the garden** faire un tour *ou* quelques pas dans le jardin

6 (*at activity*) tour *m*; *Br Theat* (*in variety show etc*) numéro *m*; **whose t. is it?** c'est à qui le tour?; **it's your t.** (*in game*) c'est votre tour, c'est à vous (de jouer); **to take turns with sb** se relayer avec qn; **they take it in turns to drive** ils se relaient au volant; **each in (his) t., t. and t. about** chacun son tour; **to do sth t. and t. about** faire qch à tour de rôle; **in t.** (*alternately*) tour à tour, à tour de rôle; **they, in t., contributed food** pour leur part, ils donnèrent de la nourriture; **she was by turns optimistic and downcast** elle était tour à tour optimiste et déprimée; **to speak out of t.** parler mal à propos

7 (*service*) **to do sb a good t.** rendre (un) service à qn; **to do sb a bad t.** jouer un mauvais tour à qn; *Prov* **one good t. deserves another** à beau jeu beau retour, un service en vaut un autre

8 *Old-fashioned* (*purpose*) **it will serve my t.** cela fera mon affaire (pour le moment)

9 (*style etc*) **t. of mind** tournure *f* d'esprit; **humorous t. of mind** esprit *m* humoristique; **t. of phrase** tournure de phrase; **to have a good t. of speed** être rapide; (*of horse*) être capable de fournir un effort à grande allure

VT 1 (*wheel, handle etc*) (faire) tourner; (*steering wheel*) braquer, tourner; (*key in lock*) (faire) tourner, faire jouer; *Fig* **to t. the knife in the wound** retourner le fer *ou* le couteau dans la plaie

2 (*page etc*) tourner; (*mattress, hay etc*) retourner; **to t. a garment inside out** retourner un vêtement; **to t. everything upside down** mettre tout sens dessus dessous; *Fam* **he didn't t. a hair** il n'a pas bronché *ou* sourcillé; **the sight/story turned my stomach** ce spectacle/l'histoire m'a soulevé le cœur

3 (*direct*) **she turned her steps towards home** elle a dirigé ses pas vers la maison; **he never turned anyone from his door** il n'a jamais fermé sa porte à personne; **to t. one's thoughts to God** tourner ses pensées vers Dieu; **to t. one's attention to …** tourner son attention vers *ou* sur …; **to t. the conversation to …** orienter la conversation vers …

4 (*head*) tourner; (*gaze*) tourner, diriger (**towards** vers); **t. your face this way** regardez de ce côté; **t. your desk this way** tournez votre bureau dans cette direction

5 (*go round*) **to t. the corner** tourner au coin de la rue; *Fig* passer le moment critique; **she's turned forty** elle a quarante ans passés, elle a passé la quarantaine; **it's turned seven** il est sept heures passées

6 (*change*) transformer, changer (**into** en); **to t. water into wine** changer l'eau en vin; **his love has been turned to hate** son amour s'est changé *ou* s'est transformé en haine; **to t. a theatre into a cinema** convertir un théâtre en cinéma; **the witch turned him into a crow** la sorcière l'a transformé en corbeau; **we've turned the attic into a study** nous avons transformé *ou* converti le grenier en bureau

7 (*cause to become*) faire devenir; **the heat has turned the milk sour** la chaleur a fait tourner le lait; **autumn turns the leaves yellow** l'automne fait jaunir les feuilles; **to t. sth green/black** rendre qch vert/noir, verdir/noircir qch; **the blood turned the water red** le sang a rougi l'eau; **Angus MacKinnon, athlete turned journalist** Angus MacKinnon, athlète reconverti dans le journalisme; **success has turned her head** le succès lui a tourné la tête

8 (make on lathe) (table leg etc) tourner, façonner au tour; Fig **a well turned sentence** une phrase bien tournée; Knitting **to t. a heel** faire le talon

vi 1 (rotate) tourner; **to t. a complete circle** faire un tour complet; **the steering wheel won't t.** le volant ne tourne pas; **my head's turning** la tête me tourne

2 to toss and t. (in bed) se tourner et se retourner (dans son lit); **to t. upside down** se retourner

3 (turn head, turn round) se retourner; **he turned to look at the landscape** il s'est retourné pour regarder le paysage; **she turned to me – what do you think?** elle se tourna vers moi – qu'est-ce que tu en penses, toi?; Mil **right t.!** à droite!; **left t!** à gauche!

4 (change direction) tourner, se diriger; **to t. to the right/the left** (of person, path etc) tourner à droite/à gauche; **he turned towards home** il s'est dirigé vers la maison; **the wind is turning** le vent tourne; **my thoughts often t. to this subject** mes réflexions se portent souvent sur ce sujet; **to t. to another subject** passer à une autre question; **the tide is turning** la marée change; **her luck has turned** sa chance a tourné

5 (for help) **to t. to sb** (for help/advice) s'adresser à qn (pour obtenir de l'aide/des conseils); **I didn't know who to t. to** je ne savais pas à qui m'adresser; **to t. to the dictionary** consulter le dictionnaire; **I don't know where** or **which way to t.** je ne sais pas à quel saint me vouer

6 (change) devenir, se transformer (**into** en); **caterpillars t. into butterflies** la chenille se métamorphose en papillon; **she's turned into a very hard-headed businesswoman** c'est devenue une femme d'affaires très réaliste; **everything he touches turns to gold** tout ce qu'il touche se change en or; **to t. (sour)** (of milk) tourner; Fig **to t. sour** tourner au vinaigre; **it's turning cold** il commence à faire froid; **the crowd turned nasty** la foule est devenue agressive; **the leaves are beginning to t.** les feuilles commencent à jaunir; **he turned red** il a rougi; **to t. red/blue** virer au rouge/bleu; **to t. sulky** devenir maussade; **to t. socialist** devenir socialiste

▸ **turn against vt insep** se retourner contre; **vt sep** (make opposed to) retourner contre; **she turns everyone against her** elle se met tout le monde à dos; **they turned his argument against him** ils ont retourné son argument contre lui

▸ **turn around vi, vt sep** = turn round

▸ **turn aside vi** se retourner; **to t. aside from the path of righteousness** se détourner du droit chemin

vt sep to t. aside a blow détourner ou faire dévier un coup

▸ **turn away vt sep 1** (direct elsewhere) (head, gaze) détourner; **police were turning drivers/people away (from the scene of the accident)** la police détournait ou écartait les automobilistes/les gens (du lieu de l'accident)

2 (refuse entry, help etc to) (of hospital, hotel etc) refuser; **to t. sb away in their hour of need** refuser de venir en aide à qn; Theat etc **to t. people away** refuser du monde; **we've been turning business away** nous avons refusé du travail

vi (look away) se détourner, détourner son regard; (go away) s'écarter; **to t. away from sb** (turn one's back on) tourner le dos à qn; (abandon) délaisser ou abandonner qn

▸ **turn back vi 1** (return in same direction) rebrousser chemin, faire demi-tour; Fig

there's no turning back now on ne peut plus faire marche arrière maintenant

2 (in book) **t. back to page ...** revenez à la page ...

vt sep 1 (of person) (cause to return in same direction) faire faire demi-tour à, faire revenir sur ses pas; **the refugees were turned back at the border** les réfugiés ont été refoulés à la frontière

2 (fold) (sheets) replier

3 (adjust to earlier time) (watch etc) retarder; **to t. the clocks back an hour** retarder les pendules d'une heure; Fig **you can't t. the clock back** on ne peut pas revenir en arrière ou revivre le passé

▸ **turn down vt sep 1** (fold down) (collar) rabattre; (page of book) plier, corner; **to t. down the bed** ouvrir le lit

2 (reduce) (heat, sound etc) baisser; **to t. down the TV/radio** baisser le son de la télé/radio

3 (refuse, reject) (offer) repousser, rejeter; (candidate, claim etc) refuser; **I've been turned down for that job** je n'ai pas été accepté pour cet emploi; **she turned me down flat** elle a refusé catégoriquement, Fam elle m'a envoyé promener; **they offered him a job but he turned them down** ils lui ont proposé un emploi mais il a rejeté leur offre

▸ **turn in vt sep 1 to t. in one's toes** tourner les pieds en dedans

2 Fam (hand in) (object) rendre, rapporter (à la police); (betray to police) (person) livrer ou vendre à la police

3 Fam (give up) (one's job) quitter, abandonner

4 Sport, Theat **to t. in a good score/performance** faire un bon score/une belle performance

vi 1 (point inwards) **his toes t. in** il a les pieds tournés en dedans

2 (go through entrance off road etc) **he turned in at the gate** arrivé à la porte, il est entré

3 Fam **I think I'll t. in (for the night)** (go to bed) je crois que je vais aller me pieuter

▸ **turn off vt sep 1** (switch off) (water, tap, gas, electricity) fermer; (light, radio, TV etc) éteindre

2 Fam (take away enthusiasm from) rebuter, refroidir; (sexually) couper l'envie à

vi 1 (leave road, street) changer de route; **I turned off to the left** j'ai pris (la route/la rue) à gauche, j'ai tourné à gauche; **he turned off onto the motorway** il s'est engagé sur l'autoroute

2 (of heater etc) se fermer

vi insep we turned off the main road nous avons quitté la grande route; **a small street turning off the High Street** une petite rue qui part de la rue principale

▸ **turn on vt sep 1** (switch on) (water, tap, gas, electricity) ouvrir; (light, radio, TV etc) allumer; **shall I t. on the light?** voulez-vous que j'allume?

2 Fam (excite) brancher; (sexually) exciter; **she turned me on to Zen Buddhism** elle m'a branché sur le bouddhisme zen

vt insep 1 (attack physically or verbally) s'attaquer à

2 (depend on) reposer sur, dépendre de; **everything turns on your answer** tout dépend de votre réponse

vi (of heater etc) se mettre en route ou en marche

▸ **turn out vt sep 1** (eject) mettre ou Fam flanquer à la porte; (tenant) déloger, évincer; (cattle) mettre au vert; Naut (men) réveiller; Mil (troops) alerter

2 (empty) (pockets etc) vider, retourner; Culin (dessert etc) démouler; **to t. out a drawer** (empty) vider un tiroir; (empty and tidy) mettre de l'ordre dans un tiroir; **to t. out a room** nettoyer une pièce à fond

3 (switch off) (gas) couper, éteindre; (light) éteindre

4 (produce) (goods) produire, fabriquer; **the factory turns them out by the thousand** l'usine en fabrique par milliers; **the sort of students that we aim to t. out here** le type d'étudiants que nous voulons former ici

5 well turned out (person) élégant, soigné

6 (point outwards) **to t. one's toes out** tourner les pieds en dehors

vi 1 (attend) (to see parade, hear speech etc) assister; (of voters) aller aux urnes; **the doctor/fire brigade had to t. out in the middle of the night** le docteur/les pompiers a/ont dû se déplacer au milieu de la nuit; **the whole town turned out to see it** toute la ville est allée le voir; **not many people turned out for his funeral/the march** il n'est pas venu beaucoup de monde à son enterrement/à la manifestation

2 (point outwards) **his toes t. out** il a les pieds tournés en dehors

3 (end) **to t. out well/badly** bien/mal tourner; **it'll t. out all right** ça s'arrangera; **how did the cake t. out?** le gâteau était-il réussi?; **I don't know how it will t. out** je ne sais pas comment cela finira; **as it turned out** en l'occurrence; **she's turned out (to be) beautiful** elle est devenue une belle femme/jeune fille

4 (transpire) **he turned out to be the son of an old friend of mine** il s'est trouvé qu'il était le fils d'un de mes anciens amis; **she turned out to be a real idiot** elle s'est avérée une vraie gourde; **it turns out that ...** il se trouve que ...; **as it turns out, we would have had time** en fait, nous aurions eu le temps

5 Fam (get out of bed) se lever, sortir du lit

▸ **turn over vt sep 1** (turn) retourner; (page) tourner; **to t. over the pages of a book** feuilleter un livre; **she turned the body over** elle a retourné le corps; Agr **to t. over the soil** retourner la terre; **to t. an idea/a plan over (in one's mind)** retourner une idée/un projet dans sa tête; **if you want a bit of time to t. it over ...** (idea, offer etc) si vous avez besoin d'un peu de temps pour y réfléchir ...; Fig **to t. over a new leaf** tourner la page

2 (surrender) **to t. sth over to sb** remettre qch entre les mains de qn; **the thief was turned over to the police** on a remis le voleur entre les mains de la police

3 (of business) rapporter; **he must be turning over a good £1,000 a week** il doit gagner ou Fam se faire au moins 1 000 livres par semaine

4 Sl (rob) (shop) dévaliser; (cheat) rouler

vi 1 (change position by turning) se tourner, se retourner; **to t. over in bed** se retourner dans son lit; **to t. (right) over** (of car etc) capoter

2 TV (change channel) changer de chaîne

3 (in reading) tourner la page

4 (of engine) tourner au ralenti

▸ **turn round vi** (rotate) tourner; (of crane etc) tourner, pivoter; (face other way) (of person) se retourner; (of vehicle) tourner; (abruptly) faire volte-face; (in one's opinions etc) tourner casaque, virer de bord; **she turned round in her chair** elle se retourna sur sa chaise; **t. round and let me see your face** tournez-vous (un peu) que je voie votre visage; **he just turned round and hit me** tout d'un coup il s'est retourné et m'a frappé; **after eight years of marriage she turned round and said she was leaving** après huit années de mariage elle annonça soudain qu'elle partait

vt sep 1 (move to face other way) retourner; **she turned the chair round** elle la retourna la chaise; **she turned the car round** elle a fait demi-tour

2 (reverse) (bad situation) renverser, retourner; **to t. the economy/a company round** remettre l'économie/une entreprise sur pied **3** Com (process, deal with) (order) traiter, s'occuper de

VT INSEP (go around) (corner) tourner

▸ **turn up** VI **1** (arrive) arriver, se présenter; **he turned up ten minutes late** il est arrivé ou Fam s'est amené dix minutes en retard; **she turned up at the party with a new boyfriend** elle est arrivée ou Fam a débarqué à la soirée avec un nouveau petit ami; **he'll t. up one of these days** il reparaîtra un de ces jours

2 I'm sure your keys will t. up (be found) je suis sûr qu'on retrouvera tes clés; **it's bound to t. up** il finira bien par réapparaître; **the pen turned up in his jacket** on a retrouvé le stylo dans sa veste; Fig **something is sure to t. up** il se présentera sûrement une occasion; **until something better turns up** en attendant mieux

3 (turn upwards) rebiquer; **her nose turns up** elle a le nez retroussé

VT SEP 1 (fold upwards) (collar) relever; (sleeves, trouser legs) retrousser; (to shorten) raccourcir en faisant un ourlet; **she turned her nose up at the job** elle a refusé l'emploi avec dédain; **don't t. your nose up like that** (at food) arrête de faire le dégoûté

2 (uncover) (card) retourner

3 (find) trouver; **the investigation has failed to t. up any new information** l'enquête n'a apporté aucun élément nouveau

4 (increase, make louder etc) augmenter; (gas) monter; **to t. the radio/radiator up** mettre la radio/le radiateur plus fort

5 Br Sl **t. it up!** (stop that) c'est fini, oui!

turnabout ['tɜːnəbaʊt] N retournement m, revirement m

turnaround ['tɜːnəraʊnd] N (of situation, opinion) retournement m, revirement m; (of ship, aeroplane etc) rotation f, Com (of an order) traitement m; Com **they offer a faster t.** leurs délais sont plus courts

▸▸ **t. time** (for order) délai m de livraison; (of ferry, plane) temps m de rotation

turncoat ['tɜːnkəʊt] N Pol etc renégat m

turndown ['tɜːndaʊn] ADJ (collar etc) rabattu

▸▸ **t. housekeeper** (in hotel) gouvernante f du soir

turned-up ['tɜːndʌp] ADJ (collar etc) relevé; (nose) retroussé

turner ['tɜːnər] N Ind tourneur m

turnery ['tɜːnərɪ] N atelier m de tourneur

turning ['tɜːnɪŋ] N **1 the t. of the tide** le changement ou renversement de la marée; Fig le renversement de tendances **2** (off road etc) tournant m; **the first t. on the right** la première route/rue à droite; Prov **it's a long road that has no t.** après la pluie le beau temps **3** (on lathe) tournage m, travail m au tour

▸▸ Br Aut **t. circle** rayon m de braquage; **t. point** (decisive moment) moment m décisif; (change) tournant m; **at the t. point of her career** au tournant de sa carrière

turnip ['tɜːnɪp] N (plant, vegetable) navet m; Hum (pocket watch) montre f de poche ou de gousset

turnkey ['tɜːnkiː] N Arch (jailer) geôlier, -ière

▸▸ **t. plant** usine f clés en main; **t. project** projet m clés en main; Comput **t. system** système m clés en main

turn-off N **1** (on motorway etc) sortie f, branchement m; **the Leeds t.** la sortie pour Leeds **2** Sl **it's a t.** (boring) c'est un ennui mortel; (sexually) c'est dégoûtant; **it's a t. for me** (sexually) cela me coupe l'envie

turn-of-the-century ADJ du début du siècle; **t. London** le Londres du début du siècle

turn-on N Sl **it's/he's a real t.** (sexually) c'est/il est vachement excitant; **is that a t.?** ça t'excite?

turnout ['tɜːnaʊt] N **1** (people present) assistance f; (at election) (taux m de) participation f; **a good/poor t.** beaucoup/peu de monde; **there was a large ou good t. at his funeral/the wedding/the meeting** il y avait beaucoup de monde à son enterrement/au mariage/à la réunion; **low turnouts at elections** faible participation f aux élections **2** (cleaning) (of room etc) nettoyage m à fond; **to give sth a good t.** nettoyer qch à fond **3** Ind (production) production f, rendement m **4** (clothes) tenue f

turnover ['tɜːnəʊvər] N **1** Fin chiffre m d'affaires, CA m; **our annual t.** notre chiffre d'affaires annuel **2** (of stock) écoulement m, rotation f, **t. of capital** roulement m de capitaux; **the (staff) t. there is very high** le taux de renouvellement du personnel y est très élevé **3** Culin chausson m; **apple t.** chausson aux pommes

▸▸ Com **t. rate** taux m de rotation; Fin **t. tax** impôt m ou taxe f sur le chiffre d'affaires

turnpike ['tɜːnpaɪk] N Am (road) autoroute f (à péage); Hist (barrier) barrière f de péage

turnround ['tɜːnraʊnd] N esp Br = **turnaround**

turnstile ['tɜːnstaɪl] N tourniquet m

turntable ['tɜːnteɪb(ə)l] N **1** Rail plaque f tournante; Mil plate-forme f tournante **2** (of record player) platine f

turn-up N **1** Br (on trousers) revers m **2** Fam **what a t. (for the book)!** ça c'est une sacrée surprise!

turpentine ['tɜːp(ə)ntaɪn] N essence f de térébenthine

▸▸ **t. substitute** white-spirit m

turpitude ['tɜːpɪtjuːd] N Fml turpitude f

turps [tɜːps] N Br Fam essence f de térébenthine

turquoise ['tɜːkwɔɪz, -kwaːz] N **1** (stone) turquoise f, **t. necklace** collier m en turquoise **2** (colour) turquoise m

ADJ turquoise inv

turret ['tʌrɪt] N Archit tourelle f, Mil, Naut (gun) **t.** tourelle f

turreted ['tʌrɪtɪd] ADJ Archit (castle) à tourelles

turtle ['tɜːt(ə)l] N (reptile) tortue f de mer

ADV to turn t. (of boat) chavirer; (of car) capoter

▸▸ **t. dove** tourterelle f des bois; Fig **a pair of t. doves** (lovers) un couple d'amoureux ou de tourtereaux; **t. neck** col m montant; **t. neck(ed) sweater** pull m à col montant; Culin **t. soup** consommé m à la tortue

Tuscan ['tʌskən] ADJ Geog, Archit toscan

N 1 (person) Toscan, -ane **2** Ling toscan m

Tuscany ['tʌskənɪ] N Toscane f

tush[1] [tʌʃ] INT Old-fashioned bah!, tarata!

tush[2] [tʊʃ] N esp Am Fam (buttocks) derrière m

tusk [tʌsk] N (of boar, elephant etc) défense f

tusker ['tʌskər] N (elephant) pachyderme m

tussle ['tʌs(ə)l] N empoignade f, lutte f au corps-à-corps; Fig lutte, bataille f, **to have a t.** en venir aux mains (**with sb** avec qn)

VI to t. with sb lutter avec qn; **to t. over sth** se disputer qch

tussock ['tʌsək] N touffe f d'herbe

tut [tʌt] INT **t. (tut)!** allons donc!

VI faire un bruit désapprobateur, émettre une exclamation désapprobatrice; **to t. at sb's behaviour** désapprouver la conduite de qn; **don't you t. t. at me!** je me passe de tes commentaires!

tutelage ['tjuːtɪlɪdʒ] N tutelle f, **to be under sb's t.** être sous la tutelle de qn

tutelar, tutelary ['tjuːtɪlər, -lərɪ] ADJ tutélaire

tutor ['tjuːtər] N **1** Br Univ directeur, -trice d'études **2 private t.** (in individual subject) professeur m particulier; (employed on permanent basis) précepteur m; **music t.** professeur de musique **3** Scot Law (of minor etc) tuteur, -trice

VT instruire; **to t. a child in French** donner à un enfant des leçons particulières de français

tutorial [tjuː'tɔːrɪəl] ADJ (work etc) de répétiteur; Univ **the t. system** = le système d'enseignement où les étudiant(e)s sont supervisé(e)s par un directeur d'études

N 1 Br Univ travaux mpl dirigés **2** Comput didacticiel m

▸▸ Comput **t. program** didacticiel

tutti-frutti ['tʊtɪ'fruːtɪ] N Culin plombières f

tutu ['tuːtuː] N (garment) tutu m

tu-whit tu-whoo [tʊ'wɪttʊ'wuː] INT hou hou!

tux [tʌks] N esp Am Fam smoking m

tuxedo [tʌk'siːdəʊ] N esp Am smoking m

TV[1] ['tiː'viː] N (abbr **television**) télé f, TV f, (television set) poste m de télévision, téléviseur m

▸▸ **TV channel** chaîne f de télévision; **TV dinner** plateau-repas m surgelé, pl plateaux-repas surgelés; **TV lounge** salle f de télévision; **TV magazine** hebdo m télé; **TV movie** téléfilm m; **TV personality** vedette f de la télévision; **TV programme** émission f télé; **TV screen** écran m de télévision; **TV set** poste de télévision, téléviseur; **TV station** station f de télévision

TV[2] N Sl (abbr **transvestite**) travelo m

TVP [tiːviː'piː] N Culin (abbr **textured vegetable protein**) protéine f végétale texturée

twaddle ['twɒd(ə)l] Fam N fadaises fpl; **to talk t.** dire ou débiter des balivernes ou des sottises

VI to t. on about sth débiter des sottises à propos de qch

twain [tweɪn] ADJ, N Arch, Lit deux m; Hum **and ne'er the t. shall meet** et ils resteront à jamais inconciliables

twang [twæŋ] N **1** (of bowstring) bruit m sec; (of guitar) son m aigu **2** (in voice) **nasal t.** ton m nasillard, nasillement m; **to speak with a t.** nasiller, parler d'une voix nasillarde

VT (drawn bowstring) lâcher; (strings etc) faire vibrer; **to t. a guitar** gratter (une guitare)

VI 1 (of string etc) vibrer; **to t. on a guitar** gratter (une guitare) **2** (speak with twang) nasiller

'twas [twɒz] CONTR Arch, Lit = **it was**

twat [twæt] N Br Sl **1** (vagina) moule f, chatte f **2** (idiot) crétin, -ine

twatted ['twætəd] ADJ Br Sl (drunk) rond comme une queue de pelle, plein comme une barrique

tweak [twiːk] N **1** (twist) **he gave her nose a t.** il lui a doucement tordu le nez **2** (adjustment) petite modification f, **to give sth a little t.** donner un petit coup à qch

VT 1 (pinch) pincer; (twist) tordre (avec les doigts); **to t. sb's ear** tirer l'oreille à qn **2** (adjust) (engine) régler; (text) apporter quelques petites modifications à

twee [twiː] ADJ Br Fam Pej mignard, gentillet

tweed [twiːd] N Tex tweed m; **t. jacket** veste f en ou de tweed; **tweeds** (suit, outfit) complet m ou costume m de ou en tweed

tweedy ['twiːdɪ] ADJ (cloth) qui tient du tweed; Fam Pej (person) qui affecte la tenue d'un propriétaire rural

'tween [twiːn] PREP Arch, Lit entre

'tween decks ['twi:ndeks] *Naut* **N** faux-pont *m, pl* faux-ponts, entrepont *m*
  ADJ, ADV dans l'entrepont

tweet [twi:t] **N** *(of bird)* pépiement *m*, gazouillement *m*
  VI *(of bird)* pépier, gazouiller

tweeter ['twi:tər] **N** *(loudspeaker)* haut-parleur *m* aigu, *pl* haut-parleurs aigus, tweeter *m*

tweezers ['twi:zəz] **NPL** brucelles *fpl*; *(for hairs)* pince *f* à épiler VOIR GRAMMAIRE A10

twelfth [twelfθ] **ADJ** douzième; **Louis the T.** Louis XII
  N 1 *(of month)* douze *m*; **(on) the t.** *(of May)* le douze (mai) **2** *(person, thing)* douzième *mf* **3** *(fraction)* douzième *m*
  ▸▸ *Cr* **t. man** joueur *m* de réserve; **T. Night** la fête des Rois

twelve [twelv] **ADJ, N** douze *m*; **t. o'clock** *(midday)* midi *m*; *(midnight)* minuit *m*

twelvemonth ['twelvmʌnθ] **N** *Old-fashioned, Lit* année *f*

twelve-tone **ADJ** *Mus* dodécaphonique
  ▸▸ **t. system** dodécaphonisme *m*

twentieth ['twentɪɪθ] **ADJ** vingtième
  N 1 *(of month)* vingt *m*; **(on) the t.** *of June* le vingt juin **2** *(person, thing)* vingtième *mf* **3** *(fraction)* vingtième *m*

twenty ['twentɪ] **ADJ, N** vingt *m*; **t.-one** vingt et un; **t.-two** vingt-deux; **about t. people** une vingtaine de personnes; **the twenties** les années vingt; **to be in one's twenties** avoir entre vingt et trente ans; **we've been working t.-four hours a day** nous avons travaillé jour et nuit; *Fam* **t.-four/seven, 24/7** sans arrêt
  ▸▸ **t.-four-hour hotline** ligne *f* directe accessible 24 heures sur 24; **t.-four hour service** service *m* vingt-quatre heures sur vingt-quatre; **t.-t. vision** vue *f* parfaite; *Rugby* **t.-two metre line** ligne *f* des vingt-deux mètres

twerp [twɜ:p] **N** *Br Fam* crétin, -ine

twice [twaɪs] **ADV** deux fois; **t. as big as sth** deux fois plus grand que qch; **t. as slow** deux fois plus lent; **t. over** à deux reprises; **to think t. before doing sth** y regarder *ou* réfléchir à deux fois avant de faire qch; **to think t. before saying sth** tourner la langue sept fois dans la bouche avant de parler; **she didn't have to think t. before accepting** elle a accepté sans hésiter; **he didn't have to be asked t.** il ne se fit pas prier

twiddle ['twɪd(ə)l] *Fam* **N** **to give sth a t.** tourner qch
  VT jouer avec, tripoter; **to t. a knob** tourner un bouton; **to t. one's thumbs** se tourner les pouces; *Fig* **I've spent the whole day twiddling my thumbs** j'ai passé la journée à me tourner les pouces
  VI **to t. with sth** jouer avec *ou* tripoter qch

twig [twɪg] **N** brindille *f*
  VT & VI (**-gg-**) *Br Fam* piger; **I soon twigged his little game** je n'ai pas tardé à voir dans son jeu

twilight ['twaɪlaɪt] **N** crépuscule *m*, demi-jour *m, pl* demi-jours; **in the (evening) t.** au crépuscule, entre chien et loup, à la brune; *Fig* **in the t. of life** au crépuscule de la vie; **the t. hours** les heures *fpl* crépusculaires; *Fig* **the t. world of the paranormal** l'entre-deux-mondes *m* du paranormal
  ▸▸ **t. zone** *(in city)* quartier *m* délabré *(qui entoure un quartier commercial)*; *(in ocean)* zone *f* crépusculaire; *Fig* zone d'ombre, zone floue

twill [twɪl] **N** *Tex* (tissu *m*) croisé *m*, sergé *m*

'twill [twɪl] **CONTR** *Arch, Lit* = **it will**

twin [twɪn] **N** jumeau, -elle
  ADJ jumeau, jumelé

VT (**-nn-**) *(towns)* jumeler; **Paisley is twinned with Furth** Paisley est jumelée avec Furth
  ▸▸ **t. beds** lits *m* jumeaux; *Obst* **t. birth** accouchement *m* de jumeaux; **t. brother** frère *m* jumeau; *Aut* **t. camshaft** double arbre *m* à cames; *Aut* **t. carburettor** carburateur *m* double-corps; **t. columns** colonnes *fpl* géminées; *Mktg* **t. plant** lot *m* de deux; **t. room** chambre *f* à deux lits; **t. sister** sœur *f* jumelle; **t. town** ville *f* jumelée *ou* jumelle; **Stirling's t. town** is Villeneuve-d'Ascq Stirling est jumelée avec Villeneuve-d'Ascq; *Aut* **t. turbo** double turbo *m*; *Aut* **t. tyres** pneus *mpl* jumelés

twin-bedded room [-bedɪd] **N** chambre *f* à lits jumeaux

twin-cam **N** *Aut* double arbre *m* à cames

twine [twaɪn] **N** *(string)* ficelle *f*
  VT *(threads)* tordre, tortiller; *(garland, fingers etc)* entrelacer
  VI **the road twined up the mountain** la route montait en lacets dans la montagne
  ▸ **twine around, twine round** **VT SEP** **to t. sth about** *or* **(a)round sth** enrouler qch autour de qch; **the honeysuckle had twined itself round the tree** le chèvrefeuille s'était enroulé autour de l'arbre
  VT INSEP s'enrouler *ou* s'enlacer autour de; **the ivy had twined around the tree** le lierre s'était enroulé autour de l'arbre

twin-engine(d) aircraft **N** avion *m* bimoteur

twinge [twɪn(d)ʒ] **N** *(of pain)* élancement *m*; *(of gout etc)* légère crise *f*; **t. of conscience** remords *m*; *Fam* **my tooth/knee still gives the odd t.** ma dent/mon genou m'élance toujours de temps en temps

twining ['twaɪnɪŋ] **ADJ** *(plant, stem)* volubile

twinjet ['twɪndʒet] **N** biréacteur *m*

twinkle ['twɪŋk(ə)l] **N** *(of stars, distant lights)* scintillement *m*, clignotement *m*; *(of eyes)* pétillement *m*; **a mischievous t. in the eye** un éclair de malice dans les yeux; *Fam* **when you were just a t. in your father's eye** quand tu n'étais pas encore de ce monde; **in a t. (of an eye)** en un clin d'œil
  VI *(of light, star)* scintiller, étinceler, clignoter; *(of eyes)* pétiller; **her eyes twinkled with amusement/mischief** ses yeux pétillaient de rire/malice

twinkling ['twɪŋklɪŋ] **ADJ** *(star etc)* scintillant, étincelant, clignotant; **t. eyes** yeux *mpl* pétillants
  N scintillement *m*, étincellement *m*, clignotement *m*; **in the t. of an eye** en un clin d'œil

twinky ['twɪŋkɪ] **N** *Am Sl (homosexual)* homo *m*

twinning ['twɪnɪŋ] **N** *(of two towns etc)* jumelage *m*; **t. of companies** jumelage d'entreprises; **t. arrangements** arrangements *mpl* en vue d'un jumelage

twinset ['twɪnset] **N** *Br (garments)* twin-set *m, pl* twin-sets; **she's very t. and pearls** ≃ elle est très BCBG

twirl [twɜ:l] **N 1** *(movement)* tournoiement *m*; *(of dancer etc)* pirouette *f* **2** *(shape) (of smoke etc)* volute *f*; *Archit* enroulement *m*, volute; *(of seashell)* spire *f*, *(in writing)* enjolivure *f* en spirale; *(in music)* fioriture *f*, **with a t. of cream on top** avec une spirale de crème dessus
  VT *(one's partner, lasso)* faire tournoyer; *(walking stick etc)* faire des moulinets avec; *(one's moustache)* tortiller
  VI *(turn round quickly)* se retourner d'un mouvement; *(when dancing)* tournoyer
  ▸ **twirl round** **VT SEP** = **twirl VT**
  VI se retourner brusquement; *(spin several times)* tournoyer

TWIST [twɪst]

N tour **1** ▪ tournure **2** ▪ torsade **3** ▪ écheveau **3**	
VT tordre ▪ tortiller ▪ dénaturer ▪ altérer	
VI se tordre ▪ se tortiller ▪ serpenter	

N 1 *(act of twisting)* *(of lid, cap)* tour *m*; **with a t. of the wrist** en un tour de main; **give the lid another t.** donne encore un tour au couvercle
  2 *(of coil)* spire *f*, **twists and turns** *(of road)* tours et détours *mpl*, *(of events etc)* tournure *f*, **final t. in a story** tour *m* inattendu à la fin d'un récit; **this adds a new t. to events** ça donne une tournure inattendue aux événements; **that's a nice t.** *(in plot)* c'est bien trouvé; *(in story, anecdote)* c'est drôle, ça!; **by a t. of fate** par un coup du sort; *Br Fam* **to be round the t.** être fou *ou* cinglé; *Fam* **to get oneself into a t.** *(upset, nervous)* se mettre dans tous ses états
  3 *(of hair)* torsade *f*, tortillon *m*; *(of wool)* écheveau *m*; *(of paper)* tortillon; **sweet in a t. of paper** bonbon dans une papillote; **a t. of lemon** une rondelle de citron; **t. of tobacco** morceau *m* de tabac
  4 *(dance)* twist *m*
  VT *(one's hair, rope etc)* tordre, tortiller; *Tex etc (thread)* retordre; *(sb's words, meaning of text)* dénaturer; *(truth, meaning of sth)* altérer; **to t. two wires together** torsader deux fils; **to t. one's ankle** se faire une entorse; *(less serious)* se fouler la cheville; **to t. sb's arm** tordre *ou* retourner le bras à qn; *Fig* exercer une pression sur qn; *Hum* **if you t. my arm** si tu insistes; **to t. one's knee** se déboîter le genou; *Fig* **to t. the knife in the wound** retourner le couteau dans la plaie
  VI se tordre; *(of worm etc)* se tortiller; *(of rope etc)* s'entortiller; *(spiral)* former une spirale; *(of smoke)* former des volutes; *(of road etc)* serpenter, faire des lacets; *(dance)* twister; **to t. and turn** *(of road etc)* serpenter
  ▸▸ **t. drill** foret *m* hélicoïdal; **t. grip** *(accelerator)* poignée *f* d'accélération; *(gear change)* poignée de changement de vitesses
  ▸ **twist off** **VI** *(of lid)* se dévisser
  VT SEP *(lid)* dévisser
  ▸ **twist round** **VT SEP 1** *(wrap around)* **to t. sth round** enrouler *ou* entortiller qch autour de qch; *Fam* **he can t. her round his little finger** il la mène par le bout du nez
  2 **she twisted her head round and stared at him** elle tourna la tête et le fixa du regard
  VI *(turn)* se retourner; **to t. round in one's seat** se retourner sur son siège
  ▸ **twist up** **VI** *(of smoke)* s'élever en spirale
  2 **VT SEP** emmêler, entortiller; **to get all twisted up** *(of cables etc)* s'emmêler, s'entortiller

twisted ['twɪstɪd] **ADJ 1** tordu; *(wire etc)* entortillé; *(rope)* tordu; *(limb)* tordu, contourné; **to get all t.** s'entortiller; **face t. with pain** traits *mpl* tordus par la douleur; **the t. wreckage of the plane/car** l'épave *f* enchevêtrée de l'avion/de la voiture **2** *Fig (disturbed) (person, character, logic, reasoning)* tordu; **to have a t. mind** avoir l'esprit tordu; **what a t. thing to do** il faut être tordu pour faire une chose pareille; **a t. way of looking at things** une façon tordue de voir les choses; **he's so bitter and t.** il est tellement amer et désabusé
  ▸▸ *Archit* **t. pillar** colonne *f* torse

twisted-pair cable **N** câble *m* en paire torsadée

twister ['twɪstər] **N** *Fam* **1** *Br (swindler)* escroc *m* **2** *esp Am (tornado)* tornade *f*

twisting ['twɪstɪŋ] **ADJ** *(path)* tortueux

twisty ['twɪstɪ] **ADJ** *(road etc)* tortueux

twit [twɪt] N *esp Br Fam* andouille *f*, imbécile *m*

▪ VT (**-tt-**) *esp Lit* narguer, taquiner (**about** à propos de)

twitch [twɪtʃ] N **1** *(jerk)* petit coup *m* sec **2** *(tic)* tic *m*; *(of limb)* mouvement *m* convulsif
▪ VT *(jerk)* tirer vivement, tirer d'un petit coup sec; **to t. its tail** *(of cat)* faire de petits mouvements de la queue
▪ VI *(of face, limb)* se contracter nerveusement; *(of eyelid, lip)* trembler; *(of hands)* se crisper nerveusement

twitcher ['twɪtʃər] N *Br Fam* dingue *mf* d'ornithologie

twitter ['twɪtər] N **1** *(of birds)* gazouillement *m*, gazouillis *m* **2** *Fam* **to be in a t.** *(of person)* être tout en émoi *ou* dans tous ses états
▪ VI *(of bird)* gazouiller; *Fig Pej (talk)* jacasser

twittering ['twɪtərɪŋ] ADJ *(bird)* gazouillant; *Fig Pej (person, voice etc)* piaillant
▪ N gazouillement *m*; *Fig Pej (talk)* jacassement *m*

'twixt [twɪkst] PREP *Arch, Lit* entre

two [tuː] N deux *m*; **twenty-t.** vingt-deux; *Gym etc* **one, t.! one, t.!** une deux! une deux!; **no t. men are alike** il n'y a pas deux hommes qui se ressemblent; **to break/fold sth in t.** casser/plier qch en deux; **to walk in twos** *or* **t. by t.** marcher deux à deux *ou* (deux) par deux; *Fig* **to put t. and t. together** en tirer les conclusions (qui s'imposent), faire le rapprochement; *Fam* **that makes t. of us** on est deux; **t. fours are eight** deux fois quatre font huit; **it's t. o'clock** il est deux heures; **to be t.** *(in age)* avoir deux ans; **a mother of t.** la mère de deux enfants; **the t. of us/them** nous/eux deux; *Cards* **t. of spades** deux de pique; *Mus* **t. part song** chanson *f* à deux voix
▪ PRON deux; **t. is not enough** deux, ce n'est pas assez
▪ ADJ deux; **t. people** deux personnes

two-bit ADJ *Am Fam* de quatre sous; *(person)* à la noix

two-colour ADJ de deux couleurs, bicolore; *(print ribbon)* bicolore
▪ ▪ *Typ* **t. printing** impression *f* en deux couleurs *ou* en bichromie, bichromie *f*; *Typ* **t. process** bichromie *f*

two-dimensional ADJ bidimensionnel; *Fig Pej (character, film etc)* simpliste, superficiel

two-door ADJ *(car)* à deux portes

two-edged ADJ *(sword, argument)* à double tranchant; *(remark, answer etc)* ambigu, -uë

two-faced [-feɪst] ADJ hypocrite

twofer ['tuːfər] N *Am Fam* deux billets *mpl etc* vendus pour le prix d'un

twofold ['tuːfəʊld] ADJ double
▪ ADV doublement; **kindness returned t.** bontés rendues au double

two-four ADJ
▪ ▪ *Mus* **t. time** mesure *f* à deux quatre; **in t. time** en deux quatre

two-handed ADJ *Cards (game)* qui se joue à deux
▪ ▪ *Tennis* **t. backhand** revers *m* à deux mains; **t. sword** épée *f* à deux mains, espadon *m*

two-headed ADJ bicéphale; *Her (eagle)* double, à deux têtes

two-horse ADJ *(carriage)* à deux chevaux; *Fig* **a t. race** une épreuve/élection qui ne comprend que deux concurrents

two-legged ADJ bipède

twonk [twɒŋk] N *Fam (fool)* andouille *f*, cruche *f*

two-part pricing N prix *mpl* à double détente

two-party ADJ *(system, politics etc)* bipartite

twopence ['tʌpəns] N *Br* deux pence *mpl*; *Fig Fam* **it isn't worth t.** ça ne vaut pas tripette

twopenny ['tʌp(ə)nɪ] ADJ *Br* à *ou* de deux pence; **a t. piece** une pièce de deux pence

twopenny-halfpenny ['tʌp(ə)nɪ'heɪpnɪ] ADJ *Br Fig Fam (person, ring etc)* à la noix, à la gomme

two-phase ADJ *Elec (current)* bi-phasé

two-piece ADJ *(suit, swimsuit)* deux pièces
▪ N *(suit) (for woman)* deux-pièces *m inv*; *(for man)* costume *m* deux pièces; *(swimsuit)* deux-pièces

two-pin ADJ
▪ ▪ *Elec* **t. plug** prise *f* à deux fiches; **t. socket** prise *f* à deux douilles

two-ply ADJ *(rope)* à deux brins; *(wool)* deux fils; *(tissue)* double épaisseur

two-seater N *(car)* voiture *f* à deux places; *(plane)* biplace *m*, avion *m* à deux places

two-sided ADJ *(contract, talks etc)* bilatéral, -aux

twosome ['tuːsəm] N **1** *(game)* jeu *m ou* partie *f* à deux joueurs; *(dance)* danse *f* à deux **2** *(pair)* paire *f*; *(of friends etc)* couple *m*; **let's just go as a t.** allons-y rien que tous le deux

two-speed ADJ *Pol (Europe)* à deux vitesses
▪ ▪ *Econ, Pol* **t. monetary union** union *f* monétaire à deux vitesses; *Aut* **t. wiper** essuie-glace *m* à deux vitesses, *pl* essuie-glaces

two-star ADJ **1** *(restaurant, hotel)* deux étoiles **2** *(petrol)* ordinaire
▪ N *(petrol)* **five litres of t.** cinq litres d'(essence) ordinaire

two-step N *Mus* pas *m* de deux

two-stroke ADJ *(motorcycle)* à deux temps
▪ ▪ **t. engine** moteur *m* à deux temps; **t. mixture** *(mélange m)* deux-temps *m inv*

two-tier ADJ *(management structure)* à deux niveaux; *(education system, health service)* à deux vitesses

two-time VT *Fam* tromper; **she had been two-timing him with his best friend** elle le trompait avec son meilleur ami

two-timer N *Fam (husband, wife, lover)* personne *f* infidèle

two-timing ADJ *Fam* infidèle; **you t. bastard!** tu es un salaud fini!

two-tone ADJ *(paint, car)* deux tons; *(klaxon etc)* à deux tons
▪ ▪ **t. horn** avertisseur *m* deux tons; *Typ* **t. printing** bichromie *f*, impression *f* en deux couleurs

two-way ADJ *(street)* à double sens; *(mirror)* sans tain; *Elec (switch)* à deux directions; *Tel* bilatéral, -aux; **any relationship is a t. thing** *or* **street** toute relation ne peut exister que si elle est réciproque
▪ ▪ **t. converter** catalyseur *m* à deux voies; *Tel* **t. radio** émetteur-récepteur *m*, *pl* émetteurs-récepteurs; **t. trade** commerce *m* dans les deux sens

two-wheel drive N deux roues motrices *fpl*

two-wheeler N deux-roues *m inv*

tycoon [taɪ'kuːn] N *Fam* magnat *m*

tying up [taɪɪŋ] N *(of capital)* immobilisation *f*

tyke [taɪk] N *Fam* **1** *(dog)* cabot *m* **2** *(person)* salaud *m*; *(small child)* môme *mf*, *(mischievous child)* diablotin *m*

tympanum, *pl* **tympana, tympanums** ['tɪmpənəm, -ə, -əmz] N *Anat, Archit* tympan *m*

type [taɪp] N **1** *(class, sort, example)* type *m*, genre *m*; **people/books of this t.** des personnes/des livres de ce genre; **people of every t.** des gens de toutes sortes; *Fam* **he's/she's not my t.** ce n'est pas mon genre; **she's not the t. to ...** elle n'est pas du genre à ...; *Fam* **he's an odd t.** *(person)* c'est un drôle de type VOIR GRAMMAIRE A13 **2** *Typ (letters)* caractères *mpl*; **to print in large t.** imprimer en gros caractères; **in t.** composé; **wait till you see it in t.** attend de le voir imprimé *ou* de voir ce que ça rend imprimé
▪ VT **1** *(write on typewriter)* taper (à la machine), dactylographier **2** *Med* **to t. blood** déterminer un groupe sanguin
▪ VI taper à la machine, dactylographier; **can you t.?** savez-vous taper à la machine?; **he types well** il tape bien
▪ ▪ *Biol* **t. genus** genre *m* type; **t. library** typothèque *f*
▪ **type in** VT SEP taper
▪ **type out** VT SEP taper à la machine
▪ **type up** VT SEP taper au propre

type-ahead N *Comput* frappe *f* en continu
▪ ▪ **t. buffer** zone *f* tampon de frappe en continu

typecase ['taɪpkeɪs] N *Typ* casse *f*

typecast ['taɪpkɑːst] VT *(pt, pp* **typecast**) *Theat, Cin (actor)* donner toujours les mêmes rôles à; **she was being t. as a dumb blonde** elle était cantonnée aux rôles de blondes écervelées; **he is always t. as a villain** on lui fait toujours jouer des rôles de bandit

typed [taɪpt] ADJ dactylographié, écrit à la machine

typeface ['taɪpfeɪs] N *(type family)* famille *f* de caractères; *(printing surface)* œil *m* (de caractère); **try another t.** essaie avec un autre caractère

typescript ['taɪpskrɪpt] N texte *m* dactylographié

typeset ['taɪpset] VT *(pt, pp* **typeset**) *Typ* composer; **t. by MWP** composition MWP

typesetter ['taɪpsetər] N *(person)* compositeur *m*; *(machine)* machine *f* à composer; *Comput (in DTP)* photocomposeuse *f*

typesetting ['taɪpsetɪŋ] N *Typ* composition *f*; **who did the t.?** qui a fait la composition?
▪ ▪ **t. machine** machine *f* à composer, composeuse *f*, **t. techniques** techniques *fpl* de composition

typesize ['taɪpsaɪz] N *(of text)* taille *f* des caractères

typewriter ['taɪpraɪtər] N machine *f* à écrire; **to write sth on a t.** écrire *ou* taper qch à la machine
▪ ▪ *Comput* **t. mode** mode *m* machine à écrire; **t. ribbon** ruban *m* de machine à écrire; *Br* **t. rubber** gomme *f* pour machine à écrire

typewriting ['taɪpraɪtɪŋ] N dactylographie *f*

typewritten ['taɪprɪt(ə)n] ADJ *(document etc)* écrit *ou* tapé à la machine, dactylographié

typhoid ['taɪfɔɪd] ADJ *Med (bacillus)* typhoïdique
▪ N *(fièvre f)* typhoïde *f*
▪ ▪ **t. fever** *(fièvre)* typhoïde

typhoon [taɪ'fuːn] N *Met* typhon *m*

typhus ['taɪfəs] N *Med* typhus *m*

typical ['tɪpɪk(ə)l] ADJ typique (**of** de); **the t. Frenchman** le Français typique; **in a t. day you can earn £300** en une journée normale vous pouvez gagner 300 livres; *Fam* **isn't that** *or* **that's t. (of him/her)!** c'est bien de lui/d'elle!; **t. man/woman!** c'est bien un homme/une femme!; **your letter took six days to get here – t.!** ta lettre a mis six jours pour arriver – ça c'est typique! *ou* ça ne m'étonne pas!

typically ['tɪpɪklɪ] ADV typiquement; **he's t. French** il est typiquement français; **the countryside is t. Mediterranean** le paysage est typiquement méditerranéen; **he made one of his t. obscure remarks** il a fait une de ses habituelles remarques obscures; **she was t. late** *(normally)* elle arrivait généralement en retard; *(as on other occasions)* conformément à son habitude elle était en retard; **she was t. rude, she was her t. rude self** comme à son habitude, elle a été très désagréable; **employees t. work a 40-hour week** les employés travaillent en moyenne 40 heures par semaine

typify ['tɪpɪfaɪ] VT *(of person) (officer etc)* personnifier; *(of specimen etc)* être caractéristique de

typing ['taɪpɪŋ] N dactylographie *f, Fam* dactylo *f*
▸▸ **t. error** faute *f* de frappe; **t. paper** papier *m* machine; **t. pool** bureau *m* ou pool *m* des

dactylos; **t. skills** compétences *fpl* en dactylographie; **t. speed** vitesse *f* de frappe

typist ['taɪpɪst] N **(copy) t.** dactylographe *mf, Fam* dactylo *mf*; **audio t.** dactylo audiomagnéto; **I'm no t.** je tape très mal; **t.'s error** faute *f* de frappe

typo ['taɪpəʊ] N *Typ Fam* coquille *f,* faute *f* de frappe

typographer [taɪ'pɒɡrəfər] N typographe *mf*

typographic(al) [taɪpə'ɡræfɪk, -ɪk(ə)l] ADJ typographique

typographically [taɪpə'ɡræfɪklɪ] ADV typographiquement

typography [taɪ'pɒɡrəfɪ] N typographie *f*
tyrannical [tɪ'rænɪk(ə)l] ADJ tyrannique
tyrannically ['tɪrænɪklɪ] ADV tyranniquement
tyrannize ['tɪrənaɪz] VT tyranniser

tyranny ['tɪrənɪ] N tyrannie *f*
tyrant ['taɪrənt] N tyran *m*
tyre ['taɪər] N *esp Br* pneu *m, pl* pneus
▸▸ **t. chain** chaîne *f* (de pneu); **t. iron, t. lever** démonte-pneu *m, pl* démonte-pneus; **t. marks** *(in mud, snow etc)* empreintes *fpl* ou traces *fpl* de pneu; **t. pressure** pression *f* des pneus; **t. pressure gauge** indicateur *m* de pression de pneu; **t. pump** pompe *f* (pour gonfler les pneus); **t. scrub** ripage *m* des pneus; **t. valve** valve *f* de gonflage; **t. wear** usure *f* des pneus

tyro ['taɪrəʊ] N novice *mf,* débutant, -ante
Tyrol (the) [ðətɪ'rəʊl] N le Tyrol
Tyrolean [tɪrə'liːən] ADJ tyrolien
▸▸ **T. hat** chapeau *m* tyrolien

tzar, tzarist *etc* = tsar, tsarist *etc*

T-zone N zones *fpl* grasses du visage *(front, nez, menton)*

U¹, u [juː] N *(letter)* U, u *m*; **two u's** deux u; *Old-fashioned Fam* **U and non U** ce qui est bien *ou* comme il faut, et ce qui ne l'est pas

U² *Br Cin (abbr* **universal)** = désigne un film tous publics en Grande-Bretagne

UAE [juːeɪˈiː] N *(abbr* **United Arab Emirates)** Émirats *mpl* arabes unis, EAU *mpl*

U-bend N **1** *(in pipe)* coude *m*; *(under sink)* siphon *m* **2** *Br (in road)* virage *m* en épingle à cheveux

UB40 [juːbiːˈfɔːtɪ] N *Br (abbr* **unemployment benefit form 40)** = carte *f* de pointage (de demandeur d'emploi); *(person)* chômeur, -euse

ubiquitous [juːˈbɪkwɪtəs] ADJ *(substance, theme, muzak)* omniprésent; *(person)* doué d'ubiquité; **the u. fast-food joint** l'inévitable fast-food

ubiquity [juːˈbɪkwɪtɪ] N omniprésence *f*, *(of person)* ubiquité *f*

U-boat N sous-marin *m* allemand, *pl* sous-marins allemands

U-bolt N étrier *m*

UCAS [ˈjuːkæs] N *Br (abbr* **Universities and Colleges Admissions Service)** = centre *m* national qui traite les demandes d'entrée à l'université

UCCA [ˈʌkə] N *Br Formerly (abbr* **Universities Central Council on Admissions)** = centre *m* national qui traitait les demandes d'entrée à l'université

UCITS [juːsiːaɪtiːˈes] N *Fin (abbr* **undertakings for collective investment in transferables)** OPCVM *m*

UDA [juːdiːˈeɪ] N *Br Formerly (abbr* **Ulster Defence Association)** = groupement *m* paramilitaire en Irlande du Nord

udder [ˈʌdər] N *(of cow etc)* mamelle *f*, pis *m*

UDI [juːdiːˈaɪ] N *(abbr* **Unilateral Declaration of Independence)** déclaration *f* unilatérale d'indépendance

UDR [juːdiːˈɑːr] N *Br Formerly (abbr* **Ulster Defence Regiment)** régiment *m* de réservistes de l'armée britannique en Irlande du Nord

UEFA [juːˈeɪfə] N *(abbr* **Union of European Football Associations)** UEFA *f*

UFO [juːeˈfəʊ, ˈjuːfəʊ] N *(abbr* **unidentified flying object)** OVNI *m*

ufologist [juːˈfɒlədʒɪst] N spécialiste *mf* des ovnis

ufology [juːˈfɒlədʒɪ] N étude *f* des ovnis

Uganda [juːˈgændə] N Ouganda *m*

Ugandan [juːˈgændən] ADJ ougandais ▸ N Ougandais, -aise

ugh [ʌg] INT pouah!, beuh!

Ugli®, *pl* **Uglis, Uglies** [ˈʌglɪ, -ɪz] N *(fruit)* tangelo *m*

uglify [ˈʌglɪfaɪ] VT enlaidir

ugliness [ˈʌglɪnɪs] N laideur *f*

ugly [ˈʌglɪ] ADJ **1** *(in appearance etc)* *(person)* laid; *(building, furniture, pattern, hat, colour)* affreux, laid; *(word)* déplaisant; *(bruise, wound, scar)* vilain, méchant; **to grow u.** enlaidir; **an u. woman** un laideron, une femme laide; **she's as u. as sin** elle est laide comme les sept péchés capitaux *ou* comme un pou *ou* à faire peur **2** *Fig (threatening) (sky, look)* menaçant; *(incident, scene)* désagréable; *Fam* **an u. customer** un sale type; *Fam* **nationalism/racism reared its u. head** le nationalisme/racisme s'est réveillé; *Fam* **to cut up** *or* **turn u.** *(of person)* devenir agressif; **the situation was starting to turn u.** la situation commençait à mal tourner; **an u. rumour** un bruit sinistre
▸▸ **u. duckling** vilain petit canard *m*

UHF [juːeɪtʃˈef] N *(abbr* **ultrahigh frequency)** UHF *f*

uh-huh INT **1** [ˈʌhʌ] *(agreeing, yes)* hmm hmm, oui oui **2** [ˈʌhʌ] *(disagreeing, no, don't)* tut-tut, non non

UHT [juːeɪtʃˈtiː] ADJ *(abbr* **ultra heat treated)**
▸▸ **U. milk** lait *m* UHT, lait longue conservation

UK [juːˈkeɪ] N *(abbr* **United Kingdom)** RU *m*, Royaume-Uni *m*; **UK sales/prices** ventes/prix au Royaume-Uni

Ukraine [juːˈkreɪn] N Ukraine *f*

Ukrainian [juːˈkreɪnɪən] ADJ ukrainien ▸ N **1** Ukrainien, -ienne **2** *Ling* ukrainien *m*

ukulele [juːkəˈleɪlɪ] N *Mus* ukulélé *m*, guitare *f* hawaïenne

ulcer [ˈʌlsər] N *Med* ulcère *m*; *(in mouth)* aphte *m*; *Fig* plaie *f*, *(ugly building etc)* verrue *f*, **peptic u.** ulcère simple de l'estomac/du duodénum

ulcerate [ˈʌlsəreɪt] *Med* VT ulcérer; **ulcerated wound** blessure *f* ulcérée *ou* ulcéreuse ▸ VI s'ulcérer

ulceration [ʌlsəˈreɪʃən] N *Med* ulcération *f*

ulcerative [ˈʌls(ə)rətɪv] ADJ *Med* ulcératif

ulcerous [ˈʌls(ə)rəs] ADJ *Med* ulcéreux

ullage [ˈʌlɪdʒ] N *(in barrel)* creux *m* du tonneau

ulna [ˈʌlnə] N *Anat* cubitus *m*

Ulster [ˈʌlstər] N **1** Ulster *m* **2 u.** *(coat)* ulster *m*

Ulsterman, *pl* **Ulstermen** [ˈʌlstəmən] N Ulstérien *m*

Ulsterwoman, *pl* **Ulsterwomen** [ˈʌlstəwʊmən, -wɪmɪn] N Ulstérienne *f*

ult [ʌlt] *Com Old-fashioned abbr* **ultimo**

ulterior [ʌlˈtɪərɪər] ADJ ultérieur
▸▸ **u. designs** desseins *mpl* secrets; **u. motive** arrière-pensée *f*, *pl* arrière-pensées; **without u. motive** sans arrière-pensée

ultimate [ˈʌltɪmət] ADJ **1** *(final)* final, -als, définitif; **the u. effect of an action** l'effet ultime d'une action; **the u. decision is his** c'est à lui qu'appartient la décision finale; **u. goal** but *m* final; **certain of u. success** certain du succès final; **the u. deterrent** l'arme *f* de dissuasion absolue; **they made the u. sacrifice** ils ont fait l'ultime sacrifice
2 *(basic, fundamental)* fondamental, -aux; **the u. constituents of matter** les constituants fondamentaux de la matière; **is this the u. physical particle?** est-ce la particule fondamentale?
3 *(supreme, best etc)* suprême, absolu; **the u. double-glazing/laser printer** le double vitrage/l'imprimante laser absolu(e); **the u. sound system** la meilleure sono qui soit; **that really is the u. cheek!** c'est vraiment le comble du culot!; **he really is the u. incompetent!** on ne fait pas plus incompétent que lui
4 *(furthest)* le plus lointain; **the u. ends of the universe** les limites externes de l'univers; **we traced our u. origins back to …** nous avons établi nos origines les plus lointaines à …
▸ N **1** *Rel, Phil* **the u.** *(the best)* l'absolu *m* **2** **the u.** *(the very best)* le fin du fin; **the u. in luxury** le summum du luxe; **it's the u. in vulgarity/bad taste** c'est le comble de la vulgarité/du mauvais goût
▸▸ *Mktg* **u. consumer** utilisateur, -trice final(e)

ultimately [ˈʌltɪmɪtlɪ] ADV **1** *(finally, in the end)* finalement; **the events which led u. to his downfall** les événements qui ont finalement conduit à sa chute **2** *(at bottom, basically)* en fin de compte; **u. it's the same thing** en fin de compte *ou* au fond c'est la même chose

ultimatum, *pl* **ultimatums, ultimata** [ʌltɪˈmeɪtəm, -təmz, -tə] N ultimatum *m*; **to deliver an u. to sb, to present sb with an u.** adresser un ultimatum à qn

ultimo [ˈʌltɪməʊ] ADV *Com Old-fashioned* du mois dernier; **on the tenth u.** le dix du mois dernier

ultra- [ˈʌltrə] PREF ultra-, hyper-

ultrafashionable [ˌʌltrəˈfæʃnəb(ə)l] ADJ à la pointe de la mode, *Fam* hyper-mode *inv*

ultrahigh [ˌʌltrəˈhaɪ] ADJ
▸▸ *Phys* **u. frequency** ondes *fpl* ultra-courtes

ultraleft [ˌʌltrəˈleft] *Pol* ADJ d'extrême gauche
▸ N extrême gauche *f*

ultramarine [ˌʌltrəməˈriːn] ADJ, N (bleu *m* d')outremer *m*
▸▸ **u. blue** (bleu d')outremer

ultramodern [ˌʌltrəˈmɒd(ə)n] ADJ ultramoderne

ultramontane [ˌʌltrəˈmɒnteɪn] ADJ, N ultramontain, -aine

ultraright [ˌʌltrəˈraɪt] *Pol* ADJ d'extrême droite
▸ N extrême droite *f*

ultrasensitive [ʌltrəˈsensɪtɪv] ADJ ultra-sensible

ultrashort [ʌltrəˈʃɔːt] ADJ *Phys* ultracourt

ultrasonic [ʌltrəˈsɒnɪk] ADJultrasonique; **u. alarm** alarme *f* à ultrasons
N ultrasonics science *f* des ultrasons VOIR GRAMMAIRE A10

ultrasound [ˈʌltrəsaʊnd] N *Med* échographie *f*, ultrason *m*
▸▸ **u. scan** échographie, ultrason

ultraviolet [ʌltrəˈvaɪələt] ADJ *Phys* ultraviolet
▸▸ **u. rays** rayons *mpl* ultraviolets; *Med* **u. treatment** traitement *m* aux (rayons) ultra-violets

ultra vires [ʌltrəˈvaɪəriːz, ʊltrəˈviːreɪz] ADJ, ADV *Law* au delà de ses pouvoirs

ululate [ˈjuːljʊleɪt] VI *Fml (of owl etc)* ululer, huer; *(of jackal etc)* hurler; *(of person, mourner)* se lamenter

ululation [juːljʊˈleɪʃən] N *Fml (of owl etc)* ululation *f*, ululement *m*; *(of jackal etc)* hurlement *m*; *(of person)* lamentation *f*

Ulysses [ˈjuːlɪsiːz] N Ulysse *m*

um [ʌm] INT *(hesitating in speaking)* heu
VI **to um and err** bafouiller

umber [ˈʌmbər] N *Art* terre *f* d'ombre *ou* de Sienne; **burnt u.** terre d'ombre brûlée
ADJ couleur *inv* d'ombre

umbilical [ʌmˈbɪlɪk(ə)l, ʌmbɪˈlaɪk(ə)l] ADJ *Anat* ombilical, -aux
▸▸ **u. cord** cordon *m* ombilical

umbilicus [ʌmˈbɪlɪkəs, ʌmbɪˈlaɪkəs] N *Anat* ombilic *m*, nombril *m*

umbrage [ˈʌmbrɪdʒ] N ombrage *m*, ressentiment *m*; **to take u. at sth** prendre ombrage de qch, se froisser de qch

umbrella [ʌmˈbrelə] N **1** parapluie *m*; **to put up** *or* **open (up) one's u.** ouvrir son parapluie; **to put down** *or* **to fold (up) one's u.** fermer *ou* replier son parapluie; **beach u.** parasol *m* **2 under the u. of the United Nations** sous la protection des Nations Unies **3** *Mil, Aviat* **air** *or* **aerial u.** parapluie *m* aérien; **nuclear u.** parapluie nucléaire **4** *(of jellyfish)* ombrelle *f*
▸▸ **u. committee** comité *m* de coordination; *Fin* **u. fund** fonds *m* de consolidation; **u. organization** organisation *f* qui en regroupe plusieurs autres; **u. stand** porte-parapluies *m inv*; *Mktg* **u. trademark** marque *f* ombrelle

Note that the French word **ombrelle** is a false friend. It means **sunshade**.

Umbria [ˈʌmbrɪə] N Ombrie *f*

Umbrian [ˈʌmbrɪən] N Ombrien, -ienne
ADJ ombrien

umlaut [ˈʊmlaʊt] N *Ling* **1** *(vowel change)* inflexion *f* vocalique, métaphonie *f* **2** *(sign)* tréma *m*

umph [hm] INT *(disbelieving, not pleased)* hum!, hmm!

umpire [ˈʌmpaɪər] *Sport etc* N arbitre *m*, juge *m*; **to be an u. at a match** arbitrer un match
VT *(match)* arbitrer
VI arbitrer (le/un match)

umpteen [ʌmpˈtiːn] ADJ *Fam* je ne sais combien de; **I've told you u. times not to** ... je t'ai dit mille *ou* je ne sais combien de fois de ne pas ...; **she's got u. books on Africa** elle a des tas de livres sur l'Afrique; **to have u. reasons for doing sth** avoir trente-six raisons de faire qch

umpteenth [ʌmpˈtiːnθ] ADJ *Fam* **that's the u. time I've told you** c'est la énième fois que je te le dis

UMTS [juːemtiːˈes] N *Tel (abbr* **Universal Mobile Telecommunications Services)** UMTS *m*

UN [juːˈen] N *(abbr* **United Nations)** ONU *f*, **UN troops/observers** soldats/observateurs de l'ONU

'un [ən] PRON *Sl (one)* **a little 'un** un petit, une petite; **he's a bad 'un** c'est un sale type

unabashed [ʌnəˈbæʃt] ADJ *(person)* aucunement décontenancé; **shocked at his u. confession of guilt** choqué de le voir avouer sa culpabilité sans aucune honte

unabashedly [ʌnəˈbæʃədlɪ] ADV *(unashamedly)* sans aucune honte; *(without being discouraged)* sans se laisser décontenancer, sans se démonter

unabated [ʌnəˈbeɪtɪd] ADJ non diminué; **for three days the storm continued u.** pendant trois jours l'orage a continué sans répit; **the riots went on u.** les émeutes continuèrent sans faiblir; **the crowd continued to cheer with u. enthusiasm** la foule continuait à pousser des acclamations avec toujours autant d'enthousiasme

unabbreviated [ʌnəˈbriːvɪeɪtɪd] ADJ non abrégé

unable [ʌnˈeɪb(ə)l] ADJ incapable; **to be u. to do sth** ne pas pouvoir faire qch; *(because of external factor)* être dans l'impossibilité de faire qch, ne pas pouvoir faire qch; **he seems u. to understand you** il semble être incapable de vous comprendre; **we are u. to help you** nous ne sommes pas en mesure de vous aider; **I was u. to persuade him** je n'ai pas pu le persuader

unabridged [ʌnəˈbrɪdʒd] ADJ non abrégé, intégral, -aux; **u. edition** édition *f* intégrale; **u. text** texte *m* intégral

unabsorbed [ʌnəbˈzɔːbd] ADJ
▸▸ *Fin* **u. cost** coût *m* non-absorbé

unaccented, unaccentuated [ʌnəkˈsentɪd, ʌnəkˈsentjʊeɪtɪd] ADJ *Ling (syllable etc)* non accentué, atone; *Mus* **u. beat** temps *m* faible

unacceptable [ʌnəkˈseptəb(ə)l] ADJ inacceptable; *(theory)* irrecevable; *(behaviour)* inadmissible; **these conditions are u. to us** nous ne pouvons pas accepter ces conditions; **it's quite u. for so many people to be homeless** il est tout à fait inacceptable *ou* inadmissible que tant de gens soient sans foyer

unacceptably [ʌnəkˈseptəblɪ] ADV **an u. high level of** ... un niveau inadmissible *ou* intolérable de ...; **what they are, quite u., demanding is** ... l'objet tout à fait inadmissible de leur demande est ...

unaccommodating [ʌnəˈkɒmədeɪtɪŋ] ADJ *(person)* peu accommodant

unaccompanied [ʌnəˈkʌmp(ə)nɪd] ADJ **1** *(person, baggage)* non accompagné **2** *Mus* sans accompagnement; **passage for u. violin** passage pour violon seul

unaccomplished [ʌnəˈkʌmplɪʃt] ADJ **1** *(not fulfilled, not completed)* *(ambition)* non réalisé; *(work)* inachevé **2** *(mediocre)* *(person, performance etc)* médiocre

unaccountable [ʌnəˈkaʊntəb(ə)l] ADJ **1** *(inexplicable)* inexplicable **2** *(not accountable)* **to be u. to sb** ne pas avoir à répondre devant qn

unaccountably [ʌnəˈkaʊntəblɪ] ADV inexpliquablement

unaccounted [ʌnəˈkaʊntɪd] ADJ **there are still several thousand soldiers who are u. for** il y a encore plusieurs milliers de soldats portés disparus; **these £10 are u. for in the balance sheet** ces 10 livres ne figurent pas au bilan; **five of the passengers are still u. for** on reste sans nouvelles de cinq passagers; **two books are still u. for** il manque toujours deux livres

unaccustomed [ʌnəˈkʌstəmd] ADJ **1** inac-

coutumé, inhabituel **2** *(person)* **u. to sth/to doing sth** peu habitué à qch/à faire qch; **as I am to public speaking** n'ayant pas l'habitude de faire des discours

unacknowledged [ʌnəkˈnɒlɪdʒd] ADJ **1** *(child, talents)* non reconnu; **to go u.** ne pas être reconnu **2** *(quotation)* dont on ne cite pas l'auteur **3** *(letter)* resté sans réponse; **you shouldn't let his letter go u.** tu ne devrais pas laisser sa lettre sans réponse

unacquainted [ʌnəˈkweɪntɪd] ADJ **to be u. with sb/sth** ne pas connaître qn/qch; **to be u. with a fact** ignorer un fait; **we are not u. with pressure** nous n'ignorons pas ce que c'est que le stress

unadapted [ʌnəˈdæptɪd] ADJ mal adapté, peu adapté (**to sth** à qch)

unaddressed [ʌnəˈdrest] ADJ *(parcel etc)* sans adresse, qui ne porte pas d'adresse

unadopted [ʌnəˈdɒptɪd] ADJ non adopté; **to remain u.** *(of measure)* rester en souffrance
▸▸ *Br* **u. road** rue *f* non prise en charge par la municipalité

unadorned [ʌnəˈdɔːnd] ADJ sans ornement, sans fioritures; *esp Lit* **her u. beauty** sa beauté sans parure *ou* sans fard; **the u. truth** la vérité pure *ou* toute nue

unadulterated [ʌnəˈdʌltəreɪtɪd] ADJ pur, sans mélange; *(wine)* non frelaté; **u. joy** joie *f* sans mélange; **the u. truth** la vérité pure et simple; **u. by Western influences** non corrompu par les influences occidentales; **this is pure u. garbage!** ceci est purement et simplement de la foutaise!; **I've never heard such u. rot!** je n'ai jamais entendu de telles foutaises!

unadventurous [ʌnədˈventʃərəs] ADJ *(life, person)* peu aventureux; *(style, performance, director, prose etc)* peu audacieux, conventionnel; **we went to Spain again – that's very u. of you** nous sommes retournés en Espagne – ce n'est pas très aventureux de votre part

unadventurously [ʌnədˈventʃərəslɪ] ADV *(produced, designed)* peu audacieusement; *(to decide, choose)* sans prendre de risques; **we very u. chose beige carpets again** nous n'avons pas pris de risques et avons encore choisi des moquettes beiges

unadvertised [ʌnˈædvətaɪzd] ADJ *(product, meeting etc)* sans publicité; *(action etc)* discret, -ète

unadvisable [ʌnədˈvaɪzəb(ə)l] ADJ *(action)* peu recommandé, imprudent; **alcohol is u. for people suffering from heart complaints** l'alcool est à déconseiller aux cardiaques

unadvised [ʌnədˈvaɪzd] ADJ *esp Lit (unwise)* imprudent

unaesthetic [ʌniːsˈθetɪk] ADJ inesthétique

unaffected [ʌnəˈfektɪd] ADJ **1** *(without affectation) (person, behaviour)* sans affectation, naturel, simple; *(style)* sans fioritures, simple; **u. joy** joie *f* qui n'a rien de simulé; **u. modesty** modestie *f* non simulée **2** *(not touched)* **to be u. by sth** *(of person)* ne pas être affecté par qch; *(of thing) (by rain, cold, heat etc)* ne pas être altéré par qch; **she remained u. by his tears** elle ne fut pas émue par ses larmes; **we were u. by the strike/recession** nous n'avons pas été affectés par la grève/récession; **there's snow everywhere, but the north-west is u.** il y a de la neige partout, mais le nord-ouest n'est pas touché
▸▸ *Med* **u. carrier** porteur *m* sain

unaffectedly [ʌnəˈfektɪdlɪ] ADV *(to behave, speak)* simplement, sans affectation; *(dressed)* sobrement

unaffiliated [ʌnəˈfɪlɪeɪtɪd] ADJ non affilié (**to** à)

unaffordable [ʌnəˈfɔːdəb(ə)l] ADJ inabordable

unafraid [ʌnə'freɪd] ADJ sans peur

unaided [ʌn'eɪdɪd] ADV sans aide, sans assistance; **he did it u.** il l'a fait tout seul *ou* à lui seul

ADJ **by my own u. efforts** par mes propres moyens; **is this your own u. work?** est-ce que tu as travaillé tout seul?

unaired [ʌn'eəd] ADJ non aéré; *(opinions etc)* non exprimé

unalike [ʌnə'laɪk] ADJ dissemblable, différent; **they are not u.** ils se ressemblent un peu, ils ne sont pas totalement dissemblables

unalleviated [ʌnə'liːvɪeɪtɪd] ADJ sans répit; **u. boredom** ennui *f* mortel

unallocated [ʌn'æləkeɪtɪd] ADJ *(rooms, places)* non assigné; *(money, grants)* non alloué

unallotted [ʌnə'lɒtɪd] ADJ *St Exch (shares)* non réparti

unalloyed [ʌnə'lɔɪd] ADJ *Lit (happiness)* parfait

unalterable [ʌn'ɔːlt(ə)rəb(ə)l] ADJ immuable; *(character)* inaltérable

unalterably [ʌn'ɔːlt(ə)rəblɪ] ADV immuablement

unaltered [ʌn'ɔːltəd] ADJ inchangé; **let's leave it u.** n'y touchons pas

unambiguous [ʌnæm'bɪgjʊəs] ADJ non équivoque; *(reply)* sans ambiguïté; **what he meant was quite u.** il a été tout à fait clair; **u. terms** termes *mpl* tout à fait *ou* on ne peut plus clairs

unambiguously [ʌnæm'bɪgjʊəslɪ] ADV *(worded etc)* sans équivoque, sans ambiguïté; **he told us quite u. to ...** il nous a dit tout à fait clairement de ...

unambitious [ʌnæm'bɪʃəs] ADJ *(person, project etc)* sans ambition, peu ambitieux

un-American [ʌn-] ADJ contraire à l'esprit américain; *(in a damaging way)* antiaméricain; **he's so u.** ce n'est vraiment pas l'Américain type

unamused [ʌnə'mjuːzd] ADJ **she was distinctly u.** visiblement, cela ne l'amusait pas

unanimity [juːnə'nɪmɪtɪ] N unanimité *f*

unanimous [jʊ'nænɪməs] ADJ unanime; **they were u. in accusing him** ils étaient unanimes à l'accuser; **to reach a u. decision** se prononcer à l'unanimité; **u. vote** résolution *f* adoptée à l'unanimité

unanimously [jʊ'nænɪməslɪ] ADV à l'unanimité

unannounced [ʌnə'naʊnst] ADJ sans être annoncé; **he marched in u.** il est entré sans se faire annoncer

unanswerable [ʌn'ɑːns(ə)rəb(ə)l] ADJ *(argument)* incontestable, irréfutable; **u. question** question *f* à laquelle on ne peut pas répondre

unanswered [ʌn'ɑːnsəd] ADJ **1** *(letter, question)* sans réponse; **I had to leave two questions u.** j'ai dû laisser deux questions sans réponse; **our letter has remained u.** notre lettre est restée sans réponse **2** *(argument)* irréfuté

unapologetic [ʌnəpɒlə'dʒetɪk] ADJ **he's an u. royalist/admirer of Hitler** il ne se cache pas d'être royaliste/d'être un admirateur d'Hitler; **they're u. about it** ils estiment qu'il n'ont pas à s'excuser

unappealing [ʌnə'piːlɪŋ] ADJ peu attrayant

unappeased [ʌnə'piːzd] ADJ *Lit (hunger, desire, lust)* inassouvi

unappetizing [ʌn'æpɪtaɪzɪŋ] ADJ peu appétissant; **this dish looks really u.** ce plat n'est pas appétissant du tout

unappreciated [ʌnə'priːʃɪeɪtɪd] ADJ peu apprécié; *(difficulty, scope of task etc)* sous-

estimé; *(hard work, capability)* non reconnu; **her efforts go u.** le mal qu'elle se donne n'est pas apprécié à sa juste valeur

unappreciative [ʌnə'priːʃɪətɪv] ADJ *(audience)* insensible; *(report etc)* peu favorable; **she was very u. of everything we had done for her** elle ne montrait aucune gratitude après tout ce qu'on avait fait pour elle; **don't be so u.!** ne sois pas si ingrat!

unapproachable [ʌnə'prəʊtʃəb(ə)l] ADJ *(person, place)* inaccessible; **an u. sort of person** une personne d'un abord difficile

unappropriated [ʌnə'prəʊprɪeɪtɪd] ADJ *Fin (money)* inutilisé, disponible; *(profit)* non distribué

unarguable [ʌn'ɑːgjʊəb(ə)l] ADJ *(case, theory)* indéfendable

unarguably [ʌn'ɑːgjʊəblɪ] ADV *(indisputably)* incontestablement

unarmed [ʌn'ɑːmd] ADJ *(person)* non armé; **I am u.** je ne suis pas armé; **I'm not going in there u.** je n'entre pas là-dedans sans arme
▸ **u. combat** combat *m* à mains nues

unashamed [ʌnə'ʃeɪmd] ADJ *(delight, joy)* non déguisé; *(greed, hypocrisy)* flagrant; **to be u. about doing sth** ne pas avoir honte de faire qch; **his u. nationalism** son nationalisme éhonté; **with u. relief** avec un soulagement non dissimulé

unashamedly [ʌnə'ʃeɪmɪdlɪ] ADV sans honte; **George was u. in favour of the war** George se déclarait ouvertement en faveur de la guerre; **he was u. open about it all** il s'est exprimé sur cette affaire avec une franchise totale; **she was quite u. relieved about not having to ...** elle ne cacha pas son soulagement à l'idée de ne pas devoir ...; **he is u. outspoken in his support of ...** il affiche (tout à fait ouvertement) son soutien à ...

unasked [ʌn'ɑːskt] ADV *(to do sth)* spontanément; **she came to help us quite u.** elle est venue nous aider sans qu'on le lui ait demandé
ADJ **u. for** *(gift etc)* spontané, qu'on n'a pas demandé; *(unwanted) (advice)* non sollicité

unaspirated [ʌn'æspɪreɪtɪd] ADJ *Ling* non aspiré

unassailable [ʌnə'seɪləb(ə)l] ADJ *(fortress, position)* imprenable; *(conclusion, argument)* irréfutable; **his reputation is u.** il a une réputation à toute épreuve

unassigned [ʌnə'saɪnd] ADJ *(office, room) (for person)* non attribué; *(for purpose)* non affecté; *(task)* non assigné
▸ *Fin* **u. revenue** recettes *fpl* non gagées

unassimilated [ʌnə'sɪmɪleɪtɪd] ADJ inassimilé; **u. knowledge** connaissances *fpl* mal assimilées

unassisted [ʌnə'sɪstɪd] ADV sans aide, sans assistance; **he did it u.** il l'a fait tout seul
ADJ **by her own u. efforts** sans l'aide de personne

unassuming [ʌnə'sjuːmɪŋ] ADJ sans prétention(s), modeste

unassumingly [ʌnə'sjuːmɪŋlɪ] ADV modestement, avec modestie

unattached [ʌnə'tætʃt] ADJ **1** *(part, wire etc)* qui n'est pas attaché (**to** à) **2** *(journalist, group etc)* indépendant (**to** de); *Mil (officer)* disponible, en disponibilité **3** *(not married etc)* **to be u.** être libre *ou* sans attaches

unattainable [ʌnə'teɪnəb(ə)l] ADJ inaccessible (**by** à)

unattended [ʌn'tendɪd] ADJ **1** *(shop, printer etc)* sans surveillance; **to leave one's car u.** laisser sa voiture sans surveillance; **do not leave your luggage u.** surveillez toujours vos bagages **2** *(person, child)* seul; **to leave a child u.** laisser un enfant sans surveillance; **don't leave the guests u. (to)** ne

négligez pas les invités, occupez-vous des invités; **the leaking pipe has gone u. (to) for months** ça fait des mois que le tuyau fuit et rien n'a été fait **3** *(queen etc)* sans escorte

unattractive [ʌnə'træktɪv] ADJ peu attrayant, sans attrait, peu séduisant; *(character)* peu sympathique; **extremely u.** pas du tout attrayant; **she is not u.** elle ne manque pas de charme

unaudited [ʌn'ɔːdɪtɪd] ADJ *(accounts)* non vérifié

unauthenticated [ʌnɔː'θentɪkeɪtɪd] ADJ dont l'authenticité n'est pas établie; *Law (document)* non légalisé

unauthorized [ʌn'ɔːθəraɪzd] ADJ non autorisé, sans autorisation; **no entry to u. persons, no u. access** *(sign)* accès interdit à toute personne étrangère au service
▸▸ *Comput* **u. access** accès *m* non autorisé

unavailability [ʌnəveɪlə'bɪlɪtɪ] N indisponibilité *f*

unavailable [ʌnə'veɪləb(ə)l] ADJ *(person, goods)* indisponible, pas disponible; *(sold out etc)* épuisé; **the minister was u. for comment** le ministre s'est refusé à tout commentaire

unavailing [ʌnə'veɪlɪŋ] ADJ inutile, vain; *(effort, attempt)* infructueux

unavailingly [ʌnə'veɪlɪŋlɪ] ADV inutilement, en vain

unavenged [ʌnə'vendʒd] ADV **it won't go u.** cela ne restera pas impuni; **the u. death of ...** la mort de ... qui n'a pas été vengée

unavoidable [ʌnə'vɔɪdəb(ə)l] ADJ inévitable; *(fate)* auquel on ne peut échapper; *(event)* qu'on ne peut prévenir; **my absence was u.** mon absence a été due à un cas de force majeure; **it is u. that ...** il est inévitable que ... + *sub*
▸▸ *Fin* **u. costs** coûts *mpl* induits

unavoidably [ʌnə'vɔɪdəblɪ] ADV inévitablement; **u. detained** retenu pour raison majeure

unaware [ʌnə'weər] ADJ ignorant, pas au courant (**of sth** de qch); **to be u. of sth** ignorer qch; **her husband was totally u. of what was going on** son mari ne se rendait absolument pas compte de ce qui se passait; **he was u. that he was being watched** il ne se rendait pas compte qu'on l'observait; **we are not u. of the need for reform** nous avons conscience de la nécessité d'une réforme; **is that so?, I was u. of that** ah oui?, je n'étais pas au courant; **you will surely not be u. of the importance of ...** l'importance de ... ne vous a certainement pas échappé; **if there are any other problems I am u. of them** s'il y a d'autres problèmes, je ne suis pas au courant; **he is sexually/politically u.** il vit dans un monde où la sexualité/ la politique n'existe pas

unawares [ʌnə'weəz] ADV *(without realizing)* inconsciemment, sans s'en rendre compte; **to take** *or* **catch sb u.** *(by surprise)* prendre qn au dépourvu

unbalance [ʌn'bæləns] VT déséquilibrer; *(sb's mind)* déranger

unbalanced [ʌn'bælənst] ADJ **1** *(person, mind etc)* déséquilibré, dérangé **2** *(distribution)* inéquitable; *(reporting)* partial **3** *(steering)* mal équilibré **4** *Fin (account)* non soldé
▸▸ *Econ* **u. growth** croissance *f* déséquilibrée

unbandage [ʌn'bændɪdʒ] VT *(wound)* débander

unbankable [ʌn'bæŋkəbəl] ADJ *Fin (bill, paper)* non bancable

unbaptized [ʌnbæp'taɪzd] ADJ non baptisé

unbar [ʌn'bɑːr] VT *(door)* débarrer

unbearable [ʌn'beərəb(ə)l] ADJ insupportable, intolérable; **the children have been u. all day** les enfants ont été insupportables toute la journée; **in this heat, the office is u.** par cette chaleur le bureau n'est pas tenable

unbearably [ʌnˈbɛərəblɪ] **ADV** **it was u. painful/hot** la douleur/chaleur était insupportable; **the last scene was u. moving** la dernière scène était d'une tristesse insupportable; **he's u. arrogant** son arrogance est insupportable

unbeatable [ʌnˈbiːtəb(ə)l] **ADJ** imbattable; *(army)* invincible; **we offer u. value** nous offrons de la qualité à des prix imbattables

unbeaten [ʌnˈbiːt(ə)n] **ADJ** *(champion, army)* invaincu; *(record)* qui n'a pas encore été battu

unbecoming [ʌnbɪˈkʌmɪŋ] **ADJ** inconvenant, malséant (**to** de la part de); *(garment)* peu seyant; *(facial hair)* peu esthétique; **it's u. of him to act in this manner** il lui sied mal d'agir de la sorte

unbeknown [ʌnbɪˈnəʊn] **ADV** **u. to me/her/** *etc* à mon/son/*etc* insu; **to do sth u. to anyone** faire qch à l'insu de tous

unbeknownst [ʌnbɪˈnəʊnst] **ADV** *esp Am* = **unbeknown**

unbelief [ʌnbɪˈliːf] **N** incrédulité *f*; **he looked at me in u.** il me regarda avec incrédulité

unbelievable [ʌnbɪˈliːvəb(ə)l] **ADJ** incroyable; **it's u. that ...** il est incroyable que ... + *sub*

unbelievably [ʌnbɪˈliːvəblɪ] **ADV** incroyablement; **u. stupid** d'une sottise incroyable

unbeliever [ʌnbɪˈliːvər] **N** incrédule *mf*

unbelieving [ʌnbɪˈliːvɪŋ] **ADJ** incrédule

unbelievingly [ʌnbɪˈliːvɪŋlɪ] **ADV** *(to say, look)* d'une manière incrédule

unbend [ʌnˈbend] (*pt, pp* **unbent** [ʌnˈbent]) **VT** *(steel rod etc)* redresser; *(leg)* déplier **VI 1** *(relax)* devenir moins strict **2** *(straighten out)* se redresser; *(of limb)* se déplier

unbending [ʌnˈbendɪŋ] **ADJ** *(character)* inflexible, rigide; **u. attitude** attitude *f* intransigeante

unbias(s)ed [ʌnˈbaɪəst] **ADJ** impartial, -aux

unbidden [ʌnˈbɪd(ə)n] **ADV** *Old-fashioned* **to do sth u.** faire qch spontanément *ou* sans y avoir été invité

unbind [ʌnˈbaɪnd] **VT** (*pt, pp* **unbound** [ʌnˈbaʊnd]) **1** *(prisoner, hands)* délier **2** *(wound)* débander

unbleached [ʌnˈbliːtʃt] **ADJ 1** écru; **u. linen** toile *f* bise *ou* écrue **2** *(coffee filters, nappies etc)* sans chlore

unblemished [ʌnˈblemɪʃt] **ADJ** sans défaut; *(reputation)* sans tache

unblinking [ʌnˈblɪŋkɪŋ] **ADJ** *(person)* impassible; *(gaze, look)* fixe; **with u. eyes** sans ciller

unblock [ʌnˈblɒk] **VT** *(road, path)* dégager; *(pipe etc)* déboucher; *Comput* débloquer

unblushing [ʌnˈblʌʃɪŋ] **ADJ** sans vergogne, éhonté; **he remained u. as she declared her love** il écoutait sa déclaration d'amour sans rougir

unblushingly [ʌnˈblʌʃɪŋlɪ] **ADV** sans rougir

unbolt [ʌnˈbəʊlt] **VT** *(door)* déverrouiller; *(rail etc)* déboulonner

unbonded warehouse [ʌnˈbɒndɪd] **N** entrepôt *m* fictif

unborn [ˈʌnbɔːn] **ADJ** qui n'est pas (encore) né; **u. child** enfant *mf* à naître; **generations yet u.** [ʌnˈbɔːn] générations *fpl* à venir, générations futures

unbosom [ʌnˈbʊzəm] **VT** *Lit* **to u. oneself to sb** ouvrir son cœur à qn

unbound [ʌnˈbaʊnd] **ADJ** *(book)* non relié, broché; *(hands)* libre; *(prisoner)* pas attaché

unbounded [ʌnˈbaʊndɪd] **ADJ** sans bornes, illimité; *(ambition etc)* démesuré

unbowed [ʌnˈbaʊd] **ADJ** invaincu, insoumis; **bloody but u.** vaincu, mais non soumis

unbranded [ʌnˈbrændɪd] **ADJ** *Mktg* sans marque

unbreakable [ʌnˈbreɪkəb(ə)l] **ADJ** incassable; *(promise, rule etc)* sacré, inviolable; *Sport (record)* imbattable; *(habit)* immuable

unbreathable [ʌnˈbriːðəb(ə)l] **ADJ** *(air)* irrespirable

unbribable [ʌnˈbraɪbəb(ə)l] **ADJ** incorruptible

unbridled [ʌnˈbraɪd(ə)ld] **ADJ 1** *(passion, greed etc)* débridé, effréné; *(capitalism)* effréné **2** *(horse)* débridé, sans bride

unbroken [ʌnˈbrəʊk(ə)n] **ADJ 1** *(plate, chair etc)* non brisé, non cassé, intact **2** *(skin, seal etc)* intact; **u. spirit** optimisme *m* intact **3** *(promise)* inviolé; *(rules)* toujours observé *ou* respecté; **the peace remained u. for ten years** la paix n'a pas été troublée pendant dix ans; *Sport* **record still u.** record qui n'a pas été battu **4** *(silence, expanse of water, years of government etc)* ininterrompu; **u. sheet of ice** nappe de glace continue **5** *(horse)* non rompu, non dressé **6** *Agr* **u. ground** terre *f* vierge

unbrotherly [ʌnˈbrʌðəlɪ] **ADJ** peu fraternel

unbuckle [ʌnˈbʌk(ə)l] **VT** *(belt)* déboucler

unbudgeted [ʌnˈbʌdʒɪtɪd] **ADJ** non prévu au budget

unbuilt [ʌnˈbɪlt, ˈʌnbɪlt] **ADJ** **u. plot, plot of u. ground** terrain *m* vague *ou* non construit

unbundle [ʌnˈbʌnd(ə)l] **VT 1** *Am (itemize)* détailler **2** *Comput* décompresser

unbundling [ʌnˈbʌndlɪŋ] **N 1** *(of goods)* séparation *f* **2** *Comput* décompression *f*

unburden [ʌnˈbɜːd(ə)n] **VT** **to u. oneself** *or* **one's heart** s'épancher; **to u. oneself to sb** se confier à qn; **to u. oneself of a secret** se soulager du poids d'un secret; **to u. one's sorrows to sb** s'épancher auprès de qn

unburied [ʌnˈberɪd] **ADJ** non enterré

unbusinesslike [ʌnˈbɪznɪslaɪk] **ADJ** *(person)* peu commerçant, qui n'a pas le sens des affaires; *(procedure, handling)* peu professionnel; **to conduct one's affairs in an u. way** mal mener ses affaires

unbutton [ʌnˈbʌt(ə)n] **VT** *(one's coat etc)* déboutonner; **to come unbuttoned** se déboutonner

unbuttoned [ʌnˈbʌt(ə)nd] **ADJ** *Fam (relaxed)* décontracté

uncallable [ʌnˈkɔːləbəl] **ADJ** *Fin (capital)* non remboursable

uncalled [ʌnˈkɔːld] **ADJ** *Fin (capital)* non appelé

uncalled-for **ADJ** *(remark)* déplacé; *(rebuke)* immérité, injustifié; *(insult)* gratuit; **that was quite u.** c'était tout à fait injustifié

uncannily [ʌnˈkænɪlɪ] **ADV** étrangement, bizarrement

uncanny [ʌnˈkænɪ] **ADJ 1** *(strange, inexplicable)* étrange, mystérieux; **it's u. how he knows where I am** c'est vraiment étrange *ou* bizarre qu'il sache où je suis; **with u. accuracy** avec une exactitude surprenante **2** *(eerie)* inquiétant

uncared-for [ʌnˈkeəd-] **ADJ** négligé; **to leave a garden u.** laisser un jardin à l'abandon

uncaring [ʌnˈkeərɪŋ] **ADJ** qui ne se soucie pas (des autres), indifférent

uncarpeted [ʌnˈkɑːpɪtɪd] **ADJ** sans tapis, sans moquette

uncashed [ʌnˈkæʃt] **ADJ** non encaissé

uncatalogued [ʌnˈkætəlɒgd] **ADJ** qui n'est pas catalogué

unceasing [ʌnˈsiːsɪŋ] **ADJ** incessant, continuel; *(work)* assidu; *(effort)* soutenu

unceasingly [ʌnˈsiːsɪŋlɪ] **ADV** sans cesse, sans arrêt

uncensored [ʌnˈsensəd] **ADJ** *(scene, version etc)* non expurgé; *(version, edition)* intégral

unceremonious [ʌnserɪˈməʊnɪəs] **ADJ** **it resulted in his u. ejection from the hall** cela a eu pour conséquence qu'il s'est fait expulser de la salle sans cérémonie; **he was packed off in a very u. way to stay with his uncle in Australia** on l'a envoyé très cavalièrement *ou* sans aucune cérémonie chez son oncle en Australie; **after his u. departure from politics** après qu'il eut peu glorieusement abandonné la politique

unceremoniously [ʌnserɪˈməʊnɪəslɪ] **ADV** sans cérémonie, brusquement; **he was u. bundled into the police van** il fut embarqué dans le fourgon de police sans cérémonie

uncertain [ʌnˈsɜːt(ə)n] **ADJ** incertain; **it's u. who will win** on ne sait pas au juste qui gagnera; **I feel u. about him** j'ai des doutes à son sujet; **he told him in no u. terms** il lui a dit sans mâcher ses mots; **to be u. what to do** ne pas savoir quoi faire; **I feel u. whether to trust him or not** je ne sais pas si je dois lui faire confiance

uncertainly [ʌnˈsɜːt(ə)nlɪ] **ADV** d'une façon incertaine; *(to look at sb)* d'un air un peu inquiet

uncertainty [ʌnˈsɜːt(ə)ntɪ] **N** incertitude *f*; **there is some u. about ...** l'incertitude règne au sujet de ...; **u. about** *or* **as to the future** incertitude quant à l'avenir; **to be in a state of u.** être dans l'incertitude; **to remove any u.** pour dissiper toute équivoque; **there's still some u. as to what was actually said** il reste quelque incertitude sur ce qui s'est réellement dit; **there are still too many uncertainties for my liking** il y a encore trop d'incertitudes à mon goût

uncertified [ʌnˈsɜːtɪfaɪd] **ADJ** non certifié

unchain [ʌnˈtʃeɪn] **VT** *(dog)* détacher; *(passions)* déchaîner

unchallengeable [ʌnˈtʃælɪndʒəb(ə)l] **ADJ** *(argument)* irréfutable; *(right)* incontestable; *(evidence, proof)* irrécusable; **to be in an u. position** *(of runner, team, politician etc)* être hors d'atteinte

unchallenged [ʌnˈtʃælɪndʒd] **ADJ 1** *(right)* indisputé, incontesté; **to let sth go** *or* **pass u.** *(statement)* ne pas relever qch; *(right)* ne pas contester qch; *(evidence)* ne pas récuser qch; **I can't let that go u.** je ne peux pas laisser passer cela; **to continue u.** continuer sans être contredit; *Sport* **his record stayed u. for several years** personne ne s'est attaqué à son record pendant plusieurs années **2** *Mil* **to let sb pass u.** laisser passer qn sans interpellation

unchangeable [ʌnˈtʃeɪndʒəb(ə)l] **ADJ** immuable

unchanged [ʌnˈtʃeɪndʒd] **ADJ** inchangé; *Med* **his condition remains u.** son état est stationnaire

unchanging [ʌnˈtʃeɪndʒɪŋ] **ADJ** immuable

uncharacteristic [ʌnkærəktəˈrɪstɪk] **ADJ** inhabituel; **it's u. of her** cela ne lui ressemble pas; **it's u. for her to make a mistake like that** ce n'est pas dans son habitude de faire une erreur pareille

uncharacteristically [ʌnkærəktəˈrɪstɪklɪ] **ADV** *(rude, late, reticent etc)* inhabituellement, anormalement; **u. (for him), he arrived late for the meeting** contrairement à son habitude, il arriva en retard à la réunion

uncharitable [ʌnˈtʃærɪtəb(ə)l] **ADJ** peu charitable; **that's rather u. of you** ce n'est pas très charitable de ta part

uncharted [ʌn'tʃɑːtɪd] **ADJ** *(unexplored)* inexploré; *(not yet mapped)* non porté sur la carte; *Fig* **these are u. waters** *(of a science etc)* ce sont des domaines inexplorés

unchaste [ʌn'tʃeɪst] **ADJ** *esp Lit (person)* non chaste, impur; *(thoughts)* impur

unchastened [ʌn'tʃeɪs(ə)nd] **ADJ** *(person)* aucunement repentant, nullement assagi; **he was u. by his experience** son expérience n'a rien rabattu de ses prétentions

unchecked [ʌn'tʃekt] **ADJ 1** *(not stopped)* *(advance)* sans (la moindre) opposition; *(passion)* effréné; *(anger)* non contenu; **we can't allow this abuse to go u.** nous ne pouvons pas permettre que ces abus continuent; **if AIDS were to spread u. ...** si le sida se propageait sans qu'on lui oppose de résistance ...; **the enemy advanced u.** l'ennemi progressait sans rencontrer de résistance **2** *(not verified)* *(report, assessment)* non vérifié **3** **u. baggage** bagages *mpl* non-enregistrés

unchivalrous [ʌn'ʃɪvəlrəs] **ADJ** peu courtois

unchristian [ʌn'krɪstjən] **ADJ** peu chrétien; **that's very u. of you** ce sont là des paroles/des pensées peu chrétiennes; *Fam* **at this u. hour** à cette heure indue

uncircumcised [ʌn'sɜːkəmsaɪzd] **ADJ** non circoncis

uncivil [ʌn'sɪv(ə)l] **ADJ** impoli

uncivilized [ʌn'sɪvɪlaɪzd] **ADJ** non civilisé, barbare; **at this u. hour** à cette heure indue; **it's very u. of you not to have any whisky in the flat!** ce n'est pas du tout civilisé de ta part de ne pas avoir une goutte de whisky chez toi!; **it's very u. of him to keep us waiting like this** ce n'est pas très correct de sa part de nous faire attendre comme ça

unclaimed [ʌn'kleɪmd] **ADJ** non réclamé; *(right)* non revendiqué; *(benefit)* non touché *ou* réclamé

unclasp [ʌn'klɑːsp] **VT** *(bracelet)* défaire; *(hand in handshake)* desserrer

unclassifiable [ʌn'klæsɪfaɪəb(ə)l] **ADJ** inclassable

unclassified [ʌn'klæsɪfaɪd] **ADJ** *(information)* non (classé), secret, -ète, non confidentiel

uncle ['ʌŋk(ə)l] **N** oncle *m*; *Fig* **rich u.** oncle d'Amérique; *Am Fam* **to cry u.** *(give up)* crier grâce
  ▸▸ **U. Sam** l'Oncle *m* Sam *(personnification des États-Unis)*; *Am Sl Pej* **U. Tom** = Noir *m* qui se comporte de façon obséquieuse avec les Blancs

unclean [ʌn'kliːn] **ADJ** *also Rel (thoughts etc)* impur; *Iron (cup etc)* souillé; **to feel u.** se sentir souillé

unclear [ʌn'klɪər] **ADJ** *(statement)* peu clair, vague; *(result)* incertain; *(prose, text)* obscur; **it's still u. what has happened** ce qui est arrivé n'est pas toujours très clair; **I'm u. about what is wanted** je ne suis pas sûr de ce qu'on demande

uncleared [ʌn'klɪəd] **ADJ 1 u. ground** terrain *m* non défriché **2** *(debt)* non liquidé **3** **u. goods** marchandises *fpl* non dédouanées **4** *(cheque)* non compensé, non crédité

unclench [ʌn'klen(t)ʃ] **VT** *(fist)* desserrer

unclimbable [ʌn'klaɪməb(ə)l] **ADJ** *(mountain)* impossible à escalader

unclimbed [ʌn'klaɪmd] **ADJ** *(mountain, peak)* invaincu *(par les alpinistes)*

uncloak [ʌn'kləʊk] **VT** *esp Lit (plans)* découvrir; *(impostor)* démasquer

unclog [ʌn'klɒg] **VT** *(-gg-)* *(machine)* débloquer; *(drain)* déboucher

unclothed [ʌn'kləʊðd] **ADJ** nu

unclouded [ʌn'klaʊdɪd] **ADJ** *(sky, future, bliss)* sans nuage(s); *(vision, liquid)* clair

uncluttered [ʌn'klʌtəd] **ADJ 1** *(desk, room)* qui n'est pas encombré **2** *(style)* dépouillé; **an u. mind** un esprit clair

unco ['ʌŋkəʊ] **ADV** *Scot Arch* très

uncoil [ʌn'kɔɪl] **VT** dérouler; *Hum* **to u. oneself from sb's arms** se dégager (avec difficulté) des bras de qn
  VI *(of snake, rope)* **to u. (itself)** se dérouler

uncollectable [ʌnkə'lektəb(ə)l] **ADJ** *(tax)* non percevable

uncollected [ʌnkə'lektɪd] **ADJ 1** *(luggage)* non réclamé **2** **u. taxes** impôts *mpl* non perçus

uncoloured, *Am* **uncolored** [ʌn'kʌləd] **ADJ** non coloré; *Fig* **u. account of sth** rapport *m* impartial sur qch

uncombed [ʌn'kəʊmd] **ADJ** *(hair, wool)* non peigné

uncomely [ʌn'kʌmlɪ] **ADJ** peu joli

uncomfortable [ʌn'kʌmf(ə)təb(ə)l] **ADJ 1** *(house, position etc)* inconfortable; *(armchair, garment)* peu confortable; **this is a very u. armchair** on est très mal (assis) dans ce fauteuil; **I'm u. in this bed** je ne suis pas bien dans ce lit; **I feel u. in this collar** je ne suis pas à l'aise avec ce col **2 to make things u. for sb** attirer *ou* créer des ennuis à qn **3 to feel** *or* **be u.** *(ill at ease)* être mal à l'aise; *(embarrassed)* se sentir gêné; **to be** *or* **feel u. about sth** être mal à l'aise à propos de qch; **to make sb feel u.** mettre qn mal à l'aise; **I'd feel u. (about) asking my parents for money** ça me gênerait de demander de l'argent à mes parents; **it's a very u. feeling, knowing you could easily have been killed** c'est un sentiment très déplaisant de savoir que tu aurais très bien pu mourir; **there was an u. silence** il y eut un silence gêné

uncomfortably [ʌn'kʌmf(ə)təblɪ] **ADV 1** *(be sitting)* inconfortablement; *(dressed)* de manière inconfortable; **it was u. stuffy in the plane** il y avait une atmosphère étouffante dans l'avion **2 to come u. close to sth** *(to bankruptcy, war, disaster etc)* s'approcher dangereusement de qch; **we came u. close to meeting them on holiday!** nous avons bien failli les rencontrer pendant les vacances!; **I was u. aware of him watching me** j'étais désagréablement conscient du fait qu'il me regardait

uncommitted [ʌnkə'mɪtɪd] **ADJ** *(person)* non engagé; *(reserves, funds, troops)* non affecté; **we are u. to any course of action** nous sommes libres de tout engagement quant à la ligne de conduite à adopter; **to remain u.** ne pas s'engager

uncommon [ʌn'kɒmən] **ADJ** peu commun; **u. word** mot peu usité; **not u.** assez fréquent
  ADV *Arch Fam* singulièrement

uncommonly [ʌn'kɒmənlɪ] **ADV 1 not u.** assez souvent **2** *Formal (very)* singulièrement; **u. good** excellent; **he took an u. long time over it** il a mis particulièrement longtemps à le faire

uncommunicative [ʌnkə'mjuːnɪkətɪv] **ADJ** peu communicatif, renfermé, taciturne; **he was very u. about it** il s'est montré très peu communicatif à ce sujet

uncomplaining [ʌnkəm'pleɪnɪŋ] **ADJ** qui ne se plaint pas, patient, résigné

uncomplainingly [ʌnkəm'pleɪnɪŋlɪ] **ADV** sans se plaindre

uncomplicated [ʌn'kɒmplɪkeɪtɪd] **ADJ** *(style, person)* simple; *(task)* facile

uncomplimentary [ʌnkɒmplɪ'ment(ə)rɪ] **ADJ** peu flatteur, -euse; **he was very u. about you** il ne s'est pas montré du tout flatteur à ton égard

uncomprehending [ʌnkɒmprɪ'hendɪŋ] **ADJ** *(person)* qui ne comprend pas; **to give sb an u. look** regarder qn sans comprendre; **in u. amazement** ahuri

uncomprehendingly [ʌnkɒmprɪ'hendɪŋlɪ] **ADV** sans comprendre

uncompromising [ʌn'kɒmprəmaɪzɪŋ] **ADJ** intransigeant; **a man of u. principles** un homme aux principes très stricts; **we took an u. stance on this** nous avons adopté une position inflexible à ce sujet; **u. honesty** honnêteté absolue; **our u. insistence on quality** notre intransigeance quant à la qualité

uncompromisingly [ʌn'kɒmprəmaɪzɪŋlɪ] **ADV** sans faire de concessions; **u. honest** d'une honnêteté absolue

unconcealed [ʌnkən'siːld] **ADJ** non dissimulé

unconcern [ʌnkən'sɜːn] **N** insouciance *f*, indifférence *f*; **to show u. in the face of danger** se montrer indifférent en face du danger

unconcerned [ʌnkən'sɜːnd] **ADJ** insouciant, indifférent; **u., he went on speaking** nullement troublé, il continua de parler; **they were quite u. about her well-being** ils ne se souciaient pas du tout de son bien-être; **he seems entirely u. about his results** il ne semble pas du tout s'inquiéter de ses résultats

unconcernedly [ʌnkən'sɜːnɪdlɪ] **ADV** d'un air indifférent, sans se (laisser) troubler

unconditional [ʌnkən'dɪʃənəl] **ADJ** inconditionnel, sans réserve
  ▸▸ *Law* **u. discharge** libération *f* inconditionnelle; **u. guarantee** garantie *f* inconditionnelle; *Fin* **u. order** ordre *m* (de payer) pur et simple; **u. surrender** reddition *f* inconditionnelle

unconditionally [ʌnkən'dɪʃənəlɪ] **ADV** inconditionnellement; *(accept)* sans réserve; **to surrender u.** se rendre sans condition

unconfirmed [ʌnkən'fɜːmd] **ADJ** non confirmé; **the report remains u.** la nouvelle n'a pas encore été confirmée
  ▸▸ *Fin* **u. letter of credit** lettre *f* de crédit révocable

uncongenial [ʌnkən'dʒiːnɪəl] **ADJ** *(person)* peu sympathique, antipathique; *(climate)* peu favorable (**to** à); *(work, atmosphere)* peu agréable

unconnected [ʌnkə'nektɪd] **ADJ** *(facts etc)* sans rapport (**with** avec); **the two events are totally u.** les deux événements n'ont aucun rapport entre eux; **this reaction was not u. with the recent ...** cette réaction n'était pas sans rapport avec le récent ...

unconquerable [ʌn'kɒŋkərəb(ə)l] **ADJ** *(enemy)* invincible; *(courage)* indomptable; *(difficulty)* insurmontable

unconquered [ʌn'kɒŋkəd] **ADJ** *(people, country)* qui n'a pas été conquis; *(peak)* invaincu, vierge

unconscionable [ʌn'kɒnʃənəb(ə)l] **ADJ** *Lit* déraisonnable, excessif; **to take an u. time doing sth** mettre un temps invraisemblable à faire qch

unconscious [ʌn'kɒnʃəs] **ADJ 1** *Med* sans connaissance; **to become u.** perdre connaissance; **to knock sb u.** assommer qn **2** *(unaware)* *(movement etc)* inconscient; *(joke, insult)* involontaire; **to be u. of doing sth** ne pas se rendre compte qu'on fait qch; **to be u. of sth** ne pas avoir conscience de qch, ne pas se rendre compte de qch; **the u. mind** l'inconscient *m*
  N *Psy* **the u.** l'inconscient *m*

unconsciously [ʌn'kɒnʃəslɪ] **ADV** inconsciemment, sans s'en rendre compte

unconsciousness [ʌnˈkɒnʃəsnɪs] N (una-wareness), Med inconscience f

unconsecrated [ʌnˈkɒnsɪkreɪtɪd] ADJ non consacré

unconsidered [ʌnkənˈsɪdəd] ADJ (remark, opinion) inconsidéré

unconsolidated [ʌnkənˈsɒlɪdeɪtəd] ADJ Fin (debt) non consolidé

unconstitutional [ʌnkɒnstɪˈtjuːʃən(ə)l] ADJ inconstitutionnel

unconstitutionally [ʌnkɒnstɪˈtjuːʃnəlɪ] ADV inconstitutionnellement

unconstrained [ʌnkənˈstreɪnd] ADJ 1 (person) sans contraintes, libre; **to be u. by convention** ne pas connaître les contraintes des conventions; (consciously reject them) faire fi des conventions 2 (act) spontané; (passion, joy etc) débordant; **u. laughter** hilarité f débordante

unconsummated [ʌnˈkɒnsəmeɪtɪd] ADJ (marriage) non consommé

uncontaminated [ʌnkənˈtæmɪneɪtɪd] ADJ (by disease, radiation), Fig non contaminé

uncontested [ʌnkənˈtestɪd] ADJ (right) incontesté; (election, seat) non disputé; **the championship has been** or **has gone u. for …** le championnat n'a pas été disputé depuis …

uncontrollable [ʌnkənˈtrəʊləb(ə)l] ADJ incontrôlable; (movement, twitch) incontrôlable, irrépressible; (desire) irrésistible, irrépressible; (inflation) irrésistible, incontrôlable; **u. laughter** fou rire m, fits of laughter; **fits of u. temper** violents accès mpl de colère; **I felt an u. urge to …** je me suis senti irrésistiblement poussé à …

uncontrollably [ʌnkənˈtrəʊləblɪ] ADV **she sobbed/laughed/coughed u.** elle ne pouvait s'arrêter de sangloter/rire/tousser; **as inflation rises u.** alors que l'inflation augmente irrésistiblement; **she was u. jealous** elle était d'une jalousie maladive

uncontrolled [ʌnkənˈtrəʊld] ADJ (anger, weeping, laughter) incontrôlé; (style) débridé; **u. inflation** inflation f incontrôlée; **u. passions** passions fpl effrénées

uncontroversial [ʌnkɒntrəˈvɜːʃəl] ADJ (subject) qui ne soulève ou ne provoque pas de controverses

unconventional [ʌnkənˈvenʃənəl] ADJ peu conventionnel, non-conformiste

unconventionally [ʌnkənˈvenʃnəlɪ] ADV de manière peu conventionnelle

unconvinced [ʌnkənˈvɪnst] ADJ sceptique (of au sujet de); **I am still u.** je ne suis toujours pas convaincu

unconvincing [ʌnkənˈvɪnsɪŋ] ADJ (evidence etc) peu convaincant; (excuse) convaincant ou vraisemblable; **he was very u. as Tartuffe** il n'était pas convaincant du tout en Tartuffe

unconvincingly [ʌnkənˈvɪnsɪŋlɪ] ADV d'une manière peu convaincante

uncooked [ʌnˈkʊkt] ADJ non cuit

uncool [ʌnˈkuːl] ADJ Fam 1 (unfashionable, unsophisticated) ringard; **it's a really u. place** c'est nul comme endroit; **what an u. thing to do!** c'est vraiment nul de faire un truc pareil! 2 (not allowed, not accepted) mal vu; **I think it's a bit u. to smoke in here** je pense pas que ce soit permis de fumer ici 3 (upset) **she was a bit u. about me moving in with them** elle tenait pas trop à ce que je m'installe chez eux

uncooperative [ʌnkəʊˈɒp(ə)rətɪv] ADJ peu coopératif; **he's being very u.** il se montre très peu coopératif

uncooperatively [ʌnkəʊˈɒp(ə)rətɪvlɪ] ADV de manière peu coopérative

uncooperativeness [ʌnkəʊˈɒp(ə)rətɪvnɪs] N manque m de coopération

uncoordinated [ʌnkəʊˈɔːdɪneɪtɪd] ADJ (manoeuvre, attack, undertaking, efforts) qui manque de coordination ou d'organisation; (movements) désordonné; **to be u.** (of person, dancer) manquer de coordination

uncork [ʌnˈkɔːk] VT (bottle) déboucher; Fig (pent-up emotions) laisser libre cours à

uncorrected [ʌnkəˈrektɪd] ADJ (exercise, proof) non corrigé; (error) non rectifié ou corrigé; Phys **result u. for temperature/for pressure** résultat m brut

uncorroborated [ʌnkəˈrɒbəreɪtɪd] ADJ non corroboré

uncorrupted [ʌnkəˈrʌptɪd] ADJ (person) non corrompu

uncountable [ʌnˈkaʊntəb(ə)l] ADJ Gram indénombrable VOIR GRAMMAIRE A9–12

uncountably [ʌnˈkaʊntəblɪ] ADV Gram **nouns which can only be used u.** noms qu'on ne peut utiliser que de façon indénombrable

uncounted [ʌnˈkaʊntɪd] ADJ (not counted) non compté

uncouple [ʌnˈkʌp(ə)l] VT (carriages, engine) dételer, découpler

uncouth [ʌnˈkuːθ] ADJ (person, behaviour) grossier; **u. manners** manières fpl gauches ou frustes

uncover [ʌnˈkʌvər] VT 1 (furniture, swimming pool) découvrir; (saucepan) enlever le couvercle de 2 (evidence, plot, conspiracy) découvrir 3 Chess (piece) découvrir, dégarnir

uncovered [ʌnˈkʌvəd] ADJ 1 non couvert, découvert 2 Fin (purchase, sale) à découvert ► ► Fin **u. advance** avance f à découvert; Fin **u. balance** découvert m; **u. cheque** chèque m sans provision; St Exch **u. position** position f non couverte

uncreasable [ʌnˈkriːsəb(ə)l] ADJ (fabric) infroissable

uncritical [ʌnˈkrɪtɪk(ə)l] ADJ dépourvu de sens ou d'esprit critique; (approach, acceptance) sans discernement; (audience) peu exigeant; **to be u. of sb/sth** ne faire preuve d'aucun sens ou esprit critique à l'égard de qn/qch

uncross [ʌnˈkrɒs] VT (legs) décroiser

uncrossed [ʌnˈkrɒst] ADJ (cheque) non barré

uncrowded [ʌnˈkraʊdɪd] ADJ (beaches) presque vide; (roads) peu encombré; **I'd never seen Heathrow so u.** je n'avais jamais vu aussi peu de monde à Heathrow

uncrowned [ʌnˈkraʊnd] ADJ sans couronne; Fig **the u. king/queen of …** le roi/la reine de …

uncrunch [ʌnˈkrʌntʃ] VT Comput décompresser, décompacter

uncrushable [ʌnˈkrʌʃəb(ə)l] ADJ (fabric) infroissable

UNCTAD [ˈʌŋktæd] N (abbr United Nations Conference on Trade and Development) CNUCED f

unction [ˈʌŋkʃən] N 1 Rel onction f 2 = unctuousness

unctuous [ˈʌŋktjʊəs] ADJ mielleux, onctueux

unctuously [ˈʌŋktjʊəslɪ] ADV d'un air/d'un ton mielleux ou onctueux

unctuousness [ˈʌŋktjʊəsnɪs] N caractère m mielleux

uncultivated [ʌnˈkʌltɪveɪtɪd] ADJ (land, person) inculte

uncultured [ʌnˈkʌltʃəd] ADJ (mind, person) inculte; (accent) peu raffiné

uncurbed [ʌnˈkɜːbd] ADJ (authority) sans restriction; (passion) déchaîné; **if these tendencies are allowed to go u.** si on ne met pas un frein à ces tendances

uncurl [ʌnˈkɜːl] VT (rope, wire) dérouler; (one's legs) déplier; **to u. oneself** s'étirer VI (of cat) s'étirer; (of snake) se dérouler

uncut [ʌnˈkʌt] ADJ 1 (hedge) non coupé; (diamond) brut, non taillé 2 (play, edition) sans coupures, intégral, -aux; **u. version** (of film) version f longue

undamaged [ʌnˈdæmɪdʒd] ADJ non endommagé, intact; (reputation) intact

undamped, undampened [ʌnˈdæmpt, ʌnˈdæmpənd] ADJ (courage) non affaibli

undated [ʌnˈdeɪtɪd] ADJ non daté, sans date

undaunted [ʌnˈdɔːntɪd] ADJ **to be u. by sth** n'être aucunement intimidé ou aucunement ébranlé par qch; (by difficulty) n'être aucunement découragé par qch; **we carried on u.** nous avons continué sans nous laisser intimider ou décourager

undeceive [ʌndɪˈsiːv] VT Lit (person) détromper

undecided [ʌndɪˈsaɪdɪd] ADJ 1 (question, problem) non résolu; **that's still u.** aucune décision n'a encore été prise 2 (person) indécis; **to be u. about sth** être indécis à propos de qch; **he was u. whether he would go or not** il se demandait s'il irait ou non; **to be u. how to act** ne pas savoir comment agir

undeclared [ʌndɪˈkleəd] ADJ (war, income) non déclaré; (love) non avoué; **u. goods** (at Customs) marchandises fpl non déclarées

undefeated [ʌndɪˈfiːtɪd] ADJ invaincu

undefended [ʌndɪˈfendɪd] ADJ 1 Mil etc sans défense; (goal) non défendu; (king at chess) non protégé 2 Law (defendant) qui n'est pas représenté par un avocat; **u. case** débats mpl non contentieux; **u. suit** cause f où le défenseur s'abstient de plaider

undefiled [ʌndɪˈfaɪld] ADJ sans souillure, immaculé; **u. by any contact with Western society** non corrompu par la civilisation occidentale

undefinable [ʌndɪˈfaɪnəb(ə)l] ADJ indéfinissable

undefined [ʌndɪˈfaɪnd] ADJ (term etc) non défini; (vague) (feeling etc) indéterminé, vague

undelete [ʌndɪˈliːt] VT Comput restaurer

undelivered [ʌndɪˈlɪvəd] ADJ non livré, non remis; (parcel) en souffrance; **if u. return to sender** en cas de non-délivrance prière de retourner à l'expéditeur

undemanding [ʌndɪˈmɑːndɪŋ] ADJ (job, book, person) peu exigeant

undemocratic [ʌndeməˈkrætɪk] ADJ antidémocratique

undemonstrative [ʌndɪˈmɒnstrətɪv] ADJ (person) peu expansif, peu démonstratif

undeniable [ʌndɪˈnaɪəb(ə)l] ADJ indéniable, incontestable; (evidence) irrécusable; **of u. worth** d'une valeur indéniable

undeniably [ʌndɪˈnaɪəblɪ] ADV incontestablement; **an u. talented man** un homme d'un talent incontestable

undenominational [ʌndɪnɒmɪˈneɪʃənəl] ADJ non confessionnel

undependable [ʌndɪˈpendəb(ə)l] ADJ (machine, trains, person) peu fiable

---

UNDER [ˈʌndər]

┌─────────────────────────────────────┐
│ **PREP** sous **1, 4, 6** ■ au-dessous de **1** │
│ ■ moins de **2** ■ conformément à **3** │
│ ■ en cours de **5** │
│ **ADV** au-dessous **1, 2** │
└─────────────────────────────────────┘

PREP 1 (beneath) sous, au-dessous de; **the dog is u. the table** le chien est sous la table;

u. water sous l'eau; **he hid u. it** il se cacha dessous; **you have to crawl u. it** il faut ramper dessous; **put it u. that** mettez-le là-dessous; **to wear a waistcoat u. one's jacket** porter un gilet sous son veston; **he pulled a stool out from u. the table** il a tiré un tabouret de sous la table; **visible u. the microscope** visible au microscope; *Agr* **field u. wheat** champ *m* mis en blé

2 *(less than)* **all their books were u. £5** tous leurs livres coûtaient moins de 5 livres; **salaries u. £10,000** salaires inférieurs à 10 000 livres; **he's u. thirty** il a moins de trente ans; **people u. thirty, the u. thirties** les moins de trente ans; **children u. ten** les enfants au-dessous de dix ans; **in u. ten minutes** en moins de dix minutes; **to speak u. one's breath** parler à mi-voix

3 *(according to)* **u. his father's will** d'après le testament de son père; **u. the terms of the agreement** d'après les termes de la convention; **u. the terms of the contract** conformément aux termes du contrat; *Com* **u. usual reserve** sauf bonne fin

4 *(under control of, subordinate to etc)* **to be u. sb** être sous les ordres de qn; **he had a hundred men u. him** il avait cent hommes sous ses ordres; **he has three sales teams u. him** il est responsable de trois équipes de ventes; **to be** *or* **to come u. the authority of the Home Office** relever du Ministère de l'Intérieur; **u. government control** soumis au contrôle de l'État; **u. Louis XIV** sous Louis XIV; **Britain u. Thatcher** la Grande-Bretagne sous Thatcher; **to study u. sb** étudier sous la direction de qn; **the orchestra, u. Alexander Gibson** l'orchestre, sous la direction d'Alexander Gibson; **she wrote it u. a pseudonym** elle l'a écrit sous un pseudonyme; **to be u. sentence of death** être condamné à mort; **to be u. orders to do sth** avoir reçu l'ordre de faire qch; **u. these conditions** dans ces conditions; **u. the circumstances** vu les circonstances

5 *(in the process of)* en cours de; **u. repair** en réparation; *Med* **u. observation** en observation; **to keep sb/sth u. observation** surveiller qn/qch; **u. construction** en construction; **the question is u. examination** la question est à l'étude

6 *(in list, directory etc)* **it's entered u. F** cela figure à la lettre F; **we're in the phone book u. Tomson** nous sommes dans l'annuaire sous le nom de Tomson; **are they u. decorators or painters?** sont-ils sous la rubrique décorateurs ou peintres?; **it's u. biology** *(in library etc)* c'est classé sous la rubrique biologie; **to look for/to file sth u.** *(the heading)* **...** chercher/classer qch sous la rubrique ...

ADV 1 *(underneath)* (au-)dessous; **to stay u. for two minutes** *(underwater)* rester deux minutes sous l'eau; **to be u.** *(anaesthetic)* être sous anesthésiant; *Fam* **to get out from u.** *(from difficult situation)* se tirer d'affaire **2** *(less)* au-dessous; **children of seven years old and u.** des enfants de sept ans et moins

underachieve [ˌʌndərə'tʃiːv] **VI** ne pas obtenir les résultats escomptés

underachiever [ˌʌndərə'tʃiːvər] **N** = personne *f* qui n'obtient pas les résultats escomptés

under-age **ADJ** mineur
▸▸ **u. drinking** consommation *f* d'alcool par les mineurs

underarm ['ʌndərɑːm] **ADV** *Cr, Tennis* **to bowl/to serve u.** lancer/servir la balle par en-dessous
ADJ 1 *Cr, Tennis (bowl, shot etc)* par en-dessous **2 u. deodorant** déodorant *m* pour les aisselles

underbelly ['ʌndəbelɪ] **N 1** *(of animal)* bas-ventre *m, pl* bas-ventres **2** *Fig* point *m* faible;

the soft u. of Europe le ventre mou de l'Europe

underbid [ʌndə'bɪd] (*pt* **underbid**; *pp* **underbid(den)** [-'bɪd((ə)n)]) **VT** *Com etc* **to u. sb** faire des soumissions *ou* offrir des conditions plus avantageuses que qn
VT & VI *Cards* **to u.** (one's hand) demander au-dessous de son jeu

underblanket ['ʌndəblæŋkɪt] **N** = couverture *f* entre le matelas et le drap de dessous

underbody ['ʌndəbɒdɪ] **N** *Aut* bas *m* de caisse

underborrow [ʌndə'bɒrəʊ] **VI** *Fin (of company)* ne pas emprunter assez

underborrowed [ʌndə'bɒrəʊd] **ADJ** *Fin (company)* sous-endetté

underborrowing [ʌndə'bɒrəʊɪŋ] **N** *Fin (of company)* sous-endettement *m*

underbrush ['ʌndəbrʌʃ] **N** sous-bois *m*

undercapitalization [ʌndəkæpɪtəlaɪ'zeɪʃən] **N** *Econ* sous-capitalisation *f*

undercapitalized [ʌndə'kæpɪtəlaɪzd] **ADJ** *(industry)* sous-capitalisé

undercarriage ['ʌndəkærɪdʒ] **N** *Aviat* train *m* d'atterrissage

undercharge [ʌndə'tʃɑːdʒ] **VT** **they undercharged him** on ne lui a pas fait payer assez; **they undercharged her** *or* **she was undercharged by £5** on aurait dû lui faire payer 5 livres de plus
VI demander trop peu (**for sth** pour qch)

underclass ['ʌndəklɑːs] **N** *(of society)* sous-prolétariat *m*, quart-monde *m*

undercloth ['ʌndəklɒθ] **N** *(on table)* sous-nappe *f, pl* sous-nappes

underclothes ['ʌndəkləʊðz] **NPL**, **underclothing** ['ʌndəkləʊðɪŋ] **N** sous-vêtements *mpl*, *(women's)* lingerie *f*, dessous *mpl*

undercoat ['ʌndəkəʊt] **N 1** *(of paint)* couche *f* de fond, première couche **2** *Am Aut* couche *f ou* revêtement *m* antirouille

undercoating ['ʌndəkəʊtɪŋ] **N** = **undercoat**

underconsumption [ʌndəkən'sʌmpʃən] **N** *Econ* sous-consommation *f*

undercook [ʌndə'kʊk] **VT** ne pas assez cuire

under-correction **N** *Aut* sous-correction *f, pl* sous-corrections, correction *f* insuffisante

undercover ['ʌndəkʌvər] **ADJ** secret, -ète, clandestin
ADV clandestinement
▸▸ **u. agent** agent *m* secret

undercurrent ['ʌndəkʌrənt] **N** *(in sea)* courant *m* sous-marin; *Fig* **u. of discontent** vague *f* de fond de mécontentement; *Fig* **but there are undercurrents** *(in relationship etc)* mais il y a des tensions sous-jacentes

undercut ['ʌndəkʌt] **N** *Culin* filet *m* (de bœuf)
VT (*pt, pp* **undercut**; *prp* **undercutting**) **1** *Sport (ball)* couper, lifter **2** *Com (competitor)* vendre moins cher que; *(prices)* casser

underdeveloped [ʌndədɪ'veləpt] **ADJ 1** *Phot* insuffisamment développé **2** *(child)* retardé; *(muscle)* pas assez développé **3** *Econ (country)* sous-développé; *(area)* insuffisamment mis en valeur; *(resources)* sous-exploité

underdog ['ʌndədɒg] **N** *Sport* outsider *m*; *(socially etc)* défavorisé, -ée; *Pol etc* **to side with the underdog(s)** prendre le parti des plus faibles; *Sport* **the underdogs won 5-2** ceux qui étaient donnés perdants à l'avance ont gagné 5 à 2

underdone [ʌndə'dʌn] **ADJ** *Culin (undercooked)* pas assez cuit; **I'd like my steak slightly u.** *(rare)* je voudrais mon steak légèrement saignant

underdrawers ['ʌndədrɔːz] **NPL** *Am* caleçon *m* (d'homme)

underdressed [ʌndə'drest] **ADJ** **to be u.** *(not warm enough)* ne pas être assez habillé *ou* couvert; *(not formal enough)* ne pas être assez bien habillé

underemployed [ʌndərem'plɔɪd] **ADJ** *(person)* sous-employé; *(resources)* sous-exploité

underemployment [ʌndərem'plɔɪmənt] **N** *(of person)* sous-emploi *m*

underestimate[1], **underestimation** [ʌndər'estɪmɪt, -estɪ'meɪʃən] **N** sous-estimation *f, pl* sous-estimations

underestimate[2] [ʌndər'estɪmeɪt] **VT** *(expenses, person)* sous-estimer; *(difficulties, opponent)* méconnaître, mésestimer

underexpose [ʌndəreks'pəʊz] **VT 1** *Phot (film)* sous-exposer **2** *(publicize insufficiently) (person, film, event)* faire insuffisamment la publicité de

underexposed ['ʌndəreks'pəʊzd] **ADJ** *Phot* sous-exposé

underexposure [ʌndəreks'pəʊʒər] **N 1** *Phot (of film)* sous-exposition *f* **2** *(to publicity)* manque *m* de publicité

underfed [ʌndə'fed] **ADJ** sous-alimenté, mal nourri

underfeeding [ʌndə'fiːdɪŋ] **N** sous-alimentation *f*

underfelt ['ʌndəfelt] **N** *(for carpet)* thibaude *f*

underfinance [ʌndə'faɪnæns] **VT** financer insuffisamment

underfloor ['ʌndəflɔːr] **ADJ**
▸▸ **u. heating** chauffage *m* par le sol

underfoot [ʌndə'fʊt] **ADV** sous les pieds; **it's wet u.** le sol est mouillé; **the snow crunched u.** la neige crissait sous les pieds; **to trample** *or* **tread sth u.** fouler qch aux pieds

underfunded [ʌndə'fʌndɪd] **ADJ** *(project etc)* insuffisamment financé

underfunding [ʌndə'fʌndɪŋ] **N** *(of industry)* insuffisance *f* de financement; **the project suffered from u.** le projet a souffert d'un financement insuffisant

undergardener **N** aide-jardinier *m, pl* aides-jardiniers

undergarment ['ʌndəgɑːmənt] **N** sous-vêtement *m, pl* sous-vêtements

undergo [ʌndə'gəʊ] **VT** (*pt* **underwent** [-'went]; *pp* **undergone** [-'gɒn]) *(change)* passer par, subir; *(hardship, examination, operation)* subir; **to u. a complete change** subir une métamorphose complète; **undergoing repairs** en réparation; *Med* **to u. treatment** suivre un traitement

undergrad [ʌndə'græd] **N** *Fam* = **undergraduate**

undergraduate [ʌndə'grædjʊɪt] **N** étudiant, -ante *(qui prépare le DEUG/la licence)*; **in my u. days** lorsque j'étais étudiant; **u. life** la vie d'étudiant; **u. newspaper** journal étudiant

underground ['ʌndəgraʊnd] **ADV 1** *(in mine etc)* sous terre **2** *Fig (secretly)* clandestinement, secrètement; **to go u.** passer dans la clandestinité
ADJ 1 *(work)* sous terre; *(pipe, lake, cable)* souterrain; **u. workings** chantier *m* souterrain, travaux *mpl* souterrains **2** *Fig (clandestine) (organization, press)* clandestin, secret, -ète
N 1 *Br Rail* métro *m* **2** *(in occupied country etc)* the u. la résistance
▸▸ **u. economy** économie *f* souterraine; **u. gallery** souterrain *m*; **u. movement** mouvement *m* clandestin; *(in occupied country)* résistance *f*; **u. passage** souterrain; *Am Hist*

The U. Railroad *(network for escaping slaves)* = réseau *m* clandestin de libération des esclaves; **u. railway** métro *m*; **u. station** station *f* de métro; **u. train** rame *f* de métro

undergrowth ['ʌndəgrəʊθ] N broussailles *fpl*, sous-bois *m*

underhand ['ʌndəhænd] ADJ *(person)* sournois; **to behave in an u. way** agir en sous-main; **u. dealings** manœuvres *fpl* clandestines, *Fam* magouilles *fpl*

underhanded [ʌndə'hændɪd] ADJ **1** = underhand **2** *Am (short of staff)* à court de personnel; *(short of workers)* à court de main-d'œuvre

underhandedly [ʌndə'hændɪdlɪ] ADV en sous-main

underinsured [ʌndərɪn'ʃɔːd] ADJ sous-assuré

underinvestment [ʌndərɪn'vestmənt] N insuffisance *f* d'investissement

underlay [¹ ['ʌndəleɪ] N *(for carpet)* thibaude *f*, *(for tiling)* assise *f*

underlay [² [ʌndə'leɪ] VT *(pt, pp* **underlaid** [-'leɪd])* **to u. sth with sth** mettre qch sous qch; **carpet underlaid with felt** moquette *f* sur thibaude

underlie [ʌndə'laɪ] VT *(pt* **underlay** [-'leɪ]; *pp* **underlain** [-'leɪn]; *prp* **underlying** [-'laɪɪŋ])* être à la base *ou* à l'origine de; **the reasons which underlay her decision** les raisons qui ont motivé sa décision

underline [¹ ['ʌndəlaɪn] N souligné *m*

underline [² [ʌndə'laɪn] VT *(word)* souligner; *Fig (fact)* souligner, appuyer sur, insister sur

underling ['ʌndəlɪŋ] N *Pej* subalterne *mf*, subordonné, -ée

underlining [ʌndə'laɪnɪŋ] N soulignement *m*, soulignage *m*

underlying [ʌndə'laɪɪŋ] ADJ *(rock, principles, causes etc)* sous-jacent;
▶▶*Fin* **u. asset** actif *m* sous-jacent; *St Exch* **u. futures contract** contrat *m* à terme sous option; *Fin* **u. mortgage** hypothèque *f* sous-jacente; *Fin* **u. security** titre *m* sous-jacent

undermanager ['ʌndəmænɪdʒər] N sous-chef *m*, *pl* sous-chefs, sous-directeur *m*, *pl* sous-directeurs

undermanned [ʌndə'mænd] ADJ à court de main-d'œuvre; **to be u.** manquer de main d'œuvre

undermanning [ʌndə'mænɪŋ] N manque *m ou* pénurie *f* de main-d'œuvre

undermentioned ['ʌndəmenʃənd] ADJ *Fml* (cité *ou* mentionné) ci-dessous; **the u. persons** les personnes dont les noms suivent

undermine [ʌndə'maɪn] VT **1** *(coast, wall)* miner, saper; *(of sea, river) (cliffs, banks)* affouiller; **foundations undermined by water** fondements minés par l'eau **2** *(principle, authority)* saper; *(sb's health)* miner; *(sb's confidence)* ébranler; **to u. the foundations of society** attaquer les bases de la société; **stop undermining me!** arrête de me faire du tort!

undermost ['ʌndəməʊst] ADJ **the u.** le plus bas, *f* la plus basse

underneath [ʌndə'niːθ] PREP au-dessous de, sous; **he pushed the letter u. the door** il a glissé la lettre sous la porte; **he pulled it (out) from u. the blanket** il l'a tiré de dessous la couverture
ADV au-dessous, dessous; **he picked up the book and found the ticket u.** il a soulevé le livre et a trouvé le billet dessous
N dessous *m*; **the u. of the box is black** le dessous de la boîte est noir
ADJ de dessous, d'en dessous

undernourished [ʌndə'nʌrɪʃt] ADJ sous-alimenté

undernourishment [ʌndə'nʌrɪʃmənt] N sous-alimentation *f*

underpaid [ʌndə'peɪd] ADJ *(work, worker)* sous-payé, sous-rémunéré

underpants ['ʌndəpænts] NPL *(for men)* slip *m*; **a pair of u.** un slip

underpart ['ʌndəpɑːt] N partie *f* inférieure

underpass ['ʌndəpɑːs] N *(for cars)* tunnel *m*; *(for pedestrians)* (passage *m*) souterrain *m*

underpay [ʌndə'peɪ] VT *(pt, pp* **underpaid** [-'peɪd])* *(worker etc)* sous-payer, sous-rémunérer

underperform [ʌndəpə'fɔːm] VI *Fin (of shares, investment)* ne pas être performant

underpin [ʌndə'pɪn] VT (-pp-) *(wall)*, *Fig (theory)* étayer; *(organization)* être à la base de; **the principles which u. Marxism-Leninism** les principes de base du marxisme-léninisme

underpinning [ʌndə'pɪnɪŋ] N étayage *m*; *(of organization, theory)* base *m*

underplay [ʌndə'pleɪ] VT **1** *(play down)* minimiser l'importance de **2** *Theat* **to u. a part** *(with subtlety)* jouer un rôle tout en nuances; *(with lack of force)* jouer un rôle de façon trop plate **3** *Fig* **to u. one's hand** ne pas être assez exigeant, ne pas demander assez; *(deliberately)* cacher son jeu

underpopulated [ʌndə'pɒpjʊleɪtɪd] ADJ sous-peuplé

underprice [ʌndə'praɪs] VT *(article)* mettre un prix trop bas à

underpriced [ʌndə'praɪst] ADJ très bon marché (par rapport à sa valeur réelle); **at £15.99 it's definitely u.** à 15,99 livres c'est vraiment donné

underpricing [ʌndə'praɪsɪŋ] N fixation *f* de prix trop bas

underprivileged [ʌndə'prɪvɪlɪdʒd] ADJ déshérité, défavorisé
NPL **the u.** les défavorisés, les économiquement faibles

underproduce [ʌndəprə'djuːs] VI *Ind* être en situation de sous-production

underproduction [ʌndəprə'dʌkʃən] N *Ind* sous-production *f*

underproductive [ʌndəprə'dʌktɪv] ADJ *Ind* sous-productif

underqualified [ʌndə'kwɒlɪfaɪd] ADJ sous-qualifié

underrate [ʌndə'reɪt] VT *(opponent, difficulty, importance of sth)* sous-estimer

under-represent VT minimiser, ne pas donner assez d'importance à

under-representation N *esp Pol* sous-représentation *f*

under-represented [-reprɪ'zentɪd] ADJ *esp Pol* sous-représenté

underscore [¹ ['ʌndəskɔːr] N trait *m* de soulignement

underscore [² [ʌndə'skɔːr] VT *(title etc)* souligner; *Fig (fact)* faire ressortir, mettre en évidence; *(importance of sth)* souligner

undersea ['ʌndəsiː] ADJ sous-marin

underseal ['ʌndəsiːl] *Br Aut* N couche *f* antirouille (pour dessous de châssis), couche anticorrosion
VT **u. (the chassis of) a car** traiter le châssis d'une voiture contre la rouille

undersecretary [ʌndə'sekrɪt(ə)rɪ] N sous-secrétaire *mf*, *Br* **permanent u.** secrétaire *m* général *(d'un ministère)*

undersell [ʌndə'sel] VT *(pt, pp* **undersold** [-'səʊld])* *Com (competition etc)* vendre moins cher que; *(goods etc)* vendre au-dessous de sa valeur; *Fig* **don't u. yourself at the interview** essaie de bien te vendre lors de l'entretien; **she tends to u. herself** elle a tendance à ne pas suffisamment se mettre en valeur

undersexed [ʌndə'sekst] ADJ de *ou* à faible libido; **he's u.** il a une faible libido

undersheet ['ʌndəʃiːt] N alaise *f*, alèse *f*

undershield ['ʌndəʃiːld] N *Aut* bouclier *m* inférieur

undershirt ['ʌndəʃɜːt] N *Am (for men)* maillot *m*

undershoot [ʌndə'ʃuːt] VT & VI *(pt, pp* **undershot** [-'ʃɒt])* *Aviat* **to u. (the runway)** se présenter *ou* atterrir trop court (sur la piste); *Fig* **to u. a production target** ne pas atteindre ses objectifs de production

underside ['ʌndəsaɪd] N dessous *m*

undersigned [ʌndə'saɪnd] ADJ, N soussigné, -ée; **I, the u.** je soussigné(e); **the u. declare that ...** les soussignés déclarent que ...

undersize(d) [ʌndə'saɪz(d)] ADJ de (trop) petite taille, trop petit

underskirt ['ʌndəskɜːt] N jupon *m*

underslung [ʌndə'slʌŋ] ADJ *Aut (chassis)* surbaissé; *(car)* à carrosserie surbaissée

understaffed [ʌndə'stɑːft] ADJ à court de personnel; **the office is u.** le bureau manque de personnel

understaffing [ʌndə'stɑːfɪŋ] N manque *m ou* pénurie *f* de personnel

understand [ʌndə'stænd] *(pt, pp* **understood** [-'stʊd])* VT **1** *(comprehend)* comprendre; **I don't u. French** je ne comprends pas le français; **he can't make himself understood in German** il ne peut pas se faire comprendre en allemand; **he understands business matters** il s'y connaît *ou* s'y entend en affaires; **this sentence can be understood in several ways** cette phrase peut s'interpréter de plusieurs façons; **no one understands me** personne ne me comprend; **to u. each other** *or* **one another** se comprendre; *(have same ideas etc)* s'entendre; **I quite u. that he must be tired** je comprends très bien qu'il soit fatigué; **I don't u. why he did it** je ne comprends pas pourquoi il l'a fait; **do you u. what he's talking about?** comprenez-vous quelque chose à ce qu'il raconte?; **what I can't u. is that ...** ce que je ne comprends pas, c'est que ... + *subj*; **I can u. your being angry** je comprends que vous soyez fâché; **I can't u. it** je ne (le) comprends pas; **I'm at a loss to u. it, I can't u. a word of it, I don't u. the first thing about it** je n'y comprends (absolument) rien; **(is that) understood?** (vous avez *ou* c'est bien) compris?, (c'est) entendu?; **that's easily understood** cela se comprend facilement

2 *(believe)* **I understood that I was to be paid for my work** j'ai cru comprendre que je devais être payé pour mon travail; **I u. (that) you're coming to work here** j'ai appris que vous veniez travailler ici; **he is understood to be abroad, it is understood that he is abroad** il serait à l'étranger; **it must be understood** *or* **you must u. that ...** il doit être (bien) entendu *ou* il faut (bien) comprendre que ...; **to give sb to u. that ...** laisser entendre à qn que ...; **I have made it understood** *or* **I have let it be understood that ...** j'ai laissé entendre que ...

3 *(sth implicit)* sous-entendre; **am I to u. that ...?** *(deduce)* dois-je en conclure que ...?; **in this sentence the verb is understood** dans cette phrase le verbe est sous-entendu; **that's understood** cela va sans dire, cela va de soi
VI comprendre; **now I u.!** je comprends *ou* j'y suis maintenant!; **you don't u.** vous n'y êtes pas; **do you u.?** vous comprenez?; **he left yesterday, I u.** il est parti hier, si j'ai bien

compris *ou* si je ne me trompe (pas); **to u. about sth** comprendre qch

understandable [ʌndəˈstændəb(ə)l] **ADJ** compréhensible; **that's u.** cela se comprend (facilement), c'est bien normal; **it's quite u. that she should be …** il est tout à fait compréhensible qu'elle soit …

understandably [ʌndəˈstændəblɪ] **ADV** naturellement, forcément; **he was u. disappointed** il était compréhensible qu'il soit déçu

understanding [ʌndəˈstændɪŋ] **ADJ** compréhensif (**about sth** au sujet de qch); *(letter, words, smile)* plein de compréhension **N 1** *(comprehension, conception)* compréhension *f*; **the age of u.** l'âge *m* de raison; **it's beyond all u.** c'est incompréhensible, c'est à n'y rien comprendre; **it's beyond my u.** cela dépasse mon entendement, je n'y comprends rien; **he showed great u.** *(sensitivity)* il s'est montré très compréhensif; **to be lacking in u. of a problem** ne pas bien comprendre un problème; **according to my u. of it** si j'ai bien compris; **my u. was that the venue would be paid for by the organizers** j'avais compris que les organisateurs paieraient pour la location des locaux **2** *(between nations etc)* entente *f*, accord *m*; *(agreement)* accord, arrangement *m*; **spirit of u.** esprit *m* d'entente; **they had an u., there was an u. between them** ils s'étaient arrangés entre eux; **to come to** *or* **to reach an u.** s'entendre *ou* s'arranger (**with sb** avec qn) **3** *(condition)* condition *f*; **on the u. that he gives it me back** à (la) condition qu'il me le rende; **on the firm u. that …** à la condition expresse que …

understandingly [ʌndəˈstændɪŋlɪ] **ADV** *(to act)* avec compréhension

understate [ʌndəˈsteɪt] **VT** minimiser; *(problem etc)* ne pas insister sur; **understated** *(make-up etc)* discret, -ète; **the deliberately understated figures in the foreground** les silhouettes volontairement estompées au premier plan

understatement [ʌndəˈsteɪtmənt] **N 1** euphémisme *m*; *Ling* litote *f*; **with typical British u.** avec un euphémisme typiquement britannique; **to say it's expensive is an u.** dire que c'est cher est un euphémisme; **that's an u. if I ever heard one!** c'est un des plus beaux euphémismes que j'aie jamais entendus; *Fam* **that's the u. of the year!** c'est le moins qu'on puisse dire! **2** *(low-key presentation) (of problem, distinction)* minimisation *f*

understeer [ʌndəˈstɪər] **VI** sous-virer; **a car which understeers** une voiture sous-vireuse

understeer(ing) [ʌndəˈstɪər(ɪŋ)] **N** sous-virage *m*, comportement *m* sous-vireur

understudy [ˈʌndəstʌdɪ] *Theat* **N** doublure *f*

VT *(actor)* doubler; *(role)* servir de doublure pour

undersubscribed [ʌndəsʌbˈskraɪbd] **ADJ** *Fin, St Exch (issue, share)* non-souscrit

undertake [ʌndəˈteɪk] **VT** *(pt* **undertook** [-ˈtʊk]; *pp* **undertaken** [-ˈteɪk(ə)n]) **1** *(journey etc)* entreprendre **2** *(task)* entreprendre; *(responsibility)* assumer; **to u. to do sth** s'engager à faire qch **3 to u. that …** garantir que … **4** *(vehicle)* doubler par l'intérieur

undertaker [ˈʌndəteɪkər] **N** entrepreneur *m* des pompes funèbres; **the u.'s** les pompes funèbres

undertaking [ʌndəˈteɪkɪŋ] **N 1** *(enterprise)* entreprise *f*; **it's quite an u.** c'est toute une affaire; **the u. of this project meant that …** la mise en œuvre de ce projet signifiait que … **2** *(promise etc)* engagement *m*, promesse *f*; *Law* soumission *f*; **he gave an u. to do it** *or*

that he would do it il s'est engagé à *ou* il a promis de le faire; **I give you my solemn u. never to …** je vous promets solennellement de ne jamais …; **I can't give you that u.** je ne peux vous faire cette promesse **3** *(profession of undertaker)* métier *m* d'entrepreneur des pompes funèbres

undertax [ʌndəˈtæks] **VT** *(something)* taxer insuffisamment; *(somebody)* ne pas faire payer assez d'impôts à

under-the-counter **ADJ** *(sales etc)* clandestin **ADV** clandestinement

undertone [ˈʌndətəʊn] **N 1 in an u.** *(to talk)* à mi-voix, à voix basse **2 an u. of menace** une note de menace; **grey with blue undertones** gris nuancé de bleu

undertow [ˈʌndətəʊ] **N** *(in water)* courant *m* (sous-marin) *(lorsqu'une vague se retire)*; *Fig* tension *f* sous-jacente

underuse[1] [ʌndəˈjuːs] **N** sous-utilisation *f*

underuse[2] [ʌndəˈjuːz] **VT** sous-utiliser

underutilization [ʌndəjuːtɪlaɪˈzeɪʃən] **N** *(of facilities, equipment)* sous-utilisation *f*

underutilize [ʌndəˈjuːtɪlaɪz] **VT** *(facilities, equipment)* sous-utiliser

undervalue [ʌndəˈvælju:] **VT** *Com (goods)* sous-évaluer; *Fig* sous-estimer, mésestimer

undervest [ˈʌndəvest] **N** *esp Br* = **vest**[1] **1**

underwater **ADJ** [ˈʌndəwɔːtər] sous-marin **ADV** [ʌndəˈwɔːtər] sous l'eau
▸▸ *Am St Exch* **u. option** option *f* à prix glissant à la baisse

underwear [ˈʌndəweər] **N** sous-vêtements *mpl*, *(for women)* lingerie *f*, dessous *mpl*

underweight [ʌndəˈweɪt] **ADJ** *(article)* d'un poids insuffisant; **to be u.** *(of person)* ne pas peser assez; **I'm ten lbs u.** ≃ il me manque cinq kilos, je devrais peser cinq kilos de plus

underwhelm [ʌndəˈwelm] **VT** *Hum* **your generosity underwhelms me** votre générosité me renverse; **he was obviously underwhelmed by his present** le cadeau l'avait laissé manifestement indifférent; **the critics were underwhelmed by his next film** son nouveau film fut accueilli avec un enthousiasme très relatif par la critique

underwired [ˈʌndəwaɪəd] **ADJ**
▸▸ **u. bra** soutien-gorge *m* avec armature, *pl* soutiens-gorge

underworld [ˈʌndəwɜːld] **N 1** *Myth* **the u.** les enfers *mpl* **2** *(of criminals)* pègre *f*, milieu *m*

underwrite [ˈʌndəraɪt] *(pt* **underwrote** [-rəʊt]; *pp* **underwritten** [-rɪt(ə)n]) **VT** *Fin (loan, new issue, policy, risk)* garantir, souscrire; **policy underwritten at Lloyd's** police garantie par Lloyd's

underwriter [ˈʌndəraɪtər] **N 1** *Fin* syndicataire *mf*, souscripteur *m*, garant *m*; **the underwriters** le syndicat de garantie **2** *(in insurance)* assureur *m*; **marine u.** assureur maritime
▸▸ *Fin* **u. agent** agent *m* souscripteur

underwriting [ˈʌndəraɪtɪŋ] **N** *Fin (of issue, policy, risk)* garantie *f*; **marine u.** assurance *f* maritime
▸▸ *Fin* **u. agent** agent *m* souscripteur; **u. commission** commission *f* de garantie; **u. syndicate** syndicat *m* de prise ferme

undeserved [ʌndɪˈzɜːvd] **ADJ** *(praise, reproach)* immérité

undeservedly [ʌndɪˈzɜːvɪdlɪ] **ADV** à tort, injustement; *(be decorated etc)* sans l'avoir mérité

undeserving [ʌndɪˈzɜːvɪŋ] **ADJ** *(person)* sans mérite; *(cause etc)* peu méritoire; **u. of attention** indigne d'attention

undesirable [ʌndɪˈzaɪərəb(ə)l] **ADJ** indésirable; **an u. character** un personnage peu

recommandable; **to have an u. influence on sb** avoir une mauvaise influence sur qn; **if you think this is u.** si vous pensez que ce n'est pas souhaitable; **it is u. that he should be sent to an adult prison** il est inadmissible qu'on l'envoie dans une prison pour adultes
N indésirable *mf*

undetected [ʌndɪˈtektɪd] **ADJ** non détecté, non décelé; **to go u.** passer inaperçu

undetermined [ʌndɪˈtɜːmɪnd] **ADJ 1** *(quality, date)* indéterminé, incertain; *(issue)* non résolu, irrésolu **2** *(not resolute)* irrésolu, indécis

undeterred [ʌndɪˈtɜːd] **ADJ to carry on u.** continuer sans se laisser décourager (**by** par); **we remained u.** nous ne nous sommes pas laissé décourager; **u. by the weather, he went out for a walk** en dépit du mauvais temps, il est sorti se promener

undeveloped [ʌndɪˈveləpt] **ADJ 1** *(ideas, suggestions)* non développé; *(land, resources)* inexploité, non exploité; *(mind)* non formé **2** *(film)* non développé

undeviating [ʌnˈdiːvɪeɪtɪŋ] **ADJ** *(course, path)* droit, direct; *(faithfulness)* qui ne se dément pas

undies [ˈʌndɪz] **NPL** *Fam* lingerie *f*, dessous *mpl*

undifferentiated [ʌndɪfəˈrenʃɪeɪtɪd] **ADJ** indifférencié
▸▸ *Mktg* **u. marketing** marketing *m* indifférencié

undigested [ʌndɪˈdʒestɪd] **ADJ** *(food)* non digéré, mal digéré; *(facts)* mal assimilé

undignified [ʌnˈdɪgnɪfaɪd] **ADJ** peu digne, qui manque de dignité; **to be u.** manquer de dignité; **what an u. way to sit!** quelle manière peu élégante de s'asseoir!; **their business venture came to an u. end** leur entreprise a échoué de façon lamentable

undiluted [ʌndaɪˈluːtɪd] **ADJ** *(liquid)* non dilué; *(acid)* concentré; *(joy, delight, pleasure)* sans mélange

undiminished [ʌndɪˈmɪnɪʃt] **ADJ** non diminué, intact; **my respect for him remains u.** mon respect pour lui n'a pas diminué *ou* est resté intact; **thirty years later, the appeal of the film remains u.** trente ans plus tard, le film n'a rien perdu de son intérêt

undiplomatic [ʌndɪpləˈmætɪk] **ADJ** peu diplomatique, peu diplomate

undiplomatically [ʌndɪpləˈmætɪklɪ] **ADV** de manière peu diplomate *ou* peu diplomatique

undipped [ʌnˈdɪpt] **ADJ** *Aut* **to drive with u. headlights** conduire en plein phares

undiscerning [ʌndɪˈsɜːnɪŋ] **ADJ** *(eater, wine-drinker)* peu raffiné, peu connaisseur, -euse; *(mind)* peu pénétrant; **to be u.** *(of person)* manquer de discernement

undischarged [ʌndɪsˈtʃɑːdʒd] **ADJ 1** *(debtor)* non libéré (d'une obligation); *(debt)* non liquidé **2** *(duty)* inaccompli
▸▸ *Law* **u. bankrupt** failli *m* non réhabilité

undisciplined [ʌnˈdɪsɪplɪnd] **ADJ** indiscipliné

undisclosed [ʌndɪsˈkləʊzd] **ADJ** non révélé
▸▸ *Com* **u. principal** acheteur *m* non identifié *ou* anonyme

undiscountable [ʌndɪsˈkaʊntəb(ə)l] **ADJ** *Fin* inescomptable

undiscovered [ʌndɪsˈkʌvəd] **ADJ** non découvert; **u. country** terre *f* inconnue; **the ruins of Troy went u. for centuries** l'emplacement des ruines de Troie est resté ignoré pendant des siècles

undiscriminating [ʌndɪsˈkrɪmɪneɪtɪŋ] **ADJ** sans discernement, qui manque de discernement

undiscriminatingly [ˌʌndɪsˈkrɪmɪneɪtɪŋlɪ] **ADV** sans discernement

undisguised [ˌʌndɪsˈgaɪzd] **ADJ** non déguisé; *(feelings)* non dissimulé

undisguisedly [ˌʌndɪsˈgaɪzɪdlɪ] **ADV** ouvertement

undismayed [ˌʌndɪsˈmeɪd] **ADJ** non découragé; **he was quite u. by the incident** l'incident ne l'a nullement découragé

undisputed [ˌʌndɪsˈpjuːtɪd] **ADJ** *(champion)* incontesté, indiscuté; *(success, failure)* incontestable

undistinguished [ˌʌndɪsˈtɪŋgwɪʃt] **ADJ 1** médiocre; *(appearance)* peu distingué **2 the novel is u. by any great originality** ce roman n'a rien de particulièrement original

undistributed [ˌʌndɪsˈtrɪbjutɪd] **ADJ** *Fin (money, earnings, profit)* non distribué

undisturbed [ˌʌndɪsˈtɜːbd] **ADJ** *(sleep)* paisible, calme; *(peace)* que rien ne vient troubler; *(papers)* non dérangé, non déplacé; **please leave us u. for fifteen minutes** veuillez ne pas nous déranger pendant quinze minutes; **she left his papers u.** elle n'a pas touché à ses papiers; **I could do with an u. night's sleep** une bonne nuit de sommeil me ferait du bien; **he was apparently u. by the news** la nouvelle ne l'a apparemment pas troublé

undivided [ˌʌndɪˈvaɪdɪd] **ADJ** non divisé; *(loyalties)* sans partage; **he gave her his u. attention/love** il lui a donné toute son attention/tout son amour

undo [ʌnˈduː] *(pt* **undid** [-ˈdɪd]*; pp* **undone** [-ˈdʌn]*)* **VT 1** *(piece of work)* détruire; *(mistake)* réparer; **you can't u. the past** ce qui est fait est fait **2** *Comput (command)* annuler, défaire; **u. changes** annuler les révisions; **u. last** annuler dernière opération; **can't u.** impossible d'annuler **3** *(knot, button, knitting)* défaire; *(fastening)* ouvrir; *(screw)* desserrer; *(parcel)* défaire, déficeler; *(shoes)* délacer; *(one's dress)* dégrafer, déboutonner
 VI *(of dress etc)* se défaire
 ▸▸ *Comput* **u. command** commande *f* d'annulation

undocumented [ʌnˈdɒkjʊmentɪd] **ADJ** *(subject, history etc)* sur lequel il n'existe pas de documentation

undoing [ʌnˈduːɪŋ] **N** *(downfall)* ruine *f*, perte *f*; **that man will be her u.** cet homme la conduira à sa perte; **drink was his u.** l'alcool a causé sa perte

undomesticated [ˌʌndəˈmestɪkeɪtɪd] **ADJ** **he's completely u.** il ne sait rien faire dans la maison

undone [ʌnˈdʌn] **ADJ 1** *(knot, button)* défait; **to come u.** *(of knot, button)* se défaire; *(of hair)* se dénouer; *(of screw)* se desserrer; *(of shoe)* se délacer; *(of dress)* se dégrafer; *(of seam)* se découdre, se défaire; *(of parcel)* se déficeler, se défaire **2** *Hum, Arch* **I am u.!** je suis perdu! **3** *(not finished, not done)* **we had to leave it u.** nous n'avons pas pu le terminer; *Lit* **we have left u. those things which we ought to have done** nous n'avons pas fait les choses que nous aurions dû faire

undoubted [ʌnˈdaʊtɪd] **ADJ** *(fact)* incontestable, indubitable

undoubtedly [ʌnˈdaʊtɪdlɪ] **ADV** indubitablement, incontestablement

undramatic [ˌʌndrəˈmætɪk] **ADJ** *(lacking in interest)* pas très intéressant; **this seemingly u. incident ...** cet incident apparemment anodin ...

undrawn [ʌnˈdrɔːn] **ADJ** **the curtains were still u.** les rideaux n'étaient toujours pas tirés

undreamed-of, undreamt-of [ʌnˈdriːmd-

DV, ʌnˈdremtɒv] ADJ *(unsuspected)* insoupçonné; *(beyond one's dreams)* inimaginable

undress [ʌnˈdres] **VI** se déshabiller
 VT déshabiller; **to get undressed** se déshabiller
 N in a state of u. en petite tenue

undressed [ʌnˈdrest] **ADJ 1** *(without clothes)* déshabillé; *(in nightdress)* en déshabillé **2** *(cloth)* inapprêté; *(wood)* en grume; **u. stone** pierre *f* non taillée **3** *Culin (meat)* non accommodé; *(lobster)* nature *inv*; *(salad)* non assaisonné **4 u. wound** blessure *f* non pansée

undrinkable [ʌnˈdrɪŋkəb(ə)l] **ADJ** *(unpleasant)* imbuvable; *(harmful)* non potable

undubbed [ʌnˈdʌbd] **ADJ** *Cin, TV* non doublé; **the u. version of the film** la version originale du film

undue [ʌnˈdjuː] **ADJ 1** *(demand)* injustifiable **2** *(haste, optimism)* exagéré, excessif; **to pay u. attention to sb** s'empresser auprès de qn

undulate [ˈʌndjʊleɪt] **VI** onduler, ondoyer

undulating [ˈʌndjʊleɪtɪŋ] **ADJ** onduleux; *(wheat)* ondoyant; **u. country** pays *m* vallonné; **an u. walk** une démarche chaloupée

undulation [ˌʌndjʊˈleɪʃən] **N** ondulation *f*

unduly [ʌnˈdjuːlɪ] **ADV** *(excessively)* à l'excès, trop; **not u. expensive/concerned** pas excessivement cher/inquiet, -ète; **an u. high price** un prix excessif; **to be u. optimistic** faire preuve d'un optimisme peu justifié; **he worries u.** *or* **he's u. worried about his health** sa santé le préoccupe trop

undying [ʌnˈdaɪɪŋ] **ADJ** immortel; *(love)* éternel

unearned [ʌnˈɜːnd] **ADJ 1** *(reward, punishment)* immérité **2** *(money)* qui ne provient pas du travail
 ▸▸ *Fin* **u. income** revenus *mpl* non professionnels, rentes *fpl*

unearth [ʌnˈɜːθ] **VT 1** *(dig out of earth)* déterrer, exhumer **2** *(find) (old photograph, hat etc)* dénicher; *Fam* dégot(t)er; *(information)* découvrir, trouver; **wherever did you u. that?** où donc as-tu déniché ça?

unearthly [ʌnˈɜːθlɪ] **ADJ 1** *(supernatural)* mystérieux; **an u. pallor** une pâleur mortelle **2** *Fam* **at an u. hour** à une heure impossible; **u. din** vacarme *m* de tous les diables; **for some u. reason** pour une raison absurde

unease [ʌnˈiːz] **N** malaise *m*

uneasily [ʌnˈiːzɪlɪ] **ADV** *(uncomfortably)* d'un air gêné; *(worriedly)* avec inquiétude; *(to sleep)* d'un sommeil agité; **the books were u. balanced on the edge of the shelf** les livres étaient en équilibre instable sur le bord de l'étagère

uneasy [ʌnˈiːzɪ] **ADJ** *(ill at ease)* mal à l'aise, gêné; *(worried)* inquiet, -ète; *(sleep)* agité; **an u. truce** une trêve précaire *ou* incertaine; **there was an u. silence** il y a eu un silence gêné; **to be u.** être inquiet *ou* anxieux *(about* au sujet de); **to be u. in one's mind about sth** ne pas avoir l'esprit tranquille au sujet de qch; **I've just got an u. feeling that it won't work** j'ai justement la fâcheuse impression que ça ne marchera pas

uneatable [ʌnˈiːtəb(ə)l] **ADJ** *(unpleasant to eat)* immangeable

uneaten [ʌnˈiːt(ə)n] **ADJ** non mangé; **u. food** restes *mpl*

uneconomic [ˌʌniːkəˈnɒmɪk] **ADJ** *(work)* pas rentable

uneconomical [ˌʌniːkəˈnɒmɪk(ə)l] **ADJ** *(method, car)* peu économique; **it's u. to do it that way** ce n'est pas économique de faire ça

unedifying [ʌnˈedɪfaɪɪŋ] **ADJ** peu édifiant

unedited [ʌnˈedɪtɪd] **ADJ** *(text)* qui n'a pas été rédigé définitivement, à l'état brut; *(un-*

expurgated) intégral, -aux; *Comput (text)* non édité; *(film)* non monté; *(recording)* à l'état brut

uneducated [ʌnˈedjʊketɪd] **ADJ** *(person)* sans instruction; *(speech, accent)* populaire; *(handwriting)* qui dénote un manque d'instruction

unelectable [ʌnɪˈlektəb(ə)l] **ADJ** inéligible

unemotional [ˌʌnɪˈməʊʃən(ə)l] **ADJ** *(person) (not feeling emotion)* peu émotif; *(not showing emotion)* impassible; *(reaction)* peu émotionnel; *(style)* neutre, dépourvu de passion; **he managed to stay quite u. about it** il a réussi à garder la tête froide

unemotionally [ˌʌnɪˈməʊʃən(ə)lɪ] **ADV** *(to react, look at things)* froidement

unemployable [ˌʌnɪmˈplɔɪəb(ə)l] **ADJ** **I'm 65 but does that make me u.?** j'ai 65 ans mais est-ce que je suis inapte à travailler pour autant?; **he's u.** *(because of criminal record etc)* personne n'est prêt à l'employer

unemployed [ˌʌnɪmˈplɔɪd] **ADJ** *(person)* au chômage, sans travail; **she was u. for months** elle est restée au chômage pendant des mois
 NPL the u. les chômeurs *mpl*
 ▸▸ *Fin* **u. capital** fonds *mpl* inactifs

unemployment [ˌʌnɪmˈplɔɪmənt] **N** chômage *m*
 ▸▸ *Br Formerly* **u. benefit,** *Am* **u. compensation** allocation *f* (de) chômage; **u. contribution** cotisation *f* chômage; **u. figures** chiffres *mpl* du chômage; **u. fund** caisse *f* de chômage; **u. insurance** assurance *f* chômage; **u. rate** taux *m* de chômage; **u. trap** cercle *m* vicieux du chômage

unencumbered [ˌʌnɪnˈkʌmbəd] **ADJ** non encombré (**by, with** de)
 ▸▸ *Law* **u. estate** propriété *f* franche d'hypothèques

unending [ʌnˈendɪŋ] **ADJ** *(controversy, list of complaints etc)* interminable, qui n'en finit plus; *(bliss etc)* éternel

unendorsed [ˌʌnɪnˈdɔːst] **ADJ** *Fin (cheque)* non endossé

unendurable [ˌʌnɪnˈdjʊərəb(ə)l] **ADJ** insupportable

unenforceable [ˌʌnɪnˈfɔːsəb(ə)l] **ADJ** inapplicable

un-English [ʌn-] **ADJ** peu anglais; **he's very u.** ce n'est pas du tout l'Anglais type

unenlightened [ˌʌnɪnˈlaɪt(ə)nd] **ADJ** *(people)* ignorant; **an u. age** une époque où régnait l'ignorance; **I remained completely u.** je suis resté dans l'ignorance la plus totale

unenlightening [ˌʌnɪnˈlaɪtnɪŋ] **ADJ** *(comment)* qui jette peu de lumière (sur une question)

unenterprising [ʌnˈentəpraɪzɪŋ] **ADJ** *(person)* peu entreprenant, qui manque d'initiative; *(plan)* qui manque d'audace; **that was very u. of you** vous avez vraiment manqué d'initiative, vous avez fait preuve d'une absence d'initiative totale

unenthusiastic [ˌʌnɪnθ(j)uːzɪˈæstɪk] **ADJ** peu enthousiaste; **he seems rather u. about it** ça n'a pas l'air de l'enthousiasmer

unenthusiastically [ˌʌnɪnθ(j)uːzɪˈæstɪklɪ] **ADV** sans enthousiasme

unenviable [ʌnˈenvɪəb(ə)l] **ADJ** peu enviable

unequal [ʌnˈiːkwəl] **ADJ 1** *(size, amount)* inégal, -aux; **an u. struggle** un combat inégal **2 he was u. to the task** il n'était pas à la hauteur de la tâche

unequalled [ʌnˈiːkwəld] **ADJ** inégalé

unequally [ʌnˈiːkwəlɪ] **ADV** inégalement

unequivocal [ʌnɪˈkwɪvək(ə)l] ADJ sans équivoque

unequivocally [ʌnɪˈkwɪvəklɪ] ADV sans équivoque

unerring [ʌnˈɜːrɪŋ] ADJ infaillible, sûr; **with u. aim, he hit the target** visant avec précision, il a touché la cible

unerringly [ʌnˈɜːrɪŋlɪ] ADV infailliblement

UNESCO [juːˈneskəʊ] N (abbr **United Nations Educational, Scientific and Cultural Organization**) UNESCO f

unescorted [ʌnɪˈskɔːtɪd] ADJ sans escorte

unessential [ʌnɪˈsenʃəl] ADJ non essentiel

unesthetic [ʌniːsˈθetɪk] ADJ Am = **unaesthetic**

unethical [ʌnˈeθɪk(ə)l] ADJ (behaviour) contraire à l'éthique

unethically [ʌnˈeθɪklɪ] ADV contrairement à l'éthique

uneven [ʌnˈiːv(ə)n] ADJ (not level, not regular) inégal, -aux; (terrain) accidenté; **the floorboards are u.** les lattes du plancher ne sont pas toutes au même niveau; **u. breathing** respiration f irrégulière; **u. temper** humeur f inégale

unevenly [ʌnˈiːv(ə)nlɪ] ADV inégalement; (to breathe) irrégulièrement; **the opponents were u. matched** les adversaires étaient de force inégale; **u. distributed load** charge f répartie inégalement

unevenness [ʌnˈiːv(ə)nnɪs] N inégalité f, (of breathing) irrégularité f

uneventful [ʌnɪˈventfʊl] ADJ (journey) sans incidents, calme; **u. life** vie f calme ou peu mouvementée

uneventfully [ʌnɪˈventfəlɪ] ADV **to pass u.** se passer sans incidents

unexceptionable [ʌnɪkˈsepʃənəb(ə)l] ADJ (behaviour) irréprochable; (person) tout à fait convenable

unexceptional [ʌnɪkˈsepʃ(ə)n(ə)l] ADJ ordinaire, qui n'a rien d'exceptionnel

unexchangeable [ʌnɪksˈtʃeɪndʒəb(ə)l] ADJ inéchangeable; Fin (securities) impermutable, inéchangeable

unexciting [ʌnɪkˈsaɪtɪŋ] ADJ (tale, film, job) insipide, peu passionnant; (person) terne, insipide; (life) monotone; **u. day** (uneventful) journée f calme; (boring) journée ennuyeuse; **this restaurant serves very u. food** on sert des repas très ordinaires dans ce restaurant

unexpected [ʌnɪksˈpektɪd] ADJ (visitor, result, success) inattendu; (event) imprévu; (departure) inopiné; (help, happiness) inespéré; **u. meeting** rencontre f inopinée; **it was completely u.** on ne s'y attendait pas du tout; **this is all so u.!** tout est si inattendu! N **the u.** l'imprévu m

unexpectedly [ʌnɪksˈpektɪdlɪ] ADV de manière inattendue; **to arrive u.** arriver à l'improviste; **they won u.** on ne s'attendait pas à ce qu'ils gagnent; **he died u.** il est mort subitement

unexpired [ʌnɪksˈpaɪəd] ADJ (lease) non expiré; (passport, ticket) non périmé, encore valable

unexplained [ʌnɪksˈpleɪnd] ADJ inexpliqué

unexploded [ʌnɪksˈpləʊdɪd] ADJ (bomb) qui n'a pas explosé

unexploited [ʌnɪksˈplɔɪtɪd] ADJ inexploité

unexplored [ʌnɪksˈplɔːd] ADJ (country etc) inexploré

unexposed [ʌnɪksˈpəʊzd] ADJ 1 Phot (film) vierge 2 (criminal) non démasqué 3 **u. to the influences of the outside world ...** qui n'est pas en contact avec le monde extérieur ...; **u. to the influence of TV** qui n'est pas soumis à l'influence de la télévision

unexpressed [ʌnɪksˈprest] ADJ inexprimé

unexpurgated [ʌnˈekspɜːgeɪtɪd] ADJ (book, text) non expurgé; **u. edition** édition f intégrale

unfading [ʌnˈfeɪdɪŋ] ADJ (memory) ineffaçable, impérissable; (hope, love) impérissable

unfailing [ʌnˈfeɪlɪŋ] ADJ 1 (loyalty) à toute épreuve; (means, remedy) infaillible; (zeal) infatigable; (memory) sans défaillance; (kindness) inaltérable; (hope, courage) inébranlable; **to be u. in one's duty** ne jamais faillir à son devoir; **to have an u. ability to do sth** avoir le don de faire qch 2 (supply etc) inépuisable

unfailingly [ʌnˈfeɪlɪŋlɪ] ADV infailliblement, immanquablement

unfair [ʌnˈfeər] ADJ injuste (to sb envers qn); (deal, arrangement) peu équitable; **to be u. to sb** (of situation) défavoriser qn; **it's u.!** ce n'est pas juste!; **to have an u. advantage over everybody else** être injustement avantagé par rapport à tous les autres; **he has been put at an u. disadvantage** il a été désavantagé
▸▸Com **u. competition** concurrence f déloyale; Ind **u. dismissal** licenciement m abusif

unfairly [ʌnˈfeəlɪ] ADV injustement, peu équitablement; (to play) déloyalement; **to be u. dismissed** être victime d'un licenciement abusif; **to act u.** se montrer injuste

unfairness [ʌnˈfeənɪs] N injustice f

unfaithful [ʌnˈfeɪθfʊl] ADJ 1 **to be u. to** (one's wife, husband) tromper, être infidèle à 2 (report) inexact, infidèle

unfaithfully [ʌnˈfeɪθfəlɪ] ADV (to betray, desert) de façon déloyale; **to act u. towards one's wife** se comporter de manière infidèle envers sa femme; **to report sth u.** faire un compte-rendu peu fidèle de qch

unfaithfulness [ʌnˈfeɪθfʊlnɪs] N infidélité f

unfaltering [ʌnˈfɔːltərɪŋ] ADJ sans défaillance; **u. steps** pas mpl assurés; **u. voice** voix f ferme

unfalteringly [ʌnˈfɔːltərɪŋlɪ] ADV sans faillir; (to speak) d'une voix ferme; (to walk) d'un pas bien assuré

unfamiliar [ʌnfəˈmɪliər] ADJ peu familier, peu connu; **to be u. with sth** ne pas connaître ou mal connaître qch, ne pas être au fait de qch; **I'm totally u. with this town** je ne connais pas du tout cette ville; **he is quite u. with this subject** il ne sait absolument rien sur ce sujet; **u. face** visage m inconnu; **the u. sounds of the language** les sonorités étranges de cette langue

unfamiliarity [ʌnfəmɪlɪˈærɪtɪ] N 1 (of place) aspect m étrange 2 (lack of knowledge) ignorance f (with de); **because of my u. with the city/terrain** parce que je ne connaissais pas très bien la ville/le terrain

unfashionable [ʌnˈfæʃənəb(ə)l] ADJ (clothes) démodé, passé de mode; (restaurant, author) qui n'est pas ou plus à la mode; (ideas) démodé

unfashionably [ʌnˈfæʃ(ə)nəblɪ] ADV (to dress etc) sans se préoccuper de la mode

unfasten [ʌnˈfɑːs(ə)n] VT (garment, bracelet) défaire, dégrafer; (safety belt) défaire, détacher; (tie, knot) défaire; (door) ouvrir, déverrouiller; **to come unfastened** (of garment) se dégrafer; (unbuttoned) se déboutonner; (of knot) se défaire, se dénouer; (of belt) se détacher; **to u. sth from sth** détacher qch de qch
VI se détacher; (of dress etc) se dégrafer

unfathomable [ʌnˈfæðəməb(ə)l] ADJ (abyss, mystery) insondable

unfathomed [ʌnˈfæðəmd] ADJ (abyss, mystery) insondé; **u. depths** profondeurs fpl inexplorées

unfavourable, Am unfavorable [ʌnˈfeɪv(ə)rəb(ə)l] ADJ défavorable, peu favorable (to à); (moment) peu propice, inopportun; (wind) contraire; (review) mauvais; (weather, report) défavorable; **to appear in an u. light** se montrer sous un jour défavorable

unfavourably, Am unfavorably [ʌnˈfeɪv(ə)rəblɪ] ADV défavorablement; **to be u. disposed towards sb/sth** être mal disposé envers qn/qch; **his work compares u. with his brother's** son travail supporte mal la comparaison avec celui de son frère

unfazed [ʌnˈfeɪzd] ADJ pas du tout impressionné

unfeeling [ʌnˈfiːlɪŋ] ADJ (person) insensible, dur

unfeelingly [ʌnˈfiːlɪŋlɪ] ADV (to act) sans pitié, impitoyablement; (to answer) durement, avec dureté

unfeigned [ʌnˈfeɪnd] ADJ non simulé, sincère

unfeignedly [ʌnˈfeɪnɪdlɪ] ADV sans simulation, sincèrement

unfeminine [ʌnˈfemɪnɪn] ADJ peu féminin

unfenced [ʌnˈfenst] ADJ (land etc) sans clôture

unfermented [ʌnfəˈmentɪd] ADJ non fermenté

unfertilized [ʌnˈfɜːtɪlaɪzd] ADJ (egg) non fécondé

unfettered [ʌnˈfetəd] ADJ sans entrave(s); (emotion) non refoulé

unfilial [ʌnˈfɪlɪəl] ADJ peu filial, -aux

unfinished [ʌnˈfɪnɪʃt] ADJ 1 (task, painting etc) inachevé; **to leave sth u.** laisser qch inachevé; **u. game** partie f interrompue; **to have some u. business** avoir quelques affaires à régler; (esp menacing) avoir des comptes à régler 2 Ind (article) semi-fini

unfit [ʌnˈfɪt] ADJ 1 (inappropriate) impropre, peu propre (for à); **u. for human consumption** impropre à la consommation; **u. to eat** non comestible; **u. to drink** (unpleasant) imbuvable; (harmful) non potable; **u. for publication** impubliable; **this house is u. for habitation** cette maison est inhabitable 2 (person) (not suitable) **u. for military service** inapte au service militaire; Mil **to be discharged as u.** être réformé; **she's u. for this type of job** elle n'est pas faite pour ce genre de travail; **to be u. to govern** ne pas être en état de gouverner 3 (physically) **to be u.** ne pas être en forme; **he's u. to travel** il n'est pas en état de voyager; **he is u. for duty** il n'est pas en état d'assurer ses fonctions

unfitness [ʌnˈfɪtnɪs] N 1 (unsuitability) **u. for sth/to do sth** inaptitude f à qch/à faire qch 2 (lack of fitness) mauvaise forme f

unfitted [ʌnˈfɪtɪd] ADJ **to be u. for sth** (of equipment) ne pas être adapté à qch; (of person) ne pas convenir à qch; (morally) être indigne de qch

unfitting [ʌnˈfɪtɪŋ] ADJ peu convenable; (remark) mal à propos, déplacé

unfittingly [ʌnˈfɪtɪŋlɪ] ADV (to behave etc) de manière peu convenable

unfix [ʌnˈfɪks] VT Mil **to u. bayonets** remettre la baïonnette

unflagging [ʌnˈflægɪŋ] ADJ (interest) soutenu; (vigour) inlassable; (optimism, courage) inébranlable

unflaggingly [ʌnˈflægɪŋlɪ] ADV inlassablement, infatigablement

unflappability [ʌnflæpəˈbɪlɪtɪ] N Fam imperturbabilité f

unflappable [ʌnˈflæpəb(ə)l] ADJ Fam imperturbable; **he is completely u.** il garde toujours son calme

unflattering [ʌnˈflætərɪŋ] ADJ peu flatteur (**to** pour); **her hat was most u.** son chapeau était loin de la mettre en valeur; **it shows him in an u. light** ça le montre sous un jour défavorable; **he was rather u. about your playing** il ne s'est pas montré très flatteur quant à votre jeu

unflatteringly [ʌnˈflætərɪŋlɪ] ADV d'une manière peu flatteuse

unfledged [ʌnˈfledʒd] ADJ **1** (*bird*) sans plumes **2** (*person*) sans expérience

unflinching [ʌnˈflɪnʃɪŋ] ADJ (*person*) qui ne bronche pas; (*resolute*) résolu; (*resolve, courage*) inébranlable

unflinchingly [ʌnˈflɪnʃɪŋlɪ] ADV sans broncher; (*resolutely*) résolument; **u. loyal** d'une loyauté à toute épreuve

unfold [ʌnˈfəʊld] VT **1** (*newspaper, serviette*) déplier; (*map*) déployer, déplier; **to u. one's arms** décroiser les bras **2** (*reveal*) (*one's intentions, plan*) révéler, exposer; (*one's plans, secret*) dévoiler
VI se déployer, se dérouler; (*of flower*) s'ouvrir, s'épanouir; (*of story, action*) se dérouler

unforced [ʌnˈfɔːst] ADJ qui n'est pas forcé, spontané; **u. laugh** rire *m* franc
▸ ▸ *Sport* **u. error** faute *f* directe

unforeseeable [ʌnfɔːˈsiːəb(ə)l] ADJ imprévisible

unforeseen [ʌnfɔːˈsiːn] ADJ imprévu, inattendu; **unless something u. happens** sauf imprévu
▸ ▸ **u. circumstances** imprévus *mpl*; *Law* force *f* majeure; **u. expenses** dépenses *fpl* non prévues au budget

unforgettable [ʌnfəˈgetəb(ə)l] ADJ inoubliable

unforgivable [ʌnfəˈgɪvəb(ə)l] ADJ impardonnable, inexcusable; **it's u. of me** je suis impardonnable

unforgivably [ʌnfəˈgɪvəblɪ] ADV **he was u. rude** il s'est montré d'une impolitesse impardonnable

unforgiven [ʌnfəˈgɪv(ə)n] ADJ impardonné

unforgiving [ʌnfəˈgɪvɪŋ] ADJ implacable, impitoyable

unforgotten [ʌnfəˈgɒt(ə)n] ADJ inoublié

unformatted [ʌnˈfɔːmætɪd] ADJ (*text*) non mis en forme; *Comput* (*disk*) non formaté;
▸ ▸ *Comput* **u. capacity** (*of disk*) capacité *f* brute

unformed [ʌnˈfɔːmd] ADJ (*bone*) qui n'est pas (encore) formé; (*mind*) inculte; (*idea*) en gestation

unformulated [ʌnˈfɔːmjʊleɪtɪd] ADJ informulé

unforthcoming [ʌnfɔːˈθkʌmɪŋ] ADJ réservé; **to be u. about sth** être *ou* se montrer réticent au sujet de qch

unfortified [ʌnˈfɔːtɪfaɪd] ADJ non fortifié, sans fortifications

unfortunate [ʌnˈfɔːtjənɪt] ADJ **1** (*unlucky*) malchanceux; **he's been most u.** il n'a vraiment pas eu de chance; **the u. people whose houses were flooded** les malheureux dont les maisons ont été inondées **2** (*accident, event*) malheureux, malencontreux; (*mistake*) regrettable; **an u. state of affairs** une situation regrettable *ou* fâcheuse; **u. choice of words** choix de mots peu heureux; **in u. circumstances** dans des circonstances regrettables; **u. consequences** conséquences *fpl* regrettables; **it's u. that she has to leave today** il est dommage qu'elle soit obligée de partir aujourd'hui; **how u.!** quel dommage!
N malheureux, -euse; **the u.** les infortunés

mpl; **a poor u.** un pauvre malheureux, une pauvre malheureuse

unfortunately [ʌnˈfɔːtjənɪtlɪ] ADV malheureusement; **an u. worded statement** une déclaration formulée d'une façon regrettable; **u. for him** malheureusement pour lui

unfounded [ʌnˈfaʊndɪd] ADJ sans fondement; **u. criticism** critique *f* injustifiée; **u. rumour** bruit *m* dénué de tout fondement

unframed [ʌnˈfreɪmd] ADJ sans cadre

unfreeze [ʌnˈfriːz] (*pt* **unfroze** [ʌnˈfrəʊz]; *pp* **unfrozen** [ʌnˈfrəʊz(ə)n]) VT (*de-ice*) dégeler; *Fin* (*credit*) dégeler, débloquer
VI dégeler

unfreezing [ʌnˈfriːzɪŋ] N (*de-icing*) dégel *m*; *Fin* (*of credit*) dégel, déblocage *m*

unfrequented [ʌnfrɪˈkwentɪd] ADJ peu fréquenté

unfriendliness [ʌnˈfrendlɪnɪs] N froideur *f* (**towards** envers, à l'égard de)

unfriendly [ʌnˈfrendlɪ] ADJ (*person*) peu sympathique; (*tone, feeling*) peu amical, -aux, inamical, -aux; **to be u. to(wards) sb** traiter qn avec froideur; **environmentally u.** nuisible à l'environnement; **u. reception** accueil *m* froid; **written in an u. style** écrit dans un style rébarbatif
▸ ▸ *Mil* **u. action** action *f* hostile

unfrock [ʌnˈfrɒk] VT (*priest etc*) défroquer

unfrozen [ʌnˈfrəʊz(ə)n] ADJ *Fin* (*credit*) dégelé, débloqué

unfruitful [ʌnˈfruːtfʊl] ADJ infructueux, vain

unfulfilled [ʌnfʊlˈfɪld] ADJ (*duty*) inaccompli; (*promise*) non tenu; (*desire*) non satisfait, inassouvi; (*ambition*) non réalisé; (*prayer*) inexaucé; **to feel u.** éprouver un sentiment d'insatisfaction

unfunded [ʌnˈfʌndɪd] ADJ sans subvention
▸ ▸ *Fin* **u. debt** dette *f* flottante *ou* non consolidée

unfunny [ʌnˈfʌnɪ] ADJ qui n'est pas drôle; **I find that distinctly u.** je ne trouve pas ça drôle du tout

unfurl [ʌnˈfɜːl] VT (*sail, flag*) déployer; (*umbrella*) ouvrir
VI se déployer

unfurnished [ʌnˈfɜːnɪʃt] ADJ non meublé

ungainliness [ʌnˈgeɪnlɪnɪs] N gaucherie *f*

ungainly [ʌnˈgeɪnlɪ] ADJ gauche

ungallant [ʌnˈgælənt] ADJ peu galant, discourtois

ungeared [ʌnˈgɪəd] ADJ *Fin* sans endettement
▸ ▸ **u. balance sheet** bilan *m* sans emprunts *ou* à faible endettement

ungenerous [ʌnˈdʒen(ə)rəs] ADJ peu généreux; (*remark*) malveillant; **that was rather u. of you** ce n'était pas très généreux de ta part

ungentlemanly [ʌnˈdʒent(ə)lmənlɪ] ADJ peu galant, discourtois; **u. behaviour** manque *m* de savoir-vivre; *Sport* **u. conduct** manque de courtoisie

ungetatable [ʌngetˈætəb(ə)l] ADJ *Fam* inaccessible

ungird [ʌnˈgɜːd] VT (*pt, pp* **ungirt** [ʌnˈgɜːt]) (*sword*) détacher

unglazed [ʌnˈgleɪzd] ADJ **1** (*window*) sans vitres **2** (*paper*) mat, non glacé **3** *Cer* non verni, non émaillé; (*brick*) non vitrifié
▸ ▸ *Cer* **u. porcelain** biscuit *m*; *Phot* **u. print** épreuve *f* mate

ungodliness [ʌnˈgɒdlɪnɪs] N impiété *f*

ungodly [ʌnˈgɒdlɪ] ADJ **1** impie, irréligieux **2** *Fam* **an u. row** un bruit de tous les diables; **he got up at an u. hour** il s'est levé à une heure impossible *ou* indue

ungovernable [ʌnˈgʌv(ə)nəb(ə)l] ADJ **1** (*people, country*) ingouvernable **2** (*desire, passion*) irrésistible; **he has u. fits of temper** il a des accès de colère incontrôlables

ungraceful [ʌnˈgreɪsfʊl] ADJ sans grâce, gauche

ungracefully [ʌnˈgreɪsfəlɪ] ADV sans grâce, gauchement

ungracious [ʌnˈgreɪʃəs] ADJ peu élégant; **it would be u. of me to refuse** j'aurais mauvaise grâce à refuser

ungraciously [ʌnˈgreɪʃəslɪ] ADV (*to refuse*) de manière peu élégante; (*to accept*) de mauvaise grâce

ungraciousness [ʌnˈgreɪʃəsnɪs] N mauvaise grâce *f*

ungrammatical [ʌngrəˈmætɪk(ə)l] ADJ (*grammaticalement*) incorrect

ungrammatically [ʌngrəˈmætɪklɪ] ADV incorrectement

ungrateful [ʌnˈgreɪtfʊl] ADJ (*person, response*) ingrat; (*task*) ingrat; **to be u. to sb** être peu reconnaissant envers qn (**for sth** de qch), se montrer ingrat envers qn (**for sth** à propos de qch); **don't be so u.!** ne sois pas si ingrat!

ungratefully [ʌnˈgreɪtfəlɪ] ADV avec ingratitude

ungratefulness [ʌnˈgreɪtfʊlnɪs] N ingratitude *f*

ungratified [ʌnˈgrætɪfaɪd] ADJ (*desire*) inassouvi

ungrudging [ʌnˈgrʌdʒɪŋ] ADJ (*assistance*) donné de bon cœur; (*admiration*) (très) sincère

ungrudgingly [ʌnˈgrʌdʒɪŋlɪ] ADV de bon cœur, généreusement

unguarded [ʌnˈgɑːdɪd] ADJ **1** (*not watched over*) non gardé; (*prisoner etc*) sans surveillance; (*town*) sans défense; *Sport* **to leave the goal u.** laisser le but vide **2** (*remark*) inconsidéré, irréfléchi; **in an u. moment** dans un moment d'inattention **3** (*mechanism*) sans dispositif protecteur; (*fire*) sans garde-feu

unguent [ˈʌŋgwənt] N onguent *m*

ungulate [ˈʌŋgjʊleɪt] ADJ, N *Zool* ongulé *m*

unhallowed [ʌnˈhæləʊd] ADJ non béni, non consacré

unhampered [ʌnˈhæmpəd] ADJ non entravé (**by** par); (*in one's movements*) libre; **u. by regulations** sans être gêné par la réglementation

unhand [ʌnˈhænd] VT *Arch, Hum* lâcher; **u. me!** lâchez-moi!

unhappily [ʌnˈhæpɪlɪ] ADV **1** (*unfortunately*) malheureusement; **u. worded** rédigé de manière malheureuse *ou* maladroite **2** (*sadly, miserably*) tristement, d'un air triste; **to live u.** ne pas être heureux; **they're u. married** ils ne sont pas heureux en ménage

unhappiness [ʌnˈhæpɪnɪs] N chagrin *m*, tristesse *f*; **the u. of her childhood** son enfance malheureuse

unhappy [ʌnˈhæpɪ] ADJ **1** (*sad*) malheureux, triste; **to make sb u.** causer du chagrin à qn; (*esp intentionally*) rendre qn malheureux; **to be u. at leaving sb** être triste de quitter qn **2** (*worried*) inquiet, -ète; **I'm u. about leaving the house empty** ça m'inquiète de laisser la maison vide **3** (*not pleased*) pas satisfait; **to be u. with sb/sth** être mécontent de qn/qch; **we're u. with the quality** nous ne sommes pas satisfaits de la qualité **4** (*remark*) malheureux, malencontreux; **an u. state of affairs** une situation regrettable

unharmed [ʌnˈhɑːmd] ADJ (*person*) sain et sauf, *f* saine et sauve, indemne; (*thing*) intact, non endommagé; **to escape u.** s'en sortir indemne

unharness [ʌn'hɑːnɪs] **VT** *(horse)* dételer

UNHCR [juːeneɪtʃsiːˈɑːr] **N** *(abbr* **United Nations High Commission for Refugees)** HCR *m*

unhealthiness [ʌn'helθɪnɪs] **N** *(of person)* mauvaise santé *f*, *(of air, place)* insalubrité *f*, *(of influence, relationship)* caractère *m* malsain

unhealthy [ʌn'helθɪ] **ADJ** *(person)* maladif; *(state of mind, influence, relationship)* malsain; *(air, place)* malsain, insalubre; **to have an u. fascination with death** avoir une fascination morbide pour la mort; **the car's sounding rather u.** la voiture fait un drôle de bruit; **u. curiosity** curiosité *f* morbide; *Fam* **it can be u. to ask too many questions** *(dangerous)* il peut être dangereux de poser trop de questions

unheard [ʌn'hɜːd] **ADJ their screams went u.** personne n'a entendu leurs cris; **the opinions of the immigrant population go u.** personne ne tient compte des opinions des immigrés; **to condemn sb u.** condamner qn sans l'avoir entendu

unheard-of ADJ 1 *(incredible)* inouï; **that's u.!** c'est vraiment incroyable! **2** *(unknown)* inconnu; **it was u. in my day** de mon temps ça n'existait pas

unheated [ʌn'hiːtɪd] **ADJ** non chauffé

unheeded [ʌn'hiːdɪd] **ADJ his warning/advice went u.** on n'a pas tenu compte de son avertissement/ses conseils

unheeding [ʌn'hiːdɪŋ] **ADJ to be u. of sb's advice** ne pas écouter les conseils de qn, ne pas tenir compte des conseils de qn

unhelpful [ʌn'helpfʊl] **ADJ** *(person)* peu serviable; *(criticism, advice)* peu utile; **that's rather u. of them** ce n'est pas très serviable de leur part; **don't be so u.!** tâche donc un peu de nous/*m*/*etc* aider!

unhelpfully [ʌn'helpfəlɪ] **ADV** de façon peu serviable; **she u. suggested that I go and see a clairvoyant** elle n'a rien trouvé de mieux que de me conseiller d'aller voir un voyant; **someone very u. left the disk on a radiator** quelqu'un de très négligent a laissé la disquette sur un radiateur

unheralded [ʌn'herəldɪd] **ADJ** *esp Lit* qui n'est pas annoncé; *(unexpected)* imprévu, inattendu

unhesitating [ʌn'hezɪteɪtɪŋ] **ADJ** *(person)* qui n'hésite pas; **u. reply** réponse *f* immédiate *ou* prompte; **my u. reaction** ma réaction immédiate; **you can count on our u. support** vous pouvez compter sur notre soutien sans faille

unhesitatingly [ʌn'hezɪteɪtɪŋlɪ] **ADV** sans hésiter, sans hésitation

unhindered [ʌn'hɪndəd] **ADJ** sans obstacle; *(not disturbed)* sans être dérangé (**by** par); **to go u.** passer librement; **u. by all that luggage** sans être encombré par tous ces bagages; **u. by petty regulations** sans être gêné par des règlements tatillons; **u. by any moral scruples** nullement encombré de scrupules

unhinge [ʌn'hɪndʒ] **VT** *(door etc)* enlever de ses gonds; *(sb's mind)* déranger, détraquer

unhinged [ʌn'hɪndʒd] **ADJ** *(person)* dérangé

unhip [ʌn'hɪp] **ADJ** *Fam* ringard

unhitch [ʌn'hɪtʃ] **VT** détacher, décrocher; *(horse)* dételer

unholy [ʌn'həʊlɪ] **ADJ 1** *Rel (place etc)* profane; **u. thoughts** des pensées *fpl* coupables **2** *Fam (mess, mix-up etc)* épouvantable, affreux; **there was an u. row** il y a eu une dispute épouvantable

unhook [ʌn'hʊk] **VT** *(picture)* décrocher; *(trailer)* décrocher, dételer; *(garment)* dégrafer; **to come unhooked** *(of dress)* se dégrafer

VT *(picture)* se décrocher; *(dress)* se dégrafer

unhoped-for [ʌn'həʊpt-] **ADJ** inespéré

unhorse [ʌn'hɔːs] **VT** désarçonner

unhurried [ʌn'hʌrɪd] **ADJ** *(manner)* posé; **she gave an u. reply** elle a pris son temps pour répondre; **in an u. way** sans se presser

unhurt [ʌn'hɜːt] **ADJ** *(person)* indemne, sain et sauf, *f* saine et sauve; **to escape u.** sortir indemne *ou* sain et sauf

unhygienic [ʌnhaɪ'dʒiːnɪk] **ADJ** non hygiénique; **it's u. to ...** il est peu hygiénique de ..., ... est contraire à l'hygiène

uni ['juːnɪ] **N** *Fam* **1** *Br (abbr* **university)** fac *f*; **he's doing law at u.** il fait une fac de droit **2** *Am (abbr* **uniform)** uniforme *m*

UNICEF ['juːnɪsef] **N** *(abbr* **United Nations International Children's Emergency Fund)** UNICEF *m*, FISE *m*

unicellular [juːnɪ'seljʊlər] **ADJ** *Biol* unicellulaire

unicorn ['juːnɪkɔːn] **N** *Myth* licorne *f*

unicycle ['juːnɪsaɪk(ə)l] **N** monocycle *m*

unidentifiable [ʌnaɪ'dentɪfaɪəb(ə)l] **ADJ** non identifiable

unidentified [ʌnaɪ'dentɪfaɪd] **ADJ** non identifié

▸▸ **u. flying object** objet *m* volant non identifié

unidirectional [juːnɪd(a)ɪ'rekʃən(ə)l] **ADJ** *Phys etc* unidirectionnel

UNIDO [juː'niːdəʊ] **N** *(abbr* **United Nations Industrial Development Organization)** UNIDO *f*

unification [juːnɪfɪ'keɪʃən] **N** unification *f*

uniform ['juːnɪfɔːm] **ADJ** *(colour, style)* uniforme; *(temperature)* constant; **these boxes are all of u. size** ces boîtes sont toutes de la même grandeur; **to make sth u.** uniformiser qch

N uniforme *m*; **in u.** en uniforme, en tenue; **out of u.** *Mil etc* en civil; *(air hostess etc)* sans son uniforme

▸▸ *Acct* **u. accounting** comptabilité *f* uniforme; *Com* **u. business rate** = taxe *f* assise sur la valeur des locaux commerciaux, ≃ taxe professionnelle; **u. rate** taux *m* uniforme

uniformed ['juːnɪfɔːmd] **ADJ** en uniforme, en tenue; **the u. branch** = la police en uniforme

uniformity [juːnɪ'fɔːmɪtɪ] **N** *(of style)* uniformité *f*, *(of current)* constance *f*

uniformly ['juːnɪfɔːmlɪ] **ADV** uniformément

unify ['juːnɪfaɪ] **VT** unifier

VI s'unifier

unifying ['juːnɪfaɪɪŋ] **ADJ** unificateur, -trice

unilateral [juːnɪ'lætərəl] **ADJ** unilatéral

▸▸ **u. disarmament** désarmement *m* unilatéral

unilaterally [juːnɪ'lætərəlɪ] **ADV** unilatéralement

unilingual [juːnɪ'lɪŋgwəl] **ADJ** unilingue

unimaginable [ʌnɪ'mædʒɪnəb(ə)l] **ADJ** inimaginable, inconcevable

unimaginably [ʌnɪ'mædʒɪnəblɪ] **ADJ** incroyablement

unimaginative [ʌnɪ'mædʒɪnətɪv] **ADJ** *(person)* qui manque d'imagination, peu imaginatif; *(cooking, solution, use of colours)* peu original, -aux; **they're very u. about their holidays** ils ne font preuve d'aucune imagination pour ce qui est de partir en vacances; **you're so u.** vous n'avez aucune imagination!

unimaginatively [ʌnɪ'mædʒɪnətɪvlɪ] **ADV** sans imagination, d'une manière peu imaginative

unimaginativeness [ʌnɪ'mædʒɪnətɪvnɪs] **N** manque *m* d'imagination

unimpaired [ʌnɪm'peəd] **ADJ** *(health, hearing, force, quality)* intact; **his mind is u.** il conserve toute sa vigueur d'esprit

unimpeachable [ʌnɪm'piːtʃəb(ə)l] **ADJ** *(reputation)* inattaquable; *(evidence, witness)* irrécusable; *(conduct)* irréprochable; **of u. character** d'un caractère irréprochable; **I have it from an u. source** je le tiens de source sûre

unimpeded [ʌnɪm'piːdɪd] **ADJ** sans entrave; **u. by ...** sans être entravé par ...

unimportant [ʌnɪm'pɔːtənt] **ADJ** sans importance; **it's quite u.** cela n'a pas la moindre importance; **it's u. what they think** leur opinion ne compte pas *ou* est sans importance

unimposing [ʌnɪm'pəʊzɪŋ] **ADJ** *(air, aspect)* peu imposant, peu impressionnant

unimpressed [ʌnɪm'prest] **ADJ** qui n'est pas impressionné, peu impressionné (**by** par); **I was u. by his speech** je n'ai pas été impressionné par son discours; **his colleagues were u. by his explanation** ses collègues n'ont pas été convaincus par son explication

unimpressive [ʌnɪm'presɪv] **ADJ** peu impressionnant; *(speech)* peu convaincant; **the countryside of the region is u.** la campagne de cette région n'a rien d'extraordinaire

uninflammable [ʌnɪn'flæməb(ə)l] **ADJ** ininflammable

uninfluential [ʌnɪnflʊ'enʃəl] **ADJ** sans influence

uninformed [ʌnɪn'fɔːmd] **ADJ** mal informé, mal renseigné (**about** sur); *(ignorant)* ignorant; *(mind)* inculte

uninhabitable [ʌnɪn'hæbɪtəb(ə)l] **ADJ** inhabitable

uninhabited [ʌnɪn'hæbɪtɪd] **ADJ** inhabité

uninhibited [ʌnɪn'hɪbɪtɪd] **ADJ** *(person)* sans inhibitions, qui n'a pas d'inhibitions; *(emotion etc)* non refréné; **she's so u.** elle est si naturelle

uninitialized [ʌnɪ'nɪʃəlaɪzd] **ADJ** *Comput* non initialisé

uninitiated [ʌnɪ'nɪʃɪeɪtɪd] **ADJ** non initié (**in** à)

NPL the u. les profanes *mpl*, les non-initiés *mpl*

uninjured [ʌn'ɪndʒəd] **ADJ** indemne; **he was shaken but u. by the accident** il a été secoué par l'accident mais n'a pas été blessé

uninspired [ʌnɪn'spaɪəd] **ADJ** *(person)* qui manque d'inspiration; *(architecture, suggestion, style)* banal, -als; **an u. performance** un spectacle peu passionnant

uninspiring [ʌn'ɪnspaɪrɪŋ] **ADJ** peu passionnant; **I find the prospect u.** l'idée ne m'inspire pas

uninstall [ʌnɪn'stɔːl] **VT** *Comput* désinstaller, supprimer

uninsured [ʌnɪn'ʃʊəd] **ADJ** non assuré (**against** contre)

unintelligent [ʌnɪn'telɪdʒənt] **ADJ** inintelligent

unintelligible [ʌnɪn'telɪdʒɪb(ə)l] **ADJ** inintelligible

unintelligibly [ʌnɪn'telɪdʒɪblɪ] **ADV** inintelligiblement

unintended [ʌnɪn'tendɪd] **ADJ** involontaire, non intentionnel; *(result)* inattendu; **the pun was quite u.** le calembour était tout à fait involontaire

unintentional [ʌnɪn'tenʃən(ə)l] **ADJ** involontaire, non intentionnel; **it was quite u.** ce n'était pas fait exprès

unintentionally [ʌnɪn'tenʃ(ə)nəlɪ] ADV involontairement; *(to annoy sb)* sans le vouloir; **he did it quite u.** il ne l'a pas fait exprès

uninterested [ʌn'ɪnt(ə)restɪd] ADJ indifférent *(in à);* **he was u. in what I was saying** il n'était pas intéressé par ce que je disais, ce que je disais ne l'intéressait pas

> Attention: ne pas confondre avec l'adjectif **disinterested**.

uninteresting [ʌn'ɪnt(ə)restɪŋ] ADJ inintéressant, sans intérêt

uninterrupted [ʌnɪntə'rʌptɪd] ADJ ininterrompu, sans interruption; **u. correspondence** correspondance suivie

uninterruptedly [ʌnɪntə'rʌptɪdlɪ] ADV sans interruption

uninvited [ʌnɪn'vaɪtɪd] ADJ *(intruder)* intrus, -use; **u. guest** visiteur, -euse inattendu(e); **to come u.** venir sans invitation; **to do sth u.** faire qch sans y avoir été invité

uninviting [ʌnɪn'vaɪtɪŋ] ADJ peu attirant, peu attrayant; *(food)* peu appétissant

union ['ju:njən] N **1** *(joining, being joined)* union *f* (**with** avec); *esp Fml (marriage)* union *f, Fig* **a u. of French and British skills** un mariage entre le savoir-faire français et britannique

2 *(harmony)* **in perfect u.** *(to live together)* en parfaite harmonie

3 the (American) U. les États-Unis *mpl,* l'Union *f* (américaine); **customs u.** union douanière

4 *(trade union)* syndicat *m* (ouvrier); **to join a u.** se syndiquer; **to form a u.** créer un syndicat; **non-u. workers** ouvriers, -ières non syndiqué(e)s; **unions and management** les syndicats et la direction, les partenaires sociaux; **increasing/decreasing u. membership** syndicalisation *f* croissante/décroissante

▸▸*Fam* **u. bashing** critiques *fpl* constantes des syndicats; **u. branch section** *f* syndicale d'entreprise; **u. card** carte *f* syndicale; **u. demands** revendications *fpl* syndicales; **the U. Jack** l'Union Jack *m (drapeau officiel du Royaume-Uni);* **u. leader** responsable *m ou* dirigeant *m* syndical; **u. meeting** réunion *f* syndicale; **u. member** *(in general)* membre *m* d'un syndicat, syndiqué, -ée; *(of particular union)* membre du syndicat, syndiqué, -ée; **u. movement** mouvement *m* syndical; *Tech* **u. nut** écrou *m* de raccord; **u. regulations** règles *fpl* syndicales; **u. representative** délégué, -ée *ou* représentant, -ante syndical(e); *Am* **u. shop** atelier *m* d'ouvriers syndiqués, union shop *m; Am* **u. suit** combinaison *f*

unionism ['ju:njənɪz(ə)m] N **1** *Ind* syndicalisme *m* (ouvrier) **2** *Pol* unionisme *m*

unionist ['ju:njənɪst] N **1** *Ind* syndicaliste *mf* **2** *Pol* unioniste *mf;* **the U. party** le parti unioniste

unionize ['ju:njənaɪz] VT *(workers)* syndiquer

uniparous [ju:'nɪpərəs] ADJ *Biol* unipare

unique [ju:'ni:k] ADJ **1** *(sole)* unique; **the sport is u. to this region** ce sport se joue exclusivement dans cette région, ce sport n'existe que dans cette région; **to be u. in doing sth** être le seul à faire qch; **you're not u.** ton cas n'est pas unique, tu n'es pas le seul **2** *(exceptional) (offer, price)* exceptionnel; *(opportunity)* unique, exceptionnel

▸▸*Mktg* **u. proposition** proposition *f* unique; *Mktg* **u. selling point, u. selling proposition** proposition unique de vente

uniquely [ju:'ni:klɪ] ADV **1** *(to correspond)* exclusivement **2** *(extremely) (suited, gifted)*

exceptionnellement; **he is u. placed to get this information** il est exceptionnellement bien placé pour obtenir ce renseignement

uniqueness [ju:'ni:knɪs] N **1** caractère *m* unique; **that's his u. as an actor** c'est ce qui en fait un acteur à part **2** *(exceptional nature) (of offer, price)* caractère *m* exceptionnel

unisex ['ju:nɪseks] ADJ *(hairdresser's, clothing)* unisexe

unison ['ju:nɪs(ə)n] N *Mus, Fig* unisson *m;* **in u.** à l'unisson (**with** de); **they all replied in u.** ils ont tous répondu en même temps; **to act in u.** agir à l'unisson

unissued [ʌn'ɪʃu:d] ADJ *St Exch (shares, share capital)* non encore émis

unit ['ju:nɪt] N **1** *(measure)* unité *f, Math* **units and tens** unités et dizaines; *Com, Ind* **each box contains a hundred units** chaque boîte contient cent unités; *Tech* **u. of energy/of work** unité d'énergie/de travail; **u. of velocity** unité de vitesse; *Phys* **u. of mass** unité de masse; *Fin* **monetary u.** unité monétaire; **standard u.** module *m;* **thermal u.** unité thermique

2 *Admin (division)* division *f*

3 *(section, department) (in hospital)* service *m; (in school, university, company)* groupe *m,* section *f, Cin, TV (team)* équipe *f, Med* **intensive care u.** centre *m* de soins intensifs; **X-ray u.** service de radiologie

4 *Mil (group)* unité *f,* **(fighting) u.,** *Am* **(combat) u.** unité de combat; **air force u.** unité *ou* groupe *m* de l'armée de l'air

5 *Tech (element)* unité *f,* élément *m;* **the engine forms a u. with the transmission** le moteur fait bloc avec la transmission; *Comput* **central processing u.** unité centrale; **input/ output u.** élément *ou* dispositif *m* (d')entrée-sortie; **(visual) display u.** console *f* de visualisation, visuel *m;* **(kitchen) u.** élément (de cuisine), placard *m;* **the knives are in the u. there** les couteaux sont dans ce placard

6 *Austr (apartment)* appartement *m*

▸▸*Fin* **u. of account** unité *f* de compte; *Tel* **u. charge** taxe *f* unitaire; *Constr* **u. construction** préfabrication *f, Com, Ind* **u. cost** coût *m* unitaire; **u. furniture** mobilier *m* par éléments; *Com, Ind* **u. labour costs** coût unitaire de travail; **u. manager** directeur *m* de service; **u. price** prix *m* unitaire *ou* à l'unité; *Br St Exch* **u. trust** fonds *m* commun de placement, ≃ SICAV *f*

Unitarian [ju:nɪ'teərɪən] ADJ, N *Rel* unitarien, -ienne, unitaire *mf*

Unitarianism [ju:nɪ'teərɪənɪz(ə)m] N *Rel* unitarisme *m*

unitary ['ju:nɪt(ə)rɪ] ADJ *(system etc)* unitaire

unite [ju:'naɪt] VT **1** *(join)* unir; **to u. one country with another** unifier deux pays; **to u. idealism with common sense** allier l'idéalisme au bon sens; **he seemed to u. all the qualities one would wish for** il paraissait réunir toutes les qualités souhaitables **2** *(unify) (people)* mettre d'accord; *(party)* unifier; **if we stay united ...** si nous restons unis ...; **more unites us than separates us** ce qui nous unit est plus fort que ce qui nous divise; **common interests that u. two countries** intérêts communs qui unissent deux pays **3** *Fml (marry)* unir (en mariage)

VI s'allier (**with** avec); *(of party, states)* s'unifier; *Chem (of atoms)* s'unir, se combiner; **to u. against** s'unir contre; *Pol (party)* faire bloc contre; **to u. in doing sth** se mettre d'accord pour faire qch

united [ju:'naɪtɪd] ADJ uni; *(unified)* unifié; **u. efforts** efforts conjugués; *Prov* **u. we stand, divided we fall** l'union fait la force; **to present a u. front** présenter un front uni

▸▸**the U. Arab Emirates** les Émirats *mpl* arabes unis; **the U. Arab Republic** la République arabe unie; **the U. Kingdom** le Royaume-Uni; **the U. Nations** les Nations *fpl* unies; **the U. States** les États-Unis *mpl*

unity ['ju:nɪtɪ] N **1** *(oneness)* unité *f,* **national/political u.** unité nationale/politique; *Prov* **u. is strength** l'union fait la force **2** *(harmony)* **there is no u. in his work** ses œuvres manquent d'unité *ou* d'harmonie; *Theat* **u. of time, place and action** unité de temps, de lieu et d'action

univ *(abbr* **university)** université *f*

univalent [ju:nɪ'veɪlənt] ADJ *Chem* univalent

universal [ju:nɪ'vɜ:s(ə)l] ADJ universel; **he's a u. favourite** tout le monde l'aime; **this proposal met with u. rejection** la proposition a été unanimement rejetée; **to meet with u. agreement** faire l'unanimité; **to meet with u. acclaim** être applaudi par tout le monde N *Phil* universel *m*

▸▸**u. bar code** code-barres *m, pl* codes-barres; *Tech* **u. joint** (joint *m* de) cardan *m;* **u. product code** code-barres, *pl* codes-barres; **u. suffrage** suffrage *m* universel

universality [ju:nɪvɜ:'sælɪtɪ] N universalité *f*

universalize [ju:nɪ'vɜ:səlaɪz] VT universaliser

universally [ju:nɪ'vɜ:səlɪ] ADV universellement

universe ['ju:nɪvɜ:s] N univers *m*

university [ju:nɪ'vɜ:sɪtɪ] N université *f;* **to go to u.** aller à l'université; **he's been to u.,** **he's had a u. education** il a fait des études supérieures; **to get a place at u.** être admis à l'université; **when I was at u.** quand j'étais à l'université; **London U.** l'université de Londres; *Fig* **the u. of life** l'école de la vie VOIR GRAMMAIRE A7

▸▸**u. professor** professeur *m* d'université; **u. student** étudiant, -ante *(à l'université), Belg, Suisse* universitaire *mf,* **u. town** ville *f* universitaire

UNIX ['ju:nɪks] N *Comput (abbr* **Uniplexed Information and Computing System)** UNIX *m;* **U.-based** à base d'UNIX

unjust [ʌn'dʒʌst] ADJ injuste *(* **to** envers, avec); **my suspicions were u.** mes soupçons n'étaient pas fondés

unjustifiable [ʌndʒʌstɪ'faɪəb(ə)l] ADJ injustifiable

unjustifiably [ʌndʒʌstɪ'faɪəblɪ] ADV sans justification

unjustified [ʌn'dʒʌstɪfaɪd] ADJ **1** *(action etc)* injustifié; **he was absolutely u. in doing that** ce qu'il a fait n'était absolument pas justifié **2** *(text)* non justifié

unjustly [ʌn'dʒʌstlɪ] ADV injustement

unkempt [ʌn'kem(p)t] ADJ *(hair)* mal peigné, hirsute; *(beard)* hirsute; *(appearance)* négligé; *(person) (with regard to hair)* dépeigné; *(in appearance)* débraillé; *(garden)* mal entretenu

unkind [ʌn'kaɪnd] ADJ *(person)* dur, méchant; *(less strong)* peu aimable, pas gentil; *(remark)* méchant; **that's very u. of him** ce n'est pas du tout gentil de sa part; **to say u. things to sb** dire des méchancetés à qn; **to be u. to animals** être cruel avec les animaux; **to be u. to sb** être méchant envers *ou* avec qn; **it's u. to one's skin/hair** cela agresse la peau/les cheveux; *Lit* **the unkindest cut of all** la pire des trahisons

unkindly [ʌn'kaɪndlɪ] ADV méchamment, durement; *(less strong)* peu aimablement; **to take u. to sth** mal accepter qch

ADJ *(person)* peu aimable, peu gentil

unkindness [ʌn'kaɪndnɪs] N *(of person)*

manque *m* de gentillesse; *(stronger)* méchanceté *f*, *(of remark)* méchanceté; *(of climate)* rigueur *f*

unknot [ʌn'nɒt] VT (**-tt-**) dénouer

unknowing [ʌn'nəʊɪŋ] ADJ inconscient; **she was the u. cause of their quarrel** sans le savoir, elle était la cause de leur dispute

unknowingly [ʌn'nəʊɪŋlɪ] ADV inconsciemment, sans le savoir

unknown [ʌn'nəʊn] ADJ inconnu (**to** de); **u. person** inconnu, -ue; *Law* **verdict against person or persons u.** verdict contre inconnu; **this is a process u. to us**, this process is **u. to us** c'est un procédé qui nous est inconnu; **it is far from u. in our country** ceci est fort bien connu dans notre pays
ADV **he did it u. to me** il l'a fait à mon insu; **u. to us, the bus had already gone** nous ne le savions pas, mais le bus était déjà parti; **u. to everyone but her …** personne à part elle ne savait que …
N **1** *(person)* inconnu, -ue **2** *Math* inconnue *f* **3 the u.** l'inconnu *m*
▸▸ *Math, Fig* **u. quantity** inconnue *f*; **he's an u. quantity** *(of uncertain value)* on ne sait pas ce qu'il vaut; *(unpredictable)* on ne sait pas ce qu'il pense; **the U. Soldier** le Soldat inconnu

unlace [ʌn'leɪs] VT *(one's shoes)* délacer, défaire

unladen [ʌn'leɪd(ə)n] ADJ *(ship, lorry)* sans charge
▸▸ **u. weight** poids *m* à vide

unladylike [ʌn'leɪdɪlaɪk] ADJ indigne d'une femme bien élevée, inélégant; *(manners)* peu distingué, inélégant; **it's u. to do that** une jeune femme qui se respecte ne fait pas cela

unlaid [ʌn'leɪd] ADJ **the table was still u.** la table n'était pas encore mise

unlamented [ʌnlə'mentɪd] ADJ non regretté; **he passed away u.** il est mort dans l'indifférence générale

unlatch [ʌn'lætʃ] VT *(door)* ouvrir
VI se déverrouiller

unlawful [ʌn'lɔːf(ʊ)l] ADJ *(possession, means, procedure)* illégal, -aux
▸▸ **u. arrest** arrestation *f* illégale; **u. detention** détention *f* abusive

unlawfully [ʌn'lɔːf(ʊ)lɪ] ADV illégalement

unleaded [ʌn'ledɪd] ADJ *(petrol)* sans plomb
N essence *f* sans plomb

unlearn [ʌn'lɜːn] VT *(pt, pp* **unlearnt** [-'lɜːnt], *occ* **unlearned** [-lɜːnd]*)* désapprendre

unlearned [ʌn'lɜːnɪd] ADJ inculte

unleash [ʌn'liːʃ] VT **1** *(dogs)* lâcher **2** *(force of army etc)* déchaîner; *(wave of repression)* provoquer, déclencher; **to u. a nuclear war** déclencher une guerre nucléaire; **to u. one's anger** déchaîner sa colère (**on sb** sur qn)

unleavened [ʌn'levənd] ADJ *(bread)* sans levain, azyme

unless [ʌn'les] CONJ à moins que + *subj*; **he will do nothing u. you ask him to** il ne fera rien à moins que vous ne le lui demandiez; **I would always be back by 6.15, u. I was working late** je rentrais toujours à 6h 15 au plus tard, sauf quand je travaillais tard; **u. I'm mistaken** à moins que je (ne) me trompe; **will you do it? – not u. you pay me** le ferez-vous? – seulement si vous me payez; **there aren't any left, not u. you want this one** il n'y en a plus, à moins que vous ne vouliez celui-ci; **u. I hear to the contrary** sauf avis contraire; **u. otherwise stated** sauf indication contraire

unlettered [ʌn'letəd] ADJ *Lit* peu lettré, inculte

unliberated [ʌn'lɪbəreɪtɪd] ADJ *(woman)*

non libéré, non émancipé; **they're very u. here** les gens ne sont pas du tout émancipés ici

unlicensed [ʌn'laɪsənst] ADJ **1** *(activity)* non autorisé, illicite; **u. taxi** taxi *m* qui opère sans licence **2** *(car)* ≃ sans vignette
▸▸ *Br* **u. premises** = établissement *m* non habilité à vendre des boissons alcoolisées

unlike [ʌn'laɪk] ADJ différent, dissemblable; **they're completely u.** ils ne se ressemblent pas du tout
PREP **to be u. sb/sth** être différent de qn/ qch; **he's not u. his sister** il ressemble assez à sa sœur; **a proposal not altogether u. yours** une proposition ne différant pas énormément de la vôtre; **he, u. his father** lui, à la différence de *ou* contrairement à son père; **it's u. him to do such a thing** cela ne lui ressemble pas de faire une chose pareille

unlik(e)able [ʌn'laɪkəb(ə)l] ADJ *(person)* antipathique, peu sympathique; *(thing)* peu agréable

unlikelihood, unlikeliness [ʌn'laɪklɪhʊd, -'laɪklɪnɪs] N improbabilité *f*

unlikely [ʌn'laɪklɪ] ADJ improbable, peu probable; *(explanation)* invraisemblable; **that's most** *or* **very** *or* **highly u.** c'est fort improbable; **it's not (at all) u.** c'est très probable, cela se pourrait bien; **it's u. to happen** il y a peu de chances pour que ça arrive; **in the u. event that they do come** au cas peu probable où ils viendraient vraiment; **he's u. to do it** il est peu probable qu'il le fasse; **he's an u. man for the job** il ne semble pas convenir pour ce travail; **we found the ring in a most u. place** nous avons retrouvé la bague dans un endroit auquel nous n'aurions jamais pensé; *Fam* **she wears the most u. clothes** elle s'habille d'une façon invraisemblable

unlimited [ʌn'lɪmɪtɪd] ADJ *(time)* illimité; *(patience)* sans borne(s); *(funds)* inépuisable; *Fin (cover)* sans limitation de somme; **u. buffet** buffet *m* à volonté; **there was u. coffee** il y avait du café à volonté; *Comput* **u. e-mail addresses** nombre *m* d'adresses électroniques illimité; **he has an u. fund of stories** il a un stock d'histoires inépuisable
▸▸ *Br Com* **u. company** société *f* à responsabilité illimitée *ou* infinie; *Br Com* **u. liability** responsabilité *f* illimitée; **u. mileage** *(of hired car)* ≃ kilométrage *m* illimité; **u. travel** *(with season ticket etc)* nombre *m* de voyages illimité

unlined [ʌn'laɪnd] ADJ **1** *(face)* sans rides **2** *(paper)* non réglé **3** *(without lining)* non doublé

unlisted [ʌn'lɪstɪd] ADJ non répertorié; *Fin (share)* incoté; *(phone number)* qui n'est pas sur l'annuaire; **she was u. in the standard reference works** son nom ne figurait pas dans les livres de référence classiques
▸▸ *St Exch* **u. market** Bourse *f* coulisse; *St Exch* **u. securities market** marché *m* hors cote, second marché; *St Exch* **u. security** valeur *f* non cotée, valeur du second marché

unlit [ʌn'lɪt] ADJ non allumé; **the u. streets** les rues obscures

unload [ʌn'ləʊd] VT **1** *(boat, car, goods)* décharger; *(from ship)* débarquer; *Fam (stolen goods)* écouler; **to u. sth onto sb** fourguer qch à qn; *Fig* **to u. one's problems onto sb** se décharger de ses problèmes sur qn **2** *(gun, camera)* décharger
VI **1** *(of lorry, ship)* décharger **2** *Am Mktg (flood market)* inonder le marché

unloaded [ʌn'ləʊdɪd] ADJ **1** *(lorry, ship)* *(with load removed)* déchargé; *(without a load)* non chargé, sans chargement **2** *(gun, camera)* non chargé; **don't worry, the gun's u.** n'aie pas peur, le fusil n'est pas chargé

unloading [ʌn'ləʊdɪŋ] N déchargement *m*; *(from ship)* débarquement *m*
▸▸ **u. dock** quai *m* de déchargement; **u. note, u. permit** permis *m* de débarquement; **u. platform** plate-forme *f* de déchargement, *pl* plates-formes de déchargement

unlock [ʌn'lɒk] VT **1** *(door)* déverrouiller **2** *(secret)* révéler, découvrir **3** *(wheel, nut)* débloquer **4** *Comput (file, diskette, keyboard)* déverrouiller **5** **to u. the steering wheel** déverrouiller le système de blocage de la direction **6** *Fin (assets)* débloquer **7** *(mobile phone)* débloquer
VI se déverrouiller

unlocked [ʌn'lɒkt] ADJ *(door)* qui n'est pas fermé à clef

unlocking [ʌn'lɒkɪŋ] N *Aut, Comput* déverrouillage *m*

unlooked-for [ʌn'lʊkt-] ADJ imprévu

unloose(n) [ʌn'luːs(n)] VT *(bolt, screw, tie)* desserrer; **to u. one's grip** lâcher prise; **to u. sb's tongue** délier la langue à qn

unlov(e)able [ʌn'lʌvəb(ə)l] ADJ peu attachant

unloved [ʌn'lʌvd] ADJ mal-aimé; **to be feeling u.** ne pas se sentir aimé, se sentir mal-aimé

unlovely [ʌn'lʌvlɪ] ADJ *(person)* disgracieux; *(sight)* laid

unloving [ʌn'lʌvɪŋ] ADJ *(person)* peu affectueux, peu aimant; *(behaviour)* froid

unluckily [ʌn'lʌkɪlɪ] ADV malheureusement, par malheur; **u. for me** malheureusement pour moi

unlucky [ʌn'lʌkɪ] ADJ **1** *(person)* malchanceux; **to be u.** ne pas avoir de chance; **talk about u.!** quelle malchance!; **you were u. not to have been chosen** tu n'as pas eu de chance de ne pas avoir été choisi; **to be u. in love** ne pas être heureux en amour; **it was u. for him that she arrived just at that moment** malheureusement pour lui, elle est arrivée à cet instant précis **2** *(coincidence, decision)* malheureux; **it had been an u. day** cela avait été un jour de malchance; **that's u.** ce n'est pas de chance **3** *(bringing bad luck)* *(number, colour etc)* qui porte malheur; **it's my u. colour** c'est la couleur qui me porte malheur; **don't walk under a ladder, it's u.** ne passez pas sous une échelle, ça porte malheur

unmade [ʌn'meɪd] ADJ qui n'est pas fait; *(bed)* défait; *(road)* non goudronné

unmade-up ADJ *(face)* non maquillé

unmake [ʌn'meɪk] VT *(pt, pp* **unmade** [-'meɪd]*)* défaire

unman [ʌn'mæn] VT (**-nn-**) *Lit (cause to lose courage)* décourager, démoraliser

unmanageable [ʌn'mænɪdʒəb(ə)l] ADJ *(person, child)* rebelle; *(horse)* indocile; *(vehicle, ship)* difficile à manœuvrer; *(large book etc)* difficile à manier, peu maniable; *(situation, problem)* ingérable; *(company)* impossible à diriger; **u. hair** cheveux difficiles à coiffer

unmanly [ʌn'mænlɪ] ADJ **1** *(effeminate)* efféminé **2** *(cowardly)* lâche

unmanned [ʌn'mænd] ADJ *(ship, spaceship)* sans équipage; *Rail (level crossing)* automatique; **all of the ticket windows were u.** il n'y avait personne derrière les guichets; **the reception desk must never be left u.** il doit toujours y avoir quelqu'un au bureau de réception
▸▸ *Astronaut* **u. flight** vol *m* inhabité *ou* non habité

unmannerliness [ʌn'mænəlɪnɪs] N *Lit* manque *m* de savoir-vivre, impolitesse *f*

unmannerly [ʌn'mænəlɪ] ADJ *Lit (behaviour, person)* impoli

unmapped [ʌnˈmæpt] ADJ **u. territory** territoire pour lequel il n'existe pas de carte

unmarked [ʌnˈmɑːkt] ADJ **1** (no scratches etc) sans marque(s); (no stains etc) sans tache(s); **u. (police) car** voiture f (de police) banalisée; **his body was bruised but his face was u.** il avait des contusions sur le corps mais son visage était intact **2** Sport (player) démarqué **3 my essay was still u.** ma dissertation n'était toujours pas corrigée

unmarketable [ʌnˈmɑːkɪtəb(ə)l] ADJ invendable, non commercialisable

unmarriageable [ʌnˈmærɪdʒəb(ə)l] ADJ immariable

unmarried [ʌnˈmærɪd] ADJ non marié; **he remained u.** il est resté célibataire, il ne s'est jamais marié
▸▸ Old-fashioned **u. mother** mère f célibataire; **u. state** célibat m

unmask [ʌnˈmɑːsk] VT démasquer; esp Lit (plot) dévoiler
VI se démasquer

unmatched [ʌnˈmætʃt] ADJ (person, ability) sans égal, incomparable; **she is u. as a novelist** comme romancière, elle n'a pas sa pareille; **he's u. for courage** son courage est inégalé

unmentionable [ʌnˈmenʃənəb(ə)l] ADJ (event, thing) dont il ne faut pas parler; (word, name) qu'il ne faut pas prononcer
NPL Old-fashioned, Hum **unmentionables** sous-vêtements mpl

unmerciful [ʌnˈmɜːsɪfʊl] ADJ impitoyable, sans pitié

unmercifully [ʌnˈmɜːsɪfəlɪ] ADV impitoyablement, sans pitié

unmerited [ʌnˈmerɪtɪd] ADJ immérité

unmetered [ʌnˈmiːtəd] ADJ Comput (Internet access) illimité

unmethodical [ʌnmɪˈθɒdɪk(ə)l] ADJ peu méthodique

unmindful [ʌnˈmaɪndf(ʊ)l] ADJ esp Lit **to be u. of sth** être peu soucieux de qch; **u. of one's own interests** sans penser à ses propres intérêts

unmistakable [ʌnmɪsˈteɪkəb(ə)l] ADJ (feeling) clair; (difference) marqué, manifeste; (person, building) que l'on ne peut pas confondre; (voice, style) reconnaissable entre mille, que l'on ne peut pas confondre; **you'll see it all right, it's u.** tu le verras sans problème, on ne peut pas le rater; **the u. smell/symptom of ...** l'odeur/le symptôme caractéristique de ...

unmistakably [ʌnmɪsˈteɪkəblɪ] ADV clairement, nettement; **the style is u. French** le style est français, il n'y a pas à s'y tromper

unmitigated [ʌnˈmɪtɪɡeɪtɪd] ADJ (evil, horror, severity) total, -aux; (used as intensifier) (idiot, cock-up) véritable; **the tedium was u. by even the slightest hint of humour** l'ennui n'était même pas allégé par la moindre pointe d'humour; **an u. lie** un pur mensonge; **an u. disaster** un échec total

unmixed [ʌnˈmɪkst] ADJ (joy) sans mélange

unmolested [ʌnməˈlestɪd] ADJ sans encombre; **to leave sb u.** (not bother) laisser qn en paix

unmortgaged [ʌnˈmɔːɡɪdʒd] ADJ non hypothéqué

unmotivated [ʌnˈməʊtɪveɪtɪd] ADJ sans mobile; (person) non motivé; (without ambition) dépourvu d'ambition; **his actions were u. by any desire for personal glory** ses actes n'étaient pas motivés par un quelconque désir de gloire personnelle

unmounted [ʌnˈmaʊntɪd] ADJ **1** (gem) non serti; (photo) non encadré **2** (not on horseback) à pied

unmourned [ʌnˈmɔːnd] ADJ non pleuré; **he died u.** personne n'a pleuré sa mort

unmoved [ʌnˈmuːvd] ADJ impassible; **u. by sth** aucunement ému de ou par qch; **he remained u. by all our arguments, all our arguments left him quite u.** tous nos arguments le laissaient indifférent ou froid

unmusical [ʌnˈmjuːzɪk(ə)l] ADJ peu mélodieux; (person) peu musicien, -ienne; **to my u. ear it sounds like ...** pour mon oreille peu musicienne ça ressemble à ...

unnameable [ʌnˈneɪməb(ə)l] ADJ innommable

unnamed [ʌnˈneɪmd] ADJ (person) anonyme; (thing) innommé

unnatural [ʌnˈnætʃərəl] ADJ **1** (not normal) anormal, -aux; (vice) contre nature; **it's u. for him** cela ne lui ressemble pas (to de) **2** (affected) (style, person) peu naturel, affecté; (laugh) forcé

unnaturally [ʌnˈnætʃərəlɪ] ADV **1** (to develop etc) anormalement; **she was u. shy** elle était anormalement timide; **not u. we turned the offer down** comme on pouvait s'y attendre nous avons rejeté cette offre; **not u. in the circumstances ...** ce qui est/était bien naturel étant donné les circonstances, ... **2** (affectedly) (to speak) avec affectation; (to act, walk) peu naturellement; **the text reads very u.** ce texte est très forcé

unnavigable [ʌnˈnævɪɡəb(ə)l] ADJ non navigable

unnecessarily [ʌnnesɪˈserɪlɪ] ADV inutilement; **you're being u. hard on yourself** tu te fais du mal pour rien

unnecessary [ʌnˈnesɪs(ə)rɪ] ADJ (costs, delay, trouble) inutile; **it was quite u. of you to say that!** tu n'avais vraiment pas besoin de dire cela!; **it's u. to change it** il n'est pas nécessaire ou ce n'est pas la peine ou il est inutile de le changer; **it's totally u. for you to come too** il est absolument inutile ou il n'est absolument pas nécessaire que tu viennes aussi

unneeded [ʌnˈniːdɪd] ADJ inutile

unnegotiable [ʌnnəˈɡəʊʃəbəl] ADJ Fin (cheque, bill) non négociable

unneighbourly, Am **unneighborly** [ʌnˈneɪbəlɪ] ADJ désobligeant; **to behave in an u. manner** manquer de respect envers ses voisins

unnerve [ʌnˈnɜːv] VT (disconcert) déconcerter; **to be unnerved by sb's presence** se sentir déstabilisé ou troublé par la présence de qn

> Note that the French verb **énerver** is a false friend. It means **to irritate** or **to make nervous**, depending on the context.

unnerving [ʌnˈnɜːvɪŋ] ADJ déconcertant

unnervingly [ʌnˈnɜːvɪŋlɪ] ADV **he can be u. flippant** il est parfois d'une désinvolture déconcertante; **there was something u. peaceful about the village** le calme du village avait quelque chose de troublant

unnoticed [ʌnˈnəʊtɪst] ADJ inaperçu, inobservé; **she left the party u.** elle a quitté la soirée sans que personne ne s'en rende compte; **to pass** or **go u.** passer inaperçu; **to let an insult pass u.** ne pas relever une insulte

unnumbered [ʌnˈnʌmbəd] ADJ **1** (page) non numéroté; (house) sans numéro **2** Lit (countless) innombrable

UNO [ˈjuːnəʊ] N (abbr United Nations Organization) ONU f

unobjectionable [ʌnəbˈdʒekʃənəb(ə)l] ADJ anodin; (person) anodin, inoffensif; **it seems u. enough** il n'y a rien à redire

unobservant [ʌnəbˈzɜːvənt] ADJ **to be u.** ne pas être observateur, -trice; **you're so u.!** tu n'es vraiment pas observateur!

unobserved [ʌnəbˈzɜːvd] ADJ (departure etc); **he went out u.** il est sorti sans que personne ne le voit

unobstructed [ʌnəbˈstrʌktɪd] ADJ (road) non encombré; **they marched on u. to ...** ils ont poursuivi leur chemin sans rencontrer d'obstacles jusqu'à ...; **u. view** vue dégagée ou libre

unobtainable [ʌnəbˈteɪnəb(ə)l] ADJ impossible à obtenir, impossible à se procurer; Tel **the number is u.** le numéro n'est pas en service actuellement

unobtrusive [ʌnəbˈtruːsɪv] ADJ (person, building) discret, -ète; **he always tried to remain u.** il cherchait toujours à s'effacer

unobtrusively [ʌnəbˈtruːsɪvlɪ] ADV discrètement

unoccupied [ʌnˈɒkjʊpaɪd] ADJ **1** (not busy) inoccupé **2** (house) inoccupé, inhabité **3** Mil occupied; **the town was still u.** la ville n'était toujours pas occupée **4** (table, seat) libre, disponible
▸▸ Mil **u. zone** zone f libre

unofficial [ʌnəˈfɪʃəl] ADJ (meeting) non officiel; (information) officieux; **in an u. capacity** à titre officieux; **from an u. source** de source officieuse; **it's still u.** on ne l'a pas encore confirmé;
▸▸ Ind **u. strike** grève f sauvage

unofficially [ʌnəˈfɪʃ(ə)lɪ] ADV non officiellement

unopened [ʌnˈəʊpənd] ADJ non ouvert, qui n'a pas été ouvert

unopposed [ʌnəˈpəʊzd] ADJ sans opposition; (to advance) sans rencontrer d'opposition ou de résistance; **we cannot allow this sort of thing to go u.** on ne peut pas laisser faire ce genre de choses; Parl **the bill was given an u. second reading** le projet de loi a été accepté sans opposition à la deuxième lecture
▸▸ Pol **u. candidate** candidat m unique

unorganized [ʌnˈɔːɡənaɪzd] ADJ (event, group, person etc) non organisé; (disorganized) désorganisé
▸▸ Ind **u. labour** main-d'œuvre f non syndiquée

unoriginal [ʌnəˈrɪdʒɪn(ə)l] ADJ sans originalité, peu original, -aux

unorthodox [ʌnˈɔːθədɒks] ADJ peu orthodoxe

unostentatious [ʌnɒstenˈteɪʃəs] ADJ (person, behaviour, house, party) simple; (dress) sobre, simple

unostentatiously [ʌnɒstenˈteɪʃəslɪ] ADV (to act) simplement; (dressed) simplement, sobrement

unostentatiousness [ʌnɒstenˈteɪʃəsnɪs] N (of person, lifestyle, house etc) manque m d'ostentation, simplicité f

unpack [ʌnˈpæk] VT (objects, books, boxes) déballer; (suitcase) défaire; (car) décharger
VI (after travelling) défaire sa valise; (after moving) déballer ou vider ses cartons

unpacking [ʌnˈpækɪŋ] N (after moving house) déballage m; **we didn't take long (after holiday)** nous n'avons pas mis longtemps à défaire nos bagages

unpaid [ʌnˈpeɪd] ADJ **1** (work, person) non payé, bénévole; (post) non rétribué, non rémunéré **2** (bill) impayé; (debt) impayé, non acquitté; **to leave an account u.** laisser arriérer un compte **3** (money) non versé; **the money is still u.** l'argent n'a toujours pas été versé
ADV **he refused to work u.** il a refusé de travailler sans être payé; **I'll work u.** je vais travailler bénévolement
▸▸ **u. bill** impayé m; **u. leave** congé m sans solde

unpaid-up share N *Fin* action *f* non libérée

unpalatable [ʌnˈpælətəb(ə)l] ADJ **1** *(food)* peu appétissant **2** *Fig (truth, facts)* désagréable, dur à avaler

unparalleled [ʌnˈpærəleld] ADJ *(beauty)* incomparable, sans égal; *(action, event)* sans précédent

unpardonable [ʌnˈpɑːd(ə)nəb(ə)l] ADJ impardonnable, inexcusable

unpardonably [ʌnˈpɑːd(ə)nəblɪ] ADV de façon impardonnable; **she was u. late** elle est arrivée avec un retard impardonnable; **he was u. harsh** il a été d'une dureté impardonnable

unparliamentary [ʌnpɑːləˈment(ə)rɪ] ADJ *Parl (language, action)* contraire au règles du parlement

unpatented [ʌnˈpeɪtəntɪd, -ˈpæt-] ADJ non breveté

unpatriotic [ʌnpeɪtrɪˈɒtɪk, -pæ-] ADJ *(person)* peu patriote; *(action)* peu patriotique; **to be u.** *(of person)* être mauvais patriote

unpatriotically [ʌnpeɪtrɪˈɒtɪklɪ, -pæ-] ADV *(to act)* en mauvais patriote

unpaved [ʌnˈpeɪvd] ADJ non pavé, sans pavés

unperceived [ʌnpəˈsiːvd] ADJ non perçu

unperforated [ʌnˈpɜːfəreɪtɪd] ADJ sans perforations

unperson [ˈʌnpɜːsən] N *Pol* non-personne *f*, *pl* non-personnes

unperturbable [ʌnpəˈtɜːbəb(ə)l] ADJ imperturbable

unperturbed [ʌnpəˈtɜːbd] ADJ impassible; **to be u. by sth** ne pas se laisser perturber par qch

unpick [ʌnˈpɪk] VT *(seam, hem)* défaire; *(garment)* découdre

unpin [ʌnˈpɪn] VT (-nn-) ôter les épingles (**from** de)

unplaced [ʌnˈpleɪst] ADJ *(competitor)* non classé; *(horse etc)* non placé

unplanned [ʌnˈplænd] ADJ *(event)* imprévu; *(child)* non prévu

unplayable [ʌnˈpleɪəb(ə)l] ADJ **1** *Sport (pitch etc)* impraticable; *(service, shot etc)* injouable; **the ball was in an u. position** la balle n'était pas jouable **2** *Mus, Theat* injouable

unpleasant [ʌnˈplezənt] ADJ *(taste, smell)* désagréable; *(person, tone, manner)* désagréable, déplaisant; **to smell u.** sentir mauvais; **to taste u.** avoir mauvais goût; **to look u.** *(of thing, person)* être laid, peu ragoûtant; **u. weather** mauvais temps *m*; **he made some u. remarks** il a dit des choses désobligeantes; **she was very u. with** *or* **to me** elle a été très désagréable avec moi; **things are getting rather u. between them** la situation est en train de se dégrader entre eux

unpleasantly [ʌnˈplezəntlɪ] ADV de façon désagréable; **the wine was u. sweet** le vin était trop sucré; **we had u. cold weather** il a fait vraiment trop froid

unpleasantness [ʌnˈplezəntnɪs] N **1** *(of person, thing)* caractère *m* désagréable; *(of place)* aspect *m* déplaisant; *(of food)* caractère peu appétissant **2** *(disagreement)* différend *m*; *(argument)* dispute *f*; **the will caused some u.** le testament a provoqué des disputes; **there was some u. between them** il y avait encore des tensions entre eux; **we managed to avoid any u.** nous avons réussi à éviter une dispute

unpleasing [ʌnˈpliːzɪŋ] ADJ déplaisant; **a not u. effect** un effet qui n'est pas désagréable

unpledged [ʌnˈpledʒd] ADJ
▸▸ *Fin* **u. revenue** recettes *fpl* non gagées

unplug [ʌnˈplʌg] VT (-gg-) **1** *(television etc)* débrancher **2** *(opening, pipe)* déboucher

unplumbed [ʌnˈplʌmd] ADJ *(depths, mystery, knowledge)* insondé

unpoetic(al) [ʌnpəʊˈetɪk, -ɪk(ə)l] ADJ peu poétique

unpolished [ʌnˈpɒlɪʃt] ADJ **1** *(surface)* non poli; *(stone)* brut; *(floor, furniture)* non ciré, non astiqué; *(shoes)* non ciré **2** *(person)* peu raffiné; *(style)* qui manque de raffinement

unpolluted [ʌnpəˈluːtɪd] ADJ non pollué

unpopular [ʌnˈpɒpjʊlər] ADJ *(decision, government)* impopulaire; **an u. make of car** une marque de voiture qui n'a pas de succès; **at school she had been an u. child** quand elle était à l'école les autres enfants ne l'aimaient pas beaucoup; **he makes himself u. with everybody** il se fait mal voir de tout le monde; **he's u. with his employees** ses employés ne l'aiment pas (beaucoup); **this decision was very u.** cette décision a été très mal accueillie *ou* très impopulaire

unpopularity [ʌnpɒpjʊˈlærɪtɪ] N impopularité *f*

unpopulated [ʌnˈpɒpjʊleɪtɪd] ADJ désert, non peuplé

unpractical [ʌnˈpræktɪk(ə)l] ADJ **1** *(person)* peu pratique; **he's completely u.** il n'a aucun sens pratique **2** *(plan)* irréalisable

unpractised, *Am* **unpracticed** [ʌnˈpræktɪst] ADJ inexpérimenté; **to be u. in the art of public speaking** ne pas avoir l'habitude de parler en public; **she's quite u. as a manager** elle n'a pas d'expérience en tant que directrice

unprecedented [ʌnˈpresɪdentɪd] ADJ *(decision)* sans précédent, exceptionnel; **this was quite u. in the continent's history** c'était du jamais vu dans l'histoire du continent

unpredictability [ʌnprɪdɪktəˈbɪlətɪ] N imprévisibilité *f*

unpredictable [ʌnprɪˈdɪktəb(ə)l] ADJ *(event, person, effect etc)* imprévisible; *(weather)* incertain

unprejudiced [ʌnˈpredʒʊdɪst] ADJ sans préjugés

unpremeditated [ʌnprɪˈmedɪteɪtɪd] ADJ *Law (offence)* non prémédité

unprepared [ʌnprɪˈpeəd] ADJ **1** *(food etc)* non préparé; *(speech)* improvisé, impromptu; **to find everything u.** ne rien trouver de prêt; **the hall was quite u. for the party** la salle n'était pas du tout prête pour la soirée **2** *(person)* **to be u. for sth** ne pas s'attendre à qch; **to go into an undertaking u.** faire qch sans être préparé; **I was quite u. for the exam** *(hadn't studied for it)* je n'étais pas du tout préparé à l'examen

unpreparedness [ʌnprɪˈpeədnɪs, -ˈpeərɪdnɪs] N impréparation *f* (**for** à)

unprepossessing [ʌnprɪpəˈzesɪŋ] ADJ *(person, building)* peu engageant; **a man of u. appearance** un homme à l'apparence peu engageante *ou* peu avenante

unpresentable [ʌnprɪˈzentəb(ə)l] ADJ pas présentable

unpretentious [ʌnprɪˈtenʃəs] ADJ *(person)* sans prétention, simple; *(tastes, house)* simple

unpretentiously [ʌnprɪˈtenʃəslɪ] ADV simplement

unpriced [ʌnˈpraɪst] ADJ *(article)* sans prix

unprincipled [ʌnˈprɪnsɪp(ə)ld] ADJ *(person)* dénué de principes, sans scrupules; *(behaviour)* sans scrupules; **what an u. thing to do** il ne faut vraiment pas avoir de scrupules pour faire une chose pareille

unprintable [ʌnˈprɪntəb(ə)l] ADJ impubliable; *Fig (comment, reply)* qu'on n'oserait

pas *ou* qu'on ne peut répéter; **what he actually said is u.** ce qu'il a vraiment dit n'est pas répétable

unprocessed [ʌnˈprəʊsest] ADJ *(film)* non développé

unproductive [ʌnprəˈdʌktɪv] ADJ *(method, capital)* improductif; *(land, conversation)* stérile; **an u. afternoon** une après-midi improductive

unprofessional [ʌnprəˈfeʃən(ə)l] ADJ *(person, action)* pas professionnel; **it looks u. not to …** ça ne fait pas très professionnel de ne pas …; **it's u. to leave a job unfinished** c'est pas professionnel de ne pas terminer un travail; **he's rather u. in his approach** il n'est pas très professionnel

unprofessionally [ʌnprəˈfeʃ(ə)nəlɪ] ADV *(to do job, work, carry out contract, behave)* de manière peu professionnelle; **he dealt with the whole situation rather u.** la façon dont il s'est occupé de l'affaire n'était pas très professionnelle

unprofitable [ʌnˈprɒfɪtəb(ə)l] ADJ *(operation, meeting)* peu fructueux; *(firm)* peu rentable; **we spent an u. morning/afternoon trying to …** nous avons perdu la matinée/l'après-midi à essayer de …

unprofitably [ʌnˈprɒfɪtəblɪ] ADV sans profit

Unprofor [ˈʌnprəfɔːr] N *(abbr* United Nations Protection Force*)* FORPRONU *f*

unpromising [ʌnˈprɒmɪsɪŋ] ADJ peu prometteur, -euse; **the weather looks u.** on dirait qu'il ne va pas faire beau; **that's an u. start** c'est un mauvais départ *ou* un départ qui augure mal de la suite

unprompted [ʌnˈprɒmptɪd] ADJ spontané; **that was quite u. by any self-interest** ce n'était motivé par aucun intérêt personnel

unpronounceable [ʌnprəˈnaʊnsəb(ə)l] ADJ imprononçable

unprotected [ʌnprəˈtektɪd] ADJ **1** *(undefended)* sans protection, sans défense; *(wood)* non traité; **u. wood will rot in this weather** si vous ne traitez pas le bois, il va pourrir avec le temps qu'il fait; **to have u. sex** avoir des rapports sexuels non protégés **2** *Tech (moving part, blade)* non protégé

unproved, unproven [ʌnˈpruːvd, -ˈpruːv(ə)n] ADJ non prouvé

unprovided-for [ʌnprəˈvaɪdɪd-] ADJ *(family)* sans ressources; *(eventuality)* non prévu; **he left his family u. in his will** il n'a rien laissé à sa famille dans son testament

unprovoked [ʌnprəˈvəʊkt] ADJ *(violence, criticism)* gratuit; **an u. attack** une agression gratuite

unpublicized [ʌnˈpʌblɪsaɪzd] ADJ non publié, inédit

unpublishable [ʌnˈpʌblɪʃəb(ə)l] ADJ impubliable

unpublished [ʌnˈpʌblɪʃt] ADJ inédit, non publié; **the u. facts** les faits qui n'ont pas été révélés au public

unpunctual [ʌnˈpʌŋktjʊəl] ADJ peu ponctuel, inexact

unpunctuality [ʌnpʌŋktjʊˈælɪtɪ] N manque *m* de ponctualité, inexactitude *f*

unpunished [ʌnˈpʌnɪʃt] ADJ *(crime, criminal)* impuni; **to go u.** rester impuni

unputdownable [ʌnpʊtˈdaʊnəb(ə)l] ADJ *Fam (book)* captivant, prenant; **I found it absolutely u.** je ne pouvais pas m'arrêter de lire

unqualified [ʌnˈkwɒlɪfaɪd] ADJ **1** *(person)* non qualifié; *(doctor, teacher)* non diplômé; **she's u. for the job** elle n'est pas qualifiée pour le poste; **to be u. to do sth** ne pas avoir la compétence nécessaire pour faire qch; **I'm quite u. to talk about it** je ne suis nullement qualifié pour en parler **2** *(unreserved)* *(accusation, support etc)* sans réserve; **to give sth one's u. support** soutenir qch complètement; **u. denial** dénégation *f* catégorique; **u. praise** éloges *mpl* sans réserve; **an u. disaster** un désastre sans nom; **it was an u. success** cela a été un succès formidable **3** *Gram (adjective)* non modifié

unquenchable [ʌnˈkwenʃəb(ə)l] ADJ *(thirst, fire)* inextinguible; *(thirst, curiosity)* insatiable

unquenched [ʌnˈkwenʃt] ADJ *(fire)* non éteint; *(thirst)* non étanché; *(desire, curiosity, passion)* inassouvi

unquestionable [ʌnˈkwestʃənəb(ə)l] ADJ indiscutable; *(right)* incontestable

unquestionably [ʌnˈkwestʃənəblɪ] ADV incontestablement, sans aucun doute

unquestioned [ʌnˈkwestʃənd] ADJ indiscuté, incontesté; **to let a statement pass** *or* **go u.** laisser passer une affirmation sans la relever

unquestioning [ʌnˈkwestʃənɪŋ] ADJ *(obedience)* aveugle; *(trust, loyalty)* absolu; **to be u. about sth** ne pas se poser de questions au sujet de qch

unquestioningly [ʌnˈkwestʃənɪŋlɪ] ADV aveuglément, sans se poser de question; **u. loyal** d'une loyauté absolue

unquiet [ʌnˈkwaɪət] ADJ *esp Lit* inquiet, -ète; **u. times** époque *f* troublée

unquote [ˈʌnkwəʊt] VI *(used only in imperative) (in quotation)* fermez les guillemets; *(in report)* fin de citation

unquoted [ʌnˈkwəʊtɪd] ADJ *Fin (share)* incoté; *(company, securities)* non coté

unratified [ʌnˈrætɪfaɪd] ADJ non ratifié

unravel [ʌnˈræv(ə)l] (-ll-, *Am* -l-) VT **1** *(fabric)* effiler, effilocher; *(knitting)* défaire; *(jumper, part of jumper)* détricoter **2** *(string)* démêler, débrouiller; *(plot)* dénouer, démêler; *(mystery)* débrouiller

VI **1 to u. (itself), to come unravelled** *(of cloth)* s'effiler, s'effilocher; *(of knitting)* se défaire; *(of jumper)* se détricoter; *(of rope)* se détordre; *Fig (of plan)* se désagréger **2** *(of facts, mystery)* s'éclaircir

unread [ʌnˈred] ADJ qui n'a pas été lu; **to leave sth u.** ne pas lire qch; **he left the magazine on the table u.** il a laissé la revue sur la table sans l'avoir lue

unreadable [ʌnˈriːdəb(ə)l] ADJ *(book, writing),* Comput illisible

unreadiness [ʌnˈredɪnɪs] N **1** *(lack of preparation)* manque *m* de préparation; **in a state of u.** sans être préparé **2** *(unwillingness)* **their u. to contribute** la mauvaise volonté qu'ils ont mise à contribuer; *(refusal)* leur refus *m* à contribuer

unready [ʌnˈredɪ] ADJ **1** *(unprepared)* **to be u. for sth** ne pas être préparé pour qch **2** *(unwilling)* **to be u. to help** n'être pas prêt à aider; **she was u. to admit that she might be wrong** elle n'était pas prête à admettre qu'elle puisse avoir tort

unreal [ʌnˈrɪəl] ADJ **1** irréel; **everything seemed u. to him** il avait l'impression de rêver **2** *Fam (very good, very bad, unbelievable) (action, situation)* dingue; *(person)* pas vrai

unrealistic [ʌnrɪəˈlɪstɪk] ADJ irréaliste

unreality [ʌnrɪˈælɪtɪ] N irréalité *f*

unrealizable [ʌnrɪəˈlaɪzəb(ə)l] ADJ irréalisable

unrealized [ʌnˈrɪəlaɪzd] ADJ **1** *(hope, wish)* irréalisé **2** *Fin (capital)* non réalisé
▸▸ *Fin* **u. gain** gain *m* latent; **u. loss** perte *f* latente

unreasonable [ʌnˈriːz(ə)nəb(ə)l] ADJ **1** *(person) (illogical)* déraisonnable; *(unfair)* injuste; **don't be u.!** sois raisonnable!; **you**

are being very u. tu es injuste; **they were quite u. in their demands** leurs exigences étaient tout à fait déraisonnables **2** *(assumption)* déraisonnable; *(demand)* immodéré; *(price)* excessif; **this would be a not u. assumption** cette supposition ne serait pas inacceptable; **surely it's not u. to expect that …** on est bien en mesure de s'attendre à ce que …; **at this u. hour** à cette heure indue

unreasonably [ʌnˈriːz(ə)nəblɪ] ADV d'une manière peu raisonnable; **that's u. expensive** c'est excessivement cher; **they asked, and not altogether u., that …** ils ont demandé, plutôt légitimement, que …

unreasoning [ʌnˈriːz(ə)nɪŋ] ADJ *(person)* qui ne raisonne pas; **u. hatred** haine *f* irraisonnée *ou* aveugle; **u. panic** peur *f* panique

unrecognizable [ʌnrekəgˈnaɪzəb(ə)l] ADJ méconnaissable

unrecognized [ʌnˈrekəgnaɪzd] ADJ **1** *(not accepted) (government)* non reconnu; *(writer, talent etc)* méconnu; **her talent went u.** son talent n'a pas été reconnu *ou* est resté méconnu **2** *(by people in street etc)* **to go u.** ne pas être reconnu; **he mingled u. in the crowd** il s'est mêlé à la foule sans qu'on le reconnaisse
▸▸ *Comput* **u. command** commande *f* inconnue

unrecorded [ʌnrɪˈkɔːdɪd] ADJ **1** *(fact, comment)* non enregistré, non noté; **the details of the case went u.** il n'y a pas eu de trace écrite sur les détails de l'affaire **2** *(music, tape)* non enregistré; *(tape)* vierge

unrecoverable [ʌnrɪˈkʌvərəb(ə)l] ADJ **1** *Comput* irrécouvrable **2** *Fin (debt)* inexigible

unrecovered debt [ʌnrɪˈkʌvəd] N créance *f* impayée

unredeemed [ʌnrɪˈdiːmd] ADJ **1** *(sinner)* non racheté; *(bad character)* non compensé **(by** par); **the film is u. by even a spark of humour** il n'y a même pas un soupçon d'humour pour racheter le film; **the town's ugliness is u. by any charm whatsoever** la ville n'a aucun charme quelconque qui puisse racheter sa laideur; **he led a life of u. evil** il a toujours vécu dans le mal **2** *(promise)* non rempli, non tenu **3** *(pawned object)* non dégagé **4** *Fin (loan)* non amorti, non remboursé; *(draft)* non honoré; *(mortgage)* non purgé; *(pledge)* non retiré

unreel [ʌnˈriːl] VT *(film, cable)* dérouler
VI se dérouler

unrefined [ʌnrɪˈfaɪnd] ADJ **1** *(sugar, petrol)* brut, non raffiné **2** *(person, taste)* peu raffiné, grossier; **u. manners** manières *fpl* frustes

unreformed [ʌnrɪˈfɔːmd] ADJ *(person)* qui ne s'est pas corrigé; *(law)* non amendé; **to remain u.** *(of person)* rester incorrigible

unrefreshed [ʌnrɪˈfreʃt] ADJ encore fatigué, non reposé

unregistered [ʌnˈredʒɪstəd] ADJ *(person)* non inscrit; *(luggage)* non enregistré; *(parcel)* non recommandé; *(car)* non immatriculé; *(birth)* non déclaré

unregretted [ʌnrɪˈgretɪd] ADJ que l'on ne regrette pas; **she died u.** personne n'a regretté sa mort

unrehearsed [ʌnrɪˈhɜːst] ADJ *(play)* joué sans répétitions; *(speech)* improvisé; **believe me, that was completely u.** crois-moi, ce n'était pas du tout prévu

unrelated [ʌnrɪˈleɪtɪd] ADJ **1** *(events)* sans rapport **(to** avec; **to each other** l'un avec l'autre); **these facts are totally u.** il n'y a aucun rapport entre ces faits **2** *(people)* **they are u.** il n'y a aucun lien de parenté entre eux

unrelenting [ʌnrɪˈlentɪŋ] ADJ *(struggle, criticism, efforts)* acharné; *(pain)* sans rémission; *(pressure, rain)* incessant; *(person,*

logic) implacable **(towards** à l'égard de); **he was u. in his insistence that I should …** il insistait avec acharnement pour que je … + *sub*; **he was u.** *(would not be persuaded, influenced)* il restait inflexible

unreliability [ʌnrɪlaɪəˈbɪlɪtɪ] N *(of undertaking, person)* manque *m* de sérieux; *(of result)* inexactitude *f*; *(of machine, car, computer)* manque *m* de fiabilité

unreliable [ʌnrɪˈlaɪəb(ə)l] ADJ *(person)* sur qui on ne peut pas compter; *(character)* instable; *(information, result, source)* douteux; *(machine, car, clock)* non fiable; **he's good but terribly u.** il est compétent mais on ne peut jamais compter sur lui

unrelieved [ʌnrɪˈliːvd] ADJ **1** *(unvarying) (monotony, ugliness, flatness)* uniforme; **she was dressed in u. black** elle était tout de noir vêtue; **u. boredom** ennui mortel; **vast expanses of grey, u. by any bright colour** de vastes étendues de gris qu'aucune couleur vive ne vient égayer **2** *(pain)* sans rémission, sans répit

unremarkable [ʌnrɪˈmɑːkəb(ə)l] ADJ *(person, film, food)* médiocre, quelconque

unremitting [ʌnrɪˈmɪtɪŋ] ADJ constant; **he was u. in his attentions** il était sans cesse plein d'attentions; **u. boredom** ennui mortel; **u. efforts** efforts soutenus

unremittingly [ʌnrɪˈmɪtɪŋlɪ] ADV sans cesse, inlassablement; *(to work)* sans relâche; **u. dull** d'un ennui mortel

unremunerative [ʌnrɪˈmjuːnərətɪv] ADJ peu rémunérateur, -trice

unrepealed [ʌnrɪˈpiːld] ADJ *(law etc)* non abrogé

unrepeatable [ʌnrɪˈpiːtəb(ə)l] ADJ **1** *(remark)* qu'on ne peut répéter, non répétable; **what he said was quite u.** ce qu'il a dit n'est pas répétable **2** *Com (price)* exceptionnel; *(offer)* unique, exceptionnel

unrepentant [ʌnrɪˈpentənt] ADJ impénitent; **to die u.** mourir dans le péché; **she was u. about what she had done** elle ne s'était pas repentie de ce qu'elle avait fait

unreported [ʌnrɪˈpɔːtɪd] ADJ *(accident, crime)* non signalé; **to go u.** *(of crime)* ne pas être signalé

unrepresentative [ʌnreprɪˈzentətɪv] ADJ peu représentatif; **it's completely u. of …** ce n'est pas du tout représentatif de …

unrepresented [ʌnreprɪˈzentɪd] ADJ non représenté; *(nation)* sans représentant, sans délégué

unrequited [ʌnrɪˈkwaɪtɪd] ADJ *(love, feelings)* non réciproque

unreserved [ʌnrɪˈzɜːvd] ADJ **1** *(outgoing) (person)* sans réserve **2** *(approval)* entier; **u. praise** éloges sans réserve; **to be u. in one's praise of sth** ne pas tarir d'éloges à propos de qch **3** *(unbooked) (seat, table)* non réservé

unreservedly [ʌnrɪˈzɜːvɪdlɪ] ADV sans réserve; **to trust sb u.** avoir pleine confiance en qn

unresisting [ʌnrɪˈzɪstɪŋ] ADJ soumis, docile

unresolved [ʌnrɪˈzɒlvd] ADJ **1** *(person)* irrésolu, indécis **2** *(problem etc)* non résolu

unresponsive [ʌnrɪˈspɒnsɪv] ADJ **1** *(engine)* qui manque de nervosité; *(steering)* qui ne répond pas bien; **u. to treatment** qui ne réagit pas au traitement; **she complains that her husband is u. in bed** elle se plaint du fait que son mari manque d'enthousiasme au lit **2** *(mentally) (to suggestion)* indifférent **(to** à); *(audience etc)* inerte, passif; **to be u. to sb's needs** ne pas répondre aux besoins de qn

unrest [ʌnˈrest] N troubles *mpl*; **social u.** agitation *f* sociale; **labour** *or* **industrial u.** agitation ouvrière; **there was u. among the workers** il y avait de l'agitation parmi les ouvriers

unrestrained [ʌnrɪ'streɪnd] ADJ non réprimé, effréné; **u. laughter** rires non réprimés

unrestrainedly [ʌnrɪ'streɪnɪdlɪ] ADV librement, sans contrainte

unrestricted [ʌnrɪ'strɪktɪd] ADJ sans restriction, illimité; *(power)* absolu; *(access)* libre; **u. by regulations** non réglementé

unrevealed [ʌnrɪ'viːld] ADJ non révélé

unrewarded [ʌnrɪ'wɔːdɪd] ADJ non récompensé; **they shouldn't go u.** on ne peut pas les laisser sans récompense

unrewarding [ʌnrɪ'wɔːdɪŋ] ADJ 1 *(financially)* peu rémunérateur, -trice 2 *(intellectually etc) (job, subject etc)* ingrat

unrhythmical [ʌn'rɪðmɪk(ə)l] ADJ *(person)* qui n'a pas le sens du rythme; *(music)* peu rythmé

unrig [ʌn'rɪg] VT **(-gg-)** *Naut (ship)* dégréer

unrighteous [ʌn'raɪtʃəs] ADJ *(person, action)* impie; *(life)* d'impiété
▪ NPL **the u.** les impies *mpl*

unripe [ʌn'raɪp] ADJ vert, qui n'est pas mûr; *(wheat)* en herbe

unrivalled, *Am* **unrivaled** [ʌn'raɪv(ə)ld] ADJ sans rival, hors pair; **our goods are u.** nos articles sont sans concurrence

unroadworthy [ʌn'rəʊdwɜːðɪ] ADJ *(vehicle)* qui n'est pas en état de rouler

unroll [ʌn'rəʊl] VT *(map, cloth)* dérouler; *(banner)* déferler
▪ VI se dérouler

unromantic [ʌnrə'mæntɪk] ADJ peu romantique; **how very u. of you!** tu n'es vraiment pas romantique!, tu manques vraiment de romantisme!

unrope [ʌn'rəʊp] VI *(in mountaineering)* se détacher (de la cordée)

unruffled [ʌn'rʌf(ə)ld] ADJ 1 *(person)* calme, serein; **u., he continued to speak** impassible, il a continué de parler 2 *(sea)* calme; *(hair, feathers)* lisse

unruled [ʌn'ruːld] ADJ *(paper)* non réglé, sans lignes

unruliness [ʌn'ruːlɪnɪs] N *(of child)* indiscipline *f*, turbulence *f*; *(of horse)* caractère *m* fougueux

unruly [ʌn'ruːlɪ] ADJ *(child)* indiscipliné, turbulent; *(horse)* fougueux; *(hair)* difficile à coiffer; **the crowd started getting u.** la foule commença à s'agiter

unsaddle [ʌn'sæd(ə)l] VT 1 *(horse)* desseller; *(donkey)* débâter 2 *(rider)* désarçonner

unsafe [ʌn'seɪf] ADJ 1 *(dangerous)* dangereux; *(bridge, structure)* peu sûr; *(chair, rope)* peu solide; *(undertaking)* hasardeux; **the chemicals are u. so close to the fire** il est dangereux de laisser ces produits chimiques si près du feu; **it's u. to leave it near the fire** c'est dangereux de le laisser près du feu 2 *(in danger) (of person)* en danger; **to feel u.** ne pas se sentir en sécurité 3 *Law* douteux
▪ ▶ **u. sex** rapports *mpl* non protégés

unsaid [ʌn'sed] ADJ **to leave sth u.** passer qch sous silence; **there was a lot that was left u. between them** il y a eu beaucoup de non-dits entre eux; **it's better left u.** mieux vaut ne rien dire; **if you don't do as I say …, he muttered, and left the rest u.** si tu ne fais pas ce que je te demande …, murmura-t-il sans finir sa phrase

unsalaried [ʌn'sælərɪd] ADJ *(position)* non rémunéré; *(person)* non salarié

unsaleable [ʌn'seɪləb(ə)l] ADJ *(goods)* invendable

unsalted [ʌn'sɔːltɪd] ADJ *(meat, fish)* sans sel
▪ ▶ **u. butter** beurre *m* doux

unsatisfactorily [ʌnsætɪs'fækt(ə)rɪlɪ] ADV d'une manière peu satisfaisante

unsatisfactory [ʌnsætɪs'fækt(ə)rɪ] ADJ *(conclusion, explanation)* non satisfaisant; *(system)* défectueux; **if this item is u. in any way …** si cet article ne vous donne pas satisfaction …; **this situation is most u.** cette situation n'est pas du tout satisfaisante

unsatisfied [ʌn'sætɪsfaɪd] ADJ 1 *(not content)* non satisfait *(with de)* 2 *(not convinced)* **I was u. with her explanation** je n'étais pas satisfait de son explication 3 *(appetite)* non rassasié; *(desire, lust)* insatisfait, inassouvi; **the meal left us u.** le repas ne nous a pas rassasiés; **her desire for novelty was still u.** son désir de nouveauté restait inassouvi

unsatisfying [ʌn'sætɪsfaɪɪŋ] ADJ 1 *(novel, ending, explanation)* peu satisfaisant 2 *(meal etc)* insuffisant

unsavoury, *Am* **unsavory** [ʌn'seɪv(ə)rɪ] ADJ 1 *(smell)* désagréable; **the food looked rather u.** la nourriture n'était pas appétissante 2 *(person, district, bar, reputation)* louche; *(scandal, details)* abject; **there were some rather u. characters in the bar** il y avait des types plutôt louches dans le bar

unsay [ʌn'seɪ] *(pt, pp* **unsaid** [ʌn'sed]) VT rétracter, retirer; **you can't u. it** tu ne peux pas retirer ce que tu as dit; **what's said cannot be unsaid** ce qui est dit est dit

unscathed [ʌn'skeɪðd] ADJ *(person)* indemne, sain et sauf; *(building)* intact; **she came through the trial with her reputation u.** sa réputation n'a pas souffert du procès

unscented [ʌn'sentɪd] ADJ *(soap etc)* sans parfum, non parfumé

unscheduled [ʌn'ʃedjuːld] ADJ *(departure, meeting)* imprévu; *(plane, train)* supplémentaire; *(stop)* non prévu

unscholarly [ʌn'skɒləlɪ] ADJ *(not appropriate for a scholar)* qui n'est pas digne d'un intellectuel; *(not written etc in a scholarly way)* peu académique

unschooled [ʌn'skuːld] ADJ 1 *Old-fashioned (person)* sans instruction; **he is u. in such matters** il est ignorant en la matière 2 *(horse)* non dressé

unscientific [ʌnsaɪən'tɪfɪk] ADJ non scientifique; **isn't that rather u.?** ce n'est pas très scientifique; **that's very u.** ce n'est pas du tout scientifique

unscientifically [ʌnsaɪən'tɪfɪklɪ] ADV peu scientifiquement

unscramble [ʌn'skræmb(ə)l] VT déchiffrer; *Tel* désembrouiller

unscrambler [ʌn'skræmblər] N *Tel* décodeur *m*

unscrambling [ʌn'skræmblɪŋ] N *Tel* décodage *m*

unscrew [ʌn'skruː] VT dévisser
▪ VI se dévisser

unscripted [ʌn'skrɪptɪd] ADJ *(dialogue in film)* improvisé; *(remark)* non préparé; **that was quite u.** c'était complètement improvisé

unscrupulous [ʌn'skruːpjʊləs] ADJ *(person)* sans scrupules; *(dealings, methods etc)* peu scrupuleux

unscrupulously [ʌn'skruːpjʊləslɪ] ADV *(to proceed, exploit)* sans scrupules

unscrupulousness [ʌn'skruːpjʊləsnɪs] N *(of person)* absence *f* de scrupules; *(of dealings)* malhonnêteté *f*

unseal [ʌn'siːl] VT *(letter)* décacheter

unsealed [ʌn'siːld] ADJ *(letter)* décacheté

unseasonable [ʌn'siːz(ə)nəb(ə)l] ADJ *(fish, fruit)* hors de saison; **this weather's very u.** ce n'est un pas un temps de saison

unseasonably [ʌn'siːz(ə)nəblɪ] ADV **it was u. warm/cold for the time of year** il faisait extrêmement chaud/froid pour la saison

unseasoned [ʌn'siːz(ə)nd] ADJ *(food)* non assaisonné; *(timber)* vert

unseat [ʌn'siːt] VT 1 *(rider)* désarçonner 2 *Parl (MP)* faire perdre son siège à

unseaworthy [ʌn'siːwɜːðɪ] N *(ship)* innavigable

unsecured [ʌnsɪ'kjʊəd] ADJ 1 *Fin (loan, overdraft)* non garanti 2 *(load)* mal attaché
▪ ▶ *Fin* **u. advance** avance *f* à découvert; *Fin* **u. creditor** créancier, -ière ordinaire *ou* chirographaire; *Fin* **u. debenture** obligation *f* non garantie; *Fin* **u. debt** créance *f* chirographaire *ou* sans garantie

unseeded [ʌn'siːdɪd] ADJ *Tennis (player)* non classé

unseeing [ʌn'siːɪŋ] ADJ **to look at sb/sth with u. eyes** regarder qn/qch sans (le) voir

unseemliness [ʌn'siːmlɪnɪs] N *(of conduct)* inconvenance *f*

unseemly [ʌn'siːmlɪ] ADJ *(behaviour)* inconvenant

unseen [ʌn'siːn] ADJ 1 *(hands, influence, force)* invisible; **u. by the guards they …** sans que les gardiens les voient, ils …; **to do sth u.** faire qch sans être vu; **to slip through u.** *(of person, mistake)* passer inaperçu 2 **to buy sth (sight) u.** acheter qch sans l'avoir vu
▪ N *Sch* version *f* non préparée
▪ ▶ *Sch* **u. translation** version non préparée

unselfconscious [ʌnself'kɒnʃəs] ADJ *(charm)* naturel; *(laugh)* spontané; **he's got a big scar on his face but he's quite u. about it** il a une grande cicatrice sur le visage mais n'est pas complexé; **he's a very u. sort of person** c'est quelqu'un de très spontané *ou* naturel

unselfconsciously [ʌnself'kɒnʃəslɪ] ADV naturellement; *(to laugh)* de façon spontanée

unselfish [ʌn'selfɪʃ] ADJ généreux; *(motive, gesture)* désintéressé; **one of the most u. people I've met** une des personnes les plus désintéressées que j'aie connues

unselfishly [ʌn'selfɪʃlɪ] ADV généreusement; **he acted u. and put his own considerations last** il a agi avec désintéressement et a fait passer ses intérêts en dernier

unselfishness [ʌn'selfɪʃnɪs] N générosité *f*; *(not putting self first)* désintéressement *m*

unsellable [ʌn'seləb(ə)l] ADJ invendable

unsentimental [ʌnsentɪ'ment(ə)l] ADJ peu sentimental, -aux; **the film remains u. throughout** le film ne verse jamais dans le mélo

unserviceable [ʌn'sɜːvɪsəb(ə)l] ADJ inutilisable

unsettle [ʌn'set(ə)l] VT *(sb's ideas)* ébranler; *(person) (less deeply)* troubler

unsettled [ʌn'set(ə)ld] ADJ 1 *(unstable, uncertain) (country)* troublé, instable; *(stock market)* instable; *(weather)* variable, changeant; *(mind)* inquiet, -ète, troublé; **I feel u. at the moment** je me sens perturbé en ce moment; **to have an u. stomach** avoir l'estomac un peu dérangé; **the u. state of the weather** l'incertitude *f* du temps 2 *(question, dispute)* irrésolu 3 *(bill)* impayé, non réglé 4 *(without settlers)* non colonisé

unsettling [ʌn'setlɪŋ] ADJ troublant, dérangeant

unsex [ʌn'seks] VT *(man)* déviriliser; *(woman)* déféminiser

unshackle [ʌnˈʃæk(ə)l] VT (prisoner) ôter les fers à; Fig libérer

unshackled [ʌnˈʃæk(ə)ld] ADJ sans entraves, libre; **to be u. by convention** ne pas porter le poids des conventions

unshakeable [ʌnˈʃeɪkəb(ə)l] ADJ inébranlable

unshaken [ʌnˈʃeɪk(ə)n] ADJ (conviction) inébranlable; **his faith was u. by ...** sa foi restait inébranlable malgré ...; **he was u. by the news** la nouvelle ne l'a pas ébranlé

unshaven, unshaved [ʌnˈʃeɪv(ə)n, -ˈʃeɪvd] ADJ (chin, armpits, legs) non rasé; **he was u.** il n'était pas rasé

unsheathe [ʌnˈʃiːð] VT (sword etc) dégainer

unsheltered [ʌnˈʃeltəd] ADJ non abrité, non protégé (**from** contre)

unship [ʌnˈʃɪp] VT (-pp-) Naut décharger, débarquer

unshod [ʌnˈʃɒd] ADJ 1 (person) sans chaussures; (having removed shoes) déchaussé 2 (horse) déferré

unsighted [ʌnˈsaɪtɪd] ADJ 1 (not visible) invisible, qui n'est pas en vue; **he was u. by one of his own team** (not able to see clearly) un membre de son équipe lui bouchait la vue 2 (sightless) aveugle

unsightliness [ʌnˈsaɪtlɪnɪs] N laideur f

unsightly [ʌnˈsaɪtlɪ] ADJ laid; (scar) vilain; (hoardings, buildings) affreux

unsigned [ʌnˈsaɪnd] ADJ non signé, sans signature

unsinkable [ʌnˈsɪŋkəb(ə)l] ADJ insubmersible

unskilful, Am **unskillful** [ʌnˈskɪlf(ʊ)l] ADJ malhabile, maladroit (**at sth** à qch); **he's u. at convincing people** il ne sait pas convaincre les gens

unskilled [ʌnˈskɪld] ADJ **to be u. in** or **at doing sth** ne pas être doué pour ce qui est de faire qch
▸▸ **u. labour** main-d'œuvre f non spécialisée; **u. worker** ouvrier m non qualifié

unskimmed [ʌnˈskɪmd] ADJ (milk) entier

unslept-in [ʌnˈslept-] ADJ (bed) non défait

unsling [ʌnˈslɪŋ] VT (pt, pp **unslung** [-ˈslʌŋ]) dégréer; (hammock) décrocher; **to u. one's rifle** enlever son fusil de l'épaule

unsmiling [ʌnˈsmaɪlɪŋ] ADJ sérieux; **he stared at me u.** il me fixait sans sourire

unsmoked [ʌnˈsməʊkt] ADJ non fumé

unsociability [ʌnsəʊʃəˈbɪlɪtɪ], **unsociableness** [ʌnˈsəʊʃəblnɪs] N manque m de sociabilité

unsociable [ʌnˈsəʊʃəb(ə)l] ADJ sauvage, peu sociable

unsocial [ʌnˈsəʊʃəl] ADJ 1 **to work u. hours** travailler en-dehors des heures habituelles 2 = **unsociable**

unsold [ʌnˈsəʊld] ADJ invendu; **u. goods** invendus mpl; **the u. copies** les invendus mpl

unsoldierly [ʌnˈsəʊldʒəlɪ] ADJ peu militaire

unsolicited [ʌnsəˈlɪsɪtɪd] ADJ (comment) non sollicité; (contribution) volontaire; (application) spontané; **to do sth u.** faire qch spontanément
▸▸ **u. manuscript** manuscrit non commandé

unsolvable [ʌnˈsɒlvəb(ə)l] ADJ insoluble

unsolved [ʌnˈsɒlvd] ADJ (problem) non résolu

unsophisticated [ʌnsəˈfɪstɪkeɪtɪd] ADJ (person, tastes, pleasures) simple, non sophistiqué; (wine) sans prétention; (machine) non sophistiqué

unsound [ʌnˈsaʊnd] ADJ 1 (kidney etc) malade; (foundations, bridge) en mauvais état; (timber) avarié; **his health was u.** il n'était pas

en bonne santé; **to be of u. mind** ne pas avoir toute sa raison 2 (theory, argument) mal fondé, peu solide; (decision, advice) peu judicieux; (investment) peu sûr, douteux; **it is financially u.** les finances ne sont pas saines; **I know it's (politically) u. to say so, but ...** je sais que cela va être mal vu de dire cela mais ...; **she regarded him as u. on social policy** elle considérait que ses vues en matière de politique sociale n'étaient pas orthodoxes; **he's still rather u. on the basics** ses bases ne sont pas encore très solides

unsparing [ʌnˈspeərɪŋ] ADJ **to be u. of one's time/with one's advice** ne pas être avare de son temps/de conseils; **to be u. in one's efforts** ne pas ménager ses efforts

unsparingly [ʌnˈspeərɪŋlɪ] ADV (to give, donate) sans compter, sans regarder à la dépense; (to work) sans ménager ses efforts

unspeakable [ʌnˈspiːkəb(ə)l] ADJ 1 (bad) (conditions, state, pain) indicible; **it's u.!** c'est innommable ou inqualifiable!; **he's really u.!** il est au-dessous de tout! 2 (joy) indicible, ineffable

unspeakably [ʌnˈspiːkəblɪ] ADV indiciblement; **to behave u.** avoir une conduite inqualifiable; **u. bad** exécrable

unspecified [ʌnˈspesɪfaɪd] ADJ non spécifié; **certain u. persons** certaines personnes, dont on taira les noms

unspectacular [ʌnspekˈtækjʊlər] ADJ peu spectaculaire

unspent [ʌnˈspent] ADJ (money) non dépensé; (cartridge) qui n'a pas servi; **to vent one's u. rage on sb** se défouler sur qn

unspoilt [ʌnˈspɔɪlt] (occ **unspoiled** [ʌnˈspɔɪld]) ADJ 1 (untouched) (countryside, view) intact; (tranquillity) parfait 2 (child) qui n'est pas gâté; **she's totally u.** ce n'est pas une enfant gâtée; **he was u. by his success** son succès ne lui a pas tourné la tête

unspoken [ʌnˈspəʊk(ə)n] ADJ (fear, thought, threat) inexprimé; (agreement) tacite; **her u. thought was that ...** intérieurement elle pensait que ...; **although his name remained u. ...** bien que son nom n'ait pas été prononcé ...

unsporting [ʌnˈspɔːtɪŋ], **unsportsmanlike** [ʌnˈspɔːtsmənlaɪk] ADJ peu sportif; **that's u.** ce n'est pas très sportif; **he was fined for u. behaviour** il a été pénalisé pour manque de sportivité

unstable [ʌnˈsteɪb(ə)l] ADJ instable
▸▸ Econ **u. equilibrium** équilibre m instable

unstained [ʌnˈsteɪnd] ADJ 1 esp Lit (reputation) sans tache 2 (wood) non teinté

unstamped [ʌnˈstæmpt] ADJ (letter) sans timbre, non affranchi; Admin, Law (document) non estampillé

unstated [ʌnˈsteɪtɪd] ADJ inexprimé

unstatesmanlike [ʌnˈsteɪtsmənlaɪk] ADJ peu digne d'un homme d'État

unsteadily [ʌnˈstedɪlɪ] ADV (to walk) d'un pas chancelant, en titubant; (to hold sth) d'une main tremblante; (to write) d'une main tremblante

unsteadiness [ʌnˈstedɪnɪs] ADJ (of table, person) déséquilibre m; (of hand) manque m de sûreté; (of drunk person) démarche f chancelante; (of dollar etc) instabilité f

unsteady [ʌnˈstedɪ] ADJ (table) instable, branlant; (legs, footsteps, person) chancelant; (hand, voice) mal assuré; (position, foothold) mal assuré, incertain; (flame) tremblant, vacillant; (economy, the dollar etc) instable; (stock market) irrégulier; **to be u. on one's legs** or **feet** ne pas tenir très bien sur ses jambes

unsterilized [ʌnˈsterɪlaɪzd] ADJ non stérilisé

unstick [ʌnˈstɪk] VT (pt, pp **unstuck** [-ˈstʌk]) décoller

unstinted [ʌnˈstɪntɪd] ADJ 1 (supplies) abondant, sans restriction 2 = **unstinting** 2

unstinting [ʌnˈstɪntɪŋ] ADJ 1 (person) **to be u. in one's praise of sb/sth** ne pas tarir d'éloges au sujet de qn/qch; **to be u. in one's efforts to do sth** faire tous ses efforts pour faire qch 2 (compliments, support) sans réserve; (admiration) sans bornes; **u. efforts** efforts illimités; **to give u. praise** ne pas ménager ses louanges

unstintingly [ʌnˈstɪntɪŋlɪ] ADV généreusement; (to help, work) sans se ménager; **to praise sb u.** ne pas tarir d'éloges sur qn

unstitch [ʌnˈstɪtʃ] VT (seam) découdre; **to come unstitched** se découdre

unstop [ʌnˈstɒp] VT (-pp-) (remove stopper from) déboucher

unstoppable [ʌnˈstɒpəb(ə)l] ADJ (shot) imparable; **he's u. now** rien ne pourra l'arrêter désormais

unstressed [ʌnˈstrest] ADJ non accentué, atone

unstring [ʌnˈstrɪŋ] VT (pt, pp **unstrung** [-ˈstrʌŋ]) 1 (bow) débander; **to u. a violin** ôter les cordes d'un violon 2 (beads etc) ôter le fil de

unstructured [ʌnˈstrʌktʃəd] ADJ (activity) non structuré; (group) non organisé; Mktg (interview) non structuré, libre

unstuck [ʌnˈstʌk] ADJ **to come u.** se décoller; Fam (of person, plan) s'effondrer; Fam **that's where they came u.** c'est là qu'ils ont cafouillé

unstudied [ʌnˈstʌdɪd] ADJ spontané, naturel

unsubdued [ʌnsəbˈdjuːd] ADJ indompté

unsubmissive [ʌnsəbˈmɪsɪv] ADJ insoumis, rebelle

unsubscribe [ʌnsəbˈskraɪb] VI Comput (from ISP) résilier son abonnement; (from mailing list) se désinscrire

unsubscribed [ʌnsəbˈskraɪbd] ADJ Fin (capital) non souscrit

unsubsidized [ʌnˈsʌbsɪdaɪzd] ADJ non subventionné

unsubstantial [ʌnsəbˈstænʃəl] ADJ (meal) peu substantiel, peu nourrissant; (novel) creux

unsubstantiated [ʌnsəbˈstænʃɪeɪtɪd] ADJ (accusation) non prouvé; (rumour) non corroboré

unsubtle [ʌnˈsʌt(ə)l] ADJ peu subtil; **how could anyone be so u.!** comment peut-on manquer de subtilité à ce point!; **u. hints** allusions fpl lourdes

unsuccessful [ʌnsəkˈsesfʊl] ADJ (effort, attempt) vain, infructueux; (outcome, marriage) malheureux; **u. applications will not be acknowledged** nous ne répondrons pas aux personnes dont les candidatures n'ont pas été retenues; **your application has been u.** votre candidature n'a pas été retenue; **it was completely u.** cela a été un échec complet; **to be u.** (of person, plan, marriage) ne pas réussir; **she was u. in practically every undertaking she embarked on** elle échouait dans pratiquement tout ce qu'elle entreprenait; **the festival was u.** le festival a été un échec; **I've tried but have been u. up till now** j'ai essayé mais je n'ai pas réussi jusqu'à présent; **u. candidate** (at election) candidat non élu

unsuccessfully [ʌnsəkˈsesfəlɪ] ADV sans succès, en vain

unsuitability [ʌns(j)uːtəˈbɪlɪtɪ] N (of per-

son) inaptitude *f* (**for sth** à qch); *(of thing)* inadéquation *f* (**for sth** à qch); **the u. of the clothes he was wearing** les vêtements inadéquats qu'il portait

unsuitable [ʌn's(j)uːtəb(ə)l] **ADJ** *(tools)* impropre, mal adapté (**for** à); *(friend, people)* peu recommandable; *(music, choice of words)* déplacé; *(time)* inopportun; *(conditions, diet)* inadéquat, non approprié; *(clothes)* inadéquat; *(climate)* peu indiqué; *(couple, partners)* mal assorti; **this is an u. environment for a child** ce n'est pas un environnement approprié pour un enfant; **this is an u. time to bring the matter up** ce n'est pas le moment de parler de cela; **I thought Wednesday was u.** je pensais que mercredi ne vous/lui/*etc* convenait pas; **they're u. for each other** ils ne vont pas ensemble; **he's u. for her** ce n'est pas l'homme qu'il lui faut; **he's quite u. for the job** ce n'est pas la personne qu'il faut pour ce poste; **u. for the occasion** qui ne convient pas à la circonstance; **you have chosen a most u. time to …** vous avez mal choisi le moment de …; **the film is u. for children** ce n'est pas un film pour les enfants; **the climate is u. for wheat** le climat ne convient pas au blé

unsuitably [ʌn's(j)uːtəblɪ] **ADV** inadéquatement; *(to behave)* de façon inappropriée; **to be u. dressed** ne pas porter les vêtements qui conviennent; **they're u. matched** *(of couple)* ils sont mal assortis

unsuited [ʌn's(j)uːtɪd] **ADJ** *(person)* inapte (**for** *or* **to sth** à qch); *(material, clothes, equipment)* inadéquat; **she's clearly u. to this type of work** il est clair qu'elle n'est pas faite pour ce genre de travail; **they are u. (to each other)** ils sont mal assortis

unsullied [ʌn'sʌlɪd] **ADJ** sans tache; **her reputation was u. by …** sa réputation n'a pas souffert de …

unsung [ʌn'sʌŋ] **ADJ** *esp Lit (deed)* non célébré
  ► ► **u. hero** héros *m* méconnu

unsupervised [ʌn'suːpəvaɪzd] **ADJ** *(child)* non surveillé; **'u. minors not admitted'** 'interdit aux enfants non accompagnés'

unsupported [ʌnsə'pɔːtɪd] **ADJ 1** *(statement, charges)* sans preuves; **the theories were u. by any evidence** ces théories n'ont été étayées par aucune preuve **2** *(structure, wall)* sans support, sans appui; **to walk u.** marcher sans se faire aider; **he could walk u. by a stick** il marchait sans canne; **to leave one's family u.** ne pas subvenir aux besoins de sa famille; **more and more students are u. by the state** de plus en plus d'étudiants ne reçoivent pas d'aide de l'État

unsure [ʌn'ʃʊər] **ADJ** *(person)* incertain (**about** de); *(position)* peu sûr, précaire; **they were u. what to do next** ils n'étaient pas sûrs de savoir quoi faire après; **I was u. what she meant by this** je n'étais pas sûr de savoir ce qu'elle voulait dire par là; **to be u. of oneself** ne pas être sûr de soi; **I'm u. about it/him** j'ai des doutes là-dessus/en ce qui concerne

unsurpassable [ʌnsə'pɑːsəb(ə)l] **ADJ** insurpassable

unsurpassed [ʌnsə'pɑːst] **ADJ** sans égal

unsurprised [ʌnsə'praɪzd] **ADJ** non surpris; **I was u. by …** je n'ai pas été surpris par …

unsurprising [ʌnsə'praɪzɪŋ] **ADJ** peu surprenant

unsurprisingly [ʌnsə'praɪzɪŋlɪ] **ADV** **u., this suggestion was rejected** comme on pouvait s'y attendre, cette suggestion fut rejetée

unsuspected [ʌnsəs'pektɪd] **ADJ** insoupçonné (**by** de)

unsuspecting [ʌnsəs'pektɪŋ] **ADJ** qui ne se

doute de rien; *(by nature)* peu soupçonneux; **he's so u.** il est si peu soupçonneux; **when he later, all u., …** quand plus tard, sans se douter de rien, il …

unsuspicious [ʌnsəs'pɪʃəs] **ADJ** peu soupçonneux

unsustainable [ʌnsə'steɪnəb(ə)l] **ADJ** non viable

unsweetened [ʌn'swiːt(ə)nd] **ADJ** non sucré

unswerving [ʌn'swɜːvɪŋ] **ADJ** *(loyalty)* constant, ferme; **they have been u. in their support (for us)** ils nous ont prêté un appui constant

unswervingly [ʌn'swɜːvɪŋlɪ] **ADV** sans s'écarter du but; *(to maintain)* sans relâche; **u. loyal** d'une loyauté absolue

unsympathetic [ʌnsɪmpə'θetɪk] **ADJ 1** *(lacking understanding)* peu compatissant; **they were very u. about our problems** nos problèmes les laissaient complètement indifférents; **the idea met with an u. reception** l'idée a reçu un accueil plutôt froid; **he was generally u. to modern art** *(didn't like)* de manière générale il appréciait peu l'art moderne; *(made critical statements about)* il n'était généralement pas tendre avec l'art moderne **2** *(unlikeable)* antipathique; **I find the characters of this novel u.** les personnages de ce roman me sont peu sympathiques

unsympathetically [ʌnsɪmpə'θetɪklɪ] **ADV** froidement; **the novel/film was u. reviewed by the critics** les critiques n'ont pas été tendres avec le roman/le film

unsystematic [ʌnsɪstə'mætɪk] **ADJ** non systématique, sans méthode; **you're too u.** tu n'es pas assez méthodique

unsystematically [ʌnsɪstə'mætɪklɪ] **ADV** sans méthode

untainted [ʌn'teɪntɪd] **ADJ** *(person, judgment)* non corrompu; *(reputation)* sans tache

untalented [ʌn'tæləntɪd] **ADJ** peu doué

untam(e)able [ʌn'teɪməb(ə)l] **ADJ** *(animal, spirit)* indomptable

untamed [ʌn'teɪmd] **ADJ** *(animal, spirit, luxuriance)* indompté

untangle [ʌn'tæŋg(ə)l] **VT** *(wool, string, hair)* démêler; *(mystery)* éclaircir; *(sth complicated)* débrouiller

untapped [ʌn'tæpt] **ADJ** *(resources)* inexploité

untarnished [ʌn'tɑːnɪʃt] **ADJ** *(metal), Fig* non terni, sans tache

untasted [ʌn'teɪstɪd] **ADJ** auquel on n'a pas goûté; **to send a dish away u.** renvoyer un plat sans y goûter

untaught [ʌn'tɔːt] **ADJ** *(person)* sans instruction; *(skill)* naturel

untaxable [ʌn'tæksəb(ə)l] **ADJ** non imposable

untaxed [ʌn'tækst] **ADJ** *(income)* exempt *ou* exempté d'impôts; *(product)* non imposé, non taxé; *(car)* ≃ sans vignette

unteachable [ʌn'tiːtʃəb(ə)l] **ADJ** *(person)* à qui l'on ne peut rien apprendre, incapable d'apprendre; *(subject, art)* impossible à enseigner

untenable [ʌn'tenəb(ə)l] **ADJ** *(position)* intenable; *(theory)* insoutenable

untenanted [ʌn'tenəntɪd] **ADJ** sans locataire(s); **these flats have been u. for years** ces appartements sont inoccupés depuis des années

untended [ʌn'tendɪd] **ADJ** *(sick person)* non soigné, sans soins; *(garden)* non entretenu

untested [ʌn'testɪd] **ADJ** inéprouvé, non prouvé; *(invention, drug)* non essayé; *(sample)* non analysé

unthinkable [ʌn'θɪŋkəb(ə)l] **ADJ** inconcevable, impensable; **it's u. that …** il est inconcevable que … + *subj*; **if the u. should happen** si l'inconcevable se produisait

unthinking [ʌn'θɪŋkɪŋ] **ADJ** *(person)* étourdi

unthinkingly [ʌn'θɪŋkɪŋlɪ] **ADV** *(to do sth)* sans réfléchir, étourdiment

unthought-of [ʌn'θɔːt-] **ADJ** auquel on n'a pas pensé

unthread [ʌn'θred] **VT** *(beads)* ôter le fil de

untidily [ʌn'taɪdɪlɪ] **ADV** en désordre; **she's always u. dressed** elle a toujours l'air débraillé

untidiness [ʌn'taɪdɪnɪs] **N** *(of room, appearance)* désordre *m*; *(of person) (characteristic)* manque *m* d'ordre

untidy [ʌn'taɪdɪ] **ADJ 1** *(room, desk)* en désordre, mal rangé; *(hair)* ébouriffé; *(writing)* brouillon; **u. appearance** tenue *f* débraillée; **his playing is u.** *(of musician)* son jeu manque de netteté; **he brings the novel to an u. end** il termine le roman d'une façon plutôt confuse; **an u. mind** un esprit brouillon; **his room/desk always gets u.** sa chambre/son bureau est toujours en désordre **2** *(person) (as characteristic)* désordonné, qui manque d'ordre; **he's such a u. sort of person** il est tellement désordonné

untie [ʌn'taɪ] **VT** *(pt, pp* untied; *prp* untying) *(shoelaces, ribbon)* défaire; *(knot)* dénouer; *(knot, parcel)* défaire, délier; *(parcel)* déficeler; *(one's hair, dog, boat)* détacher; **to u. itself, to come untied** *(of knot)* se défaire, dénouer

until [ʌn'tɪl] **PREP** VOIR GRAMMAIRE A68; A73 **1** jusqu'à; **you have u. tomorrow to finish it** tu as jusqu'à demain pour le finir; **u. 2008** jusqu'en 2008; **u. now** jusqu'ici, jusque-là; **she didn't arrive u. yesterday** elle n'est arrivée qu'hier; **u. then we'll just have to make do** en attendant il va falloir se débrouiller; *Radio, TV* **u. tomorrow, I wish you a very good night** je vous souhaite une très bonne soirée, à demain

2 not u. (after) eight o'clock pas avant huit heures *(passées)*; **not u. tomorrow** pas avant demain; **it wasn't u. after Easter that …** ce n'est qu'après Pâques que …; **I've never seen it u. now** c'est la première fois que je le vois

CONJ VOIR GRAMMAIRE A75 **1** jusqu'à ce que + *subj*; **u. all the windows are open** jusqu'à ce que toutes les fenêtres soient ouvertes; **we'll wait u. you're ready** nous attendrons que vous soyez prêt; **we waited u. the rain stopped** nous avons attendu jusqu'à ce que la pluie cesse; **wait u. the bus stops** attends que le bus soit arrêté; **he drank u. he was ill** il a bu jusqu'à s'en rendre malade; **we worked u. we dropped** nous avons travaillé jusqu'à n'en plus pouvoir; **he laughed u. he cried** il a pleuré de rire

2 he won't come u. he's invited il ne viendra pas avant d'être invité *ou* sans qu'on l'invite; **I won't leave him u. he's completely recovered** je ne le quitterai pas tant qu'il n'est pas tout à fait guéri; **don't do anything u. I say so** ne fais rien avant que je te le dise; **don't sign u. you've checked everything** ne signe rien avant d'avoir tout vérifié

untilled [ʌn'tɪld] **ADJ** non cultivé, non labouré

untimely [ʌn'taɪmlɪ] **ADJ** *(death)* prématuré; *(question, action)* inopportun, intempestif, mal à propos; **to come to an u. end** mourir avant l'âge

untiring [ʌn'taɪərɪŋ] **ADJ** infatigable, inlassable

untiringly [ʌn'taɪərɪŋlɪ] **ADV** infatigablement, inlassablement

unto [ˈʌntʊ, ˈʌntə] PREP *Arch, Lit* **to liken sth u. sth** comparer qch à *ou* avec qch; *Bible* **u. us a child is born** un enfant nous est né; *Bible* **and I say u. you …** en vérité je vous le dis …; **to turn u. sb** se tourner vers qn

untold [ʌnˈtəʊld] ADJ *(riches)* immense, énorme; **u. joy** joie *f* indicible; **u. suffering** souffrances *fpl* inouïes

untouchable [ʌnˈtʌtʃəb(ə)l] ADJ intouchable
N *(in India)* intouchable *mf*, paria *m*

untouched [ʌnˈtʌtʃt] ADJ **1** *(by hand etc)* non touché; **to be u. by the influence of …** ne pas avoir subi l'influence de …; **most of the city centre has remained u.** une grande partie du centre ville est resté intact; **u. by human hand** *(food)* non manié; **these artefacts have lain u. by human hand for thousands of years** ces objets sont restés inconnus de l'homme pendant des milliers d'années **2 he'd left the meal u.** il n'avait pas touché à son repas **3** *(safe) (person)* indemne, sain et sauf, *f* saine et sauve; *(thing)* intact **4** *(unmoved) (person)* indifférent, insensible (**by** à) **5** *(without equal)* sans égal, incomparable

untoward [ʌntəˈwɔːd, *Am* ʌnˈtɔːd] ADJ fâcheux; **I hope nothing u. has happened** j'espère qu'il n'est pas arrivé un malheur

untraceable [ʌnˈtreɪsəb(ə)l] ADJ introuvable

untrad(e)able [ʌnˈtreɪdəb(ə)l] ADJ *St Exch* incotable

untrained [ʌnˈtreɪnd] ADJ *(person)* qui n'a pas reçu de formation professionnelle; *(horse)* non dressé; **u. ear** oreille *f* inexercée

untrammelled [ʌnˈtræməld] ADJ non entravé (**by** par), libre (**by** de)

untransferable [ʌntræns'fɜːrəb(ə)l] ADJ non transmissible; *Law (right, property)* incessible

untranslatable [ʌntræns'leɪtəb(ə)l] ADJ intraduisible

untravelled [ʌnˈtrævəld] ADJ *(person)* qui n'a pas beaucoup voyagé; *(country)* inexploré, peu fréquenté; **he's relatively u.** il n'a pas beaucoup voyagé

untried [ʌnˈtraɪd] ADJ **1** *(not tried out)* qui n'a pas été essayé, non essayé **2** *(untested) (engine, system)* non testé; **u. troops** troupes qui n'ont pas encore combattu **3** *Law (prisoner, case)* qui n'a pas encore été jugé

untrodden [ʌnˈtrɒd(ə)n] ADJ *esp Lit (path)* peu fréquenté; *Fig* **democracy remains for them an u. path** ils n'ont jamais goûté à la démocratie; **u. snow** neige *f* immaculée *ou* vierge

untroubled [ʌnˈtrʌbəld] ADJ calme, tranquille; **the markets have been u. by the interest rate rise** les marchés n'ont pas été troublés par la hausse des taux d'intérêt; **he seemed u. by the news** la nouvelle ne semblait nullement le troubler

untrue [ʌnˈtruː] ADJ **1** *(incorrect)* faux, *f* fausse **2** *(unfaithful) (to wife, principles etc)* infidèle (**to** à); *(to comrades)* déloyal (**to** envers); **to be u. to oneself** trahir ses principes

untrustworthiness [ʌnˈtrʌstwɜːðɪnɪs] N *(of information, machine)* manque *m* de fiabilité; **he was noted for his u.** il avait la réputation de quelqu'un à qui on ne peut pas faire confiance

untrustworthy [ʌnˈtrʌstwɜːðɪ] ADJ *(person)* indigne de confiance; *(reference book, information)* peu fiable; *(evidence)* récusable

untruth [ʌnˈtruːθ, *pl* -ˈtruːðz] N mensonge *m*; **to tell an u.** dire un mensonge

untruthful [ʌnˈtruːθʊl] ADJ *(person)* menteur; *(story)* mensonger; **he's an u. boy** c'est un garçon qui ne dit jamais la vérité

untruthfully [ʌnˈtruːθfəlɪ] ADV de façon mensongère

untruthfulness [ʌnˈtruːθfʊlnɪs] N *(of evidence)* caractère *m* mensonger; **he was notorious for his u.** c'était un menteur notoire

untuned [ʌnˈtjuːnd] ADJ *(instrument)* non accordé; *(engine)* qui n'est pas réglé

untuneful [ʌnˈtjuːnfʊl] ADJ peu mélodieux

untutored [ʌnˈtjuːtəd] ADJ *esp Lit (person)* peu instruit; *(mind, taste)* non formé

untwine [ʌnˈtwaɪn] VT détordre, détortiller

untwist [ʌnˈtwɪst] VT *(strands)* détordre, détortiller; *(jar lid etc)* dévisser; **to u. itself, to come untwisted** se détordre
VI se détordre

untypical [ʌnˈtɪpɪk(ə)l] ADJ inhabituel; **it's very u. of her** c'est très inhabituel de sa part, cela ne lui ressemble pas

untypically [ʌnˈtɪpɪk(ə)lɪ] ADV inhabituellement

unusable [ʌnˈjuːzəb(ə)l] ADJ inutilisable

unused [ʌnˈjuːzd] ADJ **1** *(system, clothes etc)* dont on ne se sert pas; *(road)* pas fréquenté; *(talent)* non employé; *(building)* désaffecté; **her talents had gone largely u.** ses talents étaient restés inexploités; **our nuclear weapons are still u.** nos armes nucléaires n'ont encore jamais été utilisées **2** *(never yet used)* qui n'a jamais servi; *(clothes)* neuf **3** [ʌnˈjuːst] *(person)* peu habitué (**to sth** à qch); **to be u. to doing sth** ne pas avoir l'habitude de faire qch; **I'm still u. to you being here** je ne suis pas encore habitué à ce que tu sois là; **we're not u. to it** nous y sommes habitués

unusual [ʌnˈjuːʒʊəl] ADJ *(not common) (colour, style, design, thing to happen)* inhabituel, peu ordinaire; *(strange, out of the ordinary)* insolite; **an u. case of …** un cas peu commun *ou* peu ordinaire de …; **an u. lapse** une défaillance inhabituelle; **a very u. exception** une exception très inhabituelle; **what do you think of my new haircut? – well, it's certainly u.!** que penses-tu de ma nouvelle coupe de cheveux? – ah pour ça c'est original!; **he has some rather u. tastes** il a des goûts bizarres; **it's u. for her not to notice these things** c'est rare qu'elle ne remarque pas ces choses-là; **you don't want a drink?, that's u. for you** tu ne veux pas prendre un verre?, qu'est-ce qui t'arrive?; **the sort of information which is u. in most dictionaries** le genre d'information qu'on ne trouve habituellement pas dans les dictionnaires; **it's u. to see him at the theatre** il est rare qu'on le voie au théâtre; **it's not u.** ce n'est pas rare; **nothing u.** rien d'anormal; **of u. interest** d'un intérêt exceptionnel

unusually [ʌnˈjuːʒʊəlɪ] ADV inhabituellement; *(exceptionally)* exceptionnellement; **u., this language …** chose inhabituelle, cette langue …; **she stayed u. quiet** elle est restée inhabituellement calme; **an u. stupid/clever man** un homme d'une stupidité/ intelligence exceptionnelle; **u. tall** exceptionnellement grand; **it's very u. designed** c'est conçu de manière très insolite *ou* inhabituelle; **he was u. attentive** contrairement à son habitude, il a été attentif

unutterable [ʌnˈʌt(ə)rəb(ə)l] ADJ *(misery, stupidity)* innommable; *(boredom)* incroyable

unutterably [ʌnˈʌt(ə)rəblɪ] ADV **u. bored/ miserable** d'un ennui/dans une misère invraisemblable; **u. stupid** d'une stupidité innommable

unvaried [ʌnˈveərɪd] ADJ *(landscape, life)* sans variété; *(diet)* qui manque de variété

unvarnished [ʌnˈvɑːnɪʃt] ADJ *(surface)* non verni; *(pottery)* non vernissé; *Fig* **the plain u. truth** la vérité pure et simple

unvarying [ʌˈveərɪɪŋ] ADJ invariable, constant

unveil [ʌnˈveɪl] VT *(statue, plaque etc)* inaugurer; *(new car etc)* présenter; *Fig (secret, plan)* dévoiler
VI se dévoiler

unveiled [ʌnˈveɪld] ADJ sans voile

unveiling [ʌnˈveɪlɪŋ] N *(of statue, plaque etc)* inauguration *f*, *(of new car etc)* présentation *f*
▸▸ **u. ceremony** (cérémonie *f* d')inauguration

unverifiable [ʌnˈverɪfaɪəb(ə)l] ADJ invérifiable

unverified [ʌnˈverɪfaɪd] ADJ non contrôlé, non vérifié

unversed [ʌnˈvɜːst] ADJ peu versé (**in** dans)

unvoiced [ʌnˈvɔɪst] ADJ **1** *(opinion)* non exprimé **2** *Ling (vowel, consonant)* sourd, muet

unwaged [ʌnˈweɪdʒd] ADJ *(unpaid)* non rémunéré

unwanted [ʌnˈwɒntɪd] ADJ non voulu; **his help had been u.** on n'avait pas voulu de son aide; **to give away all one's u. books** se débarrasser de tous les livres dont on n'a plus besoin; **to be feeling u.** *(in the way)* se sentir de trop; *(unloved)* se sentir mal-aimé; **u. child** enfant non désiré
▸▸ **u. hair** poils *mpl* superflus

unwarlike [ʌnˈwɔːlaɪk] ADJ non belliqueux

unwarrantable [ʌnˈwɒrəntəb(ə)l] ADJ injustifiable

unwarrantably [ʌnˈwɒrəntəblɪ] ADV de manière injustifiable

unwarranted [ʌnˈwɒrəntɪd] ADJ injustifié; **u. familiarity** familiarité indue **u. insult** insulte gratuite

unwary [ʌnˈweərɪ] ADJ imprudent, imprévoyant; **an u. reader** un lecteur non averti
NPL **the u.** les imprudents *mpl*

unwashed [ʌnˈwɒʃt] ADJ non lavé
NPL *Fam Hum* **the great u.** les prolétaires *mpl*, les prolos *mpl*

unwavering [ʌnˈweɪvərɪŋ] ADJ constant; *(support, loyalty)* absolu; *(belief, conviction)* ferme; *(determination)* inébranlable; *(gaze)* soutenu

unwaveringly [ʌnˈweɪvərɪŋlɪ] ADV *(to support, be in favour of)* résolument; *(to look at sb)* sans faiblir

unweaned [ʌnˈwiːnd] ADJ *(child, kitten)* non sevré

unwearable [ʌnˈweərəb(ə)l] ADJ *(garment)* immettable

unwearying [ʌnˈwɪərɪɪŋ] ADJ inlassable, infatigable

unwed [ʌnˈwed] ADJ *Old-fashioned, Lit* qui n'est pas marié; **he remained u.** il ne s'est jamais marié

unweighted [ʌnˈweɪtɪd] ADJ *Econ (index)* non pondéré
▸▸ **u. figures** chiffres *mpl* bruts

unwelcome [ʌnˈwelkəm] ADJ *(visitor)* importun; *(news, development)* fâcheux; **to feel u.** ne pas se sentir le/la bienvenu(e); **u. visit** visite *f* importune **a not u. visit** une visite opportune; **her news could not have been more u.** les nouvelles qu'elle avait n'auraient pas pu être plus fâcheuses; **to make sb feel u.** faire sentir à qn qu'il n'est pas le bienvenu/qu'elle n'est pas la bienvenue; **the extra £50 was not u.** les 50 livres supplémentaires ne tombaient pas mal du tout

unwell [ʌnˈwel] ADJ souffrant; **are you feeling u.?** êtes-vous souffrant?

unwholesome [ʌnˈhəʊlsəm] ADJ malsain,

Com **u. demand** *(for products)* demande *f* indésirable

unwieldy [ʌnˈwiːldɪ] **ADJ** *(tool, object)* peu maniable, difficile à manier; *(method, approach)* trop complexe; *(system, bureaucracy)* lourd; *(person)* lourd et gauche

unwilling [ʌnˈwɪlɪŋ] **ADJ** *(helper)* réticent; *(consent)* donné à contrecœur; **an u. accomplice** un complice malgré moi/lui/*etc*; **to be u. to do sth** être peu disposé à faire qch, ne pas vouloir faire qch; **I was u. that my wife should know** *or* **for my wife to know** je ne voulais pas que ma femme le sache

unwillingly [ʌnˈwɪlɪŋlɪ] **ADV** à contrecœur

unwillingness [ʌnˈwɪlɪŋnɪs] **N** réticence *f*, **they showed such an u. to accept the terms that …** ils ont été tellement réticents à accepter les conditions que …; **their u. to compromise on this issue made agreement impossible** leur refus du compromis sur ce point rendait tout accord impossible

unwind [ʌnˈwaɪnd] *(pt, pp* **unwound** [-ˈwaʊnd]) **VT** dérouler; *(ball of wool)* défaire, dérouler
VI 1 *(unroll)* se dérouler; *(of ball of wool)* se défaire, se dérouler **2** *Fam (relax)* se détendre, se relaxer

unwise [ʌnˈwaɪz] **ADJ** *(person)* peu prudent, peu sage; *(action, investment)* peu judicieux; **that was very u. of you** c'était très imprudent de votre part

unwisely [ʌnˈwaɪzlɪ] **ADV** imprudemment

unwitting [ʌnˈwɪtɪŋ] **ADJ** involontaire; **if I have caused you any u. offence** si je vous ai offensé sans le vouloir

unwittingly [ʌnˈwɪtɪŋlɪ] **ADV** *(without realizing)* sans le savoir; *(without intending to)* involontairement

unwomanly [ʌnˈwʊmənlɪ] **ADJ** peu féminin

unwonted [ʌnˈwəʊntɪd] **ADJ** *esp Lit* inaccoutumé

unworkable [ʌnˈwɜːkəb(ə)l] **ADJ** *(plan)* impraticable

unworldliness [ʌnˈwɜːldlɪnɪs] **N** détachement *m* de ce monde; *(naivety)* simplicité *f*, candeur *f*

unworldly [ʌnˈwɜːldlɪ] **ADJ** détaché de ce monde; *(naive)* simple, candide; *esp Lit (beauty)* qui n'est pas de ce monde, irréel

unworn [ʌnˈwɔːn] **ADJ** *(clothes)* non porté; **these shoes look u.** on dirait que ces chaussures n'ont jamais été portées

unworthiness [ʌnˈwɜːðɪnɪs] **N** indignité *f*

unworthy [ʌnˈwɜːðɪ] **ADJ** indigne (**of sth/sb** de qch/qn); **u. of notice** qui ne mérite pas qu'on y fasse attention; **that's u. of you** c'est indigne de vous

unwounded [ʌnˈwuːndɪd] **ADJ** indemne; **to be u.** ne pas être blessé

unwrap [ʌnˈræp] **VT** (-pp-) *(parcel)* défaire; *(sweet, sandwich)* déballer; **to come unwrapped** *(of parcel)* se défaire

unwritten [ʌnˈrɪt(ə)n] **ADJ** non écrit; *(tradition)* oral, -aux; *(agreement)* verbal, -aux; **it's an u. law in this office that …** dans ce bureau on respecte la convention selon laquelle …; **he had broken one of the u. laws of the gang** il n'avait pas respecté l'une des conventions du gang

unyielding [ʌnˈjiːldɪŋ] **ADJ** *(material, surface)* qui ne cède pas, résistant; *(frozen ground)* dur; *(person, determination)* inébranlable, ferme; **u. grip** prise *f* de fer

unyoke [ʌnˈjəʊk] **VT** dételer, découpler

unzip [ʌnˈzɪp] (-pp-) **VT 1** *(garment)* descendre la fermeture éclair®️ de; **will you u. me?** tu veux bien descendre *ou* défaire ma fermeture éclair? **2** *Comput* dézipper, décompresser

VI *(of garment)* **it unzips at the side** ça s'ouvre sur le côté

UP [juːˈpiː] **N** *Com (abbr* **unit price**) PU *m*

UP [ʌp] *(when* up *is an integral part of a verb eg* **come up, go up, get up, take up,** *the user should consult the verb in question)* **ADV 1** *(at the top)* en haut; *(to the top)* vers le haut; **all the way up, the whole way up, right up (to the top)** *(of stairs, hill)* jusqu'en haut; **half way up** jusqu'à mi-hauteur; **to live three flights up** habiter *Br* au troisième *ou Am* au quatrième (étage); **to throw sth up in the air** jeter qch en l'air; **to put one's hand up** lever la main; **hands up!** haut les mains!; **what are you doing up there?** qu'est-ce que tu fais là-haut?; **up above** en haut; **up above sth** au-dessus de qch; **before the sun was up** avant le lever du soleil; **would you like the window up a bit?** *(in car)* veux-tu que je remonte un peu la vitre?; *Horseracing* **Comet with Thomas up** Comet monté par Thomas; **the river's up** la rivière est en crue; **to lay sth face up** mettre qch à l'endroit; **this side up** *(on packing case)* haut, dessus; **put it the other way up** retournez-le; **he's something quite high up in the civil service** il est haut placé dans l'administration; **to be up in arms** être en révolte; **up with …!** *(supporting)* vive …!

2 *(when travelling etc)* **to walk up and down** se promener de long en large; **to go up north** aller dans le nord; **to go up to London for the day** aller passer la journée à Londres; *Univ* **he's going up to Oxford** il va faire ses études à l'université d'Oxford; **up in London** à Londres; **up in Yorkshire** au nord dans le Yorkshire; *Univ* **up at Oxford** à l'université d'Oxford; **to come up before the judge** être cité devant les magistrats

3 *(and above)* **from £10 up** à partir de 10 livres; **suitable to children aged seven and up** convient aux enfants âgés de sept ans et plus; **all ranks from sergeant up** tous les rangs à partir de celui de sergent

4 *(on display, complete)* **to put up the results** afficher les résultats; **are the results up yet?** les résultats sont-ils déjà affichés?; **there's a big notice up at the station saying …** il y a un grand panneau à la gare disant …; **our curtains still aren't up** nous n'avons toujours pas accroché nos rideaux; **the new building is up** le nouveau bâtiment est terminé; **when the tent's up** quand la tente sera montée

5 *(for repair etc)* **this road's always up** cette route est toujours en réparation; **careful, we've got some of the floorboards up** attention au plancher, il manque des lattes; **when we've got the carpet up …** quand nous aurons enlevé la moquette …

6 *(higher)* **prices are 10% up on last year's** les prix ont augmenté de dix pour cent depuis l'année dernière; **petrol is up again** l'essence a encore augmenté; **the temperature is going up** la température monte; **business is looking up** les affaires sont à la hausse

7 *(ahead) Sport* **to be one goal up** mener par un but; *Golf* **to be one hole up** avoir un trou d'avance; **to be one up on sb** *(in point, score)* avoir un point d'avance sur qn; *Fig (have advantage)* avoir l'avantage sur qn; **his blood was up** le sang lui bouillait; **speak up!** parlez plus fort!

8 *(knowledgeable)* **to be well up in a subject** connaître un sujet à fond; **how well up are you in German?** tu t'y connais en allemand?

9 *(with proximity)* **lean up against the wall** appuyez-le contre le mur; **they were standing close up to each other** ils se tenaient tout près l'un de l'autre; **to be up against difficulties** se heurter à des diffi-

cultés; *Fig Fam* **to be up against it** être dans le pétrin

10 *(out of bed)* debout, levé; **to be up late** veiller tard; **to be up all night** ne pas se coucher de la nuit; **isn't he up yet!** il n'est pas encore levé *ou* debout!; **I was up late this morning** je me suis levé tard ce matin; **he's always up and about by seven** il est toujours debout à sept heures; **to be up and about again** *(after illness)* être de nouveau sur pied

11 *Fam (wrong)* **what's up?** qu'est-ce qui se passe?, qu'y a-t-il?; **what's up with you/him?** qu'est-ce qui te/lui prend?; **something's up** il y a quelque chose qui ne va pas; **there's something up with him** il y a quelque chose qui ne va pas chez lui; **there's something up with the TV** la télé débloque

12 *(finished)* **time is up** il est l'heure; **your time's up** c'est fini; **his time is up** *(of prisoner)* il a purgé sa peine; **his leave is up** sa permission est expirée; *Fam* **the game's up** *(we've been found out)* nous sommes faits; *(I've found you out)* vous êtes faits; *Fam* **I thought it was all up with me** j'ai cru que ma dernière heure était arrivée; *Fam* **it's all up with him** c'en est fait de lui, il a son compte

13 **up to** *(as far as)* jusqu'à; **to go up to sb** s'approcher de qn; **covered in mud up to the ears** couvert de boue jusqu'aux oreilles; **what page** *or* **where are you up to?** où en es-tu *ou* à quelle page en es-tu?; **we're up to page 50** nous en sommes à la page 50; **up to now, up to here** jusqu'ici; **up to then** jusqu'alors, jusque-là; **up to £100 a week** jusqu'à 100 livres par semaine; **up to what age?** jusqu'à quel âge?

14 **up to** *(good enough for)* **to be up to one's job** être à la hauteur de sa tâche; **he's not up to it** il n'est pas capable de le faire; **he's not up to the journey** il n'est pas à même de faire le voyage; **I don't feel up to it** je ne m'en sens pas le courage; **I don't feel up to much** je ne me sens pas bien; **it's not up to much** ça ne vaut pas grand-chose

15 *esp Pej* **he's up to something** il mijote quelque chose; **what are the children up to?** que font les enfants?; **hey you, what do you think you're up to?** eh vous là-bas, qu'est-ce que vous fabriquez?; **what's that guy over there up to?** qu'est-ce qu'il fabrique, ce type là-bas?; **what's he up to with that ladder?** qu'est-ce qu'il a l'intention de faire *ou* qu'est-ce qu'il fabrique avec cette échelle?; **what are you up to with my girlfriend?** qu'est-ce que tu lui veux à ma copine?

16 *(to be decided by)* **what shall I do? – that's up to you** qu'est-ce que je fais? – c'est à toi de décider; **it's entirely up to you whether you go or not** il ne tient qu'à toi de rester ou de partir

17 *(be the responsibility of)* **it's up to him to do it** c'est à lui de le faire; **it's up to you to tell her** c'est à toi de lui dire

18 *(phrases)* **to be up and coming** *(person, team etc)* être plein d'avenir, promettre; **to be up and running** *(of new machine etc)* être en service; *(of project)* être en route; **to get sth up and running** *(new machine)* mettre qch en service; *(project)* mettre qch en route
PREP to go up the stairs monter l'escalier; **to climb up a hill** monter *ou* grimper une colline; **to go up the street** remonter la rue; **further up the street** plus loin dans la rue; **they live further up the street** ils habitent plus loin *ou* plus haut dans cette rue; **the smoke went up my nose** la fumée m'est montée par le nez; **the gas goes up this pipe** le gaz monte par ce tuyau; **the cat is up that tree** le chat est (perché) sur cet arbre; **the cat went up a tree** le chat a grimpé à un arbre; **it's up river from here** c'est en amont d'ici; **to walk up and down the platform** aller et venir sur le quai; *(nervously etc)* arpenter le quai; **he lives up your way** il habite

par chez vous *ou* du côté de chez vous; *Br Fam* **he's up the pub** il est au pub; *Br Fam* **I'm going up the shops** je vais faire un tour en courses; *Vulg* **up yours!** va te faire enculer!

ADJ *Comput* **up arrow** flèche *f* vers le haut; **up arrow key** touche *f* flèche vers le haut; **up escalator** escalator® *m* qui monte; **he ran down the up side** il est descendu en courant du côté où l'on est censé monter; *Rail* **up line** voie *f* en direction d'une grande gare; **up train** train *m* qui va dans une grande gare

N 1 ups and downs *(of life)* hauts et bas *mpl,* vicissitudes *fpl, (in politics)* avatars *mpl, Com (of market)* oscillations *fpl, (of terrain)* ondulations *fpl;* **life is full of ups and downs** la vie est faite de hauts et de bas

2 *Fam* **to be on the up and up** *(be honest)* être clair *ou* fiable; *Br (be improving)* être en train de monter *ou* de faire son chemin

VT (**-pp-**) **1** *Fam (prices etc)* augmenter; **to up the stakes** *(at cards etc), Fig* monter la mise; **to up sticks** plier bagages; **he just upped sticks and left** il a plié bagages et est parti

2 *(swans)* recenser

VI *Fam* **to up and leave** *or* **go** partir; **they upped and went** ils sont partis très soudainement; **one day he just upped and left her** un beau jour il l'a quittée sans crier gare; **he just upped and hit him** tout à coup il (s'est levé et) l'a frappé

up-and-coming **ADJ** *(person, economy, team)* qui est plein d'avenir, prometteur, -euse; *(town)* plein d'avenir

up-and-down **ADJ** **u. movement** mouvement *m* de haut en bas

up-and-over **ADJ**
▸▸ **u. door** porte *f* basculante *(d'un garage etc)*

up-and-under **N** *Rugby* up and under *m*

upbeat [ˈʌpbiːt] **N** *Mus* levé *m*
ADJ *Fam (optimistic, cheerful)* optimiste

upbraid [ʌpˈbreɪd] **VT** faire des reproches à, réprimander

upbringing [ˈʌpbrɪŋɪŋ] **N** éducation *f,* **what sort of (an) u. has she had?** comment a-t-elle été élevée?, quelle éducation a-t-elle eu?

up-change **N** *(of gears)* passage *m* à la vitesse supérieure

upchuck [ˈʌptʃʌk] **VT & VI** *esp Am Fam (vomit)* dégobiller

upcoming [ˈʌpkʌmɪŋ] **ADJ** *Am* prochain

upcountry [ʌpˈkʌntrɪ] *esp Am, Austr* **N** intérieur *m* (du pays)
ADJ de l'intérieur (du pays)
ADV **to go u.** aller vers l'intérieur

update[1] [ˈʌpdeɪt] **N** mise *f* à jour; *Comput (of software package)* mise à jour, actualisation *f,* **to give sb an u. on sth** mettre qn au courant de qch; **a dictionary should have an u. at least every 5 years** un dictionnaire devrait être remis à jour au minimum tous les 5 ans

update[2] [ʌpˈdeɪt] **VT** *(file, record)* mettre à jour, actualiser; *(equipment etc)* moderniser; *(person)* mettre au courant; **could you u. me on what's been happening?** pourriez-vous me mettre au courant de ce qui s'est passé?; **it needs regular updating** une remise à jour régulière est nécessaire; **it hasn't been updated since 1973** il n'a pas été remis à jour depuis 1973

updating [ʌpˈdeɪtɪŋ] **N** mise *f* à jour

up-draught, *Am* **up-draft** **N** *Aviat* courant *m* d'air ascendant

upend [ʌpˈend] **VT** *(thing)* mettre debout; **to u. sb** *(turn upside down)* mettre qn les pieds en l'air, mettre qn à l'envers

up-front **ADJ 1** *Fam (honest, frank)* franc, *f*

franche, direct (**about sth** à propos de qch) **2** *(payment)* à l'avance
ADV *(to be paid etc)* à l'avance; **to ask for some of the cash u.** demander une avance

upgrade[1] [ˈʌpgreɪd] **N 1** *Am (slope)* pente *f* ascendante; *(of railway line)* montée *f* **2** *Am* **to be on the u.** *(of prices)* monter; *(of business)* reprendre, se relever; *(of invalid)* être en voie de guérison **3** *Comput (of system)* augmentation *f* de puissance; *(for software)* mise *f* à jour, actualisation *f, (for hardware) (expansion)* extension *f, (new model, processor etc)* nouvelle version *f*
▸▸ *Comput* **u. kit** ensemble *m* de mise à niveau

upgrade[2] [ʌpˈgreɪd] **VT 1** *(improve) (product)* améliorer; *Comput (of user) (software)* se procurer la dernière version de; *(hardware) (expand)* ajouter une/des extension(s) à; *(buy new and better)* remplacer par une/des nouvelle(s) version(s); *(memory)* augmenter **2** *(raise to higher rank)* nommer à un niveau supérieur, surclasser; *(civil servant)* monter en grade
VI *Comput (expand computer system)* ajouter une/des extension(s); *(buy newer and better model)* acquérir une/des nouvelle(s) version(s); **we've decided to u. to the GT model** nous avons décidé de passer à un modèle supérieur et d'acheter le GT

upgrad(e)ability [ʌpgreɪdəˈbɪlɪtɪ] **N** possibilités *fpl* d'extension

upgrad(e)able [ʌpˈgreɪdəb(ə)l] **ADJ** *Comput (hardware, system)* évolutif; *(memory)* extensible; **u. architecture** architecture *f* évolutive

upgrading [ʌpˈgreɪdɪŋ] **N 1** *(of system)* amélioration *f, Comput (expansion)* ajout *m* d'une/de plusieurs extension(s) (**of** à); *(replacement by newer and better)* acquisition *f* d'une/de nouvelle(s) version(s); *(of memory)* extension *f* **2** *(of person)* avancement *m;* **the u. of the polytechnic to university status** le reclassement de l'IUT au rang d'université

upheaval [ʌpˈhiːv(ə)l] **N** bouleversement *m;* **political u.** agitation *f* politique; **an emotional u.** un bouleversement affectif; **moving house is such an u.** déménager est un tel bouleversement *ou* chamboulement; **the u. of moving office** le tumulte qu'entraîne un déménagement dans d'autres bureaux

uphill [ˈʌphɪl] **ADJ** *(road)* qui monte; *(struggle)* pénible, difficile; **it's u. all the way** ça monte tout le long du chemin; *Fig* c'est une lutte permanente
ADV **to go u.** monter; **it's a good way u. from here** il faut monter pas mal pour y arriver; **to ski u.** skier en amont
▸▸ **u. ski** ski *m* amont

uphold [ʌpˈhəʊld] **VT** *(pt, pp* **upheld** [-ˈheld]*)* soutenir; *(opinion, principle)* défendre; *Law (decision)* confirmer; **to u. the law** faire observer la loi

upholder [ʌpˈhəʊldər] **N** *(of cause)* défenseur *m*

upholster [ʌpˈhəʊlstər] **VT** *(pad)* capitonner, rembourrer; *(cover) (sofa etc)* tapisser, garnir (**with, in** de)

upholstered [ʌpˈhəʊlstəd] **ADJ** *(padded)* capitonné, rembourré; *(covered) (sofa)* tapissé, garni; **u. in velvet/leather** garni de velours/cuir; *Fam* **she's well u.** elle est bien rembourrée

upholsterer [ʌpˈhəʊlstərər] **N** tapissier *m* en ameublement

upholstery [ʌpˈhəʊlstərɪ] **N 1** *(padding) (of armchair etc)* capitonnage *m,* rembourrage *m; (covering)* garniture *f, (in car)* garniture intérieure; **leather u.** garniture en cuir **2** *(trade)* tapisserie *f* d'ameublement

UPI [juːpiːˈaɪ] **N** *(abbr* **United Press International***)* UPI *(agence de presse)*

upkeep [ˈʌpkiːp] **N** *(of house, building, horse)* entretien *m;* **he paid nothing towards the u. of the children** il ne donnait pas d'argent pour subvenir aux besoins matériels des enfants

upland [ˈʌplənd] **N** *(usu pl)* **the uplands** le haut pays, les hauteurs *fpl*
ADJ *(village)* de montagne

uplift[1] [ˈʌplɪft] **N (moral) u.** inspiration *f* (morale)
▸▸ **u. bra** soutien-gorge *m* de maintien, *pl* soutiens-gorge de maintien

uplift[2] [ʌpˈlɪft] **VT 1** *(soul, heart)* élever **2** *Scot (collect)* récupérer

uplifted [ʌpˈlɪftɪd] **ADJ 1** *(of hand)* levé **2** *(morally, spiritually)* élevé (**by sth** par qch)

uplifting [ʌpˈlɪftɪŋ] **ADJ** *(experience, sermon etc)* édifiant

uplighter [ˈʌplaɪtər] **N** = applique *f* ou lampadaire *m* diffusant la lumière vers le haut

uplink receiver [ˈʌplɪŋk] **N** récepteur *m* de liaison terre/satellite

upload [ˈʌpləʊd] **VT** *Comput* télécharger *(vers le serveur)*

up-market **ADJ** *(product)* haut de gamme; *(district, person, accent)* bourgeois
ADV **to go u.** *(of company)* se mettre à faire du haut de gamme; *(of person)* prendre des goûts de luxe

upmost [ˈʌpməʊst] **ADJ = uppermost 1**

upon [əˈpɒn] **PREP** (**on** *and* **upon** *are interchangeable in meaning; in modern English* **upon** *is used more formally; in certain phrases, however,* **upon** *is preferable)* sur; **u. my word!** ma parole!; **the enemy was u. us** l'ennemi nous attaquait; **I came u. it by accident** je l'ai trouvé par hasard; **you brought it u. yourself** ne t'en prends qu'à toi-même!
VOIR GRAMMAIRE A73

upper [ˈʌpər] **ADJ 1** *(part, storey, deck, branch etc)* supérieur; **the u. atmosphere** les couches supérieures de l'atmosphère; **temperature in the u. twenties** température qui dépasse 25 degrés

2 *Geog* **the u. Rhine** le haut Rhin

3 **the u. end of the table** le bout de la table; **the u. echelons of the civil service** les plus hauts échelons de l'administration; **the u. classes** la haute société; **the u. middle classes** la haute bourgeoisie; **to gain the u. hand** prendre le dessus; **to let sb get the u. hand** laisser qn prendre le dessus, laisser qn dominer

4 *Mus (keyboard)* du côté droit; *(register)* aigu, -uë

N 1 *(of shoe)* empeigne *f, Fam* **to be down on one's uppers** être dans la gène **2** *Sl (drug)* amphétamine *f,* amphé *f*
▸▸ *Anat* **u. arm** bras *m; Comput* **u. ASCII** ASCII *m* supérieur; **U. Canada** le haut Canada; *Theat* **u. circle** deuxième balcon *m; Fam* **u. crust** *(of society)* la haute, le dessus du panier, la crème; **U. Egypt** la Haute-Égypte; **the U. House** la Chambre haute; *(the House of Lords)* la Chambre des lords; **u. jaw** mâchoire *f* supérieure; **u. limit** plafond *m;* **u. lip** lèvre *f* supérieure; **u. reaches** *(of river)* amont *m; Br* **u. school** grandes classes *fpl; Br Sch* **u. sixth** terminale *f*

upper-case **ADJ** *Typ (letters)* majuscule

upper-class **ADJ** *(accent, person)* aristocratique; **to be very u.** être très aristocrate
▸▸ *Fam Pej* **u. twit** = aristocrate *m* bête et prétentieux

upper-crust **ADJ** *Fam (accent, person)* aristo, de la haute; **they're frightfully u.** ils sont très aristos

uppercut [ˈʌpəkʌt] **N** *Boxing* uppercut *m*

uppermost ['ʌpəməʊst] ADJ **1** (in position) le plus haut, le plus élevé **2** (in importance) de la plus grande importance; **to be u.** tenir le premier rang; **the problem (which is) u. in our minds** le problème qui nous préoccupe au premier chef
ADV en dessus

upping ['ʌpɪŋ] N **swan u.** recensement m des cygnes

uppity ['ʌpɪtɪ], **uppish** ['ʌpɪʃ] ADJ Fam présomptueux, arrogant; **he's getting very u.** il se croit quelqu'un; **don't you get u. with me!** ne joue pas les arrogants avec moi!

upright ['ʌpraɪt] ADJ **1** (line) vertical, -aux; (wall, writing) droit **2** (honest) droit, honnête
ADV debout; **to stand u.** se tenir droit; **sitting u. on his chair** assis droit sur sa chaise; **to put** or **stand sth u.** mettre qch debout ou d'aplomb
N **1** (of door, ladder etc) montant m; Ftbl **the uprights** les montants de but **2** (piano) piano m droit
▸▸ **u. freezer** congélateur m armoire; **u. piano** piano droit

uprightly ['ʌpraɪtlɪ] ADV droitement, honnêtement

uprightness ['ʌpraɪtnɪs] N droiture f, honnêteté f

uprising ['ʌpraɪzɪŋ] N soulèvement m, insurrection f

uproar ['ʌprɔːr] N (noise) tapage m, vacarme m; (protest) tollé m; **the meeting finished in (an) u.** la réunion s'est terminée dans la confusion; **his suggestion caused an u.** (shouting, protests) sa suggestion a provoqué un tollé; **the recent u. in the press about …** la tempête qui a récemment éclaté dans la presse au sujet de …

uproarious [ʌp'rɔːrɪəs] ADJ (noisy) tumultueux; (hilarious) hilarant; **u. laughter** grands éclats de rire

uproariously [ʌp'rɔːrɪəslɪ] ADV **to laugh u.** rire à gorge déployée; **u. funny** désopilant

uproot [ʌp'ruːt] VT (plant, evil) déraciner, extirper; **to u. sb from his home** déraciner qn; **to feel uprooted** se sentir déraciné

UPS [juːpiːˈes] N Comput (abbr uninterruptible power supply) onduleur m

upsadaisy ['ʌpsədeɪzɪ] INT Fam hop là!

upset¹ ['ʌpset] N **1** (disturbance), Fig bouleversement m; **the bad news caused quite an u.** les mauvaises nouvelles ont provoqué une grande consternation; **with the fewest possible number of upsets to our plans** avec le moins de bouleversements possibles dans nos projets; **he can't stand upsets in his routine** il ne supporte pas que sa routine soit dérangée; **have you had an u. with her?** (difficulty, argument etc) est-ce que tu t'es disputé ou as eu un problème avec elle?; **losing 25-3 was something of an u.** se faire battre 25 à 3 a été une sacrée déception; **after the u. at the last match** après la déception du dernier match; **that's going to cause a bit of an u.** cela va faire du bruit **2 to have a stomach u.** avoir une grippe intestinale

upset² [ʌp'set] VT (pt, pp upset; prp upsetting) **1** (knock over, spill) renverser; (boat) (faire) chavirer **2** (plans, schedule, calculations etc) bouleverser, déranger **3** (emotionally) (person) faire de la peine à, blesser; (of sight, news, death) bouleverser; **don't mention that!, you'll u. her again** ne parle pas de ça!, tu vas encore la contrarier; **the least thing upsets him** il est très impressionnable; **don't u. yourself** arrête, tu te fais du mal **4** (stomach) déranger; (digestion) troubler

upset³ (before noun ['ʌpset], otherwise [ʌp'set]) ADJ **1** (sad) triste; (annoyed) fâché, ennuyé; (offended) vexé, blessé; **she's u. because you called her names** elle est vexée parce que tu l'as insultée; **what are you so u. about?** qu'est-ce qui te met dans cet état?; **are you still u. or are we friends again?** est-ce que tu es toujours fâché ou sommes-nous amis à nouveau?; **we'd be very u. if we missed the deadline** nous serions très ennuyés si nous dépassions l'échéance; **you'd be u. too if you'd just paid …** tu serais aussi fâché que moi si tu venais juste de payer …; **I'm u. about losing it/her** ça me fait mal au cœur de le/la perdre; **she was clearly u. by the pictures** (distraught, moved) ces images l'avaient manifestement perturbée; **we're u. about losing the order** ça nous contrarie de perdre cette commande; **I'd be very u. if you didn't come** je serais très triste si tu ne venais pas; **he was so u. he couldn't speak** il était tellement bouleversé qu'il n'arrivait pas à parler; **come on now, there's nothing to be u. about** allons, il n'y a pas de quoi en faire un drame; **don't be** or **get u.** ne t'en fais pas **2** (stomach) dérangé
▸▸ Am, Scot **u. price** mise f à prix

upsetting [ʌp'setɪŋ] ADJ (saddening) attristant, affligeant; (annoying) contrariant, fâcheux; (offending) vexant, blessant; (disturbing) troublant; (more seriously) bouleversant; **I didn't find the experience in the least u.** l'expérience ne m'a pas du tout perturbé; **viewers might find some of these scenes u.** certaines des scènes qui vont suivre peuvent être de nature à perturber les téléspectateurs

upshift ['ʌpʃɪft] N (of gears) passage m à la vitesse supérieure

upshot ['ʌpʃɒt] N résultat m; **what will be the u. of it?** cela finira comment?; **the u. of it all was that he resigned** le résultat, c'est qu'il a donné sa démission

upside ['ʌpsaɪd] ADJ
▸▸ St Exch **u. potential** potentiel m de hausse; St Exch **u. risk** risque f de hausse

upside down ADV **1** à l'envers; (person, animal) la tête en bas; **to hold sth u.** tenir qch à l'envers; **to turn u.** se retourner **2** (in disorder) en désordre; **to turn everything u.** tout bouleverser, tout mettre sens dessus dessous
ADJ renversé; **pineapple u. cake** gâteau m renversé à l'ananas

upstage [ʌp'steɪdʒ] ADJ Theat de l'arrière-scène
ADV Theat à l'arrière-scène
VT (person) éclipser

upstairs ['ʌpsteəz] ADV en haut; **he's u.** il est en haut; **she has a second living room u.** elle a un deuxième salon en haut ou à l'étage; **they live u. from us** ils habitent au-dessus de chez nous; **I'll take your things u.** je vais monter tes affaires; **to come/go u.** venir/ monter à l'étage ou en haut; **he chased me u.** il m'a poursuivi dans les escaliers; Fig Fam **to kick sb u.** donner de l'avancement à qn pour s'en débarrasser; Fam **he hasn't got much u.** (is not very clever) il n'a pas grand-chose dans le crâne
ADJ (room) d'en haut, du haut; **our u. neighbours** nos voisins du dessus; **we have an u. sitting room** nous avons un salon à l'étage
N **(the) u.** les pièces fpl d'en haut; **the house has no u.** la maison n'a pas d'étage

upstanding [ʌp'stændɪŋ] ADJ **1** (erect) droit, qui se tient bien; **a fine u. young man** un jeune homme bien comme il faut **2** (honest) honnête **3** Fml **please be u. for the toast** veuillez vous lever pour porter le toast

upstart ['ʌpstɑːt] N parvenu, -ue

upstate ['ʌpsteɪt] Am du nord; **u. New York** la partie nord de l'État de New York
ADV (to go) vers le nord

upstream ['ʌpstriːm] ADV **1** (to be) en amont (from de) **2** (to row etc) en remontant le courant, à contre-fil de l'eau; **the salmon swims u.** le saumon remonte la rivière
ADV d'amont

upstroke ['ʌpstrəʊk] N (in writing) délié m; (of piston) course f montante ou ascendante

upsurge ['ʌpsɜːdʒ] N (of enthusiasm, hatred) vague f; (of activity, interest) regain m; (of inflation) montée f soudaine

upswept ['ʌpswept] ADJ Aut, Aviat profilé; **u. hair(style)** coiffure f en hauteur

upswing ['ʌpswɪŋ] N **1** (movement) mouvement m ascendant **2** (improvement) amélioration f sensible; **business is on the u.** les affaires sont en train de redémarrer; **the economy is on the u.** il y a un redressement de l'économie

uptake ['ʌpteɪk] N **1** Fam (understanding) **to be quick on the u.** avoir l'esprit vif; **he's a bit slow on the u.** il est un peu lent à comprendre ou à la détente **2** (taking up), Biol assimilation f, Admin **the u. of benefits** la proportion des gens qui font valoir leurs droits aux allocations

uptight [ʌp'taɪt] ADJ Fam **1** (nervous) nerveux, tendu; **he's u. about the exams/about meeting them** il est nerveux ou tendu à cause des examens/à l'idée de les rencontrer **2** (inhibited) coincé; (on particular occasion) crispé, mal à l'aise; **don't be so u., everyone else is enjoying themselves** ne sois pas aussi crispé, tout le monde s'amuse **3** (conventional) (parents, attitude) dur, strict **4** Am Fam (excellent) super, génial, -aux

up-to-date ADJ (very recent) récent; (method, equipment, technology) moderne, sophistiqué; (person) qui est dans le vent ou à la mode; (information, views) à jour; **to keep one's files/accounts u.** tenir ses fichiers/ comptes à jour; **to bring sb u. on sth** mettre qn à jour sur qch; **to get the figures u.** mettre les chiffres à jour

up-to-the-minute ADJ (news, information) de dernière minute; (style) dernier cri inv

uptown ['ʌp'taʊn] esp Am ADV dans les quartiers résidentiels de la ville
N les quartiers mpl résidentiels; **u. society** les milieux chics

upturn¹ ['ʌptɜːn] N amélioration f, (in business, economy) redressement m, reprise f

upturn² [ʌp'tɜːn] VT renverser

upturned ['ʌptɜːnd] ADJ **1** (upside down) (boat, bowl) renversé **2** (nose) retroussé; **he gazed down at her u. face** il contemplait son visage, qu'elle tenait levé vers lui

upward ['ʌpwəd] ADJ montant, ascendant; **their u. progress was halted by …** leur ascension fut stoppée par …; **u. tendency** or **movement** (of prices etc) tendance f à la hausse, mouvement de hausse; **u. movement** (of piston) mouvement m ascensionnel; **u. slope** pente f ascendante; **u. trend** tendance ascensionnelle
ADV = upwards
▸▸ **u. mobility** ascension f sociale

upward-compatible ADJ Comput compatible vers le haut

upwardly ['ʌpwədlɪ] ADV **to be u. mobile** (in society) avoir la possibilité de s'élever dans la société; **the u. mobile** = les gens qui montent dans l'échelle sociale

upwards ['ʌpwədz] ADV (to move, climb etc) vers le haut; **to look u.** regarder en haut; **to put sth face u. on the table** mettre qch à l'endroit sur la table; **lying face u.** (person) couché sur le dos; **from £100 u.** à partir de 100 livres; **it costs u. of £100** ça coûte plus de 100 livres; **u. of 500 pupils** plus de 500 élèves; **children from ten (years) u.** des enfants à partir de dix ans; Comput **u. compatible** compatible avec les versions suivantes, compatible vers le haut

upwind ['ʌpwɪnd] **ADV** *(to sail)* contre le vent; *(to be)* contre le vent, au vent; **to be u. of an animal** être au vent d'un animal

Ural ['jʊərəl] **N the U. (river)** l'Oural *m*; **the U. mountains, the Urals** les monts *mpl* Oural, l'Oural

uranium [jʊ'reɪnɪəm] **N** *Chem* uranium *m*

Uranus [jʊ'reɪnəs, 'jʊərənəs] **N** *Astron* Uranus *f*; *Myth* Uranus *m*

urban ['ɜːbən] **ADJ** urbain
▸▸ **u. areas** agglomérations *fpl* urbaines; **u. clearway** rue *f* à stationnement interdit (en ville); *Aut* **u. cycle** cycle *m* urbain; **u. decay** dégradation *f* urbaine; **u. expressway** voie *f* rapide urbaine; *Aut* **u. fuel consumption** consommation *f* en ville; **u. guerilla** guerilla *f* des villes; **u. legend, u. myth** légende *f*, faux fait *m* divers; **u. planner** urbaniste *mf*; **u. renewal** rénovations *fpl* urbaines; **u. sprawl** étalement *m* urbain; **the u. sprawl of the London suburbs** la banlieue de Londres interminable

> Attention: ne pas confondre avec **urbane**.

urbane [ɜː'beɪn] **ADJ** *(person)* courtois, d'une politesse raffinée; *(wit, joke)* raffiné

> Attention: ne pas confondre avec **urban**.

urbanely [ɜː'beɪnlɪ] **ADV** courtoisement, avec urbanité

urbanism ['ɜːbənɪz(ə)m] **N** urbanisme *m*

urbanite ['ɜːbənaɪt] **N** *esp Am* citadin, -ine

urbanity [ɜː'bænɪtɪ] **N** urbanité *f*, courtoisie *f*

urbanization [ɜːbənaɪ'zeɪʃən] **N** urbanisation *f*

urbanize ['ɜːbənaɪz] **VT** urbaniser

urchin ['ɜːtʃɪn] **N** *(street)* **u.** galopin *m*; *esp Hum (child)* gamin, -ine

Urdu ['ʊədu:] **N** *Ling* ourdou *m*

urea [jʊ'ri:ə] **N** *Chem* urée *f*

ureter [jʊ'ri:tər] **N** *Anat* uretère *m*

urethra [jʊ'ri:θrə] **N** *Anat* urètre *m*

urge [ɜːdʒ] **N** *(desire)* envie *f*; *Psy* pulsion *f*; **to have an irresistible u. to do sth** avoir une envie irrésistible de faire qch; **to have a powerful u. to succeed** avoir très envie de réussir; **he's lost the u. to win** il a perdu l'envie *ou* la rage de gagner; **I had an u. to hit him** j'ai eu envie de le frapper; **I'll let you know if I ever get the u.** je te le dirai si j'en ai envie *ou* si ça me chante; *Fam* **when I get the u.** quand j'ai envie; *Fam* **the bottle's there, help yourself if you get the u.** la bouteille est là, servez-vous si ça vous dit
VT 1 *(try to persuade)* **to u. sb to do sth** conseiller vivement à qn de faire; **he urged me not to do it** il m'a vivement conseillé de ne pas le faire; **I urged him to accept** je lui ai vivement conseillé d'accepter; **they urged us to give up, but in vain** ils ont insisté pour que nous abandonnions, mais en vain
2 *(recommend earnestly)* **to u. caution** recommander *ou* conseiller la prudence; **to u. peace on the nations of the world** exhorter les nations du monde à la paix; **to u. that sth be done** recommander *ou* conseiller de faire qch
3 *(goad, encourage etc)* **to u. a horse forward** pousser un cheval; **he urged his men into battle** il poussa ses hommes dans la bataille
▸ **urge on VT SEP** *(person, team, runner)* encourager; *(horse)* pousser; **to u. sb on to do sth** pousser qn à faire qch

urgency ['ɜːdʒənsɪ] **N** urgence *f*; **it's a matter of u.** il y a urgence, c'est urgent; **could you do this as a matter of the utmost u.?** pourriez-vous faire ceci de toute urgence?; **there was a note of u. in her voice** il y avait quelque chose de pressant dans sa voix; **what's all the u.?** qu'y a-t-il de si urgent?; **there's no u.** ce n'est pas urgent, il n'y a pas urgence; **he shows no sense of u.** il ne se presse pas

urgent ['ɜːdʒənt] **ADJ** *(need, case, delivery)* urgent; *(meeting, treatment, solution, tone)* d'urgence; **to be in u. need of sth** avoir un besoin pressant de qch; **I was in u. need of a drink** il me fallait absolument quelque chose à boire; **the matter is u.** c'est urgent; **this is u.** c'est une urgence, c'est urgent; **just how u. is it?** mais est-ce vraiment urgent?; **just how u. is it that you should be there tomorrow?** qu'y a-t-il de si urgent qui exige que tu y sois demain?; **the doctor had an u. call** le médecin a été appelé d'urgence; *Fml* **at their u. request** sur leurs instances pressantes

urgently ['ɜːdʒəntlɪ] **ADV** d'urgence; **a doctor is u. required** on demande un médecin d'urgence; **to press u. for sth** réclamer qch de façon urgente *ou* instamment; **they u. called a meeting** ils ont convoqué une réunion d'urgence

uric ['jʊərɪk] **ADJ** *(acid)* urique

urinal ['jʊərɪn(ə)l, ju:'raɪn(ə)l] **N** urinoir *m*; **the urinals** l'urinoir

urinary ['jʊərɪnərɪ] **ADJ** *Anat* urinaire; **u. tract infection** infection *f* urinaire

urinate ['jʊərɪneɪt] **VI** uriner

urine ['jʊərɪn] **N** urine *f*; *Med* urines *fpl*
▸▸ **u. sample** échantillon *m* d'urine

URL [ju:ɑr'el] **N** *Comput (abbr* **uniform resource locator)** *(adresse f)* URL *m*

urn [ɜːn] **N** urne *f*; **(tea) u.** fontaine *f* à thé

urogenital [jʊərəʊ'dʒenɪt(ə)l] **ADJ** *Anat* urogénital, -aux

urological [jʊərəʊ'lɒdʒɪk(ə)l] **ADJ** urologique

urologist [jʊ'rɒlədʒɪst] **N** urologue *mf*

urology [jʊ'rɒlədʒɪ] **N** *Med* urologie *f*

Ursa ['ɜːsə] **N**
▸▸ *Astron* **U. Major** la Grande Ourse; *Astron* **U. Minor** la Petite Ourse

urticaria [ɜːtɪ'keərɪə] **N** *Med* urticaire *f*

Uruguay ['jʊərəgwaɪ] **N** Uruguay *m*

Uruguayan [jʊərə'gwaɪən] **ADJ** uruguayen **N** Uruguayen, -enne

US [ju:'es] **N** *(abbr* **United States)** USA *mpl* **ADJ** *(forces, officials etc)* américain; **US dollar** dollar *m* américain

US PERS PRON OBJECTIVE CASE 1 *(unstressed)* [əs] nous; **he sees us** il nous voit; **in front of/behind us** devant/derrière nous; **he gave it to us** il nous l'a donné; **tell us** dis-nous; **he wrote us a letter** il nous a écrit une lettre; **he stayed with us a month** il est resté chez nous pendant un mois; **there are three of us** nous sommes trois; **those of us who were left …** ceux d'entre nous qui restaient …
VOIR GRAMMAIRE A27; B18–19 2 *(stressed)* [ʌs] nous; **that concerns us alone** cela ne regarde que nous; **between them and us** entre eux et nous; **as for us Englishmen** quant à nous autres Anglais; **he couldn't believe that it was us** il ne pouvait pas croire que c'était nous **3** *Fam (me)* **let's have a look** fais-moi voir; **give us a bit** donnez-m'en un peu

USA [ju:es'eɪ] **N 1** *(abbr* **United States of America)** USA *mpl* **2** *abbr* **United States Army**

usable ['ju:zəb(ə)l] **ADJ** utilisable, employable

USAF [ju:ese'ef] **N** *abbr* **United States Air Force**

usage ['ju:sɪdʒ] **N 1** *(use)* utilisation *f*; **the machine wasn't designed for such heavy u.** la machine n'avait pas été conçue pour une utilisation aussi intensive; **this book has had some rough u.** ce livre a été maltraité **2** *(custom)* usage *m*; **an old u.** une vieille coutume; **sanctified by u.** consacré par l'usage **3** *Ling* usage *m*; **words in everyday u.** mots d'usage courant; **it's not in current u.** ce n'est pas dans l'usage courant; **a book on modern English u.** un livre sur les usages de l'anglais moderne; **it's not a u. I'm familiar with** ce n'est pas un usage que je connais

usance ['ju:səns] **N** *Banking, Fin (time limit)* usance *f*; **at thirty days' u.** à usance de trente jours
▸▸ **u. bill** effet *m* à usance

USB [ju:es'bi:] **N** *Comput (abbr* **universal serial bus)** norme *f* USB, port *m* série universel
▸▸ **U. cable** câble *m* USB; **U. port** port USB

USE¹ [ju:s]

| emploi 1 | ▪ utilisation 1 | ▪ usage 1, 2 |
| ▪ utilité 3 | | |

N 1 *(utilization)* emploi *m*, utilisation *f*; **the u. of steel in building** l'emploi de l'acier dans la construction; **one of the main uses of steel** un des principaux emplois de l'acier; **to make u. of sth** *(tool, equipment)* se servir de qch; *(word, material)* utiliser *ou* employer qch; **to make good u. of sth, to put sth to good u.** faire bon usage de qch; **I'll find a u. for it** ça peut servir; **a word in everyday u.** un mot d'usage courant; **the word is not in u. any more** ce mot ne s'emploie plus *ou* est désuet; **not in u., out of u.** *(on sign)* hors service; **for u. in case of fire** à employer en cas d'incendie; **for u. in schools** à l'usage des écoles; **directions** *or* **instructions for u.** mode *m* d'emploi; *Pharm* **for external u.** pour usage externe; **to improve with u.** s'améliorer à l'usage
2 *(ability to use)* jouissance *f*, usage *m*; *Law* usufruit *m*; **to have full u. of one's faculties** jouir de toutes ses facultés; **to lose the u. of a leg** perdre l'usage d'une jambe; **to have the u. of the bathroom** avoir le droit de se servir de la salle de bain; **you can have the u. of my car while I'm in London** tu pourras te servir de ma voiture pendant que je serai à Londres
3 *(usefulness)* utilité *f*; **to be of u.** être utile *(for sth* à qch*)*; **can I be of any u. (to you)?** puis-je vous être utile à quelque chose?; **it's of no u. to me** je n'en ai pas besoin; **it's not much u.** cela ne sert pas à grand-chose; *Fam* **a fat lot of u. that'll be to you!** si tu crois que ça va t'avancer!; *Fam Iron* **you're a lot of u.!** je te remercie de ton aide!; *Fam* **he's no u.** c'est un incapable; **he's no u. in bed** au lit, il est nul; **to have no u. for sth** ne savoir que faire de qch; **I've no further u. for it** je n'en ai plus besoin; *Fam* **I have no u. for people like that** ces gens-là ne m'intéressent pas; **it was no u.** c'était inutile; **it's no u. discussing the question** inutile de discuter la question; **it's no u. crying** cela ne sert à rien de pleurer; **it's no u. my talking** que je dis ne sert à rien; **it's no use(, I can't do it)!** c'est peine perdue(, je ne peux pas le faire)!; **is it any u. writing to him?** est-ce que ça servirait à quelque chose de lui écrire?; **what u. would that be?** à quoi cela servirait-il?; **what's the u. of doing it/of going there?** à quoi bon le faire/y aller?; **what's the u.!, give up!** à quoi bon! j'abandonne!
4 = usage

USE² [ju:z]

| se servir de 1, 3 | ▪ utiliser 1 | ▪ employer 1 | ▪ consommer 3 |

VT 1 *(object)* se servir de, utiliser; *(word)* employer, utiliser; **to be used for sth** servir à

qch; **are you using this knife?** est-ce que tu te sers de ce couteau?; **I used the money to rebuild my garage** j'ai utilisé *ou* employé l'argent pour reconstruire mon garage; **the frying pan will last a long time if you u. it carefully** cette poêle à frire durera longtemps si vous en prenez soin; **do you mind if I u. the toilet?** puis-je utiliser vos toilettes?; **this word is no longer used** ce mot est désuet *ou* n'est plus usité; **the term is used more generally to refer to ...** on utilise ce terme de manière plus générale pour désigner ...; **word used figuratively** mot employé au (sens) figuré; **to u. one's intelligence/intuition** faire marcher son intelligence/intuition; **u. your head!** fais marcher ta cervelle!; **u. your eyes!** ouvrez les yeux!; **to u. force/violence** avoir recours à la force/la violence; **to u. diplomacy** user de diplomatie; **to u. discretion** agir avec discrétion; **to u. one's influence** user de son influence; **to u. every means (at one's disposal)** employer tous les moyens (à sa disposition); *Fam* **I could u. some coffee/a holiday** j'ai besoin d'un café/de vacances **2** *(exploit)* **I feel I've been used** j'ai l'impression qu'on se sert de moi; **she doesn't care about him, she's just using him** elle ne l'aime pas, elle ne fait que se servir de lui **3** *(consume)* *(petrol, electricity etc)* consommer; **we've been using too much electricity** nous avons consommé trop d'électricité **4** *Arch* *(treat)* **to u. sb well** bien traiter qn; **to u. sb badly** maltraiter qn; **he had a reputation for using his workers well** il avait la réputation de bien traiter ses employés.

v AUX [juːst] **when we were children we used to play together** quand nous étions enfants, nous jouions ensemble; **my father used to tell me that ...** mon père me disait toujours que ...; **it used to be a pleasant town to live in** c'était autrefois une ville agréable à habiter; **things aren't what they used to be** les choses ne sont plus ce qu'elles étaient; **she used not** *or* **usedn't to like oysters** avant, elle n'aimait pas les huîtres; **I used not to like him, I didn't u. to like him** avant, je ne l'aimais pas; **do you smoke? – I do now, but I didn't u. to** est-ce que vous fumez? – je ne fumais pas mais je m'y suis mis; **do you smoke? – I used to** est-ce que vous fumez? – j'ai arrêté; **do you travel much? – I used to** vous voyagez beaucoup? – autrefois, oui VOIR GRAMMAIRE A61; B30

▸ **use up VT SEP** *(food, milk)* finir; *(funds, resources)* épuiser; *(energy)* dépenser la totalité de; *(paint, hot water, ideas, money, resources, time)* utiliser la totalité de; **she had used up all her strength** elle avait épuisé toutes ses forces; **u. up the leftovers to make soup** utiliser *ou* accommoder les restes pour faire un potage

---

Note that the French verb **user** is a false friend. Its most common meaning is **to wear out**.

---

use-by date N date *f* limite de consommation

used ADJ 1 [juːzd] *(book, car, clothes)* d'occasion; *(worn)* usé, usagé; *(stamp)* oblitéré, qui a déjà servi; **hardly u.** presque neuf **2** [juːst] *(accustomed)* **u. to (doing) sth** habitué à (faire) qch; **to get u. to sth/sb** s'habituer *ou* se faire à qch/qn; **to get sb u. to sth** habituer qn à qch; **I'm not u. to it** je n'en ai pas l'habitude; **you'll get u. to it in time** vous vous y ferez à la longue; **I'm not u. to being spoken to like that!** je n'ai pas l'habitude qu'on me parle comme ça!

useful [ˈjuːsfʊl] **ADJ 1** *(of use)* utile; **this book was very u. to me** ce livre m'a été très utile *ou* m'a rendu grand service; **it's u. to know** c'est bon à savoir; **it will come in very u.** cela rendra bien service; **a u. man to know** une relation utile, un homme qu'il est bon d'avoir dans ses relations; **to make oneself u.** se rendre utile; *Iron* **that's u.!** formidable! **2** *(skilful)* **he plays a u. game of chess** il joue bien aux échecs; **to be u. with one's fists** savoir se servir de ses poings; **to be u. with a gun** savoir manier un fusil

▸▸ **u. life** *(of product)* vie *f* utile; **this machine has a u. life of ten years** cette machine a une durée de vie de dix ans

usefully [ˈjuːsfəlɪ] **ADV** utilement; **her time had been u. employed** elle s'était occupée utilement; **one might u. write a book on ...** il serait fort utile qu'on écrive un livre sur ...; **is there anything I can u. do?** puis-je faire quelque chose pour me rendre utile?

usefulness [ˈjuːsfʊlnɪs] **N** utilité *f*; **it has outlived its u.** cela ne sert plus à rien

useless [ˈjuːslɪs] **ADJ 1** *(not useful)* inutile; *(unusable)* inutilisable; *(no good)* nul; *(remedy)* inefficace; **I hope I haven't been completely u. to you** j'espère que je ne t'ai pas été complètement inutile; **to be full of u. information** être riche en informations inutiles; **a map without a key is u.** une carte sans légende est inutilisable; *Fam* **to be worse than u.** *(of person)* être au-dessous de tout; *(of object)* ne rien valoir du tout, *Sl* ne pas valoir un pet de lapin **2** *(incompetent)* *(person)* bon à rien, incompétent, nul; **I'm u. at languages** je suis nul en langues; **he's u. in bed** au lit, il est nul; **a u. person** un bon à rien, *f* une bonne à rien **3** *(futile)* inutile; **it was u. to resist** il était inutile de résister; **it would be u. to make further requests** cela ne servirait à rien de faire d'autres demandes; **give up, it's u.!** laisse tomber, ça ne sert à rien!; **it's u. even trying to discuss it** ce n'est même pas la peine d'essayer d'en discuter

uselessly [ˈjuːslɪslɪ] **ADV** inutilement

uselessness [ˈjuːslɪsnɪs] **N** inutilité *f*, *(of person)* incompétence *f*, *(of remedy)* inefficacité *f*; **his general u.** sa nullité

Usenet [ˈjuːznet] **N** *Comput* Usenet *m*

user [ˈjuːzər] **N** *(of road, means of transport)* usager, -ère; *(of device, computer, dictionary)* utilisateur, -trice; *(of telephone)* abonné, -ée; **bus users** les usagers du bus

▸▸ *Comput* **u. group** club *m* d'utilisateurs; *Comput* **u. identification** identification *f* de l'utilisateur; *Comput* **u. identification code** code *m* d'identification de l'utilisateur; *Comput* **u. language** langage *m* utilisateur; *Comput* **u. manual** manuel *m* d'utilisation; *Comput* **u. name** nom *m* de l'utilisateur; *Comput* **u. network** réseau *m* d'utilisateurs; *Mktg* **u. panel** panel *m* d'utilisateurs; *Comput* **u. software** logiciel *m* utilisateur; *Comput* **u. support** assistance *f* à l'utilisateur

user-definable ADJ *Comput (characters, keys)* définissable par l'utilisateur

user-defined [-dɪˈfaɪnd] **ADJ** *Comput* défini par l'utilisateur

▸▸ **u. key** touche *f* personnalisée

user-friendliness N *(of software, computer)* convivialité *f*, *(of keyboard)* confort *m* d'emploi; *(of machine, dictionary, manual)* facilité *f* d'utilisation

user-friendly ADJ *(software, computer)* convivial, -aux; *(keyboard)* confortable, facile d'emploi; *(machine, technology, instruction manual, dictionary)* facile à utiliser

user-interface N *Comput etc* interface *f* utilisateur

user-programmable ADJ *Comput* programmable par l'utilisateur

user-specific ADJ spécifique à l'utilisateur

U-shaped ADJ en U; *Geog* **U-shaped valley** vallée *f* (à profil) en U

usher [ˈʌʃər] **N** *Law (in court)* (huissier *m*) audiencier *m*; *Theat, Cin* placeur *m*; *(at wedding)* garçon *m* d'honneur

VT I was ushered into the presence of the boss je fus introduit auprès du directeur; **they hastily ushered him away/out** ils le firent s'éloigner/sortir à la hâte

▸ **usher in VT SEP** introduire, faire entrer; **to u. in a new era** marquer le début d'une nouvelle époque

usherette [ʌʃəˈret] **N** *Theat, Cin* ouvreuse *f*

USM [juːesˈem] **N 1** *(abbr United States Mail)* = service *m* des postes américain **2** *Mil abbr* **United States Marines 3** *Fin abbr* **United States Mint 4** *Fin (abbr unlisted securities market)* second marché *m*

USN [juːesˈen] **N** *(abbr United States Navy)* marine *f* nationale américaine

USP [juːesˈpiː] **N** *Mktg (abbr unique selling point or proposition)* proposition *f* unique de vente

USS [juːesˈes] **N** *(abbr United States Ship)* = initiales précédant le nom des navires américains; **U. Nimitz** le Nimitz

USSR [juːeseserˈɑːr] **N** *Formerly (abbr Union of Soviet Socialist Republics)* URSS *f*

usual [ˈjuːʒəl] **ADJ** habituel; **at the u. time** à l'heure habituelle; **it's the u. practice** c'est la pratique courante; **I didn't get my u. bus this morning** je n'ai pas pris le bus que je prends d'habitude ce matin; **it wasn't the u. postman** ce n'était pas notre facteur habituel *ou Fam* de d'habitude; **u. time, u. place, OK?** même heure, même endroit, d'accord?; **she's back to her u. self again** elle a retrouvé la forme; **you're not your u. cheery self today** tu as perdu ton sourire aujourd'hui; **it's quite u. for that sort of thing to happen** ces choses-là arrivent fréquemment; **it's u. (for that to happen) with these machines** ça arrive fréquemment avec ces machines; **it's not u. to have to wait this long** d'habitude on n'attend pas aussi longtemps; **it's u. to pay in advance** il est d'usage de payer d'avance; **earlier/later than u.** plus tôt/plus tard que d'habitude; **more/less than u.** plus/moins que d'habitude; **as u.,** *Fam* **as per u.,** comme d'habitude; **business as u.** *(on sign)* ouvert pendant les réparations; **despite recent events it was business as u.** malgré les récents événements, la vie continuait comme si de rien n'était

N *Fam (in bar)* **(are you having) your u.?** comme d'habitude?; **the u. please, Jim** comme d'habitude s'il te plaît, Jim

usually [ˈjuːʒʊ(ə)lɪ] **ADV** d'habitude, habituellement; **I u. get up at seven** d'habitude je me lève à sept heures, je me lève habituellement à sept heures; **he was more than u. polite** il s'est montré encore plus poli que d'habitude; **it's not u. that difficult** ce n'est pas aussi difficile que ça d'habitude *ou* habituellement; **she's not u. like that** d'habitude elle n'est pas comme ça

usufruct [ˈjuːzjʊfrʌkt] **N** *Law* usufruit *m* (**of** de)

usufructuary [juːzjʊˈfrʌktjərɪ] **ADJ, N** *Law* usufruitier, -ière

▸▸ **u. right** droit *m* usufructuaire

usurer [ˈjuːʒərər] **N** usurier, -ière

usurious [juːˈzjʊərɪəs] **ADJ** *(interest etc)* usuraire

usurp [juːˈzɜːp, -ˈsɜːp] **VT** *(throne, title)* usurper (**from** sur)

usurpation [juːzəˈpeɪʃən, -sɜː-] **N** usurpation *f*

usurper [jʊˈzɜːpər, -sɜː-] **N** usurpateur, -trice

usury [ˈjuːʒʊrɪ] **N** usure *f*; **that's u.!** c'est du vol!

Ut *abbr* **Utah**

utensil [juːˈtens(ə)l] N ustensile m; (set of) kitchen utensils batterie f de cuisine

uterine [ˈjuːtəraɪn] ADJ utérin

uterus [ˈjuːtərəs] N Anat utérus m

utilitarian [juːtɪlɪˈteərɪən] ADJ, N utilitaire mf

utilitarianism [juːtɪlɪˈteərɪənɪz(ə)m] N utilitarisme m

utility [juːˈtɪlɪtɪ] N 1 (usefulness) utilité f 2 (public) utilities, utilities sector secteur m des services, services mpl publics
▸▸ u. car voiture f utilitaire; u. furniture = meubles mpl fonctionnels et peu chers; Sport u. player joueur, -euse polyvalent(e); Comput u. program programme m (utilitaire), utilitaire m; u. room ≃ buanderie f; Am St Exch u. stocks valeurs fpl de services publics; u. vehicle véhicule m utilitaire

utilizable [juːtɪˈlaɪzəb(ə)l] ADJ utilisable

utilization [juːtɪl(a)ɪˈzeɪʃ(ə)n] N utilisation f; better u. of resources meilleure utilisation ou meilleur emploi des ressources

utilize [ˈjuːtɪlaɪz] VT utiliser, se servir de; (take advantage of) (opportunity, situation) tirer profit de

utmost [ˈʌtməʊst] ADJ 1 (greatest) the u. le plus grand; the u. poverty la misère la plus noire; with the u. contempt avec le plus grand mépris; it is of the u. importance that he should be present il est absolument essentiel qu'il soit présent; with the u. ease avec la plus grande facilité, avec une extrême facilité; it was only with the u. difficulty that we were able to persuade them nous avons eu toutes les peines du monde à les convaincre
2 (furthest) the u. ends of the earth les confins mpl ou les extrémités fpl de la terre
▸ N 1 to live life to the u. profiter pleinement de la vie; to enjoy oneself to the u. s'amuser au plus haut point; to do sth to the u. of one's abilities faire qch au maximum de ses capacités; I'll help you to the u. of my ability je ferai tout ce qui est en mon pouvoir pour vous aider; to do one's u. to achieve sth faire tout son possible pour arriver à qch; she tried her u. to persuade him elle a fait tout ce qu'elle a pu pour le persuader
2 that's the u. we can offer c'est le maximum que nous puissions offrir; $50,000 at the u. 50 000 dollars au grand maximum

Utopia [juːˈtəʊpɪə] N utopie f

Utopian [juːˈtəʊpɪən] ADJ utopique; U. socialism socialisme m utopique
▸ N utopiste mf

utter [ˈʌtər] ADJ complet, -ète, absolu; he's an u. stranger to me il m'est complètement étranger; it's u. madness c'est de la folie totale ou pure; we were in u. darkness nous étions dans l'obscurité totale; u. boredom ennui m mortel; u. poverty la misère la plus noire; Br Fam u. rubbish (goods) de la pure camelote; (nonsense) des absurdités; what u. rubbish! quel tas de sottises!; he's an u. fool il est complètement idiot; to my u. horror comble de l'horreur; to her u. amazement à sa plus grande stupéfaction
▸ VT 1 (cry) jeter, pousser; (word) prononcer, dire; (curse) lancer; I didn't u. a word je n'ai pas desserré les dents; never u. his name in her presence il ne faut jamais prononcer son nom devant elle; if you u. another sound you're going straight to bed! et si je t'entends encore une fois tu vas directement au lit! 2 (lies) débiter 3 Fml (counterfeit money) émettre, mettre en circulation

utterance [ˈʌtərəns] N 1 (what is said) paroles fpl, propos mpl, mots mpl; Ling énoncé m; what was his last u.? quels ont été ses derniers mots?; they taped the child's first utterances ils ont enregistré les premiers mots de l'enfant; his recent utterances in the national press ses récentes déclarations dans la presse nationale 2 (expression) (of sound) expression f; on her u. of his name au moment où elle prononça son nom; to give u. to one's feelings/a thought exprimer ses sentiments/une pensée

utterly [ˈʌtəlɪ] ADV complètement, absolument; u. stupid d'une bêtise extrême

uttermost [ˈʌtəməʊst] ADJ, N = utmost

U-tube N tube m en U

U-turn N 1 Aut demi-tour m, pl demi-tours; to make a U. faire (un) demi-tour; no U-turns (sign) défense de faire demi-tour 2 Fig volte-face f inv; revirement m; the government were accused of making a U. on health policy le gouvernement a été accusé de faire volte-face en matière de politique de santé

UV [juːˈviː] ADJ (abbr ultra-violet) UV

uvula, pl **uvulas**, **uvulae** [ˈjuːvjələ, -əs, -iː] N Anat uvule f, luette f

uvular [ˈjuːvjələr] ADJ uvulaire

uxorious [ʌkˈsɔːrɪəs] ADJ Fml (husband) soumis

uxoriousness [ʌkˈsɔːrɪəsnɪs] N Fml (of husband) soumission f à sa femme

Uzbekistan [ʊzbekɪˈstɑːn] N Ouzbékistan m

V¹, v¹ [viː] N *(letter)* V, v *m*; **two v's** deux v; **to fly in a V formation** *(of birds)* voler en formant un V

V² *Elec (abbr* **volt(s))** V

v² **1** *(abbr* **verse)** v. **2** *Law, Sport abbr* **versus 3** *(abbr* **very)** t.

Va *abbr* **Virginia**

V & A [viːən'eɪ] N *Br (abbr* **Victoria and Albert Museum)** = musée *m* d'arts décoratifs, à Londres

vac [væk] N *Br Univ, Sch Fam* vacances *fpl*

vacancy ['veɪkənsɪ] N **1** *(position)* place *f* vacante, poste *m* vacant, vacance *f*; **we have a v. for ...** *(job advert)* nous recherchons ...; **to fill a v.** pourvoir un poste vacant; **v. on the board** siège *m* à pourvoir au conseil d'administration **2** *(at hotel)* chambre *f* libre; *(at camp site)* place *f* libre; **no vacancies** complet **3** *(of expression)* caractère *m* absent; **a look of sheer v.** un visage dénué de toute expression

> Note that the French word **vacances** is a false friend. It means **holiday.**

vacant ['veɪkənt] ADJ **1** *(empty)* vide; *(hotel room, seat, lavatory)* libre; *(flat)* inoccupé; *(official post)* vacant, à pourvoir; **situations v.** *(newspaper column)* offres *fpl* d'emploi; **v. site** *(for sale)* terrain *m* à vendre **2** *(mind)* vide; *(look)* *(absent-minded)* distrait, vague, sans expression; *(stupid)* niais, stupide; **with a v. expression** le regard perdu **3** *(time)* libre
> ▸▸ *Am* **v. lot** terrain vague; *Br* **v. possession** libre possession *f*

vacantly ['veɪkəntlɪ] ADV *(to gaze etc)* *(absentmindedly)* d'un air distrait *ou* absent; *(with lack of intelligence)* d'un regard perdu; *(stupidly)* d'un air stupide

vacate [və'keɪt] VT *(seat, flat, hotel room, job)* quitter; *(room)* libérer, quitter; *Law* **to v. the premises** vider les lieux

vacation [və'keɪʃən] N **1** *esp Am (holiday)* vacances *fpl*; **during** *or* **in the v.** pendant les vacances; **we spent the v. travelling around Europe** nous avons voyagé en Europe pendant nos vacances; **to take a v.** prendre des vacances; **to be on v.** être en vacances **2** *Br Univ (recess)* vacances *fpl*; *Law* vacations *fpl*, vacances judiciaires; **over the v.** pendant les vacances **3** *Fml (leaving) (of premises)* évacuation *f*; **v. of office** démission *f*
> VI *Am* prendre *ou* passer ses vacances **(at, in** à, en)
> ▸▸ *Am* **v. center** club *m* de vacances; *Am* **v. home** résidence *f* secondaire; *Am Admin* **v. leave** congé *m* annuel; *Am* **v. resort camp** *m* de vacances; *Am* **v. work** travail *m* effectué pendant les vacances *(par un étudiant)*

vacationist, vacationer [veɪ'keɪʃənɪst, -ər] N *Am* vacancier, -ière; *(in summer)* estivant, -ante

vaccinate ['væksɪneɪt] VT *Med* vacciner *(against* contre); **to get vaccinated** se faire vacciner

vaccination [væksɪ'neɪʃən] N *Med* vaccination *f*, **smallpox v.** vaccination contre la variole

vaccine ['væksiːn] N *Med* vaccin *m*

vaccinee [væksɪ'niː] N *Am* personne *f* vaccinée

vacillate ['væsɪleɪt] VI hésiter **(between** entre)

vacillating ['væsɪleɪtɪŋ] ADJ *(undecided)* irrésolu, indécis
> N *(indecision)* indécision *f*, irrésolution *f*

vacillation [væsɪ'leɪʃən] N indécision *f*

vacuity [væ'kjuːɪtɪ] N vacuité *f*, **vacuities** bêtises *fpl*, niaiseries *fpl*

vacuous ['vækjʊəs] ADJ *(look)* hébété, vide d'expression; *(remark, laugh)* niais, bête; *(book, film)* idiot; **he's completely v.** c'est un parfait idiot; **what an utterly v. thing to say** quelle niaiserie, quelle idiotie

vacuously ['vækjʊəslɪ] ADV bêtement

vacuousness ['vækjʊəsnɪs] N *(of laugh)* bêtise *f*, niaiserie *f*, *(of remark, debate)* vacuité *f*

vacuum, *pl* **vacua, vacuums** ['vækjʊm, -jʊə, -jʊmz] N **1** *Phys* vide *m*, vacuum *m*; *Fig* vide *m*; **to produce** *or* **create a v.** faire le vide; **nature abhors a v.** la nature a horreur du vide; *Fig* **a cultural/political v.** un vide sur le plan culturel/politique; **to live in a v.** vivre en vase clos; **a v. of ideas** une pénurie d'idées **2** *(machine)* aspirateur *m*; **to give the carpet a v.** passer l'aspirateur sur la moquette **3** *Aut (of venturi)* dépression *f*
> VT *(carpet)* passer l'aspirateur sur; *(room)* passer l'aspirateur dans
> ▸▸ **v. advance** avance *f* à dépression; *Am* **v. bottle** (bouteille *f*) Thermos® *f*, **v. chamber** chambre *f* à dépression; **v. cleaner** aspirateur; *Br* **v. flask** (bouteille *f*) Thermos®; **v. pack** emballage *m* sous vide; **v. pump** pompe *f* à vide; **v. tank** réservoir *m* à dépression; *Am* **v. tube** tube *m* électronique *ou* à vide

vacuuming ['vækjʊmɪŋ] N **to do the v.** passer l'aspirateur

vacuum-packed ADJ emballé sous vide

vade mecum [vɑːdɪ'meɪkəm] N vademecum *m inv*, aide-mémoire *m inv*

vagabond ['vægəbɒnd] N vagabond, -onde
> ADJ vagabond, errant

vagary ['veɪgərɪ] N caprice *m*; **the vagaries of fashion/the weather** les caprices de la mode/du temps

vagina [və'dʒaɪnə] N *Anat* vagin *m*

vaginal [və'dʒaɪn(ə)l] ADJ *Anat* vaginal, -aux
> ▸▸ **v. discharge** pertes *fpl* blanches; **v. examination** examen *m* vaginal; **v. smear** frottis *m* vaginal; **to have a v. smear taken** se faire faire un frottis vaginal

vagrancy ['veɪgrənsɪ] N *Law* vagabondage *m*; **to be arrested for v.** être arrêté pour vagabondage

vagrant ['veɪgrənt] N vagabond, -onde
> ADJ errant

vague [veɪg] ADJ *(person, look, reply)* vague; *(impression, memory)* vague, imprécis, confus; *(shape, outline)* flou, imprécis; **to bear a v. resemblance to sb/sth** ressembler vaguement à qn/qch; **there's been some v. talk of ...** on a parlé vaguement de ...; **the conditions were left deliberately v.** les conditions ont été laissées délibérément vagues; **I haven't the vaguest idea** je n'en ai pas la moindre idée; **I had a v. idea that he was dead** j'avais vaguement l'idée qu'il était mort; **he was rather v. about the date** il s'est montré assez vague à propos de la date; **she was v. (about it)** elle est restée vague là-dessus

vaguely ['veɪglɪ] ADV *(to look)* d'un air vague; *(to remember, express)* vaguement, confusément; *(to agree, resemble)* vaguement; *(slightly)* légèrement; **to be v. reminiscent of ...** rappeler vaguement ...; **their music sounds v. like the Beatles** leur musique ressemble vaguement aux Beatles

vagueness ['veɪgnɪs] N caractère *m* vague, vague *m*, imprécision *f*, *(of shape, outline, photograph)* caractère flou; *(of story, report, memory etc)* manque *m* de précision

vain [veɪn] ADJ **1** *(conceited)* vaniteux, orgueilleux; **she was v. about her beauty** elle était fière de sa beauté **2** *(unavailing)* vain, inutile, stérile; **v. efforts** efforts *mpl* vains *ou* inutiles **v. promises** vaines promesses *fpl*, promesses vaines **3** *(hope)* vain; *(pleasure)* futile **4 in v.** en vain, vainement; **to labour in v.** travailler en vain, perdre sa peine; **her efforts were in v.** ses efforts ont été inutiles; **it was all in v.** c'était peine perdue; **to take God's name in v.** invoquer le nom de Dieu en vain; *Fam* **who's taking my name in v.?** qui est-ce qui parle de moi?

vainglorious [veɪn'glɔːrɪəs] ADJ *Fml* vaniteux, orgueilleux

vaingloriously [veɪn'glɔːrɪəslɪ] ADV *Fml* vaniteusement, orgueilleusement

vainglory [veɪn'glɔːrɪ] N *Fml* vanité *f*, orgueil *m*

vainly ['veɪnlɪ] ADV **1** *(uselessly)* vainement, en vain **2** *(conceitedly)* vaniteusement, avec vanité

valance ['væləns] N *(on side of bed)* frange *f* de lit; *(for curtains)* cantonnière *f*, lambrequin *m*; *(on vehicle)* tablier *m*, doublure *f* d'aile, bouclier *m*

valanced sheet ['vælənst] N housse *f* cache-sommier

vale [veɪl] N *Arch, Lit* vallée *f*, *(small)* vallon *m*; *Fig* **this v. of tears** cette vallée de larmes

valediction [vælɪ'dɪkʃən] N **1** *(farewell)*

adieu(x) *m(pl)* **2** *Am Univ, Sch* = **valedictory** N

valedictorian [vælɪdɪk'tɔːrɪən] N *Am Univ, Sch* membre *m* d'une promotion qui prononce le discours d'adieu

valedictory [vælɪ'dɪktərɪ] ADJ *(address, dinner)* d'adieu
N *Am Univ, Sch (at graduation)* discours *m* d'adieu

valence ['veɪləns] N *Am* = **valency**

valency ['veɪlənsɪ] N *Br Chem* valence *f*

valentine ['væləntaɪn] N **1** (St) **Valentine's Day** *(14 February)* la Saint-Valentin **2** *(card)* carte *f* de la Saint-Valentin; *(recipient of card)* = celui/celle qui reçoit une carte envoyée le jour de la Saint-Valentin; **will you be my v.?** = phrase *f* écrite sur les cartes de la Saint-Valentin pour exprimer ses sentiments amoureux à l'égard du/de la destinataire; **George is my v.** c'est George que j'aime
▸ ▸ **v. card** carte de la Saint-Valentin

valerian [və'leərɪən] N *Bot, Pharm* valériane *f*

valet ['væleɪ, 'vælɪt] N *(manservant)* valet *m* de chambre; *(in hotel)* = employé *m* qui s'occupe de l'entretien des vêtements des clients; *Am (who parks car)* = employé d'un hôtel ou d'un restaurant qui se charge de garer les voitures des clients
VT (**valeted** ['vælɪtɪd]) **to v. a car** laver et nettoyer une voiture; **can I have my suit valeted?** puis-je faire nettoyer mon costume?; **valeting service** *(for clothes)* service *m* de nettoyage des vêtements; *(for car)* service de lavage et de nettoyage
▸ ▸ **v. parking** *(sign)* service de voiturier; **v. service** *(in hotel)* pressing *m* de l'hôtel

valetudinarian [vælɪtjuːdɪ'neərɪən] ADJ, N valétudinaire *mf*

Valhalla [væl'hælə] N *Myth* Walhalla *m*

valiant ['vælɪənt] ADJ courageux, vaillant, valeureux; **to make a v. effort** faire un courageux effort (**to do** pour faire)

valiantly ['vælɪəntlɪ] ADV courageusement, vaillamment, valeureusement

valid ['vælɪd] ADJ *(contract, document etc)* valide, valable; *(passport)* en règle; *(reason, objection)* valable, recevable; **ticket v. for three months** billet bon pour trois mois; **no longer v.** *(ticket, passport etc)* périmé

Note that the French word **valide** also means **able-bodied**.

validate ['vælɪdeɪt] VT **1** *(act, contract, ticket)* valider, rendre valable; *Am* **to v. an election** valider une élection **2** *(prove)* *(theory)* confirmer **3** *Comput* valider

validation [vælɪ'deɪʃən] N **1** *(of act, contract)* validation *f* **2** *(of theory)* confirmation *f* **3** *Comput* validation *f*

validator ['vælɪdeɪtər] N *(for tickets)* cachet *m*

validity [və'lɪdɪtɪ] N *(of contract, document)* validité *f*; *(of argument)* force *f*, justesse *f*; *(of claim)* bien-fondé *m*; **these objections have no v.** ces objections ne sont pas fondées

validly ['vælɪdlɪ] ADV validement, valablement

valise [və'liːs, -iːz] N *Old-fashioned (suitcase)* valise *f*; *(hand luggage)* sac *m* de voyage

Valium® ['vælɪəm] N Valium® *m*; **to be on V.** être sous Valium®; **the doctor has put her on V.** le docteur l'a mise au Valium®

Valkyrie ['vælkɪrɪ] N *Myth* Walkyrie *f*, Valkyrie *f*

valley ['vælɪ] N **1** vallée *f*; *(small)* vallon *m*; **the Rhone V.** la vallée du Rhône **2** *Constr* noue *f*, *(of roof)* cornière *f*

valor ['vælər] N *Am* = **valour**

valorization [væləraɪ'zeɪʃən] N valorisation *f*

valorize ['vælərɑɪz] VT *Com, Fin* valoriser

valorous ['vælərəs] ADJ *Fml* valeureux, vaillant

valour, *Am* **valor** ['vælər] N courage *m*, vaillance *f*, bravoure *f*; **to be decorated for v.** *(of soldier, police officer etc)* être décoré pour son courage

valuable ['væljʊəb(ə)l] ADJ *(help, time)* précieux; *(object)* précieux, de valeur, de prix; **v. gift** cadeau *m* de valeur; **nothing v. was taken** aucun objet de valeur n'a été volé; **she has given years of v. service** elle a donné des années de bons et loyaux services
NPL **valuables** objets *mpl* de valeur

valuation [vælju'eɪʃən] N *Fin* **1** *(setting of value)* évaluation *f*, estimation *f*, appréciation *f*; *Law* prisée *f* et estimation; *(by expert)* expertise *f*, rapport *m* d'expertise; **to get a v. of sth** faire expertiser qch; **to make a v. of the goods** faire l'expertise des marchandises **2** *(value)* *(of painting, house)* valeur *f* estimée; **the v. on the house was £50,000** la valeur estimée de la maison était de 50000 livres; **to set too high/too low a v. on goods** surestimer/sous-estimer des marchandises; *Fig* **to take** *or* **accept sb at his/her own v.** estimer qn selon l'opinion qu'il a de lui-même/qu'elle a d'elle-même
▸ ▸ *Fin* **v. charge** taxation *f* à la valeur

valuator ['væljʊeɪtər] N = **valuer**

value ['væljuː] N **1** *(worth)* valeur *f*; **to be of v.** *(of jewellery etc)* avoir de la valeur; **to go up/down in v.** prendre/perdre de la valeur; **of great v.** de grande *ou* haute valeur; **your help/contribution was of great v.** votre aide/contribution a été très précieuse; **she has been of great v. to the company** elle a apporté une contribution précieuse à l'entreprise; **to be of great sentimental v.** avoir une grande valeur sentimentale; **of little v.** de peu de valeur; **to be of little v.** être sans grande valeur; **her advice/help was of little v.** ses conseils n'ont/son aide n'a pas été très utile(s); **of no v.** sans valeur; **it is nothing of any v.** ce n'est rien qui ait une quelconque valeur; **to lose v., to fall in v.** se dévaluer, s'avilir; *Fin* se dévaloriser; **loss of v., fall in v.** dévalorisation *f*; **to set a v. on sth** *(evaluate)* évaluer qch; *Com* attribuer une cote de valeur à qch; **to set a high/low v. on sth** attribuer une haute/faible valeur à qch; **to set too high a v. on sth** attacher trop de valeur *ou* de prix à qch, surestimer qch; **he sets a very high v. on her** il estime que c'est une personne d'une grande valeur; **goods to the v. of ten pounds** marchandises d'une valeur de dix livres; **what will this do to the v. of property?** quel effet est-ce que ça va avoir sur le prix de l'immobilier?; **commercial** *or* **market v.** *(worth)* valeur marchande; *(price)* cours *m*; **replacement v.** valeur de remplacement; **it's good v.** c'est très avantageux; **at £2 it's very good v.** à 2 livres, c'est une bonne affaire *ou* c'est intéressant; **v. for money** *(heading on restaurant or wine review)* rapport *m* qualité/prix; **to get (good) v. for one's money** en avoir pour son argent; **he gives you v. for money** il vous en donne pour votre argent; **it's (good) v. for money** ça vaut le coup, ce n'est pas cher; **the large size gives you better v. (for your money)** le grand format est plus avantageux

2 *Math, Mus, Ling* valeur *f*; **let y have the v. 15** soit y égale 15; **to give full v. to each word** donner du poids à chaque mot

3 **values** *(standards)* valeurs *fpl*; **sense of values** sens *m* des valeurs; **moral values** valeurs morales; **according to a set of values** selon certains principes

VT **1** *(evaluate)* *(goods)* évaluer, estimer, apprécier; *Com (assess value of)* expertiser; *(property, painting)* faire l'expertise de; **to get sth valued** faire expertiser qch, faire évaluer qch; **to v. a house at £100,000** évaluer une maison à 100 000 livres; **they valued the company at $10 billion** ils ont estimé la valeur de la société à 10 milliards de dollars **2** *(appreciate)* *(person, thing)* tenir à, faire grand cas de; **to v. sb as a friend** tenir à *ou* apprécier qn en tant qu'ami; **if you v. your life** si vous tenez à la vie
▸ ▸ *Fin* **v. analysis** analyse *f* de valeur; *Mktg* **v. brand** marque *f* de valeur; *Com* **v. chain** chaîne *f* de valeur; *Fin* **v. for collection** valeur à l'encaissement; *Fin* **v. date** date *f* de valeur; *Fin* **v. day** jour *m* de valeur; *Fin* **v. engineering** analyse de valeur; *Fin* **v. in exchange** valeur d'échange, contre-valeur *f*, *pl* contre-valeurs; **v. judgement** jugement *m* de valeur; **v. marketing** marketing *m* de la valeur; *Fin* **v. at maturity** valeur à l'échéance; *Fin* **v. for money audit** = estimation *f* des performances d'une société à but non lucratif ou d'un service gouvernemental; *Fin* **v. in use** valeur d'usage

value-add N valeur *f* ajoutée

value-added ADJ *Fin (product, service etc)* à valeur ajoutée; **high v. product** produit *m* à haute valeur ajoutée
▸ ▸ *Comput* **v. network** réseau *m* à valeur ajoutée; *Br* **v. tax** taxe *f* à la valeur ajoutée, taxe sur la valeur ajoutée

valued ['væljuːd] ADJ *(contribution)* précieux; *(colleague, employee)* estimé; **my v. friend, MrThomson** M. Thomson, dont l'amitié m'est si précieuse

valueless ['væljʊlɪs] ADJ sans valeur

Attention: ne pas confondre avec **invaluable**, qui signifie **inestimable**.

valuer ['væljʊər] N *(of antique etc)* expert *m*; **official v.** commissaire-priseur *m*, *pl* commissaires-priseurs

valve [vælv] N *(in pipe, tube, air chamber)* valve *f*, *(in machine)* soupape *f*, valve; *Anat* valve; *(small)* valvule *f*; *Bot, Zool* valve; *Mus (of brass instrument)* piston *m*; *Elec (of radio)* lampe *f*, valve

valved [vælvd] ADJ *Tech* à valve(s), à soupape(s); *Mus (instrument)* à pistons

valvular ['vælvjʊlər] ADJ *Med* valvulaire

vamoose [və'muːs] VI *esp Am Fam* décamper, filer; **let's v.** filons, fichons le camp

vamp¹ [væmp] *Mus Fam* N accompagnement *m* improvisé
VI *(improvise)* improviser (au piano)

vamp² *Old-fashioned Fam* N *(woman)* femme *f* fatale, vamp *f*
VT *(of woman)* *(man)* vamper
VI *(of woman)* jouer la femme fatale
▸ **vamp up** VT SEP *Fam (building)* retaper; *(story)* enjoliver, embellir

vampire ['væmpaɪər] N *(bat, monster)* vampire *m*; *(person)* vampire, sangsue *f*
▸ ▸ *Zool* **v. bat** vampire

vampiric [væm'pɪrɪk] ADJ vampirique

vampirism ['væmpaɪərɪz(ə)m] N vampirisme *m*

vampish ['væmpɪʃ] ADJ *Old-fashioned Fam (looks, dress)* de vamp, de femme fatale

VAN [væn] N *Comput (abbr* **value-added network**) réseau *m* à valeur ajoutée

van¹ [væn] N = **vanguard**

van² N **1** *Aut (large)* camion *m*, fourgon *m*; *Br (small)* camionnette *f*, fourgonnette *f*; **furniture** *or* **removal v.** camion de déménagement; **delivery v.** camion/camionnette de livraison; *Radio, TV* **outside broadcasting v.** car *m* de radio-reportage **2** *Br Rail* wagon *m*,

fourgon *m*; **luggage v.** fourgon à bagages
▶▶*Am* **v. pool** = covoiturage *m* en minibus *(souvent aux frais de l'entreprise)*

van³ **N** *esp Br Tennis* avantage *m*; **v. in/out** avantage dedans/dehors

vanadium [vəˈneɪdɪəm] **N** *Chem* vanadium *m*

vandal [ˈvænd(ə)l] **N** vandale *mf*

vandalism [ˈvændɪlɪz(ə)m] **N** vandalisme *m*; **act of v.** acte *m* de vandalisme

vandalize [ˈvændəlaɪz] **VT** *(building, telephone etc)* saccager; **several pictures have been vandalized** plusieurs tableaux ont été mutilés (par des vandales)

vane [veɪn] **N 1** *(for indicating wind direction)* girouette *f* **2** *(of windmill)* aile *f*; *(of turbine)* aube *f*, ailette *f*, palette *f*; *(of bomb, torpedo)* ailette *f*; **the vanes** *(of turbine)* l'aubage *m*

vanguard [ˈvænɡɑːd] **N** *Mil, Fig* avant-garde *f*; *Fig* **to be in the v. of a movement** être un des pionniers d'un mouvement; **to be in the v. of technological progress** être à la pointe du progrès technologique

vanilla [vəˈnɪlə] **N** vanille *f*; **flavoured with v., v. flavoured** vanillé, (parfumé) à la vanille; **v. ice cream** crème *f* glacée à la vanille
▶▶**v. essence, v. extract** extrait *m* de vanille; **v. plant** vanille, vanillier *m*; **v. pod** gousse *f* de vanille; **v. sugar** sucre *m* vanillé; *St Exch* **v. swap** swap *m* vanilla

vanillin [vəˈnɪlɪn] **N** *Chem* vanilline *f*

vanish [ˈvænɪʃ] **VI** disparaître; *(of visions, suspicions)* se dissiper, s'évanouir; *(of difficulties)* s'aplanir; **to make sth v.** faire disparaître qch; *(of magician)* escamoter qch, faire disparaître qch; **elephants are vanishing from the earth** les éléphants sont en voie de disparition; **to v. from sight** disparaître à la vue; **to v. without trace** disparaître sans laisser de trace; **to v. into thin air** se volatiliser; **he's vanished** il a disparu; *Fam (to avoid sth, sb)* il s'est éclipsé; **she saw her last hope v.** elle a vu s'évanouir son dernier espoir

vanishing [ˈvænɪʃɪŋ] **ADJ** *Fig* **to do a v. act** s'éclipser; **he's done his famous v. act again** le voilà qui s'est encore éclipsé
▶▶*Old-fashioned* **v. cream** crème *f* de jour; **v. point** point *m* de fuite; *Fig* **profits have dwindled to v. point** les bénéfices se sont trouvés réduits à néant; **v. trick** tour *m* de passe-passe; *Fig* **he did a v. trick** *(disappeared)* il a disparu

vanity [ˈvænɪtɪ] **N 1** *(conceit)* vanité *f*, orgueil *m*; **to do sth out of v.** faire qch par vanité *ou* pour la gloriole **2** *Lit (futility)* futilité *f*; *Bible* **all is v.** tout est vanité
▶▶**v. bag** trousse *f* de toilette *(pour femme)*; **v. case** mallette *f* de toilette, vanity-case *m*, *pl* vanity-cases; *Aut* **v. mirror** miroir *m* de courtoisie; *Am Aut* **v. plate** plaque *f* d'immatriculation personnalisée; **v. press** maison *f* d'édition à compte d'auteur; **v. publishing** publication *f* à compte d'auteur; **v. table** coiffeuse *f*, table *f* de toilette; **v. unit** = meuble *m* de salle de bains avec lavabo encastré

vanquish [ˈvæŋkwɪʃ] **VT** *(person, one's passions)* vaincre, triompher de

vanquisher [ˈvæŋkwɪʃər] **N** vainqueur *m*; **Alexander, the v. of the Persians** Alexandre, celui qui a triomphé des Perses

vantage [ˈvɑːntɪdʒ] **N 1** **(point of) v., v. point** *(place)* terrain *m* avantageux, position *f* avantageuse; **to take up a v. point** choisir une position avantageuse; **from our v. point we could see …** de la position avantageuse où nous étions nous pouvions voir …; *Fig* **from the v. point of the twentieth century, it is easy to …** avec le recul qui

nous est possible au vingtième siècle, il est facile de … **2** *Tennis* avantage *m*

Vanuatu [ˌvænuːˈætuː] **N** Vanuatu

vapid [ˈvæpɪd] **ADJ** *(conversation, remark)* fade, insipide; *(style)* fade, plat; *(person)* fade, terne

vapidity [vəˈpɪdɪtɪ] **N** *(of conversation)* fadeur *f*, insipidité *f*; *(of style)* platitude *f*; *(of person)* fadeur

vapor [ˈveɪpər] **N** *Am* = **vapour**

vaporization [ˌveɪpəraɪˈzeɪʃən] **N** vaporisation *f*

vaporize [ˈveɪpəraɪz] **VT** vaporiser; *(in science fiction)* pulvériser
VI se vaporiser, se gazéifier

vaporizer [ˈveɪpəraɪzər] **N** *(spray)* atomiseur *m*, vaporisateur *m*

vaporous [ˈveɪpərəs] **ADJ** *Fml (sky, style)* vaporeux

vapour, *Am* **vapor** [ˈveɪpər] **N 1** vapeur *f* **2** *Med Old-fashioned* **to have the vapours** avoir des vapeurs
▶▶*Constr* **v. barrier** coupe-vapeur *m inv*; **v. bath** bain *m* de vapeur; *Aviat* **v. trail** traînée *f* de condensation

variability [ˌveərɪəˈbɪlɪtɪ] **N** *(of weather etc)* variabilité *f*; *Biol (of type)* inconstance *f*

variable [ˈveərɪəb(ə)l] **ADJ** *(weather, amounts etc)* variable; **rainfall is v. according to season** les précipitations varient selon les saisons; **the combinations are infinitely v.** les combinaisons peuvent varier à l'infini; **v. (at will)** réglable
N *Math, Comput* variable *f*; *Econ* **random v.** variable aléatoire
▶▶*Fin* **v. costs** coûts *mpl* variables, frais *mpl* variables; *Banking* **v. interest rate** taux *m* d'intérêt variable; *Math* **v. quantity** quantité *f* variable; *Banking* **v. rate** taux variable; **v. star** étoile *f* variable

variable-income **ADJ** *Fin (bond, investment)* à revenu variable

variable-rate **ADJ** *Banking, Fin (interest)* variable; *(security)* à revenu variable

variable-yield **ADJ** *Fin (investments, securities)* à revenu variable

variably [ˈveərɪəblɪ] **ADV** variablement

variance [ˈveərɪəns] **N 1** *(disagreement)* désaccord *m*, discordance *f*; **to be at v. with sb** être en désaccord *ou* en contradiction avec qn; **his views are totally at v. with mine** ses opinions sont totalement différentes des miennes; **historians are at v. on this point** les historiens diffèrent entre eux *ou* ne sont pas d'accord sur ce point; **this theory is at v. with the facts** cette théorie est incompatible *ou* en contradiction avec les faits **2** *(difference) (in temperature, volume etc)* variation *f*, *Chem, Math* variance *f*; *Acct* variance, écart *m*
▶▶*Acct* **v. analysis** analyse *f* des écarts

variant [ˈveərɪənt] **ADJ** différent (**from** de); **a v. interpretation** *or* **reading** une interprétation *ou* lecture différente; **a v. spelling** une variante orthographique
N variante *f*

variation [ˌveərɪˈeɪʃən] **N 1** *(difference)* variation *f*; **there was very little v. in quality** la qualité variait très peu; **v. between two readings** *(using scientific instrument)* écart *m* entre deux lectures **2** *(different version)* variation *f*, **another v. on the same theme** une autre variation sur le même thème **3** *Mus* variation *f* (**on** sur); **theme and variations** thème *m* et variations

varicoloured, *Am* **varicolored** [ˈveərɪˌkʌləd] **ADJ** *Fml* aux couleurs variées, versicolore

varicose [ˈværɪkəʊs] **ADJ** *Med* variqueux
▶▶**v. vein** varice *f*

varied [ˈveərɪd] **ADJ 1** *(diverse)* varié **2** *Biol (in colour)* multicolore, versicolore

variegated [ˈveərɪɡeɪtɪd] **ADJ 1** *Fml (diverse)* varié **2** *(multi-coloured)* bigarré, bariolé, versicolore; *Bot* panaché; **to become v.** *(of flower, leaf)* se panacher

variegation [ˌveərɪˈɡeɪʃən] **N** *(in colour)* diversité *f* de couleurs, bigarrure *f*; *Bot* panachure *f*, diaprure *f*

varietal [vəˈraɪətəl] **N** *(wine)* monocru *m*

variety [vəˈraɪətɪ] **N 1** *(diversity)* variété *f*, diversité *f*, **the hillocks give v. to the landscape** les petites collines accidentent le paysage; *Prov* **v. is the spice of life** il faut varier les plaisirs; *(a change is good)* le changement donne du piquant à la vie
2 *(assortment)* **a v. of patterns** un assortiment de modèles; **a large** *or* **wide v. of materials** *(in shop)* un grand *ou* vaste choix de tissus; **there is a v. of possible causes** il y a diverses causes possibles; **for a v. of reasons** pour des raisons diverses; **an astonishing v. of reasons was given** on a fourni des raisons incroyablement variées; **in a v. of ways** de diverses manières, diversement
3 *Bot (of flower etc)* variété *f*
4 *(sort)* type *m*
5 *Theat* variétés *fpl*; **to work in v.** travailler dans le monde des variétés
▶▶**v. artist** artiste *mf* de variétés; *Am* **v. meat** abats *mpl*; **v. show** spectacle *m* de variétés; *Am* **v. store** grand magasin *m*; **v. theatre** théâtre *m* de variétés

variola [vəˈraɪələ] **N** *Med* variole *f*, petite vérole *f*

various [ˈveərɪəs] **ADJ** divers; **of v. kinds** de diverses sortes; **to talk about v. things** parler de chose(s) et d'autre(s) *ou* de choses diverses; **her skills are many and v.** ses aptitudes sont nombreuses et diverses; **known under v. names** connu sous des noms divers; **v. people saw it** plusieurs personnes l'ont vu; **for v. reasons** pour des raisons diverses; **there are v. reasons why you shouldn't go** tu ne dois pas y aller pour plusieurs raisons; **at v. times** à diverses reprises, en diverses occasions; **in v. ways** de diverses *ou* plusieurs manières, diversement

variously [ˈveərɪəslɪ] **ADV** diversement, de diverses *ou* plusieurs manières; **v. estimated at …** estimé par diverses sources à …; **she has v. been called …** elle a été tour à tour surnommée …

varlet [ˈvɑːlɪt] **N** *Arch (rascal)* coquin *m*, vaurien *m*

varmint [ˈvɑːmɪnt] **N** *esp Am* **young v.** petit polisson *m*

varnish [ˈvɑːnɪʃ] **N** vernis *m*; *esp Br* **nail v.** vernis à ongles; **(coat of) v.** (couche *f* de) vernis; **to give sth a v.** vernir qch
VT *(wood, painting)* vernir; **to v. one's nails** se mettre du vernis à ongles
▶▶**v. remover** *(in painting)* décapant *m* pour vernis
▶ **varnish over** **VT SEP** vernir; *Fig (facts)* déguiser; *(incident)* passer sur; *(person's faults)* glisser sur, jeter un voile complaisant sur

varnisher [ˈvɑːnɪʃər] **N** vernisseur *m*

varnishing [ˈvɑːnɪʃɪŋ] **N** vernissage *m*
▶▶*Art* **v. day** (jour *m* du) vernissage

varsity [ˈvɑːsɪtɪ] **N 1** *Br Fam* université *f*, *Fam* fac *f*, **the V. match** le match entre Oxford et Cambridge **2** *Am Univ (team)* équipe *f* universitaire
ADJ universitaire

vary [ˈveərɪ] **VT** *(one's style, diet)* varier, diversifier; *(programme)* apporter de la variété à; **to v. one's methods** changer de méthodes; **to v. one's route** changer d'itinéraire de temps en temps

VI varier, changer; *Biol* s'écarter du type, présenter une variation; **the ingredients v. from place to place** les ingrédients varient d'un endroit à l'autre; **it varies with the weather** ça change en fonction du temps; **it varies** ça dépend; **to v. in quality/weight** varier en qualité/poids; **to v. from sth** s'écarter de *ou* différer de qch; **as to the date, authors v.** les auteurs ne sont pas d'accord *ou* varient quant à la date; **opinions v.** les avis sont partagés

varying ['veərɪɪŋ] **ADJ** qui varie, variable, changeant; **I've had v. reports about that restaurant** j'ai entendu des avis divergents sur ce restaurant; **they have v. opinions about this** leurs opinions divergent *ou* diffèrent sur ce point; **with v. results** avec des résultats plus ou moins satisfaisants; **with v. degrees of success** avec plus ou moins de succès

vascular ['væskjʊlər] **ADJ** *Biol* vasculaire

vascularization [væskjʊləraɪ'zeɪʃən] **N** *Med* vascularisation *f*

vas deferens [væz'defərenz] **N** *Anat* canal *m* déférent

vase [vɑːz, *Am* veɪz] **N** vase *m*; **flower v.** vase à fleurs

vasectomy [və'sektəmɪ] **N** *Surg* vasectomie *f*; **to have a v.** se faire faire une vasectomie

Vaseline® ['væsəliːn] **N** Vaseline® *f*

vasoconstricting [veɪzəʊkən'strɪktɪŋ] **ADJ** *Med* vasoconstricteur, -trice

vasoconstriction [veɪzəʊkən'strɪkʃən] **N** *Med* vasoconstriction *f*

vasoconstrictor [veɪzəʊkən'strɪktər] *Med* **N** vasoconstricteur *m*
ADJ vasoconstricteur, -trice

vasodilation [veɪzəʊdaɪ'leɪʃən] **N** *Med* vasodilatation *f*

vasodilator [veɪzəʊdaɪ'leɪtər] *Med* **N** vasodilatateur *m*
ADJ vasodilatateur, -trice

vasomotor ['veɪzəʊməʊtər] **ADJ** *Anat* vasomoteur, -trice

vassal ['væs(ə)l] **ADJ** vassal
N vassal *m*
▸▸ **v. state** pays *m* vassal

vassalage ['væsəlɪdʒ] **N** *Hist* vassalité *f*, vasselage *m*; *Fig* sujétion *f*

vast [vɑːst] **ADJ** immense; **in the v. majority of cases** dans la très grande *ou* l'immense majorité des cas; **a v. number of people** un extrêmement grand nombre de gens; **a v. expanse of territory** une immense *ou* vaste étendue de territoire; **his v. knowledge** son immense savoir; **to spend a v. amount** *or* **v. sums (of money)** dépenser de grosses sommes d'argent; **at v. expense** à grands frais; **there's a v. difference between them** il y a une différence énorme entre eux

vastly ['vɑːstlɪ] **ADV** immensément; **to be v. knowledgeable about sth** avoir des connaissances très vastes *ou* très étendues sur qch; **v. different** extrêmement différent; **they're not v. different** ils ne sont pas très différents

vastness ['vɑːstnɪs] **N** immensité *f*

VAT [viːeɪ'tiː, væt] **N** *Br* (*abbr* **value added tax**) TVA *f*; **exclusive of** *or* **excluding V.** hors TVA; **subject to V.** soumis à la TVA; **V. exempt** exonéré de TVA; **to be V. registered** être assujetti à la TVA
▸▸ **V. credit** crédit *m* de TVA; **V. exemption** franchise *f* de TVA; *Br Fam* **V. man** = inspecteur *m* de la TVA; **V. rate** taux *m* de TVA; **V. rebate** décote *f* de TVA; **V. registration number** code *m* assujetti TVA; **V. return** déclaration *f* de TVA; **V. statement** état *m* TVA

vat [væt] **N** (*container*) cuve *f*, bac *m*
▸▸ **v. dye** matière *f* colorante insoluble

vatful ['vætfʊl] **N** (*quantity*) cuvée *f*

Vatican ['vætɪkən] **N the V.** le Vatican
▸▸ **the V. City** l'État *m* de la cité du Vatican, le Vatican; *Fam Hum* **V. roulette** = méthode *f* de contraception basée sur l'abstinence périodique

VAT-registered **ADJ** assujetti à la TVA

vaudeville ['vɔːdəvɪl] **N** *Am Theat* variétés *fpl*
▸▸ **v. artist** artiste *mf* de variétés; **v. show** spectacle *m* de variétés

vault¹ [vɔːlt, vɒlt] **N 1** *Archit* voûte *f*; **tunnel v.** voûte cylindrique; **fan v.** voûte en éventail; **ribbed v.** voûte d'ogives *ou* à nervures; *Fig* **the v. of heaven** la voûte céleste **2** (*underground*) (*of country house, castle*) cave *f*, (*of church, for burial*) caveau *m*; **family v.** caveau de famille; (*bank*) **v.** chambre *f* forte
VT *Archit* **to v. (over)** (*cellar*) voûter
VI *Archit* (*of roof*) former une voûte

vault² **N** *Gym* saut *m* (*en s'aidant d'une ou de deux mains*); (*on vaulting horse*) saut au cheval d'arçons; (*pole*) **v.** saut à la perche
VI (*jump*) sauter (*en s'aidant d'une ou de deux mains*); **he vaulted over the gate** il a sauté la barrière; **to v. into the saddle** sauter en selle
VT (*barrier*) sauter, franchir d'un saut (*en s'aidant d'une ou deux mains*)

vaulted ['vɔːltɪd, 'vɒl-] **ADJ** *Archit* voûté, en (*forme de*) voûte

vaulting¹ ['vɔːltɪŋ, 'vɒl-] **N** *Archit* voûte(s) *f(pl)*; **barrel v.** voûte(s) en berceau

vaulting² **N 1** *Archit* voûte *f*, voûtes *fpl* **2** *Sport* saut *m* à la perche
ADJ 1 *Sport* (*pole*) de saut **2** *Fig Lit* (*arrogance*) outrecuidant; (*ambition*) démesuré
▸▸ **v. horse** cheval-d'arçons *m inv*

vaunt [vɔːnt] **VT** se vanter de, se faire gloire de; **our much vaunted justice** notre justice tant vantée *ou* dont on fait tant l'éloge; *esp Lit* **the city vaunts a 13th century castle** la ville s'enorgueillit de son château du XIIIᵉ siècle

VC [viː'siː] **N 1** *Br Mil* (*abbr* **Victoria Cross**) = la plus haute distinction britannique accordée pour récompenser le courage d'un militaire; **to be awarded the VC** recevoir la Victoria Cross; **John Smith VC** = John Smith, titulaire de la Victoria Cross **2** *Hist abbr* **Vietcong 3** *abbr* **vice chairman/chairwoman/chairperson** *or* **4 vice consul**

V-chip ['viːtʃɪp] **N** *Comput, TV* puce *f* antiviolence

vCJD [viːsiːdʒeɪ'diː] **N** *Med* (*abbr* **new-variant Creutzfeldt-Jakob disease**) vMCJ *m*

VCR [viːsiː'ɑːr] **N** *esp Am* (*abbr* **video cassette recorder**) magnétoscope *m*

VCT [viːsiː'tiː] **N** *Fin* (*abbr* **venture capital trust**) FCPR *m*

VD [viː'diː] **N** *Med* (*abbr* **venereal disease**) maladie *f* vénérienne; **VD clinic** centre *m* de traitement des maladies vénériennes

VDT [viːdiː'tiː] **N** *Comput abbr Br* **visual** *or Am* **video display terminal**

VDU [viːdiː'juː] **N** *Comput* (*abbr* **visual display unit**) moniteur *m*
▸▸ *Comput* **V. operator** personne *f* travaillant sur écran

veal [viːl] **N** *Culin* veau *m*
▸▸ **v. cutlet** côtelette *f* de veau

vector ['vektər] **N** *Math, Phys, Med* vecteur *m*; **v.-borne disease** maladie *f* transmise par (agent) vecteur
▸▸ **v. function** fonction *f* vectorielle; *Comput* **v. generator** générateur *m* de vecteurs; *Comput* **v. graphics** image *f* vectorielle; **v. processing** traitement *m* de vecteurs, traitement vectoriel

vectored interrupt ['vektəd] **N** *Comput* interruption *f* vectorisée

vectorial [vek'tɔːrɪəl] **ADJ** *Math* vectoriel

vee engine [viː] **N** moteur *m* en V

veep [viːp] **N** *Am Fam* vice-président, -ente, *pl* vice-président(e)s

veer [vɪər] **N** (*of wind*) changement *m* de direction; (*of ship*) virement *m* de bord; *Fig* (*of opinion*) revirement *m*
VI (*of wind*) tourner; (*of ship*) virer de bord; (*of car, road*) tourner abruptement, virer; *Naut* **to v. off course** dévier du cap fixé, dévier de sa route; *Aut* **he veered to the right** il a viré à droite; **the car veered off the road** la voiture a fait une embardée et a quitté la route; *Fig* **the conversation veered towards politics** la conversation a tourné à la politique; **to v. between two extremes** alterner entre deux extrêmes
VT (*ship*) faire virer
▸ **veer round** **VI** (*of vehicle, person*) faire demi-tour; (*of wind*) changer de direction; *Fig* (*of person*) se ranger à l'opinion contraire

veg [vedʒ] *Fam* **NPL** *Br* légumes *mpl*; **meat and two v.** = plat *m* comportant de la viande et deux légumes (*typique de la gastronomie britannique traditionnelle*)
VI (*relax*) **to v. (out)** paresser

vegan ['viːgən] **N** végétalien, -ienne

veganism ['viːgənɪz(ə)m] **N** végétalisme *m*

vegeburger ['vedʒɪbɜːgər] **N** hamburger *m* végétarien

vegetable ['vedʒtəb(ə)l] **ADJ** végétal, -aux; **the v. kingdom** le règne végétal
N 1 *Culin* légume *m*; **to grow vegetables** cultiver *ou* faire pousser des légumes; **green vegetables** légumes verts; **early vegetables** primeurs *fpl*; *Fig* **the accident has left her a v.** l'accident l'a privée de toutes ses facultés **2** *Bot* végétal *m*
▸▸ **v. dish** plat *m* à légumes, légumier *m*; **v. garden** (jardin *m*) potager *m*; **v. knife** couteau *m* à légumes, éplucheur *m*; **v. marrow** courge *f*; **v. matter** matières *fpl* végétales; **v. oil** huile *f* végétale; **v. rack** casier *m* à légumes

vegetal ['vedʒɪt(ə)l] **ADJ** *Bot* végétal, -aux

vegetarian [vedʒɪ'teərɪən] **N** végétarien, -ienne; **to be a v.** être végétarien
ADJ végétarien

vegetarianism [vedʒɪ'teərɪənɪz(ə)m] **N** végétarisme *m*

Vegetarianism
Que ce soit pour des raisons éthiques, religieuses ou diététiques, le végétarisme s'est considérablement répandu au cours des dernières années en Grande-Bretagne – sensiblement plus que dans les autres pays européens ou aux États-Unis. Aujourd'hui, la majorité des restaurants proposent un menu avec un ou plusieurs plats sans viande, et lorsque l'on invite des gens à dîner, il est d'usage de s'enquérir s'ils sont végétariens ou non.

vegetate ['vedʒɪteɪt] **VI** *Pej* végéter; **to v. in an office** végéter *ou* moisir dans un bureau

vegetation [vedʒɪ'teɪʃən] **N** végétation *f*

vegetative ['vedʒɪtətɪv, -teɪtɪv] **ADJ** *also Fig* végétatif

veggie ['vedʒɪ] **N** *Fam* **1** (*vegetarian*) végétarien, -ienne **2** *esp Am* (*vegetable*) légume *m*

veggieburger ['vedʒɪbɜːgər] **N** = **vegeburger**

vehemence ['viːɪməns] **N** (*of orator*) véhémence *f*; **with all the v. of youth** avec l'ardeur de la jeunesse

vehement ['viːɪmənt] **ADJ** (*orator*) véhément; (*desire*) passionné; (*attack, effort, dislike*) violent; **she was most v. in her**

insistence elle a insisté avec une grande véhémence

vehemently ['vi:ɪməntlɪ] ADV avec véhémence; *(to dislike)* violemment; **to be v. opposed to sth** être fortement opposé à qch

vehicle ['vi:ɪk(ə)l] N **1** véhicule *m*; **heavy vehicles turning** *(sign)* passage d'engins; **v. emissions** gaz *mpl* d'échappement; **heavy goods v.** poids *m* lourd **2** *Fig (of thought, for propaganda)* véhicule *m*; **the newspaper as a v. for advertising** le journal comme moyen de publicité; **the play is merely a v. for his talents** la pièce n'est qu'un moyen de mettre ses talents en valeur **3** *Pharm* excipient *m*
▸▸ **v. identification number** numéro *m* d'immatriculation; **v. registration document** carte *f* grise

vehicular [vɪ'hɪkjʊlər] ADJ des véhicules, des voitures
▸▸ **v. access** accès *m* aux véhicules; **v. traffic** circulation *f* automobile

veil [veɪl] N *(of nun, sign of mourning)* voile *m*; *(on hat)* voilette *f*, *Fig (of smoke, mist)* voile; *(of politeness, culture)* vernis *m*; **bridal v.** voile de mariée; *Rel* **to take the v.** prendre le voile; *Fig* **to draw** *or* **throw a v. over sth** jeter un voile sur qch; **under a v. of secrecy** sous le voile du secret
VT *(face, painting)* voiler; *(one's feelings, intentions)* voiler, cacher, dissimuler; **their plans were veiled in secrecy** leurs plans étaient gardés secrets; **to v. oneself** se voiler; **to v. one's face** se voiler le visage

veiled [veɪld] ADJ voilé, couvert d'un voile; *Fig* voilé, caché, dissimulé; *(comment, threat, allusion)* voilé; **to express oneself in v. terms** s'exprimer en termes voilés; **a thinly v. reference to** une référence à peine voilée à; **thinly v. hostility** hostilité à peine déguisée

vein [veɪn] N **1** *Anat* veine *f*, *Entom (of wing)* nervure *f*, *Bot (of leaf)* nervure, veine; **he has noble blood in his veins** il a du sang bleu dans les veines **2** *Geol, Min* veine *f*, filon *m*; *(in wood, marble)* veine; *Fig* **a v. of melancholy/humour** une pointe de mélancolie/d'humour **3** *Fig (manner, style)* veine *f*, disposition *f*, humeur *f*; **the poetic v.** la veine poétique; **other remarks in the same v.** d'autres observations faites dans le même esprit

veined [veɪnd] ADJ *(marble etc)* veiné, à veines; *Bot, Entom* nervuré

veining ['veɪnɪŋ] N **1** *(streaks)* veinure *f*, marbrure *f* **2** *Bot, Entom* nervures *fpl*

velar ['vi:lər] ADJ, N *Ling* vélaire *f*

Velcro® ['velkrəʊ] N *(bande f)* Velcro® *m*

veld(t) [velt] N veld(t) *m*

vellum ['veləm] N vélin *m*
▸▸ **v. paper** papier *m* vélin

velocipede [vɪ'lɒsɪpi:d] N *Hist* vélocipède *m*

velocity [vɪ'lɒsɪtɪ] N vélocité *f*, vitesse *f*; *Econ* **v. of circulation** vitesse de circulation de la monnaie; *Econ* **v. of money** vitesse de circulation de la monnaie

velodrome ['vi:lədrəʊm] N vélodrome *m*

velour(s) [və'lʊər] N *Tex (velvet)* velours *m* de laine; *(felt)* feutre *m* taupé

velum, *pl* **vela** ['vi:ləm, -ə] N *Anat* voile *m* du palais

velvet ['velvɪt] N **1** *Tex* velours *m*; **to have (a) skin like v.** avoir une peau de pêche; **as smooth as v.** *(skin)* doux comme du *ou* le velours; *(drink)* velouté; **black v.** *(drink)* = mélange *m* de champagne et de stout; *Fig* **to be on v.** jouer sur le velours; **to walk with a v. tread** marcher à pas de velours *ou* à pas feutrés; *Fig* **an iron hand in a v. glove** une main de fer dans un gant de velours **2** *Am Fam (profit)* bénéf *m*; *(easy money)* argent *m* facile

▸▸ *Hist* **the V. Revolution** la Révolution de Velours

velveteen [velvɪ'ti:n] N *Tex* veloutine *f*

velvety ['velvɪtɪ] ADJ *(appearance, taste)* velouté; *(wine)* velouté, qui a du velouté; *(to the touch)* velouteux, doux comme le velours

venal ['vi:n(ə)l] ADJ vénal, -aux

venality [vɪ'nælɪtɪ] N vénalité *f*

vend [vend] VT *esp Jur, Admin* vendre; **machine that vends coffee** distributeur *m* automatique (payant) de café

vendee [ven'di:] N *Law* acquéreur *m*

vendetta [ven'detə] N vendetta *f*, **to wage a v. against sb** mener une vendetta contre qn

vending ['vendɪŋ] N *Law* vente *f*
▸▸ **v. machine** distributeur *m* automatique

vendor ['vendɔ:r] N **1** *Com, Law (person)* vendeur, -euse; *Comput* fournisseur *m*, **(street) v.** marchand *m* ambulant **2** *(machine)* distributeur *m* automatique (payant)
▸▸ *Fin, Law* **v.'s lien** privilège *m* du vendeur; *Fin, Law* **v.'s shares** actions *fpl* d'apport *ou* de fondation

veneer [və'nɪər] N **1** *(covering)* placage *m*, revêtement *m*; *(material)* bois *m* de placage, bois à plaquer **2** *Fig* masque *m*, apparence *f* extérieure; *(of culture)* vernis *m*; **a v. of politeness/respectability** un vernis de politesse/respectabilité; **beneath the v. of politeness** sous le masque de politesse
VT *(wood)* plaquer (**with** avec)

venerable ['ven(ə)rəb(ə)l] ADJ *(old man etc)* vénérable

venerate ['venəreɪt] VT *(somebody, something)* vénérer

veneration [venə'reɪʃən] N vénération *f* **(for** pour); **to hold sb in v.** avoir de la vénération pour qn

venereal [vɪ'nɪərɪəl] ADJ *Med* vénérien
▸▸ **v. disease** maladie *f* vénérienne

venereology [vɪnɪərɪ'ɒlədʒɪ] N *Med* vénéréologie *f*

Venetian [vɪ'ni:ʃən] ADJ vénitien
N Vénitien, -ienne
▸▸ **V. blind** store *m* vénitien; **V. glass** verre *m* ou cristal *m* de Venise; **V. lace** point *m* de Venise

Venezuela [vene'zweɪlə] N Vénézuéla *m*

Venezuelan [vene'zweɪl(ə)n] ADJ vénézuélien
N Vénézuélien, -ienne

vengeance ['ven(d)ʒəns] N vengeance *f*, **to take v. on sb** se venger de qn; **to take v. for** tirer vengeance de; *(person's death)* venger; *Fig Fam* **with a v.** *(to set to work)* furieusement; *(to start doing sth again)* de plus belle; **to work with a v.** travailler d'arrache-pied; **the autumn set in with a v.** l'automne a fait une entrée en force; **she's back with a v.** elle fait un retour de force; **by then it was raining with a v.** à ce moment-là, la pluie tombait à torrents

vengeful ['ven(d)ʒfʊl] ADJ *(person)* vindicatif; *(look)* vengeur

vengefully ['ven(d)ʒfʊlɪ] ADV d'une manière vindicative

vengefulness ['ven(d)ʒfʊlnɪs] N *(of action)* caractère *m* vindicatif; *(of person)* esprit *m* de vengeance

venial ['vi:nɪəl] ADJ **1** *Rel (sin)* véniel **2** *(error)* sans gravité, véniel

veniality [vi:nɪ'ælɪtɪ] N caractère *m* véniel

Venice ['venɪs] N Venise *f*

venison ['venɪs(ə)n] N *Culin* venaison *f*, **haunch of v.** quartier *m* de chevreuil

venom ['venəm] N *(poison)*, *Fig* venin *m*; **to say with v.** dire avec méchanceté *ou* malveillance

venomous ['venəməs] ADJ *(snake, spider etc)* venimeux; *(plant)* vénéneux; *Fig (criticism)* venimeux, envenimé; **a v. look** un regard venimeux; *Fig* **a v. tongue** une langue de vipère

venomously ['venəməslɪ] ADV avec venin *ou* méchanceté

venous ['vi:nəs] ADJ *(system, blood)* veineux

vent[1] [vent] N **1** *(for air, gas, liquid)* orifice *m*, conduit *m*; *(in chimney)* conduit, tuyau *m*; *(in volcano)* cheminée *f*, *(in barrel)* trou *m*; *(for ventilation)* conduit d'aération; *(of fish, bird)* orifice anal **2** *Fig* **to give v. to one's grief/anger/indignation** donner libre cours à sa douleur/sa colère/son indignation; **to give v. to one's spleen** décharger sa bile
VT **1** *(pipe)* décharger, vider des gaz; *(gas from pipe, steam from boiler)* évacuer **2** *Fig (one's anger)* donner libre cours à, laisser éclater, exhaler; **to v. one's spleen/anger on sb** décharger sa bile/épancher sa colère sur qn
▸▸ **v. pipe** évent *m*

vent[2] N *(on jacket)* fente *f*

ventilate ['ventɪleɪt] VT **1** *(room)* aérer, ventiler; *(tunnel)* ventiler; *(mine)* éventer **2** *Fig (question, feelings)* mettre au grand jour

ventilated ['ventɪleɪtɪd] ADJ **1** *(aired)* aéré **2** *Br Fam (over-excited)* **to get v. about sth** se mettre dans tous ses états à propos de qch

ventilation [ventɪ'leɪʃən] N *(of room)* aération *f*, ventilation *f*, *(of mine)* aérage *m*
▸▸ *Min* **v. shaft** conduit *m* d'aération *ou* d'aérage; **v. system** système *m* d'aération *ou* de ventilation

ventilator ['ventɪleɪtər] N **1** *Tech* ventilateur *m*, aérateur *m*; *Naut* manche *f* à air **2** *Med* respirateur *m*, poumon *m* artificiel; **to be on a v.** être sur respirateur

venting screw ['ventɪŋ] N *Aut* vis *f* de mise à l'air libre *ou* de purge

ventral ['ventr(ə)l] ADJ *Anat, Biol* ventral, -aux
▸▸ **v. fin** nageoire *f* pelvienne, nageoire abdominale

ventricle ['ventrɪk(ə)l] N *Anat* ventricule *m*

ventriloquism [ven'trɪləkwɪz(ə)m] N ventriloquie *f*

ventriloquist [ven'trɪləkwɪst] N ventriloque *mf*; **v.'s dummy** marionnette *f* de ventriloque

venture ['ventʃər] N **1** *(risky undertaking)* entreprise *f* hasardeuse *ou* risquée; **this v. into advertising/fiction** cette incursion dans la publicité/fiction; **desperate v.** tentative *f* désespérée **2** *(business undertaking)* entreprise *f*, **joint v.** *(undertaking)* entreprise commune; *(company)* société *f* en participation **3** *Arch* **at a v.** *(at random)* au hasard
VT *(one's life, money)* risquer, aventurer; **to v. to do sth** se hasarder à faire qch, se risquer à faire qch; **I v. to affirm he knew nothing about it** j'ose affirmer qu'il n'en savait rien; **to v. a remark** hasarder une remarque; **I ventured the remark that ...** je me suis hasardé à faire la remarque que ...; **to v. an opinion** se hasarder *ou* se risquer à donner une opinion; *Prov* **nothing ventured nothing gained** qui ne risque rien n'a rien
VI **to v. into unknown territory** s'aventurer en terre inconnue; **this is the first time he has ventured into historical fiction** c'est sa première incursion dans la fiction historique; **to v. out of doors** se risquer à sortir; **to v. too far** s'aventurer trop loin
▸ **venture forth, venture out** VI *esp Lit (after illness, from hiding etc)* s'aventurer à sortir; **they ventured forth into the unknown** ils s'aventurèrent dans l'inconnu; **they ventured forth on their quest for ...** ils partirent à la recherche de ...

▸▸*Fin* **v. capital** capital-risque *m*; **v. capital company** société à capital-risque; **v. capital trust** fonds *m* commun de placement à risques; *Fin* **v. capitalist** pourvoyeur, -euse de capital-risque, spécialiste *mf* de la prise de risques *(dans la finance)*; *Br* **V. Scout** éclaireur *m (de grade supérieur)*

▸ **venture on, venture upon** VT INSEP se risquer à, se hasarder à

venturesome ['ventʃəsəm] ADJ **1** *(person)* aventureux, entreprenant **2** *(action)* risqué, hasardeux

venturi throat [ven'tjuːrɪ] N *Aut* col *m* du venturi

venue ['venjuː] N **1** *(hall)* salle *f*, *(for football match)* terrain *m*; **the v. for the concert will be the Albert Hall/Birmingham** le concert se déroulera à l'Albert Hall/Birmingham; **what is the v. for the match?** où est-ce que le match aura lieu?; **there has been a change of v.** ça n'a plus lieu au même endroit, ça se tiendra ailleurs **2** *Law* lieu *m* du jugement; **to change the v. of a trial** renvoyer une affaire devant une autre cour

> Note that the French word **venue** is a false friend and is never a translation for the English word **venue**. It means **coming, arrival**.

venule ['venjuːl] N *Anat* veinule *f*

Venus ['viːnəs] N *Astron, Myth* Vénus *f*
▸▸*Bot* **V. flytrap** dionée *f*

veracious [və'reɪʃəs] ADJ *Fml (person, account)* véridique

veracity [və'ræsɪtɪ], **veraciousness** [və'reɪʃəsnɪs] N *esp Fml (of person, report)* véracité *f*

veranda(h) [və'rændə] N *Archit* véranda *f*

verb [vɜːb] N *Gram* verbe *m* VOIR GRAMMAIRE A38–66; B24–53

verbal ['vɜːb(ə)l] ADJ *(agreement, promise)* verbal, -aux, oral, -aux; *(communication, skills)* verbal; *Fam* **to have v.** diarrhoea *or Am* diarrhea être atteint de diarrhée verbale
N *Br Sl* **to give sb the v.** *(shout at sb)* engueuler qn; **they were given the v.** ils se sont fait engueuler
▸▸**v. abuse** violence *f* verbale; **v. agreement** convention *f* verbale, accord *m* verbal; *Gram* **v. noun** nom *m* verbal

verbalize ['vɜːbəlaɪz] VT **1** *(idea)* exprimer par des mots; *Psy (experience)* verbaliser **2** *Gram (noun)* employer comme verbe

verbally ['vɜːbəlɪ] ADV **1** *(orally)* verbalement, oralement, de vive voix; **to be v. abused** se faire insulter verbalement; **to agree v. to do sth** se mettre d'accord verbalement pour faire qch **2** *(as a verb)* en tant que verbe

verbatim [vɜː'beɪtɪm] ADV mot à mot, textuellement; **to report a speech v.** rendre compte mot à mot d'un discours
ADJ exact, mot à mot; **to give a v. account of sth** faire un compte-rendu mot à mot de qch

verbena [vɜː'biːnə] N *Bot* verveine *f*, **lemon v.** citronnelle *f*

verbiage ['vɜːbɪɪdʒ] N verbiage *m*

verbose [vɜː'bəʊs] ADJ *(writer, style)* verbeux, diffus, prolixe

verbosely [vɜː'bəʊslɪ] ADV avec verbosité, verbeusement; **v. worded** verbeux

verbosity [vɜː'bɒsɪtɪ] N verbosité *f*, prolixité *f*

verdant ['vɜːdənt] ADJ *Fml* vert, verdoyant

verdict ['vɜːdɪkt] N **1** *Law* verdict *m*; **to bring in a v. of guilty/not guilty** rendre un verdict de culpabilité/de non-culpabilité; **to return a v.** prononcer *ou* rendre un verdict; **to reach a v.** conclure, décider; **the jury returned a v. of suicide** *(in coroner's court)* le jury

a conclu au suicide; **open v.** *(at inquest)* = jugement *m* qui ne formule aucune conclusion sur les circonstances dans lesquelles la mort a eu lieu **2** *Fig* jugement *m*, avis *m*; **to give one's v.** se prononcer *(on* sur*)*; **what's your v.?** qu'est-ce que tu en penses?

verdigris ['vɜːdɪgrɪs] N vert-de-gris *m inv*

verdure ['vɜːdʒər] N *Lit (colour)* verdure *f*, *(foliage)* verdure, feuillage *m*

verge [vɜːdʒ] N **1** *Br Aut (of road)* bas-côté *m*, *pl* bas-côtés, accotement *m*; **sitting on the grass v. of the road** assis sur l'herbe du bord de la route; **soft verges** *(road sign)* accotement instable **2** *Fig* **on the v. of tears/disaster/a nervous breakdown** au bord des larmes/du désastre/de la crise de nerfs; **on the v. of death** à la frontière de la mort; **on the v. of ruin** à deux doigts de la ruine; **to be on the v. of doing sth** être sur le point de faire qch; **on the v. of manhood** au seuil de l'âge viril **3** *esp Lit (edge)* *(of river)* bord *m*; *(of forest)* orée *f*

▸ **verge on** VT INSEP confiner à, friser; **red verging on pink** rouge qui tire sur le rose; **he was verging on sixty/hysteria** il frisait la soixantaine/l'hystérie

verger ['vɜːdʒər] N *Br Rel* bedeau *m*

Vergil ['vɜːdʒɪl] N *Antiq, Liter* Virgile *m*

verifiable [verɪ'faɪəb(ə)l] ADJ vérifiable

verification [verɪfɪ'keɪʃən] N vérification *f*; **to produce evidence in v. of a theory** fournir des preuves qui confirment *ou* vérifient une théorie

verify ['verɪfaɪ] VT *(check, prove)* vérifier; *(confirm)* vérifier, confirmer; *(information, accounts)* vérifier, contrôler; **this verifies my suspicions/my fears** cela confirme mes soupçons/mes craintes; **I can v. that Gillian Love was present** je peux confirmer que Gillian Love était bien là

verily ['verɪlɪ] ADV *Bible, Arch* en vérité, vraiment

verisimilitude [verɪsɪ'mɪlɪtjuːd] N *Fml* vraisemblance *f*

veritable ['verɪtəb(ə)l] ADJ véritable, vrai; **this is a v. disaster** c'est un véritable *ou* vrai désastre

veritably ['verɪtəblɪ] ADV véritablement

verity ['verɪtɪ] N *Lit* vérité *f*, *Rel* **the (eternal) verities** les vérités éternelles

vermicelli [vɜːmɪ'tʃelɪ] N *Culin* vermicelle(s) *m(pl)*

vermicide ['vɜːmɪsaɪd] N *Pharm* vermicide *m*

vermiculite [vɜː'mɪkjʊlaɪt] N vermiculite *f*

vermiform ['vɜːmɪfɔːm] ADJ vermiforme

vermifugal [vɜːmɪ'fjuːg(ə)l] ADJ vermifuge

vermifuge ['vɜːmɪfjuːdʒ] N vermifuge *m*

vermilion [və'mɪljən] N vermillon *m*
ADJ *(de)* vermillon *inv*; vermeil, -eille

vermin ['vɜːmɪn] N *(inv in pl)* *(insects)*, *Fig* vermine *f*, *(rodents)* animaux *mpl* nuisibles VOIR GRAMMAIRE A11

verminous ['vɜːmɪnəs] ADJ *(covered with fleas, lice etc)* couvert de vermine; *Fig (dirty)* *(coat, flat)* miteux; *Fig* **you v. little creep!** espèce de vermine!

vermouth ['vɜːmuːθ] N vermout(h) *m*

vernacular [və'nækjʊlər] ADJ **1** *Ling* vernaculaire, indigène **2** *Archit* local, -aux
N **1** *(everyday speech)* langue *f* vulgaire; **in the v.** dans la langue vulgaire; **to translate the Bible into the v.** traduire la Bible dans la langue vulgaire **2** *(dialect)* langue *f* vernaculaire *ou* indigène **3** *Archit* style *m* local **4** *(jargon)* jargon *m*; **the sporting v.** le jargon sportif

vernal ['vɜːn(ə)l] ADJ *Liter* printanier
▸▸**v. equinox** équinoxe *m* de printemps

Veronal® ['verən(ə)l] N *Pharm* véronal *m*

veronica [və'rɒnɪkə] N *Bot* véronique *f*

verruca, *pl* **verrucae** [ve'ruːkə, -kiː] N verrue *f*

versant ['vɜːsənt] N *(of mountain)* versant *m*

versatile ['vɜːsətaɪl] ADJ **1** *(person)* aux talents variés, polyvalent; *(dress, jacket) (can be worn anywhere)* passe-partout; *(has detachable parts, is reversible etc)* polyvalent; *(tool, machine)* polyvalent, d'une grande souplesse d'emploi, universel; **a v. mind** un esprit souple *ou* universel **2** *Biol* versatile

> Note that the French word **versatile** is a false friend and is never a translation for the English word **versatile**. It means **fickle, changeable**.

versatility [vɜːsə'tɪlɪtɪ] N **1** *(of person)* variété *f* de talents *ou* d'aptitudes; *(adaptability)* faculté *f* d'adaption; *(of mind)* souplesse *f*, universalité *f*, *(of tool, machine)* polyvalence *f*, grande souplesse d'emploi; **his v.** la variété de ses talents; **she has v. of mind** c'est un esprit universel **2** *Biol (of organ)* versatilité *f*

verse [vɜːs] N **1** *(poetry)* vers *mpl*; **free v.** vers libres; **light v.** poésie *f* légère **2** *(stanza) (of song)* couplet *m*; *(of poem, hymn)* strophe *f*, stance *f* **3** *(of Bible)* verset *m*

versed [vɜːst] ADJ versé *(in* en, dans*)*; **v. in the arts** versé dans les arts; **to be well v. in mathematics** être fort instruit dans les mathématiques; **I am well v. in his ways** je le connais bien, je sais bien comment il est

versification [vɜːsɪfɪ'keɪʃən] N **1** *(art)* versification *f* **2** *(metre) (of verse)* facture *f*, *(of author)* métrique *f*

versifier ['vɜːsɪfaɪər] N *Pej* versificateur *m*

versify ['vɜːsɪfaɪ] VT *(story etc)* versifier, mettre en vers
VI versifier, faire des vers

version ['vɜːʃən] N **1** *(account) (of facts)* version *f*; **he gave us a very different v. of the affair** il nous a donné de cette affaire un récit très différent; **according to his v.** d'après sa version des faits; **her v. differs from mine** sa version des faits diffère de la mienne **2** *(variation) (of car, text, recipe)* version *f*; **the military v. of this aircraft** la version militaire de cet avion; **the TV v. of a novel** l'adaptation *f* d'un roman pour la télévision **3** *(translation)* version *f*, traduction *f*; **the English v. of the Bible** la version anglaise de la Bible

verso ['vɜːsəʊ] N **1** *(of page)* verso *m* **2** *(of medal)* revers *m*

versus ['vɜːsəs] PREP *Law, Sport* contre; *Sport* **Martin v. Thomas** Martin contre Thomas; *Fig* **the advantage of a higher salary v. the loss of security** l'avantage d'un salaire plus élevé en contrepartie d'une sécurité moindre; *Fig* **the relative merits of public v. private ownership** les avantages relatifs de la propriété de l'État par opposition à la propriété privée

vertebra, *pl* **vertebrae** ['vɜːtɪbrə, -iː] N vertèbre *f*

vertebral ['vɜːtɪbrəl] ADJ vertébral, -aux
▸▸**v. column** colonne *f* vertébrale

vertebrate ['vɜːtɪbreɪt, -brɪt] ADJ *(animal)* vertébré; *(characteristic)* des vertébrés
N vertébré *m*

vertex, *pl* **vertices** ['vɜːteks, -tɪsiːz] N **1** *Geom (of angle, curve)* sommet *m* **2** *Anat* vertex *m*

vertical ['vɜːtɪk(ə)l] ADJ vertical, -aux; **a v. cliff** une falaise à pic; **in a v. position** en position verticale, à la verticale; **a v. line** une ligne *f* verticale
N *(line, position)* verticale *f*
▸▸**v. elevation** altitude *f*, *Fin* **v. equity** équité *f* verticale; *TV* **v. hold** bouton *m* de

commande de synchronisme vertical; *Com* **v. integration** intégration *f* verticale; *Typ* **v. justification** justification *f* verticale; *Aviat* **v. landing** atterrissage *m* vertical; **v. marketing** marketing *m* vertical; *Fin* **v. spread** écart *m* vertical; *Aviat* **v. take-off** décollage *m* vertical

verticality [vɜːtɪˈkælɪtɪ] N verticalité *f*

vertically [ˈvɜːtɪklɪ] ADV verticalement, à la verticale; *Aviat* **to take off/land v.** décoller/ atterrir à la verticale

vertiginous [vɜːˈtɪdʒɪnəs] ADJ vertigineux

vertigo [ˈvɜːtɪgəʊ] N *Med* vertige *m*; **to suffer from/get v.** avoir le vertige; **I had an attack of v.** j'ai été pris de vertige

verve [vɜːv] N verve *f*, brio *m*; **to play/act with v.** jouer avec verve *ou* brio

Very [ˈvɪərɪ] N
▸▸**V. light** fusée *f* éclairante; **V. pistol** pistolet *m* lance-fusées

VERY [ˈverɪ] ADV **VOIR GRAMMAIRE A22–3 1** *(extremely)* très; **v. good** *(adj phrase)* très bon, fort bon; *(adv phrase)* très bien, fort bien; **a v. good dictionary** un très *ou* fort bon dictionnaire; **v. good, captain** très bien, mon capitaine; **he is v. well known in Paris** il est très connu à Paris; **that's v. kind of you** c'est très gentil à vous; **you are v. kind** vous êtes bien bon; **so v. little** si peu; **there's v. little one can do to help** on ne peut pas faire grand-chose pour aider; **I took only a v. little** j'en ai pris très peu; **it isn't so v. difficult** ce n'est pas tellement difficile, ce n'est pas si difficile que ça; **he was not v. pleased** il n'était pas très content; **v. (v.) few people** très (très) peu de gens; **are you hungry? – yes, v.** avez-vous faim? – oui, très; **he wore a v. pleased expression** il avait l'air très satisfait; **I feel v. much better** je me sens beaucoup mieux; **it is v. much better to wait** il vaut bien mieux attendre; *Comput* **v. high level language** langage *m* très évolué; **v. large scale integration** intégration *f* à très grande échelle; *Rel* **the V. Reverend ...** le très révérend ...
2 *(emphatic use)* **the v. first** le tout premier; **we were the v. first to arrive** nous étions les tout premiers à arriver; **the v. last** le tout dernier; **the v. best** tout ce qu'il y a de mieux *ou* de meilleur; **the v. most/least** tout au plus/au moins; **at the v. latest** au plus tard; **the v. same** exactement le même; **I v. nearly died** j'ai bien failli mourir; **it was the v. last thing I expected** c'était vraiment la dernière chose à laquelle je m'attendais; **the v. next day** dès le lendemain, le lendemain même; **in the v. front row** au tout premier rang; **a room of my v. own** une pièce rien qu'à moi; **it's my v. own** c'est à moi tout seul
ADJ **1** *(emphatic use)* même; **he lives in this v. house** il habite dans cette maison même; **sitting in this v. room** assis dans cette pièce même; **by its v. nature** par sa nature même; **you are the v. man I wanted to see** vous êtes justement l'homme que je voulais voir; **come here this v. minute!** venez ici à l'instant!; **this v. day** aujourd'hui même; **it was a year ago to the v. day** c'était il y a un an jour pour jour; **these are his v. words** ce sont là ses propres paroles; **at the v. beginning** au tout début; **he knows our v. thoughts** il connaît jusqu'à nos pensées; **the v. idea frightens me** cette pensée suffit à m'effrayer; **I shudder at the v. thought of it** je frémis rien que d'y penser
2 *Rel, Arch (real, true)* vrai, véritable
▸▸**v. high frequency** très haute fréquence *f*, *(gamme f* des) ondes *fpl* métriques; **v. low frequency** très basse fréquence *f*

VESA [ˈviːsə] N *Comput (abbr* **video electronics standard association**) VESA *m*

vesical [ˈvesɪk(ə)l] ADJ *Anat, Med* vésical, -aux

vesicle [ˈvesɪk(ə)l] N *Biol, Med* vésicule *f*

vesper [ˈvespər] N *Rel* **vespers** vêpres *fpl*; **to attend vespers** aller aux vêpres; **the v. bell** la cloche des vêpres *ou* du soir

vessel [ˈves(ə)l] N **1** *Naut* bateau *m*; *(large)* navire *m* **2** *(receptacle)* récipient *m*; *Phys* **communicating vessels** vases *mpl* communicants **3** *Anat, Bot* vaisseau *m*

vest¹ [vest] N **1** *Br (for men)* maillot *m* de corps; *(for women)* chemise *f, Can* camisole *f*, *(for baby)* brassière *f*; *Sport* maillot; **string v.** gilet *m* en point noué *ou* en filet maille *(aérée)* **2** *Am (waistcoat)* gilet *m*

> Note that the French word **veste** is a false friend and is never a translation for the English word **vest**. It means **jacket**.

vest² VT **1 to v. sb with authority** investir *ou* revêtir qn d'autorité; **to v. property in sb** assigner des biens à qn; **right vested in the Crown** droit dévolu à la Couronne; **by the authority vested in me** en vertu de l'autorité dont je suis investi; **authority vested in the people** autorité exercée par le peuple **2** *Rel (clothe) (dignitary, priest)* vêtir, revêtir

vestal virgin [ˈvest(ə)l] N *Antiq* vestale *f*

vested interest [ˈvestɪd] N intérêt *m*; *(person)* = personne *f* qui a un intérêt matériel; **to have a v. in sth** avoir des intérêts dans qch; **to have a v. in sth being done** avoir intérêt à ce que qch soit fait; **to have a v. in a business** avoir des capitaux investis dans une entreprise, être intéressé dans une entreprise; **I do have a v. in the play's success** j'ai intérêt à ce que la pièce soit un succès

vestibule [ˈvestɪbjuːl] N **1** *(in house, church)* vestibule *m*; *(in hotel)* vestibule, hall *m* d'entrée **2** *Am Rail* sas *m* **3** *Anat (of ear)* vestibule *m*

vestige [ˈvestɪdʒ] N **1** *(trace) (of civilization etc)* vestige *m*; **not a v. of ...** *(truth, common sense)* pas une once de ... **2** *Biol* organe *m* rudimentaire

vestigial [vesˈtɪdʒɪəl] ADJ **1** résiduel; **the v. remains of an abbey/a civilization** les vestiges d'une abbaye/d'une civilisation; **some v. sense of decency prevented him from doing it** le peu de décence qui lui restait l'a empêché de le faire **2** *Biol (organ)* rudimentaire

vestment [ˈvestmənt] N vêtement *m* (de cérémonie); *Rel* chasuble *f*, **(church) vestments** vêtements sacerdotaux

vest-pocket *Am* N poche *f* de gilet
ADJ *(book, object)* de poche; *Fig* minuscule, tout petit

vestry [ˈvestrɪ] N *Rel* **1** *(in church)* sacristie *f* **2** *(parish council)* conseil *m* paroissial

Vesuvius [vɪˈsuːvɪəs] N le Vésuve

vet¹ [vet] N vétérinaire *mf*; **to take an animal to the v.('s)** emmener un animal chez le vétérinaire

vet² VT *(-tt-)* *(person) (for security purposes)* effectuer un contrôle de sécurité sur; *(purchases, expenditure)* contrôler; *(candidate, proposal, decision) (examine)* examiner; *(approve)* approuver; **she's been positively vetted** le contrôle de sécurité dont elle a fait l'objet s'est avéré satisfaisant; **his mother vets his girlfriends** sa mère a un droit de regard sur ses petites amies

vet³ N *Am Mil Fam (abbr* **veteran**) ancien combattant *m*

vetch [vetʃ] N *Bot* vesce *f*

veteran [ˈvet(ə)rən] N vétéran *m*, *Fam* vieux *m* de la vieille; *Mil* ancien combattant *m*; **a v. of the First World War, a First World War v.** un ancien combattant de la Première Guerre mondiale; **I have a real old v. of a typewriter** j'ai une machine à écrire, c'est une antiquité!

ADJ *(activist, opponent etc)* de longue date; *(sportsman, actor)* chevronné; **she is a v. campaigner for human rights** elle a fait campagne pour les droits de l'homme depuis très longtemps
▸▸**v. army** armée *f* de vétérans; *Br* **v. car** voiture *f* de collection *(normalement antérieure à 1905)*; **v. soldier** vieux soldat *m*

Veterans Day N *Am* ≃ l'Armistice *m*, *Can* ≃ le Jour du Souvenir

veterinarian [vet(ə)rɪˈneərɪən] N *esp Am* vétérinaire *mf*

veterinary [ˈvet(ə)rɪn(ə)rɪ] ADJ *(medicine, science)* vétérinaire; **she has a v. practice** elle a un cabinet de vétérinaire
▸▸*Br* **v. surgeon** vétérinaire *mf*

veto, *pl* **vetoes** [ˈviːtəʊ, -əʊz] N veto *m*; **right of v.** droit *m* de veto; **to have the right or power of v.** avoir le droit de veto; **to put a v. on sth** mettre *ou* opposer son veto à qch; **to use one's v.** exercer son droit de veto; *Comput* **put in v. mode** en mode sélectif
VT mettre *ou* opposer son veto à; **he vetoed it** il y a mis *ou* opposé son veto; **the spending was vetoed** cette dépense a été rejetée par veto

Vette [vet] N *Am Fam (Corvette®)* Corvette® *f*

vetting [ˈvetɪŋ] N *(examining) (of candidate, proposal, decision)* examen *m*; *(of purchases, expenditure)* contrôle *m*; *(security check)* contrôle de sécurité

vex [veks] VT ennuyer, fâcher, chagriner; **I was vexed by her attitude** son attitude m'ennuyait *ou* me chagrinait

> Note that the French verb **vexer** is a false friend. It means **to hurt somebody's feelings**.

vexation [vekˈseɪʃən] N **1** *(cause)* contrariété *f*, ennui *m* **2** *(sadness)* chagrin *m* **3** *(anger)* dépit *m*

vexatious [vekˈseɪʃəs] ADJ *esp Fml (person, thing)* contrariant, irritant, ennuyeux; *(circumstances)* fâcheux

vexed [vekst] ADJ **1** *(cross)* fâché, ennuyé, chagriné **2** **v. question** question *f* controversée *ou* très débattue *ou* non résolue; **it is a v. question whether ...** c'est une question controversée de savoir si ...

vexing [ˈveksɪŋ] ADJ contrariant, irritant, ennuyeux

VGA [viːdʒiːˈeɪ] N *Comput (abbr* **video graphics adaptor**) VGA *m*
▸▸**V. monitor** moniteur *m* VGA

VHF [viːeɪtʃˈef] ADJ *Radio, TV (abbr* **very high frequency**) VHF *f*; **to broadcast on V.** émettre en hyperfréquences
▸▸**V. radio** radio *f* en hyperfréquences

VHS [viːeɪtʃˈes] ADJ *TV (abbr* **video home system**) VHS *m*

via [ˈvaɪə, ˈviːə] PREP *(travelling)* par, via; **I found out v. Fiona/head office** j'ai découvert ça par l'intermédiaire de Fiona/du siège social

viability [vaɪəˈbɪlɪtɪ] N *(of foetus, seed, company etc)* viabilité *f*; *(of project etc)* viabilité, chances *fpl* de succès

viable [ˈvaɪəb(ə)l] ADJ *(foetus, seed, company etc)* viable; *(project etc)* viable, qui a des chances de réussir; **I can see no v. alternative** je ne vois pas d'autre moyen d'y parvenir

viaduct [ˈvaɪədʌkt] N viaduc *m*

Viagra® [vaɪˈægrə] N Viagra® *m*

vial [ˈvaɪəl] N *Fml* fiole *f*, *(for drugs)* ampoule *f*

viands [ˈvaɪəndz] NPL *Arch* aliments *mpl*

viaticum [vaɪˈætɪkəm] N *Rel* viatique *m*

vibes [vaɪbz] NPL *Fam* **1** *(atmosphere)* ambiance *f*; **the v. are good** ça marche, ça gaze; **this place gives me bad v.** cet endroit me fait un effet désagréable; **I get good v. from it** ça me branche; **I get good v. from him/her** il/elle me plaît; **I'm getting strange v. from him** je ne le sens pas très bien; **what sort of v. do you get from him?** comment tu le sens? **2** *Mus* vibraphone *m*

vibrancy ['vaɪbrənsɪ] N animation *f*, *(of colours, style)* vivacité *f*, *(of personality)* flamme *f*, fougue *f*

vibrant ['vaɪbrənt] ADJ **1** *(person, painting, description)* plein de vie; *(town, cultural scene, atmosphere)* très animé; *(style)* plein de vigueur; *(speech)* vibrant; *(new company)* très dynamique; **city v. with activity** ville palpitante d'activité **2** *(colour)* éclatant

vibraphone ['vaɪbrəfəʊn] N *Mus* vibraphone *m*

vibrate [vaɪ'breɪt] VI vibrer; *Phys* vibrer, osciller; **her voice vibrated with emotion** sa voix était vibrante d'émotion; **you're making the house v.** tu fais trembler les murs; **to v. with activity** vibrer d'activité
▶ VT faire vibrer

vibrating [vaɪ'breɪtɪŋ] ADJ vibrant
▶▶ **v. alert** *(on mobile phone)* vibration *f*

vibration [vaɪ'breɪʃən] N **1** vibration *f*; *Phys etc* oscillation *f*, pulsation *f* **2** *Fig Fam* **vibrations** = **vibes 1**

vibrato [vɪ'brɑːtəʊ] N *Mus* vibrato *m*

vibrator [vaɪ'breɪtər] N **1** *Elec* vibrateur *m*, vibreur *m* **2** *(for massage, also sexual)* vibromasseur *m*

vibratory [vaɪ'breɪtərɪ] ADJ *Phys etc* vibratoire

viburnum [vaɪ'bɜːnəm] N *Bot* viorne *f*

vicar ['vɪkər] N **1** *(in Church of England)* pasteur *m* **2 the V. of Christ** le vicaire de Jésus-Christ
▶▶ **v. apostolic** vicaire *m* apostolique; **v. general** vicaire général

vicarage ['vɪkərɪdʒ] N *(in Church of England)* presbytère *m* *(d'un pasteur)*

vicarious [vaɪ'keərɪəs, vɪ-] ADJ **1** *(at second hand)* indirect; **to lead a v. existence** vivre par procuration; **to take v. pleasure in sth** retirer indirectement du plaisir de qch; **he gets a v. thrill from watching porn films** il trouve son plaisir à regarder des films pornographiques **2** *(power, authority)* délégué **3** *(punishment)* (fait) pour autrui; *(suffering, pain)* subi pour autrui

vicariously [vaɪ'keərɪəslɪ, vɪ-] ADV **1** *(on sb's behalf)* à la place d'un autre; *(indirectly)* indirectement; **to live v.** vivre par procuration **2** *(by delegation)* par délégation, par procuration

vice¹ [vaɪs] N *(immorality)* vice *m*; **to lead a life of v.** vivre dans le vice; **to sink into v.** sombrer dans le vice; **avarice is a v.** l'avarice est un vice; *Hum* **it's my only v.** c'est mon seul vice; **there's no v. in him** il n'est pas méchant
▶▶ **v. ring** organisation *f* criminelle *(impliquée dans la prostitution, le trafic de drogue/etc)*; **the V. Squad** la brigade mondaine *ou* des mœurs, *Fam* la Mondaine, *Fam* les Mœurs *fpl*

vice², *Am* **vise** N *Tech* étau *m*; **he had a grip like a v.** il avait une poigne de fer
▶▶ **v. jaw** mâchoire *f* d'étau

vice-admiral N vice-amiral *m* d'escadre, *pl* vice-amiraux d'escadre

vice-chairman, *pl* **vice-chairmen** N vice-président, *pl* vice-présidents

vice-chairmanship N vice-présidence *f*, *pl* vice-présidences

vice-chancellor N *Pol* vice-chancelier, *pl* vice-chanceliers; *Br Univ* président *m* d'université

vice-chancellorship [vaɪs'tʃɑːnsələʃɪp] N *Pol* fonction *f ou* dignité *f* de vice-chancelier; *Br Univ* présidence *f* d'université

vice-consul N vice-consul *m*, *pl* vice-consuls

vice-consulate N *(post or premises)* vice-consulat *m*, *pl* vice-consulats

vicelike ['vaɪslaɪk] ADJ **held in a v. grip** serré dans une poigne de fer, serré comme dans un étau

vice-marshal N *Aviat* **air v.** général *m* de division aérienne

vice-presidency N vice-présidence *f*, *pl* vice-présidences; **a candidate for the v.** un candidat à la vice-présidence

vice-president N vice-président, *pl* vice-présidents

vice-presidential ADJ vice-présidentiel; **v. candidate** candidat *m* à la vice-présidence

viceroy ['vaɪsrɔɪ] N vice-roi *m*, *pl* vice-rois

vice versa ['vaɪsɪ'vɜːsə] ADV vice versa

vicinity [vɪ'sɪnɪtɪ] N **1** *(neighbourhood)* voisinage *m*; **in the v.** dans les alentours *ou* environs; **in the v. of Dover** à proximité de *ou* dans les environs de Douvres; **there was no-one in the immediate v.** il n'y avait personne dans le voisinage immédiat; **in the immediate v. of the factory** aux abords de l'usine; **in the v. of five thousand pounds** environ cinq mille livres, aux alentours de cinq mille livres **2** *Fml (nearness)* proximité *f* (**to** de)

vicious ['vɪʃəs] ADJ **1** *(harsh, violent)* rageur, violent; *(malicious)* méchant, haineux; *(struggle)* acharné; **v. blow/wind** coup *m*/vent *m* violent; **she has a v. tongue** c'est une mauvaise langue; **a v. attack** une attaque brutale; **to make a v. attack on sb's character** lancer une attaque haineuse contre la personne *ou* la réputation de qn; **v. gossip** méchants commérages *mpl* **2** *Old-fashioned, Lit (depraved)* vicieux, dépravé **3** *(horse, dog)* méchant
▶▶ **v. circle** cercle *m* vicieux

Note that the French word **vicieux** is a false friend. It means **depraved** or **underhand**, depending on the context.

viciously ['vɪʃəslɪ] ADV *(violently)* violemment; *(maliciously)* méchamment, haineusement; *(to attack)*, *Fig* férocement

viciousness ['vɪʃəsnɪs] N *(of wind, blow)* violence *f*, *(of attack)* brutalité *f*, férocité *f*, *(of criticism)* méchanceté *f*

vicissitude [vɪ'sɪsɪtjuːd] N *Lit* vicissitude *f*

victim ['vɪktɪm] N *(of attack, murder etc)* victime *f*, *(of fire)* sinistré, -ée, incendié, -ée; *(of flood)* sinistré, -ée, inondé, -ée; *(of shipwreck etc)* sinistré, -ée; **to be sb's v.** être la victime de qn; **to be the v. of an attack** être victime d'une attaque; **the v. of sb's trickery** la dupe de la fourberie de qn; **v. of an accident, accident v.** accidenté, -ée; **to fall v. to sb's charm** succomber au charme de qn; **to fall v. to a disease** être frappé d'une maladie; **she was a *or* the v. of her own success** elle a été la victime de son propre succès

victimization [vɪktɪmaɪ'zeɪʃən] N brimades *fpl* (**of** sur, contre); **this is management v.** c'est un traitement discriminatoire de la part de la direction; **it results in the v. of the lower paid** cela se traduit par la discrimination des petits salaires; **there will be no v. of workers who have gone on strike** les ouvriers qui se sont mis en grève ne souffriront aucune représaille

victimize ['vɪktɪmaɪz] VT **it victimizes the lower paid** cela constitue un traitement discriminatoire à l'égard des petits salaires, ce sont les petits salaires qui en souffrent; **he felt that he was being victimized** il se croyait victime d'un traitement discriminatoire; **I'm being victimized** on s'en prend à moi; **strikers thought that they were being victimized** les grévistes se croyaient victimes de représailles

victimless ['vɪktɪmlɪs] ADJ
▶▶ **v. crime** délit *m* sans victime

victor ['vɪktər] N *Fml* vainqueur *m*; **to emerge the clear v.** sortir grand vainqueur

Victoria [vɪk'tɔːrɪə] N *(person)* **Queen V.** la reine Victoria
▶▶ *Mil* **V. Cross** Victoria Cross *f* *(en Grande-Bretagne, la plus haute décoration militaire)*; **V. Day** = fête *f* de Victoria *(jour férié en mai)*; **V. Falls** les chutes *fpl* Victoria

victoria [vɪk'tɔːrɪə] N *(plum)* = grosse prune *f* rouge
▶▶ **v. plum** = grosse prune rouge

Victorian [vɪk'tɔːrɪən] ADJ victorien, -ienne, du règne de la reine Victoria; *(values)* victorien
▶ N Victorien, -ienne

Victoriana [vɪktɔːrɪ'ɑːnə] N antiquités *fpl* de l'époque victorienne

victorious [vɪk'tɔːrɪəs] ADJ *(army, team etc)* victorieux, vainqueur; *(struggle, campaign)* victorieux; *(day etc)* de victoire; **to be v. over sb** remporter la victoire sur qn

victoriously [vɪk'tɔːrɪəslɪ] ADV victorieusement, en vainqueur

victory ['vɪktərɪ] N victoire *f*; **to claim v.** revendiquer la victoire; **to snatch v. from the jaws of defeat** arracher la victoire; **he described the decision as a v. for common sense** il a décrit la décision comme étant une victoire du bon sens; **to gain a *or* the v.** remporter la victoire (**over** sur), être victorieux; **the Winged V. of Samothrace** la Victoire ailée de Samothrace
▶▶ **v. parade** défilé *m* de la victoire, défilé pour célébrer une victoire

victual ['vɪt(ə)l] (**-ll-**, *Am* **-l-**) VT *(ship, garrison)* ravitailler, approvisionner
▶ VI s'approvisionner, se ravitailler

victualler, *Am* **victualer** ['vɪtlər] N *Fml* fournisseur *m* de vivres; *Br Fml* **licensed v.** débitant *m* de boissons

victuals ['vɪt(ə)lz] NPL *Old-fashioned, Lit (food)* vivres *mpl*, victuailles *fpl*

vicuna [vɪ'kjuːnə] N *(animal, wool, cloth)* vigogne *f*

vid [vɪd] N *Fam (abbr* **video**) vidéo *f*, vidéocassette *f*

video ['vɪdɪəʊ] N *(medium)* vidéo *f*, *(cassette)* vidéocassette *f*, cassette *f* vidéo; *(recorder)* magnétoscope *m*; **a v. of the World Cup** une vidéo de la Coupe du Monde; **we've got a v. of the film** on a le film en vidéocassette; **to show a v.** passer une vidéo; **to have sth on v.** avoir qch sur vidéo; **they recorded the series on v.** ils ont enregistré le feuilleton au magnétoscope; **have you set the v.?** est-ce que tu as mis le magnétoscope en marche *ou* programmé le magnétoscope?; **the film went straight to v.** le film n'est jamais sorti en salle, il est sorti tout de suite sur cassette vidéo
▶ VT **1** *(record)* enregistrer (en vidéo), enregistrer sur magnétoscope, magnétoscoper **2** *(using camcorder)* filmer (à la caméra vidéo); **they didn't know they were being videoed** ils ne savaient pas qu'ils étaient filmés
▶▶ *Comput* **v. accelerator card** carte *f* vidéo accélératrice; **v. art** art *m* vidéo; *Comput* **v. board** carte vidéo; **v. camera** caméra *f* vidéo; *Comput* **v. card** carte vidéo; **v. cassette** vidéocassette; **v. cassette recorder** magné-

toscope; **v. CD** vidéodisque *m*; **v. channel** canal *m* vidéo; **v. clip** clip *m*, vidéoclip *m*, clip vidéo; **v. club** club *m* vidéo; **v. conference** vidéoconférence *f*, visioconférence *f*; **v. conferencing** vidéoconférences; **v. controller** contrôleur *m* vidéo; **v. diary** journal *m* vidéo; *Am* **v. display terminal** console *f* de visualisation; **v. editing** montage *m* vidéo; **v. film** film *m* vidéo; **v. frequency** vidéofréquence *f*; **v. game** jeu *m* vidéo; **v. installation** installation *f* vidéo; **v. library** vidéothèque *f*; **v. link** liaison *f* vidéo; **v. machine** magnétoscope; **v. maker** vidéaste *mf*; **v. memory** mémoire *f* vidéo; *Br Fam* **v. nasty** = film vidéo à caractère violent et souvent pornographique; **v. player** magnétoscope; **v. port** port *m* vidéo; **v. projector** vidéoprojecteur *m*; **v. prompter** télésouffleur *m*; **v. recorder** magnétoscope; **v. recording** enregistrement *m* sur magnétoscope; **v. rights** droits *mpl* d'exploitation vidéo; **v. shop** ≃ vidéoclub *m*, *pl* vidéo-clubs; **v. signal** signal *m* vidéo

videodisc, *Am* **videodisk** ['vɪdɪəʊdɪsk] N disque *m* vidéo, vidéodisque *m*
▶▶ **v. player** lecteur *m* de vidéodisque

videogram ['vɪdɪəʊgræm] N vidéogramme *m*

videographic ['vɪdɪəʊ'græfɪk] ADJ vidéographique

video-on-demand N vidéo *f* à la demande

videophone ['vɪdɪəʊfəʊn] N vidéophone *m*, visiophone *m*

video-selling N *Mktg* vidéovente *f*

videoshopping ['vɪdɪəʊʃɒpɪŋ] N vidéoachat *m*

videotape ['vɪdɪəʊteɪp] N bande *f* vidéo ▸ VT enregistrer sur magnétoscope

videotex ['vɪdɪəʊteks] N *Comput* vidéotex *m*

vie [vaɪ] VI (**vied** [vaɪd]; **vying** ['vaɪɪŋ]) rivaliser (**with sb** avec qn); **they are vying for the championship** ils se disputent le championnat; **to v. with each other in doing sth** rivaliser l'un avec l'autre/les uns avec les autres pour faire qch, faire qch à qui mieux mieux; **they v. with each other for cruelty** ils rivalisent de cruauté; **they were vying with one another to impress her** ils rivalisaient l'un avec l'autre pour la séduire

Vienna [vɪ'enə] N Vienne

Viennese [vɪə'niːz] ADJ viennois N Viennois, -oise

Vietcong [vjet'kɒŋ] N INV, ADJ Viêt-cong *mf*; **a prisoner of the V.** un prisonnier des Viêt-congs

Vietnam [vjet'nɑːm, -'næm] N Vietnam *m*, Viêt Nam *m*

Vietnamese [vjetnə'miːz] ADJ vietnamien N 1 Vietnamien, -ienne 2 *Ling* vietnamien *m*

Viet Vet [vjet'vet] N *Am Mil Fam* ancien *m* du Vietnam

VIEW [vjuː]

N	vue **1, 2** ▪ opinion **3**
VT	regarder **1** ▪ voir **2** ▪ considérer **3**
VI	regarder la télévision

N 1 (*sight*) vue *f* (**of** de); **exposed to/hidden from v.** exposé/caché aux regards; **to pass out of** *or* **be lost to v.** disparaître; **in v.** en vue; **in full v. of the crowd** sous les regards de la foule; **keep your hands in full v.** garde tes mains bien en vue; **they did it in full v. of the military guard** ils l'ont fait au nez et à la barbe de la sentinelle militaire; **at last a hotel came into v.** enfin j'ai/il a/*etc* aperçu un hôtel; **we were in v. of land** nous étions en vue de la terre; **to keep sth in v.** ne pas perdre qch de vue; **on v. (to the public)** (*of col-*

lection) ouvert au public; **famous people are permanently on v.** les gens célèbres sont en permanence exposés aux regards; **private v.** (*of exhibition etc*) avant-première *f*, *pl* avant-premières; (*of exhibition of paintings*) vernissage *m*; **field of v.** (*of telescope*) champ *m*; **angle of v.** angle *m* de champ

2 (*scene, prospect*) vue *f*, perspective *f*; (*photo etc*) vue; **a room with a v.** une chambre avec vue; **front v.** vue de face; **from here you have a good v. of the castle** d'ici on a une très belle vue du château; **you will get a better v. from here** vous verrez mieux d'ici; *Fig* **to take the long v.** adopter une perspective à long terme; *Archit* **front/back v.** élévation *f* du devant/du derrière; **sectional v.** vue en coupe, profil *m*

3 (*opinion*) opinion *f*, idée *f*, avis *m* (**about** au sujet de; **on** sur); **it's a widely-held v.** c'est une opinion très répandue; **point of v.** point *m* de vue; **to express a v.** exprimer une opinion *ou* un avis; **I support the v. that …** je partage l'opinion selon laquelle …; **to have very decided views on sth** avoir des idées très arrêtées sur qch; **what is your v. on the matter?** quelle est votre opinion sur la question?; **in my v.** à mon avis; **in the v. of many of our colleagues** de l'avis de nombreux de nos collègues; **our views differ** nos opinions diffèrent; **to share sb's views** partager les opinions de qn

4 (*intention*) **to have sth in v.** avoir qch en vue; **with this in v.** à cette fin; **they bought the house with a v. to letting it** ils ont acheté la maison en vue de *ou* dans le but de *ou* avec l'idée de la louer

5 (*prep phrase*) **in v. of what has happened** étant donné *ou* compte tenu de ce qui est arrivé; **in v. of these facts** compte tenu de ces faits; **in v. of the great heat** vu la grande chaleur

VT 1 (*look at, watch*) regarder; (*slides*) visionner; *TV* (*programme*) regarder; *Comput* (*codes*) regarder; **when viewed from the outside** vu de l'extérieur

2 (*inspect*) inspecter, examiner; (*exhibition, paintings*) voir; (*house for sale*) visiter, voir

3 (*consider*) considérer, voir; (*prospect*) envisager; **viewed from a commercial perspective** *or* **standpoint, the proposal …** d'un point de vue commercial, cette proposition …; **how do you v. the situation?** comment voyez-vous la situation?; **when viewed in this light** vu sous cet angle; **to v. sth with horror/delight** envisager qch avec horreur/ravissement; **the proposal was viewed unfavourably by the authorities** la proposition était considérée d'un œil peu favorable par les autorités

VI *TV* regarder la télévision

viewable area ['vjuːəbəl] ADJ *Comput* (*of monitor*) zone *f* d'affichage

viewdata® ['vjuːdeɪtə] N *Comput* vidéotex *m*

viewer ['vjuːər] N 1 *TV* téléspectateur, -trice; **I'm a regular v. of your programme** je suis un de vos fidèles téléspectateurs; **the programme has** *or* **attracts a lot of women viewers/young viewers** l'émission est beaucoup regardée par les femmes/les jeunes 2 *Phot* (*for slides*) visionneuse *f* 3 *Comput* (*program*) visualiseur *m*

viewership ['vjuːəʃɪp] N *Am TV* public *m*

viewfinder ['vjuːfaɪndər] N *Phot* viseur *m*

viewing ['vjuːɪŋ] N 1 (*of exhibition, show-house*) visite *f*; **open for v. from seven to nine** visites de sept à neuf heures; **v. is by arrangement with the owner** visite sur accord préalable du propriétaire 2 *TV* programme *m*, programmes *mpl*, émissions *fpl*; **we've got a good evening's v. tonight** il y a de bonnes choses à la télé ce soir; **this new pro-**

gramme is recommended v. cette nouvelle émission est à recommander; **the series makes for compulsive v.** c'est une série prenante *ou* captivante; **suitable for home v.** pour tout public; **the v. public** les téléspectateurs *mpl*
▶▶ *TV* **v. figures** taux *m ou* indice *m* d'écoute; *TV* **v. habits** habitudes *fpl* d'écoute; *TV* **v. hours** heures *fpl* d'écoute; **at peak v. hours** aux heures de grande écoute; *TV* **v. room** salle *f* de visionnage; *TV* **v. time** heures *f* de vision; **v. window** fenêtre *f* d'observation

viewpoint ['vjuːpɔɪnt] N 1 (*opinion*) point *m* de vue; **from the international v.** du point de vue international 2 (*lookout*) point *m* de vue

vigil ['vɪdʒɪl] N veille *f*, (*over sick person or corpse*) veillée *f*, *Rel* vigile *f*; **to keep v.** veiller

> Note that the French word **vigile** is a false friend. Its most common meaning is **security guard**.

vigilance ['vɪdʒɪləns] N vigilance *f*
▶▶ *Am* **v. committee** groupe *m* d'autodéfense

vigilant ['vɪdʒɪlənt] ADJ vigilant; **under the v. eye of …** sous l'œil vigilant de …; **to be v. for sth** être à l'affût de qch; **to keep a v. watch over sth** surveiller qch avec vigilance

vigilante [vɪdʒɪ'læntɪ] N *Pej* membre *m* d'un groupe d'autodéfense
▶▶ **v. group** groupe *m* d'autodéfense

vigilant(e)ism [vɪdʒɪ'lænt(ɪ)ɪz(ə)m] N *esp Am Pej* = tendance *f* au développement de l'autodéfense ou des milices privées

vigilantly ['vɪdʒɪləntlɪ] ADV vigilamment, avec vigilance

vignette [vɪ'njet] N 1 (*illustration*) vignette *f*, (*portrait, photo*) buste *m* sur un fond dégradé; *Fig* **this ten-minute v. of city life** cet aperçu de dix minutes de la vie dans une grande ville 2 (*camera matte*) cache *m*

vigor ['vɪgər] N *Am* = **vigour**

vigorous ['vɪgərəs] ADJ 1 (*robust*) (*person, plant*) vigoureux; (*enthusiastic*) (*person*) enthousiaste 2 (*forceful*) (*opposition, campaign, support*) vigoureux, énergique; (*denial*) formel 3 (*energetic*) (*exercise*) énergique

vigorously ['vɪgərəslɪ] ADV vigoureusement; **she v. denied the allegation** elle a vigoureusement nié

vigour, *Am* **vigor** ['vɪgər] N 1 vigueur *f*, **to deny sth with great v.** nier qch vigoureusement; **the v. of youth** la sève de la jeunesse 2 *Am* **laws in v.** lois *fpl* en vigueur

Viking ['vaɪkɪŋ] N *Hist* Viking *mf*
ADJ viking
▶▶ **V. ship** drakkar *m*

vile [vaɪl] ADJ 1 (*nasty, unpleasant*) abominable, exécrable; **the soup was v.** la soupe était infecte; **he's in a v. temper** il est d'une humeur exécrable 2 (*base, despicable*) vil, infâme, ignoble; **to be v. to sb** être ignoble envers qn; **it was a v. thing to do/say** c'est ignoble d'avoir fait/dit ça; **a v. calumny** une calomnie infâme; **the vilest of men** le dernier des hommes

vilely ['vaɪllɪ] ADV 1 (*decorated etc*) d'une manière abominable *ou* exécrable 2 (*basely, despicably*) vilement, bassement; **to behave v. towards sb** se comporter d'une manière ignoble envers qn

vileness ['vaɪlnɪs] N 1 (*nastiness*) caractère *m* exécrable; **the v. of the weather** le temps abominable 2 (*baseness*) (*of person, feeling*) bassesse *f*, caractère *m* ignoble; **her v. towards her mother** la manière ignoble dont elle traite/traitait sa mère

vilification [vɪlɪfɪˈkeɪʃən] N dénigrement m, diffamation f, calomnie f

vilify [ˈvɪlɪfaɪ] VT dénigrer, diffamer, calomnier; *(reputation, name)* salir

villa [ˈvɪlə] N *(in country)* maison f de campagne; *(in town)* pavillon m de banlieue; *(at seaside, Roman)* villa f; **to rent a v. in Spain** louer une villa en Espagne

village [ˈvɪlɪdʒ] N **1** village m; *(large)* bourg m; **I'm going into the v.** je vais au village; **the whole v. was talking about it** tout le village en parlait; **the v. church/grocer** l'église/l'épicier du village; **a v. inn** une auberge de campagne **2** *Am (municipality)* petite municipalité f
▸▸ *Br* **v. green** = pelouse f se trouvant au centre du village; **v. hall** salle f des fêtes; **v. idiot** idiot m du village

villager [ˈvɪlɪdʒər] N villageois, -oise

villain [ˈvɪlən] N *(scoundrel)* scélérat m; *Br Fam (criminal)* voyou m; *Fam* **you little v.!** petit garnement!, petit coquin!; *Theat* **the v. (of the piece)** le traître; *Fig* **so you're the v. of the piece!** alors c'est vous qui êtes responsable de tout ça!; *Fig* **why am I always the v. of the piece?** pourquoi est-ce que c'est toujours moi que l'on blâme?

villainous [ˈvɪlənəs] ADJ *(behaviour, food etc)* vil, infâme; *(weather)* exécrable; **he gave us a v. look** il nous a regardés d'un sale œil; **a v. deed** une infamie

villainously [ˈvɪlənəslɪ] ADV d'une manière infâme ou ignoble

villainy [ˈvɪlənɪ] N infamie f

villein [ˈvɪlən] N *Hist* vilain m, serf m

villus, pl **villi** [ˈvɪləs, -aɪ] N *Anat* villosité f

Vilnius [ˈvɪlnɪəs] N Vilnious

vim [vɪm] N *Fam* vigueur f, énergie f; **full of v. (and vigour)** plein d'entrain; **put a bit more v. into it!** mets-y un peu plus d'entrain!

vinaigrette [vɪnɪˈgret] N *Culin* vinaigrette f

vindaloo [vɪndəˈluː] N vindaloo m *(plat indien très épicé)*

vindicate [ˈvɪndɪkeɪt] VT *(justify) (faith, claim, report)* justifier; *(exonerate) (person)* disculper; *(uphold) (what one has said)* prouver; *(report)* appuyer; **I was vindicated by the official inquiry** l'enquête officielle m'a donné raison; **to v. one's rights** revendiquer ses droits, faire valoir son bon droit

vindication [vɪndɪˈkeɪʃən] N justification f; **in v. of his conduct** pour justifier sa conduite, en justification de sa conduite; **this is a clear v. of our policy** cela démontre le bien-fondé de notre politique

vindicator [ˈvɪndɪkeɪtər] N défenseur m

vindictive [vɪnˈdɪktɪv] ADJ *(spiteful)* vindicatif

vindictively [vɪnˈdɪktɪvlɪ] ADV vindicativement; **he had quite v. made sure she would not get the job** par esprit de vengeance, il avait tout mis en œuvre pour qu'elle n'obtienne pas le poste

vindictiveness [vɪnˈdɪktɪvnəs] N *(of reprisals, remarks)* caractère m vindicatif; **the v. in her voice** son ton vindicatif; **she did it out of (sheer) v.** elle a fait cela par esprit de vengeance

vine [vaɪn] N **1** *(grapevine)* vigne f; *Fig* **to wither on the v.** ne pas aboutir **2** *Am (climbing plant)* plante f grimpante **3** *Am Fam* **vines** *(clothes)* fringues fpl
▸▸ **v. grower** viticulteur, -trice, vigneron, -onne; **v. growing** viticulture f; **v. harvest** vendange f, vendanges fpl

vinegar [ˈvɪnɪgər] N **1** *(condiment)* vinaigre m; **wine/cider v.** vinaigre de vin/de cidre; **tarragon v.** vinaigre à l'estragon **2** *Am Fam (vitality)* vigueur f, allant m

vinegary [ˈvɪnɪg(ə)rɪ] ADJ **1** *(taste etc)* de vinaigre; *(sauce)* vinaigré; **to turn v.** *(of wine)* tourner en vinaigre **2** *Fam (tone)* acerbe, aigre

vinery [ˈvaɪnərɪ] N *(hothouse)* serre f où l'on cultive la vigne

vineyard [ˈvɪnjəd] N *(field)* (champ m de) vigne f; *(establishment)* vignoble m; **the best vineyards** les meilleurs crus mpl

viniculture [ˈvɪnɪkʌltʃər] N viticulture f

vino [ˈviːnəʊ] N *Fam (wine)* pinard m

vinous [ˈvaɪnəs] ADJ vineux

vintage [ˈvɪntɪdʒ] N **1** *(wine)* vin m de cru; *(year)* cru m, millésime m; **this claret is an excellent v.** ce bordeaux est un très grand cru; **1982 was a good v.** 1982 a été une bonne année pour le vin; **a 1983 v.** un vin de 1983; **what v. is this wine?** quel est le millésime ou quelle est l'année de ce vin? **2** *(period)* époque f; **an old radio of pre-war v.** une vieille radio d'avant-guerre; **our parents are of the same v.** nos parents sont de la même génération
ADJ **1** *(wine)* millésimé; *(port)* vieux **2** *(old)* ancien, antique **3** *(classic, superior)* classique; **the play is v. Shaw** la pièce est du meilleur Shaw
▸▸ *Br* **v. car** voiture f de collection *(normalement construite entre 1919 et 1930)*; **v. year** *(for wine)* grand millésime m, grande année f, *(for books, films)* très bonne année f; **it's been a v. year for comedy** ça a été une excellente année pour ce qui est de la comédie

vintner [ˈvɪntnər] N *Fml* négociant m en vins

vinyl [ˈvaɪnɪl] N vinyle m; *Mus Fam* **the album is available on v. and CD** l'album existe sur vinyle et en CD
ADJ *(wallpaper, tiles, coat)* de ou en vinyle; *(paint)* vinylique

viol [ˈvaɪəl] N *Mus* viole f; **bass v.** basse f de viole; *Am (double bass)* contrebasse f

viola¹ [vɪˈəʊlə] N *Mus* **1** *(violin)* alto m **2** *(viol)* viole f; **v. da gamba** viole de gambe
▸▸ **v. d'amore** viole d'amour; **v. player** altiste mf

viola² [ˈvaɪələ] N *Bot* **1** *(genus)* violacée f **2** *(flower)* violette f (de jardin)

violate [ˈvaɪəleɪt] VT **1** *(disregard)* violer; *(sanctuary)* violer, profaner; *(rule)* manquer à; *(law)* violer, enfreindre; *(sb's trust)* trahir; **to v. sb's privacy** faire intrusion auprès de qn **2** *Old-fashioned (rape)* violer, outrager

violation [vaɪəˈleɪʃən] N *(of oath, law, rights)* violation f, *(of sanctuary)* viol m, profanation f, *(of rule)* manquement m, infraction f, *(of order)* infraction f; *Am (traffic)* **v.** infraction au code de la route; **v. of territorial waters** dépassement m des eaux territoriales; **v. of sb's privacy** intrusion f auprès de qn; **it's a v. of my privacy** c'est une intrusion; **v. of rights** abus m de droits; **in v. of the treaty, they …** ils ont enfreint le traité et …; **this is in v. of the treaty** c'est une violation du traité

violator [ˈvaɪəleɪtər] N **1** *(of law)* violateur, -trice **2** *Old-fashioned (of woman)* violateur m, violeur m

violence [ˈvaɪələns] N **1** *(roughness)* violence f; **v. on television** la violence à la télévision; **to use v.** user de violence; **to resort to v.** recourir ou en venir à la violence; *Law* **to commit acts of v.** se livrer à des voies de fait; **robbery with v.** vol m avec agression ou avec coups et blessures; **he had struck his victim with great v.** il avait frappé sa victime avec une grande violence; **to do v. to sth** *(distort)* faire violence à qch; **the translation does considerable v. to the original** la traduction dénature beaucoup le texte original **2** *(intensity)* violence f, intensité f; **she said, with some v.** dit-elle avec violence; **the v. of the impact** la violence du choc

violent [ˈvaɪələnt] ADJ **1** *(fierce, rough)* violent; *(braking)* brutal, -aux; **v. storm** orage m violent, tempête f; **to die a v. death** mourir de mort violente; **to be in a v. temper** être furieux; **to become v.** *(of person)* devenir violent ou agressif **2** *(intense)* violent, vif, fort; *(coughing, fever, pain)* violent; **v. colours** couleurs fpl criardes ou crues; **to take a v. dislike to sb** se prendre d'une aversion violente ou d'une vive aversion à l'égard de qn

violently [ˈvaɪələntlɪ] ADV **1** *(fiercely, roughly)* violemment, avec violence; *(to die)* de mort violente **2** *(intensely)* vivement, extrêmement; **his heart was beating v.** son cœur battait à se rompre; **after supper I became v. ill** après le souper j'ai été terriblement malade; **she was v. sick** elle a été prise de vomissements violents; **to fall v. in love with sb** tomber follement amoureux de qn

violet [ˈvaɪələt] N **1** *(plant)* violette f; **Parma v.** violette de Parme; *Fig* **shrinking v.** personne f timide; **she is no shrinking v.** elle est loin d'être timide **2** *(colour)* violet m
ADJ violet

violin [vaɪəˈlɪn] N violon m; **first v.** premier violon, violon principal
▸▸ **v. case** étui m à violon; **v. concerto** concerto m pour violon; **v. maker** luthier m

violinist [vaɪəˈlɪnɪst] N violoniste mf

violoncellist [vaɪələnˈtʃelɪst] N violoncelliste mf

violoncello [vaɪələnˈtʃeləʊ] N violoncelle m

VIP [viːaɪˈpiː] N *(abbr* **very important person)** personnage m de marque, VIP mf inv; **to get the V. treatment** être traité comme un personnage de marque
▸▸ **V. guest** hôte m de marque; **V. list** liste f des VIP; **V. lounge** *(in airport)* = salon m d'accueil réservé aux personnages de marque

viper [ˈvaɪpər] N *(snake)*, *Fig* vipère f; **to cherish a v. in one's bosom** réchauffer un serpent dans son sein
▸▸ *Bot* **v.'s bugloss** vipérin m

viperish [ˈvaɪpərɪʃ] ADJ vipérin, de vipère; *(person)* qui a une langue de vipère; *Fig* **v. tongue** langue f de vipère

virago [vɪˈrɑːgəʊ] N *Pej* virago f, mégère f

viral [ˈvaɪrəl] ADJ *Med* viral, -aux; **a v. infection** une infection virale
▸▸ *Comput* **v. marketing** marketing m viral

Virgil [ˈvɜːdʒɪl] N *Antiq, Liter* Virgile m

virgin [ˈvɜːdʒɪn] N vierge f; *(man)* puceau m; **he/she is a v.** il/elle est vierge; **the (Blessed) V.** la Sainte Vierge; **Astron the V.** la Vierge
ADJ **1** *(sexually)* vierge **2** *(forest, soil, wool)* vierge; *(fresh)* virginal, -aux; **v. (olive) oil** huile f d'olives vierge
▸▸ *Rel* **the V. birth** l'Immaculée Conception f; **the V. Islands** les îles fpl Vierges; *Hist* **the V. Queen** *(Elizabeth I)* la Reine Vierge; **v. territory** territoire m vierge; *Fig* **this market is v. territory for the company** ce marché constitue un territoire vierge pour la société

virginal [ˈvɜːdʒɪn(ə)l] ADJ virginal, -aux, de vierge
N *Mus* **virginal(s), pair of virginals** virginal m

Virginia [vəˈdʒɪnɪə] N *Geog* la Virginie
▸▸ *Bot* **V. creeper** vigne f vierge; **V. tobacco** tabac m de Virginie, virginie m

virginity [vəˈdʒɪnɪtɪ] N virginité f; **to lose one's v.** perdre sa virginité; **to lose one's political/professional v.** perdre son innocence sur le terrain politique/professionnel

Virgo ['vɜːgəʊ] N *Astrol* Vierge f; **to be (a) V.** être (de la) Vierge

virile ['vɪraɪl, *Am* 'vɪrəl] ADJ viril

virility [vɪ'rɪlɪtɪ] N virilité f; **he's just trying to prove his v.** il essaye simplement de prouver sa virilité

virologist [vaɪ'rɒlədʒɪst] N virologiste mf, virologue mf

virology [vaɪ'rɒlədʒɪ] N virologie f

virtual ['vɜːtjʊəl] ADJ **1 it's a v. impossibility** c'est quasiment impossible; **he's a v. prisoner** il est quasiment prisonnier; **the v. extinction/monopoly** la quasi-extinction/le quasi-monopole; **he's the v. head of the business** c'est lui le vrai chef de la maison; **it was a v. failure** ce fut en fait un échec; **this was a v. admission of guilt** de fait c'était un aveu de culpabilité **2** *Phys, Comput* virtuel
▶▶ *Phys* **v. image** image f virtuelle; *Comput* **v. memory** mémoire f virtuelle; **v. reality** réalité f virtuelle; *Comput* **v. reality simulator** simulateur m de réalité virtuelle; *Comput* **v. storage** mémoire f virtuelle

virtually ['vɜːtjʊəlɪ] ADV virtuellement, pratiquement; **I'm certain of it** j'en suis virtuellement ou pratiquement certain; **v. all of them came** ils sont pratiquement tous venus

virtue ['vɜːtjuː] N **1** *(goodness, chastity)* vertu f; *Prov* **v. is its own reward** la vertu est sa propre récompense; **to make a v. of necessity** faire de nécessité vertu **2** *(advantage)* avantage m; **the hotel has the v. of being cheap** l'hôtel a l'avantage d'être bon marché; **there's no v. in just going faster** la rapidité n'a aucun mérite en soi **3** *(power)* vertu f; **the healing virtues of certain plants** les vertus curatives de certaines plantes **4** **by** *or* **in v. of** en vertu de; **by v. of one's office** à titre d'office

virtuosity [vɜːtjʊ'ɒsɪtɪ] N *Mus etc* virtuosité f

virtuoso, pl **virtuosos, virtuosi** [vɜːtjʊ-'əʊzəʊ, -zəʊz, -ziː] N *Mus etc* virtuose mf; **he gave a v. performance** *(of musician, actor)* il a joué en virtuose

virtuous ['vɜːtjʊəs] ADJ vertueux; **to feel v. about doing sth** se sentir vertueux parce qu'on fait/a fait qch; **with that oh-so-v. look on his face** avec son (petit) air de sainte nitouche ou de ne pas y toucher; **there's no need to look so v.** ce n'est pas la peine de prendre ton air de petit saint

virtuously ['vɜːtjʊəslɪ] ADV vertueusement

virulence ['vɪr(j)ʊləns] N virulence f

virulent ['vɪr(j)ʊlənt] ADJ *(disease, prejudice)* virulent; *Fig (colour)* criard; **a particularly v. strain of flu** un type de grippe particulièrement violent; **to make a v. attack on sb** lancer une attaque virulente contre qn; **she was v. in her criticism of the system** elle était virulente dans sa critique du système

virulently ['vɪr(j)ʊləntlɪ] ADV avec virulence

virus, pl **viruses** ['vaɪrəs, -əsɪz] N *Med* virus m; **there's a v. going round** il y a un virus qui sévit ou qui se promène; **I've got a v. of some kind** j'ai un virus quelconque; *Euph* **the v.** le sida **2** *Comput* virus m; **to disable a v.** désactiver un virus; **to write a v.** concevoir un virus
▶▶ *Comput* **v. attack** infection f virale; **v. author** créateur m de virus; **v. check** détection f de virus; **to run a v. check on a disk** faire tourner le programme détecteur de virus sur une disquette; **v. detection** détection f de virus; **v. detector** détecteur m de virus; **v. program** programme m virus

virus-free ADJ *Comput* dépourvu de virus

virus-infected ADJ *Comput* contaminé par un/des virus

Visa® ['viːzə] N
▶▶ **V. card** carte f Visa®

visa ['viːzə] N *(on passport, document)* visa m; **to apply for a v. for Poland** demander un visa pour la Pologne
VT **(visaed** ['viːzəd]**)** *(passport)* viser, apposer un visa à

visage ['vɪzɪdʒ] N *Fml* visage m, figure f

vis-à-vis ['viːzɑːviː] PREP *(compared with, in terms of)* par rapport à; *(about)* en ce qui concerne
N *(counterpart)* homologue mf

viscera ['vɪsərə] NPL *Anat* viscères mpl

visceral ['vɪsər(ə)l] ADJ *Anat, Fig* viscéral, -aux

viscid ['vɪsɪd] ADJ visqueux, gluant

viscidity [vɪ'sɪdɪtɪ] N viscosité f

viscose ['vɪskəʊs] N *Chem* viscose f

viscosity [vɪs'kɒsɪtɪ] N viscosité f

viscount ['vaɪkaʊnt] N vicomte m

viscountcy ['vaɪkaʊntsɪ] N vicomté m

viscountess ['vaɪkaʊntɪs] N vicomtesse f

viscounty ['vaɪkaʊntɪ] N vicomté m

viscous ['vɪskəs] ADJ visqueux
▶▶ *Tech* **v. coupling** visco-coupleur m, pl visco-coupleurs

vise [vaɪs] N *Am* = **vice²**

visibility [vɪzɪ'bɪlɪtɪ] N visibilité f; **good/bad v.** bonne/mauvaise visibilité; **v. was down to a few yards** la visibilité était réduite à quelques mètres; **v. is one hundred yards** la visibilité est de cent mètres; **the car has good front and rear v.** la voiture donne une bonne visibilité avant et arrière

visible ['vɪzɪb(ə)l] ADJ visible; **to become v.** apparaître; **the house was now v.** la maison était en vue; **v. to the naked eye** visible à l'œil nu; *Law* **to have no v. means of support** n'avoir aucun moyen apparent de subvenir à ses propres besoins; **with v. satisfaction** avec une satisfaction évidente
▶▶ *Econ* **v. assets** actif m corporel; *Com* **v. defect** défaut m apparent; *Econ* **v. earnings** gains mpl visibles; **v. horizon** horizon m

visibly ['vɪzɪblɪ] ADV visiblement, manifestement; *(to grow etc)* à vue d'œil; **she was v. moved** elle était visiblement émue

Visigoth ['vɪzɪgɒθ] N *Hist* Wisigoth, -othe

vision ['vɪʒən] N **1** *(sight)* vision f, vue f; **to have good/poor v.** avoir une bonne/une mauvaise vue; **the accident had impaired his v.** cet accident avait affaibli sa vue; **field/angle of v.** champ m/angle m visuel; *Med* **double v.** double vision, diplopie f
2 *Fig (foresight, imagination)* clairvoyance f, perspicacité f; **man/woman of v.** homme m/femme f d'une grande perspicacité ou qui voit loin dans l'avenir
3 *(dream)* vision f, *(apparition)* vision, apparition f; **to have** or **see visions** avoir des visions; **visions of wealth** visions de richesse(s); **to have visions of doing sth** se voir faire qch; **I had visions of having to walk all the way into town** je me suis vu devoir aller jusqu'en ville à pied; **I had visions of you in a police cell** je te voyais déjà dans une cellule de police; **she always had visions of owning her own business** elle avait toujours rêvé d'avoir sa propre entreprise
4 *TV* image f; **a temporary loss of v.** une perte momentanée de l'image
▶▶ **v. control** contrôle m de l'image; **v. mixer** *TV (equipment)* mixeur m, mélangeur m de signaux; *(person)* opérateur, -trice de mixage; *TV* **v. mixing** mixage m d'images

visionary ['vɪʒənərɪ] ADJ *(leader)* visionnaire
N visionnaire mf

visit ['vɪzɪt] N *(call, tour)* visite f, *(stay)* séjour m; *Comput (to Web page)* consultation f, *Am* *(talk)* causerie f, causette f *(with sb* avec qn); *(social)* **v.** visite; **courtesy v.** visite de politesse; **I had a v. from your aunt last week** j'ai eu la visite de ta tante la semaine dernière; **to pay sb a v.** faire une visite à qn, rendre visite à qn; **to return sb's v.** rendre sa visite à qn; *Fam* **to pay a v.** *(go to lavatory)* aller au petit coin; **to be on a v.** *Br* to or *Am* **with friends** être en visite chez des amis; **I'm here on a v.** je suis ici en visite, je suis de passage ici; **the last time I made a v. to London** la dernière fois que je me suis rendu à Londres; **this is my first v. to your country** c'est la première fois que je viens dans votre pays; *Naut* **right of v. (and search)** *(at sea)* droit m de visite
VT **1** *(of doctor) (patient)* visiter; *(of representative) (customer)* passer chez; *Comput (Web page)* consulter; **to v. sb** *(call on)* rendre visite à qn; *(stay with)* faire un séjour chez qn; **we're visiting relatives** nous sommes en visite chez de la famille; **we visited the museums** nous avons visité les musées; **worth visiting** *(museum etc)* qui vaut la visite ou le détour **2** *Bible (punish)* *(person, sin)* punir; **to v. the sins of the fathers upon the children** punir les enfants pour les péchés des pères
VI **1** *(be on a visit)* être en visite; **I don't live here, I'm only visiting** je n'habite pas ici, je ne suis que de passage **2** *Am (talk)* **stay and v. a while** reste à bavarder un petit moment
▶ **visit with** VT INSEP *Am* **1** *(stay with)* être en visite chez **2** *(talk with)* bavarder avec

visitation [vɪzɪ'teɪʃən] N **1** *(official visit)* visite f, *(of bishop)* visite pastorale; **the restaurant had a v. from the Department of Health** le restaurant a eu une visite d'inspection du ministère de la Santé; *Hum* **we're having a v. from the managing director next week** le directeur général nous fait l'honneur de sa visite la semaine prochaine **2** *Rel* **(the Feast of) the V.** (la fête de) la Visitation; **v. (of God)** *(punishment)* châtiment m

visiting ['vɪzɪtɪŋ] ADJ *(circus, performers)* de passage; *(lecturer)* invité; *(birds)* de passage, migrateur, -trice; *Sport* **the v. team** les visiteurs mpl
N **to go v.** aller en visites
▶▶ *Br* **v. card** carte f de visite; *Am Fam* **v. fireman** visiteur m de marque; **v. hours** heures fpl de visite; **v. lecturer** *(who gives talks)* conférencier, -ière; *Am* **v. nurse** infirmier, -ère à domicile; *Univ* **v. professor** professeur m associé ou invité; *Law* **v. rights** *(of divorced parent)* droit m de visite

visitor ['vɪzɪtər] N **1** *(guest, tourist)* visiteur, -euse; *(in hospital, prison, museum etc)* visiteur, -euse; **an unexpected v.** un visiteur inattendu; **to have visitors** *(at the moment)* avoir du monde ou des invités ou de la visite; **I rarely have visitors** c'est rare que j'aie de la visite; **you have a v.** tu as de la visite; **London will have half a million visitors this summer** 500 000 personnes visiteront Londres cette été; **she is a frequent v. to our country** elle se rend régulièrement dans notre pays; **a v. from Mars** un voyageur venu de Mars; *Br* **health v.** infirmière f à domicile ou visiteuse **2** *(bird)* oiseau m migrateur; **this species is a winter v. to Britain** cette espèce vient passer l'hiver en Grande-Bretagne; **it's a rare v. to these shores** c'est une espèce que l'on voit rarement sous ces latitudes
▶▶ **visitors' book** *(at hotel)* registre m; *(at exhibition, tourist attraction)* livre m d'or; **v. centre** *(in park, at tourist attraction etc)* centre m d'accueil pour les visiteurs; *Br* **v.'s passport** = passeport m temporaire; **visitors' tax** taxe f de séjour

visor ['vaɪzər] N *(on helmet, cap)* visière f; **to raise/lower one's v.** soulever/baisser sa visière; *Aut* **sun v.** pare-soleil m inv

vista ['vɪstə] N vue *f*, perspective *f*; *Fig* perspective; *Fig* **to open up new vistas** ouvrir de nouvelles perspectives *ou* de nouveaux horizons

vistadome ['vɪstədəʊm] N *Am Rail* vistadôme *m*

visual ['vɪzjʊəl, 'vɪʒ-] ADJ visuel; **to have a v. memory** avoir une mémoire visuelle; **her comedy is very v.** son comique repose sur les effets visuels; **his fabrics have great v. appeal** ses tissus sont très attrayants visuellement

N *(of design)* maquette *f*; **visuals** *(illustrative material)* supports *mpl* visuels

▸▸ **v. aid** support *m* visuel; **v. arts** arts *mpl* visuels; **v. check** contrôle *m* visuel; *Comput* **v. display terminal, v. display unit** visuel *m*, écran *m* de visualisation; *Cin, TV* **v. effects** effets *mpl* spéciaux; *Anat* **v. nerve** nerf *m* optique; *Mil, Naut* **v. signal** signal *m* optique; *Mil, Naut* **v. signalling** signalisation *f* optique

visualization [vɪzjʊəlaɪ'zeɪʃən, vɪʒ-] N visualisation *f*

visualize ['vɪzjʊəlaɪz, 'vɪʒ-] VT *(imagine)* se représenter; *(foresee)* envisager; **she had difficulty visualizing him without his beard** elle avait du mal à se le représenter *ou* à l'imaginer sans sa barbe

visually ['vɪzjʊəl, 'vɪʒ-] ADV visuellement; **v. handicapped** malvoyant; **the v. handicapped** les malvoyants *mpl*; **v. impaired** qui a des problèmes de vue; **the v. impaired** les personnes *fpl* qui ont des problèmes de vue

vital ['vaɪt(ə)l] ADJ **1** *(essential to life)* vital, -aux **2** *(decisive, indispensable)* essentiel, capital, -aux, vital, -aux; **it is v. that …** il est indispensable *ou* essentiel que … + *subj*; **to play a v. role** jouer un rôle capital; **a question of v. importance** une question d'une importance vitale *ou* capitale, une question de toute première importance **3** *(full of life, vigorous)* vigoureux, dynamique

N *Anat etc* **vitals** organes *mpl* vitaux

▸▸ **v. force** force *f* vitale; **v. functions** fonctions *fpl* vitales; **v. organ** organe vital; *Med* **v. signs** = température *f*, rythme *m* cardiaque et respiration *f*; **v. statistics** *(demographic)* statistiques *fpl* démographiques; *Fam (of woman)* mensurations *fpl*

vitality [vaɪ'tælɪtɪ] N *(of organism)* vitalité *f*; *(of institution)* vitalité, vigueur *f*; *(of person, style)* énergie *f*, vigueur *f*; **I wish I had her v.** j'aimerais bien avoir son énergie

vitalize ['vaɪtəlaɪz] VT vitaliser, vivifier

vitally ['vaɪt(ə)lɪ] ADV **supplies are v. needed** on a un besoin vital de vivres; **v. important question** question d'une importance vitale *ou* de toute première importance; **it is v. important that …** il est essentiel *ou* il faut absolument que … + *subj*; **v. for the British, the European Commission has agreed** la Commission Européenne a accepté, ce qui est vital *ou* capital pour les Britanniques

vitamin ['vɪtəmɪn, *Am* 'vaɪ-] N *Biol, Chem* vitamine *f*; **v. C/D** vitamine C/D; **with added vitamins** vitaminé

▸▸ **v. deficiency** carence *f* vitaminique; *(disease)* avitaminose *f*; **v. pill** comprimé *m* de vitamines

vitiate ['vɪʃɪeɪt] VT **1** *Fml (spoil, weaken)* *(blood, air)* vicier **2** *Law (contract)* vicier

vitiation [vɪʃɪ'eɪʃən] N *Fml* viciation *f*

viticulture ['vɪtɪkʌltʃər] N viticulture *f*

vitreous ['vɪtrɪəs] ADJ **1** *Chem, Geol* vitreux **2** *(enamel)* vitrifié **3** *Anat* vitré

▸▸ **v. body** *(in eye)* corps *m* vitré; **v. enamel** émail *m* vitrifié; **v. humour** humeur *f* vitrée

vitrification [vɪtrɪfɪ'keɪʃən] N vitrification *f*

vitrified ['vɪtrɪfaɪd] ADJ vitrifié

vitrify ['vɪtrɪfaɪ] VT vitrifier

VI se vitrifier

vitriol ['vɪtrɪəl] N *Chem, Fig* vitriol *m*; **to throw v. at sb** lancer du vitriol sur qn, vitrioler qn; *Fig* **the v. of her remarks** la virulence *ou* l'acerbité de ses remarques; *Fig* **the article was sheer v.** c'était un article au vitriol

vitriolic [vɪtrɪ'ɒlɪk] ADJ *(acid)* vitriolique; *Fig (attack, speech)* au vitriol; **v. criticism** critique *f* mordante

vitriolize ['vɪtrɪəlaɪz] VT vitrioler

vituperate [vɪ'tju:pəreɪt] VI *Fml* déblatérer, vitupérer (**against sb/sth** contre qn/qch)

vituperation [vɪtju:pə'reɪʃən] N *Fml* vitupération *f*

vituperative [vɪ'tju:pərətɪv] ADJ *Fml* injurieux

Vitus ['vaɪtəs] N *Med Fam* **Saint V.'s dance** danse *f* de Saint-Guy

viva¹ ['vi:və] INT, N *(cry)* vivat *m*

viva² ['vaɪvə] N *Br Univ Fam* = **viva voce** N

vivacious [vɪ'veɪʃəs] ADJ *(esp woman, girl)* vif, animé, enjoué; **she has a v. laugh** elle a un rire enjoué; **she is v.** elle a de la vivacité; **she was very v. yesterday evening** elle avait beaucoup d'entrain *ou* était très enjouée hier soir

vivaciously [vɪ'veɪʃəslɪ] ADV avec vivacité *ou* entrain; *(to laugh)* d'un air enjoué

vivacity [vɪ'væsɪtɪ] N vivacité *f*, entrain *m*; **the v. of her laugh** son rire enjoué

vivarium, *pl* **vivariums, vivaria** [vaɪ'veərɪəm, -ɪəmz, -ɪə] N *(for animals, plants)* vivarium *m*

viva voce ['vaɪvə'vəʊsɪ] *Br Univ* N épreuve *f* orale, oral *m*; *(for thesis)* soutenance *f* de thèse

ADJ oral, -aux

ADV de vive voix, oralement

vivid ['vɪvɪd] ADJ *(light, colour)* vif, éclatant, brillant; *(language, terms)* vivant, coloré; *(memory)* très vif, très clair; **v. imagination** imagination *f* vive; **v. flash of lightning** éclair *m* aveuglant; **it left a v. impression on me** ça m'a laissé une forte impression; **I have a v. recollection of the scene** j'ai un souvenir très vif *ou* très net de la scène; **v. description of sth** description *f* vivante de qch

vividly ['vɪvɪdlɪ] ADV vivement, avec éclat; *(to remember)* nettement, clairement; **to describe sth v.** décrire qch d'une manière vivante *ou* sous de vives couleurs

vividness ['vɪvɪdnɪs] N *(of light, colours)* vivacité *f*, éclat *m*; *(of memory)* netteté *f*; **the v. of his style** la vigueur *ou* le pittoresque de son style

vivify ['vɪvɪfaɪ] VT *Fml* vivifier, (r)animer

viviparous [vɪ'vɪpərəs] ADJ *Bot, Zool* vivipare

vivisect [vɪvɪ'sekt, 'vɪvɪsekt] VT *Fml* pratiquer des vivisections sur

vivisection [vɪvɪ'sekʃən] N vivisection *f*; **the v. debate** le débat sur la vivisection

vivisectionist [vɪvɪ'sekʃənɪst] N *(practitioner)* personne *f* qui pratique la vivisection

vixen ['vɪks(ə)n] N *(animal)* renarde *f*; *Pej (woman)* mégère *f*

viz [vɪz] ADV *(abbr* **videlicet)** à savoir, c'est-à-dire

vizier [vɪ'zɪər] N *Hist* vizir *m*; **grand v.** grand vizir

vizor ['vaɪzər] N = **visor**

VJ [vi:'dʒeɪ] N *(abbr* **video jockey)** présentateur, -trice de vidéoclips

VLF [vi:el'ef] N *Radio abbr* **very low frequency**

VLSI [vi:ele'saɪ] N *Comput abbr* **very large scale integration**

V-neck N encolure *f* en V

ADJ à encolure en V

V-necked ADJ à encolure en V

vocab ['vəʊkæb] N *Fam* voca(bulaire) *m*

vocabulary [və'kæbjʊlərɪ] N **1** *(glossary)* vocabulaire *m* **2** *(of person)* vocabulaire *m*; *(of language)* vocabulaire, lexique *m*; **a large/small v.** un vocabulaire étendu/limité; **to enlarge one's v.** enrichir son vocabulaire

▸▸ **v. test** test *m* de vocabulaire

vocal ['vəʊk(ə)l] ADJ **1** *Anat* vocal, -aux; **the v. organs** les organes *mpl* vocaux **2** *(music)* vocal, -aux **3** *(communication)* verbal, -aux, oral, -aux **4** *Fig (forthright) (person)* qui se fait entendre; **to be v. in one's criticisms** faire clairement entendre ses critiques; **the most v. member of the audience** le membre de l'auditoire qui s'est fait le plus entendre; **he is very v. about …** il parle beaucoup de …, il se fait entendre souvent au sujet de … **5** *(noisy) (assembly, meeting)* bruyant **6** *Ling (sound)* vocalique; *(consonant)* voisé

N *Ling* son *m* vocal; *Mus* **vocals** chant *m*, partie *f* vocale; **on vocals** au chant

▸▸ **v. cords** cordes *fpl* vocales; **v. score** partition *f* chorale

vocalic [və'kælɪk] ADJ *Ling* vocalique

vocalist ['vəʊkəlɪst] N chanteur, -euse; **who was the v. on their first album?** qui chantait sur leur premier album?; **backing v.** choriste *mf*

vocalization [vəʊkəlaɪ'zeɪʃən] N *Mus, Ling* vocalisation *f*

vocalize ['vəʊkəlaɪz] VT **1** *(articulate) (doubt, complaint)* exprimer **2** *Ling (consonant)* vocaliser

VI *Mus* faire des vocalises, vocaliser

vocally ['vəʊk(ə)lɪ] ADV vocalement, oralement; *(to protest)* à haute voix

vocation [vəʊ'keɪʃən] N vocation *f*; **to have a v.** avoir une vocation; **teaching is a v.** l'enseignement, c'est une vocation; **to miss one's v.** manquer sa vocation

vocational [vəʊ'keɪʃənəl] ADJ professionnel

▸▸ **v. course** *(short)* stage *m* de formation professionnelle; *(longer)* enseignement *m* professionnel; **v. guidance** conseiller d'orientation *m*; *Am* **v. guidance counselor** orienteur *m* professionnel; **v. qualification** qualification *f* professionnelle; **v. training** formation *f* professionnelle

vocative ['vɒkətɪv] *Gram* N vocatif *m*; **in the v.** au vocatif

ADJ **the v. case** le vocatif

vociferate [və'sɪfəreɪt] VI *(protest)* vociférer, crier (**against** contre)

vociferation [vəsɪfə'reɪʃən] N *(protest)* vocifération *f*, cri *m*

vociferous [və'sɪfərəs] ADJ vociférant, bruyant; **she was most v. in her opposition** elle s'y est opposée bruyamment

vociferously [vɒ'sɪfərəslɪ] ADV bruyamment; *(to protest)* à haute voix

VOD [vi:əʊ'di:] N *(abbr* **video on demand)** vidéo *f* à la demande

vodka ['vɒdkə] N vodka *f*; **v. and orange** vodka-orange

vogue [vəʊg] N vogue *f*, mode *f* (**for** de); **in v.** en vogue, à la mode; **to come into v.** devenir à la mode; **out of v.** démodé; **v. word** mot *m* à la mode

voice [vɔɪs] N **1** *(of person)* voix *f*; **to raise/lower one's v.** hausser/baisser la voix; **to keep one's v. down** parler à voix basse; **his v. has broken** sa voix a mué; **his v. was breaking** *(with emotion)* sa voix se brisait; **in a low v.** à voix basse, à mi-voix; **he's got a deep v.** il a une voix grave; **to speak in a**

loud v. parler à haute voix *ou* à voix haute; **at the top of one's v.** à tue-tête; **to make one's v. heard** se faire entendre; **he likes the sound of his own v.** il aime à s'entendre parler; **she's not in (good) v.** *(of singer)* elle n'est pas en voix; **to lose one's v.** perdre sa voix **2** *Fig* **a dissenting v.** un protestataire; **hers was the only dissenting v.** elle était la seule à protester; **the v. of conscience/reason** la voix de la conscience/de la raison; **a little v. inside her told her it was wrong** *(her conscience told her)* une petite voix en elle lui dit que c'était mal; **the v. of the people** la voix du peuple; **with one v.** tout d'une voix, à l'unanimité; **to give v. to one's indignation** exprimer son indignation **3** *(right to express opinion)* voix *f*, suffrage *m*; **we have no v. in the matter** nous n'avons pas voix au chapitre; **proportional representation would give small parties a greater v.** la représentation proportionnelle donnerait davantage voix au chapitre aux petits partis **4** *Gram (of verb)* voix *f*; **in the active/passive v.** à la voix active/passive, à l'actif/au passif VOIR GRAMMAIRE A40; B39

VT **1** *(opinion, one's anger etc)* exprimer; **to v. the general feeling** exprimer le sentiment général *ou* l'opinion générale **2** *Ling (consonant)* sonoriser

▸▸ **v. activation** commande *f* vocale; **v. box** larynx *m*; *Comput* **v. card** carte *f* vocale; *Comput* **v. chip** puce *f* de reconnaissance vocale; **v. coach** répétiteur *m* vocal; **v. dialling** *(on mobile phone)* numérotation *f* vocale; *Comput* **v. input** entrée *f* vocale; **v. mail** messagerie *f* vocale; **V. of America** = station *f* de radio américaine émettant dans le monde entier; *Comput* **v. recognition** reconnaissance *f* de la parole; *Comput* **v. recognition software** logiciel *m* de reconnaissance vocale; *Comput* **v. response** réponse *f* vocale; *Comput* **v. synthesizer** synthétiseur *m* de paroles; **v. test** audition *f*

voice-activated [-æktɪveɪtɪd] ADJ *(device)* commandé par la voix, à commande vocale

voiced [vɔɪst] ADJ *Ling (consonant)* sonore

-voiced [vɔɪst] SUFF **low/loud-v.** à la voix basse/forte

voiceless ['vɔɪslɪs] ADJ *Ling* sourd, non voisé

voice-over N *Cin, TV* voix *f* off, voix hors champ, voix en surimpression; **who did the v.?** qui a fait la voix off *ou* la voix hors champ?

void [vɔɪd] ADJ **1 v. of** *(lacking in)* dépourvu *ou* dénué de; **the proposal is v. of reason** la proposition est dénuée *ou* dépourvue de raison **2** *Law (deed, contract)* **(null and) v.** nul; **to make v.** annuler, frapper de nullité **3** *Lit (empty)* vide

N vide *m*; **to fill the v.** combler le vide; **the aching v. in his heart** le vide douloureux qu'il y avait dans son cœur

VT **1** *Law (contract)* résoudre, annuler **2** *(one's bowels)* évacuer

voile [vɔɪl] N *Tex* voile *m*

vol 1 *Phys (abbr volume)* vol **2** *(abbr volume) (book in series)* tome, t

volatile ['vɒlətaɪl] ADJ **1** *(person)* versatile, inconstant; *(situation)* explosif; **she's been rather v. recently** elle est d'humeur assez changeante ces temps-ci **2** *(prices, market)* volatile **3** *Chem* volatil **4** *Comput (memory)* volatil

volatility [vɒlə'tɪlɪtɪ] N **1** *(of person)* inconstance *f*, caractère *m* changeant; *(of situation)* caractère explosif; *(of prices, market)* volatilité *f*; **the v. of her moods** ses changements d'humeur **2** *Chem* volatilité *f*

volatilize [vɒ'lætɪlaɪz] *Chem* VT *(liquid)* volatiliser

VI se volatiliser

vol-au-vent ['vɒləʊvɒn] N *Culin* vol-au-vent *m inv*

volcanic [vɒl'kænɪk] ADJ *Geog, Fig* volcanique

volcano, *pl* **volcanoes** [vɒl'keɪnəʊ, -əʊz] N volcan *m*

vole [vəʊl] N *(animal)* campagnol *m*

volition [və'lɪʃən] N volition *f*, volonté *f*; **to do sth of one's own v.** faire qch de son propre gré

volley ['vɒlɪ] N **1** *(of gunfire)* volée *f*, salve *f*, *(of blows, stones etc)* volée, grêle *f*, *Fig (of insults)* volée, bordée *f*, **to fire** *or* **discharge a v.** tirer une volée *ou* une salve **2** *Sport (balle f prise de)* volée *f*, *Tennis* half v. demi-volée *f*, *pl* demi-volées

VT **1** *Mil (projectiles)* tirer une volée *ou* une salve de **2 to v. the ball** *Tennis* effectuer une volée; *Ftbl* reprendre la balle de volée; *Tennis* **to half v. the ball** effectuer une demi-volée

VI **1** *(of guns)* partir ensemble **2** *Tennis* relancer la balle à la volée; **he is volleying extremely well** sa volée est superbe

volleyball ['vɒlɪbɔːl] N *Sport* volley-ball *m*, volley *m*

▸▸ **v. player** volleyeur, -euse

volt [vəʊlt] N *Elec* volt *m*

voltage ['vəʊltɪdʒ] N *Elec* tension *f*, **high/ low v.** haute/basse tension

voltaic [vɒl'teɪɪk] ADJ *Elec* voltaïque

volte-face ['vɒltfɑːs] N volte-face *f inv*; **to make a (complete) v.** faire volte-face

voltmeter ['vəʊltmiːtər] N *Elec* voltmètre *m*

volubility [vɒljʊ'bɪlɪtɪ] N volubilité *f*

voluble ['vɒljʊb(ə)l] ADJ volubile; **he was v. in his denials** il a nié avec volubilité; **to be a v. talker** parler avec beaucoup de volubilité

volubly ['vɒljʊblɪ] ADV avec volubilité

volume ['vɒljuːm] N **1** *(book)* volume *m*, tome *m*; **v. one** tome premier, premier volume; **work in six volumes, six-v. work** ouvrage *m* en six volumes; *Fig* **to speak volumes** *(of action, remark etc)* être révélateur (**about** de), en dire long (**about** sur) **2** *(amount)* volume *m*; **v. of business/sales** volume des affaires/des ventes; **volumes of smoke** nuages *mpl* *ou* tourbillons *mpl* de fumée; **volumes of water** flots *mpl* *ou* torrents *mpl* d'eau; **a huge v. of work** une énorme quantité de travail **3** *Mus, Radio, TV* volume *m*; **to turn the v. up/down** augmenter/diminuer le volume; *Radio* **at full v.** à fond, à plein volume; **turn the radio up full v.** mets la radio à fond

▸▸ *Radio, TV* **v. control** bouton *m* de réglage du volume; *Comput* **v. label** label *m* de volume; *Mktg* **v. mailing** multipostage *m*, publipostage *m* groupé

volumetric [vɒljʊ'metrɪk] ADJ *Chem, Phys* volumétrique

▸▸ **v. analysis** analyse *f* volumétrique

voluminous [və'luːmɪnəs] ADJ **1** *(correspondence, documentation)* volumineux; *(notes)* copieux; **in v. detail** en grands détails **2** *(jacket etc)* ample

voluminously [vɒ'luːmɪnəslɪ] ADV abondamment

voluntarily [vɒlʌn'teərɪlɪ] ADV **1** *(willingly)* volontairement, de son plein gré **2** *(unpaid)* bénévolement

voluntary ['vɒlənt(ə)rɪ] ADJ **1** *(freely given) (statement, donation, gift)* volontaire, spontané **2** *(unpaid) (help, service)* bénévole; **the shop is run on a v. basis** le personnel du magasin se compose de bénévoles, le magasin est tenu par des bénévoles **3** *(optional)* facultatif; **attendance on the course is purely v.** la participation au cours est facultative **4** *Physiol* volontaire

N *Rel, Mus (on organ)* morceau *m* pour orgue; *(on trumpet)* morceau pour trompette

▸▸ *Com* **v. chain** chaîne *f* volontaire; **v. export restraint** autolimitation *f* des exportations; *Com* **v. group** groupe *m* volontaire; **v. organization** organisation *f* bénévole; *Br* **v. redundancy** départ *m* volontaire; *Com* **v. retailer chain** chaîne volontaire de détaillants; **v. service** service *m* volontaire; **v. work** travail *m* bénévole, bénévolat *m*; **v. worker** bénévole *mf*

volunteer [vɒlən'tɪər] N **1** volontaire *mf*; **can I have a v. from the audience?** y a-t-il une personne dans la salle qui voudrait bien venir sur scène? **2** *(unpaid worker)* bénévole *mf*

VT *(one's services)* offrir volontairement *ou* spontanément; *(information)* donner spontanément; **to v. advice** offrir des conseils; **she seemed unwilling to v. anything more than this** elle n'avait pas l'air de vouloir en dire plus; **'maybe I will'** was as much as he would v. pour toute réponse il déclara 'peut-être que oui'; **to v. to do sth** se porter volontaire *ou* se proposer pour faire qch; **I wish I'd never volunteered to help** si seulement je ne m'étais pas porté volontaire pour aider!; **he's always volunteering other people** il propose toujours les services des autres sans leur demander leur avis; **they volunteered their son to look after the neighbours' dog** ils ont proposé que leur fils s'occupe du chien des voisins

VI se porter volontaire; *Mil* s'engager comme volontaire (**for** pour); *(for charitable work etc)* proposer ses services (**for** pour); **why don't you v.?** pourquoi est-ce que tu ne te portes pas volontaire?; *(as audience participant)* pourquoi tu n'y vas pas?; **I wish I'd never volunteered for this** si seulement je ne m'étais pas porté volontaire!

▸▸ **v. army** armée *f* de volontaires; **v. service** service *m* volontaire

voluptuary [və'lʌptʊərɪ] N *esp Pej* voluptueux, -euse

voluptuous [və'lʌptjʊəs] ADJ **1** *(figure)* sensuel **2** *(pleasure)* voluptueux

voluptuously [və'lʌptjʊəslɪ] ADV voluptueusement

voluptuousness [və'lʌptjʊəsnɪs] N **1** *(of figure)* sensualité *f* **2** *(of pleasure)* volupté *f*

vom [vɒm] *Fam* N *(vomit)* dégueulis *m*

VI (-mm-) dégueuler, gerber

vomit ['vɒmɪt] N vomissure *f*, vomi *m*; **to choke on one's own v.** s'étouffer avec son propre vomi

VT vomir; **to v. blood** vomir du sang; **he vomits everything he eats** il vomit *ou* rejette *ou* rend tout ce qu'il mange; **to v. (forth) smoke** *(of chimney)* vomir de la fumée

VI vomir

vomiting ['vɒmɪtɪŋ] N vomissements *mpl*

voodoo ['vuːduː] N vaudou *m*

▸▸ **v. priest** prêtre *m* vaudou

voodooism ['vuːduːɪz(ə)m] N vaudou *m*

voracious [və'reɪʃəs, vɒ-] ADJ *(person, appetite)* vorace; *(hunger)* vorace, de loup; *(reader)* avide; **I was feeling quite v.** j'avais une faim de loup

voraciously [və'reɪʃəslɪ, vɒ-] ADV *(to eat)* voracement, avec voracité; *(to read)* avidement; **to be v. hungry** avoir une faim de loup

voracity [vɒ'ræsɪtɪ] N voracité *f*

vortex, *pl* **vortices, vortexes** ['vɔːteks, -ɪsiːz, -eksɪz] N *Lit (of dust, smoke)* tourbillon *m*; *(whirlpool)* gouffre *m*; *Fig* **the v. of politics** le tourbillon de la politique

votary ['vəʊtərɪ] N fervent, -ente (**of** de); *Rel* dévot, -ote (**of** à)

vote [vəʊt] N **1** *(by a group)* vote *m*, scrutin *m*;

(of individual) vote, voix *f*, suffrage *m*; *(right to vote)* droit *m* de vote; **v. by a show of hands** vote à main levée; **popular v.** consultation *f* populaire; **to put a question to the v.** soumettre une question au vote; **let's put it to the v.** votons; **to take the v.** procéder au scrutin; **to take a v. on sth** voter sur qch; **to give one's v. to sb** donner son vote *ou* sa voix à qn; **to count** *or* **tell the votes** compter les votes, dépouiller le scrutin; **they've got my v.** je vote pour eux; **can I count on your v.?** puis-je compter sur votre vote?; **to be elected by one v.** être élu à une voix de majorité; **the motion was adopted by six votes to two** la motion a été adoptée par six voix contre deux; **how many votes did she get?** combien de voix est-ce qu'elle a obtenu?; **to record** *or* **cast one's v.** voter; **the v. went against her** le vote a été en sa défaveur; **one man, one v.** suffrage universel; **to have the v.** avoir le droit de vote; **votes for women!** le droit de vote aux femmes!; **British women got the v. in 1928** les femmes britanniques ont obtenu le droit de vote en 1928; **the Republicans got 52% of the v.** les républicains ont remporté 52% du scrutin; **to increase one's (share of the) v.** obtenir de meilleurs résultats; **they increased their v. by 12%** ils ont amélioré leurs résultats de 12%; **to lose the trade union/black v.** perdre les suffrages des syndicalistes/des Noirs **2** *(of assembly)* motion *f*, résolution *f*; **v. of censure** *or* **no confidence** motion de censure; **v. of confidence** vote *m* de confiance; **to propose a v. of thanks** faire un discours de remerciement

vi voter (**for** pour; **against** contre); **to v. by (a) show of hands** voter à mains levées; **to v. in favour of a proposal** voter une proposition; **to v. Communist** voter communiste; **v. for Thomas!** votez Thomas!; *Fig* **to v. with one's feet** *(by leaving)* indiquer sa désapprobation en quittant les lieux; *(by not turning up)* indiquer sa désapprobation en ne venant pas

vt *(sum of money, credit)* voter; **to v. £50,000 for the victims of the disaster** voter 50 000 livres pour les sinistrés; **the senators voted themselves a pay rise** les sénateurs se sont voté une augmentation de salaire; **I v. (that) we go** je propose que nous y allions; **they voted the holiday a success** ils ont décidé d'un commun accord que les vacances avaient été une réussite

▸ **vote down vt sep** *(motion)* rejeter; *(candidate) (not elect)* ne pas élire; *(not re-elect)* ne pas réélire

▸ **vote in vt sep** *(candidate)* élire (**as** en tant que)

▸ **vote on vt insep** mettre au vote; **the Chairman refused to let them v. on it** le président a refusé de les laisser mettre la question au vote

▸ **vote out vt sep** *(decision, bill etc)* rejeter; *(person)* ne pas réélire

▸ **vote through vt sep** ratifier, approuver, accepter

vote-buying N achat *m* de voix *ou* de votes

vote-catcher N politique *f* électoraliste; **the government believes its new policy will be a v.** le gouvernement pense que sa nouvelle politique va lui rapporter des voix

vote-loser N = politique *f* peu populaire qui risque de faire perdre des voix; **his proposal to raise income tax is certain to be a v.** sa proposition d'augmenter l'impôt sur le revenu va très certainement lui faire perdre des voix

voter ['vəʊtər] N électeur, -trice, mandant,

-ante; **the voters** l'électorat *m*; **French voters go to the polls tomorrow** les Français vont aux urnes demain

▸▸ **v. apathy** apathie *f* électorale *ou* des électeurs; **v. registration** inscription *f* sur les listes électorales; **v. turnout** *(at election)* taux *m* de participation électorale

vote-selling N vente *f* de voix *ou* de votes

vote-trading N échange *m* de voix *ou* de votes

vote-winner N = politique *f* populaire permettant de remporter une victoire électorale; **Labour believes its plans to cut taxes were a v. at last year's elections** le Parti travailliste pense que c'est son intention de réduire les impôts qui lui a valu la victoire aux élections de l'année dernière

voting ['vəʊtɪŋ] ADJ *(assembly, member)* votant

N vote *m*; scrutin *m*; **result of the v.** résultat *m* du vote *ou* scrutin

▸▸ **v. behaviour** comportement *m* électoral; **v. booth** isoloir *m*; *Am* **v. machine** machine *f* pour enregistrer les votes; **v. method** méthode *f* électorale; **v. paper** bulletin *m* de vote; *Fin* **v. rights** droits *mpl* de vote; **v. shares** actions *fpl* donnant droit au vote

votive ['vəʊtɪv] ADJ votif

▸▸ **v. offering** ex-voto *m inv*

vouch [vaʊtʃ] **vi** **to v. for the truth of sth** témoigner de *ou* répondre de *ou* attester la vérité de qch; **to v. for sb** répondre de qn, se porter garant de qn; **I can v. for his honesty** je peux me porter garant de son honnêteté; **I can v. for the severity of the side effects** je peux témoigner de la sévérité des effets secondaires

voucher ['vaʊtʃər] N **1** *(receipt as proof of transaction)* pièce *f* justificative; *Com* pièce comptable **2** *(giving price reduction)* coupon *m*; *(to exchange for goods, service etc)* bon *m*; *(gift)* bon-cadeau *m*, *pl* bons-cadeaux; **luncheon v.** chèque-repas *m*, *pl* chèques-repas, chèque-restaurant *m*, *pl* chèques-restaurant

vouchsafe [vaʊtʃ'seɪf] **vt** *Fml* **to v. sb sth** accorder *ou* octroyer qch à qn; **to v. to do sth** *(condescend)* daigner faire qch

vow [vaʊ] N vœu *m*, serment *m*; **to take one's vows** prononcer *ou* faire ses vœux; **to make a v.** faire un vœu (**to do** de faire); **to take a v. of poverty** faire vœu de pauvreté; **to take a v. of silence** *(of monk etc)* faire vœu de silence; *(refuse to talk about sth)* promettre de ne rien dire; **to break a v.** rompre *ou* transgresser un vœu, rompre un serment; **to keep a v.** respecter un serment

vt vouer, jurer; **to v. obedience** jurer obéissance; **to v. revenge on sb** faire vœu de se venger sur qn; **to v. to do sth** faire vœu *ou* jurer de faire qch

vowel ['vaʊəl] N *Ling* voyelle *f*

▸▸ **v. shift** mutation *f* vocalique; **v. sound** son *m* vocalique

vox pop [vɒks] N forum *m* populaire; *(street interview)* micro-trottoir *m*, *pl* micros-trottoirs

voyage ['vɔɪɪdʒ] N traversée *f*; **a transatlantic v.** un voyage ou une traversée transatlantique; **to go on a v.** partir en voyage; **a round-the-world v.** un voyage autour du monde; **a v. to Jupiter** un voyage vers Jupiter **vi** *Lit* voyager; **to v. across the ocean/the desert** traverser l'océan/le désert

voyager ['vɔɪɪdʒər] N *Lit* voyageur, -euse

voyeur [vwɑː'jɜːr] N voyeur, -euse

voyeurism [vwɑː'jɜːrɪz(ə)m] N voyeurisme *m*

voyeuristic [vwɑːjɜːˈrɪstɪk] ADJ **to take a v. pleasure in sth** prendre un plaisir de voyeur à qch; **it's just v.** ce n'est que du voyeurisme

VP [viːˈpiː] N *abbr* Vice-President

VR [viːˈɑːr] *Br* *(abbr* Victoria Regina*)* la reine Victoria

VRAM ['viːræm] N *Comput (abbr* volatile or video random access memory*)* VRAM *f*

VRML [viːɑːremˈel] N *Comput (abbr* virtual reality modelling language*)* VRML *m*

vs *(abbr* versus*)* contre

V-shaped ADJ en V

V-sign N **to give the V.** *(for victory, approval)* faire le V de la victoire; *Br* **to give sb the V.** *(as insult)* ≃ faire un bras d'honneur à qn

VSO [viːesˈəʊ] N *Br abbr* Voluntary Service Overseas

VT [viːˈtiː] N *(abbr* videotape*)* bande *f* vidéo; **VT editing** montage *m* vidéo

Vt *abbr* Vermont

VTOL [viːtiːəʊˈel] N *(abbr* vertical take-off and landing*)* *(aircraft)* ADAV *m*; *(system)* décollage *m* et atterrissage *m* verticaux

VTR [viːtiːˈɑːr] N *(abbr* videotape recorder*)* magnétoscope *m*

vulcanite ['vʌlkənaɪt] N ébonite *f*

vulcanization [vʌlkənaɪˈzeɪʃən] N *Ind* vulcanisation *f*

vulcanize ['vʌlkənaɪz] VT *Ind (rubber)* vulcaniser

vulgar ['vʌlgər] ADJ **1** *(coarse)* vulgaire; **don't be v.!** ne sois pas vulgaire!; **to make v. remarks** dire des vulgarités *fpl*; **to be v. in one's speech** s'exprimer vulgairement **2** *Fml (widespread)* vulgaire, commun; **the v. tongue** la langue commune, la langue vulgaire

▸▸ **v. fraction** fraction *f* ordinaire; **V. Latin** latin *m* vulgaire

vulgarian [vʌlˈgeərɪən] N *(coarse person)* personne *f* vulgaire

vulgarism ['vʌlgərɪz(ə)m] N vulgarisme *m*; *(swearword)* vulgarité *f*, grossièreté *f*

vulgarity [vʌlˈgærɪtɪ] N vulgarité *f*, grossièreté *f*

vulgarization [vʌlgəraɪˈzeɪʃən] N vulgarisation *f*

vulgarize ['vʌlgəraɪz] VT vulgariser; *Pej (one's style etc)* vulgariser, trivialiser

vulgarly ['vʌlgəlɪ] ADV *(coarsely)* vulgairement, grossièrement; *Fml (informally)* vulgairement

Vulgate ['vʌlgɪt, -eɪt] N *Rel* **the V.** la Vulgate

vulnerability [vʌln(ə)rəˈbɪlɪtɪ] N vulnérabilité *f*

vulnerable ['vʌln(ə)rəb(ə)l] ADJ vulnérable; **he's at a v. age** il est à un âge vulnérable; **v. to criticism** sensible à la critique; **that's her v. spot** c'est son point faible *ou* son talon d'Achille; **the v. spot in our defences** le point faible de nos défenses; **this left them v. on their eastern border** cela les a laissés dans une position vulnérable sur leur frontière est

vulture ['vʌltʃər] N vautour *m*; *Fig* vautour, rapace *m*

vulva ['vʌlvə] N *Anat* vulve *f*

vulvitis [vʌlˈvaɪtɪs] N *Med* vulvite *f*

VU meter [vjuː] N *TV* vu-mètre *m*, *pl* vu-mètres

vv *abbr* verses

vying *see* vie

W¹, w [ˈdʌb(ə)lju:] **N** *(letter)* W, w *m*; **two w's** deux w

W² 1 *Elec (abbr* **watt(s))** W **2** *(abbr* **west)** O.

W3 [dʌb(ə)lju:ˈθri:] **N** *Comput (abbr* **World Wide Web)** W3 *m*, le Web *m*

WAAF [wæf] **N** *Mil (abbr* **Women's Auxiliary Air Force)** = groupe *m* de femmes, auxiliaires de l'armée de l'air britannique durant la Seconde Guerre mondiale

wack [wæk] **ADJ** *Am Fam (worthless)* nul, *f* nulle; *(mad)* cinglé, dingue; *(stupid)* débile

wack-job **N** *Am Fam* cinglé, -ée, dingue *mf*

wacko [ˈwækəʊ] *Fam* **N** cinglé, -ée, dingue *mf*
ADJ cinglé, dingue

wacky [ˈwækɪ] **ADJ** *Fam (person, sense of humour)* farfelu; *(idea, film)* loufoque
▸▸ *Hum* **w. baccy** *(marijuana)* herbe *f*

wad [wɒd] **N 1** *(of cotton wool)* tampon *m*, bouchon *m*; *(of chewing gum)* boulette *f* **2** *(of bank notes)* liasse *f*, *(of forms, documents)* paquet *m*, pile *f*, tas *m*; *esp Am* **to shoot one's w.** *Fam (spend all one's money)* claquer tout son fric, *Vulg (ejaculate)* décharger, envoyer la sauce *ou* la purée **3** *Mil (for cartridge)* bourre *f*
VT **(-dd-) 1** *Sewing* ouater, capitonner **2** *(paper)* faire un tampon de; **she wadded (up) the money and stuffed it in her pocket** elle plia les billets et les fourra dans sa poche
▸ **wad up** **VT SEP** = **wad VT**

wadding [ˈwɒdɪŋ] **N** *(material for clothes)* ouate *f*

waddle [ˈwɒd(ə)l] **N** dandinement *m*; **to walk with a w.** *(of person)* marcher en se dandinant
VI se dandiner, marcher en se dandinant; **to w. along** avancer en se dandinant

wade [weɪd] **VI 1** *(in water)* **the only way to cross the river was by wading** la seule façon de traverser la rivière était à gué; **to w. across a stream** passer un cours d'eau à gué; **he waded out to the island** il est allé jusqu'à l'île à gué; **she waded into the river to rescue him** elle s'avança dans la rivière pour le sauver **2** *esp Am (paddle)* patauger dans l'eau
VT *(stream)* passer à gué
▸ **wade in** **VI 1** *(go into water)* entrer dans l'eau **2** *Fig (to work, task)* s'y mettre; **when the fight started, everybody waded in** quand la bagarre a commencé tout le monde s'en est mêlé; **he always has to w. in with his opinion** il faut toujours qu'il donne son avis; **it would have been much better if you had let them sort it out themselves instead of wading in** tu aurais mieux fait de les laisser se débrouiller entre eux plutôt que de t'y mettre aussi
▸ **wade into** **VT INSEP** *Fig (attack) (person)* s'attaquer à, s'en prendre à; *(task)* s'attaquer à, se mettre à; **to w. into sb with one's fists** attaquer qn à coups de poings; **when Anne insulted him, he waded into her** quand Anne l'a insulté, il lui a dit ses quatre vérités; **critics have waded into his latest film** la critique a démoli son dernier film
▸ **wade through** **VT INSEP** **to w. through mud** avancer *ou* marcher péniblement dans la boue; **to w. through piles of dirty clothing** *(walk through them)* se tailler un chemin à travers les piles de linge sale; *Fam (wash them)* venir à bout de piles de linge sale; *Fam* **I'm wading through his latest novel** j'avance péniblement dans son dernier roman; *Fam* **we spent two hours wading through the agenda** il nous a fallu deux heures pour venir à bout de l'ordre du jour

wader [ˈweɪdər] **N 1** *(bird)* échassier *m* **2 waders** *(boots)* cuissardes *fpl*, bottes *fpl* de pêcheur

wadi [ˈwɒdɪ] **N** *Geog* oued *m*

wading [ˈweɪdɪŋ] **N** *(in water)* marche *f* dans l'eau
▸▸ **w. bird** échassier *m*; *Am* **w. pool** *(in swimming pool)* petit bassin *m*; *(inflatable)* piscine *f* gonflable

wafer [ˈweɪfər] **N 1** *Culin* gaufrette *f*, *Rel* hostie *f* **2** *Electron (of silicon)* tranche *f*

wafer-thin **ADJ** *(slice)* mince comme du papier à cigarette *ou* comme une pelure d'oignon; *Fig (majority)* infime; **to cut sth w.** couper qch en tranches très fines

waffle¹ [ˈwɒf(ə)l] **N** *Culin* gaufre *f*
▸▸ **w. iron** gaufrier *m*

waffle² *Br Fam* **N** *(wordiness)* verbiage *m*; **a load of (pretentious) w.** beaucoup de blabla (prétentieux); **her speech was just the usual w.** son discours n'était que du verbiage, comme d'habitude
VI parler pour ne rien dire; *(in writing)* faire du remplissage; **what did you say to that? – I just waffled** qu'est-ce que tu as répondu à ça? – j'ai baratiné; **you won't get away with waffling in this interview** tu ne pourras pas te tirer de cet entretien en faisant du baratin *ou* en parlant dans le vague; **he just waffles on** (il n'a rien à dire mais) il ne sait pas s'arrêter

waft [wɑːft, wɒft] **N** *(of wind, perfume)* bouffée *f*
VT *(of wind)* **to w. a sound/a scent through the air** porter *ou* transporter un son/un parfum dans les airs; **the music was wafted in by the breeze** la musique se faisait entendre, transportée par la brise
VI *(of smell, sound)* être porté par le vent *ou* la brise; **the scent of roses wafted in through the window** le parfum des roses entrait par la fenêtre; **her voice wafted gently down the stairs** sa voix douce parvenait jusqu'en bas de l'escalier

wag¹ [wæg] **N** *(action)* agitation *f*; **with a w. of its tail** *(of dog)* en remuant *ou* en agitant la queue
VT **(-gg-) 1** *(finger)* agiter, remuer; **to w. its tail** *(of dog, bird)* remuer *ou* agiter la queue; **to w. one's finger at sb** menacer qn du doigt; **to w. one's head** hocher la tête **2** *Br Fam* **to w. it** *(play truant)* faire l'école buissonnière
VI s'agiter, se remuer; **its tail was wagging** *(of dog)* sa queue frétillait *ou* remuait; **tongues are wagging** les langues vont bon train *(about* sur, au sujet de); **tongues were wagging about her behaviour** son comportement faisait jaser *ou* parler les gens; **if you carry on like this tongues will begin to w.** si tu continues comme ça, les gens vont jaser; **to set (people's) tongues wagging** faire jaser les gens

wag² **N** *Fam (person)* plaisantin *m*, farceur, -euse; **what w. left this here?** qui est le petit malin qui a laissé ça ici?

wage [weɪdʒ] **N** *(pay)* **wage(s)** paie *f*, salaire *m*; *(of domestic servant)* gages *mpl*; **basic w.** salaire de base; **living w.** minimum vital; **that's not even a living w.** c'est un salaire avec lequel on ne peut même pas vivre; **to get one's weekly w.** recevoir son salaire *ou* sa paie de la semaine, *Fam* toucher sa semaine; **to earn good wages** être bien payé; *Bible* **the wages of sin is death** la mort est le prix du péché VOIR GRAMMAIRE A11
VT **to w. war** faire la guerre *(with, on, against* à); **to w. a campaign against smoking** mener une campagne anti-tabac; **to w. a campaign for peace/against homelessness** faire campagne pour la paix/pour les sans-abri
▸▸ **w. bargaining** négociations *fpl* salariales; **w. bill** masse *f* salariale, charges *fpl* salariales; **w. bracket** fourchette *f* de salaire; **w. ceiling** salaire plafonné; **w. claim** revendication *f* salariale; **w.-cost inflation** inflation *f* par les salaires; **w. cut** réduction *f* de salaire, réduction salariale; **w. deductions** retenues *fpl* salariales, retenues sur salaire; *Br* **w. differential** écart *m* salarial; **w. earner** salarié, -ée; **w. freeze** gel *m* ou blocage *m* des salaires; **w. increase** augmentation *f* de salaire; **w. inflation** inflation *f* des salaires; **wages ledger** grand livre *m* de paie, journal *m* de paie, journal des salaires; *Br* **w. packet** *(envelope)* paie en espèces; *(money)* paie, salaire; **wages policy** politique *f* des salaires; **w. and price spiral** spirale *f* des prix et des salaires; **w. rise** augmentation de salaire; **wages sheet** bordereau *m* de salaires; *Fam* **w. slave** = personne *f* qui dépend entièrement de son salaire pour vivre

wager [ˈweɪdʒər] *Old-fashioned, Fml* **N** pari *m*; **to lay** *or* **make a w.** faire un pari, parier; **he did it for a w.** il l'a fait pour tenir un pari
VT *(sum of money)* parier; **to w. that ...** parier que ...; **to w. one's reputation** mettre sa réputation en jeu; **I'd w. my life on it** j'en mettrais ma main au feu

waggish [ˈwægɪʃ] **ADJ** *Old-fashioned Fam* facétieux, drôle; *(sense of humour)* blagueur

waggle ['wæg(ə)l] **VT & VI** remuer, bouger; **to w. one's eyebrows/ears** (faire) remuer ses sourcils/ses oreilles

Wag(g)on ['wægən] **N** *Astron* **the W.** la Grande Ourse

wag(g)on ['wægən] **N 1** *(horse-drawn)* chariot *m*; *Am (child's toy)* petit chariot **2** *(truck)* camionnette *f*, fourgon *m*; *Am* **(station) w. break** *m*; *Am* **(patrol) w.** voiture *f* cellulaire **3** *Br Rail* wagon *m* (de marchandises) **4** *Fig (idiom)* **to be on the w.** être au régime sec; **to fall off the w.** se remettre à boire

▸▸ **w. train** convoi *m* de chariots *(en particulier de colons américains)*

wag(g)oner ['wægənər] **N** roulier *m*, charretier *m*

wag(g)onette [wægə'net] **N** *(carriage)* break *m* attelé

wag(g)onload ['wægənləʊd] **N** *(of hay etc)* charretée *f*, *Rail* (charge *f* de) wagon *m*

Wagnerian [vɑːg'nɪərɪən] **ADJ, N** *Mus* wagnérien, -ienne

wagtail ['wægteɪl] **N** *(bird)* bergeronnette *f*, hochequeue *m*, lavandière *f*

wah-wah pedal ['wɑːwɑː] **N** *Mus* pédale *f* wah-wah *ou* wa-wa

waif [weɪf] **N** *(child)* enfant *mf* abandonné(e); *(animal)* animal *m* errant; **she looks like a w.** elle a l'air d'une petite malheureuse; **waifs and strays** miséreux *mpl*

waiflike ['weɪflaɪk] **ADJ** *(appearance)* maigrelet; **the w. look of some models** la maigreur famélique de certains mannequins

wail [weɪl] **N** cri *m* plaintif, plainte *f*, gémissement *m*; *(of newborn baby)* vagissement *m*; *(of siren etc)* hurlement *m*; **she heard a w. from upstairs, the baby had obviously woken up** elle entendit des pleurs venant d'en haut, manifestement, le bébé s'était réveillé; **a w. of complaint** un gémissement plaintif; **the child gave a w.** l'enfant se mit à hurler

VI gémir; *(of newborn child)* vagir; *(of siren)* hurler; **what's he wailing about now?** de quoi se plaint-il maintenant?; **to w. over sth** se lamenter sur qch, pleurer sur qch

wailing ['weɪlɪŋ] **ADJ** *(person)* gémissant; *(sound)* plaintif; **a w. saxophone** le son aigu d'un saxophone

N *(of person)* plaintes *fpl*, gémissements *mpl*; *(of wind)* gémissements, plainte *f*; *(of siren)* hurlement *m*, hurlements *mpl*

▸▸ **the W. Wall** le mur des Lamentations

wain [weɪn] **N** *Arch, Lit* charrette *f*; **hay w.** charrette à foin

wainscot ['weɪnskət] **N** lambris *m*, boiseries *fpl*

VT (**-t(t)-**) lambrisser

wainscot(t)ing ['weɪnskətɪŋ] **N 1** *(material)* lambris *m*, boiseries *fpl* **2** *(action)* lambrissage *m*

waist [weɪst] **N 1** *(of person, garment)* taille *f*, ceinture *f*; **down/up to the w.** jusqu'à la ceinture, jusqu'à mi-corps; **stripped to the w.** nu jusqu'à la ceinture, torse nu; **it's too tight at the w.** ça serre à la taille; **what w. are these trousers?** quel est le tour de taille de ce pantalon?; **to put one's arm round sb's w.** prendre qn par la taille **2** *(of violin)* partie *f* resserrée de la table; *(of pipe)* rétrécissement *m* **3** *Naut (of ship)* embelle *f*, passavant *m*

▸▸ **w. lock** *(in wrestling)* ceinture *f*, **w. measurement** tour *m* de taille

waistband ['weɪstbænd] **N** ceinture *f*

waistcoat ['weɪskəʊt] **N** *Br* gilet *m*

waist-deep **ADJ** *(water)* à hauteur de la taille; **the water was almost w.** l'eau arrivait à mi-corps; **to be w. in water** avoir de l'eau jusqu'à la taille *ou* jusqu'à mi-corps; *Fig* **I'm**

w. in work/files je croule sous le travail/les dossiers, je suis submergé de travail/dossiers

waisted ['weɪstɪd] **ADJ** *(coat, jacket)* cintré

waist-high **ADJ** *(grass)* à hauteur de la taille

waistline ['weɪstlaɪn] **N** *Sewing* taille *f*; **to watch one's** *or* **think of one's w.** surveiller sa ligne

WAIT [weɪt] **N 1** attente *f*; **it was quite a w.** il a fallu attendre très longtemps; **we had a long w.** nous avons dû attendre longtemps; **it was worth the w.** ça valait la peine d'attendre; **it will be a long w. before the next train** il va falloir attendre longtemps avant que le prochain train arrive; **to lie in w.** *(ambush)* se tenir en embuscade; **to lie in w. for sb** *(ambush)* attendre qn au passage; *(of military, police)* tendre un guet-apens à qn **2** *Br Old-fashioned* **waits** *(door-to-door carol singers)* chanteurs *mpl* de Noël

VI 1 attendre; **to w. for sb/sth** attendre qn/qch; **w. a moment/a minute/a bit** attendez un moment/un instant/un peu; **to w. for sth to be done** attendre que qch soit fait; **what are you waiting for?** qu'attendez-vous?; **we're waiting to be served** nous attendons qu'on nous serve *ou* qu'on s'occupe de nous; **to keep sb waiting** faire attendre qn; **w. until tomorrow** attendez jusqu'à demain; **I shall w. until she's ready** j'attendrai qu'elle soit prête; **(just) you w.!** *(threat)* attends un peu!, tu vas voir ce que tu vas voir!; **just w. till I tell you what's happened!** attends que je te dise ce qui s'est passé!; **w. for it!** *(not yet, guess what)* attends!; **I can't w. to … j'ai hâte de …; I can't w. to see him** je brûle d'impatience de le voir; **I can't w. for the weekend** vivement le weekend, j'ai hâte que le weekend arrive; **I can hardly w.** je meurs d'impatience; *Iron* n'attends que ça, je brûle d'impatience; *Com* **repairs while you w.** réparations minute; *Prov* **everything comes to him** *or* **to he who waits** tout vient à point à qui sait attendre; **we must w. and see** il faudra voir; **w. and see!** attends voir!; **w.-and-see policy** politique *f* attentiste, attentisme *m*; **a w.-and-see approach** une approche attentiste **2** **to w. at table** servir (à table), faire le service

VT *(opportunity, signal)* attendre, guetter; **w. your turn!** attendez votre tour!; **don't w. dinner for me** ne m'attendez pas pour vous mettre à table

▸▸ *Comput* **w. loop** boucle *f* d'attente; *Comput* **w. state** état *m* d'attente

▸ **wait about** **VI** attendre; **don't keep me waiting about** ne me fais pas attendre

▸ **wait behind** **VI** rester; **could you w. behind?, there's something I'd like to ask you** est-ce que vous pourriez attendre?, j'aimerais vous demander quelque chose

▸ **wait in** **VI** *(stay at home)* rester à la maison; **to w. in for sb** rester à la maison pour attendre qn

▸ **wait on** **VT INSEP** *(serve)* servir; *Am* **to w. on table** servir (à table), faire le service; **to w. on sb hand and foot** être aux petits soins pour qn

VI *(continue to wait)* continuer à attendre

▸ **wait out** **VT SEP** *(war, storm)* attendre la fin de; **to w. it out** patienter

▸ **wait up** **VI 1** *(not go to bed)* ne pas aller se coucher, veiller, rester debout; **she always waited up until her daughter was home** elle attendait toujours pour aller se coucher que sa fille rentre *ou* soit rentrée pour se coucher; **I'll w. up for you** j'attendrai que tu arrives *ou* rentres avant d'aller me coucher; **I'll be late so don't w. up for me** je rentrerai tard, couche-toi sans m'attendre

2 *Am (halt)* attendre; **w. up, I can't walk as fast as you** attends-moi, je ne peux pas marcher aussi vite que toi

waiter ['weɪtər] **N** garçon *m* (de restaurant); **head w.** maître *m* d'hôtel; **w.!** s'il vous plaît, monsieur!

▸▸ **w. service** service *m* à table

waiting ['weɪtɪŋ] **N 1** attente *f*; **it's all the w. (that) I can't stand** ce que je ne supporte pas, c'est d'avoir à attendre tout le temps; *Aut* **no w.** stationnement interdit **2 w. at table** service *m* (à table)

ADJ *(person, taxi)* qui attend; **to play a w. game** *Mil, Pol* mener une politique d'attentisme; *Fig* jouer la montre, attendre son heure

▸▸ **w. chef** chef *m* serveur; **w. list** liste *f* d'attente; **there's a two-month w. list for an operation** il faut attendre deux mois pour une opération; **w. period** période *f* d'attente; **w. room** *(in office, surgery, airport, station)* salle *f* d'attente

waitlist ['weɪtlɪst] **VT** *Am* mettre sur la liste d'attente; **I'm waitlisted for the next flight** je suis sur la liste d'attente pour le prochain vol

waitperson ['weɪtpɜːs(ə)n] **N** *Am (male)* garçon *m*, serveur *m*; *(female)* serveuse *f*

waitress ['weɪtrɪs] **N** serveuse *f*; **w.!** s'il vous plaît, mademoiselle!

▸▸ **w. service** service *m* à table

waive [weɪv] **VT** *(one's claims, rights)* renoncer à, abandonner; *(principle)* déroger à; *(condition, rule)* ne pas insister sur; **on this occasion, I think we can w. the rules** pour cette fois, je crois que nous pouvons nous permettre d'ignorer le règlement

> Attention: ne pas confondre avec **to wave**.

waiver ['weɪvər] **N** *Law* **w. of a right** renonciation *f* à un droit; **w. of a claim** désistement *m* de revendication

wake¹ [weɪk] **N** *Naut* sillage *m*; *Fig* **in the w. of sth** à la suite de qch; **in the w. of the storm** à la suite de la tempête; **the war brought famine in its w.** la guerre a amené la famine dans son sillage; *Fig* **to follow in sb's w.** marcher sur les traces *ou* dans le sillage de qn; **Steven followed in his father's w. and became a lawyer** Steven a suivi l'exemple de son père et est devenu avocat; **since then many other countries have followed in our w.** depuis lors bon nombre d'autres pays nous ont suivis; **he left the other athletes trailing in his w.** il a laissé les autres athlètes à la traîne *ou* loin derrière lui

wake² **N** *(vigil over body)* veillée *f* de corps; **to have a w. for sb** organiser une veillée de commémoration en souvenir de qn; *Fig* **it is too soon to hold a w. for the ideal of European unity** il est encore trop tôt pour enterrer l'idéal de l'unité européenne

wake³ *(pt* **woke** [wəʊk], **waked** [weɪkt]; *pp* **woke, waked, woken** ['wəʊk(ə)n]) **VI** se réveiller; **to w. with a start** se réveiller en sursaut

VT *(person)* réveiller; *(from inaction)* tirer de sa torpeur; *(emotion, memory)* éveiller, ranimer; **w. me at six** réveillez-moi à six heures; **to be hard to w.** avoir le sommeil lourd; **to make enough noise to w. the dead** faire un bruit à réveiller les morts

▸ **wake up** **VI 1** *(from sleep)* se réveiller; **come on, w. up!** allons, réveillez-vous!; *(be more alert)* remuez-vous!, secouez-vous! **2** *Fig (become aware)* prendre conscience; **it took him a while to w. up to what was going on** il lui fallut un certain temps pour comprendre *ou* réaliser ce qui se passait; **she's gradually waking up to the truth** elle commence à voir les choses telles qu'elles sont; **come on, w. up!** enfin, ouvre les yeux!

VT SEP *(person) (from sleep)* réveiller; *(from inaction)* tirer de sa torpeur, secouer; *Fig* **this**

country needs **waking up** ce pays a besoin de se réveiller; *Fig* that woke her up to what was going on ça lui a ouvert les yeux sur ce qui se passait

wakeboard ['weɪkbɔːd] N monoski *m* nautique

wakeboarding ['weɪkbɔːdɪŋ] N monoski *m* nautique

wakeful ['weɪkfʊl] ADJ 1 *(not sleepy) (person)* éveillé, peu disposé à dormir; **to have a w. night** passer une nuit blanche 2 *(vigilant)* vigilant

wakefulness ['weɪkfʊlnɪs] N 1 *(insomnia)* insomnie f 2 *(vigilance)* vigilance f

waken ['weɪk(ə)n] VT 1 éveiller, réveiller; **noise fit to w. the dead** bruit à réveiller les morts 2 *(emotion)* réveiller, ranimer
▪ VI *esp Lit* se réveiller, s'éveiller

wake-up ADJ
▸▸ **w. call** réveil *m* téléphonique; **to ask for a w. call** *(in hotel etc)* demander à être réveillé par téléphone

wakey-wakey ['weɪkɪ'weɪkɪ] INT *Fam* debout!, réveillez-vous!

waking ['weɪkɪŋ] N between sleeping and **w.** entre la veille et le sommeil; **w. hours** heures *fpl* de veille; **to spend (all) one's w. hours doing sth** passer tout son temps à faire qch

wale [weɪl] N *Fml (of whiplash)* marque f, trace f, zébrure f

Wales [weɪlz] N pays *m* de Galles; **New South W.** *(in Australia)* la Nouvelle-Galles du Sud

WALK [wɔːk]

N	marche **1** ▪ promenade **2, 5**
	▪ démarche **3**
VI	marcher **1** ▪ aller à pied **2** ▪ se
	promener **2**
VT	accompagner **2** ▪ promener **3**
	▪ faire marcher **3**

N 1 *(action)* marche f; **it's half an hour's w. from here** c'est à une demi-heure d'ici à pied *ou* une demi-heure de marche d'ici; **it's only a short w. (from here)** c'est à deux pas (d'ici) **2** *(stroll)* promenade f (à pied), tour *m*; **to go for a w.** (aller) se promener, faire un tour *ou* une promenade; **it's a lovely w. from here to the village** c'est une promenade très agréable d'ici jusqu'au village; **to take sb for a w.** emmener qn en promenade *ou* se promener; **to take the dog for a w.** sortir *ou* promener le chien; *Fam* **take a w.!** *(get lost!)* va te faire voir!, disparais!; *Fam* **it was a w. in the park** *(very easy)* c'était un jeu d'enfant **3** *(gait)* façon f de marcher, démarche f, allure f; **I know him by his w.** je le reconnais à sa démarche **4** *(speed)* **to go** *or* **move at a w.** aller *ou* avancer au pas; **to drop into a w.** *(of horse)* se mettre au pas; *(of person) (after running)* se remettre à marcher **5** *(path)* avenue f, promenade f; *(in garden)* allée f, **covered w.** allée couverte; *Archit* péristyle *m*, ambulatoire *m* **6** *Am (sidewalk)* trottoir *m*; *Am* **cross w.** passage *m* clouté (pour piétons) **7** *Fig* **w. of life** *(social class)* milieu *m*; **people from all walks of life** des gens de tous milieux

VI 1 *(move on foot)* marcher; **to w. on** *or* **in the road** marcher sur la chaussée; **to w. two paces forward** faire deux pas en avant; **to w. on all fours** marcher à quatre pattes; **is the baby walking yet?** est-ce que le bébé marche maintenant?; **to w. in one's sleep** *(be a sleepwalker)* être somnambule; **I'll w. a little way with you** je vais vous accompagner un bout de chemin; **I can't w. another step** je ne peux pas faire un pas de plus; **to w. with a**

limp boiter (en marchant); **he walks five kilometres every day** il fait cinq kilomètres à pied tous les jours; *Am* **w./don't w.** *(traffic sign)* (piétons) passez/attendez; **to w. up/down the street/the stairs** monter/descendre la rue/l'escalier; **to w. up and down** *(pace the floor)* se promener de long en large, faire les cent pas; **to w. up to sb** s'approcher de qn; **please w. in** entrez sans frapper; **to w. through the town/the crowd** traverser la ville/la foule (à pied); *Fig* **you have to w. before you can run** chaque chose en son temps; *Fig* **to w. on water** marcher sur l'eau; **as far as the party faithful are concerned, he can w. on water** aux yeux des fidèles du parti, il est capable de miracles; *Fig* **to be walking on air** être aux anges **2** *(as opposed to riding, driving etc)* aller à pied; *(for exercise, pleasure)* se promener (à pied); **to w. home/back** rentrer/retourner à pied; **I missed the bus so I had to w.** j'ai raté le bus donc j'ai dû marcher; **w.!** *(don't run)* ne cours pas! **3** *(of horse, rider)* aller au pas **4** *(of ghost)* revenir **5** *Fam (disappear, be stolen) (of money, object)* disparaître; *(disappear) (of suspected criminal)* partir; **the money seems to have walked** l'argent semble s'être envolé
VT 1 *(move along)* **to w. the streets** *(wander)* courir les rues, battre le pavé; *(of prostitute)* faire le trottoir; **to w. one's beat** *or* **one's round** *(of policeman)* faire sa ronde; *Theat* **to w. the boards** être sur les planches; *Naut* **to w. the plank** subir le supplice de la planche; *Fam* **to w. it** gagner les doigts dans le nez **2** *(accompany)* **to w. sb home** raccompagner qn; **to w. sb to the bus stop** accompagner qn jusqu'à l'arrêt de bus; **he walked me halfway home** il m'a accompagné à pied jusqu'à mi-chemin **3** *(make move)* **John walked me off my feet in London** John m'a fait marcher pendant des kilomètres à Londres; **to w. a horse** *(lead along)* conduire *ou* promener un cheval (au pas); *(bring to a walk)* mettre un cheval au pas; **to w. the dog** promener *ou* sortir le chien; **the physio walked him up and down** le kiné l'aidait à faire quelques pas

▸ **walk away** VI s'en aller, partir; *Fig* **to w. away from trouble/a problem** éviter une situation difficile/un problème; *Fig* **to w. away from a situation** se distancier d'une situation; *Fig* **just w. away from it!** laisse tomber!; **you can't just w. away from it** tu ne peux pas te dérober comme ça

▸ **walk away with** VT INSEP *Fam* **1** *(take)* prendre; **I walked away with an antique dressing table for just thirty pounds** j'ai réussi à avoir une coiffeuse ancienne pour seulement trente livres; **he walked away with a small fine** il s'en est tiré avec une petite amende **2** *(steal)* faucher **3** *(win easily) (prize, nomination)* remporter haut la main

▸ **walk in on** VT INSEP *(disturb)* déranger; **she walked in on them having sex** elle est entrée sans prévenir et les a trouvés en train de faire l'amour

▸ **walk into** VT INSEP **1** *(enter) (room)* entrer dans; **to w. straight into a job** *(after leaving school etc)* trouver *ou* obtenir facilement un emploi **2** *(collide with) (person, thing)* rentrer dans; **he walked right into me/it** il m'est rentré en plein dedans/il est rentré en plein dedans

▸ **walk off** VI s'en aller, partir
VT SEP **to w. off one's lunch** faire une promenade pour digérer

▸ **walk off with** VT INSEP *Fam* = **walk away with**

▸ **walk on** VI **1** *(continue walking)* continuer à marcher **2** *Theat (have minor stage part)* figurer, faire *ou* remplir un rôle de figurant

▸ **walk out** VI sortir (**in a rage** en colère); *(go on strike)* débrayer, se mettre en grève; **you can't just w. out as soon as things get a bit difficult** tu ne peux pas disparaître *ou* tout laisser tomber dès que les choses deviennent un peu difficiles; **to w. out on one's commitments** laisser tomber ses engagements, ne pas tenir ses engagements; **the delegates walked out of the meeting** les délégués ont quitté la réunion (en signe de protestation); *Fam* **to w. out on sb** *(desert)* abandonner qn, plaquer qn; *(leave in anger)* quitter qn en colère, partir en claquant la porte

▸ **walk over** VT INSEP **1** *Fam (treat badly)* **to w. all over sb** marcher sur les pieds de qn; **you shouldn't let him/her/people w. all over you** tu ne devrais pas te laisser marcher sur les pieds **2** *Sport* **to w. over the course** inspecter le terrain (avant l'épreuve)

▸ **walk round** VT INSEP *(museum, shops etc)* faire le tour de

▸ **walk through** VT INSEP *(one's exams etc)* réussir sans effort, *Fam* réussir les doigts dans le nez

walkabout ['wɔːkəbaʊt] N *(of aborigines)* voyage *m* dans le désert; *Fig (of politician, celebrity)* bain *m* de foule; **to go w.** *(of aborigines)* aller faire un voyage dans le désert; *Fig Fam (disappear, be stolen) (of missing object, money etc)* disparaître, s'envoler; *Fig* **to go (on a) w.** *(of politician, celebrity)* prendre un bain de foule

walkaway ['wɔːkəweɪ] N *Am Sport, Fam* victoire f facile

'walk' button N *Comput* case f 'marche'

walker ['wɔːkər] N **1** *(person), Sport* marcheur, -euse; *(for leisure)* promeneur, -euse; **I'm not much of a w.** je ne suis pas un grand marcheur; **he's a fast/slow w.** il marche vite/lentement **2** *(aid) (for infirm person)* déambulateur *m*; *(for baby)* trotte-bébé *m*, *pl* trotte-bébés, youpala *m*

walkie-talkie [wɔːkɪ'tɔːkɪ] N *Radio* talkie-walkie *m*, *pl* talkies-walkies

walk-in ADJ *(safe, wardrobe)* de plain pied; **the flat is in w. condition** l'appartement est libre d'occupation
N *(customer in hotel)* client, -ente sans réservation; *esp Am (patient)* patient, -ente sans rendez-vous
▸▸ **w. cupboard** débarras *m*; *(for clothes)* dressing *m*; **w. fridge** armoire f réfrigérante

walking ['wɔːkɪŋ] ADJ *(clothes, shoes)* de marche; **at a w. pace** au pas; **to slow (down) to a w. pace** *(after running)* se remettre à marcher; **it's within w. distance** on peut aisément s'y rendre à pied; **it's not within w. distance** on ne peut pas s'y rendre à pied; **it's ten minutes' w. distance** c'est à dix minutes à pied; **a w. holiday in the Vosges** un séjour de randonnée dans les Vosges; **we went on a w. tour of the Alps** nous avons fait de la randonnée dans les Alpes; **that man's a w. disaster area!** ce type est une catastrophe ambulante!; **she's a w. dictionary/encyclopedia** c'est un dictionnaire/une encyclopédie ambulant(e); *Am Fam* **to give sb their w. orders** *or* **papers** *(employee)* mettre *ou* flanquer qn à la porte, renvoyer qn; *(lover etc)* plaquer qn
N marche f (à pied), promenade f, promenades fpl; *(hiking)* randonnée f, *Sport* marche (athlétique); **w. is the best form of exercise** la marche est le meilleur des exercices; **two hours' w.** deux heures de marche *ou* de promenade; **I like w.** j'aime bien marcher

▸▸**w. frame** déambulateur *m*; **w. race** épreuve *f* de marche; **w. shoes** chaussures *fpl* de marche; **w. stick** canne *f*, *Mil* **w. wounded** blessés *mpl* en état de marcher

walking-out dress N *Mil* tenue *f* de ville

Walkman® ['wɔːkmən] N *(personal stereo)* Walkman® *m*, baladeur *m*

walk-on N *Theat (part)* rôle *m* de figurant ADJ *Aviat etc (flight, service)* = pour lequel il n'est pas nécessaire d'effectuer de réservation
▸▸*Theat* **w. part** rôle de figurant

walkout ['wɔːkaʊt] N *(going on strike)* débrayage *m*, mise *f* en grève; *(from meeting)* départ *m* (en signe de protestation); **to cause a w.** *(at meeting etc)* provoquer le départ d'un groupe *ou* d'une faction (en signe de protestation); **they staged a w. when their demands were refused** *(went on strike)* ils se sont mis en grève quand leurs revendications ont été refusées

walkover ['wɔːkəʊvər] N *Sport, Fam* victoire *f* facile; **it was a w.!** c'était facile *ou Fam* fastoche!

walk-through N *Theat* répétition *f* (technique)

walk-up N *(apartment)* = appartement *m ou* bureau *m* situé dans un immeuble sans ascenseur; *(building)* = immeuble *m* sans ascenseur; **they live in a third-floor w.** ils habitent un troisième étage sans ascenseur ADJ *(apartment)* situé dans un immeuble sans ascenseur; *(building)* sans ascenseur

walkway ['wɔːkweɪ] N allée *f* (couverte), passage *m* (couvert); **(moving) w.** tapis *m* roulant

wall [wɔːl] N **1** *(of house etc)* mur *m*; *(of town, city)* murs *mpl* (d'enceinte), remparts *mpl*; *(for fortification)* muraille *f*; *(of blood cell, abdomen, cave, tunnel etc)* paroi *f*; **to live outside the city walls** vivre à l'extérieur des remparts; **only the rich lived within the walls of the city** seuls les riches vivaient intra-muros; **to leave only the four walls standing** ne laisser que les quatre murs; **between these four walls** entre ces quatre murs; **what I say now must not go beyond these four walls** ce que je vais vous dire maintenant ne doit pas sortir d'ici; **the Great W. of China** la grande muraille de Chine **2** *(of tyre)* flanc *m* **3** *Fig (of ice)* muraille *f*, *(of fire)* rideau *m*, mur *m*; *(of silence)* mur; *(of policemen)* barrage *m*; **a w. of flame** un rideau de flammes; **to break down a w. of silence** abattre un mur de silence; **to come up against a blank** *or* **brick w.** se heurter à un mur; **to have one's back to the w.** avoir le dos au mur, être dans une situation désespérée; **to drive** *or* **push sb to the w.** acculer qn, mettre qn au pied du mur; **to go to the w.** *(go bankrupt)* faire faillite; **the weakest always go(es) to the w.** le plus faible est toujours battu; **to bang** *or* **beat one's head against a (brick) w.** se cogner la tête contre les murs; *Fam* **you might as well talk to a brick w.** autant parler à un mur; *Fam* **to drive** *or* **send sb up the w.** rendre qn dingue; **people like him should be put (up) against the w. (and shot)** les gens comme lui méritent la peine de mort
VT murer, entourer de murs
▸▸**w. bars** espalier *m* (pour exercices); **w. bracket** support *m* mural; **w. clock** pendule *f* murale; **w. cupboard** placard *m* mural; **w. lamp** applique *f* murale, lampe *f* murale; **w. map** carte *f* murale; **w. painting** peinture *f* murale; **W. Street** Wall Street
▸ **wall in** VT SEP murer, entourer de murs; **the park was walled in on all four sides by giant buildings** le parc était bordé sur les quatre côtés par des immeubles gigantesques; **he felt walled in by the surrounding moun-**

tains il se sentait prisonnier des montagnes qui l'entouraient
▸ **wall off** VT SEP séparer par un mur; **part of the garden was walled off from the rest** une partie du jardin était isolée du reste par un mur
▸ **wall up** VT SEP *(window, door)* murer, condamner; *Hist (prisoner)* emmurer

wallaby ['wɒləbɪ] N *(animal)* wallaby *m*

wallah ['wɒlə] N *(in India)* employé *m*, garçon *m*; *Fam* **tea w.** préposé *m* au thé; **punkah-w.** tireur *m* de panka

wallchart ['wɔːltʃɑːt] N affiche *f*, panneau *m* mural

wallcovering ['wɔːlkʌvərɪŋ] N tapisserie *f*, revêtement *m* mural

walled [wɔːld] ADJ *(garden)* clos
▸▸**w. city** ville *f* fortifiée

wallet ['wɒlɪt] N portefeuille *m*

wall-eyed ADJ *(person, fish) (with large amount of white showing)* aux yeux globuleux; *(person) (with squint)* à strabisme divergent

wallflower ['wɔːlflaʊər] N *(plant)* giroflée *f* jaune; *Fig* **to be a w.** *(at a dance)* faire tapisserie

walling up ['wɔːlɪŋ] N *(of window)* murage *m*

wall-mounted ADJ *(clock, telephone)* mural, -aux

Walloon [wɒ'luːn] ADJ wallon
N **1** Wallon, -onne **2** *Ling* wallon *m*

wallop ['wɒləp] N **1** *Fam (blow)* gros coup *m*; *(spanking)* fessée *f*; **I'll give you a w. in a minute** je vais te coller une beigne dans une minute; **she gave him a real w. across the face** elle lui a flanqué une sacrée beigne; **give it a w. with the hammer** mets-y un coup de marteau; **to pack quite a w.** *(of boxer etc)* frapper dur; *(of drink)* être fort, arracher **2** *Br Sl (beer)* bière *f*
VT *Fam (person) (one blow)* filer un gnon à; *(several blows)* battre, flanquer une raclée à; *Sport (defeat)* battre à plate(s) couture(s); **to w. the ball** *(with bat, hand)* frapper dans la balle; **she walloped him over the head with the rolling pin** elle lui donna un grand coup sur la tête avec le rouleau à pâtisserie; **w. it with the hammer** tape dessus à coup(s) de marteau; **and w.! it crashed to the ground!** et paf! il est tombé par terre!

walloping ['wɒləpɪŋ] *Fam* ADJ énorme; **a w. great lie** un gros *ou* énorme mensonge
N rossée *f*; **to give sb a w.** rosser qn; *Sport* battre qn à plate(s) couture(s); **he got a w. from his mother** il s'est fait coller une raclée par sa mère; *Sport* **we gave them a w. they'll never forget** on leur a flanqué une pâtée qu'ils ne sont pas près d'oublier

wallow ['wɒləʊ] N *(pool etc)* trou *m* bourbeux, mare *f* bourbeuse; **there's nothing like a w. in a warm bath to unwind** rien de tel qu'un bon bain pour se détendre; **to have a w. in the mud** se vautrer dans la boue; **we all enjoy a good w. in nostalgia** tout le monde aime se laisser aller à la nostalgie de temps en temps
VI *(of animal)* se vautrer; *(of ship)* être ballotté (par les flots); **to w. in self-pity** s'apitoyer sur son propre sort; **to w. in a bath** se prélasser dans un bain; **to be wallowing in luxury** baigner dans le luxe; **to w. in sin/nostalgia** se complaire dans le péché/la nostalgie

wallpaper ['wɔːlpeɪpər] N *also Comput* papier *m* peint
VT *(room)* tapisser
▸▸**w. paste** colle *f* badigeon

wallpapering ['wɔːlpeɪpərɪŋ] N **w. is easy** poser le papier peint est facile
▸▸**w. brush** *(for applying paste)* pinceau *m*

à encoller le papier peint; *(for smoothing paper)* balai *m* de colleur

wall-to-wall ADJ *(widespread, complete)* **the room was w. with people** la pièce était bondée; *Fig* **w. coverage** *(of event)* couverture *f* complète; **the sort of party where you get w. trendies** le genre de soirée bourrée de gens branchés
▸▸**w. carpet** moquette *f*, **w. carpeting** moquette *f*, **all the rooms have w. carpeting** toutes les pièces ont de la moquette

wally ['wɒlɪ] N *Br Fam (idiot)* andouille *f*, imbécile *mf*, **I felt a bit of a w.** je me suis senti un peu idiot; **he looked a real** *or* **right w.** il avait vraiment l'air d'un imbécile

walnut ['wɔːlnʌt] N **1** *(fruit)* noix *f*, **w. cake** gâteau *m* aux noix; **w. stain** brou *m* de noix **2** *(tree, wood)* noyer *m*; **w. desk** bureau *m* en noyer
▸▸**w. oil** huile *f* de noix; **w. tree** noyer

walrus ['wɔːlrəs] N *(animal)* morse *m*; **w. moustache** moustache *f* à la gauloise

Walter Mitty [wɔːltə'mɪtɪ] ADJ **to be a W. character, to live in a W. world** vivre dans un monde imaginaire

waltz [wɔːls] N valse *f*; **to play a w.** jouer une valse; **to dance a w.** danser une valse, valser; **may I have this w.?** voulez-vous danser cette valse avec moi?
VI valser; **to w. with sb** faire valser qn; *Fig* **to w. into a room** faire irruption dans une pièce; **she waltzed through the interview** elle a passé son entretien brillamment *ou Fam* les doigts dans le nez
▸ **waltz off** VI *Fam (leave)* partir, s'en aller; **to w. off with first prize** remporter le premier prix haut la main

waltzer ['wɔːlsər] N *(dancer)* valseur, -euse

wampum ['wɒmpəm] N **1** *(beads)* wampum *m (ceintures faites de coquillages servant de monnaie à certaines tribus indiennes en Amérique du Nord)* **2** *Am Fam (money)* pognon *m*, fric *m*

WAN [wæn] N *Comput (abbr wide area network)* réseau *m* longue distance

wan [wɒn] ADJ *Lit (person) (pale)* pâle, blême, blafard; *(sad)* triste; *(smile)* pâle, faible; *(light, star)* pâle

wand [wɒnd] N **1** *(magic)* baguette *f* **2** *(for bar codes)* lecteur *m* de codes barres

wander ['wɒndər] N balade *f*, **to go for a w. in the woods** aller se promener dans les bois, faire une balade dans les bois
VI **1** *(roam, stray)* errer, se promener au hasard; **we weren't allowed to w. too far from the path** nous n'avions pas le droit de nous aventurer trop loin du chemin; **don't w. too far, the bus will be here in ten minutes** ne t'éloigne pas trop, le bus sera là dans dix minutes; **they were allowed to w. wherever they wanted** ils avaient le droit d'aller là où ils voulaient; **they wandered round the town, soaking up the atmosphere** ils flânèrent dans la ville, s'imprégnant de l'atmosphère; **to w. about the house** errer dans la maison; **to w. (about) aimlessly** errer sans but; **to w. about the world** rouler sa bosse (un peu partout); **his eyes wandered over the scene** ses regards se promenaient sur cette scène **2** *(verbally)* radoter; **to w. (in one's mind)** divaguer; **to w. from the subject** sortir du sujet, digresser; **my thoughts were wandering** j'avais l'esprit ailleurs, j'étais ailleurs; **to let one's thoughts w.** laisser vaguer ses pensées; **his mind wanders at times** *or* **is apt to w.** il a des absences **3** *Fam (go)* **I think I'll be wandering off now** je crois que je vais y aller *ou* me mettre en route maintenant; **I'll just w. down to the beach later** j'irai faire un tour *ou* je descen-

drai à la plage plus tard; **could you w. round to the post office for me?** pourriez-vous passer à la poste pour moi?; **he just wandered in to the office at about 10.30** il est tranquillement arrivé au bureau à 10h30; **shall we start wandering back then?** alors, on prend doucement le chemin du retour?

VT to **w. the streets** traîner dans les rues; **to w. the world** courir le monde; **to w. the hills** se balader dans les collines

wanderer ['wɒndərər] N vagabond, -onde; **the w. returns!** voilà un revenant!

wandering ['wɒndərɪŋ] ADJ **1** (person) errant, vagabond; (tribe) nomade **2** (distracted) (mind, thoughts, attention) distrait, vagabond **3** (confused) (mind, person) qui divague, qui délire; (thoughts) incohérent

▸▸ *Fam* **w. hands** mains fpl baladeuses; **the W. Jew** le Juif errant; **w. minstrels** ménestrels mpl

wanderings ['wɒndərɪŋz] NPL **1** (roaming) pérégrinations fpl **2** (mental) **in his w.** dans ses divagations

wanderlust ['wɒndəlʌst] N désir m de voyager, passion f des voyages

wane [weɪn] N **to be on the w.** (of moon) décroître; (of person, civilization) être à ou sur son déclin; (of popularity, enthusiasm) diminuer; (of beauty) être sur le retour; (of career) être sur la pente descendante, décliner; *Fig* **his star is on the w.** son étoile pâlit

VI (of moon) décroître, décliner; (of beauty) se faner; (of enthusiasm) s'affaiblir, s'attiédir; (of popularity, power, influence) diminuer; *Fig* **his star/his glory is waning** son étoile pâlit/sa gloire diminue

wangle ['wæŋg(ə)l] *Fam* N combine f, embrouille f, truc m

VT (get) carotter, resquiller; **I wangled myself a trip to Rome** je me suis débrouillé pour obtenir un voyage à Rome; **I'll w. it somehow** je me débrouillerai; **he wangled his way onto the delegation/into the hall** il réussit à s'immiscer dans la délégation/à s'introduire dans le hall; **could you w. me a ticket?** est-ce que tu pourrais m'avoir un ticket?; **how did you w. that?** comment est-ce que tu as arrangé ça?

wangler ['wæŋglər] N *Fam* resquilleur, -euse

wangling ['wæŋglɪŋ] N *Fam* resquillage m, carottage m; **with a bit of w. I managed to get myself a ticket** j'ai eu mon ticket en faisant marcher le système D; **it just needs a bit of w.** il suffit de resquiller un peu

waning ['weɪnɪŋ] ADJ (moon) décroissant, à son déclin; (interest, power) qui diminue; (empire) sur son déclin, en déclin; **his w. influence** son influence déclinante ou décroissante; **his w. enthusiasm** son enthousiasme en baisse

N (of moon) décroissement m; (of interest, power) diminution f, (of empire) déclin m

wank [wæŋk] *Br Vulg* N **1** (masturbation) branlette f; **to have a w.** se branler, se faire une branlette; **to give sb a w.** branler qn **2** *Fig* (nonsense) conneries fpl; **he was talking a load of w.** il disait beaucoup de conneries

VI (masturbate) se branler

▸ **wank off** *Br Vulg* **VI** se branler

VT SEP to w. oneself off se branler; **to w. sb off** branler qn

wankel engine ['wæŋk(ə)l] N *Aut* moteur m wankel

wanker ['wæŋkər] N *Br Vulg* connard m

wankered ['wæŋkəd] ADJ *Br Vulg* (drunk) rond comme une queue de pelle, fin plein

wanky ['wæŋkɪ] ADJ *Br Vulg* (stupid) débile, con; **he's OK but all his friends are a bit w.** lui, ça va, mais tous ses copains sont assez cons

wanly ['wɒnlɪ] ADV (to shine) faiblement; (to smile) tristement

wanna ['wɒnə] CONTR *Fam* = **want to**, *see* **want**

wannabe ['wɒnəbi:] N *esp Am Fam* = personne f rêvant de devenir célèbre, riche etc (mais qui n'en a pas l'étoffe); **the disco was full of J-Lo wannabes** la discothèque était pleine de clones de J-Lo; **they're just a bunch of wannabes** ce n'est qu'un tas de rêveurs (qui n'arriveront jamais nulle part)

wanness ['wɒnnɪs] N pâleur f

WANT [wɒnt]

> | N | besoin **1**, **2** | ▪ manque **2**, **3** |
> |---|---|---|
> | VT | vouloir **1** | ▪ avoir besoin de **2** |
> | | ▪ demander **2** | ▪ chercher **2** |
> | VI | manquer | |

N **1** (need) besoin m; **to minister** or **attend to sb's wants** pourvoir aux besoins de qn; **my wants are few** j'ai peu de besoins

2 (poverty) misère f, besoin m; **to be in w.** être dans le besoin ou la gêne; **war on w.** lutte f contre la misère

3 (lack) manque m, défaut m; **there was no w. of volunteers** on ne manquait pas de volontaires; **to be in w. of sth** avoir besoin de qch; **w. of imagination/respect** manque d'imagination/de respect; **for w. of sth** faute de qch, à défaut de qch; **it was not for w. of trying** ce n'est pas faute d'avoir essayé; **for w. of foresight** par manque de prévoyance; **for w. of something better** faute de mieux; **for w. of something better to do** faute d'avoir quelque chose de mieux à faire; **for w. of a better word** faute d'un mot plus approprié; *Prov* **for w. of a nail the shoe was lost, for w. of a shoe the horse was lost** faute d'un point Martin perdit son âne

VT 1 (desire) vouloir; **she knows what she wants** elle sait ce qu'elle veut; **the more you get the more you w.** plus on en a, plus on en veut; **do you w. any?** en voulez-vous?; **is that all you w.?** est-ce tout ce que vous voulez?; **what more do you w.?** que voulez-vous de plus?; **what** or **how much do you w. for this armchair?** combien vendez-vous ce fauteuil?, combien voulez-vous pour ce fauteuil?; *Iron* **you don't w. much, do you!** tu es bien exigeant!; **you're wanted** on vous demande; **you're wanted on the phone** on vous demande au téléphone; **the boss wants you (in his office)** le patron veut te voir (dans son bureau); **we're not wanted here** nous sommes de trop ici; **people like you are not wanted round here** on ne veut pas de gens comme vous par ici; **they don't w. (to have) me** ils ne veulent pas de moi; **what does he w. with me?** que me veut-il?; **what does he w. me for?** qu'est-ce qu'il me veut?; **to w. sth from sb** vouloir qch de qn; **what do you w. from her?** que voulez-vous d'elle?; **to w. to do sth** vouloir faire qch; **I w. to tell you that ...** je voudrais vous dire que ...; **I w. to see the manager** je veux voir le directeur; **there's someone here who wants to see the manager** il y a quelqu'un qui veut voir ou qui demande le directeur; **he could have done it if he had wanted to** il aurait pu le faire s'il l'avait voulu; **don't come if you don't w. to** or **unless you w. to** ne venez pas si ça ne vous dit pas; **I don't w. it known** je ne veux pas que cela se sache; **what do you w. done?** que désirez-vous qu'on fasse?; **I don't w. you turning everything upside down** je ne veux pas que vous mettiez tout sens dessus dessous; **I don't w. any fuss** je ne veux pas d'histoires; **I've had enough criticism from you, I w. no more of it!** j'ai eu assez de critiques de ta part, ça suffit!

2 (need) (of person) avoir besoin de; (of

thing) exiger, réclamer, demander; **you w. good eyesight to be a pilot** il faut avoir une bonne vue pour être pilote; **that child wants taking down a peg or two** cet enfant a besoin d'être remis à sa place; **it wants a bit more red to make it the same shade** il faut un peu plus de rouge pour obtenir le même ton; **to w. rest** avoir besoin de repos; **it's a situation that wants careful handling** cette situation demande du tact ou qu'on ait du tact; **I shall w. you** j'aurai besoin de vous; **have you everything you w.?** avez-vous tout ce qu'il vous faut?; **we've more than we w.** nous en avons plus qu'il n'en faut; **you shall have as much as you w.** vous en aurez autant que vous voudrez; **I've had all I want(ed)** j'en ai eu assez; **the goods can be supplied as (and when) they are wanted** on peut fournir les articles au fur et à mesure des besoins; **that's the very thing I w., that's just what I w.** c'est juste ce qu'il me faut, cela fera parfaitement mon affaire; **I have the very thing you w.** j'ai juste ce qu'il vous faut; **the very man we w.** l'homme de la circonstance; **what does she w. with a house?** qu'est-ce qu'elle veut faire d'une maison?; **wanted, a good cook** (advertisement) on demande ou recherche une bonne cuisinière; **he's wanted by the police** il est recherché par la police; **your hair wants cutting** tu as besoin de te faire couper les cheveux, tu devrais te faire couper les cheveux; **the lawn wants cutting** la pelouse a besoin d'être tondue; **the plants w. watering about once a week** il faut arroser les plantes environ une fois par semaine

3 (giving advice, instructions) **you w. to be on your guard** il faut vous méfier; **you w. to be careful with him** il faut que tu fasses attention avec lui

VI (be lacking) manquer (**for** de); **to w. for nothing** ne manquer de rien; **her family will see to it that she doesn't w. (for anything)** sa famille veillera à ce qu'elle ne manque de rien

▸▸ *Am* **w. ad** petite annonce f

▸ **want in** **VI** *Fam* (of cat, dog) vouloir entrer; *Fig* (want to be part of sth) vouloir être inclus; **Big Vern wants in on the deal** Big Vern veut être sur le coup

▸ **want out** **VI** *Fam* (of cat, dog) vouloir sortir; *Fig* (no longer want to be part of sth) vouloir retirer ses cartes du jeu; **this has gone far enough, I w. out!** c'est allé trop loin, je laisse tomber!

wanted ['wɒntɪd] ADJ (desired) désiré, voulu; (child) désiré; (criminal) recherché par la police; **'w. for murder'** 'recherché pour meurtre'; **a w. poster** un avis de recherche; **to feel w.** se sentir apprécié

▸▸ **w. notice** avis m de recherche

wanting ['wɒntɪŋ] ADJ **1** (missing) **to be w.** faire défaut; **there is something w.** le compte n'y est pas **2** **to be w. in sth** (of person) manquer de qch; **to be w. in intelligence** être peu intelligent; **he's not w. in intelligence** il n'est pas bête; *Lit* **to be found w.** se trouver en défaut; **he was tried and found w.** il a été mis à l'épreuve et cela n'a pas été concluant

wanton ['wɒntən] ADJ **1** (action, cruelty) gratuit, sans motif; (destroyer) vicieux **2** *Old-fashioned* (licentious) (person, behaviour) licencieux, impudique

N *Old-fashioned* (woman) femme f légère; (man) libertin m

wantonly ['wɒntənlɪ] ADV **1** (to injure, insult) sans motif **2** *Old-fashioned* (licentiously) de façon dévergondée

wantonness ['wɒntənnɪs] N **1** (of insult etc) gratuité f **2** *Old-fashioned* (licentiousness) libertinage m

WAP [wæp] N *Tel (abbr* **wireless applications protocol**) WAP *m*
▸▸**W. phone** téléphone *f* WAP

wapiti ['wɒpɪtɪ] N *(deer)* wapiti *m*

War *abbr* **Warwickshire**

war [wɔːr] N **1** guerre *f*; **a state of w. now exists** l'état de guerre est déclaré (**between** entre); **in (time of) w.** en temps de guerre; **w. establishment** *or* **strength** effectif(s) *m(pl)* de guerre; **to set a unit on a w. footing** mettre une unité sur pied de guerre; **preparations for w.** préparatifs *mpl* de guerre; *Lit* **to let loose the dogs of w.** déchaîner les fureurs de la guerre; **to start a w.** déclencher une guerre; **to be at w. with a country** être en (état de) guerre avec un pays; **to make** *or* **wage w. on** *or* **against a country** faire la guerre à *ou* contre un pays; **to go to w.** se mettre en guerre (**over a territory** pour un territoire); *Fig Fam* **you look as if you've been in the wars** te voilà dans un drôle d'état; **the American Civil W.,** *Am* **the W. Between the States** la guerre de Sécession; **the Great W.** *(1914-1918)* la Grande Guerre **2** *Fig* guerre *f*, lutte *f*; **w. of nerves** guerre des nerfs; **class w.** lutte des classes; *Econ* **price w.** guerre des prix; **w. of words** dispute *f*, altercation *f*; **to wage w. on** *or* **against sb/sth** faire la guerre à *ou* contre qn/à qch, lutter *ou* militer contre qn/qch; **the w. on drugs** la lutte contre la drogue
VI **(-rr-) to w. against sb/sth** mener une campagne contre qn/qch, lutter contre qn/qch
▸▸**w. cemetery** cimetière *m* militaire; **w. chest** caisse *f* spéciale; **w. correspondent** correspondant, -ante de guerre; **w. crimes** crimes *mpl* de guerre; **w. criminal** criminel, -elle de guerre; *also Fig* **w. cry** cri *m* de guerre; **w. dance** danse *f* de guerre *ou* guerrière; **the w. effort** l'effort *m* de guerre; **w. film** film *m* de guerre; **w. game** *Mil (simulated battle with maps)* kriegspiel *m*, wargame *m*; *(manoeuvres)* manœuvres *fpl* militaires; *(game)* wargame; **w. grave** = tombeau *m* d'un soldat tombé au champ d'honneur; **w. hero** héros *m* de guerre; **w. memorial** monument *m* aux morts; *Formerly* **the W. Office** = ancien nom du ministère de la Défense britannique; **w. paint** *(of Amerindian)* peinture *f* de guerre; *Hum (of woman)* maquillage *m*; **w. risk** *(in insurance)* risques *mpl* de guerre; **w. widow** veuve *f* de guerre; **w. zone** zone *f* de guerre

warble ['wɔːb(ə)l] N *(of bird)* gazouillement *m*, gazouillis *m*
VI *(of bird)* gazouiller; *(of lark)* grisoller; *Fig (of person)* chanter
VT *Fig (of person) (song)* roucouler

warbler ['wɔːblər] N *(bird)* fauvette *f*

warbling ['wɔːblɪŋ] ADJ *(bird)* gazouillant; *(sound)* mélodieux
N = **warble** N

ward [wɔːd] N **1** *(person)* pupille *mf*, *(guardianship)* tutelle *f*; **to be in w.** être sous tutelle judiciaire **2** *Med* salle *f* d'hôpital; **which w. is she in?** dans quelle salle est-elle?; **to walk the wards** *(of medical student)* assister aux leçons cliniques **3** *Pol (electoral division)* circonscription *f* électorale
▸▸*Law* **w. of court** pupille *mf* sous tutelle judiciaire; **to be made a w. of court** être placé sous tutelle judiciaire
▸ **ward off** VT SEP *(blow)* parer, écarter; *(danger)* détourner, écarter; *(illness, accusations)* éviter

warden ['wɔːd(ə)n] N *(of institution, hostel, prison)* directeur, -trice; *(of national park)* gardien, -ienne; *Br* **Lord W. of the Cinque Ports** gouverneur *m* des Cinq Ports

warder ['wɔːdər] N *Br (in prison)* gardien, -ienne

wardress ['wɔːdrɪs] N *Br (in prison)* gardienne *f*

wardrobe ['wɔːdrəʊb] N **1** *(cupboard)* armoire *f*, garde-robe *f*, *pl* garde-robes **2** *(clothes)* (ensemble *m* de) vêtements *mpl*, garde-robe *f*, **Miss Smith's w. by ...** *(on film credits)* les costumes de Miss Smith ont été fournis par ...; **to have a large w.** avoir une garde-robe importante; **she brought half her w. with her** elle a emporté la moitié de sa garde-robe **3** *Theat* **to work in w.** être costumier, *f* costumière, s'occuper des costumes
▸▸**w. drawer** tiroir *m* d'armoire; **w. mirror** miroir *m* d'armoire; **w. mistress** costumière *f*, **w. trunk** malle *f (penderie)*

wardroom ['wɔːdruːm] N *Naut* carré *m* des officiers

wardship ['wɔːdʃɪp] N tutelle *f*

ware [weər] N **1** *(manufactured articles)* articles *mpl*; **aluminium w.** ustensiles *mpl* en aluminium; **cast-iron w.** poterie *f* en fonte **2** **wares** *(goods for sale)* marchandise *f(pl)*; *Lit* **to cry one's wares** faire l'article de *ou* vanter sa marchandise

warehouse ['¹weəhaʊs] N entrepôt *m*, dépôt *m* de marchandises; *(for furniture)* garde-meuble *m*, *pl* garde-meubles; **bonded w.** entrepôt de la douane; *Com* **ex w.** sortie *f* d'entrepôt
▸▸*Com* **w. charges** frais *mpl* d'entreposage; *Com* **w. club** club *m* de gros; **w. manager** responsable *mf* d'entrepôt; **w. party** = soirée *f* house dans un local désaffecté; *Com* **w. warrant** certificat *m* d'entreposage

warehouse ['²weəhaʊz] VT entreposer, mettre en entrepôt

warehouseman, *pl* **warehousemen** ['weəhaʊsmən] N magasinier *m*, entrepositaire *m*, manutentionnaire *m*

warehousing ['weəhaʊzɪŋ] N *(of goods)* entreposage *m*; *(of shares)* parcage *m*
▸▸**w. company** société *f* d'entrepôts; **w. costs** frais *mpl* d'entreposage

warfare ['wɔːfeər] N guerre *f*

warhead ['wɔːhed] N ogive *f*, *(on torpedo)* cône *m* de charge

warhorse ['wɔːhɔːs] N **1** *(person)* **an old w.** *Mil* un vieux soldat; *Pol* un vétéran de la politique **2** *Hist (horse)* destrier *m*, cheval *m* de bataille **3** *Mktg* cheval *m* de bataille

warily ['weərɪlɪ] ADV avec précaution; **the soldiers advanced w. through the forest** les soldats avançaient avec prudence dans la forêt; **they eyed him w. as he continued his explanation** ils le regardaient avec méfiance alors qu'il poursuivait son explication

wariness ['weərɪnɪs] N circonspection *f*, prudence *f*, **his w. of computers** sa réticence envers l'informatique

warlike ['wɔːlaɪk] ADJ *(appearance, bearing)* guerrier; *(people)* belliqueux

warlock ['wɔːlɒk] N sorcier *m*, magicien *m*

warlord ['wɔːlɔːd] N seigneur *m* de la guerre; **the local w.** le chef militaire local

warm [wɔːm] ADJ **1** *(garment, colour etc)* chaud; *(iron, oven)* assez chaud; **to be w.** *(of water)* être chaud; *(of person)* avoir chaud; **come inside, it's lovely and w.** viens à l'intérieur, il fait bon; **the water's only just w.** l'eau est à peine chaude; **to get w.** *(of person, room)* se réchauffer; *(of water)* chauffer; **the radiator was getting warmer** le radiateur commençait à chauffer; **you're getting warmer** *(in guessing game etc)* tu chauffes; **you're really w.** *(in guessing game etc)* tu brûles; **make sure you keep w.** ne prends pas froid; **to keep a dish w.** garder un plat au chaud; *Fig* **to keep a place w. for sb** *(job)* garder un emploi pour qn; **I'll do it once the**

w. weather is here je le ferai quand il commencera à faire chaud; **it's getting warmer** *(of weather)* il commence à faire plus chaud; **it's w. work** c'est une besogne qui donne soif; *Fig* **to make things** *or* **it w. for sb** mener la vie dure à qn, en faire voir de toutes les couleurs à qn; *Fig* **things were getting a bit too w.** *(dangerous)* ça commençait à chauffer
2 *(enthusiastic, kind)* chaleureux; **w. heart** cœur généreux; **w. smile** sourire accueillant; **to meet with a w. reception** être accueilli chaleureusement; **w. welcome** accueil chaleureux; **to give sb a w. welcome** accueillir qn chaleureusement
N **to have a w.** se réchauffer; **come into the w.** viens au chaud; **to give sth a w.** réchauffer qch; **to give one's hands a w. at the fire** se réchauffer les mains près du feu
VT *(faire)* chauffer; **to w. oneself by the fire/in the sun** se chauffer près du feu/au soleil; **wine/news that warms the heart** vin/nouvelle qui réchauffe le cœur; **that will w. the cockles of your heart** voilà qui vous réchauffera; **it warms the cockles of my heart to see ...** ça me réchauffe le cœur de voir ...
VI (se) chauffer, s'échauffer, se réchauffer; *Fig* **to w. to sb** (commencer à) ressentir de la sympathie pour qn; **I didn't w. to him** il ne m'a pas plu; **they warmed to one another immediately** ils se sont pris de sympathie immédiatement; **to w. to an idea** se laisser séduire par une idée; **to w. to one's theme** bien entrer dans son sujet
▸▸*Met* **w. front** front *m* chaud; *Comput* **w. start** redémarrage *m* à chaud
▸ **warm over** VT SEP **1** *esp Am (soup etc)* (faire) réchauffer **2** *Fig (novel etc)* réchauffer
▸ **warm up** VI **1** *(of weather)* faire plus chaud; *Fig (of party, audience)* s'animer; *(of discussion)* s'échauffer, s'animer **2** *(of dancer, musician, orchestra), Sport* s'échauffer; *(of engine, radio)* se mettre en route
VT SEP *(thing)* faire chauffer; *(person)* réchauffer; *Fig (party)* animer; **to w. up the engine** (faire) chauffer le moteur; **to w. up the soup** (faire) réchauffer le potage; *Fig* **to w. an audience up** chauffer le public, mettre un public en train

warm-blooded ADJ *(animal)* à sang chaud; *Fig (person)* passionné, ardent

warm-hearted [-'hɑːtɪd] ADJ *(person, welcome)* chaleureux; **we were given a very w. welcome** nous fûmes chaleureusement accueillis; **she is very w.** elle a un grand cœur

warm-heartedly [-'hɑːtɪdlɪ] ADV chaleureusement, avec chaleur

warming ['wɔːmɪŋ] ADJ *(drink)* qui réchauffe; *(thought)* qui réchauffe le cœur, réconfortant
N chauffage *m*
▸▸**w. pan** bassinoire *f*, **w. up** *(of food)* réchauffage *m*; *Sport* échauffement *m*

warmly ['wɔːmlɪ] ADV **1** *(dressed)* chaudement **2** *(to applaud)* chaudement; *(to recommend)* vivement, chaudement; *(to welcome, thank sb)* chaleureusement; **his suggestion was not w. received** sa proposition n'a pas été chaudement accueillie; **the film was w. received by the critics** le film a été accueilli par la critique avec enthousiasme

warmonger ['wɔːmʌŋgər] N belliciste *mf*

warmongering ['wɔːmʌŋg(ə)rɪŋ] N bellicisme *m*, propagande *f* de guerre

warmth [wɔːmθ] N **1** *(of sun, fire)* chaleur *f*, **we huddled together for w.** nous nous sommes blottis les uns contre les autres pour nous tenir chaud **2** *(enthusiasm)* ardeur *f*, chaleur *f*; *(of welcome)* cordialité *f*, chaleur; **to receive sth with w.** *(idea, proposal)* accueillir qch avec enthousiasme **3** *(anger)* emportement *m*, vivacité *f*; ... **she said with some w.** ... dit-elle d'un ton vif

warm-up N **1** *(of dancer, musician, orchestra)*, *Sport* échauffement *m*; **to do a w.** s'échauffer; **they get a ten-minute w.** ils ont dix minutes d'échauffement **2 come and have a w. by the fire** viens te réchauffer auprès du feu
▸ ▸ **w. exercises** exercices *mpl* d'échauffement; **w. man** personne *f* chargée de chauffer la salle; **w. match** match *m* préparatoire *ou* d'entraînement; *esp Am* **w. suit** survêtement *m*

warn [wɔ:n] VT **1** *(caution)* avertir, prévenir (that que); **he warned me not to do it** il m'a déconseillé de le faire; **to w. sb about** *or* **against sth** mettre qn en garde contre qch; **to w. sb about** *or* **against doing sth** conseiller à qn de ne pas faire qch; **he warned her against going, he warned her not to go** il lui a conseillé (fortement) de ne pas y aller; **to w. sb of a danger** avertir qn d'un danger; **they warned me about you** on m'avait mis en garde contre toi, on m'avait prévenu à ton égard; *Hum* **my parents warned me about people like you!** mes parents m'avaient bien dit de me méfier des gens comme toi!; **you have been warned!** vous voilà averti *ou* prévenu!; **I'm warning you for the last time** je te préviens pour la dernière fois; **I shan't w. you again** tenez-vous-le pour dit
2 *(alert, inform)* informer, donner l'éveil à; **she had been warned in advance** elle était prévenue; **to w. the police** alerter la police
VI **he warned of possibly serious consequences** il évoqua les graves conséquences possibles
▸ **warn off** VT SEP **1** *(tell to leave)* **he warned them off his land** il leur demanda instamment de quitter ses terres; **the signs are meant to w. people off** les panneaux sont là pour interdire aux gens d'entrer **2** *(advise against)* **to w. sb off sth** déconseiller qch à qn; **to w. sb off drink/smoking** déconseiller l'alcool/la cigarette à qn; **to w. sb off doing sth** déconseiller à qn de faire qch

warning ['wɔ:nɪŋ] N **1** *(caution)* avertissement *m*; *(alarm)* alerte *f*; **to give sb a w.** mettre qn en garde; **this is your last w.** *(to child)* c'est la dernière fois que je te le dis; *(to worker)* c'est votre dernier avertissement; **in spite of repeated warnings** malgré de nombreux avertissements; **to sound a note of w.** recommander la prudence; **he was let off with a w.** il en a été quitte pour un avertissement; **let this be a w. to you** que cela vous serve de leçon *ou* d'exemple *ou* d'avertissement; **she gave him a w. glance** elle lui lança un regard d'avertissement *ou* pour l'avertir
2 *(advance notice)* avis *m*, préavis *m*; **we only received a few days' w.** nous n'avons été prévenus que quelques jours à l'avance; **she didn't give him much w.** elle l'a prévenu assez tard; **I'm giving you fair w.** vous voilà averti!; **without w.** sans préavis, sans déclaration préalable; **he just left without w.** il est parti sans crier gare; **it just broke down without w.** elle est tombée en panne d'un seul coup; *Ind* **strike w.** préavis de grève
▸ ▸ **w. beep** signal *m* sonore; **w. bell** sonnette *f ou* sonnerie *f* d'alarme; **w. buzzer** avertisseur *m* sonore; **w. device** avertisseur *m*; **w. light** voyant *m* (avertisseur), avertisseur lumineux; *Comput* **w. message** message *m* d'avertissement; *Naut, Fig* **w. shot** coup *m* de semonce, avertissement; *Fig* **to fire a w. shot** tirer sur le signal d'alarme; **w. sign** panneau *m* avertisseur; **w. signal** signal d'alarme *ou* d'alerte; *Aut* signal de détresse; *Ind* **w. strike** grève *f* d'avertissement; **w. system** système *m ou* dispositif *m* d'alarme; *Br Aut* **w. triangle** triangle *m* de signalisation

warp [wɔ:p] N **1** *(distortion)* *(of plank)* voilure *f*, gauchissement *m*; *(in time)* brèche *f* **2** *Tex* chaîne *f*; *(for tapestry)* lisse *f*, lice *f*
VT *(distort)* *(wood, metal sheet)* gauchir, voiler; *Fig (mind, character, person)* pervertir; *(judgement)* fausser
VI *(of cupboard door etc)* se déformer, gauchir; *(of timber)* se voiler, gauchir; *(of sheet metal)* (se) gondoler

warpath ['wɔ:pɑ:θ] N **to be on the w.** *(of Amerindian etc)* être sur le sentier de la guerre; *Fig* en vouloir à tout le monde; *Fig* **the boss is on the w.** le patron est d'une humeur massacrante

warped [wɔ:pt] ADJ *(wood)* gauchi, voilé; *Fig (mind, person)* perverti, *(judgement)* faussé; **that's a very w. way of thinking** c'est une drôle de manière de voir les choses; **w. sense of humour** sens de l'humour tordu; **you must be a bit w. if you think that's funny!** tu dois être un peu tordu pour trouver ça drôle!

warping ['wɔ:pɪŋ] N *(of plank)* gauchissement *m*; *(of metal sheet)* gondolement *m*; *(of wheel)* voilure *f*, voilement *m*

warplane ['wɔ:pleɪn] N avion *m* de guerre

warrant ['wɒrənt] N **1** *Com (guarantee)* garantie *f*, *Fin* bon *m* de souscription d'actions, *Obsa m inv* **2** *Law* mandat *m*, ordre *m*; *Admin* mandat; **w. of arrest** mandat d'arrêt *ou* d'arrestation; **there's a w. out against him** *or* **for his arrest** il est sous le coup d'un mandat d'arrêt; **warehouse w.** certificat *m* d'entrepôt, warrant *m*, warrant cédule; **w. for payment** ordonnance *f* de paiement; **travel w.** feuille *f* de route
VT **1** *(justify)* justifier; **nothing can w. such conduct** rien ne justifie une pareille conduite, rien ne peut excuser une telle conduite; **his performance warranted better** sa prestation méritait mieux **2** *(guarantee)* *(something)* garantir, répondre de; *Old-fashioned* **it won't happen again, I w. you!** cela n'arrivera pas deux fois, je vous le promets! **3** *Com* warranter
▸ ▸ **w. officer** adjudant *m* (auxiliaire d'un officier)

warrantable ['wɒrəntəb(ə)l] ADJ *(justifiable)* justifiable

warrantee [wɒrən'ti:] N receveur, -euse d'une/de la garantie

warrantor ['wɒrəntɔ:r] N *Law* garant, -ante

warranty ['wɒrəntɪ] N *Com* garantie *f*, under **w.** sous garantie; **is it still under w.?** est-ce que c'est encore sous garantie?; **the iron has a one-year w.** le fer à repasser est garanti un an; **breach of w.** rupture *f* de garantie
▸ ▸ **w. certificate** certificat *m* de garantie

warren ['wɒrən] N *(of rabbit)* garenne *f*, clapier *m*; *Fig* labyrinthe *m*, dédale *m*

warring ['wɔ:rɪŋ] ADJ *(countries)* en guerre; *Fig (ideologies)* en conflit; **w. factions within the Labour Party** des factions adverses au sein du Labour Party

warrior ['wɒrɪər] N guerrier, -ière

Warsaw ['wɔ:sɔ:] N Varsovie
▸ ▸ **the W. Pact** le pacte de Varsovie; **the W. Pact nations** les nations *fpl* du pacte de Varsovie

war-scarred [-skɑ:d] ADJ *(city, country)* dévasté par la guerre

warship ['wɔ:ʃɪp] N navire *m ou* vaisseau *m* de guerre

wart [wɔ:t] N verrue *f*; **a biography of Charles de Gaulle, warts and all** une biographie de Charles de Gaulle écrite sans complaisance *ou* qui ne fait pas de cadeaux; **she'll have to accept him as he is, warts and all** il faudra qu'elle l'accepte comme il est, avec tous ses défauts

warthog ['wɔ:thɒg] N phacochère *m*

wartime ['wɔ:taɪm] N temps *m* de guerre; **in w.** en temps de guerre
▸ ▸ **w. rations** rations *fpl* de guerre

warty ['wɔ:tɪ] ADJ couvert de verrues, verruqueux

wary ['weərɪ] ADJ avisé, prudent, circonspect; **to be w. of sb/sth** se méfier de qn/qch; **I'm still w. about signing it** j'hésite encore à le signer; **to keep a w. eye on sb** surveiller qn de près

was PT *see* be

Wash *abbr* Washington

WASH [wɒʃ] N **1** *(action)* lavage *m*; **to have a w.** se laver; **give your face a w.** lave-toi le visage; **to have a w. and brush up** faire un brin de toilette; **to give sth a w.** laver qch
2 *(laundry)* lessive *f*, blanchissage *m*; **to send clothes to the w.** donner du linge à laver *ou* à blanchir; **to do the w.** faire la lessive; **your jeans are in the w.** *(being washed)* ton jean est au lavage; **it'll come out in the w.** ça partira au lavage; *Fig* **it will all come out in the w.** *(become known)* ça finira par se savoir; *(be all right)* ça finira par s'arranger
3 *Med (for wounds)* lotion *f*, *(for plants)* lessive *f* (insecticide); *(against mildew)* bouillie *f*
4 *Art (of water colour, Indian ink)* lavis *m*, **colour w.** *(for walls)* badigeon *m*
5 *(of waves, ship)* remous *m*
VT **1** *(clean)* *(car, clothes, plate, etc)* laver; **w. in cool/hot water** à laver à l'eau tiède/chaude; **hand w. only** laver à la main seulement; **to w. sth in cold water** laver qch à l'eau froide; **to w. oneself** se laver; **to w. one's face/hands/hair** se laver le visage/les mains/les cheveux; *Br Euph* **would you like to w. your hands?** *(go to lavatory)* voulez-vous que je vous montre où est la salle de bain?; *Fig* **to w. one's hands of sb/sth** se laver les mains de qn/qch; *Fig* **I w. my hands of the affair** je me lave les mains de cette affaire; *Rel* **to be washed of one's sins** être lavé de ses péchés
2 *Med (wound)* nettoyer
3 *Ind (mineral, coal)* laver; *(gas)* épurer
4 *Art (drawing)* laver; **to w. the walls** *(paint)* badigeonner les murs (**with** de)
5 *(of sea) (shore)* baigner; **to w. sb/sth ashore** rejeter qn/qch sur le rivage; **he was washed overboard** il fut emporté par une vague
VI **1** *(wash oneself)* se laver; **material that washes well** tissu qui se lave bien; **you w. and I'll dry** *(doing dishes)* tu laves et j'essuie; *Br Fam* **that won't w.!** ça ne prend pas!, ça ne marche pas!
2 **the waves washed against the cliff** les vagues baignaient la falaise
▸ ▸ *Art* **w. drawing** dessin *m* au lavis
▸ **wash away** VT SEP **1** *(remove by washing)* faire partir; **to w. one's sins away** se laver de ses péchés
2 *(of rain, flood etc)* **the flood washed away part of the river bank** l'inondation a érodé une partie de la berge; **the village was washed away by the flood** le village a été emporté par l'inondation; **heavy rains had washed away the topsoil** des pluies abondantes avaient entraîné la terre; **washed away by the tide** emporté *ou* enlevé par la mer
VI *(of mark, stain)* s'en aller *ou* partir au lavage
▸ **wash down** VT SEP **1** *(walls, car)* laver à grande eau
2 *(help to swallow)* *(pill)* faire descendre; **to w. down one's dinner with a glass of beer** boire un verre de bière en dînant
▸ **wash off** VT SEP *(remove by washing)* enlever, faire partir

VI *(of mud, dirt)* s'en aller *ou* partir au lavage
▸ **wash out** VT SEP **1** *(remove by washing)* *(stain)* enlever
2 *(clean) (cup, bottle)* laver, rincer, nettoyer; **to w. out a few clothes** *or* **things** faire une petite lessive; *Fig* **to be completely washed out** *(tired)* être complètement lessivé *ou* vanné *ou* à plat
3 *Art (colour)* dégrader; **washed out** *(of colour, material)* délavé, déteint
4 *Min* **to w. out the gold** extraire l'or
5 *(of football match etc)* **to be washed out** être annulé à cause de la pluie
6 *Geol* éroder
VI *(of stain, colour)* partir au lavage; **it will w. out** ça partira au lavage
▸ **wash over** VT INSEP *(of waves)* balayer; *Fig (have no effect on)* ne faire aucun effet à; **anything I say just washes over her** rien de ce que je lui dis ne lui fait le moindre effet
▸ **wash up** VT SEP **1** *Br* **to w. up the dishes** laver *ou* faire la vaisselle
2 *(of sea)* rejeter sur le rivage; **wreckage washed up by the sea** débris rejetés par la mer
VI **1** *Br (do dishes)* faire la vaisselle
2 *Am (have a wash)* se débarbouiller
3 *Fig (end up) (of person)* finir, échouer; **he washed up in Australia** il a échoué en Australie

washable ['wɒʃəb(ə)l] ADJ lavable
wash-and-wear ADJ lavé-repassé
washbasin ['wɒʃbeɪs(ə)n] N lavabo *m*
washboard ['wɒʃbɔːd] N planche *f* à laver
washbowl ['wɒʃbəʊl] N lavabo *m*; *(large)* bassine *f*
washcloth ['wɒʃklɒθ] N *Br (for washing dishes)* lavette *f*, *Am (face cloth)* = gant *m* de toilette
washday ['wɒʃdeɪ] N jour *m* de la lessive
washed-out ['wɒʃd-] ADJ *(faded)* délavé; *Fig (tired)* lessivé
washed-up ADJ *Fig Fam* **to be (all) w.** *(of person)* être fini *ou Fam* fichu; *(of plan)* être tombé à l'eau; **he's all w.** c'est un homme fini *ou* liquidé; **he's all w. as a boxer** il est fini comme boxeur
washer[1] ['wɒʃər] N **1** *(person)* laveur, -euse **2** *Fam (machine) (for clothes)* machine *f* à laver; *(for dishes)* lave-vaisselle *m inv*
▸ ▸ *Aut* **w. bottle** réservoir *m* de lave-glace
washer[2] N *Tech* rondelle *f*, bague *f*; **the tap needs a new w.** il faut changer la bague du robinet
washer-dryer N machine *f* à laver séchante
washer-up, *pl* **washers-up, washerupper,** *pl* **washer-uppers** N *Br Fam* laveur, -euse de vaisselle; *(in restaurant)* plongeur, -euse
washerwoman, *pl* **washerwomen** ['wɒʃəwʊmən, -wɪmɪn] N blanchisseuse *f*
wash-hand basin N lavabo *m*
washing ['wɒʃɪŋ] N **1** *(action) (of car, wall etc)* lavage *m*; *(of clothes)* lessive *f*; *(at laundry)* blanchissage *m*; *(of one's body)* toilette *f*, *Rel (of feet, hands)* lavement *m*; **to do the w.** faire la lessive; **Monday is w. day** le lundi est le jour de la lessive **2** *(dirty clothes)* linge *m* à laver; *(clean clothes)* linge lavé
▸ ▸ **w. machine** machine *f* à laver, lave-linge *m inv*; **w. powder** lessive *f ou* détergent *m* *(en poudre)*; **w. soda** cristaux *mpl* de soude
Washington ['wɒʃɪŋtən] N **1** *(state)* **W. (State)** l'État *m* de Washington **2** *(town)* **W. (DC)** Washington
washing-up N *Br* vaisselle *f*; **to do the w.** faire la vaisselle; *(in restaurant)* faire la plonge
▸ ▸ **w. bowl** cuvette *f*, bassine *f*; *Br* **w. liquid**

produit *m* pour la vaisselle, liquide *m* vaisselle; **w. water** eau *f* de vaisselle
washleather ['wɒʃleðər] N peau *f* de chamois
washout ['wɒʃaʊt] N *Fam (failure)* fiasco *m*; *(person)* raté, -ée, zéro *m*; **the whole thing's a w.** c'est une perte sèche
washrag ['wɒʃræg] N *Am* ≃ gant *m* de toilette
washroom ['wɒʃruːm] N **1** *esp Am (lavatory in hotel etc)* toilettes *fpl*; **where's the w.?** où sont les toilettes? **2** *(with toilets, washbasins etc)* salle *f* d'eau, cabinet *m* de toilette
washstand ['wɒʃstænd] N *(table)* table *f* de toilette; *Am (washbasin)* lavabo *m*
washtub ['wɒʃtʌb] N *(for clothes)* baquet *m* *(à lessive)*
washup ['wɒʃʌp] N **1** *Med Fam (before operating)* stérilisation *f* des mains **2** *Am* **to have a w.** se laver (les mains et la figure), se débarbouiller
wash-wipe N *Aut* lavage-balayage *m*
wasn't ['wɒz(ə)nt] CONTR = was not, *see* be
Wasp [wɒsp] N *Am esp Pej (abbr* White Anglo-Saxon Protestant) = Américain *m* blanc protestant d'origine anglo-saxonne
wasp [wɒsp] N *(insect)* guêpe *f*; **wasps' nest** guêpier *m*; **to have a w. waist** avoir une taille de guêpe
waspish ['wɒspɪʃ] ADJ méchant, acerbe; *(tone)* hargneux
waspishly ['wɒspɪʃlɪ] ADV *(to do)* d'une manière acerbe; *(to say)* avec hargne
wassail ['wɒseɪl] VI *Lit* chanter des chants de Noël; **to go wassailing** aller de maison en maison en chantant des chants de Noël
wastage ['weɪstɪdʒ] N **1** *(loss)* gaspillage *m*; *(of heat)* déperdition *f*, perte *f*, *Com (in shipping)* freinte *f* **2** *(what is wasted)* déchets *mpl*, rebuts *mpl*; **buy enough material to allow for w.** achetez suffisamment de tissu pour compenser les pertes **3** *(reduction of workforce)* départ *m* d'employés; **we hope to achieve this by natural w.** nous pensons y parvenir grâce à des départs volontaires
waste [weɪst] ADJ **1** *(uncultivated) (ground)* en friche; *(region)* désert, désolé; **to lay w.** *(country)* dévaster, ravager, piller
2 *(product)* non utilisé, perdu
N **1** *(of money, effort)* gaspillage *m*; **it's a terrible w. of food** c'est un terrible gâchis *ou* gaspillage de nourriture; **it's a w. of their skills** c'est gaspiller leurs talents; **w. of time** perte *f* de temps; **it's a w. of time** c'est du temps perdu; **it's a w. of time trying to convince her** je perds mon/tu perds ton/*etc* temps à essayer de la convaincre; **that film is a real w. of time** ce film ne vaut rien, ce film est nul; *Fam* **he's a w. of space** il est nul; **to go to w.** *(of food, talent)* se perdre; *(of land, garden)* partir à l'abandon
2 *(rubbish)* déchets *mpl*; *(household waste)* ordures *fpl*; *Min* déblais *mpl*
3 *(desert)* région *f* inculte, désert *m*; **the wastes of the Sahara** les étendues désertes du Sahara
VT **1** *(squander) (stocks, money)* gaspiller; *(paper)* gâcher; *(fortune)* dissiper, dilapider; *(time)* perdre, gaspiller; *(opportunity)* rater, manquer; **she felt that she had wasted her youth** *(misspent)* elle avait l'impression d'avoir gâché sa jeunesse; **nothing is wasted** rien ne se perd; **I hate wasting food** j'ai horreur de gâcher la nourriture; **to w. one's life** gâcher sa vie; **she's wasted in that job** cet emploi est bien au-dessous de ses capacités; **to w. one's words** *or* **breath** parler en pure perte; **don't w. your breath on him** ne perds pas ta salive, il ne le vaut pas; **you're wasting your breath, he won't understand** ne gaspille pas ta salive pour rien, il ne

comprend pas; **you're wasting your energy** vous vous dépensez inutilement; **I haven't any time to w. on him** je n'ai pas de temps à perdre pour lui; **we're wasting time** nous perdons notre temps; **we've already wasted too much time on this** nous avons déjà perdu trop de temps là-dessus; **to w. no time doing sth** ne pas perdre de temps pour faire qch; *Fam* **you didn't w. any time, did you!** tu n'as pas perdu de temps, hein?; **that would be wasted on me** ce serait trop beau pour moi; **expensive wine is wasted on me** *(not appreciated by)* je suis incapable d'apprécier le bon vin; **a beautiful house like that is wasted on such people** une belle maison comme ça, c'est trop beau pour des gens pareils; **the joke was wasted on him** il n'a pas compris la plaisanterie; *Prov* **w. not, want not** qui épargne gagne
2 *(consume) (person)* consumer, épuiser, faire dépérir; *(body, limb)* décharner, atrophier; **her body was wasted by disease** son corps était décharné par la maladie
3 *Sl (murder)* tuer; *(attack)* casser la gueule à, démonter le portrait à; **to w. sb's face** casser *ou* défoncer la gueule à qn, faire une tête au carré à qn
▸ ▸ **w. collection** ramassage *m* des ordures; **w. disposal** élimination *f ou* destruction *f* des déchets *ou* des ordures; **w. disposal site** dépôt *m* d'ordures; **w. disposal unit** broyeur *m* d'ordures; **w. ground** terre *f* inculte *ou* en friche; *(in town)* terrain *m* vague; **w. heat** chaleur *f* perdue; **w. heat recovery** récupération *f* de la chaleur perdue; **w. land** terre inculte *ou* en friche; *(in town)* terrain vague; **w. pipe** (tuyau *m* de) vidange *f*, **w. products** déchets; **w. water** *(domestic)* eaux *fpl* usées; *Ind* eaux résiduaires *ou* usées; **w. water treatment** traitement *m* des eaux usées
▸ **waste away** VI *(of person)* dépérir, s'affaiblir
wastebasket ['weɪstbɑːskɪt] N *esp Am* corbeille *f* (à papier); *Comput* corbeille
▸ ▸ *Comput* **w. icon** icône *f* de la corbeille
wastebin ['weɪstbɪn] N corbeille *f* à papier
wasted ['weɪstɪd] ADJ **1** *(sick person, body)* affaibli, amaigri; *(through drug use)* dévasté, ravagé; *(limb)* atrophié **2** *(money)* gaspillé; *(effort)* inutile; *(opportunity)* perdu; **it was a w. journey** c'était un voyage pour rien; **w. life** vie gaspillée; **w. time** temps perdu **3** *Fam (drunk)* pété, bourré; *(on drugs)* défoncé, raide
wasteful ['weɪstfʊl] ADJ *(person)* gaspilleur, -euse; *(expense)* excessif; *(process)* peu économique; **w. practices** gaspillage *m*; **don't be so w. with the hot water!** ne gaspillez pas l'eau chaude!; **it is w. of human resources** c'est gaspiller les ressources humaines
wastefully ['weɪstfəlɪ] ADV prodigalement, avec prodigalité; **to spend money w.** gaspiller son argent
wastefulness ['weɪstfʊlnɪs] N gaspillage *m*
wasteland ['weɪstlænd] N *(desert)* région *f* inculte, désert *m*; *(in city)* terrain *m* vague; *Fig* désert *m*; **an industrial/cultural w.** un désert industriel/culturel
wastepaper ['weɪstpeɪpər] N vieux papiers *mpl*
▸ ▸ **w. basket** corbeille *f* à papier
waster ['weɪstər] N **1** *(wasteful person)* gaspilleur, -euse; **time w.** fainéant, -ante **2** *(good for nothing)* bon *m*/bonne *f* à rien
wasting ['weɪstɪŋ] N **1** *(of resources, time)* gaspillage *m* **2** *(of body)* dépérissement *m*, amaigrissement *m*; *(of limb)* atrophie *f*; *Med* **w. of muscle** fonte *f* musculaire
▸ ▸ *Acct* **w. asset** actif *m* qui se déprécie; **w. away** *(of body)* dépérissement, amaigrissement; *(of limb)* atrophie; **w. disease** maladie *f* qui ronge

wastrel ['weɪstrəl] N *(useless person)* vaurien, -ienne, bon *m*/bonne *f* à rien

WATCH [wɒtʃ]

N	garde **1** ▪ surveillance **1**
VI	regarder **1** ▪ veiller **2**
VT	observer **1** ▪ regarder **1, 2** ▪ faire attention à **3** ▪ surveiller **4**

N 1 *(observation)* garde *f*, surveillance *f*; **to keep w.** monter la garde; **to keep a close w. on** *or* **over sb** surveiller qn de près; **to put** *or* **set a w. on sb** faire surveiller qn; **to be on the w. for sb** épier *ou* guetter qn
2 *(timepiece)* montre *f*; **it's six o'clock by my w.** il est six heures à ma montre
3 *Naut (shift)* quart *m*; *(men)* bordée *f*; **to be on w.** être de quart; **the officer of the w.** l'officier *m* du quart
4 *Hist (guard)* **the w.** la garde, le guet
5 *(vigil)* veille *f*; *Lit* **in the watches of the night** pendant les heures de veille; **to keep w. at sb's bedside** veiller au chevet de qn
VI 1 *(look on)* regarder; **they watched help-lessly as the wall came tumbling down** ils regardèrent, impuissants, le mur qui s'écroulait; **they're watching to see if you make a mistake** ils surveillent pour voir si tu fais une erreur
2 *(keep vigil)* veiller; **to w. by a sick person** veiller auprès d'un malade
VT 1 *(observe)* observer, regarder attentivement; **I'm not going to stand back and w. him make a fool of himself** je ne vais pas juste le regarder se ridiculiser; **I want to w. what happens when you tell him the news** je veux voir ce qui se passe quand tu lui annonceras la nouvelle; **to w. sb closely** ne pas quitter qn des yeux; *(of police, secret service)* surveiller qn de près; **to have sb watched** faire surveiller qn; **we are being watched** on nous observe; **to w. birds** observer les oiseaux; **you're not doing it properly, w. me** tu t'y prends mal, regarde-moi faire; *Prov* **a watched pot never boils** plus on désire une chose plus elle se fait attendre
2 *(look at, monitor)* regarder; **I watched her working** je la regardais travailler; **to w. television** regarder la télévision; **is there anything worth watching on TV?** est-ce qu'il y a quelque chose de bien (à regarder) à la télévision?; **to w. a football match** *(attend)* assister à un match de football; *(on television)* regarder un match de football; **to w. the course of events/sb's career** suivre le cours des événements/la carrière de qn; *Pej* **to w. the clock** avoir les yeux rivés à *ou* fixés sur l'heure; **to w. the world go by** regarder passer la foule VOIR GRAMMAIRE A41; B35
3 *(be careful of)* faire attention à; **we shall have to w. the expenses** il nous faudra faire attention aux dépenses; **we'll have to w. the time** *(so as not to be late)* il va falloir que nous fassions attention à l'heure; **w. what you say about ...** fais attention à ce que tu dis au sujet de ...; **w. you don't say anything stupid** fais attention à ne pas dire quelque chose de stupide; **w. where you're going!** *(or you'll fall)* regarde où tu vas!; *(or you'll bump into somebody)* regarde devant toi!; **w. your language!** surveille ton langage!; **to w. one's weight** surveiller sa ligne; **w. the step!** *(fais)* attention à la marche!; **w. your step!** *(don't fall)* fais attention de ne pas tomber!; *(step carefully)* fais attention où tu mets les pieds!; *(be careful)* fais attention!; *Fam* **w. it!** fais gaffe!
4 *(keep an eye on) (children, luggage etc)* surveiller; **our neighbour is watching the flat while we're away** notre voisin s'occupe de notre appartement pendant que nous sommes en voyage
5 *(be mindful of)* **to w. one's opportunity/time** guetter l'occasion/le moment propice

▸▸**w. chain** chaîne *f* de montre; **w. night** nuit *f* de la Saint-Sylvestre; **w. night service** messe *f* (de minuit) de la Saint-Sylvestre; **w. pocket** gousset *m*; *Comput* **w. pointer** pointeur-montre *m*, *pl* pointeurs-montres; **w. spring** ressort *m* de montre
▸**watch for** VT INSEP **something to w. for this month is the London marathon** la chose à ne pas rater ce mois, c'est le marathon de Londres; **w. for the moment when he realizes she may be the killer** regarde bien la scène où il comprend qu'elle est peut-être l'assassin
▸**watch out** VI faire attention; **you'd better w. out, the boss knows** tu devrais te méfier, le patron est au courant; **w. out!** attention!, prenez garde!
▸**watch out for** VT INSEP **1** *(look for)* **ask the garage to w. out for a decent second-hand car** demande au garage d'essayer de trouver une bonne voiture d'occasion; **w. out for trouble when Fred gets out of prison** méfiez-vous quand Fred sortira de prison
2 *Am (take care of) (person)* s'occuper de
3 *(keep watch) (for return of)* attendre; *(for approach of)* guetter
4 *(be careful of)* faire attention à; **w. out for Ronnie!** gare à Ronnie!
▸**watch over** VT INSEP *(guard, protect) (person)* veiller sur; *(person's interest, welfare)* veiller à

watchband ['wɒtʃbænd] N bracelet *m* de montre

watchdog ['wɒtʃdɒg] N chien *m* de garde; *Fig (person)* contrôleur *m*; *(organization)* organisme *m* de surveillance *ou* de contrôle; **(consumer) w.** protecteur *m* des intérêts du consommateur; *(organization)* organisme protégeant les intérêts du consommateur; **the committee acts as w. on environmental issues** le comité veille aux problèmes d'environnement
▸▸*Comput* **w. program** programme *m* sentinelle

watcher ['wɒtʃər] N *(of political etc scene)* observateur, -trice; **Downing Street/Kremlin watchers** les observateurs de Downing Street/du Kremlin

watchful ['wɒtʃfʊl] ADJ vigilant, alerte, attentif; **to be w.** être sur ses gardes; **to keep a w. eye on** *or* **over sb** surveiller qn de près; **under the w. eye of his grandmother** sous l'œil vigilant de sa grand-mère; **we're keeping a w. eye on the situation** nous suivons la situation de près; **to be w. of sb** observer *ou* épier qn d'un œil méfiant *ou* jaloux

watchfully ['wɒtʃfəlɪ] ADV avec vigilance, d'un œil attentif

watching brief ['wɒtʃɪŋ] N **to have a w.** avoir un mandat de contrôle

watchmaker ['wɒtʃmeɪkər] N horloger, -ère

watchmaking ['wɒtʃmeɪkɪŋ] N horlogerie *f*

watchman, *pl* **watchmen** ['wɒtʃmən] N gardien *m*

watchstrap ['wɒtʃstræp] N bracelet *m* de montre

watchtower ['wɒtʃtaʊər] N tour *f* d'observation *ou* de guet; *(in prison camp)* mirador *m*

watchword ['wɒtʃwɜːd] N mot *m* de passe; *(slogan)* mot d'ordre

water ['wɔːtər] N **1** eau *f*; **is the w. safe to drink?** est-ce que l'eau est potable?; **to take** *or* **drink the waters** *(mineral springs)* prendre les eaux, faire une cure; *Fig* **to get into hot w.** se mettre dans de mauvais draps; **to drink a glass of cold w.** boire un verre d'eau fraîche; *Fig* **to pour cold w. on a scheme** se montrer très négatif à l'égard d'un projet; **to**

put w. in one's wine couper son vin d'eau; **the wine flowed like w.** le vin a coulé à flots; *Fig* **to spend money like w.** jeter l'argent par les fenêtres; *Prov* **you can lead a horse to w. but you cannot make him drink** on ne saurait faire boire un âne qui n'a pas soif; *Fig* **to hold w.** *(of argument etc)* tenir debout; **my shoes let in w.** mes chaussures prennent l'eau; **to take w. on** *(of ship)* embarquer son eau, faire de l'eau; **the waters of the Danube** les eaux du Danube; **to feel like a fish out of w.** se sentir perdu *ou* hors de son élément; *Prov* **still waters run deep** il faut se méfier de l'eau qui dort; **the steeple of the church was all that remained above w.** seul le clocher de l'église était hors de *ou* au-dessus de l'eau; **to keep oneself** *or* **one's head above w.** se maintenir à la surface *ou* sur l'eau; *Fig* garder la tête hors de l'eau; *(financially)* faire face à ses engagements; **by w.** en bateau; *(to transport goods)* par voie d'eau; **under w.** *(land, roots)* inondé; *(submarine)* en plongée; *(to swim)* sous l'eau; *Fig* **that's all w. under the bridge now** c'est du passé tout ça; *Fig* **a lot of w. has flowed under the bridge since then** il y a de l'eau qui a coulé sous les ponts depuis; **she's a real w. baby** c'est un vrai petit poisson; **high/low w.** marée *f* haute/basse; *Chem* **w. soluble** hydrosoluble; **hot w. bottle** bouillotte *f*
2 *Med* **w. on the brain** hydrocéphalie *f*, **w. on the knee** hydarthrose *f* du genou, épanchement *m* de synovie; *Obst* **breaking of the waters** perte *f* des eaux; **her waters have broken** elle a perdu les eaux; **to pass** *or* **make w.** uriner
3 *(of diamond)* **a diamond of the first w.** un diamant de première eau; *Old-fashioned Fig* **a villain of the first w.** une canaille de premier ordre
VT 1 *(plant, garden)* arroser; **an area watered by many rivers** une région arrosée par de nombreuses rivières
2 *(liquid)* diluer, délayer; **to w. one's wine** couper son vin
3 *(animals)* faire boire, donner à boire à, abreuver
VI *(of eyes)* pleurer, larmoyer; **it makes my mouth w.** cela me fait venir l'eau à la bouche
▸▸**w. bed** lit *m* à matelas d'eau; **w. bird** oiseau *m* aquatique; **w. birth** accouchement *m* sous l'eau; *Br* **w. biscuit** = biscuit *m* salé croquant; **w. blister** ampoule *f*, *Spec* phlyctène *f*, *Br Admin* **w. board** service *m* des eaux; *Entom* **w. boatman** notonecte *f*, **w. bottle** bouteille *f* d'eau; *(soldier's, worker's)* bidon *m* à eau; *(in leather)* gourde *f*, **w. buffalo** *(in India)* buffle *m* d'Inde; *(in Malaysia)* karbau *m*, kérabau *m*; *(in Asia)* buffle d'Asie; **w. butt** citerne *f* (à eau de pluie); **w. cannon** canon *m* à eau; **w. carrier** *(container)* bidon à eau; *(person)* porteur, -euse d'eau; **w. chestnut** châtaigne *f* d'eau; **w. chute** *(in swimming-pool)* toboggan *m*; *Old-fashioned* **w. closet** W.C. *mpl*, toilettes *fpl*, cabinets *mpl*; **w. cooler** distributeur *m* d'eau fraîche; *TV Fam* **w. cooler show** = émission *f* dont tout le monde parle; **w. cooling** refroidissement *m* par eau; *Am* **w. cracker** = biscuit salé croquant; **w. cures** thermalisme *m*, cures *fpl* thermales; **w. damage** dégâts *mpl* des eaux; **w. gun** pistolet *m* à eau; **w. hammer** *(in pipes)* cognements *mpl* dans la canalisation; **w. heater** chauffe-eau *m inv*; **w. hen** poule *f* d'eau; *Br* **w. ice** sorbet *m*; **w. jacket** chemise *f* d'eau; *Aut* **w. jet** gicleur *m* d'eau; **w. jump** brook *m*; **w. level** *(of river, sea)* niveau *m* de l'eau; *(in tank)* niveau d'eau; *Bot* **w. lily** nénuphar *m*; **w. line** ligne *f* de flottaison; **w. main** conduite *f* d'eau; **w. mattress** matelas *m* à eau; **w. meadow** prairie *f* (souvent inondée); **w. meter** compteur *m* d'eau; **w. mill** moulin *m* à eau; **w. park** parc *m* aquatique; **w. pipe**

Constr conduite *ou* canalisation *f* d'eau; *(hookah)* narguilé *m*; **w. pistol** pistolet *m* à eau; **w. plant** plante *f* aquatique; **w. polo** water-polo *m*; **w. power** énergie *f* hydraulique, houille *f* blanche; **w. pump** pompe *f* à eau; *Zool* **w. rat** rat *m* d'eau; *Br* **w. rate** taxe *f* sur l'eau; **w. shortage** pénurie *f* d'eau; **w. ski** ski *m* nautique; **w. skiing** ski nautique; *Zool* **w. snail** hélice *f* aquatique; **w. sports** *(water skiing, windsurfing etc)* sports *mpl* nautiques; *Vulg* = pratique *f* sexuelle qui consiste à uriner sur son ou sa partenaire; *Myth* **w. sprite** ondin, -ine; **w. supply** *(for campers, troops)* provision *f* d'eau; *(to house)* alimentation *f* en eau; *(to area, town)* distribution *f* des eaux, approvisionnement *m* en eau; **w. table** niveau *m* de la nappe phréatique; **w. tank** réservoir *m* d'eau, citerne *f*; **w. tower** château *m* d'eau; **w. transport** transport *m* par voie d'eau; **w. wheel** roue *f* à eau, roue hydraulique; **w. wings** *(for swimming)* flotteurs *mpl*

▸ **water down** VT SEP **1** *(liquid)* diluer, délayer **2** *Fig (expression, remark, accusation)* atténuer; **to w. down one's claims** en rabattre, mettre de l'eau dans son vin; **to w. down an article** rendre un article moins virulent; **a watered-down version of sth** une version édulcorée de qch

waterborne ['wɔːtəbɔːn] ADJ **1** *(vessel)* à flot, flottant **2** *(goods)* transporté par voie d'eau **3** *(disease)* d'origine hydrique

watercolour, *Am* **watercolor** ['wɔːtəkʌlər] N *(picture)* aquarelle *f*, *(paint)* couleur *f* pour aquarelle, peinture *f* à l'eau; **to paint in watercolours** faire de l'aquarelle
▸ ▸ **w. artist** aquarelliste *mf*

water-cooled [-kuːld] ADJ refroidi par eau
▸ ▸ **w. engine** moteur *m* à refroidissement d'eau

watercourse ['wɔːtəkɔːs] N cours *m* d'eau

watercress ['wɔːtəkres] N *Bot, Culin* cresson *m* de fontaine

watered ['wɔːtəd] ADJ
▸ ▸ *Tex* **w. silk** soie *f* moirée; *Fin* **w. stock** titres *mpl* dilués

waterfall ['wɔːtəfɔːl] N chute *f* d'eau, cascade *f*

Waterford crystal ['wɔːtəfəd] N = cristal *m* fabriqué à Waterford en Irlande

waterfowl ['wɔːtəfaʊl] N **1** *(bird)* oiseau *m* aquatique **2** *(no pl)* *(birds)* gibier *m* d'eau, sauvagine *f*

waterfront ['wɔːtəfrʌnt] N *(seafront)* front *m* de l'eau; *(at harbour)* quais *mpl*; **on the w.** *(on seafront)* face à la mer; *(at harbour)* sur les quais

wateriness ['wɔːtərɪnɪs] N *(of soup, sth boiled)* insipidité *f*, fadeur *f*, *(of colour)* ton *m* délavé

watering ['wɔːtərɪŋ] N **1** *(of plant)* arrosage *m*; *(of fields)* irrigation *f* **2** *(of animals)* abreuvage *m* **3** *(of eyes)* larmoiement *m* **4** *Tex (of silk)* moirage *m*
▸ ▸ **w. can** arrosoir *m*; **w. hole** *(for animals)* point *m* d'eau; *Fam Hum (pub)* troquet *m*; *Fam* **this was my favourite w. hole** c'est là que j'allais régulièrement me rincer le gosier; **w. place** *(waterhole)* point d'eau; *Br (spa)* station *f* thermale; *Br (seaside resort)* station balnéaire

waterlogged ['wɔːtəlɒgd] ADJ *(boat, carpet)* plein d'eau; *(wood)* imprégné d'eau; *(shoes, clothes)* trempé; *(land)* détrempé, imbibé d'eau; *(subsoil)* détrempé

Waterloo [wɔːtə'luː] N **the Battle of W.** la bataille de Waterloo; *Fig* **to meet one's W.** *(come up against unresolvable situation)* avoir son compte; *(come up against unbeatable opponent)* trouver son maître; **it's like W. station here** *(noisy and busy)* c'est une vraie maison de fous ici

watermark ['wɔːtəmɑːk] N **1** *Naut (for high or low water)* laisse *f* **2** *(on paper, bank note)* filigrane *m*
VT filigraner

watermelon ['wɔːtəmelən] N pastèque *f*, melon *m* d'eau

waterproof ['wɔːtəpruːf] ADJ *(clothing, material)* imperméable; *(watch, container, seal)* étanche; **w. sheet** bâche *f* étanche
N imperméable *m*; **waterproofs** vêtements *mpl* imperméables
VT imperméabiliser

waterproofing ['wɔːtəpruːfɪŋ] N *(action)* imperméabilisation *f*, *(substance)* imperméabilisant *m*

water-repellent ADJ imperméable, hydrofuge; *(product, spray)* imperméabilisant
N imperméabilisant *m*

water-resistant ADJ qui résiste à l'eau, résistant à l'eau

watershed ['wɔːtəʃed] N **1** *Geog (line)* ligne *f* de partage des eaux; *Am (area)* bassin *m* hydrographique **2** *Fig* point *m* décisif, tournant *m*; *TV* **the (nine o'clock) w.** = l'heure *f* après laquelle l'émission de programmes destinés aux adultes est autorisée; **at this w. in her life** à ce moment critique de sa vie; **the decision proved to be a w.** la décision s'est avérée marquer un grand tournant

waterside ['wɔːtəsaɪd] N bord *m* de l'eau
ADJ *(house, path)* au bord de l'eau; *(flower)* du bord de l'eau; **w. residents** riverains *mpl*
▸ ▸ *Am* **w. workers** dockers *mpl*

waterspout ['wɔːtəspaʊt] N **1** *Met* trombe *f* **2** *(pipe)* tuyau *m*, descente *f* (d'eau)

watertight ['wɔːtətaɪt] ADJ **1** étanche (à l'eau); **to be w.** *(keep water in)* retenir l'eau **2** *Fig (alibi)* en béton; *(argument, reasoning)* inattaquable, indiscutable
▸ ▸ *Naut* **w. bulkhead** cloison *f* étanche

waterway ['wɔːtəweɪ] N voie *f* navigable

waterworks ['wɔːtəwɜːks] NPL **1** *(establishment)* usine *f* de distribution d'eau **2** *Br Fam (urinary system)* voies *fpl* urinaires; **he's having a bit of trouble with his w.** il a des problèmes de vessie **3** *Fam* **to turn on the w.** *(start to cry)* se mettre à pleurer, ouvrir la fontaine

watery ['wɔːtərɪ] ADJ **1** *(surroundings, world)* aquatique; *(ground, soil)* détrempé, saturé d'eau; **the sailors found a w. grave** les marins ont été ensevelis par les eaux **2** *(eyes)* larmoyant, humide **3** *(coffee, tea)* trop léger; *(soup)* trop liquide; *(milk)* qui a trop d'eau; *(vegetables, beer)* insipide; *(taste)* fade, insipide **4** *(light, sun, smile)* faible; *(colour)* délavé, pâle; *(sky)* chargé de pluie; **she gave a w. smile** elle sourit à travers ses larmes

watt [wɒt] N *Elec* watt *m*

wattage ['wɒtɪdʒ] N *Elec* puissance *f* ou consommation *f* en watts

watt-hour N *Elec* wattheure *m*

wattle¹ ['wɒt(ə)l] N **1 w.-and-daub wall** mur *m* en clayonnage revêtu de boue *ou* d'argile **2** *Austr (tree)* acacia *m*

wattle² N *(of bird)* caroncule *f*, *(of fish)* barbillon *m*

wave [weɪv] N **1** *Naut* vague *f*, lame *f*, *Fig* vague; **the pain came in waves** la douleur venait par vagues; *Art* **new w.** nouvelle vague; **w. of crime/refugees/enthusiasm** vague de criminalité/de réfugiés/d'enthousiasme; **w. of anger** bouffée *f* de colère; **a w. of bitterness swept over her** un flot d'amertume l'envahit; *Fam* **to make waves** *(cause trouble)* créer des remous
2 *Phys (electric, magnetic)* onde *f*, **radio waves** ondes radio; **long waves** grandes ondes; **medium/short waves** ondes moyennes/courtes

3 *(in hair)* ondulation *f*, **to have a natural w. (in one's hair)** avoir les cheveux qui ondulent naturellement; **her hair fell in waves to her waist** ses cheveux ondulaient jusqu'à sa taille
4 *(movement)* balancement *m*, ondoiement *m*; *(of hand, hat)* geste *m*, signe *m*; **with a w. of his hand** d'un geste *ou* d'un signe de la main; **the Queen gave them a w. from the car** la Reine les salua de la main depuis la voiture; **with a w. of her magic wand** d'un coup de baguette magique
VI **1** *(of person)* faire signe; *(of flag)* flotter (au vent); *(of corn, grass, plume)* ondoyer, onduler; **to w. to sb** *(signal to)* faire signe à qn; *(greet)* saluer qn de la main; **the kids went to the window to w.** *(goodbye/hello)* les gosses sont allés à la fenêtre pour faire au revoir/bonjour de la main; **the President stepped onto the balcony to w. to the crowd** le président est sorti sur le balcon pour saluer la foule; **he waved to us as he left** il nous fit au revoir de la main en partant; **I waved to him to stop** je lui ai fait signe d'arrêter
2 my hair waves naturally mes cheveux ondulent naturellement
VT **1** *(arm, handkerchief)* agiter; *(umbrella, walking stick)* brandir; **to w. a flag** agiter un drapeau; **to w. one's hand** faire signe de la main; **to w. one's arms about** agiter les bras; **stop waving that gun about** cesse d'agiter ce pistolet dans tous les sens; **to w. a magic wand** agiter une baguette magique; *Fig* **to do sth by waving a magic wand** faire qch d'un coup de baguette magique; **to w. goodbye to sb** agiter la main en signe d'adieu à (l'adresse de) qn, faire au revoir de la main à qn; **w. Mummy goodbye** fais au revoir à maman; *Fig* **you can w. your money goodbye** tu peux abandonner tout espoir de récupérer ton argent
2 *(hair)* **to have one's hair waved** se faire faire une mise en plis
▸ ▸ **w. machine** machine *f* à vagues; **w. power** énergie *f* des vagues
▸ **wave aside** VT SEP **to w. sb aside** faire signe à qn de s'écarter; **to w. aside an objection** écarter une objection
▸ **wave down** VT SEP **to w. a car/sb down** faire signe à une voiture/qn de s'arrêter
▸ **wave on** VT SEP **to w. a car on** faire signe à une voiture de continuer; **he waved us on** de la main il nous a fait signe de continuer

Attention: ne pas confondre avec **to waive**.

waveband ['weɪvbænd] N *Radio* gamme *f* d'ondes, plage *f* (d'ondes)

wavelength ['weɪvleŋθ] N *Radio, Fig* longueur *f* d'onde; *Fig* **we weren't on the same w.** nous n'étions pas sur la même longueur d'onde

waver ['weɪvər] VI *(falter)* *(of person)* vaciller; *(of voice)* trembler; *(of courage)* faiblir; *(of gaze)* flotter; *(of troops)* fléchir; *(of flame)* vaciller; **they never wavered in their support, their support never wavered** leur soutien n'a jamais faibli; **to w. in one's resolution** chanceler dans sa résolution; **the price wavered around the £46 per kilo mark** le prix tournait autour des 46 livres le kilo; **to w. between** hésiter entre; **to w. over** hésiter sur; **they wavered over whether to tell their parents** ils se demandèrent s'ils allaient en parler à leurs parents

waverer ['weɪvərər] N indécis, -ise

wavering ['weɪvərɪŋ] ADJ *(person, mind)* irrésolu, indécis, vacillant; *(voice)* tremblant; *(courage)* faiblissant; *(flame)* vacillant, tremblotant; **their w. resolution** leur détermination chancelante

N *(of person)* hésitation *f,* irrésolution *f; (of voice)* tremblement *m; (of courage)* défaillance *f; (of flame)* tremblement, vacillement *m*

waviness ['weɪvɪnɪs] **N** *(of surface)* caractère *m* onduleux *ou* ondulé; *(of hair)* ondulations *fpl* naturelles

waving ['weɪvɪŋ] **ADJ** *(fields, corn)* ondulant, ondoyant

wavy ['weɪvɪ] **ADJ** *(line, surface, hair)* ondulé

wax¹ **N** cire *f, (for skis)* fart *m; (in ears)* cérumen *m;* **(paraffin) w.** cire (minérale), paraffine *f;* **to mould sb like w.** façonner *ou* former (le caractère de) qn comme de la cire
VT 1 *(floor, furniture)* cirer, encaustiquer; *(furniture)* astiquer; *Ski* farter **2** *(in order to remove hairs)* épiler (à la cire); **to w. one's legs** s'épiler les jambes (à la cire)
▸▸ *Am* **w. beans** haricots *mpl* beurre; **w. crayon** crayon *m* gras; **w. museum** musée *m* de cire

wax² **VI 1** *(of the moon)* croître; **to w. and wane** croître et décroître **2** *esp Fml (be, become)* **to w. eloquent in support of sth** déployer toute son éloquence en faveur de qch; **he waxed indignant** il s'indigna; **to w. lyrical/poetical** devenir lyrique/poétique **(about** à propos de)

waxed [wækst] **ADJ** *(floor, tablecloth)* ciré; *(thread)* poissé; *(moustache)* gominé
▸▸ **w. cotton** coton *m* ciré, **w. jacket** veste *f* en toile huilée

waxen ['wæks(ə)n] **ADJ 1** *(candle, figure)* de cire, en cire **2** *(face, complexion)* cireux

waxing¹ ['wæksɪŋ] **N** *(of floor, furniture)* cirage *m,* encaustiquage *m; (of skis)* fartage *m*

waxing² **N 1** *(of moon)* croissance *f* **2** *Aut (of diesel)* paraffinage *m*

waxwing ['wækswɪŋ] **N** *(bird)* jaseur *m*

waxwork ['wækswɜːk] **N** *(object)* objet *m* de ou en cire; *(statue of person)* statue *f* de cire

waxworks ['wækswɜːks] **N** musée *m* de cire

waxy ['wæksɪ] **ADJ** *(texture, complexion)* cireux; *(potato)* ferme, pas farineux

---

WAY [weɪ]

N rue **1**	chemin **1–3**	route **2**
direction **4**	sens **4**	moyen **5**
façon **6**	manière **6**	égard **7**
état **10**		

N 1 *(street)* rue *f; (path)* chemin *m;* **over or across the w.** de l'autre côté du chemin *ou* de la rue; **the house/the people over or across the w.** la maison/les gens d'en face **2** *(route)* chemin *m;* **the w. to the station** le chemin qui mène *ou* qui conduit à la gare, le chemin de la gare; **to show sb the w.** montrer la route *ou* le chemin à qn; **to ask one's w.** demander son chemin; **to lose one's w.** s'égarer, se perdre; **that's the w. to ruin** c'est le chemin de la ruine; **the right w.** le bon chemin, la bonne route; **to go the wrong w.** se tromper de chemin, faire fausse route; **to go the nearest or shortest w.** prendre le plus court chemin; **to know one's w. about a place** connaître un endroit; **you'll soon find your w. about** tu trouveras bientôt ton chemin tout seul; *Fig* **he knows his w. about or around** il sait se débrouiller, il est débrouillard; **to prepare the w.** préparer la voie; **on the w.** en cours de route, en chemin, chemin faisant; **to stop on the w.** s'arrêter en chemin; **to start on one's w.** se mettre en route; **to be on one's or the w. to Paris** être en route pour Paris; **on my or the w. home** en revenant chez moi, en rentrant; **I must be on my w.** je dois partir; **I'm on my w.** *(coming)* j'arrive; *(going)* je pars; **he's well on the w. to doing it** il est en bonne voie de le faire; **the building is well on the w. to**

completion l'édifice est bien avancé; *Fam* **there's a baby on the w.** elle attend un bébé; **to lead the w. in research** être à la pointe de la recherche; **to lead the w. in fighting inflation** être le chef de file dans la lutte contre l'inflation; **to go the w. of all things** *or* **of all flesh** aller où va toute chose, mourir; **we went our separate ways** nous avons suivi chacun notre chemin; **to go one's own w.** *(follow own wishes)* faire à sa guise; *(differ from others)* faire bande à part, suivre son chemin; **to go out of one's w.** s'écarter de son chemin, dévier de sa route, faire un détour; *Fig* **to go out of one's w. to oblige sb** se donner de la peine pour être agréable à qn; **the w. to a man's heart is through his stomach** = pour conquérir le cœur d'un homme, il faut lui faire de bons petits plats; **the village is rather out of the w.** le village est un peu isolé; **that's nothing out of the w.** rien d'extraordinaire à cela; *Rel* **the W. of the Cross** le chemin de la Croix; **w. in** entrée *f,* **w. out** sortie *f,* **to find a w. out/in** trouver moyen de sortir/d'entrer; **w. through** passage *m;* **to find a w. out of a deadlock** trouver une issue à une impasse; **to find a w. out of a problem** trouver une solution à un problème; **to leave sb a w. out** laisser à qn le moyen de sortir d'une difficulté; **easy w. out** solution *f* de facilité; **to find one's w. to a place** se rendre quelque part; **can you find your w. there?** est-ce que tu sais y aller tout seul?; **I can't find my w. back to the hotel** je n'arrive pas à retrouver l'hôtel; **can you find your w. out?** vous connaissez le chemin pour sortir?; **I can find my own w. out** *(out of house etc)* je trouverai mon chemin; **however did it find its w. into print?** comment en est-on venu à l'imprimer?; **she made her w. to the door/the bar** elle se dirigea vers la porte/se rendit au bar; **to make one's w. towards sb** se diriger vers qn; **to make or work or push one's w. through the crowd** se frayer un chemin à travers la foule; **she made her w. into the house** elle a pénétré dans la maison; **to make one's w. back/out/home** revenir/sortir/rentrer; **how to make one's w. (in the world)** comment réussir; **to work one's w. up** s'élever (à force de travail); **to pay one's w.** *(of company)* se suffire; *(contribute to expenses)* payer sa part; **to see one's w. (clear) to doing sth** être à même de faire qch; **couldn't you see your w. (clear) to doing it?** ne trouveriez-vous pas moyen de le faire?; **to stand in sb's w.** être dans le chemin de qn, barrer le passage à qn; **I don't wish to stand in the w. of your happiness** je ne voudrais pas faire obstacle à votre bonheur; **to stand in the w. of a scheme** s'opposer à un projet; **the obstacles that stand in our w.** les obstacles qui se dressent sur notre chemin; **to put difficulties in sb's w.** opposer *ou* créer des difficultés à qn; **to get in one another's w.** se gêner (les uns les autres); **work gets in the w. of my social life** le travail m'empêche de sortir autant que je voudrais; **to be in sb's w.** gêner qn; **this table is in the w.** cette table gêne le passage *ou* est encombrante; **you're in the w.** tu gênes le passage; *Fig* tu gênes, tu me/nous/*etc* déranges; **to get out of the w.** *(to let sb pass)* se ranger, s'ôter du chemin, s'écarter; **(get) out of the w.!** poussez-vous!, ôtez-vous de là *ou* de mon chemin!; **to get out of sb's w.** s'ôter *ou* s'écarter du chemin de qn; *Fig (in relationship)* laisser le champ libre à qn; **to get sb out of the w.** se débarrasser de qn, écarter *ou* éloigner qn; **to get sth out of the w.** enlever *ou* pousser qch; *Fig* **let's get the subject of holidays out of the w. first** réglons d'abord la question des vacances; **to keep out of the w.** se tenir à l'écart; **to keep out of sb's w.** éviter qn; **to make w. for sb** laisser passer qn, faire place à qn; **clear the**

w.! poussez-vous!; **the agreement will clear the w. for the company's expansion** l'accord déblaiera le terrain pour permettre l'expansion de la société; *Fig* **the w. is clear** la voie est libre; **he is retiring to make w. for a younger man** il prend sa retraite pour céder la place à un plus jeune; **the cinema is going to be demolished to make w. for a supermarket** le cinéma va être démoli et sera remplacé par un supermarché
3 *(distance)* **to go a little w.** *or* **part of the w. with sb** faire un bout de chemin avec qn; **all the w.** tout le long du chemin; *(to the end)* jusqu'au bout; **he talked the entire or whole w.** il a parlé pendant tout le trajet; *Fam* **to go the whole w.** *or* **all the w.** *(sexually)* aller jusqu'au bout; *Fig* **I'm with you all the w.** *(agree)* je suis tout à fait d'accord (avec toi); **I flew most of the w.** j'ai fait la plupart du voyage en avion; **I've come a long w.** j'ai fait un long voyage, j'arrive de loin; *Fig* **she's come a long w.** *(been successful)* elle a bien réussi (dans la vie); *Fig* **she'll go a long w.** elle ira loin; **it's a long w. to London, London's a long w. from here** Londres est bien loin d'ici; **it's a long w. from Paris to Rome** la route est longue de Paris à Rome; **to have a long w. to go** avoir un long chemin à faire; **a little or short w. off** à peu de distance; **it's only a short w. (off)** c'est assez proche; **Christmas is still a long w. off** Noël est encore loin; **a little understanding goes a long w.** un peu de compréhension facilite bien les choses; **a little of it goes a long w.** *(it's very economical, strong-tasting)* il en faut très peu; **I like it but a little goes a long w.** *(of rich food)* j'aime ça mais à petites doses; **a little of him goes a long w.** on en a vite assez de lui; **you can make a little meat go a long w. by doing this** utilisez au mieux un petit morceau de viande en faisant ceci; **to make one's money go a long w.** savoir ménager ses sous; **by a long w.** de beaucoup; **not by a long w.** il s'en faut de beaucoup; **you're a long w. out** *or* **out by a long w.** vous êtes loin du compte, vous vous trompez de beaucoup
4 *(direction)* côté *m,* direction *f,* sens *m;* **which w. is the wind blowing?** d'où vient *ou* souffle le vent?; **which w. does the tap turn?** dans quel sens faut-il tourner le robinet?; *Fig* **so that's the w. the wind's blowing!** ça se passe donc comme ça!; **this w.** de ce côté-ci, par ici; **that w.** de ce côté-là, par là; **(step) this w.!** venez *ou* passez par ici!; **is this the w.?** c'est par ici?; **which w. is the library from here?** par où faut-il passer pour aller à la bibliothèque?; **which w. did you come?** par où êtes-vous venu?; **which w. did she go?** par où est-elle passée?; **which w. do we go?** de quel côté *ou* par où allons-nous?; **this w. and that** de-ci de-là, de tous (les) côtés; **he didn't know which w. to look** il ne savait pas où regarder; **to look the other w.** détourner les yeux; **I've nothing to say one w. or the other** je n'ai rien à dire pour ou contre; **they set off, each going his own w.** ils sont partis chacun de leur côté; **I'm going your w.** je vais de votre côté; **the next time you're that w.** la prochaine fois que vous passerez par là; *Fam* **down our w.** chez nous; *Fam* **she lives out Hampstead w.** elle habite du côté de Hampstead; **if the chance comes your w.** si l'occasion se présente à vous; **that works both ways** ça vaut *ou* marche dans les deux sens; *Fig Fam* **to swing both ways** *(be bisexual)* être *ou* marcher à voile et à vapeur; **the wrong w.** à contre-sens; *Fig Fam* **to rub sb up the wrong w.** prendre qn à rebrousse-poil; **the wrong w. up** sens dessus dessous, à l'envers; **to hold sth (the) right w. up** tenir qch dans le bon sens; **to split a sum of money three ways** partager une somme en trois; *Am* **every which w.** dans tous les sens

5 *(means)* moyen *m*; **to find a w. of doing sth** trouver (le) moyen de faire qch; *Admin* **ways and means** voies et moyens; **there are ways and means** il y a des moyens; *Parl* **Committee of Ways and Means** Commission *f* du Budget

6 *(manner)* façon *f*, manière *f*; **in this w.** de cette façon; **in a friendly w.** amicalement; *(to treat sb)* en ami; **speaking in a general w.** (parlant) d'une façon générale; **in such a w. as to ...** de façon à ..., de telle sorte que ...; *Fam* **no w.!** jamais de la vie!, pas question!, *Fam* des clous!; *Fam* **there's no w.** he'll ... il est absolument impossible qu'il ... + *subj*, *Fam* **there's no w. that's Jeanne Moreau!** tu rigoles?, ce n'est pas Jeanne Moreau!; **without in any w.** wishing to criticize sans aucunement vouloir critiquer; **either w.** *(whatever you decide)* quoi que tu décides; *(whatever happens)* quoi qu'il arrive; **that's the w.!** ça y est!, voilà!, à la bonne heure!; **in such and such a w.** de telle et telle façon; **to go** *or* **set about it the right w.** s'y prendre de la bonne manière *ou* comme il faut; **you're going the right w. to make her angry** ça, c'est la meilleure manière de la mettre en colère; **the best w. is to say nothing** le mieux est de ne rien dire; **in one w. or another** d'une façon ou d'une autre; **there are no two ways about it** il n'y a pas à discuter; **we can't go on in the same old w.** nous ne pouvons pas (toujours) continuer comme ça; **I don't like the w. things are going** je n'aime pas la tournure que prennent les choses; **they'll never finish it the w. things are going** ils n'en finiront jamais, au train où vont les choses; **w. of doing sth** manière *ou* façon de faire qch; **w. of speaking/writing** façon de parler/d'écrire; **w. of living** style *m* de vie; **her w. of looking at things** sa manière de voir (les choses); **it isn't what he says, it's the w. he says it** ce n'est pas ce qu'il dit mais la manière dont il le dit; **I don't like the w. you talk to her** je n'aime pas la manière dont tu lui parles; **to my w. of thinking** selon moi, à mon sens; **that's not my w. (of doing things)** ce n'est pas mon genre, ce n'est pas ma façon de faire; **that's her w.** c'est sa façon de faire; **that's always the w. when you're in a hurry** c'est toujours comme ça quand on est pressé; **that's always the w. with him** il est toujours comme ça, c'est toujours comme ça avec lui; **to do things in one's own w.** faire les choses à sa façon *ou* à sa manière; **to have a w. of one's own** *or* **one's own w. of doing sth** avoir une façon à soi de faire qch, avoir sa méthode pour faire qch; **he's a genius in his w.** c'est un génie dans son genre; **she does what she can for them in her small w.** elle les aide dans la mesure de ses moyens; **the restaurant is doing quite well in a small w.** le restaurant marche bien à son échelle; **he started out in a small w.** *(of businessman)* il a commencé petit; **one's ways** *(behaviour)* ses manières; **you'll soon get into our ways** vous vous ferez bientôt à nos habitudes; **engaging ways** petites façons engageantes; **I know his little ways** je connais ses petites manies; **to get** *or* **fall into the w. of doing sth** *(through habit)* prendre l'habitude de faire qch, s'habituer à faire qch; *(through practice)* apprendre à faire qch; **you'll get into the w. of it** vous vous y ferez; **that's one w. of looking at it!** c'est une façon de voir!; **he has a w. with children** il sait s'y prendre avec les enfants; **to have one's (own) w.** en faire à sa tête; **to get one's (own) w.** arriver à ses fins; **she wants her (own) w.** elle veut n'en faire qu'à sa tête; **if I had my w.** si on me laissait faire; **have it your (own) w.** *(do as you like)* faites ce que vous voulez *ou* à votre guise; *(if you insist)* soit; **she had it all her (own) w.** elle a fait exactement ce qu'elle a voulu;

you can't have it both ways on ne peut pas avoir le beurre et l'argent du beurre; *Old-fashioned, Hum* **he had his w. with her** *(sexually)* il a obtenu ses faveurs

7 *(respect)* égard *m*; **in many ways** à bien des égards; **in some ways** à certains points de vue; **in every w.** sous tous les rapports, en tous points; **in one w.** d'un certain point de vue; **you're right in a w.** d'une certaine manière vous avez raison; **in no w.** en aucune façon, nullement; **she is in no w. or not in any w. to blame** elle n'est aucunement *ou* elle n'est en aucune façon responsable; **this should in no w. be regarded as a victory** cela ne doit en aucune façon être considéré comme une victoire

8 *(sphere)* **I met him in the ordinary w. of business** je l'ai rencontré dans le courant de mes affaires

9 *(progress) Naut* erre *f*; **to get under w.** *(of person)* se mettre en route; *(of ship)* appareiller; *(of meeting)* commencer; *(of campaign etc)* démarrer; **the ship was under w.** le navire était en marche *ou* en route; **an important experiment is under w.** une expérience importante est en cours; **the project is well under w.** le projet est bien avancé

10 *(state, condition)* état *m*; **to be in a good/bad w.** être bien/mal en point; **things seem in a bad w.** les choses ont l'air d'aller mal; **his business is in a bad w.** ses affaires vont mal *ou* périclitent; **to be in a fair w. to do sth** être en bonne voie de *ou* en (bonne) passe de faire qch; **to put sb in the w. of earning a few pounds** donner à qn l'occasion de gagner quelques livres

11 by the w., ... au fait ..., à propos ...; **to mention sth by the w.** mentionner qch en passant *ou* incidemment; **(let it be said) by the w.** soit dit en passant; **all this is by the w.** tout ceci est entre parenthèses; **by the w., did you see him yesterday?** à propos, l'avez-vous vu hier?; **by w. of** *(via)* par, via; **(with the intention of)** à titre de; **by w. of introduction/warning** à titre d'introduction/d'avertissement; **he asked after her dog by w. of changing the conversation** il a demandé des nouvelles de son chien, histoire de changer de sujet; **what do you have by w. of** *or* **in the w. of fruit?** qu'est-ce que vous avez comme fruits?

ADV *Fam* **(a lot)** très; **w. ahead** très avancé (of sur); **he is w. crazy** il est vachement atteint; **it was w. back in the twenties** cela remonte aux années vingt; **Mary and I go w. back** *or* **are friends from w. back** Mary et moi sommes amies de longue date; **w. down south** là-bas dans le sud; **to be w. out** *(mistaken) (of person)* faire une grosse erreur, se tromper sérieusement; **your guess was w. out** vous étiez très loin de la vérité; **it's w. more than I can afford** c'est beaucoup plus que je ne peux payer

▸▸ *Am* **w. station** *Rail* petite gare *f*, *Fig* étape *f*, *Am Rail* **w. train** (train *m*) omnibus *m*

waybill ['weɪbɪl] **N** *Com* feuille *f* de route, connaissement *m*, bulletin *m ou* bordereau *m* d'expédition

wayfarer ['weɪfeərər] **N** voyageur, -euse (à pied)

wayfaring ['weɪfeərɪŋ] **N** voyages *mpl* (à pied)

ADJ voyageur; **a w. life** une vie de voyages; **w. man** voyageur *m* (à pied)

waylay [weɪ'leɪ] **VT** *(pt, pp* **waylaid** [weɪ-'leɪd]*)* **1** *(attack)* attaquer, agresser; **to be waylaid** se faire agresser **2** *(in order to speak to)* arrêter au passage

way-out **ADJ 1** *Fam (weird, eccentric)* dingue **2** *Old-fashioned Sl (great)* géant

wayside ['weɪsaɪd] **N** bord *m* de la route; **to fall by the w.** *(not keep up)* rester en chemin;

(become dishonest), Hum s'écarter du droit chemin

ADV au bord de la route; **a w. inn** une auberge au bord de la route; **w. flowers** les fleurs qui bordent la route

wayward ['weɪwəd] **ADJ** capricieux; **to be w.** *(of person)* n'en faire qu'à sa tête

waywardness ['weɪwədnɪs] **N** caractère *m* difficile; **a certain w. became apparent in his character** il est apparu comme quelqu'un qui n'en faisait qu'à sa tête

wazz [wæz] *Br Sl* **N to have a w.** *(urinate)* faire la petite commission; **to go for a w.** aller faire la petite commission

VI *(urinate)* faire la petite commission

wazzock ['wæzək] **N** *Br Sl* andouille *f*, cloche *f*

WC [dʌb(ə)lju:'si:] **N** *(abbr* water closet) WC *mpl*; **where is the WC?** où sont les WC?

we [wi:] **PERS PRON PL** VOIR GRAMMAIRE A27–8 **1** *(unstressed)* nous; **we were playing** nous jouions; **here we are!** nous voilà!; **we both thank you** nous vous remercions tous (les) deux

2 *(stressed)* nous; **we are English, they are French** nous, nous sommes anglais, eux, ils sont français; **you don't think that we did it!** vous ne pensez pas que c'est nous qui l'avons fait?; **we English** nous autres Anglais **3** *(indefinite)* on; **how are we this morning, Mrs Smith?** comment ça va ce matin, Mme Smith?; **as we say in England** comme on dit en Angleterre; **we all make mistakes sometimes** tout le monde peut se tromper VOIR GRAMMAIRE A28

4 *(plural of majesty, editorial* we*)* nous; **we are convinced that ...** nous sommes convaincus que ...

w/e *(abbr* **week ending**) semaine se terminant

weak [wi:k] **ADJ 1** *(person, currency)* faible; *(in character)* faible (mentalement), mou, *f* molle; *(health)* fragile, délicat; *(body)* fragile; *(argument)* faible, peu convaincant; *(style)* mou; *(decision)* qui dénote de la faiblesse; **to grow w.** *(of person)* s'affaiblir, faiblir; **to be w. in body** être physiquement faible; **to have a w. heart** avoir le cœur faible; **to have a w. (eye)sight** avoir une mauvaise vue; **to have a w. stomach** avoir un estomac délicat; **w. with hunger** affaibli par la faim; **to feel as w. as a kitten** se sentir mou comme une chiffe; *Fam* **to be w. in the head** être faible d'esprit; *Fam* **you must be w. in the head if you believe that** tu dois être dérangé pour croire ça; *Old-fashioned* **the weaker sex** le sexe faible; **in a w. moment** dans un moment de faiblesse; **his w. side** *or* **spot** son point faible; **to find sb's w. spot** trouver le point faible de qn; **she gave a w. smile** elle a eu un faible sourire; **the weaker pupils** les élèves moins doués; **to be w. in French** être faible en français; **the play is w. in character analysis** la pièce est faible du point de vue de l'analyse des personnages; **to have a w. chin/mouth** avoir le menton fuyant/la bouche tombante; **I feel all w. at the knees** j'ai les jambes en coton; **he makes me go all w. at the knees** j'ai les jambes en coton rien que de le voir; *Mus* **w. beat** temps *m* faible; *Radio* **w. signal** signal *m* faible

2 *(solution)* dilué, étendu; *(tea, coffee)* léger; *Aut* **w. mixture** mélange *m* pauvre

3 *Gram (verb)* faible; *Ling (syllable)* non accentué

weaken ['wi:k(ə)n] **VT** affaiblir; *(foundations of house)* miner; *Aut* **to w. the mixture** appauvrir le mélange

VI *(of person, authority, argument)* s'affaiblir, faiblir; *(of sound)* fléchir; *(of currency)* s'affaiblir; **don't w.** ne faiblis pas!; **her courage weakened** son courage a fléchi *ou* faibli,

the pound has weakened against the dollar la livre est en baisse par rapport au dollar

weakening ['wiːk(ə)nɪŋ] **ADJ** *(makes lose strength)* affaiblissant; *(losing strength)* faiblissant

N affaiblissement *m*; *(of will, resistance)* fléchissement *m*; *(of current, currency)* affaiblissement, fléchissement

weakhearted [wiːk'hɑːtɪd] **ADJ** sans courage

weak-kneed [-'niːd] **ADJ** *Fig (person)* lâche, mou, *f* molle; *(decision)* lâche

weakling ['wiːklɪŋ] **N** *(morally)* mauviette *f*, faible *mf*; *(physically)* gringalet *m*

weakly ['wiːklɪ] **ADJ** *(person)* débile, chétif **ADV 1** *(lacking strength)* faiblement **2** *(lacking energy)* sans énergie, mollement; **she protested w.** elle protesta mollement

weak-minded **ADJ 1** *(unintelligent)* faible d'esprit **2** *(lacking character)* irrésolu, indécis, qui manque de résolution

weakness ['wiːknɪs] **N 1** *(of body, character, link, argument)* faiblesse *f*; *Aut (of mixture)* pauvreté *f* **2** *(fault)* point *m* faible; **we all have our own weaknesses** nous avons tous nos faiblesses; **to have a w. for sth/sb** *(like)* avoir un faible pour qch/qn

weak-willed [-'wɪld] **ADJ** faible, sans volonté

weal¹ [wiːl] **N** *(from whip)* marque *f ou* trace *f* de coup

weal² **N** *Arch* **the common w.** le bien commun

wealth [welθ] **N 1** *(riches)* richesse(s) *f(pl)*; **he was a man of great w.** il était très riche **2** *(abundance) (of details etc)* abondance *f*, profusion *f*; **a w. of information** une mine d'informations; **this job offers a w. of opportunity for travel** cet emploi offre de nombreuses occasions de voyage; **she has had a w. of opportunities to prove it** elle a eu une quantité d'occasions de le prouver
▸▸ **w. creation** création *f* de richesses; *Fin* **w. tax** impôt *m* de solidarité sur la fortune

wealth-creating [-kriːeɪtɪŋ] **ADJ** générateur, -trice de richesses

wealthy ['welθɪ] **ADJ** riche, opulent; **a w. heiress** une riche héritière
NPL the w. les riches *mpl*

wean [wiːn] **VT** *(baby)* sevrer; *Fig* **youngsters today are being weaned on computers** les jeunes d'aujourd'hui sont nourris d'informatique; **she had been weaned on Mozart** elle a grandi sur les airs de Mozart; *Fig* **to w. sb from** *ou* **off a bad habit** détacher *ou* détourner qn d'une mauvaise habitude; *Fig* **he was trying to w. himself off cigarettes** il essayait de se passer peu à peu de la cigarette

weaner ['wiːnər] **N** *(pig)* = porcelet *m* venant d'être sevré et pesant moins de 40 kg

weaning ['wiːnɪŋ] **N** sevrage *m*

weapon ['wepən] **N** *Mil, Fig* arme *f*; **the carrying of weapons is illegal** le port d'armes est prohibé; **he was carrying a w.** il avait une arme sur lui; *Fig* **it is an important w. in the fight against inflation** c'est une arme importante dans la lutte contre l'inflation
▸▸ **weapons inspection** inspecteur *m* du désarmement; **weapons inspector** inspecteur *m* du désarmement; **weapons of mass destruction** armes de destruction massive

weaponry ['wepənrɪ] **N** *(weapons)* armes *fpl*, armement *m*

WEAR [weər]

| **N** | usure **2** ▪ usage **2** |
| **VT** | porter **1** ▪ avoir **1** ▪ user **2** |

N 1 *(clothing)* vêtements *mpl*; **children's w.** vêtements pour enfants; **for country w.** pour la campagne

2 *(use, deterioration)* usure *f*, détérioration *f* *(par usure)*; *(of machine)* fatigue *f*; *(of road)* dégradation *f*; **to stand hard** *or* **heavy w.** *(of material)* être d'un bon usage; **those shoes still have some w. in them** ces chaussures sont toujours mettables; **my shoes are showing signs of w.** mes chaussures commencent à s'user; **you'll get lots of w. out of it** *(it will last for a long time)* vous le porterez longtemps; *(it is versatile, can be worn often)* vous le porterez beaucoup; **they get very heavy w.** *(of shoes etc)* ils ont la vie dure; **w. and tear** usure *f*, **fair** *or* **normal w. and tear** usure normale; **living in the big city puts a lot of w. and tear on people** les grandes villes sont une source de stress pour leurs habitants; **to be the worse for w.** *(of garment, sofa etc)* être usé *ou* défraîchi; *(of machine)* être abîmé; *Fig (of person) (tired)* être épuisé; *(bruised)* être amoché; *(hung over)* avoir la gueule de bois; **the next morning he was looking a bit the worse for w.** le lendemain matin il avait l'air plutôt en travers

VT *(pt* **wore** [wɔːr]; *pp* **worn** [wɔːn])* **1** *(garment, glasses, watch, beard etc) (have on)* porter; *(put on)* mettre; *(look, smile)* avoir; **he was wearing glasses/his new jacket** il portait des lunettes/sa nouvelle veste; **w. your glasses/your new jacket** mets tes lunettes/ta nouvelle veste; **she wasn't wearing make-up** elle n'était pas maquillée; **she never wears make-up** elle ne se maquille pas; **she was wearing eye-shadow/lipstick** elle avait de l'ombre à paupières/du rouge à lèvres; **I never w. eye-shadow/lipstick** je ne mets jamais d'ombre à paupières/de rouge à lèvres; **his face wore a smile** il souriait; **his face wore a dubious look** son visage affichait un air dubitatif, il avait un air dubitatif; **skirts are being worn long this year** les jupes sont longues cette année; **to w. black** porter du noir; **I've nothing (fit) to w.** je n'ai rien à me mettre, je n'ai rien de mettable; **he was wearing his slippers** il était en pantoufles; **to w. one's hair long** avoir les cheveux longs; **to w. one's hair in pigtails/in a bun** porter des nattes/un chignon; **you must w. your seat belt** tu dois attacher ta ceinture de sécurité; **she wears her age well** elle porte bien son âge; *Br Fig Fam* **they won't w. it** ça ne marchera pas avec eux; *Br Fig Fam* **she won't w. that argument** ne lui fera pas avaler cet argument

2 *(use, rub etc)* user; **to w. holes in sth** faire des trous à qch (à force d'usage); **to w. a hole/a track in sth** faire un trou/creuser un sillon dans qch; **the water had worn grooves in the rock** l'eau avait creusé des rigoles dans le rocher; **worn with anxiety** usé par les soucis; **the surface has been worn smooth** la surface est devenue lisse (à force d'usure); **to be worn to a shadow** *(of person)* ne plus être que l'ombre de soi-même; **to w. a surface flat** araser une surface; **a path had been worn across the lawn** des centaines d'allées et venues avaient fait un chemin dans la pelouse

VI 1 *(become rubbed etc)* s'user; **to w. smooth** *(of stone)* devenir lisse (par frottement); **my patience is wearing thin** je suis bientôt à bout de patience; **his jokes are wearing a bit thin** ça commence à bien faire avec ses blagues

2 *(last)* **to w. well** *(of material)* être de bon usage, faire bon usage; *Fam (of person)* bien porter son âge; **jeans w. well** *(look good after much use)* les jeans vieillissent bien; **this coat has worn well** ce manteau m'a bien servi *ou* m'a fait de l'usage; **the film has not worn well** le film n'a pas bien vieilli; **it will w. for ever** c'est inusable

3 to w. to a close *or* **an end** toucher à sa fin
▸ **wear away** **VT SEP** user, ronger; **much of**

the detail has been worn away les détails ont été en grande partie effacés; **the pattern on the carpet has been worn away** le motif du tapis s'est effacé

VI *(of material)* s'user; *(of pattern)* s'effacer; **the stone has worn away** la pierre s'est érodée

▸ **wear down** **VT SEP** user; **to w. one's heels down** user ses talons; **to w. down the enemy's resistance** user *ou* épuiser peu à peu la résistance de l'ennemi; *Fig* **to w. sb down** faire céder qn, *Fam* avoir qn à l'usure
VI s'user

▸ **wear off** **VI 1** *(be removed) (of colour, pattern)* s'effacer, disparaître

2 *(decrease) (of pain)* se calmer; *(of anaesthetic)* cesser de faire effet; **the novelty soon wore off** l'attrait de la nouveauté a vite passé; **it'll w. off** ça passera

▸ **wear on** **VI** *(of time)* s'écouler (lentement), avancer (lentement); **as the evening wore on** à mesure que la soirée avançait

▸ **wear out** **VT SEP 1** *(one's clothes etc)* user

2 *(exhaust) (person, sb's patience)* épuiser; **I'm worn out** je suis crevé; **to w. oneself out** s'user, s'épuiser; **to w. oneself out with work** se tuer au travail *ou* à travailler

VI 1 *(of material)* s'user; **this material will never w. out** ce tissu ne s'use pas *ou* est inusable

2 *(of patience)* s'épuiser

wearable ['weərəb(ə)l] **ADJ** *(garment)* mettable

wearer ['weərər] **N** **a jacket that is too heavy for the w.** une veste trop lourde à porter; **designed with the w.'s comfort in mind** conçu pour le confort de celui qui le portera

wearily ['wɪərɪlɪ] **ADV 1** *(to smile etc)* d'un air las, avec lassitude; *(to answer)* d'un ton las **2** *(to walk etc)* péniblement

weariness ['wɪərɪnɪs] **N 1** *(tiredness)* fatigue *f*, lassitude *f*; **a general air of w. has settled over the country** un sentiment général de morosité s'est emparé du pays **2** *(discontent)* ennui *m*, lassitude *f*

wearing ['weərɪŋ] **ADJ** fatigant, lassant; *(stronger)* épuisant; **their company is rather w.** je trouve leur présence assez pénible; **a very w. day** une journée très fatigante

wearisome ['wɪərɪs(ə)m] **ADJ** fatigant, ennuyeux; **his w. insistence on …** sa façon pénible d'insister sur …

weary ['wɪərɪ] **ADJ 1** *(tired) (physically)* fatigué, las, *f* lasse; *(mentally)* las, dégoûté (**of** de); **in their present w. state** dans l'état de fatigue où ils sont pour le moment; **he had grown w. of listening to their complaints** il s'était lassé de les écouter se plaindre; **to feel w.** se sentir las; **to look w.** avoir l'air fatigué; **to be w. of war/solitude** être las de la guerre/de la solitude; **to be w. of life** être dégoûté de la vie; **to grow w. of waiting** se lasser d'attendre; **a w. smile** un sourire las

2 *(tiring)* fatigant, ennuyeux; **a w. day** une journée fatigante; **it was a w. climb** la montée était pénible

VI se lasser, se fatiguer (**of** de); **to w. of doing sth** se lasser de faire qch

VT lasser, fatiguer; **he wearies me with all his complaints** je suis las de l'entendre se plaindre, il me lasse avec ses plaintes

wearying ['wɪərɪɪŋ] **ADJ** fatigant, ennuyeux; **I find her quite w.** je la trouve très pénible; **I find it very w.** cela me fatigue beaucoup

weasel ['wiːz(ə)l] **N** *(animal)* belette *f*, *Fig Fam (person)* personne *f* sournoise
▸▸ *Fam* **w. words** paroles *fpl* ambiguës
▸ **weasel out** **VI** *Fam* **to w. out of an obligation** se débrouiller pour éviter une obligation; **you're not going to w. out of it this time!** tu ne vas pas te défiler cette fois!

weather ['weðər] N temps *m*; **in all wea-thers** par tous les temps; **in (the) hot/cold w.** par temps chaud/froid; **the w. is settled, we're in for a spell of fine w.** le temps est au beau; **we had good w. for the time of year** nous avons eu du beau temps pour la saison; **what kind of w. did you have on your holiday?** quel temps avez-vous eu pendant vos vacances?; **what's the w. like?** quel temps fait-il?; **in spite of bad w.** en dépit du mauvais temps; **in this** *or* **such w.** par un temps pareil; **w. permitting** si le temps le permet; *Fig* **to make heavy w. (of doing sth)** *(make a fuss)* faire un tas d'histoires (pour faire qch); *(find difficulty)* avoir toutes les peines du monde (à faire qch); **to make heavy w. (of ship)** bourlinguer; *Fig* **to keep one's w. eye open** veiller au grain; *Fig* **to be under the w.** *(ill)* ne pas se sentir bien, ne pas être très bien; *(depressed)* être déprimé

SEE GRAMMAR B29

VT **the rocks had been weathered by wind and rain** le vent et la pluie avaient érodé les rochers; *Naut* **to w. a storm** étaler une tempête; *Fig* **to w. the storm** tenir le coup; *Pol* tenir le coup, surmonter la crise

VI *(of rock)* s'éroder; *(of copper)* se couvrir de patine, se patiner; *(fade) (of paintwork, stonework etc)* vieillir; **the brickwork has weathered to a pleasant shade of pink** la brique a pris une jolie couleur rose avec le temps; **a stone that weathers well** une pierre qui supporte bien le passage du temps; *Fig* **he has weathered well** il a bien vieilli; **the theory has weathered well** la théorie a bien résisté au temps

▸▸ **w. bulletin** bulletin *m* météorologique; **w. chart** carte *f* météorologique; **w. forecast** prévisions *fpl* météorologiques, météo *f*; **what's the w. forecast for tomorrow?** quelle est la météo pour demain?; **w. map** carte *f* météorologique; **w. report** bulletin *m* météorologique; **w. satellite** satellite *m* météorologique; **w. ship** navire *m* météorologique; **w. side** *(of house etc)* côté exposé au vent; *Naut* bord du vent; **w. station** station *f ou* observatoire *m* météorologique; **w. strip** *(for door, window)* bourrelet *m* isolant, calfeutrage *m*; **w. vane** girouette *f*; **w. warning** alerte *f* météorologique; **to issue a w. warning** lancer une alerte météorologique

weatherbeaten ['weðəbi:t(ə)n] ADJ *(person, face)* hâlé, basané; *(cliffs, rocks, castle)* battu par le vent et la pluie

weatherboarding ['weðəbɔ:dɪŋ] N *Constr* planches *fpl* à recouvrement

weatherbound ['weðəbaʊnd] ADJ retenu *ou* arrêté par le mauvais temps

weathercock ['weðəkɒk] N *(on roof)*, *Fig* girouette *f*

weathergirl ['weðəgɜ:l] N présentatrice *f* de météo

weathering ['weðərɪŋ] N *(of rocks)* érosion *f*; *(fading) (of paintwork, stonework)* vieillissement *m*

weatherman, *pl* **weathermen** ['weðəmæn, -men] N *TV, Radio* monsieur *m* météo; **what did the w. say?** qu'est-ce qu'ils ont dit à la météo?

weatherproof ['weðəpru:f] ADJ *(paint, coating)* résistant à l'eau; *(fabric)* imperméable; *(windows, house)* étanche; *(equipment, machinery)* qui résiste aux intempéries

VT *(fabric)* imperméabiliser; *(house)* rendre étanche

weatherstrip ['weðəstrɪp] VT *(window)* calfeutrer

weave [wi:v] N *Tex (pattern)* tissage *m*; **a tight/loose w.** un tissage serré/lâche

VT *(pt* **wove** [wəʊv]; *pp* **woven** ['wəʊv(ə)n]) *Tex* tisser; *(garland, basket)* tresser; *(strands, small branches)* entrelacer; **to w. yarn into cloth** tisser du fil; **to w. a garland out of flowers** tresser une guirlande de fleurs; *Fig* **skilfully woven plot** intrigue bien tissée *ou Fam* ficelée; **to w. a spell** composer un charme; **to w. one's way through sth** se faufiler entre *ou* parmi qch; **she weaves the various strands of the story into a satisfying whole** elle tisse les différents fils de l'histoire en un tout satisfaisant; **political elements have been woven into the plot** des éléments politiques ont été introduits dans *ou* intégrés à l'intrigue

VI **1** *Tex* tisser **2** *Fig* **to w. through the traffic** se frayer un chemin parmi les voitures; **to w. in and out of the crowd** se faufiler dans la foule *ou* parmi la foule **3** *Fam* **to get weaving** *(start)* s'y mettre; **get weaving!** vas-y!

weaver ['wi:vər] N *Tex* tisserand, -ande, tisseur, -euse

weaver(bird) ['wi:və(bɜːd)] N *Tex* tisserin *m*

weaving ['wi:vɪŋ] N *Tex* tissage *m*

Web [web] N *Comput* **the W.** le Web, la Toile

▸▸ **W. address** adresse *f* de site Internet; **W. authoring** création *f* de pages Web; **W. authoring tool** outil *m* de création de pages Web; **W. browser** navigateur *m*, logiciel *m* de navigation; **W. designer** concepteur, -trice de sites Web; **W. forum** forum *m* Internet; **W. hosting** hébergement *m* de sites Web; **W. master** Webmaster *m*, Webmestre *m*, responsable *mf* de site Web; **W. page** page *f* Web; **W. phone** téléphone *m* par Internet; **W. publishing** édition *f* sur le Web; **W. server** serveur *m* Web; **W. site** site *m* Web, site Internet; **W. space** espace *m* Web; **W. streaming** streaming *m*

web [web] N **1** *(fabric)* tissu *m* **2** *(of spider)* toile *f* **3** *Fig (of lies)* tissu *m*; *(of intrigue)* réseau *m* **4** *Biol (on feet) (of duck, frog)* palmure *f*, *(of human)* palmature *f* **5** *Typ* bande *f* de papier continue

webbed [webd] ADJ palmé; **to have w. feet or toes** *(duck, frog)* avoir les pattes palmées; *(human)* avoir une palmature

webbing ['webɪŋ] N **1** *(of chair, bed etc)* sangles *fpl* **2** *(fabric)* toile *f* à sangles **3** *Biol* palmure *f* **4** *Mil* sangles *fpl*

webcam ['webkæm] N caméra *f* Internet

webcast ['webkɑ:st] N webcast *m*
VT diffuser sur Internet

webcaster ['webkɑ:stər] N diffuseur *m* sur Internet

webcasting ['webkɑ:stɪŋ] N webcasting *m*

web-footed, **web-toed** ADJ palmipède, aux pieds palmés

weblog ['weblɒg] N *Comput* weblog *m*

web-offset printing N impression *f* (offset) continue

webzine ['webzi:n] N webzine *m*

Wed *abbr* **Wednesday**

wed [wed] *(pt, pp* **wedded,** *occ* **wed**; *prp* **wedding**) VT **1** *(get married to)* épouser; *Fig* **to be wedded to one's work** faire passer son travail avant tout; **they're wedded to the idea of ...** ils tiennent absolument à l'idée de ...; **the fate of the project was wedded to that of the Chairman** la destinée du projet était liée à celle du Président **2** *(of priest) (couple)* marier; **he wanted to see all his daughters w. before he died** il voulait voir toutes ses filles mariées avant sa mort

VI se marier

we'd [wi:d] CONTR **1** = **we had,** *see* **have**
2 = **we would,** *see* **would**

wedded ['wedɪd] ADJ *(person)* marié; **my (lawful) w. wife/husband** mon épouse/époux légitime; **w. bliss** bonheur *m* conjugal

wedding ['wedɪŋ] N mariage *m*, noces *fpl*; **I've been invited to a w.** j'ai été invité à un mariage; **the w. guests** les invités *mpl* (au mariage)

▸▸ **w. anniversary** anniversaire *m* de mariage; **w. band** alliance *f*; **w. breakfast** repas *m* de noces; **w. cake** gâteau *m* de noces, ≃ pièce *f* montée; **w. day** jour *m* du mariage; **on my w. day** le jour de mon mariage; **w. dress** robe *f* de mariée; **w. invitation** invitation *f* de mariage; **w. list** liste *f* de mariage; **w. march** marche *f* nuptiale; **w. night** nuit *f* de noces; **w. planner** organisateur, -trice de mariages; **w. present** cadeau *m* de mariage; **w. ring** alliance *f*; *Fam Hum* **w. tackle** *(man's genitals)* bijoux *mpl* de famille

wedge [wedʒ] N **1** *Tech (for keeping sth in place)* cale *f*, *(for cutting wood)* coin *m*; **to drive in a w.** enfoncer un coin; *Fig* **it has driven a w. between them** ça a mis une distance entre eux; *Fig* **it's the thin end of the w.** c'est s'engager sur une mauvaise pente; **w.-heeled shoes** chaussures *fpl* à semelles compensées **2** **w. of cake** morceau *m* (triangulaire) de gâteau, part *f* (de gâteau); **a w. of cheese** un morceau de fromage **3** *Br Sl (money)* fric *m*, flouze *m*, pognon *m*

VT *Tech* coincer; **to w. a door open** maintenir une porte ouverte avec une cale; **to w. a piece of paper in a crack** coincer *ou* enfoncer un bout de papier dans une fente; **I was wedged (in) between two large women** je me suis trouvé coincé entre deux grosses femmes

wedge-shaped ADJ en (forme de) coin; **a w. piece of cheese/land** un triangle de fromage/de terre

wedgie ['wedʒɪ] N *Fam* **to have a w.** avoir le slip coincé entre les fesses; **to give sb a w.** = remonter brusquement le slip de quelqu'un pour le lui coincer entre les fesses

wedlock ['wedlɒk] N *Law* mariage *m*; **to be born out of w.** être un enfant illégitime

Wednesday ['wenzdɪ] N mercredi *m*; **W. 9 September** mercredi 9 septembre; **W. morning/evening** mercredi matin/soir; **it's W. today** nous sommes mercredi aujourd'hui; **on Wednesdays** le mercredi; **they're coming on W.** ils viennent mercredi; **every W.** tous les mercredis VOIR GRAMMAIRE A81–2; B61–2

wee¹ [wi:] ADJ *esp Scot Fam* petit; **a w. bit** un petit peu; **a w. drop of whisky** un doigt *ou* une larme de whisky

wee² N, VI *Br Fam* = **wee-wee**

weed [wi:d] N **1** *(in garden)* mauvaise herbe *f*; **the garden was overgrown with weeds** le jardin était envahi par les mauvaises herbes **2** *Old-fashioned Fam* **the w.** *(tobacco)* le tabac; **to give up the w.** arrêter de fumer **3** *Fam (marijuana)* marijuana *f*, herbe *f* **4** *Pej (person) (in build)* personne *f* chétive, gringalet *m*; *(in character)* mauviette *f*; **don't be such a w.!** arrête de faire la mauviette!

VT *(garden)* désherber; *(path)* arracher les mauvaises herbes de

VI arracher *ou* enlever les mauvaises herbes; *(with hoe)* sarcler

▸ **weed out** VT SEP *Fig (weak candidates)* éliminer; **to w. out the bad (from the good)** éliminer *ou* rejeter ce qui est de mauvaise qualité

weeding ['wi:dɪŋ] N désherbage *m*; *(with hoe)* sarclage *m*

weedkiller ['wi:dkɪlər] N herbicide *m*, désherbant *m*

weeds [wi:dz] NPL *Old-fashioned (widow's)* vêtements *mpl* de deuil

weedy ['wi:dɪ] ADJ **1** *(garden etc)* couvert de mauvaises herbes **2** *Pej (person, arms)* malingre, chétif **3** *(feeble) (sound of instrument)* faible

weegie ['wi:dʒɪ] *Br Fam Pej* N habitant, -ante de Glasgow
  ADJ de Glasgow

week [wi:k] N semaine *f*; **what day of the w. is it?** quel jour de la semaine sommes-nous?; **next/last w.** la semaine prochaine/dernière; **the w. before last** pas la semaine dernière, celle d'avant; **the w. after next** pas la semaine prochaine, celle d'après; **w. in w. out** toutes les semaines que Dieu nous envoie; **I haven't seen her for** *or* **in weeks** ça fait des semaines que je ne l'ai pas vue, je ne l'ai pas vue depuis des semaines; *Rel* **Holy W.** la semaine sainte; **once/twice a w.** une/deux fois par semaine; **every w.** tous les huit jours; **within a w.** sous huitaine; **a w. from now, today w., in a w.'s time** aujourd'hui en huit, dans une huitaine; **tomorrow/Tuesday w.** demain/mardi en huit; **yesterday w.** il y a eu hier huit jours; **in a w. or so** dans une huitaine; **it'll take a w. to get there** il faudra une semaine pour arriver là-bas; **in six weeks' time** dans six semaines; **a w. ago today** il y a (aujourd'hui) huit jours; **I'm taking a w.'s holiday** *or* **a w. off** je vais prendre huit jours de congé; *Ind etc* **forty-hour w.** semaine de quarante heures; **a w.'s wages** le salaire d'une semaine, une semaine de salaire, *Fam* une semaine; **this dress cost me a w.'s wages** cette robe m'a coûté une semaine de salaire; **to be paid by the w.** être payé à la semaine

weekday ['wi:kdeɪ] N jour *m* ouvrable; **on weekdays** en semaine; **weekdays only** en semaine uniquement, tous les jours sauf samedi et dimanche

weekend [wi:k'end] N week-end *m*, *pl* week-ends, *Can* fin *f* de semaine; **to have one's weekends free** être libre le week-end; **have a good w.!** bon week-end!, *Can* bonne fin de semaine!; **I'll do it at** *or* **esp Am on the w.** je le ferai pendant ce week-end; *Br* **what do you do at the weekend(s)?**, *esp Am* **what do you do (on) weekends?** qu'est-ce que vous faites le week-end?; **what are you doing at the w.?** qu'est-ce que vous faites ce week-end?; **to make a w. visit to relations** rendre visite à de la famille pendant le week-end
  VI passer le week-end *ou Can* la fin de semaine
  ▸▸ **w. break** = séjour *m* d'un week-end; **w. cottage** maison *f* secondaire *ou* de campagne *(où on passe le week-end)*; *Br Rail* **w. return** = billet *m* aller-retour valable du vendredi au dimanche soir

weekender [wi:k'endər] N = personne *f* en voyage pour le week-end; **they're weekenders** ils viennent/vont y passer le week-end

weekly ['wi:klɪ] **ADJ** *(magazine, visit, payment)* hebdomadaire; *(pay)* de la semaine; *(tenant)* à la semaine; **these incidents were an almost w. occurrence** ces incidents avaient lieu presque chaque semaine
  N (journal *m* / revue *f*) hebdomadaire *m*; **the weeklies** la presse hebdomadaire
  ADV *(every week)* toutes les semaines, tous les huit jours, chaque semaine; **twice w.** deux fois par semaine; **to be paid w.** être payé à la semaine

weeknight ['wi:knaɪt] N soir *m* de semaine; **at seven on weeknights** à sept heures les soirs de semaine; **I'm not letting you go to a party on a w.** je ne vais pas te permettre d'aller à une soirée pendant la semaine

weenie ['wi:nɪ] N *Am* = **wiener**

weeny ['wi:nɪ] **ADJ** *Fam* minuscule

weeny-bopper [-bɒpər] N *Fam* = très jeune fan *f* de musique pop

weep [wi:p] N **to have a good w.** pleurer un bon coup; **a good w. would help you** pleure

un bon coup, ça ira mieux; **to have a little w.** verser quelques larmes
  VI *(pt, pp* **wept** [wept]*)* **1** *(of person)* pleurer; **to w. bitterly** pleurer à chaudes larmes; **to w. for joy** pleurer de joie; **to w. for sb** *(mourn)* pleurer (la mort de) qn; *(feel sorry for)* pleurer sur le sort de qn; **to w. for one's lost youth** pleurer sa jeunesse perdue; **it's enough to make you w.** c'est à faire pleurer; **I could have wept to see it** j'en aurais pleuré (en le voyant) **2** *(of wall, rock)* suinter, suer; *(of sore)* couler, exsuder; **the smoke was making my eyes w.** la fumée me faisait pleurer les yeux
  VT to w. tears of joy pleurer de joie; **to w. one's heart** *or* **one's eyes out** pleurer à chaudes larmes

weeping ['wi:pɪŋ] **ADJ 1** *(child)* qui pleure **2** *Med (eczema)* suintant
  N *(of person)* pleurs *mpl*, larmes *fpl*; **we could hear w. from the next room** on pouvait entendre quelqu'un qui pleurait dans la pièce d'à côté; **the sound of w.** des pleurs; **a fit of w.** une crise de larmes
  ▸▸ **w. willow** saule *m* pleureur

weepy ['wi:pɪ] *Fam* **ADJ 1** *(book, film)* larmoyant, mélo; **there's a w. bit coming next** il y a un passage mélo après **2** **to feel w.** avoir envie de pleurer; **it makes me go all w.** ça me fait pleurer
  N *(book, film)* mélo *m*, livre *m* / film *m* à faire pleurer dans les chaumières

weevil ['wi:vɪl] N *(beetle)* charançon *m*

wee-wee *Br Fam* N *(in children's language)* pipi *m*; **to have a w.** faire pipi; **do you want to go w.?** tu veux faire pipi?
  VI faire pipi

WEF [dʌb(ə)lju:i:'ef] N *(abbr* **World Economic Forum)** Forum *m* mondial de l'économie

weft [weft] N *Tex* trame *f*

weigh [weɪ] **VT 1** *(package etc)* peser; **to w. sth in one's hand** soupeser qch; **to w. oneself** se peser
  2 *(consider) (one's words)* peser, mesurer, ménager; **to w. sth in one's mind** considérer qch; **to w. the consequences** calculer les conséquences *(of sth* de qch*)*; **to w. the pros and (the) cons** peser le pour et le contre; **to w. the risks/the evidence** évaluer les risques/les preuves; **to w. one thing against another** mettre deux choses en balance
  3 *Naut* **to w. anchor** lever l'ancre, appareiller
  VI 1 *(of person, parcel etc)* peser; **it weighs two kilos** ça pèse deux kilos; *Fam* **this case weighs a ton** cette valise pèse une tonne; **how much do you w.?** combien est-ce que tu pèses?
  2 **it's weighing on my mind** cela me trouble *ou* me tracasse; **it weighed heavy on his conscience** cela pesait sur sa conscience
  3 *(have influence)* **her qualifications weighed in her favour** ses qualifications ont fait pencher la balance en sa faveur *ou* ont joué en sa faveur; **his past record weighed against him** son passé a joué en sa défaveur
  ▸ **weigh down VT SEP** surcharger; **in order to w. the body down** pour alourdir le corps; **branch weighed down with fruit** branche surchargée de fruits; *Fig* **weighed down by** *or* **with heavy responsibilities** accablé de grosses responsabilités; *Fig* **to be weighed down by** *or* **with grief** être accablé par la tristesse
  ▸ **weigh in VI 1** *(of jockey, boxer) (before race or match)* se faire peser; **he weighed in at 75 kilos** il faisait 75 kilos à la pesée **2** *Fam (enter fight, debate)* intervenir; **to w. in (with an argument)** intervenir (en présentant un argument)

  ▸ **weigh out VT SEP** peser; **w. out 200 grams of flour for me** pèse-moi 200 grammes de farine
  ▸ **weigh up VT SEP** **to w. up the situation** peser la situation; **to w. sb up** *(their character)* estimer la valeur de qn; *(their intentions)* estimer les intentions de qn; **to w. up one's chances of doing sth** calculer ses chances de faire qch; **to w. up the advantages and disadvantages of sth** peser le pour et le contre de qch

weighbridge ['weɪbrɪdʒ] N pont-bascule *m*, *pl* ponts-bascules

weigh-in N *Boxing, Horseracing* pesée *f*

weighing ['weɪɪŋ] N pesage *m*
  ▸▸ **w. in** *(of jockey, boxer)* pesage; **w.-in room** pesage; **w. machine** *(for people)* balance *f*, *(for loads)* bascule *f*

weight [weɪt] N **1** *(of person, parcel etc)* poids *m*; **to feel the w. of sth** *(in hand)* soupeser qch; **that case must be quite a w.** cette valise doit être drôlement lourde; **to sell by w.** vendre au poids; **to give short w.** tricher sur le poids; **it's ten pounds in w.** cela pèse dix livres; **it's twice the w. of the other one** ça pèse deux fois plus que l'autre; **they're the same w.** ils font le même poids; **it's worth its w. in gold** cela vaut son pesant d'or; **what a w.!** que ça pèse lourd!, que c'est lourd!; **to lose w.** perdre du poids; **to gain** *or* **put on w.** prendre du poids; **to watch one's w.** surveiller son poids; **to have a w. problem** avoir un problème de poids; **to be a w. watcher** surveiller son poids; *Fig* **to pull one's w.** y mettre du sien; *Fig* **you're not pulling your w.** tu ne fais pas assez d'effort; *Horseracing* **to carry w.** être handicapé
  2 *(for weighing)* poids *m*; **set of weights** série *f* de poids; **weights and measures** poids et mesures *fpl*
  3 *(object) (of clock)* poids *m*; *(for fishing net)* lest *m*; **don't lift any heavy weights** ne soulève pas de poids trop lourds
  4 *(load)* charge *f*; **this pillar bears the w. of the whole building** cette colonne soutient tout le bâtiment; **to give way under the w. of sth** fléchir sous le poids de qch; **he feels the w. of his responsibilities** ses responsabilités lui pèsent; **that is** *or* **takes a w. off my mind** cela me soulage, ça m'ôte un poids; *Fam* **I'm going to take the w. off my feet for a bit** je vais me reposer un peu
  5 *(of blow)* force *f*; **his blow had no w. behind it** son coup était sans force; **you'll feel the w. of my hand, my lad!** tu vas recevoir une claque, mon gars!
  6 *Fig (importance)* importance *f*; **to give w. to an argument** donner du poids à un argument; **what he says carries w.** sa parole a du poids *ou* de l'autorité; **she doesn't carry much w. with the committee** elle n'a pas beaucoup d'influence auprès du comité; **the w. of the evidence was against him** les témoignages pesaient contre lui; **he threw his w. behind the other candidate** il a soutenu l'autre candidat à fond; *Fam* **to throw one's w. about** *or* **around** faire l'important; **they won the battle by sheer w. of numbers** ils ont gagné la bataille parce qu'ils avaient l'avantage numérique
  VT 1 *(fix a weight to)* attacher un poids à; *(net, rope)* lester, plomber; *(walking stick)* plomber
  2 *Econ (index, average etc)* pondérer; *Fig* **the circumstances are weighted in his favour** les circonstances pèsent en sa faveur *ou* lui sont favorables; **the electoral system is weighted against small parties** le système électoral défavorise les petits partis
  ▸▸ **w. allowance** *(in aeroplane)* poids *m* de bagages autorisé; **w. charge** taxation *f* au poids; **w. loss** perte *f* de poids; **w. training** entraînement *m* aux haltères; **to do w. training** faire des haltères

▶ **weight down** VT SEP *(hold down)* retenir *ou* maintenir avec un poids; **the body had been weighted down with stones** le corps avait été alourdi de pierres

weighted ['weɪtɪd] ADJ **1** *(with a weight)* chargé d'un poids; *(balloon)* lesté; *(walking stick)* plombé **2** *(average, index)* pondéré
▶▶ *Fin* **w. average** moyenne *f* pondérée; *Acct* **w. average cost** coût *m* moyen pondéré; *Mktg* **w. distribution** distribution *f* valeur

weightily ['weɪtɪlɪ] ADV *(to reason)* puissamment, avec force

weighting ['weɪtɪŋ] N *Econ (of index etc)* pondération *f*, coefficient *m*; *Admin* **London w.** indemnité *f* de résidence à Londres

weightless ['weɪtlɪs] ADJ *Astronaut* en état d'apesanteur
▶▶ **w. conditions** état *m* d'apesanteur

weightlessness ['weɪtlɪsnɪs] N *Astronaut* apesanteur *f*

weightlifter ['weɪtlɪftər] N haltérophile *mf*

weightlifting ['weɪtlɪftɪŋ] N haltérophilie *f*

weighty ['weɪtɪ] ADJ **1** *(heavy)* pesant, (très) lourd **2** *Fig (motive)* grave, important, sérieux; *(reasoning)* puissant, d'un grand poids; *(argument)* de poids

weir [wɪər] N *(across river etc)* barrage *m*

weird [wɪəd] ADJ **1** *(eerie)* mystérieux, inquiétant **2** *(odd)* étrange, bizarre; **he went a bit w. after his parents died** il est devenu un peu bizarre après la mort de ses parents; **that's w.** c'est bizarre
▶ **weird out** VT SEP *Am Fam* faire flipper

weirdie ['wɪədɪ] N *Fam* = **weirdo**

weirdly ['wɪədlɪ] ADV *(oddly)* étrangement, bizarrement

weirdness ['wɪədnɪs] N *(oddness) (of person, clothing)* caractère *m* étrange *ou* bizarre

weirdo, weirdy ['wɪədəʊ, -dɪ] N *Fam* excentrique *mf*, drôle d'oiseau *m*; *(frightening etc)* type *m* bizarre

WELCOME ['welkəm] ADJ **1** *(person)* bienvenu; **to make sb w.** faire bon accueil à qn; **you're always w.** vous êtes toujours le bienvenu; **any friend of Bob's is always w. here** les amis de Bob sont toujours les bienvenus ici; **I did not feel w.** je ne me suis pas senti le bienvenu; **the card is w. in over 1,000 outlets** la carte est acceptée dans plus de 1000 points de vente; **w.!** soyez le bienvenu!; **w. to England!** bienvenue en Angleterre!; **w. back!** nous sommes heureux de vous revoir!; *Radio, TV (after commercial)* re-bonjour!/re-bonsoir!; **w. home!** bienvenue à la maison!
2 *(agreeable)* agréable; **a w. cup of coffee** une bonne tasse de café; **this is a very w. development** c'est un grand progrès; **this is w. news** je me réjouis/nous nous réjouissons de cette nouvelle; **the hotel was a w. sight** on a aperçu l'hôtel avec plaisir; **that would be most w.** *(coffee, brandy, sandwich)* ça me ferait le plus grand bien; **this cheque is most w.** ce chèque est vraiment bienvenu *ou* tombe à merveille; **a w. change** un changement opportun; **the laid-back atmosphere of Somerset made a w. change from London** l'atmosphère détendue de Somerset nous changeait en bien de Londres
3 *(free)* **to be w. to do sth** être le bienvenu à faire qch; **you're w. to ask any questions** vos questions seront les bienvenues; **anybody is w. to attend** c'est ouvert à tous; **you're w. to borrow any of my books** ma bibliothèque est à votre disposition; **they're w. to stay with us** ils peuvent venir chez nous; **you're w. to it** je t'en prie (ne te gêne pas); *Iron* je te le/la laisse; **you're w. to try** libre à vous

d'essayer; **you're w.!** *(on being thanked)* je vous en prie!, de rien!, ce n'est rien!; **tell her she's w.** dis-lui que ce n'est rien!
N accueil *m*; **we were given a wonderful w.** nous avons été merveilleusement bien accueillis; **the whole town prepared a w. for him** la ville entière se préparait à l'accueillir; **to extend a w. to sb** souhaiter la bienvenue à qn; **to give sb a warm w.** faire un accueil chaleureux à qn; **he gave us a very poor or cold w.** il nous a reçus froidement, il nous a mal reçus; **w. bouquet** bouquet *m* d'accueil; **w. drink** cocktail *m* de bienvenue, pot *m* d'accueil
VT **1** *(person) (wish welcome)* souhaiter la bienvenue à; *(greet)* faire bon accueil à, bien accueillir, accueillir *ou* recevoir avec plaisir; **to w. the/an opportunity to do sth** se réjouir de *ou* saluer l'occasion de faire qch; **I w. every chance of getting out of the house** je suis content de sortir de la maison chaque fois que c'est possible; **his efforts weren't welcomed** ses efforts ont reçu peu d'encouragement; *Radio, TV* **I am pleased to w. back Billy Bragg** j'ai le plaisir d'accueillir à nouveau Billy Bragg
2 *(receive)* accueillir; **to w. sb warmly** faire un accueil chaleureux à qn; **the announcement was welcomed with indifference** la nouvelle a été accueillie avec indifférence
▶▶ **w. committee** comité *m* d'accueil; **w. mat** paillasson *m*; *Fig* **they put out the w. mat for him** ils l'ont accueilli à bras ouverts; **w. pack** *(at conference, in hotel)* documentation *f* *(remise à l'accueil)*; **w. reception** réception *f* de bienvenue

welcoming ['welkəmɪŋ] ADJ *(smile, person, atmosphere)* accueillant; *(speech, committee)* d'accueil

weld [weld] N *(joint)* soudure *f*
VT **to w. (together)** *(pieces of metal)* souder; *(pieces of plastic)* unir à chaud; *Fig* **to w. employees into a team** réunir des employés en une équipe bien soudée; **he has welded his players into a formidable unit** il a soudé ses joueurs pour former une équipe formidable
▶▶ **w. spot** point *m* de soudure

welder ['weldər] N soudeur, -euse; **w.'s mask** masque *m* protecteur pour la soudure

welding ['weldɪŋ] N soudure *f*, soudage *m*; **arc w.** soudure à l'arc
▶▶ **w. torch** chalumeau *m*

welfare ['welfeər] N **1** *(wellbeing)* bien-être *m*; **to have sb's w. at heart** avoir à cœur le bonheur *ou* le bien-être de qn; **the w. of the nation** le bien public **2** *Am (social security)* aide *f* sociale; **to be on w.** toucher les allocations; **the w. lines are lengthening** la masse des gens qui touchent le chômage augmente; **to stand in the w. line** recevoir les allocations chômage
▶▶ *Am* **w. benefits** avantages *mpl* sociaux; **w. centre** ≃ centre *m* d'assistance sociale; *Am* **w. check** *(chèque m d')allocations fpl*; **the W. State** *(concept)* l'État *m* providence; **w. work** travail *m* social; **w. worker** assistant, -ante social(e)

well[1] [wel] N **1** *(of water, oil)* puits *m*; **we get our water from a w.** notre eau vient d'un puits; **to drive/sink a w.** forer/creuser un puits **2** *(shaft) (for lift)* puits *m*, cage *f*; *(stairwell)* cage, jour *m*; *(sump)* fond *m* de carter; *(on fishing boat)* vivier *m*, réservoir *m*; *Br Law* **the w. of the court** le barreau; *Culin* **make a w. in the flour** faire une fontaine dans la farine **3** *Arch (spring)* source *f*, fontaine *f*
▶▶ **w. digger** puisatier *m*

WELL[2] *(comp* **better**; *superl* **best)** ADJ **1** *(in good health)* **to be w.** être bien portant *ou* en bonne santé, se porter *ou* aller bien; **to sound w.** avoir l'air en forme; **are you okay?,**

you don't sound very w. ça va?, tu n'as pas l'air bien; **how are you? – w., thank you** comment allez-vous? – bien, merci; **he's not very w.** il n'est pas très bien; **to get w.** guérir, se rétablir, se remettre; **you look w.** tu as l'air en forme; **he's not a w. man** il ne se porte pas bien, il n'a pas une bonne santé
2 it is w. to … *(advisable)* il est opportun de …; **it would be w. to …** il serait bon *ou* utile *ou* recommandable de …; **it would be w. not to mention it again** il vaudrait mieux ne plus en reparler; **it would be just as w. if you were present** ce serait mieux si vous étiez présent, vous feriez mieux d'être présent; **it is just as w. we did leave without her** c'est aussi bien que nous soyons partis sans elle; **it might be as w. to …** il faudrait peut-être …, il serait peut-être bon de …; **it was w. for him that nobody saw him** heureusement pour lui que personne ne l'a vu; *Prov* **all's w. that ends w.** tout est bien qui finit bien; **all's w.!** tout va bien!; **that's all very w., but …** c'est bien beau *ou* joli, tout ça, mais …; **it is all very w. for you to say that** tu peux bien dire ça, toi; **w. and good!** soit!, bon!; **that's all very w. and good, but …** c'est très bien, tout ça, mais …
ADV **1** *(satisfactorily etc)* bien; **to work w.** bien travailler; **to do as w. as one can** faire de son mieux; **this boy will do w.** ce garçon ira loin; **to be doing w.** *(after operation etc)* aller bien; **mother and baby are both doing w.** la mère et l'enfant se portent bien; **w. done!** bravo!, très bien!; **w. played!** bien joué!; **the government hasn't come out of it very w.** le gouvernement n'en est pas sorti grandi; **to do oneself w.** *(indulge oneself)* bien se soigner; *(in restaurant etc)* bien manger (et bien boire); **it wouldn't look w. if we refused** si on refusait cela ferait mauvaise impression; **you would do w. to be quiet (about it)** vous feriez bien *ou* le mieux serait de vous taire; **I know her w.** je la connais bien; **I know only too w. what patience it needs** je ne sais que trop quelle patience cela exige; **I can't very w. do it** il ne m'est guère possible de le faire; **he apologized, as w. he might** il s'est excusé, ce qui était la moindre des choses; **one might as w. say that black is white** autant dire que blanc est noir; **you might as w. stay** *(there's no point in going now)* tu ferais aussi bien de rester; **I might (just) as w. do it myself** je ferais aussi bien de le faire moi-même; **very w.!** *(OK)* (très) bien!, entendu!; **everyone speaks w. of him** tout le monde dit du bien de lui; **she is very w. thought of** on pense beaucoup de bien d'elle; **to do w. by sb** se montrer généreux envers qn; **he meant w.** il voulait bien faire; **he means w.** ses intentions sont bonnes; **you're w. out of it** soyez heureux d'en être quitte; **the fête went off w.** la fête s'est bien passée; *Arch* **w. met!** heureuse rencontre!, vous arrivez bien à propos!
2 *(intensive)* bien; **it is w. known that …** tout le monde sait que …; **it's w. worth trying** cela vaut bien la peine *ou* *Fam* le coup d'essayer; **she's w. able to look after herself** elle est tout à fait capable de se débrouiller toute seule; **I can w. believe it** je veux bien le croire; **I am w. aware of that** j'en suis bien conscient; **we'll be w. away by the time she wakes up** nous serons déjà loin quand elle se réveillera; *Br Fam* **w. away** *(drunk)* parti; **it's w. after six** il est six heures bien sonnées; **buy your tickets w. ahead of time** *ou* **w. in advance** achetez vos billets bien à l'avance; **he's w. over fifty** il a largement dépassé la cinquantaine; **to be w. up in a subject** bien posséder un sujet; **leave w. enough alone** ne t'en mêle pas; *Br Fam* **w. and truly** bel et bien; *Hum* **w. padded** *or* **upholstered** *(plump)* bien rembourré
3 pretty w. all presque tout; **it's pretty w.**

finished c'est presque *ou* pratiquement terminé; *Fam* **it serves him damn w.** *or* **jolly w. right!** il l'a bien cherché *ou* mérité!, c'est bien fait pour lui!

4 as w. *(also)* aussi; **take me as w.** emmenez-moi aussi; **I need some as w.** il m'en faut également; **as w. as** *(in addition to)* de même que, comme, ainsi que; **by day as w. as by night** de jour comme de nuit, le jour comme la nuit

5 *(introducing remark)* eh bien, donc; *(exclamatory)* ça alors!, pas possible!; **w., as I was telling you** eh bien *ou* donc comme je vous disais; **w., who was it?** eh bien, qui était-ce?; **w., here we are (at last)!** enfin nous voilà!; **you told her?, (oh** *or* **ah) w.!** vous le lui avez dit?, eh bien!; **w., w.!** *(expressing resignation)* tant pis!, que voulez-vous!; *(surprise)* tiens, tiens!; **w. then** eh bien, alors!; **w. I never!** ça alors!; **w., that's life!** c'est la vie!; **w. then, why worry about it?** eh bien *ou* alors, pourquoi se faire du mauvais sang?

N 1 **the w. and the sick** *(pl)* les bien portants *mpl* et les malades

2 **to wish sb w.** vouloir du bien à qn; *(in attitude)* être bien disposé envers qn

▸ **well out** *vi (of liquid)* jaillir

▸ **well over** *vi (of tears)* jaillir

▸ **well up** *vi (of water, spring)* jaillir, *Lit* monter; **tears welled up in her eyes** les larmes lui sont montées aux yeux

we'll [wi:l] **CONTR 1** = **we shall,** *see* **shall 2** = **we will,** *see* **will**[2]

well-adjusted **ADJ** équilibré

well-advised [-əd'vaɪzd] **ADJ** sage, prudent, judicieux; **you would be w. to say yes** tu aurais (tout) intérêt à dire oui; **it was not very w. of you to annoy her like that** ce n'était pas très malin de l'ennuyer comme ça

well-appointed **ADJ** *(house)* bien aménagé

well-argued [-'ɑːgjuːd] **ADJ** bien argumenté

well-attended [-ə'tendɪd] **ADJ** bien suivi; **the classes were not w.** les cours étaient peu suivis

well-balanced **ADJ** *(person, debate)* équilibré; *(coverage)* impartial, -aux; **I think she's fairly w.** je pense qu'elle est plutôt bien équilibrée

well-behaved **ADJ** *(child)* sage; *(animal)* bien dressé

wellbeing ['welbiːɪŋ] **N** bien-être *m*; **physical and moral w.** santé *f* physique et morale

well-born **ADJ** de bonne famille; **she was not sufficiently w. to marry him** elle n'était pas assez bien née pour l'épouser

well-bred [-bred] **ADJ** *(polite)* bien élevé; *(of good family)* de bonne famille

well-built **ADJ** *(building)* bien construit, solide; *(machine, car)* de bonne fabrication; *(person)* solide, bien bâti

well-chilled [-tʃɪld] **ADJ** *(wine)* frais, *f* fraîche

well-chosen **ADJ** bien choisi; **a few w. words** quelques mots bien choisis

well-connected **ADJ** **to be w.** avoir des relations

well-defined [-dɪ'faɪnd] **ADJ** bien défini

well-developed [-dɪ'veləpt] **ADJ** bien développé

well-disposed **ADJ** *(person)* bien disposé (**towards** envers)

well-documented [-'dɒkjʊmentɪd] **ADJ** bien documenté

well-done [-dʌn] **ADJ** *Culin* bien cuit

well-dressed [-drest] **ADJ** bien habillé

well-earned **ADJ** bien mérité

well-educated **ADJ** instruit, cultivé

well-endowed [-ən'daʊd] **ADJ** *(physically)* *(man)* bien monté; *(woman)* bien roulé

well-equipped **ADJ** bien équipé

well-established **ADJ** bien implanté

well-fed **ADJ** bien nourri

well-fixed **ADJ** *Am Fam* riche

well-founded [-'faʊndɪd] **ADJ** *(suspicion)* fondé

well-groomed **ADJ** *(person)* soigné; *(horse)* bien pansé

well-grounded **ADJ** fondé

wellhead ['welhed] **N** *Petr* tête *f* de puits

well-heeled [-hiːld] **ADJ** *Fam* riche, cossu

well-hung **ADJ** *Sl (man)* bien monté

wellied ['welɪd] **ADJ** *Br Fam (drunk)* bourré comme un coing, rond comme une queue de pelle

well-in **ADJ** *Fam* **1** *Br* **to be w. with sb** être bien avec qn **2** *Austr (rich)* riche

well-informed **ADJ** *(about specific event etc)* informé; *(generally) (person, mind)* au courant; **to be w. on a subject** bien posséder un sujet

wellington ['welɪŋtən] **N** *Br (boot)* botte *f* en caoutchouc

▸▸ **w. boot** botte en caoutchouc

well-intentioned [-ɪn'tenʃənd] **ADJ** bien intentionné

well-judged [-dʒʌdʒd] **ADJ** judicieux; *(shot, pass)* bien visé, bien vu

well-kept **ADJ** *(garden)* bien (entre)tenu, soigné; *(hands)* soigné; *(secret)* bien gardé

well-known **ADJ** (bien) connu, célèbre; *(expert)* réputé; **a w. liar** un fameux menteur; **it is w. that …** il est bien connu que …

well-liked [-laɪkt] **ADJ** apprécié

well-loved [-lʌvd] **ADJ** très aimé

well-made **ADJ** *(furniture)* bien fait, de fabrication soignée; *(garment)* de coupe soignée; *(play)* bien construit

well-mannered **ADJ** poli, bien élevé

well-matched [-mætʃt] **ADJ** *(couple)* bien assorti; *(teams)* de force égale; **Bob can't possibly be as boring as Sarah – oh yes he is, they're very w.** Bob ne peut pas être aussi ennuyeux que Sarah – et pourtant si, ils se sont bien trouvés

well-meaning **ADJ** *(person)* bien intentionné; *(remark)* fait avec les meilleures intentions; **she's very w.** elle est pleine de bonnes intentions

well-nigh **ADV** presque, pratiquement; **it's w. impossible** c'est presque *ou* quasi impossible

well-off **ADJ** riche; **to be very w.** avoir de la fortune, *Fam* avoir de quoi; **you don't know when you're w.** vous ne connaissez pas votre bonheur; **to be w. for books/cupboards/paper** avoir beaucoup de livres/placards/papier

NPL **the w.** les riches *mpl*

well-oiled **ADJ** *Fig Fam (drunk)* soûl, parti

well-paid **ADJ** bien payé, bien rétribué

well-preserved **ADJ** bien conservé; *Fig* **she's w.** elle est bien conservée

well-proportioned **ADJ** bien proportionné

well-read [-red] **ADJ** *(person)* instruit, cultivé

well-respected **ADJ** respecté

well-rounded **ADJ** *(education, course etc)* complet

well-spent **ADJ** *(money, time)* bien utilisé, bien employé; **it was time w.** je n'ai/il n'a/*etc* pas perdu mon/son/*etc* temps; **I'm not sure this is time w.** je crains que ça ne soit une perte de temps

well-spoken **ADJ** qui parle bien

well-stacked [-stækt] **ADJ** *Sl (woman)* bien balancé, bien roulé, bien foutu; **she's w.!** il y a du monde au balcon!

well-stocked [-stɒkt] **ADJ** *(shop)* bien approvisionné

well-thought-of **ADJ** apprécié

well-thought-out **ADJ** *(plan etc)* bien pensé

well-thumbed [-θʌmbd] **ADJ** *(book, magazine)* qui a fait de l'usage, écorné

well-timed [-taɪmd] **ADJ** opportun, bien calculé

well-to-do **ADJ** aisé, riche, cossu

NPL **the w.** les riches *mpl*, les fortunés *mpl*

well-tried **ADJ** *(remedy)* éprouvé, qui a fait ses preuves

well-trodden [-'trɒdən] **ADJ** **a w. path** un chemin très fréquenté; *Fig* **a w. path to fame** une voie très fréquentée qui mène vers la célébrité

well-turned [-tɜːnd] **ADJ** *(speech)* bien tourné; *(ankle)* galbé

well-versed **ADJ** versé (**in** dans)

wellwisher ['welwɪʃər] **N** *(of cause etc)* partisan, -ane; **a w.** *(at end of anonymous letter)* un ami qui vous veut du bien; **surrounded by wellwishers** entouré d'admirateurs

well-woman clinic **N** clinique *f* pour femmes; *(session)* consultations *fpl* dans la clinique pour femmes

well-worn **ADJ** *(garment)* très usé; *(argument)* rebattu, usé jusqu'à la corde

well-written **ADJ** bien écrit

welly ['welɪ] **N** *Br Fam (boot)* botte *f* en caoutchouc; **to give it some w.** mettre le paquet; **he really gave the ball some w.** il a tapé dans le ballon de toutes ses forces

Welsh [welʃ] **ADJ** gallois, du pays de Galles

N 1 **the W.** *(pl)* les Gallois *mpl* **2** *Ling* gallois *m*

▸▸ **the Welsh Assembly** l'Assemblée *f* du pays de Galles; **W. dresser** vaisselier *m*; **W. rabbit** ≃ croque-monsieur *m inv*; **W. rarebit** ≃ croque-monsieur

Welsh Assembly

L'assemblée nationale du pays de Galles fut établie dans le cadre de la décentralisation engagée par le gouvernement travailliste et fut inaugurée à Cardiff en mai 1999. Les soixante membres de l'assemblée forment le "Welsh Cabinet" et siègent sous la houlette du "First Secretary" qui représente les intérêts gallois au parlement de Westminster. L'assemblée nationale du pays de Galles, la première depuis six siècles, a toutefois moins de pouvoirs que le parlement écossais mis en place en même temps.

▸ **welsh on** **VT INSEP** *Fam* **to welsh on sb** faire faux bond à qn; **to welsh on a bet** ne pas tenir un pari

Welshman, *pl* **Welshmen** ['welʃmən] **N** Gallois *m*

Welshwoman, *pl* **Welshwomen** ['welʃwʊmən, -wɪmɪn] **N** Galloise *f*

welt [welt] **N 1** *(of shoe)* trépointe *f* **2** *(left by blow)* marque *f* ou trace *f* de coup

welter[1] ['weltər] **N** **a w. of** *(details, statistics)* une pléthore de; *(forms)* une masse de; **a w. of blood and guts** une marée de sang

welter[2] **VI** *Lit (in mud)* se vautrer, se rouler; *(in blood)* nager, baigner

welterweight ['weltəweɪt] **N** *Boxing* poids *m* mi-moyen, poids welter; **to fight as a** *or* **at w.** boxer dans la catégorie des poids welters

▸▸ **w. match** match *m* de poids welters

wen [wen] N *Med* kyste *m* sébacé, *Fam* loupe *f*

wench [wentʃ] N **1** *Hum Fam* (*young woman*) (jeune) fille *f*, jeune femme *f*; **great strapping w.** grande gaillarde *f* **2** *Arch* (**serving**) **w.** (*in inn*) serveuse *f*; **kitchen w.** fille *f* de cuisine

  VI *Arch, Hum* **to go wenching** courir le jupon

wencher [ˈwentʃər] N *Arch, Hum* coureur *m* de jupons

wend [wend] VT **to w. one's way** se diriger, s'acheminer (**to** vers); **to w. one's way homeward** prendre le chemin du retour

Wendy house® [ˈwendɪ] N *Br* = maison *f* en modèle réduit pour enfants

Wensleydale [ˈwenzlɪdeɪl] N = fromage *m* anglais à pâte dure originaire de Wensleydale

went PT *see* go

wept PT, PP *see* weep

were PT *see* be

we're [wɪər] CONTR = we are, *see* be

weren't [wɜːnt] CONTR = were not, *see* be

werewolf, *pl* **werewolves** [ˈwɪəwʊlf, -wʊlvz] N *Myth* loup-garou *m*, *pl* loups-garous

Wesleyan [ˈweslɪən] ADJ, N wesleyen, -enne

west [west] N ouest *m*; **the house faces the w.** la maison est exposée à l'ouest; **on the w., to the w.** (**of** de); **the W.** (*the Occident*) l'Occident *m*, les pays *mpl* occidentaux; (*in United States*) l'Ouest *m* (*États situés à l'ouest du Mississippi*); *Am* **the Far W.** le Far-West; *Am* **the Mid W.** les États de la Prairie

  ADV à l'ouest; **to travel w.** voyager vers l'ouest; *Old-fashioned* **Fam** (*die*) casser sa pipe, passer l'arme à gauche; *Fam* **there's another plate gone w.!** encore une assiette de cassée!

  ADJ *inv*; (*wind*) d'ouest; (*wall, window*) qui fait face *ou* qui est exposé à l'ouest; **the w. coast** la côte ouest

  ▸▸ **W. Africa** Afrique *f* occidentale; **the W. Bank** la Cisjordanie; *Formerly* **W. Berlin** Berlin *m* Ouest; **the W. Coast** la côte ouest (*des États-Unis*); **the W. Country** = le sud-ouest de l'Angleterre (Cornouailles, Devon et Somerset); *Br* **W. End** (*in general*) quartiers *mpl* ouest; (*of London*) West End *m* (*centre touristique et commercial de la ville de Londres connu pour ses théâtres*); **in the W. End** dans le West End; *Formerly* **W. Germany** Allemagne *f* de l'Ouest; **the W. Indies** les Antilles *fpl*; **W. Point** = importante école *f* militaire américaine; *Am* **the W. Side** les quartiers *mpl* ouest de New York

westbound [ˈwestbaʊnd] ADJ (*traffic*) en direction de l'ouest; (*lane, carriageway*) de l'ouest; (*road*) qui va vers l'ouest; **w. traffic is subject to delays** la circulation est ralentie dans le sens ouest; **there's a jam on the w. carriageway** il y a un bouchon en direction de l'ouest

westerly [ˈwestəlɪ] ADJ (*wind*) d'ouest, qui vient de l'ouest; (*current*) qui se dirige vers l'ouest; **w. point** point *m* situé à *ou* vers l'ouest

  ADV vers l'ouest

  N vent *m* d'ouest

western [ˈwestən] ADJ ouest *inv*, de l'ouest; (*wind*) d'ouest; *esp Pol* occidental, -aux; *Pol* **the W. powers** les puissances occidentales

  N *Cin* western *m*; (*novel*) roman-western *m*, *pl* romans-westerns

  ▸▸ **W. Australia** l'Australie-Occidentale *f*; **W. Europe** Europe *f* occidentale; **W. Isles** Hébrides *fpl*; *Sport* **w. roll** rouleau *m* costal

Westerner [ˈwestənər] N **1** *Pol* occidental, -aux **2** *Geog* habitant, -ante de l'ouest

westernization [westənaɪˈzeɪʃən] N occidentalisation *f*

westernize [ˈwestənaɪz] VT (*people*) occidentaliser; **to become westernized** s'occidentaliser

Westminster [ˈwestmɪnstər] N Westminster (*siège du gouvernement britannique*)

Westminster

C'est dans ce quartier que se trouvent le Parlement et le palais de Buckingham. Le nom de "Westminster" est également employé pour désigner le Parlement lui-même.

---

westward [ˈwestwəd] ADJ vers l'ouest, en direction de l'ouest

  ADV = westwards

westwards [ˈwestwədz] ADV vers l'ouest, en direction de l'ouest

wet [wet] ADJ (*comp* **wetter;** *superl* **wettest**) **1** (*soaked*) mouillé; (*damp*) humide; (*weather*) pluvieux; **to get w.** se mouiller; **to get one's feet w.** se mouiller les pieds; **to be w. through** *or* **w. to the skin** être trempé *ou* mouillé jusqu'aux os; **her cheeks were w. with tears** ses joues étaient baignées de larmes; **the ink/paint was still w.** l'encre/la peinture n'était pas encore sèche; *Fig* **he's (still) w. behind the ears** il manque de maturité, il n'est pas mûr; **when you're a bit less w. behind the ears** quand tu seras un peu plus mûr; **three w. days** trois jours de pluie; **the wettest summer on record** l'été le plus humide dont on se souvienne; **when it's w.** (*raining*) quand il pleut; **the w. season** la saison des pluies; **a w.-look hairstyle** une coiffure à l'aspect mouillé; **a w.-look coat** un manteau moiré *ou* brillant; **w. paint** (*notice*) peinture fraîche

  2 *Br Fam* (*silly*) bête, idiot; (*excuse*) faible; (*weak, pathetic*) lamentable; *Pol* modéré; **don't be so w.!** (*stupid*) ne sois pas si bête!; (*lacking in physical courage*) du nerf!; **he thinks it's w. to discuss emotions** il trouve ça mièvre de parler des sentiments

  3 (*allowing alcohol sales*) (*country, state*) qui permet la vente des boissons alcoolisées

  N **1** (*dampness*) humidité *f*

  2 (*rain*) pluie *f*; *Austr* **the w.** (*season*) la saison des pluies; **to go out in the w.** sortir sous la pluie

  3 *Br Pol Fam* modéré, -ée

  VT (**-tt-**) mouiller, humecter; (*sponge*) imbiber; (*pastry*) mouiller; (*clay*) humidifier, mouiller; **to w. the bed** (*of child*) faire pipi au lit; **to w. one's pants** *or* **oneself** mouiller sa culotte, faire pipi dans sa culotte; *Fig Fam* pisser dans sa culotte; *Hum Fam* **to w. one's whistle** se rincer *ou* s'humecter le gosier; *Fig Fam* **we'll have to w. the baby's head** il faudra qu'on arrose la naissance du bébé

  ▸▸ *Fam* **w. blanket** rabat-joie *m inv*; *Elec* **w. cell** pile *f* à élément humide; **w. dock** bassin *m* à flot; **w. dream** éjaculation *f ou* pollution *f* nocturne; **w. fish** poisson *m* frais; **w. lease** (*for aircraft*) location *f* d'avion avec équipage; **w. nurse** nourrice *f*; **w. rot** moisissure *f* humide; **w. suit** combinaison *f ou* ensemble *m* de plongée

wetback [ˈwetbæk] N *Am Pej* = ouvrier *m* agricole mexicain entré illégalement aux États-Unis

wether [ˈweðər] N (*ram*) bélier *m* châtré

wetlands [ˈwetləndz] NPL marais *mpl*

wetness [ˈwetnɪs] N humidité *f*; **renowned for the w. of its climate** connu pour son climat pluvieux

wetting [ˈwetɪŋ] N **to get a w.** se faire mouiller; **w. the bed can be a sign that …** l'incontinence nocturne peut indiquer que …

  ▸▸ *Chem* **w. agent** (agent *m*) mouillant *m*

wet-weather tyre N pneu *m* pluie

WEU [dʌb(ə)ljuːiːˈjuː] N *Pol* (*abbr* Western European Union) UEO *f*

we've [wiːv] CONTR = we have, *see* have

WFP [dʌb(ə)ljuːefˈpiː] N (*abbr* World Food Programme) PAM *m*

whack [wæk] *Fam* N **1** (*blow*) (*with stick*) coup *m* retentissant *ou* bien appliqué; (*with hand*) claque *f*, taloche *f*; **to give sb a w.** donner un grand coup à qn; *Fig* **to have a w. at doing sth** (*try*) essayer de faire qch; **to have a whack** tenter le coup

  2 (*share*) part *f*; **all I want is a fair w.** tout ce que je veux, c'est ma part; **he didn't get his w.** il n'a pas eu sa part; **you're already earning (the) top w. for this job** tu gagnes déjà le maximum pour ce travail; **we can offer you £50,000, top w.** (*no more*) nous ne pouvons vous offrir 50 000 livres, dernier prix *ou* grand maximum

  INT v'lan!, vlan!

  VT **1** (*hit*) (*person*) (*one blow*) filer un gnon à; (*several blows*) battre, *Fam* cogner; (*ball*) (*of tennis player, golf player*) donner un grand coup dans; (*of football player*) donner un grand coup de pied dans; **to w. sb over the head** frapper qn sur la tête; **to w. sb with a stick/ruler** donner un coup de bâton/de règle à qn; **Pele whacked the ball into the net** Pele a envoyé le ballon d'un grand coup de pied dans le filet

  2 *Sport* (*defeat*) (*one's opponents*) battre à plate(s) couture(s), piler

  VI **to w. at sth with a stick** donner un coup de bâton à qch

  ▸ **whack off** VI *Sl* (*masturbate*) se branler

whacked [wækt] ADJ *Br Fam* (*exhausted*) vanné, crevé

whacker [ˈwækər] N *Fam* **1** (*large thing*) **what a w.!, isn't it a w.!** (*piece of meat, vegetable, fish*) quel morceau!, c'est un sacré morceau!; **he's got a w. of a nose** il a un nez énorme **2** *Old-fashioned* (*lie*) gros mensonge *m*

whacking [ˈwækɪŋ] *Fam* ADJ énorme

  ADV vachement; **a w. great dog** un chien énorme; **a w. great lie** un gros mensonge

  N **1** (*beating*) rossée *f*, raclée *f*; **his father gave him a w.** son père lui a donné une raclée **2** *Sport* (*defeat*) **we gave them a w.** on leur a mis la pâtée

whacko [ˈwækəʊ] ADJ *Fam* = wacky

  INT *Old-fashioned Br Sl* magnifique!

whacky [ˈwækɪ] ADJ *esp Am Fam* = wacky

whale [weɪl] N **1** baleine *f*; **blue w.** baleine bleue; **white w.** bél(o)uga *m* **2** *Fam* **we had a w. of a time** on s'est drôlement bien amusé

  VI pêcher la baleine, aller à la pêche à la baleine

  ▸▸ **w. calf** baleineau *m*; **w. hunter** baleinier *m*; **w. oil** huile *f* de baleine

whaleboat [ˈweɪlbəʊt] N baleinier *m*

whalebone [ˈweɪlbəʊn] N (*in corset*) busc *m*, baleine *f*

whaler [ˈweɪlər] N (*person, vessel*) baleinier *m*

whaling [ˈweɪlɪŋ] N pêche *f ou* chasse *f* à la baleine

  ▸▸ **w. ship** baleinier *m*

wham [ˈwæm] *Fam* INT v'lan!, vlan!

  VI (**-mm-**) rentrer (**into** dans); **the ball whammed into the back of the net** le ballon a filé dans les buts; **her fist whammed into his face** son poing s'est écrasé sur son visage; **she whammed into the wall** elle s'est écrasée contre le mur; **the car whammed into the lamppost** la voiture est rentrée dans le réverbère

  VT enfoncer; **to w. the ball into the net** envoyer le ballon dans le filet à toute volée

wharf, *pl* **wharfs, wharves** [wɔːf, -s, wɔːvz] N quai *m*; *Com* **ex w.** à prendre sur quai

wharfage ['wɔːfɪdʒ] N droits *mpl* de quai *ou* de bassin

WHAT [wɒt]

> ADJ quel **2, 3**
> PRON ce qui **1, 3** ▪ ce que **1, 3** ▪ qu'est-ce qui **2** ▪ qu'est-ce que **2** ▪ que **2** ▪ quoi **2** ▪ combien **2** ▪ comment **2**

ADJ **1** (*rel*) **he took w. little I had left** il m'a pris le peu qui me restait; **I'll give you w. money I have** je vais vous donner ce que j'ai comme argent VOIR GRAMMAIRE A33

2 (*interr direct or indirect*) **quel, quelle,** *pl* **quels, quelles; w. time is it?** quelle heure est-il?; **w. date is it (today)?** quelle est la date (d'aujourd'hui)?; **tell me w. books you want** dites-moi quels livres vous désirez; **w. right has she to give orders?** de quel droit donne-t-elle des ordres?; **w. good** *or* **use is this?** à quoi ça sert?; **w. sort of (a) book is it?** quelle sorte de livre est-ce?; **w. colour/ size is it?** c'est de quelle couleur/de quelle taille? VOIR GRAMMAIRE A31–2; B16

3 (*exclamatory*) **w. an idea!** quelle idée!; **w. a fool he is!** qu'il est bête!, comme il est bête!; **w. a fuss about nothing!** voilà bien du bruit pour rien!; **w. a question!** quelle question!; **w. a man!** quel homme!; **w. a pity!** quel dommage!; **w. a (long) time you're taking to get dressed!** qu'est-ce que vous êtes long à vous habiller!; **w. a lot of people!** que de gens!, que de monde! VOIR GRAMMAIRE A5; B17

PRON **1** (*rel*) (*subject*) ce qui; (*object*) ce que; **w. is done cannot be undone** ce qui est fait est fait; **I don't know w. has happened** je ne sais pas ce qui est arrivé; **w. I like is a detective story** moi, ce que j'aime, ce sont les romans policiers; **w. is most remarkable is that …** ce qu'il y a de plus remarquable c'est que …; **this is w. it's all about** voici ce dont il s'agit; **but that's not w. I said** mais ce n'est pas ce que j'ai dit; **come w. may** advienne que pourra; **he never talks about w. he has gone through** il ne parle jamais de ce qu'il a enduré; **w. with golf and tennis I have no time to write** entre le golf et le tennis je n'ai pas le temps d'écrire; *SI* **to give sb w. for** (*scold*) passer un savon à qn; (*beat*) flanquer une bonne raclée à qn SEE GRAMMAR B23

2 (*interr direct*) (*subject*) qu'est-ce qui; (*object*) qu'est-ce que, que, quoi; **w. has happened?** qu'est-ce qui est arrivé?; **w.'s happening?** que se passe-t-il?; *Fam* **w.'s up?** comment ça va?; **w. do you want?** qu'est-ce que vous voulez?; **w. on earth are you doing here?** qu'est-ce que vous pouvez bien faire ici?; **w. is it?** (*identify it*) qu'est-ce que c'est?; (*what is wrong*) qu'est-ce qu'il y a?; **w.'s that?** (*identify it*) qu'est-ce que c'est que ça?; (*what did you say*) quoi?; **w.'s that you're telling me?** qu'est-ce que vous me dites?; **w. will become of her?** que deviendra-t-elle?; **w.'s the matter?** qu'est-ce qu'il y a?, qu'y a-t-il?; **w.'s the date (today)?** quel jour sommes-nous?; **w.'s her address?** quelle est son adresse?; **w.'s his name?** quel est son nom?, comment s'appelle-t-il?; **w.'s that to you?** qu'est-ce que cela vous fait?, est-ce que ça vous regarde?; **w. is she to you that you're so concerned about her?** il faut qu'elle soit bien importante pour toi pour que tu sois aussi inquiet à son sujet; **w. is there to see in this town?** qu'y a-t-il à voir dans cette ville?; **w.'s the good** *or* **the use?** à quoi bon?; **w.'s to be done?** que faire?; **w. did I tell you?** qu'est-ce que je vous avais dit?, je vous l'avais bien dit!; **w. will people say?** que dira-t-on?, que vont dire les gens?; **w.'s the French for 'dog'?** comment dit-on

'dog' en français?; **w. else could bring me here?** quoi d'autre pourrait me faire venir ici?; **w. could be more beautiful?** quoi de plus beau?; **w. do seven and eight make?** combien font sept plus huit?; **w. is the rent?** à combien s'élève le loyer?; **w. do I owe you?** qu'est-ce que je vous dois?; (*in shop*) c'est combien?, ça fait combien?; **w. is he like?** comment est-il?; **w. do you take me for?** pour qui me prenez-vous?; **w.'s it made of?** en quoi est-ce que c'est fait?, c'est fait en quoi?; **w. are you thinking of?** à quoi pensez-vous?; **w. were you thinking of, letting her go out on her own?** qu'est-ce qui t'a pris de la laisser sortir toute seule?; **w. about the ten pounds I lent you?** et les dix livres que je vous ai prêtées?; **w. about a game of bridge?** si on faisait une partie de bridge?; **w. about you?** et vous?; **w. about that coffee?** et ce café?; **w.'s that for?** à quoi ça sert-il?, à quoi ça sert?; **w. did he do that for?** pourquoi a-t-il fait cela?; **w. for?** pourquoi?; **w. on earth for?** mais pourquoi donc?; **and w. if she hears about it?** et si elle l'apprend?; **w. then?** et après?; *Fam* **so w.?** et alors?; *Fam* **d'you think I'm mad or w.?** tu crois que je suis fou ou quoi?; **w. did you say?** vous disiez?, pardon?; **w. of it?** qu'est-ce que cela fait?, eh bien, et après?; **well, w. of it?** et bien?, et après? VOIR GRAMMAIRE A31–2; B17

3 (*indirect*) (*subject*) ce qui; (*object*) ce que; **tell me w.'s happened** dites-moi ce qui s'est passé; **I don't know w. you want** je ne sais pas ce que vous désirez; **he didn't know w. to say/do** il ne savait que dire/faire; **there were books and I don't know w.** il y avait des livres et je ne sais quoi d'autre *ou* encore; *Fam* **paper, pens, pencils, and w.** not *or* and w. have you du papier, des stylos, des crayons et d'autres choses encore *ou* et je ne sais quoi encore; **tell me w. you're crying for** dites-moi pourquoi vous pleurez; **tell me w.'s to be done** dis-moi ce qu'il y a à faire; **I'll tell you w.** je vais vous dire, écoutez; **he knows w.'s w.** (*in a subject*) il s'y connaît; **I've still to find out w.'s w.** (*how things work etc*) il faut que je trouve comment ça marche; (*what the situation is*) il faut que je me mette au courant de la situation; **I'll show him w.'s w.!** je vais lui montrer de quel bois je me chauffe!

4 (*exclamatory*) **w. she has suffered!** ce qu'elle a souffert!; **w. next (I ask myself)!** ça par exemple!, et puis quoi encore!; **w.! you can't come!** comment! vous ne pouvez pas venir!; **w.! no eggs!** quoi! pas d'œufs!; *Old-fashioned Fam* **nice girl, w.!** joli brin de fille, hein!

what-d'ye-call-her ['wɒtjəkɔːlər] N *Fam* (*person*) Machine *f*

what-d'ye-call-him ['wɒtjəkɔːlɪm] N *Fam* (*person*) Machin *m*

what-d'ye-call-it ['wɒtjəkɔːlɪt] N *Fam* (*thing*) machin *m*, truc *m*

whate'er [wɒtˈeər] PRON *Lit* = whatever

whatever [wɒtˈevər] VOIR GRAMMAIRE A32; A33 PRON **1** (*rel*) (*subject*) tout ce qui; (*object*) tout ce que; **w. you like** tout ce qui vous plaira, tout ce que vous voudrez

2 (*no matter what*) quoi que + *subj*, **w. it is** *or* **may be** quoi que ce soit; **w. happens, keep calm** quoi qu'il survienne, restez calme; **he shall have w. he wants** quoi qu'il désire, il l'aura; **w. she says** *or* **may say** en dépit de ce qu'elle dit; **use w. you can find** utilise ce que tu trouveras; **w. can she have said to make him so angry?** qu'est-ce qu'elle a bien pu dire pour le mettre dans une telle colère?

3 *Fam* **pens, pencils, paper and w.** des stylos, des crayons, du papier et tout ce que vous voulez; **… or w.** (*something similar*) … ou quelque chose de ce genre; (*anything you like*) … ou tout ce que vous voulez

ADJ **1** (*no matter what*) **w. price they are asking** quel que soit le prix qu'ils demandent; **w. mistakes I (may) have made** quelles que soient les erreurs que j'ai faites

2 (*emphatic*) **under any pretext w.** sous quelque prétexte que ce soit; **no hope w.** pas le moindre espoir, pas l'ombre d'un espoir; **is there any hope w.?** y a-t-il l'ombre d'un espoir?; **none w.** pas un seul; **nothing w.** absolument rien

what-ho INT *Br Old-fashioned* **1** eh bien!, tiens! **2** (*greeting*) bonjour!, salut!

whatnot ['wɒtnɒt] N **1** (*for ornaments*) étagère *f* **2** *Fam* (*thing*) machin *m*, truc *m*; (*person*) chose *mf*, machin *m*, machine *f* **3** *Fam* **… and w.** … et ainsi de suite, … et tout ce qui s'ensuit; **there was champagne, caviar and w.** il y avait du champagne, du caviar et tout le tralala

what's-her-name, what's-his-name, what's-its-name ['wɒtsə-, -ɪz-, -ɪtsneɪm] N = **what-d'ye-call-her, what-d'ye-call-him, what-d'ye-call-it**

whatsit ['wɒtsɪt] N *Fam* machin *m*, truc *m*

whatsoever [wɒtsəʊˈevər] PRON *Lit* **w. it may be** quoi que ce soit
ADJ (*emphatic*) = **whatever** ADJ 2

wheat [wiːt] N blé *m*, froment *m*; **to plant land with w.** mettre une terre en blé; *Agr, Fig* **to separate the w. from the chaff** séparer le bon grain de l'ivraie
▸▸ **w. field** champ *m* de blé

wheatear ['wiːtɪər] N (*bird*) traquet *m* (motteux), cul-blanc *m*, *pl* culs-blancs

wheaten ['wiːt(ə)n] ADJ (*bread*) de froment, de blé

wheatgerm ['wiːtdʒɜːm] N germes *mpl* de blé

wheatmeal ['wiːtmiːl] N farine *f* grossière, grosse farine de froment
▸▸ **w. bread** pain *m* de froment

wheatsheaf ['wiːtʃiːf] N gerbe *f* de blé

wheedle ['wiːd(ə)l] VT **1** to w. sb into doing sth faire faire qch à qn à force de cajoleries; **she wheedled me into agreeing** elle m'a cajolé tant et si bien que j'ai fini par accepter **2** **to w. sth out of sb** obtenir *ou* soutirer qch de qn par des cajoleries; **he wheedled his way into the old lady's confidence** il s'est assuré la confiance de la vieille dame à force de cajoleries

wheedling ['wiːd(ə)lɪŋ] ADJ (*manner etc*) enjôleur, cajoleur; **a w. voice** une voix pateline
N cajoleries *fpl*

wheel [wiːl] N **1** (*on car, printer etc*) roue *f*, (*small*) roulette *f*; **on wheels** sur roues/roulettes; *Br* **meals on wheels** = repas *mpl* livrés à domicile (*aux personnes âgées etc*); *Fam* **my wheels** (*my car*) ma bagnole; *Fig* **the fifth w.** la cinquième roue du carrosse; *Am Fam* **to feel like a fifth w.** être la cinquième roue du carrosse; *Aviat* **landing wheels** roues (du train) d'atterrissage; *Aviat* **nose w.** roue (d'atterrisseur) avant; **the wheels** (*of mechanism, watch*) les rouages *mpl*; *Fig* **the wheels of government** les rouages du gouvernement; *Fig* **there are wheels within wheels** c'est une affaire très compliquée *ou* dont il faut connaître les dessous, c'est plus compliqué que cela n'en a l'air; *Fig* **the w. has come full circle** la boucle est bouclée; *Hist* **to condemn a criminal to the w.** condamner un criminel à la roue; *Hist* **to break sb on the w.** rouer qn; **big w.** (*at fair*) grande roue; *Am Fam* (*important person*) gros bonnet *m*, huile *f*; **the w. of fortune** la roue de la fortune

2 (*for steering*) *Aut* volant *m* (de direction); *Naut* roue *f* du gouvernail, barre *f*; **to be at the w.** *Aut* être au volant; *Naut* tenir la barre *ou* le gouvernail; *Fig* tenir la barre; **the man at the w.** *Aut* le conducteur, l'homme au volant; *Naut* l'homme de barre; *Fig* l'homme qui mène la barque, *Fam* le grand patron; **do you want to take a turn at the w.?** tu veux me remplacer au volant?; *Naut* tu veux me remplacer à la barre?

3 *Mil etc (movement)* (mouvement *m* de) conversion *f*; **left/right w.** conversion à gauche/à droite

vt (barrow, bicycle) pousser; **to w. sth in a barrow** transporter qch en brouette; **to w. a child in a pram** promener un enfant dans son landau

vi **1** *(circle) (of birds)* tournoyer; *(of plane)* tourner **2** *Mil* opérer *ou* effectuer une conversion; **left w.!** par file à gauche, gauche! **3** *Fam* **to w. and deal** brasser des affaires (plus ou moins louches); **after spending the whole week wheeling and dealing** après une semaine complète de tractations

▸▸*Aut* **w. alignment** parallélisme *m* des roues; *Aut* **w. arch** passage *m* de roue; *Aut* **w. bolt** boulon *m* de roue; *Aut* **w. brace** clef *f* en croix; *Aut* **w. chain** chaîne *f* (de pneu); *Aut* **w. cover** enjoliveur *m*; *Aut* **w. cylinder** cylindre *m* de roue; *Aut* **w. disc** enjoliveur; *Aut* **w. hop** rebond *m* des roues; *Aut* **w. lock(-up)** blocage *m* des roues; *Aut* **w. nut** écrou *m* de roue; *Aut* **w. rim** jante *f* de roue; *Aut* **w. shimmy** phénomène *m* de shimmy; *Aut* **w. spin** patinage *m* de roues; *Aut* **w. track** alignement *m* des roues; *Aut* **w. trim** enjoliveur de roues; *Aut* **w. wobble** flottement *m* des roues

▸ **wheel about, wheel around** *vi* **1** *(turn)* faire demi-tour *ou* se retourner (brusquement); **she wheeled around to face him** elle s'est retournée brusquement pour lui faire face **2** *(circle)* tourner en rond *ou* en cercle, tournoyer; **vultures wheeling about in the sky** des vautours qui tournoient dans le ciel *vt sep (turn)* tourner; *(dancing partner)* faire tourner

▸ **wheel in** *vt sep* **1** *(in wheelchair)* faire entrer en fauteuil roulant **2** *Br Fam (show in)* faire entrer; **w. him in as soon as he arrives** faites-le entrer dès qu'il arrive

▸ **wheel round** *vi, vt sep* = **wheel about**

wheelbarrow ['wi:lbærəʊ] *n* brouette *f*

wheelbase ['wi:lbeɪs] *n Aut* empattement *m*

wheelchair ['wi:ltʃeər] *n* fauteuil *m* roulant; **she'll be in a w. for the rest of her life** elle sera dans un fauteuil roulant pour le reste de ses jours; **access is difficult for people in wheelchairs** l'accès est difficile pour les personnes en fauteuil roulant

▸▸ **w. access** accès *m* aux handicapés

wheelclamp ['wi:lklæmp] *Aut* **n** sabot *m* de Denver

vt mettre un sabot de Denver à; **I got wheelclamped last week** je me suis pris un sabot la semaine dernière

wheeled [wi:ld] *adj* à roues; *(on castors)* à roulettes

-wheeled [-wi:ld] *suff* **two/three-w.** à deux/trois roues

-wheeler [-'wi:lər] *suff* **two/three-w.** voiture *f*/bicyclette *f* à deux/trois roues, véhicule *m* à deux/trois roues

wheeler-dealer *n Fam* brasseur *m* d'affaires, *Pej* magouilleur, -euse

wheelhouse ['wi:lhaʊs] *n Naut* abri *m* de navigation

wheelie ['wi:lɪ] *n Br Fam* **to do a w.** = rouler sur la roue arrière d'une bicyclette *ou* d'une moto

wheeling ['wi:lɪŋ] *n* **1** *(of birds etc)* tournoiement *m* **2** **w. and dealing** brassage *m* d'affaires, *Pej* tractations *fpl*, magouilles *fpl*

wheelmouse ['wi:lmaʊs] *n Comput* souris *f* à molette

wheelwright ['wi:lraɪt] *n* charron *m*

wheeze [wi:z] *n* **1** *(noise)* respiration *f* sifflante **2** *Br Fam (trick)* ruse *f*, truc *m*; **a good w.** une bonne astuce, une bonne combine *vi* respirer péniblement

wheezing ['wi:zɪŋ] *n (of person)* respiration *f* difficile; *Med* sibilance *f* respiratoire

wheezy ['wi:zɪ] *adj (person, voice)* asthmatique, poussif; **she's still a little bit w. after her cold** elle a encore un peu de mal à respirer après son rhume; *Fig* **a w. old barrel organ** un vieil orgue de Barbarie asthmatique

whelk [welk] *n* buccin *m*

whelp [welp] *n (dog)* jeune chien *m*, chiot *m*; *(of big cat)* petit *m*; *Old-fashioned Fam (youth)* garnement *m* *vi (of animals)* mettre bas

WHEN [wen]

ADV	quand **1** ▪ où **2**
CONJ	quand **1, 2** ▪ lorsque **1** ▪ alors que **3**
PRON	quand **1**

ADV **1** *(interr)* quand; **w. will you come?** quand viendrez-vous?; **w. will the wedding be?** à quand le mariage?; **w. ever** *or* **w. on earth will he come?** quand donc *ou* quand diable viendra-t-il?; *Fam* **say w.!** *(when pouring drink)* dites-moi stop! **2** *(rel)* **the day w. I first met her** le jour où je l'ai rencontrée pour la première fois; **one day w. I was on duty** un jour que j'étais de service; **at the very time w. …** au moment même où …, alors même que …

CONJ VOIR GRAMMAIRE A75; B31–2 **1** *(at the time that)* quand, lorsque; **w. I came into the room** quand *ou* lorsque je suis entré dans la pièce; **w. I think of what she must have suffered!** quand je pense à ce qu'elle a dû souffrir!; **I get very irritated w. talking to her** je m'énerve chaque fois que je lui parle; *Culin* **w. cool, turn out onto a dish** une fois refroidi, démouler sur un plat

2 *(at which time)* **the prince will arrive on the 10th, w. he will open the new university** le prince arrivera le dix et inaugurera la nouvelle université; **I had just gone to bed w. the phone rang** je venais de me mettre au lit quand le téléphone sonna

3 *(though)* **he walked there w. he could have taken the car** il y est allé à pied, alors qu'il aurait pu prendre la voiture

4 *(since)* **what's the good of telling you w. you won't listen to me?** à quoi bon vous le dire puisque vous ne voulez pas m'écouter?

PRON **1** *(interr)* **until w. can you stay?** jusqu'à quand pouvez-vous rester?; **since w. have you been living in Paris?** depuis quand habitez-vous Paris?; *Iron* **since w. have you been interested in opera?** depuis quand est-ce que tu t'intéresses à l'opéra?

2 *(rel)* **since w. I have always bought a car of that make** depuis lors je n'achète que des voitures de cette marque; **until w. I shall stay in Paris** d'ici là je reste à Paris

n **the w. and the how of it** quand et comment cela s'est-il passé/se passera-t-il

whence [wens] *adv Arch, Lit* d'où; **no one knows w. he comes** personne ne sait d'où il vient; **w. I conclude that …** d'où je conclus que …

whenever, *Lit* **whene'er** [wen'evər, -'eər] *conj, adv* VOIR GRAMMAIRE A75 **1** *(every time)* toutes les fois *ou* chaque fois que; **w. I see it I think of you** chaque fois que je le vois je pense à vous; **I go w. I can** j'y vais aussi souvent que possible **2** *(any time)* à n'importe quel moment; **come w. you like** venez quand vous voudrez *ou* à n'importe quel

moment; **Sunday, Monday or w.** dimanche, lundi, ou n'importe quel jour; **next month or w.** le mois prochain ou n'importe quand **3** *(interr)* quand; **w. did you find (the) time to do all that?** quand avez-vous trouvé le temps de faire tout cela?

WHERE [weər]

INTERR ADV	où **1**
CONJ	où ▪ là où ▪ là que

INTERR ADV **1** *(in what place or direction)* où; **w. am I?** où suis-je?; **tell me w. she is** dites-moi où elle est; **w. did you put it?** où l'avez-vous mis?; **w. are you going to?** où allez-vous?; **w. does he come from?** d'où vient-il?; **w. have you got to?, w. are you?** *(in work, book etc)* où en êtes-vous?; *(when looking for someone)* où êtes-vous passé?, où êtes-vous?; **w. should I be if I had followed your advice?** qu'est-ce que je serais devenu si j'avais suivi vos conseils?

2 w. is the use *or* **the good of it?** à quoi bon (faire) cela?

REL CONJ, REL ADV (in, at, to the place which) (là) où; **I'll stay w. I am** je resterai (là) où je suis; **go w. you like** allez où vous voudrez; **that's w. we've got to** voilà où nous sommes; **that is w. you are mistaken** c'est là que vous vous trompez, voilà où vous vous trompez; **he came to (the place) w. I was fishing** il est venu à l'endroit où je pêchais; **I can see it from w. we are** je le vois d'où nous sommes; **delete w. inapplicable** *(on form)* rayer les mentions inutiles; **the house w. I was born** la maison où *ou* dans laquelle je suis né; **they went to Paris, w. they stayed a week** ils sont allés à Paris et y sont restés huit jours VOIR GRAMMAIRE A75

n **the w. and the when** le lieu et la date/ l'heure

whereabouts *adv* [weərə'baʊts] où; **do you know w. the town hall is?** savez-vous de quel côté se trouve l'hôtel de ville?; **w. in France do you live?** où est-ce que tu habites en France?

npl ['weərəbaʊts] **nobody knows her w., her w. are unknown** personne ne sait où elle est; **we are still unsure of his exact w.** on ignore encore le lieu où il se trouve exactement; **the precise w. of the control centre** le lieu précis où se trouve le centre de contrôle

whereafter [weər'ɑ:ftər] *rel adv Arch, Lit* après quoi, à la suite de quoi

whereas [weər'ræz] *conj* **1** *Law etc (introducing preamble)* attendu que, vu que, puisque **2** *(on the other hand)* alors que, tandis que

whereat [weər'ræt] *adv, conj Arch, Lit* à quoi, sur quoi; **w. he replied that …** (ce) à quoi il a répondu que …

whereby [weər'baɪ] *adv Arch, Fml* par quoi, par quel moyen; **we have a situation here w. …** nous sommes ici en présence d'une situation dans laquelle …; **a scheme w. we can …** un plan par lequel nous pouvons …

wherefore ['weəfɔ:r] *adv Arch, Lit* **1** *(interr)* pourquoi, pour quelle raison **2** *(rel)* donc, pour cette raison

n **the why and the w.** le pourquoi et le comment

wherein [weər'ɪn] *adv Arch, Lit* en quoi; **w. the difficulty lies** où se trouve la difficulté

whereof [weər'ɒv] *adv Arch, Lit (interr)* en quoi, de quoi; *(rel)* dont; **a matter w. I know nothing** une affaire dont j'ignore tout

whereon [weər'ɒn] *adv Arch, Lit* sur lequel; **the day w. …** le jour où …; **w. he left us** sur quoi il nous a quittés

wheresoever, **wheresoe'er** [weəsəʊ'evər, -'eər] *adv, conj esp Lit* = **wherever**

whereupon [weərə'pɒn] ADV, CONJ *Lit (at which point)* sur quoi, après quoi; **w. he left us** sur quoi il nous a quittés

wherever [weə'revər] CONJ, ADV VOIR GRAMMAIRE A75 **1** *(every place)* partout où, n'importe où; **I shall remember it w. I go** où que j'aille, je m'en souviendrai; **I'll go w. you want (me to)** j'irai partout où vous voudrez (que j'aille); **w. possible** partout où cela est possible; *Fam* **at home, in the office or w.** à la maison, au bureau ou n'importe où **2** *(whichever place)* **they come from w.** d'où qu'ils viennent; **he comes from Glossop, w. that may be** il est originaire d'un bled qui s'appelle Glossop, et ne me demandez pas où cela se trouve **3** *(interr)* où; **w. can he be?** où peut-il bien être?

wherewithal ['weərwɪðɔːl] N **the w.** l'argent *m*, le nécessaire, les moyens *mpl*; **I haven't the w. to buy it** je n'ai pas de quoi l'acheter

whet [wet] VT (-tt-) **1** *(sharpen) (tool, blade)* aiguiser, affûter, repasser **2** *(stimulate) (appetite)* stimuler, aiguiser; **the weekend break in Florence had whetted her appetite for travel** ce week-end à Florence lui avait donné soif de voyages

whether ['weðər] CONJ VOIR GRAMMAIRE A74 **1** *(indirect question)* si; **I don't know w. it's true** je ne sais pas si c'est vrai; **it's doubtful** *or* **uncertain w. ...** il est douteux *ou* peu certain que ... + *subj*; **I doubt w. he'll come** je doute qu'il vienne; **I want to know w. ... or w. ...** je voudrais savoir si ... ou si ...; **it depends on w. you're in a hurry or not** cela dépend (de) si vous êtes pressé ou non **2** *(conditional)* **w. it rains or (whether it) snows, he always goes out** qu'il pleuve ou qu'il neige, il sort toujours; **w. she comes or not we shall leave** qu'elle vienne ou non *ou* qu'elle vienne ou qu'elle ne vienne pas, nous partirons; **w. or not this is true** qu'il en soit ainsi ou non; **everyone, w. rich or poor, needs it** chacun, qu'il soit riche ou pauvre, en a besoin; **you'll listen to me w. you like it or not** tu vas m'écouter, que tu le veuilles ou non; **w. he likes it or not** que cela lui plaise ou non

whetstone ['wetstəʊn] N pierre *f* à aiguiser *ou* à repasser

whew [hjuː] INT **1** *(relief, fatigue)* ouf! **2** *(astonishment)* mon Dieu!

whey [weɪ] N petit-lait *m*, *pl* petits-laits

WHICH [wɪtʃ] VOIR GRAMMAIRE A31–2

ADJ	quel **1** ▪ lequel **2**
PRON	lequel **1, 3** ▪ qui **2** ▪ que **2** ▪ ce qui **2** ▪ ce que **2**

ADJ 1 *(interr)* quel, *f* quelle, *pl* quels, quelles; **w. colour do you like best?** quelle couleur aimez-vous le mieux?; **w. way do we go?** par où allons-nous?; **w. way is the wind blowing?** d'où vient le vent?; **w. one?** lequel?, laquelle?; **w. ones?** lesquels?, lesquelles?; **I know w. one you want** je sais lequel vous désirez VOIR GRAMMAIRE A31–2; B16 **2** *(rel)* lequel, laquelle, *pl* lesquels, lesquelles; **he stayed here two weeks, during w. time he never left the house** il est resté ici deux semaines, et pendant (tout) ce temps il n'a pas quitté la maison; **she came at noon, at w. time I'm usually in the garden** elle est venue à midi, heure à laquelle je suis habituellement au jardin VOIR GRAMMAIRE A33

PRON 1 *(interr)* lequel, laquelle, *pl* lesquels, lesquelles; **w. have you chosen?** lequel/laquelle/lesquels/lesquelles avez-vous choisi(e)(s)?; **w. of you?** lequel d'entre vous?; **w. of the two (girls) is the prettier?** laquelle des deux (filles) est la plus jolie?; **w. would you rather have?** lequel préféreriez-vous

(avoir)?; **I can never tell w. is w.** je ne sais jamais les distinguer, je ne sais jamais lequel est l'un et lequel est l'autre; **I don't know w. to choose** je ne sais (pas) lequel choisir; **I don't mind w.** n'importe (lequel) SEE GRAMMAR B17 **2** *(rel) (subject)* qui; *(object)* que; *(referring to whole clause) (subject)* ce qui; *(object)* ce que; **the house w. is for sale** la maison qui est à vendre; **the book w. I bought yesterday** le livre que j'ai acheté hier; **he looked like a retired colonel, w. in fact he was** il avait l'air d'un colonel en retraite, ce qu'il était en effet; **she was back in London, w. I didn't know** elle était de retour à Londres, fait que *ou* ce que j'ignorais VOIR GRAMMAIRE A32–3; B22–3 **3** *(with prepositions)* lequel, laquelle, *pl* lesquels, lesquelles; **to w., at w.** auquel, à laquelle, *pl* auxquels, auxquelles; **of w., from w.** duquel, de laquelle, *pl* desquels, desquelles; **the house of w. I am speaking** la maison dont je parle; **the countries to w. we are going** *or* **w. we're going to** les pays où nous allons; **the pen with w. I'm writing, the pen w. I'm writing with** le stylo avec lequel j'écris; **the town in w. we live, the town w. we live in** la ville où nous habitons *ou* que nous habitons *ou* dans laquelle nous habitons; **he insists that actors should have talent, in w. he is right** il exige que les acteurs aient du talent, (ce) en quoi il a raison; **there are no trains on Sunday, w. I hadn't thought of** il n'y a pas de trains le dimanche, ce à quoi je n'avais pas pensé; **after w. he went out** après quoi il est sorti

whichever [wɪtʃ'evər] VOIR GRAMMAIRE A33 **PRON 1** *(any) (subject)* celui qui, *f* celle qui, *pl* ceux qui, celles qui; *(object)* celui que *etc*; **take w. you like best** prenez celui que vous préférez; **w. of you comes in first** celui (d'entre vous) qui arrive le premier; **the 30th or the last Friday in the month, w. comes first** le 30 *ou* le dernier vendredi du mois, suivant lequel de ces deux jours survient le premier **2** *(no matter which)* **w. of the measures they adopt ... (one)** quelle que soit la mesure qu'ils adoptent ..., quelque mesure qu'ils adoptent ..., qu'ils adoptent une mesure ou une autre ..., ils peuvent adopter n'importe quelle mesure ...; *(more than one)* quelles que soient les mesures qu'ils adoptent ..., quelques mesures qu'ils adoptent ..., ils peuvent adopter n'importe quelles mesures ...; **w. you choose, you will have a good bargain** quel que soit celui/quelle que soit celle/*etc* que vous choisissiez *ou* vous pouvez choisir n'importe lequel/laquelle/*etc*, vous ferez une bonne affaire **3** *(interr)* lequel, laquelle, *pl* lesquels, lesquelles; **w. shall I choose?** lequel vais-je choisir? VOIR GRAMMAIRE A32 **ADJ 1** *(the one/ones which)* **buy w. model is cheapest** achète le modèle qui est le moins cher(, peu importe lequel); **take w. ties you prefer** prends les cravates que tu préfères (, peu importe lesquelles); **I'll have w. cake Mary doesn't want** je prendrai le gâteau que Mary ne veut pas; **you should write to w. organization you think best** vous devriez écrire à l'organisme qui vous paraît le meilleur **2** *(no matter which)* **w. candidate wins the election, he will have to ...** quel que soit le candidat qui remporte l'élection, il lui faudra ...; **w. road you take, it'll take you two hours** quelle que soit la route que tu prennes *ou* quelque route que tu prennes *ou* que tu prennes une route ou une autre *ou* tu peux prendre n'importe quelle route, tu mettras deux heures; **in w. company you work ...** quelle que soit l'entreprise dans laquelle tu travailles ..., dans quelque entre-

prise que tu travailles ..., que tu travailles dans une entreprise ou dans une autre ..., tu peux travailler dans n'importe quelle entreprise ...; **w. way you turn ...** de quelque côté que vous vous tourniez ..., que vous vous tourniez d'un côté ou d'un autre ..., vous pouvez vous tourner de n'importe quel côté ...

whiff [wɪf] N *(smell) (of wine, socks, incense etc)* odeur *f*, *Fig* **a w. of scandal** un parfum de scandale; **to catch a w. of sth** *(smell)* sentir qch; *Fig (hear rumours about)* avoir vent de qch; **he had caught a w. of something suspicious** il avait senti que quelque chose de louche était dans l'air; **there mustn't be the slightest w. of suspicion that I'm involved** rien ne doit laisser penser que je suis impliqué; *Fam* **what a w.!** *(bad smell)* qu'est-ce que ça pue!

whiffy ['wɪfɪ] ADJ *Br Fam* puant, qui pue; **the dog's a bit w.** ce chien sent fort; **it's a bit w. in here, don't you think?** ça schlingue par ici, tu ne trouves pas?

Whig [wɪg] N *Pol, Hist* whig *m*

while [waɪl] N **1** *(time)* (espace *m* de) temps *m*; **a short w.** un petit moment; **some w. later** *(soon after)* un moment plus tard; *(longer)* quelque temps plus tard; **after a w.** au bout de quelque temps, quelque temps après; **after a little w., a little w. later** peu de temps après; **for a (short) w.** pendant un moment; **in a short** *or* **little w.** sous peu, avant peu; **a short** *or* **little w. ago** il y a peu de temps; **a long w.** longtemps; **a long w. ago** il y a longtemps; **a good w.** pas mal de temps; **it lasted a good w.** ça a duré un bon moment; **it will be a good w. before you see him again** vous ne le reverrez pas de si tôt; **it will take me quite a w.** cela me prendra un certain temps *ou* pas mal de temps; **it took me a w. to realize what she meant** j'ai mis un certain temps à comprendre ce qu'elle voulait dire; **stay a little w. longer** restez encore un peu; **all the w.** tout le temps; **once in a w.** de temps en temps, de temps à autre; *Arch* **the w.** en attendant, pendant ce temps

2 to be worth (one's) w. valoir la peine, *Fam* valoir le coup; **it's not worth our w. waiting** cela ne vaut pas *ou* ce n'est pas la peine que nous attendions; **it is perhaps worth w. pointing out that ...** cela vaut peut-être la peine de faire remarquer que ...; **I'll make it worth your w.** vous serez bien récompensé de votre peine

CONJ **1** *(during the time that)* pendant que, tandis que; **don't speak w. the performance is in progress** ne parlez pas pendant le spectacle; **he drowned w. he was having a bath** il s'est noyé en prenant un bain; **w. (he was) here** pendant qu'il était ici; **w. in Paris** pendant mon/son/*etc* séjour à Paris; **w. reading I fell asleep** tout en lisant, je me suis endormi; **w. this was going on** sur ces entrefaites; **w. you're at** *or* **about it, could you photocopy this too?** pendant que tu y es, peux-tu aussi me photocopier cela? VOIR GRAMMAIRE B31–2

2 *(as long as)* tant que

3 *(although)* quoique + *subj*, bien que + *subj*; **w. I admit it's difficult** quoique j'admette que c'est difficile

4 *(whereas)* tandis que; **one of the sisters was in white, w. the other was all in black** une des sœurs était vêtue de blanc, tandis que l'autre était tout en noir

▸ **while away** VT SEP *(time)* faire passer, tuer; *(hour)* tuer; **we whiled away the hours by playing cards** on faisait passer le temps en jouant aux cartes; **I played patience to w. away the time** j'ai fait des réussites pour m'occuper

whilst [waɪlst] CONJ *esp Br* = **while**

whim [wɪm] N caprice *m*, fantaisie *f*, lubie *f*,

passing w. toquade f; **to do sth on a w.** faire qch sur un coup de tête; **it was just a w.** ce n'était qu'un caprice; **it was a sudden w. of his** c'était un de ses caprices; **she indulges his every w.** elle lui passe tous ses caprices

whimper ['wɪmpər] **N** (crying) pleurnicherie f, pleurnichement m; (of dog) petit cri m plaintif; Fig (complaint) geignement m, plainte f; **without so much as a w.** sans se plaindre

VI (of person) pleurnicher, geindre; (of dog) pousser de petits cris plaintifs; **the dog's whimpering to be let in** le chien gémit pour qu'on le laisse entrer

whimpering ['wɪmpərɪŋ] **ADJ** pleurnicheur, gémissant; (dog) qui pousse de petits cris plaintifs

N (crying) pleurnichement m, pleurnicheries fpl; (of dog) petits cris mpl plaintifs; Fig (complaints) plaintes fpl

whimsey ['wɪmzɪ] **N** = **whimsy**

whimsical ['wɪmzɪk(ə)l] **ADJ** (person) capricieux, fantasque; (playful) malicieux, (behaviour, sense of humour, story, remark) farfelu; (smile) malicieux

whimsicality [wɪmzɪ'kælɪtɪ] **N** (of person) caractère m capricieux ou fantasque; (playfulness) malice f, (of behaviour, sense of humour, story, remark) caractère farfelu

whimsically ['wɪmzɪklɪ] **ADV** (capriciously) capricieusement; (playfully) malicieusement; (directed, written) de façon farfelue; (to smile) malicieusement

whimsy ['wɪmzɪ] **N 1** (capricious idea) fantaisie f, **she dismissed the idea as a mere piece of w.** elle rejeta cette idée qui lui parut de la plus haute fantaisie **2** (playfulness) malice f

whin [wɪn] **N** (plant) ajonc m, genêt m épineux

whine [waɪn] **N 1** (crying) (of child) gémissement m; (of dog) gémissement m, geignement m **2** (of engine etc) bruit m strident

VI 1 (cry) (of child) pleurnicher; (of person, dog) gémir; (in pain etc) geindre **2** (complain) se plaindre; **she's always whining about something** elle est toujours en train de se lamenter à propos d'une chose ou d'une autre; **you've nothing to w. about** il n'y a pas de quoi vous plaindre; **stop whining!** assez de jérémiades!

whinge [wɪndʒ] Fam **N** (complaint) plainte f, **to have a w. about sth** se plaindre (à propos) de qch

VI 1 (cry) (of child) pleurnicher, gémir **2** (complain) se plaindre; **stop whingeing!** assez de jérémiades!; Austr a whingeing pom un Anglais qui se plaint toujours

whinger ['wɪndʒər] **N** Fam geignard, -arde

whining ['waɪnɪŋ] **ADJ** (voice) geignard; (child) pleurnicheur; (tone) plaintif

N 1 (of person, dog) gémissement m; (in pain etc) geignement m **2** (complaining) jérémiades fpl, plaintes fpl; **stop your w.!** assez de jérémiades!; **I've had enough of his w.** j'en ai assez de ses jérémiades

whinny ['wɪnɪ] **N** (of horse) hennissement m

VI (of horse) hennir; Fig (of person) brailler

whinnying ['wɪnɪɪŋ] **ADJ a w. laugh** un rire qui ressemble à un hennissement; **he gave a w. laugh** il se mit à rire en hennissant

whiny ['waɪnɪ] **ADJ** pleurnichard

whip [wɪp] **N 1** (lash) fouet m; Fig Fam **to give sb a fair crack of the w.** donner toutes ses chances à qn; Fig Fam **to get a fair crack of the w.** avoir toutes ses chances; Fig **to have or hold the w. hand** avoir l'avantage, avoir le dessus; Fig **to have the w. hand over sb** avoir barre(s) sur qn

2 Parl (person) chef m de file, whip m; (or-

der) appel m aux membres d'un groupe **3** (movement) (of cable etc) mouvement m brusque

4 Culin mousse f, **strawberry/raspberry w.** mousse aux fraises/framboises

VT (**-pp-**) **1** (horse) fouetter; (child) donner le fouet à; Culin (egg whites) battre en neige; (cream) fouetter, battre; **to w. a top** fouetter ou faire aller un sabot; **whipped cream** crème fouettée; Fig **he whipped the crowd into a frenzy with his speech** son discours rendit la foule frénétique; **the rain was whipping the window panes** la pluie fouettait ou cinglait les vitres

2 Fam (defeat) battre à plate(s) couture(s); **I know when I'm whipped** je sais quand déclarer forfait

3 Sewing **to w. a seam** surjeter une couture, faire un surjet

4 (move quickly) **she whipped it out of sight** elle l'a caché d'un mouvement rapide; **she's been whipped into hospital** elle a été transportée à l'hôpital de toute urgence

5 Fam (steal) faucher, piquer; **someone's whipped my wallet** on m'a piqué mon portefeuille

VI fouetter; **the rain was whipping against the panes** la pluie fouettait ou cinglait les vitres

▸ **whip away VT SEP** Fam (remove quickly) enlever brusquement ou d'un geste rapide

▸ **whip back VI** Fam (return) retourner rapidement; **w. back and get it** retournez-y en vitesse le chercher

▸ **whip in VI** Fam (go in, drop in) **I'll just w. in and buy some bread** je vais juste passer acheter du pain

VT SEP (of huntsman) rassembler

▸ **whip off VT SEP** Fam (remove) (clothes) ôter ou enlever rapidement, se débarrasser de

▸ **whip out** Fam **VT SEP** (extract) sortir rapidement; **he whipped out a revolver** il a sorti brusquement un revolver; **to w. out sb's appendix** enlever l'appendice de qn

VI (go out) sortir en vitesse; **I'm just whipping out to the library** je file à la bibliothèque

▸ **whip round VI** Fam **1** (turn) se retourner vivement **2** (go quickly) **w. round to the chemist's for me** fais un saut à la pharmacie pour moi

▸ **whip up VT SEP 1** (arouse) (horse) toucher (du fouet); Fig **to w. up an audience** galvaniser ou exalter un public **2** Parl (summon) (members of party) faire passer un appel urgent à; **to w. up support for sth** susciter un soutien en faveur de qch **3** Culin (egg whites) battre en neige; (cream) battre, fouetter; Fam **I'll w. you up something to eat** je vais te préparer ou te faire quelque chose à manger en vitesse; Fam **I'll see what I can w. up** je vais voir ce que je peux préparer en vitesse

whipcord ['wɪpkɔːd] **N 1** (on whip) mèche f de fouet **2** Tex whipcord m; **w. trousers** pantalon m en whipcord

whiplash ['wɪplæʃ] **N 1** (stroke of whip) coup m de fouet; Fig **tongue like a w.** langue cinglante **2** Med (injury) coup m du lapin, Spec syndrome m cervical traumatique

▸▸ Med **w. effect** effet m du coup du lapin; Med **w. injury** coup du lapin, Spec syndrome cervical traumatique

whipper-in [wɪpər-] **N** (of hounds) piqueur m

whippersnapper ['wɪpəsnæpər] **N** Fam petit malin m

whippet ['wɪpɪt] **N** (dog) whippet m

whipping ['wɪpɪŋ] **N** correction; **to give sb a w.** donner une correction à qn

▸▸ **w. boy** bouc m émissaire; **w. cream** ≃ crème f fraîche (à fouetter)

whippoorwill ['wɪpʊəwɪl] **N** Am (bird) en-

goulevent m de Virginie, Can engoulevent bois-pourri

whipround ['wɪpraʊnd] **N** Br Fam quête f, collecte f; **to have a w. for sb** organiser une collecte pour qn

whir [wɜːr] **N, VI** = **whirr**

whirl [wɜːl] **N** (of wheel) mouvement m giratoire; (of leaves, dust) tourbillon m, tournoiement m; Fig Fam **would you like to give it a w.?** tu veux essayer?; Fig Fam **I'll have a w. at it** je vais tenter le coup; **a w. of activity** un tourbillon d'activités; **my head's in a w.** la tête me tourne; **the social w.** les tourbillons de la vie mondaine

VI (of dead leaves etc) tourbillonner, tournoyer; (of propeller etc) tourner; (of top) tournoyer; **whirling dervish** derviche m tourneur; **my head's whirling** la tête me tourne; **the thoughts that were whirling through my head** les pensées qui tourbillonnaient dans ma tête

VT (dead leaves etc) faire tournoyer, faire tourbillonner; **to w. sb/sth around** (of person) faire tournoyer qn/qch autour de soi; **he whirled her onto the dance floor** il l'a entraînée en tournoyant sur la piste de danse

▸ **whirl along VI** filer à toute vitesse ou à toute allure

VT SEP entraîner à toute vitesse ou à fond de train; **the train whirled us along** le train nous emportait à grande allure

▸ **whirl round VI** (of person) se retourner brusquement; (of dancer) pirouetter; (of leaves) tourbillonner, tournoyer; **she whirled round and round in the middle of the dance floor** elle tournait et tournait au milieu de la piste de danse

VT SEP to w. sb round faire tournoyer qn

whirligig ['wɜːlɪgɪg] **N** (top) tourniquet m; (merry-go-round) manège m de chevaux de bois

whirlpool ['wɜːlpuːl] **N** tourbillon m (d'eau), gouffre m; Fig **a w. of violence** un tourbillon de violence

▸▸ **w. bath** bain m à remous, Jacuzzi® m

whirlwind ['wɜːlwɪnd] **N** tourbillon m (de vent), trombe f (de vent); **to come in like a w.** entrer comme une tornade

▸▸ **w. romance** aventure f enivrante; **w. tour** visite f éclair

whirlybird ['wɜːlɪbɜːd] **N** Old-fashioned Fam (helicopter) hélico m

whirr [wɜːr] **N** (of machines) ronflement m, ronronnement m; (of propeller etc) vrombissement m

VI (of machinery etc) ronfler, ronronner; (of propeller) vrombir

whisk [wɪsk] **N 1** (for beating eggs) fouet m, batteur m **2** (action) **give the eggs a w.** battre les œufs; **a w. of the tail/the duster** un coup de queue/de chiffon

VT 1 to w. its tail (of cow etc) agiter sa queue; **to w. a duster over the table** donner un coup de chiffon sur la table **2** (move quickly) **he was whisked to hospital** il a été transporté à l'hôpital de toute urgence; **she whisked it out of sight** elle l'a caché d'un mouvement rapide **3** Culin (eggs) battre; (cream) fouetter

VI she whisked past me elle est passée devant moi comme un éclair

▸ **whisk away, whisk off VT SEP** (thing) enlever d'un geste rapide; (person) emporter très rapidement; **to w. away a fly** chasser une mouche; **the president was whisked away in a helicopter** le président a été emmené à toute vitesse en hélicoptère; **he was whisked away to hospital in an ambulance** il a été transporté de toute urgence en ambulance à l'hôpital

▸ **whisk up VT SEP** Culin (eggs) battre; (cream) fouetter

whisker ['wɪskər] N **whiskers** *(of man) (side whiskers)* favoris *mpl*, *(moustache)* moustache *f*, *(beard)* barbe *f*, *(of cat, mouse etc)* moustache(s) *f(pl)*; *Sport Fig* **to win by a w.** gagner d'un poil *ou* de justesse; *Fig* **to escape death by a w.** frôler la mort, échapper de justesse à la mort

whiskered ['wɪskəd] ADJ *(man)* qui porte des favoris

whisky, *Ir, Am* **whiskey** ['wɪskɪ] N whisky *m*; **two whiskies** deux whiskies; **a w. and soda** un whisky soda; **w. on the rocks** whisky avec des glaçons, *Can* whisky sur glace *ou* aux glaçons
▸▸ **w. company** société *f* de fabrication de whisky; **w. distillery** distillerie *f* de whisky; **w. glass** verre *m* à whisky; **w. mac** = boisson *f* à base de whisky et d'alcool au gingembre; **w. sour** = cocktail *m* à base de whisky et de jus de citron

whisper ['wɪspər] N **1** *(of person speaking)* chuchotement *m*; *esp Lit (of wind in leaves)* bruissement *m*; **to speak in a w.** *or* **in whispers** chuchoter, parler en chuchotant; **to say sth in a w.** chuchoter qch, dire qch tout bas; **… she said in a loud w.** … chuchota-t-elle assez fort **2** *(rumour)* rumeur *f*, bruit *m*; **I've heard whispers** *or* **a w. that …** j'ai entendu dire que …; **and remember, not a w. of it to anyone!** et souviens-toi, pas un mot à qui que ce soit!
VI *(of person speaking)* chuchoter, parler bas; *esp Lit (of wind in leaves)* bruire; **to w. to sb** chuchoter à l'oreille de qn, parler à voix basse à qn; **stop whispering, Evans!** ça suffit les messes basses, Evans!
VT **1 to w. sth to sb** chuchoter qch à qn, dire qch à voix basse à qn; **what were you whispering to her?** qu'est-ce que tu lui disais à l'oreille?; **whispered conversation** conversation à voix basse **2** *(as rumour)* **it is being whispered that …** le bruit court que …, on dit que …

whispering ['wɪspərɪŋ] N **1** *(of person speaking)* chuchotement *m*; *esp Lit (of wind)* bruissement *m*; **stop that w.!** ça suffit les messes basses! **2** *Pej (rumours)* rumeur *f*
▸▸ **w. campaign** campagne *f* de diffamation; *Archit* **w. gallery** galerie *f* à écho

whist [wɪst] N *Cards* whist *m*; **to have a game of w.** faire une partie de whist; **to play w.** jouer au whist
▸▸ **w. drive** tournoi *m* de whist; **w. player** joueur, -euse de whist

whistle ['wɪs(ə)l] N **1** *(noise)* sifflement *m*; *(blow on a whistle)* coup *m* de sifflet; **she gave a w. of surprise** elle a sifflé de surprise; *Sport* **final w.** coup de sifflet final **2** *(object)* sifflet *m*; **to blow a w.** donner un coup de sifflet; *Sport* **to blow the w. for a foul/for half-time** siffler une faute/la mi-temps; *Fig Fam* **to blow the w. on sth** révéler *ou* dévoiler qch; *Fig Fam* **to blow the w. on sb** dénoncer qn; *Fig Fam* **who blew the w.?** qui a vendu la mèche?
VI *(of person, bird, wind etc)* siffler; *(on whistle)* donner un coup de sifflet; **she whistled in surprise** elle a sifflé de surprise; **the bullet whistled past his ear** la balle a passé en sifflant tout près de son oreille; *Fig* **to w. in the dark** essayer de se rassurer; **to w. for one's dog/a taxi** siffler son chien/un taxi; *Fig Fam* **he can w. for his money** il peut courir après son argent; *Fig Fam* **you can w. for it!** tu peux toujours courir!
VT *(tune)* siffler, siffloter; *Sport* **to w. half-time** siffler la mi-temps
▸ **whistle up** VT SEP *Fam* **I'll w. up a few friends to help us** je vais trouver quelques amis pour nous aider; **can you w. up some more sandwiches?** peux-tu nous avoir *ou* dégoter encore quelques sandwichs?

whistle-blower N *Fig Fam* personne *f* qui vend la mèche; **we need a few more whistle-blowers like her** il faudrait d'autres personnes comme elle pour tirer sur la sonnette d'alarme

whistler ['wɪslər] N **1** *(person)* siffleur, -euse **2** *(bird)* oiseau *m* siffleur **3** *(animal)* siffleur *m*, marmotte *f* canadienne, *Can* siffleux *m*

whistle-stop N **1** *Am Rail* arrêt *m* facultatif **2** *(town)* village *m* perdu
ADJ **she made a w. tour of Europe** elle a fait une tournée rapide en Europe
VI *Am Pol* = faire une tournée électorale en passant par des petites villes
▸▸ **w. town** village perdu

whistling ['wɪslɪŋ] N sifflement *m*

Whit [wɪt] N Pentecôte *f*
▸▸ **W. Monday** lundi *m* de Pentecôte; **W. Sunday** dimanche *m* de Pentecôte

whit [wɪt] N *(usu in neg)* brin *m*; **it won't make a w. of difference** ça ne changera rien à rien; **it doesn't matter a w.** ça n'a aucune espèce d'importance; **she doesn't care a w. about him or anyone else** elle se fiche de lui comme du reste; **he's not a w. the better for it** il ne s'en porte nullement mieux; **I don't care a w.** je m'en moque comme de ma première chemise *ou* comme de l'an quarante

white [waɪt] ADJ blanc, *f* blanche; **as w. as snow** blanc comme la neige; **we had a w. Christmas** on a eu de la neige à Noël; **to turn** *or* **go w.** *(of face)* devenir blanc *ou* pâle *ou* blême; *(of hair)* blanchir; **he's going w.** *(hair)* il commence à blanchir; **he went w. overnight** ses cheveux sont devenus blancs du jour au lendemain; **w. with fear** blanc de peur; **w. as a ghost/sheet** pâle comme la mort/un linge; *Fig* **whiter than w.** *(person)* blanc comme neige; **do you take your coffee w.?** tu prends du lait dans ton café?; **a w. man** un Blanc; **the w. man's burden** = obligation *f* pour les blancs d'assurer l'instruction des habitants noirs de leurs colonies
N **1** *(colour)* blanc *m*; **dressed in w.** habillé en blanc *ou* de blanc; **whites** *(linen)* blanc; *Sport* tenue *f* de sport blanche; **wash your whites with Jizmo** lavez votre linge avec Jizmo **2** *(person)* blanc *m*, blanche *f* **3** *(of egg, eyes)* blanc *m*
VT *Rel, Fig* **whited sepulchre** sépulcre *m* blanchi
▸▸ **w. alloy** métal *m* blanc; **w. ant** fourmi *f* blanche, termite *m*; **w. blood cell** globule *m* blanc, leucocyte *m*; **w. chocolate** chocolat *m* blanc; **w. coat** blouse *f* blanche; *Med Fam* **w.-coat syndrome** syndrome *m* de la blouse blanche; **w. coffee** café *m* au lait; *Astron* **w. dwarf** naine *f* blanche; **w. elephant** *(useless construction)* = réalisation *f* de prestige dont l'utilité ne justifie pas le coût; **the fear is that the new museum will turn out to be another w. elephant** on craint que le nouveau musée ne soit une nouvelle construction coûteuse et peu utile; *Br* **w. elephant stall** *(at fair, jumble sale)* stand *m* de bibelots; *Naut* **w. ensign** pavillon *m* blanc; *Hist* **w. feather** = symbole *m* de lâcheté; *Br* **w. fish** poisson *m* à chair blanche; **w. flag** drapeau *m* blanc; **w. flour** farine *f* de ménage; **w. gold** or *m* blanc; **w. goods** *(household equipment)* appareils *mpl* ménagers; *(linen)* linge *m* de maison, blanc *m*; **w. hope** espoir *m*; **w. horses** *(waves)* moutons *mpl*; **the W. House** la Maison-Blanche; *Fig* **w. knight** sauveur *m*, chevalier *m*; **w. lie** pieux mensonge *m*; *Fam* **w. lightning** tord-boyaux *m inv (distillé illégalement)*; **w. magic** magie *f* blanche; **w. meat** viande *f* blanche; *(of poultry)* blanc; **w. metal** métal *m* blanc; *Br* **w. meter heating** = système *m* de chauffage permettant d'ac-

cumuler la chaleur pendant les heures creuses; **w. noise** bruit *m* de fond; *Am* **W. Out®** correcteur *m* liquide; *Br* **w. paper** *(government report)* livre *m* blanc; **w. pepper** poivre *m* blanc; *Culin* **w. pudding** boudin *m* blanc; **W. Russia** Russie *f* Blanche; *Am* **w. sale** promotion *f* sur le blanc; **w. sauce** sauce *f* blanche; **w. shark** requin *m* blanc; **w. slavery** traite *f* des blanches **w. space** *(on page)* espace *m* blanc; **w. spirit** white-spirit *m*; **w. stick** *(of blind person)* canne *f* blanche; **w. supremacist** partisan, -ane de la suprématie (de la race) blanche; **w. supremacy** suprématie *f* (de la race) blanche; *Aviat Sl* **w. tail** = avion *m* n'appartenant encore à aucune compagnie aérienne; **w. tie** *(formal clothes)* habit *m*; *(on invitation)* ≃ tenue de soirée exigée; *Pej* **w. trash** Blancs *mpl* pauvres; **w. water** eau *f* vive; **w. wedding** mariage *m* en blanc; **she's having a w. wedding** elle se marie en blanc; **w. whale** bélouga *m*, béluga *m*
▸ **white out** VT SEP *(delete)* masquer au vernis correcteur blanc

whitebait ['waɪtbeɪt] N *(fish)* blanchaille *f*, **a dish of w.** un plat de friture

whiteboard ['waɪtbɔːd] N tableau *m* blanc

whitebread ['waɪtbred] ADJ *Am Pej* conventionnel

whitecaps ['waɪtkæps] NPL *(waves)* moutons *mpl*

white-collar ADJ
▸▸ **w. crime** délits *mpl* financiers; **w. union** syndicat *m* d'employés de bureau; **w. worker** employé *m* de bureau, col *m* blanc

white-faced [-'feɪst] ADJ au visage pâle

whitefish ['waɪtfɪʃ] N corégone *m*

white-haired ADJ aux cheveux blancs
▸▸ *Am Fig* **w. boy** chouchou *m*

Whitehall ['waɪthɔːl] N *(British government)* l'Administration *f* britannique

> **Whitehall**
> De nombreux services gouvernementaux ont leurs bureaux dans cette rue londonienne dont le nom est souvent employé pour désigner le gouvernement lui-même.

white-headed ADJ **1** *(animal)* à tête blanche **2** *(person)* aux cheveux blancs
▸▸ *Am Fig* **w. boy** chouchou *m*

white-hot ADJ chauffé *ou* porté à blanc

white-knuckle ADJ *Fam* **I'm a w. flyer** j'ai la trouille en avion; **a w. ride** *(at fair etc)* un manège terrifiant

white-livered [-lɪvəd] ADJ *Fig (person)* poltron

whiten ['waɪt(ə)n] VT **1** *(hair, linen, shoes)* blanchir **2** *(with whitewash)* blanchir à la chaux, badigeonner de chaux
VI blanchir; *(with fear etc)* pâlir, blêmir

whiteness ['waɪtnɪs] N *(of snow, skin)* blancheur *f*, *(of face)* pâleur *f*

white-on-black N *Typ* noir au blanc *m*

whiteout ['waɪtaʊt] N visibilité *f* nulle (à cause de la neige); **in w. conditions** dans des conditions de visibilité nulle

white-slaver N personne *f* qui se livre à la traite des blanches

whitethorn ['waɪtθɔːn] N *(tree)* aubépine *f*

whitethroat ['waɪtθrəʊt] N *(bird)* fauvette *f* grisette

whitewall ['waɪtwɔːl] N **w. (tyre** *or Am* **tire)** pneu *m* à flanc blanc

whitewash ['waɪtwɒʃ] N **1** *(paint)* blanc *m* ou lait *m* de chaux, badigeon *m* à la chaux; **to give a wall a coat of w.** badigeonner un mur (à la chaux) **2** *Fig (dishonest exonera-*

tion) blanchiment *m*; **a w. (job)** une opération de blanchiment **3** *Sport Fam* défaite *f* à zéro, raclée *f*

vt 1 *(paint)* peindre *ou* blanchir à la chaux, badigeonner en blanc **2** *Fig (exonerate dishonestly)* blanchir; *(events, episode)* maquiller **3** *Sport Fam (one's opponents)* battre à plate couture, donner une raclée à

whitewashing ['waɪtwɒʃɪŋ] **N 1** *(painting)* peinture *f* à la chaux, badigeonnage *m* **2** *Fig (of sb's reputation)* blanchiment *m*

whitewood ['waɪtwʊd] **N** bois *m* blanc

whitey ['waɪtɪ] **N** *Am Pej* blanc *m*, blanche *f*, *(npl)* les blancs

whither ['wɪðər] **ADV, CONJ** *Arch, Lit* **1** *(interr)* où, vers quel lieu; **w. Britain?** où va la Grande-Bretagne? **2** *(rel)* (là) où; **I shall go w. fate leads me** j'irai là où me mènera le destin

whiting ['waɪtɪŋ] **N** *(fish)* merlan *m*

whitish ['waɪtɪʃ] **ADJ** blanchâtre

whitlow ['wɪtləʊ] **N** *Med* panaris *m*

Whitney system ['wɪtnɪ] **N** *(in hotel)* planning *m* Whitney

Whitsun(tide) ['wɪtsən(taɪd)] **N** (la fête *ou* la saison de) la Pentecôte

whittle ['wɪt(ə)l] **vt** *(stick)* tailler (au couteau)

▶ **whittle away vt sep** *(one's capital)* rogner, manger; *(resistance)* faire tomber petit à petit; **our capital/lead has been whittled away** notre capital/avance a été réduit(e) à presque rien

▶ **whittle down vt sep** *(one's capital)* rogner, manger; **we've whittled down the number of candidates** nous avons réduit le nombre des candidats; **can you w. it down by another 5%?** peux-tu le réduire d'encore 5%?

Whitworth thread ['wɪtwəθ] **N** *Tech* filetage *m* Whitworth

whizz [wɪz] **INT** pan!

N 1 *(of bullet)* sifflement *m* **2** *Fam (expert)* as *m*, crack *m* (**at** en); **he's a real w. in the kitchen** il cuisine comme un chef; **she's a real w. with computers** c'est un as en informatique **3** *Br Sl (amphetamines)* amphés *fpl*, amphets *fpl* **4** *Am Sl* **to take a w.** *(urinate)* faire pipi

vi 1 *(of bullet etc)* siffler **2** *Fam (move quickly)* **we were whizzing along at top speed** on fonçait; **the cars whizzed past** les voitures passaient à toute allure; **she whizzed back into the house to get some money** elle retourna dare-dare à la maison chercher de l'argent

▶▶ *Fam* **w. kid** jeune prodige *m*

▶ **whizz by vi** *Fam (of traffic)* passer à toute vitesse; *(of holiday, time etc)* passer à toute vitesse, filer

▶ **whizz through vt insep** *Fam (work)* faire à toute vitesse; *(meal)* avaler; *(book)* lire à toute vitesse

WHO [dʌb(ə)ljuːeɪtʃ'əʊ] **N** *(abbr* **World Health Organization)** OMS *f*

who [huː] **PRON 1** *(interr) (subject)* qui, qui est-ce qui; *(object)* qui, qui est-ce que; **w. is it?** qui est-ce?; **w. with?** avec qui?; **w. is that woman?** qui est cette femme?; **w. on earth told you that?** qui diable vous a dit cela?; *Tel* **w.'s speaking?** qui est à l'appareil?; *Tel* **may I ask w.'s speaking?** *(when taking call for another)* c'est de la part de qui?; **w. is this?** *(on telephone)* qui êtes-vous?; **w. did you say?** qui ça?; **w. does he think he is?** pour qui se prend-il?; **w. of us can still remember it?** qui parmi nous *ou* lesquels d'entre nous se le rappelle(nt) encore?; **w. do you want?** qui voulez-vous?; **w. were you talking to?** à qui parliez-vous?; **to know w.'s w.** *(the right people)* avoir des relations; **you'll soon find out w.'s w.** *(who people are)*

tu connaîtras très vite tout le monde; **tell me w.'s w.** dites-moi qui est qui VOIR GRAMMAIRE A31; B17

2 *(rel)* qui; *(to avoid ambiguity), Fml* lequel, laquelle, *pl* lesquels, lesquelles; *(independent rel)* (celui/celle/*etc*) qui; **the friends w. came yesterday** les amis qui sont venus hier; **Louise's father, w. is very rich** le père de Louise, qui *ou Fml* lequel est très riche; **deny it w. will** le nie qui voudra VOIR GRAMMAIRE A32–3; B22–3

whoa [wəʊ] **INT** *(to horse)* ho!, holà!; *Fam (to person)* doucement!, attendez!

whodun(n)it [huː'dʌnɪt] **N** *Fam (novel)* roman *m* policier; *(film)* film *m* policier

whoever [huː'evər] **PRON 1** *(anyone that)* celui/celle/*etc* qui, quiconque; **w. finds it may keep it** celui qui le trouvera pourra le garder **2** *(no matter who)* qui que + *subj*; **w. you are, speak!** qui que vous soyez, parlez!; **w. wrote that letter** qui que ce soit qui ait écrit cette lettre; *Fam* **... or w.** ... ou qui que ce soit; **w. she marries** qui que ce soit qu'elle épousera, celui qu'elle épousera; **w. you like** qui vous voudrez VOIR GRAMMAIRE A33 **3** *(intensive)* **w. can that be at this time of night?** qui cela peut-il bien être à cette heure tardive? VOIR GRAMMAIRE A32

whole [həʊl] **ADJ 1** *(entire)* entier, complet, -ète; **cook the fish w.** faites cuire le poisson entier; **he swallowed it w.** *(food)* il l'a avalé sans le mâcher; *Fig* il a pris ça pour de l'argent comptant; **a w. loaf** un pain entier; **to tell the w. truth** dire toute la vérité; **the w. world** le monde entier; **do you have to tell the w. world?** est-ce que tu tiens à ce que tout le monde le sache?; **to last a w. week** durer toute une semaine; **I never saw her the w. evening** je ne l'ai pas vue de (toute) la soirée; **w. families died of it** des familles entières en sont mortes; *Fam* **to go the w. hog** aller jusqu'au bout; **they went the w. hog for the party** ils n'ont pas fait les choses à moitié pour la fête VOIR GRAMMAIRE A36

2 *(emphatic)* tout, entier, tout entier; **I don't think it will make a w. lot of difference** je ne pense pas que ça fasse une énorme différence; **we've had a w. heap of problems** nous avons eu tout un tas de problèmes; **the w. lot of you** vous tous; **there's still a w. lot left** il en reste encore plein; **for a w. lot of reasons** pour tout un tas de raisons

3 *(intact) (thing)* intact; *Bible* **his hand was made w.** sa main fut guérie

N tout *m*, totalité *f*, ensemble *m*; **the w. of the school** l'école entière, toute l'école; **nearly the w. of our resources** la presque totalité de nos ressources; **he spent the w. of that year in London** il a passé toute cette année-là à Londres; **the w. amounts to ...** le total se monte à ...; **to buy/sell sth as a w.** acheter/vendre qch en bloc; **taken as a w.** pris dans sa totalité; **on the w.** dans l'ensemble; **the w. is greater than the sum of its parts** le tout est plus grand que la somme des parties

▶▶ **w. milk** lait *m* entier; *Math* **w. number** *(integer)* nombre *m* entier

wholefood ['həʊlfuːd] **N** aliments *mpl* complets; **w. shop** magasin *m* diététique

wholehearted [həʊl'hɑːtɪd] **ADJ** *(enthusiasm, support etc)* sans réserve; *(laugh)* qui vient du cœur; **she was less than w. in her endorsement of him** elle ne l'approuvait qu'à moitié; **a w. admirer** un admirateur inconditionnel; **she had never really been w. in her commitment to Europe** elle n'a jamais été convaincue à 100% par l'Europe

wholeheartedly [həʊl'hɑːtɪdlɪ] **ADV** de bon *ou* de grand *ou* de tout cœur; *(to agree)* de tout cœur; **to support sb w.** soutenir qn sans réserve *ou* inconditionnellement; **I admire you w.** je vous admire sans réserve

wholemeal ['həʊlmiːl] **ADJ** *Br (bread, flour)* complet, -ète

wholeness ['həʊlnɪs] **N** intégralité *f*, intégrité *f*

wholesale ['həʊlseɪl] **N** (vente *f* en) gros *m*; **w. and retail** gros et détail

ADJ 1 *Com* de gros, en gros **2** *Fig* **by w. borrowing** en empruntant de tous côtés; **a w. slaughter** un massacre, une tuerie en masse

ADV 1 to sell/buy w. vendre/acheter en gros; **I can get it for you w.** je peux vous l'avoir au prix de gros **2** *Fig* en masse, en bloc; **communities have been destroyed w.** des communautés entières ont été détruites

▶▶ *Fin* **w. bank** banque *f* de gros; **w. co-operative** coopérative *f* d'achats; **w. customer** client, -ente qui achète en gros; **w. dealer** grossiste *mf*, commerçant, -ante en gros; **w. distribution** distribution *f* en gros; **w. goods** marchandises *fpl* de gros; *Banking* **w. market** marché *m* de gré à gré entre banques; **w. merchant** grossiste, commerçant, -ante en gros; **w. price** prix *m* de gros; **w. price index** indice *m* des prix de gros; **w. trade** commerce *m* de gros; **w. trader** grossiste

wholesaler ['həʊlseɪlər] **N** grossiste *mf*, commerçant, -ante en gros

▶▶ **w. margin** marge *f* du grossiste

wholesaling ['həʊlseɪlɪŋ] **N** vente *f* en gros

wholesome ['həʊlsəm] **ADJ** *(food)* sain; *(air, climate)* salubre; *(person, appearance)* comme il faut; **a very w. young man** un petit jeune homme propre sur lui; **she has a w. appearance** elle a l'air rangé, elle a l'air (bien) comme il faut

wholesomeness ['həʊlsəmnɪs] **N** *(of food)* nature *f* saine; *(of air)* salubrité *f*, **the w. of her appearance** son côté rangé *ou* (bien) comme il faut

wholewheat ['həʊlwiːt] **ADJ** *Am (bread, flour)* complet(ète)

wholly ['həʊllɪ] **ADV** tout à fait, complètement, entièrement

wholly-owned subsidiary N *Com* filiale *f* à 100%

whom [huːm] **PRON** *(objective case) often Fml* **1** *(interr)* qui, qui est-ce que; **w. did you see?** qui avez-vous vu?, qui est-ce que vous avez vu?; **to w./of w. are you speaking?** à qui/de qui parlez-vous?; **I don't know to w. to turn** je ne sais à qui m'adresser VOIR GRAMMAIRE A31; B17 **2** *(rel) (direct object)* que, lequel, laquelle, *pl* lesquels, lesquelles; *(indirect object and after prep)* qui; **the woman w. you saw** la femme que vous avez vue; **somebody to w. he could talk** quelqu'un à qui il pouvait parler; **the friend of w. I speak** l'ami dont je parle; **these two men, both of w. were quite young** ces deux hommes, qui l'un et l'autre étaient tout jeunes VOIR GRAMMAIRE A32; B22 **3** *(independent rel)* celui/celle/*etc* que, qui; **those w. the gods love die young** qui est aimé des dieux meurt jeune

whomsoever [huːmsəʊ'evər] **PRON** *Fml* **1** *(any person whom)* celui (quel qu'il soit) que; **w. they choose** celui qu'ils choisiront **2** *(no matter whom)* qui que ce soit que

whoop N 1 [wuːp] *(shout)* cri *m* (de joie); *Am (of owl)* (h)ululement *m*; *esp Am Iron* **big w.!** la belle affaire! **2** [huːp] *Med (in whooping cough)* quinte *f*

vi 1 [wuːp] *(shout)* crier, pousser des cris (de joie); *Am (of owl)* (h)ululer; *Fam* **to w. it up** *(have good time, celebrate)* faire la noce **2** [huːp] *Med* = tousser convulsivement à cause d'une coqueluche; **she's been whooping all night** elle a eu des quintes de toux toute la nuit

whoopee [wʊ'piː] **INT** youpi

['wʊpiː] **N** *Old-fashioned Fam* **to make w.**

(enjoy oneself) faire la noce *ou* la bombe; *(sexually)* faire l'amour

whooper ['hu:pər] N
  ▸▸ **w. swan** cygne *m* chanteur *ou* sauvage

whooping cough ['hu:pɪŋ] N coqueluche *f*

whoops [wʊps] INT houp-là!

whop [wɒp] VT (**-pp-**) *Fam* **1** *(hit)* battre, rosser **2** *(defeat)* battre à plates coutures, massacrer

whopper ['wɒpər] N *Fam* **1** *(huge thing)* quelque chose de colossal *ou* d'énorme; **a w. of a fish** un poisson énorme *ou* maous(se); **it's a real w.!** il est énorme! **2** *(lie)* énorme *ou* gros mensonge *m*

whopping ['wɒpɪŋ] *Fam* ADJ énorme; **it costs a w. £3,000** ça coûte la coquette somme de trois mille livres
  ADV **a w. great lie** un mensonge énorme; **that was a w. huge mistake!** c'était une sacrée bourde!

whore [hɔ:r] N prostituée *f*, *Sl* putain *f*
  VI *Old-fashioned, Lit (of man)* **to w., to go whoring** fréquenter les prostituées

whorehouse ['hɔ:haʊs] N *Fam* bordel *m*

whoremonger ['hɔ:mʌŋgər] N *Arch* habitué *m* des lieux de débauche; **he was a w.** il fréquentait les filles de petite vertu

whoring ['hɔ:rɪŋ] N *Old-fashioned, Lit* **1** *(by woman)* prostitution *f* **2** *(by man)* **because of all his w.** parce qu'il n'arrêtait pas de fréquenter les prostituées

whorl [wɜ:l] N **1** *Bot* verticille *m* **2** *(turn of spiral)* spire *f*, volute *f*; *(of shell)* spire, enroulement *m*; *(of fingerprint)* sillon *m*

whorled [wɜ:ld] ADJ *(flower)* verticillé; *(shell)* convoluté

whortleberry ['wɜ:t(ə)lberɪ] N *(fruit)* airelle *f* myrtille

whose [hu:z] POSS PRON **1** *(interr)* de qui; *(ownership)* à qui; **w. are these gloves?** à qui sont ces gants?; **w. daughter are you?** de qui êtes-vous la fille?; **w. fault is it?** à qui la faute?; **w. book did you borrow?** à qui avez-vous emprunté ce livre?; **w. is this?** à qui est-ce? VOIR GRAMMAIRE A31 **2** *(rel)* dont; *(after prep)* de qui, duquel, de laquelle, *pl* desquels, desquelles; **the pupil w. work I showed you** l'élève dont je vous ai montré le travail; **the man to w. wife I gave the money** l'homme à la femme de qui *ou* duquel j'ai donné l'argent VOIR GRAMMAIRE A33; B23

whosoever [hu:səʊ'evər] PRON *Arch, Fml* = **whoever**

Who's Who N *Br* ≃ Bottin *m* mondain

why [waɪ] ADV, CONJ **1** *(interr)* pourquoi, pour quelle raison?; **w. (ever) didn't you say so?** pourquoi ne l'avez-vous pas dit?; **w. not?** pourquoi pas?; **w. not agree?** pourquoi ne pas accepter?; **w. bother?** à quoi bon (s'en donner la peine)?; **w. get angry?** à quoi bon se mettre en colère? VOIR GRAMMAIRE A41

  2 *(rel)* pourquoi; **that is (the reason) w. ...** voilà pourquoi ..., c'est pourquoi ...; **w. he should always be late I do not understand** qu'il soit toujours en retard, je ne me l'explique pas; **I'll tell you w.** je vais vous dire pourquoi
  N *(pl* **whys**) pourquoi *m*, raison *f*; **I like to know the whys and wherefores of things** j'aime connaître le pourquoi et le comment des choses
  INT **1** *(surprise)* **w., it's David!** tiens, mais c'est David!; **w., you're not afraid, are you?** vous n'avez tout de même pas peur, si?
  2 *(protest)* **w., it's simple** allons, c'est simple; **w., what's the harm?** mais quel mal y a-t-il?
  3 *(hesitation)* **w., I really don't know** vraiment *ou* franchement je ne sais pas

4 *(introducing consequence)* **if this doesn't do, w. we must try something else** si ceci ne réussit pas, alors *ou* eh bien il faudra essayer autre chose

WI [dʌb(ə)lju:'aɪ] N **1** *Br abbr* **Women's Institute 2** *abbr* **West Indies**

wick [wɪk] N **1** *(of lamp, candle)* mèche *f* **2** *Br Sl* **she gets on my w.** elle me tape sur les nerfs; **it gets on my w. that he's always there** ça me tape sur les nerfs qu'il soit toujours là

wicked ['wɪkɪd] ADJ **1** *(evil)* mauvais, méchant; *(crime)* atroce, affreux; **what a w. thing to do!** qu'est-ce que c'est méchant!; **a w. lie** un affreux mensonge; *Fam* **you w. little thing!** *(to child)* petit vilain!/petite vilaine!
  2 *Fig (dreadful) (weather)* affreux, atroce; *(pain)* cruel, atroce; **he's got a w. temper** il a très mauvais caractère; **it's w. to waste so much food** c'est un crime de gaspiller tant de nourriture; **they're asking a w. price for their house** ils ont mis leur maison en vente à un prix exorbitant; **it's a w. shame that ...** il est scandaleux que ... + *sub*
  3 *Fig (mischievous)* malicieux, espiègle
  4 *Sl (good)* génial, -aux, super; **she makes a w. curry** elle fait un curry d'enfer
  NPL **the w.** les méchants *mpl*; *Hum* **(there's) no rest for the w.** pas de répit pour les braves

wickedly ['wɪkɪdlɪ] ADV **1** *(evilly)* méchamment **2** *Fig (extremely)* terriblement, affreusement; **w. expensive** hors de prix; **w. funny** à mourir de rire; **she makes a w. good curry** elle fait un curry d'enfer **3** *(mischievously)* malicieusement; **she was smiling w.** elle souriait d'un air malicieux

wickedness ['wɪkɪdnɪs] N méchanceté *f*, perversité *f*; *(of crime)* atrocité *f*

wicker ['wɪkər] N osier *m*; **a w. basket/chair** un panier/une chaise en osier

wickerwork ['wɪkəwɜ:k] N *(material)* osier *m*; *(objects)* vannerie *f*; **is the chair made of w.?** est-ce que la chaise est en osier?; **they sell w.** ils vendent de la vannerie

wicket ['wɪkɪt] N **1** *(beside large door etc) (door)* porte *f* à piétons; *(gate)* petite porte à claire-voie **2** *Am (in bank, post office etc)* guichet *m* **3** *Cr (sticks)* guichet *m*; *(area)* terrain *m* entre les guichets; **to take/lose a w.** prendre/perdre un guichet; **to keep w.** garder les guichets
  ▸▸ **w. door** porte à piétons; **w. gate** petite porte à claire-voie

wicketkeeper ['wɪkɪtki:pər] N *Cr* gardien *m* de guichet

widdle ['wɪdəl] *Br Fam* N **to have a w.** *(urinate)* faire pipi
  VI faire pipi

wide [waɪd] ADJ **1** *(broad) (road, river)* large; *(desert, ocean)* vaste; *(garment)* ample, large; **the road gets wider after the village** la route s'élargit après le village; **to be five metres w.** faire cinq mètres de large *ou* de largeur; **how w. is the room?** quelle est la largeur de la pièce?, combien est-ce que la pièce fait de large?; **to travel the w. world** parcourir le vaste monde; **in the whole w. world** dans le monde entier; **to give a w. yawn** bâiller en ouvrant largement la bouche; *Phot* **w. angle of view** grand angle de champ

  2 *(extensive) (range, experience, knowledge)* étendu, vaste, ample; *(influence)* répandu; **there is a w. difference between ...** il y a une grande différence entre ...; **in a wider sense** dans un sens plus large, par extension; **in the widest sense of the word** dans l'acception la plus large du mot
  3 *Br Fam (cocky)* culotté, gonflé
  ADV **1** *(far)* loin; **w. apart** espacé; **with one's**

legs w. apart les jambes très écartées
  2 *(to open etc)* largement, grandement; **to fling the door open w.** *or* **w. open** ouvrir la porte toute grande; **w.-open door** porte toute grande ouverte; **to open one's eyes w.** ouvrir les yeux tout grands; **to be w. awake** être réveillé *ou* bien éveillé; *Fig* avoir l'esprit vif; *Boxing* **to leave oneself w. open** se découvrir; *Fig* **to leave oneself w. open to criticism** prêter le flanc *ou* s'exposer à la critique; **this town is very w. open (to attack)** cette ville est très exposée (aux attaques); *Aut* **to take a bend w.** prendre un virage large
  3 *(to fall, shoot)* loin du but; **w. of the mark** *(far from target)* loin du but; *(far from truth)* loin de la réalité *ou* de la vérité
  N *Cr* balle *f* écartée *ou* qui passe hors de la portée du batteur
  ▸▸ *Comput* **w. area network** réseau *m* longue distance; *Br Fam Pej* **w. boy** escroc *m*, fricoteur *m*; *Aut* **w. load** *(notice on vehicle)* = convoi exceptionnel; *Cin, TV* **w. shot** plan *m* d'ensemble

wide-angle ADJ
  ▸▸ **w. lens** grand-angle *m*, *pl* grands-angles, grand-angulaire *m*, *pl* grands-angulaires; *Cin, TV* **w. shot** panoramique *m*

wide-body ADJ
  ▸▸ *Aviat* **w. aircraft** avion *m* à fuselage élargi, gros-porteur *m*, *pl* gros-porteurs

wide-eyed ADJ les yeux grands ouverts, les yeux écarquillés; **he looked at me in w. amazement** il m'a regardé avec des yeux grands comme des soucoupes, il m'a regardé les yeux écarquillés

widely ['waɪdlɪ] ADV **1** *(extensively)* largement; **she has travelled w.** elle a beaucoup voyagé; **it is w. thought** *or* **believed that ...** on pense couramment *ou* communément que ...; **w. known** très connu, connu partout; **w. different versions of what happened** des versions très différentes des événements **2** *(broadly)* **to smile w.** faire un grand sourire; **to yawn w.** bâiller profondément; **the houses were w. scattered/spaced** les maisons étaient très dispersées/espacées

widely-read [-red] ADJ **to be w.** *(of person)* avoir beaucoup lu; *(of author)* avoir un public très étendu; *(of book, newspaper)* être très lu; **the Bible remains the most w. of all books** la Bible demeure le livre le plus lu

widen ['waɪd(ə)n] VT **1** *(road, channel, garment, hole)* élargir **2** *(influence, limits of sth)* étendre
  VI **1** s'élargir; **the breach is widening** la rupture s'accentue **2** *(of influence)* s'étendre
  ▸ **widen out** VI *(of road, river, valley)* s'élargir

wideness ['waɪdnɪs] N largeur *f*

widening ['waɪd(ə)nɪŋ] N **1** *(of road, channel)* élargissement *m* **2** *(of influence)* extension *f*

widescreen ['waɪdskri:n] N grand écran *m*
  ▸▸ **w. television** téléviseur *m* grand écran

widespread ['waɪdspred] ADJ *(belief, poverty)* répandu; **w. damage** des dégâts importants; **w. opinion** opinion largement répandue *ou* généralement admise

widgeon ['wɪdʒən] N *(bird)* canard *m* siffleur

widget ['wɪdʒɪt] N *Br Fam* truc *m*

widow ['wɪdəʊ] N *also Typ* veuve *f*; **she was left a w. at (the age of) thirty** elle a été veuve à l'âge de trente ans; *Fam* **golf w.** = femme *f* délaissée par son mari qui joue constamment au golf
  VT **to be widowed** *(of man)* devenir veuf; *(of woman)* devenir veuve
  ▸▸ *Bible Fig* **w.'s mite** denier *m* de la veuve; **w.'s peak** = ligne *f* de cheveux sur le front en

forme de v; **w.'s pension** allocation *f* veuvage; **w.'s weeds** deuil *m* de veuve

widowed ['wɪdəʊd] ADJ *(man)* veuf; *(woman)* veuve; **his w. mother** sa mère qui est/était veuve

widower ['wɪdəʊər] N veuf *m*

widowhood ['wɪdəʊhʊd] N veuvage *m*

width [wɪdθ] N 1 *(of road, chest)* largeur *f*, *(of garment)* ampleur *f*, *(of tyre)* grosseur *f*, *(of cloth, wallpaper)* lé *m*, laize *f*, largeur *f*, *Typ (of letter)* chasse *f*; **to be three metres in w.** avoir trois mètres de large **2** *(of knowledge)*, *Mktg (of product range)* largeur *f* **3** *(of swimming pool)* largeur *f*; **to swim six widths (of the pool)** nager six largeurs

widthways ['wɪdθweɪz], **widthwise** ['wɪdθwaɪz] ADV dans la largeur, en largeur

wield [wiːld] VT **1** *(handle) (sword, pen)* manier; *Fig (power, influence)* exercer **2** *(brandish) (weapon, stick)* brandir

Wiener ['viːnər]
▸▸ *Culin* **W. schnitzel** escalope *f* viennoise

wiener ['wiːnər] N *Am* **1** saucisse *f* de Francfort **2** *Sl (penis)* zizi *m*
▸▸ **w. roast** barbecue *m* de saucisses de Francfort

wife, *pl* **wives** [waɪf, waɪvz] N **1** femme *f* (mariée); *esp Admin* épouse *f*; **Mr Martin and his w.** M. Martin et sa femme; **she was his second w.** c'était sa deuxième femme; **the baker's w.** *(who is also a baker)* la boulangère; *(who is not a baker)* la femme du boulanger; *Br Fam* **the w.** ma/ta/*etc* moitié **2** *Arch (woman)* femme *f*

wifely ['waɪflɪ] ADJ de bonne épouse

wife-swapping [-swɒpɪŋ] N échangisme *m*
▸▸ **w. party** soirée *f* échangiste

wig [wɪg] N *(full length)* perruque *f*, *(hairpiece)* postiche *m*; *Br (for lawyers)* perruque *f*; **she's wearing a w.** elle porte une perruque
▸ **wig out** VI *Am Fam (get angry)* piquer une crise, péter les plombs; *(go mad)* devenir cinglé, perdre la boule; *(get excited)* devenir dingue

wigeon ['wɪdʒən] N *(bird)* canard *m* siffleur

wigged [wɪgd] ADJ *(judge etc)* à perruque

wigging ['wɪgɪŋ] N *Old-fashioned Br Fam* réprimande *f*; **to give sb a good w.** attraper qn; **to get a good w.** se faire passer un savon

wiggle ['wɪg(ə)l] N *(of body etc)* tortillement *m*; **to give sth a w.** agiter *ou* remuer qch; **she gave her hips a seductive w.** elle marchait en tortillant les fesses
VT agiter, remuer; **he wiggled his backside** il remuait du derrière; **to w. one's toes** remuer ses orteils; **to w. one's hips** tortiller des hanches
VI *(of person, snake)* se remuer, se tortiller; *(of fish)* frétiller; **stop wiggling!** arrête de te tortiller!; *Fig* **to try to w. out of it** chercher une échappatoire

wiggly ['wɪglɪ] ADJ *Fam (snake etc)* qui se remue *ou* se tortille; **a w. line** un trait ondulé

wiggy ['wɪgɪ] ADJ *Am Fam (mad)* cinglé, tapé; *(eccentric)* loufoque, allumé

wigmaker ['wɪgmeɪkər] N perruquier, -ière *m,f*

wigwam ['wɪgwæm] N wigwam *m*

wilco ['wɪlkəʊ] INT *esp Radio* j'exécute

WILD [waɪld] ADJ **1** *(animal, plant)* sauvage; **w. and woolly** *(untamed)* frustre, rustre; *(not thought out)* irréfléchi; *Fig* **w. horses wouldn't drag it out of me** rien au monde ne me le ferait dire; *Pol* extrémiste *m*; *Fig* **to sow one's w. oats** jeter sa gourme
2 *(wind)* furieux, violent; **the weather's been pretty w.** les éléments se sont déchaînés; *Naut* **in w. weather** par gros temps;

w. sea mer agitée; **a w. (and stormy) night** une nuit de tempête
3 *(unrestrained) (person)* dissipé, dissolu; *(adolescent)* indiscipliné; *(behaviour)* déréglé; *(idea)* délirant, abracadabrant; *(project)* insensé, extravagant; *(party)* fou, *f* folle, déchaîné; **he's got some pretty w. friends** certains de ses amis sont de vrais casse-cou; **what a w. thing to do!** quelle inconscience!; **I'm worried by all his w. talk** tous ses propos irréfléchis m'inquiètent; **having so much money is beyond my wildest dreams** même dans mes rêves les plus fous je n'aurais jamais espéré posséder autant d'argent; **to make a w. rush at sth** se ruer sur qch; **w. applause** applaudissements frénétiques; **w. eyes** yeux égarés; **w. enthusiasm** enthousiasme délirant *ou* débordant; **w. with joy/rage** fou de joie/rage; **it makes me w. to think that ...** j'enrage *ou* cela me met en rage quand je pense que ...; **to drive sb w.** mettre qn en fureur; **w. promises** promesses extravagantes *ou* insensées; **w. rumour** bruit extravagant *ou* sans fondation
4 *(random)* **it was just a w. guess** c'était un coup au hasard; **to make a w. guess (at the answer)** répondre à tout hasard *ou* à l'aveuglette; **some of the estimates were pretty w.** certaines des estimations étaient complètement à côté
5 *Cards* libre; **the joker is w.** le joker peut être joué n'importe quand
6 *Fam (enthusiastic)* **to be w. about sb/sth** être emballé par qn/qch, être dingue de qn/qch; **I'm not w. about it** ça ne m'emballe pas
ADV **to grow w.** *(of plant)* pousser à l'état sauvage; **to run w.** *(of children)* mener une vie sans discipline; *(of hooligans)* se livrer à des actes de violence; *(of escaped bull etc)* s'emballer; *(of garden)* être laissé à l'abandon, être abandonné; **their children are allowed to run w.** leurs enfants peuvent faire tout et n'importe quoi
N **in the w.** *(of animal)* à l'état sauvage; **the call of the w.** l'appel de la nature; **in the wilds** dans une région sauvage *ou* déserte; **he lives in the wilds of Africa/Ealing** il habite au fin fond de l'Afrique/d'Ealing
VI *Am Sl* = effectuer, en bande, des actes de violence extrême contre des personnes
▸▸ **w. card** *(in card games)* joker *m*; *Comput* joker; *Sport (player)* = sportif *m* invité à participer à une compétition sans s'être qualifié; *(in American football)* = équipe *f* qualifiée pour la finale sans pour autant avoir remporté sa poule; *Comput* **w. card character** caractère *m* joker; **w. cherry** *(fruit)* merise *f*, *(tree)* merisier *m*; **w. dog** chien *m* sauvage; **w. flowers** fleurs *fpl* des champs *ou* sauvages; **w. goose** oie *f* sauvage; **w. man** *(savage)* sauvage *m*; *Culin* **w. rice** zizania *m*, riz *m* sauvage; **W. West** Far West *m*

wildcard ['waɪldkɑːd] N *Comput* joker *m*
▸▸ **w. character** caractère *m* joker

wildcat ['waɪldkæt] N **1** *(animal)* chat *m* sauvage; *Fig* **she's a w.** c'est une tigresse **2** *Am Petr (well)* forage *m* d'exploration **3** *Mktg (product)* dilemme *m*
ADJ *(imprudent, ill-considered)* aléatoire, hasardeux
VI *Am Petr* faire un forage d'exploration
▸▸ **w. strike** grève *f* sauvage; *Am Petr* **w. well** forage d'exploration

wildcatter ['waɪldkætər] N *Am Petr (company)* entrepreneur *m* de forage d'exploration; *(driller)* ouvrier *m* qui effectue des forages d'exploration

wildebeest ['wɪldɪbiːst, 'vɪl-] N *(animal)* gnou *m*

wilder ['waɪldər] N *Am Sl* = membre *m* d'une bande de jeunes voyous effectuant des ac-

tes de violence extrême contre des personnes

wilderness ['wɪldənɪs] N **1** *(desert)* désert *m*; **an economic w.** un désert économique; **a voice in the w.** une voix qui prêche dans le désert; *Fig* **to be in the w.** *(of politician, party)* faire sa traversée du désert; *Fig* **during his w. years** pendant sa traversée du désert; **the party believes that the w. years may be about to end** le parti pense que sa traversée du désert touche à sa fin **2** *(overgrown garden)* jungle *f*, **the garden is turning into a w.** le jardin est en train de se transformer en jungle

wildfire ['waɪldfaɪər] N **to spread like w.** *(of news)* se répandre comme une traînée de poudre; *(of disease)* se propager très rapidement

wildfowl ['waɪldfaʊl] N gibier *m* d'eau, sauvagine *f*

wild-goose chase N fausse piste *f*, **the search for the information was a real w.** on a cherché en vain les renseignements; **I've been on a w. round town trying to get the fabric** j'ai couru toute la ville pour rien à la recherche du tissu; **to go on a w.** faire fausse piste; **to send sb on a w.** mettre qn sur une fausse piste

wilding ['waɪldɪŋ] N *Am Sl* = actes *mpl* de violence extrême effectués par une bande de voyous contre des personnes

wildlife ['waɪldlaɪf] N *(wild animals)* faune *f*, *(wild animals and plants)* la faune et la flore
▸▸ **w. park** réserve *f* naturelle; **w. programme** émission *f* sur la nature; **w. reserve** réserve animale; **w. sanctuary** réserve animale

wildly ['waɪldlɪ] ADV **1** *(without control) (to behave)* sans contraintes; *(to cheer)* frénétiquement; *(to applaud)* à tout rompre; **to talk w.** dire des folies; **to talk w. of suicide** tenir des propos insensés de suicide; **the children had been behaving w. all afternoon** les enfants ont été intenables toute l'aprèsmidi; **to rush about w.** courir comme un fou; **her heart was beating w.** son cœur battait à tout rompre; **prices have been fluctuating w.** les prix ont subi des fluctuations violentes
2 *(at random) (to answer, guess)* au hasard, au petit bonheur; **by now it was clear that he was guessing w.** il était clair qu'il répondait au hasard; **to hit out w.** lancer des coups au hasard
3 *(as intensifier) (expensive, funny etc)* extrêmement; **w. inaccurate** dramatiquement inexact; **w. happy** follement heureux, aux anges; **to be w. excited** être surexcité; **it's not w. encouraging** ça n'est pas franchement encourageant; **w. exaggerated** follement exagéré; **I'm not w. enthusiastic about it** je ne suis pas franchement emballé

wildness ['waɪldnɪs] N **1** *(of country, animal)* état *m* sauvage; *(of region)* état inculte **2** *(of wind, waves)* fureur *f*, violence *f*, *(of storm)* violence **3** *(of applause)* frénésie *f*; *(of ideas, words)* extravagance *f*

wiles [waɪlz] NPL ruses *fpl*, artifices *mpl*; **he used all of his w. to persuade her** il l'a persuadée à force de ruse(s) *ou* d'artifice(s); **to fall victim to sb's w.** succomber aux séductions de qn

wilful, *Am* **willful** ['wɪlfʊl] ADJ **1** *(stubborn)* obstiné, entêté, volontaire **2** *(deliberate)* délibéré, intentionnel, volontaire; *Law* **w. murder** homicide *m* volontaire *ou* prémédité; **w. damage** bris *m*, dommage *m* délibéré; **with w. intent** délibérément

wilfully, *Am* **willfully** ['wɪlfəlɪ] ADV **1** *(stubbornly)* obstinément, avec entêtement; **she has behaved quite w. over this issue** elle n'en a fait qu'à sa tête pour cette question **2** *(deliberately)* délibérément; **are you being w. obtuse?** est-ce que tu fais exprès de faire l'idiot?

wilfulness, *Am* **willfulness** ['wɪlfʊlnɪs] **N 1** *(stubbornness)* obstination *f*, entêtement *m*; **the sheer w. of his refusal** son refus obstiné *ou* entêté **2** *(deliberateness)* caractère *m* délibéré

wiliness ['waɪlɪnɪs] **N** astuce *f*, caractère *m* rusé

WILL¹ [wɪl] **N 1** *(faculty, determination)* volonté *f*, **to have a strong/weak w.** avoir beaucoup/peu de volonté; **w. of iron, iron w.** volonté de fer; **he has a w. of his own** il sait ce qu'il veut, il est volontaire; **strength of w.** force *f* de volonté; **the w. to live** la volonté de survivre; **she seems to have lost the w. to live** elle semble avoir perdu sa volonté de vivre; **good/ill w.** bienveillance *f*/malveillance *f*, **to show good w.** faire preuve de bonne volonté; **I bear her no ill w.** *(have no wish for revenge)* je ne lui en veux pas; *(do not dislike her)* je ne lui veux aucun mal; **to work with a w.** travailler de bon cœur *ou* avec détermination; **with the best w. in the world** avec la meilleure volonté du monde; *Prov* **where there's a w. there's a way** vouloir c'est pouvoir

2 *(desire, wish)* volonté *f*, désir *m*; **the w. of the people** la volonté du peuple; **to impose one's w. on sb** imposer sa volonté à qn; **at w.** *(to choose, fire)* à volonté; *(to depart etc)* quand on veut; **free w.** libre arbitre *m*; **to do sth of one's own free w.** faire qch de son plein gré; **to do sth against one's w.** faire qch contre son gré *ou* à contrecœur; *Bible* **Thy w. be done** que ta volonté soit faite

3 *Law* testament *m*; **the last w. and testament of ...** les dernières volontés de ...; **to make one's w.** faire son testament; **to mention sb in one's w.** mettre *ou* coucher qn sur son testament

vT (*-ll-*) **1 to w. sb to do** *or* **into doing sth** faire faire qch à qn (par la volonté), souhaiter ardemment que qn fasse qch; *(by hypnotism)* suggestionner à qn de faire qch; **the crowd was willing him to win** la foule voulait absolument qu'il gagne; **she was willing her child to live** elle souhaitait de toutes ses forces que son enfant survive; **you can't just w. these things to happen** on ne peut pas faire arriver ces choses par un simple acte de volonté; **to w. oneself to do sth** faire un effort de volonté pour faire qch; *Arch, Lit* **God so willed it** Dieu l'a voulu ainsi

2 *Law (leave in one's will)* **to w. sth** léguer qch, disposer de qch par testament; **to w. sth to sb** léguer qch à qn

WILL² MODAL AUX V VOIR GRAMMAIRE A57–8 (**I will, you/he/we/etc will;** *Arch* **thou wilt;** *pt, cond* **would** [wʊd], **I will, he will** *etc are often contracted to* **I'll** [aɪl], **he'll** [hiːl] *etc*; **I would, they would** *etc to* **I'd** [aɪd], **they'd** [ðeɪd] *etc*; **will not** *and* **would not** *to* **won't** [wəʊnt], **wouldn't** ['wʊd(ə)nt]) **1** *(expressing future)* **I'll do it tomorrow** je le ferai demain; **he won't do it again** il ne le fera plus; **w. he be there?** – **he w.** y sera-t-il? – oui (il y sera); **w. he be there?** – **no, he won't** y sera-t-il? – non (il n'y sera pas); **but I'll starve!** – **no, you won't mais je vais mourir de faim!** – mais non!; **you won't forget, w. you?** vous n'oublierez pas, hein?; **you'll write to me, won't you?** vous m'écrirez, n'est-ce pas?; **we w. be there** nous serons là; **Mr Long w. explain the situation to you** *(immediate future)* M. Long va vous expliquer la situation VOIR GRAMMAIRE A50–1

2 *(consent)* **I w. not do it** je refuse de le faire; **I w. not have that said of me** je ne veux pas qu'on dise cela de moi; *Fam* **w. do!** d'accord!; **the engine won't start** le moteur ne veut pas

démarrer; **it won't open** ça ne s'ouvre pas, ça ne veut pas s'ouvrir; **just wait a moment, w. you?** pouvez-vous attendre un instant?; *(emphatic)* voulez-vous bien attendre un instant?; **won't you sit down?** asseyez-vous, je vous en prie

3 *(emphatic)* **accidents will happen** on ne peut pas éviter les accidents; **she will go out in spite of her cold** elle persiste à sortir malgré son rhume; **he will get in my way** il est toujours dans mon chemin; **the doctor will have his little joke** il aime (à) plaisanter, le docteur; **I will not have it!** je ne permettrai pas cela!; **will you be quiet!** voulez-vous bien vous taire!

4 *(habit)* **this hen w. lay up to six eggs a week** cette poule pond jusqu'à six œufs par semaine

5 *(conjecture)* **you'll be tired** vous devez être fatigué

6 *(wish)* vouloir; **do as you w.** faites comme vous voudrez; **say what you w., you won't be believed** quoi que vous disiez, on ne vous croira pas

7 *(injunction)* **you'll be here at three** soyez ici à trois heures

willful *etc Am* = **wilful** *etc*

William the Conqueror ['wɪlɪəm] **N** Guillaume le Conquérant

willie ['wɪlɪ] **N** *Br Fam (penis)* zizi *m*

willies ['wɪlɪz] **NPL** *Fam* **to have the w.** avoir le trac *ou* la frousse; **this place gives me the w.** cet endroit me fiche la frousse *ou* me donne les chocottes; **I had a bad case of the w.** j'avais une frousse incroyable

willing ['wɪlɪŋ] **ADJ 1** *(compliant)* de bonne volonté, bien disposé; *Fig* **w. horse** bonne poire **2** *(ready)* **to be w. to do sth** bien vouloir faire qch, être disposé à faire qch; **w. to help** prêt à rendre service, serviable; **she's always w. to lend a hand** elle est toujours prête à rendre service; **I am more than w. to come with you** je ne demande pas mieux que de vous accompagner; **I am w. and able to help them** je peux les aider et je le ferai très volontiers; **she wasn't very w. to tell me what had happened** elle ne tenait pas vraiment à me dire ce qui s'est passé; **w. or not** bon gré mal gré; **God w.** s'il plaît à Dieu; *Fam* **to show w.** faire preuve de bonne volonté

willingly ['wɪlɪŋlɪ] **ADV 1** *(voluntarily)* volontairement; **he came along quite w.** il est venu de son plein gré; **she had not gone there w.** elle n'y était pas allée de son plein gré **2** *(with pleasure)* volontiers, avec plaisir

willingness ['wɪlɪŋnɪs] **N 1** *(compliance)* bonne volonté *f*, **with the utmost w.** de très bon cœur **2** *(readiness)* empressement *m* (**to do sth** à faire qch)

will-o'-the-wisp [wɪlədə'wɪsp] **N** *also Fig* feu *m* follet

willow ['wɪləʊ] **N 1** *(tree)* saule *m* **2** *Cr Old-fashioned Fam* **the w.** la batte
▸▸ **w. pattern** = motif *m* de céramique; **w. pattern plates** des assiettes *fpl* à motifs chinois; **w. tree** saule

willowy ['wɪləʊɪ] **ADJ** *(person)* souple, svelte, élancé

willpower ['wɪlpaʊər] **N** volonté *f*, **through w. alone** par ma/sa/etc seule volonté; **lack of w.** manque *m* de volonté

willy ['wɪlɪ] **N** = **willie**

willy-nilly [-'nɪlɪ] **ADV 1** *(without order, randomly)* au hasard; **the editor just altered a few words w.** le rédacteur a simplement changé quelques mots au hasard **2** *(willingly or not)* bon gré mal gré

wilt¹ [wɪlt] **vI 1** *(of plant)* se flétrir, se faner **2** *Fig (of person) (with heat, fatigue)* dépérir, languir; *(at reproach)* perdre contenance;

(lose courage) se dégonfler; **I'm beginning to w.** *(become tired)* je commence à fatiguer; **he tends to w. under pressure** il ne résiste pas à la pression
▸ **vT** *(of heat) (flowers)* faner, dessécher

wilt² *see* **will²**

Wilts *abbr* **Wiltshire**

wily ['waɪlɪ] **ADJ** rusé, astucieux, malin, *f* -igne, roublard; **he's a w. old bird** *or* **fox** c'est un vieux roublard

wimp [wɪmp] **N** *Fam* poule *f* mouillée, mauviette *f*
▸ **wimp out** **vI** *Fam* se dégonfler; **he wimped out of the fight** il s'est dégonflé au dernier moment à a refusé de se battre; **he wimped out of telling her the truth** finalement il a eu la trouille de lui dire la vérité

wimpish ['wɪmpɪʃ], **wimpy** ['wɪmpɪ] **ADJ** *Fam (behaviour, attitude)* de poule mouillée, de mauviette; **you didn't go because it was raining?, how w.!** tu n'y es pas allé à cause de la pluie?, quelle mauviette!

wimple ['wɪmp(ə)l] **N** *(worn by nun)* guimpe *f*

win [wɪn] **N** *Sport etc* victoire *f*, **to have three wins in succession** emporter trois victoires consécutives; **to back a horse for a w.** jouer un cheval gagnant
▸ **vT** (*pt, pp* **won** [wʌn]; *prp* **winning**) **1** *(be successful in) (battle, race, bet)* gagner; **to w. an election** remporter une élection; **to w. an argument** avoir le dessus dans une discussion; *Fam* **you can't w. them all, you w. some you lose some** on ne peut pas toujours gagner

2 *(obtain) (prize)* remporter, gagner; **to w. a contract** remporter un marché; **I won 500 pounds off him at poker** j'ai gagné 500 livres en jouant au poker contre lui; **the Greens have won ten seats** les Verts ont gagné dix sièges; **they won the seat from Labour** ils ont enlevé le siège aux Travaillistes

3 *(acquire) (popularity, sb's good will)* acquérir; *(sb's attention)* captiver; *(sb's confidence)* gagner; **to w. fame** trouver la gloire; **she was desperate to w. his favour** elle cherchait désespérément à attirer ses bonnes grâces; **to w. a reputation for sth** se faire une réputation de qch; **to w. the right to do sth** obtenir le droit de faire qch; **to w. sb's love** se faire aimer de qn; **to w. recognition** parvenir à être reconnu; **he has finally won recognition for his work** son travail a finalement été reconnu; **she was gradually winning recognition as a talented young poet** elle commençait à se faire connaître en tant que jeune poète; **you've just won yourself a friend** tu viens juste de te faire un ami; **how to w. friends and influence people** comment se faire des amis et influencer les gens; **to w. sb away from sth** détourner *ou* détacher qn de qch; **she won her way to the top of her profession** elle a réussi à atteindre le sommet de sa profession

▸ **vI** gagner; *Sport* **to w. by a length** gagner d'une longueur; **to back a horse to w.** jouer un cheval gagnant; *Fam* **you (just) can't w.** j'aurai/tu auras/etc toujours tort; *Fam* **to w. hands down** gagner les doigts dans le nez *ou* les mains dans les poches; **w. or lose, I'm sure I'll enjoy this match** que je gagne ou que je perde je suis certain que je vais m'amuser pendant ce match

▸ **win back** **vT SEP** *(territory, championship)* reprendre (**from** à), reconquérir (**from** sur); *(esteem, friendship)* reconquérir; *(money)* regagner

▸ **win out** **vI** *(succeed)* y arriver, réussir

▸ **win over, win round** **vT SEP** **I think we should manage to w. her over** *or* **round in the end** je pense qu'on devrait finir par la persuader; **to w. sb round** or **over to one's position** gagner qn à sa cause; **see whether you can w. him over** essayez de le persuader de se mettre avec nous; **I won him round to my point of view** j'ai réussi à le rallier à mon point de vue

▸ **win through** VI (succeed) y arriver, réussir; Sport **to w. through to the second round** passer le premier tour

wince [wɪns] N (of pain etc) crispation f
VI (with pain) tressaillir; (with embarrassment) se crisper; **the remark made him w.** il s'est crispé en entendant cette remarque

winceyette [wɪnsɪ'et] N Br Tex flanelle f de coton

winch [wɪntʃ] N treuil m; (on boat) winch m
▸ **winch in** VT SEP amener ou rentrer à l'aide d'un treuil
▸ **winch up** VT SEP soulever ou hisser ou monter à l'aide d'un treuil; **the crew were winched up by helicopter** l'équipage a été hissé à l'aide d'un hélicoptère ou a été hélitreuillé

wind[1] [wɪnd] N 1 (air) vent m; **strong winds** vents forts ou violents; **there's quite a w.** il y a beaucoup de vent; Naut **to sail against the w.** avoir le vent debout; Naut **to sail** or **run before the w.** avoir ou être vent arrière; Naut **to sail with w. and tide** avoir vent et marée; **in the teeth of the w.** contre le vent; **to sail into the w.** venir ou aller au lof; Fig **to sail close to the w.** jouer un jeu dangereux; (when telling joke) friser l'indécence; (in business dealings) friser la malhonnêteté; Fig **my friends are all scattered to the four winds** mes amis sont dispersés aux quatre coins du monde; Fig **to throw caution to the w.** oublier toute prudence; Fig **to see** or **find out which way the w. blows** voir d'où vient le vent; Fig **there's something in the w.** il se prépare ou se mijote quelque chose; Fig **a w.** or **the winds of change** un vent de changement; Fig **to go like the w.** aller comme le vent; Old-fashioned Fam **to raise the w.** rassembler des fonds; Fig Fam **to put the w. up sb** faire une peur bleue à qn; Fig Fam **to have** or **get the w. up** avoir le trac ou la frousse; (stronger) avoir une peur bleue; Fig **to take the w. out of sb's sails** déjouer les projets de qn, couper l'herbe sous le pied à qn
2 (scent) vent m; Fig **to get w. of sth** avoir vent de qch
3 Med (flatulence) vent(s) m(pl), flatuosité f; **to break w.** lâcher un vent; **to have w.** avoir des gaz; **beans give you w.** les haricots donnent des gaz; **the baby's got w.** le bébé n'a pas fait son rot; **to get the baby's w. up** faire faire son rot au bébé; Fam **to be full of w.** (useless talk) parler à tort et à travers ou pour ne rien dire; (boastful talk) être vantard
4 (breath) souffle m, respiration f, **let me get my w.** laissez-moi souffler ou reprendre mon souffle
5 Mus **the w.** (in orchestra) les instruments mpl à vent
6 Ind vent m, air m ou vent de soufflerie
VT (of blow) (person) couper la respiration ou le souffle à; (of race) (person, horse) essouffler; (baby) faire faire son rot à; **I was badly winded** (by blow) j'avais le souffle coupé; (by race) j'étais très essoufflé
▸▸ Mus **w. chest** (of organ) laie f, sommier m; **w. chimes** carillon m éolien; **w. energy** énergie f éolienne; **w. ensemble** ensemble m d'instruments à vent; **w. farm** parc m d'éoliennes; **w. gag** (on microphone) anti-vent m, pl anti-vents; **w. gauge** anémomètre m; Aviat **w. indicator** indicateur m de direction du vent; Mus **w. instrument** instrument m à vent; Theat **w. machine** machine f à souffler le vent; Aut **w. noise** bruit m aérodynamique; **w. power** énergie du vent ou éo-

lienne; **w. pump** éolienne f, Aut **w. roar** bruit m du vent; Aviat **w. sleeve** manche f à air; **w. tunnel** tunnel m aérodynamique; **w. turbine** éolienne f

wind[2] [waɪnd] N **to give the clock a w.** remonter la pendule
VI (pt, pp **wound** [waʊnd]) tourner; (of path, river) serpenter; (of staircase) monter en colimaçon; **the road winds up/down the hill** le chemin monte/descend en serpentant
VT 1 (roll) enrouler; Tex (thread, silk) dévider; **to w. wool into a ball** enrouler de la laine (pour en faire une pelote); **to w. cotton on a reel** bobiner du coton; Fishing **to w. in the line** ramener la ligne; **to w. a bobbin** enrouler le fil sur une bobine; Elec **to w. a dynamo** armer une dynamo **2** (clock) remonter **3** (handle) tourner
▸ **wind down** VT SEP 1 (car window) baisser **2** (reduce) réduire progressivement ou graduellement
VI 1 (of party, meeting etc) tirer à sa fin; **the party didn't begin to w. down until nearly 4 am** la fête n'a commencé à diminuer en intensité que vers 4 heures du matin **2** Fam (relax) décompresser, se détendre
▸ **wind round** VT SEP enrouler autour de; **to w. a scarf round one's neck** enrouler une écharpe autour de son cou; **she wound her arms round the child** elle a entouré l'enfant de ses bras
VT INSEP (of thread) s'enrouler autour de
▸ **wind up** VT SEP 1 (car window) remonter **2** (rope etc) enrouler **3** (clock) remonter; (spring) bander; Fig **to be all wound up** (of person) être excité ou énervé **4** (end) finir, terminer; Com (company) liquider, dissoudre; (account) régler, clôturer; **she wound up her speech by announcing that …** elle a terminé son discours en annonçant que …; **she winds up the book with a chapter on …** elle boucle son livre sur un chapitre sur … **5** Br Fam (tease) faire marcher; **they're only winding you up** ils te font marcher, ils essaient seulement de te mettre en boîte; **don't you know when you're being wound up?** tu ne te rends même pas compte quand on te fait marcher ou quand on essaie de te mettre en boîte? **6** Br Fam (irritate) foutre en rogne
VI 1 (end speech etc) conclure **2** Fam (end up) **he'll w. up in prison** il finira en prison; **we usually w. up back at my place** généralement nous finissons chez moi; **we wound up working for the same company** nous nous sommes retrouvés à travailler pour la même société

windbag [wɪndbæg] N Fam moulin m à paroles; **what a w.!** quel bavard!

windblown [wɪndbləʊn] ADJ (hair) ébouriffé par le vent; (trees) fouetté ou cinglé par le vent

wind-borne ADJ porté par le vent

windbreak [wɪndbreɪk] N brise-vent m inv

windcheater [wɪndtʃiːtər] N (jacket) blouson m, Can coupe-vent m inv

wind-chill ADJ
▸▸ **w. factor** facteur m d'abaissement de la température provoqué par le vent

winder [waɪndər] N 1 (device) Tex bobinoir m, dévidoir m; (on clock, watch) remontoir m **2** Aut (on car door) lève-glace m inv **3** (person) Tex bobineur, -euse, dévideur, -euse; (of clocks) remonteur, -euse

windfall [wɪndfɔːl] N 1 (in garden, orchard etc) fruit m abattu par le vent, fruit tombé **2** Fig aubaine f, bonne fortune f, (legacy) héritage m inattendu; **I've had a bit of a w. from my aunt** j'ai eu la chance d'hériter d'un peu d'argent de ma tante
▸▸ **w. profits** bénéfices mpl exceptionnels; **w. tax** impôt m sur les bénéfices exceptionnels

winding [waɪndɪŋ] ADJ (road, street) tortueux, sinueux; (river) sinueux; (staircase) en hélice, en colimaçon
N 1 (process) enroulement m; Elec (wire) bobinage m, enroulement m **2** (in a river) méandres mpl, coudes mpl; (in a road) zigzags mpl
▸▸ **w. gear** (of lift) treuil m; Mining appareils mpl ou machine f d'extraction; **w. sheet** linceul m

winding-up N (of business etc) liquidation f, dissolution f, (of speech) fin f, conclusion f, (of account) clôture f

windjammer [wɪnddʒæmər] N Naut grand voilier m

windlass [wɪndləs] N treuil m

windmill [wɪndmɪl] N moulin m à vent; Fig **to tilt at windmills** se battre contre des moulins à vent

window [wɪndəʊ] N 1 (of house etc) fenêtre f, **to look in at/out of the w.** regarder par/à la fenêtre; **to break a w.** casser une vitre ou un carreau; Fig Fam **to throw money out of the w.** jeter l'argent par les fenêtres; Fig Fam **that's my holiday out of the w.** voilà mes vacances fichues en l'air; **that's her chances of qualifying out of the w.** voilà ses chances de qualification qui partent en fumée; Fig **a w. on sth** un aperçu de qch; **w. of opportunity** ouverture f
2 Comput fenêtre f
3 (of ticket office) guichet m
4 (of shop) vitrine f, devanture f
5 (of car, train) vitre f, glace f
6 (on envelope) fenêtre f
▸▸ **w. box** jardinière f, **w. cleaner** (person) laveur, -euse de vitres ou de carreaux; (substance) nettoyant m pour vitres; **w. display** étalage m, **w. envelope** enveloppe f à fenêtre; **w. frame** châssis m de fenêtre; **w. ledge** (inside) appui m de fenêtre; (outside) rebord m de fenêtre; **w. seat** (in room) banquette f sous la fenêtre; (in train, plane) place f côté fenêtre; **w. tab** (on suspension file) onglet m à fenêtre; Aut **w. winder** lève-vitre m, pl lève-vitres

window-dress VT (accounts, balance sheet) camoufler, habiller

window-dresser N étalagiste mf

window-dressing N (art m de l')étalage m; Fig façade f, décor m de théâtre, camouflage m; **w. of a balance sheet** habillage m ou camouflage de bilan; **no amount of w. can hide the fact that the party is in crisis** rien ne pourra camoufler l'état de crise dans lequel se trouve le parti; Fig **it's just w.** ce n'est qu'une façade

windowing [wɪndəʊɪŋ] N Comput fenêtrage m

windowless [wɪndəʊlɪs] ADJ sans fenêtres

windowpane [wɪndəʊpeɪn] N vitre f, carreau m

window-shop VI faire du lèche-vitrines; **to w. for a coat** faire du lèche-vitrines pour trouver un manteau

window-shopper N personne f qui fait du lèche-vitrines; **the streets were full of window-shoppers** les rues étaient pleines de gens en train de faire du lèche-vitrines

window-shopping N lèche-vitrines m; **to go w.** faire du lèche-vitrines

windowsill [wɪndəʊsɪl] N (outside) rebord m de fenêtre; (inside) appui m ou tablette f de fenêtre

windpipe [wɪndpaɪp] N Anat trachée f

wind-pollinated [-pɒlɪneɪtɪd] ADJ pollinisé par le vent

wind-pollination N pollinisation f par le vent

windscreen ['wɪndskriːn] N *Br Aut* pare-brise *m inv*
▸▸ **w. cleaner** lave-glace *m*, *pl* lave-glaces; **w. washer** lave-glace; **w. wiper** essuie-glace *m*, *pl* essuie-glaces

windshield ['wɪndʃiːld] N *Am* = **windscreen**

windsock ['wɪndsɒk] N *Aviat* manche *f* à air, *Sl* biroute *f*

windstorm ['wɪndstɔːm] N tempête *f* de vent

windsurf ['wɪndsɜːf] VI faire de la planche à voile

windsurfer ['wɪndsɜːfər] N *Sport* **1** *(board)* planche *f* à voile **2** *(person)* véliplanchiste *mf*

windsurfing ['wɪndsɜːfɪŋ] N *(sport)* planche *f* à voile; **to go w.** faire de la planche à voile

windswept ['wɪndswept] ADJ *(place)* balayé par le vent; *(hair)* ébouriffé par le vent; **you're looking very w.** tu as l'air tout ébouriffé par le vent

wind-up ['waɪnd-] N *Br Fam* **is this a w.?** tu me fais marcher?

windward ['wɪndwəd] ADJ au vent
ADV contre le vent; **to sail w.** avoir le vent debout
N côté *m* au vent; **lying to (the) w. of …** situé au vent de …
▸▸ **the W. Islands** les îles *fpl* du Vent

windy¹ ['wɪndɪ] ADJ **1** *(day)* de grand vent; **it's very w.** il fait beaucoup de vent; **March is usually a w. month** en général il y a du vent au mois de mars **2** *(place)* balayé par le vent, exposé au vent *ou* aux quatre vents; **the W. City** = surnom donné à Chicago **3** *Old-fashioned Br Fam* **to be w.** *(afraid)* avoir le trac *ou* la frousse

windy² ['waɪndɪ] ADJ *(road etc)* sinueux

wine [waɪn] N **1** vin *m*; **a bottle/glass of w.** une bouteille/un verre de vin; **red/white w.** vin rouge/blanc; **the wines of Spain** les vins espagnols; **wines and spirits** *(shop sign)* vins et spiritueux **2** *(colour)* lie *f* de vin
VT **to w. and dine sb** fêter qn
▸▸ **w. bar** bistrot *m*; **w. box** Cubitainer® *m*; **w. cellar** cave *f* (à vin), cellier *m*; **w. cooler** *(container)* seau *m* à rafraîchir (le vin); *Am (drink)* = mélange de de vin, de jus de fruit et d'eau gazeuse; **w. list** carte *f* des vins; **w. merchant** *(shopkeeper)* marchand, -ande de vin(s); *(wholesaler)* négociant, -ante en vin(s); **w. rack** casier *m* à vin; **w. route** route *f* des vins; *Am* **w. steward** sommelier *m*; **w. tasting** dégustation *f* (de vins); **w. vinegar** vinaigre *m* de vin; **w. waiter** sommelier

wine-coloured, *Am* **wine-colored** ADJ lie de vin *inv*

wineglass ['waɪnglɑːs] N verre *m* à vin

winepress ['waɪnpres] N pressoir *m*

wing [wɪŋ] N **1** *(of bird, insect, plane)* aile *f*; *Fig* **to take sb under one's w.** prendre qn sous son aile *ou* sous sa protection; *Lit* **fear lent him wings** la peur lui donnait des ailes; **to shoot a bird on the w.** tirer un oiseau au vol *ou* à la volée; **to be on the w.** *(of bird)* voler; **to take w.** s'envoler, prendre son vol *ou* son essor; *Fig* **to spread** *or* **stretch one's wings** élargir son horizon; *Fig* **on a w. and a prayer** Dieu sait comment; *Aviat* **wings** *(insignia)* insigne *m* de pilote
2 *(of building)* aile *f*; *(of hospital)* pavillon *m*; *(of door)* battant *m*; *Theat* **the wings** la coulisse, les coulisses; **to be standing** *or* **waiting in the wings** *Theat* attendre dans les coulisses; *Fig* rester dans les coulisses
3 *Mil (of army)* aile *f*, flanc *m*; *Sport* aile; *(player)* ailier *m*; **the w. halves** les demis *mpl* aile; **she plays on the w.** elle est ailier;

Pol **the left w. of the party** l'aile gauche du parti
4 *(of nut)* oreille *f*, ailette *f*
5 *Br (of car)* aile *f*
6 *Mil, Aviat (unit)* escadre *f* aérienne; *Am* brigade *f* aérienne
VT **1** *(injure) (bird)* frapper *ou* blesser à l'aile; **I've winged him** je lui ai mis du plomb dans l'aile
2 *Fam* **to w. it** improviser
3 **to w. its/one's way towards** *(of bird)*, *Fig (of person)* voler vers; **my report should be winging its way towards you now** mon rapport devrait te parvenir incessamment sous peu
▸▸ **w. chair** bergère *f* à oreilles; **w. collar** col *m* cassé; **w. commander** ≃ lieutenant-colonel *m*, *pl* lieutenants-colonels; **w. flap** *(of plane)* volet *m*; **w. forward** *(in rugby)* ailier *m*; **w. mirror** rétroviseur *m* extérieur; **w. nut** papillon *m*, écrou *m* à ailettes; *Rugby* **w. threequarter** trois-quarts aile *m*

wingding ['wɪŋdɪŋ] N *Am Fam (party)* fête *f*, bringue *f*

winged [wɪŋd, *Lit* often 'wɪŋɪd]
ADJ *(possessing wings)* ailé
▸▸ *Lit* **w. words** paroles *fpl* ailées

-winged [wɪŋd] SUFF **red/white/**etc**-w.** aux ailes rouges/blanches/*etc*

winger ['wɪŋər] N *Ftbl, Rugby* ailier *m*

wingless ['wɪŋlɪs] ADJ sans ailes, aptère

wingspan ['wɪŋspæn], **wingspread** ['wɪŋspred] N *(of bird, plane)* envergure *f*; **the eagle has a w. of two metres** l'aigle a une envergure de deux mètres

wink [wɪŋk] N clignement *m* d'œil, clin *m* d'œil; **to give sb a w.** faire un clin d'œil à qn; **with a w.** en clignant de l'œil; *Fig Fam* **to tip sb the w.** prévenir *ou* avertir qn *(about* de*)*; **I didn't sleep a w.** *or* **didn't get a w. of sleep all night** je n'ai pas fermé l'œil *ou* dormi de toute la nuit; **it was all over in the w. of an eye** tout était fait en un clin d'œil; **a nod's as good as a w. to him** il comprend à demi-mot
VI cligner de l'œil *ou* des yeux; *(of star, light)* clignoter; **it's as easy as winking** c'est simple comme bonjour
VT **she winked an eye** elle a fait un clin d'œil
▸ **wink at** VT INSEP *(person)* faire un clin d'œil à; *Fig (abuse, illegal practice)* fermer les yeux sur

winker ['wɪŋkər] N *Br Aut Fam* clignotant *m*

winking ['wɪŋkɪŋ] ADJ *(light)* clignotant

winkle ['wɪŋk(ə)l] N **1** *(mollusc)* bigorneau *m* **2** *Fam (penis)* zizi *m*
▸▸ *Br Fam* **w. pickers** chaussures *fpl* à bout pointu
▸ **winkle out** VT SEP *Br Fam (something)* extraire; **I finally winkled the information out of him** j'ai fini par lui tirer les vers du nez; **it's no good trying to w. any money out of me** ce n'est pas la peine d'essayer de me soutirer de l'argent

winner ['wɪnər] N **1** *(person)* vainqueur *m*, gagnant, -ante; *(horse)* *(cheval m)* gagnant; **the w. of the big prize** *(in lottery)* le gagnant du gros lot; **to back a w.** *Horseracing* jouer un cheval gagnant; *Fig* jouer gagnant, bien miser; **every one's a w.!** *(at fair, in raffle etc)* à tous les coups (l')on gagne! **2** *Fig (successful novel, play)* roman *m*/pièce *f* à grand succès; **this book will be a w.** ce livre a un succès assuré; **to be onto a w.** jouer gagnant *ou* la bonne carte

winning ['wɪnɪŋ] ADJ **1** *(victorious)* gagnant; **the w. side** les vainqueurs *mpl*; **to be on a w. streak** remporter victoire sur victoire; **w. number** *(in lottery)* numéro *m* gagnant *ou* sortant **2** *(attractive)* attrayant, séduisant; *(smile)* engageant, charmant;

that child has a w. way with her cette enfant est très gracieuse
N **1** *(of sth)* acquisition *f* **2** *(usu pl)* **winnings** *(at races etc)* gains *mpl*
▸▸ **w. post** poteau *m* d'arrivée; **he was first past the w. post** il est arrivé premier

winnow ['wɪnəʊ] VT *Agr (grain)* vanner; **to w. the chaff from the grain** séparer le bon grain de l'ivraie; *Fig* **to w. the evidence** passer les témoignages au crible *ou* au peigne fin

winnowing ['wɪnəʊɪŋ] N *Agr* vannage *m*; *Fig* examen *m* minutieux; **winnowings** *(of grain)* vannure *f*
▸▸ **w. basket** van *m*

wino ['waɪnəʊ] N *Fam* ivrogne *mf*, soûlard, -arde

winsome ['wɪnsəm] ADJ charmant, séduisant

winsomely ['wɪnsəmlɪ] ADV d'une manière séduisante, de façon charmante

winter ['wɪntər] N hiver *m*; **in w.** en hiver; **she was born in the w. of 1946** elle est née pendant l'hiver 1946; **a cold w.'s day** une froide journée d'hiver; *Lit* **he has seen sixty winters** il compte soixante hivers VOIR GRAMMAIRE A7
VI *(of people)* passer l'hiver *(at* à*)*; *(of cattle)* hiverner
VT *(livestock)* hiverner
▸▸ **w. clothing** vêtements *mpl* d'hiver; **w. corn** semis *m* d'hiver; **w. garden** *(conservatory)* jardin *m* d'hiver; **w. holiday** vacances *fpl* d'hiver; **the W. Olympics** les jeux *mpl* Olympiques d'hiver; **w. quarters** quartiers *mpl* d'hiver; **w. resort** station *f* de sports d'hiver; **w. season** saison *f* d'hiver; **w. solstice** solstice *m* d'hiver; **w. sports** sports *mpl* d'hiver

winter-flowering ADJ *(plant)* hibernal, -aux, hiémal, -aux

wintergreen ['wɪntəgriːn] N *(plant)* gaulthérie *f*

winterize ['wɪntəraɪz] VT *esp Am (car, house etc)* mettre en état pour passer l'hiver, *Can* hivériser

wintertime ['wɪntətaɪm], *Lit* **wintertide** [-taɪd] N hiver *m*

winterweight ['wɪntəweɪt] ADJ *(coat etc)* d'hiver

wint(e)ry ['wɪnt(ə)rɪ] ADJ hivernal, -aux; *Fig (smile, look)* glacial, -aux; **it's quite w. this morning** c'est presque un jour d'hiver, ce matin; **because of the w. conditions** parce qu'il fait/faisait un temps d'hiver

WIP [dʌb(ə)ljuːaɪ'piː] N *Acct (abbr* **work in progress)** travail *m* en cours, encours *m* de production de biens

wipe [waɪp] N **1** *(action) (with cloth, handkerchief, sponge)* coup *m* de torchon/de mouchoir/d'éponge; **to give sth a w. (over/round)** essuyer qch, donner un coup de torchon/d'éponge à qch **2** *(moist tissue)* lingette *f* **3** *TV, Cin* volet *m*
VT **1** *(table, plate)* essuyer; **to w. one's face/hands/eyes** s'essuyer la figure/les mains/les yeux; **to w. oneself, to w. one's bottom** s'essuyer les fesses, se torcher; *Vulg* **it's not fit to w. your arse with** c'est de la merde; *Fig Fam* **we wiped the floor with them** nous n'en avons fait qu'une bouchée **2** *(erase recording etc from)* effacer; **the tape has been wiped** la bande a été effacée
VI **1** *(when washing up, dusting)* essuyer **2** **the windscreen wiper isn't wiping** l'essuie-glace ne marche pas
▸ **wipe away** VT SEP *(tears)* essuyer; *(mark)* enlever, ôter; *Fig (memories)* effacer
▸ **wipe off** VT SEP **1** *(splash)* enlever, essuyer **2** *(sth from blackboard)* effacer; *(marks)* enlever; *Fam* **that'll w. the smile off his face** ça

va lui enlever le sourire; *Fam* **w. that smile off your face!** arrête de sourire comme ça!; **to w. a town off the map** *or* **off the face of the earth** rayer une ville de la carte **3** *Fin (debt)* annuler; **several millions of pounds were wiped off the value of shares** la valeur des actions a baissé de plusieurs millions de livres

VI *(of stain etc)* s'enlever

▸ **wipe out VT SEP 1** *(bath etc)* nettoyer **2** *(debt)* liquider, amortir; **his gambling debts wiped out his entire fortune** ses dettes de jeu ont eu raison de toute sa fortune; **many small traders were wiped out in the recession** de nombreux petits commerçants ont été balayés par la récession **3** *(memory, one's past)* effacer **4** *(army)* exterminer; **whole families were wiped out by the disease** des familles entières ont été exterminées par la maladie; **the fire wiped out the whole district** l'incendie a détruit tout le quartier **5** *Fam (exhaust)* lessiver; **I feel wiped out after interviewing so many people** ça m'a crevé *ou* lessivé de faire passer tous ces entretiens

▸ **wipe up VT SEP** *(dirt)* nettoyer, enlever; *(liquid)* essuyer; *(dishes)* essuyer

VI essuyer la vaisselle

wiped [waɪpt] **ADJ** *Fam (exhausted)* lessivé, crevé

wiper ['waɪpər] **N** *Aut (for windscreen)* essuie-glace *m*, *pl* essuie-glaces

▸▸ **w. blade** balai *m* d'essuie-glace

wiping out ['waɪpɪŋ] **N 1** *(of debt)* liquidation *f*, amortissement *m* **2** *(of memory)* effacement *m*

wire ['waɪər] **N 1** fil *m* métallique, fil de fer; *Elec* fil (électrique); **cheese w.** fil à couper le beurre; **the high w.** *(in circus)* la corde raide; *Fig* **to get one's wires crossed** mal se comprendre; *esp Am Fam* **to pull the wires** tirer les ficelles, faire jouer ses pistons

2 *esp Am (finishing line)* ligne *f* d'arrivée; *Fig* **down to the w.** jusqu'à la dernière minute; **to get an application in under the w.** soumettre une demande juste à temps; *Fig* **to (just) get in under the w.** *(of application etc)* arriver de justesse

3 *Fam (hidden microphone)* **he agreed to wear a w.** il accepta de porter un micro

4 *Old-fashioned (telegram)* télégramme *m*

VT 1 *(fix with wire)* attacher avec du fil de fer; *(jaw)* mettre en place avec du fil de fer; *(flowers etc)* monter sur fil de fer; *(close off with wire) (opening)* grillager; **wired glass** verre armé

2 *Elec (house)* faire l'installation électrique de; **to w. a hall for sound** sonoriser une salle **3** *esp Am Fam (police officer)* munir d'un micro

4 *(send telegram to)* envoyer un télégramme à; *(message)* télégraphier; **he wired that he would arrive at twelve** il a télégraphié qu'il arriverait à midi

▸▸ **w. brush** brosse *f* métallique; *Mil* **w. entanglements** barbelés *mpl*; **w. fence** clôture *f* en fil de fer; **w. mesh** grillage *m*, treillis *m* métallique; **w. netting** grillage, treillis métallique; **w. rope** câble *m* métallique; *Am* **w. service** agence *f* de presse *(envoyant des dépêches télégraphiques)*; *Aut* **w. wheel** roue *f* avec jante à rayons; **w. wool** éponge *f* métallique

▸ **wire into VT INSEP** *Fam* **he wired into his colleagues about their failure to keep him informed** il est rentré dans ses collègues en leur reprochant leur mauvaise communication avec lui; **they wired into the food as if they hadn't eaten for days** ils ont attaqué la nourriture comme s'ils n'avaient pas mangé depuis des jours; **they got wired into the backlog of work** ils ont attaqué le *ou* se sont attelés au travail en retard

▸ **wire up VT SEP** *Comput, Elec (devices)* brancher (**to** sur); *(put electronic bugs in) (room)* installer des micros dans

wirecutter ['waɪəkʌtər] **N** coupe-fil *m inv*, **(pair of) wirecutters** pince(s) *f(pl)* coupante(s)

wired ['waɪəd] **ADJ** *Fam (highly strung)* sur les nerfs, à cran; *(after taking drugs)* défoncé *(après avoir pris de la cocaïne ou des amphétamines)*

wire-haired **ADJ** *(terrier)* à poil dur

wireless ['waɪəlɪs] **ADJ** sans fil

N *Br Old-fashioned* T.S.F. *f*, poste *m* de T.S.F., radio *f*; **they communicated by w.** ils communiquaient par radio

▸▸ *Comput* **w. keyboard** clavier *m* sans fil; *Comput* **w. mouse** souris *f* sans fil; **w. network** réseau *m* sans fil; **w. network card** carte *f* de réseau sans fil; *Br Old-fashioned* **w. set** T.S.F., poste de T.S.F.

wirepuller ['waɪəpʊlər] **N** *esp Am Fam* personne *f* qui a du piston

wirepulling ['waɪəpʊlɪŋ] **N** *esp Am Fam* intrigues *fpl*; **a bit of w. would help his cousin get the job** un peu de piston pourrait aider son cousin à avoir le poste

wiretap ['waɪətæp] **N** **they've put a w. on him** *or* **his telephone** on a mis sa ligne sur écoute

VT *(telephone line)* mettre sur écoute

wiretapping ['waɪətæpɪŋ] **N** mise *f* sur écoute d'une ligne téléphonique

wireworm ['waɪəwɜːm] **N** *(pest)* larve *f* de taupin; *(millipede)* iule *m*

wiring ['waɪərɪŋ] **N** installation *f* électrique; **the house needs new w.** il faut refaire l'installation électrique *ou* l'électricité dans la maison

▸▸ **w. diagram** schéma *m* de branchement, schéma de câblage

wiry ['waɪərɪ] **ADJ 1** *(hair)* raide **2** *(person)* vigoureux, (sec et) nerveux

Wis *abbr* Wisconsin

wisdom ['wɪzdəm] **N** *(knowledge)* sagesse *f*, *(advisability)* sagesse, prudence *f*; **the received** *or* **conventional w.** l'opinion communément admise; **to question the w. of a decision** mettre en cause la sagesse d'une décision

▸▸ **w. tooth** dent *f* de sagesse

wise[1] [waɪz] **ADJ** *(knowledgeable)* sage; *(advisable)* prudent; **a w. man** un sage; **the Three W. Men** les (Rois) Mages *mpl*; **to get** *or* **grow wise(r)** *(learn more)* s'assagir; *(gain experience)* acquérir de l'expérience; **it wouldn't be w. to do it** ça ne serait pas sage *ou* prudent (de le faire); **w. after the event** sage après coup; **everyone can be w. after the event** c'est facile d'avoir raison après coup; **I'm no wiser than you** je n'en sais pas plus long que vous; **she's none** *or* **not any the wiser (for it)** elle n'est pas plus avancée; **without anyone being (any) the wiser** à l'insu de tout le monde, sans que personne ne sache; **no one will be any the wiser** personne n'en saura rien; *Fam* **to get w. to a fact** se rendre compte d'un fait; *Fam* **to get w. to sb** se rendre compte de *ou* réaliser ce que qn fait; *Fam* **I'm w. to his tricks** je connais ses combines; *Fam* **to put sb w. to sth** avertir qn de qch; *Fam* **to put sb w. to sb** prévenir qn contre qn

▸▸ *Fam* **w. guy** malin, -igne; **don't be a w. guy!** ne fais pas le malin!

▸ **wise up** *esp Am Fam* **VT SEP** mettre au courant; **w. me up about it** mets-moi au courant

VI **to w. up to sb** se rendre compte du petit jeu de qn; **to w. up to the fact that …** se rendre compte du fait que …; **w. up!** ouvre les yeux!

wise[2] **N** *Lit (way)* manière *f*, façon *f*; **in no w.**

en aucune manière *ou* façon, nullement, aucunement

-wise [waɪz] **SUFF 1** *(indicating direction)* dans le sens de …; **lengthw.** dans le sens de la longueur **2** *Fam (with reference to)* en ce qui concerne …, du point de vue de …, **côté** …; **healthw.** en ce qui concerne la santé, côté santé; **salaryw.** en ce qui concerne le salaire, côté salaire VOIR GRAMMAIRE A20

wiseacre ['waɪzeɪkər] **N** *(person who wants to seem wise)* petit malin *m*

wiseass ['waɪzæs] **N** *Am Sl* je-sais-tout *mf inv*

wisecrack ['waɪzkræk] *Fam* **N** vanne *f*, blague *f*; **to make a w.** faire *ou* lancer une vanne; **I don't want any more wisecracks** je ne veux plus entendre une seule vanne

VI sortir une/des vanne(s), faire de l'esprit

wisecracking ['waɪzkrækɪŋ] **ADJ** *Fam* blagueur

wisely ['waɪzlɪ] **ADV 1** sagement, prudemment

2 **to shake one's head w.** secouer la tête d'un air entendu

▐**WISH** [wɪʃ]

| **N** désir **1** ▪ vœu **2** ▪ souhait **2** |
| ▪ amitiés **3** |
| **VI** vouloir ▪ souhaiter |
| **VT** vouloir **1, 2** ▪ souhaiter **1–3** |

N 1 *(desire)* désir *m*; **I have no w. to go/to see it** je n'ai pas envie d'y aller/de le voir; **I have no w. to offend you, but …** je n'ai aucune envie de te blesser, mais …; **to express a w. to do sth** exprimer le désir de faire qch; **the w. to please** le désir de plaire; **by my father's w.** sur le désir de mon père; *Hum* **your w. is my command** vos désirs sont des ordres; **it was done against** *or* **contrary to my wishes** cela s'est fait à l'encontre de mon désir *ou* contre mon gré; **to make a w.** faire un vœu; **your w. will come true** ton vœu se réalisera

2 *(what is desired)* **his w. will come true** votre vœu sera exaucé; **his great w. was to see his son become president** son plus grand souhait *ou* désir était de voir son fils président

3 *(greeting)* **they send you their best wishes** ils te font leurs amitiés; **please give your parents my best wishes** *(said verbally)* fais toutes mes amitiés à tes parents; *(in writing)* transmets mes meilleures pensées à tes parents; **with best wishes** *(at end of letter)* (bien) amicalement; **with best wishes for a speedy recovery** avec tous mes/ nos meilleurs vœux de prompt rétablissement; **to send all good wishes to sb** présenter ses souhaits à qn

VI **to w. for sth** désirer *ou* vouloir *ou* souhaiter qch; **to w. for happiness/peace** désirer *ou* souhaiter le bonheur/la paix; **to have everything one can** *or* **could w. for** avoir tout pour être heureux; **I couldn't w. for anything better** je ne pourrais désirer mieux; **what more can** *or* **could you w. for?** que souhaiter de plus?; **as you w.** comme vous voulez

VT 1 *(want)* vouloir; **to w. to do sth** désirer *ou* vouloir faire qch; **I w. it to be done** je désire *ou* vouloir que ce soit fait; **I w. them to be here tomorrow** je désire *ou* je souhaite qu'ils soient là demain; **it is to be wished that …** il est à souhaiter que …

2 *(want sth impossible, unlikely)* **I w. I were a bird!** je voudrais être un oiseau!; **I w. I were in your place** je voudrais bien être à votre place; **I w. I had seen it!** j'aurais bien voulu voir cela!, si seulement j'avais pu le voir!; **I w. I hadn't left so early** je regrette d'être parti si tôt, si seulement je n'étais pas parti si tôt; **I**

w. she would come j'aimerais bien qu'elle vienne; **how I w. I could (do it)!** si seulement je pouvais (le faire)!; **I w. he wouldn't say things like that!** il ne pourrait pas éviter de dire des choses pareilles!; **w. you were here!** (on postcard) je pense à vous

3 (have feelings towards, greet) **he wishes me well** il est bien disposé envers moi; **he wishes nobody ill** il ne veut de mal à personne; **w. me luck** souhaite-moi bonne chance; **to w. sb a pleasant journey** souhaiter bon voyage à qn; **to w. sb goodnight** souhaiter bonne nuit à qn, dire bonsoir à qn; Iron **I w. you joy of it** je te souhaite bien du plaisir

▶▶ Psy **w. fulfilment** accomplissement m d'un désir

▶ **wish away** VT SEP faire disparaître comme par enchantement; **you can't w. your problems away** tu ne vas pas te débarrasser de tes problèmes d'un coup de baguette magique; **to w. one's life away** souhaiter que sa vie soit différente

▶ **wish on** VT SEP **to w. sth on sb** obliger qn à accepter qch; **it was wished on me by my boss** j'ai été obligé de l'accepter à cause de mon patron, mon patron m'a obligé à l'accepter; **the boss wished his son on the head of marketing** le patron a imposé son fils au directeur du marketing; **I wouldn't w. this on my worst enemy** je ne souhaiterais pas cela à mon pire ennemi; **it's not an experience I would w. on anyone** c'est une expérience que je ne souhaiterais à personne; **can we w. the children on you for the day?** est-ce qu'on peut vous laisser les enfants pour la journée?

wishbone ['wɪʃbəʊn] N fourchette f, bréchet m; esp Am (on surfboard) wishbone m; **to pull a w. with sb** = faire un vœu avec qn en essayant de casser le bréchet du poulet

▶▶ Aut **w. suspension** suspension f triangulée

wishful thinking ['wɪʃfʊl] N **that's a bit of w.** c'est prendre ses désirs pour des réalités

wishy-washy ['wɪʃɪwɒʃɪ] ADJ Fam (style) fade, insipide; (person) indécis; (compromise) insatisfaisant; **a w. liberal** un libéral mou

wisp [wɪsp] N (strand) (of straw, wool) brin m; **w. of smoke** trainée f de fumée; **w. of hair** mèche f de cheveux; **a little w. of a girl** un tout petit bout de fille; **a w. of cloud** un filet de nuage

wispy ['wɪspɪ] ADJ (beard, hair) fin; (cloud) vaporeux

wisteria [wɪs'tɪərɪə] N (plant) glycine f

wistful ['wɪstfʊl] ADJ nostalgique; (look, air, smile) mélancolique; **he sounded w. when he spoke of her** il parlait d'elle avec une nuance de regret dans la voix

wistfully ['wɪstfəlɪ] ADV avec nostalgie, avec regret; **she looked w. at the children playing in the street** (wanting to join them) elle regardait avec envie les enfants qui jouaient dans la rue; (thinking of the baby she never had) elle regardait avec regret les enfants qui jouaient dans la rue

wit [wɪt] N **1** (intelligence) (often pl) esprit m, entendement m, intelligence f; **he hasn't the w. to see it** il n'est pas assez intelligent pour s'en apercevoir; **he didn't have the w. to come and tell me** il n'a pas eu la présence d'esprit de me le dire; **he hasn't the w. he was born with!** il n'a pas inventé la poudre!; **to have quick wits** avoir l'esprit vif; **to have lost one's wits** avoir perdu l'esprit ou la raison; **to collect or gather one's wits** se ressaisir, reprendre ses esprits; **to have/keep one's wits about one** avoir/conserver toute sa présence d'esprit; **you need your wits about you in this job** il faut avoir de la présence d'esprit dans ce métier; **she has all her wits about her** c'est une maligne ou une fine; **to be at one's w.'s end** ne plus savoir que faire; **to have** or **engage in a battle of wits** jouer au plus fin; **to live by one's wits** vivre d'expédients; **to scare sb out of his/her wits** faire une peur bleue à qn; **to put one's wits to work on a problem** s'attaquer à un problème

2 (humour) esprit m, vivacité f d'esprit; **in a speech full of his usual w.** dans un de ses discours très spirituels; **flash of w.** trait m d'esprit; **sparkling with w.** étincelant d'esprit

3 (person) bel esprit m, homme m/femme f d'esprit; **what a w.!** toujours le mot pour rire!

wit² ADV Law **to w.** à savoir ..., c'est-à-dire ...

witch [wɪtʃ] N sorcière f, Fig Pej garce f, chameau m; **old w.** vieille sorcière

▶▶ **w. doctor** sorcier m guérisseur; **w. hazel** (plant) hamamélis m

witchcraft ['wɪtʃkrɑ:ft] N sorcellerie f, **to practise w.** pratiquer la sorcellerie

witchery ['wɪtʃərɪ] N **1** (practice) ensorcellement m, enchantement m **2** (influence, charm) envoûtement m, fascination f

witch-hunt N Pol chasse f aux sorcières

witch-hunting N Pol chasse f aux sorcières

witching ['wɪtʃɪŋ] ADJ Lit, Hum **the w. hour** minuit m, l'heure f du crime

WITH [wɪð]

| ▪ avec **1, 3, 5** ▪ à **2** ▪ chez **1, 3** ▪ de **5** |

PREP **1** (expressing accompaniment) avec; **to travel/work w. sb** voyager/travailler avec qn; **he is staying w. friends** il est chez des amis; **to mingle w. the crowd** se mêler à la foule; **I have nobody to go out w.** je n'ai personne avec qui sortir; **here I am w. nobody to talk to** me voilà sans personne à qui parler; **I'll be w. you in a moment** je serai à vous dans un instant; **some cheese to eat w. it** du fromage pour manger avec; **this is a problem that will always be w. us** ce problème sera toujours d'actualité; **she came in w. a suitcase** elle est entrée avec une valise; **I'm sorry I don't have a handkerchief w. me** je suis désolé, je n'ai pas de mouchoir; **do you have a pencil w. you?** avez-vous un crayon sur vous?; **to leave a child w. sb** laisser un enfant à la garde de qn; **the decision rests** or **lies w. you** c'est à vous de décider; **what will happen to her w. both her parents dead?** (now that they are dead) que va-t-elle devenir maintenant que son père et sa mère sont morts?

2 (having) à; **a knife w. a silver handle** un couteau à manche d'argent; **a girl w. blue eyes** une jeune fille aux yeux bleus; **a child w. a cold** un enfant enrhumé; **w. his/her hat on** le chapeau sur la tête; **w. his (over)coat on** en pardessus; **w. your intelligence you'll easily guess what followed** intelligent comme vous l'êtes vous devinerez facilement la suite; Arch **w. child** (of woman) enceinte

3 (expressing association) avec; **to correspond w. sb** correspondre avec qn; **to have to do w. sb** avoir à faire avec qn; **to have nothing to do w. sb** n'avoir rien à faire avec qn; **the next move is w. him** c'est à lui d'agir maintenant; **w. him all men are equal** tous les hommes sont égaux à ses yeux ou pour lui; **to be patient w. sb** être patient avec qn; **to be honest w. oneself** être honnête envers ou avec soi-même; **it's a habit w. me** c'est une habitude chez moi; **to use one's influence w. sb** agir auprès de qn; **all is well w. her** elle va bien; **I sympathize w. you** je vous plains; **I don't agree w. you** je ne suis pas d'accord avec vous; **I'm w. you** (I support you) je suis de votre côté; (I understand) je vous suis, je comprends; **I'm not w. you** (I don't understand) je ne (vous) suis pas, je ne comprends pas; Fam **to be w. it** (fashionable) être à la page ou dans le vent; Fam **I'm not w. it today** je n'y suis pas aujourd'hui; **to rise w. the lark** se lever au chant du coq; **w. these words/w. that he dismissed me** sur ces mots/là-dessus, il m'a congédié; **she said this w. a smile** elle a dit ça avec un sourire ou en souriant; **w. a cry** en poussant un cri; **to compete w. sb** concourir avec qn; **to fight w. sb** se battre contre ou avec qn; Fam **get w. it** (become alert) réveille-toi; (realize what's happening) ouvre les yeux

4 (despite) malgré; **w. all his faults** malgré tous ses défauts; **w. the best will in the world** avec la meilleure volonté du monde

5 (expressing instrument, agent) **to cut sth w. a knife** couper qch avec un couteau ou au couteau; **to walk w. (the aid of) a stick** marcher avec une canne; **to fight w. swords** se battre à l'épée; **to take sth w. both hands** prendre qch à deux mains; **to strike w. all one's might** frapper de toutes ses forces; **to tremble w. rage** trembler de rage; **to be stiff w. cold** être engourdi par le froid; **to be ill w. measles** avoir la rougeole; **to fill a vase w. water** remplir un vase d'eau; **lorry loaded w. timber** camion chargé de bois; **it's pouring w. rain** il pleut à verse

6 (forming adv phrase) **to work w. a will** travailler avec courage ou ardeur; **to receive/welcome sb w. open arms** recevoir/accueillir qn à bras ouverts; **w. all due respect** avec tout le respect que je vous dois; **w. your permission** avec votre permission; **w. this object (in view)** dans ce but; **I say it w. regret** je le dis à regret; **w. a few exceptions** à part quelques exceptions, quelques exceptions mises à part; **away w. care!** plus de soucis!, ça suffit, les soucis!; **down w. the police!** à bas les flics!; Fam **to hell w. him!** qu'il aille au diable!, qu'il aille se faire voir!

withal [wɪ'ðɔ:l] ADV Arch de plus

withdraw [wɪð'drɔ:] (pt withdrew [-'dru:]; pp withdrawn [-'drɔ:n]) VT **1** (one's hand, support) retirer; **the government has withdrawn funding from the project** le gouvernement a arrêté de financer le projet **2** (troops) retirer **3** (money) retirer; **to w. coins from circulation** retirer des pièces de la circulation, démonétiser des pièces **4** (offer, remark, candidacy) retirer; (promise) retirer, revenir sur; (claim) renoncer à; **to w. a charge** se rétracter; **to w. an order** Com annuler une commande; Admin rapporter un décret; Law **to w. one's action** retirer sa plainte; Fml **to w. one's labour** faire la grève; **the right to w. one's labour** le droit de grève VI **1** (also after sex act) se retirer (**from** de); **he withdrew ten paces** il a reculé de dix pas; **to w. in favour of sb** (of candidate) se désister en faveur de qn; **to w. into oneself** se replier sur soi-même; **to w. into silence** se renfermer dans le silence **2** Mil se retirer

withdrawal [wɪð'drɔ:(ə)l] N **1** (of one's troops) retrait m; (by troops) retraite f; **to make a w.** (of troops) se retirer, battre en retraite; Fig **to make a w. from one's position** battre en retraite

2 Banking retrait m; **cash w.** retraite m en espèces; **to make a w.** faire un retrait; **w. of capital** retrait de fonds; **w. from circulation** démonétisation f

3 Psy repli m sur soi; (from drugs) (état m ou

crise *f* de) manque *m*; **the boy is showing signs of w.** le jeune garçon présente des signes de repli sur lui-même

4 *(of decree, order)* rappel *m*; *(of promise, accusation)* rétractation *f*, *(of complaint)* retrait *m*; **w. of a candidate** désistement *m* d'un candidat

5 *(after sex act)* retrait *m*

►► *Banking* **w. limit** plafond *m* (d'autorisation) de retrait; **w. method** *(of contraception)* coït *m* interrompu; *Banking* **w. notice** avis *m* de retrait; *Banking* **w. slip** bordereau *m* de retrait; **w. symptoms** symptômes *mpl* de manque; **to suffer w. symptoms** *(of alcoholic, drug addict)* être en manque; *Fig* se sentir perdu

withdrawn [wɪð'drɔːn] **ADJ** *(reserved)* replié sur soi-même

wither ['wɪðər] **VI** *(of plant)* se dessécher, se flétrir, se faner; *(of limb)* s'atrophier; *Fig (of beauty)* passer, (se) faner; *(of hope)* s'évanouir; *(of person, company)* dépérir; **without the steel industry the region will simply w. and die** sans l'industrie sidérurgique, la région va mourir lentement; **the party gradually withered and died** le parti s'est peu à peu éteint

VT *(of wind, heat)* *(plant)* dessécher, flétrir, faner; *(limb)* atrophier; *Fig* **to w. sb with a look** foudroyer qn du regard

► **wither away**, **wither up** **VI** = wither

withered ['wɪðəd] **ADJ 1** *(plant)* desséché, flétri, fané; *(face, cheek)* fané, flétri; **he was old and w.** il était vieux et complètement desséché **2** *(arm)* atrophié

withering ['wɪðərɪŋ] **ADJ** *(heat)* qui dessèche, qui flétrit; *Fig (look)* foudroyant; *(tone)* de mépris; **w. sarcasm** sarcasme cinglant; **to give sb a w. look** foudroyer qn du regard

witheringly ['wɪðərɪŋlɪ] **ADV** *(to look at)* avec mépris; *(to say)* d'un ton méprisant

withers ['wɪðəz] **NPL** *(of horse)* garrot *m*

withershins ['wɪðəʃɪnz] **ADV** *Scot* à contre-sens

withhold [wɪð'həʊld] **VT** *(pt, pp withheld* [-'held]*)* **1** *(not give) (consent, help)* refuser; *(money)* retenir; *(taxes)* prélever; **to w. recognition of a country** ne pas reconnaître un pays **2** *(suppress) (fact etc)* taire, supprimer; *(information)* retenir, bloquer; **I managed to w. my indignation/laughter** j'ai réussi à contenir mon indignation/rire; **to w. the truth from sb** cacher la vérité à qn **3** *Law (property)* détenir

withholding [wɪð'həʊldɪŋ] **N 1** *(of help, aid, loan)* refus *m*; *(of taxes)* prélèvement *m*, retenue *f* **2** *(of information, facts)* rétention *f*

within [wɪð'ɪn] **ADV** **from w.** de l'intérieur; **seen from w.** vu de l'intérieur *ou* du dedans; **staff required, apply w.** *(notice in shop window)* on recherche du personnel, se présenter à l'intérieur

PREP 1 *(not beyond)* **w. reason** dans des limites raisonnables; **to keep w. the law** rester dans (les limites de) la légalité; **it is quite w. the realms of possibility** c'est dans les limites du possible; **to keep** *or* **live w. one's income** vivre selon ses moyens; **w. sight** en vue; **to keep sb/sth w. sight** avoir qn/qch à portée de vue; **to be w. sight of the shore** avoir la côte en vue; **w. call** à portée de (la) voix; **w. two miles of the town** à moins de deux milles de la ville; **w. a radius of ten kilometres** dans un rayon de dix kilomètres; **I live w. walking distance of the office** je peux aller au travail à pied; **is it w. walking distance?** est-ce qu'on peut y aller à pied?; **we were w. an inch of death** nous étions à deux doigts de la mort

2 *(in expressions of time)* **w. an hour** en moins d'une heure; **it will be ready w. an** *or* **the hour** ça sera prêt d'ici une heure; **w. a**

week *(in the space of)* en moins d'une semaine; *(by the time a week has passed)* d'ici une semaine; **w. the week** avant la fin de la semaine, dans la semaine; **w. a year of his death** *(after he died)* moins d'un an après sa mort; *(before he died)* moins d'un an avant sa mort; **w. the next week** dans le courant de la semaine prochaine; **w. the next five years, w. five years from now** d'ici cinq ans; **w. the required time** dans le délai prescrit; **w. twenty-four hours** dans les vingt-quatre heures; **w. ten days of receipt of your order** dans un délai de dix jours à compter de la réception de votre commande; **w. a short time** *(soon)* à court délai; *(soon after)* peu de temps après; **her time was w. a few seconds of the world record** son temps était à quelques secondes du record du monde

3 *Old-fashioned, Lit (inside)* à l'intérieur de, en dedans de; **w. these four walls** entre ces quatre murs; **the enemy is w. our frontiers** l'ennemi est dans nos frontières; **a voice w. me** une voix intérieure

without [wɪð'aʊt] **PREP 1** sans; **she did it w. asking/being asked** elle l'a fait sans demander/sans qu'on le lui demande; **to be w. a care in the world** n'avoir aucun souci; **w. a tail/coat/hope** sans queue/manteau/espoir; **to be w. food** manquer de nourriture; **he came back w. any money** il est revenu sans argent; **w. any difficulty** sans aucune difficulté; **the rumour is w. foundation** la rumeur est dénuée de fondement *ou* n'est pas fondée; **not w. difficulty** non sans difficulté; **w. end** sans fin; **he passed by w. seeing me/being seen** il est passé sans me voir/être vu; **it goes w. saying that ...** il va sans dire *ou* de soi que ...; **can you do it w. her knowing about it?** pouvez-vous le faire sans qu'elle le sache?; **they are w. any knowledge of French** ils n'ont aucune connaissance du français; **to do** *or* **go w. sth** se passer de qch; **I don't want her to go w. anything** je ne veux pas qu'elle manque de quoi que ce soit; **w. so much as saying goodbye/asking permission** sans même dire au revoir/demander la permission **2** *Arch (outside)* en dehors de

ADV *Arch* à l'extérieur, au dehors; **from w.** de l'extérieur; **seen from w.** vu de l'extérieur *ou* du dehors

with-pack premium **N** *Mktg* prime *f* directe

with-profits **ADJ** *Fin (pension fund)* avec participation aux bénéfices

withstand [wɪð'stænd] **VT** *(pt, pp withstood* [-'stʊd]*)* *(person, pain, pressure)* résister à; **to w. the heat** supporter la chaleur; *Mil etc* **to w. an attack** soutenir une attaque

withy ['wɪðɪ] **N** brin *m* *ou* lien *m* d'osier

witless ['wɪtlɪs] **ADJ** stupide, sot, *f* sotte; *Fam* **to scare sb w.** faire une peur bleue à qn

witness ['wɪtnɪs] **N 1** *(person)* témoin *m*; *(to will)* témoin testamentaire; **will you act as a w. at our wedding?** est-ce que vous voulez bien être témoin à notre mariage?; **I gave my name as a w.** j'ai donné mon nom en tant que témoin; *Law* **w. to a document** *or* **a deed** témoin instrumentaire, témoin à un acte; *Law* **to call sb as w.** citer qn comme témoin; *Law* **w. for the defence/prosecution** témoin à décharge/charge

2 *(testimony)* témoignage *m*; **to give w. on behalf of the accused** rendre témoignage pour l'accusé, témoigner en faveur de l'accusé; **to bear w. to sth** rendre *ou* porter témoignage de qch, témoigner de qch, attester qch; **this situation bears w. to the need to ...** cette situation témoigne de la nécessité de ...; *Rel* **to bear false w.** porter un faux témoignage; **I call you to w.** j'en appelle à votre témoignage

VT *(scene)* être spectateur *ou* témoin de; *(interview etc)* assister à; *Law (deed)* attester; *Law (signature)* certifier; **I witnessed the whole thing** j'ai assisté à tout ce qui s'est passé; **this house has witnessed many deaths** cette maison a vu de nombreux décès; **we are witnessing a historic event** nous assistons à un événement historique; **he had witnessed the entire scene from his window** il avait vu *ou* assisté à toute la scène depuis sa fenêtre; **never in my entire life have I witnessed such stupidity** je n'ai jamais, de ma vie entière, vu une telle stupidité

VI *Law* **to w. to sth** témoigner de qch; **to w. against/for sb** témoigner contre/en faveur de qn

►► *Br* **w. box** barre *f* des témoins

-witted [-'wɪtɪd] **SUFF** slow/quick/etc-**w.** qui a l'esprit lent/vif/etc

witter ['wɪtər] **VI** *Br Fam* **to w. (on)** parler interminablement, parler pour ne rien dire; **to w. (on) about sth** parler interminablement de qch; **what's he wittering (on) about now?** qu'est-ce qu'il est encore en train de raconter?

wittering ['wɪtərɪŋ] **N** *Br Fam* bavardage *m*; **his constant w. gets on my nerves** son papotage me tape sur les nerfs

witticism ['wɪtɪsɪz(ə)m] **N** mot *m* d'esprit, bon mot

wittily ['wɪtɪlɪ] **ADV** spirituellement, avec esprit

wittiness ['wɪtɪnɪs] **N** *(of remark etc)* esprit *m*, sel *m*

wittingly ['wɪtɪŋlɪ] **ADV** *(intentionally)* sciemment, en connaissance de cause, intentionnellement

witty ['wɪtɪ] **ADJ** spirituel, plein d'esprit

wizard ['wɪzəd] **N 1** sorcier *m*, magicien *m*; *Fig* génie *m*; **he's a real w. with figures/ computers** c'est un as des chiffres/des ordinateurs; **to be a financial w.** avoir le génie de la finance *ou* des affaires; **she's a w. on the violin** c'est une violoniste géniale *ou* de génie; **to be a w. with a sewing needle** avoir des doigts de fée (pour la couture) **2** *Comput* assistant *m*

ADJ *Old-fashioned Br Fam* épatant, excellent

wizardry ['wɪzədrɪ] **N** sorcellerie *f*, magie *f*; *Fig* génie *m*, habileté *f*; **her financial w.** son talent génial en matière de finance; **that was sheer w. with the ball** c'était un jeu subtil et simplement génial

wizened ['wɪzənd] **ADJ** ratatiné; *(cheeks)* parcheminé; *(apple)* ratatiné, ridé; **to become w.** *(of person, apple)* se ratatiner; *(of skin)* se parcheminer

wk *abbr* week

WO [dʌb(ə)lju:'əʊ] **N** *Br Mil abbr* warrant officer

wo(a) ['wəʊ(ə)] **INT** *(to horse)* ho!, holà!

woad [wəʊd] **N** guède *f*

wobble ['wɒb(ə)l] **N 1** *(swaying)* **the chair/ desk has got a bit of a w.** la chaise/le bureau est légèrement bancal(e) *ou* branlant(e); **there is a slight w. in the front wheel of the bike** la roue avant du vélo a un léger jeu; *Aut* **front-wheel w.** shimmy *m* **2** *(of voice)* tremblement *m*

VI 1 *(sway) (of flame)* vaciller, osciller; *(of jelly, thighs etc)* trembler; *(of table)* branler; *(of person)* chanceler; *(of building, tooth)* bouger; *(of wheel)* avoir du jeu **2** *(of voice etc)* trembler, chevroter **3** *Fam (hesitate)* hésiter

wobbly ['wɒblɪ] **ADJ 1** *(table, chair)* branlant; *(flame)* vacillant; *(person)* chancelant; **the whole structure is slightly w.** toute la structure bouge légèrement; **my legs** *or* **I feel w.** j'ai les jambes en coton; *Fam* **I'm a**

bit w. on irregular verbs je ne maîtrise pas vraiment les verbes irréguliers **2** *(voice etc)* chevrotant, tremblotant

▪ N *Br Fam* **to throw a w.** piquer une *ou* sa crise

wodge [wɒdʒ] N *Br Fam (of bread)* gros morceau m; *(of money)* gros paquet m; **a huge w. of time** un bon bout de temps

woe [wəʊ] N *Lit* malheur m, chagrin m, peine f; **to tell a tale of w.** raconter ses malheurs; **to recount one's woes** égrener ses malheurs; **w. is me!** pauvre de moi!, malheureux que je suis!; **w. betide you if you're late** malheur à toi si tu es en retard

woebegone ['wəʊbɪgɒn] ADJ *(look, face)* désolé, abattu; **to look w.** avoir l'air désolé

woeful ['wəʊfʊl] ADJ **1** *(bad)* déplorable, mauvais; **w. standard of workmanship** qualité f de travail déplorable **2** *Lit (look)* affligé, malheureux; *(news)* attristant, affligeant; **the Knight of the W. Countenance** le chevalier à la Triste Figure

woefully ['wəʊfəlɪ] ADV **1** *(bad, ill-equipped, inadequate etc)* terriblement; *(low)* déplorablement; **a w. inadequate husband** un très mauvais mari **2** *(to say, look at)* tristement

wog [wɒg] N *Br Offensive Sl* métèque m

wok [wɒk] N wok m, poêle f chinoise

wold [wəʊld] N *Geog* plateau m

wolf, pl **wolves** [wʊlf, wʊlvz] N **1** loup m; **she w.** louve f; **to be as hungry as a w.** avoir une faim de loup; *Fig* **that will keep the w. from the door** cela vous/nous/*etc* mettra à l'abri du besoin; *Fig* **to throw sb to the wolves** sacrifier qn; **a w. in sheep's clothing** un loup déguisé en agneau; **to cry w.** crier au loup **2** *Fam (womanizer)* coureur m de jupons
▸▸ *Old-fashioned Br Fam* **W. Cub** *(scout)* louveteau m; **w. whistle** sifflement m *(au passage d'une femme)*
▸ **wolf down** VT SEP engloutir, dévorer

wolfhound ['wʊlfhaʊnd] N chien-loup m, pl chiens-loups; **Irish w.** lévrier m d'Irlande

wolfish ['wʊlfɪʃ] ADJ de loup; *(appetite)* vorace; **a w. grin** un sourire aux dents longues

wolfram ['wʊlfrəm] N *Miner* wolfram m

wolfsbane ['wʊlfsbeɪn] N *(plant)* aconit m

wolf-whistle VT & VI siffler; **to get wolf-whistled** se faire siffler

wolverine ['wʊlvəri:n] N glouton m

woman, pl **women** ['wʊmən, 'wɪmɪn] N *VOIR GRAMMAIRE A13* femme f; **an old w.** une vieille femme, *Pej* une vieille; *Fam (man)* un chipoteur; **the other w.** l'autre femme; **they have a w. in to do the cleaning** ils ont quelqu'un qui vient faire le ménage; **she's his w.** c'est sa compagne; **he's got women all over the place** il a des maîtresses partout; *Old-fashioned Fam* **the little w.** *(my wife)* ma femme; *Fam* **get in the car, w.!** allez femme, en voiture!; **to run after women** courir le jupon; **a w.'s place is in the home** une femme doit rester à la maison; *Prov* **a w.'s work is never done** = les femmes sont constamment occupées (à la maison); **the women's movement,** *Fam* **women's lib** le Mouvement pour la libération de la femme; *Fam Pej* **women's libber** féministe f; *Journ* **women's page** page f des lectrices; **women's magazines** magazines féminins, revues féminines; **women's problems** ennuis *ou* problèmes de femmes *ou* féminins; **women's refuge, women's shelter** centre m d'accueil pour les femmes
▸▸ **w. artist** femme f peintre; **w. doctor** (femme) médecin m; **w. driver** conductrice f; **it was a w. driver** c'était une femme qui conduisait; **w. friend** amie f

womanhater ['wʊmənheɪtər] N misogyne m

womanhood ['wʊmənhʊd] N féminité f; **to grow to w.** devenir femme

womanish ['wʊmənɪʃ] ADJ *Pej (characteristic of a woman)* de femme; *(man)* efféminé

womanize ['wʊmənaɪz] VI courir les femmes, courir le jupon

womanizer ['wʊmənaɪzər] N coureur m (de femmes)

womanizing ['wʊmənaɪzɪŋ] N aventures fpl; **she was fed up with his w.** elle en avait assez qu'il coure le jupon

womankind ['wʊmənkaɪnd] N *(no pl)* les femmes fpl

womanliness ['wʊmənlɪnɪs] N féminité f

womanly ['wʊmənlɪ] ADJ féminin

womb [wu:m] N *Anat* utérus m; **the child she carried in her w.** l'enfant qu'elle portait dans son ventre m; **while still in his mother's w.** quand il était encore dans le ventre de sa mère

wombat ['wɒmbæt] N wombat m, phascolome m

women ['wɪmɪn] NPL *see* **woman**

womenfolk ['wɪmɪnfəʊk] N *(no pl)* les femmes fpl; **the settlers brought their w.** les colons ont amené leurs femmes et leurs filles

won PT, PP *see* **win²**

wonder ['wʌndər] N **1** *(miracle)* merveille f, miracle m, prodige m; **to work** or **do wonders** faire des merveilles *ou* des miracles; **the seven wonders of the world** les sept merveilles du monde; **one of the wonders of the world** une des merveilles du monde; **it's a w. (that) he hasn't lost it** c'est un miracle qu'il ne l'ait pas perdu; **no** or **little** or **small w. that the plan failed** il n'est guère *ou* pas étonnant que le projet n'ait pas réussi; **she's angry and no** or **little w.** elle est en colère et ce n'est pas étonnant; **a nine-day(s') w.** la merveille d'un jour; **w. cure** traitement m miracle; **w. drug** remède m miracle
2 *(astonishment)* étonnement m, surprise f; *(admiration)* émerveillement m, admiration f; **in w.** émerveillé; **to look at sb in w.** regarder qn avec émerveillement; **to fill sb with w.** émerveiller qn; **an expression** or **look of w.** un air émerveillé, une expression d'émerveillement; **I looked at it with a sense of w.** je l'ai regardé, émerveillé; **he has no sense of w.** il n'a aucune capacité d'émerveillement

VI *(be amazed)* s'étonner, s'émerveiller (at de); *Iron* **I really w. at you sometimes!** tu me surprendras toujours!; **I w. at how he manages to do it** je suis étonné par sa façon de s'y prendre; **I w. about her sometimes** je me pose des questions à son sujet parfois; **I was wondering about buying a new car** je songeais à acheter une nouvelle voiture; **I don't w. at it** cela ne m'étonne pas *ou* ne me surprend pas; **it's not to be wondered at that she left** il n'est pas étonnant qu'elle soit partie, rien d'étonnant à ce qu'elle soit partie

VT **1** *(be amazed)* **to w. that …** s'étonner que … + *subj*; **I w. that nobody thought of it before** je m'étonne que personne n'y ait pensé avant; **can you w. that he refused?** comment s'étonner qu'il ait refusé?
2 *(ask oneself)* se demander; **I w.** *(if he/she/etc will do that)* je me le demande; **one wonders!** c'est à se demander!; **it makes you w. how safe these power stations are** on en vient à se demander si ces centrales électriques sont vraiment sûres; **I w. whether he'll come** je me demande *ou* je voudrais bien savoir s'il viendra; **one wonders whether …** c'est à se demander si …; **I shouldn't w. if he were already married** cela ne m'étonnerait pas *ou* ne me surprendrait pas qu'il soit

déjà marié; **she knows a lot more, I shouldn't w.** cela ne m'étonnerait pas qu'elle en sache beaucoup plus long que ça; **I w. who invented that** je suis curieux de savoir qui a inventé cela; **I w. why!** je voudrais bien savoir pourquoi!; **their son will help them – I w.!** leur fils leur viendra en aide – vous croyez?; **I was wondering if you were free tonight** je me demandais si vous étiez libre ce soir; **oh, I just wondered** *(answering question 'why do you ask?')* oh, pour rien, comme ça; **I was just wondering where you'd got to** j'étais en train de me demander où tu étais

Wonderbra® ['wʌndəbrɑ:] N Wonderbra® m

wonderful ['wʌndəfʊl] ADJ merveilleux, prodigieux, admirable; *(film, book)* remarquable, formidable; **it's w. weather** il fait un temps fantastique; **a w. meal** un excellent *ou* délicieux repas; **she's a w. mother** c'est une mère merveilleuse; **she's a w. person** elle est fantastique; **it was w.!** c'était merveilleux *ou* magnifique!; **we had a w. time** nous nous sommes très bien amusés

wonderfully ['wʌndəfʊlɪ] ADV merveilleusement; **he sings w.** il chante merveilleusement *ou* remarquablement (bien); **it was w. hot** il faisait délicieusement chaud; **w. well** merveilleusement bien, à merveille; **a w. good book** un livre absolument génial; **we had some w. good food** nous avons très bien mangé

wondering ['wʌndərɪŋ] ADJ *(amazed)* étonné, émerveillé; **the child's w. eyes** les yeux émerveillés de l'enfant

wonderingly ['wʌndərɪŋlɪ] ADV avec étonnement, d'un air étonné

wonderland ['wʌndəlænd] N pays m des merveilles; **Alice in W.** Alice au Pays des Merveilles

wonderment ['wʌndəmənt] N *Lit* émerveillement m; **she looked at him with** or **in w.** elle l'a regardé avec émerveillement

wondrous ['wʌndrəs] *Arch, Lit* ADJ merveilleux
ADV merveilleusement

wondrously ['wʌndrəslɪ] ADV *Arch, Lit* merveilleusement

wonga ['wɒŋgə] N *Br Fam (money)* fric m, flouze m, pognon m

wonk [wɒŋk] N *Am (student)* bûcheur, -euse; *(intellectual, expert)* intello mf (qui n'intéresse qu'à sa discipline)

wonky ['wɒŋkɪ] ADJ *Br Fam (machine)* détraqué, déglingué; *(gadget, zip, switch etc)* qui débloque; *(collar, picture etc)* de travers; *(wardrobe, shelves)* branlant; *(one leg short)* *(chair, table)* boiteux; *(idea)* fumeux; **to feel w.** *(of person)* se sentir patraque; **this sentence is a bit w.** il y a quelque chose qui cloche dans cette phrase; **my grammar's a bit w.** ma grammaire cloche un peu; **the floorboards are a bit w.** le plancher n'est pas dans un état merveilleux

wont [wəʊnt] *Lit* ADJ **to be w. to do sth** avoir coutume *ou* l'habitude de faire qch; **he is w. to panic** il a tendance à paniquer, il panique facilement
N coutume f, habitude f; **according to his w., as is/was his w.** selon sa coutume, à *ou* selon *ou* suivant son habitude

won't [wəʊnt] CONTR = **will not,** *see* **will²**

wonted ['wəʊntɪd] ADJ *Lit* habituel, accoutumé

woo [wu:] VT **1** *Fig (potential employee, supporter, company)* courtiser; *(fame)* rechercher; **they wooed voters with promises of reforms** *(tried to attract)* ils ont essayé d'attirer des électeurs avec des promesses de réforme; *(succeeded in attracting)* ils se sont assuré les voix des électeurs avec des promesses de réforme; **they wooed him away from their rivals by promising him more money** ils lui ont fait quitter leurs concurrents en lui promettant plus d'argent **2** *Arch, Lit (court) (woman)* faire la cour à, courtiser

wood [wʊd] **N 1** *(group of trees)* bois *m*; **a walk in the woods** une promenade en forêt; *Fig* **you can't see the w. for the trees** les arbres cachent la forêt; **his problem is that he can't see the w. for the trees** son problème, c'est que les arbres lui cachent la forêt; *Fig* **we're not out of the w. yet** nous ne sommes pas encore tirés d'affaire

2 *(material)* bois *m*; **made of w.** fait de bois, en bois; *Fig* **touch w.!**, *Am* **knock on w.!** touchons du bois!; *Am* **to put the w. to sb** *Fam (beat up)* tabasser qn; *(defeat)* battre qn à plates coutures; *Vulg (have sex with)* tringler qn; *Vulg* **to get w.** *(erection)* bander

3 *(in wine making)* **the w.** le tonneau, le fût; **wine in the w.** vin *m* en tonneau *ou* en fût; **beer (drawn) from the w.** bière tirée au fût **4** *Golf* bois *m*; **a number 4 w.** un bois numéro 4

5 *(in game of bowls)* boule *f*

6 *Mus* = **woodwind**

▸▸**w. alcohol** esprit-de-bois *m*, alcool *m* méthylique; *Bot* **w. anemone** anémone *f* des bois; **w. ash** cendre *f* de bois; **w. block** planche *f*, bois; **w. carver** sculpteur *m* sur bois; **w. carving** sculpture *f* sur bois; **w. chisel** ciseau *m* à bois; **w. fire** feu *m* de bois; **w. nymph** nymphe *f* des bois, dryade, *f*; **w. panelling** boiserie *f*; *Orn* **w. pigeon** ramier *m*; **w. pulp** pâte *f* à papier; **w. stove** poêle *m* à bois

woodbine ['wʊdbaɪn] **N** *(honeysuckle)* chèvrefeuille *m* des bois; *Am (Virginia creeper)* vigne *f* vierge

woodchuck ['wʊdtʃʌk] **N** marmotte *f* d'Amérique

woodcock ['wʊdkɒk] **N** *(usu inv in pl)* bécasse *f* (des bois)

woodcraft ['wʊdkrɑːft] **N 1** *(knowledge of forest)* connaissance *f* de la forêt **2** *(woodwork)* (pratique *f* du) travail *m* sur bois

woodcut ['wʊdkʌt] **N** gravure *f* sur bois

woodcutter ['wʊdkʌtər] **N** bûcheron *m*

woodcutting ['wʊdkʌtɪŋ] **N 1** *Art (process, object)* gravure *f* sur bois **2** *(in forest)* abattage *m* du bois

wooded ['wʊdɪd] **ADJ** boisé; **densely w.** très boisé

wooden ['wʊd(ə)n] **ADJ 1** *(made of wood)* de bois, en bois; **the W. Horse of Troy** le cheval de Troie **2** *Fig (movement, manner)* raide, gauche; *(look)* impassible; *(performance, actor)* peu naturel; **w. smile** sourire *m* forcé ▸▸*Fam Hum* **w. overcoat** *(coffin)* costume *m* de sapin; **w. pallet** palette *f* en bois; **w. spoon** cuillère *f* en bois; *Fig* prix *m* de consolation

wooden-headed **ADJ** *Fam (stupid)* stupide, bouché

woodenness ['wʊdənnɪs] **N** *Fig (of manner)* raideur *f*, *(of actor, performance)* manque *m* de naturel

woodfree ['wʊdfriː] **ADJ** *(paper)* sans bois

woodie ['wʊdɪ] **N** *Am Sl (erection)* érection *f*, bandaison *f*; **to have a w.** bander

woodland ['wʊdlənd] **N** région *f* boisée, bois *mpl* ▸▸ **ADJ** *(fauna)* des bois; **w. scenery** paysage *m* boisé

woodlark ['wʊdlɑːk] **N** alouette *f* des bois

woodlouse, *pl* **woodlice** ['wʊdlaʊs, -laɪs] **N** cloporte *m*

woodman, *pl* **woodmen** ['wʊdmən] **N** *(logger)* bûcheron *m*

woodpecker ['wʊdpekər] **N** pic *m*

woodpile ['wʊdpaɪl] **N** tas *m ou* monceau *m* de bois

woodshed ['wʊdʃed] **N** remise *f* à bois; *Fig* **there's something nasty in the w.** il se passe du vilain

woodsman, *pl* **woodsmen** ['wʊdzmən] **N** *esp Am (hunter)* chasseur *m* (en forêt); *(for skins)* trappeur *m*; *(in forestry)* forestier *m*

woodstack ['wʊdstæk] **N** = **woodpile**

woodwind ['wʊdwɪnd] **N** *Mus (single instrument)* bois *m*; *(family of instruments)* bois *mpl* ▸▸ **w. instrument** bois *m*; **w. section** bois

woodwork ['wʊdwɜːk] **N 1** *(action)* travail *m* du bois; *(smaller scale)* menuiserie *f*, ébénisterie *f*; *(school subject)* menuiserie **2** *(carved wood)* bois *m* travaillé; *(ornamental)* boiserie *f*, *(structural)* charpente *f*; **that's a fine piece of w.** c'est de la belle menuiserie; *Fig Pej* **to come out of the w.** sortir d'on ne sait où; *Sport* **to hit the w.** heurter les bois

woodworm ['wʊdwɜːm] **N** ver *m* à bois; **this table's got w.** cette table est vermoulue; **it's full of w.** c'est rongé par les vers

woody ['wʊdɪ] **ADJ 1** *(countryside)* boisé **2** *Bot* ligneux **3** *(smell, texture)* de bois

wooer ['wuːər] **N** *Old-fashioned, Lit* prétendant *m*

woof[1] [wʊf] **N** *(of dog)* aboiement *m*; **the doggie goes w. (w.)** *(in children's language)* le toutou fait oua-oua ▸▸ **VI 1** *(of dog)* aboyer, faire oua-oua **2** *Am Sl (boast, bluff)* frimer, flamber

woof[2] [wuːf] **N** *Tex* trame *f*

woofer ['wuːfər] **N** *(in stereo equipment)* haut-parleur *m* de basses, *pl* hauts-parleurs de basses, boomer *m*, woofer *m*

woofter ['wʊftər] **N** *Br Offensive Sl (homosexual)* tante *f*, tapette *f*

wool [wʊl] **N 1** *(material)* laine *f*; **pure** *or* **all w. suit** complet *m* pure laine; **a ball of w.** une pelote de laine; *Fig* **to pull the w. over sb's eyes** jeter de la poudre aux yeux de qn; *Fig* **you can't pull the w. over my eyes** on ne peut pas me faire croire n'importe quoi **2** *(of animal)* pelage *m* **3** *Tech* **steel** *or* **wire w.** paille *f* de fer ▸▸ **ADJ 1** *(made of wool) (cloth)* de laine; *(socks, dress)* en laine **2** *(relating to wool)* **the w. industry** l'industrie *f* lainière; **the w. trade** commerce des laines; **w. shop** magasin *m* de laines

woolen, wooly *etc Am* = **woollen, woolly** *etc*

woolgathering ['wʊlgæð(ə)rɪŋ] **N** *Fam* **1** *(daydreaming)* rêvasserie *f* **2** *(used as a verb)* **to be w.** rêvasser, être dans les nuages; **he's always w.** il a toujours l'esprit ailleurs, il est toujours ailleurs

woollen, *Am* **woolen** ['wʊlən] **ADJ** *(dress etc)* en laine; **w. materials** laines *fpl*, lainages *mpl* ▸▸ **NPL woollens** lainages *mpl*

woolliness, *Am* **wooliness** ['wʊlɪnɪs] **N 1** *(of reasoning, style)* imprécision *f*, *(of ideas)* caractère *m* confus; *(of outline)* manque *m* de netteté, flou *m* **2** *(resemblance to wool)* nature *f* laineuse (**of** de)

woolly, *Am* **wooly** ['wʊlɪ] **ADJ 1** *(resembling wool)* laineux, de laine; **w. clouds** nuages ouatés; **w. hair** cheveux crépus **2** *Fig (vague)* peu net; *(outline)* flou; **w. ideas** idées vagues *ou* nébuleuses; **w.-minded** aux idées imprécises *ou* vagues; **w. style** style qui manque de précision; **a w. liberal** un libéral aux idées vagues ▸▸ **N** *Fam (garment)* tricot *m*, laine *f*; **winter woollies** vêtements chauds d'hiver

Woolsack ['wʊlsæk] **N** *Br Parl* **the W.** = le siège du Lord Chancellor (à la Chambre des Lords)

woozy ['wuːzɪ] **ADJ** *Fam (person)* dans les vapes, patraque; **I feel a bit w.** je me sens un peu patraque, je me sens tout chose

wop [wɒp] **N** *Offensive Sl* macaroni *m*, rital *m*

Worcs *abbr* Worcestershire

WORD [wɜːd]

N mot **1, 5, 9** ▪ nouvelle **3** ▪ parole **4, 7** ▪ ordre **6**
VT formuler

N 1 mot *m*; **w. for w.** *(to repeat sth)* mot pour mot; *(to translate sth)* mot à mot, textuellement; **in a w.** en un mot, (en) bref; **in a w., no** en un mot, non; **in a few words** en quelques mots; **in other words** en d'autres termes, autrement dit; **those were her very words** ce sont ses propres mots; **I told him what I thought of him in so many words** je lui ai dit clairement ce que je pensais de lui; **did she say you could take it? – well, not in so many words** est-ce qu'elle a dit que tu pouvais le prendre? – eh bien, pas exactement; **in the strict sense of the w.** au sens strict du mot; **he doesn't know a w. of German** il ne sait pas un mot d'allemand; **'robbery' would be a better w. for it** 'vol' serait un mot plus approprié; **'bad' isn't the w. for it** 'mauvais' n'est pas le mot; **that's the wrong** *or* **not the right w. (for it)** ce n'est pas le mot qui convient; **there's a w. for it in Russian** il y a un mot pour exprimer cela en russe; **the Spanish w. for 'mouse'** 'mouse' en espagnol; **he was reserved – that's one w. for it!** il était réservé – c'est le moins qu'on puisse dire!; **there's a w. for people like you, it's 'thief'** les gens dans ton genre, on les appelle des voleurs; **she used a less flattering w.** elle a utilisé un terme moins flatteur; **what's the w. I'm looking for?** quel est le mot que je cherche?; **there's no other w. for it** il n'y a pas d'autre mot; **the spoken/ written w.** la parole/les écrits *mpl*; **in the words of Voltaire** selon (l'expression de) Voltaire, comme l'a dit Voltaire; **that is your w., not mine** c'est toi qui as dit cela, pas moi; **in your own words** selon tes propres mots; **a 600-w. article** un article de 600 mots; **I can't put it into words** je n'arrive pas à l'exprimer par des mots; **he's a man of few words** c'est un homme qui parle peu *ou* qui ne parle pas beaucoup; **I can't get a w. out of her** je ne peux pas en tirer un mot; **I couldn't get a w. in (edgeways)** je n'ai pas pu placer un mot; **he didn't say a w.** il n'a rien dit, il n'a pas soufflé mot; **not a w.!** pas un mot!, bouche cousue!; **without a w.** sans mot dire; **with these words, he went** sur ces mots *ou* là-dessus, il est parti; **words fail me!** j'en perds la parole!; **too ridiculous for words** d'un ridicule sans nom; *Am Fam* **w. (up)!** *(I agree)* parfaitement!; *(it's true)* sans dec!; **too stupid for words** d'une bêtise indicible; **too beautiful for words** d'une beauté ineffable; **fine words, but we'll see if their actions match them** belles paroles, mais nous verrons si l'on peut en dire de même de leurs actes; **kind words** des mots aimables; **words per minute** *(of printer, typist)* mots par minute; **to be w. perfect** *(of actor)* savoir son rôle sur le bout du doigt

2 *(remarks, conversation)* **may I have a w. with you?, I'd like a w. with you** puis-je vous parler un instant?; **I'll have a w. with her about it** je lui en toucherai deux mots; **I have been asked to say a few words of introduction** on m'a demandé de dire quelques mots d'introduction; **you're putting words into my mouth** vous me faites dire des choses que je ne veux pas dire; **you've taken the**

words (right) out of my mouth tu me l'as retiré de la bouche; **to put in a good w. for sb** dire *ou* glisser un mot en faveur de qn; **he never has a good w. for anyone** il ne peut pas s'empêcher de dire du mal des gens; **a w. in/out of season** un conseil opportun/ inopportun; **a w. of warning** une mise en garde; **I gave him a w. of warning** je lui ai mis en garde; **can I offer you a w. (or two) of advice?** puis-je vous donner un petit conseil?; **they had few words of comfort for her** ils ne lui ont pas dit grand-chose pour la consoler; **a w. of sympathy** un mot de condoléances

3 *(no pl) (message)* nouvelle *f*, *(official etc)* avis *m*, déclaration *f*; **to send sb w. of sth** faire part à qn de qch; *(officially, formally)* faire savoir qch à qn; **they sent w. that ...** ils ont fait savoir que ...; **we received w. that ...** on nous a apporté la nouvelle que ...; **have you had any w. yet?** *(of how they are etc)* est-ce que tu as eu des nouvelles?; **there's (been) no w. from Moscow** on n'a pas de nouvelles de Moscou; **by w. of mouth** *(to tell somebody something)* verbalement; *(to spread) (of rumours)* de bouche à oreille; **w.-of-mouth advertising** publicité *f* de bouche à oreille; **the w. is that he's retiring** on raconte qu'il va prendre sa retraite; **the w. on the street is that the Mafia did it** le bruit court que c'est la Mafia qui l'a fait; **she left w. with George for them to join her** elle a demandé à George de leur dire de la rejoindre

4 *(promise)* parole *f*; **one's w. of honour** sa parole d'honneur; **to give sb one's w.** donner sa parole à qn; **to keep one's w.** tenir (sa) parole; **to break one's w.** manquer à sa parole; **to go back on one's w.** revenir sur sa parole; **I give you my w., (you can) take my w. for it** je vous en donne ma parole, je vous en réponds; **I'll take your w. for it** je vous crois sur parole, je m'en rapporte à vous; **we've only got her w. for it** du moins, c'est ce qu'elle nous a dit; **it's your w. against his** c'est votre parole contre la sienne; **he's a man of his w.** c'est un homme de parole; **she's as good as her w.** elle tient parole; **she was better than her w.** elle a fait mieux que tenir ses promesses; **his w. is as good as his bond** sa parole vaut sa signature; **they took her at her w.** ils l'ont prise au mot; **we will hold you to your w.** nous vous obligerons à tenir parole; **my w.!** ma parole!

5 to have words with sb *(argue)* se disputer *ou* se quereller avec qn; **they had words** ils ont eu des mots

6 *(order)* **w. of command** ordre *m*; **to give the w. to do sth** *(give order)* donner l'ordre de faire qch; *(give signal)* donner le signal de faire qch; **if you want any more paper just say the w.** si tu veux encore du papier, dis-le

7 *Rel* **the w. of God** la parole de Dieu; **theW.** *(Christ)* le Verbe; **to spread the w.** *(proselytize)* annoncer la bonne parole

8 *Comput* mot *m*

9 words *(lyrics)* paroles *fpl*; **words and music by Ian Smith** paroles *fpl* et musique *f* par Ian Smith; **listen to the words** écoute les paroles

VT *(document etc)* formuler, rédiger; *(comment)* formuler, exprimer; **it could have been better worded** il aurait/tu aurais/*etc* pu mieux le formuler; **be careful how you w. it** fais attention à la manière dont tu le formules; **a cleverly worded contract** un contrat habilement formulé

▸▸**w. association** association *f* d'idées par les mots; *Typ* **w. break** césure *f*, *Comput* **w. count** nombre *m* des mots; **to do a w. count** compter les mots; **w. count facility** fonction *f* de comptage de mots; **w. group** groupe *m* de mots, membre *m* de phrase; **w. list** liste *f*

de mots; *(content of dictionary)* nomenclature *f*, **w. order** ordre *m* des mots; **w. picture** description *f* imagée *ou* pittoresque; *(of person)* portrait *m* en prose; **w. processing** traitement *m* de texte; **w. processor** logiciel *m* de traitement de texte; *Typ* **w. split** coupure *f* de mot

---

wordbook ['wɜːdbʊk] N vocabulaire *m*, lexique *m*

wordiness ['wɜːdɪnɪs] N verbosité *f*, prolixité *f*

wording ['wɜːdɪŋ] N **1** *(choice of words) (of article, document)* formulation *f*, (choix *m* de) termes *mpl*; *(of problem)* énoncé *m*; *(of banker's draft, bill of exchange)* libellé *m*; **the w. was ambiguous** les termes étaient ambigus, la formulation était ambiguë; **it is important to get the w. right** il est important de choisir les termes appropriés **2** *(action) (of document)* rédaction *f*

wordless ['wɜːdlɪs] ADJ *esp Lit* sans paroles, muet

wordlessly ['wɜːdlɪslɪ] ADV sans dire un mot

word-process VT réaliser par traitement de texte; **word-processed text** texte *m* écrit au traitement de texte
VI travailler sur traitement de texte

wordsmith ['wɜːdsmɪθ] N **he's a real w.** il sait manier les mots

wordwrap ['wɜːdræp] N *Comput* passage *m* automatique à la ligne suivante

wordy ['wɜːdɪ] ADJ verbeux, prolixe, diffus

wore PT *see* **wear**

WORK [wɜːk]

N travail **1, 2, 4, 5** ▪ besogne **2** ▪ œuvre **3** ▪ ouvrage **3** ▪ emploi **4** ▪ usine **5** ▪ travaux **6, 7** ▪ mécanisme **8**
VI travailler **1, 2** ▪ fonctionner **3** ▪ marcher **3, 4**
VT faire travailler **1** ▪ faire marcher **2** ▪ travailler **5** ▪ exploiter **5**

N **1** *(labour)* travail *m*, -aux; **to be at w.** être au travail; **they are at w. on a new book** ils sont en train de travailler à un nouveau livre; **the forces at w.** les forces en jeu; **there are evil forces at w.** des forces maléfiques sont à l'œuvre; **to be hard at w.** être en plein travail; **he was hard at w. gardening** il était en plein jardinage; **to start w., to set** *or* **get to w.** se mettre au travail; **they set to w. digging the hole** ils se sont mis à creuser le trou; **they put him to w. in the kitchen** ils l'ont mis au travail dans la cuisine; **she was set to w. cataloguing the collection** on lui a donné pour tâche de répertorier la collection; **to stop w.** cesser le travail; *(for the day)* suspendre le travail; **w. in progress** *Acct* produits *mpl* en cours; *(actual work)* travaux en cours

2 *(task)* travail *m*, -aux, ouvrage *m*, besogne *f*, tâche *f*; **I've (got) w. to do** j'ai (du travail) à faire; **to have too much w. to do** avoir trop de travail à faire; **to get through a lot of w.** abattre de la besogne; **to give sb some w. to do** donner du travail à faire à qn; **there's a lot of w. to be done** il y a beaucoup (de travail) à faire; **it will take a lot of w. to make a team out of them** ça va être un drôle de travail de faire d'eux une équipe; **she put a lot of w. into her exams** elle a beaucoup travaillé à ses examens; **they're doing some w. for an American firm** *(of subcontractor)* ils travaillent pour une firme américaine; **very little w. has been done on this disease** peu de travail a été effectué sur cette maladie; **let's get down to w.!** mettons-nous au travail!; **a fine piece of w.** un beau travail; **the brandy had**

done its w. l'eau-de-vie avait fait son effet; **I'll have my w. cut out to finish in time** je vais en baver pour finir à l'heure; **you'll have your w. cut out with him** il vous donnera du fil à retordre; **he made quick w. of the ironing** il est rapidement venu à bout du repassage; **to make w. for sb** compliquer la vie à qn; **day's w.** (travail d'une) journée *f*; **it's all in a day's w.** ça n'a rien d'exceptionnel; **good w.!** bien fait!; **it was thirsty w.** c'était un travail qui donnait soif; **the w. of a professional** le travail *ou* l'œuvre *f* d'un professionnel; **this break-in is the w. of a professional** cette effraction est l'œuvre d'un professionnel

3 *(product, achievement)* ouvrage *m*, œuvre *f*; **the works of God** les œuvres de Dieu; **good works** bonnes œuvres; **the (complete) works of Shakespeare** les œuvres *ou* l'œuvre *m ou f* de Shakespeare; **a w. of art/genius** une œuvre d'art/de génie; **his early works** ses premières œuvres; **w. of fiction** ouvrage de fiction; **is this all your own w.?** est-ce que vous avez fait ça tout seul?; **her w. sells well** ses ouvrages se vendent bien; **very detailed/delicate w.** *(embroidery, carving etc)* ouvrage très détaillé/délicat

4 *(employment)* travail *m*, emploi *m*; **I need w.** il me faut du travail; **what kind of w. are you looking for?** quel genre de travail recherchez-vous?; **cleaning w.** nettoyage *m*; **I'm looking for translation w.** je cherche du travail dans la traduction; **office w.** travail de bureau; **manual w.** travail manuel; **skilled w.** travail qualifié; **the factory will provide w. for a hundred people** l'usine fournira du travail à cent personnes; **to be off w.** ne pas travailler *(parce qu'on est malade)*; **to be out of w.** *(unemployed)* être en ou au chômage; **she's not in w. at the moment** elle ne travaille pas en ce moment; *Fam* **nice w. if you can get it** il y en a qui ne s'embêtent pas!; *Br Fam* **he's a nasty bit** *or* **piece of w.** c'est un sale type; *Br Fam* **their daughter is a nasty bit** *or* **piece of w.** leur fille est une sale gosse

5 *(workplace)* (lieu *m* de) travail *m*; **works** *(factory)* usine *f*; **he's not at w. today** il ne travaille pas aujourd'hui; **on my way to w.** en allant travailler *ou* au travail; **someone at w. told me** quelqu'un au travail me l'a dit; **someone from w.** quelqu'un du travail; **someone from your w. called** quelqu'un de ton travail a appelé; **works council** comité *m* d'entreprise; **works outing** sortie *f* annuelle des employés *ou* des ouvriers

6 *Mil (usu pl)* **works** ouvrages *mpl*, travaux *mpl*; **field works** travaux de campagne

7 *Constr (usu pl)* **works** travaux *mpl*; **public works** travaux publics; **road works ahead!** attention travaux!; *Am* **w. zone!** travaux!, chantier!

8 *(mechanism) (usu pl)* **works** *(of watch etc)* rouages *mpl*, mécanisme *m*

9 *Fam* **they had eggs, bacon, toast, the works** ils avaient des œufs, du bacon, du pain grillé, tout, quoi!; *Fam* **the whole works** tout le bataclan, tout le tralala; **in his autobiography we are given the full works** *(full details of life)* son autobiographie nous livre tous les dessous de sa vie; **I treated myself to the full works at the beauty parlour** je me suis payé une séance de luxe chez l'esthéticienne; *Sl* **to give sb the works** *(beating)* passer qn à tabac; *(luxury treatment)* jouer le grand jeu à qn; *esp Am Fam* **to shoot the works** *(spend all one's money)* claquer tout son fric; **to be in the works** *(in preparation)* être en cours

VI **1** *(of person)* travailler; *(for good of other people)* œuvrer; **to w. hard** travailler dur; **to w. like a slave** *or* **a dog** *or* **a Trojan** *or* **a beaver** travailler comme un forçat *ou* comme un bœuf; **to w. a 40-hour week** faire une semaine de 40 heures; **to w. long hours** faire de grandes journées de travail; *Ind* **to w. to rule** faire la grève du zèle; **to w. in leather/brass** travailler dans le cuir/cuivre; **she works in publishing** elle travaille dans l'édition; **to w. on** *or* **for a newspaper** collaborer à un journal; **to w. for a good cause** travailler pour une bonne cause; **he worked with the poor and the sick** il travaillait avec les pauvres et les malades; **the city council, working to improve the quality of life** le conseil municipal, à l'œuvre pour l'amélioration de la qualité de la vie; **all her life she worked for peace/to bring the two countries together** toute sa vie elle a œuvré pour la paix/pour unir les deux pays; **we are working towards a peaceful solution** nous œuvrons en vue d'une solution pacifique; **to w. against sb** intriguer *ou* travailler contre qn; **their earlier popularity was now working against them** leur popularité des débuts jouait maintenant en leur défaveur; **let your body weight w. for you rather than against you** laisse ton poids jouer en ta faveur plutôt que contre toi; **her age worked in her favour** son âge a joué en sa faveur; **working from the principle that ...** partant du principe que ...; **I am working on the assumption that you can type** je pars du principe que vous savez taper à la machine

2 *(be employed)* travailler, avoir un emploi; **who do you w. for?** chez qui est-ce que vous travaillez?; **she works for Smith and Wilson** elle travaille chez Smith and Wilson; **she works for the water board** elle travaille au service des eaux

3 *(function) (of machine, system)* fonctionner, marcher; **the pump isn't working** la pompe ne marche *ou* ne fonctionne pas; **the lift isn't working** l'ascenseur est hors de service *ou* est en panne; **the system works well** le système fonctionne bien; **I can't get this machine to w.** je n'arrive pas à faire marcher cette machine; **they soon got** *or* **had it working** ils sont vite parvenus à le faire fonctionner; **can you show me how the photocopier works?** est-ce que tu peux me faire voir comment marche la photocopieuse?; **it works like this, here's how it works** *(of machine, system)* cela marche de la façon suivante, voilà comment ça marche; **it works both ways** ça marche dans les deux sens; **to w. as sth** *(serve the function of)* faire office de qch; **high unemployment works as a brake on wage claims** le taux élevé de chômage freine la hausse des salaires; **the clock works off electricity** la pendule marche à l'électricité; **these tools w. by compressed air** ces outils sont actionnés par *ou* marchent à l'air comprimé

4 *(have effect, succeed) (of drug, cleaning product)* faire effet; *(of plan, method)* marcher, y faire; *(of yeast)* fermenter; **the drug works in most cases** le médicament fait de l'effet dans la plupart des cas; **rubbing the stain won't w.** frotter la tache ne servira à rien; **she tried everything she could think of but nothing worked** elle a essayé tout ce à quoi elle pouvait penser mais rien n'a marché; **this isn't working** ça ne marche pas; **his plan didn't w.** son projet a échoué *ou* n'a pas réussi; **that/flattery won't w. with me** ça/la flatterie ne prend pas avec moi

5 *(of face, features)* remuer, s'agiter

6 *(move)* **to w. upstream** remonter le courant; **a band of rain working across the country** un front de pluie qui traverse le pays; **the infection has worked downwards** l'infection a progressé vers le bas; **I knew what he was trying to w. round to** je savais où il voulait en venir; **he finally worked round to asking her out** il l'a finalement invitée à sortir; **I haven't done it yet but I'm working round to it** je ne l'ai pas encore fait,

mais je vais m'en occuper; **to w. loose** *(of nut etc)* se desserrer

VT 1 *(person, horse etc)* faire travailler; **he works his employees/himself very hard** il exige beaucoup de travail de son personnel/lui-même; **to w. oneself to death** se tuer à force de travailler; **don't w. yourself to death!** ne va pas te tuer à la tâche *ou* à l'ouvrage!; *Iron* ne te fais pas trop mal, surtout!

2 *(operate) (machine etc)* faire travailler, faire fonctionner, faire marcher; **it is worked by steam/electricity** cela marche à la vapeur/à l'électricité

3 *(bring about) (miracle, cure)* opérer; *(change)* amener; **the beauty of the place was beginning to w. its magic on her** la beauté de l'endroit commençait à exercer sa magie sur elle; **the destruction wrought by the fire** la dévastation causée par l'incendie; **I'll w. it** *or* **things so that they pay in advance** je ferai de sorte qu'ils paient à l'avance; **his keys had worked a hole in his pocket** ses clefs avaient fini par faire un trou dans sa poche

4 *(move)* **to w. one's hands free** parvenir à dégager ses mains; **she worked the ropes loose** elle a réussi à desserrer les cordes petit à petit; **to w. one's way down/up** descendre/monter petit à petit *ou* avec précaution; **his hand worked its way up my leg** sa main remontait progressivement sur ma jambe; **he worked his way towards her** il s'est avancé vers elle petit à petit; **they worked their way through the crowd** ils se sont frayé un chemin à travers la foule; **they worked their way through the list** ils ont traité chaque élément de la liste tour à tour; **we're working our way through the French subjunctive** nous sommes en train d'étudier le subjonctif en français; **he's worked his way through the whole grant** il a épuisé toute la subvention; **they have worked themselves into a corner** ils se sont mis dans une impasse

5 *(mine, quarry)* exploiter; *(land)* travailler; *Com* **to w. the south-east** *(of representative)* couvrir le sud-est

6 *Naut* **to w. one's passage** payer son passage par son travail; **he worked his passage to Rio** il a payé son passage à Rio en travaillant; **to w. one's way through university** *(of student)* travailler pour payer ses études

7 *Sewing (design, initials)* broder; **the flowers are worked in silk** les fleurs sont brodées en soie

▸ ▸ **w. area** *(in school, home)* coin *m* de travail; *Comput* zone *f* de travail; *Comput* **w. file** fichier *m* de travail; **w. group** groupe *m* de travail; **w. permit** permis *m* de travail; **w. rate** cadence *f ou* rythme *m* de travail; **w. standard** norme *f* de travail

▸ **work in** VT SEP *(include, introduce) (incident in novel etc)* introduire; *(mix in)* incorporer, mélanger; **to w. in a reference to unemployment** faire une allusion au chômage; **to w. the other ingredients in** incorporer les autres ingrédients

▸ **work into** VT SEP **gently w. the cream into your hands** massez-vous les mains pour faire pénétrer la crème; **w. the dye into the surface of the leather** faites pénétrer la teinture dans le cuir; **he worked several references to her into his speech** il a glissé plusieurs allusions à elle dans son discours; **she worked the clay into the shape of a giraffe** elle modela l'argile pour en faire une girafe; **his oratory had them worked into a frenzy** sa virulence oratoire les avait rendus frénétiques; **it takes a while to w. yourself into the right frame of mind** il faut un certain temps pour se mettre dans le bon état d'esprit

▸ **work off** VT SEP *(one's anger, bad mood)*

évacuer (**by doing** en faisant); **to w. off one's anger on sb** passer sa colère sur qn; **I want to w. off some fat** je veux perdre du poids

▸ **work on** VI *(continue to work)* continuer à travailler

VT INSEP **1** *(be involved in)* travailler à *ou* sur; **he's working on an edition of Hamlet** il travaille à *ou* prépare une édition de Hamlet; **we're working on it** nous travaillons là-dessus; **a detective is working on this case** un détective est sur cette affaire; **he's been working on his breaststroke/emotional problems** il a travaillé sa brasse/essayé de résoudre ses problèmes sentimentaux

2 *(use as basis)* **have you any data to w. on?** avez-vous des données sur lesquelles vous fonder?

3 *(somebody) (persuade)* influencer, agir sur (l'esprit de); *(attempt to persuade)* travailler

▸ **work out** VT SEP **1** *(calculate) (cost, distance, sum)* calculer; **from this information, w. out the answer** à partir de cette information, déduisez la réponse; **it took me ages to w. out the right answer** j'ai mis un temps fou pour trouver la réponse exacte; **to w. out the total** faire la somme; **I w. it out at £22** d'après mes calculs, ça fait 22 livres; **the dog had worked out how to open the door** le chien avait compris comment ouvrir la porte; **he's a strange person – I'd worked that out!** il est bizarre – je m'en étais rendu compte!; **well, you can w. it out for yourself** alors, pas besoin que je te fasse un dessin

2 *(devise) (way of doing sth)* trouver, mettre au point; *(scientific method etc)* élaborer

3 *(resolve) (problem)* résoudre; **we must try to w. out our differences** nous devons essayer de résoudre nos désaccords; **I'm sure we can w. this thing out** *(your problem)* je suis sûr que nous pouvons arranger ça; *(our argument)* je suis sûr que nous finirons par nous mettre d'accord

4 *(understand)* comprendre; **I can't w. her out** je n'arrive pas à la comprendre; **she couldn't w. it out** elle n'y comprenait rien

5 *(of mine, seam)* **to be worked out** être épuisé

VI **1** *(be resolved)* **I wonder how it will all w. out** je me demande comment cela finira *ou* va finir; **it** *or* **things worked out very well for me** ça a *ou* les choses ont très bien marché pour moi; **it worked out well** *or* **all right for us** ça s'est bien passé pour nous, les choses se sont bien tourné pour nous; **but it didn't w. out that way** mais il en a été tout autrement; **it worked out badly for them** les choses ont mal tourné pour eux

2 *(succeed) (of marriage, arrangement)* marcher; **they started a business together, but it didn't w. out** ils ont monté une affaire ensemble, mais ça n'a pas marché; **I don't like my job, but things may w. out** je n'aime pas mon travail, mais ça peut-être s'arranger; **how is the new system working out?** est-ce que le nouveau système marche?; **are things working out for you OK?** est-ce que ça se passe bien pour toi?; **how's the new manager working out?** comment est-ce que le nouveau directeur se débrouille?

3 *(amount to)* **how much does it all w. out at?** ça fait combien en tout?; **it** *or* **the cost works out at £150 a head** cela fait 150 livres par personne; **it'll w. out more expensive like that** ça reviendra plus cher comme ça

4 *Sport* s'entraîner

▸ **work up** VT SEP **1** *(develop)* **to w. up an appetite** s'ouvrir l'appétit; **I can't w. up much enthusiasm/interest for the idea** j'ai du mal à m'enthousiasmer pour/à m'intéresser à cette idée

2 *(arouse)* **he worked the crowd up into a frenzy** il a rendu la foule frénétique; **she**

had worked herself up into a dreadful rage elle s'était mise dans une rage terrible; **to get worked up** *(upset)* se rendre malade (**about** au sujet de); *(angry)* se fâcher (**about** au sujet de); *(excited)* se mettre dans tous ses états (**about** au sujet de); **he's all worked up** il est dans tous ses états; **I'm too worked up to do it now** je suis trop énervé *ou* trop à cran pour le faire maintenant ▪ **VI** *(of skirt)* remonter

▸ **work up to VT INSEP** *(move towards) (something)* avancer par degrés à; **what are you working up to?** où voulez-vous en venir?; **he was working up to a discussion of his salary** il amenait progressivement la discussion sur le sujet de son salaire; **the symphony was working up to its finale** la symphonie allait crescendo, annonçant le finale

workability [wɜːkə'bɪlɪtɪ] **N** *Tech* maniabilité *f*

workable ['wɜːkəb(ə)l] **ADJ 1** *Tech (material)* maniable **2** *(mine)* exploitable **3** *(project)* réalisable, possible; **it isn't a w. proposition** ce n'est pas une proposition réalisable

workaday ['wɜːkədeɪ] **ADJ** *(clothes, routine)* de tous les jours; *(man)* ordinaire, banal, -als; *(incident)* courant, banal; **the w. world of the office** la routine du bureau

workaholic [wɜːkə'hɒlɪk] **N** *Fam* bourreau *m* de travail

workbag ['wɜːkbæg] **N** *Sewing* sac *m* à ouvrage

workbasket ['wɜːkbɑːskɪt] **N** *Sewing* corbeille *f* à ouvrage

workbench ['wɜːkbentʃ] **N** établi *m*

workbook ['wɜːkbʊk] **N** cahier *m* d'exercices

workbox ['wɜːkbɒks] **N** *Sewing* boîte *f* à ouvrage

workday ['wɜːkdeɪ] **N** *(weekday)* jour *m* ouvrable; *(day of work)* journée *f* de travail

worker ['wɜːkər] **N 1** travailleur, -euse; *Ind* ouvrier, -ière; **hard w.** travailleur assidu; **to be a hard w.** être un bon travailleur; **Workers of the world unite!** travailleurs de tous les pays, unissez-vous!; **the workers** *(as opposed to management)* le personnel; **workers and management** partenaires *mpl* sociaux; **workers' control** autogestion *f* **2** *Entom* ouvrière *f*

▸ ▸ *Entom* **w. ant** (fourmi *m*) ouvrière; *Entom* **w. bee** (abeille *f*) ouvrière; **w. director** = ouvrier qui fait partie du conseil d'administration; **w. participation** participation *f* ouvrière

worker-priest **N** prêtre-ouvrier *m, pl* prêtres-ouvriers

workfare ['wɜːkfeə(r)] **N** *Pol* = principe *m* selon lequel les bénéficiaires de l'allocation de chômage doivent fournir un travail en échange

workflow ['wɜːkfləʊ] **N** rythme *m* de travail ▸ ▸ **w. schedule** plan *m* de travail

workforce ['wɜːkfɔːs] **N** main-d'œuvre *f*; *(non-industrial)* personnel *m*

workhorse ['wɜːkhɔːs] **N** cheval *m* de labour; *Fig* **to be a w.** travailler comme un cheval *ou* une bête; **she's a willing w.** elle est toujours prête à faire n'importe quelle tâche

workhouse ['wɜːkhaʊs] **N 1** *Hist (for the poor)* asile *m* des pauvres **2** *Am Old-fashioned (prison)* maison *f* de correction

workie ['wɜːkɪ] **N** *Br Fam* ouvrier *m*

working ['wɜːkɪŋ] **ADJ 1** *(person)* qui travaille; *(population)* actif; **he's very hard-w.** il est très travailleur, il travaille très dur **2** *(day, hours)* **w. day** journée *f* de travail; *Admin* jour *m* ouvrable; **the w. week** la semaine de travail; **throughout her w. life** tout

au long de sa vie active *ou* de sa vie professionnelle **3** *(machine etc)* qui fonctionne; **in w. order** en état de fonctionnement *ou* marche; **to be in good w. order** bien fonctionner; **w. parts of a machine** mécanisme *m* d'une machine **4** *(clothes, conditions)* de travail; **the two leaders have a good w. relationship** les deux dirigeants ont une bonne relation de travail; **a relaxed w. environment** un milieu professionnel détendu **5 w. agreement** modus vivendi *m*; **to have a w. knowledge of French/the law** posséder une connaissance suffisante du français/ du droit ▪ **N 1** *(work)* travail *m*; **w. at home** le travail à domicile **2** *(of mine, forest)* exploitation *f*; *Min* **workings** chantiers *mpl* d'exploitation; **old mine workings** anciens chantiers d'exploitation d'une mine **3** *(operation) (of machine etc)* manœuvre *f* **4** *(mechanism) (usu pl)* **workings** mécanisme *m*, rouages *mpl*; *(of organization, system)* rouages; **I can't fathom the workings of her mind** je ne comprends pas ce qui se passe dans sa tête

▸ ▸ *Fin* **w. account** compte *m* d'exploitation; *Acct* **w. assets** actif *m* circulant; *Fin* **w. capital** fonds *mpl* de roulement, capital *m* de roulement; *Fin* **w. capital cycle** cycle *m* du besoin en fonds de roulement; *Fin* **w. capital fund** compte d'avances; **the w. class** la classe ouvrière; **the w. classes** la classe ouvrière; **w. copy** *(of document, text)* copie *f* de travail; *Comput* **w. file** fichier *m* de travail; **w. girl** *(prostitute)* professionnelle *f*; **w. lunch** déjeuner *m* d'affaires *ou* de travail; **w. majority** majorité *f* suffisante; *Br* **w. men's club** = club *m* pour ouvriers; **w. model** modèle *m* qui fonctionne; **w. mother** mère *f* de famille qui travaille; *Math* **w. out** *(of problem)* résolution *f*; **w. party** *(committee for study)* groupe *m* de travail; *(for enquiry)* commission *f* d'enquête; *(group of prisoners, soldiers)* groupe *m* de travail; **w. speed** vitesse *f* de régime; **w. theory** théorie *f* qui donne des résultats; **w. title** titre *m* provisoire; **w. woman** *(worker)* ouvrière *f*, employée *f*, *(woman with job)* femme *f* qui travaille

working-class **ADJ** *(family etc)* ouvrier; *(accent)* prolétaire, *Fam* prolo; **he's very w.** il fait très prolétaire

workload ['wɜːkləʊd] **N** quantité *f* de travail; **to have a heavy w.** avoir beaucoup de travail

workman, *pl* **workmen** ['wɜːkmən] **N** ouvrier *m*; **he's a good/bad w.** c'est un bon/ mauvais ouvrier; *Prov* **a bad w. always blames his tools** les mauvais ouvriers ont toujours de mauvais outils; **workmen's compensation** indemnité *f* d'invalidité (pour les ouvriers)

workmanlike ['wɜːkmənlaɪk] **ADJ** *(job)* bien fait, de professionnel; **to do sth in a w. manner** faire qch de façon professionnelle; **w. performance** représentation *f* honnête

workmanship ['wɜːkmənʃɪp] **N** *(of sth made)* travail *m*; *(of clothes)* façon *f*; **sound w.** fabrication *ou* exécution soignée; **fine *(piece of)* w.** beau travail; **the w. on this furniture is superb** ce meuble est fait de façon superbe; **poor w.** travail de mauvaise qualité; **he was famous for his w.** il était connu pour la finesse de son travail; **Swiss w. is second to none** la fabrication suisse est la meilleure du monde; **you don't get any w. these days** la qualité n'est plus ce qu'elle était

workmate ['wɜːkmeɪt] **N** *esp Br* collègue *mf* de travail

work-out **N** *Sport* séance *f* d'entraînement

workpeople ['wɜːkpiːp(ə)l] **NPL** ouvriers *mpl*

workplace ['wɜːkpleɪs] **N** lieu *m* de travail

workroom ['wɜːkruːm] **N** atelier *m ou* salle *f* de travail

workshare ['wɜːkʃeər] **N** travail *m* en temps partagé; *(person)* travailleur, -euse en temps partagé; **workshares are becoming more common** le partage du travail devient de plus en plus courant

worksharing ['wɜːkʃeərɪŋ] **N** partage *m* du travail; **we have a w. arrangement** nous avons un système de partage du travail; **w. is becoming popular** le partage du travail est de plus en plus courant

workshop ['wɜːkʃɒp] **N** atelier *m*; **a music/ an acting w.** un atelier de musique/de théâtre

workshy ['wɜːkʃaɪ] **ADJ** fainéant; **to be w.** bouder *ou* renâcler à la besogne

workspace ['wɜːkspeɪs] **N** *Comput* espace *m* de travail

workstation ['wɜːksteɪʃən] **N** *Comput* station *f ou* poste *m* de travail

worktable ['wɜːkteɪb(ə)l] **N** table *f* de travail; *Sewing* table à ouvrage

worktop ['wɜːktɒp] **N** *(in kitchen)* plan *m* de travail

work-to-rule **N** *Ind* grève *f* du zèle; **to operate a w.** faire une grève du zèle

workweek ['wɜːkwiːk] **N** *esp Am* semaine *f* de travail; **a four-day w.** une semaine (de travail) de quatre jours; **the forty-hour w.** la semaine de quarante heures

WORLD [wɜːld] **N 1** monde *m*; **in this w.** en ce monde; **the other** *or* **next w.**, **the w. to come** l'autre monde; *Rel* **the w.**, **the flesh and the devil** le monde, la chair et le diable; **he's not long for this w.** il n'en a pas pour longtemps à vivre; **to bring a child into the w.** *(of mother, midwife, doctor)* mettre un enfant au monde; **she came into the w. on 22nd May 1973** elle est venue au monde le 22 mai 1973; **he wants the best of both worlds** il veut tout avoir; **the end of the w.** la fin du monde; *Fam* **it's not the end of the w.** ce n'est pas la fin du monde, ce n'est pas une catastrophe; *Rel* **w. without end** pour les siècles des siècles; **the whole w.** le monde entier; **there isn't a nicer spot in the whole w.** il n'y a pas d'endroit plus agréable au monde; **to be alone in the w.** être seul au monde; **you're not the only person in the w.!** tu n'es pas seul au monde!; **the happiest man in the w.** l'homme le plus heureux du monde; **he's the w.'s worst letter-writer** il n'y a pas pire correspondant que lui au monde; **you're the w.'s worst!** il n'y a pas pire que toi!; **she lives in a w. of her own** elle vit dans un monde à part; **you live in a dream** *or* **fantasy w.** tu vis dans un monde imaginaire; **the w. we live in is not like that** le monde dans lequel nous vivons n'est pas comme ça; **it's a different w. up north** c'est complètement différent au nord; **the book takes us into a w. of corruption and intrigue** le livre nous entraîne dans un monde de corruption et d'intrigues; *Fam* **it's out of this w.** c'est (quelque chose d')extraordinaire *ou* épatant; *Fam* **it was out of this w.** *(of experience, holiday etc)* c'était fabuleux; *Fam* **the mountains were out of this w.** les montagnes étaient d'une beauté extraordinaire; **what in the w. is the matter with you?** que pouvez-vous bien avoir?; **where in the w. is that?** où est-ce que ça peut bien être?; **I wouldn't do it for (anything in) the w.** je ne le ferais pour rien au monde; **nothing in the w. could make me leave** rien au monde ne pourrait me faire partir; **what I want most of all in the w. is for you to be happy** ce que je souhaite le plus au monde, c'est que tu sois heureux; **it's**

been happening ever since the w. began ça se passe comme ça depuis que le monde est monde; **to go round the w.** faire le tour du monde; **round-the-w. trip** *or* **tour** voyage *m* autour du monde; **he has seen the w.** il a vu du pays; **map of the w.** carte *f* du monde; *(in two hemispheres)* mappemonde *f*, **(all) the w. over, all over the w.** dans le monde entier; **people are the same the w. over** les gens sont partout pareils; **to the end of the w.** jusqu'au bout du monde; **it's a small w.!** (que) le monde est petit!; **the Old/New W.** l'ancien/le nouveau monde; **the ancient** *or* **classical w.** l'antiquité *f*; **the English-speaking w.** le monde anglophone; **the richest nation in the w.** la nation la plus riche au monde

2 *(society)* monde *m*; **it's the way of the w.** ainsi va le monde; **what is the w. coming to?** où allons-nous?; **man of the w.** homme *m* qui connaît la vie *ou* qui a l'expérience du monde; **she doesn't care what the w. thinks** elle se moque de ce que les gens pensent; **he's gone up in the w.** il a fait du chemin; **to come down in the w.** déchoir; **all the w. knows** c'est bien connu, tout le monde le sait; *Fam* **the w. and his wife seemed to be there** tout le monde sans exception semblait être présent; **the singer had the w. at her feet** la chanteuse avait tout le monde à ses pieds

3 *(circle, field)* **the w. of literature** *or* **of letters, the literary w.** le milieu *ou* monde littéraire; **the theatrical w.** le milieu *ou* monde du théâtre

4 *(great deal)* **that will do you a w. of good** cela vous fera le plus grand bien; **there's a w. of difference between ...** il y a une différence énorme entre ...; **their opinions are worlds apart** leurs opinions sont totalement différentes; **she thinks the w. of him** elle l'admire énormément; **she means the w. to them** elle compte énormément à leurs yeux; **I'd give the w. to know what he's thinking** je donnerais n'importe quoi pour savoir ce qu'il pense; **they kept on talking, for all the w. as if nothing had happened** ils ont continué à parler comme s'il ne s'était rien passé

▸▸ **the W. Bank** la Banque mondiale; **w. champion** champion *m* du monde; **w. championship** championnat *m* du monde; **the W. Cup** la Coupe du monde; **w. domination** domination *f* du monde; **they have w. domination in gymnastics** ils dominent le monde de la gymnastique; **W. Economic Forum** Forum *m* économique mondial; **W. Fair** exposition *f* universelle; **W. Food Programme** Programme *m* alimentaire mondial; **the W. Health Organization** l'Organisation *f* mondiale de la santé; **w. history** histoire *f* universelle; **w. map** carte du monde; *(in two hemispheres)* mappemonde *f*; *Com* **w. market** marché *m* mondial *ou* international; **w. opinion** l'opinion internationale; **w. politics** politique *f* mondiale; **w. power** puissance *f* mondiale; **w. record** record *m* mondial; *Fin* **w. reserves** réserves *fpl* mondiales; **w. rights** droits *mpl* d'exploitation pour le monde entier; **the W. Series** = le championnat américain de baseball; *Radio* **the W. Service** = service *m* étranger de la BBC; **w. television** mondovision *f*, **w. trade** commerce *m* international; **the W. Trade Organization** l'Organisation mondiale du commerce; **w. tour** voyage autour du monde; **w. war** guerre *f* mondiale; *Comput* **the W. Wide Web** le World Wide Web

---

world-beater N **a w.** le meilleur/la meilleure du monde, le leader mondial; **we've got a real w. here** c'est le nouveau leader mondial

world-beating [-bi:tɪŋ] ADJ meilleur du monde; **of w. quality** d'une qualité inéga-

lée; **the new w. X52** le X52, nouveau leader mondial

world-famous ADJ de renommée mondiale, célèbre dans le monde entier

worldliness ['wɜːldlɪnɪs] N **1** *(knowledge of world)* connaissance *f* du monde; **there was an air of w. about her** elle avait l'air de quelqu'un qui a l'expérience du monde **2** *(materialism)* matérialisme *m*, attachement *m* aux biens de ce monde

worldly ['wɜːldlɪ] ADJ **1** *(of this world)* de ce monde, matériel; **all his w. goods** toute sa fortune; **he's a child in w. matters** il n'a aucune expérience du monde; **w. pleasures** les plaisirs de ce monde; **w. wisdom** la sagesse du monde *ou* du siècle **2** *(knowledgeable)* qui a l'expérience du monde, qui connaît le monde; **she was very w. for one so young** elle avait une bien grande expérience du monde pour quelqu'un d'aussi jeune **3** *(materialistic)* matérialiste

worldly-wise ADJ qui a l'expérience du monde, qui connaît le monde; **with a w. air** avec l'air de quelqu'un qui connaît le monde

world-weary ADJ las, *f* lasse de ce monde

worldwide ['wɜːldwaɪd] ADJ mondial, -aux ADV dans le monde entier; **the Olympics are watched w.** on regarde les Jeux Olympiques dans le monde entier

▸▸ **w. rights** droits *mpl* d'exploitation pour le monde entier

WORM [wɜːm] *Comput* (*abbr* **write once read many times**) WORM

worm [wɜːm] N **1** ver *m*; *(maggot)* asticot *m*; *Fig* **the w. has turned** j'en ai/elle en a/*etc* assez de se laisser mener par le bout du nez; *Fig* **even a w. will turn** il y a une limite à tout; **he's a w.** c'est un minable; **w.'s-eye view** *(from below)* perspective *f* vue d'en bas; *(from lowly position)* perspective au ras des pâquerettes; *Cin, Phot, TV* contre-plongée *f*, *pl* contre-plongées; **to get a w.'s-eye view of the theatre/catering industry** voir le monde du théâtre/de la restauration au ras des pâquerettes *ou* d'un point de vue restreint; *Fig* **the w. in the bud** le ver dans le fruit; **that's opening a real can of worms** nous allons nous fourrer dans un véritable guêpier; *Med, Vet* **to have worms** avoir des vers; *Fam* **to be food for worms** bouffer les pissenlits par la racine; **meal w.** ver de farine

2 *Tech (of screw)* filet *m*; **w. and roller steering** direction *f* à vis et galet

3 *Comput (invasive program)* ver *m*

VT **1** **he wormed himself** *or* **his way along the tunnel** il a avancé dans le tunnel en rampant *ou* en se tortillant; **to w. one's way out of/into sth** se faufiler hors de/dans qch; *Fig* **I'd like to see her w. her way out of that one** j'aimerais bien voir comment elle va s'en tirer; **to w. oneself into sb's favour/confidence** s'insinuer dans les bonnes grâces de qn/la confiance de qn; **to w. a secret out of sb** tirer un secret de qn, arracher un secret à qn; **I'll w. it out of him** je saurai lui tirer les vers du nez

2 *Vet* **to w. a dog** débarrasser un chien de ses vers

▸▸ *Tech* **w. drive** transmission *f* par vis sans fin; *Tech* **w. gear** engrenage *m* de vis sans fin; **w. powder** poudre *f* à vers, poudre *f* vermifuge; **w. tablets** comprimés *mpl* vermifuges

wormcast ['wɜːmkɑːst] N déjection *f* de ver de terre

wormeaten ['wɜːmiːtən] ADJ *(wood)* vermoulu; *(fruit)* véreux; *Fig (hat, slippers)* miteux

wormhole ['wɜːmhəʊl] N *(in wood, ground)* trou *m* de ver; *(in cloth, wood)* piqûre *f* (de ver)

wormwood ['wɜːmwʊd] N *Bot* armoise *f* (amère); *Lit* **life to him was gall and w.** la vie pour lui n'était qu'amertume et dégoût

wormy ['wɜːmɪ] ADJ *(furniture)* infesté *ou* plein de vers; *(fruit)* véreux; *(wood, cloth)* piqué des vers

worn [wɔːn] PP *see* **wear**

ADJ **1** *(weary)* las, *f* lasse; **w. with anxiety** usé par les soucis **2** *(with use) (shoes, edges etc)* usé

worried ['wʌrɪd] ADJ **1** *(look, expression, letter)* inquiet, -ète; *(person)* tracassé, soucieux; **I'm w. about this** cela m'inquiète *ou* me tracasse; **he was w. by these developments** ces développements l'inquiétaient; **she's w. about the car** elle est inquiète au sujet de la voiture; **they're w. sick about her** ils sont malades d'inquiétude à son sujet; **he looks w.** il a l'air préoccupé *ou* soucieux **2** *(weaker sense)* **I was w. it would be the wrong size** j'avais peur que ce ne soit pas la bonne taille

worriedly ['wʌrɪdlɪ] ADV avec inquiétude

worrier ['wʌrɪər] N anxieux, -ieuse; **he's such a w.** il se fait tellement de soucis; **don't be such a w.** arrête de t'inquiéter comme ça

worrisome ['wʌrɪsəm] ADJ tracassant, inquiétant

worry ['wʌrɪ] N souci *m*, tracas *m*; **financial worries** soucis d'argent; **it's causing me a lot of w.** cela m'inquiète beaucoup; **that's the least of my worries** c'est le moindre *ou* le dernier de mes soucis; *Fam* **what's your w.?** qu'est-ce qui ne va pas?; *Austr Fam* **no worries!** pas de problème!

VT **1** *(cause anxiety to)* inquiéter; **these events worried her greatly** ces événements l'ont beaucoup inquiétée; **that boiler worries me, suppose it blows up?** la chaudière m'inquiète, si elle explosait?; **Janet worries me sometimes, she's not like other little girls** Janet m'inquiète parfois, elle n'est pas comme les autres petites filles; **something is worrying her** il y a quelque chose qui la préoccupe *ou* qui la travaille; **tell me what's worrying you** dites-moi ce qui vous préoccupe; **it doesn't w. me what other people think** je ne me soucie pas de ce que les autres pensent; **it worried him that he was getting older** le fait de vieillir le préoccupait; **it doesn't seem to w. you if other people get hurt** que d'autres souffrent ne semble pas te préoccuper; **doesn't it w. you, your daughter being out this late?** ça ne vous inquiète pas que votre fille ne soit pas rentrée à cette heure tardive?; **it doesn't w. her who she upsets** elle ne se préoccupe pas des gens qu'elle froisse; **it worries me to think of them all on their own** ça m'inquiète de penser qu'ils sont tout seuls; **to w. oneself sick** *or* **to death about sb/sth** se rendre malade d'inquiétude *ou* mourir d'inquiétude au sujet de qn/qch

2 *(bother, disturb)* ennuyer; **he doesn't want to be worried with these minor details** il ne veut pas être embêté par ces petits détails; **don't w. him about it, I'll do it** ne l'ennuie pas avec ça, je m'en occuperai; **don't w. yourself about it** ne t'embête pas avec ça; **don't you w. your pretty little head about it** ne te fais pas de soucis, mignonne!

3 *(of dog, wolf)* *(harass)* *(sheep)* attaquer, harceler; *(bite)* secouer entre ses dents

VI se tracasser, s'inquiéter, se faire du souci *ou* de la bile *ou* du mauvais sang; **don't tell them, they'll only w.** ne le leur dis pas, ça ne fera que les inquiéter; **don't (you) w.!** not to w.! ne vous tracassez ou n'inquiétez pas!, ne vous en faites pas!; **sorry, I forgot the milk – don't w. (about it)** je suis désolée, j'ai oublié le lait – ne vous inquiétez pas (pour ça); **not to w.! it'll wash out** ce n'est rien, ça partira au lavage; **don't (you) w. about me** ne t'inquiète pas pour moi; **there's plenty more beer, don't you w.** il reste plein de bière, ne t'en fais pas; **you'll find out soon enough,** don't you w. vous n'allez pas tarder à le savoir, ne vous en faites pas; **there's** or **it's nothing to w. about** il n'y a pas de quoi se faire du souci; **it's only a scratch, nothing to w. about** ce n'est qu'une égratignure, pas de quoi s'inquiéter; **what's the use of worrying?** à quoi bon se tourmenter?; *Fam* **I should w.!** ce n'est pas mon affaire!

▸▸**w. beads** ≃ komboloï *m (pour s'occuper les mains)*

worryguts ['wʌrɪgʌts] N *Br Fam* bileux, -euse; **don't be such a w.** arrête de te tracasser autant

worrying ['wʌrɪɪŋ] ADJ tracassant, inquiétant

N tracas *m*, tourment *m*, inquiétude *f*; **all this w. will get you nowhere** à quoi bon se tourmenter?

worrywart ['wʌrɪwɔːt] N *Am Fam* = **worryguts**

WORSE [wɜːs]

ADJ	pire ▪ plus mauvais ▪ plus mal
N	pire
ADV	plus mal

ADJ *(comp of bad)* pire, plus mauvais (**than** que); **I'm a w. player than he is** or **him** or *Fml* **he** je joue plus mal que lui; **your problems are w. than ours** vos problèmes sont pires que les nôtres; **the situation was w. than (it had been) before** la situation était pire qu'avant; **there's nothing w. than arriving too early** il n'y a rien de pire que d'arriver trop tôt; **you're bad at French but he's w.** tu es mauvais en français mais il est plus mauvais que toi; **in w. condition** dans un plus mauvais état; **this is getting w. and w.** c'est ou ça va de mal en pis; **how are things? – no w. than before** comment ça va? – pas plus mal qu'avant; **things could be w.** ça pourrait être pire; **you're only making things** or **matters w.** vous ne faites qu'aggraver les choses; **to make things** or **matters w. ...** par ou pour surcroît de malheur ...; **it'll just make it w.** if you tell them ça ne va faire qu'empirer les choses si tu le leur dis; **you'll only make matters w. for yourself by offending them** tu ne feras qu'aggraver ton cas en les blessant; **it will be even w. for them if she finds out** ça va être encore pire pour eux si elle l'apprend; **it might** or **could have been w.** ça aurait pu être pire; **he escaped with nothing w. than a fright** il en fut quitte pour la peur; **what is w. ...** ce qui est plus grave ...; **to go from bad to w.** aller de mal en pis; **to get w.** *(deteriorate)* s'altérer; *(of illness)* s'aggraver, empirer; **the situation is getting w.** la situation s'aggrave; **his memory's got a lot w.** sa mémoire s'est beaucoup amoindrie; **how do you feel today? – w.** comment ça va aujourd'hui? – pire; **things will get w. before they get better** les choses vont empirer avant de s'améliorer; **I'm none the w. for it** je ne m'en trouve pas plus mal; **they were none the w. for their experience** ils ne s'en sont pas trouvés plus mal pour autant; **I think none the w. of him because he accepted** ce n'est pas parce qu'il a accepté que j'ai une moins bonne opinion de lui; **so much the w. for them!** tant pis pour eux!; **she was the w. for drink** elle était éméchée; **a sofa somewhat the w. for wear** un sofa un peu défraîchi; **he was rather the w. for wear** il était en mauvais état; **she was looking the w. for w.** elle avait l'air en travers; *Fam* **w. things happen at sea** ce n'est pas la fin du monde; **w. luck!** hélas!

N **there was w. to follow** or **to come** le pire était encore à venir; **I have seen w.** j'en ai vu bien d'autres, j'ai vu pire; **to change for the w.** s'altérer; **a change for the w.** un changement en mal; **he has taken a sudden turn for**

the w. son état s'est subitement aggravé

ADV *(comp of badly)* plus mal, *Lit* pis; **w. still** pire encore; **you could do (a lot) w.** *(than accept offer)* ce n'est vraiment pas si mal; *(than marry him or her)* tu aurais pu tomber plus mal; **he could do w. than accept their offer** il pouvait faire pire que d'accepter leur proposition; **to think w. of sb for doing sth** estimer qn moins pour avoir fait qch; **I don't think any w. of her for it** je n'ai pas une plus mauvaise opinion d'elle pour autant; **he is w. off than before** *(in worse situation)* sa situation a empiré; *(even poorer)* il est encore plus pauvre qu'avant; **the noise went on w. than ever** le vacarme a repris de plus belle

worsen ['wɜːs(ə)n] VT *(situation)* empirer; *(crisis, infection, bad mood)* aggraver; *(relations, driving conditions)* rendre plus difficile

VI *(of situation)* empirer, devenir pire; *(of health)* s'aggraver, empirer; **the situation has since worsened** la situation a empiré depuis; **the worsening situation** la situation qui est en train de s'aggraver; **her worsening memory** sa mémoire faiblissante

worsening ['wɜːs(ə)nɪŋ] N aggravation *f*

Worship ['wɜːʃɪp] N *esp Br (title)* **His W. the Mayor** monsieur le maire; **yes, your W.** oui, Votre Honneur

worship ['wɜːʃɪp] N **1** *Rel* culte *m*; **divine w.** le culte divin; **hours of w.** heures *fpl* des offices; **place of w.** lieu *m* consacré au culte; **to be an object of w.** être un objet d'adoration **2** *(love, adoration)* adoration *f*

VT *(-pp-)* **1** *Rel (god, idol)* rendre ou vouer un culte à, adorer; **to w. the golden calf** adorer le veau d'or **2** *(love, adore)* adorer, vouer un culte à; **she worshipped her mother** elle adorait sa mère; **he worships Elvis Presley** il voue un culte à Elvis Presley; **he worships the ground she walks on** il vénère jusqu'au sol qu'elle foule; **to w. money** vouer un culte à l'argent

VI **the church where his family has worshipped for years** l'église où sa famille fait ses dévotions depuis des années; **where does he w.?** à quelle église/à quel temple/à quelle synagogue/à quelle mosquée va-t-il?

worshipful ['wɜːʃɪpfʊl] ADJ *esp Br* honorable *(titre des membres des Corporations de Londres, des juges de paix)*

worshipper ['wɜːʃɪpə(r)] N adorateur, -trice; **the worshippers** *(in church)* les fidèles *mpl*

WORST [wɜːst]

ADJ	le pire ▪ le plus mauvais
N	le pire
ADV	le plus mal

ADJ *(superl of bad)* (le) pire, (le) plus mauvais; **that was his w. mistake** c'était sa plus grave erreur; **his w. enemy** son pire ennemi; **you're your own w. enemy** tu es ton plus grand ennemi; **the w. thing about it was the heat** le pire c'était la chaleur; **the w. weather was in the south** c'était dans le sud qu'il faisait le plus mauvais temps; **the w. possible situation** la pire situation possible

N **the w. that could happen** le pire ou la pire chose qui puisse arriver; **the w. of it is that ...** le pire c'est que ...; **that's the w. of cheap shoes** c'est l'inconvénient des chaussures bon marché; **when things are at their** or **the w.** quand les choses vont au plus mal; **to get the w. of it** *(in a fight)* avoir le dessous; **he's prepared for the w.** il s'attend au pire; **at the w., if it comes to the w., if the w. comes to the w.** au pire; **if it comes to the w., we can always take the train** dans le pire des cas, nous pouvons toujours prendre le train; **at the w. there's still the possibility of finding another actor** au pire, il y a tou-

jours la possibilité de trouver un autre acteur; **the w. is yet to come** on n'a pas encore vu le pire, et ce n'est pas fini; **do your w.!** allez-y!, essayez toujours!; **the w. is over** le plus mauvais moment est passé; **the w. of the storm is over** le plus fort de l'orage est passé; **the w. has happened!** c'est la catastrophe!; **and that's not the w. of it!** et ce n'est pas le pire!, et il y a pire encore!; **I'm at my w. in the morning** le matin est mon plus mauvais moment de la journée; **you haven't seen her at her w.** tu ne l'as pas vue dans ses mauvais moments; **even at her w. she is still a brilliant player** même quand elle joue mal, elle reste une joueuse fantastique

ADV *(superl of badly)* (le) plus mal, *Lit* (le) pis; **out of all of us I played w.** j'ai joué le plus mal de nous tous; **that frightened me w. of all** c'est ce qui m'a fait le plus peur; **the w. possible situation** la pire situation possible; **the elderly are the w. off** les personnes âgées sont les plus mal loties; **they are the w. paid** ce sont les plus mal payés; **the w. dressed men in Europe** les hommes les plus mal habillés d'Europe

VT *Old-fashioned* battre, vaincre, défaire; **to be worsted** avoir le dessous

worst-case ADJ **w. scenario** scénario *m* catastrophe; **what's the w. scenario?** quel est le pire qui puisse se produire?

worsted ['wʊstɪd] N *Tex* laine *f* peignée, peigné *m*

WORTH [wɜːθ] ADJ **1** *(having a value of)* valant; **to be w. ...** valoir ...; **to be w. a lot of money** *(of thing)* valoir cher, avoir beaucoup de valeur; *(of person)* être riche; **this ring is w. $500** cette bague vaut 500 dollars; **how much** or **what is this painting w.?** combien vaut ce tableau?; **it's not w. anything** cela ne vaut pas quatre sous; **the house isn't w. what they paid for it** la maison ne vaut pas le prix qu'ils ont payé pour l'avoir; **this cheque/contract isn't w. the paper it's printed on** ce chèque/contrat n'a aucune valeur; **she's w. ten of you** elle en vaut dix comme toi; **to be w. nothing** ne rien valoir; **what is the euro w.?** combien vaut l'euro?; **it's not w. much** cela ne vaut pas grand-chose; **to be w. sth to sb** valoir qch pour qn; **this old book is w. a lot to me** ce vieux livre a beaucoup de valeur pour moi; **what's my silence w. to you?** tu donnerais combien pour que je me taise?; **whatever it may be w.** quoi que cela vaille; **I'll tell you this for what it's w.** je vous dis ça pour ce que ça vaut; **she's a lawyer, for what that's w.** elle est avocate, pour ce que cela vaut; **for what it's w., I think they're wrong** pensez-en ce que vous voulez mais je crois qu'ils ont tort; **that's my advice, for what it's w.** c'est mon conseil, il vaut ce qu'il vaut; **it would be as much as my life is w.** ce serait risquer ma vie; **it would be more than my job's w.** ça me coûterait mon emploi, *Fig* **it's not w. the candle** le jeu ne vaut pas la chandelle

2 *(meriting)* **it's not w. the trouble** cela ne ou n'en vaut pas la peine; **is it w. while?, is it w. it?** cela (en) vaut-il la peine?; **it's not w. my/your/etc while doing it** ça ne vaut pas la peine que je le fasse/tu le fasses/etc; **it isn't w. it** ça ne vaut pas le coup; **don't get upset, he isn't w. it** ne te rends pas malade, il n'en vaut pas la peine; **you're w. it** tu en vaux la peine; **this novel is not w. reading** ce roman ne vaut pas la peine ou ne mérite pas d'être lu; **it's so late, it's not w. going** il est si tard, ça ne vaut pas la peine ou *Fam* le coup d'y aller; **something w. having** une chose précieuse; **without you, life wouldn't be w. living** sans toi, la vie ne vaudrait pas la peine d'être vécue; **your life won't be w. living** *(if you get on the wrong side of him etc)* ça sera invivable pour toi; **it's the only thing that makes their lives w. living** c'est la seule chose qui donne de la valeur à leur vie; **it's w. thinking about** cela mérite réflexion; **it's w. knowing** c'est bon à savoir; **the castle is w. a visit** le château vaut la visite; **your friendship/opinion is w. a lot to me** ton amitié/ton opinion représente beaucoup pour moi

3 (having money) **he's w. millions** il est riche à millions; **that is all I am w.** voilà toute ma fortune; Fig **he was pulling for all he was w.** il tirait de toutes ses forces

N valeur f; **of great/little/no w.** de grande/de peu de/d'aucune valeur; **give me £40 w. of petrol** donnez-moi (pour) 40 livres d'essence; **to have/want one's money's w.** en avoir/en vouloir pour son argent; **a day's w. of food/water** un jour de vivres/d'eau; **an hour's w. of my time** une heure de mon temps; **she has no sense of her own w.** elle n'est pas consciente de sa propre valeur

---

worthily ['wɜ:ðɪlɪ] ADV (to live) dignement, honorablement; (to donate, sacrifice) honorablement

worthiness ['wɜ:ðɪnɪs] N mérite m

worthless ['wɜ:θlɪs] ADJ **1** (object) sans valeur, qui ne vaut rien **2** **he's completely w.** c'est un vaurien

> Attention: ne pas confondre avec l'adjectif **priceless**, qui signifie **inestimable**.

worthlessness ['wɜ:θlɪsnɪs] N **1** (of object) peu m de valeur **2** (of person) nature f méprisable

worthwhile [wɜ:θ'waɪl] ADJ qui en vaut la peine ou Fam le coup; **at last I've found a w. job** j'ai enfin trouvé un poste qui me donne satisfaction; **she didn't think it w. replacing the van** elle ne pensait pas que cela valait la peine de remplacer la camionnette

worthy ['wɜ:ðɪ] ADJ **1** (distinguished, meriting respect) digne; **a w. man** un homme respectable ou estimable; **a w. life** une vie honorable ou vertueuse **2** **w. of** (deserving, meriting) digne de; **surely my letter was at least w. of an answer?** ma lettre méritait quand même une réponse, non?; **w. of respect** digne de respect; **you're not w. of your father** tu n'es pas digne de ton père; **her remarks are w. of contempt** ses remarques sont dignes de mépris; **he is a w. winner** il a mérité sa victoire; **to be w. to do sth** être digne de faire qch; **I am not w. to kiss your hand** je ne suis pas digne de baiser ta main; **it is w. of note that …** il est à noter que …; **the town has no museum w. of the name** la ville n'a aucun musée digne de ce nom

N (of place) personnage m; Hum **the village worthies** les notables mpl du village

wotcher ['wɒtʃər] INT Br Fam salut!

WOULD [wʊd] MODAL AUX V VOIR GRAMMAIRE A57–8 (**I would, they would** etc are often contracted to **I'd** [aɪd], **they'd** [ðeɪd] etc, **would not** to **wouldn't** ['wʊd(ə)nt]) **1** (expressing future) **she told me she w. be there** elle m'a dit qu'elle serait là

2 (consent) **I wouldn't do it for anything** je ne le ferais pour rien au monde; **w. you pass the mustard please?** voudriez-vous bien me passer la moutarde?; **the wound wouldn't heal** la blessure ne voulait pas se cicatriser, la blessure ne se cicatrisait pas

3 (emphatic) **I quite forgot! – you would!** j'ai oublié! – c'est bien de vous! ou ça ne m'étonne pas de vous!; **you would insist on going** évidemment, il a fallu que tu insistes pour y aller; Fam **I wouldn't know** (I don't know) je ne saurais dire

4 (habit) **she w. often return home exhausted** elle rentrait souvent très fatiguée

5 (conjecture) **w. that be your cousin you have in mind?** c'est à votre cousin que vous pensez?; **that w. be your job, am I right?** et ce serait toi qui t'occuperais de cela, non?

6 (wish) vouloir; **what w. you have me do?** que voulez-vous que je fasse?; **he w. if he could** il le ferait s'il le pouvait; Lit **w. (that) I were a bird!** je voudrais être un oiseau!; **w. to God it wasn't true!** plût à Dieu que cela ne fût pas vrai!

7 (conditional) **she w. come if you invited her** elle viendrait si vous l'invitiez; **had he or if he had let go, he w. have fallen** s'il avait lâché prise il serait tombé VOIR GRAMMAIRE A52–3; B34

would-be ADJ prétendu; Pej soi-disant; (housebuyer, student) potentiel; (musician, actor) en herbe; **troops seized the w. assassin** les militaires ont attrapé l'assassin avant qu'il ne commette le crime; **the w. burglar was tied up to a chair** le cambrioleur, pris sur le fait, était attaché à une chaise

wound¹ [wu:nd] N **1** Med blessure f; **bullet w.** blessure par balle **2** Fig plaie f; **to reopen a w.** ou **an old w.** rouvrir une plaie; **to rub salt in the w.** retourner le fer ou le couteau dans la plaie

VT **1** blesser; **to be badly wounded** être gravement blessé; **wounded in the shoulder** blessé ou atteint à l'épaule **2** Fig (of accusation etc) blesser; **to w. sb's pride** blesser qn dans son amour-propre; **to w. sb's feelings** blesser les susceptibilités de qn, froisser ou heurter qn; **my feelings were wounded** j'ai été froissé ou heurté

VI causer une blessure

wound² [waʊnd] PT, PP see **wind²**

wounded ['wu:ndɪd] ADJ **1** blessé; **the w. man** blessé **2** Fig (feelings, pride) blessé

NPL **the w.** les blessés mpl

wounding ['wu:ndɪŋ] ADJ blessant; **he found it w. to his pride** cela a blessé son amour-propre

wove PT see **weave**

woven PP see **weave**

wow¹ [waʊ] Fam INT oh là là!

N (success) succès m fou; **it's a w.** c'est sensationnel; **this is a w. of a show** c'est un spectacle sensationnel

VT emballer

wow² N (in sound system) pleurage m

WP [dʌb(ə)lju:'pi:] N Comput **1** abbr **word processing 2** abbr **word processor**

wp (abbr **weather permitting**) si le temps le permet

WPC [dʌb(ə)lju:pi:'si:] N Br (abbr **woman police constable**) femme-agent f, pl femmes-agents

wpm [dʌb(ə)lju:pi:'em] (abbr **words per minute**) mots par minute

WRAC [ræk] N Br (abbr **Women's Royal Army Corps**) ≃ AFAT

wrack¹ [ræk] N (seaweed) varec(h) m

wrack² N = **rack¹**

WRAF [ræf] N Br Mil (abbr **Women's Royal Air Force**) = section f féminine de l'armée de l'air britannique

wraith [reɪθ] N apparition f

wraithlike ['reɪθlaɪk] ADJ (appearance) semblable à une apparition ou un spectre, spectral

wrangle ['ræŋɡ(ə)l] N dispute f, querelle f

VI se disputer, se quereller, se chamailler (over à propos de)

VT Am (livestock) garder

wrangler ['ræŋɡlər] N **1** (quarreller) querelleur, -euse **2** Am (cowboy) cowboy m **3** Cin (animal trainer) animalier m

wrangling ['ræŋɡlɪŋ] N (quarrelling) disputes fpl, querelles fpl; **there has been a lot of**

w. over who to give the job to il y a eu beaucoup de querelles pour décider à qui donner le poste

wrap [ræp] N (blanket) (for journey) couverture f; (shawl) châle m; (cloak) pèlerine f, manteau m; Fig **to keep sth under wraps** garder qch secret; Fig **the wraps were taken off the new car today** la voiture a été montrée au public pour la première fois aujourd'hui; **it's a w.!** Cin c'est dans la boîte!; Fam (it's complete) ça y est, c'est fini!

VT (-pp-) envelopper, emballer; **to w. sth in paper** envelopper ou empaqueter qch dans du papier; **the cheese was wrapped in plastic** le fromage était emballé ou enveloppé sous plastique; **would you like it wrapped?** (of gift) c'est pour offrir?; **to w. a baby in a shawl** emmitoufler un bébé dans un châle; Fig **wrapped in mystery** enveloppé ou entouré de mystère

VI **1** Comput (of lines) se boucler **2** Cin finir de tourner

▶ **wrap round** VT SEP **to w. sth round sth** enrouler ou entortiller qch autour de qch; **w. this blanket round you/your shoulders** enroule cette couverture autour de toi/de tes épaules; **he wrapped the bandage round my finger** il a enroulé le bandage autour de mon doigt; **the cable wrapped itself round the …** le câble s'est enroulé autour du …; Fam **he wrapped his car round a tree** il a encadré un arbre

▶ **wrap up** VT SEP **1** (parcel, present) envelopper; **to w. sth up in sth** envelopper qch dans qch; **w. yourself up well** (dress warmly) emmitoufle-toi bien; **wrapped up** (person) emmitouflé **2** Fig **to be wrapped up in sth** (absorbed) être uniquement préoccupé de qch; **he is wrapped up in his work** il est entièrement absorbé par son travail; **she is too wrapped up in herself/in her own problems** elle est trop préoccupée par elle-même/par ses propres problèmes; **they are wrapped up in each other** ils sont uniquement préoccupés l'un par l'autre **3** Fam (bring to an end) (deal, negotiations, discussion) conclure; **well that about wraps it up for today** voilà, c'est à peu près tout pour aujourd'hui

VI **1** (put on warm clothes) (bien) s'emmitoufler **2** Br Fam (stop talking) se taire; **w. up!** ferme-la!, écrase!

wraparound ['ræpəraʊnd] N = **wraparound** N

▶ ▶ **w. bumper** pare-chocs m enveloppant; **w. sunglasses** lunettes fpl panoramiques

wrapover ['ræpəʊvər] N (skirt) jupe f portefeuille

ADJ (dress, skirt etc) portefeuille inv

wrapped [ræpt] ADJ (bread, sweets etc) emballé

wrapper ['ræpər] N **1** (packaging) (papier m d')emballage m; (of sweet) papier m; (of cigar) emballage m; **her pocket was full of old sweet wrappers** sa poche était pleine de vieux papiers de bonbons **2** (of book) couverture f, couvre-livre m, pl couvre-livres; (to protect jacket) liseuse f, (of newspaper being mailed) bande f **3** Old-fashioned (dressing gown) saut-de-lit m, pl sauts-de-lit

wrapping ['ræpɪŋ] N (material) emballage m

▶ ▶ **w. paper** (for gift) papier m cadeau; (for parcel) papier d'emballage

wraparound ['ræpraʊnd] N (in word processing) bouclage m, renouement m (des mots)

▶ ▶ Aut **w. rear window** lunette f arrière panoramique; **w. windscreen** pare-brise m panoramique

wrath [rɒθ] N Lit courroux m; **the w. of God** la colère de Dieu

wrathful ['rɒθfʊl] ADJ Lit courroucé, en colère

wreak [ri:k] VT (havoc) entraîner; **to w. (one's) vengeance upon sb** exercer ou assouvir sa vengeance sur qn; **the hurricane**

wreaked terrible destruction on the island l'ouragan a entraîné de terribles destructions sur l'île

wreath [ri:θ, *pl* ri:ðz, ri:θs] N **1** *(of flowers)* couronne *f*, guirlande *f*; **(funeral) w.** couronne mortuaire; **w. of poppies** couronne de coquelicots; **he laid a w. on her grave** il a déposé une couronne sur sa tombe **2** *(of smoke, mist)* volute *f*

wreathe [ri:ð] VT **1** *(encircle)* enguirlander; *(sb's head)* couronner; **the mountain was wreathed with mist** la montagne était entourée de brouillard; **her face was wreathed in smiles** son visage était rayonnant **2** *(entwine) (flowers)* enrouler (**round** autour de) VI *(of smoke)* tourbillonner

wreck [rek] N **1** *(ship)* navire *m* naufragé, épave *f*; *(car, lorry, train, plane)* voiture *f*/camion *m*/train *m*/avion *m* accidenté(e), épave; **my car's a total w.** ma voiture est bonne pour la casse; **the burnt-out w. of a bus** les restes calcinés d'un bus; **human wrecks** épaves (humaines); *Fig* **to be a physical/nervous w.** avoir la santé détraquée/les nerfs détraqués; **the man's an emotional w.** le type est une loque, au niveau émotionnel; *Fig* **after two hours with those kids I was a total w.** après deux heures avec ces gamins j'étais complètement épuisé **2** *(destruction) (of ship)* naufrage *m*; **to be saved from the w.** échapper au naufrage VT **1** *(ship)* faire faire naufrage à, causer le naufrage de; **to be wrecked** *(of ship, person)* faire naufrage; **the ship was wrecked on these rocks** le bateau a fait naufrage sur ces rochers **2** *(car)* démolir; *(building)* démolir, détruire; **vandals have wrecked the building/train** les vandales ont abîmé le bâtiment/le train; **to w. one's health** se ruiner la santé **3** *Fig (undertaking)* faire échouer, saboter; *(person's hopes)* détruire, ruiner, briser; *(chances)* ruiner; **to w. sb's plans** faire échouer les projets de qn; **to w. sb's marriage** ruiner *ou* détruire le mariage de qn; **this defeat has wrecked the team's chances** cette défaite a anéanti les chances de l'équipe; **the accident wrecked her hopes** l'accident a anéanti ses espoirs; **you wrecked his life/career** tu as brisé sa vie/sa carrière

wreckage ['rekɪdʒ] N *(no pl) (of ship)* épave *f*; *(of aircraft, train, car)* débris *mpl*; **piece of w.** épave; **documents were found in the w.** on a trouvé des documents parmi les débris; *Fig* **she hoped to salvage something from the w. of her career** elle espérait sauver quelque chose de ce qui restait de sa carrière

wrecked [rekt] ADJ *Fam (drunk)* bourré, pété; *(on drugs)* défoncé, raide; *(exhausted)* crevé, claqué

wrecker ['rekər] N **1** *Constr (of buildings)* démolisseur *m* **2** *(salvager)* sauveteur *m* d'épaves **3** *Am Aut (vehicle)* dépanneuse *f*, camion *m* de dépannage; *(person)* dépanneur *m* **4** *Hist (person who causes shipwrecks)* naufrageur *m*, pilleur *m* d'épave

wrecking truck, wrecking car ['rekɪŋ] N *Am* camion *m* de dépannage, dépanneuse *f*

Wren [ren] N *Br Fam* = membre *m* du Women's Royal Naval Service; **the Wrens** = section *f* féminine de la marine britannique

wren [ren] N troglodyte *m*

wrench [rentʃ] N **1** *(twist)* mouvement *m* violent de torsion; **to give sth a w.** tordre qch violemment; **he gave his ankle a w.** il s'est fait une entorse; *(less serious)* il s'est foulé la cheville **2** *Fig (emotional)* **the separation was a terrible w.** la séparation fut un déchirement affreux; **it will be a w. to leave the old house** il m'en/nous en/*etc* coûtera de quitter la vieille maison **3** *(tool)* clef *f*; **adjustable w.** clef à ouverture variable, clef universelle

VT *(twist)* tordre *ou* tourner violemment; **to w. one's ankle/shoulder** se fouler la cheville/l'épaule; **to w. the lid open** forcer le couvercle; **to w. off/out** arracher *ou* enlever (avec un violent effort de torsion); **to w. sth (away) from sb** arracher qch à qn; **she wrenched herself free** d'une secousse elle se dégagea; *Fig* **nothing could w. her away from her book** rien ne pouvait l'arracher à son livre

wrest [rest] VT arracher (**from** à); **she wrested the knife from him** *or* **his grip** elle lui a arraché le couteau; **to w. a confession from sb** arracher un aveu à qn; **we could w. no meaning from the coded message** nous n'avons pu tirer aucun sens du message codé; **I managed to w. her attention away from the tennis** j'ai réussi à l'arracher au tennis qui occupait toute son attention

wrestle ['res(ə)l] VI **1** *(physically)* lutter (**with** avec, contre); **to w. together** lutter, se prendre corps à corps; **the two men wrestled briefly** les deux hommes ont brièvement lutté; *Fig* **to w. with one's umbrella** se (dé)battre avec son parapluie; *Fig* **he wrestled with the zip/knot in the darkness** il luttait avec la fermeture éclair®/le nœud dans le noir **2** *Fig* **to w. with** *(difficulties, temptation)* lutter contre; *(adversity)* être aux prises avec; *(problem)* s'attaquer à; **they've been wrestling with the problem for years** ils sont aux prises avec ce problème depuis des années; **to w. with one's conscience** être aux prises avec sa conscience VT lutter avec *ou* contre; **he wrestled his attacker to the ground** il a jeté son attaquant au sol dans la lutte

N *(fight)*, *Fig* lutte *f* (corps à corps), corps à corps *m* (**with** contre); **after a w. with the knot, she was free** après s'être débattue avec le nœud, elle était libre; *Fig* **after a w. with his conscience, he agreed** après une lutte avec sa conscience, il a accepté

► **wrestle down** VT SEP *(one's opponent)* terrasser *(à la lutte)*

wrestler ['reslər] N lutteur, -euse

wrestling ['reslɪŋ] N lutte *f*; *(professional)* catch *m*; **Sumo w.** lutte *f* Sumo
► ► **w. match** match *m* de catch

wretch [retʃ] N **1** *(pitiable person)* malheureux, -euse; **poor w.** pauvre diable *m* **2** *(despicable person)* misérable *mf*; **you w.!** misérable!; **you little w.!** petit fripon!

wretched ['retʃɪd] ADJ **1** *(miserable)* misérable; **to feel w.** *(ill)* être mal en train; *(depressed)* avoir le cafard; *(guilty)* s'en vouloir; **to lead a w. existence** mener une existence misérable; **to be in w. poverty** être dans une misère affreuse **2** *(bad, pitiful)* pitoyable, lamentable; *(meal)* triste, pauvre; **the animal/house was in a w. state** l'animal/la maison était dans un état lamentable; **this coffee is w. stuff!** ce café est abominable; **what w. weather!** quel temps abominable!, quel temps de chien!; **it's a w. business** c'est une affaire *ou* une histoire lamentable; **she's a w. singer** c'est une piètre chanteuse; **w. hovel** taudis *m* **3** *(despicable)* misérable; **it was a w. thing to do/say** c'est immonde d'avoir fait/dit ça **4** *Fam (expressing anger, contempt etc)* fichu; *Old-fashioned* damné, sacré; **I can't find that w. umbrella** je ne retrouve pas ce fichu parapluie

wretchedly ['retʃɪdlɪ] ADV **1** *(as intensifier)* *(cold, poor, unhappy)* terriblement, affreusement; **to be w. poor** être dans une misère affreuse; **to be w. ill** être malade à faire pitié **2** *(in an unhappy fashion)* de façon pitoyable, pitoyablement

wretchedness ['retʃɪdnɪs] N **1** *(misfortune)* misère *f* **2** *(sadness)* tristesse *f* **3** *(of clothes, living conditions)* extrême pauvreté *f*

wriggle ['rɪg(ə)l] N tortillement *m* du corps;

VT *(twist)* tordre *ou* tourner violemment; **to w. one's ankle/shoulder** se fouler la cheville/l'épaule; **to** w. one's ankle/shoulder
VI **1** *(of worm, person)* se tortiller; *(of fish)* frétiller; **stop wriggling!** arrête de t'agiter!; **to w. through a hedge** se faufiler à travers une haie (en se tortillant); **he managed to w. into the sweater** il a réussi à enfiler le pull en se tortillant; **to w. free** se libérer en se faufilant **2** *Fig* **to w. out of a difficulty** se tirer d'affaire; **I'd like to see him w. out of this one!** j'aimerais savoir comment il va s'en sortir!; **w. out of that one if you can!** à toi de t'en sortir!; **to try to w. out of it** chercher une échappatoire; **he tried to w. out of his promise** il a essayé de se dégager de sa promesse

VT *(fingers)* tortiller; *(legs)* agiter; **she wriggled her way along the tunnel** elle s'est faufilée le long du tunnel; *Fig* **to w. one's way out of a situation/a problem/a commitment** se dérober devant *ou* se dégager d'une situation/d'un problème/d'un engagement; *Fig* **I'd like to see him w. his way out of that!** j'aimerais bien voir comment il va se sortir de cette situation!

wriggler ['rɪglər] N **he's a terrible w.** il gigote tout le temps

wriggling ['rɪg(ə)lɪŋ] ADJ = **wriggly** N tortillement *m*; **a w. movement** un tortillement

wriggly ['rɪglɪ] ADJ *(person)* qui gigote; **the children started getting w.** les enfants commençaient à gigoter; **the fish was wet and w.** le poisson était humide et frétillant; **a w. worm** un ver qui se tortille

wring [rɪŋ] N **to give the clothes a w.** tordre le linge; *(by machine)* essorer le linge; **he gave my hand a w.** il m'a donné une vigoureuse poignée de main

VT *(pt, pp* wrung [rʌŋ]*)* tordre; *(washing)* tordre; *(by machine)* essorer; **do not w.** *(on garment label)* ne pas essorer; **to w. sb's hand** serrer (longuement) la main de qn; **to w. one's hands (in despair)** se tordre les mains (de désespoir); **to w. a bird's neck** tordre le cou à une volaille; *Fam* **I'd like to w. his neck** j'ai envie de lui tordre le cou; **to w. a secret from sb** arracher un secret à qn; **to w. money from sb** arracher *ou* extorquer de l'argent à qn; **to w. tears from sb** arracher des larmes à qn; **to w. the last drop of pathos from a situation** extraire la dernière goutte de pathos d'une situation

► **wring out** VT SEP *(washing)* tordre; *(by machine)* essorer; **to w. the water out** *(from clothes)* exprimer l'eau; **to feel wrung out** se sentir lessivé *ou* moulu

wringer ['rɪŋər] N essoreuse *f* (à rouleaux); **he put the clothes through the w.** il passa les vêtements à l'essoreuse; *Fig Fam* **to put sb through the w.** faire passer un mauvais quart d'heure à qn

wringing ['rɪŋɪŋ] ADJ **w. (wet)** *(clothes)* complètement trempé; *(person)* complètement trempé, trempé jusqu'aux os; **the shirt was w. with sweat** la chemise était trempée de sueur

N *(of washing)* tordage *m*; *(by machine)* essorage *m*; **she told us the news, with much w. of hands** elle nous a annoncé la nouvelle, en se tordant les mains

wrinkle ['rɪŋk(ə)l] N **1** *(on skin)* ride *f*; *(in cloth, paper, carpet)* faux pli *m* **2** *Old-fashioned Fam (tip)* renseignement *m* utile, tuyau *m*

VT *(skin)* rider, plisser; *(dress)* froisser, chiffonner, faire des plis à; **to w. one's forehead** froncer les sourcils; **to w. one's nose** froncer le nez; **her stockings were wrinkled** ses bas faisaient des plis

VI *(of skin)* se rider, se plisser; *(of dress)* se plisser, faire des plis; *(of fruit)* se rider, se ratatiner

wrinkled ['rɪŋk(ə)ld] ADJ *(forehead)* plissé;

(skin) ridé; *(dress)* froissé, chiffonné; *(fruit)* ridé, ratatiné; **a w. old man** un vieil homme (tout) fripé

wrinkly ['rɪŋklɪ] ADJ *(skin) (after bath)* fripé; *(with old age)* ridé, fripé; *(blouse)* froissé; **to go all w.** *(of fruit)* se ratatiner; *(of skin, fingers)* se friper, devenir tout fripé

N *esp Br Fam Pej, Hum (old person)* croulant, -ante

wrist [rɪst] N *(of hand, dress etc)* poignet m
▸▸ *Comput* **w. rest** repose-poignets m inv

wristband ['rɪstbænd] N **1** *(on shirt)* poignet m, manchette f **2** *(sweatband)* bracelet m en éponge; *Gym (of leather)* bracelet de force (en cuir) **3** *(of watch)* bracelet m

wristbone ['rɪstbəʊn] N *Anat* os m du carpe

wristlet ['rɪstlɪt] N bracelet m

wristlock ['rɪstlɒk] N *(in wrestling)* clef f de poignet; **to put a w. on sb** faire une clef de poignet à qn

wristwatch ['rɪstwɒtʃ] N montre-bracelet f, pl montres-bracelets, bracelet-montre m, pl bracelets-montres

writ¹ [rɪt] N *Law* acte m judiciaire, mandat m, ordonnance f; *(summons)* assignation f; **to serve a w. on sb, to issue a w. against sb** assigner qn (en justice); **his w. no longer runs in this part of the country** cette région n'est plus sous son pouvoir; *Rel* **Holy W.** les saintes Écritures fpl, l'Écriture sainte
▸▸ **w. of attachment** ordonnance de saisie; **w. of possession** envoi m en possession

writ² PP *see* **write**

WRITE [raɪt] *(pt* **wrote** [rəʊt]; *pp* **written** ['rɪt(ə)n], *Arch* **writ** [rɪt]) VT **1** *(one's name, novel, letter, piece of music etc)* écrire; *(article)* rédiger; *(cheque)* faire, écrire; *Com* libeller; **can I w. you a cheque for it?** est-ce que je peux vous faire un chèque?; **w. the answer in the space provided** écrivez la réponse dans l'espace réservé à cet effet; **that was not written by me** cela n'est pas écrit de ma main; **do you w. it with a capital?** ça s'écrit avec une majuscule?, ça prend une majuscule?, tu l'écris avec une majuscule?; **the paper is written all over** la feuille est couverte d'écritures; **embarrassment was written all over her (face)** la gêne se lisait sur son visage; **his guilt was written on his face** sa culpabilité se lisait sur son visage; *Fam* **he's got journalist written all over him** on voit tout de suite que c'est un journaliste; *Fig* **writ large** *(obvious)* écrit en gros, écrit en grosses lettres; **this is Conservative policy writ large** c'est la politique conservatrice tout crachée; **it is written that …** il est écrit que …; *Comput* **to w. sth to disk** écrire qch sur disque

2 *esp Am (write a letter to)* écrire à; **I wrote them to complain** je leur ai écrit pour me plaindre

VI écrire; **w. and tell me what you think** écris pour me dire ce que tu en penses; **she writes well** *(of author)* elle écrit bien; *(expresses herself well in writing)* elle a un beau style; *(has good handwriting)* elle a une belle écriture; **he can w. in Italian** il sait écrire l'italien; **they can read and w.** ils savent lire et écrire; **please w. in black ink** prière d'écrire en noir; **this pen won't w.** ce stylo ne marche pas *ou* n'écrit pas; **she writes** *(is an author)* elle écrit; **to w. for children** écrire des livres pour enfants; **to w. for a paper** écrire dans *ou* collaborer à un journal; **he writes on** *or* **about gardening** il écrit des articles sur le jardinage; **to w. to sb** écrire à qn; **I wrote (to them) to complain** je leur ai écrit pour me plaindre; **we still w.** *(to each other)* nous nous écrivons toujours; **he writes home regularly** il écrit à sa famille régulièrement; *Fig* **that's nothing to w. home about** il n'y a pas de quoi s'en relever la

nuit *ou* s'extasier; **w. for our catalogue/more information** nous écrire pour obtenir un catalogue/plus d'informations
▸▸ *Comput* **w. access** accès m en écriture; *Comput* **w. area** zone f d'écriture; *Comput* **w. density** densité f d'écriture; *Tech* **w. head** tête f d'enregistrement; *Comput* **w. protection** protection f contre l'écriture *ou* en écriture; *Comput* **w. speed** vitesse f d'écriture

▸ **write away for** VT INSEP écrire pour demander; **w. away for a free sample** écrire pour obtenir un échantillon gratuit

▸ **write back** VI répondre; **she wrote back to say that …** elle a répondu (à la lettre) pour dire que …

▸ **write down** VT SEP **1** *(in order to remember)* noter; *(one's name)* écrire; **to w. down one's thoughts/ideas** mettre ses pensées/ses idées par écrit
2 *Fin (capital)* réduire; *Acct* déprécier

▸ **write in** VT SEP *(enter in writing) (correction)* insérer; **w. in the correct answer** mettez *ou* écrivez la bonne réponse; *Am* **to w. in a complaint** envoyer une plainte à la direction; *Am Pol* **to w. sb in** inscrire qn
VI *(send letter)* écrire; **many (of our) viewers wrote in with suggestions** de nombreux téléspectateurs nous ont envoyé leurs suggestions; **to w. in for** *(catalogue, free gift etc)* demander par courrier

▸ **write off** VT SEP **1** *Fin (capital)* réduire, amortir; *(debt)* amortir; **to w. £1000 off for wear and tear** déduire 1000 livres pour l'usure; *Com* **to w. off a bad debt** défalquer une mauvaise créance, passer une créance aux profits et pertes
2 *Br Fam* **my car was written off** ma voiture était bonne pour la casse; *Br* **she wrote off her father's car** elle a bousillé la voiture de son père; *Fam* **the critics wrote the play off** les critiques ont démoli la pièce; **they had written her off as a has-been** ils l'avaient cataloguée comme une ringarde
VI *(send letter)* écrire; **to w. off for a catalogue** demander *ou* commander un catalogue par courrier

▸ **write out** VT SEP **1** *(write in full)* transcrire; *(copy)* mettre au net; **w. this out neatly** écris *ou* recopie cela au propre; **to w. sth out in full** écrire qch en toutes lettres
2 *(write) (cheque)* faire; *Med (prescription)* rédiger
3 *TV, Radio (remove from script) (character)* supprimer (le rôle de)

▸ **write up** VT SEP **1** *(prepare) (news item, report)* écrire, rédiger; **w. up your notes** mettez vos notes au propre
2 *(praise)* faire l'éloge de
3 *(update) (diary, accounts)* mettre à jour
4 *Fin (capital, stocks)* augmenter; *Acct (asset)* revaloriser

write-back N *Acct* **w. of provisions** reprises fpl sur provisions

write-down N *Fin* dépréciation f

write-off N **1** *Acct* annulation f par écrit; **w. of expenditure** amortissement m de dépenses **2** *(car)* épave f; *Fam (project etc)* perte f sèche; **my car was a (complete) w.** ma voiture a été complètement détruite *ou* n'était plus qu'une épave

write-protect VT *Comput* protéger contre l'écriture

write-protected ADJ *Comput* protégé en écriture

writer ['raɪtər] N **1** *(professional)* écrivain m; *(of novel, scenario, letter etc)* auteur m (**of** de); **woman w.** femme f écrivain; **w.'s block** vertige m de la page blanche; **w.'s cramp** crampe f des écrivains; **the present w., the w. (of this letter)** celui qui écrit, l'auteur (de cette lettre); **I'm not a good letter w.** *(I don't write often)* la correspondance n'est

pas mon fort; *(I don't write well)* je n'ai pas la plume facile; **to be a good/bad w.** bien/mal écrire **2** *Scot Law* notaire m; **W. to the Signet** ≃ avoué m

writer-director N *Cin, TV* auteur-réalisateur, -trice, pl auteurs-réalisateurs, -trices

write-up N **1** *Journ* article m; **the play got a good w.** la pièce a eu une bonne critique **2** *Fin (of stock)* augmentation f de la valeur comptable

writhe [raɪð] VI *(of person)* se contorsionner; *(with pain)* se tordre; *(of snakes, worms)* grouiller; **to w. in agony** se tordre dans des souffrances atroces; **the remark made him w.** *(with shame, embarrassment)* en entendant la remarque, il ne savait plus où se mettre; *(with indignation, anger)* en entendant la remarque, il s'est raidi d'indignation/de colère; **the memory still makes me w. with embarrassment** ce souvenir me fait encore rougir

writing ['raɪtɪŋ] N **1** *(action)* écriture f; **the art of w.** l'art de l'écriture; **I'm very bad about letter w.** je suis très mauvais correspondant; **at the time of w.** au moment où j'écris/il écrit/etc; *Journ* à l'heure où nous rédigeons ceci; **that's my w.** *(handwriting)* c'est mon écriture; **his w. is bad** *(illegible)* il écrit mal; *Fig* **the w. is on the wall** la catastrophe est imminente; **the w. was on the wall for the Roman Empire** la fin de l'empire romain était imminente; **I could see the w. on the wall** je savais à quoi m'attendre; **in w.** *(to put sth, answer)* par écrit; **I won't be satisfied until I see it in w.** je ne serai pas satisfait tant que ce ne sera pas écrit noir sur blanc; **can I have that in w.?** est-ce que vous pouvez me mettre cela par écrit?; **to commit the facts to w.** consigner les faits par écrit; **to take up w.** *(of author)* commencer à écrire **2** *(work)* littérature f, œuvre f littéraire; **the writings of an author** les écrits mpl *ou* l'œuvre m d'un auteur; **selected writings** morceaux mpl choisis; **a fine piece of w.** *(passage)* un beau passage; *(book, article)* quelque chose de très bien écrit **3** *(style)* style m; **his w. has matured** son style a mûri
▸▸ **w. case** nécessaire m de correspondance; **w. desk** secrétaire m *(meuble)*; *Acct* **w. off** *(of debt)* amortissement m; **w. pad** bloc-notes m, pl bloc-notes; **w. paper** papier m à lettres; **w. table** secrétaire *(meuble)*

written ['rɪt(ə)n] PP *see* **write**
ADJ écrit; *(in writing)* par écrit; **w. confirmation** confirmation f écrite *ou* par écrit; **the w. word** le mot écrit; **w. consent** consentement m par écrit; **w. law** loi f écrite; *Sch etc* **w. examination** épreuve f écrite

written-down cost, written-down value N *Fin* valeur f amortie

WRNS [renz] N *Br Mil (abbr* **Women's Royal Naval Service)** = section f féminine de la marine britannique

WRONG [rɒŋ]

ADJ	mauvais **1, 2** ▪ faux **2** ▪ mal **1, 2, 4, 5** ▪ tort **3**
N	mal **1** ▪ tort **2, 3**
ADV	mal **1, 2**
VT	faire du tort à

ADJ **1** *(morally bad) (judgement etc)* mauvais; **it is w. to steal, stealing is w.** c'est mal de voler; **it was w. of you not to tell me!** c'était très mal de votre part de ne pas m'en parler!; **it is w. for people to have to pay for hospital care** il n'est pas normal que les gens doivent payer les soins hospitaliers; **it's w. that they should suffer because of other people's incompetence** il n'est pas normal qu'ils pâtissent de l'incompétence des autres

2 *(incorrect, mistaken)* faux, f fausse; *(atti-*

tude, sort, key, bus, road) mauvais; (answer) mauvais, incorrect; **my watch is w.** ma montre n'est pas à l'heure; **w. use of a word** emploi abusif d'un mot; **don't get the w. idea** ne te fais pas de fausses idées; **his ideas are all w.** il a des idées tout de travers; **to be in the w. place** ne pas être à sa place; **to drive on the w. side of the road** conduire du mauvais côté de la route; Fig **to get out of bed on the w. side** se lever du pied gauche; esp Br Fig **to get on the w. side of sb** se faire mal voir de qn; **your sock is the w. side out** ta chaussette est à l'envers; **to be (the) w. side up** être à l'envers; **to be on the w. side of forty** avoir (dé)passé la quarantaine; **to take the w. train** se tromper de train; also Fig **to back the w. horse** miser sur le mauvais cheval; **to take the w. road** se tromper de chemin ou de direction; **this is the w. road for Munich** ce n'est pas la bonne route pour aller à Munich; **she gave me the w. address** elle ne m'a pas donné la bonne adresse, elle m'a donné une mauvaise adresse; **to put sb on the w. track** mettre qn sur une fausse piste; **to be on the w. scent** or **track** suivre une mauvaise piste, faire fausse piste; **you've got the w. man**, Jack Taylor **isn't a murderer** vous faites erreur, Jack Taylor n'est pas un meurtrier; **to come at the w. time** venir à un mauvais moment ou mal à propos; **to do/say the w. thing** commettre un impair, dire/faire ce qu'il ne faut pas, Fam faire une gaffe, mettre les pieds dans le plat; **I'm the w. person to ask** il ne faut pas me demander ça à moi; **you're talking to the w. person** (ask sb else) ce n'est pas à moi qu'il faut demander ça; Tel **w. number** mauvais numéro m; **to dial the w. number** composer un mauvais numéro; **I think you've got the w. number** je crois que vous n'avez pas fait le bon numéro; **it was the w. number** (I didn't dial correctly) ce n'était pas le bon numéro; **who was that? – nobody, it was a w. number** qui était-ce? – personne, c'était une erreur de numéro ou un mauvais numéro; Mus **w. note** fausse note; Fig **her speech hit the w. note** son discours n'était pas dans la note

3 to be w. (of person) avoir tort, se tromper, être dans l'erreur; **they were w. to assume** or **in assuming that …** ils ont eu tort de supposer que …; **that's just where you are w.** c'est justement ce qui vous trompe, c'est justement là que vous vous trompez; **to be w. about sb/sth** se tromper sur le compte de qn/sur qch; **you were w. about the price** tu avais tort en ce qui concerne le prix; **I was w. about her** je me suis trompé sur son compte ou sur elle; **you were w. to contradict him** vous avez eu tort de le contredire

4 we went the w. way nous nous sommes trompés de chemin; **I was sent the w. way** on m'a mal dirigé; **if you want to impress him you're going the w. way about it!** si tu veux l'impressionner tu t'y prends mal!; **you're setting about it in the w. way** vous vous y prenez mal ou de travers; **to take sth the w. way** prendre quelque chose à contrepied; **it went down the w. way** (of food) je l'ai/il l'a/etc avalé de travers; **to stroke a cat the w. way** caresser un chat à rebrousse-poil

5 (amiss) **what's w.?** qu'est-ce qui ne va pas?; **is there something** or **anything w.?** quelque chose ne va pas?; **what's w. with you?** qu'avez-vous?, qu'est-ce qui ne va pas?; **what's w. with these people?** (that they don't understand) qu'est-ce qu'ils ont qui ne va pas, ces gens?; **there's something w. with me** (ill) j'ai quelque chose qui ne va pas; **there must be something w. with me** (that people don't like me) il doit y avoir quelque chose qui ne va pas chez moi; Fam **he's w. in the head** il a quelque chose qui ne

tourne pas rond dans sa tête, il est un peu timbré; **there was something w. with our car** nous avons eu des ennuis avec la voiture; **there's nothing w. with the engine** le moteur fonctionne normalement; **there's something w. somewhere** il y a quelque chose qui cloche ou qui ne tourne pas rond; **I hope there's nothing w.** j'espère qu'il n'est rien arrivé; Fam **what's w. with that?** qu'avez-vous à redire à cela?; **there's nothing w. about wanting a holiday without the kids** il n'y a pas de mal à vouloir des vacances sans les enfants; **what's w. with going to France?** quel mal y a-t-il à aller en France?; **what's w. with my idea?** qu'est-ce qu'elle a qui ne va pas, mon idée?

N 1 (immoral action) mal m; **to know right from w.** distinguer le bien du mal; **in her eyes he can do no w.** il trouve toujours grâce à ses yeux; **the president can do no w.** le président ne peut pas mal faire

2 (unjust action) tort m, injustice f; **to right a w.** réparer une injustice; **two wrongs do not make a right** on ne répare pas le mal par le mal; **to do sb w.**, **to do w. to sb** faire tort à qn; **you do her great w. in accusing her of not caring** tu lui as fait beaucoup de tort en l'accusant de se moquer

3 (mistake) **to be in the w.** (because of an action) être dans son tort; (be mistaken) avoir tort; **to put sb in the w.** mettre qn dans son tort

ADV 1 (morally) mal; **you did w.** vous avez mal agi

2 (incorrectly) mal, incorrectement; **to guess w.** mal deviner; **you've added it up w.** vous avez mal calculé; **you have spelt my name w.** vous avez mal orthographié mon nom; **she got the time/address/name w.** (was mistaken about) elle s'est trompée d'heure/d'adresse/de nom; (misunderstood) elle a mal compris l'heure/l'adresse/le nom; Fam **don't get me w.**, **I'm not saying …** comprenez-moi bien, je ne dis pas …; Fam **you've got me w.** vous m'avez mal compris; esp Am **to get in w. with sb** se faire mal voir de qn

3 to go w. (of mechanism) se dérégler, se détraquer; (of business) aller mal, aller de travers; (mistake route) se tromper de chemin, Fig se fourvoyer, faire fausse route; (go morally astray) se dévoyer, mal tourner; (be mistaken) se tromper, commettre une erreur; **then things started to go terribly w.** et puis les choses ont commencé à aller très mal; **his son went w.** son fils a mal tourné; **we went w. at that crossroads** nous nous sommes trompés à ce carrefour; **it's at the end of this road, you can't go w.** c'est au bout de cette route, vous ne pouvez pas vous tromper; **where I went w. was in being too kind to him** là où j'ai commis une erreur, c'est en me montrant trop gentil avec lui; **you can't go w. buying secondhand** vous ne faites pas d'erreur en achetant d'occasion, vous faites forcément le bon choix en achetant d'occasion; **the clock's gone w. again** la pendule s'est déréglée encore une fois; **something went w. with the lighting** nous avons/il a/etc eu un problème avec l'éclairage; **all our plans went w.** tous nos projets ont échoué; **things have gone w.** les choses ont mal tourné; **she used to be a normal, happy little girl, but something went w.** c'était une petite fille normale et heureuse mais quelque chose a mal tourné; **the space flight went disastrously w.** le vol spatial a tourné à la catastrophe

VT faire (du) tort à, léser, être injuste pour ou envers; **he feels wronged** il se sent lésé

wrongdoer ['rɒŋduːər] **N 1** (of immoral action) auteur m d'une injustice; **they did not**

regard themselves as wrongdoers ils ne se considéraient pas comme coupables **2** (of illegal action) malfaiteur m

wrongdoing ['rɒŋduːɪŋ] **N 1** (immoral action) (usu pl) **wrongdoings** méfaits mpl **2** (illegal action) infraction f à la loi

wrong-foot **VT** Sport prendre à contrepied; Fig prendre à l'improviste ou au dépourvu ou au pied levé

wrongful ['rɒŋfʊl] **ADJ** (unjust) injuste; (unjustified) injustifié; (illegal) illégal, -aux, illicite
▶▶ Law **w. arrest** arrestation f arbitraire; Ind **w. dismissal** renvoi m injustifié; **w. imprisonment** emprisonnement m injustifié

wrongfully ['rɒŋfəlɪ] **ADV** injustement, à tort, de façon arbitraire

wrong-headed **ADJ** buté

wrongly ['rɒŋlɪ] **ADV 1** (unjustly) à tort, à faux; **I've been w. accused** on m'a accusé injustement ou à tort ou à faux; **rightly or w.** à tort ou à raison **2** (incorrectly) mal, incorrectement; **to choose w.** mal choisir

wrongness ['rɒŋnɪs] **N 1** (incorrectness) erreur f, inexactitude f **2** (injustice) (of accusation etc) injustice f

wrote **PT** see **write**

wrought [rɔːt] **PT, PP** see **work**
ADJ (silver, gold) travaillé, ouvragé, façonné; (metal) ouvré, forgé; Fig **finely w. phrase** phrase finement ciselée
▶▶ **w. iron** fer m forgé

wrought-iron **ADJ** en fer forgé

wrought-up **ADJ** (nervous, anxious) anxieux; (angry, upset) en colère, dans tous ses états; **there's no need to get so w. about it!** pas la peine de vous faire de soucis pour ça!; **she's still pretty w. over her son's death** elle est encore très affectée par la mort de son fils

WRVS [dʌb(ə)ljuːɑːrviːˈes] **N** Br abbr **Women's Royal Voluntary Service**

wry [raɪ] **ADJ** (comp **wrier**, **wryer**) (smile, comment) ironique; (humour) pince-sansrire; **to pull a w. face** faire la grimace; **she's w. but never bitter** elle est désabusée mais jamais amère

wryly ['raɪlɪ] **ADV** (to remark etc) avec ironie; **to smile w.** avoir un sourire ironique; **her w. observed portrait** son portrait ironique

wt (abbr **weight**) p.

WTO [dʌb(ə)ljuːtiːˈəʊ] **N** (abbr **World Trade Organization**) OMC f

wulfenite ['wʊlfənaɪt] **N** wulfénite f

wunderkind ['wʌndəkɪnd, 'vʊndəkɪnt] **N** enfant mf prodige

wuss [wʊs] **N** Fam mauviette f, lavette f

wussy ['wʊsɪ] Fam **N** mauviette f, lavette f
ADJ mou, f molle, mollasson

WVa abbr **West Virginia**

WW abbr **World War**

WWF [dʌb(ə)ljuːdʌb(ə)ljuːˈef] **N** (abbr **World Wildlife Fund, Worldwide Fund for Nature**) WWF m

WWW [dʌb(ə)ljuːdʌb(ə)ljuːˈdʌb(ə)ljuː] **N** Comput (abbr **World Wide Web**) WWW m, W3 m

wych-elm [wɪtʃ-] **N** orme m blanc ou de(s) montagne(s)

wynd [waɪnd] **N** Scot venelle f

Wyo abbr **Wyoming**

WYSIWYG ['wɪzɪwɪg] **N** Comput (abbr **what you see is what you get**) tel écran-tel écrit m, tel-tel m, Wysiwyg m
▶▶ **W. display** affichage m tel écran-tel écrit ou tel-tel ou Wysiwyg

X, x [eks] N *(letter)* X, x *m*; **X marks the spot** l'endroit est marqué d'une croix; **for x number of years** pendant x années
▸ ▸ *Cin Formerly* **X (certificate) film** = film *m* interdit aux moins de 18 ans; **the film was an X** le film a été interdit aux moins de 18 ans; *Biol* **X chromosome** chromosome *m* x

x-axis N *Math* axe *m* des X, abscisse *f*

X-Dax ['eksdæks] N *St Exch* **the X-Dax (index)** le X-Dax, l'indice *m* X-Dax

xenon ['zenɒn] N *Chem* xénon *m*

xenophobe ['zenəfəʊb] N xénophobe *mf*

xenophobia [zenə'fəʊbɪə] N xénophobie *f*

xenophobic [zenə'fəʊbɪk] ADJ xénophobe

xerography [zɪə'rɒgrəfɪ] N xérographie *f*

Xerox® ['zɪərɒks] N photocopie *f*
VT photocopier

Xetra-Dax ['ekstrədæks] N *St Exch* **the X. index** l'indice *m* Xetra-Dax

XL ['ek'sel] *(abbr* **extra large)** XL

Xmas ['krɪsməs, 'eksməs] N *(abbr* **Christmas)** Noël *m*

XML [eksem'el] N *Comput (abbr* **Extensible Markup Language)** XML *m*

X-rated ADJ *Cin Formerly* interdit aux moins de 18 ans; *Fig* obscène, indécent

X-ray N **1** *(radiation)* rayon *m* X; *Fig Fam* **you must have X. eyes!** tu es médium! **2** *(picture)* radio *f*; *Med* **to have/take an X.** passer/faire une radio
VT *Med (person, chest)* radiographier; **to be**
X-rayed se faire radiographier, *Fam* passer à la radio
▸ ▸ *Med* **x. diagnosis** radiodiagnostic *m*; **X. machine** machine *f* à rayon X; *Med* **x. photograph** radiographie *f*, radio *f*; **X. photography** radiographie, radio; **X. therapy** radiothérapie *f*, *Med* **x. unit** service *m* de radiologie

xylograph ['zaɪləʊgrɑːf] N xylographie *f*

xylographic [zaɪləʊ'græfɪk] ADJ xylographique

xylography [zaɪ'lɒgrəfɪ] N xylographie *f*

xylophone ['zaɪləfəʊn] N *Mus* xylophone *m*

xylophonist [zaɪ'lɒfənɪst] N *Mus* joueur, -euse de xylophone

Y, y [waɪ] N *(letter)* Y, y m, i m grec; **two y's** deux y

▸▸ *Biol* **Y chromosome** chromosome m y

Y2K [waɪtuːˈkeɪ] ADJ *(abbr year 2000)* de l'an 2000; **Y. compliant** *or* **compatible** conforme à l'an 2000

yacht [jɒt] N yacht m; **(sailing) y.** voilier m; **racing y.** yacht de course

VI faire de la voile

▸▸ **y. club** yacht-club m, pl yacht-clubs; **y. race** régate f

yachting [ˈjɒtɪŋ] N voile f; **to go y.** faire de la voile;

▸▸ **y. cap** casquette f de yachtman

yachtsman, pl **yachtsmen** [ˈjɒtsmən] N yacht(s)man m, pl yacht(s)men; *(in yacht race)* régatier m; *(for amusement)* plaisancier m; **round-the-world y.** navigateur m qui fait/a fait/*etc* le tour du monde

yachtswoman, pl **yachtswomen** [ˈjɒtswʊmən, -wɪmɪn] N yacht(s)woman f, pl yacht(s)women; *(in yacht race)* régatière f; *(for amusement)* plaisancière f; **round-the-world y.** navigatrice f qui fait/a fait/*etc* le tour du monde

yack [jæk] *Fam* N jacasserie f; **to have a y. about sth/sb** jacasser au sujet de qch/qn; **it's ages since we've had a really good y.** ça fait longtemps qu'on ne s'est pas taillé une bonne bavette

VI jacasser; **it's y., y., y. all day long!** elle n'arrête/ils n'arrêtent/*etc* pas de jacasser toute la journée

yackety-yack [ˈjækətɪ-] ADV *Fam* **to go y.** jacasser

yah [jɑː] INT *(in affirmation)* oui (évidemment)

N *Fam (loud upper-class person)* bourge mf

yahoo [jəˈhuː] N *Fam* brute f

yak¹ [jæk] N *(animal)* ya(c)k m

yak² N, VI *Fam* = **yack**

yam [jæm] N *(plant, tuber)* igname f

yammer [ˈjæmər] *Fam* N boucan m; **a terrible y. of voices** un brouhaha terrible

VI *(complain)* pleurnicher, geindre; **what's he yammering on about?** *(going on about)* qu'est-ce qu'il raconte?

yang [jæŋ] N *Phil* yang m

Yank, Yankee [jæŋk, ˈjæŋkɪ] *Fam* N **1** *(from the US)* Ricain, -aine, Amerloque mf, Yankee mf **2** *Am esp Pej (from the Northern US)* = habitant, -ante des États du Nord

ADJ **1** *(from the US)* ricain, amerloque **2** *Am esp Pej (from the Northern US)* qui habite les États du Nord

yank [jæŋk] *Fam* N **to give sth a y.** tirer qch un bon coup; **she gave his hair a y.** elle lui a tiré les cheveux; *Vulg* **to have a y.** *(masturbate)* se tirer sur l'élastique, se taper sur la colonne

VT tirer (d'un coup sec); **to y. the door open**
ouvrir la porte d'un coup sec; **to y. sth loose/out/off** arracher qch d'un coup sec; **to y. out a tooth** arracher une dent (d'un seul coup); *Fam* **to y. sb's chain** *(tease)* faire marcher qn

VI *Vulg (masturbate)* se tirer sur l'élastique, se taper sur la colonne

yap [jæp] N **1** *(of dog)* jappement m **2** *Fam (mouth)* clapet m, gueule f; **shut your y.!** ferme ton clapet!, la ferme! **3** *Am Fam (idiot)* andouille f, truffe f; *(country bumpkin)* pécore mf, péquenaud, -aude

VI *(-pp-)* **1** *(of dog)* japper **2** *Fig Fam (of person)* jacasser; **the shop assistants were yapping away instead of serving** les vendeuses jacassaient au lieu de servir la clientèle; **what's he yapping on about now?** qu'est-ce qu'il est encore en train de raconter?

yapping [ˈjæpɪŋ] ADJ *(dog)* jappeur

N *(no pl)* **1** *(of dog)* jappement m; **I wish that dog would stop its y.!** si ce chien pouvait arrêter ses jappements! **2** *Fig Fam (of person)* jacasseries fpl

yappy [ˈjæpɪ] ADJ *Fam (dog)* jappeur

yard¹ [jɑːd] N **1** *(measurement)* yard m *(0,914m)*; *Can* verge f; **square y.** yard carré *(0,836m²)*; *Fig* **his face was a y. long** il faisait une tête de trois pieds de long; *Fig* **yards of statistics, statistics by the y.** des statistiques à n'en plus finir **2** *Naut (spar)* vergue f

yard² N **1** *(of house, farm, stable etc)* cour f; *Am (garden)* jardin m; *Sch* cour, préau m; *Austr (cattle enclosure)* parc m à bétail *ou* à bestiaux **2** *Ind (for working)* chantier m; **timber** *or* **lumber y.** chantier de bois; **builder's y.** chantier (de construction); *Naut* **repair y.** chantier de radoub; **(ship) y.** chantier naval; **naval (dock)yard,** *Am* **navy y.** chantier naval de l'État, arsenal m maritime *ou* de la marine **3** *(for storage)* dépôt m de marchandises **4** *Br Fam* **the Y.** *(Scotland Yard)* ≃ la Sûreté

▸▸ *Am* **y. sale** vide-greniers m inv; **y. work** jardinage m

yardage [ˈjɑːdɪdʒ] N ≃ métrage m

yardarm [ˈjɑːdɑːm] N *Naut* bout m de vergue

yardie [ˈjɑːdɪ] N *Fam* = membre m d'une organisation criminelle fondée en Jamaïque

yardman [ˈjɑːdmæn] N *Am* jardinier m

yardstick [ˈjɑːdstɪk] N *(ruler)* yard m; *Fig (standard of comparison)* critère m, point m de référence; *Fig* **to measure others by one's own y.** mesurer les autres selon ses propres valeurs

yarmulka [ˈjɑːmʊlkə] N *(Jewish skullcap)* kippa f

yarn [jɑːn] N **1** *Tex* fil m; *(cotton)* filé m **2** *Fam (unbelievable story)* histoire f à dormir debout; *(long story)* longue histoire; **to spin a y.** raconter une histoire à dormir debout

VI *Fam* débiter des histoires, bavasser
yarrow [ˈjærəʊ] N *(plant)* achillée f, millefeuille f

yashmak [ˈjæʃmæk] N *(Muslim veil)* litham m

yaw [jɔː] N *Naut* embardée f; *Aviat (movement m de)* lacet m

VI *Naut* faire une embardée; *Aviat* faire un *(mouvement de)* lacet

yawl [jɔːl] N *Naut (sailing vessel)* sloop m, yawl m; *(small boat)* yole f

yawn [jɔːn] N **1** bâillement m; **to give a y.** bâiller; **to let out a y.** laisser échapper un bâillement **2** *Fig (boring thing)* plaie f; **the book/film is one long y.** le livre/film est ennuyeux à mourir

VI **1** *(with tiredness etc)* bâiller *(with* de*)* **2** *Fig (of chasm etc)* être béant, béer; **the gulf yawned at his feet** le gouffre s'ouvrait *ou* béait à ses pieds

VT *Fam* **to y. one's head off** bâiller à se décrocher la mâchoire

yawning [ˈjɔːnɪŋ] ADJ **1** *(person)* qui bâille **2** *Fig (chasm)* béant, ouvert; *(difference, gap)* énorme

N bâillement m

yaws [jɔːz] NPL *Med* pian m

y-axis N *Math* axe m des Y *ou* des ordonnées

yay [jeɪ] N *Am Sl (cocaine)* coco f, neige f

yd N *(abbr yard)* yard m *(0,914m)*

ye¹ [jiː] DEF ART *Arch, Hum* le, la, les; **Ye Olde Shoppe** la Vieille Boutique

ye² PERS PRON **1** pl *Arch, Lit* vous; **seek and ye shall find** cherchez et vous trouverez; *Fam* **ye gods!** grand Dieu! **2** sing *Fam, Dial* tu, vous; **how d'ye do?** comment vas-tu?, comment allez-vous?

yea [jeɪ] ADV *Bible, Lit* **1** *(yes)* oui **2** *(truly, indeed)* en vérité

N oui m; *Am Pol* **yeas and nays** voix fpl pour et contre

yeah [jeə] ADV *Fam* ouais; **oh y.?** *(in disbelief, challenging)* vraiment?, ah ouais?; **y. y.!, y., right!** *(in disbelief)* ouais, c'est ça!

year [jɪər] N SEE GRAMMAR B61 **1** an m, année f; **in the y.** *(Arch* of our Lord *or* of grace)* **1850** en l'an *ou* en l'année (du Seigneur *ou* de grâce) 1850; **a ticket valid for one** *or* **a y.** un billet valable (pour) un an; **I've known him for ten years** je le connais depuis dix ans; *Hist* **the Thirty Years' War** la Guerre de Trente Ans; **sentenced to ten years' imprisonment** condamné à dix ans de prison; **he got five years** *(prison sentence)* il en a pris pour cinq ans; **a y.'s work/ salary** un an de travail/de salaire; **a y. last/ next September** il y a eu/il y aura un an en septembre; **it will be a y. in April** *(answering question 'how long?')* ça va faire un an en avril; **we're going/we went to Greece this y.** nous allons/nous sommes allés en Grèce cette année; **last y.** l'an dernier, l'année dernière; **next y.** l'an prochain, l'année prochaine; **this day next y.** dans un an jour pour jour; **every y.** tous les ans, chaque année, *Fml* annuellement; **twice a y.** deux fois par an; **to earn £10,000 a y.** gagner 10 000 livres par an; **a y.-old child, a one-y.-old (child)** un enfant (âgé) d'un an; **to be ten years old** avoir dix ans; *Fml* **she's in her eightieth y.** elle est dans sa quatre-vingtième année; **new y.** nouvel an; **we'll see you in the new y.** nous vous verrons au début de l'année prochaine; **New Y.'s Day** le jour de l'An, le 1er de l'An; **Am New Y.'s** *(New Year's Day)* le jour de l'An, le 1er de l'An; *(New Year's Eve)* le 31 décembre, la Saint-Sylvestre; **Happy New Y.!** bonne année!; **to see the old y. out** *or* **the new y. in** faire la veillée *ou* le réveillon de la Saint-Sylvestre, réveillonner; **for many long years** pendant de longues années; **for many years now we have been promised a new road** ça fait maintenant de nombreuses années qu'on nous promet une nouvelle route; **all (the) y. round** (pendant) toute l'année; **y. in (and) y. out** une année après l'autre; **y. by y.** d'année en année; **over the years** au fil des ans *ou* années; **in the early years of the century/their marriage** au cours des premières années de ce siècle/de leur mariage; **years ago** il y a bien des années; **this is where I met him, all those years ago** c'est ici que je l'ai rencontré il y a tant d'années; **it's years since I saw him, I haven't seen him for** *or* **in years** *(for many years)* ça fait des années que je ne l'ai pas vu, je ne l'ai pas vu depuis des années; *Fam (for a long time)* il y a une éternité que je ne l'ai vu; **it seemed like years rather than hours** les heures m'ont semblé des années; **years and years** des années et des années; **the best years of our lives** les plus belles années de notre vie; **from his earliest years** dès son plus jeune âge; **to be old for one's years** *(of child)* être précoce; *(of adult)* faire plus vieux que son âge; **to be young for one's years** faire jeune pour son âge; **to be getting on in years** prendre de l'âge; **advanced in years** âgé; **smoking can take years off your life** fumer peut raccourcir la durée de votre vie; *Fam* **those kids have taken years off my life!** ces gamins m'ont fait prendre dix ans d'un coup!; **working there put years on him** le fait de travailler là l'a vieilli; **that dress takes years off her** cette robe la fait paraître des années plus jeune *ou* la rajeunit beaucoup; **calendar** *or* **civil y.** année civile; **financial** *or* **fiscal** *or* **tax y.** année budgétaire, exercice *m* (financier); **leap y.** année bissextile; *Astron* **light y.** année-lumière *f, pl* années-lumière, année de lumière; **school y.** année scolaire; **solar/lunar y.** année solaire/lunaire

2 *(at school, university etc)* année *f*; **third-y. student** étudiant, -ante de troisième année; **he was in my y.** *(at school)* il était dans ma classe; *(at university)* il était de ma promotion; **she was in the y. above/below me** elle était dans la classe au-dessus/en dessous de la mienne

3 *(of wine)* millésime *m*, année *f*; **a good y. for claret** une bonne année *ou* un bon millésime pour le bordeaux rouge; *Fig* **it was a good y. for apples/French cinema** ça a été une bonne année pour les pommes/le cinéma français

4 *Comput* **y. 2000 compatible** *or* **compliant** conforme à l'an 2000

▸▸ *Fin* **y. of assessment** année *f* d'imposition; *Fin* **y. end** fin *f* d'exercice

When translating the word **year**, note that the French words **an** and **année** are not interchangeable. **Année** is used when the emphasis is on duration, while in cases where it is preceded by a number, **year** is usually translated by **an**.

yearbook ['jɪəbʊk] N annuaire *m*, almanach *m*

year-end N *Acct* de fin d'exercice;
▸▸ **y. accounts** compte *m* de résultats; **y. audit** vérification *f* comptable de fin d'exercice; **y. closing of accounts** clôture *f* annuelle des livres; **y. loss** perte *f* de fin d'exercice; **y. profits** bénéfices *mpl* de fin d'exercice

yearling ['jɪəlɪŋ] N *(in general)* animal *m* d'un an; *(horse)* poulain *m* d'un an; *(thoroughbred)* yearling *m*
ADJ d'un an

yearlong ['jɪəlɒŋ] ADJ qui dure/a duré un an *ou* toute l'année; **they had a y. wait** ils ont attendu une année entière *ou* toute une année

yearly ['jɪəlɪ] ADJ annuel
ADV *(once a year)* annuellement, une fois par an; *(every year)* annuellement, tous les ans
N *(publication)* publication *f* annuelle

yearn [jɜːn] VI **to y. for** *or* **after sb/sth** languir après qn/qch; **they y. for their own country** ils ont la nostalgie de leur propre pays; **to y. to do sth** brûler de faire qch

yearning ['jɜːnɪŋ] N désir *m* (**for** de); **he felt a great y. to …** il ressentit un désir ardent de …

yearningly ['jɜːnɪŋlɪ] ADV avec un désir ardent

year-round ADJ ininterrompu; **California enjoys y. sun** en Californie il y a du soleil toute l'année

yeast [jiːst] N levure *f*; **brewer's y.** levure de bière

yeasty ['jiːstɪ] ADJ de levure

yell [jel] N **1** hurlement *m*, grand cri *m*; **to give a y.** pousser un grand cri *ou* un hurlement; **yells of laughter** hurlements de rire **2** *Am (organized shout) (of students etc)* cri *m* de guerre ou de bataille
VI hurler, crier à tue-tête; **to y. at sb** hurler après qn; **to y. with pain/laughter** hurler de douleur/de rire
VT to y. (out) *(song)* hurler, beugler; *(order)* hurler, *Fam* gueuler

yelling ['jelɪŋ] N hurlements *mpl*; **there was a lot of y. going on next door** ça hurlait *ou* *Fam* gueulait pas mal à côté

yellow ['jeləʊ] ADJ **1** *(in colour)* jaune; **to turn** *or* **go y.** jaunir **2** *Fam (cowardly)* trouillard, lâche; **he says you're y.!** il dit que tu n'es qu'un trouillard *ou* un lâche!; **to turn** *or* **go y.** se dégonfler; **to have a y. streak** être un peu trouillard sur les bords
N 1 *(colour)* jaune *m* **2** *(yolk)* jaune *m* (d'œuf)
VT & VI jaunir; **papers yellowed with age** papiers jaunis par le temps
▸▸ **y. card** *(in football, rugby)* carton *m* jaune; *Belg* **carte** *f* jaune; **y. fever** fièvre *f* jaune; *Am* **y. light** feu *m* orange; **y. line** bande *f* jaune; *Br* **to park on a double y. line** = se garer sur une zone de stationnement interdit; **y. metal** *(brass)* cuivre *m* jaune, laiton *m*; *(gold)* métal *m* jaune, or *m*; **Y. Pages®** Pages *fpl* jaunes; *Old-fashioned* **y. peril** péril *m* jaune

Yellow lines

En Grande-Bretagne, une ligne jaune parallèle au trottoir signifie "arrêt autorisé réglementé"; une double ligne jaune signifie "stationnement interdit".

yellowbelly ['jeləʊbelɪ] N *Fam (coward)* froussard, -arde, trouillard, -arde

yellowhammer ['jeləʊhæmər] N *(bird)* bruant *m* jaune

yellowish ['jeləʊɪʃ] ADJ jaunet, -ette, *Pej* jaunâtre

yellowness ['jeləʊnɪs] N **1** *(colour)* ton *m* jaune, teinte *f* jaune; *(of person)* teint *m* jaune; **judging by the y. of her skin** à en juger par son teint jaune **2** *(cowardice)* lâcheté *f*

yelp [jelp] N jappement *m*, glapissement *m*; **to let out a y.** laisser échapper un jappement *ou* un glapissement
VI japper, glapir; **to y. with pain** gémir de douleur

yelping ['jelpɪŋ] N *(no pl)* jappements *mpl*, glapissements *mpl*

Yemen (the) ['jɑːmen] N le Yémen

Yemeni(te) ['jeminɪ, -aɪt] ADJ yéménique, yéménite
N Yéménite *mf*

yen¹ [jen] N *(currency)* yen *m*

yen² N *(desire)* envie *f*; **to have a y. for sth/to do sth** avoir envie de qch/de faire qch

yeoman, pl yeomen ['jəʊmən] N **1** *Hist (small freeholder)* franc-tenancier *m, pl* francs-tenanciers; *Fig* **to do y. service** rendre des services inestimables **2** *Br Mil, Hist* soldat *m* du yeomanry; **Y. of the Guard** = hallebardier *m* à la Tour de Londres

yeomanry ['jəʊmənrɪ] N *(no pl)* **1** *Hist (small freeholders)* francs-tenanciers *mpl* **2** *Br Mil, Hist* = corps *m* de cavalerie composé de volontaires

yep [jep] ADV *esp Am Fam* ouais

yes [jes] ADV **1** oui; *(contradicting negation)* si; **to answer y. or no** répondre par oui ou (par) non; **to say y.** dire oui, dire que oui; **y., certainly!, oh y.!** mais oui!; **are you hungry? – y. (I am)** avez-vous faim? – oui; **you didn't hear me? – y., I did** vous ne m'avez pas entendu? – (mais) si; **would you like some cake? – y. please** *or esp Am* **thanks** est-ce que vous voulez du gâteau? – oui, s'il vous plaît; **could I have a glass of water? – y., of course** est-ce que je pourrais avoir un verre d'eau? – oui, bien sûr; **y. sir/madam** *(I'm coming)* voilà, monsieur/madame; *Mktg* **y./no question** *(in survey)* question *f* fermée SEE GRAMMAR B64 **2** *(interrogatively)* **y.?** *(are you sure)* vraiment?; *(go on)* et puis après?; *(to sb waiting to speak)* oui?, vous désirez?
N *(pl yeses* ['jesɪz]) oui *m inv*; **an emphatic y.** un oui énergique

yes-man, *pl* **yes-men** ['jesmæn, -men] N *Fam* béni-oui-oui *m*

yesterday ['jestəd(e)ɪ] ADV, N hier *m*; **the day before y.** avant-hier; **a week ago y.** il y a eu hier huit jours; **y. week, a week (from) y.** d'hier en huit; **y.'s paper/milk** le journal/le lait d'hier; **y. morning/evening** hier matin/soir; **I can remember it as clearly as if it had happened y.** je m'en souviens comme si c'était hier; *Pej* **y.'s men/designers** les hommes/designers qui appartiennent au passé; **y.'s heroes** les héros *mpl* de jadis; *Lit* **our yesterdays** les jours *mpl* d'autrefois *ou* d'antan

yesteryear ['jestəjɪər] N *Lit* of **y.** d'antan; **the snows of y.** les neiges *fpl* d'antan

yet [jet] ADV **1** *(still)* encore; **we've got ten minutes y.** nous avons encore dix minutes; **jobs y. to be done** tâches encore à faire; **y. again** encore une fois; **y. more** encore plus; **y. greater advantages** des avantages encore plus grands; **y. another mistake** encore une erreur; **y. one more** encore un(e) autre **2** *(in neg phrases)* encore; *(in questions) (already)* déjà; **I haven't finished y.** je n'ai pas encore fini; **we're not ready y.** nous ne sommes pas encore prêts; **have they decided y.?** est-ce qu'ils ont déjà décidé?; **are you ready y.?** tu es prêt?; **not y.** pas encore; **don't go y.** ne partez pas encore; **it will not happen just y.** cela n'arrivera pas tout de suite; **we're not going just y.** nous ne partons pas tout de suite; **as y. nothing has been done** jusqu'à présent *ou* jusqu'ici rien n'a été fait; **not as y.** pas encore; **as y. unexplored jungle** jungle pas encore explorée

3 *(in spite of everything)* malgré tout; **I shall catch him y.!** je finirai bien par l'attraper!; **I'll do it y.!** j'y arriverai!

4 *Old-fashioned (even)* **not finished nor y. started** pas achevé ni même commencé **CONJ** néanmoins, cependant, tout de même; **and y. I like him** et cependant *ou* et malgré tout *ou* néanmoins il me plaît, mais il me plaît tout de même

yeti ['jetɪ] **N** yeti *m*

yew [ju:] **N** *(tree)* if *m*; *(wood)* (bois *m* d')if

Y-fronts® ['waɪ'frʌnts] **NPL** slip *m* ouvert

YHA [waɪeɪtʃ'eɪ] **N** *(abbr Youth Hostels Association)* FUAJ *f*

Yid [jɪd] **N** *Offensive Sl* youpin, -ine

Yiddish ['jɪdɪʃ] **ADJ, N** *Ling* yiddish *m*

yield [ji:ld] **N 1** *(of field, machine)* rendement *m*; *(of fruit tree, capital outlay, land etc)* rapport *m*; *(of mine)* production *f*, produit *m*, débit *m*; **this tree gives a better/poor y.** cet arbre donne un meilleur/un faible rapport

2 *Fin (from investments)* rapport *m*, rendement *m*; *(profit)* bénéfice *m*, bénéfices *mpl*; *(from tax)* recette *f*, rapport *m*; **the y. on these shares is large** ces actions rapportent beaucoup

VT 1 *(give)* rapporter, produire, donner; **shares that y. high interest** actions à gros rendement; **to y. a profit** rapporter *ou* dégager un bénéfice; **these remarks y. an insight into his motives** ces remarques donnent une idée de ses motifs; **further investigations yielded no new information** des recherches supplémentaires n'ont fourni aucune information nouvelle

2 *(concede) (fortress to enemy, right etc)* céder; **to y. ground** céder du terrain; **to y. a point to sb** céder à qn sur un point; *also Sport* concéder un point à qn; *Lit* **to y. (up) the ghost** *or* **one's soul** rendre l'âme

VI 1 *(surrender)* céder (**to** à); *(of army, enemy)* se rendre; **to y. to force** céder devant la force; **to y. to reason** se rendre à la raison; **we shall not y. to threats** nous ne céderons pas aux menaces; **I had to y. to them on that point** j'ai dû leur céder sur ce point; **to y. to temptation** succomber *ou* céder à la tentation; **to y. to sb's wishes** consentir *ou* céder aux désirs de qn

2 *(of rope etc)* céder; *(of beam etc)* s'affaisser, fléchir; **the plank yielded under our weight** la planche a manqué *ou* cédé sous notre poids

3 *Am Aut* **y.!** *(on sign)* vous n'avez pas la priorité!

▸▸ *Fin* **y. capacity** productivité *f*; **y. curve** courbe *f* des taux; *Fin* **y. gap** prime *f* de risque

yielding ['ji:ldɪŋ] **ADJ 1** *(person)* facile, complaisant, accommodant; **the management hasn't been very y.** la direction n'a pas été très accommodante **2** *(substance)* souple, élastique, flexible

yikes [jaɪks] **INT** *Fam* mince!

yin [jɪn] **N** *Phil* yin *m*; **y. and yang** le yin et le yang

yippee [jɪ'pi:] **INT** *Fam* hourra!, bravo!

Y-junction **N** fourche *f*

YMCA [waɪemsiː'eɪ] **N** *(abbr Young Men's Christian Association)* Union *f* chrétienne de jeunes gens

yo [jəʊ] **INT** hé!, eh!

yob [jɒb], **yobbo** ['jɒbəʊ] **N** *Br Fam* voyou *m*, loubar(d) *m*; **the y. culture that prevails in this country today** l'aggressivité et l'anti-intellectualisme qui règnent aujourd'hui dans notre pays

yobbish ['jɒbɪʃ] **ADJ** *Br Fam* de voyou; **it**

makes you look y.** ça te donne l'air d'un voyou; **don't be so y.** arrête de jouer les voyous

yodel ['jəʊd(ə)l] *Mus* **N** (chant *m* à la) tyrolienne *f*

VI (**-ll-**, *Am* **-l-**) jodler, iodler

yod(el)ler, *Am* **yodler, yodeler** ['jəʊd(ə)lər] **N** jodleur, -euse, iodleur, -euse

yoga ['jəʊgə] **N** yoga *m*

yoghurt, yoghourt ['jɒgət, 'jəʊ-] **N** yaourt *m*, yog(h)urt *m*

▸▸ **y. drink** yaourt à boire

yogi ['jəʊgɪ] **N** yogi *m*

yogurt ['jɒgət, 'jəʊ-] **N = yoghurt**

yoke¹ [jəʊk] **N 1** *(for ox), Fig* joug *m*; *Fig* **the y. of convention** le joug des conventions; *Fig* **to throw off the y.** secouer le joug, s'affranchir du joug **2** *(for carrying)* palanche *f* **3** *Sewing* empiècement *m* **4** *Elec (of dynamo)* carcasse *f*, bâti *m*

VT 1 *(oxen)* accoupler, atteler (**to the plough** à la charrue); *Fig* lier; *Fig* **to y. together** *(in marriage)* unir **2** *Tech (pieces of equipment)* accoupler

yokel ['jəʊk(ə)l] **N** *Pej* rustre *m*, campagnard, -arde

yolk [jəʊk] **N 1** *Culin (of egg)* jaune *m*; **take the y. of an egg** prenez un jaune d'œuf **2** *Biol* vitellus *m*; **y. bag** *or* **sac** membrane *f* vitelline

Yom Kippur [jɒmkɪ'pʊər] **N** *Rel* Yom Kippour *m*

yomp [jɒmp] **VI** *Mil* crapahuter; **a group of hikers was yomping towards us** un groupe de marcheurs se dirigeait vers nous avec tout leur chargement

yon [jɒn] **ADJ, ADV** *Arch, Dial* **= yonder**

yonder ['jɒndər] *Lit* **ADV** (**down/over**) **y.** là-bas

ADJ ce … -là, cette … -là, *pl* ces … -là; **y. elms** ces ormes là-bas, ces ormes-là

yonks [jɒŋks] **NPL** *Fam* une éternité; **we've been waiting for y.** ça fait une éternité qu'on attend; **I haven't been there in y.** ça fait une paye que je n'y suis pas allé; **that was y. ago** ça fait une paye

yoohoo ['ju:hu:] **INT** ohé!

yore [jɔ:r] **N** *Arch, Lit* **of y.** (d')autrefois, d'antan; **in days of y.** au temps jadis, autrefois

Yorkshire ['jɔ:kʃɪər] **N** le Yorkshire

▸▸ **Y. pudding** = crêpe *f* épaisse salée traditionnellement servie avec du rôti de bœuf; **Y. terrier** yorkshire-terrier *m*, *pl* yorkshire-terriers, yorkshire *m*

Yoruba ['jɒrʊbə] **N 1** *(person)* Yor(o)uba *mf* **2** *Ling* yor(o)uba *m*

ADJ yor(o)uba

you [ju:] **PERS PRON** SEE GRAMMAR B67 **1** *(subject)* sing, *pl* vous; sing *(when addressing relatives, intimate friends, children, animals, deities)* tu; **y. are very kind** vous êtes/tu es bien aimable(s); **how are y.?** comment allez-vous?/vas-tu?; **there y. are** *(here's what you wanted, it's done, see what I mean)* et voilà; *(I was looking/waiting for you)* vous/te voilà; **y. all know who I mean** vous savez tous de qui je veux parler VOIR GRAMMAIRE A27-9; A43; B18-21

2 *(as object of verb)* vous/te, *pl* vous; **I hope to see y. tomorrow** j'espère vous/te voir demain; **I'll give y. some** je vous en/t'en donnerai; **I told y. so!** je vous/te l'avais bien dit! SEE GRAMMAR B18-19

3 *(after preposition)* vous/toi, *pl* vous; **between y. and me** *(when confiding)* entre vous et moi/entre toi et moi, entre nous soit dit; **I gave them to y.** je te/vous les ai donnés; **away with y.!** allez-vous-en!/va-t'en!; **all of y.** vous tous; **to/for y. and yours** à/pour toi et les tiens/vous et les vôtres; **now there's a**

singer for y.!** ah, voilà un chanteur!; **now there's a typical politician for y.** voilà un politicien type; **now there's manners for y.!** au moins c'est quelqu'un de bien élevé/ce sont des gens bien élevés!; *Iron* en voilà des manières!

4 *(stressed)* vous/toi, *pl* vous; **y. and I will go by train** vous et moi/toi et moi nous irons par le train; **is that y.?** c'est vous/toi?; **oh, it's y.** ah, c'est vous/toi; **I am older than y.** je suis plus âgé que vous/que toi; **if I were y.** (si j'étais) à votre/ta place; **hey! y. there!** eh! dites donc, là-bas!; **poor old y.!** mon pauvre vieux!, ma pauvre vieille!; **silly/lucky (old) y.!** quel gros bêta/veinard tu fais!; *Fam* **that jacket/job wasn't y.** cette veste/ce travail n'était pas ton style; **y. two are very different** vous êtes très différents tous les deux; **y. four! come with me** vous quatre! venez avec moi; **where are y. two going?** où est-ce que vous allez, tous les deux?; **how long have y. two been married?** cela fait combien de temps que vous êtes mariés tous les deux?

5 *(in the imperative)* **don't y. cry!** ne pleure pas!; **don't y. dare!** ne t'avise surtout pas de faire ça!; **y. sit down and eat your lunch!** toi, assieds-toi et mange ton déjeuner!; **never y. mind!** ne t'occupe pas de ça, toi!; **now you tell a joke** à ton tour *ou* à toi de raconter une blague maintenant; **don't you start!** ne commence pas, toi!, ne t'y mets pas, toi!; **just y. try!** essaye un peu pour voir!

6 *(in apposition)* **y. lawyers/Englishmen** vous autres avocats/Anglais; *Fam* **y. lot** vous; **y. idiot(, y.)!** idiot que tu es!, espèce d'idiot!; **y. darling(, y.)!** tu es un amour!

7 *(indefinite)* on; **y. never can tell** on ne sait jamais; **the joy y. feel when …** la joie qu'on ressent quand …; **exercise is good for y.** (prendre de) l'exercice est bon pour la santé VOIR GRAMMAIRE A29; B16

you-all [j(ə)'ɑ:l] **PERS PRON** *Am Fam (used in Southern US)* vous tous; *(speaking to one person)* vous

you'd [ju:d] **CONTR 1 = you had,** *see* **have 2 = you would,** *see* **will²**

you-know-who **N** qui-vous-savez *mf*; **yesterday I had a telephone call from y.** hier, j'ai reçu un coup de téléphone de qui-vous-savez

you'll [ju:l] **CONTR 1 = you will,** *see* **will² 2 = you shall,** *see* **shall**

young [jʌŋ] **ADJ 1** *(person, animal)* jeune; *(baby animal)* petit; **younger** plus jeune; **younger son/daughter** fils cadet/fille cadette; **my younger brother** mon frère cadet; **the youngest** le/la plus jeune, le cadet/la cadette; **this is my youngest, Vicki** voici ma cadette *ou* ma dernière, Vicki; **he's younger than me** *or* **I (am)** il est plus jeune *ou* moins âgé que moi, il est mon cadet; **she's two years younger than me** elle est plus jeune que moi *ou* elle est ma cadette de deux ans; **they wanted someone younger** ils voulaient quelqu'un de plus jeune; **when I was twenty years younger** quand j'avais vingt ans de moins; **if I were twenty years younger!** si j'avais vingt ans de moins!; **you're only y. once** on n'est jeune qu'une fois, la jeunesse ne dure qu'un temps; **she's too y. for alcohol/to get married** elle est trop jeune pour boire de l'alcool/se marier; **don't be too hard on him, he's only y.** ne sois pas trop sévère avec lui, il est encore bien jeune; **I am not as y. as I used to be** je n'ai plus mes jambes de vingt ans; **y. man** jeune homme; **y. woman** jeune femme; **now you listen to me, y. man/woman** écoute-moi un peu jeune homme/ma petite dame; **he's her y. man** c'est son petit ami; **a y. couple/mother** un jeune couple/une jeune mère; **a y. family** des enfants en bas âge; **y. people** jeunes gens *mpl*, jeunes *mpl*; **Pliny the Younger** Pline le Jeune; **the younger generation** la jeune génération; **in his younger days** dans son jeune temps, dans sa jeunesse; **in my young(er) days** dans ma jeunesse; **a y. country/company** un pays/une société de création récente; **a y. wine** un vin vert; **the night is y.!** j'ai/nous avons toute la soirée devant moi/nous!

2 *(youthful)* jeune; **y. for his age** *or* **years** jeune pour son âge; **y. in spirit** *or* **at heart** jeune d'esprit; **to grow** *or* **get y. again, to grow younger** rajeunir; **you look younger than ever!** tu parais plus jeune que jamais!; **she's a y. forty** elle ne fait pas ses quarante ans; **thirty's still y.!** trente ans c'est encore jeune!

N 1 *(people)* **the y.** les jeunes (gens) *mpl*, la jeunesse; **books for the y.** livres pour la jeunesse; **it appeals to y. and old alike** ça plaît aux jeunes comme aux moins jeunes

2 an animal and its y. un animal et ses petits; **a mare with y.** *(pregnant)* une jument pleine

▸ ▸ *Br Pol* **Y. Conservatives** jeunes conservateurs *mpl*; **Y. Liberals** jeunes libéraux *mpl*; *Br* **Y. Offenders' Institution** = centre *m* de détention pour mineurs

youngish ['jʌŋɪʃ] ADJ assez jeune, *Fam* jeunet, -ette; **he's a y. fifty** il ne fait pas tout à fait ses cinquante ans

youngster ['jʌŋstər] **N 1** *(young person)* jeune *mf*, jeune personne *f* **2** *(child)* petit, -ite, *Fam* gosse *mf*

your [jɔːr] POSS ADJ **1** *sing, pl* votre, *pl* vos; *sing (when addressing relatives, intimate friends, children, animals, deities)* ton, ta, *pl* tes; **y. friends** vos/tes ami(e)s; **y. house** votre/ta maison; **y. father and mother** votre père et votre mère/ton père et ta mère; *(formal)* vos père et mère; **the most recent of y. books, y. most recent book** votre/ton livre le plus récent; **have you hurt y. hand?** vous vous êtes/tu t'es fait mal à la main?; **turn y. head(s)** tourne(z) la tête; **y. turn!** *(to play etc)* à vous/toi!; **I like y. London buses** j'aime bien les bus que vous avez à Londres; **I object to y. visiting the children** je m'oppose à ce que tu rendes visite aux enfants VOIR GRAMMAIRE A30; B21

2 *(indefinite)* son, sa, *pl* ses; **you cannot alter y. nature** on ne peut pas changer son caractère

3 *Fam* **y. (typical** *or* **average) Frenchman** le Français moyen; **of course, y. kings and queens don't do that** bien sûr, les rois et les reines ne font pas ça

4 *(in titles)* **Y. Highness** Votre Majesté *(à un roi, une reine, un prince ou une princesse)*; **Y. Holiness** Très Saint Père; **Y. Honour** Votre Honneur; **Y. Majesty** Votre Majesté *(à un roi ou une reine uniquement)*

you're [jɔːr] CONTR = **you are,** *see* **be**

yours [jɔːz] POSS PRON SING, PL VOIR GRAMMAIRE A30; B21–2 **1** le vôtre, la vôtre, *pl* les vôtres; *sing (when addressing relatives, intimate friends, children)* le tien, la tienne, *pl* les tiens, les tiennes; **this is y.** ceci est à vous/à toi, c'est le vôtre/le tien; **these are y.** ceux-ci sont à toi/à vous, ceux-ci sont les tiens/les vôtres;

you and y. vous et les vôtres/toi et les tiens; **the bathroom's all y.** la salle de bains est libre maintenant; **can I use your telephone? – it's all y.** est-ce que je peux utiliser ton téléphone? – vas-y; *Com, Fml* **in reply to y. of the 14th November** en réponse à votre lettre en date du 14 novembre; **y. is a nation of travellers** vous êtes une nation de voyageurs; **y. was no easy task** ta tâche n'était pas facile; **he is a friend of y.** c'est un de vos/tes amis, c'est un ami à vous/toi; **that's no business of y.** cela ne vous/te regarde pas, ce n'est pas votre/ton affaire; *Pej* **that dog of y.** votre/ton sacré *ou* fichu *ou* foutu chien **2** *(in letter)* **y., Peter** ≃ bien à vous *ou* à bientôt, Peter; **y. sincerely, y. faithfully** *(in letters)* ≃ je vous prie d'agréer, Madame/Monsieur, l'expression de mes sentiments distingués

yourself [jɔːˈself], *pl* **yourselves** [jɔːˈselvz] PERS PRON VOIR GRAMMAIRE A29–30 **1** *(emphatic) sing, pl* vous-même(s); *sing (when addressing relatives, intimate friends, children, deities)* toi-même; **you said y.** *or* **you y. said it was cheap** tu as dit toi-même/vous avez dit vous-même que ce n'était pas cher; **tell her y.** dis-lui toi-même/dites-lui vous-même; **you don't look quite y.** vous avez/tu as l'air mal en train; **just be y.** contente-toi d'être toi-même/contentez-vous d'être vous-même

2 *(reflexive)* vous/te, *pl* vous; **are you enjoying y.?** tu t'amuses/vous vous amusez bien?; **have you hurt y.?** vous êtes-vous/tu t'es fait mal?; **I see you've got y. a wife/you've bought y. a car** je vois que tu t'es trouvé une femme/que tu t'es acheté une voiture; *Fam* **have y. a good time** amuse-toi bien; **and you call y. a Christian/socialist!** et vous vous dites/tu te dis chrétien/socialiste! SEE GRAMMAR B28

3 *(after preposition)* **see for y.** vois toi-même/voyez vous-même; **see for yourselves** voyez vous-mêmes; **tell us something about y.** parle-nous de toi/parlez-nous de vous; **what about y.?** et toi/vous?; **speak for y.!** parle pour toi!/parlez pour vous!; **keep it for y.** garde-le pour toi/gardez-le pour vous; **do you live by y.?** vous vivez/tu vis (tout) seul?; **did you do this by y.?** est-ce que vous avez/tu as fait ça tout seul?; **among yourselves** *(reciprocal)* entre vous

4 *(used impersonally)* soi-même; *(reflexive)* se; **you have to do it y.** il faut le faire soi-même; **you can't take y. too seriously** il ne faut pas se prendre trop au sérieux

youth [juːθ, *pl* juːðz] **1** VOIR GRAMMAIRE A11 *(no pl) (period)* jeunesse *f*, jeune âge *m*; **in his early y.** dans sa première jeunesse; **she is not in the first flush of y., she is past her first y.** elle n'est pas de la première jeunesse; **lost y.** jeunesse perdue; *Myth* **the fountain of Y.** la Fontaine de Jouvence; **y. will have its way** *or* **its fling** il faut que jeunesse se passe **2** *(male teenager)* jeune homme *m*, adolescent *m* **3** *(no pl) (young people) (of village etc)* jeunes gens *mpl*, jeunesse *f*; **inner-city y.** la jeunesse des quartiers déshérités; **the y. of today** la jeunesse *ou* les jeunes d'aujourd'hui

▸ ▸ *Br* **y. club** ≃ maison *f* des jeunes; **y.**

culture culture *f* des jeunes; **y. fare** tarif *m* jeune; **y. hostel** auberge *f* de jeunesse; **Y. Hostels Association** association *f* des auberges de jeunesse; *Mktg* **y. market** marché *m* de la jeunesse; *Mktg* **y. marketing** marketing *m* de la classe des jeunes, marketing des juniors; **y. orchestra** orchestre *m* de jeunes

youthful ['juːθfʊl] ADJ **1** *(person, face, fashion etc)* jeune; **to look y.** avoir l'air jeune; **y. good looks** *(of men)* air *m* de jeune homme; **he is a y. fifty-two** il est jeune pour ses cinquante-deux ans **2** *(error)* de jeunesse; *(enthusiasm, impetuousness)* juvénile

youthfulness ['juːθfʊlnɪs] **N** jeunesse *f*; *(youthful appearance)* air *m* de jeunesse, air jeune

you've [juːv] CONTR = **you have,** *see* **have**

yowl [jaʊl] **N** *(of dog)* hurlement *m*; *(of cat)* miaulement *m*; **there was a y. of protest/pain from him** il a émis un cri de protestation/douleur

VI *(of dog, person)* hurler; *(of cat)* miauler

yo-yo® ['jəʊjəʊ] **N 1** yo-yo® *m inv*; *Fam* **he was jumping up and down like a y.** il sautait sur place comme s'il était monté sur un ressort; *Fam* **I've been up and down the stairs like a y. all day** je n'ai pas arrêté de monter et de descendre l'escalier toute la journée **2** *Am Fam (fool)* abruti, -ie

yr *(abbr* **year)** a.

YTS [waɪtiːˈes] **N** *Br (abbr* **Youth Training Scheme)** *(person)* TUC *mf*; *(job)* TUC *m*

yuan [juːˈæn] **N INV** yuan *m*

yucca ['jʌkə] **N** *(plant)* yucca *m*; **a y. plant** un yucca

yuck [jʌk] **INT** *Fam* pouah!, berk!

yucky ['jʌkɪ] ADJ *Fam* dégoûtant; **to feel y.** *(not well)* se sentir patraque

Yugoslav ['juːgəʊslɑːv] ADJ yougoslave **N** Yougoslave *mf*

Yugoslavia [juːgəʊˈslɑːvɪə] **N** *Formerly* Yougoslavie *f*; **the ex-Y.** l'ex-Yougoslavie

Yugoslavian [juːgəʊˈslɑːvɪən] ADJ *Formerly* yougoslave

yule [juːl] **N** *Arch, Lit* Noël *m*

▸ ▸ **y. log** bûche *f* de Noël

yuletide ['juːltaɪd] **N** *Arch, Lit* période *f* de Noël; **y. festivities** fêtes *fpl* de Noël

yummy ['jʌmɪ] ADJ *Fam* délicieux; *(person)* sexy *inv*; **y.!** miam-miam!

yum-yum [jʌmˈjʌm] **INT** *Fam* miam-miam!

yup [jʌp] ADV *Am Fam* ouais

yuppie ['jʌpɪ] **N** *usu Pej (abbr* **young upwardly mobile professional)** yuppie *mf*, ≃ jeune cadre *m* dynamique
ADJ *(club)* pour jeunes cadres dynamiques; *(lifestyle, neighbourhood)* de yuppies

▸ ▸ **y. flu** encéphalomyélite *f* myalgique

yuppify ['jʌpɪfaɪ] **VT** *Fam* rendre chic et branché; **the area/pub has become rather yuppified** ce quartier/pub est plein de yuppies maintenant

YWCA [waɪdʌb(ə)ljuːsiːˈeɪ] **N** *(abbr* **Young Women's Christian Association)** Union *f* chrétienne de jeunes femmes

Z, z [zed, *Am* ziː] N *(letter)* Z, z *m*; **two z's** deux z

Zaire [zɑːˈɪər] N Zaïre *m*

Zairean [zɑːˈɪərɪən] ADJ zaïrois N Zaïrois, -oise

Zambezi (the) [ðəzæmˈbiːzɪ] N le Zambèze

Zambia [ˈzæmbɪə] N Zambie *f*

Zambian [ˈzæmbɪən] ADJ zambien N Zambien, -ienne

zaniness [ˈzeɪnɪnɪs] N *Fam* loufoquerie *f*

zany [ˈzeɪnɪ] ADJ *Fam* loufoque

zap [zæp] *Fam* INT *(esp in comic books)* paf!
N *(energy)* punch *m*; **to be full of z.** avoir une pêche d'enfer
VT **1** *(destroy, stun, disable) (with ray gun, by bombing etc)* détruire; *(person)* éliminer
2 *(put, send)* **z. it in the microwave** balance-le au micro-ondes; **we'll z. it across to you by courier** on vous l'enverra *ou* expédiera vite fait par courrier; **they zapped him off to the TV studios** ils l'ont emmené vite fait *ou* sur les chapeaux de roues aux studios de la télé
3 *Comput (delete)* effacer
4 *(hit)* donner un coup à, cogner
VI **1** *(change channel on TV)* zapper, *Can* pitonner **2** *(move fast)* **he's been zapping in and out of his office all morning** il n'arrête pas d'entrer et de sortir de son bureau depuis ce matin; **the project's really zapping along** le projet avance vraiment à fond de train; **z., z. and it's done!** tac tac et c'est fini!
▸ **zap up** VT SEP *Fam (make more exciting)* **to z. up one's style** rendre son style plus coloré *ou* vivant; **to z. up the colour scheme** *(in house etc)* rehausser les couleurs

zapped [zæpt] ADJ *Fam (exhausted)* crevé, claqué

zapper [ˈzæpər] N *Fam (for TV)* télécommande *f*

zapping [ˈzæpɪŋ] N *(changing TV channels)* zapping *m*

zappy [ˈzæpɪ] ADJ *Fam (fast) (car, computer)* rapide; *(stylish, punchy) (prose, manager, style)* énergique, qui a du punch

ZBB [zedbiːˈbiː, *Am* ziːbiːˈbiː] N *Fin (abbr* zero-base budgeting) BBZ *m*

Z chart N tableau *m* en Z

zeal [ziːl] N zèle *m*, ardeur *f*, *(religious)* zèle *m*, ferveur *f*, **to show excessive z.** faire preuve d'un zèle excessif

zealot [ˈzelət] N **1** *Bible, Hist* Z. zélote *mf* **2** *Fig* fanatique *mf*, *Lit* zélateur, -trice (**for** de)

zealotry [ˈzelətrɪ] N fanatisme *m*, ferveur *f*

zealous [ˈzeləs] ADJ zélé; *(campaigner, advocate)* fervent; **z. to do sth** empressé *ou* à faire qch; **to be z. in doing sth** faire qch avec zèle

zealously [ˈzeləslɪ] ADV avec zèle

zebra [ˈzebrə, ˈziːbrə] N **1** *(animal)* zèbre *m* **2** *Am Sl (in American football)* arbitre *m*

▸▸ *Br* **z. crossing** passage *m* clouté *ou* pour piétons

zebu [ˈziːbuː] N *(animal)* zébu *m*

zed [zed] N *Br (letter)* z *m*

zeds [zedz] NPL *Fam (sleep)* **to catch some z.** faire un roupillon

zee [ziː] N *Am (letter)* z *m*
▸▸ **z. chart** tableau *m* en Z

zees [ziːz] NPL *Am Fam (sleep)* **to catch some z.** faire un roupillon

Zen [zen] N zen *m*
ADJ zen *inv*
▸▸ **Z. Buddhism** le bouddhisme zen, les préceptes *mpl* du zen; **Z. Buddhist** bouddhiste *mf* zen

zenith [ˈzenɪθ] N *Astron, Fig* zénith *m*; *Fig* **at the z. of his fame** à l'apogée *ou* au sommet de sa gloire

zephyr [ˈzefər] N *Lit* zéphyr *m*

zeppelin [ˈzepəlɪn] N *Aviat, Hist* zeppelin *m*

zero [ˈzɪərəʊ] N *Math, Comput* zéro *m*; **z. point two (0.2)** zéro virgule deux (0,2); *Comput* **with z. wait states** sans état d'attente; **the thermometer is at z./four below z.** le thermomètre est à zéro/à quatre au-dessous de zéro; **the temperature fell below z.** la température est tombée au-dessous de zéro; **exports are down to z.** les exportations sont tombées à zéro; **I'd put your chances at z.** je dirais que tes chances sont nulles ̲V̲O̲I̲R̲ ̲G̲R̲A̲M̲M̲A̲I̲R̲E̲ ̲A̲7̲7̲
ADJ *Fam* **he's got z. intelligence/charm** il n'a aucun(e) intelligence/charme
VT *(instrument etc)* (re)mettre à zéro
▸▸ **z. altitude** altitude *f* zéro; *Fin* **z. coupon bond** obligation *f* à coupon zéro; *Mktg* **z. defects** zéro défaut *m*; *Mktg* **z. defects purchasing** achats *mpl* de qualité à 100%, achats zéro défaut; **z. gravity** apesanteur *f*, **z. hour** heure *f* H; **z. growth** croissance *f* zéro; *Pol* **the z. option** l'option *f* zéro; **z. point** *(on graduated scale)* zéro; **z. rating** imposition *f* nulle. **z. tolerance** = politique *f* d'intransigeance à l'égard de toute infraction à la loi ou au règlement
▸ **zero in** VT SEP *Mil (gun)* régler le tir de
VI *(of missile etc)* se régler sur une/la cible
▸ **zero in on** VT INSEP *Mil (target)* régler le tir sur; *(of missile etc)* se régler sur; *Fig (concentrate on) (subject, problem)* se concentrer sur; *(identify)* aller droit sur; **they zeroed in on the one weak point of the argument** ils ont été droit sur le seul point faible de l'argument

zero-base budgeting N *Fin* budget *m* base zéro, budgétisation *f* base zéro

zeroed [ˈzɪərəʊd] ADJ *(milometer)* à zéro

zeroing [ˈzɪərəʊɪŋ] N *Comput* initialisation *f* du compteur

zero-rated ADJ *(without VAT)* exempt *ou* exonéré de TVA; **in Britain, books are z.** en Grande-Bretagne, les livres sont exempts *ou* exonérés de TVA

zero-rating N franchise *f* de TVA, taux *m* zéro, taux nul

zest [zest] N **1** *(enjoyment)* enthousiasme *m*, entrain *m*; *(in speaking)* verve *f*, **with z.** *(to fight etc)* avec élan, avec entrain; *(to eat)* avec appétit, de bon appétit; **her z. for life** sa joie de vivre **2** *(interest)* saveur *f*, goût *m*; **to add z. to the adventure** donner du piquant à l'aventure **3** *(of orange, lemon)* zeste *m*

zestful [ˈzestfʊl] ADJ *(person)* plein d'enthousiasme *ou* d'entrain; *(in speaking)* plein de verve; *(approach)* enthousiaste; *(performance)* plein de vie

zeugma [ˈzjuːɡmə] N zeugma *m*, zeugme *m*

zigzag [ˈzɪɡzæɡ] N *(in design)* zigzag *m*; *(on road)* lacet *m*
ADJ *(path, line)* en zigzag; *(pattern)* à zigzag *ou* zigzags; **the path follows a z. course across the fields** le chemin traverse les champs en zigzaguant
ADV en zigzag
VI *(-gg-) (of road, line)* zigzaguer, faire des zigzags

zigzagging [ˈzɪɡzæɡɪŋ] N zigzags *mpl*

zilch [zɪltʃ] N *Sl* zéro *m*, que dalle

zillion [ˈzɪljən] N *Fam* des millions *mpl* (et des millions)

Zimbabwe [zɪmˈbɑːbweɪ] N Zimbabwe *m*

Zimbabwean [zɪmˈbɑːbweɪən] ADJ zimbabwéen N Zimbabwéen, -éenne

Zimmer® [ˈzɪmər] N Z.® (frame) déambulateur *m*

zinc [zɪŋk] N zinc *m*
▸▸ **z. ointment** pommade *f* à l'oxyde de zinc; **z. oxide** oxyde *m* de zinc; **z. white** blanc *m* de zinc, oxyde de zinc

zincblende [ˈzɪŋkblend] N *Miner* blende *f*

zing [zɪŋ] *Fam* N **1** *(zest)* punch *m* **2** *(sound)* sifflement *m*
VI *(of projectile)* siffler, passer dans un sifflement; **the bullet zinged past me** la balle est passée à côté de moi dans un sifflement
VT *Am (tease)* vanner, chambrer

zinnia [ˈzɪnɪə] N *(flower)* zinnia *m*

Zion [ˈzaɪən] N Sion *m*

Zionism [ˈzaɪənɪz(ə)m] N *Pol* sionisme *m*

Zionist [ˈzaɪənɪst] ADJ, N *Pol* sioniste *mf*

zip [zɪp] N **1** fermeture *f* éclair®, fermeture à glissière, *Belg* tirette *f* **2** *Fam (vigour)* énergie *f*, vitesse *f*, **put some z. into it!** mets-y du nerf!; **your style needs more z.** ton style a besoin d'un peu plus de punch **3** *(of bullet)* sifflement *m*
VI *(-pp-) (like bullet)* siffler; **to z. past** *(of car etc)* passer en trombe
VT **1** *Comput* zipper, compresser **2** *Sl* **z. it!** la ferme!, ferme ton clapet!

▸▸ *Am* **z. code** code *m* postal; *Br* **z. fastener** fermeture éclair®, fermeture à glissière, *Belg* tirette; *Comput* **z. file** fichier *m* zippé; *Am Fam* **z. gun** pistolet *m* rudimentaire *(à ressort)*

▸ **zip along** VI foncer, aller à fond de train

▸ **zip in** VT SEP *(lining)* attacher à l'aide d'une fermeture éclair® *ou* à glissière

VI s'attacher à l'aide d'une fermeture éclair® *ou* à glissière

▸ **zip into** VT INSEP **to z. into the chemist's** faire un saut à la pharmacie

VT SEP **they zipped themselves into their sleeping bags** ils ont fermé leurs sacs de couchage; **to z. oneself into one's tent/overalls** fermer la fermeture éclair® de sa tente/combinaison; **she zipped the baby into his anorak** elle a enfilé le bébé dans son anorak et a fermé la fermeture éclair®

▸ **zip on** VT SEP attacher à l'aide d'une fermeture éclair® *ou* à glissière

VI s'attacher à l'aide d'une fermeture éclair®

▸ **zip through** VT INSEP *Fam (do quickly)* faire à toute vitesse; *(read quickly)* lire à toute vitesse

▸ **zip up** VT SEP *(clothes)* remonter *ou* fermer la fermeture éclair® *ou* à glissière de; **z. me up** remonte ma fermeture

VI **1** *(clothes)* se fermer à l'aide d'une fermeture éclair® *ou* à glissière **2** *Sl* **z. up!** la ferme!, ferme ton clapet!

Zip® disk N *Comput* cartouche *f* Zip®

Zip® drive N *Comput* lecteur *m* Zip®

zipper ['zɪpər] N *esp Am* fermeture *f* éclair® *inv ou* à glissière, *Belg* tirette *f*

▸▸ **z. bag** (sac *m*) fourre-tout *m inv* à fermeture éclair® *ou* à glissière

zipping ['zɪpɪŋ] N *(with tape)* avance *f* rapide

zippy ['zɪpɪ] ADJ *Fam* plein d'énergie *ou* d'entrain *ou* de punch; **a z. little car** une petite voiture nerveuse; **look z.!** grouille-toi!

zircon ['zɜːkɒn] N *Miner* zircon *m*

zit [zɪt] N *Am Fam (pimple)* bouton *m*

zither ['zɪðər] N *Mus* cithare *f*

zizz [zɪz] N *Br Fam* somme *m*; **to have a z.** faire un petit somme

zodiac ['zəʊdɪæk] N *Astrol* zodiaque *m*; **the signs of the z.** les signes *mpl* du zodiaque

zodiacal [zəʊ'daɪək(ə)l] ADJ zodiacal, -aux

zombi(e) ['zɒmbɪ] N *Rel, Fig* zombi *m*; **he walks about like a z.** il a tout le temps l'air abruti *ou* l'air d'un zombi; **I feel like a z.** je me sens complètement abruti

zonal ['zəʊn(ə)l] ADJ zonal, -aux

zone [zəʊn] N **1** zone *f*; *Admin* **no parking z.** zone d'interdiction de stationner; **parking meter z.** ≃ zone bleue; *Mil* **battle/war z.** zone de l'avant/de guerre; **danger z.** zone dangereuse; **z. of vision** *(when driving)* périmètre *m* de vision **2** *Am* **(postal delivery) z.** zone *f* (de distribution) postale **3** *Am Sl* **to be in a z.** *(dazed)* être dans le coaltar; *(after taking drugs)* être raide, planer; *Sport* **to be in the z.** être au top de sa forme

VT *(town etc)* répartir en zones

zoning ['zəʊnɪŋ] N répartition *f* en zones; *(in town planning)* zonage *m*

zonked (out) [zɒŋkt('aʊt)] ADJ *Sl (drugged)* défoncé; *(drunk)* pété, bourré; *(exhausted)* crevé, vanné

zoo [zuː] N jardin *m* zoologique, *Fam* zoo *m*

zookeeper ['zuːkiːpər] N gardien, -ienne de zoo

zoological [zəʊə'lɒdʒɪk(ə)l, zuː-] ADJ zoologique

▸▸ **z. gardens** jardin *m ou* parc *m* zoologique

zoologist [zəʊ'ɒlɒdʒɪst, zuː-] N zoologiste *mf*

zoology [zəʊ'ɒlɒdʒɪ, zuː-] N zoologie *f*

zoom [zuːm] N **1** *(noise)* bourdonnement *m*; *(louder)* vrombissement *m* **2** *Cin, TV (lens, effect)* zoom *m*

VI **1 to z. along** *or* **past/through** passer/traverser en trombe *ou* comme une flèche; **the cars are zooming along the road** les voitures passent en trombe sur la route; **children were zooming around on skateboards** des enfants passaient à toute vitesse sur des planches à roulettes **2** *Aviat (climb steeply)* monter en chandelle

▸▸ *Comput* **z. box** case *f* zoom; **z. lens** zoom *m*

▸ **zoom in** VI *Cin, TV* faire un zoom; **the camera zoomed in on the laughing children** la caméra a fait un zoom sur les enfants en train de rire

▸ **zoom off** VI déguerpir, partir en vitesse; **they're zooming off on holiday tomorrow** ils filent en vacances demain

▸ **zoom out** VI *Cin, TV* faire un zoom arrière

▸ **zoom up** VI *(of plane)* monter en chandelle; *(of rocket etc)* s'élever; *(of hit record etc)* monter comme une flèche; *(of prices etc)* monter en flèche

zooming ['zuːmɪŋ] N *Phot* changement *m* de focale

zoophyte ['zəʊəfaɪt] N *Biol* zoophyte *m*

zooted ['zuːtɪd] ADJ *Am Fam (drunk)* bourré, pété; *(on drugs)* raide, défoncé

zoot suit ['zuːtsuːt] N = costume *m* tapageur des années 40, rembourré aux épaules

zounds [zaʊndz] INT *Arch* morbleu!, sacrebleu!

zowie ['zaʊɪ] INT *Am Fam* oh là là!, la vache!

zucchini [zʊ'kiːnɪ, zuː-] N *Am* courgette *f*

Zulu ['zuːluː] ADJ zoulou

N **1** Zoulou, -oue **2** *Ling* zoulou *m*

Zululand ['zuːluːlænd] N Zoulouland *m*

zwieback ['zwiːbæk] N *Am* biscotte *f*

zygote ['zaɪgəʊt] N *Biol* zygote *m*

200 EXPRESSIONS ANGLAISES À CONNAÎTRE

L'amour et l'affection

she is the apple of his eye
il tient à elle comme à la prunelle de ses yeux

> ✋ L'expression anglaise est toujours au singulier (the apple of his/her eye) et s'applique toujours à une personne, jamais à une chose.

to sweep somebody off their feet
faire perdre la tête à quelqu'un

to carry a torch for someone
avoir un faible pour quelqu'un

to fall head over heels for someone
tomber follement amoureux de quelqu'un

Aimer/ne pas aimer

to be in someone's good books
être dans les petits papiers de quelqu'un

to have been bitten by the bug
avoir la folie de quelque chose

to get on like a house on fire
s'entendre à merveille

to turn one's nose up at something
dédaigner quelque chose

to give someone the cold shoulder
snober quelqu'un

to make someone's toes curl
donner des frissons de plaisir à quelqu'un

to ruffle someone's feathers
froisser quelqu'un

to get up someone's nose
taper sur les nerfs à quelqu'un

to look daggers at someone
foudroyer quelqu'un du regard

S'amuser

to let one's hair down
se détendre, se laisser aller

> ✋ Cette expression fait référence au fait qu'autrefois les femmes ne laissaient retomber leurs cheveux que dans l'intimité.

to have a blast
s'éclater

to paint the town red
faire la noce

to be out on the tiles
sortir faire la bringue

> ✋ L'expression compare ceux qui sortent s'amuser aux chats qui se promènent sur les toits la nuit.

Le bonheur

to be on top of the world
être en pleine forme

to be walking on air
to be on cloud nine
to be over the moon
être ravi, être aux anges

La tristesse

with one's heart in one's boots
complètement abattu

to hit rock bottom
toucher le fond

to be down in the mouth
être déprimé

to be in the doldrums
avoir le moral à zéro

 Le terme "doldrums" désigne la zone des calmes équatoriaux, où les vents sont faibles et où les bateaux à voiles ont donc du mal à avancer.

La colère

to hit the ceiling
péter les plombs

to go off at the deep end
piquer une crise

to blow one's top
sortir de ses gonds

to go ballistic
piquer une crise

to be like a red rag to a bull to somebody
avoir le don de mettre quelqu'un hors de soi

to get hot under the collar
se mettre en rogne

to be at the end of one's tether
être à bout

 Littéralement: avoir atteint le bout de sa longe. Quand l'herbe à portée de l'animal attaché est épuisée, il tire sur sa longe pour tenter de brouter plus loin.

Attention: cette expression n'est pas l'équivalent du français "être au bout du rouleau".

La mauvaise humeur

to be like a bear with a sore head
être d'humeur massacrante

to get out of bed on the wrong side
se lever du pied gauche

Les critiques

to drive a coach and horses through something
tailler quelque chose en pièces

to haul someone over the coals
démolir quelqu'un (en le critiquant)

the pot calling the kettle black
l'hôpital qui se moque de la charité

to give someone the rough side of one's tongue
parler brutalement à quelqu'un

to cut someone down to size
remettre quelqu'un à sa place

to pick holes in something
relever des erreurs dans quelque chose

to take a pot shot at someone
lancer une critique à quelqu'un

Les réprimandes

to throw the book at someone
passer un savon à quelqu'un

 L'expression fait référence au code pénal.

to send someone away with a flea in their ear
envoyer quelqu'un promener

to bite someone's head off
rembarrer quelqu'un

to jump down someone's throat
rabrouer quelqu'un

to have someone's guts for garters
massacrer quelqu'un

 Cette expression s'emploie toujours sous forme de menace.

to get it in the neck
en prendre pour son grade

La peur

to brick it
avoir les jetons

to get cold feet
avoir la frousse

to scare the pants off someone
faire une peur bleue à quelqu'un

to have one's heart in one's mouth
avoir le cœur qui bat la chamade

to get the wind up
avoir une peur bleue

Les opinions

to nail one's colours to the mast
afficher ses opinions

 Au cours d'une bataille navale, un navire voulant abandonner le combat descendait jadis son pavillon en signe de défaite. Impossible de déclarer forfait lorsque le pavillon est cloué au mât.

to get on one's soapbox
haranguer les foules

 Littéralement: monter sur sa caisse à savon (soapbox), c'est-à-dire sur une tribune improvisée, pour faire un discours.

to be in bed with someone
être allié avec quelqu'un de façon officieuse

to see eye to eye (with someone)
voir les choses du même œil (que quelqu'un)

to vote with one's feet
indiquer sa désapprobation en quittant les lieux

to change horses in midstream
se raviser en cours de route

to stick to one's guns
rester sur ses positions, tenir bon

 L'expression fait référence au soldat qui continue à tirer au lieu de s'enfuir devant l'ennemi.

to stick one's oar in
mettre son grain de sel

Contrôle et manipulation

to have someone eating out of one's hand
faire faire ce qu'on veut à quelqu'un

to wrap someone round one's little finger
faire ce qu'on veut de quelqu'un

to be in the saddle
tenir les rênes

to run a tight ship
mener tout le monde à la baguette

to twist someone's arm
exercer une pression sur quelqu'un

La tromperie

a wolf in sheep's clothing
un loup déguisé en agneau

to lead someone up the garden path
duper quelqu'un, faire marcher quelqu'un

to sell someone down the river
trahir quelqu'un, vendre quelqu'un

 Cette expression idiomatique fait allusion aux esclaves que l'on transportait sur le Mississippi jusqu'aux marchés aux esclaves de la Nouvelle-Orléans.

to pull the wool over someone's eyes
faire croire n'importe quoi à quelqu'un

 "The wool" était une perruque portée autrefois par les riches. Un voleur ou un plaisantin pouvait les désorienter en tirant la perruque sur leur visage.

L'âge

to have been around the block a few times
ne plus être de la première jeunesse

to be over the hill
commencer à se faire vieux

to be as old as the hills
dater de Mathusalem

to be long in the tooth
ne plus être tout jeune

 On peut estimer l'âge d'un cheval à la longueur de ses dents. En général, plus les dents sont longues, plus le cheval est âgé.

L'entraide

to bend over backwards
se mettre en quatre

to give someone a hand
donner un coup de main à quelqu'un

to get someone off the hook
tirer quelqu'un d'affaire

to give someone a leg up
donner un coup de pouce à quelqu'un

L'apparence

to look like death warmed up
avoir une mine de déterré

to be knee-high to a grasshopper
être haut comme trois pommes

to look like something the cat brought in
être en piteux état

to look like a million dollars
être superbe

L'argent

to be made of money
être plein aux as, rouler sur l'or

to bring home the bacon
faire bouillir la marmite

to laugh all the way to the bank
s'en mettre plein les poches

to cost an arm and a leg
coûter les yeux de la tête

to pay through the nose for something
payer quelque chose les yeux de la tête

it's daylight robbery
c'est du vol organisé

to cut corners
faire des économies exagérées

to push the boat out
ne pas regarder à la dépense

to throw money around
jeter l'argent par les fenêtres

to go Dutch
payer chacun sa part

to take someone to the cleaners
nettoyer quelqu'un, plumer quelqu'un

Boisson et ivresse

to drink like a fish
boire comme un trou

to be on the wagon
être au régime sec

> À l'origine, cette expression d'origine américaine était "on the water wagon", terme qui désignait le chariot qui transportait la citerne d'eau.

to wet one's whistle
se rincer le gosier

to be three sheets to the wind
avoir du vent dans les voiles

La prise de risques

a leap in the dark
un saut dans l'inconnu

to sail close to the wind
jouer un jeu dangereux

> Si on navigue au plus près, c'est-à-dire presque contre le vent, le bateau risque de chavirer.

better the devil you know
mieux vaut se contenter de ce que l'on a plutôt que de risquer de trouver pire

> L'expression anglaise est la forme tronquée du proverbe "better the devil you know than the devil you don't know": mieux vaut un danger que l'on connaît qu'un danger que l'on ne connaît pas.

on a wing and a prayer
Dieu sait comment

> Il s'agit d'une référence à une chanson des années 40 à propos d'un pilote d'avion.

to dice with death
risquer sa vie

to go out on a limb
prendre des risques

> Dans cette expression, l'image est celle d'une personne s'aventurant sur une branche d'arbre.

to skate on thin ice
toucher à un sujet délicat

to stick one's neck out
prendre des risques

Le changement et la continuité

to break the mould
rompre avec la tradition

to turn the tables
retourner la situation

the worm has turned
j'en ai/il en a/etc... assez de se laisser mener par le bout du nez

to be in a rut
être enlisé dans la routine

to turn the clock back
revenir en arrière

you can't teach an old dog new tricks
on ne peut pas apprendre un nouveau métier à quelqu'un une fois passé un certain âge

La supériorité

to be head and shoulders above someone
surpasser quelqu'un

to have someone for breakfast
ne faire qu'une bouchée de quelqu'un

to knock spots off someone
être bien supérieur à quelqu'un

to put somebody/something in the shade
éclipser quelqu'un/quelque chose

to make mincemeat of someone
démolir quelqu'un, écraser quelqu'un

to wipe the floor with someone
ne faire qu'une bouchée de quelqu'un

Ressemblances et différences

to be cut from the same cloth
être coulé dans le même moule

to be as alike as two peas in a pod
se ressembler comme deux gouttes d'eau

it's a different kettle of fish
c'est une autre affaire

to be poles apart
être diamétralement opposés

to be like chalk and cheese
c'est le jour et la nuit

Compréhension et incompréhension

to get one's head around something
piger quelque chose

the penny dropped
j'ai/il a/etc... fini par comprendre

to put two and two together
faire le rapprochement

to get hold of the wrong end of the stick
mal comprendre

to get one's wires crossed
mal se comprendre

S'informer

to pick someone's brains
avoir recours aux lumières de quelqu'un

to have one's ear to the ground
se tenir aux écoutes

Les Indiens d'Amérique sont souvent représentés l'oreille au sol en train d'estimer la position de personnes ou d'animaux.

to put out feelers
tâter le terrain

Les "feelers" sont les antennes d'un insecte.

to keep abreast of something
se tenir au courant de quelque chose

to see how the land lies
tâter le terrain

to get wind of something
avoir vent de quelque chose

Savoir

to know one's onions
connaître son affaire

 Cette expression n'a rien à voir avec "s'occuper de ses oignons".

to know something like the back of one's hand
connaître quelque chose comme sa poche

to hear something on the grapevine
apprendre quelque chose par le téléphone arabe

 Les premières lignes télégraphiques aux États-Unis étaient si mal installées que parfois les fils s'entremêlaient et l'ensemble ressemblait à des pieds de vigne. D'où le terme "grapevine telegraph" qui est à l'origine de l'expression.

to read someone like a book
savoir toujours ce que pense quelqu'un

to hear something from the horse's mouth
apprendre quelque chose de source sûre

 Pour se faire une idée de l'âge d'un cheval, la meilleure façon est de lui examiner les dents.

to be in the picture
être au courant

La détermination

to bite the bullet
serrer les dents

 Littéralement: mordre la balle. Lorsque les produits anesthésiques n'existaient pas, les médecins des armées demandaient à leurs patients de mordre une balle de fusil de façon à mieux supporter la douleur.

to grasp the nettle
prendre le taureau par les cornes

to leave no stone unturned
remuer ciel et terre

to put one's foot down
faire preuve de fermeté

come hell or high water
quoi qu'il arrive

La parole

to shoot the breeze
bavarder

to bend someone's ear
casser les oreilles à quelqu'un, pomper l'air à quelqu'un

to talk through one's hat
parler à tort et à travers

to talk the hind legs off a donkey
être bavard comme une pie

to shoot one's mouth off
ouvrir sa grande gueule, l'ouvrir

to spin a yarn
raconter une histoire à dormir debout

to put a sock in it
la fermer

to spill the beans
révéler un secret

 Il faut noter que l'expression anglaise ne signifie pas nécessairement "trahir un secret".

to be all mouth and no trousers
être une grande gueule

L'effort

to bust a gut
se décarcasser, se donner un mal de chien

to sing for one's supper
donner quelque chose en échange

to put one's shoulder to the wheel
se mettre à l'œuvre avec énergie

Réussite et échec

to be cooking with gas
marcher très fort

 Selon une vieille réclame américaine, rien ne valait la cuisine au gaz.

to bring the house down
casser la baraque, faire un tabac

 Il s'agit d'une allusion aux applaudissements qui font trembler les murs d'une salle de spectacle.

to set the world alight
faire sensation

to go belly up
faire faillite

to bite the dust
mordre la poussière, être battu

to go by the board
être abandonné, tomber à l'eau

to go great guns
marcher très fort

 Le terme "great guns" désignait l'artillerie lourde par opposition aux armes légères.

to come up roses
marcher parfaitement

to make the grade
se montrer à la hauteur

 Le terme "grade" désigne un tronçon de voie ferrée en pente raide. Aux États-Unis, "to make the grade" se disait d'un train qui pouvait monter cette côte.

La folie

to be out to lunch
débloquer

to have a screw loose
avoir une case de vide

to be barking mad
être complètement cinglé

to lose one's marbles
perdre la boule

Difficultés et problèmes

out of the frying pan into the fire
tomber de Charybde en Scylla

 L'expression anglaise s'utilise beaucoup plus fréquemment que sa traduction habituelle "tomber de Charybde en Scylla".

to go through the mill
en baver

 L'image est celle du grain écrasé par la meule du moulin.

to go to hell and back
connaître des moments très difficiles (mais s'en sortir)

to paint oneself into a corner
se mettre dans une impasse

to tie oneself in knots
s'embrouiller

to shoot oneself in the foot
faire une gaffe

to score an own goal
se faire du tort à soi-même

to leave someone holding the baby
refiler le bébé à quelqu'un

to cook someone's goose
couler quelqu'un

to pull the rug from under someone's feet
faire capoter les projets de quelqu'un

a hard nut to crack
un problème difficile à résoudre

a hot potato
un sujet délicat

to be an albatross around someone's neck
être un boulet pour quelqu'un

 Dans le poème de Coleridge *The Rime of the Ancient Mariner* (La Chanson du vieux marin), le mauvais sort s'abat sur un navire après qu'un marin a abattu un albatros. L'équipage force alors le coupable à porter l'oiseau mort autour du cou.

to cut off one's nose to spite one's face
se punir soi-même

La vanité

to be too big for one's boots
avoir les chevilles qui enflent

to blow one's own trumpet
chanter ses propres louanges

to throw one's weight around
faire l'important

to think one is the bee's knees
ne pas se prendre pour n'importe qui

Les relations

to play the field
papillonner, avoir de nombreuses aventures amoureuses

to have been left on the shelf
être en passe de devenir vieille fille

to tie the knot
se marier

to take the plunge
se marier

to sow one's wild oats
jeter sa gourme

to make a pass at someone
draguer quelqu'un

to get one's oats
prendre son pied

Les gaffes

to have egg on one's face
s'être couvert de ridicule

to blot one's copybook
se faire mal voir

to put one's foot in one's mouth
faire une gaffe

La mort

to pop one's clogs
casser sa pipe

to be pushing up the daisies
manger les pissenlits par la racine

to be as dead as a doornail
être mort et bien mort

to kick the bucket
casser sa pipe

200 ESSENTIAL FRENCH IDIOMS

Anger

péter les plombs
to blow one's top

> ✋ Here, the word 'plombs' refers to the fuses that melt in order to avoid a short-circuit.

sortir de ses gonds
to fly off the handle

> ✋ The image is that of a door that has come off its hinges.

se fâcher tout rouge
to go up the wall

j'ai la moutarde qui me monte au nez
I'm beginning to lose my temper

monter sur ses grands chevaux
to get on one's high horse

prendre la mouche
to fly off the handle

> ✋ This expression is close to 'quelle mouche vous a piqué?' (what's with you?). The idea is that a person's sudden outburst is the result of having being stung by an insect.

être hors de soi
to be beside oneself (with rage)

être vert de rage
to be livid with rage

avoir les nerfs en pelote
to be on edge, to be nervy

> ✋ Although this expression is reminiscent of the English 'to be a bundle of nerves', it is used to describe someone's exasperation, and not a permanent state.

se mettre en boule
to fly off the handle

se mettre en pétard
to blow one's top

se lever du pied gauche
to get out of bed on the wrong side

être soupe au lait
to flare up very easily

> ✋ This expression comes from the fact that soup with added milk boils over quickly.

ne pas être à prendre avec des pincettes
to be like a bear with a sore head

> ✋ Originally the expression 'être à prendre avec des pincettes' ('to have to be handled with tongs') was used about people who were unspeakably dirty or immoral.

avoir la tête près du bonnet
to have a short fuse

être de mauvais poil
to be in a bad mood

Telling somebody off

faire passer un mauvais quart d'heure à quelqu'un
to give somebody a bad time

remonter les bretelles à quelqu'un
to bawl somebody out

> ✋ The image is that of someone shaking someone else violently by their braces.

passer un savon à quelqu'un
to give somebody a telling-off

souffler dans les bronches à quelqu'un
to bawl somebody out

fusiller quelqu'un du regard
to look daggers at someone

Criticizing

casser du sucre sur le dos de quelqu'un
to bad-mouth somebody

tailler un costard à quelqu'un
to slag somebody off

> ✋ The idea here is that once you have a bad reputation, it is difficult to lose it, in the same way that a suit cannot be altered once it has been cut to a certain shape.

descendre quelqu'un en flammes
to shoot somebody down in flames

Annoyance

casser les pieds à quelqu'un
to do somebody's head in

courir sur le haricot à quelqu'un
to get up somebody's nose

rendre quelqu'un chèvre
to drive somebody up the wall

faire tourner quelqu'un en bourrique
to drive somebody round the bend

Getting along (and not)

s'entendre comme larrons en foire
to be as thick as thieves

être comme cul et chemise
to be inseparable

être comme les doigts de la main
to be very close

être dans les petits papiers de quelqu'un
to be in somebody's good books

 Here 'petits papiers' refers to fictitious notes that people would keep about who they liked and disliked.

je ne peux pas le voir en peinture
I can't stand the sight of him

se regarder en chiens de faïence
to glare at one another

This is a reference to china dogs which were sometimes used to decorate mantelpieces, one being placed at either end.

je l'ai dans le nez
he gets up my nose

il me sort par les trous de nez
I can't stand the sight of him

Love

avoir le coup de foudre
to fall in love at first sight

être un bourreau des cœurs
to be a ladykiller

avoir un cœur d'artichaut
to be fickle (in love)

The full form of this expression used to be 'cœur d'artichaut, une feuille pour tout le monde' (in an artichoke heart, there's a leaf for everyone), suggesting fickleness in love.

avoir quelqu'un dans la peau
to be crazy about somebody

être mordu
to be madly in love

en pincer pour quelqu'un
to be crazy about somebody

It is believed that this expression might come from the image of someone serenading their loved one while playing a stringed instrument.

avoir un faible pour quelqu'un
to have a soft spot for somebody

Truth and lies

mentir comme un arracheur de dents
to be a compulsive liar

In the days before anaesthetic, patients were wise enough not to believe the dentist when he said 'relax, you won't feel a thing'.

raconter des salades
to tell fibs

mener quelqu'un en bateau
to take somebody for a ride

faire avaler des couleuvres à quelqu'un
to take somebody in

ne pas savoir si c'est du lard ou du cochon
to wonder what to make of it

This expression – the literal meaning of which is 'not to know if this is bacon or pork'– is used in situations where the significance of an event is open to only a few different interpretations.

mener quelqu'un par le bout du nez
to have someone wrapped around one's little finger

une histoire à dormir debout
a cock-and-bull story

Appearance

être une grande perche
to be a beanpole

avoir un œil qui dit merde à l'autre
to have a squint

être haut comme trois pommes
to be knee-high to a grasshopper

avoir les dents du bonheur
to have a gap between one's teeth

se mettre sur son trente-et-un
to get all dressed up

être tiré à quatre épingles
to be dressed up to the nines

This is a reference to the fact that four pins are needed to stretch a piece of fabric and eliminate creases.

avoir les cheveux en bataille
to have dishevelled hair

être fagoté comme l'as de pique
to be dressed any old how

c'est une armoire à glace
he's built like a tank

A variant of this expression is 'être bâti comme une armoire normande' – to be built like a Norman wardrobe – such items of furniture being particularly large and sturdy.

être laid comme un pou
to be as ugly as sin

être joli comme un cœur
to be as pretty as a picture

avoir une mine de déterré
to look like death warmed up

Embarrassment

être dans ses petits souliers
to feel awkward

 In this expression embarrassment is likened to the sort of discomfort one experiences when wearing shoes that are too small.

il ne savait plus où se mettre
he didn't know where to put himself

être rouge comme une tomate
to be as red as a beetroot

Fear and worry

ne pas en mener large
to have one's heart in one's boots

serrer les fesses
to have the wind up

avoir les jetons
to have the jitters

avoir une peur bleue
to be scared to death

avoir les foies
to be scared out of one's wits

donner la chair de poule à quelqu'un
to make someone's flesh creep

se faire des cheveux (blancs)
to worry oneself (sick)

se faire un sang d'encre
to worry oneself (sick)

This expression – which means literally 'to worry so much that one's blood turns the colour of ink'– is similar to 'se faire du mauvais sang' (in both cases worry is believed to alter the quality of one's blood) and to 'se faire de la bile' (to produce bile).

Directness

ne pas y aller par quatre chemins
to go straight to the point

ne pas tourner autour du pot
not to beat around the bush

 The expression evokes the directness of someone going straight to the cooking pot to check its contents instead of wondering what's for dinner.

ne pas y aller de main morte
not to pull one's punches

ne pas mâcher ses mots
not to mince one's words

être franc du collier
to be very frank and open

ne pas y aller avec le dos de la cuillère
not to go for half-measures

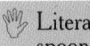 Literally, 'not to dish things out using the back of a spoon'.

Speaking and keeping silent

tenir la jambe à quelqu'un
to bore somebody with one's talk

être un moulin à paroles
to be a chatterbox

soûler quelqu'un
to bore somebody silly

avoir la langue bien pendue
to have the gift of the gab

ne pas avoir sa langue dans sa poche
never to be at a loss for words

discuter le bout de gras
to chew the fat

tailler une bavette
to have a chat

se mettre à table
to come clean

cracher le morceau
to spill the beans

 The origin of the expressions 'se mettre à table' and 'manger le morceau', which both mean 'to confess', dates back to the time when suspects were deliberately starved by the police in order to force them to confess. They were only given food once they had agreed to confess, hence the expression.

vendre la mèche
to give the game away

ne pas desserrer les dents
not to open one's mouth

avoir perdu sa langue
to have gone all quiet

tenir sa langue
to keep a secret

Surprise

couper le sifflet à quelqu'un
to shut somebody up

en boucher un coin à quelqu'un
to take the wind out of somebody's sails

en rester comme deux ronds de flan
to be flabbergasted

tomber de haut
to be dumbfounded

tomber des nues
to be flabbergasted

je n'en reviens pas
I can't get over it

il y a de quoi tomber à la renverse
it's staggering

Happiness

être au septième ciel
to be in seventh heaven

être aux anges
to be walking on air

être comme un coq en pâte
to be in clover

être heureux comme un poisson dans l'eau
to be in one's element

être bien dans ses baskets
to be sorted

Sadness

être malheureux comme les pierres
to be utterly miserable

broyer du noir
to be down in the dumps

être au trente-sixième dessous
to be extremely depressed

pleurer comme une madeleine
to cry one's heart out

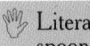 This expression has nothing to do with the fairy cakes called 'madeleines' but is a biblical allusion to Mary Magdalene, who cried over the body of Christ after his crucifixion.

aller comme une âme en peine
to wander around like a lost soul

avoir le cafard
to feel down

avoir une tête d'enterrement
to look sombre

avoir le moral à zéro
to be feeling down in the dumps

Laughter

s'en payer une tranche
to have the time of one's life

se fendre la pipe
to split one's sides (laughing)

être plié en deux
to be doubled up with laughter

rire comme un bossu/comme une baleine
to laugh one's head off

> It is believed that 'rire comme une baleine' (to laugh like a whale) might have derived from 'se tordre comme une baleine de parapluie retourné', playing on the words 'se tordre' which means both 'to bend' and 'to laugh' (in colloquial language), and 'baleine', which of course means 'whale', but which also means 'umbrella rib'.

rire à s'en décrocher la mâchoire
to split one's sides (laughing)

Madness

il ne tourne pas rond
he's not all there

travailler du chapeau
to have a screw loose

avoir un petit vélo dans la tête
to be off one's rocker

perdre la boule
to go round the bend

être marteau
to be nuts

être tombé sur la tête
to have a screw loose

avoir une araignée au plafond
to have bats in the belfry

être timbré
to be cracked

Stupidity

il n'a pas inventé l'eau chaude/la poudre
he'll never set the Thames on fire

être bête à manger du foin
to be as thick as two short planks

> This expression plays on the two meanings of the word 'bête'; as a noun it means 'animal' but as an adjective it means 'stupid'.

être bête comme ses pieds
to be unbelievably stupid

raisonner comme un tambour
to talk through one's hat

> This expression plays on the verbs 'raisonner' (to think) and 'résonner' (to echo). The hollowness of the drum (tambour) also suggests a person of little intelligence.

avoir une case de vide
to have a screw loose

avoir une cervelle de moineau
to be feather-brained

être dur à la détente
to be slow on the uptake

 The image is that of a weapon that is difficult to fire because of a stiff trigger.

Hunger and eating

avoir l'estomac dans les talons
to be ravenous

avoir les crocs
to be famished

avoir la dalle
to be hungry

avoir une faim de loup
to be ravenous

avoir les dents du fond qui baignent
to have stuffed oneself

tu as les yeux plus grands que le ventre
your eyes are bigger than your belly

manger sur le pouce
to have a quick snack

Drinking

boire comme un trou
to drink like a fish

avoir la gueule de bois
to be hungover

avoir du vent dans les voiles
to be three sheets to the wind

 This expression likens the teetering drunkard to a ship that is buffeted by the wind.

lever le coude
to booze

ne pas sucer que de la glace
to drink like a fish

Doing things easily

ce n'est pas la mer à boire
it's no big deal

c'est du gâteau
it's a piece of cake

faire quelque chose les doigts dans le nez
to do something very easily

ce n'est pas le bout du monde
it's no big deal

 Do not confuse with the expression 'ce n'est pas la fin du monde', which means 'it isn't the end of the world'.

c'est simple comme bonjour
it's as easy as pie

Leaving

prendre ses jambes à son cou
to take to one's heels

mettre les bouts/les voiles
to skedaddle

prendre le large
to clear off

prendre la poudre d'escampette
to make off

 The word 'escampette' only occurs in this expression and derives from 'escamper', an old French verb which means 'to flee'.

se faire la malle
to clear off

filer à l'anglaise
to sneak off, to take French leave

 Interestingly, but unsurprisingly, the French and the English credit each other with this type of rude behaviour.

prendre ses cliques et ses claques
to pack one's bags and go

Work and effort

mettre la main à la pâte
to lend a hand

 In this expression the word 'pâte' refers to the dough prepared and kneaded by bakers.

retrousser ses manches
to roll up one's sleeves

en mettre un coup
to pull out all the stops

mettre les bouchées doubles
to really get a move on

être un bourreau de travail
to be a workaholic

un travail de Romain
a Herculean task

se mettre en quatre pour faire quelque chose
to do one's utmost to do something

faire des pieds et des mains pour faire quelque chose
to move heaven and earth to do something

Laziness

avoir les côtes en long
to be bone-idle

Literally, this expression means 'to have vertical ribs', a condition that would make it impossible to bend over and do any kind of physical work.

se tourner les pouces
to twiddle one's thumbs

peigner la girafe
to do damn all

ne pas se fouler la rate
not to strain oneself

les avoir palmées
to be a complete layabout

This expression means 'to have webbed hands', a condition that would, obviously, make work somewhat difficult.

avoir un poil dans la main
to be workshy

Success

marcher comme sur des roulettes
to be going very smoothly

casser la baraque
to bring the house down

faire un malheur
to be a sensation

avoir le vent en poupe
to have the wind in one's sails

Failure

battre de l'aile
to be in a bad way

faire chou blanc
to draw a blank

tomber à l'eau
to fall through

s'en aller en eau de boudin
to go down the drain

rester le bec dans l'eau
to be left high and dry

c'est la fin des haricots
we've had it now

It is believed that this expression came to describe a hopeless situation because beans used to be the main staple of a soldier's diet and running out of beans was therefore considered a disaster.

Money

ne pas attacher son chien avec des saucisses
to be tight with one's money

Obviously, using link sausage as a lead for one's dog would be a sign that one doesn't care too much about money.

être près de ses sous
to be a penny-pincher

avoir des oursins dans le porte-monnaie
to be tight-fisted

Literally, 'to have sea urchins in one's purse'. The idea is that someone does not want to put his hand into his purse because the spikes of the sea urchins might hurt him.

coûter les yeux de la tête/la peau des fesses
to cost an arm and a leg

jeter l'argent par les fenêtres
to throw money down the drain

l'argent lui fond entre les doigts
money runs through his fingers

être un panier percé
to be a spendthrift

plaie d'argent n'est pas mortelle
money isn't everything

être plein aux as
to be rolling in it

rouler sur l'or
to be rolling in money

tirer le diable par la queue
to be hard up

mener la vie de château
to lead a life of luxury

s'en mettre plein les poches
to make a packet

un chèque en bois
a rubber cheque

être sans un radis
to be stony broke

être raide (comme un passe-lacets)
to be stony broke

être sur la paille
to be on one's uppers

plumer quelqu'un
to fleece somebody

Death

casser sa pipe
to kick the bucket

passer l'arme à gauche
to snuff it

The expression 'passer l'arme à gauche' meaning 'to die' comes from military terminology, referring to the position in which soldiers hold their weapons when they stand at ease; this is because in French the expression for 'to stand at ease' is 'être au repos' which can also mean 'to be at rest', ie dead.

manger les pissenlits par la racine
to be pushing up the daisies

lâcher la rampe
to kick the bucket

GRAMMAIRE ANGLAISE

ENGLISH GRAMMAR

TABLE DES MATIÈRES

1 GLOSSAIRE DES TERMES GRAMMATICAUX

ABSTRAIT
Un nom abstrait est un nom qui ne désigne pas un objet physique ou une personne, mais une qualité ou un concept. *Bonheur*, *vie*, *longueur*, ou en anglais kindness (*gentillesse*), love (*amour*), etc. sont des exemples de noms abstraits.

ACTIF
La voix active (ou l'actif) correspond aux phrases dont le sujet est considéré comme agissant, par exemple *mon père lave la voiture*. Elle s'oppose à la forme passive : *la voiture est lavée par mon père*. Voir PASSIF.

ADJECTIF
Mot adjoint au nom pour le décrire ou le déterminer. Parmi les adjectifs, on distingue les adjectifs qualificatifs (*une petite maison*), les adjectifs démonstratifs (*cette maison*), les adjectifs possessifs (*ma maison*), etc.

ADJECTIF SUBSTANTIVÉ
C'est un adjectif employé comme nom. Par exemple les adjectifs *jeune*, *réel*, *virtuel*, etc. peuvent aussi s'employer comme noms : *les jeunes*, *le réel*, *le virtuel*. De même en anglais, the blind (*les aveugles*), the homeless (*les sans-abri*), etc.

ADVERBE
Les adverbes accompagnent le plus souvent un verbe pour ajouter une information supplémentaire en indiquant comment l'action est accomplie (adverbe de manière), **quand**, **où** et **avec quelle intensité** l'action est accomplie (adverbes de temps, de lieu et d'intensité), etc. Certains adverbes peuvent aussi s'employer avec un adjectif ou un autre adverbe (par exemple *une fille très mignonne*, *il y va trop souvent*).

ANTÉCÉDENT
Mot auquel renvoie un pronom. Par exemple, dans *je connais l'homme qui a fait ça*, *l'homme* est l'antécédent du pronom relatif *qui*.

APPOSITION
On dit qu'un mot ou une proposition est en apposition par rapport à un autre mot ou une autre proposition lorsque l'un ou l'autre est placé directement après le nom ou la proposition, sans y être relié par aucun mot (par exemple *M. Duclos, notre directeur, a téléphoné ce matin*).

ARTICLE DÉFINI
Les articles définis sont *le*, *la*, *les* en français. Ils correspondent tous à the en anglais.

ARTICLE INDÉFINI
Les articles indéfinis sont *un*, *une* (et *des* au pluriel) en français. Ils correspondent à a (ou an devant une voyelle ou un h muet) en anglais.

ASPECT
L'aspect correspond à la manière dont on envisage l'action exprimée par le verbe : dans sa durée, son déroulement, son achèvement, etc. On distingue en anglais l'aspect simple, l'aspect progressif (ou continu) et le "perfect".

Voir FORME PROGRESSIVE et PERFECT.

ATTRIBUT
Nom ou, le plus souvent, adjectif, relié au sujet ou au complément d'objet par le verbe *être* ou un autre verbe d'état. Par exemple, **I am** tired (*je suis fatigué*), **it seems** interesting (*cela semble intéressant*). Voir aussi ÉPITHÈTE.

AUXILIAIRE
Les auxiliaires sont employés pour former les temps composés d'autres verbes, par exemple dans he has **gone** (*il est parti*), l'auxiliaire employé est have (et être en français). En anglais, on distingue les auxiliaires ordinaires (have, be, do) et les auxiliaires modaux (can, could, may, etc.). Voir MODAL.

CARDINAL
Les nombres cardinaux sont *un*, *deux*, *trois*, etc. Ils expriment la quantité. On les oppose aux nombres ordinaux. Voir ORDINAL.

COLLECTIF
Un collectif est un mot qui est au singulier mais qui désigne un groupe de gens ou de choses. Par exemple, crowd (*foule*), flock (*troupeau*) et fleet (*flotte*) sont des noms collectifs.

COMPARATIF
Le comparatif des adjectifs et des adverbes permet d'établir une comparaison entre deux personnes, deux choses ou deux actions. En français, on emploie *plus... que* (comparatif de supériorité), *moins... que* (comparatif d'infériorité) et *aussi... que* (comparatif d'égalité).

COMPLÉMENT D'OBJECT DIRECT
Groupe nominal qui accompagne un verbe (= verbe transitif direct), sans préposition entre les deux. Par exemple, *j'ai rencontré un ami*. Les pronoms peuvent aussi s'employer comme compléments d'objet direct : *je l'ai rencontré*.

COMPLÉMENT D'OBJECT INDIRECT
Groupe nominal ou pronom qui suit un verbe (= verbe transitif indirect), normalement séparé de ce dernier par une préposition (en général à en français) : *je parle à mon ami*. Vous noterez qu'en français comme en anglais, on omet souvent la préposition devant un pronom. Par exemple, dans *je lui ai envoyé un cadeau*, *lui* est l'équivalent de *à lui* : c'est le complément d'objet indirect. De même, him correspond à to him dans la phrase équivalente anglaise I **sent** him a **present**.

CONDITIONNEL
Mode verbal employé pour exprimer ce que quelqu'un ferait ou ce qui arriverait si une condition était remplie, par exemple *il viendrait s'il le pouvait ; la chaise se serait cassée s'il s'était assis dessus*.

CONJONCTION
Les conjonctions sont des mots qui relient deux mots ou propositions. On distingue les conjonctions de coordination, comme *et*, *ou*, *or*, et les conjonctions de subordination comme *parce que*, *après que*, *bien que*, qui introduisent une proposition subordonnée. Voir SUBORDONNÉE.

CONTINU
Voir FORME PROGRESSIVE.

DÉMONSTRATIF
Les adjectifs démonstratifs (*ce*, *cette*, *ces*, etc.) et les pronoms démonstratifs (*celui-ci*, *celui-là*, etc.) s'emploient pour désigner une personne ou un objet bien précis.

DÉNOMBRABLE
Un nom est dénombrable s'il peut avoir un pluriel et si on peut l'employer avec un article indéfini. Par exemple house (*maison*), car (*voiture*), dog (*chien*). On les oppose aux noms indénombrables. Voir INDÉNOMBRABLE.

ÉPITHÈTE
Adjectif ou nom qui n'est pas relié au nom par un verbe, par opposition à l'attribut. Par exemple, an interesting film (*un film intéressant*). Voir aussi ATTRIBUT.

FORME PROGRESSIVE
La forme progressive (ou forme continue) d'un verbe exprime l'action dans sa durée. Elle se forme avec to be + participe présent : I am thinking (*je pense*), he has been writing all day (*il a passé la journée à écrire*), will she be staying with us? (*est-ce qu'elle va loger chez nous ?*).

GÉNITIF
Le génitif anglais (ou cas possessif) permet d'exprimer l'appartenance ou la dépendance. Il se forme avec 's après un nom singulier (my father's car *la voiture de mon père*) et simplement avec l'apostrophe après un nom pluriel (my parents' car, *la voiture de mes parents*).

GÉRONDIF
Le gérondif anglais est une forme verbale ayant une fonction nominale. On l'appelle aussi "verbe substantivé". Il se forme en ajoutant la terminaison -ing au radical du verbe. Par exemple, skiing is fun (*c'est amusant de faire du ski*). Il peut aussi être précédé d'une préposition : I'm fed up with waiting (*j'en ai assez d'attendre*). Attention à ne pas le confondre avec le participe présent anglais qui se forme de la même manière.

IDIOMATIQUE
Se dit d'un emploi ou d'une expression propres à une langue donnée et qui ne peuvent donc pas se traduire mot à mot dans une autre langue. Par exemple, he thinks he's the cat's whiskers correspond en français à *il se croit sorti de la cuisse de Jupiter*.

IMPÉRATIF
Mode qui permet d'exprimer un ordre (*va-t'en, tais-toi !*) ou de faire des suggestions (*allons-y*).

INDÉFINI
Les pronoms et les adjectifs indéfinis sont des mots qui ne se rapportent pas à des personnes ou à des choses précises (par exemple *chaque, quelqu'un*, etc.).

INDÉNOMBRABLE
Les indénombrables sont des noms qui n'ont pas de pluriel et ne peuvent normalement pas être précédés de l'article indéfini ou d'un adjectif cardinal. Par exemple *le beurre, la paresse* en français, et advice (*conseil*), travel (*voyage*) en anglais. On les oppose aux noms dénombrables. Voir DÉNOMBRABLE.

INDICATIF
Mode qui permet de décrire l'action ou l'état de manière neutre : *j'aime, il est venu, nous essayons*. Il s'oppose au subjonctif, au conditionnel et à l'impératif.

INFINITIF
Forme de base du verbe qui ne porte pas d'indication de personne et qui, en anglais, peut être précédée ou non de to. Le verbe à l'infinitif employé sans to s'appelle le "radical". Par exemple, to eat ou eat (*manger*).

INTERROGATIF
Les pronoms interrogatifs sont employés pour formuler une question. Il peut s'agir d'une question directe (*quand arriveras-tu ?*) ou d'une question indirecte (*je ne sais pas quand il arrivera*). Voir QUESTION.

INTRANSITIF
Se dit d'un verbe qui n'a pas de complément d'objet et dont l'action se limite au sujet, par opposition à un verbe transitif. Par exemple, *marcher* est un verbe intransitif. Voir TRANSITIF.

MODAL
Les auxiliaires modaux permettent de modifier un verbe en exprimant différentes notions : la capacité, la possibilité, l'obligation, etc. Les auxiliaires modaux anglais sont can/could, may/might, must/had to, shall/should, will/would, ought to. On trouve aussi les "semi-auxiliaires" : used to, dare et need. Une des caractéristiques des auxiliaires modaux est que, aux formes interrogative et négative, ils se construisent sans do.

MODE
Le mode représente l'attitude du sujet parlant vis-à-vis de l'action dont il est question dans la phrase. Voir aussi INDICATIF, SUBJONCTIF, CONDITIONNEL, IMPÉRATIF.

NOM
Un nom (ou substantif) est un mot qui sert à désigner une chose, un être animé, un lieu ou des idées abstraites. Par exemple *passeport, chat, magasin, vie*. On distingue aussi les dénombrables, les indénombrables et les collectifs. Voir DÉNOMBRABLE, INDÉNOMBRABLE et COLLECTIF.

NOM COMPOSÉ
Nom formé de deux mots distincts ou plus, comme *ouvre-boîte* et *tiroir-caisse* en français, ou table napkins (*serviettes de table*) et mother-in-law (*belle-mère*) en anglais.

NOMBRE
Le nombre d'un nom indique si celui-ci est **singulier** ou **pluriel**. Un nom singulier fait référence à une seule chose ou à une seule personne (*train, garçon*), et un nom pluriel à plusieurs (*trains, garçons*).

OBJET DIRECT
Voir COMPLÉMENT.

OBJET INDIRECT
Voir COMPLÉMENT.

ORDINAL
Les nombres ordinaux sont *premier, deuxième, troisième*, etc. Ils expriment l'ordre, le classement. On les oppose aux nombres cardinaux. Voir CARDINAL.

PARTICIPE PASSÉ
Forme verbale qui se place après l'auxiliaire pour former les temps composés (*il a mangé, ils sont arrivés*) ou la voix passive (*la maison vient d'être vendue*). Le participe passé anglais se forme en ajoutant la terminaison -d ou -ed au radical (participes passés réguliers) et s'emploie après l'auxiliaire have, pour former le "perfect" et après l'auxiliaire be dans les phrases au passif. Voir PASSIF et PERFECT. Pour la liste des participes passés irréguliers, voir pp. A63-5.

PARTICIPE PRÉSENT
Le participe présent en anglais est la forme verbale qui se termine en -ing. Il permet par exemple d'exprimer la manière : they went running out of the house (*ils sont partis de la maison en courant*). Il sert aussi à for-

mer l'aspect progressif. Voir FORME PRO-GRESSIVE.

PARTITIF
En français, l'article partitif *de* (ou *du, de la*) permet de désigner une partie par rapport à un tout qu'on ne peut pas dénombrer. Par exemple, *j'ai de l'argent, il nous faut du bois*, etc.

PASSIF
Un verbe est au passif ou à la voix passive lorsque le sujet n'accomplit pas l'action mais la subit. En français, le passif se forme avec le verbe être + participe passé du verbe, par exemple, *il est aimé, les tickets sont vendus à l'entrée*, etc. En anglais, la voix passive se forme avec le verbe to be + participe passé du verbe, par exemple **he was rewarded** (*il fut récompensé*). Voir ACTIF.

PAST PERFECT
Voir PERFECT.

PERFECT
C'est l'aspect qui permet d'exprimer une action accomplie dans le passé ayant des conséquences au moment de l'énonciation ou une action commencée dans le passé et qui se poursuit dans le présent. Il se forme avec to have + participe passé. On distingue le "present perfect", comme dans **I have arrived** (*je suis arrivé*) ou **I have seen** (*j'ai vu*), et le "past perfect" (ou "pluperfect") comme dans **I had arrived** (*j'étais arrivé*) ou **I had seen** (*j'avais vu*).

PLUPERFECT
Voir PERFECT.

POSSESSIF
Les adjectifs et les pronoms possessifs s'emploient pour indiquer la possession ou l'appartenance. Ce sont des mots comme *mon/le mien, ton/le tien, notre/le nôtre*, etc.

PRÉPOSITION
Les prépositions introduisent le complément d'un nom, d'un verbe, d'un adjectif ou d'un adverbe. Ce sont des mots tels que *avec, dans, vers, à*, etc. Ils sont normalement suivis d'un nom ou d'un pronom.

PRESENT PERFECT
Voir PERFECT.

PRINCIPALE
Au sein d'une phrase, la proposition principale est celle dont dépendent les autres propositions (dites subordonnées). Par exemple *il a dit* dans *il a dit qu'il viendrait*. Voir SUBORDONNÉE.

PRONOM
Mot qui remplace un nom. Les principales catégories de pronoms sont les :
* pronoms personnels (*je, me, moi, tu, te, toi*, etc.)
* pronoms démonstratifs (*celui-ci, celui-là*, etc.)
* pronoms relatifs (*qui, que*, etc.)
* pronoms interrogatifs (*qui ?, quoi ?, lequel ?*, etc.)
* pronoms possessifs (*le mien, le tien*, etc.)
* pronoms réfléchis (*me, te, se*, etc.)
* pronoms indéfinis (*quelque chose, tout*, etc.)

PROPOSITION
Une proposition est un groupe de mots qui contient au moins un sujet et un verbe : *il chante* est une proposition. Une phrase peut être composée de plusieurs propositions : *il chante | quand il prend sa douche | et qu'il est content.*

QUESTION
Il existe deux types de questions : les questions au style **direct**, qui sont retranscrites telles qu'elles ont été posées, avec un point d'interrogation (par exemple, *quand viendra-t-il ?*) ; les questions au style **indirect**, qui sont introduites par une proposition et ne nécessitent pas de point d'interrogation (par exemple, *je me demande quand il viendra*).

RADICAL
Voir INFINITIF.

RÉFLÉCHI
Les verbes réfléchis "renvoient" l'action sur le sujet (par exemple *je me suis habillé*). En anglais, on emploie les pronoms réfléchis **myself, yourself**, etc. : **enjoy yourself** (*amuse-toi bien*). Les verbes réfléchis sont moins nombreux en anglais qu'en français.

SUBJONCTIF
Mode employé pour exprimer un souhait, un doute ou une possibilité, etc. Par exemple, le verbe *venir* est au subjonctif dans la phrase *il se peut qu'il vienne*. En anglais, on le trouve notamment dans les propositions conditionnelles (**if I were you, I would tell him** *si j'étais toi, je lui dirais*) mais de manière générale, son emploi n'est pas très courant.

SUBORDONNÉE
Au sein d'une phrase, la subordonnée est une proposition qui dépend de la proposition principale. Sans cette dernière, la subordonnée ne formerait pas une phrase complète du point de vue syntaxique. Par exemple, dans *il a dit qu'il viendrait, qu'il viendrait* est la proposition subordonnée.

SUBSTANTIF
Voir NOM.

SUPERLATIF
C'est le degré le plus élevé de la comparaison. On distingue d'une part le superlatif relatif qui se construit en français avec *le plus..., le moins...*, et d'autre part le superlatif absolu (*très sympathique*).

TEMPS COMPOSÉ
Les temps composés sont des temps verbaux formés de plus d'un élément. En anglais, ils se forment avec l'**auxiliaire + participe présent** ou **passé** du verbe conjugué. Par exemple **I am reading** (*je suis en train de lire*), **he has gone** (*il est parti*).

TRANSITIF
Se dit d'un verbe qui se construit avec un complément d'objet. Les verbes transitifs s'opposent aux verbes intransitifs. Les verbes transitifs directs régissent leur complément (complément d'objet direct) sans intermédiaire ; c'est le cas de *manger*. Les verbes transitifs indirects régissent leur complément (complément d'objet indirect) par l'intermédiaire d'une préposition ; par exemple, *parler à*. Voir INTRANSITIF.

VERBE COMPOSÉ
Les verbes composés anglais ou verbes à particules (en anglais "phrasal verbs") sont des verbes dont le sens n'équivaut pas forcément à la somme du sens des deux éléments qui les composent. Par exemple, **run up** peut avoir le sens de "monter en courant" ou de "laisser s'accumuler" (**I've run up a huge overdraft** *j'ai un découvert énorme*). Les verbes composés forment donc un tout ; la particule est indispensable, elle permet de modifier le sens du verbe principal.

2 LES ARTICLES

A LES FORMES

a) L'article indéfini "un/une" se traduit par a devant une consonne et an devant une voyelle :

a **cat**	un chat
a **dog**	un chien
an **owl**	une chouette
an **umbrella**	un parapluie

Il est cependant important de se souvenir que l'on emploie a/an selon que l'initiale du mot qui suit se prononce comme une voyelle ou non. Ainsi, le "h" muet des trois mots suivants (ainsi que ceux de la même famille) est précédé de an :

an **hour** ['aʊə(r)]	une heure
an **heir** [eə(r)]	un héritier
an **honest man** ['ɒnɪst]	un honnête homme

Il en est de même pour les abréviations commençant phonétiquement par une voyelle :

| an **MP** ['em'piː] | un député |

En revanche, la diphtongue se prononçant "iou" et qui s'écrit "eu" ou "u" est précédée de a :

a **university** ['juːnɪ'vɜːsətɪ]	une université
a **eucalyptus tree** ['juːkə'lɪptəs]	un eucalyptus
a **union** ['juːnjən]	un syndicat

Avec le mot **hotel**, on peut employer a ou an, bien qu'à l'oral on préfère l'emploi de a. Les deux formes de l'article indéfini sont également possibles devant les adjectifs **historic** et **historical**, même si à l'écrit ou dans un style littéraire on dira plutôt **an historic**.

b) L'article défini "le/la/les" se traduit toujours par **the** :

the **cat**	le chat
the **owl**	la chouette
the **holidays**	les vacances

On peut prononcer le e de **the** un peu comme un "i" français lorsque le mot qui suit commence phonétiquement par une voyelle (voir a) ci-dessus), comme pour **the owl**, ou lorsqu'il est accentué :

he's definitely the man for the job
voilà vraiment l'homme qu'il faut pour ce travail

B LA POSITION DE L'ARTICLE

L'article précède le nom et tout adjectif (avec ou sans adverbe) placé devant un nom :

a good book/the good book
un bon livre/le bon livre

a very good book/the very good book
un très bon livre/le très bon livre

Cependant **all** et **both** précèdent l'article défini :

they drank all the wine
ils ont bu tout le vin

both the men (= both men) **were guilty**
les deux hommes étaient tous les deux coupables

L'adverbe **rather** peut se placer avant ou après l'article, sans qu'il y ait de différence de sens :

it was rather a good play/a rather good play
c'était une assez bonne pièce

that was a rather unfortunate remark/rather an unfortunate remark
c'était une remarque plutôt malencontreuse

À la différence de **rather**, l'adverbe **quite** ne signifie pas la même chose lorsqu'il est placé avant ou après l'article. Il a le même sens que **rather** (*assez*) quand il précède l'article, mais il signifie "complètement", "tout à fait", quand il se trouve entre l'article et l'adjectif. Comparez :

it was quite a good play
c'était une assez bonne pièce

that would be a quite useless task
ce serait une tâche tout à fait inutile

Les adverbes **too**, **so** et **as** précèdent l'adjectif et l'article indéfini. On a donc la construction **too/so/as** + adjectif + article + nom :

if that is not too great a favour to ask
si ce n'est pas trop vous demander

never have I seen so boring a film
je n'ai jamais vu de film aussi ennuyeux

I have never seen as fine an actor as Olivier
je n'ai jamais vu d'acteur aussi bon qu'Olivier

On peut aussi trouver **many a** (*plus d'un*), **such a** (*un tel*) et **what a** (*quel !*) :

many a man would do the same
plus d'un homme ferait la même chose

| **she's such a fool** | **what a joke!** |
| *elle est tellement idiote* | *quelle blague !* |

Remarquez qu'avec **such** l'adjectif suit l'article indéfini, tandis qu'avec **so** il le précède (voir aussi ci-dessus) :

I have never seen such a beautiful painting
je n'ai jamais vu une peinture aussi belle

I have never seen so beautiful a painting
je n'ai jamais vu une peinture aussi belle

Half (*la moitié de*) aussi précède en général l'article :

half the world knows about this
presque tout le monde est au courant

I'll be back in half an hour
je reviens dans une demi-heure

Lorsque **half** fait partie d'un nom composé (**half-bottle**, **half-brother**, etc.), l'article se place bien sûr en premier :

why don't you buy a half-bottle of rum?
pourquoi tu n'achètes pas une demi-bouteille de rhum ?

Comparez avec :

he drank half a bottle of rum
il a bu la moitié d'une bouteille de rhum

C L'EMPLOI DES ARTICLES

1 L'article indéfini (a, an)

L'article indéfini ne s'emploie normalement que pour les noms dénombrables, bien que la distinction "dénombrable/indénombrable" ne soit pas toujours évidente, comme nous le verrons p. A9.

a) Devant un nom générique, pour faire référence à une catégorie ou à une espèce :

a mouse is smaller than a rat
une souris est plus petite qu'un rat

A mouse et **a rat** représentent les souris et les rats en général. Avec une légère différence de sens, l'article défini peut aussi s'employer devant un terme générique. Voir 2b).

Remarquez que le terme générique **man** représentant l'humanité (à la différence de **a man** = "un homme", "une personne de sexe masculin") ne prend pas d'article :

this could be considered man's greatest achievement
on pourrait considérer ça comme le plus grand exploit de l'homme

b) Avec des noms attributs du sujet ou dans des appositions, ou bien après as (en particulier avec des noms de métiers, à la différence du français) :

he is a hairdresser
il est coiffeur

she has become a Member of Parliament
elle est devenue députée

John McIntyre, a journalist with over twenty years' experience, seems the best candidate for the job
John McIntyre, journaliste ayant plus de vingt ans d'expérience, semble être le meilleur candidat pour ce travail

her brother, a retired police officer, was able to give her advice on making her home more secure
son frère, policier à la retraite, a pu la conseiller sur la manière de rendre sa maison plus sûre

he used to work as a skipper
il travaillait comme capitaine

L'article indéfini s'emploie lorsque le nom fait partie d'un groupe. S'il n'y a pas d'appartenance à un groupe, on omet l'article, comme dans l'exemple suivant, où la personne mentionnée est unique :

she is now Duchess of York
elle est maintenant duchesse d'York

Professor Draper, head of the English department
le professeur Draper, chef du département d'anglais

Si on a une liste de mots en apposition, on peut omettre l'article :

Olivia Ford, actress, charity worker and campaigner, died yesterday after a long illness
Olivia Ford, actrice, bénévole et militante, est morte hier après une longue maladie

Mais on emploiera l'article défini the pour une personne célèbre (ou pour distinguer deux personnes ayant le même nom) :

Nicole Kidman, the actress
Nicole Kidman, l'actrice

c) Comme préposition :

L'article indéfini peut s'employer dans le sens de "par", comme dans les exemples suivants :

the haddock is £6 a kilo
le haddock est à 6 livres le kilo

take two tablets twice a day
prenez deux comprimés deux fois par jour

d) Avec little (*peu de* + indénombrable) et few (*peu de* + dénombrable) :

L'article indéfini qui accompagne ces deux mots indique un sens positif (*un peu de*). Employés seuls, little et few ont un sens négatif :

she needs a little attention (= some attention)
elle a besoin d'un peu d'attention

she needs little attention (= hardly any attention)
elle a besoin de peu d'attention

they have a few paintings (= some)
ils ont quelques tableaux

they have few paintings (= hardly any)
ils ont peu de tableaux

Only a little/only a few signifient plus ou moins la même chose que little/few, qui sont moins courants :

I have only a little coffee left (= hardly any)
il ne me reste presque plus de café

I can afford only a few books (= hardly any)
je ne peux me permettre d'acheter que quelques livres

Remarquez aussi l'expression a good few, qui équivaut à "pas mal de" en français :

there are a good few miles to go yet
il y a encore pas mal de kilomètres à faire

he's had a good few to drink
il a pas mal bu

2 L'article défini (the)

a) L'article défini s'emploie avec des noms dénombrables et des noms indénombrables :

the butter (*indénombrable*)	*le beurre*
the cup (*sing. dénombrable*)	*la tasse*
the cups (*pl. dénombrable*)	*les tasses*

b) Comme l'article indéfini, l'article défini peut s'employer devant un nom générique. Il semble alors plus scientifique :

the mouse is smaller than the rat (comparez avec 1a) ci-dessus)
la souris est plus petite que le rat

when was the potato first introduced to Europe?
quand est-ce que la pomme de terre fut introduite en Europe pour la première fois ?

c) Si un groupe prépositionnel est placé après le nom et qu'il a pour fonction de définir de manière précise le nom auquel on fait référence, il faut employer l'article défini. Cet article désigne alors un objet ou une personne en particulier :

she has just met the man of her dreams
elle vient juste de rencontrer l'homme de sa vie

the money from my parents hasn't arrived yet
l'argent que mes parents m'ont envoyé n'est pas encore arrivé

Si par contre le groupe prépositionnel sert à décrire le nom de manière générale et que la phrase exprime un fait général, on omet normalement l'article. Comparez l'exemple qui suit avec le dernier des exemples précédents :

I often receive money from my parents
je reçois souvent de l'argent de mes parents

knowledge of a second language would be an advantage
la connaissance d'une deuxième langue serait un avantage

presence of mind is what he needs
ce qu'il lui faut, c'est de la présence d'esprit

Dans la phrase :

the presence of mind that she showed was extraordinary
la présence d'esprit dont elle a fait preuve était extraordinaire

l'emploi de the est obligatoire car la proposition relative (that she showed) permet de faire référence à un exemple de présence d'esprit bien précis.

Cependant, quand le complément du nom introduit par of sert à la fois à définir et à décrire le nom, on emploie l'article défini :

the women of Paris (= women from Paris, in general)
les femmes de Paris

the children of such families (= children from such families)
les enfants de telles familles

d) L'omission de l'article défini :

À la différence du français, l'omission de l'article défini en anglais est très fréquente. Ainsi, un grand nombre de noms ne sont pas précédés de l'article s'ils font référence à une fonction ou à des caractéristiques générales, plutôt qu'à l'objet. On n'emploie pas l'article défini pour :

i) les institutions, par exemple :

church	*l'église*
prison	*la prison*
college	*l'établissement d'enseignement supérieur*

school	l'école
court	le tribunal
university	l'université
hospital	l'hôpital

Exemples:

do you go to church?
tu vas à la messe ?, tu es pratiquant ?

she's in hospital/in prison **Tom is at university**
elle est à l'hôpital/en prison *Tom est à l'université*

aren't you going to school today?
tu ne vas pas à l'école aujourd'hui ?

Cependant, en anglais américain, on préfère l'emploi de l'article défini devant **hospital** :

Caroline is back in the **hospital**
Caroline est de retour à l'hôpital

Si le nom fait référence au bâtiment plutôt qu'à sa fonction, on emploie alors **the** :

walk up to the **church and turn right**
allez jusqu'à l'église, puis tournez à droite

the taxi stopped at the **school**
le taxi s'est arrêté devant l'école

The s'emploie aussi pour désigner un nom défini ou précisé par le contexte :

at the **university where his father studied**
à l'université où son père a étudié

she's at the **university**
elle est à l'université (dans cette ville, etc.)

Pour faire référence à l'institution en général, on emploie l'article :

the **Church was against it**
l'Église était contre

ii) les moyens de transport précédés de **by** :

we always go by **bus/car/boat/train/plane**
nous partons toujours en bus/en voiture/en bateau/en train/en avion

iii) les repas :

can you meet me before **lunch?**
tu peux me voir avant le déjeuner ?

buy some chicken for **dinner, will you?**
tu veux bien acheter du poulet pour le dîner ?

Mais si l'on fait référence à une occasion précise, on emploie l'article. Ainsi, il y a une différence entre :

I enjoy lunch et : **I enjoyed** the **lunch**
j'aime le déjeuner *j'ai apprécié ce déjeuner*

Dans le premier cas, on fait référence au plaisir de manger à midi ; dans le second cas, on parle d'un repas particulier.

iv) les moments de la journée et de la nuit, après une préposition autre que **in** et **during** :

I don't like going out at **night**
je n'aime pas sortir le soir/la nuit

these animals can often be seen after **dusk**
on peut souvent voir ces animaux après le crépuscule

they go to bed around **midnight**
ils vont se coucher vers minuit

mais :

see you in **the morning!**
à demain matin !

if you feel peckish during **the day, have an apple**
si tu as un petit creux dans la journée, mange une pomme

v) les saisons, en particulier pour exprimer un contraste par rapport à une autre saison plutôt que pour faire référence à une période de l'année. Ainsi :

spring is here! (winter is over)
le printemps est là ! (l'hiver est fini)

it's like winter today
on se croirait en hiver aujourd'hui

mais :

the **winter was spent at expensive ski resorts**
on passait l'hiver dans des stations de ski de luxe

he needed the **summer to recover**
il avait besoin de l'été pour récupérer

Après **in**, on emploie parfois l'article défini, avec très peu de différence de sens entre les deux cas :

most leaves turn yellow in **(the) autumn**
la plupart des feuilles deviennent jaunes en automne

En anglais américain, on préfère l'emploi de **the**.

vi) les expressions de temps avec **next** et **last** :

Si de telles expressions sont envisagées par rapport au présent, on n'emploie normalement pas l'article :

can we meet next **week?**
est-ce qu'on peut se voir la semaine prochaine ?

he was drunk last **night**
il était soûl hier soir

Dans les autres cas, on emploie l'article :

we arrived on 31 March and the **next day was spent relaxing by the pool**
nous sommes arrivés le 31 mars et on a passé le jour suivant à se relaxer près de la piscine

vii) les noms abstraits :

a talk about politics
un discours sur la politique

a study of human relationships
une étude sur les relations humaines

suspicion is a terrible thing
le soupçon est quelque chose de terrible

Mais, bien sûr, lorsque le mot est précisé, on emploie l'article (voir 2c) ci-dessus) :

the **politics of disarmament**
la politique de désarmement

viii) certaines maladies :

he has diabetes **I've got jaundice**
il a du diabète *j'ai la jaunisse*

Cependant, pour certaines maladies courantes, on peut employer l'article dans un anglais un peu plus familier :

she has (the) flu **he's got (the) measles**
elle a la grippe *il a la rougeole*

ix) les noms de couleurs :

red is my favourite colour
le rouge est ma couleur préférée

x) les noms de matériaux, d'aliments, de boissons, de corps chimiques, etc. :

concrete is used less nowadays
on utilise moins le béton de nos jours

oxygen is crucial to life
l'oxygène est indispensable à la vie

I prefer gold jewellery
je préfère les bijoux en or

xi) les noms de langues (qui prennent des majuscules en anglais) et de matières scolaires :

German is harder than English
l'allemand est plus difficile que l'anglais

I hate maths
je déteste les maths

xii) les noms pluriels pris dans un sens général :

he loves antiques
il adore les antiquités

he's frightened of dogs
il a peur des chiens

e) L'article défini n'est normalement pas employé lorsque l'on fait référence à des noms de pays, de comtés, d'États :

Switzerland *la Suisse*   **Sussex** *le Sussex*
England *l'Angleterre*   **Texas** *le Texas*

he went to South America   **I live in France**
il est parti en Amérique du Sud   *j'habite en France*

i) mais il existe quelques exceptions :

(the) **Yemen** *le Yémen*   (the) **Sudan** *le Soudan*
(the) **Gambia** *la Gambie*   (the) **Lebanon** *le Liban*

Et l'on emploie l'article lorsque le nom du pays est qualifié :

the Republic of Ireland
la République d'Irlande

the People's Republic of China
la République populaire de Chine

ii) les noms de lieux au pluriel prennent l'article :

the Philippines   *les Philippines*
the Azores   *les Açores*
the Shetlands   *les Shetlands*
the Midlands   *les Midlands*
the Netherlands   *les Pays-Bas*
the United States   *les États-Unis*
the Borders   *la région des Borders*

iii) les fleuves, les rivières et les océans prennent l'article :

the Thames *la Tamise*   **the Pacific** *le Pacifique*
the Danube *le Danube*   **the Atlantic** *l'Atlantique*

iv) les noms de régions prennent l'article :

the Tyrol *le Tyrol*   **the Ruhr** *la Ruhr*
the Orient *l'Orient*   **the Crimea** *la Crimée*
the City (of London)
la Cité de Londres

v) les noms de montagnes et de lacs ne prennent pas l'article :

Ben Nevis *le Ben Nevis* **K2** *le K2*
Loch Ness *le loch Ness* **Lake Tahoe** *le lac Tahoe*

Mais les chaînes de montagnes sont précédées de l'article :

the Himalayas *l'Himalaya* **the Alps** *les Alpes*

Cependant, il existe des exceptions :

the Matterhorn *le mont*   **the Eiger** *l'Eiger*
                  Cervin

vi) les noms de rues, de parcs, de places, etc. ne prennent normalement pas l'article :

they met in Hyde Park
ils se sont rencontrés à Hyde Park

he lives in Wilton Street
il habite Wilton Street

there was a concert in Trafalgar Square
il y avait un concert à Trafalgar Square

Mais il existe des exceptions où l'article fait partie intégrante du nom :

the Strand   *le Strand*

Et parfois on trouve des exceptions fondées sur un usage purement local :

the Edgware Road   *l'Edgware Road*

f) On omet l'article dans les **énumérations** (même à deux termes) :

the boys and girls
les garçons et les filles

the hammers, nails and screwdrivers
les marteaux, les clous et les tournevis

g) Les noms d'hôtels, de pubs, de restaurants, de théâtres, de cinémas, de musées sont normalement précédés de **the** :

the Caledonian (Hotel)   **the Red Lion**
the Copper Kettle   **the Old Vic**
the Odeon   **the Tate (Gallery)**

h) On trouve l'article défini dans les titres de journaux (**the Observer, the Independent, the Guardian**, etc.) et de quelques magazines (**the Spectator, the Economist**, etc.)

Cependant, la plupart des magazines ne sont pas précédés de l'article : **FHM, Vanity Fair, Punch, Private Eye**, etc.

i) Les instruments de musique :

L'article défini s'emploie lorsqu'on fait référence à une aptitude

she plays the clarinet
elle joue de la clarinette

Cependant, lorsqu'on fait référence à une occasion précise plutôt qu'à une aptitude d'ordre général, on omet l'article :

in this piece he plays bass guitar
il joue de la basse dans ce morceau

j) Les noms de titres sont normalement précédés de l'article défini :

the Queen   *la reine*
the President   *le président*

Cependant, on omet l'article défini lorsque le titre est suivi du nom de la personne :

Doctor MacPherson   *le docteur MacPherson*
Queen Elizabeth   *la reine Élisabeth*
Prime Minister Churchill   *le Premier ministre Churchill*

Remarquez :

Christ   *le Christ*

k) L'omission de l'article défini pour produire un effet particulier :

i) dans des phrases auxquelles on veut donner de l'importance ou dans un jargon :

all pupils will assemble in hall
tous les élèves se rassembleront dans le hall

the number of delegates at conference
le nombre des délégués à la conférence

ii) dans les gros titres de journaux (omission aussi de l'article indéfini a/an) :

Attempt To Break Record Fails
La tentative de pulvériser le record échoue

New Conference Centre Planned
Projet pour un nouveau Palais des Congrès

iii) dans les instructions (omission aussi de l'article indéfini a/an) :

break glass in emergency
casser la vitre en cas d'urgence

Pour la traduction de l'article partitif, voir **some, any, no** et **none** pp. A34-5. Pour les articles employés avec les parties du corps, voir p. A30.

3   LES NOMS

A   LES TYPES DE NOMS

es noms anglais n'ont pas de genre grammatical ("le" et "la" se
sent the).

Les noms concrets et les noms abstraits

n peut classer les noms de différentes manières. On peut ainsi les
viser en noms concrets, c'est-à-dire des noms qui font référence à
s êtres animés ou à des choses, comme **woman** (*femme*), **cat**
hat) et **stone** (*pierre*), et en noms abstraits, c'est-à-dire des noms
i expriment des concepts, des caractéristiques ou des activités :
ve (*l'amour*), **ugliness** (*la laideur*), **classification** (*la classifi-
tion*).

n grand nombre de noms abstraits se forment en ajoutant une ter-
inaison (suffixe) à un adjectif, à un nom ou à un verbe. Cepen-
nt, beaucoup de noms abstraits ne prennent pas cette terminaison.
'est le cas, par exemple, de **love** (*l'amour*), **hate** (*la haine*), **con-
pt** (*le concept*). Voici quelques terminaisons de noms abstraits
uramment employées (certaines peuvent aussi s'employer pour des
ms concrets).

Les noms abstraits formés à partir d'autres noms

-age	percent + -age	percentage	*pourcentage*
-cy	democrat + -cy	democracy	*démocratie*
-dom	martyr + -dom	martyrdom	*martyre*
-hood	child + -hood	childhood	*enfance*
-ism	alcohol + -ism	alcoholism	*alcoolisme*
-ry	chemist + -ry	chemistry	*chimie*

Les noms abstraits formés à partir d'adjectifs

-age	short + -age	shortage	*pénurie*
-cy	bankrupt + -cy	bankruptcy	*faillite*
	normal + -cy	normalcy (*Am*)	*normalité*
-hood	likely + -hood	likelihood	*probabilité*
-ism	social + -ism	socialism	*socialisme*
-ity	normal + -ity	normality	*normalité*
-ness	kind + -ness	kindness	*gentillesse*

Les noms abstraits formés à partir de verbes

-age	break + -age	breakage	*rupture*
-al	arrive + -al	arrival	*arrivée*
-ance	utter + -ance	utterance	*déclaration*
-(at)ion	starve + -ation	starvation	*famine*
	operate + -ion	operation	*opération*
-ing	voir le gérondif, p. A43		
-ment	treat + -ment	treatment	*traitement*

emarquez que la terminaison du nom, de l'adjectif ou du verbe
it parfois subir quelques changements avant l'ajout du suffixe
kely → likelihood, arrive → arrival, etc.). Voir chapitre 19,
A79

2   Les noms communs et les noms propres

On peut aussi classer les substantifs en noms communs et en noms
propres, ces derniers faisant référence à des noms de personnes ou à
des noms géographiques, de jours et de mois. Ils s'écrivent avec une
majuscule.

COMMUNS		PROPRES	
cup	*tasse*	**Peter**	*Pierre*
palace	*palais*	**China**	*la Chine*
cheese	*fromage*	**Wednesday**	*mercredi*
time	*le temps*	**August**	*août*
love	*l'amour*	**Christmas**	*Noël*

3   Les noms dénombrables et les noms indénom-brables

Une classification, déterminante pour l'absence ou la présence de
l'article indéfini, permet de distinguer les noms dénombrables et les
noms indénombrables. Un nom dénombrable à part entière peut,
bien sûr, être considéré comme une "unité" (c'est-à-dire qu'il peut
être précédé de l'article indéfini ou de tout adjectif numéral), et doit
avoir une forme au singulier et au pluriel (il peut être précédé de
these/few/many, etc.). Les noms indénombrables à part entière ne
sont quant à eux ni au singulier, ni au pluriel, puisque par définition
on ne peut les compter, bien qu'ils soient suivis d'un verbe au singulier (ils peuvent être précédés de **this/little/much**, etc.). On dit
qu'ils représentent une "totalité" :

DÉNOMBRABLES

a/one pen/three pens	*un crayon/trois crayons*
a/one coat/three coats	*un manteau/trois manteaux*
a/one horse/three horses	*un cheval/trois chevaux*
a/one child/three children	*un enfant/trois enfants*

INDÉNOMBRABLES

furniture	*les/des meubles*	**rubbish**	*les/des ordures*
spaghetti	*les/des spaghettis*	**information**	*les/des informa-tions*
spinach	*les/des épinards*	**news**	*les/des nouvelles*
fish	*les/des poissons*	**progress**	*les/des progrès*
fruit	*les/des fruits*	**violence**	*la violence*

Lorsque l'on veut faire référence à une unité de chacun de ces noms
indénombrables, il faut faire précéder le nom indénombrable d'un
autre nom qui soit dénombrable. Ainsi on emploie, par exemple,
piece pour indiquer une ou plusieurs unités :

a piece of furniture/two pieces of furniture
un meuble/deux meubles

De même, on dira **an act of violence** (*un acte de violence*), **an
item of news** (*une nouvelle*), **a strand of spaghetti** (*un
spaghetti*), où **act**, **item** et **strand** sont des dénombrables tout à
fait normaux. Le dénombrable qui accompagne **cattle** est **head**, qui
ne prend jamais de **-s** dans ce sens : **ten head of cattle** (*dix têtes
de bétail*).

Voici d'autres exemples de noms indénombrables à part entière :
baggage (*les bagages*), **luggage** (*les bagages*), **garbage** (*les
ordures*), **advice** (*les conseils*).

Pour **accommodation**, voir p. A11.

a) *Les noms pouvant être dénombrables ou indénombrables*

i) Certains noms peuvent être dénombrables ou indénombrables, suivant que leur sens fait référence à une "unité"
ou une "totalité". De tels noms font souvent référence à
la nourriture ou aux matériaux :

DÉNOMBRABLES	**INDÉNOMBRABLES**
that sheep has only one lamb	**we had lamb for dinner**
ce mouton n'a qu'un agneau	*nous avons eu de l'agneau au dîner*

would you like a glass of wine?
prendrez-vous un verre de vin ?

the table is made of glass
c'est une table en verre

mumps is **not a life-threatening disease**
les oreillons ne sont pas une maladie mortelle

he bought a paper
il a acheté un journal

I need some wrapping paper
il me faut du papier cadeau

darts is **still played in many pubs**
on joue encore aux fléchettes dans beaucoup de pubs

she's a beauty
c'est une beauté

beauty **is only skin-deep**
la beauté n'est pas tout

d) *Noms de "paires"*

Certains noms au pluriel faisant référence à des objets compos
de deux parties identiques n'ont pas de forme au singulier et
doivent être précédés de a pair of si l'on veut mettre l'accent su
leur nombre :

ii) Comme en français, les noms indénombrables deviennent dénombrables lorsqu'ils signifient "un verre de", "une variété de", etc. :

I'd like a coffee
je voudrais un café

two white wines, please
deux vins blancs, s'il vous plaît

Britain has a large selection of cheeses
la Grande-Bretagne a une grande variété de fromages

a very good beer
une très bonne bière

a pair of trousers
un pantalon

two pairs of trousers
deux pantalons

this is a nice pair of trousers
c'est un beau pantalon

those are nice trousers
c'est un beau pantalon

de même :

bellows *soufflet*	pyjamas ou pajamas (*Ar*
binoculars *jumelles*	pyjama
breeches *culotte*	scissors *ciseaux*
glasses *lunettes*	shears *cisailles*
knickers *culotte, slip*	shorts *short*
pants *culotte* (*Br*), *pantalon* (*Am*)	spectacles *lunettes*
pincers *tenailles*	tights *bas*
pliers *pinces, tenailles*	tongs *fer à friser*
	tweezers *pince à épiler*

iii) Certains noms habituellement indénombrables peuvent s'employer au pluriel dans quelques expressions figées et idiomatiques :

EMPLOI NORMAL

EMPLOI PARTICULIER

my shoes let in water
mes chaussures prennent l'eau

the boat has just entered Japanese waters
le bateau vient d'entrer dans les eaux (territoriales) japonaises

it's beautiful weather
il fait beau

in all weathers
par tous les temps

e) *Noms habituellement employés au pluriel*

i)

arms *armes*	odds *chances, cote (d'un*
arrears *arriéré(s)*	*cheval, etc.)*
auspices *auspices*	outskirts *environs, ban-*
banns *bans (de mariage)*	*lieue(s)*
clothes *vêtements*	pains *peine, effort*
customs *douane(s)*	premises *locaux*
dregs *la lie*	quarters *résidence(s)*
earnings *revenus*	remains *restes*
entrails *entrailles*	riches *richesse(s)*
goods *biens, marchandise(s)*	spirits *humeur, alcool*
greens *légumes verts*	(soap) suds *mousse (de*
guts (*Fam*) *boyaux, courage*	*savon)*
lodgings *logement(s)*	surroundings *environs,*
looks *apparence(s)*	*cadre*
manners *manières*	tropics *tropiques*
means *moyens (financiers)*	valuables *objets de valeu*

iv) Certains noms abstraits indénombrables (**indignation, hate, anger,** etc.) sont précédés de l'article indéfini lorsqu'ils sont accompagnés d'un adjectif ou d'un groupe adjectival qui permet de qualifier et de spécifier le nom :

he expressed an indignation so intense that people were taken aback
il exprima une indignation si véhémente que les gens en furent stupéfaits

Ces noms sont normalement accompagnés d'un verbe au pluriel.

Quelques noms doivent se mettre au singulier dans certai
contextes et au pluriel dans d'autres. Le changement de
nombre apporte des nuances différentes mais le sens de
base reste le même :

b) *Les noms en -ics*

Lorsque ces noms sont considérés comme des concepts abstraits, ils sont indénombrables et suivis d'un verbe au singulier :

economics is a difficult subject
l'économie est une matière difficile

En revanche, on préférera un verbe au pluriel lorsque le nom en -ics est utilisé dans un sens concret, et non plus de manière générale :

the economics of the project are to be considered
il faut considérer l'aspect financier du projet

what are your politics?
quelles sont vos opinions politiques ?

contents (*le contenu*) mais content (*la quantité qui pe
être contenue*) :

show me the contents of your bag
montrez-moi le contenu de votre sac

spinach has a high iron content
les épinards contiennent beaucoup de fer

funds (*des fonds*) mais fund (*un fonds*) :

I'm a bit short of funds
je n'ai pas beaucoup d'argent

we started a church roof repair fund
*nous avons commencé à faire une collecte pour réparer l
toit de l'église*

c) *Les indénombrables se terminant par -s*

Certains noms se terminant par ce qui semble être le -s du pluriel sont indénombrables. C'est le cas des noms en -ics que nous venons de voir, mais aussi du mot news (*nouvelles*), des maladies telles que measles (*rougeole*), mumps (*oreillons*), rickets (*rachitisme*), shingles (*zona*) et de quelques noms de jeux tels que billiards (*billard*), bowls (*boules*), darts (*fléchettes*), dominoes (*dominos*), draughts (*Br*) ou checkers (*Am*) (*dames*) :

thanks (*les remerciements*) : vous noterez la possibilité
d'employer l'article indéfini devant un adjectif (pas de sin
gulier dans ce cas) :

the news hasn't arrived yet
la nouvelle n'est pas encore arrivée

a very special thanks to our sponsor
un grand merci à notre sponsor

wages (*le salaire, la paie*) : souvent au singulier aussi, particulièrement lorsqu'il est précédé d'un adjectif :

all we want is a decent wage
tout ce que nous voulons, c'est un salaire correct

accommodations (*l'hébergement*) est employé en anglais américain. En anglais britannique, on emploie accommodation comme indénombrable pour désigner un logement.

ii) Quelques noms pluriels ne portent jamais la marque du pluriel :

cattle *bétail*	police *police, policiers*
clergy *(membres du) clergé*	vermin *vermine, parasites*
livestock *(têtes de) bétail*	

Mais même clergy et police peuvent parfois être accompagnés d'un article indéfini, s'ils sont qualifiés par un adjectif, par un groupe prépositionnel ou par une proposition relative. Dans de tels cas, il existe une différence de sens importante entre clergyman (*ecclésiastiques*) et body of clergymen (*ensemble du clergé*), et policemen (*policiers*) et police force (*la police*). Comparez :

seventy-five clergy were present
soixante-quinze membres du clergé étaient présents

the problem is whether the country needs a clergy with such old-fashioned views
le problème est de savoir si le pays a besoin d'un clergé aux idées aussi dépassées

at least thirty police were needed for that task
on a eu besoin d'au moins trente policiers pour cette tâche

the country had a semi-military police
le pays avait une police semi-militaire

Le nom pluriel folk (*gens, personnes*) ne prend normalement pas de -s en anglais britannique :

some folk just don't know how to behave
certaines personnes ne savent pas se tenir

Dans un registre plus familier, on pourrait également employer folks dans l'exemple ci-dessus. Folks désigne aussi familièrement "la famille", "les parents" (my folks are from Chicago *ma famille est de Chicago*).

Les noms collectifs

i) Ce sont des noms qui, au singulier, désignent un groupe de personnes ou de choses. Ils sont accompagnés d'un verbe au singulier quand le nom désigne un ensemble, ou d'un verbe au pluriel si l'on désire mettre l'accent sur les membres du groupe :

the jury is one of the safeguards of our legal system (sing)
le jury est garant de notre système législatif

the jury have returned their verdict (pl)
le jury a rendu son verdict

Les pronoms et les adjectifs possessifs s'accordent normalement en nombre avec le verbe (voir their dans l'exemple ci-dessus).

L'emploi du verbe au pluriel est plus répandu en anglais britannique qu'en anglais américain.

Les mots suivants sont des exemples typiques de noms collectifs :

army	*armée*	government	*gouvernement*
audience	*public*	group	*groupe*
choir	*chorale*	majority	*majorité*
chorus	*chœur*	minority	*minorité*
class	*classe*	orchestra	*orchestre*
committee	*comité*	Parliament	*Parlement*
enemy	*ennemi*	proletariat	*prolétariat*
family	*famille*	public	*public*
firm	*firme*	team	*équipe*
gang	*gang*		

(younger/older) generation
(*jeune/ancienne*) *génération*

● Les mots crew (*équipage*), staff (*personnel*), people (*peuple*) sont souvent des noms collectifs, comme dans :

the crew is excellent (sing)
l'équipage est excellent

the crew have all enjoyed themselves (pl)
l'équipage s'est bien amusé

the staff of that school has a good record (sing)
le personnel de cette école a obtenu de bons résultats

the staff don't always behave themselves (pl)
le personnel ne se conduit pas toujours bien

it is difficult to imagine a people that has suffered more (sing)
il est difficile d'imaginer un peuple qui ait plus souffert

the people have not voted against the re-introduction of capital punishment (pl)
le peuple n'a pas voté contre le rétablissement de la peine capitale

Ces trois mots diffèrent des autres noms collectifs par le fait qu'ils peuvent être des dénombrables à part entière, avec ou sans la terminaison -s au pluriel, suivant leur sens. Si le pluriel est en -s, il est le même que le pluriel en -s d'autres noms collectifs : five crews/staffs/peoples (*nations*)/ armies/governments, etc.

Cependant, le pluriel sans -s fait référence à des membres individuels :

the captain had to manage with only fifteen crew
le capitaine a dû se débrouiller avec seulement quinze membres d'équipage

the English Department had to get rid of five staff
le département d'anglais a dû renvoyer cinq personnes

he spoke to six people about it
il a parlé à six personnes à ce sujet

On peut tout aussi bien dire crew members, staff members ou members of staff au pluriel.

Pour clergy et police, voir e) ii) ci-dessus.

● Youth (*la jeunesse, les jeunes*) peut être suivi aussi bien d'un verbe au singulier que d'un verbe au pluriel :

our country's youth has/have little to look forward to
la jeunesse de notre pays a peu de perspectives d'avenir

mais il est dénombrable dans le sens de "jeune homme" :

they arrested a youth/two youths
ils ont arrêté un jeune/deux jeunes

● Le nom pluriel media (*les médias, la presse*) se comporte comme un nom collectif. Il s'emploie très souvent au singulier, mais il peut aussi être suivi du pluriel :

the media follows/follow her everywhere
les journalistes la suivent partout

Le mot data (*données*), du latin datum (sing), peut s'utiliser au pluriel (these data are...) mais il est très souvent employé comme indénombrable (this/much/little data is...) : on considère que les données forment un tout. On devra donc utiliser le terme piece pour dissocier les données (seven pieces of data).

ii) Les pays :

Les noms de nations faisant référence à une équipe (sportive) sont normalement accompagnés d'un verbe au pluriel en anglais britannique :

France have beaten England
la France a battu l'Angleterre

bien que le singulier et le pluriel soient tout aussi corrects.

Remarquez que les noms de pays au pluriel sont suivis d'un verbe au singulier :

the United States exerts a great influence on the world political stage
les États-Unis exercent une grande influence sur la scène politique internationale

Il en est de même pour **the Bahamas, the Philippines**, etc.

B LES FORMES DU PLURIEL

1 Les pluriels en -(e)s

a) La marque du pluriel est normalement -(e)s en anglais :

soup	→	**soups**	*soupe*
peg	→	**pegs**	*pince à linge*
bus	→	**buses**	*bus*
quiz	→	**quizzes**	*jeu télévisé*
bush	→	**bushes**	*buisson*
match	→	**matches**	*allumette*
page	→	**pages**	*page*

-es s'emploie pour des mots en -s, -x, -z, -ch ou -sh. On le prononce alors /ɪz/.

Remarquez que les noms de famille au pluriel prennent -(e)s en anglais, alors qu'ils sont invariables en français :

the Smiths
les Smith

b) Pour les noms se terminant par une consonne + -y, le -y se transforme en -ies :

lady	→	**ladies**	*dame, demoiselle*
fairy	→	**fairies**	*fée*

Mais les noms qui se terminent par une voyelle + -y ont un pluriel régulier en -s :

trolley	→	**trolleys**	*chariot*

Pour plus de détails, voir le chapitre 19, p. A79.

c) Les noms en -o prennent parfois un -s, parfois -es au pluriel. Il est difficile d'établir des règles précises dans ce cas ; toutefois, on peut dire que l'on ajoute seulement un -s si :

le -o suit une autre voyelle : embryo → **embryos** (*embryons*), studio → **studios** (*studios*)

le nom est une abréviation : photo → **photos**, piano → **pianos** (de pianoforte)

Dans d'autres cas, il est difficile de généraliser, bien que l'on puisse observer une préférence pour le -s avec des mots qui ont encore une connotation étrangère pour les Britanniques :

avec -es : echo, cargo (*cargaison*), hero, mosquito (*moustique*), Negro, potato (*pomme de terre*), tomato, torpedo (*torpille*)

avec -s : canto (*chant*), memento, proviso (*stipulation*), quarto, solo, zero, zoo

avec -s ou -es : banjo, buffalo (*buffle*), commando,

flamingo (*flamand rose*), motto, volcano

d) Pour certains noms en -f(e), le -f se transforme en -ve au pluriel :

calf	→	**calves**	*veau*

Il en est de même pour :

elf	*elfe*	self	*soi*
half	*moitié*	sheaf	*gerbe*
knife	*couteau*	shelf	*étagère*
leaf	*feuille d'arbre*	thief	*voleur*
life	*vie*	wife	*épouse*
loaf	*pain*	wolf	*loup*

Certains peuvent avoir un pluriel en -ves ou en -s :

dwarf	→	**dwarfs/dwarves**	*nain*
hoof	→	**hoofs/hooves**	*sabot*
scarf	→	**scarfs/scarves**	*écharpe*
wharf	→	**wharfs/wharves**	*quai*

Un grand nombre de ces mots conservent le -f :

belief	→	**beliefs**	*croyance*

Il en est de même pour :

chief	*chef*	roof	*toit*
cliff	*falaise*	safe	*coffre-fort*
proof	*preuve*	sniff	*reniflement, etc.*

e) Quelques mots français se terminant avec un -s muet au singulier ne changent pas leur pluriel à l'écrit ; on ajoute cependant le son /z/ au pluriel à l'oral : corps (*sing* [kɔː(r)], *pl* [kɔːz]).

f) Les mots français en -eu ou -eau prennent un -s ou un -x (que l'on prononce tous les deux /z/), par exemple :

adieu, bureau, tableau

gateau prend normalement un -x.

g) Les noms d'animaux

Certains noms d'animaux, notamment les noms de poissons, se comportent (presque toujours) comme les noms mentionnés dans la section 3a) ci-dessous, c'est-à-dire qu'ils ne prennent pas la marque du pluriel :

cod	*morue*	salmon	*saumon*
hake	*colin*	trout	*truite*
herring	*hareng*	deer	*cerf*
mackerel	*maquereau*	sheep	*mouton*
pike	*brochet*	grouse	*coq de bruyère*

D'autres noms d'animaux au pluriel prennent un -s dans certains cas et n'en prennent pas dans d'autres. Dans le contexte de la chasse, on omet souvent le -s. Comparez :

these antelopes have just been bought by the zoo
le zoo vient juste d'acheter ces antilopes

they went to Africa to shoot antelope
ils sont allés en Afrique pour chasser l'antilope

Il en est de même pour :

buffalo	*buffle*	fowl	*volaille*
giraffe	*girafe*	partridge	*perdrix*
lion	*lion*	pheasant	*faisan*
duck	*canard*	et bien d'autres	

Le pluriel régulier de fish est fish, mais fishes s'emploie pour faire référence à des espèces de poissons (**cod and haddock are two different fishes that can be found in British waters**).

h) Les adjectifs numéraux

i) **hundred** (*cent*), **thousand** (*mille*), **million, dozen** (*douzaine*), **score** (*vingt*) et **gross** (*douze douzaines*) n'ont pas de pluriel en -s lorsqu'ils sont précédés d'un autre adjectif numéral. Remarquez la différence de construction avec le français pour "million", "milliard" et "douzaine" :

five hundred/thousand/million people
cinq cents personnes/cinq mille personnes/cinq millions de personnes

two dozen eggs
deux douzaines d'œufs

we'll order three gross
nous en commanderons trente-six douzaines

mais :

there were hundreds/thousands/millions of them
il y en avait des centaines/milliers/millions

I've told you dozens of times
je te l'ai dit des dizaines de fois

Peter and Kate have scores of friends
Peter et Kate ont des tas d'amis

ii) Les unités de mesure **foot** et **pound** peuvent être soit au pluriel, soit au singulier :

Kate is five foot/feet eight
Kate mesure un mètre soixante-douze

that comes to three pound(s) fifty
ça fait trois livres cinquante

2 Les pluriels avec un changement de voyelle

existe un petit groupe de mots dont le pluriel se forme au moyen 'un changement de voyelle :

foot	→	feet	*pied*
goose	→	geese	*oie*
louse	→	lice	*pou*
man	→	men [men]	*homme*
mouse	→	mice	*souris*
tooth	→	teeth	*dent*
woman	→	women ['wɪmɪn]	*femme*

3 Les pluriels invariables

) singulier et pluriel sans -s :

aircraft (*avion*), **counsel** (*avocat*), **offspring** (*progéniture*), **quid** (*Fam livre sterling*), par exemple :

we saw a few aircraft   **these are my offspring**
nous avons vu quelques avions   *c'est ma progéniture*

both counsel asked for an adjournment
les deux avocats ont demandé un renvoi

this will cost you ten quid
ça te coûtera cent livres

Les mots **kind, sort, type** (*genre, sorte, type*), apparaissant dans une phrase du type **these/those** + nom + **of**, ne prennent souvent pas de -s :

these kind of people always complain
ce genre de personne se plaint toujours

she always wears those sort of clothes
elle porte toujours ce genre de vêtements

) singulier et pluriel en -s :

barracks	*caserne*	means*	*moyen*
crossroads	*carrefour*	series	*série*
gallows	*potence*	shambles	*désordre*
headquarters	*quartier*	species	*espèce*
	général	works	*usine*
innings	*tour de batte*		

*Comparez avec **means** (= moyens financiers) p. A10.

Voici quelques exemples :

every means was tried to improve matters
on a usé de tous les moyens pour améliorer les choses

this is a dreadful shambles
c'est un désordre abominable

they have built a new gasworks north of here
ils ont construit une nouvelle usine à gaz au nord d'ici

Certains de ces noms, en particulier **barracks, gallows, headquarters, works** peuvent aussi s'employer dans un sens singulier avec un verbe au pluriel :

these are the new steelworks
c'est la nouvelle aciérie

On fait référence ici à une seule usine.

c) dice et pence

Dice, pluriel irrégulier de **die** (*dé*), est également devenu le terme communément employé au singulier, **die** ne s'utilisant plus que dans les expressions idiomatiques telles que **the die is cast** (*les dés sont jetés*) ou **straight as a die** (*d'une grande honnêteté, franc comme l'or*). On a donc, avec **dice**, la même forme au singulier et au pluriel :

he threw the dice
il a lancé le dé ou les dés

Lorsque l'on parle de la monnaie et de la valeur de l'argent, le pluriel de **penny** est irrégulier (**pence**). Par ailleurs, il n'est pas rare d'entendre **one pence** plutôt que **one penny** quand on parle du coût de quelque chose. Cependant, lorsque l'on désigne une pièce d'un **penny** (ou d'un **cent** aux États-Unis), le pluriel est régulier :

these are 18th-century pennies
ce sont des pennies du XVIIIe siècle

4 Les pluriels en -en

Il n'en existe que trois, et un seul est commun :

child	→	children	*enfant*

Les autres sont :

ox	→	oxen	*bœuf*
brother	→	brethren	*frère*

ce dernier faisant référence aux membres d'une congrégation religieuse, comme dans :

our Catholic brethren from other countries
nos frères catholiques d'autres pays

Le pluriel normal de **brother** est **brothers**.

5 Les pluriels en -a ou -s

Ce sont des noms latins au singulier en -um ou des noms grecs au singulier en -on. Beaucoup d'entre eux ont un pluriel en -s, en particulier s'ils sont employés couramment, par exemple :

museum (*musée*), **stadium** (*stade*), **demon, electron**

Certains, souvent employés dans un langage scientifique et dont le singulier est -um/-on, ont un pluriel en -a, par exemple :

an addendum   *un addenda (ou addendum)*

numerous addenda   *de nombreux addenda*

De même, on a **bacterium** (*bactérie*), **curriculum** (*programme d'étude*), **erratum, ovum** (*ovule*), **criterion** (*critère*), **phenomenon**

Certains mots acceptent les deux formes du pluriel (en -s et en -a) :

memorandum, millennium (*millénaire*)**, symposium, automaton** (*automate*)

Le pluriel de **medium** est toujours **mediums** lorsque ce mot fait référence à un extralucide. Lorsqu'il signifie "moyen", le pluriel est **media** ou **mediums**.

Pour **media** et **data**, voir p. A11.

6 Les pluriels en -e ou -s

Ces noms sont latins ou grecs et ont une terminaison en -a au singulier. Ceux qui sont fréquemment employés ont un pluriel en -s, comme **arena** et **drama**. Les noms plus techniques ou scientifiques ont tendance à avoir un pluriel en -e (on obtient alors la terminaison -ae prononcée /iː/ ou /aɪ/ selon le mot), par exemple **alumna** (*ancienne élève* ou *étudiante*) et **larva**.

La terminaison de certains noms varie selon leur sens et le contexte. Ainsi, **antenna** prend toujours un -e lorsqu'il fait référence aux insectes, mais un -s lorsqu'il signifie "antenne de télévision" en américain. Il en est de même pour **formula** qui prend un -e ou -s lorsqu'il s'agit d'une formule de chimie, de mathématiques, etc., mais qui a toujours un pluriel en -s quand le terme désigne une expression.

7 Les pluriels en -i ou -s (mots italiens)

Quelques mots empruntés à l'italien, notamment **libretto**, **tempo** et **virtuoso**, peuvent conserver leur pluriel italien en -i /iː/ ou prendre le -s du pluriel régulier anglais.

Vous noterez que **confetti**, **graffiti**, **macaroni**, **ravioli**, **spaghetti**, etc. sont indénombrables, c'est-à-dire qu'ils sont suivis d'un verbe au singulier.

8 Les pluriels en -i ou -es (mots latins)

Ceux qui sont courants prennent normalement la terminaison -es au pluriel, comme :

campus, **chorus** (*refrain, chœur*), **virus**

Ceux qui appartiennent au langage plus érudit gardent en général leur pluriel latin en -i (que l'on prononce /iː/ ou /aɪ/ selon le mot) comme par exemple :

alumnus (*ancien élève* ou *étudiant*), **bacillus** (*bacille*), **stimulus** (*stimulant, stimulus*)

D'autres prennent les deux formes au pluriel : **cactus**, **fungus** (*champignon, fongus*), **nucleus** (*noyau*), **syllabus** (*programme d'enseignement*). Il en est de même pour les noms grecs latinisés : **hippopotamus** et **papyrus**.

Le pluriel de **genius** est **geniuses** au sens de "personne extrêmement intelligente", mais **genii** lorsqu'il signifie "(bon/mauvais) esprit".

9 Les pluriels des noms en -ex ou -ix

Ces noms latins peuvent conserver leur pluriel d'origine, leur singulier en -ex/-ix se transforme alors en -ices au pluriel, ou bien ils prennent -es, par exemple :

index → **ind**ices ou **index**es

Il en est de même pour **appendix**, **matrix**, **vortex**.

Mais remarquez que **appendixes** est le seul pluriel pour la partie du corps, tandis que **appendixes** et **appendices** peuvent s'employer pour désigner les parties d'un livre ou d'une thèse.

10 Le pluriel des noms grecs en -is

La terminaison -is /ɪs/ de ces mots se transforme en -es /iːz/ au pluriel, par exemple :

an analysis   *une analyse*
different analyses   *différentes analyses*

Il en est de même pour : **axis**, **basis**, **crisis**, **diagnosis**, **hypothesis**, **oasis**, **parenthesis**, **synopsis**, **thesis**.

Mais remarquez : **metropol**is → **metropol**ises

11 Les pluriels en -im ou -s

Les mots hébreux **kibbutz**, **cherub** (*chérubin*) et **seraph** (*séraphin*) peuvent prendre soit -(e)s (pluriel régulier), soit -im au pluriel.

12 Les pluriels des noms composés

a) *Le pluriel porte sur le deuxième élément*

Lorsque le deuxième élément est un nom (et qu'il n'est pas précédé d'une préposition) :

lip balms (*baumes pour les lèvres*), **lion cubs** (*lionceaux*), **pencil sharpeners** (*taille-crayon*), **table napkins** (*serviettes de table*), **road users** (*usagers de la route*), etc.

et lorsque le mot composé est formé d'un verbe + adverbe :

lay-bys (*aires de stationnement*), **lie-ins** (*grasses matinées*), **sit-ins**, **stand-bys**, **tip-offs** (*tuyaux*)

Remarquez que les noms de mesures se terminant par -ful peuvent avoir un -s à la fin de l'un ou l'autre de leurs éléments : **spoonfuls** ou **spoonsful**.

b) *Le pluriel porte sur le premier élément*

Lorsque le deuxième élément est un groupe prépositionnel :

editors-in-chief   *rédacteurs en chef*
fathers-in-law*   *beaux-pères*
aides-de-camp   *aides de camp*
men-of-war   *bâtiments de guerre*

*Remarquez que **law** se met au pluriel dans l'expression familière **in-laws**, forme abrégée de **parents-in-law** (**my in-laws are coming this weekend** *mes beaux-parents viennent ce week-end*).

Mais si le premier élément ne désigne pas une personne, on place le -s sur le dernier élément, comme dans :

will-o'-the-wisps   **jack-in-the-boxes**
feux follets   *diables à ressort*

Les noms composés formés d'un nom (dérivé d'un verbe) et d'un adverbe prennent eux aussi un -s à la fin du premier élément (à la différence de ceux composés d'un verbe + adverbe, voir a) ci-dessus) :

hangers-on   **passers-by**
parasites   *passants*

Les noms composés avec -to-be prennent un -s à la fin du premier élément :

brides-to-be   **mothers-to-be**
futures mariées   *futures mamans*

Le premier élément porte aussi la marque du pluriel si le second élément est un adjectif :

Lords temporal and spiritual
membres laïques et ecclésiastiques de la Chambre des lords

Mais beaucoup peuvent aussi porter la marque du pluriel sur le deuxième élément (ce qui est de plus en plus courant) :

attorneys general ou **attorney generals**
directors general ou **director generals**
poets laureate ou **poet laureates**
courts-martial ou **court-martials**

C USAGE : PLURIEL OU SINGULIER ?

a) *Le pluriel distributif*

i) type 1, dans un groupe nominal

Dans la plupart des cas, l'anglais préfère le pluriel :

between the ages of 30 and 45
entre l'âge de 30 et 45 ans

the reigns of Henry VIII and Elizabeth I
le règne d'Henri VIII et celui d'Élisabeth Iʳᵉ

ii) type 2, dans une proposition

En anglais, lorsque le sujet d'une phrase est pluriel, on a très souvent un pluriel dans la proposition complément d'objet, contrairement au français :

cats seem to spend their lives **sleeping**
les chats semblent passer leur vie à dormir

many people are unhappy about their careers
beaucoup de gens ne sont pas satisfaits de leur carrière

they both broke their legs
ils se sont tous les deux cassé la jambe

we took off our coats
nous avons enlevé notre manteau

we changed our minds
nous avons changé d'avis

Dans certaines expressions, on peut employer soit le pluriel avec un adjectif possessif, soit le singulier avec l'article défini :

they were up to their waists/the waist **in water**
l'eau leur arrivait à la ceinture

they were up to their necks/the neck **in debt**
ils étaient endettés jusqu'au cou

b) *Le complément du nom placé avant ou après le nom*

i) Lorsqu'un nom est suivi d'un complément du nom au pluriel, ce dernier est toujours singulier devant le nom car il a valeur d'adjectif (voir p. A17) :

a collection of bottles → **a bottle collection**
une collection de bouteilles

ii) En anglais, il est possible de mettre des compléments du nom commençant par un nombre en position adjectivale. Dans ce cas-là, le nom qui fait partie du syntagme adjectival ne prend pas de -s et les différents termes doivent être séparés par un trait d'union :

a girl of eight (= eight years old) → **an eight-year-old girl**
une fille de huit ans

a baby of twelve months → **a twelve-month-old baby**
un bébé de douze mois

Cette construction est très courante et, dans certains cas, l'emploi d'un complément du nom avec of ne semblerait pas naturel. On dira par exemple :

a thirty-minute talk
un exposé de trente minutes

a two-week holiday
deux semaines de vacances

a two-mile walk
une promenade de trois kilomètres

Comparez aussi avec l'emploi du génitif expliqué au paragraphe D 2b).

D LE GÉNITIF

1 Les formes

a) Le génitif singulier se forme en ajoutant -'s après le nom du "possesseur" :

the cat's tail　　　　　　　*la queue du chat*

et le génitif pluriel en ajoutant seulement l'apostrophe au pluriel :

the cats' tails　　　　　　*la queue des chats*

Il y a souvent confusion au sujet de la position de l'apostrophe. Comparez ces deux exemples :

the boy's school　　　　　*l'école du garçon*
the boys' school　　　　　*l'école de garçons*

Dans le premier exemple, **boy** est au singulier, on parle donc de l'école d'un garçon en particulier. Dans le deuxième exemple, le nom **boys** est au pluriel, on parle donc de l'école de garçons en général.

Si le pluriel ne se termine pas en -s, le génitif pluriel se forme avec -'s comme le singulier :

the men's toilet　　　　*les toilettes pour hommes*
the children's room　　*la chambre des enfants*

b) Cas particuliers

i) La forme du génitif des noms propres se terminant par -s varie en fonction de la longueur et de l'accentuation des mots. Les noms d'une ou deux syllabes prennent 's (prononcé /ɪz/) :

Dickens's (ou Dickens') novels
les romans de Dickens

Ross's/James's/Thomas's car
la voiture de Ross/James/Thomas

Les noms de plus de deux syllabes et ceux qui se terminent par le son /iːz/ ne prennent que l'apostrophe :

Hercules' labours ['hɜːkjʊliːz]　**Socrates' wife** ['sɒkrətiːz]
les travaux d'Hercule　　　　　*l'épouse de Socrate*

Mais les noms de plus de deux syllabes accentués sur l'avant-dernière syllabe (la pénultième) prennent -'s :

Dionysus's mother ['daɪə'naɪsəsɪz]
la mère de Dionysos

Ce sont là les règles de base, mais le génitif des noms propres dépend aussi de l'usage.

ii) Avant le mot sake (*amour de/nom de*), le génitif singulier n'est normalement indiqué que par l'apostrophe avec des noms communs se terminant par -s :

for goodness' sake! (mais **for God's/Christ's/heaven's sake!**)
pour l'amour du ciel ou de Dieu !

for politeness' sake
par politesse

c) Pour les types de noms composés mentionnés au paragraphe B 12 du génitif au deuxième élément, même si c'est le premier élément qui porte la marque du pluriel -s :

I met the editor-in-chief's wife
j'ai rencontré la femme du rédacteur en chef

my parents-in-law's house is huge
la maison de mes beaux-parents est immense

2 Le génitif avec of

a) *Les êtres animés (personnes, animaux)*

Le génitif est très courant avec les personnes :

John's car　　　　　　**my mother's ring**
la voiture de John　　　*la bague de ma mère*

L'emploi de la préposition of ne semblerait pas naturel dans ces deux exemples.

Avec les animaux, on peut employer le génitif ou la construction avec of :

the wings of an insect/an insect's wings
les ailes d'un insecte

the movements of the worm/the worm's movements
les mouvements du ver de terre

b) *Les objets inanimés, les concepts, etc.*

La construction normale se forme avec **of** :

the pages of the book
les pages du livre

the roof of the car
le toit de la voiture

Cependant, souvenez-vous qu'en anglais on utilise très souvent la forme composée :

the laptop screen
l'écran de l'ordinateur portable

Le génitif est également possible avec certains noms :

the mind's ability to forget
la capacité de l'esprit à oublier

the nation's strength lies in its young people
ce sont les jeunes qui font la force du pays

en particulier si de tels noms font référence à des lieux ou à des institutions :

England's heritage (= **the heritage of England**)
l'héritage de l'Angleterre

the University's catering facilities (= **the catering facili-ties of the University**)
le service de restauration de l'université

Les noms faisant référence au temps et à la valeur de l'argent sont souvent accompagnés du génitif :

today's menu
le menu du jour

two months' work
deux mois de travail

you've had your money's worth
tu en as eu pour ton argent

Comparez ce dernier exemple avec l'emploi de la structure adjectivale expliqué au paragraphe C b) ii).

Les mesures de distances sont parfois au génitif, en particulier dans des expressions figées :

a stone's throw (away)
à deux pas (d'ici)

at arm's length
à distance

3 Le génitif sans nom

a) Si le nom déterminé par le génitif a déjà été mentionné ou si le contexte est assez clair, on n'est pas obligé de le rajouter :

it's not my father's car, it's my mother's
ce n'est pas la voiture de mon père, c'est celle de ma mère

On omet aussi le nom après le génitif lorsqu'il est sous-entendu. C'est le cas des noms de lieux :

at the baker's (= **baker's shop**)
chez le boulanger

at Alex's (= **at Alex's place**)
chez Alex

b) Le "double génitif" (c'est-à-dire la construction avec **of** et le génitif dans la même phrase) est fréquent si le génitif fait référence à une personne bien définie. Mais le premier nom est normalement précédé d'un article indéfini, d'un pronom indéfini ou d'un adjectif numéral :

they are relatives of Karen's
ils font partie de la famille de Karen

he's a friend of Peter's
c'est un ami de Peter

he's an acquaintance of my father's
c'est une connaissance de mon père

he's an uncle of Mrs Pitt's
c'est un oncle de Mme Pitt

Un pronom démonstratif peut parfois précéder le premier nom. Ceci implique un certain degré de familiarité :

that car of your father's, how much does he want for it?
cette voiture, ton père, combien est-ce qu'il la vend ?

L'article défini ne peut normalement pas s'employer avec le pre-mier nom, à moins qu'une proposition relative (ou autre déter-minatif) ne suive le génitif :

the poem of Larkin's we read yesterday is lovely
le poème de Larkin que nous avons lu hier est très joli

this is the only poem of Larkin's to have moved me
c'est le seul poème de Larkin qui m'ait ému

c) On trouve souvent le "groupe génitif" dans deux types de cons-tructions : (1) nom + déterminatif introduit par une préposi-tion, et (2) noms reliés par **and**. Dans de telles combinaisons, on peut ajouter le **-'s** au dernier élément :

John and Kate's new house
la nouvelle maison de John et de Kate

the head of department's office
le bureau du chef de service

an hour and a half's work
un travail d'une heure et demie

the Queen of Holland's yacht
le yacht de la reine de Hollande

Si le nom du possesseur est au pluriel, on emploie normalement la construction avec **of** :

the regalia of the Queens of Holland
les insignes royaux des reines de Hollande

Cependant, si les deux noms ne forment pas une unité, ils pren-nent chacun la marque du génitif **-'s** :

Shakespeare's and Marlowe's plays
les pièces de Shakespeare et de Marlowe

E LE FÉMININ

En anglais, on trouve énormément de noms communs qui s'em-ploient à la fois pour un homme et pour une femme :

artist	*artiste*	neighbour	*voisin(e)*
banker	*banquier(-ère)*	novelist	*romancier(-ère)*
cousin	*cousin(e)*	teacher	*enseignant(e)*
friend	*ami(e)*	zoologist	*zoologiste*
lawyer	*avocat(e)*	etc.	

Mais il existe certains cas où l'on emploie différentes terminaisons pour déterminer le genre d'un nom :

MASCULIN			FÉMININ	
actor	*acteur*	→	**actress**	*actrice*
duke	*duc*	→	**duchess**	*duchesse*
god	*dieu*	→	**goddess**	*déesse*
hero	*héros*	→	**heroine**	*héroïne*
prince	*prince*	→	**princess**	*princesse*
widower	*veuf*	→	**widow**	*veuve*
businessman	*homme d'affaires*	→	**businesswoman**	*femme d'affaires*

Mais on peut aussi dire **she is a good actor** (*c'est une très bonne actrice*), ou bien **she was the hero of the day** (*ce fut l'héroïne du jour*).

On utilise aussi des termes complètement différents pour distinguer le féminin du masculin : **son/daughter** (*fils/fille*), **bull/cow** (*tau-reau/vache*), etc.

Pour les noms qui ont normalement la même forme au masculin et au féminin, il est possible de rajouter les adjectifs **male/female** ou les noms **man/woman** si l'on veut absolument identifier le sexe d'une personne :

a female friend	*une amie*	**a male friend**	*un ami*
a female stu-dent	*une étudiante*	**a male student**	*un étudiant*
a man doctor	*un médecin*	**a woman doctor**	*une femme médecin*

Mais attention, cet emploi est maintenant considéré comme extrême-ment sexiste. Il est préférable d'employer le mot neutre **person**, qui s'utilise aussi lorsque l'on ne connaît pas le sexe de la personne en question :

a chairman/chairwoman → a chairperson *un(e) président(e)*

a salesman/saleswoman → a salesperson *un(e) représentant(e) de commerce*

a spokesman/spokeswoman → a spokesperson *un porte-parole*

4 LES ADJECTIFS

! Les adjectifs anglais ne s'accordent jamais avec le nom.

L'adjectif se place toujours devant le nom, en dehors de certaines exceptions (voir 2b) et c) ci-dessous).

1 Épithète et attribut

Les termes "épithète" et "attribut" font référence à la position de l'adjectif par rapport au nom. Si l'adjectif est placé devant le nom, il est épithète (**this old car** *cette vieille voiture*). S'il est placé après le verbe, il est attribut (**this car is old** *cette voiture est vieille*).

Certains adjectifs (ou certains sens d'un adjectif) sont uniquement épithètes, alors que d'autres ne peuvent être qu'attributs.

a) *Épithète seulement*

i) Certains adjectifs ayant un rapport très étroit avec le nom auquel ils se rapportent dans des constructions toutes faites sont uniquement épithètes. Par exemple :

he's a moral philosopher
c'est un philosophe spécialiste en éthique

ii) Les participes passés sont parfois employés comme adjectifs épithètes :

a disabled toilet (= toilet for disabled people)
des toilettes pour handicapés

iii) On emploie très souvent en anglais des noms faisant fonction d'adjectifs :

a logistics problem
un problème de logistique

a polystyrene container   a cardboard box
un emballage en polstyrène   une boîte en carton

a foreign affairs correspondent
un correspondant à l'étranger

Pour l'emploi des compléments du nom en position adjectivale, voir aussi p. A15.

b) *Attribut seulement*

Les adjectifs qui sont uniquement attributs qualifient généralement une condition physique ou un état mental, comme afraid (*effrayé*), ashamed (*honteux*), faint (*prêt à s'évanouir*), fond (*attaché*), poorly (*souffrant*), (un)well (*en mauvaise/bonne santé*) :

the children need not feel ashamed
les enfants ne doivent pas avoir honte

my uncle is fond of me   the girl is afraid
mon oncle m'aime beaucoup   la fille a peur

he suddenly felt faint
tout à coup, il se sentit mal ou il fut pris d'un malaise

our mother has been unwell for some time
cela fait quelque temps que notre mère est souffrante

Mais remarquez l'expression suivante construite avec une épithète :

he's not a well man
il ne se porte pas bien du tout

2 La position de l'adjectif

a) Si plus d'un adjectif précède le nom, celui ou ceux qui peuvent être aussi attributs se placent en premier. Les adjectifs uniquement épithètes ont un rapport trop étroit avec le nom pour qu'un autre mot puisse se placer entre eux et le nom :

he is a young parliamentary candidate
c'est un jeune candidat parlementaire

they have employed a conscientious social worker
ils ont employé une assistante sociale consciencieuse

a big old red brick house
une grande et vieille maison de brique rouge

Remarquez que les adjectifs old et little changent de sens selon leur position. Lorsqu'ils sont employés au sens propre, c'est-à-dire qu'ils signifient respectivement "vieux" et "petit", ils peuvent se placer devant un autre adjectif (et pourraient aussi être attributs) :

I'll just wear my old black shoes
je vais mettre mes vieilles chaussures noires

pass me that little black notebook
passe-moi ce petit cahier noir

Mais lorsque l'adjectif little signifie "petit" dans le sens de "plus jeune", il ne peut pas être séparé du nom par un autre adjectif car il forme une unité sémantique (little brother). De même, old et little employés au sens figuré dans des expressions marquant l'affection doivent précéder le nom. Dans les exemples suivants, little et old ne peuvent être qu'épithètes :

my greedy little brother ate all the ice cream
mon petit frère, gourmand comme tout, a mangé toute la glace

you poor old thing!   you poor little thing!
mon pauvre vieux !   mon pauvre petit !

b) L'adjectif peut parfois se mettre en apposition, c'est-à-dire directement après le nom sans qu'un verbe soit nécessaire. La fonction et l'emploi de ces adjectifs (et toute qualification supplémentaire éventuelle) sont similaires à ceux des propositions relatives :

this is a custom peculiar to Britain
c'est une coutume propre à la Grande-Bretagne

this is a man confident of success
c'est un homme sûr de réussir

Seuls les adjectifs qui s'emploient aussi comme attributs (après un verbe) peuvent se mettre en apposition. La mise en apposition est fréquente lorsque les adjectifs sont suivis d'un groupe prépositionnel, comme on le voit dans les exemples ci-dessus. Mais on trouve aussi des adjectifs en apposition employés dans un but emphatique, toujours employés par deux et plus :

her expression, cold and untrusting, spoke volumes
l'expression de son visage, froide et méfiante, en disait long

the building, tall and imposing, was visible from almost anywhere in the city
cet édifice, haut et imposant, se voyait pratiquement de n'importe quel endroit en ville

Il est à noter que l'emploi des adjectifs entre virgules est assez rare en anglais, contrairement au français.

La mise en apposition de l'adjectif est également possible après des mots imprécis comme things et matters. Cependant, cet emploi est assez rare et souvent littéraire :

his interest in matters linguistic
son intérêt pour tout ce qui touche à la linguistique

she has an abhorrence of things English
elle a horreur de tout ce qui est anglais

Enfin, les adjectifs en -able ou -ible peuvent se mettre après le nom, surtout si celui-ci est précédé de only (*seul, unique*) ou d'un superlatif :

he's the only person responsible
c'est la seule personne responsable

they committed the worst atrocities imaginable
ils commirent les pires atrocités imaginables

this is the most inexpensive model available
c'est le modèle disponible le moins cher

c) Certains adjectifs d'origine française ou latine se placent après le nom auquel ils se rapportent, comme en français, et dans des expressions toutes faites comme :

devil incarnate *diable incarné*
letters patent *lettres patentes*
lion rampant *lion rampant*
Lords Spiritual = *membres ecclésiastiques de la Chambre des lords*
Lords Temporal = *membres laïques de la Chambre des lords*
poet laureate *le poète lauréat*
the Princess Royal *la Princesse Royale*

3 **Les adjectifs employés comme noms**

a) Les adjectifs peuvent s'employer comme noms. Cet emploi concerne en général les concepts et les classes ou groupes de gens (en général ou dans un contexte particulier) :

i) Classes ou groupes de gens :

she gives money to the homeless **every month**
elle donne de l'argent tous les mois aux sans-abri

the government must do more to help the poor
le gouvernement doit faire davantage pour aider les pauvres

he does charity work for the blind
il fait du bénévolat pour les aveugles

a game suitable for young **and** old **alike**
un jeu pour les jeunes et les moins jeunes

Remarquez qu'en anglais ces mots ont un sens de pluriel collectif (voir p. A11). Pour désigner une personne dans un groupe, on ajoute man, woman, person, etc. :

a blind woman   **three deaf people**
une aveugle   *trois sourds*

ii) Concepts abstraits :

it's not always easy to distinguish the true **from** the false
il n'est pas toujours facile de distinguer le vrai du faux

Cet emploi est néanmoins assez rare.

b) Normalement, un adjectif ne peut pas remplacer un nom singulier dénombrable. Dans ce cas, il est nécessaire d'employer one (mais voir aussi One, pp. A37-8) :

I don't like the striped shirt; I prefer the plain one
je n'aime pas la chemise à rayures, je préfère l'unie

of all the applicants, the French one **was the best**
de tous les candidats, le Français était le meilleur

Cependant, il existe un certain nombre de participes passés que l'on peut utiliser (avec l'article défini) à la place d'un nom dénombrable. Par exemple :

the accused   the deceased
l'accusé/les accusés   *le mort/les morts*

the accused's family was with him in court
la famille de l'accusé était avec lui au tribunal

the deceased's possessions were sold
les biens du mort furent vendus

Ces adjectifs substantivés ne prennent pas de -s au pluriel.

c) Pour les exemples au pluriel en a), on n'ajoutait pas de -s à l'adjectif. Mais il arrive parfois que la conversion d'un adjectif en nom soit totale et que l'adjectif prenne un -s au pluriel :

the Blacks against the Whites in South Africa
les Noirs contre les Blancs en Afrique du Sud

the Reds
les rouges (les communistes)

here come the newlyweds
voilà les jeunes mariés

put all the empties in a box
mets toutes les bouteilles vides dans un carton

d) Nationalités

i) En anglais, les adjectifs et les noms désignant la nationalité prennent une majuscule (ainsi que les noms de langues) :

an American car   **an American**
une voiture américaine   *un Américain*

ii) On peut classer les nationalités en quatre groupes, selon la forme de l'adjectif et du nom :

GROUPE 1   adjectif ordinaire

GROUPE 2   adjectif et nom identiques (se terminant par -ese et -s)

GROUPE 3   comme le groupe 2, mais le nom prend un -s au pluriel (adjectifs se terminant par -an, -i, etc.)

GROUPE 4   adjectif et nom différents (mais au pluriel, le nom + -s est aussi possible)

GROUPE 1

adjectif :   **English literature**
           la littérature anglaise

employé comme nom lorsqu'il se réfère à une nation :

the English are rather reserved
les Anglais sont plutôt réservés

Les adjectifs du Groupe 1 ne peuvent pas s'utiliser comme noms pour faire référence à des individus. Dans ce cas, il faut ajouter la terminaison -man (ou -woman) :

we spoke to two Englishmen/Englishwomen
nous avons parlé à deux Anglais/Anglaises

De même pour :

Dutch	*hollandais*	Irish	*irlandais*
French	*français*	Welsh	*gallois*

GROUPE 2

adjectif :   **Japanese art**
           l'art japonais

employé comme nom lorsqu'il se réfère à une nation :

the Japanese are famous for their technology
les Japonais sont célèbres pour leur technologie

et lorsqu'il se réfère à des individus (sans -s au pluriel) :

their new au pair is a Japanese
leur nouvelle fille au pair est japonaise

I've got six Japanese in my class
il y a six Japonais dans ma classe

De même pour :

Burmese	*birman*	Swiss	*suisse*
Chinese	*chinois*	Vietnamese	*vietnamien*
Portuguese	*portugais*		

GROUPE 3

adjectif : **German institutions**
les institutions allemandes

employé comme nom (avec un **-s** au pluriel) lorsqu'il fait référence à une nation :

the Germans produce some fine cars
les Allemands produisent de belles voitures

et lorsqu'il se réfère à des individus (avec un **-s** au pluriel) :

he was having a conversation with a German
il était en conversation avec un Allemand

we met quite a few Germans on our holiday
nous avons rencontré un bon nombre d'Allemands pendant nos vacances

De même, ceux qui se terminent en **-an**, par exemple :

African	*africain*	**European**	*européen*
American	*américain*	**Hungarian**	*hongrois*
Asian	*asiatique*	**Indian**	*indien*
Australian	*australien*	**Iranian**	*iranien*
Belgian	*belge*	**Italian**	*italien*
Brazilian	*brésilien*	**Norwegian**	*norvégien*
Canadian	*canadien*	**Russian**	*russe*

(mais notez que **Arabian** (*arabe*) appartient au Groupe 4 ci-dessous)
et ceux qui se terminent en **-i** :

Bangladeshi	*bangladais*	**Israeli**	*israélien*
Iraqi	*iraquien*	**Pakistani**	*pakistanais*

On trouve aussi dans ce groupe :

Cypriot	*chypriote*	**Greek**	*grec*
Czech	*tchèque*		

GROUPE 4

adjectif : **Danish furniture**
les meubles danois

employé comme nom lorsqu'il fait référence à une nation :

the Danish enjoy good food
les Danois apprécient la bonne chère

Mais il y a un nom différent qui peut aussi être utilisé pour faire référence à la nation :

the Danes enjoy good food
les Danois apprécient la bonne chère

et qui est la seule forme admise pour désigner les individus :

I met a Dane on the bus
j'ai fait la connaissance d'un Danois dans le bus

there were two Danes in the cast
il y avait deux Danois parmi les acteurs

De même pour :

British/Briton	*Britannique*	**Spanish/Spaniard**	*Espagnol*
Finnish/Finn	*Finlandais*	**Swedish/Swede**	*Suédois*
Polish/Pole	*Polonais*		

Cas particulier : **Arabian, Arabic** et **Arab**

L'adjectif courant est **Arabian** (*The Arabian Nights* les Mille et Une Nuits) sauf si l'on parle de la langue ou des chiffres :

do you speak Arabic?
est-ce que vous parlez arabe ?

this figure should be written in Arabic numerals, not Roman ones
ce nombre devrait être écrit en chiffres arabes, et non en chiffres romains

Arab est employé pour désigner les individus des pays de culture arabe, sauf si **Saudi** le précède. Dans ce cas, on emploie

Saudi Arabian ou **Saudi** :

he's worked a lot with Arabs
il a beaucoup travaillé avec des Arabes

the hotel has been hired by Saudi Arabians (ou **Saudis**)
l'hôtel a été loué par des Saoudiens

iii) Remarques sur **Scottish, Scots** et **Scotch** (*écossais*) :

Aujourd'hui, **Scotch** est rarement utilisé, sauf dans des locutions (concernant souvent la nourriture ou les boissons), telles que **Scotch egg** (= œuf dur entouré de chair à saucisse et enrobé de chapelure), **Scotch whisky**, **Scotch broth** (= soupe écossaise à base de légumes et d'orge perlée) et **Scotch terrier**.

Dans les autres cas, on utilise normalement l'adjectif **Scottish** comme dans a **Scottish bar** (*un bar écossais*), **Scottish football supporters** (*supporters de football écossais*), même si **Scots** est parfois utilisé pour les personnes : a **Scots lawyer** (*un avocat écossais*). On distingue aussi le **Scottish English** (= l'anglais parlé avec un accent écossais) du **Scots** (= le dialecte écossais).

Pour désigner la nation, on emploie **the Scots** (*les Écossais*) (parfois **the Scottish**). L'individu est a **Scot** (au pluriel **Scots**) ou a **Scotsman/Scotswoman** (au pluriel **Scotsmen/Scotswomen**).

5 LES ADVERBES

Par adverbe, on entend un seul mot (par exemple **happily**) et par groupe adverbial ou proposition adverbiale, on entend un groupe de mots ayant une fonction adverbiale (par exemple **in a friendly way**).

A LES DIFFÉRENTS TYPES

On peut classer les adverbes en différentes catégories, selon leur forme ou leur sens.

a) *Forme*

On distingue deux sortes d'adverbes suivant leur forme : les adverbes "en tant que tels" et les adverbes "dérivés".

Les adverbes dérivés sont ceux qui dérivent de mots issus d'une autre catégorie grammaticale et auxquels on ajoute une terminaison particulière (voir B) :

happily *heureusement*, de l'adjectif **happy**
hourly *par heure*, du nom **hour** ou de l'adjectif **hourly**
moneywise *en ce qui concerne l'argent*, du nom **money**

Parmi les adverbes en tant que tels, on trouve :

here	*ici*	**often**	*souvent*
there	*là-bas*	**never**	*jamais*
now	*maintenant*	**soon**	*bientôt*
then	*alors*	**very**	*très*

b) *Sens*

Les adverbes peuvent se diviser en divers types selon leur sens. Les adverbes suivants sont particulièrement courants :

i) Adverbes de temps :

now (*maintenant*), **then** (*alors*), **once** (*une fois*), **soon** (*bientôt*), **always** (*toujours*), **briefly** (*brièvement*)

I saw her once
je l'ai vue une fois

you always say that
tu dis toujours ça

ii) Adverbes de lieu :

here (*ici*), **there** (*là-bas*), **everywhere** (*partout*), **up** (*en haut*), **down** (*en bas*), **back** (*derrière*)

come here
viens ici

iii) Adverbes de manière :

well (*bien*), **clumsily** (*maladroitement*), **beautifully** (*merveilleusement*), etc.

what's worth doing is worth doing well
ce qui vaut la peine d'être fait vaut la peine d'être bien fait

iv) Adverbes d'intensité :

rather (*plutôt*), **quite** (*assez*), **very** (*très*), **hardly** (*à peine*), **extremely** (*extrêmement*)

this gravy is rather good
cette sauce est plutôt bonne

B LES DIFFÉRENTES FORMES

a) *Les adverbes en -ly*

On ajoute normalement cette terminaison directement à l'adjectif :

sweet → **sweet**ly
gentil   *gentiment*

Mais si l'adjectif se termine en **-ic**, on ajoute **-ally** :

intrinsic → **intrinsically**   **drastic** → **drastically**
intrinsèque   *intrinsèquement*   *radical* → *radicalement*

Les seules exceptions sont :

public → **publicly**
public   *publiquement*

politic → **politicly** (*rarement employé*)
judicieux   *judicieusement*

Pour les changements orthographiques (comme dans **happy** → **happily** ou **noble** → **nobly**), voir p. A79.

Remarquez que l'on prononce toujours la voyelle **-e** (c'est-à-dire le son /ɪ/) de **-ed** à l'intérieur d'un adverbe, qu'on la prononce dans l'adjectif correspondant ou pas :

assured [əˈʃʊəd]   →   **assuredly** [əˈʃʊərɪdlɪ]
assuré   *assurément*

offhanded [ɒfˈhændɪd] → **offhandedly** [ɒfˈhændɪdlɪ]
désinvolte   *avec désinvolture*

b) *Même forme que l'adjectif*

Certains adverbes ont la même forme que l'adjectif correspondant, par exemple :

in the far distance (*adj*)
tout au loin

you don't have to go far (*adv*)
tu n'as pas besoin d'aller très loin

Voir la liste d'adverbes et les exemples donnés dans la section C, 2 de ce chapitre.

c) **-wise**

On peut ajouter le suffixe **-wise** à des noms pour former un adverbe qui a le sens général de "en ce qui concerne" (quel que soit le nom) :

how's he feeling? – do you mean mentally or healthwise?
comment se sent-il ? – tu veux dire mentalement ou côté santé ?

Bien que cette construction soit très courante, elle a tendance à être plus employée à l'oral qu'à l'écrit, et elle n'est pas toujours

considérée comme particulièrement élégante :

things are going quite well schedule-wise
les choses se passent assez bien en ce qui concerne nos prévisions

we're not really short of anything furniture-wise
nous ne manquons pas de grand-chose côté meubles

the town's quite good restaurant-wise
la ville a pas mal de restaurants

C L'EMPLOI

1 Fonctions de l'adverbe et des constructions adverbiales

Les adverbes et les groupes adverbiaux s'emploient pour modifier :

a) des verbes :

he spoke well
il a bien parlé

he spoke in a loud voice
il a parlé à haute voix

b) des adjectifs :

that's awfully nice of you
c'est vraiment gentil à vous

this isn't good enough
ça n'est pas assez bien

c) d'autres adverbes :

she didn't sing well enough
elle n'a pas assez bien chanté

it happened extremely quickly
ça s'est passé extrêmement vite

(Remarquez que **enough** suit l'adjectif ou l'adverbe qu'il modifie ; voir 3d) vi) p. A23)

d) des noms :

this is rather a mess
c'est plutôt en désordre

he's quite a hero
c'est un vrai héros

e) toute la phrase :

fortunately they accepted the verdict
par bonheur, ils ont accepté le verdict

amazingly enough, it was true
aussi incroyable que cela puisse paraître, c'était vrai

2 Les adverbes ayant la même forme que l'adjectif

Parmi ceux-ci on trouve :

far (*lointain – loin*) (voir B, b) ci-dessus), **fast** (*rapide – vite*), **hard** (*dur, difficile – dur*), **little** (*petit – peu*), **long** (*long – longtemps*), **early** (*matinal, en avance – tôt*), **only** (*seul – seulement*)

et un certain nombre en **-ly** dérivés de noms (faisant souvent référence au temps), par exemple :

daily (*quotidien – tous les jours*), **monthly** (*mensuel – tous les mois*), **weekly** (*hebdomadaire – toutes les semaines*), **deathly** (*cadavérique – comme la mort*), **leisurely** (*tranquille – sans se presser*)

ADJECTIF	ADVERBE
this is a fast train *c'est un train rapide*	**you're driving too fast** *vous roulez trop vite*
it's a hard question *c'est une question difficile*	**he worked hard** *il a travaillé dur*
he bought a little house *il a acheté une petite maison*	**little do you care!** *ça t'importe peu !*
she was wearing a long dress *elle portait une longue robe*	**have you been here long?** *tu es là depuis longtemps ?*
you'll have to catch the early plane *il faudra que tu prennes le premier avion*	**they arrived early** *ils sont arrivés tôt*

she's an only child
elle est fille unique

I've only got two tickets
je n'ai que deux billets

do you get a daily newspaper?
vous achetez un quotidien ?

there's a flight twice daily
il y a un vol deux fois par jour

you'll receive this in monthly instalments
vous le recevrez en versements mensuels

the list will be updated monthly
la liste sera mise à jour tous les mois

a deathly silence fell on the spectators
un silence de mort s'abattit sur les spectateurs

she was deathly pale
elle avait le teint blafard

we took a leisurely stroll after lunch
nous sommes allés faire une petite balade tranquille après manger

we spent a month travelling leisurely through the Loire Valley
nous avons passé un mois à voyager tranquillement dans la vallée de la Loire

3 La position de l'adverbe

En anglais, l'adverbe ne peut pas se placer entre le verbe et le complément. On dira toujours :

they speak English well (*et jamais* **they speak well English**)
ils parlent bien anglais

Il faut donc faire attention à ne pas garder systématiquement la structure française. Lorsqu'il peut se placer au milieu d'une phrase, l'adverbe anglais se mettra toujours **devant** le verbe (ou entre l'auxiliaire et le verbe principal pour les temps composés) :

we often go to the cinema (*et jamais* **we go often to the cinema**)
on va souvent au cinéma

Certains adverbes peuvent se placer au début, au milieu ou à la fin de la phrase, alors que le choix est beaucoup plus restreint pour d'autres. Vous trouverez ci-dessous les différentes positions possibles des adverbes les plus courants.

a) *Les adverbes de temps*

i) S'ils font référence à un moment précis, on les place en début ou en fin de phrase (et non au milieu) :

tonight the shops close at 8
ce soir, les magasins ferment à 8 heures

I'll come and see you tomorrow
je viendrai te voir demain

Mais l'adverbe **now** est possible aux trois endroits dans la phrase car il peut aussi précéder le verbe :

I now see the point
je vois maintenant ce que vous voulez dire

ii) Si l'on fait référence à un moment imprécis, l'adverbe peut aussi se placer avant le verbe principal :

we soon got to know him
on a vite appris à le connaître

we have often talked about it
on en a souvent parlé

they have frequently discussed such matters
ils ont fréquemment discuté de tels sujets

Remarquez que les adverbes de fréquence **never** et **always** se placent toujours avant le verbe :

I always buy my shirts here
j'achète toujours mes chemises ici

we'll never know the truth
on ne connaîtra jamais la vérité

Mais les adverbes de fréquence se placent normalement après le verbe **to be** :

he's never late
il n'est jamais en retard

he was frequently in trouble with the police
il avait souvent des ennuis avec la police

S'il y a plus d'un auxiliaire, ces adverbes peuvent se mettre entre les deux auxiliaires ou devant le verbe principal :

she has frequently been/has been frequently visited by distant relatives
des parents lointains lui ont fréquemment rendu visite

b) *Les adverbes de lieu*

Ils ne peuvent pas se mettre au milieu de la phrase (entre le sujet et le verbe). Ils se placent en général en fin de phrase, c'est-à-dire qu'ils suivent le verbe (et le complément d'objet) :

they travelled everywhere
ils ont voyagé partout

I saw you there
je vous ai vu là-bas

he's doing some gardening outside
il est en train de jardiner dehors

Mais remarquez la position en début de phrase devant **be**, **come** et **go** :

there's the postman
voilà le facteur

here are your books
voici tes livres

here comes the bus
voilà le bus qui arrive

et devant des pronoms personnels avec ces mêmes verbes :

there he is
le voilà

here she comes
la voilà (qui arrive)

c) *Les adverbes de manière*

i) La position d'un adverbe de manière ne change pas le sens général de la phrase, sauf dans les cas où l'adverbe peut modifier le verbe ou la phrase entière (voir iv) ci-dessous). On peut souvent le placer où l'on veut, suivant les nuances ou le ton que l'on souhaite donner à la phrase. Néanmoins, la position en début de phrase est assez rare (voir iii) ci-dessous) :

they stealthily crept upstairs
they crept stealthily upstairs
they crept upstairs stealthily
ils ont monté les escaliers furtivement

stealthily, they crept upstairs
furtivement, ils ont monté les escaliers

she carefully examined the report
she examined the report carefully
elle examina le rapport avec attention

Mais, lorsque l'adverbe donne une information importante dans le contexte, il se met en fin de phrase. Comparez :

I quickly packed my bags and left
j'ai fait mes valises en vitesse et je suis parti

I packed my bags quickly, that's why I forgot my passport
j'ai fait mes valises en vitesse, voilà pourquoi j'ai oublié mon passeport

Dans la phrase suivante, une seule position est possible car l'adverbe constitue l'information générale :

they fought the war intelligently
ils ont mené la guerre avec intelligence

ii) Si le complément d'objet direct est extrêmement long, on évite de placer l'adverbe en fin de phrase :

she carefully examined the report sent to her by the Minister
elle examina attentivement le rapport envoyé par le ministre

iii) La position en tête de phrase est très descriptive et emphatique :

clumsily, he made his way towards the door
maladroitement, il se dirigea vers la porte

iv) Les adverbes de manière modifiant les phrases ou seulement les verbes :

Suivant la place qu'il a dans la phrase, l'adverbe va modifier la phrase entière ou bien le verbe seul. Comparez les phrases suivantes :

she spoke wisely at the meeting
elle a parlé avec sagesse durant la réunion

she wisely spoke at the meeting
elle a eu la sagesse de parler à la réunion

Voici des exemples analogues :

she spoke naturally and fluently (*modifie le verbe*)
elle parla avec naturel et aisance

she naturally assumed it was right (*modifie la phrase*)
elle supposa naturellement que c'était vrai

naturally, she assumed it was right (*modifie la phrase*)
naturellement, elle supposa que c'était vrai

she understood it clearly (*modifie le verbe*)
elle l'a bien compris

she clearly understood it (*modifie la phrase ou le verbe*)
de toute évidence, elle l'a compris
elle l'a bien compris

clearly, she understood it (*modifie la phrase*)
de toute évidence, elle l'a compris

Le mot **enough** peut aussi s'employer après un adverbe pour marquer le fait que l'adverbe est employé pour modifier la phrase :

funnily (enough), they both spoke at the meeting
aussi drôle que cela puisse paraître, ils ont tous les deux parlé lors de la réunion

d) *Les adverbes d'intensité*

i) Si les adverbes d'intensité modifient d'autres adverbes, des adjectifs ou des noms, ils viendront se placer juste devant ces mots :

she played extremely well
elle a joué extrêmement bien

it's too difficult to define   **it's rather a shame**
c'est trop difficile à définir   *c'est bien dommage*

Remarquez que les adverbes tels que **well** et **badly**, qui permettent d'évaluer la qualité de quelque chose, se placent toujours en fin de phrase :

she plays tennis badly
elle joue mal au tennis

sauf dans les tournures passives où l'adverbe viendra se placer entre l'auxiliaire **to be** et le verbe principal :

the bridge was badly built
le pont a été mal construit

ii) Sinon, les adverbes d'intensité (ainsi que ceux qui permettent d'attirer l'attention sur un élément de la phrase : just,

also, only, etc.) précèdent normalement le verbe principal :

we very much enjoyed your book
nous avons beaucoup apprécié votre livre

I could hardly remember a thing
je ne me souvenais de presque rien

we just want to know the time of departure
nous voulons juste connaître l'heure du départ

they also went to France last year
ils sont aussi allés en France l'année dernière

Mais contrairement à **also**, l'adverbe **too** suit normalement les mots qu'il modifie et peut donc se placer aussi en fin de phrase :

you too should go and see the exhibition
toi aussi, tu devrais aller voir cette exposition

you should go and see that exhibition too
tu devrais aussi aller voir cette exposition

iii) **Only** (*seulement*)

Only est en général placé avant le verbe, mais il peut aussi se mettre en début de phrase lorsqu'il fait référence au sujet :

only James came to visit her in hospital
seul James est venu la voir à l'hôpital

Cet adverbe pose rarement problème à l'oral, car le contexte, l'accentuation et l'intonation permettent de déduire son sens :

(a) **Jayne only saw Gillian today**
Jayne a seulement vu Gillian aujourd'hui
(mais elle ne lui a pas parlé)

(b) **Jayne only saw Gillian today**
Jayne n'a vu que Gillian aujourd'hui
(elle n'a vu personne d'autre)

(c) **Jayne only saw Gillian today**
Jayne n'a vu Gillian qu'aujourd'hui
(elle l'a vue seulement aujourd'hui)

Mais de telles différences sont difficiles à cerner à l'écrit, à moins que le contexte ne soit bien clair. Ainsi, dans l'exemple (b) à l'écrit, on changerait la place de l'adverbe de la façon suivante :

Jayne saw only Gillian today
Jayne n'a vu que Gillian aujourd'hui

et (c) deviendrait :

it was only today that Jayne saw Gillian
ce n'est qu'aujourd'hui que Jayne a vu Gillian

Pour l'exemple (a), on écrirait probablement le mot accentué en italique :

Jayne only *saw* Gillian today
Jayne n'a fait que voir Gillian aujourd'hui

iv) **Very** ou **much** ? (*très/beaucoup*)

● Devant des adjectifs dans leur forme de base, on emploie **very** :

these are very nice
ils sont très beaux

ainsi que devant des superlatifs en **-est** :

these are the very nicest flowers I've seen
ce sont les plus belles fleurs que j'aie jamais vues

Cependant, dans la construction au superlatif qui suit, **much** s'emploie devant le **the** du superlatif :

this is much the best **example in the book**
c'est de loin le meilleur exemple du livre

Pour le superlatif, voir le chapitre 6, pp. A24-7.

● Le comparatif est accompagné de much :

she's much taller **than you**
elle est bien plus grande que toi

she's much more **particular**
elle est beaucoup plus pointilleuse

Pour le comparatif, voir le chapitre 6, pp. A24-7.

● Il en est de même avec les adverbes :

you do it very well, but I do it much better
tu le fais très bien, mais je le fais bien mieux

● Les verbes sont accompagnés de much (qui est lui-même modifié par very) :

I love you very much
je t'aime énormément

● Avant les participes passés :

S'ils ont la fonction d'adjectif, on emploie very :

they were very offended   **I'm** very tired
ils étaient extrêmement vexés   je suis très fatigué

we're very interested **in this house**
nous sommes très intéressés par cette maison

I'm very pleased **to meet you**
je suis très heureux de faire votre connaissance

these suitcases are looking very used
ces valises ont l'air très usées

Mais s'ils ne sont pas considérés comme adjectifs en tant que tels, ou s'ils gardent leur fonction verbale, on emploie alors much, et non very :

these suitcases haven't been much used
ces valises n'ont pas été très utilisées

he has been much maligned
on l'a beaucoup calomnié

this has been much spoken **about**
on en a beaucoup parlé

his new house is much admired **by people round here**
les gens du coin ont beaucoup d'admiration pour sa nouvelle maison

Dans un langage légèrement familier, on préfère employer a lot à la place de much, en particulier à la forme affirmative (a lot se met après le verbe) :

these have been used a lot
ceux-ci ont été beaucoup utilisés

v) All (*tout*)

All peut s'employer comme adverbe d'intensité et signifie alors "tout", "complètement". Il peut se placer devant un adjectif, un participe passé, un adverbe ou un groupe prépositionnel :

she was all alone (+ *adjectif*)
elle était toute seule

he was all covered **in mud** (+ *participe passé*)
il était tout couvert de boue

that's what I've been saying all along (+ *adverbe*)
c'est ce que je dis depuis le début

I forgot all about **the meeting** (+ *préposition*)
j'ai complètement oublié qu'il y avait une réunion

et devant des comparatifs :

I've stopped smoking and feel all the better **for it**
j'ai arrêté de fumer et je me sens tellement mieux

it makes her all the more **interesting**
ça la rend encore plus intéressante

vi) Enough (*assez*)

Lorsqu'il est employé comme adverbe, enough se place après l'adjectif :

he isn't big enough **for that yet**
il n'est pas encore assez grand pour ça

On l'emploie aussi après un nom employé comme adjectif attribut :

he isn't man enough **for the job**
il n'a pas la carrure suffisante pour ce travail

Remarquez que enough peut séparer l'adjectif du nom :

it's a decent enough **town**
c'est pas mal comme ville

e) *Les adverbes modifiant toute la phrase*

i) Tout comme la plupart des adverbes de manière (voir c) i) ci-dessus), ces adverbes peuvent se placer à différents endroits dans la phrase, selon l'importance que l'on veut leur donner :

fortunately, **he stopped in time**
heureusement, il s'est arrêté à temps

he fortunately **stopped in time**
il s'est heureusement arrêté à temps

he stopped in time, fortunately
il s'est arrêté à temps, heureusement

ii) Les adverbes probably, certainly et definitely se placent presque toujours au milieu de la phrase (juste avant le verbe) :

he'll probably **come later**
il va probablement venir plus tard

I definitely **saw him yesterday**
je suis sûre de l'avoir vu hier

Mais surely et perhaps se mettent habituellement en début de phrase :

surely **you must be joking!**   perhaps **he'll come**
vous plaisantez, j'espère ?   *il va peut-être venir*

f) *La place de l'adverbe de négation* not

i) Not précède le groupe adverbial qu'il modifie :

is he here? – not yet
est-ce qu'il est là ? – pas encore

do you mind? – not at all
ça ne te dérange pas ? – pas du tout

he speaks not only **English, but also French**
il parle non seulement anglais, mais aussi français

he lives not far **from here**
il n'habite pas loin d'ici

Dans l'exemple suivant, c'est absolutely (*absolument*) qui qualifie not, et non le contraire :

have you said something to her? – absolutely not
tu lui as dit quelque chose ? – absolument pas

ii) Not suit le verbe to be :

he is not **hungry**
il n'a pas faim

iii) À la forme négative, on ajoute **not** après l'auxiliaire ou **-n't** directement à l'auxiliaire. **Not** (ou **-n't**) se met normalment après le premier auxiliaire :

he does not/doesn't smoke
il ne fume pas

they would not/wouldn't have seen her
ils ne l'auraient pas vue

Mais dans des questions, la forme complète de **not** suit le sujet, tandis que **-n't** le précède, puisqu'il est lié à l'auxiliaire :

did they not go there last year?
didn't they go there last year?
n'y sont-ils pas allés l'an dernier ?

have they not already been there?
haven't they already been there?
ne sont-ils pas déjà allés là-bas ?

iv) En anglais américain, **not** peut précéder un subjonctif :

it is important that he not be informed of this
il est important qu'il n'en soit pas informé

v) Remarquez aussi les emplois suivants :

did you do it? – not me (*Fam*)
c'est toi qui l'as fait ? – non, c'est pas moi

will she come? – I hope not
est-ce qu'elle viendra ? – j'espère que non

Ici **not** est la négation de **will come** (**I hope she won't come** *j'espère qu'elle ne viendra pas*). Pour cet emploi de **not** avec **hope**, voir p. A38.

g) *L'emploi de* **some/any, something/anything** *comme adverbes*

i) **Some** est utilisé comme adverbe :

devant des nombres = "à peu près", "autour de" :

some fifty people were present
il y avait une cinquantaine de personnes présentes

avec **more** :

talk to me some more
parle-moi encore un peu

seul, en anglais américain :

we talked some
on a un peu parlé

ii) **Any** est utilisé comme adverbe devant les comparatifs :

he isn't any less of a friend in spite of this
malgré cela, il n'en est pas moins mon ami

I refuse to discuss this any further
je refuse de continuer cette discussion

iii) **Something** et **anything** sont aussi employés comme adverbes devant **like**. **Something** a alors le sens de "plutôt" ou "environ" et **anything** le sens de "rien" :

it looks something like a Picasso
ça ressemble à du Picasso

something like fifty or sixty people were present
il y avait environ cinquante à soixante personnes présentes

it wasn't anything like I had imagined
ça n'avait rien à voir avec ce que j'avais imaginé

On entend parfois des expressions dans lesquelles **some-thing** est utilisé comme adverbe d'intensité. Il s'agit là d'un emploi régional ou familier, grammaticalement in-correct :

it hurts something awful!
ça fait vachement mal !

she fancies him something rotten
elle est dingue de lui

Pour l'emploi de **some/any** comme adjectifs ou pronoms indéfinis et de **something/anything** comme pronoms, voir pp. A34-5.

h) *L'emploi de* **no** *et* **none** *comme adverbes*

i) **No** est adverbe lorsqu'il est employé devant un comparatif :

he earns no more than £15,000 a year
il ne gagne pas plus de 15 000 livres par an

ii) **None** est aussi adverbe devant **the** + comparatif :

she's none the worse for her adventure
son aventure ne lui a pas fait de mal

he's taken some medicine but is feeling none the bet-ter
il a pris des médicaments, mais il ne se sent pas mieux pour autant

after his explanation we were all none the wiser
malgré ses explications, nous n'étions pas plus avancés

Dans ce dernier exemple, on aurait aussi pu dire : **none of us was any the wiser after his explanation** (voir g) ii) ci-dessus).

Pour l'emploi de **no** comme adjectif et de **none** comme pronom, voir p. A35.

i) *L'emploi de* **either, neither** *et* **nor** *comme adverbes*

i) L'adverbe **either** n'est utilisé que dans des propositions négatives. Dans les phrases affirmatives, on emploiera **too** (voir d) ii) p. A22) :

I can't do it either   **I can do it too**
je ne peux pas le faire non plus   *je peux le faire aussi*

ii) Les adverbes **neither** et **nor** sont utilisés dans les proposi-tions qui suivent les propositions négatives. Attention à l'in-version sujet-auxiliaire :

I can't swim and neither/nor can she
je ne sais pas nager, et elle non plus

I can't swim – neither/nor can I (*ou* **me neither** *dans un style familier*)
je ne sais pas nager – moi non plus

I don't like coffee, nor do I like tea
je n'aime pas le café et je n'aime pas le thé non plus

I don't like coffee, (and) nor/neither does she
je n'aime pas le café, et elle non plus

Voir aussi **Les conjonctions**, p. A74, ainsi que **Les pronoms et les adjectifs indéfinis**, p. A37.

6 LA COMPARAISON

1 Les formes

Le comparatif et le superlatif des adjectifs et des adverbes se forment de la même manière.

a) Il existe trois degrés de comparaison : **le positif** (forme de base), **le comparatif** et **le superlatif** :

sweet   **beautiful**   (positif)
doux   *beau*

sweeter   more **beautiful**   (comparatif)
plus doux   *plus beau*

sweetest   the most **beautiful** (superlatif)
le plus doux   *le plus beau*

Pour les changements orthographiques résultant de l'addition de -er, -est (happy - happier ou big - bigger), voir pp. A79-80.

b) -er/-est ou more/most ?

i) Plus l'adjectif est court, plus il est probable que son comparatif et son superlatif se forment en ajoutant -er et -est. Ceci concerne tout particulièrement les adjectifs monosyllabiques, comme keen, fine, late, wide, neat, etc. Des adjectifs très courants tels que big ou fast prennent toujours la forme -er/-est. Il en est de même pour les adverbes qui ont la même forme que l'adjectif correspondant (voir pp. A20-1) :

a faster car *(adj)*
une voiture plus rapide

I can run faster than you think *(adv)*
je peux courir plus vite que tu ne crois

if he could just work a little harder! *(adv)*
si seulement il pouvait travailler un peu plus !

Si les adjectifs ont deux syllabes, on trouve les formes -er/-est et more/most, les suffixes -er/-est étant particulièrement courants avec les adjectifs qui se terminent en -y, -le, -ow, -er :

noisy :   **this is the noisiest pub I've ever seen**
          c'est le pub le plus bruyant que j'aie jamais vu

feeble :   **this is the feeblest excuse I've heard**
          c'est la plus mauvaise excuse que j'aie entendue

shallow : **the stream is shallower up there**
          le ruisseau est moins profond en amont

clever :   **she's the cleverest of them all**
          c'est la plus intelligente de tous ou de toutes

Les adjectifs formés à partir d'autres adjectifs dissyllabiques peuvent prendre -er/-est ou s'employer avec more/most :

she's unhappier than she has ever been
elle est plus malheureuse que jamais

he's got the untidiest room in the whole house
il a la chambre la plus mal rangée de toute la maison

ii) Les adjectifs de plus de deux syllabes s'utilisent avec more au comparatif et the most au superlatif :

this is the most idiotic thing I ever heard!
c'est la chose la plus idiote que j'aie entendue !

I prefer a more traditional Christmas
je préfère un Noël plus traditionnel

she's getting more and more predictable
il devient de plus en plus facile de deviner ce qu'elle va faire

iii) Les adjectifs formés à partir de participes passés s'emploient avec more et the most :

she's more gifted than her sister
elle est plus douée que sa sœur

the most advanced students
les étudiants les plus avancés

that's the most bored I've ever been!
je ne me suis jamais autant ennuyé !

Tired peut prendre les terminaisons -er/-est.

iv) Les adverbes formés à partir de l'adjectif + -ly ont un comparatif et un superlatif construits avec more et the most :

the most recently published works in this field
les ouvrages publiés le plus récemment dans ce domaine

Mais early, qui n'est pas dérivé d'un adjectif sans -ly, prend -er/-est. Il a la même forme que l'adjectif et se comporte donc de la même manière (voir l'explication concernant les adjectifs dissyllabiques, b) ii) ci-dessus) :

we arrived earlier than we expected
nous sommes arrivés plus tôt que prévu

v) Si la comparaison se fait entre deux adjectifs (comme choix de mots), on ne peut employer que more :

this sauce is more sweet than sour
cette sauce est plus douce qu'aigre

c) Les comparatifs et superlatifs irréguliers

Quelques adjectifs et adverbes ont un comparatif et un superlatif irréguliers.

bad *(adj)*	worse	the worst
mauvais	*pire*	*le pire*
badly *(adv)*	worse	the worst
mal	*pire*	*le pire*
far *(adj)*	further/farther	the furthest/the farthest
éloigné, lointain	*plus éloigné*	*le plus éloigné*
far *(adv)*	further/farther	the furthest/the farthest
loin	*plus loin*	*le plus loin*
good *(adj)*	better	the best
bon	*meilleur*	*le meilleur*
well *(adv)*	better	the best
bien	*meilleur*	*le meilleur*
little *(adj)*	less/lesser	the least
peu de, petit	*moins de/moindre*	*le moins de/moindre*
little *(adv)*	less	the least
peu	*moins*	*le moins*
many *(adj)*	more	the most
beaucoup de	*plus de*	*le plus de*
much *(adv ou adj*)*	more	the most
beaucoup (de)	*plus (de)*	*le plus (de)*

*much peut être adjectif avec les indénombrables (voir p. A35) et dans les structures interrogatives ou négatives (there isn't much cake left *il ne reste pas beaucoup de gâteau*). Le contraire de much est l'adjectif little.

Le comparatif régulier de late (*tard*) est later (*plus tard*) et le superlatif, the latest (*le plus récent*). Remarquez aussi que late possède un comparatif et un superlatif irréguliers avec des significations différentes : latter (*le second*) et the last (*le dernier*).

De même, old (*vieux*) possède un comparatif et un superlatif réguliers, older (*plus vieux*) et the oldest (*le plus vieux*), ainsi qu'une forme irrégulière : elder (*plus vieux*) et the eldest (*aîné*).

Pour les différences d'usage entre the latest et the last, the oldest et the eldest, further/the furthest et farther/the farthest, voir les cas particuliers p. A26.

Pour l'emploi du comparatif et du superlatif (et les variantes), voir ci-dessous et pp. A22-3.

d) Le comparatif d'égalité

On forme le comparatif d'égalité avec la construction as... as :

he's as funny as his father
il est aussi drôle que son père

e) Les comparatifs d'infériorité et superlatifs d'infériorité

Le comparatif d'infériorité se forme avec **less... than**, et le superlatif d'infériorité avec **the least** + adjectif :

he's less successful than his brother
il a moins de succès que son frère

he is the least successful of the three brothers
c'est celui des trois frères qui a le moins de succès

On peut également exprimer l'infériorité en employant le comparatif d'inégalité, **not as/so... as** :

he's not as/so successful as his brother
il n'a pas autant de succès que son frère

Remarquez que **so** ne peut être utilisé qu'à la forme négative.

f) "plus/moins…, plus/moins…"

Pour traduire la tournure française "plus/moins…, plus/moins…" l'anglais utilise le comparatif précédé de **the** :

the hotter it gets, the less I want to work
plus il fait chaud, moins j'ai envie de travailler

the less I see of him the better!
moins je le vois, mieux je me porte !

Remarquez les expressions proverbiales :

the more the merrier   **the sooner the better**
plus on est de fous, plus on rit   *le plus tôt sera le mieux*

2 L'emploi

a) Dans les comparaisons, **than** se traduit par "que" :

it's hotter here than in Spain
il fait plus chaud ici qu'en Espagne

b) Le comparatif est employé quand deux personnes ou deux choses sont comparées :

of the two, she is the cleverer
des deux, elle est la plus intelligente

Dans l'anglais parlé d'aujourd'hui, certains emploient aussi le superlatif :

of the two, she is the cleverest
des deux, elle est la plus intelligente

sauf, bien sûr, quand **than** suit (**she is cleverer than her brother** *elle est plus intelligente que son frère*).

c) Quand plus de deux personnes ou choses sont comparées, on emploie le superlatif :

she is the cleverest in the class
c'est la plus intelligente de la classe

d) Dans certains cas, le comparatif est employé non pas pour marquer le degré, mais le contraste. Cela s'applique surtout pour les adjectifs qui n'ont pas de forme de base :

former/latter   **inner/outer**
premier/dernier   *intérieur/extérieur*

upper/lower   **lesser/greater**
supérieur/inférieur   *petit/grand*

Ces adjectifs, dans ce sens, sont toujours épithètes.

e) Le superlatif absolu :

Il permet de renforcer un adjectif, et non de comparer des choses ou des personnes. On emploie normalement **most** au lieu de **-est**, même avec des adjectifs monosyllabiques (cet emploi de **most** fait partie d'un registre soutenu ou littéraire) :

this is most kind!
c'est très gentil !

I thought his lecture was most interesting
j'ai trouvé que sa conférence était des plus intéressantes

Mais on peut également employer un superlatif en **-est** comme épithète :

she was rather plain but had the sweetest smile
elle n'était pas très jolie, mais elle avait un sourire magnifique

please accept my warmest congratulations!
veuillez accepter mes plus chaleureuses félicitations !

3 Cas particuliers

a) Further/the furthest et farther/the farthest

Further est d'un usage plus courant que **farther** quand on fait référence à la distance (et lorsqu'il est employé comme adverbe) :

this is the furthest (farthest) point
c'est le point le plus éloigné

(En tant qu'adverbe : **I can't go any further (farther)** *je ne peux pas aller plus loin*)

Si on fait référence au temps ou à un nombre, on ne peut employer que **further** :

any further misdemeanours and you're out
une autre incartade et tu sors

this must be delayed until a further meeting
ceci doit être reporté à un prochain meeting

anything further can be discussed tomorrow
pour le reste, on verra demain

et comme adverbe :

don't try my patience any further
n'abuse pas de ma patience

the police want to question him further
la police veut encore l'interroger

b) Later/latest et latter/last

Later et **latest** font référence au temps, **latter** et **last** à un ordre, à une série :

(a) his latest book is on war poetry
  son dernier livre en date est sur la poésie en temps de guerre

(b) his last book was on war poetry
  son dernier livre était sur la poésie en temps de guerre

Latest en (a) a le sens de "le plus récent", alors que **last** en (b) fait référence au dernier d'une série de livres.

Pour **latter**, voir **Les nombres**, p. A77. Notez, de plus, que **latter** sous-entend une division en deux, comme dans **the latter part of the century** (*la deuxième moitié du siècle*).

c) Less/lesser

Less est quantitatif, **the lesser** est qualitatif :

use less butter   **the lesser of two evils**
prenez moins de beurre   *le moindre mal*

it'll take less time if you go by train
vous mettrez moins de temps en train

there's a lesser degree of irony in this novel
il y a moins d'ironie dans ce roman

d) Older/oldest et elder/eldest

Elder et **eldest** ne font en général référence qu'aux liens familiaux :

this is my elder/eldest brother
c'est mon frère aîné

bien que **older** puisse aussi s'utiliser dans ce contexte. Si **than** (*que*) suit, seul **older** est possible :

my brother is older than I am
mon frère est plus vieux que moi

Remarquez l'emploi de **elder** comme nom :

listen to your elders
écoute tes aînés

the elders of the tribe
les anciens de la tribu

she is my elder by two years
elle est mon aînée de deux ans

7 LES PRONOMS PERSONNELS

	SINGULIER	PLURIEL
1ère	**I/me**	**we/us**
2ème	**you**	**you**
3ème	**he/him, she/her, it**	**they/them**

Voir p. A78 pour l'ordre des pronoms personnels dans une phrase.

Dans le tableau ci-dessus, la première forme de chaque paire est la forme du sujet, la seconde étant celle des autres emplois :

she's not here yet *(sujet)*
elle n'est pas encore là

Jane didn't see her *(complément d'objet direct)*
Jane ne l'a pas vue

Jane wrote her a letter *(complément d'objet indirect)*
Jane lui a écrit une lettre

it's her!   with/for her
c'est elle !   *avec/pour elle*

You correspond, en français, à toutes les formes de la deuxième personne du singulier et du pluriel (*tu, toi, te, vous*)

a) *Pronoms sujets ou pronoms compléments ?*

   i) Les pronoms **I, you, he, she, it, we, they** s'utilisent comme sujets :

       my wife and I are always there
       ma femme et moi, nous sommes toujours là

       Mais on entend parfois à l'oral des phrases incorrectes où le pronom complément est employé à la place du pronom sujet :

       me and my wife are always there *(Fam)*

       Mais, de manière générale, on utilise souvent en anglais le pronom complément (me, you, him, her, it, us, them) là où en français on utilise les pronoms "moi", "toi", etc. :

       who is it? – it's me   who did it? – me (ou I did)
       qui est-ce ? – c'est moi   *qui a fait cela ? – moi*

       Cependant, si une proposition relative suit, il est assez courant d'utiliser la forme sujet, à condition que le pronom relatif fasse fonction de sujet. Ainsi, on dira :

       it was I who did it   ou :   it was me that did it *(Fam)*
                                     c'est moi qui l'ai fait

       mais toujours :   it was me (that) you spoke to
                              c'est à moi que vous avez parlé

       Comme en français, le pronom complément s'utilise après une préposition :

       we have a long day in front of us
       nous avons une longue journée devant nous

       have you got any cash on you?
       avez-vous du liquide sur vous ?

he has his whole life before him
il a toute la vie devant lui

   ii) On place généralement le pronom complément après than et as (si aucun verbe ne suit) :

       she's not as good as him, but she's better than me
       elle n'est pas aussi bonne que lui, mais elle est meilleure que moi

       mais si un verbe suit, c'est le pronom sujet qui doit être employé :

       she's not as good as he is, but she's better than I am
       elle n'est pas aussi bonne que lui, mais elle est meilleure que moi

       Cependant, dans un style plus soutenu, le pronom sujet peut être placé en position finale après than et as, et surtout après than :

       he is a better player than I
       il joue mieux que moi

b) *Omission du pronom sujet*

   On omet bien sûr les pronoms sujets à l'impératif :

   don't say a word!
   ne dis rien !

   Mais on peut les utiliser pour renforcer le sens de l'impératif (par exemple, pour proférer une menace) :

   don't you say a word!
   je t'interdis de dire quoi que ce soit !

c) *He, she ou it ?*

   Le pronom it s'emploie pour désigner des choses et des animaux alors que les pronoms he (him, his) ou she (her) s'emploient pour des personnes. Cependant, he (him, his) ou she (her) peuvent s'utiliser à la place de it dans des cas bien particuliers :

   i) Les animaux :

       On emploie it lorsque l'on parle d'un animal en général (c'est-à-dire de l'espèce), et he/she quand on connaît bien l'animal dont il est question :

       have you seen the cat? — I think she's gone out
       est-ce que tu as vu la chatte ? – je crois qu'elle est sortie

       the dog is hungry, would you mind feeding him?
       le chien a faim, est-ce que tu veux bien lui donner à manger ?

   ii) Les moyens de transport :

       Le pronom qui s'utilise habituellement pour désigner un moyen de transport est it :

       where's the car? – it's in the driveway
       où est la voiture ? – elle est dans l'allée

       this ship is larger than that one, and it has two funnels
       ce bateau est plus grand que celui-là, et il a deux cheminées

       Cependant, on peut trouver parfois le pronom féminin pour une voiture. Par cet emploi, le locuteur montre qu'il est attaché à sa voiture :

       she's been a long way, this old car
       elle en a fait du chemin, cette vieille voiture

       Il arrive aussi que le féminin soit employé pour un bateau, dans un style très soutenu ou littéraire :

       I saw the QE2 when she first sailed
       j'ai vu le Queen Elizabeth II lors de sa première sortie en mer

iii) Les pays :

On emploie pratiquement toujours **it** pour les pays, mais on peut trouver aussi le pronom féminin (emploi rare et littéraire) :

Denmark will remember those who died for her
le Danemark se souviendra de ceux qui sont morts pour lui

d) **It** *sans référence*

i) Comme en français, on peut utiliser en anglais le pronom impersonnel **it** pour parler du temps, donner des jugements, décrire des situations, etc. :

it's raining	**it's freezing in here**
il pleut	*on se gèle ici*
it's wrong to steal	**what's it like outside today?**
il ne faut pas voler	*il fait quel temps dehors aujourd'hui ?*
it's very cosy here	**it's clear that they don't like it**
c'est très confortable ici	*il est clair que ça ne leur plaît pas*

it's not easy to raise that sort of money
ce n'est pas facile de trouver une telle somme d'argent

it looks as if they've left
on dirait qu'ils sont partis

Et aussi pour faire référence à un point précis dans l'espace ou dans le temps :

it's ten o'clock	**it's 10th June**
il est dix heures	*c'est le 10 juin*
it's time to go	**it's at least three miles**
il est temps de partir	*ça fait au moins cinq kilomètres*

Mais si on évoque la durée, on emploie **there** :

there's still time to put things right
il reste du temps pour arranger les choses

Remarquez aussi la phrase **it says** (*on dit, il est dit*) pour faire référence à un texte :

it says in today's newspaper that they're getting divorced
on dit dans le journal d'aujourd'hui qu'ils vont divorcer

ii) **It** peut aussi être utilisé de façon impersonnelle, surtout dans des expressions toutes faites :

that's it! (= that's right)	**beat it!** (*Fam*)
c'est ça !	*va-t'en !*
she thinks she's it (*Fam*)	**she has it in for him** (*Fam*)
elle s'y croit	*elle a une dent contre lui*

e) *Emploi collectif*

You, **we** et **they** sont souvent employés de façon collective pour désigner les gens en général. Le pronom **they** exclut normalement le locuteur :

you don't see many phone boxes any more
on ne voit plus beaucoup de cabines téléphoniques

I'm afraid we simply don't treat animals very well
j'ai bien peur qu'on ne traite pas très bien les animaux

they say he won the lottery
il paraît qu'il a gagné au loto

i) **You** est employé pour faire une remarque sur une situation :

you never can find one when you need one
on n'en trouve jamais quand on en a besoin

you never can be too careful
on n'est jamais trop prudent

ii) **You** est également employé pour donner des instructions :

you first crack the eggs into a bowl
cassez d'abord les œufs dans un saladier

you must look both ways before crossing
il faut regarder des deux côtés avant de traverser

Pour l'emploi de **one**, voir h) ci-dessous.

f) *Un emploi particulier de* **we**

We s'utilise parfois à la place de la deuxième personne du singulier et du pluriel (= *tu, vous*) et équivaut au "nous" de condescendance ou ironique :

have we all done our homework, class?
alors, on a tous fait ses devoirs ?

how are we feeling today, then?
eh bien, comment allons-nous aujourd'hui ?

g) *Emploi de* **they**

i) L'emploi de **they** collectif est devenu très courant, pour renvoyer à **somebody, someone, anybody, anyone, everybody, everyone, nobody, no one**. Le **they** collectif évite le **he or she** maladroit (parfois écrit **s/he**).

Certains considèrent malheureux l'emploi de **he** seul comme pronom collectif signifiant "les gens". Le **they** (**their, them(selves)**) collectif est maintenant courant dans l'anglais parlé et parfois écrit (même si on ne fait référence qu'à un sexe) et offre un moyen pratique d'éviter de s'exprimer d'une façon qui pourrait être jugée sexiste :

if anybody has anything against it, they should say so
si certains sont contre, qu'ils le disent

everybody grabbed their possessions and ran
tout le monde a ramassé ses affaires et s'est enfui

somebody has left their bike right outside the door
quelqu'un a laissé son vélo juste devant la porte

Cet emploi est de plus en plus courant avec des noms précédés **any**, **some** ou **no**.

some person or other has tampered with my files – they'll be sorry
quelqu'un a touché à mes dossiers sans permission – il va le regretter

no child is allowed to leave until they have been seen by a doctor
aucun enfant ne pourra sortir avant d'avoir été examiné par un médecin

Pour l'emploi de **one**, voir h) ci-dessous.

ii) **They** est employé pour faire référence à une (ou plusieurs) personne(s) que l'on ne connaît pas, mais qui représente(nt) l'autorité, le pouvoir, le savoir :

they're going to have to close the factory
ils vont devoir fermer l'usine

they should be able to repair it
ils devraient pouvoir le réparer

they will be able to tell you at the advice centre
on pourra vous renseigner au bureau d'information

when you earn a bit of money they always find a way of taking it off you
quand on gagne un peu d'argent, ils trouvent toujours un moyen pour vous en prélever

h) *Le pronom personnel indéfini* **one**

One peut s'employer comme sujet et comme complément d'objet. La forme possessive est **one's** et la forme réfléchie, **oneself**. L'emploi de **one** est soutenu ; ce pronom ne s'utilise que très rarement aujourd'hui.

i) Si **one** est pris dans un sens collectif, le locuteur s'inclut dans "les gens en général" :

well, what can one do?
eh bien, qu'est-ce qu'on peut faire ?

one is not supposed to do that
on n'est pas censé faire ça

Il est à noter qu'en anglais américain, le pronom masculin de la troisième personne peut suivre **one** :

one shouldn't take risks if he can avoid it
on ne devrait pas prendre de risques si on peut l'éviter

One offre un moyen pratique d'éviter les erreurs d'interprétation de **you**. En effet, l'emploi collectif **you** est parfois source d'ambiguïté. Dans la phrase suivante par exemple, on ne sait pas si **you** est utilisé de manière générale ou s'il renvoie à l'interlocuteur :

you need to be ruthless if you want to get anywhere in this world
tu dois être impitoyable si tu veux réussir dans la vie

Pour être plus précis, un locuteur désirant énoncer une généralité, et non pas faire référence à un individu en particulier, préférera utiliser la phrase suivante :

one needs to be ruthless if one wants to get anywhere in this world
il faut être impitoyable si l'on veut réussir dans la vie

ii) L'emploi de **one** pour la première personne, c'est-à-dire à la place de I (*je*) ou we (*nous*), est maintenant considéré comme un style précieux :

seeing such misery has taught one to appreciate how lucky one is in one's own country
le spectacle de tant de misère nous a appris à apprécier la chance que nous avons dans notre pays

i) It *ou* so ?

Pour l'emploi de **so** comme pronom, voir p. A38.

Le pronom personnel **it** ne s'utilise pas de la même manière que **so**. Comparez :

(a) I can't believe he said it
je n'arrive pas à croire qu'il l'ait dit

(b) you'll do it because I said so
tu vas le faire parce que je l'ai dit

En (a), le pronom **it** est un complément d'objet ; il renvoie à quelque chose de très précis. En (b), **so** est plus vague ; il renvoie au **fait** que le locuteur l'ait dit.

8 LES PRONOMS RÉFLÉCHIS

	SINGULIER	PLURIEL
1ère	**myself** *(moi-même)*	**ourselves**
2ème	**yourself**	**yourselves**
3ème	**himself, herself, itself, oneself**	**themselves**

a) *Employés comme attributs, compléments d'objet direct, compléments d'objet indirect et après des prépositions pour renvoyer au sujet*

I am not myself today (*attribut*)
je ne me sens pas bien aujourd'hui

she has burnt herself (*complément d'objet direct*)
elle s'est brûlée

we gave ourselves a treat (*complément d'objet indirect*)
on s'est fait plaisir

why are you talking to yourself? (*après une préposition*)
pourquoi est-ce que tu parles tout seul ?

b) *Emploi d'intensité*

Lorsque le locuteur souhaite donner une certaine intensité à ce dont il parle, il emploie souvent un pronom réfléchi :

you're quite well-off now, aren't you? – you haven't done so badly yourself
tu es plutôt riche maintenant, n'est-ce pas ? – tu ne t'es pas si mal débrouillé non plus

only they themselves know whether it is the right thing to do
eux seuls savent si c'est la bonne chose à faire

get me a beer, will you? – get it yourself
tu vas me chercher une bière, s'il te plaît ? – va te la chercher toi-même

La position du pronom réfléchi peut modifier le sens de la phrase :

the Queen wanted to speak to him herself
la Reine a voulu lui parler elle-même

mais :

the Queen herself wanted to speak to him
la Reine elle-même a voulu lui parler (c'est-à-dire la Reine en personne)

c) *Après* as, like, than *et* and

Après ces mots, il n'est pas rare de voir les pronoms réfléchis utilisés à la place des pronoms personnels car on hésite parfois entre la forme sujet et la forme complément (voir **Les pronoms personnels** p. A27). Mais cet emploi est familier et grammaticalement incorrect :

he's not quite as old as myself
il n'est pas aussi âgé que moi

like yourself, I also have a few family problems
comme vous, j'ai aussi quelques problèmes familiaux

d) *Verbes réfléchis*

i) Quelques rares verbes ne sont que réfléchis, par exemple :

absent oneself *s'absenter*   **ingratiate oneself** *se faire*
avail oneself of *utiliser*   *bien voir*
demean oneself *s'abaisser*   **perjure oneself** *se parjurer*
                                    pride oneself *se fier*

ii) D'autres ont des significations totalement différentes lorsqu'ils sont réfléchis et lorsqu'ils ne le sont pas :

he applied for the post
il a posé sa candidature pour le poste

he should apply himself more to his studies
il devrait se consacrer davantage à ses études

the jury acquitted him at the trial
le jury l'a acquitté au procès

he acquitted himself well in the recent championships
il s'en est bien sorti lors des récents championnats

iii) Et il existe plusieurs verbes dont le sens demeure le même, que le verbe soit réfléchi ou non :

they always behave (themselves) in public
ils se conduisent toujours bien en public

we found it very difficult to adjust (ourselves) to the humid climate
nous avons trouvé très difficile de nous adapter au climat humide

Notez que l'élément réfléchi peut ajouter la notion de détermination. Comparez :

(a) he proved to be useful
il a fini par être utile

(b) he'll have to prove himself more useful if he wants to keep his job
il va falloir qu'il se montre plus utile s'il veut garder son travail

(c) the crowd pushed forward
la foule avançait

(d) the crowd pushed itself forward
la foule s'avançait

Dans l'exemple (d), il y a plus de détermination que dans l'exemple (c).

9 LES POSSESSIFS

a) *Forme et emploi des possessifs*

LES ADJECTIFS POSSESSIFS

	SINGULIER	PLURIEL
1ère	my *(mon, ma, mes)*	our *(notre, nos)*
2ème	your *(ton, ta, tes ; votre, vos)*	your *(votre, vos)*
3ème	his *(son, sa, ses)*	their *(leur, leurs)*
	her *(son, sa, ses)*	
	its *(son, sa, ses)*	

LES PRONOMS POSSESSIFS

	SINGULIER	PLURIEL
1ère	mine *(le mien,* etc.)	ours
2ème	yours	yours
3ème	his, hers, its	theirs

! Il existe trois formes à la troisième personne du singulier ; on les utilise selon que le possesseur est de sexe masculin ou féminin ou qu'il est neutre. Il est important de se souvenir qu'il n'y a pas de genres grammaticaux en anglais et que le choix entre his/her dépend uniquement du sexe du possesseur. Pour les objets et les animaux, on emploie its (voir ci-dessous) :

who is that man?
qui est cet homme ?

what is his name?
quel est son nom ?

who is that woman?
qui est cette femme ?

what is her name?
quel est son nom ?

what street is this?
quelle est cette rue ?

what is its name?
quel est son nom ?

Dans les cas particuliers où he/she désignent des animaux ou des objets (voir **Les pronoms personnels** p. A27), on emploie les possessifs correspondants :

our dog's hurt his/its paw
notre chien s'est fait mal à la patte

the lion is hunting its prey
le lion chasse sa proie

Les pronoms possessifs anglais ne permettent pas de distinguer le nombre du nom auquel ils renvoient (la forme du pronom est la même, que l'antécédent soit singulier ou pluriel). Cette infor-

mation nous est donnée par les pronoms personnels, les verbes qui suivent ou le contexte. Par ailleurs, si l'on veut traduire la phrase anglaise, il est nécessaire de connaître l'antécédent pour savoir le genre que l'on doit utiliser en français :

mine is this one
le mien/la mienne, c'est celui-ci/celle-ci

mine are these ones
les miens/les miennes, ce sont ceux-là/celles-là

ours is much younger (= our daughter)
la nôtre est beaucoup plus jeune

ours are much younger (= our children)
les nôtres sont beaucoup plus jeunes

they've bought their tickets *(adj)*/they've bought theirs *(pron)*
ils ont acheté leur(s) billet(s)/ils ont acheté le(s) leur(s)

Dans ce dernier exemple, la phrase anglaise ne permet pas de savoir s'ils ont acheté un billet chacun ou plusieurs. Seul le contexte peut nous renseigner. Cet emploi du pluriel distributif après l'adjectif possessif anglais est expliqué pp. A14-15.

Remarquez le "double génitif" (voir p. A16) avec les pronoms possessifs :

he's an old friend of mine
c'est un vieil ami à moi ou un de mes vieux amis

that mother of hers is driving me mad
sa mère me rend fou

b) *Adjectif possessif ou article ?*

L'adjectif possessif anglais correspond très souvent en français à l'article défini, notamment lorsque l'on parle d'une partie du corps ou d'un vêtement :

he put his hands behind his back
il a mis les mains derrière le dos

my head is spinning
j'ai la tête qui tourne

she's broken her leg
elle s'est cassé la jambe

what have you got in your pockets?
qu'est-ce que tu as dans les poches ?

En général, on emploie l'article défini après une préposition (bien que l'adjectif possessif soit aussi possible) :

he grabbed her by the hair
il l'a attrapée par les cheveux

he was punched on the nose
il a reçu un coup de poing dans le nez

Mais si le mot est qualifié par un adjectif, on emploiera l'adjectif possessif à la place de l'article :

he grabbed her by her long hair
il l'a attrapée par ses longs cheveux

Voir aussi "le pluriel distributif" pp. A14-15.

10 LES DÉMONSTRATIFS

SINGULIER	PLURIEL
this, that	these, those

Les formes sont les mêmes pour l'adjectif démonstratif (*ce, cette, ces,* etc.) et le pronom démonstratif (*celui-ci, celle-ci, celle-là,* etc.).

a) This et these renvoient à quelque chose qui se trouve près du locuteur, ou qui a un rapport immédiat avec le locuteur, alors que that et those ont un rapport plus distant avec lui :

(a) this pen is mine; that one is yours
ce crayon-ci est à moi ; celui-là est à toi

(b) that pen is mine; this one is yours
ce crayon-là est à moi ; celui-ci est à toi

En (a), le crayon mentionné en premier se trouve plus près du locuteur que l'autre crayon ; en (b), c'est le contraire.

De même au téléphone :

hi, this is Christine, is that Joanna?
bonjour, c'est Christine, c'est Joanna à l'appareil ?

La distinction entre this/these et that/those se fait aussi en fonction de la distance dans le temps :

honestly, teenagers these days!
vraiment, les adolescents d'aujourd'hui !

in those days it wasn't possible
à cette époque-là, ce n'était pas possible

Remarquez que la même phrase peut prendre un sens différent selon le démonstratif employé :

(a) this is what I want you to do
voici ce que je veux que tu fasses

(b) that's what I want you to do
c'est ça que je veux que tu fasses

En (a), le locuteur est sur le point de dire à l'interlocuteur ce dont il s'agit, tandis qu'en (b) l'explication vient juste d'être mentionnée.

Quand ils sont pronoms, les démonstratifs ne renvoient jamais à des personnes, sauf dans les phrases où ils sont sujets (this is Carla *c'est Carla*) et dans les questions (who is this? *qui est-ce ?*).

b) **This/these** *indéfinis*

L'emploi de this/these comme pronoms indéfinis est très courant en anglais familier, quand on raconte une histoire ou une blague par exemple :

the other day these guys came up to me...
l'autre jour, des types se sont approchés de moi...

this Irishman was sitting in a pub when...
un Irlandais était assis dans un pub quand...

c) **That/this** *adverbes*

That/this sont souvent utilisés comme adverbes, dans un sens proche de so (*si*), avant un adjectif ou un autre adverbe :

I like a red carpet but not one that red
j'aime bien les tapis rouges, mais pas aussi rouges que ça

I don't like doing it that/this often
je n'aime pas le faire si souvent

now that we've come this far, we might as well press on
maintenant qu'on en est là, autant continuer

I don't want that/this much to eat!
je ne veux pas manger autant que ça !

she doesn't want to marry him, she's not that stupid
elle ne veut pas se marier avec lui, elle n'est pas si stupide

11 LES INTERROGATIFS

Les interrogatifs anglais sont :

who/whom/whose, which, what et toutes les formes composées avec le suffixe -ever, par exemple : whichever.

Les interrogatifs peuvent s'employer comme pronoms ou comme adjectifs (sauf who et whom qui ne s'emploient que comme pronoms) :

which do you want? *(pron)*   which flavour do you
lequel veux-tu ?   want? *(adj)*
                                      quel parfum veux-tu ?

Remarquez qu'ils sont invariables. Le premier exemple pourrait tout aussi bien se traduire par "laquelle/lesquels/lesquelles veux-tu ?"

a) **Who** *et* **whom**

Who et whom sont toujours des pronoms (c'est-à-dire qu'ils ne sont jamais suivis par un nom) et ils renvoient à des personnes :

who are you?
qui êtes-vous ?

to whom were your remarks addressed?
à qui s'adressaient vos remarques ?

Whom est utilisé dans un style soutenu, lorsqu'il est complément d'objet (direct ou indirect) ou qu'il suit une préposition :

whom did she embrace?
qui a-t-elle embrassé ?

to whom did he give his permission?
à qui a-t-il donné la permission ?

I demanded to know to whom he had spoken
ou :
I demanded to know whom he had spoken to
j'ai exigé de savoir à qui il avait parlé

En anglais parlé d'aujourd'hui, on utilise en général who (au lieu de whom) pour toutes les fonctions grammaticales. Whom reste obligatoire lorsqu'il est placé directement après une préposition, même si ce genre de tournure ne s'emploie plus tellement à l'oral. Par exemple :

who did you see at the party?
tu as vu qui à la soirée ?

I want to know who you spoke to just now
I want to know to whom you spoke just now *(style soutenu)*
je veux savoir avec qui tu étais en train de parler

b) **Whose**

C'est la forme au génitif de who. Il peut être pronom ou adjectif :

whose are these bags? *(pron)*   whose bags are these?
à qui sont ces sacs ?   *(adj)*
                                  ce sont les sacs de qui ?

c) **Which/what**

Au contraire de who(m), which peut être adjectif ou pronom, et peut renvoyer à une personne ou à un objet :

which actor do you mean? *(adj)* which album do you pre-
de quel acteur parles-tu ?   fer? *(adj)*
                                  quel album tu préfères ?

which of the actors do you mean? *(pron)*
duquel des acteurs parles-tu ?

of these two albums, which do you prefer? *(pron)*
de ces deux albums, lequel tu préfères ?

La différence entre which et who/what est que which est restrictif : il invite celui à qui on parle à faire un choix parmi un certain nombre de choses précises.

Comparez :

what would you like to drink?
qu'est-ce que tu veux boire ?

I've got coffee or tea, which would you like?
j'ai du café ou du thé, qu'est-ce que tu veux ?

Si l'objet du choix n'est pas identifié avant la question, on ne peut employer que what :

what would you like to drink? I've got beer, red wine or mineral water
qu'est-ce que tu veux boire ? j'ai de la bière, du vin rouge ou de l'eau minérale

d) **What**

Lorsqu'il est **pronom**, what ne renvoie jamais à une personne :

what's this book? | **don't ask me what I did**
qu'est-ce que c'est que ce livre ? | *ne me demande pas ce que j'ai fait*

Lorsqu'il est **adjectif**, what peut renvoyer à une personne, à un animal ou à une chose :

what child does not like sweets?
quel enfant n'aime pas les bonbons ?

what kind of soap do you use?
quelle sorte de savon utilisez-vous ?

Pour la différence entre which et what, voir c) ci-dessus.

Remarquez l'emploi de what dans les exclamations :

what awful weather! | **what a dreadful day!**
quel temps affreux ! | *quelle journée épouvantable !*

what must they think!
qu'est-ce qu'ils doivent penser !

e) *Avec -ever*

Le suffixe -ever exprime la surprise, la confusion ou la gêne, l'agacement :

whatever do you mean? *(confusion ou gêne)*
qu'est-ce que tu veux dire ?

whoever would have thought that? *(surprise)*
qui donc aurait pu penser cela ?

whatever did you do that for? *(agacement)*
pourquoi donc as-tu fait ça ?

12 LES RELATIFS

Les relatifs anglais sont :

who/whom/whose, which, what, that et toutes les formes composées avec le suffixe -ever, par exemple : whichever.

Les pronoms relatifs (sauf what) ont en général un antécédent auquel ils se rapportent.

Dans :

she spoke to the man who/that sat beside her
elle a parlé à l'homme qui était assis à côté d'elle

who/that est le pronom relatif et the man, l'antécédent.

a) *Déterminative et explicative*

Une proposition relative peut être déterminative ou explicative.

Si elle est déterminative, elle est nécessaire au sens de la phrase complète par le lien qui l'unit à l'antécédent ; elle restreint le sens de l'antécédent :

that's the man who asked to see you
c'est l'homme qui a demandé à vous voir

Si elle est explicative, elle a un rapport moins étroit avec l'antécédent et son rôle est similaire à celui d'une parenthèse. Par exemple :

Janice, who came to see us yesterday, told us she was expecting a baby
Janice, qui est venue nous voir hier, nous a annoncé qu'elle attendait un enfant

Au contraire des propositions déterminatives, les propositions explicatives doivent être précédées d'une virgule. Cependant, la virgule est souvent oubliée, ce qui entraîne parfois une ambiguïté au niveau du sens de la phrase. Ainsi, la proposition de l'exemple suivant :

he helped the woman who had cried out
il aida la femme qui avait appelé au secours

peut être soit déterminative (= il aida la femme qui avait appelé au secours et non celle qui ne l'avait pas fait), soit explicative (= il aida la femme (qui, par ailleurs, avait appelé au secours)).

! Le pronom relatif that est uniquement employé dans des propositions relatives déterminatives. Who et which peuvent être utilisés dans les deux cas.

b) **Who/whom/that**

Who ou that sont utilisés comme pronoms sujets (*qui*) :

the woman who/that called was his sister
la femme qui a appelé était sa sœur

Who(m) ou that sont utilisés comme compléments (*que*) :

the man who(m)/that she rescued was a tourist
l'homme qu'elle a sauvé était un touriste

Whom est utilisé dans un style plus soutenu (voir **Les interrogatifs**, p. A31)

c) **Who/which/that**

i) **Who/that**

Ces formes renvoient à des personnes ou, dans certains cas, à des animaux (voir **Les pronoms personnels** p. A27) :

we ignored the people who/that were late
nous n'avons pas tenu compte des gens qui étaient en retard

our cat, who is two years old, keeps sharpening his claws on the curtains
notre chat, qui a deux ans, n'arrête pas de faire ses griffes sur les rideaux

Remarquez que seul who, et non that, peut être employé dans le second exemple, qui est une proposition relative explicative, voir b) ci-dessus.

Pour les noms collectifs (voir p. A11), on emploie who ou that si l'on veut leur donner un caractère individuel. Mais si l'on considère le groupe de manière moins personnelle, on emploie which ou that :

the crowd who/that had gathered were in great spirits *(aspect personnalisé)*
la foule qui s'était rassemblée était très enthousiaste

the crowd which/that had gathered was enormous *(aspect collectif)*
la foule qui s'était rassemblée était énorme

ii) Which/that

Which ou that renvoient à des objets, des concepts, etc. :

the car which/that drove into me
la voiture qui m'est rentrée dedans

the disks which/that I sent you
les disquettes que je t'ai envoyées

! Bien que les pronoms personnels puissent être utilisés pour des moyens de transport, comme on l'a vu p. A27, cette personnalisation ne s'applique pas aux pronoms relatifs, c'est-à-dire que who ne pourra jamais renvoyer à des véhicules, etc.

d) Whose

La forme au génitif whose renvoie à des personnes et à des animaux, mais elle est aussi souvent employée, à la place de of which, pour un objet ou une chose :

this is the girl whose mother has just won the lottery
c'est la fille dont la mère vient juste de gagner au loto

that's that new machine whose cover is damaged
c'est la nouvelle machine dont le couvercle est abîmé

the department, whose staff are all over 50, is likely to be closed down
ce service, dont tout le personnel a plus de 50 ans, risque de fermer

the vehicles, the state of which left a good deal to be desired, had been in use throughout the year
les véhicules, dont l'état laissait à désirer, avaient été en service pendant toute l'année

e) Which

i) Which ne renvoie jamais aux personnes, mais toujours aux objets, aux idées, etc. :

I received quite a few books for Christmas, which I still haven't read
j'ai reçu un bon nombre de livres pour Noël, que je n'ai pas encore lus

Mais il peut renvoyer à une caractéristique d'une personne :

she complains that her husband is a bit insensitive, which in fact he is
elle se plaint que son mari est un peu insensible, ce qui d'ailleurs est vrai

ii) On ne trouve which utilisé comme adjectif qu'après une préposition ou lorsque son antécédent est une chose. L'emploi de which comme adjectif est d'un style soutenu et littéraire, surtout quand il n'est pas accompagné d'une préposition :

he returned to Nottingham, in which city he was born and bred
il revint à Nottingham, ville dans laquelle il avait grandi

he rarely spoke in public, which fact only added to his obscurity
il parlait très peu en public, particularité qui contribuait à le laisser dans l'ombre

f) What

i) What est le seul relatif qui ne prend pas d'antécédent. Il peut être pronom ou adjectif. Quand il est pronom, il fait normalement référence à une chose et a souvent le sens de that which (*ce qui/que*), ou au pluriel, de the things which (*les choses qui/que*) :

show me what did the damage
montre-moi ce qui a causé les dégâts

Quand il est adjectif, il peut renvoyer à une personne ou à une chose, et il correspond à the + nom + who/which :

show me what damage was done
montre-moi quels dégâts ont été faits

with what volunteers they could find, they set off for the summit
avec les volontaires qu'ils ont pu trouver, ils sont partis à la conquête du sommet

what money they had left, they spent on drink
l'argent qu'il leur restait, ils le dépensèrent en alcool

ii) What ou which ?

Seul which peut renvoyer à une proposition complète alors que what n'a pas d'antécédent. Mais le pronom what peut annoncer ou introduire une proposition sujet ou complément :

she left the baby unattended, which was a silly thing to do
elle a laissé le bébé tout seul, ce qui était inconscient de sa part

what you need is a hot bath (*proposition sujet*)
ce qu'il vous faut, c'est un bon bain chaud

she has what it takes to succeed (*proposition complément*)
elle a ce qu'il faut pour réussir

g) Avec -ever

Au contraire des pronoms interrogatifs (voir p. A32), -ever n'exprime pas la surprise, la confusion ou l'agacement quand il est associé à un relatif ; il permet seulement de les renforcer dans le sens de no matter who/which/what (*qui/quoi que ce soit*) :

take whichever tool is best (*adj*)
prends l'outil qui convient le mieux

take whichever is best (*pron*)
prends celui qui convient le mieux

I'll do it whatever happens (*pron*)
je le ferai quoi qu'il arrive

do whatever you like (*pron*)
fais ce que tu veux

whatever problems we may have to face, we'll solve them (*adj*)
quels que soient les problèmes que nous ayons à affronter, nous les résoudrons

h) Omission du relatif

Le pronom relatif peut être omis (ce qui est très souvent le cas à l'oral) dans les propositions relatives déterminatives, sauf s'il est sujet ou s'il est précédé d'une préposition :

these are the things (which/that) we have to do
ce sont les choses que nous devons faire

I saw the boy (who/that) you met last night
j'ai vu le garçon que tu as rencontré hier soir

is this the sales assistant (who/that) you spoke to?
est-ce à cette vendeuse que tu as parlé ?

who's the girl (who/that) you came to the party with?
qui est la fille avec qui tu es venu à la soirée ?

Remarquez que la construction assez soutenue :

who are the people with whom you are doing business?
qui sont les gens avec qui vous travaillez ?

peut être évitée si l'on change de place la préposition (with) :

who are the people you are doing business with?

13 LES PRONOMS ET LES ADJECTIFS INDÉFINIS

a) Some *et* any

i) Some et any s'emploient avec des indénombrables et des noms pluriels. Avec les noms dénombrables singuliers, on emploiera l'article indéfini a (**do you have** a **car?** *est-ce que tu as une voiture ?*). Some et any peuvent être pronoms ou adjectifs :

I have some **money** *(adj)*　　**I have** some *(pron)*
j'ai de l'argent　　　　　　　　*j'en ai*

do you have any **friends?**　　**do you have** any? *(pron)*
(adj)　　　　　　　　　　　　*en avez-vous ?*
est-ce que vous avez des amis ?

Les formes composées avec les suffixes -body, -one, -thing sont toujours des pronoms :

did you speak to anybody?　**tell me** something
as-tu parlé à quelqu'un ?　　*dis-moi quelque chose*

ii) Some/any comme adjectifs :

De manière générale, some s'emploie dans les phrases affirmatives et any dans les propositions négatives, interrogatives et conditionnelles :

I have some **money**　　　**I haven't got** any **money**
j'ai de l'argent　　　　　　*je n'ai pas d'argent*

have you got any **money?**
est-ce que tu as de l'argent ?

if you've got any **money, could you lend it to me?**
si tu as de l'argent, tu peux m'en prêter ?

Any s'utilise aussi dans les phrases affirmatives qui ont un sens négatif (c'est-à-dire avec des adverbes, des prépositions ou des verbes négatifs) :

I've got hardly any money
je n'ai presque pas d'argent

you never asked me for any **help**
tu ne m'as jamais demandé de t'aider

I can do it without any difficulty
je peux le faire sans aucune difficulté

the noise outside prevented me from doing any **work**
le bruit qu'il y avait dehors m'a empêché de travailler

ou lorsqu'il a le sens de "n'importe quel" :

you can choose any **number**
tu peux choisir n'importe quel nombre

La différence entre some et any est souvent subtile. Some est aussi très fréquent dans les propositions interrogatives et conditionnelles ; le locuteur sous-entend alors quelque chose de légèrement différent.

Comparez :

(a) **shall I buy** some **wine for dinner?**
dois-je acheter du vin pour le dîner ?

(b) **will you give** some **money to the kids?**
tu veux bien donner un peu d'argent aux enfants ?

(c) **if there's** some **chocolate left, can I have it?**
s'il reste du chocolat, est-ce que je peux le manger ?

(d) **have we got** any **wine in the house?**
est-ce qu'on a du vin à la maison ?

(e) **did you take** any **money from my purse?**
est-ce que tu as pris de l'argent dans mon porte-monnaie ?

(f) **if there was** any **chocolate left, he would have eaten it**
s'il restait du chocolat, il l'aurait mangé

En (a)-(c), some veut dire "un peu de" ou "quelques", alors qu'en (d)-(f), any signifie "du tout". On a tendance à employer some dans les phrases interrogatives ou conditionnelles lorsqu'on attend une réponse positive de la part de l'interlocuteur, ou lorsqu'on veut l'encourager à dire "oui".

iii) Some/any comme pronoms et leurs composés :

Comparez :

(a) **has she written** any? (any = **books, chapters,** etc.)
est-ce qu'elle en a déjà écrit ?

(b) **has she written** anything?
est-ce qu'elle a déjà écrit quelque chose ?

En (a), le nom auquel any fait référence est sous-entendu et a été évoqué un peu plus tôt, tandis qu'en (b) anything est plus vague ; il ne renvoie à rien de spécifique.

Les pronoms some et any peuvent renvoyer à des noms indénombrables :

I've run out of coffee, have you got any?
je n'ai plus de café, tu en as ?

Remarquez que some est pronom quand il a le sens de "certains" :

some **say it wasn't an accident**
certains disent que ce n'était pas un accident

iv) Some(thing)/any(thing) + of + nom :

Some et any suivis d'une locution commençant par of ont un sens quantitatif, alors que something et anything suivis d'une locution commençant par of sont qualitatifs. Comparez :

(a) **give me** some **of that cheese**
donne-moi un peu de ce fromage

(b) **he hasn't got** any **of her qualities**
il n'a aucune de ses qualités

(c) **there is** something **of the artist in her**
il y a quelque chose d'artistique chez elle

(d) **he hasn't got** anything **of her qualities**
il n'a en rien ses qualités

En (a) et (b), some et any signifient "une part de", "un peu de", alors qu'en (c) et (d) ils ont le sens de "quelque chose dans la manière de" ou "quelque chose qui relève de".

Remarquez que la construction any of + nom ou pronom au pluriel peut être suivie d'un verbe au singulier ou au pluriel, si une ou plusieurs personnes sont sous-entendues :

if any **of your friends wants the ticket, phone me**
si un de tes amis veut le billet, appelle-moi

if any **of your friends want to come, they're welcome**
si certains de tes amis veulent venir, ils sont les bienvenus

v) Some = "un(e) certain(e)" :

On a vu plus haut (en ii) ci-dessus) que some est utilisé dans un contexte positif avec des noms au pluriel (**would you like some biscuits?**) ou des noms indénombrables (**he stayed here for** some **time**). Lorsqu'il est placé devant un nom dénombrable au singulier, il fait référence à quelqu'un ou quelque chose que l'on ne connaît pas et veut souvent dire "un certain" :

some person (or other) must have taken it
quelqu'un l'aura pris

some fool left the door open
un imbécile a laissé la porte ouverte

he's gone to some **town in the north**
il est parti dans une ville quelque part dans le nord

come and see me some **day**
il faudra que tu viennes me voir un jour

Comparez avec l'emploi de any + nom dénombrable singulier (= n'importe quel) :

come and see me any **day**
viens me voir n'importe quel jour

vi) Some = "un mauvais" ou "un bon" :

En anglais familier, on utilise souvent some pour exprimer soit son mépris, son irritation, soit son admiration :

some husband you are, forgetting my birthday like that!
quel mauvais mari tu fais, oublier mon anniversaire, quand même !

this really is some **party!**
c'est vraiment une soirée excellente !

Pour l'emploi de some/any, something/anything comme adverbes, voir p. A24.

b) **Many et much**

Many et much s'emploient surtout dans les phrases interrogatives ou négatives. Dans les phrases affirmatives, ils permettent de créer un style un peu plus soutenu que a lot of ou lots of.

On emploie many avec des noms pluriels dénombrables et much avec des indénombrables :

ii) **Many/much comme adjectifs :**

how many students came?
combien d'étudiants sont venus ?

she got cards from all her many admirers
elle a reçu des cartes de ses nombreux admirateurs

there isn't much money left
il ne reste pas beaucoup d'argent

we don't have much time
on n'a pas beaucoup de temps

iii) **Many/much comme pronoms :**

many of the audience were children
il y avait beaucoup d'enfants dans l'assistance

we can only fit in so many
nous n'avons de place que pour un certain nombre de personnes

we spent much of the time arguing
on a passé la plupart du temps à se disputer

he didn't have much to say on the subject
il n'avait pas grand-chose à dire à ce sujet

Pour l'emploi de much comme adverbe, voir pp. A22-3.

c) **No et none**

No et none ont le même sens que not any, mais ils permettent parfois d'insister davantage ou de formuler une phrase de manière plus soutenue :

he doesn't have any **money** *il n'a pas d'argent*	**he has** no **money** *il n'a pas d'argent*
he doesn't have any **left** *il n'en a plus*	**he has** none **left** *il n'en a plus*

i) No est un adjectif :

he has no **house,** no **money,** no **friends**
il n'a pas de maison, pas d'argent, pas d'amis

ii) None est un pronom :

do you have any cigarettes? – no, I've none **left**
est-ce que vous avez des cigarettes ? – non, je n'en ai plus

I tried on a lot of jumpers but none **(of them) fitted**
j'ai essayé beaucoup de pulls, mais aucun ne m'allait

Remarquez qu'une phrase comme **I have none** (je n'en ai pas) est plus soutenue que celle employée couramment, **I don't have any.**

Quand on fait référence à des gens, none of them/us/you (aucun d'eux/de nous/de vous) est plus courant que none (aucun, personne) à l'oral :

none of us knew where he had filed it
aucun de nous ne savait où il l'avait classé

I waited for them for hours, but none of them **came**
je les ai attendus pendant des heures, mais aucun d'eux n'est venu

many have set out to climb this mountain but none **have ever returned**
nombreux sont ceux qui sont partis à la conquête de cette montagne, mais aucun n'en est jamais revenu

Quand on veut donner à une phrase un ton emphatique, on peut employer la construction not one :

not one (of them) was able to tell me the answer!
pas un seul (d'entre eux) n'a été capable de me répondre !

iii) None : singulier ou pluriel ?

Le sens littéral de none étant no one (*pas un*), le verbe qui suit doit toujours être au singulier :

none of them has seen it before
aucun d'eux ne l'a jamais vu

Cependant, on rencontre parfois le pluriel (**none of them have seen it before**), mais il s'agit là d'un usage incorrect.

Pour l'emploi de no et none comme adverbes, voir p. A24.

d) **Every et each**

i) Each (*chaque*) peut être pronom ou adjectif ; every (*tout*) est toujours adjectif. Ils font tous les deux uniquement référence à des noms dénombrables :

each child was given a Christmas present *(adj)*
on a donné un cadeau de Noël à chaque enfant

each of them was given a Christmas present *(pron)*
on a donné un cadeau de Noël à chacun d'eux

each was given a Christmas present *(pron)*
on a donné un cadeau de Noël à chacun

every child was given a Christmas present *(adj)*
on a donné un cadeau de Noël à tous les enfants

Every renvoie à la totalité des enfants (il n'y a pas d'exception) alors que each permet de les individualiser. Dans les exemples avec **each**, on insiste davantage sur le fait qu'ils ont reçu un cadeau "les uns après les autres". **Every** est plus général ; il désigne "tous les enfants".

Remarquez que **every** peut être précédé d'un génitif ou d'un adjectif possessif :

Wendy's every move was commented on
on commenta chacun des faits et gestes de Wendy

her every move was commented on
on commenta chacun de ses faits et gestes

et notez son emploi avec les nombres et avant **other** :

she goes to the dentist every three months
elle va chez le dentiste tous les trois mois

I call my parents every two days
j'appelle mes parents tous les deux jours

every other day something goes wrong
un jour sur deux, il y a quelque chose qui ne va pas

Dans la plupart des cas, **every two** et **every other** sont interchangeables. Mais **every two** insiste davantage sur la régularité des faits (expression prise au sens littéral), tandis que **every other** peut avoir soit le sens de "tous les deux (jours, etc.)", soit un sens plus vague, comme dans le dernier exemple ci-dessus dans lequel **every other day** signifie "souvent" et ne doit pas être pris au sens littéral de "un jour sur deux".

Remarquez aussi son emploi adverbial :

every now and then
every now and again
every so often
de temps en temps

ii) **Everybody/everyone** et **everything** sont des pronoms et sont toujours suivis d'un verbe au singulier mais, comme les autres pronoms indéfinis, **everybody** peut être suivi de **they**, **them(selves)** ou **their** (voir **Les pronoms personnels**, p. A28).

e) **All**

i) **All** peut être adjectif ou pronom ; il renvoie à des noms dénombrables et indénombrables. Remarquez que, lorsqu'un article défini, un pronom personnel ou un adjectif démonstratif ou possessif est utilisé, il se place entre **all** et le nom :

all expenses will be reimbursed
tous les frais seront remboursés

I want all the/those/their biscuits
je veux tous les/ces/leurs biscuits

all his energy was spent
il a dépensé toute son énergie

I want them all/all of them   **I want it all/all of it**
je les veux tous   *je le veux en entier*

ii) **All** et **everything** :

La différence entre ces deux pronoms est souvent assez subtile. Remarquez que **all that**, employé en début de phrase, signifie "la seule chose qui/que". Seul **all** peut renvoyer à des noms indénombrables.

we ate everything that was on the table
nous avons mangé tout ce qui était sur la table

all that was on the table was a single vase
il n'y avait qu'un vase sur la table

did you eat the ice-cream? – not all of it
as-tu mangé la glace ? – pas tout

they believed everything/all he said
ils croyaient tout ce qu'il disait

did he say anything? – all that he said was 'do nothing'
est-ce qu'il a dit quelque chose ? – tout ce qu'il a dit, c'est "ne faites rien"

iii) **All** et **whole** :

La différence principale entre **all** et l'adjectif **whole** réside dans le fait que **whole** insiste davantage sur le nom qu'il qualifie, en apportant souvent une nuance différente au niveau du sens :

he ate all (of) the cake   **he ate the whole cake**
il a mangé tout le gâteau   *il a mangé le gâteau en entier*

don't interrupt me all the time
ne m'interromps pas tout le temps

she said nothing the whole time we were there
elle n'a rien dit tout le temps que nous étions là

All the time exprime la répétition tandis que **the whole time** insiste sur la durée.

Mais **whole** s'emploie uniquement devant les noms dénombrables :

the whole town/all the town *(dénombrable)*
toute la ville

all the butter *(indénombrable)*
tout le beurre

Remarquez que **whole** ne s'emploie pas avec un nom au pluriel. On emploie par exemple :

he read all the books in their entirety
il a lu tous les livres en entier

Pour l'emploi de **all** en tant qu'adverbe, voir p. A23.

f) **Other(s)** *et* **another**

i) **Another**, qui peut être adjectif ou pronom, s'emploie uniquement pour les noms singuliers dénombrables. Seul l'adjectif **other** peut être suivi d'un nom pluriel ; **others** est toujours pronom (d'un antécédent au pluriel) :

I want another hamburger *(adj)***/I want another** *(pron)*
je veux un autre hamburger/j'en veux un autre

other children get more money *(adj)*
les autres enfants ont plus d'argent

I like these colours – don't you like the others? *(pron)*
j'aime ces couleurs – tu n'aimes pas les autres ?

ii) Avec la construction nom + **than**, on peut placer **other** avant ou après le nom :

there are difficulties other than those mentioned by the government
there are other difficulties than those mentioned by the government
il y a d'autres difficultés que celles qui sont mentionnées par le gouvernement

Mais **other** est toujours placé après **none** :

who should arrive? none other than the Prime Minister himself
et qui est arrivé ? le Premier ministre en personne

iii) On utilise parfois **no other** à la place de **not another** :

he has no other coat/he doesn't have another coat *(adj)*
il n'a pas d'autre manteau

for this reason, if for no other/if not for another (pron)
pour cette raison, à défaut d'une autre

iv) Remarquez la construction avec some et ses composés, quand some veut dire "un(e) certain(e)..." (comparez avec a) v) ci-dessus). On ajoute or other pour intensifier le caractère vague de ce dont on parle :

he married some girl or other from the Bahamas
il s'est marié avec une fille des Bahamas

somebody or other must have betrayed her
quelqu'un a dû la trahir

we'll get there somehow or other (*emploi adverbial*)
on y arrivera d'une manière ou d'une autre

v) Avec one :

One... another et one... the other ont en général la même signification :

one day after another went by
one day after the other went by
les jours se sont écoulés petit à petit

Mais si l'on ne fait référence qu'à deux choses ou à deux personnes, on préférera employer one... the other :

the two brothers worked well together: one would sweep the yard while the other chopped the wood
les deux frères travaillaient bien ensemble : l'un balayait la cour pendant que l'autre coupait le bois

Cependant, si le second élément est précédé d'une préposition, comme dans le premier exemple, on peut aussi employer one... another :

they would sit there and repeat, one after another, every single word of the lesson
ils s'asseyaient là et répétaient, l'un après l'autre, chaque mot de la leçon

On trouve aussi parfois la combinaison the one... the other, qui aurait pu être employée dans l'exemple des deux frères ci-dessus.

Dans la locution on the one hand... on the other hand..., l'article est obligatoire devant one :

on the one hand, you'd earn less, on the other hand, your job satisfaction would be greater
d'un côté tu gagnerais moins d'argent, mais de l'autre, tu aurais une plus grande satisfaction professionnelle

g) Either *et* neither

i) Either a souvent le sens de "l'un ou l'autre" en parlant de deux choses ou de deux personnes (on utilisera any s'il y en a plus de deux). Il peut être adjectif ou pronom :

you can take either route (*adj*)
tu peux prendre l'un ou l'autre de ces chemins

either bus will get you there (*adj*)
les deux bus y vont

you can take either (*pron*)
vous pouvez prendre l'un ou l'autre/n'importe lequel (des deux)

Either employé comme adjectif peut aussi vouloir dire "chaque" ou "les deux" :

there were candles at either end of the table
il y avait des bougies aux deux bouts/à chaque bout de la table

Cependant, il est parfois préférable d'éviter cet emploi de either dans le sens de each et both, car il peut être ambigu :

vehicles may be parked on either side of the road
il est possible de se garer des deux côtés de la rue ou il est possible de se garer d'un côté

ii) Neither est la forme négative de either :

neither bag is big enough (*adj*)
aucun des deux sacs n'est assez grand

which do you prefer? — neither! (*pron*)
lequel des deux préfères-tu? — ni l'un ni l'autre !

iii) On emploie toujours un verbe au singulier après either et neither suivis de of + nom pluriel :

neither of the boys is likely to have done it
il est peu probable que l'un des deux garçons l'ait fait

either of the boys is likely to have done it
il est probable que l'un des deux garçons l'ait fait

Pour l'emploi de either et neither comme adverbe, voir p. A24.

h) Both

Both fait référence à deux choses ou à deux personnes et signifie "l'un et l'autre", "les deux". Il est soit adjectif, soit pronom, et comme pour all, il peut être suivi d'un adjectif démonstratif ou possessif, d'un pronom personnel, d'un article défini :

I like both jackets *j'aime ces deux vestes*	I like both those/of those jackets *j'aime l'une et l'autre de ces vestes*
I love both my parents *j'aime mon père et ma mère*	I love both (of them)/them both *je les aime tous les deux*

both (the/of the) versions are correct
les deux versions sont correctes

i) One

i) Ce pronom est employé dans le sens de "une seule chose/personne" en référence à ce qui a été évoqué dans une phrase ou une proposition précédente :

I love dogs but I've never owned one
j'aime bien les chiens mais je n'en ai jamais eu

he's got a lot of cousins, but I've only got one
il a beaucoup de cousins, mais moi, je n'en ai qu'un

his case is a sad one
son cas est triste

this solution is one of considerable ingenuity
c'est une solution remarquablement ingénieuse

Il peut aussi être employé au pluriel (ones) :

she goes to a lot of restaurants, especially Italian ones
elle va dans beaucoup de restaurants différents, notamment dans les restaurants italiens

ii) L'emploi restrictif

The one s'emploie lorsque l'on fait un choix parmi un certain nombre de choses précises et signifie alors "celui que/qui", etc. :

which cat do you prefer? – the white one
quel chat préférez-vous ? – le blanc

I prefer the pen you gave me to the one my mother gave me
je préfère le stylo que vous m'avez donné à celui que ma mère m'a donné

these are the ones I meant
ce sont celles dont je parlais

these burgers are better than the ones you make
ces hamburgers sont meilleurs que ceux que tu fais

iii) Comme le montre le premier exemple du ii) ci-dessus,

one(s) s'emploie en général après des adjectifs qui font référence à des noms dénombrables :

I asked for a large whisky and he gave me a small one
je lui ai demandé un grand whisky, et il m'en a donné un petit

which shoes do you want? the grey ones?
quelles chaussures voulez-vous ? les grises ?

Cependant, si deux adjectifs opposés se suivent, on peut parfois se dispenser d'utiliser one(s) :

I drink a lot of wine, both red and white
je bois beaucoup de vin, aussi bien du rouge que du blanc

she stood by him in good times and bad
elle est restée à ses côtés dans les bons et les mauvais moments

today I wish to talk about two kinds of climate, the temperate and the tropical
je vais vous parler aujourd'hui de deux sortes de climats, le climat tempéré et le climat tropical

Si aucun nom n'a été mentionné de manière précise et que seul un terme général est sous-entendu (men, etc.), l'adjectif fonctionne comme un nom, et one(s) n'a pas besoin d'être employé. On remarque notamment cette absence de one(s) dans les expressions idiomatiques :

the survival of the fittest   **fortune favours** the brave
la persistance du plus apte   *la chance sourit aux braves*

Il est évident que one ne peut pas renvoyer à un nom indénombrable :

do you want white sugar or brown?
voulez-vous du sucre blanc ou du roux ?

iv) One est parfois employé dans un sens proche de "quelqu'un" ou "une personne", comme dans :

I'm not one for big parties
je ne raffole pas des grandes fêtes

I'm not one to complain
je ne suis pas du genre à me plaindre

v) One pris dans un sens collectif, voir pp. A28-9.

j) **So**

So est un pronom quand il renvoie à une affirmation ou à une question ; il permet d'éviter de répéter les termes venant d'être énoncés et remplace donc une proposition relative introduite par that :

did she manage to escape? – I believe so (= I believe that she managed to escaped)
est-elle parvenue à s'échapper ? – je crois bien que oui

has he left? – it seems so (= it seems that he has left)
il est parti ? – on dirait bien

I knew it would happen, I told you so (= I told you that it would happen)
je savais bien que ça arriverait, je te l'avais dit

So ne s'utilise qu'après certains verbes dont les plus courants sont : appear, believe, expect, guess, hope, imagine, seem, reckon, suppose, think.

Remarquez que ces verbes peuvent se construire de deux manières différentes à la forme négative (verbe à la forme négative + so ; verbe à la forme affirmative + not), sauf pour hope et guess qui n'acceptent que la structure avec not. Par ailleurs, cet emploi de not est beaucoup moins courant avec les verbes think, believe et seem :

I believe so   **I don't believe so (= I believe not**, *plus*
je crois (que oui)   *soutenu*)
                                  je ne crois pas

I think so   **I don't think so (= I think not**, *plus*
je pense (que oui)   *soutenu*)
                              je ne pense pas

I hope so   **I hope not**
j'espère bien   *j'espère que non*

14 LES VERBES

A LES DIFFÉRENTS TYPES

On peut distinguer trois types de verbes : les verbes réguliers, les verbes irréguliers et les auxiliaires.

1 Les verbes réguliers

Ces verbes forment leur prétérit et leur participe passé en ajoutant -(e)d au radical du verbe :

		PRÉTÉRIT	PARTICIPE PASSÉ
seem	*sembler*	**seemed**	**seemed** [si:md]
kiss	*embrasser*	**kissed**	**kissed** [kɪst]
plant	*planter*	**planted**	**planted** ['plɑːntɪd]
manage	*diriger*	**managed**	**managed** ['mænɪdʒd]

Pour les modifications orthographiques, voir p. A79.

2 Les verbes irréguliers

Les verbes irréguliers se caractérisent par leurs formes particulières au prétérit et au participe passé, qui font apparaître parfois un changement de voyelle :

parler speak, spoke, spoken *gâter* spoil, spoilt, spoilt
voir   see, saw, seen   *couper* cut, cut, cut
aller   go, went, gone

Vous trouverez la liste des verbes irréguliers pp. A63-5.

3 Les auxiliaires

Un auxiliaire modifie le verbe principal de la phrase. Dans he can sing (*il sait chanter*), l'auxiliaire est can et le verbe principal est sing. On fait la distinction entre les auxiliaires "ordinaires" et les auxiliaires modaux.

a) Les **auxiliaires ordinaires** sont be, have et do.

On les appelle "ordinaires" parce qu'ils fonctionnent aussi comme verbes à part entière, signifiant alors *être* (be), *avoir* (have) et *faire* (do) :

he does not sing (does = auxiliaire, sing = verbe principal)
il ne chante pas

he does the washing up (does = verbe principal)
il fait la vaisselle

Voir aussi les sections 9, 17 et 23 de la partie C de ce chapitre.

b) Les **auxiliaires modaux** sont appelés ainsi car ils remplacent le mode du subjonctif dans de nombreux cas (voir p. A53). En voici la liste :

can - could	pouvoir (capacité)
may - might	pouvoir (possibilité - permission)
shall - should	futur - conditionnel, devoir (moral), conseil etc.
will - would	futur - conditionnel, ordre, etc.
must	devoir (obligation)
ought to	devoir (moral)

Les auxiliaires modaux peuvent s'employer seuls lorsque le verbe ordinaire est sous-entendu :

can you come at 8 p.m.? – yes, I can
est-ce que tu peux venir à 20 heures ? – oui

Pour l'emploi des auxiliaires modaux, voir pp. A57-61.

B LES FORMES

1 L'infinitif

On distingue l'infinitif complet (avec **to**) et l'infinitif sans **to** :

he is trying **to** sing   he can sing
il essaie de chanter   *il sait chanter*

Dans ces deux phrases le mot **sing** est à l'infinitif.

Pour l'infinitif passé et la voix passive, voir sections 7 et 9 ci-dessous.

2 Le participe présent

Il se forme à partir du radical + **-ing** :

they were **whispering**
ils murmuraient

Le participe présent sert notamment à former l'aspect progressif. Pour son emploi, voir pp. A44-5. Pour les modifications orthographiques, voir p. A79.

3 Le participe passé

Le participe passé des verbes réguliers est identique à leur prétérit (radical du verbe + **-ed**) :

they have **watched** it on TV
ils l'ont regardé à la télé

Les verbes irréguliers ont un grand nombre de formes différentes au participe passé. Voir A2 ci-dessus, ainsi que la liste des verbes irréguliers pp. A63-5.

Pour l'emploi du participe passé, voir p. A46.

4 Le gérondif

Le gérondif, comme le participe présent, se forme à partir du radical + **-ing**. Il a une fonction nominale :

I like **picking** strawberries
j'aime cueillir les fraises

sailing is a very popular sport in Greece
la voile est un sport très populaire en Grèce

Pour l'emploi du gérondif, voir p. A43. Pour la comparaison entre le gérondif et le participe présent, voir pp. A45-6.

5 Le présent

À la 3ème personne du singulier, il se construit avec le radical + **-(e)s** (pour les modifications orthographiques, voir p. A79). La forme du verbe au présent est la même pour toutes les autres personnes :

	Singulier		
1ère	**I**	sing	*je chante*
2ème	**you**	sing	*tu chantes*
3ème	**he/she/it**	sings	*il/elle chante*
	Pluriel		
1ère	**we**	sing	*nous chantons*
2ème	**you**	sing	*vous chantez*
3ème	**they**	sing	*ils/elles chantent*

Les auxiliaires modaux ne changent pas de forme à la 3ème personne du singulier. Il en est de même pour les verbes **dare** et **need** lorsqu'ils sont employés comme auxiliaires :

he may come   how **dare** he come here!
il se peut qu'il vienne   *comment ose-t-il venir ici !*

Les auxiliaires ordinaires ont des formes irrégulières, voir la liste p. A66. Pour **dare** et **need**, voir p. A61.

6 Le prétérit

Le prétérit des verbes réguliers est identique à leur participe passé (radical du verbe + **-ed**) :

they **kicked** the ball
ils ont donné un coup de pied dans le ballon

Pour les verbes irréguliers et les auxiliaires, voir A2 et 3 ci-dessus, ainsi que la liste des verbes irréguliers et des auxiliaires pp. A63-6. La forme du verbe est la même à toutes les personnes :

		RÉGULIER *(embrasser)*	IRRÉGULIER *(chanter)*	AUXILIAIRE *(pouvoir)*
	Singulier			
1ère	**I**	kissed	sang	could
2ème	**you**	kissed	sang	could
3ème	**he/she/it**	kissed	sang	could
	Pluriel			
1ère	**we**	kissed	sang	could
2ème	**you**	kissed	sang	could
3ème	**they**	kissed	sang	could

7 Les temps et les aspects

La plupart des temps peuvent avoir différents aspects, considérant un événement dans le temps de trois manières différentes. On distingue donc l'aspect simple, l'aspect progressif (ou continu) et le perfect (ou passé).

La forme progressive, qui exprime l'action dans sa durée, se construit avec l'auxiliaire **be** + participe présent.

Le perfect, qui exprime une action accomplie ou une action du passé ayant des conséquences au moment de l'énonciation, se forme avec l'auxiliaire **have** + participe passé.

Pour la conjugaison des auxiliaires **be** et **have**, voir p. A66.

Dans la liste ci-dessous les traductions sont données à titre indicatif :

infinitif	**(to) watch** *(regarder)*
infinitif progressif	**(to) be watching** *(être en train de regarder)*
infinitif passé	**(to) have watched** *(avoir regardé)*
infinitif passé progressif	**(to) have been watching** *(avoir été en train de regarder)*
présent simple	**(I/you/he, etc.) watch(es)** *(je/tu/il, etc. regarde(s))*
présent progressif	" **am/are/is watching** *(" suis/es/est, etc. en train de regarder)*
passé simple (ou prétérit)	" **watched** *(je regardai, etc.)*
passé progressif	" **was/were watching** *(j'étais, etc. en train de regarder)*
present perfect	" **have/has watched** *(j'ai regardé, etc.)*
present perfect progressif	" **have/has been watching** *(j'ai, etc. été en train de regarder)*
past perfect	" **had watched** *(j'avais regardé, etc.)*
past perfect progressif	" **had been watching** *(j'avais, etc. été en train de regarder)*
futur simple	" **will watch** *(je regarderai, etc.)*
futur progressif	" **will be watching** *(je serai, etc. en train de regarder)*
futur antérieur	" **will have watched** *(j'aurai, etc. regardé)*

futur antérieur progressif	" will have been watching *(j'aurai, etc. été en train de regarder)*
conditionnel présent	" would watch *(je regarderais, etc.)*
conditionnel présent progressif	" would be watching *(je serais, etc. en train de regarder)*
conditionnel passé	" would have watched *(j'aurais, etc. regardé)*
conditionnel passé progressif	" would have been watching *(j'aurais, etc. été en train de regarder)*

8 Les modes

Les modes font référence à l'attitude d'une personne par rapport aux propos qu'elle rapporte. Il existe quatre modes :

- l'**indicatif** pour exprimer des faits réels

- le **subjonctif** pour exprimer un souhait, une incertitude ou une possibilité, etc.

- le **conditionnel** pour exprimer l'éventualité ou le résultat d'une condition

- l'**impératif** pour exprimer des ordres et des suggestions.

La seule différence de forme entre l'indicatif et le subjonctif réside dans la présence de -(e)s à la 3ᵉᵐᵉ personne du singulier au présent de l'indicatif :

God save the Queen!
vive la reine !

Le subjonctif de **to be** est **be** à toutes les personnes du présent et **were** à toutes les personnes du passé :

they are welcome to attend, whether they be members or not
ils peuvent venir, qu'ils soient membres ou pas

if I were you, I'd leave him
si j'étais toi, je le quitterais

Le conditionnel se forme généralement avec l'auxiliaire **would** dans la proposition principale (voir aussi l'exemple précédent) :

if I had a car, I would go and visit her more often
si j'avais une voiture, j'irais la voir plus souvent

Comme le montre cet exemple, c'est souvent le subjonctif passé que l'on trouve dans la proposition subordonnée. Mais il est possible d'employer d'autres temps. Voir pp. A52-3.

Pour le mode impératif, on emploie le radical du verbe seul :

give it to me!   **somebody go and get it!**
donne-le-moi !   *que quelqu'un aille le chercher !*

9 Les voix (actif et passif)

Les deux "voix" sont la voix active et la voix passive. À la voix active, le sujet accomplit l'action :

the new members signed the contract
les nouveaux membres ont signé le contrat

À la voix passive, le sujet subit l'action :

the contract was signed by the new members
le contrat a été signé par les nouveaux membres

La voix passive est plus courante en anglais qu'en français.

Le passif se forme avec l'auxiliaire **be** + participe passé (pour la conjugaison de **be**, voir p. A66) :

infinitif	(to) be watched *(être regardé)*
infinitif passé	(to) have been watched *(avoir été regardé)*
infinitif progressif	(to) be being watched *(être en train d'être regardé)*

présent simple	am/are/is watched *(suis/es/est, etc. regardé)*
présent progressif	am/are/is being watched *(suis/es/est, etc. en train d'être regardé)*
passé simple (ou prétérit)	was/were watched *(étais, etc. regardé)*
passé progressif	was/were being watched *(étais, etc. en train d'être regardé)*
present perfect	have/has been watched *(ai, etc. été regardé)*
present perfect progressif	have/has been being watched *(ai, etc. été en train d'être regardé)*
past perfect	had been watched *(avais, etc. été regardé)*
past perfect progressif	had been being watched *(avais, etc. été en train d'être regardé)*
futur simple	will be watched *(serai, etc. regardé)*
futur progressif	will be being watched *(serai, etc. en train d'être regardé)*
futur antérieur	will have been watched *(aurai, etc. été regardé)*
conditionnel présent	would be watched *(serais, etc. regardé)*
conditionnel présent progressif	would be being watched *(serais, etc. en train d'être regardé)*
conditionnel passé	would have been watched *(aurais, etc. été regardé)*

Quelques exemples :

it was hidden under some old papers
il était caché sous de vieux papiers

it was thought to have been hidden by the Romans
on pensait qu'il avait été caché par les Romains

it had deliberately been hidden by his assistant
il avait délibérément été caché par son assistant

you'll be closely watched
tu seras surveillé de près

the programme will have been watched by ten million viewers in total
l'émission aura été regardée en tout par dix millions de téléspectateurs

if he had made any comment it would have been ignored
s'il avait fait des commentaires, ils n'en auraient pas tenu compte

Le passif de l'infinitif progressif est plutôt rare. Il en est de même pour le passif du present perfect progressif :

he may have been being operated on by then
il était peut-être en train de se faire opérer à ce moment-là

C EMPLOIS

1 L'infinitif

a) *L'infinitif sans* **to**

i) Après l'auxiliaire **do** et les auxiliaires modaux :

I don't know
je ne sais pas

I must go
il faut que je m'en aille

ii) Après **dare** et **need** lorsqu'ils sont employés comme auxiliaires (voir p. A61) :

how dare you talk to me like that!
comment oses-tu me parler ainsi !

you needn't talk to me like that
tu n'as pas besoin de me parler comme ça

iii) Après **had better** et **had best** (ou **would best** en anglais américain) :

you'd better apologize
tu ferais mieux de t'excuser

you'd best ask the manager
tu ferais mieux de demander au directeur

iv) Dans la construction complément d'objet direct : nom/pronom + infinitif. Comparez avec b) ii) ci-dessous :

● Après **let** (*laisser*), **make** (*faire*) et **have** (*faire* dans ce cas) dans les tournures anglaises qui signifient "laisser faire" ou "faire faire" (voir aussi pp. A56-7) :

we let him smoke
nous l'avons laissé fumer

I made him turn round
je l'ai fait se retourner

we had him say a few words
nous lui avons fait dire quelques mots

● Après les verbes de perception **feel** (*sentir*), **hear** (*entendre*), **see** (*voir*), **watch** (*regarder*) :

I felt the floor tremble
j'ai senti trembler le sol

they saw him die
ils l'ont vu mourir

we heard her tell the manager
on l'a entendue le dire au directeur

we watched the train approach the platform
on a regardé le train s'approcher du quai

Pour **feel** (*penser, avoir l'impression que*), voir b) ii) ci-dessous.

Remarquez que ces verbes peuvent aussi être suivis du participe présent qui met l'accent sur la durée de l'action :

I felt her creeping up behind me
je sentais qu'elle s'approchait de moi à pas de loup

we heard her crying bitterly in the next room
nous l'avons entendue pleurer amèrement dans l'autre pièce

she saw smoke coming from the house
elle a vu de la fumée venir de la maison

they watched him slowly dying
ils l'ont vu mourir petit à petit

● On peut trouver les deux formes de l'infinitif après **help** :

we helped him (to) move house
nous l'avons aidé à déménager

Pour les constructions passives correspondantes employées avec ces verbes, voir b) ii) ci-dessous.

v) Après **why** ou **why not** :

why stay indoors in this lovely weather?
pourquoi rester à l'intérieur par ce beau temps ?

why not try our cream cakes?
pourquoi ne pas essayer nos gâteaux à la crème ?

b) *L'infinitif avec* **to**

i) L'infinitif avec **to** peut s'employer comme sujet, comme attribut ou comme complément d'objet direct. La phrase suivante contient les trois emplois (dans cet ordre) :

to die is to cease to exist
mourir, c'est cesser d'exister

ii) Comme complément d'objet direct, comparez avec a) iv) ci-dessus.

● Après des verbes exprimant un désir ou une antipathie, en particulier **want** (*vouloir*), **wish** (*souhaiter*), **like** (*aimer*), **prefer** (*préférer*), **hate** (*détester*, ici *ne pas vouloir*) :

I want you to remember this
je veux que tu t'en souviennes

we wish you to leave
nous souhaitons que vous partiez

we would like you to come with us
nous aimerions que vous veniez avec nous

we prefer your cousin to stay here
nous préférons que ton cousin reste ici

I would hate you to think I was avoiding you
je ne voudrais pas vous donner l'impression que je cherchais à vous éviter

● Dans un niveau de langue assez soutenu, on trouve souvent **to be** et **to have** après des verbes exprimant une opinion, un jugement, une supposition ou une affirmation :

we believe this to be a mistake
nous pensons qu'il s'agit d'une erreur

we believe this to have some serious consequences
nous pensons que cela va avoir de graves conséquences

we considered/judged it to be of little use
nous considérions/jugions cela peu utile

I felt/knew it to be true
j'avais l'impression/je savais que c'était vrai

he maintained these accusations to be false
il soutenait que ces accusations étaient fausses

En anglais plus courant, on préférera une simple proposition relative, introduite ou non par **that** :

we believe (that) this is a mistake
nous croyons que c'est une erreur

I know (that) it's true
je sais que c'est vrai

he maintained that these accusations were false
il a soutenu que ces accusations étaient fausses

● Dans la construction passive correspondante, on emploie l'infinitif complet :

this was believed to be a mistake
on pensait que c'était une erreur

● Remarquez l'expression courante **be said to**, pour laquelle il n'existe pas d'équivalent à la voix active en anglais :

it is said to be true
il paraît que c'est vrai

he's said to be rich
il paraît qu'il est riche

this hotel is said to have the most beautiful gardens
il paraît que cet hôtel a des jardins absolument magnifiques

● La forme **to** + infinitif doit aussi être employée dans des constructions passives avec les verbes mentionnés en a) iv) ci-dessus :

she was made to do it
on l'a forcée à le faire

the aircraft was seen to crash just after take-off
on a vu l'avion s'écraser juste après le décollage

iii) Employé après des noms, des pronoms et des adjectifs :

he has a tendency to forget **there are things to be**
things   done
il a tendance à tout oublier   *il y a des choses à faire*

we shall remember this in years to come
on se rappellera cela pendant des années

we were afraid to ask
nous avions peur de demander

this game is easy to understand
ce jeu est facile à comprendre

there is that to take into consideration
il y a ça à prendre en considération

pleased to meet you!
heureux de faire votre connaissance !

De telles constructions sont particulièrement courantes après des superlatifs et après only :

this is the latest book to appear on the subject
c'est le livre le plus récent qui soit paru sur ce sujet

she's the only person to have got near him
elle est la seule personne à avoir pu l'approcher

iv) Correspondant à une proposition subordonnée :

● Pour exprimer le but ou la conséquence (l'infinitif pouvant être précédé de in order ou so as (but) ou only (conséquence) pour souligner ses propos) :

he left early to/in order to/so as to get a good seat for the performance
il est parti tôt pour/afin d'être bien placé au spectacle

they arrived (only) to find an empty house
à leur arrivée, la maison était vide

● Dans des propositions interrogatives indirectes :

tell me what to do
dis-moi ce que je dois faire

I didn't know where to look
je ne savais pas où regarder

we didn't know who to ask
nous ne savions pas à qui demander

we weren't sure whether to tell him or not
nous ne savions pas si nous devions le lui dire ou non

● Pour exprimer le temps ou la circonstance :

I shudder to think of it (= ... when I think of it)
j'en tremble rien que d'y penser

to hear him speak, one would think he positively hates women (= when one hears him speak...)
à l'entendre parler, on dirait vraiment qu'il déteste les femmes

v) Dans des exclamations :

to think she married him!
et dire qu'elle l'a épousé !

vi) Dans des phrases elliptiques exprimant des événements à venir. Cet emploi de l'infinitif est courant dans le langage journalistique :

Blair to Make Speech on Iraq
Blair doit s'exprimer sur l'Irak

Chirac to Visit Disaster Zone
Chirac doit se rendre dans la zone sinistrée

vii) On peut aussi trouver l'infinitif avec césure : un adverbe vient s'intercaler entre to et le radical du verbe. Cette forme est devenue très courante, mais peu appréciée de beaucoup, qui soutiennent qu'il ne faut jamais séparer to du radical :

nobody will ever be able to fully comprehend his philosophy
personne ne sera jamais capable de comprendre complètement sa philosophie

Comparez les deux exemples suivants :

the way out of this is to really try and persuade him
le moyen de s'en sortir, c'est de vraiment essayer de le persuader

the way out of this is really to try and persuade him
le moyen de s'en sortir, c'est en fait d'essayer de le persuader

Dans le premier exemple, l'adverbe really signifie "beaucoup" et il renforce try, tandis que dans le deuxième exemple, il signifie "en fait" et modifie toute la phrase.

viii) On emploie souvent to sans le radical du verbe dans une répétition, plutôt que l'infinitif complet :

why haven't you tidied your room? I told you to
pourquoi n'as-tu pas rangé ta chambre ? je t'ai dit de le faire

I did it because she encouraged me to
je l'ai fait parce qu'elle m'y a encouragé

ix) Dans la construction for + nom/pronom + infinitif avec to :

it took an hour for the taxi to get to the station
le taxi a mis une heure pour aller jusqu'à la gare

there's no need for you to worry
il n'y a aucune raison de vous inquiéter

he waited for her to finish
il attendit qu'elle ait fini

Cette construction grammaticale et idiomatique exprime souvent la condition, le but ou encore la circonstance, et peut même être sujet de la phrase :

for the university to function properly, more money is needed
afin que l'université fonctionne bien, il faut plus d'argent

for me to say nothing would be admitting defeat
(sujet)
ne rien dire serait admettre ma défaite

for a man to get custody of his children used to be difficult *(sujet)*
à l'époque, il était difficile pour un homme d'obtenir la garde de ses enfants

x) En anglais parlé, on remplace très souvent le to de l'infinitif par and après des verbes tels que try, go, come ou stay :

try and be there around 6 (= try to be there around 6)
essaie d'arriver vers 18 heures

Cette structure avec try ne peut s'employer qu'à l'infinitif, alors qu'il est possible d'utiliser les verbes suivants au passé ou à la 3ème personne du présent :

you should go and see this film (= you should go to see this film)
tu devrais aller voir ce film

he went and saw it   **he goes and sees her every week**
il est allé le voir   *il va la voir toutes les semaines*

come and have dinner with us (= come to have dinner with us)
viens manger avec nous un soir

he usually comes and has dinner with us on Sundays
en général, il vient manger avec nous tous les dimanches soir

he came and had dinner with us yesterday
il est venu manger avec nous hier soir

2 Le gérondif

Le gérondif (ou verbe substantivé) possède des caractéristiques propres aux noms et aux verbes.

a) *Caractéristiques nominales*

i) Un gérondif peut être sujet, attribut ou complément d'objet :

surfing is difficult *(sujet)*
le surf, c'est difficile

that's cheating *(attribut)*
c'est de la triche

I love reading *(complément)*
j'adore lire

Comme on l'a vu, ce sont là des fonctions communes à l'infinitif (voir p. A41) ; pour les différences d'emploi, voir section 4 ci-dessous.

ii) Il peut être placé après une préposition (contrairement à l'infinitif) :

he's thought of leaving
il a pensé partir

his back hurt from lifting heavy boxes
il avait mal au dos après avoir soulevé de gros cartons

iii) Il peut être précédé d'un article puis suivi d'un groupe prépositionnel (c'est-à-dire introduit par **of**) :

the timing of his remarks was unfortunate
il a mal choisi son moment pour faire des remarques

Et il peut être modifié par un adjectif ou un possessif :

careless writing leaves a bad impression
une écriture peu soignée fait mauvaise impression

the soprano's singing was wonderful
le chant du soprano était magnifique

do you remember his trying to persuade her?
tu te souviens qu'il a essayé de la persuader ?

b) *Caractéristiques verbales*

i) Un gérondif peut avoir un sujet :

the thought of John doing that is absurd
penser que John ait pu faire ça est absurde

ii) Il peut être suivi d'un complément d'objet ou d'un attribut :

hitting the wing mirror was unavoidable
nous n'avons pas pu éviter le rétroviseur

becoming an expert took him more than twenty years
il lui a fallu plus de vingt ans pour devenir expert en la matière

iii) Il peut être modifié par un adverbe :

she was afraid of totally disillusioning him
elle avait peur de lui faire perdre toutes ses illusions

3 Le possessif et le gérondif

Devant un gérondif, il n'est pas rare d'hésiter entre l'emploi d'une forme complément ou celui d'une forme possessive :

do you remember him/his trying to persuade her?
tu te souviens qu'il a essayé de la persuader ?

Les deux formes sont ici correctes. Mais il existe parfois des différences d'emploi entre les deux. Il convient de noter les exemples suivants :

a) *Le gérondif sujet ou attribut*

Dans ce cas, on emploie normalement le possessif (un adjectif possessif ou le génitif) :

your trying to persuade me will get you nowhere
tu auras beau essayer, tu n'arriveras pas à me convaincre

it was John's insisting that we went there that saved the situation
c'est grâce à l'insistance de John qui voulait que nous y allions que la situation fut sauvée

b) *Le gérondif complément ou placé après une préposition*

Dans ce cas, il est possible d'employer soit un nom/pronom complément d'objet direct, soit la forme possessive :

you don't mind me/my turning up so late, do you?
ça ne te dérange pas que j'arrive si tard, n'est-ce pas ?

they spoke at great length about him/his being elected president
ils parlèrent longtemps de son élection comme président

they spoke at great length about Richard/Richard's being elected president
ils parlèrent longtemps de l'élection de Richard comme président

Remarquez que l'emploi du possessif est plus soutenu que celui du nom/pronom complément. On aura donc tendance à employer la forme complément à l'oral ou dans un style plus familier :

they laughed their heads off at him falling into the river
ils riaient à n'en plus pouvoir parce qu'il était tombé dans la rivière

On a également plus tendance à employer le possessif devant le gérondif en anglais américain qu'en anglais britannique.

Pour la comparaison entre le gérondif et le participe présent et les ambiguïtés éventuelles, voir section 6, p. A45.

c) *Le facteur d'emphase*

Si le sujet du gérondif est accentué, on préférera l'emploi de la forme complément à celui de la forme possessive :

just to think of HIM marrying Karen!
que ce soit lui qui épouse Karen, je n'arrive pas à le croire !

4 Comparaison entre le gérondif et l'infinitif

a) *Emploi identique*

On a vu que l'infinitif et le gérondif ont des caractéristiques nominales du fait qu'ils peuvent fonctionner comme sujet, complément d'objet ou attribut. Il y a donc souvent peu ou pas de différence de sens entre les deux :

we can't bear seeing you like this
we can't bear to see you like this
nous ne supportons pas de te voir comme ça

I prefer being called by my first name
I prefer to be called by my first name
je préfère qu'on m'appelle par mon prénom

En anglais américain, l'infinitif est souvent utilisé là où en anglais britannique on emploierait un gérondif :

I like cooking *(Br)*
I like to cook *(Am)*
j'aime faire la cuisine

b) *Différents sens*

i) Quand le verbe **try** signifie simplement "essayer", on peut souvent employer l'infinitif ou le gérondif :

I tried to make a chocolate cake, but it wasn't very good
I tried making a chocolate cake, but it wasn't very good
j'ai essayé de faire un gâteau au chocolat, mais il n'était pas très bon

Mais ces formes verbales ne sont pas toujours interchangeables. Lorsque **try** a le sens de "faire un effort, essayer quelque chose de difficile", on emploie l'infinitif :

I really tried to understand
j'ai vraiment cherché à comprendre

Si *try* a le sens de "tenter quelque chose pour voir ce qui va se passer", on emploie le gérondif :

I tried sending her a letter of apology, but it didn't work
j'ai essayé de lui envoyer une lettre pour m'excuser, mais ça n'a pas marché

ii) Après **forget** (*oublier*) et **remember** (*se souvenir*), l'infinitif fait référence au futur, le gérondif au passé :

I won't forget to ask her to dinner (*dans le futur*)
je n'oublierai pas de l'inviter à dîner

I won't forget asking her to dinner (*dans le passé*)
je n'oublierai pas que je l'ai invitée à dîner

will she remember to meet me? (*dans le futur*)
est-ce qu'elle se souviendra de notre rendez-vous ?

will she remember meeting me? (*dans le passé*)
est-ce qu'elle se souviendra d'avoir fait ma connaissance ?

iii) Vous verrez dans le point c) ci-dessous une liste de verbes après lesquels l'infinitif et le gérondif sont employés comme compléments d'objet direct. Il en est de même pour le gérondif dans la phrase suivante :

I stopped looking at her
je me suis arrêté de la regarder

Mais l'infinitif n'est pas complément d'objet direct dans :

I stopped to look at her
je me suis arrêté pour la regarder

Ici, l'infinitif fonctionne comme un complément circonstanciel de but, ce qui explique la différence considérable de sens entre les deux phrases. La différence est la même entre les deux exemples suivants :

he was too busy talking to her
il était trop occupé à lui parler

he was too busy to talk to her
il était trop occupé pour lui parler

iv) Il est aussi important de faire la distinction entre **to**, marque de l'infinitif, et **to**, préposition. Après une préposition, on trouvera toujours le gérondif :

I'm tired of watching television
j'en ai assez de regarder la télévision

what do you think about getting a loan?
qu'est-ce que tu dirais de faire un emprunt ?

Ceci, bien sûr, concerne aussi la préposition **to** :

they are committed to implementing the plan
ils se sont engagés à réaliser le projet

we're looking forward to receiving your letter
nous attendons votre lettre avec impatience

they object to working overtime
ils ne sont pas d'accord pour faire des heures supplémentaires

we're not used to getting up at this hour
nous ne sommes pas habitués à nous lever à cette heure-ci

c) *L'infinitif seulement ou le gérondif seulement*

i) L'infinitif seulement :

Certains verbes ne peuvent être suivis que de l'infinitif, par exemple : **demand** (*exiger*), **deserve** (*mériter*), **expect** (*s'attendre à*), **hope** (*espérer*), **want** (*vouloir*), **wish** (*souhaiter*) :

I want/wish to leave   **he deserves to be punished**
je veux/souhaite partir   *il mérite d'être puni*

we hope to be back by five
nous espérons être de retour vers cinq heures

ii) Le gérondif seulement :

D'autres verbes ne sont suivis que du gérondif, par exemple : **avoid** (*éviter*), **consider** (*considérer*), **dislike** (*ne pas aimer*), **enjoy** (*apprécier*), **finish** (*finir*), **keep** (*continuer*), **mind** (*déranger, gêner*), **practise** (*faire, pratiquer*), **risk** (*risquer*) :

he avoided answering my questions
il évitait de répondre à mes questions

will you consider taking some time off work?
est-ce que vous songez à prendre des congés ?

I dislike flying
je n'aime pas prendre l'avion

we enjoy having friends round to dinner
nous aimons recevoir des amis pour le dîner

she finished writing her e-mail
elle a fini d'écrire son e-mail

they keep teasing him
ils n'arrêtent pas de le taquiner

do you mind going out when the weather's cold?
est-ce que cela vous ennuie de sortir quand il fait froid ?

you must practise playing the piano more often
tu dois travailler ton piano plus souvent

I don't want to risk upsetting Jennifer
je ne veux pas risquer de contrarier Jennifer

Il faut noter aussi que l'adjectif **worth** et la préposition **like** ne peuvent être suivis que du gérondif :

that suggestion is worth considering
cette proposition vaut la peine d'être examinée

that's just like wishing for the moon
c'est comme si je demandais la lune

5   Le participe présent

Le participe présent s'emploie comme forme verbale ou comme adjectif.

a) *Comme forme verbale*

i) Le participe présent s'emploie après **be** pour former l'aspect progressif :

he is/was/has been/had been running
il court/courait/a couru/avait couru

ii) Le participe présent s'emploie souvent pour former une proposition relative elliptique (sans pronom relatif et sans auxiliaire) :

I saw the people coming out of the theatre (= who were coming)
j'ai vu les gens qui sortaient du théâtre

iii) Le participe présent peut avoir pour sujet celui de la proposition principale. Dans ce cas, il est précédé d'une virgule. Le participe présent peut s'employer après une proposition principale au présent ou au passé :

she turned towards the man, looking pleasantly surprised
elle se tourna vers l'homme, l'air agréablement surpris

Dans cet exemple, le sujet de **looking** est **she** ; mais si l'on omet la virgule, le sujet de **looking** est **the man**, et la phrase appartient alors au type ii) ci-dessus (= **the man who is/was looking pleasantly surprised**).

Ce participe présent peut précéder son sujet :

looking pleasantly surprised, she **turned towards the man**
l'air agréablement surpris, elle se tourna vers l'homme

La proposition introduite par un participe présent équivaut souvent à une proposition subordonnée de cause, de condition ou de temps :

living alone, she often feels uneasy at night (= because/since/as she lives alone...)
vivant seule, elle est souvent inquiète le soir

it might be more expensive, living alone (= ...if you lived alone)
ce doit être plus cher de vivre seul

driving along, I suddenly saw him standing at the side of the road (= as/while I was driving along...)
j'étais en train de conduire, quand soudain je l'ai vu sur le bord de la route

Mais il correspond aussi parfois à une proposition indépendante :

she walked away from him, shouting that she never wanted to see him again (= and (she) shouted that...)
elle est partie en criant qu'elle ne voulait plus jamais le revoir

living in London, he is an artist who has organized many cultural events (= he lives in London and (he) is...)
vivant à Londres, c'est un artiste qui a organisé de nombreuses manifestations culturelles

Dans tous ces exemples, le sujet du participe est le même que celui de la proposition principale. Comparez avec les exemples du point v) ci-dessous dans lesquels le participe présent a son propre sujet.

iv) Le participe présent "non rattaché" :

Un participe présent est considéré comme "non rattaché" si son sujet est différent de celui du verbe de la proposition principale :

coming down the staircase carrying an umbrella, one of the cats tripped him up
un des chats le fit trébucher alors qu'il descendait l'escalier, un parapluie à la main

Dans cet exemple, on peut facilement deviner que le sujet de **coming** est en fait le complément d'objet de la principale (**him**). Mais il est préférable d'éviter cette structure de phrase grammaticalement incorrecte et souvent source d'ambiguïté.

L'emploi du participe présent est toutefois normal et très courant lorsqu'un sujet indéfini est sous-entendu, comme le *we* indéfini ou le "on" français. On trouve surtout cet emploi dans des expressions figées :

generally speaking, British cooking is much better than it used to be
d'une manière générale, la cuisine britannique s'est beaucoup améliorée

judging by the way she dresses, she must have a lot of confidence
à voir ou à en juger par sa façon de s'habiller, elle doit avoir une grande confiance en elle

v) Comme en français, le sujet du participe (différent de celui de la principale) peut le précéder dans ce qu'on appelle la "construction absolue". La proposition contenant le participe présent équivaut là aussi à une proposition subordon-née causale (voir iii) ci-dessus) :

the lift being out of order, we had to use the stairs
l'ascenseur étant en panne, nous avons dû monter par les escaliers

she being the hostess, any kind of criticism was out of the question
étant donné que c'était elle qui recevait, il était hors de question de faire quelque critique que ce soit

b) *Comme adjectif*

she has always been a loving **child**
elle a toujours été une enfant aimante

her appearance is striking
elle a une allure frappante

she finds Steven very charming
elle trouve Steven très charmant

De cette fonction adjectivale dérive la fonction adverbiale :

he is strikingly **handsome**
il est d'une beauté saisissante

Remarquez que cette structure est bien plus courante en anglais qu'en français :

a self-adjusting mechanism
un mécanisme à autoréglage

the falling **birth rate**   **increasing sales**
le taux de natalité en baisse   *des ventes en hausse*

6 Comparaison entre le participe présent et le gérondif

a) *Ambiguïté*

La phrase suivante peut se comprendre de deux manières différentes :

I hate | people | trying to get in without paying
je déteste les gens qui essaient d'entrer sans payer

Si **trying** est un gérondif, le sens de la phrase est : **I hate the fact that (some) people try to get in without paying** (*je n'aime pas le fait que certaines personnes essaient d'entrer sans payer*). Grammaticalement, on pourrait couper la phrase au niveau de la barre bleue.

Si c'est un participe présent, le sens devient : **I hate people who try to get in without paying** (*je n'aime pas les gens qui essaient d'entrer sans payer*). Grammaticalement, on pourrait couper la phrase au niveau de la barre noire.

Mais si la forme en *-ing* est précédée d'un adjectif possessif, il ne peut s'agir que d'un gérondif (voir p. A43) :

I hate their trying to get in without paying
je n'aime pas qu'ils essaient d'entrer sans payer

De même, dans la phrase suivante, la forme en *-ing* ne peut être qu'un gérondif ; sa fonction nominale entraîne un verbe au singulier :

children suffering like that is on our conscience (= the suffering of children)
la souffrance de ces enfants pèse sur notre conscience

Au contraire, le pluriel de la phrase suivante montre que **suffering** est un participe présent :

children suffering like that are on our conscience (= children who suffer)
les enfants qui souffrent comme cela pèsent sur notre conscience

b) *Accentuation*

Quand un gérondif modifie un nom, seul le gérondif est accentué dans le discours, et non le nom :

a living room [ə ˈlɪvɪŋ rʊm]   **a walking stick** [ə ˈwɔːkɪŋ stɪk]
un salon   *une canne*

Mais quand l'élément modificateur est un participe présent, celui-ci et le nom sont accentués de la même manière :

a living animal [ə ˈlɪvɪŋ ˈænɪml]
un animal vivant

the walking wounded [ðə ˈwɔːkɪŋ ˈwuːndɪd]
les blessés qui peuvent encore marcher

Remarquez que ces deux derniers adjectifs sont des participes présents car "l'action" est accomplie par le nom ("un animal qui vit", etc.), ce qui n'est pas le cas des deux premiers adjectifs. Ces derniers sont des gérondifs : ils qualifient les noms en indiquant leur rôle (= "une pièce pour vivre", "un bâton pour marcher").

7 Le participe passé

Parmi les emplois suivants, beaucoup peuvent être comparés avec ceux du participe présent. Voir 5 pp. A44-5.

a) *Comme forme verbale*

   i) Le participe passé s'emploie après l'auxiliaire **have** pour former le present perfect et le past perfect :

   he has/had arrived
   il est/était arrivé

   et après l'auxiliaire **be** pour former la voix passive :

   she is/was admired
   elle est/était admirée

   et avec les deux auxiliaires pour former le passif au present perfect et au past perfect :

   she has/had been admired
   elle a/avait été admirée

   ii) Le participe passé est souvent employé pour former une proposition relative elliptique (sans pronom relatif et sans auxiliaire) :

   they go to all the concerts given by the local orchestra (= which are given)
   ils vont à tous les concerts donnés par l'orchestre local

   they went to all the concerts given by the local orchestra (= which were/had been given)
   ils sont allés à tous les concerts donnés par l'orchestre local

   Il peut aussi avoir la fonction de subordonnée de cause, de condition ou de temps. Des conjonctions (en particulier **if** et **when**), non obligatoires en début de phrase, permettent de rendre le sens plus explicite :

   watched over by her family, Monica felt safe but unhappy (= because/since/as she was watched over...)
   surveillée par sa famille, Monica se sentait en sécurité, mais malheureuse

   (if) treated with care, CDs should last indefinitely
   si l'on en prend soin, les CD ne s'usent jamais

   CDs should last indefinitely if treated with care
   les CD ne s'usent jamais si l'on en prend soin

   (when) asked why, he refused to answer
   quand on lui demanda pourquoi, il refusa de répondre

   he refused to answer when asked why
   il refusa de répondre lorsqu'on lui demanda pourquoi

   Ou il peut avoir valeur de proposition indépendante :

   born in Aberdeen, he now lives in Perth with his wife (= he was born in Aberdeen and he now lives...)
   né à Aberdeen, il habite maintenant à Perth avec sa femme

   iii) On trouve parfois des phrases avec un participe passé non rattaché au sujet de la phrase (appelé en anglais **dangling participle**). Cependant, il est préférable d'éviter cette structure de phrase grammaticalement incorrecte et qui donne souvent lieu à des ambiguïtés (voir 5a) iv) p. A45) :

   told to cancel the meeting, his project was never discussed

   On pourrait exprimer ceci de manière plus élégante :

   his project was never discussed as he was told to cancel the meeting
   son projet ne fut jamais examiné car on lui demanda d'annuler la réunion

   iv) Dans la "construction absolue", le participe passé a son propre sujet et il équivaut à une proposition subordonnée (voir 5a) v) p. A45) :

   the problems solved, they went their separate ways (= when the problems were solved...)
   les problèmes résolus, ils sont partis chacun de leur côté

   that done, he left (= once that was done...)
   une fois que ce fut terminé, il est parti

b) *Comme adjectif*

   the defeated army retreated   **I am very tired**
   l'armée vaincue battit en retraite   *je suis très fatigué*

   Remarquez que l'on peut placer l'adverbe **very** avant un participe passé adjectif. Lorsque l'on insiste plus sur le caractère verbal du participe passé, on emploie **much**, et non **very** :

   I am much obliged
   je vous suis très obligé

   Pour la différence d'emploi entre **very** et **much**, voir pp. A22-3.

   Lorsque **aged** (*âgé*), **beloved** (*bien-aimé*), **blessed** (*sacré*), **cursed** (*maudit*) et **learned** (*érudit*) sont des adjectifs épithètes, on prononce normalement -ed /ɪd/. Mais lorsque ce sont des verbes, on adopte la prononciation régulière /d/ ou /t/ :

   he has aged [eɪdʒd]   **a man aged 50** [eɪdʒd]
   il a vieilli   *un homme âgé de 50 ans*

   mais :

   an aged man [ˈeɪdʒɪd]
   un homme âgé

   La prononciation /ɪd/ est toutefois rare et littéraire.

8 Les questions

a) *Phrases complètes*

   i) On emploie l'auxiliaire **do** pour former les questions à moins que la phrase ne contienne un autre auxiliaire (**have**, **will**, etc.), auquel cas l'auxiliaire précède le sujet, ou que le sujet ne soit un pronom interrogatif. **Do** se met au présent ou au passé, et le verbe principal est à l'infinitif. Le sujet se place entre l'auxiliaire et le verbe :

   he always arrives late → **does he always arrive late?**
   il arrive toujours en retard   *est-ce qu'il arrive toujours en retard ?*

   she often goes there → **does she go there often?**
   elle y va souvent   *est-ce qu'elle y va souvent ?*

   he saw her → **did he see her?**
   il l'a vue   *est-ce qu'il l'a vue ?*

   you said that... → **what did you say?**
   tu as dit que...   *qu'est-ce que tu as dit ?*

   how do we get to Oxford Street from here?
   comment fait-on pour aller d'ici à Oxford Street ?

Quand d'autres auxiliaires sont employés, ce sont eux qui précèdent le sujet :

they are trying to... → **are they trying to call us?**
ils essaient de... *est-ce qu'ils essaient de nous appeler ?*

he's taking her to... → **where is he taking her?**
il l'emmène à... *où est-ce qu'il l'emmène ?*

they've seen us → **have they seen us?**
ils nous ont vus *est-ce qu'ils nous ont vus ?*

you'll help us → **will you help us?**
tu nous aideras *tu pourras nous aider ?*

you can come at eight → **can you come at eight?**
tu peux venir à huit heures *est-ce que tu peux venir à huit heures ?*

Quand on a un pronom interrogatif sujet et qu'il n'y a pas d'auxiliaire existant, la question se forme sans l'auxiliaire do :

who said that? **what happened?**
qui a dit ça ? *qu'est-ce qui s'est passé ?*

Pour dare et need, voir p. A61. Pour have, voir pp. A55-7.

ii) En anglais parlé, où l'on distingue une proposition interrogative d'une proposition affirmative par l'intonation, on peut employer l'ordre des mots d'une affirmative dans une interrogative (emploi moins fréquent en anglais, qu'en français) :

you just left him standing there?
tu l'as laissé planté là ?

Dans des propositions interrogatives indirectes, l'ordre des mots est identique à celui de la proposition affirmative directe. Mais attention à la concordance des temps :

when are you leaving? *(style direct)*
quand est-ce que tu pars ?

he asked her **when she was leaving** *(style indirect)*
il lui a demandé quand elle partait

b) *Les question-tags*

Le question-tag, équivalent du "n'est-ce pas ?" français, est une tournure interrogative très courante en anglais, qui se place en fin de phrase et qui permet généralement de demander confirmation. Il se compose d'un pronom personnel et d'un auxiliaire.

i) Une proposition affirmative est suivie d'un tag à la forme négative et vice versa :

you can see it, can't you? **you can't see it, can you?**
tu le vois, n'est-ce pas ? *est-ce que tu peux le voir ?*

Lorsqu'un tag est emphatique, c'est-à-dire lorsqu'il sert à renforcer le sens de la phrase principale plutôt qu'à poser une question ou demander confirmation, on emploie un tag à la forme affirmative après une proposition affirmative :

so you've seen a ghost, have you? *(incrédulité ou ironie)*
alors comme ça, tu as vu un fantôme ?

you think that's fair, do you? *(ressentiment)*
tu crois que c'est juste, hein ?

you've bought a new car, have you? *(surprise ou intérêt)*
alors, tu as acheté une nouvelle voiture ?

ii) Le question-tag reprend le temps employé dans la principale. Si la proposition précédente est au présent simple ou au prétérit, et donc sans auxiliaire, on utilisera do dans le question-tag :

you want to meet him, don't you? *(présent)*
tu veux le rencontrer, n'est-ce pas ?

you wanted to meet him, didn't you? *(passé)*
tu voulais le rencontrer, n'est-ce pas ?

you'll want to meet him, won't you? *(futur)*
tu voudras le rencontrer, n'est-ce pas ?

iii) Si, comme dans ce dernier exemple, la proposition qui précède est régie par un auxiliaire, il faut le répéter dans le tag :

you have seen it before, haven't you?
tu l'as déjà vu, n'est-ce pas ?

they aren't sold yet, are they?
ils n'ont quand même pas déjà été vendus ?

you will help me, won't you?
tu m'aideras, n'est-ce pas ?

I shouldn't say anything to him, should I?
je ne devrais rien lui dire, n'est-ce pas ?

iv) Lorsque le tag suit un impératif, on emploie un auxiliaire à la forme affirmative (en particulier will/would). Ces tags permettent souvent de nuancer l'impératif, d'éviter un ton trop sec :

leave the cat alone, will you?
laisse le chat tranquille, tu veux ?

take this to Jackie, would you?
tu veux bien apporter ça à Jackie ?

La forme négative won't indique une invitation :

help yourselves to drinks, won't you?
servez-vous à boire, je vous en prie

9 Les négations

a) *La négation des formes conjuguées*

i) On emploie l'auxiliaire do avec not pour former la négation, à moins que la proposition ne contienne un autre auxiliaire (should, will, etc.). En anglais, on utilise pratiquement tout le temps les formes contractées (don't, won't, can't, etc.), mais elle doivent toutefois être évitées dans un style soutenu à l'écrit :

we accept traveller's cheques → **we do not/don't accept traveller's cheques**
nous acceptons les chèques de voyage
nous n'acceptons pas les chèques de voyage

Lorsque l'on a déjà un auxiliaire, on doit le reprendre à la forme négative :

he should come → **he should not/shouldn't come**
il devrait venir *il ne devrait pas venir*

ii) Dans une question négative, not se place après le sujet, à moins que la forme contractée ne soit utilisée :

do they not accept traveller's cheques?
don't they accept traveller's cheques?
ils n'acceptent pas les chèques de voyage ?

should you not try his office number?
shouldn't you try his office number?
ne devrais-tu pas essayer son numéro au bureau ?

iii) Les verbes exprimant un point de vue believe, suppose, think, etc. sont normalement à la forme négative, même si la négation porte logiquement sur le verbe dans la proposition complément d'objet :

I don't believe we have met
je ne crois pas que nous nous soyons déjà rencontrés

I don't suppose you could lend me a fiver?
ça t'embêterait de me prêter un billet de 5 livres ?

I didn't think these papers were yours
je ne pensais pas que ces papiers étaient à toi

mais **hope** est plus logique :

I hope it won't give me a headache
j'espère que ça ne me donnera pas mal à la tête

et il n'est pas accompagné de **do** lorsqu'il est employé seul :

is she ill? – I hope not
elle est malade ? – j'espère que non

De nombreuses formes sont possibles pour des réponses courtes avec des verbes tels que **believe**, **suppose** et **think** :

will she marry him?
va-t-elle l'épouser ?

I don't believe/think so *(couramment employé)*
je ne crois pas/ne pense pas

I believe/think not *(moins courant, plus soigné)*

I don't suppose so *(couramment employé)*

I suppose not *(couramment employé)*

Voir aussi p. A38.

b) *La négation des infinitifs et des gérondifs*

On forme la négation des infinitifs et des gérondifs en plaçant **not** devant :

we tried not to upset her
nous avons essayé de ne pas la contrarier

I want you to think seriously about not going
je veux que tu songes sérieusement à ne pas partir

not eating enough fruit is a cause of vitamin deficiency
ne pas manger assez de fruits peut entraîner une carence en vitamines

L'exemple avec l'infinitif ci-dessus a bien sûr un sens différent de la phrase suivante, où c'est **try** qui est à la forme négative :

we didn't try to upset her
nous n'avons pas essayé de la contrarier

Remarquez l'expression idiomatique **not to worry = don't worry** :

I won't manage to finish it by tomorrow – not to worry
je n'arriverai pas à terminer avant demain – ce n'est pas grave

c) *La négation des impératifs*

i) La négation des impératifs se forme avec l'auxiliaire **do**. **Do not** a pour forme contractée **don't** :

don't worry   **don't be silly**
ne t'inquiète pas   *ne sois pas bête*

L'emploi de la forme complète **do not** est courant dans les déclarations officielles, dans les modes d'emploi, sur les panneaux, etc. :

do not fill in this part of the form
ne pas remplir cette partie du formulaire

do not feed the animals
prière de ne pas donner à manger aux animaux

do not exceed the stated dose
ne pas dépasser la dose prescrite

La forme complète s'emploie aussi à l'oral pour rendre un impératif plus emphatique :

I'll say it again: do not touch!
je te le redis encore : ne touche pas !

Dans la forme de l'impératif **let's**, employée pour des suggestions, l'ordre des mots est le suivant :

don't let's wait any longer
n'attendons pas plus longtemps

Mais cette tournure est assez rare. On emploiera normalement :

let's not wait any longer
n'attendons pas plus longtemps

ii) On peut également exprimer la négation à l'impératif en employant uniquement **not** après le verbe. Cette structure, soutenue et littéraire, peut aussi s'employer sur un ton humoristique :

worry not, I'll be back soon
ne t'inquiète pas, je reviendrai bientôt

fear not, the situation is under control
n'aie pas peur, je maîtrise la situation

d) Never

L'adjectif négatif **never** n'est normalement pas accompagné de **do** :

we never accept traveller's cheques
nous n'acceptons jamais les chèques de voyage

I never said a word
je n'ai rien dit

On trouve l'auxiliaire **do** après **never** uniquement lorsque l'on veut insister sur le verbe (pour l'emploi de **do** comme auxiliaire emphatique, voir p. A57) :

you never did like my cooking, did you?
tu n'as jamais aimé ma cuisine, hein ?

Si **never** est en début de phrase, on emploiera **do** avec une inversion sujet-auxiliaire (style soutenu) :

never did it taste so good!
ça n'a jamais été aussi bon !

never did their courage waver
à aucun moment leur courage n'a faibli

Dans le premier de ces deux exemples, la phrase est plus une exclamation qu'une négation, et dans la seconde, le style est poétique ou rhétorique.

Cette inversion est possible avec d'autres adverbes négatifs (voir p. A78).

e) *La traduction des formes négatives françaises*

i) ne... jamais

he never speaks to me
he doesn't ever speak to me
il ne me parle jamais

ii) ne... rien

I saw nothing
I didn't see anything
je n'ai rien vu

iii) ne... personne

she agrees with nobody/no-one
she doesn't agree with anybody/anyone
elle n'est d'accord avec personne

iv) ne... plus

I don't smoke any more/any longer
I no longer smoke
je ne fume plus

words which are no longer used
words which aren't used any longer
des mots qui ne sont plus employés

Voir aussi le chapitre **Les adverbes**, pp. A23-4.

10 Pour exprimer le présent

On peut exprimer le présent de différentes façons selon que l'on fait référence à des événements habituels et d'ordre général, ou à des événements précis, et selon que l'on considère ces événement précis comme des actions en cours ou des événements ponctuels. Cette section décrit les emplois des formes verbales appropriées.

a) *Le présent simple*

i) Pour des événements habituels ou d'ordre général, ou pour des vérités universelles :

I get up at seven o'clock every morning
je me lève à sept heures tous les matins

she teaches French at the local school
elle enseigne le français dans l'école du quartier

the earth revolves round the sun
la terre tourne autour du soleil

ii) Avec des verbes qui n'impliquent pas d'idée de progression dans le temps. Ces verbes, parfois appelés "verbes statiques", expriment souvent un sentiment, une opinion, ou font référence aux sens :

I (dis)like/love/hate/want that girl
j'aime (je n'aime pas)/j'adore/je déteste/je veux cette fille

I believe/suppose/think you're right
je crois/suppose/pense que vous avez raison

we hear/see/feel the world around us
nous entendons/voyons/sentons le monde qui nous entoure

it tastes good/it smells good
c'est bon/ça sent bon

Remarquez que ces verbes statiques peuvent devenir des "verbes dynamiques", si l'on considère l'action dans son déroulement ou dans sa durée. Dans de tels cas, on emploie le présent progressif (voir b) ci-dessous) :

what are you thinking about?
à quoi penses-tu ?

how are you feeling today?
comment vous sentez-vous aujourd'hui ?

we're tasting the wine to see if it's all right
nous goûtons le vin pour voir s'il est bon

b) *Le présent progressif*

i) Le présent progressif est employé avec des verbes dynamiques, c'est-à-dire des verbes qui renvoient à des événements en cours et normalement temporaires :

don't interrupt while I'm talking to somebody else
ne m'interromps pas quand je parle à quelqu'un d'autre

please be quiet; I'm watching a good programme
tais-toi, s'il te plaît ; je suis en train de regarder une émission intéressante

he's trying to get the car to start
il essaie de faire démarrer la voiture

not now, I'm thinking
pas maintenant, je réfléchis

Comparez :

I live in London (*présent simple*)
je vis à Londres

I'm living in London (*présent progressif*)
je vis à Londres (maintenant)

La deuxième phrase implique que le locuteur n'est pas installé à Londres de façon permanente et définitive ; ce n'est que temporaire.

ii) Les adverbes de fréquence s'emploient généralement avec le présent simple :

he always goes to bed after midnight
il se couche toujours après minuit

Mais on trouve parfois ces adverbes employés avec le présent progressif. Cet aspect sous-entend que l'action ou le fait en question se produit souvent, mais de manière inattendue ou non intentionnelle. Dans l'exemple suivant, on ne peut employer que le présent progressif avec **forever** :

John is forever forgetting his car keys
John oublie toujours ses clés de voiture

Comparez les deux phrases suivantes :

he always meets her in this pub
il la retrouve ou rejoint toujours dans ce pub

he's always meeting her in this pub
il la rencontre ou croise toujours dans ce pub

Dans le premier exemple, l'aspect simple permet de décrire quelque chose de prévu (= ils se donnent toujours rendez-vous dans ce pub). L'aspect progressif du deuxième exemple permet de deviner qu'il s'agit du verbe **meet** employé dans le sens de "rencontrer par hasard".

Mais dans certains cas, il n'y a pas de différence de sens entre l'aspect simple et l'aspect progressif :

you always say that!	**he always criticizes me**
you're always saying that!	**he's always criticizing me**
tu dis toujours ça !	*il me critique tout le temps*

11 Pour exprimer le passé

a) *Le prétérit*

On emploie le prétérit lorsque l'on veut mettre l'accent sur l'accomplissement d'une action qui s'est déroulée à un moment précis, souvent indiqué par un adverbe :

he caught the train yesterday
il a pris le train hier

he didn't say a word at the meeting
il n'a pas dit un mot pendant la réunion

she sang at the Lyric Opera only a few times
elle ne chanta/n'a chanté à l'Opéra qu'en de rares occasions

Pour les verbes irréguliers au prétérit, voir la liste pp. A63-5.

b) Used to/would

Lorsque l'on souhaite faire référence à un événement habituel dans le passé, on emploie souvent **used to** ou **would** :

on Sundays we used to go to my grandmother's
on Sundays we would go to my grandmother's
le dimanche, on allait chez ma grand-mère

Pour cet emploi de l'auxiliaire **would**, voir p. A57. Pour l'emploi de **used to** et la distinction que l'on peut faire entre les deux, voir p. A61.

c) *Le passé progressif*

Ce temps permet d'insister sur la continuité d'une action ou d'un événement :

what were you doing last night when I called?
qu'est-ce que tu faisais hier soir quand j'ai appelé ?

sorry, could you say that again? I wasn't listening
pardon, est-ce que tu peux répéter ? je n'écoutais pas

she was watching her favourite programme when the phone rang
elle était en train de regarder son émission préférée quand le téléphone a sonné

I was having **dinner** when he came **home**
j'étais en train de dîner quand il est arrivé à la maison

Le passé simple et le passé progressif sont souvent employés pour mettre en valeur le lien qui existe entre deux faits du passé. Le passé progressif s'emploie pour des événements servant de toile de fond à d'autres événements de courte durée, pour lesquels on préfère l'aspect simple. Dans le dernier exemple ci-dessus, une action ponctuelle (he came home) s'oppose à une action qui dure (I was having dinner). Comparez avec cette phrase :

I had **dinner** when he was **coming home**
j'ai dîné pendant qu'il rentrait à la maison

Le sens est différent : l'action qui dure se trouve dans la proposition subordonnée (he was coming home). La proposition principale (I had dinner) fait référence à quelque chose qui a lieu à un moment précis pendant le déroulement d'une action plus longue.

d) *Le present perfect (progressif)*

On emploie le present perfect pour des actions du passé ou des événements qui ont un lien avec le présent :

she has read **a lot of books to prepare for this exam**
(c'est-à-dire qu'elle est prête)
elle a lu beaucoup de livres pour préparer cet examen

Comparez le present perfect avec le prétérit dans les phrases qui suivent :

have you heard **the news this morning?** (c'est encore la matinée)
tu as entendu les informations ce matin ?

did you hear **the news this morning?** (c'est maintenant l'après-midi ou le soir)
tu as entendu les informations ce matin ?

he has **just arrived** (il est là maintenant)
il vient d'arriver

he arrived **a moment ago** (accent sur le moment du passé)
il est arrivé il y a un instant

Mrs Smith **has died** (elle est morte maintenant)
Mme Smith est morte

Mrs Smith **died a rich woman** (au moment où elle est morte, elle était riche)
Mme Smith est morte riche

Pour insister sur le fait qu'une action est continue, on peut employer l'aspect progressif :

I've been living **in this city for ten years**
cela fait dix ans que je vis dans cette ville

Cependant, on peut également employer ici la forme simple dans le même sens :

I've lived **in this city for ten years**

Remarquez que "depuis" se traduit par for devant un nombre, c'est-à-dire lorsqu'il s'agit d'une période de temps, mais par since lorsque l'on fait référence à un moment précis dans le temps. Par ailleurs, le present perfect employé avec for et since se traduit en général par un présent en français :

I've been living **here** since **1991**
je vis ici depuis 1991

I've been waiting **for three hours**/since **5 o'clock**
j'attends depuis trois heures (durée)/depuis 17 heures

e) *Le past perfect (progressif)*

Le past perfect permet de décrire des actions et des événements passés survenus avant d'autres événements passés. Il exprime un passé par rapport à un autre passé. Comparez avec le prétérit :

she had **left** when I **arrived** (*past perfect*)
elle était partie lorsque je suis arrivé

she left **when I arrived** (*prétérit*)
elle est partie lorsque je suis arrivé

L'aspect progressif permet d'insister sur la durée de l'action :

she had been trying **to contact me for hours when I finally turned up**
cela faisait des heures qu'elle essayait de me contacter lorsque je suis enfin arrivé

I had been meaning **to contact him for ages**
cela faisait très longtemps que j'avais l'intention de le contacter

Pour le past perfect dans les propositions conditionnelles, voir p. A53.

12 Pour exprimer le futur

a) Will *et* shall

i) Pour exprimer le futur à la 1ère personne du singulier ou du pluriel, on emploie will ou shall devant le verbe. L'emploi de shall est néanmoins peu fréquent. Will et shall se contractent en 'll, et will not/shall not en won't/shan't :

I will/I'll/I shall **inform Mr Thompson of her decision**
je ferai part de sa décision à M. Thompson

we won't/shan't **be long**
nous n'en avons pas pour longtemps

ii) Aux autres personnes, on emploie will :

he will/he'll **get angry if you tell him this**
il va se mettre en colère si tu lui dis cela

you will/you'll **be surprised when you see him**
vous serez surpris quand vous le verrez

! Remarquez qu'après when l'anglais emploie un présent pour faire référence au futur, comme dans l'exemple ci-dessus. Ceci s'applique aussi pour d'autres conjonctions de temps, par exemple :

I'll do it **as soon as I get home**
je le ferai dès que j'arriverai à la maison

it'll be easy **once you get there**
une fois que tu seras arrivé là-bas, ce sera facile

while you're **in London you should visit the British Museum**
pendant que vous serez à Londres, vous devriez visiter le British Museum

iii) Si le locuteur exprime une intention à la 2ème ou 3ème personne (souvent une promesse ou une menace), on rencontre alors parfois shall, mais cet emploi est aujourd'hui bien moins courant que celui de will :

you shall **get what I promised you**
tu auras ce que je t'ai promis

they shall **pay for this!**
ils vont me le payer !

Si le futur dépend de l'intention ou de la volonté d'une personne autre que le locuteur, on emploie will ('ll) :

he will/he'll **do it, I'm sure**
il le fera, j'en suis sûr

iv) On emploie shall pour faire des propositions, des suggestions :

shall we go?   shall I do it for you?
on y va ?   *tu veux que je te le fasse ?*

Will ne pourrait pas s'employer dans ces deux exemples.

v) On emploie will pour demander à quelqu'un de faire quelque chose :

will you please put your cigarette out?
pouvez-vous éteindre votre cigarette, s'il vous plaît ?

ou pour donner des ordres :

you'll be here at three
soyez ici à trois heures

vi) Pour exprimer l'avenir immédiat, on préférera l'emploi de will à celui de shall. La forme contractée est ici très courante :

leave that, I'll do it　　**try some, you'll like it**
laisse, je vais le faire　　*goûte, tu vas aimer*

I'll have a beer, please
je prendrai une bière, s'il vous plaît

b) *Le futur progressif*

i) Will et shall peuvent être suivis de la forme progressive (be + forme en -ing) si le locuteur veut insister sur la continuité de l'action, sur le fait que l'action sera en cours à un moment précis du futur :

this time next Saturday I'll be sunbathing
samedi prochain à cette heure-ci, je serai en train de me faire bronzer

I'll be marking essays and you'll be looking after the baby
je corrigerai les dissertations et tu t'occuperas du bébé

ii) La forme progressive s'emploie aussi pour indiquer un arrangement préalable :

she'll be giving two concerts in London next week (= she is due to give...)
elle donnera deux concerts à Londres la semaine prochaine

iii) Le futur progressif permet également de formuler des questions sur un ton plus poli, moins direct. Par ailleurs, il y a parfois des nuances différentes entre le futur simple et le futur progressif. Comparez aussi les exemples suivants :

will you speak to him about it? *(simple)*
tu lui en parleras ?

will you be speaking to him about it? *(progressif)*
tu comptes lui en parler ?

L'emploi de la forme progressive dans le second exemple indique que le locuteur ne fait pas une demande directe (comme dans le premier exemple), mais qu'il demande simplement et objectivement si la personne à laquelle il s'adresse a l'intention de "lui en parler".

c) Be going to

i) Il n'y a souvent aucune différence entre be going to et will :

I wonder if this engine is ever going to start (= ... will ever start)
je me demande si le moteur va finir par démarrer

you're going to just love it (= you'll just love it)
tu vas adorer ça

what's he going to do about it? (= what'll he do about it?)
qu'est-ce qu'il a l'intention de faire ?

ii) Be going to est plus courant que will ou shall pour indiquer une intention :

we're going to sell the house after all
en fin de compte, nous allons vendre la maison

he's going to sue us
il va nous intenter un procès

I'm going to go to London tomorrow
je vais aller à Londres demain

iii) On préférera employer be going to plutôt que will lorsque les raisons justifiant les prévisions sont directement liées au présent :

it's going to rain (look at those clouds)
il va pleuvoir (regarde ces nuages)

I know what you're going to say (it's written all over your face)
je sais ce que tu vas dire (ça se lit sur ton visage)

d) *Le présent simple*

i) Comme en français, le présent simple peut exprimer le futur lorsque l'on fait référence à un programme établi, à un événement prévu, à un horaire, etc. :

when does university start?
quand a lieu la rentrée universitaire ?

classes start on 6 October
les cours reprennent le 6 octobre

the train for London leaves at 11 a.m.
le train qui va à Londres part à 11 heures

ii) Lorsque la proposition principale est au futur, on emploie le présent simple dans les propositions subordonnées temporelles (voir a) iii) ci-dessus) ou conditionnelles :

you'll like him when you see him
il te plaira quand tu le verras

if he turns up, will you speak to him?
tu lui en parleras s'il vient ?

Ne confondez pas les propositions de ce type commençant par when et if et les propositions interrogatives indirectes. Dans ces dernières, la forme du verbe est la même que celle du verbe de l'interrogation directe correspondante ; il est donc possible d'employer le futur :

when will they be here? → **I know when they'll be here**
quand vont-ils arriver ?　　*je sais quand ils vont arriver*

will she be there? → **I wonder if she'll be there**
est-ce qu'elle y sera ?　　*je me demande si elle y sera*

e) *Le présent progressif*

i) Le présent progressif s'emploie souvent de façon semblable à be going to pour exprimer une intention :

I'm taking this book with me (= I'm going to take...)
j'emporte ce livre (= je vais emporter...)

what are you doing over Christmas? (= what are you going to do...) *qu'est-ce que tu fais à Noël ? (= qu'est-ce que tu vas faire... ?)*

ii) Le présent progressif peut aussi être employé pour faire référence à un événement organisé ou prévu dans le futur, son emploi étant alors similaire à celui du futur progressif ou du présent simple :

she's giving two concerts in London next week
elle donne deux concerts à Londres la semaine prochaine

the train for London is leaving soon
le train pour Londres part bientôt

f) Be to

On emploie souvent be to pour faire référence à des projets d'avenir spécifiques, en particulier des projets qui dépendent de la décision d'autres personnes :

the President is to visit the disaster zone (pour le style journalistique, voir aussi p. A42)
le président doit se rendre dans la zone sinistrée

we are to be there by ten o'clock (soutenu)
nous devons y être pour dix heures

g) **Be about to**

Be about to exprime le futur très proche :

you are about to meet a great artist
vous êtes sur le point de rencontrer un grand artiste

please take your seats, the play is about to start
veuillez vous asseoir, la pièce va maintenant commencer

Be about to peut aussi s'employer pour exprimer les intentions futures d'une personne :

I'm not about to sign a contract like that!
je ne signerai pas un tel contrat !

h) *Le futur antérieur (progressif)*

On emploie le futur antérieur pour faire référence à une action qui s'achèvera avant une autre action dans le futur :

by the time we get there he will already have left
le temps que nous arrivions, il sera déjà parti

by then we'll have been working on this project for five years (forme progressive)
nous aurons alors travaillé pendant cinq ans sur ce projet

On emploie aussi le futur antérieur pour exprimer des suppositions quant au présent ou au passé :

I expect you'll have been wondering why I asked you here
je suppose que vous vous êtes demandé pourquoi je vous ai convoqué

13 Pour exprimer la condition

Dans les phrases conditionnelles, on exprime la condition dans une proposition subordonnée placée avant ou après la proposition principale et commençant normalement par if :

if the train is late, we'll miss our plane
si le train a du retard, nous raterons notre avion

we'll miss our plane if the train is late
nous raterons notre avion si le train a du retard

Pour les conditions négatives, on emploie parfois unless + forme affirmative (si... ne, à moins que) :

unless the train is on time, we'll miss our plane
if the train isn't on time, we'll miss our plane
si le train n'est pas à l'heure, nous raterons notre avion

Étant donné que l'action de la principale dépend de la condition de la subordonnée, cette action doit être au futur (pour les exceptions voir a) i) ci-dessous).

La forme des verbes varie selon le temps auquel ils font référence et selon le degré de probabilité de la condition.

a) *Pour faire référence au présent/futur*

i) Possibilité vraisemblable :

Le verbe de la proposition subordonnée est au présent ou au present perfect. La proposition principale comprend la construction will + infinitif (quelquefois shall + infinitif à la 1ère personne) :

if you see her, you will not recognize her
si tu la vois, tu ne la reconnaîtras pas

if you are sitting comfortably, we will begin
si vous êtes assis confortablement, nous allons commencer

if you have completed the forms, I will send them off
si vous avez rempli les formulaires, je les enverrai

if he comes back, I shall ask him to leave
s'il revient, je lui demanderai de partir

Il y a trois exceptions importantes :

● Si le verbe de la principale est aussi au présent, on sous-entend une conséquence logique, un résultat automatique ou habituel. Dans ces phrases, if a presque le sens de when(ever) (quand, à chaque fois que) :

if the sun shines, people look happier
quand le soleil brille, les gens ont l'air plus heureux

if you're happy, I'm happy
si ça te va, ça me va

if you don't increase your bid, you don't get the house
si vous n'offrez pas plus, vous n'aurez pas la maison

● Lorsque will est aussi employé dans la subordonnée, le locuteur fait alors référence à la bonne volonté d'une personne ou à son intention de faire quelque chose :

if you will be kind enough to stop singing, we will/shall be able to get some sleep
si vous vouliez bien arrêter de chanter, que nous puissions dormir

if you will insist on driving home, you'll have to stay on soft drinks all night
si tu tiens vraiment à rentrer à la maison en voiture, il faudra ne pas boire de toute la soirée

Lorsque cette forme est employée pour demander à quelqu'un de faire quelque chose, on peut rendre la phrase plus polie en employant would :

if you would be kind enough to stop singing, we would/should be able to get some sleep
si vous aviez la bonté d'arrêter de chanter, nous pourrions dormir

● Lorsque l'on emploie should dans la subordonnée (à toutes les personnes), on sous-entend que la condition est moins probable, qu'elle a moins de chance de se réaliser. Ces propositions avec should sont souvent suivies de l'impératif, comme c'est le cas dans les deux premiers exemples :

if you should see him, ask him to call
au cas où vous le verriez, demandez-lui de m'appeler

if he should turn up, please tell him I want to see him
si jamais il vient, dis-lui que je veux le voir, s'il te plaît

if they should attack you, you will have to fight them
s'ils en venaient à vous attaquer, il vous faudrait vous défendre

Dans un style légèrement plus soutenu, on peut omettre if et faire commencer la phrase par should avec une inversion sujet-auxiliaire :

should the matter arise again, telephone me at once
si le problème devait se présenter de nouveau, téléphonez-moi immédiatement

ii) Possibilité peu probable ou irréelle :

L'expression "possibilité peu probable ou irréelle" signifie que l'on s'attend à ce que la condition ne se réalise pas ou qu'on l'oppose à des faits connus. Le verbe de la proposition subordonnée est au passé ; la principale comprend la construction would + infinitif (ou aussi should + infinitif à la 1ère personne) :

if you saw her, you would not recognize her
si tu la voyais, tu ne la reconnaîtrais pas

if she had a car, she would visit you more often
si elle avait une voiture, elle viendrait te voir plus souvent

if I won that amount of money, I would/should just spend it all
si je gagnais une telle somme d'argent, je dépenserais tout

if the lift was working properly, there would not be so many complaints
si l'ascenseur marchait correctement, il n'y aurait pas autant de plaintes

Néanmoins, ce type de phrase n'exprime pas toujours une possibilité peu probable ou irréelle. Elle présente souvent peu de différence avec la construction du type a) i) ci-dessus :

if you worked harder, you would pass the exam
if you work harder, you will pass the exam
si tu travaillais davantage, tu réussirais ton examen

L'emploi du passé peut donner à la phrase un ton un peu plus amical, moins direct et plus poli.

b) *Pour faire référence au passé*

i) Dans ce cas-là, la condition ne s'est pas réalisée puisque ce qui est exprimé dans la subordonnée ne s'est pas produit. Le verbe de la subordonnée est au past perfect ; la principale comprend la construction **would** + infinitif passé (ou aussi **should** + infinitif passé à la 1ère personne) :

if you had seen her, you would not have recognized her
si tu l'avais vue, tu ne l'aurais pas reconnue

if I had been there, I would/should have ignored him
si j'avais été là, j'aurais fait semblant de ne pas le voir

Dans un style légèrement plus soutenu, on peut omettre if et faire commencer la phrase par had avec une inversion sujet-auxiliaire:

had I been there, I would/should have ignored him

ii) Exceptions :

● Si la proposition principale fait référence à la non-réalisation dans le présent d'une condition dans le passé, on peut aussi employer **would** + infinitif :

if I had studied harder, I would be an engineer today
si j'avais étudié davantage, je serais ingénieur maintenant

● On emploie le passé dans les deux propositions si, comme c'est le cas en a) i) ci-dessus, on sous-entend une conséquence logique, un résultat automatique ou habituel (if = when(ever)) :

if people got ill in those days, they often died
si les gens tombaient malades à cette époque-là, ils mouraient souvent

if they tried to stand up to the boss, they were fired
s'ils essayaient de tenir tête au patron, ils étaient virés

● Si la condition est censée s'être réalisée, les restrictions quant à la concordance des temps indiquées en a) et b) ci-dessus ne s'appliquent plus. Dans ce cas-là, if signifie souvent "comme" ou "puisque". Remarquez, par exemple, la diversité des formes verbales employées dans les propositions principales qui suivent les propositions subordonnées (qui sont toutes au passé) :

if he was rude to you, why did you not walk out?
s'il a été grossier avec toi, pourquoi est-ce que tu n'es pas parti ?

if he was rude to you, why have you still kept in touch?
if he was rude to you, why do you still keep in touch?
s'il a été grossier avec toi, pourquoi est-ce que tu es resté/restes en contact avec lui ?

if he told you that, he was wrong
s'il t'a dit ça, il a eu tort

if he told you that, he is a fool
s'il t'a dit ça, c'est un imbécile

if he told you that, he has broken his promise
s'il t'a dit ça, il a manqué à sa promesse

14 Le subjonctif

Par opposition à l'indicatif, qui est le mode du réel, le subjonctif est le mode du non-réel, exprimant le souhait, l'espoir, la possibilité, etc. (Voir Les modes p. A40).

Le présent du subjonctif est identique par sa forme à l'infinitif (sans **to**) aux trois personnes du singulier et du pluriel. Autrement dit, la seule différence entre les formes du présent du subjonctif et celles du présent de l'indicatif est l'omission du -s à la 3ème personne du singulier.

L'imparfait du subjonctif (ou subjonctif passé) est identique par sa forme au prétérit, sauf pour le verbe **to be** qui devient **were** à la 1ère et 3ème personne du singulier. Cependant, dans le langage de tous les jours, on emploie de préférence **was** (voir aussi b) vi) ci-dessous).

a) *Le subjonctif dans les propositions principales*

Cet emploi du subjonctif est limité à des locutions fixes et idiomatiques exprimant, par exemple, l'espoir ou le souhait :

God save the Queen!   **long live the King!**
vive la Reine !   *vive le Roi !*

Heaven be praised!
Dieu soit loué !

b) *Le subjonctif dans les propositions subordonnées*

i) Dans les propositions conditionnelles, le subjonctif passé est très courant (voir 13a) ii) ci-dessus). L'emploi du présent du subjonctif appartient à un niveau de langue très soutenu ou à un style littéraire :

if this be true, old hopes are born anew *(littéraire)*
si c'était vrai, tous les espoirs renaîtraient

if this were/was true, I'd be so happy *(courant)*
si c'était vrai, je serais vraiment contente

On trouve aussi le subjonctif présent dans l'expression consacrée **if need be** (*s'il le faut, si besoin est*) :

if need be, we can sell the furniture
s'il le faut, nous pouvons vendre les meubles

Remarquez aussi l'emploi du subjonctif présent dans les tournures concessives, avec l'inversion sujet-verbe :

they are all interrogated, be they friend or foe *(littéraire)*
ils sont tous interrogés, qu'ils soient amis ou ennemis

ii) Les propositions comparatives, introduites par **as if** ou **as though**, contiennent souvent, mais pas dans tous les cas, un subjonctif passé :

he treats me as if I was/were a child
il me traite comme si j'étais un gamin

iii) Le subjonctif passé est employé après **if only** et dans les propositions compléments d'objet direct qui suivent **wish** et **had rather**. Toutes ces propositions expriment le souhait ou le désir :

if only we had a bigger house, life would be perfect
si seulement nous avions une maison plus grande, tout serait parfait

are you going abroad this year? – I wish I were/was
est-ce que tu pars à l'étranger cette année ? – si seulement je pouvais !

where's your passport? – I wish I knew
où est ton passeport ? – si je le savais !

do you want me to tell you? – I'd rather you didn't
tu veux que je te le dise ? – je n'aime mieux pas !

iv) Dans un langage soutenu ou juridique, on rencontre parfois le présent du subjonctif dans les propositions compléments d'objet direct qui suivent les expressions impersonnelles ("il est souhaitable", "il est important", etc.) ou les verbes indiquant une suggestion ou un souhait :

it is important that he take steps immediately
il est important qu'il prenne immédiatement des mesures

it is imperative that this matter be discussed further
il est impératif de discuter davantage de cette affaire

we propose that the clause be extended to cover such eventualities
nous proposons que la clause soit élargie pour couvrir ces éventualités

Dans ces propositions, le subjonctif est d'un emploi plus courant en anglais américain qu'en anglais britannique et il n'est pas rare de le rencontrer en dehors du langage des négociations ou du langage juridique. En anglais britannique, on préférera l'emploi de should + infinitif :

we suggest that the system (should) be changed
nous suggérons que le système soit changé

I am adamant that this (should) be put to the vote
j'insiste pour que cela soit soumis au vote

it is vital that he (should) start as soon as possible
il est primordial qu'il commence aussi vite que possible

v) On emploie aussi le subjonctif passé après it's time, lorsque le locuteur veut insister sur le fait que quelque chose devrait être fait :

it's time we spoke to him
il est temps que nous lui parlions

it's high time they stopped that
il est grand temps qu'ils arrêtent

Comparez avec l'emploi de l'infinitif qui ne fait qu'exprimer l'opportunité du moment :

it's time to speak to him about it
c'est le moment de lui en parler

vi) If I was/if I were

Les confusions sont fréquentes quant à l'emploi correct de if I was/if I were.

Lorsque la condition à laquelle on fait référence n'est en aucun cas une condition irréelle, on ne peut employer que if I was :

if I was mistaken about it then I can only apologize
si je me suis trompé, eh bien je ne peux que m'excuser

Le locuteur ne met pas en cause le fait qu'il se soit trompé. Comparez avec la phrase suivante :

if I were mistaken about it, surely I would have realized
si je m'étais trompé, je m'en serais certainement aperçu

Ici, le locuteur émet un doute quant à la réalité de l'erreur, d'où l'emploi du subjonctif were. Mais dans un niveau de langue moins soutenu, on pourrait également employer was dans cette phrase.

15 Un emploi particulier du passé

Nous avons vu dans les sections 13 et 14 comment le subjonctif passé peut faire référence au présent dans des propositions condition-

nelles ou autres. Outre ces emplois du subjonctif passé, le passé peut faire référence au présent dans les propositions principales exprimant une attitude plus hésitante et donc plus polie et respectueuse. Ainsi :

did you want to see me?
vous vouliez me voir ?

est plus poli ou moins direct que :

do you want to see me?
vous voulez me voir ?

Remarquez aussi l'emploi du passé progressif dans l'expression I was wondering, qui permet de demander quelque chose de manière plus polie :

I was wondering if you could help me do this (= I wonder if you could help me do this)
est-ce que vous pourriez m'aider à faire cela ?

L'expression I was hoping, qui permet aussi de formuler indirectement et poliment une requête, n'a pas de construction correspondante au présent :

I was hoping you could help me
est-ce que vous pourriez m'aider ?

16 La voix passive

Pour les différences de forme entre la voix active et la voix passive, voir p. A40.

a) *Le passif direct et le passif indirect*

Dans la phrase à la voix active :

they sent him another bill
ils lui ont envoyé une autre facture

another bill est le complément d'objet direct et him, le complément d'objet indirect. Si dans une construction correspondante à la voix passive, le complément d'objet direct de la phrase à la voix active devient le sujet de la phrase à la voix passive, on a alors un "passif direct" :

another bill was sent to him
une autre facture lui a été envoyée

Un "passif indirect" aurait pour sujet le complément d'objet indirect de la phrase à la voix active :

he was sent another bill
on lui a envoyé une autre facture

b) *Le passif d'état et le passif d'action*

Dans la phrase suivante, le verbe exprime un état :

the shop is closed
la boutique est fermée

tandis que, dans l'exemple suivant, il exprime une action :

the shop is closed by the manager at the end of the day
la boutique est fermée par le gérant à la fin de la journée

Dans la première phrase, le verbe est appelé "verbe d'état" ; dans la deuxième phrase, il est appelé "verbe d'action". C'est le contexte qui nous renseigne et non la forme. La forme du verbe reste la même. L'absence de formes distinctes peut parfois donner lieu à des ambiguïtés, comme par exemple :

his neck was broken when they lifted him

Cette phrase signifie soit "son cou était cassé quand ils l'ont soulevé" (passif d'état), soit "son cou s'est cassé quand ils l'ont soulevé" (passif d'action). Cependant, si l'on souhaite insister sur le passif d'action (souvent plus vivant), on peut employer get comme auxiliaire à la place de be, notamment dans le langage courant :

his neck got broken when they lifted him
il a eu le cou cassé quand ils l'ont soulevé

they finally got caught
ils ont fini par se faire prendre

On peut aussi employer le verbe have pour exprimer un passif d'action :

he had his neck broken when they lifted him
il a eu le cou cassé quand ils l'ont soulevé

they've had their house burgled three times
ils se sont fait cambrioler trois fois

c) *Voix passive ou voix active ?*

i) Si la personne qui fait l'action est moins importante que l'action elle-même, on préfère souvent la voix passive à la voix active :

his invitation was refused
son invitation a été refusée

Ici, d'après le locuteur, l'identité de la personne qui refuse l'invitation n'a pas d'importance. Ce qui est important, c'est le fait qu'elle ait été refusée.

Dans certains cas, notamment dans le domaine scientifique, on emploie de très nombreuses tournures passives parce que l'on considère que mentionner l'agent ou celui qui fait l'action manque d'objectivité :

the experiment was conducted in darkness (*objectivité*)
l'expérience a été effectuée dans le noir

I conducted the experiment in darkness (*subjectivité*)
j'ai effectué l'expérience dans le noir

ii) De nombreux verbes peuvent également s'employer à la voix active, tout en ayant un sens passif :

the theatre runs at a profit (= the theatre is run at a profit)
le théâtre fait des bénéfices

her eyes filled with tears (= her eyes were filled with tears)
elle avait les larmes aux yeux

Dans ces deux exemples, on pourrait tout aussi bien employer les formes passives données entre parenthèses. Mais certains verbes intransitifs à sens passif ne peuvent pas s'employer d'une autre manière :

a cloth which feels soft   **it flies beautifully**
un tissu qui est doux au toucher   *il se pilote très bien*

silk blouses do not wash well
les chemisiers en soie ne se lavent pas bien

this essay reads better than your last one
cette dissertation se lit mieux que la dernière que vous avez écrite

where is the film showing?   **he photographs well**
dans quel cinéma passe ce film ?   *il est photogénique*

iii) On trouve également des infinitifs à sens passif dans les constructions du type there is + nom/pronom + infinitif :

when we get home there'll be suitcases to unpack
quand nous rentrerons à la maison, il y aura les valises à défaire

there was plenty to eat
il y avait beaucoup de choses à manger

have you got anything to wash?
est-ce que tu as quelque chose à laver ?

Dans certains cas, on peut employer indifféremment l'infinitif actif ou l'infinitif passif :

there's nothing else to say/to be said
il n'y a rien d'autre à dire

is there anything to gain/to be gained from it?
est-ce qu'il y a quelque chose à y gagner ?

there is work to do/to be done
il y a du travail à faire

Mais lorsque ces constructions suivent les pronoms **something, anything, nothing**, il peut y avoir une différence entre l'infinitif actif (à sens passif) et l'infinitif passif de **do**. Comparez par exemple :

there is always something to do
on trouve toujours à s'occuper

there is always something to be done
il y a toujours du travail à faire

iv) "On"

Le passif est bien plus employé en anglais qu'en français. Le français préfère souvent une construction avec le pronom personnel indéfini "on" :

he was spotted leaving the bar
on l'a vu sortir du bar

that's already been done
on l'a déjà fait/ça a déjà été fait

I hadn't been told that
on ne m'avait pas dit ça

17 Be, have, do

a) Be

i) Be s'emploie comme auxiliaire avec le participe passé pour former le passif (voir p. A40 et section 16 ci-dessus). Be peut parfois remplacer have en tant qu'auxiliaire pour l'aspect "perfect" (ou passé), comme dans :

are you finished? (= have you finished?)
est-ce que tu as fini ?

his voice is gone (= his voice has gone)
il a une extinction de voix

Dans ces cas-là, on insiste particulièrement sur l'état présent plutôt que sur l'action.

ii) Comme les autres auxiliaires modaux, be n'est pas accompagné de do dans les négations et les interrogations (**he isn't Spanish, is he Spanish?**, etc.). Mais lorsque be se comporte comme un verbe indépendant et non pas comme un auxiliaire, on emploie do dans les impératifs à la forme négative :

don't be silly
ne dis pas n'importe quoi

iii) Lorsque be est un verbe ordinaire, et non un auxiliaire, il ne s'emploie à l'aspect progressif que lorsqu'il fait uniquement référence au comportement. Comparez :

you are funny   **you are being funny**
tu es drôle (= de nature)   *tu es drôle (= en ce moment)*

he is annoying   **he is being annoying**
il est énervant   *il devient énervant*

b) Have

i) Have est employé avec le participe passé pour former l'aspect "perfect" (voir p. A39).

En tant que verbe ordinaire, il permet parfois d'exprimer une activité, quelque chose dont on fait l'expérience (des difficultés, etc.) ou des impressions que l'on ressent, comme dans les expressions idiomatiques :

to have dinner   **to have a shower**
dîner   *prendre une douche*

to have a chat   **to have a good time**
bavarder   *s'amuser*

A55

to have difficulty (doing something)
avoir du mal (à faire quelque chose)

Lorsque have n'exprime pas une activité, il fait normalement référence à la possession, à un état ou à quelque chose de prévu :

to have a farm   **to have an appointment**
avoir une ferme   *avoir un rendez-vous*

to have toothache
avoir mal aux dents

to have time (for something/to do something)
avoir le temps (pour quelque chose/de faire quelque chose)

On désignera le verbe have sous le nom de have 1 lorsque son emploi correspond aux exemples du premier type et de have 2 lorsqu'il est employé comme dans les exemples du deuxième type.

ii) Have 1 :

● Il se comporte comme les verbes ordinaires normaux dans les interrogations et dans les négations (ainsi que dans les question-tags), c'est-à-dire qu'il est accompagné de do :

did you have the day off yesterday?
est-ce que tu étais en congé hier ?

we don't have fun any more
on ne s'amuse plus tellement maintenant

we had a marvellous time, didn't we?
nous avons vraiment passé un très bon moment, n'est-ce pas ?

● Il peut s'employer à l'aspect progressif :

he telephoned as we were having lunch
il a téléphoné pendant que nous déjeunions

I'm having problems with Carol these days
j'ai des problèmes avec Carol en ce moment

iii) Have 2 :

● Au lieu de have 2, l'anglais britannique emploie souvent have got, notamment à l'oral, et surtout au présent :

he has/he has got/he's got a large garden
il a un grand jardin

Au passé, on emploie normalement had ou used to have, cette dernière forme insistant davantage sur l'idée de possession, sur la répétition ou l'habitude :

they all had flu in July last year
ils ont tous eu la grippe en juillet l'année dernière

he had/used to have a large garden once
autrefois, il avait un grand jardin

we had/used to have lots of problems in those days
à cette époque-là, nous avions beaucoup de problèmes

● Dans les interrogations, le sujet et have peuvent être inversés :

have you any other children?
avez-vous d'autres enfants ?

Dans les négations, not peut s'employer sans do :

he hasn't a garden
il n'a pas de jardin

On considère parfois ces phrases comme appartenant à un niveau de langue plutôt soutenu, et dans le langage de tous les jours, on préfère employer have... got ou une construction avec do :

have you got/do you have any other children?
he hasn't got/doesn't have a garden

La tournure en do, qui était avant un emploi exclusivement américain, est maintenant très courante, notamment lorsque l'on fait référence à quelque chose d'habituel, de permanent. Comparez :

have you got/do you have any sweets?
est-ce que tu as des bonbons ?

do you always have sweets in the cupboard?
est-ce que tu as toujours des bonbons dans ton placard ?

De même :

have you got/do you have a pain in your chest?
est-ce que vous ressentez une douleur dans la poitrine ?

do you frequently have a pain in your chest?
est-ce que vous ressentez souvent une douleur dans la poitrine ?

Remarquez aussi que les deux auxiliaires sont possibles dans les réponses à la forme négative :

have you a minute? – no, I haven't
have you a minute? – no, I don't
tu as une minute ? – non

Dans les question-tags après have, on peut employer have ou do puisque, comme nous l'avons vu, have peut s'employer avec ou sans do dans les interrogations. Do est particulièrement courant au passé, mais on le trouve aussi au présent :

he has a dog, hasn't/doesn't he?
il a un chien, n'est-ce pas ?

they had a large garden once, hadn't they/didn't they?
ils avaient un grand jardin autrefois, n'est-ce pas ?

Mais après have got, on ne peut employer que have dans les questions-tags :

he's got a dog, hasn't he?
il a un chien, n'est-ce pas ?

● On ne peut employer l'aspect progressif avec have 2 que lorsqu'on fait référence au futur. Ainsi :

they are having a baby

ne signifie en aucun cas "ils ont un bébé", mais "ils vont avoir un bébé".

iv) L'emploi causatif de have :

Le verbe have est employé dans la construction du type "faire faire quelque chose", qui se forme avec have + complément d'objet direct + participe passé. Par exemple :

they're having a conservatory built
ils se font construire une véranda

could you have these photocopied?
est-ce que vous pouvez faire photocopier cela ?

I'll have it done immediately
je vais le faire faire immédiatement

we'll have to have it fixed
il va falloir que nous le fassions réparer

Remarquez que get peut s'employer à la place de have dans tous ces exemples.

Cette construction n'a pas toujours le sens littéral de "faire faire quelque chose". Dans l'exemple suivant, la construction signifie simplement "demandez-lui d'entrer" :

Mr Braithwaite is here – ah, have him come in
M. Braithwaite est là – ah, faites-le entrer

On emploie aussi **have** ou **get** + infinitif pour dire "faire faire quelque chose à quelqu'un" :

I'll have the kitchen send it up to your room, madam
I'll get the kitchen to send it up to your room, madam
je vais demander à la cuisine de vous le monter dans votre chambre, madame

Notez que l'infinitif après **have** est employé sans **to**, ce qui n'est pas le cas de **get**.

v) Constructions à la voix passive :

Le verbe **have** s'emploie aussi pour former un type de construction passive, notamment lorsque l'on sous-entend que le sujet de la phrase a souffert d'une manière ou d'une autre (voir aussi 16b)) :

he's had all his money stolen
il s'est fait voler tout son argent

c) **Do**

Nous avons vu l'emploi de **do** dans les interrogations et les négations dans les sections 8 et 9 de ce chapitre. Pour son emploi dans les autres cas d'inversion, voir **La structure de la phrase**, p. A78.

i) **Do** emphatique :

Dans les phrases qui ne sont ni interrogatives ni négatives, on peut marquer l'emphase en employant l'auxiliaire **do** (que l'on accentue à l'oral) devant le verbe principal :

oh, I do like your new jacket!
oh, j'aime beaucoup ta nouvelle veste !

do try to keep still !
essaye de rester tranquille !

he doesn't know any German but he does know a few words of French
il ne comprend pas l'allemand, mais par contre il connaît quelques mots de français

I didn't manage to get tickets for Saturday night, but I did get some for Monday
je n'ai pas réussi à avoir de billets pour samedi soir, mais j'en ai pris pour lundi

Et le verbe ordinaire **do** (*faire*) peut s'employer avec **do** en tant qu'auxiliaire emphatique. Mais cette construction, qui n'est pas très élégante, est assez rare :

we don't do everything but what we do do, we do well
nous ne faisons pas tout, mais ce que nous faisons, nous le faisons bien

ii) **Do** pour remplacer le verbe :

L'auxiliaire **do** peut s'employer seul lorsque le verbe principal a déjà été énoncé. On pourrait répéter à la place le verbe principal précédé de l'auxiliaire (voir l'emploi emphatique ci-dessus) ou parfois sans l'auxiliaire :

she never drinks! – oh yes, she does (= oh yes, she does drink)
elle ne boit jamais ! – bien sûr que si !

can I help myself to another cream cake? – please do (= please do help yourself)
est-ce que je peux avoir un autre gâteau à la crème ? – mais je vous en prie !

do you both agree? – I do, but she doesn't (= I agree, but she doesn't)
vous êtes tous les deux d'accord ? – moi oui, mais pas elle

Voir aussi la section traitant des question-tags (p. A47).

18 Les auxiliaires modaux

Ce sont les auxiliaires **will–would**, **shall–should**, **can–could**, **may–might**, **must–had to**, **ought to**.

a) Will–would

Les formes négatives contractées sont **won't–wouldn't**.

i) Pour l'emploi du futur, voir pp. A50-2.

ii) Pour les phrases au conditionnel, voir pp. A52-3.

iii) Pour donner des ordres, exprimer l'obligation ou la détermination :

you will do as you are told!   will you stop that!
tu feras ce qu'on te dit !   arrête ça !

new recruits will report to headquarters on Tuesday
les jeunes recrues se présenteront au quartier général mardi

I will not stand for this!   I will be obeyed!
je ne le supporterai pas !   je veux qu'on m'obéisse !

Dans ces phrases, **will** apporte des nuances différentes ; il fait plus qu'exprimer un simple futur.

iv) Pour faire appel, sur un ton plutôt cérémonieux, aux souvenirs ou aux connaissances de quelqu'un :

you will recall last week's discussion about the purchase of a computer
vous vous souvenez certainement de notre discussion de la semaine dernière concernant l'achat d'un ordinateur

you will all know that the company has just been sold
vous savez certainement tous que l'entreprise vient d'être vendue

v) Pour faire des suppositions :

there's the telephone, Mary! – oh, that will be John
le téléphone sonne, Mary ! – oh, ça doit être John

they'll be there by now
ils doivent être arrivés maintenant

how old is he now? – he'll be about 45
quel âge a-t-il maintenant ? – il doit avoir à peu près 45 ans

vi) Pour insister sur la notion de capacité, d'inclination naturelle ou inhérente, d'habitude ou de comportement caractéristique :

cork will float on water   the car won't start
le liège flotte sur l'eau   la voiture ne veut pas démarrer

the Arts Centre will hold about 300 people
le centre culturel peut contenir environ 300 personnes

John will sit playing quietly on his own for hours
John peut rester tranquillement assis à jouer tout seul pendant des heures

it's so annoying, he will keep interrupting! (accent sur **will** à l'oral)
c'est énervant, il n'arrête pas de m'interrompre !

De même **would**, pour faire référence au passé :

when he was little, John would sit playing quietly on his own for hours
quand il était petit, John restait tranquillement assis à jouer tout seul pendant des heures

she created a scene in public – she would!
elle a fait une scène en public – c'est bien elle !

vii) Pour poser des questions ou proposer quelque chose de manière légèrement soutenue :

will you have another cake? – thank you, I will
voulez-vous un autre gâteau ? – oui, merci, je veux bien

won't you try some of these?
vous ne voulez pas y goûter ?

viii) Pour demander à quelqu'un de faire quelque chose :

will you move your car, please?
est-ce que vous pouvez déplacer votre voiture, s'il vous plaît ?

On peut poser la même question de façon légèrement plus polie et moins directe avec **would** :

would you move your car, please?
est-ce que vous pourriez déplacer votre voiture, s'il vous plaît ?

b) **Shall–should**

Les formes négatives contractées sont **shan't–shouldn't**.

i) Pour **shall** exprimant le futur, voir pp. A50-2.

ii) Pour les phrases au conditionnel, voir pp. A52-3.

iii) Pour **should**, équivalent du subjonctif, voir p. A54.

iv) Dans le langage juridique ou officiel, **shall** (uniquement) s'emploie fréquemment pour exprimer une obligation. Ce sens de **shall** est très semblable à celui de **must** (voir p. A60) :

the committee shall consist of six members
le comité sera constitué de six membres

the contract shall be subject to English law
le contrat sera régi par la loi anglaise

v) Pour exprimer une obligation, souvent morale (uniquement **should**) :

you should lose some weight
tu devrais perdre du poids

he shouldn't be allowed to
il ne devrait pas y être autorisé

you really should see this film
tu devrais essayer de voir ce film

something was not quite as it should be
il y avait quelque chose qui n'allait pas

what do you think I should do?
à ton avis, qu'est-ce que je devrais faire ?

vi) Pour exprimer la déduction, la probabilité (uniquement **should**) :

it's ten o'clock, they should be back any minute
il est dix heures, ils devraient rentrer d'un moment à l'autre

John should have put up those shelves by now
John devrait maintenant avoir fini d'installer ces étagères

are they there? – I don't know, but they should be
ils sont là ? – je ne sais pas, mais ils devraient

vii) Pour donner son avis de manière hésitante (uniquement **should**) :

I should just like to say that...
j'aimerais simplement dire que...

I should hardly call him a great intellectual but...
je ne dirais pas vraiment que c'est un grand intellectuel, mais...

will he agree? – I shouldn't think so
est-ce qu'il sera d'accord ? – je ne pense pas

viii) **Should** est souvent employé pour faire référence à la notion (par opposition à la réalité concrète) d'une action. Cet emploi de **should** est parfois qualifié de "putatif" :

that she should want to take early retirement is quite understandable
il est tout à fait compréhensible qu'elle veuille prendre sa retraite anticipée

Comparez ce dernier exemple avec :

it is quite understandable that she wanted to take early retirement
il est tout à fait compréhensible qu'elle ait voulu prendre sa retraite anticipée

Dans le premier cas, la proposition subordonnée est au présent. Dans le second cas, elle est au passé.

Il est important de remarquer que ce **should** est neutre pour ce qui est du temps. Le premier exemple pourrait tout aussi bien faire référence au passé (**she has taken early retirement**) ou au futur (**she will be taking early retirement**) suivant le contexte. Le second exemple ne peut bien sûr que faire référence au passé.

L'emploi putatif peut être comparé à l'emploi de **should** après les tournures impersonnelles ou les verbes indiquant la suggestion, le souhait ou l'ordre, dont il est question dans la section sur le subjonctif, p. A54.

Dans l'exemple ci-dessus, l'emploi putatif de **should** est apparu dans une proposition subordonnée, mais on le trouve aussi dans des propositions principales, qui expriment souvent l'agacement, la surprise, etc. :

where have I put my glasses? – how should I know?
où est-ce que j'ai mis mes lunettes ? – comment veux-tu que je le sache ?

as we were sitting there, who should walk by but George !
nous étions assis là, et devine qui est passé ?... George !

c) **Can–could**

Les formes négatives contractées sont **can't–couldn't**. La forme négative non contractée de **can** est **cannot**.

i) Pour exprimer la capacité, le fait de pouvoir faire quelque chose (= **be able to**) :

I can't afford it   **I can swim**
je ne peux pas me le permettre   *je sais nager*

when I was young, I could swim for hours
quand j'étais jeune, je pouvais nager pendant des heures

Ce dernier exemple est au passé. Cependant, dans les propositions conditionnelles, **could** + infinitif fait référence au présent et au futur (comparez avec **would** dans la section 13 p. A53) :

you could do a lot better if you'd only try
tu pourrais faire bien mieux si seulement tu faisais un effort

Be able to (*pouvoir, être capable de*) permet d'exprimer la capacité à d'autres temps :

I'll be able to tell you the answer tomorrow
je pourrai te donner la réponse demain

I've never been able to understand her
je n'ai jamais pu la comprendre

ii) Pour demander ou donner la permission :

can/could I have a sweet? **you can come with me**
je peux avoir un bonbon ?   *tu peux venir avec moi*

Remarquez que **could** fait autant référence au présent ou au futur que **can** lorsque l'on demande la permission de faire quelque chose. La seule différence réside dans le fait que **could** est un peu plus poli.

Mais **could** peut s'employer pour exprimer une permission dans un contexte au passé :

for some reason we couldn't smoke in the waiting room before, but now we can
pour une raison que j'ignore, on ne pouvait pas fumer avant dans le salon, mais maintenant on peut

Be allowed to (*pouvoir, être autorisé à*) permet d'exprimer la permission à tous les temps :

we weren't allowed to smoke in the lounge
nous n'avions pas le droit de fumer dans le salon

will they be allowed to change the rules?
est-ce qu'ils auront le droit de changer les règles ?

Lorsqu'ils signifient "avoir le droit de", **may** est plus poli et plus soutenu que **can** (voir d) i) ci-dessous).

iii) Pour exprimer la possibilité :

what shall we do tonight? – we can/could watch a film
qu'est-ce qu'on va faire ce soir ? – on pourrait regarder un film

Là encore, remarquez que **could** ne fait pas référence au passé, mais au présent ou au futur. Pour faire référence au passé, on doit employer **could** + infinitif passé :

instead of going out, we could have watched a DVD
au lieu de sortir, nous aurions pu regarder un DVD

I could have (could've) gone there if I'd wanted to, but I didn't
j'aurais pu y aller si j'avais voulu, mais je n'en avais pas envie

Could et **may** sont parfois interchangeables lorsqu'ils expriment la possibilité, l'éventualité :

you could/may be right
vous avez peut-être raison

Mais il existe parfois une différence importante entre **can** et **may** : **can** indique souvent une conséquence logique ou un simple fait, tandis que **may** exprime l'incertitude, le hasard ou la probabilité d'un événement :

(a) **your comments can be overheard**
on peut entendre vos remarques

(b) **your comments may be overheard**
on pourrait entendre vos remarques

En (a), il est possible d'entendre les remarques (parce qu'elles sont faites à voix haute, par exemple), mais cela ne signifie pas forcément que quelqu'un les entendra. En (b), il existe une probabilité, une chance que les remarques soient réellement entendues.

La différence est la même dans les propositions à la forme négative :

he can't have heard us (= it is impossible for him to have heard us)
il ne peut pas nous avoir entendus

he may not have heard us (= it is possible that he did not hear us)
il se peut qu'il ne nous ait pas entendus

iv) Pour faire des suggestions (uniquement **could**) :

you could try a supermarket
tu peux essayer d'aller voir au supermarché

they could always sell their second house
ils peuvent toujours vendre leur maison secondaire

v) Pour faire des reproches (uniquement **could**) :

you could have let us know!
tu aurais pu nous le dire !

he could have warned us!
il aurait pu nous prévenir !

d) May–might

La forme négative contractée **mayn't** exprimant la "permission négative" (= l'interdiction) n'est pas très courante. On emploie à la place **may not** ou **must not/mustn't** ou encore **can't**. La forme négative contractée de **might** est **mightn't**, mais elle ne s'emploie pas pour exprimer l'interdiction.

i) Pour demander ou donner la permission (ou exprimer l'interdiction) :

you may sit down
vous pouvez vous asseoir

may I open a window? – no, you may not!
est-ce que je peux ouvrir une fenêtre ? – non, pas question !

Comparez avec **can** dans c) ii) ci-dessus. **May** est plus soutenu que **can**.

Remarquez que l'on emploie **may not** dans les réponses aux questions commençant par l'auxiliaire **may** (voir le dernier exemple ci-dessus), mais que dans les simples phrases négatives, on emploiera en général **must not/mustn't** :

you must not/mustn't open the windows in here
tu ne dois pas ouvrir les fenêtres ici

L'emploi de **might** pour exprimer la permission est plus poli que **can**, **could** ou **may** :

I wonder if I might have another glass of wine
pourrais-je avoir un autre verre de vin, s'il vous plaît ?

might I suggest we adjourn the meeting?
puis-je suggérer que nous ajournions la réunion ?

Notez que **might** fait référence au présent et au futur. Il s'utilise très rarement au passé lorsqu'il est employé dans une proposition principale. Comparez :

he then asked if he might smoke (*emploi soutenu de* **might** *dans la proposition subordonnée*)

he then asked if he was allowed to smoke
il a alors demandé s'il pouvait fumer

et : **he wasn't allowed to smoke**
il n'avait pas le droit de fumer, il ne pouvait pas fumer

On ne peut pas employer **might** dans le dernier exemple. **Might** ne s'emploie dans une proposition principale au passé que dans certaines tournures de phrase, par exemple après l'adverbe **nor** (attention à l'inversion sujet-auxiliaire après cet adverbe ; voir aussi p. A78) :

in those days we were told not to drink; nor might we smoke or be out after 10 o'clock
à cette époque, nous n'avions pas le droit de boire, pas plus que de fumer ou de rentrer après dix heures

Une manière plus courante et moins littéraire de formuler cette phrase serait :

in those days we were told not to drink; nor were we allowed to smoke or be out after 10 o'clock

ii) Pour exprimer la possibilité :

it may/might rain	**they may/might be right**
il va peut-être pleuvoir	*il se peut qu'ils aient raison*

it may not/mightn't be so easy as you think
ce ne sera peut-être pas aussi facile que vous le pensez

she may/might have left already
elle est peut-être déjà partie

Might exprime généralement une possibilité moins forte.

iii) Pour exprimer la surprise, l'amusement ou l'agacement, comme dans les tournures idiomatiques suivantes :

and who may/might you be?
à qui ai-je l'honneur ?

and who may/might you be to give out orders?
et pour qui est-ce que tu te prends pour donner des ordres ?

iv) Pour formuler des suggestions (uniquement **might**) :

you might help me dry the dishes
tu pourrais m'aider à essuyer la vaisselle

well, you might at least try!
tu pourrais au moins essayer, enfin !

you might have a look at chapter 2 for next Wednesday
vous voudrez bien lire le chapitre 2 pour mercredi prochain

he might be a little less abrupt
il pourrait être un peu moins brusque

v) Pour faire des reproches (uniquement **might**) :

you might have warned us what would happen!
vous auriez pu nous prévenir de ce qui allait se produire !

he might have tried to stop it!
il aurait pu essayer d'arrêter cela !

vi) Pour exprimer des souhaits :

may the best man win!
que le meilleur gagne !

may you be forgiven for telling such lies!
que le bon Dieu te pardonne de tels mensonges !

might I be struck dumb if I tell a lie!
que le diable m'emporte si je mens !

Attention à bien respecter l'ordre des mots : auxiliaire-sujet-verbe.

Cet usage est normalement réservé à des expressions consacrées (comme dans les deux premiers exemples) ou considérées comme étant d'un style quelque peu ampoulé ou littéraire (comme dans le dernier).

e) **Must–had to**

La forme négative contractée de **must** est **mustn't**. Pour les formes contractées de **have**, voir p. A66.

i) Pour exprimer l'obligation :

you must try harder
il faut que tu fasses un effort

I must stop spending so much money
je dois arrêter de dépenser autant d'argent

Au passé, on utilise **had to**. On ne peut employer **must** qu'au discours indirect passé, mais même dans ce cas, **had to** est beaucoup plus courant :

you said the other day that you had to/must clean out the garden shed
tu as dit l'autre jour qu'il fallait que tu nettoies la cabane du jardin

Au présent, on peut aussi employer **have to**, ou dans un style plus familier **have got to**. La différence entre **must** et **have (got) to** réside généralement dans le fait que **must** exprime des sentiments personnels d'obligation ou de contrainte tandis que **have (got) to** est plus souvent employé lorsqu'une obligation extérieure est sous-entendue. Comparez :

I must go to the dentist (= I have toothache, etc.)
il faut que j'aille chez le dentiste (= j'ai mal aux dents, etc.)▮

I have (got) to go to the dentist (= I have an appointment)
je dois aller chez le dentiste (= j'ai rendez-vous)

ii) Pour exprimer l'interdiction ou l'absence d'obligation (formes négatives) :

On ne peut employer **must not/mustn't** que pour exprimer l'interdiction (= "une obligation de ne pas faire quelque chose") :

we mustn't park the car here (= we're not allowed to park here)
nous ne devons pas nous garer ici (= nous n'avons pas le droit de nous garer ici)

you mustn't take so many pills (= do not take so many pills)
il ne faut pas que tu prennes autant de comprimés

Don't have to ou **haven't got to** sont employés pour indiquer, non pas l'interdiction, mais l'absence d'obligation c'est-à-dire qu'il n'est pas nécessaire ou obligatoire de faire quelque chose :

we don't have to park here, we could always drive ▮ little further
nous ne sommes pas obligés de nous garer ici, nous pouvons aller un peu plus loin

you don't have to take so many pills (= you needn'▮ take…)
tu n'as pas besoin de prendre autant de comprimés

we haven't got to be there before nine
nous n'avons pas besoin d'y être avant neuf heures

iii) Pour exprimer la déduction, la probabilité :

if they're over 65, they must be entitled to benefits
s'ils ont plus de 65 ans, ils doivent avoir droit à des prestations

they must have been surprised to see you
ils ont dû être surpris de te voir

hello, you must be Susan	**you must be joking**
bonjour, vous devez être Susan	*tu veux rire !*

Have to s'emploie aussi souvent dans ce sens :

you have to be kidding!
tu veux rire !

de même que **have got to**, notamment en anglais britannique :

well if she said so, it's got to be true (it's = it has)
si elle l'a dit, c'est que c'est vrai

À la forme négative, on emploie **can** :

he can't be that old!
il ne peut pas être si vieux que ça !

f) **Ought to**

La forme négative contractée est **oughtn't to**. L'infinitif placé après **ought** est précédé de **to**, contrairement aux autres auxiliaires modaux.

i) Pour exprimer l'obligation :

Ought to a le même sens que **should** lorsqu'ils expriment▮ l'obligation :

I ought to be going now
il faudrait que je m'en aille maintenant

I know I really ought to, but I don't want to
je sais bien que je devrais, mais je n'en ai pas envie

you oughtn't to **speak to her like that**
tu ne devrais pas lui parler de cette façon

Mais **ought to** est moins fort que **must** dans ce sens. Comparez :

I must/have to avoid fatty foods (*obligation ferme ou nécessité*)
je dois éviter les matières grasses

I ought to avoid fatty foods (*obligation moins stricte*)
je devrais éviter les matières grasses

Should remplace normalement **ought to** dans les questions :

should you visit your mother every Sunday?
est-ce que tu dois aller voir ta mère tous les dimanches ?

ii) Pour exprimer la déduction, la probabilité :

they ought to have reached the summit by now
ils devraient maintenant avoir atteint le sommet

£20 ought to be enough
20 livres, ça devrait suffire

Comparez **ought to** et **must** exprimant la probabilité :

if they have three cars and a holiday home in France, they must be rich (*déduction logique*)
s'ils ont trois voitures et une résidence secondaire en France, ils doivent être riches

if they have three cars and a holiday home in France, they ought to be happy (*prévision ou probabilité logique – ou obligation morale*)
s'ils ont trois voitures et une résidence secondaire en France, ils devraient être heureux

g) **Used to**

Used to (pour exprimer une habitude ou un fait durable dans le passé) peut être considéré comme une sorte de semi-auxiliaire, puisque l'emploi de **do** est normalement facultatif dans les phrases interrogatives et négatives (même s'il est en fait rarement omis) :

he used not to visit us so often (*très rare*)
he didn't use to visit us so often (*emploi habituel*)
(autrefois), il ne venait pas nous voir aussi souvent

À la forme interrogative, la forme sans **do** est possible, mais elle ne s'emploie jamais à l'oral et que très rarement à l'écrit :

used you to live abroad? (*très rare*)
did you use to live abroad? (*emploi habituel*)
est-ce que vous habitiez à l'étranger (autrefois) ?

On emploie souvent **never** à la place de **not** :

he never used to visit us so often
(autrefois), il ne venait pas nous voir aussi souvent

Comme **used to**, **would** peut exprimer une action habituelle dans le passé (voir a) vi) ci-dessus) :

he used to/would visit us every week
avant, il venait nous voir toutes les semaines

La différence entre les deux est que **used to** peut s'utiliser à la fois pour des actions habituelles et pour des faits ou des situations dans le passé, tandis que **would** ne s'emploie que pour des actions habituelles et répétitives, des comportements typiques ou caractéristiques. On ne pourrait donc pas employer **would** dans les phrases suivantes car il s'agit de faits, et non d'actions :

John used to play badminton when he was younger
John jouait au badminton lorsqu'il était plus jeune

I used to live abroad
autrefois, je vivais à l'étranger

do you smoke? – I used to
est-ce que tu fumes ? – plus maintenant

19 Dare, need

Ces verbes peuvent se comporter soit comme des verbes ordinaires, soit comme des auxiliaires modaux. Lorsqu'ils sont auxiliaires :

● ils ne prennent pas de **-s** à la troisième personne du singulier du présent

● on n'emploie pas **do** dans les phrases interrogatives ou négatives

● s'ils sont suivis d'un infinitif, celui-ci n'est pas précédé de **to**.

a) *Comme verbes ordinaires*

nobody dares to contradict her
personne n'ose la contredire

he didn't dare to speak
il n'osait pas parler/il n'a pas osé parler

does he really dare to talk openly about it?
est-ce qu'il ose vraiment en parler ouvertement ?

all he needs to do now is buy the tickets
tout ce qu'il a à faire maintenant, c'est d'acheter les billets

you don't need to pay for them now
ce n'est pas la peine que tu les paies maintenant

does he really need all this money?
est-ce qu'il a vraiment besoin de tout cet argent ?

Cependant, **dare** peut avoir des caractéristiques à la fois du verbe ordinaire (par exemple avec **do** dans les phrases interrogatives ou négatives) et de l'auxiliaire (suivi d'un infinitif sans **to**) :

does he really dare talk openly about it?
est-ce qu'il ose vraiment en parler ouvertement ?

mais on doit employer l'infinitif avec **to** après le participe présent :

not daring to speak to her, he quietly left the room
n'osant pas lui parler, il sortit de la pièce silencieusement

Dans les propositions principales à la forme affirmative (c'est-à-dire les propositions principales qui ne sont ni interrogatives ni négatives), **need** se comporte toujours comme un verbe ordinaire :

I need to go to the dentist
il faut que j'aille chez le dentiste

b) *Comme auxiliaires modaux*

this is as much as I dare spend on it
je ne peux pas me permettre de dépenser plus

he dared not speak
il n'osait pas parler/il n'a pas osé parler

dare he talk openly about it?
est-ce qu'il ose en parler ouvertement ?

all he need do now is buy the tickets
tout ce qu'il a à faire maintenant, c'est d'acheter les billets

you needn't pay for them right now
ce n'est pas la peine que tu les paies maintenant

need I pay for this now?
est-ce qu'il faut que je paie ça maintenant ?

Notez l'expression idiomatique **I dare say** (= *probablement*) :

I dare say he'll forget
je suppose qu'il va oublier

is it going to rain, do you think? – I dare say it will
est-ce que tu crois qu'il va pleuvoir ? – probablement

20 Les verbes composés

Les verbes composés ou verbes à particules (phrasal verbs) sont une spécificité de la langue anglaise, une structure verbale réputée difficile. Les verbes composés forment un tout ; la particule est indispensable, elle permet de modifier le sens du verbe principal.

a) *Les verbes composés inséparables*

i) Il est important de faire la distinction entre un "verbe + préposition introduisant un complément", (a) et (c) ci-dessous, et un "verbe composé + complément d'objet direct", (b) et (d). Dans ce dernier cas, la préposition fonctionne comme une particule faisant partie intégrante du verbe. Comparez les deux phrases :

(a) they | danced | after dinner (*sujet* | *verbe* | *complément de temps*)
ils ont dansé après le dîner

(b) they | looked after | the child (*sujet* | *verbe* | *complément d'objet direct*)
ils se sont occupés de l'enfant

La structure de ces deux phrases n'est pas la même. Les deux mots **look after** forment une seule unité verbale (comparez avec **they nursed the child** *ils ont soigné l'enfant*), ce qui n'est pas le cas pour **danced after** : **after dinner** est un complément de temps introduit par une préposition distincte du verbe, tandis qu'en (b), **the child** est le complément d'objet direct de **look after**. Grammaticalement, on pourrait couper les phrases au niveau des barres verticales.

On observe la même différence dans les deux exemples suivants :

(c) they | went | through Germany
ils sont passés par l'Allemagne

(d) they | went through | the accounts
ils ont examiné la comptabilité

ii) **Look after** et **go through** (*examiner*) sont des verbes composés inséparables : le complément d'objet direct vient après la particule ; il ne peut jamais séparer le verbe de la particule. Ces verbes sont très souvent idiomatiques, c'est-à-dire qu'on ne peut pas les traduire littéralement car leur sens n'équivaut pas forcément à la somme du sens des deux éléments qui les composent. Voici d'autres exemples :

go by (*suivre des instructions*)

pick on (*chercher querelle à, s'en prendre à*)

get at (*Fam*) (*attaquer ; graisser la patte à*)

you can't do your own thing; you have to go by the book
tu ne peux pas faire ce que tu veux ; il faut agir selon les règles

the teacher's always picking on him
le professeur s'en prend toujours à lui

my mother is always getting at me
ma mère est toujours sur mon dos

I'm sure the jury have been got at
je suis sûr qu'on a graissé la patte au jury

iii) Puisque les verbes composés sont suivis d'un complément d'objet direct, ils admettent l'emploi des pronoms interrogatifs compléments **who(m)** et **what** (voir **Les interrogatifs**, pp. A31-2) :

they looked after the girl → **who(m) did they look after?**
ils se sont occupés de la petite fille
de qui se sont-ils occupés ?

they went through the accounts → **what did they go through?**
ils ont examiné la comptabilité
qu'est-ce qu'ils ont examiné ?

the police officer grappled with the thug → **who(m) did he grapple with?**
l'agent de police a lutté avec le voyou
avec qui a-t-il lutté ?

Mais on ne pourrait pas former des phrases interrogatives commençant par **where**, **when**, **how** avec des verbes com-

posés, car ces adverbes permettent de poser une question sur un complément circonstanciel introduit par une préposition, et non sur un complément d'objet direct. Les verbes suivants ne sont donc pas des verbes composés :

they went through Germany → **where did they go?**
ils sont passés par l'Allemagne
par où est-ce qu'ils sont passés ?

they danced after dinner → **when did they dance?**
ils ont dansé après le dîner
quand ont-ils dansé ?

they worked with great care → **how did they work?**
ils ont travaillé avec beaucoup de soin
comment ont-ils travaillé ?

Les particules des verbes inséparables précèdent les pronoms relatifs, ce qui n'est jamais le cas des verbes composés séparables (pour les verbes séparables, voir b) ci-dessous) :

this is a man on whom you can rely
c'est un homme sur lequel vous pouvez compter

iv) Un verbe composé étant considéré comme une seule unité, on peut souvent l'employer dans une construction passive :

the child has been looked after very well indeed
on s'est vraiment très bien occupé de l'enfant

the accounts have been gone through
la comptabilité a été examinée

do you feel you're being got at?
est-ce que tu as l'impression que tout le monde est après toi ?

v) Certains verbes transitifs inséparables sont composés de trois mots, c.-à-d. qu'ils ont deux particules, par exemple :

come up with (*trouver, concocter*)

Avec ces verbes, le complément d'objet ne peut jamais séparer le verbe et ses particules (on ne peut PAS dire : **have you come it up with?**). Le complément d'objet direct doit toujours suivre la dernière particule.

we've come up with a great solution
nous avons trouvé une solution idéale

Les deux particules ne peuvent pas non plus précéder un pronom relatif. Ainsi, on mettra toujours les particules à la fin de la proposition :

is there anything else (which) you can come up with?
est-ce que tu peux trouver quelque chose d'autre ?

Autres exemples de verbes composés à deux particules :

make off with (*voler, partir avec*)
live up to (*se montrer à la hauteur de*)
stand up for (*défendre, prendre le parti de*)
crack down on (*sévir contre*)

somebody made off with her suitcase
quelqu'un est parti avec sa valise

it was difficult for him to live up to this reputation
il lui était difficile d'être à la hauteur de cette réputation

why didn't you stand up for me if you knew I was right?
pourquoi est-ce que tu n'as pas pris mon parti si tu savais que j'avais raison ?

the police are cracking down on petty criminals
la police est en train de sévir contre les délinquants

b) *Les verbes composés séparables*

i) Au contraire des verbes composés inséparables, les verbes composés séparables peuvent admettre un complément d'objet direct avant la particule (entre le verbe et la particule) ou après :

turn down the television
turn the television down
baisse la télévision

look up these words
look these words up
cherche ces mots (dans le dictionnaire)

have you switched on the computer?
have you switched the computer on?
est-ce que tu as allumé l'ordinateur ?

have you tried on any of your new clothes?
have you tried any of your new clothes on?
est-ce que tu as essayé quelques-uns de tes nouveaux vêtements ?

Si le complément d'objet direct est un pronom, on doit placer la particule après celui-ci :

look them up   **turn it down**   **switch it on**
cherche-les   *baisse-la*   *allume-le*

ii) Tandis que les verbes composés inséparables sont toujours transitifs (lorsqu'on les considère comme unités complètes), certains verbes composés séparables sont toujours transitifs et d'autres peuvent être transitifs ou intransitifs :

back up (*soutenir – seulement transitif*) :
he always backs her up
il la soutient toujours

call back (*rappeler – transitif*) :
he said he'll call you back later
il a dit qu'il te rappellerait plus tard

call back (*rappeler – intransitif*) :
can you call back later?
est-ce que vous pouvez rappeler plus tard ?

iii) Comme de nombreux verbes composés inséparables (voir a) ii) ci-dessus), les verbes composés séparables sont très idiomatiques :

square up (*régler – des dettes, etc.*)
bring round (*faire reprendre connaissance à ; convertir à un point de vue*)
set back (*Fam*) (*coûter – de l'argent à quelqu'un*) :

if you pay now, we can square up later
si tu payes maintenant, on réglera nos comptes plus tard

give him a brandy; that'll bring him round
donne-lui un cognac pour qu'il reprenne ses esprits

do you think anything will bring him round to our point of view?
est-ce que tu crois qu'on pourrait l'amener à penser comme nous ?

that car must have set you back at least £25,000
cette voiture doit vous avoir coûté au moins 25 000 livres

Les verbes composés seulement intransitifs

Il y a aussi des verbes composés intransitifs, qui ne sont bien entendu jamais séparables puisque, par définition, ils n'appellent pas de complément d'objet direct :

he got off at Victoria Station
il descendit à la gare Victoria

do you mind if I listen in while you talk?
ça vous dérange si j'écoute votre conversation ?

the entire species is on the verge of dying out
l'espèce entière est sur le point de disparaître

À la différence des verbes composés inséparables, ces verbes n'ont jamais de forme passive.

21 Le temps au discours indirect

Le discours indirect permet de rapporter les paroles de quelqu'un. La concordance des temps en anglais dans le dis-

cours indirect a les mêmes caractéristiques qu'en français :

Henry said/had said, "I am unhappy" (*direct*)
Henry a dit/avait dit : "je suis malheureux"

Henry said/had said (that) he was unhappy (*indirect*)
Henry a dit/avait dit qu'il était malheureux

22 Liste des verbes irréguliers

Les américanismes sont indiqués par *. Les formes peu courantes, archaïques ou littéraires sont données entre parenthèses. Les traductions ci-dessous ne sont pas restrictives et ne donnent qu'un des sens de base.

INFINITIF		PRÉTÉRIT	PARTICIPE PASSÉ
abide	supporter	(abode) [1]	abided
arise	surgir	arose	arisen
awake	s'éveiller	awoke, awaked	awoken, (awaked)
bear	porter	bore	borne [2]
beat	battre	beat	beaten [3]
become	devenir	became	become
befall	arriver	befell	befallen
beget	engendrer	begot	begotten
begin	commencer	began	begun
behold	apercevoir	beheld	beheld
bend	courber	bent	bent [4]
bereave	priver	bereaved	bereft [5]
beseech	implorer	besought	besought
bestride	chevaucher	bestrode	bestridden
bet	parier	bet, betted	bet, betted
bid	offrir	bid	bid
bid	commander	bade	bidden
bind	attacher	bound	bound
bite	mordre	bit	bitten
bleed	saigner	bled	bled
blow	souffler	blew	blown
break	casser	broke	broken [6]
breed	élever	bred	bred
bring	apporter	brought	brought
broadcast	diffuser	broadcast	broadcast
build	construire	built	built
burn	brûler	burnt, burned	burnt, burned
burst	éclater	burst	burst
buy	acheter	bought	bought
cast	jeter	cast	cast
catch	attraper	caught	caught
chide	gronder	chid, chided	chid, (chidden), chided
choose	choisir	chose	chosen
cleave	fendre	clove, cleft	cloven, cleft [7]
cleave	adhérer	cleaved, (clave)	cleaved
cling	s'accrocher à	clung	clung
clothe	habiller	clothed, (clad)	clothed, (clad)
come	venir	came	come
cost	coûter	cost	cost
creep	ramper	crept	crept
crow	chanter	crowed, (crew)	crowed
cut	couper	cut	cut
dare	oser	dared, (durst)	dared, (durst)
deal	traiter	dealt	dealt

INFINITIF		PRÉTÉRIT	PARTICIPE PASSÉ	INFINITIF		PRÉTÉRIT	PARTICIPE PASSÉ
dig	fouiller	dug	dug	let	laisser	let	let
dive	plonger	dived, dove*	dived	lie	coucher	lay	lain
draw	dessiner, tirer	drew	drawn	light	allumer	lit, lighted	lit, lighted [1]
dream	rêver	dreamt, dreamed	dreamt, dreamed	lose	perdre	lost	lost
				make	faire	made	made
drink	boire	drank	drunk [8]	mean	signifier	meant	meant
drive	conduire	drove	driven	meet	rencontrer	met	met
dwell	demeurer	dwelt, dwelled	dwelt, dwelled	melt	fondre	melted	melted, molten [15]
eat	manger	ate	eaten	mow	faucher	mowed	mown, mowed
fall	tomber	fell	fallen				
feed	nourrir	fed	fed	pay	payer	paid	paid
feel	sentir	felt	felt	plead	plaider	pled*, pleaded	pled*, pleaded [16]
fight	battre	fought	fought				
find	trouver	found	found	put	poser	put	put
fit	aller à	fit*, fitted	fit*, fitted	quit	quitter	quit, (quitted)	quit, (quitted) [17]
flee	s'envoler	fled	fled				
fling	lancer	flung	flung	read	lire	read	read
fly	voler	flew	flown	rend	déchirer	rent	rent
forbear	s'abstenir	forbore	forborne	rid	débarrasser	rid, (ridded)	rid
forbid	interdire	forbad(e)	forbidden	ride	monter à	rode	ridden
forget	oublier	forgot	forgotten	ring	sonner	rang	rung
forgive	pardonner	forgave	forgiven	rise	se lever	rose	risen
forsake	abandonner	forsook	forsaken	run	courir	ran	run
freeze	geler	froze	frozen	saw	scier	sawed	sawn, sawed
get	obtenir	got	got, gotten* [9]	say	dire	said	said
gild	dorer	gilt, gilded	gilt, gilded [10]	see	voir	saw	seen
gird	ceindre	girt, girded	girt, girded [10]	seek	chercher	sought	sought
give	donner	gave	given	sell	vendre	sold	sold
go	aller	went	gone	send	envoyer	sent	sent
grind	grincer	ground	ground	set	mettre	set	set
grow	pousser	grew	grown	sew	coudre	sewed	sewn, sewed
hang	accrocher, suspendre	hung, hanged [11]	hung, hanged [11]	shake	secouer	shook	shaken
hear	entendre	heard	heard	shear	tondre	sheared	shorn, sheared [18]
heave	lever	hove, heaved [12]	hove, heaved [12]	shed	perdre	shed	shed
hew	tailler	hewed	hewn, hewed	shine	briller	shone [19]	shone [19]
hide	cacher	hid	hidden	shoe	chausser	shod, shoed	shod, shoed [20]
hit	frapper	hit	hit	shoot	abattre, tirer	shot	shot
hold	tenir	held	held	show	montrer	showed	shown, showed
hurt	blesser	hurt	hurt				
keep	garder	kept	kept	shrink	rétrécir	shrank, shrunk	shrunk, shrunken [21]
kneel	s'agenouiller	knelt, kneeled	knelt, kneeled	shut	fermer	shut	shut
knit	tricoter	knit, knitted [13]	knit, knitted [13]	sing	chanter	sang	sung
know	savoir, connaître	knew	known	sink	couler	sank	sunk, sunken [22]
lay	coucher	laid	laid	sit	s'asseoir	sat	sat
lead	mener	led	led	slay	tuer	slew	slain
lean	s'appuyer	leant, leaned	leant, leaned	sleep	dormir	slept	slept
leap	sauter	leapt, leaped	leapt, leaped	slide	glisser	slid	slid
				sling	lancer	slung	slung
learn	apprendre	learnt, learned	learnt, learned	slink	se glisser furtivement	slunk	slunk
leave	laisser	left	left	slit	fendre	slit	slit
lend	prêter	lent	lent	smell	sentir	smelt, smelled	smelt, smelled

INFINITIF		PRÉTÉRIT	PARTICIPE PASSÉ		INFINITIF		PRÉTÉRIT	PARTICIPE PASSÉ
smite	frapper	smote	smitten [23]		win	gagner	won	won
sneak	se faufiler, se glisser	snuck*, sneaked	snuck*, sneaked		wind	remonter	wound	wound
sow	semer	sowed	sown, sowed		wring	tordre	wrung	wrung
					write	écrire	wrote	written
speak	parler	spoke	spoken					
speed	aller vite	sped, speeded	sped, speeded					
spell	écrire	spelt, spelled	spelt, spelled					
spend	dépenser	spent	spent					
spill	renverser	spilt, spilled	spilt, spilled					
spin	filer	spun	spun					
spit	cracher	spat, spit*	spat, spit*					
split	se briser	split	split					
spoil	abîmer	spoilt, spoiled	spoilt, spoiled					
spread	étendre	spread	spread					
spring	bondir	sprang	sprung					
stand	se tenir	stood	stood					
steal	voler	stole	stolen					
stick	enfoncer, coller	stuck	stuck					
sting	piquer	stung	stung					
stink	puer	stank	stunk					
strew	répandre	strewed	strewn, strewed					
stride	marcher à grands pas	strode	stridden					
strike	frapper	struck	struck, stricken [24]					
string	enfiler	strung	strung					
strive	s'efforcer	strove	striven					
swear	jurer	swore	sworn					
sweat	suer	sweat*, sweated	sweat*, sweated					
sweep	balayer	swept	swept					
swell	gonfler	swelled	swollen, swelled [25]					
swim	nager	swam	swum					
swing	se balancer	swung	swung					
take	prendre	took	taken					
teach	enseigner	taught	taught					
tear	déchirer	tore	torn					
tell	dire	told	told					
think	penser	thought	thought					
thrive	fleurir	thrived, (throve)	thrived, (thriven)					
throw	jeter	threw	thrown					
thrust	pousser	thrust	thrust					
tread	marcher	trod	trodden					
understand	comprendre	understood	understood					
undertake	s'engager	undertook	undertaken					
wake	se réveiller	woke, waked	woken, waked					
wear	porter	wore	worn					
weave	tisser	wove [26]	woven [26]					
weep	pleurer	wept	wept					
wet	mouiller	wet*, wetted [27]	wet*, wetted [27]					

1 Régulier dans la construction **abide by** *se conformer à, suivre* : **they abided by the rules.**

2 Mais **born** au passif = *né* ou comme adjectif : **he was born in France; a born gentleman.**

3 Remarquez la forme familière **this has me beat/you have me beat** there *cela me dépasse/tu m'as posé une colle* et **beat** dans le sens de "très fatigué, épuisé" : **I'm (dead) beat.**

4 Remarquez la phrase **on one's bended knees** *à genoux.*

5 Mais **bereaved** dans le sens de "endeuillé", comme dans **the bereaved received no compensation** *la famille du disparu ne reçut aucune indemnité.* Comparez : **he was bereft of speech** *il en perdit la parole.*

6 Mais **broke** quand il s'agit d'un adjectif = *fauché* : **I'm broke.**

7 **Cleft** n'est employé qu'avec le sens de "coupé en deux". Remarquez **cleft palate** *palais fendu* et **to be caught in a cleft stick** *être dans une impasse,* mais **cloven foot/hoof** *sabot fendu.*

8 Quand il s'agit d'un adjectif épithète (placé devant le nom) désignant une personne, il est possible d'employer **drunken (a lot of drunk(en) people** *beaucoup de gens ivres*). Mais il doit toujours être employé devant les noms de choses, d'objets inanimés, etc. (**drunken parties** *des soirées bien arrosées*).

9 Mais **have got to** s'emploie aussi en américain avec le sens de "devoir, être obligé de" : **I've got to go** *je dois y aller.* Comparez avec : **she has gotten into a bit of a mess** *elle s'est fourrée dans le pétrin.*

10 Les formes du participe passé **gilt** et **girt** s'emploient comme adjectifs épithètes : **gilt mirrors** *des miroirs dorés,* **a flower-girt grave** *une tombe entourée de fleurs* (mais toujours **gilded youth** *la jeunesse dorée,* où **gilded** est employé au sens figuré).

11 Régulier quand il signifie *pendre quelqu'un.*

12 **Hove** est utilisé dans le domaine nautique comme dans l'expression **heave into sight** (*poindre à l'horizon*), également employée au sens figuré : **and suddenly, she hove into sight** *et tout à coup, elle apparut.*

13 Irrégulier quand il a le sens de "unir" (**a close-knit family** *une famille unie*), mais régulier lorsqu'il a le sens de "fabriquer en laine" et quand il fait référence aux os (= *se souder*).

14 Lorsque le participe passé est employé comme adjectif épithète, on préfère souvent **lighted** à **lit** : **a lighted candle** *une bougie allumée* (mais : **the candle is lit** *la bougie est allumée,* **she has lit a candle** *elle a allumé une bougie*). Dans les noms composés, on emploie généralement **lit** : **well-lit streets** *des rues bien éclairées.* Au sens figuré (avec **up**), c'est uniquement **lit** qui est employé au prétérit et au participe passé : **her face lit up when she saw me** *son visage s'illumina lorsqu'elle me vit.*

15 On emploie **molten** uniquement comme adjectif épithète, et seulement lorsqu'il signifie "fondu à très haute température", par exemple : **molten lead** *du plomb fondu* (mais **melted butter** *du beurre fondu*).

16 En anglais d'Écosse et en américain, on emploie **pled** au passé et au participe passé.

17 En américain, les formes régulières ne sont pas employées, et elles sont de plus en plus rares en anglais britannique.

18 Le participe passé est normalement **shorn** devant un nom

(newly-shorn lambs *des agneaux tout juste tondus*) et toujours dans l'expression **to be shorn of** *être privé de* : **shorn of his riches he was nothing** *privé de ses richesses, il n'était plus rien.*

19 Mais régulier quand il a le sens de "cirer, astiquer" en américain.

20 Quand il est adjectif, on n'emploie que **shod** : **a well-shod foot** *un pied bien chaussé.*

21 **Shrunken** n'est employé que lorsqu'il est adjectif : **shrunken limbs/her face was shrunken** *des membres rabougris/son visage était ratatiné.*

22 **Sunken** ne s'emploie que comme adjectif : **sunken eyes** *des yeux enfoncés.*

23 Verbe archaïque dont le participe passé **smitten** s'emploie encore comme adjectif : **he's completely smitten with her** *il est complètement fou d'elle.*

24 **Stricken** n'est utilisé qu'au sens figuré (**stricken with grief** *accablé par le chagrin*). Il est très courant dans les noms composés (*accablé par*) : **poverty-stricken, fever-stricken, grief-stricken, horror-stricken** (aussi **horror-struck**), **terror-stricken** (aussi **terror-struck**), mais on dit toujours **thunder-struck** *abasourdi.*

C'est aussi un emploi américain : **the remark was stricken from the record** *la remarque a été rayée du procès-verbal.*

25 **Swollen** est plus courant que **swelled** comme verbe (**her face has swollen** *son visage a gonflé*) et comme adjectif (**her face is swollen/a swollen face**). **To have a swollen head** (*avoir la grosse tête*) devient **to have a swelled head** en américain.

26 Mais il est régulier lorsqu'il a le sens de "se faufiler" : **the motorbike weaved through the traffic** *la moto se faufila entre les voitures.*

27 Mais irrégulier aussi en anglais britannique lorsqu'il a le sens suivant : **he wet his bed** *il a fait pipi au lit.*

23 Les formes des auxiliaires be, have, do

BE

	PRÉSENT	PRÉTÉRIT	PARTICIPE PASSÉ
1ère	I am	I was	been
2ème	you are	you were	
3ème	he/she/it is	he/she/it was	
1ère	we are	we were	
2ème	you are	you were	
3ème	they are	they were	

Formes contractées avec le sujet :

I'm = I am
you're = you are
he's/John's = he is/John is
we're/you're/they're = we are/you are/they are

Formes contractées avec **not** :

aren't I? (questions seulement) = am I not?
you/we/they aren't = you/we/they are not
he isn't = he is not
I/he wasn't = I/he was not
you/we/they weren't = you/we/they were not

On a aussi : **I'm not ; you're not**, etc.

Pour le subjonctif, voir pp. A53-4.

HAVE

	PRÉSENT	PRÉTÉRIT	PARTICIPE PASSÉ
1ère	I have	I had	had
2ème	you have	you had	
3ème	he/she/it has	he/she/it had	
1ère	we have	we had	
2ème	you have	you had	
3ème	they have	they had	

Formes contractées avec le sujet :

I've/you've/we've/they've = I have, etc.
he's = he has
I'd/you'd/he'd/we'd/they'd = I had, etc.

Vous noterez que **he's/she's** ne sont normalement pas contractés lorsqu'ils sont employés comme verbes en tant que tels, et non comme auxiliaires, au présent :

I've two cars   he has two cars
j'ai deux voitures   *il a deux voitures*

Formes contractées avec **not** :

haven't = have not
hasn't = has not
hadn't = had not

DO

	PRÉSENT	PRÉTÉRIT	PARTICIPE PASSÉ
1ère	I do	I did	done
2ème	you do	you did	
3ème	he/she/it does	he/she/it did	
1ère	we do	we did	
2ème	you do	you did	
3ème	they do	they did	

Formes contractées avec **not** :

don't = do not
doesn't = does not
didn't = did not

15 LES PRÉPOSITIONS

1 Les prépositions servent à relier grammaticalement ou sémantiquement les noms ou pronoms devant lesquels elles sont placées, à un autre élément de la phrase. Elles permettent d'exprimer des relations de temps, de lieu, de provenance, de possession, etc.

after (*après*)	**I'll see you after the show** *je te verrai après le spectacle*
on (*sur*)	**the keys are on the table** *les clefs sont sur la table*
from (*de*)	**I have just arrived from London** *j'arrive juste de Londres*
of (*de*)	**would you like a cup of tea?** *est-ce que tu veux une tasse de thé ?*

Cependant, dans certaines constructions les prépositions anglaises peuvent se placer en fin de proposition :

the people I came here with
les gens avec lesquels je suis venu

something I had never dreamed of
quelque chose dont je n'avais jamais rêvé

Voir aussi **Les verbes composés**, pp. A61-3, ainsi que **Les interrogatifs** et **Les relatifs**, pp. A31-3.

2 Voici une liste des prépositions les plus couramment employées. La plupart des prépositions ayant différents sens et emplois, seuls les usages les plus importants et ceux particulièrement intéressants ou susceptibles de poser problème sont mentionnés ci-dessous.

ABOUT ET AROUND

i) dans les environs, dans tous les sens :

Il n'y a souvent pas de différence entre about et around, bien qu'en anglais américain on préfère around :

they walked about/around town
ils se sont promenés dans la ville

he must be about/around somewhere
il doit être dans les parages

the dog was racing about/around in the garden
le chien courait dans tous les sens dans le jardin

ii) au coin, autour de :

he lives just around the corner
il habite au coin de la rue

when I arrived they were all seated around the table
quand je suis arrivé, ils étaient tous assis autour de la table

iii) environ, à peu près :

I have about £15 on me
j'ai environ quinze livres sur moi

he's about/around your age
il a à peu près votre âge

iv) au sujet de, sur (seulement about) :

what's the book about? – it's a story about nature
de quoi parle le livre ? – c'est une histoire sur la nature

v) sur le point de (seulement about) :

I was just about to leave
j'allais partir/j'étais sur le point de partir

what were you about to say?
qu'est-ce que vous alliez dire ?

ABOVE

Above exprime normalement le fait d'être "situé au-dessus de" dans un sens purement physique :

the shirts had been placed in the wardrobe above the socks
les chemises avaient été placées dans l'armoire au-dessus des chaussettes

Il y a en général peu de différence entre above et over lorsque ce dernier signifie "au-dessus de" :

he has a lovely mirror above/over the mantelpiece
il a un très joli miroir au-dessus de la cheminée

mais contrairement à over, above ne peut pas avoir le sens de "sur" :

he flung his coat over a chair
il a jeté son manteau sur une chaise

ACROSS

i) d'un côté à l'autre :

he swam across the lake
il a traversé le lac à la nage

ii) de l'autre côté de :

we live across the street from them
nous habitons en face de chez eux

iii) à travers :

the study of literature across cultures
l'étude de la littérature à travers différentes cultures

Across et over ont souvent un sens très proche, mais across a tendance à indiquer une dimension horizontale (sur la largeur de) :

he laid out his suit across the bed
il étendit son costume en travers du lit

AFTER

i) après (dans le temps et dans l'espace) :

I'll call him after breakfast
je l'appellerai après le petit déjeuner

the shopping centre is just after the church
le centre commercial est juste après l'église

ii) après, derrière :

close the door after you
fermez la porte après vous

iii) à la recherche de (toujours utilisé avec le verbe to be) :

the police are after him　　**she's after a full-time**
il est recherché par la police　　**job**
　　　　　　　　　　　　　　　　elle cherche un travail à
　　　　　　　　　　　　　　　　temps plein

iv) After peut être employé comme particule de verbes composés (voir p. A62), par exemple dans la construction to ask after. Remarquez dans ce cas, les différences d'emploi entre les verbes to ask after et to ask for, qui peuvent avoir un sens similaire ou complètement différent :

he asked after you　　　**he asked for you**
il m'a demandé de tes nouvelles　*il a demandé à te parler*

tell him I'm asking for him
dis-lui bonjour de ma part

v) Dans un sens temporel, on pourrait comparer after et since. La différence entre les deux apparaît dans l'emploi des temps : prétérit (after) et present perfect (since). Comparez :

he wasn't well after his journey
il ne se sentait pas très bien après son voyage

he hasn't been well since his journey
il ne se sent pas très bien depuis son voyage

AGAINST

i) contre (pour indiquer une position ou un choc) :

he leant his bike against the wall
il appuya son vélo contre le mur

he knocked his head against the wall
il s'est cogné la tête contre le mur

ii) en sens inverse :

we're sailing against the current
nous naviguons à contre-courant

iii) contre, à l'encontre de (pour indiquer l'opposition ou une opinion contraire) :

it's against the law　　　**they voted against it**
c'est illégal ou *contraire à la loi*　*ils ont voté contre*

iv) contre, sur (pour indiquer un contraste) :

he stood against the light
il était à contre-jour

she was silhouetted against the snow
sa silhouette se découpait sur la neige

v) contre (pour un match, une guerre, etc.) :

United against Everton
United contre Everton

they fought against them
ils ont combattu contre eux

vi) contre (pour indiquer une mesure de précaution ou de protection) :

our car is insured against accidents
notre voiture est assurée contre les accidents

his coat protected him against the cold
son manteau le protégeait du froid

AMONG(ST)

au milieu de, parmi, entre (voir aussi **between**) :

she was lost among the crowd
elle était perdue dans la foule

I count her among my friends
je la compte parmi mes amis

she said, among other things, that she would be late
elle a dit, entre autres, qu'elle serait en retard

share out the sweets among the children
partagez les bonbons entre les enfants

AT

i) à (pour faire référence à un point précis dans le temps et dans l'espace) :

I'm meeting him at six o'clock
je dois le retrouver à six heures

I like studying at night
j'aime étudier la nuit

they waited at the bus stop
ils attendaient à l'arrêt de bus

he was sitting at the table
il était assis à table

Pour les noms de villes, on utilise habituellement la préposition **in**, sauf dans certains cas particulier. Dans l'exemple suivant, les villes sont des étapes sur un itinéraire.

the train stops at Dundee, Edinburgh and York
le train s'arrête à Dundee, Édimbourg et York

ii) à l'âge de :

he started working at 15
il a commencé à travailler à (l'âge de) 15 ans

iii) vers, dans la direction de :

look at this!
regarde ça!

he shot at the rabbit
il a tiré sur le lapin

iv) à (pour indiquer une activité) :

my parents are at work
mes parents sont au travail

v) à (pour indiquer un prix, une vitesse, une température, un taux, etc.) :

it's a bargain at £5
à 5 livres, c'est une bonne affaire

he drove at 50 mph
il faisait du 80 (à l'heure)

the temperature stands at 30°
la température est de 30 °

vi) en (pour introduire le complément d'un adjectif) :

he's hopeless at maths
il est nul en maths

BEFORE

i) avant, auparavant :

be there before six o'clock
sois là avant six heures

before that, she was a teacher
auparavant, elle était professeur

I saw him the day before yesterday
je l'ai vu avant-hier

Dans le sens temporel de **before**, comparez son emploi et celui de **until** avec des verbes à la forme négative. **Before** signifie

"plus tôt que" et **until** "jusqu'à (un certain temps)" :

(a) **you will not get the letter before Monday**
tu ne recevras pas la lettre avant lundi

(b) **you will not get the letter until Monday**
tu ne recevras pas la lettre avant lundi

En (a), la lettre arrivera lundi ou n'importe quel jour après lundi (mais pas avant); en (b), la lettre arrivera lundi.

ii) avant (dans un ordre de préférence) :

her name came before mine in the list
son nom était avant le mien sur la liste

iii) devant (dans l'espace et au sens figuré) :

the accident happened before my very eyes
l'accident s'est déroulé sous mes propres yeux

we have a difficult task before us
nous avons une tâche difficile devant nous

iv) devant, en présence de :

he said it before witnesses
il l'a dit devant ou en présence de témoins

Lorsque la préposition **before** est employée pour indiquer la position au sens littéral, on peut la remplacer par **in front of**, qui est plus courant et moins soutenu que **before** :

he was standing in front of the judge in the queue
il se tenait devant le juge dans la file

Mais lorsque **before** n'est pas pris au sens littéral, il n'est pas possible d'employer **in front of** :

he was brought before the judge
il a été amené à comparaître devant le juge

BELOW

i) au-dessous de, en dessous de, sous :

he lives in the flat below ours
il habite dans l'appartement au-dessous ou en dessous du nôtre

there was a feeling of anxiety lying below the surface
on sentait une angoisse sous-jacente

ii) au-dessous de, inférieur à :

his grades are below average
ses notes sont au-dessous de la moyenne

En général, **below** est le contraire de **above** (*au-dessus de*), et **under** (*sous*) est le contraire de **over** ou **on** (*sur*). Mais remarquez l'emploi de **below** dans le sens de "en aval", et non de "au-dessous de" :

he was sitting under the bridge
il était assis sous le pont

below the bridge the water gets deeper
en aval du pont, l'eau est plus profonde

BESIDE

i) à côté de, près de :

come and sit beside me
viens t'asseoir à côté de moi

ii) par rapport à, comparé à :

these results don't look very good beside last year's
ces résultats n'ont pas l'air très bons par rapport à ceux de l'année dernière

iii) à part, excepté :

other people beside ourselves might need it
d'autres (personnes) que nous pourraient en avoir besoin

iv) être loin de (au sens figuré) :

that is **beside** the point
cela n'a rien à voir (avec l'affaire en question)

BESIDES

en plus de, à part :

there were three guests there **besides** him and me
il y avait trois invités à part lui et moi

BETWEEN

i) entre (dans le temps et dans l'espace) :

I'll be home **between** six and seven
je serai à la maison entre six et sept heures

the crowd stood **between** him and the door
la foule le séparait de la porte

Remarquez que **between** ne s'emploie qu'avec deux éléments. Lorsque l'on veut désigner plus de deux éléments, on emploiera **among(st)** :

he sat **between** John and Joan   he sat **among(st)** his
il était assis entre John et Joan   friends
                                    il était assis parmi ses amis

ii) entre (pour une tranche d'âge, une fourchette, etc.) :

the theatre company is for children **between** the ages of 8 and 12
c'est une troupe de théâtre pour enfants de 8 à 12 ans

iii) entre (pour indiquer une relation entre deux personnes/choses) :

it's a half-hour drive **between** home and the office
il y a une demi-heure de route entre la maison et le bureau

he felt things weren't right **between** them
il sentait que ça n'allait pas entre eux

iv) entre (pour indiquer un choix, une alternative) :

I had to choose **between** going with them and staying at home
il fallait que je choisisse entre les accompagner et rester à la maison

v) entre (pour indiquer le partage) :

they shared the cake **between** them
ils se sont partagé le gâteau

BUT

Lorsqu'il est employé comme préposition, **but** signifie "sauf", "à part". Il se place généralement après des pronoms indéfinis ou interrogatifs, ou des adverbes comme **anywhere, where**, etc. :

she wouldn't see anyone **but** her lawyer
elle ne voulait voir personne sauf ou à part son avocat

where **but** in America could you find such a gadget?
il n'y a qu'en Amérique qu'on trouve un tel gadget

Dans la plupart des cas, on peut employer **except** à la place de **but** :

nobody **but/except** you would think of that
personne à part toi ne penserait à ça

where else **but/except** in France would you...?
où, sinon en France, est-ce qu'on pourrait... ?

BY

i) près de, à côté de, devant :

he was sitting **by** the table
il était assis près de la table

she parked her car **by** the kerb
elle gara sa voiture au bord du trottoir

I drive **by** the school every day
je passe (en voiture) devant l'école tous les jours

ii) par :

she left **by** the back door
elle est partie par la porte de derrière

iii) par, en (pour indiquer le moyen de paiement, de communication, de transport) (comme en français, le nom qui suit ne prend pas d'article) :

to pay **by** cheque   **by** letter/phone
payer par chèque   *par courrier/téléphone*

to go **by** bus/car/plane/train
aller en autobus/voiture/avion/train

iv) par (au passif pour introduire le complément d'agent) :

the house was surrounded **by**   I was shocked **by** his
  police   reaction
la police a cerné la maison   *sa réaction m'a choqué*

v) en (avec un participe présent) :

he learned to cook **by** watching his mother
il a appris à faire la cuisine en regardant sa mère

vi) avant, pas plus tard que :

be there **by** six o'clock
sois là avant ou pour six heures

Comparez avec **at** qui s'emploie pour faire référence à un point précis dans le temps :

be there **at** six o'clock
sois là à six heures

vii) selon, d'après :

it's 6:15 **by** my watch
il est 6 h 15 à ma montre

viii) de (en ce qui concerne) :

he's an actor **by** profession
il est acteur de profession

Remarquez aussi les verbes composés **to live by** et **to live on**. **To live by** signifie "gagner sa vie d'une occupation", tandis que **to live on** signifie "vivre avec un revenu de" ou "se nourrir de". L'emploi de **by** insiste sur le moyen :

he lives **by** acting in commercials
il gagne sa vie en jouant dans des pubs

he lives **on** fruit
il se nourrit de fruits

he lives **by** his pen   he lives **on** £100 a month
il vit de sa plume   *il vit avec 100 livres par mois*

To live by signifie aussi "vivre selon les règles de" :

it is difficult to live **by** such a set of doctrines
il est difficile de vivre en appliquant un tel ensemble de doctrines

ix) à, par, en (pour indiquer la fréquence, le taux, la vitesse, etc.) :

little **by** little   day **by** day   year **by** year
peu à peu   *jour par jour ou*   *d'année en année*
                      de jour en jour

DURING

pendant, au cours de (voir aussi **for**) :

they met **during** the war
ils se sont rencontrés pendant la guerre

EXCEPT

sauf (voir aussi **but**) :

everybody was there **except** him
tout le monde était là sauf lui

FOR

i) pour (pour indiquer un but, une fonction) :

we were in Vienna for work
nous étions à Vienne pour le travail

ii) pour, à l'intention de :

these flowers are for her
ces fleurs sont pour elle

iii) pour, dans la direction de :

they left for Spain
ils sont partis pour l'Espagne

iv) à :

for rent   **for sale**
à louer   *à vendre*

v) pour, pendant (pour une période dans le futur ou dans le passé) ; depuis (pour une action qui n'est pas encore terminée) :

they're going away for the   **I lived there for one**
weekend   **month**
ils partent pour le week-end   *j'y ai vécu pendant un mois*

I've been playing tennis for years
je joue au tennis depuis des années

Pour la différence de temps entre l'anglais et le français dans ce dernier exemple, voir l'emploi du present perfect p. A50.

Lorsque **for** est employé comme préposition de temps, il est utile de le comparer à **during** (*pendant*) et **in** (*en*). **For** insiste sur l'idée de durée (pendant combien de temps ?), tandis que **during** indique la période au cours de laquelle des actions se produisent (quand ?) :

he let the cat out for the night
il a fait sortir le chat pour la nuit

he let the cat out during the night
il a fait sortir le chat pendant/dans la nuit

On peut aussi comparer **for** (utilisé pour indiquer une durée) à **in**, qui signifie "dans une période" :

I haven't seen her for five years
je ne l'ai pas vue depuis cinq ans

he didn't see her once in five years
il ne l'a pas vue une seule fois en cinq ans

Cependant, on pourrait maintenant aussi employer **in** dans le premier exemple :

I haven't seen her in five years
ça fait cinq ans que je ne l'ai pas vue

Pour l'emploi de **for/since** avec des expressions de temps, voir p. A50.

vi) pendant (pour indiquer la distance) :

we walked for several miles
nous avons marché pendant plusieurs kilomètres

vii) **For** s'utilise également dans des constructions avec des verbes à l'infinitif :

it's not for him to decide
il ne lui appartient pas ou ce n'est pas à lui de décider

FROM

i) de, à partir de, depuis (pour indiquer la provenance ou un point de départ, dans l'espace et dans le temps) :

her parents came from France
ses parents venaient de France

she was unhappy from her first day at boarding school
elle a été malheureuse dès son premier jour à l'internat

the price has gone up from 50 pence to 60 pence
le prix a augmenté de 50 pence à 60 pence

ii) de (pour indiquer la cause) :

she died from multiple injuries
elle n'a pas survécu à ses blessures multiples

iii) de (pour indiquer un endroit) :

from the top of the hill you can see the whole city
du haut de la colline on voit toute la ville

iv) après l'adjectif **different** (on trouve parfois **different** suivi de **to**, mais cette construction est incorrecte) :

yours is different from mine
le tien est différent du mien

what he just said is different from what he had said before
ce qu'il vient de dire est différent de ce qu'il avait dit auparavant

En anglais américain, on emploie **different than.**

IN FRONT OF

devant (voir aussi **before**) :

she was sitting in front of the TV
elle était assise devant la télé

IN

(voir aussi **at** et **for**)

i) dans (pour indiquer un lieu, un moment précis dans le temps, etc.) :

what have you got in your pockets?
qu'est-ce que tu as dans tes poches ?

we swam in the sea
nous nous sommes baignés dans la mer

throw the letter in the bin   **I'll be back in five minutes**
jette la lettre à la poubelle   *je reviens dans cinq minutes*

she could see a reflection in the mirror
elle voyait un reflet dans la glace

ii) à (avec des noms de villes) :

he lives in Paris
il habite à Paris

iii) en (avec les pays, les vêtements, les saisons, les années ; pour indiquer la durée, le moyen, etc.) :

they live in Spain   **he was in a suit**
ils habitent en Espagne   *il était en costume*

in (the) spring/summer/autumn/winter
au printemps, en été/automne/hiver

he cooked the meal in ten minutes
il prépara le repas en dix minutes

she paid in cash   **he writes in English**
elle a payé en liquide   *il écrit en anglais*

iv) à, en (pour faire référence à des institutions) :

he spent five years in prison   **she's in hospital**
il a passé cinq ans en prison   *elle est à l'hôpital*

he teaches in a language school
il enseigne dans une école de langues

INTO

(voir aussi **in**)

i) dans (pour indiquer une direction, un mouvement) :

come into my office
venez dans mon bureau

On emploie donc **into** après un verbe de mouvement et **in** simplement pour indiquer l'endroit :

he was sitting in the living room
il était assis dans la salle de séjour

he went into the living room
il est entré dans la salle de séjour

Ainsi, lorsque le verbe to be a le même sens que to go, on pourra employer la préposition into :

you've been in the bathroom for an hour
tu es dans la salle de bains depuis une heure

have you been into/in the bathroom yet?
est-ce que tu es allé dans la salle de bains ?

• dans, contre (pour indiquer une collision) :

the truck ran into the wall
le camion est rentré dans le mur

) en (pour indiquer un changement, une transformation) :

he's grown into a man
c'est un homme maintenant

) dans (pour donner une indication de temps) :

we worked well into the night
nous avons travaillé (jusque) tard dans la nuit

avec le verbe to be dans le sens de "bien aimer" *(Fam)* :

he's into fast cars at the moment
il est branché voitures de sport en ce moment

OF

de (pour indiquer la quantité, la possession, etc.) :

he bought a pound of onions
il a acheté une livre d'oignons

there are six of us (et jamais **we are six**)
nous sommes six

I need a map of Spain   **he's a friend of mine**
il me faut une carte d'Espagne   *c'est un ami à moi*

• de (pour exprimer une attitude, une émotion ou pour décrire une qualité) :

I'm proud of it   **he is a man of courage**
j'en suis fier   *c'est un homme de courage*

) de (pour indiquer la cause) :

he never thought about the consequence of his actions
il n'a pas pensé à la conséquence de ses actes

) de (pour indiquer un moment précis dans l'espace ou dans le temps) :

it was the happiest day of his life
c'était le plus beau jour de sa vie

there was a cat in the middle of the road
il y avait un chat au milieu de la chaussée

OFF

de (pour indiquer un mouvement) :

he fell off his chair
il est tombé de sa chaise

de (pour quelque chose que l'on enlève) :

I've stripped the wallpaper off the walls
j'ai décollé le papier peint des murs

) de (pour indiquer la provenance) :

a cool breeze off the sea
une brise fraîche venant du large

• pour indiquer un lieu :

just off Oxford Street there's a pretty little square
à deux pas d'Oxford Street il y a une petite place ravissante

v) pour indiquer l'absence de quelque chose ou de quelqu'un:

you need a few days off work
vous avez besoin de quelques jours de congé

Mr Dale is off work today
M. Dale est absent aujourd'hui

ON

(voir aussi by et upon)

i) sur (pour indiquer une position, un lieu, etc.) :

the vase is on the shelf   **they live on a farm**
le vase est sur l'étagère   *ils habitent une ferme*

the child fell on the floor   **I'm on the bus/train**
l'enfant est tombé par terre   *je suis dans le bus/train*

Pour indiquer un lieu, on peut employer in à la place de on si l'idée d'intérieur domine :

it's often cold in British trains
il fait souvent froid dans les trains britanniques

ii) sur, à propos de, au sujet de :

I watched a film on the French Revolution
j'ai regardé un film sur la Révolution française

we all agree on that point
nous sommes tous d'accord sur ce point

Remarquez que on (*au sujet de, sur*) peut être plus technique, plus académique que about :

he gave a paper on Verdi and Shakespeare
il a fait un exposé sur Verdi et Shakespeare

a book on English history
un livre sur l'histoire anglaise

iii) selon :

everyone will be judged on their merits
chacun sera jugé selon ses mérites

iv) à (pour un moyen, une source d'énergie, la simultanéité de deux événements, etc.) :

he came on foot   **it runs on electricity**
il est venu à pied   *ça marche à l'électricité*

he'll deal with it on his return   **who's on bass?**
il s'en occupera à son retour   *qui est à la basse ?*

v) à (pour les moyens de communication) :

it's the first time she's been on television
c'est la première fois qu'elle passe à la télévision

I heard it on the radio   **he's on the phone**
je l'ai entendu à la radio   *il est au téléphone*

vi) par (pour indiquer une cause) :

I shall refuse on principle
je refuserai par principe

vii) pour indiquer une activité, un intérêt :

they went on safari
ils ont fait un safari

he's good on music
il a de bonnes connaissances côté musique

Remarquez que la préposition on dans ce dernier exemple n'a pas le même sens que la préposition at. La phrase **he's good at music** implique qu'il sait bien jouer d'un instrument.

viii) devant les jours de la semaine :

can you come on Saturday?
tu peux venir samedi ?

ix) en (avec un participe présent) :

she cried on hearing the news
elle a pleuré en apprenant la nouvelle

OPPOSITE

en face de :

> **they live just opposite**
> *ils habitent juste en face*

Lorsqu'il indique une position, il peut toujours être accompagné de **to** :

> **the house opposite (to) ours is being pulled down**
> *on est en train de démolir la maison en face de la nôtre*

Mais il est impossible d'utiliser **to** dans la phrase suivante :

> **she played opposite Richard Burton in many films**
> *elle fut la partenaire de Richard Burton dans de nombreux films*

OUTSIDE

dehors, en dehors de, à l'extérieur de :

> **nobody is allowed outside (of) the house**
> *personne n'a le droit de quitter la maison*

Remarquez que **outside** est souvent accompagné de **of** en anglais américain (ce qui est peu fréquent en anglais britannique).

En outre, il peut parfois avoir le sens de "devant" :

> **they met outside the cathedral**
> *ils se sont retrouvés devant la cathédrale*

OVER

(voir aussi **above** et **across**)

i) au-dessus de :

> **they live over the shop**
> *ils habitent au-dessus du magasin*

ii) sur, par-dessus :

> **she wore a cardigan over her dress**
> *elle portait un gilet par-dessus sa robe*

> **he was watching me over his newspaper**
> *il m'observait par-dessus son journal*

iii) plus de (avec un nombre) :

> **he must be over thirty**
> *il doit avoir plus de trente ans*

iv) au sujet de:

> **they disagree over the working conditions**
> *ils ont un conflit portant sur les conditions de travail*

OWING TO

en raison de, à cause de, grâce à :

> **this was owing to his alertness of mind**
> *c'était grâce à sa vivacité d'esprit*

> **owing to bad weather they arrived late**
> *ils sont arrivés en retard à cause du mauvais temps*

SINCE

depuis (voir aussi **after**) :

> **he has been talking about it since yesterday**
> *il en parle depuis hier*

Remarquez également la préposition **ever since** (depuis) :

> **ever since that day he's been afraid of dogs**
> *depuis ce jour-là, il a peur des chiens*

TILL

jusqu'à (+ complément de temps) (voir **until**)

TO

(voir aussi **for** et **until**)

i) à, jusqu'à, en, pour (pour indiquer une direction, un lieu, une période, etc.) :

> **what's the best way to the station?**
> *quel est le meilleur chemin pour aller à la gare ?*

> **I'm off to Paris**
> *je pars à/pour Paris*

> **I will be away from Tuesday night to Thursday morning**
> *je serai absent du mardi soir (jusqu')au jeudi matin*

ii) jusqu'à (pour un niveau, un âge, un montant, etc.) :

> **the snow came (up) to her knees**
> *la neige lui arrivait aux genoux*

> **it's accurate to the millimetre**
> *c'est exact au millimètre près*

iii) avant (pour une date, etc.) :

> **there's only two weeks to Christmas**
> *il ne reste que deux semaines avant Noël*

iv) pour (pour indiquer une intention) :

> **I did it to annoy her**
> *je l'ai fait exprès pour l'énerver*

v) pour (pour indiquer un avis, une opinion) :

> **it sounds suspicious to me**
> *cela me semble bizarre*

> **to be honest, I don't think he will come**
> *pour être franc, je ne crois pas qu'il viendra*

vi) pour, contre, dans, etc. (pour indiquer la composition, la proportion) :

> **use one cup of sugar to every three cups of fruit**
> *mettez une tasse de sucre pour trois tasses de fruits*

> **the vote was 6 to 3**
> *il y avait 6 voix contre 3*

vii) à (pour indiquer la comparaison) :

> **they often compare his work to Coppola's**
> *on a souvent comparé ses films à ceux de Coppola*

> **that's nothing (compared) to what I've seen**
> *ce n'est rien à côté de ce que j'ai vu*

viii) de (dans le sens de **of** ou **for**) :

> **here is the key to the front door**
> *voici la clé de la porte d'entrée*

> **her husband is the French ambassador to Algeria**
> *son mari est l'ambassadeur français en Algérie*

Pour l'emploi de l'infinitif avec **to**, voir pp. A41-2.

TOWARD(S)

i) dans la direction de, vers :

> **he turned towards her**
> *il s'est tourné vers elle*

ii) envers (pour faire référence à une attitude) :

> **she's very hostile towards me**
> *elle est très hostile à mon égard*

iii) pour (en contribution à) :

> **I'll give you something towards your expenses**
> *je vous donnerai quelque chose pour payer une partie de vos frais*

Toward s'emploie normalement en anglais américain et **towards** en anglais britannique.

UNDER

(voir aussi **below**)

i) sous :

the newspaper was under the chair
le journal était sous la chaise

ii) moins de, au-dessous de :

everything is under £5
tout est à moins de 5 livres

iii) dans (pour indiquer une condition ou des circonstances particulières) :

she was murdered under strange circumstances
elle a été tuée dans d'étranges circonstances

iv) en cours de :

this building is under construction
cet immeuble est en cours de construction

UNTIL

jusqu'à (+ complément de temps) (voir aussi **before**)

she was here (up) until February
elle a été ici jusqu'en février

On peut aussi employer **until** après la préposition **from**. Comparez avec l'emploi de **from... to** ; la différence est la même qu'en français (*à/jusqu'à*) :

the shop is closed from 1 to 2 p.m.
le magasin ferme de 13 heures à 14 heures

last night I worked from eight until/till midnight
hier soir j'ai travaillé de huit heures jusqu'à minuit

Il n'y a pas de différence de sens entre **until** et **till**.

UPON

(voir aussi **on**)

La préposition **upon** a le même sens que **on**, mais elle fait partie d'un niveau de langue plus soutenu.

i) sur :

she had a sad look upon her face
elle avait l'air triste

ii) contre :

attacks upon old people are on the increase
les agressions contre les personnes âgées sont de plus en plus fréquentes

iii) lorsque, en (avec un participe présent) :

upon hearing the news, he rang home
lorsqu'il a appris la nouvelle, il a appelé chez lui

WITH

i) avec :

she filled the vase with water
elle a rempli le vase d'eau

she went out with her friend
elle est sortie avec son amie

stop fighting with your brother
arrête de te battre avec ton frère

he spoke with ease
il s'exprima avec aisance

ii) à :

a boy with green eyes
un garçon aux yeux verts

iii) chez :

I'm staying with friends
je loge chez des amis

isn't he with Ford anymore?
ne travaille-t-il plus chez Ford ?

iv) de (dans des expressions idiomatiques) :

he was white with fear
il était blanc de peur

I was sick with worry
j'étais malade d'inquiétude

WITHOUT

sans :

we couldn't have done it without you
on n'aurait pas pu le faire sans vous

I knocked without getting a reply
j'ai frappé sans obtenir de réponse

16 LES CONJONCTIONS

Les conjonctions sont des mots qui servent à relier deux mots ou deux propositions. On distingue deux types de conjonctions :

Les **conjonctions de coordination** relient des mots ou des propositions qui ont une même fonction. Elles servent à marquer l'union (**and**), l'opposition (**but**), l'alternative (**or**), la négation (**nor**), etc.

Les **conjonctions de subordination** relient des propositions qui **dépendent** d'autres mots ou propositions. Elles servent à marquer la cause (**because**), la comparaison (**as if**), la concession (**although**), le lieu (**where**), etc.

Voir aussi **La structure de la phrase**, pp. A78-9.

1 Les conjonctions de coordination

Elles peuvent être simples :

and *et*   **but** *mais*   **or** *ou/ni*   **nor** *ni*

ou corrélatives :

both... and *à la fois... et*
either... or *ou... ou, soit... soit, ni... ni (avec une négation)*
neither... nor *ni... ni*
not only... but also *non seulement... mais aussi*

a) *Exemples de conjonctions de coordination simples*

i) **And** peut relier deux noms, deux adjectifs, deux adverbes, deux verbes ou deux propositions :

she's old and fragile
elle est âgée et frêle

you need butter and flour
tu as besoin de beurre et de farine

she spoke naturally and fluently
elle parla avec naturel et aisance

they ate and drank a great deal
ils ont beaucoup mangé et beaucoup bu

they finished their work and then went out to dinner
ils ont terminé leur travail et puis ils sont sortis dîner

ii) **But** et **or** offrent les mêmes possibilités de combinaison que **and**, par exemple :

he came home tired but happy
il est rentré fatigué mais heureux

I can go today or tomorrow
je peux y aller aujourd'hui ou demain

iii) **Nor** s'emploie devant le second élément (ou le troisième, etc.) lorsque la proposition principale est à la forme négative :

I don't eat sweets, nor **chocolate,** nor **any kind of sugary thing**
je ne mange pas de bonbons, ni de chocolat, ni aucunes sucreries

On peut aussi employer or dans cette même construction :

I don't eat sweets, or **chocolate,** or **any kind of sugary thing**

b) *Exemples de conjonctions de coordination corrélatives*

i) Both... and permettent de relier deux noms, deux adjectifs ou deux verbes :

you need both **butter** and **flour**
vous avez besoin de beurre et de farine

she's both **old** and **fragile**
elle est (à la fois) âgée et frêle

the film made me both **laugh** and **cry**
le film m'a fait à la fois rire et pleurer

ii) De manière générale, on emploiera either... or dans les phrases affirmatives et neither... nor lorsque le sens est négatif :

you need either **butter** or **margarine**
tu as besoin soit de beurre, soit de margarine

they're either **very rich** or **very stupid**
ils sont soit très riches, soit très bêtes

she was travelling either **to** or **from Aberdeen**
elle allait à Aberdeen ou bien elle en revenait

I have neither **the time** nor **the inclination to do it**
je n'ai ni le temps ni l'envie de le faire

she neither **drinks** nor **smokes**
elle ne boit ni ne fume

Mais on peut aussi employer either... or dans une phrase négative. Dans ce cas-là, il ne faut pas oublier le not de la négation :

I've not **met** either **him** or **his brother**
je n'ai rencontré ni lui ni son frère

iii) Si (n)either... (n)or relient deux noms, le verbe s'accorde en nombre avec le nom le plus proche du verbe :

either the turntable or the speakers have to be replaced
either the speakers or the turntable has to be replaced
il faut remplacer soit les enceintes, soit la platine

Lorsque les deux noms ou pronoms sont singuliers, le verbe qui suit doit se mettre au singulier (même si l'on trouve parfois un verbe au pluriel dans un langage familier et incorrect) :

neither he nor his wife has ever spoken to me
ni lui ni sa femme ne m'ont jamais adressé la parole

iv) Not only... but also

she plays not only **the guitar,** but also **the piano**
elle joue non seulement de la guitare, mais aussi du piano

Remarquez aussi l'emploi avec l'adverbe too :

she's not only **bright, she's funny** too
elle est non seulement intelligente, mais en plus elle est drôle

c) *Les différents emplois de* or

i) Or peut exprimer l'alternative ou avoir un sens exclusif :

he lives in Liverpool or **Manchester, I can't remember which**
il habite à Liverpool ou à Manchester, je ne me souviens plus exactement

ii) Il sert aussi à relier deux synonymes :

bovine spongiform encephalopathy, or **BSE**
l'encéphalite spongiforme bovine, ou ESB

iii) Il peut avoir le sens de "sinon" lorsqu'il relie deux propositions :

apologize to her, or **she'll never speak to you again**
excuse-toi auprès d'elle, ou elle ne te parlera plus jamais

2 Les conjonctions de subordination

Il existe un grand nombre de conjonctions de subordination. Certaines sont simples :

because *parce que*	so that *si bien que*
although *bien que*	when *quand* etc.

D'autres sont corrélatives :

as... as *aussi... que*
more... than *plus... que*
so... that *afin... que* etc.

a) *Introduisant une proposition substantive*

Les propositions substantives ont la même fonction dans la phrase que les noms ou pronoms et les groupes nominaux :

(a) I told him that **they had done it**
je lui ai dit qu'ils l'avaient fait

(b) I told him the facts
je lui ai dit les faits

En (a), le complément d'objet direct de told est une proposition substantive, alors qu'en (b) c'est un groupe nominal.

Les conjonctions qui introduisent des propositions substantives sont :

that *que*   whether *si (+ choix)*   if *si*   how *comment*

That peut être omis si la proposition subordonnée est le complément d'objet direct de la phrase, mais jamais si elle en est le sujet :

he said (that) he wanted to see me *(complément d'objet)*
il a dit qu'il voulait me voir

that such films can be made is unbelievable *(sujet)*
que l'on puisse faire de tels films est incroyable

he asked me if/whether I had any money *(complément d'objet)*
il m'a demandé si j'avais de l'argent (ou pas)

whether I have any money or not is none of your business *(sujet)*
que j'aie de l'argent ou non, ça ne te regarde pas

he told us how he had seen his child being born *(complément d'objet)*
il nous a raconté qu'il avait vu naître son enfant

how it's done is immaterial *(sujet)*
la manière dont c'est fait est sans importance

Cet emploi de if, whether et how est différent de celui décrit ci-dessous, où ces conjonctions ont pour rôle d'introduire un groupe adverbial (voir ci-dessous).

b) *Introduisant une proposition adverbiale*

Voir aussi **Les adverbes**, p. A19.

Il existe un grand nombre de conjonctions qui introduisent des propositions adverbiales. On peut trouver des noms qui servent de conjonctions :

he arrived the minute the clock struck twelve (= when, *conjonction de temps*)
il est arrivé à la minute où la pendule sonnait midi

he didn't explain it the way you did (= how, *conjonction de manière*)
il ne l'a pas expliqué de la manière dont tu l'as fait

ou des participes passés ou présents :

provided you keep quiet, you can stay (= if, *conjonction de condition*)
du moment que tu restes sage, tu peux rester

he's doing well considering he's been here for only a week (= although/even if, *conjonction de concession*)
il se débrouille bien si l'on considère qu'il n'est ici que depuis une semaine

Voici les principales conjonctions adverbiales :

i) Conjonctions de temps :

   after *après que*   **until** *jusqu'à ce que*
   as *alors que*   **when** *lorsque*
   before *avant que*   **whenever** *chaque fois que*
   since *depuis que*   **while** *tandis que*

L'idée de futur dans les subordonnées introduites par l'une de ces conjonctions est exprimée par un présent en anglais (voir p. A51).

he came back after the show had finished
il est revenu après que le spectacle fut fini

the phone rang as he was having a bath
le téléphone a sonné alors qu'il prenait son bain

before you sit down, you must see the bedroom
avant que tu ne t'asseyes, il faut que tu voies la chambre

they've been crying (ever) since their parents left
ils pleurent depuis que/le moment où leurs parents sont partis

he talked non-stop until it was time to go home
il n'a pas arrêté de parler jusqu'à ce qu'il fût l'heure de partir

when he's ready we'll be able to get going at last
(*présent dans la subordonnée*)
quand il sera prêt, on pourra enfin se mettre en route

whenever we go on a picnic, it rains
chaque fois qu'on part en pique-nique, il pleut

will you go and see him while you're in Barcelona?
(*présent dans la subordonnée*)
est-ce que vous irez le voir quand vous serez à Barcelone ?

ii) Conjonctions de lieu :

   where *où*
   wherever *où que, partout où*

plant them where there is a lot of shade
plante-les là où il y a beaucoup d'ombre

wherever you go it's the same thing
où que vous alliez c'est la même chose

wherever we went, he complained about the food
partout où on est allés, il s'est plaint de la nourriture

iii) Conjonctions de manière, de comparaison ou d'intensité :

   as *comme*   **how** *comment, comme*
   as if *comme si*   **however** *de quelque*
   as though *comme si*   *manière que*

he does it as he's always done it
il le fait comme il l'a toujours fait

he behaved as if/as though there was (were) something wrong
il s'est comporté comme s'il y avait quelque chose qui n'allait pas

tell me how you do it
dites-moi comment vous faites

you can pay how you want
tu peux payer comme tu veux

it'll be fine, however you do it
de quelque manière que vous le fassiez, ça ira

iv) Conjonctions de cause :

   as *étant donné que*   **for** *car, parce que*
   because *parce que*   **since** *puisque*

as there was nothing in the fridge, we went out to eat
comme il n'y avait rien dans le frigo, nous sommes sortis dîner

he came because it was his duty
il est venu parce que c'était son devoir

I was surprised when he arrived punctually, for he was usually late (*soutenu*)
je fus surpris de le voir arriver à l'heure, car il était souvent en retard

since you've been so kind to me, I want to give you a present
puisque tu as été si gentil avec moi, je veux te faire un cadeau

v) Conjonctions de concession :

   (al)though *bien que*   **even though** *bien que*
   even if *même si*   **whether** *que*

although I've never liked him, I do respect him
bien que je ne l'aie jamais aimé, je le respecte

you can stay, even if you haven't been invited
tu peux rester, même si tu n'as pas été invité

even though she explained it in detail, I couldn't understand
bien qu'elle l'ait expliqué en détail, je n'ai pas réussi à comprendre

I'm going whether you like it or not
je vais y aller que ça te plaise ou non

vi) Conjonctions de but :

   in order to *afin de*
   lest *de peur/crainte que/de*
   so that *afin que*

they went to the stage door in order to get a glimpse of him
ils sont allés à l'entrée des artistes afin de pouvoir l'apercevoir

he did it so that she would be happy
il l'a fait afin qu'elle soit heureuse

they whispered lest the children should hear
ils parlèrent à voix basse de peur que les enfants ne les entendent

Remarquez que **lest** a tendance à être employé dans un style littéraire. Il est possible d'employer **so that... not** à la place :

they whispered so that the children wouldn't hear
ils parlèrent à voix basse afin que les enfants ne les entendent pas

vii) Conjonctions de conséquence :

   so that *si bien que, de façon à ce que*

she didn't eat enough, so that in the end she fell ill
elle ne mangeait pas assez, si bien qu'elle a fini par tomber malade

viii) Conjonctions de condition :

   if *si*
   so/as long as *à condition que, pourvu que*
   unless *à moins que*

if he comes, we'll ask him
s'il vient, on lui demandera

you can have it as long as you give me it back
vous pouvez le prendre à condition que vous me le rendiez

tell me, unless you don't want to
dis-le-moi, à moins que tu ne le veuilles pas

c) **But** *comme conjonction de subordination*

i) L'emploi de **but** comme conjonction de subordination signifiant "sans que" (après les adverbes négatifs **never, barely, hardly**, etc.) est d'un style soutenu et littéraire :

she never hears his name but she starts to weep
elle ne peut entendre son nom sans verser des larmes

barely/hardly a day goes by but he receives another invitation
il ne se passe pas un jour sans qu'il reçoive une nouvelle invitation

ii) **But** peut aussi s'employer comme conjonction de subordination devant **that** après certains noms précédés de **no** :

there's no doubt (but) that he's responsible
il n'y a aucun doute que c'est lui le responsable

d) *Introduisant des propositions comparatives*

Les propositions subordonnées comparatives ne modifient pas d'autres propositions (comme le font les propositions adverbiales). Elles modifient des éléments de la proposition : groupes nominaux, adverbiaux et adjectivaux.

Les conjonctions comparatives sont corrélatives (comparez avec les conjonctions de coordination, p. A73) :

more... than *plus... que*
less... than *moins... que*
as... as *autant/aussi... que*

i) Modifiant un nom :

we invited more people than we had planned to
nous avons invité plus de gens que prévu

he has as much money as we do
il a autant d'argent que nous

ii) Modifiant un adjectif :

it was less interesting than we'd thought
c'était moins intéressant que nous n'avions pensé

it was as interesting as we thought
c'était aussi intéressant que nous le pensions

iii) Modifiant un adverbe :

she paints better than she sculpts
elle peint mieux qu'elle ne sculpte

she sang as well as she could
elle chanta aussi bien qu'elle put

Remarquez l'absence de négation dans les exemples anglais.

Voir aussi **La comparaison**, pp. A24-7.

17 LES NOMBRES

1 Les nombres cardinaux et les nombres ordinaux

CARDINAUX		ORDINAUX	
1	one	1st	first
2	two	2nd	second
3	three	3rd	third
4	four	4th	fourth
5	five	5th	fifth
6	six	6th	sixth
7	seven	7th	seventh
8	eight	8th	eighth
9	nine	9th	ninth
10	ten	10th	tenth
11	eleven	11th	eleventh
12	twelve	12th	twelfth
13	thirteen	13th	thirteenth
14	fourteen	14th	fourteenth
15	fifteen	15th	fifteenth
16	sixteen	16th	sixteenth
17	seventeen	17th	seventeenth
18	eighteen	18th	eighteenth
19	nineteen	19th	nineteenth
20	twenty	20th	twentieth
21	twenty-one	21st	twenty-first
30	thirty	30th	thirtieth
40	forty	40th	fortieth
50	fifty	50th	fiftieth
60	sixty	60th	sixtieth
70	seventy	70th	seventieth
80	eighty	80th	eightieth
90	ninety	90th	ninetieth
100	a/one hundred	100th	(one) hundredth
101	a/one hundred and one	101st	(one) hundred and first
200	two hundred	200th	two hundredth
1,000	a/one thousand	1,000th	(one) thousandth
1,345	a/one thousand, three hundred and forty-five	1,345th	one thousand, three hundred and forty-fifth

1,000,000	a/one million	millionth
1,000,000,000 (10⁹)	a/one billion	billionth
1,000,000,000,000 (10¹²)	a/one trillion	trillionth

Remarquez qu'en anglais britannique **a thousand million** était autrefois 10^9 (un milliard), **a billion** 10^{12} et **a trillion** 10^{18}. Aujourd'hui, on n'emploie que les valeurs données dans la liste, qui étaient à l'origine américaines.

Remarquez également l'emploi de la virgule pour indiquer les milliers, là où en français on a un espace.

2 Les fractions

a) *Les fractions ordinaires*

Comme en français, on écrit les fractions avec un nombre cardinal (ou parfois **a** à la place de **one**) + un nombre ordinal :

$1/5$	=	**a/one fifth** *un cinquième*
$3/8$	=	**three eighths** *trois huitièmes*
$3\,4/9$	=	**three and four ninths** *trois exposant quatre neuvièmes*
$1/2$	=	**a/one half** *un demi*
$1/4$	=	**a quarter** *un quart*
$3/4$	=	**three quarters** *trois quarts*
$1\,1/4$ **hours**	=	**an/one hour and a quarter** ou **one and a quarter hours** *(une heure et quart)*

Voir aussi **Les expressions de temps**, p. A80.

Remarquez que le **-s** est maintenu lorsque les fractions sont employées comme adjectifs :

they had a two-thirds majority
ils ont eu une majorité de deux tiers

L'emploi des fractions ordinaires est très courant en anglais.

b) *Les nombres décimaux*

Alors que dans les autres pays européens on utilise une virgule pour les nombres décimaux, les anglophones se servent du point :

25.5 = twenty-five point five

Les décimales sont énumérées une à une après le point :

25.552 = twenty-five point five five two

3 Nought, zero, 0, nil

a) *Anglais britannique*

   i) Nought et zero sont utilisés pour le chiffre 0. Dans les calculs, on emploie habituellement **nought** :

   add another nought (ou zero) to that number
   ajoute un autre zéro à ce chiffre

   put down nought and carry one
   je pose zéro et je retiens un

   0.6 = nought point six ou **zero point six**
   zéro virgule six

   ii) Pour un nombre sur une échelle, on préfère **zero** :

   it's freezing, it's 10 below zero
   il gèle, il fait moins 10

   De même, on emploiera **zero** en anglais scientifique ou économique, dans le sens de **nothing** (*rien*) :

   given zero conductivity
   étant donné une conductivité de zéro

   a country striving for zero inflation
   un pays qui se bat pour atteindre une inflation zéro

   production was soon reduced to zero (ou nil)
   la production fut rapidement réduite à zéro/à néant

   iii) Pour les numéros de téléphone, on prononce le chiffre comme la lettre o, mais on emploie aussi maintenant **zero** (voir le point 4 ci-dessous).

   iv) **Nil** est toujours utilisé pour les points ou les scores :

   Arsenal won four nil/by four goals to nil (= 4-0)
   Arsenal a gagné quatre zéro/quatre buts à zéro

   sauf au tennis, où l'on utilise **love** :

   Hewitt leads forty-love
   Hewitt mène quarante zéro

b) *Anglais américain*

   Zero s'utilise dans presque tous les cas :

   how many zeros are there in a billion?
   combien y a-t-il de zéros dans un milliard ?

   my telephone number is 721002 (= seven two one zero zero two)

   Chicago Cubs zero – Detroit Tigers six *(au base-ball)*

   Cependant, on utilise toujours le mot **love** au tennis.

4 Les numéros de téléphone

Les numéros de téléphone se lisent chiffre par chiffre :

   1567 = one five six seven
   40032 = four zero zero three two *(Am, Br)* **four double 'o' three two** *(Br)*

Remarquez l'emploi de **double** en anglais britannique lorsqu'on a deux chiffres identiques. Cependant, cet emploi n'est pas systématique ; on peut aussi répéter les deux chiffres.

À l'écrit, on regroupe normalement les chiffres en fonction des différents codes régionaux. À l'oral, on marquera une pause après chaque groupe de chiffres :

   0141-221-5266 = 'o' one four one – double two one ou **two two one – five two double six** ou **six six**

5 Les adresses

En Amérique du Nord, les numéros de rue à quatre chiffres se lisent comme les dates (voir **Les expressions de temps**, p. A81), c'est-à-dire deux par deux :

   3445 Sherbrooke Street = thirty-four forty-five

6 Les opérations

Il existe plusieurs façons d'exprimer les opérations arithmétiques. Voici les plus courantes :

   12 + 19 = 31
   twelve plus nineteen is/equals thirty-one

   19 – 7 = 12
   nineteen minus seven is/equals twelve
   seven from nineteen is/leaves twelve
   nineteen take away seven is/leaves twelve *(emploi enfantin)*

   2 x 5 = 10   **4 x 5 = 20**
   twice five is ten   **four times five is/equals**
   two fives are ten   **twenty**
                             four fives are twenty

   36 x 41 = 1476
   thirty-six times forty-one is/equals one thousand four hundred and seventy-six
   thirty-six multiplied by forty-one is/equals one thousand four hundred and seventy-six

   10 ÷ 2 = 5
   ten divided by two is/equals five
   two into ten goes five *(emploi plus familier)*

7 L'emploi du pluriel

Pour hundred, thousand, million (billion, trillion) avec ou sans -s, voir **Les noms**, pp. A12-13.

Voici quelques exemples où l'on utilise le pluriel :

   there were tens of thousands of refugees
   il y avait des dizaines de milliers de réfugiés

   she's now in her eighties
   elle est maintenant octogénaire (elle a entre 80 et 90 ans)

   in the 1950s (= nineteen fifties) ou **in the 50s (= fifties)**
   dans les années cinquante

Voir aussi p. A81.

8 The former et the latter

Au lieu d'employer **the first**, on emploie **the former** si l'on fait référence à une personne/chose parmi deux qui viennent juste d'être énoncées ; et **the latter** (au lieu de **the last**) quand on fait référence à la dernière de deux personnes/choses :

   Lauren and Alison are both good candidates for the job, but the former is more experienced than the latter
   Lauren et Alison sont de bonnes candidates pour ce poste, mais la première a plus d'expérience que la seconde

De ces expressions, **the latter** est la plus souvent utilisée, et elle peut aussi renvoyer à la dernière chose d'une énumération qui comprend plus de deux éléments :

   Spain, Italy, Greece: of these countries the latter is still the most interesting as regards...
   l'Espagne, l'Italie, la Grèce : de tous ces pays, le dernier est le plus intéressant en ce qui concerne...

The former/the latter peuvent avoir une fonction adjectivale, c'est-à-dire qu'ils peuvent en effet être suivis d'un nom :

   of dogs and cats, the former animal makes a better pet
   du chien ou du chat, c'est le premier qui est le meilleur animal domestique

9 Once et twice

Once signifie "une fois" et **twice**, "deux fois". **Thrice** (*trois fois*) est archaïque :

   I've been there once before
   j'y suis déjà allé une fois

   I've only seen her twice
   je ne l'ai vue que deux fois

18 LA STRUCTURE DE LA PHRASE

1 Le sujet

En général, le sujet précède l'auxiliaire et le verbe :

I can swim
je sais nager

L'inversion du sujet et du verbe a lieu dans les cas suivants (s'il y a plus d'un auxiliaire, seul le premier auxiliaire précède le sujet) :

a) dans les questions :

may I?
puis-je ?

(when) can you come?
(quand) peux-tu venir ?

would you have liked to come with us?
tu aurais aimé venir avec nous ?

b) dans les propositions conditionnelles, lorsque if est omis :

had I got there in time, she'd still be alive
si j'étais arrivé à temps, elle serait encore en vie

should that be true, I'd be most surprised
si c'était vrai, je serais vraiment surpris

c) quand la phrase commence avec un mot dont le sens est négatif (comme never, seldom) :

I can't swim – nor/neither can I
je ne sais pas nager – moi non plus

never did I think this would happen
je n'aurais jamais pensé que cela arriverait

little did I think this would happen
je ne me doutais pas du tout que cela arriverait

hardly had he entered the room, when the phone rang
à peine était-il entré dans la pièce que le téléphone sonna

seldom have I enjoyed a meal so much
j'ai rarement autant apprécié un repas

Mais après **nevertheless/nonetheless** et **only**, qui renvoient à la proposition précédente, il n'y a pas d'inversion :

I know he's not very nice, nevertheless/nonetheless he should be invited
je sais bien qu'il n'est pas très sympa, mais on devrait quand même l'inviter

we'd like you to come, only we haven't got enough room
nous aimerions que vous veniez, mais nous n'avons pas assez de place

d) souvent quand une phrase commence avec un adverbe d'intensité :

so marvellously did he play that it brought tears to my eyes
il a joué tellement bien que j'en avais les larmes aux yeux

only too well do I remember those words
je m'en souviens trop bien, de ces paroles

e) parfois lorsque la phrase commence par un complément circonstanciel ou un complément d'objet indirect et que l'on veut insister sur le sujet ou le complément d'objet (le verbe étant moins important) :

in that year came the announcement that the space shuttle would be launched
cette année-là fut annoncé le lancement de la navette spatiale

on the stage stood the three main actors
sur la scène se tenaient les trois acteurs principaux

to his brave efforts do we owe our happiness (*littéraire*)
c'est à son grand courage que nous devons notre bonheur

Remarquez aussi que l'on peut placer out, in, etc. devant le verbe pour insister ou donner un effet stylistique dans une narration. Il s'agit là d'un emploi assez courant :

a big black car pulled up and out jumped Margot
une grosse voiture noire s'arrêta et Margot en sortit avec précipitation

out came a scream so horrible that it made my hair stand on end
on entendit tout à coup un cri si horrible que j'en eus la chair de poule

Le pronom se place avant le verbe :

in you go!
entre !

out you get!
sors !

f) après so placé en position initiale (= aussi) :

I'm hungry – so am I
j'ai faim – moi aussi

g) au discours direct :

Après le discours direct, le verbe de parole précède parfois son sujet, surtout si celui-ci est un nom (plus le nom ou le groupe nominal est important, plus on aura tendance à inverser l'ordre des mots) :

"you're late again", said John/John said
"tu es encore en retard", dit John

"you're late again!", boomed the furious sergeant/the furious sergeant boomed
"tu es encore en retard", hurla le sergent, furieux

Mais il n'y a pas d'inversion du sujet avec les temps composés :

"you're late again", John had said
"tu es encore en retard", avait dit John

Si le sujet est un pronom, il se met normalement avant le verbe :

"you're late again", he said
"tu es encore en retard", dit-il

Le verbe précède le pronom lorsqu'une proposition relative suit ou lorsque l'on veut donner un ton humoristique à la phrase :

"you're late again", said I, who had been waiting for at least two hours
"tu es encore en retard", ai-je dit ; ça faisait au moins deux heures que j'attendais

S'il y a un adverbe, l'inversion est moins courante, mais possible :

"you're back again", said John tentatively/John said tentatively
"tu es de retour", fit John d'un ton hésitant

Mais s'il y a un complément d'objet, après ask ou tell par exemple, on ne fait pas l'inversion :

"she's late again", John told the waiting guests
"elle est encore en retard", dit John aux invités qui attendaient

2 Le complément d'objet

a) Le complément d'objet suit normalement le verbe, mais il est en position initiale dans les cas suivants :

i) dans les questions qui commencent par un pronom interrogatif complément d'objet :

who(m) did you meet?
qui as-tu rencontré ?

ii) dans les propositions subordonnées interrogatives et relatives (les pronoms étant compléments d'objet) :

please ask him what he thinks
demande-lui, s'il te plaît, ce qu'il en pense

he brought back what she'd given him
il a ramené ce qu'elle lui avait donné

iii) pour renforcer un complément d'objet, surtout quand celui-ci est that :

that I couldn't put up with   **that I don't know**
cela, je ne pouvais pas l'accepter   *ça, je ne sais pas*

but his sort I don't like **at all**
son genre, je ne l'aime pas du tout

- L'ordre des compléments d'objet direct et indirect

i) Le complément d'objet indirect précède le complément d'objet direct quand celui-ci est un nom (ice-cream), que le complément indirect soit un pronom ou un nom (him, the children) :

she gave him an ice-cream
elle lui a donné une glace

she gave the children some ice-cream
elle a donné de la glace aux enfants

Mais si le complément d'objet indirect est introduit par une préposition, il vient se placer après le complément d'objet direct :

she gave some ice-cream to the children
elle a donné de la glace aux enfants

ii) Quand les deux compléments sont des pronoms, le complément d'objet indirect précède le complément d'objet direct :

he wouldn't sell me them   **would you give** me one?
il ne voulait pas me les vendre   *tu veux bien m'en donner un ?*

could you please send her   **well, tell** them that, **then**
these?   *tu peux les lui envoyer, s'il te*
eh bien, dis-le-leur   *plaît ?*

Mais les phrases où l'on emploie le pronom personnel it après les verbes give, lend, etc. peuvent se construire des deux manières suivantes :

could you give him it **when you see him?**
could you give it to him **when you see him?**
tu veux bien le lui donner quand tu le verras ?

Avec la préposition to, l'ordre des mots est semblable à celui de l'exemple ci-dessus :

he wouldn't sell them to me
il ne voulait pas me les vendre

would you give one to me?
tu veux bien m'en donner un ?

19 LES CHANGEMENTS ORTHOGRAPHIQUES

y devient i

n y placé après une **consonne** se change en i devant les termi-isons suivantes :

-able, -ed, -er *(adjectifs ou noms)*
-est, -es *(noms et verbes)*
-ly et -ness

ply	→	**plies, pliable**
cry	→	**cried, cries, crier**
happy	→	**happier, happiest, happily, happiness**

Exceptions :

shyly *(timidement)* et slyly *(sournoisement)* (on évite d'employer slily qui est rare). Par contre, drily est plus courant que dryly.

Les noms propres qui se terminent en -y prennent seulement -s :

there were two Henrys **at the party**
il y avait deux Henri à la soirée

Les composés en -by prennent -s :

standbys *remplaçants*

On trouve aussi parmi les exceptions les noms dyer *(teinturier)* et parfois flyer *(aviateur)* (aussi flier).

Mais y précédé d'une voyelle ne change pas et la terminaison des noms ou des verbes est -s au lieu de -es :

play	→	**plays, playable, player**
coy	→	**coyer, coyest, coyly, coyness**

Mais remarquez les verbes irréguliers :

lay	→	**laid**	**say** →	**said**
pay	→	**paid**		

ainsi que les adverbes formés à partir des adjectifs :

day	→	**daily**	**gay** →	**gaily** (aussi **gayly**).

2 ie **devient** y

Ce changement a lieu devant -ing :

die	→	**dying**	**lie** →	**lying**

3 Chute de la voyelle finale -e

On enlève normalement le -e si l'on ajoute une syllabe commençant par une voyelle :

love	→	**loving, lovable**	**stone** →	**stony**

Exceptions :

Parmi les exceptions principales, on peut citer :

matey *copain*
likeable *aimable*
mileage *distance parcourue en miles*
dyeing *teinture* (à ne pas confondre avec dying = *mourir*)
hoeing *binage*
swingeing *énorme* (à ne pas confondre avec swinging = *dans le vent*)

Si le mot se termine en -ce ou en -ge, alors le -e est maintenu devant -a et -o :

irreplaceable, changeable, outrageous

Si la syllabe suivante commence par une consonne, on conserve normalement le -e :

love	→	**lovely**	**bore** →	**boredom**

Mais là encore, il existe des exceptions importantes, notamment :

argue	→	**argument**	**true** →	**truly**
due	→	**duly**	**whole** →	**wholly**

4 -our ou -or

Quand on ajoute un suffixe à certains mots se terminant par -our, le -u tombe :

humour	→ **humorist**	**vigour**	→ **vigorous**

Mais l'exception importante concerne le mot colour :

colour → **colourful, colourlessness, colourist**

En anglais américain, la terminaison -our devient -or. On aura donc toujours -or pour les noms avec ou sans suffixe :

humor	→	**humorist**
vigor	→	**vigorous**
color	→	**colorful**, etc.

5 Doublement des consonnes

Après une voyelle courte accentuée, on double la consonne finale lorsqu'elle est placée devant -er, -est, -ed, -ing :

big [bɪg]	→	**bigger, biggest**
fit [fɪt]	→	**fitter, fittest, fitted, fitting**
begin [bɪ'gɪn]	→	**beginner, beginning**

On double aussi le -r dans les mots qui se terminent par -ur ou -er (voyelles longues accentuées) :

blur [blɜː(r)]	→	**blurred, blurring**
occur [əˈkɜː(r)]	→	**occurred, occurring**
refer [rɪˈfɜː(r)]	→	**referred, referring**

Mais on ne double pas la consonne dans les monosyllabes à voyelle longue ou à diphtongue (= voyelle qui change de timbre au cours de son émission) :

keep [kiːp]	→	**keeper, keeping**
cure [kjʊə(r)]	→	**cured, curing**

et dans les dissyllabes accentués sur la première syllabe :

vomit [ˈvɒmɪt]	→	**vomited, vomiting**

En anglais britannique, le -l est doublé même dans une syllabe non accentuée :

revel [ˈrevəl]	→	**revelled, reveller, revelling**
travel [ˈtrævəl]	→	**travelled, traveller, travelling**

Mais ce doublement n'a pas lieu en anglais américain :

travel	→	**traveled, traveler, traveling**

Remarquez aussi :

kidnap [ˈkɪdnæp] →		**kidnapped, kidnapper** (*Br*)
kidnap	→	**kidnaped, kidnaper** (*Am*)

6 c devient ck

Le -c final d'un mot devient -ck devant -ed, -er, -ing :

frolic →	**frolicked, frolicking**
picnic →	**picnicked, picnicker, picnicking**

7 Anglais américain

En plus des variantes américaines données en 4 et 5 ci-dessus, il faut noter les différences suivantes entre l'orthographe britannique et l'orthographe américaine :

a) Anglais britannique -gue, anglais américain -g :

catalogue (*Br*) – catalog (*Am*)

b) Anglais britannique -tre, anglais américain -ter :

centre (*Br*) – center (*Am*)

metre (*Br*) – meter (*Am*)

c) Anglais britannique -nce, anglais américain -nse :

defence (*Br*) – defense (*Am*)

offence (*Br*) – offense (*Am*)

pretence (*Br*) – pretense (*Am*)

d) Quelques mots qui s'écrivent différemment :

Br	Am
cheque	check
pyjamas	pajamas
practise (*pratiquer*)	practice (le nom se termine en -ce des deux côtés de l'Atlantique)
programme	program (de même en anglais britannique dans le domaine de l'informatique)
tyre (*pneu*)	tire

20 LES EXPRESSIONS DE TEMPS

A L'HEURE

what's the time?, what time is it?	what time do you make it?
quelle heure est-il ?	*quelle heure avez-vous ?*

a) *Les heures*

it's one/two (o'clock)	it's 12 (o'clock)/midnigh
il est une heure/deux heures	*il est minuit*
it's 12 (o'clock)/noon/12 noon/midday	
il est midi	

b) *Les demi-heures*

it's half past one, it's one thirty (*Am*), it's half one (*Fam*)
il est une heure et demie

it's half past midnight	it's half past twelve
il est minuit et demi	*il est midi/minuit et demi*

On peut ajouter in the afternoon et at night soit pour insister, soit pour éviter toute ambiguïté lorsque le contexte ne perm pas de savoir s'il s'agit de "midi" ou "minuit" :

it was half past twelve in the at afternoon	it was half past twelve night
il est midi et demi	*il est minuit et demi*

c) *Les quarts d'heure*

it's (a) quarter past two	at (a) quarter to two
il est deux heures et quart	*à deux heures moins le quart*

d) *Les minutes*

it's twenty-three minutes past four (= 4.23)
il est quatre heures vingt-trois

it's twenty to five (= 4.40)
il est cinq heures moins vingt

En anglais américain, on emploie after au lieu de past (it's twenty after five *il est cinq heures vingt*) et of au lieu de to (it's twenty of five *il est cinq heures moins vingt*).

e) a.m. *et* p.m.

a.m.	p.m.
du matin	*de l'après-midi/du soir*
it's 6.50 a.m.	it's 7.10 p.m.
il est 6 h 50	*il est 7 h 10 (du soir)/19 h 10*

A.m. et p.m. s'utilisent surtout lorsque le contexte ne permet pas de savoir s'il s'agit du matin ou de l'après-midi/du soir et que l'on veut éviter toute ambiguïté.

Les expressions du type "quinze heures" (à la place de "trois heures") ne s'emploient pas en anglais de tous les jours. Cependant, on les rencontre parfois dans les horaires et dans le langage militaire (souvent suivis de hours) :

fifteen hundred hours	fifteen thirty hours
quinze heures	*quinze heures trente*

'o' five hundred hours
cinq heures du matin

L'emploi de 'o', pour désigner le zéro devant le chiffre, est uniquement militaire. Dans les horaires, on emploiera simplement five hundred hours.

Pour les moyens de transport, on peut aussi dire :

we took the sixteen-twenty to Brighton
nous avons pris le train de 16 h 20 pour Brighton

Remarquez les abréviations : 7.15 = 7 h 15.

B LA DATE

Les mois, les jours et les saisons

es jours et les mois prennent une majuscule en anglais.

• *Les mois* (the months)

January	janvier	July	juillet
February	février	August	août
March	mars	September	septembre
April	avril	October	octobre
May	mai	November	novembre
June	juin	December	décembre

• *Les jours de la semaine* (the days of the week)

Monday	lundi	Friday	vendredi
Tuesday	mardi	Saturday	samedi
Wednesday	mercredi	Sunday	dimanche
Thursday	jeudi		

• *Les saisons* (the seasons)

spring	le printemps	autumn	l'automne
summer	l'été	winter	l'hiver

En anglais américain, "l'automne" se dit aussi fall. Pour l'emploi de l'article, voir p. A7.

Les dates

Les années

Pour lire les années, on sépare les deux premiers chiffres des deux derniers :

1945 (19|45) = nineteen forty-five (littéralement *dix-neuf, quarante-cinq*)

L'emploi de hundred est possible, mais plus rare ; il s'utilisera dans un style très soutenu :

1945 = nineteen hundred and forty-five (*dix-neuf cent quarante-cinq*)

Mais les dates suivantes se disent pratiquement toujours de la même manière :

811* = eight hundred and eleven
1026 = ten twenty-six
1000* = one thousand
2000* = two thousand
2005 = two thousand and five

*Pour les années qui précèdent l'an 1000, ainsi que pour l'an 1000 et l'an 2000, on ajoute en général the year devant l'année (= the year 2000).

Les jours et les mois

En anglais, on emploie souvent les nombres ordinaux pour les dates (contrairement au français) :

14th July (qui se dit **"the fourteenth of July"**)
le 14 juillet

2nd November (qui se dit **"the second of November"**)
le 2 novembre

I wrote to you on 3rd March (qui se dit **"on the third of March"**)
je vous ai écrit le 3 mars

Mais il y a en fait différentes manières d'écrire la date :

12(th) May   **May 12(th)**

L'emploi du nombre cardinal est beaucoup plus courant que celui du nombre ordinal en anglais américain. En anglais britannique, il est aussi parfaitement possible d'employer le nombre cardinal.

En anglais américain, on omet pratiquement tout le temps le the à l'oral quand on commence par le mois :

May 12 se dit **May twelfth/May twelve**

En anglais britannique, on écrit les dates en mettant le jour en premier (comme en français), alors que c'est l'inverse en anglais américain :

10/4/92 = 10th April 1992, anglais britannique
4/10/92 = 10th April 1992, anglais américain (**10/4/92 = 4th October 1992** en américain)

Pour les nombres ordinaux, voir **Les nombres** p. A76.

C EXPRESSIONS IDIOMATIQUES

at 5 o'clock	*à cinq heures*
at about 11 o'clock	*à onze heures environ*
at about midnight	*vers minuit*
at about 10 o'clock	*vers (les) dix heures*
it's past six o'clock	*il est six heures passées*
at exactly four o'clock	*à quatre heures précises/ pile*
on the stroke of three	*sur le coup de trois heures*
from 9 o'clock onwards	*à partir de neuf heures*
shortly before seven	*peu avant sept heures*
shortly after seven	*peu après sept heures*
it's late	*il est tard*
he's late	*il est en retard*
the train is twenty minutes late	*le train a vingt minutes de retard*
my watch is six minutes slow	*ma montre retarde de six minutes*
my watch is six minutes fast	*ma montre avance de six minutes*
one day/morning/evening	*un jour/matin/soir*
this evening, tonight	*ce soir*
tomorrow evening, tomorrow night	*demain soir*
yesterday evening, last night	*hier soir*
Saturday evening, Saturday night	*samedi soir*
I'm going out on Saturday night ou evening	*je sors samedi soir*
on Saturday evening	*dans la soirée de samedi*
during Saturday night	*dans la nuit de samedi (à dimanche)*
tomorrow morning	*demain matin*
yesterday morning	*hier matin*
Monday morning	*lundi matin*
I'm going (on) Monday morning	*j'y vais lundi matin*
the next day	*le lendemain*
the next morning	*le lendemain matin*
a week on Monday, Monday week	*lundi en huit*
a fortnight on Monday	*lundi en quinze*
next week	*la semaine prochaine*
this (coming) week	*la semaine qui vient*
last week	*la semaine dernière*
I saw him the other Saturday	*je l'ai vu l'autre samedi*
I'm starting on Monday	*je commence lundi*
he comes on Mondays, he comes on a Monday	*il vient le lundi*
come one Monday	*viens un lundi*
he comes in the afternoon(s)	*il vient l'après-midi*
come one afternoon	*viens un après-midi*

A81

every other Monday, every second Monday — *un lundi sur deux*

every Saturday — *tous les samedis*

every Saturday evening ou night — *tous les samedis soir*

I spent the whole Sunday doing the cleaning — *j'ai passé tout mon dimanche à faire le ménage*

all her Sundays — *tous ses dimanches*

in the early afternoon/evening — *en début d'après-midi/de soirée*

I'll phone him first thing in the morning — *je lui téléphonerai à la première heure demain matin*

in the middle of June, mid-June — *au milieu du mois de juin, (à la) mi-juin*

in the middle of winter, mid-winter — *au milieu de l'hiver*

I've a meeting late morning — *j'ai une réunion à la fin de la matinée ou en fin de matinée*

at the end of winter — *à la fin de l'hiver*

we'll talk about it again at the end of January — *on en reparlera fin janvier ou à la fin du mois de janvier*

what day is it today? — *quel jour sommes-nous aujourd'hui ?*

what's the date? — *le combien sommes-nous ?*

it's the third of April — *c'est le trois avril*

in February — *au mois de/en février*

in 1996 — *en 1996*

in the summer of 1996, in summer 1996 — *l'été 1996*

in the sixties, in the 60s, in the 1960s — *dans les années soixante*

in the early/late sixties — *au début/à la fin des années soixante*

in the seventeenth century — *au dix-septième siècle*

in the 17th C — *au XVIIe s.*

FRENCH GRAMMAR

GRAMMAIRE FRANÇAISE

CONTENTS

1 GLOSSARY OF GRAMMATICAL TERMS

ADJECTIVE
An adjective provides supplementary information about a noun, describing what something is like, eg *a small house, a red car, an interesting pastime.*

ADVERB
Adverbs are normally used with a verb to add extra information by indicating **how** the action is done (adverbs of manner), **when, where** or **with how much intensity** the action is done (adverbs of time, place and intensity), or **to what extent** the action is done (adverbs of quantity). Adverbs may also be used with an adjective or another adverb, eg *a very attractive girl, very well.*

AGREEMENT
In French, words such as adjectives, articles and pronouns must agree in number and gender with the noun or pronoun to which they refer. This means that their spelling changes according to the **number** of the noun (singular or plural) and according to its **gender** (masculine or feminine).

ANTECEDENT
The antecedent of a relative pronoun is the word or words to which the relative pronoun refers. The antecedent is usually found directly before the relative pronoun, eg in the sentence *I know the man who did this*, the man is the antecedent of *who*.

APPOSITION
A word or a clause is said to be in apposition to another when it is placed directly after it without any joining word, eg *Mr Jones, our bank manager, rang today.*

ARTICLE
See DEFINITE ARTICLE, INDEFINITE ARTICLE and PARTITIVE ARTICLE.

ASPIRATE H
If a word begins with an aspirate h in French, it means that there is no liaison between it and the word preceding it, eg in les **h**aricots the s of les is not pronounced. Similarly, there is no contraction in spelling, eg la **h**aine and not l'haine. See SILENT H.

AUXILIARY
The French auxiliary verbs are avoir (*to have*) and être (*to be*). They are used to make up the first part of compound tenses, the second part being a past participle, eg *j'ai mangé, il est allé.*

CARDINAL
Cardinal numbers are numbers such as *one, two, ten, fourteen*, as opposed to ORDINAL numbers, eg *first, second.*

CLAUSE
A clause is a group of words which contains at least a subject and a verb: *he said* is a clause. A clause often contains more than this basic information, eg *he said this to her yesterday*. Sentences can be made up of several clauses, eg *he said/he'd call me/if he were free*. See SENTENCE.

COMPARATIVE
The comparative forms of adjectives and adverbs allow two things, persons or actions to be compared. In English, *more ... than, ...er than, less ... than* and *as ... as* are used for comparison.

COMPOUND
Compound tenses are verb tenses consisting of more than one element. In French, the compound tenses of a verb are formed by the auxiliary verb and the past participle: *j'ai visité, il est venu.*

CONDITIONAL
This mood is used to describe what someone would do, or something that would happen if a condition were fulfilled, eg *I would come if I were well; the chair would have broken if he had sat on it.*

CONJUGATION
The conjugation of a verb is the set of different forms taken in the particular tenses of that verb.

CONJUNCTION
Conjunctions are used to link different clauses. They may be coordinating or subordinating. Coordinating conjunctions are words like *and, but, or*; subordinating conjunctions are words like *because, after, although.*

DEFINITE ARTICLE
The definite article is *the* in English and *le, la* and *les* in French.

DEMONSTRATIVE
Demonstrative adjectives such as *this, that, these* and pronouns such as *this one, that one* are used to point out a particular person or object.

DIRECT OBJECT
A direct object is a noun or a pronoun which in English follows a verb without any linking preposition, eg *I met a friend.*

ELISION
Elision consists in replacing the last letter of certain words (*le, la, je, me, te, se, de, que*) with an apostrophe before a word starting with a vowel or a silent h, eg *l'eau, l'homme, j'aime.*

ENDING
The ending of a verb is determined by the person (1st/2nd/3rd) and number (singular/plural) of its subject. In French, most tenses have six different endings. See PERSON and NUMBER.

EXCLAMATION
An exclamation is a word or sentence used to express surprise or wonder, eg *what!, how!, how lucky!, what a nice day!*

FEMININE
See GENDER.

GENDER
The gender of a noun indicates whether the noun is masculine or feminine (all French nouns are either masculine or feminine).

IDIOMATIC EXPRESSIONS
Idiomatic expressions (or idioms) are expressions which cannot normally be translated word for word. For example, *it's raining cats and dogs* is translated by *il pleut des cordes.*

IMPERATIVE
This mood is used for giving orders, eg *eat!, don't go!*

INDEFINITE
Indefinite pronouns and adjectives are words that do not refer to a definite person or object, eg *each, someone, every.*

INDEFINITE ARTICLE
The indefinite article is *a* in English and *un, une* and *des* in French.

INDICATIVE
The indicative is the normal form of a verb as in *I like, he came, we are trying*. It is opposed to the subjunctive, conditional and imperative.

INDIRECT OBJECT
An indirect object is a pronoun or noun which follows a verb indirectly, with a linking preposition (usually to), eg *I spoke to my friend/him.*

INFINITIVE
The infinitive is the basic form of the verb as found in dictionaries. Thus *to eat, to finish, to take* are infinitives. In French, the infinitive is recognizable by its ending (-er, -ir or -re, eg *manger, finir, prendre*).

INTERROGATIVE
Interrogative words are used to ask a question. This may be a direct question (*when will you arrive?*) or an indirect question (*I don't know when he'll arrive*). See QUESTION.

MASCULINE
See GENDER.

MOOD This is the name given to the four main areas within which a verb is conjugated. See INDICATIVE, SUBJUNCTIVE, CONDITIONAL, IMPERATIVE.

NOUN A noun is a word or group of words which refers to a living creature, a thing, a place or an abstract idea, eg *postman, cat, shop, passport, life*.

NUMBER The number of a noun indicates whether the noun is singular or plural. A singular noun refers to one single person or thing, eg *boy, train* and a plural noun to more than one, eg *boys, trains*.

ORDINAL Ordinal numbers are *first, second, third, fourth* and all other numbers which end in -th. In French, all ordinal numbers, except for *premier* (first) and *second* (second), end in -ième.

PARTITIVE ARTICLE The partitive articles are *some* and *any* in English and *du, de la, de l'* and *des* (as in *du pain, de la confiture, de l'eau, des bananes*) in French.

PASSIVE A verb is used in the passive when the subject of the verb does not perform the action but is subjected to it. The passive is formed with the verb *to be* and the past participle of the verb, eg *he was rewarded*.

PAST PARTICIPLE The past participle of a verb is the form which is used after *to have* in English, eg *I have eaten, I have said, you have tried*.

PERSON In any tense, there are three persons in the singular (1st: *I* ... , 2nd: *you* ... , 3rd: *he/she* ...), and three in the plural (1st: *we* ... , 2nd: *you* ... , 3rd: *they* ...). See also ENDING.

PERSONAL PRONOUNS Personal pronouns stand for a noun. They usually accompany a verb and can be either the subject (*I, you, he/she/it, we, they*) or the object of the verb (*me, you, him/her/it, us, them*).

PLURAL See NUMBER.

POSSESSIVE Possessive adjectives and pronouns are used to indicate possession or ownership. They are words like *my/mine, your/yours, our/ours*.

PREPOSITION Prepositions are words such as *with, in, to, at*. They are followed by a noun or a pronoun.

PRESENT PARTICIPLE The present participle is the verb form which ends in -ing in English and -ant in French.

PRONOUN This is a word which stands for a noun. The main categories of pronouns are:

* Relative pronouns (eg *who, which, that*)

* Interrogative pronouns (eg *who?, what?, which?*)

* Demonstrative pronouns (eg *this, that, these*)

* Possessive pronouns (eg *mine, yours, his*)

* Personal pronouns (eg *you, him, us*)

* Reflexive pronouns (eg *myself, himself*)

* Indefinite pronouns (eg *something, all*)

QUESTION There are two question forms: **direct** questions stand on their own and require a question mark at the end, eg *when will he come?*; **indirect** questions are introduced by a clause and require no question mark, eg *I wonder when he will come*.

REFLEXIVE Reflexive verbs 'reflect' the action back onto the subject, eg *I dressed myself*. They are always found with a reflexive pronoun and are much more common in French than in English.

SENTENCE A sentence is a group of words made up of one or more clauses (see CLAUSE) and which makes a complete grammatical structure. The end of a sentence is indicated by a punctuation mark (usually a full stop, a question mark or an exclamation mark).

SILENT H The term 'silent h' is actually misleading since an h is never pronounced in French. The point is that when a silent h occurs, any preceding vowel is not pronounced either. For example, the h in *j'habite* is silent (note the *j'*). The h in *je hurle*, however, is **aspirate**, and so there is no contraction in spelling.

SIMPLE TENSE Simple tenses are tenses in which the verb consists of one word only, eg *j'habite, Maurice partira*.

SINGULAR See NUMBER.

SUBJECT The subject of a verb is the noun or pronoun which performs the action. In the sentences, *the train left early* and *she bought a record*, the train and she are the subjects.

SUBJUNCTIVE The subjunctive is a verb form which is rarely used in English, eg *if I were you, God save the Queen*, but common in French.

SUPERLATIVE The superlative is the form of an adjective or an adverb which, in English, is marked by *the most ... , the ...est* or *the least ...*

TENSE Verbs are used in tenses, which tell us whether an action takes place in the present, the past or the future.

VERB A verb is a word which describes the performance of an action, eg *to sing, to work, to watch* or the existence of a state, eg *to be, to have, to hope*.

2 ARTICLES

A THE DEFINITE ARTICLE

1 Forms

In English, there is only one form of the definite article: **the**. In French, there are three forms, depending on the gender and number of the noun following the article:

- with a masculine singular noun: le
- with a feminine singular noun: la   } the
- with a plural noun (masc or fem): les

MASC SING	FEM SING	PLURAL
le **chauffeur**	la **secrétaire**	les **étudiants**
the driver	*the secretary*	*the students*
le **salon**	la **cuisine**	les **chambres**
the living-room	*the kitchen*	*the bedrooms*

Note: le and la both change to l' before a vowel or a silent h:

	MASCULINE	FEMININE
BEFORE VOWEL	l'avion	l'odeur
	the plane	*the smell*
BEFORE SILENT H	l'homme	l'hôtesse
	the man	*the hostess*

Pronunciation: the s of les is pronounced z when the noun following it begins with a vowel or a silent h.

2 Forms with the prepositions 'à' and 'de'

When the definite article is used with à or de, the following spelling changes take place:

a) with à (to, at)

à + le → au
à + les → aux

à + la and à + l' do not change

au restaurant
at/to the restaurant

aux enfants
to the children

à la plage
at/to the beach

à l'aéroport
at/to the airport

Pronunciation: the x of aux is pronounced z when the noun following it begins with a vowel or a silent h.

b) with de (of, from)

de + le → du
de + les → des

de + la and de + l' do not change

du directeur
of/from the manager

des chômeurs
of/from the unemployed

de la région
of/from the area

de l'usine
of/from the factory

Pronunciation: the s of des is pronounced z when the noun following it begins with a vowel or a silent h.

3 Use

As in English, the definite article is used when referring to a particular person or thing, or particular persons or things:

les amis dont je t'ai parlé
the friends I told you about

le café est prêt
the coffee is ready

However, the definite article is used far more frequently in French than in English. It is used in particular in the following cases where English uses no article:

a) when the noun is used in a general sense

  i) to refer to all things of a kind:

vous acceptez les chèques?
do you take cheques?

le sucre est mauvais pour les dents
sugar is bad for the teeth

  ii) to refer to abstract things:

le travail et les loisirs
work and leisure

la musique classique
classical music

  iii) when stating likes and dislikes:

j'aime la viande mais je préfère le poisson
I like meat, but I prefer fish

je déteste les tomates
I hate tomatoes

b) with geographical names

  i) continents, countries and areas:

le Canada
Canada

la France
France

l'Europe
Europe

la Bretagne
Brittany

l'Afrique
Africa

les États-Unis
the United States

But: the article la is omitted with the prepositions en and de when used with feminine country names:

j'habite en France
I live in France

il vient d'Italie
he comes from Italy

With masculine country names, the corresponding prepositions à and de follow the normal rules:

j'habite au Portugal/aux États-Unis
I live in Portugal/in the United States

je viens du Japon/des Pays-Bas
I come from Japan/the Netherlands

A very few country names do not require an article, eg Panamá, Cuba, Taïwan, Singapour.

  ii) mountains, lakes and rivers:

le mont Everest
Mount Everest

le lac de Genève
Lake Geneva

c) with names of seasons

l'automne *autumn/Am fall*
l'hiver *winter*
le printemps *spring*
l'été *summer*

But: **en automne/été/hiver**
in autumn/summer/winter

au printemps
in spring

un jour d'été
a summer's day

d) with names of languages

j'apprends le français
I'm learning French

But: **ce film est en anglais**
this film is in English

e) with parts of the body

j'ai les cheveux roux
I've got red hair

ouvrez la bouche
open your mouth

les mains en l'air!
hands up!

l'homme à la barbe noire
the man with the black beard

f) with names following an adjective

le petit Pierre
little Pierre

la pauvre Isabelle
poor Isabelle

g) with titles

le docteur Coste
Doctor Coste

le commandant Cousteau
Captain Cousteau

h) with days of the week to express regular occurrences

que fais-tu le samedi?
what do you do on Saturdays?

le docteur reçoit le lundi et le vendredi
the doctor sees patients on Mondays and Fridays

i) with names of subjects or leisure activities

les maths *maths*
l'histoire et la géographie *history and geography*

la natation, la lecture, le football
swimming, reading, football

j) in expressions of price, quantity etc

c'est combien le kilo/la douzaine/la bouteille?
how much is it for a kilo/dozen/bottle?

B THE INDEFINITE ARTICLE

1 Forms

In French, there are three forms of the indefinite article, depending on the number and gender of the noun it accompanies:

- with a masculine singular noun: un *a*
- with a feminine singular noun: une *a*
- with a plural noun (masc or fem): des *some*

Note: des is often not translated in English:

il y a **des** nuages dans le ciel
there are clouds in the sky

2 Use

a) On the whole, the French indefinite article is used in the same way as its English equivalent:

un **homme**	une **femme**	des **hommes/femmes**
a man	*a woman*	*(some) men/women*
un **livre**	une **tasse**	des **livres/tasses**
a book	*a cup*	*(some) books/cups*

b) However, the English indefinite article is not always translated in French:

i) when stating someone's profession or occupation:

mon **père est** architecte
my father is an architect

elle **est** médecin
she is a doctor

Note, however, that the article is used after **c'est**, **c'était** etc:

c'est un **acteur célèbre**
he's a famous actor

ce sont des **fraises**
these are strawberries

ii) with nouns in apposition:

Madame Leclerc, employée de bureau
Mrs Leclerc, an office worker

iii) after **quel** in exclamations:

quel **dommage**!	quelle **surprise**!
what a pity!	*what a surprise!*

c) In negative sentences, **de** (or **d'**) is used instead of **un**, **une**, **des**:

je n'ai pas **d'amis**	je n'ai plus **de voiture**
I don't have any friends	*I don't have a car any more*

d) In French (but not in English), the indefinite article is used with abstract nouns followed by an adjective:

avec une patience remarquable
with remarkable patience

elle a fait **des** progrès étonnants
she's made amazing progress

Note, however, that the article is not used when there is no adjective:

avec plaisir	**sans** hésitation
with pleasure	*without hesitation*

C THE PARTITIVE ARTICLE

1 Forms

There are three forms of the French partitive article, which corresponds to 'some'/'any' in English:

- with a masculine singular noun: **du**
- with a feminine singular noun: **de la**
- with plural nouns (masc or fem): **des**

du **vin**	de la **bière**	des **fruits**
some wine	*some beer*	*some fruit*

Note that **de l'** is used in front of masculine or feminine singular nouns beginning with a vowel or a silent **h**:

de l'**argent**	de l'**eau**	de l'**helium**
some money	*some water*	*some helium*

2 Use

a) On the whole, the French partitive article is used as in English.

However, English tends to omit the partitive article where French does not:

achète **du pain**	vous avez **du beurre**?
buy (some) bread	*do you have (any) butter?*
je voudrais de la **viande**	tu veux de la **soupe**?
I'd like some meat	*do you want (any) soup?*
tu dois manger des **légumes**	as-tu acheté des **poires**?
you must eat (some) vegetables	*did you buy any pears?*

b) The partitive article is replaced by **de** (or **d'**) in the following cases:

i) in negative expressions:

il n'y a plus **de café**	je n'ai pas **de frères**
there isn't any coffee left	*I don't have any brothers*
nous n'avons plus **d'argent**	je n'ai pas **d'enfants**
we don't have any money left	*I don't have any children*

Note, however, that when the clause is introduced by **c'est**, **il est** etc, the partitive article remains:

ce n'est pas **du** cuir, c'est **du** plastique
it's not leather, it's plastic

ii) after expressions of quantity (see also p B60):

il boit trop **de café**	il gagne assez **d'argent**
he drinks too much coffee	*he earns enough money*

iii) after **avoir besoin de**:

j'ai besoin **d'argent**	tu as besoin **de timbres**?
I need (some) money	*do you need (any) stamps?*

iv) where an adjective is followed by a plural noun:

de **petites villes**	d'**énormes mensonges**
(some) small towns	*outrageous lies*

Note, however, that if the adjective comes after the noun, **des** does not change:

des **résultats encourageants**
encouraging results

3 Partitive or definite article?

When no article is used in English, it is not always clear which is the right article in French: **le/la/les** or **du/de la/des**.

If **some/any** can be inserted before the English noun, the French partitive article should be used. But if the noun is used in a general sense and inserting **some/any** in front of the English noun does not make sense, the definite article must be used:

did you buy fish? (ie any fish)
tu as acheté **du** poisson?

yes, I did; I like fish (ie fish in general)
oui; j'aime **le** poisson

3 NOUNS

A noun is a word or group of words which refers to a person, an animal, a thing, a place or an abstract idea.

A GENDER

All French nouns are either masculine or feminine; there is no neuter as in English. Though no absolute rule can be stated, the gender can often be determined either by the meaning or the ending of the noun.

1 Masculine

a) *by meaning*

i) words referring to men and male animals:

un homme	le boucher	le tigre
a man	*the butcher*	*the tiger*

ii) names of common trees and shrubs:

le chêne	le sapin	le laurier
the oak	*the fir tree*	*the laurel*

iii) days, months, seasons:

lundi	mars	le printemps
Monday	*March*	*spring*

iv) languages:

le français	le polonais	le russe
French	*Polish*	*Russian*

v) rivers and countries not ending in a silent e:

le Nil	le Portugal	le Danemark
the Nile	*Portugal*	*Denmark*

Note, however, that there are exceptions to this rule:

le Danube	le Rhône	le Mexique
the Danube	*the Rhone*	*Mexico*

b) *by ending*

-acle	**le spectacle** (show)
	But: **une débâcle** (shambles)
-age	**le fromage** (cheese)
	But: **la cage** (cage), **une image** (picture), **la nage** (swimming), **la page** (page), **la plage** (beach), **la rage** (rage, rabies)
-é	**le marché** (market)
	But: nouns ending in -té and -tié are usually feminine (see 2b)
-eau	**le chapeau** (hat)
	But: **l'eau** (water), **la peau** (skin)
-ège	**le piège** (trap), **le collège** (secondary school)
-ème	**le thème** (theme, topic)
	But: **la crème** (cream)
-isme, -asme	**le communisme** (communism), **le tourisme** (tourism), **l'enthousiasme** (enthusiasm)
-o	**le numéro** (the number)
	But: **la dynamo** (dynamo) and most abbreviated expressions: **une auto** (car), **la météo** (weather forecast), **la photo** (photograph), **la radio** (radio), **la sténo** (shorthand), **la stéréo** (stereo)

Nouns ending in a consonant are usually *masculine*.

Notable exceptions are:

i) most nouns ending in -tion, -sion, -ation, -aison, -ison

ii) most abstract nouns ending in -eur (see 2b)

iii) the following nouns ending in a consonant:

la clef (key)	la nef (nave)
la soif (thirst)	la faim (hunger)
la fin (end)	la façon (manner)
la leçon (lesson)	la boisson (drink)
la moisson (harvest)	la rançon (ransom)
la mer (sea)	la cuiller (spoon)
la chair (flesh)	la basse-cour (farmyard)
la cour (yard)	la tour (tower)
la brebis (ewe)	une fois (once)
la vis (screw)	la souris (mouse)
la part (share)	la plupart (majority, most)
la dent (tooth)	la dot (dowry)

la forêt (forest)	la jument (mare)
la mort (death)	la nuit (night)
la croix (cross)	la noix (nut)
la paix (peace)	la perdrix (partridge)
la toux (cough)	la voix (voice)

2 Feminine

a) *by meaning*

i) words referring to women and female animals:

la mère	la bonne	la génisse
the mother	*the maid*	*the heifer*

ii) names of rivers and countries ending with a silent e:

la Seine	la Russie	la Belgique
the Seine	*Russia*	*Belgium*

iii) saints' days and festivals:

la Toussaint	la Pentecôte
All Saints' Day	*Whitsun*

Note, however, that **Noël** (Christmas) is masculine except when used with the definite article: **à la Noël** (at Christmas)

b) *by ending*

-ace	**la place** (square, seat)
	But: **un espace** (space)
-ade	**la salade** (salad)
	But: **le grade** (degree, rank), **le stade** (stadium)
-ance, -anse	**la puissance** (power), **la danse** (dancing)
-ée	**la soirée** (evening), **la journée** (day)
	But: **le musée** (museum), **le lycée** (secondary school)
-ence, -ense	**une évidence** (evidence), **la défense** (defence)
	But: **le silence** (silence)
-ère	**la lumière** (light)
	But: **le mystère** (mystery), **le caractère** (character)
-eur	**la peur** (fear)
	But: **le bonheur** (happiness), **le chœur** (choir), **le cœur** (heart), **un honneur** (honour), **le labeur** (toil), **le malheur** (misfortune)
-ie	**la pluie** (rain)
	But: **le génie** (genius), **un incendie** (fire), **le parapluie** (umbrella)
-ière	**la bière** (beer)
	But: **le cimetière** (cemetery)
-oire	**la gloire** (glory)
	But: **le laboratoire** (laboratory), **le pourboire** (tip)
-tion, -sion, -ation, -aison, -ison	**la fiction** (fiction), **la nation** (nation), **la raison** (reason), **la prison** (prison)
-té	**la bonté** (goodness)
	But: **le côté** (side), **le comté** (county), **le traité** (treaty), **le pâté** (pâté)
-tié	**la moitié** (half), **la pitié** (pity)

Most nouns ending in a silent e following two consonants are feminine:

la botte (boot), **la couronne** (crown), **la terre** (earth), **la masse** (mass), **la lutte** (struggle)

But: **le verre** (glass), **le parterre** (flower-bed), **le tonnerre** (thunder), **un intervalle** (interval), **le carrosse** (carriage)

3 Difficulties

a) Some nouns may have either gender depending on the sex of the person to whom they refer:

un artiste	une artiste
a (male) artist	*a (female) artist*

le Russe | la Russe
the Russian (man) | *the Russian (woman)*

similarly:

un aide/une aide — *an assistant*
un camarade/une camarade — *a friend*
un domestique/une domestique *a servant*
un enfant/une enfant — *a child*
un malade/une malade — *a patient*
un propriétaire/une propriétaire *an owner*

b) Others have only one gender for both sexes:

un ange | un amateur | un auteur
an angel | *an amateur* | *an author*

une connaissance | une dupe | un écrivain
an acquaintance | *a dupe* | *a writer*

une personne | le médecin | le peintre
a person | *the doctor* | *the painter*

la recrue | le sculpteur | la sentinelle
the recruit | *the sculptor (sculptress)* | *the sentry*

le témoin | la victime | la vedette
the witness | *the victim* | *the (film) star*

Note, however, that modern French tends to use feminine forms for many different functions. La ministre, la juge and la professeur can now be commonly found in the press, and new forms such as une écrivaine have also begun to appear.

c) The following nouns change meaning according to gender:

	MASCULINE	FEMININE
aide	*male assistant*	*assistance, female assistant*
crêpe	*mourning band*	*pancake*
critique	*critic*	*criticism*
faux	*forgery*	*scythe*
livre	*book*	*pound*
manche	*handle*	*sleeve*
manœuvre	*labourer*	*manoeuvre*
mémoire	*memorandum*	*memory*
mode	*method, way*	*fashion*
mort	*dead man*	*death*
moule	*mould*	*mussel*
page	*pageboy*	*page*
pendule	*pendulum*	*clock*
physique	*physique*	*physics*
poêle	*stove*	*frying pan*
poste	*post (job), set*	*post office*
somme	*nap*	*sum*
tour	*trick, tour*	*tower*
trompette	*trumpeter*	*trumpet*
vapeur	*steamer*	*steam*
vase	*vase*	*silt*
voile	*veil*	*sail*

d) A few words vary in gender according to their usage. The plural noun gens is regarded as feminine when it follows an adjective, and masculine when it precedes it:

de bonnes gens | des gens ennuyeux
good people | *boring people*

amour, délice and orgue are masculine when used in the singular and feminine when used in the plural:

un amour de jeunesse | des amours maheureuses
an old flame | *unhappy love affairs*

un délice inoubliable | des délices infinies
an unforgettable delight | *infinite delights*

un orgue électrique | les grandes orgues
an electric organ | *the great organ*

e) City names

Some city names are traditionally feminine:

La Rochelle | La Haye | Alger la Blanche
La Rochelle | *The Hague* | *Algiers, the white city*

Others are masculine in everyday usage:

le Paris des années 30 | le Londres de mon souvenir
Paris in the 30s | *the London I remember*

le vieux Nice | Berlin fut totalement détruit
old Nice | *Berlin was completely destroyed*

In literary French, however, city names are feminine:

Caen fut prise après de terribles bombardements
Caen was taken after a terrible bombardment

B THE FORMATION OF FEMININES

The feminine of nouns may be formed in the following ways:

1 By adding an e to the masculine form:

un ami | une amie
a (male) friend | *a (female) friend*

un Hollandais | une Hollandaise
a Dutchman | *a Dutch woman*

Note that nouns which end in -e in the masculine form do not change:

un élève | une élève
a (male) pupil | *a (female) pupil*

Note also that the addition of an e often entails an alteration of the masculine form:

i) nouns ending in -t and -n double the final consonant:

le chien | la chienne *(dog/bitch)*
le chat | la chatte *(cat)*

ii) nouns ending in -er add a grave accent to the e immediately preceding the r:

un ouvrier | une ouvrière *(workman/female worker)*

iii) nouns ending in -eur change into -euse:

le vendeur | la vendeuse *(male/female shop assistant)*

However, a few nouns ending in -eur change into -eresse:

le pécheur | la pécheresse *(sinner)*

iv) nouns ending in -teur change into -teuse or -trice according to the following guidelines:

if the stem of the word is also that of a present participle the feminine form ends in -euse:

le chanteur | la chanteuse *(male/female singer)*

if the stem is not that of a present participle, the feminine form ends in -trice:

le lecteur | la lectrice *(male/female reader)*

v) nouns ending in -f change into -ve:

le veuf | la veuve *(widower/widow)*

vi) nouns ending in -x change into -se:

un époux | une épouse *(husband/wife)*

vii) nouns ending in -eau change into -elle:

le jumeau | la jumelle *(male/female twin)*

2 By using a different word (as in English):

le beau-fils | la belle-fille *(son-/daughter-in-law)*
le beau-père | la belle-mère *(father-/mother-in-law)*
le bélier | la brebis *(ram/ewe)*

le bœuf	la vache (ox/cow)
le canard	la cane (drake/duck)
le cheval	la jument (horse/mare)
le cerf	la biche (stag/hind)
le coq	la poule (cock/hen)
le fils	la fille (son/daughter)
le frère	la sœur (brother/sister)
un homme	une femme (man/woman)
un jars	une oie (gander/goose)
le mâle	la femelle (male/female)
le neveu	la nièce (nephew/niece)
un oncle	une tante (uncle/aunt)
le parrain	la marraine (godfather/godmother)
le père	la mère (father/mother)
le porc	la truie (pig/sow)
le roi	la reine (king/queen)

3 By adding the word femme (or femelle for animals):

une femme **médecin** (doctor)
un perroquet femelle (female parrot)

4 *Irregular feminine forms*

un abbé	une abbesse (abbot/abbess)
un âne	une ânesse (donkey)
le comte	la comtesse (count/countess)
le dieu	la déesse (god/goddess)
le duc	la duchesse (duke/duchess)
un Esquimau	une Esquimaude (Eskimo)
le fou	la folle (madman/mad woman)
un Grec	une Grecque (Greek)
un héros	une héroïne (hero/heroine)
un hôte	une hôtesse (host/hostess)
le maître	la maîtresse (master/mistress)
le prêtre	la prêtresse (priest/priestess)
le prince	la princesse (prince/princess)
le tigre	la tigresse (tiger/tigress)
le Turc	la Turque (Turk)
le vieux	la vieille (old man/old woman)

C THE FORMATION OF PLURALS

1 Most nouns form their plural by adding s to the singular:

| le vin | les vins | wine |
| un étudiant | des étudiants | student |

2 Nouns ending in -s, -x or -z remain unchanged:

le bras	les bras	arm
la voix	les voix	voice
le nez	les nez	nose

3 Nouns ending in -au, -eau and -eu add x to the singular:

le tuyau	les tuyaux	drainpipe
le bateau	les bateaux	boat
le jeu	les jeux	game

But: le landau | les landaus | pram |
| le bleu | les bleus | bruise |
| le pneu | les pneus | tyre |

4 Nouns ending in -al change to -aux:

| le journal | les journaux | newspaper |

But: le bal | les bals | dance |
| le carnaval | les carnavals | carnival |
| le festival | les festivals | festival |

5 Nouns ending in -ail change to -aux:

le bail	les baux	lease
le travail	les travaux	work
le vitrail	les vitraux	stained-glass window

But: le détail | les détails | detail |
| l'épouvantail | les épouvantails | scarecrow |
| l'éventail | les éventails | fan |

| le rail | les rails | rail |

6 Nouns ending in -ou:

a) Seven nouns ending in -ou add x in the plural:

le bijou	les bijoux	jewel
le caillou	les cailloux	pebble
le chou	les choux	cabbage
le genou	les genoux	knee
le hibou	les hiboux	owl
le joujou	les joujoux	toy
le pou	les poux	louse

b) Other nouns ending in -ou add s:

| le clou | les clous | nail |

7 Plural of compound nouns:

Each noun ought to be checked individually in a dictionary:

eg | le chou-fleur | les choux-fleurs | cauliflower |
| le beau-père | les beaux-pères | father-in-law |

But: un essuie-glace | des essuie-glaces | windscreen wiper |
| le tire-bouchon | les tire-bouchons | corkscrew |

8 Irregular plurals:

un œil	des yeux	eye
le ciel	les cieux	sky
Monsieur	Messieurs	Mr
Madame	Mesdames	Mrs
Mademoiselle	Mesdemoiselles	Miss

9 Collective nouns:

a) Some nouns are singular in French but plural in English:

le bétail	cattle
la recette	takings
la police	police

la police a arrêté certains grévistes
the police have arrested some strikers

b) Others are plural in French but singular in English:

le nouvelles	news
les capitaux	capital
les cheveux	hair

les nouvelles sont bonnes
the news is good

10 Proper nouns:

a) Ordinary family names are invariable:

j'ai rencontré les Leblanc
I met the Leblancs

b) Historical names add -s:

| les Stuarts | les Bourbons | les Tudors |
| *the Stuarts* | *the Bourbons* | *the Tudors* |

4 ADJECTIVES

Adjectives usually accompany a noun (or a pronoun) and provide extra information about what someone or something is like:

une grande ville
a large city

un film intéressant
an interesting film

elle est espagnole
she is Spanish

c'était ennuyeux
it was boring

A AGREEMENT OF ADJECTIVES

In French, adjectives agree in number and gender with the noun or pronoun to which they refer. Therefore French adjectives have four different forms which are determined by the noun they accompany:

- masculine singular (basic form, found in the dictionary)
- feminine singular
- masculine plural
- feminine plural

un passeport vert
a green passport

une voiture verte
a green car

des gants verts
green gloves

des chaussettes vertes
green socks

Note that if two singular words share the same adjective, the adjective will be in the plural:

un foulard et un bonnet rouges
a red scarf and (a red) hat

If one of these words is feminine and the other masculine, the adjective will be in the masculine plural:

une robe et un manteau noirs
a black dress and (a black) coat

B FEMININE FORMS OF ADJECTIVES

1 General rule

Add the letter e to the masculine singular form:

MASCULINE	FEMININE
grand	grande
amusant	amusante
anglais	anglaise
bronzé	bronzée

un livre amusant
an amusing book

une histoire amusante
an amusing story

il est bronzé
he is suntanned

elle est bronzée
she is suntanned

2 Adjectives already ending in -e

These do not change:

MASCULINE	FEMININE
rouge	rouge
jeune	jeune
malade	malade

mon père est malade
my father is ill

ma mère est malade
my mother is ill

3 Others

The spelling of some adjectives changes when the e is added:

a) The following masculine endings generally double the final consonant before adding e:

MASCULINE ENDING	FEMININE ENDING
-el	-elle
-eil	-eille
-en	-enne
-on	-onne
-as	-asse
-et	-ette

MASCULINE		FEMININE
réel	*(real)*	réelle
cruel	*(cruel)*	cruelle
pareil	*(similar)*	pareille
ancien	*(old)*	ancienne
italien	*(Italian)*	italienne
bon	*(good)*	bonne
gras	*(greasy)*	grasse
bas	*(low)*	basse

muet	*(dumb)*	muette
net	*(clear)*	nette

un problème actuel
a topical problem

la vie actuelle
present-day life

un bon conseil
good advice

c'est une bonne recette
it's a good recipe

Note, however, that the feminine ending of some common adjectives in -et is -ète instead of -ette:

MASCULINE		FEMININE
complet	*(complete)*	complète
incomplet	*(incomplete)*	incomplète
concret	*(concrete)*	concrète
discret	*(discreet)*	discrète
inquiet	*(worried)*	inquiète
secret	*(secret)*	secrète

b) | MASCULINE IN -er | | FEMININE IN -ère |
|---|---|---|
| cher | *(dear)* | chère |
| fier | *(proud)* | fière |
| dernier | *(last)* | dernière |

c) | MASCULINE IN -x | | FEMININE IN -se |
|---|---|---|
| heureux | *(happy)* | heureuse |
| malheureux | *(unhappy)* | malheureuse |
| sérieux | *(serious)* | sérieuse |
| jaloux | *(jealous)* | jalouse |

But: | doux | *(soft)* | douce |
|---|---|---|
| faux | *(false)* | fausse |
| roux | *(red-haired)* | rousse |
| vieux | *(old)* | vieille |

d) | MASCULINE IN -eur | | FEMININE IN -euse |
|---|---|---|
| menteur | *(lying)* | menteuse |
| trompeur | *(deceitful)* | trompeuse |

This rule, however, applies only when the stem of the adjective is also the stem of a present participle (eg mentant, trompant). The following five adjectives simply add an e to the feminine, -eur becoming -eure:

MASCULINE		FEMININE
extérieur	*(external)*	extérieure
intérieur	*(internal)*	intérieure
inférieur	*(inferior)*	inférieure
supérieur	*(superior)*	supérieure
meilleur	*(better)*	meilleure

The feminine ending of the remaining adjectives in -teur is -trice:

MASCULINE		FEMININE
protecteur	*(protective)*	protectrice
destructeur	*(destructive)*	destructrice

e) | MASCULINE IN -f | | FEMININE IN -ve |
|---|---|---|
| neuf | *(new)* | neuve |
| vif | *(lively)* | vive |
| naïf | *(naive)* | naïve |
| actif | *(active)* | active |
| passif | *(passive)* | passive |
| positif | *(positive)* | positive |
| bref | *(brief)* | brève *(note the è)* |

f) | MASCULINE IN -c | | FEMININE IN -che or -que |
|---|---|---|
| blanc | *(white)* | blanche |
| franc | *(frank)* | franche |
| sec | *(dry)* | sèche *(note the è)* |
| public | *(public)* | publique |
| turc | *(Turkish)* | turque |
| grec | *(Greek)* | grecque *(note the c)* |

g) The following five common adjectives have an irregular feminine form and two forms for the masculine singular; the second masculine form, based on the feminine form, is used before words starting with a vowel or a silent h:

MASCULINE	FEMININE	MASCULINE 2
beau	belle	bel
(beautiful)		
nouveau	nouvelle	nouvel
(new)		
vieux	vieille	vieil
(old)		
fou	folle	fol
(mad)		
mou	molle	mol
(soft)		

un beau lac	une belle vue	un bel enfant
a beautiful lake	*a beautiful view*	*a beautiful child*
un nouveau disque	la nouvelle année	un nouvel ami
a new record	*the new year*	*a new friend*
un vieux tableau	la vieille ville	un vieil homme
an old painting	*the old town*	*an old man*

h) Other irregular feminines:

MASCULINE		FEMININE
favori	*(favourite)*	favorite
gentil	*(nice)*	gentille
nul	*(no)*	nulle
frais	*(fresh)*	fraîche
malin	*(shrewd)*	maligne
sot	*(foolish)*	sotte
long	*(long)*	longue
aigu	*(sharp)*	aiguë
ambigu	*(ambiguous)*	ambiguë
chic	*(elegant)*	chic
châtain	*(chestnut)*	châtain

C PLURALS OF ADJECTIVES

1 General rule

The masculine and feminine plural of adjectives is formed by adding an s to the singular form:

un vélo neuf	des vélos neufs
a new bike	*new bikes*
une belle fleur	de belles fleurs
a beautiful flower	*beautiful flowers*
le livre intéressant	les livres intéressants
the interesting book	*the interesting books*

2 Adjectives ending in -s or -x

If the masculine singular ends in -s or -x, the plural form does not take an s:

il est heureux	ils sont heureux
he's happy	*they are happy*
un touriste anglais	des touristes anglais
an English tourist	*English tourists*

3 Others

A few masculine plurals are irregular (the feminine plurals are all regular):

a) | SINGULAR IN | | PLURAL IN |
|-------------|------|-----------|
| -al | | -aux |
| normal | *(normal)* | normaux |
| brutal | *(brutal)* | brutaux |
| loyal | *(loyal)* | loyaux |
| *But:* fatal | *(fatal)* | fatals |
| natal | *(native)* | natals |
| naval | *(naval)* | navals |

Note that the adjective final (final) has two masculine plural forms: finals and finaux.

b) | SINGULAR IN | | PLURAL IN |
|-------------|------|-----------|
| -eau | | -eaux |
| beau | *(beautiful)* | beaux |
| nouveau | *(new)* | nouveaux |

D POSITION OF ADJECTIVES

1 Unlike English adjectives, French adjectives usually follow the noun:

un métier intéressant	des parents modernes
an interesting job	*modern parents*

Adjectives of colour and nationality always follow the noun:

des chaussures rouges	le drapeau britannique
red shoes	*the British flag*

2 However, the following common adjectives generally come before the noun:

beau	beautiful
bon	good
court	short
gentil	nice
grand	big, tall
gros	fat
haut	high
jeune	young
joli	pretty
long	long
mauvais	bad
méchant	nasty, naughty
meilleur	better
moindre	lesser, least
petit	small
pire	worse
vieux	old
vilain	nasty, ugly

3 Some adjectives have a different meaning according to their position:

	BEFORE NOUN	AFTER NOUN
ancien	*former*	*ancient*
brave	*good*	*brave*
certain	*some*	*sure*
cher	*dear*	*expensive*
dernier	*last (final)*	*last (latest)*
grand	*great (people only)*	*big, tall*
même	*same*	*very*
pauvre	*poor (pitiable)*	*poor (not rich)*
propre	*own*	*clean*
seul	*single, only*	*alone, lonely*
simple	*mere*	*simple*
vrai	*real*	*true*

mon ancien métier	un tableau ancien
my former job	*an old painting*
un brave type	un homme brave
a nice fellow	*a brave man*
un certain charme	un fait certain
a certain charm	*a definite fact*
chère Brigitte	un cadeau cher
dear Brigitte	*an expensive present*
la dernière séance	le mois dernier
the last performance	*last month*
une grande vedette	un homme assez grand
a great star	*a fairly tall man*
le même endroit	la vérité même
the same place	*the truth itself*
mon pauvre ami!	des gens pauvres
my poor friend!	*poor people*
mon propre frère	une chambre propre
my own brother	*a clean room*

mon seul **espoir**	**un homme** seul
my only hope	*a lonely man*
un simple employé	**des goûts** simples
an ordinary employee	*simple tastes*
un vrai **casse-pieds**	**une histoire** vraie
a real bore	*a true story*

If a noun is accompanied by several adjectives, the same rules apply to each of them:

le bon vieux temps
the good old days

un joli foulard rouge
a pretty red scarf

E COMPARATIVE AND SUPERLATIVE OF ADJECTIVES

Persons or things can be compared by using:

1. *the comparative form of the adjective:*

   more ... than
   ...er than
   less ... than
   not as ... as
   as ... as

2. *the superlative form of the adjective:*

   the most ...
   the ...est
   the least ...

1 The comparative

The French comparative is formed as follows:

plus ... (que)	plus **long**	plus **cher**
more ... (than)	*longer*	*more expensive*
... er (than)		
moins ... (que)	moins **long**	moins **récent**
less ... (than)	*less long*	*less recent*
not as ... (as)		
aussi ... (que)	aussi **bon**	aussi **important**
as ... (as)	*as good*	*as important*

une plus grande **maison**   **un village** plus ancien
a larger house   *an older village*

le football est-il plus populaire **que le rugby?**
is football more popular than rugby?

ces gants sont moins **chauds** que **les autres**
these gloves are less warm than the other ones

elle est beaucoup/bien moins **patiente** que **lui**
she's far less patient than he is

le problème de la pollution est tout aussi **grave**
the pollution problem is just as serious

2 The superlative

a) *Formation*

le/la/les plus ...	*the most ... , the ...est*
le/la/les moins ...	*the least ...*
le plus grand **pays**	la plus grande **ville**
the largest country	*the largest city*
les plus grands **acteurs**	les plus grandes **voitures**
the greatest actors	*the largest cars*

b) *Word order*

i) The normal rules governing word order of adjectives apply. When a superlative adjective comes after the noun, the article is used twice, before the noun and before the adjective:

le plat le plus **délicieux**
the most delicious dish

l'histoire la plus **passionnante**
the most exciting story

ii) When a possessive adjective is used, there are two possible constructions, depending on the position of the adjective:

ma plus forte matière
my best subject

or: **mon besoin** le plus **urgent est de trouver un emploi**
my most urgent need is to find a job

c) 'in' is normally translated by de:

la plus jolie maison du **quartier/de** la **ville**
the prettiest house in the area/town

le restaurant le plus **cher de France**
the most expensive restaurant in France

Note that verbs following the superlative usually take the subjunctive (see p B33).

3 Irregular comparatives and superlatives

ADJECTIVE	COMPARATIVE	SUPERLATIVE
bon	meilleur	le meilleur
good	*better*	*best*
mauvais	pire	le pire
bad	plus mauvais	le plus mauvais
	worse	*the worst*
petit	moindre	le moindre
small	plus petit	le plus petit
	smaller, lesser	*the smallest, the least*

Note that pire and le pire are, strictly speaking, the correct comparative and superlative forms of **mauvais**. **Plus mauvais** and **le plus mauvais** can also be found in everyday French, however, with a slight difference in meaning: pire and le pire express the absolute (ie one cannot conceive of a worse example of ...) while **plus mauvais** and **le plus mauvais** indicate a comparison of a lesser degree:

il n'y a pas de pire **professeur que lui**
he is the worst teacher of all

c'est la pire **chose qui pouvait lui arriver**
it's the worst thing that could happen to him

ma note est plus mauvaise **que la tienne**
my mark is worse than yours

c'est le plus mauvais **élève de la classe**
he's the worst pupil in the class

Note, too, that moindre usually means 'less in importance', and plus petit 'less in size':

le moindre **de mes soucis**
the least of my worries

elle est plus petite **que moi**
she is smaller than I (am)

F ADJECTIVES OF NATIONALITY

1. French, unlike English, does not use capital letters for adjectives of nationality. Only nouns indicating nationality are written with a capital letter in French:

une voiture anglaise   **une Anglaise**
an English car   *an English woman*

2. An adjective of nationality in English is sometimes best translated by a genitive construction in French:

l'ambassade de France	**l'équipe de France de rugby**
the French embassy	*the French rugby team*
l'équipe de Nantes	**l'équipe de Glasgow**
the Nantes team	*the Glasgow or Glaswegian team*

le championnat de France
the French league

la Coupe de France de foot-ball
the French football cup

la Grand Prix du Brésil
the Brazilian Grand Prix

la terre de France
French soil

la couronne de France
the French crown, the crown of France

les côtes de France
the French coastline

une grammaire de l'anglais
an English grammar

5 ADVERBS

Adverbs are normally used with a verb to express:

		ADVERBS OF
how		*manner*
when		*time*
where	an action is done	*place*
with how much intensity		*intensity*
to what extent		*quantity*

A ADVERBS OF MANNER

These are usually formed by adding -ment to the adjective (like -ly in English):

1 If the adjective ends in a consonant, -ment is added to its feminine form:

ADJECTIVE (masc, fem)	ADVERB
doux, douce *(soft)*	doucement *(softly)*
franc, franche *(frank)*	franchement *(frankly)*
final, finale *(final)*	finalement *(finally)*

2 If the adjective ends in a vowel, -ment is added to its masculine form:

ADJECTIVE	ADVERB
absolu *(absolute)*	absolument *(absolutely)*
désespéré *(desperate)*	désespérément *(desperately)*
vrai *(true)*	vraiment *(truly)*
simple *(simple)*	simplement *(simply)*

But: gai *(cheerful)* — gaiement or gaîment *(cheerfully)*

nouveau *(new)* — nouvellement *(newly)*
fou *(mad)* — follement *(madly)*

3 Many adverbs have irregular forms:

a) Some change the e of the feminine form of the adjective to é before adding -ment:

ADJECTIVE	ADVERB
commun *(common)*	communément *(commonly)*
précis *(precise)*	précisément *(precisely)*
profond *(deep)*	profondément *(deeply)*
énorme *(enormous)*	énormément *(enormously)*
aveugle *(blind)*	aveuglément *(blindly)*

b) Adjectives which end in -ent and -ant change to -emment and -amment. Note that both endings are pronounced like amant:

ADJECTIVE	ADVERB
prudent *(careful)*	prudemment *(carefully)*
évident *(obvious)*	évidemment *(obviously)*
brillant *(brilliant)*	brillamment *(brilliantly)*

But: lent *(slow)* — lentement *(slowly)*

4 Some adverbs are completely irregular, including some of the most commonly used ones:

ADJECTIVE	ADVERB
bon *(good)*	bien *(well)*
bref *(brief)*	brièvement *(briefly)*
gentil *(kind)*	gentiment *(kindly)*
mauvais *(bad)*	mal *(badly)*
meilleur *(better)*	mieux *(better)*

5 Some adjectives are also used as adverbs in certain set expressions:

parler bas/haut *or* fort	*to speak softly/loudly*
coûter/payer cher	*to cost/pay a lot*
s'arrêter net	*to stop short*
couper court	*to cut short*
voir clair	*to see clearly*
marcher droit	*to walk straight*
travailler dur	*to work hard*
chanter faux/juste	*to sing off key/in tune*
sentir mauvais/bon	*to smell bad/good*
refuser net	*to refuse point blank*

6 After verbs relating to saying something or looking at something in French an adverbial phrase is often preferred to an adverb:

'tu m'écriras?' dit-il d'une voix triste
'will you write to me?' he said sadly

elle nous a regardés d'un air dédaigneux
she looked at us disdainfully

7 English adverbs may be expressed in French by a preposition followed by a noun:

sans soin	*carelessly*
avec fierté	*proudly*
avec amour	*lovingly*

B ADVERBS OF TIME

These are not usually formed from adjectives. The commonest ones are the following:

alors	*then*
après	*afterwards*
aujourd'hui	*today*
aussitôt	*at once*
bientôt	*soon*
d'abord	*first*
déjà	*already*
demain	*tomorrow*
encore	*still, again*
pas encore	*not yet*
enfin	*at last, finally*
hier	*yesterday*
parfois	*sometimes*
rarement	*seldom*
souvent	*often*
tard	*late*
tôt	*early*
toujours	*always*
tout de suite	*immediately*

c'est déjà Noël!
it's Christmas already!

tu as déjà essayé?
have you tried before?

il mange encore!
he's still eating!

elle n'est pas encore arrivée
she hasn't arrived yet

C ADVERBS OF PLACE

Like adverbs of time, these are not usually formed from adjectives. The commonest ones are the following:

ailleurs	somewhere else, elsewhere
ici	here
là	there
loin	far away
dessus	on top, on it
au-dessus	over, above
dessous	underneath
au-dessous	below
dedans	inside
dehors	outside
devant	in front, ahead
derrière	behind
partout	everywhere

ne restez pas dehors!
don't stay outside!

mon nom est marqué dessus
my name is written on it

qu'est-ce qu'il y a dedans?
what's inside?

passez devant
go in front

D ADVERBS OF INTENSITY AND QUANTITY

These may be used with a verb, an adjective or another adverb. The commonest ones are the following:

à peine	hardly
assez	enough, quite
autant	as much/many
beaucoup	a lot, much/many
combien	how much/many
comme	how
moins	less
plus	more
presque	nearly
peu	little
seulement	only
si	so
tant	so much/many
tellement	so much/many
très	very
trop	too, too much/many
un peu	a little

vous avez assez bu!
you've had enough to drink!

il ne fait pas assez chaud!
it's not warm enough

nous avons beaucoup ri
we laughed a lot

comme c'est amusant!
how funny!

je vais un peu mieux
I'm feeling a little better

c'est si fatigant!
it's so tiring!

elle parle trop
she talks too much

il est très timide
he's very shy

Note that all of these adverbs, except à peine, comme, presque, , très and seulement, may be followed by de and a noun to express a quantity (see p B60).

E POSITION OF ADVERBS

Adverbs usually follow verbs:

je vais rarement au théâtre
I seldom go to the theatre

comme vous conduisez prudemment
you do drive carefully!

With compound tenses, shorter adverbs usually come between the auxiliary and the past participle:

j'ai enfin terminé
I have finished at last

il me l'a déjà dit
he's already told me

nous y sommes souvent allés
we've often gone there

elle avait beaucoup souffert
she had suffered a lot

3 Adverbs of place and many adverbs of time, however, follow the past participle:

je l'ai rencontré hier
I met him yesterday

elle avait cherché partout
she had looked everywhere

mettez-le dehors
put it outside

tu t'es couché tard?
did you go to bed late?

4 Adverbs usually come before adjectives or other adverbs, as in English:

très rarement
very seldom

trop vite
too quickly

elle est vraiment belle
she is really beautiful

F COMPARATIVE AND SUPERLATIVE OF ADVERBS

1 The comparative and superlative of adverbs are formed in the same way as those of adjectives:

ADVERB	COMPARATIVE	SUPERLATIVE
souvent *often*	plus **souvent (que)** *more often (than)*	le plus **souvent** *(the) most often*
	moins **souvent (que)** *less often (than)* *not as often (as)*	le moins **souvent** *(the) least often*
	aussi **souvent (que)** *as often (as)*	

Note that the superlative of the adverb always takes the masculine singular article le:

je le vois plus souvent qu'avant
I see him more often than I used to

il conduit moins prudemment que moi
he drives less carefully than I do
he doesn't drive as carefully as I do

c'est lui qui conduit le moins prudemment
he's the one who drives the least carefully

je sais cuisiner aussi bien que toi!
I can cook as well as you!

Note:

a) 'as ... as possible' is translated either by aussi ... que possible or by le plus ... possible:

as far as possible

aussi loin que possible
le plus loin possible

b) after a negative, aussi is often replaced by si:

pas si vite!
not so fast!

c) In French, the idea of 'not so', 'not as' is often expressed by moins *(less)*:

parle moins fort!
don't talk so loud!

2 Irregular comparatives and superlatives

ADVERB	COMPARATIVE	SUPERLATIVE
beaucoup *much, a lot*	plus *more*	le plus *(the) most*

bien	mieux	le mieux
well	*better*	*(the) best*
mal	pis	le pis
	plus mal	le plus mal
badly	*worse*	*(the) worst*
peu	moins	le moins
little	*less*	*(the) least*

il est mieux payé que moi
he is better paid than me

c'est lui le mieux payé
he's the best paid

Note:

a) mieux/le mieux must not be confused with meilleur/le meilleur which are adjectives, used in front of a noun.

elle chante mieux que toi
she sings better than you (do)

c'est elle qui chante le mieux
she sings best

elle est meilleure chanteuse que toi
she is a better singer than you

c'est la meilleure chanteuse
she is the best singer

b) pis/le pis are only found in certain set expressions or in literary French:

tant pis
too bad

de mal en pis
from bad to worse

il n'y a rien de pis que cela
there is nothing worse than that

on en dit pis que pendre
nobody has a good word to say about it

6 PRONOUNS AND CORRESPONDING ADJECTIVES

A DEMONSTRATIVES

1 Demonstrative adjectives

a) *CE*

ce is often used to point out a particular person or thing, or persons or things. It is followed by the noun to which it refers and agrees in number and gender with that noun:

- with a masculine singular noun: ce (cet)   *this/that*
- with a feminine singular noun: cette   *this/that*
- with a plural noun (masc or fem): ces   *these/those*

ce roman m'a beaucoup plu   **il a neigé ce matin**
I really liked this novel   *it snowed this morning*

cette chanson m'énerve   **cette fois, c'est fini!**
that song gets on my nerves   *this time, it's over!*

tu trouves que ces lunettes me vont bien?
do you think these glasses suit me?

cet is used instead of ce in front of a masculine singular word that begins with a vowel or a silent h:

cet été   **cet hôtel**
this summer   *that hotel*

b) *-CI and -LÀ*

French does not have separate words to distinguish between 'this' and 'that'. However, when a particular emphasis is being placed on a person or object, or when a contrast is being made between persons or objects, -ci and -là are added to the noun:

-ci translates the idea of   *this/these*
-là translates the idea of   *that/those*

je suis très occupé ces jours-ci
I'm very busy these days

que faisiez-vous ce soir-là?
what were you doing that evening?

tu préfères cette robe-ci ou cette robe-là?
do you prefer this dress or that dress?

2 Demonstrative pronouns

Demonstrative pronouns are used instead of a noun with ce/cette/ces. They are:

celui, celle, ceux, celles
ce
ceci, cela, ça

a) *CELUI*

celui agrees in number and gender with the noun it refers to. It has four different forms:

	MASCULINE	FEMININE
SINGULAR	celui	celle
PLURAL	ceux	celles

celui, celle, ceux and celles cannot be used on their own. They are used:

- with -ci or -là, for emphasis or for contrast:

celui-ci	celle-ci	*this (one)*
celui-là	celle-là	*that (one)*
ceux-ci	celles-ci	*these (ones)*
ceux-là	celles-là	*those (ones)*

j'aime bien ce maillot mais celui-là est moins cher
I like this swimsuit, but that one is cheaper

je voudrais ces fleurs – lesquelles? celles-ci ou celles-là?
I'd like these flowers – which ones? these or those?

- with de + noun, to express possession:

je préfère mon ordinateur à celui de Jean-Claude
I prefer my computer to Jean-Claude's

range ta chambre plutôt que celle de ta sœur
tidy your own bedroom rather than your sister's

mes parents sont moins sévères que ceux de Nicole
my parents aren't as strict as Nicole's

les douches municipales sont mieux que celles du camping
the public showers are better than those at the campsite

- with the relative pronouns qui, que, dont to introduce a relative clause (for use of these relative pronouns, see p B22):

celui/celle/ceux/celles qui	*the one(s) who/which*
celui/celle/ceux/celles que	*the one(s) whom/which*
celui/celle/ceux/celles dont	*the one(s) of which/whose*

lequel est ton père? celui qui a une moustache?
which one is your father? the one with the moustache?

regarde cette voiture! celle qui est garée au coin
look at that car! the one which is parked at the corner

deux filles, celles qu'il avait rencontrées la veille
two girls, the ones he had met the day before

voilà mon copain, celui dont je t'ai parlé l'autre jour
here's my friend, the one I told you about the other day

b) *CE*

ce (meaning 'it' or 'that') is normally used with the verb être:

c'est	**ce serait**	**c'était**
it's/that's	*it/that would be*	*it/that was*

Note that ce changes to c' before an e or an é.

● with a noun or pronoun, ce is used to identify people or things, or to emphasize them; it is translated in a variety of ways:

qu'est-ce que c'est? – c'est mon billet d'avion
what's that? – it's my plane ticket

qui est-ce? – c'est moi	**ce doit être lui**
who is it? – it's me	*that must be him*

c'est un artiste bien connu	**c'était une bonne idée**
he's a well-known artist	*it was a good idea*

ce sont mes amis	**c'est la dernière fois!**
they're my friends	*it's the last time!*

c'est elle qui l'a fait	**c'est celui que j'ai vu**
she's the one who did it	*he's the one I saw*

ce sont des gens sympathiques	**ce ne sont pas mes chaussures**
they're nice people	*those aren't my shoes*

● before an adjective, ce is used to refer to an idea, an event or a fact which has already been mentioned; it does not refer to any specific noun:

c'était formidable	**ce serait amusant**
it was great	*it would be funny*

oui, c'est vrai	**c'est sûr?**
yes, that's true	*is that definite?*

ce n'est pas grave	**c'est bon à entendre**
it doesn't matter or it's not serious	*that's good to hear*

c'est exact!	**c'est rare qu'il pleuve en juin**
that's right!	*it doesn't often rain in June*

Note that the translation of it is an area of some difficulty for students of French, as it is sometimes translated by ce and sometimes by il/elle; see p B66 for further information.

c) *CECI, CELA, ÇA*

ceci (this), cela (that) and ça (that) are used to refer to an idea, an event, a fact or an object. They never refer to a particular noun already mentioned.

non, je n'aime pas ça!	**ah, bon? cela m'étonne**
no, I don't like that!	*really? that surprises me*

ça, c'est un acteur!	**souvenez-vous de ceci**
that's what I call an actor!	*remember this*

ça m'est égal	**cela ne vous regarde pas**
I don't mind	*that's none of your business*

buvez ceci, ça vous fera du bien
drink this, it'll do you good

ça alors!
well, really!

cela s'appelle comment, en anglais?
what do you call this in English?

Note that ceci is not very common in French; cela and ça are often used to translate 'this' as well as 'that'; ça is used far more frequently than cela in spoken French.

B INDEFINITE ADJECTIVES AND PRONOUNS

1 Indefinite adjectives

They are:

Masculine	Feminine	
autre(s)	autre(s)	*other*
certain(s)	certaine(s)	*certain*
chaque	chaque	*each, every*
même(s)	même(s)	*same*
plusieurs	plusieurs	*several*
quelque(s)	quelque(s)	*some*
tel(s)	telle(s)	*such*
tout (tous)	toute(s)	*all, every*

Note that, when used as indefinite adjectives, all the above adjectives are placed before the nouns to which they refer. Certain and même can be found after the noun but they will then have a different meaning (see p B10).

a) *CHAQUE and PLUSIEURS*

chaque (each) is always singular, plusieurs (several) always plural; the feminine form is the same as the masculine form:

j'y vais chaque jour	**chaque personne**
I go there every day	*each person*

plusieurs années	**il a plusieurs amis**
several years	*he's got several friends*

b) *AUTRE, MÊME and QUELQUE*

autre (other), même (same) and quelque (some) agree in number with the noun that follows; the feminine is the same as the masculine:

je voudrais un autre café	**d'autres couleurs**
I'd like another coffee	*other colours*

la même taille	**les mêmes touristes**
the same size	*the same tourists*

quelque temps après	**à quelques kilomètres**
some time later	*a few kilometres away*

c) *CERTAIN, TEL and TOUT*

certain (certain, some), tel (such) and tout (all) agree in number and gender with the noun; they have four different forms:

un certain charme	**une certaine dame**
a certain charm	*a certain lady*

à certains moments	**certaines personnes**
at (certain) times	*some people*

un tel homme	**une telle aventure**
such a man	*such an adventure*

de tels avantages	**de telles difficultés**
such advantages	*such difficulties*

quoi! tu as mangé tout le fromage et tous les fruits?
what! you've eaten all the cheese and all the fruit?

toute la journée	**toutes mes matières**
all day long	*all my subjects*

Note:

i) tel: the position of the article un/une with tel is not the same as in English: un tel homme = *such a man*.

ii) tel cannot qualify another adjective; when it is used as an adverb, 'such' is translated by si or tellement:

c'était un si bon repas/un repas tellement bon!
it was such a good meal!

iii) tous les/toutes les are often translated by 'every':

tous les jours	**toutes les places**
every day	*all seats, every seat*

B15

2 Indefinite pronouns

a) These are:

MASCULINE	FEMININE	
aucun	aucune	none, not any
autre(s)	autre(s)	another one, other ones
certains	certaine(s)	certain, some
chacun	chacune	each one, every one
on		everyone, one, someone, you, they, people, we
personne		nobody
plusieurs	plusieurs	several (ones)
quelque chose		something, anything
quelqu'un		someone
quelques-uns	quelques-unes	some, a few
rien		nothing
tout (tous)	toute(s)	everything, every one, all

pas celui-là, l'autre
not that one, the other one

où sont les autres?
where are the others?

certains disent que ...
some say that ...

personne n'est venu
no one came

qui est là? – personne
who's there? – nobody

qu'as-tu? – rien
what's wrong? – nothing

plusieurs d'entre eux
several of them

chacun pour soi!
every man for himself!

il manque quelque chose?
is anything missing?

dis quelque chose!
say something!

quelqu'un l'a averti
someone warned him

il y a quelqu'un?
is anyone in?

j'ai tout oublié
I've forgotten everything

c'est tout, merci
that's all, thanks

elles sont toutes arrivées
they've all arrived

allons-y tous ensemble
let's all go together

b) Points to note

i) aucun(e), personne and rien: these can be used on their own, but they are more often used with a verb and the negative word ne (see negative expressions, pp B62-3):

personne n'habite ici
no one lives here

il n'y a rien à manger
there's nothing to eat

ii) aucun(e), un(e) autre, d'autres, certain(e)s, plusieurs and quelques-un(e)s: when these pronouns are used as direct objects, the pronoun en must be used before the verb:

je n'en ai lu aucun
I haven't read any (of them)

donne-m'en une autre
give me another one

j'en ai vu d'autres qui étaient moins chers
I saw other ones which were cheaper

j'en connais certains
I know some of them

il y en a plusieurs
there are several

tu m'en donnes quelques-uns?
will you give me a few?

achètes-en quelques-unes
buy a few

iii) personne, quelque chose, rien, plusieurs: when these are followed by an adjective, the preposition de (or d') must be used in front of the adjective:

il n'y a personne de libre
there's no one available

quelque chose de mieux
something better

il y en avait plusieurs de cassés
several of them were broken

rien de grave
nothing serious

iv) autre is commonly used in the following expressions:

quelqu'un d'autre	**quelque chose d'autre**	**rien d'autre**
someone else	something else	nothing else

c) *ON*

This pronoun is used in a variety of ways in French. It can mean:

i) *one/you/they/people* in a general sense:

en France, on roule à droite
in France, they drive on the right

on ne sait jamais
you/one never know(s)

on ne doit pas mentir
you shouldn't lie

ii) *someone* (an undefined person)

In this sense, on is often translated by the passive (see p B39):

on me l'a déjà dit
someone's already told me
I've already been told

on vous l'apportera
someone will bring it to you
it will be brought to you

iii) *we*

In spoken French, on is frequently used instead of nous; although it refers to a plural subject, it is followed by the third person singular:

qu'est-ce qu'on fait?
what shall we do?

fais vite, on t'attend!
hurry up, we're waiting for you!

Note that in compound tenses with the auxiliary être, the agreement of the past participle with on is optional:

on est allé au cinéma
on est allés au cinéma
we went to the cinema

on est rentré en taxi
on est rentrées en taxi
we went home by taxi

C INTERROGATIVE AND EXCLAMATORY ADJECTIVES AND PRONOUNS

1 The interrogative adjective QUEL?

a) Forms

quel (*which, what*) agrees in number and gender with the noun it refers to. It has four forms:

- with a masculine singular noun: quel?
- with a feminine singular noun: quelle?
- with a masculine plural noun: quels?
- with a feminine plural noun: quelles?

b) Direct questions:

quel est votre passe-temps favori?
what's your favourite pastime?

quelle heure est-il?
what time is it?

quels jours as-tu de libres?
which days have you got free?

quelles affaires comptes-tu prendre avec toi?
what/which things do you intend to take with you?

c) Indirect questions:

je ne sais pas quel CD choisir
I don't know which CD to choose

il se demande quelle veste lui va le mieux
he's wondering which jacket suits him best

2 The exclamatory adjective QUEL!

quel! has the same forms as the interrogative adjective quel?:

quel **dommage!**
what a pity!

quelle **belle maison!**
what a beautiful house!

quels **imbéciles!**
what idiots!

quelles **jolies chaussures!**
what lovely shoes!

3 Interrogative pronouns

These are:

lequel/laquelle/ lesquels/lesquelles?	which (one(s))?
qui?	who?/whom?
que?	what?
quoi?	what?
ce qui	what
ce que	what

ce qui and ce que are used only in indirect questions; all other interrogative pronouns can be used both in direct and indirect questions.

a) LEQUEL?

i) forms

lequel (*which?*, *which one?*) agrees in gender and in number with the noun it stands for:

● with a masculine singular noun: lequel? *which (one)?*
● with a feminine singular noun: laquelle? *which (one)?*
● with a masculine plural noun: lesquels? *which (ones)?*
● with a feminine plural noun: lesquelles? *which (ones)?*

After the prepositions à and de, the following changes occur:

à + lequel?	→	auquel?
à + lesquels?	→	auxquels?
à + lesquelles?	→	auxquelles?
de + lequel?	→	duquel?
de + lesquels?	→	desquels?
de + lesquelles?	→	desquelles?

Note that à/de + laquelle? do not contract.

ii) direct questions:

je cherche un hôtel; lequel **recommandez-vous?**
I'm looking for a hotel; which one do you recommend?

nous avons plusieurs couleurs; vous préférez laquelle?
we have several colours; which one do you prefer?

lesquels **de ces livres sont à toi?**
which of these books are yours?

je voudrais essayer ces chaussures – lesquelles?
I would like to try these shoes on – which ones?

iii) indirect questions:

demande-lui lequel **de ces ordinateurs est le moins cher**
ask him/her which (one) of these computers is the cheapest

c'est dans une de ces rues mais je ne sais plus laquelle
it's in one of these streets, but I can't remember which one

b) QUI?

qui (*who?*, *whom?*) is used to refer to people; it can be both subject and object and can be used after a preposition:

qui **t'a accompagné?**
who came/went with you?

qui **as-tu appelé?**
who did you call?

tu y vas avec qui?
who are you going with?

c'est pour qui?
who is it for?

pour qui **vous prenez-vous?**
who do you think you are?

à qui **l'as-tu donné?**
who did you give it to?

Note that qui does not contract to qu' before a vowel or a silent h:

qui est-ce **qu'elle attend?**
who is she waiting for?

qui? can be replaced by qui est-ce qui? (subject) or qui est-ce que? (object) in direct questions:

qui est-ce qui **veut du café?**
who wants coffee?

qui est-ce que **tu as vu?**
who did you see?

avec qui est-ce que **tu sors ce soir?**
who are you going out with tonight?

Note, however, that qui cannot be replaced by qui est-ce qui or qui est-ce que in indirect questions:

j'aimerais savoir qui **vous a dit ça**
I'd like to know who told you that

elle se demandait de qui **étaient les fleurs**
she was wondering who the flowers were from

For more details on the use of qui/que as relative pronouns, see p B22.

c) QUE?

que (*what?*) is used to refer to things. It is only used in direct questions, is always a direct object and cannot be used after prepositions:

que **désirez-vous?**
what do you wish?

qu'**a-t-il dit?**
what did he say?

que? is rather formal and is usually replaced by qu'est-ce qui? or qu'est-ce que? in spoken French.

Note that que becomes qu' before a vowel or a silent h.

d) QU'EST-CE QUI?

qu'est-ce qui? (*what?*) is used as the subject of a verb; it cannot refer to a person:

qu'est-ce qui **t'est arrivé?**
what happened to you?

qu'est-ce qui **la fait rire?**
what makes her laugh?

e) QU'EST-CE QUE?

qu'est-ce que? (*what?*) replaces que? as the object of a verb; it becomes qu'est-ce qu' before a vowel or a silent h:

qu'est-ce que **tu aimes lire?**
what do you like reading?

qu'est-ce qu'**il va faire pendant les vacances?**
what's he going to do during the holidays?

f) QUOI?

quoi? (*what?*) refers to things; it is used:

i) instead of que or qu'est-ce que after a preposition:

à quoi **penses-tu?**
what are you thinking about?

dans quoi **l'as-tu mis?**
what did you put it in?

ii) in indirect questions:

demandez-lui de quoi **il a besoin**
ask him what he needs

je ne sais pas à quoi **ça sert**
I don't know what it's for

g) CE QUI, CE QUE

ce qui and ce que (*what*) are only used in indirect questions; they replace qu'est-ce qui and (qu'est-ce) que.

They are used in the same way as the relative pronouns ce qui and ce que (see p B23).

i) ce qui is used as the subject of the verb in the indirect question (ce qui is the subject of s'est passé in the following example):

nous ne saurons jamais ce qui s'est passé
we'll never know what happened

ii) **ce que** (**ce qu'** before a vowel or a silent h) is used as the object of the verb in the indirect question (ce que is the object of il faisait in the following example):

je n'ai pas remarqué ce qu'il faisait
I didn't notice what he was doing

D PERSONAL PRONOUNS

There are four categories of personal pronouns:

- subject pronouns
- object pronouns
- disjunctive pronouns
- reflexive pronouns

For reflexive pronouns, see p B28.

1 Subject pronouns

PERSON	SINGULAR		PLURAL	
1st	je (j')	*I*	nous	*we*
2nd	tu	*you*	vous	*you*
3rd	il	*he, it*	ils	*they*
	elle	*she, it*	elles	*they*
	on	*one, we, they*		

Note:

a) je changes to j' before a vowel or a silent h:

j'ai honte   **j'adore les frites**
I'm ashamed   *I love chips*

j'habite en Écosse
I live in Scotland

b) **tu and vous**

vous can be plural or singular; it is used when speaking to more than one person (plural), or to a stranger or an older person (singular):

pourriez-vous m'indiquer   **vous venez, les gars?**
la gare?   *are you coming, guys?*
could you show me the way
to the station?

tu is used when speaking to a friend, a relative, a younger person, or someone else you know well:

tu viens, Marc?
are you coming, Marc?

c) **il/ils, elle/elles** may refer to people, animals or things, and must be of the same gender as the noun they replace:

ton stylo? il est là   **ta montre? elle est là**
your pen? there it is   *your watch? there it is*

tes gants? ils sont là   **tes lunettes? elles sont là**
your gloves? there they are   *your glasses? there they*
                                  are

When referring to several nouns of different genders, French uses the masculine plural **ils**:

j'ai trouvé dans mon sac un stylo et une montre. Ils ne m'appartiennent pas
I found a pen and a watch in my bag. They don't belong to me

d) **on**: see p B16.

2 Object pronouns

There are three types of object pronouns:

- direct object pronouns
- indirect object pronouns
- the pronouns en and y

a) *Forms*

PERSON		DIRECT	INDIRECT
SING	1st	me (m')	me (m')
		me	*(to) me*
	2nd	te (t')	te (t')
		you	*(to) you*
	3rd	le (l')	lui
		him, it	*(to) him*
		la (l')	lui
		her, it	*(to) her*
PLUR	1st	nous	nous
		us	*(to) us*
	2nd	vous	vous
		you	*(to) you*
	3rd	les	leur
		them	*(to) them*

Note:

i) **me, te, le** and **la** change to **m', t'** and **l'** before a vowel or a silent h:

il m'énerve!   **je m'habituerai à lui**
he gets on my nerves!   *I'll get used to him*

ii) **te** and **vous**: the same distinction should be made as between the subject pronouns tu and vous (see D 1b).

iii) **le** is sometimes used in an impersonal sense to refer to a fact, a statement or an idea which has already been expressed; it is usually not translated in English:

j'irai aux États-Unis un jour; en tout cas je l'espère
I'll go to the States one day; I hope so anyway

elle a eu un bébé – je le sais, elle me l'a dit
she's had a baby – I know, she told me

iv) when used as an indirect object pronoun, **lui** can be masculine or feminine:

pose-lui la question
ask him/her the question

j'ai décidé de lui offrir un cadeau
I've decided to give him/her a present

v) when they are used with imperatives, **moi** and **toi** are used instead of me and te, except when en follows:

écris-moi bientôt   **donne m'en**
write to me soon   *give me some*

b) *Position*

In French, object pronouns come immediately before the verb they refer to. With a compound tense, they come before the auxiliary:

on t'attendra ici   **je l'ai rencontrée en ville**
we'll wait for you here   *I met her in town*

Note that when there are two verbs, the pronoun comes immediately before the verb to which it refers:

j'aimerais lui demander   **tu l'as entendu chanter?**
I'd like to ask him/her   *have you heard him sing?*

In positive commands (the affirmative imperative) the pronoun follows the verb and is joined to it by a hyphen:

regarde-les!   **parle-lui!**
look at them!   *speak to him/her!*

dis-nous ce qui s'est passé
tell us what happened

c) *Direct pronouns and indirect pronouns*

i) Direct object pronouns replace a noun which directly follows the verb. They answer the question 'who(m)?' or 'what?'

WHO(M) did you see?	I saw my friend; I saw him
qui as-tu vu?	**j'ai vu mon ami; je l'ai vu**
tu me connais	**j'aime le voir danser**
you know me	*I like to see him dance*
je les ai trouvés	**ne nous ennuie pas!**
I found them	*don't bother us!*

ii) Indirect object pronouns replace a noun which follows the verb with a linking preposition (usually à, to whom?). They answer the question 'who to?'

WHO did you speak to?	I spoke to Marc; I spoke to him
à qui as-tu parlé?	**j'ai parlé à Marc; je lui ai parlé**
elle lui a menti	**je te donne ce CD**
she lied to him/her	*I'm giving this CD to you*
je ne leur parle plus	
I'm not talking to them any more	

iii) le/la/les or lui/leur?

Direct pronouns differ from indirect pronouns only in the 3rd person and great care must be taken to use the correct one.

English indirect object pronouns often look like direct objects; this becomes obvious when the object is placed at the end of the clause, after a linking preposition:

I showed him your photo = *I showed your photo to him*
je lui ai montré ta photo

This is particularly the case with the following verbs:

acheter	*to buy*	**offrir**	*to offer, to give*
donner	*to give*	**prêter**	*to lend*
montrer	*to show*	**vendre**	*to sell*

je lui ai acheté un livre	**ne leur prête pas mes affaires**
I bought him/her a book	
= *I bought a book for him/her*	*don't lend them my things*
	= *don't lend my things to them*

Some verbs take a direct object in English and an indirect object in French (see p B53):

je ne lui ai rien dit	**je leur demanderai**
I didn't tell him/her anything	*I'll ask them*
tu lui ressembles	**téléphone-leur**
you look like him/her	*phone them*

Some verbs take a direct object in French and an indirect object in English (see p B53):

je l'attends	**écoutez-les!**
I'm waiting for him/her	*listen to them!*

d) *Order of object pronouns*

When several object pronouns are used together, they come in the following order:

i) Before the verb:

1	me	te	nous	vous
2	le	la	les	
3	lui	leur		

il me l'a donné	**je vais vous les envoyer**
he gave it to me	*I'll send them to you*
ne la leur vends pas	**je le lui ai acheté**
don't sell it to them	*I bought it for him/her*

ii) After the verb:

With a positive command (the affirmative imperative), the order is as follows:

1	le	la	les	
2	moi (m')	toi (t')	nous	vous
3	lui	leur		

apporte-les-moi!	**prête-la-nous!**
bring them to me!	*lend it to us!*
dites-le-lui!	**rends-la-leur!**
tell him/her!	*give it back to them!*

3 The pronoun EN

a) *Use*

en is used instead of de + noun. Since de has a variety of meanings, en can be used in a number of ways:

i) It means 'of it/them', but also 'with it/them', 'about it/them', 'from it/there', 'out of it/there':

tu es sûr du prix? – j'en suis sûr
are you sure of the price? – I'm sure of it

je suis content de ce cadeau; j'en suis content
I'm pleased with this present; I'm pleased with it

elle est folle des animaux; elle en est folle
she's crazy about animals; she's crazy about them

il est descendu du train; il en est descendu
he got off the train; he got off it

il revient de Paris; il en revient
he's coming back from Paris; he's coming back from there

ii) Verbal constructions

Particular care should be taken with verbs and expressions which are followed by de + noun. Since de is not always translated in the same way, en may have a number of meanings:

il a envie de ce livre; il en a envie
he wants this book; he wants it

je te remercie de ton aide; je t'en remercie
thank you for your help; thank you for it

tu as besoin de ces papiers? tu en as besoin?
do you need these papers? do you need them?

elle a peur des chiens; elle en a peur
she's afraid of dogs; she's afraid of them

tu te souviens de ce film? tu t'en souviens?
do you remember this film? do you remember it?

iii) 'some'/'any'

en replaces the partitive article (du, de la, des) + noun; it means 'some'/'any':

tu veux du café? – non, je n'en veux pas
do you want (any) coffee? – no, I don't want any

j'achète des fruits? – non, j'en ai chez moi
shall I buy (some) fruit? – no, I've got some at home

il y a de la place? – en voilà là-bas
is there any room? – there's some over there

iv) Expressions of quantity

en must be used with expressions of quantity not followed by a noun. It replaces de + noun and means 'of it/them', but is seldom translated in English:

tu as pris assez d'argent? tu en as pris assez?
did you take enough money? did you take enough?

vous avez combien de frères? – j'en ai deux
how many brothers do you have? – I've got two

j'ai fini mes cigarettes; je vais en acheter un paquet
I've finished my cigarettes; I'm going to buy a packet

b) *Position*

Like object pronouns, en comes immediately before the verb, except with positive commands (the affirmative imperative), where it comes after the verb and is linked to it by a hyphen:

j'en veux un kilo
I want a kilo (of it/them)

j'en ai marre!
I'm fed up (with it)!

prends-en assez!
take enough (of it/them)!

laisses-en aux autres!
leave some for the others!

When used in conjunction with other object pronouns, it always comes last:

ne m'en parlez pas!
don't tell me about it!

je vous en donnerai
I'll give you some

prête-lui-en!
lend him/her some!

gardez-nous-en!
keep some for us!

4 The pronoun Y

a) *Use*

y is used instead of à + noun, but never refers to a person. It is used:

i) As the indirect object of a verb. Since the preposition à is translated in a variety of ways in English, y may have various meanings (*it, of it/them, about it/them* etc):

tu joues au tennis? – non, j'y joue rarement
do you play tennis? – no, I seldom play (it)

je pense à mon pays natal; j'y pense souvent
I'm thinking about my home country; I often think about it

il s'intéresse à la photo; il s'y intéresse
he's interested in photography; he's interested in it

ii) To mean 'there':

j'ai passé deux jours à Londres; j'y ai passé deux jours
I spent two days in London; I spent two days there

il est allé en Grèce; il y est allé
he went to Greece; he went there

Note that y must always be used with the verb aller (to go) when the place is not mentioned in the clause. It is often not translated in English:

comment vas-tu à l'école? – j'y vais en bus
how do you get to school? – I go (there) by bus

allons-y!
let's go!

on y va demain
we're going (there) tomorrow

iii) To replace the prepositions en, dans, sur + noun; y then means 'there', 'in it/them', 'on it/them':

je voudrais vivre en France; je voudrais y vivre
I'd like to live in France; I'd like to live there

je les ai mis dans ma poche; je les y ai mis
I put them in my pocket; I put them there

sur la table? – non, je ne l'y vois pas
on the table? no, I don't see it there

b) *Position*

Like other object pronouns, y comes immediately before the verb, except with a positive command (the affirmative imperative), where it must follow the verb:

j'y réfléchirai
I'll think about it

il s'y est habitué
he got used to it

pensez-y!
think about it!

n'y allez pas!
don't go!

When used with other object pronouns, y comes last:

il va nous y rencontrer
he'll meet us there

je l'y ai vu hier
I saw him there yesterday

5 Disjunctive pronouns

a) *Forms*

PERSON	SINGULAR	PLURAL
1st	moi	nous
	me	*us*
2nd	toi	vous
	you	*you*
3rd (masculine)	lui	eux
	him	*them*
(feminine)	elle	elles
	her	*them*
(impersonal)	soi	
	oneself	

Note:

i) toi/vous: the same difference should be made as between tu and vous (see p B18).

ii) soi is used in an impersonal, general sense to refer to indefinite pronouns and adjectives (on, chacun, tout le monde, personne, chaque etc); it is mainly found in set phrases, such as:

chacun pour soi
every man for himself

cela va de soi
that goes without saying

b) *Use*

Disjunctive pronouns, also called emphatic pronouns, are used instead of object pronouns when referring to persons in the following cases:

i) In answer to a question, alone or in a phrase without a verb:

qui est là? – moi
who's there? – me

j'ai aimé ce film; et toi?
I liked that film; did you?

qui préfères-tu, lui ou elle? – elle, bien sûr
who do you prefer, him or her? – her, of course

ii) After c'est/ce sont, c'était/c'étaient etc:

ouvrez, c'est moi!
open up, it's me!

non, ce n'était pas lui
no, it wasn't him

iii) After a preposition:

vous allez chez lui?
are you going to his place?

tu y vas avec elle?
are you going with her?

regarde devant toi!
look in front of you!

oh, c'est pour moi?
oh, is that for me?

iv) With verbal constructions. Special care should be taken when the verb is followed by a preposition:

tu peux compter sur moi
you can count on me

quoi! tu as peur de lui?
what! you're afraid of him?

il m'a parlé de toi
he told me about you

je pense souvent à vous
I often think about you

Note that emphatic pronouns are only used when referring to people. In other cases y or en must be used.

v) For emphasis, particularly when two pronouns are contrasted. The unstressed subject pronoun is usually included:

vous, vous m'énervez!
you get on my nerves!

lui, il joue bien; elle, non
he plays well; she doesn't

moi, je n'aime pas l'hiver
I don't like winter

eux, ils sont partis
they've left

vi) In the case of multiple subjects (two pronouns or one pronoun and one noun):

lui et son frère sont dans l'équipe
he and his brother are in the team

ma famille et moi allons très bien
my family and I are very well

vii) As the second element of a comparison:

il est plus sympa que toi	**elle chante mieux que lui**
he is nicer than you	*she sings better than he does*

viii) Before a relative pronoun:

c'est lui que j'aime	**c'est toi qui l'as dit**
he's the one I love	*you're the one who said it*

lui qui n'aime pas le vin blanc en a bu six verres
he who doesn't like white wine had six glasses

ix) With -même(s) (-self, -selves), aussi (too), seul (alone):

faites-le vous-mêmes	**j'irai moi-même**
do it yourselves	*I'll go myself*
lui aussi est parti	**elle seule le sait**
he too went away	*she alone knows*

x) To replace a possessive pronoun (see E2):

c'est le mien; il est à moi
it's mine; it belongs to me

cette valise n'est pas à lui?
doesn't that suitcase belong to him?

E POSSESSIVE ADJECTIVES AND PRONOUNS

1 Possessive adjectives

a) *Forms*

Possessive adjectives always come before their related noun. Like other adjectives, they agree in gender and number with the noun; the masculine and feminine plural forms are identical:

SINGULAR		PLURAL	
MASC	FEM	(MASC AND FEM)	
mon	ma	mes	*my*
ton	ta	tes	*your*
son	sa	ses	*his/her/its/ one's*
notre	notre	nos	*our*
votre	votre	vos	*your*
leur	leur	leurs	*their*

j'ai mis mon argent et mes affaires dans mon sac
I've put my money and my things in my bag

comment va ton frère? et ta sœur? et tes parents?
how's your brother? and your sister? and your parents?

notre rue est assez calme	**ce sont vos amis**
our street is fairly quiet	*they're your friends*

Note that mon/ton/son are used instead of ma/ta/sa when the next word starts with a vowel or silent h:

mon ancienne maison	**ton amie Christine**
my old house	*your friend Christine*

son haleine sentait l'alcool
his/her breath smelled of alcohol

b) *Use*

i) The possessive adjective is repeated before each noun and agrees in number and gender with it:

mon père et ma mère sont sortis
my mother and father have gone out

ii) son/sa/ses

son, sa and ses can all mean 'his', 'her' or 'its'. In French, the form of the adjective is determined by the gender and number of the noun that follows, and not by the possessor:

il m'a prêté sa mobylette et son casque
he lent me his moped and his helmet

elle s'entend bien avec sa mère mais pas avec son père
she gets on well with her mother, but not with her father

elle vit pour son travail; lui pour ses enfants
she lives for her job; he lives for his children

iii) ton/ta/tes and votre/vos

The two sets of words for 'your', ton/ta/tes and votre/vos, correspond to the two different forms of tu and vous; they must not be used together with the same person:

tu as parlé à ton patron?
have you spoken to your boss?

Monsieur, vous oubliez votre parapluie!
excuse me, sir, you've forgotten your umbrella!

iv) In French, the possessive adjective is replaced by the definite article (le/la/les) with the following:

● parts of the body:

il s'est essuyé les mains	**elle a haussé les épaules**
he wiped his hands	*she shrugged (her shoulders)*

● descriptive phrases at the end of a clause, where English adds 'with':

il marchait lentement, les mains dans les poches
he was walking slowly, with his hands in his pockets

elle l'a regardé partir, les larmes aux yeux
she watched him leave with tears in her eyes

2 Possessive pronouns

SINGULAR		PLURAL	
MASC	FEM	(MASC AND FEM)	
le mien	la mienne	les mien(ne)s	*mine*
le tien	la tienne	les tien(ne)s	*yours*
le sien	la sienne	les sien(ne)s	*his/hers/its*
le nôtre	la nôtre	les nôtres	*ours*
le vôtre	la vôtre	les vôtres	*yours*
le leur	la leur	les leurs	*theirs*

Possessive pronouns are used instead of a possessive adjective + noun. They agree in gender and in number with the noun they stand for, and not with the possessor (it is particularly important to remember this when translating 'his' and 'hers'):

j'aime bien ton appartement mais je préfère le mien
I quite like your flat, but I prefer mine

on prend quelle voiture? la mienne ou la tienne?
which car shall we take? mine or yours?

comment sont vos profs? les nôtres sont sympas
what are your teachers like? ours are nice

j'avais mon passeport mais Brigitte avait oublié le sien
I had my passport, but Brigitte had forgotten hers

j'ai gardé ma moto mais Paul a vendu la sienne
I've kept my motorbike but Paul has sold his

à or de + possessive pronoun

The prepositions à and de combine with the articles le and les in the usual way:

à + le mien	→	au mien
à + les miens	→	aux miens
à + les miennes	→	aux miennes
de + le mien	→	du mien
de + les miens	→	des miens
de + les miennes	→	des miennes

demande à tes parents, j'ai déjà parlé aux miens
ask your parents, I've already spoken to mine

leur appartement ressemble beaucoup au nôtre
their flat is very similar to ours

j'aime bien les chiens mais j'ai peur du tien
I like dogs, but I'm afraid of yours

Note that after the verb être, the possessive pronoun is often replaced by à + emphatic pronoun (see p B21):

à qui est cette écharpe? – elle est à moi
whose scarf is this? – it's mine

ce livre est à toi? – non, il est à elle
is this book yours? – no, it's hers

c'est à qui? à vous ou à lui?
whose is this? yours or his?

F RELATIVE PRONOUNS

1 Definition

Relative pronouns are words which introduce a relative clause. In the sentence:

I bought the book which you recommended

'which' is the relative pronoun, 'which you recommended' is the relative clause and 'the book' is the antecedent (ie the noun to which the relative pronoun refers).

2 Form

Relative pronouns are:

qui	*who/which*	lequel	*which*
que	*who(m)/which*	dont	*of which/whose*
quoi	*what*	ce qui	*what*
où	*where*	ce que	*what*

qui, que, quoi, lequel, ce qui and ce que can also be used as interrogative pronouns (see p B17) and must not be confused with them.

3 Use

a) *QUI*

qui is used as the subject of a relative clause. It means:

i) 'who', 'that' (referring to people):

est-ce que tu connais le monsieur qui habite ici?
do you know the man who lives here?

ce n'est pas lui qui a menti
he's not the one who lied

ii) 'which', 'that' (referring to things):

tu as pris le journal qui était sur la télé?
did you take the paper which/that was on the TV?

b) *QUE*

que (which contracts to qu' before a vowel or a silent h) is used as the object of a relative clause; it is often not translated. It means:

i) 'who(m)', 'that' (referring to people):

la fille que j'aime ne m'aime pas
the girl (that) I love doesn't love me

ii) 'which', 'that' (referring to things):

j'ai perdu le briquet qu'il m'a offert
I've lost the lighter (which/that) he gave me

c) *QUI or QUE?*

qui (subject) and que (object) are translated by the same words in English (who, which, that). To use the correct pronoun in French, it is essential to know whether a relative pronoun is the object or the subject of the relative clause:

i) when the verb of the relative clause has its own subject, the object pronoun que must be used:

c'est un passe-temps que j'adore
it's a pastime (that) I love (the subject of 'adore' is 'je')

ii) otherwise the relative pronoun is the subject of the verb in the relative clause and the subject pronoun qui must be used:

j'ai trouvé un manteau qui me plaît
I've found a coat that I like (the subject of 'plaît' is 'qui')

d) *LEQUEL*

i) *forms*

lequel (which) has four different forms, as it must agree with the noun to which it refers:

	SINGULAR	PLURAL	
MASCULINE	lequel	lesquels	} *which*
FEMININE	laquelle	lesquelles	

lequel etc combines with the prepositions à and de as follows:

à + lequel	→	auquel
à + lesquels	→	auxquels
à + lesquelles	→	auxquelles
de + lequel	→	duquel
de + lesquels	→	desquels
de + lesquelles	→	desquelles

à + laquelle and de + laquelle do not change.

quels sont les sports auxquels tu t'intéresses?
what sports are you interested in?

voilà le village près duquel on campait
here's the village which we camped near

ii) qui or lequel with a preposition

When a relative pronoun follows a preposition, the pronoun used is either qui or lequel. In English, the relative pronoun is seldom used and the preposition is frequently placed after the verb or at the end of the sentence.

qui is generally used after a preposition when referring to people:

où est la fille avec qui je dansais?
where's the girl I was dancing with?

montre-moi la personnne à qui tu as vendu ton vélo
show me the person you sold your bike to

lequel is often used after a preposition when referring to things:

l'immeuble dans lequel j'habite est très moderne
the building (which) I live in is very modern

je ne reconnais pas la voiture avec laquelle il est venu
I don't recognize the car (which) he came in

lequel is also used when referring to persons after the prepositions entre (between) and parmi (among):

elle observait les invités parmi lesquels elle ne reconnaissait personne
she was watching the guests, none of whom she recognized

il y avait deux candidats, entre lesquels nous avons dû choisir
there were two candidates, between whom we had to choose

e) *DONT*

dont is frequently used instead of **de qui, duquel** etc. It means:

i) of which/of whom:

un métier dont il est fier
a job (which) he is proud of

Care must be taken with verbs that are normally followed by **de** + object: de is not always translated by 'of' in English, and is sometimes not translated at all (see section on verbal constructions p B53):

voilà les choses dont j'ai besoin
here are the things (which) I need

les gens dont tu parles ne m'intéressent pas
I'm not interested in the people you're talking about

l'enfant dont elle s'occupe n'est pas le sien
the child she is looking after is not hers

ii) whose

dont is also used to translate the English pronoun 'whose'. In French, the construction of the clause that follows dont differs from English in two ways:

the noun which follows dont is used with the definite article (le, la, les, l'):

mon copain, dont le père a eu un accident
my friend, whose father had an accident

the word order in French is dont + subject + verb + object:

je te présente Hélène, dont tu connais déjà le frère
this is Hélène, whose brother you already know

c'était dans une petite rue dont j'ai oublié le nom
it was in a small street the name of which I've forgotten

Note that dont cannot be used after a preposition:

une jolie maison, près de laquelle il y a un petit lac
a pretty house, next to which there is a small lake

f) *OÙ*

i) où generally means 'where':

l'hôtel où on a logé était très confortable
the hotel where we stayed was very comfortable

ii) où often replaces a preposition + lequel, and means 'in/to/on/at which' etc:

c'est la maison où je suis né
that's the house in which/where I was born

une soirée où il a invité tous ses amis
a party to which he invited all his friends

iii) où is also used to translate 'when' after a noun referring to time:

le jour où   **la fois où**   **le moment où**
the day when   *the time when*   *the moment when*

tu te rappelles le soir où on a raté le dernier métro?
do you remember the evening when we missed the last train?

le jour où j'ai eu mon permis de conduire
the day when I got my driving licence

g) *CE QUI, CE QUE*

ce is used before qui and que when the relative pronoun does not refer to a specific noun. Both ce qui and ce que mean 'that which', 'the thing which', and are usually translated by 'what':

i) ce qui

ce qui is followed by a verb without a subject (qui is the subject):

ce qui s'est passé ne vous regarde pas
what happened is none of your business

ce qui m'étonne, c'est sa patience
what surprises me is his patience

Note that in French, this structure requires a comma between the two clauses, and the second clause must be introduced by c'est/c'était/ce sera depending on the tense being used.

ii) ce que

ce que (ce qu' before a vowel or a silent h) is followed by a verb with its own subject (que is the object):

fais ce que tu veux   **c'est ce qu'il a dit?**
do what you want   *is that what he said?*

ce que vous me demandez est impossible
what you're asking me is impossible

iii) tout ce qui/que

tout is used in front of ce qui/que in the sense of 'all that', 'everything that':

c'est tout ce que je veux   **tout ce que tu as fait**
that's all I want   *everything you did*

tu n'as pas eu de mal; c'est tout ce qui compte
you weren't hurt; that's all that matters

iv) ce qui/que are often used in indirect questions (see p B17):

je ne sais pas ce qu'ils vont dire
I don't know what they'll say

v) when referring to a previous clause, ce qui and ce que are translated by 'which':

elle est en retard, ce qui arrive souvent
she's late, which happens often

vi) ce qui/que are used with a preposition; ce qui is used as the subject of the verb in the relative clause and ce que is used as the object of the verb in the relative clause:

ce n'est pas étonnant, après ce qui nous est arrivé
it's not surprising, after what happened to us

il y a du vrai dans ce que vous dites
there is some truth in what you say

When a preposition is required by the verb in the relative clause, eg **penser à, s'expliquer sur**, quoi is used instead of ce que and comes after the preposition:

c'est ce à quoi je pensais
that's what I was thinking about

voici ce sur quoi il devra s'expliquer
this is what he'll have to explain

ce dont is used instead of de + ce que when de is the preposition required by the verb in the relative clause, eg **avoir peur de, avoir besoin de**:

c'est ce dont j'avais peur
that's what I was afraid of

tu as trouvé ce dont tu avais besoin?
did you find what you needed?

7 VERBS

A REGULAR CONJUGATIONS

1 Conjugations

There are three main conjugations in French, which are determined by the infinitive endings. The first conjugation verbs, by far the largest category, end in -er, eg **aimer** and will be referred to as -er verbs; the second conjugation verbs end in -ir, eg **finir** and will be referred to as -ir verbs; the third conjugation verbs, the smallest category, end in -re, eg **vendre** and will be referred to as -re verbs.

2 Simple tenses

The simple tenses in French are:

- present
- imperfect
- future
- conditional
- past historic
- present subjunctive
- imperfect subjunctive

For the use of the different tenses, see pp B30-2.

3 Formation of tenses

The tenses are formed by adding the following endings to the stem of the verb (usually the stem of the infinitive) as set out in the following section:

a) PRESENT: stem of the infinitive + the following endings:

-er verbs	-ir verbs	-re verbs
-e, -es, -e,	-is, -is, -it,	-s, -s, ø,
-ons, -ez, -ent	-issons, -issez, -issent	-ons, -ez, -ent

AIMER	FINIR	VENDRE
j'aime	je finis	je vends
tu aimes	tu finis	tu vends
il aime	il finit	il vend
elle aime	elle finit	elle vend
nous aimons	nous finissons	nous vendons
vous aimez	vous finissez	vous vendez
ils aiment	ils finissent	ils vendent
elles aiment	elles finissent	elles vendent

b) IMPERFECT: stem of the first person plural of the present indicative (ie the 'nous' form minus -ons) + the following endings:

-ais, -ais, -ait, -ions, -iez, -aient

j'aimais	je finissais	je vendais
tu aimais	tu finissais	tu vendais
il aimait	il finissait	il vendait
elle aimait	elle finissait	elle vendait
nous aimions	nous finissions	nous vendions
vous aimiez	vous finissiez	vous vendiez
ils aimaient	ils finissaient	ils vendaient
elles aimaient	elles finissaient	elles vendaient

Note that the only irregular imperfect is **être**: **j'étais** etc.

c) FUTURE: infinitive + the following endings:

-ai, -as, -a, -ons, -ez, -ont

Note that verbs ending in -re drop the final e of the infinitive.

j'aimerai	je finirai	je vendrai
tu aimeras	tu finiras	tu vendras
il aimera	il finira	il vendra
elle aimera	elle finira	elle vendra
nous aimerons	nous finirons	nous vendrons
vous aimerez	vous finirez	vous vendrez
ils aimeront	ils finiront	ils vendront
elles aimeront	elles finiront	elles vendront

d) CONDITIONAL: infinitive + the following endings:

-ais, -ais, -ait, -ions, -iez, -aient

Note that verbs ending in -re drop the final e of the infinitive.

j'aimerais	je finirais	je vendrais
tu aimerais	tu finirais	tu vendrais
il aimerait	il finirait	il vendrait
elle aimerait	elle finirait	elle vendrait
nous aimerions	nous finirions	nous vendrions
vous aimeriez	vous finiriez	vous vendriez
ils aimeraient	ils finiraient	ils vendraient
elles aimeraient	elles finiraient	elles vendraient

e) PAST HISTORIC: stem of the infinitive + the following endings:

-er verbs	-ir verbs	-re verbs
-ai, -as, -a, -âmes, -âtes, -èrent	-is, -is, -it, -îmes, -îtes, -irent	-is, -is, -it, -îmes, -îtes, -irent

j'aimai	je finis	je vendis
tu aimas	tu finis	tu vendis
il aima	il finit	il vendit
elle aima	elle finit	elle vendit
nous aimâmes	nous finîmes	nous vendîmes
vous aimâtes	vous finîtes	vous vendîtes
ils aimèrent	ils finirent	ils vendirent
elles aimèrent	elles finirent	elles vendirent

f) PRESENT SUBJUNCTIVE: stem of the first person plural of the present indicative (ie the 'nous' form minus -ons) + the following endings:

-e, -es, -e, -ions, -iez, -ent

j'aime	je finisse	je vende
tu aimes	tu finisses	tu vendes
il aime	il finisse	il vende
elle aime	elle finisse	elle vende
nous aimions	nous finissions	nous vendions
vous aimiez	vous finissiez	vous vendiez
ils aiment	ils finissent	ils vendent
elles aiment	elles finissent	elles vendent

g) IMPERFECT SUBJUNCTIVE: stem of the first person singular of the past historic + the following endings:

-er verbs	-ir verbs	-re verbs
-asse, -asses, -ât, -assions, -assiez, -assent	-isse, -isses, -ît, -issions, -issiez, -issent	-isse, -isses, -ît, -issions, -issiez, -issent

j'aimasse	je finisse	je vendisse
tu aimasses	tu finisses	tu vendisses
il aimât	il finît	il vendît
elle aimât	elle finît	elle vendît
nous aimassions	nous finissions	nous vendissions
vous aimassiez	vous finissiez	vous vendissiez
ils aimassent	ils finissent	ils vendissent
elles aimassent	elles finissent	elles vendissent

B STANDARD SPELLING IRREGULARITIES

Spelling irregularities affect only -er verbs.

1 Verbs ending in -cer and -ger

a) Verbs ending in -cer require a cedilla under the c (ç) before an a or an o to preserve the soft sound of the c: eg **commencer** *(to begin)*; il commença *(he began)*.

b) Verbs ending in -ger require an -e after the g before an a or an o to preserve the soft sound of the g: eg **manger** *(to eat)*; je **mangeais** *(I was eating)*.

Changes to -cer and -ger verbs occur in the following tenses: present, imperfect, past historic, imperfect subjunctive and present participle.

COMMENCER

MANGER

PRESENT

je commence	je mange
tu commences	tu manges
il commence	il mange
elle commence	elle mange
nous commençons	nous mangeons
vous commencez	vous mangez
ils commencent	ils mangent
elles commencent	elles mangent

IMPERFECT

je commençais	je mangeais
tu commençais	tu mangeais
il commençait	il mangeait
elle commençait	elle mangeait
nous commencions	nous mangions
vous commenciez	vous mangiez
ils commençaient	ils mangeaient
elles commençaient	elles mangeaient

PAST HISTORIC

je commençai	je mangeai
tu commenças	tu mangeas
il commença	il mangea
elle commença	elle mangea
nous commençâmes	nous mangeâmes
vous commençâtes	vous mangeâtes
ils commencèrent	ils mangèrent
elles commencèrent	elles mangèrent

IMPERFECT SUBJUNCTIVE

je commençasse	je mangeasse
tu commençasses	tu mangeasses
il commençât	il mangeât
elle commençât	elle mangeât
nous commençassions	nous mangeassions
vous commençassiez	vous mangeassiez
ils commençassent	ils mangeassent
elles commençassent	elles mangeassent

PRESENT PARTICIPLE

commençant	mangeant

2 Verbs with other -er endings

a) *Verbs ending in* -eler

Verbs ending in -eler double the l before a silent e (ie before -e, -es, -ent of the present indicative and subjunctive, and throughout the future and present conditional): eg **appeler** *(to call)*.

PRESENT INDICATIVE	PRESENT SUBJUNCTIVE
j'appelle	j'appelle
tu appelles	tu appelles
il appelle	il appelle
elle appelle	elle appelle
nous appelons	nous appelions
vous appelez	vous appeliez
ils appellent	ils appellent
elles appellent	elles appellent

FUTURE	CONDITIONAL
j'appellerai	j'appellerais
tu appelleras	tu appellerais
il appellera	il appellerait
elle appellera	elle appellerait
nous appellerons	nous appellerions
vous appellerez	vous appelleriez
ils appelleront	ils appelleraient
elles appelleront	elles appelleraient

Note, however, that some verbs in -eler, including the following, are conjugated like **acheter** (see p B26):

celer	to conceal
congeler	to (deep-)freeze
déceler	to detect, to reveal
dégeler	to defrost
geler	to freeze
harceler	to harass
marteler	to hammer
modeler	to model
peler	to peel

b) *Verbs ending in* -eter

Verbs ending in -eter double the t before a silent e (ie before -e, -es, -ent of the present indicative and subjunctive, and throughout the future and conditional): eg **jeter** *(to throw)*.

PRESENT INDICATIVE	PRESENT SUBJUNCTIVE
je jette	je jette
tu jettes	tu jettes
il jette	il jette
elle jette	elle jette
nous jetons	nous jetions
vous jetez	vous jetiez
ils jettent	ils jettent
elles jettent	elles jettent

FUTURE	CONDITIONAL
je jetterai	je jetterais
tu jetteras	tu jetterais
il jettera	il jetterait
elle jettera	elle jetterait
nous jetterons	nous jetterions
vous jetterez	vous jetteriez
ils jetteront	ils jetteraient
elles jetteront	elles jetteraient

Note, however, that some verbs in -eter, including the following, are conjugated like **acheter** (see p B26):

crocheter	to pick (lock)
fureter	to ferret about
haleter	to pant
racheter	to buy back

c) *Verbs ending in* -oyer *and* -uyer

In verbs ending in -oyer and -uyer the y changes to i before a silent e (ie before -e, -es, -ent of the present indicative and subjunctive, and throughout the future and conditional): eg **employer** *(to use)* and **ennuyer** *(to bore)*.

PRESENT INDICATIVE	PRESENT SUBJUNCTIVE
j'emploie	j'emploie
tu emploies	tu emploies
il emploie	il emploie
elle emploie	elle emploie
nous employons	nous employions
vous employez	vous employiez
ils emploient	ils emploient
elles emploient	elles emploient

FUTURE	CONDITIONAL
j'emploierai	j'emploierais
tu emploieras	tu emploierais
il emploiera	il emploierait
elle emploiera	elle emploierait
nous emploierons	nous emploierions
vous emploierez	vous emploieriez
ils emploieront	ils emploieraient
elles emploieront	elles emploieraient

Note that **envoyer** *(to send)* and **renvoyer** *(to dismiss)* have an irregular future and conditional: j'enverrai, j'enverrais; je renverrai, je renverrais.

d) *Verbs ending in -ayer*

In verbs ending in -ayer, eg **balayer** *(to sweep)*, **payer** *(to pay)*, **essayer** *(to try)*, the change from y to i is optional:

eg	je balaie	or	je balaye
	je paie	or	je paye
	j'essaie	or	j'essaye

e) *Verbs in e- + consonant + -er*

Verbs like **acheter, enlever, mener, peser** change the (last) e of the stem to è before a silent e (ie before -e, -es, -ent of the present indicative and subjunctive and throughout the future and conditional):

PRESENT INDICATIVE	PRESENT SUBJUNCTIVE
j'achète	j'achète
tu achètes	tu achètes
il achète	il achète
elle achète	elle achète
nous achetons	nous achetions
vous achetez	vous achetiez
ils achètent	ils achètent
elles achètent	elles achètent

FUTURE	CONDITIONAL
j'achèterai	j'achèterais
tu achèteras	tu achèterais
il achètera	il achèterait
elle achètera	elle achèterait
nous achèterons	nous achèterions
vous achèterez	vous achèteriez
ils achèteront	ils achèteraient
elles achèteront	elles achèteraient

Verbs conjugated like **acheter** include:

achever *to complete*	haleter *to pant*
amener *to bring*	harceler *to harass*
celer *to conceal*	lever *to lift*
crever *to burst*	marteler *to hammer*
crocheter *to pick (lock)*	mener *to lead*
élever *to raise*	modeler *to model*
emmener *to take away*	peler *to peel*
enlever *to remove*	peser *to weigh*
étiqueter *to label*	se promener *to go for a*
fureter *to ferret about*	*walk*
geler *to freeze*	semer *to sow*
	soulever *to lift*

f) *Verbs in é- + consonant + -er*

Verbs like **espérer** *(to hope)* change é to è before a silent e in the present indicative and subjunctive. Note, however, that in the future and conditional é is retained.

PRESENT INDICATIVE	PRESENT SUBJUNCTIVE
j'espère	j'espère
tu espères	tu espères
il espère	il espère
elle espère	elle espère
nous espérons	nous espérions
vous espérez	vous espériez
ils espèrent	ils espèrent
elles espèrent	elles espèrent

FUTURE	CONDITIONAL
j'espérerai	j'espérerais
tu espéreras	tu espérerais
il espérera	il espérerait
elle espérera	elle espérerait
nous espérerons	nous espérerions
vous espérerez	vous espéreriez
ils espéreront	ils espéreraient
elles espéreront	elles espéreraient

Verbs conjugated like **espérer** include verbs in -éder, -érer, -éter etc:

accéder	*to accede to*
céder	*to yield*
célébrer	*to celebrate*
compléter	*to complete*
considérer	*to consider*
décéder	*to die*
digérer	*to digest*
gérer	*to manage*
inquiéter	*to worry*
libérer	*to free*
opérer	*to operate*
pénétrer	*to penetrate*
persévérer	*to persevere*
posséder	*to possess*
précéder	*to precede*
préférer	*to prefer*
protéger	*to protect*
récupérer	*to recover*
refréner	*to curb*
régler	*to rule*
régner	*to reign*
répéter	*to repeat, to rehearse*
révéler	*to reveal*
sécher	*to dry*
succéder	*to succeed*
suggérer	*to suggest*
tolérer	*to tolerate*

C AUXILIARIES AND THE FORMATION OF COMPOUND TENSES

1 Formation

a) The two auxiliary verbs avoir and être are used with the past participle of a verb to form compound tenses.

b) *The past participle*

The regular past participle is formed by taking the stem of the infinitive and adding the following endings:

-er	-ir	-re
aim(er) + é	fin(ir) + i	vend(re) + u
aimé	fini	vendu

For the agreement of past participles see p B38.

c) *Compound tenses*

In French there are seven compound tenses: perfect, pluperfect, future perfect, past conditional (conditional perfect), past anterior, perfect subjunctive, pluperfect subjunctive.

2 Verbs conjugated with AVOIR

PERFECT	PLUPERFECT
present of avoir + past participle	imperfect of avoir + past participle
j'ai aimé	j'avais aimé
tu as aimé	tu avais aimé
il a aimé	il avait aimé
elle a aimé	elle avait aimé
nous avons aimé	nous avions aimé
vous avez aimé	vous aviez aimé
ils ont aimé	ils avaient aimé
elles ont aimé	elles avaient aimé

FUTURE PERFECT	PAST CONDITIONAL
future of avoir + past participle	conditional of avoir + past participle
j'aurai aimé	j'aurais aimé
tu auras aimé	tu aurais aimé
il aura aimé	il aurait aimé
elle aura aimé	elle aurait aimé

nous aurons aimé
vous aurez aimé
ils auront aimé
elles auront aimé

nous aurions aimé
vous auriez aimé
ils auraient aimé
elles auraient aimé

nous soyons arrivé(e)s
vous soyez arrivé(e)(s)
ils soient arrivés
elles soient arrivées

nous fussions arrivé(e)s
vous fussiez arrivé(e)(s)
ils fussent arrivés
elles fussent arrivées

PAST ANTERIOR

past historic of avoir +
past participle

j'eus aimé
tu eus aimé
il eut aimé
elle eut aimé
nous eûmes aimé
vous eûtes aimé
ils eurent aimé
elles eurent aimé

PERFECT SUBJUNCTIVE

present subjunctive of
avoir + past participle

j'aie aimé
tu aies aimé
il ait aimé
elle ait aimé
nous ayons aimé
vous ayez aimé
ils aient aimé
elles aient aimé

PLUPERFECT SUBJUNCTIVE

imperfect subjunctive of
avoir + past participle

j'eusse aimé
tu eusses aimé
il eût aimé
elle eût aimé
nous eussions aimé
vous eussiez aimé
ils eussent aimé
elles eussent aimé

3 Verbs conjugated with ÊTRE

PERFECT

present of être +
past participle

je suis arrivé(e)
tu es arrivé(e)
il est arrivé
elle est arrivée
nous sommes arrivé(e)s
vous êtes arrivé(e)(s)
ils sont arrivés
elles sont arrivées

PLUPERFECT

imperfect of être +
past participle

j'étais arrivé(e)
tu étais arrivé(e)
il était arrivé
elle était arrivée
nous étions arrivé(e)s
vous étiez arrivé(e)(s)
ils étaient arrivés
elles étaient arrivées

FUTURE PERFECT

future of être +
past participle

je serai arrivé(e)
tu seras arrivé(e)
il sera arrivé
elle sera arrivée
nous serons arrivé(e)s
vous serez arrivé(e)(s)
ils seront arrivés
elles seront arrivées

PAST CONDITIONAL

conditional of être +
past participle

je serais arrivé(e)
tu serais arrivé(e)
il serait arrivé
elle serait arrivée
nous serions arrivé(e)s
vous seriez arrivé(e)(s)
ils seraient arrivés
elles seraient arrivées

PAST ANTERIOR

past historic of être +
past participle

je fus arrivé(e)
tu fus arrivé(e)
il fut arrivé
elle fut arrivée
nous fûmes arrivé(e)s
vous fûtes arrivé(e)(s)
ils furent arrivés
elles furent arrivées

PERFECT SUBJUNCTIVE

present subjunctive of
être + past participle

je sois arrivé(e)
tu sois arrivé(e)
il soit arrivé
elle soit garrivée

PLUPERFECT SUBJUNCTIVE

imperfect subjunctive of
être + past participle

je fusse arrivé(e)
tu fusses arrivé(e)
il fût arrivé
elle fût arrivée

4 AVOIR or ÊTRE?

a) *Verbs conjugated with* avoir

The compound tenses of most verbs are formed with avoir:

j'ai marqué un but
I scored a goal

elle a dansé toute la nuit
she danced all night

b) *Verbs conjugated with* être

i) all reflexive verbs (see p B28):

je me suis baigné
I had a bath

ii) the following verbs (mainly of motion):

aller	to go
arriver	to arrive
descendre	to go/come down
entrer	to go/come in
monter	to go/come up
mourir	to die
naître	to be born
partir	to leave
passer	to go through, to drop in
rester	to remain
retourner	to return
sortir	to go/come out
tomber	to fall
venir	to come

and most of their compounds:

revenir	to come back
devenir	to become
parvenir	to reach, to manage to
rentrer	to return home
remonter	to go up again
redescendre	to go down again

Note, however, that prévenir *(to warn)* and subvenir *(to provide for)* are conjugated with avoir:

je t'avais prévenu!
I did warn you!

elle avait subvenu à toutes les dépenses
she met all the expenses

Note too that passer can also be conjugated with avoir:

il a passé par Paris
he went via Paris

Some of the verbs listed above can take a direct object. In such cases they are conjugated with avoir and will have a different meaning:

descendre	to take/bring down, to go down (the stairs, a slope)
monter	to take/bring up, to go up (the stairs, a slope)
rentrer	to take/bring/put in
retourner	to turn over
sortir	to take/bring out

les élèves sont sortis à midi
the pupils came out at midday

les élèves ont sorti leurs livres
the pupils took out their books

elle n'est pas encore descendue
she hasn't come down yet

elle a descendu un vieux tableau du grenier
she brought an old painting down from the loft

elle a descendu l'escalier
she came down the stairs

les prisonniers sont montés sur le toit
the prisoners climbed on to the roof

le garçon a monté les bouteilles de vin de la cave
the waiter brought the bottles of wine up from the cellar

nous sommes rentrés tard
we got home late

j'ai rentré la voiture dans le garage
I put the car in the garage

je serais retourné à Paris
I would have returned to Paris

le jardinier a retourné le sol
the gardener turned over the soil

ils sont sortis de la piscine
they got out of the swimming pool

il a sorti les mains de ses poches
he took his hands out of his pockets

D REFLEXIVE VERBS

1 Definition

Reflexive verbs are so called because they 'reflect' the action back onto the subject. Reflexive verbs are always accompanied by a reflexive pronoun, eg in the following sentence:

I look at myself in the mirror

'myself' is the reflexive pronoun.

je lave la voiture	je me lave
I'm washing the car	*I'm washing myself*
j'ai couché le bébé	je me suis couché
I put the baby to bed	*I went to bed (I put myself to bed)*

2 Reflexive pronouns

They are:

PERSON	SINGULAR	PLURAL
1st	me (m') *myself*	nous *ourselves*
2nd	te (t') *yourself*	vous *yourself/selves*
3rd	se (s') *himself, herself, itself, oneself*	se (s') *themselves*

Note:

a) m', t' and s' are used instead of me, te and se in front of a vowel or a silent h:

tu t'amuses? – non, je m'ennuie
are you enjoying yourself? – no, I'm bored

il s'habille dans la salle de bain
he gets dressed in the bathroom

b) French reflexive pronouns are often not translated in English:

je me demande si ...	ils se moquent de moi
I wonder if ...	*they're making fun of me*

c) Plural reflexive pronouns can also be used to express reciprocal actions; in this case they are translated by 'each other' or 'one another':

nous nous détestons	ils ne se parlent pas
we hate one another	*they're not talking to each other*

d) se can mean 'ourselves' or 'each other' when it is used with the pronoun on meaning 'we' (see p B16):

on s'est perdu	on se connaît
we got lost	*we know each other*

3 Position of reflexive pronouns

Reflexive pronouns are placed immediately before the verb, except in positive commands, where they follow the verb and are linked to it by a hyphen:

tu te dépêches?	dépêchons-nous!
will you hurry up?	*let's hurry!*
ne t'inquiète pas	ne vous fiez pas à lui
don't worry	*don't trust him*

Note that reflexive pronouns change to emphatic (disjunctive) pronouns in positive commands:

elle doit se reposer	repose-toi
she needs to rest	*have a rest*

4 Conjugation of reflexive verbs

a) *Simple tenses*

These are conjugated in the same way as non-reflexive verbs, except that a reflexive pronoun is used.

b) *Compound tenses*

These are conjugated using the auxiliary être followed by the past participle of the verb.

A full conjugation table is given on p B47.

5 Agreement of the past participle

a) In most cases, the reflexive pronoun is a direct object and the past participle of the verb agrees in number and in gender with the reflexive pronoun:

il s'est trompé	elle s'est endormie
he made a mistake	*she fell asleep*
ils se sont excusés	elles se sont assises
they apologized	*they sat down*

b) When the reflexive pronoun is used as an indirect object, the past participle does not change:

nous nous sommes écrit	elle se l'est acheté
we wrote to each other	*she bought it for herself*
elles se sont parlé	les années se sont succédé
they spoke to each other	*one year followed another*

When the reflexive verb has a direct object, the reflexive pronoun is the indirect object of the reflexive verb and the past participle does not agree with it:

Caroline s'est tordu la cheville
Caroline sprained her ankle

vous vous êtes lavé les mains, les filles?
did you wash your hands, girls?

elles se sont égratigné les genoux
they scratched their knees

6 Common reflexive verbs

s'en aller *to go away*	s'éloigner (de) *to move away (from)*	se moquer de *to laugh at*
s'amuser *to have fun*	s'endormir *to fall asleep*	s'occuper de *to take care of*
s'appeler *to be called*	s'ennuyer *to be bored*	se passer *to happen*
s'approcher (de) *to come near*	s'étonner (de) *to be surprised (at)*	se passer de *to do without*
s'arrêter *to stop*	s'excuser (de) *to apologize (for)*	se promener *to go for a walk*
s'asseoir *to sit down*	se fâcher *to get angry/fall out*	se rappeler *to remember*

s'attendre à *to expect*	**s'écrier** *to cry out/exclaim*	**se raser** *to shave*
se baigner *to have a bath*	**s'habiller** *to get dressed*	**se renseigner** *to make enquiries*
se battre *to fight*	**se hâter** *to hurry*	**se ressembler** *to look alike*
se blesser *to hurt oneself*	**s'inquiéter** *to worry*	**se retourner** *to turn round*
se coucher *to go to bed*	**s'installer** *to settle down*	**se réveiller** *to wake up*
se débarrasser de *to get rid of*	**se laver** *to wash*	**se sauver** *to run away*
se demander *to wonder*	**se lever** *to get up*	**se souvenir (de)** *to remember*
se dépêcher *to hurry*	**se mêler de** *to meddle with*	**se taire** *to be/keep quiet*
se déshabiller *to undress*	**se mettre à** *to start*	**se tromper** *to be mistaken*
se diriger vers *to move towards*	**se mettre en route** *to set off*	**se trouver** *to be (situated)*

E IMPERSONAL VERBS

1 Conjugation

Impersonal verbs are used only in the third person singular and in the infinitive. The subject is always the impersonal pronoun il (= it).

il neige *it's snowing*	**il y a du brouillard** *it's foggy*

2 List of impersonal verbs

a) *verbs describing the weather:*

i) faire + adjective:

il fait beau/chaud *it's fine/warm*	**il fait frais/froid** *it's cool/cold*
il fera beau demain *the weather will be good tomorrow*	**il va faire très froid** *it will be very cold*

ii) faire + noun:

il fait beau temps *the weather is nice*	**il fait mauvais temps** *the weather is bad*
il fait jour *it's daylight*	**il fait nuit** *it's dark*

iii) other impersonal verbs and verbs used impersonally to describe the weather:

il gèle	(geler)	*it's freezing*
il grêle	(grêler)	*it's hailing*
il neige	(neiger)	*it's snowing*
il pleut	(pleuvoir)	*it's raining*
il tonne	(tonner)	*there's thunder*

Note that some of these verbs may be used personally:

je gèle	*I'm freezing*

iv) il y a + noun:

il y a des nuages	*it's cloudy*
il y a du brouillard	*it's foggy*
il y a du verglas	*it's icy*

b) être

i) il est + noun:

il est cinq heures *it's five o'clock*	**il était une fois un géant** *once upon a time there was a giant*

ii) il est + adjective + de + infinitive:

il est **difficile** de	*it's difficult to*
il est **facile** de	*it's easy to*
il est **nécessaire** de	*it's necessary to*
il est **inutile** de	*it's useless to*
il est **possible** de	*it's possible to*

il est **difficile** d'en parler *it's difficult to talk about it*

Note that the indirect object pronoun in French corresponds to the English 'for me', 'for him' etc:

il m'est difficile d'en parler
it's difficult for me to talk about it

iii) il est + adjective + que:

il est **douteux** que	*it's doubtful that*
il est **évident** que	*it's clear that*
il est **possible** que	*it's possible that*
il est **probable** que	*it's probable that*
il est **peu probable** que	*it's unlikely that*
il est **vrai** que	*it's true that*

Note that que may be followed by the indicative or the subjunctive (see p B32):

il est probable qu'il ne viendra pas
he probably won't come

il est peu probable qu'il vienne
it's unlikely that he'll come

c) arriver, se passer *(to happen)*

il est arrivé **une chose curieuse** *a strange thing happened*	**que** se passe-t-il? *what's happening?*

d) exister *(to exist)*, rester *(to remain)*, manquer *(to be missing)*

il existe trois exemplaires de ce livre
there are three copies of this book

il me restait **un euro** *I had one euro left*	il me manque **4 euros** *I am 4 euros short*

e) paraître, sembler *(to seem)*

il paraîtrait/semblerait qu'il ait changé d'avis
it would appear that he has changed his mind

il paraît qu'il va se marier
it seems he's going to get married

il me semble que le professeur s'est trompé
it seems to me that the teacher has made a mistake

f) other common impersonal verbs

i) s'agir de *(to be a matter of)* may be followed by a noun, a pronoun or an infinitive:

il s'agit **de ton avenir** *it's about your future*	**de quoi** s'agit-il? *what's it about?*

il s'agit de trouver le coupable
we must find the culprit

ii) falloir *(to be necessary)* may be followed by a noun, an infinitive or the subjunctive:

il faut deux heures pour aller à Paris
it takes two hours to get to Paris

il me faut plus de temps
I need more time

il faudra rentrer plus tôt ce soir
we'll have to come home earlier tonight

il faut que tu parles à Papa
you have to speak to Dad

iii) **suffire** (*to be enough*) may be followed by a noun, an
infinitive or the subjunctive:

il suffit de peu de choses pour être heureux
it doesn't take much to be happy

il suffit de passer le pont
you just have to cross the bridge

il suffira qu'ils te donnent le numéro de téléphone
they will only have to give you the telephone number

iv) **valoir mieux** (*to be better*) may be followed by an infinitive or the subjunctive:

il vaudrait mieux prendre le car
it would be better to take the coach

il vaut mieux que vous ne sortiez pas seule le soir
you'd better not go out alone at night

F TENSES

For the formation of the different tenses, see pp B24 and B26-8.

Note that French has no continuous tenses (as in 'I am eating', 'I
was going', 'I will be arriving'). The 'be' and '-ing' parts of English
continuous tenses are not translated as separate words. Instead, the
equivalent tense is used in French:

je mange	**je mangerai**
I am eating	*I will be eating*

1 PRESENT

The present is used to describe what someone does/something that
happens regularly, or what someone is doing/something that is happening at the time of speaking.

a) *regular actions*

il travaille dans un bureau
he works in an office

je lis rarement le journal
I seldom read the paper

b) *continuous actions*

ne le dérangez pas, il travaille
don't disturb him, he's working

je ne peux pas venir, je garde mon petit frère
I can't come, I'm looking after my little brother

Note that the continuous nature of the action can also be
expressed by using the phrase **être en train de** (*to be in the
process of*) + infinitive:

je suis en train de cuisiner
I'm (busy) cooking

c) *immediate future*

je pars demain
I'm leaving tomorrow

However, the present cannot be used after **quand** and other
conjunctions of time when the future is implied (see p B31):

je le ferai quand j'aurai le temps
I'll do it when I have the time

d) *general truths*

la vie est dure
life is hard

2 IMPERFECT

The imperfect is a past tense used to express what someone was
doing or what someone used to do, or to describe something in the
past. The imperfect refers particularly to something that continued
over a period of time, as opposed to something that happened at a
specific point in time.

a) *continuous actions*

The imperfect describes an action that was happening, often

when something else took place:

il prenait un bain quand le téléphone a sonné
he was having a bath when the phone rang

excuse-moi, je pensais à autre chose
I'm sorry, I was thinking of something else

Note that the continuous nature of the action can be emphasized
by using **être en train de** + infinitive:

j'étais en train de faire le ménage
I was (busy) doing the housework

b) *regular actions in the past*

je le voyais souvent quand il habitait dans le quartier
I used to see him often when he lived in this area

quand il était plus jeune il voyageait beaucoup
when he was younger he used to travel a lot

c) *description in the past*

il faisait beau ce jour-là	**c'était formidable!**
the weather was good that day	*it was great!*
elle portait une robe bleue	**elle donnait sur la rue**
she wore a blue dress	*it looked onto the street*

3 PERFECT

The perfect tense is a compound past tense, used to express single
actions which have been completed. What someone did, has done or
has been doing, or something that has happened or has been happening are all expressed using the perfect tense:

je l'ai envoyé lundi	**on est sorti hier soir**
I sent it on Monday	*we went out last night*
tu t'es bien amusé?	**je ne l'ai pas vu de toute**
did you have a good time?	**la journée**
	I haven't seen him all day
j'ai lu toute la journée	**tu as déjà mangé?**
I've been reading all day	*have you eaten?*

In English, the simple past ('did', 'went', 'prepared') is used to
describe both single and repeated actions in the past. In French, the
perfect only describes single actions in the past, while repeated
actions are expressed by the imperfect (they are sometimes signposted by 'used to'). Thus 'I went' should be translated 'j'allais' or
'je suis allé' depending on the nature of the action:

après dîner, je suis allé en ville
after dinner I went into town

l'an dernier, j'allais plus souvent au théâtre
last year I went to the theatre more often

4 PAST HISTORIC

This tense is used in the same way as the perfect tense, to describe a
single, completed action in the past (what someone did or something
that happened). It is a literary tense, not common in everyday spoken French; it is found mainly as a narrative tense in written form:

le piéton ne vit pas arriver la voiture
the pedestrian didn't see the car coming

5 PLUPERFECT

This compound tense is used to express what someone had done/had
been doing or something that had happened or had been happening:

il n'avait pas voulu aller avec eux
he hadn't wanted to go with them

elle était essoufflée parce qu'elle avait couru
she was out of breath because she'd been running

However, the pluperfect is not used as in English with **depuis** (*for*,
since), or with **venir de** + infinitive (*to have just done something*).
For details see p B31:

il neigeait depuis une semaine
it had been snowing for a week

les pompiers venaient d'arriver
the firemen had just arrived

6 FUTURE

This tense is used to express what someone will do or will be doing or something that will happen or will be happening:

je ferai la vaisselle demain
I'll do the dishes tomorrow

j'arriverai tard
I'll be arriving late

Note that the future and not the present, as in English, is used in time clauses introduced by **quand** *(when)* or other conjunctions of time where the future is implied (see section 11):

il viendra quand il le pourra
he'll come when he can

French makes frequent use of **aller** + infinitive *(to be about to do something)* to express the immediate future:

je vais vous expliquer ce qui s'est passé
I'll explain (to you) what happened

il va déménager la semaine prochaine
he's moving house next week

7 FUTURE PERFECT

This compound tense is used to describe what someone will have done or will have been doing in the future or to describe something that will have happened in the future:

j'aurai bientôt fini
I will soon have finished

In particular, it is used instead of the English perfect in time clauses introduced by **quand** or other conjunctions of time where the future is implied (see section 11):

appelle-moi quand tu auras fini
call me when you've finished

on rentrera dès qu'on aura fait les courses
we'll come back as soon as we've done the shopping

8 PAST ANTERIOR

This tense is used instead of the pluperfect to express an action that preceded another action in the past (ie a past in the past). It is usually introduced by a conjunction of time (translated by 'when', 'as soon as', 'after' etc) and the main verb is in the past historic:

il se coucha dès qu'ils furent partis
he went to bed as soon as they'd left

à peine eut-elle raccroché que le téléphone sonna
she'd hardly hung up when the telephone rang

9 Use of tenses with 'depuis' (for, since)

a) The present must be used instead of the perfect to describe actions which started in the past and are still continuing:

il habite ici depuis trois ans
he's been living here for three years

elle t'attend depuis ce matin
she's been waiting for you since this morning

Note, however, that the perfect, not the present, is used when the clause is negative or when the action has been completed:

il n'a pas pris de vacances depuis longtemps
he hasn't taken any holidays for a long time

j'ai fini depuis un bon moment
I've been finished for quite a while

Note:

i) **il y a ... que** or **voilà ... que** are also used with the present tense to translate 'for':

it's been ringing for ten minutes
ça sonne depuis dix minutes
il y a dix minutes que ça sonne
voilà dix minutes que ça sonne

ii) **depuis que** is used when 'since' introduces a clause, ie when there is a verb following depuis:

elle dort depuis que vous êtes partis
she's been sleeping since you left

iii) Do not confuse **depuis** *(for, since)* and **pendant** *(for, during)*: depuis refers to the starting point of an action which is still going on and pendant refers to the duration of an action which is over and is used with the perfect:

il vit ici depuis deux mois
he's been living here for two months

il a vécu ici pendant deux mois
he lived here for two months

b) The imperfect must be used instead of the pluperfect to describe an action which had started in the past and was still going on at a given time:

elle le connaissait depuis son enfance
she had known him since her childhood

il attendait depuis trois heures quand on est arrivé
he had been waiting for three hours when we arrived

Note, however, that if the sentence is negative or if the action has been completed, the pluperfect and not the imperfect is used:

je n'étais pas allé au théâtre depuis des années
I hadn't been to the theatre for years

il était parti depuis peu
he'd been gone for a short while

Note:

i) **il y avait ... que** + imperfect is also used to translate 'for':

she'd been living alone for a long time
elle habitait seule depuis longtemps
il y avait longtemps qu'elle habitait seule

ii) **depuis que** is used when 'since' introduces a clause; if it describes an action which was still going on at the time, it can be followed by the imperfect, otherwise it is followed by the pluperfect:

il pleuvait depuis que nous étions en vacances
it had been raining since we had been on holiday

il pleuvait depuis que nous étions arrivés
it had been raining since we arrived

iii) Do not confuse **depuis** and **pendant**: depuis refers to the starting point of an action which is still going on and pendant refers to the duration of an action which is over; pendant is used with the pluperfect:

j'y travaillais depuis un an
I had been working there for a year

j'y avais travaillé pendant un an
I had worked there for a year

10 Use of tenses with 'venir de'

venir de + infinitive means 'to have just done'.

a) If it describes something that has just happened, it is used in the present instead of the perfect:

l'avion vient d'arriver
the plane has just arrived

je viens de te le dire!
I've just told you!

b) If it describes something that had just happened, it is used in the imperfect instead of the pluperfect:

le film venait de commencer
the film had just started

je venais de rentrer
I'd just got home

11 Use of tenses after conjunctions of time

quand	when
tant que	as long as
dès/aussitôt que	as soon as
lorsque	when
pendant que	while

Verbs which follow these conjunctions must be used in the following tenses:

a) future instead of present:

je te téléphonerai quand **je serai prêt**
I'll phone you when I'm ready

elle ira le voir dès qu'elle le pourra
she'll go to see him as soon as she can

b) future perfect instead of perfect when the future is implied:

on rentrera dès qu'on aura fini **les courses**
we'll come back as soon as we've done the shopping

je t'appellerai dès qu'il sera arrivé
I'll call you as soon as he's arrived

c) conditional present/perfect instead of perfect/pluperfect in indirect speech:

il a dit qu'il sortirait quand **il aurait fini**
he said that he would come out when he had finished

For the tenses of the subjunctive and conditional, see G1 and G3.

G MOODS

1 THE SUBJUNCTIVE

In everyday spoken French, the only two subjunctive tenses that are used are the present and the perfect. The imperfect and the pluperfect subjunctive are found mainly in literature or in texts of a formal nature.

The subjunctive is always preceded by the conjunction **que** and is used in subordinate clauses when the subject of the subordinate clause is different from the subject of the main verb.

Some clauses introduced by **que** take the indicative. The subjunctive must be used after the following:

a) Verbs of emotion:

être content que	to be pleased that
être désolé que	to be sorry that
être étonné que	to be surprised that
être heureux que	to be happy that
être surpris que	to be surprised that
être triste que	to be sad that
avoir peur que ... ne	to be afraid/to fear that
craindre que ... ne	to be afraid/to fear that
regretter que	to be sorry that

ils étaient contents que j'aille les voir
they were pleased (that) I went to visit them

je serais très étonné qu'il mente
I would be very surprised if he was lying

je regrette que tu ne puisses pas y aller
I'm sorry (that) you can't go

Note that ne is used after several verbs in the subjunctive mood but it does not have a negative meaning in itself and is not translated in English:

je crains que l'avion ne soit en retard
I'm afraid (that) the plane will be late

j'ai bien peur qu'il ne soit déjà trop tard
I'm very much afraid (that) it's already too late

pour éviter que la situation ne s'aggrave
to prevent the situation from getting any worse

b) Verbs of wishing and willing:

aimer que	to like
désirer que	to wish (that)
préférer que	to prefer (that)
souhaiter que	to wish (that)
vouloir que	to want

Note that in English, such verbs are often used in the following type of construction: verb of willing + object + infinitive (eg I'd like you to listen); this type of construction is impossible in French, where a subjunctive clause has to be used:

je souhaite que tu réussisses
I hope you will succeed

il aimerait que je lui écrive plus souvent
he'd like me to write to him more often

voulez-vous que je vous y amène en voiture?
would you like me to drive you there?

préférez-vous que je rappelle demain?
would you rather I called back tomorrow?

c) Impersonal constructions (expressing necessity, possibility, doubt, denial, preference):

il faut que	it is necessary (that) (must)
il est nécessaire que	it is necessary that (must)
il est important que	it is important (that)
il est possible que	it is possible that (may)
il se peut que	it is possible that (may)
il est impossible que	it is impossible (that) (can't)
il est douteux que	it is doubtful whether
il est peu probable que	it is unlikely that
il semble que	it seems (that)
il est préférable que	it is preferable (that)
il vaut mieux que	it is better (that) (had better)
c'est dommage que	it is a pity (that)

Note that these expressions may be used in any appropriate tense:

il faut absolument que je le leur dise
I simply must tell them

il était important que tu le saches
it was important that you should know

il se pourrait qu'elle change d'avis
she might change her mind

il est peu probable qu'ils s'y intéressent
they're unlikely to be interested in that

il semble qu'elle ait raison
she appears to be right

il vaudrait mieux que tu ne promettes rien
you'd better not promise anything

c'est dommage que vous vous soyez manqués
it's a pity you missed each other

d) Some verbs and impersonal constructions expressing doubt or uncertainty (mainly used negatively or interrogatively):

douter que	to doubt (that)
(ne pas) croire que	(not) to believe (that)
(ne pas) penser que	(not) to think (that)
(ne pas) être sûr que	(not) to be sure that
il n'est pas certain que	it isn't certain that
il n'est pas évident que	it isn't obvious that
il n'est pas sûr que	it isn't certain that
il n'est pas vrai que	it isn't true that

je doute fort qu'il veuille t'aider
I very much doubt whether he'll want to help you

croyez-vous qu'il y ait des places libres?
do you think there are any seats available?

on n'était pas sûr que ce soit le bon endroit
we weren't sure that it was the right place

il n'était pas certain qu'elle puisse gagner
it wasn't certain whether she could win

e) attendre que (to wait until someone does something or something happens, to wait for someone to do something or for something to happen):

attendons qu'il revienne
let's wait until he comes back

f) Some subordinating conjunctions:

bien que	*although*
quoique	*although*
sans que	*without*
pour que	*so that*
afin que	*so that*
à condition que	*provided that*
pourvu que	*provided that*
jusqu'à ce que	*until*
en attendant que	*until*
avant que ... (ne)	*before*
à moins que ... (ne)	*unless*
de peur que ... ne	*for fear that*
de crainte que ... ne	*for fear that*
de sorte que	*so that*
de façon que	*so that*
de manière que	*so that*

Note that when ne is shown in brackets, it may follow the conjunction, although it is seldom used in spoken French; it does not have a negative meaning, and is not translated in English.

il est allé travailler bien qu'il soit **malade**
he went to work although he was ill

elle est entrée sans que je la voie
she came in without me seeing her

voilà de l'argent pour que tu puisses **aller au cinéma**
here's some money so that you can go to the cinema

d'accord, pourvu que tu me promettes **de ne pas le répéter**
all right, as long as you promise not to tell anyone

tu l'as revu avant qu'il (ne) parte?
did you see him again before he left?

je le ferai demain, à moins que ce (ne) soit **urgent**
I'll do it tomorrow, unless it's urgent

elle n'a pas fait de bruit de peur qu'il ne se réveille
she didn't make any noise in case he woke

parle moins fort de sorte qu'elle ne nous entende pas
talk more quietly so that she doesn't hear us

Note that when de façon/manière que *(so that)* expresses a result, as opposed to a purpose, the indicative is used instead of the subjunctive:

il a fait du bruit de sorte qu'elle l'a entendu
he made some noise, and as a result she heard him

g) A superlative or adjectives like premier *(first)*, dernier *(last)*, seul *(only)* followed by qui or que:

c'était le coureur le plus rapide que j'aie **jamais vu**
he was the fastest runner I ever saw

Note, however, that the indicative is used with a statement of fact rather than the expression of an opinion:

c'est lui qui me l'a dit
it was he who told me

h) Negative and indefinite pronouns (eg rien, personne, quelqu'un) followed by qui or que:

je ne connais personne qui fasse **aussi bien les crêpes**
I don't know anyone who can make such good crêpes

il n'y a aucune chance qu'il réussisse
he hasn't got a chance of succeeding

ils cherchent quelqu'un qui puisse **garder le bébé**
they're looking for someone who can look after the baby

2 AVOIDING THE SUBJUNCTIVE

Note, however, that the subjunctive is not used if the verbs in both clauses have the same subject. The infinitive will be used in the subordinate clause instead, sometimes introduced by a preposition (à or de) (see pp B35-7).

a) de + infinitive replaces the subjunctive after:

i) verbs of emotion:

j'ai été étonné d'apprendre **la nouvelle**
I was surprised to hear the news

il regrette de ne pas être arrivé **plus tôt**
he's sorry he didn't arrive earlier

tu as peur de ne pas **avoir assez d'argent?**
are you worried you won't have enough money?

ii) attendre *(to wait)* and douter *(to doubt)*:

j'attendrai d'avoir bu **mon café**
I'll wait until I've drunk my coffee

iii) most impersonal constructions:

il serait préférable de les en **informer tout de suite**
it would be better to let them know immediately

il est indispensable de parler **une langue étrangère**
it's essential to be able to speak a foreign language

iv) most conjunctions:

il est resté dans la voiture afin de ne pas **se mouiller**
he stayed in the car so as not to get wet

j'ai lu avant de **m'endormir**
I read before falling asleep

tu peux sortir à condition de **rentrer avant minuit**
you can go out, as long as you're back before midnight

b) à + infinitive replaces the subjunctive after:

i) de façon/manière

mets la liste sur la table de manière à ne pas l'oublier
put the list on the table so that you won't forget it

ii) premier, seul, dernier

il a été le seul à s'excuser
he was the only one who apologized

c) The infinitive without any linking preposition replaces the subjunctive after:

i) verbs of wishing and willing:

je voudrais sortir **avec toi**
I'd like to go out with you

ii) il faut, il vaut mieux:

il vous faudra prendre **des chèques de voyage**
you'll have to take some traveller's cheques

il lui a fallu recommencer **à zéro**
he had to start all over again

il vaudrait mieux lui apporter **des fleurs que des bonbons**
it would be better to take her flowers than sweets

Note that il faut + infinitive is used to state a generality. If one particular person etc is the subject of the action, an indirect object is used:

il faut réserver **à l'avance**
you have to book in advance

il lui faut se dépêcher
he has to hurry

iii) verbs of thinking:

je ne crois pas le connaître
I don't think I know him

tu penses être chez toi à cinq heures?
do you think you'll be home at five?

iv) pour and sans:

le car est reparti sans nous attendre
the coach left without waiting for us

j'économise pour pouvoir **acheter une moto**
I'm saving up to buy a motorbike

3 THE CONDITIONAL

a) *The conditional present*

i) The conditional present is used to describe what someone would do or would be doing, or what would happen (if something else were to happen):

si j'avais de l'argent, je ferais le tour du monde
if I had money, I would travel around the world

Note that when the main verb is in the conditional present, the verb after **si** is in the imperfect.

ii) It is also used in indirect questions or reported speech instead of the future:

il ne m'a pas dit s'il viendrait
he didn't tell me whether he would come

b) *The conditional perfect (or past conditional)*

The conditional perfect or past conditional is used to express what someone would have done or would have been doing or what would have happened:

si j'avais su, je n'aurais rien dit
if I had known, I wouldn't have said anything

qu'aurais-je fait sans toi?
what would I have done without you?

Note that if the main verb is in the conditional perfect, the verb introduced by **si** is in the pluperfect.

c) *Tenses after* **si**

The tense of the verb introduced by **si** is determined by the tense of the verb in the main clause:

MAIN VERB		VERB FOLLOWING 'SI'
conditional present	→	imperfect
conditional perfect	→	pluperfect

je te le dirais si je le savais
I would tell you if I knew

je te l'aurais dit si je l'avais su
I would have told you if I had known

The conditional and the future should never be used with **si** unless **si** means 'whether' (ie when it introduces an indirect question):

je me demande si j'y serais arrivé sans toi
I wonder if I would have managed without you

4 THE IMPERATIVE

a) *Definition*

The imperative is used to give commands or polite instructions, or to make requests or suggestions; these can be positive ('do!') or negative ('don't!'):

mange ta soupe!
eat your soup!

n'aie pas peur!
don't be afraid!

partons!
let's go!

entrez!
come in!

faites attention!
be careful!

n'hésitez pas!
don't hesitate!

tournez à droite à la poste
turn right at the post office

b) *Forms*

The imperative has only three forms, which are the same as the **tu**, **nous** and **vous** forms of the present tense, but without the subject pronoun:

	-ER VERBS	-IR VERBS	-RE VERBS
'tu' form:	regarde	choisis	attends
	watch	choose	wait
'nous' form:	regardons	choisissons	attendons
	let's watch	let's choose	let's wait
'vous' form:	regardez	choisissez	attendez
	watch	choose	wait

Note:

i) The -s of the **tu** form of -er verbs is dropped, except when **y** or **en** follow the verb:

parle-lui!
speak to him!

parles-en avec lui
speak to him about it

achète du sucre!
buy some sugar!

achètes-en un kilo
buy a kilo (of it)

ii) The distinction between the subject pronouns **tu** and **vous** (see p B18) applies to the **tu** and **vous** forms of the imperative:

prends ta sœur avec toi
take your sister with you

prenez le plat du jour, Monsieur; c'est du poulet rôti
have today's special, sir; it's roast chicken

ouvrez vos livres à la page 24
open your books at page 24

c) *Negative commands*

In negative commands, the verb is placed between **ne** and **pas** (or the second part of other negative expressions):

ne fais pas ça!
don't do that!

ne dites rien!
don't say anything!

d) *Imperative with object pronouns*

In positive commands, object pronouns come after the verb and are attached to it by a hyphen. In negative commands, they come before the verb (see pp B18-20):

dites-moi ce qui s'est passé
tell me what happened

attendons-les!
let's wait for them

prends-en bien soin, ne l'abîme pas!
take good care of it, don't damage it!

ne le leur dis pas!
don't tell them (that)!

ne les écoutez pas
don't listen to them

e) *Imperative of reflexive verbs*

The position of the reflexive pronoun of reflexive verbs is the same as that of object pronouns:

tais-toi!
be quiet!

levez-vous!
get up!

méfiez-vous de lui
don't trust him

arrêtons-nous ici
let's stop here

ne nous plaignons pas
let's not complain

ne t'approche pas plus!
don't come any closer!

f) *Alternatives to the imperative*

i) infinitive

the infinitive is often used instead of the imperative in written instructions and in recipes:

s'adresser au concierge
see the caretaker

ne pas fumer
no smoking

verser le lait et bien mélanger
pour in the milk and mix well

ii) subjunctive

as the imperative has no third person (singular or plural), **qu** + subjunctive is used for giving orders in the third person:

que personne ne me dérange! qu'il entre!
don't let anyone disturb me! *let him (come) in!*

qu'elle parte, je m'en fiche!
I don't care if she goes!

g) *Idiomatic usage*

The imperative is used in spoken French in many set phrases. Here are some of the most common ones:

allons donc!
you don't say!

dis/dites donc!
by the way!
hey! (protest)

tiens/tenez!
here you are!

tiens! voilà le facteur
ah! here comes the postman

tiens (donc)!
(oh) really?

tiens! tiens!
well, well!

voyons!
come (on) now!

voyons donc!
let's see now

H THE INFINITIVE

1 The infinitive is the basic form of the verb. It is recognizable by its ending, which is found in three forms corresponding to the three conjugations: -er, -ir, -re.

These endings give the verb the meaning 'to ... ':

acheter
to buy

choisir
to choose

vendre
to sell

Note that although this applies as a general rule, the French infinitive will often be translated by a verbal construction ending in -ing (see p B65).

2 Uses of the infinitive

The infinitive can follow a preposition, a verb, a noun, a pronoun, an adverb or an adjective.

a) *After a preposition*

The infinitive can be used after some prepositions (pour, avant de, sans, au lieu de, afin de etc):

sans attendre
without waiting

avant de partir
before leaving

b) *After a verb*

There are three main constructions when a verb is followed by an infinitive:

i) Verbs followed by the infinitive with no linking preposition:

● verbs of wishing and willing, eg:

vouloir *to want*
souhaiter *to wish*
désirer *to wish, to want*
espérer *to hope*

voulez-vous manger maintenant ou plus tard?
do you want to eat now or later?

je souhaite parler au directeur
I wish to speak to the manager

● verbs of seeing, hearing and feeling, eg:

voir *to see*
écouter *to listen to*
regarder *to watch*
sentir *to feel, to smell*
entendre *to hear*

je l'ai vu jouer
I've seen him play

tu m'as regardé danser?
did you watch me dance?

j'ai entendu quelqu'un crier
I heard someone shout

● verbs of motion, eg:

aller *to go*
monter *to go/come up*
venir *to come*
entrer *to go/come in*
rentrer *to go/come home*
sortir *to go/come out*
descendre *to go/come down*

je viendrai te voir demain
I'll come and see you tomorrow

il est descendu laver la voiture
he went down to wash the car

va acheter le journal
go and buy the paper

Note that in English, 'to come' and 'to go' may be linked to the verb that follows by 'and'; 'and' is not translated in French.

aller + infinitive can be used to express a future action:

qu'est-ce que tu vas faire demain?
what are you going to do tomorrow?

● modal auxiliary verbs (see pp B39-40)

● verbs of liking and disliking, eg:

aimer *to like*
adorer *to love*
aimer mieux *to prefer*
détester *to hate*
préférer *to prefer*

tu aimes voyager?
do you like travelling?

je déteste aller à la campagne
I hate going to the country

j'adore faire la grasse matinée
I love having a lie-in

j'aime mieux attendre
I'd rather wait

● some impersonal verbs (see p B29)

● a few other verbs, eg:

compter *to intend to*
sembler *to seem*
laisser *to let, to allow*
faillir *'to nearly' (do)*
oser *to dare*

ils l'ont laissé partir
they let him go

je n'ose pas le leur demander
I daren't ask them

tu sembles être malade
you seem to be ill

je compte partir demain
I intend to leave tomorrow

j'ai failli manquer l'avion
I nearly missed the plane

● in the following set expressions:

aller chercher *to go and get, to fetch*
envoyer chercher *to send for*
entendre dire (que) *to hear (that)*
entendre parler de *to hear about*
laisser tomber *to drop*

venir chercher   *to come and get*
vouloir dire   *to mean*

va chercher ton argent
go and get your money

j'ai entendu dire qu'il était journaliste
I've heard that he's a journalist

tu as entendu parler de ce film?
have you heard about this film?

ne le laisse pas tomber!
don't drop it!

ça veut dire 'demain'
it means 'tomorrow'

ii) Verbs followed by à + infinitive:

A list of these is given on p B52:

je dois aider ma mère à préparer le déjeuner
I must help my mother prepare lunch

il commence à faire nuit
it's beginning to get dark

alors, tu t'es décidé à y aller?
so you've made up your mind to go?

je t'invite à venir chez moi pour les vacances de Noël
you are welcome to come to my house for the Christmas holidays

je passe mon temps à lire et à regarder la télé
I spend my time reading and watching TV

cela sert à ouvrir les bouteilles
this is used for opening bottles

iii) Verbs followed by de + infinitive:

A list of these is given on p B52:

je crois qu'il s'est arrêté de pleuvoir
I think it's stopped raining

tu as envie de sortir?
do you feel like going out?

le médecin a conseillé à Serge de rester au lit
the doctor advised Serge to stay in bed

j'ai décidé de rester chez moi
I decided to stay at home

essayons de faire du stop
let's try and hitch-hike

demande à Papa de t'aider
ask Dad to help you

n'oublie pas d'en acheter!
don't forget to buy some!

je vous prie de m'excuser
please forgive me

tu as fini de m'ennuyer?
will you stop annoying me?

je t'interdis d'y aller
I forbid you to go

j'ai refusé de le faire
I refused to do it

il vient de téléphoner
he's just phoned

c) *After a noun, a pronoun, an adverb or an adjective*

There are two possible constructions:

i) with the linking preposition à:

il avait plusieurs clients à voir
he had several customers to see

c'est difficile à dire
it's difficult to say

une maison à vendre
a house for sale

j'ai des examens à préparer
I've got exams to prepare

il nous a indiqué la route à suivre
he showed us the road to follow

il n'y a pas de temps à perdre
there's no time to lose

c'était une occasion à ne pas manquer
it was an opportunity not to be missed

● à conveys the idea of something to do or to be done after the following:

beaucoup	*a lot*
plus	*more*
tant	*so much*
trop	*too much*
assez	*enough*
moins	*less*
rien	*nothing*
tout	*everything*
quelque chose	*something*

il y a trop de livres à lire
there are too many books to read

il n'y a rien à ajouter
there's nothing further to add

elle a quelque chose à nous annoncer
she has something to tell us

● à is used in a passive sense (when something is being done) and after c'est:

un livre agréable à lire
a pleasant book to read

il est facile à satisfaire
he is easily satisfied

c'est intéressant à savoir
that's interesting to know

c'était impossible à faire
it was impossible to do

ii) with the linking preposition de:

je suis content de te voir
I am pleased to see you

● de is used after nouns of an abstract nature, usually with the definite article, eg:

l'habitude de	*the habit of*
l'occasion de	*the opportunity to*
le temps de	*the time to*
le courage de	*the courage to*
l'envie de	*the desire to*
le besoin de	*the need to*
le plaisir de	*the pleasure of*
le moment de	*the time to*

il n'avait pas l'habitude d'être seul
he wasn't used to being alone

je n'ai pas le temps de leur expliquer
I don't have time to explain it to them

avez-vous eu l'occasion de la rencontrer?
did you have the opportunity to meet her?

ce n'est pas le moment de le déranger
now is not the time to disturb him

je n'ai pas eu le courage de te le dire
I didn't have the courage to tell you

● de is used after **il est** in an impersonal sense (see p B29):

il est intéressant de savoir **que ...**
it is interesting to know that ...

For information on the use of **c'est** and **il est**, see p B66.

● de is used after many adjectives, and is frequently used to translate 'of' in English, eg:

certain/sûr de	*certain of/to*
capable de	*capable of*
incapable de	*incapable of*
coupable de	*guilty of*

j'étais sûr de réussir
I was sure of succeeding

il est incapable d'y arriver **seul**
he is incapable of managing on his own

● de is also used with adjectives relating to emotions and states of mind, eg:

content de	*pleased/happy to*
surpris/étonné de	*surprised to*
fier de	*proud to*
heureux de	*happy to*
fâché de	*annoyed to/at*
triste de	*sad to*
gêné de	*embarrassed to*
désolé de	*sorry for/to*

j'ai été très content de recevoir ta lettre
I was very pleased to get your letter

elle sera surprise de **vous** voir
she will be surprised to see you

nous avons été très tristes d'apprendre **la nouvelle**
we were very sad to hear the news

Note, however, that à is used with **prêt à** (*ready to*) and **disposé à** (*willing to*):

es-tu prêt à partir?
are you ready to go?

je suis tout disposé à vous aider
I'm very willing to help you

d)   **faire** + *infinitive*

faire is followed by an infinitive without any linking preposition to express the sense of 'having someone do something' or 'having something done'; two constructions are possible, depending on whether there are one or two objects:

i)   when only one object is used, it is a direct object:

je dois le faire réparer
I must have it fixed

il veut faire repeindre **sa voiture**
he wants to have his car resprayed

cette veste est sale, il faut la faire nettoyer
this jacket's dirty, I'll have to have it cleaned

tu m'as fait attendre!	**je le ferai parler**
you kept me waiting!	*I'll make him talk*

Note the following set expressions:

faire entrer	*to show in*
faire venir	*to send for*

faites entrer ce monsieur	**je vais** faire venir **le docteur**
show this gentleman in	*I'll send for the doctor*

ii)   when both **faire** and the following infinitive have an object, the object of **faire** is indirect:

elle m'a fait prendre une douche
she made me take a shower

je leur ai fait ranger leur chambre
I made them tidy their room

e)   *Infinitive used as subject of another verb:*

trouver un emploi n'est pas facile
finding a job isn't easy

devenir pilote était mon rêve
my dream was to become a pilot

3   The perfect infinitive

a)   *Form*

The perfect or past infinitive is formed with the infinitive of the auxiliary **avoir** or **être** as appropriate (see pp B26-8), followed by the past participle of the verb, eg:

avoir **mangé**	être **allé**	s'être **levé**
to have eaten	*to have gone*	*to have got up*

b)   *Use*

i)   after the preposition **après** (*after*):

après avoir attendu une heure, il est rentré chez lui
after waiting for an hour, he went back home

j'ai compris la remarque après avoir relu **le livre**
I understood the remark after reading the book again

ii)   after certain verbs:

se souvenir de	*to remember*
remercier de	*to thank for*
regretter de	*to regret, to be sorry for*
être désolé de	*to be sorry for*

je vous remercie de m'avoir invité
thank you for inviting me

il regrettait de leur avoir menti
he was sorry he had lied to them

tu te souviens d'avoir fait cela?
do you remember doing this?

I   PARTICIPLES

1   The present participle

a)   *Formation*

Like the imperfect, the present participle is formed by using the stem of the first person plural of the present tense (the **nous** form without the **-ons** ending) to which **ant** (like English 'ing') is added. The following three verbs, however, have irregular present participles:

INFINITIVE	PRESENT PARTICIPLE
avoir *to have*	ayant *having*
être *to be*	étant *being*
savoir *to know*	sachant *knowing*

b)   *Use as an adjective*

Used as an adjective, the present participle agrees in number and in gender with its noun or pronoun:

un travail fatigant	**la semaine** suivante
tiring work	*the following week*

ils sont très exigeants	**des nouvelles** sur-prenantes
they're very demanding	*surprising news*

c)   *Use as a verb*

The present participle is used far less frequently in French than in English, and English present participles in '-ing' are often not translated by a participle in French (see pp B65-6).

i)   Used on its own, the present participle corresponds to the English present participle:

ne voulant plus attendre, ils sont partis sans moi
not wanting to wait any longer, they left without me

pensant bien faire, j'ai insisté
thinking I was doing the right thing, I insisted

ii) en + present participle

When the subject of the present participle is the same as
that of the main verb, this structure is often used to express
simultaneous actions (ie 'while doing something'), manner
(ie 'by doing something') and to translate English phrasal
verbs expressing motion.

● simultaneous actions

In English this structure is translated by:

while/when/on + present participle (eg 'on arriving')
while/when/as + subject + verb (eg 'as he arrived')

il est tombé en descendant l'escalier
he fell as he was going down the stairs

en le voyant, j'ai éclaté de rire
when I saw him, I burst out laughing

elle lisait le journal en attendant l'autobus
she was reading the paper while waiting for the bus

Note that the adverb tout is often used before en to
emphasize the fact that the actions are simultaneous, especially when there is an element of contradiction:

elle écoutait la radio tout en faisant ses devoirs
she was listening to the radio while doing her homework

tout en protestant, je les ai suivis
under protest, I followed them

● manner

When expressing how an action is done, en + participle is
translated by 'by' + participle, eg:

il gagne sa vie en vendant des voitures d'occasion
he earns his living (by) selling second-hand cars

j'ai trouvé du travail en lisant les petites annonces
I found a job by reading the classified ads

● phrasal verbs of motion

en + present participle is often used to translate English
phrasal verbs expressing motion, where the verb expresses
the means of motion and a preposition expresses the direction of movement (eg 'to run out', 'to swim across').

In French, the English preposition is translated by a verb,
while the English verb is translated by en + present participle.

il est sorti du magasin en courant
he ran out of the shop

elle a traversé la route en titubant
she staggered across the road

2 The past participle

a) *Forms*

For the formation of the past participle see p B26.

b) *Use*

The past participle is mostly used as a verb in compound tenses
or in the passive, but it can also be used as an adjective. In
either case, there are strict rules of agreement to be followed.

i) When it is used as an adjective, the past participle always
agrees with the noun or pronoun to which it refers:

un pneu crevé
a burst tyre

ils étaient épuisés
they were exhausted

une pomme pourrie
a rotten apple

des photos prises à la nuit tombée
photos taken at nightfall

Note that in French, the past participle is used as an adjective to describe postures or attitudes of the body, where
English uses the present participle. The most common of
these are:

accoudé	*leaning on one's elbows*
accroupi	*squatting*
agenouillé	*kneeling*
allongé	*lying (down)*
appuyé (contre)	*leaning (against)*
couché	*lying (down)*
étendu	*lying (down)*
penché	*leaning (over)*
(sus)pendu	*hanging*

il est allongé sur le lit
he's lying on the bed

une femme assise devant moi
a woman sitting in front of me

ii) In compound tenses:

● With the auxiliary avoir the past participle agrees in
number and gender with the direct object only when the
direct object comes before the participle, ie in the following
cases:

in a clause introduced by the relative pronoun que:

le jeu vidéo que j'ai acheté
the video game I bought

la valise qu'il a perdue
the suitcase he lost

with a direct object pronoun:

je ne trouve pas la disquette; où l'as-tu mise?
I can't find the floppy disk; where did you put it?

**merci pour tes suggestions, je les ai trouvées très
utiles**
thank you for your suggestions; I found them very useful

in a clause introduced by combien de, quel or lequel:

combien de pays as-tu visités?
how many countries have you visited?

laquelle avez-vous choisie?
which one did you choose?

Note that if the direct object comes after the past participle,
the participle remains in the masculine singular form:

on a rencontré des gens très sympathiques
we met some very nice people

● With the auxiliary être the past participle agrees with the
subject of the verb:

quand est-elle revenue?
when did she come back?

elle était déjà partie
she'd already left

ils sont passés te voir?
did they come to see you?

elles sont restées là
they stayed here

Note that this rule also applies when the verb is in the passive:

elle a été arrêtée
she's been arrested

● With reflexive verbs the past participle normally agrees
with the reflexive pronoun if the pronoun is a direct object;
since the reflexive pronoun refers to the subject, the number
and gender of the past participle are determined by the subject:

Jacques s'est trompé
Jacques made a mistake

Marie s'était levée tard
Marie had got up late

ils se sont disputés?
did they have an argument?

elles se sont vues
they saw each other

Michèle et Marie, vous vous êtes habillées?
Michèle and Marie, have you got dressed yet?

Note, however, that the past participle does not agree when the reflexive pronoun is an indirect object:

elles se sont écrit
they wrote to each other

elle s'est lavé les cheveux
she washed her hair

ils se sont serré la main
they shook hands

J THE PASSIVE

1 Formation

The passive is used when the subject does not perform the action, but is subjected to it, eg:

the house has been sold   *he was made redundant*

Passive tenses are formed with the corresponding tense of the verb être ('to be', as in English), followed by the past participle of the verb, eg:

j'ai été invité
I was invited

The past participle must agree with its subject, eg:

il sera puni
he will be punished

elle a été renvoyée
she has been dismissed

ils seront déçus
they will be disappointed

elles ont été vues
they were seen

2 Avoidance of the passive

The passive is far less common in French than in English. In particular, an indirect object cannot become the subject of a sentence in French; the following sentence, where 'he' is an indirect object, has no equivalent in French:

he was given a book (ie a book was given to him)

In general, French tries to avoid the passive wherever possible. This can be done in several ways.

a) *By using the pronoun* on

on m'a volé mon portefeuille
my wallet has been stolen

on construit une nouvelle piscine
a new swimming pool is being built

en France, on boit beaucoup de vin
a lot of wine is drunk in France

b) *By making the agent the subject of the verb*

If the agent, that is the real subject, is mentioned in English, it can become the subject of the French verb:

la nouvelle va les surprendre
they will be surprised by the news

mon correspondant m'a invité
I've been invited by my penfriend

mon cadeau te plaît?
are you pleased with my present?

) *By using a reflexive verb*

Reflexive forms can be created for a large number of verbs, particularly in the third person:

elle s'appelle Anne
she is called Anne

ton absence va se remarquer
your absence will be noticed

ce plat se mange froid
this dish is eaten cold

cela ne se fait pas ici
that isn't done here

d) *By using* se faire + *infinitive (when the subject is a person)*

il s'est fait renverser par une voiture
he was run over by a car

je me suis fait couper les cheveux
I've had my hair cut

3 Conjugation

For the complete conjugation of a verb in the passive, see être aimé *(to be loved)* p B41.

K MODAL AUXILIARY VERBS

The modal auxiliary verbs are always followed by the infinitive. They express an obligation, a probability, an intention, a possibility or a wish rather than a fact.

The five modal auxiliary verbs are: devoir, pouvoir, savoir, vouloir and falloir.

1 Devoir (for conjugation see p B44) is used to express the following:

a) *obligation*

nous devons arriver à temps
we must arrive in time

nous avions dû partir
we had (had) to go

demain tu devras prendre le bus
tomorrow you'll have to take the bus

j'ai dû avouer que j'avais tort
I had to admit that I was wrong

In the conditional, devoir may be used for advice, ie to express what should be done (conditional present) or should have been done (conditional past):

vous devriez travailler davantage
you ought to/should work harder

tu ne devrais pas marcher sur l'herbe
you shouldn't walk on the grass

tu aurais dû tout avouer
you should have admitted everything

tu n'aurais pas dû manger ces champignons
you shouldn't have eaten those mushrooms

Note that the French infinitive is translated by a past participle in English: manger = eaten.

b) *probability*

il doit être en train de dormir
he must be sleeping (he's probably sleeping)

j'ai dû me tromper de chemin
I must have taken the wrong road

Note that in a past narrative sequence in the distant past, 'must have' is translated by a pluperfect in French:

il dit qu'il avait dû se tromper de chemin
he said he must have taken the wrong road

c) *intention, expectation*

je dois aller chez le dentiste
I am supposed to go to the dentist

le train doit arriver à 19h30
the train is due to arrive at 7.30 p.m.

2 Pouvoir (for conjugation see p B48) is used to express the following:

a) *capacity/ability*

il peut rester plusieurs jours sans dormir
he can go without sleep for several days

cette voiture peut faire du 150
this car can go up to 93 mph

il était si faible qu'il ne pouvait pas sortir de son lit
he was so weak that he couldn't get out of bed

b) *permission*

puis-je entrer?
may I come in?

puis-je vous offrir du thé?
may I offer you some tea?

c) *possibility*

cela peut arriver
it can happen

ça peut n'avoir aucune importance
it might not be at all important

Note that pouvoir + the infinitive is usually replaced by peut-être + the finite tense, eg il s'est peut-être trompé de livres *(he may have taken the wrong books).*

In the conditional, pouvoir is used to express something that could or might be (conditional present) or that could or might have been (conditional past):

tu pourrais t'excuser
you might apologize

j'aurais pu vous prêter mon téléphone portable
I could have lent you my mobile phone

Note that with verbs of perception, eg entendre *(to hear)*, sentir *(to feel, to smell)*, voir *(to see)*, pouvoir is often omitted.

j'entendais le bruit des vagues
I could hear the sound of the waves

3 **Savoir** (for conjugation see p B49) is used to express 'to know how to':

je sais/savais conduire une moto
I can/used to be able to ride a motorbike

elle sait parler plusieurs langues
she can speak several languages

4 **Vouloir** (for conjugation see p B51) is used to express the following:

a) *desire*

je veux partir
I want to go

voulez-vous danser avec moi?
will you dance with me?

b) *wish*

je voudrais être riche
I wish I were rich

je voudrais trouver un travail intéressant
I'd like to find an interesting job

j'aurais voulu te donner un coup de poing
I would have liked to punch you

c) *intention*

il a voulu sauter par la fenêtre
he tried to jump out of the window

Note that veuillez, the imperative of vouloir, is used as a polite form to express a request *('would you please ... ')*:

veuillez ne pas déranger
please do not disturb

5 **Falloir** (for conjugation see p B46) is used to express necessity:

il faut manger pour vivre
you must eat to live

il faudrait y aller tout de suite
we should go right away

il aurait fallu apporter des sandwichs
we should have brought sandwiches

Note that some of the above verbs can also be used without infinitive constructions in which case they have a different meaning, eg devoir = *to owe*, savoir = *to know*.

je te dois 20 euros
I owe you 20 euros

elle le sait par cœur
she knows it by heart

L CONJUGATION TABLES

The following verbs provide the main patterns of conjugation including the conjugation of the most common irregular verbs. They are arranged in alphabetical order:

-er verb (see p B24)	AIMER
-ir verb (see p B24)	FINIR
-re verb (see p B24)	VENDRE
Reflexive verb (see pp B28-9)	SE MÉFIER
Verb with auxiliary être (see p B27)	ARRIVER
Verb in the passive (see p B39)	ÊTRE AIMÉ
Auxiliaries (see pp B26-8)	AVOIR
	ÊTRE
Verb in -eler/-eter (see p B25)	APPELER
Verb in -e + consonant + er (see p B26)	ACHETER
Verb in é + consonant + er (see p B26)	ESPÉRER
Modal auxiliaries (see p B39)	DEVOIR
	POUVOIR
	SAVOIR
	VOULOIR
	FALLOIR
Irregular verbs	ALLER
	CONDUIRE
	CONNAÎTRE
	CROIRE
	DIRE
	DORMIR
	ÉCRIRE
	FAIRE
	METTRE
	OUVRIR
	PRENDRE
	RECEVOIR
	TENIR
	VENIR
	VIVRE
	VOIR

ACHETER   *to buy*

PRESENT	IMPERFECT	FUTURE	SUBJUNCTIVE	IMPERATIVE
j'achète	j'achetais	j'achèterai	**PRESENT**	achète
tu achètes	tu achetais	tu achèteras	j'achète	achetons
il achète	il achetait	il achètera	tu achètes	achetez
nous achetons	nous achetions	nous achèterons	il achète	
vous achetez	vous achetiez	vous achèterez	nous achetions	
ils achètent	ils achetaient	ils achèteront	vous achetiez	
			ils achètent	*INFINITIVE*
PAST HISTORIC	**PERFECT**	**PLUPERFECT**	**IMPERFECT**	**PRESENT**
j'achetai	j'ai acheté	j'avais acheté	j'achetasse	acheter
tu achetas	tu as acheté	tu avais acheté	tu achetasses	
il acheta	il a acheté	il avait acheté	il achetât	**PAST**
nous achetâmes	nous avons acheté	nous avions acheté	nous achetassions	avoir acheté
vous achetâtes	vous avez acheté	vous aviez acheté	vous achetassiez	
ils achetèrent	ils ont acheté	ils avaient acheté	ils achetassent	
	CONDITIONAL		**PERFECT**	*PARTICIPLE*
PAST ANTERIOR	**PRESENT**	**PAST**	j'aie acheté	**PRESENT**
j'eus acheté etc	j'achèterais	j'aurais acheté	tu aies acheté	achetant
	tu achèterais	tu aurais acheté	il ait acheté	
	il achèterait	il aurait acheté	nous ayons acheté	**PAST**
	nous achèterions	nous aurions acheté	vous ayez acheté	acheté
FUTURE PERFECT	vous achèteriez	vous auriez acheté	ils aient acheté	
j'aurai acheté etc	ils achèteraient	ils auraient acheté		

AIMER   *to like/to love*

PRESENT	IMPERFECT	FUTURE	SUBJUNCTIVE	IMPERATIVE
j'aime	j'aimais	j'aimerai	**PRESENT**	aime
tu aimes	tu aimais	tu aimeras	j'aime	aimons
il aime	il aimait	il aimera	tu aimes	aimez
nous aimons	nous aimions	nous aimerons	il aime	
vous aimez	vous aimiez	vous aimerez	nous aimions	
ils aiment	ils aimaient	ils aimeront	vous aimiez	
			ils aiment	*INFINITIVE*
PAST HISTORIC	**PERFECT**	**PLUPERFECT**	**IMPERFECT**	**PRESENT**
j'aimai	j'ai aimé	j'avais aimé	j'aimasse	aimer
tu aimas	tu as aimé	tu avais aimé	tu aimasses	
il aima	il a aimé	il avait aimé	il aimât	**PAST**
nous aimâmes	nous avons aimé	nous avions aimé	nous aimassions	avoir aimé
vous aimâtes	vous avez aimé	vous aviez aimé	vous aimassiez	
ils aimèrent	ils ont aimé	ils avaient aimé	ils aimassent	
	CONDITIONAL		**PERFECT**	*PARTICIPLE*
PAST ANTERIOR	**PRESENT**	**PAST**	j'aie aimé	**PRESENT**
j'eus aimé etc	j'aimerais	j'aurais aimé	tu aies aimé	aimant
	tu aimerais	tu aurais aimé	il ait aimé	
	il aimerait	il aurait aimé	nous ayons aimé	**PAST**
	nous aimerions	nous aurions aimé	vous ayez aimé	aimé
FUTURE PERFECT	vous aimeriez	vous auriez aimé	ils aient aimé	
j'aurai aimé etc	ils aimeraient	ils auraient aimé		

ÊTRE AIMÉ   *to be loved*

PRESENT	IMPERFECT	FUTURE	SUBJUNCTIVE	IMPERATIVE
je suis aimé(e)	j'étais aimé(e)	je serai aimé(e)	**PRESENT**	sois aimé(e)
tu es aimé(e)	tu étais aimé(e)	tu seras aimé(e)	je sois aimé(e)	soyons aimé(e)s
il (elle) est aimé(e)	il (elle) était aimé(e)	il (elle) sera aimé(e)	tu sois aimé(e)	soyez aimé(e)(s)
nous sommes aimé(e)s	nous étions aimé(e)s	nous serons aimé(e)s	il (elle) soit aimé(e)	
vous êtes aimé(e)(s)	vous étiez aimé(e)(s)	vous serez aimé(e)(s)	nous soyons aimé(e)s	
ils (elles) sont aimé(e)s	ils (elles) étaient aimé(e)s	ils seront aimé(e)s	vous soyez aimé(e)(s)	
			ils (elles) soient aimé(e)s	*INFINITIVE*
PAST HISTORIC	**PERFECT**	**PLUPERFECT**	**IMPERFECT**	**PRESENT**
je fus aimé(e)	j'ai été aimé(e)	j'avais été aimé(e)	je fusse aimé(e)	être aimé(e)(s)
tu fus aimé(e)	tu as été aimé(e)	tu avais été aimé(e)	tu fusses aimé(e)	
il (elle) fut aimé(e)	il (elle) a été aimé(e)	il (elle) avait été aimé(e)	il (elle) fût aimé(e)	**PAST**
nous fûmes aimé(e)s	nous avons été aimé(e)s	nous avions été aimé(e)s	nous fussions aimé(e)s	avoir été aimé(e)(s)
vous fûtes aimé(e)(s)	vous avez été aimé(e)(s)	vous aviez été aimé(e)(s)	vous fussiez	
ils (elles) furent aimé(e)s	ils (elles) ont été aimé(e)s	ils (elles) avaient été aimé(e)s	ils (elles) fussent aimé(e)s	
	CONDITIONAL		**PERFECT**	*PARTICIPLE*
PAST ANTERIOR	**PRESENT**	**PAST**	j'aie été aimé(e)	**PRESENT**
j'eus été aimé(e) etc	je serais aimé(e)	j'aurais été aimé(e)	tu aies été aimé(e)	étant aimé(e)(s)
	tu serais aimé(e)	tu aurais été aimé(e)	il (elle) ait été aimé(e)	
	il (elle) serait aimé(e)	il (elle) aurait été aimé(e)	nous ayons été aimé(e)s	**PAST**
	nous serions aimé(e)s	nous aurions été aimé(e)s	vous ayez été aimé(e)(s)	été aimé(e)(s)
FUTURE PERFECT	vous seriez aimé(e)(s)	vous auriez été aimé(e)(s)	ils (elles) aient été aimé(e)s	
j'aurai été aimé(e) etc	ils (elles) seraient aimé(e)s	ils (elles) auraient été aimé(e)s		

ALLER · *to go*

PRESENT	IMPERFECT	FUTURE		SUBJUNCTIVE	IMPERATIVE
je vais	j'allais	j'irai		**PRESENT**	va
tu vas	tu allais	tu iras		j'aille	allons
il va	il allait	il ira		tu ailles	allez
nous allons	nous allions	nous irons		il aille	
vous allez	vous alliez	vous irez		nous allions	
ils vont	ils allaient	ils iront		vous alliez	
				ils aillent	

PAST HISTORIC	PERFECT	PLUPERFECT	IMPERFECT	INFINITIVE
j'allai	je suis allé(e)	j'étais allé(e)	j'allasse	**PRESENT**
tu allas	tu es allé(e)	tu étais allé(e)	tu allasses	aller
il alla	il (elle) est allé(e)	il (elle) était allé(e)	il allât	
nous allâmes	nous sommes allé(e)s	nous étions allé(e)s	nous allassions	**PAST**
vous allâtes	vous êtes allé(e)(s)	vous étiez allé(e)(s)	vous allassiez	être allé(e)(s)
ils allèrent	ils (elles) sont allé(e)s	ils (elles) étaient allé(e)s	ils allassent	

CONDITIONAL

			PERFECT	PARTICIPLE
PAST ANTERIOR	**PRESENT**	**PAST**	je sois allé	**PRESENT**
je fus allé(e) etc	j'irais	je serais allé(e)	tu sois allé(e)	allant
	tu irais	tu serais allé(e)	il (elle) soit allé(e)	
	il irait	il (elle) serait allé(e)	nous soyons allé(e)s	**PAST**
	nous irions	nous serions allé(e)s	vous soyez allé(e)(s)	allé
FUTURE PERFECT	vous iriez	vous seriez allé(e)(s)	ils (elles) soient allé(e)s	
je serai allé(e) etc	ils iraient	ils (elles) seraient allé(e)s		

APPELER · *to call*

PRESENT	IMPERFECT	FUTURE		SUBJUNCTIVE	IMPERATIVE
j'appelle	j'appelais	j'appellerai		**PRESENT**	appelle
tu appelles	tu appelais	tu appelleras		j'appelle	appelons
il appelle	il appelait	il appellera		tu appelles	appelez
nous appelons	nous appelions	nous appellerons		il appelle	
vous appelez	vous appeliez	vous appellerez		nous appelions	
ils appellent	ils appelaient	ils appelleront		vous appeliez	
				ils appellent	

PAST HISTORIC	PERFECT	PLUPERFECT	IMPERFECT	INFINITIVE
j'appelai	j'ai appelé	j'avais appelé	j'appelasse	**PRESENT**
tu appelas	tu as appelé	tu avais appelé	tu appelasses	appeler
il appela	il a appelé	il avait appelé	il appelât	
nous appelâmes	nous avons appelé	nous avions appelé	nous appelassions	**PAST**
vous appelâtes	vous avez appelé	vous aviez appelé	vous appelassiez	avoir appelé
ils appelèrent	ils ont appelé	ils avaient appelé	ils appelassent	

CONDITIONAL

			PERFECT	PARTICIPLE
PAST ANTERIOR	**PRESENT**	**PAST**	j'aie appelé	**PRESENT**
j'eus appelé etc	j'appellerais	j'aurais appelé	tu aies appelé	appelant
	tu appellerais	tu aurais appelé	il ait appelé	
	il appellerait	il aurait appelé	nous ayons appelé	**PAST**
	nous appellerions	nous aurions appelé	vous ayez appelé	appelé
FUTURE PERFECT	vous appelleriez	vous auriez appelé	ils aient appelé	
j'aurai appelé etc	ils appelleraient	ils auraient appelé		

ARRIVER · *to arrive/to happen*

PRESENT	IMPERFECT	FUTURE		SUBJUNCTIVE	IMPERATIVE
j'arrive	j'arrivais	j'arriverai		**PRESENT**	arrive
tu arrives	tu arrivais	tu arriveras		j'arrive	arrivons
il arrive	il arrivait	il arrivera		tu arrives	arrivez
nous arrivons	nous arrivions	nous arriverons		il arrive	
vous arrivez	vous arriviez	vous arriverez		nous arrivions	
ils arrivent	ils arrivaient	ils arriveront		vous arriviez	
				ils arrivent	

PAST HISTORIC	PERFECT	PLUPERFECT	IMPERFECT	INFINITIVE
j'arrivai	je suis arrivé(e)	j'étais arrivé(e)	j'arrivasse	**PRESENT**
tu arrivas	tu es arrivé(e)	tu étais arrivé(e)	tu arrivasses	arriver
il arriva	il (elle) est arrivé(e)	il (elle) était arrivé(e)	il arrivât	
nous arrivâmes	nous sommes arrivé(e)s	nous étions arrivé(e)s	nous arrivassions	**PAST**
vous arrivâtes	vous êtes arrivé(e)(s)	vous étiez arrivé(e)(s)	vous arrivassiez	être arrivé(e)(s)
ils arrivèrent	ils (elles) sont arrivé(e)s	ils (elles) étaient arrivé(e)s	ils arrivassent	

CONDITIONAL

			PERFECT	PARTICIPLE
PAST ANTERIOR	**PRESENT**	**PAST**	je sois arrivé(e)	**PRESENT**
je fus arrivé(e) etc	j'arriverais	je serais arrivé(e)	tu sois arrivé(e)	arrivant
	tu arriverais	tu serais arrivé(e)	il (elle) soit arrivé(e)	
	il arriverait	il (elle) serait arrivé(e)	nous soyons arrivé(e)s	**PAST**
	nous arriverions	nous serions arrivé(e)s	vous soyez arrivé(e)(s)	arrivé
FUTURE PERFECT	vous arriveriez	vous seriez arrivé(e)(s)	ils (elles) soient arrivé(e)s	
je serai arrivé(e) etc	ils arriveraient	ils (elles) seraient arrivé(e)s		

AVOIR   *to have*

PRESENT	IMPERFECT	FUTURE	SUBJUNCTIVE	IMPERATIVE
j'ai	j'avais	j'aurai	**PRESENT**	aie
tu as	tu avais	tu auras	j'aie	ayons
il a	il avait	il aura	tu aies	ayez
nous avons	nous avions	nous aurons	il ait	
vous avez	vous aviez	vous aurez	nous ayons	
ils ont	ils avaient	ils auront	vous ayez	
			ils aient	

PAST HISTORIC	PERFECT	PLUPERFECT	IMPERFECT	INFINITIVE
j'eus	j'ai eu	j'avais eu	j'eusse	**PRESENT**
tu eus	tu as eu	tu avais eu	tu eusses	avoir
il eut	il a eu	il avait eu	il eût	
nous eûmes	nous avons eu	nous avions eu	nous eussions	**PAST**
vous eûtes	vous avez eu	vous aviez eu	vous eussiez	avoir eu
ils eurent	ils ont eu	ils avaient eu	ils eussent	

CONDITIONAL

PAST ANTERIOR	PRESENT	PAST	PERFECT	PARTICIPLE
j'eus eu etc	j'aurais	j'aurais eu	j'aie eu	**PRESENT**
	tu aurais	tu aurais eu	tu aies eu	ayant
	il aurait	il aurait eu	il ait eu	
	nous aurions	nous aurions eu	nous ayons eu	**PAST**
FUTURE PERFECT	vous auriez	vous auriez eu	vous ayez eu	eu
j'aurai eu etc	ils auraient	ils auraient eu	ils aient eu	

CONDUIRE   *to lead/to drive*

PRESENT	IMPERFECT	FUTURE	SUBJUNCTIVE	IMPERATIVE
je conduis	je conduisais	je conduirai	**PRESENT**	conduis
tu conduis	tu conduisais	tu conduiras	je conduise	conduisons
il conduit	il conduisait	il conduira	tu conduises	conduisez
nous conduisons	nous conduisions	nous conduirons	il conduise	
vous conduisez	vous conduisiez	vous conduirez	nous conduisions	
ils conduisent	ils conduisaient	ils conduiront	vous conduisiez	
			ils conduisent	

PAST HISTORIC	PERFECT	PLUPERFECT	IMPERFECT	INFINITIVE
je conduisis	j'ai conduit	j'avais conduit	je conduisisse	**PRESENT**
tu conduisis	tu as conduit	tu avais conduit	tu conduisisses	conduire
il conduisit	il a conduit	il avait conduit	il conduisît	
nous conduisîmes	nous avons conduit	nous avions conduit	nous conduisissions	**PAST**
vous conduisîtes	vous avez conduit	vous aviez conduit	vous conduisissiez	avoir conduit
ils conduisirent	ils ont conduit	ils avaient conduit	ils conduisissent	

CONDITIONAL

PAST ANTERIOR	PRESENT	PAST	PERFECT	PARTICIPLE
j'eus conduit etc	je conduirais	j'aurais conduit	j'aie conduit	**PRESENT**
	tu conduirais	tu aurais conduit	tu aies conduit	conduisant
	il conduirait	il aurait conduit	il ait conduit	
	nous conduirions	nous aurions conduit	nous ayons conduit	**PAST**
FUTURE PERFECT	vous conduiriez	vous auriez conduit	vous ayez conduit	conduit
j'aurai conduit etc	ils conduiraient	ils auraient conduit	ils aient conduit	

CONNAÎTRE   *to know*

PRESENT	IMPERFECT	FUTURE	SUBJUNCTIVE	IMPERATIVE
je connais	je connaissais	je connaîtrai	**PRESENT**	connais
tu connais	tu connaissais	tu connaîtras	je connaisse	connaissons
il connaît	il connaissait	il connaîtra	tu connaisses	connaissez
nous connaissons	nous connaissions	nous connaîtrons	il connaisse	
vous connaissez	vous connaissiez	vous connaîtrez	nous connaissions	
ils connaissent	ils connaissaient	ils connaîtront	vous connaissiez	
			ils connaissent	

PAST HISTORIC	PERFECT	PLUPERFECT	IMPERFECT	INFINITIVE
je connus	j'ai connu	j'avais connu	je connusse	**PRESENT**
tu connus	tu as connu	tu avais connu	tu connusses	connaître
il connut	il a connu	il avait connu	il connût	
nous connûmes	nous avons connu	nous avions connu	nous connussions	**PAST**
vous connûtes	vous avez connu	vous aviez connu	vous connussiez	avoir connu
ils connurent	ils ont connu	ils avaient connu	ils connussent	

CONDITIONAL

PAST ANTERIOR	PRESENT	PAST	PERFECT	PARTICIPLE
j'eus connu etc	je connaîtrais	j'aurais connu	j'aie connu	**PRESENT**
	tu connaîtrais	tu aurais connu	tu aies connu	connaissant
	il connaîtrait	il aurait connu	il ait connu	
	nous connaîtrions	nous aurions connu	nous ayons connu	**PAST**
FUTURE PERFECT	vous connaîtriez	vous auriez connu	vous ayez connu	connu
j'aurai connu etc	ils connaîtraient	ils auraient connu	ils aient connu	

CROIRE — *to believe*

PRESENT	IMPERFECT	FUTURE	SUBJUNCTIVE	IMPERATIVE
			PRESENT	crois
je crois	je croyais	je croirai	je croie	croyons
tu crois	tu croyais	tu croiras	tu croies	croyez
il croit	il croyait	il croira	il croie	
nous croyons	nous croyions	nous croirons	nous croyions	
vous croyez	vous croyiez	vous croirez	vous croyiez	
ils croient	ils croyaient	ils croiront	ils croient	

PAST HISTORIC	PERFECT	PLUPERFECT	IMPERFECT	INFINITIVE
				PRESENT
je crus	j'ai cru	j'avais cru	je crusse	croire
tu crus	tu as cru	tu avais cru	tu crusses	
il crut	il a cru	il avait cru	il crût	**PAST**
nous crûmes	nous avons cru	nous avions cru	nous crussions	avoir cru
vous crûtes	vous avez cru	vous aviez cru	vous crussiez	
ils crurent	ils ont cru	ils avaient cru	ils crussent	

	CONDITIONAL		PERFECT	PARTICIPLE
				PRESENT
	PRESENT	**PAST**	j'aie cru	
PAST ANTERIOR	je croirais	j'aurais cru	tu aies cru	croyant
j'eus cru etc	tu croirais	tu aurais cru	il ait cru	
	il croirait	il aurait cru	nous ayons cru	**PAST**
	nous croirions	nous aurions cru	vous ayez cru	cru
	vous croiriez	vous auriez cru	ils aient cru	
FUTURE PERFECT	vous croiriez	vous auriez cru		
j'aurai cru etc	ils croiraient	ils auraient cru		

DEVOIR — *to owe/to have to*

PRESENT	IMPERFECT	FUTURE	SUBJUNCTIVE	IMPERATIVE
			PRESENT	dois
je dois	je devais	je devrai	je doive	devons
tu dois	tu devais	tu devras	tu doives	devez
il doit	il devait	il devra	il doive	
nous devons	nous devions	nous devrons	nous devions	
vous devez	vous deviez	vous devrez	vous deviez	
ils doivent	ils devaient	ils devront	ils doivent	

PAST HISTORIC	PERFECT	PLUPERFECT	IMPERFECT	INFINITIVE
				PRESENT
je dus	j'ai dû	j'avais dû	je dusse	devoir
tu dus	tu as dû	tu avais dû	tu dusses	
il dut	il a dû	il avait dû	il dût	**PAST**
nous dûmes	nous avons dû	nous avions dû	nous dussions	avoir dû
vous dûtes	vous avez dû	vous aviez dû	vous dussiez	
ils durent	ils ont dû	ils avaient dû	ils dussent	

	CONDITIONAL		PERFECT	PARTICIPLE
			j'aie dû	**PRESENT**
	PRESENT	**PAST**	tu aies dû	devant
PAST ANTERIOR	je devrais	j'aurais dû	il ait dû	
j'eus dû etc	tu devrais	tu aurais dû	nous ayons dû	**PAST**
	il devrait	il aurait dû	vous ayez dû	dû (due, dus)
	nous devrions	nous aurions dû	ils aient dû	
FUTURE PERFECT	vous devriez	vous auriez dû		
j'aurai dû	ils devraient	ils auraient dû		

DIRE — *to say*

PRESENT	IMPERFECT	FUTURE	SUBJUNCTIVE	IMPERATIVE
			PRESENT	dis
je dis	je disais	je dirai	je dise	disons
tu dis	tu disais	tu diras	tu dises	dites
il dit	il disait	il dira tu dises	il dise	
nous disons	nous disions	nous dirons	nous disions	
vous dites	vous disiez	vous direz	vous disiez	
ils disent	ils disaient	ils diront	ils disent	

PAST HISTORIC	PERFECT	PLUPERFECT	IMPERFECT	INFINITIVE
				PRESENT
je dis	j'ai dit	j'avais dit	je disse	dire
tu dis	tu as dit	tu avais dit	tu disses	
il dit	il a dit	il avait dit	il dît	**PAST**
nous dîmes	nous avons dit	nous avions dit	nous dissions	avoir dit
vous dîtes	vous avez dit	vous aviez dit	vous dissiez	
ils dirent	ils ont dit	ils avaient dit	ils dissent	

	CONDITIONAL		PERFECT	PARTICIPLE
			j'aie dit	**PRESENT**
	PRESENT	**PAST**	tu aies dit	disant
PAST ANTERIOR	je dirais	j'aurais dit	il ait dit	
j'eus dit etc	tu dirais	tu aurais dit	nous ayons dit	**PAST**
	il dirait	il aurait dit	vous ayez dit	dit
	nous dirions	nous aurions dit	ils aient dit	
FUTURE PERFECT	vous diriez	vous auriez dit		
j'aurai dit etc	ils diraient	ils auraient dit		

DORMIR — *to sleep*

PRESENT	IMPERFECT	FUTURE	SUBJUNCTIVE	IMPERATIVE
je dors	je dormais	je dormirai	**PRESENT**	dors
tu dors	tu dormais	tu dormiras	je dorme	dormons
il dort	il dormait	il dormira	tu dormes	dormez
nous dormons	nous dormions	nous dormirons	il dorme	
vous dormez	vous dormiez	vous dormirez	nous dormions	
ils dorment	ils dormaient	ils dormiront	vous dormiez	
			ils dorment	

PAST HISTORIC	PERFECT	PLUPERFECT	IMPERFECT	INFINITIVE
je dormis	j'ai dormi	j'avais dormi	je dormisse	**PRESENT**
tu dormis	tu as dormi	tu avais dormi	tu dormisses	dormir
il dormit	il a dormi	il avait dormi	il dormît	
nous dormîmes	nous avons dormi	nous avions dormi	nous dormissions	**PAST**
vous dormîtes	vous avez dormi	vous aviez dormi	vous dormissiez	avoir dormi
ils dormirent	ils ont dormi	ils avaient dormi	ils dormissent	
	CONDITIONAL		**PERFECT**	*PARTICIPLE*

PAST ANTERIOR	PRESENT	PAST	j'aie dormi	**PRESENT**
j'eus dormi etc	je dormirais	j'aurais dormi	tu aies dormi	dormant
	tu dormirais	tu aurais dormi	il ait dormi	
	il dormirait	il aurait dormi	nous ayons dormi	**PAST**
	nous dormirions	nous aurions dormi	vous ayez dormi	dormi
FUTURE PERFECT	vous dormiriez	vous auriez dormi	ils aient dormi	
j'aurai dormi etc	ils dormiraient	ils auraient dormi		

ÉCRIRE — *to write*

PRESENT	IMPERFECT	FUTURE	SUBJUNCTIVE	IMPERATIVE
j'écris	j'écrivais	j'écrirai	**PRESENT**	écris
tu écris	tu écrivais	tu écriras	j'écrive	écrivons
il écrit	il écrivait	il écrira	tu écrives	écrivez
nous écrivons	nous écrivions	nous écrirons	il écrive	
vous écrivez	vous écriviez	vous écrirez	nous écrivions	
ils écrivent	ils écrivaient	ils écriront	vous écriviez	
			ils écrivent	

PAST HISTORIC	PERFECT	PLUPERFECT	IMPERFECT	INFINITIVE
j'écrivis	j'ai écrit	j'avais écrit	j'écrivisse	**PRESENT**
tu écrivis	tu as écrit	tu avais écrit	tu écrivisses	écrire
il écrivit	il a écrit	il avait écrit	il écrivît	
nous écrivîmes	nous avons écrit	nous avions écrit	nous écrivissions	**PAST**
vous écrivîtes	vous avez écrit	vous aviez écrit	vous écrivissiez	avoir écrit
ils écrivirent	ils ont écrit	ils avaient écrit	ils écrivissent	
	CONDITIONAL		**PERFECT**	*PARTICIPLE*

PAST ANTERIOR	PRESENT	PAST	j'aie écrit	**PRESENT**
j'eus écrit etc	j'écrirais	j'aurais écrit	tu aies écrit	écrivant
	tu écrirais	tu aurais écrit	il ait écrit	
	il écrirait	il aurait écrit	nous ayons écrit	**PAST**
	nous écririons	nous aurions écrit	vous ayez écrit	écrit
FUTURE PERFECT	vous écririez	vous auriez écrit	ils aient écrit	
j'aurai écrit etc	ils écriraient	ils auraient écrit		

ESPÉRER — *to hope*

PRESENT	IMPERFECT	FUTURE	SUBJUNCTIVE	IMPERATIVE
j'espère	j'espérais	j'espérerai	**PRESENT**	espère
tu espères	tu espérais	tu espéreras	j'espère	espérons
il espère	il espérait	il espérera	tu espères	espérez
nous espérons	nous espérions	nous espérerons	il espère	
vous espérez	vous espériez	vous espérerez	nous espérions	
ils espèrent	ils espéraient	ils espéreront	vous espériez	
			ils espèrent	

PAST HISTORIC	PERFECT	PLUPERFECT	IMPERFECT	INFINITIVE
j'espérai	j'ai espéré	j'avais espéré	j'espérasse	**PRESENT**
tu espéras	tu as espéré	tu avais espéré	tu espérasses	espérer
il espéra	il a espéré	il avait espéré	il espérât	
nous espérâmes	nous avons espéré	nous avions espéré	nous espérassions	**PAST**
vous espérâtes	vous avez espéré	vous aviez espéré	vous espérassiez	avoir espéré
ils espérèrent	ils ont espéré	ils avaient espéré	ils espérassent	
	CONDITIONAL		**PERFECT**	*PARTICIPLE*

PAST ANTERIOR	PRESENT	PAST	j'aie espéré	**PRESENT**
j'eus espéré etc	j'espérerais	j'aurais espéré	tu aies espéré	espérant
	tu espérerais	tu aurais espéré	il ait espéré	
	il espérerait	il aurait espéré	nous ayons espéré	**PAST**
	nous espérerions	nous aurions espéré	vous ayez espéré	espéré
FUTURE PERFECT	vous espéreriez	vous auriez espéré	ils aient espéré	
j'aurai espéré etc	ils espéreraient	ils auraient espéré		

ÊTRE   *to be*

PRESENT	IMPERFECT	FUTURE	SUBJUNCTIVE	IMPERATIVE
je suis	j'étais	je serai	**PRESENT**	sois
tu es	tu étais	tu seras	je sois	soyons
il est	il était	il sera	tu sois	soyez
nous sommes	nous étions	nous serons	il soit	
vous êtes	vous étiez	vous serez	nous soyons	
ils sont	ils étaient	ils seront	vous soyez	
			ils soient	

PAST HISTORIC	PERFECT	PLUPERFECT	IMPERFECT	INFINITIVE
je fus	j'ai été	j'avais été	je fusse	**PRESENT**
tu fus	tu as été	tu avais été	tu fusses	être
il fut	il a été	il avait été	il fût	
nous fûmes	nous avons été	nous avions été	nous fussions	**PAST**
vous fûtes	vous avez été	vous aviez été	vous fussiez	avoir été
ils furent	ils ont été	ils avaient été	ils fussent	
	CONDITIONAL		PERFECT	*PARTICIPLE*
PAST ANTERIOR	PRESENT	PAST	j'aie été	**PRESENT**
j'eus été etc	je serais	j'aurais été	tu aies été	étant
	tu serais	tu aurais été	il ait été	
	il serait	il aurait été	nous ayons été	**PAST**
	nous serions	nous aurions été	vous ayez été	été
FUTURE PERFECT	vous seriez	vous auriez été	ils aient été	
j'aurai été etc	ils seraient	ils auraient été		

FAIRE   *to do/to make*

PRESENT	IMPERFECT	FUTURE	SUBJUNCTIVE	IMPERATIVE
je fais	je faisais	je ferai	**PRESENT**	fais
tu fais	tu faisais	tu feras	je fasse	faisons
il fait	il faisait	il fera	tu fasses	faites
nous faisons	nous faisions	nous ferons	il fasse	
vous faites	vous faisiez	vous ferez	nous fassions	
ils font	ils faisaient	ils feront	vous fassiez	
			ils fassent	

PAST HISTORIC	PERFECT	PLUPERFECT	IMPERFECT	INFINITIVE
je fis	j'ai fait	j'avais fait	je fisse	**PRESENT**
tu fis	tu as fait	tu avais fait	tu fisses	faire
il fit	il a fait	il avait fait	il fît	
nous fîmes	nous avons fait	nous avions fait	nous fissions	**PAST**
vous fîtes	vous avez fait	vous aviez fait	vous fissiez	avoir fait
ils firent	ils ont fait	ils avaient fait	ils fissent	
	CONDITIONAL		PERFECT	*PARTICIPLE*
PAST ANTERIOR	PRESENT	PAST	j'aie fait	**PRESENT**
j'eus fait etc	je ferais	j'aurais fait	tu aies fait	faisant
	tu ferais	tu aurais fait	il ait fait	
	il ferait	il aurait fait	nous ayons fait	**PAST**
	nous ferions	nous aurions fait	vous ayez fait	fait
FUTURE PERFECT	vous feriez	vous auriez fait	ils aient fait	
j'aurai fait etc	ils feraient	ils auraient fait		

FALLOIR   *to be necessary*

PRESENT	IMPERFECT	FUTURE	SUBJUNCTIVE	IMPERATIVE
il faut	il fallait	il faudra	**PRESENT**	
			il faille	

PAST HISTORIC	PERFECT	PLUPERFECT	IMPERFECT	INFINITIVE
il fallut	il a fallu	il avait fallu	il fallût	**PRESENT**
				falloir
				PAST
				avoir fallu
	CONDITIONAL		PERFECT	*PARTICIPLE*
PAST ANTERIOR	PRESENT	PAST	il ait fallu	**PRESENT**
il eut fallu	il faudrait	il aurait fallu		
FUTURE PERFECT				**PAST**
il aura fallu				fallu

FINIR   *to finish*

PRESENT	IMPERFECT	FUTURE	SUBJUNCTIVE	IMPERATIVE
je finis	je finissais	je finirai	**PRESENT**	finis
tu finis	tu finissais	tu finiras	je finisse	finissons
il finit	il finissait	il finira	tu finisses	finissez
nous finissons	nous finissions	nous finirons	il finisse	
vous finissez	vous finissiez	vous finirez	nous finissions	
ils finissent	ils finissaient	ils finiront	vous finissiez	
			ils finissent	

PAST HISTORIC	PERFECT	PLUPERFECT	IMPERFECT	INFINITIVE
je finis	j'ai fini	j'avais fini	je finisse	**PRESENT**
tu finis	tu as fini	tu avais fini	tu finisses	finir
il finit	il a fini	il avait fini	il finît	
nous finîmes	nous avons fini	nous avions fini	nous finissions	**PAST**
vous finîtes	vous avez fini	vous aviez fini	vous finissiez	avoir fini
ils finirent	ils ont fini	ils avaient fini	ils finissent	
	CONDITIONAL		PERFECT	PARTICIPLE
PAST ANTERIOR	PRESENT	PAST	j'aie fini	**PRESENT**
j'eus fini etc	je finirais	j'aurais fini	tu aies fini	finissant
	tu finirais	tu aurais fini	il ait fini	
	il finirait	il aurait fini	nous ayons fini	**PAST**
	nous finirions	nous aurions fini	vous ayez fini	fini
FUTURE PERFECT	vous finiriez	vous auriez fini	ils aient fini	
j'aurai fini etc	ils finiraient	ils auraient fini		

SE MÉFIER   *to be suspicious*

PRESENT	IMPERFECT	FUTURE	SUBJUNCTIVE	IMPERATIVE
je me méfie	je me méfiais	je me méfierai	**PRESENT**	méfie-toi
tu te méfies	tu te méfiais	tu te méfieras	je me méfie	méfions-nous
il se méfie	il se méfiait	il se méfiera	tu te méfies	méfiez-vous
nous nous méfions	nous nous méfiions	nous nous méfierons	il se méfie	
vous vous méfiez	vous vous méfiiez	vous vous méfierez	nous nous méfiions	
ils se méfient	ils se méfiaient	ils se méfieront	vous vous méfiiez	
			ils se méfient	

PAST HISTORIC	PERFECT	PLUPERFECT	IMPERFECT	INFINITIVE
je me méfiai	je me suis méfié(e)	je m'étais méfié(e)	je me méfiasse	**PRESENT**
tu te méfias	tu t'es méfié(e)	tu t'étais méfié(e)	tu te méfiasses	se méfier
il se méfia	il (elle) s'est méfié(e)	il (elle) s'était méfié(e)	il se méfiât	
nous nous méfiâmes	nous ns. sommes méfié(e)s	nous nous étions méfié(e)s	nous nous méfiassions	**PAST**
vous vous méfiâtes	vous vs. êtes méfié(e)(s)	vous vous étiez méfié(e)(s)	vous vous méfiassiez	s'être méfié(e)(s)
ils se méfièrent	ils (elles) se sont méfié(e)s	ils (elles) s'étaient méfié(e)s	ils se méfiassent	
	CONDITIONAL		PERFECT	PARTICIPLE
PAST ANTERIOR	PRESENT	PAST	je me sois méfié(e)	**PRESENT**
je me fus méfié(e) etc	je me méfierais	je me serais méfié(e)	tu te sois méfié(e)	se méfiant
	tu te méfierais	tu te serais méfié(e)	il (elle) se soit méfié(e)	
	il se méfierait	il (elle) se serait méfié(e)	nous ns. soyons méfié(e)s	**PAST**
	nous nous méfierions	nous nous serions méfié(e)s	vous vs. soyez méfié(e)(s)	méfié
FUTURE PERFECT	vous vous méfieriez	vous vous seriez méfié(e)(s)	ils (elles) se soient méfié(e)s	
je me serai méfié(e) etc	ils se méfieraient	ils (elles) se seraient méfié(e)s		

METTRE   *to put*

PRESENT	IMPERFECT	FUTURE	SUBJUNCTIVE	IMPERATIVE
je mets	je mettais	je mettrai	**PRESENT**	mets
tu mets	tu mettais	tu mettras	je mette	mettons
il met	il mettait	il mettra	tu mettes	mettez
nous mettons	nous mettions	nous mettrons	il mette	
vous mettez	vous mettiez	vous mettrez	nous mettions	
ils mettent	ils mettaient	ils mettront	vous mettiez	
			ils mettent	

PAST HISTORIC	PERFECT	PLUPERFECT	IMPERFECT	INFINITIVE
je mis	j'ai mis	j'avais mis	je misse	**PRESENT**
tu mis	tu as mis	tu avais mis	tu misses	mettre
il mit	il a mis	il avait mis	il mît	
nous mîmes	nous avons mis	nous avions mis	nous missions	**PAST**
vous mîtes	vous avez mis	vous aviez mis	vous missiez	avoir mis
ils mirent	ils ont mis	ils avaient mis	ils missent	
	CONDITIONAL		PERFECT	PARTICIPLE
PAST ANTERIOR	PRESENT	PAST	j'aie mis	**PRESENT**
j'eus mis etc	je mettrais	j'aurais mis	tu aies mis	mettant
	tu mettrais	tu aurais mis	il ait mis	
	il mettrait	il aurait mis	nous ayons mis	**PAST**
	nous mettrions	nous aurions mis	vous ayez mis	mis
FUTURE PERFECT	vous mettriez	vous auriez mis	ils aient mis	
j'aurai mis etc	ils mettraient	ils auraient mis		

OUVRIR — *to open*

PRESENT	IMPERFECT	FUTURE	SUBJUNCTIVE	IMPERATIVE
j'ouvre	j'ouvrais	j'ouvrirai	**PRESENT**	ouvre
tu ouvres	tu ouvrais	tu ouvriras	j'ouvre	ouvrons
il ouvre	il ouvrait	il ouvrira	tu ouvres	ouvrez
nous ouvrons	nous ouvrions	nous ouvrirons	il ouvre	
vous ouvrez	vous ouvriez	vous ouvrirez	nous ouvrions	
ils ouvrent	ils ouvraient	ils ouvriront	vous ouvriez	
			ils ouvrent	

PAST HISTORIC	PERFECT	PLUPERFECT	IMPERFECT	INFINITIVE
j'ouvris	j'ai ouvert	j'avais ouvert	j'ouvrisse	**PRESENT**
tu ouvris	tu as ouvert	tu avais ouvert	tu ouvrisses	ouvrir
il ouvrit	il a ouvert	il avait ouvert	il ouvrît	
nous ouvrîmes	nous avons ouvert	nous avions ouvert	nous ouvrissions	**PAST**
vous ouvrîtes	vous avez ouvert	vous aviez ouvert	vous ouvrissiez	avoir ouvert
ils ouvrirent	ils ont ouvert	ils avaient ouvert	ils ouvrissent	
	CONDITIONAL		PERFECT	*PARTICIPLE*
PAST ANTERIOR	PRESENT	PAST	j'aie ouvert	**PRESENT**
j'eus ouvert etc	j'ouvrirais	j'aurais ouvert	tu aies ouvert	ouvrant
	tu ouvrirais	tu aurais ouvert	il ait ouvert	
	il ouvrirait	il aurait ouvert	nous ayons ouvert	**PAST**
	nous ouvririons	nous aurions ouvert	vous ayez ouvert	ouvert
FUTURE PERFECT	vous ouvririez	vous auriez ouvert	ils aient ouvert	
j'aurai ouvert etc	ils ouvriraient	ils auraient ouvert		

POUVOIR — *to be able to*

PRESENT	IMPERFECT	FUTURE	SUBJUNCTIVE	IMPERATIVE
je peux	je pouvais	je pourrai	**PRESENT**	
tu peux	tu pouvais	tu pourras	je puisse	
il peut	il pouvait	il pourra	tu puisses	
nous pouvons	nous pouvions	nous pourrons	il puisse	
vous pouvez	vous pouviez	vous pourrez	nous puissions	
ils peuvent	ils pouvaient	ils pourront	vous puissiez	
			ils puissent	

PAST HISTORIC	PERFECT	PLUPERFECT	IMPERFECT	INFINITIVE
je pus	j'ai pu	j'avais pu	je pusse	**PRESENT**
tu pus	tu as pu	tu avais pu	tu pusses	pouvoir
il put	il a pu	il avait pu	il pût	
nous pûmes	nous avons pu	nous avions pu	nous pussions	**PAST**
vous pûtes	vous avez pu	vous aviez pu	vous pussiez	avoir pu
ils purent	ils ont pu	ils avaient pu	ils pussent	
	CONDITIONAL		PERFECT	*PARTICIPLE*
PAST ANTERIOR	PRESENT	PAST	j'aie pu	**PRESENT**
j'eus pu etc	je pourrais	j'aurais pu	tu aies pu	pouvant
	tu pourrais	tu aurais pu	il ait pu	
	il pourrait	il aurait pu	nous ayons pu	**PAST**
	nous pourrions	nous aurions pu	vous ayez pu	pu
FUTURE PERFECT	vous pourriez	vous auriez pu	ils aient pu	
j'aurai pu etc	ils pourraient	ils auraient pu		

PRENDRE — *to take*

PRESENT	IMPERFECT	FUTURE	SUBJUNCTIVE	IMPERATIVE
je prends	je prenais	je prendrai	**PRESENT**	prends
tu prends	tu prenais	tu prendras	je prenne	prenons
il prend	il prenait	il prendra	tu prennes	prenez
nous prenons	nous prenions	nous prendrons	il prenne	
vous prenez	vous preniez	vous prendrez	nous prenions	
ils prennent	ils prenaient	ils prendront	vous preniez	
			ils prennent	

PAST HISTORIC	PERFECT	PLUPERFECT	IMPERFECT	INFINITIVE
je pris	j'ai pris	j'avais pris	je prisse	**PRESENT**
tu pris	tu as pris	tu avais pris	tu prisses	prendre
il prit	il a pris	il avait pris	il prît	
nous prîmes	nous avons pris	nous avions pris	nous prissions	**PAST**
vous prîtes	vous avez pris	vous aviez pris	vous prissiez	avoir pris
ils prirent	ils ont pris	ils avaient pris	ils prissent	
	CONDITIONAL		PERFECT	*PARTICIPLE*
PAST ANTERIOR	PRESENT	PAST	j'aie pris	**PRESENT**
j'eus pris etc	je prendrais	j'aurais pris	tu aies pris	prenant
	tu prendrais	tu aurais pris	il ait pris	
	il prendrait	il aurait pris	nous ayons pris	**PAST**
	nous prendrions	nous aurions pris	vous ayez pris	pris
FUTURE PERFECT	vous prendriez	vous auriez pris	ils aient pris	
j'aurai pris etc	ils prendraient	ils auraient pris		

RECEVOIR   *to receive*

PRESENT	IMPERFECT	FUTURE		SUBJUNCTIVE	IMPERATIVE
je reçois	je recevais	je recevrai		**PRESENT**	reçois
tu reçois	tu recevais	tu recevras		je reçoive	recevons
il reçoit	il recevait	il recevra		tu reçoives	recevez
nous recevons	nous recevions	nous recevrons		il reçoive	
vous recevez	vous receviez	vous recevrez		nous recevions	
ils reçoivent	ils recevaient	ils recevront		vous receviez	
				ils reçoivent	

PAST HISTORIC	PERFECT	PLUPERFECT		IMPERFECT	INFINITIVE
je reçus	j'ai reçu	j'avais reçu		je reçusse	**PRESENT**
tu reçus	tu as reçu	tu avais reçu		tu reçusses	recevoir
il reçut	il a reçu	il avait reçu		il reçût	
nous reçûmes	nous avons reçu	nous avions reçu		nous reçussions	**PAST**
vous reçûtes	vous avez reçu	vous aviez reçu		vous reçussiez	avoir reçu
ils reçurent	ils ont reçu	ils avaient reçu		ils reçussent	

CONDITIONAL

PAST ANTERIOR	PRESENT	PAST		PERFECT	PARTICIPLE
j'eus reçu etc	je recevrais	j'aurais reçu		j'aie reçu	**PRESENT**
	tu recevrais	tu aurais reçu		tu aies reçu	recevant
	il recevrait	il aurait reçu		il ait reçu	
	nous recevrions	nous aurions reçu		nous ayons reçu	**PAST**
FUTURE PERFECT	vous recevriez	vous auriez reçu		vous ayez reçu	reçu
j'aurai reçu etc	ils recevraient	ils auraient reçu		ils aient reçu	

SAVOIR   *to know*

PRESENT	IMPERFECT	FUTURE		SUBJUNCTIVE	IMPERATIVE
je sais	je savais	je saurai		**PRESENT**	
tu sais	tu savais	tu sauras		je sache	sache
il sait	il savait	il saura		tu saches	sachons
nous savons	nous savions	nous saurons		il sache	sachez
vous savez	vous saviez	vous saurez		nous sachions	
ils savent	ils savaient	ils sauront		vous sachiez	
				ils sachent	

PAST HISTORIC	PERFECT	PLUPERFECT		IMPERFECT	INFINITIVE
je sus	j'ai su	j'avais su		je susse	**PRESENT**
tu sus	tu as su	tu avais su		tu susses	savoir
il sut	il a su	il avait su		il sût	
nous sûmes	nous avons su	nous avions su		nous sussions	**PAST**
vous sûtes	vous avez su	vous aviez su		vous sussiez	avoir su
ils surent	ils ont su	ils avaient su		ils sussent	

CONDITIONAL

PAST ANTERIOR	PRESENT	PAST		PERFECT	PARTICIPLE
j'eus su etc	je saurais	j'aurais su		j'aie su	**PRESENT**
	tu saurais	tu aurais su		tu aies su	sachant
	il saurait	il aurait su		il ait su	
	nous saurions	nous aurions su		nous ayons su	**PAST**
FUTURE PERFECT	vous sauriez	vous auriez su		vous ayez su	su
j'aurai su etc	ils sauraient	ils auraient su		ils aient su	

TENIR   *to hold*

PRESENT	IMPERFECT	FUTURE		SUBJUNCTIVE	IMPERATIVE
je tiens	je tenais	je tiendrai		**PRESENT**	
tu tiens	tu tenais	tu tiendras		je tienne	tiens
il tient	il tenait	il tiendra		tu tiennes	tenons
nous tenons	nous tenions	nous tiendrons		il tienne	tenez
vous tenez	vous teniez	vous tiendrez		nous tenions	
ils tiennent	ils tenaient	ils tiendront		vous teniez	
				ils tiennent	

PAST HISTORIC	PERFECT	PLUPERFECT		IMPERFECT	INFINITIVE
je tins	j'ai tenu	j'avais tenu		je tinsse	**PRESENT**
tu tins	tu as tenu	tu avais tenu		tu tinsses	tenir
il tint	il a tenu	il avait tenu		il tînt	
nous tînmes	nous avons tenu	nous avions tenu		nous tinssions	**PAST**
vous tîntes	vous avez tenu	vous aviez tenu		vous tinssiez	avoir tenu
ils tinrent	ils ont tenu	ils avaient tenu		ils tinssent	

CONDITIONAL

PAST ANTERIOR	PRESENT	PAST		PERFECT	PARTICIPLE
j'eus tenu etc	je tiendrais	j'aurais tenu		j'aie tenu	**PRESENT**
	tu tiendrais	tu aurais tenu		tu aies tenu	tenant
	il tiendrait	il aurait tenu		il ait tenu	
	nous tiendrions	nous aurions tenu		nous ayons tenu	**PAST**
FUTURE PERFECT	vous tiendriez	vous auriez tenu		vous ayez tenu	tenu
j'aurai tenu etc	ils tiendraient	ils auraient tenu		ils aient tenu	

VENDRE   *to sell*

PRESENT	IMPERFECT	FUTURE
je vends	je vendais	je vendrai
tu vends	tu vendais	tu vendras
il vend	il vendait	il vendra
nous vendons	nous vendions	nous vendrons
vous vendez	vous vendiez	vous vendrez
ils vendent	ils vendaient	ils vendront

SUBJUNCTIVE

PRESENT
je vende
tu vendes
il vende
nous vendions
vous vendiez
ils vendent

IMPERATIVE
vends
vendons
vendez

PAST HISTORIC	PERFECT	PLUPERFECT
je vendis	j'ai vendu	j'avais vendu
tu vendis	tu as vendu	tu avais vendu
il vendit	il a vendu	il avait vendu
nous vendîmes	nous avons vendu	nous avions vendu
vous vendîtes	vous avez vendu	vous aviez vendu
ils vendirent	ils ont vendu	ils avaient vendu

IMPERFECT
je vendisse
tu vendisses
il vendît
nous vendissions
vous vendissiez
ils vendissent

INFINITIVE

PRESENT
vendre

PAST
avoir vendu

CONDITIONAL

PAST ANTERIOR	PRESENT	PAST
j'eus vendu etc	je vendrais	j'aurais vendu
	tu vendrais	tu aurais vendu
	il vendrait	il aurait vendu
	nous vendrions	nous aurions vendu
FUTURE PERFECT	vous vendriez	vous auriez vendu
j'aurai vendu etc	ils vendraient	ils auraient vendu

PERFECT
j'aie vendu
tu aies vendu
il ait vendu
nous ayons vendu
vous ayez vendu
ils aient vendu

PARTICIPLE

PRESENT
vendant

PAST
vendu

VENIR   *to come*

PRESENT	IMPERFECT	FUTURE
je viens	je venais	je viendrai
tu viens	tu venais	tu viendras
il vient	il venait	il viendra
nous venons	nous venions	nous viendrons
vous venez	vous veniez	vous viendrez
ils viennent	ils venaient	ils viendront

SUBJUNCTIVE

PRESENT
je vienne
tu viennes
il vienne
nous venions
vous veniez
ils viennent

IMPERATIVE
viens
venons
venez

PAST HISTORIC	PERFECT	PLUPERFECT
je vins	je suis venu(e)	j'étais venu(e)
tu vins	tu es venu(e)	tu étais venu(e)
il vint	il (elle) est venu(e)	il (elle) était venu(e)
nous vînmes	nous sommes venu(e)s	nous étions venu(e)s
vous vîntes	vous êtes venu(e)(s)	vous étiez venu(e)(s)
ils vinrent	ils (elles) sont venu(e)s	ils (elles) étaient venu(e)s

IMPERFECT
je vinsse
tu vinsses
il vînt
nous vinssions
vous vinssiez
ils vinssent

INFINITIVE

PRESENT
venir

PAST
être venu(e)(s)

CONDITIONAL

PAST ANTERIOR	PRESENT	PAST
je fus venu(e) etc	je viendrais	je serais venu(e)
	tu viendrais	tu serais venu(e)
	il viendrait	il (elle) serait venu(e)
	nous viendrions	nous serions venu(e)s
FUTURE PERFECT	vous viendriez	vous seriez venu(e)(s)
je serai venu(e) etc	ils viendraient	ils (elles) seraient venu(e)s

PERFECT
je sois venu(e)
tu sois venu(e)
il (elle) soit venu(e)
nous soyons venu(e)s
vous soyez venu(e)(s)
ils (elles) soient venu(e)s

PARTICIPLE

PRESENT
venant

PAST
venu

VIVRE   *to live*

PRESENT	IMPERFECT	FUTURE
je vis	je vivais	je vivrai
tu vis	tu vivais	tu vivras
il vit	il vivait	il vivra
nous vivons	nous vivions	nous vivrons
vous vivez	vous viviez	vous vivrez
ils vivent	ils vivaient	ils vivront

SUBJUNCTIVE

PRESENT
je vive
tu vives
il vive
nous vivions
vous viviez
ils vivent

IMPERATIVE
vis
vivons
vivez

PAST HISTORIC	PERFECT	PLUPERFECT
je vécus	j'ai vécu	j'avais vécu
tu vécus	tu as vécu	tu avais vécu
il vécut	il a vécu	il avait vécu
nous vécûmes	nous avons vécu	nous avions vécu
vous vécûtes	vous avez vécu	vous aviez vécu
ils vécurent	ils ont vécu	ils avaient vécu

IMPERFECT
je vécusse
tu vécusses
il vécût
nous vécussions
vous vécussiez
ils vécussent

INFINITIVE

PRESENT
vivre

PAST
avoir vécu

CONDITIONAL

PAST ANTERIOR	PRESENT	PAST
j'eus vécu etc	je vivrais	j'aurais vécu
	tu vivrais	tu aurais vécu
	il vivrait	il aurait vécu
	nous vivrions	nous aurions vécu
FUTURE PERFECT	vous vivriez	vous auriez vécu
j'aurai vécu etc	ils vivraient	ils auraient vécu

PERFECT
j'aie vécu
tu aies vécu
il ait vécu
nous ayons vécu
vous ayez vécu
ils aient vécu

PARTICIPLE

PRESENT
vivant

PAST
vécu

VOIR — to see

PRESENT	IMPERFECT	FUTURE	SUBJUNCTIVE	IMPERATIVE
je vois	je voyais	je verrai	**PRESENT**	vois
tu vois	tu voyais	tu verras	je voie	voyons
il voit	il voyait	il verra	tu voies	voyez
nous voyons	nous voyions	nous verrons	il voie	
vous voyez	vous voyiez	vous verrez	nous voyions	
ils voient	ils voyaient	ils verront	vous voyiez	
			ils voient	

PAST HISTORIC	PERFECT	PLUPERFECT	IMPERFECT	INFINITIVE
je vis	j'ai vu	j'avais vu	je visse	**PRESENT**
tu vis	tu as vu	tu avais vu	tu visses	voir
il vit	il a vu	il avait vu	il vît	
nous vîmes	nous avons vu	nous avions vu	nous vissions	**PAST**
vous vîtes	vous avez vu	vous aviez vu	vous vissiez	avoir vu
ils virent	ils ont vu	ils avaient vu	ils vissent	
	CONDITIONAL		**PERFECT**	**PARTICIPLE**
PAST ANTERIOR	**PRESENT**	**PAST**	j'aie vu	**PRESENT**
j'eus vu etc	je verrais	j'aurais vu	tu aies vu	voyant
	tu verrais	tu aurais vu	il ait vu	
	il verrait	il aurait vu	nous ayons vu	**PAST**
	nous verrions	nous aurions vu	vous ayez vu	vu
FUTURE PERFECT	vous verriez	vous auriez vu	ils aient vu	
j'aurai vu etc	ils verraient	ils auraient vu		

VOULOIR — to want

PRESENT	IMPERFECT	FUTURE	SUBJUNCTIVE	IMPERATIVE
je veux	je voulais	je voudrai	**PRESENT**	veuille
tu veux	tu voulais	tu voudras	je veuille	veuillons
il veut	il voulait	il voudra	tu veuilles	veuillez
nous voulons	nous voulions	nous voudrons	il veuille	
vous voulez	vous vouliez	vous voudrez	nous voulions	
ils veulent	ils voulaient	ils voudront	vous vouliez	
			ils veuillent	

PAST HISTORIC	PERFECT	PLUPERFECT	IMPERFECT	INFINITIVE
je voulus	j'ai voulu	j'avais voulu	je voulusse	**PRESENT**
tu voulus	tu as voulu	tu avais voulu	tu voulusses	vouloir
il voulut	il a voulu	il avait voulu	il voulût	
nous voulûmes	nous avons voulu	nous avions voulu	nous voulussions	**PAST**
vous voulûtes	vous avez voulu	vous aviez voulu	vous voulussiez	avoir voulu
ils voulurent	ils ont voulu	ils avaient voulu	ils voulussent	
	CONDITIONAL		**PERFECT**	**PARTICIPLE**
PAST ANTERIOR	**PRESENT**	**PAST**	j'aie voulu	**PRESENT**
j'eus voulu etc	je voudrais	j'aurais voulu	tu aies voulu	voulant
	tu voudrais	tu aurais voulu	il ait voulu	
	il voudrait	il aurait voulu	nous ayons voulu	**PAST**
	nous voudrions	nous aurions voulu	vous ayez voulu	voulu
FUTURE PERFECT	vous voudriez	vous auriez voulu	ils aient voulu	
j'aurai voulu etc	ils voudraient	ils auraient voulu		

M VERBAL CONSTRUCTIONS

There are two main types of verbal construction:

1 Verbs followed by an infinitive

There are three main types of construction when a verb is followed by an infinitive. For examples of all three types, see pp B35-7.

a) *Verbs followed by an infinitive without any linking preposition*

These include verbs of wishing and willing, of movement and of perception:

adorer *to love*	**aimer** *to like*	**aimer mieux** *to prefer*
aller *to go (and)*	**compter** *to intend to*	**descendre** *to go down (and)*
désirer *to wish*	**détester** *to hate*	**devoir** *to have to*
écouter *to listen to*	**entendre** *to hear*	**entrer** *to go in (and)*
envoyer *to send*	**espérer** *to hope to*	**faire** *to make*
falloir *to have to*	**laisser** *to let*	**monter** *to go up (and)*
oser *to dare*	**pouvoir** *to be able to*	**préférer** *to prefer to*
regarder *to watch*	**rentrer** *to go in/back (and)*	**savoir** *to know how to*
sembler *to seem to*	**sentir** *to feel*	**sortir** *to go out (and)*
souhaiter *to wish to*	**valoir mieux** *to be better to*	**venir** *to come (and)*
voir *to see*	**vouloir** *to want to*	

b) *Verbs followed by* à + *infinitive:*

aider à	*to help (to do)*
s'amuser à	*to enjoy (doing)*
apprendre à	*to learn (to do)*
s'apprêter à	*to get ready (to do)*
arriver à	*to manage (to do)*
s'attendre à	*to expect (to do)*
autoriser à	*to allow (to do)*
chercher à	*to try (to do)*
commencer à	*to start (doing)*
consentir à	*to agree (to do)*
consister à	*to consist in (doing)*
continuer à	*to continue (to do)*
se décider à	*to make up one's mind (to do)*
encourager à	*to encourage (to do)*
enseigner à	*to teach how (to do)*
forcer à	*to force (to do)*
s'habituer à	*to get used (to doing)*
hésiter à	*to hesitate (to do)*
inciter à	*to prompt (to do)*
s'intéresser à	*to be interested in (doing)*
inviter à	*to invite (to do)*
se mettre à	*to start (doing)*
obliger à	*to force (to do)*
parvenir à	*to succeed (in doing)*
passer son temps à	*to spend one's time (doing)*
perdre son temps à	*to waste one's time (doing)*
persister à	*to persist in (doing)*
pousser à	*to urge (to do)*
se préparer à	*to get ready (to do)*
renoncer à	*to give up (doing)*
rester à	*to be left (to do)*
réussir à	*to manage (to do)*
servir à	*to be used for (doing)*
songer à	*to think of (doing)*

tarder à	*to delay/be late in (doing)*
tenir à	*to be keen (to do)*

c) *Verbs followed by* de + *infinitive:*

accepter de	*to agree (to do)*
accuser de	*to accuse of (doing)*
achever de	*to finish (doing)*
s'arrêter de	*to stop (doing)*
avoir besoin de	*to need (to do)*
avoir envie de	*to feel like (doing)*
avoir peur de	*to be afraid (to do)*
cesser de	*to stop (doing)*
se charger de	*to undertake (to do)*
commander de	*to order (to do)*
conseiller de	*to advise (to do)*
se contenter de	*to make do with (doing)*
craindre de	*to be afraid (to do)*
décider de	*to decide (to do)*
déconseiller de	*to advise against (doing)*
défendre de	*to forbid (to do)*
demander de	*to ask (to do)*
se dépêcher de	*to hasten (to do)*
dire de	*to tell (to do)*
dissuader de	*to dissuade from (doing)*
s'efforcer de	*to strive (to do)*
empêcher de	*to prevent (from doing)*
s'empresser de	*to hasten (to do)*
entreprendre de	*to undertake (to do)*
essayer de	*to try (to do)*
s'étonner de	*to be surprised (at doing)*
éviter de	*to avoid (doing)*
s'excuser de	*to apologize for (doing)*
faire semblant de	*to pretend (to do)*
feindre de	*to pretend (to do)*
finir de	*to finish (doing)*
se garder de	*to be careful not to (do)*
se hâter de	*to hasten (to do)*
interdire de	*to forbid (to do)*
jurer de	*to swear (to do)*
manquer de	*'to nearly' (do)*
menacer de	*to threaten (to do)*
mériter de	*to deserve (to do)*
négliger de	*to fail (to do)*
s'occuper de	*to undertake (to do)*
offrir de	*to offer (to do)*
omettre de	*to omit (to do)*
ordonner de	*to order (to do)*
oublier de	*to forget (to do)*
permettre de	*to allow (to do)*
persuader de	*to persuade (to do)*
prier de	*to ask (to do)*
promettre de	*to promise (to do)*
proposer de	*to offer (to do)*
recommander de	*to recommend (to do)*
refuser de	*to refuse (to do)*
regretter de	*to be sorry (to do)*
remercier de	*to thank for (doing)*
résoudre de	*to resolve (to do)*
risquer de	*to risk (doing)*
se souvenir de	*to remember (doing)*
suggérer de	*to suggest (doing)*
supplier de	*to implore (to do)*
tâcher de	*to try (to do)*
tenter de	*to try (to do)*
venir de	*to have just (done)*

2 Verbs followed by an object

In general, verbs which take a direct object in French also take a direct object in English, and verbs which take an indirect object in French (ie verb + preposition + object) also take an indirect object in English.

There are, however, some exceptions:

a) *Verbs followed by an indirect object in English but not in French* (the English preposition is not translated):

attendre	to wait for
chercher	to look for
demander	to ask for
écouter	to listen to
espérer	to hope for
payer	to pay for
regarder	to look at
reprocher	to blame for

on a demandé l'addition
we asked for the bill

j'attendais l'autobus
I was waiting for the bus

je cherche mon frère
I'm looking for my brother

tu écoutes la radio?
are you listening to the radio?

b) *Verbs which take a direct object in English, but an indirect object in French:*

convenir à	to suit
se fier à	to trust
jouer à	to play (game, sport)
jouer de	to play (musical instrument)
obéir à	to obey
désobéir à	to disobey
pardonner à	to forgive
renoncer à	to give up
répondre à	to answer
résister à	to resist
ressembler à	to resemble (to look like)
téléphoner à	to phone

tu peux te fier à moi
you can trust me

tu joues souvent au tennis?
do you often play tennis?

il joue bien de la guitare
he plays the guitar well

tu as répondu à ma lettre?
did you answer my letter?

téléphonons au médecin
let's phone the doctor

obéis à ton père!
obey your father!

c) *Verbs which take a direct object in English but de + indirect object in French:*

s'apercevoir de	to notice
s'approcher de	to come near
avoir besoin de	to need
changer de	to change
douter de	to doubt
se douter de	to suspect
s'emparer de	to seize, to grab
jouir de	to enjoy
manquer de	to lack, to miss
se méfier de	to mistrust
se servir de	to use
se souvenir de	to remember
se tromper de ...	to get the wrong ...

je dois changer de train?
do I have to change trains?

il ne s'est aperçu de rien
he didn't notice anything

méfiez-vous de lui
don't trust him

je me servirai de ton vélo
I'll use your bike

tu te souviens de Jean?
do you remember Jean?

il s'est trompé de numéro
he got the wrong number

d) *Some verbs take à or de before an object, whereas their English equivalent uses a different preposition:*

i) Verb + à + object:

croire à	to believe in
s'intéresser à	to be interested in
penser à	to think of/about
songer à	to think of
rêver à	to dream of/about
servir à	to be used for

je m'intéresse au football et à la course automobile
I'm interested in football and in motor-racing

à quoi penses-tu?
what are you thinking about?

ça sert à quoi?
what is this used for?

ii) Verb + de + object:

dépendre de	to depend on
être fâché de	to be annoyed at
féliciter de	to congratulate for
parler de	to speak of/about
remercier de	to thank for
rire de	to laugh at
traiter de	to deal with, to be about
vivre de	to live on

cela dépendra du temps
it'll depend on the weather

il m'a parlé de toi
he told me about you

tu l'as remercié du cadeau qu'il t'a fait?
did you thank him for the present he gave you?

3 Verbs followed by one direct object and one indirect object

a) In general, these are verbs of giving or lending, and their English equivalents are constructed in the same way, eg:

donner quelque chose à quelqu'un
to give something to someone

il a vendu son ordinateur à son voisin
he sold his computer to his neighbour

Note that after such verbs, the preposition 'to' is often omitted in English but à, however, cannot be omitted in French. Particular care must be taken when object pronouns are used with these verbs (see p B18).

b) With verbs expressing 'taking away', à is translated by 'from' (*qn* stands for 'quelqu'un' and *sb* for 'somebody'):

acheter à qn	to buy from sb
cacher à qn	to hide from sb
demander à qn	to ask sb for
emprunter à qn	to borrow from sb
enlever à qn	to take away from sb
ôter à qn	to take away from sb
prendre à qn	to take from sb
voler à qn	to steal from sb

à qui as-tu emprunté cela?
who did you borrow this from?

il l'a volé à son frère
he stole it from his brother

4 Verb + indirect object + 'de' + infinitive

Some verbs which take a direct object in English are followed by à + object + de + infinitive in French:

commander à qn de faire	to order sb to do
conseiller à qn de faire	to advise sb to do
défendre à qn de faire	to forbid sb to do
demander à qn de faire	to ask sb to do
dire à qn de faire	to tell sb to do
ordonner à qn de faire	to order sb to do
permettre à qn de faire	to allow sb to do
promettre à qn de faire	to promise sb to do
proposer à qn de faire	to offer to do for sb, to suggest to sb to do

je leur ai conseillé de ne pas essayer
I advised them not to try

demande à ton fils de t'aider
ask your son to help you

j'ai promis à mes parents de ne jamais recommencer
I promised my parents never to do this again

8 PREPOSITIONS

Prepositions in both French and English can have many different meanings, which presents considerable difficulties for the translator. The following guide to the most common prepositions sets out the generally accepted meanings on the left, with a description of their use in brackets, and an illustration. The main meanings are given first. Prepositions are listed in alphabetical order.

À

at	(place)	**au troisième arrêt** *at the third stop*
	(date)	**à Noël** *at Christmas*
	(time)	**à trois heures** *at three o'clock*
	(idiom)	**au hasard** *at random*
		au travail *at work*
in	(place)	**à Montmartre** *in Montmartre*
		à Lyon *in Lyons*
		au supermarché *in the supermarket*
		à la campagne *in the country*
		au lit *in bed*
		au loin *in the distance*
	(manner)	**à la française** *in the French way*
		à ma façon *my way*
to	(place)	**aller au théâtre** *to go to the theatre*
		aller à Londres *to go to London*
	(+ infinitive)	**c'est facile à faire** *it is easy to do (see p B36)*
away from	(distance)	**à 3 km d'ici** *3 km away*
by	(means)	**aller à vélo** *to go by bike*
		je l'ai reconnu à ses habits *I recognized him by his clothing*
	(manner)	**fait à la main** *hand-made*
	(rate)	**à la centaine** *by the hundred*
		100 km à l'heure *100 km per hour*
for/up to	(+ pronoun)	**c'est à vous de jouer** *it's your turn*
		c'est à nous de te le dire *it's up to us to tell you*
	(purpose)	**une tasse à café** *a coffee cup*
from		**il l'a caché à ses parents** *he hid it from his parents*

his/her/my etc	(possessive)	**son sac à elle** *her bag*
on	(means)	**aller à cheval/à pied** *to go on horseback/on foot*
	(place)	**à la page 12** *on page 12*
		à droite/à gauche *on/to the right/left*
	(time)	**à cette occasion** *on this occasion*
with	(descriptive)	**un homme aux cheveux blonds** *a man with blond hair*
		l'homme à la valise *the man with the case*
	(idiom)	**à bras ouverts** *with open arms*

For use of the preposition à with the infinitive see verbal constructions p B52.

APRÈS

after	(time)	**après votre arrivée** *after your arrival*
	(sequence)	**24 ans après la mort du président** *24 years after the death of the President*
		je suis allé au lit après avoir fini le livre *I went to bed after I finished the book*
		après s'être séparée de son mari *after separating from her husband*

AUPRÈS DE

beside		**il s'assit auprès de sa mère** *he sat down beside his mother*
compared to		**ce n'est rien auprès de ce que tu as fait** *it's nothing compared to what you've done*

AVANT

before	(time)	**avant cet après-midi** *before this afternoon*
		avant ce soir *before tonight*
		avant de s'asseoir *before sitting down*
	(preference)	**la famille avant tout** *the family comes first (above all else)*

AVEC

with	(association)	**je viendrai avec lui** *I'll come with him*
	(means)	**elle marche avec une canne** *she walks with a stick*

CHEZ

at	(place)	**chez moi/toi** *at/to my/your house*
		chez mon oncle *at my uncle's*
		chez le pharmacien *at the chemist's*

among		chez les Écossais *among the Scots*
about		ce qui m'énerve chez toi, c'est *what annoys me about you is ...*
in		chez Sartre *in Sartre's work*

CONTRE

against	(place)	contre le mur *against the wall*
with	(after verb)	je suis fâché contre elle *I'm angry with her*
for		elle a échangé un billet contre des pièces *she changed a note for coins*

DANS

in	(position)	dans ma serviette *in my briefcase*
	(time)	je pars dans deux jours *I'm leaving in two days' time*
	(idiom)	dans l'attente de vous voir *looking forward to seeing you*
from	(removal)	prendre quelque chose dans l'armoire *to take something from the cupboard*
on	(position)	dans le train *on the train*
out of	(idiom)	boire dans un verre *to drink out of a glass*

DE

from	(place)	je suis venu de Glasgow *I have come from Glasgow*
	(date)	du 5 février au 10 mars *from 5 February to 10 March*
		d'un week-end à l'autre *from one weekend to another*
of	(adjectival)	un cri de triomphe *a shout of triumph*
	(contents)	une tasse de café *a cup of coffee*
	(cause)	mourir de faim *to die of hunger*
	(measurement)	long de 3 mètres *3 metres long*
	(time)	ma montre retarde de 10 minutes *my watch is 10 minutes slow*
	(price)	le montant est de 20 euros *the total is 20 euros*
	(possessive)	la père de mon ami *my friend's father*
	(adjectival)	les vacances de Pâques *the Easter holidays*
	(after 'quelque chose')	quelque chose de bon *something good*
	(after 'rien')	rien de nouveau *nothing new*
	(after 'personne')	personne d'autre *nobody else*
	(quantity)	beaucoup de, peu de *many, few*
by	(idiom)	je le connais de vue *I know him by sight*

in	(manner)	de cette façon *in this way*
	(after superlatives)	la plus haute montagne d'Écosse *the highest mountain in Scotland*
on	(position)	de ce côté *on this side*
than	(comparative)	moins de 2 euros *less than 2 euros*
		plus de 3 litres *more than 3 litres*
to	(after adjectives)	ravi de vous voir *delighted to see you*
		il est facile de se tromper *it is easy to make a mistake*
	(after verbs)	s'efforcer de *to try to*
with	(cause)	tomber de fatigue *to drop with exhaustion*

DEPUIS

for	(time)	j'étudie le français depuis 3 ans *I have been studying French for 3 years*
		j'étudiais le français depuis 3 ans *I had been studying French for 3 years*
		je n'y ai pas joué depuis des années *I haven't played for years*
from	(place)	depuis ma fenêtre, je vois la mer *from my window I can see the sea*
	(time)	depuis le matin jusqu'au soir *from morning till evening*
since		depuis dimanche *since Sunday*

DERRIÈRE

behind	(place)	derrière la maison *behind the house*

DÈS

from	(time)	dès six heures *from six o'clock onwards*
		dès 1934 *as far back as 1934*
		dès le début *from the beginning*
		dès maintenant *from now on*
	(place)	dès Édimbourg *from (the moment of leaving) Edinburgh*

DEVANT

in front of	(place)	devant l'école *in front of the school*
before	(place)	sur la table devant eux *on the table before them*

EN

in	(place)	être en ville *to be in town*
		en Angleterre *in England*

	(colour)	**un mur peint en jaune** *a wall painted yellow*
	(material)	**une montre en or** *a gold watch*
by	(means)	**en auto/en avion** *by car/by plane*
	(dates, seasons)	**en quelle année?** *in what year?*
		en 2004 *in 2004*
		en été *in the summer*
		en juillet *in July*
	(dress)	**en jupe** *in a skirt*
	(language)	**en chinois** *in Chinese*
	(time)	**j'ai fait mes devoirs en 20 minutes** *I did my homework in 20 minutes*
like, as		**il s'est habillé en femme** *he dressed as a woman*
on	(idiom)	**en vacances** *on holiday*
		en moyenne *on average*
	(+ present participle)	**en faisant** *on/while/by doing*

Note that en is not used with the definite article except in certain expressions: **en l'an 2020** *(in the year 2020)*, **en l'honneur de** *(in honour of)* and **en la présence de** *(in the presence of)*.

EN TANT QUE

| *as/in one's capacity as* | **en tant que professeur**
as a teacher |

ENTRE

among		**être entre amis** *to be among friends*
between	(place)	**entre Londres et Paris** *between London and Paris*
	(time)	**entre 6 et 10 heures** *between 6 and 10 o'clock*
	(idiom)	**entre nous** *between you and me*
in	(punctuation)	**entre guillemets** *in inverted commas*
		entre parenthèses *in brackets*

D'ENTRE

| *of/from among* | **certains d'entre eux**
some of them |

ENVERS

| *to/towards* | **être bien disposé envers quelqu'un**
to be well-disposed towards someone |

HORS DE

| *out of* | **hors de danger**
out of danger |

JUSQUE

up to/as far as	(place)	**jusqu'à la frontière espagnole** *as far as the Spanish border*
	(time)	**jusqu'ici** *up to now*
		jusque-là *up till then*
till		**jusqu'à demain** *till tomorrow*

MALGRÉ

| *in spite of* | **malgré la chaleur**
in spite of the heat |

PAR

by	(agent)	**la décision fut prise par le président** *the decision was made by the President*
	(means of transport)	**par le train** *by train*
	(distributive)	**trois fois par semaine** *three times a week*
		deux par deux *two by two*
	(place)	**par ici/là** *this/that way*
in/on	(weather)	**par un temps pareil** *in such weather*
		par un beau jour d'hiver *on a beautiful winter's day*
through/out of	(place)	**regarder par la fenêtre** *to look out of the window*
		jette-le par la fenêtre *throw it out of the window*
to/on		**tomber par terre** *to fall to the ground*
		étendu par terre *lying on the ground*
	(+ infinitive)	**commencer/finir par faire** *to begin/end by doing*

PARMI

| *among* | **parmi mes ennemis**
among my enemies |

PENDANT

| *for* | (time) | **il l'avait fait pendant 5 ans**
he had done it for 5 years |
| *during* | | **pendant l'été**
during the summer |

POUR

for		**ce livre est pour vous** *this book is for you*
		mourir pour la patrie *to die for one's country*
	(purpose)	**c'est pour cela que je suis venu** *that's why I've come*
	(emphatic)	**pour moi, cet argument ne tient pas** *if you ask me, this argument isn't valid*
	(time)	**j'en ai pour une heure** *it'll take me an hour*

je suis en vacances pour 2
semaines
I'm on holiday for 2 weeks

(pour stresses intention and future time: see depuis and pendant,
pp B55 and B56)

	(idiom)	c'est bon pour la santé *it's good for your health*
to	(+ infinitive)	il était trop paresseux pour réussir ses examens *he was too lazy to pass his exams*

PRÈS DE

near	(place)	près du marché *near the market*
nearly	(time)	il est près de minuit *it's nearly midnight*
	(quantity)	près de cinquante *nearly fifty*

QUANT À

as for		quant à moi *as for me*

SANS

without	(+ noun)	sans espoir *without hope*
	(+ pronoun)	je n'irai pas sans vous *I won't go without you*
	(+ infinitive)	sans parler *without speaking*
		sans s'arrêter *without stopping*

SAUF

except for		ils sont tous partis, sauf John *everyone left except John*
barring		sauf accidents/sauf imprévu *barring accidents/the unexpected*

SELON

according to		selon le président *according to the President*
		selon moi *in my opinion*

SOUS

under	(physical)	sous la table *under the table*
	(governed by)	sous Élisabeth II *under Elizabeth II*
in	(weather)	sous la pluie *in the rain*
	(idiom)	sous peu *before long/shortly*
		sous la main *to hand*
		sous tous rapports *in all respects*
		sous mes yeux *before my eyes*

SUR

on/upon	(place)	le chat est sur le toit *the cat's on the roof*
off		je l'ai pris sur l'étagère *I took it off the shelf*

out of	(proportion)	neuf sur dix *nine out of ten*
		une semaine sur trois *one week in three*
over	(place)	le pont sur la Loire *the bridge over the Loire*
		l'emporter sur quelqu'un *to prevail over someone*
about	(idiom)	une enquête sur ... *an enquiry about ...*
at		sur ces paroles *at these words*
		sur ce, il est sorti *at this he went out*
by		quatre mètres sur cinq *four metres by five*
in		sur un ton amer *in a bitter tone (of voice)*

VERS

towards	(place)	vers le nord *towards the north*
	(time)	vers la fin du match *towards the end of the match*
about	(time)	vers 10 heures *about 10 o'clock*

VOICI/VOILÀ

here		le voici qui vient *here he comes*
there		voilà où il demeure *that's where he lives*

9 CONJUNCTIONS

Conjunctions are words or expressions which link words, phrases or clauses. They fall into two categories, coordinating conjunctions and subordinating conjunctions:

A COORDINATING CONJUNCTIONS

1 Definition

These link two similar words or groups of words, eg nouns, pronouns, adjectives, adverbs, prepositions, phrases or clauses. The principal coordinating conjunctions (or adverbs used as conjunctions) are:

et *and*	mais *but*	ou *or*
ou bien *or (else)*	soit *either*	ni *neither*
alors *then*	aussi *therefore*	donc *then, therefore*
puis *then (next)*	car *for (because)*	or *now*
cependant *however*	néanmoins *nevertheless*	pourtant *yet, however*
toutefois *however*		

il est malade mais il ne veut pas aller au lit
he's ill but he won't go to bed

il faisait beau alors il est allé se promener
it was nice weather so he went for a walk

2 Repetition

a) Some coordinating conjunctions are repeated:

soit ... soit ...   either ... or ...
ou (bien) ... ou (bien) ...   either ... or ...

prenez soit l'un soit l'autre
take one or the other

soit tu viens avec nous, soit tu restes ici mais tu te décides
either you come with us or you stay here, but you have to decide

ou tu t'habitues ou tu démissionnes
either you get used to it or you resign

ni ... ni ...   neither ... nor ...

le vieillard n'avait ni amis ni argent
the old man had neither friends nor money

b) et and ou can be repeated in texts of a literary nature:

et ... et ...   both ... and ...
ou ... ou ...   either ... or ...

elle ne cessa et de crier et de pleurer
she didn't stop shouting and crying

ou c'est lui ou c'est moi !
it's either him or me!

3 Aussi

aussi means 'therefore' only when placed before the verb. The subject pronoun is placed after the verb (see p B62).

il pleuvait, aussi Pascal n'est-il pas sorti
it was raining, so Pascal didn't go out

When aussi follows the verb it means 'also':

j'ai aussi emporté des pulls, au cas où
I also brought some jumpers, just in case

B SUBORDINATING CONJUNCTIONS

These join a subordinate clause to another clause, usually a main clause. The principal subordinating conjunctions are:

comme	as	parce que	because
puisque	since	ainsi que	(just) as
à mesure que	as	tant que	as long as
avant que	before	après que	after
jusqu'à ce que	until	depuis que	since
pendant que	while	tandis que	whereas
si	if	à moins que	unless
pourvu que	provided that	quoique	although
bien que	although	quand	when
lorsque	when	dès que	as soon as
aussitôt que	as soon as	pour que	in order that
afin que	so that	de sorte que	so that
de façon que	so that	de peur que (+ ne)	for fear that, lest

Note that some subordinating conjunctions require the subjunctive (see p B33).

C QUE

1 Coordinating (see pp B11 and B13-14)

que is a coordinating conjunction when used in comparisons:

il est plus fort que moi
he is stronger than I

elle est plus courageuse que tu ne crois
she's braver than you think

2 Subordinating

a) *meaning 'that':*

elle dit qu'elle l'a vu
she says she has seen him

je pense que tu as raison
I think you're right

il faut que tu viennes
you'll have to come

il paraît qu'elle a gagné
it seems she's won

b) *replacing another conjunction:*

When a conjunction introduces more than one verb, que usually replaces the second subordinating conjunction and any subsequent ones to avoid repetition:

comme il était tard et que j'étais fatigué, je suis rentré
as it was late and I was tired, I went home

s'il fait beau et que tu es libre, nous irons à la piscine
if the weather's nice and you're free, we'll go to the swimming pool

nous sortirons lorsque nous aurons déjeuné et que tu te seras reposé
we'll go out when we've had lunch and you've had a rest

10 NUMBERS AND QUANTITY

A CARDINAL NUMBERS

0	zéro	40	quarante
1	un (une)	50	cinquante
2	deux	60	soixante
3	trois	70	soixante-dix
4	quatre	71	soixante et onze
5	cinq	72	soixante-douze
6	six	80	quatre-vingt(s)
7	sept	90	quatre-vingt-dix
8	huit	99	quatre-vingt-dix-neuf
9	neuf	100	cent
10	dix	101	cent un(e)
11	onze	102	cent deux
12	douze	121	cent vingt et un(e)
13	treize	122	cent vingt-deux
14	quatorze	200	deux cents
15	quinze	201	deux cent un(e)
16	seize	1000	mille
17	dix-sept	1988	mille neuf cent quatre-vingt-huit
18	dix-huit		
19	dix-neuf	2000	deux mille
20	vingt	10 000	dix mille
30	trente	1 000 000	un million

Note:

a) un is the only cardinal number which agrees with the noun in gender:

un kilo   une pomme
a kilo   *an apple*

b) hyphens are used in compound numbers between 17 and 99 except where et is used (this also applies to compound numbers after 100: cent vingt-trois 123).

c) cent and mille are not preceded by un as in English (one hundred).

d) vingt and cent multiplied by a number take an s when they are not followed by another number.

il a quatre-vingts ans
he's eighty

elle a remporté quatre-vingt-deux victoires
she has notched up eighty-two wins

c'est une civilisation vieille de huit cents ans
it's a civilization which is eight hundred years old

ce livre compte trois cent cinq pages
this book has three hundred and five pages

e)   **mille** is invariable.

trente mille personnes ont assisté à la rencontre
thirty thousand people went to the match

B ORDINAL NUMBERS

		abbreviation
1st	premier/première	1er/1ère
2nd	deuxième/second	2^e
3rd	troisième	3^e
4th	quatrième	4^e
5th	cinquième	5^e
6th	sixième	6^e
7th	septième	7^e
8th	huitième	8^e
9th	neuvième	9^e
10th	dixième	10^e
11th	onzième	11^e
12th	douzième	12^e
13th	treizième	13^e
14th	quatorzième	14^e
15th	quinzième	15^e
16th	seizième	16^e
17th	dix-septième	17^e
18th	dix-huitième	18^e
19th	dix-neuvième	19^e
20th	vingtième	20^e
21st	vingt et unième	21^e
22nd	vingt-deuxième	22^e
30th	trentième	30^e
100th	centième	100^e
101st	cent unième	101^e
200th	deux centième	200^e
1000th	millième	1000^e
10,000th	dix millième	10 000^e

Note:

a)   ordinal numbers are formed by adding -ième to cardinal numbers, except for premier and second; cinq, neuf and numbers ending in e undergo slight changes: cinquième, neuvième, onzième, douzième etc.

b)   ordinal numbers agree with the noun in gender and number:

le Premier ministre   **la première fleur**
the Prime Minister   **du printemps**
                                 the first flower of spring

c)   there is no elision with huitième and onzième:

le huitième jour   **du onzième candidat**
the eighth day   *of the eleventh candidate*

d)   cardinal numbers are used for monarchs, except for 'first':

Charles deux   **Charles premier**
Charles II   *Charles I*

C FRACTIONS AND PROPORTIONS

1 Fractions

Fractions are expressed as in English: cardinal followed by ordinal:

deux cinquièmes
two fifths

But: ¼ **un quart**   ½ **un demi, une demie**

⅓ **un tiers**   ¾ **trois quarts**

2 Decimals

The English decimal point is conveyed by a comma in French:

un virgule huit (1,8)
one point eight (1.8)

3 Approximate numbers

une huitaine   **une dizaine**
about eight   *about ten*

une trentaine   **une centaine**
some thirty   *about a hundred*

But: **un millier**
about a thousand

Note that **de** is used when the approximate number is followed by a noun:

une vingtaine d'enfants
about twenty children

4 Arithmetic

Addition:	**deux plus quatre**	2 + 4
Subtraction:	**cinq moins deux**	5 - 2
Multiplication:	**trois fois cinq**	3 x 5
Division:	**six divisé par deux**	6 ÷ 2
Square:	**deux au carré**	2^2
Power:	**deux puissance six**	2^6

D MEASUREMENTS AND PRICES

1 Measurements

a)   *Dimensions*

long(ue)/de longueur/de long	*long*
profond(e)/de profondeur/de profond	*deep*
épais(se)/d'épaisseur	*thick*
haut(e)/de hauteur/de haut	*high*

la salle de classe est longue de 12 mètres
la salle de classe a/fait 12 mètres de longueur/de long
the classroom is 12 metres long

ma chambre fait quatre mètres sur trois
my bedroom is about four metres by three

b)   *Distance*

à quelle distance sommes-nous de la gare?
how far are we from the station?

nous sommes à deux kilomètres de la gare
we are two kilometres from the station

combien y a-t-il d'ici à Blois?
how far is it to Blois?

2 Price

ce pull m'a coûté 50 euros
this sweater cost me 50 euros

j'ai payé ce pull 50 euros
I paid 50 euros for this sweater

des pommes à 2 euros le kilo
apples at 2 euros a kilo

du vin blanc à 5 euros la bouteille
white wine at 5 euros a bottle

cela fait/revient à 6 euros
that comes to 6 euros

ils coûtent 4 euros pièce
they cost 4 euros each

E EXPRESSIONS OF QUANTITY

Quantity may be expressed by an adverb of quantity, eg 'a lot', 'too much' or by a noun which names the actual quantity involved, eg 'a bottle', 'a dozen'.

1 Expression of quantity + 'de' + noun

Before a noun, adverbs and other expressions of quantity are followed by de (d' before a vowel or a silent h) and never by du, de la or des, except for bien des and la plupart du/des:

assez de *enough*	**autant de** *as much/many*
beaucoup de *a lot of/much/many*	**combien de** *how much/many*
moins de *less/fewer*	**plus de** *more*
peu de *little/few*	**un peu de** *a little*
tant de *so much/many*	**tellement de** *so much/many*
bien du/de la/des *many/a lot of*	**la plupart du/de la/des** *most*
trop de *too much/many*	

il y a assez de **fromage?** *is there enough cheese?*	**autant de gens** *as many people*
je n'ai pas beaucoup de **temps** *I haven't got much time*	**il y a** combien de **pièces?** *how many rooms are there?*
j'ai mis moins de **temps que lui** *I took less time than him*	**mange** plus de **légumes!** *eat more vegetables!*
peu de gens le savent *not many people know that*	**tu veux** un peu de **pain?** *would you like a little bread?*
il y a tant d'**années** *so many years ago*	**j'ai** tellement de **travail** *I've got so much work*
bien des gens *a good many people*	**la plupart des Français** *most French people*
tu as bien de la **patience** *you have a lot of patience*	**il y a** trop de **voitures** *there are too many cars*

2 Noun expressing quantity + 'de' + noun

une boîte de *a box/tin/can/jar of*	**une bouteille de** *a bottle of*
une bouchée de *a mouthful of (food)*	**une cuillerée de** *a spoonful of*
une douzaine de *a dozen*	**une gorgée de** *a mouthful of (drink)*
un kilo de *a kilo of*	**un litre de** *a litre of*
une livre de *a pound of*	**un morceau de** *a piece of*
un paquet de *a packet of*	**une paire de** *a pair of*
une part de *a share/helping of*	**une tasse de** *a cup of*
une tranche de *a slice of*	**un verre de** *a glass of*

je voudrais une boîte de **thon et** un litre de **lait**
I'd like a tin of tuna and a litre of milk

il y a une boîte de **limonade dans le frigo**
there's a can of lemonade in the fridge

j'ai pris deux parts de **choucroute**
I took two helpings of sauerkraut

il a mangé une douzaine d'**œufs et** six morceaux de **poulet**
he ate a dozen eggs and six pieces of chicken

3 Expressions of quantity used without a noun

When an expression of quantity is not followed by a noun, de is replaced by the pronoun en (see pp B19-20):

il y avait beaucoup de neige; il y en avait beaucoup
there was a lot of snow; there was a lot (of it)

elle a mangé trop de chocolats; elle en a trop mangé
she's eaten too many chocolates; she's eaten too many (of them)

11 EXPRESSIONS OF TIME

A THE TIME

quelle heure est-il?	*what time is it?*

a) *Full hours*

il est midi/minuit *it is 12 noon or midday/ midnight*	**il est une heure** *it is 1 o'clock*

b) *Half-hours*

il est minuit et demi(e) *it is 12.30 a.m.*	**il est midi** et demi(e) *it is 12.30 p.m.*
il est une heure et demie *it is 1.30*	

c) *Quarter-hours*

il est deux heures un/ et quart *it is a quarter past two*	**il est deux heures** moins le quart *it is a quarter to two*

d) *Minutes*

il est quatre heures vingt-trois *it is 23 minutes past 4*	**il est cinq heures** moins vingt *it is 20 to 5*

Note that minutes is usually omitted; heures is never omitted.

e) *A.m. and p.m.*

du matin *a.m., in the morning*	**de l'après-midi/du soir** *p.m., in the evening*

il est sept heures moins dix du soir
t is 7.10 p.m. or in the evening

il est sept heures dix du matin
it is 6.50 a.m. or in the morning

The 24-hour clock is commonly used:

dix heures trente *10.30 a.m.*	**quatorze heures trente- cinq** *2.35 p.m.*
dix-neuf heures dix *7.10 p.m.*	

Note that times are often abbreviated as follows:

dix-neuf heures dix	**19h10**

B THE DATE

1 Names of months, days and seasons

a) *Months*

janvier	*January*
février	*February*

mars	*March*
avril	*April*
mai	*May*
juin	*June*
juillet	*July*
août	*August*
septembre	*September*
octobre	*October*
novembre	*November*
décembre	*December*

b) *Days of the week*

lundi	*Monday*
mardi	*Tuesday*
mercredi	*Wednesday*
jeudi	*Thursday*
vendredi	*Friday*
samedi	*Saturday*
dimanche	*Sunday*

c) *Seasons*

le printemps	*spring*
l'été	*summer*
l'automne	*autumn*
l'hiver	*winter*

For prepositions used with the seasons see p B4.

Note that in French, months and days are masculine and do not have a capital letter unless they begin a sentence.

2 Dates

a) Cardinals (eg deux, trois) are used for the dates of the month except the first:

le quatorze juillet
the fourteenth of July

le deux novembre
the second of November

But: **le premier février**
the first of February

The definite article is used as in English; French does not use prepositions ('on' and 'of' in English):

je vous ai écrit le trois mars
I wrote to you on the third of March

b) **mil** *(a thousand)* is used instead of mille in dates from 1001 onwards:

mil neuf cent quatre-vingt sept
nineteen hundred and eighty-seven

l'an deux mil deux
the year two thousand and two

3 Année, journée, matinée, soirée

Année, journée, matinée, soirée (the feminine forms of an, jour, matin and soir) are usually found in the following cases:

a) *when duration is implied:*

pendant une année	*for a (whole) year*
toute la journée	*all day long, the whole day*
dans la matinée	*in the (course of the) morning*
passer une soirée	*to spend an evening*
l'année scolaire/universitaire	*the school/academic year*

b) *with an ordinal number or an indefinite expression:*

la deuxième année	*the second year*
dans sa vingtième année	*in his twentieth year*
plusieurs/quelques années	*several/a few years*
bien des/de nombreuses années	*many years*
environ une année	*about a year*

c) *with an adjective:*

de bonnes/mauvaises années	*good/bad years*

C IDIOMATIC EXPRESSIONS

à cinq heures	*at five o'clock*
à onze heures environ	*(at) about eleven o'clock*
vers minuit	*(at) about midnight*
vers (les) dix heures	*(at) about ten o'clock*
il est six heures passées	*it's past six o'clock*
à quatre heures précises ou pile	*at exactly four o'clock*
sur le coup de trois heures	*on the stroke of three*
à partir de neuf heures	*from nine o'clock onwards*
peu avant sept heures	*shortly before seven*
peu après sept heures	*shortly after seven*
tôt ou tard	*sooner or later*
au plus tôt	*at the earliest*
au plus tard	*at the latest*
il est tard	*it is late*
il est en retard	*he is late*
il se lève tard	*he gets up late*
il est arrivé en retard	*he arrived late*
le train a vingt minutes de retard	*the train is twenty minutes late*
ma montre retarde de six minutes	*my watch is six minutes slow*
ma montre avance de six minutes	*my watch is six minutes fast*
ce soir	*this evening, tonight*
demain soir	*tomorrow evening, tomorrow night*
hier soir	*yesterday evening, last night*
samedi soir	*Saturday evening*
je sors samedi soir	*I'm going out on Saturday night or evening*
dans la soirée de samedi	*on Saturday evening*
dans la nuit de samedi (à dimanche)	*during Saturday night*
demain matin	*tomorrow morning*
hier matin	*yesterday morning*
lundi matin	*Monday morning*
j'y vais lundi matin	*I'm going there on Monday morning*
demain en huit	*tomorrow week*
le lendemain	*the next day*
le lendemain matin	*the next morning*
hier matin	*yesterday morning*
la semaine dernière	*last week*
la semaine prochaine	*next week*
la semaine qui vient	*this coming week*
je l'ai vu l'autre samedi	*I saw him the other Saturday*
lundi	*on Monday*
le lundi	*on Mondays*
je commence lundi	*I'm starting (on) Monday*
il vient le lundi	*he comes on Mondays, he comes on a Monday*
vient un lundi	*come one Monday*
un lundi sur deux	*every other Monday, every second Monday*
tous les lundis	*every Monday*
tous les lundis soirs	*every Monday evening or night*
tous mes lundis	*all my Mondays*
lundi en huit	*a week on Monday, Monday week*
lundi en quinze	*a fortnight on Monday*
il y a trois semaines	*three weeks ago*
il vient l'après-midi	*he comes in the afternoon(s)*
viens un après-midi	*come one afternoon*
une demi-heure	*a half-hour, half an hour*
un quart d'heure	*a quarter of an hour*
trois quarts d'heure	*three quarters of an hour*
passer son temps (à faire)	*to spend one's time (doing)*
perdre son temps	*to waste one's time*
de temps en temps	*from time to time*

de temps à autre	from time to time
dans les temps	on time
au début de l'après-midi/ de la soirée, en début d'après-midi/de soirée	in the early afternoon/ evening
je te téléphonerai en début de matinée	I'll phone you first thing in the morning
au début du mois	at the beginning of the month
j'ai une réunion au milieu de la matinée ou en milieu de matinée	have a meeting mid-morning
au milieu (du mois) de juin, (à la) mi-juin	in the middle of June, mid-June
au milieu de l'hiver	in the middle of winter, midwinter
j'ai une réunion à la fin de la matinée ou en fin de matinée	I have a meeting late morning
à la fin de l'hiver	at the end of the winter
on en reparlera fin janvier ou à la fin du mois de janvier	we'll talk about it again at the end of January
quel jour sommes-nous aujourd'hui?	what day is it today?
le combien sommes-nous aujourd'hui?	what's the date today?, what's today's date?
nous sommes/c'est le trois avril	it's the third of April
aujourd'hui nous sommes samedi	today is Saturday, it's Saturday today
vendredi 11 janvier 2004	Friday, 11 January 2004
nous nous sommes vus le vendredi 11 janvier	we saw each other on Friday, 11th January
le vendredi treize juillet	Friday the thirteenth of July
en février/au mois de février	in February/in the month of February
en février 2004	in February 2004
l'été 2004	in the summer of 2004, in summer 2004
en 2004	in 2004
dans les années soixante	in the sixties, in the 60s, in the 1960s
au début/à la fin des années soixante	in the early/late sixties
au dix-septième siècle	in the seventeenth century
au XVIIe	in the 17th century
le jour de l'An	New Year's Day
avoir treize ans	to be thirteen (years old)
être âgé de quatorze ans	to be fourteen (years old)
elle fête ses vingt ans	she's celebrating her twentieth birthday
elle a une vingtaine d'années	she's around twenty (years old)
un plan quinquennal	a five-year plan
une année bissextile	a leap year
une année civile	a calendar year
une année-lumière	a light year

12 THE SENTENCE

A WORD ORDER

Word order is usually the same in French as in English, except in the following cases:

1 Adjectives

Many French adjectives follow the noun (see p B10):

de l'argent suisse
(some) Swiss money

j'ai les yeux bleus
I've got blue eyes

2 Adverbs

In simple tenses, adverbs usually follow the verb (see p B13):

j'y vais rarement
I seldom go there

il fera bientôt nuit
it will soon be dark

3 Object pronouns

Object pronouns usually come before the verb (see p B18):

je t'attendrai
I'll wait for you

il la lui a vendue
he sold it to him

4 Noun phrases

Noun phrases are formed differently in French (see p B67):

une chemise en coton
a cotton shirt

le père de mon copain
my friend's father

5 Exclamations

The word order is not affected after **que** or **comme** (unlike after 'how' in English):

que tu es bête!
you are silly!
(how silly you are!)

qu'il fait froid!
it's so cold!

comme il chante mal!
he sings so badly!

comme c'est beau!
that's so beautiful!

6 DONT

dont must be followed by the subject of the clause it introduces; compare:

l'ami dont j'ai perdu l'adresse
the friend whose address I lost

l'ami dont l'adresse a changé
the friend whose address has changed

7 Inversion

In certain cases, the subject of a French clause is placed after the verb. Word order is effectively that of an interrogative sentence (see pp B63-4). This occurs:

a) *after the following, when they occur at the beginning of a clause:*

à peine	aussi	peut-être
hardly	*therefore*	*maybe, perhaps*

à peine Alain était-il sorti qu'il a commencé à pleuvoir
Alain had barely gone out when it started raining

il y avait une grève du métro, aussi a-t-il pris un taxi
there was an underground strike, so he took a taxi

peut-être vont-ils téléphoner plus tard
maybe they'll phone later

But: **Alain était à peine sorti qu'il a commencé à pleuvoir**
ils vont peut-être téléphoner plus tard

b) *when a verb of saying follows direct speech:*

'si tu veux,' a répondu Marie
'if you want,' Marie replied

'attention!' a-t-elle crié
'watch out!' she shouted

'j'espère que non,' dit-il
'I hope not,' he said

'répondez!' ordonna-t-il
'answer!' he ordered

B NEGATIVE EXPRESSIONS

1 Main negative words

a)
ne ... pas	*not*
ne ... point	*not (literary)*
ne ... plus	*no more/longer, not ... any more*
ne ... jamais	*never*
ne ... rien	*nothing, not ... anything*
ne ... guère	*hardly*

b)
ne ... personne	*nobody, no one, not ... anyone*
ne ... que	*only*
ne ... ni (ni ... ni)	*neither ... nor*

ne ... aucun(e) — *no, not any, none*
ne ... nul(le) — *no*
ne ... nulle part — *nowhere, not ... anywhere*

Note:

i) ne becomes n' before a vowel or a silent h.

ii) aucun and nul, like other adjectives and pronouns, agree with the word they refer to; they are used only in the singular.

2 Position of negative expressions

a) *with simple tenses and with the imperative*

Negative words enclose the verb: ne comes before the verb, and the second part of the negative expression comes after the verb:

je ne la connais pas
I don't know her

n'insistez pas!
don't insist!

je n'ai plus d'argent
I haven't any money left

tu ne le sauras jamais
you'll never know

ne dis rien
don't say anything

il n'y a personne
no one's here

je n'avais que 3 euros
I only had 3 euros

il n'est nulle part
it isn't anywhere

tu n'as aucun sens de l'humour
you have no sense of humour

il n'est ni bête ni crédule
he's neither stupid nor gullible

b) *with compound tenses*

With ne ... pas and the other expressions in list 1a), the word order is: ne + auxiliary + pas + past participle:

il n'est pas revenu
he didn't come back

je n'ai plus essayé
I didn't try any more

je n'avais jamais vu Paris
I had never seen Paris

on n'a rien fait
we haven't done anything

With ne ... personne and the other expressions in list 1b), the word order is: ne + auxiliary + past participle + personne/que/ni etc:

il ne l'a dit à personne
he didn't tell anyone

tu n'en as acheté qu'un?
did you only buy one?

je n'en ai aimé aucun
I didn't like any of them

il n'est allé nulle part
he hasn't gone anywhere

c) *with the infinitive*

i) ne ... pas and the other expressions in list 1a) are placed together before the verb:

je préfère ne pas y aller
I'd rather not go

essaye de ne rien perdre
try not to lose anything

ii) ne ... personne and the other expressions in list 1b) enclose the infinitive:

il a été surpris de ne voir personne
he was surprised not to see anybody

j'ai décidé de n'en acheter aucun
I decided not to buy any of them

d) *at the beginning of a sentence*

When personne, rien, aucun and ni ... ni ... begin a sentence, they are followed by ne:

personne ne le sait
nobody knows

rien n'a changé
nothing has changed

ni Paul ni Simone ne sont venus
neither Paul nor Simone came

aucun secours n'est arrivé
no help arrived

3 Combination of negative expressions

Negative expressions can be combined:

ne ... plus jamais
ne ... plus rien
ne ... plus personne
ne ... plus ni ... ni
ne ... plus que

ne ... jamais rien
ne ... jamais personne
ne ... jamais ni ... ni
ne ... jamais que

on ne l'a plus jamais revu
we never saw him again

il n'y a plus rien
there isn't anything left

plus personne ne viendra
no one will come any more

tu ne dis jamais rien
you never say anything

je ne bois jamais que de l'eau
I only ever drink water

je ne vois jamais personne
I never see anybody

je ne pardonnerai jamais ni n'oublierai
I will never forgive nor forget

4 Negative expressions without a verb

a) pas

pas *(not)* is the most common of all negatives; it is frequently used without a verb:

tu l'aimes? – pas beaucoup
do you like it? – not much

ah non, pas lui!
oh no, not him!

non merci, pas pour moi
no thanks, not for me

un roman pas très long
not a very long novel

lui, il viendra, mais pas moi
he will come, but I won't

j'aime ça; pas toi?
I like that; don't you?

b) ne

ne is not used when there is no verb:

qui a crié? – personne
who shouted? – nobody

jamais de la vie!
not on your life!

rien! je ne veux rien!
nothing! I want nothing!

rien du tout
nothing at all

c) non

non *(no)* is always used without a verb:

tu aimes la natation? – non, pas du tout
do you like swimming? – no, not at all

tu viens, oui ou non? – je crois que non
are you coming, yes or no? – I don't think so

Note that non plus means 'neither':

je ne le crois pas – moi non plus
I don't believe him – neither do I

je n'ai rien mangé – nous non plus
I haven't eaten anything – neither have we

C DIRECT AND INDIRECT QUESTIONS

1 Direct questions

There are three ways of forming direct questions in French:

a) *subject + verb (+ question word)*

The word order remains the same as in statements (subject + verb) but the intonation changes: the voice is raised at the end of the sentence. This is by far the most common question form in conversational French:

tu l'as acheté où?
where did you buy it?

je peux téléphoner d'ici?
can I phone from here?

vous prendrez quel train?
which train will you take?

tu me fais confiance?
do you trust me?

c'était comment?
what was it like?

la gare est près d'ici?
is the station near here?

le train part à quelle heure?
what time does the train leave?

cette robe me va?
does this dress suit me?

b) (*question word*) + est-ce que + *subject* + *verb*

This question form is also very common in conversation:

qu'est-ce que tu as?   **est-ce qu'il est là?**
what's the matter with you?   *is he in?*

est-ce que ton ami s'est amusé?
did your friend have a good time?

où est-ce que vous avez mal?
where does it hurt?

c) *inversion*

This question form is the most formal of the three, and the least commonly used in conversation:

i) If the subject is a pronoun, the word order is as follows:

(question word) + verb + hyphen + subject

où allez-vous?   **voulez-vous commander?**
where are you going?   *do you wish to order?*

quand est-il arrivé?   **avez-vous bien dormi?**
when did he arrive?   *did you sleep well?*

ii) If the subject is a noun, a pronoun referring to the noun is inserted after the verb, and linked to it with a hyphen:

(question word) + noun subject + verb + hyphen + pronoun

où ton père travaillait-il?   **Nicole en veut-elle?**
where did your father work?   *does Nicole want any?*

iii) -t- is inserted before il and elle when the verb ends in a vowel:

comment va-t-il voyager?   **aime-t-elle le café?**
how will he travel?   *does she like coffee?*

pourquoi a-t-il refusé?   **Marie viendra-t-elle?**
why did he refuse?   *will Marie be coming?*

Note that when a question word is used, modern French will often just invert the verb and the noun subject, without adding a pronoun; no hyphen is then necessary:

où travaille ton père?
where does your father work?

2 Indirect questions

a) *Definition*

Indirect questions follow a verb and are introduced by an interrogative word, eg:

ask him when he will arrive   *I don't know why he did it*

b) *Word order*

i) The word order is usually the same as in statements: question word + subject + verb:

je ne sais pas s'il voudra   **dis-moi où tu l'as mis**
I don't know if he'll want to   *tell me where you put it*

il n'a pas dit quand il appellerait
he didn't say when he would phone

ii) If the subject is a noun, the verb and subject are sometimes inverted:

demande-leur où est le camping
ask them where the campsite is

But: **je ne comprends pas comment l'accident s'est produit**
I don't understand how the accident happened

il ne savait pas pourquoi elle avait l'air triste
he didn't know why she looked sad

3 Translation of English question tags

Examples of question tags are: isn't it? aren't you? doesn't he? won't they? haven't you? is it? did you? and so on. Question tags are not used in French as often as they are in English. Some of them can, however, be translated in the following ways:

a) n'est-ce pas?

n'est-ce pas? is used at the end of a sentence when confirmation of a statement is expected:

c'était très intéressant, n'est-ce pas?
it was very interesting, wasn't it?

tu voudrais partir en vacances, n'est-ce pas?
you'd like to go on holiday, wouldn't you?

vous n'arriverez pas trop tard, n'est-ce pas?
you won't be arriving too late, will you?

b) hein? *and* non?

In conversation hein? and non? are often used after affirmative statements instead of n'est-ce pas:

il fait beau, hein?   **il est amusant, non?**
the weather's nice, isn't it?   *he's funny, isn't he?*

D ANSWERS ('YES' AND 'NO')

1 OUI, SI and NON

a) oui and si mean 'yes' and are equivalent to longer affirmative answers such as 'yes, it is', 'yes, I will', 'yes, he has' etc:

tu m'écriras? – oui, bien sûr!
will you write to me? – (yes) of course I will

b) non means 'no' and is equivalent to longer negative answers such as 'no, it isn't', 'no, I didn't' etc:

c'était bien? – non, on s'est ennuyé
was it good? – no, it wasn't, we were bored

2 OUI or SI?

oui and si both mean 'yes', but oui is used to answer an affirmative question, and si to contradict a negative question:

cette place est libre? – oui
is this seat free? – yes (it is)

tu n'aimes pas lire? – si, bien sûr!
don't you like reading? – yes, of course (I do)

13 TRANSLATION PROBLEMS

A GENERAL TRANSLATION PROBLEMS

1 French words not translated in English

Some French words are not translated in English, particularly:

a) *Articles*

Definite and indefinite articles are not always translated (see p B3-5):

dans la société moderne
in modern society

les gens en ont assez!
people have had enough!

ah non! encore du riz! je déteste le riz!
oh no! rice again! I hate rice!

b) **que**

que meaning 'that' as a conjunction (see p B58) or 'that'/'which'/'whom' as a relative pronoun (see p B22) cannot be omitted in French:

j'espère que tu vas mieux
I hope you're better

elle pense que c'est vrai
she thinks it's true

celui que j'ai vu
the one I saw

c'est un pays que j'aime
it's a country I like

c) *Prepositions*

Some French verbs are followed by a preposition (+ indirect object) when their English equivalent takes a direct object without a preposition (see p B53):

elle a téléphoné au médecin
she phoned the doctor

tu l'as dit à ton père?
did you tell your father?

d) **le**

When le *(it)* is used in an impersonal sense (see p B18), it is not translated:

oui, je le sais
yes, I know

dis-le-lui
tell him

2 English words not translated in French

Some English words are not translated in French, for example:

a) *Prepositions*

i) with verbs which take an indirect object in English, but a direct object in French (see p B53):

tu l'as payé combien?
how much did you pay for it?

écoutez cette chanson
listen to this song

ii) in certain expressions (see p B61):

je viendrai te voir lundi soir
I'll come and see you on Monday night

b) *'can'*

'can' + verb of hearing or seeing (see pp B39-40):

je ne vois rien!
I can't see anything!

tu entends la musique?
can you hear the music?

3 Other differences

a) *English phrasal verbs*

Phrasal verbs are verbs which, when followed by a preposition, take on a different meaning, eg 'to give up', 'to walk out'. They do not exist in French and are translated by simple verbs or by expressions:

to give up
abandonner

to run away
s'enfuir

to run across
traverser en courant

b) *English possessive adjectives*

English possessive adjectives (my, your etc) are translated by the French definite article (le/la/les) when parts of the body are mentioned (see p B21):

brush your teeth
brosse-toi les dents

he hurt his foot
il s'est fait mal au pied

c) *'from'*

'from' is translated by à with verbs referring to taking something away (see p B53):

he hid it from his parents
il l'a caché à ses parents

borrow some from your dad
empruntes-en à ton père

B SPECIFIC TRANSLATION PROBLEMS

1 Words ending in -ing

The English verbal form ending in **-ing** is translated in a number of ways in French:

a) *by the appropriate French tense* (see p B30):

he's speaking (present tense)	**il parle**
he was speaking (imperfect)	**il parlait**
he will be speaking (future)	**il parlera**
he has been speaking (perfect)	**il a parlé**
he had been speaking (pluperfect)	**il avait parlé**
he would be speaking (conditional)	**il parlerait**

b) *by a French present participle* (see p B37)

i) as an adjective:

un livre amusant
a funny book

c'est effrayant
it's frightening

ii) as a verb, with en (while/on/by doing something; see p B38):

'ça ne fait rien', dit-il en souriant
'it doesn't matter', he said smiling

j'ai vu mes copains en sortant du lycée
I saw my friends when I was coming out of school

Note, however, that en + present participle cannot be used when the two verbs have different subjects, eg:

I saw my brother coming out of school
j'ai vu mon frère sortir du lycée/qui sortait du lycée

c) *by a present infinitive* (see pp B35-7):

i) after a preposition:

au lieu de rire
instead of laughing

avant de traverser
before crossing

ii) after verbs of perception:

je l'ai entendu appeler
I heard him calling

je l'ai vue entrer
I saw her going in

iii) after verbs of liking and disliking:

j'adore faire du camping
I love camping

tu aimes lire?
do you like reading?

iv) after verbs followed by à or de:

tu passes tout ton temps à ne rien faire
you spend all your time doing nothing

il a commencé à neiger
it started snowing

continuez à travailler
go on working

tu as envie de sortir?
do you feel like going out?

il doit finir de manger
he must finish eating

v) when an English verb in **-ing** is the subject of another verb:

attendre serait inutile
waiting would be pointless

écrire est une corvée!
writing is a real chore!

vi) when an English verb in **-ing** follows 'is' or 'was' etc:

mon passe-temps favori, c'est de lire
my favourite pastime is reading

d) *by a perfect infinitive* (see p B37)

i) after après *(after)*:

j'ai pris une douche après avoir nettoyé ma chambre
I had a shower after cleaning my room

ii) after certain verbs:

regretter	remercier de	se souvenir de
to regret	*to thank for*	*to remember*

j'ai regretté de leur en avoir parlé
I regretted speaking to them about it

il m'a remercié d'être allé le chercher
he thanked me for going to pick him up

e) *by a noun*

particularly when referring to sports, activities, hobbies etc:

le ski	la natation	l'équitation
skiing	*swimming*	*horse-riding*
la voile	le patinage	le canoë
sailing	*skating*	*canoeing*
la lecture	la planche à voile	la cuisine
reading	*windsurfing*	*cooking*
la boxe	la lutte	la marche à pied
boxing	*wrestling*	*walking*

2 IT IS (IT'S)

'it is' (it's) can be translated in three ways in French:

a) il *or* elle (see p B18)

il or elle are used with the verb être to translate 'it is', 'it was' etc (+ adjective) when referring to a particular masculine or feminine noun (a thing, a place etc):

merci de ta carte; elle était très amusante
thanks for your card; it was very funny

regarde ce blouson; il n'est vraiment pas cher
look at this jacket; it really isn't that expensive

b) ce (see p B15)

ce (c' before a vowel) is used with the verb être to translate 'it is', 'it was' etc in two cases:

i) If être is followed by a word which is not an adjective on its own, ie by a noun, a pronoun, an expression of place etc:

c'était ta voix	**c'est une grande maison**
it was your voice	*it's a big house*
c'est moi! c'est Claude!	**c'est le tien?**
it's me! it's Claude!	*is it yours?*
c'est en France que tu vas?	**c'est pour lundi**
is it France you're going to?	*it's for Monday*

ii) If être is followed by an adjective which refers to something previously mentioned, such as an idea, an event or a fact, but not to a specific noun:

l'homme n'ira jamais sur Saturne; ce n'est pas possible
Man will never go to Saturn; it's not possible

j'ai passé mes vacances en Italie; c'était formidable!
I spent my holidays in Italy; it was great!

oh, je m'excuse! – ce n'est pas grave
oh, I'm sorry! – it's all right

c) il (see pp B29-30)

il is used to translate 'it is', 'it was' etc in three cases:

i) With être followed by an adjective + de or que, ie referring to something that follows, but not to a specific noun:

il est impossible de connaître l'avenir
it's impossible to know the future

il est évident que tu ne me crois pas
it's obvious you don't believe me

ii) To describe the weather (see p B29):

il y a du vent	**il faisait très froid**
it's windy	*it was very cold*

iii) With être to tell the time and in phrases relating to the time of day, or in such expressions as il est temps de (it's time to):

il est deux heures du matin	**il est tard!**
it's two in the morning	*it's late!*

il est temps de partir
it's time to go

Note that with other expressions of time, c'est is used:

c'est lundi ou mardi aujourd'hui?	**c'était l'été**
is it Monday or Tuesday today?	*it was summer*

3 TO BE

Although 'to be' is usually translated by être, it can also be translated in the following ways:

a) avoir

i) avoir is used instead of être in many set expressions:

avoir faim/soif	*to be hungry/thirsty*
avoir chaud/froid	*to be warm/cold*
avoir peur/honte	*to be afraid/ashamed*
avoir tort/raison	*to be wrong/right*

ii) avoir is also used for age:

quel âge as-tu?	**j'ai vingt-cinq ans**
how old are you?	*I'm twenty-five*

b) aller

aller is used for describing health:

je vais mieux	**tout le monde va bien**
I am/feel better	*everyone's fine*

c) faire

faire is used in many expressions to describe the weather (see p B29):

il fait beau	**il fera chaud**
the weather's nice	*it will be hot*

Note that il y a can also be used to describe the weather, but only before du/de la/des:

il y a du vent/des nuages/de la tempête
it's windy/cloudy/stormy

d) *untranslated*

'to be' is not translated when it is the first part of an English continuous tense; instead, the appropriate tense is used in French (see p B30):

I'm having a bath	*he was driving slowly*
je prends un bain	**il conduisait lentement**

4 ANY

'any' can be translated in three different ways:

a) du/de la/des *or* de (see p B5)

The partitive article is used with a noun in negative and interrogative sentences:

il ne mange jamais de viande	**tu veux du pain?**
he never eats meat	*do you want any bread?*

b) en (see pp B19-20)

en is used to translate 'any' when it occurs without a noun in negative and interrogative sentences:

je n'en ai pas
I haven't got any

il en reste?
is there any left?

c) **n'importe quel(le)/quel(les) or tout(e)/tou(te)s**

these are used to translate 'any' (and 'every') when they mean 'no matter which':

il pourrait arriver à n'importe quel moment
he could arrive any time

prends n'importe quelle couleur, je les aime toutes
take any colour, I like them all

5 ANYONE, ANYTHING, ANYWHERE

Like 'any', these can be translated in different ways:

a) *in interrogative sentences:*

il y a quelqu'un?
is anyone in?

tu l'as vu quelque part?
did you see it anywhere?

il a dit quelque chose?
did he say anything?

b) *in negative sentences:*

il n'y a personne
there isn't anyone

je ne le vois nulle part
I can't see it anywhere

je n'ai rien fait
I didn't do anything

c) *in the sense of 'any' (and 'every'), 'no matter which':*

n'importe qui peut le faire
anyone can do that

il croit n'importe quoi
he believes anything

j'irai n'importe où
I'll go anywhere

n'importe quand
anytime

6 YOU, YOUR, YOURS, YOURSELF

French has two separate sets of words to translate 'you', 'your', 'yours', 'yourself':

- **tu, te (t'), toi, ton/ta/tes, le tien etc**
- **vous, votre/vos, le vôtre etc**

For their respective meanings and uses, see pp B18, B20-1.

a) **tu** *etc*

tu, te, ton etc correspond to the tu form of the verb (second person singular) and are used when speaking to one person you know well (a friend, a relative) or to someone younger. They represent the familiar form of address:

si tu viens au concert avec ton copain, je t'achète deux places; une pour toi et une pour lui
if you're coming to the concert with your boyfriend, I'll get you two tickets; one for you and one for him

b) **vous** *etc*

vous, vos etc correspond to the vous form of the verb (second person plural) and are used:

i) when speaking to more than one person:

dépêchez-vous, les gars! Vous allez manquer le train
hurry up, boys! You'll miss the train

ii) when speaking to one person you do not know well or to someone older. They represent the formal or polite form of address:

je regrette, Monsieur, mais vous ne pouvez pas garder votre chien avec vous dans ce restaurant
I'm sorry, sir, but you can't keep your dog with you in this restaurant

c) when speaking or writing to one person, you must not mix words from both sets, but decide whether you are being formal or familiar, and use the same form of address throughout:

**Cher Michel,
Merci pour ta lettre. Comment vas-tu? ...**
*Dear Michel,
Thanks for your letter. How are you? ...*

**Monsieur,
Pourriez-vous me réserver une chambre dans votre hôtel pour le 8 juin?**
*Dear Sir,
Could you book a room for me in your hotel for 8th June?*

vous etc and tu etc can only be used together when vous is plural (ie when it refers to more than one person):

tu sais, Jean, toi et ta sœur, vous vous ressemblez
you know, Jean, you and your sister look like each other

7 Noun phrases

A noun phrase is a combination of two nouns used together to name things or people. In English, the first of these nouns is used to describe the second one, eg 'a love story'. In French, however, the position of the two nouns is reversed, so that the describing noun comes second and is linked to the first one by the preposition de (or d'):

une histoire d'amour
a love story

une feuille d'impôts
a tax form

un magasin de disques
a record shop

un acteur de cinéma
a film actor

un arrêt d'autobus
a bus stop

un film d'aventure
an adventure film

un coup de soleil
sunstroke

une boule de neige
a snowball

un roman de science-fiction
a science-fiction novel

un match de football
a football match

le château d'Édimbourg
Edinburgh castle

un conte de fées
a fairy tale

un joueur de rugby
a rugby player

un employé de bureau
an office worker

Note that when the describing noun refers to a type of material, the preposition en is often used instead of de:

un pull en laine
a woollen jumper

un pantalon en cuir
leather trousers

une bague en or
a gold ring

un sac en plastique
a plastic bag

8 Possession

In English, possession is often expressed by using a noun phrase and tagging 's at the end of the first word, eg:

my friend's cat

This is translated in French by: object + de + possessor:

le chat de mon ami

Note the use of the article le/la/les:

le fiancé de ma sœur
my sister's fiancé

les amis de Claire
Claire's friends

les événements de la semaine dernière
last week's events

When 's is used to refer to someone's house or shop etc, it is translated by the preposition chez:

je téléphone de chez Paul
I'm telephoning from Paul's (house)

chez le dentiste
at/to the dentist's

FRANÇAIS–ANGLAIS

FRENCH–ENGLISH

A, a [ɑ] NM (lettre) A, a; **connaître un sujet de A (jusqu')à Z** to know a subject inside out or from A to Z or from beginning to end; **prouver qch par A plus B** to prove sth in a logical or scientific fashion

A [a]

to **1, 3, 5, 9, 11, 13, 14**	▪ at **1–3, 8, 10**	▪ in **2, 9** ▪ by **4, 8** ▪ from **5** ▪ with **6, 8** ▪ for **7, 10, 11** ▪ on **8, 9** ▪ + infinitif **12**

PRÉP SEE GRAMMAR B54 (contracts with the article **le** into **au**, with the article **les** into **aux**) **1** (direction) **il est venu à moi** he came (up) to me; **revenir à la surface** to come back (up) to the surface, to resurface; **aller à l'église/au collège/au cinéma/au marché** to go to church/to school/to the cinema/to the market; **se mettre** ou **s'asseoir au piano** to sit down at the piano; **monter au premier étage** to go up to the first floor; **partir à la recherche de ses ancêtres** to begin a search for one's ancestors; **de Paris à Lyon** from Paris to Lyons; **se rendre au Japon/aux Antilles/à la Guadeloupe/à Terre-Neuve** to travel to Japan/to the West Indies/to Guadeloupe/to Newfoundland; **au lit!** off to bed!; **au feu!** fire!; **au voleur!** stop thief!; **courir à sa perte** to head for disaster; **(de) vingt à trente personnes** between twenty and thirty people

2 (position) **au coin de la rue** at the corner of the street, at the street corner; **vivre à Montpellier/à la campagne** to live in Montpellier/in the country; **à l'horizon** on the horizon; **à la page deux** on page two; **à l'ombre** in the shade; **au grenier** in the attic; **à la maison** at home; **au théâtre** at the theatre; **au Canada** in Canada; **aux États-Unis** in the United States; **à la Jamaïque** in Jamaica; **à Cuba** in Cuba; **à Paris** in Paris; **se tenir à la fenêtre** to stand at the window; **à 2 kilomètres d'ici** 2 kilometres (away) from here; **avoir mal aux dents/yeux/pieds/au ventre** to have toothache/sore eyes/sore feet/stomach ache; **à la télévision/à la radio** on (the) television/on the radio; **le sourire aux lèvres** with a smile on his/her/etc lips; **un livre à la main** a book in his/her/etc hand; **au fond** basically, fundamentally; **au fond, il n'est pas méchant** deep down, he's not a bad person

3 (dans le temps) **du matin au soir** from morning to or till night; **remettre une affaire à plus tard** to put something off (until later), to postpone something; **à jamais** for ever; **à demain!/mardi!** see you tomorrow!/on Tuesday!; **du lundi au vendredi** from Monday to Friday, Am Monday to or thru Friday; **je serai chez elle de lundi à vendredi** I'll be at her house from Monday to Friday; **il sera là à 8 heures/à la tombée de la nuit/au petit matin** he'll be there at 8 o'clock/at nightfall/in the early hours; **à temps** on time; **à un certain moment** at some moment; **au prin-**

temps in (the) spring; **le 2 au soir** on the evening of the 2nd; **à Noël** at Christmas; **au revoir** goodbye (for now); **à ces mots** at these words; **au premier mot** at the first word; **à première vue** on first sight; **à mon arrivée** on my arrival; **à deux heures** at two o'clock; **à toute heure du jour et de la nuit** at all hours of the day and night; **au vingtième siècle** in the twentieth century; **à l'avenir** in (the) future; **à l'aube** at dawn

4 (distribution) **faire du 10 litres aux 100 (km)** to do 100 kilometres on 10 litres; **faire du 90 km à l'heure** to do 90 km an or per hour; **payé au mois/au forfait** paid monthly or by the month/at a fixed rate; **travailler à la pièce** to do piecework; **vendre des oranges à la pièce** to sell oranges separately or individually; **vendre des huîtres à la douzaine** to sell oysters by the dozen; **entrer deux à deux** to come in two by two; **se battre d'homme à homme** to fight man to man; Tennis **quinze à** fifteen all; **monter l'escalier quatre à quatre** to go upstairs four (steps) at a time; **peu à peu, petit à petit** little by little, gradually

5 (avec complément d'objet indirect) **attacher un cheval à un arbre** to tie a horse to a tree; **aspirer au calme** to long for peace and quiet; **échapper à qch** to escape from sth; Fig **avoir un fil à la patte** to be tied down; **attacher de l'importance à qch** to attach importance to sth; **s'adresser à qn** to address sb, to speak to sb; **lettre ouverte à ...** open letter to ...; **donner qch à qn** to give sth to sb, to give sb sth; **parler à qn** to speak to sb; **dire qch à qn** to say sth to sb, to tell sb sth; **penser à qn/qch** to think of or about sb/sth; **s'habituer à qch** to become used to sth; **à quoi cela sert-il?** what's that used for?; (quel intérêt?) what's the good of that?; **survivre à qn/qch** to survive or outlive sb/sth; **prendre qn à témoin** to call sb to witness or as a witness; **s'opposer à qch** to oppose sth; **résister à qn/qch** to resist sb/sth; **cacher/voler qch à qn** to hide/steal sth from sb; **prendre qch à qn** to take sth from sb; **boire à (même) la bouteille** to drink (straight) from the bottle; **faire faire qch à qn** to make sb do sth, to get sb to do sth; **faire savoir qch à qn** to tell sb about sth, to inform sb of sth; **laisser croire à qn que ...** to let sb think or believe that ...; **c'est à vous de décider** it's for you or up to you to decide; **c'est à vous** (de jouer etc) it's your turn; Radio **à vous** over (to you); **la parole est à M. Dupont** Mr Dupont will now speak; **c'est aimable à vous d'être venu** it's kind or good of you to have come

6 (possession, attributs etc) **ce livre est à Paul** this book is Paul's, this is Paul's book, this book belongs to Paul; **un ami à moi** a friend of mine; Fam **la sœur à Anne** Anne's sister; **enfant aux yeux bleus** child with blue eyes, blue-eyed child; **homme à barbe noire** man with a black beard; **une expression**

bien à Anne a typically Anne expression; **chambre à deux lits** room with twin beds; **voiture à toit ouvrant** car with a sunroof

7 (destination, usage) for; **affaire à suivre** something worth watching or keeping an eye on; **c'est à voir** it remains to be seen; **bon à jeter** fit for the dustbin; **une machine à coudre** a sewing machine; **j'ai une veste à nettoyer** I have a jacket to be cleaned; (c'est moi qui vais le faire) I have a jacket to clean; **j'ai une lettre à écrire** I have a letter to write; **je voudrais quelque chose à boire** I'd like something to drink; **maison à vendre** house for sale; **tasse à thé** teacup; **brosse à dents** toothbrush; **moulin à vent** windmill; **moulin à café** coffee grinder; **pompe à vélo** bicycle pump; **poudre à récurer** scouring powder; **pompe à eau** water pump SEE GRAMMAR B36

8 (manière) **à pied** on foot; **écrire à la machine** to type; **montre à quartz** quartz watch; **ça fonctionne à l'électricité** it runs on electricity; **à la main** by hand; **fait à la main** handmade; **peint à la main** hand-painted; **jouer un air au violon** to play a tune on the violin; **arriver à l'improviste** to arrive unexpectedly; **à toute allure** at top speed; **à ce rythme, nous y sommes encore demain** the way we're going or at this rate, we'll still be at it tomorrow; **recevoir qn à bras ouverts** to receive sb with open arms; **cuisine à l'huile** cooking with oil; **à l'espagnole** in the Spanish manner or way; **un repas à l'anglaise** a typical(ly) English meal; Fam **encore une histoire à la Marie** another one of Marie's typical stories; **manger à sa faim** to eat one's fill; (autant que possible) to eat as much as one can; **faire qch à sa manière** ou **façon** to do sth (in) one's own way; **nous l'avons fait à trois** there were three of us doing it; **se mettre à plusieurs pour faire qch** to team up or to get together with several people to do sth; Sport **rugby à quinze/treize** Rugby Union/League

9 **à mon avis** in my opinion; **à ce qu'il dit** according to him or to what he says, from what he says; **au reste** moreover, besides; **à cette condition** on this condition; **cela se fera à une seule condition** that will be done on one condition; **à la demande générale** by popular request; **à ma grande surprise** to my great surprise

10 (expression du prix) **vendre qch à dix euros le kilo** to sell sth for or at ten euros a kilo; **à quel prix vendez-vous cela?** how much are you asking for that?; **un timbre à deux euros** a two-euro stamp; **à ce prix, on ne peut pas se plaindre** at that price, you can't complain

11 (après adjectif) **indispensable à qn/qch** indispensable or essential to sb/for sth; **parallèle à** parallel to; **hostile à** hostile to; **utile à** useful for

12 (avec le verbe à l'infinitif) **penser à faire qch** (envisager) to think of doing sth; (se souvenir) to remember to do sth; **songer à faire**

qch to dream of or about doing sth; **consentir à faire qch** to consent or agree to do sth; **encourager qn à faire qch** to encourage sb to do sth; **c'est à refaire** it will have to be done again; **il me reste à faire une dissertation de philo** I still have to do a philosophy essay; **il ne me reste qu'à vous remercier** it only remains for me to thank you; **commencer à faire qch** to begin to do sth, to start doing sth; **apprendre à lire** to learn to read SEE GRAMMAR B33; B36

13 (conséquence) **laid à faire peur** frightfully ugly; **s'ennuyer à mourir** to be bored to death; **c'était à mourir de rire** it was hilarious; **jolie à croquer** pretty as a picture; **il est à croquer dans son petit costume de marin** he looks good enough to eat in his little sailor suit; **c'est à se demander si elle sait de quoi elle parle** you begin to wonder if she knows what she's talking about; **geler à pierre fendre** to freeze hard; **à quoi bon le lui dire?** what's the good or use of telling him/her?

14 je suis prêt à vous écouter I'm willing to listen to you; **facile à comprendre** easy to understand; **il est homme à se défendre** he's the kind of man who will hit back; **elle est à plaindre** she is or deserves to be pitied; **être le seul à faire qch** to be the only one to do sth; **le troisième à arriver** the third to arrive **15 à partager les mêmes périls, ils ont appris à s'estimer** by or through sharing the same dangers, they gained respect for each other; **à rouler trop vite, tu vas finir par avoir un accident** if you go on driving too fast, you're going to end up having an accident; **à en juger par ...** judging by ..., to judge by ...; **à les en croire** according to them, if we are to believe them

AA [ɑɑ] NF Banque, Bourse (notation) AA AA (rating), double-A rating

AAA [ɑɑɑ] NF Banque, Bourse (notation) A. AAA (rating), triple-A rating

A3 [atrwa] NM A3

A4 [akatr] NM A4

abaissant [abɛsɑ̃] ADJ degrading

abaisse [abɛs] NF Culin thinly rolled pastry

abaisse-langue NM INV Méd spatula, tongue depressor

abaissement [abɛsmɑ̃] NM **1** (d'un store etc) lowering, pulling down; (du niveau d'un fleuve etc) lowering **2** (chute) fall; (du sol, d'un bâtiment) subsidence, sinking; (de la température, des prix) fall, drop; (des prix) reduction **3** Litt (humiliation) abasement, humiliation

abaisser [abese] VT **1** to lower; (store) to pull down; (pont-levis) to let down; **a. son regard** to look down; **a. un mur** to pull down a wall **2** (prix) to lower; (prix, coût, pression etc) to reduce **3** Litt (humilier) to lower, to abase **4** Math **a. une perpendiculaire à une ligne** to drop a perpendicular to a line; **a. le chiffre des dizaines** (dans une division) to bring down the figure in the tens column **5** Culin **a. une pâte** to roll out pastry
  VPR **s'abaisser 1** to fall away, to dip, to slope down, to go down; (s'effondrer) to subside; **la fenêtre s'abaisse quand on appuie sur ce bouton** the window slides down when you press this button **2** (chuter) to drop, to fall **3** **s'a. jusqu'à faire qch** (consentir) to stoop so low as to do sth; (d'une personne orgueilleuse) to condescend to do sth; **s'a. à des compromissions** to stoop to compromise **4** **s'a. devant Dieu** to humble oneself before God

abaisseur [abɛsœr] NM Anat depressor
  ADJ Élec (transformateur) step-down

abandon [abɑ̃dɔ̃] NM **1** (de biens) surrender; (de droits) renunciation, surrender; Fin **a. de**

créances debt forgiveness; **faire a. de qch à qn** to make over or relinquish or surrender sth to sb
  2 Sport (au cours d'une épreuve) retirement, withdrawal; (avant la course) withdrawal **3** Jur (d'enfants) desertion, abandonment; (de fonction) desertion, dereliction; **a. du domicile conjugal** desertion **4** (état) neglect; **finir sa vie dans l'a.** to end one's life alone; **à l'a.** (jardin) (completely) neglected; Naut adrift, derelict **5** (détente) lack of restraint; **parler avec un complet a.** to speak quite freely or without restraint; **dans un moment d'a.** in a moment of abandon or freedom **6** Ordinat abort **7** Bourse **a. de l'option, a. de prime** relinquishment or abandonment of the option

abandonné, -ée [abɑ̃dɔne] ADJ (personne) abandoned, deserted; (air) untidy; **navire a. en mer** derelict; **maison abandonnée** deserted house

abandonner [abɑ̃dɔne] VT **1** (personne) to desert, to abandon, Litt to forsake; Naut **a. un homme** to maroon a man; Naut **a. le bâtiment** to abandon ship; Aviat **a. le bord** ou **un avion en vol** to bale out; Mil **a. son poste** to desert one's post
  2 (délaisser) (voiture) to abandon; (village) to abandon, to desert; **mes forces m'abandonnent** my strength is failing me **3** (renoncer à) (quelque chose) to surrender, to renounce, to give up; **a. la course** to abandon or withdraw from the race; **a. un projet** to abandon a project; **il a abandonné les études à quatorze ans** he dropped out (of school) when he was fourteen; **a. la partie** to throw in one's hand; **a. sa part d'héritage (à sa sœur)** to forgo one's share of an inheritance (in favour of one's sister); **a. ses prétentions** to renounce or surrender one's claims **4** Ordinat to abort **5** Bourse **a. l'option** ou **la prime** to relinquish or abandon or surrender the option
  VI to give up; Sport to give up, to retire; Fam **c'est trop dur, j'abandonne** it's too hard, I give up
  VPR **s'abandonner 1** (se laisser aller) to let oneself go, Fml to be unconstrained; **s'a. au chagrin** to give oneself up to or to abandon oneself to grief; **s'a. au sommeil** to abandon oneself to sleep **2** (s'en remettre à) **s'a. à son sort** to resign oneself to one's fate **3** (se confier) to open up

abaque [abak] NM **1** (boulier) abacus, counting frame **2** Math chart, graph **3** Archit abacus

abasourdir [abazurdir] VT to deafen; Fig to astound, to stun; Fig **nous sommes restés abasourdis par la nouvelle** we were flabbergasted or astounded or stunned by the news

abasourdissant [abazurdisɑ̃] ADJ (bruit) deafening; Fig (nouvelle) stunning, astounding

abasourdissement [abazurdismɑ̃] NM bewilderment, stupefaction

abat [aba] NM **1** Arch slaughter **2** **pluie d'a.** sudden shower
  NMPL **abats** offal, Am variety meat; (de volaille) giblets

abâtardi [abatardi] ADJ degenerate

abâtardir [abatardir] VT (espèce) to cause to degenerate; (qualité) to debase
  VPR **s'abâtardir** to degenerate, to deteriorate

abâtardissement [abatardismɑ̃] NM degeneracy

abat-jour NM INV lampshade; Fig **mettre la main en a.** to shade one's eyes with one's hand

abattage [abataʒ] NM **1** (de bâtiments) knocking down, pulling down; (d'arbres etc) felling, cutting down, clearing; Min cutting, working; Min **face d'a.** working face; Naut **a. en carène** careening; **avoir de l'a.** Vieilli to be full of energy; Fig (d'un acteur, d'un politicien etc) to have charisma **2** (d'animal) slaughtering, killing; **grand a. de gibier** heavy bag of game **3** Com **vente à l'a.** sale at knock-down prices

abattant [abatɑ̃] ADJ **siège a.** tip-up seat
  NM (d'un comptoir, d'une table) flap

abattement [abatmɑ̃] NM **1** (physique) exhaustion, Fml prostration **2** (moral) despondency, dejection, depression, low spirits **3** Fin (d'impôts) **a.** fiscal tax allowance; **a. forfaitaire** fixed-rate rebate

> Il faut noter que le nom anglais **abatement** est un faux ami. Il signifie **apaisement**.

abatteur, -euse [abatœr, -øz] N **1 a. de besogne** hard worker, Fam slogger **2** (d'arbres) feller **3** (d'animaux) slaughterer

abattis [abati] NM **1** (des arbres) felling, clearing **2** Région heap of felled trees; **a. de maisons** heap of fallen houses
  NMPL **1** Culin giblets **2** Arg limbs, hands and feet; **si tu viens te battre avec moi, commence par numéroter tes a.!** if you're going to pick a fight with me, you can say your prayers right now!

abattoir [abatwar] NM slaughterhouse, abattoir; Fig **envoyer des hommes à l'a.** to send men to the slaughter or to be slaughtered or butchered

abattre [abatr] (conj like **battre**) VT **1** (faire tomber) to knock down, to throw down, to pull down; (régime) to overthrow; **a. son rival** to floor or fell one's opponent, to knock down one's opponent; **a. une maison/un mur** to pull or knock down a house/a wall; **a. de la besogne** to get through a lot of work **2** (arbres) to fell, to cut down, to clear; **a. du minerai** to break down or to stope ore **3** (tuer) (personne, cochon, bœuf) to slaughter, to kill; (animal malade ou dangereux) to destroy; Arg (personne) to bump off; **a. un avion** to bring down or shoot down an aircraft; **c'est un homme à a.** this man is on the hit-list **4** (poussière, vent) to lay; Prov **petite pluie abat grand vent** a soft answer will turn away wrath **5** (du vent) (arbre) to blow down; (blé) to flatten; Naut **a. navire en carène** to careen a ship **6** Fig (fatiguer) (de la chaleur) to drain of energy; (d'une maladie) to lay low **7** (démoraliser) to dishearten, to depress; **ne vous laissez pas a.!** keep your chin or spirits up!; **cette nouvelle l'a profondément abattu** this news has really crushed or demoralized him **8** Cartes **a. ses cartes** ou **son jeu** to lay one's cards on the table, to lay down one's hand; Fig to lay one's cards on the table **9** Naut to pay off
  VPR **s'abattre 1** (tomber) to fall, to crash down, to collapse; **le pilier s'abattit** the pillar came crashing down **2 s'a. sur qch** to pounce on sth; (d'un oiseau) to swoop down on(to) sth; **les précipitations qui se sont abattues sur la région** the torrential rain which has been falling on the region; **les injures n'ont pas cessé de s'a. sur l'orateur** insults rained down constantly on the speaker; **le malheur s'abattra sur toi et ta descendance** misfortune will descend upon you and your offspring!

abattu [abaty] ADJ dejected, dispirited, low-spirited; **a. par la chaleur** limp with the heat;

a. par l'échec depressed *or* demoralized by the failure; **visage a.** drawn face
NM fusil à l'a. uncocked rifle

abbatial, -iale, -iaux, -iales [abasjal, -jo] **ADJ terres abbatiales** abbey lands; **église abbatiale** abbey (church)
NF abbatiale abbey (church)

abbaye [abei] NF abbey

abbé [abe] NM **1** *(supérieur d'une abbaye)* abbot **2** *(prêtre)* **j'en parlerai à monsieur l'a.** I'll mention it to the priest; **(Monsieur) l'a.** Constantin Father Constantin

abbesse [abɛs] NF abbess

abc [abese] NM INV **1** *(livre pour apprendre à lire)* ABC, alphabet (book); *(livre scolaire)* primer **2** *Fig (d'une science)* rudiments; **apprendre l'a. du métier** to learn the rudiments *or* basics of the job

abcès [apsɛ] NM abscess; **a. à la gencive** gumboil; *Fig* **crever** *ou* **vider l'a.** to resolve the situation

abdication [abdikasjɔ̃] NF *(d'un monarque, d'une autorité)* abdication; *(d'une autorité, de droits)* renunciation, surrender

abdiquer [abdike] VT *(trône, autorité)* to abdicate; *(droits etc)* to renounce, to surrender
VI to abdicate

abdomen [abdɔmɛn] NM *Anat* abdomen

abdominal, -ale, -aux, -ales [abdɔminal, -o] ADJ abdominal
NMPL **abdominaux** abdominal *or* stomach muscles; **faire des abdominaux** to do exercises for the stomach muscles

abdos [abdo] NMPL *Fam* stomach muscles; **faire des a.** to do exercises for the stomach muscles

abducteur [abdyktœr] *Anat* ADJ *(muscle)* abductor
NM abductor muscle

abécédaire [abesedɛr] ADJ *Vieilli* alphabetical
NM ABC, alphabet book

abeille [abɛj] NF *(insecte)* bee; **a. mâle** drone; **a. mère** queen bee; **nid d'abeilles** bees' nest, honeycomb; *Aut* **radiateur nid d'abeilles** honeycomb radiator; *Fam* **elle ne cesse de travailler, c'est une vraie petite a.** she never stops working, she's a real busy bee; *très Fam* **avoir les abeilles** to be hacked off *or* cheesed off
▸▸ **a. domestique** hive *or* honey bee; **a. neutre** *ou* **ouvrière** worker (bee)

aber [abɛr] NM *Géog* deep estuary

aberrant [abɛrɑ̃] ADJ **1** *Biol* aberrant **2** *(absurde) (comportement)* aberrant, illogical; *(remarque)* nonsensical; **avoir une conduite aberrante** to behave illogically; **c'est a.!** it's absurd!

aberration [abɛrasjɔ̃] NF *(de l'esprit, du comportement)*, *Astron, Biol, Math, Opt* aberration; **a. chromosomique** chromosome abnormality; **dans un moment d'a.** in a moment of aberration; **c'est une a.!** it's absurd!

abêtir [abɛtir] VT **a. qn** to make sb stupid; **la télévision abêtit les enfants** television deadens *or* stultifies children's minds
VI to addle the brain
VPR **s'abêtir** to grow *or* become stupid

abêtissant [abetisɑ̃] ADJ mind-destroying, mindless

abhorrer [abɔre] VT *Litt* to abhor, to loathe

abîme [abim] NM **1** *(de l'océan)* abyss, chasm, depth(s); *Fig* gulf; *Géol* swallowhole; **les abîmes de l'océan** the ocean depths; *Fig* **un a. nous sépare** we are separated by a gulf, there is a gulf between us; **plonger dans les abîmes de l'angoisse** to plunge into the depths of anguish; *Fig* **le livre est un a. d'ennui** this book is extremely boring *or* deadly dull; *Fig* **un a. de science** a person of im-

mense learning; *(qui peut fournir beaucoup de renseignements)* a mine of information; *Litt* **les abîmes de l'histoire** the earliest beginnings of history, the mists of time
2 *(moral)* despair; **il est au bord de l'a.** he is on the brink *or* verge of depression *or* despair
3 *(financier)* ruin; **courir à l'a.** to be on the road to ruin, to be heading for ruin

abîmer [abime] VT *(objet)* to spoil, to damage; *Fam (personne)* to injure; **livre abîmé par la pluie** book spoilt by the rain; **a. ses affaires** to damage one's belongings; **abîmé en cours de transit** damaged in transit; *Fam* **se faire a. (le portrait)** to get beaten up *or* knocked about
VPR **s'abîmer 1** *Litt* **s'a. dans les flots** to sink, *Litt* to be engulfed by *or* swallowed up by the sea; *Fig* **s'a. dans la douleur/dans ses pensées** to be sunk in grief/lost in thought **2** *(d'un fruit)* to spoil, to go bad; *(de chaussures)* to wear out; **s'a. facilement** not to wear well **3** **s'a. la santé** to damage one's health; **tu t'abîmes les yeux** you're ruining your eyes *or* eyesight

abject [abʒɛkt] ADJ *Litt (pauvreté)* abject; *Péj (personne, comportement)* mean, contemptible, despicable

abjectement [abʒɛktəmɑ̃] ADV *Litt* abjectly; *Péj* contemptibly, despicably

abjection [abʒɛksjɔ̃] NF *Litt* abjectness, abjection; **se conduire avec a.** to behave abjectly

abjuration [abʒyrasjɔ̃] NF abjuration; *(d'un serment)* renunciation; *(d'une menace, d'une hérésie)* recantation

abjurer [abʒyre] VT to abjure, to forswear; *(serment)* to renounce; *(hérésie)* to recant; *(insulte, confession)* to retract

ablatif, -ive [ablatif, -iv] *Gram* ADJ ablative
NM ablative case; **à l'a.** in the ablative; **a. absolu** ablative absolute

ablation [ablasjɔ̃] NF ablation; *Méd* **a. des amygdales** removal of the tonsils, tonsillectomy

ablette [ablɛt] NF *(poisson)* bleak

ablution [ablysjɔ̃] NF washing, *Fml* ablution; *Fam* **faire ses ablutions** to wash, *Hum* to perform one's ablutions

abnégation [abnegasjɔ̃] NF abnegation, self-sacrifice

aboi [abwa] NM *Chasse* bay; **aux abois** *(cerf, ennemi)* at bay; *Fig (dans un état désespéré)* hard-pressed, with one's back to *or* against the wall; *Fig* **ils sont aux abois** they are in desperate *or* dire straits

aboiement [abwamɑ̃] NM *(d'un chien)* barking; *(des chiens de la meute)* baying; **il fit entendre un a. timide** he gave a timid little bark; **les aboiements de votre chien** your dog's barking; *Fig Péj* **les aboiements de la presse** the rantings of the press

abolir [abɔlir] VT to abolish, to suppress; *(dette etc)* to cancel; **le téléphone abolit les distances** the telephone makes distances irrelevant

abolissement [abɔlismɑ̃] NM, **abolition** [abɔlisjɔ̃] NF abolition, suppression; *(d'un décret)* repeal, annulment; **l'a. de l'esclavage** the abolition of slavery

abolitionnisme [abɔlisjɔnism] NM *Hist* abolitionism

abolitionniste [abɔlisjɔnist] ADJ, N *Hist* abolitionist

abominable [abɔminabl] ADJ abominable, foul; *(crime)* heinous; *(odeur)* foul; **une fin** *ou* **mort a.** a horrible death; **l'a. homme des neiges** the abominable snowman; **temps a.** abominable *or* filthy weather

abominablement [abɔminabləmɑ̃] ADV abominably

abomination [abɔminasjɔ̃] NF **1** abomination, abhorrence; **avoir qn/qch en a.** to loathe sb/sth **2** *(chose atroce)* abomination; **ne l'écoute pas, elle ne dit que des abominations** don't listen to her, she has a foul tongue; **ce café est une a.** this coffee is abominable; **c'est une a.!** it's abominable!, it's atrocious!

abominer [abɔmine] VT to abominate, to loathe

abondamment [abɔ̃damɑ̃] ADV abundantly, plentifully, copiously; **manger/boire a.** to eat/drink in copious amounts; **se servir a. de pain/dans la caisse du magasin** to help oneself to plenty of bread/from the till; **il a plu a. toute la nuit** it rained heavily all night; **peu a.** scantily; **dossier a. documenté** well-researched file; **se documenter a.** to gather large amounts of information *or* material; **parler a.** to talk a great deal

abondance [abɔ̃dɑ̃s] NF **1** *(profusion)* abundance, plenty; **on trouve des pommes en a. sur le marché** there is an abundant *or* a plentiful supply of apples on the market; **il y a une a. de fautes** there are numerous mistakes; **une a. de fruits** an abundance of fruit; **corne d'a.** cornucopia, horn of plenty **2** *(d'informations, de détails)* wealth; **vivre dans l'a.** to live in affluence; **parler avec a.** to speak volubly; *Litt* **parler d'a.** to speak off the cuff, to speak extempore

abondant [abɔ̃dɑ̃] ADJ abundant, copious, plentiful; *(style, vocabulaire)* rich; *(feuillage)* luxuriant; *(repas)* copious, hearty; *(excuses, saignement)* profuse; *(pluie)* heavy; **une chevelure abondante** a thick head of hair; **chevelure peu abondante** thin hair; **une récolte peu abondante** a poor *or* scanty harvest; **elle m'a donné d'abondants conseils** she gave me a great deal of advice

abondement [abɔ̃dmɑ̃] NM *Fin* = employer's contribution to company savings scheme

abonder [abɔ̃de] VI **1** *(foisonner)* to be plentiful, to abound (**en** in); **le raisin abonde cet automne** the grapes are plentiful this autumn **2** **rivière qui abonde de** *ou* **en poissons** river that abounds in fish; **votre texte abonde en images** your text abounds *or* is rich in imagery; **a. de biens** to be blessed with riches **3** **a. dans le sens de qn** to be entirely of sb's opinion, to agree entirely *or* thoroughly with sb

abonné, -ée [abɔne] N *(à un journal etc)* subscriber; *Rail, Théâtre* season-ticket holder; *Admin* **abonnés du gaz/de l'électricité** gas/electricity consumers; *Tél* **il n'y a pas d'a. au numéro que vous avez demandé** = the number you have dialled has not been recognized; **a. numérique** digital subscriber
ADJ *(à un journal)* subscribing; *Rail, Théâtre* holding a season ticket; **les membres abonnés au théâtre** members holding a season ticket for the theatre; *Admin* **être a. au téléphone/gaz** to be a telephone subscriber/gas consumer; *Fig* **j'ai l'habitude de ce genre d'ennui, j'y suis a.!** I'm used to this kind of problem, it's the story of my life!

abonnement [abɔnmɑ̃] NM **1** *(à un journal etc)* subscription; **prendre un a. au Figaro** to subscribe to *or* take out a subscription to the Figaro; **sur a.** on subscription **2** *Admin* **a. au téléphone** (telephone) line rental; **a. à un service en ligne** on-line subscription; *Rail, Théâtre* **(carte d')a.** season ticket; **a. collectif** group subscription; **a. saisonnier** season ticket; **prendre un a.** to take out a season ticket

abonner [abɔne] VT *(à une revue etc)* to take out a subscription for; **être abonné à qch** to subscribe to sth, to have a subscription to sth; **je vais vous a. à cette revue** I'll take out a subscription to that magazine for you

VPR s'abonner 1 s'a. à une revue to take out a subscription to a magazine **2** *Rail, Théâtre* to take out a season ticket; *Admin* **s'a. au téléphone** to be a telephone subscriber

abord [abɔr] NM **1** *(à terre)* access, approach; **île d'un a. difficile** island that is difficult to approach; *Fig* **un auteur d'un a. difficile** an author who is difficult to get to grips with *or* not very accessible **2 abords** approaches (**d'un endroit** to a place); *(d'une ville)* outskirts **3** *(façon d'accueillir)* approachability; **être d'un a. rude/chaleureux** to have a rough/welcoming manner (with people); **être d'un a. facile/difficile** to be approachable/unapproachable

ADV **d'a., tout d'a.** at first, to begin with; *(tout de suite)* straight away, at once; *(première-ment)* first, in the first place, first and foremost; **dès l'a.** from the (very) first, from the outset; **au premier a., de prime a.** at first sight; **d'a., elle ne dit jamais merci** for a start, she never says thank you; **toi, d'a., je ne te parle plus!** I'm not talking to you, so there!

abordable [abɔrdabl] ADJ **1** *(piste d'atterrissage etc)* easy to land on; *(côte, rivage)* easy to approach; *(lieu)* easily accessible **2** *(prix)* reasonable, affordable; **vos prix ne sont pas abordables** your prices are unreasonable **3** *(personne)* approachable; **peu a.** aloof, standoffish; *(grincheux)* grumpy

abordage [abɔrdaʒ] NM *Naut* **1** *(manœuvre de guerre)* boarding; **monter** *ou* **sauter à l'a.** **(d'un navire)** to board a ship; **à l'a.!** get ready to board! **2** *(collision)* collision; **il y a eu un a. causé par le brouillard** two ships collided in the fog **3** *(pour attaquer)* *(autre bateau)* boarding; *(pour s'amarrer)* coming alongside

aborder [abɔrde] VI *Naut* to land, to make land; *(dans un port)* to berth; *Vieilli* **a. à un port** to reach a port

VT **1** *(personne)* to accost; **se faire a. dans la rue** to be approached in the street **2** *(question, difficulté)* to tackle **3** *Naut* *(navire dans un combat)* to board, to grapple; *(se mettre côte à côte de)* *(bateau)* to come alongside **4** *Naut* *(rentrer en collision avec)* *(bateau)* to collide with *or* run foul of *or* run down

aborigène [abɔriʒɛn] ADJ native, indigenous (**de** to); *(relatif aux peuplades australiennes)* Aboriginal

N *(d'un pays)* native; **les aborigènes d'Australie** the (Australian) Aborigines

abortif, -ive [abɔrtif, -iv] ADJ **1** abortive **2** *Méd* **pilule abortive** abortion pill; *Jur* **manœuvres abortives** (procuring of) abortion

NM *Méd* abortifacient

aboucher [abuʃe] VT **1** *(faire rencontrer)* *(personnes)* to put in touch *or* contact **2** *Tech* **a. le tuyau au robinet** to connect the pipe (up) to the tap

VPR s'aboucher 1 *(rencontrer)* **s'a. avec qn** to get in touch with sb, to contact sb **2** *Tech* **le tuyau s'abouche sur l'aspirateur** the tube is connected *or* connects to the vacuum cleaner

Aboukir [abukir] N Ab(o)ukir; *Hist* **la bataille d'A.** the battle of the Nile

abouler [abule] *Arg* VT to bring; *(donner)* to hand over; **aboule ça ici!** bring it here!, hand it over!

VPR s'abouler *(arriver)* to turn up, to show up

about [abu] NM *Tech* butt

abouter [abute] VT *Tech* *(poutres etc)* to join end to end, to butt(-joint)

aboutir [abutir] VI **1 a. à qch** *(mener à)* *(d'un chemin, escalier)* to lead to sth; *(de différentes directions)* to converge on sth, to lead

to sth; *Fig* *(d'une tentative, d'efforts)* to result in sth; **n'a. à rien** *(d'un projet)* to come to nothing, *Fam* to go up in smoke; **leur raison-nement aboutit à une évidence** their reasoning leads to an obvious conclusion; **pour a. aux fins que nous poursuivons** to attain the end (which) we have in view; **a. dans un champ/sur la place du village** *(d'une personne)* to end up in a field/in *or* at the village square; *Fig* **j'ai abouti à la conclusion que … I** finally concluded that …; *Fig* **nous n'avons abouti à aucun résultat** in the end, we didn't get any result **2** *(d'un projet etc)* to succeed; **ne pas a.** to fail, to fall through; **faire a. qch** to bring sth to a successful conclusion

aboutissants [abutisɑ̃] NMPL **connaître les tenants et les a. d'une affaire** to know the ins and outs of an affair, to know all there is to know about an affair

aboutissement [abutismɑ̃] NM *(d'un effort etc)* result, outcome

aboyer [abwaje] VI **(j'aboie; j'aboierai)** *(d'un chien)* to bark; *(chien de meute)* to bay; *Fig* **a. après qn** to shout *or* yell at sb

aboyeur, -euse [abwajœr, -øz] ADJ *(chien)* barking

N *Fam* tout, *Am* barker

NM *(oiseau)* sandpiper

abracadabra [abrakadabra] NM abracadabra

abracadabrant [abrakadabrɑ̃] ADJ *Fam (histoire)* cock-and-bull

abraser [abraze] VT *Tech* to abrade

abrasif, -ive [abrazif, -iv] ADJ, NM *Tech* abrasive

abrasion [abrazjɔ̃] NF *Tech* abrasion; *Géol* **a. de la roche par l'eau** abrasion of the rock by the water

abrégé [abreʒe] NM précis, summary; *(d'un roman)* abridg(e)ment; *(d'une thèse)* abstract; **a. d'histoire de France** short history of France; **a. de philosophie** short guide to philosophy; **voici les faits en a.** here are the facts in a few words *or* in brief; **en a.** in abridged *or* abbreviated form; **écrire en a.** to write in abbreviated form

abrègement [abrɛʒmɑ̃] NM **1** *(d'un discours etc)* summarizing; *(d'une syllabe)* shortening; **a. d'un délai** shortening of the amount of time allowed for sth **2** *(texte)* summary, précis; *(d'un roman)* abridg(e)ment; *(d'un mot)* abbreviation; **a. (d'un ouvrage)** abridged edition (of a work)

abréger [abreʒe] **(j'abrège, n. abrégeons; j'abrégerai)** VT **1** *(vie, travail etc)* to shorten, to cut short; **pour a. votre attente** so as not to keep you waiting **2** *(article)* to abridge, to cut down; *(mot)* to abbreviate

VI to be brief; **pour a.** to be brief, to cut it short; *Fam* **allez, abrège!** come on, get *or* come to the point!

abreuvement [abrœvmɑ̃] NM *(des animaux)* watering

abreuver [abrœve] VT **1** *(chevaux, bétail etc)* to water **2** *(pré etc)* to flood, to irrigate; *(pompe)* to prime; *(tonneaux)* to season; **l'Égypte est abreuvée par le Nil** Egypt is watered by the Nile; *Fig* **a. qn d'injures** to shower *or* cover sb with insults, to heap insults on sb; *Fig* **les téléspectateurs sont abreuvés de publicité** the viewers are swamped *or* bombarded with advertising

VPR s'abreuver *(d'un cheval)* to drink; *Fam (d'une personne)* to knock it back

abreuvoir [abrœvwar] NM *(dans un cours d'eau, une mare)* watering place; *(baquet)* drinking trough; **mener les chevaux à l'a.** to lead the horses to water

abréviation [abrevjasjɔ̃] NF abbreviation

abri [abri] NM shelter, cover; *(écran, paravent)* screen; *(pour les plantes)* (tent) cloche;

a. à outils/à vélos tool/bike shed; **a. public** public shelter; **a. de sous-marins** submarine pen; **a. bétonné** bunker; **a. sous roche** rock shelter; **famille sans a.** homeless family; **à l'a.** sheltered, under shelter, under cover; **mettre qch à l'a.** to shelter *or* screen sth; **se mettre à l'a.** to take shelter; **à l'a. de qch** sheltered *or* screened from sth; **se mettre à l'a. de la pluie** to (take) shelter from the rain; **se mettre à l'a. de l'auvent** to shelter in the doorway; **a. contre le vent** windscreen; *Fig* **à l'a. de toute suspicion** free from (all) suspicion; *Fig* **personne n'est à l'a. d'une erreur** anybody can make a mistake; **il sera toujours à l'a. du besoin** he will always be protected from hardship, he will never experience hardship; *Naut* **à l'a. de la côte** under the lee of the shore

▸ ▸ **a. antinucléaire** (nuclear) bunker; **a. fiscal** tax shelter; **a. souterrain** air-raid shelter

Abribus® [abribys] NM bus shelter

abricot [abriko] NM apricot

ADJ INV apricot-coloured

abricoté [abrikɔte] ADJ apricot-flavoured

abricotier [abrikɔtje] NM apricot tree

abricotine [abrikɔtin] NF *Suisse* apricot brandy

abrier (s') [sabrije] VPR *Can* to wrap up (well)

abri-garage, *pl* **abris-garages** NM carport

abriter [abrite] VT **1** *(protéger)* to shelter, to screen, to shield, to protect; *(yeux)* to shade; **a. ses yeux du soleil** to shade one's eyes from the sun; **cet auvent nous abrite des regards indiscrets** the awning shields us from prying eyes **2** *(héberger)* to house; **cet hôtel peut a. cent personnes** the hotel can accommodate a hundred people

VPR s'abriter *(de la pluie)* to (take) shelter (**de** from); *(des tirs)* to take cover; **s'a. derrière qn** to shelter behind sb; *Fig* **il s'abrite derrière le règlement** he shelters *or* hides behind the rules

abrivent [abrivɑ̃] NM windbreak

abrogation [abrɔgasjɔ̃] NF *(de la loi etc)* abrogation, rescinding, repeal

abrogeable [abrɔʒabl] ADJ repealable

abroger [abrɔʒe] VT **(j'abrogeai(s); n. abrogeons)** *(loi etc)* to abrogate, to rescind, to repeal

abrupt [abrypt] ADJ **1** *(rocher, pente)* sheer, steep **2** *Fig (manière)* abrupt, blunt; **répondre d'un ton a.** to give an abrupt *or* short answer, to answer abruptly *or* shortly

NM steep slope

abruptement [abryptəmɑ̃] ADV **1** steeply, abruptly **2** *Fig* abruptly

abruti, -ie [abryti] ADJ **1** stupefied, dazed; *(par la chaleur)* exhausted; **j'étais complète-ment a. après cette séance** my mind *or* brain was totally dead after that session; **a. par l'alcool** stupefied *or* sodden with drink **2** *Fam* stupid, idiotic, moronic; **avoir un air a.** to look stupid *or* moronic

N *Fam* idiot, fool

abrutir [abrytir] VT **1** *(abêtir)* *(personne)* to exhaust; **ce travail m'abrutit** this work's addling my brain; **la chaleur m'abrutissait** my brain couldn't work in that heat; **je suis abruti de travail** my brain's dead from too much work **2** *(de l'alcool etc)* to stupefy; **les buveurs, que l'alcool abrutit** drinkers, whose minds are (being) numbed *or* deadened by alcohol

VPR s'abrutir 1 *(se fatiguer)* **s'a. de travail/de discussions** to work oneself to the point of exhaustion/to wear oneself out with discussion **2** *(devenir stupide)* to become dazed *or* stupefied; **on s'abrutit à trop regarder la télévision** too much television addles the brain

abrutissant [abrytisã] ADJ **1** *(fatigant)* exhausting, wearing; *(bruit)* deafening **2** *(abêtissant)* mind-destroying

abrutissement [abrytismã] NM *(abêtissement)* **a. de qn** reducing of sb to a mindless state; **propagande qui cause l'a. des masses** propaganda that stops people thinking for themselves

ABS [abeɛs] NM *Aut* (*abrév* **Antiblockiersystem**) **système A.** ABS

abscisse [apsis] NF abscissa

abscons [apskɔ̃] ADJ *Péj* obscure, abstruse

absence [apsɑ̃s] NF **1** *(de personne)* absence; **en** *ou* **pendant mon a.** in *or* during my absence, when I am/was/*etc* away; **en l'a. de ma secrétaire** while *or* when my secretary is away; **nous avons regretté votre a.** we were sorry that you weren't with us; **nous regrettons tous les jours son a.** *(d'un mort)* we miss him every day; **briller par son a.** to be conspicuous by one's absence; **a. de l'école** non-attendance at *or* absence from school; **comment expliquez-vous toutes ces absences?** how do you explain all these absences? **2** *(manque)* *(de meubles, de principes, du père etc)* lack; **a. de demande** absence *or* lack of demand; **a. de goût** lack of taste, tastelessness; **a. d'imagination** lack of imagination; **a. d'esprit** absent-mindedness; **j'ai eu une a. d'esprit et j'ai oublié ...** I absent-mindedly forgot ...; **il a des absences** he's apt to be absent-minded, he has *or* is prone to memory lapses; **dans un moment d'a.** in a moment of absent-mindedness, in an absent-minded moment; *(de négligence, de manque d'attention)* without thinking **3** *Méd* **a. (épileptique)** petit mal fit ▸▸ *Mil etc* **a. illégale** absence without leave; **a. non rémunérée** unpaid leave; **a. rémunérée** paid leave

absent, -ente [apsã, -ãt] ADJ **1** absent, away; **il est a. de Paris en ce moment** he isn't in Paris at the moment; **quand ma femme est absente** when my wife's away; *Mil* **a. sans permission** absent without leave, AWOL **2** *(qui n'existe pas)* absent, missing; **une déclaration d'où tout humour était a.** a statement totally lacking in humour; **chez cet animal, les dents sont absentes** this animal has no teeth **3** *(distrait, rêveur)* absent; **son esprit est a.** his mind is far away, *Fam* he's miles away; **il avait un air a.** he was miles away
N *(à une réunion etc)* absentee; **les Russes ont été les grands absents lors de la Coupe du monde** the Russians were the most notable absentees from the World Cup; *Prov* **les absents ont toujours tort** it's always the people who are not there that get blamed; **il ne faut pas dire du mal des absents** you shouldn't say bad things about people when they're not there to defend themselves

absentéisme [apsɑ̃teism] NM absenteeism

absentéiste [apsɑ̃teist] ADJ (regularly) absent; **propriétaire a.** absentee landlord
N (regular) absentee

absenter (s') [sapsɑ̃te] VPR *(de chez soi)* to go away; *(de l'école)* to stay away; **je ne me suis pas absenté de toute la journée** I haven't been out all day; **il a dû s'a. pour quelques heures** he had to go somewhere for a few hours, *Fam* he had to pop out for a few hours; **son mari s'absente beaucoup** her husband is away a lot

absidal, -ale, -aux, -ales [apsidal, -o] ADJ apsidal

abside [apsid] NF *Archit* apse

absidiole [apsidjɔl] NF *Archit* apsidal chapel

absinthe [apsɛ̃t] NF **1** *(boisson)* absinthe **2** *(plante)* wormwood

absolu [apsɔly] ADJ **1** absolute; **zéro a.** abso-
lute zero; **poser une règle absolue** to lay down a hard-and-fast rule; **refus a.** flat refusal; **majorité absolue** absolute majority **2** *(total)* absolute; **nous sommes dans l'impossibilité absolue de vous donner des réponses définitives** we are quite unable to give you any definite answers; **pouvoir a.** absolute power; **caractère a.** autocratic nature; **liberté absolue** absolute *or* total freedom
3 *(ton, voix)* peremptory
4 *Gram* absolute
NM *Phil* **l'a.** the absolute; **juger qch dans l'a.** to judge sth in the absolute *or* out of context

absolument [apsɔlymã] ADV **1** *(complètement)* absolutely; **a.!** absolutely!; **a. pas!** absolutely not!; **a. rien** nothing whatsoever **2** *(strictement)* *(parler)* peremptorily; **c'est a. défendu** it is absolutely *or* strictly forbidden; **je le veux a.** I insist on it; **nier a. qch** to deny sth flatly **3** *(sans faute)* simply, absolutely; **vous devez a. y aller!** you simply *or* absolutely must go! **4** *(sans limite)* **régner a.** to reign as an absolute monarch; **a. parlant** speaking generally **5** *Gram* absolutely

absolution [apsɔlysjɔ̃] NF **1** *Rel* absolution **2** *Jur* discharge, acquittal

absolutisme [apsɔlytism] NM *Pol* absolutism

absorbant [apsɔrbã] ADJ **1** *(matériau, qualités)* absorbent **2** *(livre, tâche)* absorbing, engrossing

absorber [apsɔrbe] VT **1** *(d'une éponge etc)* *(eau etc)* to absorb, to soak up; *Chimie (gaz)* to occlude; **le noir absorbe la lumière** black absorbs light **2** *(nourriture)* to consume; *(boisson)* to drink; *(médicament)* to take; *Écon* **la multinationale va a. cette entreprise** the multinational is going to take over *or Fam* swallow up the firm; **les travaux ont absorbé toutes mes économies** the repairs have used up all my savings **3** *(d'une lecture)* to absorb, to engross; **son travail l'absorbe** he/she is completely wrapped up in his/her work; **cette pensée m'absorbe complètement** I think about it constantly; **être absorbé dans ses pensées** to be lost in thought
VPR **s'absorber** to become absorbed *or* engrossed (**dans** in); **s'a. dans la lecture d'un livre** to be absorbed *or* lost in a book

absorption [apsɔrpsjɔ̃] NF absorption; **a. de médicaments** (the) taking of medicines; *Écon* **a. d'une petite société par une grosse** the takeover of a small company by a large one

absorption-fusion, *pl* **absorptions-fusions** NF *Écon* merger

absoudre [apsudr] VT *(prp* **absolvant**; *pp* **absous**, *f* **absoute**; *pr ind* **j'absous, il absout**, n. **absolvons, ils absolvent**; *pr sub* **j'absolve**; *p hist & pr sub are lacking*; *fu* **j'absoudrai**) **1 a. qn de qch** to forgive sb sth; *Rel* **a. qn de ses péchés** to absolve sb from his sins, to forgive sb his sins; *Rel* **je vous absous** I absolve you **2** *Jur (personne)* to absolve, to acquit

abstenir (s') [sapstǝnir] VPR *(conj like* **tenir**) to stand aside *or* aloof; *Pol* to abstain (from voting); **s'a. de qch** to abstain from sth, to forgo sth; **s'a. de faire qch** to refrain *or* abstain from doing sth; **s'a. de commentaires** to refrain from comment; **s'a. de manger du chocolat/de boire de l'alcool** to keep off chocolate/alcohol; **dans le doute, abstiens-toi** when in doubt, don't

abstention [apstɑ̃sjɔ̃] NF abstention (**de** from)

abstentionnisme [apstɑ̃sjɔnism] NM *Pol (de vote etc)* abstention

abstentionniste [apstɑ̃sjɔnist] N *Pol* abstainer; **le nombre des abstentionnistes** the number of abstentions

abstinence [apstinɑ̃s] NF abstinence; *(qualité d'une personne)* abstemiousness; *Rel* **jour d'a.** day of abstinence; **faire a. le vendredi** to abstain from eating meat on Fridays; **a. (sexuelle)** (sexual) abstinence

abstinent, -ente [apstinã, -ãt] ADJ abstemious
N abstainer; *(qui ne boit pas d'alcool)* teetotaller; *Rel* person who practises abstinence

abstraction [apstraksjɔ̃] NF **1** *Phil* abstraction; **un esprit capable d'a.** a mind capable of abstract thought **2 faire a. de qch** to disregard sth; **a. faite du style** style apart **3** *(idée abstraite)* abstract idea, abstraction; **se perdre dans des abstractions** to lose oneself in abstractions

abstraire [apstrɛr] *(conj like* **traire**) VT to separate, to isolate; *Phil* to abstract
VPR **s'abstraire** **s'a. dans qch** to become engrossed in sth

abstrait [apstrɛ] ADJ *(idée, art etc)* abstract; *(question)* abstruse, deep
NM **1** *(abstraction)* abstract, abstraction; **dans l'a.** in the abstract, in theory **2** *Beaux-Arts* abstract art; *(artiste)* abstract artist; *(tableau)* abstract (painting)

abstraitement [apstrɛtmã] ADV **1** *(en théorie)* in the abstract; **parler a.** to talk in the abstract *or* in abstract terms **2** *(distraitement)* abstractedly, absentmindedly

abstrus [apstry] ADJ abstruse, recondite

absurde [apsyrd] ADJ absurd, preposterous; **votre conduite est totalement a.!** your behaviour is totally preposterous!; **elle est complètement a.** she's completely ridiculous
NM **l'a.** absurdity; *Phil* the absurd; **réduire une théorie à l'a.** to reduce a theory ad absurdum; *Phil* **démonstration par l'a.** reductio ad absurdum; **l'a. de la situation** the absurdity *or* absurdness of the situation, the absurd thing about the situation; **le théâtre de l'a.** the theatre of the absurd

absurdement [apsyrdǝmã] ADV absurdly, preposterously

absurdité [apsyrdite] NF **1** *(caractère absurde)* absurdity, preposterousness; **l'a. de l'existence** the absurdity of existence **2** *(chose absurde)* piece of nonsense; **cette réaction est une a.** this reaction is completely absurd; **dire des absurdités** to talk nonsense

abus [aby] NM **1** *(mauvais emploi)* abuse, misuse (**de** of); *(excès)* overindulgence (**de** in); **l'a. de médicaments** the misuse of pharmaceutical drugs; **l'a. de boissons** alcohol abuse; **faire a. de qch** to indulge too freely in sth; **faire a. de son autorité** to abuse one's authority; **employer un terme par a.** to misuse a term
2 *Jur (de droits)* violation; **a. de confiance** breach of trust; **a. d'autorité/de pouvoir** abuse *or* misuse of (one's) authority/power; **a. de biens sociaux** misuse of a company's assets; **a. de droits sociaux** misappropriation of corporate funds
3 *(pratique)* abuse, corrupt practice; **un écrivain connu pour ses a. de langage** a writer known for his abuse of the language *or Fam* for murdering the language; **réformer un a.** to remedy an abuse; **je ne supporte plus ses a.!** I can't stand his/her outrageous behaviour any longer!; **faire quelques a.** to overdo it, to overindulge; *Fam* **il y a de l'a.!** that's going too far!

abuser [abyze] VI **a. de qch** to misuse sth; *(exploiter)* to take (unfair) advantage of sth; **vous abusez de vos forces** you're overtaxing yourself; **a. du tabac** to smoke too much; **il ne faut pas a. des bonnes choses** good things should be enjoyed in moderation, enough is as good as a feast; **a. de l'amabilité de qn** to impose on sb *or* on sb's kindness; **a. de la confiance de qn** to abuse sb's confidence; **j'abuse de votre temps** I am taking up too much of your time; **n'abusez point** be moderate; **je ne voudrais pas a., j'ai peur d'a.** I don't want to cause you any inconvenience; **c'est un peu fort, elle abuse!** she's going a bit (too) far!; **vous abusez!** that's a bit much!; **a. de qn** to sexually abuse sb

vt to deceive; **il ne nous abusera pas par de belles paroles** he will not deceive us with fine words

vpr s'abuser to be mistaken; **je vous ai déjà rencontré, si je ne m'abuse** I've met you before, if I'm not mistaken

Il fait noter que le verbe anglais **to abuse** ne s'emploie jamais dans le sens d'**exagérer**.

abusif, -ive [abyzif, -iv] **ADJ 1** *(emploi d'un mot)* incorrect; **il serait a. de l'affirmer** it would be an exaggeration to say that **2** *(excessif)* excessive; **emploi a. de la force** excessive *or* unwarranted use of force; **mère abusive** possessive *or* domineering mother

abusivement [abyzivmã] **ADV** incorrectly, wrongly; **employer un mot a.** to use a word incorrectly *or* wrongly; **elle a profité a. de la situation** she took unfair advantage of the situation

abuter [abyte] **VT a. un camion à un quai** to back a lorry against a platform

abyme [abim] **NM tableau/film/pièce avec structure en a.** painting within a painting/ film within a film/play within a play

abyssal, -ale, -aux, -ales [abisal, -o] **ADJ** *(faune etc)* abyssal; *Fig (profondeurs)* unfathomable; **les fosses abyssales** the troughs of the ocean depths

abysse [abis] **NM** *Géog* abyssal zone; *Fig* **les abysses du désespoir** the depths of despair

Abyssinie [abisini] **NF** Abyssinia

abyssinien, -ienne [abisinjɛ̃, -jɛn] **ADJ** Abyssinian

n A. Abyssinian

A.C. [ase] *abrév* **appellation contrôlée**

acabit [akabi] **NM** *Péj* **ils sont du même a.** they're tarred with the same brush; **je me méfie des gens de cet a.** I don't trust people like that; **des drogués, des dealers et autres paumés de cet a.** drug addicts, dealers and other dropouts of the same type

acacia [akasja] **NM** *(arbre)* **a. vrai** acacia; *(robinier)* **a. vulgaire, faux a.** locust tree, false acacia

académicien, -ienne [akademisjɛ̃, -jɛn] **N** *(membre d'une académie)* academician; *(membre de l'Académie française)* member of the Académie française

académie [akademi] **NF 1** *(des lettres, des sciences, d'art)* society; **l'A. française** the French Academy **2** *(école)* school, academy; **a. de musique** music school, school of music; **a. de danse** dancing school; **a. de dessin** school of art, art school **3** *Admin (en France)* educational district **4** *(de Platon etc)* academy **5** *(étude)* nude

Académie française

The Académie was originally a group of men of letters who were encouraged by Cardinal Richelieu in 1635 to become an official body. Consisting of forty distinguished writers ("les Quarante" or "les Immortels"), the Académie's chief task was, and is, to produce a definitive dictionary and to be the ultimate authority in matters concerning the French language.

académique [akademik] **ADJ 1** academic; **les palmes académiques** = insignia of decoration granted by the French Ministry of Education; **séance a.** sitting *or* meeting of an Academy; **occuper un fauteuil a.** *(de l'Académie française)* to be a member of the Académie française; *Littér Péj* **style a.** pedantic style; **débat a.** academic discussion **2** *Admin* **inspection a.** board of school inspectors **3** *Beaux-Arts* **figure a.** nude **4** *Belg, Suisse, Can Univ* **l'année a.** the academic year

académisme [akademism] **NM** *Beaux-Arts Péj* academicism

Acadie [akadi] **NF** *Hist* Acadia

acadien, -ienne [akadjɛ̃, -jɛn] **ADJ** Acadian
NM *Ling* Acadian
n A. Acadian

acajou [akaʒu] **NM 1** mahogany; **table en a.** mahogany table **2 noix d'a.** cashew nut; **a. à noix** cashew nut tree
ADJ INV reddish-brown, auburn

acanthe [akɑ̃t] **NF** *Bot, Archit* acanthus

a cappella [akapɛla] **ADV** *Mus* a cappella; **chanter a c.** to sing a cappella

acariâtre [akarjatr] **ADJ** bad-tempered, cantankerous; **être d'humeur a.** to be bad-tempered

acarien [akarjɛ̃] **NM** *(insecte)* dust mite

accablant [akablɑ̃] **ADJ 1** *(malchance, témoignage, responsabilités)* overwhelming; *(chaleur)* overpowering, oppressive **2** *(témoignage)* damning

accablé [akable] **ADJ** *(de travail etc)* overwhelmed; *(de peine)* overcome, weighed down; **a. de fatigue** overwhelmed with fatigue; **a. par la chaleur** overwhelmed *or* overcome by the heat; **a. de dettes** burdened with debt

accablement [akabləmɑ̃] **NM** dejection, despondency, depression

accabler [akable] **VT 1** to overpower, to overwhelm; **être accablé de douleur** to be grief-stricken; **il m'accable de travail** he piles work on me; **il m'accable de questions** he bombards me with questions; **a. qn d'injures** to heap abuse on sb; **elle nous accable de recommandations** she heaps advice on us **2** *(fournir des preuves contre)* to damn

accalmie [akalmi] **NF** lull; **dans un moment d'a.** in a calm moment, in a moment of respite

accaparant [akaparɑ̃] **ADJ** demanding; **un emploi a.** a demanding job; **leurs enfants sont très accaparants** their children take up a lot of their time

accaparement [akaparmɑ̃] **NM** monopolizing; *(des stocks)* buying up; *(des marchandises)* cornering

accaparer [akapare] **VT** *(stocks)* to buy up; *(marchandises)* to corner, to hoard; *(pouvoir)* to seize; **a. le marché de l'automobile** to corner the automobile market; **a. la conversation** to monopolize the conversation; **a. les meilleures places** to secure *or* corner the best seats; **son travail l'accapare trop** his/her work takes up too much of his/her time; **je ne voudrais pas vous a. toute la soirée** I don't want to monopolize you for the whole evening

accapareur, -euse [akaparœr, -øz] **N** *(de nourriture etc)* buyer-up; *(société)* monopolist, *Péj* grabber
ADJ *(personne)* possessive

accastillage [akastijaʒ] **NM** *Naut (d'un navire)* fittings

accastiller [akastije] **VT** *Naut (navire)* to fit out

accédant, -e [aksedɑ̃, -ɑ̃t] **N a. à la propriété** first-time buyer, new home owner

accéder [aksede] **VI** (**j'accède, n. accédons; j'accéderai**) **1** *(atteindre)* to have access (à to); **on accède à la porte par un escalier** a flight of steps leads to the door; *Ordinat* **a. à un programme** to access a program
2 *(accepter)* to comply, to agree; **a. à une requête** to comply with a request; **a. à une condition** to agree *or* assent to a condition **3** *(parvenir)* to accede; **a. à de hautes responsabilités** to acquire important responsibilities; **a. à un poste important** to obtain *or* to get an important job; **a. au trône** to accede to the throne; **a. à la propriété** *(d'un appartement, d'une maison)* to be a first-time buyer; **pour permettre aux jeunes ménages d'a. à la propriété** to allow young couples to buy their first home

accélérateur, -trice [akseleratœr, -tris] **ADJ** accelerating
NM *Aut, Ordinat* accelerator; *Nucl* **a. de particules** particle accelerator; **a. d'électrons** betatron; **Aut appuyer sur l'a.** to accelerate; *Ordinat* **a. graphique** graphic(s) accelerator

accélération [akselerasjɔ̃] **NF** acceleration; *(du travail)* speeding up; **a. de la pesanteur** gravitational acceleration; *Aut* **pédale d'a.** accelerator (pedal); *Aut* **en a. partielle** part-throttle; **avoir une bonne a.** to have good acceleration

accéléré [akselere] **ADJ** quick, fast, rapid; *(mouvement)* accelerated; **un cours a.** a crash course
NM *Cin, TV* accelerated motion, time lapse

accélérer [akselere] (**j'accélère, n. accélérons; j'accélérerai**) **VT** to accelerate, to speed up; **a. le mouvement** to speed up
VI dépêche-toi, accélère! hurry up, get a move on!; *Aut* **passe en seconde et accélère** go into second and accelerate; **a. à vide** to rev the engine
VPR s'accélérer to accelerate, to speed up; *(du pouls)* to go faster, to speed up

accent [aksɑ̃] **NM 1** *(phonétique)* accent, stress; **a. d'intensité** *ou* **tonique** tonic accent **2** *Gram* accent; **a. aigu/grave** acute/grave (accent); **e a. circonflexe** e circumflex **3** *(prononciation)* accent; **parler le français avec un. a. anglais** to speak French with an English accent; **il n'a pas l'a. ou d'a.** he doesn't have an accent **4** *(inflexion)* tone of voice; *Fig* **son récit a l'a. de la vérité** his account rings true; *Ling* **a. de phrase** sentence stress; *Fig* **mettre l'a. sur la présentation du produit** to put the emphasis on *or* to emphasize the presentation of the product **5 les accents du désespoir** the accents of despair; **il parlait avec des accents de rage/de terreur dans la voix** his voice was angry/terror-stricken; **les accents de la Marseillaise** the strains of the Marseillaise

accentuation [aksɑ̃tɥasjɔ̃] **NF 1** *(des syllabes etc)* stressing; **les règles de l'a. espagnole** the stress rules in Spanish **2** *Gram* accentuation, placing of the grammatical accents; **faire des fautes d'a.** to put accents in the wrong place **3** *(d'un phénomène)* growth

accentué [aksɑ̃tɥe] **ADJ** stressed, accented; *Fig* pronounced, marked; **traits fortement accentués** pronounced *or* strongly marked features; **les traits accentués par la fatigue** features drawn with fatigue

accentuer [aksɑ̃tɥe] **VT 1** *(syllabes etc)* to stress; **syllabe non accentuée** unstressed syllable **2** *Gram* **a. une voyelle** to mark a vowel with an accent **3** *Fig* to emphasize, to accentuate; **son conseil/cet incident n'a fait qu'a. leurs problèmes** his advice/this incident has only added to their problems; **a. le chômage** to increase *or* add to unemployment

VPR s'accentuer to become more pronounced *or* marked

acceptabilité [aksɛptabilite] NF *Gram* acceptability; *Mktg* **a. de la marque** brand acceptability

acceptable [aksɛptabl] ADJ **1** acceptable (**à** to); **offre a.** reasonable offer **2** *(voiture, maison, machine)* in fair condition; *(performance)* reasonably good

acceptablement [aksɛptabləmɑ̃] ADV acceptably, in an acceptable manner

acceptant, -ante [aksɛptɑ̃, -ɑ̃t] ADJ, N *Com, Jur* acceptant

acceptation [aksɛptasjɔ̃] NF acceptance; **a. sous condition** conditional acceptance; **sous réserve d'a.** subject to a favourable report; *Fin* **a. bancaire** banker's acceptance

accepter [aksɛpte] VT to accept; *(défi)* to take up; *(pari)* to take on; *(chèque, effet)* to accept, to sign, to honour; **il n'accepte pas l'échec/la difficulté** he refuses to acknowledge failure/the existence of problems; **elle n'arrive pas à a. le mariage de sa fille** she can't come to terms with her daughter's marriage; **je n'accepte pas votre conduite d'hier soir** I find your behaviour last night unacceptable; **je n'accepte pas cette théorie** I don't accept that theory, I don't agree with that theory; **a. de faire qch** to agree to do sth; **elle n'accepte pas que son mari soit au chômage** she can't *or* won't accept the fact that her husband is unemployed; **a. qn comme ou pour arbitre** to accept sb as an arbitrator; **il a été accepté dans la famille** he was accepted into the family; **acceptez-vous Gérard Manvussat pour époux?** ≃ do you take this man, Gérard Manvussat, as your lawfully wedded husband?

accepteur [aksɛptœr] NM **1** *Com (d'une facture)* acceptor, drawee **2** *Chimie, Électron* acceptor

acception [aksɛpsjɔ̃] NF *Fml* **1** *(d'un mot etc)* meaning, sense, *Fml* acceptation **2 sans a. de race/de sexe** *(dans une offre d'emploi)* open to candidates of all races/of both sexes, irrespective of race/sex

accès [aksɛ] NM **1** *(approche)* access, approach; **les a. de la gare** the station approaches, the approaches to the station; **le refuge est facile d'a.** the shelter is easily accessible *or* easy to reach; **avoir a. à qch** to have access to sth; **donner a. à qch** to give access *or* to lead to sth; **ce diplôme donne a. à toute une gamme de professions passionnantes** this diploma opens the door to a wide range of exciting professions; **trouver a. auprès de qn** to be admitted to sb's presence; **être d'a. facile/difficile** *(d'une personne)* to be approachable/unapproachable; *(d'un auteur, d'un livre etc)* to be accessible/not very accessible; **facile/difficile d'a.** *(lieu)* easy/hard to reach, easy/hard to get to; **l'a. à la profession de médecin devient de plus en plus difficile** entry into the medical profession is becoming more and more difficult; **l'a. au statut de membre de l'Union européenne** entry into the European Union; *Rail* **a. aux quais** to the trains **2** *(poussée)* fit, attack, outburst; **a. de fièvre** attack *or* bout of fever; **des a. de toux** fits of coughing, coughing fits; **a. de faiblesse** fainting fit; **a. d'enthousiasme** burst *or* fit of enthusiasm; **a. de tristesse/découragement** wave of sadness/discouragement; **a. de colère/folie** fit of anger/madness; **travailler par a.** to work by *or* in fits and starts **3** *Ordinat* access; *(à une page Web)* hit; **avoir a. à** to be able to access; **code d'a.** access code; **à a. multiple** multi-access; **temps d'a.** access time; **a. aléatoire** random access; **a. au bus local** local bus access; **a. commuté, a.**

par ligne commutée dial-up access; **a. direct à la mémoire** direct memory access; **a. à distance** remote access; **a. en écriture** write access; **a. rapide** high-speed access, fast access; **a. sécurisé par mot de passe** password-protected access; **a. sélectif** selective access; **a. séquentiel** sequential access; **a. au système** system access

accessibilité [aksɛsibilite] NF accessibility

accessible [aksɛsibl] ADJ **1** *(où l'on peut arriver)* accessible; **séminaire a. à tous les licenciés** seminar open to all graduates; **endroit a.** accessible place, place that can be reached easily; **parc a. à tous** park open to everybody; *Fig* **les prix sont très accessibles** the prices are within everyone's reach, the prices are very affordable; **un livre tout à fait a.** a very accessible book **2** *(personne)* approachable; **a. à la pitié** open to pity; **a. à la flatterie** susceptible to flattery

accession [aksesjɔ̃] NF **1** *(au pouvoir etc)* accession; **faciliter l'a. des femmes à la politique** to make it easier for women to enter politics; **a. à la propriété** home ownership; **l'a. à la propriété est rendue possible à tous** home ownership is within everyone's reach; **a. au trône** accession to the throne; **l'a. du pays à l'indépendance a eu lieu en 1968** the country became independent *or* gained independence in 1968; **a. au statut de membre de l'Union européenne** entry into the European Union **2** *(à un contrat, un parti)* adherence, adhesion

accessit [aksesit] NM *(dans un examen)* honourable mention; **remporter un a. en musique** to get an honourable mention in music

accessoire [aksɛswar] ADJ accessory; *Compta (frais)* incidental; **jouer un rôle a.** to play a subordinate role; **c'est un détail a.** it's an incidental detail

NM **1** *(objet)* accessory, *Fml* appurtenance; **voiture vendue sans accessoires** car sold without accessories; **chapeau et accessoires coordonnés** hat and matching accessories; **a. d'objectif** lens attachment; *Ordinat* **a. de bureau** desk accessory **2** *Théâtre etc* **accessoires** properties, *Fam* props; **magasin des accessoires** property room **3** *(ce qui est accessoire)* *(minor)* details; **on s'occupera de l'a. plus tard** we'll take care of the (minor) details later

accessoirement [aksɛswarmɑ̃] ADV *(si besoin est)* if necessary, if need be; **je m'occupe a. de la comptabilité** I look after the accounts in addition to my main duties

accessoiriser [aksɛswarize] VT *(vêtements etc)* to accessorize

accessoiriste [aksɛswarist] N *Théâtre etc* props (man, *f* woman), property man, *f* mistress; *TV* props buyer

accident [aksidɑ̃] NM **1** *(événement imprévisible)* accident; *(contretemps)* mishap; **je l'ai retrouvé par a.** I found it by accident, I found it accidentally; **nous sommes arrivés sans a.** we arrived safely *or* safe and sound; **la cérémonie s'est déroulée sans a.** the ceremony went off without a hitch **2** *(collision, malheur)* crash, accident; **a. de chemin de fer** railway accident; **a. d'avion** plane *or* air crash; **a. de voiture** car accident *or* crash; **a. de la route** road accident; **a. de la circulation** traffic accident; **a. mortel** fatal accident, fatality; **être victime d'un a.** to meet with an accident **3** *Méd* **a. cardiaque** cardiac arrest, heart attack; **a. vasculaire** vascular accident **4** *Mus* accidental **5 a. de terrain** unevenness *or* irregularity of the ground ►► **a. de parcours** hitch; *Fig* **son échec n'est qu'un a. de parcours** his failure is just a tem-

porary hitch *or* setback; **a. du travail** industrial accident, accident in the workplace

accidenté, -ée [aksidɑ̃te] ADJ **1** *(terrain)* uneven, broken **2 voiture accidentée** damaged car

N victim of an accident; **les accidentés** the injured, the casualties; **accidentés de la route** road accident victims; **les accidentés du travail** victims of industrial accidents

accidentel, -elle [aksidɑ̃tɛl] ADJ **1** *(imprévu)* accidental; **une rencontre accidentelle** a chance *or* an accidental meeting; **je le rencontrai de façon purement accidentelle** I met him quite by accident; **mort accidentelle** *(dans un accident)* accidental death **2** *Mus* **signes accidentels** accidentals; *(armature constante)* key signature

accidentellement [aksidɑ̃tɛlmɑ̃] ADV accidentally; *(mourir)* in an accident, as a *or* the result of an accident

accidenter [aksidɑ̃te] VT *(voiture)* to damage, *Fam* to prang

accidentologie [aksidɑ̃tɔlɔʒi] NF study of road accidents

accidentologue [aksidɑ̃tɔlɔg] N accident researcher, person who specializes in the study of road accidents

acclamation [aklamasjɔ̃] NF acclamation, cheering; **les acclamations de la foule** the cheers *or* acclamations of the crowd; **discours salué d'acclamations** speech greeted with cheers; **elle fut élue par a.** she was elected by acclamation

acclamer [aklame] VT *(personne, discours)* to acclaim, to cheer; *(en tapant dans les mains)* to applaud; *(saluer qn, discours)* to greet with cheers; **a. qn empereur** to acclaim sb emperor

acclimatable [aklimatabl] ADJ acclimatizable, *Am* acclimatable

acclimatation [aklimatasjɔ̃] NF acclimatization, *Am* acclimation; **jardin d'a.** zoological gardens

acclimatement [aklimatmɑ̃] NM acclimatization, *Am* acclimation

acclimater [aklimate] VT to acclimatize, *Am* to acclimate (**à** to); *Fig (usages)* to introduce **VPR s'acclimater** to become *or* get acclimatized *or Am* acclimated

accointance [akwɛ̃tɑ̃s] NF *Péj* accointances dealings, relations; **avoir des accointances dans le milieu des affaires** to have contacts in the business world

accointer (s') [akwɛ̃te] VPR *Péj Vieilli* **s'a. avec qn** to take up with sb

accolade [akɔlad] NF **1** *(embrassade)* *(formal)* embrace; **donner/recevoir l'a.** to embrace/to be embraced **2** *Hist* accolade; **recevoir l'a.** ≃ to be knighted **3** *Mus* brace; *Typ* curly bracket, brace **4** *Archit* **(arc en) a.** ogee arch

accolement [akɔlmɑ̃] NM joining, bracketing

accoler [akɔle] VT **1** *(joindre côte à côte)* to join side by side, to couple; *Typ* to brace, to bracket; **le nom de l'épouse est accolé à celui du mari** the wife's surname is joined *or* added to that of the husband; **accolé aux murs** built on the walls **2** *(vigne)* to tie up **VPR s'accoler** *(de plantes)* to intertwine, to cling

accommodant [akɔmɔdɑ̃] ADJ accommodating; **a. en affaires** easy to do business with

accommodation [akɔmɔdasjɔ̃] NF **1** *(adaptation)* adapting; **a. d'une pièce aux usages d'un bureau** adaptation *or* conversion of a room for office use **2** *Physiol (des yeux)* accommodation

accommodement   [akɔmɔdmɑ̃]   NM

compromise, arrangement, agreement; **en venir à un a.** to come to a compromise or arrangement, to come to terms (**avec** with); **politique d'a.** give-and-take policy; Com **a. avec ses créanciers** composition with one's creditors

accommoder [akɔmɔde] **VT 1** Culin (nourriture) to prepare; **a. les restes** to use up the leftovers; **a. une salade** to dress a salad **2 a. qch à qch** to fit or adapt sth to sth; **a. une pièce à un usage particulier** to adapt a room to or for a particular purpose; Opt **a. l'objectif sur l'infini** to set or adjust the lens to infinity

VI Opt to focus

VPR s'accommoder 1 Litt **s'a. à qch** to adapt to sth; **il s'accommode à toutes les circonstances** he's very adaptable; **je m'accommode à tout** anything will do for me **2 s'a. de qch** to make the best of sth, to put up with sth; **il vous faudra vous a. de cette pièce pour dormir** you'll have to make do with sleeping in this room **3 s'a. avec qn** to come to an agreement with sb; (par un compromis) to compromise with sb; (créancier) to compound with sb **4** Arch (dans un fauteuil etc) to make oneself comfortable, to settle down

Il faut noter que le verbe anglais **to accommodate** est un faux ami. Il ne signifie jamais **accommoder**.

accompagnateur, -trice [akɔ̃paɲatœr, -tris] **N 1** Mus accompanist **2** (d'un voyage organisé) courier, tour guide, tour leader; (de sortie scolaire) accompanying adult **3** Belg Rail **a. de train** ticket inspector

accompagnement [akɔ̃paɲmɑ̃] **NM 1** Mus accompaniment; **chanter sans a.** to sing unaccompanied **2** Mil etc close support; **tir d'a.** supporting fire; Aviat **chasseur d'a.** escort fighter **3** Culin (servi avec la viande etc) accompaniment, trimmings; **qu'y a-t-il comme a.?** what does it come with?, what is it served with?; **servi avec des frites en a.** served with chips

accompagner [akɔ̃paɲe] **VT 1** (venir avec, aller avec) (personne) to go or come with, surtout Fml to accompany; **il est arrivé accompagné de ses amis** he arrived with his friends; **accompagné de sa secrétaire** accompanied by his secretary; **est-ce que tu vas m'a.?** are you coming with me?; **a. qn jusqu'à la gare** to see sb to the station; **a. qn un bout de chemin** to go part of the way with sb; **l'angoisse qui accompagne ses pensées** the anguish which accompanies his thoughts **2** (escorter) to escort; (groupe de touristes) to act as courier or tour guide to; (groupe d'enfants) to accompany; **accessible aux enfants accompagnés uniquement** children must be accompanied by an adult **3** Mus **a. qn au piano** to accompany sb on the piano **4** (ajouter à) **il a accompagné ses mots d'un sourire** he said it with a smile; **il a accompagné le bouquet de fleurs d'une carte** he enclosed a card with the bouquet of flowers; Culin **a. une viande de pommes de terre** to serve potatoes with meat

VPR s'accompagner 1 Mus **elle s'accompagne elle-même** she plays her own accompaniment **2** Culin (avec des légumes etc) to be served; **le porc s'accompagne bien de pommes** apples go well with pork **3** (advenir en même temps que) to be accompanied by, to come with; **ces maux de tête s'accompagnent souvent de saignements de nez** these headaches are often accompanied by nosebleeds

accompli [akɔ̃pli] **ADJ** (musicien, linguiste, menteur etc) accomplished; **fait a.** fait accompli, accomplished fact; **on le mit devant**

le fait a. he was presented with a fait accompli; **il a quarante ans accomplis** he's turned forty; **à quarante ans accomplis, il serait temps que tu prennes une décision** now you've turned forty, it's time you made a decision

accomplir [akɔ̃plir] **VT 1** (but etc) to accomplish, to achieve; (tâche) to carry out; (formalités) to go through; (souhait, promesse) to fulfil; **a. son devoir** to perform one's duty **2** (apprentissage etc) to complete, to finish; **c'est une mauvaise action que tu as accomplie là** it was very wrong of you to do that; **a. un geste** to make a gesture

VPR s'accomplir to be realized, to come true; **notre souhait s'est accompli** our wish came true; Rel **que la volonté du Seigneur s'accomplisse** the Lord's will be done

accomplissement [akɔ̃plismɑ̃] **NM 1** (d'une tâche, d'une fonction) accomplishment, performance, carrying out; (d'un souhait) fulfilment; **c'était l'a. de plusieurs années de travail** it was the result of several years' work **2** (d'un apprentissage) completion

accord [akɔr] **NM 1** (traité) agreement; (non formel) understanding; (transaction commerciale) bargain; (pour résoudre un conflit) settlement; **conclure un a.** to enter into an agreement; **a. de principe** agreement in principle; **arriver ou parvenir à un a.** to come to an agreement, to reach (an) agreement; **un a. est intervenu d'après lequel ...** an agreement has been reached by which ...

2 (entente) agreement (**sur** on); **vivre en ou de bon a.** to live in harmony; **l'a. parfait qui règne entre nous deux** the perfect harmony between us; **être en a. avec la nature** to be in harmony or at one with nature; **vivre en a. avec ses principes** to live by one's principles; **être en a. avec soi-même** to be true to oneself; **en a. avec qn** in agreement with sb; **mettre d'a. deux points de vue** to reconcile two points of view; **se mettre d'a. ou tomber d'a. avec qn** to come to an agreement with sb; **être d'a. avec qn** to agree with sb; **les témoins ne sont pas d'a.** the witnesses disagree or differ; **mes comptes sont d'a.** my accounts balance; **tout est d'a.** everything is settled or arranged; **c'est d'a., d'a.!** all right!, OK!; **d'un commun a.** by common consent, by mutual agreement

3 (autorisation) consent; **il a donné son a.** he gave his consent; **la décision doit être prise en a. avec les différents intéressés** the decision must be made with the agreement or the consent of the different parties involved

4 Gram agreement, concordance (**avec** with); **l'a. de l'adjectif avec le nom** the agreement of the adjective with the noun; **les règles d'a.** the rules of agreement

5 Mus chord; **a. parfait** common chord; **faux a.** discord; **a. arpégé ou brisé ou figuré** broken chord; **a. de sensible** dominant seventh (chord)

6 (réglage) Mus pitch; Tech tuning; Mus **tenir l'a.** (d'un piano etc) to keep or stay in tune

▶▶ Com **a. d'achat et de vente** buy-sell agreement; Électron **a. d'antenne** alignment input; Com, Pol **a. d'association** partnership agreement; Com, Pol **a. bilatéral** bilateral agreement; Com **a. de clearing** clearing agreement; Com **a. commercial** trade agreement; Com **a. de compensation** offset agreement; Com, Pol **a. de coopération** cooperation agreement; Com **a. de crédit** credit agreement; Com **a. de distribution exclusive** exclusive distribution agreement; Com **a. d'exclusivité** exclusivity arrangement; Com **a. de franchise** franchise agreement; **A. général sur les tarifs et le commerce** General Agreement on Tariffs

and Trade; **accords d'Helsinki** Helsinki Agreement or Accord; Com **a. de libre-échange** Free Trade Agreement; Com **A. de libre-échange nord-américain** North American Free Trade Agreement; Com **a. de licence** licensing agreement; UE **A. monétaire européen** European monetary agreement; Com **a. multilatéral** multilateral agreement; Com **a. multilatéral sur l'investissement** multilateral investment agreement; Com **a. de partenariat** partnership agreement; UE **a. de préadhésion** pre-accession agreement; Radio **a. précis** fine tuning; Com **a. de représentation** agency agreement; Com **a. de reprise** buyback arrangement; **a. salarial** pay or wage agreement; **a. verbal** verbal agreement

accordage [akɔrdaʒ], **accordement** [akɔrdəmɑ̃] **NM** Mus tuning

accord-cadre, pl **accords-cadres NM** outline agreement

accordéon [akɔrdeɔ̃] **NM** accordion; **a. à touches ou à boutons/diatonique** piano/diatonic accordion; Fig **en a.** (chaussettes) wrinkled, coming down; **plissé ou plissage a.** accordion pleats; Fig **voiture en a.** concertinaed car

accordéoniste [akɔrdeɔnist] **N** accordionist, accordion player

accorder [akɔrde] **VT 1** (ennemis) to reconcile

2 Gram **a. le verbe avec le sujet** to make the verb agree with the subject

3 Mus (instrument de musique) to tune; **a. les violons au ton du piano** to tune the violins to the pitch of the piano; Fig **il faudrait a. vos violons** (de deux personnes ou plus) you'd better get your story straight

4 (faveur, pardon etc) to grant; (découvert bancaire) to allow, to give; (prêt) to authorize, to extend; **a. des dommages-intérêts** to award damages; **a. un escompte** to allow a discount; Com **a. une licence à qn** to license sb; **pouvez-vous m'a. quelques minutes?** can you spare me a few minutes?; **je n'ai pas essayé très longtemps, je vous l'accorde** I didn't try for very long, I grant you or I admit; **je t'accorde qu'il a tout pour plaire** he's very attractive, I('ll) grant you that; **a. à qn de faire qch** to give sb permission to do sth; **elle accorde la plus grande importance à ce travail** she attaches the greatest importance to this job; **il n'accorde pas la moindre valeur à ce que je dis** he doesn't attach the slightest value to anything I say; **c'est à peine s'il m'a accordé un regard** he barely glanced my way; **on m'a accordé huit jours de congé** I have been given a week's leave

5 (harmoniser) to match (up)

VPR s'accorder 1 (se mettre d'accord) (sur quelque chose) to agree, to come to an agreement (**avec qn** with sb); **s'a. sur le prix** to agree (on) the price; **s'a. à ou pour faire qch** to agree to do sth; **on s'accorde à penser que la maladie sera curable d'ici là** there is a general belief or it is generally believed that the disease will be curable by then; **tout le monde s'accorde à dire qu'elle est stupide** everyone agrees that she's stupid

2 (s'entendre) to get on (**avec qn** with sb); **ils s'accordent mal** they don't get on (at all) well; **ils s'accordent très bien** they get on very well (together)

3 (aller avec, correspondre) to correspond; (de couleurs etc) to harmonize; (de chiffres) to tally; (de témoignages) to square; (d'un projet) to fit in (**avec** with); **cette action ne s'accorde pas avec son caractère** this action is not in keeping or in line with his/her character; **cela ne s'accorde pas avec mes idées** it doesn't fit in with my ideas; Com **faire a. les livres** to agree the books; **il faut que la pratique s'accorde avec la théorie** the practice should correspond to *or* with the theory; **cette ceinture s'accorde à toutes les tenues** this belt goes with *or* can be worn with everything

4 *Gram* to agree; **le verbe s'accorde avec le sujet** the verb agrees with the subject

5 *(se donner)* to allow *or* grant oneself; **s'a. dix minutes de repos** to allow *or* give oneself ten minutes' rest

accordeur [akɔrdœr] NM (piano) tuner

accordoir [akɔrdwar] NM (piano) tuning key

accort [akɔr] ADJ *Litt* winsome

accostable [akɔstabl] ADJ *Naut* **plage a.** beach suitable for mooring

accostage [akɔstaʒ] NM **1** *Fam (de personne)* accosting **2** *Naut (du quai)* drawing alongside **3** *Astronaut* docking

accoster [akɔste] VT **1** *(personne)* to go *or* come up to, to accost; *(pour l'agresser)* to accost **2** *Naut* **a. un bateau le long du quai** to bring a boat alongside (the quay); **le bateau nous a accostés** the boat came alongside us ▸ VI *Naut (navire)* to come on board; *(d'un navire)* to berth, to dock; *Astronaut* to dock

accotement [akɔtmã] NM **1** *(de la route)* verge, *Am* berm; **a. non stabilisé** soft verge *or* shoulder **2** *Rail* shoulder

accoter [akɔte] VT to lean (**contre** against); *(navire, mur etc)* to shore up; **accoté contre qch** leaning against sth; **a. une échelle à** *ou* **contre un mur** to lean a ladder against a wall ▸ VPR **s'accoter** to lean; **s'a. à** *ou* **contre un mur** to lean against a wall

accotoir [akɔtwar] NM armrest, elbow rest; *(pour la tête)* headrest

accouchée [akuʃe] NF mother *(of newborn child)*; *Méd* **salle des accouchées** maternity ward

accouchement [akuʃmã] NM childbirth; **elle a eu un a. difficile** she had a difficult birth; **ce médecin fait plusieurs accouchements par jour** this doctor carries out *or* performs several deliveries a day; **on a dû provoquer l'a.** she had to be induced; *Fig* **il a enfin fini son texte, ce fut un véritable a.!** he really laboured to finish his text!
▸▸ **a. aux forceps** forceps delivery; **a. avant terme** premature delivery *or* birth; **a. naturel** natural childbirth; **a. prématuré** premature delivery *or* birth; **a. sans douleur** natural childbirth; **cours d'a. sans douleur** natural childbirth classes; **a. à terme** full-term delivery

accoucher [akuʃe] VI **1** to give birth; **a. d'un garçon** to give birth to a boy; **elle doit a. dans un mois** her baby's due in a month's time; **a. chez soi** to have a home birth *or* confinement **2** *Fam* **mais accouche donc!** come on, out with it! *or* spit it out!; **il a accouché de ce recueil de nouvelles** he has laboured to produce this collection of short stories
▸ VT to deliver

accoucheur, -euse [akuʃœr, -øz] N *(médecin)* obstetrician
▸ NF **accoucheuse** *(sage-femme)* midwife

accouder (s') [sakude] VPR to lean on one's elbow(s); **s'a. à la fenêtre** to lean out of the window; **s'a. sur son bureau** to be sitting with one's elbows on one's desk, to lean (one's elbows) on one's desk

accoudoir [akudwar] NM **1** *(de fauteuil)* armrest, elbow rest **2** *Archit* balustrade

accouple [akupl] NF leash

accouplement [akupləmã] NM **1** coupling, join(ing), link(ing); *Élec* connecting; *(de bœufs)* yoking **2** *(d'animaux)* pairing, mating
▸▸ *Aviat* **a. bendix** bendix drive; *Tech* **a. à débrayage** disengaging gear, clutch coupling; *Aut* **a. direct** direct drive; *Aut* **a. à glissement** slip clutch; *Aviat* **a. à griffe(s)** dog clutch, coupling

accoupler [akuple] VT **1** *(unir par deux)* to couple, to join; *(pièces)* to couple (up); *Élec (batteries etc)* to connect, to group; *(bœufs)* to yoke; **a. un moteur à une batterie** to connect an engine up to a battery **2** *(animaux)* to mate
▸ VPR **s'accoupler** to mate, to pair; *(avoir des relations sexuelles)* to copulate

accourir [akurir] VI *(conj like* **courir**; *aux* **avoir** *or* **être***)* to run (up), to rush up; **à mes cris, ils ont accouru** *ou* **sont accourus** they came running when they heard my cries; **ils ont accouru** *ou* **sont accourus à mon secours** they ran *or* came running to help me

accoutrement [akutrəmã] NM *Péj* dress, garb, *Fam* get-up

accoutrer [akutre] VT *souvent Péj* to rig out (**de** in); **accoutré d'une vieille capote** rigged out in an old army greatcoat; **tu ne peux pas l'a. ainsi, il est ridicule!** you can't rig him out like that, it looks ridiculous!
▸ VPR **s'accoutrer** to rig oneself out (**de** in)

accoutumance [akutymãs] NF **1** *(adaptation)* familiarization (**à** with); *(à la douleur etc)* inurement (**à** to); *Méd* **a. (à une drogue)** tolerance (to a drug); **l'effet d'a. des drogues dures** the habit-forming effect of hard drugs **2** *Litt (habitude)* habit, usage

accoutumé [akutyme] ADJ usual, habitual; **à l'heure accoutumée** at the usual time
▸ ADV **à l'accoutumée** usually; **il est arrivé à huit heures comme à l'accoutumée** he arrived at eight o'clock as usual

accoutumer [akutyme] VT **a. qn à qch** to accustom sb to sth, to get sb used to sth; **être accoutumé à qch** to be accustomed *or* used to sth
▸ VPR **s'accoutumer s'a. à** to get *or* become used *or* accustomed to; **s'a. à la fatigue** to become accustomed *or* used *or* hardened to fatigue; **je ne peux pas m'y a.** I can't get used to it

accouvage [akuvaʒ] NM artificial incubation

accréditation [akreditasjɔ̃] NF *(d'un ambassadeur, d'un journaliste)* accreditation, accrediting

accrédité, -ée [akredite] ADJ of good standing, accredited; **notre représentant a.** our authorized representative
▸ N agent; *Fin* beneficiary, payee

accréditer [akredite] VT **1** *(ambassadeur, journaliste)* to accredit; *(dans le générique d'un film etc)* to acknowledge; **je suis accrédité pour mener les négociations** I have been appointed to lead the negotiations; *Fin* **a. un client** to open an account for a client; *Fin* **être accrédité auprès d'une banque** to have credit facilities at a bank **2** *(rendre plausible)* to substantiate, to give credence to; **cette rumeur est accréditée par ses dernières actions** this rumour is substantiated *or* backed up by his latest actions
▸ VPR **s'accréditer** *(d'une rumeur etc)* to gain ground, to spread

accréditif [akreditif] NM credential; *(lettre de crédit)* letter of credit

accro [akro] *Fam* ADJ *(à la drogue, à une activité)* *Fig* addicted (**à** to), hooked (**à** on); **il va à tous les matchs de foot, il est a.** he goes to all the football matches, he's a real addict
▸ N *(à une activité)* addict

accroc [akro] NM **1** *(dans les vêtements etc)* tear, *Fml* rent **2** *Fig* hitch, difficulty, snag; **la cérémonie s'est déroulée sans a.** the ceremony went off without a hitch; **faire un a. à sa réputation** to spoil one's reputation, *Fam* to blot one's copybook

accrochage [akrɔʃaʒ] NM **1** *Aut* minor accident; *Boxe* clinch **2** *Rail* hitching on, coupling **3** *(d'un tableau etc)* hanging (up); *(dans*

un musée) (small) exhibition **4** *Radio (d'une station)* picking up **5** *(dispute)* altercation, squabble; *Mil* brush, skirmish

accroche [akrɔʃ] NF *(titre d'appel)* blurb; *(verbale)* striking (publicity) slogan, catch phrase

accroche-casseroles [akrɔʃkasrɔl] NM INV saucepan rack

accroche-cœur, *pl* **accroche-cœurs** NM kiss curl; **se faire des accroche-cœurs** to put one's hair into kiss curls

accrocher [akrɔʃe] VT **1** *(retenir)* to hook, to catch; **a. un asticot à son hameçon** to attach a maggot to one's fishing hook; **a. sa robe à des ronces** to catch one's dress on brambles; *Aut* **il a accroché mon pare-chocs** he caught *or* hit my bumper; **titre qui accroche le lecteur** striking *or* eye-catching title; **vitrine qui accroche le regard** eye-catching window display; *Fam* **a. qn** to buttonhole *or* corner sb

2 *Rail (wagon)* to hitch on, to couple **3** *(navire)* to grapple **4** *(suspendre)* to hang up; *Constr (porte)* to hang; **a. son manteau** to hang up one's coat; *Fig* **il faut avoir le cœur bien accroché** you need a strong stomach *or* strong nerves; *Arg* **a. sa montre** to put one's watch in hock, to pop one's watch **5** *Radio* **a. une station** to tune in to a station
▸ VI *(aux vêtements etc)* to stick, to catch; *Fig* **les négociations ont accroché** there has been a hitch in the negotiations; **ça ne marche pas très bien entre eux, ça accroche souvent** things aren't very good between them, they argue a lot; **ça n'a pas du tout accroché** *(entre deux personnes)* they didn't get on, *Fam* they didn't click
▸ VPR **s'accrocher 1 s'a. à qn/qch** to hold on to sb/sth; *(ne pas lâcher)*, *Fig* to cling on to sb/sth; **accroche-toi à la rampe** hold on tight *or* hang on to the handrail; *Fig* **elle s'accroche à lui, il est son seul espoir** she's clinging to him as her only hope; *Fig* **s'a. à des illusions** to cling to illusions; *Fig Fam* **accroche-toi, tu n'as pas tout entendu!** brace yourself, you haven't heard everything yet!

2 *(se fixer)* **ça s'accroche au mur par un clou** you fasten *or* attach it to the wall with a nail **3** *(tenir)* to stick at it, *Fam* to hang in there **4** *Boxe* to clinch; *Fig* **les deux voitures se sont accrochées** the two cars clipped each other **5** *Fam (se disputer)* to have a row; **s'a. avec qn** to have a row with sb, to clash with sb **6** *Fam* **tu peux te l'a.!** you can kiss goodbye to that!, you've had it!

accrocheur, -euse [akrɔʃœr, -øz] ADJ **1** *(tenace)* tenacious, stubborn **2** *(titre, slogan etc)* eye-catching, catchy
▸ N **c'est un a.** he's a fighter

accroire [akrwar] VT **faire a. à qn que ...** to make sb believe that ...; **elle veut nous en faire a.** *(abuser de notre crédulité)* she's trying to fool us; *(se faire valoir)* she's trying to impress us

accroissement [akrwasmã] NM **1** increase (**de** in); **les nouveaux équipements ont permis un a. de la productivité** the new equipment has led to an increase in productivity; **taux d'a.** rate of increase; *Math* **a. d'une fonction** increment of a function; *Fin* **a. global net** aggregate net increment **2** *(d'une plante etc)* growth

accroître [akrwatr] *(prp* **accroissant**; *pp* **accru**; *pr ind* **j'accrois, il accroît, n. accroissons, ils accroissent;** *impf* **j'accroissais;** *p hist* **j'accrus;** *fu* **j'accroîtrai***)* VT to increase, to enlarge, to add to; *(réputation)* to enhance
▸ VPR **s'accroître** to increase, to grow

accroupir (s') [sakrupir] VPR to squat

(down), to crouch (down); **accroupi** squatting, crouching

accroupissement [akrupismɑ̃] NM crouching, squatting

accru [akry] NM *Bot* sucker

accu [aky] NM *Élec* battery; *Fig* **recharger ses accus** to recharge one's batteries

accueil [akœj] NM *(façon d'accueillir)* reception, welcome, greeting; *(lieu)* reception; **tenir l'a.** to be on reception; **hôtesse d'a.** receptionist; **centre d'a.** reception centre; **passez à l'a.** go to the reception desk, go to reception; **a. handicapés** services for the disabled; **faire bon a. à qn/qch** to welcome sb *or* give sb a warm welcome/to welcome sth; **faire mauvais a. à qn** to give sb a cool reception; **ils ont fait un a. très mitigé à notre proposition** they gave our proposal a very mixed reception; **a. hostile** *ou* **défavorable** hostile reception; **discours/cérémonie d'a.** welcoming speech/ceremony; *Com* **faire (bon) a. à une traite** to honour a bill

accueillant [akœjɑ̃] ADJ welcoming

accueillir [akœjir] VT *(conj like* **cueillir***) (personne, nouvelle idée)* to receive, to greet; **(bien) a. qn** to welcome sb, to give sb a warm welcome; **mal a. qn** to give sb a bad reception; **a. qn à bras ouverts** to welcome sb with open arms; **cet hôtel peut a. jusqu'à 500 visiteurs** the hotel can accommodate up to 500 visitors; **j'ai un ami qui pourrait vous a. pendant un certain temps** I have a friend who could put you up for a while; **se faire a. par des volées de pierre** to be greeted with *or* by volleys of stones; **le film a été mal accueilli par le public** the film got a bad reception from the public; *Com* **a. une traite** to meet *or* honour a bill

acculer [akyle] VT *(personne)* to drive back (**contre** against); *(animal)* to bring to bay *or* to a stand; *Fig (personne)* to drive to the wall; *Fig* **être acculé aux aveux/à la ruine** to be forced into a confession/into bankruptcy

acculturation [akyltyrasjɔ̃] NF acculturation

accumulateur [akymylatœr] NM *Élec* battery, accumulator; *Aut* **a. de carburant** fuel accumulator

accumulation [akymylasjɔ̃] NF **1** *(action)* accumulation; *(d'énergie)* storage; *(d'argent)* hoarding; *(de dettes)* accumulation; *(en magasin)* stockpiling; *Fin* **a. de capital** capital accumulation; **a. des intérêts** accrual of interest; **chauffage par a.** storage heating; **chauffage à a. nocturne** (night) storage heating **2** *(stock)* accumulation; *(d'argent, de nourriture)* hoard; *(d'objets)* collection; *(d'erreurs)* series

accumuler [akymyle] VT to accumulate, to amass; *(nourriture, argent)* to hoard; *(dettes)* to accumulate; *(énergie)* to accumulate, to store; *(entasser)* to heap up, to pile up; *(en magasin)* to stockpile; **les médailles** to accumulate medals; **intérêts accumulés** accrued interest; **a. les preuves/renseignements** to gather evidence/information; **a. les gaffes/erreurs** to make a series of blunders/mistakes; **quand je suis fatigué, j'accumule les erreurs** I make lots of mistakes when I'm tired; *Fam* **tu les accumules!** you're making quite a habit of it!
VPR **s'accumuler** to accumulate; *(de nuages)* to gather, to build up; *Fin (des intérêts)* to accrue; *(des dettes)* to accumulate, to pile up; **les plaintes s'accumulent sur mon bureau** complaints are piling up on my desk; **les preuves s'accumulent contre elle** the evidence is building up against her

accusateur, -trice [akyzatœr, -tris] ADJ *(regard, doigt)* accusing, *Fml* accusatory; *(preuve)* incriminating; **j'ai pointé vers lui un**

index **a.** I pointed an accusing finger at him
N accuser; *(d'un officiel)* impeacher, arraigner; *Hist* **a. public** public prosecutor

accusatif [akyzatif] NM *Gram* accusative (case); **mot à l'a.** word in the accusative

accusation [akyzasjɔ̃] NF **1** *(condamnation)* accusation; **lancer** *ou* **porter une a. contre qn** to bring an accusation against sb **2** *Jur* **mettre qn en a.** to commit sb for trial; **quels sont les chefs** *ou* **les sujets d'a.?** what are the charges? **3** *Pol* impeachment, arraignment; **faire une a. contre la politique extérieure actuelle** to deliver an indictment against current foreign policy

accusé, -ée [akyze] ADJ *(trait etc)* prominent, pronounced, bold; *(baisse, hausse)* sharp; **rides très accusées** very deep wrinkles
N *(d'un crime)* accused; *(au tribunal)* defendant, prisoner at the bar
NM **a. de réception** *(pour une lettre)* acknowledgement (of receipt); *(d'un colis)* receipt; *Ordinat* acknowledge, acknowledgement, confirmation page

accuser [akyze] VT **1** *(incriminer)* to accuse; **a. qn de (faire) qch** to accuse sb of (doing) sth; **on l'accuse de meurtre** he is (being) accused of murder; *Fig* **a. le sort** to blame fate **2** *(tendance, baisse etc)* to show; **paroles qui accusent une grande ignorance** words that betray *or* show *or* reveal great ignorance; **la Bourse accuse une forte baisse** the Stock Market is registering big losses; **elle accuse trente ans** she looks (at least) thirty; **il commence à a. son âge** he's starting to look his age; **il accuse le coup** *Boxe* he's feeling that one; *Fig* he's obviously shaken **3** *(faire ressortir)* to define, to show up, to accentuate; **esquisse qui accuse tous les muscles** sketch that brings out every muscle; **le temps a accusé son avarice** he has got meaner with time **4** **a. réception de qch** to acknowledge (receipt of) sth
VPR **s'accuser 1** *(se rendre coupable)* to admit, to confess; **il s'est accusé du crime pour protéger son frère** he confessed to the crime to protect his brother **2** *(se renforcer)* to become more pronounced *or* marked

acerbe [asɛrb] ADJ sharp, harsh, acerbic; **réprimande a.** sharp reprimand; **discussion a.** ill-tempered discussion; **parler d'un ton a.** to speak sharply

acéré [asere] ADJ *(lame etc)* sharp; *Fig (remarque)* cutting, scathing; **langue acérée** sharp tongue; **il écrit des satires d'une plume acérée** he writes satire with a scathing pen

acérer [asere] VT *(j'acère; j'acérerai) (rare)* to sharpen, to give a keen edge to

acériculteur, -trice [aserikyltœr] N *Can* maple syrup and sugar producer

acériculture [aserikyltyr] NF *Can* production of maple syrup and sugar

acétate [asetat] NM *Chimie* acetate; **a. de cuivre** copper acetate; *Tex* **a. de cellulose** cellulose acetate

acétique [asetik] ADJ *Chimie* acetic; **odeur a.** vinegary smell

acétocellulose [asetɔselyloz] NF *Chimie* cellulose acetate

acétone [asetɔn] NF *Chimie* acetone

acétylène [asetilɛn] NM *Chimie* acetylene; **lampe à a.** acetylene lamp *or Am* torch

acétylsalicylique [asetilsalisilik] ADJ *Pharm* **acide a.** acetylsalicylic acid

ACF [aseɛf] NM *(abrév* **Automobile Club de France***)* = automobile association of France

achalandage [aʃalɑ̃daʒ] NM *Jur, Com* custom, customers, clientele; *(fonds de commerce)* goodwill

achalandé [aʃalɑ̃de] ADJ **bien a.** well-stocked; *Vieilli (ayant nombreux clients)* with a large clientele; **mal a.** *Vieilli (ayant peu de clients)* with a small clientele; *(mal approvisionné)* poorly-stocked

achalander [aʃalɑ̃de] VT *Fam (magasin)* to stock

achaler [aʃale] VT *Can* to annoy, to bother

achards [aʃar] NMPL *Culin* relish

acharné [aʃarne] ADJ *(enragé, furieux) (lutte)* desperate, bitter; *(concurrence)* cut-throat; *(travail)* relentless; *(joueur)* inveterate; **meute acharnée à la poursuite** pack in hot *or* eager pursuit; **hommes acharnés les uns contre les autres** men fighting desperately against each other; **ils sont acharnés à se faire du mal** they're bent on hurting each other, they're desperately trying to hurt each other

acharnement [aʃarnəmɑ̃] NM relentlessness; **a. au** *ou* **pour le travail** passion for work; **avec a.** relentlessly; **se battre avec a.** to fight tooth and nail; *Pharm* **a. thérapeutique** = use of intensive medication to keep a person alive

acharner [aʃarne] VPR **s'acharner s'a. après** *ou* **contre** *ou* **sur qn** *(persécuter)* to be always after sb; **le meurtrier s'est acharné sur sa victime** the murderer savaged his victim; **les examinateurs se sont acharnés sur le candidat** the examiners really stuck the knife into the candidate; **pourquoi t'acharnes-tu à essayer de le lui faire comprendre?** why are you so determined to try to make him understand?; **le malheur s'acharne après lui** he is dogged by misfortune; **s'a. à** *ou* **sur qch** to work desperately hard at sth, to slave (away) at sth; **il s'acharne à vous nuire** he is set on harming you; **elle ne se décourage pas, elle s'acharne** she doesn't let herself be discouraged, she just keeps at it *or Fam* keeps plugging away
VT *Vieilli* **a. la meute après une bête** to set the pack on (the track of) a quarry; **a. un chien** to flesh *or* blood a hound

achat [aʃa] NM **1** *(action)* purchase, buying; **faire un a.** to make a purchase, to buy something; **faire l'a. de qch** to buy sth; **aller faire ses achats** to go shopping; **pouvoir d'a.** purchasing power; **prix d'a.** purchase price; **centrale d'a.** central purchasing office; *Can* **agent d'a.** procurement officer **2** *(ce qu'on a acheté)* purchase; **ses achats** one's shopping, *surtout Fml* one's purchases; **tu me montres tes achats?** show me what you've bought

▸▸ **a. au comptant** *ou* **contre espèces** *ou* **en espèces** cash purchase; **a. à crédit** purchase on credit, credit purchase; **a. de droits** rights buying; **a. d'espace** media buying; **a. impulsif** impulse buy; **achats institutionnels** institutional buying; *Com* **a. juste à temps** just-in-time purchasing; **a. non prémédité** impulse buy; **a. renouvelé** repeat purchase; **a. spontané** impulse buy; *Com* **a. de système** systems buying; *Fin* **a. à terme** forward purchase; **achats centralisés** centralized purchasing; *Mktg* **achats comparatifs** comparison shopping; **achats directs** direct purchasing; **achats à domicile** teleshopping; **achats hors taxes** tax-free shopping; **achats regroupés** one-stop buying *or* shopping; **achats spéculatifs** speculative buying; *Bourse* **a. à terme** forward buying

acheminement [aʃminmɑ̃] NM **1** *(progrès)* step, progress (**à, vers** towards) **2** *(de marchandises, paquets)* forwarding, shipment; **l'a. des marchandises se fait par Calais** the goods are routed through Calais; **a. du courrier** mail delivery *or* handling

acheminer [aʃmine] VT **1** *(conduire) (personne)* to set on his way (**sur, vers** towards)

2 *(marchandises etc)* to dispatch, to convey, to forward (**sur, vers** to); *(courrier)* to handle **VPR s'acheminer s'a. vers** to set out for, to make one's way towards; **s'a. vers le succès** to be heading for success; **nous nous acheminons vers de grands changements structurels** we are moving towards great structural changes

acheter [aʃte] *(j'achète, n. achetons; j'achèterai)* **VT 1 a. qch** to buy sth, *Fml* to purchase sth; **a. qch à qn** to buy sth from sb; **a. qch à** *ou* **pour qn** to buy sth for sb; **je vais lui a. un livre** I'm going to buy him/her a book; **a. en gros/au détail** to buy wholesale/retail; **a. qch par correspondance** to buy sth by mail order; **a. qch à crédit/au comptant** to buy sth on credit/for cash; **a. qch à tempérament** to buy sth on hire purchase *or Am* on the installment plan; *Fin* **a. à terme** to buy forward; **j'ai acheté ce livre 10 euros** I bought this book for 10 euros; **je ne l'ai pas acheté cher** I didn't pay much for it *or* a high price for it; **a. qch (à) bon marché** to buy sth cheap; *Fig* **a. qch chèrement** to pay a high price for sth; *Fig* **c'est une façon bien basse d'a. votre pardon** it's a very low way of buying forgiveness; **a. chat en poche** to buy a pig in a poke

2 *Fam (personne)* to bribe, to buy off; **a. la complicité de qn** to buy sb's silence; **se faire a.** to be bribed

VPR s'acheter ça s'achète en pharmacie you can buy it/them in any pharmacy; **ces choses-là ne s'achètent pas** such things cannot be bought *or* are not for sale; *Fig* **s'a. une conduite** to turn over a new leaf

acheteur, -euse [aʃtœr, -øz] **N** buyer, purchaser; *Jur* vendee; *Com* **elle est acheteuse pour Prisunic®** she is a buyer for Prisunic®; *Mktg* **a. impulsif** impulsive buyer, impulse buyer; **a. industriel** business buyer; **je suis a.!** I'm in the market!, I'm interested!

achevé [aʃve] **ADJ** *(artiste, style etc)* accomplished; *(travail)* perfect; *(perfection)* absolute; **il est d'un ridicule a.** he's utterly ridiculous; *Fam* **sot a.** utter *or* absolute fool; **menteur a.** *(accompli)* consummate *or* accomplished liar; *(sans honte)* out and out liar

achèvement [aʃɛvmɑ̃] **NM** *(de travaux)* completion, finishing; **date d'a.** target *or* completion date

> Il faut noter que le nom anglais **achievement** est un faux ami. Il signifie **réussite**.

achever [aʃve] *(j'achève, n. achevons; j'achèverai)* **VT 1** *(finir) (discours)* to end, to conclude; *(travail etc)* to finish (off), to complete; **laisse-lui le temps d'a. sa phrase** let him finish what he's saying; **toutes nos peines sont loin d'être achevées** our troubles are all far from over; **avant d'a. ma lettre** before closing *or* finishing my letter; **a. ses jours** *ou* **sa vie** to end one's days; **a. de faire qch** to finish doing sth; **achève de boire ton café** drink up *or* finish your coffee

2 *(mettre à mort) (personne)* to finish off; *(animal)* to put out of its misery *or* out of pain; *Fam* **cette grosse perte l'a achevé** this heavy loss was the end of him; *Fam* **ça m'a achevé** that really finished me (off)

VPR s'achever 1 *(finir)* to draw to a close, to end; **c'est ainsi que l'histoire s'achève** that's how the story finishes *or* ends; **le jour s'acheva tristement** the day closed *or* ended sadly *or* on a sad note **2** *(d'un travail)* to reach completion

> Il faut noter que le verbe anglais **to achieve** est un faux ami. Il ne signifie jamais **achever**.

achigan [aʃigɑ̃] **NM** *Can (poisson)* (black) bass

Achille [aʃil] **N** Achilles

achoper [aʃɔpe] **VI** *Can Fig* **a. sur qch** to stumble over sth

achoppement [aʃɔpmɑ̃] **NM** *Litt* obstacle, difficulty; **pierre d'a.** stumbling block

achopper [aʃɔpe] **VI** **c'est là que ça achoppe** that's the stumbling block; **a. au problème de …** to come to grief over the problem of …; **a. sur un mot** to stumble over a word

achromatique [akromatik] **ADJ** achromatic

achrome [akrom] **ADJ** *Phot* achromous, achromatous

acide [asid] **ADJ** acid(ic); *(au goût)* tart, sour; *Fig (personne)* witty; *Fig (propos, remarques)* acid, cutting; **une pomme a.** a sour apple; *Biol* **milieu a.** acidic environment; **savon a.** acidic soap

NM *(drogue), Chimie* acid; **a. désoxyribonucléique** deoxyribonucleic acid; **a. folique** folic acid; **a. gras** fatty acid

acidificateur [asidifikatœr] **NM** acidifier, acidifying agent

acidification [asidifikasjɔ̃] **NF** acidification

acidifier [asidifje] **VT** to acidify

VPR s'acidifier to become acid, to turn sour

acidité [asidite] **NF** acidity; *(d'une etc)* sourness, tartness; *Fig (d'un commentaire)* wittiness; *Chimie* **l'a. d'une solution** the acidity of a solution; *Méd* **a. gastrique** stomach, hyperacidity

acidose [asidoz] **NF** *Méd* acidosis

acidulé [asidyle] **ADJ** acidulous; **bonbons acidulés** acid drops

acier [asje] **NM** steel; **lame d'a.** *ou* **en a.** steel blade; **a. au chrome/au nickel** chrome/nickel steel; *Fig* **avoir un moral d'a.** to be very resilient, *Fam* to be a tough cookie; *Fig* **regard d'a.** steely look

▶ ▶ **a. au carbone** carbon steel; **a. cémenté** case-hardened steel; **a. embouti** pressed steel; **a. galvanisé** galvanized steel; **a. inoxydable** stainless steel; **a. à ressort** spring steel; **a. trempé** hardened *or* tempered steel

aciérie [asjeri] **NF** steel works

aciériste [asjerist] **N** steel maker *or* manufacturer

acmé [akme] **NM OU NF** *Litt* acme, peak; *Méd* crisis

acné [akne] **NF** acne; **a. juvénile** *ou* **vulgaire** teenage acne; **avoir de l'a.** to have *or* suffer from acne; **traitement contre l'a.** acne treatment

acolyte [akɔlit] **NM 1** *Péj* confederate, accomplice **2** *Rel* acolyte

acompte [akɔ̃t] **NM** instalment, *Am* installment; *(avance, premier versement)* payment on account, down payment; **payer par acomptes** to pay by *or* in instalments; **recevoir un a.** to receive something on account; **verser un a.** to make a down payment; **a. de** *ou* **sur dividende** interim dividend; *Fin* **a. provisionnel** interim payment; **a. mensuel** monthly instalment, monthly payment; **recevoir un a. sur son salaire** to receive an advance on one's salary; *Fig* **j'ai pris un petit a.** I had a little taster

aconit [akɔnit] **NM** *(plante)* aconite

a contrario [akɔ̃trarjo] **ADV** **raisonnement a c.** converse reasoning

acoquiner (s') [sakɔkine] **VPR** *Péj* to team up, to fall in (**avec** with)

Açores [asɔr] **NFPL les A.** the Azores

à-côté, *pl* **à-côtés** [akote] **NM 1** *(verbal)* aside **2** *(élément secondaire)* **les à-côtés d'une question** the side issues of a question; **les à-côtés de l'histoire** sidelights on history **3** *Fam (financier etc)* extra; **il a quelques à-côtés** he makes a bit on the side

à-coup, *pl* **à-coups** [aku] **NM** jerk, jolt, jar,

shock; *Élec* surge (of current); **il y eut des à-coups lorsque la voiture démarra** the car jerked *or* jolted as it set off; **il travaille par à-coups** he works by *or* in fits and starts; *Aut* **le moteur a des à-coups** the engine judders; **sans à-coups** smoothly

acousticien, -ienne [akustisjɛ̃, -jɛn] **N** acoustician

acoustique [akustik] **ADJ** acoustic; **cornet a.** ear trumpet; **tuyau a.** speaking tube; **voûte a.** whispering gallery; **les phénomènes acoustiques** acoustics

NF *Phys* acoustics; **a. d'une salle** acoustics of a hall; **avoir une bonne/mauvaise a.** to have good/bad acoustics

acquéreur [akerœr] **NM** purchaser, buyer; *Jur* vendee; **notre voiture n'a pas trouvé a.** we couldn't find a buyer for our car

acquérir [akerir] *(prp* **acquérant**; *pp* **acquis**; *pr ind* **j'acquiers, il acquiert, n. acquérons, ils acquièrent**; *pr sub* **j'acquière, n. acquérions**; *impf* **j'acquérais**; *p hist* **j'acquis**; *fu* **j'acquerrai**) **VT 1** *(obtenir)* to acquire, to obtain, to get; *(habitude)* to get into; *(expérience, confiance)* to acquire, to gain; **nous avons acquis la certitude de son innocence** we have established beyond doubt that he/she is innocent; **l'expérience acquise au long d'une carrière** the experience gained in the course of one's career; **a. de mauvaises habitudes** to get into bad habits; *Prov* **un bien en acquiert un autre** money attracts money

2 *(prendre)* to acquire; **a. de la valeur** to go up *or* increase in value

3 *(devenir propriétaire de)* to acquire; *(acheter)* to purchase, to buy; **a. une terre d'un voisin** to purchase *or* buy land from a neighbour; **a. un bien par héritage** to come into *or* to inherit some property

4 **a. qch à qn** to bring sth to sb, to bring sb sth

VPR s'acquérir 1 *(se prendre)* **cette habitude s'acquiert facilement** it's easy to get into this habit; **une fortune peut s'a. de différentes manières** there are different ways of making one's fortune **2** *(s'attirer)* to win, to gain

acquêt [akɛ] **NM** *Jur* acquisition, *(fortuit)* windfall; **communauté réduite aux acquêts** = marriage settlement whereby only goods acquired since the marriage are deemed to be held in common

acquiescement [akjɛsmɑ̃] **NM** acquiescence; *Jur* **a. licite/conditionnel** lawful/conditional consent; **hocher la tête en signe d'a.** to nod one's agreement

acquiescer [akjɛse] **VI** *(j'acquiesçai(s); n. acquiesçons)* **a. à qch** *(se résigner)* to acquiesce in sth; *(consentir)* to agree *or* assent to sth; **a. d'un signe de tête** to agree with a nod of the head, to nod one's approval; **elle a acquiescé d'un sourire** she gave a smile of agreement, she smiled her agreement; *Jur* **a. à un acte** to consent (fully) to an act

acquis [aki] **ADJ** *(savoir, caractères etc)* acquired; **fait a.** established *or* accepted fact; **tenir pour a.** to take for granted; **son aide nous est acquise** we can take it for granted that he will help us; **droits a.** vested interests; **cela est a.** that's been established; **ce droit lui est a.** he/she has an established right in this respect; **je vous suis tout a.** I entirely agree

NM *(connaissances)* knowledge; *(réussite)* attainments, achievements; **a. sociaux** social benefits that have been won

acquisitif, -ive [akizitif, -iv] **ADJ** *Jur* acquisitive

acquisition [akizisjɔ̃] **NF 1** *(fait)* acquisition; **faire l'a. de qch** *(entrer en possession de)* to acquire sth; *(acheter)* to purchase sth **2** *(bien acquis)* acquisition; *(bien acheté)* purchase; **c'est ma dernière a.** it's my latest acquisition

3 *UE* **a. intracommunautaire** intra-Community acquisition

acquit [aki] **NM 1** *Com* receipt; **donner a. de qch** to give a receipt for sth; **pour a.** received (with thanks), paid; **a. de douane** customs receipt; **a. de paiement** receipt; **a. de transit** transshipment note **2** *(d'un navire)* clearance **3** *(d'une promesse)* discharge, release; **par a. de conscience** to ease one's conscience, to put one's mind at rest; **faire qch par manière d'a.** to do sth as a matter of form **4** *Jur* sentence *ou* ordonnance **d'a.** order of acquittal

acquit-à-caution, *pl* **acquits-à-caution** [akiakosjɔ̃] **NM** bond note

acquittement [akitmɑ̃] **NM 1** *(d'une dette etc)* discharge, payment; *(d'effet)* acquittal **2** *Jur* acquittal; **verdict d'a.** verdict of not guilty

acquitter [akite] **VT 1 a. qn** *(d'une obligation etc)* to release sb **2** *Jur* **a. un accusé** to acquit *or* discharge a defendant **3** *(obligation)* to fulfil; *(dette)* to discharge, to pay off; *(chèque)* to endorse **4** *(facture)* to receipt, to pay **VPR s'acquitter s'a. d'une obligation/d'un devoir** to fulfil *or* carry out *or* discharge an obligation/a duty; **s'a. de son devoir** to do one's duty; **s'a. d'une facture** to pay a bill; **comment pourrai-je m'a. envers vous?** how can I repay you?

acre [akr] **NF** *Hist* acre
NM *Can* acre

âcre [akr] **ADJ** *(goût)* bitter; *(odeur)* pungent, acrid; *Fig (souvenir)* bitter; *(propos, humeur)* caustic

âcreté [akrəte] **NF** *(d'un goût)* bitterness; *(d'une odeur)* pungency; *Fig (de la jalousie, la douleur)* bitterness; *(de propos)* caustic nature

acrimonie [akrimɔni] **NF** *(mauvaise humeur)* acrimony; *(d'un discours, d'une querelle)* acrimoniousness, bitterness

acrimonieux, -ieuse [akrimɔnjø, -jøz] **ADJ** *(mots, querelle etc)* acrimonious, bitter

acrobate [akrɔbat] **N** acrobat; *Fig* **c'est un a.** he can wriggle out of anything
NM *(mammifère)* flying squirrel

acrobatie [akrɔbasi] **NF 1** *(art)* acrobatics; **numéro** *ou* **tour d'a.** acrobatic feat; **faire des acrobaties** to do *or* perform acrobatics; **a. aérienne** stunt flying, aerobatics **2** *Fig (virtuosité)* clever trick; **a. intellectuelle** intellectual acrobatics; **il s'en sortira par une a.** he'll wriggle out of it somehow

acrobatique [akrɔbatik] **ADJ** acrobatic

acronyme [akrɔnim] **NM** *Ling* acronym

acropole [akrɔpɔl] **NF** acropolis; **l'A.** the Acropolis

acrostiche [akrɔstiʃ] **NM** acrostic

acrylique [akrilik] **ADJ** *Chimie, Tex* acrylic
NM *Tex* acrylic; **pull en a.** acrylic pullover

ACT [asete] **NM** *(abrév* **arbre à cames en tête)** ohc

acte [akt] **NM 1** *(action)* action, act, deed; **moins de paroles, des actes!** let's have less talk and more action!; **a. de courage** act of bravery *or* courage, brave *or* courageous act *or* action; **faire a. de bonne volonté** to show willing *or* good will; **faire a. d'autorité** to use *or* exercise one's authority; **passer aux actes** to take action; **il menace de se suicider, j'ai peur qu'il passe aux actes** I'm scared that he'll carry out his threats of suicide; **faire a. de présence** to put in an appearance; **faire a. de candidature à un emploi** to submit an application *or* to apply for a job; **faire a. de souverain** to exercise the royal prerogative; **faire a. d'héritier** to come forward as an heir; **a. de terrorisme** act of terrorism; **a. de guerre** act of war; **être facturé à l'a.** to be billed on a usage basis

2 *Jur* instrument; *(establishing ownership)* deed, title; **a. authentique** *ou* **notarié, a. sur papier timbré** deed executed and authenticated by a notary; **dont a.** duly noted *or* acknowledged **3** *(certificat)* record; **prendre a. de qch** to record *or* note *or* take a note of *or* set down sth; *Fml* **nous prenons a. de votre candidature** we acknowledge your application; **donner a. de qch** to grant sth, to admit sth **4** **actes** *(de procès etc)* records; *(d'un organisme scientifique etc)* transactions; *(d'un colloque)* proceedings

5 *Théâtre* act; **tragédie en trois actes** three-act tragedy, tragedy in three acts; **dans le second a.** in the second act
▸▸ *Jur* **a. d'accusation** bill of indictment, charges; *Bible* **Actes des Apôtres** Acts of the Apostles; *Jur* **a. d'association** partnership deed; *Jur* **a. de cession** deed *or* certificate of transfer; *Rel* **a. de contrition** act of contrition; **a. de décès** death certificate; *Jur* **a. de dernière volonté** last will and testament; **a. d'état civil** = certificate of birth/marriage/death; *Rel* **a. de foi** act of faith; *Jur* **a. hypothécaire** mortgage deed; *Jur* **a. judiciaire** writ; **a. de mariage** marriage certificate; **a. médical** medical treatment; **a. de naissance** birth certificate; *Jur* **a. notarié** notarized deed; *Jur* **a. de propriété** title deed; *Jur* **a. sous seing privé** private agreement; **a. unique européen** Single European Act; *Jur* **a. de vente** bill of sale, deed of sale

acter [akte] **VT** *Belg (noter)* to take a note of, to note; *Jur* to record

acteur, -trice [aktœr, -tris] **N 1** *Théâtre, Cin* actor, *f* actress; **a. de cinéma** screen actor, movie *or Br* film actor; **se faire a.** to go on the stage; **a. comique** comic actor; **a. de composition** feature player; **a. de théâtre** stage actor; **a. à transformations** quick-change artist; **a. virtuel** virtual-reality actor, *Fam* synthespian **2** *(d'un événement)* participant; *(sur le marché)* player; **les différents acteurs de la négociation** the different participants in *or* parties involved in the negotiation; **a. économique** economic agent *or* player; **a. du marché** market participant, market player; **les acteurs sociaux** = employers, workers and trade unions

actif, -ive [aktif, -iv] **ADJ 1** *(défenseur, participation)*, *Gram (verbe, voix)* active; *(substance etc)* potent, active; **le principe a. d'un produit** the active ingredient of a product; *Écon* **population active** labour force; **femme active** working woman; *Mil* **armée active** regular army; **service a.** (active) service; **citoyen a.** person with the right to vote **2** *(personne)* active; **sa grand-mère est très active pour son âge** his grandmother is very sprightly for her age; **faire un commerce a.** to do brisk trade **3** *Com, Jur* **dettes actives** accounts receivable **4** *Ordinat (fichier, fenêtre)* active; **rendre a.** *(unité etc)* to activate
NM 1 *Com* assets; *(moyens financiers)* credit (account); **mettre qch à l'a. de qn** to credit sb with sth; *Fig* **il faut mettre sa patience à son a.** you have to give him credit for patience; *Fig* **avoir plusieurs prix à son a.** to have several prizes to one's name *or* credit; *Fig* **avoir plusieurs infractions à son a.** to have several offences to one's name
2 *Gram* **verbe à l'a.** verb in the active voice
VOIR GRAMMAIRE A40
N active person; **c'est un a.** he likes to do things, he's a doer
▸▸ *Compta* **a. brut** gross assets; **a. circulant** circulating *or* floating *or* current assets; **a. corporel** tangible asset; **a. disponible liquide** available assets; **a. fictif** fictitious asset; **a. immobilisé** fixed *or* capital asset; **a.**

incorporel intangible asset; **a. liquide** liquid assets; **a. net** net assets *or* worth; **a. réel** real assets; **a. de roulement** current assets; **a. sous-jacent** underlying asset; **a. soustractif** depreciated credit balance; **a. stable** fixed *or* long-term asset

action [aksjɔ̃] **NF 1** *(acte)* action, act; **l'a. de marcher** the act of walking; **commettre** *ou* **faire une a. insensée** to commit a senseless act; **commettre** *ou* **faire une bonne/mauvaise a.** to do a good/bad deed; **a. d'éclat** brilliant feat

2 *(influence, effet) (d'une substance)* action, effect; **a. sur qch** action *or* effect on sth; **ce désherbant n'a aucune a. sur le liseron** this weedkiller has no effect on bindweed; **exercer une a. sur qn** to have influence over sb; **sans a.** ineffectual, ineffective; **a. de l'eau** effect of water; **par l'a. personnelle d'un membre du club** through the personal intervention of a club member

3 *(activité) (d'une machine etc)* action, motion, working, functioning; **entrer en a.** *(d'une loi etc)* to come into force *or* effect; *Pol* **recourir à l'a. directe** to resort to direct action; **hors d'a.** out of action; **développer son champ d'a.** to expand one's sphere of activity *or* field of operations, to expand the scope of one's activities; **homme d'a.** man of action, action man; **passer à l'a.** to take action, to act; **mettre qch en a.** to set sth in motion, to put sth into operation

4 *(d'un orateur etc)* action, gesture **5** *(intrigue)* action; *(d'une pièce, d'un roman)* plot; **scène qui retarde l'a.** scene that delays the action; **un film d'a.** action-packed movie; *(genre)* action movie; *TV, Cin* **a.!** action!; **l'a. se déroule à Prague** the action is set in Prague

6 *Fin* share; *(document)* share certificate; **actions** shares, *esp Am* stock; **avoir des actions dans** to have shares *or* a shareholding in; **détenir des actions d'une société** to have shares in a company; **compagnie par actions** joint-stock company; **hausse/baisse des actions** rise/fall in the value of shares; *Fig* **les actions du ministre montent/baissent** the minister's stock is rising/falling

7 *Jur* action, lawsuit, trial; **intenter une a. judiciaire** *ou* **en justice** to take legal action; **mener une a. contre qch** to take action against sth; *(pour de l'argent)* to sue sb; **a. en divorce** divorce suit

8 *Mil* action, fight, engagement; **dans le feu de l'a.** *(pendant la guerre)* in the heat of battle; *Fig* in the heat of the moment **9** *Suisse (vente promotionnelle)* **acheter qch en a.** to buy sth on special offer; **acheter une a.** to buy something on special offer
▸▸ *Fin* **a. d'attribution** bonus share; *Fin* **a. de capitalisation** capital share; *Fin* **a. cotée (en Bourse)** quoted share; *Fin* **a. de distribution** income share; *Fin* **a. gratuite** bonus share; *Fin* **a. de jouissance** dividend share; *Ordinat* **a. logique** logical operation; *Fin* **a. nominative** bearer registered share; *Fin* **a. ordinaire** ordinary share, *Am* common stock; *Fin* **a. au porteur** bearer stock share; *Fin* **a. privilégiée** preference share, *Am* preferred stock; *Mktg* **a. de stimulation** sales stimulation campaign; *Mktg* **a. de vente** sales campaign *or* drive *or* action

actionnaire [aksjɔner] **N** *Fin* shareholder, *Am* stockholder; **a. majoritaire/minoritaire** majority/minority shareholder, *Am* majority/minority stockholder; **a. de référence** major shareholder *or Am* stockholder

actionnariat [aksjɔnarja] **NM** *Fin* shareholding; **a. intermédiaire** nominee shareholding; **a. ouvrier** workers' shareholding, worker share ownership

actionnement [aksjɔnmɑ̃] **NM** activation; **a. à distance** remote-control operation

actionner [aksjɔne] **VT 1** *(mettre en marche)* to start up, to turn on; *(faire fonctionner)* to operate, to drive, to run; *Tech* to actuate; **actionné à la main** hand operated; **a. les freins** to put on *or* apply the brakes **2** *Jur* to sue, to bring an action against; **a. qn en dommages-intérêts** to sue sb for damages

actionneur [aksjɔnœr] **NM** *Tech* actuator

activation [aktivasjɔ̃] **NF** activation

activé [aktive] **ADJ** *Chimie* activated; *Ordinat* active

activement [aktivmɑ̃] **ADV** actively, briskly, busily; **prendre a. qch en charge** to take an active responsibility for sth; **s'occuper a. de qch** to be actively engaged in sth; **vivre a.** to lead an active life

activer [aktive] **VT 1** *(presser)* to stimulate, to rouse; *(accélérer)* to speed up; *(feu)* to stoke; **a. un ouvrage** to press on with *or* to speed up a piece of work; *Fam* **activez!** get a move on! **2** *Chimie, Nucl etc* to activate **3** *Ordinat* to activate; **a. une option** to select an option
▸ **VPR s'activer** to be busy, to busy oneself, to bustle about; **s'a.** to get on *or* press on (**à qch** with sth)

activisme [aktivism] **NM** *Pol* activism

activiste [aktivist] **ADJ, N** *Pol* activist

activité [aktivite] **NF** activity; *(d'une substance)* potency; **l'a. d'une ville** the (amount of) activity in a city; **elle déploie une grande a. au travail** she invests a lot of energy in her work; **maintenir l'a. industrielle** to keep industry going; **une région reconnue pour son a.** a region known for its industrial/cultural/*etc* activity; **en a.** in action, in operation, in progress; *(personne)* working, employed; **en pleine a.** *(entreprise)* in full operation *or* production, fully operational; *(personne)* very busy; *(secteur économique, hôtel etc)* very busy, bustling; **un moment de grande a.** a very busy time; **marché sans a.** dull market; **l'usine est en a.** the factory is working *or* is in production; **volcan en a.** active volcano; **le temps d'a. d'un employé** the length of (active) service of an employee; **être en a. (de service)** to be on active duty *or* on the active list; **je ne connais pas ses activités** I know nothing about his activities; **le centre de jeunes propose les activités suivantes** the following activities are available at the youth centre
▸ ▸ **a. économique** economic activity; **a. de plein air** outdoor activity; **a. professionnelle** occupation; **a. solaire** solar activity; **a. sportive** sport, sporting activity; *Scol etc* **activités dirigées** project work, projects

actrice [aktris] **NF** actress *(voir aussi* **acteur 1***)*

actuaire [aktɥɛr] **N** actuary

actualisation [aktɥalizasjɔ̃] **NF 1** *(de textes etc)* updating, update **2** *Écon* discounting; **taux d'a.** rate of discount **3** *Phil* actualization **4** *Ordinat* refresh

actualiser [aktɥalize] **VT 1** *(texte, méthode de travail)* to update **2** *Écon* to discount **3** *Phil* **a. qch** to turn sth into a reality, to actualize sth **4** *Ordinat* to refresh
▸ **VPR s'actualiser 1** *(se moderniser)* to become more up to date **2** *Phil* to become a reality, to come into being

actualité [aktɥalite] **NF 1** topicality; **l'a., les questions d'a.** current affairs; **l'a. politique française** the current French political scene; **cette question est toujours d'a.** this is still a topical question; **question d'une a. brûlante** burning question; **les actualités** *(dans la presse)* current events *or* affairs; *TV, Radio* news; **il est passé aux actualités** he was on the news; **actualités filmées** newsreel; **actualités télévisées** television news **2** *Phil* actuality, reality

actuariat [aktɥarja] **NM** actuarial profession

actuariel, -ielle [aktɥarjɛl] **ADJ** actuarial

actuel, -elle [aktɥɛl] **ADJ** present, current; **le gouvernement a.** the present government; **l'état a. du pays** the present *or* current state of the country; **valeur actuelle** present *or* current value; **à l'heure actuelle** at the present time; **dans la situation actuelle** as things are *or* stand at the moment; **cette question est toujours actuelle** this is still a topical question, the question is still relevant today

> Il faut noter que l'adjectif anglais **actual** est un faux ami. Il ne signifie jamais **actuel**.

actuellement [aktɥɛlmɑ̃] **ADV** now, at present, currently, at the present time

> Il faut noter que l'adverbe anglais **actually** est un faux ami. Il signifie **en fait**.

acuité [akɥite] **NF** *(de la douleur etc)* acuteness, sharpness, keenness; *(d'un argument)* sharpness; **il a analysé le problème avec une a. remarquable** his analysis of the problem was remarkably shrewd; **a. d'un son** high pitch of a sound; **a. visuelle** keenness of vision *or* eyesight; **a. intellectuelle** sharpness of intellect

acuponcteur, -trice, acupuncteur, **-trice** [akypɔ̃ktœr, -tris] **N** *Méd* acupuncturist

acuponcture, acupuncture [akypɔ̃ktyr] **NF** *Méd* acupuncture; **se soigner à l'a.** to have acupuncture treatment

acutangle [akytɑ̃gl] **ADJ** *Math* acute-angled

ADAC [adak] **NM** *(abrév* **avion à décollage et atterrissage courts)** STOL

adage [adaʒ] **NM** adage, (common) saying; **selon l'a.** as the saying goes

adagio [adadʒjo] **ADV, NM** *Mus* adagio

Adam [adɑ̃] **N** Adam; *Fam* **en costume d'A.** in one's birthday suit; **pomme d'A.** Adam's apple

adaptabilité [adaptabilite] **NF** adaptability (**à** to)

adaptable [adaptabl] **ADJ** adaptable

adaptateur, -trice [adaptatœr, -tris] **NM 1** *Élec, Tech, Phot, Ordinat* adapter; **a. (secteur)** (mains) adapter; *Ordinat* **a. graphique amélioré** enhanced graphics adapter, EGA; *Phot* **a. graphique couleur** colour graphics adapter; **a. femelle/mâle** female to male adapter; **a. vidéo** video adapter **2** *Radio* convertor
N *(d'un roman pour le cinéma etc)* adapter

adaptation [adaptasjɔ̃] **NF 1** adaptation (**à** to); **faire un effort d'a.** to make an effort to adapt; **faculté d'a.** adaptability **2** *TV, Cin, Théâtre* adaptation; **a. d'une nouvelle au théâtre/pour la télévision** adaptation of a short story for the stage/for television; *TV, Cin* **a. à l'écran** screen adaptation; *TV* **a. en feuilleton** *(d'un roman etc)* serialization; **faire une nouvelle a. de 'Macbeth'** to do a new adaptation of 'Macbeth'; **a. théâtrale** stage adaptation

adapter [adapte] **VT 1 a. qch à qch** to adapt sth to sth; **a. un règlement à un cas personnel** to adapt a rule to (fit) individual circumstances; **est-ce vraiment adapté à la situation?** is it really suitable for the situation?; **a. un tube à un autre** to make one tube fit another **2** *TV, Cin, Théâtre* **a. un roman à la scène** to adapt a novel for the stage; *TV* **a. en feuilleton** to serialize
▸ **VPR s'adapter** to adapt; **la prise s'adapte à toutes les télévisions** the plug fits all types of television; **s'a. aux conditions nouvelles** to adapt (oneself) *or* adjust to new conditions; **il sait s'a.** he's very adaptable *or* flexible

ADAV [adav] **NM** *(abrév* **avion à décollage et atterrissage verticaux)** VTOL

addenda [adɛ̃da] **NM INV** addendum (**à** to)
VOIR GRAMMAIRE A13

additif, -ive [aditif, -iv] **ADJ** additive
NM 1 supplement, addition; *(à un texte)* additional clause; **a. à un budget** addition to a budget **2** *Chimie etc* additive; **sans additifs** additive free; **a. antidétonant** anti-knock additive; **a. antigivre** antifreeze additive; **a. anti-mousse** anti-foam additive; **a. antioxydant** oxidation inhibitor; **a. détergent** detergent additive

addition [adisjɔ̃] **NF 1** *(fait d'ajouter)* addition, adding (to); *(pour faire un total)* adding up; **apprendre à faire les additions** to learn how to do addition *or* how to add up; **faire l'a. des chiffres** to add up *or* *Fam* tot up the figures; **l'a. d'un paragraphe à un texte** the addition *or* adding of a paragraph to a text; **l'a. de thym améliorera le ragoût** adding some thyme will improve the stew **2** *(extension)* addition, extension; **faire une a. à une maison** to build an extension to a house; **en a. à** in addition to **3** *Math* addition SEE GRAMMAR A77; B59 **4** *(au restaurant etc)* bill, *Am* check **5** *Typ* note

additionnel, -elle [adisjɔnɛl] **ADJ** additional, extra; *Ordinat* add-on

additionner [adisjɔne] **VT** to add (up), *Fam* to tot up; **a. un alcool d'un peu d'eau** to add a little water to a drink; **lait additionné d'eau** watered down milk; **café additionné d'eau-de-vie** coffee laced with spirits
VI to add (up)
▸ **VPR s'additionner** to add up; **aux longues heures de travail s'additionnent celles passées dans le métro** along with the long working hours, there are those spent on the underground *or* *Am* subway

additionneur [adisjɔnœr] **NM** *Ordinat* adder

additionneuse [adisjɔnøz] **NF** adding machine, adder

adducteur, -trice [adyktœr, -tris] **ADJ** *Anat etc* adducent; **canal a.** feeder canal
NM 1 *Anat* adductor **2** *Constr* supply main

adduction [adyksjɔ̃] **NF 1** *Anat* adduction **2** *Tech* admission, intake; *Constr* **a. d'eau** canalization; **adductions d'eau** water supply

adénoïde [adenɔid] **ADJ** *Méd* **végétations adénoïdes** adenoids

adénopathie [adenɔpati] **NF** adenopathy

adent [adɑ̃] **NM** *Menuis* dovetail

adepte [adɛpt] **N 1** *(partisan)* follower, adherent; **un a. de la non-violence** a supporter of non-violence; **les adeptes de la marche à pied** walking enthusiasts; **a. du cinéma** film fan *or* buff; **a. des ordinateurs** computer buff; **c'est une a. du ski** she loves skiing; **faire des adeptes** to attract followers *or* a following **2** *(rare) (personne initiée)* adept, initiate

adéquat [adekwa] **ADJ** *(personne, lieu, expression, méthode)* appropriate, suitable; *(montant, quantité)* adequate

adéquation [adekwasjɔ̃] **NF** appropriateness, suitability; *Fin* **a. des fonds propres** capital adequacy; **l'a. entre l'offre et la demande favorise la stabilité des prix** the balance between supply and demand encourages stable prices

adhérence [aderɑ̃s] **NF** adhesion, adherence; **a. des pneus (à la route)** grip of the tyres (on the road); **cette voiture a une excellente a. à la route** this car has excellent road-holding

adhérent, -ente [aderɑ̃, -ɑ̃t] **ADJ** *(substance, propriétés)* adhesive
N member; **a. d'un parti** member of a party;

(partisan) supporter of a party; **carte d'a.** membership card

adhérer [adere] **VI 1** (**j'adhère, n. adhérons; j'adhérerai**) **1** to adhere, to stick (**à** to); **a. à la route** *(des pneus)* to grip the road **2** (*à une opinion, un idéal etc*) to adhere, to hold, to subscribe (**à** to) **3** *(s'inscrire)* **a.** (**à un parti**) to join (a party)

adhésif, -ive [adezif, -iv] **ADJ** adhesive, sticky; **pansement a.** sticking plaster; **papier a.** sticky(-backed) paper
NM adhesive

adhésion [adezjɔ̃] **NF 1** *(fait de coller)* adhesion, sticking; *(des pneus)* grip(ping), road-holding; **force d'a.** adhesiveness **2** *(accord)* agreement, approval; **donner son a. à un projet** to support *or* give one's support to a plan **3** *(inscription)* adhesion, adherence (**à** to); *(d'un parti)* membership; **après leur a. à l'UE** after joining the EU; **le nombre des adhésions augmente** the number of new members is increasing

ad hoc [adɔk] **ADJ, ADV** ad hoc

adieu, *pl* **-eux** [adjø] **INT 1** *Arch* goodbye!, *Arch* farewell!; **dire a. à qn** to say goodbye to sb; *Fig Fam* **dire a. à qch** to kiss sth goodbye, to say goodbye to sth **2** *Région (bonjour)* hello!, hi!; **allez a., à demain!** bye then, see you tomorrow!
NM farewell; **des adieux déchirants/émouvants** heart-rending/emotional farewells *or* partings; **faire ses adieux** to make one's farewells, to say one's goodbyes; **faire ses adieux à qn** to say goodbye to sb; **faire ses adieux à la scène** to make one's final appearance on stage; **baiser d'a.** goodbye kiss; *(à tout jamais)* parting *or* farewell kiss

adipeux, -euse [adipø, -øz] **ADJ** *(tissu etc)* adipose, fatty; **un visage pâle et a.** a pale, bloated face

adiposité [adipozite] **NF** adiposity

adjacent [adʒasɑ̃] **ADJ** adjacent (**à** to); *Math* **angles adjacents** adjacent angles

adjectif, -ive [adʒɛktif, -iv] **ADJ** *(expression, locution etc)* adjectival
NM adjective; **a. attribut** predicative adjective; **a. épithète** attributive adjective; **a. déterminatif** determiner; **a. verbal** present participle; **a. substantivé** adjective used as a noun SEE GRAMMAR A17–19; B8–12

adjectival, -ale, -aux, -ales [adʒɛktival, -o] **ADJ** adjectival

adjectiver [adʒɛktive] **VT** to use as an adjective

adjoindre [adʒwɛ̃dr] *(conj like* **joindre)** **VT 1 a. qch à qch** to unite *or* associate sth with sth; **a. un mode d'emploi à un appareil** to include *or* enclose an instruction booklet with an appliance **2 a. qn à qn** to give sb to sb as an assistant; **a. qn à un comité** to add sb to a committee
VPR s'adjoindre *(assistant)* to engage, to take on; **s'a. d'autres** to join (in) with others

adjoint, -ointe [adʒwɛ̃, -wɛ̃t] **ADJ** assistant, deputy; *(directeur etc)* associate; *Can* **Sous-ministre a.** Assistant Deputy Minister
N assistant; **a. au maire** deputy mayor

adjonction [adʒɔ̃ksjɔ̃] **NF 1** *(fait d'ajouter)* adding, addition; **produit sans a. de sucre** product with no added sugar **2** *(élément adjoint) (à un texte etc)* addition; *(d'un hôpital)* annexe

adjudant [adʒydɑ̃] **NM 1** *Mil* warrant officer class II, *Am* warrant officer (junior grade); **a.-chef** warrant officer class I, *Am* chief warrant officer; **(capitaine) a.-major** adjutant, *Am* executive officer **2** *(oiseau)* adjutant bird

adjudicataire [adʒydikatɛr] **N** *(d'un contrat)* successful tenderer; *(aux enchères)* highest bidder, purchaser; **être l'a.** to be awarded the contract

adjudicateur, -trice [adʒydikatœr, -tris] **N** adjudicator; *(d'un contrat etc)* awarder

adjudication [adʒydikasjɔ̃] **NF** adjudication, allocation; *(d'un contrat)* award; *(vente aux enchères)* selling *or* sale by auction; **mettre qch en a.** *(marché administratif)* to invite tenders for sth; *(aux enchères)* to put sth up for (sale by) auction; **a. forcée** compulsory sale

adjuger [adʒyʒe] (**j'adjugeai(s); n. adjugeons**) **VT a. qch à qn** to award sth to sb; *(allouer)* to allocate sth to sb; *(aux enchères)* to knock sth down to sb; **une fois! deux fois! trois fois! adjugé! vendu!** going! going! gone!
VPR s'adjuger s'a. qch to appropriate sth, to take possession of sth; **elle s'est adjugé la plus belle part** she took the biggest share for herself

adjuration [adʒyrasjɔ̃] **NF** entreaty, plea

adjurer [adʒyre] **VT a. qn de faire qch** to implore *or* entreat sb to do sth

adjuvant [adʒyvɑ̃] **NM 1** *Méd* adjuvant **2** *Chimie, Tech* additive (**de** to); *Pétr* dope **3** *Fig* stimulus

ADM [adeɛm] **NFPL** *(abrév* **armes de destruction massive)** weapons of mass destruction, WMD

admettre [admɛtr] **VT** *(conj like* **mettre)** **1** *(accueillir)* **a. qn** to admit sb, to let sb in; **les chiens ne sont pas admis** *(sur la porte d'un magasin etc)* no dogs allowed; **a. qn chez soi** to let sb into one's house; **être admis à un club** to be admitted to a club; **être admis à l'université** to be accepted for university; **être admis à un examen** to pass an examination; *Bourse* **a. une société à la cote** to list a company
2 *(accepter)* **a. qn à siéger** to admit sb as a (new) member; **a. qch** to admit *or* admit of *or* permit *or* allow sth; **je n'admets pas qu'on me mente** I won't tolerate being lied to; **il n'admet pas mes explications** he doesn't *or* won't accept my explanations; **elle n'admet pas la discussion** she won't allow *or* permit any discussion; **cette règle n'admet aucune exception** the rule admits of *or* allows no exceptions, there can be no exceptions to the rule; **l'usage admis** the accepted custom; **non, cela je ne l'admets pas!** no, I don't agree with that!; **cela je ne l'admettrai pas** I won't allow it, I'm not having it
3 *(reconnaître)* to admit, to acknowledge; **il admet que c'est vrai** he admits *or* acknowledges that it is true; **admettons que j'aie tort** assuming *or* supposing (that) I'm wrong **4** *Jur* **a. un appel** to grant leave to appeal **5** *(laisser entrer) (vapeur, pétrole)* to let in; **l'essence est admise dans le moteur par ce conduit** the petrol enters the engine through this pipe

administrateur, -trice [administratœr, -tris] **N 1** administrator; **a. foncier** land agent; *(qui vend des maisons, des appartements)* estate agent **2** *(d'une société, d'une banque etc)* director **3** *(de fondation)* trustee
▸▸ **a. délégué** executive director; **a. judiciaire** official receiver; *TV, Cin* **a. de la production** production accountant; *Ordinat* **a. de réseau** network manager; *Ordinat* **a. de serveur** server administrator; **a. du système** systems administrator

administratif, -ive [administratif, -iv] **ADJ** administrative
N administrative worker; **les administratifs** the administrative staff

administration [administrasjɔ̃] **NF 1** *(d'affaires etc)* administration, direction, management; *(d'un pays)* governing; **conseil d'a.** board of directors; **elle a confié l'a. de son affaire à des collaborateurs** she entrusted the handling of her business to colleagues;

mauvaise a. *(d'une société)* mismanagement **2** *(ensemble des directeurs)* board of directors; *(d'une institution)* governing body; **l'a. est en délibération** the board is meeting **3** *(service public)* government service; *(fonctionnaires)* authorities, officials; **l'a. publique, l'A.** ≃ the Civil Service; **entrer dans l'a.** ≃ to become a civil servant; **travailler dans l'a.** ≃ to work in the Civil Service
▸▸ **a. communale** local government; **a. des Douanes** Customs and Excise; **l'a. des Eaux et Forêts** *Br* ≃ the Forestry and Wildlife Commission; **a. fiscale** tax authorities; **a. locale** local authority; **a. municipale** local government; **a. du personnel** personnel management; **a. portuaire** port authorities; **a. privée** private administration; *Ordinat* **a. de réseau** network management; **a. des ventes** sales management

administrativement [administrativmɑ̃] **ADV** administratively

administré, -ée [administre] **N** citizen

administrer [administre] **VT 1** *(affaire, propriété)* to administer, to manage; *(affaire)* to conduct; *(pays)* to govern **2** *(justice)* to dispense; *Rel (sacrements)* to administer; **a. un malade** to administer *or* give the last rites to a sick person; **a. un remède à un malade** to administer medication to a patient; **je vais lui a. une bonne correction** I'm going to give him/her a good hiding **3** *Jur* **a. des preuves** to produce proofs

admirable [admirabl] **ADJ** admirable; *(très bon)* *(cuisinière, père de famille)* wonderful; **elle a été a. de courage/volonté** she showed admirable courage/willpower

admirablement [admirabləmɑ̃] **ADV** admirably; *(très bien)* *(chanter, cuisiner)* wonderfully; **ça fonctionne a. bien** it's working perfectly

admirateur, -trice [admiratœr, -tris] **N** admirer; *(d'une vedette de variété etc)* fan

admiratif, -ive [admiratif, -iv] **ADJ** *(geste etc)* admiring

admiration [admirasjɔ̃] **NF** admiration; **avoir de l'a. pour qn** to admire sb, to be full of *or* filled with admiration for sb; **être en a. devant qch** to be filled with admiration for sth; **il est en a. devant sa fille** he is full of *or* filled with admiration for his daughter; **tomber en a.** to be filled with admiration for; **tu fais l'a. de plus d'un** many people admire you; **cette peinture a fait l'a. de tout le monde** this painting was admired by everybody; **soulever l'a. de qn** to be admired by sb

admirer [admire] **VT** to admire; **admiré de tous** admired by all; *Iron* **j'admire la légèreté avec laquelle tu parles de la famine dans ton pays!** I admire the way you speak so casually about famine in your country!

admis, -ise [admi, -iz] **ADJ 1** *(reçu)* accepted **2** *(autorisé à entrer)* admitted, allowed (in) **3** *(accepté)* allowed, acceptable; **c'est chose communément admise ici** it's a widely accepted fact here; **c'est l'opinion communément admise** it's the commonly held opinion **4** **il a été a. à passer les épreuves à la session de septembre** *(autorisé à)* he was allowed *or* permitted to take the tests in September
N *Univ (à un examen)* successful candidate

admissibilité [admisibilite] **NF** admissibility; *(à un emploi)* eligibility; *Scol* **épreuves d'a.** (**à l'examen oral**) written examinations (to gain admission to the oral examination)

admissible [admisibl] **ADJ** *(excuse, preuve, conduite)* admissible, allowable; *Jur (preuve)* admissible; **a. à un emploi** eligible for a job; *Scol* **(candidats) admissibles** candidates who have qualified for the oral examination

admission [admisjɔ̃] **NF 1** admission (**à,**

dans to); **l'a. des pays de l'Est dans l'Union européenne** the entry *or* admission of Eastern European countries into the European Union; **demande d'a. dans un club** club membership application; **a. à un club** admission to a club; **cotisation d'a.** entrance *or* admission fee

2 *Com (de marchandises)* entry; **a. en franchise** duty-free entry; **a. temporaire** temporary entry

3 *(entrée) Tech* intake; *Aut* induction; *(temps moteur)* induction *or* intake stroke; **période d'a.** induction stroke; **soupape d'a.** inlet valve

4 *Bourse* **a. à la cote** admission to quotation; **faire une demande d'a. à la cote** to seek admission to quotation

5 *Univ* pass; **le nombre des admissions à un concours** the number of passes *or* successful candidates at a competitive examination; **il a eu son a. à Centrale** he was accepted into Centrale

admixtion [admiksjɔ̃] NF admixture (**à** with)

admonestation [admɔnɛstasjɔ̃] NF admonishing

admonester [admɔnɛste] VT to admonish

admonition [admɔnisjɔ̃] NF admonition

ADN [adeen] NM *(abrév* **acide désoxyribonucléique)** DNA

ado [ado] N *Fam (adolescent)* teenager; **magazine/club/musique pour ados** teenage magazine/club/music

adobe [adɔb] NM *(brique, maison)* adobe

adolescence [adɔlesɑ̃s] NF adolescence; **pendant l'a.** during adolescence *or* one's teenage years *or* one's teens

adolescent, -ente [adɔlesɑ̃, -ɑ̃t] ADJ adolescent, teenage

N adolescent, teenager

adon [adɔ̃] NM *Can Fam* coincidence

Adonis [adɔnis] N *Myth* Adonis

adonis [adɔnis] NM **1** *(bel homme)* Adonis; **je ne suis pas vraiment un a.!** I'm no Adonis!, I'm no oil painting! **2** *(insecte)* adonis

adonner [adɔne] V IMPERS *Can* to suit, to be convenient; **viens me voir quand ça t'adonnera** come and see me whenever it suits you

VI *Can* **a. avec qch** *(vêtements etc)* to go with sth

VPR **s'adonner s'a. à qch** to give oneself up to sth; **s'a. à l'étude** to devote oneself to study; **s'a. à une profession** to take up a profession; **s'a. à la boisson** to take to drink; **s'a. à une vie de plaisirs** to abandon oneself to a life of pleasure

adoptant, -ante [adɔptɑ̃, -ɑ̃t] ADJ adoptive

N adoptive parent

adopté, -ée [adɔpte] ADJ adopted

N adopted child

adopter [adɔpte] VT **1** *(prendre sous sa tutelle) (enfant)* to adopt; *Fig* **nous l'avons adopté comme un fils** we treated him like a son

2 *(accepter)* **a. qn pour ami** to choose sb as a friend, to befriend sb; **il a très vite été adopté par ses nouveaux collègues** he was very quickly accepted by his new colleagues

3 *(choisir) (produit)* to adopt; *(nom)* to adopt, to assume; *(cause)* to adopt, to take up, to embrace; **a. un produit comme norme** to standardize on a product

4 *(approuver, voter)* **a. un projet de loi/une résolution** to adopt *or* pass *or* carry a bill/a resolution; **adopté à l'unanimité** carried unanimously

adopteur [adɔptœr] NM *Mktg (d'un produit)* adopter; **a. précoce** early adopter

adoptif, -ive [adɔptif, -iv] ADJ *(enfant, pays)* adopted; *(parent)* adoptive

adoption [adɔpsjɔ̃] NF *(d'un enfant, d'une proposition, d'une idée, d'une mode)* adop-

tion; **procédure d'a.** adoption procedure; *Parl (d'un projet de loi)* adoption, carrying; **mon pays d'a.** my country of adoption, my adopted country

adorable [adɔrabl] ADJ adorable, charming; **vous êtes a. dans cette robe** you look charming in that dress

adorablement [adɔrabləmɑ̃] ADV adorably

adorateur, -trice [adɔratœr, -tris] N **1** *(d'une religion)* worshipper **2** *(d'un chanteur)* ardent admirer, fan; *(d'une femme)* admirer

adoration [adɔrasjɔ̃] NF **1** *(d'une divinité)* adoration, worship **2** *(attachement très profond)* profound admiration **(de** for); **vouer une véritable a. à qn** to nurse a feeling of adoration for sb; **être en a. devant son bébé** to worship one's baby

adorer [adɔre] VT **1** *(divinité)* to adore, to worship **2** *(personne, chose)* to love; *(plus fort)* to adore; *(star du cinéma, petit ami etc)* to idolize; *Euph* **Joseph Beuys?, bof, je n'adore pas** Joseph Beuys?, well, I wouldn't call him my favourite; **j'adore monter à cheval** I adore *or* love riding

VPR **s'adorer** to adore each other

adossé [adose] ADJ **1** *(dos contre dos)* back to back **2 a. à qch** *(personne)* with one's back against sth, leaning against sth; *(édifice etc)* backed on to sth

adosser [adose] VT **1 a. deux choses** to place two things back to back **2 a. qch à** *ou* **contre qch** to place *or* lean *or* rest sth (with its back) against sth; **a. une chaise à qch** to put a chair with its back against sth

VPR **s'adosser s'a. à** *ou* **contre qch** to lean (up) against sth; **le village s'adosse à la colline** the village is built against the hillside

adouber [adube] VT **1** *Échecs (pièce)* to adjust **2** *Arch (chevalier)* to dub

adoucir [adusir] VT **1** *(voix, eau, tissu, peau)* to soften; *(contraste, couleur)* to tone down; *(lumière)* to subdue; *(boisson, goût)* to sweeten; **sa nouvelle coiffure adoucit son expression** her new haircut softens her face

2 *(tempérer) (douleur, chagrin etc)* to alleviate, to relieve, to ease; **a. une situation tendue** to ease *or* alleviate a tense situation; *Prov* **la musique adoucit les mœurs** music hath charms to soothe the savage breast

3 *(personne)* to pacify, to mollify

4 *(surface, bois etc)* to smooth, to soften; *(angle)* to smooth off; *(verre)* to (rough-)polish

5 *Métal* to temper; *(fonte de fer)* to soften

VPR **s'adoucir 1** *(d'une voix)* to grow softer, to soften, to mellow **2** *(du temps)* to get *or* grow milder **3** *(de la douleur)* to decrease **4** *(du caractère)* to mellow; **il s'est adouci avec l'âge** he has mellowed with age; **ce cognac s'adoucit avec le temps** this brandy mellows with age

adoucissage [adusisaʒ] NM **1** *Métal* tempering; *(de fonte de fer)* softening **2** *(de glace, de marbre)* polishing **3** *(des couleurs)* toning down

adoucissant [adusisɑ̃] ADJ softening; **crème adoucissante pour les mains** hand cream; **produit a. pour le linge** fabric softener

NM *(pour le linge)* fabric softener

adoucissement [adusismɑ̃] NM **1** *(de la voix etc)* softening; *(du caractère)* calming; *(de la température)* rise; **on prévoit un a.** milder weather is forecast **2** *(de la douleur etc)* alleviation **3** *(de surfaces, d'angles)* smoothing **4** sweetening; *(de l'eau)* softening **5** *Métal* annealing

adoucisseur [adusisœr] NM (water) softener

ad patres [adpatrɛs] ADV **envoyer qn a.** to send sb to meet his maker

ad(r). *abrév* **adresse**

adrénaline [adrenalin] NF *Méd* adrenalin(e)

adressable [adrɛsabl] ADJ *Ordinat* addressable

adressage [adrɛsaʒ] NM *Ordinat* addressing; **mode d'a.** address mode; **a. direct** direct addressing

adresse [adrɛs] NF **1** address; **nom, profession et a.** name, address and occupation; **nous avons échangé nos adresses** we exchanged addresses; **a. personnelle** home address; **a. au bureau** office address; **a. de facturation** invoicing address, address for invoicing; **a. de livraison** delivery address; *(d'objets volumineux)* shipping address; **a. du siège social** head office *or* registered office address; **carnet d'adresses** address book; **changer d'a.** to change one's address; **faire son changement d'a.** *(à la poste)* to have one's mail redirected; *Fig* **tu te trompes d'a.** you've come to the wrong person, you're knocking at the wrong door; **il m'a donné une bonne a.** *(de restaurant, de magasin etc)* he recommended a good restaurant/shop/ *etc*; **inconnu à cette a.** not known at this address; *Fig* **une observation à votre a.** *(intention)* a remark aimed at *or* meant for you; **je l'ai dit à l'a. de ceux qui …** I said it for the benefit of those who … **VOIR GRAMMAIRE A77**

2 *(dans une assemblée)* (formal) address **3** *(habileté)* skill, dexterity; *(savoir faire)* diplomacy; **jongler avec a.** to juggle skilfully *or* with dexterity; **faire des tours d'a.** to perform tricks; **dénué d'a.** bungling; **il lui faudra une sacrée a. pour se tirer de cette situation** he'll have to be damn clever to get out of this situation

4 *Ordinat* address; **a. absolue** absolute *or* specific address; *Can* **a. de courriel** e-mail address; **a. électronique** e-mail address; **a. Internet** Internet *or* web address; **a. IP** IP address; **a. de mémoire** memory address; **a. URL** URL; **a. virtuelle** virtual address

adresser [adrɛse] VT **1** *(lettre etc)* to address; **la lettre lui fut adressée dans sa résidence d'été** the letter was addressed to (him at) his summer residence; **lettre mal adressée** incorrectly addressed letter

2 *(envoyer)* to send *or* to refer **(qn à qn** sb to sb); **on m'a adressé à vous** *(par le biais d'un médecin etc)* I have been recommended to come and see you, I have been referred to you; **le médecin m'a adressé à un spécialiste** the doctor sent *or* referred me to a specialist

3 *(remarques etc)* to address, to aim; **a. des remerciements à qn** to deliver thanks to sb; **cette remarque était adressée à Martin** this remark was aimed at *or* meant for Martin; **a. un sourire à qn** to smile at sb; **elle ne m'adresse plus la parole depuis notre dispute** she hasn't spoken to me since our argument

VPR **s'adresser s'a. à qn** *(d'une remarque, recommandation etc)* to apply to sb; *(d'une personne)* to speak to sb; **s'a. ici** apply within; *(pour des renseignements)* enquire within; **adressez-vous à l'agent** ask the policeman; **s'a. à l'imagination/au bon sens de qn** to appeal to sb's imagination/common sense; **le livre s'adresse aux enfants** the book is aimed at children

Adriatique [adriatik] ADJ Adriatic

NF **l'A.** the Adriatic

Adrien [adriɛ̃] N Adrian; *(en histoire romaine)* Hadrian

adroit [adrwa] ADJ **1** *(habile)* dexterous, deft; **être a. de ses mains** to be clever *or* good with one's hands **2** *(réponse, diplomate)* shrewd, clever, skilful, *Am* skilful; **il le lui a annoncé de but en blanc, ce qui n'est pas très a.** he informed him quite bluntly, which wasn't very tactful; **phrase adroite** neatly turned phrase, neat turn of phrase

adroitement [adrwatmɑ̃] ADV *(fabriqué)*

skilfully, *Am* skillfully, cleverly; *(juger)* shrewdly; *(finir un discours etc)* neatly; **se défendre a.** to defend oneself skilfully *or* adroitly

adr. tél. *abrév* **adresse télégraphique**

ADSL [adɛesɛl] NF *(abrév* **Asynchronous Digital Subscriber Line)** ADSL

adsorber [atsɔrbe] VT *Phys, Biol* to adsorb

adsorption [atsɔrpsjɔ̃] NF *Phys, Biol* adsorption

adulateur, -trice [adylatœr, -tris] N *Litt* adulator; *(flatteur)* sycophant

adulation [adylasjɔ̃] NF *Arch* adulation, flattery *(de* of); *Péj* sycophancy

aduler [adyle] VT to idolize

adulte [adylt] ADJ *(personne)* adult, grown-up; *(plante, animal)* mature, fully grown; **l'âge a.** adulthood; **atteindre l'âge a.** to reach adulthood; **à l'âge a.** when fully grown; **ça n'est pas très a., cette réaction** that is not a very mature way to react N adult, grown-up

adultère [adyltɛr] ADJ adulterous N adulterer, *f* adulteress NM *(infidélité)* adultery; **commettre un a.** to commit adultery; **pour cause d'a.** for reasons of adultery, on grounds of adultery

adultérin [adylterɛ̃] ADJ *Jur* **enfant a.** child conceived in adultery, adulterine child

ad valorem [advalɔrɛm] ADJ, ADV ad valorem

advenir [advənir] V IMPERS *(conj like* **venir**) to occur, to happen, *Litt* to befall, to chance; **or, il advint que ...** now it came to pass that ...; **quoi qu'il advienne** no matter what happens; **advienne que pourra** come what may

adventice [advɑ̃tis] ADJ *(imprévu)* adventitious; *(sans cause ou but précis)* casual

adventif, -ive [advɑ̃tif, -iv] ADJ *Bot (racine etc)* adventitious; *Géol (cône)* parasitic

adverbe [adverb] NM adverb; **a. de manière/de temps** adverb of manner/time SEE GRAMMAR A19–24; B12–14

adverbial, -iale, -iaux, -iales [adverbjal, -jo] ADJ adverbial; **locution adverbiale** adverbial phrase

adversaire [adverser] N adversary, opponent; *(dans un conflit, une guerre)* enemy

adverse [advers] ADJ *(hostile)* adverse, unfavourable, *Am* unfavorable; **fortune a.** bad luck; **critique a.** unfavourable criticism; *Jur* **la partie a.** the opposing party, the other side; *Sport* **le camp a.** the opposing side

adversité [adversite] NF *Litt* **1** *(sort)* adversity, adverse circumstances **2** *(malheur)* misfortune, trial; **lutter contre l'a.** to fight in the face of adversity

advertorial [advɛrtɔrjal] NM *Journ* advertorial

ad vitam aeternam [advitametɛrnam] ADV *Fam* from here to eternity, till kingdom come

AELE [aəelə] NF *(abrév* **Association européenne de libre-échange)** EFTA

aérage [aeraʒ] NM **1** *(d'une pièce etc)* ventilation, airing **2** *(de l'eau)* aeration

aérateur [aeratœr] NM ventilator, (air) vent

aération [aerasjɔ̃] NF = **aérage**

aéré [aere] ADJ airy, well-ventilated

aérer [aere] (**j'aère, n. aérons; j'aérerai**) VT **1** *(mine)* to ventilate; *(pièce, linge)* to air **2** *(eau)* to aerate **3** *(rendre moins dense)* *(texte, exposé etc)* to lighten VPR **s'aérer** to get some fresh air; **avoir besoin de s'a.** to need some fresh air *or* a breath of fresh air

aérien, -ienne [aerjɛ̃, -jɛn] ADJ **1** air; *(plante, racine)* aerial; *(phénomène etc)* atmospheric; *Mil* **les forces aériennes** the air force; **défense/attaque aérienne** air de-

---

fence/raid; *Aviat* **compagnie aérienne** airline; **poste aérienne** airmail; **expédier par fret a.** to airfreight **2** *(texture etc)* (light and) airy; *(grâce, allure, démarche etc)* light, floating; **marcher d'un pas a.** to have a spring in one's step **3** *(câble etc)* overhead; *(voie ferrée)* elevated

aérium [aerjɔm] NM (open-air) sanatorium

aéro- [aerɔ, -o] PRÉF aero-

aérobic [aerobik] NM aerobics; **professeur/cours d'a.** aerobics teacher/class; **faire de l'a.** to do aerobics

aérobie [aerobi] ADJ aerobic

aérocâble [aerokɑbl] NM cableway

aéro-club, *pl* **aéro-clubs** NM flying *or* aero club

aérodrome [aerodrom] NM aerodrome, airfield, *Am* airdrome

aérodynamique [aerodinamik] ADJ aerodynamic; *(forme, voiture)* streamlined NF aerodynamics

aérodynamisme [aerodinamism] NM aerodynamics

aérodyne [aerodin] NM aerodyne

aérofrein [aerofrɛ̃] NM *Aviat* air brake

aérogare [aerogar] NF air terminal, terminal building

aérogastrie [aerogastri] NF *Méd* aerogastria

aéroglisseur [aeroglisœr] NM hovercraft

aérogramme [aerogram] NM airmail letter

aérographe [aerograf] NM airbrush; **retoucher qch à l'a.** to airbrush sth; **ajouter/effacer qch à l'a.** to airbrush sth in/out

aérologie [aerɔlɔʒi] NF aerology

aéromodélisme [aeromɔdelism] NM model aircraft making

aéromoteur [aeromɔtœr] NM wind engine

aéronaute [aeronot] N aeronaut

aéronautique [aeronotik] ADJ aeronautic(al) NF aeronautics; **ingénieur d'a.** aeronautical engineer

aéronaval, -ale, -als, -ales [aeronaval] ADJ *(forces etc)* air and sea NF **l'Aéronavale** *Br* ≃ the Fleet Air Arm, *Am* ≃ the Naval Air Service

aéronef [aeronɛf] NM aircraft; *(dirigeable)* airship

aérophagie [aerofaʒi] NF **avoir** *ou* **faire de l'a.** to suffer from flatulence

aérophotographie [aerofotografi] NF aerial photography

aéroplane [aeroplan] NM *Vieilli* aeroplane, *Am* airplane

aéropoint [aeropwɛ̃] NM *Aviat* ≃ airmile; **accumuler des aéropoints** to collect airmiles

aéroport [aeropɔr] NM airport; **a. de destination** airport of destination, destination airport; **a. de départ** airport of departure, departure airport; **a. de déroutement** diverting airport; **a. de remplacement** alternative airport; **Aéroports de Paris** Paris Airports Authority

aéroporté [aeropɔrte] ADJ airborne

aéroportuaire [aeropɔrtɥɛr] ADJ *(équipement, installations etc)* airport

aéropostal, -ale, -aux, -ales [aeropɔstal, -o] ADJ airmail NF *Hist* **l'Aéropostale** the (French) airmail service

aérosol [aerosɔl] NM aerosol; **vendu en a.** sold in aerosol *or* spray form ADJ INV aerosol; **bombe a.** aerosol (can)

aérospatial, -iale, -iaux, -iales [aerospasjal, -jo] ADJ *(équipement etc)* aerospace

aérostat [aerosta] NM balloon, aerostat

aérostatique [aerostatik] ADJ aerostatic NF aerostatics

---

aérostier [aerostje] NM balloonist

Aérotrain® [aerotrɛ̃] NM hovertrain

aérotransporté [aerotrãsporte] ADJ *(marchandises, passagers, troupes)* airborne

AF *abrév* **1 allocations familiales 2 Air France**

AFB [ɑɛfbe] NF *(abrév* **Association française des banques)** = French Bankers' Association

affabilité [afabilite] NF graciousness, affability *(* **avec, envers** to, towards); **être d'une grande a.** to be very gracious *or* affable

affable [afabl] ADJ gracious, affable *(* **envers, avec** to, towards, with)

affablement [afabləmã] ADV graciously, affably

affabulateur, -trice [afabylatœr, -tris] ADJ **qu'est-ce que tu peux être a.** you're too fond of telling tall stories N fibber, storyteller

affabulation [afabylasjɔ̃] NF fabrication(s), distortion(s); **les résultats publiés ne sont qu'une a.** the published results are pure invention

affabuler [afabyle] VI to invent things, to make things up

affacturage [afaktyraʒ] NM *Com* factoring

affactureur [afaktyrœr] NM *Com* factor

affadir [afadir] VT *(nourriture etc)* to make insipid *or* tasteless; *(couleur, style, personnalité etc)* to make dull *or* uninteresting VPR **s'affadir** *(nourriture etc)* to become insipid; *(couleur, style, personnalité etc)* to become dull *or* uninteresting

affaiblir [afeblir] VT **1** *(réduire)* to lessen, to reduce; **l'usage a affaibli le sens du mot** the meaning of the word has become weakened through overuse; **a. le courage de qn** to dampen sb's courage; *Phot* **a. un cliché** to reduce (the contrasts of) a negative **2** *(d'une maladie)* to weaken, *Fml* to enfeeble, to debilitate; **affaibli par la maladie** weakened by illness VPR **s'affaiblir 1** *(devenir faible)* to grow *or* become weak(er) *or* feeble(r), to lose one's strength; *(d'un son)* to become *or* grow fainter; **ma vue s'affaiblit rapidement** my eyesight is deteriorating *or* failing rapidly; **mes forces s'affaiblissaient** my strength was failing; **la tempête s'affaiblit** the storm is abating **2** *(s'atténuer)* **le sens du mot s'affaiblit au XVIᵉ siècle** the word took on a weaker meaning in the 16th century

affaiblissement [afeblismã] NM **1** weakening; *(de la force etc)* diminution; *(du sens d'un mot)* weakening; *TV (de signaux)* attenuation; **a. de la lumière** dimming (of the light) **2** *(faiblesse)* weakness; *Méd* debility

affaiblisseur [afeblisœr] NM *Phot* reducer

affaire [afɛr] NF **1** business, concern; **ce n'est pas votre a.** it's not your business, it's none of your business; **occupez-vous de vos affaires** mind your own business; **ça, c'est mon a.** that's my business; *(je m'en occupe)* (you can) leave that to me; **mettre le nez dans les affaires de qn** to stick one's nose into sb's business; **mettre de l'ordre dans ses affaires** to put one's affairs in order; **ce n'est pas l'a. de tout le monde** not everybody can do that; **c'est l'a. d'un médecin** it's a case for a doctor; **a. d'argent** money matter; **a. de cœur** love affair; **a. d'honneur** duel; **a. de conscience** matter of conscience; **a. difficile** difficult question *or* matter; **c'est (une) a. de goût** it's a matter *or* question of taste; **ce n'est que l'a. d'un instant** it won't take a minute; **ça, c'est une autre a.** that's another question *or* another matter; **avoir a. à** to deal with; **nous avons eu a. à un homme charmant** we were dealt with by a charming man; **s'il continue à mentir, il aura a. à moi!** if he keeps on lying, he'll have me to contend with *or* me to answer to!

2 *(compte)* **ça fait mon a.** that's just what I need *or* what I was looking for; **cela ne fera pas l'a.** that won't do; **il fera votre a.** he's just the man for you; **cela devrait tout à fait faire mon a.** that should do the trick; **faire son a. à qn** *Fam* to give sb what he deserves *or* what he's asking for *or* what was coming to him; *Arg (le tuer)* to do sb in, to bump sb off **3** *(ennui)* (difficult *or* serious) business; **c'est une a. de pots-de-vin qui a fait la une des journaux** it's a case of bribery which made the headlines; **c'est une sale/drôle a.** it's a nasty/funny business; **il cherche à étouffer l'a.** he's trying to hush up the whole affair; **ce n'est pas une petite a., c'est toute une a.** it's quite a business; **je n'en fais pas une a.** I'm not making an issue of it; **en voilà une a.!** here's a nice mess *or* a nice kettle of fish!; *(ce n'était pas la peine)* it's a lot of fuss about nothing!; **la belle a.!** is that all?, so what?; **se tirer d'a.** to get out of a difficulty; **tirer qn d'a.** to get sb out of trouble *or* out of the woods; **les médecins vont pouvoir le tirer d'a.** the doctors will be able to pull him through; **se faire une a. de qch** to get all worked up about sth; *Pol* **l'a. de Suez** the Suez crisis; **l'a. est encore chaude** *(toute la presse en parle)* it's still very much in the news, it's still hot news **4** *(transaction)* (business) transaction, deal; *(achat à bon marché)* bargain; **une bonne/mauvaise a.** a good/bad deal; **on fait des affaires dans ce magasin** you get good bargains in this shop; **être dur en affaires** *(homme)* to be a hard-headed businessman; *(femme)* to be a hard-headed businesswoman; **ils font des affaires en or** they're coining it, they're making money hand over fist, they're raking it in; **faire a. avec qn** to do a deal with sb; **faire des affaires avec qn** to do business with sb; **il est sur une a. avec le Mozambique** he's doing a deal with Mozambique; **chiffre d'affaires** turnover; **homme d'affaires** businessman; *(d'un sportif etc)* business manager; **femme d'affaires** businesswoman; **voyage d'affaires** business trip; **déjeuner d'affaires** business *or* working lunch; **droit des affaires** corporate law; **avocat d'affaires** corporate lawyer **5 les affaires** business; **être dans les affaires** to be a businessman/businesswoman; **comment vont les affaires?** how's business?; **parler affaires** to talk business *or* *Fam* shop; **les affaires sont les affaires (et on ne fait de cadeaux à personne)** business is business and nobody gets any favours *or* anything for nothing) **6** *(entreprise)* firm, business; **une grosse a.** a large firm **7 affaires** *(effets personnels)* things, possessions, belongings; **tu peux mettre tes affaires dans le vestibule** you can put your things in the hall; **ranger ses affaires** to put one's things away, to tidy one's things; **mettre de l'ordre dans ses affaires** to tidy up; **mets tes petites affaires dans ce sac** put your small things in this bag; *Hum* **il est en train de préparer ses petites affaires** he's sorting out his bits and pieces **8** *Pol* **les affaires de l'État** affairs of state; **ce n'est pas une a. d'État** it's of no great importance; **on ne va pas en faire une a. d'État** we're not going to make a big issue of it; **le ministère des Affaires étrangères** *Br* ≃ the Foreign (and Commonwealth) Office, *Am* ≃ the State Department; **ministre des Affaires étrangères** *Br* ≃ Foreign (and Commonwealth) Secretary, *Am* ≃ Secretary of State; *Can* **Ministère des Affaires extérieures** External Affairs Department

affairé [afere] ADJ busy; **ils entraient et sortaient d'un air a.** they were bustling in and out; **être a. à faire qch** to be busy doing sth

affairement [afermɑ̃] NM bustle, bustling activity

affairer (s') [safere] VPR to be busy, to busy oneself; **s'a. autour de qn** to fuss (a)round sb; **s'a. à tout remettre en place** to be busy tidying up

affairisme [aferism] NM *Péj* wheeling and dealing

affairiste [aferist] N *Péj* wheeler-dealer; **ce n'est qu'un a.** he thinks of nothing but making money *or* getting rich *or* *Am* making a fast buck

affaissement [afesmɑ̃] NM **1** *(de terrain)* subsidence, sinking; *(d'une fondation)* settling; *(du plancher, d'une poutre)* sagging; **il y a eu un a. de terrain** there was (land) subsidence **2** *(accablement)* depression, dejection, despondency; *Méd* prostration, collapse; **l'a. de l'enthousiasme** the waning of enthusiasm; **l'a. du moral** the collapse of morale

affaisser (s') [safese] VPR **1** *(du terrain)* to subside; *(d'une poutre, d'un fauteuil etc)* to sag **2** *(tomber, s'écrouler) (dans une chaise)* to sink down *or* back; *(de fatigue etc)* to collapse **3** *Fig Litt (décliner)* to decline, to sink; **il s'affaisse de jour en jour** he is declining *or* sinking day by day

affaler [afale] VT *(objet)* to lower; *Naut* **a. la voile** to lower the sail; **affale!** lower away!
VPR **s'affaler** to collapse; **s'a. par terre** to sink to the ground; **s'a. dans un fauteuil** to sink *or* *Fam* flop into an armchair

affamé, -ée [afame] ADJ hungry, *Fam* starving, ravenous, famished; *(mourant de faim)* starving; **regarder qch d'un œil a.** to look hungrily at sth; *Fig* **être a. de succès/d'argent** to be hungry for success/money
N **les affamés** the hungry, the starving

affamer [afame] VT to starve

affectation [afɛktasjɔ̃] NF **1** *Péj (pose)* affectation, affectedness; *(simulacre)* pretence, affectation; **parler avec a.** to speak affectedly; **être sans a.** to be without affectation, to be unaffected; **sans a.** *(dire etc qch)* without affectation, unaffectedly; **avec une a. de générosité** with a show of generosity **2** *(fait de désigner)* assignment, allocation, allotment; **l'a. de subventions à une association** the allocation of subsidies to an association; **a. des places** seating plan **3** *Mil etc* assignment, posting; **avoir une** *ou* **être en a. spéciale** ≃ to be in a reserved occupation **4** *Ordinat (de touche)* assignment; **a. de mémoire** memory allocation
▸▸ **affectations budgétaires** budget appropriations; **a. de fonds** appropriation of funds; **a. hypothécaire** mortgage charge

affecté [afɛkte] ADJ *Péj (personne, manière)* affected

affecter [afɛkte] VT **1** *(destiner)* to assign (à to), to allocate, to earmark; **a. des fonds à** to allocate funds to **2** *(désigner) (employé)* to assign, to appoint; *Mil (soldat, détachement)* to detail, to post, to draft; *Naut* **être affecté à un navire** to be posted to a ship **3** *(feindre)* to feign, to affect; **a. de faire qch** to pretend to do sth; **a. la désinvolture la plus complète** to feign *or* affect an extremely offhand attitude **4** *(toucher) (personne)* to affect, to move; **vivement affecté par la nouvelle** greatly moved by the news **5** *(agir sur) (carrière, santé etc)* to affect, to have an effect on; **la grève a affecté plusieurs usines** the strike has affected *or* hit several factories; **les pluies qui affectent le nord de l'Europe** the rain affecting *or* over northern Europe

6 *(prendre) (forme, couleur etc)* to assume, to take on
VPR **s'affecter** to be troubled *or* unsettled; **elle s'affecte de la moindre dispute** she is upset by the slightest argument

affectif, -ive [afɛktif, -iv] ADJ emotional, *Spéc* affective; **sa vie affective** his emotional life

affection [afɛksjɔ̃] NF **1** *(attachement)* affection, fondness, liking (**pour** for); **une preuve d'a.** a show of affection; **en manque d'a.** in need of affection; **prendre qn en a.** to become attached to *or* fond of sb; **terme d'a.** term of affection; **avoir de l'a. pour qn** to feel *or* have affection for sb, to be fond of sb; **avec a.** affectionately **2** *Méd* disease, complaint, ailment; **a. cutanée** skin disorder *or* complaint

affectionné [afɛksjɔne] ADJ affectionate, loving; **votre cousin(e) affectionné(e)** *(dans une lettre)* your affectionate cousin

affectionner [afɛksjɔne] VT *(ami, connaissance etc)* to be attached to, to be fond of; *(chiens etc)* to like; **affectionné de tous** loved by all; **le genre de petits plats qu'il affectionne** the type of food he likes *or* is fond of

affectivité [afɛktivite] NF affectivity

affectueusement [afɛktɥøzmɑ̃] ADV affectionately; **a. à tous** *(dans une lettre)* love to all

affectueux, -euse [afɛktɥø, -øz] ADJ affectionate, loving

afférent [aferɑ̃] ADJ **1** *Jur* **la part afférente à** the portion accruing to **2 a. à** *(concernant)* relating to, relevant to, pertaining to **3** *Méd* afferent

affermage [afermaʒ] NM **1** *(d'un bien rural)* tenant farming **2** *(d'un emplacement publicitaire)* contracting

affermer [aferme] VT *(ferme etc)* to lease, to rent; *(terre etc)* to take on lease; *(emplacement publicitaire)* to contract for

affermir [afermir] VT **1** *(fondations etc)* to strengthen, to make firm; **crème pouvant a. les chairs** toning *or* firming cream **2** *(pouvoir, croyance)* to strengthen, to consolidate; *(santé)* to improve; **a. sa voix** to strengthen one's voice; **a. qn dans sa position** to strengthen *or* consolidate sb in his/her position
VPR **s'affermir** to become stronger, to strengthen; *(du ciment)* to harden; *(des chairs, des muscles)* to firm up

affermissement [afermismɑ̃] NM strengthening; *(du pouvoir etc)* consolidation; *(d'un ciment)* hardening; *(des chairs, des muscles)* firming up

affichage [afiʃaʒ] NM **1** *(pose d'affiches)* billsticking, billposting; **a. interdit** stick *or* *Am* post no bills; **tableau** *ou* **panneau d'a.** notice board, *Am* bulletin board; *(dans aéroport, gare)* arrivals and departures (board) **2** *Ordinat* display; **horloge/montre à a. digital** *ou* **numérique** digital clock/watch **3** *Cin* billing **4** *Aviat* visual indicator
▸▸ *Ordinat* **a. couleur** colour display; **a. à cristaux liquides** liquid crystal display; **a. digital** digital display *or* readout; **a. dynamique** *(publicité)* mobile advertising; *Ordinat* **a. graphique** graphics display; *Ordinat* **a. inversé** reverse video; **a. mobile** *(publicité)* mobile advertising; *Ordinat* **a. non entrelacé** non-interlaced display; *Ordinat* **a. numérique** digital display; **a. à plasma** plasma display; **a. des prix** price display; **a. routier** *(publicité)* roadside advertising; **a. rural** *(publicité)* rural advertising; *Ordinat* **a. tel écran-tel écrit, a. tel-tel** WYSIWYG; *Ordinat* **a. TFT** TFT display; **a. transport** *(publicité)* public transport advertising, transportation advertising; **a. urbain** *(publi-*

cité) urban (poster) advertising; *Ordinat* **a. vectoriel** vector graphics

affiche [afiʃ] **NF** poster, bill; *(de protestation)* placard; *(de publicité)* advertisement; **colleur d'affiches** billsticker, bill poster; **a. à la main** handbill; **a. électorale** election poster; **affiches publicitaires** advertisements; **a. de théâtre** playbill; **être à l'a.** *(de spectacle)* to be on, to be showing; **les pièces à l'a.** the plays now on *or* now showing; **la pièce a tenu l'a.** *ou* **est restée à l'a. pendant deux ans** the play ran for two years; **tenir longtemps l'a.** to have a long run; **qui tient l'a.** long-running; **mettre à l'a.** to put on, to stage; **quitter l'a.** to close; **être en tête d'a.** to be top of the bill, to have top billing

afficher [afiʃe] **VT 1** *(annonce, affiche)* to stick (up), to post (up); *(prix)* to display; **a. une vente** to advertise a sale, *Am* to post a sale; **défense d'a.** stick *or Am* post no bills; **a. complet** *(d'un spectacle)* to be sold out **2** *(montrer, étaler)* to parade, to show off, to flaunt, to make a display of; *(mépris, indifférence)* to put on; **a. son savoir** to air *or* flaunt one's knowledge; **a. son ignorance** to display *or* expose *or* betray one's ignorance; **a. sa pauvreté** to plead poverty; **derrière cette nonchalance affichée** behind this outwardly casual air; **a. son nouvel amant** to flaunt *or* parade one's latest lover; *Com* **a. un déficit/un excédent** to show a deficit/a surplus **3** *Ordinat (message)* to display; *(fichiers, articles)* to show; **l'écran affiche …** the on-screen message appears …, the screen displays the message …

VPR s'afficher 1 *(d'une personne)* **elle s'affiche avec un homme plus âgé qu'elle** she's flaunting herself with an older man **2** *(sur un écran)* to be displayed **3** *Fam (se ridiculiser)* to make an idiot of oneself; **il a fait tomber ses lunettes dans le bol de punch; je te dis pas comment il s'est affiché!** his glasses fell off into the punch bowl, what an idiot he made of himself!

affichette [afiʃɛt] **NF** small poster *or* advertisement

afficheur [afiʃœr] **NM 1** *(colleur d'affiches)* billsticker, billposter; *(entreprise d'affichage)* poster advertising company **2** *Ordinat* VDU, visual display unit; **a. LCD** LCD display; **a. à cristaux liquides** liquid crystal display

affichiste [afiʃist] **N** poster designer

affidavit [afidavit] **NM** *Jur* affidavit

affidé, -ée [afide] **N** *Péj* accomplice

affilage [afilaʒ] **NM** sharpening, whetting

affilée (d') [dafile] **ADV** **cinq heures d'a.** five hours at a stretch *or* at a time *or* on end; **lire vingt chapitres d'a.** to read twenty chapters in one go *or* straight off *or* at one sitting

affiler [afile] **VT** *(lame etc)* to sharpen, to whet, to put an edge on; *Fig* **avoir la langue bien affilée** *(être méchant)* to have a sharp *or* wicked tongue

affiliation [afiljasjɔ̃] **NF** affiliation; **demander son a. à un club** to apply for membership to a club; **l'a. d'un membre à un club** a member's affiliation to a club

affilié, -ée [afilje] **ADJ** affiliated **N** affiliated member

affilier [afilje] **VT** to affiliate (**à** to, with) **VPR s'affilier** to join; *(d'une organisation)* to become affiliated; **s'a. à un parti** to join a party

affin [afɛ̃] **ADJ** *Ling* related, cognate; *Math* affine

affinage [afinaʒ] **NM** *Métal* refining; *(de l'acier, du fer)* smelting; *(du vin, du fromage)* maturing

affinement [afinmɑ̃] **NM** refinement

affiner [afine] **VT 1** *(purifier)* to improve, to refine, to make better; *(fer, or)* to refine; *(fromage etc)* to ripen, to mature **2** *(intelligence)* to sharpen; *(goût, plaisir etc)* to refine; **ces livres ont affiné son jugement** these books have sharpened his judgment

VPR s'affiner 1 *(d'une personne)* to become more refined; *(des traits)* to become finer; *(de l'intelligence)* to become sharper; **elle s'est affinée en suivant un nouveau régime** she has lost weight *or* slimmed down on her new diet **2** *(du fromage etc)* to ripen, to mature

affinité [afinite] **NF 1** *(entre personnes)* affinity (**entre** between); *(physique)* resemblance; *(de caractère)* similarity of character; **nous avons une grande a. de goûts** we have many tastes in common **2** *Chimie* attraction; **a. pour un corps** affinity for a body

affirmatif, -ive [afirmatif, -iv] **ADJ 1** affirmative, positive; **réponse affirmative** affirmative answer, answer in the affirmative; **signe a.** nod (of agreement); **faire un signe a. de la tête** to nod in agreement **2** *(personne)* assertive, positive; **il a été très a.** he was very definite

NF l'affirmative the affirmative; **dans l'affirmative** if so, if the answer is yes, if you can; **répondre par l'affirmative** to answer in the affirmative, to say *or* answer yes

INT affirmative

affirmation [afirmasjɔ̃] **NF** affirmation, assurance, assertion, statement; **a. trop générale** sweeping statement; **a. de soi** self-assertion; **a. de la personnalité** assertion of one's personality

▸▸ *Jur* **a. de créance** proof of debt; **a. sous serment** affidavit; *(lors d'un procès etc)* statement on oath

affirmativement [afirmativmɑ̃] **ADV** in the affirmative

affirmer [afirme] **VT 1** *(soutenir)* to maintain; **il affirme vous connaître** he maintains that he knows you; **je ne peux rien a.** I can't say anything for certain; **je n'affirmerais pas que …** I wouldn't swear to it that …; **a. qch sous serment** to state sth on oath *or* on affidavit **2** *(manifester, prouver)* to assert; **a. son autorité** to assert one's authority, to make one's authority felt; **a. son amitié** to declare one's friendship

VPR s'affirmer 1 *(s'exprimer pleinement) (d'une personne)* to assert oneself **2** *(se révéler)* **son talent s'affirme peu à peu** his/her talent is gradually expressing itself *or* becoming apparent; **beaucoup de vos observations se sont affirmées justes** many of your observations have proved correct *or* have been confirmed; **cet ordinateur s'est affirmé le plus performant de tous** this computer has established itself as the best performer

affleurement [aflœrmɑ̃] **NM** *Géol* outcrop

affleurer [aflœre] **VT** *(bois de charpente etc)* to bring to the same level, to make flush; **a. à qch** to be level *or* even *or* flush with sth **VI** *aussi Fig* to float *or* rise to the surface; *Géol (d'un filon)* to outcrop; *Fig* **l'espace d'une seconde il laissa a. ses sentiments** for a second he let his feelings show through

affliction [afliksjɔ̃] **NF** affliction, sorrow; **plongé dans l'a.** deeply distressed

affligé, -ée [afliʒe] **ADJ 1** *(atteint)* afflicted, troubled (**de** with) **2** *(peiné)* grieved, distressed

N les affligés the afflicted

affligeant, -e [afliʒɑ̃] **ADJ** *(nouvelle, vision)* distressing, painful; **manque d'imagination a.** pitiful *or* appalling lack of imagination

affliger [afliʒe] *(j'affligeai(s); n. affligeons)* **VT 1** *(attrister)* to afflict (**de** with); **région que le choléra afflige** area afflicted with cholera; **la nature l'a affligé d'un grand nez**

nature has cursed him with a big nose **2** *(attrister)* to distress, to grieve; **la nouvelle l'a profondément affligé** the news deeply distressed him *or* caused him great distress

VPR s'affliger to be grieved *or* distressed (**de qch** about sth); **ne vous affligez pas ainsi** don't take it so much to heart

affluence [aflyɑ̃s] **NF** *(de personnes)* crowd; *(de marchandises)* abundance; **heures d'a.** *(transports)* rush hours; *(dans les magasins etc)* peak hours

affluent [aflyɑ̃] **NM** *(d'une rivière)* tributary

affluer [aflye] **VI** *(d'un liquide)* to flow (**vers** towards; **dans** into); *(du sang)* to rush, to flow (**à** to); **a. ou dans un endroit** to crowd *or* flock to a place

afflux [afly] **NM** *Méd etc (de sang)* rush; *Élec (de courant)* surge; *(de visiteurs)* crowd; *Compta* **a. de capitaux** inflow *or* influx of capital, capital inflow

affolant [afɔlɑ̃] **ADJ** *(spectacle, nouvelle)* distressing, horrifying; *Fam* **c'est a.** *(ce qu'elle a grandi etc)* it's frightening *or* incredible

affolé [afɔle] **ADJ 1** demented, frantic, panic-stricken; **il était a.** he was scared out of his wits **2** *Tech (aiguille du compas)* spinning, crazy

affolement [afɔlmɑ̃] **NM 1** *(de personne)* panic, *Fam* flap; **voyons, pas d'a.** come on, there's no need to panic; **dans un moment d'a.** in a moment of panic, in a panic-stricken moment **2** *(d'une aiguille magnétique)* perturbation, unsteadiness, spinning **3** *(d'un moteur, d'une hélice etc)* racing; *(d'une poulie etc)* disconnecting

affoler [afɔle] **VT 1** *(personne)* to madden, to drive crazy *or* to distraction; *(foule)* to throw into a panic **2** *(aiguille de compas)* to disturb, to perturb

VPR s'affoler 1 *(paniquer)* to panic, to get in(to) a panic, *Fam* to lose one's head; **s'a. pour un rien** to get into a flap about nothing **2** *(d'une aiguille de compas)* to spin **3** *(d'une machine)* to begin to race

affouiller [afuje] **VT** *(de l'eau)* **(rive, fondation etc)** to undermine, to erode, to wash away, to lay bare

affranchi, -ie [afrɑ̃ʃi] **ADJ 1** *(esclave)* free(d), emancipated; *Fig* **un esprit a.** an open mind; **un esprit a. des préjugés** a mind free from prejudice **2** *(lettre)* stamped, with a stamp on; **lettre bien/mal affranchie** letter with/without enough stamps on it

N 1 *(esclave)* emancipated slave **2** *(marginal)* free spirit

affranchir [afrɑ̃ʃir] **VT 1** *(esclave etc)* to free, to set free, to emancipate; **a. qn/qch de qch** to free *or* release sb/sth from sth; **par son attitude très cordiale, il nous a affranchis de toute gêne** his friendly attitude ensured that we didn't feel in the least awkward **2** *(envoi)* to pay the postage on; *(tamponner) (lettre)* to frank, to stamp; **colis affranchi** pre-paid parcel; **machine à a. (les lettres)** franking machine, franker **3** *Cartes (couleur)* to unblock **4** *Fam (renseigner)* **a. qn** to put sb in the picture

VPR s'affranchir s'a. du joug to cast off the yoke; **s'a. d'une habitude** to break (oneself of) a habit; **s'a. d'idées préconçues** to rid oneself of preconceived ideas

affranchissement [afrɑ̃ʃismɑ̃] **NM 1** *(d'un esclave etc)* emancipation, setting free **2** *(de lettre)* prepayment; *(fait de tamponner)* stamping, franking; *(montant payé) (de lettre, de paquet etc)* postage, carriage; **tarif d'a.** postage rate

affranchisseuse [afrɑ̃ʃisøz] **NF** franking machine, franker

affres [afr] NFPL *Litt (angoisse)* (spasm of) anguish; *(du doute etc)* agonies, horrors; **a. de la mort** death throes; **a. de la faim** pangs of hunger, hunger pangs; **découvrir toutes les a. de l'humiliation** to discover the agonies of humiliation

affrètement [afretmɑ̃] NM charter, *Fml* affreightment; **a. au voyage** trip charter; **a. à temps** time charter

affréter [afrete] VT (**j'affrète, n. affrétons; j'affréterai**) *(navire, avion)* to charter

affréteur [afretœr] NM *Naut* charterer; *Aut* **a. routier** road haulier

affreusement [afrøzmɑ̃] ADV *(en retard)* terribly, frightfully; *(blessé, torturé)* horribly; *(défiguré)* horribly, shockingly; **je suis a. coiffée** my hair's a mess; **il parle a. mal l'anglais** his English is awful

affreux, -euse [afrø, -øz] ADJ **1** *(laid)* horrible, hideous, dreadful, ghastly; **un visage a.** a horrible *or* hideous face; **il est a.** he's terribly *or* horribly ugly; **un a. petit chapeau/chien** a horrible *or* an ugly little hat/dog **2** *(atroce) (nouvelles, pauvreté, crime etc)* awful, horrible, dreadful, shocking **3** *Fam (détestable)* awful, dreadful; **mal de tête a.** splitting headache; **qu'est-ce que ça a augmenté, c'est a.!** it's dreadful *or* shocking how the price has gone up!; **c'est a. ce qu'il y a comme monde!** it's dreadfully *or* awfully busy!; **ce gamin est un a. jojo** that child is a (frightful) little horror; **temps a.** filthy *or* shocking weather
  ▪ N **1** *Mil Fam* white mercenary *(usually in Africa)* **2** *Fam (vilain personnage)* **c'est un a.** he's a nasty piece of work

affriander [afrijɑ̃de] VT *Litt* to entice, to allure

affriolant [afrijɔlɑ̃] ADJ *(décolleté, vêtement)* alluring, tantalizing; **ce travail n'a rien d'a.** it's not the world's most exciting job

affrioler [afrijɔle] VT to excite, to tempt

affriquée [afrike] NF *Ling* affricate (consonant)

affront [afrɔ̃] NM affront, insult, *Fam* slap in the face; **subir un a.** to be affronted *or* insulted; **faire** *ou* **infliger un a. à qn** to affront *or* insult sb; *(snober qn)* to snub sb; **doubler ses torts d'un a.** to add insult to injury

affrontement [afrɔ̃tmɑ̃] NM **1** *(de l'ennemi, du danger etc)* confrontation, confronting, clash; **l'a. de deux personnalités différentes** the clash *or* conflict of two different personalities **2** *(de deux choses)* joining edge to edge; *Chir* bringing into apposition

affronter [afrɔ̃te] VT **1** *(personne, chose)* to face, to confront, to brave, to tackle; **a. une épreuve avec courage** to face *or* meet an ordeal bravely; **a. la colère de qn** to brave the wrath of sb **2** *(mettre de front)* to join face *or* edge to edge; *(plaques de métal etc)* to bring together; *Chir* to bring into apposition **3** *Sport* to clash with
  ▪ VPR **s'affronter** *(d'ennemis etc)* to clash, to confront each other; *Sport (de deux équipes, joueurs etc)* to meet, to clash; **leurs personnalités s'affrontent constamment** their personalities clash constantly; **deux thèses s'affrontent** there are two conflicting theories

affubler [afyble] *Péj* VT **a. qn de qch** to dress sb up in sth, to deck *or* rig sb out in sth; **elle m'affublait toujours des pires guenilles** she always made me wear the most awful old rags
  ▪ VPR **s'affubler** to rig *or* deck oneself out, to get oneself up (**de** in); **il s'affuble souvent des vêtements les plus ridicules** he often gets himself all rigged out in the most ridiculous clothes

affût [afy] NM **1** *(guet)* hiding place; *(pour observatoire d'oiseaux etc)* hide; **chasse au cerf à l'a.** deer stalking; **être** *ou* **se mettre à l'a. de** *(personne)* to lie in wait for; *(être vigilant) (vis-à-vis de qn, qch)* to be on the watch *or* lookout for; *Fig* **être à l'a. de qch** to be on the lookout for sth **2** *Mil* carriage; *(d'un télescope etc)* mounting

affûtage [afytaʒ] NM **1** *(d'outils)* sharpening, grinding; *(d'une scie)* setting **2** set of bench tools

affûter [afyte] VT *(outil)* to grind, to sharpen, to whet; *(scie)* to set; *Fig (esprit)* to sharpen; *Courses de chevaux* **a. un cheval** to bring a horse to the top of its form

affûteur [afytœr] NM *(tool)* grinder, sharpener; *(de scies)* setter

affûteuse [afytøz] NF grinding machine

afghan, -ane [afgɑ̃, -an] ADJ Afghan
  ▪ N **A.** Afghan
  ▪ NM *Ling* Afghan

Afghanistan [afganistɑ̃] NM Afghanistan

aficionado, -os [afisjɔnado, -os] NM aficionado; **les aficionados du vélo** cycling enthusiasts

afin [afɛ̃] ADV **1 a. de faire qch** (in order) to, so as to do sth **2 a. que** + *sub* so that, in order that, *Fml, Litt* that; **a. que les autres puissent le voir** so that the others may see it SEE GRAMMAR A74; B58

AFNOR [afnɔr] NF *(abrév* **Association française de normalisation***)* French industrial standards authority, *Br* ≃ BSI, *Am* ≃ ANSI

à-fond, *pl* **à-fonds** [afɔ̃] NM *Belg* **faire un à.** to down one's drink in one
  ▪ NMPL *Suisse* **à-fonds** spring-cleaning; **faire les à-fonds** to spring-clean, to do the spring-cleaning

a fortiori [afɔrsjɔri] ADV a fortiori, all the more so

AF-P [aɛfpe] NF *abrév* Agence France-Presse

AFPA [afpa] NF *abrév* Association pour la formation professionnelle des adultes

AFR [aɛfɛr] NF *abrév* allocation de formation reclassement

africain, -aine [afrikɛ̃, -ɛn] ADJ African
  ▪ N **A.** African

africanisation [afrikanizasjɔ̃] NF *Pol* Africanization

africaniser [afrikanize] VT to Africanize
  ▪ VPR **s'africaniser** to become Africanized

africaniste [afrikanist] N student of African races and languages

afrikaans [afrikɑ̃s] NM *Ling* Afrikaans

Afrikander [afrikɑ̃dɛr] N Afrikaner

Afrique [afrik] NF Africa; **l'A. du Nord** North Africa; **l'A. du Sud** South Africa

afro [afro] ADJ *(coupe de cheveux)* Afro; **avoir une coiffure a.** to have an Afro; **à l'a.** *(style)* **les cheveux à l'a.** Afro hair

afro-américain, -aine, *pl* **afro-américains, -aines** ADJ Afro-American, Black American
  ▪ N **A.** Afro-American, Black American

afro-asiatique, *pl* **afro-asiatiques** ADJ Afro-Asian
  ▪ N **A.** Afro-Asian

afro-cubain, -aine, *pl* **afro-cubains, -aines** ADJ Afro-Cuban
  ▪ N **A.** Afro-Cuban

after-shave [aftœrʃɛv] NM INV aftershave
  ▪ ADJ INV **lotion a.** aftershave (lotion)

A.G. [aʒe] *abrév* assemblée générale

agaçant [agasɑ̃] ADJ annoying, irritating, aggravating

agacement [agasmɑ̃] NM irritation, annoyance; **dire/témoigner son a.** to express/show one's annoyance *or* irritation

agacer [agase] VT (**j'agaçai(s); n. agaçons**) **1** *(dents)* to set on edge; *(nerfs)* to grate on, to set on edge **2** *(énerver)* **a.** to annoy sb, to irritate sb, to aggravate sb, to get on sb's nerves; **ça m'agace de t'entendre dire encore la même chose** it annoys me *or* gets on my nerves to hear you saying the same thing again; **a. un chien** to tease a dog; **il m'agace avec ses questions** he's getting on my nerves, asking all those questions; **elle m'agace, avec sa façon de faire l'enfant tout le temps** she gets on my nerves, the way she acts so childishly all the time

agaceries [agasri] NFPL charms, wiles; **faire des a.** to use one's charm(s) *or* wiles

agaceur, -euse [agasœr, -øz] ADJ *Can* irritating, annoying; **ce qu'il peut être a.!** he can be so annoying!

agapanthe [agapɑ̃t] NF *Bot* agapanthus

agape [agap] NF *Hum* agapes feast, spread; **nous allons faire des agapes chez Jeannot** we're going to have a real feast *or Fam* slap-up meal at Jeannot's

agar-agar, *pl* **agars-agars** [agaragar] NM agar-agar

agaric [agarik] NM *(champignon)* agaric

agate [agat] NF **1** *Minér* agate; **a. noire** *ou* **d'Islande** obsidian; **a. onyx** sardonyx **2** *(bille)* glass marble

agave, agavé [agav, agave] NM *(plante)* agave; **a. d'Amérique** American aloe, sisalhemp

AGC [aʒese] NM *Phot (abrév* **adaptateur graphique couleur***)* CGA

AGE [aʒeə] NF *(abrév* **assemblée générale extraordinaire***)* EGM

âge [aʒ] NM **1** *(d'une personne)* age; **quel â. avez-vous?** how old are you?; **quand j'avais votre â.** when I was your age; **à ton â., je travaillais** when I was your age, I was working; **à ton â., on ne pleure plus** you're old enough now not to cry, at your age, you shouldn't be crying; **nous avons le même â., nous sommes du même â.** we are the same age; **à l'â. de six ans** at the age of six; **quel â. lui donnez-vous?** how old do you think he is *or* would you say he was?; **on ne lui donne pas du tout son â.** he doesn't look his age at all; **je ne sais pas quel â. lui donner** I don't know how old he can be; **accuser** *ou* **faire son â.** to look one's age; **dès son â.** le plus tendre *ou* **dès son plus jeune â.** from his/her earliest years; **un homme d'un certain â.** a middle-aged man; **en dépit de son grand â.** in spite of his/her great age; **mourir à un grand â.** *ou* **à un â. avancé** *ou* **à un bel â.** to die at a ripe old age; **un homme d'un grand â.** a very old man; **faire plus jeune que son â.** to look younger than one really is, not to look one's age; **il n'a pas d'â., on ne peut pas dire quel â. il a** it is difficult to tell how old he is; **être d'â. légal** to be of age; **être en â. de faire qch, être d'â. à faire qch** to be old enough to do sth; **j'ai passé l'â. de ce genre de choses** I've grown out of that kind of thing; **fréquenter des gens de son â.** to see people of one's own age; **ce n'est plus de mon â.** I'm too old for that type of thing; **être en â. de se marier** to be old enough *or* of an age to marry; **un whisky de 15 ans d'â.** a 15-year-old whisky; **hors d'â.** *(cheval)* aged; **le bas â.** infancy; **enfant en bas â.** infant; **le premier â.** childhood; *(tout premier)* infancy; **couches premier/deuxième â.** nappies for children up to 12 months old/between 12 and 18 months old; **le bel â.** youth; **l'â. ingrat** the awkward *or* difficult age; **sans â.** ageless; **avoir l'â. de raison** to have reached the age of reason; **l'â. d'homme** manhood; **l'â. adulte** adulthood; **être d'â. mûr** *ou* **entre deux âges** *ou* **d'un certain â.** to be middle-aged; **elle est bien pour son â.** she's marvellous for her age; **les maux qui viennent avec**

l'â. the aches and pains that come with old age; **un homme d'â.** an old man; **le troisième â.** retirement age; *(personnes)* the over-sixties; **les gens du troisième â.** the elderly, senior citizens, *Am* golden agers; **à l'â. que j'ai, à mon â.** at my age, at my time of life; **mourir avant l'â.** to die before one's time, to die young; **â. mental** mental age; **avoir un â. mental de six ans** to have a mental age of six; *Fig* **être dans** *ou* **à la fleur de l'â.** to be in the bloom *or* flower of youth; *Fig* **être dans la force de l'â.** to be in one's prime *or* the prime of life; *Fig* **le retour d'â.** the change of life **2** *(génération)* generation; **d'â. en â.** from generation to generation

3 *Hist* age, period, epoch; *Archéol* **l'â. de (la) pierre** the Stone Age; **l'â. de la pierre taillée** the Palaeolithic age; **l'â. de la pierre polie** the Neolithic age; **l'â. de** *ou* **du bronze** the Bronze Age; **l'â. de** *ou* **du fer** the Iron Age; *Hist* **le Moyen Â.** the Middle Ages; **costumes du Moyen Â.** medi(a)eval costumes; *Myth* **l'â. d'or** the golden age; **l'â. d'or du cinéma muet** the golden age of silent movies; **c'est une tradition qui est venue du fond des âges** it's a tradition which has come down through the ages

âgé [aʒe] ADJ **1** *(qui a tel âge)* old, aged; **â. de dix ans** ten years old, ten years of age, aged ten; **je suis plus/moins â. que vous** I am older/younger than you **2** *(vieux)* old, *Litt* aged ['eidʒid]; **assez â.** elderly; **les personnes âgées** old *or* elderly people, senior citizens

Aged [aʒed] NF *abrév* allocation de garde d'enfant à domicile

agence [aʒɑ̃s] NF **1** agency, bureau; **a. d'intérim** temping agency; **a. de publicité/de traduction** advertising/translation agency; **a. de renseignement(s)** information bureau; **a. de placement** employment agency *or* bureau; **a. de presse** press *or* news agency; **a. commerciale** *(d'agence de voyages etc)* public sales office; **a. conseil en communication** public relations *or* PR consultancy; *Com* **a. de distribution physique** physical distribution agency; **A. France-Presse** Agence France-Presse *(French national news agency)*; **a. maritime** shipping agency, forwarding agency; **Agence nationale pour l'emploi** *Br* ≃ Jobcentre, *Can* ≃ CEC; **a. de notation** credit rating agency, *Am* credit bureau; **a. de promotion des ventes** sales promotion agency; **a. de réceptif** ground handling agency, ground operator; **a. de réservation** booking agency; **a. de voyages de discompte** discount travel agency, bucket shop; **a. distributrice** *(d'agence de voyages)* retail travel agency; **a. photographique** photographic agency; **a. réceptive** ground handling agency; **a. de presse de télévision** television news agency; **a. de tourisme** *ou* **de voyages** travel agency *or* agent's; **a. immobilière** estate agency *or* agency; **a. de recouvrements** debt collection agency **2** *(de banque)* branch office; **a. bancaire** bank branch

agencé [aʒɑ̃se] ADJ *Suisse (cuisine)* fitted

agencement [aʒɑ̃smɑ̃] NM **1** arrangement; *(des pièces d'une machine etc)* fitting (together); *(d'une maison, d'une radio, d'un embrayage etc)* layout; **a. de l'intrigue** *(d'un roman etc)* construction of the plot; **l'a. d'un spectacle** the way a show is put together **2** *(éléments)* fixtures, fittings

agencer [aʒɑ̃se] VT **(j'agençai(s); n. agençons)** *(maison etc)* to lay out, to design; *(pièces de machine etc)* to fit (together), to adjust; **local bien agencé** well-designed premises; **phrases mal agencées** badly constructed sentences

▸ VPR **s'agencer** to be laid out; **les parties du discours s'agencent bien/mal** the different

parts of the speech go/don't hang well together

agencier [aʒɑ̃sje] NM *Journ* news agency journalist

agenda [aʒɛ̃da] NM *(pour noter des rendez-vous, journal)* diary; *Ordinat* organizer, planner; **a. de poche/de bureau** pocket/desk diary; **a. organisateur** personal organizer, Filofax®; **a. de réservation** book *or* hotel register, reservations book; **a. électronique** personal organizer, electronic organizer

> Il faut noter que le nom anglais **agenda** est un faux ami. Il signifie **ordre du jour**.

agender [aʒɑ̃de] VT *Suisse (rendez-vous, date)* to note down (in a diary *or* *Am* notebook)

agenouiller (s') [saʒnuje] VPR to kneel (down); **s'a. devant un autel** to kneel at *or* before an altar

agenouilloir [aʒnujwar] NM prie-dieu; *(coussin)* hassock; *(planche)* kneeling bench

agent [aʒɑ̃] NM **1** *(facteur)* agent, agency, medium; **a. économique/atmosphérique** economic/atmospheric factor; **a. chimique** chemical agent; **a. monétaire** circulating medium **2** *Gram* agent; **complément d'a.** agent **3** *(personne)* agent; **un a. de la CIA** CIA agent; **a. (de police)** police officer *or* constable; **a. de la circulation** traffic policeman; **pardon, monsieur l'a.** excuse me, officer

▸▸ *Com* **a. d'affaires** business agent; *Com* **a. agréé** registered agent; **a. d'ambiance** = policeman assigned to patrol in dangerous areas; **a. d'assurance(s)** insurance broker *or* agent; **a. de change** *Fin* stockbroker, exchange broker; *Com* mercantile broker; *Com* **a. autorisé** authorized representative; *Com* **a. commercial** sales agent, sales representative, sales rep; *Com* **a. commissionnaire** commission agent; *Com* **a. de contact** contact; *Com* **a. direct** commission agent; *Com* **a. de distribution à l'export** export distribution agent; **a. en douanes** customs broker; **a. double** double agent; *Com* **a. exclusif** sole agent; *Com* **a. exportateur** export agent; *Com* **a. de fret** freight forwarder, forwarding agent; **a. du fisc** tax official; *Com* **a. général** agent; **a. immobilier** estate agent; *Com* **a. importateur** importer; *Com* **a. indépendant** free agent; *Com* **a. intermédiaire** agent middleman; **a. de liaison** *Com* contact; *Mil* liaison officer; *Com* **a. lié** tied agent; *Com* **a. de ligne** forwarding agent; **a. littéraire** literary agent; **a. de maîtrise** foreman; *Com* **a. mandataire** authorized representative; **a. maritime** shipping agent; **a. publicitaire, a. de publicité** advertising agent, publicity agent; **a. de réceptif** ground handling agency; **a. de recouvrements** debt collector; **a. de réservation** reservation agent; **a. secret** secret agent; **a. de sécurité** security officer; *Com* **a. technico-commercial** sales technician; **a. de transmission** runner, dispatch rider, messenger; **a. du trésor** government broker; **a. de voyages** travel agent

AGETAC [aʒetak] NM *(abrév* **Accord général sur les tarifs et le commerce)** GATT

aggiornamento [a(d)ʒjɔrnamento] NM adaptation to new circumstances; **le parti doit faire son a.** the party has to move with the times

agglomérant [aglɔmerɑ̃] ADJ *(matériau)* binding

NM binding material, binder

agglomérat [aglɔmera] NM agglomerate

agglomération [aglɔmerasjɔ̃] NF **1** *(de ville)* agglomeration, built-up area; **vitesse limi-**

tée dans les agglomérations speed restriction in built-up areas; **les grandes agglomérations** the great urban centres; **l'a. lyonnaise/parisienne** Lyons/Paris and its suburbs; **l'a. londonienne** Greater London **2** *(de fuel etc)* caking

aggloméré [aglɔmere] ADJ conglomerate; **panneau de fibres agglomérées** fibreboard

NM **1** *Géol, Constr* conglomerate **2** *(briquette)* compressed fuel, briquette **3** *(de bois)* fibreboard; **a. de liège** agglomerated cork

agglomérer [aglɔmere] (**j'agglomère, n. agglomérons; j'agglomérerai**) VT to agglomerate; **toute la population est agglomérée dans le ...** the entire population is packed together in the ...

VPR **s'agglomérer** to agglomerate; *(d'un mélange, de substances différentes)* to cohere, to bind; *(de fuel etc)* to cake; **les populations pauvres s'agglomèrent dans les favelas** the poor population is packed together in the shanty towns

agglutinant [aglytinɑ̃] ADJ **1** *(adhésif)* agglutinant, adhesive **2** *Ling (langues)* agglutinative

NM *(de conglomérats)* bond

agglutination [aglytinasjɔ̃] NF **1** *(action)* agglutination, caking; *(d'un mélange, de substances différentes)* binding **2** *(de microbes)* clump **3** *Ling* **phénomène d'a.** agglutination

agglutiner [aglytine] VT to agglutinate; *(mélange etc)* to bind

VPR **s'agglutiner 1** *(de personnes)* to congregate, to gather **2** *Méd (des bords d'une plaie)* to join, to unite

aggravant [agravɑ̃] ADJ *Méd, Jur etc (symptôme, circonstances)* aggravating

aggravation [agravasjɔ̃] NF **1** *(d'une maladie etc)* aggravation; *(du temps, d'un conflit etc)* worsening **2** *(d'une peine)* increase

aggraver [agrave] VT **1** *(maladie, crime)* to worsen, to make worse, to aggravate; **pour a. les choses** to make matters worse **2** *(peine)* to increase, to augment; *(difficultés, imposition)* to increase

VPR **s'aggraver** to worsen, to become worse, to deteriorate; **la situation s'aggrave de jour en jour** the situation is getting *or* becoming worse by the day; **son état s'est aggravé** his condition has deteriorated, he has taken a turn for the worse; **les choses s'aggravent** things are getting worse

agile [aʒil] ADJ *aussi Fig* agile, nimble; *(démarche)* nimble; **elle est a. de ses doigts** she has nimble fingers

agilement [aʒilmɑ̃] ADV agilely, nimbly

agilité [aʒilite] NF *(physique, mentale)* agility; **a. d'un raisonnement** agility of an argument

agios [aʒjo] NMPL *Fin* premium; *(dans un échange de devises)* agio; *(quand on est à découvert)* bank charges; *(d'un emprunt)* interest payments

agiotage [aʒjɔtaʒ] NM *Bourse* stock jobbing, agiotage; *(truquage)* rigging the market; *(en prenant des risques financiers)* speculating, gambling

agioter [aʒjɔte] VI *Bourse* to speculate, to gamble

agioteur, -euse [aʒjɔtœr, -øz] N *Bourse* speculator, gambler

agir [aʒir] VI **1** *(faire quelque chose)* to act; **a. de soi-même** to act on one's own initiative; **a. sur le conseil de qn** to act on sb's advice; **maintenant agissons** now let's get going, now let's get down to it; **il est temps d'a.** it's time to take action *or* to act; **faire a. qn** to get sb to act *or* to take action; **je vais a. en votre faveur (auprès du ministre)** I am going to intervene on your behalf (with the minister); **faire a. qch** to set sth going *or* working, to put sth in motion; **a. en connaisseur** to know what one is doing; **a. en sage** to act wisely; **bien/mal a. envers qn** to act *or* behave well/badly towards sb; **je n'aime pas sa façon** *ou* **manière d'a.** I don't like the way he goes about things; **est-ce ainsi que vous agissez envers moi?** is this how you treat me?

2 *(produire un effet)* to act, to operate, to take effect; **médicament qui agit vite** quick-acting medicine, medicine that acts *or* takes effect quickly; **a. sur qch** to act on sth; **les mauvaises conditions de travail finissent par a. sur le moral/la santé** bad working conditions will end up affecting one's morale/health; **a. sur qn** to exercise an influence on sb; **a. sur les sentiments de qn** to work on sb's feelings; *Bourse* **a. sur le marché** to rig the market

3 *Jur* **a. au nom de qn** to act on behalf of sb; **a. civilement contre qn** to sue sb; **a. au criminel/civil** to prosecute/to sue

V IMPERS s'agir (de) SEE GRAMMAR B29 **1** *(être question de)* **de quoi s'agit-il?** what's the matter?, what's it all about?, *Fam* what's up?; **il ne veut pas me dire de quoi il s'agit** he won't tell me what the matter is; **je ne sais pas vraiment de quoi il s'agit** I don't really know what it's about; **l'affaire dont il s'agit** the matter in hand; **il ne s'agit pas d'argent** it's not a question of money; **il ne s'agit pas de cela** that is not the question *or* not the point, that's neither here nor there; **il s'agit de lui** it concerns him, it is about him; **quand il s'agit d'aider, il est toujours occupé!** when it comes to helping, he always seems to be busy!; **s'agissant de ...** as for ..., as far as ... is concerned

2 *(falloir)* to be a question of ...; **il ne s'agit que de les rendre heureux** it is only a question of making them happy; **il s'agirait de savoir si ...** the question is whether ...; **il s'agirait de se dépêcher** we've got to hurry; *(c'est notre dernière chance)* it's a case of now or never; **il s'agit de savoir ce que tu veux!** make up your mind!

âgisme [aʒism] NM agism

agissant [aʒisɑ̃] ADJ effective, efficient; **un remède a.** an effective remedy

agissements [aʒismɑ̃] NMPL *souvent Péj* dealings, manoeuvres, machinations

agitateur, -trice [aʒitatœr, -tris] N *Pol* agitator

NM **1** *Chimie* stirring *or* glass rod **2** *(appareil)* stirring machine, agitator, mixer

agitation [aʒitasjɔ̃] NF **1** *(de la mer)* roughness, choppiness **2** *(inquiétude)* agitation; *(bougeotte)* restlessness, agitation, fidgeting; *(excitation)* excitement; *Pol* unrest; *Psy* *(state of)* perturbation *or* disturbance; **l'a. de la ville** the bustle of the city; **ville en pleine a.** bustling town; **il l'a trouvée dans un état de grande a.** he found her greatly excited; **cette nouvelle a provoqué l'a. des esprits** the news greatly upset *or* worried people; **l'a. ouvrière** (labour) unrest; **a. sociale** civil commotion

agité, -ée [aʒite] ADJ **1** *(mer)* choppy, rough; *(ciel)* wild **2** *Méd (patient)* feverish, restless; *(nuit)* restless, sleepless; *(sommeil)* broken, fitful **3** *(foule)* agitated, tumultuous; *(personne)* restless, excited, fidgety; *(esprit)* perturbed, troubled; *(époque)* unsettled; **vie agitée** hectic life

N restless *or* unsettled person; *Méd* **pavillon des agités** security wing, wing for dangerous patients; *Fam Hum* **a. du bocal** nutter, *Am* wacko

agiter [aʒite] VT **1** *(mouchoir, drapeau, bras)* to wave; *(bouteille)* to shake; *(aile, éventail)*

to flutter; *(du vent) (arbre, branches)* to sway; *(mer)* to rouse; *(mélange)* to stir; *(air)* to fan; **a. la queue** *(d'un chien)* to wag its tail; *(d'un cheval)* to flick its tail; **a. avant usage/de consommer** shake before use

2 *(inquiéter)* to perturb, to trouble; *(malade)* to agitate, to excite; **cette nouvelle risque de l'a. encore plus** this news could upset him even more; **malade agité par la fièvre** patient restless with fever; **elle est agitée par cette rencontre** the meeting has upset her *or* has got her (all) worked up; **a. le peuple** *ou* **les masses** to stir up the masses

3 *(idée)* to discuss, to debate

VPR **s'agiter 1** to be agitated; *(s'affairer)* to bustle around; **s'a. dans l'eau** to splash about in the water; **s'a. dans son sommeil** to toss (about) *or* thrash around in one's sleep

2 *(s'énerver)* to become agitated *or* excited, to get upset *or* worked up; *(de la mer)* to get rough; **il ne faut pas que le malade s'agite** care should be taken not to upset *or* excite the patient

agit-prop [aʒitprɔp] NF INV agit-prop

agneau, -eaux [aɲo] NM lamb; **(peau d')a.** lambskin; **laine d'a.** lamb's wool; *Fig* **c'est un a.** he is as meek as a lamb; *Fig* **mon a.** my (pet) lamb; **doux comme un a.** as gentle as a lamb; *Rel* **l'A. sans tache** the Lamb (of God); *Culin* **côtelette d'a.** lamb chop; *Culin* **gigot d'a.** leg of lamb

agnelage [aɲəlaʒ] NM **1** *(mise à bas)* lambing **2** *(saison)* lambing season

agneler [aɲəle] VI **(elle agnèle; elle agnèlera)** to lamb

agnelet [aɲəlɛ] NM lambkin, young lamb

agneline [aɲəlin] NF lamb's wool

agnelle [aɲɛl] NF ewe lamb

agnosticisme [agnɔstisism] NM agnosticism

agnostique [agnɔstik] ADJ, N agnostic

agonie [agɔni] NF death agony *or* struggle, pangs of death; **être à l'a.** to be at one's last gasp *or* at death's door; *Fig* to be suffering agonies; **lente a.** lingering death; *Fig* **l'a. d'un régime** the death throes of a regime

> Il faut noter que le nom anglais **agony** est un faux ami. Il signifie **douleur atroce** ou **angoisse**, selon le contexte.

agonir [agɔnir] VT **a. qn d'injures/d'insultes** to heap insults *or* abuse on sb, to hurl insults *or* abuse at sb; **se faire a.** to be loudly insulted *or* abused

agonisant, -ante [agɔnizɑ̃, -ɑ̃t] ADJ dying, in the throes of death; **de sa voix agonisante** with his dying breath; *Fig* **un règne a.** a reign in its dying moments *or* death throes

N dying person; **prières pour les agonisants** prayers for the dying

agoniser [agɔnize] VI to be dying *or* at the point of death; *Fig (d'une entreprise)* to be on its last legs

> Il faut noter que le verbe anglais **to agonize** est un faux ami. Il signifie **se tourmenter**.

agoraphobe [agɔrafɔb] ADJ, N *Méd* agoraphobic

agoraphobie [agɔrafɔbi] NF *Méd* agoraphobia; **souffrir d'a.** to be agoraphobic

agrafage [agrafaʒ] NM fastening; *(de feuilles de papier)* stapling; *(d'un objet sur un établi etc)* clamping; *Tech* dowelling; *(de vêtements)* fastening, hooking

agrafe [agraf] NF **1** fastener; *(d'une médaille, d'un album)* clasp; *(d'une sangle)* buckle; *(de bureau)* staple; *Chir etc* suture clip; **a. de diamants** diamond clasp; **agrafes et portes (de couturière)** hooks and eyes; *Com* **a. antivol**

anti-theft *or* security tag **2** *Constr* clamp, cleat, cramp iron **3** *(d'une fenêtre etc)* hasp, catch **4** *Archit (d'une voûte)* keystone

agrafer [agrafe] VT **1** *(accrocher)* to fasten, to clip together; *(avec une agrafeuse)* to staple; *(robe)* to hook up; *(ceinture)* to buckle; **j'ai tellement grossi que je n'arrive plus à a. mes vêtements!** I've put on so much weight that I can't do up *or* fasten my clothes!; *Fam* **aide-moi à a. ma robe!** do me up! **2** *Constr* to clamp, to cramp **3** *Fam (de la police) (arrêter)* to nab, to nick; **il va finir par se faire a.** he's going to end up getting nabbed *or* nicked

agrafeuse [agraføz] NF stapler

agraire [agrɛr] ADJ agrarian; **réforme a.** land reform; **mesures agraires** land measures; *Jur* **loi a.** land act

agrammatical, -ale, -aux, -ales [agramatikal, -o] ADJ *Ling* ungrammatical

agrandir [agrɑ̃dir] VT **1** *(rendre plus grand)* to make larger, to enlarge; *(photographie etc)* to enlarge; *(sur écran)* to magnify; *Ordinat (fenêtre)* to maximize; *(influence, cercle de relations)* to increase, to extend; **a. une maison/un appartement** to extend a house/flat; **a. qch en long/en large** to lengthen/widen sth

2 *(faire paraître plus grand)* to make appear larger, to magnify; **ce papier peint agrandit la pièce** this wallpaper makes the room look larger

3 *(développer) (affaire)* to expand

4 *(esprit etc)* to uplift

VPR **s'agrandir** *(devenir plus grand)* to grow larger; *(en quantité)* to become greater, to increase; *(prendre du volume)* to expand; **nous allons nous a.** we are going to enlarge our premises; **elle veut s'a.** *(dans son appartement)* she wants more space

agrandissement [agrɑ̃dismɑ̃] NM **1** *(extension)* enlargement, extension, expansion; **a. en long/en large** lengthening/widening; **travaux d'a.** extension work **2** *(d'une entreprise etc)* extension; *(d'un holding etc)* increase **3** *Phot* enlargement

agrandisseur [agrɑ̃disœr] NM *Phot* enlarger

agrarien, -ienne [agrarjɛ̃, -jɛn] ADJ, N *Pol* agrarian

agréable [agreabl] ADJ pleasant, agreeable; *(apparence, arrangement)* pleasing; *(manière etc)* nice, pleasant; **un jeune homme très a.** a very pleasant *or* nice young man; **se rendre a. à qn** to be pleasant to sb; **a. au goût** pleasant to the taste; **a. à voir** pleasing to the eye; **peu a.** disagreeable

NM **joindre l'utile à l'a.** to combine business with pleasure

N **faire l'a.** to make oneself pleasant (**auprès de** to)

agréablement [agreabləmɑ̃] ADV pleasantly, agreeably; **nous avons été a. surpris par ta décision** we were pleasantly surprised by your decision

agréé [agree] ADJ *(échantillon etc)* approved; *Com* recognized, authorized; *Can* **comptable a.** chartered *or Am* certified accountant

agréer [agree] VT *(fournisseur, équipement)* to approve; **a. un contrat** to approve an agreement; **veuillez a. l'assurance de mes salutations distinguées** *(dans une lettre)* *(à une personne dont on connaît le nom)* yours sincerely; *(à une personne dont on ne connaît pas le nom)* yours faithfully

VI to please; **si cela vous agrée** if that suits you

agrég [agrɛg] NF *Univ Fam* = **agrégation 1**

agrégat [agrega] NM aggregate

agrégatif, -ive [agregatif, -iv] N agrégation exam candidate

agrégation [agregasjɔ̃] NF **1** *Univ* **(concours**

de) l'a. = competitive examination for posts on the teaching staff of lycées and universities **2** *Constr* aggregation, binding; **matière d'a.** *(pour une route etc)* binding material

---

Agrégation

This is a prestigious professional qualification for teachers in France. Those who pass the challenging competitive exam for the "agrég" become teachers in secondary education or universities and are entitled to higher pay and a less onerous timetable than those who have passed the **CAPES** *(see box at this entry).*

---

agrégé, -ée [agreʒe] *Univ* **ADJ** = who has passed the agrégation examination
N = graduate who has passed the agrégation examination

agréger [agreʒe] **VT 1** *(rassembler)* **les cristaux agrégés dans la roche** the crystals incorporated in the rock **2** *(admettre) (société)* to incorporate; *(individu)* to admit
VPR s'agréger 1 to combine, to merge **2 s'a. à un groupe** to join a group

agrément [agremã] **NM 1** *(plaisir)* pleasure, amusement; **voyage d'a.** pleasure trip; **arts d'a.** amateur artistic pursuits; **livres d'a.** light reading
2 *(charme)* attractiveness, pleasantness, charm; **une ville sans a.** an unattractive town; **agréments** *(d'un lieu)* amenities; *(d'une personne)* charm
3 *Mus* **notes d'a.** grace notes
4 *(accord)* approval, consent; **nous avons besoin de l'a. de la Sécurité sociale pour commencer à vous soigner** the Social Security must give us their approval or consent before we can begin to treat you
5 *Com (d'agence de voyages)* agency appointment; *(garantie financière)* bonding scheme

---

Il faut noter que le nom anglais **agreement** est un faux ami. Il signifie **accord**.

---

agrémenter [agremãte] **VT** to ornament, to decorate; *(robe etc)* to trim; **texte agrémenté de citations** text laced with quotations

agrès [agrɛ] **NMPL 1** *Naut* tackle **2** *Sport* (gymnastics) apparatus; **faire des a.** to do exercises on the apparatus

agresser [agrese] **VT** to attack (without provocation), to assault; *(yeux, tympans)* to assault; **le soleil agresse la peau** the sun damages the skin or has a damaging effect on the skin; **se faire a.** to be attacked; *(dans un lieu public et pour son argent)* to be mugged; **arrête de m'a., ce n'est pas de ma faute!** stop being so aggressive towards me, it's not my fault!; *Fam* **ne te sens pas agressé** don't think you're being got at

agresseur [agresœr] **NM** attacker, aggressor, assailant

agressif, -ive [agresif, -iv] **ADJ** *(ton, personne, couleur etc)* aggressive

agression [agresjɔ̃] **NF 1** *(agressivité)* aggression **2** *(acte) (sur un passant etc)* mugging *(de* of); *(d'un pays)* act of aggression *(de* against); **ce genre de publicité est une véritable a.** this kind of advertising is extremely aggressive; **être victime d'une a.** to be attacked; *(dans un lieu public et pour son argent)* to be mugged; **a. de la peau par les intempéries** damaging effects of bad weather on the skin; **le bruit est une réelle a.** noise is a real act of aggression; **les agressions de la vie moderne** the stresses of modern life

agressivement [agresivmã] **ADV** aggressively

agressivité [agresivite] **NF** aggressiveness

agreste [agrɛst] **ADJ** *Litt* **1** rustic; *(site)* rural **2** *(personne, manières)* uncouth

agricole [agrikɔl] **ADJ** *(produit, nation etc)* agricultural; **comice(s) agricole(s)** agricultural show; **exploitation a.** farming; *(ferme)* farm; **petite exploitation a.** small farm, smallholding; **travail a.** farmwork, farming; **ouvrier a.** farm worker or hand; **la population a.** the farming population

agriculteur, -trice [agrikyltœr, -tris] **N** farmer

agriculture [agrikyltyr] **NF** agriculture, farming

agripper [agripe] **VT** *(personne, objet)* to clutch (at), to grip; *(saisir) (objet)* to seize (hold of)
VPR s'agripper to cling; **il s'agrippait au bord de la fenêtre** he was clinging to the windowsill

agritourisme [agriturism] **NM** agritourism

agro [agro] **NM** *Fam abrév* **Institut national agronomique**

agro-alimentaire [agroalimãter] **ADJ** *(industrie, secteur)* food-processing
NM food-processing industry, agribusiness

agrochimie [agroʃimi] **NF** agrochemistry

agrochimiste [agroʃimist] **N** agrochemist

agronome [agronom] **N** agronomist, agricultural economist; **ingénieur a.** agricultural engineer or scientist

agronomie [agronomi] **NF** agronomy; *Écon* agronomics

agronomique [agronomik] **ADJ** agronomic(al); **l'Institut national a.** = (university level) college for students of agronomics

agrume [agrym] **NM** citrus fruit

agrumicole [agrymikɔl] **ADJ** citrus fruit-producing

aguerrir [agerir] **VT** *(personne)* to harden, to toughen; *(troupes)* to train (for battle)
VPR s'aguerrir s'a. à ou **contre qch** to become hardened to sth; *(apprendre à accepter, se débrouiller)* to learn to take sth in one's stride; **ça va te permettre de t'a.** *(d'aller en pension etc)* it will toughen you up a bit

aguets [agɛ] **NMPL aux a.** on the watch, on the lookout; **être** ou **se tenir aux a.** to be on the watch or on the lookout; **avoir l'oreille aux a.** to keep one's ears open

aguichant [agiʃã] **ADJ** seductive, provocative

aguiche [agiʃ] **NF** *(publicité)* teaser

aguicher [agiʃe] **VT** to excite, to arouse, *Fam* to lead on

aguicheur, -euse [agiʃœr, -øz] **ADJ** seductive, provocative; **une fillette aguicheuse** a little tease, a nymphet
NF aguicheuse provocative woman, tease

Ah *(abrév* **ampère-heure)** Ah

ah [ɑ] **INTJ** ah!; *(exprimant la surprise)* oh!; **ah, que c'est beau!** isn't it beautiful!; **ah oui!** well yes, of course!; **ah ça non/oui!** certainly not/certainly!; *Iron* **ah ah! je savais bien que tu me cachais quelque chose!** aha! I knew that you were hiding something from me!
NM INV pousser des oh et des ah to oooh and ah

ahaner [aane] **VI** *Litt* to puff and pant

ahuri, -ie [ayri] **ADJ** *(regard)* astounded; *(personne)* stupefied, *Fam* flabbergasted; **avoir l'air a.** to look astounded or stupefied
N idiot, numbskull

ahurir [ayrir] **VT** to astound, to stupefy

ahurissant [ayrisã] **ADJ** astounding, incredible, stupefying; *Fam* **il a un culot a.** he's got one hell of a cheek

ahurissement [ayrismã] **NM** stupefaction; **il ne revient pas de son a.** he can't get over it

aï [ai] **NM** *(mammifère)* three-toed sloth

AIDA [aida] **NM** *Mktg (abrév* **attention-intérêt-désir-action)** AIDA

aide¹ [ɛd] **NF** help, assistance; *(humanitaire)* aid; **j'ai dû lui demander de l'a.** I had to ask him for help; **appeler à l'a.** to call for help; **donner son a. à qn** to help sb; **venir en a. à qn, apporter son a. à qn** to come to sb's assistance or aid; **recourir à l'a. d'un médecin** to call in a doctor; **à l'a.!** help!; **à l'a. de qch** with the help or assistance of sth; **avec l'a. de qn** with the help or assistance of sb; **faire qch sans a.** to do sth without help or on one's own
▸▸ *Ordinat* **a. à la césure** hyphenation help; *Ordinat* **a. contextuelle** context-sensitive help; *Écon* **a. au développement** foreign aid (to developing countries); **a. de l'État** = national assistance; **a. financière** financial aid or assistance; *Compta* **a. fiscale** tax credit; **a. gouvernementale** government aid; **a. judiciaire** legal aid; *Ordinat* **a. en ligne** online help; **a. au logement** accommodation allowance; **a. publique au développement** official development assistance; **a. au retour** = voluntary repatriation allowances for immigrant workers leaving France; **a. sociale** *Br* social security, *Am* welfare

aide² **N** assistant, helper; *Naut* mate; *(de géomètre)* chainman
▸▸ *Mil* **a. de camp** aide-de-camp; **a. de cuisine** assistant cook, kitchen hand; **a. familiale** ou **maternelle** mother's help; **a. de laboratoire** laboratory assistant; **a. ménagère** home help

aidé [ede] **ADJ 1** *(assisté)* **elle n'est pas très aidée** she doesn't have much help (around the house); **elle est très aidée par cette femme** she gets a lot of help from this woman **2** *Admin* **contrat a.** = employment contract whereby part of an employee's salary is paid by the state **3** *Fig* **il n'est pas très a.** *(pas très intelligent)* he's not very smart, he's a bit of a dimwit

aide-comptable, *pl* **aides-comptables N** assistant accountant, accounts clerk

aide-cuisinier, *pl* **aides-cuisiniers N** kitchen assistant

aide-éducateur, *pl* **aides-éducateurs N** = in the French educational system, assistant helping with pupil activities and supervision

aide-électricien, *pl* **aides-électriciens NM** *Cin, TV* best boy

aide-gouvernante, *pl* **aides-gouvernantes NF** assistant housekeeper

aide-mécanicien, *pl* **aides-mécaniciens NM** garage hand

aide-mémoire NM INV aide-memoire; *TV* prompt card; *Ordinat* quick reference guide; **j'ai besoin d'un a.** I need something to jog my memory

aide-monteur *pl* **aides-monteurs NM** *Cin, TV* assistant film editor

aide-opérateur *pl* **aides-opérateurs NM** *Cin, TV* assistant cameraman

aider [ede] **VT** to help, to assist, to aid; **attends, je vais t'a.** hold on, I'll help you or I'll give you a hand; **que puis-je faire pour vous a.?** how may I help you?; **je me suis fait a. par un ami** I got a friend to help me or to give me a hand; **tu ne peux pas t'occuper de ta maison toute seule, fais-toi a.** you can't look after the house on your own, get some help or get someone to help you; **a. qn à faire qch** to help sb to do sth; **a. qn à monter/descendre/entrer/sortir** to help sb up/down/in/out; **a. qn à mettre/ôter son pardessus** to help sb on/off with his/her coat; **Dieu aidant** with God's help; *Iron* **tu veux que je t'aide?** stop that **VOIR GRAMMAIRE A41**

VI a. à qch to contribute to(wards) sth; **elle n'aide jamais!** she never helps (out), she never lends a hand

VPR s'aider 1 *Prov* **aide-toi et le ciel t'aidera** God helps those who help themselves; **il faut s'a. les uns les autres** we must help one another **2 s'a. de qch** to make use of sth; **s'a. d'un dictionnaire** to consult a dictionary; **marcher en s'aidant d'une canne/de béquilles** to walk with the aid of a stick/crutches

aide-serveur, *pl* **aides-serveurs NM** waiter's assistant, *Am* busboy

aide-soignant, -ante, *pl* **aides-soignants, -antes N** nursing auxiliary, auxiliary nurse

aïe [aj] **INT** *(cri de douleur)* ow!, ouch!; *Fig* **a.! j'ai fait une gaffe!** oh no *or* oh dear, I've put my foot in it!; **a. a. a.!** boy oh boy!

AIEA [aiəa] **NF** *Nucl (abrév* **Agence internationale de l'énergie atomique)** IAEA

aïeul, -eule [ajœl, ajø] **N 1** *(pl* **aïeux)** *(ancêtre)* ancestor; *Fam* **mes aïeux!** goodness me! **2** *Vieilli (pl* **aïeuls)** grandfather, f grandmother

aigle [ɛgl] **NM 1** *(oiseau)* eagle; **a. royal** *ou* **fauve** *ou* **doré** golden eagle; **grand a. des mers** erne, sea eagle; *Fig* **un œil d'a.** a keen *or* penetrating glance; *Fig* **avoir un œil d'a.** to be eagle-eyed; **nez en bec d'a.** hook *or* aquiline nose **2** *Fig* genius, mastermind; **ce n'est pas un a.** he's no genius **3** *(lutrin)* lectern **4** *(poisson)* **a. de mer** eagle ray **5** *(en patinage)* **grand a.** spread-eagle

NF 1 *Hér* eagle; **a. de sable éployée** eagle displayed sable; **double a., a. à deux têtes** double-headed eagle **2** *Mil* eagle, standard; **les aigles romaines** the Roman eagles; **l'a. impériale (des armées napoléoniennes)** the imperial eagle

aiglefin [ɛɡləfɛ̃] **NM** *(poisson)* haddock

aiglette [ɛglɛt] **NF** *Hér* eaglet

aiglon, -onne [ɛglɔ̃, -ɔn] **N** *(oiseau)* eaglet, young eagle; *Hist* **L'A.** Napoleon II

aigre [ɛgr] **ADJ** *(goût etc)* sour, sharp, acid, tart; *(lait)* sour; *Fig (propos)* cutting; *(personne)* sour; *(éprouvant du ressentiment)* bitter; *(vent, froid)* bitter; *(son)* harsh, shrill; **parler d'un ton a.** to speak sharply

NM tourner à l'a. *(d'un aliment etc)* to turn sour; *Fig (d'une discussion)* to turn nasty

aigre-doux, -douce *pl* **aigres-doux, -douces ADJ** *(sauce)* sweet and sour; *Fig (remarque)* snide, *Fam* catty

aigrefin [ɛgrəfɛ̃] **NM** *Péj* swindler, (financial) shark

aigrelet, -ette [ɛgrəlɛ, -ɛt] **ADJ** *(vin, goût)* (rather) sour; *(son, voix)* harsh, reedy

aigrement [ɛgrəmɑ̃] **ADV** acrimoniously, bitterly

aigrette [ɛgrɛt] **NF 1** *(d'un héron)* aigrette; *(d'un perroquet etc)* crest; *(d'une chouette)* horn; *(de cheveux, de fourrure)* tuft **2** *(panache)* aigrette, plume; **a. de diamants** spray of diamonds **3** *Bot* egret; *(du maïs)* tassel **4** *Élec (décharge)* aigrette, brush **5** *(oiseau)* egret

aigreur [ɛgrœr] **NF 1** *(d'un goût)* sourness, tartness, acidity; *Fig (du tempérament)* sourness; *(d'une remarque)* sharpness, bitterness; **il en parle encore avec a.** he's still very bitter about it **2** *Méd* **aigreurs (d'estomac)** acidity, excess stomach acid

aigri [egri] **ADJ** embittered, soured

aigrir [egrir] **VT a. qch** to turn sth sour; *Fig* **a. qn** to embitter sb, to make sb bitter

VI to turn *or* grow sour; *(du lait)* to turn

VPR s'aigrir *(devenir acide)* to turn sour; *Fig* **son caractère s'est aigri** he has become embittered

aigu, -uë [egy] **ADJ 1** *(douleur)* acute, sharp; *(curiosité)* intense; *(conflit, jalousie)* bitter; *(regard)* penetrating; *(esprit, sensation, intelligence)* keen, sharp; **elle a un sens a. du rôle de chacun** she has a keen sense of what everybody's role should be **2** *(instrument)* sharp, pointed; *(dans le réglage de la tonalité)* treble; *Math* **angle a.** acute angle **3** *(son)* shrill, sharp, high-pitched **4** *Gram* **accent a.** acute (accent)

NM les aigus the treble; **il y a trop d'aigus** the treble is too high

aigue-marine, *pl* **aigues-marines** [ɛgmarin] **NF** aquamarine

aiguillage [egɥijaʒ] **NM 1** *Rail (manœuvre)* switching *or* shifting of points; *(d'un train)* shunting; **poste d'a.** signal box **2** *Rail (appareil)* points, *Am* switches; **a. à deux voies** two-way switch **3** *Fig* orientation; **faire une erreur d'a.** to take the wrong turning *or* course

aiguille [egɥij] **NF 1** needle; **a. à coudre/repriser/tricoter** sewing/darning/knitting needle; **travail à l'a.** needlework; **a. à passer** *ou* **à lacet** bodkin; *Méd* **a. hypodermique** hypodermic needle; *Fig* **chercher une a. dans une botte de foin** to look for a needle in a haystack; *Fig* **de fil en a. nous en sommes venus à parler de notre enfance** one thing led to another and we got talking about our childhood

2 *Ordinat* pin; **imprimante à aiguilles** 24-pin printer

3 a. de glace icicle; *Géol* **a. (rocheuse)** needle; *(d'un sommet)* spine; **a. de pin** pine needle; **a. de mer** *(poisson)* pipe fish, garfish; **a. à tracer** scriber; **a. de graveur** etching needle

4 *Rail* tongue rail, point rail, blade; **a. de raccordement** points, *Am* switches

5 *(d'un obélisque, d'un pic etc)* needle, point; *(d'une église)* (church) spire

6 *(de boussole, de compteur de vitesse etc)* needle; *(d'une montre, d'une horloge)* hand; **petite a.** hour hand; **grande a.** minute hand; **a. trotteuse** second hand

aiguillée [egɥije] **NF** (short) piece of thread

aiguiller [egɥije] **VT** *Rail (train)* to shunt, *Am* to switch; *Fig* **a. la police sur une fausse piste** to put the police on a false scent; *Fig* **on l'a aiguillé vers la profession de banquier** he was steered into banking; *Fig* **il a été mal aiguillé dans ses études** he was badly advised about his studies; *Fig* **a. ses recherches vers un certain domaine** to orient(ate) *or* direct one's research towards a particular field

aiguilleur [egɥijœr] **NM** *Rail* pointsman, *Am* switchman; *Aviat* **a. du ciel** air traffic controller

aiguillon [egɥijɔ̃] **NM 1** *(pique-bœuf)* goad; *Fig* incentive, spur, stimulus; *Fig* **sa remarque me fit l'effet d'un a.** his/her remark spurred me on **2** *Bot* prickle, thorn; *(d'une guêpe)* sting

aiguillonner [egɥijɔne] **VT** *(bœufs)* to goad; *Fig (personne) (de la jalousie, de l'ambition)* to spur on; *(d'une personne)* to urge on; *Fig* **l'appât du gain l'aiguillonne** the lure of money spurs him on

aiguisé [egize] **ADJ** *(couteau)* sharp; *Fig (appétit, intérêt)* keen

aiguiser [egize] **VT 1** *(couteau etc)* to sharpen, to put an edge on, to grind; *(scie, rasoir)* to set; *(faux)* to whet; *(outil)* to sharpen to a point **2** *Fig (curiosité, jalousie)* to arouse; *(appétit)* to whet; *(intelligence)* to sharpen

aiguiseur, -euse [egizœr, -øz] **N** *(d'outils etc)* grinder, sharpener

aiguisoir [egizwar] **NM** *(outil)* (knife) sharpener, steel; *(pierre à aiguiser)* whetstone

aïkido [ajkido] **NM** *Sport* aikido; **faire de l'a.** to do aikido

ail, *pl* **ails** [aj] *Vieilli* **aulx** [o] **NM 1** *Culin* garlic; **une gousse d'a.** a clove of garlic; **un bulbe** *ou* *Fam* **une tête d'a.** a head of garlic **2** *(plante)* allium

aile [ɛl] **NF 1** *(d'oiseau, de papillon etc)* wing; *(de manchot)* flipper; **battre des ailes** to beat *or* flap its wings; **battre de l'a.** *(d'un oiseau)* to flutter; *Fig (d'une personne)* to be flustered *or* embarrassed; **l'entreprise bat de l'a.** the firm is struggling (to survive) *or* is in a bad way; **avoir du plomb dans l'a., en avoir dans l'a.** *(d'un oiseau)* to be winged; *Fig (d'une personne)* to be hard hit; *Fig* **la théorie a du plomb dans l'a.** the theory doesn't stand up; *Fig* **la peur nous donnait des ailes** fear lent us wings; *Fig* **voler de ses propres ailes** to stand on one's own (two) feet; *Fig* **vouloir voler avant d'avoir ses ailes** to want to run before one can walk; *Fig* **rogner les ailes à qn** to clip sb's wings; *Fig Fam* **avoir un coup dans l'a.** to have had a bit too much to drink; *Fig* **prendre qn sous son a.** to take sb under one's wing; *Fig* **travailler sous l'a. d'un grand professeur** to be the protégé of an eminent professor

2 *Aut* wing, *Am* fender; *(d'un bâtiment, de la scène)* wing; *(d'une armée)* wing, flank; *(d'un moulin)* sail; *(d'un sémaphore)* arm; *(d'une hélice, d'une turbine)* blade; *(d'une oreille)* helix; *(du nez)* wing; *(d'une poutre)* flange

3 *Aviat* wing, aerofoil, *Am* airfoil; **a. courbe** cambered wing; **a. en flèche** swept-back wing; **a. à fente** slotted wing; **a. en delta** delta wing; **a. cantilever, a. en porte à faux** cantilever wing

4 *Rugby, Ftbl* wing; **les demi ailes** the wing halves; **jouer trois quarts a.** to play three-quarters; **à l'a. gauche** on the left wing

5 *Sport* **a. volante** *ou* **libre** *(sport)* hang-gliding; *(objet)* hang-glider; **faire de l'a. volante** to hang-glide, to go hang-gliding

ailé [ele] **ADJ** winged, feathered, *Spéc* alate

aileron [ɛlrɔ̃] **NM 1** *(d'oiseau)* pinion; *(de requin etc)* fin **2** *Aviat* aileron **3** *Aviat etc* fin; **a. stabilisateur** stabilizer fin; **stabilisateur à a.** fin stabilizer **4** *Aut* wing, *Am* fender; *(de voiture de course)* aerofoil; **a. arrière** rear wing **5** *(de roue à eau)* paddle board **6** *(d'un sous-marin)* fin keel; *(d'une planche à voile)* skeg

ailette [ɛlɛt] **NF 1** *(d'un radiateur)* radiating plate, fin; *Aut* **a. de refroidissement** cooling fin; **tube à ailettes** fanned *or* gilled tube **2** *(d'une pièce de machine)* lug, tenon; *(d'un coquillage)* stud; **vis à ailettes** wing nut, thumbscrew **3** *(d'une torpille, d'un éventail, d'un ventilateur etc)* vane; *(d'une bombe, d'une missile)* wing, fin; *(d'un avion)* fin; *(d'une turbine)* blade; **à ailettes** *(roue etc)* bladed; *(bombe, missile)* winged

ailier [elje] **NM** *Sport* winger

ailler [aje] **VT** *Culin* to add garlic to

ailleurs [ajœr] **ADV 1** *(à un autre endroit)* elsewhere, somewhere else; **elle vient d'a.** she's not from here, she's not from these parts; **c'est dit a. dans le texte** it's mentioned somewhere else in the text; **on a dû passer par a.** we had to come a different way; *Fig* **être a.** to be miles away; **partout a.** everywhere else; *(n'importe où)* anywhere else; **nulle part a.** nowhere else; **vous mangerez ici comme nulle part a.** you'll eat better here than you will anywhere else; *Fam* **va voir a. si j'y suis** take a walk or hike

2 besides, anyway, *surtout Fml* moreover; *(quoi qu'il en soit)* however; *(au fait)* come to that, for that matter; **d'a., j'avais quelque chose à te dire à ce sujet** by the way, I had something to tell you about this

3 par a. in other respects; *(par qn d'autre etc)* from another source; *(d'ailleurs)* moreover

NM il avait quitté son pays en quête d'un a. où la vie serait meilleure he had left his country in search of a better life elsewhere *or* somewhere else

ailloli [ajɔli] **NM** = aïoli

aimable [ɛmabl] **ADJ 1** *(gentil)* kind, pleasant, agreeable; **vous êtes bien a., c'est très a. de votre part** it's very kind of you, it's very good of you; **peu a.** disagreeable; *(remerciements, propos etc)* ungracious; **échanger quelques mots aimables avec qn** to exchange a few kind words with sb **2** *Arch (que l'on peut aimer facilement)* lovable, attractive

aimablement [ɛmabləmã] **ADV** kindly, pleasantly

aimant¹ [ɛmã] **NM** magnet; **a. supraconducteur** superconducting magnet

aimant² [ɛmã] **ADJ** *(parent etc)* loving

aimantation [ɛmãtasjɔ̃] **NF** magnetization

aimanter [ɛmãte] **VT** to magnetize

aimer [eme] **VT 1** *(d'amour)* to love; **a. qn (d'amour)** to love sb, to be in love with sb; **tu crois qu'il m'aime?** do you think he loves me?

2 *(apprécier, avoir de l'affection pour)* *(personne, chose)* to like, to be fond of; **il te téléphone encore, ouh, je n'aime pas ça!** he's calling you again, oh I don't like that at all!; **elle n'aime pas la viande crue** she doesn't like raw meat; **a. qn d'amitié** to be good friends with sb; **je n'aime guère Pierre** I don't like Pierre very much, I don't care for Pierre very much; **j'aime beaucoup Pierre** I like Pierre very much, I'm very fond of Pierre; **j'aime beaucoup la musique** I'm very fond of music; **je t'aime bien** I like you a lot; **se faire a. de qn** to win sb's affection; **plante qui aime un sol calcaire** plant that likes a chalky soil; **tu sais que nous n'aimons pas ce genre de choses** you know we don't like that sort of thing; **a. (à) faire qch** to like doing sth; **j'aurais aimé le voir** I would like to have seen him; *Prov* **qui m'aime aime mon chien** love me, love my dog; **je vais prendre un pot – qui m'aime me suive!** I'm going for a drink – anyone want to join me?; **j'aime autant le cidre que le vin** I like cider just as much as wine; **j'aime(rais) autant rester ici** I would just as soon stay here (**que de ... ** as ...); **j'aime autant qu'il ne m'attende pas** I would just as soon he didn't wait for me; **a. mieux** to prefer; **ah, j'aime mieux ça, j'ai cru que tu avais oublié de les inviter** that's just as well, I thought you'd forgotten to invite them; **j'aime** *ou* **j'aimerais mieux rester ici** I would rather *or* sooner stay here; *Fam* **j'aime mieux pas** I'd rather not

VPR s'aimer 1 *(être attaché par amour)* to love each other, to be in love (with each other); *(avoir des relations sexuelles)* to make love; **ils s'aiment** they are in love (with each other) **2** *(être fier de soi)* to think a lot of oneself; *(à une occasion particulière)* to be pleased with oneself; **je ne m'aime pas dans cette veste** *(ne me plais pas)* I don't like myself in this jacket

aine [ɛn] **NF** *Anat* groin

aîné, -ée [ene] **ADJ** *(de deux personnes)* elder; *(de plus que deux personnes)* eldest; **mon frère a.** my elder brother; *(plus de deux frères)* my eldest brother; **la branche aînée de la famille** the elder *or* senior branch of the family VOIR GRAMMAIRE A26–7

N elder *or* eldest (child); **il ne va pas encore à l'école** the eldest doesn't go to school yet; **nos aînés** our elders; **il est mon a.** he is older than me; **il est mon a. de deux ans** he is two years older than me

aînesse [enɛs] **NF** **droit d'a.** law of primogeniture

ainsi [ɛ̃si] **ADV 1** *(de cette façon)* like this, like that, in this *or* that way, *Fml* thus; **c'est a. que commence la chanson** the song starts like this, this is how the song starts; **c'est a. qu'il est devenu soldat** and that is *or* was how he became a soldier; **s'il en est a.** if that is the case, if (it is) so; **puisqu'il en est a., je n'ai plus rien à dire** under the circumstances, I have nothing more to say; **les choses étant a.** if that's the way *or* how things are; **et a. de suite** and so on, and so forth; **pour a. dire** so to speak, as it were; *Rel* **a. soit-il** so be it; **a. donc so; a. donc tu nous quittes** so you're leaving us then?

2 *(par exemple)* for example, for instance; **il m'arrive des aventures, a., l'autre jour ...** things happen to me, for instance, the other day ...

CONJ 1 so; **a. vous ne venez pas?** so you're not coming? **2** as well as, and; **cette règle a. que la suivante me paraît** *ou* **paraissent inutile(s)** this rule, as well as *or* and the next, seems to me to be unnecessary

AIO [ajo] **NM** *Mktg (abrév* **activités, intérêts et opinions)** AIO

aïoli [ajɔli] **NM** *Culin* garlic mayonnaise

AIR [ɛr] **NM 1** *(gaz)* air, atmosphere; **une bouffée d'a. pur** a breath of fresh air; *Fig* **cette discussion a été comme une bouffée d'a. pur** this discussion has been like a breath of fresh air; **privé d'a., sans a.** airless; **cela manque d'a. ici** it's stuffy in here; **j'ouvre la porte pour faire de l'a.** I'll open the door to let some air in; **l'a. de la mer/des montagnes** (the) sea/mountain air; **donner de l'a. à** *(pièce)* to ventilate, to air; *(personne)* to give some (fresh) air; **à a. conditionné** air conditioned; **avoir l'a. conditionné** to have air conditioning; **sortir prendre l'a.** to go out for some fresh air; *Fig* **vivre de l'a. du temps** to live on (next to) nothing *or* on fresh air; **ne pas laisser à l'a.** not to be exposed to the air; **allez, de l'a.!** go on, clear off!; **au grand a., en plein a., à l'a. libre** in the fresh air, in the open air; **vie au grand a.** open-air life; **vie de plein a.** outdoor life; **concert en plein a.** open-air concert; **libre comme l'a.** free as a bird; *Typ* **donner de l'a. à la composition** to lead out *or* space out the type

2 *(ciel)* **l'a.** the air; **la conquête de l'a.** the conquest of the air; **prendre l'a.** *(d'un avion)* to take off; **la navette spatiale s'éleva dans les airs** the space shuttle rose into the air; **tenir l'a.** to keep flying; *(être en état de voler)* to be airworthy; **ministère de l'A.** = ministry responsible for air defence; **Armée de l'A.** Air Force; **École de l'A.** = training college for the French air force, *Br* ≃ RAF College, *Am* ≃ USAF Academy; **hôtesse de l'a.** air hostess; **jouer les filles de l'a.** to vanish into thin air; **mal de l'a.** air sickness; **en l'a.** in the air; **regarder en l'a.** to look up; *Fig* **être en l'a.** *(en désordre)* to be in a mess; **il a mis toute la maison/mon bureau en l'a.** he made an awful mess of the house/my office; *Fig* **ficher qch en l'a.** to mess sth up; **mes projets sont fichus en l'a. à cause de lui** my plans have all gone up in smoke because of him; *Fig* **elle veut tout envoyer** *ou Fam* **foutre en l'a.** she wants to throw it all up *or Fam* chuck *or* jack it all in; *Fig* **paroles en l'a.** idle talk; *Fig* **parler en l'a.** to talk wildly *or* rashly; *Fig* **j'ai dit ça en l'a.** I was talking off the top of my head; *Fig* **c'est une tête en l'a.** he's got his head in the clouds

3 *Fig (atmosphère)* **elle est passée prendre l'a. de l'atelier** she looked in at the workshop to see how things were; **changer d'a.** to have a change of scene; **il y a quelque chose dans l'a.** there's something in the air *or* wind; **il y a de la dispute/de l'orage dans l'a.** there's an argument/a storm brewing; **c'est dans l'a. du temps** *(de se préoccuper de l'environnement etc)* it's the in thing

4 *(vent)* wind; **courant d'a.** draught; **il ne fait pas d'a.** there's not a breath of air

5 *(allure)* appearance, look; **avoir bon** *ou* **grand a.** *(d'une personne)* to look distinguished; *(d'une robe etc)* to be smart; *(être seyant)* to be becoming; **a. de famille** family likeness; **un jeune homme à l'a. très comme il faut** a very respectable-looking young man; **avoir un faux a. de ...** to have a vague *or* slight resemblance to ..., to look vaguely like ...; **il a un drôle d'a.** he looks odd *or* funny; **cette fillette a un petit a. malin** that little girl looks very mischievous; **la ville a un a. de fête** the town is looking festive, the town has a festive look about it; **elle, avec son a. de ne pas y toucher** her, with her innocent look; **se donner** *ou* **prendre des airs** to give oneself *or* to put on airs, to (try to) look important; **prendre des airs entendus** to have a knowing look; **ne prends pas tes grands airs!** don't get on your high horse!

6 **avoir l'a.** to look, to seem; **avoir l'a. fatigué/déçu/de s'ennuyer/d'être intéressé** to look tired/disappointed/bored/interested; **sa voiture a l'a. ancienne** his car looks old; **Marie a l'a. contente** Marie looks happy; *Fam* **avoir l'a. fin** to look daft; **il a l'a. d'un étranger** he looks like a foreigner; **ils ont l'a. d'avoir peur** they look as if they're afraid; **tu as l'a. de ne pas comprendre le problème** you look as if you don't understand the problem; **cela en a tout l'a.** it looks like it; **n'avoir l'a. de rien** *(d'une personne)* to seem *or* appear insignificant, to seem *or* appear of no importance; *(d'une maison etc)* to be unpretentious, to look nothing much (from the outside); *(d'un travail)* to look (deceptively) easy; **il n'a l'a. de rien, mais il est d'une force extraordinaire** he doesn't look much, but he's unbelievably strong; **le temps a l'a. d'être à la pluie** it looks like rain

7 *Mus* tune, air, melody; **un a. à la mode** a popular tune; **a. varié** theme with variations; **un a. d'opéra** an (operatic) aria

8 *Équitation* **les airs du manège** the paces of a horse

►► a. comprimé compressed air; **a. liquide** liquid air; **a. recyclé** recirculated air; **a. refroidi** cooled air

airain [ɛrɛ̃] **NM** *(cuivre et étain)* bronze; *(cuivre et zinc)* brass; *Écon* **la loi d'a.** (Lassalle's) iron law of wages

air-air [ɛrɛr] **ADJ INV** *Mil* air-to-air; **missile a.** air-to-air missile

Air Bag® [ɛrbag] **NM 1** *(dispositif)* Airbag® **2** *Fam* **air bags** *(seins)* tits, jugs

Airbus® [ɛrbys] **NM** *Aviat* Airbus®

aire [ɛr] **NF 1** *(surface plane)* (plane) surface; *(plancher)* floor; *(d'un pont)* roadway, floor; **a. (d'une grange)** threshing floor **2** *(d'un champ, d'un triangle, d'un bâtiment etc)* area; *Fig* **a. d'influence** sphere of influence; *Ling* **a. linguistique** linguistic region; *Géog* **a. de drainage** drainage area, basin **3** *(d'un aigle)* eyrie **4** *Naut* **les aires de vent** the points of the compass

►► ** *Aviat* **a. d'atterrissage landing area; *Géog* **a. continentale** continental shield; **a. de dédouanement** customs clearance area; **a. de jeux** play area; *Astronaut* **a. de lancement** launching site; **a. de lavage** *Aut* car wash, washing bay, *Am* wash rack; *Aviat* washdown; *Aviat* **a. de manœuvre** apron; **a. de pique-nique** picnic site *or* area; **a. de repos** *(sur l'autoroute)* parking *or* picnic area; **a. de services (principale)** service area; *(panneau indicateur)* services; **a. de stationnement** *Aviat* tarmac, apron; *Aut* parking area, lay-by

airedale [ɛrdɛl] **NM** Airedale (terrier)

airelle [ɛrɛl] NF (plante) a. **myrtille** blueberry, bilberry; a. **coussinette** cranberry

air-sol [ɛrsɔl] ADJ INV Mil air-to-ground; **missile a.** air-to-ground missile

ais [ɛ] NM Typ wetting board; (en reliure) press board

aisance [ɛzɑ̃s] NF **1** (facilité) ease; (de mouvement etc) freedom; **faire qch avec a.** to do sth easily or with ease; **donner de l'a. à qch** to ease sth; **parler ou s'exprimer avec a.** to speak or express oneself with great ease or facility; **jouir de l'a., être dans l'a.** to be well off or comfortably off; **vivre dans l'a.** to live comfortably **2 fosse d'aisances** cesspool; Vieilli **lieu ou cabinet d'aisances** public convenience or lavatory
▸▸ Jur a. **de voirie** easement

aise [ɛz] NF ease, comfort; **être à l'a. ou à son a.** (bien installé) to be comfortable; (avoir beaucoup de place) to have (elbow) room; (financièrement) to be well off; **tu serais plus à l'a. si tu lui en parlais une bonne fois pour toutes** you'd feel more comfortable or more at ease if you told him once and for all; **tu seras bien plus à l'a. dans cette pièce** you'll be much more comfortable in this room; **on tient à l'a. à six dans cette voiture** this car holds six comfortably; Fam **à l'a.!** easy!, no problem!, it's a piece of cake or Br a doddle!; **à ton a.!** suit yourself!; **ne pas être à son a., se sentir mal à l'a.** to feel awkward, to feel uncomfortable, to feel ill at ease; (physiquement) to feel indisposed or off colour; **être (très) à l'a.** to be relaxed; **je l'ai mis à l'a. en l'appelant Roger** I put him at his ease by calling him Roger; Iron **elle peut en parler à son a.!** it's easy (enough) or it's all right for her to talk!; **mettez-vous à votre a.** make yourself comfortable; **il en prend à son a. avec ses collègues** he takes his colleagues for granted; **faire qch à son a.** to do sth at one's own convenience; **aimer ses aises** to like one's comforts; **il prend ses aises** he makes himself at home; Fam **et lui se tournait les pouces, à l'a., Blaise!** and there he was, twiddling his thumbs without a care in the world!
ADJ Litt **je suis bien ou tout a. de l'entendre parler ainsi** I'm delighted to hear him talk this way

aisé [ɛze] ADJ **1** (manière) easy, free; (vêtement, situation) comfortable; (personne) (financièrement) comfortably off, well-to-do, Fam well heeled; **parler d'un ton a.** to speak in a natural way **2** (tâche) easy

aisément [ezemɑ̃] ADV (facilement) easily, readily

aisselle [ɛsɛl] NF **1** Anat armpit **2** Bot axilla

AITA [aitea] NF (abrév Association internationale des transports aériens) IATA

Aix-la-Chapelle [ɛkslaʃapɛl] N Aachen, Aix-la-Chapelle

ajiste [aʒist] N (youth) hosteller

ajointer [aʒwɛ̃te] VT to join up; (planches, tuyaux etc) to fit end to end

ajonc [aʒɔ̃] NM (plante) furze, gorse

ajour [aʒur] NM (laissant passer la lumière) opening, hole, orifice; (en sculpture etc) (ornamental) perforation, openwork; Couture **ajours** hemstitching; (dans une dentelle etc) openwork

ajouré [aʒure] ADJ perforated; (motif) openwork; **travail a.** Menuis fretwork; Couture drawn-thread work

ajourer [aʒure] VT **1** (pour laisser passer la lumière) to pierce with an opening; a. **une mansarde** to make a window in an attic **2** (d'un ornement) to perforate, to pierce; Couture to hemstitch

ajournement [aʒurnəmɑ̃] NM **1** (d'une réunion) postponement; (après le début de la séance) adjournment; Scol (d'un candidat) referring; Mil (d'un conscrit) deferment **2** Jur writ of summons (to appear), subpoena

ajourner [aʒurne] VT **1** (réunion, décision, voyage etc) to postpone, to put off, to defer; (après le début de la séance) to adjourn; (projet) to delay; Pol (projet de loi) to table; Scol (candidat) to refer; Mil (conscrit) to grant deferment to **2** Jur (personne) to subpoena

ajout [aʒu] NM (à un texte) addition; (à un bâtiment) extension; Mktg a. **à la gamme** range addition; Mktg a. **à la ligne** line addition; Ordinat a. **de mémoire** memory upgrade

ajoute [aʒut] NF Belg (ajout) addition

ajouté [aʒute] NM (à un manuscrit, un contrat) addition

ajouter [aʒute] VT **1** to add; Ordinat (à une base de données) to append; a. **qch à qch** to add sth to sth; **sans a. que ...** not to mention the fact that ...; a. **aux embarras de qn** to add to sb's difficulties; **'venez aussi,' ajouta-t-il** 'you come too,' he added; **nous devons a. que ...** it should also be stated that ...; **je dois a. qu'il m'a été très utile** I must add or I must also say that he has been very useful to me **2** a. **foi à qch** to believe sth, to have faith in sth
VI a. **à** to add to
VPR **s'ajouter** to be added (à to); **à ceci viennent s'a. les frais de déplacement** on top of this there are travel expenses (to be added)

ajustable [aʒystabl] ADJ adjustable

ajustage [aʒystaʒ] NM **1** (d'une robe etc) fitting **2** (d'une machine) assembly; **atelier d'a.** fitting shop; a. **mécanique** machining **3** fit; a. **serré** tight fit; a. **lâche** ou à jeu loose fit

ajustement [aʒystəmɑ̃] NM **1** (d'un appareil, des prix etc) adjusting, adjustment; (fait de régler) arrangement; a. **des salaires** wage adjustment; Com a. **fret** bunker adjustment factor; a. **saisonnier** seasonal adjustment; Mktg a. **stratégique** strategic or marketing fit **2 ajustements** fittings

ajuster [aʒyste] VT (appareil, outil) to adjust; (monter) (machine) to set up; (pièce) to gauge; (salaire, prix, monnaie) to adjust; **nous ajustons la moquette aux dimensions de la pièce** we're altering the carpet to fit the dimensions of the room; a. **le tir** to aim; **feu bien ajusté** well aimed fire; a. **son coup** to have a precise target (in mind); a. **qch à qch** to fit or adjust or adapt sth to sth; **on a fait a. la veste à la taille de ma sœur** we had the jacket altered to fit my sister; **veste (bien) ajustée** close- or tight-fitting jacket; a. **son chapeau devant le miroir** to adjust one's hat in front of the mirror; Fam **comme vous voilà ajusté!** what a sight you look!; a. **la théorie à la pratique** to adapt the theory to the practice
VPR **s'ajuster 1** (de personne) to straighten one's clothes, to tidy oneself up **2 l'embout s'ajuste sur le tuyau** the nozzle fits the pipe; **cette clef s'ajuste à chacune des serrures** this key fits each of the locks

ajusteur [aʒystœr] NM a. **sur métaux, a. mécanicien** (metal) fitter, filer, bench hand; a. **de tubes (de chaudières)** tube setter

alacrité [alakrite] NF Litt liveliness, alacrity

Aladin [aladɛ̃] N Aladdin

alaire [alɛr] ADJ Aviat **charge a.** wing load(ing); **surface a.** wing area

alaise [alɛz] NF drawsheet

alambic [alɑ̃bik] NM Chimie, Ind still; **passer qch par ou à l'a.** to distil or Am distill sth

alambiqué [alɑ̃bike] ADJ (texte) abstruse, overcomplicated; (esprit) oversubtle; (explication, système etc) convoluted, involved

alangui [alɑ̃gi] ADJ languid

alanguir [alɑ̃gir] VT to make languid; (affaiblir) to enfeeble, to make feeble; **la chaleur alanguit les ouvriers** the heat is making the workers lethargic or listless
VPR **s'alanguir** to grow languid, to flag, to droop, to wilt

alanguissement [alɑ̃gismɑ̃] NM languor

alarmant [alarmɑ̃] ADJ alarming, frightening; **son état est a.** his condition is giving serious cause for concern

alarme [alarm] NF (alerte) alarm; **donner/sonner l'a.** to give/sound the alarm; **signal d'a.** alarm; Rail **tirer la sonnette d'a.** to pull the communication cord; Fig **à la prochaine a., il faudra vous amener à l'hôpital** if there's another scare or alarm, you'll have to be taken to hospital; Fig **une fausse a.** a false alarm; **état d'a.** state of alarm
▸▸ a. **antivol** anti-theft alarm; a. **incendie** fire alarm; a. **lumineuse** warning light; Aut a. **périmétrique** perimeter alarm; a. **sonore** beep; a. **télécommandée** remote-control alarm; a. **à ultrasons** ultrasonic alarm

alarmer [alarme] VT to alarm, to frighten; (d'un bruit) to startle; **la nouvelle ne nous a pas alarmés** we were not alarmed at or by the news
VPR **s'alarmer** to take fright; **il s'alarme pour un rien** the least thing frightens him; **il n'y a pas lieu de s'a.** there is no cause for alarm or concern

alarmisme [alarmism] NM alarmism

alarmiste [alarmist] ADJ alarmist; **la presse a.** the sensational press
N alarmist

Alaska [alaska] NM Alaska; **en A.** in Alaska

albanais, -aise [albanɛ, -ɛz] ADJ Albanian
NM Ling Albanian
N A. Albanian

Albanie [albani] NF Albania

albanophone [albanɔfɔn] ADJ (communauté, populations) Albanian-speaking
N Albanian speaker

albâtre [albɑtr] NM alabaster; **peau d'a.** alabaster skin, skin like alabaster

albatros [albatrɔs] NM (oiseau) albatross

albigeois, -oise [albiʒwa, -waz] NPL Hist **les A.** the Albigenses, the Albigensians

albinisme [albinism] NM albinism

albinos [albinos] ADJ INV albino; **un lapin a.** an albino rabbit
N INV albino

Albion [albjɔ̃] NF Hist Albion, Britain; Litt **la perfide A.** perfidious Albion

album [albɔm] NM **1** Phot, Mus etc album; a. **de timbres/de photos** stamp/photo album **2** Ordinat (sur Macintosh) scrapbook

albumen [albymen] NM Biol albumen

albumine [albymin] NF Chimie albumin

alcali [alkali] NM Chimie alkali

alcalin [alkalɛ̃] ADJ Chimie alkaline

alcaloïde [alkalɔid] NM Chimie alkaloid

alchimie [alʃimi] NF alchemy

alchimiste [alʃimist] NM alchemist

alcolo [alkɔlo] N Fam = alcoolo

alcool [alkɔl] NM **1** alcohol; **lampe à a.** spirit lamp, Am alcohol lamp **2** (boisson) alcohol; (whisky, eau-de-vie etc) spirits, hard liquor, Fam the hard stuff; **je ne bois jamais d'a.** I don't drink (anything alcoholic); **il ne tient pas l'a.** he can't hold his drink; **l'a. au volant accroît considérablement les risques d'accidents** drink-driving greatly increases the risk of accidents; a. **de poire** pear brandy; **vous prendrez bien un petit a.?** would you like a liqueur or a brandy or something?
▸▸ a. **à 90°** surgical spirit, Am rubbing alcohol; a. **absolu** pure or absolute alcohol; a. **blanc** (kirsch etc) clear spirits; a. **à brûler** methylated spirits; Ind a. **dénaturé** methylated spirits; a. **éthylique** ethyl alcohol

alcoolémie [alkɔlemi] NF *Méd* presence of alcohol in the blood; **taux d'a.** level of alcohol in the blood

alcoolique [alkɔlik] ADJ alcoholic N alcoholic; **être un a.** to be an alcoholic

alcoolisation [alkɔlizasjɔ̃] NF alcoholization

alcoolisé [alkɔlize] ADJ *(boisson)* alcoholic

alcooliser [alkɔlize] VT *(vin)* to fortify VPR **s'alcooliser** to drink too much, to get drunk

alcoolisme [alkɔlism] NM alcoholism

alcoolo [alkɔlo] N *Fam* alcoholic, drunk

alcoologie [alkɔlɔʒi] NF *Méd* alcohology

alcoologue [alkɔlɔg] N *Méd* alcohologist

alcoomètre [alkɔmetr] NM alcohol(o)meter

Alcootest® [alkɔtest] NM breathalyser test; **faire passer** *ou* **subir un A. à un conducteur** to breathalyse *or* breath-test a motorist

alcôve [alkov] NF alcove; **a. de dortoir** cubicle; **secrets d'a.** pillow talk

aldéhyde [aldeid] NM *Chimie* aldehyde; **a. formique** formaldehyde

al dente [aldɛnte] ADJ *Culin (pâtes)* al dente

aldin [aldɛ̃] ADJ *Typ (édition, caractère)* Aldine

ALE [ɑɛlə] NF *(abrév* **Association de libre-échange)** FTA

ale [ɛl] NF (light) ale

aléa [alea] NM risk, hazard, chance; **l'affaire présente trop d'aléas** it's too risky a business; **les aléas de la vie** the hazards of life

aléatoire [aleatwar] ADJ *(échantillon)* random; *(résultat)* unpredictable, chancy, uncertain; *Jur (contrat etc)* aleatory; *Math* **fonction/variable a.** random function/variable; *Ordinat* **accès a.** random access

alémanique [alemanik] ADJ *Ling* **Suisse a.** German-speaking Switzerland

ALENA [alena] NM *(abrév* **Accord de libre-échange nord-américain)** NAFTA

alène [alɛn] NF awl; **a. plate** bradawl

alentour [alɑ̃tur] ADV around, round about; **les villages a.** the surrounding *or* neighbouring villages; **le pays d'a.** the surrounding *or* neighbouring countryside
NMPL **alentours** surroundings, vicinity; **aux alentours de la ville/300 euros** in the vicinity of the town/300 euros; **il n'y avait personne aux alentours** there was no one around *or* in the vicinity; **il est arrivé aux alentours de midi** he arrived (some time) around midday

aléoute [aleut], **aléoutien, -ienne** [aleusjɛ̃, -jɛn] ADJ Aleutian; **les (îles) Aléoutiennes** the Aleutian Islands
N **A.** Aleut(ian)

alerte¹ [alɛrt] NF alarm; **donner/sonner l'a.** to give/sound the alarm; **fausse a.** false alarm; **a. (aérienne)** air-raid warning; **à la première a.** as soon as the alarm goes; **en cas d'a.** if the alarm sounds; **état d'a.** state of alert; **l'état d'a. est déclaré** a state of alert has been declared; **être en a.** to be on the alert; *Mil* **fin d'a.** all clear; *Aviat* **a. en piste** scramble; **côte d'a.** danger level; **l'a. fut chaude** it was a narrow escape; *Méd* **nous avons eu une a. en septembre** we had a warning sign *or* a scare in September
INT look out!, *Arch* to arms!
▸▸ **a. à la bombe** bomb scare; **a. rouge** red alert

alerte² ADJ **1** alert; *(démarche)* brisk; *(personne)* sprightly, alert; **style a.** *(écrit)* lively style; **il est paralysé mais son esprit est très a.** he's paralysed but his mind is (still) very alert **2** *Arch* vigilant, watchful

alerter [alɛrte] VT *(troupes, opinion publique etc)* to alert; **a. qn sur qch** to alert sb to sth

alésage [alezaʒ] NM *Métal* **1** *(opération)* boring (out); *(d'un cylindre)* reaming **2** *(diamètre)* *(d'un canon de fusil)* bore; *(d'un moteur à combustion)* bore; *(d'un cylindre etc)* internal diameter

alèse [alɛz] NF *Méd* drawsheet, undersheet

aléser [aleze] VT *Métal* to bore (out); *(élargir)* to ream

aléseuse [alezøz] NF *Métal* borer; *(pour élargir)* reamer

alester [alɛste], **alestir** [alɛstir] VT *Naut (gréement)* to trim up, to tidy up

alevin [alvɛ̃] NM alevin, fry, young fish

alevinage [alvinaʒ] NM *(d'une rivière etc)* stocking with young fish

aleviner [alvine] VT to stock a river with young fish

alevinier [alvinje] NM, **alevinière** [alvinjɛr] NF breeding pond, nursery

Alexandre [alɛksɑ̃dr] N **A. le Grand** Alexander the Great

Alexandrie [alɛksɑ̃dri] N Alexandria

alexandrin [alɛksɑ̃drɛ̃, -in] ADJ **1** *Littér* alexandrine; **poème en vers alexandrins** poem in alexandrine verse *or* in alexandrines **2** *Géog* Alexandrian; *Fig* **des discussions alexandrines** convoluted discussions
NM *Littér* alexandrine (verse)

alexie [alɛksi] NF *Méd* word blindness, alexia

alezan [alzɑ̃, -an] ADJ *(cheval)* chestnut
NM **a. châtain** chestnut sorrel; **a. roux** red bay

alfa [alfa] NM *Bot* esparto (grass); **papier d'a.** esparto paper; **tiré sur a.** printed on esparto paper

algarade [algarad] NF row, quarrel; **nous avons eu une a.** we've had a row

algèbre [alʒɛbr] NF algebra; **a. booléenne** Boolean algebra; **résoudre un problème par l'a.** to solve a problem algebraically; *Fig* **c'est de l'a. pour moi** it's all Greek to me

algébrique [alʒebrik] ADJ algebraic

Alger [alʒe] N Algiers; *Hist* (the Department of) Alger

Algérie [alʒeri] NF Algeria; **en A.** in Algeria

algérien, -ienne [alʒerjɛ̃, -jɛn] ADJ Algerian
N **A.** Algerian

algérois, -oise [alʒerwa, -waz] ADJ of *or* from Algiers
N **A.** inhabitant *or* native of Algiers

algie [alʒi] NF ache, pain

algol [algɔl] NM *Ordinat* ALGOL

algonkien, -ienne [algɔ̃kjɛ̃, -jɛn] *Géol* ADJ Algonkian
NM Algonkian

algonquin, -ine [algɔ̃kɛ̃, -in] ADJ *(peuple)* Algonquin
NM *Ling* Algonquian
N **A.** Algonquin

algorithme [algɔritm] NM *Math, Ordinat* algorithm; *Ordinat* **a. de chiffrement** coding *or* encryption algorithm; *Ordinat* **a. de tri** sorting algorithm

algorithmique [algɔritmik] ADJ *Math, Ordinat* algorithmic

algothérapie [algɔterapi] NF = alternative medicine based on marine plant extracts

algue [alg] NF (piece of) seaweed, *Spéc* alga; **algues** seaweed, *Spéc* algae

alias [aljas] NM *Ordinat (de courrier électronique, de bureau)* alias
ADV alias, otherwise *or* also known as; *Ordinat* alias; **Joe Balance, a. le Braqueur** Joe Balance, alias *or* aka the Robber

aliassage [aljasaʒ] NM *Ordinat* aliasing

alibi [alibi] NM alibi; **il a invoqué un a. absurde pour justifier son absence** he gave an absurd alibi to explain his absence

alicament [alikamɑ̃] NM nutraceutical

aliénable [aljenabl] ADJ *Jur* alienable, transferable

aliénant [aljenɑ̃] ADJ alienating

aliénation [aljenasjɔ̃] NF **1** *(de l'esprit)* alienation; **conditions d'a.** alienating conditions; *Psy* **a. mentale** insanity **2** *Jur (des droits, de biens etc)* alienation, transfer; *(de liberté)* loss

aliéné, -ée [aljene] *Psy* ADJ mad, insane
N insane person; **les aliénés** the insane; **hospice d'aliénés** mental hospital

aliéner [aljene] (**j'aliène**; **n. aliénerons**) VT **1** *(sentiments etc)* to alienate, to estrange; **ce commentaire vous a aliéné la sympathie de l'auditoire** that comment lost you the audience's sympathy; **ces conditions de vie ne peuvent qu'a. les jeunes** such living conditions can only alienate young people **2** *Jur (biens, droits etc)* to alienate, to transfer; **a. sa liberté** to give up one's freedom **3** *(psychisme)* to derange, to unhinge
VPR **s'aliéner** *(objet)* to lose; *(personne)* to alienate (oneself from); **s'a. la sympathie de l'électorat** to lose the goodwill of the electorate; **s'a. un ami** to alienate a friend; **s'a. l'amitié de qn** to lose sb's friendship; **s'a. par le travail** to be alienated by work

aliéniste [aljenist] N *Méd* alienist

alignement [aliɲ(ə)mɑ̃] NM **1** *(opération)* alignment, aligning; *Mil (d'une ligne)* dressing; *Compta (d'un compte etc)* making up, balancing; *(de son, image)* tracking; **être dans l'a.** to be in a line; **maison frappée d'a.** house scheduled for realignment; **se mettre à l'a.** to fall into line, to line up; *Mil* **à droite a.!** right dress!; *Écon* **a. monétaire** alignment of currencies; *Com* **a. des prix** alignment of prices, price alignment; **l'a. des salaires sur le coût de la vie** bringing salaries into line with the cost of living; *Pol* **l'a. du parti sur la politique des États-Unis** the party's alignment with US policy
2 *(d'un mur etc)* alignment, line; **un a. de menhirs** a line of menhirs; *Constr* **déborder** *ou* **dépasser l'a.** to project beyond the building line; **prendre des alignements** to get one's bearings
3 *Rail (ligne droite)* straight stretch
4 *Ordinat* alignment

aligner [aliɲe] VT **1** *(mettre en ligne)* to align, to line up, to put in a line; *(arranger)* to lay out; *Mil* to dress (a line); *Compta (compte)* to balance; **a. un terrain** to mark out a plot (of ground); *Typ* **a. des caractères** to align *or* range type; *Pol* **a. sa politique sur celle des États voisins** to fall into line with the policy of neighbouring states; *Écon* **a. une monnaie** to align a currency; **les petits commerçants ne peuvent pas a. leurs prix sur ceux des grandes surfaces** small shopkeepers can't bring their prices into line with those of hypermarkets
2 *(dire, faire à la suite)* *(arguments)* to marshal; **a. des phrases** to string sentences together; **je passe ma journée à a. des chiffres** I spend my day producing lists of figures; *Fam* **les a.** *(payer)* to pay up, to cough up
3 *Fam (réprimander)* **a. qn** to tell sb off; **il s'est fait a. par un flic en moto** a motorcycle cop slapped a fine on him
4 *Ordinat* to align
VPR **s'aligner** **1** *(se mettre en ligne)* *(enfants)* to line up; *Mil (soldats)* to dress **2** *(d'un pays, d'une personne)* to fall into line; *Pol (sur un pays, une politique)* to align oneself (**sur** in); *Arg* **tu peux toujours t'a.!** *(tu n'es pas à la hauteur)* just you try it!

aliment [alimɑ̃] NM **1** food; **a. pauvre/riche** food that is low/high in nutritional value; **des aliments en conserve/surgelés** tinned/frozen food; **a. périssable** perishable food;

Physiol a. **complet** complete food; *Fig* **cette histoire a servi d'a. à la presse** the press made a meal out of the story **2** *Jur* **aliments** alimony

alimentaire [alimɑ̃tɛr] ADJ **1** *(denrée, plante etc)* nutritious; **produits alimentaires** food, foodstuffs; **conserves alimentaires** tinned *or* canned food(s); **régime a.** diet; *Admin, Hist* **carte a.** ration card; **surveiller son bol a.** to watch what one eats; **mauvaises habitudes alimentaires** bad eating habits **2** *Jur* **pension** *ou* **provision a.** alimony, maintenance; **payer** *ou* **verser une pension a.** to pay alimony *or* maintenance; **il est en retard dans le paiement de la pension a.** he's late with his *or* the alimony; *Fig* **travail** *ou* **occupation a.** job that keeps body and soul together **3** *Physiol* **canal** *ou* **tube a.** alimentary canal; **pompe a.** feed pump

alimentation [alimɑ̃tasjɔ̃] NF **1** *(régime alimentaire)* food, nourishment; *Biol* nutrition; **avoir une a. équilibrée** to have a balanced diet; **a. défectueuse** malnutrition; **surveillez votre a.** watch what you eat, watch your diet; **article d'a.** foodstuff; **(magasin d')a.** grocer's shop; **(rayon d')a.** grocery department, food counter
2 *(action) (de plantes, d'animaux etc)* feeding; *(de ville, de marché etc)* supply; **l'a. d'une ville en eau** the water supply to a town
3 *Tech (d'une chaudière etc)* feed(ing); *(d'un fusil)* feed mechanism; *(en électricité)* power supply; **pompe d'a.** feed pump; **a. par pesanteur** *ou* **par gravité** gravity feed; *Aut* **a. par injection** fuel injection; *Élec* **bloc d'a.** power supply; **câble** *ou* **fil d'a.** feeder; **a. papier** *(d'une imprimante)* sheetfeed, paper feed; **a. feuille à feuille** *ou* **page par page** *(d'une imprimante)* cut sheet *or* single sheet feed; *Ordinat* **a. ininterruptible** uninterruptible power supply

alimenter [alimɑ̃te] VT *(personne)* to feed, to nourish; *(marché)* to supply with food; *(chaudière)* to feed; **ruisseaux qui alimentent une rivière** streams that feed a river; *Élec* **a. une usine en courant** to supply a factory with power; *Fig* **a. la curiosité de qn** to feed sb's curiosity; *Fig* **a. la conversation par des anecdotes** to keep the conversation going with anecdotes; *Fig* **ces petits incidents risquent d'a. la discorde entre elles** these little incidents are likely to fuel the discord between them; **a. un compte** to pay money into an account
VPR s'alimenter to eat; *(d'un malade)* to take (solid) food

alinéa [alinea] NM *Typ* **1** *(renfoncement)* paragraph indent, indent; **mettre à l'a., faire un a.** to indent; **a. négatif** hanging indent **2** *(texte)* paragraph, *Fam* para; **sans a.** full-out

alité [alite] ADJ confined to (one's) bed, *Fam* laid up; *(infirme)* bedridden

alitement [alitmɑ̃] NM confinement to bed; **trois jours d'a.** three days in bed

aliter [alite] VT **a. qn** to confine sb to bed, to keep sb in bed
VPR s'aliter *(se mettre au lit)* to take to one's bed

alizé [alize] ADJ, NM **les (vents) alizés** the trade winds

Allah [ala] N Allah

allaitant [alɛtɑ̃] ADJ suckling, nursing; **mère allaitante** nursing mother

allaitement [alɛtmɑ̃] NM feeding, nursing, suckling; **a. au biberon** bottle-feeding; **a. mixte** mixed feeding; **a. naturel** breastfeeding; **durant l'a.** during breastfeeding

allaiter [alete] VT *(enfant)* to breastfeed, to nurse; *(enfant, petit)* to suckle

allant [alɑ̃] ADJ *(personne)* active, busy, live-ly; *(personne âgée)* active, mobile, able to move *or* walk about
NM initiative, drive, energy; **avoir de l'a., être plein d'a.** to be full of go *or* (drive and) energy; **elle travaille avec a.** she works energetically *or* with gusto

alléchant [aleʃɑ̃] ADJ *(offre, plat)* attractive, alluring, enticing, tempting; *(odeur etc)* appetizing

allécher [aleʃe] VT *(j'allèche, n. alléchons; j'allécherai)* to attract, to entice, to tempt, to allure; **j'étais alléché par cette proposition** I was tempted by the proposal

allée [ale] NF **1** *(dans un jardin, menant à une maison)* path; *(permettant le passage de voitures)* drive; *(entre deux immeubles)* passage, alley; *(dans une ville)* street, avenue; *(longée d'arbres)* walk; **a. (cavalière)** bridle path; **a. de circulation** *(d'un magasin)* aisle **2** **allées et venues** coming(s) and going(s), running about; **j'ai dû faire de nombreuses allées et venues pour obtenir ce visa** I had to run all over the place to get this visa; **qu'est-ce que signifient ces allées et venues à cette heure tardive?** what's the meaning of all these comings and goings at this time of night?

allégation [alegasjɔ̃] NF allegation

allégé [aleʒe] ADJ *(yaourt, chips)* low-fat, diet; *(confiture)* low-sugar

allège [alɛʒ] NF **1** *Naut* lighter, hopper, barge; *Com* **frais d'a.** lighterage; **franco a.** free over side **2** *(de fenêtre)* window breast, (window)sill

allégeance [aleʒɑ̃s] NF **1** *(nationalité)* nationality; **avoir la double a.** to have dual nationality **2** *Arch* **serment d'a.** oath of allegiance; **faire a. à …** to pledge one's allegiance to … **3** *Naut* handicap

allégement, allègement [aleʒmɑ̃] NM **1** *(d'impôts, charges etc)* reduction; **a. fiscal** tax relief **2** *(de véhicule, fardeau)* lightening

alléger [aleʒe] VT *(j'allège, n. allégeons; j'allégeai(s); j'allégerai)* **1** *(impôts, charges etc)* to reduce; *(douleur, chagrin)* to alleviate, to relieve, to soothe **2** *(véhicule, fardeau etc)* to lighten; *(poutres de charpente etc)* to ease the strain on; *Scol* **a. un programme scolaire** to lighten a school syllabus **3** *Tech (objet)* to reduce the volume of; *(bois)* to plane down; *(métal)* to file down, to fine down

allégorie [alegɔri] NF allegory; **par a.** allegorically

allégorique [alegɔrik] ADJ allegorical

allégoriquement [alegɔrikmɑ̃] ADV allegorically

allègre [alɛgr] ADJ lively, jolly, cheerful; *(musique)* lively; **parler d'un ton a.** to speak cheerfully *or* light-heartedly; **caractère a.** cheerful disposition; **avoir le cœur a.** to be light-hearted; **marcher d'un pas a.** to walk with a spring in one's step

allègrement [alɛgrəmɑ̃] ADV cheerfully; *Iron* blithely; *(marcher)* with a spring in one's step; **il s'est a. moqué de nous** he has been quite blithely making fools of us

allégresse [alegrɛs] NF joy, cheerfulness, liveliness; **plein d'a.** full of joy; **a. générale** general rejoicing; **cris d'a.** cries of joy

allegretto [alegretto] ADV, NM *Mus* allegretto

allegro [alegro] ADV, NM *Mus* allegro

alléguer [alege] VT *(j'allègue, n. alléguons; j'alléguerai)* **1** *(invoquer)* to allege, to plead; **a. l'ignorance** to plead ignorance; **a. une excuse/une raison** to put forward *or* offer *or* give an excuse/a reason; **a. comme raison que le temps manquait** to give lack of time as one's reason; **il allégua que personne ne l'avait informé de ce projet** he alleged that

no one had informed him of the plan **2** *(auteur, texte etc)* to cite, to quote

alléluia [aleluja] INT, NM *Rel* alleluia, hallelujah

Allemagne [aləmaɲ] NF Germany; *Anciennement* **l'A. de l'ouest/de l'est** West/East Germany; *Anciennement* **les deux Allemagnes** the two Germanies; **l'ambassadeur d'A.** the German ambassador

allemand, -ande [almɑ̃, -ɑ̃d] ADJ German; **la langue allemande** the German language, German
NM *Ling* German, the German language
N **A.** German; *Anciennement* **A. de l'Est/de l'Ouest** East/West German
NF **allemande** *Mus* allemande

ALLER¹ [ale]

VI to go **1, 2, 4, 6, 7, 9, 13, 15** ▪ to go + *adv* **3** ▪ *future tense* **14** ▪ to walk **2** ▪ to lead **4** ▪ to work **7** ▪ to fit *(aller à)* **8, 11** ▪ to suit *(aller à)* **11** ▪ to match *(aller avec)* **12** ▪ to go well with *(aller avec)* **12** ▪ *interjection* **16**	
VPR to go away **1** ▪ to come off **3**	

VI *(prp* **allant**; *pp* **allé**; *pr ind* **je vais** *(Arch, Région* **je vas**), **tu vas, il va, n. allons, v. allez, ils vont**; *pr sub* **j'aille, n. allions, ils aillent**; *imp* **va (vas-y), allons, allez**; *impf* **j'allais**; *p hist* **j'allai**; *fu* **j'irai**; *the aux is* **être**) **1** *(se rendre)* to go; **a. à Paris** to go to Paris; **navire allant à Bordeaux** ship bound for Bordeaux; **a. chez le coiffeur/médecin/au marché** to go to the hairdresser's/to the doctor/to the market; **a. en course/à la chasse/à la pêche/à cheval/en voiture/au galop/au trot** *voir ces mots*; **a. aux champignons** to go mushroom-picking; **on va sur Lyon** we're going to *or* as far as Lyons; **a. de ville en ville** to go from town to town; **a. devant/derrière/à côté de qn** to go in front of/behind/beside sb; **a. chez qn** to go to sb's house, to call on *or* visit sb, to go and see sb; **je vais chez lui pour dîner ce soir** I'm going to his house for dinner this evening; **je vais chez ma grand-mère quand je suis à Paris** I call on *or* visit my grandmother whenever I'm in Paris; **nous allons toujours chez Maxim's** we always go to Maxim's; **a. jusqu'à qch/qn** to go as far as sth/to go up to sb; **qui va là?** who goes there?; **ne faire qu'a. et venir** to be always on the go *or* on the move; **je n'ai fait qu'a. et venir ce matin pour obtenir les papiers** I did nothing but run all over the place this morning to get the papers; **je ne ferai qu'a. et revenir** I shall come straight back; **où allons-nous?** where are we going?; *Fig (qu'est-ce qu'on va devenir?)* what are things coming to?; *Fam* **où tu vas?** are you mad?, have you got a screw loose?, *Br* are you off your head?; **je suis allé aux nouvelles** I went to find out what was happening; **il va sur ses quarante ans** he is getting on for forty, he is nearly forty (years old); **il ira loin** he will go far *or* will distinguish himself; **insulter un agent de police? ça peut a. loin, ça** insulting a policeman can have serious consequences; **vous allez trop loin** you're going too far; **vous n'irez pas loin avec 50 euros** 50 euros won't get you very far, you won't get very far on 50 euros; **soyez tranquille, cela n'ira pas plus loin** don't worry, it won't go any further; **cette vieille voiture n'ira pas loin** this old car won't get very far; **a. jusqu'au bout** to see it through; *(avoir des rapports sexuels)* to go the whole way; **nous irons jusqu'au bout** we shall carry on to the end; **a. au fond des choses** to get to the bottom of things; **décontractez-vous, laissez-vous a.** relax, let yourself go; **il faut apprendre à laisser a. les choses** you must learn to let things take their course; **reprends-toi, tu ne dois pas te lais-**

ser a. pull yourself together, you mustn't let yourself go; **se laisser a. à la tendresse/à de meilleurs sentiments** to give way to tenderness/better feelings; **sa remarque m'est allée droit au cœur** his remark went straight to my heart; **l'eau va jusqu'à la taille** the water is waist-deep; **l'eau lui allait jusqu'à la taille** the water came up to his/her waist; **ses cheveux vont jusqu'à la taille** her hair goes down to her waist, she has waist-length hair

2 *(se déplacer)* to go, to move; *(à pied)* to walk; **on y va à pied** we're walking there; **a. en vélo/voiture/avion/bateau** to go by bike/car/plane/boat; **on va à la catastrophe** we're heading for disaster; **j'y suis allé très lentement** I went very slowly; **j'y suis allé en deux heures** it took me two hours to get there

3 *(with adv)* **a. bon train** to go at a good pace; **a. grand train** to race along; **la voiture va vite** the car goes fast

4 *(mener)* to lead, to go; **chemin qui va à la gare** road leading to the station; *Prov* **tous les chemins vont à Rome** all roads lead to Rome

5 *(être conçu pour)* **ces ciseaux vont bien pour couper les roses** these scissors are good for cutting roses; **plat qui va au feu** *ou* **allant au feu** *ou* **au four** fireproof *or* ovenproof dish

6 *(marcher) (bien, mal)* to go; **tout va bien** everything is going well *or* is fine; **tout va mal** things are going badly, things aren't going at all well; **non, ça ne va pas du tout** *(ce n'est pas ce que j'ai demandé)* no, that won't do at all; **ça va!** *(d'accord)* OK!; **ça va, ça va, on te pardonne** OK, OK, you're forgiven; *Fam* **non, mais ça va pas (la tête)?!** are you crazy?!, what's wrong with you?!; **ça ira!** we'll/I'll/*etc* manage!; **ça va comme ça** it's all right *or* it's fine *or* that will do (as it is); **merci, ça va comme ça, j'ai eu assez à manger** that will do *or* that's fine, thanks, I've had enough to eat; **faire a.** to get by, to struggle along; **ça n'irait pas du tout** that would never do; **ça va a. mal si tu me mens** if you've been lying to me, there'll be trouble; **il y a quelque chose qui ne va pas** there's something wrong; **tout a l'air d'a. bien entre eux** everything seems to be fine between them; **je vous en offre 100 euros, ça va?** I'll give you 100 euros for it, OK?; **ça va tout seul** it's a piece of cake; **cela ne va pas tout seul** it's not (that) easy, it's not an easy job

7 *(d'un appareil, d'une horloge etc)* to go, to work, to run; **la pendule va bien/mal** the clock is/isn't working (properly); **quand le bâtiment va, tout va** what's good for the construction industry is good for us all; **les affaires vont/ne vont pas** business is good/slack; **faire a. un commerce** to run a business; **tout va comme sur des roulettes** everything is going like clockwork

8 *(être de la bonne taille etc)* to fit; **ce veston ne va pas bien** this jacket doesn't fit well

9 *(tenir)* **c'est trop grand pour a. dans le panier** it's too big to go *or* get *or* fit into the basket; **je ne sais pas où vont les assiettes** I don't know where the plates go

10 *(se porter)* comment **allez-vous?** how are you?; **je vais bien,** *Fam* **ça va** I'm well, I'm all right, I'm fine; **cela va mieux** I'm better; **cela ne va pas** I'm not feeling very well

11 a. à qn *(de couleurs etc)* to suit sb; *(de vêtements)* to fit sb; *(de climat, de denrées)* to agree with sb; *(d'un projet etc)* to suit sb; **cela vous va comme un gant** *(d'une robe etc)* it fits you like a glove; *(d'une situation etc)* it suits you down to the ground; **cette robe te va mal** *(elle te grossit)* that dress doesn't suit you; **la chemise ne me va pas** *(elle est trop petite)* the shirt doesn't fit me; **ça me va!** *(d'accord)* agreed!, done!; **ça te va bien de**

me **conseiller** you're a fine one to give me advice

12 *(être assorti)* **a. avec qch** *(de couleurs etc)* to go well with sth, to match sth; **a. (bien) ensemble** to go well together; **chaussettes qui ne vont pas ensemble** odd socks

13 *(aller + inf)* **a. voir qn** to go and *or* to see sb, to call on sb; **a. trouver qn** to go and find sb; **va voir si quelqu'un n'a pas sonné à la porte** go and see if that was someone ringing the doorbell; **a. se promener** to go for a walk; **va donc le lui dire!** go and tell him then!; **n'allez pas vous imaginer que …** don't imagine that …, don't go imagining that …, don't get it into your head that …; **allez donc savoir!** how are you (supposed) to know?; *Fam* **allez vous faire voir!** go to hell!

14 *(utilisé comme auxiliaire)* to be going, to be about (to do sth); **il va s'en occuper** he is going to see about it, he'll deal with it; **je vais te dire quelque chose** let me tell you something; **je sais ce que tu vas me dire** I know what you're about to tell me; **il va venir** he'll be coming; **je vais devoir prendre une décision** I'm going to have to make a decision; **il va pouvoir acheter la voiture dont il rêve** he's going to be able to buy the car of his dreams; **elle allait tout avouer** she was about to confess everything; **sa santé va (en) empirant** his/her health is steadily deteriorating

15 *(avec 'y')* **j'y vais!, on y va!** coming!; **j'y vais** *(ouvrir la porte)* I'll get it; **est-ce comme ça que vous y allez?** is that how you go about it *or* do it?; **allez-y doucement!** easy *or* gently (does it)!; **il y va fort** he's going a bit too far, he's going a bit over the top; **y a. de tout son cœur** to put one's heart and soul into it; **y a. carrément** *ou* **franchement** to make no bones about it; **vas-y, dis-moi ce que tu as à dire!** go on then, say what you've got to say!; **maintenant allons-y!** now (let's get down) to it!; **allons-y!** well, here goes!; **vas-y!/allez-y!** go!, on you go!; *(au travail etc)* get on with it!; *(pose-moi ces questions)* fire away!; *Fam* **y a. de qch** to lay *or* stake sth; **il y est allé de ses économies** he staked his savings; **y a. de son reste** to stake one's all; **y a. de sa personne** to take a hand in it oneself, *Fam* to do one's bit; **il y est allé de son histoire/sa petite chanson** he gave us his story/little song

16 *(interjection)* **allons, dépêchez-vous!** come on, hurry up!; **allez, s'il te plaît, viens avec moi!** oh go on, come with me, please!; **allons donc!** *(c'est vrai?)* (well I) never!; **allez, je vous écoute** go ahead, I'm listening; **allez, c'est oublié** don't worry, it's all forgotten; **allons bon!** there now!; *(exprimant de l'irritation)* oh no!; **allons, sois un peu raisonnable!** come on now, be reasonable!; **allons, allons, calme-toi** come on now, calm down; **va pour une soirée au cinéma** OK then, a night out at the cinema it is; **allez, allez, débarrasse la table!** come on *or* along (now), clear the table!; *Fam* **va donc, eh patate!** if you don't like it, you can lump it!; **va donc eh, vieux crétin!** get lost, you idiot!

VPR s'en aller *(pr ind* **je m'en vais;** *imp* **va-t'en, allons-nous-en, allez-vous-en, ne t'en va pas, ne nous en allons pas;** *perf* **je m'en suis allé(e), nous nous en sommes allé(e)s)**
1 *(partir)* to go away, to leave; **les voisins s'en vont** the neighbours are moving; **s'en a. en vacances** to go away on holiday; **elle s'en est allée** *ou Fam* **s'est en allée** assez satisfaite she went away fairly satisfied; **allez-vous-en!** go away!; **allons-nous-en!** let's go!; **s'en a. en fumée** to go up in smoke; **à demain, je m'en vais** I'm off, see you tomorrow; **il faut que je m'en aille** I must be going; **ses forces s'en allaient** his strength was failing
2 *(mourir)* to pass away, to die; **le malade s'en va** the patient is sinking (fast)

3 *(disparaître)* **les taches ne veulent pas s'en a.** the stains won't come off *or* out
4 *(+ inf)* **s'en a. faire qch** to go off and *or* to do sth; **je m'en vais lui dire ce que je pense** I'm going to tell him exactly what I think; **va savoir s'il ne ment pas!** how am I/are we/*etc* supposed to know if he's telling the truth or not?; **je m'en vais vous raconter ça** I'll tell you all about it

V IMPERS il va sans dire *ou* **il va de soi que …** it stands to reason *or* it goes without saying that …; **il va sans dire qu'elle a refusé** it goes without saying that she refused, needless to say, she refused; **il en va de même pour lui/moi** it's the same with him/me; **il n'en va pas de même pour eux** things are different for them; **il en va de sa réputation** his reputation is at stake; **il y va de vingt mille euros** it's a matter of twenty thousand euros; **il y allait de sa vie** it was a matter of life and death (for him), his life was at stake; **il y va de sa place** his job is at stake; **il y va de votre santé** your health is at risk, you're risking your health

---

aller² NM going; *(d'un aller retour)* outward journey; **a. retour, voyage d'a. (et) retour** round trip, return journey, journey there and back; *Naut* voyage out and home; **billet a. retour** return ticket, *Am* round-trip ticket; *Fam* **un a.** a single ticket, *Am* a one-way ticket; **deux allers et un a. retour pour Marseille, s'il vous plaît** two singles and a return to Marseilles, please; *Bourse* **a. et retour** bed and breakfasting; **à l'a.** on the way there; **je me suis arrêté en route à l'a.** I stopped on my *or* the way (there); **cargaison d'a.** outward cargo; *Sport* **match a.** away match; **a. retour du piston** up and down stroke; *Fam* **si tu continues, tu vas recevoir un a. et retour dont tu te souviendras** if you carry on, you'll get a clip round the ear that you won't forget in a hurry

allergène [alɛrʒɛn] NM *Méd* allergen

allergénique [alɛrʒenik] ADJ *Méd* allergenic

allergie [alɛrʒi] NF *Méd* allergy; **avoir une a. au poil de chat** to have an allergy *or* to be allergic to cat hair; *Fig* **elle a fini par faire** *ou* **avoir une véritable a. au travail** she eventually became completely allergic to work

allergique [alɛrʒik] ADJ *Méd* allergic (**à** to); *Fig* **il est a. aux maths** he's allergic to maths

allergologiste [alɛrgɔlɔʒist], **allergologue** [alɛrgɔlɔg] N *Méd* allergist

alliage [aljaʒ] NM *Métal* alloy; **sans a.** pure, unalloyed; *Fig* **un a. d'idées fausses** a mishmash *or* hotchpotch of mistaken ideas

alliance [aljɑ̃s] NF **1** *(entente)* alliance; *(d'un couple)* marriage, union; **conclure une a.** to enter into *or* forge an alliance; **faire a. avec/contre qn** to ally *or* team up with/against sb; **entrer par a. dans une famille** to marry into a family; **faire a. avec une autre famille** to be joined to another family by marriage; **parent par a.** relation by marriage; **traité d'a.** treaty of alliance; *Mktg* **a. de marques** co-branding **2** *(bague)* wedding ring **3** *(combinaison) (de parfums etc)* combination; **une a. de termes très réussie** a very effective juxtaposition of terms; **a. de mots** *(figure de style)* oxymoron

---

> ### Alliance française
> In many respects, the activities of the Alliance française are similar to those of the British Council, although it is a private body. It organizes classes in French language and civilization and has branches all over the world.

allié, -ée [alje] ADJ **1** *(nation etc)* allied **2** *(dans une famille)* related by marriage; **être bien a.** to be well connected
N ally; *(de famille)* relation by marriage; *(moins précis)* family connection; **invitation lancée aux parents et alliés** invitation sent out to immediate family and close relatives; **il est d'accord avec nous, c'est un a.** he agrees with us, he's on our side; *Hist* **les Alliés** the Allies

allier [alje] *(impf, pr sub n.* **alliions,** *v.* **alliiez)** VT **1** *(unir)* to ally, to unite; **intérêts communs qui allient deux pays** common interests that unite two countries; **a. une famille à** *ou* **avec une autre** to unite one family with another by marriage **2** *(métaux)* to alloy, to mix; *(couleurs)* to harmonize, to blend, to match; *(qualités, mots etc)* to combine **(à** with); **a. l'intelligence à la beauté** to combine intelligence and beauty
VPR **s'allier 1** *(s'unir)* to form an alliance, to become allies, to ally **(avec qn** with sb); **s'a. à une famille** to marry into a family; **s'a. contre qn/qch** to unite against sb/sth **2** *(de liquides)* to mix; *(de métaux)* to alloy; *(de couleurs)* to harmonize, to blend; *(de goûts, de qualités)* to combine

alligator [aligatɔr] NM alligator

allitératif, -ive [aliteratif, -iv] ADJ alliterative

allitération [aliterasjɔ̃] NF alliteration; **a. en s** alliteration of (the letter) s

allô, allo [alo] INT *Tél* hello!

alloc [alɔk] NF *Fam* benefit; **les allocs** *(allocations familiales)* child benefit

allocataire [alɔkatɛr] N beneficiary; *(à la Sécurité sociale etc)* claimant, recipient

allocation [alɔkasjɔ̃] NF **1** *(d'argent, de terres, de marchandises etc)* allocation, granting; *Fin (de titres etc)* allotment, allocation **2** *(prestation financière)* allowance, grant; **elle touche les allocations (familiales)** she gets child benefit
▸▸ **a. (de) chômage** unemployment benefit; **a. de garde d'enfant à domicile** = allowance paid to working parents who employ a childminder at home; **a. (de) logement** housing benefit, *Am* rent subsidy; **a. (de) maternité** maternity benefit; **allocations familiales** child benefit, family allowance(s), *Am* dependents' allowances; **a. de formation reclassement** = allowance paid to employees requiring further training or new qualifications; **a. de parent isolé** = allowance paid to single parents; **a. de rentrée scolaire** = allowance paid to parents to help cover costs incurred at the start of the school year; **a. de solidarité spécifique** = allowance paid to long-term unemployed people who are no longer entitled to unemployment benefit; **a. vieillesse** old-age pension

allocution [alɔkysjɔ̃] NF **1** short speech, address; **prononcer une a.** to make a speech **2** *Rel, Jur (par un évêque, un juge aux jurés)* charge

allogène [alɔʒɛn] ADJ *(population etc)* non-indigenous, non-native

allogreffe [alɔgref] NF *Chir* allograft, homograft

allonge [alɔ̃ʒ] NF **1** *(d'une table)* (extension) leaf; *(d'un tuyau, d'une cornue etc)* extension; *(de machine)* coupling rod; **mettre une a. à qch** to put an extension to sth, to lengthen sth; **a. de tige** extension rod; **a. de boucher** meathook **2** *Boxe* reach; **il a une bonne a.** he has a long reach

allongé, -ée [alɔ̃ʒe] ADJ long; *(forme, silhouette)* elongated; **avoir le visage a.** to have a long face; *Méd* **les malades allongés** recumbent patients; *Anat* **la moelle allongée**

the medulla oblongata; *Sport* **coup a.** follow through
N *Méd* recumbent patient

allongement [alɔ̃ʒmɑ̃] NM **1** *(d'un canal etc)* lengthening, extension; *(d'une robe)* lengthening; *(de métaux etc)* elongation, strain; *Mil (des tirs)* lifting **2** *(de temps)* protraction, extension; **a. de la journée de travail** lengthening *or* extension of the working day; **a. de l'espérance de vie des femmes** increase in women's life expectancy **3** *Aviat (des ailes)* aspect ratio

allonger [alɔ̃ʒe] *(*j'allongeai(s); n. allongeons)* VT **1** *(rendre plus long)* to lengthen; *(forme, silhouette)* to elongate; *(vêtement)* to let down; *Mil (tirs)* to lift; **cette robe allonge votre silhouette** this dress makes you look taller; *Culin* **a. la sauce** to thin (down) the sauce; *Fig* to spin it out **2** *(bras)* to stretch out; *(cou)* to crane; **a. le pas** to quicken one's pace *or* step(s); *Sport* **a. l'allure** to increase the pace **3 a. un malade** to lay a sick person down; *Fam* **a. qn** to knock sb down, to floor sb; **a. un coup à qn** to aim a blow at sb; *Fam* **je lui ai allongé une gifle dont il se souviendra** I gave him a slap he'll remember for a long time; *Fam* **a. l'argent** *(payer)* to hand over *or* fork out the money **4** *(conversation, période, délai etc)* to protract, to prolong
VPR **s'allonger 1** *(des jours etc)* to grow longer, to lengthen; *(d'un enfant)* to get taller, to grow; **elle a changé de corps, elle commence à s'a.** her body has changed, she's starting to stretch out **2** *(se coucher)* to stretch (oneself) out, to lie down
VI to extend; *Sport* **le peloton des coureurs allonge derrière** the field is strung out behind; **les jours commencent à a.** the days are starting to get longer, the days are drawing out

allopathe [alɔpat] *Méd* ADJ allopathic
N allopath, allopathist

allopathie [alɔpati] NF *Méd* allopathy

allouer [alwe] VT *Admin (salaire, pension, etc)* to award, to grant; *(actions, rations etc)* to allocate, to apportion; **on lui a alloué un délai supplémentaire de deux jours** he was granted *or* allowed a two-day extension; **a. une dépense/un budget** to allow *or* pass an item of expenditure/a budget; *Jur* **a. une somme à qn à titre de dommages-intérêts** to award sb damages; **pendant le temps alloué** *(faire qch)* within the allotted time, within the time allowed

allouf [aluf] NF match *(for lighting fire)*

allumage [alymaʒ] NM *(d'une lampe, d'un feu)* lighting; *(d'une lampe électrique)* switching on; *(d'un moteur à combustion)* ignition; *(d'une mine)* firing; *Aut* **a. par bobine batterie** battery-coil ignition; **a. par compression** compression ignition; **a. à déclenchement statique** breakerless ignition; **a. défectueux** misfiring; **a. électronique** electronic *or* breakerless ignition; **a. par magnéto haute tension** high-tension magneto ignition; **a. prématuré** pre-ignition; **a. sans rupteur** breakerless ignition; **a. à rupteur transistorisé** transistorized ignition; **a. statique** breakerless ignition; **a. transistorisé** transistorized ignition

allumé, -ée [alyme] ADJ **1** alight, burning; *(d'un haut fourneau)* in blast **2** *Fam (ivre)* tiddly, tipsy **3** *Fam (dingue)* crazy, off one's head *or* rocker
N *Fam* nutcase, nutter

allume-cigare, *pl* **allume-cigares** [alymsigar] NM cigar lighter

allume-gaz [alymgaz] NM INV *(pour cuisinière)* gas lighter

allumer [alyme] VT **1** *(lampe à pétrole, feu, pipe)* to light; *(lampe, télévision, électricité)* to switch on, to turn on; *Ordinat* to power up; **tu pourrais a. la chambre?** could you switch on *or* turn on *or* put on the light in the bedroom?; **veux-tu a. la lumière?** will you switch on *or* turn on *or* put on the lights?; **a. une pompe** to prime a pump
2 *Fig (passions, personnes)* to inflame, to excite, to stir up, to arouse; **a. l'imagination** to fire the imagination; **elle allume les hommes** she excites men, she turns men on; **se faire a.** *(séduire)* to get aroused, *Fam* to get turned on; *(reprendre)* to get a ticking *or* telling off; *(tuer)* to get bumped off
VPR **s'allumer** *(de la lumière)* to come on; *Fig (des yeux)* to light up; *Ordinat* to power up; **ça ne s'allume pas** the light's not working; **où est-ce que ça s'allume?** where does it switch *or* turn on?; **ça s'allume et ça s'éteint** the light's going on and off; **s'a. prématurément** *(d'un moteur)* to backfire
VI to switch on *or* turn on *or* put on the light(s)

allumette [alymɛt] NF **1** match; **a. de sûreté** safety match; **pochette/boîte d'allumettes** book/box of matches; **frotter une a.** to strike a match; *Fam* **des jambes comme des allumettes** legs like matchsticks **2** *Culin* **a. au fromage** cheese straw; **pommes allumettes** thinly cut chips

allumeur [alymœr] NM **1** *(appareil)* lighter, igniting device; *(de moteur)* distributor; *Aut* **a.-distributeur** distributor unit **2** *Arch* lighter, igniter; **a. de réverbère** lamplighter

allumeuse [alymøz] NF *Fam (femme séductrice)* tease

allure [alyr] NF **1** *(vitesse)* pace, speed; **marcher à (une) vive a.** to walk at a brisk pace; **à toute a.** at full *or* top speed; *Sport* at full stretch; **pleine a.** maximum speed
2 *(démarche)* walk, gait; *(manière de se tenir)* bearing, appearance; **allures d'un cheval** paces of a horse; **cela lui donne une belle a.** that makes her look nice
3 *(manière de se présenter)* manner; *(manière d'agir)* way(s) of doing things; *(d'une personne, d'événements etc)* appearance, look; **il prend** *ou* **se donne des allures de roi quand il est en visite** he acts *or* behaves like royalty when he's visiting; **elle/la voiture a de l'a.** she's/the car's got (real) style; **l'a. des affaires** the way things are going; **prendre bonne a.** to look promising, to look well
4 *(d'un fourneau, d'un moteur etc)* working; **a. régulière** smooth running; **a. de marche** rating; **a. normale** normal speed; **a. économique de croisière** cruising speed

> Il faut noter que le nom anglais **allure** est un faux ami. Il signifie **attrait**.

allusif, -ive [alyzif, -iv] ADJ allusive; **sois moins a.!** be more specific!

allusion [alyzjɔ̃] NF allusion *(à* to); *Péj* innuendo; **faire a. à qn/qch** to refer to *or* to allude to *or* to make an allusion to sb/sth; **c'est à vous que s'adresse cette a.** that's a dig at you, that's meant for you; **cette a. m'échappe** I can't see what he's/she's/you're/*etc* getting at

allusivement [alyzivmɑ̃] ADV allusively

alluvial, -iale, -iaux, -iales [alyvjal, -jo] ADJ *Géol* alluvial

alluvions [alyvjɔ̃] NFPL *Géol* alluvium

alma mater [almamater] N *Belg, Can, Suisse* Alma Mater; **l'université de Genève est mon a.** Geneva University is my Alma Mater

almanach [almana] NM *(calendrier)* almanac, yearbook

aloès [alɔɛs] NM *(plante)* aloe; *Pharm* **amer d'a.** bitter aloes

aloi [alwa] NM **1** *(de chose, de personne)* de bon a. genuine; **une plaisanterie de mauvais a.** an unsavoury joke, a joke in bad taste; **des résultats de mauvais a.** unpromising results; **un succès de bon a.** a well-deserved *or* worthy success **2** *(titre)* = proportion of precious metal in an alloy

alopécie [alɔpesi] NF *Méd* alopecia

alors [alɔr] ADV **1** *(à cette époque-là) (dans le passé)* then, at that time, at the time; *(dans le futur)* then; **elle était a. institutrice** she was a teacher then *or* at the time; **a. nous nous marierons** then we'll get married; **que faisiez-vous a.?** what were you doing then or at the time?; **jusqu'a.** until then; **la vie d'a.** life then *or* in those days; **le ministre d'a.** the minister at the time, the then minister

2 *(dans ce cas)* (well) then, in that case, in such a case; **s'il mourait, a., elle devrait reprendre son travail** if he died, then she would have to go back to work; **a. vous viendrez?** well then, you're coming?; **et (puis) a.?, a. quoi?** and what then?; *(qu'est-ce que ça peut faire?)* so what?; *Fam* **non mais a., pour qui te prends-tu?** really!, just who do you think you are?; **je ne suis pas le banquier de tout le monde, non mais a.!** honestly! I'm not made of money, you know!; **a., tu viens?** are you coming then?; **merde a.!** shit!; **a. ... right ..., now then ...; a. Sophie, tu es prête?** OK *or* right Sophie, are you ready?, are you ready then, Sophie?

3 *(donc)* therefore, so; **il n'était pas là, a. je suis revenu** he wasn't there, so I came back CONJ **a. (même) que** (at the very time) when, even when; *(bien que)* even though; **vous dépensez, a. qu'il faudrait économiser** you're spending, when you should be saving; **a. même que je le pourrais** even though I could

alouette [alwɛt] NF **1** *(oiseau)* lark; **a. des champs** skylark; **a. des bois** woodlark; **a. de mer** summer snipe, sea lark, dunlin **2** *Culin* **a. sans tête** veal olive

alourdi [alurdi] ADJ heavy, dull; **a. de sommeil** drowsy; **a. par le sommeil** heavy with sleep; **style a. par trop de tournures compliquées** style weighed down by too many complicated expressions; *Fin* **le marché est a.** the market is dull

alourdir [alurdir] VT **1** *(rendre plus lourd)* *(objet)* to make heavy; *(personne, objet)* to weigh down; *Fig (sens)* to dull; *(phrase)* to make cumbersome *or* unwieldy; **les abus de toutes sortes ont alourdi ses traits** over-indulgence has thickened his features **2** *(alourdir) (charges, impôts)* to increase VPR **s'alourdir** to grow *or* become heavy

alourdissement [alurdismɑ̃] NM *(process of)* growing heavy; *(des membres etc)* growing heaviness; *(des sens)* dulling; **sensation d'a.** feeling of heaviness

aloyau, -aux [alwajo] NM *Culin (de bœuf)* sirloin; **bifteck d'a.** T-bone (steak)

alpaga [alpaga] NM *Zool, Tex* alpaca

alpage [alpaʒ] NM *(pâturage)* alp, mountain pasture; *(droit) (dans les pâturages)* right of pasture; *(saison)* = season spent by livestock in mountain pastures

alpaguer [alpage] VT *Fam* to nab, to collar; **se faire a. par la police** to get nabbed *or* collared by the police

alpe [alp] NF **1** *Région (pâturage)* alp, mountain pasture **2 les Alpes** the Alps; **les Alpes suisses** the Swiss Alps; **cor des Alpes** alpenhorn

alper [alpe] VI *Suisse* = to move cattle up to higher mountain pastures at the beginning of summer

alpestre [alpɛstr] ADJ *(paysage, climat etc)* alpine; **plante a.** alpine (plant)

alpha [alfa] NM **1** *(lettre de l'alphabet grec)* alpha; *Fig* **l'a. et l'oméga** alpha and omega, the beginning and the end; *Fig* **connaître l'a. et l'oméga de qch** to know sth from beginning to end **2** *(particule, rayons, radiation)* alpha

alphabet [alfabɛ] NM **1** alphabet; **apprendre son a. à un enfant** to teach a child the alphabet **2** *Scol* spelling book

alphabétique [alfabetik] ADJ alphabetical; **par ordre a.** in alphabetical order, alphabetically; **classer qch par ordre a.** to put sth in alphabetical order, to alphabetize sth; **index a.** index in alphabetical order

alphabétiquement [alfabetikmɑ̃] ADV alphabetically

alphabétisation [alfabetizasjɔ̃] NF **l'a. de la population** teaching the population to read and write; **taux d'a.** literacy rate

alphabétiser [alfabetize] VT to teach to read and write

alpha-hydroxy-acide [alfaidrɔksiasid] NM alpha hydroxy acid

alphanumérique [alfanymerik] ADJ alphanumeric

Alphapage® [alfapaʒ] NM bleeper

alpha-test, *pl* **alpha-tests** NM *Ordinat* alpha test; **alpha-tests** alpha testing

alpin [alpɛ̃] ADJ *(plante, chasseurs)* alpine; **la chaîne alpine, le massif a.** the Alps; **ski a.** downhill skiing

alpinisme [alpinism] NM *Sport* mountaineering, climbing; **faire de l'a.** to go mountaineering *or* climbing

alpiniste [alpinist] N mountaineer, climber

Alsace [alzas] NF Alsace

alsacien, -ienne [alzasjɛ̃, -jɛn] ADJ from Alsace, Alsatian
 NM *Ling* Alsatian (dialect)
 N **A.** inhabitant of Alsace, Alsatian

altérable [alterabl] ADJ liable to deterioration; **marchandise a.** perishable goods

altéragène [alteraʒɛn] ADJ *(substance)* harmful to the environment, noxious

altérant [alterɑ̃] ADJ thirst-producing, thirst-making

altération [alterasjɔ̃] NF **1** change (for the worse); *(de la santé etc) (par un agent extérieur)* impairment; *(de denrées, de la santé etc)* deterioration; *Ordinat (de fichier)* corruption; **a. de la voix** breaking of the voice **2** *(falsification) (de monnaie, document etc)* falsification; *(de denrées)* adulteration; *(de texte)* garbling; *(de faits)* misrepresentation **3** *Mus* sharp/flat sign, inflection; *(dans le courant du morceau)* accidental **4** *(soif)* great thirst

altercation [alterkasjɔ̃] NF altercation, dispute; **avoir une a. avec qn** to have a quarrel *or* a row with sb

altéré [altere] ADJ **1** *(couleur)* faded; *(visage)* drawn, haggard; **voix altérée par l'émotion** voice strained *or* faltering with emotion; **les faits sont altérés** the facts have been distorted **2** *Ordinat* corrupt **3** *Litt (assoiffé)* thirsty; **a. de sang** thirsting for blood, bloodthirsty; **être a. de pouvoir** to thirst *or* hunger for power

alter ego [alterego] NM INV alter ego

altérer [altere] (**j'altère,** *n.* **altérons; j'altérerai**) VT **1** *(détériorer)* to change (for the worse); *(viande, vin)*, *Fig (tempérament)* to spoil, to taint; *(vin, alimentation)* to adulterate; *(santé)* to impair **2** *Ordinat* to corrupt **3** *(fausser) (dispositif)* to tamper with; *(document)* to falsify; *(texte, histoire)* to garble; *(monnaie)* to falsify; **a. la vérité** to twist the truth **4** *Mus* **a. une note** to inflect a note **5** **a. qn** to make sb thirsty
 VPR **s'altérer** to deteriorate; *(de couleurs)* to fade; *Ordinat* to go corrupt

altérité [alterite] NF *Phil* otherness

altermondialisation [altɛrmɔ̃djalizasjɔ̃] NF ethical globalization

alternance [alternɑ̃s] NF **1** *(des saisons, des feuilles etc)* alternation; **a. des cultures** crop rotation; **en a.** alternately; **nous venons en a. un jour sur deux** we come on alternate days; **formation en a.** = training given partly in an educational institution and partly in the workplace **2** *Pol (des membres du gouvernement)* alternation; **a. du pouvoir** changeover of political power; **pratiquer l'a.** to take turns running a country **3** *Élec* alternation; **redresseur à deux alternances** full-wave rectifier

alternateur [alternatœr] NM *Élec* alternating-current generator, alternator

alternatif, -ive [alternatif, -iv] ADJ **1** *(successif, périodique)* alternative **2** *Élec (courant)* alternating; *(moteur, scie, mouvement)* reciprocating **3** *(projet, médecine etc)* alternative
 NF **alternative 1** *(succession)* alternation, succession; **des alternatives de lumière et d'obscurité** alternation(s) of light and shade **2** *(choix)* alternative, option, choice; **vous pouvez accepter ou refuser, voilà l'alternative** take it or leave it, there's no other choice; **être dans une alternative** to have to choose one way or the other; **alternatives économiques** economic alternatives; **l'alternative verte** *ou* **écologique** the green alternative *or* option

alternativement [alternativmɑ̃] ADV alternately, in turn

alterne [altern] ADJ *(feuilles, angles etc)* alternate

alterner [alterne] VI **1** *(se succéder)* to alternate **2** *(avec qn)* to take turns, to take it in turns *(pour* to *+ inf)*; **ils alternent pour veiller** they take it in turns to sit up; **a. à la surveillance** to take (it in) turns to keep watch
 VT *(cultures)* to rotate

altesse [altɛs] NF highness; **son A. impériale** His/Her Imperial Highness

altier, -ière [altje, -jɛr] ADJ *(ton, port)* haughty, proud, arrogant

altimètre [altimɛtr] NM altimeter, altitude indicator; *Aviat* **a. à contact** altitude switch

altiport [altipɔr] NM high altitude airport

altiste [altist] N *Mus* viola player

altitraceur [altitrasœr] NM altitude recorder

altitude [altityd] NF altitude; **à basse/haute a.** at low/high altitude; **à 100 mètres d'a.** at an altitude of 100 metres; **en a.** at (a high) altitude; *Aviat* **prendre de l'a.** to climb; **vol à haute a.** altitude flight; **a. limite** ceiling; *Méd* **cure d'a.** high-altitude treatment; **mal d'a.** altitude sickness; **ivresse d'a.** altitude narcosis

alto [alto] NM *Mus* **1** alto, counter-tenor (voice) **2** *(instrument à cordes)* viola; *(saxophone)* alto

altocumulus [altokymylys] NM INV *Météo* altocumulus

altostratus [altostratys] NM INV *Météo* altostratus

altruisme [altrɥism] NM altruism

altruiste [altrɥist] ADJ altruistic
 N altruist

Altuglas® [altyglas] NM = thick form of Perspex®

alumine [alymin] NF *Chimie* alumina, aluminium oxide

aluminé [alymine] ADJ aluminized

aluminium [alyminjɔm] NM aluminium, *Am* aluminum; **sulfate d'a.** aluminium sulphate

alun [alœ̃] NM alum; **pierre d'a.** styptic pencil

alunir [alynir] VI to land on the moon

alunissage [alynisaʒ] **NM** moon landing

alvéolaire [alveɔlɛr] **ADJ** cellular; *(motif)* honeycomb; *(nerf, veine, consonne)* alveolar

alvéole [alveɔl] **NF 1** *(pulmonaire)* alveolus; *(de cire d'abeilles etc)* cell; *(d'un bureau etc)* pigeonhole; *(d'un revolver)* chamber; **alvéoles pulmonaires** alveoli of the lungs **2** *(de dent)* socket; *(de diamant)* socket, seat(ing) **3** *(de pierre etc)* cavity, pit; *Élec* **alvéoles d'un grillage** interstices of an accumulator grid **4** *Mil* gun pit

alvéolé [alveɔle] **ADJ** honeycomb(ed), *Spéc* alveolate; **carton a.** corrugated cardboard

AM [ɑɛm] **NF 1** *(abrév assurance maladie)* health insurance **2** *(abrév amplitude modulation)* AM

amabilité [amabilite] **NF** friendliness, amiability; *(bonté)* kindness; **dans un ton plein d'a.** in a friendly tone *(of voice)*; **auriez-vous l'a. de me dire …?** would you be good *or* kind enough to tell me …?; **faites mes amabilités à …** give my kindest regards to …

amadou [amadu] **NM** tinder

amadouement [amadumã] **NM** *(fait d'enjôler)* wheedling, coaxing; *(apaisement)* softening

amadouer [amadwe] **VT** *(enjôler, gagner)* to coax, to wheedle, to persuade; *(apaiser)* to soften; **elle essaie de l'a. pour qu'il accepte** she's trying to coax *or* to wheedle him into accepting

amagnétique [amaɲetik] **ADJ** non-magnetic

amaigrir [amegrir] **VT 1** to make thin; **la maladie l'a amaigri** his illness has made him lose weight **2** *Agr (sol)* to impoverish **3** *Constr (colonne, poutre etc)* to thin down, to reduce

VPR s'amaigrir to grow thin, to lose weight

amaigrissant [amegrisã] **ADJ** *(régime)* slimming

amaigrissement [amegrismã] **NM 1** *(non volontaire)* weight loss, growing thin; *(volontaire)* slimming; **cure d'a.** slimming cure **2** *(dans l'épaisseur)* reducing; *(d'une poutre etc)* thinning down

amalgamation [amalgamasjɔ̃] **NF** amalgamation

amalgame [amalgam] **NM 1** *(dentaire)*, *Chimie* amalgam; *Fig* confusion; **il est tentant de faire l'a. de ces deux idées** these two ideas are easily confused **2** *(alliage)* mixture

amalgamer [amalgame] **VT 1** *(or, argent)*, *Élec (plaque de zinc)* to amalgamate **2** *(banques, sociétés etc)* to amalgamate, to merge; **il a tendance à a. les deux partis** *(il ne voit pas la différence)* he tends to get confused between the two parties; *(il les considère comme un seul parti)* he tends to think of the two parties as one

VPR s'amalgamer to merge, to amalgamate

amanché [amãʃe] **ADJ** *Can* **mal a.** badly dressed

amande [amãd] **NF** *(fruit)* almond; *(dans un noyau d'abricot etc)* kernel; **amandes amères/douces** bitter/sweet almonds; **amandes pilées** ground almonds; **pâte d'amandes** almond paste; *Fig* **les yeux en a.** almond(-shaped) eyes

amandier [amãdje] **NM** *(arbre)* almond tree

amanite [amanit] **NF** *(champignon)* **a. phalloïde** death cap; **a. tue-mouches** fly agaric

amant, -ante [amã, -ãt] **N** lover; **a. de la nature** nature-lover

NM lover; **prendre un a.** to take a lover

amarante [amarãt] **NF** *(fleur)* amaranth(h); **a. commune** *ou* **à fleurs en queue** love-lies-bleeding

amariner [amarine] **VT** *Naut* **1** *(navire enne-*

mi) to man **2** *(homme, équipage)* to accustom to life at sea

VPR s'amariner to find *or* get one's sea legs

amarrage [amaraʒ] **NM** *Naut* **1** mooring, fastening; *(lieu)* berth, moorings; **droits d'a.** berthing dues **2 faire un a. sur une corde** to lash a rope

amarre [amar] **NF 1** (mooring) rope; *(d'avant)* painter; **navire sur ses amarres** ship at her moorings; **rompre ses amarres** *(d'un navire)* to break adrift, to break its moorings; **larguer les amarres** to cast off; *Fig* to break one's moorings **2** *(câble)* cable, hawser; **a. de retenue** guy

amarrer [amare] **VT** *Naut etc* **1** *(navire etc)* to make fast, to moor; **navire amarré à quai** boat berthed *or* lying at the quay **2** *(cordage, chaîne)* to make fast **3** *(haussières etc)* to seize, to lash

amaryllis [amarilis] **NF** *(fleur)* amaryllis; **a. belle-dame** belladonna lily

amas [ama] **NM 1** *(tas)* heap, pile, accumulation; **des a. de glace** packs of ice; *Anat* **a. graisseux** lump of fat **2** *Astron* cluster, constellation; **a. globulaire** globular cluster **3** *(de cristal)* colony **4** *Min* lode

amasser [amase] **VT 1** *(amonceler)* to amass, to heap up, to pile up **2** *(de l'argent)* to hoard (up); **a. une belle somme** to amass a tidy sum **3** *(rassembler)* to collect; *(troupes etc)* to gather together

VPR s'amasser to build up, to pile up; **une foule s'amassait** a crowd was gathering; **les preuves s'amassent contre vous** the evidence is building up *or* piling up against you

amateur [amatœr] **NM 1** *(passionné)* lover; **a. de vieux meubles/de vieilles photos** lover of old furniture/old photos; **a. d'art** art lover; **a. d'oiseaux** bird fancier; **édition d'a.** collector's *or* booklover's edition; **a. de cinéma** film buff; **être a. de qch** to be fond of *or* to have a taste for sth **2** *(dans une vente)* bidder; **est-ce qu'il y a des amateurs?** any takers? **3** *(non-professionnel)* amateur; **photographe/théâtre a.** amateur photographer/theatre; **elle joue bien pour un a.** she plays well for an amateur; *Sport* **championnat d'amateurs** amateur championship; **faire qch en a.** to do sth as a hobby, to dabble in sth; **il fait de la photo en a.** he's an amateur photographer; **travail d'a.** work done by an amateur; *Péj* amateurish work

amateurisme [amatœrism] **NM** *Sport etc* amateurism; *Péj* amateurishness, amateurism

amazone [amazon] **NF 1** *Myth* Amazon **2 l'A.** the (river) Amazon **3** *(cavalière)* horsewoman; **monter en a.** to ride side-saddle **4** *(jupe)* riding habit

Amazonie [amazɔni] **NF** Amazonia

ambages [ɑ̃baʒ] **NFPL** *(seulement dans l'expression)* **parler sans a.** to speak plainly, not to beat about the bush; **il me l'a dit sans a.** he told me quite plainly *or* without beating about the bush

ambassade [ɑ̃basad] **NF 1** *(mission)* embassy; *(moins importante)* mission; **envoyer une a. extraordinaire** to send a special mission; **être envoyé en a. auprès de qn** to be sent on a mission to sb **2** *(édifice)* embassy; *(personnel)* ambassador's staff, embassy; **l'a. de France/du Canada** the French/Canadian embassy; **a. de Tunisie en France** the Tunisian embassy in France; **obtenir une a.** to be appointed ambassador

ambassadeur [ɑ̃basadœr] **NM** ambassador; *(représentant)* envoy; **a. extraordinaire** ambassador extraordinary; **l'a. de Grande-Bretagne** the British ambassador; **a. auprès du roi/de la reine d'Angleterre** Ambassador to *or* at the Court of St James; *Fig* **l'a. de la poé-**

sie indienne the ambassador of Indian poetry; *Fig* **vous êtes les ambassadeurs de votre pays** you are ambassadors for your country

ambassadorial, -iale, -iaux, -iales [ɑ̃basadɔrjal, -jo] **ADJ** ambassadorial

ambassadrice [ɑ̃basadris] **NF 1** *(diplomate)* (woman) ambassador; *Fig* ambassadress **2** *(femme de l'ambassadeur)* ambassador's wife

ambiance [ɑ̃bjɑ̃s] **NF** *(environnement)* surroundings, environment; *(atmosphère)* atmosphere, ambiance; *Cin* room tone; **une a. de travail** a working atmosphere; **l'a. au travail** the atmosphere at work; **musique d'a.** atmospheric music, *Péj* Muzak®; **régulateur d'a.** thermostat; *Fin* **l'a. générale** the prevailing tone; *Fam* **il y a de l'a. ici** there's a cheerful *or* good atmosphere here; **il y a beaucoup d'a.** it's very lively, there's a very good atmosphere; **mettre de l'a.** to liven things up, to create a good atmosphere

ambiant [ɑ̃bjɑ̃] **ADJ** *(atmosphère etc)* surrounding; *Cin* ambient; **milieu a.** environment; **température ambiante** room temperature; *Tech* ambient temperature

ambidextre [ɑ̃bidɛkstr] **ADJ** ambidextrous

ambigu, -uë [ɑ̃bigy] **ADJ** ambiguous

ambiguïté [ɑ̃biguite] **NF** ambiguity; **répondre sans a.** to give an unambiguous *or* unequivocal answer

ambigument [ɑ̃bigymɑ̃] **ADV** ambiguously

ambitieusement [ɑ̃bisjøzmɑ̃] **ADV** ambitiously; *Péj* pretentiously

ambitieux, -ieuse [ɑ̃bisjø, -jøz] **ADJ** ambitious

N ambitious person; *Péj* careerist

ambition [ɑ̃bisjɔ̃] **NF** ambition (**de faire** to do); **elle manque d'a.** she lacks ambition; **être dévoré par l'a.** to be consumed with ambition; **un homme sans a.** an unambitious man; **mettre toute son a. à un travail** to put everything one has into a piece of work, *Fam* to give it one's all; **avoir de l'a.** to have ambition, to be ambitious

ambitionner [ɑ̃bisjɔne] **VT** to set one's heart on (**qch** sth; **de faire qch** doing sth)

ambivalence [ɑ̃bivalɑ̃s] **NF** ambivalence

ambivalent [ɑ̃bivalɑ̃] **ADJ** ambivalent

amble [ɑ̃bl] **NM** *Équitation* amble, pace, *Am* single-foot; **a. rompu** rack; **aller l'a.** to amble

ambler [ɑ̃ble] **VI** *(d'un cheval etc)* to amble (along)

ambre [ɑ̃br] **NM 1 a. gris** ambergris; **pomme d'a.** pomander **2 a. jaune** (yellow) amber; **un collier en a.** an amber necklace

ADJ INV amber

ambré [ɑ̃bre] **ADJ 1** perfumed with amber(-gris) **2** amber-coloured, *Am* -colored; *(complexion, couleur)* warm; **un vin a.** an amber-coloured wine

ambroisie [ɑ̃brwazi] **NF** ambrosia; *Fig* **c'est de l'a.!** it's like nectar!

ambulance [ɑ̃bylɑ̃s] **NF** ambulance; *Fig* **il a assez souffert sans que les médias s'y mettent, on ne tire pas sur une a.** he's suffered enough without the media having a go at him, you shouldn't kick a man when he's down; **il faut soutenir l'ONU au lieu de la critiquer, on ne tire pas sur une a.** the UN should be supported instead of criticized, one shouldn't make a difficult situation worse

ambulancier, -ière [ɑ̃bylɑ̃sje, -jɛr] **N** ambulance man, *f* ambulance woman; *(conducteur)* ambulance driver

ambulant [ɑ̃bylɑ̃] **ADJ** itinerant, travelling; **épicier a.** mobile grocer; **comédiens ambulants** strolling players; **marchand a.** itinerant dealer, hawker; **cirque a.** travelling circus; *Méd* **érysipèle a.** migrant erysipelas;

Fam **c'est un cadavre a.** he's a walking corpse, he looks like death warmed up; **c'est un dictionnaire a.** he's a walking dictionary ▸ NM *Admin (de taxes, de douanes etc)* itinerant collector

ambulatoire [ũbylatwar] ADJ ambulatory; *Méd* **malade a.** out-patient; **(fièvre) typhoïde a.** ambulant typhoid; **traitement a.** outpatient treatment

AME [aɛmə] NM *(abrév* **Accord monétaire européen)** EMA

âme [ɑm] NF **1** *Rel, Phil* soul; *(motif) (d'une entreprise)* inspiration, soul, life; **se donner corps et â. à qch** to give oneself body and soul to sth; **rendre l'â.** to give up the ghost; **de toute mon â.** with all my heart; **elle a l'â. d'une artiste** she has the soul of an artist; **il est peintre dans l'â.** he's a painter through and through *or* to the core; **il jouait de la flûte avec â.** he played the flute with great feeling; **une déclaration sans â.** an unfeeling *or* a soulless declaration; **Dieu ait son â.** God rest his soul; **les âmes en peine** the souls in Purgatory; **aller comme une â. en peine** to wander around like a lost soul; **avoir l'â. chevillée au corps** to have nine lives; **chercher la paix de l'â.** to seek spiritual peace; **â. sœur** kindred soul *or* spirit, soul mate; **en mon â. et conscience** to the best of my knowledge and belief; **cet homme est d'une grandeur d'â. extraordinaire** that man has an extraordinary nobility of spirit; **état d'â.** state of mind, mood; **elle était l'â. de notre organisation** she was the heart and soul of our organization

2 *(personne)* **une bonne â.** a well-meaning person, a good soul; **ne pas rencontrer â. qui vive** not to meet a (living) soul; **un hameau de 50 âmes** a hamlet of some 50 inhabitants; *Iron* **il y a toujours de bonnes âmes pour conseiller quand c'est trop tard!** there are always plenty of people ready with helpful advice when it's too late!; **c'est une â. généreuse** he has great generosity of spirit; **je connais quelques grandes âmes** I know a few high-minded people; **avoir charge d'âmes** *Rel* to have the cure of souls; *(d'enfants, de passagers etc)* to have lives in one's care

3 *(d'un fusil, d'une pompe)* bore; *(d'une statue, d'un câble)* core; *(d'une poutre de bois ou métallique)* web; *(de rail)* centre rib; *Aviat (des ailes)* web; *Mus (d'un violon)* sound post

améliorable [ameljɔrabl] ADJ capable of being improved, improvable; **le système est a.** the system could be improved

améliorant [ameljɔrã] ADJ *Agr* soil-improving; **culture** *ou* **plante améliorante** cover crop

amélioration [ameljɔrasjɔ̃] NF **1** improvement, change for the better; *Ordinat (d'image, de qualité)* enhancement; **on note une nette a. dans les relations des deux pays** there has been a distinct improvement in the relations between the two countries; **l'a. de son état de santé** the improvement in his condition; **il y a de l'a.** there's some improvement; **il y a de l'a. dans les affaires** business is improving; **faire des améliorations dans qch** to make improvements to sth; **travaux d'a.** improvements; *Mktg* **a. du produit** product augmentation *or* improvement **2** *Jur (de biens etc)* appreciation

amélioré [ameljɔre] ADJ improved; *(modèle, version)* enhanced; **un petit mousseux a.** a very good quality sparkling wine

améliorer [ameljɔre] VT **1** *(propriété, sol, traduction etc)* to improve; *(service, chambre d'hôtel)* to upgrade; **a. son état** to improve one's situation **2** *Ordinat (logiciel)* to upgrade; *(image, qualité)* to enhance
▸ VPR **s'améliorer** to get better, to improve; **sa**

santé/le temps s'améliore his health/the weather is improving; **ça ne s'améliore pas** it's not getting any better

amen [amɛn] NM INV amen; *Fig* **il s'attend à ce que je dise a. à tout ce qu'il dit!** he expects me to agree with everything he says!

aménagement [amenaʒmã] NM **1** *(disposition)* arrangement, layout; *Can* **a. paysager** open-plan offices

2 aménagements fittings, fixtures, installations; *Naut, Aviat* accommodation, berthing; **les nouveaux aménagements dans un quartier** new developments in a district

3 *(action)* equipping, arranging; *(d'un navire)* fitting out; **a. d'une usine** equipping *or* fitting out of a factory

4 *Écon, Admin* **a. urbain et rural** town and country planning; *Écon, Admin* **a. du territoire** regional development, physical planning; **a. forestier** forest management

5 *(amendement)* adjustment; **un a. dans un contrat** an adjustment to a contract; **a. fiscal** tax adjustment

6 *Ordinat* housekeeping

aménager [amenaʒe] VT **(j'aménageai(s); n. aménageons) 1** *(maison, navire etc)* to fit out; **étable aménagée** converted cowshed; **a. une cuisine en salle à manger** to convert a kitchen into a dining room; **a. une douche dans une salle de gymnastique** to install *or Am* instal a shower in a gym; **route aménagée** made-up road; **a. un emploi du temps** to adjust a timetable **2** *(ville)* to plan; *(approvisionnement etc)* to divide, to distribute; **a. une forêt** to manage a forest

amende [amãd] NF **1** fine, penalty; **mettre une a. à qn** to fine sb; **être condamné à l'a.** *ou* **à une a.** to be fined; *Fam* **mettre qn à l'a.** to fine sb; **200 euros d'a.** a 200 euro fine; **défense d'entrer sous peine d'a.** trespassers will be prosecuted; **a. fiscale** tax penalty; **a. pour stationnement interdit** parking fine; **a. immédiate** on-the-spot fine **2 faire a. honorable** to make amends

amendement [amãdmã] NM **1** *(du sol etc)* improvement **2** *(engrais)* (soil) conditioner **3** *Pol (à un projet de loi etc)* amendment; *(clause)* additional clause; **proposer un a.** to move an amendment; **(à qch** to sth); **a. constitutionnel** constitutional amendment; **a. européen** European amendment

amender [amãde] VT **1** to make better; *(sol etc)* to improve **2** *Pol (projet de loi etc)* to amend **3** *Suisse (infliger une amende à)* to fine
▸ VPR **s'amender** to turn over a new leaf

amène [amɛn] ADJ pleasing, agreeable; **peu a.** unpleasant, disagreeable

amenée [amne] NF **1 tuyau** *ou* **conduite d'a.** *Constr* branch pipe; *(d'eau)* supply pipe; *Élec* lead **2** *(d'air)* inlet, intake

amener [amne] **(j'amène, n. amenons; j'amènerai)** VT **1** *(personne)* to bring; *Mil (réserves etc)* to bring up; *(eau, gaz etc)* to lay on; **amenez votre ami/chien avec vous** bring your friend/dog (with you); **quel bon vent vous amène?** what brings you here?; **les oléoducs amènent le pétrole à la raffinerie** the pipelines carry the oil to the refinery; *Culin* **a. l'eau à ébullition** to bring the water to the boil; **a. qn à faire qch** to get *or* induce sb to do sth; **et ceci nous amène à parler de la ponctualité** which brings us to the question of punctuality; **a. qn à son opinion** to bring sb round to one's point of view; **a. un sujet** to bring up *or* raise a subject; **a. la conversation sur un sujet** to bring the conversation round to a subject; **un bon auteur sait a. le dénouement de son récit** a good author knows how to bring his story to a conclusion; **a. une querelle** to bring about *or* lead to a quarrel; **a. une mode** to bring in a fashion

2 *Naut (signal)* to haul down; *(couleurs)* to strike; *(bateau, drapeau, voile)* to lower

3 *(tirer à soi)* to draw in, to bring in; **le pêcheur amène les filets** the fisherman draws in the nets
▸ VPR **s'amener** *Fam* to turn up; **amène-toi ici!** come (over) here!

> Do not confuse **amener** and **apporter**. The former should be used with animate objects and the latter with inanimate objects.

aménité [amenite] NF **1** *(de manières, d'un accueil etc)* charm, graciousness; *(de style)* charm, grace; **nous avons été traités sans a.** we were treated ungraciously **2** *Iron* aménités insults, uncomplimentary remarks

aménorrhée [amenɔre] NF *Méd* amenorrhoea

amenuisement [amənɥizmã] NM *(des ressources)* diminishing, dwindling; *(des espoirs)* dwindling

amenuiser [amənɥize] VT to reduce, to thin (down), to whittle down; **a. ses économies/ses réserves** to whittle down one's savings/supplies
▸ VPR **s'amenuiser** *(d'une valeur)* to decline; *(de l'espoir, des chances)* to fade; *(économies, provisions)* to dwindle, to run low

amer¹, -ère [amɛr] ADJ *(goût)*, *Fig (souvenirs, personne)* bitter
▸ NM *(boisson)* bitters

amer² NM *Naut* seamark, landmark

amèrement [amɛrmã] ADV bitterly

américain, -aine [amerikɛ̃, -ɛn] ADJ American; **cuisine américaine** = kitchen with a bar separating the cooking and eating areas
▸ N **A.** American
▸ NM **1** *Ling* American (English) **2** *Belg Culin Fam (steak tartare)* steak tartare
▸ NF **américaine 1** *Culin* **homard à l'américaine** lobster américaine **2** *Cyclisme* track relay (race) **3** *Aut* American car

américanisation [amerikanizasjɔ̃] NF Americanization

américaniser [amerikanize] VT to Americanize
▸ VPR **s'américaniser** to become Americanized

américanisme [amerikanism] NM *Ling* Americanism

américaniste [amerikanist] N specialist in American studies

amérindien, -ienne [amerɛ̃djɛ̃, -jɛn] ADJ Amerindian, American Indian
▸ N **A.** Amerindian, American Indian

Amérique [amerik] NF America; **l'A. du Nord/du Sud** North/South America; **l'A. latine** Latin America; **l'A. centrale** Central America; **les Amériques** the Americas

Amerlo(t) [amerlo], **Amerloque** [amerlɔk] N *Fam* Yank

amerrir [amerir] VI **1** *Aviat* to land on the sea, to make a sea landing **2** *(d'un vaisseau spatial)* to splash down

amerrissage [amerisaʒ] NM *Aviat* landing on the sea, sea landing; *(d'un vaisseau spatial)* splashdown; *Aviat* **a. forcé** ditching

amertume [amɛrtym] NF bitterness

améthyste [ametist] NF amethyst

ameublement [amœbləmã] NM **1** *(action de meubler)* furnishing **2** *(meubles)* set *or* suite of furniture; **un a. très simple** very simple furniture; **magasin d'a.** furniture store; **tissu d'a.** furnishing fabric

ameublir [amœblir] VT **1** *Agr (sol)* to loosen, to break up **2** *Jur (biens immobiliers)* to convert into personalty, to bring into the communal estate

ameublissement [amœblismã] NM **1** Agr (du sol) loosening, breaking up **2** Jur (biens immobiliers) conversion into personalty, inclusion in the communal estate

ameuter [amøte] VT **1** (gens) to bring out; **a. une foule** to draw a crowd; **elle va a. tout le voisinage si elle continue à hurler comme ça!** she'll have the whole neighbourhood out if she carries on shouting like that! **2** (chiens) to form into a pack, to pack
VPR **s'ameuter** to form a mob

AMI [aɛmi] NM (abrév **accord multilatéral sur l'investissement**) MAI

ami, -ie [ami] N friend; **un de mes meilleurs amis** one of my best friends; **a. intime** close friend; **a. d'enfance** childhood friend; **un a. de la maison** a friend of the family; **en a.** as a friend; **mon a.** (entre amis) my dear fellow; (entre époux) my dear; **mon amie** my dear, my love; **être sans amis** to be friendless, to have no friends; **faire a.-a.** (de deux personnes) to decide to be pals; (se réconcilier) to make up (**avec** with); **les amis de mes amis sont mes amis** any friend of yours/his/etc is a friend of mine; **son a.** her boyfriend; (amant) her lover; Fam **sa petite amie** his girlfriend; **son amie** (sa maîtresse) his mistress; **eh l'a.! viens donc m'aider!** hey, you (over) there, come and give me a hand!; **un a. des arts** a patron of the arts; **les amis de la nature/des bêtes** nature/animal lovers; Ling **faux amis** false friends, faux amis; Géog **les îles des Amis** the Friendly Islands, Tonga; **Société des Amis** Society of Friends, Quakers
ADJ friendly (**de** to); (vent) favourable; **un visage a.** a friendly face; **peuple a.** ally, friendly state

amiable [amjabl] ADJ Jur friendly, conciliatory, amicable; **partage a.** amicable sharing arrangement; **a. compositeur** arbitrator
ADV **à l'a.** amicably; Jur **arranger une affaire à l'a.** to settle a difference out of court; **s'arranger à l'a.** to settle out of court; **divorce à l'a.** no-fault divorce; **arrangement à l'a.** amicable arrangement; **vente à l'a.** private sale, sale by private contract

amiante [amjãt] NM Minér asbestos; **plaque d'a.** asbestos mat; **fibres d'a.** asbestos fibres

amibe [amib] NF amoeba, Am ameba

amibiase [amibjaz] NF Méd amoebiasis, Am amebiasis

amibien, -ienne [amibjɛ̃, -jɛn] ADJ Méd amoebic, Am amebic; **dysenterie amibienne** amoebic dysentery

amical, -ale, -aux, -ales [amikal, -o] ADJ (conseil, ton etc) friendly; (relations) amicable; **être a. avec qn** to be friendly towards sb; **peu a.** unfriendly; Sport **match a.** friendly (match); **association amicale** association
NF **amicale** association; Br Scol old-boys'/-girls' or former pupils' association; Am Univ alumni association

amicalement [amikalmã] ADV in a friendly way; **discuter a.** to have a friendly chat; **bien a. à vous** (dans une lettre) yours (ever)

amide [amid] NM Chimie amide

amidon [amidɔ̃] NM starch

amidonnage [amidɔnaʒ] NM starching

amidonner [amidɔne] VT to starch

amieuter(s') [samjøte] VPR Can to improve, to get better

amigne [amiɲ] NM Suisse = grape variety from the Valais canton, and white wine produced from these grapes

amincir [amɛ̃sir] VT to make thinner; (bois) to fine down, to thin down; (métal) to machine down; **cette robe t'amincit** that dress makes you look thinner or slimmer
VPR **s'amincir** to get thinner
VI to get slimmer

amincissant [amɛ̃sisã] ADJ slimming; **régime a.** (slimmer's or slimming) diet

amincissement [amɛ̃sismã] NM (de choses) thinning down; (du métal) machining down; (d'une personne) growing thinner or slimmer; **a. rapide** rapid loss of weight

amine [amin] NF Chimie, Pharm **a. de réveil** amphetamine

aminé [amine] ADJ Chimie **acide a.** amino acid

aminoacide [aminoasid] NM Chimie amino acid

amiral, -ale, -aux, -ales [amiral, -o] ADJ **vaisseau a.** (en mer) flagship; (dans un port) guardship
NM **1** Mil admiral, flag officer; **a. de la flotte** admiral of the fleet **2** (coquillage) admiral shell

amirale [amiral] NF admiral's wife

amirauté [amirote] NF **1** Mil Admiralty; **conseil d'a.** Br ≃ Admiralty Board; Jur High Court of Admiralty **2 îles de l'A.** the Admiralty Islands; **île de l'A.** (Colombie-Britannique) Admiralty Island

amitié [amitje] NF **1** (sentiment) friendship; **éprouver de l'a. ou un sentiment d'a. pour ou envers qn** to have friendly feelings towards sb; **étroite a.** close friendship; **concevoir de l'a. pour qn, prendre qn en a.** to take a liking to sb, to take to sb; **se lier d'a. avec qn** to make friends with sb, to become friendly with sb; **par a.** out of friendship; **une très ancienne a.** a long-standing friendship; **a. particulière** homosexual relationship; Pol **l'a. qui existe entre nos deux pays** the friendship between our two countries **2** (marque) kindness, favour; **faites-moi l'a. de le lui dire** do me the favour of telling him so; **mes amitiés à votre sœur** my best wishes to your sister; **sincères amitiés de …** best wishes from …

amitieux, -euse [amitjø, -øz] ADJ Belg friendly, affectionate

ammoniac, -iaque [amɔnjak] Chimie ADJ **gaz a.** ammonia; **sel a.** sal ammoniac
NM ammonia

ammoniacal, -ale, -aux, -ales [amɔnjakal, -o] ADJ Chimie of ammonia

ammoniaque [amɔnjak] NF Chimie ammonia

ammoniaqué [amɔnjake] ADJ ammoniated

ammonite [amɔnit] NF (fossile) ammonite

amnésie [amnezi] NF Méd amnesia; **souffrir d'a.** to have amnesia

amnésique [amnezik] Méd ADJ amnesic; **être a.** to have amnesia
N amnesia case, amnesiac

amniocentèse [amnjosɛtɛz, amnjosãtɛz] NF Méd amniocentesis; **se faire faire une a.** to have an amniocentesis

amnioscopie [amnjɔskɔpi] NF Méd amnioscopy

amniotique [amnjɔtik] NF Physiol amniotic; **liquide a.** amniotic fluid

amnistie [amnisti] NF amnesty; **accorder une a.** to grant an amnesty

Amnistie
Parking fines as well as some prison sentences are traditionally waived by the French president immediately after a presidential election. The latter is known as "la grâce présidentielle".

amnistier [amnistje] VT (pr sub, impf n. amnistiions, v. amnistiiez) to grant amnesty to, to pardon

amocher [amɔʃe] Arg VT **a. qn** to knock or bash sb about, to beat sb up; **la voiture est**

sérieusement amochée the car's really been bashed up, the car's (in) one hell of a mess; **se faire a.** to get bashed up or beaten up
VPR **s'amocher elle s'est bien amochée en tombant** she smashed herself up when she fell

amoindrir [amwɛ̃drir] VT to decrease, to lessen, to diminish; (affaiblir) to weaken; (mal) to mitigate; (déconsidérer) (personne) to belittle; **la fièvre amoindrit ses forces** the fever is sapping his strength; **a. la puissance de qn** to curtail sb's power
VPR **s'amoindrir** to diminish, to grow less

amoindrissement [amwɛ̃drismã] NM lessening, decrease, diminution

amollir [amɔlir] VT (substance etc) to soften; **pareille chaleur m'amollit** heat like this makes me feel weak
VPR **s'amollir** to soften, to become soft; (du courage etc) to flag, to weaken

amollissement [amɔlismã] NM (du courage etc) softening, weakening, flagging; **pareille chaleur entraîne l'a. général** heat like this makes everyone feel weak

amonceler [amɔ̃sle] (**j'amoncelle, n. amoncelons; j'amoncellerai**) VT to pile up, to heap up, to accumulate, to amass; **a. des preuves** to pile up or amass evidence
VPR **s'amonceler** to pile up, to accumulate

amoncellement [amɔ̃sɛlmã] NM **1** (action) heaping (up), piling (up), accumulation; (des nuages) banking up **2** (pile) heap, pile; **a. de neige** covering of snow

amont [amɔ̃] NM **1** (d'une rivière) upper waters, upstream side; **en a., vers l'a.** upstream, up river; **la Seine en a. de Paris** the Seine above Paris; **vent d'a.** off-shore wind; **le ski a.** the uphill ski **2** Com **activités d'a.** upstream activities; **en a.** upstream

amoral, -ale, -aux, -ales [amɔral, -o] ADJ amoral

amoralité [amɔralite] NF amorality

amorçage [amɔrsaʒ] NM **1** (d'une pompe, d'un moteur, d'une cartouche etc) priming; (d'un champ magnétique) building up; Ordinat booting; Méd (du sommeil) induction; **le système d'a. d'une bombe** the detonating system of a bomb **2** (d'un crochet, d'un cordage) baiting

amorce [amɔrs] NF **1** beginning; (d'une route etc en travaux) initial section; **a. de négociations** preliminary talks **2** (détonateur) primer, fuse, detonator; (d'une petite arme) percussion or cartridge cap; Élec fuse; (d'une pompe) priming; (d'une soudure) scarf; **pistolet à amorces** cap gun **3** Pêche bait **4** Cin leader

amorcer [amɔrse] (**j'amorçai(s); n. amorçons**) VT **1** (bâtiment, route, attaque, discours etc) to begin, to start; **a. des négociations** to initiate negotiations; **a. de nouveau** to reboot **3** (pompe) to prime, to fetch; (coquillage) to cap; Élec (dynamo) to start, to excite; (arc) to strike; (soudure) to scarf; (bombe) to fuse **4** (cordage, piège etc) to bait **5** Vieilli (animal, personne) to entice
VPR **s'amorcer** to begin; Ordinat to boot (up); **une baisse des cours s'amorce** stocks and shares are showing a downward trend

amorçoir [amɔrswar] NM **1** Pêche ground-baiting appliance **2** (vrille) auger, twist bit, boring bit

amorphe [amɔrf] ADJ **1** Chimie, Minér, Biol amorphous **2** (sans énergie) lifeless, apathetic; **cette chaleur me rend totalement a.** this heat is making me lethargic or listless

amorti [amɔrti] ADJ **1** Phys (vague) damped **2 marteau a.** cushioned hammer **3** Fin (bien) depreciated; (capital) amortized
NM Tennis etc drop shot; Ftbl trap

amortir [amɔrtir] **vt 1** *(bruit)* to deaden, to muffle; *(lumière)* to subdue; *(douleur)* to dull; *(ardeur)* to damp; *(passion)* to damp, to cool; *(couleur)* to tone down; *(chute)* to break; *(choc)* to absorb, to deaden; *(coup)* to break the force of; *Ftbl (ballon)* to trap; *Tennis (balle)* to kill; *Aut (secousses)* to damp **2** *Fin (rembourser) (dette, prêt)* to redeem, to pay off, to amortize; *Compta* to write off, to amortize **3** *Fin (rentabiliser)* **il a amorti sa nouvelle voiture en six mois** he recouped the cost of his new car in six months; **le matériel a été amorti dès la première année** the equipment paid for itself by the end of the first year **4** *Phys (oscillations)* to damp down *or* out **5** *Constr* to slack, to slake (lime)
▸ **vpr s'amortir 1** *(dépenses, investissement etc)* to pay for itself **2** *(de bruits etc)* to fade, to die down

amorti-sacrifice, *pl* **amortis-sacrifices** **nm** *Sport* squeeze-bunt

amortissable [amɔrtisabl] **adj** *Fin* redeemable

amortissant [amɔrtisɑ̃] **adj** *Aut* shock-absorbent

amortissement [amɔrtismɑ̃] **nm 1** *Fin (d'une dette)* redemption, paying off, liquidation; **l'a. est plus rapide** *(d'une voiture)* it pays for itself faster; **fonds** *ou* **caisse d'a.** sinking fund; *Compta* **a.-dépenses** amortization *or* write-off of expenditure **2** *Compta (perte de valeur)* depreciation; **provision pour a.** depreciation allowance; **a. dégressif** accelerated depreciation; **a. dérogatoire** excess tax depreciation over normal; **a. linéaire** straightline depreciation; **amortissements cumulés** cumulative depreciation; **amortissements différés** deferred depreciation **3** *(d'une chute)* breaking; *(d'un choc)* absorption; *Aut* damping; *(du son)* deadening

amortisseur [amɔrtisœr] **nm 1** *Aut etc* shock absorber, *Am* snubber; **a. de commande sur carburateur** carburettor damper; **a. de vibrations** vibration damper; **a. hydraulique** hydraulic shock absorber, hydraulic damper; **a. à gaz** gas strut; **a. hydro-élastique** hydroelastic displacer unit **2** *Tech* **a. à moulinet** air brake; **a. pneumatique** air cushion **3** *Élec* damper

amour [amur] **nm** *(f in pl)* **1** *(sentiment)* love; **aimer qn d'a.** to be in love with sb; **ils filent le parfait a.** they are completely in love (with each other); **l'a. d'une mère** a mother's love; **l'a. maternel/paternel/filial** a mother's/father's/child's love; **l'a. du prochain** love of one's neighbour; **avec a.** lovingly; *(traiter, soigner)* with loving care; **a. platonique** platonic love; **s'aimer d'a. platonique** to love each other platonically; **l'a. libre** free love; **elle est folle d'a. pour lui** she's madly in love with him; **a. intéressé** cupboard love; **alors, c'est le grand a.?** so, it's true love then?, *Fam* so, it's the real thing then?; **chanson d'a.** love song; **enfant de l'a.** love child; **se marier par a.** to marry for love; **faire qch par a.** to do sth out of love; **mariage d'a.** love match; **roman/film d'a.** romantic novel/film; **histoire d'a.** love story; *Fig* **c'est une véritable histoire d'a. qui me lie à cette ville** I have a love affair with this city; **faire l'a.** to make love (**avec** with); **l'a. de Dieu** the love of God; **pour l'a. du Ciel, tiens-toi bien!** for heaven's sake, sit up straight!; *Can* **être/tomber en amour (avec qn)** to be/fall in love (with sb) **2** **amours** *(vie amoureuse)* love life; **les premières amours** first love, calf love; **à tes amours!** *(en buvant)* your health!, cheers!; *(à qn qui éternue)* bless you!; **où en sont tes amours?** how's your love life? **3** *(personne)* **mon a.** my love, my darling; **une de mes anciennes amours** an old flame

of mine; **les voitures sont ses seul(e)s amours** cars are his/her sole passion **4 A.** Cupid, Eros, the god of Love; **beau comme l'A.** handsome as a Greek god; **quel a. d'enfant!** what an adorable child!; **tu es un a.!** you('re an) angel!; **sois un a.!** be a dear!, be an angel!; **tu serais un a. si tu voulais me chercher mes cigarettes** be an angel and fetch my cigarettes; **un a. d'histoire** a very sweet story
5 *(goût)* **l'a. (pour qch)** love (of sth), passion (for sth); **l'a. de la nature** love of nature; **l'a. de la justice** passion for justice; **faire qch avec a.** to do sth lovingly *or* with love
▸ **nmpl** *Suisse (vin)* **les amours** = the last drops of wine in a bottle

amouracher (s') [samuraʃe] **vpr s'a. de qn** to become infatuated with sb

amourette [amurɛt] **nf 1** *(entre deux personnes)* little fling **2** *Culin* **amourettes** marrowbone jelly

amoureusement [amurøzmɑ̃] **adv** *(avec tendresse)* lovingly; *(avec passion)* amorously

amoureux, -euse [amurø, -øz] **adj 1** *(soin, regard, geste)* loving; **vie amoureuse** love life; **tomber a.** to fall in love; **être a. de qn** to be in love with sb; *Fig* **il est a. de cette petite maison** he's in love with this little house; **être a. de qch** to be a lover of sth; **je suis a. de cette région** I love that part of the country; **je suis a. de la nature** I'm a nature-lover **2** *(passionné) (regard, geste)* amorous
▸ **n** lover, man/woman in love; **pour les a. de la nature** for nature-lovers *or* lovers of nature; **c'est mon a.** he's my boyfriend

amour-propre [amurprɔpr] **nm** *(dignité)* self-respect, pride; **il n'a aucun a.** he has no self-respect *or* pride; **blesser l'a. de qn** to hurt *or* wound sb's pride; **elle est blessée dans son a.** her pride is hurt; **pétri d'a.** eaten up with conceit

amovible [amɔvibl] **adj 1** detachable; *Ordinat (disque dur)* removable; **siège a.** sliding seat **2** *Jur (fonctionnaire)* removable; **fonction a.** = office that may be withdrawn from the holder (and given to another person)

ampérage [ɑ̃peraʒ] **nm** *Élec* amperage

ampère [ɑ̃pɛr] **nm** *Élec* ampere

ampère-heure, *pl* **ampères-heures** **nm** ampere-hour

ampèremètre [ɑ̃permɛtr] **nm** *Élec* ammeter

amphé [ɑ̃fe] **nf** *Fam (amphétamine)* speed

amphétamine [ɑ̃fetamin] **nf** amphetamine

amphi [ɑ̃fi] **nm** *Univ Fam (salle)* lecture hall; *(cours)* lecture

amphibie [ɑ̃fibi] **adj** *Biol (plante, animal)* amphibious; **appareil** *ou* **voiture a.** amphibian; *Mil* **opération a.** combined operation
▸ **nm** *(véhicule etc), Biol* amphibian

amphibiens [ɑ̃fibjɛ̃] **nmpl** *Zool* amphibians, Amphibia

amphithéâtre [ɑ̃fiteatr] **nm 1** *Univ* lecture hall **2** *Théâtre* gallery, *Fam* the gods **3** *Archit* amphitheatre, *Am* amphitheater; **en a.** in tiers, tier upon tier

amphore [ɑ̃fɔr] **nf** jar; *Archéol* amphora

ample [ɑ̃pl] **adj 1** *(robe, jupe etc)* full **2** *(magasin, théâtre etc)* roomy, spacious **3** *(récit)* full; *(approvisionnement)* plentiful, ample; **jusqu'à plus a. informé** until fuller *or* more information is available; **le sujet est a.** the subject is a wide one; **je vais vous donner de plus amples détails** I will give you fuller *or* more details

amplement [ɑ̃pləmɑ̃] **adv** amply, fully; **nous avons a. le temps** we have plenty of time; **je vous ai a. servi** I have given you

plenty; **il nous a a. renseigné/conseillé** has given us plenty of information/advice; **c'est a. suffisant** it's more than enough

ampleur [ɑ̃plœr] **nf 1** *(d'un vêtement)* width, fullness; *(de la voix)* volume, fullness; **ça manque un peu d'a. au bras** it's not quite full enough in the arm **2** *(importance)* scale, extent; **le mouvement politique prend de l'a.** the (political) movement is growing in size *or* is taking on new dimensions; **devant l'a. du désastre** in view of the extent *or* the scope of the disaster; *Mktg* **a. de gamme** breadth of range; *Mktg* **a. de la ligne de produits** product-line length

ampli [ɑ̃pli] **nm** *Fam* amplifier

amplificateur, -trice [ɑ̃plifikatœr, -tris] **adj** *Radio etc* amplifying; *Opt* magnifying
▸ **nm** amplifier; **a. de puissance** power amplifier

amplification [ɑ̃plifikasjɔ̃] **nf 1** *(d'un sujet)* amplification, development; *(d'un mouvement politique, phénomène)* growth; *(exagération)* exaggeration **2** *Radio etc* amplification; *Opt* magnification

amplifier [ɑ̃plifje] *(impf, pr sub n.* **amplifiions,** *v.* **amplifiiez)** **vt 1** *(bruit, son, idée etc)* to amplify; *(histoire)* to embroider on; *(scandale)* to magnify, to blow up; **a. les échanges commerciaux** to increase trade **2** *Opt* to magnify; *Élec* to amplify
▸ **vpr s'amplifier** *(en taille, en étendue etc)* to grow; **le bruit s'amplifie** the noise is growing *or* getting louder; **les revendications ouvrières s'amplifient** the workers' demands are increasing, the workers are increasing their demands

ampliforme [ɑ̃plifɔrm] **adj** *(soutien-gorge)* padded

amplitude [ɑ̃plityd] **nf 1** *(d'une oscillation)* amplitude; *Radio* **modulation d'a.** amplitude modulation **2** *(variation)* range; **a. thermique** temperature range **3** *Litt (de l'espace etc)* amplitude, vastness; *(d'un désastre, d'une catastrophe)* magnitude, scale

ampoule [ɑ̃pul] **nf 1** *(d'une lampe électrique)* (light) bulb; *(d'un thermomètre)* bulb; *(d'une Thermos®)* container; **une a. de 75 watts** a 75 watt bulb; **a. à baïonnette/vis** bayonet/screw-in (light) bulb; *Aut* **a. de détection de chaleur** heat-sensing bulb; *Phot* **a. de flash** flashbulb, flashlight **2** *(de la peau, du métal etc)* blister; *Hum* **il ne risque pas de se faire des ampoules** he's not going to die of exhaustion **3** *(fiole)* phial

ampoulé, -ée [ɑ̃pule] **adj** *Péj (discours)* inflated, bombastic

amputation [ɑ̃pytasjɔ̃] **nf 1** *(d'un membre etc)* amputation **2** *Fig (d'un livre etc)* cutting down; *(d'une revendication)* reduction; **cet article a subi de sérieuses amputations** this article has been drastically cut; **c'est une sérieuse a. à sa fortune** it has cut into his fortune

amputé, -ée [ɑ̃pyte] **n** amputee

amputer [ɑ̃pyte] **vt 1** *(membre)* to amputate; **il fut amputé du bras gauche** his left arm was amputated **2** *Fig (article etc)* to cut down; *(revendication)* to cut, to reduce (**de** by); **a. un capital** to make inroads into one's/sb's capital

amulette [amylɛt] **nf** amulet, charm

amusant [amyzɑ̃] **adj** amusing, funny; *(divertissant)* entertaining; **comme c'est a., je n'avais pas remarqué ...** that's funny, I hadn't noticed ...; **je ne trouve pas ça très a.** I don't find that very funny *or* amusing, *Hum* I am not amused; **c'était très a.** it was great fun
▸ **nm le plus a., c'est que ...** the funniest *or* most amusing thing is that ...; **l'a. de l'histoire** the amusing part of the story, what was funny *or* amusing about the story

amuse-gueule [amyzgœl] NM INV cocktail snack, nibble; *Fig* appetizer

amusement [amyzmã] NM amusement; **avoir besoin d'a.** to need amusement *or* entertainment; **faire qch pour son a.** to do sth for one's own amusement; *Iron* **tu parles d'un a.!** what fun!

amuser [amyze] VT to amuse; *(divertir)* to entertain; **l'histoire m'a beaucoup amusé** I found the story really funny; *(divertissante)* I found the story really entertaining; **en attendant, il faut a. la salle** in the meantime, we must keep the audience amused; **si tu penses que ça m'amuse!** if you think I enjoy (doing) it!; **tu crois que ça m'amuse, ce genre de situations?** do you think I enjoy this kind of situation?; **ah ça t'amuse, toi!** you think that's funny, do you?; **fais-le si ça t'amuse** do it if it amuses you; **il avait un regard amusé quand il nous a dit bonjour** he looked amused *or* as if something was amusing him when he said hello to us
   VPR **s'amuser** *(se distraire)* to enjoy oneself, to have a good time; **je ne me suis jamais aussi bien amusé** I've had the time of my life; **les enfants s'amusent dans le jardin** the children are playing in the garden; **amusez-vous bien!** have fun!, enjoy yourselves!; **s'a. aux dépens de qn** to amuse oneself at sb's expense; **s'a. avec qn** to have fun with sb; **s'a. de qn/de qch** to make fun of sb/sth; **s'a. à faire qch** to have fun doing sth; **faire qch pour s'a.** to do sth for fun *or* for the fun of it; *Fam* **ne t'amuse pas à recommencer** don't you dare do that again; **si tu crois que je vais m'a. à faire ça** if you think I've nothing better to do than that; **nous n'avons pas le temps de nous a. en chemin/à faire ça** we can't afford to waste time on the way/doing that

> Il faut noter que le verbe anglais **to amuse oneself** est un faux ami. Il signifie **s'occuper, passer le temps.**

amusette [amyzɛt] NF **1** *Vieilli* pastime, diversion **2** *Belg* frivolous person

amuseur, -euse [amyzœr, -øz] N entertainer

amygdale [ami(g)dal] NF tonsil; **inflammation des amygdales** tonsillitis; **se faire opérer des amygdales** to have one's tonsils out; *Fam* **se sucer les amygdales** to snog (furiously)

amygdalectomie [ami(g)dalɛktɔmi] NF *Chir* tonsillectomy

amygdalite [ami(g)dalit] NF *Méd* tonsillitis; **faire une a.** to have tonsillitis

an [ã] NM year; **tous les trois ans** every three years; **dans trois ans** in three years' time, three years from now; **l'an passé** *ou* **dernier** last year; **l'an prochain** next year; **par an** per year; *Fin* per annum; **j'ai deux semaines de vacances par an** I have two weeks' holiday per *or* a year; **deux fois par an** twice a year; **un prêt sur vingt ans** a loan over twenty years; **tous les ans** every year; **avoir dix ans** to be ten (years old); *(d'une machine)* to be ten years old; **je gagne tant par an** I earn so much a year; **ami de vingt ans** friend of twenty years' standing; **bon an, mal an** on average over the years; **le jour** *ou* **le premier de l'an, le Nouvel An** New Year's day; **l'an II de la République** Year Two of the Republic; **en l'an 2005** in the year 2005; **je m'en moque comme de l'an 40** I couldn't give a damn about it, I couldn't care less

anabaptisme [anabatism] NM Anabaptism

anabaptiste [anabatist] ADJ, N Anabaptist

anabolisant [anabɔlizã] NM *Méd* anabolic steroid
   ADJ anabolic

anabolisme [anabɔlism] NM *Méd* anabolism

anacarde [anakard] NM cashew nut

anacardier [anakardje] NM cashew tree

anachorète [anakɔrɛt] NM recluse; *Rel* anchorite; *Fig* **il mène une vie d'a.** he lives the life of a recluse

anachronique [anakrɔnik] ADJ anachronistic

anachronisme [anakrɔnism] NM anachronism

anacoluthe [anakɔlyt] NF anacoluthia

anaconda [anakɔda] NM anaconda

anaérobie [anaerɔbi] ADJ anaerobic

anagrammatique [anagramatik] ADJ anagrammatic(al)

anagramme [anagram] NF anagram

ANAH [ana] NF *(abrév* **Agence nationale pour l'amélioration de l'habitat)** = housing department

anal, -ale, -aux, -ales [anal, -o] ADJ *Anat, Psy* anal

analeptique [analɛptik] ADJ, NM *Pharm* analeptic

analgésie [analʒezi] NF *Méd* analgesia

analgésique [analʒezik] ADJ, NM *Pharm* analgesic

anallergique [analɛrʒik] ADJ *(produit cosmétique)* hypoallergenic

analogie [analɔʒi] NF analogy; **raisonner par a.** to argue from analogy; **par a. avec** by analogy with

analogique [analɔʒik] ADJ **1** analogical; **dictionnaire a.** analogical dictionary **2** *Électron* analogue, *Am* analog; **calculatrice a.** analog computer; **montre a.** analogue watch

analogue [analɔg] ADJ analogous (**à** to, **with**), similar (**à** to); **dans des conditions analogues** in similar conditions
   NM analogue, *Am* analog, parallel; **ce mot anglais n'a pas d'a. en français** this English word has no equivalent in French

analphabète [analfabɛt] ADJ, N illiterate (person)

analphabétisme [analfabetism] NM illiteracy

analysable [analizabl] ADJ analysable, *surtout Am* analyzable

analyse [analiz] NF **1** *(étude)* analysis; **en dernière a.** in the last *or* final analysis, when all is said and done, all things considered; **avoir l'esprit d'a.** to have an analytical mind; **faire l'a. de qch** to analyse sth; **roman/film d'a.** psychological novel/film; **a. de la situation** situation(al) analysis VOIR GRAMMAIRE A14
   2 *Méd* test; **laboratoire d'analyses** pathology laboratory; **a. de sang/d'urine** blood/urine test; **faire des analyses de sang** to undergo blood tests
   3 *Psy* (psycho)analysis; **être en a.** to be in analysis; **commencer/finir son a.** to begin *or* go into analysis/to finish *or* come out of analysis
   ▸ ▸ *Mktg* **a. des attraits et des atouts** opportunity and issue analysis; *TV, Radio* **a. de l'audience** audience research *or* analysis; **a. des besoins** needs analysis; **a. du chemin critique** critical path analysis; **a. des coûts** cost analysis; **a. de coût et d'efficacité** cost-effectiveness; **a. coût-profit** cost-benefit analysis; **a. de la demande** demand analysis; **a. de données** data analysis; **a. des écarts** variance analysis; *Écon* **a. économique** economic analysis; *Ordinat* **a. factorielle** factor analysis; **a. fonctionnelle** systems analysis; *Mktg* **a. des forces et faiblesses** strengths and weaknesses analysis; *Mktg* **a. des forces, faiblesses, opportunités et menaces** SWOT analysis; *Ling* **a. grammaticale** parsing; *Ling* **faire l'a. grammaticale d'une phrase** to parse a sentence; *Math* **a. infinitésimale** *(différentielle et intégrale)* calculus; *Ling* **a. logique** analysis; *Ling* **faire l'a. logique d'une phrase** to analyse a sentence; **a. du marché** market analysis; **a. des médias** media analysis; *Mktg* **a. d'un modèle de décision en arborescence** decision-tree analysis; *Ordinat* **a. numérique** numerical analysis; *Mktg* **a. des opportunités et des menaces** opportunity and threat analysis; *Ordinat* **a. organique** systems design; *Ordinat* **a. des performances du système** system evaluation; **a. de portefeuille** portfolio analysis; **a. prévisionnelle** predictive analysis; **a. qualitative** qualitative analysis; *Chimie* **a. quantitative** quantitative analysis; **a. du rendement** rate-of-return analysis; **a. des risques** risk analysis; **a. par secteur d'activité** segment reporting; **a. par segment** cluster analysis; **a. de séries temporelles** time-series analysis; **a. statistique** statistical analysis; **a. du style de vie** lifestyle analysis; *Ordinat* **a. syntaxique** parsing; **a. de système, a. systémique** systems analysis; **a. du ton de la voix** voice pitch analysis; **a. de la valeur** value analysis; **a. de la valeur perçue** perceived value analysis; **a. vectorielle** vector analysis; **a. des ventes** sales analysis; **a. volumétrique** volumetric analysis

analyser [analize] VT **1** *(faits etc)* to analyse, *esp Am* to analyze; *Méd (sang, urine etc)* to test; *Ordinat* to parse; **a. une phrase** *Gram* to parse a sentence; *(en propositions)* to analyse a sentence **2** *Psy* to (psycho)analyse; **se faire a.** to be (psycho)analysed
   VPR **s'analyser** to analyse one's feelings; **elle s'analyse trop** she goes in for too much self-analysis

analyseur [analizœr] NM analyser, *surtout Am* analyzer; *TV* scanner; *Ordinat* **a. syntaxique** parser; *Ordinat* **a. logique** logic analyzer

analyste [analist] N *Ordinat etc* analyst; *Psy* (psycho)analyst; **être un bon a. de ses sentiments** to be good at analysing one's feelings; *Mktg* **a. du marché** market analyst; **a. des médias** media analyst; *Mktg* **a. mercaticien** marketing analyst; *Fin* **a. en placements financiers** investment analyst

analyste-programmeur, *pl* **analystes-programmeurs** NM *Ordinat* systems analyst

analytique [analitik] ADJ analytical; **géométrie a.** analytic geometry; **un esprit a.** an analytical mind; *Psy* **suivre un traitement a.** to have psychoanalytical treatment
   NF analytics

analytiquement [analitikmã] ADV analytically

anamnèse [anamnɛz] NF *Méd* anamnesis

anamorphique [anamɔrfik] ADJ *Cin, TV* anamorphic

anamorphose [anamɔrfoz] NF anamorphosis

ananas [anana(s)] NM *(fruit)* pineapple; *(plante)* pineapple plant; **serre à a.** pinery; **a. frais/en conserve** fresh/tinned *or* canned pineapple

anaphore [anafɔr] NF anaphora

anaphorique [anafɔrik] ADJ anaphoric

anaphylactique [anafilaktik] ADJ anaphylactic; **choc a.** anaphylactic shock

anar [anar] N *Fam* = **anarchiste**

anarchie [anarʃi] NF *Pol, Fig* anarchy

anarchique [anarʃik] ADJ *(comportement)* anarchic(al); *(philosophie, système)* anarchistic

anarchiquement [anarʃikmã] ADV anarchically, in an anarchic(al) manner; *Fig* chaotically, in a chaotic manner

anarchisant [anarʃizã] ADJ with anarchist tendencies *or* leanings

anarchisme [anarʃism] NM anarchism

anarchiste [anarʃist] *Pol* **ADJ** anarchist; *Fig* chaotic, disorderly; *(personne)* rebellious, non-conformist
N anarchist; *Fig* rebel, non-conformist

anarcho-syndicaliste, *pl* **anarcho-syndicalistes** [anarkosɛ̃dikalist] **N** anarchosyndicalist

anathématiser [anatematize] **VT** to curse, *Fml* to anathematize

anathème [anatɛm] **NM** anathema

anatife [anatif] **NM** *(crustacé)* barnacle

anatomie [anatɔmi] **NF** anatomy; *Méd* **a. pathologique** morbid anatomy; *Fam* **une belle a.** a great body; **pièce d'a.** anatomical figure; **avoir une a. d'athlète** to have the body of an athlete

anatomique [anatɔmik] **ADJ** anatomical

anatomiquement [anatɔmikmā] **ADV** anatomically

anatomiste [anatɔmist] **N** anatomist

ancestral, -ale, -aux, -ales [āsɛstral, -o] **ADJ** ancestral

ancêtre [āsɛtr] **NM** ancestor; *Fam (vieillard)* old man; **la maison de ses ancêtres** his family home; *(château etc)* his ancestral home; **être sur les traces de ses ancêtres** to be tracking down one's ancestors; **nos ancêtres les Gaulois** our ancestors *or* forefathers the Gauls; **Bartok est l'a. de la musique contemporaine** Bartok is the father of contemporary music; **c'est l'a. de la vidéo** it's the forerunner of the video

anche [āʃ] **NF** *Mus (de hautbois, de clarinette etc)* reed, tongue; **jeu d'anches** *(d'un orgue)* reed-stop

anchois [āʃwa] **NM** *(poisson)* anchovy; **a. de Norvège** sprat; **beurre d'a./sauce aux a.** anchovy paste/sauce; **filets d'a.** anchovy fillets; *Fam* **serrés comme des a.** packed like sardines

ancien, -ienne [āsjɛ̃, -jɛn] **ADJ** SEE GRAMMAR B10 **1** *(vieux)* ancient, old, antique; **monument a.** ancient monument; **meubles anciens** antique furniture; **anciens meubles** old furniture
2 *Hist* ancient, old(en), early, bygone, past; **les peuples anciens** people of antiquity; **le grec a.** ancient *or* classical Greek; **dans l'a. temps** in the old(en) days, in bygone days, in days gone by; **l'A. Testament** the Old Testament; **c'est de l'histoire ancienne** *(c'est oublié)* that's ancient history
3 *(révolu)* *(professeur, élève etc)* former, old, ex-; *(d'avant)* *(voiture, maison etc)* old; **a. président** former *or* past president; **a. élève** *(d'une école)* old pupil, old boy; *Am Univ* alumnus; **je suis un de vos anciens élèves** I'm a former pupil of yours; **anciens combattants** ex-servicemen, *Am* veterans; **mon a. époux** my ex-husband; **c'est un a. boxeur** he's a former boxer, he used to be a boxer
4 *(capitaine, officier etc)* senior; **je suis plus a. que vous dans la profession** I've been in the profession longer than you; **il est votre a.** he is senior to you
NM 1 *Hist* **les anciens** the ancients
2 *Rel, Pol* elder; **les anciens du village** the older inhabitants of the village; **les anciens de la tribu** the elders of the tribe; **respecter les anciens** to respect one's elders; *Fam* **l'a.** *(père)* the old man
3 **aimer l'a.** *(meubles)* to like antique furniture *or* antiques; *(architecture)* to like old buildings
4 *Vieilli (de scouts)* patrol leader
N *(par l'expérience)* **c'est une ancienne dans la maison** she's been with the firm a long time; **les anciens de l'entreprise** the company's long-time *or* long-serving employees

> Il faut noter que le mot anglais **ancient** est un faux ami. Il correspond au français **antique**.

anciennement [āsjɛnmā] **ADV** formerly

ancienneté [āsjɛnte] **NF 1** *(d'un monument, d'une race etc)* age, antiquity; **de toute a.** from time immemorial **2** *(par l'expérience)* seniority, length of service; **a. de grade** seniority in rank; **avoir 15 ans d'a. dans une entreprise** to have 15 years' service with a firm; **avancer à l'a.** to be promoted by seniority; **il a plus d'a. que moi** he's been with the company longer than I have

ancillaire [āsilɛr] **ADJ** ancillary; **amours ancillaires** love affairs with a servant/servants

ancolie [ākɔli] **NF** *(fleur)* aquilegia, columbine

ancrage [ākraʒ] **NM 1** *Naut* anchoring; *(attache)* anchorage; **(droits d')a.** anchorage dues **2** *Constr etc (action)* anchoring, anchorage, fixing; *(d'un mur)* bracing, staying; *(dispositif)* wall tie; **plaque/tige d'a.** anchor plate/tie; **point d'a.** *(d'un câble)* cable anchorage; *Fig* base; *Fig* **ce studio à Londres est son point d'a., c'est à partir de là qu'il rayonne** this studio in London is his base for touring around; *Fig* **l'a. de nouvelles idées** the taking root of new ideas **3** *Ordinat* justification; **a. à droite/gauche** right/left justification

ancre [ākr] **NF 1** anchor; **a. de veille** sheet anchor; **lever l'a.** to weigh anchor; *Fig Fam (partir)* to get moving, to hit the road; **jeter l'a.** to anchor; *Fig* to settle down; *Aviat* **a. de ballon** balloon anchor, grapnel; *Naut Arch* **a. de miséricorde** sheet anchor **2** *Constr etc (d'un mur, d'un fourneau etc)* anchor, cramp iron, tie (plate); *(d'une chaudière)* brace, stay **3** *Ordinat* anchor

ancrer [ākre] **VT 1** *(navire, montgolfière)* to anchor; *Fig* **il faut lui a. cette idée dans la tête** we/you/*etc* have to get that into his head; *Fig* **je ne sais pas qui lui a ancré cette idée dans la tête, mais il n'en démord pas** I don't know who put that idea in his head, but he won't let go of it; **cette idée est profondément ancrée en lui** this idea is firmly rooted in his mind **2** *Constr (cheminée, moteur, chaudière etc)* to brace, to tie, to stay, to anchor
VPR **s'ancrer** *(d'une idée, d'un concept)* to stick, to become rooted; *Fig* **elle a décidé de s'a. dans cette région** she has decided to put down roots in the region; *Fig* **je m'ancrais dans mon intention première** I stuck fast to my original intention; *Fig* **celui en qui s'ancre la foi …** he whose faith is steadfast …

andain [ādɛ̃] **NM** swathe

andalou, -ouse [ādalu, -uz] **ADJ** Andalusian **NM 1** *Ling* Andalusian (dialect) **2** *(cheval)* Andalusian horse
N A. Andalusian

Andalousie [ādaluzi] **NF** Andalusia

andante [ādāt(e)] **ADV, NM** *Mus* andante

andantino [ādātino] **ADV, NM** *Mus* andantino

Andes [ād] **NFPL** **les A.** the Andes; **la Cordillère des A.** the Andean *or* the Great Cordillera

andin [ādɛ̃] **ADJ** Andean

andorran, -ane [ādɔrā, -an] **ADJ** Andorran
N A. Andorran

Andorre [ādɔr] **N** Andorra; **le val/la principauté d'A.** the Vale/Principality of Andorra

andouille [āduj] **NF 1** *Culin* chitterlings sausage **2** *Fam (imbécile)* fool, twit; **faire l'a.** to play the fool

andouiller [āduje] **NM** *(d'un cervidé)* antler

andouillette [ādujɛt] **NF** *Culin* = small chitterlings sausage (for frying)

androgène [ādrɔʒɛn] **ADJ** androgenic
NM androgen, male hormone

androgyne [ādrɔʒin] **ADJ** androgynous
N androgyne

androïde [ādrɔid] **NM** android

andrologie [ādrɔlɔʒi] **NF** andrology

andrologue [ādrɔlɔg] **NM** andrologist

Andromaque [ādrɔmak] **N** Andromache

Andromède [ādrɔmɛd] **N** Andromeda

andropause [ādrɔpoz] **NF** male menopause

âne [ɑn] **NM 1** donkey, *Litt, Vieilli* ass; **â. mâle** jackass; **promenade à dos d'â.** donkey ride; **se promener à dos d'â.** to go for a donkey ride; *Prov* **on ne saurait faire boire un â. qui n'a pas soif** you may lead a horse to water but you cannot make him drink; **être comme l'â. de Buridan** to be unable to make up one's mind between two things; *Fig* **le coup de pied de l'â.** the final insult, the last straw **2** *Fam (idiot)* ass; *(ignare)* dunce; **bonnet d'â.** dunce's cap; **espèce d'â. bâté!** stupid ass!

anéantir [aneātir] **VT** to annihilate; **a. les espérances de qn** to dash sb's hopes, to put an end to sb's hopes; *Fig* **la nouvelle l'a anéantie** she was staggered by the news
VPR **s'anéantir 1** *(disparaître)* *(d'espoir, de chances de succès)* to be dashed **2** *Rel (devant Dieu)* to humble *or* abase oneself

anéantissement [aneātismā] **NM 1** *(de l'espoir etc)* destruction; *(d'un empire etc)* annihilation, destruction; **l'a. de l'individu/de la personnalité** the annihilation of the individual/the personality **2** *(abattement)* **dans un état d'a. total** completely shattered

anecdote [anɛkdɔt] **NF** anecdote

anecdotique [anɛkdɔtik] **ADJ** anecdotal

anémie [anemi] **NF** *Méd* anaemia, *Am* anemia; **faire de l'a.** to have anaemia; **a. pernicieuse** pernicious anaemia; *Fig* **l'a. d'un secteur** the enfeebled state of an industrial sector

anémier [anemje] **VT** **a. qn** to make sb anaemic *or Am* anemic; *Fig* **la crise a anémié la sidérurgie** the crisis has severely weakened the steel industry
VPR **s'anémier** to become anaemic *or Am* anemic; *Fig* **un secteur qui s'anémie** an industrial sector that is falling into decline

anémique [anemik] **ADJ** *(personne)* anaemic, *Am* anemic; *Fig* feeble, weak

anémomètre [anemɔmɛtr] **NM** anemometer, wind gauge; **a. badin** airspeed indicator

anémone [anemɔn] **NF** anemone; **a. sylvie** wood anemone; **a. de mer** sea anemone

ânerie [ɑnri] **NF** *Fam* **1** *(stupidité, bêtise)* stupidity; **il est d'une â.!** what an idiot!; **quelle â.!** *(ta décision etc)* how idiotic! **2** *(action, propos)* **je crois que je viens de dire/faire une â.** I think I've just said/done something silly; **faire des âneries** to make an ass *or* a fool of oneself; **dire des âneries** to talk tripe *or* rubbish

anéroïde [anerɔid] **ADJ** *Météo (baromètre)* aneroid

ânesse [ɑnɛs] **NF** she ass, jenny; **lait d'â.** ass's milk

anesthésiant [anɛstezjā] **ADJ, NM** *Méd* anaesthetic, *Am* anesthetic

anesthésie [anɛstezi] **NF** *Méd* anaesthesia, *Am* anesthesia; **a. générale/locale** general/local anaesthetic; **on va vous faire une a. locale/générale** we're going to give you a local/general anaesthetic; **mettre un malade sous a.** to anaesthetize a patient, to put a patient under anaesthetic; **elle est encore sous a.** she's still under (the) anaesthetic

anesthésier [anɛstezje] **VT** *Méd* to anaesthetize, *Am* to anesthetize; *Fig (crainte)* to deaden; *(opinion publique)* to anaesthetize

anesthésiologie [anɛstezjɔlɔʒi] **NF** *Méd* anaesthetics, *Am* anesthesiology

anesthésique [anɛstezik] ADJ, NM *Méd* anaesthetic, *Am* anesthetic

anesthésiste [anɛstezist] N *Méd (médecin)* anaesthetist, *Am* anesthetologist; *Am (infirmière)* anesthetist

aneth [anɛt] NM *(plante)* dill

anévrisme, anévrysme [anevrism] NM *Méd* aneurism, aneurysm

anfractuosité [ãfraktɥozite] NF crevice, crack

ange [ãʒ] NM *Rel* angel; **un visage d'a.** an angelic face; *Beaux-Arts* **a. joufflu** chubby little cherub; **être le bon a. de qn** to be sb's good angel; **être le mauvais a. de qn** to be a bad influence on sb; **être aux anges** to be in seventh heaven, to be walking on air; **rire aux anges** to smile contentedly; *Fam* **faiseuse d'anges** backstreet abortionist; *Fam* **un a. passe** silence is wonderful; **un a. passa** there was a sudden silence in the conversation; *Fig* **discuter du sexe des anges** to talk round in circles; **oui, mon a.** yes (my) angel; **tu es un a.** you're an angel; **tu serais un a. si tu allais me chercher mes cigarettes** be an angel and fetch me my cigarettes; **beau comme un a.** pretty as a picture; **sage comme un a.** (as) good as gold; **une patience d'a.** the patience of a saint; **une douceur d'a.** angelic sweetness
▸▸ **a. déchu** fallen angel; **a. gardien** guardian angel; *Iron* bodyguard; *Vieilli* **a. tutélaire** guardian angel

angéiologie [ãʒejoloʒi] NF *Méd* angiology

angélique [ãʒelik] ADJ angelic(al); *Rel* **la salutation a.** the Hail Mary; **être d'une patience a.** to have the patience of a saint
NF *Culin* angelica

angélisme [ãʒelism] NM saintliness

angelot [ãʒlo] NM **1** little angel, cherub **2** *(poisson)* monkfish, angel fish *or* ray *or* shark

angélus [ãʒelys] NM *Rel* angelus (bell)

angevin, -ine [ãʒvɛ̃, -in] ADJ Angevin, (of *or* from) Angers/Anjou
N **A.** Angevin, person from Angers/Anjou

angine [ãʒin] NF *Méd* sore throat, *Fam* strep throat; *(des amygdales)* tonsillitis; **avoir une a.** to have a sore throat/to have tonsillitis; **a. de poitrine** angina (pectoris)

angiogenèse [ãʒjoʒənɛz] NF *Méd* angiogenesis

angiographie [ãʒjografi] NF *Méd* angiography

angiome [ãʒjom] NM *Méd* angioma

angioplastie [ãʒjoplasti] NF *Méd* angioplasty

anglais, -aise [ãglɛ, -ɛz] ADJ English; *(incorrect au sens strict) (armée, marchandises etc)* British
NM English (language); **l'a. correct** the King's *or* Queen's English; **a. britannique/américain** British/American English
N **A.** Englishman, *f* Englishwoman; *(incorrect au sens strict)* Briton; **les A.** the English; *(incorrect au sens strict)* the British; **les A. ont débarqué, Can j'ai la visite des A.** I have my period
NF **anglaise** *Culin* **pommes de terre à l'anglaise** boiled potatoes
NFPL **anglaises** ringlets

angle [ãgl] NM **1** *(d'un mur, d'une pièce etc)* corner, angle; **la maison qui fait l'a. appartient à mon oncle** the house on the corner belongs to my uncle; **armoire d'a.** corner cupboard; **l'a. de la rue** the street corner; **à l'a. du chemin** at the bend of the road; **l'a. de la table** the corner of the table; *Fig* **arrondir les angles** to smooth things over; **c'est toujours elle qui arrondit les angles** she's always the one who smooths things over

2 *(point de vue)* angle, point of view; **nous ne voyons pas les choses sous le même a.** we don't see things from the same angle *or* in the same way; **sous cet a.-là** from that angle, from that point of view; **vu sous cet a.** seen from that angle; **a. d'attaque** *(d'un sujet)* line of attack, approach

3 *Géom* angle; **a. aigu/obtus** acute/obtuse angle; **a. plat/droit** straight angle/right angle; **les rues se coupent à angles droits** the roads cross at right angles; **former un a. avec qch** to be at right angles to sth

4 *Menuis etc* **abattre les angles de qch** to chamfer sth; **soudure d'a.** fillet weld; **roue d'a.** bevel wheel, mitre wheel; **a. oblique** bevel rule, mitre square; **engrenage d'a.** bevel gear; **fer d'a.** angle iron

5 *(d'un outil)* edge; **à angles vifs** with sharp edges
▸▸ *Aut* **a. de braquage** turning circle; **a. de cap** track course; *Aut* **a. de chasse** caster angle; *Aviat* **a. critique** stalling angle; *Opt* **a. d'incidence** angle of incidence; *Mil* **a. de mire** angle of sight; **a. mort** *(au tir)* dead angle; *(dans un rétroviseur etc)* blind spot; *TV, Cin* **a. plongée** high angle; *TV, Cin* **a. de prise de vue** shooting *or* camera angle; *Opt* **a. de réfraction** angle of refraction; *TV, Cin* **a. de vue** angle of view

angledozer [ãglədozɛr] NM angledozer

Angleterre [ãglətɛr] NF England; *(incorrect au sens strict)* Britain; *Hist* **la bataille d'A.** the Battle of Britain; *Couture* **point d'A.** Brussels (bobbin) lace

anglican, -ane [ãglikã, -an] *Rel* ADJ Anglican; **l'Église anglicane** the Church of England, the Anglican Church
N Anglican

anglicanisme [ãglikanism] NM *Rel* Anglicanism

anglicisant, -ante [ãglisizã, -ãt] N student of English, English scholar

angliciser [ãglisize] VT *(mot etc)* to anglicize
VPR **s'angliciser** to become anglicized

anglicisme [ãglisism] NM *Ling* Anglicism

angliciste [ãglisist] N *(étudiant)* student of English; *(spécialiste)* specialist in English, Anglicist

anglo- [ãglo] PRÉF Anglo-

anglo-américain, -aine, *pl* **anglo-américains, -aines** ADJ Anglo-American
NM *Ling* American English
N **A.** Anglo-American

anglo-catholique, *pl* **anglo-catholiques** *Rel* ADJ Anglo-Catholic
N Anglo-Catholic

anglo-irlandais, -aise, *pl* **anglo-irlandais, -aises** ADJ Anglo-Irish; **l'Accord a.** the Anglo-Irish Agreement
N **A.** Anglo-Irishman, -woman

anglomane [ãgloman] N anglomaniac

anglomanie [ãglomani] NF anglomania

anglo-normand, -ande, *pl* **anglo-normands, -andes** ADJ **1** **les îles Anglo-Normandes** the Channel Islands **2** *Hist* Anglo-Norman
NM *Ling* Anglo-Norman

anglophile [ãglofil] ADJ anglophile, pro-English
N anglophile

anglophilie [ãglofili] NF anglophilia

anglophobe [ãglofɔb] ADJ anglophobic
N anglophobe

anglophobie [ãglofɔbi] NF anglophobia

anglophone [ãglofɔn] ADJ English-speaking, *Can* anglophone
N English-speaking person, *Can* Anglophone

anglo-saxon, -onne, *pl* **anglo-saxons, -onnes** [ãglosaksɔ̃, -ɔn] ADJ Anglo-Saxon; **les pays anglo-saxons** the English-speaking countries
NM *Ling* Anglo-Saxon
N **A.** English speaker; *Hist* Anglo-Saxon

> **Anglo-saxon**
>
> Note that the adjective "anglo-saxon" and the noun "Anglo-Saxon" are often used in French to refer to British and American people, culture, customs etc: "la musique anglo-saxonne", "la littérature anglo-saxonne".

angoissant [ãgwasã] ADJ *(nouvelles)* distressing; *(attente)* agonizing; *(film, livre)* frightening; *(moment)* tense, anxious; *(situation, expérience)* alarming; **le fait d'être au chômage peut être très a.** being out of work can be very distressing

angoisse [ãgwas] NF anguish, distress; *(douleur)* agony; *Méd* **une crise d'a.** an anxiety attack; **les angoisses de la mort** the pangs of death; **vivre dans l'a. de la mort** to live in fear of dying; **considérer qch avec a.** *(à l'avenir)* to dread sth; *(au passé)* to look back on sth with anguish; *Fam* **c'est l'a.!, bonjour l'a.!** what a pain *or* drag *or* bummer!

angoissé [ãgwase] ADJ distressed, anxious; **j'étais a.** my heart was in my mouth
N anxious person

angoisser [ãgwase] VT **a. qn** to fill sb with anxiety *or* distress *or* anguish; *Fam* **ça m'angoisse d'entrer dans un supermarché/d'être seul avec lui** I can't face going into a supermarket/being alone with him; **ce n'est tout de même pas ça qui t'angoisse!** you're not getting all worked up over a thing like that, are you?
VI *Fam* to worry, to get worked up; **j'angoisse à mort** I'm worried to death, I'm worried stiff
VPR **s'angoisser** to get anxious, *Fam* to get worked up; **elle s'angoisse pour un rien** she gets worked up over nothing

Angola [ãgola] NM Angola

angolais, -aise [ãgɔlɛ, -ɛz], **angolan, -ane** [ãgɔlã, -an] ADJ Angolan
N **A.** Angolan

angora [ãgɔra] ADJ *(souvent inv) (laine, pull)* angora; **poil de chèvre a.** mohair
NM **1** *(lapin)* angora rabbit; *(chat)* Persian cat; *(chèvre)* angora **2** *Tex* angora (wool)

angstrœm, angström [ãgstrœm] NM *Phys* angström

anguille [ãgij] NF *(poisson)* eel; **a. de mer** conger eel; *Fig* **il y a a. sous roche** there's something fishy going on, I smell a rat; *Fam* **elle a filé comme une a.** she ran off like greased lightning; **être souple comme une a.** to be (as) flexible as rubber, to be made of rubber

angulaire [ãgylɛr] ADJ angular; *Constr* **pierre a.** cornerstone; *Fig* **la pierre a. d'une théorie/de la société** the cornerstone of a theory/of society
NM *Phot* **grand a.** wide-angle lens

anguleux, -euse [ãgylø, -øz] ADJ *(visage, silhouette etc)* angular, bony; *(contours etc)* rough, rugged; *Fig* **caractère a.** awkward disposition

anicroche [anikrɔʃ] NF difficulty, hitch, snag; **se passer sans a.** to go smoothly *or* without a hitch

aniline [anilin] NF *Chimie* aniline

animal, -ale, -aux, -ales [animal, -o] NM animal; **société protectrice des animaux** society for the prevention of cruelty to animals; **a. domestique** pet; **l'homme est un a. social** man is a social animal; **il en a de la chance, cet a.-là!** what a lucky beggar!; **c'est un drôle d'a.** he's a funny old beggar; *Fam*

quel a.! what a brute!, what a beast!; **espèce d'a.!** you pig! VOIR GRAMMAIRE A12; A15; A27

ADJ 1 *(règne, question etc)* animal; **chaleur animale** animal warmth **2** *(instinct etc)* animal; **avoir une confiance animale en qn** to trust sb instinctively

animalerie [animalri] NF animal room; *(bâtiment séparé)* animal house

animalier [animalje] ADJ *(peinture etc)* animal; **peintre a.** animal painter

NM **1** *(peintre)* painter or sculptor of animals **2** *(dans un laboratoire)* animal keeper

animalité [animalite] NF animality, animal nature; *(des êtres humains)* animal side

animateur, -trice [animatœr, -tris] ADJ *(énergie, pouvoir)* life-giving

N **1** *Radio, TV* presenter; *(d'émission de variétés)* host, compère, MC, *Am* emcee; *(de jeu télévisé ou radiophonique)* quiz or question master; *Radio* presenter, radio personality; *(d'une émission de musique pop)* disc jockey, DJ, deejay; *(d'un débat)* moderator **2** *(sur un bateau)* entertainments officer; *(de centre aéré)* organizer; **l'animatrice d'un centre de jeunes** the organizer or youth leader of a youth club; *Mktg* **a. d'une réunion de groupe** group discussion moderator **3** *Cin* animator **4** *(personne qui a de l'entrain)* stimulating person; **il a d'excellents talents d'a.** he's extremely good at livening things up

▸▸**a. socioculturel** = community worker in social and cultural activities; **a. sportif** sports presenter; *TV* **a. vedette** star presenter; **a. des ventes** marketing executive

animation [animasjɔ̃] NF **1** *(vie)* animation, liveliness; **l'a. des rues** the bustle in the streets; **mettre de l'a. dans une soirée** to liven up a party; **il parle avec beaucoup d'a.** he speaks with great animation; **ville pleine d'a.** town full of life; *Fin* **a. du marché** buoyancy of the market; *Com* **a. des ventes** sales drive or promotion **2** *(divertissements)* activities; **faire de l'a.** to organize activities in a community **3** *Cin* animation; **film d'a.** animated film; **a. de photos** photo-animation; **a. par ordinateur** computer animation **4** *Météo* **a. satellite** satellite picture

animatique [animatik] NF *Ordinat* animation; *TV, Cin* animatic

animé [anime] ADJ **1** *(personne, discussion etc)* animated, spirited, lively; *(agité) (discussion)* heated; *(rue, quartier etc)* busy, bustling; *Fin* **marché a.** brisk or buoyant market **2** *Cin* **dessin a.** cartoon

animer [anime] VT **1** *(stimuler) (personne, chose)* to animate, to give life to; **la passion du travail l'anime** he is driven by his passion for work; **animé par un nouvel espoir** buoyed up with new hope

2 *(mener, diriger)* to move, to propel; *(discussion)* to lead, to conduct; *(entreprise)* to lead, to mastermind; *(machine)* to drive; **animé d'un sentiment de jalousie** prompted by feelings of jealousy; **animé de bonnes intentions** motivated by good intentions

3 *(rendre plus vivant) (conversation)* to enliven; *(quartier, pièce)* to liven up; *(pièce)* to brighten up

4 *Cin* to animate; *TV, Radio* **a. une émission** to present a programme

VPR **s'animer** to come to life; **la conversation s'animait** the conversation was getting more lively or was warming up; **la ville s'anime avec le marché** the town comes to life on market day; **la rue s'anime le soir** the street wakes up at night; **son visage s'anima** his face lit up; **les esprits s'animent, il va y avoir de la bagarre** people are getting worked up, there's going to be trouble

animisme [animism] NM animism

animiste [animist] ADJ, N animist

animosité [animozite] NF animosity *(contre*

for, towards), hostility *(contre* towards); **être plein d'a. envers** ou **contre** ou **pour qn** to feel great hostility towards sb; **avoir de l'a. contre** ou **pour qn** to feel animosity towards sb; **garder de l'a. contre qn** to nurse a grudge against sb; **agir par a.** to act out of spite

anion [anjɔ̃] NM *Phys* anion

anis [ani(s)] NM *(plante)* anise; *(boisson)* **(sirop d')a.** aniseed cordial; *Culin* **(graine d')a.** aniseed; **à l'a.** aniseed-flavoured

aniser [anize] VT *Culin* to flavour with aniseed

anisette [anizɛt] NF anisette

ankylose [ɑ̃kiloz] NF stiffness; *Méd* ankylosis; **une sorte d'a. gagne peu à peu tous ses membres** his limbs are gradually stiffening up

ankyloser [ɑ̃kiloze] VT *Méd* to ankylose; **être ankylosé** to be stiff

VPR **s'ankyloser** to become or get stiff; *Fig (dans un métier etc)* to get into a rut

annal, -ale, -aux, -ales [anal, -o] ADJ *Jur* valid for one year; **location annale** yearly letting

annales [anal] NFPL annals, (public) records; **les a. du crime** the annals of crime; **les a. du bac** = past examination papers (with annotations); **a. de géographie/littéraires** geographical/literary review; *Fig* **ça restera dans les a.** it will go down in (the annals of) history

annamite [anamit] ADJ Annamese, Annamite

NM *Ling* Annamese

N **A.** person from Annam

anneau, -eaux [ano] NM **1** *(cercle, bague)* ring; **a. de rideau** curtain ring; **avoir des petits anneaux d'or aux oreilles** to have little gold rings or hoops in one's ears; **toutes ses clés sont sur un même a.** *(d'un porte-clés)* all his keys are on the same ring; *Gym* **les anneaux** the rings; *Gym* **exercices aux anneaux** ring exercises; **jeu des anneaux** hoop-la

2 *Bot* annulus

3 *(de chaîne)* link; *(de cheveux)* ringlet, curl; *(d'un serpent)* coil; *(d'une clé)* bow

4 *Tech* ring, collar; *(d'un moyeu etc)* hoop; *(d'un cordage)* sling; **a. brisé** key or split ring; **a. à fiche** ring-bolt, eye-bolt; *Aut* **a. de retenue de charge** load restraining eye

5 *Naut* **a. de port** = berth with facilities for hooking up to land-based power and water supplies

▸▸**a. épiscopal** episcopal or bishop's ring; **a. nuptial** ou **de mariage** wedding ring; *Astron* **a. de Saturne** ring of Saturn

année [ane] NF SEE GRAMMAR B61 year; **Bonne A.!** Happy New Year!; **fin d'a.** end of the year; **une a. de vacances** a year's holiday; **payer à l'a.** to pay by the year; **a. après a.** year after year; **d'a. en a.** year by year; **une a. après l'autre** year in year out; **nous nous connaissons depuis bien des années** we've known each other for years; **il y a des années que je ne l'ai pas vue** I haven't seen her for years; **les années 80** the eighties, the 80s; **en quelle a. Charlemagne a-t-il été couronné?** in what year was Charlemagne crowned?; **l'a. prochaine/dernière** next/last year; **pendant les années de guerre/d'occupation** during the war years/the years of occupation; **quelle est son a. de naissance?** what year was he/she born?; **elle entre dans sa trentième a.** she'll be thirty (on her) next birthday; *Univ* **entrer en troisième a. de médecine** to go into one's third year of medicine; *Univ* **les classes de deuxième a.** the second year students, *Am* the sophomores

▸▸**a. bissextile** leap year; **a. budgétaire** financial year; **a. civile** calendar year; **a. comptable** accounting or financial year,

Am fiscal year; **a. fiscale** tax year; **a. d'imposition** year of assessment

année-lumière, *pl* **années-lumière** NF light year; **à des années-lumière** *(étoile etc)* light years away; *Fig* **nous sommes à des années-lumière l'un de l'autre** we're light years away from each other, we're worlds apart

annelé [anle] ADJ *(colonne, ver etc)* ringed

annexe [anɛks] NF **1** *(bâtiment)* annex(e); *(de ferme, château)* outbuilding **2** *(de projet de loi)* rider; *(de loi)* schedule; *(de livre, rapport)* appendix; *(de lettre)* enclosure; **en a. à ma lettre** enclosed with my letter; **en a., veuillez trouver ...** please find enclosed ...; **annexes** *Compta* notes to the accounts; *(d'un livre)* back matter, appendices **3** *Rel* chapel of ease **4** *(d'un État)* dependency **5** *Naut (d'un bateau)* dinghy

ADJ **établissement a.** annex(e); **lettre a.** covering letter; **industries annexes** subsidiary industries; **revenus annexes** supplementary income

annexer [anɛkse] VT **1** *Pol (territoire)* to annex **2** *(document etc)* to append, to attach; **pièces annexées** *(à une lettre)* enclosures

VPR **s'annexer s'a. qch** to acquire sth for oneself; **il s'est annexé la meilleure place** he grabbed the best seat for himself

annexion [anɛksjɔ̃] NF annexation

Annibal [anibal] N *Antiq* Hannibal

annihilation [aniilasjɔ̃] NF annihilation; *(des efforts, effets etc)* destruction

annihiler [aniile] VT **1** *(armée etc)* to annihilate, to destroy; *(efforts, travail etc)* to destroy; **toute forme d'agressivité l'annihile** he goes to pieces when faced with any form of aggressive behaviour **2** *Jur* to annul, to cancel

anniversaire [anivɛrsɛr] ADJ *(cérémonie)* anniversary; **la date a.** *(de la Libération etc)* the anniversary

NM *(d'une naissance)* birthday; *(d'une victoire, d'une mort etc)* anniversary; *(d'un mariage)* (wedding) anniversary; **le cinquantième a. de leur mariage** their fiftieth wedding anniversary; **c'est mon a.** it's my birthday; **mon vingtième a., l'a. de mes vingt ans** my twentieth birthday; **bon a.!** happy birthday!; **gâteau/carte d'a.** birthday cake/card

Attention: ne pas confondre **anniversary** et **birthday** lorsqu'on traduit **anniversaire**. **Birthday** s'utilise pour l'anniversaire d'une personne et **anniversary** pour celui d'un événement.

annonce [anɔ̃s] NF **1** announcement; *(surtout par écrit)* notification, notice; *Cartes* declaration, bid; *Fig* sign, indication; *Rel* **faire l'a. d'un mariage** to publish the banns; **faire une a.** to make an announcement; **les annonces de la semaine** the weekly notices; *Fig* **le retour des hirondelles est l'a. du printemps** it's a sign of spring when the swallows return; *TV, Radio* **a. de continuité** continuity announcement; *TV* **a. de programme** programme trail **2** *(de publicité etc)* advertisement; **passer une (petite) a. dans un journal/sur Minitel®** to put an ad(vert) in a newspaper/on Minitel®; **petites annonces** classified advertisements, small ads; **annonces classées** classified ads

annoncer [anɔ̃se] (j'annonçai(s); n. annonçons) VT **1** *(déclarer)* to announce, to give notice of; **a. une mauvaise nouvelle à qn** to break bad news to sb; **a. ses fiançailles en public** to announce one's engagement publicly

2 *(dans journal) (soldes etc)* to advertise **3** *(indiquer)* to promise, to foretell, to herald; **tout semble a. le succès** everything points to success; **cela n'annonce rien de bon** it looks unpromising, no *or* nothing good will come of that; **l'hirondelle annonce le printemps** the swallow is a sign that spring is on its way, the swallow heralds the approach of spring

4 a. qn to show sb in; *(lors d'une occasion officielle)* to announce sb; **se faire a.** to give one's name

VPR s'annoncer 1 *(prévenir de sa visite)* to give notice of one's arrival **2** *(se présenter) (de la situation)* **cela s'annonce bien** it looks promising; **cela s'annonce mal** it looks unpromising, no good *or* nothing good will come of that; **l'avènement de la démocratie s'annonce partout en Europe** there are signs all over Europe of the advent of democracy **3** *Suisse (se présenter, s'adresser à)* to go, to report; **annoncez-vous à la réception** report to reception

annonceur, -euse [anɔ̃sœr, -øz] N *Radio, TV (speaker)* announcer
NM *(de publicité)* advertiser

annonciateur, -trice [anɔ̃sjatœr, -tris] ADJ **signes annonciateurs du printemps** signs that spring is on the way, signs that herald the approach of spring

annonciation [anɔ̃sjasjɔ̃] NF *Rel* annunciation; **fête de l'A.** Feast of the Annunciation, Lady Day

annotateur, -trice [anɔtatœr, -tris] N *(d'un texte etc)* annotator, commentator

annotation [anɔtasjɔ̃] NF **1** *(action)* annotating, making notes **2** *(note)* annotation, note; **faire des annotations dans un texte** to annotate a text

annoter [anɔte] VT *(texte)* to annotate; *(livre)* to write notes in; *(épreuves)* to mark up

annuaire [anɥɛr] NM annual; *(d'un organisme international)* yearbook; *Ordinat* directory; **l'a. du téléphone** *ou* **téléphonique** the telephone directory; *Fam* the phone book; **je suis dans l'a.** I'm in the book; **je ne suis pas dans l'a., je suis sur la liste rouge** I'm not in the (phone) book, I'm ex-directory; **a. du commerce** trade directory; **a. papier** printed directory; **a. électronique** electronic directory; **a. des marées** tide table; **l'A. militaire** the Army list, *Am* the Army Register; **l'A. de la Marine** the Navy List; **a. de l'université** university calendar

annualisation [anɥalizasjɔ̃] NF annualization; **l'a. du temps de travail permettra de répondre à une demande saisonnière** calculating working hours across the year will enable us to meet seasonal demand

annualiser [anɥalize] VT to annualize

annuel, -elle [anɥɛl] ADJ annual, yearly; **budget a.** annual budget; **chiffre d'affaires a.** annual *or* yearly turnover; **congé a.** annual leave; **plante annuelle** annual; **rente annuelle** annuity; **magistrature annuelle =** judicial office held only for one year

annuellement [anɥɛlmɑ̃] ADV annually, yearly

annuitaire [anɥiter] ADJ *Compta, Fin (dette)* redeemable by yearly payments

annuité [anɥite] NF **1** *(dans le remboursement d'un emprunt)* annual instalment *or Am* installment *or* repayment; *Compta* **a. constante** *(de remboursement)* fixed annual payment; *Compta* **a. d'amortissement** annual depreciation *or* writedown **2** *Can, Suisse (rente)* annuity

annulaire [anɥler] ADJ annular, ring-shaped
NM ring finger, third finger

annulation [anylasjɔ̃] NF **1** *(d'un contrat, d'une commande, de vacances etc)* cancelling, cancellation; *Jur etc (d'un mariage)* annulment; *(d'un jugement)* quashing, setting aside; *(d'un acte judiciaire)* annulment, re-

peal; *(d'un contrat)* voidance; *(d'un testament)* setting aside; *Com* **a. rétroactive** retroactive cancellation; **a. de dernière minute** late cancellation **2** *Ordinat* deletion; **a. d'entrée** *(commande)* cancel entry; **a. des révisions** *(commande)* undo changes

annuler [anyle] VT **1** *(contrat, commande etc)* to cancel; *(dette)* to cancel, to write off; *(marché)* to call off; *Jur (mariage)* to annul; *(loi, jugement)* to render void, to repeal, to rescind; *(testament)* to set aside; **a. un ordre de grève** to call off a strike **2** *Banque (chèque etc)* to cancel **3** *(remplacer)* to supersede, to cancel; **ce catalogue annule les précédents** this catalogue supersedes all previous issues **4** *Ordinat* to cancel; *(opération)* to undo; **a. les révisions** *(commande)* undo changes **5** *Ftbl (but)* to disallow
VPR s'annuler to cancel each other out

anoblir [anɔblir] VT **a. qn** to ennoble sb, to raise sb to the peerage

> Do not confuse with **ennoblir**, which means **to elevate morally**.

anoblissement [anɔblismɑ̃] NM ennoblement (**de** of); **lettres d'a.** letters patent of nobility

anode [anɔd] NF *Élec* anode

anodin [anɔdɛ̃] ADJ harmless, innocuous; *(blessure, changement)* slight, minor; *(infection)* mild; **cette remarque n'était pas anodine** this remark was not as innocent as it might seem; **une personne tout à fait anodine** a totally insignificant person; *Méd* **remèdes anodins** painkillers; *Fig* **moyen/ remède a.** ineffective method/remedy; **mensonge a.** white lie

anodique [anɔdik] ADJ *Élec* anodic, anodal; *(courant)* anode

anomalie [anɔmali] NF *Gram, Astron, Biol* anomaly; *Méd* disorder; **si vous remarquez la moindre a. dans la comptabilité** if you should notice the slightest irregularity in the accounting; **il y a une a. dans le fonctionnement de la machine** the machine has a malfunction

ânon [anɔ̃] NM little donkey; *(très jeune)* baby donkey

ânonnement [anɔnmɑ̃] NM mumbling, faltering tone

ânonner [anɔne] VT *(paroles)* to stumble *or* blunder through; **â. une récitation** to recite sth falteringly
VI to mumble

anonymat [anɔnima] NM anonymity; **garder l'a.** to remain anonymous; **faire qch dans l'a. le plus complet** to do sth anonymously

anonyme [anɔnim] ADJ *(écrivain, lettre etc)* anonymous; *Fig (décor, intérieur)* impersonal, anonymous

anonymement [anɔnimmɑ̃] ADV anonymously

anophèle [anɔfɛl] NM *Zool* anopheles mosquito

anorak [anɔrak] NM anorak

anorexie [anɔrɛksi] NF *Méd* anorexia; **a. mentale** anorexia nervosa; **faire de l'a.** to suffer from anorexia

anorexique [anɔrɛksik] ADJ, N *Méd* anorexic

anormal, -ale, -aux, -ales [anɔrmal, -o] ADJ **1** *(non-conforme)* abnormal; **personne d'une maigreur anormale** abnormally thin person; **évolution anormale d'une maladie** unexpected development of an illness; **enfants anormaux** *(en intelligence)* educationally subnormal children; **il fait un temps a.** the weather is abnormal, *Fam* the weather is all wrong for this time of year; **il fait une chaleur anormale** it's abnormally hot **2** *(injuste)* unjust, unfair; **il est a. que ... +** *subjt*

is unfair that ... **3** *(extraordinaire)* extraordinary; **ce qu'il y a d'a., c'est que ...** the strange *or* extraordinary thing is that ...
N *Méd, Psy* mentally defective person; *Fam* **c'est un a.** he's round the bend
NM **l'a..., c'est que ...** *(injuste)* what's unjust is that ...; *(extraordinaire)* what's unusual is that ...

anormalement [anɔrmalmɑ̃] ADV abnormally

anormalité [anɔrmalite] NF abnormality

ANPE [aɛnpeø] NF *(abrév* **Agence nationale pour l'emploi)** *Br* ≃ Jobcentre, *Can* ≃ CEC; **être à l'A.** ≃ to be registered with the Jobcentre

ANRS [aɛnɛres] NF *(abrév* **Agence nationale de recherches sur le sida)** Aids research institute

anse [ɑ̃s] NF **1** *(d'une cruche, d'un panier)* handle; *(d'un cadenas)* shackle; *Fig* **faire danser** *ou* **valser l'a. du panier** *(d'un domestique etc)* to fiddle the books; *Archit* **voûte en a. de panier** basket-handle arch; *Fig* **faire le pot** *ou* **le panier à deux anses** to have someone on each arm **2** *(d'une corde etc)* loop, bight; *Anat* loop; **a. à vis** screw eye (bolt) **3** *Géog* cove

antagonique [ɑ̃tagɔnik] ADJ *(forces, personnes etc)* antagonistic; *(intérêts, influences)* conflicting

antagonisme [ɑ̃tagɔnism] NM *(de personne), Physiol* antagonism

antagoniste [ɑ̃tagɔnist] ADJ antagonistic, opposed; **avoir des positions antagonistes** to have opposing *or* conflicting opinions; **les partis antagonistes** the opposing parties; **force a.** antagonistic force; *(de contrôle)* controlling force, countercheck; *Anat* **muscles antagonistes** antagonists; **couple a.** opposing couple
N antagonist, opponent

antalgique [ɑ̃talʒik] ADJ, NM *Pharm* analgesic

antan [ɑ̃tɑ̃] ADV *Arch, Litt* **d'a.** of yesteryear; **où sont les neiges d'a.?** where are the snows of yesteryear?

antarctique [ɑ̃tarktik] *Géog* ADJ Antarctic; **cercle a.** Antarctic circle
NM **l'A.** Antarctica, the Antarctic; **une expédition dans l'A.** an Antarctic expedition

anté- [ɑ̃te] PRÉF ante-, pre-

antécédence [ɑ̃tesedɑ̃s] NF *Phil, Géog* antecedence

antécédent [ɑ̃tesedɑ̃] ADJ previous, antecedent, anterior (**à** to)
NM *Ling, Phil* antecedent SEE GRAMMAR A32-3; B22-3
NMPL **antécédents** previous history, past record, *Fml* antecedents; **antécédents médicaux** medical history; **il y a des antécédents cancéreux dans ma famille** my family has a history of cancer; **avoir de bons/mauvais antécédents** to have a good/bad record

antéchrist [ɑ̃tekrist] NM antichrist

antédiluvien, -ienne [ɑ̃tedilyvjɛ̃, -jɛn] ADJ antediluvian; *Fam* **ma télévision est antédiluvienne** my television is an antique; *Fam* **c'est une relation antédiluvienne** I've known him/her for donkey's years

antémémoire [ɑ̃tememwar] NF *Ordinat* cache (memory); **mettre en a.** to cache

anténatal, -ale, -aux, -ales [ɑ̃tenatal, -o] ADJ *Méd* antenatal

antenne [ɑ̃ten] NF VOIR GRAMMAIRE A14 **1** *Radio* aerial, antenna; *(d'un satellite, d'un robot)* antenna; **a. de télévision** television aerial; **à l'a.** on-air; **être à l'a.** to be on the air; **on est à l'a. dans cinq minutes** we'll be on the air in five minutes; **prendre/garder l'a.** to go/stay on the air; **passer à l'a.** *(d'une émission)* to be broadcast *or* televised;

(*d'une personne*) to be on television/radio; **rendre l'a.** (*d'un présentateur etc*) to go back, to return (to the studio/*etc*); **je dois rendre l'a.** I have to hand over now; **je vous passe l'a., à vous l'a.!** (I'll hand) over to you; **hors a.** off-air; **déclarer hors a. que …** to declare off the air that …; **sur notre a.** *Radio* on this station; *TV* on this channel

2 (*d'un insecte*) antenna, feeler; *Fig* **avoir des antennes** to have a sixth sense, to be perceptive, to pick up on things; *Fig* **avoir ses antennes quelque part** to have one's feelers out, to have informers

3 *Mil* **a. chirurgicale** advanced surgical unit

4 (*de société*) branch

▸▸ **a. en cadre** loop aerial; *TV* **a. collective** shared aerial; *Aut* **a. électrique** electric aerial; **a. d'émission** broadcast antenna; **a. fermée** loop aerial; *Aut* **a. manuelle** manual aerial; **a. parabolique** (satellite) dish, *Am* dish antenna; *Aviat* **a. pendante** trailing aerial; **a. de réception** receiver aerial, receiving aerial *or* antenna; **a. satellite** satellite antenna; **a. télescopique** telescopic mast; **a. terrestre** ground antenna; **a. en V** rabbit's ears

antépénultième [ātepenyltjɛm] ADJ antepenultimate, third (from) last

antérieur [āterjœr] ADJ **1** (*période*) former; (*date*) earlier; (*année*) previous; (*engagement*) prior; **tous ces événements sont antérieurs à la révolution** all these events took place before the revolution; **cela est a. à ma naissance** that was before I was born; **a. au mariage** premarital; **dans une vie antérieure** in a previous life *or* existence; *Gram* **futur a.** future perfect VOIR GRAMMAIRE A52; *Gram* **passé a.** past anterior SEE GRAMMAR B31

2 (*muscle*) anterior; (*membre etc*) fore; (*mur, voyelle etc*) front

antérieurement [āterjœrmā] ADV previously, earlier; **cela s'est passé a. à notre rencontre** that happened before we met

antériorité [āterjɔrite] NF precedence; *Gram* anteriority

anthère [āter] NF *Bot* anther

anthologie [ātɔlɔʒi] NF anthology

anthracite [ātrasit] NM **1** *Minér* anthracite **2** (*couleur*) charcoal grey
▪ ADJ INV charcoal grey

anthrax [ātraks] NM *Méd* carbuncle; **a. malin** anthrax

anthropique [ātrɔpik] ADJ anthropogenic

anthropocentrique [ātrɔpɔsātrik] ADJ anthropocentric

anthropocentrisme [ātrɔpɔsātrism] NM anthropocentrism

anthropoïde [ātrɔpɔid] ADJ anthropoid
▪ NM anthropoid ape

anthropologie [ātrɔpɔlɔʒi] NF anthropology

anthropologique [ātrɔpɔlɔʒik] ADJ anthropological

anthropologiste [ātrɔpɔlɔʒist], **anthropologue** [ātrɔpɔlɔg] N anthropologist

anthropométrie [ātrɔpɔmetri] NF anthropometry

anthropométrique [ātrɔpɔmetrik] ADJ anthropometric(al); *Admin* **service a.** criminal anthropometry department, *Br* ≃ Criminal Records Office; **fiche a.** ≃ record containing fingerprints and details of height, weight etc

anthropomorphe [ātrɔpɔmɔrf] ADJ anthropomorphic

anthropomorphisme [ātrɔpɔmɔrfism] NM anthropomorphism

anthropophage [ātrɔpɔfaʒ] ADJ cannibalistic, man-eating
▪ N cannibal

anthropophagie [ātrɔpɔfaʒi] NF cannibalism

anti[1] [āti] PRÉF anti-

anti[2] PRÉF ante-

antiacnéique [ātiakneik] ADJ (*médicament, crème, traitement*) anti-acne

antiadhésif [ātiadezif] ADJ (*revêtement etc*) nonstick
▪ NM antiadhesive; **casserole recouverte d'un a.** nonstick saucepan

antiaérien, -ienne [ātiaerjɛ̃, -jɛn] ADJ (*arme, défense*) anti-aircraft; **abri a.** air-raid shelter

anti-âge ADJ INV (*traitement, crème*) anti-ageing

antialcoolique [ātialkɔlik] ADJ (*ligue etc*) temperance

antialcoolisme [ātialkɔlism] NM temperance, teetotalism

anti-aliassage [ātialjasaʒ] NM *Ordinat* anti-aliasing

antiallergique [ātialɛrʒik] ADJ hypoallergenic

antiasthénique [ātiastenik] ADJ *Méd* antiasthenic

antiatomique [ātiatɔmik] ADJ antinuclear; **abri a.** fall-out shelter; **manifestation a.** ban-the-bomb *or* anti-nuclear demonstration

antibactérien [ātibakterjɛ̃] ADJ antibacterial
▪ NM antibacterial product

antibalistique [ātibalistik] ADJ (*missile*) antiballistic

antibiogramme [ātibjɔgram] NM *Méd* antibiogram

antibiotique [ātibjɔtik] *Pharm* ADJ antibiotic; **un traitement a.** a course of antibiotics
▪ NM antibiotic; **être sous antibiotiques** to be on antibiotics

antiblocage [ātiblɔkaʒ] NM *Aut* **a. de freins** anti-lock braking system, anti-lock brakes; **a. des roues** anti-lock brakes

antibrouillage [ātibrujaʒ] NM *Radio etc* anti-jamming

antibrouillard [ātibrujar] ADJ, NM *Aut* (*phare*) **a.** fog lamp

antibruit [ātibrɥi] ADJ INV (*mur*) soundproof; **lutte a.** noise abatement campaign

antibuée [ātibɥe] ADJ, NM *Aut* (*dispositif*) **a.** demister

anticalcaire [ātikalkɛr] NM (*qui empêche les dépôts*) scale preventer; (*qui détartre*) scale remover

anticancéreux, -euse [ātikāserø, -øz] ADJ **centre/sérum a.** cancer hospital/serum

anticasseurs [ātikasœr] ADJ INV *Pol* **Loi a. =** law banning violent behaviour during demonstrations

anticathode [ātikatɔd] NF anticathode

antichambre [ātiʃābr] NF waiting room, antechamber; **pilier d'a.** (*d'un ministre etc*) hanger-on; **faire a.** to hang around in the waiting room; *Fig* to wait patiently to see sb

antichar [ātiʃar] *Mil* ADJ anti-tank
▪ NM anti-tank device

antichoc [ātiʃɔk] ADJ INV shock-proof; *Méd* **traitement a.** anti-shock treatment

antichute [ātiʃyt] ADJ **traitement a.** treatment to stop hair loss

anticipatif, -ive [ātisipatif, -iv] ADJ anticipatory, anticipative; **paiement a.** prepayment

anticipation [ātisipasjɔ̃] NF anticipation; **payer par a.** to pay in advance; **demander l'a. d'un paiement** to ask for payment in advance; **littérature d'a.** science fiction; **film d'a.** science-fiction film

anticipé [ātisipe] ADJ (*paiement*) advance; (*départ, retour*) early; **prendre sa retraite anticipée** to take early retirement; **avec mes remerciements anticipés** thanking you in advance

anticiper [ātisipe] VT to forecast; (*réaction, réponse*) to anticipate; (*action*) to forestall; **plaisir anticipé** anticipated pleasure; **j'anticipais déjà le pire** I was expecting the worst; *Fin* **dividende anticipé** advance dividend; **remboursement anticipé** redemption before due date; **a. un paiement** to pay in advance
▪ VI to anticipate, to look *or* think ahead; *Sport etc* to anticipate one's opponent's moves; **n'anticipons pas** let's not look *or* think too far ahead; **a. sur les événements** to anticipate events; **je ne voudrais pas a. sur ce qui sera dit plus tard** I don't wish to anticipate *or* guess what will be said later; **a. sur ses revenus** to spend one's income in advance

anticlérical, -ale, -aux, -ales [ātiklerikal, -o] ADJ, N anticlerical

anticléricalisme [ātiklerikalism] NM anticlericalism

anticlinal, -aux [ātiklinal, -o] NM *Géol* anticline

anticoagulant [ātikɔagylā] ADJ, NM *Pharm* anticoagulant

anticolonialisme [ātikɔlɔnjalism] NM anticolonialism

anticolonialiste [ātikɔlɔnjalist] ADJ anticolonialist

anticommercial, -iale, -iaux, -iales [ātikɔmɛrsjal, -jo] ADJ (*attitude, pratique*) unbusinesslike

anticommunisme [ātikɔmynism] NM *Pol* anticommunism; **faire de l'a. primaire** to be a dyed-in-the-wool anticommunist

anticommuniste [ātikɔmynist] ADJ, N *Pol* anticommunist

anticonceptionnel, -elle [ātikɔ̃sɛpsjɔnɛl] ADJ (*pilule*) contraceptive; (*mesures etc*) contraceptive, birth-control

anticonformisme [ātikɔ̃fɔrmism] NM nonconformism; **faire de l'a.** to be a nonconformist

anticonformiste [ātikɔ̃fɔrmist] ADJ, N nonconformist

anticonstitutionnel, -elle [ātikɔ̃stitysjɔnɛl] ADJ anticonstitutional, unconstitutional

anticonstitutionnellement [ātikɔ̃stitysjɔnɛlmā] ADV unconstitutionally

anticorps [ātikɔr] NM antibody; **a. monoclonal** monoclonal antibody

anti-corrosion ADJ corrosion-resistant

anti-crevaison ADJ *Aut* (*pneu*) run-flat

anticyclique [ātisiklik] ADJ anticyclic

anticyclonal, -ale, -aux, -ales [ātisiklɔnal, -o] ADJ *Météo* anticyclonic; **aire anticyclonale** high-pressure area

anticyclone [ātisiklon] *Météo* NM anticyclone
▪ ADJ **abri a.** cyclone cellar

anticyclonique [ātisiklɔnik] ADJ *Météo* anticyclonic

antidate [ātidat] NF antedate

antidater [ātidate] VT to backdate; (*contrat etc*) to antedate

antidéflagrant [ātideflagrā] ADJ explosion-proof

antidémarrage [ātidemaraʒ] NM *Aut* engine immobilizer; **a. codé** (security-coded) immobilizer

antidémocratique [ātidemɔkratik] ADJ antidemocratic, undemocratic

antidépresseur [ātideprɛsœr] ADJ, NM antidepressant

antidérapant [ãtiderapã] *Aut* ADJ *(pneu, route)* non-skid; *(semelle, tapis)* non-slip NM *(pneu)* non-skid tyre; *(revêtement)* non-slip coating

antidétonant [ãtidetɔnã] ADJ, NM anti-knock

antidiphtérique [ãtidifterik] ADJ vaccin a. diphtheria vaccine

antidiscriminatoire [ãtidiskriminatwar] ADJ *(mesures, politique)* anti-discriminatory

antidopage [ãtidɔpaʒ] NM, **antidoping** [ãtidɔpiŋ] NM *Sport* contrôle a. drug(s) test; être positif au contrôle a. to fail a drugs test

antidote [ãtidɔt] NM *Méd, Fig* antidote (contre for)

antidumping [ãtidœmpiŋ] ADJ *(loi, législation)* anti-dumping

anti-éblouissant ADJ *Aut (phares)* anti-dazzle

antiéconomique [ãtiekɔnɔmik] ADJ *(mesure)* uneconomic

antiémétique [ãtiemetik] ADJ, NM *Méd* antiemetic

antiémeute [ãtiemøt] ADJ antiriot

antienne [ãtjɛn] NF antiphon; *Fig* c'est toujours la même a. he says that all the time, it's always the same old tune; *Fig* chanter toujours la même a. to be always harping on the same subject

antiesclavagisme [ãtiesklavaʒism] NM *Pol* anti-slavery movement, abolitionism

antiesclavagiste [ãtiesklavaʒist] ADJ anti-slavery, abolitionist N person opposed to slavery, abolitionist

antifading [ãtifadiŋ] NM INV automatic volume control

antifasciste [ãtifasist, -ʃist] ADJ, N *Pol* antifascist

antifongique [ãtifɔ̃ʒik] ADJ *Méd* fungicidal NM fungicide

anti-friction NM INV babbit, bearing *or* white metal

anti-g [ãtiʒe] ADJ INV *Aviat* vêtement *ou* combinaison a. (anti) G suit

antigang [ãtigãg] ADJ brigade a. = police squad concerned with combating terrorism and organized crime

antigaz [ãtigaz] ADJ anti-gas

antigel [ãtiʒel] NM antifreeze

antigène [ãtiʒɛn] NM *Méd* antigen

antigivre [ãtiʒivr] ADJ *Aviat* anti-icing; *Aut* de-icing NM *Aviat* anti-icer; *Aut* de-icer

antiglisse [ãtiglis] ADJ INV vêtements/tissu a. non-slip clothing/material

antigrippal, -ale, -aux, -ales [ãtigripal, -o] ADJ *(médicament, remède etc)* anti-flu

antihalo [ãtialo] NM *Phot* anti-halo

antihéros [ãtiero] NM antihero

antihistaminique [ãtiistaminik] ADJ, NM *Méd* antihistamine

antihygiénique [ãtiiʒjenik] ADJ unhygienic, insanitary

anti-inflammatoire ADJ *Méd* anti-inflammatory

anti-inflationniste ADJ *Écon* anti-inflation(ary)

antillais, -aise [ãtijɛ, -ɛz] ADJ West Indian N A. West Indian

Antilles [ãtij] NFPL les A. the (French) West Indies; la mer des A. the Caribbean (Sea)

antilog [ãtilɔg] NM *Math Fam* antilog

antilogarithme [ãtilɔgaritm] NM *Math* antilogarithm

antilope [ãtilɔp] NF antelope VOIR GRAMMAIRE A12

antimagnétique [ãtimaɲetik] ADJ anti-magnetic

antimatière [ãtimatjɛr] NF antimatter

antimilitarisme [ãtimilitarism] NM anti-militarism

antimilitariste [ãtimilitarist] ADJ, N anti-militarist

antimissile [ãtimisil] ADJ anti-missile; missile a. anti-missile missile

antimite(s) [ãtimit] ADJ *(vêtement)* moth-proof; *(produit)* moth-repellent; bombe a. mothkiller NM antimite mothkiller, moth-repellent

antimoine [ãtimwan] NM *Chimie* antimony

antimonarchique [ãtimɔnarʃik] ADJ anti-monarchic(al)

antimonarchisme [ãtimɔnarʃism] NM antimonarchism

antimonarchiste [ãtimɔnarʃist] N anti-monarchist

antimondialisation [ãtimɔ̃djalizasjɔ̃] NF antiglobalization

antimondialiste [ãtimɔ̃djalist] ADJ antiglobalist N *(personne)* antiglobalist

anti-mousse ADJ INV *(pouvoir, agent)* anti-foam

antimycosique [ãtimikɔzik] ADJ, NM *Méd* antimycotic

antinazi, -ie [ãtinazi] ADJ, N anti-Nazi

antinévralgique [ãtinevralʒik] ADJ, NM *Pharm* antineuralgic

antinomie [ãtinɔmi] NF antinomy

antinomique [ãtinɔmik] ADJ antinomic

antinucléaire [ãtinykleer] ADJ anti-nuclear

Antiope ® [ãtjɔp] NM *TV* = information system available via the French television network, *Br* ≃ Teletext®

antioxydant [ãtiɔksidã] NM anti-oxidant

anti-paludéen, -enne *Pharm* ADJ anti-malarial NM antimalarial (drug)

antipaludique [ãtipalydik] *Pharm* ADJ antimalaria(l) NM antimalarial (drug)

antipape [ãtipap] NM *Hist, Rel* antipope

antiparasitage [ãtiparazitaʒ] NM *Radio, Élec* suppression

antiparasite [ãtiparazit] *Radio, Aut etc* NM suppressor, interference eliminator ADJ dispositif a. suppressor, interference eliminator

antiparlementaire [ãtiparləmãter] ADJ *Pol* antiparliamentary

antiparlementarisme [ãtiparləmãtarism] NM antiparliamentarianism

antipathie [ãtipati] NF antipathy; avoir *ou* éprouver de l'a. pour qn to have antipathy for *or* feel antipathy towards sb; éprouver une grande a. pour qn to have great antipathy for *or* feel great antipathy towards sb

antipathique [ãtipatik] ADJ unpleasant; je le trouve très a. I don't like him at all; je ne le trouve pas du tout a. I quite like him

antipelliculaire [ãtipelikyler] ADJ shampooing a. (anti-)dandruff shampoo

antipersonnel [ãtipersɔnel] ADJ INV *Mil* antipersonnel

antiphone [ãtifɔn] NM *Rel* antiphon

antiphrase [ãtifraz] NF *Ling* antiphrasis; dire qch par a. to say sth ironically

antipodal, -ale, -aux, -ales [ãtipɔdal, -o] ADJ antipodean

antipode [ãtipɔd] NM *Géog* antipodes; la Nouvelle-Zélande est l'a. *ou* aux antipodes de la France New Zealand is on the other side of the world from France; aux antipodes at *or* in the antipodes; *Fig* diametrically opposed, poles apart; *Fig* son opinion est à l'a. *ou* aux antipodes de la mienne his opinion is quite the opposite of mine *or* is poles apart from mine

antipoétique [ãtipɔetik] ADJ unpoetic

antipoison [ãtipwazɔ̃] ADJ *Méd* centre a. poisons unit

antipoliomyélite [ãtipɔljɔmjelit] ADJ vaccination a. polio vaccination

antipollution [ãtipɔlysjɔ̃] ADJ INV *(mesures)* anti-pollution

antiprogressif, -ive [ãtiprɔgresif, -iv] ADJ reactionary

antiprotectionniste [ãtiprɔtɛksjɔnist] ADJ *(ligne d'action)* free-trade N antiprotectionist, free trader

antipsychiatrie [ãtipsikjatri] NF antipsychiatry

antipyrétique [ãtipiretik] ADJ, NM *Méd* antipyretic, antifebrile

antipyrine [ãtipirin] NF *Méd* antipyrine

antiquaille [ãtikaj] NF *Péj* worthless old junk

antiquaire [ãtiker] N antique dealer

antique [ãtik] ADJ old, ancient; *(mobilier)* antique, *Péj* old-fashioned, antiquated; la Grèce a. ancient *or* classical Greece NM 1 *(art)* art from the antiquity; *(objets d'art de l'Antiquité)* works of art from the antiquity 2 l'a. the antique, classical antiquity 3 *Typ* antique

antiquité [ãtikite] NF 1 *(ancienneté)* antiquity 2 *(temps anciens)* ancient times, antiquity; ça remonte à la plus haute a. that goes back *or* dates back to time immemorial; connu de toute a. known (about) since time immemorial 3 *Hist* l'a. grecque ancient Greek civilization 4 antiquités *(meubles etc anciens)* antiques; magasin d'antiquités antique shop 5 les antiquités the works of classical antiquity

antirabique [ãtirabik] ADJ *Méd (vaccin)* anti-rabies

antirachitique [ãtiraʃitik] ADJ *Méd* antirachitic

antiracisme [ãtirasism] NM antiracialism, anti-racism

antiraciste [ãtirasist] ADJ, N antiracist, antiracialist

antiradar [ãtiradar] ADJ anti-radar NM anti-radar device

antireflet [ãtiraflɛ] ADJ INV nonreflective; *Ordinat* non-reflecting, antiglare

antiréglementaire [ãtireglǝmãter] ADJ against regulations

antireligieux, -ieuse [ãtirǝliʒjø, -jøz] ADJ antireligious

antirépublicain, -aine [ãtirepyblikɛ̃, -ɛn] ADJ, N antirepublican

antirétroviral, -ale, -aux, -ales [ãtiretroviral, -o] ADJ *(molécule, traitement)* antiretroviral

antirévolutionnaire [ãtirevɔlysjɔner] ADJ, N antirevolutionary

antirides [ãtirid] ADJ INV *(crème)* anti-wrinkle

anti-roman, pl anti-romans NM *Littér* anti-novel

antirouille [ãtiruj] NM rust preventive ADJ INV *(métal)* rustproof, non-rusting; *(produit, traitement)* rust-preventing

antiroulis [ãtiruli] NM *Naut, Aviat* (gyro) stabilizer; *Aut* anti-roll bar

anti-scintillements ADJ *Ordinat* flicker-free

antiscorbutique [ãtiskɔrbytik] ADJ, NM *Pharm* antiscorbutic

antisèche [ãtisɛʃ] NF *Fam* crib sheet

antiségrégationniste [ãtisegregasjɔnist] ADJ, N antisegregationist

antisémite [ɑ̃tisemit] **ADJ** anti-semitic
N anti-semite

antisémitique [ɑ̃tisemitik] **ADJ** anti-semitic

antisémitisme [ɑ̃tisemitism] **NM** anti-semitism

antisepsie [ɑ̃tisɛpsi] **NF** *Méd* antisepsis

antiseptique [ɑ̃tisɛptik] **ADJ, NM** *Méd* antiseptic

antisérum [ɑ̃tiserɔm] **NM** *Méd* antiserum

antisionisme [ɑ̃tizjɔnism] **NM** anti-Zionism

antisioniste [ɑ̃tizjɔnist] **ADJ, N** anti-Zionist

antisocial, -iale, -iaux, -iales [ɑ̃tisɔsjal, -jo] **ADJ** antisocial

antisolaire [ɑ̃tisɔlɛr] **ADJ** sun-reflective

anti-sous-marin **ADJ** *Mil* anti-submarine

antisoviétique [ɑ̃tisɔvjetik] **ADJ** anti-Soviet

antispasmodique [ɑ̃tispasmɔdik] **ADJ, NM** *Pharm* antispasmodic

antisportif, -ive [ɑ̃tispɔrtif, -iv] **ADJ** (*opposé au sport*) anti-sport; (*contraire à l'esprit du sport*) unsportsmanlike, unsporting

antistrophe [ɑ̃tistrɔf] **NF** antistrophe

antisudoral, -aux [ɑ̃tisydɔral, -o] **ADJ, NM** antiperspirant

antitabac [ɑ̃titaba] **ADJ INV** (*lutte, campagne*) anti-smoking

antiterroriste [ɑ̃titɛrɔrist] **ADJ** anti-terrorist, anti-terrorism

antitétanique [ɑ̃titetanik] *Méd* **ADJ** antitetanus
NM antitetanus serum

antithèse [ɑ̃titɛz] **NF** antithesis; *Fig* **je suis l'a. de ma sœur** I'm the opposite of my sister

antithétique [ɑ̃titetik] **ADJ** antithetic(al)

antitoxine [ɑ̃titɔksin] **NF** *Méd* antitoxin

antitoxique [ɑ̃titɔksik] **ADJ** *Méd* antitoxic

antitrust [ɑ̃titrœst] **ADJ INV** anti-monopoly, antitrust; **lois a.** anti-monopoly *or* antitrust laws

antituberculeux, -euse [ɑ̃titybɛrkylø, -øz] **ADJ** *Méd* antitubercular; **centre a.** tuberculosis centre

antitussif, -ive [ɑ̃titysif, -iv] **ADJ, NM** *Méd* **sirop a.** cough mixture *or* syrup *or* medicine

antivariolique [ɑ̃tivarjɔlik] **ADJ** *Méd* **vaccin a.** smallpox vaccine

antivénérien [ɑ̃tivenerjɛ̃] **ADJ** *Méd* antivenereal

antivenimeux, -euse [ɑ̃tivənimø, -øz] **ADJ** antivenin

anti-vent, *pl* **anti-vents NM** (*pour microphone*) wind gag

antivieillissement [ɑ̃tivjejismɑ̃] **NM** (*produit qui ralentit le vieillissement*) anti-ageing product; **traitement a.** anti-ageing treatment

antiviral, -ale, -aux, -ales [ɑ̃tiviral, -o] **ADJ** *Méd* antivirus

antivirus [ɑ̃tivirys] **NM** antivirus

antivivisection(n)iste [ɑ̃tivivisɛksjɔnist] **N** antivivisectionist
ADJ antivivisection(ist); **société a.** antivivisection society

antivol [ɑ̃tivɔl] **ADJ INV** (*équipement*) anti-theft; (*serrure*) thief-proof; *Aut* **alarme a.** car alarm
NM (*pour les cycles*) lock; (*pour les voitures*) steering lock; *Aut* **a. de direction** steering column lock; *Aut* **a.-contact** ignition lock

antonomase [ɑ̃tɔnɔmaz] **NF** *Litt* antonomasia

antonyme [ɑ̃tɔnim] **ADJ** antonymous
NM antonym

antre [ɑ̃tr] **NM 1** (*caverne*) cave, cavern; (*d'animaux, de brigands*), *Fig* (*d'une personne*) den, lair; **un a. de voleurs** a den of thieves **2** *Anat* antrum, sinus

anurie [anyri] **NF** *Méd* anuria

anus [anys] **NM** *Anat* anus; *Chir* **a. artificiel** colostomy

Anvers [ɑ̃vɛr(s)] **N** Antwerp

anversois, -oise [ɑ̃vɛrswa, -waz] **ADJ** of/from Antwerp
N A. (*natif*) native of Antwerp; (*habitant*) inhabitant of Antwerp

anxiété [ɑ̃ksjete] **NF** anxiety; **éprouver de l'a.** to feel anxious; **avec a.** anxiously

anxieusement [ɑ̃ksjøzmɑ̃] **ADV** anxiously

anxieux, -ieuse [ɑ̃ksjø, -jøz] **ADJ 1** (*inquiet*) anxious, uneasy **2 a. de faire qch** anxious *or* impatient to do sth; **il est a. de partir** he's anxious *or* impatient to leave
N worrier

anxiogène [ɑ̃ksjɔʒɛn] **ADJ** causing anxiety

anxiolytique [ɑ̃ksjɔlitik] **ADJ** anxiolitic
NM tranquillizer

AOC [aose] **NF** (*abrév* **appellation d'origine contrôlée**) = guarantee of quality

aorte [aɔrt] **NF** *Anat* aorta

aortique [aɔrtik] **ADJ** *Anat* aortic, aortal

août [u(t)] **NM** August; **en a., au mois d'a.** in (the month of) August; **le premier/le sept a.** (on) the first/the seventh of August, (on) August the first/the seventh, *Am* (on) August first/seventh; **le quinze a.** the Assumption, Assumption Day; **à la mi-a.** in mid-August SEE GRAMMAR A81–2; B60–2

aoûtat [auta] **NM** harvest mite, *Am* chigger

aoûtien, -ienne [ausjɛ̃, -jɛn] **N** August holidaymaker *or Am* vacationer

apache [apaʃ] **NM A.** Apache

apaisant [apɛzɑ̃] **ADJ** (*geste, paroles*) appeasing; (*nouvelles, effet etc*) soothing, calming

apaisement [apɛzmɑ̃] **NM** (*d'une personne en colère, des dieux*) appeasement, appeasing; (*d'une personne en colère ou inquiète*) calming (down) (*de la douleur*) alleviation; **donner des apaisements à qn** (*paroles*) to give (re)assurance to sb, to (re)assure sb

apaiser [apeze] **VT** (*personne en colère, dieux*) to appease, to pacify; (*personne en colère ou inquiète*) to calm (down); (*douleur, enfant*) to soothe; (*faim*) to appease, to satisfy; (*soif*) to quench; (*craintes*) to calm, to allay
VPR **s'apaiser** (*d'une personne*) to calm down; (*du vent*) to drop, to subside; (*de la douleur, des craintes*) to subside; **la foule s'apaisait** the crowd was calming down *or* becoming quieter

apanage [apanaʒ] **NM** prerogative; **elle croit avoir l'a. de la sagesse** she thinks she has a monopoly on wisdom

aparté [aparte] **NM 1** *Théâtre* aside, stage whisper; **en a.** aside, in a stage whisper **2** (*entre deux personnes*) private conversation; **en a.** in private, as an aside; **il le lui a dit en a.** he took him/her aside *or* to one side to tell him/her

apartheid [aparted] **NM** apartheid

apathie [apati] **NF** apathy, listlessness; **le malade est dans une a. totale** the patient is completely listless; **il sombra dans une complète a.** he sank into a state of complete apathy

apathique [apatik] **ADJ** apathetic, listless

apatride [apatrid] **ADJ** stateless
N *Jur* stateless person

apatridie [apatridi] **NF** *Jur* statelessness

APE [apeə] **NF** (*abrév* **Assemblée parlementaire européenne**) EP

APEC [apɛk] **NF** (*abrév* **Association pour l'emploi des cadres**) = agency providing information on recruitment and training opportunities for professionals

Apennins [apenɛ̃] **NMPL** Apennines

aperception [apɛrsɛpsjɔ̃] **NF** *Phil* apperception

apercevoir [apɛrsəvwar] (*prp* **apercevant;** *pp* **aperçu;** *pr ind* **j'aperçois, n. apercevons, ils aperçoivent;** *pr subj* **j'aperçoive, n. apercevions;** *impf* **j'apercevais;** *p hist* **j'aperçus;** *fu* **j'apercevrai**) **VT** to perceive, to see; (*soudain, rapidement*) (*personne, chose*) to catch sight of, to catch a glimpse of; **je n'ai fait que l'a.** I only caught a glimpse of him/her; **elle cherche à ne pas laisser a. sa fatigue** she's trying not to let her tiredness show; **je commence à a. ses raisons** I'm starting to see his reasons; **si on y pense bien, on aperçoit des difficultés** if you think about it, you start to see difficulties
VPR **s'apercevoir 1** (*être visible*) to be noticeable; **cela ne s'aperçoit pas** it isn't visible *or* noticeable **2** (*comprendre, réaliser*) **s'a. de qch** to realize *or* notice sth, to become aware *or* conscious of sth; **il s'est aperçu qu'il n'avait pas ses clés** he realized that he hadn't got his keys with him; **sans s'en a.** without being aware of it, without noticing it **3** (*se voir*) (*de deux personnes*) to catch a glimpse of each other; (*soi-même*) to catch sight of oneself

aperçu [apɛrsy] **NM 1** (*coup d'œil*) glimpse; **a. sur la campagne** glimpse of the countryside **2** (*idée générale*) general idea, outline, summary; **par a.** at a rough estimate; **ça te donnera un a. du travail à faire** that'll give you an idea of the work to be done; *Ordinat* **a. avant impression** print preview **3** (*intuition*) insight (**sur** into)

apériodique [aperjɔdik] **ADJ** *Élec* aperiodic

apéritif [aperitif] **NM** aperitif; **viens prendre l'a. chez moi demain soir** come round and have an early evening drink tomorrow
ADJ *Litt* (*promenade etc*) pre-prandial

Apéritif

In France, the "apéritif", or "apéro", is an informal social ritual. It is quite usual to invite people for before-dinner drinks without actually providing dinner, or to arrange to meet someone in a café "pour l'apéritif" before going out for a meal.

apéro [apero] **NM** *Fam* = **apéritif**

aperture [apɛrtyr] **NF** *Ling* aperture

apesanteur [apəzɑ̃tœr] **NF** weightlessness; **en état d'a.** in weightless conditions

à-peu-près **NM INV** approximation, rough estimate, guess; **calculer une somme par à.** to make a rough calculation; **il y a trop d'à. dans votre exposé** there is too much woolliness in your report

apeuré [apœre, -øre] **ADJ** scared, frightened

apeurer [apœre] **VT** to frighten, to scare

APEX [apɛks] **NM** (*ticket*) APEX

apex [apɛks] **NM** apex

aphasie [afazi] **NF** *Méd* aphasia

aphasique [afazik] *Méd* **ADJ** aphasi(a)c
N aphasic

aphis [afis] **NM** aphis, greenfly

aphone [afɔn] **ADJ** *Méd* voiceless; **elle était a. pour avoir trop crié** she'd lost her voice through shouting too much

aphonie [afɔni] **NF** *Méd* loss of voice; **être atteint d'a.** to have lost one's voice

aphorisme [afɔrism] **NM** aphorism; *Péj* **s'exprimer par aphorismes** to speak in platitudes

aphrodisiaque [afrɔdizjak] **ADJ, NM** *Pharm* aphrodisiac

aphte [aft(ə)] **NM** *Méd* mouth ulcer

aphteux, -euse [aftø, -øz] ADJ *Méd, Vét* **fièvre aphteuse** foot-and-mouth disease

API [apei] NF *abrév* allocation de parent isolé

à-pic [apik] NM *INV* cliff, bluff

apicole [apikɔl] ADJ apiarian; **exploitation a.** honey farm

apiculteur, -trice [apikyltœr, -tris] N beekeeper, apiarist

apiculture [apikyltyr] NF beekeeping, apiculture

apitoiement [apitwamã] NM pity, compassion; **porté à l'a.** compassionate; **pas d'a.!** *(à mon égard)* don't commiserate (with me)!, don't be sympathetic!; **leurs apitoiements** their pity *or* compassion

apitoyer [apitwaje] *(j'apitoie, n. apitoyons; j'apitoierai)* VT **a. qn** to move sb (to pity), to incite sb to pity

VPR **s'apitoyer s'a. sur qn** to pity sb, to feel pity for sb; **s'a. sur (le sort de) qn** to commiserate with sb; **s'a. sur soi-même** *ou* **sur son sort** to feel sorry for oneself; **ça ne sert à rien de s'a. sur soi-même** feeling sorry for yourself/himself/*etc* won't help, self-pity won't help

ap. J.-C. = apr. J.-C.

APL [apeɛl] NF *abrév* Aide personnalisée au logement) ≃ housing benefit

aplanir [aplanir] VT *(surface)* to flatten, to smooth; *(bois)* to plane; *(métal)* to planish; *(route etc)* to level; *(imperfections)* to smooth out; *Fig (difficultés)* to iron out; *Fig (conflit)* to settle

VPR **s'aplanir** *(du sol)* to become level; **les problèmes se sont aplanis d'eux-mêmes** the problems have ironed *or* smoothed themselves out

aplanissement [aplanismã] NM *(du sol)* levelling; *(des difficultés)* ironing out

aplat [apla] NM *Ordinat* solid (figure)

aplati [aplati] ADJ **1** flattened, flat; *(nez)* flat **2** *(sphère etc)* oblate

aplatir [aplatir] VT *(objet)* to flatten, to make flat; *(angle)* to blunt; *Métal (rivet)* to clench; *(tête de rivet)* to hammer down; **a. au fer** to press; **a. qch à coups de marteau** to hammer sth flat; *Fig Fam* **a. qn** *(casser la figure à qn)* to flatten sb; **il l'a aplati d'un coup de poing** he knocked him down *or* flattened him with one punch

VI *Rugby* to score a try, to touch down

VPR **s'aplatir** *(de coiffure)* to go flat; *(d'un chapeau)* to get flattened; **s'a. par terre** to lie down flat on the ground; *Fam (tomber)* to come a cropper; **s'a. contre un mur** to flatten oneself against a wall; *Fig* **s'a. devant qn** to grovel to sb

aplatissage [aplatisaʒ] NM *Tech* pressing; *(d'une surface, d'une couture)* flattening; *(d'un rivet)* hammering down

aplatissement [aplatismã] NM **1** flatness; **l'a. de la Terre aux pôles** the flattening of the earth at the poles **2** *Fig (abaissement)* grovelling

aplomb [aplɔ̃] NM **1** perpendicularity; **d'a.** upright, vertical(ly), plumb; **mets la bouteille d'a., elle va tomber** straighten up the bottle, it's going to fall; **les étagères ne sont pas d'a.** the shelves are out of plumb *or* off plumb; **bien d'a. sur ses pieds** steady on one's feet; *Fig Fam* **je ne suis pas d'a. aujourd'hui** I'm out of sorts *or* off colour today; *Fig* **voilà qui vous remettra d'a.** that will revive you, *Fam* that will buck you up; *Fig* **il me faut deux mille euros pour me remettre d'a.** I need two thousand euros to set me back on my feet; **hors d'a.** out of plumb, out of true; **à l'a. de qch** straight above/below/on sth; *Tech* plumb with sth **2** *(assurance)* (self-)assurance, coolness; **perdre son a.** to lose one's self-assurance; *Péj* **avoir l'a. de dire/de faire**

qch to have the cheek *or* nerve to say/do sth; **il ne manque pas d'a.** he's got a nerve *or* a cheek

aplomber [aplɔ̃be] *Can* VT *(verticalement)* to make straight; *(horizontalement)* to make level

VPR **s'aplomber** to straighten up

apnée [apne] NF *Méd* apnoea, *Am* apnea; **plongée en a.** apnoea diving, breath-holding diving; **plonger en a.** to dive without breathing apparatus

apnéiste [apneist] N apnoea diver, breath-holding diver

apocalypse [apɔkalips] NF apocalypse, revelation; *Bible* **l'A.** the Book of Revelation, the Apocalypse; **les quatre cavaliers de l'A.** the four horsemen of the Apocalypse; *Fig* **vision d'a.** apocalyptic vision; *Fig* **un paysage d'a.** a post-holocaust landscape

apocalyptique [apɔkaliptik] ADJ apocalyptic(al); *Fig* **silence/paysage a.** doom-laden silence/post-holocaust landscape

apocope [apɔkɔp] NF *Ling* apocope

apocryphe [apɔkrif] ADJ apocryphal, *Péj* of doubtful authenticity

NMPL *Bible* **les Apocryphes** the Apocrypha

apogée [apɔʒe] NM *Astron* apogee; **la lune est à son a.** the moon is at its apogee; *Fig* **à l'a. de sa gloire** at the height of one's fame; *Fig* **être à l'a. de sa carrière** to be at the height *or* pinnacle of one's career; *Fig* **atteindre son a.** to reach one's peak

apolitique [apɔlitik] ADJ apolitical

apolitisme [apɔlitism] NM apolitical attitude

Apollon [apɔlɔ̃] N *Myth* Apollo; *Beaux-Arts* **A. du Belvédère** Apollo Belvedere

apollon [apɔlɔ̃] NM *Fig* Adonis, Greek god; **ce n'est pas vraiment un a.!** he's no Adonis!, he's no oil painting!

apologétique [apɔlɔʒetik] ADJ apologetic NF *Rel* apologetics

apologie [apɔlɔʒi] NF *(défense)* apologia **(de** for), defence; *(éloge)* encomium, eulogy; **faire l'a. de qn/qch** to justify *or* defend sb/sth; *(louer)* to eulogize sb/sth

> Il faut noter que le nom anglais **apology** est un faux ami. Il signifie **excuses**.

apologiste [apɔlɔʒist] N apologist

apologue [apɔlɔg] NM apologue

apophyse [apɔfiz] NF *Phys* apophysis

apoplectique [apɔplɛktik] ADJ, N *Méd* apoplectic

apoplexie [apɔplɛksi] NF *Méd* apoplexy; **attaque d'a.** apoplectic seizure, stroke

apostasie [apɔstazi] NF *Rel* apostasy; **faire acte d'a.** to apostatize, to become an apostate; *Fig* to renounce one's party *or* principles, to desert the cause

apostasier [apɔstazje] VI *(pr sub, impf n. apostasiions, v. apostasiiez)* to apostatize, to become an apostate; *Fig* to renounce one's party *or* principles, to desert the cause

apostat, -ate [apɔsta, -at] ADJ apostate, renegade; **curé a.** renegade priest

N apostate; *Fig* **ce politicien est un a.** that politician has renounced his principles

a posteriori [apɔsterjɔri] ADV with hindsight, after the event; *Phil* a posteriori; **a. je me suis rendu compte que c'était moi qui avais raison** with hindsight, I realized that I was right

ADJ INV **méthode a.** a posteriori method

apostolat [apɔstɔla] NM *Rel* apostolate; *Fig* **cette profession est un a.** this job is a real vocation

apostolique [apɔstɔlik] ADJ *(temps, église etc)* apostolic; **vicaire a.** vicar apostolic; **pères apostoliques** apostolic fathers

apostrophe [apɔstrɔf] NF **1** *Ling, Gram* apostrophe; **le vocatif est le cas de l'a.** the vocative is the case of direct address **2** *(interpellation)* reproach, reprimand; **les apostrophes des conducteurs énervés** the rude remarks of angry motorists

apostrophe [apɔstrɔf] NF *Gram (signe)* apostrophe; **s apostrophe** s apostrophe

apostropher [apɔstrɔfe] VT **a. qn** *(pour attirer l'attention)* to shout to sb; *(être impoli envers lui)* to address sb rudely, to shout at sb

VPR **s'apostropher** to shout at one another; **les supporters des équipes de foot s'apostrophent** the football supporters hurl abuse at each other

apothéose [apɔteoz] NF **1** apotheosis, deification; *Fig (consécration)* crowning moment *or* glory; **cette promotion est l'a. de sa carrière** this promotion is the crowning moment of his/her career; **l'a. du cinéma français** the supreme achievement *or* the crowning glory of French cinema; **finir en a.** to end in triumph **2** *Théâtre* grand finale

apothicaire [apɔtikɛr] NM *Vieilli* apothecary; *Fig* **tenir des comptes d'a.** to know where every penny goes

apôtre [apotr] NM apostle; *Fig* **se faire l'a. du recyclage** to become an advocate of recycling; *Fig* **il fait toujours le bon a.** he always puts on such a saintly air

Appalaches [apalaʃ] NMPL **les (monts) A.** the Appalachian Mountains, the Appalachians

appalachien, -ienne [apalaʃjɛ̃, -jɛn] ADJ Appalachian; **relief a.** Appalachian relief

apparaître [aparɛtr] *(conj like paraître; the auxiliary is être, sometimes avoir)* VI **1** *(devenir visible)* to appear; **il lui est apparu en rêve** he came *or* appeared to her in a dream; **a. à travers le brouillard** to loom out of the fog; **un spectre lui était apparu** a ghost had appeared to him **2** *(se révéler)* to become evident *or* apparent; **cette décision m'est apparue évidente** it seemed the obvious decision **3** *(sembler)* **le projet lui apparaissait impossible** the plan seemed impossible to him; **il m'apparaît comme le seul capable d'y parvenir** he seems to me to be the only person capable of doing it

VI IMPERS **il apparaît que vous avez été souvent absent** it appears that you have frequently been absent; **selon les statistiques, il apparaîtrait que ...** according to the statistics, it would appear that ...

apparat [apara] NM pomp, show, display; **tenue d'a.** ceremonial dress; **en grand a.** with great pomp and ceremony; **dîner d'a.** banquet; **discours d'a.** ceremonial speech; **lettres d'a.** illuminated letters

apparatchik [aparatʃik] NM apparatchik

apparaux [aparo] NMPL **1** *Naut* tackle, gear; **les gros a.** the purchase **2** *Gym* apparatus

appareil [aparɛj] NM **1** *(instrument)* apparatus, equipment; *Ind (sing or pl)* plant; **appareils ménagers** household appliances; **appareils de laboratoire** laboratory apparatus; **a. auxiliaire** *ou* **de secours** stand-by equipment; **a. de pêche** fishing tackle; *Min* **a. de forage** drilling rig; **a. d'enregistrement** recorder; **a. de lecture** *(de microfilm)* reader; *Tech* **a. de levage** lifting tackle; *Cin* **a. de projection** film projector; **a. à gaz** gas appliance; *Rail* **a. de voie** switch gear; **a. de prothèse** prosthesis, artificial limb/*etc*; **a. (dentaire)** *(correctif)* brace; *(dentier)* dentures; **a. à sous** slot machine, fruit machine, one-armed bandit

2 *Tél* telephone; **Marcelline à l'a.** Marcelline speaking *or* here; **qui est à l'a.?** who's speaking?; **a. mains libres** free-hands device

3 *Aviat* aircraft, plane; **a. de chasse** fighter; **a. d'école** training aircraft, trainer **4** *Phot* **a. (photographique), a. photo** camera; **a. photo numérique** digital camera; **a. reflex** reflex camera **5** *(administration etc)* bodies, authorities; **mettre en jeu l'a. de la justice** to put the machinery of the law in motion; **l'a. du parti** the party machine *or* apparatus; *Ind* **a. de production** production facilities; **a. commercial** commercial structure **6** *Méd* dressing; *(pour fracture)* splint, plaster **7** *Anat* system, apparatus; **a. digestif** digestive system; **a. respiratoire** respiratory system **8** *Constr (de pierres)* height; *(agencement)* bond; **assise de grand a.** course of large stones **9** *(d'un texte)* **a. critique** critical apparatus **10** *Litt* display, magnificence, pomp; *Fig* **dans le plus simple a.** in the nude

appareillage [apaʀεjaʒ] NM **1** *Naut* getting under way, weighing (anchor), setting sail **2** *(matériel)* fittings, equipment, accessories; *Ind* plant; **a. électrique** electrical equipment **3** *(d'un atelier etc)* installation, fitting (up), setting up **4** *Constr (de pierres, de briques)* bonding

appareillement [apaʀεjmɑ̃] NM *(d'animaux pour la reproduction)* pairing, mating; *(de bœufs)* pairing

appareiller [apaʀeje] VT **1** *Naut* **a. un navire** to rig a boat out **2** *Constr (pierres, briques)* to bond **3** *(filet)* to spread **4** *(atelier etc)* to install, to fit up *or* out **5** *Méd (handicapé)* to fit up; **a. un sourd** to fit a deaf person with a hearing aid **6** *(assortir)* **a. une lampe** to find a match for a lamp ▸ VI *Naut* to get under way

appareilleur [apaʀεjœʀ] NM *(de pierres etc)* trimmer, fitter, dresser; *Constr* foreman mason

apparemment [apaʀamɑ̃] ADV apparently; **a. tout allait bien** everything seemed to be going well

apparence [apaʀɑ̃s] NF **1** *(air, aspect extérieur)* appearance, look; **cette maison/voiture a une belle a.** this house/car looks nice; **donner une belle a. à sa maison en la repeignant** to make one's house look nice by repainting it; **quelque a. de (la) vérité** some semblance of truth; **un homme à l'a. négligée/soignée** an untidy-looking *or* an unkempt(-looking) man/a tidy-looking *or* a neat(-looking) man; **selon toute a.** to all appearances; **contre toute a.** against all expectations **2** *(aspect trompeur)* **il ne faut pas se fier aux apparences** appearances can be deceptive; **prendre l'a. pour réalité** to confuse appearance with reality; **sous de fausses apparences** under false pretences; **sous une a. de douceur se cache une grande fermeté** beneath a mild-mannered exterior there lies great strength of will; **il a l'air gentil, mais ce n'est qu'une (fausse) a.** he seems nice, but it's only a façade; **il ne faut pas juger sur les apparences** you shouldn't judge by *or* on appearance(s) (alone); **il ne faut pas s'arrêter à l'a.** you should look beyond the façade; **en a.** outwardly, on the surface; **plus difficile en a. qu'en réalité** less difficult than it looks; **pour sauver les apparences** for the sake of appearances; *(pour éviter une humiliation)* to save face **3** *(trace)* semblance, vestige; **elle n'a plus la moindre a. de respect pour lui** she no longer has the slightest vestige of respect for him

apparent [apaʀɑ̃] ADJ **1** *(visible)* visible, apparent; **peu a.** hardly noticeable; **sans raison apparente** for no apparent reason **2**

(prétendu) apparent, not real; **c'est la raison apparente, mais la vérité est autre** that's the ostensible reason, but the truth is quite different; **mouvement a. du soleil** apparent movement of the sun; **sous cette apparente bonté se cache un grand égoïsme** beneath that kind exterior there lies great selfishness; **piété apparente** outward piety **3** *Jur* **héritier a.** heir apparent

apparenté [apaʀɑ̃te] ADJ **1** *(par le mariage)* related; *(qui a des liens avec)* related, connected; **bien a.** well connected **2** *Pol* **candidat a. au Parti socialiste** = candidate who, though not a member of the Socialist Party, can count on its support in an election **3** *Chimie* **éléments apparentés** related *or* affinitive elements

apparentement [apaʀɑ̃təmɑ̃] NM *Pol* = practice of forming electoral alliances (under proportional representation)

apparenter (s') [sapaʀɑ̃te] VPR **1** to marry (**à une famille** into a family) **2** *Pol* to form an alliance (**à** with) **3** *Fig* to have sth in common (**à** with); **les deux tendances s'apparentent en de nombreux points** the two trends have many things in common

apparier [apaʀje] *(impf & pr sub n.* **apparions,** *v.* **appariiez)** VT **1** *(oiseaux pour la reproduction)* to couple, to pair, to mate **2** *(chaussettes, chevaux etc)* to match, to pair; *(adversaires)* to pair off ▸ VPR **s'apparier** *(des oiseaux)* to mate

appariteur [apaʀitœʀ] NM *(d'université)* mace bearer

apparition [apaʀisjɔ̃] NF **1** appearance; *(d'une fièvre)* outbreak; **l'a. des boutons/des symptômes** the appearance of the spots/symptoms; **faire une courte a.** *(d'une personne)* to make a brief appearance; **brève a.** *(à l'écran)* short *or* cameo appearance, cameo; **la star a finalement fait son a. vers 18 heures** the star finally appeared *or* made his/her appearance around 6 o'clock **2** *(de fantôme)* apparition; *(d'un ange)* appearance; **avoir des apparitions** to see things

appartement [apaʀtəmɑ̃] NM **1** flat, *Am* apartment; *(dans un hôtel etc)* suite, set of rooms; **a. de passage** pied-à-terre; **a. de fonction** company flat; **a. témoin** show flat, *Am* model apartment; **vivre en a.** to live in a flat; **plantes d'a.** indoor *or* house *or* pot plants **2** *(dans un château etc)* **les grands appartements** the state apartments

appartenance [apaʀtənɑ̃s] NF **1** **a. à qch** (the fact of) belonging to sth *or* being part of sth; *Math* **a. à un ensemble** membership of a set; **a. à un parti** membership of a party **2** **appartenances** *(d'une maison, d'un château)* appurtenances

appartenir [apaʀtəniʀ] *(conj like* **tenir)** VI **1** *(être la possession de)* to belong (**à** to), to be owned (**à** by); **cette maison lui appartient en propre** this house is his own personal property **2** *(dépendre)* **pour des raisons qui t'appartiennent** for your own private reasons; **cela n'appartient pas à mes fonctions** this does not come within the scope of my duties **3** *(par famille etc)* **a. à qch** to be part of sth, to belong to sth, to be a member of sth; *Math* **a. à un ensemble** to be a member of a set; **elle appartient à une famille très riche** she comes from a very wealthy family ▸ VPR **s'appartenir je ne m'appartiens pas** I'm not my own master; *(je n'ai pas de temps à moi)* I've no time to call my own ▸ V IMPERS **à tous ceux qu'il appartient** to all whom it may concern; **il appartient au comité de prendre la décision** it is for the committee *or* up to the committee to decide, the decision lies with the committee; **il ne m'appartient pas de le critiquer** it is not for me to criticize him; *Iron* **il vous appartient**

bien de me critiquer you're a fine one to criticize me

appas [apɑ] NMPL *Litt* charms

appât [apɑ] NM **1** *(de pêche)* bait; *Fig (du succès)* lure; **a. de fond** ground bait; **mettre l'a. à la ligne** to bait the line; **mordre à l'a.** *(d'un poisson), Fig (d'une personne)* to rise to the bait; *Fig* animé par l'a. du gain** driven by the lure of money **2** *(pour la volaille)* soft food

appâter [apɑte] VT **1** *(poissons, oiseaux etc)* to lure with bait; *Fig (personne)* to entice; *Fig* **a. qn par des promesses** to entice sb with promises **2** *(hameçon etc)* to bait **3** *Vieilli (volaille)* to force-feed

appauvrir [apovʀiʀ] VT to impoverish; *Méd* **a. le sang** to thin the blood; **a. la constitution de qn** to weaken sb's constitution ▸ VPR **s'appauvrir** to grow poorer; *(du sol)* to lose its fertility, to become impoverished; **la langue risque de s'a.** there is a risk that the language will become impoverished

appauvrissement [apovʀismɑ̃] NM *(d'un pays, du sol etc)* impoverishment; *(d'une race)* degeneration; *(de la santé, des stocks)* deterioration; *(du sang)* thinning; *(d'une entreprise)* decline in the financial position

appeau, *pl* **appeaux** [apo] NM bird call; *Fig* **servir d'a. à qn** to act as a decoy for sb

appel [apɛl] NM **1** *(invitation, sollicitation)* appeal; *(d'un spécialiste etc)* calling in; **faire a. à qn** to call on sb; *(faire venir) (plombier etc)* to send for sb; **faire a. à la générosité de qn** to appeal to sb's generosity; **cette formation fait a. à des connaissances commerciales** this training course calls for *or* requires some knowledge of business; **faire a. à tout son courage** to summon up all one's courage; **il faut faire a. à tous vos souvenirs** you have to search your memory; **l'a. à la révolte** the call to revolt; **l'a. du Général de Gaulle** General de Gaulle's appeal *or* call to the French nation; *Radio* **nous lançons un a. à tous les automobilistes sur la R.N. 7** here is a message for all motorists on the RN 7 **2** *Jur* appeal (at law); **avis d'a.** notice of appeal; **Cour d'a.** Court of Appeal; **faire a. d'une décision** to appeal (against) a decision; **juger en a. (d'une décision)** to hear an appeal (from a decision); **casser un jugement en a.** to quash a sentence on appeal; **jugement sans a.** final judgment; *Fig* **c'est ce que j'ai décidé, et c'est sans a.** that's my decision and it's final *or Fam* that's that **3** *(attirance)* call; *(voix)* voice; **l'a. du printemps** the call of spring; **l'a. du large** ou **de la mer** the call of the sea; **l'a. de la nature** the call of the wild; **l'a. de la conscience** the voice of conscience **4** *(cri)* call, shout; **cri d'a.** call for help; **entendre un a. au secours** to hear a cry for help; **a. d'incendie** fire alarm; **accourir à un a.** to run in answer to sb's call; *Fig* **il m'a fait un a. du regard pour que je lui vienne en aide** his eyes pleaded with me to help; *Fig* **faire un a. du coude à qn** *(pour attirer son attention sur qch)* to nudge sb; *Aut* **faire un a. de phares** to flash one's headlights (**à qn** at sb) **5** *Fin* **faire un a. de fonds** to call up capital; *Com* **faire un a. d'offres** to invite bids *or* tenders; **a. de couverture** ou **de garantie** ou **de marge** margin call; *Mktg* **a. à froid** cold call; *Com* **produit d'a.** loss leader **6** *Mil* **l'a. aux armes** the call to arms; **devancer l'a.** to join up before being enlisted; **a. de mobilisation** mobilization order **7** *Tél* **touche d'a.** call key; **signal d'a.** call waiting service; **numéro d'a.** (telephone) number; **a. téléphonique** (tele)phone call; **a. de réveil** wake-up *or* alarm call; *Vieilli* **a. interurbain** trunk call, long-distance call;

a. matinal early morning call; **a. national** national call; **a. gratuit** freecall; *Mktg* **a. à froid** cold call; **il y a eu un a. pour vous** there was a (telephone) call for you; **a. avec préavis** person to person call; *Radio* **indicatif d'a.** call sign

8 *Aviat* **a. particulier** selective calling

9 *(pour vérifier)*, *Scol* roll call, register; **faire l'a. (des écoliers)** to take *or* call the register; **répondre à l'a.** to be present; **feuille/cahier d'a.** roll, register; *Mil* **l'a. du soir** tattoo; **manquant à l'a.** missing

10 *Tech* **a. d'air** intake of air; **vitesse d'a.** inflow; **a. d'un aimant** pull of a magnet; **le moteur part au premier a.** the engine starts at the first touch of the switch

11 *Typ* **a. de note** footnote reference, superior figure

12 *Sport* take-off; **quel est le pied d'a.?** which is the take-off foot?; **un bon coup d'a. sur le tremplin** a good kick off from the springboard

13 *(signal)* signal, call; **l'a. à la prière** (Muslim) call to prayer

14 *Ordinat* call; *(de commande)* selection; **a. automatique** automatic dial

appelant, -ante [aplɑ̃, -ɑ̃t] ADJ *Jur (partie etc)* appealing

▪ N **1** *Jur* appellant (against a judgment); **se porter a.** to appeal **2** *Tél* caller

appelé [aple] NM **1** *Mil* conscript; *Fig* **il y a beaucoup d'appelés, mais peu d'élus** many are called, but few are chosen **2** *Tél* party called

appeler [aple] (**j'appelle, n. appelons; j'appellerai**) VT **1** *(personne, chien)* to call (to); *(taxi)* to call, to hail; **a. au secours** to call for help; **a. qn dans la rue** to call to sb in the street; **a. qn de la main** *ou* **du geste** to beckon (to) sb; **les noms sont appelés un à un** the names are called out one by one; *Jur* **a. une cause** to call (out) a case

2 *Tél* **a. qn (au téléphone)** to ring sb (up), to call sb; **a. Paris** to call Paris; **a. un taxi/un médecin** to phone for a taxi/a doctor

3 *(convoquer)* to call in, to send for, to summon; *Jur* **a. qn (en justice)** to summon(s) sb; *(poursuivre)* to sue sb; **a. qn à témoin** to call sb to witness; **a. les pompiers** to call the fire brigade; **faire a. un médecin** to call in *or* send for a doctor; **a. l'ascenseur** to call the lift; **elle a été appelée auprès de son père mourant** she was called to her dying father's bedside; *Mil* **a. qn sous les drapeaux** to call sb up, to conscript sb; *aussi Hum* **le devoir t'appelle** duty calls; *Fin* **capital appelé** called-up capital

4 **a. qn à** *(fonction etc)* to appoint *or* assign sb to; **être appelé à qch** to be destined for sth; **cette technique est appelée à se développer partout dans le monde** the technique is destined *or* set to spread throughout the world; **son courage l'appelle à ce genre d'action** his courage inspires him to that kind of action; **il fut appelé à travailler à l'étranger** he was called to work overseas

5 *(donner un nom à)* to call; **nous l'avons appelé David** we have called him David; **tu l'appelles par son prénom?** do you call him by his first name?; **j'appelle cela une bêtise** I call that *or* that's what I call a stupid mistake; **voilà ce que j'appelle un homme** now that's what I call a man; **vous appelez cela danser?** (do) you call that dancing?; **a. un chat un chat, a. les choses par leur nom** to call a spade a spade

6 *(demander, réclamer)* to call for; *(critique)* to invite; **ce problème appelle une solution immédiate** the problem calls for an immediate solution; **a. qn à faire qch** to call on *or* invite sb to do sth; **je vous appelle tous à y réfléchir** I call on *or* invite you all to think about it

7 *(entraîner)* to provoke, to arouse, to attract; *Prov* **un malheur en appelle un autre** misfortunes never come singly; **la violence appelle la violence** violence breeds *or* begets violence

8 *Ordinat (fichier)* to call up

VI **1** *(crier)* to call, to shout; **il arrive qu'il appelle la nuit** he sometimes calls out *or* shouts out in the night; **elle appelait à l'aide** *ou* **au secours** she was calling *or* shouting for help; **si tu as un problème, tu appelles** if you have a problem, just shout

2 *Tél* to call, to phone; **laisse-la a. la première** wait for her to call *or* phone you

3 **en a. à qn** to appeal to sb; **j'en appelle à votre bon sens** I appeal to your common sense; **j'en appelle de votre décision** I challenge your decision; *Jur* **a. d'un jugement** to appeal against a sentence; **en a.** to appeal

VPR **s'appeler 1** *(avoir pour nom)* to be called; **comment vous appelez-vous?** what is your name?; **je m'appelle David** my name is David; **cela s'appelle un plaqueminier** it's called a persimmon; *Fam* **voilà qui s'appelle pleuvoir!** it's raining with a vengeance!; **nous nous appelons par nos prénoms** we call each other by our first names, we're on first-name terms

2 *Tél (entre plusieurs individus)* **alors, on s'appelle, hein?** talk to you on the phone

> Il faut noter que le verbe anglais **to appeal** est un faux ami. Il ne signifie jamais **appeler.**

appellation [apɛlɑsjɔ̃] NF name; *(de produit)* designation, *Fml* appellation; **vin sans a.** non-vintage wine; **a. injurieuse** abusive term

▸▸**a. contrôlée** *(de vin)* guaranteed vintage; **a. d'origine** designation *or* label of origin

appendice [apɛ̃dis] NM **VOIR GRAMMAIRE A14 1** *Anat* appendix; *Zool, Bot* appendage; **se faire enlever l'a.** to have one's appendix out; *Hum* **quel a. nasal!** what a conk *or* hooter! **2** *(d'un livre)* appendix, supplement **3** *Vieilli (d'un bâtiment)* annex(e) **4** *(d'un ballon)* neck

appendicectomie [apɛ̃disɛktɔmi] NF *Chir* append(ic)ectomy

appendicite [apɛ̃disit] NF *Méd* appendicitis; **crise d'a.** appendicitis; **a. chronique** grumbling appendix; **se faire opérer de l'a.** to have an operation for appendicitis, to have one's appendix out

appentis [apɑ̃ti] NM *Constr (bâtiment)* lean-to; *(toit)* lean-to, sloping roof; *(remise)* outhouse, shed

appesantir [apəzɑ̃tir] VT *(rendre moins agile)* to slow down, to weigh down; **l'âge a appesanti sa démarche** old age has slowed his step; **paupières appesanties par le sommeil** eyes heavy with sleep

VPR **s'appesantir** to grow heavier; **son pas s'appesantit avec la fatigue** his step grew slower *or* heavier through fatigue; *Fig* **la main de fer de l'Inquisition s'appesantit sur ...** the iron fist of the Inquisition weighed down on ...; *Fig* **la nuit s'appesantit sur la ville** black night fell over the town; *Fig* **s'a. sur un sujet** to dwell on a subject; *Fig Fam* **pas la peine de s'a., passons à autre chose** there's no point in dwelling on it, let's get on to something else

appesantissement [apəzɑ̃tismɑ̃] NM *(de la marche, des recherches)* slowing (down); *(des pas)* (growing) heaviness

appétence [apetɑ̃s] NF *Litt* penchant, partiality; **une a. d'aventure** a penchant for adventure

appétissant [apetisɑ̃] ADJ *(nourriture)* appetizing, tempting; *Fig (femme)* alluring

appétit [apeti] NM **1** *(de nourriture)* appetite; **couper l'a. à qn** to spoil *or* take away sb's appetite; **donner de l'a. à qn** to give sb an appetite; **mettre qn en a.** to give sb an appetite; **manger de bon a.** *ou* **avec a.** to eat heartily *or* with relish, *Fam* to tuck in; **avoir un a. d'oiseau** to have a small *or* poor appetite, to peck at one's food; **avoir bon** *ou* **un gros a.** to have a hearty appetite; **bon a.!** enjoy your meal!, bon appetit!; **manger sans a.** *(sans plaisir)* not to enjoy one's food; *(picorer)* to pick at one's food; *Prov* **l'a. vient en mangeant** only when you start eating do you realize you're hungry; *Fig* **the more you get the more you want 2** *(désir)* desire, craving *(de* for); **a. sexuel** sexual desire; **a. du gain** craving for money; **l'a. de la connaissance** a thirst *or* hunger for knowledge

applaudimètre [aplodimɛtr] NM clapometer

applaudir [aplodir] VT to applaud; **se faire a. à tout rompre** to get tremendous applause, to bring the house down; *Fig* **je vous applaudis de tout cœur** I congratulate you with all my heart

VI to applaud, to clap; **a. à tout rompre** to applaud *or* clap thunderously; *Fig* **nous applaudissons à la reprise des relations entre nos deux pays** we welcome the resumption of relations between our two countries; *Fig* **a. à une décision/un changement** to applaud *or* welcome a decision/a change

VPR **s'applaudir s'a. (d'avoir fait qch)** to congratulate oneself, to pat oneself on the back (for having done sth)

applaudissement [aplodismɑ̃] NM *(souvent pl)* **1** applause, clapping; **un tonnerre** *ou* **une tempête d'applaudissements** thunderous applause; **soulever des applaudissements** to be applauded **2** *Litt* approval

applicable [aplikabl] ADJ applicable; **cette règle est a. à tous les cas** this rule applies to all cases; **a. à partir du 1er janvier** to take effect from 1 January

applicateur [aplikatœr] NM *(dispositif)* applicator; **tampon avec a.** applicator tampon ADJ **pinceau a.** applicator

application [aplikɑsjɔ̃] NF **1** *(de peinture etc)* application, applying; **première a. de peinture** first coat of paint; *Couture* **broderie d'a.** appliqué (work); **bois d'a.** veneer

2 *(d'un règlement)* application; *(de la loi)* enforcement; **mettre une théorie en a.** to put a theory into practice; **mettre une loi en a.** to enforce *or* implement a law; **entrer en a.** to come into force; **a. d'une somme d'argent à un projet** use of a sum of money for a project; **en a. de ce décret** in pursuance of this decree; *Mil etc* **école d'a.** school of instruction

3 *(débouché)* application; *(de la matière première)* use

4 *(assiduité)* application (to one's work), industriousness; **travailler avec a.** to apply oneself to one's work, to work diligently

5 *Ordinat* **a. bureautique** business application; **a. phare** killer app; **a. en service** current application; **a. graphique** graphics application; **logiciel d'a.** application software

applique [aplik] NF **1** *(lampe)* wall light **2** *Couture* appliquéd ornament

appliqué [aplike] ADJ **1** *(personne)* hardworking, diligent; *(écriture)* careful **2** *(sciences)* applied; **informatique appliquée à la gestion** computer technology applied to management

appliquer [aplike] VT **1** *(mettre)* to apply *(* sur on); **a. une couche de peinture sur qch** to put a coat of paint on sth, *surtout Fml* to apply a coat of paint to sth; **a. une oreille au mur** to put one's ear to the wall, to listen through the wall; **un coup bien appliqué** a well-planted or well-aimed blow; **elle lui fit une bise bien appliquée** she planted a kiss on his cheek

2 (mettre en œuvre) to apply; (peine) to enforce; (sanctions, règlement, mesures) to enforce, to apply; (idée, réforme) to put into practice, to implement; (recette, méthode) to use; **a. une loi à un cas particulier** to apply a law to a particular case; **a. (les dispositions de) la loi** to apply the law; **a. un traitement à une maladie** to apply a treatment to an illness; **a. une recette particulière** to use a particular recipe; Jur **a. le maximum de la peine** to impose the maximum penalty

3 (concentrer) to apply; **a. toute son attention à un problème** to devote or apply all one's attention to a problem; **a. son esprit à ses études** to apply one's mind to one's studies

VPR s'appliquer 1 (se concentrer) to apply oneself, to take pains; **elle doit s'a. davantage** she has to apply herself more; **s'a. à qch** to apply oneself to sth, to take pains over sth; **il s'applique à vérifier toutes les dates** he's taking pains to check all the dates; **elle s'applique à me contredire** she is making a point of contradicting me; **il s'applique à apprendre le français** he is making a serious effort to learn French

2 (d'un règlement etc) to apply (à to); **à qui s'applique cette remarque?** who is that remark intended for?; **le règlement s'applique pour tous** the rule applies to everybody

3 (se placer) to be applied; **le cataplasme s'applique directement sur la peau** the poultice should be applied directly (on)to the skin

appoint [apwɛ̃] NM **1** Com, Fin exact money or change; **faire l'a.** (ajouter le reste) to make up the full amount, to give the exact change; (donner la somme exacte) to pay the exact amount; **ressources d'a.** additional (sources of) income; **ce travail à mi-temps lui fait un petit a.** this part-time job brings him a little extra income; **chauffage/éclairage d'a.** additional heating/lighting; **siège d'a.** extra chair; **un travail d'a.** a second job **2** (contribution) contribution; **apporter son a. à qch** to contribute to sth, to take part in sth

appointements [apwɛ̃tmɑ̃] NMPL salary; **toucher ses a.** to draw one's salary

Il faut noter que le nom anglais **appointment** est un faux ami. Il signifie **rendez-vous** ou **nomination**, selon le contexte.

appointer [apwɛte] VT **1** (payer) (personne) to pay (a salary to); **être appointé à la semaine** to be paid weekly or by the week **2** (crayon etc) to sharpen

appondre [apɔ̃dr] VT Suisse to join (together)

appontage [apɔ̃taʒ] NM (d'un porte-avions) landing (on an aircraft carrier); **officier d'a.** landing officer; **crosse** ou **crochet d'a.** arrester hook

appontement [apɔ̃tmɑ̃] NM Naut (de bois) jetty, pier, landing stage

apponter [apɔ̃te] VI (sur un porte-avions) to land (on an aircraft carrier)

apport [apɔr] NM **1** (fait d'apporter) contribution, contributing; Écon inflow, influx; **a. de capitaux** contribution of capital; Compta **a. en capital** capital contribution; Compta **a. en numéraire** cash contribution; Compta **a. d'argent frais** injection of new money; Compta **apports libérés** fully paid-up capital; **capital d'a.** initial capital; **actions d'a.** founder's or promoter's shares; **l'a. du tourisme dans une région** the financial contribution made by tourism to a region; **sans a. extérieur,**

nous étions perdus without outside (financial) help, we'd have been ruined; Jur **a. de pièces** (dans une enquête) deposit(ing) of documents; Jur **biens d'a.** estate brought in by husband/wife on marriage; **a. en communauté** = goods contributed by husband and wife to the joint estate; **terres d'a.** earthworks; **l'a. de la civilisation grecque** the contribution made by Greek civilization

2 (contribution) contribution; Fin initial share; **un a. en nature** a contribution in kind; **les fruits donnent un a. de vitamines indispensable** fruit provides essential vitamins; **l'a. en vitamines du foie** the vitamins provided by liver, the vitamins present in liver; Agr **un a. d'engrais** a heavy dressing of manure; **a. de chaleur, a. calorifique** heat supply or input

3 Tech coating, layer, deposit

▸▸ Jur **a. dotal** dowry, marriage portion

apporter [apɔrte] VT **1** to bring (**qch à qn** sth to sb); **je t'ai apporté la cassette vidéo** I've brought you the video; **si tu vas la voir, apporte-lui des fleurs** if you go to see her, take her some flowers; Fin **a. des capitaux** to bring in capital

2 a. du soin/un grand intérêt à faire qch to do sth carefully/with great interest

3 (donner) (bonheur, soulagement etc) to bring; **cette démonstration n'apporte aucune preuve supplémentaire** this demonstration gives or provides no additional proof; **cette expérience lui a beaucoup apporté** the experience has been very beneficial for him; **qu'est-ce que ça peut t'a.?** what good can that do you?; **notre relation ne m'apporte plus rien** I'm not getting anything out of our relationship any more, our relationship doesn't do anything for me any more; **tu ne m'apportes plus rien** you've got nothing to offer me any more, I've outgrown you; **ce travail ne m'apporte pas grand-chose** I don't get very much out of this work **4** (changements etc) to cause, to bring about; **ce que l'avenir apportera** what the future has in store

Do not confuse **apporter** and **amener**. The former should be used with inanimate objects and the latter with animate objects.

apposer [apoze] VT to place, to put, Fml to affix; **a. une affiche sur un mur** to stick a poster on a wall; Jur **a. les scellés** (pour interdire tout accès) to affix the seals; Jur **a. sa signature** to put one's signature to; Jur **a. sa signature à un acte** to append or affix one's signature to a deed; **a. une clause à un acte** to insert a clause or add a clause to an act

apposition [apozisjɔ̃] NF **1** Admin (d'un sceau, de scellés, de signature etc) affixing, appending **2** Gram apposition; **mot en a.** word in apposition SEE GRAMMAR A6; B5

appréciable [apresjabl] ADJ **1** (par les sens) perceptible **2** (évolution, changement etc) appreciable, noticeable; **une différence à peine a.** a barely perceptible difference; **la différence est difficilement a.** it's difficult to tell the difference **3** (non négligeable) considerable, appreciable (usu attrib); **à une distance a.** at an appreciable or considerable distance **4** (louable) (motivations) praiseworthy; **ses qualités de dirigeant ont été fort appréciables** his leadership qualities were greatly appreciated; **le changement de temps est tout à fait a.** (bienvenu) the change in the weather is very welcome

appréciateur, -trice [apresjatœr, -tris] N appreciator (**de** of); Com etc appraiser, valuer; **a. du talent** person who recognizes talent, good judge of talent

appréciatif, -ive [apresjatif, -iv] ADJ (re-

gard, silence) appreciative; Com **devis a.** estimate

appréciation [apresjasjɔ̃] NF **1** (évaluation) valuation, estimation, estimate; (d'une distance) judging; **faire l'a. des marchandises** to value or to make a valuation of goods; **a. des risques** risk assessment **2** (opinion) judgment, opinion; (d'une œuvre d'art, d'un repas etc) appreciation; **les appréciations sont notées dans la marge** the comments are in the margin; **je laisse cette tapisserie/ce problème à votre a.** I'll leave you to form an opinion on this piece of tapestry/this problem **3** (augmentation de valeur) appreciation, rise in value; **a. monétaire** currency appreciation

apprécier [apresje] (pr sub, impf n. **appréciions,** v. **appréciiez**) VT **1** (évaluer) to appraise; (peinture etc) to estimate the value of, to value; **tu ne l'apprécies pas à sa juste valeur** you don't appreciate his/her true worth

2 (déterminer) to determine; (approximativement) (température, son) to estimate; (distance) to judge; (différences, nuances) to appreciate, to judge

3 (aimer) to appreciate; **un bon repas entre amis, voilà ce que j'apprécie le plus** having a good meal with friends is what I enjoy doing most or is what I like most; **je n'apprécie pas ce genre de plaisanterie** I don't appreciate or I don't care for that kind of joke; **elle ne l'apprécie pas du tout** she doesn't like him at all; **elle l'apprécie, sans plus** she just likes him; (ils ne sont pas amants) she's just good friends with him

VI Fam **elle n'a pas apprécié** she didn't appreciate that, she wasn't very amused or pleased

VPR s'apprécier 1 (de personnes) to like each other

2 (de monnaie) to appreciate; **l'euro s'est apprécié par rapport au dollar** the euro has risen against the dollar

appréhender [apreɑ̃de] VT **1** Jur **a. qn (au corps)** to arrest or apprehend sb **2** (craindre) to dread, to fear; **j'appréhende de rentrer** ou **le retour** I'm dreading going back; **j'appréhende toujours un peu les voyages en avion** I'm always a bit apprehensive about travelling by air **3** (notion) to grasp

VI to be apprehensive

appréhensif, -ive [apreɑ̃sif, -iv] ADJ apprehensive

appréhension [apreɑ̃sjɔ̃] NF **1** (crainte) apprehension (**de** of); **avoir des appréhensions** to be apprehensive **2** (d'une notion) grasp

apprenant, -ante [aprənɑ̃, -ɑ̃t] N learner

apprendre [aprɑ̃dr] (conj like **prendre**) VT **1** (leçon, commerce, langue, méthode etc) to learn; **il n'a jamais rien appris à l'école** he didn't learn a thing at school

2 (nouvelles etc) to learn, to hear (of), to get to know of; **comment l'avez-vous appris?** how did you hear or find out?; **nous l'avons appris à la radio/aux informations** we heard it on the radio/on the news; **j'ai appris que tu allais te marier** I've heard that you're getting married; **je l'ai appris de bonne source** I have it on good authority

3 (enseigner) **a. qch à qn** to teach sb sth; **a. à qn à faire qch** to teach or show sb how to do sth; **il m'a tout appris** he taught me everything I know

4 (informer) **a. qch à qn** to inform sb of sth, to tell sb sth; Fam **vous ne m'apprenez rien!** you're telling me!, you're not telling me anything new!; **il faut tout lui a., il ne sait rien** he has to be told everything, he hasn't a clue

VI to learn; **a. facilement** to find learning easy; **a. vite/lentement** to be a fast/slow learner; **a. à faire qch** to learn how to do sth; **a. à lire/skier** to learn to read/(how) to ski; *Prov* **on apprend à tout âge** it is never too late to learn, you're never too old to learn; *Fam* **je vous apprendrai à me parler de la sorte!** I'll teach you to speak to me like that!; *Fam* **ça vous apprendra!** serve(s) you right!, that'll teach you!; *Fam* **je vais lui a. à vivre** I'm going to teach him a few manners

VPR **s'apprendre** **ça s'apprend vite** it's easy to learn, it can be learned quickly; **le chinois ne s'apprend pas facilement** it isn't easy to learn Chinese

apprenti, -ie [aprãti] N apprentice; *Jur* articled clerk; **une apprentie couturière** an apprentice dressmaker; **a. menuisier** carpenter's apprentice; **je ne suis qu'un a.** I'm only a beginner *or* a novice

▸▸ **a. conducteur** learner (driver); **a. sorcier** sorcerer's apprentice; *Fig* **cesse donc de jouer les apprentis sorciers!** stop meddling with things that you know nothing about!

apprentissage [aprãtisaʒ] NM training; *(chez un artisan)* apprenticeship; **centre d'a.** training school; **contrat d'a.** contract of apprenticeship; **mettre qn en a. chez un patron** to apprentice sb to an employer; **être en a. chez qn** to be apprenticed to sb; **faire l'a. de la vie** to gain some experience of life, *Fam* to go through the university of life; **faire l'a. de la douleur** to become acquainted with grief

apprêt [aprɛ] NM **1** *(opération)* *(de tissus, de cuirs etc)* dressing, finishing **2** *(substance)* *(de tissu etc)* finish, dress; *(de peinture)* primer, size; **a. anti-corrosion** anti-corrosion primer **3** *(affectation)* affectation, affectedness; **style sans a.** unaffected style

apprêtage [apretaʒ] NM *Tech* **1** *(de tissu)* dressing, finishing **2** *(de peinture)* priming, sizing

apprêté [aprete] ADJ **1** *(style, attitude etc)* affected, stiff; **coiffure apprêtée** fussy hairstyle **2** **papier a.** glossy paper

apprêter [aprete] VT **1** *(repas etc)* to prepare; **a. un enfant** to get a child ready, to dress a child; **les femmes apprêtent la mariée** the women help the bride to dress *or* get ready **2** *(tissus etc)* to dress, to finish, to stiffen; *(cuir)* to finish **3** *(surface)* to prime

VPR **s'apprêter** *(s'habiller)* to get dressed; *(se donner un coup de peigne etc)* to tidy oneself (up); **s'a. à faire qch** to be getting ready *or* preparing to do sth, to be on the point of doing sth

apprivoisable [aprivwazabl(ə)] ADJ tameable

apprivoisé [aprivwaze] ADJ tame

apprivoisement [aprivwazmã] NM taming, domestication

apprivoiser [aprivwaze] VT *(animal)* to tame; *Fig (personne)* to win over; *Fig* **je veux a. cette peur** I want to conquer this fear

VPR **s'apprivoiser** *(d'un animal)* to become domesticated *or* tame; *Fig (d'une personne)* to become more sociable; *Fig Litt* **s'a. à une idée** to get used to *or* come round to an idea

approbateur, -trice [aprɔbatœr, -tris], **approbatif, -ive** [aprɔbatif, -iv] ADJ *(geste, sourire etc)* approving; **regard a.** look of approval

approbation [aprɔbasjɔ̃] NF approval *(de qch* of sth); *(de documents officiels, de comptes rendus)* certifying, approval; **donner son a. à qch** to give one's approval to sth, to approve sth; **le film a reçu l'a. du public** the film was well received by the public; **a. tacite** tacit approval; **votre conduite est digne d'a.** your behaviour is commendable; **cette étude mérite l'a. de tous** this study merits general approval; *Com* **pour a.** for approval; **a. des comptes** approval of the accounts

approchable [aprɔʃabl] ADJ *(endroit, personne)* approachable, accessible; **le refuge n'est pas a. en voiture** the shelter is not accessible *or* cannot be reached by car; **elle n'est pas a. aujourd'hui** *(elle est de mauvaise humeur)* she's not very approachable today

approchant [aprɔʃã] ADJ similar, approximate *(de* to); **offre approchante** near offer; **je n'ai jamais rien vu d'a.** I've never seen anything like it *or* anything approaching it; **voilà ce qu'il a dit, ou quelque chose d'a.** that is what he said, or something like it; **je cherche qch d'a.** I'm looking for something similar

ADV *Suisse* about, around; **gagner a. cinq mille francs** *ou* **cinq mille francs a.** to earn about five thousand francs

approche [aprɔʃ] NF **1** approach; **l'a. de l'hiver** the approach of winter; **à l'a. de la vieillesse** as old age draws/drew near; **aux approches de la trentaine** as you/etc near *or* approach thirty; **à son a.** as he came up, as he approached; **d'une a. difficile** *(lieu)* hard to get to, not easily accessible; *(personne)* unapproachable; *(livre etc)* hard to understand; **à l'a. de la difficulté, elle abandonne** she gives up whenever a difficulty arises; **un homme d'a. facile** an approachable man

2 *(manière d'aborder)* **une nouvelle a. du problème** a new approach to the problem; **travail d'a.** manoeuvre, *Am* maneuver; **cette étude a nécessité un long travail d'a.** the study required a great deal of preliminary work; *Mktg* **a. bayésienne** Bayesian theory; *Aviat* **a. à vue** visual approach; **chasse à l'a.** deerstalking

3 *(environs)* **les approches d'une ville** the approaches of a town; **aux approches du village** on the outskirts of the village

4 *Typ (faute)* = extra space wrongly inserted between two letters; *(signe)* close-up sign *or* mark

5 *Zool* mating

approché [aprɔʃe] ADJ *(résultat, valeur)* approximate

approcher [aprɔʃe] VT **1** *(personne, objet)* to approach, to come near, to come close to; **a. qch de qn/qch** to bring *or* draw sth near (to) sb/sth; **approchez votre chaise** pull up your chair; **a. sa chaise de la lampe** to move one's chair nearer the lamp; **ne m'approchez pas** don't come near me; **elle approche les plus grands noms du spectacle** she rubs shoulders with the biggest names in showbusiness; **a. des lions d'assez près** to get quite close to some lions; **on ne peut pas l'a.** you can never see him; *(parce qu'il ne le veut pas)* you can't get near him, he's unapproachable; **le président? on ne peut pas l'a. comme ça!** you can't just walk up to the president!

2 *(faire des démarches auprès de)* *(personne)* to approach; **il a été approché par diverses sociétés** he was approached by various companies

VI **1** to approach, to draw near(er), to come nearer; **l'heure** *ou* **le moment approche** it will soon be time; **la nuit approchait** night was falling, it was beginning to get dark; **faites-le a.** ask him to come closer; **approche!** **je vais te montrer quelque chose!** come (over) here! I've something to show you!; **a. de qn/qch** to approach sb/sth; **nous approchons de Paris** we are approaching *or* getting near Paris; **a. du but** to be nearing one's goal; **il approche de la trentaine** he's getting on for *or* nearing *or* approaching thirty; **nous approchions alors les 200 km/heure** we were going at almost 200 km an hour

2 a. de qch to be *or* to come close to sth; **ça en approche** it's close, it's getting close (to it); **son art approche de la perfection** his

art comes close to perfection; **tu approches de la vérité** you're getting close to the truth; **son comportement approche de la folie** his behaviour borders on insanity

3 *Zool* to mate

VPR **s'approcher** to come *or* go closer *or* nearer, to draw near(er), to approach; **je n'ai pas pu m'a. de la scène, il y avait trop de monde** I couldn't get near the stage, there were too many people; **je me suis approché pour voir** I went closer to have a look; **s'a. de qn/qch** to come *or* go up to sb/sth; **ne t'approche pas du chien** don't go near the dog; **il faut t'a.!, viens!** come on!, come closer!; **le navire s'approchait de la terre** the ship was nearing land; **s'a. de la perfection** to be almost perfect, to be close to perfection

approfondi [aprɔfɔ̃di] ADJ *(recherche)* elaborate, detailed, extensive; *(enquête)* detailed, in-depth; *(connaissances)* thorough, in-depth

approfondir [aprɔfɔ̃dir] VT **1** *(lit de la rivière etc)* to deepen, to excavate **2** *(examiner)* *(problème)* to go deeply *or* thoroughly into; *(sujet)* to study thoroughly; **a. une affaire** to get to the root of a matter; **sans a. la question** *ou* **le sujet** without going into too much detail; **laissez-moi le temps d'a. la question** give me time to examine the question in detail

VPR **s'approfondir** to become deeper, to deepen

approfondissement [aprɔfɔ̃dismã] NM **1** *(d'un canal etc)* deepening, excavating, excavation **2** *(d'une question)* in-depth analysis; *(d'une étude)* further development

appropriation [aprɔprijasjɔ̃] NF **1** *(de biens etc)* appropriation; **a. par violence** forcible seizure; **a. de fonds** embezzlement, misappropriation of funds **2** *Arch, Belg* cleaning, tidying up

approprié [aprɔprije] ADJ appropriate *(à* for)

approprier [aprɔprije] *(pr sub, impf n. appropriions, v. appropriiez)* VT **1** *(adapter)* **a. qch** to arrange sth, to suit sth; **a. qch à qch** to adapt sth to sth; **a. son style à un public** to adapt one's style to (suit) an audience **2** *Arch, Belg (nettoyer)* to clean; *(ranger)* to tidy

VPR **s'approprier 1** *(s'adjuger)* **s'a. qch** to appropriate sth **2** *(s'adapter)* **s'a. à qch** to be suitable *or* appropriate for sth, to be in keeping with sth, to suit sth; **cette musique s'approprie à la situation** this music is suitable for the occasion

approuver [apruve] VT **a. qch** to approve of sth; **a. qch de la tête** to nod approval; **a. qn** to agree with sb; **a. qn de faire/d'avoir fait qch** to think sb is right for doing/having done sth; **elle approuve tout ce qu'il dit/fait** she agrees with everything he says/does; **nous vous approuvons dans votre choix** we approve of your choice; **a. qch officiellement** to agree formally to sth; *Com* **a. une facture** to pass an invoice; **a. un contrat** to ratify a contract; *Com* **a. et contre-argumenter** to agree and counter; *Admin* **a. une nomination** to confirm an appointment; **a. un appel** to endorse an appeal; **lu et approuvé** read and approved; **lessive approuvée par un grand nombre de fabriquants** washing powder recommended by a large number of manufacturers; *Méd* **médicament approuvé** approved drug *or* medicine

approvisionné [aprɔvizjɔne] ADJ stocked, supplied *(de, en* with); **bien a.** well-stocked; **magasin bien/mal a. en ...** shop with a good/poor stock of ...

approvisionnement [aprɔvizjɔnmã] NM **1** *(ravitaillement)* *(d'une ville, d'une armée)* supplying; *(d'une personne)* catering; *(d'un magasin)* stocking; **l'a. de la ville en produits frais** the supply(ing) of fresh produce to the town **2** *(provisions)* supply, stock, provisions; **faire un a. de qch** to stock up with sth

approvisionner [aprɔvizjɔne] VT **1** *(ravitailler, fournir)* to supply (**en** with); *(personne)* to cater for; *(magasin)* to stock; **a. une île en produits frais** to supply an island with fresh produce **2** *Banque* **a. son compte** to pay money into one's account; **son compte en banque n'est plus approvisionné** his bank account is no longer in credit

VPR **s'approvisionner** to lay in provisions, to get a stock *or* a supply (**en** of); **s'a. chez qn** to get one's supplies from sb; *(d'une ménagère etc)* to shop at sb's; **s'a. au marché** to shop *or* to do one's shopping *or* to buy one's provisions at the market; **s'a. en qch** to stock up on sth

approximatif, -ive [aprɔksimatif, -iv] ADJ *(calcul, estimation)* approximate, rough; **ce chiffre est très a.** this figure is only a rough estimate; **nous nous sommes exprimés dans un anglais a.** we expressed ourselves in broken English

approximation [aprɔksimasjɔ̃] NF approximation, rough estimate; *Math* approximation

approximativement [aprɔksimativmɑ̃] ADV approximately, roughly; **dans une heure a.** in an hour or so

appt *abrév* **appartement**

appui [apɥi] NM **1** *(support)* support, prop; *Archit* balustrade; **mur d'a.** supporting *or* retaining wall; **barre d'a.** handrail; **point d'a.** *(d'un levier)* fulcrum; *Mil (d'opérations)* base; **à hauteur d'a.** elbow high; **mettre un a. à un mur** to shore up a wall; **prendre a. sur qch** to be supported by *or* on sth; *(d'une personne)* to support oneself on sth; **prendre a. sur le pied gauche** *(pour sauter)* to take off from the left foot; **a. de fenêtre** window ledge *or* sill; **a. de porte** door sill **2** *(aide)* support, backing; **a. moral** moral support; **a. financier** (financial) backing; **la société ne bénéficie pas d'un a. financier suffisant** the company does not have sufficient financial backing; **prêter son a. à qn** to support *or* lend support to sb, to back sb up; **vous avez mon a.** you have my support *or* backing; **être sans appui(s)** to be friendless; **avoir des appuis en haut lieu** to have friends in high places; **à l'a.** *(de qch)* in support; **à l'a., il me montra tes lettres** to support *or* to back up what he said, he showed me your letters; **avec preuves à l'a.** with supporting evidence; **à l'a. d'un témoignage** in support of testimony **3** *Mil* **a. direct** close *or* Am direct support; **tir d'a.** covering fire; **a. tactique/aérien** tactical/air support **4** *Ordinat* **a. droite** flush right; **texte en a. droite** right justified text

appui-bras, *pl* **appuis-bras** NM armrest

appuie- [apɥi] *(compound nouns of which the first element is* **appui-** *have an alternative form* **appuie-,** *in which case they are invariable)*

appui-jambes, *pl* **appuis-jambes** NM leg rest

appui-nuque, *pl* **appuis-nuque** NM headrest

appui-queue, *pl* **appuis-queue** NM *Billard* (cue) rest, *Fam* jigger

appui-tête, *pl* **appuis-tête** NM headrest, head restraint

appuyé [apɥije] ADJ *(plaisanterie, ironie)* laboured, *Am* labored, heavy; **regard a.** (fixed) stare; **il lui lançait des regards appuyés** he stared at him intently

appuyer [apɥije] (j'**appuie,** n. **appuyons;** j'**appuierai)** VT **1** *(mettre contre)* to lean, to rest (**qch contre qch** sth against sth); **a. sa**

tête contre la fenêtre to lean one's head against the window; **a. sa tête sur l'épaule de qn** to rest one's head on sb's shoulder; *Fig* **a. son opinion sur qch** to base one's opinion on sth; *Fig* **théorie appuyée sur des faits** theory supported by facts

2 *(exercer une pression sur)* **a. qch sur qch** to press sth on sth; **a. son pied sur la pédale de frein** to put one's foot on the brake; *Fig* **a. son regard sur qn** to stare intently at sb

3 *(mur, solive etc)* to support, to prop (up)

4 *Fig (soutenir)* **a. une pétition** to support a petition (**par** by); **a. une proposition** to second a proposal; **a. un candidat** to back *or* support a candidate; **a. la demande de qn** to support sb's request; **a. qn financièrement** to back sb (financially), to give sb financial backing

VI **1** *(reposer)* to bear (**sur** on); **poutre qui appuie sur deux montants** beam resting *or* bearing on two uprights

2 *(presser)* to depress; **a. sur la valise pour la fermer** to press down on the suitcase to close it; **a. sur le point sensible** to press the sore spot; **a. sur son stylo** to press on one's pen; **a. sur le bouton** to press the button; *Aut Fam* **a. sur le champignon** *(accélérer)* to step on it, to put one's foot down; **a. sur une syllabe** to stress a syllable; *Mus* **a. sur une note** to hold a note; **a. sur l'urgence d'un problème** to stress the urgency of a problem; *Fam* **inutile d'a. là-dessus, on a compris** you don't need to keep going on about it, we understand; **appuyez à droite à la sortie du village** bear right as you leave the village

VPR **s'appuyer 1** *(reposer)* **s'a. sur** *ou* **contre** *ou* **à qch** to lean *or* rest on *or* against sth; **s'a. sur** *ou* **contre le bras de qn** to lean on sb's arm; **s'a. sur qn** to lean on sb; *Fig* to lean *or* to rely *or* depend on sb; **s'a. sur son expérience pour conseiller qn** to draw on *or* to use one's experience to advise sb; **ses recherches s'appuient sur des découvertes récentes** his research is based on recent discoveries

2 *Fam* **s'a. une corvée** to be lumbered with a chore; **c'est toujours moi qui m'appuie la vaisselle!** it's always me who gets lumbered with the dishes!; **s'a. un bon dîner/un gentil petit voyage** to treat oneself to *or* stand oneself a good dinner/a nice little trip

âpre [apr] ADJ **1** *(aigre)* rough, harsh; **voix â.** rasping voice; **goût â.** sour taste; **vin â.** rough wine **2** *(temps, vent)* raw **3** *(dégoût)* bitter, biting, sharp; *(ironie)* scathing **4** *(lutte)* bitter **5** *(concurrence etc)* keen; **homme â. (au gain)** grasping man; **être â. au gain** to be grasping *or* money-grabbing

âprement [aprəmɑ̃] ADV *(défendu)* fiercely; *(se disputer)* violently

après [aprɛ] PRÉP **1** *(dans le temps, dans l'espace)* after; **il est arrivé a. moi** he arrived after me; **a. tout** after all; **fermé a. 20 heures** closed from 8 o'clock (onwards); **a. bien des discussions, nous avons décidé de …** after a great deal of discussion, we decided to …; **jour a. jour** day after day; **a. vous, monsieur/madame!** after you!; **et a. cela, madame?** *(au restaurant)* and to follow, madam?; **a. quoi** after which; **je suis** *ou* **viens a. lui** I am *or* come after him; **tourner à droite a. la poste** turn right just past the post office; *Fam* **courir a. qn** to run after sb; **les chiens risquent de nous courir a.** the dogs might run after us; *Fig Fam* **ces garçons qui te courent a.** those boys who are (always) chasing (after) you; *Fig Fam* **tout le monde leur court a.** everybody runs after them; **jurer/maugréer a. qn** to swear/grumble at sb; **il est toujours a. moi** he's always nagging at me *or* getting at me; *Fam* **en**

avoir **a. qn** to have it in for sb; **les jeux passent a. le travail** work comes before play; **ça passe a. tout le reste** everything else comes first

2 d'**a.** according to; **d'a. ce qu'elle a dit** going by *or* according to what she said; **d'a. l'horloge, il est trois heures** according to the clock, it's three; **peint d'a. nature** painted from life; **paysage d'a. Turner** landscape after Turner; **texte d'a. Cicéron** text adapted from Cicero; **d'a. l'article 12** under article 12; **d'a. vos instructions** in accordance with your instructions

3 (+ *inf*) **a. avoir dîné** after dinner; **a. manger** after eating

ADV afterwards, later; **parlez d'abord, je parlerai a.** you speak first, I'll speak afterwards; **six semaines a.** six weeks later; **les vacances, ça passe a.** holidays are not a priority; **avec lui, la famille, ça passe a.** his family takes second place; **le jour (d')a.** the next *or* following day, the day after; **la page d'a.** the next *or* following page; **nous eûmes des huîtres, et a. du saumon** we had oysters, followed by salmon; **et a.?** what then?; **et a., qu'est-ce qu'il a dit?** and then what did he say?; *Fam* **eh bien, et puis a.?** well, what of it?, what about it?, so what?

CONJ **a. que** after, when; **a. que je fus** *ou Fam* **sois parti** after I had gone; *Vieilli* **a. que j'aurai fini** when I have finished

après- [aprɛ] PRÉF post-…; **la période de l'a.-soixante-huit** the period after 1968, the post-1968 period; **le Moscou de l'a.-Gorbatchev** Moscow in the post-Gorbachev era; **les jeunes de l'a.-sida** the post-Aids generation

après-demain ADV the day after tomorrow

après-dîner, *pl* **après-dîners** NM evening; **discours d'a.** after-dinner speech

après-guerre, *pl* **après-guerres** NM post-war period

après-midi NM INV OU NF INV afternoon; **trois heures de l'a.** three (o'clock) in the afternoon, three pm

après-rasage, *pl* **après-rasages** ADJ INV lotion **a.** aftershave (lotion)
NM aftershave

après-ski NM INV *(chaussure)* snowboot

Il faut noter que le nom anglais **après-ski** est un faux ami. Il désigne les activités récréatives auxquelles on se livre après une séance de ski.

après-vente ADJ INV *Com* service **a.** after-sales service

âpreté [aprəte] NF **1** *(du vin, de la voix, de l'hiver etc)* roughness, harshness; *(du froid)* sharpness; *(d'un fruit)* sourness, tartness **2** *(du ton etc)* bitterness; *(des reproches)* sharpness, bitterness; *(de la concurrence)* fierceness

a priori [apriɔri] ADJ INV a priori; **raisonnement a.** a priori reasoning
ADV a priori; **a. ça me paraît possible** in principle, I think it's possible
NM INV preconception, apriorism; **avoir des a. (contre/en faveur de qch)** to be biased *or* prejudiced (against/in favour of sth); **être sans a.** to be impartial

apr. J.-C. *(abrév* **après Jésus-Christ)** AD

à-propos NM *(d'une expression etc)* aptness, appropriateness, relevance; **avoir l'esprit d'à.** to have presence of mind; **répondre avec à.** to give a suitable *or* an appropriate reply; **il fait des commentaires sans le moindre à.** he makes comments that aren't the slightest bit relevant; **votre observation manque d'à.** your remark is not to the point *or* is irrelevant; **son manque d'à. lui joua des tours** the fact that he always does/says the wrong thing is going to cause him problems

apte [apt] ADJ **a. à faire qch/à qch** fit or suited or qualified to do sth/for sth; **peu a. (à faire qch)** unsuitable, ill-equipped (to do sth); **a. à accomplir une tâche** well-suited or qualified to carry out a task; **a. à naviguer** seaworthy; *Mil* **a. au service** fit for military service; *Jur* **a. à hériter** entitled to inherit

aptère [aptɛr] ADJ wingless; *Beaux-Arts* **victoire a.** wingless victory

aptéryx [apteriks] NM *(oiseau)* kiwi

aptitude [aptityd] NF **1** *(capacité)* aptitude, ability (**à, pour** to); **il a des aptitudes manuelles** he's good with his hands; **avoir des aptitudes intellectuelles** to have intellectual skills; **avoir une a. pour qch** *(être doué)* to have a gift for sth; **test d'a.** aptitude test; **certificat d'a. professionnelle** = vocational training certificate **2** *Jur* capacity

apurement [apyrmɑ̃] NM **1** *(d'un compte)* auditing, agreeing **2** *(d'une dette, du passif)* discharge

apurer [apyre] VT **1** *(comptes)* to audit **2** *(dette, passif)* to discharge

aquaculteur, -trice [akwakyltœr, -tris] N fish farmer

aquaculture [akwakyltyr] NF aquaculture; *(de poissons)* fish farming

aquaplanage [akwaplanaʒ] NM *Aut* aquaplaning

aquaplane [akwaplan] NM *Sport* aquaplaning; *(planche)* aquaplane

aquaplaning [akwaplaniŋ] NM *Aut* = aquaplanage

aquaplaniste [akwaplanist] N *Sport* aquaplaner

aquarelle [akwarɛl] NF *Beaux-Arts* watercolour, *Am* watercolor; **peindre à l'a.** to paint in watercolours; **une a. de Matisse** a watercolour by Matisse, a Matisse watercolour

aquarelliste [akwarɛlist] N watercolourist, *Am* watercolorist

aquarium [akwarjɔm] NM aquarium; **a. d'eau de mer** oceanarium

aquatinte [akwatɛ̃t] NF aquatint

aquatique [akwatik] ADJ **1** *(oiseau, plante, sport)* aquatic **2** *(sol)* marshy, watery

aqueduc [ak(ə)dyk] NM **1** *(construction)* aqueduct **2** *Anat* aqueduct, canal

aqueux, -euse [akø, -øz] ADJ **1** *(boisson, fruit etc)* watery; *(sol)* waterlogged **2** *Anat, Chimie etc* aqueous, water; **humeur aqueuse** aqueous humour

à quia [akɥija] ADV *Litt* **être à.** to be at a loss for words or a reply; **mettre qn à.** to render sb speechless, to nonplus sb

aquiculture [akɥikyltyr] NF = aquaculture

aquifère [akɥifɛr] ADJ *Géol* **nappe a.** aquifer

aquilin [akilɛ̃, -in] ADJ *(profil etc)* aquiline; **nez a.** aquiline or hook or Roman nose

aquilon [akilɔ̃] NM north wind

Aquin [akɛ̃] N **Saint Thomas d'A.** St Thomas Aquinas

aquitain, -aine [akitɛ̃, -ɛn] ADJ of or from Aquitaine
  N A. *(natif)* native of Aquitaine; *(habitant)* inhabitant of Aquitaine

Aquitaine [akitɛn] NF *Hist* (province of) Aquitaine; **bassin d'A.** Basin of Aquitaine

A.R. *(abrév* **aller retour)** return

ara [ara] NM *(oiseau)* macaw

arabe [arab] VOIR GRAMMAIRE A19 ADJ *(monde, littérature, pays)* Arab, Arabic; *(chiffres, langue etc)* Arabic; *(cheval)* Arab; *(coutumes, civilisation etc)* Arabian, Arabic
  NM *Ling* Arabic
  N **A.** Arab

Arabe

Note that in a French context this word usually refers to people from the former colonies of North Africa, who make up the largest ethnic minority in France.

---

arabesque [arabɛsk] ADJ *(architecture etc)* arabesque, Arabian
  NF *(danse, ornement)* arabesque; **la fumée monte en arabesques** the smoke curls up

arabica [arabika] NM *(café)* arabica

Arabie [arabi] NF Arabia; **A. saoudite** Saudi Arabia; **le désert d'A.** the Arabian desert

arabique [arabik] ADJ **gomme a.** gum arabic

arabisant, -ante [arabizɑ̃, -ɑ̃t] N Arabic scholar, Arabist

arabisation [arabizasjɔ̃] NF Arabization

arabiser [arabize] VT to Arabize

arable [arabl] ADJ *(terre etc)* arable

arabophone [arabɔfɔn] ADJ Arabic-speaking
  N Arabic speaker

arachide [araʃid] NF *(plante)* peanut, groundnut, *Br Fam* monkey nut; **huile d'a.** groundnut oil; **beurre d'a.** peanut butter

arachnéen, -enne [araknee, -ɛn] ADJ *(de l'araignée)* of spiders; *Litt* **légèreté arachnéenne** gossamer lightness; **être d'une légèreté arachnéenne** to be as light as thistledown

arachnides [araknid] NMPL *Zool* Arachnida

arachnoïde [araknɔid] NF *Anat* arachnoid *(membrane)*

araignée [arɛɲe] NF **1** spider; **toile d'a.** cobweb, spider's web; *Fam* **avoir une a. au plafond** to have a screw loose, to have bats in the belfry; *Fig* **a. du matin, chagrin, a. du soir, espoir** = seeing a spider in the morning will bring bad luck, seeing a spider in the evening will bring good luck **2** *Ordinat* spider
  ▸▸ *Zool* **a. d'eau** water spider; **a. de mer** *(crustacé)* spider crab; *(poisson)* weever *(fish)*

araire [arɛr] NM *Agr* swing or ard plough

araméen, -enne [aramee, -ɛn] ADJ, NM *Ling* Aramaic

arasé [araze] ADJ flush; **armoire arasée** built-in cupboard

araser [araze] VT **1** *Constr* **a. un mur** to level (off) a wall; **a. deux pierres** to make two stones flush; **a. une planche** to plane a plank down **2** *Géol (roche)* to erode, to weather

aratoire [aratwar] ADJ *(outils, instruments)* agricultural

araucaria [arokarja] NM *(arbre)* araucaria, monkey puzzle (tree)

arbalète [arbalɛt] NF crossbow

arbalétrier [arbaletrije] NM **1** *Constr (d'un toit etc)* principal rafter **2** *(soldat)* crossbowman

arbitrage [arbitraʒ] NM **1** *Sport (au tennis)* umpiring; *(au football)* refereeing; *(dans un conflit social)* arbitration; **conseil d'a.** *(dans un conflit social)* conciliation or arbitration board; **soumettre un litige à l'a. d'un tiers** to take a dispute to arbitration by a third party; *Sport* **erreur d'a.** mistake by the referee or umpire **2** *Banque etc* arbitrage
  ▸▸ **a. de change** arbitration of exchange; *Bourse* **a. en reports** jobbing in contango(e)s

arbitragiste [arbitraʒist] N *Bourse* arbitrager

arbitraire [arbitrɛr] ADJ **1** *(nom, choix etc)* arbitrary; *(punition etc)* discretionary **2** *(gouvernement, pouvoir, action etc)* arbitrary, despotic, high-handed; *(ordre)* arbitrary
  NM arbitrariness, arbitrary nature; **laisser qch à l'a. de qn** to leave sth to sb's discretion

arbitrairement [arbitrɛrmɑ̃] ADV arbitrarily

arbitral, -ale, -aux, -ales [arbitral, -o] ADJ *Jur* arbitration; **tribunal a.** tribunal, court of arbitration; **solution arbitrale, règlement a.** settlement by arbitration; **commission arbitrale** board of referees

arbitre [arbitr] NM **1** *Jur* arbitrator, referee, adjudicator **2** *Sport* referee; *Tennis* umpire; **a. de touche** *Ftbl* linesman; *Rugby* touch judge **3** *Fig (de la mode, dans une dispute etc)* arbiter **4** *Phil* **libre a.** free will
  ▸▸ **a. rapporteur** *(dans un conflit commercial)* arbitrator

arbitrer [arbitre] VT **1** *Jur* to arbitrate **2** *Sport (match de football)* to referee; *(match de tennis)* to umpire **3** *Bourse* **a. des valeurs** to do arbitrage trading

arboré [arbɔre] ADJ planted with trees

arborer [arbɔre] VT **1** *(dresser)* to raise, to erect, to set up; *(drapeau)* to hoist; *Naut (mât)* to step; **a. l'étendard de la révolte** to raise the standard of revolt **2** *(porter, exhiber)* **a. une cravate rouge/une rose à la boutonnière** to wear or sport a red tie/a rose in one's buttonhole; **elle arbore un sourire triomphant** she is wearing a triumphant smile; **a. un air de mépris** to affect an air of disdain; **a. certaines idées** to parade certain ideas

arborescence [arbɔresɑ̃s] NF **1** *Bot* arborescence **2** *Ordinat (structure)* tree diagram or structure, directory structure; *(chemin)* directory path; **a. des répertoires** directory tree

arborescent [arbɔresɑ̃] ADJ **1** *Bot* arborescent; **fougère arborescente** tree fern **2** *Math, Ordinat* **structure arborescente** tree diagram or structure, directory structure

arborétum [arbɔretɔm] NM *Bot* arboretum

arboricole [arbɔrikɔl] ADJ **1** *(technique etc)* arboricultural **2** *(animal)* tree-dwelling, arboreal

arboriculteur, -trice [arbɔrikyltœr, -tris] N nurseryman, nurserywoman

arboriculture [arbɔrikyltyr] NF arboriculture; **a. fruitière** fruit growing

arborisation [arbɔrizasjɔ̃] NF *(de cristaux)* arborization; *(du givre sur les vitres)* tree-like markings

arborisé [arbɔrize] ADJ **1** *Minér* dendritic **2** *Suisse (boisé)* planted with trees

arbouse [arbuz] NF arbutus berry

arbousier [arbuzje] NM *(arbre)* arbutus; **a. commun** strawberry tree

arbre [arbr] NM **1** *(végétal)* tree; **jeune a.** sapling; **a. fruitier** fruit tree; **arbres d'agrément** ornamental trees; **a. à feuille(s) caduque(s)** deciduous tree; **a. résineux** softwood (tree); **a. feuillu** hardwood (tree); **a. vert** evergreen (tree); *Fig* **faire l'a. fourchu** to do a headstand *(with one's legs apart)*; *Prov* **entre l'a. et l'écorce, il ne faut point mettre le doigt** don't get involved in other people's affairs; *Fig* **les arbres cachent la forêt** you can't see the wood for the trees; *Fig* **les arbres lui cachent la forêt** he can't see the wood for the trees; *Fig* **couper l'a. pour avoir le fruit** to kill the goose that lays the golden egg SEE GRAMMAR B6
  2 *Ordinat* tree; *Math, Ordinat* **structure en a.** tree diagram
  3 *Tech* shaft, spindle, axle; *(d'horloge etc)* arbor
  ▸▸ **a. d'accouplement** coupling shaft; *Aut* **a. arrière** back axle shaft; **a. à cames** camshaft; *Aut* **a. à cames en tête** overhead camshaft; **a. à caoutchouc** rubber tree; **a. à cardan** ou **de cardan(s)** cardan shaft; **a. coudé** ou **vilebrequin, a.-manivelle** crankshaft; **a. creux** hollow spindle, tubular shaft; **l'a. de la Croix**

the Rood; **a. de culbuteur** rocker shaft; *Mktg* **a. de décision** decision tree; *Aut* **a. de distribution** distributor shaft, camshaft; *Aut* **a. d'entrée** input *or* primary shaft; **a. d'entraînement** drive shaft; *Aut* **a. d'essieu** axle shaft; **a. à excentrique(s), a. excentré** *ou* **excentrique** eccentric shaft; **a. fou** loose shaft; **a. généalogique** family tree; **faire son a. généalogique** to trace one's family tree; **a. de l'hélice, a. porte-hélice** propeller shaft; *Élec* **a. d'induit** armature shaft; *Aut* **a. intermédiaire** layshaft, countershaft; **a. de Jessé** tree of Jesse; **a. de Judée** Judas tree; **a. de la liberté** tree of liberty; **a. moteur** *ou* **de commande** main *or* driving shaft; **a. de Noël** Christmas tree; **a. à pain** bread(fruit) tree; **a. de plein vent** standard; *Aut* **a. de pompe** pump shaft; *Aut* **a. primaire** primary *or* input shaft; *Aut* **a. principal** mainshaft, third motion shaft; *Aut* **a. de renvoi** layshaft; *Anat* **a. respiratoire** respiratory system; *Aut* **a. de roue** axle shaft; *Aut* **a. secondaire** secondary shaft, layshaft; *Aut* **a. de sortie** output shaft; **a. de tour** lathe spindle, mandrel; **a. de transmission** line shaft; *Aut* propeller *or* transmission shaft, propshaft; **a. de vie** tree of life

arbrisseau, -eaux [arbriso] NM shrub; **plantation d'arbrisseaux** shrubbery

arbuste [arbyst] NM bush, shrub; **plantation d'arbustes** shrubbery

arc [ark] NM **1** *(arme)* bow; **tir à l'a.** archery; **tirer à l'a.** to do archery; **tu sais tirer à l'a.?** can you use a bow and arrow?; **à la portée de l'a.** within bowshot; **corde de l'a.** bowstring; *Fig* **avoir plusieurs cordes à son a.** to have more than one string to one's bow; **ressort à a.** bow spring; **scie à a.** bow saw **2** *Archit, Anat* arch; **l'a. des sourcils/de l'aorte** the arch of the eyebrows/of the aorta; **a. dentaire** dental arch **3** *Géom* **a. de cercle** arc of a circle; **assis en a. de cercle** sitting in a semicircle **4** *Élec* **a. voltaïque** voltaic arc; **a. électrique** electric arc; **soudure en a.** arc welding; **lampe à a.** arc lamp ▸▸ **a. brisé** *ou* **aigu** gothic arch; **a. en fer à cheval** horseshoe arch; **a. en plein cintre, a. roman** semicircular arch; **a. de triomphe** triumphal arch

arcade [arkad] NF **1** *Archit* archway; **a. feinte** blind arcade; **arcades** arcade; **se promener sous les arcades** to walk through the arcade **2** *Anat* **a. dentaire/orbitaire** dental/orbital arch; **a. sourcilière** the arch of the eyebrows **3** *Suisse (local commercial)* shop, store

arcadé [arkade] ADJ *(allée, promenade etc)* arcaded

arcane [arkan] NM mystery; **les arcanes de la politique/du pouvoir** the arcane mysteries of politics/of power

arcature [arkatyr] NF *Archit* arcature, blind arcade

arc-boutant, *pl* **arcs-boutants** [arkbutã] NM **1** *Archit* flying buttress **2** *Constr* abutment pier

arc-bouter [arkbute] VT **1** *(mur)* to buttress, to support with flying buttresses **2** *(étayer) (mur etc)* to prop up, to shore up
VPR **s'arc-bouter** to brace oneself; **s'a. sur ses jambes** to brace one's legs

arc-doubleau, *pl* **arcs-doubleaux** [arkdublo] NM *Archit* transverse rib

arceau, -eaux [arso] NM **1** *(d'une voûte)* arch **2** *(croquet)* hoop; *Méd* (bed-)cradle; *Aut* **a. de sécurité** roll bar, roll-over framework

arc-en-ciel, *pl* **arcs-en-ciel** [arkãsjɛl] NM rainbow

archaïque [arkaik] ADJ *(style, expression etc)* archaic

archaïsant [arkaizã] ADJ archaistic

archaïsme [arkaism] NM archaism

archange [arkãʒ] NM archangel

arche[1] [arʃ] NF *Rel* ark; **l'a. de Noé** Noah's ark; **l'a. d'alliance, l'a. sainte** the Ark of the Covenant

arche[2] NF *(d'un pont etc)* arch; *Géol* **a. naturelle** natural arc

archéologie [arkeɔlɔʒi] NF arch(a)eology

archéologique [arkeɔlɔʒik] ADJ arch(a)eological

archéologue [arkeɔlɔg] N arch(a)eologist

archer [arʃe] NM archer, bowman

archet [arʃɛ] NM **1** *(de violon etc)* bow; **scie à a.** bow saw; **avoir un bon coup d'a.** *(d'un violoniste)* to be a good violinist; *(d'un violoncelliste)* to be a good cellist **2** *Rail* pantograph

archétypal, -ale, -aux, -ales [arketipal, -o] ADJ archetypal

archétype [arketip] ADJ archetypal
NM archetype, prototype; **c'est l'a. du père de famille** he is the archetypal father figure

archevêché [arʃəveʃe] NM **1** *(territoire)* archbishopric, archdiocese **2** *(fonction)* archbishopric **3** *(résidence)* archbishop's palace

archevêque [arʃəvɛk] NM archbishop

archiconnu [arʃikɔny] ADJ *Fam* very well known; **c'est a.** everybody knows that

archicube [arʃikyb] NM *Scol Fam* graduate of the École normale supérieure

archidiacre [arʃidjakr] NM *Rel* archdeacon

archidiocèse [arʃidjɔsɛz] NM *Rel* archdiocese, archbishopric

archiduc [arʃidyk] NM archduke

archiduchesse [arʃidyʃɛs] NF archduchess

Archie [arʃi] NM *Ordinat* Archie

archiépiscopal, -ale, -aux, -ales [arʃiepiskɔpal, -o] ADJ archiepiscopal

archiépiscopat [arʃiepiskɔpa] NM archiepiscopate, archiepiscopacy

archifaux, -fausse [arʃifo, -fos] ADJ *Fam* dead wrong

Archimède [arʃimɛd] N *Hist* Archimedes; *Phys* **le principe d'A.** Archimedes' principle; *Tech* **vis d'A.** Archimedean screw

archimillionnaire [arʃimiljɔnɛr] ADJ, N *Fam* multimillionaire

archipel [arʃipɛl] NM *Géog* archipelago

archisec, -sèche [arʃisɛk, -sɛʃ] ADJ *Fam* bone-dry

archisecret, -ète [arʃisəkrɛ, -ɛt] ADJ *Fam* top secret, hush-hush

architecte [arʃitɛkt] N *(d'un immeuble)*, *Fig (d'une réforme)* architect; **a. paysagiste** landscape architect; **a. naval** naval architect; *Ordinat* **a. de réseaux** network architect; **a. urbaniste** town planner

architectonique [arʃitɛktɔnik] ADJ architectonic
NF architectonics

architectural, -ale, -aux, -ales [arʃitɛktyral, -o] ADJ architectural

architecture [arʃitɛktyr] NF *(d'une ville, d'un ordinateur etc)* architecture; **a. navale/industrielle/religieuse** naval/industrial/religious architecture; **cette maison a une très belle a.** this house is beautifully designed; *Fig* **l'a. du corps** the way the body is designed, the structure of the body; *Ordinat* **a. client-serveur** client-server architecture; *Ordinat* **a. évolutive** upgradable architecture; *Ordinat* **a. à micro-canaux** microchannel architecture

architecturer [arʃitɛktyre] VT *(discours, roman, texte)* to structure; *Ordinat* **architecturé autour de ...** with its architecture built around ...

architrave [arʃitrav] NF *Archit* architrave

archivage [arʃivaʒ] NM archiving, filing

archive [arʃiv] NF *Ordinat* archive

archiver [arʃive] VT to archive, to file

archives [arʃiv] NFPL archives, records; **exemplaire des a.** file copy; **les a. nationales** ≃ the (Public) Record Office; **a. audiovisuelles/sonores** audiovisual/sound archives; **a. de coupures de presse** cuttings library; **a. photographiques** photographic archives; *Fam* **ça restera dans les a.** that'll go down in history, wonders will never cease

archiviste [arʃivist] N archivist; *(fonction publique)* keeper of public records; *Com etc* clerk (in charge of records), filing clerk

arçon [arsɔ] NM **1** *(de selle)* saddle bow; **vider les arçons** to fall off one's horse; **être ferme sur ses arçons** to be steady in the saddle; *Fig* **Vieilli Fam** to have fixed opinions; *Gym* **cheval d'arçons** (vaulting) horse **2** *Tex* bow

arçonner [arsɔne] VT *Tex (coton, laine etc)* to card *or* clean with a bow

arctique [arktik] ADJ arctic; **cercle a.** Arctic Circle
NM **l'A.** the Arctic

ardemment [ardamã] ADV *(aimer)* ardently, passionately; *(travailler)* enthusiastically, eagerly; **désirer qch a.** to crave sth; **désirer a. faire qch** to yearn to do sth

Ardennes [arden] NFPL **les A.** the Ardennes; **la Bataille des A.** the Battle of the Bulge

ardent [ardã] ADJ **1** *(feu etc)* burning hot, scorching, blazing; **soleil a.** scorching *or* blazing sun; **soif ardente** raging thirst; **cheveux d'un blond/roux a.** strawberry *or* reddish blond/fiery red hair; **rouge a.** fiery red **2** *(passionné)* fiery, passionate, ardent; **désir a.** burning desire; **jeune homme a.** hot-blooded *or* passionate young man; **ardente conviction** deep-seated conviction; **j'en ai l'ardente conviction** I am firmly convinced of it; **socialiste a.** red-hot Socialist; **a. sportif** keen sportsman **3** *(vif) (intérêt)* keen; *(imagination)* vivid; *(curiosité)* burning; *Fam (lutte)* fierce; **être dans une colère ardente** to be in a furious rage

ardeur [ardœr] NF **1** *(du soleil, du feu etc)* heat **2** *(enthousiasme)* eagerness, ardour, *Am* ardor, fervour, *Am* fervor; **cheval plein d'a.** high-spirited *or* high-mettled horse; **travailler avec a.** to work hard *or* enthusiastically; **soutenir son opinion avec a.** to argue one's case with passion *or* passionately; **modère tes ardeurs!** calm down!, don't get excited!; **les ardeurs de la passion** the heat of passion; **son a. à lire** his passion for reading

ardoise [ardwaz] NF **1** *Minér* slate; **(feuille d')a.** slate; **maison au toit d'ardoises** house with a slate roof; **couvrir un toit d'a.** to slate a roof **2** **a. (à écrire)** (writing) slate; *Fam (compte)* bill, cost; **crayon d'a.** slate pencil; *Fam* **mets ça sur mon a.** put it on my slate *or* bill *or* tab; *Fam* **il a des ardoises dans tous les bars de la ville** he owes money in all the bars in town; *Fam* **j'ai quelques ardoises à régler** I've got a few bills to pay; *TV, Cin* **a. d'identification** identifying head slate; *Ordinat* **a. électronique** notepad computer
ADJ **(couleur) gris a.** slate grey (colour)

ardoisé [ardwaze] ADJ slate-colour(ed), bluish-grey

ardoisier, -ière [ardwazje, -jɛr] ADJ slaty; **schiste a.** slate clay, shale
NM *(exploitant)* owner of a slate quarry; *(ouvrier)* slate worker *or* quarryman
NF **ardoisière** slate quarry

ardt *abrév* arrondissement

ardu [ardy] ADJ **1** *(tâche etc)* difficult, hard, arduous **2** *Rare (pente etc)* steep

are [ar] NM *Agr* are (= 100 square metres)

arec [arɛk] NM **1** areca palm (tree) **2** (**noix d'**)a. areca or betel nut

areligieux, -ieuse [arəliʒjø, -jøz] ADJ not religious

aréna [arena] NF *Can* arena

arène [arɛn] NF **1** (d'amphithéâtre) arena; (de tauromachie) bullring; **les arènes d'Arles** the amphitheatre of Arles; *Fig* **descendre dans l'a.** to enter the ring or the fray, to take up the challenge; *Fig* **l'a. politique** the political arena **2** *Arch, Litt* sand

arénicole [arenikɔl] ADJ that lives in sand

aréole [areɔl] NF *Anat, Bot, Méd* areola

aréomètre [areɔmɛtr] NM hydrometer

aréométrie [areɔmetri] NF hydrometry

aréopage [areɔpaʒ] NM *Fig* learned gathering or assembly

arête [arɛt] NF **1** (de poisson) (fish) bone; **c'est du poisson pané, garanti sans arêtes** it's breaded fish, guaranteed boneless; **enlever toutes les arêtes d'un poisson** to bone a fish; **poisson plein d'arêtes** bony fish; **grande a.** (d'un poisson) backbone; **dessin en a. de hareng** ou *Archit* de poisson herringbone pattern **2** (du nez) bridge **3** *Constr etc* line; **a. d'un comble** hip of a roof; **pierre d'a.** quoin stone; **a. de voûte** groin **4** *Aviat* **dorsale** (du fuselage) dorsal fin **5** *Géog* ridge **6** (de graminées etc) beard **7** (de la lame d'une épée, d'une baïonnette) ridge, rib

argent [arʒã] NM **1** (métal) silver; **vaisselle d'a.** (silver) plate; **couverts en a.** silver cutlery; **a. en feuille** silver foil, silver leaf; **bijoux en a.** silver jewellery; *Prov* **la parole est d'a., le silence est d'or** speech is silver, silence is golden; *Sport* **gagner la médaille d'a.** to win the silver (medal); *Fig* **cheveux d'a.** silvery(-grey) hair; **reflets d'a. sur le lac** silvery glints on the lake

2 *Fin* money; **avoir de l'a.** (être riche) to have money; (sur soi) to have some money; *Compta* **en caisse** cash in hand; (recettes) takings; **payer a. comptant** to pay (in) cash; *Fam* **se faire un a. fou** to make lots or loads of money; **placer son a.** to invest one's money; **les puissances de l'a.** the rich and powerful; **a. à bon marché** cheap money; *Fig* **l'a. lui fond entre les mains** money just slips through his fingers; **elle le fait pour l'a.** she does it for the money; **attendre une rentrée d'a.** to be waiting for money to come in; *Fig* **jeter de l'a. par les fenêtres** to throw money down the drain, to throw money away; **en avoir pour son a.** to have or get one's money's worth, to get good value for (one's) money; *Fig* **plaie d'a. n'est pas mortelle** money isn't everything, it's only money; *Fig* **prendre tout pour a. comptant** to take everything at face value; **le temps, c'est de l'a.** time is money

▸▸**a. électronique** e-cash, electronic money; **a. liquide** cash (in hand), ready money or cash; **a. de poche** pocket money; **a. à vue** call money

argenté [arʒãte] ADJ **1** (couleur) silver, silvery; **gris a.** silver-grey; **reflet a.** silvery glint, glint of silver; **renard a.** silver fox **2** (plaqué, couvert) silver-plated **3** *Fam* (riche) well-heeled, loaded; **je ne suis pas très a. en ce moment** I'm not in funds at the moment, I'm a bit hard up at the moment, I'm a bit strapped at the moment

argenter [arʒãte] VT to silver(-plate); *Fig* **la lune argente le lac de ses reflets** the moon gives the lake a silvery sheen

argenterie [arʒãtri] NF (silver) plate, silverware

argenteur [arʒãtœr] NM silverer, silver plater

argentier [arʒãtje] NM **1** (meuble) silver ca-

binet **2** *Hist* = superintendent of the Royal Household **3** *Fam* **le Grand a.** (ministre) the Finance Minister

argentin¹ [arʒãtɛ̃] ADJ (voix, rire, vagues) silvery; (cloche) tinkling

argentin², -ine [arʒãtɛ̃, -in] ADJ Argentinian, Argentine; **la République Argentine** Argentina, the Argentine (Republic)
N **A.** Argentinian, Argentine
NF **l'Argentine** Argentina, the Argentine (Republic)

argile [arʒil] NF clay; **a. à blocaux** boulder clay; **a. schisteuse** shale; **traitement par l'a.** mud-pack treatment; **masque d'a.** mud-pack; **a. cuite** terracotta, earthenware; *Fig* **une statue** ou **un colosse aux pieds d'a.** an idol with feet of clay

argileux, -euse [arʒilø, -øz] ADJ clayey

argon [argɔ̃] NM *Chimie* argon

argonaute [argɔnot] NM **1** *Myth, Fig* Argonaut **2** (mollusque) argonaut, paper nautilus

argot [argo] NM slang; **parler a.** to talk (in) slang; **mot d'a.** slang word; **l'a. (parisien)** Paris(ian) slang; **a. des voleurs** thieves' cant; **a. du milieu** underworld slang; **a. scolaire** school slang

> **Argot**
>
> This term can refer both to "la langue verte" (the slang of the underworld) or the jargon of particular social or professional groups (such as butchers, soldiers, students etc). Some "argot" has evolved from being part of the secret language of a select group to becoming part of everyday speech, while other terms have become obsolete, supplanted by **verlan** (see box at this entry), the slang used by young people in the suburbs of big cities.

argotique [argɔtik] ADJ (langue) slangy; **expression a.** (propre à un milieu) cant phrase; (familière) slang expression

argotisme [argɔtism] NM slang expression

arguer [arg(ɥ)e] (**j'argue** [ʒargy], **n. arguons** [nuzargɥjɔ̃]) VT **1** *Litt* to infer, to assert, to deduce; **que peut-il a. de ce fait?** what can he deduce or infer from this fact?, what conclusion(s) can he draw from this fact?; **il argue qu'on ne l'avait pas prévenu** his excuse is that he was not informed **2** *Jur* **a. une pièce de faux** to assert a deed to be forged
VI **a. de qch** to give sth as a reason; **elle argua du manque d'informations fournies** she argued that insufficient information had been provided

argument [argymã] NM **1** (démonstration) argument; **tirer a. de qch** to use sth as an argument; **a. de vente** selling point; **arguments de vente** sales pitch **2** (d'un livre etc) outline; (d'un article, d'un film) synopsis **3** *Math* argument

argumentaire [argymãtɛr] NM (sales) blurb; *Com* **rédiger un a.** to draw up a list of selling points; **l'a. est très convaincant** the sales pitch is very convincing

argumentateur, -trice [argymãtatœr, -tris] *Péj* ADJ argumentative
N arguer

argumentation [argymãtasjɔ̃] NF **1** argument; **une a. serrée** a series of closely argued points **2** *Com* sales pitch

argumenter [argymãte] VI to argue (**contre** against); *Fam* to be argumentative; **on ne peut pas a. de ce fait** you can't base an argument on that fact; **discours/démonstration bien argumenté(e)** well-argued speech/demonstration

Argus [argys] NM **1** *Myth* Argus **2** **l'A. (de l'Automobile)** = guide to used car prices; **être/**

ne plus être coté à l'A. to be listed/not be listed any more in the guide to used car prices; **acheter/vendre qch à l'A.** to buy/sell sth for the book price

argutie [argysi] NF quibble; **mettre fin à des arguties** to stop quibbling

aria [arja] NF *Mus* aria

aride [arid] ADJ (pays, sujet) arid, dry, barren; (œuvre) dry; (cœur) unfeeling; **une imagination a.** an unfertile imagination

aridité [aridite] NF aridity, aridness, barrenness; **l'a. d'un sujet** the dryness or aridity of a topic

arien, -ienne [arjɛ̃, -jɛn] ADJ Aryan
N **A.** Aryan

ariette [arjɛt] NF *Mus* arietta, ariette

aristo [aristo] N *Fam* nob, toff

aristocrate [aristɔkrat] N aristocrat

aristocratie [aristɔkrasi] NF aristocracy

aristocratique [aristɔkratik] ADJ aristocratic

Aristote [aristɔt] N *Phil* Aristotle; **la logique d'A.** Aristotelian logic

aristotélicien, -ienne [aristɔtelisjɛ̃, -jɛn] ADJ, N *Phil* Aristotelian

arithméticien, -ienne [aritmetisjɛ̃, -jɛn] N arithmetician

arithmétique [aritmetik] ADJ arithmetical
NF **1** (matière, calculs) arithmetic; **a. en virgule fixe** fixed point arithmetic; **a. en virgule flottante** floating point arithmetic SEE GRAMMAR A77; B59 **2** (livre) arithmetic book

arlequin [arləkɛ̃] NM *Théâtre* Harlequin; **habillé en a.** in Harlequin costume; **manteau d'a.** proscenium arch

arlequinade [arləkinad] NF *Théâtre* harlequinade; *Fig* (piece of) buffoonery

arlésien, -ienne [arlezjɛ̃, -jɛn] ADJ Arlesian, of or from Arles
N **A.** (natif) native of Arles; (habitant) inhabitant of Arles; *Fig* **c'est l'Arlésienne!** (d'une femme) does this girl really exist?; (d'un homme) does this man really exist?

armada [armada] NF *Hist* armada; **l'Invincible A.** the Invincible Armada; *Fig Fam* **une a. de photographes** an army of photographers

armagnac [armaɲak] NM Armagnac

armailli [armaji] NM *Suisse* shepherd

armateur [armatœr] NM *Naut* (d'un navire, d'une expédition) fitter-out; (propriétaire) shipowner

armature [armatyr] NF **1** (dans le béton) reinforcement; (d'une poutre etc) truss; (d'une fenêtre etc) frame, brace; **soutien-gorge à a.** underwired bra; *Fig* **l'a. de nos principes moraux** the basis or the underpinnings of our moral principles **2** (d'un câble électrique) armouring, sheathing **3** *Élec* (d'un aimant, d'une petite dynamo, d'un magnétophone) armature; (d'un condensateur) plate; **a. de soupape/de pompe** valve/pump gear **4** *Mus* key signature

arme [arm] NF **1** arm, weapon; (en escrime) sword; **salle d'armes** armoury; (d'escrime) fencing school; **l'a. du crime** the murder weapon; **port d'a.** carrying of weapons; **porter une a. sur soi** to carry a weapon; **prendre le pouvoir par les armes** to take power by force; **nation en** ou **sous les armes** nation in arms; **prendre les armes** to take up arms, to rise up in arms (**contre** against); *Mil* to parade under arms; **déposer les armes** to lay down one's arms, to surrender; **porter les armes** to be a soldier; *Mil* **aux armes!** to arms!, guard turn out!; **le métier** ou **la carrière des armes** the military profession, soldiering; **suspension d'armes** cessation of hostilities; **frères d'armes** brothers in arms; **place d'ar-**

mes parade ground; **passer qn par les armes** to send sb to the firing squad; **sans armes** unarmed; *Fig* **passer l'a. à gauche** to snuff it, to kick the bucket; *(dans un accident)* to cop it; *Fig* **il fait ses premières armes** he's earning his spurs; *Fig* **fournir des armes à qn** to provide sb with ammunition; *Fig* **le cynisme est son a. favorite** cynicism is his favourite weapon; *Fig* **l'indépendance est une a. à double tranchant** independence is a two-edged sword; *Fig* **la télévision est l'a. absolue des politiciens** television is the politician's ultimate weapon; *Fig* **à armes égales** on equal terms; *Fig* **avec armes et bagages** (with) bag and baggage
  2 *(section de l'armée)* arm, branch, service; **a. de l'infanterie** infantry; **douze mille hommes de toutes armes** twelve thousand men of all arms *or* services
  3 *Hér* **armes** (coat of) arms
  ▸▸ **a. atomique** atomic weapon; **a. biologique** biological weapon; **a. blanche** knife; **combat à l'a. blanche** knife fight; **a. chimique** chemical weapon; **armes classiques** conventional weapons; **armes conventionnelles** conventional weapons; **armes de destruction massive** weapons of mass destruction; **a. de dissuasion** deterrent; **a. à feu** firearm; **a. non classique** non-conventional weapon, advanced weapon; **a. non conventionnelle** non-conventional weapon, advanced weapon; **a. nucléaire** nuclear weapon; **armes portatives** small arms; **armes traditionnelles** conventional weapons

armé [arme] ADJ **1** armed; **troupe armée** body of troops; **vol à main armée** hold-up, armed robbery; **animal a. de piquants/d'une carapace** animal with spines/a shell; **a. d'une canne/d'un dictionnaire/d'un guide touristique** armed with a stick/a dictionary/a guidebook; **a. jusqu'aux dents** armed to the teeth; **sortir a. de chez soi** to go out carrying a weapon; *Fig* **être bien/mal a. pour partir dans la vie** to be well/badly equipped to make one's way in the world; *Fig* **mes enfants partiront armés dans le monde du travail** my children will be well qualified to find a job **2** *(renforcé)* fortified, strengthened; **poutre armée** trussed beam; **béton a.** reinforced concrete; **verre a.** wired glass **3** *(arme à feu)* cocked; **pistolet à demi a.** pistol at half cock
  NM à l'a. *(arme à feu)* cocked

armée [arme] NF **1** *Mil* army; **partir à l'a.** to join the army; *(pour faire son service militaire)* to start one's military service; **a. de métier** professional *or* regular army; **a. d'occupation** army of occupation; **lever une a.** to raise an army; **a. permanente** standing army; **a. régulière** *ou* **active** regular army; **l'a. de terre** the army, the land forces; **l'a. de l'air** the air force; **l'a. de mer** the navy, the naval forces; **a. de secours** relieving army; **les armées alliées** the allied armies *or* forces; **être dans l'a.** to be in the army; **la 8ème a.** the 8th army; **le Dieu des armées** the Lord of Hosts; **groupe d'a.** army group VOIR GRAMMAIRE A11 **2 l'A. du salut** the Salvation Army **3** *(foule)* **quelle a. d'incapables!** what a shower (of incompetents)!; **toute une a. de fonctionnaires** a whole army of officials; **une a. d'insectes ravageurs** an army of marauding insects

armement [arməmã] NM **1** *(d'une armée)* *(action)* arming, equipping; *(équipement)* armament, equipment; *(armes)* **armements** armaments, weaponry; **officier d'a.** ordnance officer; **vente d'armements** sale of arms; **la vente d'armements a diminué** arms sales have decreased; **réduction des armements** arms reduction; **course aux armements** arms race

2 *(d'une poutre etc)* strengthening, bracing; *(d'un câble etc)* sheathing
  3 *Naut (action)* commissioning, fitting out; *(équipement)* equipment, gear, stores; **mettre un navire en a.** to put a ship in commission; **port d'a.** port of registry
  4 *(en personnel)* manning
  5 *Com (profession)* merchant shipping
  6 *(d'un fusil)* loading; *(d'un fusible)* arming; *(d'un appareil photo etc)* setting; *(d'une arme à feu chargée)* cocking; *(d'une machine etc)* mounting, fitting up

Arménie [armeni] NF Armenia

arménien, -ienne [armenjɛ̃, -jɛn] ADJ Armenian
  NM *Ling* Armenian
  N **A.** Armenian

armer [arme] VT **1** *(munir d'armes) (soldats)* to arm (**de** with); **je sors toujours armé** I always carry a weapon when I go out; *Fig* **a. qn contre les difficultés de la vie** to equip sb to deal with the difficulties of life; *Fig* **il est armé d'un solide bagage universitaire** he's equipped with a good university education; *Fig* **cette position l'arme de tous les pouvoirs** this job puts him in a position of real power
  2 *(ville)* to fortify, *(solive)* to strengthen, to brace; *(dynamo)* to wind; *(câble)* to sheathe, to armour; **a. du béton** to reinforce concrete
  3 *Naut (navire)* to equip, to fit out, to commission; *(bateau etc)* to man; *(cabestan)* to rig; **a. les avirons** to ship the oars
  4 *(fusible)* to arm; *(appareil)* to set; *(arme à feu)* to cock; *(canons, pompe)* to man; *(machine, artillerie)* to mount; *(machine)* to fit up; **a. son appareil photo** to set one's camera
  5 *Hist* **a. qn chevalier** to knight sb
  6 *Mus* **a. la clef** *(d'un morceau de musique)* to put the key signature
  VI *Naut* **le navire arme à Brest** the ship is being commissioned at Brest; **a. sur un navire** to serve on a vessel
  VPR **s'armer** to arm oneself; *Fig* **je me suis armé de mon livre préféré pour attendre** I armed myself with my favourite book to read while I waited; *Fig* **s'a. de courage/de patience** to summon up (one's) courage/patience

armistice [armistis] NM armistice; *(temporaire)* truce; **journée** *ou* **anniversaire de l'A.** Armistice Day, Remembrance Day, *Am* Veterans' Day

armoire [armwar] NF *(placard)* cupboard, *surtout Am* closet; *(pour les vêtements)* wardrobe, *surtout Am* closet; **a. à linge** linen cupboard; **a. à provisions** store cupboard; **a. à pharmacie** medicine chest *or* cabinet; **a. frigorifique** cold store; **a. de toilette** *ou* **de salle de bain** bathroom cabinet; **a. ignifugée** fireproof cabinet; **a. à fournitures** stationery supplies cupboard; **a. de cuisine** kitchen cupboard; **a. normande** large wardrobe; **a. à glace** mirrored wardrobe; *Fig Hum* **c'est une a. à glace** he's built like a tank

armoiries [armwari] NFPL *Hér* (coat of) arms, armorial bearings

armorial, -iale, -iaux, -iales [armɔrjal, -jo] ADJ armorial

armoricain, -aine [armɔrikɛ̃, -ɛn] ADJ Armorican; **massif a.** Armorican massif
  N *Hist* **A.** Armorican, ancient Breton

Armorique [armɔrik] NF Armorica

armoriste [armɔrist] NM heraldic artist

armure [armyr] NF **1** *(cuirasse etc)* armour; *(d'animaux)* defence; **a. complète** suit of armour; **a. d'un navire de guerre** armour (plating) of a warship; *Fig* **cette insolence est une a., elle s'en protège** she uses insolence as a defence mechanism **2** *Tex* weave, pattern, design; **a. toile** plain weave **3** *Élec (d'une dynamo)* pole piece, armouring; *(d'un câble)* sheathing **4** *Mus* key signature

armurier [armyrje] NM **1** *(fabricant etc)* arms manufacturer; *(de pistolets etc)* gunsmith; *(vendeur)* gun dealer **2** *Mil etc* armourer

ARN [aɛrɛn] NM *(abrév* **acide ribonucléique)** RNA

arnaque [arnak] NF *Fam* swindle, rip-off; **attention à l'a.!** be careful you don't get ripped off!; **c'est de l'a.!** what a rip-off!

arnaquer [arnake] VT *Fam* to cheat, to swindle, to rip off; **se faire a.** to get ripped off

arnaqueur, -euse [arnakœr, -øz] N *Fam* swindler, rip-off merchant

arnica [arnika] NF *Bot, Pharm* arnica

arobase [arɔbaz] NF at-sign

aromate [arɔmat] NM *(herbe)* herb; *(épice)* spice

aromathérapie [arɔmaterapi] NF *Méd* aromatherapy

aromatique [arɔmatik] ADJ **1** aromatic; *(saveur)* spicy; **plantes aromatiques** aromatic plants **2** *Chimie* **carbures aromatiques** aromatics

aromatisation [arɔmatizasjɔ̃] NF *Chimie* aromatization

aromatiser [arɔmatize] VT **1** *Culin* to flavour, *Am* to flavor; **aromatisé à la vanille** vanilla-flavoured **2** *Chimie* to aromatize

arome, arôme [arom] NM aroma; *(goût)* flavour, *Am* flavor; **crème glacée, a. vanille** vanilla flavour ice cream

aronde [arɔ̃d] NF *Menuis* queue d'a. dovetail; **assembler qch en queue d'a.** to dovetail sth

arpège [arpɛʒ] NM *Mus* arpeggio

arpéger [arpeʒe] VT *Mus* **a. un accord** to play a chord in *or* as an arpeggio

arpent [arpɑ̃] NM *Hist* arpent (= one acre)

arpentage [arpɑ̃taʒ] NM surveying, land measuring; **faire l'a. d'un terrain** to measure a piece of ground

arpenter [arpɑ̃te] VT **1** *(terre)* to survey, to measure **2** *(parcourir rapidement)* **a. le terrain** to stride over the ground; **il arpentait le quai** he was pacing up and down the platform

arpenteur [arpɑ̃tœr] NM (land) surveyor

arpion [arpjɔ̃] NM *Arg (pied)* hoof; *(orteil)* toe; **tu vas quand même pas te laisser marcher sur les arpions par ce minable?** you're not going to let that pathetic specimen walk all over you, surely?

arqué [arke] ADJ arched, curved; *(poutre etc)* cambered; *(nez)* high-bridged; *(cheval)* bandy-legged; **jambes arquées** bow legs

arquebuse [arkəbyz] NF (h)arquebus

arquebusier [arkəbyzje] NM *(soldat)* (h)arquebusier

arquer [arke] VT *(bois, fer etc)* to bend, to arch, to curve; *(surface)* to camber; **a. le dos** to arch one's back
  VI **1** *(fléchir)* to bend, to sag, to buckle **2** *Fam (marcher)* to walk; **je ne pouvais plus a.** *(j'étais épuisé)* I couldn't walk another step, I couldn't put one foot in front of the other
  VPR **s'arquer** to bend, to become bent *or* arched

arr *abrév* = **arrt**

arrachage [araʃaʒ] NM *(des plantes etc)* pulling up, uprooting; *(des pommes de terre)* lifting; *(d'une dent, d'un clou etc)* pulling out, extraction; *(en imprimerie)* picking

arraché [araʃe] NM *Sport (en haltérophilie)* snatch; *Fig* **obtenir un accord à l'a.** to obtain a deal after much effort; *Fig* **gagner à l'a.** to snatch a victory

arrache-agrafes [araʃagraf] NM INV staple remover

arrache-clou, *pl* **arrache-clous** [araʃklu] NM claw hammer

arrachement [araʃmɑ̃] NM **1** (d'un arbre etc) uprooting **2** Fig (déchirure) wrench; **l'a. du départ** the wrench of leaving; **nous ne pouvons quitter Paris sans a.** it will be a wrench leaving Paris **3** Constr toothing **4** (en mécanique) tearing, wrenching, stripping; **effort d'a.** wrenching force **5** Méd etc wrench

arrache-moyeu, pl **arrache-moyeux** [araʃmwajø] NM Aut **a. universel** universal hub puller

arrache-pied (d') [daraʃpje] ADV without interruption, relentlessly; **travailler d'a.** to work steadily; (excessivement) to slave away

arracher [araʃe] VT **1** (enlever) to pull out; (arbre) to pull up, to uproot; (pommes de terre) to lift; Fig (argent, promesse, secret) to extract (de from); (dent) to extract, to pull out; (affiche) to tear down, to pull down; **a. qch à qn/des mains de qn** to snatch sth from sb/from sb's hands; Fig **on est quand même parvenu à lui a. quelques paroles** we did manage to get a few words out of him; Fig **nous sommes parvenus à lui a. cet aveu** we managed to extract that confession from him; **se faire a. une dent** to have a tooth extracted or out; **a. les yeux à qn** to tear sb's eyes out; Fig **j'avais envie de lui a. les yeux** I wanted to strangle him; Fig **il faut a. son masque** we/they/etc must unmask him

2 (déchirer) **cela m'arrache le cœur** it breaks my heart; très Fam **la tequila pure, ça arrache la gueule!** pure tequila will blow your head off!; très Fam **ça t'arracherait la gueule de dire merci/de t'excuser?** it wouldn't kill you to say thanks/to apologize

3 Fig (personne) **a. qn de son foyer** (armée d'occupation, police) to drag or uproot sb from his home; **a. qn à la mort** to snatch or rescue sb from the jaws of death; **a. qn au sommeil** to rouse sb from (his) sleep; **la sonnerie du réveil m'a arraché du lit** the alarm dragged me out of bed; **a. qn à son travail/à la télé** to tear or drag sb away from his work/the TV

VI **1** Arg (alcool fort, piment) **ça arrache!** that's dynamite!

2 Can **en a.** to have difficulties

VPR **s'arracher** (se déchirer) Fig **je n'y comprends rien, je m'arrache les cheveux!** I don't understand it at all, I'm tearing my hair out!; Fig **c'est à s'a. les cheveux!** it's enough to make you tear your hair out!; Fig **tout le monde la demande, on se l'arrache** she's very much in demand, they're even fighting over her; **on se l'arrache** (d'un livre etc) copies are being snatched up; Fig **impossible de m'a. de ce pays** I could never tear myself away from this country; Fig **s'a. à sa rêverie** to wake from one's daydream; Arg **alors, on s'arrache?** time to go?

arrache-roulement, pl **arrache-roulements** [araʃrulmɑ̃] NM Aut **a. universel** universal bearing puller

arracheur, -euse [araʃœr, -øz] N (de pommes de terre etc) lifter; Fig **mentir comme un a. de dents** to lie through one's teeth

NF Agr **arracheuse** (outil) grubbing plough, grubber; (de pommes de terre) (potato) lifter; (de betteraves) (beet) puller

arrachoir [araʃwar] NM Agr (de pommes de terre) (potato) lifter; (de betteraves) (beet) puller

arraisonnement [arɛzɔnmɑ̃] NM Naut (d'un navire) boarding; **a. de la patente (d'un navire)** examination of the bill of health, sanitary report

arraisonner [arɛzɔne] Naut VT **a. un navire** to hail a vessel; (l'aborder) to stop and examine a ship

VI **a. avec les autorités du port** to report to the port authorities

arrangeant [arɑ̃ʒɑ̃, -ɑ̃t] ADJ accommodating, helpful

arrangement [arɑ̃ʒmɑ̃] NM **1** (fait d'arranger) arranging, putting in order; (manière d'être arrangé) (du mobilier etc) arrangement; **l'a. des fleurs dans un vase** the arrangement of flowers in a vase; **l'a. de ses cheveux demande un soin constant** his hairstyle demands constant attention; **l'a. des mots dans une phrase** the word order in a sentence **2** Mus **a. pour violon** arrangement for violon **3** (accord) agreement, settlement; (officieux) understanding; **mal prendre ses arrangements** to arrange or plan things badly; **sauf a. contraire** unless otherwise agreed; **essayer de trouver un a. financier avec son banquier** to try to come to (some kind of) an arrangement with one's banker; Jur **a. à l'amiable** out of court settlement

arranger [arɑ̃ʒe] (j'arrangeais; n. arrangeons) VT **1** (meubles etc) to arrange; (livres, pièce) to put in order; (pièce) to tidy (up); (cravate etc) to straighten; Fam **le voilà bien arrangé!** what a mess he looks!; **ils l'ont drôlement arrangé, il a des bleus partout** they've given him a good going over, he's covered in bruises; **a. qn de la belle manière** (physiquement, en dire du mal) to have a go at sb; Fam **on vous a arrangé** (volé) you've been had or done, you've been ripped off; **voilà un bouge où on vous arrange le client** it's a rip-off joint; Arg **se faire a.** (tuer) to get bumped off

2 (voiture, montre etc) to repair, to overhaul; (montre) to mend; **je vais t'a. ça** I'll fix it for you **3** (concert etc) to arrange, to organize; **a. qch d'avance** to arrange or plan sth in advance; **il arrange bien sa vie** he's got his life well organized; **je vous ai arrangé un entretien avec lui** I've arranged a meeting with him for you; **ne t'en fais pas, j'ai tout arrangé** don't worry, I've made all the arrangements

4 (conflit etc) to settle; **je vais essayer d'a. les choses** I'll try to put things right; **cela n'arrangera rien** that won't (be much) help; **cela n'arrange pas nos affaires** that's no good (to us), that doesn't help (us)

5 (plaire à, satisfaire) (personne) to suit, to be convenient for; **ça t'arrangerait que je vienne te chercher?** would it suit you or would it be convenient if I came to collect you?; **faire qch pour a. qn** to do sth to help sb; **on ne peut pas a. tout le monde** you can't please everybody; **tu ne fais que ce qui t'arrange** you only do what suits you; **ça t'arrange?** does that suit you?

6 Mus (morceau pour violon etc) to arrange

VPR **s'arranger 1** (s'organiser etc) to manage; **si vous pouvez vous a. pour le voir** if you can manage to see him or make the time to see him; **arrangez-vous pour être là** make sure you're there; Fam **je ne sais pas comment tu t'arranges, mais tu es toujours en retard** I don't know how you manage it, but you're always late

2 (se contenter) **il s'arrange de tout** he's very adaptable; **s'a. d'un vieux lit** to make do with an old bed

3 (sa tenue, son apparence) to tidy oneself up; **tu as vu comment tu t'es arrangé!** have you seen the state you're in?!

4 (se mettre d'accord) **s'a. avec qn** to come to an agreement or to terms with sb; **arrange-toi avec elle, elle peut peut-être te prêter sa voiture** sort things out with her, maybe she can lend you her car; **arrangez-vous** settle it among yourselves; **on s'est arrangé à l'amiable** we came to an amicable arrangement or agreement

5 (s'améliorer) to work out; **cela s'arrangera** things will turn out all right; **cela s'arrangera tout seul** that will sort itself out; **ça ne s'arrange pas!** it's not getting any better!; **elle ne fait rien pour s'a.** she doesn't do anything to make the most of herself; **ça n'a pas l'air de s'a. entre eux** things don't seem to have got any better between them

arrangeur, -euse [arɑ̃ʒœr, -øz] N Mus arranger

arrérages [arera3] NMPL **1** (de salaires, du loyer etc) arrears **2** (intérêt) back interest; **coupon d'a.** interest or dividend warrant

arrestation [arɛstasjɔ̃] NF arrest; **procéder à l'a. de qn** to arrest sb; **mettre qn en état d'a.** to place sb under arrest; **en état d'a.** under arrest; **a. préventive/provisoire** custodial/conditional arrest

arrêt [arɛ] NM **1** (interruption) stop, stoppage, stopping; **a. de travail** (grève) stoppage; (congé) sick leave; (certificat) doctor's or medical certificate; **être en a. de travail** to be on sick leave; **a. maladie** sick leave; **être en a. maladie** to be on sick leave; **véhicule à l'a.** stationary vehicle; **a. d'urgence** emergency stop; **point d'a.** stopping place or point; Mus (pendant une pause) pause; **faire un a. au cours de son voyage** to break one's journey, to stop over; **nous avons fait plusieurs arrêts pendant le voyage** we made several stops during the journey; **a. en cours de route** break of journey, stopover; **trajet sans a.** non-stop journey; **New York est un a. obligatoire** New York is an absolute must; **il neige sans a. depuis mercredi** it's been snowing non-stop or continuously since Wednesday; **la machine tombe sans a. en panne** the machine is constantly or continually breaking down; **c'est ce que je lui dis sans a.** that's what I tell him over and over again; **dix minutes d'a.** ten minutes' stop; (pour café, repos etc) ten minutes' break; **temps d'a.** pause, halt; **chien d'a.** setter, pointer; Fig **rester** ou **tomber en a. devant qn/qch** to stop and stare at sth/sb; **marquer un temps d'a.** to pause, to halt, to mark time; **a. de paiement** stoppage of payment(s); **a. des comptes** closing (off) the accounts; Méd **a. du cœur** heart failure; **a. (inopiné)** breakdown; Radio, TV **a. d'émission** break in transmission; Ordinat **a. de fin de session** shutdown; TV, Cin **a. sur image** freeze frame, stop frame; **faire un a. sur image** to freeze a frame; Ordinat **a. anormal du système** system crash; Ordinat **a. de défilement** scroll lock; Ordinat **a. de l'impression** (commande) stop printing

2 (de bus etc) **a. de bus** bus stop; **a. facultatif** request stop; **ne pas descendre avant l'a.** do not get off before the bus/train/etc has come to a complete stop; **le train est sans a. jusqu'à l'aéroport** the train goes non-stop to the airport

3 (d'une porte etc) stop, catch; (d'un verrou) tumbler; **cran d'a.** safety catch; **a. de pied** toeclip

4 Jur (prononcé par la cour d'assises, cour d'appel ou cour de cassation) judgment, adjudication; **prononcer** ou **rendre un a.** to pronounce or deliver judgment; **a. par défaut** judgment by default; **a. de défense** stay of execution; **a. de mort** death sentence; Fig **les arrêts de la Providence** the decrees of Providence; Fig **les arrêts de la mode** the dictates of fashion

5 (arrestation) arrest; **ordre** ou **mandat d'a.** (d'une personne) warrant for the arrest; **mettre un officier aux arrêts** to put an officer under arrest; **arrêts à la chambre, arrêts domestiques** house arrest; **être en maison d'a.** to be in prison, to be under or to be held in detention

6 (saisie) seizure, impounding, attachment; **faire a. sur des marchandises** to impound or seize goods

7 *Ftbl* tackle; *Rugby* **a. de volée** mark; **faire un a. de volée** to make a mark **8** *Naut (d'un navire)* detention

arrêt-court, *pl* **arrêts-courts** [arɛkur] NM *Can Sport* shortstop

arrêté [arete] ADJ **1** *(idées etc)* fixed, decided; **homme aux opinions arrêtées** dogmatic man, man with set ideas; *(décidé)* man with decided views; **c'est une chose arrêtée** it's already been decided; **dessein a.** settled design **2** *Sport* **départ a.** standing start

NM **1** *Admin* decision, order, decree; **a. ministériel** departmental order (signed by a minister); **a. municipal** by-law; **a. préfectoral** by-law; **a. d'exécution** = decree providing for the enforcement of a law **2** *Com* **a. de compte(s)** closing off of an account

arrêter [arete] VT **1** *(stopper) (personne)* to stop; *(véhicule)* to bring to a stop or to a standstill; *(appareil)* to turn off; *(fuite)* to stem; *Ordinat* to halt; *(système)* to shut down; **là je vous arrête, je ne suis pas d'accord!** stop right there, I don't agree!; **tu pourrais m'a. au bureau de tabac?** could you drop me off at the tobacconist's?; **a. un cheval** to pull up a horse; **rien ne l'arrêtera** nothing will stop him, he will stop at nothing; **quel obstacle vous arrête?** what's stopping you?; **a. le vent** to break (the force of) the wind; *Aut* **a. le moteur** to switch off the engine; **a. la croissance** to arrest growth; **le brouillard/la neige a complètement arrêté toute circulation** fog/snow has brought traffic to a (complete) standstill; *Ftbl* **a. un tir** to save or stop a shot; **a. le gibier** *(d'un chien)* to point game

2 *(fixer) (volet, planche etc)* to fix, to fasten, to secure; *Fig* **a. l'attention** to draw or catch attention; *Fig* **je voudrais a. votre attention sur ce point** I'd like to draw your attention to this point; *Fig* **ce détail arrêta mon attention** this detail caught my attention; *Couture* **a. un point** to fasten off a stitch; *Tricot* **a. les mailles** to cast off

3 *(criminel)* to arrest, to seize; *(contrebande, livres etc)* to seize; **l'assassin n'a pas encore été arrêté** the murderer is still at large

4 *(déterminer)* to decide; **a. un jour** to fix or appoint a day; **la date n'a pas encore été arrêtée** the date has not yet been decided on or fixed; **a. un prix** to fix a price; **a. un programme/un projet** to draw up a programme/plan; **il a été arrêté que la séance débuterait à 14 heures** it has been decided that the meeting will begin at 2 o'clock; **a. un marché** to close a deal

5 *Com (compte)* to make up, to close (off)

VI to stop, to halt; **dites au chauffeur d'a. devant l'hôtel de ville** tell the driver to stop at or in front of the town hall; **elle n'arrête jamais de parler** she never stops talking; **elle est toujours occupée à laver, elle n'arrête pas** she's always washing something or other, she never stops; **arrête!, arrêtez!** stop (it)! that's enough!

VPR **s'arrêter 1** *(s'immobiliser)* to stop, to come to a stop or a standstill; *(d'un corps mobile)* to come to rest; *Ordinat (système)* to shut down; **s'a. court** to stop short; **ma montre s'est arrêtée** my watch has stopped; **la voiture s'est arrêtée** the car stopped or pulled up; *(en s'approchant)* the car drew up; **s'a. en route** to break one's journey; **nous nous sommes arrêtés dans un village pittoresque** we stopped in a picturesque village; **s'a. chez qn** to call at sb's house/*etc*; **passer sans s'a.** to pass without stopping

2 *(cesser)* to stop; **la pluie va s'a.** the rain will stop or it will stop raining soon; **s'a. de faire qch** to stop doing sth; **s'a. de fumer** to give up smoking

3 *(faire attention à)* to fix one's attention (à qch on sth), to dwell, to insist (à qch on sth); **il ne faut pas s'a. aux apparences** one should not go by appearances

arrhes [ar] NFPL deposit; **verser des a.** to pay a deposit; **stipulation d'a.** = right to annul a sale by paying a fine

arriération [arjerasjɔ̃] NF *Psy* **a. mentale** retardation; *(d'un enfant etc)* backwardness

arrière [arjer] ADV **1** **en a.** *(à une certaine distance)* behind; **rester en a.** *(ne pas aller, sortir)* to remain or stay behind; *(en se promenant avec d'autres personnes)* to lag behind; *Naut* **avoir le vent en a.** to have the wind astern; **en a. de qn/qch** behind sb/sth; **il est resté en a. de sa classe** he stayed at the bottom of the class; **en a. de son siècle** *ou* **de son temps** behind the times

2 *(en retard)* **locataire en a. pour ses loyers** tenant in arrears with his/her rent

3 *(derrière)* backwards; **a.!** (stand) back!; **a., Satan!** get thee behind me, Satan!; **cheveux en a.** hair brushed or combed back, hair swept back; **revenir en a.** to come back; *Fig* **j'ai l'impression de revenir en a., c'est tout à fait comme dans mon enfance** I feel like I've gone or stepped back in time, it's exactly how it was in my childhood; **pencher la tête en a.** to lean one's head back; **retourner en a.** to go or turn back; *Fig* **il faut remonter loin en a. pour trouver une épidémie de ce genre** you have to go back a long way (in history) to find such an epidemic; *Fig* **vous revenez en a., nous avons déjà parlé de ça** you're going (back) over previous ground, we've already talked about or covered that; *Fig* **pas la peine de revenir en a., c'est oublié** there's no point in looking back, it's all been forgotten; **regarder en a.** to look back; *Naut* **en a. (à) toute (vitesse)!** full speed astern!

ADJ INV back; **faire marche a.** to reverse, to back; *Naut* **faire marche** *ou* **machine a.** to go astern; *Fig* to back down, to backtrack; *Aut* **où est la marche a.?** where is reverse (gear)?; *Aut* **essieu a.** back or rear axle; **lunette a.** rear window; **feu a.** rear light; **à moteur a.** rear-engined; **siège** *ou* **banquette a.** *(d'une voiture)* back seat; *Couture* **point a.** backstitch

NM **1** *(d'une maison etc)* back, back part, rear; *Aut* tail; **assis à l'a. de la voiture** sitting in the back of the car; *Aut* **un modèle tout à l'a.** a rear-engined model

2 *Naut (d'un navire)* stern; **vers l'a.** aft; **sur l'a.** astern; **aller à l'a.** to go aft

3 *Mil* **l'a.** the rear; *Fig* **protéger ses arrières** to protect one's rear, to leave oneself a way out

4 *Ftbl* (full) back; *Rugby* full back; *Ftbl* **a. gauche** left back; **à l'a.** at full back

arriéré, -ée [arjere] ADJ **1** *(dû)* late, behind, in arrears; **paiement a.** overdue or outstanding payment **2** *(dépassé, démodé)* **être a.** *(d'une personne)* to be behind the times; **idées arriérées** old-fashioned ideas; *Écon* **pays arriérés** underdeveloped or backward countries **3** *(attardé) (enfant)* backward

NM *(d'un compte etc)* arrears; *(de travail, d'une correspondance etc)* backlog; **a. du loyer** rent arrears, arrears of rent; **a. d'impôts** tax arrears, back taxes; **il y a un a. de 5000 euros** 5,000 euros are still outstanding; **avoir des arriérés** to be in arrears; *Mil* **a. de solde** back pay; **a. de permissions** accumulated leave

N backward or retarded person

arrière-ban, *pl* **arrière-bans** NM *Fig* **tout le monde était là, le ban et l'a.** they were all there, the world and his wife; **le ban et l'a. de LVMH** the entire LVMH clan

arrière-bassin, *pl* **arrière-bassins** NM inner dock

arrière-bouche, *pl* **arrière-bouches** NF back of the mouth, *Spéc* fauces

arrière-boutique, *pl* **arrière-boutiques** NF back shop, *Am* back store

arrière-cour, *pl* **arrière-cours** NF backyard

arrière-cuisine, *pl* **arrière-cuisines** NF scullery, back kitchen

arrière-défense, *pl* **arrière-défenses** NF *Ftbl* (the) back four (defence), the backs

arrière-fond, *pl* **arrière-fonds** NM innermost depth(s)

arrière-garde, *pl* **arrière-gardes** NF *Mil* rearguard; *Naut* rear squadron; *Fig* **c'est un professeur d'a.** he's a teacher of the old guard

arrière-gorge, *pl* **arrière-gorges** NF back of the throat; **voix d'a.** throaty voice

arrière-goût, *pl* **arrière-goûts** NM *aussi Fig* aftertaste (**de** of); **ce vin a un a. de fruit** this wine leaves a fruity aftertaste

arrière-grand-mère, *pl* **arrière-grands-mères** NF great-grandmother

arrière-grand-oncle [arjergrɑ̃tɔ̃kl], *pl* **arrière-grands-oncles** [arjergrɑ̃zɔ̃kl] NM great-great-uncle

arrière-grand-père, *pl* **arrière-grands-pères** NM great-grandfather

arrière-grands-parents NMPL great-grandparents

arrière-grand-tante, *pl* **arrière-grands-tantes** NF great-great-aunt

arrière-main, *pl* **arrière-mains** NM *Tennis etc* **(coup d')a.** backhand (stroke) NF *(d'un cheval)* (hind)quarters

arrière-neveu, *pl* **arrière-neveux** NM great-nephew

arrière-nièce, *pl* **arrière-nièces** NF great-niece

arrière-pays NM INV hinterland

arrière-pensée, *pl* **arrière-pensées** NF ulterior motive

arrière-petite-fille, *pl* **arrière-petites-filles** NF great-granddaughter

arrière-petite-nièce, *pl* **arrière-petites-nièces** NF great-great-niece

arrière-petit-fils, *pl* **arrière-petits-fils** NM great-grandson

arrière-petit-neveu, *pl* **arrière-petits-neveux** NM great-great-nephew

arrière-petits-enfants [arjerpətizɑ̃fɑ̃] NMPL great-grandchildren

arrière-plan, *pl* **arrière-plans** NM *aussi Ordinat* background; **à l'a.** in the background; *(derrière, en arrière)* at the back; *Théâtre* upstage; *Fig* **ce projet est passé à l'a.** this plan has been put on the back burner; *Fig* **mettre qch à l'a.** to put sth on the back burner; *Fig* **rester à l'a.** to remain in the background; **se trouver relégué à l'a.** to be pushed into the background; *Théâtre, Fig* to be upstaged

arrière-pont, *pl* **arrière-ponts** NM *Naut* afterdeck

arrière-port, *pl* **arrière-ports** NM inner harbour

arriérer [arjere] (j'**arrière**, n. **arriérons**; j'**arriérerai**) VT *(paiement etc)* to postpone, to delay, to defer VPR **s'arriérer** to fall into arrears

arrière-saison, *pl* **arrière-saisons** NF **1** late season, late autumn or Am fall **2** *Agr* **les pêches sont chères dans l'a.** peaches are expensive at the end of the season

arrière-salle, *pl* **arrière-salles** NF back room

arrière-train, *pl* **arrière-trains** NM *(d'un animal)* (hind)quarters; *Fam (d'une personne)* rump, rear

arrimage [arimaʒ] NM *Naut etc* **1** *(du chargement d'un navire etc)* stowing; **bois d'a.** dunnage **2** *(chargement)* stowage **3** *(d'une navette spatiale)* docking

arrimer [arime] VT **1** *Naut etc (cargaison etc)* to stow **2** *(fixer)* to secure *or* fasten; **a. un chargement sur le toit d'une voiture** to secure *or* fasten a load to the roof of a car
VI *Astronaut* to dock

arrimeur [arimœr] NM *Naut* stevedore

arrivage [arivaʒ] NM *(de marchandises)* consignment; **nous attendons un a. (de produits) venant de France** we're expecting a consignment *or* delivery from France; *Iron, Péj* **t'as vu le nouvel a.?** *(vacanciers etc)* have you seen the new arrivals *or* the new lot?; *Fin* **a. de fonds de l'étranger** accession of funds from abroad

arrivant, -ante [arivɑ̃, -ɑ̃t] N arrival; **le dernier a.** the last person to arrive; **les nouveaux arrivants** the new arrivals, the newcomers

arrivé, -ée [arive] ADJ **être a.** *(socialement)* to have made it in society; **il fait très quadragénaire a.** he looks a real forty-something nouveau riche

N *(personne)* **un nouvel a.** a newcomer, a new arrival; **le dernier a.** the last (person) to arrive; **le dernier a. a un gage!** = last one there's a cissy!

arrivée [arive] NF **1** *(de personne etc)* arrival, coming; *(d'une situation, d'une nouvelle étape)* advent; **on attend son a. pour la semaine prochaine** he/she is expected to arrive next week; **depuis son a. au pouvoir** since his coming to power; **depuis son a. à la direction** since he joined the management; **a. matinale** early morning arrival; **a. tardive** late arrival; **à mon a.** when I arrived; **arrivées** arrivals; **tableau des arrivées** arrivals board; **heures d'a.** *(du courrier)* times of delivery; **l'a. du printemps** the coming *or* arrival *or* onset of spring; **l'a. de nouveaux produits sur le marché** the arrival of new products onto the market **2** *Tech* inlet; *(pour la vapeur etc)* intake, admission; **a. (d'huile)** (oil) feed; *Aut* **a. d'essence** petrol inlet; *Aut* **a. de carburant** fuel inlet **3** *Sport* (winning) post, finish; **ligne d'a.** finishing line

arriver [arive] VI *(aux être)* **1** *(parvenir à destination)* to arrive, to come; *(dans un hôtel)* to arrive, to check in; **a. en voiture** to come by car; **a. par le train/le bateau** to come by train/boat; **il est arrivé en courant** he came running up; **il arrive de voyage** he is just back from a journey; **a. chez soi** to arrive home, to get back home; **a. à temps** to arrive *or* to be *on* or in time; **a. en retard** to be late; **a. le premier** to be the first to arrive, to come *or* be first; **a. dans les premiers** to be among the first to finish; **le printemps est arrivé!** spring is here!, spring has arrived!; **l'avion devait a. à midi** the plane was due at midday; **j'arrive!** (I'm) coming!, I'll be with you in a moment!, I'll be right there!; **c'est à cette heure-là que tu arrives?** and what time do you call this to be turning up?; **arrivez (vite)!** hurry up!; **nous sommes presque arrivés** we're almost there; **mangeons, ça la fera peut-être a.** let's start eating, maybe that'll make her come

2 a. à un endroit to reach *or* get to *or* arrive at a place; **a. à quai** to berth, to dock; **a. à bon port** to arrive safely; **le paquet m'est arrivé trop tard** the parcel reached me too late; **l'eau m'arrive aux chevilles** the water comes up to my ankles; **ma fille m'arrive déjà à l'épaule** my daughter comes up to my shoulder already; **ses cheveux lui arrivent aux épaules** her hair comes down to her shoulders *or* is shoulder-length; **le bruit arrivait jusqu'à ma chambre** the noise reached my bedroom; *Fig* **elle ne lui arrive pas à la cheville** she's not in the same class as him, he's head and shoulders above her

3 j'en étais arrivé là quand … I had got to that point when …; **j'en arrive à me demander s'il n'est pas stupide** I'm beginning to wonder whether he's stupid *or* something; *Fam* **si c'est pas malheureux d'en a. là!** it's such a pity to be reduced to that!, what a pity it's come to that!; **en a. aux coups** to come to blows

4 *(socialement)* to succeed; **c'est un homme qui arrivera** he is a man who will succeed *or* get on *or* do well

5 *(parvenir à un but)* to succeed; **a. à ses fins** to succeed in one's aims *or* plans; **avec du courage on arrive à tout** with courage one can achieve anything; **a. à faire qch** to succeed in doing sth; **je n'arrive pas à le faire toute seule** I can't do *or* manage it on my own; **pour a. à le lui faire accepter, tu devras être patient** to get him to accept it, you'll just have to be patient; **je n'arrive pas à y croire** I just can't believe it; **j'arrive au même résultat que tout à l'heure** I get the same result as before; *Fig* **a. à la vérité** to arrive at *or* get at the truth; *Fig* **a. au fait** to come to the point; **et pour ma voiture? – j'y arrive** what about my car? – I'm (just) coming to that; **tu n'y arriveras pas!** you'll never do it!; **comment y a.?** how can it be done?; **tu n'arriveras jamais à rien!** you'll never amount to anything!, you'll never get anywhere in life!; *Fam* **tu y arrives?** can you do *or* manage *or* get *or* make it?; **a. à échéance** to fall due; *(d'un bail)* to expire; *(d'un prêt)* to mature

6 *(se produire)* to happen, to occur; **ça t'est déjà arrivé?** has that ever happened to you (before)?; **cela arrive tous les jours** it happens every day; *Prov* **un malheur n'arrive jamais seul** misfortunes never come singly; **ça n'arrive qu'aux autres** it's something that happens to other people; **cela ne nous arrivera jamais** it will never happen to us; **cela n'arrive qu'à nous!** just our luck!; **il lui est arrivé un accident** he had an accident; **je ne voudrais pas qu'il lui arrive quelque chose** I don't want anything to happen to him; **cela arrive à tout le monde** it can happen to anyone; **quoi qu'il arrive** whatever happens, whatever may happen, come what may; **devine ce qu'il m'arrive!** guess what!, guess what's happened (to me)!; **mais qu'est-ce qu'il t'arrive en ce moment?** what's wrong with you at the moment?; **il m'arrive souvent d'oublier** I often forget, I'm apt to forget; **il nous arrive rarement d'aller au restaurant** we rarely go to restaurants; **il pourrait a. qu'il se trompe** he might have made a mistake, it could be that he's made a mistake; **s'il vous arrivait de la voir, dites-le-lui** if you (should) happen to see her, tell her SEE GRAMMAR B29

arrivisme [arivism] NM *Péj* pushiness, ambitiousness

arriviste [arivist] N *Péj* careerist

arrogance [arɔgɑ̃s] NF arrogance; **parler avec a.** to speak arrogantly

arrogant, -ante [arɔgɑ̃, -ɑ̃t] ADJ arrogant, overbearing
N arrogant person

arroger (s') [saroʒe] VPR (**je m'arrogeai(s);** n. n. **arrogeons**) **s'a. un droit/un privilège** to assume *or* claim a right/a privilege

arrondi [arɔ̃di] ADJ **1** rounded, round; **visage a.** round face; **chiffre a.** rounded-off number **2** *Ling* **voyelle arrondie** rounded vowel
NM **1** roundness, rounded form; *(d'une bordure etc)* round-off; *Aviat* fillet, fillet radius; **l'a. du visage** the round shape *or* roundness of the face **2** *Aviat* flare out; **atterrissage avec a.** flared landing **3** *(d'une jupe)* hemline

arrondir [arɔ̃dir] VT **1 a. qch** to round sth (off), to make sth round; **la grossesse commence à a. son ventre** her pregnancy is beginning to make her stomach swell; **cette coupe de cheveux arrondit ton visage** that haircut makes your face look round(er); **a. une jupe** to level a skirt; **a. son bras** to flex one's (arm) muscles; **les yeux arrondis par l'étonnement** in wide-eyed astonishment; *Fig* **a. les angles** to smooth down the rough edges, to smooth things over
2 *Ling* **a. une voyelle** to round a vowel
3 *Fin etc (vers le haut)* to round up; *(vers le bas)* to round down; **a. sa fortune** to amass a considerable sum of money; *Fam* **a. ses fins de mois** to supplement one's income; **a. une somme/un poids** to round off a sum/a weight; **vous pouvez a. à 200 euros** you can round it up to 200 euros; **a. à l'euro supérieur/inférieur** to round up/down to the nearest euro; **a. son champ** to add to *or* to round off one's land; *Math* **a. un résultat** to correct a result (to the nearest whole number *or* to so many decimal places)
4 *Naut* **a. un cap** to round *or* double a cape
5 *Aviat (avant l'atterrissage)* to flare out
VPR **s'arrondir** to become rounded; *(du visage)* to round out, to fill out; **pendant la grossesse, elle s'est arrondie** she swelled up during her pregnancy; **son visage s'est arrondi** his face has become round(er) *or* has filled out; **sa fortune s'arrondit** his fortune is growing

arrondissement [arɔ̃dismɑ̃] NM **1** *Admin (à Paris, Marseille, Lyon)* = administrative district **2** *(d'un territoire etc)* rounding (off)

> ### Arrondissement
> In Paris, Lyons and Marseilles, the number of the "arrondissement" corresponds to the last two figures in a postcode: thus, you can tell from the postcode 75012 that it refers to the 12th arrondissement of Paris.

arrosage [arozaʒ] NM **1** *(des plantes)* watering; *(d'une pelouse etc)* sprinkling, spraying; *Culin (de la pâte etc)* wetting, moistening; *Fam* **un bon a.** a good soaking; **a. des rues** watering of the streets; **voiture d'a.** water cart; **tuyau d'a.** hose **2** *(publicité)* bombardment, flood; **l'a. continuel par les médias** the constant media bombardment **3** *(d'un pré)* irrigation **4** *(du vin etc)* watering, diluting **5** *Mil* heavy bombing *or* shelling

arroser [aroze] VT **1** *(rues, plantes)* to water; *(pelouse)* to sprinkle, to spray; *Culin* **a. un rôti** to baste a joint; *Fam* **j'ai été bien arrosé** I got soaking wet; **vous allez vous faire a.** you're going to get soaked; **ville très peu arrosée** town with little rainfall; **repas (abondamment) arrosé de vin** meal washed down with (plenty of) wine; **café arrosé** laced coffee; *Vieilli* **visage arrosé de larmes** face bathed in tears
2 a. une prairie to irrigate a meadow; **rivière qui arrose une région** river that waters a district; **la Seine arrose Paris** the Seine flows through Paris
3 *(vin, lait)* to water down, to dilute
4 *(de la publicité)* to bombard
5 *Mil* **a. une ville** to bomb *or* shell a town; **a. des troupes de projectiles** to spray troops with missiles
6 *Fig Fam (soudoyer)* **a. qn pour obtenir qch de lui** to grease sb's palm to get sth from him; **on a dû l'a. pour qu'il accepte** we had to bribe him into accepting
VPR **s'arroser 1 ça ne s'arrose pas** *(plante)* it doesn't need watering **2 ça s'arrose!** that calls for a drink!

arroseur [arozœr] NM *(appareil)* sprinkler;

Fig **c'est (le gag de) l'a. arrosé** the boot's on the other foot

arroseuse [arozøz] NF *(de rue)* water(ing) cart, street sprinkler

arrosoir [arozwar] NM watering can

arrt *abrév* arrondissement

ARS [aɛres] NF *abrév* allocation de rentrée scolaire

arsenal, -aux [arsənal, -o] NM **1** *Mil* arsenal; **a. maritime** *ou* **de la marine** naval dockyard **2** *(dépôt d'armes)* **a. d'artillerie** gun factory; **découverte d'un a. chez un particulier** discovery of an arsenal of weapons in sb's house **3** *Fam (attirail)* gear, paraphernalia; **un a. d'outils** a whole range of tools; **il emporta son a. de drogues** he took his whole stock of drugs with him; **l'a. des lois** the weight of the law

arsenic [arsənik] NM *Chimie* arsenic

art [ar] NM **1** *(technique)* art, craft; **l'a. militaire** *ou* **de la guerre** the art of war; **l'a. oratoire** (the art of) public speaking; **l'a. culinaire** the art of (good) cooking; **dans les règles de l'a.** by the book, according to the rules **2** *(esthétique)* art; **l'a. pour l'a.** art for art's sake; **pour l'amour de l'a.** for art's sake; **a. égyptien/italien** Egyptian/Italian art; **l'a. antique/baroque/de la Renaissance** antique/baroque/Renaissance art; **musée d'a. contemporain** museum of modern art; **beaux-arts** fine arts; *Beaux-Arts, Fig* **œuvre d'a.** work of art; **l'a. poétique** poetics; **ville d'a.** city of artistic interest; **livre d'a.** art book; **histoire de l'a.** history of art; **c'est du grand a.!** it's a work of art! **3** **le septième/le huitième/le neuvième a.** cinema/television/cartoons; **cinéma d'a. et d'essai** art cinema **4** *(savoir-faire)* **l'a. de ...** the art of ...; **elle a l'a. des soirées réussies** she's got a flair *or* a knack for organizing successful parties; **les Français ont l'a. de vivre** French people know how to live *or* how to enjoy life; **il a l'a. et la manière pour parler aux femmes** he has a way with women; *Fam* **il a l'a. de m'énerver** he's got a gift for getting up my nose **5** *(adresse)* skill; **faire qch avec a.** to do sth skilfully **6** *Can Scol* **maître ès arts** Master of Arts **7** *Constr* **travaux** *ou* **ouvrages d'a.** civil engineering structures *or* works ▸▸ **a. déco** art deco; **a. dramatique** dramatic art; **a. du feu** ceramics; **a. nouveau** art nouveau; **l'a. sacré** *ou* **religieux** religious art; **arts décoratifs** decorative arts; **arts graphiques** graphic arts; **arts martiaux** martial arts; **arts plastiques** fine arts; **a. vidéo** video art

Arte [arte] N = French-German cultural TV channel

artefact [artefakt] NM artefact, artifact

artère [arter] NF **1** *Anat* artery; **a. aorte** aorta; **a. pulmonaire** pulmonary artery; **on a l'âge de ses artères** you're as old as you feel **2** *Fig (route etc)* main highway, arterial road; *(en ville)* main thoroughfare

artériel, -ielle [arterjɛl] ADJ *Physiol* arterial; **tension artérielle** blood pressure

artériole [arterjɔl] NF *Anat* arteriole

artériosclérose [arterjɔskleroz] NF *Méd* arteriosclerosis, hardening of the arteries

artésien, -ienne [artezjɛ̃, -jɛn] ADJ *(puits)* Artesian

arthrite [artrit] NF *Méd* arthritis; **a. sèche** *ou* **déformante** rheumatoid arthritis

arthritique [artritik] *Méd* ADJ arthritic N arthritic (patient), sufferer from arthritis

arthro- [artrɔ] PRÉF arthro-

arthropode [artrɔpɔd] NM arthropod

arthrose [artroz] NF *Méd* osteoarthritis

Arthur [artyr] N *Fam* **je vais me faire appeler A.!** I'll catch it!

artichaut [artiʃo] NM *(légume)* globe artichoke; *Culin* **fonds d'artichauts** artichoke hearts; *Fig* **c'est un cœur d'a.** he/she flits from one affair to another

artiche [artiʃ] NM *Fam* dough, bread, *Br* dosh, *Am* bucks

article [artikl] NM **1** *Com* article, commodity; **articles** goods, wares; **articles de luxe** luxury goods; **a. en réclame** special offer; **nous ne suivons** *ou* **faisons plus cet a.** we don't stock that item any more; **articles de voyage** travel goods; **articles de ménage** household requisites; **articles de bureau** office supplies; **articles de toilette** toiletries; **articles pour hommes/femmes** menswear/ladies' wear; **a. bas de gamme** bottom of the range item; **a. démarqué** markdown; **a. haut de gamme** top of the range item; **a. de marque** branded article; **a. à forte rotation** fast mover; **articles de consommation** consumables, consumer goods; **faire l'a.** to make a sales pitch; *Mktg* **a. d'appel** traffic builder; *Mktg* **de caisse** check-out display item **2** *(d'une facture etc)* item; *(de compte)* entry; **articles divers** sundries **3** *(dans un journal etc)* article; **a. de journal** newspaper article; *Journ* **a. de tête** editorial, leader, leading article; **un a. de dictionnaire** a dictionary entry; *Journ* **a. clé en main** rip 'n' read article; *Journ* **a. d'appel** lead(ing) story; *Journ* **a. de fond** feature (article); *Journ* **a. nécrologique** obituary; *Journ* **a. principal** lead(ing) story, main feature **4** *(d'un traité etc)* article, clause; *(sujet)* point; **il est très ferme sur cet a.** he's very strict about that *or* on that point; **a. de foi** article of faith **5** *(point critique)* critical point; **ce qu'il a dit à l'a. de la mort** what he said just before he died; **être à l'a. de la mort** to be at the point of death **6** *Entom* joint **7** *Gram* **a. défini/indéfini** definite/indefinite article SEE GRAMMAR A5–8; B3–5 **8** *Ordinat (dans base de données)* record; *(commande)* command; **a. 'annuler'** undo command; **a. contrasté** highlighted command; **a. de menu** command, menu item

articulaire [artikyler] ADJ *Anat* articular, articulatory; *Méd* **rhumatisme a.** rheumatoid arthritis

articulation [artikylasjɔ̃] NF **1** *Anat etc* joint, *Spéc* articulation; *Bot* node; *Anat* **a. du doigt** knuckle; **a. à** *ou* **par emboîtement** ball-and-socket joint **2** *Tech* connection, joint; **accouplement à a.** jointed coupling; **a. à rotule** ball-and-socket joint **3** *(prononciation)* articulation **4** *(organisation)* **l'a. des idées d'un texte** the structuring of ideas in a text **5** *Jur (des faits)* numeration

articulé [artikyle] ADJ **1** articulate(d), jointed; *(membre, articulation etc)* hinged; **poupée articulée** doll with movable joints; *Tech* **courroie articulée** chain *or* link belt **2** *Ling (discours)* articulate

articuler [artikyle] VT **1** *(assembler)* to articulate, to hinge, to link, to joint; **a. des idées dans un texte** to organize ideas in a text **2** *Ling* to articulate; *Fig (dire)* **il n'a même pas pu a. son nom, tant il était terrorisé** he was so afraid, he couldn't even say his own name **3** *Jur (faits)* to enumerate, to set forth; *(fait)* to state clearly *or* definitely VPR **s'articuler** to be joined together; **la façon dont les os s'articulent** the way the bones are joined together; **ces deux parties s'articulent assez bien** the two parts of the text hang together well; **son raisonnement s'articule autour d'un point central** his argument is based on a central point; *Ling* **le j espagnol s'articule dans le fond de la gorge** the Spanish j is pronounced in the back of the throat VI to articulate; **mal a.** to mumble; **articule!** speak clearly!, *Fml* articulate!

artifice [artifis] NM **1** *(ruse)* trick, contrivance; **user de tous les artifices pour ...** to resort to every trick (in the book) in order to ...; **les artifices de la toilette** the little tricks women use to make themselves (look) beautiful **2** *(pyrotechnique)* **pièce d'a.** firework

artificialité [artifisjalite] NF artificiality

artificiel, -ielle [artifisjɛl] ADJ **1** *(non naturel)* *(lumière, fleurs, goût etc)* artificial; *(lac)* artificial, man-made; *(perle etc)* imitation; *(dent etc)* false; *Fig (personne)* artificial, false; **jambe artificielle** artificial leg; **colorant a.** artificial colouring; **rire a.** forced laugh **2** *(arbitraire)* arbitrary; **classification artificielle** arbitrary classification

artificiellement [artifisjɛlmɑ̃] ADV artificially; *(arbitrairement)* arbitrarily

artificier [artifisje] NM *(fabricant)* firework manufacturer; *(dans un feu d'artifice)* master of ceremonies

artificieusement [artifisjøzmɑ̃] ADV *Litt* deceitfully, craftily

artificieux, -ieuse [artifisjø, -jøz] ADJ *Litt* deceitful, wily

artillerie [artijri] NF **1** artillery, ordnance; **a. de campagne** field artillery; **a. légère/lourde** light/heavy artillery; **a. navale** naval artillery; **a. motorisée** motorized artillery; **a. antichars, Belg a. anti-blindés** anti-tank artillery; **a. antiaérienne** anti-aircraft artillery; **a. d'assaut** assault artillery *or* guns; **tir d'a.** artillery fire; **pièce d'a.** artillery cannon; *Aut* **roue type a.** artillery type wheel **2** *(collectif)* gunnery

artilleur [artijœr] NM artilleryman, gunner

artimon [artimɔ̃] NM *Naut* mât d')a. mizzenmast; **voile d'a.** mizzen (sail); **a. de cape** storm mizzen

artisan, -ane [artizɑ̃, -an] N artisan, craftsman, *f* craftswoman; *Fig* **il est l'a. de sa réussite** he brought about his own success, he's the author *or* architect of his own success

artisanal, -ale, -aux, -ales [artizanal, -o] ADJ **métier a.** craft; **production artisanale** small-scale production (by craftsmen); **magasin a.** craft shop; **poterie artisanale** hand-made pottery; **fait de façon artisanale** made in the traditional way; **leur maison d'édition est restée très artisanale** their publishing house has remained very small-scale

artisanalement [artizanalmɑ̃] ADV **fait a.** hand-crafted, made by craftsmen

artisanat [artizana] NM *(profession)* craft industry; **l'a. indigène** the native craftsmen; **encourager l'a.** to encourage small-scale industry *or* the craft industries; **a. d'art** arts and crafts; **produits d'a. régional** local handicrafts

artiste [artist] N **1** *(esprit créatif)* artist; *Fig* **avoir une sensibilité d'a.** to have an artistic temperament, to be artistic; **c'est un a., il a une mentalité d'a.** he's a real eccentric; *Fig* **eh l'a.! viens par là!** hey, smarty pants! come over here! **2** *Théâtre, Mus* performer; *Théâtre* actor, *f* actress; *(chanteur)* singer; *(danseur)* dancer; **a. peintre** painter; **représentation** *ou* **vue d'a.** artist's impression; **entrée des artistes** stage door ADJ *(tempérament, style)* artistic; **se donner un genre a.** to try to look all arty

Il faut noter que le terme anglais **artist** désigne généralement un peintre, un dessinateur ou un sculpteur.

artistement [artistəmɑ̃] ADV artistically

artistique [artistik] ADJ artistic

artistiquement [artistikmɑ̃] ADV artistically

arum [arɔm] NM *(fleur)* arum

arvine [arvin] NF *Suisse* = grape variety from the Valais canton, and white wine produced from these grapes

aryen, -enne [arjɛ̃, -ɛn] ADJ Aryan
N A. Aryan

AS *abrév* assurances sociales

as [ɑs] NM **1** *Cartes etc* ace; **amener deux as** to throw two aces; **as de pique** ace of spades; *Culin Fam (dans la volaille)* parson's nose; *Fig Fam* **être ficelé** *ou* **fichu comme l'as de pique** to be dressed any old how; *Fig Fam* **être coiffé comme l'as de pique** to have hair like a bird's nest; *Arg Fig* **être aux as** *ou* **plein aux as** to be rolling (in it); *Fam* **ma prime est passée à l'as** my bonus never materialized; *Fam* **les vacances sont passées à l'as** that's the holidays out of the window **2** *(dominos)* one; **l'as blanc** one blank **3** *Fam (champion)* ace; *(aux jeux)* crack player, star; **au tennis c'est un as** he's an ace at tennis; **as du volant** *ou* **de la route** crack (racing) driver, ace driver; **Pierre c'est un as, il sait tout faire** Pierre's ace, he can do anything

a/s *(abrév* **aux soins de)** c/o

asbeste [azbɛst] NM *Minér* asbestos

asbestose [azbɛstoz] NF *Méd* asbestosis

ASBL [aɛsbeɛl] NF *(abrév* **association sans but lucratif)** non-profit-making organization, *Am* not-for-profit organization

ascendance [asɑ̃dɑ̃s] NF **1** *Astron* ascent **2** *(de famille etc)* ancestry; **l'une et l'autre famille avaient une a. canadienne** both families were of Canadian ancestry *or* descent; **a. maternelle** ancestry on his/her/*etc* mother's side; **être d'a. noble** to be of noble ancestry **3** *Phys* **a. thermique** thermal (current)

ascendant [asɑ̃dɑ̃] ADJ *(mouvement, courant, échelle, série)* ascending; *(mouvement etc)* upward; *Aviat* **vol a.** climbing flight; **course ascendante** *(d'un piston)* up stroke; **tuyau a.** standpipe
NM **1** *Astron etc* ascendant; **astre qui est à l'a.** star in the ascendant **2** *(influence)* ascendancy, influence; **avoir de l'a. sur qn** to have influence over sb; **elle subit l'a. de son mari** she's dominated by her husband **3** **ascendants** *(famille)* ancestry **4** *Astrol* rising sign; **Verseau a. Cancer** Aquarius with Cancer as his rising sign *or* with Cancer in the ascendant

ascenseur [asɑ̃sœr] NM **1** lift, *Am* elevator; **a. de marchandises** goods hoist; **a. de service** service lift; **a. à bagages** baggage lift; **a. à tous les étages** lift to all floors; **a. à sas** canal lift; *Fig* **renvoyer l'a.** to return the favour **2** *Ordinat* scroll box

ascension [asɑ̃sjɔ̃] NF **1** *(montée, escalade)* ascent; *Aviat* climb; **faire l'a. d'une montagne** to climb a mountain; **une a. facile** an easy climb; **l'a. du mont Blanc** the climbing *or* ascent of Mont Blanc; *Aviat* **angle d'a.** climbing angle; *Aviat* **a. verticale** vertical climb; *Astron* **right ascension**; *Rel* **fête** *ou* **jeudi de l'A.** Ascension Day; **l'île de l'A.** Ascension Island **2** *Astron* **a. d'un astre** ascension of a star; **a. verticale** right ascension **3** *Fig* progress, ascent, rise; **l'a. professionnelle de qn** sb's climb up the professional ladder; **l'a. de Bonaparte** the rise of Bonaparte

Ascension
Ascension Day is on the fortieth day after Easter and is a public holiday in France. Many people take an extended weekend break during this period.

ascensionnel, -elle [asɑ̃sjɔnɛl] ADJ *(mouvement)* upward; *Aviat* **force ascensionnelle** lifting power, lift; **vitesse ascensionnelle** rate of climb, climbing speed; **mouvement a.** upstroke; *Sport* **parachutisme a.** parascending

ascensionner [asɑ̃sjɔne] VI to climb

ascensionniste [asɑ̃sjɔnist] N climber, mountaineer

ascèse [asɛz] NF asceticism; **mener une vie d'a.** to live an ascetic life

ascète [asɛt] N ascetic

ascétique [asetik] ADJ ascetic; **vie a.** ascetic life

ascétisme [asetism] NM asceticism

ASCII [aski] NM *Ordinat (abrév* **American Standard Code for Information Interchange)** ASCII; **A. inférieur** lower ASCII; **A. supérieur** upper ASCII

ascorbique [askɔrbik] ADJ *(acide)* ascorbic

asdic [asdik] NM *Naut (abrév* **Allied Submarine Detection Investigation Committee)** ASDIC

ASE [aɛsə] NF *(abrév* **Agence spatiale européenne)** ESA

asepsie, aseptie [asɛpsi] NF *Méd* asepsis

aseptique [asɛptik] ADJ *Méd* aseptic

aseptisation [asɛptizasjɔ̃] NF *(d'une blessure, d'un pansement)* sterilization, asepsis; *(d'une pièce)* disinfection

aseptiser [asɛptize] VT *Méd (blessure)* to sterilize; *(pièce)* to disinfect; *Fig Péj* **un univers aseptisé** a sterile *or* sanitized environment

asexué [asɛksɥe], **asexuel, -elle** [asɛksɥel] ADJ *Biol* asexual

asiatique [azjatik] ADJ Asian, Asiatic; **grippe a.** Asian flu
N A. Asian, Asiatic

Il faut noter qu'en anglais britannique le nom **Asian** désigne le plus souvent une personne originaire du sous-continent indien.

Asiatique
This word tends to refer to Oriental people (ie from countries such as China, Japan, Vietnam etc), rather than Asia as a whole. Note that it does not refer to the British English sense of "Asian" meaning someone from the Indian subcontinent.

Asie [azi] NF Asia; **l'A. Mineure** Asia Minor; **A. du Sud-Est** South-East Asia

asile [azil] NM **1** *Jur* sanctuary; **droit d'a.** right of sanctuary; **a. politique/diplomatique** political/diplomatic asylum; **demander l'a. politique** to ask for political asylum **2** *(abri)* shelter, refuge, retreat; **lieu d'a.** (place of) refuge; **sans a.** without refuge; *Arch* **a. des pauvres** ≃ workhouse; **a. de nuit** night shelter, *Fam* dosshouse; **a. des marins** sailors' home; **a. (d'aliénés)** mental hospital, *Vieilli* lunatic asylum; *Fam* **il faut le mettre à l'a.!** he belongs in the loony bin *or* at the funny farm!, he ought to be locked away!; *Litt* **a. de paix** haven of peace; **le dernier a.** the grave **3** *Mktg (document publicitaire)* stuffer, insert

asinien, -ienne [azinjɛ̃, -jɛn] ADJ asinine

asocial, -iale, -iaux, -iales [asɔsjal, -jo] ADJ maladjusted
N misfit, maladjusted person

asparagus [asparagys] NM asparagus fern

aspartam(e) [aspartam] NM aspartame

aspect [aspɛ] NM **1** *(vue)* sight, *Fml* aspect **2** *(air)* appearance, look; **avoir un a. imposant** to look imposing; **je n'aime pas l'a. de cette affaire** I don't like the look of the thing; **un démon qui pouvait prendre tous les aspects** a demon who could take on any appearance **3** *(angle)* angle, point of view; **considérer une affaire sous tous ses aspects** to look at a problem from every angle *or* from all points of view; **vu sous cet a.** seen from this angle *or* point of view **4** *Astrol (des étoiles)* aspect, relative positions **5** *Gram* aspect; **a. perfectif** perfective VOIR GRAMMAIRE A39

asperge [aspɛrʒ] NF **1** *(plante)* asparagus; **a. plumeuse** asparagus fern; **une botte d'asperges** a bunch of asparagus; **pointe** *ou* **tête d'a.** asparagus tip; **plant d'asperges** asparagus bed **2** *Fam (personne)* beanpole

asperger [aspɛrʒe] VT **(j'aspergeai(s); n. aspergeons)** *(linge etc)* to sprinkle with water; **a. qn d'eau bénite** to sprinkle sb with holy water; **une voiture nous a aspergés d'eau** a (passing) car sprayed us with water; **se faire a.** to get splashed

aspergès [aspɛrʒɛs] NM *Rel* **1** *(goupillon)* aspergillum, holy-water sprinkler **2** *(rite)* asperges

aspérité [asperite] NF **1** *(d'une surface etc)* unevenness, ruggedness, roughness **2** *(d'un caractère, d'une voix)* asperity, harshness, sharpness

asperme [aspɛrm] ADJ *Bot* seedless

aspersion [aspɛrsjɔ̃] NF sprinkling; *Agr* drench

aspersoir [aspɛrswar] NM **1** *Rel* aspergillum **2** *(d'un arrosoir)* rose

asphaltage [asfaltaʒ] NM *Constr etc* asphalting

asphalte [asfalt] NM *Minér* asphalt; **a. minéral** pitch, bitumen; **route en a.** asphalt road; *Fam* **arpenter l'a.** to pace up and down the streets

asphalter [asfalte] VT *(route etc)* to asphalt

asphodèle [asfɔdɛl] NM *(plante)* asphodel; **a. rameux** branched lily, king's rod; **a. blanc** king's spear

asphyxiant [asfiksjɑ̃] ADJ **1** asphyxiating, suffocating; **gaz a.** poison gas **2** *Fig (atmosphère etc)* stifling, suffocating

asphyxie [asfiksi] NF asphyxia, asphyxiation, suffocation; *Min etc* gassing; **mourir d'a.** *ou* **par a.** to die of asphyxiation; *Fig* **a. économique** economic strangulation

asphyxié [asfiksje] ADJ *(personne)* asphyxiated, suffocated; *Min etc* gassed; **mourir a.** to die of asphyxiation

asphyxier [asfiksje] *(pr sub, impf* **n. asphyxiions, v. asphyxiiez)** VT to asphyxiate, to suffocate; *Min etc* to gas; *Fig* **elle se sent asphyxiée par sa famille** she feels suffocated *or* stifled by her family
VPR **s'asphyxier** *(accidentellement)* to be asphyxiated, to suffocate; *(au gaz)* to be gassed; *(pour se suicider)* to suffocate oneself; *(au gaz)* to gas oneself

aspic [aspik] NM **1** *(serpent)* asp **2** *Culin* aspic

aspidistra [aspidistra] NM *(plante)* aspidistra

aspirant, -ante [aspirɑ̃, -ɑ̃t] ADJ sucking; **pompe aspirante** suction pump; **ventilateur a.** suction fan; **course aspirante** induction *or* admission stroke
N candidate (**au** for)
NM *Naut* midshipman; *Mil* officer cadet; *Naut* **a. pilote** apprentice pilot

aspirateur, -trice [aspiratœr, -tris] ADJ aspiratory; *(mécanisme)* suction
NM *(pour la maison)* vacuum (cleaner), Hoover®; *Chimie, Ind, Méd (de gaz, d'air)* exhauster, aspirator; **passer l'a. dans la maison** to vacuum(-clean) *or* hoover the house; **passer une pièce/moquette à l'a.** to vacuum(-clean) *or* hoover a room/rug; **un coup d'a.** a quick once-over with the vacuum (cleaner)

or Hoover®; **a. à céréales** grain elevator; **a. de buées** extractor fan

aspiration [aspirasjɔ̃] NF **1** *Physiol* inhaling (of air into the lungs), *Spéc* inspiration; *Tech (d'eau dans pompe etc)* suction, sucking up; *Aut* aspiration; *Aut* **à a. naturelle** naturally aspirated, unblown; **ventilateur à a.** exhaust fan; *(d'un moteur à combustion interne)* admission, induction; **clapet d'a.** intake valve **2** *(désir, ambition)* aspiration, yearning (**à, vers** for, after); **aspirations à la scène** ambitions to go on the stage **3** *Ling* aspiration

aspiré [aspire] ADJ *Ling* aspirate(d)

aspirée [aspire] NF *Ling* aspirate

aspirer [aspire] VI **1** *(inspirer)* to breathe in, to inhale **2** *(ambitionner)* to aspire (**à** to); **a. à la gloire/la célébrité** to aspire to glory/fame; **a. à un poste** to covet a post; **a. à faire qch** to long to do sth; **elle aspire à devenir actrice** she longs to become an actress
▪ VT **1** *(air, parfum etc)* to inhale, to breathe (in); *(poudre etc)* to sniff up **2** *(eau etc) (d'une pompe)* to suck up, to suck in, to draw (up) **3** *Ling (un son)* to aspirate, to breathe; **l'h est aspiré en allemand** the h is aspirated in German

aspirine [aspirin] NF *Pharm* aspirin; **un cachet d'a.** an aspirin; **prenez deux aspirines** take two aspirin(s)

aspiro-batteur, *pl* **aspiro-batteurs** [aspirobatœr] NM beating vacuum cleaner

ASS [aɛɛs] NF *abrév* allocation de solidarité spécifique

assagir [asaʒir] VT to quieten down; **le mariage l'a assagi** marriage has calmed him down; **voilà qui l'assagira** that will knock some sense into him; **le temps assagit les passions** passions will cool with time
▪ VPR **s'assagir** to settle down

assagissement [asaʒismɑ̃] NM quietening (down), calming (down); *(des esprits)* calming (down)

assaillant, -ante [asajɑ̃, -ɑ̃t] N assailant, attacker

assaillir [asajir] VT *(prp* **assaillant**; *pp* **assailli**; *pr ind* **j'assaille**, *n.* **assaillons**, **ils assaillent**; *impf* **j'assaillais**; *p hist* **j'assaillis**; *fu* **j'assaillirai**) to assault, to attack; *Fig (de difficultés, remords etc)* to beset; **à mon retour, j'ai été assailli de questions** when I came back, I was bombarded with questions

assainir [asenir] VT *(maison, murs)* to clean up; *(atmosphère etc)* to cleanse, to purify; *(étable)* to clean, to disinfect; *(marais)* to drain; *(ville)* to improve the sanitation of; *(monnaie, marché etc)* to stabilize; *Compta (bilan)* to balance; **a. les finances/l'administration** to reorganize finance/administration; **a. une rivière** to clean up a river
▪ VPR **s'assainir** *(d'atmosphère)*, *Fig (de marché)* to become healthier; *Fig* **la situation s'est assainie** the situation has improved

assainissant [asenisɑ̃] ADJ cleansing, purifying

assainissement [asenismɑ̃] NM *(d'atmosphère)* cleansing, purifying; *(de terrain)* drainage; *(de ville)* improving of the sanitation; *Fin* stabilization; **a. monétaire** stabilization of the currency; **travaux d'a.** drainage work

assaisonnement [asɛzɔnmɑ̃] NM **1** *(de plat)* seasoning, flavouring; *(de salade)* dressing; **je n'aime pas ce plat, l'a. est trop fade** I don't like this dish, it's under-seasoned **2** *(aromate etc)* seasoning, flavouring

assaisonner [asɛzɔne] VT **1** *Culin* to season, to flavour (**de** with); *(salade)* to dress; *Fig Fam* **se faire a.** *(réprimander)* to get a good telling-off; **le président a vraiment été assai-**

---

sonné dans le journal de ce matin the president really got it in the paper this morning **2** *Fam (faire payer plus)* to rip off; **je me suis fait assaisonner** I got ripped off

assassin, -ine [asasɛ̃, -in] NM murderer, *f* murderess; *(d'une personnalité politique etc)* assassin; **à l'a.!** murder!; **l'a. est Madame Duval** the murderer is Mrs Duval
▪ ADJ **1** *(horde etc)* murderous **2** *Fig (sourire)* provocative, bewitching; **elle lance des œillades assassines à tous les hommes** she's always making eyes at men

assassinat [asasina] NM murder; *(d'une personnalité politique etc)* assassination; *Jur* premeditated murder, *Am* murder in the first degree

assassiner [asasine] VT to murder; *(homme politique etc)* to assassinate; *Fam (chanson etc)* to murder; *Fig* **si je rentre en retard, je vais me faire a. par mes parents** if I get home late, my parents will murder me; *Fig* **je ne vais pas vous a., c'est seulement 10 euros** I'm not going to charge you the earth, it's only 10 euros

assaut [aso] NM **1** *(attaque)* assault, attack; *surtout Mil* charge, onslaught; **canon d'a.** assault gun; **troupes d'a.** assault *or* storm troops; **a. à la baïonnette** bayonet charge; **donner l'a. à** to storm, to launch an attack on; *Fig* **partir à l'a. du mont Blanc/d'une entreprise** to set out to conquer Mont Blanc/to take over a firm; **les meilleures places ont été prises d'a.** everybody made a rush for the best seats; **les assauts répétés d'une maladie** the repeated attacks *or* onslaughts of a disease **2** *(combat)* match, bout; **a. de lutte** wrestling bout; **a. de boxe** boxing match; **faire a. d'élégance/de zèle/de courtoisie** to (try to) outdo each other in elegance/zeal/politeness

assèchement [asɛʃmɑ̃] NM *(de route)* drying; *(de terrain, mare etc)* draining, drainage; *(de mine)* pumping dry

assécher [aseʃe] VT *(marais etc)* to drain; *(mine etc)* to pump dry *or* out
▪ VPR **s'assécher** to become dry, to dry up

ASSEDIC [asedik] NFPL *(abrév* **Associations pour l'emploi dans l'industrie et le commerce)** = French unemployment benefits department; *Br* ≃ Unemployment Benefit Office, *Am* Unemployment Office; **toucher les A.** to get unemployment benefit; **faire un dossier aux A.** to apply for unemployment benefit

assemblage [asɑ̃blaʒ] NM **1** *(de personnes)* gathering; *(d'objets)* collection, combination; **a. de circonstances** combination of circumstances **2** *(d'éléments de machine etc)* assembling, assembly; *Menuis* joint, joining; *Couture* sewing together; *Tricot* making up; *(de feuillets)* gathering, collating **3** *(structure)* assembly; **un a. de tiges métalliques** an assembly *or* structure of metal shafts; **a. en queue d'aronde** dovetail joint; **a. par vis/à rivets** screw/rivet assembly; **a. à tenon et mortaise** mortise-and-tenon joint **4** *Ordinat* **programme d'a.** assembler **5** *Élec* connection; **a. en quantité** parallel connection **6** *(par soudure)* bond

assemblée [asɑ̃ble] NF **1** *(réunion)* assembly; *(plus petite)* meeting; **se réunir en a.** to assemble (for a meeting) **2** *Pol* **A. nationale** National Assembly, *Br* ≃ House of Commons, *Am* ≃ House of Representatives; **A. parlementaire européenne** European Parliamentary Assembly **3** *(foule)* gathering; **une nombreuse a.** a large gathering; **a. des fidèles** the congregation
▪▶ **a. des actionnaires** shareholders' meeting; **a. annuelle/extraordinaire** annual/extraordinary general meeting; **a. générale**

---

annual general meeting; **a. générale d'actionnaires** general meeting of shareholders; **a. générale annuelle** annual general meeting; **a. générale extraordinaire** extraordinary general meeting; **a. générale ordinaire** annual general meeting

> ### Assemblée nationale
> The French parliament has two chambers: the National Assembly and the Senate. The members of the National Assembly (the "députés") are elected in the "élections législatives" held every five years.

assembler [asɑ̃ble] VT **1** to assemble; *(personnes)* to call together, to assemble; *(comité etc)* to convene; *(ingrédients, idées, ce dont on a besoin etc)* to collect, to gather (together); *Naut* **a. l'équipage** to muster the crew **2** *(machine, meuble en kit etc)* to assemble, to put *or* fit together; *(documents)* to collate; *(feuillets)* to collate, to gather **3** *Menuis, Tech etc* to join (up), to joint; **a. deux morceaux à plat** to butt-joint two pieces; **a. deux pièces par soudure/collage** to weld/glue two parts together **4** *Ordinat (programme)* to assemble; *(modules)* to link **5** *Élec (cellules)* to connect, to join up
▪ VPR **s'assembler** to assemble, to meet, to gather; *(d'une foule)* to gather; **s'a. devant un spectacle insolite** to gather in front of an unusual sight; **les membres s'assemblent deux fois par an** the members meet twice a year; *Prov* **qui se ressemble s'assemble** birds of a feather flock together

assembleur, -euse [asɑ̃blœr, -øz] N assembler; *(de machines etc)* fitter
▪ NF **assembleuse** *(machine)* gatherer
▪ NM *Ordinat* assembler

asséner [asene] VT (**j'assène**, *n.* **assénons**; **j'assénerai**) *(coup)* to strike; **coup bien asséné** telling *or* well-aimed blow; **a. une réplique** to answer back like a shot; **la façon dont la propagande est assénée** the way propaganda is thrust at you; **on nous assène des publicités toute la journée** we are bombarded with adverts all day long; **c'est là qu'il lui a asséné l'argument final** that's when he hurled the final argument at him

assentiment [asɑ̃timɑ̃] NM assent, consent, agreement; **donner/refuser son a. (à qch)** to give/withhold one's assent (to sth); **avoir l'a. de tous** to be supported unanimously; **sourire d'a.** smile of agreement

asseoir [aswar] *(prp* **asseyant**; *pp* **assis**; *pr ind* **j'assieds** [asje], **il assied**, *n.* **asseyons**, **ils asseyent** *or* **j'assois, il assoit, ils assoient** *or* **j'asseye**, *n.* **asseyions** *or* **j'assoie**; *imp* **assieds, asseyons, asseyez**; *impf* **j'asseyais** *or* **j'assoyais**; *p hist* **j'assis**; *impf sub* **j'assisse**; *fu* **j'assiérai** *or* **j'assoirai**) VT **1** *(installer)* to seat, to sit; **asseyez-le sur le gazon** sit him down on the grass; **faire a. qn** to ask sb to sit down *or* to take a seat **2** *(fondations etc)* to place, to lay; **a. une pierre** to bed a stone; **a. une statue sur un piédestal** to stand a statue on a pedestal; **a. une tente/un camp** to pitch a tent/(a) camp; *Fig* **a. son autorité/sa réputation** to establish one's authority/reputation; *Fig* **a. une théorie sur des résultats scientifiques** to base a theory on scientific results; *Fin* **a. l'impôt sur le revenu** to base taxation on income **3** *Fig (étonner)* to amaze, to stagger; **ça m'assoit complètement de voir qu'il réussit aussi vite** I'm staggered to see him succeeding so quickly
▪ VPR **s'asseoir** to sit (down); **asseyez-vous** *(à de nombreuses personnes)* sit down, be seated; *(à une ou deux personnes)* sit down, have *or* take a seat; **asseyez-vous, je vous en prie** please sit down *or* take a seat; **vous**

permettez que je m'asseye *ou* **m'assoie?** may I sit down?; **s'a. sur une chaise/dans un fauteuil** to sit on a chair/in an armchair; **s'a. (sur son séant)** *(d'une position allongée)* to sit up; *Fig Fam* **s'a. sur qn** to ignore sb; *Fig Fam* **les ordres du patron, moi, je m'assois dessus!** I don't give a damn about the boss's orders!

assermentation [asɛrmɑ̃tasjɔ̃] NF *Can, Suisse* swearing in, taking of an oath

assermenté [asɛrmɑ̃te] ADJ sworn (in); *(témoin etc)* on oath; **fonctionnaire a.** sworn official; *Hist* **(prêtre) non a.** non-juring (priest)

assermenter [asɛrmɑ̃te] VT *(personne)* to swear in; *(témoin etc)* to administer the oath to

assertion [asɛrsjɔ̃] NF assertion

asservi [asɛrvi] ADJ *(appareil)* servo; **moteur a.** servomotor

asservir [asɛrvir] VT **1** *(assujettir)* to enslave, to subjugate, to subdue; *(nation)* to reduce to slavery; **a. ses instincts** to control one's instincts, to keep one's instincts under control; **être asservi à la mode** to be a slave to fashion **2** *(de mécanisme de commande etc) (pièce)* to control
▸ VPR **s'asservir** to submit, to bow (à to)

asservissant [asɛrvisɑ̃] ADJ enslaving; **avoir un emploi a.** to be a slave to one's job

asservissement [asɛrvismɑ̃] NM **1** *(assujettissement) (d'un pays)* subjection (à to), reduction to slavery, enslavement; *(envers qn de plus fort)* subservience; **vivre dans l'a. des médias** to believe everything the newspapers and television say **2** *Tech* control; *(de mécanisme)* servo control

assesseur [asɛsœr] NM **1** *Jur (juge)* **a.** *(auprès d'un magistrat etc)* assessor **2** **être secondé par ses assesseurs** to be supported by one's assistants

assez [ase] ADV **1** *(suffisamment)* enough; **vous travaillez bien a.** you work quite enough; **elle parle a. bien l'anglais pour ce poste** she speaks English well enough for the job; **(c'est) a. parlé!** that's enough talking!; **nous sommes a. de trois, nous n'avons pas besoin de toi** three's enough, we don't need you; **il est a. bête pour la croire!** he's stupid enough to believe her!; **il n'est pas a. bête pour dire oui** he's not so stupid as to say yes; **être a. près pour voir** to be near enough to see; **il n'avait pas a. pour vivre/pour acheter des cigarettes** he hadn't enough to live on/enough (money) to buy cigarettes; **a.!** that's enough!, stop!; **a.! je ne veux plus t'entendre!** that's enough! I don't want to hear another sound out of you!; **j'en ai a.!** I've had enough (of it)!, I'm sick *or* tired of it!, I'm fed up!; **en voilà a. (sur ce sujet)!** that's enough (about that)!; **c'en est a.!** that's enough of that!; **j'en ai plus qu'a. de ses sautes d'humeur!** I've had more than enough of his moods VOIR GRAMMAIRE A23
2 a. de *(+ n)* enough; **il y a a. de pain pour tous** there's enough bread for everybody; **avez-vous a. d'argent?** have you enough money?; **a. de promesses! des actes!** enough (of) promises! let's see some action! **3** *(plutôt)* quite, rather, fairly; **elle est a. jolie** she's quite pretty; **je suis a. de votre avis** I'm rather inclined to agree with you; **je suis a. content de ma carrière** I'm quite *or* fairly happy with my career; **arriver a. tard** to arrive rather *or* fairly late; **j'ai dû attendre a. longtemps** I had to wait quite a long time; **il parle a. peu** he doesn't talk much VOIR GRAMMAIRE A5

assidu [asidy] ADJ assiduous, *(employé, élève etc)* industrious, hard-working; *(soin, attention)* constant; *(visiteur)* regular, constant; **efforts assidus** untiring efforts; **travailleur a.** hard worker; **présence assidue aux cours** regular attendance at classes; **le médecin est a. auprès de ses malades** the doc-

tor takes good care of *or* is very attentive to his patients; **faire une cour assidue à qn** to court sb persistently; *Vieilli* **un amoureux a.** a persistent suitor

assiduité [asidɥite] NF **1** assiduity, perseverance; *Scol etc* regular attendance; **a. à (faire) qch** assiduity in (doing) sth; **a. au travail** devotion to work **2** *(fréquence)* constant attention(s), constant care; **fréquenter qn avec a.** to be a frequent visitor at sb's house **3** **il la poursuit de ses assiduités depuis des années** he's been forcing his attentions on her for years

assidûment [asidymɑ̃] ADV assiduously, unremittingly; *(fréquenter un lieu)* regularly; **il y travaille a.** he is hard at work on it

assiégé, -ée [asjeʒe] ADJ besieged
▸ NPL **les assiégés** the besieged

assiégeant, -ante [asjeʒɑ̃, -ɑ̃t] ADJ *(armée etc)* besieging
▸ N besieger

assiéger [asjeʒe] VT **(assiégeant; j'assiège, n. assiégeons; j'assiégerai)** *(ville, château)* to besiege, to lay siege to; *(personne)* to surround, to crowd round; *Fig* **les journalistes ont assiégé l'hôtel** journalists besieged *or* laid siege to the hotel; *Fig* **assiégé par l'inondation** hemmed in by flood water; *Fig* **la ville est assiégée par les touristes** the town is overrun with *or* by tourists; *Fig* **a. qn de demandes** to pester sb with requests

assiette [asjɛt] NF **1** *(vaisselle)* plate; **manger dans une a.** to eat off *or* from a plate; **ne mange pas avec le nez dans ton a.** don't eat like that with your nose right in your plate **2** *(fondation) (de bâtiment etc)* situation, site; *(de camp)* disposition; *(du terrain)* lie; *(de pierre, poutre etc)* set; *(d'un impôt, d'un taux)* base; *(d'une route)* foundation, bottom, bed **3** *(d'un cavalier)* seat; *(de bateau)* trim; *Aviat, Naut* **angle d'a.** trim angle; **avoir une bonne a.** *Équitation* to have a good seat; *Naut* to be in good trim; *Fam* **ne pas être dans son a.** to be out of sorts *or* off colour *or* under the weather; **prendre son a.** *(de fondation, canon etc)* to set, to settle, to bed down
▸▸ *Culin* **a. anglaise** assorted cold meat(s), cold cuts; *Fam* **a. au beurre** cushy job; **a. des coupes** felling plan; **a. creuse** soup dish; **a. à dessert** dessert plate; **a. fiscale, a. de l'impôt** tax base; **a. plate** dinner plate; *Belg* **a. profonde** soup dish; **a. à soupe** soup dish *or* plate

assiettée [asjete] NF plate(ful)

assignable [asiɲabl] ADJ *(limite)* assignable; *(cause, raison)* ascribable, attributable

assignataire [asiɲatɛr] ADJ **banque a.** warrant bank

assignation [asiɲasjɔ̃] NF **1** *Fin (de parts, fonds)* assignment, transfer (à to); *Bourse* exercise notice **2** *Jur (action)* serving of a writ *or* summons *or* process; *(acte)* (writ of) summons, subpoena; **signifier** *ou* **faire** *ou* **donner** *ou* **envoyer une a. à** to serve a writ on, to issue a summons to; *(témoin)* to subpoena
▸▸ **a. à comparaître** summons; **a. à résidence** house arrest

assigner [asiɲe] VT **1** to assign; *(heure etc)* to fix, to appoint; *(cause)* to attribute, to ascribe (à to); **a. une tâche à qn** to assign *or* allot a job to sb; **a. une somme à un paiement** to earmark a sum for a payment, to allocate a sum to a payment; **a. une dépense sur le trésor public** to charge an expense to public funds **2** *Jur (témoin etc)* to summon, to subpoena, to cite; **a. qn en justice** *(de la cour)* to issue a writ against sb; *(d'un demandeur)* to have a writ issued against sb; *(d'un huissier)* to serve a writ on sb; **a. qn à résidence** to place sb under house arrest

assimilable [asimilabl] ADJ **1** *(absorbable) (connaissances, aliment)* easily assimilated *or* absorbed; **population très a.** population that assimilates *or* integrates easily **2** *(comparable)* **une maladie a. à une autre** an illness comparable to another

assimilation [asimilasjɔ̃] NF **1** *(absorption, Fig)* assimilation; **l'a. chlorophyllienne** photosynthesis; *Ling* **a. de phonèmes** assimilation of phonemes; **politique d'a.** policy of assimilation **2** *(comparaison)* comparison

assimilé [asimile] ADJ **1** *(immigrés etc)* assimilated **2** *(de même nature)* related; **le sucre et produits assimilés** sugar and related products **3** *Mil, Naut* **être a. à …** to rank as *or* with …, to be ranked as …; **a. au grade de capitaine** ranking *or* ranked as a captain
▸ NM *Journ* = press employee entitled to carry a press card; **cadres et assimilés** executives and their equivalents; **officiers et assimilés** officers and equivalent

assimiler [asimile] VT **1** *(absorber) (aliment), Fig (connaissances, immigrés etc)* to assimilate **2** *(comparer)* to assimilate, to compare (à to, with); **a. qch à** to class sth as, to put sth in the same category as
▸ VPR **s'assimiler 1** *(des aliments etc)* to be assimilated; *(d'immigrants etc)* to assimilate, to become assimilated; **ces minéraux s'assimilent facilement** these minerals are easily assimilated **2** *(être comparable)* to be comparable (à to)

assis [asi] ADJ sitting, seated; **nous étions a. auprès du feu** we were sitting *or* seated round the fire; *Fig Fam* **en rester a.** to be flabbergasted; *Fig* **il a une situation bien assise** he has a secure job; *Rail, Théâtre etc* **places assises** seats; **il n'y a plus de places assises** standing room only; *Jur* **la magistrature assise** the Bench

Assise [asiz] N Assisi; **St François d'A.** St Francis of Assisi

assise [asiz] NF **1** *(des fondations)* bed; *(de moteur etc)* bed(plate); *Géol* bed, stratum; *Fig (d'un raisonnement, d'une théorie)* basis, foundation; **ajuster l'a. d'une soupape** to seat a valve **2** *Constr (de maçonnerie)* course; *(de ciment)* layer **3** *Jur* **les assises** the assizes; **cour d'assises** Assize Court; **être envoyé devant la cour d'assises** to be committed for trial; **avocat d'assises** criminal lawyer **4** **assises** *(d'un congrès)* sittings; *(d'un syndicat)* conference; **tenir ses assises** *(d'un parti)* to hold a conference; *(d'un club)* to hold a general meeting

assistanat [asistana] NM **1** *(aide)* aid **2** *Univ* assistantship

assistance [asistɑ̃s] NF **1** *(assemblée)* audience; *Sport* spectators; *(lors d'une manifestation etc)* onlookers; *Rel* congregation; **je demande un peu de calme à l'a.** could the audience please be quiet; **y a-t-il un médecin dans l'a.?** is there a doctor in the house? **2** *(aide)* assistance, help, aid; **demander l'a. de qn** to ask for sb's assistance *or* help; **prêter (son) a.** to assist; **faire qch sans a.** to do sth unaided *or* without help **3** **elle est à l'A. (publique) depuis l'âge de trois ans** she's been in care since she was three; **les enfants de l'A. (publique)** children in care **4** *(de magistrat, prêtre)* presence, attendance
▸▸ **a. dépannage** roadside assistance; *Aut* **a. des freins** power braking; **a. judiciaire** *ou* **juridique** legal aid; *Com* **a. maritime** salvage; **a. médicale** *(à un pays du tiers-monde)* medical aid *or* assistance; *Méd* **a. respiratoire** artificial respiration; **a. sanitaire** medical care; **a. sociale** welfare work; **a. technique** *(à un pays du tiers-monde)* technical aid *or* assistance; *Ordinat* technical assistance; **a.**

technique aux véhicules roadside assistance; *Ordinat* a. à l'utilisateur user support

assistant, -ante [asistã, -ãt] N **1** *(aide)* assistant; *(à l'école)* language assistant; *Univ (de travaux pratiques)* demonstrator, laboratory assistant; **l'a. du metteur en scène** assistant producer; **maître a.** ≃ senior lecturer, *Am* assistant professor **2 assistants** members of the audience; *Sport* spectators ►► *TV, Cin* **a. cadreur, a. cameraman** assistant cameraman; **a. du chef de cuisine** sous chef; **a. de direction** personal assistant, PA; *Ordinat* **a. numérique** personal digital assistant, PDA; **a. opérateur** camera assistant; **a. personnel** personal assistant; **a. de production** production *or* producer's assistant, PA; *TV, Cin* **a. réalisateur** assistant director; **assistante sociale** social worker, welfare worker *or* officer; *(à l'hôpital)* medical social worker

assisté [asiste] ADJ **1** *Admin (personne)* on social security; **enfants assistés** children in care **2** *Aut* **freins assistés** power-assisted brakes; **direction assistée** power steering **3** *Ordinat* **a. par ordinateur** *(enseignement, fabrication etc)* computer-aided *or*-assisted ▸ N person on social security; *Péj* person living on hand-outs; **avoir une mentalité d'a.** to expect everything to be handed to one on a plate

assister [asiste] VI **a. à qch** to be (present) at sth; *(cérémonie)* to attend sth; **je ne peux pas vous répondre, je n'ai pas assisté à la scène** I can't give you an answer, I wasn't at the scene ▸ VT *(personne)* to help, to assist; *(soutenir financièrement)* to help (financially); **dans cette entreprise, je ne me sens pas assisté du tout** I don't feel I'm getting any help in this company at all; **tu devrais te faire a.** you ought to get help, you ought to get somebody to help you; **a. qn de ses conseils** to give sb some helpful advice; **prêtre assisté de deux enfants de chœur** priest attended by two altar boys

Il faut noter que le verbe anglais **to assist** n'a jamais le sens d'**être présent** (à un événement).

associatif, -ive [asɔsjatif, -iv] ADJ *Math* **loi associative** associative law; **mouvement a.** association; **mémoire associative** involuntary memory

association [asɔsjasjɔ̃] NF **1** *(groupe, société)* society, association; *Com* partnership **2** *(réunion) (de mots, d'idées)* association; **cette a. a été très bénéfique pour les deux entreprises** this association has been very beneficial for both companies; **a. capital-travail** profit-share scheme; **l'a. de ces deux aliments** the combination of these two foods ►► **a. d'automobilistes** motoring organization; **a. de bienfaisance** charity, charitable organization *or* institution; **a. à but non lucratif** non-profit-making *or Am* not-for-profit organization; **a. commerciale** trade association; **a. de consommateurs** consumer association; **a. de défense des consommateurs** consumer protection association; **A. européenne de libre-échange** European Free Trade Association; **A. française des banques** French Bankers' Association; **A. internationale des transports aériens** International Air Transport Association; **a. loi 1901** = type of non-profit-making organization; *Jur* **a. de malfaiteurs** conspiracy; **a. de parents d'élèves** parent-teacher association; **a. professionnelle** trade association; **a. sportive** sports club; **a. syndicale** trade union; **a. d'utilité publique** public utility

associé, -ée [asɔsje] ADJ associated; *surtout*

Fin, Bourse joint; *Fin* **porteurs** *ou* **souscripteurs associés** joint holders (of stock); *Admin* **territoires associés** associated territories ▸ N associate, honorary member; *Com* partner, business associate; **a. gérant** active partner; **a. principal** senior partner; **a. commandité** active partner; **a. commanditaire** sleeping partner; **a. en second** junior partner

associer [asɔsje] *(pr sub, impf n. associions, v. associiez)* VT **1** *(joindre, lier)* to associate, to unite, to join; **comment peux-tu a. deux thèses aussi différentes?** how can you compare two such different theories?; **a. les travailleurs aux profits de leur entreprise** to allow workers to share in their firm's profits; **il a associé son frère à son expédition** he brought his brother in on his expedition; **son entreprise est associée au projet** his company is taking part in the project **2** *(mentalement)* to associate; **j'ai toujours associé la neige à Noël** I've always associated snow with Christmas; **a. des idées** to associate ideas ▸ VPR **s'associer 1 s'a. à qch** to share *or* participate *or* join in sth; **s'a. à un voyage** to come *or* go along on a trip; **je m'associe à votre douleur** I share (in) your grief; **s'a. à un crime** to be a party to a crime **2 s'a. à** *ou* **avec qn** *(dans une lutte etc)* to join forces with sb; *Com etc* to enter into partnership with sb; **s'a. qn** to take sb on as a partner; **les deux pays se sont associés** the two countries have joined forces **3** *(s'allier)* to combine; **les deux parfums s'associent merveilleusement bien** these two fragrances combine wonderfully *or* go wonderfully well together

assoiffant [aswafã] ADJ *(travail)* thirsty

assoiffé [aswafe] ADJ thirsty; *Fig* **a. de sang** bloodthirsty; *Fig* **a. de savoir/de vengeance** thirsty *or* hungry for knowledge/revenge

assoiffer [aswafe] VT to make thirsty

assolement [asɔlmã] NM *Agr (des cultures)* rotation; **a. triennal** three course system

assoler [asɔle] VT *Agr* to rotate

assombrir [asɔ̃brir] VT to darken, to obscure; *Fig* to cast a shadow over; **cette triste nouvelle a assombri le repas** the sad news cast a shadow over the meal; **nous avons passé des vacances merveilleuses sans rien qui vienne les a.** nothing spoiled *or* marred our wonderful holidays; **ciel assombri** cloudy *or* overcast sky; **visage assombri** gloomy face ▸ VPR **s'assombrir** *(du ciel)* to become dark; *(du ciel, d'un visage)* to cloud over; **il s'assombrit en me voyant** he glowered when he saw me

assombrissement [asɔ̃brismã] NM *(du ciel, de l'humeur)* darkening, clouding over; *(d'une pièce)* darkening

assommant [asɔmã] ADJ *Fam* boring, tedious, deadly dull; **il est a., cet enfant-là!** that child is a real pain!

assommer [asɔme] VT **1 a. un bœuf** to fell an ox; **a. qn** *(l'étourdir)* to knock sb senseless, to stun sb; *Fig* **arrête ou je t'assomme!** stop that or I'll knock your block off!; **la chaleur m'assomme** the heat's overpowering **2** *Fam (ennuyer)* to bore (to death); *(harceler)* to pester; **tu m'assommes à toujours demander la même chose** you're getting on my nerves always asking the same thing

assommeur, -euse [asɔmœr, -øz] N slaughterer

assommoir [asɔmwar] NM **1** *(arme)* club, bludgeon; *(plus petit)* cosh, *Am* blackjack; *Fam* **porter un coup d'a. à qn** to deal sb a knock-out blow **2** *(bar)* dive

assomption [asɔ̃psjɔ̃] NF **1** *Rel* **(fête de) l'A. (de la Vierge Marie)** (feast of) the Assumption (of the Blessed Virgin) **2** *Géog* **A.** Asunción **3** *(hypothèse)* assumption

Assomption

The Feast of the Assumption, on the 15th of August, is a Catholic feast day and an important holiday in France.

assonance [asɔnãs] NF *Ling* assonance

assorti [asɔrti] ADJ **1** *(en harmonie)* matched, matching; **bien a.** well-matched; **couple mal a.** ill-matched *or* ill-assorted couple; **couleurs assorties** colours that match, matching colours; **pull avec jupe assortie** jumper with matching skirt **2** *(bonbons, clous etc)* assorted, mixed; **fromages assortis** choice of cheeses; *(au restaurant)* cheese board *or* platter **3 bien a.** *(magasin etc)* well-stocked **4** *(accompagné)* **a. de** accompanied by, along with; **une peine de prison, assortie d'une amende de 2000 euros** a prison sentence, accompanied by a fine of 2,000 euros; **un accord a. de plusieurs conditions** an agreement with several conditions

assortiment [asɔrtimã] NM **1** *(ensemble) (de marchandises etc)* assortment, variety, collection; *(d'outils)* set; *(de produits)* mix, selection; **ample a. d'échantillons** wide range of patterns; **a. de charcuterie** assorted cold meats **2** *(action)* matching; **a. parfait de couleurs** perfect match(ing) of colours

assortir [asɔrtir] *(j'assortis, n. assortissons)* VT **1** *(couleurs etc)* to match; **a. les accessoires à sa robe** to match one's accessories to *or* with one's dress; **elle n'a pas su a. les invités** she didn't manage to choose a good mix of guests; **nos mentalités sont bien/mal assorties** we think/don't think the same way **2** *Com* to restock ▸ VPR **s'assortir 1** *(être en harmonie)* to match, to blend, to go well together; **la ceinture s'assortit à la robe** the belt goes well with the dress **2** *(s'accompagner)* **le texte s'assortit d'illustrations** the text is accompanied with *or* by illustrations

assoupi [asupi] ADJ dozing, *Fml* somnolent; *(volcan, passion)* dormant

assoupir [asupir] VT *(personne)* to make drowsy *or* sleepy, to send to sleep; *(la douleur, les sens)* to calm, to deaden, to dull; **a. une dispute** to calm a dispute ▸ VPR **s'assoupir** to drop off to sleep, to doze off; *(de la douleur, du chagrin)* to die down

assoupissant [asupisã] ADJ soporific

assoupissement [asupismã] NM *(somnolence)* drowsiness

assouplir [asuplir] VT to soften; *(cuir)* to make supple; *Fig (réglementation, règlement)* to relax, to make less strict; **cette lessive va a. votre linge** this washing powder will make your clothes feel soft; *Fig* **cela va finir par a. son caractère** it'll eventually make him more flexible ▸ VPR **s'assouplir** *(du cuir, d'une personne)* to become supple; *(du caractère)* to become more flexible; **s'a. les muscles** to limber up

assouplissant [asuplisã] ADJ **liquide a. (pour le linge)** fabric softener ▸ NM fabric softener

assouplissement [asuplismã] NM softening; *Fig (de la réglementation, des contrôles)* relaxing; **exercices d'a., assouplissements** limbering-up exercises; **a. du crédit** easing of credit

assouplisseur [asuplisœr] NM *(fabric)* softener

assourdir [asurdir] VT **1** *(personne)* to make deaf, to deafen **2** *(son)* to deaden, to muffle; *(tambour, cloche, oreilles)* to muffle; *(violon)* to mute; *Ling (consonne)* to unvoice **3** *(lumière, couleur)* to soften, to subdue, to tone down

VPR s'assourdir *Ling* to become unvoiced *or* voiceless

assourdissant [asurdisã] **ADJ** *(bruit etc)* deafening

assourdissement [asurdismã] **NM** *(de personne) (processus)* deafening; *(résultat)* temporary deafness; *(de son)* deadening; *(de tambour)* muffling; *Ling (de consonne)* unvoicing

assouvir [asuvir] **VT** *(faim, désir)* to satisfy, to appease, to assuage; **a. sa soif** to quench one's thirst; **a. sa curiosité** to satisfy one's curiosity

VPR s'assouvir *(faim)* to be satisfied *or* assuaged; *(passions)* to be assuaged

assouvissement [asuvismã] **NM** *(de la faim, du désir etc)* satisfying, satisfaction; *(de la soif)* quenching; **un sentiment d'a.** a feeling of satisfaction, a satisfied feeling

assuétude [asɥetyd] **NF** *Méd* addiction

assujetti, -ie [asyʒeti] **ADJ** *(peuple)* subject, subjugated (à to); **tous les citoyens sont assujettis à l'impôt** all citizens are subject *or* liable to tax

N person liable for tax

assujettir [asyʒetir] **VT 1** *(province etc)* to subdue, to subjugate **2** *(personne)* to subject, to make liable (à to); **a. qn à faire qch** to compel *or* oblige sb to do sth; **a. une population à des lois** to subject a population to laws; **a. une population à l'impôt** to make a population liable for tax **3** *(objet)* to fix, to fasten (à to), to make secure; **les planches sont assujetties par des clous** the planks are held in place with nails

VPR s'assujettir to submit (à to)

assujettissant [asyʒetisã] **ADJ** *(travail)* exacting, demanding

assujettissement [asyʒetismã] **NM 1** *(action)* subjection, subjugation **2** *(état)* subjection, subservience (à to) **3** *(contrainte)* tie **4** *(à l'impôt)* liability (à for)

assumer [asyme] **VT 1** *(droit, responsabilité etc)* to assume, to take on, to take upon oneself; **a. les frais** to meet the costs *or* expenses, to bear the costs; **a. un risque** to take a risk; **a. un poste** to hold a post; **a. son service** to take up one's duties *(accepter) (conséquences)* to bear, to take on board

VI *Fam* **il va falloir que tu assumes** you'll have to live with it

VPR s'assumer to come to terms with oneself

> Il faut noter que le verbe anglais **to assume** est un faux ami. Il signifie le plus souvent **supposer**.

assurable [asyrabl] **ADJ** insurable

assurance [asyrãs] **NF 1** *(confiance)* (self-)assurance, (self-) confidence; **parler avec a.** to speak confidently *or* with confidence; **perdre son a.** to lose one's self-assurance; **vous pouvez l'acheter en toute a.** you can buy it with complete confidence

2 *(garantie)* security, pledge; **elle vivait dans l'a. de la réussite** she was assured of success; **je vous donne l'a. que tout sera fait d'ici demain** I assure you *or* I guarantee (you) that everything will be done by tomorrow; **demander/recevoir des assurances** to ask for/to receive assurance; **recevez l'a. de mes sentiments distingués** *(dans une lettre)* yours faithfully

3 *Com* insurance; **police d'a.** insurance policy; **prime d'a.** insurance premium; **compagnie** *ou* **société d'assurances** insurance company; **agent d'assurance(s)** insurance agent; **courtier d'assurance(s)** insurance

broker; *Fam* **je vais écrire à mon a.** I'll write to my insurance company; **contracter une a.** to take out insurance, to take out an insurance policy

4 *(en alpinisme)* **(point d')a.** *(d'alpiniste)* belay

▸▸ **a.-accident, a. contre les accidents** accident insurance; **a. 'ad valorem'** replacement value insurance; **a. automobile** car *or* motor insurance; **a. bagage(s)** baggage insurance; *Suisse Aut* **a. casco** comprehensive *or* all-risks insurance; *Com* **a. catalogue coface** standard export guarantee insurance; **a. catalogue évolutif** upgradable standard insurance; **a. chômage** *(payée par le patron et le salarié)* ≃ unemployment insurance; *(reçue par le chômeur)* ≃ unemployment benefit(s); **a. collective** group insurance; **a. confiscation** confiscation insurance; **a. contre les accidents du travail** employers' liability insurance; **a. crédit** credit *or* loan insurance; **a. décès-invalidité** whole life and disability insurance; **a. dépannage** car breakdown and recovery insurance; **a. foire** exhibition insurance; **a. garantie constructeur** manufacturer's guarantee insurance; **a.-incendie, a. contre l'incendie** fire insurance; **a. invalidité** ≃ disability pension; **a. maintenance étendue** extended maintenance insurance; **a. maintenance visite** call-out maintenance insurance; **a. maladie** health insurance; **a. maritime** marine insurance; **a. maternité** ≃ maternity benefit(s); **a. médicale** medical insurance; **a. multirisque** comprehensive insurance; **a. offre** tender insurance; **a. offre coface** Export Credit Guarantee tender insurance; **a. panne mécanique** mechanical breakdown insurance; **a. perte de l'exploitation** insurance for loss of trade; **a. de portefeuille** portfolio insurance; **a. prospection** market exploration insurance; **a. responsabilité civile** public liability insurance; **a. responsabilité produit** product liability insurance; *Admin* **assurances sociales** ≃ national insurance; **a. au tiers** third-party insurance; **a. tous risques** comprehensive *or* all-risks insurance; **a. tous risques chantiers** comprehensive site insurance; **a. transport** transportation insurance; **a. vacances** holiday insurance; **a. vieillesse** ≃ retirement pension; *Suisse* **a. vieillesse et survivants** ≃ Swiss pension scheme; **a. sur la vie, a.-vie** life insurance, *Br* life assurance; **prendre une a.-vie** to take out life insurance; **a. vol** theft insurance

assuré, -ée [asyre] **ADJ 1** *(plein d'assurance) (pas, voix etc)* firm, sure; *(air, personne)* assured, confident; **voix mal assurée** unsteady *or* quavering voice; **d'une main assurée** with a steady hand **2** *(certain) (remède)* certain; *(retraite)* secure, safe; **il n'y a encore rien d'a.** there is nothing fixed yet; **tenez pour a. qu'il vous écrira** rest assured that he will write to you; **la victoire est assurée** we/they/*etc* are certain of victory

N l'a. the policy holder, the insured; *Admin* **les assurés sociaux** ≃ national insurance contributors, those who pay national insurance

assurément [asyremã] **ADV** assuredly, surely, undoubtedly, certainly; **il le fera a.** he's certain to do it; **a. non!** certainly not!; **oui, a.!** yes, of course!

assurer [asyre] **VT 1** *(immobiliser)* to make firm *or* steady; *(attacher)* to fix, to secure, to fasten; *(échelle)* to steady; *(mur)* to prop up; *(corde)* to make fast; *(alpiniste)* to belay; **a. qn sec** to give sb a tight rope; **a. ses arrières** *Mil* to protect one's rear; *Fig* to protect oneself against any eventuality; **a. la sécurité d'un pays** to make a country secure; **a. sa fortune** to consolidate one's fortune

2 *(se charger de)* to look after; **le courrier littéraire sera assuré par M. Leclerc** the literary column will be looked after by Mr Leclerc; **la France assure le rapatriement des touristes** the French government is repatriating the tourists; **un service régulier est assuré entre Paris et Londres** there is a regular service between Paris and London; **la sécurité est assurée par des soldats de métier** professional soldiers are providing the security cover *or* are responsible for security; **la secrétaire assurera la permanence de neuf heures à midi** the secretary will be there from nine till twelve; **a. la défense de qn** to defend sb; **a. une rente à qn** to settle an annuity on sb

3 *(garantir)* to ensure, to guarantee; **cette formation vous assure un avenir brillant** this type of training will ensure *or* guarantee you a brilliant future; **ma retraite m'assure de quoi vivre** my pension gives me enough to live on; **ce but assure la victoire des Allemands** this goal assures the Germans of victory; **a. une créance** to stand security for *or* to guarantee a debt

4 *(certifier)* **a. qch à qn, a. qn de qch** to assure sb of sth; **il m'a assuré qu'il voulait bien le faire** he assured me that he was willing to do it; **il m'a assuré de son amitié** he assured me of his friendship; **c'est bien vrai, je te l'assure** *ou Fam* **je t'assure** it's quite true, I (can) assure you; **je t'assure que ce n'est pas amusant** I (can) assure you it's not funny; **il vient de nous a. de sa participation** he's just assured us that he will be taking part

5 *(par contrat d'assurance)* **a. qn** to insure sb; **se faire a. sur la vie** to take out a life insurance (policy); **a. un immeuble contre l'incendie** to insure a building against fire; **êtes-vous assuré?** are you insured?; **a. qch pour deux millions d'euros** to insure sth for two million euros

VI *Fam* to cope well; **j'assure pas du tout en maths** I'm hopeless at maths, I'm no good at maths; **elle assure, cette nana, avec les mecs** she has a real way with the men, that girl; **t'as pas amené les sandwichs? vraiment, t'assure pas!** didn't you bring the sandwiches? honestly, you're hopeless!; **ça assure!** brilliant!, wicked!; **a. comme une bête** to do brilliantly; *Fam* **à l'entretien, j'ai assuré un max** I did brilliantly at the interview

VPR s'assurer 1 *(vérifier)* **s'a. de qch** to make sure *or* certain of sth; **je vais m'en a.** *(le vérifier)* I'll check; *(faire en sorte que ça soit fait)* I'll make sure of it; **assurez-vous que c'est encore possible** make sure *or* check that it's still possible; **s'a. du transport** to make sure one has transport; **il faut que nous nous assurions de la véracité de ses dires** we must ensure that he is speaking the truth

2 *(par contrat d'assurance)* to take out insurance, to insure oneself (**contre** against); **s'a. au tiers/sur la vie** to take out third-party/life insurance

3 *(se pourvoir)* **tu aurais dû t'a. de l'aide** you should have got help; **s'a. la collaboration de qn** to secure sb's collaboration; **s'a. du silence de qn** to secure sb's silence; **les Allemands se sont assuré la victoire** the Germans have ensured themselves of victory

4 *(s'affirmir)* to settle oneself firmly; *(d'un alpiniste)* to belay oneself; **s'a. sur ses pieds** to steady oneself on one's feet

assureur [asyrœr] **NM** underwriter; *(agent)* insurance agent; *(compagnie)* insurance company; *(courtier)* insurance broker

assureur-conseil, *pl* **assureurs-conseils** **NM** insurance adviser

Assyrie [asiri] **NF** Assyria

assyrien, -ienne [asirjɛ̃, -jɛn] **ADJ** Assyrian **NM** *Ling* (ancient) Assyrian **N A.** Assyrian

aster [aster] NM aster; **a. de Chine** China aster; **a. œil-du-Christ** Michaelmas daisy, *Am* aster

astérisque [asterisk] NM *Typ* asterisk

astéroïde [asteroid] NM *Astron* asteroid

asthénie [asteni] NF *Méd* tiredness, *Spéc* asthenia

asthmatique [asmatik] ADJ, N *Méd* asthmatic

asthme [asm] NM *Méd* asthma; **être atteint d'a., avoir** *ou* **faire de l'a.** to suffer from *or* to have asthma; **crise d'a.** attack of asthma, asthma attack

asticot [astiko] NM maggot; *Fam (type)* bloke, geezer

asticoter [astikɔte] VT *Fam* to needle, to bug, to bait

astigmate [astigmat] ADJ, N *Méd, Opt* astigmatic

astigmatisme [astigmatism] NM *Méd, Opt* astigmatism

astiquage [astikaʒ] NM polishing

astiquer [astike] VT *(maison)* to clean; *(sol)* to polish; *(casserole)* to scour

astragale [astragal] NM **1** *Anat* ankle bone **2** *Archit (de colonne etc)* astragal

astrakan [astrakɑ̃] NM astrakhan (fur); **manteau d'a.** astrakhan coat

astral, -ale, -aux, -ales [astral, -o] ADJ *(influence, corps etc)* astral; **esprits astraux** astral spirits; **thème a.** (astrological) star chart

astre [astr] NM star, heavenly body; **contempler les astres** to look at the stars, to stargaze; **consulter les astres** to consult the stars; **beau comme un a.** (as) handsome as a Greek god; **né sous un a. favorable** born under a lucky star

astreignant [astrɛɲɑ̃] ADJ exacting, demanding

astreindre [astrɛ̃dr] *(prp* **astreignant;** *pp* **astreint;** *pr ind* **j'astreins, il astreint,** *n.* **astreignons;** *impf* **j'astreignais;** *p hist* **j'astreignis;** *fu* **j'astreindrai)** VT to compel, to oblige *(à faire qch* to do sth), to tie down *(à un devoir* to a duty); **astreint au service militaire** liable for military service
▸ **VPR s'astreindre s'a. à un régime sévère** to keep to a strict diet; **s'a. à faire du sport** to force oneself to do sport

astreinte [astrɛ̃t] NF obligation; **les astreintes de la vie moderne** the pressures of modern life

astringence [astrɛ̃ʒɑ̃s] NF astringency

astringent [astrɛ̃ʒɑ̃] ADJ, NM astringent

astro- [astro] PRÉF astro-

astrolabe [astrolab] NM spacelab

astrologie [astrɔlɔʒi] NF astrology

astrologique [astrɔlɔʒik] ADJ astrological

astrologue [astrɔlɔg] N astrologer

astronaute [astronot] N astronaut

astronautique [astronotik] NF astronautics

astronef [astronef] NM spaceship

astronome [astronɔm] N astronomer

astronomie [astronɔmi] NF astronomy

astronomique [astronɔmik] ADJ *Astron, Fig* astronomical; **heure a.** sidereal time; *Fig Fam* **pratiquer des prix astronomiques** *(d'un magasin)* to charge astronomical prices

astronomiquement [astronɔmikmɑ̃] ADV astronomically

astrophysicien, -ienne [astrofizisjɛ̃, -jɛn] N astrophysicist

astrophysique [astrofizik] ADJ astrophysical
▸ NF astrophysics VOIR GRAMMAIRE A10

astuce [astys] NF **1** *(finesse)* astuteness, shrewdness; **elle a répondu avec beaucoup**

d'a. she answered very astutely *or* shrewdly; **c'est un enfant plein d'a.** he/she is a very sharp child **2** *(truc)* trick; *(conseil)* tip; **il doit y avoir une a.** there must be a trick to it; **l'a., c'est de ne pas pointer en sortant** the trick is not to clock off when you leave; **les astuces du métier** the tricks of the trade; **a. du vendeur** sales acumen; **Windows® XP: 50 astuces** Windows® XP: 50 tips **3** *(plaisanterie)* witticism; *(jeu de mots)* pun; **je ne saisis pas l'a.** I don't get it

astucieusement [astysjøzmɑ̃] ADV astutely, shrewdly; **il a arrangé sa petite chambre très a.** he has arranged his little room very cleverly

astucieux, -ieuse [astysjø, -jøz] ADJ *(personne, comportement)* astute, shrewd, clever; *(solution, méthode)* clever, cunning; **réponse astucieuse** crafty *or* clever answer

asymétrie [asimetri] NF asymmetry

asymétrique [asimetrik] ADJ asymmetrical

asymptomatique [asɛ̃ptɔmatik] ADJ *Méd (maladie)* asymptomatic; **porteur a.** carrier without symptoms

asymptote [asɛ̃ptɔt] NF *Math* asymptote

asynchrone [asɛ̃kron] ADJ *Ordinat* asynchronous

asyntaxique [asɛ̃taksik] ADJ *Gram* asyntactic

atavique [atavik] ADJ atavistic; *Biol* **retour a.** throwback

atavisme [atavism] NM atavism; **faire qch par a.** to do sth because it's in one's genes

atchoum [atʃum] INT *(éternuement)* atishoo!

atelier [atəlje] NM **1** *(work)shop; (dans une maison)* workroom; *(d'artiste)* studio; **a. de réparations** repair shop; *Tech* **a. de montage** *ou* **d'assemblage** assembly shop; **a. d'ajustage** fitting shop; **a. de constructions mécaniques** machine shop; **a. de tissage** weaving shed; **a. de constructions navales** shipyard; *Aut* **a. de carrosserie** bodyshop; *Aut* **a. de peinture** paint shop; *TV, Cin* **a. de décors** scenic workshop; *TV, Cin* **a. de production** production workshop, graphics studio; *Ordinat* **a. de flashage** bromide bureau; **chef d'a.** foreman; **il est devenu contremaître après cinq ans d'a.** he became a foreman after five years on the factory *or* shop floor; **camion a.** repair van **2** *(ensemble du personnel d'un atelier)* staff **3** *(groupe de travail)* (work-)group; **les enfants travaillent en ateliers de trois** the children work in groups of three **4** *(loge maçonnique)* lodge

atemporel, -elle [atɑ̃pɔrɛl] ADJ timeless

atermoiement [atɛrmwamɑ̃] NM **1** *Com, Jur* = arrangement with creditors for extension of time for payment; **a. d'une lettre de change** renewal of a bill **2** *Fam* **atermoiements** delays, procrastination, shillyshally(-ing); **après mille atermoiements, elle a dit oui** after much shillyshallying, she said yes; **sans atermoiements** without a moment's hesitation

atermoyer [atɛrmwaje] VI to procrastinate

ATF [ateɛf] NM *Bourse (abrév* **accord de taux futur)** forward rate agreement, future rate agreement

athée [ate] ADJ *(personne, argument)* atheistical
▸ N atheist

athéisme [ateism] NM atheism

athénée [atene] NM **1** Athenaeum **2** *Belg (state)* secondary school

Athènes [atɛn] N Athens

athénien, -ienne [atenjɛ̃, -jɛn] ADJ Athenian
▸ N **A.** Athenian; *Hum* **et c'est là que les Athéniens s'atteignirent** and at that point things started to get rather complicated

athlète [atlɛt] N athlete; **avoir un corps d'a.** to have the body of an athlete *or* an athletic body

athlétique [atletik] ADJ athletic

athlétiquement [atletikmɑ̃] ADV athletically

athlétisme [atletism] NM athletics, track and field; **épreuves d'a.** athletic events, track and field events

Atlantide [atlɑ̃tid] NF Atlantis

atlantique [atlɑ̃tik] ADJ Atlantic; **l'océan A.** the Atlantic (Ocean)
▸ NM **l'A.** the Atlantic (Ocean); **Organisation du traité de l'A. Nord** North Atlantic Treaty Organization

atlas [atlas] NM **1** *(recueil de cartes)* atlas **2** *Myth, Géog* **A.** Atlas **3** *Anat* atlas

atmosphère [atmɔsfɛr] NF **1** atmosphere; **humidité de l'a.** atmospheric humidity; **Fig vivre dans l'a. de qn** to breathe the same air as sb; *Fig* **une a. de vacances** a holiday atmosphere *or* feeling; *Fig* **avoir besoin de changer d'a.** to need a change of atmosphere *or* scene(ry) **2** *Phys (unité)* atmosphere

atmosphérique [atmɔsferik] ADJ atmospheric; *Radio* **parasites atmosphériques** atmospherics; **perturbations atmosphériques** atmospheric disturbances

atoca [atɔka] NM *Can (plante)* cranberry

atoll [atɔl] NM *Géog* atoll

atome [atom] NM particle, bit; *Phys* atom; **atomes de poussière** specks of dust; *Fig* **avoir des atomes crochus avec qn** to hit it off with sb, to get on very well with sb; *Fig* **nous n'avons aucun a. crochu** we have nothing in common; *Fig* **pas un a. de vérité** not an ounce *or* iota of truth

atome-gramme, *pl* **atomes-grammes** NM *Phys* gram-atom

atomicité [atomisite] NF *Chimie* atomicity

atomique [atomik] ADJ *(théorie, poids etc)* atomic; **masse a.** atomic mass; **nombre** *ou* **numéro a.** atomic number; **sciences atomiques** atomics; **bombe a.** atom(ic) bomb; **guerre a.** atomic war(fare); **énergie a.** atomic energy; **sous-marin à propulseur** *ou* **propulsion a.** nuclear(-powered *or* -propelled) submarine; **pile a.** atomic reactor; **centre a.** atomic research station; **usine a.** atomic energy plant; **l'époque a.** the nuclear *or* atomic age; **Commissariat à l'énergie a.** *Br* ≃ Atomic Energy Authority, *Am* ≃ Atomic Energy Commission

atomisation [atomizasjɔ̃] NF atomization; *Pol Péj* **a. du pouvoir** dispersal of power

atomisé, -ée [atomize] N victim of a nuclear attack
▸ ADJ *Aut* atomized

atomiser [atomize] VT **1** *(pulvériser)* to atomize; **a. de l'eau sur les fleurs** to mist the flowers **2** *Mil* to destroy with nuclear warheads, *Fam* to nuke; *(à la bombe)* to drop a nuclear bomb on; *Fig* to smash to smithereens

atomiseur [atomizœr] NM atomizer, spray; *Aut* atomizer; *(injecteur)* sprayer; **parfum en a.** spray perfume

atomisme [atomism] NM *Phil* atomism

atomiste [atomist] N **1** *Phys* nuclear *or* atomic physicist **2** *Phil* atomist

atomistique [atomistik] NF nucleonics, nuclear engineering, atomic science
▸ ADJ atomic; *Phil* **théorie a.** atomistic theory

atonal, -ale, -aux, -ales [atonal, -o] ADJ *(musique)* atonal

atonalité [atonalite] NF atonality

atone [aton] ADJ **1** *(regard)* dull, vacant, lacklustre; **un individu a.** a lacklustre individual **2** *Méd* atonic **3** *Ling* unstressed, unaccented

atonie [atɔni] **NF 1** *(mollesse)* lethargy, listlessness, lack of vitality **2** *Méd* poor physical condition, *Spéc* atony

atours [atur] **NMPL** adornments, finery; **parée de ses plus beaux a.** in all her finery

atout [atu] **NM 1** *Cartes* trump; *Fig* asset, advantage; **a. maître** master trump; **jouer a.** to play a trump, to play trumps; *Cartes, Fig* **avoir tous les atouts dans son jeu** to hold all the winning cards; *Fig* **ce candidat a des atouts** this candidate has a lot going for him; *Fig* **c'est un a. que de savoir l'anglais** a knowledge of English is an asset **2** *Fam (coup)* clout, thump; **prendre un a.** to get clouted *or* thumped

atoxique [atɔksik] **ADJ** *Biol* non-poisonous, non-toxic

âtre [atr] **NM 1** *(cheminée)* fireplace, hearth; **au coin de l'â.** by *or* round the fireplace **2** *Ind (de forge etc)* hearth; *(du forgeron)* (blacksmith's) forge

atriqué [atrike] **ADJ** *Can* **mal a.** badly dressed

atroce [atrɔs] **ADJ** *(crime etc)* atrocious, heinous; *(terrible)* dreadful, horrible; **douleur a.** excruciating *or* agonizing pain; **j'avais une peur a. de le rencontrer** I dreaded meeting him; **d'une laideur a.** hideously ugly; **une odeur a.** a foul *or* an awful *or* a horrible smell; **il fait un temps a.** the weather is shocking *or* dreadful; **elle a fait un a. cauchemar** she had an awful nightmare

atrocement [atrɔsmɑ̃] **ADV** *(cruellement)* atrociously, shockingly; *(horriblement)* dreadfully, awfully, horribly, terribly; **elle a été a. torturée** she was hideously tortured; **elle a a. mal** she's in dreadful *or* terrible pain; **ça sentait a. mauvais** it smelled awful *or* horrible; **il a fait a. froid** it was dreadfully cold

atrocité [atrɔsite] **NF 1** *(cruauté)* atrociousness; *(d'un crime)* atrocity; **leurs exactions sont d'une a. indescriptible** their acts of violence are indescribably atrocious **2** *(acte)* atrocity; **les atrocités commises pendant la guerre** the atrocities committed during the war; *Fam* **on m'a raconté des atrocités sur votre compte** I have been hearing dreadful things about you; *Fam* **ce tableau est une a.** this picture is a real horror *or* an atrocity

atrophie [atrɔfi] **NF** *Méd (d'un membre, du foie)* atrophy; **a. intellectuelle** intellectual atrophy

atrophié [atrɔfje] **ADJ** *(foie, intelligence)* atrophied; *(membre)* wasted, withered

atrophier [atrɔfje] **VT** *(membre, intelligence)* to atrophy

VPR s'atrophier *(d'un membre)* to wither away; *Fig (de l'intelligence)* to atrophy

atropine [atrɔpin] **NF** *Chimie* atropin(e)

attabler (s') [satable] **VPR** to sit down at the (dinner *etc*) table; **veuillez vous a. pour que nous commencions à dîner** please sit down at the table so that we can begin to eat

attachant [ataʃɑ̃] **ADJ 1** *(livre)* captivating **2** *(personnalité)* engaging, attractive

attache [ataʃ] **NF 1** *(fixation)* point d'a. connection; **pièce d'a.** fastening; **rivets d'a.** jointing rivets; *Naut* **droit d'a.** mooring right; **droits d'a.** *(frais)* mooring dues, moorage; **port d'a.** home port, port of registry; *Fig* home base; **borne d'a.** *Naut* bollard; *Élec* terminal **2** *(lien)* tie, fastener, fastening; *(pour réparer la porcelaine)* rivet; *Élec* (wire) clamp; *(sur les vêtements)* loop, tab; **a. de diamants** diamond clasp; *Rail* **a. de rail** rail fastening; **a. de bureau** clip; *Fig* **nos attaches dans ce pays** our close ties *or* links with this country;

Fig **sans attaches** unattached, unconnected; *Fig* **je n'avais plus aucune a. dans cette ville** there was nothing to keep me in the town; *Fig* **j'ai gardé beaucoup d'attaches en France** I have kept many ties with France **3** *Anat (de muscle)* origin, attachment; **a. de la main/du pied** wrist/ankle joint; **avoir les attaches fines** to have delicate wrists and ankles **4** *Constr etc* connection, bond, brace; *(de poutre en béton armé)* binder **5** *Bot* tendril

attaché, -ée [ataʃe] **ADJ 1** *(enchaîné)* fastened, tied up; *(chien)* chained up; **on l'a laissé a. au radiateur pendant une semaine** he was left tied (up) to the radiator for a week **2** *(lié affectivement)* attached; **être a. à qn/qch** to be attached *or* devoted to sb/sth; **être très a. à une région/à ses responsabilités** to be very attached to a region/very devoted to one's duties **3** *(dépendant)* linked, attached; **les avantages attachés à une fonction** the benefits going with a post; **mon bonheur est a. au vôtre** my happiness is bound up with yours; *Bourse* **coupon a.** cum dividend

N attaché; **a. militaire** military attaché; **a. commercial** *(d'une ambassade)* commercial attaché; *(d'une entreprise)* sales representative; **a. de presse** press attaché *or* officer; **a. d'administration** junior civil servant

attaché-case, *pl* **attachés-cases** [ataʃekes] **NM** attaché case

attachement [ataʃmɑ̃] **NM 1** *(pour quelqu'un, quelque chose)* attachment (**pour** to), affection (**pour** for) **2** *Constr* = daily statement of work carried out and expenses incurred **3** *Mktg* **a. à la marque** brand bonding

attacher [ataʃe] **VT 1** *(fixer, enchaîner)* to attach, to fasten (**qch à qch** sth to sth); *(avec ficelle, corde)* to tie (up), to do up; *(avec une chaîne)* to chain (up); **a. un cheval** to tie up *or* tether a horse; **a. qch avec une boucle** to buckle sth; **a. qch avec des clous/épingles** to nail/pin sth on; **a. deux choses avec des clous/épingles** to nail/pin two things together; **a. ses cheveux avec un ruban** to tie a ribbon in one's hair; **a. ses cheveux** to tie one's hair back; **a. une étiquette à un paquet** to stick a label on a parcel; **il faut bien a. le paquet** you should tie up the parcel securely; **a. un prisonnier au poteau** to tie a prisoner to the stake; **attachez vos ceintures** fasten your seat belts; **tu peux m'a. ma robe?** can you fasten my dress?, can you do up my dress?, can you do me up?; **a. ses lacets** *ou* **chaussures** to do up *or* tie (up) *or* fasten one's shoelaces

2 *(accorder)* **a. de l'importance à qch** to attach importance to sth; **a. du prix** *ou* **de la valeur à** to attach great value to; **a. une signification à un fait/un acte** to read into a fact/an act

3 **a. un nouveau secrétaire à une ambassade** to attach a new secretary to an embassy; **ce domestique est attaché au service de la famille depuis cinquante ans** this servant has been in the family's employment for fifty years

4 *(lier sentimentalement)* to attach; **ce qui m'attache à lui** what attaches me to him; **tout ce qui nous attache à la vie** everything we hold dear in life

5 **a. ses yeux** *ou* **ses regards sur** to fix one's eyes on

VI *Culin Fam* **les pommes de terre ont attaché** the potatoes have stuck (to the pan); **casserole qui n'attache pas** non-stick saucepan

VPR s'attacher 1 *(d'une chose)* to cling, to stick (**à** to); *(ne pas s'enlever)* to be attached *or* stuck (**à** to); *(avec une agrafe etc)* to be fastened (**à** to); *(avec ficelle, corde etc)* to be tied

(à on, to); **les manifestants se sont attachés aux grilles avec des menottes et des chaînes** the protesters handcuffed and chained themselves to the railings; **la sangsue s'attacha à son mollet** the leech clung *or* stuck to his calf; **le lierre s'attache aux arbres** ivy clings to trees; **collier qui s'attache avec une agrafe** necklace that fastens with a clip; **la jupe s'attache par derrière** the skirt fastens (up) *or* does up at the back; *Fig* **s'a. aux pas de qn** to follow sb closely

2 *(se lier sentimentalement)* **tu t'attaches trop aux gens que tu rencontres** you get too attached to the people you meet; **elle s'est beaucoup attachée à cette vieille dame** she has got *or* become very attached to that old lady; **s'a. à qn** to become *or* grow fond of *or* attached to sb; **s'a. à une région** to become attached to a region; **je ne veux pas m'a.** I don't want to tie myself down *or* get involved *or* commit myself; **elle sait s'a. ses élèves** she knows how to gain her pupils' affection

3 *(se concentrer sur)* **s'a. aux faits** to stick to the facts; **ce n'est pas la peine de s'a. aux détails** there's no point getting caught up in details; **s'a. à une tâche** to apply oneself to a job; **s'a. à qch** to pay particular attention to sth; **s'a. à bien faire son travail** to take particular care over one's work; **s'a. à l'honnêteté/l'éducation** to attach great importance to *or* to set great store by honesty/education

attaquable [atakabl] **ADJ 1** *Mil* open to attack, attackable **2** *(fait, opinion etc)* contestable; *(testament etc)* open to attack

attaquant, -ante [atakɑ̃, -ɑ̃t] **ADJ** attacking **N** assailant, attacker; *Sport* striker

attaque [atak] **NF 1** *Mil etc* attack, assault; *(d'une voiture, d'un train etc)* hold-up (**de** of); **à l'a.!** attack!; **a. concertée** concerted attack; **reprise d'a.** renewed attack; **corps d'a.** attacking party; *aussi Fig* **passer à l'a.** to go on to the offensive; *Fig* **il a attendu de la connaître un peu mieux pour passer à l'a.** he waited until he knew her a bit better before he moved in for the kill; **repasser à l'a.** to return to the attack; **monter une a.** to mount an attack; **a. frontale** *ou* **de front** frontal *or* head-on attack; **subir une a.** to be attacked; *Fig* **les attaques de la presse** attacks by the press; *Fig* **diriger de violentes attaques contre qn** to attack sb violently; **a. de côté** flank attack; **a. latérale** flank attack; **a. par encerclement** encirclement attack

2 *Sport* attack; *(à l'aviron)* catch; *Cartes* lead **3** **d'a.** vigorously; **se sentir d'a.** to feel in good shape, *Am* to feel bright-eyed and bushy-tailed; **se sentir d'a. pour faire qch** to feel up to *or* ready to do sth; **être d'a.** *(en pleine forme)* to be on top form; **il est toujours d'a.** he is still going strong; **il n'est plus assez d'a. pour faire de longues marches** he's no longer up to going for long walks

4 *Méd (de maladie douloureuse)* attack; *(de fièvre, grippe)* bout; **a. d'épilepsie** epileptic fit; **a. d'apoplexie** (apoplectic) stroke; **a. de nerfs** fit of hysterics; **une a.** *(crise cardiaque)* a heart attack

5 *Tech* **a. directe** *(de moteur)* direct drive; **pignon d'a.** driving pinion; *Aviat, Naut* **bord d'a.** *(d'aile, d'hélice)* leading edge; **angle d'a.** leading angle

6 *(d'un article)* intro; *Mus (d'un instrument)* entry; *(d'une note)* attack; **chef d'a.** *(de l'orchestre)* first violin, leader

▶ ▶ *Aviat* **a. aérienne** air raid *or* strike; **a. à la bombe** bomb attack, bombing; **a. à main armée** armed robbery

attaquer [atake] **VT 1** *(personne, ennemi, place forte etc)* to attack; *(personne, ennemi)* to set upon, to assault; *(de l'acide)* *(métal)* to attack, to eat into, to corrode; *Mil* **a. de front** to make *or* to launch a frontal attack on; **at-**

taquez! engage!; être attaqué par les moustiques to be attacked by mosquitoes; a. qn à coup de poings to lay into sb, to go for sb with one's fists; *Fig* a. les abus/les préjugés to attack injustice/prejudices; *Fig* a. qn sur un sujet to tackle sb on a subject; *Jur* a. (la validité d')un testament to contest a will; *Jur* a. qn en justice to prosecute sb, to bring an action against sb; *Fig* a. la réputation/l'honneur de qn to attack sb's reputation/honour; *Méd* le poumon droit est attaqué the right lung is affected

2 (repas, sujet, travail etc) to tackle, to get to work on; nous attaquons demain l'ascension du mont Blanc tomorrow we('ll) attack or tackle Mont Blanc; attaquons le repas avant que ça ne refroidisse let's tuck in or get stuck in before it gets cold

3 *Mus* (note) to attack; (morceau) to strike up; bien a. la note to hit the note well or clearly

VI 1 to attack; qui a attaqué le premier? (à deux enfants qui se battent) who started it?; *Mktg* a. de front to launch a frontal attack; *Mktg* a. latéralement to launch a flank attack **2** *Mus* a. faux to hit the wrong note **3** *Cartes* a. trèfle/de la reine to lead clubs/the queen

4 (d'acides etc) to corrode

VPR s'attaquer s'a. à qn/qch to attack or make an attack on or tackle sb/sth; elle s'attaque à tout le monde she's always having a go at people; s'a. à une difficulté/un problème to grapple with or to tackle a difficulty/a problem

attardé, -ée [atarde] ADJ **1** il ne restait plus que quelques passants attardés there were only a few people out late; il profite de la pénombre pour attaquer les promeneurs attardés he takes advantage of the dim light to attack people who are out walking late **2** (dans le temps) behind the times; ma grandmère est complètement attardée my grandmother is completely behind the times or old-fashioned; idées ou conceptions attardées old-fashioned or outmoded ideas **3** *Psy* (mentalement) (enfant) (mentally) retarded

N 1 *Psy* a. (mental) (mentally) retarded person **2** (dans une course etc) les attardés the laggards, those that bring up the rear

attarder [atarde] VT to keep late, to delay; une crevaison nous a attardés we were delayed by a puncture

VPR s'attarder to linger, to loiter; (en se promenant) to lag behind, to dawdle; s'a. en route to dawdle on the way; ne nous attardons pas let's not linger, *Fam* let's not hang about; nous nous sommes attardés chez nos amis we stayed on late at our friends' house; elle s'est attardée au travail she stayed late at work; s'a. pour regarder le paysage to linger to look at the scenery; s'a. à qch to linger over sth; *Péj* to waste one's time on sth; ne nous attardons pas sur ce point let's not dwell on this point; inutile de s'a. là-dessus there's no point in dwelling on it

atteindre [atɛ̃dr] (prp atteignant; pp atteint; pr ind j'atteins, il atteint, n. atteignons; impf j'atteignais; p hist j'atteignis; fu j'atteindrai) VT **1** (parvenir à) to reach, *Fml* to attain; a. la ville to reach the town, to get to the town; a. la plus haute étagère to reach the top shelf; je ne peux pas l'a. I can't reach it; a. qn to catch sb up; a. l'ennemi to catch up with the enemy; a. son but to attain or achieve one's aim; a. l'âge de soixante ans to reach the age of sixty

2 (s'élever à) to reach; le nombre des participants atteint le millier the number of participants is nearing or reaching the thousand mark; très peu de montagnes at-

teignent 8000 mètres very few mountains reach (a height of) 8,000 metres; la pollution atteint la cote d'alerte pollution is reaching danger level; a. un prix élevé to reach or fetch a high price

3 (toucher) to hit, to reach; a. le but to hit the target or the mark; ne pas a. le but to fall short of the mark; a. une couche pétrolifère to strike oil; être atteint (par une balle) à la jambe to be shot in the leg; être atteint d'une maladie to be struck down by a disease; (d'arbres etc) to be attacked by a disease; le poumon est atteint the lung is affected; un malade très atteint a seriously ill patient; *Fam* il est complètement atteint (fou) he's completely cracked or potty; *Fig* tu peux le lui dire, mais cela ne l'atteint pas you can tell him, but it doesn't have any effect; *Fig* rien ne l'atteint nothing affects him, he's impervious to everything; *Fig* elle est atteinte dans son amour-propre her pride has been wounded or hurt; *Fig* une perte qui m'a profondément atteinte a loss which affected me very badly

VI a. à qch to reach or attain sth; **a. à son but** to achieve one's aim; son travail atteint à la perfection his work is close to or is nearing perfection

atteinte [atɛ̃t] NF **1** (portée) reach; hors d'a. (fuyard etc) beyond reach, out of reach; *Fig* sa réputation est hors d'a. his reputation is beyond attack or is unassailable; se dérober ou se soustraire à l'a. de la loi to circumvent or get round or *Fam* dodge the law; (s'échapper) to get out of the clutches of the law

2 (attaque) blow, stroke, attack; légère a. au bras slight blow on the arm; les premières atteintes d'une maladie the first attacks of an illness; a. au crédit de qn blow to sb's credit; porter a. à l'autorité de qn to undermine sb's authority; a. portée aux privilèges breach of privilege; porter a. aux intérêts de qn to interfere with sb's interests, to affect sb's interests; je considère que c'est une a. à mon honneur I consider it an attack on or a blow to my honour; porter a. à la réputation de qn to damage sb's reputation

attelage [atlaʒ] NM **1** (action d'atteler) harnessing; (de bœufs) yoking; *Constr etc* attachment; (de remorques etc) tying, fastening; (avec un crochet) hooking on; *Rail* coupling; *Astronaut* l'a. d'engins spatiaux the docking of spacecraft **2** (animaux) team; (de chevaux) pair; (de bœufs) yoke; (voiture) carriage (and horses)

atteler [atle] (j'attelle, n. attelons; j'attellerai) VT **1** (chevaux etc) to harness; (bœufs) to yoke; *Fig* toujours attelé à son travail always hard at work or hard at it **2** a. une voiture to attach horses to a carriage; voiture attelée de quatre chevaux carriage drawn by four horses; *Sport* course de trot attelé trotting race; *Rail* a. des wagons to couple (up) wagons

VPR s'atteler le gouvernement doit s'a. au problème du chômage the government must tackle the problem of unemployment; s'a. à une tâche/un travail to buckle down or get down to a task/a job; je m'y attelle tous les jours I force myself to do it every day

attelle [atɛl] NF *Méd* splint

attenant [at(ə)nɑ̃] ADJ adjacent (à to), adjoining, bordering; deux chemins attenants two intersecting paths

attendre [atɑ̃dr] VT to wait for; *Fml, Litt* to await; qu'attendez-vous? what are you waiting for?; le déjeuner nous attend lunch is ready; une surprise vous attend there's a surprise in store for you, you've got a surprise waiting for you; l'avenir nous attend the future lies before us; j'attends midi pour lui téléphoner I'll wait until twelve o'clock before I telephone him; aller a. qn à la gare

to go to meet or to go and meet sb at the station; a. la fin de l'histoire to wait for or until the end of the story; il se fait a. he's keeping us waiting; la réponse ne s'est pas fait a. the reply wasn't long in coming; tu t'es fait a.! and about time too!; nous n'attendions que toi now you're here, we can start/go/etc; on l'attend la semaine prochaine he is expected next week; je l'attends d'un moment à l'autre I'm expecting him any minute now; nous l'attendions tous avec impatience we were all looking forward to seeing him; nous attendons les résultats avec impatience we can't wait to get the results; j'attends des explications I'm waiting for an explanation; je n'en attends rien de bon I'm not expecting anything good to come of it; a. un bébé, *Belg* a. famille to be expecting (a baby); attendez voir just wait, wait and see; (laissez-moi réfléchir) let me see; on ne t'attendait plus we'd given up on you; qu'attend-il de moi? what does he want or expect from me?; elle n'attend que ça that's (just) what she wants or is waiting for; je n'attends qu'une chose, les vacances I (just) can't wait for the holidays to begin; a. que qn fasse qch to wait for sb to do sth; j'attendrai (jusqu'à ce) qu'il soit prêt I shall wait until he's ready; *Fig* a. qn au tournant to be waiting to catch sb out; a. son tour to wait one's turn; qu'est-ce que tu attends pour aller porter plainte? what are you waiting for? go and complain

VI 1 to wait; perdre son temps à a. to waste one's time waiting; désolé de vous avoir fait a. sorry to have kept you waiting; le train n'attendra pas the train won't wait; j'attends de voir pour juger I'll wait and see before I pass judgment; a. de faire qch to wait (until it is time) to do sth; attendons jusqu'à demain let's wait until tomorrow; *Fam* on ne va pas a. 107 ans we're not going to wait forever; *Iron* j'ai failli a.! nice of you to turn up!; attends un peu que je t'attrape! just you wait till I catch you!; attendez (donc)! hang or hold on!, wait (a bit)!, just a moment or a minute!; sans plus a. without further ado; *Prov* tout vient à point à qui sait a. everything comes to him who waits; il vaut mieux a. encore un peu it would be better to wait a bit longer; a. une heure to wait (for) an hour; il ne perd rien pour a. he's got it coming to him; un plat qui n'attend pas a dish that won't wait, a dish you have to eat straight away

2 *Fam* a. après qn/qch to wait for or to need sb/sth; porte-lui ce livre, il attend après take this book to him, he is waiting for it

3 en attendant meanwhile, in the meantime; un remplaçant va arriver mais, en attendant, c'est nous qui devons tout faire a replacement will arrive, but in the meantime we have to do everything; en attendant son arrivée until he arrives, while waiting for him to arrive; en attendant de vous voir until I/we/etc see you; il te dit peut-être qu'il t'aime, mais en attendant il vit avec une autre maybe he does say he loves you, but he's living with somebody else all the same

VPR s'attendre s'a. à qch to expect sth; il ne faut pas s'a. à des miracles you can't expect miracles; il faut s'a. à tout one must be prepared or ready for anything; je m'y attendais I expected as much; il fallait s'y a. it was only to be expected; je m'attendais à ce que tu me le dises I was expecting you to tell me; je ne m'attendais pas à ça I wasn't expecting or hadn't expected that

---

Il faut noter que le verbe anglais **to attend** est un faux ami. Il signifie le plus souvent **être présent, assister à.**

---

attendri [atɑ̃dri] ADJ regard a. fond or tender look

attendrir [atɑ̃drir] **VT 1** *(le cœur de qn)* to soften; *(personne)* to move, to touch; **cela attendrirait un cœur de pierre** it would melt a heart of stone; **s'il espère m'a. avec ses cadeaux, il se trompe** if he's hoping to soften me up with his presents, he's got another think coming **2** *(viande)* to make tender, to tenderize

VPR s'attendrir to be moved *or* touched; **les médecins ne peuvent se permettre de s'a.** doctors cannot allow themselves to get emotionally involved; **s'a. sur qch** to be moved (to tears) *or* touched by sth; **s'a. sur un bébé** to gush over a baby; **s'a. sur soi-même** *ou* **sur son propre sort** to feel sorry for oneself; **il s'attendrit facilement** he is very emotional

attendrissant [atɑ̃drisɑ̃] **ADJ** moving, touching; **sa crédulité est attendrissante** his/her naivety is touching

attendrissement [atɑ̃drismɑ̃] **NM** tenderness; **allons, pas d'a.!** come on, let's not get emotional!; **larmes d'a.** tender tears of emotion

attendrisseur [atɑ̃drisœr] **NM** (meat) tenderizer

attendu [atɑ̃dy] **ADJ** expected; **le jour tant a. est arrivé** the long-awaited *or* much-awaited day arrived; **le train est a. pour cinq heures** the train is expected at five o'clock

PRÉP *(les circonstances)* considering; *(les événements)* owing to; *(ses services)* in consideration of; **a. son attitude envers moi** considering *or* in view of his attitude towards me

CONJ a. que + *ind* considering that, seeing that; *Jur* whereas

attentat [atɑ̃ta] **NM** attack; **a. contre la vie de qn** attempted murder on sb, attempt on sb's life; *Pol* assassination attempt on sb; **victime d'un a.** victim of an attack

▸▸ **a. à la liberté** violation *or* infringement of liberty; *Jur* **a. aux mœurs** indecent behaviour, public indecency; **a. à la pudeur** indecent assault; **a. à la sûreté de l'État** high treason

attentatoire [atɑ̃tatwar] **ADJ** *Jur* **action a. à l'autorité** action that is a challenge to *or* in contempt of authority; **mesure a. à la liberté** measure that constitutes an infringement of *or* an attack on liberty

attente [atɑ̃t] **NF 1** *(fait d'attendre)* waiting; *(période)* wait; **je ne supporte plus cette a.** I can't stand this waiting any longer; **vous devez compter une a. de quatre heures** you should expect a four-hour wait; **être dans l'a. de qch** to be waiting for sth; **salle d'a.** waiting room; **rester en a.** to be held over; **liste d'a.** waiting list; **file d'a.** *Br* queue, *Am* line; *Ordinat* **liste de fichiers à imprimer en a.** print queue; *Mil* **combat d'a.** delaying action; *Chir* **ligature d'a.** temporary ligature; *Aviat* **circuit d'a.** holding pattern, stack

2 *(espoir)* expectation(s), anticipation; **contre toute a.** contrary to all expectations; **remplir l'a. de qn, répondre à l'a. de qn** to come up *or* live up to sb's expectations; **dans l'a. de votre réponse/de vous rencontrer** *(dans une lettre)* awaiting your reply/looking forward to meeting you

attenter [atɑ̃te] **VI** to make an attempt (**à** on, against); **a. à la vie de qn** to make an attempt on sb's life; **a. à ses jours** to attempt suicide; **a. à la liberté de qn** to infringe upon sb's liberty

attentif, -ive [atɑ̃tif, -iv] **ADJ 1** *(en alerte)* **soyez attentifs!** pay attention!; **il n'est pas a.** he doesn't pay attention; **être (très) a. aux autres** to be (very) attentive to others; **écouter d'un air a./d'une oreille attentive** to listen attentively; **être a. à qch** to look after sth, to see to sth; **être a. à ses intérêts** to

look after one's (own) interests; **être a. à sa santé** to look after oneself *or* one's health; **a. aux prix** price-conscious **2** *(appliqué)* careful; **examen a.** careful examination

attention [atɑ̃sjɔ̃] **NF 1** attention; **appliquer toute son a. à qch** to devote one's undivided attention to sth; **faute d'a.** through not paying attention; **faire un effort d'a.** to try to be more attentive, to try to concentrate; **écouter avec a.** to listen attentively; **porter** *ou* **tourner** *ou* **diriger son a. vers** *ou* **sur qch** to turn one's attention to sth; **attirer l'a.** *(d'un objet ou d'un fait)* to attract attention; **c'est ce détail qui a attiré mon a.** it's this detail which attracted *or* caught my attention; **attirer l'a. de qn sur qch** to draw sb's attention to sth; **puis-je avoir votre a., s'il vous plaît** (may I have) your attention, please; **faire a. à sa santé** to take care of one's health; **ne faire aucune a. à qn/qch, ne pas prêter la moindre a. à qn/qch** to take no *or* to take not the slightest notice of sb/sth; **il a fait très a. de ne pas la blesser** he took great care not to hurt her; **(faites) a.!** take care!, look out!, watch it!; **a. à la peinture** mind the paint; *(écriteau)* wet paint; *Rail* **a. à la fermeture des portières!, au départ!** ≃ stand clear of the doors!, mind the doors!; **a. au train** beware of (the) trains; **a., verglas** caution, ice; **a. aux travaux** caution, road works ahead; **il a une petite amie/une bagnole, a. les yeux!** you should see his girlfriend/car!, his girlfriend/car is an absolute *Br* cracker *or Am* crackerjack; **faites a. à** *ou* **de ne pas vous perdre** be careful not to get lost; **faites a. (à ce) que personne ne sorte** take care *or* be sure that no one leaves (the house); **à l'a. de Marie Berne** for the attention of Marie Berne **2** *(amabilité)* attention(s), consideration; **être plein d'attention(s) envers qn** to be full of consideration for sb, to be very attentive towards sb; **il a eu l'a. de m'avertir** he was considerate enough to warn me

attentionné [atɑ̃sjone] **ADJ** attentive; **être a. envers qn** to be full of consideration for sb, to be very attentive towards sb

attentisme [atɑ̃tism] **NM** wait-and-see policy

attentiste [atɑ̃tist] **ADJ** *(politique)* wait-and-see

N advocate of a wait-and-see policy

attentivement [atɑ̃tivmɑ̃] **ADV** attentively, carefully; *(regarder)* closely

atténuant [atenɥɑ̃] **ADJ** *Jur (circonstances)* mitigating, extenuating

atténuateur [atenɥatœr] **NM** attenuator

atténuation [atenɥasjɔ̃] **NF 1** diminishing, reducing, lessening; *(de lumière)* dimming, subduing; *(de couleur)* toning down; *(d'une chute)* breaking; *(d'un châtiment, d'une sentence)* mitigation, reduction; *(de la douleur)* easing, relief **2** *Phot (de négatif)* reduction; *(des contrastes)* softening **3** *(d'un crime)* extenuation

atténué [atenɥe] **ADJ** attenuated, diminished; *Jur* **responsabilité atténuée** diminished responsibility

atténuer [atenɥe] **VT 1** to diminish, to reduce, to lessen; *(couleur)* to tone down; *(lumière)* to dim, to subdue; *(châtiment, conséquences)* to mitigate; *(douleur)* to ease, to relieve; **a. une chute** to break a fall **2** *Phot (négatif etc)* to reduce; *(contrastes)* to soften, to tone down **3** *(offense)* to extenuate; *(crime etc)* to make less serious; **sa situation n'atténue en rien la gravité de ce qu'il a fait** his situation in no way lessens *or* reduces the seriousness of what he has done

VPR s'atténuer to lessen; *(de la lumière)* to fade

atterrant [atɛrɑ̃] **ADJ** overwhelming; *(nouvelle)* shattering

atterrer [atere] **VT** to appal; **sa naïveté m'atterre** I am appalled *or* staggered by his/her naivety; **ils se regardent atterrés** they look at each other aghast

atterrir [aterir] **VI 1** *Naut (voir la terre)* to make *or* sight land, to make a landfall; *(toucher le fond)* to ground, to run ashore **2** *Aviat* to land; **l'avion a dû a. en catastrophe** the aeroplane had to make an emergency landing; **a. trop court** to undershoot; **a. trop long** to overshoot; **a. brutalement** to crash (land), to make a rough *or* bumpy landing; *Fam* **a. dans un bar/dans un fossé/à l'hôpital** to land up *or* end up *or* finish up in a bar/a ditch/hospital; *Fam* **atterris, mon vieux!** you dozy thing!

atterrissage [aterisaʒ] **NM 1** *Aviat* landing, touchdown; *Fig Fam* **elle a cru qu'il l'aimait et l'a. a été difficile** she thought he loved her but she came down to earth with a bump; **a. trop long** overshoot; **a. trop court** undershoot; **a. forcé** forced landing; **a. à vue** visual landing; **a. aux instruments** instrument landing; **a. sans visibilité** blind landing; **a. brutal** rough *or* bumpy landing; **a. en catastrophe** emergency landing; **terrain d'a.** *(ensemble des pistes)* landing strip *or* field; **pont d'a.** *(de porte-avions)* landing deck; **a. en douceur** soft landing **2** *Naut* making (the) land, landfall; *(en touchant le fond)* grounding, running ashore **3** *Tél (de câble marin)* landing

attestation [atɛstasjɔ̃] **NF** *(action)* attestation; *(certificat)* certificate; **demander l'a. du professeur** to ask for a reference from the teacher; **a. du médecin/de l'employeur** doctor's/employer's certificate; **a. d'assurance** certificate of insurance; **a. de rejet** *(de chèque)* notification of returned cheque; *Jur* **a. du titre** warranty of title; **a. sous serment** *ou* **sur l'honneur** affidavit

attester [atɛste] **VT 1 a. qch** to attest *or* certify sth, to testify to sth; *(la réputation de qn)* to vouch for sth; *(sortie d'argent)* to confirm sth; **a. que qch est vrai** to attest *or* certify that sth is true; **c'est un fait attesté** it is an established fact, it is beyond doubt; **sa réponse atteste sa mauvaise foi** his reply bears witness to *or* demonstrates his bad faith; **nous pensons tous qu'il a menti et la bande enregistrée en atteste** we all think he lied and the tape recording proves it; *Ling* **forme attestée** attested form; **ce mot n'est attesté dans aucun dictionnaire** this word isn't attested *or* doesn't occur in any dictionary

2 *(prendre à témoin)* **a. qn** to call sb to witness (**de qch** to sth); **a. l'autorité de qn en faveur d'une affirmation** to advance a statement on the authority of sb

attiédir [atjedir] **VT** *(eau chaude etc)* to cool; *(eau froide)* to warm, to take the chill off; *Fig* **a. les passions de qn** to calm *or* cool sb's passions

VPR s'attiédir *(de l'eau chaude)* to cool down, to become tepid *or* lukewarm; *(de l'eau froide)* to warm up; *Fig (des passions)* to cool

attiédissement [atjedismɑ̃] **NM** *(de l'eau chaude)* cooling down; *(de l'eau froide)* warming up; *Fig (des passions)* cooling

attifer [atife] **VT** *Fam* to rig out, to get up, to deck out (**de** in); **elle est toujours attifée de manière impossible** she's always rigged out in the most ridiculous fashion; **elle attife ses enfants n'importe comment** she dresses her children any old how; **comme le voilà attifé!** what a sight he looks!

VPR s'attifer **elle s'attife toujours bizarrement** she's always wearing strange rig-outs

attiger [atiʒe] **VI 1** *(j'attigeais; n. attigeons)* *Arg Vieilli (exagérer)* to go over the top, to go too far; **tu attiges!** come off it!

attique [atik] ADJ *Antiq* Attic, Athenian ▸ NM **1** *Archit (étage)* attic **2** *Suisse* **appartement en a.** top-floor flat

attirail [atiraj] NM **1** equipment, gear; *(d'outils etc)* set; *(de cuisine)* utensils; *(de jardin)* tools; **a. de pêche** fishing tackle **2** *Fam* paraphernalia; **avant d'acheter la moto, il s'est acheté tout l'a.** before buying the motorbike, he bought himself all the right gear; **elle est arrivée avec tout un a. de photographe** she arrived with a lot of photographer's paraphernalia

attirance [atirɑ̃s] NF attraction (**vers** to); *(du plaisir, d'un endroit etc)* lure, fascination; **éprouver de l'a. pour qn** to be drawn *or* attracted to sb; **je n'ai aucune a. vers** *ou* **pour les mathématiques** maths does not appeal to me in the least

attirant [atirɑ̃] ADJ attractive; *(force etc)* drawing; *(manières, sourire)* alluring, engaging

attirer [atire] VT **1** *(d'un aimant, du soleil etc)* to attract, to draw; **quelque chose les attire l'un vers l'autre** something draws them together, there is some kind of attraction between them; **ce qui m'attire dans ce projet** what attracts me *or* what I find attractive about this project; **je ne sais pas ce qui m'attire en** *ou* **chez elle** I don't know what attracts me to her; **la Grèce, ça ne vous attire pas?** doesn't Greece appeal to you?; **sa pièce attire un grand public** his play draws a large audience; **a. qn dans un coin** to draw *or* take sb into a corner; **a. qch à** *ou* **sur qn** to bring sth on sb; **cela risque de vous a. des ennuis/des ennemis** that may cause you problems/make enemies for you; **avec ton insolence, tu vas nous a. des ennuis** your insolence is going to cause us problems; **a. la colère de qn sur qn** to bring down sb's wrath on sb; **je voudrais a. votre attention sur ce point** I'd like to draw your attention to this point; **c'est vraiment quelqu'un qui attire la sympathie** he/she is someone who gains a lot of sympathy; **son roman a attiré de violentes critiques** his novel has come in for *or* has attracted harsh criticism; **affiche qui attire les regards** eye-catching poster
2 *(séduire)* to attract; **elle attire les hommes d'un certain âge/paumés** she attracts middle-aged men/losers; **a. qn dans un piège** to lure sb into a trap; **a. qn par des promesses** to entice sb with promises
▸ VPR **s'attirer 1** *(mutuellement)* to attract each other; **ils s'attirent** they're attracted to each other; **les contraires s'attirent** opposites attract (each other)
2 *(sur soi)* **s'a. des critiques/des éloges** to come in for criticism/praise; **je me suis attiré la colère de mon père** I incurred my father's anger; **il s'est attiré la reconnaissance du patron** he earned his boss's gratitude; **s'a. des sympathies/des ennemis** to gain sympathy/to make enemies

attiser [atize] VT **1** *(feu)* to stir (up), to poke; *Ind etc* to stoke **2** *Fig (désir, mécontentement)* to fan the flames of, to fuel; **a. les haines/le racisme** to stir up hatred/racism

attitré [atitre] ADJ *(chargé d'une fonction)* appointed, recognized; *(journaliste)* accredited; **fournisseurs attitrés de Sa Majesté** purveyors by appointment to His/Her Majesty; *(habituel)* **mon marchand de légumes a.** my usual *or* regular greengrocer; **mon fauteuil a.** my chair, the chair I sit in

attitrer [atitre] VT *(ambassadeur)* to appoint

attitude [atityd] NF **1** *(disposition)* attitude; **a. hostile/intransigeante** hostile/uncompromising attitude *(envers, à l'égard de, pour, en face de* towards); **quelle est votre a. vis-à-vis de ce problème?** what is your stance *or* position on this problem?, how

do you stand on this problem? **2** *(conduite)* attitude; **je n'aime pas son a.** I don't like his attitude; **tu as eu une a. déplorable au cours de cette réunion** you behaved appallingly during the meeting, your behaviour during the meeting was appalling; **ce n'est qu'une a.** it's only an act *or* a pose **3** *(port)* attitude; **il prit une a. décontractée** he struck a casual pose

attouchement [atuʃmɑ̃] NM **1** *(pour guérir)* laying on of hands **2** *(sexuel)* **se livrer à des attouchements sur qn** to fondle sb; *Jur* to interfere with sb

attractif, -ive [atraktif, -iv] ADJ **1** *Phys (pouvoir)* attractive, drawing, *(force)* gravitational **2** *Fig (prix, vertu)* attractive

attraction [atraksjɔ̃] NF **1** *(d'un aimant etc)* attraction, pull; *Phys* **a. universelle** gravitation; **a. moléculaire** molecular attraction **2** *(d'un endroit, d'une personne etc)* attraction; **l'a. de deux personnes l'une pour l'autre** the attraction between two people; **exercer une a. sur qn** to attract sb; **l'a. qui me porte vers cet endroit** the attraction this place has for me; **les automobiles allemandes suscitent une a. très marquée chez les Britanniques** German cars are very popular with the British **3** *(de cabaret)* number; *Fam* **c'est la grosse a.** he/she is the big attraction **4** **attractions** attractions; *(à la foire)* sideshows; *Théâtre* variety show; *(au restaurant)* cabaret show; **parc d'attractions** amusement park; **les attractions passent à 21 heures** the show starts at 9 o'clock; **a. touristique** tourist *or* visitor attraction

attrait [atrɛ] NM **1** *(chose)* attraction, lure; *(état)* attractiveness; *(de la jeunesse etc)* charm; **l'a. de la mer** the call of the sea; **a. touristique** *(charme)* tourist appeal; **l'a. de l'aventure** the lure of adventure; **les attraits d'une carrière dans le commerce** the attraction of a business career; *Mktg* **a. commercial** market appeal; **dépourvu d'a.** unattractive, devoid of attraction; **ressentir de l'a. pour qn** to feel attracted by sb **2** **attraits** *(d'une femme)* charms

attrapade [atrapad] NF, **attrapage** [atrapaʒ] NM *Fam* **1** *(dispute)* quarrel, set-to **2** *(réprimande)* ticking-off, telling-off; **j'ai eu droit à un(e) bon(ne) a.** I got a right telling-off

attrape [atrap] NF **1** *(farce)* trick, hoax; **faire une a. à qn** to play a trick *or* a practical joke on sb; *(tromper)* to take sb in; **c'est une a.** there's a catch in it; **magasin de farces et attrapes** joke shop **2** *Arch (à oiseaux etc)* trap, gin snare

attrape-couillon, *pl* **attrape-couillon(s)** NM *Fam* gimmick

attrape-mouche, *pl* **attrape-mouches** NM **1** *(piège)* flypaper **2** *(fleur)* Venus flytrap, Venus's flytrap

attrape-nigaud, *pl* **attrape-nigauds** NM trick

attraper [atrape] VT **1** *(capturer) (personne, animal)* to catch
2 *(saisir) (ballon, voleur etc)* to catch; *(se saisir de)* to grab; **les voleurs se sont fait a.** the thieves were caught; **attention si je t'attrape!** if I catch you, there'll be trouble!; **il l'attrapa par le poignet** he grabbed *or* caught her (by the) wrist; **tu peux m'a. le torchon?** could you grab that cloth for me?; **a. un autobus/un train** to catch a bus/a train; **je n'ai pu a. que quelques secondes/bribes de leur conversation** I could only catch a few seconds/snatches of their conversation
3 *(prendre, contracter)* **a. froid** to catch a chill; **a. un bon coup de soleil** to get badly sunburned; **a. un rhume** to catch (a) cold; **j'ai attrapé mal à la tête** I've got a headache; **a. mal** to catch a cold; **en a. pour dix ans** to get ten years' (imprisonment); *Aut etc* **a. une**

contravention to get a ticket, to pick up a ticket; **a. un accent** to pick up an accent
4 *(tromper)* **a. qn** to trick *or* cheat sb, to take sb in; **là, vous êtes bien attrapé** you fell for it hook, line and sinker *or* good and proper
5 *(surprendre)* to catch; *Fam* **a. qn à faire qch** to catch sb doing sth; **et méfie-toi, si je t'y attrape encore une fois …!** don't let me catch you (at it) again, or else …!; **a. qn sur le fait** to catch sb in the act, to catch sb redhanded
6 *Fam (gronder)* **a. qn** to scold sb, to give sb a good talking to; **se faire a.** to get told off, to catch it
▸ VPR **s'attraper 1** *(d'une maladie etc)* to be caught; **le sida ne s'attrape pas par la salive** you can't catch AIDS through saliva; **ça s'attrape facilement** it's very catching **2** *(se disputer)* to scold each other

attrape-touristes NM INV *Fam* tourist trap

attrayant [atrɛjɑ̃] ADJ attractive, appealing; **peu a.** unattractive

attribuable [atribɥabl] ADJ attributable, ascribable (**à** to)

attribuer [atribɥe] VT **1** *(allouer)* to assign, to allot (**à** to), to confer (**à** (up)on); *(prix, récompense)* to award; *Fin (actions)* to allot; *Ordinat (mémoire)* to allocate; **a. des rôles** *ou* **des fonctions** to allocate duties (**à** to); *Théâtre* **a. un rôle à qn** to cast sb for a part; **a. le rôle de Cyrano à qn** to cast sb as Cyrano **2** *(fait, livre etc)* to attribute, to ascribe (**à** to); *(crime, erreur)* to blame (**à** on); *(de l'importance à qch)* to attach; **on attribue l'incendie à une inattention** the fire has been blamed on carelessness; **ne m'attribue pas des motivations qui sont les tiennes** don't project your motives onto me; **a. un projet à qn** to give sb the credit for a plan; **tableau attribué à Hogarth** painting attributed to Hogarth
▸ VPR **s'attribuer** *(un devoir)* to take upon oneself; **s'a. qch** to claim *or* lay claim to sth; **il s'est attribué tout le mérite** he claimed *or* took all the credit

attribut [atriby] VOIR GRAMMAIRE A17 NM attribute; *Mktg* **a. du produit** product attribute; *Ordinat* **a. de fichier** file attribute; *Ordinat* **a. de mise en forme** formatting parameter ▸ ADJ *Gram* attributive; **nom a.** attributive noun

attribution [atribysjɔ̃] NF **1** assigning, attribution, attributing (**à** to); *(des tâches)* allocation, allocating; *(de bourses d'étude etc)* awarding; *Théâtre (des rôles)* casting; *Fin (d'actions)* allotment; *(d'un salaire, d'une prime)* assigning, allocation; *Bourse* **actions d'a.** bonus shares; **avis d'a.** letter of allotment; **a. (d'essence/de sucre)** quota, ration (of petrol/sugar); **attributions** prerogative, competence, powers; *(de fonction)* duties, functions, responsibilities; **cela entre dans ses attributions** this comes within his competence *or* is part of his duties **2** *(d'une œuvre)* attribution; **l'a. de cette œuvre à Maillol est inexacte** this work is wrongly attributed to Maillol **3** *Gram* **complément d'a.** indirect object

attriqué [atrike] ADJ *Can* **mal a.** badly dressed

attristant [atristɑ̃] ADJ *(nouvelle etc)* saddening, depressing

attristé [atriste] ADJ *(visage)* sad; *(regard)* sorrowful; **contempler qch d'un œil a.** to gaze sadly at sth

attrister [atriste] VT to sadden, to grieve; **cette décision m'attriste** I am saddened by this decision; **cela m'attriste de voir …** it makes me sad *or* saddens me to see …
▸ VPR **s'attrister** to be sad (**de qch** about sth); **je m'attriste de les voir si démunis** I'm sad *or* saddened to see them so helpless

attroupement [atrupmɑ̃] NM *(de manife-*

stants etc) crowd; *Jur* unlawful *or* riotous assembly; **leur éclat dans la rue a provoqué un a.** their scene in the street drew a crowd; **la loi contre les attroupements** ≃ the Riot Act; **un a. pacifique** a peaceful assembly

attrouper [atʀupe] **VT** *(foule etc)* to gather together; **arrêtez de crier, vous allez a. les passants** stop shouting, you'll draw a crowd
VPR s'attrouper to gather, to assemble; **les manifestants s'attroupaient** the demonstrators were gathering

atypique [atipik] **ADJ** atypical

au [o] *voir* **à**

aubade [obad] **NF** dawn serenade; **donner l'a. à qn** to serenade sb

aubaine [obɛn] **NF 1** *(chance etc)* windfall, godsend; **c'était vraiment une a. de vendre ton salon à ce prix-là** it was a real godsend to be able to sell your suite for that price; **profiter de l'a.** to take advantage of one's good luck; **quelle a.!** what a stroke of luck! **2** *Can (occasion)* bargain, good buy

aube¹ [ob] **NF 1** *(matin)* dawn; **à l'a. (du jour)** at dawn, at daybreak; **partir dès l'a.** to leave at dawn; *Fig* **l'a. de la civilisation** the dawn of civilization **2** *Rel* alb

aube² **NF 1** *Naut (de roue)* paddle, blade; **roue à aubes** paddle (wheel); **vapeur à roue à aubes** paddleboat **2** *(de turbine)* blade, vane; *(de ventilateur)* vane

aubépine [obepin] **NF** *(arbuste)* hawthorn, may (tree); **fleurs d'a.** may (blossom)

aubère [obɛʀ] **ADJ** red roan
NM red roan (horse)

auberge [obɛʀʒ] **NF** inn; **a. rurale** *ou* **de campagne** country inn; **tenir a.** to keep an inn; *Fig* **c'est un peu une a. espagnole** what you get out of it depends on what you put in; **a. de jeunesse** youth hostel; **il prend notre maison pour une a.** he treats our house like a hotel; *Fig Fam* **on n'est pas sorti de l'a.** we're not out of the wood(s) yet

aubergine [obɛʀʒin] **NF 1** *(plante)* aubergine, *Am* eggplant **2** *Fig Fam Vieilli (contractuelle)* (female) traffic warden
ADJ INV aubergine

aubergiste [obɛʀʒist] **N** innkeeper

aubette [obɛt] **NF** *surtout Belg* newspaper kiosk; *(Abribus®)* bus shelter

aubriétie [obʀiesi] **NF** *(plante)* aubrietia

auburn [obœʀn] **ADJ INV** auburn

AUCUN, -UNE [okœ̃, -yn] **PRON** SEE GRAMMAR A35; B16; B63 **1** *(avec négation exprimée ou sous-entendue, accompagné de 'ne' ou 'sans')* *(être humain)* no one, nobody; *(chose)* none, not any; **lequel des deux veux-tu? – a.** which of the two do you want? – neither; **je ne me fie à a. d'entre eux** I don't trust any of them; **a. (des deux) ne viendra** neither (of them) will come; **de tous ces élèves, a. n'a répondu** not one of these pupils answered **2** *(avec négation implicite)* **de tous vos soi-disant amis, a. interviendra-t-il?** will any of your so-called friends intervene? **3** *(positif)* anyone; **il travaille plus qu'a.** he works more than anyone (else) **4** *Litt* **d'aucuns** some people; **d'aucuns prétendent qu'il est encore en vie** there are some who maintain that he is still alive
ADJ 1 *(positif, interrogatif)* any; **un des plus beaux livres qui aient été écrits sur a. sujet** one of the finest books written on any subject; **plus rapide qu'a. autre coureur** faster than any other runner; **avez-vous aucune intention de le faire?** have you any intention of doing it? **2** *(négatif)* no, not any; **je n'ai aucune idée** I don't have any idea, I have no idea; **sans aucune exception** without any exception; **le fait n'a aucune importance** the fact is of no importance; **oui, sans a. doute** yes, without

a *or* any doubt; **en aucune façon je ne l'aiderai** I will not help him in any way (at all); **sans mentionner a. nom** mentioning no names, without mentioning any names; **réparer qch sans a. mal** to repair sth with no difficulty at all *or* without any difficulty at all; **il n'a jamais fait a. mal à personne** he never did anyone any harm

aucunement [okynmɑ̃] **ADV** in no way, not at all, by no means, not in the slightest, not in the least; **je n'en suis a. étonné** I am not the slightest surprised; **je ne la connais a.** I don't know her at all; **je ne m'attendais a. à ce qu'il vînt** I never expected him to come

audace [odas] **NF 1** *(courage, assurance)* audacity, boldness, daring; **il faut beaucoup d'a. pour le faire/réussir** you need to be very bold *or* very daring to do it/to succeed **2** *(culot)* audacity, impudence; **vous avez l'a. de me dire cela!** you have the audacity *or* impudence *or* cheek *or* nerve to tell me that!; **ah! tu ne manques pas d'a.!** you've got the cheek of the Devil! **3** *(action audacieuse)* **elle est jeune, elle a toutes les audaces** she is young and daring; **une a. de style** daring unconventionality of style, stylistic daring

audacieusement [odasjøzmɑ̃] **ADV 1** *(avec courage)* audaciously, boldly, daringly; **elle a a. demandé un rendez-vous avec le grand patron** she boldly requested a meeting with the big boss **2** *(avec culot)* impudently

audacieux, -ieuse [odasjø, -jøz] **ADJ 1** *(courageux)* audacious, bold, daring; **il fait des harmonies de couleurs très audacieuses** he uses very bold combinations of colour **2** *(culotté)* impudent; *(mensonge etc)* brazen

au-deçà *Arch* **ADV** on this side
PRÉP a. de on this side of

au-dedans **ADV** inside
PRÉP a. de inside, within

au-dehors **ADV** outside
PRÉP a. de outside, beyond

au-delà **ADV** beyond; **il est très connu dans la région et même a.** he is very well-known in the region and even further afield; **jusqu'à une certaine somme, mais pas a.** up to a certain sum, but no further
NM l'a. the next world, the hereafter
PRÉP a. de beyond, on the other side of; **n'allez pas a. de 100 euros** don't go above *or* beyond 100 euros

au-dessous [odəsu, otsu] **ADV** below, underneath; **sur la table et a.** on the table and under it; **les locataires a.** the tenants below *or* downstairs; **les enfants âgés de sept ans et a.** children of seven (years) and under; **on en trouve à 10 euros et même a.** you can get them for 10 euros or even less; **musique transposée deux tons a.** music transposed two tones lower *or* two tones down
PRÉP a. de below, under; **50 kilomètres a. de Paris** 50 kilometres south of Paris; **a. du genou** below the knee; **les locataires a. de nous** the tenants below *or* underneath us; **15 degrés a. de zéro** 15 degrees below zero; **a. de la moyenne/du pair** below average/par; *Litt* **il est a. de lui de se plaindre** it is beneath him to complain; **a. de cinq ans** under five (years of age); **quantités a. de 30 kilos** quantities of less than 30 kilos; **a. de 100 euros** less than *or* under *or* below 100 euros; **acheter qch a. de sa valeur** to buy sth for less than it is worth; **son travail était a. de mon attente** his work fell short of what I expected; **je suis a. de la tâche** I'm not up to the job; **être a. de tout** to be beneath contempt VOIR GRAMMAIRE A68

au-dessus [odəsy, otsy] **ADV** above; **une terrasse avec une marquise a.** a terrace with an awning over it *or* above (it); **la salle de bains est a.** the bathroom is upstairs; **1000 euros et a.** 1,000 euros and up(wards); **la qualité**

a. the next grade up; **tout ce qui est a. est bien meilleur** everything up-market of this is a lot better; **musique transposée un ton a.** music transposed a tone higher *or* up a tone
PRÉP a. de above; **le château est situé a. du village** the castle stands above the village; **il a son nom a. de la porte** his name is above *or* over the door; **les avions volaient a. de nos têtes** the planes were flying overhead; **l'eau leur montait jusqu'a. des genoux** the water came up above their knees; **2 degrés a. de zéro** 2 degrees above zero; **a. de 50 euros** more than 50 euros, over 50 euros; **50 kilomètres a. de Paris** 50 kilometres north of Paris; **a. de la moyenne** above average; **a. de cinq ans** over five (years of age); **le colonel est a. du commandant** a colonel is higher than a major; **la tâche est a. de leurs forces** the job is too much for them *or* is beyond them; **vivre a. de ses moyens** to live beyond one's means; **je suis a. de ça** I'm above that, I wouldn't stoop to that VOIR GRAMMAIRE A67

au-devant [odvɑ̃] *(utilisé uniquement dans les prépositions telles que* **aller** *ou* **courir** *ou* **se jeter** *ou* **se précipiter au-devant)* **ADV** **quand il y a du danger, je vais a.** when there is danger ahead, I go to meet it; **quand je prévois une objection, je vais a.** when I anticipate an objection, I take steps in advance
PRÉP **aller/courir a. de qn** to go/run to meet sb; **aller a. des désirs de qn** to anticipate sb's wishes; **aller a. d'un danger** to anticipate a danger; **aller a. d'un complot** to forestall a plot; **aller a. du danger/d'une défaite** to court danger/failure

audibilité [odibilite] **NF** audibility

audible [odibl] **ADJ** audible

audience [odjɑ̃s] **NF 1** *Jur* hearing, session, court; **plaider en pleine a.** *ou* **en a. publique** to plead in open court; **a. à huis clos** hearing in camera; **tenir a.** to hold a court *or* a sitting; **l'a. est suspendue** the case is adjourned; **l'a. est reprise** the case is resumed **2** *(intérêt du public)* following; **ce cinéaste a trouvé a. auprès des jeunes** this film-maker has gained a following among young people **3** *Mktg (public)* audience; **a. captive** captive audience; **a.-cible** target audience; **a. cumulée** cumulative audience (size); **a. télévisuelle** television audience; **a. utile** *(d'un support, d'un média)* addressable audience; **a. utile nette** *(d'un support, d'un média)* net addressable audience reached **4** *(entrevue)* audience, hearing; **recevoir qn sur lettre d'a.** to interview sb by appointment; **tenir une a.** *(roi)* to hold an audience; **donner une a. à qn** to grant sb an audience

Do not confuse with **auditoire**.

audiencier [odjɑ̃sje] **NM** *Jur* huissier a. court crier, usher

Audimat® [odimat] **NM** *(appareil)* = device installed in homes for calculating television audience ratings; *(résultats)* audience ratings, audience viewing figures; **cette émission a un bon A.** this programme attracts a large audience

audimètre [odimɛtʀ] **NM** audiometer, people meter, setmeter

audimétrie [odimetʀi] **NF** = calculation of audience ratings

audio [odjo] **ADJ** audio

audiocassette [odjokasɛt] **NF** (audio) cassette

audioconférence [odjokɔ̃feʀɑ̃s] **NF** audioconference; **a. multipoint** multipoint audioconference; **a. point à point** point-to-point audioconference

audiofréquence [odjofʀekɑ̃s] **NF** audiofrequency

audiomètre [odjomɛtr] NM audiometer

audionumérique [odjonymerik] ADJ digital audio; **disque a.** compact disc; **a. DAB** digital audio broadcasting, DAB

audio-oral, -ale, -aux, -ales [odjɔɔral, -o] ADJ *(méthode, exercice)* audio

audiophone [odjofɔn] NM **1** *(de malentendant)* hearing aid **2** *(lors d'une visite de musée)* audiophone

audioprothésiste [odjoprotezist] N hearing-aid specialist

audiotypie [odjotipi] NF audiotyping

audiotypiste [odjotipist] N audiotypist

audio(-)visuel, -elle [odjovizɥɛl] ADJ **1** *Scol etc (méthodes etc)* audiovisual **2** *TV, Radio* television and radio
▪ NM **1** *Scol etc* audiovisual aids **2** *TV, Radio* television and radio

audiphone [odifɔn] NM *Tél* = pre-recorded telephone message service

audit [odit] NM audit; **cabinet d'a.** firm of auditors; **être chargé de l'a. d'une société** to audit a company; **a. social** = management consultancy report; **a. de diagnostic** diagnostic audit; **a. de qualité** quality audit; **a. de vente** sales audit; *Mktg* **a. des détaillants** retail audit; **a. marketing** *ou* **mercatique** marketing audit; **a. consommateur** consumer audit; **a. opérationnel** operational audit

auditer [odite] VT *(entreprise)* to audit

auditeur, -trice [oditœr, -tris] N **1** listener; **les auditeurs** the audience; *Radio, TV* **programme des auditeurs** request programme; *Univ* **suivre un cours en a. libre** = to follow a university course without being officially registered as a student, *Am* to audit a course **2** *Admin* **a. à la Cour des comptes** = Commissioner of Audit **3** *(chargé de l'audit)* auditor; **a. mercatique** marketing auditor; **a. externe/interne** external/internal auditor

auditif, -ive [oditif, -iv] ADJ *(nerf)* auditory; **avoir des problèmes auditifs** to have hearing problems; **prothèse** *ou* **aide auditive** hearing aid; **mémoire auditive** aural memory

audition [odisjɔ̃] NF **1** *(de chanteur etc)* audition; **passer une a.** to have an audition; **faire passer une a. à qn** to audition sb **2** *(écoute)* hearing; **juger d'un opéra à la première a.** to judge an opera at the first hearing **3** *Jur* **a. des témoins** hearing *or* examination of the witnesses; **nouvelle a.** rehearing **4** *(concert)* **a. de piano** (private) piano recital

auditionner [odisjɔne] VT **1** *Théâtre* to audition **2** *Jur* to hear
▪ VI *Théâtre etc* to have an audition, to audition (**pour un rôle** for a part)

auditoire [oditwar] NM **1** audience **2** *Jur* court; *Belg, Suisse* auditorium, lecture hall

> Do not confuse with the French noun **audience**.

auditorium [oditɔrjɔm] NM auditorium; *Radio, TV* (broadcasting, television) studio; **a. d'enregistrement** sound studio

auge [oʒ] NF **1** *(pour animaux)* trough; **a. d'écurie** manger; *Fam* **amène ton a.!** *(assiette)* pass me your plate **2** *(pour mener l'eau au moulin)* flume, channel **3** *(d'un concasseur)* hopper

auget [oʒɛ] NM **1** (small) trough; *(d'une cage d'oiseau)* seed *or* water trough **2** *(de roue à eau)* bucket; **roue à augets** bucket *or* overshot wheel

augmentation [ɔgmɑ̃tasjɔ̃] NF **1** increase, growth; *Admin (de salaire)* increment; **a. des dépenses/du chômage/de la consommation** increase in expenditure/unemployment/consumption; **a. de salaire** (pay-)rise, rise *or* increase in wages, *Am* raise; **a. de bé-** néfices earnings growth; **a. du capital** increase in capital; **demander une a.** to ask for a (pay-)rise *or Am* a raise; **a. de prix** price increase; **a. du prix de vente** mark-up; **être en a.** to be rising, to be on the increase; **les chiffres du chômage sont en nette a.** there is a marked increase in the unemployment figures **2** *Ordinat* **a. de puissance** upgrade, upgrading **3** *Mus* augmentation **4** *Tricot* **faire une a.** to make a stitch, to make one

augmenter [ɔgmɑ̃te] VT to increase; **a. la durée de cuisson** to increase the cooking time; **édition augmentée** enlarged edition; **a. une douleur** to aggravate a pain; **cela risque d'a. sa colère** that is liable to make him/her even more angry; **a. le prix de qch** to put up *or* increase *or* raise the price of sth; **a. qn** to raise *or* increase sb's salary *or* wages
▪ VI **1** to increase; **la criminalité augmente** crime is increasing *or* on the increase; **empêcher les frais d'a.** to keep expenses down; **tout augmente!** everything's going up!; **le prix a augmenté de 10% par rapport à l'année dernière** the price is up 10% on last year; **la douleur augmente** the pain is worsening; **la chaleur augmente** it is getting hotter; **un conflit qui va en augmentant** an escalating conflict **2** *Tricot* to make a stitch, to make one; **a. de deux mailles au commencement du rang suivant** increase two at the beginning of the next row **3** *Mus* **en augmentant** crescendo
▪ VPR **s'augmenter** **notre société s'est augmentée d'une nouvelle part de capital/de trois nouveaux cadres/de filiales à l'étranger** our firm has acquired new capital/three new managers/branches abroad

augure [ogyr] NM **1** *Antiq (devin)* augur; **consulter les augures** to consult the oracle; **le Collège des augures** the College of Augurs **2** *(présage)* augury, omen; **de bon a.** auspicious; **ce beau temps me paraît de bon a.** this nice weather seems to be a good omen; **de mauvais a.** ominous; **prendre les augures** to take the auguries; *Fig* **oiseau de mauvais a.** bird of ill omen

augurer [ogyre] VT to augur, to forecast; **a. l'avenir** to forecast *or* foresee the future; **a. bien/mal de qch** to bode well/not to bode well for sth, to augur well/ill for sth; **une querelle le premier jour, voilà qui augure mal de leur mariage** a quarrel on the first day doesn't bode well for their marriage; **que peut-on a. de cette rencontre prochaine?** what does this next meeting hold in store?; **je n'augure rien de bon de tout cela** I don't see any good coming of all this

Auguste [ogyst] NM **1** *Hist* Augustus; **le siècle d'A.** the Augustan Age **2** **l'a.** *(au cirque)* the clown

auguste [ogyst] ADJ august, majestic; **une a. assemblée** an august *or* illustrious assembly

Augustin [ogystɛ̃] ADJ *Rel* Augustinian
▪ NM **1** Augustine **2** *Rel* Augustinian (friar); **les Augustins** the Augustin friars

augustinien, -ienne [ogystinjɛ̃, -jɛn] ADJ *Phil* Augustinian

auj *abrév* **aujourd'hui**

aujourd'hui [oʒurdɥi] ADV **1** *(ce jour)* today; **quel jour sommes-nous a.?** what day is it today, what's today?; **c'est a. le cinq/dimanche** today is the fifth/is Sunday, it's the fifth/Sunday; **le journal d'a.** today's paper; **ce sera tout pour a.** that's all for today; **(d')a. en huit/en quinze** a week/two weeks today, *Br* today week/fortnight; **il y a a. huit jours** a week ago today; **ce n'est pas d'a. que je la** connais I have known her for a long time; *Fam* **c'est pour a. ou pour demain?** I/we haven't got all day!; *Belg* **a. matin** this morning; *Belg* **a. soir** this evening, tonight **2** *(à l'heure actuelle)* nowadays, these days; **les jeunes gens d'a.** (the) young people (of) today; **l'Europe d'a.** modern-day *or* present-day Europe, the Europe of today

aula [ola] NF *Suisse (dans une école)* (conference) hall

aulne [on] NM *(arbre)* alder

aulx *voir* **ail**

aumône [omon] NF alms; **demander l'a.** to beg *or* ask for charity; **faire l'a. à qn** to give money to sb; **donner qch en a. à qn** to give sb sth out of charity; **réduit à l'a.** reduced to begging; *Fig* **faire l'a. d'un regard à qn** to spare sb a glance, to condescend *or* deign to look at sb

aumônier [omonje] NM chaplain; **a. militaire** army chaplain

aune [on] NM *(arbre)* alder

aune² NF *Arch* ell (= 1.188 m); *Vieilli Fig* **figure longue d'une a.** face as long as a fiddle

auparavant [oparavɑ̃] ADV before(hand), previously; **a., il faut s'assurer de …** first, we/you must make sure of …; **l'année a.** the preceding year, the year before; **comme a.** as before; **mais a. nous devons parler** but we must have a talk first *or* beforehand

auprès de [oprɛ də] PRÉP **1** *(près de)* close to, (close) by, beside, near; **tout auprès de qn/qch** close to *or* beside sb/sth; **il a toujours une garde-malade auprès de lui** he always has a nurse with him *or* at hand **2** *(indiquant une relation)* **agir auprès de qn** to use one's influence with sb; **se renseigner auprès de qn** to ask sb; **se renseigner auprès d'un service** to enquire at a department; **être bien auprès de qn** to be in favour with sb, to be in sb's good books; **trouver grâce auprès de qn** to be in favour with sb, to find favour with sb; **je sais que je passe pour un idiot auprès d'eux** I know that they take me for an idiot; **ambassadeur auprès du roi de Suède** ambassador to the King of Sweden; **avocat auprès du tribunal** advocate attached to the tribunal **3** *(comparé à)* compared with, in comparison with, next to

auquel [okɛl] *voir* **lequel**

aura [ɔra] NF aura; *Méd* **a. épileptique** epileptic aura

auréole [ɔreol] NF **1** *(de saint, de la lune)* halo; *(du soleil)* corona; *Fig* **il pare son épouse d'une a.** he puts his wife on a pedestal; **entouré de l'a. de la gloire/réussite** bathed in glory/flushed with success **2** *(trace)* ring, mark; **le tableau a laissé une a. sur le mur** the picture has left a ring on the wall; **son matelas est couvert d'auréoles** his mattress is covered in dirty marks; **détachant qui ne laisse pas d'a.** stain remover that doesn't leave rings

auréoler [ɔreole] VT *(d'un peintre)* to surround with a halo; *Fig* to exalt, to glorify; **elle est auréolée de génie** she positively radiates genius
▪ VPR **s'auréoler** to be crowned (**de** with)

auréomycine [ɔreomisin] NF *Méd* aureomycin

auriculaire [ɔrikylɛr] ADJ *(confession etc)* auricular; *Anat* **appendice a.** auricular appendix; *Mil etc* **protecteur a.** ear protector
▪ NM little finger

auricule [ɔrikyl] NF **1** *Anat (du cœur)* auricle; **a. de l'oreille** lower lobe of the ear **2** *Bot, Zool* auricula, auricle; *(de mollusque)* auricula

auriculothérapie [ɔrikyloterapi] NF *Méd* aural acupuncture

aurifère [ɔrifɛr] **ADJ** gold-bearing; **champ** *ou* **gisement a.** goldfield

aurifier [ɔrifje] **VT** *(une dent)* to put a gold filling in

Aurigny [ɔriɲi] **NM** Alderney; **vache d'A.** Alderney (cow)

auriol [ɔrjɔl] **NM** *(oiseau)* oriole

aurique [ɔrik] **ADJ** *Naut* **voile a.** gaffsail; **gréement a.** gaff rig; **à gréement a.** gaff-rigged

aurochs [ɔrɔks] **NM** aurochs, wild ox

aurore [ɔrɔr] **NF 1** dawn, daybreak, break of day; **aux aurores** at the crack of dawn; **l'a. commence à paraître** *ou* **à poindre** dawn is breaking; *Fig* **l'a. de la civilisation** the dawn of civilization **2** *(papillon)* orange tip
ADJ INV *(saffron or golden)* yellow
▸▸ **a. australe** aurora australis, southern lights; **a. boréale** aurora borealis, northern lights; **a. polaire** aurora polaris, polar light

auscultation [ɔskyltasjɔ̃] **NF** *Méd* auscultation

ausculter [ɔskylte] **VT** *Méd (patient etc)* to auscultate, to sound

auspices [ɔspis] **NMPL 1** *(présage)* auspice, omen; **mauvais a.** ill *or* bad omen; **l'année commence sous d'heureux/de fâcheux a.** the year begins auspiciously/inauspiciously **2** *(appui)* **sous les a. de qn** under the auspices of sb

aussi [osi] **ADV 1** *(également)* also, too; **c'est a. ce que je pense** that's what I think too; **vous venez a.** you are coming too; **elle fait du grec, et a. du latin** she's doing Greek, and Latin too; **je suis fatigué – toi a.?** I'm tired – you too?; **gardez a. ceux-là** keep those too, keep those as well; **moi a.** me too, so am I/so can I/so do I/so shall I/so did I/so was I/*etc*; **et moi a. je suis peintre** I'm a painter too *or* as well; **j'écoute du classique a. bien que du jazz** I listen to classical music as well as jazz, I listen to (both) classical music and jazz

2 *(tellement)* so; **après avoir attendu a. long-temps** after waiting so long *or* for such a long time; **je ne pensais pas que tu étais a. sensible** I didn't think you were so *or* that sensitive; **une a. bonne affaire, ça ne se manque pas** a deal as good as that shouldn't be passed up; **un homme a. travailleur que vous** a man as hardworking as you; **d'a. belles journées** such nice days; **avez-vous jamais entendu une symphonie a. bizarre?** have you ever heard such a peculiar symphony? VOIR GRAMMAIRE A5

3 *(dans les phrases comparatives)* as; **pas a. gros que** not so big as, not as big as; **il est a. grand que son frère** he is as tall as his brother; **tout a. au sud/à l'est que Paris** as far south/east as Paris; **ma méthode est tout a. bonne que la vôtre** my method is just *or* every bit as good as yours; **on pourrait a. bien rester là ce soir** we might as well stay here this evening; **je le connais a. peu que son frère** I don't know him any better than I know his brother

4 *(quelque)* however; **a. bizarre que cela soit/semble** however odd it may be/seem, (as) strange as it my be/seem
CONJ therefore, consequently, so; **la vie est chère ici, a. nous devons** *ou* **devons-nous économiser** the cost of living is high here, so we have to economize; **il ne regarde pas où il met les pieds, a. il tombe tout le temps** he doesn't watch where he's going, so he falls over all the time; *Fam* **a., c'est ta faute** after all, it's your fault SEE GRAMMAR B57; B62

aussitôt [osito] **ADV** immediately, straight away, at once; **a. dit, a. fait** no sooner said than done; **a. l'argent reçu, je vous paierai** as soon as I get the money, I will pay you; **a. après** immediately after; **a. après son retour,**

je suis parti as soon or the minute he returned, I left
CONJ a. que + *ind* as soon as; **il se repentit de ses paroles a. qu'il les eut prononcées** he regretted his words as soon as he had said them; **a. que le train est parti, je me suis aperçu que ...** no sooner had the train left than I realized ... SEE GRAMMAR B31–2

austère [oster] **ADJ** *(vie)* austere; *(jeûne)* strict; *(style)* severe, austere; *(expression)* stern; *(robe)* plain, severe

austèrement [ostermɑ̃] **ADV** austerely; **elle s'habille a.** she dresses very austerely *or* plainly

austérité [osterite] **NF 1** austerity; **vivre dans l'a.** to live in austerity; **la période d'a.** the days of austerity; **mesures d'a.** austerity measures **2 austérités** asceticism, mortification of the flesh

austral, -ale, -als *ou* **-aux, -ales** [ostral, -o] **ADJ** *(hémisphère)* southern

Australasie [ostralazi] **NF** Australasia

australasien, -ienne [ostralazjɛ̃, -jɛn] **ADJ** Australasian
N A. Australasian

Australie [ostrali] **NF** Australia

australien, -ienne [ostraljɛ̃, -jɛn] **ADJ** Australian
N A. Australian

austro-hongrois, -oise, *pl* **austro-hongrois, -oises** [ostroɔ̃grwa, -waz] *Hist* **ADJ** Austro-Hungarian
N A. Austro-Hungarian

AUTANT [otɑ̃] **ADV 1** *(intensité)* **je ne savais pas qu'il avait a. souffert** I did not know he had suffered so or as much; **je ne le savais pas a. respecté** I did not know he was so greatly respected; **travailles-tu toujours a.?** *(qu'aujourd'hui)* do you always work so or as or this hard?; *(qu'avant)* are you working as hard as ever?; **a. en emporte le vent** it's all idle talk; **a. vous l'aimez, a. il vous hait** he hates you as much as you love him; **tout a.** quite as much; **il m'en veut, mais je lui en veux tout a.** he's angry with me, but I'm just as angry with him; **encore a.** as much again

2 *(quantité)* **tout a.** quite as much; *(de choses individuelles)* quite as many; **encore a.** as much/many again; **je n'en ai pas assez, remettez m'en encore a.** I don't have enough, give me as much/many again *or* the same again; **tous les salariés ont été augmentés d'a.** all the employees received the same pay rise, everybody's salary went up by the same amount; **le coût de la vie a augmenté de 5%, mais les salaires n'ont pas augmenté d'a.** the cost of living has increased by 5%, but salaries have not risen accordingly *or* have not risen in line; **a. pour moi!** I stand corrected!

3 *(de même)* the same, likewise; **on ne peut pas en dire a. de tout le monde** you can't say as much *or* the same for everybody; **essaie un peu d'en faire a.** try to do the same; **peux-tu en dire a.?** can you say as much?

4 ils disent qu'ils réfléchissent, a. dire qu'ils ont accepté they say they're thinking about it, in other words they've accepted; **j'aime a. vous dire que je n'apprécie pas vos manières!** I don't mind telling you that I don't care for your manners!; **j'aime a. vous le dire tout de suite** I might as well tell you right away; **j'aimerais a. aller au cinéma** I would just as soon go to the cinema; **a. le faire tout de suite** better do it right away; **a. ne rien faire du tout** we might as well do nothing at all; **a. rester ici** we may as well stay here; **a. dire que ...** one might as well say that ...; **a. dire que c'était difficile/que je n'étais pas content** as you can imagine, it was difficult/I wasn't happy

5 a. que as much as; *(de choses in-*

dividuelles) as many as; **a. que possible** as far as possible; **sois à l'heure a. que possible** do your best to be on time; **faites a. que vous pourrez** do as much as you can; **(pour) a. que je sache** as far as I know, to the best of my knowledge; **j'en sais a. que toi** your guess is as good as mine, I know as much (about it) as you do; **c'est a. ta faute que la mienne** it is as much your fault as mine, you're as much to blame as I am; **il est a. à craindre qu'elle** he is as much to be feared as she is; *Fam* **a. ça qu'autre chose** it's all the same to me; **a. que j'en puis(se) juger** as far as I can judge; **pour a. qu'il est en mon pouvoir** to the best of my ability; **a. que faire se peut** as much as possible, as much as can be; **je me suis dépêché a. que faire se peut** I hurried as fast as I could

6 a. de as much, so much; *(de choses individuelles)* as many, so many; **a. de filles que de garçons** as many girls as boys; **ils ont a. de terrain/d'amis que vous** they have as much land/as many friends as you; *Litt* **ce sont a. de (voleurs/*etc*)** they are nothing better than (a pack of thieves/*etc*); **ce sera a. de moins à payer** it will be so much the less to pay; **c'est a. de gagné** that's so much gained, that's that much to the good

7 d'a. (plus) que especially *or* particularly since; **d'a. plus/moins (que)** all the more/less (because); **j'en suis surpris, d'a. plus qu'au fond il est honnête** I am all the more surprised because basically he is honest; **elle travaille d'a. mieux qu'elle se sait surveillée** she works all the better for knowing that someone's keeping an eye on her; **cela vous sera d'a. plus facile que vous êtes jeune** it will be all the easier for you since you are young

8 pour a. for all that; **j'ai plus de travail, mais ce n'est pas pour a. que j'ai plus d'argent** just because I have more work doesn't mean that I have more money; **elle est très riche, elle n'est pas plus heureuse pour a.** she's very rich, but she isn't any the happier for it *or* but that doesn't mean she's any the happier; **elle ne s'en fait pas pour a.** she doesn't worry about it

autarcie [otarsi] **NF** *Pol* autarky; **une communauté qui vit en a.** a self-sufficient community

autarcique [otarsik] **ADJ** *Pol* autarkic

autel [otɛl] **NM** *aussi Fig* altar; **maître a.** high altar; **a. latéral** side altar; **nappe d'a.** altar cloth; **pierre d'a.** altar stone *or* table; **tableau d'a.** altarpiece; **conduire sa fille à l'a.** to give one's daughter away (in marriage); **suivre qn à l'a.** to walk up the aisle with sb, to marry sb

auteur [otœr] **NM 1** *(de livre)* author, writer; *(de chanson)* composer; *(de tableau)* painter; **droit d'a.** copyright; **droits d'a.** royalties; **un droit d'a. de 10%** a 10% royalty; *Fig* **citer ses auteurs** to quote one's authorities **2** *(responsable)* author; *(d'un crime)* perpetrator; *(d'un projet)* promoter, sponsor; *Jur* principal; **a. d'un accident** party at fault in an accident; *Fig* **être l'a. de la ruine de qn** to be the cause of sb's downfall; **qui est l'a. de cette plaisanterie?** whose idea was that joke?; *Hum* **je vous présente l'a. de mes jours** this is my beloved father/mother

auteur-compositeur, *pl* **auteurs-compositeurs NM** songwriter

authenticité [otɑ̃tisite] **NF** authenticity; **on conteste l'a. de ce tableau** the authenticity of this painting is in doubt

authentification [otɑ̃tifikasjɔ̃] **NF** authentication; **cachet d'a.** approved stamp

authentifier [otɑ̃tifje] **VT** to authenticate

authentique [otɑ̃tik] **ADJ** authentic, genuine; **c'est un fait a.** it's a true fact; **bourgo-**

gne a. genuine Burgundy; *Jur* **acte a.** instrument drawn up by a solicitor; **copie a.** certified copy; *Fam* **je ne te mens pas, c'est a.! c'est ce qu'il a dit!** I'm not lying to you, it's true! that's what he said!

authentiquement [otãtikmã] ADV authentically, genuinely

authentiquer [otãtike] VT *Vieilli (document etc)* to authenticate, to certify, to legalize

autisme [otism] NM *Psy* autism

autiste [otist] ADJ, N *Psy* autistic

autistique [otistik] ADJ *Psy* autistic

auto [oto] NF (motor)car; **les autos tamponneuses** Dodgems®, bumper cars; **jouer avec des petites autos** to play with toy cars
ADJ INV **assurance a.** car insurance; **budget a.** car budget

auto- PRÉF auto-, self-

auto-accusation, *pl* **auto-accusations** NF self-accusation

auto-adhésif, -ive ADJ self-adhesive; **bande auto-adhésive** adhesive tape

auto-allumage, *pl* **auto-allumages** NM running-on, self-ignition, post-ignition

auto-amorçage, *pl* **auto-amorçages** NM automatic *or* self priming

auto-antigène, *pl* **auto-antigènes** NM *Physiol* autoantigen

autoberge [otobɛrʒ] NF = highway running along a river embankment

autobiographie [otobjografi] NF autobiography

autobiographique [otobjografik] ADJ autobiographical

autobronzant [otobrɔ̃zã] ADJ self-tanning
NM self-tanning cream; *Fam* fake tan

autobus [otobys] NM bus

autocar [otokar] NM coach, bus; **a. de luxe** luxury coach

autocariste [otokarist] NM coach tour operator

autocassable [otokasabl] ADJ **ampoule a.** easy-to-open *or* break-open phial

autocélébrer (s') [sotoselebre] VPR to sing one's own praises

autocensure NF self-censorship; **faire de l'a.** to practise self-censorship

autocensurer (s') [sotosãsyre] VPR to practise self-censorship

autochenille [otoʃnij] NF half-track vehicle

autochrome [otokrom] ADJ *(pellicule, film)* colour

autochtone [otɔkton] ADJ aboriginal, *Can* native; *Géol* **terrain a.** autochthonous rock
N native, *Admin* non-alien, *Spéc* autochthon; *Can* **Conseil national des autochtones du Canada** Native Council of Canada; *Hum* **les autochtones ne sont pas très accueillants** the natives aren't very friendly

autocinétique [otosinetik] ADJ autokinetic

autoclave [otoklav] ADJ hermetically sealed, pressure-sealed; **marmite a.** autoclave, digester
NM **1** *Chimie, Ind* autoclave, digester **2** *Méd* sterilizer **3** *Culin Vieilli* pressure cooker

autocode [otokɔd] NM *Ordinat* assembly language

autocollant [otokɔlã] ADJ self-adhesive; *(enveloppe)* self-sealing
NM sticker

autocommutateur [otokɔmytatœr] NM *Ordinat* autoswitch; **a. privé** PBX, private branch exchange

autoconduction [otokɔ̃dyksjɔ̃] NF *Électron* mutual induction

autoconsommation [otokɔ̃sɔmasjɔ̃] NF subsistence farming; **économie d'a.** subsistence economy

autocopiant [otokɔpjã] ADJ self-copying

autocopie [otokɔpi] NF *(de documents)* duplicating

autocopier [otokɔpje] VT *(pr sub, impf n. autocopiions,* v. **autocopiiez**) to duplicate

autocorrecteur [otokɔrɛktœr] ADJ *Ordinat* self-correcting

autocorrection [otokɔrɛksjɔ̃] NF self-correction; **faire de l'a.** to do one's own correction

autocouchette ADJ INV **train a.** = car-sleeper train

autocrate [otokrat] N *Pol* autocrat

autocratie [otokrasi] NF *Pol* autocracy

autocratique [otokratik] ADJ autocratic

autocratiquement [otokratikmã] ADV autocratically

autocritique [otokritik] NF self-criticism; **faire son a.** to criticize oneself

autocuiseur [otokɥizœr] NM pressure cooker

autodafé [otodafe] NM *Hist* auto-da-fé; **faire un a. de livres rares** to burn rare books

autodébrayage [otodebrɛjaʒ] NM *Aut* automatic clutch

autodéfense [otodefɑ̃s] NF self-defence

autodestructeur, -trice [otodɛstryktœr, -tris] ADJ self-destructive

autodestruction [otodɛstryksjɔ̃] NF self-destruction

autodétermination [otodetɛrminasjɔ̃] NF *Pol* self-determination

autodidacte [otodidakt] ADJ self-taught, self-educated
N autodidact

autodrome [otodrom] NM motor-racing track; *(pour les essais)* car-testing track

auto-école, *pl* **auto-écoles** NF school of motoring, driving school

autoérotique [otoerotik] ADJ *Psy* autoerotic

autoérotisme [otoerotism] NM *Psy* autoeroticism

autofécondation [otofekɔ̃dasjɔ̃] NF *Bot* self-pollination

autofiction [otofiksjɔ̃] NF autofiction

autofinancé [otofinãse] ADJ *Fin* financed from cashflow

autofinancement [otofinãsmã] NM *Fin* self-financing, financing from cashflow

autofinancer (s') [sotofinãse] VPR *Fin* to be self-financing

autofocus [otofokys] *Phot* NM autofocus
ADJ autofocus; **appareil a.** autofocus camera

autogène [otoʒɛn] ADJ **1** *Physiol* **faire du training a.** to learn how to relax **2** *Tech* **soudure a.** autogenous weld

autogenèse [otoʒənɛz] NF *Biol* autogenesis

autogéré [otoʒere] ADJ self-managed

autogestion [otoʒɛstjɔ̃] NF self-management

autogestionnaire [otoʒɛstjɔnɛr] ADJ self-managing

autogire [otoʒir] NM *Aviat* autogyro

autograissage [otogrɛsaʒ] NM *Tech* self-lubrication

autograisseur, -euse [otogrɛsœr, -øz] ADJ *(roulement, palier etc)* self-lubricating

autographe [otograf] ADJ autograph; *(lettre etc)* handwritten
NM autograph

autogreffe [otogrɛf] NF *Chir* autograft

autoguidage [otogidaʒ] NM **(retour par) a.** homing; **cellule d'a.** homing eye

autoguidé [otogide] ADJ *(missile)* self-directional, homing

auto-immun ADJ *Méd* autoimmune

auto-immunisation, *pl* **auto-immunisations** NF autoimmunization

auto-induction, *pl* **auto-inductions** NF *Électron* self-induction

auto-intoxication, *pl* **auto-intoxications** NF autointoxication, autotoxaemia

autolimitation [otolimitasjɔ̃] NF setting of voluntary limits

autolimiter [otolimite] VT to set voluntary limits to; **les Japonais autolimitent leurs exportations de voitures** the Japanese set voluntary limits to their car exports

autolubrifiant [otolybrifjã] ADJ self-lubricating

autolubrification [otolybrifikasjɔ̃] NF self-lubrication

autolyse [otoliz] NF autolysis

auto-marché, *pl* **auto-marchés** NM car mart

automate [otomat] NM **1** automaton, robot; **marcher comme un a.** to walk like a robot; **vivre comme un a.** to live like an automaton VOIR GRAMMAIRE A13 **2** *Suisse (distributeur)* vending machine; *(distributeur de billets)* cash dispenser

automation [otomasjɔ̃] NF automation

automatique [otomatik] ADJ *(action)* automatic; *(appareil)* self-acting; **'attention à la fermeture a. des portières'** 'danger, automatically closing doors'; **à mise en marche a.** self-starting; **réflexe a.** automatic reflex; *Méd* involuntary reflex; **payer l'électricité par prélèvement a.** to pay one's electricity bill by direct debit; *Fam* **votre dossier est envoyé à Paris, c'est a.** your file has been sent to Paris, that's the usual procedure; **il va vouloir te voir, c'est a.** he'll want to see you, it's a dead cert
NM **1** *(téléphone)* direct dialling **2** *(pistolet)* automatic
NF **1** *Tech* automatics, automation **2** *Aut* automatic

automatiquement [otomatikmã] ADV automatically; **votre nom est inséré a. dans le fichier** your name is automatically entered in the file; *Fam* **si vous ne payez pas vos impôts, vous agissez a. contre la loi** by not paying your tax you are automatically breaking the law

automatisable [otomatizabl] ADJ automatable

automatisation [otomatizasjɔ̃] NF automation

automatiser [otomatize] VT to automate

automatisme [otomatism] NM **1** *Physiol, Méd* automatism; **agir par a.** to act automatically; **fermer la porte à double tour est devenu un a.** double-locking the door has become automatic **2** *(fonctionnement)* automatic working *or* functioning **3** *(dispositif)* automatic device

automédication [otomedikasjɔ̃] NF self-medication

automitrailleuse [otomitrajøz] NF armoured car

automnal, -ale, -aux, -ales [otɔ(m)nal, -o] ADJ autumnal

automne [otɔn] NM VOIR GRAMMAIRE A7 autumn, *Am* fall; **l'équinoxe d'a.** the autumnal equinox; **en a., à l'a.** in autumn; **une soirée d'a.** an autumn evening; *Fig* **à l'a. de sa vie** in the autumn of his/her life

automobile [otomɔbil] ADJ **1** *(à moteur)* self-propelling, automotive; **voiture a.** motor vehicle; **canot a.** motor boat *(relatif à la voiture)* **club a.** automobile club; **assurance a.** car *or* motor insurance; **industrie a.** automobile *or* car industry; **accessoires automobiles** car accessories

NF (motor)car, *Am* automobile; *Mil* a. **blindée** armoured car; **salon de l'a.** motor show; **l'a. marche bien en France** the car industry is doing well in France

automobilisme [otomɔbilism] NM motoring

automobiliste [otomɔbilist] N motorist

automoteur, -trice [otomɔtœr, -tris] ADJ *(véhicule)* self-propelling, automotive; *(valve etc)* self-acting; **train a.** multiple unit (Diesel) train
  NF **automotrice** railcar
  NM *Naut* self-propelled barge

automutilation [otomytilasjɔ̃] NF self-mutilation

autoneige [otonɛʒ] NF *Can* snowmobile

autonettoyant [otonetwajɑ̃] ADJ **four a.** self-cleaning oven

autonome [otɔnɔm] ADJ autonomous, self-governing; *(État, région etc)* independent; *(appareil)* self-contained; *(personne)* self-sufficient; *Ordinat* **calculateur a.** stand-alone (computer)

autonomie [otɔnɔmi] NF **1** *Pol* autonomy, self-government **2** *(de personne)* self-sufficiency; **ma fille veut avoir son a.** my daughter wants her independence **3** *Aviat* cruising radius, range; *(de voiture)* range; **l'avion a deux heures/800 km d'a.** the aircraft has a range of two hours/800 km **4** *(de batterie)* battery life, life; *(d'un téléphone portable)* talktime

autonomiste [otɔnɔmist] N *Pol* autonomist

autopalpation [otopalpasjɔ̃] NF *Méd* self-examination

auto-patrouille, *pl* **auto-patrouilles** NF *Can* police car

autopont [otopɔ̃] NM flyover

autoportant [otopɔrtɑ̃], **autoporteur**[1], **-euse** [otopɔrtœr, -øz] ADJ *Archit* self-supporting

autoporteur[2] ADJ *Aut* integral, integrated; *(carrosserie)* frameless

autoportrait [otopɔrtrɛ] NM self-portrait

autopropulsé [otoprɔpylse] ADJ self-propelled

autopropulsion [otoprɔpylsjɔ̃] NF self-propulsion

autopsie [otɔpsi] NF autopsy; **a. (cadavérique)** postmortem (examination); **pratiquer une a.** to carry out a postmortem (examination); *Fig* **faire l'a. d'une œuvre** to examine a work critically

autopsier [otɔpsje] VT to perform a postmortem (examination) on, to autopsy

autopunition [otopynisjɔ̃] NF *Psy* self-punishment

autoradio [otoradjo] NM car radio

autorafraîchissement [otorafrɛʃismɑ̃] NM *Ordinat* auto-refresh

autorail [otoraj] NM railcar

auto-régénérateur, -trice [otoreʒeneratœr, -tris] ADJ *Nucl (réacteur etc)* breeder

autoréglage [otoreglaʒ] NM *Tech* self-regulation

autorégulateur, -trice [otoregylatœr, -tris] ADJ self-regulating
  NM self-acting regulator

autorégulation [otoregylasjɔ̃] NF self-regulation

autoreverse [otorəvɛrs] ADJ **appareil a.** auto-reverse
  NM auto-reverse

autorisation [otorizasjɔ̃] NF **1** authorization, authority, permission; **donner à qn l'a. de faire qch** to authorize sb to do sth, to give sb permission to do sth; **demander l'a. de faire qch** to ask permission to do sth; *surtout*

Mil, Admin etc to request authority to do sth; **je n'ai pas eu l'a. de sortir ce soir** I didn't get permission to go out tonight; **il nous manque encore l'a. du conseil municipal pour ouvrir le restaurant** we still need the council's authorization to open the restaurant; **avoir l'a. de bâtir** to have planning permission **2** *(document)* licence; **montrez-moi votre a.** show me your permit
  ▸ ▸ *Ordinat* **a. d'accès** access authorization; **a. de crédit** credit line; **a. de découvert** overdraft facility; **a. de dédouanement** customs clearance authorization; *TV, Cin* **a. d'exploitation** rights; **a. d'exporter** export permit; **a. de prélèvement** direct debit mandate; *Admin* **a. de sortie du territoire** = parental authorization for a minor to travel abroad; *Aviat* **a. de vol** flight clearance

autorisé [otorize] ADJ **1** *(qualifié)* authorized; **tenir qch d'une source autorisée** to have sth from an authoritative source; **les milieux autorisés** (the) official circles **2** *(permis)* permitted, permissible, allowed; **tournure autorisée par l'usage** turn of phrase sanctioned *or* hallowed by usage; **il se croit tout a.** he thinks he can get away with anything **3** *(étalon)* approved

autoriser [otorize] VT **1** **a. qn à faire qch** to authorize *or* permit sb to do sth, to give sb the authority to do sth; **je vous autorise à sortir de table** you may have my permission to leave the table; **l'alcool ne lui est pas autorisé** he/she is not allowed (to drink) alcohol; **a. la pêche** to allow fishing **2** *(justifier) (une action)* to justify, to authorize, to sanction; **ces découvertes autorisent à penser que ...** these discoveries entitle us to believe that ...; **rien ne nous autorise à le croire** nothing entitles us to believe that
  VPR **s'autoriser je m'autorise de ces résultats pour ...** on the basis of these results, I feel entitled to ...

autoritaire [otoritɛr] ADJ authoritarian

autoritairement [otoritɛrmɑ̃] ADV authoritatively, *Péj* in an authoritarian manner

autoritarisme [otoritarism] NM authoritarianism

autorité [otorite] NF **1** *(domination)* authority; **exercer son a. sur qn** to exercise authority over sb; **il n'a aucune a. sur ses élèves** he can't keep order *or* he has no control over his pupils; **a. parentale** parental authority; **être sous l'a. de qn** to be under sb's authority; **il veut tout emporter d'a.** he wants his own way in everything, *Fam* he wants to run the whole show; **agir de pleine a.** to act with full powers; **faire qch d'a.** to do sth on one's own (responsibility), to take it upon oneself to do sth; **de sa propre a.** on one's own authority; **territoire soumis à l'a. de ...** area within the jurisdiction of ...; *Jur* **l'a. de la loi** the force of the law
  2 *(poids)* authority; **avoir de l'a. sur qn** to have influence *or* authority over sb; **faire a. en qch** to be an authority on sth; **il fait a. en matière de physique nucléaire** he is an authority on nuclear physics; **ce livre fait a. dans le milieu** this book is taken as the authority here; *Jur* **cas d'espèce qui font a.** leading cases; **parler avec a.** to speak authoritatively *or* with authority
  3 *(gouvernement)* **l'a.** the authorities; **les représentants de l'a.** the representatives of authority; **l'a. fiscale** the tax authorities; **les autorités** the authorities, the powers that be; **les autorités locales/religieuses** the local/religious authorities; **autorités portuaires** port authorities
  4 *(personne)* **citer une a.** to quote an authority; **c'est une a., elle est très écoutée** she's an authority, people take a lot of notice of what she says

autoroute [otorut] NF **1** *Aut* motorway, *Am* freeway, *Am* thruway; **prendre l'a.** to take the motorway; **a. à péage** toll motorway, *Am* turnpike (road) **2** *Ordinat* **a. de l'information** information (super)highway; **a. interactive** interactive highway; **a. électronique** electronic highway, superhighway

autoroutier, -ière [otorutje, -jɛr] ADJ **système a.** motorway *or Am* freeway system *or* network

autosatisfaction [otosatisfaksjɔ̃] NF self-satisfaction

auto-stop NM hitchhiking, *Fam* hitching; **faire de l'a.** to hitchhike, *Fam* to hitch, to thumb a lift; **prendre qn en a.** to pick up a hitchhiker; **je ne voyage qu'en a.** I hitchhike everywhere I go; **faire le tour de l'Europe en a.** to hitchhike around Europe

auto-stoppeur, -euse, *pl* **auto-stoppeurs, -euses** N hitchhiker, *Fam* hitcher

autosuffisance [otosyfizɑ̃s] NF *Écon* self-sufficiency

autosuggestion [otosygʒɛstjɔ̃] NF auto-suggestion

autotest [ototɛst] NM *Ordinat* self-test

autotester (s') [ototɛste] VPR *Ordinat* to self-test, to auto-test

autour[1] [otur] ADV around; **une ville avec des murs tout a.** a town with walls all around it
  PRÉP **a. de** around, *surtout Br* round, about; **nous nous sommes assis a. de la table** we sat down round the table; **discuter qch a. d'un verre** to discuss sth over a drink; **enrouler qch a. de son cou** to coil sth round one's neck; **ce qui se passe a. de nous** what is going on around *or* round about us; *Fam* **il a a. de vingt ans** he is (somewhere) about twenty, he's twentyish; **tourner a. de la question** *ou* **du pot** to beat about the bush; **tout a. de ... all around ...**   VOIR GRAMMAIRE A67

autour[2] NM *(oiseau)* **a. (des palombes)** goshawk

autovaccin [otovaksɛ̃] NM *Méd* autovaccine

AUTRE [otr] VOIR GRAMMAIRE A36–7; B15–16

┌───┐
ADJ other **1, 4** ▪ another **1, 3, 4**
▪ something else *(autre chose)* **5**
PRON another **2–4, 6–8** ▪ both *(l'un et l'autre)* **4** ▪ either *(l'un ou l'autre)* **5, 6**
▪ each other *(l'un l'autre)* **7** ▪ else **9, 10**
└───┘

ADJ 1 other; **l'a. côté** the other side; **une a. semaine/un a. jour** another week/another day; **une a. fois** another time; **toute a. femme aurait agi de la même façon** any other woman would have acted in the same way; **les choux et autres légumes** cabbages and (all) other vegetables; **des choux et d'autres légumes** cabbages and some other vegetables; **tous les autres verbes que ceux en -er** all verbs other than those in -er; **je ne pourrai pas y aller, entre autres raisons je suis à court d'argent** I can't go, for one thing I'm short of money; **l'a. monde** the next world; **sans faire d'a. observation** without making any further observation; **sans a. perte de temps** without further loss of time; **l'a. lundi** the other Monday; *(prochain)* Monday week; **je l'ai vu l'a. jour/soir** I saw him the other day/evening

2 vous autres hommes, vous êtes seuls coupables it is you men alone who are to blame; **nous autres Anglais** we English (people); **vous autres** you others, all of you; **eh, vous autres! venez par ici!** hey, you lot! come over here!

3 *(second)* **il se croit un a. Napoléon** he thinks he is a second *or* another Napoleon; **mon frère, c'est un a. moi-même** my brother is just another me

4 *(différent)* other, different; **donnez-moi un**

a. torchon give me another cloth; *Prov* **autres temps, autres mœurs** other days, other ways; **il est a. que je ne le pensais** he is different from what I thought; **elle est devenue a.** she has changed, she has become different; **cela a fait de lui un a. homme** it made a new man of him; **une tout a. femme** quite a different woman; **j'ai des idées autres** I have different ideas, my ideas are different; **être d'une a. opinion** to think otherwise *or* differently

5 a. chose *(en plus)* something else; *(en remplacement)* something different; **j'ai a. chose d'important à vous dire** I have something else of importance to tell you; **avez-vous a. chose à faire?** have you anything else to do?; **ce qu'il éprouve pour elle, ce n'est pas a. chose que de l'amour** what he feels for her is nothing other than love; *Fam* **a. chose, ma mère est partie hier** not only that, but my mother left yesterday; **c'est tout a. chose!** that's quite a different thing!; **une chose est de parler, a. chose est d'agir** it's one thing to talk, it's another to act; **a. part** somewhere else

PRON 1 les défauts des autres the failings of others; **d'autres vous diront que ...** others *or* other people will tell you that ...; **tous les autres sont là** all the others are there; **encore un a.** one more, another (one); **encore bien d'autres** many more besides

2 cela peut arriver d'un jour à l'a. it may happen any day; **je l'attends d'un moment à l'a.** I expect him/her any moment; **je le vois de temps a a.** I see him from time to time *or* now and again *or* now and then; **un jour ou l'a.** one day or another, one of these days; **d'un bout à l'a.** from one end to the other, from start to finish, from end to end; **il a menti d'un bout à l'a.** he lied from start to finish

3 la science est une chose, l'art en est une a. science is one thing, art is another; **il parle d'une façon et agit d'une a.** he says one thing and does another

4 l'un et l'a. both; **les uns et les autres** *(tout le monde)* all (and sundry), one and all; *(deux groupes)* both parties; **il a parlé aux uns et aux autres** he spoke to them all; **l'un et l'a. ont été punis** both were punished; **il passe son temps chez l'un ou l'a.** he spends his time with one friend or another

5 l'un ou l'a. either; **c'est l'un ou l'a.!** it's either or!, it's one thing or the other!; **c'est tout l'un ou tout l'a.** there is no happy medium, it's either one extreme or the other; **ni l'un ni l'a.** neither; **ni l'un ni l'a. ne sont venus** neither of them came; **je ne les connais ni l'un ni l'a.** I don't know either of them; **je n'ai vu ni les uns ni les autres** I didn't see any of them

6 l'un ..., l'a. ... one ..., the other ...; **l'un dit ceci, l'a. dit cela** one says this and the other says that; **les uns ..., les autres ...** some ..., others ..., some ..., some ...; **ils s'en allèrent, les uns par ci, les autres par là** they went off, some one way, some another; **sans prendre parti ni pour les uns ni pour les autres** without taking either side; **l'un ne va pas sans l'a.** you can't have one without the other, the two go hand in hand; **qui voit l'un voit l'a.** there's no difference between them, you can't tell the two apart; **l'un vaut l'a.** there's no difference between them, the one's just as good/bad as the other

7 l'un l'a. each other, one another; **on va s'aider l'un l'a.** we'll help each other; **elles se moquent les unes des autres** they make fun of each other; **vivre l'un pour l'a.** to live for each other; **aller l'un à côté de l'a.** to walk side by side; **ils dépendent l'un de l'a.** they depend on each other; **l'un auprès de l'a., auprès l'un de l'a.** near each other, near one another

8 l'un dans l'a., il se fait mille euros with one

thing and another, he earns a thousand euros; **une année dans l'a.** taking one year with another

9 d'a. else; **il y a quelque chose d'a. dans la boîte? – non, rien d'a.** is there anything else in the box? – no, nothing else; **il n'y en a pas d'a.** there's no other; **parler de choses et d'autres** to talk about this and that; **personne d'a. ne le sait** nobody else knows; **quelqu'un d'a.** somebody else; **je ne demande rien d'a.** I don't ask for anything more, I ask for nothing more; **c'est de la stupidité et rien d'a.** it's stupidity and nothing else, it's nothing but stupidity, it's sheer stupidity; **que pouvait-il faire d'a.?** what else could he do?; **que pouvaient-ils faire d'a. que de l'inviter?** what else could they do but invite him/her?; **qui d'a. que lui aurait pu le faire?** who else (but him) could have done it?; **(dites cela) à d'autres!** who do you think you're kidding?, get away!; *Fam* **j'en ai vu bien d'autres** I've been through worse than that

10 *(personne)* someone *or* somebody else; **adressez-vous à un a.** ask someone else *or* somebody else; **je l'ai pris pour un a.** I mistook him for someone else; **c'était un touriste comme un a.** he was just an ordinary tourist; **c'est une raison comme une a.** it's as good a reason as any; **c'est un homme pas comme les autres** he is not like other men; **peut m'importe ce que pensent les autres** I don't care what anyone else thinks *or* what other people think; *Fam* **comme dit l'a.** as the saying goes, as they say; *Fam* **dis donc! t'as vu l'a.?** God! did you see him/her there?; *Fam* **et l'a. qui fait encore son cirque!** and that one making his/her usual scene!; **il n'est pas plus bête qu'un a.** he is no more stupid than anyone else; **nul a. ne l'a vu** no one else *or* nobody else saw him; **tout a. le comprendrait** anyone else would understand it; **il y avait des Écossais, entre autres** there were some Scots, among others

autrefois [otrəfwa] **ADV** formerly, in the past; *(à une époque particulière)* once; **c'est ce qu'on faisait a. à la maison, avant l'accident** that's what we used to do at home, before the accident; **a., il était plus bavard** he was more talkative before *or* in the past, he used to be more talkative; **il y avait a. un roi** once upon a time there was a king; **c'était l'usage a.** it was the custom in former times *or* in olden days; **d'a.** of long ago; **sa vie d'a.** his past life; **les hommes d'a.** men of old *or* of olden times; **des chants d'a.** old-time songs

autrement [otrəmã] **ADV 1** *(différemment)* otherwise, differently; **il me l'a raconté a. que vous** the way he told it was different from the way you told it; **faisons a.** let's do *or* set about it (in) another way; **Alain, a. appelé Jojo** Alain, otherwise known as Jojo; **le bouton d'or, a. appelé ...** the buttercup, otherwise known as ..., the buttercup, or ...; **a. dit** in other words, put differently; **tu ne viendras pas demain? a. dit, tu ne veux plus me voir!** so you're not coming tomorrow? in other words, you don't want to see me any more!; **il ne put faire a. que d'obéir** he had no alternative but to obey; **à chaque fois que je le vois, je pleure, je n'arrive pas à faire a.** every time I see him I cry, I can't help myself; *Fam* **pas moyen de faire a.** there's no alternative, there's no other way; **pas moyen de faire a. que de l'emmener** there's no alternative *or* there's nothing else to do *or* nothing else for it but to take him along

2 *(plus)* (far) more; **elle est a. intelligente** she is far more intelligent, she is more intelligent by far; **c'est bien a. sérieux** that is far more serious

3 *(sinon)* otherwise, or (else); **venez demain, a. il sera trop tard** come tomorrow,

otherwise it will be too late; **explique-lui, a. elle n'arrivera pas à le faire** explain it to her, otherwise *or* or (else) she won't be able to do it; **les verres n'étaient pas propres, a. c'était pas mal** the glasses weren't clean, but otherwise it wasn't bad

4 pas a. not particularly; **cela ne me surprend pas a.** that does not particularly surprise me

Autriche [otriʃ] **NF** Austria

autrichien, -ienne [otriʃjɛ̃, -jɛn] **ADJ** Austrian

N A. Austrian

autruche [otryʃ] **NF** *(oiseau)* ostrich; **œuf d'a.** ostrich egg; **chaussures/sac en a.** ostrich-skin shoes/handbag; *Fig Fam* **avoir un estomac d'a.** to have a cast-iron stomach; *Fig* **pratiquer la politique de l'a., faire l'a.** to bury one's head in the sand

autrui [otrɥi] **PRON INDÉF** others, other people; **convoiter le bien d'a.** to covet one's neighbour's property; **ne fais pas à a. ce que tu ne voudrais pas qu'on te fît** do as you would be done by

auvent [ovã] **NM 1** porch roof; **un toit en a.** a sloping roof; **s'abriter sous l'a.** to shelter in the porch **2** *(de tente)* canopy, awning **3** *Ind* *(au-dessus de l'âtre etc)* hood; *Aut* **auvents de capot** bonnet louvres

auvergnat, -ate [ovɛrɲa, -at] **ADJ** of Auvergne

NM *Ling* Auvergne dialect

N A. *(natif)* native of Auvergne; *(habitant)* inhabitant of Auvergne

aux [o] *voir* à

auxiliaire [oksiljɛr, o-] **ADJ** *(verbe, troupes etc)* auxiliary; **machine a.** auxiliary engine; **bureau a.** sub-office; **services auxiliaires de l'armée** non-combatant services; **maître a.** supply teacher

N *(aide)* auxiliary, helper, assistant; *Admin* temporary civil servant; *(aux PTT)* non-permanent employee; *Com* facilitator; **c'est un a. précieux** he's a valuable helper

NM 1 *Naut* auxiliary cruiser **2** *Aviat, Naut* **auxiliaires** the auxiliary engines **3** *Mil* **auxiliaires** auxiliaries **4** *Gram* auxiliary verb SEE GRAMMAR A38–9; A55–61; B26–8

▸ ▸ a. familiale ≃ mother's help; **a. de justice** representative of the law; **a. médical** medical auxiliary

auxquels [okɛl] *voir* lequel

AV *(abrév* avant*)* front

av. *abrév* avenue

avachi [avaʃi] **ADJ 1** *(vêtements, bottes etc)* *(déformé par l'usage)* out of shape, shapeless; **elle traîne toujours son vieux manteau tout a.** she wears her shapeless old coat everywhere she goes **2** *(posture)* sloppy; *(personne, muscles)* flabby; **être a. dans un fauteuil** to be slumped in an armchair

avachir [avaʃir] **VT 1** *(vêtements etc)* to make shapeless; *(cuir)* to soften **2** *(personne, muscles)* to make flabby; **la chaleur m'avachit** the heat makes me feel quite limp *or* floppy

VPR s'avachir 1 *(du cuir)* to soften, to become soft; *(des vêtements)* to become shapeless, to lose its shape **2** *(de personne)* to become flabby; *(se laisser aller)* to let oneself go, to go to seed; **s'a. dans un fauteuil** to flop into an armchair

avachissement [avaʃismã] **NM** *(de cuir)* softening; *(des vêtements)* losing shape; *(de posture)* sloppiness; *(de personne, muscles)* flabbiness

aval¹, -als [aval] **NM** *Fin* *(d'un effet de commerce)* endorsement; **a. bancaire** bank guarantee, aval; **pour a.** for approval; **donner son a. à un billet** to endorse *or* back a bill; **donneur d'a.** guarantor, backer; *Fig* **donner son a. à un projet** to give a project one's backing or support

aval² NM **1** downstream side; **les villages d'a.** the villages downstream; **canal d'a.** (d'écluse) tail race; **porte d'a.** tail or aft gate; **en a.** downstream, downriver; Rail down the line; **en a. du village/du torrent** downstream of the village/torrent; **le ski a.** the downhill ski **2** Com **stade a.** (de la production) downstream; **en a.** downstream **3** Tél down side

avalanche [avalɑ̃ʃ] NF avalanche; **a. de pierres** avalanche of stones; **a. boueuse** avalanche of mud; **couloir d'a.** avalanche corridor; **a. électronique/ionique** avalanche of electrons/ions; Fig **a. d'injures/de compliments** shower of insults/compliments; Fig **ce fut une a. de lettres** letters came pouring in, there was a flood of letters

avalancheux, -euse [avalɑ̃ʃø, -øz] ADJ prone to avalanches; **couloir a.** avalanche corridor

avaler [avale] VT **1** (absorber) to swallow (down); **a. son repas sans mâcher** to swallow down one's meal without chewing it; **a. son repas** to bolt one's meal; **j'avale mon repas et j'arrive** I'll just get my food down, then I'll be along; **a. son vin d'un trait** to swallow one's wine in one gulp; **j'ai avalé de travers** it went down the wrong way; **a. qch tout rond** to swallow sth whole; **je meurs de faim, je n'ai rien avalé depuis hier** I'm starving, I haven't had a thing to eat since yesterday; Fig **a. ses mots** to swallow one's words; **a. la fumée** to inhale; Fig **j'ai cru qu'elle allait m'a. tout cru** I thought she was going to bite my head off; **a. une carte de crédit** (d'un distributeur automatique) to eat or swallow a credit card; **je préfère a. ma salive et penser à autre chose** I prefer to grin and bear it and think of something else; **on dirait qu'il a avalé son parapluie!** he's as stiff as a poker!; **les kilomètres** to eat up the miles; **il a avalé 'Vol de Nuit' en une soirée** he read or devoured 'Vol de Nuit' in an evening

2 Fig **a. le morceau** ou **la pilule** to take one's medicine or one's punishment; **celle-là est dure à a.** that's a tall story, I can hardly swallow that; **tu auras du mal à leur faire a. ça** you'll have a job getting them to swallow that; **on peut lui faire a. n'importe quoi, il est tellement naïf** he's so naive he'll swallow anything; Fam **tu as avalé ta langue?** have you lost your tongue?, has the cat got your tongue?; Fam **a. son acte de naissance** to kick the bucket, to pop one's clogs VI to swallow; Fam **qu'est-ce qu'il avale!** he doesn't half put it away!

avaleur [avalœr] NM **a. de sabres** sword-swallower

avaliser [avalize] VT Fin to avalize; Com (effet de commerce) to endorse, to back; (signature) to guarantee; Fig **a. un projet** to back a project

avaliste [avalist] NM Jur endorser, guarantor, backer

à-valoir NM INV (paiement) advance

[avɑ̃s] NF **1** (marche) advance; **l'a. d'une armée/d'un mouvement indépendantiste** the advance of an army/of an independence movement; **l'a. rapide de l'indice du coût de la vie** the rapid rise or climb of the cost of living index; Élec **a. d'une magnéto** magneto lead; **a. rapide** (sur magnétophone) fast-forwarding; **mettre une cassette en a. rapide** to fast-forward a cassette, to put a cassette on fast forward

2 (dans le temps, l'espace, avantage) lead; **avoir une a. de 2 minutes/2 km** to have a 2-minute/2-km lead; **avoir 2 minutes/2 km d'a. sur qn** to have a 2-minute/2-km lead over sb; (en début de course) to have a 2-minute/

2-km head start on sb; Sport **un trou/but/set d'a.** one hole/goal/set up; **j'ai fini le projet avec deux jours d'a. sur le programme** I finished the project two days ahead of schedule; **j'ai fini le contrôle avec un quart d'heure d'a.** I finished the test a quarter of an hour ahead of time; **arriver avec cinq minutes d'a.** to arrive five minutes early; **il vaut toujours mieux arriver à la gare avec quelques minutes d'a.** it's always better to arrive at the station a few minutes early or with a few minutes to spare; **nous avons pris de l'a. sur nos poursuivants/concurrents** we've pulled away from our pursuers/competitors; **accentuer/conserver/perdre son a. sur qn** to increase/maintain/lose one's lead over sb; Sport **donner de l'a. à qn** to give sb a head start; **je vais le laisser prendre de l'a. dans la ligne droite** I'll let him get ahead in the straight; **grâce à l'a. acquise pendant les deux premières heures de la course** thanks to the lead he/she/etc established or built up during the first two hours of the race; **Paris-St-Germain cherche à préserver son a. au classement** Paris-St-Germain are trying to hold on to or maintain their lead in the league; **l'a. des Français au niveau de la recherche** the French lead in the sphere of research; **une mauvaise gestion peut nous faire perdre notre a.** we may lose our lead through bad management; Fam **la belle a.!** much good that will do/did/is doing you!

3 Tech (d'un outil) feed movement, travel; **mécanisme d'a.** feed mechanism

4 Aut **a. à l'allumage** ignition advance; **mettre de l'a. à l'allumage** to advance the ignition; **réduire l'a.** to retard the ignition; **levier d'a.** ignition lever; **a. à l'échappement** exhaust lead

5 Fin **a. (de fonds)** advance; **a. à découvert** unsecured or uncovered advance; **a. en devises** foreign currency loan; **a. en numéraire** cash advance; **a. de trésorerie** cash advance; **par a., à titre d'a.** as an advance; **faire une a. de mille euros à qn** to give sb an advance of a thousand euros; **demander une a. sur salaire** to ask for an advance on one's salary; **faire les avances d'une entreprise** to advance funds for an enterprise; Cin **a. sur recette(s)** (d'acteur) advance payment; (de metteur en scène) = money invested in the production of a film, to be recouped from the box office takings

6 **faire des avances à qn** to approach sb; (sexuellement) to make advances to sb; **ne réponds jamais aux avances de ce monsieur!** don't ever respond to that man's advances!

7 Suisse **faire de l'a.** (prendre de l'avance) (sur un travail, des devoirs, etc) to get ahead (sur in, with)

8 Ordinat **a. automatique** automatic feed

9 **d'a., à l'a., par a.** in advance; **payer qn d'a.** ou **à l'a.** to pay sb in advance; **payable à l'a.** payable in advance; **retenir** ou **louer une place huit jours à l'a.** to book a seat a week in advance; **et pourtant, je les ai prévenus deux mois à l'a.** I did warn them two months in advance or beforehand; **entrer à l'école primaire avec un an d'a.** to go to primary school a year early; Scol **avoir un an d'a.** to be a year ahead; **je vous remercie d'a., par a., merci** (dans une lettre) thanking you in advance or in anticipation; **je m'en réjouis d'a.** I'm greatly looking forward to it; **je savourais à l'a. le plaisir de …** I was relishing (in anticipation) the thought of …, I was relishing the prospect of …

10 **en a.** early; **je suis en a. d'une demi-heure** I am half an hour early; **je suis arrivé très en a.** I arrived very early; **elle sait déjà lire, elle est très en a. pour son âge** she can already read, she's very advanced for her age; **être en a. sur son temps** to be ahead of

one's time; **la moisson est en a. cette année** the harvest is early this year; Fam **je vous préviens, nous ne sommes pas en a.!** I'm warning you, we're not exactly running on time!

avancé [avɑ̃se] ADJ **1** (dans l'espace) advanced; **position avancée** advanced or forward position; Rail **signal a.** distant signal; **j'étais trop a. sur ma route pour pouvoir faire demi-tour** I had gone too far along the road to be able to turn back

2 (précoce) forward; **les pommiers sont bien avancés cette année** the apple trees are early this year; **c'est un esprit a.** he's a progressive thinker; **élève a.** pupil ahead of his class; **opinions avancées** advanced or progressive ideas

3 (dans le temps) **à une heure avancée de la nuit** late in the night, well on in the night; **à une heure peu avancée** quite early on; Can **heure avancée** daylight saving time; **l'été est bien a.** summer is well advanced; **à un âge a.** late in life, at an advanced age

4 (fruit) overripe; **viande avancée** rotten meat

5 (presque à terme) (far) advanced; **à un stade a. du projet** at an advanced stage in the project; **je ne suis pas assez a. dans mon travail pour pouvoir sortir ce soir** I'm not far enough ahead with my work to be able to go out tonight; Fam **vous voilà bien a.!** a lot of good that's done you!; **tu es bien a. maintenant que tu l'as renvoyé: tu n'as personne pour le remplacer!** a lot of good it's done you firing him, you've got no one to replace him!; **vous n'en êtes pas plus a.** you're no further forward

avancée [avɑ̃se] NF **1** (saillie) bulge, projection, protuberance; Constr **a. du toit** eaves **2** (de la mer, du désert), Fig (des nationalistes etc) advance **3** (d'une ligne de pêche) leader, trace

avancement [avɑ̃smɑ̃] NM **1** (mouvement) advancing, putting forward **2** Ordinat etc **a. automatique** automatic feed; **a. ligne par ligne** line feed; **a. du papier** paper feed; **a. par friction** friction feed **3** (de projet) advancement, furtherance; **état d'a. des travaux** progress report **4** (promotion) promotion; **a. à l'ancienneté** promotion by seniority; **avoir** ou **obtenir de l'a.** to be promoted **5** (progrès) advance(ment), progress; **l'a. des sciences** the advance or progress of science **6** Jur **a. d'hoirie** = part of inheritance given in advance

[avɑ̃se] (j'avançai(s); n. avançons)

VT to move forward **1** ▪ to put forward **2** ▪ to bring forward **3** ▪ to lend **4** ▪ to further **5**			
VI to move forward **1** ▪ to advance **1, 3** ▪ to progress **2** ▪ to be fast **4** ▪ to jut out **5**			
VPR to move forward **1** ▪ to make headway **2** ▪ to jut out **4**			

VT **1** (mettre en avant) to move forward; (la main) to stretch out, to hold out; **avance un peu ton pied, tu écrases la queue du chien** move your foot (forward) a bit, you're crushing the dog's tail; **a. sa chaise pour mieux voir** to pull up or forward one's chair to see better; **il avança son verre** he held out his glass; **elle avança son petit visage vers moi** she moved her little face towards me; **a. une voiture jusqu'au portail** to drive a car up to the door; Fml, Hum **l'automobile de Monsieur est avancée** Sir's carriage awaits; Fam **laisse-moi t'a. jusqu'au métro** let me take you as far as the underground; Échecs **a. un pion** to advance a pawn

2 Fig **a. une proposition** to put forward or advance a proposal; **a. ses raisons** to produce *or* set out one's reasons; **comment peut-il prouver ce qu'il avance?** how can he prove his assertion?; **comme l'ont avancé certains chercheurs …** as some researchers have proposed …

3 *(dans le temps)* to bring forward; **la réunion a été avancée du 14 au 7** the meeting has been brought forward from the 14th to the 7th; **a. l'heure du dîner** to put dinner forward; **a. une montre d'une heure** to put a watch forward one hour

4 a. de l'argent à qn to advance money to sb; *(prêter)* to lend sb money; **tu peux m'a. (l'argent de) mon train?** could you lend me my train fare?

5 *(promouvoir)* to further; **être avancé** to be promoted, to get promotion; **a. ses recherches** to push on with *or* get ahead with one's research; **a. une plante** to bring on *or* force a plant; **est-ce que ça t'avancerait si je faisais les courses?** would it help you along if I did the shopping?; **à quoi cela vous avancera-t-il?** what good will that do you?, how much better (off) will you be for it?; **ça ne t'avancera à rien de te mettre en colère** losing your temper won't get you anywhere; **je lui ai posé des questions, mais ses réponses ne m'ont pas beaucoup avancé** I asked him some questions, but his answers got me no further forward *or* left me none the wiser

VI 1 *(aller de l'avant)* to move *or* go forward; *(d'un bateau)* to make headway; *(d'une armée)* to advance; **a. à grands pas** to stride along; **a. à pas de loup** to creep along; **a. à tâtons** to feel *or* grope one's way; **a. d'un pas** to take a *or* one step forward; **avancez vers moi** come towards me; **chaque année, la mer avance un peu plus sur notre terrain** each year, the sea encroaches a little further on our land; **faire a. qn** to help sb along; *(en le poussant)* to push sb along; **faire a. une chaise roulante** to push a wheelchair; *Mil* **faire a. les troupes** to advance the troops, to move the troops forward; **faire a. sa voiture jusqu'à la porte** to drive one's car up to the door; **vous ne pouvez pas a., s'il vous plaît?** je ne peux pas passer could you move, please? I can't get past; **tu n'avances pas assez vite, on ne sera jamais à l'heure** you're not going fast enough, we'll never be on time; **allez avance! on va être en retard** come on, move! we're going to be late; **aux heures de pointe, on n'avance pas sur cette route** during the rush hours, you can't move on this road; **nous n'avancions pas d'un centimètre** we weren't moving an inch; **nous avancions péniblement dans les marais** we struggled our way through the swamp; **le vieil homme avançait en traînant les pieds** the old man shuffled along

2 *(faire des progrès)* to progress, to get on; **le travail avance** the work is progressing *or* getting on *or* coming along; **depuis sa démission, ça n'avance plus** since he/she resigned, things have been at a standstill *or* have ground to a halt; *Fam* **alors, ça avance?** so how's it coming along?; **je n'avance pas dans mon livre** I'm not making any headway with this book; **mon livre n'avance pas** my book isn't coming along at all; **on sentait en lui le désir de faire a. les choses** you could tell he wanted to get things moving (along); **faire a. la cause de la démocratie** to advance the cause of democracy, to further democracy; **faire a. la science** to bring about scientific progress; **a. en âge** to be getting on; **la nuit avance** it's getting late; **la matinée avançait péniblement** the morning was dragging on *or* wore on

3 *(dans une carrière etc)* to advance; **en grade** to get promoted; *Mil* to rise in rank

4 *(dans le temps)* *(d'une montre)* to be fast; **l'horloge avance** the clock is fast; **montre qui avance d'une minute par jour** watch that

gains a minute a day; **vous avancez de dix minutes** your watch is ten minutes fast

5 *(de promontoire, toit etc)* to jut out, to project, to protrude; **les rochers avançaient sur la mer** the rocks jutted out into the sea; **le balcon avançait sur la baie** the balcony jutted out over the bay

VPR s'avancer 1 *(aller devant)* to move forward; **s'a. vers qch** to make one's way *or* to head towards sth; **s'a. d'un pas** to take a *or* one step forward; **avance-toi si tu veux voir** move forward if you want to see; **s'a. péniblement** to drag oneself along

2 *(dans une tâche)* to make headway; **elle en a profité pour s'a. dans son travail** she made use of this to get ahead in her work

3 *Fig* **il s'est trop avancé pour reculer** he has gone too far to take it back; **elle refuse de s'a. sur ce point** she won't be drawn on this matter; **je crois que je me suis trop avancé en disant que mes parents leur prêteraient leur maison** I think I went too far when I said my parents would lend them their house; **tu t'avances un peu en disant que je vais avoir ce boulot** you're getting ahead of yourself a bit in saying that I'm going to get this job

4 *(de promontoire etc)* to jut out; **une langue de terre s'avance dans la mer** a strip of land juts out *or* runs out into the sea

avanie [avani] NF *Litt* snub; **subir** *ou* **essuyer une a.** to be snubbed

---

AVANT [avɑ̃]

PRÉP before **1–6** ▪ by **1** ▪ within **1** ▪ until **4, 5** ▪ by the time **5**				
ADV before **1, 2** ▪ beforehand **1** ▪ far **3** ▪ late **4**				
ADJ INV front				
NM front **1, 3** ▪ forward **1**				

PRÉP SEE GRAMMAR A68; B54 **1** *(dans le temps)* before; **venez a. midi** come before twelve o'clock; **il sera ici a. une heure** he will be here by one o'clock; *(dans moins d'une heure)* he will be here within an *or* the hour; **je le verrai a. quinze jours** I shall see him within *or* in less than a fortnight; **pas a. lundi** not before Monday; **pas a. de nombreuses années** not for many years to come; **il a terminé la course a. moi** he finished the race before me *or* ahead of me; **a. son arrivée** before his arrival, before his arrival; **juste a. la pluie** just before it started to rain, just before the rain started; **800 a. Jésus-Christ** 800 BC; **a. imposition** *ou* **impôt** before tax

2 *(dans l'espace)* before; **la maison est a. la boucherie** the house is before the butcher's; **l'article se place a. le nom** the article is placed before the noun *or* in front of the noun

3 *(priorité)* **a. la ceinture noire, il y a la ceinture bleue** the blue belt comes before the black belt; **mettre** *ou* **faire passer la santé a. le reste** to put one's health above *or* before all else; **pour lui, la famille passe a. tout** for him, (the) family comes first; **a. tout** first of all, above all; **a. toute chose** before anything else, in the first place; **a. tout, il faut que tu sois satisfait** above all (else) *or* first and foremost, we want you to be satisfied

4 a. de faire before doing; **je vous reverrai a. de partir** I shall see you before I leave; **ne fais rien a. d'être tout à fait sûr** do not do anything until you are quite certain; **lave-toi les mains a. de manger** wash your hands before eating *or* you eat; *Litt* **a. que de mourir** before dying

5 je vous reverrai a. que vous (ne) partiez I shall see you again before you leave; **je serai parti a. que vous ayez fini** I shall be gone by the time (that) you have finished; **ne partez pas a. qu'on vous le dise** don't go until you are told; *Fam* **celle-là, a. qu'elle arrive!** the

time it takes (for) her to get here!

6 il est à quelques mètres en a. de nous he's a few metres in front of us; **en a. du village se trouvait une petite église** there was a little church just before the village; *Litt* **avec rien que la mort en a. de nous** with nothing but death awaiting *or* before us

ADV 1 *(auparavant)* before; *(par rapport à un événement futur)* beforehand; **a. j'avais les cheveux longs** I used to have long hair; **a. je voulais être prof** I wanted to be a teacher before; **il était arrivé quelques mois a.** he had arrived some months before *or* earlier; **réfléchis a., tu parleras après** think first, speak later; **on commencera mardi, que tout le monde ait lu la pièce a.** we'll start on Tuesday, (so) everyone make sure you've read the play beforehand; **tu ferais mieux de téléphoner a.** you'd better phone beforehand; **du pain comme on le faisait a.** bread the way they used to make it; **bien/peu a.** well/shortly before; **juste a.** just before; **il l'a mentionné a. dans la préface** he mentioned it before *or* earlier in the preface; **le jour d'a., tout était calme** the day before, everything was quiet

2 *(dans l'espace)* **n'allez pas jusqu'à l'église, sa maison est a.** don't go as far as the church, his house is before (you come to) it

3 *(loin)* far, deep; **pénétrer très a. dans les terres** to penetrate far inland; **le harpon pénétra très a. dans les chairs** the harpoon sank deep into the flesh; *Fig* **tu t'es engagé trop a.** you've got too involved, you're in too deep; **on l'a empêché de pousser plus a. son enquête** he was prevented from taking his investigation(s) any further

4 *(tard)* far, late; **très a. dans la journée** very late in the day; *Litt* **on dut attendre fort a. dans le siècle la diffusion du vaccin** vaccinations did not become readily available until well on into the century

5 en a. in front, ahead; *Mil* **en a.!** forward!; *Mil* **en a., marche!** forward march!; **en a. toute!** *Naut* full steam ahead!; *Fig* forward march!; **en a. la musique!** *(on y va)* let's be off!; *(ça recommence)* here we go again!; **il est parti en a. pour reconnaître le chemin** he set off ahead to reconnoitre the route; **envoyer qn en a.** to send sb ahead *or* on (in front); **aller en a.** to go to the front; **elle marche toujours quelques mètres en a.** she always walks a few yards in front *or* ahead; **se pencher en a.** to lean forward(s); **tomber en a.** to fall forwards; **faire deux pas en a.** to take two steps forward, to move forward two steps; *Fig* **mettre qn en a.** to push sb forward; *Fig* **mettre le règlement/la loi en a.** to hide behind the rule book *or* the law; *Fig* **mettre en a. une question** to bring up a question

ADJ INV front; **la partie a. du navire** the fore part of the ship; **roue a.** front wheel; *Aut* **à traction a.** with front-wheel drive

NM 1 *Aut, Rail, Aviat* front; *Naut* bow; *(de piston)* crank end; **l'a. de la voiture est complètement défoncé** the front of the car is completely smashed in; **les enfants ne doivent pas s'asseoir à l'a.** children may not sit in (the) front; **tu seras mieux à l'a.** you'll be better in (the) front; **le logement de l'équipage est à l'a.** the crew's quarters are forward; *Naut* **présenter l'a. à la lame** to be head to sea; **aborder un navire par l'a.** to collide with a ship head on; **par tribord a.** on the starboard bow; **sur** *ou* **à l'a. du mât** before the mast; **aller de l'a.** to go *or* forge ahead; *Fig* **lui, au moins, il allait de l'a.** at least he always forged ahead

2 *Ftbl etc* forward; **la ligne des avants** the forward line; *Rugby* **a. de deuxième ligne** second-row forward, lock (forward); **il joue a.** he plays up front

3 *Mil* **l'a.** the front

avantage [avɑ̃taʒ] NM **1** (*profit*) advantage; **a. pécuniaire** monetary gain; **a. en nature** benefit in kind, *Fam* perk; **avantages acquis** long-service benefits; **a. concurrentiel** competitive advantage; **avantages et coûts comparatifs** comparative advantages and costs; **a. fiscal** tax benefit, tax incentive; **a. matériel/personnel** material/personal gain; **avantages sociaux** social security benefits; **il ne m'en revient aucun a.** I'm not getting any advantage *or* benefit from it; **être à l'a. de qn** to be to sb's advantage; **la situation tourne à votre a.** the situation is turning to your advantage; **et voilà que Vincent cherche encore à tirer a. de la situation** there's Vincent trying to turn the situation to his advantage again; **trouver de l'a. à faire qch** to find it an advantage *or* advantageous to do sth

2 (*atout*) advantage; **présenter un a.** to have an advantage; **cette solution a l'a. d'être rapide et efficace** this solution has the advantage of being quick and effective; **les avantages que vous procure un appartement en ville** the benefits *or* advantages gained from having a flat in town; **posséder un ordinateur est un a. certain** owning a computer is a definite advantage; **sa connaissance du français lui est un a. précieux** his knowledge of French is a great asset to him; **avoir un a. sur qn** to have an advantage over sb; **avoir (sur qn) l'a. du nombre/de l'âge** to have the advantage of number/age (over sb)

3 *Jur* gift, donation; **à titre d'a.** as a gift

4 *Sp, Tennis, Fig* advantage; **donner l'a. à qn** to give sb a head start; **je vais lui donner l'a. dans la ligne droite** I'll let him go in front of me in the straight; **c'est tout à ton a. d'être arrivé en avance** it's to your advantage that you arrived early; **il a changé à son a.** he has changed for the better; **s'habiller à son a.** to dress to one's best advantage; **paraître à son a.** (*physiquement*) to look one's best; (*à un entretien*) to be at one's best; **il est à son a. en uniforme** he looks his best in uniform; **parler à l'a. de qn** to speak in sb's favour; **avoir l'a. sur qn** to have the advantage of *or* over sb; **prendre l'a.** *Sport* to go into the lead; (*sur un marché*) to become the leader; **conserver l'a.** *Sport* to stay in the lead; (*sur un marché*) to hold onto one's lead; **prendre l'a. sur qn** to take the lead from sb; **il a l'a.** the odds are in his favour; *Tennis* **a. (au) service** (*Mauresmo au service*) advantage Mauresmo; *Tennis* **a. dehors** (*Pierce au service, Mauresmo en face*) advantage Mauresmo; *Tennis* **a. Williams** advantage Williams

5 il y a a. à + *inf* it is best to, it is worth one's while to + *inf*, **il y aura a. à ce que vous soyez présent** it will be a good thing *or* just as well if you are present; **tu aurais a. à être poli la prochaine fois** you would do well to be polite next time

6 *Fml* **à quoi dois-je l'a. de votre venue?** to what do I owe the honour of your visit?; **je n'ai pas l'a. de vous connaître** I have not had the honour of making your acquaintance

avantagé [avɑ̃taʒe] ADJ **être fort a. par rapport aux autres** to enjoy many advantages over others; **a. par la nature** (*physiquement*) well endowed; *Péj* **la pauvre, elle n'a pas été avantagée par la nature!** the poor thing, nature hasn't been too kind to her!; *Sport* **joueur a.** player who has been given a start

avantager [avɑ̃taʒe] VT (**j'avantageai(s); n. avantageons**) **1** (*favoriser*) to favour, to give an advantage to; **ton expérience t'avantage par rapport aux autres candidats** your experience gives you an advantage over the other candidates; **son bégaiement ne l'avantage pas** his stammer doesn't help

him **2** (*physiquement*) **l'uniforme l'avantage** he looks his best in uniform; **cette coiffure ne l'avantage vraiment pas** that hairstyle really doesn't flatter her

avantageusement [avɑ̃taʒøzmɑ̃] ADV advantageously, to advantage; **elle sait mettre a. son décolleté en valeur** she knows how to show off her cleavage to advantage; **parler de qn a.** to speak favourably of sb

avantageux, -euse [avɑ̃taʒø, -øz] ADJ **1** (*intéressant*) advantageous, favourable; (*bon marché*) good value; *Com* **prix a.** reasonable price **2** (*flatteur*) **parler de qn en termes a.** to speak favourably of sb; **robe avantageuse** becoming dress; **portrait a.** flattering portrait **3** **poitrine avantageuse** well-developed bust **4** *Péj* (*vaniteux*) conceited, vain; **prendre un ton a.** to adopt a superior tone

avant-aile, *pl* **avant-ailes** NM *Rugby* wing-forward, flanker

avant-bassin, *pl* **avant-bassins** NM *Naut* outer basin, dock

avant-bras NM INV *Anat* forearm

avant-cale, *pl* **avant-cales** NF *Naut* fore hold

avant-centre, *pl* **avants-centres** NM *Ftbl* centre forward

avant-corps NM INV *Archit* (*d'un bâtiment*) projecting part

avant-cour, *pl* **avant-cours** NF *Archit* forecourt

avant-coureur, *pl* **avant-coureurs** NM forerunner, precursor; *Mil* scout

ADJ (*symptôme*) warning; **choc a. (de séisme)** preliminary tremor; **les signes avant-coureurs du changement** the harbingers of change

avant-dernier, -ière, *pl* **avant-derniers, -ières** ADJ last but one, second (to) last, *Fml* penultimate; **l'avant-dernière fois** the time before last

N last but one, second (to) last, next to last

avant-garde, *pl* **avant-gardes** NF **1** *Mil* advance(d) guard; **détachement d'a.** advance(d) party **2** **hommes d'a.** men in the van, pioneers; *Pol* **les éléments d'a.** the avant-garde; **livre d'a.** avant-garde book; **les découvertes de l'a.** the discoveries of the avant-garde; **technique d'a.** avant-garde technique; **être à l'a. de la mode/du progrès** to be in the vanguard *or* at the forefront of fashion/progress

avant-gardisme, *pl* **avant-gardismes** [avɑ̃gardism] NM avant-gardism

avant-gardiste, *pl* **avant-gardistes** [avɑ̃gardist] ADJ avant-garde
N avant-gardiste

avant-goût, *pl* **avant-goûts** NM foretaste, anticipation, first impression; **cela m'a donné un a. de ce qu'allait être ma vie/mon travail** it gave me a taste *or* foretaste of my life to come/of what my work would be like

avant-guerre, *pl* **avant-guerres** NM OU NF pre-war period; **la mode d'a.** pre-war fashion

avant-hier [avɑ̃tjɛr] ADV the day before yesterday; **a. au soir** the night *or* evening before last

avant-main, *pl* **avant-mains** NM **1** (*de cheval*) forequarters, forehand **2** *Tennis* **coup d'a.** forehand (stroke)

avant-midi [avɑ̃midi] NM OU NF INV *Belg, Can* morning

avant-plan, *pl* **avant-plans** NM *Beaux-Arts, Phot etc* foreground

avant-pont, *pl* **avant-ponts** NM *Naut* foredeck

avant-port, *pl* **avant-ports** NM *Naut* outer harbour

avant-poste, *pl* **avant-postes** NM *Mil* outpost

avant-première, *pl* **avant-premières** NF private view *or* viewing, preview; *Théâtre* dress rehearsal; **présenté en a.** (*film, pièce etc*) previewed, given an advanced showing

avant-programme, *pl* **avant-programmes** NM (*d'un festival*) synopsis of events

avant-propos NM INV (*de livre*) preface, foreword; *Fig* **après quelques a.** after a few preliminary remarks; **en a. à cette conférence** before the lecture gets underway, as a prelude to this lecture

avant-scène, *pl* **avant-scènes** NF *Théâtre* **1** *Antiq* proscenium, apron, forestage **2** (**loge d'**)**a.** stage box

avant-spectacle, *pl* **avant-spectacles** NM pre-show performance; **en a.** as a curtain-raiser

avant-titre, *pl* **avant-titres** NM (*d'un livre*) half-title

avant-toit, *pl* **avant-toits** NM eaves; **comble avec a.** umbrella roof

avant-train, *pl* **avant-trains** NM **1** *Aut* front-axle unit **2** (*d'une charrue*) wheels **3** *Mil* limber

avant-veille, *pl* **avant-veilles** NF two days before; **l'a. de Noël** two days before Christmas

avare [avar] ADJ **1** (*mesquin*) mean, miserly, *Fam* tight **2** **il n'est pas a. de compliments** he's generous *or* lavish with his compliments; **il n'est pas a. de ses conseils** he's only too happy to offer advice
N miser

avarice [avaris] NF avarice, miserliness; **au diable l'a.!** you can't take it with you!, to hell with the expense!

avaricieux, -ieuse [avarisjø, -jøz] ADJ miserly, avaricious, *Fam* stingy
N miser, skinflint; **un vieil a.** an old miser

avarie [avari] NF **1** (*à un bateau, moteur etc*) damage; **subir une a.** to be damaged; **faire subir une a. à qch** to damage sth **2** **déclaration d'avaries** (ship's) protest; **avaries matérielles de mer** damage done by sea water **3** **avaries-frais** average; **règlement d'avaries** adjustment of average; **répartiteur d'avaries** average adjuster

avarié [avarje] ADJ (*marchandises etc*) damaged, spoiled; (*viande, poisson etc*) rotten

avarier [avarje] (*pr sub, impf* n. **avariions**, v. **avariiez**) VT (*marchandises etc*) to damage
VPR **s'avarier** (*nourriture etc*) to go off, to go bad, to rot; (*denrées non comestibles*) to be damaged

avatar [avatar] NM **1** (*transformation*) transformation, change, metamorphosis; **avatars** (*de la vie politique etc*) ups and downs, vicissitudes **2** (*mésaventure*) mishap, misadventure **3** (*incarnation*) avatar, incarnation **4** *Ordinat* avatar

Ave [ave] NM Ave; **l'A. Maria** the Hail Mary

AVEC [avɛk]

| PRÉP with **1-5, 7-9** ▪ in spite of **5** ▪ to **8** |

PRÉP **1** with; **je vous ai vu a. lui** I saw you with him; **je crois a. vous que ...** like you, I believe that ...; **le public est a. nous** the public is with *or* behind us; **a. qui viendras-tu?** who are you coming with?, *Fml* with whom are you coming?; **être bien/mal a. qn** to be getting on well/badly with sb; **un pavillon a. garage** a detached house with a garage; **elle ressemble à sa sœur, a. des traits plus réguliers** she is like her sister, but with more regular features

2 (*manière*) **a. enthousiasme/tristesse** enthusiastically/sadly, with enthusiasm/sadness; **a. beaucoup de gentillesse** very kindly, with great kindness; **a. beaucoup de franchise** very candidly; **elle danse a. beaucoup de grâce** she dances very gracefully; **c'est a. émotion que j'accepte le poste** I'm thrilled to accept the job; **mots dits a. colère** words spoken in anger

3 *(simultanéité)* **la capacité pulmonaire diminue a. l'âge** lung capacity decreases with age; **l'oxygène se raréfie a. l'altitude** air becomes thinner with altitude; **cela viendra a. le temps** that will come in *or* with time; **il se lève a. le soleil** he gets up at sunrise; **il est arrivé a. la nuit** he arrived when it was getting dark, he arrived at nightfall; **le paysage change a. les saisons** the countryside changes with the seasons

4 *(à cause de)* **a. tous les ennuis qu'il a eus, il ne sait plus où donner de la tête** with all the problems he's had, he doesn't know whether he's coming or going; **a. cette sécheresse, rien ne pousse** nothing will grow with this drought; **impossible de sortir a. cette pluie/ce temps** it's impossible to go out in *or* with this rain/weather

5 *(malgré)* **a. tous ses défauts, il a quand même réussi à se faire accepter** with *or* in spite of all his faults, he has still managed to become accepted; **a. tout le respect que je vous dois** with all due respect

6 *(moyen)* **a. l'aide de qn** with sb's help; **ouvrir une porte a. une clef** to open a door with a key; **a. 2000 euros par mois, on s'en sort très bien** you can get by *or* manage perfectly well on *or* with 2,000 euros per month; **je fais toujours mes devoirs a. de la musique** I always have music on when I'm doing my homework; **aujourd'hui, on va faire notre gymnastique a. de la musique** today we're going to do our gymnastics to music; **je m'endors mieux a. de la musique** I fall asleep more quickly with music on; **je préfère travailler a. la lumière du jour** I prefer to work in daylight; **j'ai eu un accident a. cet avion** I had an accident in this plane

7 *(contre)* **lutter a. qch** to struggle with sth; **se battre a. qn** to fight (with) sb

8 *(à l'égard de)* **elle est toujours gentille a. moi/les enfants** she's always nice to me/ children; **c'est un amour a. sa femme** he's a darling to his wife; **être dur a. qn** to be hard on sb; **être franc a. qn** to be frank with sb

9 *(en ce qui concerne)* **a. elle, on ne sait jamais** you never can tell with her; **a. toi, c'est toujours pareil** it's always the same with you, it's always the same old story with you; **tu sais bien qu'a. lui on peut avoir confiance** you know that he can be trusted; **a. le caractère qu'elle a** with her character; *Fam* **il nous embête a. ses problèmes de famille!** he's driving us mad with all his family problems!

10 *Fam* **elle est grande, mince, athlétique, et sympa a. ça** she's tall, slim, athletic, and what's more, she's nice; **et a. (tout) ça, il n'est pas content!** and he still isn't happy!; **... et ne me dis pas a. (tout) ça qu'il n'a pas triché!** ... and don't tell me after all that that he didn't cheat!; **et a. cela** *ou* **ceci, madame?** anything else, madam?

11 *(à partir de)* **d'a.** from; **distinguer** *ou* **séparer le bon d'a. le mauvais** to distinguish (the) good from (the) bad; **divorcer d'a. sa femme** to divorce one's wife

ADV *Fam* with it; with them; **il a pris la caisse et s'est sauvé a.** he ran off with the takings; **j'espérais qu'il laisserait sa femme à la maison, malheureusement, il est venu a.** I was hoping he'd leave his wife at home, unfortunately he brought her with him; **nous n'avions qu'un vieux tourne-disque, il a bien fallu faire a.** we only had an old record player so we had to make do (with it); *Région* **tu viens a.?** are you coming too?

aveline [avlin] **NF** *(fruit)* hazel nut, cob (nut)

avelinier [avlinje] **NM** *(arbre)* hazel

aven [avɛn] **NM** *Géol* swallowhole

avenant [avnɑ̃] **ADJ** *(personne, manières etc)* pleasant, gracious

NM 1 à l'a. in keeping, correspondingly; **ils se sont conduits à l'a.** they acted accordingly; **le bâtiment est beau et le jardin est à l'a.** the building is beautiful and the garden is in keeping with it **2** *(de traité)* codicil **3** *(de police d'assurance)* additional clause, endorsement **4** *(de verdict)* rider

avènement [avɛnmɑ̃] **NM 1** *(du Christ etc)* advent; *(d'un messie)* coming; **depuis l'a. de l'automobile** since the advent of the (motor)car **2** *(accession)* advent, coming, arrival; **a. au trône** accession to the throne

avenir[1] [av(ə)nir] **NM** future; **qu'est-ce que l'a. nous réserve?** what does the future hold for us?, what has the future in store for us?; **prédire l'a.** to predict the future; **jeune homme d'un grand a.** *ou* **de beaucoup d'a.** young man with a great future ahead of him; **c'est un homme d'a.** he's an up-and-coming man *or* a man with a (promising) future; *Sport* **un joueur d'a.** a coming player; **un métier d'a.** a career with good prospects; **un avocat d'a.** a lawyer with a great future (ahead of him), an up-and-coming lawyer; **situation sans a.** job with no future *or* prospects, dead-end job; **assurer l'a. de qn** to make provision for sb; **dans l'a.** in the future, at some future date; **dans un a. très prochain** in the very near *or* in the immediate future; **à l'a., je serai plus circonspect** in future, I shall be more cautious

avenir[2] **NM INV** *Jur (à l'avocat de la partie adverse)* writ of summons; **signifier un a. à la partie adverse** to serve a writ on the other party

Avent [avɑ̃] **NM** *Rel* Advent

aventure [avɑ̃tyr] **NF 1** adventure; **tu ne peux pas savoir l'a. qui m'est encore arrivée** you can't imagine the adventure I've just had *or* what's just happened to me; **homme d'aventures** adventurous man, adventurer; **film d'aventures** adventure film; **a. effrayante** terrifying experience; **pour trouver des fruits en hiver, c'est toute une a.** it's quite a business *or Fam* a heck of a job finding fruit in winter

2 *(liaison)* (love) affair; **il collectionne les aventures (amoureuses)** he has one affair after another

3 *(hasard)* chance, luck; **tenter l'a.** to try one's luck; **vie d'a.** life of adventure; **l'a. est au coin de la rue** the unexpected is always round the corner; **à l'a.** at random; **aller** *ou* **errer à l'a.** to wander about aimlessly; **partir à l'a.** to set off in search of adventure; **vivre à l'a.** to live in a happy-go-lucky fashion; *Litt* **par a., d'a.** by chance

4 la bonne a. fortune-telling; **dire** *ou* **tirer la bonne a. à qn** to tell sb's fortune; **diseuse de bonne a.** fortune teller

aventuré [avɑ̃tyre] **ADJ** risky, chancy

aventurer [avɑ̃tyre] **VT** *(sa vie etc)* to risk; **a. une grosse somme d'argent** to risk *or* venture a large sum of money

VPR s'aventurer to venture (**dans** into); **s'a. en pays inconnu** to venture into an unknown country; *Fig* **s'a. en terrain glissant** to venture into dangerous territory; **je ne m'aventurerai pas à dire que ...** I won't go so far as to say ...

aventureusement [avɑ̃tyrøzmɑ̃] **ADV** adventurously

aventureux, -euse [avɑ̃tyrø, -øz] **ADJ** adventurous; **homme a. au jeu** reckless gambler; **projet a.** hazardous *or* risky plan

aventurier, -ière [avɑ̃tyrje, -jɛr] **N** adventurer, *f* adventuress

aventurisme [avɑ̃tyrism] **NM** *Pol* adventurism

avenue [avny] **NF** *(de ville)* avenue; *(menant à une maison)* drive(way); **les avenues du pouvoir** the paths to power

avéré [avere] **ADJ** *(fait)* recognized, established; **ennemi a.** avowed enemy; **marxistes avérés** professed Marxists; **il est a. que ...** it is confirmed that ...

avérer [avere] (**j'avère, n. avérons; j'avérerai**) **VT** *Jur Vieilli (fait)* to aver

VPR s'avérer to be proved (correct), to be confirmed; **elle s'est avérée indispensable dans l'équipe** she's proved to be *or* turned out to be an essential member of the team; **il s'est avéré que ...** it's turned out that ..., as it's turned out, ...

avers [aver] **NM** *(de monnaie)* obverse

averse [avers] **NF** sudden shower, downpour; **essuyer une a.** to be caught in a shower; *Fig* **une a. de félicitations** a flood *or* stream of congratulations

aversion [aversjɔ̃] **NF** aversion (**pour** to, for), dislike (**pour** for, of); **avoir une a.** *ou* **de l'a. pour** *ou* **contre qn** to have an aversion to *or* for sb, to have a dislike for sb; **prendre qn en a.** to take a dislike to sb

averti [averti] **ADJ** *(bien informé)* (well-)informed; *(expérimenté)* experienced; **un homme a.** an experienced man, an expert; *Prov* **un homme a. en vaut deux** forewarned is forearmed; **a. de qch** aware *or* warned of sth; **se tenir pour a.** to take a warning; **vous voilà a.!** I give you fair warning!, don't say I haven't warned you!

avertir [avertir] **VT a. qn de qch** to inform sb of sth; **a. qn du danger d'une situation** to warn *or* tell sb of *or* about the danger(s) of a situation; **je l'en avais averti** I had warned him of *or* against it; **je vous en avertis!** I give you fair warning!; **je vais me mettre en colère, je t'avertis!** I'm going to get angry, I'm warning you!; *Ordinat* **a. de la réception de** to acknowledge

> Il faut noter que le verbe anglais **to advertise** est un faux ami. Il ne signifie jamais **avertir**.

avertissement [avertismɑ̃] **NM 1** *(avis préalable)* warning; **renvoyer qn sans a. préalable** to discharge sb at a moment's notice; **lettre envoyée à titre d'a.** letter sent as a reminder; *(avis)* warning letter **2** *(réprimande)* warning, reprimand; *Sport (de l'arbitre)* warning, caution **3** *(signal)* danger signal *or* sign, warning signal; **a. de tempête** gale warning; **a. (au lecteur)** foreword (to book); *Ordinat* **a. de réception** *(de message)* acknowledgement; *Ordinat* **a. à réception d'un courrier** mail received message **4** *Jur* **billet d'a.** summons to appear before a magistrate **5** *Admin* demand note

> Il faut noter que le nom anglais **advertisement** est un faux ami. Il signifie **publicité** ou **annonce**, selon le contexte.

avertisseur, -euse [avertisœr, -øz] **NM 1** *(dispositif)* warning signal, alarm; *Aut* horn; *Ind* hooter; *Rail* signal; **a. d'incendie** fire alarm; **a. sonore** warning buzzer; *(Klaxon®)* horn; **avertisseurs sonores interdits après 22.00 heures** no sounding of horns after 10 p.m.; *Aut* **a. de marche arrière** reversing beeper; *Aut* **a. deux tons** two-tone horn; **a. lumineux** warning light; **a. optique** warning light **2** *Théâtre* callboy

ADJ signal a. warning signal

aveu, -eux [avø] **NM 1** *(confession)* confession, acknowledgement; *Jur* admission; **faire l'a. d'une erreur** to own up *or* confess to a mistake; **passer aux aveux** to make a confession; **faire des aveux complets** to make a full confession; **de son a. même, il est ruiné** on his own admission, he's bankrupt; **je dois vous faire un a., je n'y étais pas non plus** I must confess or admit, I wasn't there either, I have to tell you, I wasn't there either; **arracher des aveux à un accusé** to drag or wring or wrest a confession out of or from a defendant; **il est certain, de l'a. de tout le monde, que ...** it is commonly acknowledged that ... **2** *Jur* consent, authorization; **obtenir l'a. de qn pour faire qch** to obtain sb's consent to do sth **3** *Hist* recognition between a vassal and his overlord; **homme sans a.** vagabond, vagrant

aveuglant [avœglɑ̃] **ADJ** blinding, dazzling; *Fig* **une évidence/preuve aveuglante** a glaringly or patently or blindingly obvious fact/proof

aveugle [avœgl] **ADJ 1** *(atteint de cécité)* blind; **devenir a.** to go blind; **a. d'un œil** blind in one eye; **être a. de naissance, naître a.** to be born blind, to be blind from birth; *Opt* **point a.** blind spot **2** *Archit Fig* **fenêtre/arcade a.** blind window/arch; **mur a.** blind wall; *Tech* **écrou a.** blind nut; **trou a.** dead hole; **bout a. (d'un tuyau)** blind end **3** *(haine)* blind, unreasoning; *(confiance)* implicit; **avoir une confiance a. en qn** to trust sb implicitly or unreservedly; **obéissance a.** blind or unquestioning obedience; **son amour pour elle le rend a.** he's blinded by his love for her
▪ **N** blind man, *f* blind woman; **les aveugles** the blind; *Fig* **suivre qn en a.** to follow sb blindly; *Vieilli* **aller à l'a.** to grope one's way

aveuglement [avœɡləmɑ̃] **NM 1** *(moral, mental)* blindness; **l'a. de la passion/de la colère** the blindness of passion/of anger **2** *Arch* blinding; **depuis son a.** since his blindness

aveuglément [avœɡlemɑ̃] **ADV** blindly; **obéir a.** to obey blindly

aveugle-né, -née, *pl* **aveugles-nés, -nées** **ADJ** *(homme, femme)* blind from birth
▪ **N** congenitally blind person, person blind from birth

aveugler [avœgle] **VT 1** *(rendre aveugle)* to blind **2** *(de la lumière etc)* to blind, to dazzle; *Fig* **aveuglé par la colère** blind with rage; *Fig* **son amour pour elle l'aveugle** he's blinded by his love for her **3** *Naut* **a. une voie d'eau** to stop a leak **4** *(boucher)* to plug, to stop (up), to block up; **a. une fenêtre** to wall up or block a window
▪ **VPR s'aveugler** *Fig* to be blind, to shut one's eyes (**sur qch** to sth); **il ne faut pas t'a., ça ne sera pas facile** don't delude yourself or *Fam* kid yourself, it won't be easy; **s'a. sur les défauts de qn** to shut one's eyes or turn a blind eye to sb's faults

aveuglette (à l') [alavœglɛt] **ADV** blindly; **aller à l'a.** to feel or grope one's way; **avancer à l'a. vers qch** to feel or grope one's way to(-wards) sth; *Fig* **choisir qch à l'a.** to choose sth at random or in the dark or blindly; **lancer des coups à l'a.** to hit out blindly; *Aviat* **voler à l'a.** to fly blind

aveulir [avølir] **VT** *Litt* to enervate; *(sentiments)* to deaden
▪ **VPR s'aveulir** to be effete

aveulissement [avølismɑ̃] **NM** effeteness

aviaire [avjɛr] **ADJ** **peste a.** fowl plague or pest

aviateur, -trice [avjatœr, -tris] **N** aviator

aviation [avjasjɔ̃] **NF 1** *(activité)* flying, aviation; **aimer l'a.** to like flying; **il fait de l'a. le week-end** he goes flying at the weekends; **école d'a.** flying school, school of aviation **2** *(secteur)* aviation; **a. civile/commerciale** civil/commercial aviation; **a. de tourisme** civil aviation; **champ** *ou* **terrain d'a.** airfield; **usine d'a.** aircraft factory; **compagnie d'a.** airline **3** *Mil* air force; **base d'a.** air base

avicole [avikɔl] **ADJ** **élevage a.** *(activité)* poultry farming; *(établissement)* poultry farm

aviculteur, -trice [avikyltœr, -tris] **N** poultry farmer

aviculture [avikyltyr] **NF 1** *(d'oiseaux)* aviculture **2** *(de volailles)* poultry farming

avide [avid] **ADJ 1** *(passionné)* eager, avid, greedy; **a. de qch** *(âpre)* greedy for sth; *(plein d'enthousiasme)* eager for sth; **espérances avides** eager hopes; **a. de sang** bloodthirsty; **a. de tout savoir** eager for knowledge **2** *Péj* greedy, covetous (**de** of); *(mains, nature)* grasping

avidement [avidmɑ̃] **ADV** greedily, hungrily; **écouter a.** to listen eagerly or avidly

avidité [avidite] **NF** avidity, greed(iness); *(de nourriture)* greed, gluttony; **manger avec a.** to eat greedily; **écouter avec a.** to listen eagerly or avidly

Avignon [aviɲɔ̃] **NF** *Géog* Avignon; **à** *ou* **en Avignon** in Avignon; *Théâtre* **le festival d'Avignon** the Avignon festival

Le festival d'Avignon

Founded by Jean Vilar in 1947 and held every summer in Avignon in the South of France, this arts festival is a showcase for new theatre and dance performances: "La pièce sera donnée d'abord en Avignon". Along with the programme of official shows ("le in") performed in prestigious venues such as the Court of Honour of the "Palais des Papes", a programme comprising numerous fringe shows, referred to as "le off", has also been performed since the 1970s.

avili [avili] **ADJ 1** *(personne)* degraded, debased, demeaned **2** *Com (monnaie, système monétaire)* debased; *(biens)* depreciated

avilir [avilir] **VT 1** *(dégrader)* to degrade, to debase, to lower **2** *Com (monnaie, prix etc)* to depreciate, to lower, to bring down
▪ **VPR s'avilir 1** *(d'une personne)* to lower or demean oneself **2** *(de biens)* to depreciate, to come down (in value)

avilissant [avilisɑ̃] **ADJ** debasing, degrading

avilissement [avilismɑ̃] **NM 1** *(dégradation)* debasement, degradation **2** *Com* depreciation; *(de prix)* fall

aviné [avine] **ADJ** *(attrib)* intoxicated, inebriated; **haleine avinée** breath reeking of wine

aviner [avine] **VT** *(tonneau)* to impregnate with wine

avion [avjɔ̃] **NM** aeroplane, aircraft, plane, *Am* airplane; **j'ai fait une partie du trajet en a.** I flew part of the journey; **par a.** (by) airmail; **voyager en a.** to travel by plane or air, to fly; **prendre l'a. pour aller à Londres** to get or take the plane to London, to fly to London; **accident d'a.** plane crash; **détournement d'a.** hijacking, hijack, skyjacking
▪▶ **a. d'attaque au sol** ground attack aircraft; **a. bimoteur** twin-engine aircraft; **a. de bombardement** bomber; **a. charter** charter plane; **a. de chasse** fighter (plane); **a. commercial** commercial aircraft; **a. à décollage et atterrissage courts** short take-off and landing aircraft; **a. à décollage et atterrissage verticaux** vertical take-off and landing aircraft; **a. furtif** stealth bomber; **a. à géométrie variable** swing-wing aircraft; **a. gros porteur** jumbo jet, wide bodied aircraft; **a. à hélices** prop jet; **a. de ligne** airliner, passenger aircraft; **a. mixte** passenger and cargo plane; **a. moyen porteur** regular bodied aircraft; **a. de pénétration** intruder; **a. petit porteur** narrow bodied aircraft; **a. ravitailleur** tanker; **a. à réaction** jet, jet plane, jet aircraft; **a. de reconnaissance** reconnaissance aircraft; **a. supersonique** supersonic aircraft; **a. de tourisme** private aircraft; **a. transbordeur** air ferry; **a. de transport** transport aircraft

avion-cargo, *pl* **avions-cargos** **NM** freight plane, cargo plane

avion-citerne, *pl* **avions-citernes** **NM** *Aviat* tanker (aircraft)

avion-école, *pl* **avions-écoles** [avjɔ̃ekɔl] **NM** trainer, training aircraft

avion-espion, *pl* **avions-espions** [avjɔ̃ɛspjɔ̃] **NM** spy plane

avionique [avjɔnik] **NF** *Aviat* avionics

avionneur [avjɔnœr] **NM 1** *(concepteur)* airframe designer **2** *(constructeur)* airframe manufacturer

avion-suicide, *pl* **avions-suicides** **NM** suicide plane

avion-taxi, *pl* **avions-taxis** **NM** air taxi, taxiplane

aviron [avirɔ̃] **NM 1** *(rame)* oar, *Can* (canoe) paddle; **a. de couple** scull; **avirons de couple** *ou* **accouplés** double-banked oars; **avirons de** *ou* **en pointe** single-banked oars; **a. de galère** sweep; **les avirons dans l'eau!** hold water!; **engager son a.** to catch a crab; **coup d'a.** stroke **2** *Sport* **l'a.** rowing; **cercles d'a.** rowing clubs; **faire de l'a.** to row

avironner [avirɔne] **VI** *Can (en canoë)* to paddle

avis [avi] **NM 1** *(opinion)* opinion, judg(e)ment; **a. d'expert** expert advice or opinion; **exprimer** *ou* **émettre un a.** to express a view or an opinion; **être du même a. que qn** to be of the same opinion as sb; **ne pas être du même a. que qn** to disagree with sb; **sauf meilleur a., je crois que ...** with all due deference, I think that ...; *Prov* **deux a. valent mieux qu'un** two heads are better than one; **à** *ou* **selon mon a.** in my opinion; **à mon humble a. ...** in my humble opinion ...; *Fam* **on ne t'a pas demandé ton a.!** nobody asked you!, mind your own business!, nobody asked your opinion!; **de l'a. de tous** in the opinion or judgment of all; **on dit qu'il est généreux, mais ce n'est pas l'a. de tout le monde** he's said to be generous, but not everyone would agree with that; **je suis tout à fait de votre a.** I entirely agree with you; **j'ai changé d'a.** I have changed my mind; *Hum* **elle change d'a. comme de chemise** she changes her mind like she changes her underwear; **être d'a. de faire qch** to be of a mind to do sth; **êtes-vous d'a. de rester ici?** are you for staying here?
2 *(conseil)* advice; **donner des a. à qn sur qch** to give sb some advice on or about sth; **prendre** *ou* **demander l'a. de qn** to ask sb's advice
3 *(avertissement)* notice, announcement; **a. (au public)** public notice, notice (to the public); **donner a. de qch** to give notice of sth; **donner a. à qn de qch** to advise sb of sth; *aussi Iron* **a. aux amateurs!** any takers?; **a. par écrit** notice in writing; **jusqu'à nouvel a.** until further notice, until you hear further; **à moins d'a. contraire** unless I/you/etc hear to the contrary; *Com* **au** *ou* **lettre d'a.** advice note; **suivant a.** as per advice
▪▶ *Bourse* **a. d'attribution** allotment letter; **a. de la banque** bank notification or advice; **a. de crédit** credit advice; **a. de débit** debit advice; *Com* **a. de domiciliation** domiciliation advice; *Journ* **a. éditorial** editorial opinion; *Bourse* **a. d'exécution** contract note; **a. d'expédition** *(de marchandises)* dispatch or consignment note; **a. d'expédition stan-**

dard *(de marchandises)* standard shipping note; **a. d'imposition** tax assessment; **a. de licenciement** redundancy notice; **a. de livraison** delivery note; **a. de paiement** payment advice; **a. de prélèvement** direct debit advice; **a. de réception** acknowledgement (of receipt); **a. de rejet** *(de chèque)* notice of returned cheque; *Banque* **a. de virement** (bank) transfer advice

avisé [avize] **ADJ** sensible, wise, prudent; **être trop a. pour faire qch** to be too sensible *or* cautious *or* wary to do sth; **il est trop a. pour ...** he knows better than to ...; **acheteur a.** discriminating purchaser; **bien a.** well-advised; **mesures mal avisées** ill-advised measures; **tu serais mal a. de ...** you'd be ill-advised to ...

aviser [avize] **VT 1** *(informer)* to inform, to notify, to advise; **a. qn de qch** to inform *or* warn *or Com* advise sb of sth; **a. qn de faire qch** to give sb notice to do sth; **a. qn que ... +** *ind* to warn sb that ... **2** *Arch, Litt (entrevoir)* to perceive, to catch a glimpse of
VI a. à *(situation etc)* to decide what to do about, to see about *or* to; **vous ferez bien d'y a.** you had better look into it; **a. à faire qch** to see about doing sth; **a. à ce que qch se fasse** to take steps to have sth done; **il est temps d'a.** it is time to decide *or* to make up one's mind; **j'aviserai en temps voulu** I'll see to that when it's necessary
VPR s'aviser 1 s'a. de qch to think of sth; **il ne s'avise de rien** he's not aware of anything; **s'a. que** to notice that, to become aware that, to realize that **2 s'a. de faire qch** to take it upon oneself to do sth; **ne vous en avisez pas!** don't dare to do such a thing!, don't you dare!, you'd better not!; **et ne t'avise pas de recommencer!** don't (you) dare start again!

aviso [avizo] **NM** *Naut* sloop; **a.-torpilleur** torpedo gunboat; **a. d'escorte** corvette; **canonnière-a.** gunboat

avitaminose [avitaminoz] **NF** vitamin deficiency, avitaminosis

aviver [avive] **VT 1** *(couleurs)* to brighten; *(image)* to touch up; *(plaie, blessure)* to irritate; *(passion)* to excite, to stir up; *(feu)* to fan, to revive, to stir up; *(appétit)* to sharpen; *(querelle)* to stir up; **a. d'anciennes rancunes** to revive ancient grudges **2** *(ferronnerie)* to burnish; *(marbre)* to polish **3** *(surfaces à souder)* to clean up **4** *(outil etc)* to put a keen edge on, to whet
VPR s'aviver *(souvenirs, controverse etc)* to be stirred up, to be revived; *(couleur)* to become brighter

av. J.-C. *(abrév* avant Jésus-Christ) BC

avocat¹, -ate [avɔka, -at] **N 1** *Jur* lawyer, *surtout Am* attorney; *(à la barre) Br* barrister, *Am* trial lawyer *or* attorney; **plaider par a.** to be represented by counsel; **elle est a. ou avocate** she's a lawyer **2** *Fig* advocate; **a. du diable** devil's advocate
▶▶**a. conseil** legal adviser; **a. consultant** counsel in chamber; **a. général** assistant public prosecutor (in a court of appeal)

avocat² **NM** *(fruit)* avocado (pear)

avocat-avoué, *pl* **avocats-avoués NM** ≃ attorney

avocatier [avɔkatje] **NM** *(arbre)* avocado (tree)

avocette [avɔsɛt] **NF** *(oiseau)* avocet

avoine [avwan] **NF 1** oats; **a. commune** common oats; **farine d'a.** oatmeal; **flocons d'a.** porridge oats; **bouillie d'a.** (oatmeal) porridge; **galette d'a.** oatcake **2** *Arg (argent)* dough, *Br* dosh

AVOIR¹ [avwar] *(prp* ayant; *pp* eu; *pr ind* j'ai, tu as, il a, n. avons, v. avez, ils ont; *pr sub* j'aie, tu aies, il ait, n. ayons, v. ayez, ils aient; *imp* aie, ayons, ayez; *impf* j'avais; *p hist* j'eus,

tu eus, il eut, n. eûmes, v. eûtes, ils eurent; *impf sub* j'eusse; *fu* j'aurai; avoir *is the auxiliary of all transitive and of many intransitive verbs)*

VT to have **1, 2, 4, 7, 10** ▪ to get **2, 5** ▪ to be **3, 8** ▪ to hit **5** ▪ to make **6** ▪ to give **6**
V IMPERS to be **1, 4**
V AUX to have

VT VOIR GRAMMAIRE A55–7 **1** *(maison, télévision, sœur, enfant, animal domestique)* to have; **tu ne veux pas a. d'enfants?** do you not want to have children?; **elle vient d'a. un enfant** she's just had a child; **quel diplôme avez-vous?** what degree have you got?, what degree do you have?; **il donnerait tout ce qu'il a pour ...** he'd give everything he's got *or* he has to ...; **on a 4 heures d'anglais par semaine** we have *or* we've got 4 hours (of) English a week; *Fam* **faut que j'y aille, j'ai math!** I've got to go, I've got maths!; **j'ai Monsieur Lê comme professeur de math** I've got *or* I've got maths; **j'ai Bill pour ami/voisin** Bill is a friend/neighbour of mine; **a. un entretien/une dispute/une conversation avec qn** to have an interview/an argument/a conversation with sb; **j'ai rendez-vous chez le médecin** I have *or* I've got a doctor's appointment; **a. des amis à dîner** to have friends to *or* for dinner; **je te rappelle que nous avons des amis à dîner ce soir** remember we're having friends to *or* for dinner tonight; **as-tu de quoi manger/vivre?** have you (got) enough to eat/live on?, do you have enough to eat/live on?; **ça coûte cher d'a. une voiture** it's expensive to run a car; **qu'est-ce que vous avez là?** what have you (got) there?; **c'est un joli collier que vous avez là** that's a pretty necklace you have *or* you've got there; **il a encore son père** his father is still alive, he's still got his father; **Dieu ait son âme** God rest his/her soul
2 *(obtenir)* to get; **j'ai eu sa réponse ce matin** I had *or* got his answer this morning; **pourriez-vous m'a. ce renseignement?** could you get that information for me?; **j'ai eu du mal à a. Paris/le numéro** *(au téléphone)* I've had trouble getting (through to) Paris/the number; **c'est lui que j'ai eu au téléphone hier** he's the one I talked to *or* had on the phone yesterday; **j'ai bien eu mon train ce matin** I caught my train all right this morning; **j'ai eu ce réfrigérateur à bon marché** I got *or* bought this refrigerator cheap; **celui-là, je l'aime et je l'aurai!** *(je le séduirai)* I love that man and I'll get him! *or* I'm going to have him!
3 *(mesure, âge)* **a. dix ans** to be ten (years old); **le mur a trois mètres de haut** the wall is three metres high; **a. plusieurs centaines de mètres de profondeur/de longueur/de largeur** to be several hundred metres deep/long/broad
4 *(dans les descriptions physiques et morales)* to have; **a. les yeux bleus** to have blue eyes; **a. de grandes mains/de beaux yeux** to have big hands/beautiful eyes; **a. les cheveux longs** to have long hair; **je commence à a. des cheveux blancs** I'm starting to get a few grey hairs; **a. du charme** to have charm, to be full of charm; **elle a du talent** she has (got) talent; **il a beaucoup d'ambition** he's got a lot of ambition; **elle a beaucoup d'humour** she has (got) a good sense of humour; **elle avait un foulard sur les cheveux** she had a scarf in her hair; **elle avait une jolie robe bleue** she had a pretty blue dress on; **il avait un bébé dans les bras** he had a baby in his arms
5 *(toucher)* to hit, to get; *Fam (duper)* to take for a ride, to con; **je crois que je l'ai eue** *(cible)* I think I hit *or* got it; **on les aura!** we'll get them!; **il finira par se faire a.** *(par la po-*

lice) he'll end up getting done (by the police); **on l'a eu!** *(dupé)* he's been had!, he's been taken for a ride!; **je t'ai eu!** got you!; **tu m'as bien eu cette fois-ci!** you really got me that time!, I really fell for it that time!; **se faire a.** to be had, to be taken for a ride; **je veux acheter une voiture d'occasion, mais je ne veux pas me faire a.** I want to buy a second-hand car, but I don't want to get ripped off *or* done *or* conned; **je me suis fait a. de 50 euros** I got done out of 50 euros
6 *(faire)* **il eut un mouvement brusque** he made a sudden movement; **il eut un sourire** he gave a smile; **il eut un cri de surprise** he gave a cry of surprise; **il eut un petit rire moqueur** he gave a mocking little laugh; **il eut un regard étrange** he gave a strange look
7 *(souffrir de)* to have; **a. un rhume/la grippe/le hoquet** to have a cold/(the) flu/(the) hiccups; **a. du diabète/du cholestérol** to have diabetes/excess cholesterol; **a. mal au cœur** to feel sick; **a. de la fièvre** to have a *or* be running a temperature; **a. la rougeole** to have measles
8 *(éprouver)* **qu'avez-vous?, qu'est-ce que vous avez?** what's wrong *or* the matter *or* up (with you)?; **je ne sais pas ce que j'ai, je ne me sens pas bien du tout** I don't know what's wrong *or* the matter with me, I don't feel at all well; **mais qu'est-ce qu'elle a, cette auto?** what's wrong *or* the matter with this car?; **qu'est-ce que tu as? – j'ai que je suis en colère!** what's wrong with you? – I'm angry, that's what's wrong with me!; **mais qu'est-ce qu'elle a à râler tout le temps?** what's the matter with her, moaning all the time?; **a. de la peine** to be upset; **a. des soucis** to be worried; **a. des doutes** to have misgivings; **a. des remords** to feel remorse
9 *(après en)* **nous en avons pour deux heures** it will take us two hours, we'll be two hours; **j'en ai pour une minute** I won't be a minute; **tu en auras pour combien de temps?** how long will you be?, how long will it take you?; **j'en ai assez, je n'en veux plus** I've had enough, I don't want any more; **j'en ai assez** *ou Fam* **marre** *ou Fam* **ras le bol** I've had enough *or Fam* I've had it up to here *or Fam* I'm sick (to the back teeth) of it; **j'en ai eu pour 100 euros** *(c'est le prix)* it cost me 100 euros; *(en quantité)* I had 100 euros' worth; **en a. contre** *ou* **après qn** to have it in for sb
10 a. qch à faire to have sth to do; **pourquoi tu t'en vas? – parce que j'ai à faire** why are you leaving? – because I have things to do; **je n'ai rien à faire** I have nothing to do; **j'ai à travailler** I've work to do; **vous n'avez pas à vous inquiéter** you have no need to worry; **tu n'as pas à te mêler de cette histoire** you shouldn't get mixed up in this matter; **je n'ai que faire de cela** I don't need that
11 for the verbal phrases **a. affaire, faim, froid, pitié, raison** etc, see under these words SEE GRAMMAR B66

V IMPERS il y a 1 *(être présent)* **il y a un problème** there is a problem; **il y a des problèmes** there are problems; **qu'est-ce qu'il peut (bien) y a. dans ce tiroir?** I wonder what's in this drawer; **qu'est-ce qu'il y a à voir?** what is there to see?; **combien y a-t-il de blessés?** how many wounded are there?; **il n'y en a qu'un** there is only one; **il n'y en aura pas assez pour tout le monde** there won't be enough for everyone; **il n'y en a que pour elle** she gets all the attention; **un homme comme il y en a peu** a man in a million; **une petite fille tout ce qu'il y a de gentil** the nicest little girl you've ever seen; **il y a du soleil aujourd'hui** it's sunny today, the sun is shining today; **il n'y a pas de quoi!** please don't mention it!, you're welcome!; *Fam* **quand (il) y en a pour deux, (il) y en a pour trois** there's more than enough to go round; *Fam* **quand (il n')y en a plus, (il) y en**

a encore there'll be plenty more when that's finished; *(comme on apporte encore de la nourriture)* as soon as one lot is finished, another one is on its way; **il y a hôpital et hôpital!** there are hospitals and hospitals!; **il y en a qui disent que ...** there are people who say that ..., some people say that ...; **il y en a un qui va être surpris** someone is in for a surprise; **il n'y a que lui qui ... + subj** he's the only one who ..., it's only him that ...; **il n'y a qu'à demander** you only have to ask, just ask; **il n'y a pas à hésiter, il faut lui parler** there's no point in hanging about, I/you/we/*etc* have to talk to him; *Fam* **il n'y a pas à dire, tu es plus fort que moi** there's no denying it *or* there's no question, you're stronger than I am; **à l'entendre, y'a qu'à faire ceci, y'a qu'à faire cela, c'est trop simple** listening to him and his just do this, just do that, it's all too easy

2 *(se passer)* **il doit y a. quelque chose** there must be something wrong; **qu'y a-t-il à présent?** what now?; **qu'est-ce qu'il y a?** what's the matter?, what's up?; **il y a qu'on t'attendait hier** we were expecting you yesterday, that's what's wrong *or* that's what's the matter

3 *(temps)* **il y a deux ans** two years ago; **il y avait six mois que j'attendais** I had been waiting for six months; **il y a des années qu'on ne s'est pas vus** we haven't seen each other for years; *Fam* **il y a une éternité** ages ago

4 *(distance)* **combien y a-t-il d'ici à Londres?** how far is it (from here) to London?; **il y a 5 km d'ici à Londres** it's 5 km (from here) to London

v AUX **j'ai fini** I have *or* I've finished; **j'ai fini ce matin** I finished this morning; **je n'ai pas compris** I did not *or* didn't understand; **je l'ai déjà vu** I have already seen him, I have seen him before; **l'avez-vous lu?** have you read it?; **je l'ai vu/vue hier** I saw him/her yesterday; **attendez que nous ayons fini** wait until we've finished; **j'ai eu vingt ans hier** I was twenty yesterday; **j'ai eu bientôt fini de m'habiller** I (had) soon finished dressing; **quand il eut** *ou* **a eu fini de parler** when he had finished speaking; **j'aurai bientôt fini** I shall soon have finished `SEE GRAMMAR B26–8; B38`

avoir² NM *(biens)* property, possessions; *(de société)* assets *pl*; *(capital)* capital; *(sur compte)* credit; *(attestation de crédit)* credit note; **a. de compte** account credit; **a. en banque** bank credit; *Compta* **a.-client** customer credit; *Compta* **a.-fournisseur** supplier credit; **a. en devises** foreign currency holding; **a. disponible** liquid assets; **a. fiscal** tax credit; **tout mon a.** all I possess *or* have; *Com* **doit et a.** debit and credit; **obtenir un a.** to be given credit, to obtain *or* to get credit; **je ne peux pas vous rembourser, mais je peux vous faire un a.** I can't give you your money back, but I can give you a credit note

avoirdupoi(d)s [avwardypwa] NM avoirdupois

avoisinant [avwazinã] ADJ neighbouring, nearby; **il a cinquante ans ou un âge a.** he's fifty or thereabout(s); **il a volé une somme avoisinante de 500 euros** he has stolen a sum of around 500 euros *or* close to 500 euros

avoisiner [avwazine] VT **a. qch** to be near *or* close to *or* adjacent to sth, to border on sth; **il a volé une somme avoisinant les 500 euros** he has stolen a sum of around 500 euros *or* close to 500 euros; **cela avoisine la malhonnêteté** it's bordering on dishonesty

avortement [avɔrtəmã] NM **1** *(chez une femme)* **a. spontané** miscarriage; **a. provoqué** abortion; **a. thérapeutique** termination *or* abortion (for medical reasons) **2** *(chez un animal)* casting **3** *Fig (de projet etc)* failure, falling through

avorter [avɔrte] VI **1** *(d'une femme) (faire une fausse couche)* to miscarry; **elle veut a.** she wants (to have) an abortion; **faire a. qn** to give sb an abortion; *(d'une injection etc)* to induce a miscarriage in sb **2** *(d'un animal)* to cast **3** *Bot* to develop imperfectly, to fail to abort; **arbres avortés** stunted trees **4** *Fig* **projet qui a avorté** plan that fell through

vt *(médecin)* to abort; **se faire a.** to have an abortion

avorteur, -euse [avɔrtœr, -øz] N abortionist

avorton [avɔrtɔ̃] NM *(personne, animal)* runt; *(plante)* stunted plant; *Péj* **espèce d'a.!** you little shrimp *or* squirt!

avouable [avwabl] ADJ *(fait, motif)* avowable; **c'est un métier plus a.** it's a more respectable trade

avoué¹ [avwe] NM *Jur Br* ≃ solicitor, *Am* ≃ attorney

avoué² ADJ **1** *(fait)* acknowledged, admitted **2** *(auteur, partisan)* confessed; **il est le père a. de cette petite fille** he admits he's the father of this little girl **3** *(but)* confessed; **il est allé là-bas dans le but a. de se venger** he went there ostensibly *or* supposedly for revenge

avouer [avwe] VT *(faute etc)* to confess, to admit, to own up to; **elle ne veut pas a. que c'est elle qui a pris l'argent** she won't admit that she took the money; **elle avoue avoir trente ans** she admits to being thirty; **ceci me surprend, je l'avoue** this surprises me, I must confess *or* admit *or* say; **il faut bien a. que c'est lui qui avait raison** it must be admitted *or* said that he was right; **a. avoir fait qch** to confess *or* to own up to having done sth

vi to confess

vpr **s'avouer** to admit (to being + *adj*); **s'a. coupable** to admit one's guilt; **s'a. vaincu** to acknowledge oneself beaten, to acknowledge defeat

avril [avril] NM April; **en a.** in April; **au mois d'a.** in the month of April; **pluie d'a.** April showers; **le sept a.** (on) the seventh of April, (on) April (the) seventh; **le premier a.** *(jour des farceurs)* April Fools' Day; **poisson d'a.!** April fool! `SEE GRAMMAR A81–2; B60–2`

AVS [aveɛs] NF *Suisse (abrév* **assurance vieillesse et survivants)** = Swiss pension scheme

avunculaire [avɔ̃kylɛr] ADJ avuncular

axe [aks] NM **1** *Géom (de plante, de la terre, d'ellipse etc)* axis; **grand/petit a.** major/minor axis; **a. de rotation** axis of rotation; *Constr* **a. d'une route/d'un pont** centre line of a road/bridge; *Aut* **a. routier** trunk road; **les grands axes de la circulation** trunk *or* major roads; *Fig* **les grands axes de sa politique** the main thrust of his policy; *Math* **a. des x/des y** x-axis/y-axis; **a. des abscisses/des ordonnées** x-/y-axis; **axes de coordonnées** co-ordinate axes; *Tech* **axes principaux d'un corps** principal axes of a body; **cristal à deux axes** biaxial crystal `VOIR GRAMMAIRE A14`

2 *Tech etc* axle, spindle, pin; *(de roue de vélo)* axle (pin); **a. de pompe** pump spindle; **a. d'une grue** pin of a crane; **a. du piston** *(d'un moteur)* gudgeon pin; *Aut* **a. de fusée** king pin; **a. transversal** cross-shaft; **a. roulis** roll axis

3 *Hist* axis; **les Puissances de l'A.** the Axis powers

4 *Mil* **a. de progression** main direction of advance; **a. (principal) de ravitaillement** main line of supply, main supply route

5 *Aviat* **a. de sustentation** lift axis; **a. de descente** glide path, line of descent; **a. balisé** radio range course; **a. balisé d'atterrissage** radio landing beam; **a. de référence** datum line

axer [akse] VT to centre, *Am* to center; **être**

axé sur *ou* **autour de** to centre on; **sa philosophie est axée sur le don de soi** his philosophy is centred *or* based on self-denial; **toute sa vie est axée là-dessus** it's his whole life, his whole life revolves around it; **il a toujours été axé sur le travail/l'argent** he has always been work-oriented/money-oriented; **il a toujours été axé sur la religion/la recherche du plaisir** for him, everything has always revolved around religion/pleasure-seeking; **une visite touristique axée sur ...** a guided tour focusing on ...; **axé sur le profit** profit-oriented; **l'expansion de la compagnie sera axée sur ...** the central thrust of company expansion will be ...

axial, -iale, -iaux, -iales [aksjal, -jo] ADJ *(ligne, plan)* axial; **effort de compression axiale** collapsible load; *Géol* **plan a.** axial plane; **éclairage a.** *(des rues)* central overhead lighting

axillaire [aksilɛr] ADJ *Anat, Bot* axillary

axiomatique [aksjɔmatik] ADJ axiomatic

axiome [aksjom] NM axiom

axis [aksis] NM *Anat* axis

ayant cause, *pl* **ayants cause** [ɛjã koz] NM *Jur (bénéficiaire de testament)* legal successor, successor in title, legatee; *(bénéficiaire de cadeau)* donee; *(bénéficiaire de transfert)* assignee; *(acheteur)* vendee; *(agent désigné)* executor, trustee

ayant-compte, *pl* **ayants-comptes** NM *Banque* account holder

ayant droit, *pl* **ayants droit** [ɛjãdrwa] NM *Jur* eligible party, entitled beneficiary

ayatollah [ajatɔla] NM ayatollah

azalée [azale] NF *(plante)* azalea

Azerbaïdjan [azɛrbajdʒã] NM Azerbaijan

azerbaïdjanais, -aise [azɛrbajdʒanɛ, -ɛz]
ADJ Azerbaijani
N **A.** Azerbaijani

azéri, -ie [azeri] ADJ Azeri
NM *Ling* Azerbaijani
N **A.** Azeri

azimut [azimyt] NM *Astron etc* azimuth; *Naut etc* **prendre un a.** to take a bearing; *Fam* **dans tous les azimuts** everywhere, all over the place; *Fig Fam* **y aller tous azimuts** to go flat out *or* all out, to go at it hammer and tongs; *Fig* **une campagne électorale tous azimuts** an all-out electoral campaign

azimutal, -ale, -aux, -ales [azimytal, -o] ADJ azimuth(al); **cercle a.** azimuth circle; **compas a.** azimuth compass

azimuté [azimyte] ADJ *Fam* crazy, round the bend

azotate [azɔtat] NM *Chimie* nitrate; **a. de potasse** nitre, saltpetre

azote [azɔt] NM *Chimie* nitrogen

azoté [azɔte] ADJ nitrogenous; **engrais azotés** nitrate fertilizers, nitrates

azoter [azɔte] VT to nitrogenize

azotique [azɔtik] ADJ *Chimie* nitric

azotite [azɔtit] NM *Chimie* nitrite

AZT® [azɛdte] NM *Pharm (abrév* **azidothymidine)** AZT

aztèque [aztɛk] ADJ Aztec
N **A.** Aztec

azur [azyr] NM **1** *(couleur)* azure, sky-blue **2** *Géog* **la Côte d'A.** the French Riviera **3** *Litt* **l'a.** *(le ciel)* the sky **4** *Hér* **champ d'a.** field azure **5** **pierre d'a.** lapis lazuli **6** *Com (pour linge)* blue

azuré [azyre] ADJ **1** (sky-)blue, azure **2** *Litt* tinged with blue

azurer [azyre] VT **1** *(linge etc)* to blue **2** *Litt* to tinge with blue

azyme [azim] ADJ **pain a.** unleavened bread
NM *Rel* **fête des Azymes** feast of unleavened bread, Passover

B, b [be] NM **1** *(lettre)* B, b **2** *Chimie (symbole du bore)* B

B.A. [bea] NF *(abrév* **bonne action)** good deed; **faire sa/une B.A.** to do one's good deed for the day/a good deed

baba¹ [baba] NM *Culin* **b. au rhum** (rum) baba; *Fam* **elle l'a eu dans le b.** she came unstuck

baba² ADJ INV *Fam* dumbfounded, flabbergasted; **j'en suis resté b.** I was absolutely flabbergasted; **j'en suis complètement b.** I'm absolutely flabbergasted

b.a.-ba [beaba] NM *Fam* ABC, *Am* ABCs, rudiments; **je ne connais que le b. de la comptabilité** I only know the rudiments of accountancy; **c'est le b. de la physique quantique** *(livre)* it's the idiot's guide to quantum physics

baba cool N hippie

Babel [babɛl] N Babel; **la tour de B.** the Tower of Babel; *Fig* **c'est une vraie tour de B.** you hear every language under the sun there

babeleer [babəler] N *Belg Fam* chatterbox

babeurre [babœr] NM buttermilk

babil [babi(l)] NM *(d'un enfant)* prattle, prattling; *(des oiseaux)* twittering; *(d'un ruisseau)* babbling

babillage [babijaʒ] NM **1** = babil **2** *Psy* lallation

babillard, -arde [babijar, -ard] ADJ *(personne)* chattering; *(enfant)* prattling; *(bébé)* babbling; *Fig* **ruisseau b.** babbling brook
▪ N *(personne)* chatterbox
▪ NM **1** *Can Scol* flannel board **2** *Ordinat* bulletin board, BBS

babillement [babijmɑ̃] NM = babil

babiller [babije] VI *(d'une personne)* to chatter; *(d'un enfant)* to prattle; *(d'un ruisseau)* to babble; *(d'un oiseau)* to twitter

babines [babin] NFPL *Zool* chops; *Fam (d'une personne)* chops, lips; **s'essuyer les b.** to wipe one's chops or lips; **d'avance, je m'en lèche les b.** my mouth's watering in anticipation

babiole [babjɔl] NF **1** *(bibelot)* knick-knack, trinket **2** *(incident)* trifle

bâbord [babɔr] NM *Naut* port (side); **la barre à b. toute!, b. toute!** hard a-port!; **la terre par b.!** land on the port side!; **aviron de b.** stroke side-oar

babouche [babuʃ] NF Turkish slipper

babouin [babwɛ̃] NM baboon

baboune [babun] NF *Can Fam* **faire la b.** to sulk

baby [bebi] ADJ INV **taille b.** baby-size(d); **whisky b.** small whisky
▪ NM small whisky

baby-boom, *pl* **baby-booms** NM baby boom; **enfants du b.** baby-boomers

baby-foot [babifut] NM INV table football; *(table)* football table

Babylone [babilɔn] N *Antiq* Babylon

Babylonie [babilɔni] NF *Antiq* Babylonia

babylonien, -ienne [babilɔnjɛ̃, -jɛn] *Antiq* ADJ Babylonian
▪ N B. Babylonian

babyphone [babifɔn] NM baby monitor

baby-sitter, *pl* **baby-sitters** [bebisitœr, babi-] N baby-sitter

baby-sitting [bebisitiŋ, babi-] NM baby-sitting; **faire du b.** to baby-sit

bac¹ [bak] NM **1** *(bateau)* ferry (boat); **b. à piétons** passenger ferry; **passer qn dans un b.** to ferry sb across; *Jur* **droit de b.** ferry (right) **2** *(récipient) (pour liquides)* tank, vat; *(d'une cellule électrique)* pot; *(d'un accumulateur, pour la nourriture etc)* box, container; *(de mineur)* truck, tub; *(d'imprimeur, de photographe)* tray
▪ ▪ *Ordinat* **b. d'alimentation** sheet feed; *Aut* **b. à cartes** map pocket; **b. à correspondance** correspondence tray; *Ordinat* **b. feuille à feuille** cut sheet feeder; *Ordinat* **b. de feuilles** paper tray; **b. à glace** ice tray; **b. introducteur** *(de feuillets)* sheet feed; **b. à laver** wash tub; **b. à légumes** salad drawer or crisper; *Belg* **b. à ordures** *Br* dustbin, *Am* garbage or trash or ash can; **b. de** ou **à papier** *(d'imprimante)* paper tray; **b. de papier A4** A4 paper tray; *Aut* **b. de rangement** stowage bin; **b. roulant** file trolley; **b. à sable** sandpit

bac² NM *Fam* = secondary school examination qualifying for entry to university, *Br* ≃ A levels, *Am* ≃ high school diploma; *Scot* ≃ Scottish Higher Certificate of Education; *Ir* ≃ School Leaving Certificate; **passer le b.** to take or *Br* sit one's baccalauréat; **préparer le b.** to study for one's baccalauréat; **b. + 3** *(dans une annonce)* three years of higher education required

baccalauréat [bakalɔrea] NM **1** = secondary school examination qualifying for entry to university, *Br* ≃ A levels, *Am* ≃ high school diploma; *Scot* ≃ Scottish Higher Certificate of Education; *Ir* ≃ School Leaving Certificate **2** *Anciennement* **b. en droit** = degree granted when a student has passed his first two examinations for the Licence en Droit **3** *Can Univ* bachelor's degree; **b. ès arts/ès sciences** Bachelor of Arts/Science

Baccalauréat

The "baccalauréat", or "bac", is taken by pupils who have completed their final year at the "lycée"; successful candidates may go to university. Depending on which subjects pupils choose to study at "lycée", they prepare for a "baccalauréat général", "technologique" (vocational) or "professionnel" (vocational and including professional training). Since the last major reform, in 1995, there have been three main

types of "baccalauréat général", each corresponding to a specific field: "bac L" (arts subjects), "bac ES" (economics and social studies) and "bac S" (sciences).

baccara(t)¹ [bakara] NM *Cartes* baccarat

baccarat² NM *(cristal)* Baccarat crystal

bacchanale [bakanal] NF **1** *(orgie)* orgy; *(débauche)* drunken revel; *(danse)* bacchanalian dance **2** *Antiq* **les bacchanales** the bacchanalia

bacchante [bakɑ̃t] NF **1** *Antiq* bacchante **2** *Fam* **bacchantes** moustache

bâche [baʃ] NF **1** *Tech (réservoir)* tank, cistern **2** *(serre)* forcing frame **3** *(toile)* tarpaulin, canvas cover; **b. de campement** ground sheet
▪ ▪ **b. d'alimentation** feed tank; **b. goudronnée** tarpaulin

bachelier, -ière [baʃəlje, -jɛr] N *Scol* student who has passed the baccalauréat

bâcher [baʃe] VT **b. qch** to cover sth (with a tarpaulin)
▪ VPR **se bâcher** *Fam* to hit the sack or the hay

bachi-bouzouk, *pl* **bachi-bouzouks** [baʃibuzuk] NM *Hist* Bashi-Bazouk; *Fam* **espèce de b.!** you crackpot!

bachique [baʃik] ADJ Bacchic; **scène b.** bacchanalian scene; **chanson b.** drinking song

bachot¹ [baʃo] NM *Naut* skiff, wherry

bachot² NM *Fam* = baccalauréat; **boîte à b.** crammer

bachotage [baʃɔtaʒ] NM *Scol Fam* cramming, *Br* swotting; **faire du b.** to do some cramming

bachoter [baʃɔte] VI *Scol Fam* to cram, *Br* to swot

bachoteur, -euse [baʃɔtœr, -øz] N *Scol Fam* student cramming or *Br* swotting for an exam

bacillaire [basilɛr] ADJ bacillary
▪ N tubercular patient

bacille [basil] NM **1** *Biol* bacillus VOIR GRAMMAIRE A14 **2** *(insecte)* stick insect

bacillose [basiloz] NF *Méd* bacillosis, bacillus infection; **b. pulmonaire** pulmonary tuberculosis

background [bakgrawnd] NM background

back-office, *pl* **back-offices** [bakɔfis] NM *Banque* back office

bâclage [baklaʒ] NM *Fam (d'un travail)* botching (up)

bâcle [bakl] NF *(d'une porte, fenêtre)* bar

bâclé [bakle] ADJ *(travail etc)* botched (up), slapdash

bâcler [bakle] VT **1** *Fam (travail)* to botch (up); **b. sa toilette** to give oneself a quick wash **2** *Arch (porte, fenêtre)* to bar
▪ VI to do a botched job

bacon [bekɔn] NM *Culin* bacon; **œufs au b.** bacon and eggs

bactéricide [bakterisid] ADJ bactericidal NM bactericide

bactérie [bakteri] NF bacterium, *pl* -ia

bactérien, -ienne [bakterjɛ̃, -jɛn] ADJ bacterial

bactériologie [bakterjɔlɔʒi] NF bacteriology

bactériologique [bakterjɔlɔʒik] ADJ bacteriological; **guerre b.** bacteriological *or* germ warfare

bactériologiste [bakterjɔlɔʒist], **bactériologue** [bakterjɔlɔg] N bacteriologist

bactériophage [bakterjɔfaʒ] NM bacteriophage

badaboum [badabum] INT *Fam* **et b., il est tombé** he fell down, crash, bang, wallop

badaud, -aude [bado, -od] ADJ gawping, *Am* rubbernecking
N 1 *(promeneur)* stroller; *(curieux)* gawper, *Am* rubberneck 2 *Ordinat (sur Internet)* lurker

badauder [badode] VI *Vieilli (se promener)* to stroll about (idly); *(regarder)* to gawp, *Am* to rubberneck

baderne [badɛrn] NF *Fam Péj* **une (vieille) b.** an old fogey, an old fossil, an old stick-in-the-mud

badge [badʒ] NM badge, *Am* button; *(pour scouts)* badge

badigeon [badiʒɔ̃] NM *(pour les murs etc)* (colour)wash, distemper; **b. à la chaux** whitewash; *Méd* **faire un b. de teinture d'iode sur une blessure** to paint a wound with tincture of iodine

badigeonnage [badiʒɔnaʒ] NM 1 *(de mur etc)* colourwashing, distempering; *(à la chaux)* whitewashing 2 *Méd (avec de l'iode etc)* painting

badigeonner [badiʒɔne] VT 1 **b. une surface de qch** to daub a surface with sth; **b. un mur en blanc/en couleur** to whitewash/to colourwash a wall, to distemper a wall; **b. la tourte de jaune d'œuf** to brush the pie with egg yolk 2 *Méd* to paint (**d'iode, à l'iode** with iodine)

badin[1] [badɛ̃] ADJ playful, light-hearted

badin[2] NM *Aviat* airspeed indicator

badinage [badinaʒ] NM banter, jesting; **sur un ton de b.** in a bantering *or* playful tone

badine [badin] NF cane, switch

badiner [badine] VI to jest, to joke; **b. de tout** to turn everything into a joke; **on ne badine pas avec l'amour** love is not something to be trifled with; **il ne faut pas b. avec ce genre de choses** these things are no laughing matter; **il ne badine pas avec la ponctualité** he's very strict about *or* he's a real stickler for punctuality

badinerie [badinri] NF jest

bad-lands [badlɑ̃ds] NFPL badlands

badminton [badminton] NM *Sport* badminton

bâdrant [bɑdrɑ̃] ADJ *Can* bothersome

bâdrer [bɑdre] VT *Can Fam* **b. qn** to bug sb, *Am* to give sb a pain (in the neck)

baffe [baf] NF *Fam (gifle)* slap, clout, clip on the ear; **recevoir/donner une paire de baffes** to get/give a couple of slaps; **tu veux une b. ou quoi?** do you want a clip on the ear?

baffer [bafe] VT *Fam* to clout, to cuff

Baffin [bafɛ̃] NM **la terre de B.** Baffin Island

baffle [bafl] NM *Électron (enceinte)* speaker; *(dans une enceinte)* baffle

bafouer [bafwe] VT *(personne)* to ridicule, to jeer at; *(règlement, autorité)* to flout; **mari bafoué** cuckold

bafouillage [bafujaʒ] NM *Fam (défaut de prononciation)* stammering, spluttering; *(propos incohérents)* gibberish, nonsense; *(de moteur)* misfiring, missing

bafouille [bafuj] NF *Arg* letter

bafouiller [bafuje] VI *Fam (mal prononcer)* to stammer, to splutter; *(être incohérent)* to talk gibberish *or* nonsense; *(d'un moteur)* to misfire, to miss
VT to stammer (out), to splutter (out); **je ne sais pas ce qu'il m'a bafouillé** I don't know what he was babbling about

bâfrer [bɑfre] *Arg* VI to stuff oneself, to guzzle, to pig out
VT *(nourriture)* to guzzle, to wolf

bâfreur, -euse [bɑfrœr, -øz] N *Arg* glutton, *Br* greedy-guts

bagage [bagaʒ] NM 1 *(équipement)* kit; **plier b.** to pack one's bags *or Mil* one's kit 2 **bagages** luggage, *surtout Am* baggage; **retrait des bagages** baggage (re)claim; **fourgon à bagages** luggage van, *Am* baggage car; **voyager avec peu de bagages** to travel light; **faire ses bagages** to pack one's bags 3 *Fig (connaissance)* knowledge (**en** of); **avoir un bon b. en sciences éco** to know a lot about economics; **son b. en physique est nul** he doesn't know any physics
▶▶ **bagages accompagnés** accompanied luggage *or* baggage; **bagages non accompagnés** unaccompanied luggage *or* baggage, luggage *or* baggage in advance; **bagages enregistrés** checked luggage *or* baggage; **bagages non-enregistrés** unchecked luggage *or* baggage; **bagages à main** hand luggage *or* baggage, cabin *or* carry-on baggage; **bagages de soute** hold luggage *or* baggage

bagagerie [bagaʒri] NF luggage room

bagagiste [bagaʒist] NM 1 *(dans une gare, un aéroport)* luggage *or* baggage handler 2 *(fabricant de bagages)* luggage manufacturer, travel goods manufacturer

bagarre [bagar] NF fight, brawl; **b. de rue** street fight; **il va y avoir de la b.** there's going to be a fight; **il cherche la b.** he's looking *or* spoiling for a fight; *Fig* **entre eux, c'est la b.** they've got it in for each other, they're at daggers drawn

bagarrer [bagare] *Fam* VI to fight, to battle (**pour** for); **aimer b.** to like a fight; *Fig* **il faudra b. pour l'avoir** you'll have to fight *or* battle to get it
VPR **se bagarrer** *(physiquement)* to fight, to scrap, to brawl; *(se quereller)* to quarrel, to argue

bagarreur, -euse [bagarœr, -øz] *Fam* ADJ *(personne, caractère)* aggressive; *Fig* **elle est bagarreuse** *(elle ne se laisse pas faire)* she's a fighter
N brawler; *Fig* **c'est une bagarreuse** she's a fighter

bagatelle [bagatɛl] NF 1 *(chose sans importance)* trifle, bagatelle; **se fâcher pour une b.** to take offence at a (mere) trifle; **elle perd son temps à des bagatelles** she's frittering away her time, she's wasting her time on trifles; **pour la b. de mille euros** for a mere thousand euros 2 *(plaisir sexuel)* lovemaking; **il ne pense qu'à la b.** he's got a one-track mind

bagnard [baɲar] NM convict

bagne [baɲ] NM *Hist (prison)* convict prison; **b. flottant** hulks; **condamné à cinq ans de b.** sentenced to five years' penal servitude; *Fig Fam* **c'est le b., la vie avec elle!** life with her is torment *or* a real nightmare!

bagnole [baɲɔl] NF *Fam* car; *Péj* **(vieille) b.** (old) jalopy, *Br* (old) banger; **ça, c'est de la b.!** that's some car!

bagou(t) [bagu] NM *Fam* glibness (of tongue); **avoir du b.** to have the gift of the gab

baguage [bagaʒ] NM *(des oiseaux, des arbres)* ringing

bague [bag] NF 1 *(bijou)* ring; **porter des bagues** to wear rings; **b. en argent/en or** silver/gold ring; **avoir la b. au doigt** to be married; **passer à qn la b. au doigt** to put a ring on sb's finger 2 *(d'une boîte de conserve)* ring-pull; *(de cigare)* band 3 *Tech* bush, ring 4 *(d'oiseau)* ring
▶▶ **b. d'appui** washer; **b. d'assemblage** collar, sleeve; **b. à bride** adapter; **b. d'espacement** sleeve; **b. de fiançailles** engagement ring; **b. (de garniture)** de piston piston ring, packing ring; **b. rallonge** *(d'une caméra)* extender lens; **b. de réglage** setting ring; **b. de roulement** ball race, bearing race; **b. de serrage** jubilee clip

baguenauder [bagnode] *Fam* VI to stroll *or* wander around
VPR **se baguenauder** to stroll *or* wander around

baguer[1] [bage] VT *(oiseau, arbre)* to ring; **cigare bagué d'or** cigar with a gold band

baguer[2] VT *Couture (plis etc)* to tack, to baste

baguette [bagɛt] NF 1 *(tige)* switch, stick; *(pain)* French stick; **baguettes** *(pour manger)* chopsticks; **tu ne crois pas que tout va changer, comme ça, d'un coup de b.?** surely you don't believe everything's going to change, just like that, as if by magic *or* as if by the wave of a magic wand?; *Fig* **avoir les cheveux raides comme les baguettes (de tambour)** to have hair that's as straight as a poker; *Fam* **commander** *ou* **mener** *ou* **faire marcher qn à la b.** to rule sb with a rod of iron *or* with an iron hand; **être sous la b. de qn** to be under someone's thumb; **passer par les baguettes** to run the gauntlet 2 *Menuis etc* moulding, beading 3 *(de bas, chaussette)* clock 4 *Aut* **b. de pavillon** roof bar; **b. de protection latérale** side-impact bar
▶▶ **b. de chef d'orchestre** conductor's baton; **b. magique** magic wand; **d'un coup de b. magique** with a wave of my/his/*etc* magic wand; **baguettes de tambour** drumsticks

baguier [bagje] NM ring case

bah [ba] INT bah!, pooh!

Bahamas [baamas] NFPL **les (îles) B., l'archipel des B.** the Bahamas VOIR GRAMMAIRE A11–12

Bahreïn [barajn], **Bahrayn** [barɛ̃] NM Bahrain, Bahrein

bahut [bay] NM 1 *(coffre)* (round-topped) chest; *(buffet)* sideboard 2 *Arg (collège, lycée)* school 3 *Arg (taxi)* cab, taxi

bai [bɛ] ADJ *(cheval)* bay; **b. châtain** chestnut bay

baie[1] [bɛ] NF *Géog* bay; **une petite b. abritée** a sheltered cove; **la grande b. australienne** the Great Australian Bight; **la b. d'Hudson** Hudson Bay

baie[2] NF 1 *Archit* opening; **b. vitrée** picture window 2 *Ordinat* bay

baie[3] NF *Bot* berry

baignade [bɛɲad] NF 1 *(activité)* swimming, *Br* bathing; **b. interdite** no swimming *or Br* bathing 2 *(endroit)* swimming *or Br* bathing place

baigner [bɛɲe] VT *(pieds, doigt etc)* to bathe; *(bébé, chien etc)* to bath *or Am* bathe; *(de la mer)* *(côte etc)* to wash; *(d'une rivière)* *(région)* to water; *Fig* **baigné de soleil** bathed in sunlight; **pièce baignée de lumière** room flooded with *or* bathed in light; **il était baigné de sueur** he was dripping with *or* bathed in sweat; **son visage est baigné de larmes** his face is bathed in tears
VI *(tremper)* to soak, to steep (**dans** in); **les légumes baignent dans une sauce à la tomate** the vegetables are swimming in a tomato sauce; *Fam* **ça baigne (dans l'huile)!**

everything's great or fine!; **OK, ça baigne!** OK, no problem!; **il baignait dans son sang** he was lying in a pool of his own blood; **la ville baigne dans la brume** the town is shrouded or swathed in mist; **maison qui baigne dans la lumière** house that is flooded with or bathed in light; **cette histoire/maison baigne dans le mystère** this story/house is shrouded in mystery

VPR se baigner 1 (se laver) to have or take a bath, Br to bath, Am to bathe **2** (nager) (dans la mer, un lac etc) to have a swim, Br to (have a) bathe; (dans une piscine) to have a swim, to swim; **on va se b.?** shall we go for a swim?, shall we go swimming?

baigneur, -euse [bɛɲœr, -øz] N Vieilli swimmer, Br bather
NM (en porcelaine ou en plastique) doll

baignoire [bɛɲwar] **NF 1** (dans la salle de bains) bath, (bath)tub **2** Théâtre ground-floor box **3** Naut (de sous-marin) upper part of the conning tower
▸▸**b. encastrée** sunken bath; **b. sabot** hip bath

bail, pl **baux** [baj, bo] **NM** lease; **b. commercial** commercial lease; **b. à ferme** farming lease; **b. emphytéotique** long lease; **b. à loyer** rental agreement, lease; **prendre une maison à b.** to take a lease on or to lease a house; **donner une maison à b.** to lease (out) a house; **renouveler un b.** to renew a lease; **résilier un b.** to cancel a lease; Fam **ça fait un b. que je ne l'ai pas vu** I haven't seen him for ages

baille [baj] **NF** Naut (baquet) bucket; (mauvais bateau) tub; Fam **la (grande) b.** the drink, the sea; **tomber à la b.** to fall into the drink

bâillement [bɑjmɑ̃] **NM 1** (de personne) yawn; **étouffer un b.** to stifle a yawn; **bâillements** yawning, yawns **2** (d'une couture etc) gaping; **b. des rideaux** gap between the curtains

bâiller [bɑje] **VI 1** (d'une personne) to yawn; **b. de sommeil/d'ennui/de fatigue** to yawn drowsily/with boredom/with tiredness; Fig **son histoire me fait b.** his/her story is one big yawn; Fam **b. à s'en** ou **se décrocher la mâchoire** to yawn one's head off **2** (des coutures, d'un col etc) to gape; (d'une porte) to be or stand ajar

bâilles [bɑj] **NFPL** Belg **faire des b.** to yawn

bailleur, -eresse [bɑjœr, bɑjrɛs] N **1** Jur lessor **2** Com **b. de fonds** (investisseur) (financial) backer, sponsor; (associé passif) Br sleeping partner, Am silent partner; **b. de licence** licensor, licenser

bailli [baji] **NM** Hist bailiff

bailliage [bajaʒ] **NM** Hist (district) bailiwick; (tribunal) bailiff's court

bâillon [bɑjɔ̃] **NM** gag; **mettre un b. à qn** to gag sb; **mettre un b. à la presse/l'opposition** to gag or muzzle the press/the opposition

bâillonner [bɑjone] **VT** to gag; **b. la presse/l'opposition** to gag or muzzle the press/the opposition

bain [bɛ̃] **NM 1** (pour se laver) bath; (baignoire) bath(tub); **prendre un b.** to have or take a bath, Br to bath, Am to bathe; **donner un b. à qn** to give sb a bath, to bath or bathe sb; **salle de bain(s)** bathroom; **peignoir** ou **sortie de b.** bathrobe; **le b. est rempli/vidé** the bath is full/empty; **fais-moi couler un b.** run me a bath; Fig Fam **être dans le b.** (être compromis) to be implicated; (être habitué) to be in the swing of things; **elle n'a pas eu de mal à se mettre dans le b.** she had no trouble getting into the swing of things; Fig **ils sont dans le même b.** they're in the same boat; **on peut les mettre dans le même b.** you can lump them all together; **je dé-**

teste les bains de foule I hate crowds; **prendre un b. de foule** (d'une personne célèbre) to go on a walkabout; (d'un politicien) to press the flesh; **petit b.** (à la piscine) small or children's pool; **grand b.** (à la piscine) large pool
2 (à la mer etc) swim, Br bathe; **bains de mer** swimming in the sea, Br sea bathing; Vieilli (lieu) seaside resort; **b. en piscine** swimming or Br bathing in a pool
3 Phot bath; **b. révélateur** ou **de développement** developing bath; **b. de fixage** ou **fixateur** fixing bath
4 Tex dye; **ce n'est pas le même b.** it's not the same dye lot
5 (pour moutons) (sheep) dip
▸▸**b. d'arrêt** stop bath; **b. de bouche** mouthwash; **faire un b. de bouche** to use a mouthwash; **b. de boue** mud bath; **b. bouillonnant** spa bath; Phot **b. de fixateur** fixing bath; Fig **b. de jouvence** rejuvenating experience; **ça m'a fait l'effet d'un b. de jouvence** it rejuvenated me, it made me feel years younger; **b. moussant** bubble bath; **b. de pieds** footbath; **prendre un b. de pieds** to soak or bathe one's feet; **b.-de-soleil** (corsage) halter top; **b. de soudure** solder bath; **b. turc** Turkish bath; **b. de vapeur** steam bath; **bains (publics)** (public) baths, Am bathhouse; **bains romains** Roman baths; **bains de soleil** sunbathing; **prendre un b. de soleil** ou **des bains de soleil** to sunbathe

bain-marie, pl **bains-marie** [bɛ̃mari] **NM** bain-marie, double saucepan or boiler; **faire cuire qch au b.** to cook sth in a bain-marie

baïonnette [bajonɛt] **NF** bayonet; **mettre/remettre la b.** to fix/unfix bayonets; **charge à la b.** bayonet charge; Tech **joint en b.** bayonet joint; Élec **douille à b.** bayonet socket; Élec **ampoule à b.** bulb with a bayonet fitting

baïram [bairam] **NM** Bairam

baisable [bɛzabl] **ADJ** Vulg fuckable, Br shaggable

baise [bɛz] **NF 1** Vulg (acte sexuel) screwing; **il ne pense qu'à la b.** all he ever thinks of is screwing **2** Belg (baiser) kiss

baise-en-ville **NM INV** Fam overnight bag; (pochette) (man's) handbag

baisemain [bɛzmɛ̃] **NM** hand kissing, kissing of hands; **faire le b. à qn** to kiss sb's hand

baiser[1] [bɛze] **VT 1** (embrasser) to kiss; **b. qn au front** to kiss sb on the forehead; **elle lui baisa les pieds** she kissed his feet **2** Vulg (coucher avec) to fuck, to screw **3** Arg (tromper) to screw; **il m'a bien baisé** he screwed me good and proper; **se faire b.** to be or get screwed **4** Arg (comprendre) **qu'est-ce qu'il dit? on n'y baise rien** what's he saying? you can't make head nor tail of it
VI Vulg **elle baise bien** she's a good screw or fuck

baiser[2] **NM** kiss; **gros baisers** (dans une lettre) love and kisses; **b. de paix** kiss of peace; **b. d'adieu** parting or goodbye or farewell kiss; **b. de Judas** Judas kiss; **faire un b. à qn** to give sb a kiss

baiseur, -euse [bɛzœr, -øz] N Vulg **c'est un sacré b./une sacrée baiseuse** he's/she's a great screw

baisse [bɛs] **NF** fall, drop, downturn; (de la marée) ebb; **la b. de la natalité** the fall or drop in the birthrate; **la b. du niveau scolaire** the fall in educational standards; **b. des prix** fall or drop in prices, price cut; (action) price cutting; Bourse **b. sensible (des cours)** sharp fall (in prices); **être en b.** (de la température, du nombre d'adhésions etc) to be falling or dropping; (de la popularité de qn) to be on the decline or the wane; (d'une rivière) to subside; **le moral du malade est en b.** the patient's morale is sinking; Bourse **spéculations à la b.** bear speculations; **jouer à la b.**

to bear; **revoir à la baisse** to revise downwards; **actions en b.** falling shares

BAISSER [bese] **VT** (rideau) to lower; (store) to lower, to pull down; (vitre de voiture) to open, to lower; **b. une étagère d'un cran** to lower a shelf by one notch; Aut **b. ses phares** to dip or Am dim one's headlights; **le store est baissé** the blind is down or lowered; **b. la lumière** to turn down or dim the light; **b. la radio/le chauffage** to turn down the radio/the heating; **b. pavillon** Naut to strike one's flag, to surrender; Fig (céder) to admit defeat, to give in; **b. la tête** ou **le front** to bend or lower one's head; (de honte, découragement etc) to hang one's head; **b. brusquement la tête** to duck; **donner tête baissée dans un piège** to fall headlong into a trap; **b. les yeux** to look down, to lower one's eyes; **les yeux baissés** with downcast eyes; **b. le nez** to hang one's head in shame; Fig **il ne faut pas b. les bras, battez-vous!** don't give in, fight!; **b. la voix** to lower one's voice; **b. le ton** (après une dispute) to climb down; **je vous prie de b. le ton!** please keep your voice down!; **b. le prix de qch** to lower or reduce or cut the price of sth
VI 1 (de la température) to fall, to go or come down; (de la marée) to ebb; (du feu) to burn low, to burn down; (de la vue, de la mémoire) to fail; Théâtre **les lumières baissent** the lights are going down; **le baromètre baisse** the barometer is falling; **le jour baisse** night is falling, it's getting dark
2 (s'affaiblir) (d'un malade) to get weaker, to deteriorate; (de l'enthousiasme) to fall off, to decline, to weaken; **il a beaucoup baissé dernièrement** (physiquement) he has got a lot weaker lately, he has deteriorated a lot lately; (intellectuellement) his mind has been going or deteriorating a lot lately; **le moral baisse** morale is sinking; **elle a baissé dans mon estime** she's gone down in my estimation
3 (des prix) to fall, to come or go down; **la valeur de ces maisons a baissé** these houses have gone down in value; **faire b. les prix** to bring down prices; **le dollar a baissé** the dollar has weakened; **le niveau scolaire a beaucoup baissé** educational standards have fallen a lot
VPR se baisser to bend down, to stoop; (pour éviter un coup etc) to duck; **c'est en se baissant qu'il s'est cogné** he banged himself as he bent down; Fig **il n'y a qu'à se b. pour les ramasser** there are loads of them around

baissier [besje] Bourse **NM** bear
ADJ bearish

bajoues [baʒu] **NFPL** (d'animal) chops; Péj (d'une personne) flabby cheeks

bakchich [bakʃiʃ] **NM** Fam Br backhander, bung, Am payoff

Bakélite® [bakelit] **NF** Bakelite®; **téléphone en B.** Bakelite® telephone

baklava [baklava] **NM** Culin baklava, baclava

bal, pl **bals** [bal] **NM 1** (fête) (populaire) dance; (chic) ball, dance; **b. costumé** ou **masqué** ou **travesti** fancy dress ball; **donner un b.** to give a dance; **aller au b.** to go dancing; **robe de b.** ball gown, evening dress; **ouvrir le b.** to open the ball; Fig to set the ball rolling **2** (endroit) dance hall
▸▸**b. populaire** = free, open-air dance to popular music; **b. public** public dance

balade [balad] **NF** Fam (à pied) walk, stroll; (en voiture) drive, run; **faire une b.** (à pied) to go for a walk or stroll; (en voiture) to go for a drive or run (in the car); **être/partir en b.** (à pied) to be out for/go off for a walk; (en voiture) to be out for/go off for a drive

balader [balade] Fam **VT** (personne, chien) to take (out) for a walk; (avoir avec soi) (objet)

to carry or drag around; **il balade toujours cette vieille valise avec lui** he always carries or drags that old suitcase around with him
VPR se balader (à pied) to go for a walk; (en voiture) to go for a drive; **se b. en montagne** to walk in the mountains; **tu ne vas pas te b. en ville avec cette casquette?** surely you're not going to walk around town in that cap?; **ses affaires se baladent dans la maison** his things are lying around all over the house

baladeur, -euse [baladœr, -øz] ADJ (instinct) wandering, roving; **j'ai l'âme baladeuse** I'm a wanderer at heart; (en ce moment) I want to be up and away; Fam **avoir les mains baladeuses** to have wandering hands; Tech **train b.** sliding gear
NF baladeuse (lampe) portable lamp, inspection lamp
NM personal stereo, Walkman®

baladin [baladɛ̃] NM strolling player, wandering actor

baladisque [baladisk] NM portable compact disc player, Discman®

balafre [balafr] NF 1 (coupure) gash, slash, cut; (au sabre) sabre cut 2 (cicatrice) scar

balafré [balafre] NM scarface

balafrer [balafre] VT to slash, to gash, to cut; **les agresseurs lui ont balafré le visage** the attackers slashed his face; **visage balafré** scarred face

balai [balɛ] NM 1 (de ménage) broom; **passer le b.** to sweep the floor, to give the floor a sweep; **donner un coup de b. dans** ou **à la cuisine** to give the kitchen a sweep, to sweep the kitchen; Fig **donner un coup de b.** (dans une entreprise) to have a shake-out; Fig **il y a eu un coup de b.** there's been a shake-out; **(allez,) du b.!** clear off!, scram!; Arg **con comme un b.** as stupid as they come, bloody stupid, Br as daft as a brush 2 Fam (voiture-) **b.** (autobus) last bus; (métro) last underground or Am subway 3 Élec brush 4 Aut (d'essuie-glace) blade 5 Fam (an) year; **il a cinquante balais** he's fifty
▸▸ **b. mécanique** carpet sweeper

balai-brosse, pl **balais-brosses** NM (long-handled) scrubbing brush

balaise [balɛz] ADJ, N Fam = **balèze**

balalaïka [balalaika] NF Mus balalaika

balan [balɑ̃] NM Suisse **être sur le b.** (être sur le point de tomber) to be tottering; (hésiter) to be indecisive; (être inquiet quant à son sort) to wait nervously

balance [balɑ̃s] NF 1 (appareil) (pair of) scales; (publique) weighing machine; **monter sur la b.** to stand on the scales VOIR GRAMMAIRE A10
2 Astron, Astrol **la B.** Libra, the Scales; **être (du signe de la) B.** to be Libra or a Libran
3 Fig **candidat mis en b.** candidate who is still being considered; **la victoire/la décision restait en b.** victory/the decision hung in the balance; **mettre qch en b.** to weigh up the pros and cons of sth; **il faut mettre ces deux arguments en b.** you have to weigh each argument against the other; **ce facteur pèse dans la b.** this is an important factor; **cet argument est un poids dans la b.** this argument has great weight; **il y a divers facteurs à mettre dans la b.** there are various factors to take into account; **faire pencher** ou **incliner** ou **emporter la b.** to tip the scales or balance; **votre qualification fera pencher la b. en votre faveur** your qualification will tip the balance in your favour
4 Compta, Com **d'un compte** balance or balancing of an account; **faire la b.** to make up the balance (sheet); **la b. de l'actif et du passif** the balance of assets and liabilities, credit and debit balance; **compte en b.** ac-

count that balances; **la b. est en excédent** there is a surplus
5 Pêche shrimp net
6 Fam (mouchard) squealer, Br grass
▸▸ **b. automatique** shop scales; **b. avant inventaire** pre-inventory balance; **b. à bascule** weighbridge; Cin, TV **b. des blancs** white balance; **b. du commerce** ou **commerciale** trade balance, balance of trade; **b. créditrice** credit balance; **b. de cuisine** ou **de ménage** kitchen scales; **b. déficitaire** trade deficit; Pol **b. des forces** ou **des pouvoirs** balance of power; **b. d'inventaire** inventory balance; **b. du main courantier de nuit** (dans un hôtel) night auditor's report; **b. des paiements** balance of payments; **b. de Roberval** Roberval's balance; **b. romaine** steelyard; **b. de salle de bains** bathroom scales; **b. de vérification** trial balance

> Il faut noter que le nom anglais **balance** est un faux ami. Il signifie le plus souvent **équilibre** et ne s'emploie jamais pour désigner un instrument de mesure.

balancé [balɑ̃se] ADJ **(bien) b.** (phrase, tournure) well-balanced; Fam **elle est bien balancée** she's got a great figure

balancelle [balɑ̃sɛl] NF (de jardin) Br swing chair, Am glider

balancement [balɑ̃smɑ̃] NM 1 (de bateau, de train, des arbres etc) swaying, rocking; (des hanches) swaying; **balancements** (en politique) wavering, shilly-shallying 2 Beaux-Arts, Littér (équilibre) balance

balancer [balɑ̃se] (je **balançai(s); n. balançons**) VT 1 (bras, jambes, trompe) to swing; (personne dans un hamac) to rock; (hanches) to sway; **tu pourrais me b.?** (sur la balançoire) can you push me or give me a push?; **b. un enfant sur ses genoux** to rock a child on one's knees
2 Fam (lancer) (pierres, stylo etc) to chuck, to throw; **tu pourrais me b. le journal** can you chuck or throw me the paper?; **b. des pierres à qn** to chuck or throw stones at sb; **il est toujours en train de b. des vannes** he's always making snide remarks
3 Com **b. un compte** to balance an account; Fig **b. le pour et le contre** to weigh up the pros and cons; **tout bien balancé, c'est d'accord** all things considered, I agree
4 Fam (se débarrasser de) (objet) to chuck or throw out or away; **b. qn** to give sb the push or Br the elbow; **elle a tout balancé** (tout abandonné) she's given it all up
5 Fam (moucharder) to squeal on, Br to grass on, Br to shop
VI Litt (hésiter) to waver, to hesitate
VPR **se balancer 1** (d'arbres, de blés etc) to sway; **se b. sur ses ancres** (d'un navire) to ride at anchor; **se b. sur sa chaise** to rock (backwards and forwards) on one's chair; **se b. d'un pied sur l'autre** to rock from one foot to the other
2 (sur une balançoire) to swing; (sur une bascule) to see saw
3 Arg **je m'en balance!** I don't give a damn!, I couldn't care less!; **je me balance complètement de ce qu'ils pensent** I really don't give a damn or I really couldn't care less what they think
4 Fam **il s'est balancé du haut de la tour Eiffel** he chucked or threw himself off the top of the Eiffel Tower

balancier [balɑ̃sje] NM 1 (d'un funambule) balancing pole 2 (dans une horloge) pendulum; (d'une montre) balance wheel 3 (d'une pompe) handle

balançoire [balɑ̃swar] NF (bascule) seesaw; (suspendue) swing; (dans une foire) swing-boat; **faire de la b.** to have a go on the seesaw/the swing

balayage [balɛjaʒ] NM 1 (d'une pièce etc) sweeping; (de la saleté etc) sweeping up; **b. intermittent** (d'essuie-glace) intermittent wipe; **b. unique** (d'essuie-glace) flick wipe 2 Radio, Électron, TV scan(ning), sweep; **fréquence de b.** sweep frequency; TV **b. de télévision** raster scan; TV **b. de trame** raster scan 3 (de cheveux) streaks; **se faire faire un b.** to have streaks put in one's hair, to have one's hair streaked

balayer [balɛje] VT (je **balaie, je balaye; je balaierai, je balayerai**) 1 (pièce etc) to sweep (out); (saleté etc) to sweep up; **le vent a balayé les nuages** the wind has swept the clouds away; **b. l'ennemi** to drive away the enemy; **b. les critiques/objections/obstacles** to brush aside criticism/objections/obstacles; **les communistes ont été balayés aux dernières élections** the Communists were swept from power or were swept out at the last elections; Fig **b. devant sa porte** to put one's (own) house in order; **cette nouvelle a balayé tous mes soucis** this news has swept away all my worries
2 Radio, Électron, TV to scan, to sweep; (caméra) to pan across; **le radar balaie jusqu'à 100 km** the radar has a sweep of 100 kilometres; **les projecteurs de la prison balaient les champs tout autour** the prison searchlights sweep the fields all around
3 Aut to scavenge

balayette [balɛjɛt] NF (small) brush

balayeur, -euse [balɛjœr, -øz] N (personne) (road) sweeper
NF balayeuse 1 (machine) road sweeper 2 Can (aspirateur) vacuum cleaner

balayures [balɛjyr] NFPL sweepings

balbutiant [balbysjɑ̃] ADJ (voix) stuttering, stammering; **il répondit, tout b.** he stammered an answer; Fig **la psychanalyse, encore toute balbutiante** psychoanalysis, still in its infancy or still in its early stages

balbutiement [balbysimɑ̃] NM stuttering, stammering; (dans sa barbe) mumbling, muttering; **les balbutiements d'un jeune enfant** the babbling of a young child; Fig **l'informatique n'était alors qu'à ses balbutiements** data processing was then only in its infancy or in its early stages

balbutier [balbysje] (pr sub, impf n. **balbutiions, v. balbutiiez**) VI to stutter, to stammer; (parler dans sa barbe) to mumble, to mutter VT (des excuses) to stammer (out); (en parlant dans sa barbe) to mumble, to mutter

balcon [balkɔ̃] NM 1 Archit balcony; Fam **il y a du monde au b.** she's well endowed, she's a big girl 2 Théâtre circle; **premier b.** dress circle; **nous étions placés au deuxième b.** we were in the upper circle

balconnet [balkɔnɛ] NM half-cup bra

baldaquin [baldakɛ̃] NM (de lit) tester, canopy; (de trône) canopy, baldachin; **lit à b.** tester bed

Bâle [bɑl] N Basle, Basel

Baléares [balear] NFPL **les B.** the Balearic Islands, the Balearics

baleine [balɛn] NF 1 Zool whale; **b. à bosse** humpbacked whale; **b. blanche** white whale; **blanc de b.** spermaceti; Fig **rire comme une b.** to laugh like a drain 2 (d'un corset etc) (whale)bone; (d'un parapluie) rib

baleiné [balene] ADJ (soutien-gorge) boned; (col) stiffened

baleineau, -eaux [baleno] NM whale calf

baleinier, -ière [balenje, -jɛr] ADJ (bateau, industrie) whaling
NF baleinière whaleboat, whaler; **baleinière de sauvetage** lifeboat

balèze [balɛz] Fam ADJ (grand et fort) hefty, brawny; Fig **elle est vraiment b.!** (intelli-

gente) she's so brainy!; **b. en maths** brilliant at maths

N *(personne grande et forte)* hefty *or* brawny sort; *(personne intelligente)* brainy sort

balier [balje] *Can Fam* **VT** *(nettoyer) (plancher, pièce)* to sweep (up *or* out); *(tapis)* to brush, to sweep
VI to sweep up

balisage [balizaʒ] **NM 1** *(signaux), Naut* beacons, buoys; *Aviat* lights; *Radio* beacons; **projecteur de b.** direction beacon **2** *(action), Naut* beaconing, buoying; *Aviat* lighting; *Radio* marking out with beacons

balise [baliz] **NF 1** *Naut* beacon, buoy; *Aviat* light; *Radio* beacon; *(de piste de ski, d'épave)* marker; *Naut* **b. flottante** buoy; *Radio* **b. radar** radar beacon **2** *Ordinat (d'un texte)* tag; **traitement de texte à balises** word processing with embedded visible commands

baliser [balize] **VT** *Naut (chenal)* to beacon, to buoy, to mark out; *Aviat (aéroport)* to equip with lights; *(route)* to mark out with beacons; **b. une piste de ski** to mark out a ski run
VI *Fam (avoir peur)* to have the jitters (**pour qch** about sth); **ne m'en parle pas, ça me fait b.** don't talk to me about it, it gives me the jitters

baliseur [balizœr] **NM 1** *(bateau)* **b.** buoy-laying boat **2** *(personne)* person who lays buoys

balistique [balistik] **ADJ** ballistic; **engin b.** ballistic missile
NF ballistics

baliverne [balivern] **NF** stupid remark; **balivernes** twaddle, nonsense; **débiter des balivernes** to talk twaddle *or* nonsense

balkanique [balkanik] **ADJ** Balkan

balkanisation [balkanizasjɔ̃] **NF** *Pol, Fig* Balkanization

Balkans [balkɑ̃] **NMPL** **les B.** the Balkans

ballade [balad] **NF** *(poème court)* ballade; *(poème long), Mus* ballad

ballant [balɑ̃] **ADJ** *(bras, jambes)* swinging, dangling; **assis les pieds ballants** sitting with one's feet dangling
NM 1 *(mouvement) (d'un véhicule)* sway, roll **2** *Naut (d'un cordage)* slack

ballast [balast] **NM 1** *Constr (d'une route, d'une voie ferrée)* ballast **2** *Naut* ballast tank

ballaster [balaste] **VT 1** *Constr (voie ferrée etc)* to ballast **2** *Naut (remplir)* to ballast; *(vider)* to unballast

balle¹ [bal] **NF 1** *(pour jouer)* ball; **b. de golf/de tennis/de ping-pong** golf/tennis/table-tennis ball; **jouer à la b.** to play ball; **b. au mur** ≃ fives, *Am* handball; *Can* **b. de neige** snowball; *Sport* **renvoyer/lancer la b.** to return the ball/to serve; *Sport Fam* **c'est une belle b.!** good shot *or* ball!; *Tennis* **faire des ou quelques balles** to have a knock-up; *Fig* **prendre ou saisir la b. au bond** to seize the opportunity *or* chance; *Fig* **se renvoyer la b.** to pass the buck; *Fig* **renvoyer la b. à qn** *(dans un débat)* to answer sb back; *Fig* **la b. est dans votre camp** the ball's in your court **2** *(d'arme)* bullet; **b. de fusil** rifle bullet; *Fam* **recevoir douze balles dans la peau** to go before the firing squad; **à l'épreuve des balles** bullet-proof
▸▸**b. de filet** net (ball); **b. de match** match point; **b. morte** spent bullet; **b. perdue** stray bullet; **b. plastique** plastic bullet, baton round; **b. de set** set point; **b. traçante** tracer bullet

balle² **NF 1** *Com (de coton, laine etc)* bale **2** *Arg (visage)* mug, *Br* dial; **il a une drôle de b.** he's an odd-looking guy; **quelle b.!** what an ugly mug!

balle³ **NF** *(de blé)* husk, chaff; *Bot (de fleur)* glume

baller [bale] **VI** *(de bras, jambes)* to dangle; *(de tête)* to hang

ballerine [balrin] **NF 1** *Théâtre* ballerina, ballet dancer **2** *(chaussure)* pump

balles [bal] **NFPL** *Anciennement Fam* francs; **je te le vends pour deux cents b.** I'll sell it to you for two hundred francs; **t'as pas cent b.?** *(dit dans la rue etc)* ≃ have you got any (spare) change?

ballet [bale] **NM** *Théâtre* ballet; **maître de b.** ballet master; **les ballets du Bolshoï** the Bolshoi Ballet; *Pol Fig* **le b. de ministres** the ministerial merry-go-round; **le b. diplomatique** diplomatic to-ings and fro-ings

ballon [balɔ̃] **NM 1** *(aéronef, vessie)* balloon; **faire un voyage en b.** to make a balloon journey; **monter en b.** to go up in a balloon; **envoyer ou lancer un b. d'essai** to send up a pilot balloon; *Fig* to put out feelers, to fly a kite; **marchand de ballons** balloon-seller
2 *Sport etc (pour jouer)* ball; *(au base-ball) (chandelle)* highball; **b. de football/de rugby/de volley** football/rugby ball/volleyball; **jouer au b.** to play with a ball; **b. d'entraînement (pour boxeurs)** punchball
3 *(de bande dessinée)* balloon
4 *(pour boire) (verre)* **b.** round wine glass; **un b. de vin blanc** a glass of white wine; *Suisse* **un b.** *(de vin)* = decilitre of wine
5 *Chimie* balloon flask; *Ind* carboy
6 **b. (d'Alcootest®)** (breathalyser) bag; **souffler dans le b.** to blow into the bag
7 *Suisse (petit pain)* (bread) roll
▸▸**b. de barrage** barrage balloon; **b. dirigeable** airship, dirigible; **b. gonflable** balloon; *(de football etc)* inflatable ball; **b. d'observation** observation balloon; **b. ovale** rugby ball; *(sport)* rugby; *Méd* **b. d'oxygène** oxygen bottle; **b. de protection** barrage balloon; **b. rond** football; *(sport)* football

ballonné [balɔne] **ADJ** *(bombé, arrondi) (joues)* chubby, round; *(nuages)* puffy; *(ventre)* bloated, distended

ballonnement [balɔnmɑ̃] **NM** *(du ventre, de l'estomac)* distending; **avoir des ballonnements** to feel bloated

ballonner [balɔne] **VT** *(gonfler) (cape, jupe, joues)* to puff out; *(ventre, estomac)* to distend; **manger ce genre de choses me ballonne** eating that kind of thing makes me feel bloated *or* gives me wind; **cette herbe risque de b. les bêtes** this grass is liable to bloat the livestock

ballon-panier **NM** **INV** *Can Sport* basketball

ballon-sonde, *pl* **ballons-sondes** **NM** *Météo* sounding balloon

ballot [balo] **NM 1** *(paquet)* bundle, package **2** *Fam (imbécile)* twit, wally
ADJ *Fam* **t'es pas b.?** are you mad?; **c'est vraiment b. de l'avoir prévenu** it's really crazy to have warned him

ballotin [balotɛ̃] **NM** sweet *or Am* candy box; **b. de chocolats** small box of chocolates

ballottage [balɔtaʒ] **NM** *Pol etc* **scrutin de b.** second ballot, run-off; **il y a b.** there will be a second ballot *or* a run-off; **M. Martin est en b.** Mr Martin has to stand again *or Am* run again in a second ballot

ballottement [balɔtmɑ̃] **NM** *(de train)* rocking, swaying; *(des passagers)* shaking, jolting; *(de porte)* swinging to and fro; *(de navire)* tossing

ballotter [balɔte] **VT** *(bateau)* to toss (about); *(passagers)* to shake *or* jolt (about); **être ballotté par des sentiments opposés** to be pulled this way and that by contradictory feelings; **un enfant ballotté entre ses parents** a tug-of-love child; **un enfant ballotté entre des écoles/villes** a child that has been

moved around from school to school/from town to town
VI *(de bagages)* to be tossed about; *(de porte)* to swing to and fro; *(de bateau)* to toss (about); *(de poitrine)* to bounce (up and down)

ballottine [balɔtin] **NF** *Culin* meat roll

balloune [balun] **NF** *Can Fam* **être en b.** *(enceinte)* to be in the (pudding) club

ball-trap, *pl* **ball-traps** [baltrap] **NM** *(sport)* clay-pigeon shooting, skeet shooting; *(appareil)* trap

balluchon [balyʃɔ̃] **NM** *Fam (de vêtements)* bundle; **faire son b.** to pack one's bags

balnéaire [balneɛr] **ADJ** **station b.** seaside resort

balnéothérapie [balneoterapi] **NF** *Méd* balneotherapy

baloche [balɔʃ] **NM** *Fam* local dance

balourd, -ourde [balur, -urd] **ADJ** *(personne)* awkward, clumsy; *(peu délicat)* loutish, uncouth
N *(maladroit)* clumsy oaf; **un grand b.** *(grand gars)* a great hulking fellow; **c'est le roi des balourds** he's a great oaf
NM *Tech* unbalance

balourdise [balurdiz] **NF 1** *(manque de finesse)* awkwardness, clumsiness **2** *(gaffe)* stupid blunder, *Fam* clanger

balsa [balza] **NM** balsa (wood)

balsamier [balzamje] **NM** balsam tree

balsamine [balzamin] **NF** *(plante)* balsam

balte [balt] **ADJ** Baltic; **les pays baltes** the Baltic States

balthazar [baltazar] **NM** *(de champagne)* Balthazar

Baltique [baltik] **NF** **la (mer) B.** the Baltic (Sea)

baluchon [balyʃɔ̃] **NM** *Fam* = **balluchon**

balustrade [balystrad] **NF 1** *Archit* balustrade **2** *(clôture)* railing

balustre [balystr] **NM** *Archit* baluster

balzacien, -ienne [balzasjɛ̃, -jɛn] **ADJ** *Littér* typical of Balzac; **une description très balzacienne** a description very typical of Balzac; **dans le plus pur style b.** in a style that is pure Balzac

balzan [balzɑ̃] **ADJ** **cheval b.** horse with white stockings

balzane [balzan] **NF** *(de cheval)* white stocking

bambin, -ine [bɑ̃bɛ̃, -in] **N** *Fam* toddler

bamboche [bɑ̃bɔʃ] **NF** *Fam* spree, lark; **faire b.** to live it up

bambocher [bɑ̃bɔʃe] **VI** *Fam* to live it up

bambocheur, -euse [bɑ̃bɔʃœr, -øz] **N** *Fam* reveller; **c'est un b.** he likes living it up

bambou [bɑ̃bu] **NM** *(plante)* bamboo; *Culin* **pousses de b.** bamboo shoots; *Fig Fam* **coup de b.** *(insolation)* sunstroke; *Fam* **il a le coup de b.** *(fou)* he's nuts *or* crazy; *(épuisé)* he's shattered *or* whacked; *Fam* **c'est le coup de b.** *(très cher)* it's a rip-off

bamboula [bɑ̃bula] **NF** *Fam* spree, lark; **faire la b.** to live it up

ban [bɑ̃] **NM 1** *(bannissement)* banishment; **mettre qn au b.** to banish sb; **pratique mise au b.** outlawed practice; **être au b. de la société** to be outlawed by society; **être en rupture de b.** to have illegally returned from banishment; *Fig* **être en rupture de b. avec** to have broken with **2 bans** *(de mariage)* banns; **publier les bans** to publish the banns **3 le b. et l'arrière-b.** *Hist* the ban and the arrière-ban; *Fig (tout le monde)* the world and his wife **4** *(applaudissements)* round of applause; **faire un b. pour qn** to give sb a round of applause, to applaud sb; **un b. pour Monsieur le maire!** a round of applause for the mayor!, ≃ three cheers for the mayor! **5** *(avant une annonce officielle)* drum roll; *Arch (d'un événement)* (public) proclamation

banal [banal] ADJ **1** *(pl* **banals)** *(objet)* ordinary, commonplace; *(gens, occupation)* ordinary, run-of-the-mill; *(idée, remarque, style)* trite, banal; *(accident, exemple, excuse)* common; **parler de choses banales** to engage in small talk; **ça, c'est peu b.!** that's unusual, that's a bit out of the ordinary!; **c'est d'un b.!** it's dead ordinary!; *(idée)* it's so trite! **2** *(pl* **banaux)** *Hist (moulin, fournil)* communal

banalement [banalmɑ̃] ADV in an ordinary manner; **notre rencontre s'est passée très b.** our meeting took place in very ordinary circumstances

banalisation [banalizasjɔ̃] NF **1** *(de la violence, du sexe dans les médias)* trivialization; **la b. des transports aériens** the fact that air travel has become commonplace *or* has become an everyday phenomenon; **la b. des voitures de police** the use of unmarked police cars **2** *Rail (pour une voie à deux sens)* signalling for two-way working; **la b. d'une locomotive** the manning of an engine by several crews

banaliser [banalize] VT **1** *(sexe, violence etc)* to trivialize; **voiture** *ou* **véhicule banalisé(e)** unmarked police car **2** *Rail (voie ferrée)* to signal for two-way working; **b. une locomotive** to have an engine manned by several crews
▪ VPR **se banaliser** to become commonplace

banalité [banalite] NF **1** *(caractère)* *(d'objet, de gens, d'occupation)* ordinariness; *(d'idée, de remarque, de style)* triteness, banality; *(d'accident, d'exemple)* commonness **2** **banalités** small talk, *Péj* platitudes; **un tissu** *ou* **ramassis de banalités** a collection of platitudes

banane [banan] NF **1** *(fruit)* banana **2** *Mil Fam (médaille)* medal, *Br* gong **3** *Aviat Fam (hélicoptère)* chopper **4** *(coiffure)* quiff; **porter la b.** to have a quiff **5** *(petit sac)* bum-bag, *Am* fanny pack

bananier, -ière [bananje, -jɛr] NM **1** *(arbre)* banana tree **2** *Naut* banana boat
▪ ADJ *(plantation, production)* banana; **république bananière** banana republic

banc [bɑ̃] NM **1** *(siège)* bench, seat **2** *(de rocher etc)* layer, bed; *Min (de charbon)* seam; *Naut* **toucher au b.** to run aground **3** *(colonie)* *(de poissons)* shoal, school; **b. d'huîtres** oyster bed **4** *(de brume)* bank; **b. de brouillard** fog bank **5** *Tech* (work)bench; *(d'un tour)* bed
▪▶ *Jur* **b. des accusés** dock; *Géog* **b. continental** continental shelf; **b. à coulisses** *(à l'aviron)* sliding seat; **b. d'école** school bench; **ils se sont connus sur les bancs de l'école** they got to know each other at school; **b. d'église** pew; **b. d'essai** *Ind* test bed; *Mktg* benchtest; *Ordinat* benchmark; *Fig* testing ground; **faire passer au b. d'essai** to benchtest; **mettre qch au b. d'essai** to test sth (out); **b. de glace** ice floe, ice field; **b. de jardin** garden bench *or* seat; *Jur* **b. des magistrats** magistrates' bench; *Ordinat* **b. de mémoire** memory bank; *Pol* **le b. des ministres** *Br* ≃ the (government) front bench; *TV, Cin* **b. de montage** editing desk, edit controller; *Can* **b. de neige** snowbank; **b. d'œuvre** churchwardens' pew; *Jur* **b. des prévenus** dock; **b. de roches** reef; **b. de sable** sandbank; **b. des témoins** witness box *or Am* witness stand; **le B. de Terre-Neuve** the Banks (of Newfoundland); **b. de vase** mudbank

bancable [bɑ̃kabl] ADJ *Fin* bankable, negotiable

bancaire [bɑ̃kɛr] ADJ bank(ing); **opérations bancaires** bank(ing) transactions; **chèque b.** bank cheque; **compte b.** bank account; **informatique b.** computerized banking

bancal, -ale, -als, -ales [bɑ̃kal] ADJ *(personne)* lame; *(meuble etc)* wobbly, rickety; *Fig (raisonnement, idée)* shaky, unsound; *(projet)* unsound

bancarisation [bɑ̃karizasjɔ̃] NF **la b. de l'économie** the growing role of banks in the economy; **la b. de la population française** the spread of the use of banking services amongst the French population

bancarisé [bɑ̃karize] ADJ **être b.** to have an account with a bank, to use the banking system; **presque toutes les PME sont bancarisées** almost all small businesses have accounts with a bank *or* use the banking system

bancassurance [bɑ̃kasyrɑ̃s] NF *Banque* bancassurance

bancassureur [bɑ̃kasyrœr] NM insurance banker

bancatique [bɑ̃katik] NF electronic *or* computerized banking

banco [bɑ̃ko] NM *Cartes* banco; **faire b.** to go banco

bancomat [bɑ̃komat] NM *Suisse* ATM, cash dispenser

banc-titre, *pl* **bancs-titres** NM *Cin, TV* rostrum camera

bandage [bɑ̃daʒ] NM **1** *(pansement)* bandage; *(action)* *(d'une blessure)* bandaging, binding up; **b. herniaire** truss **2** *(d'une roue)* *(en caoutchouc)* tyre, *Am* tire; *(en métal)* hoop, band **3** *(d'un ressort)* tightening; *(d'un arc)* bending

bandagiste [bɑ̃daʒist] N *Méd* truss manufacturer *or* supplier

bandana [bɑ̃dana] NM bandan(n)a

bandant [bɑ̃dɑ̃] ADJ *Vulg* sexy; *Fig* orgasmic; **une proposition bandante** a turn-on; **ce n'est pas très b., comme idée de vacances** it doesn't really turn me on, as holiday ideas go

BANDE¹ [bɑ̃d] NF **1** *(de tissu, de papier, de métal etc)* strip, band; *(de terre)* strip, stretch, belt; *(motif)* stripe; *Fig* **par la b.** in a roundabout way, indirectly; **mettre un journal sous b.** to put a wrapper round a newspaper; **b. de téléimprimeur** ticker tape; *Agr* **culture en bandes de niveau** strip contour farming **2** *Méd* bandage; **mettre une b. à qn** to put a bandage on sb, to bandage sb **3** *(magnétique)* tape; *(pellicule)* film; **tourner une b. d'essai** to have a screen test; **faire tourner une b. d'essai à qn** to give sb a screen test **4** *(de roue)* hoop, band **5** *Tél, Ordinat* **à large b.** broadband **6** *Billard* cushion **7** *Opt (du spectre)* band **8** *(d'une mitrailleuse)* (feeding) belt **9** *Hér* bend **10** *Naut (de navire)* side; *(inclinaison)* list; **donner de la b.** to list, to have a list
▪▶ *Cin* **b. amorce** (film) leader; **b. d'arrêt d'urgence** hard shoulder; *Cin* **b. audionumérique** digital audio tape, DAT; **b. en bobine** open-reel tape, reel-to-reel tape; *Ordinat* **b. en cassettes** cassette tape; **b. cyclable** cycle lane; *Ordinat* **b. de défilement** scroll bar; *Cin* **b. démo** demo tape; **b. dessinée** comic strip, strip cartoon; *Ordinat* **b. de données** data tape; **b. enregistrée** recorded tape; *Aviat* **b. d'envol** airstrip, landing strip; **b. ferrique** ferric tape; *Fin* **b. de fluctuation** *(d'une monnaie)* fluctuation band; *Ordinat* **b. sans fin** endless tape; *Radio* **b. de fréquences** frequency band; **b. illustrée** comic strip, strip cartoon; *TV, Cin* **b. internationale** music and effects track, M&E track; *Radio* **b. latérale** sideband; **b. magnétique** magnetic tape; **b. magnétique au-**dio audio tape; **b. maîtresse** *ou* **mère** master tape; *Aut* **b. médiane** *(sur la route)* central (white) line; *Mil* **b. molletière** puttee; **b. noire** terrorist gang; **b. originale (d'un film)** original (film) soundtrack; *Ordinat* **b. de papier** paper tape; *Aut* **b. pare-soleil** shadeband; *Cin* **b. parole** dialogue track; *Électron, Ordinat* **b. passante** bandwidth; *Ordinat* **b. perforée** perforated tape, *Br* punched paper tape; **b. de présentation** *(d'une chanson etc)* demo tape; *Aut* **b. de protection latérale** side-impact bar; **b. de roulement** *(de pneu)* tread; **b. son** *ou* **sonore** sound reel *or* track; *Aut* **b. de stationnement** layby, *Am* rest stop; **b. Velpeau®** crepe bandage; **b. vidéo** videotape; **b. vidéo promotionnelle** promotional video; **b. vierge** blank tape; **bandes vierges** (film) stock

---

bande² NF **1** *(de personnes)* band, group; **b. d'amis** group of friends; **b. de voleurs** gang *or* band of thieves; **b. armée** armed gang; **elle fait b. à part** she keeps (herself) to herself; **viens avec nous, ne fais pas b. à part** come with us, don't stay all on your own *or* all by yourself; **cet artiste fait un peu b. à part dans le mouvement minimaliste français** this artist is rather a special case *or* is something of an exception in the French minimalist movement; **faire qch en b.** to do sth in a group; **être de la b. de qn** to belong to sb's gang; **toute la b.** the whole gang, the whole lot of them; **une b. de fous/d'incapables** a bunch of madmen/incompetents; **b. d'imbéciles!** you bunch of idiots! **2** *(d'oiseaux)* flock, flight; *(de loups)* pack; *(de buffles)* herd; *(de marsouins)* school; *(de lions)* pride

bandé [bɑ̃de] ADJ **1** *(main, cheville etc)* bandaged; **les yeux bandés** blindfold(ed) **2** *Hér* bendy

bande-annonce, *pl* **bandes-annonces** NF *Cin* trailer, *Am* preview (**de** for)

bandeau, -eaux [bɑ̃do] NM **1** *(pour les cheveux)* headband; **cheveux en bandeaux** hair parted in the middle and swept back round the sides **2** *(sur les yeux)* blindfold; **mettre un b. à qn** to blindfold sb, to put a blindfold on sb; *Fig* **avoir un b. sur les yeux** to be blind **3** *Archit* string course **4** *Journ (titre)* streamer **5** *Ordinat (dans un site web)* banner

bandelette [bɑ̃dlɛt] NF *(de tissu)* strip, band; **bandelettes** *(des momies)* bandages, wrappings; **b. réactive** *Méd* testing strip; *(pour analyse d'urine)* dipstick; *Aut* **b. talon** chafer strip

bander [bɑ̃de] VT **1** *(blessure, main etc)* to bandage (up), to put a bandage on; **b. les yeux à** *ou* **de qn** to blindfold sb, to put a blindfold on sb **2** *(ressort)* to tighten; **b. un arc** to bend a bow; **b. ses muscles** to tense one's muscles
▪ VI *Vulg* to have a hard-on *or* an erection; *Fig* **faire b. qn** to excite sb; **le théâtre, ça la fait b.** she gets a real buzz from the theatre

banderille [bɑ̃drij] NF *(en tauromachie)* banderilla

banderole [bɑ̃drɔl] NF banderole; *(publicitaire)* streamer; *(de manifestant)* banner

bandit [bɑ̃di] NM *(escroc)* crook, swindler, rogue; *Vieilli (brigand)* bandit, brigand; **b. de grand chemin** highwayman

banditisme [bɑ̃ditism] NM crime; **recrudescence du b.** crime wave; **le grand b.** organized crime

bandonéon [bɑ̃doneɔ̃] NM bandoneon

bandouiller [bɑ̃duje] VI *Vulg* to have a semi

bandoulière [bɑ̃duljɛr] NF **1** *(d'un sac etc)* shoulder strap; **porter/mettre qch en b.** to carry/sling sth over *or* across one's shoulder; **le sac en b.** with one's bag slung over *or* across one's shoulder **2** *Mil* bandolier

bang [bãg] NM INV Aviat (super)sonic boom

Bangladesh [bãglade∫, bẽglade∫] NM Bangladesh

banian [banjã] NM banyan (tree)

banjo [bãn(d)ʒo] NM Mus banjo VOIR GRAMMAIRE A12

banlieue [bãljø] NF suburbs pl; la grande/petite b. the outer/inner suburbs; vivre en b. to live in the suburbs or in suburbia; maisons de b. suburban houses; Rail ligne/gare de b. suburban line/station; b. rouge communist-voting suburb
NM Belg stopping train

> **Banlieue**
> In France the word "banlieue" often refers not to the upmarket areas of a city – as the word "suburbia" can suggest in English-speaking countries – but to the impoverished suburban areas on the outskirts of some cities. These neighbourhoods are culturally and ethnically diverse and are frequently associated with social problems such as delinquency, unemployment and unrest.

banlieusard, -arde [bãljøzar, -ard] N Fam suburbanite

banne [ban] NF 1 (pour le charbon etc) cart 2 (panier) (wicker) basket 3 (de magasin etc) awning, canopy

banneret [banrε] NM Hist banneret; chevalier b. knight banneret

banneton [bantɔ̃] NM 1 (pour le pain) basket 2 (pour la pêche) corf

banni, -ie [bani] ADJ (personne) banished, exiled
N exile

bannière [banjεr] NF (étendard) banner; il s'est rangé sous la b. des écologistes he's joined the ranks of the ecologists; la b. étoilée the Star-Spangled Banner; Fig c'est la croix et la b. pour le faire manger it's a devil of a job or a heck of a job getting him to eat; c'est la croix et la b., ce job! this job is a real devil!

bannir [banir] VT (personne) to banish, to exile; bannissez les pensées négatives de votre esprit banish negative thoughts from your mind; il a complètement banni la cigarette he has completely given up smoking; vous devez b. le sucre de votre alimentation you must exclude sugar from your diet, you must cut sugar out of your diet

bannissement [banismã] NM banishment

banquable [bãkabl] ADJ Fin bankable, negotiable

banque [bãk] NF 1 (commerce) banking; (établissement) bank; avoir de l'argent à la b. to have money in the bank; porter un chèque à la b. to bank a cheque; opération de b. bank(ing) transaction; billet de b. banknote, Am bank bill; chèque de b. Br bank cheque; carnet ou livret de b. bankbook; travailler dans la b. to be in banking; avoir un compte en b. chez ... to have an account or to bank with ...; employé/directeur de b. bank clerk/manager; b. privée/de l'État privately owned/State bank 2 Cartes bank; tenir la b. to be (the) banker; faire sauter la b. to break the bank
▸▸ b. d'acceptation Br accepting or Am acceptance house; b. d'affaires investment bank, Br merchant bank; b. centrale central bank; B. centrale européenne European Central Bank; b. commerciale commercial bank; b. compensatrice clearing bank; b. confirmatrice confirming bank; b. de crédit credit bank; b. de dépôt clearing bank; b. de détail retail bank; (activité) retail banking; b. à distance direct banking; b. à domicile tele-

banking, home banking; Ordinat b. de données data bank; b. d'émission bank of issue; b. d'entreprise corporate banking; b. d'épargne savings bank; b. d'escompte discount house or bank; B. européenne d'investissement European Investment Bank; B. européenne pour la reconstruction et le développement European Bank for Reconstruction and Development; B. de France Bank of France; b. de gestion de patrimoine trust bank; b. de gros wholesale bank; b. d'images Ordinat image bank; TV television archives, image bank; B. internationale pour la reconstruction et le développement International Bank for Reconstruction and Development; la B. mondiale the World Bank; b. notificatrice advising bank; b. de placement issuing bank or house; Radio, TV b. de programmes programme library, programme archives; b. de recouvrement collecting agency or bank; Méd b. de ou du sang blood bank; b. du sperme sperm bank; b. statistique statistics bank; b. des yeux eye bank

banquer [bãke] VI Fam to cough up, Br to stump up; c'est toujours moi qui banque it's always me that has to cough up

banqueroute [bãkrut] NF Jur bankruptcy; faire b. to go bankrupt

banqueroutier, -ière [bãkrutje, -jεr] N bankrupt; (frauduleux) fraudulent bankrupt

banquet [bãkε] NM banquet, feast; salle de b. banqueting hall

banquette [bãkεt] NF 1 (siège) seat; b. de piano piano stool; Aut la b. arrière the back seat 2 Constr (de terre etc) bank; (de pont, de tunnel) (foot)path; Archit b. de fenêtre window seat 3 (d'un couloir d'autobus) = kerb separating a bus lane from the rest of the roadway

banquier, -ière [bãkje, -jεr] N Fin, Cartes banker; Fig crois-tu que je vais être ton b.? do you think I'm going to finance or Am bankroll you?; je ne suis pas b. I'm not made of money
▸▸ b. d'affaires merchant banker; b. prêteur lending bank

banquise [bãkiz] NF ice floe, pack ice, ice pack

bantou, -oue [bãtu] ADJ Bantu
N B. Bantu

bantoustan [bãtustã] NM Bantustan, Bantu Homeland

baobab [baɔbab] NM baobab (tree)

baptême [batεm] NM 1 Rel baptism, christening; conférer ou donner le b. à qn to baptize or christen sb; recevoir le b. to be baptized or christened; nom de b. Christian name, first or Am given name 2 (d'une cloche) blessing; (d'un navire) naming, christening
▸▸ b. de l'air first flight; Mil b. du feu baptism of fire; Naut b. de la ligne crossing of the line

baptiser [batize] VT 1 Rel (personne) to baptize, to christen; (surnommer) to christen, to nickname; ses parents l'ont baptisée Léa her parents christened her Léa; on l'avait baptisé 'le Balafré' they had christened or nicknamed him 'Scarface'; b. son vin/son lait to water down one's wine/milk 2 Rel (cloche) to bless; (navire) to name

baptismal, -ale, -aux, -ales [batismal, -o] ADJ baptismal

baptisme [batism] NM baptism

baptistaire [batistεr] ADJ registre b. register of baptisms; extrait b. certificate of baptism

baptiste [batist] ADJ, N Rel Baptist

baptistère [batistεr] NM Rel baptist(e)ry

baquer (se) [səbake] VPR Fam to go for a dip

baquet [bakε] NM 1 (cuve) tub 2 Aut (siège en) b. bucket seat

bar¹ [bar] NM (poisson) bass; b. commun sea perch

bar² [bar] NM (café, comptoir) bar; le b. du coin the bar on the corner, the local; prendre une consommation au b. to have a drink at the bar; b. américain (dans une cuisine) bar; b.-tabac = bar where tobacco, stamps and lottery tickets are also sold over the counter; b. à vin wine bar

bar³ NM Météo bar

barachois [bara∫wa] NM Can (dans une rivière) sandbar

baragouin [baragwẽ] NM Fam gibberish, gobbledegook

baragouinage [baragwinaʒ] NM Fam jabbering

baragouiner [baragwine] Fam VT (langue étrangère) to speak badly; b. l'anglais to talk broken English; qu'est-ce qu'il baragouine? what's he jabbering (on) about?
VI to jabber (on)

baragouineur, -euse [baragwinœr, -øz] N Fam jabberer

baraka [baraka] NF Fam (good) luck; avoir la b. to be lucky

baraque [barak] NF 1 (logement provisoire) hut, shack, shed 2 Fam (foyer) place; Péj (lieu) hole, dump; casser la b. to bring the house down; il n'y a rien à manger dans cette b.! there's nothing to eat in this joint! 3 (de foire etc) stall, stand

> Il faut noter que le nom anglais **barracks** est un faux ami. Il signifie **caserne**.

baraqué [barake] ADJ Fam hefty

baraquement [barakmã] NM shacks; Mil camp

baraquer [barake] VI (d'un chameau) to kneel down

baratin [baratẽ] NM Fam (bavardage) chatter; (d'un vendeur) sales talk, patter, spiel; (pour draguer) sweet or smooth talk; b. publicitaire (écrit) blurb; (parlé) sales pitch; quel b.! (je n'y comprends rien) what gibberish!; faire du b. (à qn) to spin (sb) a yarn, to shoot (sb) a line; ce type me fait du b. (pour draguer) this guy's chatting me up or Am hitting on me; faire son b. à un client to give a customer the patter or sales talk or spiel; avoir du b. to be a smooth talker

baratiner [baratine] Fam VI (parler beaucoup) to chatter; (parler sans sincérité) to shoot a line, to spin a yarn; (d'un vendeur) to give one's patter or sales talk or spiel
VT to sweet-talk; b. un client to give a client the patter or sales talk or spiel; b. une fille to chat up or Am hit on a girl

baratineur, -euse [baratinœr, -øz] N Fam smooth talker, smoothie

baratte [barat] NF churn

baratter [barate] VT (lait) to churn

barbacane [barbakan] NF 1 (ouvrage) barbican, outwork; (meurtrière) loop(hole) 2 (canalisation) drainage channel

Barbade [barbad] NF Barbados

barbant [barbã] ADJ Fam boring

barbaque [barbak] NF Fam meat; (de mauvaise qualité) lousy meat

barbare [barbar] ADJ (cruel, sauvage) barbaric, barbarous; Fam il écoute de la musique b. he's listening to that awful racket he calls music
N barbarian

barbaresque [barbarεsk] Vieilli ADJ Berber; les États barbaresques the Barbary States
N B. Berber

Barbarie [barbari] NF Vieilli la B. the Barbary States

barbarie [barbari] NF **1** *(cruauté, action cruelle)* barbarity **2** *(manque de civilisation)* barbarism

barbarisme [barbarism] NM *Gram* barbarism

barbe¹ [barb] NF **1** *(d'homme)* beard; **sans b.** *(adulte)* clean-shaven; *(jeune adolescent)* beardless; **avoir de la b.** *(d'un homme)* to need a shave; *(d'un adolescent)* to have some hairs on one's chin; **se faire pousser la b.** to grow a beard, to let one's beard grow; **faire la b. à qn** to shave sb; **il avait une b. de huit jours** he had a week's beard *or* growth; **tu n'as pas encore de b. au menton et tu crois tout savoir** you're still in short pants and you think you know everything; **brosse/savon à b.** shaving brush/soap; **parler dans sa b.** to mutter, to mumble; **femme à b.** bearded lady; *Fig* **faire qch à la b. de qn** to do sth right under sb's nose; **rire dans sa b.** to laugh up one's sleeve; *Fam* **quelle b.!** what a drag!, what a bore!; *Fam* **la b.!** shut it!, shut up!; *Fam* **vieille b.** old fogey
2 *(de chèvre, d'oiseau etc)* beard; *(de chat)* whiskers; *(de poisson)* barbel, wattle; *(de plume, d'hameçon)* barb; *(du blé)* beard
3 *Tech (sur moulage etc)* bur(r); **barbes** *(sur papier)* deckle edge
▸▸ **b. à papa** candy floss, *Am* cotton candy

barbe² NM **(cheval) b.** barb, Barbary horse

barbeau [barbo] NM **1** *(poisson)* **b. commun** barbel; **b. de mer** red mullet **2** *Bot* cornflower **3** *Arg (souteneur)* pimp
ADJ INV **(bleu) b.** cornflower blue

Barbe-Bleue N Bluebeard

barbecue [barbəkju] NM barbecue; **faire un b.** to have a barbecue

barbelé [barbəle] ADJ *(flèche)* barbed; **fil de fer b.** barbed wire
NMPL **barbelés** barbed wire; *Mil* barbed wire entanglement; **être derrière les barbelés** to be in a prison camp

barber [barbe] *Fam* VT *(personne)* to bore stiff, to bore to death
VPR **se barber** to be bored stiff *or* bored to death

barbeux, -euse [barbø, -øz] *Can Fam* ADJ **être b.** to be a pain (in the neck)
NM pain (in the neck)

barbiche [barbiʃ] NF goatee (beard)

barbichette [barbiʃɛt] NF *Fam* small goatee (beard)

barbichu [barbiʃy] ADJ with a goatee (beard)
NM man with a goatee (beard)

barbier [barbje] NM **1** *Vieilli (qui rase le visage)* barber **2** *Can (coiffeur pour hommes)* (men's) hairdresser, barber; **salon de b.** (men's) hairdresser's, barber's, barbershop

barbillon [barbijɔ̃] NM **1** *(d'un poisson)* barbel; **barbillons** *(de cheval, bœuf)* barbs **2** *(poisson)* barbel; **b. de mer** red mullet

barbital, *pl* **barbitals** [barbital] NM *Pharm* barbitone, *Am* barbital

barbiturique [barbityrik] *Pharm* ADJ barbituric
NM barbiturate

barbiturisme [barbityrism] NM *Méd* barbiturate poisoning; *(dépendance)* barbiturism, addiction to barbiturates

barbon [barbɔ̃] NM *Litt* **vieux b.** greybeard

barbotage [barbɔtaʒ] NM *(dans l'eau)* paddling, splashing (about); *Chimie (d'un gaz dans un liquide)* bubbling

barboter [barbɔte] VI *(dans l'eau)* to paddle, to splash (about); *(du gaz)* to bubble *(through liquid)*; **les enfants barbotent dans la piscine** the children are splashing about in the swimming pool
VT *Arg (voler)* to pinch, *Br* to nick; **quelqu'un m'a barboté mon stylo** someone's pinched my pen

barboteur, -euse [barbɔtœr, -øz] N **1** *(dans l'eau)* paddler **2** *Arg (voleur)* thief
NM *Chimie* bubbler, blower
NF barboteuse playsuit, rompers

barbotin [barbɔtɛ̃] NM *Tech* sprocket wheel

barbouillage [barbujaʒ] NM **1** *(action de peindre)* daubing, smearing; *(action d'écrire)* scrawling, scribbling **2** *(mauvaise peinture)* daub; *(griffonnage)* scrawl, scribble

barbouiller [barbuje] VT **1** *(avec de la peinture)* to daub, to smear; *(salir) (visage)* to smear; *(papier avec de l'encre)* to blot; **visage barbouillé de larmes/de chocolat** tear-stained face/face smeared with chocolate; **b. des toiles** to do a bit of painting **2** *(griffonner)* to scribble, to scrawl; **b. un article** to dash off an article **3** *Fam* **ça me barbouille l'estomac** *ou* **le cœur** it makes me feel sick, it turns my stomach; **avoir l'estomac barbouillé** to feel queasy

barbouilleur, -euse [barbujœr, -øz] N **1** *(de peinture)* dauber, so-called artist **2 b.** *(de papier)* scribbler, hack

barbouze [barbuz] NF *Fam* **1** *(barbe)* beard **2** *(agent secret)* secret agent

barbu, -ue [barby] ADJ bearded
NM **1** bearded man **2** *Fam (fondamentaliste islamique)* Islamic fundamentalist **3** *Vulg (poils pubiens de la femme)* bush
NF **barbue** *(poisson)* brill

barcarolle [barkarɔl] NF *Mus* barcarol(l)e

barcasse [barkas] NF *Naut* launch, boat

Barcelone [barsəlɔn] N Barcelona

barda [barda] NM *Arg* gear, kit, stuff; *Mil* kit

bardage [bardaʒ] NM **1** *(de matériaux lourds)* hand transport **2** *(pour protéger un tableau etc)* boarding; *(d'un bâtiment)* weatherboarding, *Am* siding

bardane [bardan] NF *(plante)* burdock

bardas [barda] NM *Can (pagaille)* shambles; **être de b.** *(déranger)* to be a nuisance

barde¹ [bard] NF **1** *Culin (sur un rôti)* bard **2** *Hist (protégeant les chevaux de bataille)* bard

barde² NM bard, poet

bardeau, -eaux [bardo] NM **1** *Constr* shingle; **toit de bardeaux** shingle roof **2** *Zool* hinny **3** *Can Fam* **manquer un b.** to be not quite right in the head, to have a slate loose

barder¹ [barde] V IMPERS *Fam* **ça va b.!** there's going to be trouble!; **c'est là que ça a commencé à b.!** and then the fun began!, and then the sparks flew!

barder² VT **1** *Culin (volaille etc)* to bard **2** *Hist (cheval)* to bard; **chevalier bardé de fer** steel-clad knight; *Fig* **malle bardée d'étiquettes** trunk stuck all over with labels; **il est bardé de diplômes/décorations** he's got a whole string of qualifications/decorations

bardot [bardo] NM *Zool* hinny

barème [barɛm] NM **1** *(de notes, de salaires)* scale; **b. fiscal** *ou* **d'imposition** tax schedule, tax scale; **b. des prix** price list, schedule of prices **2** *(pour calcul rapide)* ready reckoner

barge¹ [barʒ] NF *Naut* barge, lighter

barge² ADJ *voir* **barjo**

baril [baril] NM *(de vin)* cask, barrel; *(de poudre)* keg; *(d'anchois)* barrel; *Pétr* barrel *(42 gallons)*; **b. de lessive** drum of washing powder

barillet [barijɛ] NM **1** *(petit baril)* small barrel *ou* cask **2** *(d'une pompe)* barrel piston chamber; *(d'un revolver, d'une serrure)* cylinder, barrel; **il n'y avait rien dans le b.** the gun was empty; **b. (de ressort)** *(dans une horloge)* spring box, spring drum; **serrure à b.** cylinder lock, Yale® lock

bariolage [barjɔlaʒ] NM *(de peinture)* painting *or* daubing with bright colours; *Fig (de couleurs)* medley, riot; *Péj (motif)* gaudy colour scheme

bariolé [barjɔle] ADJ *(tissu)* multicoloured, *Péj* gaudy; **audience bariolée** colourfully dressed audience

barioler [barjɔle] VT to paint *or* daub in bright *or Péj* gaudy colours

bariolure [barjɔlyr] NF bright *or Péj* gaudy colours

barjo(t) [barʒo] *Fam* N nut, *Br* nutter
ADJ crazy

barmaid [barmɛd] NF barmaid

barman, *pl* **barmen, barmans** [barman, -mɛn] NM barman

barn [barn] NM *Phys* barn

barographe [barɔgraf] NM *Météo* barograph

baromètre [barɔmɛtr] NM *Météo, Fig* barometer; **b. anéroïde** aneroid barometer; **b. enregistreur** recording barometer

barométrique [barɔmetrik] ADJ barometric

baron [barɔ̃] NM **1** *(seigneur)* baron; *Fig* **les barons de la finance/de l'industrie** financial/industrial tycoons **2** *Arg (protecteur)* protector; *(compère)* plant **3** *Culin* **b. d'agneau** baron of lamb

baronnage [barɔnaʒ] NM *(titre)* barony, baronage

baronne [barɔn] NF baroness

baronnet [barɔnɛ] NM baronet

baronnie [barɔni] NF *Hist* barony

baroque [barɔk] ADJ *(idées etc)* bizarre, odd, strange; *Archit, Beaux-Arts, Mus* baroque; *(perle)* tear-shaped
NM Baroque

baroud [barud] NM *Mil Fam* fighting; **b. d'honneur** last-ditch battle, last stand

barouder [barude] VI *Fam (voyager)* to knock about

baroudeur [barudœr] NM *Mil Fam (qui aime le combat)* (keen) fighter; **c'est un b.** *(voyageur)* he's knocked about a bit

barouf(le) [baruf(l)] NM *Fam* din, row, racket; **faire du b.** to make a din *or* row *or* racket

barque [bark] NF *Naut* **1** *(embarcation)* boat; **b. de pêcheur** fishing boat; **patron de b.** skipper; *Fig* **bien mener** *ou* **bien conduire sa b.** to manage one's affairs well; *Fig* **c'est elle qui mène la b.** she's the boss, she's in charge; **charger la b.** to overdo it **2 trois-mâts b.** barque

barquette [barkɛt] NF **1** *(récipient) (pour plat à emporter etc)* container; *(de fraises, framboises etc)* punnet **2** *(gâteau)* pastry boat

barracuda [barakyda] NM barracuda

barrage [baraʒ] NM **1** *(fait de bloquer) (d'une route, rue)* blocking (off), closing; *(d'un port)* blocking; *(d'une vallée)* damming; **faire b. à qn/qch** to block sb/sth **2** *(fermeture)* barrier, obstruction; *(d'un port)* boom; **b. routier** *ou* **de route** roadblock; **b. de police** police roadblock, police cordon; **b. (de retenue)** dam, barrage; *(de petite taille)* weir; *Mil* **b. aérien** anti-aircraft barrage; **(tir de) b.** barrage (fire)

BARRE [bar] NF **1** *(de métal)* bar, rod; *(de bois etc)* rod; *Sport* bar; *(de danse)* barre; *Fam* **c'est le coup de b.** it's a rip-off; *Fig Fam* **avoir un coup de b.** to be shattered *or* whacked; **s'exercer à la b., faire des exercices à la b.** to do exercises at the barre; **avoir barre(s) sur qn** to have an advantage over sb; **passer la b./sous la b. de 1000 euros** to rise above/drop below the 1,000 euro mark; *Archit* **b. (de) HLM** ≃ large block of council flats **2** *Naut (de bateau)* tiller; *(de navire)* helm; **homme de b.** helmsman; **être à** *ou* **tenir la b.**

to be at the helm; **prendre la b.** to take the helm; *Fig* **à partir d'aujourd'hui, je prends la b.** as from today, I'm in charge

3 *Jur (d'un tribunal)* bar; **b. des témoins** witness box *or Am* stand; **paraître à la b.** to appear before the court *or* at the bar; **être appelé à la b.** to be called to the witness box *or* stand

4 *(d'une rivière, d'un port)* (sand)bar; *(artificielle)* boom; **b. d'eau** (tidal) bore; **b. de flot** tidal wave; **b. de plage** surf

5 *(trait)* line, dash, stroke; **b. d'un t** cross(-bar) of a t; **mettre une b. à un t** to cross a t; *Mus* **b. de mesure** bar (line); **double b.** double bar

6 *(de cheval)* bar

7 *Hér* bend sinister

8 jeu de barres = prisoners' base

▸▸**b. d'accouplement** tie rod, coupling bar; *(de direction)* steering rod; *Aut* **b. antidévers** *ou* **anti-roulis** anti-roll bar; *Aut* **b. antivol** locking bar; **b. d'appui** *(d'une fenêtre)* rail; **barres asymétriques** asymmetric bars; *Aut* **b. de calandre** nudge bar; **b. de chocolat** bar of chocolate; **b. chocolatée** chocolate bar; *Aut* **b. de connexion** *(de la boîte de direction)* crossbar, tie rod; *Typ, Ordinat* **b. d'espacement** space bar; *Ordinat* **b. d'état** status bar; **b. de défilement** scroll bar; *Gym* **b. fixe** horizontal bar; *Ordinat* **b. d'icônes** icon bar; *Ordinat* **b. de menu** menu bar; *Ordinat* **b. de navigation** navigation bar; *Typ* **b. oblique** oblique, slash; *Typ* **b. oblique inversée** backslash; *Ordinat* **b. d'outils** tool bar; **barres parallèles** parallel bars; *Aut* **b. de remorquage** towing rod, towbar; *Aut* **b. de renfort latéral** side-impact bar; **b. de savon** bar of soap, cake of soap; *Ordinat* **b. de sélection** menu bar; *Aut* **b. stabilisatrice** stabilizer bar; *Ordinat* **b. de style** style bar; *Ordinat* **b. de titre** title bar; *Aut* **b. de toit** roof bar; *Aut* **b. de torsion** torsion bar, torque strut

barré [bɑʀe] ADJ **1** *(chemin, passage, route)* closed; **'route barrée'** 'road closed' **2 chèque b.** crossed cheque *or Am* check; **chèque non b.** open cheque **3 dent barrée** impacted tooth **4** *(à l'aviron)* **un deux b.** a coxed pair **5** *Fam* **on est mal b.** things don't look good

barreau, -eaux [baʀo] NM **1** *(d'une fenêtre, cage)* bar; *(d'une échelle)* rung; *(d'une chaise)* rung, crosspiece; *Fig* **b. de chaise** fat cigar; **fenêtre garnie de barreaux** barred window, window with bars; **être derrière les barreaux** to be behind bars **2** *Jur* **le b.** the bar; **être reçu** *ou* **admis au b.** to be called to the bar; **radier qn du b.** to disbar sb

barrement [baʀmɑ̃] NM *(d'un chèque)* crossing

barrer [baʀe] VT **1** *(porte, fenêtre)* to bar; *Can (fermer à clef)* to lock; *(route, passage, chemin)* to block (off), to close; **b. le passage** *ou* **la route à qn** to block *or* bar sb's way; *Fig* to stand in sb's way, to block sb, to thwart sb **2** *(chèque)* to cross; **b. un t** to cross a t **3** *(mot etc)* to cross out, to strike out; **je vais pouvoir b. ça de ma liste** I can cross that off my list **4** *Naut (bateau)* to steer; *(à l'aviron)* to cox

VPR **se barrer** *Fam* to clear off, to beat it, to scram

barrette¹ [baʀɛt] NF *Rel* biretta

barrette² NF **1** *(pour les cheveux)* (hair) slide, *Am* barrette **2** *(broche)* brooch; *(de médaille)* bar **3** *Fam (de haschich)* thin strip

▸▸*Ordinat* **b. de mémoire vive** RAM module; *Aut* **b. verticale** overrider

barreur [baʀœʀ] NM **1** *Naut* helmsman **2** *(à l'aviron)* cox; **un deux sans b.** a coxless pair

barricade [baʀikad] NF **b. (de rue)** (street) barricade; *Fig* **de l'autre côté de la b.** on the opposing side, on the other side of the fence

barricader [baʀikade] VT *(route, porte etc)* to barricade

VPR **se barricader** to barricade oneself in; **se b. dans une chambre** to barricade oneself in a room (**contre** against); *(pour ne pas être dérangé)* to shut *or* lock oneself up in a room

barrière [baʀjɛʀ] NF **1** *(obstacle)* barrier; *(clôture)* fence; *(dans le métro)* gate, barrier; *(d'un passage à niveau)* gate; **barrières culturelles/sociales** cultural/social barriers; *Géog* **b. naturelle** natural barrier; **la Grande B.** the Great Barrier Reef **2** *Hist (d'une ville, d'un château etc)* gate; *(péage)* toll gate, turnpike

▸▸*Com* **b. d'accès** access barrier; *Aviat* **b. antisouffle** blast wall; **b. à bascule** drop-arm barrier; **b. commerciale** trade barrier; *Aut* **b. de dégel** = ban on the use of a road by heavy traffic during a thaw; *Com* **barrières douanières** trade barriers; *Com* **b. à l'entrée** entry barrier; *Com* **b. non tarifaire** non-tariff barrier; *Phys* **b. de potentiel** potential barrier; *Com* **b. à la sortie** exit barrier; *Phys* **b. thermique** thermal barrier, heat barrier; **b. Vauban** security barrier

barrique [baʀik] NF barrel, cask *(containing approx 200 litres)*; *Fam* **il est gros comme une b.** he's as round as a barrel; *Fig Fam* **plein** *ou* **rond comme une b.** blind drunk, (as) drunk as a lord

barrir [baʀiʀ] VI *(d'un éléphant)* to trumpet

barrissement [baʀismɑ̃], **barrit** [baʀi] NM *(d'un éléphant)* trumpeting

bartavelle [baʀtavɛl] NF **(perdrix) b.** rock partridge

barycentre [baʀisɑ̃tʀ] NM *Math* barycentre

baryte [baʀit] NF *Chimie, Minér* baryta, barium oxide

baryté [baʀite] ADJ *Méd* **bouillie barytée** barium meal

baryton [baʀitɔ̃] *Mus* ADJ *(voix)* baritone NM baritone

baryum [baʀjɔm] NM *Chimie, Minér* barium

barzoï [baʀzɔj] NM *(chien)* borzoi

BAS [beɑɛs] NM *Admin (abrév* **Bureau d'aide sociale)** welfare office

BAS¹, BASSE [bɑ, bɑs]

ADJ	low **1, 2, 4** ▪ late **3** ▪ mean **4** ▪ petty **4**	
ADV	low **1, 4** ▪ down **5, 6**	
NM	bottom **1**	

ADJ **1** *(de peu de hauteur, d'altitude)* low; *(station de ski etc)* low(-lying); *(baromètre, température, prix)* low; **maison basse de toit** *ou* **à toit b.** low-roofed house, house with a low roof; **b. de plafond** low-ceilinged; *(d'une ville, Fig)* low ceiling; **b. sur pattes** short-legged; *Boxe, Fig* **coup b.** blow below the belt; **enfant en b. âge** infant; **avoir la vue basse** to be short-sighted *or* near-sighted; **basse saison** low season; **à b. prix** cheaply, for a low price; **maintenir les prix b.** to keep prices down *or* low; **prix les plus b.** rock-bottom prices, lowest possible prices; **en ce b. monde** here on earth; **au b. mot** at the very least, at the lowest estimate; **le soleil est b.** the sun is low; *Météo* **plafond b.** low ceiling (of cloud); **mer basse** low water *or* tide; **quand la mer est basse** when it's low tide, when the tide is low *or* out; **la marée est basse** the tide is out *or* low; **à marée basse** at low tide; *Fig* **la tête basse** with a hang-dog look; **le moral est très b.** morale is very low; **elle est au plus b.** she's really low, she's at a very low ebb; **terres** *ou* **régions basses** lowlands; **le b. Rhin** the lower Rhine; **la basse Normandie** Lower Normandy; **les Bas Bretons** the inhabitants of Lower Britanny

2 *(dans hiérarchie)* lower; **les basses classes** *(de la société)* the lower classes; *Pol* **la Chambre basse** the Lower House; **la partie basse d'une ville, la basse ville** the lower (part of a) town

3 *(dans le temps)* late; **le b. Moyen Âge** the late Middle Ages; **le B.-Empire** the Late Empire **4** *Péj (acte)* mean, base, low; *(besognes)* menial; **motif b.** base *or* contemptible motive; **terme/style b.** vulgar expression/style; **c'est une basse vengeance** that was a petty revenge; **c'est vraiment b. de sa part** it's really mean of him; **de basse naissance** of low(ly) birth; **de basse condition** from a poor family **5** *(son, note)* low; *(voix)* low, deep; *(dans le réglage de la tonalité)* bass; **parler à voix basse** to speak in a low voice *or* in a whisper *or* under one's breath; **clarinette basse** bass clarinet

ADV **1** *(dans l'espace)* low (down); **être assis trop b.** to be sitting too low (down); **mettre une étagère plus b.** to put a shelf lower (down); **quelques marches plus b.** a few steps lower down *or* farther down; **plus b. dans la rue** farther down the street; **dix lignes plus b.** ten lines (further) down; **les hirondelles volent b.** the swallows are flying low; **voir plus b.** see below; *Fig* **mettre qn plus b. que terre** to treat sb like dirt; *Bourse* **les cours sont tombés très b.** shares are well down; **la température est tombée b. pendant la nuit** the temperature plummeted during the night; **comment a-t-elle pu tomber si b.?** how could she sink so low?; **le malade est bien b.** the patient is very low **2 chapeau b.!** *(bravo)* bravo!; *Fam* **b. les mains** *ou* **les pattes!** hands off!, keep your paws off!; **b. les pattes!** *(à un chien)* paws (down)!; *Naut* **mettre b. une voile** to haul down a sail; **mettre pavillon b.** *Naut* to lower *or* strike the colours; *Fig Fam* to climb down **3** *(des animaux)* **mettre b.** to give birth, *Spéc* to drop (its young); *(d'une jument)* to foal; *(d'une brebis)* to lamb; *(d'une chèvre)* to kid; *(d'une chienne)* to pup, to whelp; *(d'une truie)* to farrow; **mettre b. avant terme** to cast *or* slip its young **4** *(en intensité)* low; **vous chantez trop b.** you are singing too low; *(dans le registre)* you are singing too softly; *(doucement)* you are singing too softly; **parler (tout) b.** to (speak in a) whisper; **parlez plus b., je vous prie** please speak more quietly, please lower your voice; **rire tout b.** to chuckle *or* laugh to oneself; **tu pourrais mettre la télévision/le chauffage plus b.?** could you turn down the television/the heating?

5 en b. *(à l'étage inférieur)* downstairs; **aller en b.** to go downstairs *or* down; **les gens d'en b.** the people below *or* downstairs; **ça a l'air de venir d'en b.** it seems to come from below *or* from downstairs; **agiter les bras de haut en b.** to move one's arms up and down; **de haut en b.** from top to bottom, downwards; **regarder qn de haut en b.** to look sb up and down, to look at sb from head to foot *or* toe; **il est vêtu de neuf de haut en b.** he's dressed from head to toe in new clothes; **de b. en haut** upwards; **la tête en b.** upside down; **ce vase est plus large en b.** this vase is wider at the bottom; **la jupe tombe mal en b.** the skirt hangs wrong at the bottom; **en** *ou* **au b. de** at the bottom of; *(escalier, page)* at the foot *or* bottom of; **en b. du village** at the lower end of the village

6 à b. la dictature/la police! down with dictatorship/the police!; **à b. Martin!** down with Martin!; **mettre** *ou* **jeter à b.** *(maison)* to pull down, to demolish; *(personne, gouvernement)* to bring down, to overthrow; **mettre b. les armes** *Mil* to lay down one's arms; *Fig (dans une dispute)* to give in

NM **1** *(partie inférieure)* bottom; *(d'une colline, échelle, page)* foot, bottom; **les gens du b.** the people below *or* downstairs; **l'étagère**

du b. the bottom shelf; **la boulangerie du b.** the bakery at the bottom (of street, village); **b. du dos** small of the back; **le** ou **les b. du navire** the ship's bottom **2** Aut **b. de caisse** underbody; **b. de marche** sill; **b. de porte** doorsill **3 les hauts et les b.** (de la vie etc) the ups and downs; **avoir des hauts et des b.** to have ups and downs or highs and lows ► ► **b. allemand** low German; **le b. clergé** the lower clergy; **b. de gamme** bottom-of-the-range, down-market; **b. latin** low Latin; Culin **b. morceaux** (de viande) cheap cuts; Typ **b. de page** footer; **les b. quartiers** (d'une ville) the poor districts

bas ² NM (de femme) stocking; **b. de soie/de Nylon®** silk/nylon stocking; **b. fin** ou **voile** sheer stocking; **b. mousse** stretch stocking; **b. 15 deniers** 15-denier stocking; **b. sans couture** seamless stocking; **b. filet** ou **résille** fishnet or mesh stocking; Méd **b. de contention** elastic stocking; Méd **b. élastique** elastic or support stocking; **b. de laine** woollen stocking; Fig nest egg; Méd **b. à varices** elastic or support stocking

basalte [bazalt] NM Géol basalt

basaltique [bazaltik] ADJ Géol basaltic

basané [bazane] ADJ (bronzé) (sun)tanned, sunburnt; (tanné) weatherbeaten; (naturellement) swarthy

basaner [bazane] VT (visage etc) to tan

bas-bleu, pl **bas-bleus** NM Péj bluestocking

bas-côté, pl **bas-côtés** NM **1** (d'une route etc) verge, shoulder, side; **défense de stationner sur les bas-côtés** no parking on the verge **2** (d'une église) (side) aisle

basculant [baskylɑ̃] ADJ **benne basculante** (de camion) tipping or dump body; **pont b.** drawbridge, bascule bridge; **siège b.** tip-up seat; **fenêtre basculante** tilt window

bascule [baskyl] NF **1** (pièce mobile) rocker; **mouvement de b.** rocking motion; **(jeu de) b.** seesaw; **fauteuil/cheval à b.** rocking chair/horse; Fig **politique de b.** balancing act **2 (balance à) b.** weighbridge, weighing machine; **b. automatique** ou **du pharmacien** weighing machine; **wagon à b.** tip wagon **3** Aut toggle; Ordinat toggle; (circuit) flip-flop (circuit); Électron **(montage en) b.** bistable trigger circuit, flip-flop circuit

basculement [baskylmɑ̃] NM (renversement) knocking over; (des intentions de vote) swing, reversal

basculer [baskyle] VT **1** (culbuter) to rock; **levier basculé par une came** lever rocked by a cam **2** (renverser) (charrette etc) to tip (up); (fardeau, chargement) to tip off **3** Tél (appel) to transfer VI **1** (tomber) to fall over, to topple over; **faire b.** (personne) to knock over, to knock off balance; (chargement) to tip over; **ce pays risque de b. dans la dictature** the country is in danger of tipping into dictatorship; **il a basculé dans l'opposition** he moved over or went over to the opposition; Pol **b. dans l'extrême droite** to swing (over) to the far right; Fig **nous étions heureux, et puis tout a basculé** we were happy, then everything turned upside down **2** Ordinat to toggle

basculeur [baskylœr] NM **1** (de wagon etc) tipper **2** Élec rocker switch; Ordinat toggle (key)

bas-de-casse NM INV Typ lower case; **en b.** lower-case, in lower case; **mettre qch en b.** to put sth into lower case

base [baz] NF **1** (d'une montagne) base, foot, bottom; (d'un bâtiment) base, foundation(s); Anat, Math (du cœur, d'un triangle etc) base; (en arpentage) base (line); (d'une machine) base plate; **jeter** ou **poser les bases de qch** to lay the foundations for sth **2** Mil etc (d'opérations) base; **b. de ravitaille-** ment supply base; **b. aérienne/navale** air/naval base; **b. de lancement (d'engins)** (missile) launch(ing) site; **b. arrière** rear base **3** (principe) basis; **être à la b. de qch** to be at the root or heart of sth; **argument qui pèche par la b.** fundamentally unsound argument; **sur la b. de qch** on the basis of sth; **vocabulaire/l'anglais de b.** basic vocabulary/English; **les produits de b. pour la maison** basic household goods, basics; **denrées de b.** staple commodities, staples; **avoir des connaissances de b. en informatique** to have an elementary or a basic knowledge of information technology; **traitement de b.** basic salary; **produits à b. d'amidon** starch-based products; **boisson à b. de gin** gin-based drink; **alimentation à b. de légumes** vegetable-based diet; **à b. d'Unix** Unix-based; **ordinateur à b. de 486** 486-based computer; **documents/données de b.** source documents/data; Pol etc **la b.** (d'un syndicat etc) the rank and file, the grassroots; **militant de b.** grassroots activist VOIR GRAMMAIRE A14

4 Math (d'un système de notation) base, radix; (d'un logarithme) radix, root, basis; **calculer en b. 3** to do calculations in base 3 **5** Chimie base **6** Électron (d'un transistor) base (electrode); Ordinat (d'imprimante laser) engine ► ► Compta **b. amortissable** basis for depreciation; Compta **b. de calcul** basis of calculations; Ordinat **b. de connaissances** knowledge base; Ordinat **b. de données** database; **mettre qch dans une b. de données** to enter sth into a database; Ordinat **b. de données client-serveur** client-server database; **b. de données de consommateurs** customer database; **b. de données relationnelle** relational database; **b. hors taxe** (de TVA) amount exclusive of VAT; **b. d'imposition** taxable base; **b. de loisirs** country park; **b. de maquillage** (make-up) base; Mktg **b. de sondage** sample base; Cin, TV **b. de temps** time code; **b. de vernis à ongles** nail varnish or Am polish base

base-ball [bɛzbol] NM Sport baseball

baser [baze] VT to base (sur on); **cette opinion n'est pas basée sur la réalité** this opinion is not based on reality; **entièrement basée sur le commerce** based wholly on trade, wholly trade-based; **avions américains basés en Grande-Bretagne** American aircraft based in Great Britain VPR se baser **se b. sur qch** to base one's argument on sth; **sur quoi te bases-tu pour dire que …?** what basis do you have or what's your basis for saying that …?

bas-fond, pl **bas-fonds** NM **1** (creux) low ground, hollow; Fig **les bas-fonds de la société** the dregs of society; **les bas-fonds d'une ville** the seedy districts of a town **2** (dans la mer, la rivière) shallow, shoal

Basic [bazik] NM Ordinat BASIC

basilic ¹ [bazilik] NM (plante) basil

basilic ² NM Zool, Myth basilisk

basilical, -ale, -aux, -ales [bazilikal, -o] ADJ Archit basilical

basilique [bazilik] NF Archit basilica

basin [bazɛ̃] NM Tex cotton damask

basique [bazik] ADJ **1** Chimie, Métal (sel, procédé etc) basic; **scorie b.** basic slag **2** (faits etc) basic; Fam **des connaissances/produits basiques** basic knowledge/products

basket [baskɛt] NF **une paire de baskets** a pair of baseball boots; Fam Fig **lâche-moi les baskets** don't hassle me, get off my back; Fam Fig **être bien dans ses baskets** to be Br sorted (in one's head) or Am very together NM Sport basketball

basket-ball [baskɛtbol] NM Sport basketball

basketteur, -euse [baskɛtœr, -øz] N Sport basketball player

bas-mât, pl **bas-mâts** NM Naut lower mast

basquaise [baskɛz] ADJ f **poulet b.** Basque chicken (cooked in a tomato and ham sauce)

basque ¹ [bask] ADJ Basque; **le Pays b.** the Basque country NM Ling Basque N B. Basque

basque ² NF (d'une veste etc) basque; Fig **être toujours pendu aux basques de qn** to be always at sb's heels

bas-relief, pl **bas-reliefs** NM Archit etc bas relief, low relief

basse [bɑs] ADJ voir bas¹ NF **1** Mus (partie) bass part; (voix, chanteur) bass; **b. chiffrée** ou **continue** ou **figurée** figured bass, basso continuo; **b. chantante** basso cantante, singing bass; **b. profonde, b. noble** basso profundo; **voix de b.** bass voice **2** (contrebasse) (double) bass; (saxophone) bass saxophone; (guitare) bass (guitar); (d'un instrument) bass strings **3** Naut shoal, flat, sandbank ► ► **b. de hautbois** bassoon; **b. de viole** bass viol

basse-contre, pl **basses-contre** NF Mus basso profundo

basse-cour, pl **basses-cours** NF **1** (cour) farmyard **2** (volaille) poultry

basse-fosse, pl **basses-fosses** NF dungeon

bassement [bɑsmɑ̃] ADV basely, meanly; **elle s'est b. vengée** she took a petty revenge

bassesse [basɛs] NF **1** (d'une expression, d'une action, du caractère de qn etc) baseness; **c'est d'une b.!** how low can you get?; **il est d'une b. sans nom** he's the lowest of the low; Vieilli **on lui reproche la b. de sa naissance** his low(ly) birth is held against him **2** (action) base or mean or contemptible action; **faire des bassesses** to behave contemptibly; **homme prêt à toutes les bassesses** man who would stoop to anything

basset ¹ [basɛ] NM (chien) basset (hound); **b. allemand** dachshund

basset ² NM Mus **cor de b.** tenor clarinet in F, basset horn

basse-taille, pl **basses-tailles** NF Mus basso cantante, singing bass

bassin [basɛ̃] NM **1** (récipient) basin, bowl; (d'une balance) pan; Méd **b. (de lit)** bedpan **2** (dans un jardin) ornamental lake; (plus petit) pond; (de fontaine) basin; (réservoir) tank; **petit b.** (de la piscine) small or children's pool; **grand b.** (de la piscine) large pool; **les bassins du Luxembourg** the pools in the Luxembourg Gardens **3** (d'un port) dock, basin; **entrer au b.** to dock; **b. à flot** wet dock; **b. à marée** tidal dock; **b. de radoub** dry dock, graving dock; **b. naturel/artificiel** natural/artificial basin; **b. de décantation** settling tank; **b. filtrant** filter bed **4** Géol basin; (dépression) depression; **le B. parisien** the Paris Basin; **le b. de la Tamise** the Thames Basin; **b. de réception** catchment area **5** Anat pelvis ► ► TV **b. d'audience** audience pool; **b. houiller** coal basin; **b. minier** mining area

bassinant [basinɑ̃] ADJ Fam boring

bassine [basin] NF (en cuivre) pan; (en plastique) bowl; **b. à confitures** preserving pan; **b. (à vaisselle)** washing-up bowl; **une (pleine) b. de confiture** a panful of jam

bassiner [basine] VT **1** (blessure etc) to bathe; (plate-bande, fleurs) to spray lightly **2** Arg (personne) to bore; **elle nous bassine avec ses histoires de bureau** we're bored stiff hearing about her work at the office **3 b. un**

lit to warm a bed (with a warming pan)

bassinet [basinɛ] NM 1 *Anat (du rein)* pelvis 2 *(d'armure)* basinet 3 *Fam* **cracher au b.** to cough up, *Br* to stump up

bassinoire [basinwar] NF 1 *(instrument)* warming pan 2 *Arg (importun)* bore, pain in the neck

bassiste [basist] N *Mus (contrebassiste)* (double) bass player; *(joueur de guitare basse)* bass guitarist

basson [basɔ̃] NM *Mus* 1 *(instrument)* bassoon 2 *(joueur)* bassoonist

bassoniste [basɔnist] N bassoonist

basta [basta] INT *Fam* that's enough!

bastide [bastid] NF 1 *(en Provence) (maison)* country house; *(ferme)* farm 2 *Hist (en Provence) (ville fortifiée)* fortified town

bastille [bastij] NF fortress; *Hist* **la B.** the Bastille; **la prise de la B.** the storming of the Bastille

bastingage [bastɛ̃gaʒ] NM *Naut* 1 *(garde-corps)* rail; **accoudé aux bastingages** leaning over the rails 2 *Hist* bulwark

bastion [bastjɔ̃] NM bastion; *Fig (de la liberté etc)* bastion, stronghold

baston [bastɔ̃] NM OU NF *Fam* fight, *Br* punch-up

bastonnade [bastɔnad] NF beating (with sticks), bastinado

bastonner [bastɔne] *Fam* V IMPERS **ça a bastonné** there was a scuffle *or Br* a punch-up *or Am* a fist fight
▪ VPR **se bastonner** to have a scuffle *or Br* a punch-up *or Am* a fist fight

bastos [bastos] NM *Arg (balle)* slug, bullet

bastringue [bastrɛ̃g] NM *Fam* 1 *(lieu)* (cheap) dance hall; *(orchestre)* (dance) band; *(bruit)* din, racket 2 *(affaires)* gear, stuff, *Br* clobber; **prendre tout son b.** to pack up all one's gear *or* stuff; **et tout le b.** and the whole bag of tricks, and the whole caboodle

bas-ventre, *pl* **bas-ventres** NM *Anat* lower abdomen

BAT [beate] NM *Typ (abrév* **bon à tirer**) press proof, final corrected proof; **donner le B.** to pass for press

bât [ba] NM packsaddle; **cheval de b.** packhorse; *Fig* **c'est là que le b. blesse** that's where the shoe pinches

bataclan [bataklɑ̃] NM *Fam* paraphernalia, *Br* clobber; **et tout le b.** and the whole caboodle, and whatever else; **vendez tout le b.!** sell the whole lot!

bataille [bataj] NF 1 *(combat)* battle, fight; **b. de rue** street fight; **b. terrestre/aérienne/navale** land/air/naval battle; **au (plus) fort de la b.** in the thick of the battle; **champ de b.** *Mil* battlefield; *Fig* mess; **cheval de b.** warhorse; *Fig* hobby-horse; **livrer b. à** to give battle to, to join battle with; *Fig* **c'est une b. constante** it's a constant battle, it's an endless struggle; **la vie est une dure b.** life is a struggle; **la b. contre l'inflation** the battle *or* fight against inflation; **une b. d'idées** a battle of ideas; **une b. politique/électorale** a political/an electoral contest; *Mil* **en b.** in battle order *or* formation, *Arch* in battle array; **stationnement en b.** angled parking; **voitures garées en b.** cars parked at an angle; *Fig* **il portait son chapeau en b.** his hat was all crooked *or* askew; **cheveux en b.** dishevelled hair 2 *Cartes* beggar-my-neighbour

batailler [bataje] VI to fight, to battle; **il est toujours prêt à b.** he's always spoiling for a fight; *Fam* **j'ai dû b. pendant une heure pour ouvrir la porte** I had to battle (away) for an hour to get the door open

batailleur, -euse [batajœr, -øz] ADJ aggres-

sive, quarrelsome, pugnacious
▪ N fighter, battler

bataillon [batajɔ̃] NM *Mil* battalion; *Fam (grand nombre)* crowd, swarm (**de** of); **commandant de b.** battalion commander; **b. d'Afrique** = French disciplinary battalion (formerly stationed in North Africa); *Fam* **elle a un b. de petits chats** she has a whole load of kittens

bâtard, -arde [batar, -ard] ADJ *(enfant)* illegitimate, *Péj* bastard; *(architecture, produit, solution etc)* hybrid; **chien b.** mongrel; **écriture bâtarde** slanting round-hand writing; *Typ* **format b.** bastard size; **pain b.** = short stick of French bread
▪ NM *(chien)* mongrel; *(pain)* = short stick of French bread
▪ N *(enfant)* illegitimate child, *Péj* bastard

bâtardise [batardiz] NF illegitimacy, *Péj* bastardy; **la b. de cette solution** the hybrid nature of this solution

batavia [batavja] NF batavia lettuce

Bat d'Af [batdaf] NM = the bataillon d'Afrique, a disciplinary battalion originally stationed in North Africa

bateau, -eaux [bato] NM 1 boat; **b. à voiles** sailing boat, *Am* sailboat; **b. à vapeur** steamboat, steamer; **b. à moteur** motorboat; **b. à rames** rowing boat, *Am* rowboat; **b. de plaisance** pleasure boat; **b. de pêche** fishing boat; **b. de sauvetage** lifeboat; **b. pneumatique** rubber dinghy; **b. de guerre** warship, battleship; **faire du b.** to go boating; **faire du b. à voiles/à rames** to go sailing/rowing; **b. d'excursion** pleasure boat; **b. de croisière** cruise ship; **b. mixte** passenger and cargo boat; **b. à fond de verre** glass-bottomed boat; *Rail* **le train du b.** the boat train; **prendre le b.** to take the boat, to go by boat; **je suis venu en ou par b.** I came by boat; *Fam* **monter un b. à qn** to have *or Am* put sb on, to pull sb's leg; **encolure b.** *(d'une robe, d'un pull etc)* boat neck, scoop neck 2 *(sur le trottoir)* driveway entrance
▪ ADJ *Fam* hackneyed; **un sujet b.** a subject that's been done to death, a hackneyed subject
▪ ▪ **b.-citerne,** *pl* **bateaux-citernes** tanker; **b.-école,** *pl* **bateaux-écoles** training ship; **b.-feu,** *pl* **bateaux-feux** lightship; **b.-hôtel,** *pl* **bateaux-hôtels** botel; *Hist* **b.-lavoir,** *pl* **bateaux-lavoirs** wash-house; **b.-mouche,** *pl* **bateaux-mouches** river boat *(on the Seine)*; **b.-phare,** *pl* **bateaux-phares** lightship; **b.-pilote,** *pl* **bateaux-pilotes** pilot boat; **b.-pompe,** *pl* **bateaux-pompes** fire boat

batelage¹ [batlaʒ] NM *Naut* **(frais de) b.** lighterage, *Br* waterage (charges)

batelage² NM *(art du jongleur)* juggling; *(acrobatique)* tumbling, acrobatics

bateleur, -euse [batlœr, -øz] N *Arch (jongleur)* juggler; *(acrobate)* tumbler, acrobat

batelier, -ière [batəlje, -jɛr] N boatman, waterman, f boatwoman; *(sur un bac)* ferryman, f ferrywoman; **b. de chaland** bargeman, bargee, lighterman

batellerie [batɛlri] NF 1 *(transport)* inland water transport 2 *(ensemble de bateaux)* small craft

bat-flanc [baflɑ̃] NM INV 1 *(dans un dortoir, une prison)* wooden partition 2 *(d'une stalle)* swinging bail

bath [bat] ADJ INV *Arg Vieilli* super, fantastic, fabulous

bathymètre [batimɛtr] NM bathometer, bathymeter

bathymétrie [batimetri] NF bathymetry

bathyscaphe [batiskaf] NM bathyscape, bathyscaph(e)

bathysphère [batisfɛr] NF bathysphere

bâti [bati] NM 1 *Menuis* frame(work); **b. de fenêtre** window frame; **b. moteur** engine mounting 2 *Couture* tacking, basting

batifolage [batifɔlaʒ] NM *Fam* 1 *(jeu)* larking *or* playing about *or* around 2 *(flirt)* flirting

batifoler [batifɔle] VI *Fam* to lark *or* play about *or* around

batik [batik] NM batik; **une jupe en b.** a batik skirt

bâtiment [batimɑ̃] NM 1 **le b.,** **l'industrie du b.** building, the building trade; **b. et travaux publics** building and civil engineering; **être dans le b.** to be in the building trade, to be a builder; **peintre en b.** (house) painter; *Fig* **il est du b.** he's in the same line of business; *(il s'y connaît)* he knows what he's doing; **quand le b. va, tout va** when the building trade is doing well, the whole economy is doing well 2 *(construction)* building; **b. d'habitation** residential building; **bâtiments de ferme** farm buildings; **usine en trois corps de b.** factory in three main buildings; **elle habite dans ces grands bâtiments** she lives in one of those high-rise blocks *or Br* tower blocks 3 *Naut* ship, vessel; **b. de guerre** warship, battleship
▪ ▪ *Naut* **b.-école,** *pl* **bâtiments-écoles** training ship

bâtir [batir] VT 1 *(construire) (maison etc)* to build; **(se) faire b. une maison** to have a house built; **terrain à b.** building land *or* site; **b. une fortune** to build up a fortune; *Fig* **b. sur le sable** to build on sand; **b. une théorie/une hypothèse** to build up *or* develop a theory/a hypothesis; **b. une interprétation sur qch** to build up *or* construct an interpretation on sth; **terrain bâti** developed *or* built-up site; **maison bien/mal bâtie** well/poorly built *or* constructed house; **homme bien bâti** well-built man; **un homme bâti comme moi** a man of my build 2 *Couture* to tack, to baste; **coton à b.** tacking thread
▪ VPR **se bâtir** 1 *(se construire)* to be built; **ces maisons se sont bâties en moins d'un mois** these houses were built *or* were put up *or* went up in less than a month 2 *(établir)* **se b. une réputation** to build up a reputation *(de* as)

bâtisse [batis] NF 1 *(partie en maçonnerie)* masonry 2 *(bâtiment)* big building; **ce n'est qu'une grande b.** it's a great (ugly) barracks of a place

bâtisseur, -euse [batisœr, -øz] N builder; *Fig* **un b. d'empires** an empire-builder

batiste [batist] NF *Tex* batiste, lawn, cambric

batoille [batɔj] NF *Suisse Fam (personne bavarde)* chatterbox; **ce type, quelle b.!** what a chatterbox that man is!

batoiller [batɔje] VI *Suisse Fam (bavarder)* to chatter

bâton [batɔ̃] NM 1 *(en bois etc)* stick; *(d'agent de police)* truncheon, *Am* nightstick; **b. d'une croix** staff of a cross; **b. de pavillon** flagstaff, flagpole; **son fils est son b. de vieillesse** his son is the support *or* prop of his old age; *Can* **aller au b.** to face the music; **donner des coups de b. à qn** to beat sb (with a stick); *Fam* **il faut le faire travailler à coups de b.** he won't work unless he's pushed; **il va goûter du b.** he'll get a beating; *Fig* **mettre des bâtons dans les roues** to throw a spanner *or Am* (monkey) wrench in the works; **mettre des bâtons dans les roues à qn** to put a spoke in sb's wheel; *Can* **tenir le mauvais bout du b.** to get the short end of the stick; **travailler à bâtons rompus** to work by fits and starts; **parler à bâtons rompus** to talk about this and that, to make small talk; **conversation à bâtons rompus** rambling conversation
    2 *(de colle, de craie, de réglisse, de dyna-*

mite) stick; **b. de rouge (à lèvres)** lipstick
3 *(trait) (de crayon etc)* (vertical) line; **apprendre à un enfant à faire des bâtons** to teach a child to write; *Typ* **capitale b.** block letter
4 *Anciennement Fam (dix mille francs)* ten thousand francs
▸▸**b. d'agent de police** truncheon, *Am* nightstick; **b. de chaise** chair rung *or* crosspiece; *Fam* **mener une vie de b. de chaise** to lead a wild life; **b. de chef d'orchestre** conductor's baton; **b. ferré** alpenstock; **b. de maréchal** marshal's baton; *Fig* **ce poste fut son b. de maréchal** this post was the peak *or* high point of his career; **b. de pèlerin** pilgrim's staff; *Fig* **prendre son b. de pèlerin** to set out on *or* go on a crusade; **bâtons de ski** ski sticks *or* poles

bâtonner [batɔne] **VT** *Vieilli* to beat, to cudgel, to cane

bâtonnet [batɔnɛ] **NM 1** *(petit bâton)* small stick; **b. d'encens** stick of incense **2** *Biol* rod bacterium; *Anat* rodlike cell; **bâtonnets de la rétine** retinal rods **3** *Ordinat* **b. magnétique** magnetic stripe

bâtonnier [batɔnje] **NM** = leader of the barristers attached to a French lawcourt, ≃ President of the Bar

batraciens [batrasjɛ̃] **NMPL** *Zool* batrachians

battage [bataʒ] **NM 1** *(d'un tapis etc)* beating; *(du beurre)* churning; *(du blé)* threshing; **b. de l'or** gold beating; **b. des pieux** pile driving **2** *Fam (d'un produit, d'une personne)* hype, publicity (campaign); **faire du b. autour de qch** to hype sth (up); **il faudra faire beaucoup de b. pour vendre le livre** it will take a lot of hype *or* publicity to sell the book; **un grand b. publicitaire** a major publicity *or* promotional campaign; **b. médiatique** media hype

battant, -ante [batɑ̃, -ɑ̃t] **ADJ** **pluie battante** driving *or* pelting *or* lashing rain; **porte battante** *(qui claque)* banging door; *(automatique)* swing door; **le cœur b.** with a pounding heart; *Fig* **faire qch tambour b.** to do sth at the double; **mener les choses tambour b.** to hurry *or* hustle things along; **(tout) b. neuf** brand new; **à onze heures b. ou battantes** on the stroke of eleven
NM 1 *(d'une cloche)* clapper, tongue; *(d'un loquet)* lift; *Naut (d'un drapeau)* fly; *(d'une voile)* slab **2** *(d'une table, d'un comptoir etc)* flap; *(d'une porte, d'un volet)* leaf; *(d'un placard)* door; **porte à deux battants** double door; **ouvrir la porte à deux battants** to open both sides of the door **3** *Fam (cœur)* ticker
N *Sport etc* fighter, battler; **c'est une battante, elle va réussir** she's a fighter, she'll succeed

batte [bat] **NF 1** *(action)* beating; **b. de l'or** gold beating **2** *(instrument) (de tapis etc)* beater; *(maillet)* mallet; *(massue)* club **3** *Sport* bat; **une b. de base-ball/cricket** a baseball/cricket bat

battement [batmɑ̃] **NM 1** *(de tambour)* beat(ing); *(de pieds)* tap(ping); *(de mains)* clapping; *(d'ailes)* flapping, flutter(ing); *(de voiles)* flapping; *(de porte)* banging; *(de volets)* banging, rattling; *(d'un pendule)* swing(-ing); *(d'une horloge)* ticking; *(d'un danseur)* high kick; *Cartes* shuffling; *Phys (d'oscillations)* beating, pulsation; **chaque b. de cœur** every heartbeat; **avoir des battements de cœur** to suffer from palpitations; *Fig* to be in a flutter; *Fig* **donner des battements de cœur à qn** to make sb's heart pound **2** *(entre deux événements ou deux)* interval; **il y a quelques jours de b. avant d'attaquer le projet** we have a few days' break *or* there are a few days clear before we get stuck into the pro-

ject; **deux heures de b.** two clear hours; **b. de cinq minutes entre les deux trains** five minutes' wait between the two trains **3** *(sur une fenêtre)* shutter catch

batterie [batri] **NF 1** *Mus (de tambour)* beat; *(de caisse claire)* roll; *(suite de notes)* quick succession of notes; *(instruments) (dans orchestre classique)* percussion instruments; *(dans orchestre de jazz, de rock)* drums; **tenir la b.** to be on drums; **il joue de la b.** he plays the drums; **à la b., Jean-Pierre!** Jean-Pierre on drums!
2 *Mil* battery; **b. antiaérienne/antichars** anti-aircraft/anti-tank battery; **pièces en b.** guns in firing position *or* in action; **en b.!** action!; **b. d'instruction** training battery; *Fig* **dévoiler ses batteries** to show one's hand; *Fig* **changer de batteries** to change one's plan of attack
3 *(ensemble, groupe)* battery; **b. de chaudières/de fours à coke** battery *or* range *or* bank of boilers/of coke ovens; **b. de projecteurs** bank *or* battery of spotlights; **poulet de b.** battery hen; **élevage en b.** *(de poulets etc)* battery farming; **b. de cuisine** (set of) kitchen utensils; *Fig Fam* medals, *Br* gongs; **on lui a fait passer toute une b. de tests** he was subjected to a whole battery of tests; **il a dû répondre à toute une b. de questions** he had to answer a whole battery of questions
4 *Élec* battery; **b. de rechange** *(pour torche etc)* replacement battery; **fonctionnant sur b.** battery-operated, battery-powered; **b. au cadmium-nickel** nickel cadmium battery; **b. au plomb** lead-acid battery; **b. de cellules photoélectriques** photoelectric cell battery; **b. de secours** emergency battery; **b. sans entretien** no-maintenance battery, maintenance-free battery; **b. à entretien réduit** low-maintenance battery

batteur, -euse [batœr, -øz] **NM 1** *Mus (dans un groupe de rock etc)* drummer; *(au cricket)* batsman; *(au base-ball)* batter, striker; *Chasse* beater; **b. d'or** gold beater; **b. en grange** thresher; *Fam* **b. de pavé** loafer, idler **2** *Agr (d'une batteuse)* beater drum; *Culin* **b. électrique** electric mixer; **b. (à œufs)** (egg) whisk **3** **b. de coton** cotton breaker *or* shaker
NF *Agr* **batteuse** threshing machine, thresher; *Métal* beater

battoir [batwar] **NM** *(pour les tapis)* (carpet) beater; *Vieilli (pour le linge)* beetle; *Fam (grande main)* great paw *or* mitt

BATTRE [batr] *(prp* **battant**; *pp* **battu**; *pr ind* **je bats** [ba], **tu bats**, **il bat**, **n. battons**, **v. battez**, **ils battent**; *p hist* **je battis**; *fu je battrai)* **VT 1** *(frapper) (personne, chien)* to beat, to hit; *(tapis, or)* to beat; *(blé)* to thresh; *(beurre)* to churn; *(œufs, préparation culinaire)* to beat, to whisk; **b. qn à coups de poing/avec une canne** to punch/cane sb; **b. qn à mort** to beat *or* batter sb to death; **b. qn comme plâtre** to beat the living daylights out of sb; **il bat sa femme** he beats his wife, he is a wife-beater; **il me donne envie de le b. parfois!** I want to hit him sometimes!; **b. le tambour** to beat the drum; **b. le fer (avec un marteau)** to hammer iron; **b. le fer à froid** to cold-hammer iron; **la cape lui bat les talons** his cloak is flapping round his heels; *Prov* **b. le fer quand ou pendant qu'il est chaud** to strike while the iron is hot; **b. monnaie** to mint coins; *Culin* **b. les blancs en neige** to beat the whites until stiff; **b. l'air en agitant les mains** to saw the air (with one's hands); **la pluie bat les carreaux** the rain is beating *or* lashing against the windowpanes; **la mer bat les rochers** the sea breaks against *or* batters the rocks; **île battue par les flots/les vents** island battered by the waves/the winds; **il avançait, le visage battu par le vent** he moved forward, his face whipped by the

wind; *Mil* **b. une position** to fire on a position; *Mus* **b. la mesure** to beat time; **b. la semelle** to stamp one's feet (to keep warm); *Mil* **b. le réveil/la retraite** to beat *or* sound the reveille/retreat; **b. le rappel** to call to arms; *Fig* to call everyone together; *Rel* **b. sa coulpe** to beat one's breast; **b. la campagne** to scour *or* comb the countryside; *Fig* **son esprit commence à b. la campagne** his mind is beginning to wander; **b. un bois/les buissons** to beat a wood/the bushes; *Naut* **b. un pavillon** to fly a flag; **b. pavillon français** to fly the French flag; *Cartes* **b. les cartes** to shuffle the cards
2 *(vaincre) (adversaire)* to beat, to defeat; *(record)* to beat; **b. qn à plate(s) couture(s)** to beat sb hollow; *Fam* **je te bats, je gagne 500 euros de plus que toi!** I earn 500 euros more than you, that's one up to me!
3 *très Fam* **j'en ai rien à b.** I don't give a shit
VI 1 *(de cœur)* to beat; *(de porte)* to bang; *(de volet)* to bang, to rattle; *(de voile)* to flap; **il a le cœur qui bat quand il la voit** his heart pounds whenever he sees her; **la nouvelle nous fit b. le cœur** we were thrilled at the news; **le vent faisait b. les volets** the shutters were banging *or* rattling in the wind
2 **b. des mains** to clap one's hands; *(applaudir)* to clap, to applaud; **b. du pied** *(en cadence)* to tap (with) one's foot; **l'oiseau battait des ailes** the bird was flapping *or* beating its wings; **b. des paupières** to blink
VPR **se battre** to fight; **se b. avec ou contre qn** *(physiquement)* to fight (with *or* against) sb; *(verbalement)* to argue *or* fight with sb; **se b. comme des chiffonniers** to fight like demons; **se b. au couteau** to fight with knives; **se b. en duel** to fight a duel; **se b. contre qch** to fight against sth; **il faut se b. pour réussir** you've got to fight if you want to succeed; **voyons, ne vous battez pas,** il y en a pour tout le monde now don't quarrel *or* fight (over it), there's enough for everyone; **je me suis battu pour obtenir ce visa/avec ce tournevis** I had a lot of trouble getting this visa/with that screwdriver; **il se bat avec ses devoirs** he's struggling *or* having trouble with his homework; *très Fam* **je m'en bats l'œil** I don't give a damn, I couldn't care less; *très Fam* **tout le monde s'en bat de ces histoires** nobody gives a damn about these stories; *Vulg* **je m'en bats les couilles** I couldn't give a monkey's *(fart)*

battu [baty] **ADJ** beaten; **enfant/femme battu(e)** battered child/wife; **chien b.** mistreated dog; **un air ou regard de chien b.** a hangdog look; **S.O.S. femmes battues** = battered wives' helpline; **avoir les yeux battus** to have rings *or* circles round one's eyes; **armée battue** defeated *or* beaten army; **ne pas se tenir pour b.** not to admit defeat, not to admit oneself beaten; **fer b.** wrought iron; **or b.** beaten gold; *Tennis* **court en terre battue** clay court; **jouer sur terre battue** to play on clay; **chemin b.** well-trodden path; **suivre les sentiers battus ou le chemin b.** to follow the beaten track; **hors des sentiers battus** off the beaten track; **œufs battus en neige** stiffly beaten egg whites; **pas b.** *(en danse)* pas battu

battue [baty] **NF** *Chasse* battue, beat; *Fig (pour retrouver qn)* search

batture [batyr] **NF** *Can* sandbank

bau, pl **baux** [bo] **NM** *Naut* beam; **maître b.** midship beam

baud [bo(d)] **NM** *Tél, Ordinat* baud; **à (une vitesse de) 1200 bauds** at (a speed of) 1,200 baud

baudet [bodɛ] **NM 1** *(âne)* ass, donkey; **chargé comme un b.** loaded down, weighed down **2** *Menuis* sawhorse, trestle

baudrier [bodrije] **NM** shoulder belt; *(pour*

épée) baldric; *Sport* **b. d'escalade** climbing harness; *Astron* **le B. d'Orion** Orion's belt

baudroie [bodrwa] NF *(poisson)* monkfish, anglerfish

baudruche [bodryʃ] NF bladder; *Fig Péj (homme)* empty windbag; **ballon de b.** balloon

bauge [boʒ] NF **1** *(d'un sanglier)* wallow; *Fig Fam* **c'est une vraie b.** it's a real pigsty **2** *Constr* clay and straw mortar

baume [bom] NM **1** *(substance)* balm, balsam; **b. de** *ou* **du Canada** Canada balsam; *Pharm* **b. de benjoin** friar's balsam **2** *Fig Litt* balm, consolation; **mettre du b. au cœur de qn** *(des propos, l'arrivée de qn etc)* to be a consolation for sb; *(d'une personne)* to console sb **3** *(plante)* **b. sauvage** *ou* **des champs** wild mint; **b. vert** garden mint, spearmint

baumier [bomje] NM balsam (tree)

baux [bo] *voir* **bail, bau**

bauxite [boksit] NF *Minér* bauxite

bavard, -arde [bavar, -ard] ADJ **1** *(qui parle beaucoup)* talkative, garrulous, gabby; **il est b. comme une pie** he'd talk the hind legs off a donkey; **une analyse bavarde** a wordy analysis **2** *(indiscret)* indiscreet ▪ N **1** *(qui parle beaucoup)* chatterbox **2** *(personne indiscrète)* gossip, *Fam* blabbermouth ▪ NM *Fam (avocat)* lawyer ▪ NF **bavarde** *Fam (langue)* tongue; **tenir sa bavarde** to hold one's tongue, to keep one's mouth shut

bavardage [bavardaʒ] NM **1** *(action)* chattering, *Br* nattering; *(commérage)* gossiping; **envoyé au coin pour b.** sent into the corner for talking in class **2** *(paroles)* chatter; *(commérage)* gossip, tittle-tattle; **ce ne sont que des bavardages** that's just gossip **3** *Ordinat (sur Internet)* chat

bavarder [bavarde] VI **1** *(parler)* to chatter, *Br* to natter **2** *(commérer)* to gossip **3** *(être indiscret)* to talk, *Fam* to blab **4** *Ordinat (sur Internet)* to chat

bavarois, -oise [bavarwa, -waz] ADJ Bavarian ▪ N **B.** Bavarian ▪ NF *Culin* **bavaroise** Bavarian cream

bavasser [bavase] VI *très Fam* to gossip

bave [bav] NF *(de personne)* dribble, slobber; *(de chien)* slobber, slaver; *(de cheval, de chien enragé)* froth, foam; *(d'escargot)* slime; *(de crapaud)* spittle; *Fig* spiteful *or* malicious talk

baver [bave] VI *(d'une personne)* to dribble, to slobber; *(d'un chien)* to slobber, to slaver; *(d'un chien enragé)* to foam at the mouth; *(d'un stylo)* to leak, to run; *(de l'encre)* to smudge; *Fam* **cela me fait b. de jalousie/de rage/d'admiration** it makes me green with envy/makes me hopping mad/leaves me speechless with admiration; *Fam* **en b. d'envie** he's drooling over it; *Fam* **en b.** to have a rough time of it; **elle m'en a fait b.!** she gave me a rough time ▪ VT *Fam* **1 en b. des ronds de chapeau** to have a rough time of it; *Vieilli (être étonné)* to have eyes like saucers **2** *(dire)* **qu'est-ce que tu baves?** what are you rambling *or* jabbering *or Br* wittering on about? **3** *Can (embêter)* to mess around, *Br* to wind up; **se faire b.** to get messed around, *Br* to be wound up

bavette [bavɛt] NF **1** *(d'un bébé, d'un tablier)* bib **2** *Culin* skirt (of beef); **b. d'aloyau** undercut of the sirloin; **dans la b., s'il vous plaît** from the flank, please **3** *Fam* **tailler une b.** to have a chat *or Br* a natter **4** *Aut* mud flap, mud guard

baveux, -euse [bavø, -øz] ADJ *(bouche)* dribbling, slobbery; *(enfant)* dribbling; *(chien)* slobbering, slavering; **omelette ba-**

veuse runny omelette; *Typ* **lettres baveuses** blurred *or* smeared letters ▪ N *Fam* **1** *Can (morveux)* pain, pest **2** *(journal)* newspaper, rag **3** *(baiser)* sloppy kiss

Bavière [bavjɛr] NF Bavaria

bavocher [bavɔʃe] VI *Typ* to smear

bavocheux, -euse [bavɔʃø, -øz] ADJ *Typ* mackled

bavochure [bavɔʃyr] NF *Typ* smear

bavoir [bavwar] NM bib

bavure [bavyr] NF **1** *Métal (de moulage etc)* burr, wire edge; *(de métal)* barb **2** *(tache)* smudge, smear; *(erreur)* slip-up, mistake; **sans bavure(s)** *(emploi adjectival)* faultless; *Fig* impeccable; *(emploi adverbial)* faultlessly; *Fig* impeccably; **un coup sans b.** *(cambriolage etc)* a perfect job; **les bavures de la police** police misconduct

bayer [baje] VI *(je baye, je baie, n. bayons; je bayerai, je baierai)* **b. aux corneilles** to stand gaping

bazar [bazar] NM **1** *(marché)* (oriental) bazaar **2** *(magasin)* general shop *or* store; **de b.** shoddy, (of) poor quality; **littérature de b.** pulp literature **3** *Fam (désordre)* shambles; *(bruit)* din, racket; **tout son b.** *(affaires)* all one's things *or* gear; **et tout le b.** and the whole caboodle; **il a mis un sacré b. dans mes papiers** he made a hell of a mess of my papers; **quel b., cette chambre!** this room is a shambles! **4** *Belg Fam* thing, thingy

bazarder [bazarde] VT *Fam (se débarrasser de)* to get rid of; *(jeter)* to chuck out; *(vendre)* to sell off, *Br* to flog

bazooka [bazuka] NM *Mil* bazooka

BBS [bebeɛs] NM *Ordinat (abrév* **bulletin board system)** BBS

BBZ [bebezɛd] NM *(abrév* **budget base zéro)** ZZB

BCBG [besebeʒe] ADJ *(abrév* **bon chic bon genre)** ≃ Sloany, *Am* ≃ preppy

BCE [beseə] NF *(abrév* **Banque centrale européenne)** ECB

BCG [beseʒe] NM *Méd* BCG

BD [bede] NF **1** *(abrév* **bande dessinée)** comic strip, strip cartoon; *(livre)* comic book **2** *Ordinat (abrév* **base de données)** dbase

---

BD

This is a common abbreviation for "bande dessinée", or "comic book". Considered a serious and important art form in France, the comic book has become popular among teenagers and intellectuals alike. An annual festival of comic book art is held in Angoulême.

---

bd *abrév* **boulevard**

bdc NM *Typ (abrév* **bas-de-casse)** lc

B. de F. NF *(abrév* **Banque de France)** Bank of France

bê [be] INT baa!

beach-volley [bitʃvɔlɛ] NM beach volleyball

beagle [bigl] NM beagle

béant [beɑ̃] ADJ *(bouche, porte)* wide open; *(blessure)* gaping, open; *(gouffre, entrée de grotte)* yawning, gaping

béarnais, -aise [bearnɛ, -ɛz] ADJ Béarn; *(personne)* from the Béarn; *Culin* **sauce béarnaise** béarnaise (sauce) ▪ NF *Culin* **béarnaise** béarnaise (sauce) ▪ N **B.** *(natif)* native of the Béarn; *(habitant)* inhabitant of the Béarn

béat [bea] ADJ *Rel* blessed; *(heureux)* blissfully happy; *Péj (niais)* *(air, sourire)* vacuous; **être b. d'admiration** to be open-mouthed in admiration; **elle nous observait d'un air b.** she watched us open-mouthed

béatement [beatmɑ̃] ADV blissfully; **il la regardait b.** he looked at her with a blissfully stupid expression

béatification [beatifikasjɔ̃] NF *Rel* beatification

béatifier [beatifje] VT *(pr sub, impf n.* **béatifiions, v. béatifiiez)** *Rel* to beatify

béatifique [beatifik] ADJ *Rel (vision)* beatific

béatitude [beatityd] NF **1** *Rel* beatitude; **les (huit) Béatitudes** the Beatitudes **2** *(bonheur parfait)* bliss

beatnik [bitnik] ADJ, N beatnik; **la génération b.** the beat generation

BEAU, BELLE [bo, bɛl] *(the form* **bel** [bɛl] *is used before m sing nouns beginning with a vowel or a mute h, in the expressions* **bel et bien, Charles le Bel** *and* **Philippe le Bel)**

> ADJ beautiful **1** ▪ good-looking **1**
> ▪ handsome **1** ▪ fine **1–3, 5, 7, 12**
> ▪ great **3, 5** ▪ smart **4** ▪ awful **7**
> NM beauty **2**

ADJ **1** *(physiquement)* *(femme, enfant)* beautiful, good-looking; *(homme)* handsome, good-looking; *(objet, produit, maison, arbre etc)* lovely, beautiful; **un bel homme** a fine figure of a man; **une belle femme** a beautiful *or* good-looking woman; *(sculpturale)* a fine figure of a woman, a handsome woman; **ça n'est pas b. à voir** that's not a pretty *or* an attractive sight; **mettre ses plus beaux habits** to put on one's best *or* finest clothes; *Hist* **Philippe le Bel** Philip the Fair; **la mer est belle** the sea is beautiful; *(calme)* the sea is calm; **le temps est b.** the weather is fine; **nous avons eu (du) b. temps** we had fine weather; **ami des beaux jours** fairweather friend; **un (de ces) beau(x) jour(s)** one (of these) fine day(s); **et un b. jour, il est arrivé** then one (fine) day, he arrived; **oh la belle bleue!** *(de feu d'artifice)* what a lovely blue!; *(jeune fille)* hi, gorgeous!

2 *(moralement)* fine; **de beaux sentiments** fine *or* noble feelings; **belle action** fine deed; **une belle vie** a full life; **trouver une belle mort** to die a glorious death; *Fam* **elle a le b. rôle** she's got it *or* things easy, she's sitting pretty; **cela n'est pas b. de votre part** that wasn't very nice of you; **ce n'est pas b. de mentir** it isn't nice to tell lies; *Fam* **ce n'est pas b. de parler la bouche pleine** it isn't polite *or* nice to speak with your mouth full; **il est b. joueur** he's a good loser

3 *(excellent)* *(œuvre, artiste, film, match etc)* fine, excellent; *(occasion)* wonderful; **une belle page de littérature** a fine piece of writing; **un b. talent** a talented *or* gifted artist/ writer/*etc*; **il a un b. talent de peintre** he has a great gift as a painter, he's a very gifted painter; **20 ans! le bel âge!** twenty! a great age (to be)!; **avoir une belle santé** to be very healthy; **il a une belle situation** he has an excellent job; **ils font un b. couple** they make a fine couple; **oh la belle balle!** what a good *or* lovely shot *or* ball!; **c'est trop b. pour être vrai** it's too good to be true; **ce serait trop b.!** that would be too much (to hope for)!; **le plus b. jour de ma vie** the best day of my life; *Cartes* **avoir (un) b. jeu** to have good cards *or* a good hand

4 *(élégant)* *(monsieur, dame)* smart, elegant; **se faire b.** to smarten oneself up; **sois belle et tais-toi** = women should be seen but not heard; **vous voilà b.!** you do look smart!

5 *Iron* **le bel avantage, ma foi!** well, that's a great advantage!; **tout cela est bien b., mais ...** that's all very fine *or* well, but ...; **vous avez fait du b. travail!** you have done well!

6 *(intensif)* **au b. milieu de la rue** right *or* bang in the middle of the road; **il y a b. temps**

qu'il est parti he left a long time ago *or* ages ago; **une belle tranche de tarte** a nice slice of tart; **une belle paie** a good salary, good wages; **c'est une belle sole** that's a lovely piece of sole; **belle fortune** large *or* tidy fortune; **b. poulet** good-sized *or* sizeable chicken; **un b. kilo** a good kilo

7 *(mauvais)* **une belle congestion pulmonaire** a bad attack of pneumonia; **belle correction** good thrashing; **b. tapage** terrific din *or* racket; **il a fait un b. désordre** he made a terrible mess; **un b. gâchis** a fine mess; **son bras est dans un bel état** his arm is in an awful *or* a terrible state; **j'ai eu une belle peur** I had an awful *or* a terrible fright; *Arg* **un b. salaud** a real *or* right bastard

8 bel et bien well and truly; **il est bel et bien venu** he really did come; **tu l'avais bel et bien dit** you definitely said so; **vous voilà bel et bien grand-père!** so you've actually become a grandfather!

9 tout b.! steady (on)!, gently!

10 de plus belle with a vengeance; **il reprit l'entraînement de plus belle** he resumed training with a vengeance, more enthusiastically than ever; **les discussions/batailles ont recommencé de plus belle** the arguing/fighting has started again with a vengeance, worse than ever

11 je l'ai échappé belle I had a narrow escape *or* a close shave

12 il ferait b. voir cela that would be a fine thing to see

13 j'ai b. le lui dire, il ne veut rien entendre it's no good my trying *or* however much I try to tell him, he just won't listen; **j'avais b. chercher, je ne trouvais rien** however hard I looked *or* no matter how hard I looked *or* look as I might, I found nothing; **vous avez b. parler …** you can talk until you're blue in the face …

NM 1 un vieux b. an old roué; **faire le b.** *(d'un chien)* to sit up and beg; *Can (d'un homme)* to strut about; *Arch* **un b.** a dandy, a beau, a buck

2 *(beauté)* **le b.** the beautiful, beauty; **l'amour du b.** the love of beauty; **le b., le bien et le vrai** beauty, goodness and truth

3 le b. de l'histoire, c'est que … the best bit *or* part of the story is that …; **mais le plus b., c'est que …** but the best bit *or* part is that …; *Fam Iron* **c'est du b.!** that's great!

4 *Météo* **le temps est au b. (fixe)** the weather is set fair; *Fig* **avoir l'humeur au b. fixe** to be permanently in a good mood

5 *(beaux objets)* **le b.** beautiful things; **ne vouloir/vendre que du b.** to want/sell only *or* nothing but the best

NF belle 1 *(jolie femme)* beauty, belle; *(amie, amante)* lady friend; **la Belle et la Bête** the Beauty and the Beast; **la Belle au bois dormant** Sleeping Beauty; **allez ma belle, ça suffit** now that's quite enough, my dear

2 *Sport* decider, deciding game; *Cartes* rubber game; **jouer** *ou* **faire la b.** *Sport* to play the decider *or* the deciding game; *Cartes* to play the rubber game

3 *Naut (d'un navire)* waist; **en b.** abeam

4 *Fam* **se faire la b.** *(de prison)* to break out, to escape

5 *Fam* **il en dit de belles!** he comes out with some good ones!, he really comes out with them!; **j'en ai entendu de belles sur votre compte!** I've heard some nice things about you!; **vous en avez fait une b.!** you've put your foot in it!

▸▸ **un bel âge** a ripe old age; **le b. monde** fashionable society; *Iron* **pour satisfaire tout ce b. monde** in order to satisfy all these fine people; **beaux quartiers** fashionable *or* smart districts; **le b. sexe** the fair sex

---

La Belle Époque

This term refers to the period of apparent stability and prosperity from the closing years of the 19th century to the beginning of the First World War, which found its expression in café and theatre society, fashion, art and architecture. Its chief surviving monument is the area on the south side of the Champs-Élysées containing the "Petit Palais" and the "Grand Palais", erected at the time of the Universal Exhibition of 1900.

BEAUCOUP [boku] ADV VOIR GRAMMAIRE A22–3

(une grande quantité) a lot, a great deal; **il reste encore b. à faire** there's still a lot *or* a great deal *or* much to do; **b. de** *(nombre)* a lot of, (a great) many; *(quantité)* a lot of, a great deal of, much; **b. de monde** a lot of people; **b. de vin/chance** a lot of *or* a great deal of wine/luck; **avoir b. d'argent** to have plenty of *or* a lot of money; **ils n'ont pas b. d'argent** they don't have much *or* a lot of *or* a great deal of money; **je n'ai pas eu b. d'occasions** *ou* **l'occasion de le faire** I haven't had much (of an) opportunity to do it; **avec b. de soin** very carefully; **avoir besoin de b. d'attention/d'eau** to need a lot of attention/water; **j'en veux b., 20!** I want a lot, 20!; **il n'en reste pas b.** *(de la tarte etc)* there's not much left; *(des bonbons etc)* there aren't many left; **y a-t-il b. de champignons cette année? – oui, b./non, pas b.** are there many *or* a lot of mushrooms this year? – yes, there are/no, there aren't; **b. plus/moins de temps/de sel** a lot *or* much more/less time/salt; **b. plus/moins d'enfants/de livres** a lot *or* many more/fewer children/books; **elle veut b.** she wants a lot out of life; **c'est déjà b. s'il veut bien** *ou* **qu'il veuille bien vous parler** it's (quite) something that he condescended to speak to you; **b. pensent que …** a lot of *or* many people think that …; **il y est pour b.** he has had a great deal to do with it; **b. d'entre nous/d'entre vous** many *or* a lot of us/you; **de b.** by far; **c'est de b. le meilleur** it's by far *or* it's far and away the best, it's the best by a long chalk; **il s'en faut de b. que je sois riche** I'm far from being rich; **elle vous aime b.** she is very fond of you, she likes you a lot *or* a great deal; **il parle b.** he talks a lot *or* a great deal; **il a b. voyagé/lu** he has travelled/read a lot *or* a great deal; **elle ne lit pas b.** she doesn't read much *or* a lot *or* a great deal; **il parle b. trop** he talks far too much; **je me sens b. mieux** I feel a lot better; **ambitieuse, elle l'est, et b.** she's ambitious, very ambitious; **b. moins/plus vite** a lot *or* much slower/faster; **il est b. plus âgé que sa femme** he is much *or* a lot older than his wife; **ça te plaît? – pas b.** do you like it? – not much *or* not a lot; **j'y tiens b.** it means a lot to me

---

beauf [bof] *Fam* NM **1** *(beau-frère)* brother-in-law **2** *Fig Péj* narrow-minded middle-class type

ADJ *Fig Péj* **il est un peu b.** he's a bit of a narrow-minded middle-class type

beau-fils, *pl* **beaux-fils** NM **1** *(gendre)* son-in-law **2** *(après remariage)* stepson

beau-frère, *pl* **beaux-frères** NM brother-in-law

beaujolais [boʒɔlɛ] NM Beaujolais

beaujolpif [boʒɔlpif] NM *Fam* Beaujolais

beau-père, *pl* **beaux-pères** NM **1** *(père du conjoint)* father-in-law **2** *(après remariage)* stepfather

beaupré [bopre] NM *Naut* bowsprit

beauté [bote] NF **1** *(de femme, paysage etc)* beauty; **apparaître dans toute sa b.** to appear in all one's beauty; **être en b.** to be look-

---

ing one's best; **une femme/une vue de toute b.** a magnificent woman/view; *Fam* **finir en b.** to end with a flourish *or* on a high note; **faire qch pour la b. du geste** to do sth for its own sake; **grain de b.** beauty spot, mole; **institut de b.** beauty parlour; **produits de b.** beauty products, cosmetics; **la b. du diable** youthful beauty; *Fam* **se (re)faire une b.** to do one's face, to put one's face on **2** *(femme)* beauty **3 les beautés artistiques de l'Italie** the art treasures of Italy; **les beautés touristiques** the sights

beaux-arts [bozar] NMPL fine arts; *Univ* **l'École des b.,** *Fam* **les B.** the Art School

beaux-parents NMPL parents-in-law, *Fam* in-laws

bébé [bebe] NM **1** *(nourrisson)* baby; **avoir/vouloir un b.** to have/want a baby; **attendre un b.** to be expecting (a baby); *Fig* **c'est un vrai b., il ne sait rien faire seul** he's a real baby *or* he's just like a child, he can't do anything for himself; **faire le b.** to behave childishly *or* like a baby; **il/elle est très b.** he/she is very childish *or* babyish **2** *Com (poupée)* (baby) doll **3** *Zool* **b. gazelle/lapin** baby gazelle/rabbit

bébé-éprouvette, *pl* **bébés-éprouvette** NM test-tube baby

bébelle [bebɛl] NF *Can (gadget)* gadget; *(bibelot)* ornament

bébelleux, -euse [bebɛlø, -øz] ADJ *Can* gadget mad; *(bibelots)* ornament mad

bébête [bebɛt] *Fam* ADJ silly; **rire b.** giggle, titter

NF little insect, *Br* creepy-crawly

bec [bɛk] NM **1** *(d'oiseau)* beak, bill; *(de tortue, pieuvre etc)* beak; **au b. long/court/jaune** long-/short-/yellow-billed; **coup de b.** peck; **donner un coup de b. à qn** to peck sb; *Fig Fam* to have a dig at sb; **l'oiseau se fait le b.** the bird is sharpening its beak; *Fig* **se défendre b. et ongles** to fight tooth and nail

2 *Fam (bouche)* mouth, *Br Fam* gob; **claquer du b.** to be starving; **fin b.** gourmet; **être** *ou* **rester le b. dans l'eau** to be left high and dry; **il n'a pas ouvert le b. de la journée** he hasn't said a single word all day, there hasn't been a peep out of him all day; **il n'ouvre pas beaucoup le b., ton copain** your friend hasn't got much to say for himself, not the world's greatest talker, your friend, is he?; **avoir la cigarette/pipe au b.** to have a cigarette/one's pipe in one's mouth; **ferme ton b.!** shut up!, shut your mouth *or* gob!; **clouer** *ou* **clore le b. à qn** to shut sb up; **avoir bon b.** to have the gift of the gab; **prise de b.** quarrel, slanging match

3 *(d'outil)* nose; *(de tube)* nozzle; *(de pot)* lip; *(de cafetière)* spout; *(de selle de bicyclette)* peak; *(de clarinette, flûte etc)* mouthpiece; *Arg* **tomber sur un b.** to come a cropper; *Aviat* **b. d'attaque** *(d'une aile)* leading edge; **b. de plume** pen nib

4 *Géog (nom de localité)* bill; **le B. de Portland** Portland Bill

5 *Belg, Can, Suisse Fam (baiser)* kiss, peck; **donner un b. à qn** to give sb a kiss *or* peck; *Can* **b. pincé** snob

▸▸ **b. Bunsen** Bunsen burner; **b. à gaz** gas jet *or* burner; **b. de gaz** gas lamp; **b. verseur** lip

bécane [bekan] NF *Fam (vélo)* bike; *(machine, ordinateur)* machine

bécarre [bekar] *Mus* ADJ *(signe)* natural; **mi b.** E natural

NM natural

bécasse [bekas] NF **1** *(oiseau)* **b. (des bois)** woodcock; **b. de mer** oystercatcher **2** *Fam (idiote)* silly woman/girl, silly goose

bécasseau, -eaux [bekaso] NM *(échassier)*

sandpiper; *(petit de la bécasse)* young woodcock

bécassine [bekasin] **NF 1** *(oiseau)* snipe **2** *Fam (fille niaise)* silly naive girl

bec-croisé, *pl* **becs-croisés NM** *(oiseau)* crossbill

bec-de-cane, *pl* **becs-de-cane NM 1** *(serrure)* catch **2** *(poignée)* (door) handle

bec-de-lièvre, *pl* **becs-de-lièvre NM** *Méd* harelip

becfigue [bɛkfig] **NM** *(oiseau)* (garden) warbler; *(fauvette)* blackcap; *(jaseur)* waxwing; *(pipi)* pipit

bêchage [bɛʃaʒ] **NM** *(de la terre)* digging (over), turning over

béchamel [beʃamɛl] **ADJ, NF** *Culin* **(sauce) b.** béchamel sauce, white sauce

bêche [bɛʃ] **NF** spade

bêcher [beʃe] **VT 1** *(terre)* to dig (over), to turn over; *(plate-bande)* to dig (over) **2** *Fam (personne)* to run down, to pull to pieces ▸ **VI** *Fam* to put on airs

bêcheur, -euse [beʃœr, -øz] **N** *Fam* **1** *(critiqueur)* knocker **2** *(snob)* stuck-up person

bécot [beko] **NM** *Fam* kiss, peck; **gros b.** smacker

bécoter [bekɔte] *Fam* **VT** to kiss ▸ **VPR se bécoter** to smooch, to kiss (and cuddle)

becquée [beke] **NF** beakful; *Fam* **encore une b.!** *(à un enfant)* another little mouthful!; **donner la b. à son bébé** to feed one's baby

becquerel [bɛk(ə)rɛl] **NM** *Nucl* becquerel

becquet [bekɛ] **NM 1** *Aut* spoiler **2** *Typ* paste-on

becquetance [bɛktãs] **NF** *Arg* grub, *Br* nosh

becqueter [bɛkte] **VT** (**je becquette, n. becquetons; je becquetterai**) *(d'un oiseau)* to peck at; *Arg (d'une personne)* to eat; **il n'y a rien à b.** there's no grub *or Br* nosh; **on a bien becqueté** we had a good feed

bectance [bɛktãs] **NF** *Arg* grub, *Br* nosh

becter [bɛkte] **VT** = **becqueter**

bedaine [bədɛn] **NF** *Fam* pot(belly), paunch; **avoir de la b.** to be pot-bellied *or* paunchy; **prendre de la b.** to get a paunch

bédane [bedan] **NM** mortise, (cold) chisel

bédé [bede] **NF** *Fam* comic strip

bedeau, -eaux [bədo] **NM** *Rel* verger

bédéphile [bedefil] **N** *Fam* comic-strip freak

bedon [bədõ] **NM** *Fam* pot(belly), paunch

bedonnant [bədɔnã] **ADJ** *Fam* potbellied, paunchy

bedonner [bədɔne] **VI** *Fam* to get a paunch

bédouin, -ouine [bedwɛ̃, -win] **ADJ** Bedouin ▸ **N B.** Bedouin

bée [be] **ADJ** **bouche b.** gaping, open-mouthed; **rester bouche b. devant qch** to stand gaping *or* open-mouthed in front of sth; **j'en suis resté bouche b.** I was flabbergasted (by it) *or* gobsmacked, it staggered me; **son culot me laisse bouche b.** I am staggered *or* flabbergasted by his cheek; **regarder qch bouche b.** to gape at sth

béer [bee] **VI** *Litt* **1 b. d'étonnement/d'admiration** to gape in astonishment/admiration **2** *(être grand ouvert)* to be wide open

beffroi [befrwa] **NM 1** *(tour)* belfry **2** *(cloche)* **entendre sonner le b.** to hear the bell sound

bégaiement [begɛmã] **NM 1** *(pathologique)* stuttering, stammering **2** *(des petits enfants)* lispings **3** *Fig* **bégaiements** hesitant *or* tentative beginnings

bégayant [begɛjã] **ADJ** *(involontairement)* stuttering, stammering; *Fig Litt* hesitant, faltering

bégayer [begɛje] (**je bégaye, je bégaie, n. bégayons; je bégayerai, je bégaierai**) **VI 1** *(pathologiquement)* to stutter, to stammer **2** *(des petits enfants)* to lisp ▸ **VT** to stammer (out); **b. une excuse** to stammer out an excuse

bégayeur, -euse [begɛjœr, -øz] **ADJ** stuttering, stammering

bégonia [begɔnja] **NM** *(plante)* begonia

bègue [bɛg] **ADJ** stuttering, stammering ▸ **N** stutterer, stammerer

bégueule [begœl] **ADJ** prudish; **ne sois pas b.** don't be prudish, don't be a prude ▸ **NF** prude

béguin [begɛ̃] **NM 1** *Fam* **avoir le b. pour qn/qch** to have a crush on sb/to have taken a fancy to sth; **voilà son nouveau b.** that's his/her latest crush **2** *(pour un petit enfant)* bonnet; *Rel* hood

béguinage [beginaʒ] **NM** *Rel* Beguine convent

béguine [begin] **NF** *Rel* Beguine (nun)

bégum [begɔm] **NF** begum

behaviorisme [biavjɔrism, biev-] **NM** *Psy* behaviourism, *Am* behaviorism

behavioriste [biavjɔrist, biev-] *Psy* **ADJ** behaviourist(ic), *Am* behaviorist(ic) ▸ **N** behaviourist, *Am* behaviorist, behavioural *or Am* behavioral scientist

BEI [beəi] **NF** *(abrév* **Banque européenne d'investissement** *)* EIB

beige [bɛʒ] **ADJ, NM** beige

beigne¹ [bɛɲ] **NF** *Arg* slap, clout; **filer** *ou* **flanquer une b. à qn** to give sb a clout, to clout sb one

beigne² [bɛɲ] **NM** *Can, Région* doughnut, *Am* donut

beignet [bɛɲɛ] **NM** fritter; *(au sucre, à la confiture)* doughnut, *Am* donut; **b. de** *ou* **aux pommes** apple fritter; **b. de crevettes** prawn cracker; *(avec de la pâte)* prawn fritter

beïram [biram] **NM** = **baïram**

béké [beke] **N** white Creole (in the French Indies)

bel¹ [bɛl] **NM** *Phys* bel

bel² **ADJ** *voir* **beau**

bélandre [belãdr] **NF** canal barge

bêlant [belã] **ADJ** *aussi Fig* bleating

bel canto [bɛlkãto] **NM** *Mus* bel canto

bêlement [bɛlmã] **NM** *Zool, Fig* bleating

bélemnite [belɛmnit] **NF** *(fossile)* belemnite

bêler [bele] **VI** *Zool, Fig* to bleat; *Fig* **qu'est-ce que vous avez à b. comme ça?** what on earth are you bleating about?

bel-étage, *pl* **beaux-étages** [beletaʒ, boze-taʒ] **NM** *Belg (rez-de-chaussée surélevé)* mezzanine ground floor, *Am* mezzanine first floor

belette [bəlɛt] **NF 1** *Zool* weasel **2** *Fam (jeune femme)* *Br* bird, *Am* chick

Belga [bɛlga] **NF** *Journ* = Belgian press agency

belge [bɛlʒ] **ADJ** Belgian; **histoire b.** = joke told at the expense of the Belgians, *Br* ≃ Irish joke, *Am* ≃ Polish joke, *Can* ≃ Newfie joke ▸ **N B.** Belgian

belgicain, -aine [bɛlʒikɛ̃, -ɛn] *Belg Péj* **ADJ** **être b.** *(partisan de l'unité belge)* to be in favour of a united Belgium; *(attaché aux traditions nationales)* to be attached to conservative (Belgian) tradition ▸ **N** *(partisan de l'unité belge)* Belgian nationalist *(in favour of national unity)*; *(personne attachée aux traditions nationales)* conservative (Belgian)

belgicisme [bɛlʒisism] **NM** *(mot)* Belgian-

French word; *(tournure)* Belgian-French expression

Belgique [bɛlʒik] **NF** Belgium

Belgrade [bɛlgrad] **N** Belgrade

bélier [belje] **NM 1** *(animal)* ram **2** *Mil* battering ram **3** *Constr* **b. (à pilotage)** pile driver, ram(mer); **b. mécanique** bulldozer **4 b. hydraulique** hydraulic ram; **coup de b.** water hammer **5** *Astron, Astrol* **le B.** Aries, the Ram; **être (du signe du) B.** to be (an) Aries

bélière [beljɛr] **NF 1** *(d'une cloche)* clapper ring; *(d'une montre etc)* ring **2** *(du bélier qui conduit le troupeau)* (sheep) bell

Belize [beliz] **NM** Belize

belladone [beladɔn] **NF** *(plante)* belladonna, deadly nightshade

bellâtre [belɑtr] **NM** *Péj* smoothie

belle [bɛl] **ADJ, NF** *voir* **beau**

belle-dame, *pl* **belles-dames NF 1** *(plante)* deadly nightshade **2** *(papillon)* painted lady

belle-de-jour, *pl* **belles-de-jour NF** *(plante)* convolvulus, bindweed

belle-de-nuit, *pl* **belles-de-nuit NF 1** *(plante)* marvel of Peru, four o'clock **2** *Fam (prostituée)* lady of the night

belle-doche, *pl* **belles-doches** [bɛldɔʃ] **NF** *Fam* mother-in-law

belle-famille, *pl* **belles-familles NF** *(de l'époux)* wife's family, *Fam* in-laws; *(de l'épouse)* husband's family, *Fam* in-laws

belle-fille, *pl* **belles-filles NF 1** *(épouse du fils)* daughter-in-law **2** *(après remariage)* stepdaughter

bellement [bɛlmã] **ADV** *Arch* well and truly; **voilà la vérité, tout b.** that's the simple truth

belle-mère, *pl* **belles-mères NF 1** *(mère du conjoint)* mother-in-law **2** *(après remariage)* stepmother

belle-sœur, *pl* **belles-sœurs NF** sister-in-law

bellicisme [belisism] **NM** bellicosity, warmongering

belligérance [beliʒerãs] **NF** belligerence

belligérant, -ante [beliʒerã, -ãt] **ADJ** belligerent ▸ **N** belligerent, combatant

belliqueux, -euse [bel(l)ikø, -øz] **ADJ** *(nation, pays, peuple)* warlike, bellicose; *(personne etc)* aggressive, quarrelsome; *(humeur, tempérament)* aggressive; **tenir des propos b.** to speak aggressively

belote [bəlɔt] **NF** *Cartes* belote *(card game)*; *Fam* **faire une b.** to have a game of belote

bélouga, béluga [beluga] **NM 1** *(mammifère)* beluga, white whale **2** *(caviar)* beluga (caviar)

belvédère [bɛlvedɛr] **NM 1** *(construction)* belvedere, gazebo **2** *(sur un site naturel)* viewpoint

Belzébuth [bɛlzebyt] **N** *Bible* Beelzebub

bémol [bemɔl] **NM** *Mus* flat; **clarinette en si b.** B-flat clarinet; *Fig* **mettre un b. à ses critiques** to tone down one's criticism; *Fig Fam* **mettre un b.** to tone it down

bémoliser [bemɔlize] **VT** *Mus (note)* to flatten, *Am* to flat

ben [bɛ̃] **ADV** *Arg* = **bien; b. oui!** well, yes!; **b. voilà, euh …** yeah, well, er …

bénarde [benard] **NF** pin key lock, double-sided lock

bène [bɛn] **NM** *Fam* trousers, keks, *Am* pants

bénédicité [benedisite] **NM** *(avant le repas)* grace; **dire le b.** to say grace

bénédictin, -ine [benediktɛ̃, -in] *Rel* **ADJ** *(moine, sœur)* Benedictine ▸ **N** Benedictine; *Fig* **un vrai b.** a painstaking scholar; **un travail de b.** a work of painstaking scholarship ▸ **NF Bénédictine®** *(liqueur)* Benedictine

bénédiction [benediksjɔ̃] NF *Rel* blessing, benediction; *Fig* blessing; *(d'une église, des couleurs)* consecration; **donner la b.** *(d'un prêtre)* to give *or* pronounce the blessing; *Fig* **vous avez ma b.** you have my blessing; **il a donné sa b. au projet** he gave the plan his blessing; **quelle b.!** what a blessing!, what a godsend!; **il a dit oui, c'est une b.!** it's a blessing he said yes!

bénef [benɛf] NM *Arg* profit; **petits bénefs** perks; **faire 50 euros de b.** to make 50 euros profit

bénéfice [benefis] NM **1** *(gain)* profit; **b. brut/net** gross/net profit; **bénéfices non commerciaux** non-trading profits; **réaliser de gros bénéfices** to make large *or* handsome profits; **rapporter des bénéfices** to yield a profit; **faites-vous du b.?** do you make a *or* any profit?; **participation aux bénéfices** profit-sharing; **être intéressé aux bénéfices** to share in the profits; **petits bénéfices** perquisites, *Fam* perks; **avec b.** *(investir)* profitably; **vendre qch à b.** to sell sth at a profit **2** *(avantage)* benefit, advantage; **tirer un certain b. de qch** to derive some benefit *or* advantage from sth; **c'est tout à son b. de suivre cette formation** it's wholly to his benefit *or* advantage to do this training; **c'est tout b.** it's all to his/their/*etc* advantage; **quel b. aurais-je à te mentir?** what good would it do me to lie to you?, what advantage *or* benefit would I get from lying to you?; **avoir le b. de l'âge** to have the benefit of age; *Jur* **b. du doute** benefit of the doubt; **on peut lui accorder** *ou* **laisser le b. du doute** we can give him the benefit of the doubt; *Théâtre, Sport* **représentation/match à b.** benefit performance/match; **concert donné au b. de la Croix-Rouge** concert given in aid of the Red Cross; *Can* **concert/repas-b.** fund-raising concert/dinner **3** *Rel* living, benefice
▸▸ **b. par action** earnings per share; **b. brut avant impôt** pre-tax profit; **b. brut d'exploitation** gross operating profit; *Mktg* **b. consommateur** *(d'un produit)* consumer benefit; **b. cumulé** cumulative profit; **b. escompté** desired profit; **bénéfices exceptionnels** windfall profit; **b. d'exploitation** operating profit; **b. imposable** taxable profit; **b. transféré** profit transferred

bénéficiaire [benefisjɛr] ADJ *Com* **solde b.** profit balance; **compte b.** account in credit, account showing a credit balance; **marge b.** profit margin
N *(d'un chèque etc)* recipient, payee; *Rel, Jur etc* beneficiary; **b. conjoint** joint beneficiary

bénéficier [benefisje] VT *(impf, pr sub n. bénéficiions, v. bénéficiiez)* to benefit *(de* from); **faire b. qn de son expérience** to give sb the benefit of one's experience; **cette carte d'abonnement vous fait b. d'une remise de 20 pour cent** this season ticket entitles you to a 20 per cent reduction; **à qui vont b. ces mesures?** who are these measures going to benefit?, who is going to benefit from these measures?; **cet article bénéficie d'une remise de dix pour cent** this article carries a ten per cent discount, there is a discount of ten per cent on this article; *Jur* **il a bénéficié d'une ordonnance de non-lieu** he was discharged

bénéfique [benefik] ADJ beneficial *(à* to); *Astrol (planète)* beneficent; **ce séjour à la montagne vous sera b.** this stay in the mountains will do you good *or* will be beneficial to you

Benelux [benelyks] NM **le B.** Benelux

benêt [bənɛ] ADJ silly, stupid
NM simpleton

bénévolat [benevɔla] NM voluntary work; **faire du b.** to do voluntary work

bénévole [benevɔl] ADJ **1** *(service, travail, conseiller, infirmière)* voluntary, unpaid; **aide b.** voluntary help; **organisation b.** voluntary organization **2** *Litt (bienveillant) (personne)* benevolent, kindly
N volunteer, voluntary worker

bénévolement [benevɔlmɑ̃] ADV **1** *(sans être payé)* voluntarily, without pay, unpaid; **il travaille b.** he does voluntary work **2** *Litt (avec bienveillance)* benevolently, kindly

Bengale [bɛ̃gal] NM **1** Bengal **2** **feu de B.** Bengal light

bengali [bɛ̃gali] ADJ Bengali, Bengalese
NM *Ling* Bengali
N **B.** Bengali

bénignité [beninite] NF **1** *(du climat, d'une maladie)* mildness **2** *Litt (d'une personne)* benignity, kindness

Bénin [benɛ̃] NM Benin

bénin, -igne [benɛ̃, -iɲ] ADJ **1** *(accident)* slight, minor; *(opération)* minor; **tumeur bénigne** benign *or* non-malignant tumour; **forme bénigne de (la) rougeole** mild form of measles **2** *Litt (personne, tempérament, critique etc)* benign, kindly

béninois, -oise [beninwa, -waz] ADJ Beninese
N **B.** Beninese

béni-oui-oui [beniwiwi] NM INV *Fam* yes-man

bénir [benir] VT *aussi Fig* to bless; *(église, pain etc)* to consecrate; **(que) Dieu vous bénisse!** (may) God bless you!; **le ciel en soit béni!** thank heaven(s)!; **je bénis cette journée où …** I bless the day when …; **b. la mémoire de qn** to glorify sb's memory; **je bénis cette occasion de parler avec elle** I'm thankful *or* grateful for this opportunity of speaking to her

bénit [beni] ADJ consecrated; **pain b.** consecrated bread, holy bread; **eau bénite** holy water

bénitier [benitje] NM **1** *Rel* stoup, stoop, holy-water basin; *(pour le baptême)* font **2** *(mollusque)* giant clam

benjamin, -ine [bɛ̃ʒamɛ̃, -in] N youngest child; **le b. de la famille** the youngest of the family

benjoin [bɛ̃ʒwɛ̃] NM *(gum)* benzoin, benjamin

benne [bɛn] NF *Min etc* tub, truck; *(d'une grue)* scoop; *(d'une dragueuse)* bucket; *(de ski etc)* (cable) car; *(de camion)* tipping *or* dump body; **camion à b. (basculante)** tip(per) truck, dump(er) truck

Benoist, Benoît [bənwa] NM *Fam* **j'te crois, B!** tell me about it!

benoît [bənwa] ADJ ingratiating

benthique [bɛ̃tik] ADJ *(faune etc)* benthic

benthos [bɛ̃tɔs] NM benthos

benzène [bɛ̃zɛn] NM *Chimie* benzene

benzine [bɛ̃zin] NF **1** *(mélange d'hydrocarbures)* benzine **2** *Suisse (essence)* petrol, *Am* gas

benzol [bɛ̃zɔl] NM *Chimie* benzol(e)

benzolisme [bɛ̃zɔlism] NM *Méd* benzole poisoning

béotien, -ienne [beɔsjɛ̃, -jɛn] ADJ *Péj* philistine

BEP [beəpe] NM *Scol abrév* **brevet d'études professionnelles**

BEPC [beəpese] NM *Scol Anciennement abrév* **brevet d'études du premier cycle**

béquet [bekɛ] NM *Typ* paste-on

béquille [bekij] NF **1** *Méd* crutch; *Fig* prop; **marcher avec des béquilles** to walk on crutches **2** *(d'une moto)* stand; *Aviat* tail skid; *Naut* shore, prop; *(du gouvernail)* tiller **3** *(de serrure)* catch; *(poignée)* (door) handle

béquiller [bekije] VT *Naut (bateau)* to shore up, to prop up
VI *Fam Arch* to walk on crutches

berbère [bɛrbɛr] ADJ Berber
NM *Ling* Berber
N **B.** Berber

bercail [bɛrkaj] NM *(de l'Église etc)* fold; **ramener au b. la brebis égarée** to bring the lost sheep back to the fold; *Fam* **rentrer au b.** to go (back) home; *(d'un mari etc qui a abandonné le foyer)* to return to the fold

berçante [bɛrsɑ̃t] ADJ, NF *Can* **(chaise) b.** rocking chair

berce [bɛrs] NF **1** *(plante)* **b. commune** hogweed **2** *Belg (berceau)* cradle

berceau, -eaux [bɛrso] NM **1** *(de bébé)* cradle; **dès le b.** from the cradle, from birth; *Fig* **le b. d'un mouvement populaire** the birthplace *or* cradle of a popular movement; *Fam* **il les prend au b.** he's a cradle-snatcher **2** *Typ* cradle, bed, support; *Mil (d'un fusil)* cradle; *(treillage)* bower, arbour, *Am* arbor, *Aut, Aviat* **b. (du) moteur** engine cradle; *Archit* **voûte en b.** barrel vault; **b. de verdure** leafy bower

bercelonnette [bɛrsələnɛt] NF rocking cradle

bercement [bɛrsəmɑ̃] NM rocking

bercer [bɛrse] *(je berçai(s), n. berçons)* VT **1** *(bébé, passager)* to rock; **bateau bercé par la houle** boat rocked by the waves **2** *Litt (calmer) (chagrin)* to soothe **3** **b. qn de promesses/de belles paroles** to delude sb with promises/fine words
VPR **se bercer 1 se b. d'illusions** to delude oneself, to give oneself false hopes; **se b. d'un espoir** to indulge in a hope **2** *Can (se balancer)* to rock (back and forth) *(in a rocking chair)*

berceur, -euse [bɛrsœr, -øz] ADJ soothing, lulling
NF **berceuse** *Can (fauteuil)* rocking chair; *(chanson)* lullaby, cradle song; *Mus* berceuse

BERD [bɛrd] NF *(abrév* **Banque européenne pour la reconstruction et le développement)** EBRD

béret [berɛ] NM **b. (basque)** beret

bergamasque [bɛrgamask] NF bergamask

bergamote [bɛrgamɔt] NF bergamot; **thé à la b.** Earl Grey tea, tea with bergamot

berge¹ [bɛrʒ] NF *(de rivière, de voie ferrée, de route)* bank; *(d'une vallée)* slope, side; **voie sur b.** embankment road

berge² NF *Fam* **il a quarante berges** he's forty; **un type de trente-cinq berges** a guy of thirty-five

berger, -ère [bɛrʒe, -ɛr] N shepherd, f shepherdess; *Rel* shepherd, pastor; **chien de b.** sheepdog; **l'étoile du b.** the evening star
NM **(chien) b. allemand** German shepherd, *Br* Alsatian
NF **bergère** *(fauteuil)* wing chair

bergerette [bɛrʒərɛt] NF *(oiseau)* wagtail

bergerie [bɛrʒəri] NF **1** *(pour moutons etc)* sheepfold, sheep pen; *Fig* **enfermer le loup dans la b.** to set the fox to mind the geese **2** *Beaux-Arts, Littér (tableau, poème etc)* pastoral

bergeronnette [bɛrʒərɔnɛt] NF *(oiseau)* wagtail

béribéri [beriberi] NM *Méd* beriberi; **avoir le b.** to have beriberi

Béring [beriŋ] N **le détroit de B.** the Bering Strait; **la mer de B.** the Bering Sea

berk [bɛrk] INT yuk!

berkélium [bɛrkeljɔm] NM *Chimie* berkelium

berlander [bɛrlɑ̃de] VI *Can* to dawdle, to waste time

Berlin [bɛrlɛ̃] N Berlin; *Anciennement* B.-Ouest/-Est West/East Berlin

berline [bɛrlin] NF *Min* truck, tub; *Aut* (four-door) saloon, *Am* (four-door) sedan; *Arch* (*voiture à cheval*) berlin(e); **b. familiale** family saloon; **b. trois/cinq portes** (three-/five-door) hatchback

berlingot [bɛrlɛ̃go] NM **1** (*bonbon*) boiled sweet, *Am* hard candy; (*à la menthe*) humbug **2** (*de lait*) (pyramid-shaped) carton; (*de shampoing*) sachet; (*de liquide ménager*) pack

berlinois, -oise [bɛrlinwa, -waz] ADJ of/from Berlin
N **B.** Berliner

berlue [bɛrly] NF **avoir la b.** to be seeing things; (*se faire des illusions*) to delude or deceive oneself

berme [bɛrm] NF (*ouvrage*) berm; (*le long d'un canal, d'un fossé etc*) (foot)path, verge

bermuda [bɛrmyda] NM Bermuda shorts, Bermudas

Bermudes [bɛrmyd] NFPL **les (îles) B.** Bermuda

bernache [bɛrnaʃ], **bernacle** [bɛrnakl] NF **1** (*crustacé*) barnacle **2** (*oiseau*) barnacle goose

bernardin, -ine [bɛrnardɛ̃, -in] N *Rel* Bernardine, Cistercian

bernard-l'(h)ermite [bɛrnarlɛrmit] NM INV (*crustacé*) hermit crab

Berne [bɛrn] N Bern

berne [bɛrn] NF **1** *Naut* **pavillon en b.** flag at half mast or *Am* half staff **2** *Mil* **drapeau en b.** furled flag

berner [bɛrne] VT **1** (*duper*) to fool, to hoax; (*ridiculiser*) to ridicule **2** *Arch* (*brimer*) to toss in a blanket

bernicle [bɛrnikl], **bernique**[1] [bɛrnik] NF (*mollusque*) limpet

bernique[2] INT *Fam* nothing doing!

bernois, -oise [bɛrnwa, -waz] ADJ Bernese
N **B.** Bernese

berrichon, -onne [beriʃɔ̃, -ɔn] ADJ from Berry

Berry [beri] NM **le B.** Berry (*region in central France*)

bertillonnage [bɛrtijɔnaʒ] NM (*en anthropométrie*) Bertillon system

béryl [beril] NM *Minér* bery!

béryllium [beriljɔm] NM *Chimie* beryllium

berzingue [bɛrzɛ̃g] NM *Fam* **à tout b.** at full speed, double quick

besace [bəzas] NF *Arch* (*de mendiant*) bag; (*de pèlerin*) scrip

bésef [bezɛf] ADV *Fam* = **bézef**

besicles [bəzikl], **bésicles** [bezikl] NFPL *Fam* specs; *Arch* spectacles

bésigue [bezig] NM *Cartes* bezique

besogne [bəzɔɲ] NF (*piece of*) work, task, job; **se mettre à la b.** to set to work; **rude b.** hard job; **aller vite en b.** to get things done quickly; *Fam Péj* to rush things; **il est allé vite en b.!** he didn't hang about or mess about!; **abattre de la b.** to get through a lot of work; **voilà de la belle b.!** here's a fine mess!; *Fig* **mâcher la b. à qn** to spoon-feed sb

besogner [bəzɔɲe] VI *Péj* to slave away, to toil away
VT *Vulg* to hump, to screw, *Br* to shaft

besogneux, -euse [bəzɔɲø, -øz] ADJ **1** (*travailleur lent*) plodding; **faire son travail de façon besogneuse** to plod away (at one's work) **2** *Arch* (*dans le besoin*) poor

N **1** (*travailleur lent*) plodder **2** *Arch* (*dans le besoin*) poor person

besoin [bəzwɛ̃] NM **1** (*nécessité*) need; **un b. de chaleur humaine** a need for human warmth; **éprouver le b. de faire qch** to feel the need to do sth; **b. d'appartenance** need to belong; **pourvoir** ou **subvenir aux besoins de qn** to provide for sb's needs; **si le b. s'en faisait sentir** if the need or necessity arose; **pour les besoins de la cause** for the sake of the cause; **cet enfant a de grands besoins** this child is very demanding; *Fam* **faire ses besoins** (*d'une personne*) to relieve oneself; (*d'un animal*) to do its business; **au b.** if necessary, if need(s) be; **en cas de b.** in an emergency; **avoir b. de qn/qch** to need sb/sth; **j'en ai b. pour lundi** I need it for Monday; **j'ai grand b. de son aide** I'm badly in need of or I really need his help; **avoir b. de faire qch** to need to do sth; **il n'a pas b. de venir lundi** he needn't come or there's no need for him to come on Monday; **cette maison a grand b. d'être nettoyée** this house really needs to be cleaned or is badly in need of a clean; (**il n'y a** ou **je n'ai) pas b. de dire qu'elle était là** needless to say (that) or it goes without saying (that) she was there; **j'ai b. que tu me laisses tranquille maintenant** I need to be left alone now; **elle a b. qu'on lui parle** she needs someone to talk to; **vous aviez bien b. d'aller lui parler de cela!** you would go and tell him about that!; **tu n'as pas b. de me parler sur ce ton!** there's no need to talk to me in that tone of voice!; *Litt* **il n'est pas b. d'insister** there is no need to insist; **s'il (en) est b., si b. (en) est** if necessary, if need(s) be; *Compta* **b. en fonds de roulement** working capital requirements; **besoins de trésorerie** cash requirements VOIR GRAMMAIRE A40–1 **2** (*misère*) need, poverty, indigence; **être dans le b.** to be in need; **vieillards dans le b.** needy or impoverished old people, old people in need

bessemer [besmɛr] NM *Tech* (**convertisseur**) **b.** Bessemer converter

bestiaire [bɛstjɛr] NM *Litt* bestiary

bestial, -iale, -iaux, -iales [bɛstjal, -jo] ADJ (*personne, colère, air*) brutish; **sensualité bestiale** animal sensuality

bestialement [bɛstjalmɑ̃] ADV brutishly

bestialité [bɛstjalite] NF brutishness; (*perversion*) bestiality

bestiaux [bɛstjo] NMPL livestock; **parqués comme des b.** herded together like cattle

bestiole [bɛstjɔl] NF (*bête*) small or tiny animal or creature; (*insecte*) insect, bug

best of [bɛstɔf] NM INV greatest hits compilation; **un b. des Rolling Stones** a compilation of the greatest hits of the Rolling Stones

best-seller, pl **best-sellers** [bɛstsɛlœr] NM bestseller

bêta[1] **, -asse** [bɛta, -as] *Fam* ADJ silly, stupid
N twit, idiot; **oh le gros b.!** (*à un enfant*) you silly billy!

bêta[2] [beta] NM **1** (*lettre de l'alphabet grec*) beta **2** *Nucl* **particules/rayons b.** beta particles/rays

bêtabloquant [betablɔkɑ̃] NM *Pharm* beta-blocker

bétail [betaj] NM livestock; **gros b.** livestock (*including cattle, horses, asses, mules*); **menu** ou **petit b.** smaller livestock; *Fig* **on était traité comme du b.** we were treated like cattle VOIR GRAMMAIRE A11

bétaillère [betajɛr] NF cattle truck

bêta-test, pl **bêta-tests** NM *Ordinat* beta test; **bêta-tests** beta testing

bêtatron [betatrɔ̃] NM *Nucl* betatron

bête [bɛt] NF **1** (*animal*) animal, *Litt* beast; **b. à cornes** horned animal; **b. de trait** draught

animal; **les bêtes** (*à la ferme*) the animals, the livestock; *Fam* **reprendre du poil de la b.** (*reprendre le dessus*) to perk up, to pick up; **les bêtes féroces** wild animals; **une b. sauvage** a wild animal; **nos amies les bêtes** our animal friends, our four-legged friends; **sale b.** nasty little animal; **elle m'a regardé comme une b. curieuse** she looked at me as if I was from another planet; *Fam* **c'est une b. en maths!** he/she's a genius or a wiz at maths!; **travailler comme une b.** to work all out or flat out; **c'est une bonne b.** he's/she's a good sort; **grosse b.!** you silly(billy)!

2 (*insecte*) insect, bug; **petites bêtes** insects; (*nocives*) vermin; *Fig* **chercher la petite b.** to be over-critical, *Fam* to nit-pick; **jouer à la b. qui monte, qui monte** = to play 'round and round the garden like a teddy bear'

3 (*idiot*) fool, idiot, twit; **faire la b.** to act stupid, to pretend to be stupid; (*sans le vouloir*) to act stupidly or foolishly

ADJ stupid, silly, foolish; **que je suis b.!** how silly or stupid of me!; **ce que tu peux être b. parfois!** you can be really stupid sometimes!; **pas si b.!** I'm/she's/*etc* not such a fool (as all that)!; **c'est vraiment b., j'ai oublié mes clés** how stupid, I've forgotten my keys; **c'est trop b., tu aurais dû venir** that's a pity or a shame, you should have come; **c'est b., on a loupé le film!** what a pity or a shame, we've missed the film!; **il n'est pas si b. qu'il en a l'air** he's not as stupid or silly as he looks; **elle est loin d'être b.** she's no fool; *Fam* **elle est b. comme un âne** ou **comme ses pieds** ou **à manger du foin** she's as thick as a brick or *Br* as two short planks; **une histoire/une fille b. à pleurer** a pitifully stupid story/girl, a story/girl that is too stupid for words; **mon Dieu qu'il est b.!** God he's stupid!; **l'âge b.** the difficult age; **b. et méchant** stupid and nasty; **c'est b. comme chou, c'est tout b.** it's as easy as pie or as anything; **ce n'est pas b.** that's not a bad idea, *Br* that's not daft; *Can* **rester tout b.** (*décontenancé*) to be stupefied; **une mort b.** a stupid or senseless death

▸▸ **b. à bon Dieu** ladybird, *Am* ladybug; *Péj* **b. à concours** swot, *Am* grind; **b. noire:** *Fig* **c'est sa b. noire** (*personne*) he's/she's his bête noire; **les maths, c'est ma b. noire** maths are my pet aversion or hate or my bête noir; **b. de scène** complete performer; **b. de somme** beast of burden

bétel [betɛl] NM (*plante*) betel

bêtement [bɛtmɑ̃] ADV stupidly, foolishly, idiotically; **mourir b.** to die senselessly; **tout b.** quite simply, purely and simply

Bethléem [betleɛm] N *Bible* Bethlehem

bêtifiant [betifjɑ̃] ADJ idiotic

bêtifier [betifje] (*pr sub, impf* n. **bêtifiions,** v. **bêtifiiez**) VT to make stupid
VPR **se bêtifier ils se bêtifient à trop regarder la télévision** too much television is bad for their minds
VI to talk nonsense; (*faire l'idiot*) to act or play the fool; **quand il parle à un enfant, il bêtifie** he uses baby-talk to children

bêtise [betiz] NF **1** (*imbécillité*) stupidity, silliness; **être d'une rare b.** to be exceptionally stupid; **elle a eu la b. de dire oui** she was stupid enough to say yes; **tu ne crois pas que c'est de la b. de l'acheter?** don't you think it's a stupid idea or it's stupid to buy it?

2 (*action idiote*) stupid thing (to do); (*parole idiote*) stupid remark, stupid thing to say; **dire des bêtises** to talk nonsense or *Br* rubbish; **quelle b.!** what nonsense!, how ridiculous!; **faire des bêtises** to do silly things; **ne faites pas de bêtises, les petits** don't do anything silly, children; **faire une (grosse) b.** to do something (very) stupid or silly; **ça, c'est une grosse b.** that is/was very stupid; **il**

ne faudrait pas qu'elle fasse une b. we don't want her to do anything silly; **se disputer pour des bêtises** to argue over nothing; **perdre son temps à des bêtises** to waste one's time on trifles; **dépenser tout son argent en bêtises** to fritter away one's money; **elle achète énormément de bêtises** she buys lots of rubbish or Am trash
3 Can **bêtises** (injures) insults
4 bêtises de Cambrai ≃ mint humbugs, Am ≃ hard mint candies

bêtisier [betizje] NM (sous forme écrite) collection of howlers; (émission de télévision) compendium of out-takes

béton [betɔ̃] NM **1** Constr concrete; **b. armé** reinforced concrete; Fig **des muscles en b.** rock-hard muscles; Fam **un alibi en b.** a cast-iron alibi; **il est b., leur dossier** their dossier is watertight **2** Ftbl **faire le b.** to pack the defence **3** Fam **laisse b.!** let it drop!, drop it!

bétonnage [betɔnaʒ] NM **1** Constr concreting **2** Ftbl packing the defence

bétonner [betɔne] VT **1** Constr to concrete **2** Fam (préparer avec soin) to work hard on; **il a bétonné son discours/son dossier** he's worked really hard on his speech/his application
VI Ftbl to pack the defence

bétonneuse [betɔnøz], **bétonnière** [betɔnjɛr] NF cement mixer, concrete mixer

bette [bet] NF (spinach) beet; **b. à carde (blanche), b. à côtes** seakale beet, Swiss chard

betterave [betrav] NF **b. (rouge)** beetroot, Am beet; **b. sucrière** sugar beet; **b. fourragère** mangel-wurzel

betteravier, -ière [betravje, -jɛr] ADJ **l'industrie betteravière** the beet industry
NM sugar beet grower

beuglant [bøglɑ̃] NM Fam Vieilli (café-concert) dive, Am honky-tonk

beuglante [bøglɑ̃t] NF Fam (cri) yell; (chanson) song; **pousser une b.** (crier) to shout one's head off; (chanter) to bawl out a song

beuglement [bøgləmɑ̃] NM (du bétail) lowing; (du taureau) bellow(ing); Fam (d'une personne) bawling, bellowing; (de la radio etc) blaring; **pousser des beuglements** to bawl, to bellow

beugler [bøgle] VI (du bétail) to low; (d'un taureau) to bellow; Fam (d'une personne) to bawl, to bellow; (de la radio etc) to blare; **pas la peine de b., je t'entends!** no need to yell, I can hear you!; **les voisins font b. leur télévision** the neighbours have got their television blaring away
VT Fam **b. une chanson** to bawl out or bellow out a song

beur [bœr] NM = young man born in France, of North African immigrant parents
ADJ INV (culture, mode, musique) = of North Africans born in France, of immigrant parents

beurette [bœret] NF = young woman born in France, of North African immigrant parents

beurre [bœr] NM butter; **b. salé/demi-sel** salted/slightly salted butter; **b. fondu** melted butter; **une motte de b.** a lump of butter; Culin **au b.** (pâtisserie) made with butter; (légumes) with melted butter; **faire la cuisine au b.** to cook with butter; **crème au b.** butter cream; **au b. noir** with black butter; **avoir un œil au b. noir** to have a black eye; **c'est entré comme dans du b.** it went in very easily; Fam **cela compte pour du b.** that doesn't count; Fam **il a fait son b.** he's made a packet; **ça mettra du b. dans les épinards** that will improve matters or ease the situation; **elle veut le b. et l'argent du b.** she wants to have her cake and eat it

▸▸**b. d'anchois** anchovy butter; **b. de cacahouètes** peanut butter; **b. de cacao** cocoa butter

beurrée [bœre] NF Can (tartine) slice of bread and butter

beurre-frais ADJ INV buttercup-yellow

beurrer [bœre] VT (pain, plat etc) to butter; Arg **être complètement beurré** to be plastered or smashed
VPR **se beurrer** Arg to get plastered or smashed

beurrerie [bœrri] NF **1** (laiterie) dairy **2** (industrie) butter industry

beurrier, -ière [bœrje, -jɛr] ADJ **l'industrie beurrière** the butter industry; **région beurrière** butter-producing region
NM butter dish

beuverie [bøvri] NF binge, drinking session, Br Fam booze-up

bévatron [bevatrɔ̃] NM Nucl bevatron

bévue [bevy] NF blunder, mistake, slip; **commettre une b.** to blunder, to make a blunder

bey [bɛ] NM bey

Beyrouth [berut] N Beirut

bézef [bezef] ADV Fam **il n'y en a pas b.** (non comptable) there's not much or a lot (of it); (comptable) there aren't many or a lot (of them)

BF [beef] NF (abrév **Banque de France**) Bank of France

BFCE [beefseə] NF (abrév **Banque française du commerce extérieur**) French foreign trade bank

Bhoutan [butɑ̃] NM Bhutan

bi [bi] NM Can **donner** ou **faire un bi** to lend a hand

bi- [bi-] PRÉF bi-; **bilatéral/bipartisan/etc** bilateral/bipartisan/etc

biacide [biasid] ADJ, NM Chimie diacid

biais [bjɛ] ADJ Archit oblique, slanting; **voûte biaise** skew(ed) arch
NM **1** (d'un outil, d'une arche) skew; (d'un mur) slant; **en b.** at an angle, slantwise; Couture **tailler un tissu dans le b.** to cut material on the bias **2** (moyen) way; (détour) expedient; **par le b. de son voisin** through his neighbour; **aborder** ou **prendre de b. une personne/une question** to approach a person/a question indirectly or in a roundabout way; **regarder qn de b.** to look sideways or askance at sb **3** (aspect) angle; **par quel b. envisager la chose?** from what angle should we look at the issue? **4** Couture bias binding

biaiser [bjeze] VI **1** (obliquer) to be on the slant; (vers qch) to veer off **2** Fig to dodge the issue; **pour éviter cela, il va falloir b.** we'll have to manoeuvre to avoid that
VT **l'échantillon a été biaisé** the sample has been distorted

biathlon [biatlɔ̃] NM Sport biathlon

bibande [bibɑ̃d] Tél ADJ dual-band
NM (téléphone portable) dual-band mobile phone or Am cellphone

bibasique [bibazik] ADJ Chimie dibasic

bibelot [biblo] NM curio, knick-knack; **bibelots sans valeur** trinkets

biberon [bibrɔ̃] NM (baby's or feeding) bottle; **nourrir** ou **élever un enfant au b.** to bottle-feed a child; **il est encore au b.?** is he still being bottle-fed?; **il prend trois biberons par jour** he has three feeds a day; **l'heure du b.** feeding time

biberonner [bibrɔne] VI Fam to booze, to tipple

bibi [bibi] NM **1** Arg (moi) yours truly; **et ça, c'est pour b.** that's for yours truly **2** Fam (chapeau) (woman's) hat

bibine [bibin] NF Fam (boisson) dishwater; **c'est de la b., cette bière** this beer is (like) dishwater

bibite [bibit] NF Can Arg bug, insect

bible [bibl] NF bible; **la B.** the Bible; **la b. du bricoleur** the DIY bible; Ordinat **b. de paragraphes** library of standard paragraphs

bibliobus [biblijɔbys] NM mobile library, Am bookmobile

bibliographe [biblijɔgraf] N bibliographer

bibliographie [biblijɔgrafi] NF bibliography

bibliographique [biblijɔgrafik] ADJ bibliographical

bibliomane [biblijɔman] N book lover, Fml bibliomaniac

bibliomanie [biblijɔmani] NF love of books, Fml bibliomania

bibliophile [biblijɔfil] N bibliophile, book lover

bibliophilie [biblijɔfili] NF love of books, Fml bibliophily

bibliothécaire [biblijɔtekɛr] N librarian

bibliothéconomie [biblijɔtekɔnɔmi] NF library science

bibliothèque [biblijɔtɛk] NF **1** (bâtiment, salle) library; **b. de prêt** lending library; **b. municipale** municipal or public library; **b. universitaire** university library; **B. nationale** the former national library in Paris (now part of the Bibliothèque nationale de France); **B. nationale de France** = the French national library in Paris **2** (meuble) bookcase **3** (série), Ordinat library; **la b. verte/rose** = series of books aimed at 7- to 15-year-olds/at 5- to 7-year-olds; Fam **c'est une b. ambulante** ou **vivante** he's a walking encyclopaedia; Ordinat **b. de programmes** program library

biblique [biblik] ADJ biblical

Bi-bop® [bibɔp] NM Tél = mobile telephone system run by France Télécom

Bic® [bik] NM **pointe B.** ballpoint pen, Fam Biro®

bic® ADJ **stylo b., pointe b.** ballpoint pen, Br Biro®
NM ballpoint, Br Biro®

bicaméral, -ale, -aux, -ales [bikameral, -o] ADJ Pol (système etc) bicameral

bicaméralisme [bikameralism], **bicamérisme** [bikamerism] NM Pol bicameral system

bicarbonate [bikarbɔnat] NM Chimie bicarbonate; **b. de soude** bicarbonate of soda, sodium bicarbonate

bicentenaire [bisɑ̃tnɛr] NM bicentenary, Am bicentennial

bicéphale [bisefal] ADJ (animal) two-headed, Spéc bicephalous

biceps [bisɛps] Anat ADJ (muscle) biceps
NM biceps; Fam **avoir des b.** to have muscles

biche [biʃ] NF **1** (mammifère) hind, doe; **ventre de b.** (couleur) reddish-white; **table à pieds de b.** table with cabriole legs; **aux yeux de b.** doe-eyed **2** Fam **ma b.** my darling, my dear

bicher [biʃe] VI Fam **1** (aller bien) **ça biche?** how's things? **2** (se réjouir) to be tickled pink, Br to be as pleased as Punch

bichette [biʃet] NF **1** (mammifère) young or small hind **2** Fam **ma b.** my darling, my dear

bichlorure [biklɔryr] NM Chimie bichloride, dichloride

bichon, -onne [biʃɔ̃, -ɔn] N **1** (chien) lapdog, toy dog **2** Fam **mon b.** my darling, my love, my dear

bichonner [biʃɔne] VT **1** (préparer) (personne) to make spruce or smart **2** (soigner) (personne) to pamper, to mollycoddle
VPR **se bichonner** to spruce oneself up

bichromate [bikrɔmat] NM *Chimie* bichromate, dichromate

bichromie [bikrɔmi] NF *Typ* two-colour *or Am* two-color *or* two-tone printing

biclic [biklik] NM *Ordinat* double click

bicliquer [biklike] VI *Ordinat* to double-click

biclo [biklo], **biclou** [biklu] NM *Fam* bike

bicolore [bikɔlɔr] ADJ two-colour(ed) *or Am* -color(ed), two-tone

biconcave [bikɔ̃kav] ADJ biconcave

biconvexe [bikɔ̃vɛks] ADJ biconvex

bicoque [bikɔk] NF *(maison)* shack

bicorne [bikɔrn] ADJ *Biol, Anat* two-horned; *Spéc* bicorn(u)ate
NM cocked hat

bicot [biko] NM **1** *(biquet)* kid **2** *Fam (terme injurieux) (Arabe)* Arab, *Br* ≃ wog

bicross [bikrɔs] NM *Sport* cyclo-cross bicycle; **faire du b.** to cyclo-cross, to go cyclo-crossing

biculturalisme [bikyltyralism] NM biculturalism

biculturel, -elle [bikyltyrɛl] ADJ bicultural

bicyclette [bisiklɛt] NF bicycle; **aller en ville à** *ou Fam* **en b.** to cycle to town, to go to town by bicycle; **faire de la b. tous les week-ends** to go cycling *or* to cycle every weekend; **il ne sait pas faire de la b.** he can't ride a bicycle

bidasse [bidas] NM *Mil Arg* squaddie, *Am* GI

bide [bid] NM *Arg* **1** *(ventre)* belly; **avoir/prendre du b.** to have/develop a belly; *Fig* **c'est du b.** it's a load of baloney *or Br* codswallop **2 la pièce/le film a fait un b.** the play/film flopped *or* bombed; **un b. complet** a total flop

bidet [bidɛ] NM **1** *(de toilette)* bidet **2** *Vieilli Fam (cheval)* nag

bidimensionnel, -elle [bidimɑ̃sjɔnɛl] ADJ bidimensional

bidirectionnel, -elle [bidirɛksjɔnɛl] ADJ bidirectional; *Tél* **b. simultané** full duplex

bidoche [bidɔʃ] NF *Arg* meat

bidon [bidɔ̃] NM **1** *(d'huile, d'essence)* can; *Mil etc (gourde)* water bottle; **b. d'essence** petrol can, jerry can; **b. à lait** milk churn **2** *très Fam (ventre)* belly; **se remplir le b.** to stuff oneself; **c'est du b.** it's a load of baloney *or Br* codswallop; **c'est pas du b.** it's the honest truth
ADJ *Fam* phoney, fake; *(élections)* rigged
NMPL *Belg Fam* **bidons** *(frusques)* togs, gear, threads; *(affaires)* things, stuff

bidonnant [bidɔnɑ̃] ADJ *Arg* hilarious, screamingly funny; **c'est b.** it's a scream

bidonner [bidɔne] VI *Fam* to create false news
VT *Fam (truquer)* to fake
VPR **se bidonner** *Fam* to laugh one's head off, to split one's sides (laughing)

bidonville [bidɔ̃vil] NM shantytown

bidouillage [biduja3] NM *Fam* **1** *(bricolage)* **c'est du b.** it's just been thrown together **2** *Ordinat* patching

bidouiller [biduje] VT *Fam* to patch up; *Ordinat (programme)* to patch

bidouilleur, -euse [bidujœr, -øz] N *Ordinat* hacker, expert user

bidule [bidyl] NM *Arg* thingy, thingummy, whatsit; **j'ai vu B.** I saw whats-his-name, *f* whats-her-name

bief [bjɛf] NM **1** *(portion du cours d'eau)* reach **2** *(d'un moulin)* millcourse, millrace

bielle [bjɛl] NF *Aut* connecting rod, conrod; *Tech (sous tension)* (tie) rod; *(sous compression)* push rod, crank arm; *Aut* **b. d'accouplement** track link; **tête de b.** crank head; *(de*

moteur) big end; **pied de b.** crosshead; *(de moteur)* little end; *Aut* **b. de connexion** track rod; *Aut* **b. pendante** drop arm, drag link bar

biellette [bjɛlɛt] NF *Tech (petite bielle)* small rod; *Aut* **b. de direction** drag link, track rod

biélorusse [bjelorys] ADJ B(y)elorussian
N **B.** B(y)elorussian

Biélorussie [bjelorysi] NF B(y)elorussia

<u>BIEN</u> [bjɛ̃]

| ADV well **1, 3, 11** ▪ right **2, 3** ▪ really **3** ▪ very **4** ▪ a lot **5** ▪ although *(bien que)* ▪ **8** ▪ otherwise *(ou bien)* ▪ **10** |
| INT well |
| ADJ INV good **1, 4** ▪ comfortable **2** ▪ well **3** ▪ good-looking **4** |
| NM good **1** ▪ possession **2** ▪ property **2** |

ADV **1** *(convenablement)* well; **livre b. écrit** well-written book; **c'est du travail b. fait** it's a fine *or* well-executed piece of work; **j'aime le travail b. fait** I like work that's done well; **il parle b.** he is a good speaker, he speaks well; **on y mange très b.** the food there is very good, you eat very well there; **cette couleur/ce rôle lui va b.** this colour/this role suits him well; **ça te va b. de critiquer le travail des autres sans rien faire** you're a fine one to criticize the work of others without doing anything yourself; **aller** *ou* **se porter b.** to be well *or* in good health; **tout va b.** all's well, everything's OK *or* fine; **s'y prendre b.** to go about it the right way; *Iron* **voilà qui commence b.!** that's a good *or* fine start!; **vous arrivez b.** you've come just at the right moment; **b.!** good!; *(ça suffit)* that's enough!, that will do!; *(entendu)* all right!; **très b.!, fort b.!** very good!, well done!; *(signalant son accord avec le locuteur)* hear, hear!; **écoutez b. ceci** now listen carefully to this; **il faut b. les soigner** they must be well looked after

2 *(moralement)* **vous avez b. fait** you did the right thing, you did right; **se conduire** *ou* **se tenir b.** to behave (well); **veux-tu te conduire b.!** will you behave!; **c'est b. fait (pour lui)** it serves him right; **voilà qui est b. dit!** well said!; **tu fais b. de me le dire** it's a good thing *or* job you've told me, you've done well to tell me; **tu ferais b. de te méfier** you would do well to beware

3 *(emphatique)* **est-ce b. raisonnable?** is that really reasonable?; **c'est b. cela** that's right; **il y a b. deux ans que je ne l'ai vue** it's at least *or* it must be two years since I (last) saw her; **j'ai b. dû lire dix de ses livres** I must have read at least ten of his books; **je l'ai regardé b. en face** I looked him full *or* right in the face; **j'irais b. avec vous, mais …** I'd love to go with you, but …; **j'y suis b. obligé** I just *or* really have to; **conduis b. à droite** drive well over on the right; **b. au milieu** right *or Fam* bang in the middle; **être b. d'accord** to be entirely *or* completely in agreement, to be in complete agreement; **c'est b. d'accord/compris?** is that agreed/understood?; **b. à vous** *(dans une lettre)* yours; **je veux b. le croire** I can quite believe it; **je sais b.** I know full well, I'm well aware of it; **qu'est-ce que ça peut b. être/vouloir dire?** whatever can it be/mean?, what on earth can it be/mean?; **je me demande b. ce qu'il pouvait en penser** I really wonder what he might think of it; **c'est b. lui** it *is* him; **ce sont b. mes lunettes** those *are* my glasses; **c'est b. une erreur** that's definitely a mistake; **c'est b. de lui** it's just like him, that's typical of him; *Fam* **c'est b. à moi, ça?** that's really mine?; **est-ce b. le train pour Paris?** is this the right train for Paris?, is this train OK for Paris?; **c'est b. Apollinaire qui a écrit ces poèmes?** am I right in thinking Apollinaire wrote these poems?, Apollinaire did write

these poems, didn't he?; **je l'avais b. dit!** didn't I say so?; **on vous avait b. dit que tous les magasins seraient fermés** you were told all the shops would be shut; **voulez-vous b. vous taire!** do shut up!, will you *please* be quiet!; **il est b. entendu que …** it is understood, of course, that …; **b. entendu, b. sûr, b. évidemment** of course; **je m'en doutais b.** I thought as much; **c'est b. ce que je pensais** that's just what I thought; **il faut b. qu'on mange quelque chose** we really must eat something; **il est b. venu, mais j'étais occupé** he did come, but I was busy; **je ne veux pas que tu fasses cela – mais vous le faites b., vous!** I don't want you to do that – but *you* do it, don't you?; *Iron* **c'est b. le moment de parler comme ça!** a fine time *or* what a time to talk like that!; **c'est b. ma chance!** (it's) just my luck!; **c'était b. la peine** it wasn't worth the trouble; **voilà b. les hommes!** just like men!, that's men all over!

4 *(très)* very; **b. malheureux** very unhappy; **vous venez b. tard** you're very late; **b. souvent** quite often; **c'est b. loin de Paris** it's a long way (away) from Paris; **b. loin de moi l'idée de vous accuser** far be it from me to accuse you; **c'est b. gentil, mais …** that's very kind, but …; **c'est b. simple** it's quite *or* very simple; **je voudrais que ce soit b. clair entre nous** I want us to be quite clear on this

5 *(beaucoup) (souffrir, réfléchir, changer etc)* a lot, a great deal; **b. plus** much *or* a lot more; **b. moins** much *or* a lot less; **tu t'es b. amusé** did you have a good time?, did you enjoy yourself?; **b. de …** a lot of …, a great deal of …; **b. des …** a lot of …, a good many …; **j'ai eu b. de la peine** *ou* **du mal à la convaincre** I had a lot of *or* a great deal of trouble convincing her; **j'ai reçu b. des lettres** I received a lot of *or* a good many letters; **nous avons eu b. des inquiétudes à son sujet** he caused us a lot of *or* a great deal of worry; **je l'ai vu b. des fois** I have seen him many times; **b. d'autres** many others, lots more

6 **aussi b.** just as well, just as easily; **on fera aussi b. d'y aller par nous-mêmes** we can just as well *or* just as easily go there by ourselves

7 tant b. que mal somehow (or other), after a fashion; **je m'en suis acquitté tant b. que mal** I got through

8 b. que + *sub* although, though; **je le respecte, b. qu'il ne me soit pas sympathique** I respect him (even) though I don't like him
SEE GRAMMAR B33

9 si b. que + *ind* and so; **il ne reparut plus, si b. qu'on le crut mort** he failed to come back, and so he was thought dead

10 ou b. or else, otherwise; **il faut le lui dire ou b. il l'apprendra par quelqu'un d'autre** we'll have to tell him or else *or* otherwise he'll hear about it from someone else; **viens à la maison, ou b. on se retrouve dans un café** come to my place, or (else) we could meet in a café; **ou b. … ou b. …** either … or …

INT **eh b.!** well!; **eh b. donc!** well then!; **eh b. ça alors!** well, fancy that!

ADJ INV **1** *(satisfaisant)* good; *Scol (sur un devoir)* good; **c'est b.!** good!; **ce serait b. si …** it would be good if …; **comme c'est b. à vous d'être venu!** how good of you to come!; **ce n'est pas b. de vous moquer de lui** it's not nice *or* kind of you to make fun of him; **des gens b.** nice *or* decent people; **il est très b., le nouvel assistant** the new assistant is very good; **il est très b., ce petit gars** he's a nice fellow; **il me faut quelque chose de b.** I'm looking for something good

2 *(à l'aise)* **êtes-vous b. dans ce fauteuil/ces chaussures?** are you comfortable in that armchair/those shoes?; **qu'est-ce qu'on serait b., dans une maison comme la tienne!** I'd really feel at home in a house like yours!;

se sentir b. dans un pays to like it *or* to feel at home in a country; **je suis b. partout** I'm at home anywhere; **ne t'occupe pas de moi, je suis b. comme ça** don't worry about me, I'm fine *or* all right as I am; **nous voilà b.!** we're in a right mess!; **être b. avec qn** to be on good terms with sb, to be well in with sb; **se mettre b. avec qn** to get into sb's good books, to get well in with sb

3 *(en forme)* well; **je ne me sens pas très b.** I don't feel very well; **vous vous sentez b. maintenant?** do you feel better now?; **il est moins b.** he's not as well (as he was)

4 *(beau) (personne)* good-looking, attractive; **il est b. de sa personne** he's a fine figure of a man; **tu es très b. dans cette robe** you look very good in that dress, that dress suits you very well; **elle est b. sur cette photo** she looks good in this photo

NM 1 *Phil, Rel etc* good; **le b. et le mal** good and evil, right and wrong; **faire le b.** to do good; **homme de b.** good *or* upright man; **le b. public** the public good; **c'est pour votre b.** it's for your own good; **cela m'a fait beaucoup de b.** it did me a lot of good; **ça pourrait peut-être faire du b. à mes rhumatismes** that could perhaps do my rheumatism some good; **faire le plus grand b. à qn** to do sb a great deal of good; **grand b. vous fasse!** much good may it do you!; **vouloir du b. à qn, vouloir le b. de qn** to wish sb well; **je ne veux que votre b.** I only want the best for you; **un ami qui vous veut du b.** a well-wisher; **tout le monde dit du b.** *ou* **parle en b. de lui** everyone speaks well of him; **on m'a dit beaucoup de b. de vous/de ce produit** I've heard a lot of good things about you/about this product; **je trouve qu'il a changé en b.** I think he's changed for the better; **mener une affaire à b.** to bring a matter to a satisfactory conclusion

2 *(chose matérielle)* possession, property; *Jur* assets; *(argent)* wealth, fortune; **biens** possessions, property; **il a du b. (au soleil)** he's a man of property, he has property; **c'est mon b. le plus cher** it's my dearest possession; **biens et services** goods and services

3 *Fam* **en tout b. (et) tout honneur** with the best of intentions

► ► **biens capitaux** capital goods *or* items; **collectif** collective good; **b. commun** common good; **biens consommables** consumables; **biens de consommation** consumer goods *or* products; **biens de consommation durables** consumer durables; **biens de consommation finale** final consumer goods; **biens de consommation intermédiaire** intermediate consumer goods; **biens de consommation non durables** disposable goods, non-durable consumer goods; **biens corporels** tangible assets; **biens dotaux** dowry; **biens durables** (consumer) durables; **biens d'équipement** capital equipment *or* goods; **biens fonciers** landed property; **biens immeubles** *or* **immobiliers** real estate *or* property; **b. industriel** industrial good; **biens intermédiaires** semi-finished goods; **biens meubles** *ou* **mobiliers** personal property *or* estate; **biens de première nécessité** staples; **biens de production** capital goods; *Compta* **biens sociaux** corporate assets *or* funds; **biens successoraux** hereditaments; **biens tangibles** physical goods; **biens vacants** ownerless property

bien-aimé, -ée, *pl* **bien-aimés, -ées** [bjɛ̃neme] ADJ beloved; **mon ami b.** my very dear friend

N beloved; *Hist (Louis)* **le Bien-Aimé** Louis XV

bien-être [bjɛ̃netr] NM INV **1** well-being; *(d'une population etc)* welfare; **sentiment de b.** feeling of well-being; **b. du consommateur** consumer welfare **2** *Can* **b. social** *Br* social security, *Am* welfare

bienfaisance [bjɛ̃fəzɑ̃s] NF *(générosité)* benevolence; *(charité)* charity; **bureau de b.** welfare office; **organisation** *ou* **œuvre de b.** charitable organization, charity

bienfaisant [bjɛ̃fəzɑ̃] ADJ **1** *(personne)* charitable, kindly **2** *(remède etc)* beneficial, salutary; *(vent, pluie)* refreshing

bienfait [bjɛ̃fɛ] NM **1** *(avantage)* benefit; **les bienfaits de la technique/du traitement** the benefits of technology/of the treatment **2** **un b. du ciel** a godsend; *Prov* **un b. n'est jamais perdu** a good deed will have its reward

bienfaiteur, -trice [bjɛ̃fɛtœr, -tris] N benefactor, *f* benefactress; **b. du peuple** people's friend

bien-fondé, *pl* **bien-fondés** NM *(d'une opinion, d'un argument, d'une revendication)* validity, merits; *Jur* cogency

bien-fonds, *pl* **biens-fonds** NM real estate, landed property

bienheureux, -euse [bjɛ̃nørø, -øz] ADJ **1** *(heureux)* blissful, happy **2** *Rel* blessed

N *Rel* blessed person; **dormir comme un b.** to sleep the sleep of the just; **les b.** the blessed, the blest

bien-jugé NM INV *Jur* just and lawful decision

biennal, -ale, -aux, -ales [bjenal, -o] ADJ biennial, two-yearly; **contrat b.** two-year contract; **fonction biennale** two-year post; **exposition biennale** biennial exhibition

NF **biennale** biennial

bien-pensant, -ante, *pl* **bien-pensants, -antes** ADJ *(personne)* right-thinking, right-minded, *Péj* self-righteous

N *Péj* self-righteous person, prig

bienséance [bjɛ̃seɑ̃s] NF propriety, decorum; **respecter les bienséances** to observe the proprieties

bienséant [bjɛ̃seɑ̃] ADJ decorous, proper; **il est b. aux jeunes gens de respecter la vieillesse** it is right and proper for young people to respect old age; **il n'est pas b. de manger avec ses doigts** it is not proper *or* it is not the done thing to eat with your fingers

bientôt [bjɛ̃to] ADV soon, before long; **on est b. arrivé?** are we nearly there?, will we soon be there?; **il est b. deux heures** it's soon be two o'clock; **tu vas b. arrêter de répéter la même chose?** will you please stop repeating the same thing?; **à b.!** see you soon!, goodbye for now!; **on s'est dit à b.** we said we'd see each other soon; **on se dit adieu ou on se dit à b.?** is it goodbye or just au revoir?; **les beaux jours seront b. là** the fine days will soon be here; **c'est pour b., ce bébé?** is the baby due soon?; *Litt* **b. après** soon after(wards); *Vieilli* **c'est b. dit!** that's easier said than done! VOIR GRAMMAIRE A21

bienveillance [bjɛ̃vɛjɑ̃s] NF benevolence, kindness (**envers, pour** to); **avec b.** kindly

bienveillant [bjɛ̃vɛjɑ̃] ADJ kind, kindly, benevolent (**envers, pour** to); **examinateur b.** lenient examiner

bienvenu, -ue [bjɛ̃vny] ADJ *(remarque)* opportune, apposite; *(repas, explication etc)* welcome

N **soyez le b./la bienvenue!** welcome!; **vous êtes toujours le b.** you're always welcome; **votre proposition est la bienvenue** your suggestion is welcome

bienvenue [bjɛ̃vny] NF welcome; **souhaiter la b. à qn** to welcome sb; **b. à nos amis de Russie!** welcome to our Russian friends!; **b. à Nice!** welcome to Nice!; **allocution de b.** welcoming speech

INT *Can (de rien)* you're welcome!

bière¹ [bjɛr] NF *(boisson)* beer; **b. blonde** lager; **b. brune** brown ale, *Am* dark beer; **b. pression** draught *or* *Am* draft beer; *Fig* **ça n'est pas de la petite b.** it's no small matter; **c'est de la petite b.** it's small beer

bière² NF *(cercueil)* coffin, *Am* casket; **assister à la mise en b.** to be present when the body is placed in the coffin

biffe [bif] NF *Mil Arg* infantry

biffer [bife] VT *(mot etc)* to cross out, to strike out, to put a line through; **tu peux b. ce nom de ta liste** you can cross *or* strike this name off your list

biffeton [biftɔ̃] NM = **bifton**

biffin [bifɛ̃] NM **1** *Arg (chiffonnier)* ragman, *Br* rag-and-bone man **2** *Mil Fam* infantryman

biffure [bifyr] NF crossing out, striking out

bifide [bifid] ADJ bifid

bifidus [bifidys] NM *Biol* live culture

bifocal, -ale, -aux, -ales [bifɔkal, -o] ADJ *(lentille etc)* bifocal; **lunettes bifocales** bifocals

bifteck [biftɛk] NM (beef)steak; **b. de cheval** horse(meat) steak; *Fam* **gagner son b.** to earn a living

bifton [biftɔ̃] NM *Fam (billet de banque)* note, *Am* greenback; *(de transport, de spectacle)* ticket

bifurcation [bifyrkasjɔ̃] NF *(d'une route)* junction, fork; *(d'un tronc d'arbre etc)* fork; *(professionnelle)* change of direction; **tournez à droite à la b.** take the right fork

bifurquer [bifyrke] VI *(d'une route, d'un chemin)* to fork, to divide, to branch off; **nous avons bifurqué vers** *ou* **sur la ville** we turned *or* forked off towards the town; **bifurquez à droite** take the right fork; **b. vers la politique/dans la recherche** to branch out into politics/research

bigame [bigam] ADJ bigamous

N bigamist

bigamie [bigami] NF bigamy

bigarade [bigarad] NF *(fruit)* bitter *or* Seville orange

bigarré [bigare] ADJ *(tissu, chemise etc)* multicoloured, *Am* multicolored; *(groupe, société etc)* mixed; *(foule)* motley, mixed

bigarreau, -eaux [bigaro] NM *(cerise)* bigarreau

bigarrer [bigare] VT to colour *or Am* to color in many shades

bigarrure [bigaryr] NF mixture *or* medley of colours *or Am* colors; *(d'un groupe, style etc)* variety, motley nature; **les bigarrures du costume d'Arlequin** Harlequin's multicoloured *or Am* multicolored costume; **une b. de gens** a motley collection of people

big band [bigbɑ̃d] NM *Mus* big band

big(-)bang [bigbɑ̃g] NM *Astron* big bang

bigle [bigl] *Vieilli, Hum* ADJ cross-eyed

N cross-eyed person

bigler [bigle] *Fam* VI *(loucher)* to squint, to have a squint; **b. sur qch** to squint at sth

VT *(quelque chose)* to squint at; *(fille)* to eye (up)

bigleux, -euse [biglø, -øz] *Fam* ADJ *(personne) (qui louche)* cross-eyed; *(myope)* short-sighted; **t'es b.?** are you blind?

N *(qui louche)* cross-eyed person; *(qui est myope)* short-sighted person

bigophone [bigɔfɔn] NM *Fam (téléphone)* phone, *Br* blower; **passer un coup de b. à qn** to give sb a buzz *or Br* a ring

bigophoner [bigɔfɔne] VI *Fam* to make a phone call; **b. à qn** to give sb a buzz *or Br* a bell

bigorneau, -eaux [bigɔrno] NM *(mollusque)* winkle

bigorner [bigɔrne] VT *Métal* to work on an anvil; *Arg (abîmer)* to smash up

VPR **se bigorner** *Arg* to have a punch-up, to scrap

bigot, -ote [bigo, -ɔt] *Péj* **ADJ** excessively devout, zealously religious
N religious zealot

> Il faut noter que le terme anglais **bigot** est un faux ami. Il se rapporte au sectarisme religieux et non à une attitude excessivement dévote.

bigoterie [bigɔtri] **NF** *Péj* (religious) bigotry

bigoudi [bigudi] **NM** (hair) curler, (hair) roller; **se mettre des bigoudis** to put one's hair in curlers *or* rollers; **tu ne vas pas sortir en bigoudis!** you're not going out in (your) curlers!

bigre [bigr] **INT** *Fam Vieilli* gosh!, *Br* crikey!

bigrement [bigrəmɑ̃] **ADV** *Fam* **vous avez b. raison!** you're dead right!; **il fait b. froid** it's awfully cold; **il a b. changé/grandi** he's changed/grown a heck of a lot; **il était b. surpris** he was dead surprised; **tu étais content? – oui, et b.!** were you satisfied? – yes, and how!

biguine [bigin] **NF** *Mus* beguine

bihebdo [biɛbdo] **NM** biweekly

bihebdomadaire [biɛbdɔmadɛr] **ADJ** *(magazine etc)* twice-weekly, biweekly

bijection [biʒɛksjɔ̃] **NF** *Math* bijection

bijou, -oux [biʒu] **NM** jewel; **bijoux** jewellery, *Am* jewelry, jewels; **un b. fantaisie** a piece of costume jewellery; *Fig* **c'est un b.** it's a gem; **cette montre est un b. d'exactitude/de précision** this watch is a marvel of accuracy/precision; **bijoux de famille** family jewels, *Fig Arg (sexe masculin)* family jewels, *Br* wedding tackle; *Fam* **mon b.!** my precious!, my pet!

bijouterie [biʒutri] **NF 1** *(boutique)* jeweller's *or Am* jeweler's (shop); *(commerce, fabrication)* jeweller's trade *or* business **2** *(bijoux)* jewellery, *Am* jewelry, jewels **3** *(art)* jewellery-making, *Am* jewelry-making

bijoutier, -ière [biʒutje, -jɛr] **N** jeweller, *Am* jeweler

Bikini® [bikini] **NM** bikini

bilabial, -iale, -iaux, -iales [bilabjal, -jo] *Ling* **ADJ** bilabial
NF bilabiale bilabial

bilan [bilɑ̃] **NM 1** *Fin (état)* balance sheet; **faire** *ou* **dresser un b.** to draw up a balance sheet; **déposer son b.** to file one's petition (in bankruptcy); **déposer le b.** to file for bankruptcy; **un dépôt de b.** a petition in bankruptcy **2** *(appréciation) (d'une situation, de faits)* assessment, evaluation; *(résultats)* results; **faire le b. de la situation** to take stock of *or* assess *or* evaluate the situation; **arrivé à 40 ans, on fait souvent le b.** you often stop to take stock when you reach 40; **'accident sur l'autoroute, b. quatre morts'** 'motorway accident, four dead'; **le b. d'un tremblement de terre** the toll of an earthquake
▸▸ *Mktg* **b. annuel** annual accounts; **b. commercial** market report; **b. de compétences** = summary of one's skills; **b. comptable** balance sheet; *Compta* **b. condensé** summary balance sheet; **b. financier** financial statement; *Compta* **b. intérimaire** interim statement; **b. de liquidation** statement of affairs; *Compta* **b. d'ouverture** opening balance sheet; *Compta* **b. prévisionnel** forecast balance sheet; **b. de santé** complete (medical) check-up; **votre b. de santé est excellent** your state of health is excellent, you are in excellent health; **faire le b. de santé de qn** to give sb a (medical) check-up; **faire le b. de santé d'une entreprise** to assess *or* evaluate the state of a company; *Compta* **b. social** social report

bilantiel [bilɑ̃sjɛl] **ADJ** balance-sheet

bilatéral, -ale, -aux, -ales [bilateral, -o]

ADJ *(paralysie, traité, discussions etc)* bilateral, two-sided; **stationnement b.** parking on both sides (of the road)

bilboquet [bilbɔkɛ] **NM 1** *(jouet)* = cup-and-ball; *(poussah)* tumbler **2** *Typ* small job

bile [bil] **NF 1** *Physiol* bile **2** *(colère)* **échauffer la b. de** *ou* **à qn** to rouse sb's anger; **décharger sa b. sur qn** to vent one's spleen on sb **3** *(inquiétude)* **se faire de la b.** to fret, to be worried sick (**pour** about); **elle ne se fait pas de b.** she doesn't let things get on top of her; **ne te fais pas de b.!** don't fret!; **ses humeurs de b. noire** his black moods

biler (se) [səbile] **VPR** *Fam* to get worked up, to get all hot and bothered; *(être inquiet)* to be worried sick, to fret; **ne te bile pas!** don't fret!; **elle ne se bile pas, elle!** she's not bothered!

bileux, -euse [bilø, -øz] **ADJ** *Fam* easily upset; **elle n'est pas bileuse** she doesn't let things worry her *or* get on top of her

biliaire [biljɛr] **ADJ** *Anat (vaisseaux etc)* biliary; *Méd* **calcul b.** gallstone, *Spéc* biliary calculus; **vésicule b.** gall bladder; **cirrhose b.** cirrhosis (of the liver)

bilieux, -ieuse [biljø, -jøz] **ADJ 1** *(tempérament, teint)* bilious **2** *(personne) (colérique)* irritable, irascible; *(inquiet)* sick with worry

bilingue [bilɛ̃g] **ADJ 1** *(personne, dictionnaire etc)* bilingual **2** *Can Fam (bisexuel)* bi

bilinguisme [bilɛ̃gɥism] **NM** bilingualism

billard [bijar] **NM 1** *(jeu)* billiards; **jouer au b.** to play billiards; **faire un b.** *ou* **une partie de b.** to play *or* have a game of billiards VOIR GRAMMAIRE A10 **2** *(table)* billiard table; *Fig Fam* **monter** *ou* **passer sur le b.** to have an operation, to be operated on **3** *(salle)* billiard saloon; *(dans une maison)* billiard room
▸▸ **b. américain** pool; **b. électrique** pinball; **b. russe** bar billiards

bille¹ [bij] **NF 1** *(pour le billard)* (billiard) ball **2** *Arg (visage)* mug, face; **il a une bonne b.** he looks pleasant enough; **une b. de clown** a funny face; **quelle b., il ne comprend rien!** what a mug, he just doesn't twig! **3** *(de verre)* marble; **jouer aux billes** to play marbles; *Fig* **reprendre ses billes** to pull out; *Fam* **elle touche sa b. en informatique** she knows a thing or two about computers; *Fam* **il ne touche pas une b. au flipper** he's hopeless *or* lousy at pinball; *Fig* **savoir placer ses billes** to play one's cards right **4** *Tech* ball; **roulement à billes** ball bearing; **stylo (à) b.** ballpoint (pen), *Br* Biro®; **flacon (à) b.** roll-on (bottle); **déodorant à b.** roll-on deodorant

bille² **NF** *(pièce de bois)* billet

billet [bijɛ] **NM 1 b. (de banque)** (bank)note, *Am* bill; **un faux b.** a forged banknote; **un b. de cent euros** a hundred-euro note; *Fam* **je te fiche mon b. qu'il pleuvra!** I bet my bottom dollar it'll rain! **2** *Com, Fin (effet)* note, bill **3** *(pour voyager)* ticket; **prendre un b. pour Valence** to buy a ticket for Valence **4** *Théâtre etc* ticket; **b. de théâtre** theatre ticket **5** *Litt (lettre)* note, short letter **6** *Journ* diary column
▸▸ *Scol* **b. d'absence** absence slip; **b. d'aller** single *or Am* one-way ticket; **b. d'aller (et) retour** return *or Am* round-trip ticket; **b. d'avion** plane ticket; **b. bradé** discounted ticket; **b. circulaire** round-trip ticket; **b. de complaisance** accommodation bill; **billets complémentaires** conjunction tickets; **b. demi-tarif** half-fare ticket; **b. doux** love letter, billet doux; *Vieilli* **b. de faire-part** = card announcing a birth/wedding/death in the family; **b. 'famille nombreuse'** = special SNCF rates for families with 3 children or more; **b. de faveur** complimentary ticket;

Mil **b. de logement** billet; **b. de naissance** birth certificate; **b. neutre** blank ticket; **b. open** (open)(-date) ticket; *Fin* **b. à ordre** promissory note; **b. ouvert** open ticket; *Fin* **b. au porteur** bill payable to bearer; **b. de première** first class ticket; **b. de reconnaissance de dettes** IOU; *Scol* **b. de retard** = note given to pupil who is late, specifying the time of arrival; **b. de retour** return *or Am* round-trip ticket; **b. sans condition** flexible ticket; **b. de santé** certificate *or* bill of health; **b. de seconde** second class ticket; **b. simple** single *or Am* one-way ticket; *Scol* **b. de sortie** pass, *Br Fml* exeat; **b. souple** flexible ticket; **b. de train** train ticket; **b. de transport** ticket; **b. du Trésor** Treasury bill; *Fin* **b. de trésorerie** commercial paper; **b. vert** dollar, *Am Fam* greenback

billétique [biʒetik] **NF** *Banque, Ordinat* cash dispenser technology

billette [bijɛt] **NF 1** *(du bois de chauffage, du métal)* billet **2** *Archit* billet (moulding)

billetterie [bijɛtri] **NF 1** *(opérations)* ticketing; *(lieu)* ticket office **2** *(distributeur de billets de banque)* cash dispenser; **b. automatique** automatic ticket machine

billettiste [bijɛtist] **N** ticketing clerk; *Journ* diary column writer

billevesées [bilvəze] **NFPL** nonsense, *Fam* twaddle; **b. que tout cela!** that's absolute nonsense!

billion [biljɔ̃] **NM** VOIR GRAMMAIRE A76 **1** *(million de millions)* trillion, *Br Vieilli* billion **2** *Arch (milliard)* billion, *Br Vieilli* milliard

billot [bijo] **NM** *(de boucher, bourreau)* block; *(dans la cuisine)* butcher's block table; *(de cordonnier)* last; **b. d'enclume** anvil block *or* stock; **périr** *ou* **mourir sur le b.** to be beheaded, to die on the block; *Fam* **j'en mettrais ma tête sur le b.** I'd stake my life on it

bilobé [bilobe] **ADJ** *Archit, Biol* bilobate, bilobed

bimane [biman] *Zool* **ADJ** bimanous
N bimanous animal

bimbeloterie [bɛ̃blɔtri] **NF 1** *(fabrication, commerce)* fancy goods business *or* trade **2** *(objets)* fancy goods, knick-knacks, odds and ends

bimbelotier [bɛ̃blɔtje] **NM** *(fabricant)* maker of fancy goods; *(vendeur)* dealer in fancy goods

bi-média [bimedja] **ADJ** bi-media

bimensuel, -elle [bimɑ̃sɥɛl] **ADJ** bimonthly, *Br* fortnightly, *Am* semimonthly
NM bimonthly (magazine), *Br* fortnightly magazine

bimestriel, -ielle [bimɛstriɛl] **ADJ** bimonthly
NM bimonthly

bimétallique [bimetalik] **ADJ** bimetallic

bimétallisme [bimetalism] **NM** *Écon* bimetallism

bimillénaire [bimilenɛr] **ADJ** bimillenary

bimoteur [bimɔtœr] **ADJ, NM (avion) b.** twin-engine (aircraft)

binage [binaʒ] **NM** *Agr* harrowing, hoeing; *(de jardin)* hoeing

binaire [binɛr] **ADJ** *Math etc* binary; **langage b.** binary notation

biner [bine] **VT** *Agr (sol)* to harrow, to hoe; *(jardin)* to hoe
VI *Rel* to celebrate Mass twice in one day

binette [binɛt] **NF 1** *Agr* hoe **2** *Arg (visage)* mug, face **3** *Can, Suisse Ordinat* smiley, emoticon

bineuse [binøz] **NF** *Agr* cultivator

bing [biŋ] **INT** bam!, wham!

bingo [biŋgo] **NM** bingo; **jouer au b.** to play bingo

biniou [binju] NM **1** *Mus* Breton bagpipes **2** *Fam (téléphone)* phone, *Br* blower; **donner un coup de b. à qn** to give sb a buzz *or* a call *or Br* a ring

binoclard, -arde [binɔklar, -ard] N *Fam* specs wearer; **hé, b.!** hey, four-eyes!

binocle [binɔkl] NM pince-nez; *Fam* **binocles** *(lunettes)* specs

binoculaire [binɔkylɛr] ADJ *(vision, microscope etc)* binocular

binôme [binom] NM **1** *Math* binomial; **le b. de Newton** the binomial theorem **2** **travailler en b.** *(d'étudiants etc)* to work in twos

binomial, -iale, -iaux, -iales [binɔmjal, -jo] ADJ *Math* binomial

binot [bino] NM *Agr* = **bineuse**

binz [bins] NM *Fam* **1** *(chose compliquée)* **quel b. pour trouver sa maison!** it was a real hassle finding his/her house! **2** *(désordre)* shambles

bio [bjo] *Fam* ADJ *(abrév* **biologique)** *(produits, agriculture)* organic
  NF *(abrév* **biographie)** biog; **une b. d'Elvis** an Elvis biog

biocarburant [bjokarbyrɑ̃] NM biofuel

biochimie [bjoʃimi] NF biochemistry

biochimique [bjoʃimik] ADJ biochemical; **demande b. en oxygène** biochemical oxygen demand

biochimiste [bjoʃimist] N biochemist

bioclimat [bjoklima] NM bioclimate

bioclimatique [bjoklimatik] ADJ bioclimatic

bioclimatologie [bjoklimatɔlɔʒi] NF bioclimatology

biodégradable [bjodegradabl] ADJ biodegradable

biodiversité [bjodivɛrsite] NF biodiversity

bioénergétique [bjoenɛrʒetik] ADJ bioenergetic
  NF bioenergetics

bioéthique [bjoetik] NF *Méd* bioethics

biogenèse [bjoʒɔnɛz] NF *Biol* biogenesis

biographe [bjograf] N biographer

biographie [bjografi] NF biography

biographique [bjografik] ADJ biographical

bio-industrie [bjoɛ̃dystri] NF biotechnology industry

bio-informatique [bjoɛ̃fɔrmatik] NF bio-IT, bio-information technology

biologie [bjɔlɔʒi] NF biology

biologique [bjɔlɔʒik] ADJ biological; **horloge b.** biological clock; **parents biologiques** biological parents; **agriculture/jardinage b.** organic farming/gardening; **aliments biologiques** organic food

biologiste [bjɔlɔʒist] N biologist

biomasse [bjomas] NF biomass

biomatériau [bjomaterjo] NM biomaterial

biomédical, -ale, -aux, -ales [bjomedikal, -o] ADJ biomedical

biométrie [bjometri] NF biometrics

biomoléculaire [bjomolekylɛr] ADJ biomolecular

bionique [bjonik] NF bionics

biophysicien, -ienne [bjofizisjɛ̃, -jɛn] N biophysicist

biophysique [bjofizik] NF biophysics

biopsie [bjɔpsi] NF *Chir* biopsy

biopuce [bjopys] NF biochip

biorythme [bjoritm] NM biorhythm

BIOS [bjos] NM *Ordinat* BIOS

biosphère [bjosfɛr] NF biosphere

biosynthèse [bjosɛ̃tɛz] NF biosynthesis

biotechnique [bjotɛknik] NF, **biotechnolo-**

gie [bjotɛknɔlɔʒi] NF *Pharm, Chimie* biotechnology

biotechnologique [bjotɛknɔlɔʒik] ADJ biotechnological

bioterrorisme [bjotɛrɔrism] NM bioterrorism

bioterroriste [bjotɛrɔrist] N bioterrorist

biothérapie [bjoterapi] NF biotherapy

biotope [bjɔtɔp] NM biotope

biovigilance [bjoviʒilɑ̃s] NF biovigilance

bioxyde [bjoksid] NM *Chimie* dioxide

bip [bip] INT beep
  NM **1** *(son)* beep; **après le b. sonore** after the beep; **faire b.** to beep; *TV, Radio* **b. de censure** censor bleep **2** *(appareil)* beeper, pager, bleeper

bipale [bipal] ADJ *(hélice)* twin-bladed

biparti [biparti] ADJ bipartite

bipartisme [bipartism] NM *Pol* bipartite system

bipartite [bipartit] ADJ = **biparti**

bip-bip, *pl* **bips-bips** NM beep

bipède [bipɛd] ADJ, NM biped

biper [bipe] VT *(personne)* to page

biphasé [bifaze] *Élec* ADJ *(courant)* two-phase, diphase
  NM two-phase *or* diphase current

biplace [biplas] ADJ, NM *Aut, Aviat* two-seater

biplan [biplɑ̃] ADJ, NM **(avion) b.** biplane

bipolaire [bipɔlɛr] ADJ *Élec, Phys etc* bipolar, two-pole

bipolarisation [bipɔlarizasjɔ̃] NF *Pol* separation into two blocs

bipolarité [bipɔlarite] NF bipolarity

biquadratique [bikwadratik] *Math* ADJ *(équation)* biquadratic
  NF biquadratic

bique [bik] NF *Fam* **1** *(chèvre)* nanny goat; **peau de b.** goatskin **2** *Péj (femme)* **vieille b.** old bag *or* hag

biquet, -ette [bikɛ, -ɛt] N **1** *(petit de la chèvre)* kid **2** *Fam* **mon b.** my pet, my love

biquotidien, -ienne [bikɔtidjɛ̃, -jɛn] ADJ twice-daily

birbe [birb] NM *Fam* **vieux b.** old fogey, old fuddy-duddy

BIRD [bird] NF *(abrév* **Banque internationale pour la reconstruction et le développement)** IBRD

bircher [birʃɛr] NM *Suisse* muesli

biréacteur [bireaktœr] NM twin-jet (aircraft)

biréfringence [birefrɛ̃ʒɑ̃s] NF *Opt* double refraction, birefringence

biréfringent [birefrɛ̃ʒɑ̃] ADJ *Opt* doubly refractive, birefringent

birman, -ane [birmɑ̃, -an] ADJ Burmese
  NM *Ling* Burmese
  N B. Burmese

Birmanie [birmani] NF Burma

biroute [birut] NF **1** *Mil, Aviat Fam* (wind) sock, wind sleeve **2** *Arg (pénis)* dick, cock

bis[1] [bi] ADJ greyish-brown, brownish-grey; **teint b.** dark *or* swarthy complexion; **toile bise** unbleached linen; **pain b.** brown bread

bis[2] [bis] ADV **1** *Théâtre* encore; *Mus* repeat **2** *(dans une adresse)* **10 b.** 10A **3 itinéraire b.** alternative route

bisaïeul, -eule, *pl* **bisaïeuls, -eules** [bizajœl] N *Litt* great-grandfather, *f* great-grandmother

bisannuel, -elle [bizanɥɛl] ADJ biennial; **plante bisannuelle** biennial (plant)

bisbille [bisbij] NF *Fam* squabble, petty quarrel, tiff; **être en b. avec qn** not to see eye to eye with sb, to be at odds with sb

Biscaye [biskaj] N Biscay; **le golfe de B.** the Bay of Biscay

biscôme [biskom] NM *Suisse* = Swiss gingerbread

biscornu [biskɔrny] ADJ **1** *(de forme) (chapeau)* crooked; *(personne, nain)* crooked, misshapen; *(sac, maison, bâtiment, cactus)* oddly shaped **2** *Fam (idées)* bizarre, weird, cranky; *(raisonnement, esprit)* tortuous

biscoteaux [biskoto] NMPL *Fam* biceps; **avoir des b.** to have bulging biceps

biscotte [biskɔt] NF rusk

biscuit [biskɥi] NM **1** *Culin* biscuit, *Am* cookie; **b. au chocolat** chocolate biscuit; **b. au fromage** cheese biscuit **2** *Cér* biscuit, bisque; **un b.** a piece of biscuitware
  ▸▸ **b. à la cuiller** sponge finger, *Am* lady finger; **b. de fourrage** *(d'avoine etc)* cake; **b. de mer** ship's biscuit; **b. pour chien** dog biscuit; **b. de Savoie** sponge cake; **b. salé** cracker

biscuiterie [biskɥitri] NF **1** *(usine)* biscuit *or Am* cookie factory **2** *(commerce)* biscuit *or Am* cookie trade **3** *(fabrication)* biscuit *or Am* cookie making

bise[1] [biz] NF *(vent)* north wind

bise[2] NF *Fam (baiser)* kiss; **donner** *ou* **faire une b. à qn** to give sb a kiss, to kiss sb; **on se fait la b.** we give each other a kiss, we kiss each other; **grosses bises** *(sur une lettre)* love and kisses

biseau, -eaux [bizo] NM **1** *Menuis etc (bord)* chamfer, bevel, chamfered *or* bevelled edge; **taillé en b.** bevel-edged, bevelled, chamfered **2** *(d'horloge etc)* bezel; *Mus (d'instrument à vent)* lip **3** *(outil)* bevel

biseautage [bizotaʒ] NM **1** *Menuis etc* bevelling, chamfering **2** *(de cartes à jouer)* marking

biseauter [bizote] VT **1** *Menuis etc* to bevel, to chamfer **2** *(cartes à jouer)* to mark

biser[1] [bize] VI *Agr (du grain)* to darken, to deteriorate

biser[2] VT *Fam* to kiss

biset [bizɛ] NM *(oiseau)* rock pigeon

bisexualité [bisɛksɥalite] NF bisexuality

bisexué [bisɛksɥe] ADJ bisexual; **animal b.** hermaphrodite

bisexuel, -elle [bisɛksɥɛl] ADJ bisexual

bismuth [bismyt] NM bismuth

bison [bizɔ̃] NM *Zool* bison, buffalo VOIR GRAMMAIRE A12

Bison Futé NM *Aut* = body which advises drivers of road conditions and congestion on French motorways

bisou [bizu] NM *Fam* kiss; **faire un b. à son papa** to give Daddy a kiss

bisque [bisk] NF *Culin* bisque; **b. de homard** lobster bisque

bisquer [biske] VI *Fam* to be riled; **ça va le faire b.** that'll rile him, *Br* that'll get right up his nose

bissecteur, -trice [bisɛktœr, -tris] ADJ *(ligne etc)* bisecting
  NF **bissectrice** bisector, bisecting line

bissection [bisɛksjɔ̃] NF *Math* bisection

bisser [bise] VT **1** *(d'un artiste) (chanson etc)* to give an encore of, to repeat **2** *(d'un spectateur) (chanson, artiste etc)* to call on to give an encore **3** *Belg Scol (redoubler)* to repeat

bissextile [bisɛkstil] ADJ **année b.** leap year

bistandard [bistɑ̃dar] ADJ *TV* dual-standard

bistouquette [bistukɛt] NF *Fam Br* willy, *Am* peter

bistouri [bisturi] NM *Chir* lancet, *Spéc* bistoury

bistre [bistr] ADJ bistre, blackish-brown; **teint b.** swarthy *or* dark complexion
  NM bistre

bistré [bistre] ADJ *(peau)* swarthy, dark

bistrer [bistre] VT *(teint)* to darken, to tan

bistro(t) [bistro] NM *Fam* ≃ café

> ### Bistrot
> This word can refer either to a small café or to a cosy restaurant, especially one frequented by regulars. These establishments are usually less classy than bistros in English-speaking countries. The "style bistrot" refers to a style of furnishing inspired by the chairs, tables and zinc countertops typical of the traditional "bistrot".

bisulfate [bisylfat] NM *Chimie* bisulphate

bisulfite [bisylfit] NM *Chimie* bisulphite

bisulfure [bisylfyr] NM *Chimie* disulphide, bisulphide

BIT [beite] NM *(abrév* **Bureau international du travail)** ILO

bit [bit] NM *Ordinat* bit; **b. d'arrêt** stop bit; **b. de contrôle** control bit, check bit; **b. de départ** start bit; **b. de parité** parity bit; **bits par seconde** bits per second

bite [bit] NF *Vulg (pénis)* cock, prick, dick

biter [bite] VT *Vulg* **j'y bite rien** I don't understand a bloody *or Am* goddamn thing

biterrois, -oise [biterwa, -waz] **1** ADJ of/ from Béziers
  N **B.** *(natif)* native of Béziers; *(habitant)* inhabitant of Béziers

bitmap [bitmap] *Ordinat* ADJ bitmap
  NM bitmap

bitonal, -ale, -aux, -ales [bitɔnal, -o] ADJ *Tél* **sonnerie bitonale** two-tone ring

bitoniau [bitɔnjo] NM *Fam* thingy, whatsit

bitte¹ [bit] NF *Vulg* = **bite**

bitte² NF *Naut (sur un bateau)* bitt; **b. d'amarrage** bollard

bitter [bitɛr] NM bitters

bitture [bityr] NF **1** *Naut* range of cable **2** *Arg* **prendre une b.** to get plastered *or* canned; **il tient une sacrée b.** he's absolutely plastered, *Br* he's paralytic

bitturer (se) [səbityre] VPR *Arg* to get plastered *or* canned

bitumage [bitymaʒ] NM **1** *(de route)* asphalting **2** *(de papier etc)* tarring

bitume [bitym] NM *Minér* **1** *(asphalte)* bitumen, asphalt; *Fam* **arpenter le b.** to walk the streets **2** *(goudron)* bitumen, tar

bitumer [bityme] VT **1** *(route)* to asphalt **2** *(goudronner)* to tar; **carton bitumé** tarred felt

bitum(in)eux, -euse [bitym(in)ø, -øz] ADJ *Minér* bituminous

biture [bityr] NF = **bitture**

biturer (se) [səbityre] VPR *Arg* = **bitturer (se)**

biunivoque [biynivɔk] ADJ *Math* one-to-one

bivalent [bivalɑ̃] ADJ *Chimie etc* bivalent, divalent

bivalve [bivalv] ADJ, NM bivalve

bivouac [bivwak] NM bivouac; **faire un b.** to bivouac; **feu de b.** watchfire; **cet endroit sera un excellent b.** this will be an excellent place to bivouac

bivouaquer [bivwake] VI to bivouac

bizarre [bizar] ADJ odd, strange, peculiar, bizarre; **c'est b., ce n'est pas ce qu'elle m'avait dit** that's odd *or* strange, that's not what she told me; **le plus b., c'est que …** the strangest *or* oddest *or* funniest thing of all is that …
  NM **le b.** the bizarre; **le b. de l'affaire, c'est que …** the strange *or* odd *or* funny thing is that …

bizarrement [bizarmɑ̃] ADV strangely, oddly, peculiarly; **et b., elle est venue toute seule** and for some strange reason, she came all alone

bizarrerie [bizarri] NF *(de situation, d'idée, d'attitude etc)* strangeness, oddness, peculiarity; *(de personne)* eccentricity; **bizarreries** oddities; *(de personne)* eccentricities

bizarroïde [bizarɔid] ADJ *Fam* weird; **ce type est b.** that guy's a weirdo

bizut [bizy] NM *Univ Fam* fresher, *Am* freshman

bizutage [bizytaʒ] NM *Univ Fam (des nouveaux arrivés)* ragging, *Am* hazing

> ### Bizutage
> In some French schools and colleges, students in fancy-dress take to the streets and play practical jokes, sometimes of a very cruel nature, on each other and on passers-by at the beginning of the school year. This is part of the traditional initiation ceremony known as "bizutage". As a consequence of the excessive behaviour to which it has often led, a law was passed in 1998 to make it an offence.

bizuter [bizyte] VT *Univ Fam (nouvel arrivé)* to rag, *Am* to haze

bizuth [bizy] NM *Univ Fam* = **bizut**

blabla(bla) [blabla(bla)] NM *Fam* claptrap, baloney; *(dans un discours, texte etc)* padding, waffle

blablater [blablate] VI *Fam* to waffle on, *Br* to witter on

black [blak] *Fam* N *(personne de race noire)* Black
  NM **travailler au b.** *(clandestinement)* = to work without declaring one's earnings; *(en plus de son travail habituel)* to moonlight

blackboulage [blakbulaʒ] NM blackballing; *Fam (d'un candidat à un examen)* failing

blackbouler [blakbule] VT to blackball; *Fam (à un examen)* to fail; **se faire b. d'un bureau à l'autre** to get shunted from one office to another

black-out [blakawt] NM INV blackout; *Fig* **faire le b. sur un scandale** to hush up *or* cover up a scandal; **c'est le b. total, on ne sait rien** there's a complete blackout, we don't know a thing

blad [blad] NM *Typ* blad

blafard [blafar] ADJ *(lune, lumière, teint etc)* pallid, wan, pale

blague [blag] NF **1** *(plaisanterie)* joke; *(tour)* (practical) joke, trick, hoax; **faire une b. (à qn)** to play a joke *or* trick (on sb); **il m'a fait une sale b.** he played a dirty trick on me; **tout ça, c'est de la b.** it's all bunkum *or* nonsense; **ne racontez pas de blagues** you're kidding (me), you're having *or Am* putting me on; **b. à part** seriously, joking apart; **sans b.?** really?, no kidding? **2 b. (à tabac)** *(tobacco)* pouch **3** *Vieilli (erreur)* mistake, blunder

blaguer [blage] *Fam* VI to joke; **il aime bien b.** he likes a joke; **là, tu es en train de b.!** you're joking *or* kidding!, you're having *or Am* putting me on!
  VT *(personne)* to tease, to make fun of

blagueur, -euse [blagœr, -øz] *Fam* N *(qui dit des blagues)* joker, comedian; *(qui fait des blagues)* practical joker, prankster
  ADJ *(remarque)* teasing, bantering; **il est très b.** he really likes a joke

blair [blɛr] NM *Arg (nez)* conk, *Br* hooter

blaireau, -eaux [blɛro] NM **1** *(mammifère)* badger **2** *(pour se raser)* shaving brush **3** *Beaux-Arts* (badger-hair) brush **4** *Fam (imbécile)* nerd, prat

blairer [blere] VT *Arg* **je ne peux pas le b.** I can't stick *or* stand *or* stomach him

blâmable [blɑmabl] ADJ blameworthy; **vous n'êtes pas b.** you're not to blame

blâme [blɑm] NM **1** *(reproche)* blame; **rejeter le b. de qch sur qn** to lay the blame for sth on sb; **s'attirer le b. de ses parents** to incur one's parents' disapproval **2** *Admin (sanction)* reprimand; **donner un b. à qn** to reprimand sb, to give sb a reprimand; **recevoir un b.** to be reprimanded

blâmer [blɑme] VT **1** *(condamner) (personne, gouvernement, acte etc)* to blame; **b. qn de faire/d'avoir fait qch** to blame sb for doing/having done sth **2** *Admin (réprimander)* to reprimand
  VPR **se blâmer** to blame oneself; **je ne peux que me b. d'avoir dit oui** I can't forgive myself for having said yes

blanc, blanche [blɑ̃, blɑ̃ʃ] ADJ **1** *(drap, pain, vin, chocolat etc)* white; **b. comme (la) neige** *(tissu, drap etc)* white as snow, snow-white; *Fig* **il est sorti du procès b. comme neige** he came out of the trial whiter than white; **vieillard à cheveux blancs** white-haired old man, old man with white hair; **fromage b.** cream cheese; **verre b.** colourless *or Am* colorless glass; **bruit b.** white noise

2 *(peau)* pale, light-coloured, *Am* light-colored; *(pas bronzé)* white; **la race blanche** the white race; **b. de peur** white with fear; **b. de colère** livid with anger; **b. comme un linge** as white as a sheet; **b. comme un cachet d'aspirine** completely white; **il a la peau blanche** *(fragile)* he has a pale skin

3 *Litt (innocent)* innocent, pure; **j'ai les mains blanches** my hands are clean, I'm innocent

4 *(vierge) (page etc)* blank; *(papier)* plain, unlined; **j'ai besoin d'une feuille blanche** I need a clean piece of paper; **nuit blanche** sleepless night; **examen b.** mock (examination); *Scol* **rendre copie blanche** to hand in a blank paper; **mariage b.** unconsummated marriage; **voix blanche** toneless voice; **vers blancs** blank verse; *Tennis* **jeu b.** love game
  NM **1** *(couleur)* white; **b. éclatant** brilliant white; **robe d'un b. sale** dingy white dress; **peint en b.** painted white; **être habillé de b., être en b.** to be dressed in white; **mariage en b.** white wedding; **le b. est très à la mode** white is very fashionable; **je vous l'écris noir sur b.** I'm putting it in black and white for you

2 *(d'une cible)* bull's-eye; **donner** *ou* **mettre dans le b.** to hit the bull's-eye

3 *(espace)* blank, space, gap; *Ordinat* blank; **laisser des blancs** to leave blanks *or* spaces *or* gaps; **chèque en b.** blank cheque *or Am* check

4 *(aux dominos)* blank; **double b.** double blank

5 saigner qn à b. to bleed sb white; **chauffer un métal à b.** to bring a metal to a white heat; **chauffé à b.** white-hot; **cartouche à b.** blank (cartridge); **tirer à b.** to fire a blank/ blanks

6 *Culin* **b. de poulet** breast of chicken, chicken breast; **tu veux le b. ou la cuisse?** would you like breast or leg *or Am* white meat or dark?

7 *(colorant)* **b. de billard** billiard chalk; **b. de chaux** whitewash; **b. de zinc** zinc white, oxide of zinc; **b. de céruse** *ou* **d'argent** *ou* **de plomb** white lead; **b. d'Espagne** whiting, whitening

8 *(linge)* **(articles de) b.** linen; **il est préférable de laver le b. séparément** it's preferable to wash whites separately; **magasin de b.** linen shop; **vente de b.** white *or* linen sale

9 *(vin)* white wine; **du rouge ou du b.?** red or white?; **b. de b.** = white wine made from white grapes

10 b. du rosier/de la vigne rose/vine mildew **11** *TV, Radio* drop-out **12** *Can, Suisse (trou de mémoire)* blank; **avoir un b.** to have a blank **NF blanche 1** *Billard* white (ball) **2** *Mus* minim, *Am* half note **N B.** White (man, *f* woman); **réservé aux Blancs** reserved for Whites ►► **b. cassé** off-white; *Typ* **b. de grand fond** gutter, fore-edge; *Typ* **b. de petit fond** gutter, back margin; **b. d'œuf** egg white; **le b. des yeux** the white of the eye; **regarder qn dans le b. des yeux** to look sb straight in the eye

blanc-bec, *pl* **blancs-becs NM** *Péj* greenhorn; *(adolescent)* callow youth

blanchaille [blɑ̃ʃɑj] **NF 1** *Pêche (poisson)* small fry, bait **2** *Culin* whitebait

blanchâtre [blɑ̃ʃɑtr] **ADJ** whitish, off-white

Blanche-Neige [blɑ̃ʃnɛʒ] **N** Snow White; **B. et les sept nains** Snow White and the Seven Dwarfs

blanchet [blɑ̃ʃɛ] **NM** *Typ* blanket

blancheur [blɑ̃ʃœr] **NF** whiteness; *Fig* purity, innocence; **d'une b. de perle** pearl-white; **sa peau est d'une telle b.!** his skin is so white!

blanchiment [blɑ̃ʃimɑ̃] **NM 1** *(d'un plafond, mur etc)* whitewashing **2** *Culin (de légumes)* blanching **3** *Tex* bleaching **4** *(de l'argent)* laundering

Do not confuse with **blanchissement**.

blanchir [blɑ̃ʃir] **VT 1** *(dents etc)* to whiten, to make white; **b. (à la chaux)** *(plafond, mur etc)* to whitewash; **la neige qui blanchit les sommets** the snow that turns the peaks white; *Typ* **b. la composition** to space out the matter **2** *(linge)* to launder; *Tex* to bleach; **donner du linge à b.** to send clothes to the laundry; *Fig* **cette déclaration l'a blanchi complètement** this statement has completely exonerated him *or* completely cleared his name; **b. de l'argent** to launder money **3** *Culin (légumes)* to blanch; *Ind (sucre)* to refine **4** *Can Sport (équipe)* to shut out **5** *Typ (texte, page)* to space, to space out **6** *Phot* to bleach out **VI 1** *(devenir blanc)* to turn *or* go white **2** *(pâlir)* to blanch, to turn pale **VPR se blanchir** to clear oneself *or* one's name, to exonerate oneself; **se b. d'une accusation** to clear oneself of *or* exonerate oneself from a charge

blanchissage [blɑ̃ʃisaʒ] **NM 1** *(du linge etc)* laundering; **liste de b.** laundry list **2** *Ind (du sucre)* refining **3** *Can Sport* shutout

blanchissant, -e [blɑ̃ʃisɑ̃] **ADJ 1** *(chevelure)* whitening; *(peau etc)* paling; **l'aube blanchissante** the brightening dawn **2 agent b.** whitener

blanchissement [blɑ̃ʃismɑ̃] **NM 1** *(des cheveux)* whitening **2** *(de la peau)* blanching, turning pale

Do not confuse with **blanchiment**.

blanchisserie [blɑ̃ʃisri] **NF 1** *Com* laundry **2** *Tex* bleachery

blanchisseur, -euse [blɑ̃ʃisœr, -øz] **N** launderer, laundryman, *f* laundress, *Vieilli* washerwoman

blanchon [blɑ̃ʃɔ̃] **NM** *Can* whitecoat *(seal pup)*

blanc-manger, *pl* **blancs-mangers NM** *Culin* = almond milk jelly, *Arch* blancmange

blanc-seing, *pl* **blancs-seings NM** signature to a blank document; *Fig* **donner un b. à qn** to give sb a free hand

blanquette¹ [blɑ̃kɛt] **NF** *Culin (de veau)* blanquette

blanquette² **NF** **b. de Limoux** = sparkling white wine from Limoux

blasé, -ée [blɑze] **ADJ** blasé **N** blasé person; **faire le b.** to act all blasé

blaser [blɑze] **VT** *(personne)* to make blasé; **être blasé de qch** to be indifferent to sth **VPR se blaser** to become blasé; **se b. de qch** to become indifferent to sth

blason [blazɔ̃] **NM** *Hér* **1** *(armes)* coat of arms, armorial bearings, blazon **2** *(héraldique)* heraldry

blasonner [blazɔne] **VT** *Hér* **b. un écu** to blazon an escutcheon

blasphémateur, -trice [blasfematœr, -tris] **N** blasphemer **ADJ** blaspheming, blasphemous

blasphématoire [blasfematwar] **ADJ** blasphemous

blasphème [blasfɛm] **NM** blasphemy; **dire** *ou* **prononcer des blasphèmes** to blaspheme

blasphémer [blasfeme] *(je blasphème, n. blasphémons; je blasphémerai)* **VI** to blaspheme *(contre against)* **VT** *Vieilli* to blaspheme; **b. le nom de Dieu** to take the Lord's name in vain

blastoderme [blastɔdɛrm] **NM** *Biol* blastoderm

blatérer [blatere] **VI** *(il blatère; il blatérera)* *(d'un chameau)* to roar; *(d'un bélier)* to bleat

blatte [blat] **NF** *(insecte)* cockroach, black beetle

blaze [blaz] **NM** *Arg* **1** *(nez)* conk, *Br* hooter **2** *(nom)* name, handle

blazer [blazœr] **NM** blazer

bld *abrév* **boulevard**

blé [ble] **NM 1** *(céréale)* wheat, *Br* corn; **b. dur** hard *or* durum wheat; **b. tendre** soft wheat; **champ de b.** wheatfield; **grenier à b.** granary; **halle aux blés** corn exchange; **b. en herbe** wheat in the blade; *Fig* **manger son b. en herbe** to eat one's seed corn **2** *Fam Fig (argent)* bread, dough, *Br* lolly ►► *Can* **b. d'Inde** maize, *Am* (Indian) corn; **b. noir** buckwheat

bled [blɛd] **NM** *(en Afrique du Nord)* inland country, interior; *Fam (région ou village reculé(e))* backwater, place in the middle of nowhere; *(petite ville)* one-horse town; *Fam* **dans mon b.** in my part of the country; *Fam Péj* **un sale b.,** **un b. perdu** a godforsaken place, a dump, a hole

blême [blɛm] **ADJ 1** *(personne, visage, teint)* pallid, wan; **b. de peur** white with fear; **un visage de fatigue** a tired, wan face; **b. de rage/colère** white with rage/anger; **elle est devenue b. quand je le lui ai dit** she went white *or* she blanched when I told her **2** *Fig* **lueur b.** pale *or* wan light; **matin b.** pale morning

blêmir [blemir] **VI 1** *(de personne)* to turn *or* go pale; **b. de rage/colère** to turn *or* go livid *or* white with rage/anger **2** *Fig (de la lumière)* to grow dim *or* faint *or* wan

Il faut noter que le verbe anglais **to blemish** est un faux ami. Il ne signifie jamais **devenir pâle**.

blêmissement [blemismɑ̃] **NM** paling, turning pale

blennorragie [blenɔraʒi] **NF** *Méd* gonorrhoea

blennorragique [blenɔraʒik] *Méd* **ADJ** gonorrhoeal **N** gonorrhoea sufferer

blépharite [blefarit] **NF** *Méd* blepharitis

blèsement [blɛzmɑ̃] **NM** lisping, lisp

bléser [bleze] **VI** *(je blèse, n. blésons; je bléserai)* to lisp

blésité [blezite] **NF** lisping

blessant, -e [blesɑ̃] **ADJ** *(remarque etc)* hurtful, cutting; *(personne)* hurtful

blessé, -ée [blese] **ADJ** *(par arme)* wounded; *(dans un accident)* injured, hurt; *(moralement)* hurt, upset **N** *(victime d'une agression)* wounded person, casualty; *(victime d'un accident)* injured person, casualty; **les blessés** the wounded/injured, the casualties; **les blessés légers** the slightly wounded/injured; **les grands blessés** the severely wounded/injured; **un mort et trois blessés** one dead and three wounded/injured; **les blessés de guerre** the war wounded; **b. de la face** person with facial wounds/injuries

blesser [blese] **VT 1** *(par arme)* to wound; *(dans un accident)* to injure, to hurt; **la chute l'a grièvement blessée** she was severely injured *or* hurt in the fall; **vous êtes blessé?** are you hurt?; **ces souliers me blessent** these shoes hurt me; **il a été blessé au bras** *(par arme)* he was wounded in the arm; *(dans un accident)* his arm was injured; **être blessé à mort** *(par arme)* to be fatally wounded; *(dans un accident)* to be fatally injured **2** *(moralement) (personne)* to offend, to hurt, to upset; **b. la vue** *ou* **les yeux/l'oreille** to offend the eye/to grate on the ear; **b. qn au vif** to cut sb to the quick; **b. l'amour-propre de qn, b. qn dans son orgueil** *ou* **amour-propre** to hurt *or* injure sb's pride *or* self-esteem; **cette suspicion de ta part me blesse** I resent your suspiciousness; **cela blesse notre sens des convenances** that offends (against) our sense of propriety **VPR se blesser** *(physiquement) (avec une arme)* to wound oneself; *(dans un accident)* to hurt *or* injure oneself *(avec with)*; **il s'est blessé à la tête** *(avec une arme)* he's wounded himself in the head; *(dans un accident)* he's hurt *or* injured his head

blessure [blesyr] **NF** *(par arme)* wound; *(dans un accident)* injury; **faire une b. à qn** to wound sb; **b. légère** *ou* **superficielle** slight *or* flesh wound; **b. profonde** deep wound; *Jur* **coups et blessures** assault and battery; **une b. d'amour-propre** a blow to one's pride *or* self-esteem; *Fig* **rouvrir une b.** to open an old wound

blet, blette¹ [blɛ, blɛt] **ADJ** *(fruit)* overripe, soft

blette² [blɛt] **NF** = bette

blettir [bletir] **VI** *(d'un fruit)* to become overripe, to go soft

blettissement [bletismɑ̃] **NM** *(d'un fruit)* overripeness

bleu, -e [blø] **ADJ** blue; *(bifteck)* very rare; **avoir les yeux bleus** to have blue eyes, to be blue-eyed; **b. de froid** blue with cold; *Can* **un froid b.** extreme cold; **il fait un froid b.** it's freezing (cold); **colère bleue** towering rage; **j'en suis resté b.** I was flabbergasted; *Méd* **maladie bleue** blue disease, *Spéc* cyanosis; *Méd* **enfant b.** blue baby; *Aut* **zone bleue** restricted parking area **NM 1** *(couleur)* blue; *Fig* **n'y voir que du b.** not to catch on, *Br* not to twig; **le b. du ciel** the blue(ness) of the sky; *Mil* **tirer dans le b.** to fire at random; **b. (de lessive)** blue, blueing; **passer du linge au b.** to blue laundry; *Tex* **b. de teinturier** blue, blueing **2** *(ecchymose)* bruise; **j'ai le bras couvert de bleus** my arm's covered with bruises, my arm's black and blue; **se faire un b.** to bruise oneself **3** *Fam (novice)* novice, greenhorn, *Am* tenderfoot; *Mil* raw recruit, rookie **4** *(fromage)* blue cheese **5** *Culin* **truite au b.** trout au bleu *(boiled alive in vinegar bouillon)* **6 bleu(s) (de chauffe** *ou* **de travail)** *(combi-*

naison) overalls, *Br* boiler suit; *(salopette)* dungarees; *(à deux pièces)* overalls
7 *Tech* blueprint
8 *Can Pol* Conservative
9 *Vieilli* **petit b.** telegram
▸▸**b. ciel** sky blue; **b. clair** light blue; **b. foncé** dark blue; **b. horizon** sky blue; **b. marine** navy (blue); **b. d'outremer** ultramarine; **b. de Prusse** Prussian blue; **b. roi** royal blue; **b.-noir** bluish-black; **encre b.-noir** blue-black ink; **b.-nuit** midnight blue

bleuâtre [bløatr] ADJ bluish

bleuet [bløɛ] NM **1** *(plante)* cornflower **2** *Can (baie)* blueberry

bleuetière [bløɛtjɛr] NF *Can* blueberry field

bleuir [bløir] VT to turn *or* make blue
VI to turn *or* go blue

bleuissement [bløismɑ̃] NM turning blue

bleuté [bløte] ADJ *(lumière, couleur etc)* bluish, blue-tinged; *(verres de lunettes etc)* blue-tinted

bleuter [bløte] VT *(verre, acier etc)* to give a blue tinge to

blindage [blɛ̃daʒ] NM **1** *Constr, Min (d'une tranchée)* timbering, sheeting **2** *Mil etc* armour(-plate *or* -plating), *Am* armor(-plate *or* -plating); **plaque de b.** armour-plate **3** *Élec (d'une valve etc)* screen(ing); *(d'un transformateur etc)* shrouding; *Ordinat* shield

blinde [blɛ̃d] NF *Fam* **à toute b.** at full speed, like lightning, *Br* like the clappers

blindé [blɛ̃de] ADJ **1** *Mil etc* armoured, armour-plated, *Am* armored, *Am* armor-plated; *(division, train)* armoured; **porte blindée** steel security door; **abri b.** bombproof shelter; **non b.** *(véhicule)* soft-skinned **2** *Fam* **je suis b.** *(ce n'est pas la première fois que ça m'arrive)* I'm hardened *or* immune to it; **b. contre qch** hardened *or* immune to sth **3** *Arg (ivre)* blind drunk, plastered **4** *Élec (valve)* screened; *(transformateur)* shrouded
NMPL *Mil* **les blindés** the armour, *Am* the armor

blinder [blɛ̃de] VT **1** *Constr, Min (tranchée, puits de mine etc)* to sheet, to timber **2** *Mil etc* to armour(-plate), *Am* to armor(-plate); *(abri)* to make bombproof; **b. sa porte** to reinforce one's door (with steel) **3** *Élec* to screen, to shroud **4** *Fam (personne)* to harden, to make immune (**contre qch** to sth)
VPR **se blinder 1** *(s'endurcir)* to harden oneself, to become thick-skinned **2** *Fam (s'enivrer)* to get plastered *or* wasted

blinis [blini(s)] NM *Culin* blini

blinquer [blɛ̃ke] *Belg Fam* VT to polish
VI to shine

blister [blistɛr] NM *Com* blister pack; **marchandise vendue sous b.** goods sold in blister packs

blizzard [blizar] NM blizzard

bloblote [blɔblɔt] NF *Fam* **avoir la b.** to have the shakes

bloc [blɔk] NM **1** *(de bois, de pierre etc)* block, lump; **taillé d'un seul b.** cut from a solid block; **elle s'est retournée tout d'un b. et l'a giflé** she turned round smartly and slapped him in the face; **coulé en b.** cast in one piece; **acquérir des droits en b.** to buy rights outright; **il a tout refusé/critiqué en b.** he rejected/criticized everything in its entirety; **visser ou serrer qch à b.** to screw sth (up) as tightly as possible; **serrer les freins à b.** to jam the brakes on hard; *Fam* **gonflé à b.** full of beans, raring to go
2 *(de maisons)* block; **il habite dans ce b.** he lives in this block
3 *Pol etc* bloc, group, coalition; **faire b.** to join forces, to unite (**avec** with; **contre** against); **les deux partis font b.** the two parties have formed a bloc *or* group *or* coali-

tion; **former un b.** to make up *or* form a group; **le b. occidental** the Western bloc; **le b. des gauches** the left-wing bloc *or* group *or* coalition
4 *(de papier)* pad; **b. à dessin** sketch pad, drawing pad; **b. de papier à lettres** writing pad; **b. de bureau** office pad, desk pad
5 *(ensemble d'éléments)* unit; *Cin* **b. sonore** sound unit; **former un b.** to make up *or* form a unit
6 *Fam (prison)* clink, *Br* nick; **être au b.** to be in the clink *or* the nick
7 *Ordinat* block; **quelle commande faut-il utiliser pour déplacer un b.?** what's the command for moving a block?; **b. d'alimentation secteur** mains power unit; **b. de données** data block; **b. numérique** numeric keypad; **b. de texte** text block, block of text; **b. de touches** keypad
▸▸**b. adresse** address block; *Fin* **b. de contrôle** controlling shareholding; *Sport* **b. de départ** starting block; *Aut* **b. des feux arrière** rear light cluster; **b. logique** package; **b. monétaire** currency bloc; **b. opératoire** theatre block, operating theatre *or Am* room; *Aut* **b. optique** sealed beam unit; **b. sanitaire** toilet block; **b. technique** *(d'une usine etc)* technical services block; **b. de titres** block of securities

blocage [blɔkaʒ] NM **1** *(de mécanismes etc)* jamming, sticking; *(des freins)* locking, seizing; *Écon, Fin* freezing; *Sport (du ballon)* blocking; *Psy* block; **b. des prix et des salaires** wage and price freeze; *Psy* **il a ou fait un b.** he's got a (mental) block; *Aut* **b. des roues** wheel lock, wheel lock-up; *Aut* **b. du volant** steering wheel clamp; *Aut* **b. de maintien du corps** bodylock seat restraints; **vis de b.** locking screw **2** *Constr* rubble (stone); *Typ (des lettres)* turning; *Ordinat* **b. majuscule** caps lock **3** *Ordinat (dans réseau)* lockout

blocaille [blɔkaj] NF *Constr* rubble (stone)

bloc-appartement, *pl* **blocs-appartements** NM *Can Br* block of flats, *Am* apartment building

bloc-cuisine, *pl* **blocs-cuisines** NM kitchen unit

bloc-cylindres, *pl* **blocs-cylindres** NM *Aut* cylinder block

bloc-diagramme, *pl* **blocs-diagrammes** NM *Géog* block diagram

bloc-évier, *pl* **blocs-éviers** NM sink unit

blockbuster [blɔkbœstœr] NM *Cin* blockbuster

blockhaus [blɔkos] NM **1** *Mil* blockhouse, pillbox **2** *Naut* armoured *or Am* armored tower; **b. de commandement** conning tower

bloc-moteur, *pl* **blocs-moteurs** NM *Aut* engine block

bloc-notes, *pl* **blocs-notes** NM notepad, memo pad; *Ordinat* notepad, scratchpad; **mémoire b.** scratchpad memory; **b. électronique** electronic notepad

bloc-sièges NM INV block of seats

bloc-système, *pl* **blocs-systèmes** NM *Rail* block system

blocus [blɔkys] NM **1** blockade; **faire le b. d'un port** to blockade a port; **lever/forcer le b.** to raise/to run the blockade

blond, -onde [blɔ̃, -ɔ̃d] ADJ *(cheveux)* fair, blond; *(personne)* fair(-haired), blond; *(sable, blés)* golden; **être b. comme les blés** *(des cheveux)* to be golden(-blond), *Litt* to be corn-coloured; *(d'une personne)* to have golden(-blond) hair, to be golden-haired; **bière blonde** lager; **un demi de blonde** = a half of lager; **(cigarette) blonde** Virginia cigarette; **tabac b.** Virginia tobacco
N *(personne)* **un b.** a fair(-haired) man; **une blonde** a blonde, a fair(-haired) woman; **blonde décolorée** peroxide blonde; *Can*

Fam **il va voir sa blonde** he's off to see his girl(friend)
NM **cheveux (d'un) b. doré** golden(-blond) hair; **se teindre (les cheveux) en b.** to dye one's hair blond
▸▸**b. ardent** auburn; **b. cendré** ash blond; **b. platine** platinum blond; **b. vénitien** strawberry blond, Titian red

blondasse [blɔ̃das] ADJ *(cheveux)* washed-out blond

blondeur [blɔ̃dœr] NF *(des cheveux)* blondness, fairness; *(du sable, des blés)* goldenness, gold

blondin¹, -ine [blɔ̃dɛ̃, -in] N fair-haired child

blondin² NM *Tech* cableway

blondinet, -ette [blɔ̃dinɛ, -ɛt] N fair-haired child

blondir [blɔ̃dir] VI *(des cheveux)* to go *or* turn blond, to get fairer *or* lighter; *(d'une personne)* to go *or* turn blond; **il faut faire b. les oignons dans du beurre** cook the onions in butter until they turn pale yellow
VT *(cheveux)* to bleach; **l'eau de mer blondit les cheveux** sea water bleaches the hair
VPR **se blondir elle s'est blondi les cheveux** she's bleached her hair

bloquer [blɔke] VT **1** *(mécanisme etc)* to jam; *(porte)* to jam, to wedge; *(port etc)* to blockade; **b. les roues** to lock (up) the wheels; **b. les freins** to jam the brakes on; **bloqué par la neige/le brouillard** snowbound/fogbound; **il m'a bloqué contre un mur** he jammed me up against a wall; *Fam* **me voilà bloqué à l'hôpital** here I am stuck in hospital
2 *(réunir)* to group together; **les cours sont bloqués sur six jours** the classes are grouped together over six days; **b. ses jours de congés** to lump together one's days off
3 *Constr (mur)* to block up *or* fill up (with rubble); *Typ* **b. une lettre** to turn a letter
4 *(chèque)* to stop; *(compte en banque)* to block; *(prix, salaires)* to freeze; *(négociations)* to hold up, to block
5 *(route etc)* to block; *Sport (ballon)* to block; **b. le chemin** *ou* **le passage à qn** to block *or* be in sb's way
6 *Belg Fam (sujet)* to bone up on, *Br* to swot up
7 *Can Fam (échouer à) (examen)* to fail, to flunk
8 *Psy* **ça me bloque de me sentir observé** I get a (mental) block if I feel I'm being watched; **être bloqué** to have a (mental) block
VPR **se bloquer 1** *(de machine, d'ascenseur etc)* to get stuck; *(d'une carte à puce)* to be automatically invalidated; *(de papier)* to jam **2** *Psy* to have *or* get a (mental) block

blottir (se) [səblɔtir] VPR to snuggle up, to curl up; **se b. dans son lit** to curl up *or* snuggle up *or* snuggle down in bed; **se b. contre qn/dans les bras de qn** to snuggle up to sb/ in sb's arms; **blottis les uns contre les autres** huddled up *or* snuggled up together; **blotti dans un coin** huddled *or* huddling in a corner; **village blotti au fond de la vallée** village tucked away *or* nestling in the valley

blousant [bluzɑ̃] ADJ loose-fitting

blouse [bluz] NF **1** *(d'écolier, de femme de ménage, de mécanicien etc)* overall; *(de médecin)* (white) coat; *(de paysan)* smock; **b. (de laboratoire)** (lab) coat **2** *(chemisier)* blouse

blouser [bluze] VT *Fam (personne)* to con, to take in, to cheat
VI *(d'un corsage etc)* to be loose-fitting
VPR **se blouser** *Fam* to make a mistake *or* a blunder

blouson [bluzɔ̃] NM (lumber)jacket; *(plus léger)* blouson; **b. en** *ou* **de cuir** leather jacket; **b. d'aviateur** bomber jacket; *Fam* **b. noir** young hoodlum *(wearing a black leather jacket)*, *Br* rocker

blue chip [blutʃip] NM *Bourse* blue chip

blue-jean(s), *pl* **blue-jeans** [blu(d)ʒin(z)] NM jeans

blues [bluz] NM *Mus* blues

Bluetooth [blutus] NM *Tél* Bluetooth

bluff [blœf] NM bluff; **faire du b.** to bluff; **c'est un coup de b.** it's all bluff, he's/they're/*etc* bluffing *or Br* trying it on; **il faut y aller au b.** you'll have to try and bluff

bluffer [blœfe] VT 1 *(tromper)* to take in, to trick; *Cartes* to bluff 2 *Fam (impressionner)* to blow away; **ils m'ont vraiment bluffé lors du concert qu'ils ont donné à Paris** they really blew me away when they played Paris VI to bluff; **il ne fait que b.** he's only bluffing, *Br* he's just trying it on

bluffeur, -euse [blœfœr, -øz] N bluffer

blush [blœʃ] NM *(fard)* blusher

blutage [blytaʒ] NM *(de la farine)* bolting

bluter [blyte] VT *(farine)* to bolt

BMTN [beemteeɛn] NM *Fin (abrév* **bon à moyen terme négociable)** MNT

BN [beeɛn] NF *abrév* **Bibliothèque nationale**

BNF [beeɛnef] NF *abrév* **Bibliothèque nationale de France**

BO [beo] NF *abrév* **bande originale** NM *abrév* **Bulletin officiel**

boa [boa] NM 1 *(serpent)* boa; **b. constricteur** boa constrictor 2 *(tour de cou)* boa

boat people [botpipœl] NMPL boat people

bob [bɔb] NM *Fam* 1 *Sport* bob(sleigh) 2 *(chapeau)* sun hat

bobard [bɔbar] NM *Fam* tall story

bobet [bɔbɛ] *Suisse Fam* ADJ stupid NM idiot

bobinage [bɔbinaʒ] NM 1 *(opération)* winding, reeling 2 *Élec* coil

bobinard [bɔbinar] NM *très Fam* whorehouse, *Br* knocking shop

bobine [bɔbin] NF 1 *(de ruban, fil etc)* reel; *(dans une machine à coudre)* bobbin; *(de machine à écrire, d'appareil photo etc)* spool; *(de papier)* roll; *Cin, Phot* reel; **une b. de pellicule** a roll of film; *Cin, Phot* **à bobines** reel-to-reel 2 *Élec* coil; **b. de dérivation** shunt coil; **b. d'allumage** ignition coil; **b. HT** tesla coil; **b. d'induction** induction coil; **b. exploratrice** pick-up coil; **b. haute tension** high-tension coil; **b. magnétique** magnet coil; **b. réceptrice** pick-up coil; **b. à faible inductance** low-inductance coil 3 *Arg (visage)* mug, face; **elle a fait une drôle de b.** she pulled a (funny) face

bobiner [bɔbine] VT *(fil de coton etc)* to wind, to reel; *(fil de fer etc)* to coil

bobineur, -euse [bɔbinœr, -øz] N *Tex, Élec* winder NF **bobineuse** winding machine, winder

bobinoir [bɔbinwar] NM *Tex, Élec* winding machine, winder

bobinot [bɔbino] NM *Cin, TV* reel

bobo [bobo] NM *Enf (blessure légère)* cut; **ça fait b.?** does it hurt?, is it sore?; **j'ai un b. au doigt** my finger hurts; **se faire b.** to hurt oneself N *Fam (abrév* **bourgeois(e) bohème)** bobo

bobonne [bɔbɔn] NF 1 *Arg Péj* missus, old girl; **il est toujours accompagné de b.** he always has his missus *or* old girl with him 2 *Belg Fam* grand-mama, grandma

bobsleigh [bɔbslɛ(g)] NM *Sport* bobsleigh

bobtail [bɔbtɛjl] NM *(chien)* Old English sheepdog

boc [bɔk] NM *Suisse* goatee (beard)

bocage [bɔkaʒ] NM 1 *Litt (bois)* copse 2 *Géog* bocage *(countryside with many hedges, trees and small fields)*

bocager, -ère [bɔkaʒe, -ɛr] ADJ wooded

bocal, -aux [bɔkal, -o] NM jar; **mettre des fruits en bocaux** to bottle fruit; **b. à poissons rouges** goldfish bowl

bocard [bɔkar] NM *Métal* ore crusher, stamping mill

Boccace [bɔkas] N Boccaccio

BOCE [beosea] NM *(abrév* **Bulletin officiel des communautés européennes)** = official listing of all new EC directives

boche [bɔʃ] *Fam Péj* ADJ Boche, Kraut N **B.** Boche, Kraut

bock [bɔk] NM 1 *(verre)* beer glass 2 *(contenu)* glass of beer (c) *Fam* **aller pisser un b.** to go for a pee

bocson [bɔksɔ̃] NM *Fam* **quel b.!** what a shambles!; **ils ont mis le b. dans la chambre** they make a real mess in the room

body [bɔdi] NM *(vêtement)* body

body-building NM *Sport* body building; **faire du b.** to do body building

boentje [buntja] N *Belg Fam (attirance)* **avoir un b. pour qn** to have a crush on sb

Boer [bur] ADJ, N Boer

boët(t)e [bwɛt] NF *Pêche* bait

bœuf, *pl* **bœufs** [bœf, bø] NM 1 *(mammifère)* bullock, steer; *(de trait)* ox; **bœufs à l'engrais** beeves; **b. gras** fatted ox, prize ox; **bœufs de boucherie** beef cattle; **fort comme un b.** as strong as an ox; *Fam* **on n'est pas des bœufs** I'm/we're not superhuman; **avoir un b. sur la langue** to keep mum VOIR GRAMMAIRE A13 2 *(viande)* beef 3 *Mus* jam session; **faire un b.** to have a jam session, to jam ADJ INV *Fam* fantastic, tremendous, amazing; **il a eu un succès b.** he was incredibly successful; **ça a fait un effet b.** it made a really big impression

▶▶ *Zool* **b. à bosse** zebu; **b. bourguignon** bœuf bourguignon; **b. gros sel** boiled beef; *Culin* **b. (à la) mode** stewed beef; **b. musqué** musk ox

bof [bɔf] INT **ça te plaît? – b., pas tellement** do you like it? – not really, no; **ça te dirait de venir avec nous? – b.** would you like to come with us? – I don't know *or* I'm not bothered; **il est chouette, hein, mon nouveau pull? – b.** my new sweater's great, isn't it? – I suppose so

boggie [bɔgi], **bogie** [bɔʒi] NM *Rail* bogie, bogy

Bogota [bɔgɔta] N Bogota

bogue¹ [bɔg] NF *Bot* chestnut bur, *Am* shuck

bogue² NM *Ordinat* bug; **dépourvu/plein de bogues** bug-free/-ridden; **b. de logiciel** software bug; **le b. de l'an 2000** the millennium bug

bogué [bɔge] ADJ *Ordinat* bug-ridden

boguet [bɔgɛ] NM *Suisse (cyclomoteur)* moped

bohème [bɔɛm] ADJ bohemian; **un esprit b.** an unconventional thinker N bohemian; **mener une vie de b.** to lead a bohemian *or* an unconventional life NF **la b.** *(milieu)* bohemia

Bohème [bɔɛm] NF Bohemia

bohémien, -ienne [bɔemjɛ̃, -jɛn] ADJ Bohemian N gipsy

boire [bwar] *(prp* buvant; *pp* bu, bue; *pr ind* je bois [bwa], il boit, n. buvons, ils boivent; *pr sub* je boive, n. buvions; *impf* je buvais; *p hist* je bus, n. bûmes; *fu* je boirai) VT 1 *(avaler)* to drink; **b. qch à petits coups** to sip sth; **b. qch d'un (seul) trait** *ou* **d'un seul coup** to drink sth at one gulp, to swig sth down, *Br* to knock sth back; **je ne bois pas d'alcool** I don't drink (alcohol); **b. une bouteille à quatre** to drink a bottle between four; **b. un verre jusqu'à la dernière goutte** to drain a glass; *Fam* **b. un coup** to have a drink; **il a bu un coup (de trop)** he's had one too many; **tu viens b. un verre?** are you coming for a drink?; *Fig* **b. les paroles de qn** to drink in sb's every word; *Fam* **b. la** *ou* **une tasse** *(en nageant)* to get a mouthful; *Fig Fam* **ce n'est pas la mer à b.** it's not that bad, it's no big deal; **b. un bouillon** *(en nageant)* to get a mouthful; *Fin* to make a big loss, to come a cropper; *Fig* **il boit du petit lait** *(il est content)* he's as pleased as Punch; **quand on le flatte, il boit du petit lait** when people flatter him, he laps it up

2 *(des plantes, des matières poreuses etc)* *(eau)* to soak up, to absorb

VI 1 *(d'une personne)* to drink; *(des plantes)* to soak up *or* absorb water; *Can (d'un bébé)* to feed; **b. à la bouteille** to drink from the bottle; **b. à sa soif, b. jusqu'à plus soif** to drink one's fill; **b. à la santé de qn** to drink (to) sb's health; **b. au succès de qch** to drink to the success of sth; **faire b. qn** to give sb a drink *or* something to drink; **faire b. les chevaux** to water the horses; *Fig* **il y a à b. et à manger là-dedans** it's got its good and its bad points, it's a bit of a mixed bag; *Prov* **qui a bu boira** old habits die hard; **il a commandé à b.** *(pour lui)* he ordered a drink; *(pour deux, trois etc)* he ordered the drinks; **vous avez commandé à b.?** have you ordered something to drink?

2 *(d'un alcoolique)* to drink; **tu bois trop** you drink too much; **elle boit comme un trou** she drinks like a fish; **je ne sais pas b.** I'm not much of a drinker

NM **le b. et le manger** food and drink, eating and drinking; *Fig* **il était si triste qu'il en avait perdu le b. et le manger** he was so upset that he couldn't eat or drink; *Can* **c'est l'heure de son b.** *(tétée)* it's his feeding time

VPR **se boire** *(de boisson)* to be drunk; **les vins sucrés se boivent au dessert** sweet wines are drunk with dessert; **ce vin se boit bien** *ou* **se laisse b.** this wine is very drinkable *or* goes down well

bois [bwa] NM 1 *(forêt)* wood; **petit b.** grove, *Br* spinney; **b. de chênes/sapins** oak/fir wood; **Robin des B.** Robin Hood; **je n'aimerais pas le rencontrer un soir au coin d'un b.** I wouldn't like to meet him in a dark alley

2 *(arbres)* timber (trees); **abattre** *ou* **couper le b.** to cut down *or* fell timber; *Fam* **casser du b.** *(d'un avion)* to crash-land

3 *(matériau)* wood; **petit b.** kindling; **chantier de b.** timber yard; **travail du b.** woodwork; **train de b.** float *or* raft of timber; **jambe de b.** wooden leg; **meubles en b.** wooden furniture; *Can* **maison en b. rond** log house; *Fig* **elle n'est pas de b.** she's only human; *Fig* **être du b. dont on fait les flûtes** to be easy-going; *Fig* **je leur ferai voir de quel b. je me chauffe** I'll show them (what I'm made of); *Fam* **touchez du b.!** touch wood!, *Am* knock on wood!; *Fam* **chèque en b.** rubber cheque, cheque that bounces; *Fam* **ça envoie le b.** *(c'est excellent)* it's the business

4 *(gravure)* woodcut

5 *(de chaise, raquette etc)* frame; *Tennis* **faire un b.** to hit the ball off the wood *or* the frame

6 *Mus* **les b.** the woodwind

7 **les b.** *(d'un cerf)* the antlers

▶▶ **b. blanc** deal, whitewood; **b. à brûler** firewood; **b. de charpente** timber, *Am* lumber; **b. de chauffage** firewood; *surtout Can* **b. debout** standing timber; **b. dur** hardwood; *Can* **b. franc** hardwood; **b. des îles** West Indian hardwood; **b. de lit** bedstead; **b. de mai** hawthorn; **b. mort** deadwood; **b. d'œuvre** timber, *Am* lumber; **b. de rose** rosewood; **b. de** sapin deal, whitewood; **b. tendre** softwood; **b. vert** unseasoned or green timber

boisage [bwazaʒ] NM Min **1** (action) (d'un puits, d'une galerie etc) timbering **2** (ensemble des bois) timbering, timber work

boisé [bwaze] ADJ (région) wooded; **pays b.** woodland(s), wooded country

boisement [bwazmã] NM (d'une région) afforestation

boiser [bwaze] VT **1** (planter d'arbres) to afforest, to plant with trees **2** (mine, galerie) to timber

boiserie [bwazri] NF Constr woodwork, wainscot(ing), panelling

boisseau, -eaux [bwaso] NM **1** Can, Arch (mesure) bushel; Fig **mettre la lumière sous le b.** to keep things hidden **2** Tech (tuyau) drain tile; (de cheminée) chimney (flue) tile; (de moteur) throttle chamber

boisson [bwasõ] NF **1** (liquide à boire) drink, Fml beverage; **b. gazeuse** fizzy drink; **b. fraîche** cold drink; **boissons alcoolisées/non alcoolisées** alcoholic/soft drinks; **b. chaude** hot drink **2** (alcool) drink; **il s'est adonné à la b.** he's taken to drink; **pris de b.** inebriated, intoxicated; **débit de boissons** bar **3** Can (spiritueux) hard liquor, spirits; **être/se mettre en b.** to be/get drunk

boîte [bwat] NF **1** (récipient) box; (de conserves) can, Br tin; **b. à bijoux** jewel box; **b. à couture** ou **ouvrage** sewing box; **b. en fer** tin; **une b. de chocolats** a box of chocolates; **des haricots en b.** canned or Br tinned beans; TV, Cin **en b.** in the can; **mettre en b.** (marchandises) to box; (sardines, légumes etc) to can, Br to tin; Fig Fam **mettre qn en b.** to pull sb's leg; **b. à violon** violin case; Fig Fam **fermer sa b.** to shut one's trap or mouth **2** Tech (de serrure) case **3** Fam (entreprise) firm; (école) school; **je travaille dans une b. d'informatique** I work for a computer firm or company; **sale b.** rotten hole **4 b. (de nuit)** nightclub; **aller** ou **sortir en b.** to go (out) to a nightclub

▸▸ **b. d'allumettes** (pleine) box of matches; (vide) matchbox; **b. de conserve** can, Br tin; **ils se nourrissent de boîtes de conserve** they live on canned or Br tinned food; Anat **b. crânienne** ou **du crâne** cranium; **b. de dérivation** junction box; Ordinat **b. de dialogue** dialog box; **b. de l'embrayage** clutch casing; Rail **b. de l'essieu** axle box; **b. à feu** firebox; Élec **b. à fusibles** fuse box; Aut **b. à gants** glove compartment; **b. à** ou **aux lettres** (pour envoyer) letterbox, postbox, pillarbox, Am mailbox; (chez soi) letterbox, Am mailbox; Ordinat **b. à lettres électronique** (electronic) mailbox, e-mail box; **b. à malice** secret toy box; **b. à musique** music box, Br musical box; Aviat **b. noire** flight recorder, black box; **b. à outils** (sens informatique également) toolbox; **b. à pain** bread bin; **b. postale** Post Office box; **b. à rythmes** drum machine; **b. de secours** first-aid box; **b. à vapeur** steam chest; Aut **b. de vitesses** gearbox; **b. vocale** voice mail

boîte-pont, pl **boîtes-ponts** NF Aut transaxle

boiter [bwate] VI (en marchant) to limp, to walk with a limp; **b. d'un pied** to be lame in one foot; **b. bas** to limp badly

boiterie [bwatri] NF lameness

boiteux, -euse [bwatø, -øz] ADJ (personne, cheval) lame; Fig (meuble) wobbly, rickety; (explication) lame; (raisonnement, projet) shaky; (traduction, phrase) iffy; (paix) fragile, uncertain; (période) uncertain; **le facteur est b.** the postman walks with or has a limp; **vers b.** limping verses; **cette phrase est**

---

un peu boiteuse this sentence doesn't hang together very well or doesn't work very well
N **lame man,** f **lame woman**

boîtier [bwatje] NM case, casing, housing; Phot (camera) body; **b. de montre** watch case; **b. de chirurgien** surgeon's instrument case

▸▸ Ordinat **b. de commande** command box; Ordinat **b. commutateur** data switch; Ordinat **b. compact** compact case; Aut **b. de direction** steering box; Aut **b. de direction à crémaillère** rack and pinion steering box; Ordinat **b. grande tour** large tower case; Ordinat **b. mini-tour** minitower case; Ordinat **b. moyenne tour** miditower case; Ordinat **b. de partage** (pour imprimante) data switch; Aut **b. de raccordement** junction box; **b. de télécommande** remote control; Ordinat **b. vertical** tower

boitillement [bwatijmã] NM slight limp

boitiller [bwatije] VI to limp slightly, to have a slight limp

boit-sans-soif [bwasãswaf] NM INV Arg boozer, tippler

bol [bɔl] NM **1** Physiol **b. alimentaire** (alimentary) bolus **2** Pharm, Vét bolus, pellet

bol NM **1** (pièce de vaisselle) bowl **2** Arg (chance) luck; **manque de b.** bad luck; **coup de b.** stroke of luck; **ne pas avoir de b.** to be unlucky, to be out of luck; **pas de b.!** what rotten luck! **3** (contenu) bowl(ful); **avaler son b. de café** to drink one's coffee; **on a pris un b. d'air frais** ou **pur** we got a good breath of fresh air

bolchevik, bolchevique [bɔlʃəvik] ADJ, N Bolshevik, Bolshevique

bolchevisme [bɔlʃəvism] NM Bolshevism

bolcheviste [bɔlʃəvist] ADJ, N Bolshevik, Bolshevist

bolduc [bɔldyk] NM gift-wrap ribbon

bolée [bɔle] NF (de cidre etc) bowl(ful)

boléro [bɔlero] NM (vêtement), Mus bolero

bolet [bɔlɛ] NM (champignon) boletus

bolide [bɔlid] NM (voiture de course) racing car; Astron meteor, fireball, Spéc bolide; **lancé comme un b. sur la route** hurtling along the road; **s'éloigner** ou **partir comme un b.** to shoot off like a rocket; **il est arrivé comme un b.** he arrived at top speed

bolivar [bɔlivar] NM (monnaie) bolivar

Bolivie [bɔlivi] NF Bolivia

bolivien, -ienne [bɔlivjɛ̃, -jɛn] ADJ Bolivian
N **B.** Bolivian

bolognais, -aise [bɔlɔɲɛ, -ɛz] ADJ Bolognese; Culin **spaghetti bolognaise** spaghetti bolognese; **sauce bolognaise** bolognese sauce
N **B.** Bolognese

Bologne [bɔlɔɲ] N Bologna

bombage [bõbaʒ] NM Fam (aerosol) graffiti; **faire des bombages sur un mur** to spray-paint a wall with graffiti

bombance [bõbãs] NF Fam feast; **faire b.** to go on a spree or a binge; (manger) to have a feast

bombardement [bõbardəmã] NM **1** (avec des obus) bombardment, shelling; (avec des bombes) bombing, bombardment; (avec des pierres etc) pelting; **b. de questions** flood of questions; **b. aérien** air raid; **avion de b.** bomber; **le b. atomique d'Hiroshima** the dropping of the atomic bomb on Hiroshima **2** Phys bombardment

bombarder [bõbarde] VT **1** (avec des obus) to bombard, to shell; (avec des bombes) to bomb, to bombard; **maison bombardée** shelled/bombed house; **b. qn de pierres** to pelt sb with stones; **b. qn de questions** to fire questions at sb, to bombard sb with ques-

---

tions; **être bombardé de lettres/coups de téléphone** to be bombarded or inundated with letters/phone calls **2** Phys (de neutrons etc) to bombard (**de** with) **3** Fam **on l'a bombardé ministre** he's been pitchforked into the post of minister or made a minister out of the blue
VI Fam (fumer beaucoup) to smoke like a chimney

bombardier [bõbardje] NM Mil **1** Aviat (avion) bomber; (aviateur) bombardier **2** Arch bombardier

bombe [bõb] NF **1** Mil etc bomb; **b. de fabrication artisanale** home-made bomb; **attaque** ou **attentat à la b.** bomb attack; **lâcher** ou **larguer une b.** to release or drop a bomb; Fam **entrer en** ou **comme une b.** to come bursting in; Fig **cela a fait l'effet d'une b.** it was a real bombshell **2** (atomiseur) spray, aerosol; **b. de peinture/d'insecticide** paint/fly spray; **déodorant en b.** deodorant spray **3** Équitation riding hat or cap **4** Fam **faire la b.** to live it up **5** Can (bouilloire) kettle

▸▸ **b. A** A bomb; **b. atomique** atom(ic) bomb; Méd **b. au cobalt** cobalt bomb; **b. à eau** water bomb; **b. à fragmentation** fragmentation or scatter bomb; **b. fumigène** smoke bomb; Culin **b. glacée** bombe glacée; **b. H** H bomb; **b. à hydrogène** hydrogen bomb; **b. incendiaire** fire bomb, incendiary bomb; **b. lacrymogène** tear-gas grenade; **b. au plastic** plastic bomb; **b. à retardement** time bomb, delayed-action bomb; **b. volante** flying bomb, Fam doodlebug

bombé [bõbe] ADJ bulging; (forme) rounded, curved; **avoir le front b.** to have a bulging forehead; **se tenir droit, la poitrine bombée** to stand up straight with one's chest thrown out; **chaussée bombée** cambered road

bombement [bõbmã] NM bulge, bulging; (d'une route) camber

bomber [bõbe] VT **1** (gonfler) to cause to bulge; (route) to camber; **b. la poitrine** ou **le torse** to throw out one's chest; Fig to swagger (around) **2** (écrire à la bombe) to spray; **b. des graffiti/des slogans** to spray graffiti/slogans
VI **1** (d'un mur etc) to bulge (out) **2** Fam (aller très vite) to bomb along, to belt along

bombinette [bõbinet] NF Fam **1** (petite bombe) little bomb **2** (petite voiture très nerveuse) nippy little car

bombonne [bõbon] NF = **bonbonne**

bôme [bom] NF Naut boom

| ADJ good **1–7, 9–11, 13** ■ nice **2** ■ kind **5** ■ right **4, 13** ■ fit **7** |
| ADV good |

ADJ **1** (moralement) good; **le b. M. Seguin** good old Mr Seguin; **mon b. monsieur** my dear sir; **défendre la bonne cause** to fight the good fight; **bonne action** good deed; Fam **b. chic b. genre** ≃ Sloany, Am ≃ preppy; **la bonne société** polite society

2 (agréable) (livre, histoire, odeur, ambiance, travail etc) good; **bonne soirée** pleasant evening; **installé dans un b. fauteuil** settled in a nice or comfortable armchair; **j'ai trouvé b. le rôti** I enjoyed the roast, I thought the roast was good; **je ne trouve pas ça très b.** I don't think it's very good, I don't much like it; **qu'est-ce que c'est b.!** that's really good!; **l'eau est bonne** (en se baignant) the water's great; **elle est bonne?** (en se baignant) what's the water like?; **ils aiment les bonnes choses** they like the good things in life; **elle lui fait de bons petits plats** she makes him nice little meals; **être en bonne compagnie** to be in good company;

être de bonne compagnie to be good company

3 *(capable, apte)* good; **un b. médecin/père** a good doctor/father; **les bons élèves** the good *or* bright pupils; **b. en anglais** good at English; *Fin* **b. pour aval** guaranteed by

4 *(correct) (travail, qualité etc)* good; *(réponse, clé, côté, bus etc)* right; **si j'ai bonne mémoire** if my memory serves me (well); **c'est de la bonne qualité** it's good quality; **oui, c'est b.** yes, that's right; **maintenant, c'est b.** *(à qn qui fixe une étagère etc)* it's right *or* fine now; **pour le b. fonctionnement de l'appareil** to ensure the appliance functions correctly; **pour lui, tous les moyens sont bons pour réussir** he'll do anything to succeed, he'll stop at nothing to succeed; **prends le marteau par le b. bout** hold the hammer the right way round; **tourner dans le b. sens** to turn in the right direction; **un intellectuel, dans le b. sens du terme** an intellectual in the true sense of the term; **en b. état** in good condition; *Fig* **frapper/ne pas frapper à la bonne porte** to come to the right/wrong person; *Fig* **la bonne voie** *ou* **route** the right path *or* track; **il a encore de bonnes jambes** he still has a good pair of legs; **avoir une bonne vue** to have good eyesight; **sa vue n'est plus très bonne** he doesn't see too well any more; *Tennis* **la balle est bonne** the ball is in *or* good; **les yaourts sont-ils encore bons?** are the yoghurts still good *or* all right?; **le fusible n'est plus b., il faut le changer** the fuse has gone, we'll have to change it

5 *(généreux)* good, kind (**pour, envers, avec** to); **c'est un b. garçon** *ou* *Fam* **type** *ou* **gars** he's a good sort, he's all right; **tu es trop bonne pour moi** you're too good to me; **être b. avec** *ou* **envers les animaux** to be kind to animals; **c'est parti d'une bonne intention, l'intention était bonne** the intention was good; **être b. public** to be a good audience; **vous êtes bien b. de m'inviter** it's very good *or* kind of you to invite me; *Fam Iron* **tu es b.!** oh **very** funny!

6 *(profitable, utile) (investissement etc)* good; **bonne affaire** bargain; **c'est b. à savoir/à se rappeler** it's worth knowing/remembering; **c'est toujours b. à avoir** it's always worth having; **à quoi b.?** what's the point?, what's the good of it?; **à quoi b. se plaindre?** what's the use *or* the good or the point of complaining?; **c'est un b. conseil** it's a good piece of advice; **quelle bonne idée!** what a good idea!; **puis-je vous être b. à quelque chose?** can I do anything for you?, can I be of any help (to you)?; **cet exercice est b. pour le dos** this exercise is good for the back; **ce qui est b. pour les uns n'est pas toujours b. pour les autres** what is good for some is not necessarily good for others

7 **b. à manger** good to eat; *(comestible)* fit *or* safe to eat; **b. pour le service** *Mil* fit for duty; *Fig* serviceable; **c'est b. pour les nerfs** it's good for your nerves; **il n'est b. qu'à cela** that's all he's fit for; **elle n'est bonne à rien** she's useless, she's good for nothing, she's no good at anything; **c'est b. à jeter** you can throw that away, *Fam* chuck it out

8 *(souhaitable)* **si b. vous semble** if you think it advisable; **il est b. de s'en informer tout de suite** it's best to get information straightaway; **il est b. que vous le sachiez** it's just as well that you should know; **juger** *ou* **croire** *ou* **trouver b. de faire qch** to think it best *or* advisable to do sth

9 *(présage)* good, favourable, *Am* favorable; **souhaiter une** *ou* **la bonne année à qn** to wish sb a happy New Year; **b. Noël** Merry Christmas; **b. anniversaire!** happy birthday!; **avoir la bonne vie** to have it easy; **b. week-end!**, *Can* **bonne fin de semaine!** have a good weekend!; **bonne chasse!** good hunt-

ing!; **b. voyage!** have a good trip!, bon voyage!; **bonne journée!** have a good *or* nice day!; **b. appétit!** bon appetit!; *(surtout dans un restaurant)* enjoy your meal!, *Am Fam* enjoy!; **bonne nuit** good night; **bonnes vacances!** have a good *or* enjoy your holiday!

10 *(caution, crédit etc)* good; **billet b. pour trois mois** ticket valid *or* good for three months; **ta carte d'étudiant n'est plus bonne** your student card isn't valid any more *or* is out of date; *Com* **b. pour une entrée gratuite/cinq euros de réduction sur votre prochain achat** this entitles you to free admission/to five euros off your next purchase; **son affaire est bonne!, son compte est b.!** he's in for it!; **elle est bonne pour deux mois de prison** she's looking at *or* she's going to get two months in prison; **tu es b. pour la contravention** you're in for a fine; *Fam* **on est b.!** *(c'est raté)* we've had it!

11 *(intensif)* good; **j'ai attendu deux bonnes heures** I waited a full *or* a good two hours, I waited (for) two solid hours; **deux bons kilos** two good kilos; **il m'a fallu un b. moment pour comprendre** it took me a (good *or* little) while to understand; **arriver b. premier** to come in an easy first; **il était b. dernier** he was way behind all the others, he brought up the rear; **b. nombre de** a number of, a good many; **prendre une bonne moitié de qch** to take a good half of sth; **donner bonne mesure** to give good *or* full measure; **elle a reçu une bonne fessée** she got a good spanking; **b. gros rire** big resounding laugh; **un b. rhume** a bad cold; **il faudrait qu'on ait une bonne discussion** we must have a good *or* proper discussion *or* talk; **une bonne fois pour toutes** once and for all

12 *Litt* **tout de b.** in earnest, really; **est-ce pour de b.?** are you serious?; **on se quitte pour de b.** we're splitting up for good; **il pleut pour de b.** it's raining in real earnest; **cette fois, elle pleure pour de b.** this time she's really crying

13 **b.!** right!, good!, fine!; **b., je viendrai** right *or* good *or* fine, I'll come; **il est malade, allons b.?** he's ill, eh?; **ah b., je ne le savais pas** oh, I didn't know; **b., b., d'accord** all right, all right, OK, OK; **c'est b., j'ai compris** all right *or* OK, I understand

ADV **tenir b.** *(résister)* to stand fast, to hold one's own; **tenez b.!** hold tight!, hold on (tight)!; **(ne lâchez pas)** don't give up *or* in; **sentir b.** to smell good; **il fait b. vivre** it's good to be alive; **un pays où il fait b. vivre** a country that's good to live in; **il ne fait pas b. se promener dans ce quartier** it's not safe to walk in this district

N **les bons** the good, the righteous; *Fam (dans un film etc)* the goodies; **une histoire de bons et de méchants** a goodies and baddies story; **un b./une bonne à rien** a good-for-nothing

NM **cela a du b.** it has its good points, it has some advantages, there's some good in it; **il y a du b. à ne pas travailler** there's something to be said for not working; **le b. de l'histoire** the best part of the story

NF **bonne** *voir* **bonne**

---

bon² **NM 1** *(billet)* voucher, coupon, slip **2** *Fin* bond, bill; **b. d'exécution de contrôle** performance bond

▶▶**b. d'achat** gift voucher; **b. d'agence** *(d'une agence de voyages)* travel agent's voucher; **b. d'annulation** cancellation form; **b. de caisse** *(justifiant sortie de fonds)* cash voucher; *Compta* interest-bearing note; *Typ* **b. à clicher** machine proof; **b. de commande** order form; *Typ* **b. à copier** machine proof; **b. de débours** *(pour services aux clients d'un hôtel)* visitors paid out voucher, VPO voucher; **b. de décaissement** disbursement voucher, paid out voucher; **b. à délivrer**

freight release; **b. d'échange** *(d'une agence de voyages)* (travel agent's) voucher; *Com* **b. d'entrée** stock received docket/form; **b. d'épargne** savings certificate; **b. d'essence** petrol coupon; *Com* **b. d'expédition** dispatch note, consignment note; **b. de garantie** guarantee; *Com* guarantee slip; *Com* **b. de livraison** delivery note; **b. au porteur** bearer bond; **b. de réception des marchandises** receipt note; **b. de réduction** money-off coupon *or* voucher, discount voucher; *Com* **b. de remboursement** money-off voucher; **b. de réservation** reservation form; *Com* **b. de sortie** stock issued docket/form; *Fin* **b. de souscription d'actions** warrant; *Tex* **b. teint** colourfast, *Am* colorfast; *(couleur)* fast; *Fig (syndicaliste, socialiste etc)* dyed-in-the-wool, staunch; **b. à tirer** press proof, final corrected proof; **donner le b. à tirer** to pass the proofs for press; **b. du Trésor** treasury bond, exchequer bill; **b. vacances** = voucher supplied by holiday associations to less well-off families to help cover holiday expenses

bonace [bɔnas] **NF** lull, calm *(before or after a storm)*

bonapartisme [bɔnapartism] **NM** Bonapartism

bonapartiste [bɔnapartist] **ADJ, N** Bonapartist

bonard [bɔnar] **ADJ** *Fam* great

bonasse [bɔnas] **ADJ** *Péj* soft, mild; **il est b.** he's too easy-going *or* too soft; **répondre d'un ton b.** to answer mildly

bonbon [bɔ̃bɔ̃] **NM 1** sweet, *Am* candy, *Austr* lolly; **b. anglais** fruit drop; **b. acidulé** acid drop; **b. à la menthe** mint **2** *Belg (biscuit)* biscuit, *Am* cookie

ADV *Fam* **coûter b.** to cost an arm and a leg *or* a bundle

bonbonne [bɔ̃bɔn] **NF 1** *Ind* carboy **2** *(récipient)* demijohn; **b. en verre** glass demijohn; **une b. de vin** a demijohn of wine

bonbonnière [bɔ̃bɔnjɛr] **NF 1** *(pour les bonbons)* sweet *or Am* candy box, bonbonnière **2** *Fig* bijou residence

bond [bɔ̃] **NM 1** *(saut)* leap, bound, spring, jump; **faire un b.** to leap up, to jump up; **franchir qch d'un b.** to clear sth at one bound *or* leap *or* jump; **se lever d'un b.** to spring *or* to leap *or* to jump to one's feet; **les loyers/prix ont fait un b.** rents/prices have shot up; **progresser par bonds** to advance by leaps and bounds; **b. en avant** *(technologique etc)* breakthrough **2** *(d'une balle etc)* bounce, rebound; **saisir** *ou* **prendre la balle au b.** to catch the ball on the bounce *or* the rebound; *Fig* to seize *or* grasp the opportunity; **faire faux b. à qn** to leave sb in the lurch, to let sb down

bonde [bɔ̃d] **NF 1** *(bouchon)* **(**d'un évier, d'une baignoire) plug; *(d'un tonneau)* bung; *(d'un bassin)* sluice gate; **lâcher** *ou* **lever la b.** to pull the plug out; *Fig* **lâcher la b. à sa colère** to give vent to one's anger **2** *(trou d'évacuation)* **(**d'un évier, d'une baignoire) plughole; *(d'un tonneau)* bunghole; *(d'un bassin)* drainage hole, outlet

bondé [bɔ̃de] **ADJ** *(bus, cinéma, ville etc)* packed, jam-packed; **des trains bondés de vacanciers** trains packed *or* crammed with holiday-makers; *Théâtre* **salle bondée** packed house

bondieuserie [bɔ̃djøzri] **NF** *Péj* **1** *(bigoterie)* religiosity, over-religious zeal **2** *(objet)* devotional object, religious knick-knack

bondir [bɔ̃dir] **VI 1** *(sauter)* to leap (up), to spring (up), to jump (up); **b. en avant/arrière** to leap *or* spring *or* jump forward/back; **b. sur qn/qch** to pounce on sb/sth; *Fig* **il a bondi de colère** he flew into a rage; *Fig* **cela me**

fait b. it makes me mad, it makes me see red **2** *(courir)* to rush (off), to dash (off); **j'ai bondi jusqu'à la poste la plus proche** I rushed (off) *or* dashed (off) to the nearest post office; **b. au secours de qn** *ou* **pour aider qn** to spring *or* leap to sb's assistance **3** *(gambader)* to gambol, to leap (about), to skip (about) **4** *(d'une balle etc)* to bounce

bondissement [bɔ̃dismɑ̃] NM **1** *(saut)* bound, leap **2** *(des agneaux etc)* gambolling, frisking

bon enfant [bɔnɑ̃fɑ̃] ADJ INV *(personne, manières etc)* easy-going, good-natured; *(atmosphère)* easy-going

bonheur [bɔnœr] NM **1** *(chance)* good fortune, (good) luck; **j'ai eu le b. de la connaître** I had the good fortune to know her; **porter b. à qn** to bring sb (good) luck; **il ne connaît pas son b.** he doesn't know how lucky he is, he doesn't know his luck; **quel b.!** how marvellous!; **par b.** luckily, fortunately, as luck would have it; **au petit b. (la chance)** at random **2** *(bien-être)* happiness; **la recherche du b.** the quest for happiness; **le b. de vivre** the joy of living; **faire le b. de qn** to make sb happy; **ces chocolats font mon b.** I adore these chocolates; **l'argent ne fait pas le b.** money can't buy you happiness; **il fait tout pour mon b.** he does everything he can to make me happy; **j'ai eu le b. de voir ma fille naître** I had the joy of seeing my daughter being born; **quel b. de voyager en avion** what a pleasure *or* delight it is to travel by air **3** *Litt (réussite)* **avec b.** felicitously; **texte écrit avec b.** felicitous text; **le salé et le sucré s'allient avec b.** savoury and sweet combine happily *or* are a happy combination

bonheur-du-jour, *pl* **bonheurs-du-jour** NM escritoire

bonhomie [bɔnɔmi] NF good-heartedness, good-naturedness, bonhomie; **avec b.** goodnaturedly

bonhomme, *pl* **bonshommes** [bɔnɔm, bɔ̃zɔm] NM *Fam* (homme, type) fellow, guy, *Br* chap, *Br* bloke; **un petit b.** a little fellow; **un vilain b.** a nasty piece of work; **c'est un sacré b.** he's a hell of a guy; **pourquoi pleures-tu, mon b.?** *(à un petit garçon)* what are you crying for, little fellow?; *Fig* **il va son petit b. de chemin** he's jogging along nicely; **dessiner des bonshommes** to draw little people ▶▶**b. de neige** snowman; **faire un b. de neige** to make *or* build a snowman; **b. de** *ou* **en pain d'épice** gingerbread man; *Tech* **b. de verrouillage** plunger

boni [bɔni] NM *(bénéfice)* profit; *(excédent)* surplus, balance in hand

boniche [bɔniʃ] NF *Péj* (maid)servant, *Br* skivvy; **je ne suis pas ta b., fais-le tout seul!** I'm not your servant, do it yourself!; **faire la b. pour qn** to do sb's menial jobs for them, *Br* to skivvy for sb

bonification [bɔnifikasjɔ̃] NF **1** *(d'une terre, d'un vin)* improvement **2** *Com* bonus; **b. pour non sinistre** no claims bonus **3** *Sport* advantage

bonifié [bɔnifje] ADJ *(prêt)* at a reduced rate of interest

bonifier [bɔnifje] *(pr sub, impf n. bonifiions, v. bonifiiez)* VT **1** *(terre, caractère etc)* to improve **2** *Com (pénurie etc)* to make up, to make good ▶**se bonifier** VPR *(d'une personne, du vin etc)* to improve; **ses humeurs vont se b. avec le temps** his/her nature will improve with time

boniment [bɔnimɑ̃] NM **1** *Com* sales talk *or* pitch, patter; **faire du b. à qn** *(d'un vendeur)* to give sb the sales talk *or* the patter; **faire du b. à une femme** to chat a woman up; **faire**

du b. à qn pour qu'il fasse qch to try to coax *or* talk sb into doing sth **2** *Fam (blague)* tall story; **tout ça, c'est du b.** that's all eyewash *or* claptrap

bonimenter [bɔnimɑ̃te] VI *Fam* to dish out the sales talk *or* the patter

bonite [bɔnit] NF *(poisson)* bonito

bonjour [bɔ̃ʒur] NM **1** hello, *Fam* hi, *Fml* good day; *(le matin)* good morning; *(l'après-midi)* good afternoon; *(quand on est présenté à qn)* hello, how do you do?; *Can (au revoir) (pendant la journée)* goodbye, bye, see you later; **dis b. à la dame** *(à un enfant)* say hello to the lady; **(dis) b. à ta mère (de ma part)** (give) my regards to your mother, say hello to your mother for me; **c'est facile** *ou* **simple comme b.** it's as easy as pie, it's child's play **2** *Fam Iron* **b. les dégâts!** what a mess!; *(ça va aller mal)* there'll be trouble!; **b. la soirée/ l'odeur!** what an evening/a smell!; **b. la propreté ici!** I don't think much of the way things are cleaned round here!; **le périphérique le soir à six heures, b.!** the ring road at six o'clock at night, no way *or* forget it!

bon marché ADJ INV cheap; **acheter/vendre qch (à) b.** to buy/sell sth cheap(ly)

bonnard [bɔnar] ADJ *Fam* great; **c'est b.!** cool!

bonne [bɔn] NF **1** *(domestique)* maid, *Vieilli* maidservant; **b. à tout faire** general help, *Vieilli* maid of all work; **b. d'enfants** nurse, *Br* nanny **2 en voilà une (bien) b.!** that's a good one!; **il en a de bonnes!** he must be joking *or* kidding!; **tu en as de bonnes!** you're having a laugh, aren't you?; **il m'en a raconté de bonnes sur toi!** he told me some interesting things about you!; **avoir qn à la b.** *(d'un employeur, d'un professeur)* to have a soft spot for sb; *Fam* **il t'a à la b.** you're well in with him

Bonne-Espérance N cap **de B.** Cape of Good Hope

bonne-main, *pl* **bonnes-mains** NF *Suisse* tip

bonne-maman, *pl* **bonnes-mamans** NF *Vieilli* grandmama

bonnement [bɔnmɑ̃] ADV **tout b.** simply; **je lui ai dit tout b. que ...** I simply *or* just told him that ...

bonnet [bɔnɛ] NM **1** *(coiffure)* hat; *(de bébé)* bonnet; **b. de ski** ski cap; *Fig* **prendre qch sous son b.** *(faire de sa propre initiative)* to take it upon oneself to do sth, *Fam* to do sth off one's own bat; *(prendre la responsabilité)* to take on the responsibility for sth, to take sth on; **opiner du b.** to nod (one's) assent, to nod in agreement; *Fig* **avoir la tête près du b.** to have a short fuse; *Fig* **jeter son b. par-dessus les moulins** to kick over the traces, to throw caution to the winds; **c'est b. blanc et blanc b.** it's six of one and half a dozen of the other; *Fig Fam* **gros b.** big shot, big noise, bigwig; *Fam* **te casse pas le b.!** don't worry about it, don't let it bother you! **2** *(d'un soutien-gorge)* cup; **quelle profondeur de b.?** what size cup? **3** *Zool (d'un ruminant)* second stomach, reticulum, honeycomb ▶▶**b. de bain** bathing *or* swimming cap; **b. de douche** shower cap; **b. d'évêque** bishop's mitre; **b. de nuit** nightcap; **être triste comme un b. de nuit** to be as cheerful as the grave; **b. phrygien** *ou* **rouge** Phrygian cap *(in French Revolution)*; *Mil* **b. de police** forage cap

bonneterie [bɔnɛtri] NF **1** *(bas)* hosiery **2** *(commerce)* hosiery trade; *(magasin)* hosier's (shop)

bonnetier, -ière [bɔntje, -jɛr] N hosier

bonnette [bɔnɛt] NF *(objectif)* supplementary lens; *(de micro)* windshield; **b. anti-vent** *(d'un microphone)* windscreen, windshield

bonniche [bɔniʃ] NF *Péj* = **boniche**

bonobo [bɔnɔbo] NM *Zool* bonobo

bon-papa, *pl* **bons-papas** NM *Vieilli* grandpapa

bonsaï [bɔnzaj, bɔ̃zaj] NM *(arbre)* bonsai

bonsoir [bɔ̃swar] NM *(pour saluer en arrivant)* good evening; *(en partant le soir)* goodbye; *(quand on prend congé tard le soir)* goodnight; **dire b.** *ou* **souhaiter le b. à qn** to say good evening/goodnight to sb

bonté [bɔ̃te] NF **1** *(qualité)* kindness, goodness, kindliness; **une femme d'une grande b.** a very kind *or* good woman; **sourire plein de b.** kind(ly) *or* benevolent smile; **ayez la b. de me dire qui ...** be so good as to tell me who ..., please tell me who ...; **auriez-vous la b. de ...?** would you be so good as to ...?; **faire qch par b. d'âme** to do sth out of the goodness *or* kindness of one's heart; *Fam* **b. divine** *ou* **du ciel!** good heavens! **2 bontés** kindnesses, acts of kindness, kind acts; **avoir des bontés pour qn** to show kindness towards sb; **remercier qn pour ses bontés** to thank sb for his/her kindness; **je ne m'attendais pas à tant de bontés** I didn't expect such kindness **3** *Vieilli (de choses)* goodness, excellence

bonus [bɔnys] NM *(dans les assurances)* no-claims bonus

bonus-malus [bɔnysmalys] NM INV *(en assurances)* no-claims bonus system

bon vivant ADJ **il est b.** he enjoys life NM man who enjoys life; **des bons vivants** people who enjoy life

bonze [bɔ̃z] NM **1** *Rel* Buddhist priest *or* monk, bonze **2** *Fig Fam (personnage important)* big shot, bigwig **3** *Fam* **vieux b.** bigheaded old fool

bonzerie [bɔ̃zri] NF Buddhist monastery

bonzesse [bɔ̃zɛs] NF Buddhist nun, bonze

boogie-woogie, *pl* **boogie-woogies** [bugiwugi] NM *Mus* boogie-woogie

book¹ [buk] NM *(d'un mannequin, d'un artiste etc)* portfolio; **b. de contacts** contacts book

bookmaker [bukmɛkœr], *Fam* **book²** [buk] NM bookmaker, *Fam* bookie

bookmark [bukmark] NM *Ordinat* bookmark

booléen, -éenne [buleɛ̃, -ɛɛn] ADJ *Math, Ordinat* Boolean

boom [bum] NM *Com, Fin* boom

boomerang [bumrɑ̃g] NM boomerang; **avoir un effet b.** to have a boomerang effect; *Fam* **son projet a fait b.** his plan boomeranged *or* backfired

booster¹ [bustœr] NM *(amplificateur), Astronaut* booster

booster² [buste] VT *Fam (stimuler)* to boost

booter [bute] VI *Ordinat* **b. (sur le lecteur B)** to boot (off the B drive)

boots [buts] NMPL ankle boots

boquer [bɔke] VI *Can (s'entêter)* to dig one's heels in

borate [bɔrat] NM *Chimie* borate

borax [bɔraks] NM *Chimie* borax

borborygme [bɔrbɔrigm] NM *(usu pl) (de l'estomac)* rumbling(s), gurgling(s); *Fig* **je ne comprenais pas ses borborygmes** I didn't understand his mumblings *or* mutterings; **borborygmes de la plomberie** gurgling noises in the plumbing

bord [bɔr] NM **1** *Naut (d'un navire)* side; **jeter qch/tomber** *ou* **passer par-dessus b.** to throw sth/to fall overboard; **moteur hors b.** outboard motor; **les hommes du b.** the ship's company, the crew; *Fig* **être du même b.** to be on the same side *or* of the same opinion; *Can* **se trouver du bon/mauvais b.** to be on the right/wrong side; **à b. d'un navire/d'un avion** on board *or* aboard a ship/a plane; **monter à b. (d'un bateau/d'un avion)** to go/come on board *or* aboard (a boat/a plane), to board (a boat/a plane); **prendre qn à son b.** to take sb on board *or* aboard; *Fig* **vous êtes (le) seul maître à b.** you're the one in charge **2** *Naut (bordée)* tack; **courir** *ou* **tirer un b.** to tack, to make a tack

3 *(d'une table, d'une assiette, d'un biscuit, des paupières)* edge; *(d'un vêtement)* border, hem; *(d'une falaise, d'un chemin)* edge, verge; *(d'un chapeau)* brim; *(d'un vase, d'une tasse)* rim, brim; *(d'une blessure)* lip; *(de l'œil)* rim; **b. du trottoir** kerb, *Am* curb; **remplir un verre jusqu'au** *ou* **à ras b.** to fill a glass to the brim; **sur le** *ou* **au b. de la route** at *or* on the roadside, at *or* on the side of the road; *Can* **de l'autre b. de la rue** on the other side of the street; **auberge au b.** *ou* **sur le b. de la route** wayside *or* roadside inn; **hôtel au b. du lac** lakeside hotel; **se promener au b. du lac** to walk along the edge of the lake; **je l'ai trouvé au b. de la rivière** I found it on the river bank; **se promener au b. de la mer** to walk by the sea; **maison au b. de la mer** house by the sea, seaside house; **maison sur le** *ou* **en b. de mer** house on the sea front *or* the (sea)shore; **vivre au b. de la mer** to live at the seaside *or* by the sea; **le b. de mer est très construit** there is a lot of development along the sea front; **b. à b.** edge to edge; *Can* **de b. en b.** from end to end; **chapeau à larges bords** broad- *or* wide-brimmed hat; *Fig* **au b. de la tombe** at death's door; **au b. des larmes** on the verge of tears; **au b. de la crise de nerfs/du désespoir/de la catastrophe** on the verge *or* brink of hysteria/of despair/of disaster; **un peu voleur/bête sur les bords** a bit light-fingered/stupid; **il est un peu menteur/provocateur sur les bords** he's a bit of a liar/an agitator

▸▸ *Aviat* **b. d'attaque** *(d'une aile)* leading edge; **b. de fuite** *(d'une aile)* trailing edge; *Ordinat* **b. de reliure** inside margin

bordage [bɔrdaʒ] **NM 1** *Couture* edging; **b. de pierres** stone kerb *Am* curb **2** *Can* **bordages** *(glace)* inshore ice **3** *Naut (d'un navire) (en bois)* planking; *(en fer)* plating

bordé [bɔrde] **ADJ** edged, bordered (**de** with); **mouchoir b. de dentelle** lace-edged handkerchief; **boulevard b. d'arbres** tree-lined boulevard

NM 1 *Couture* edging, border **2** *Naut (d'un navire)* planking, planks; *(en fer)* plating

bordeaux [bɔrdo] **NM** Bordeaux (wine); **b. rouge** claret

ADJ INV claret(-coloured), maroon

bordée [bɔrde] **NF 1** *Naut (de coups de feu)* broadside; **lâcher une b.** to let fly a broadside; *Fig* **b. de jurons** *ou* **d'injures** torrent *or* hail of abuse **2** *Naut (distance)* tack; **courir une b.** to tack, to make a tack; **tirer des bordées** to tack; *Fam Fig* **tirer** *ou* **courir une b.** to go on a binge; *Fam* **être en b.** to be on a binge **3** *Naut (équipe)* watch; **b. de tribord/de bâbord** starboard/port watch **4** *Can* **b. (de neige)** heavy snowfall

bordel [bɔrdɛl] **NM** *très Fam (hôtel de passe)* brothel; *Arg (désordre)* mess; **quel b.!** what a mess!, what a shambles!; **tu as rangé ton b.?** have you cleared up your mess?; **mettre** *ou* **foutre le b. dans qch** to make a mess of sth, to mess sth up; *(dans une pièce)* to make a mess in sth; **tout le b.** the whole damn lot; **b.!** hell!; *Arg* **b. de merde!** shit!; *Vulg* **putain de b. de merde!** fucking hell!, fuck!; **mais qu'est-ce qu'il fout, bordel!** what the fuck is he doing?

bordelais, -aise [bɔrdəlɛ, -ɛz] **ADJ** of/from Bordeaux

NM le B. *(région)* the Bordeaux region

NF bordelaise *(futaille)* = cask of about 225 litres; *(bouteille)* = type of bottle for Bordeaux wine

N B. *(natif)* native of Bordeaux; *(habitant)* inhabitant of Bordeaux

bordélique [bɔrdelik] **ADJ** *Fam (pièce, bureau, organisation etc)* shambolic; **tu es très b.** you're a real slob

border [bɔrde] **VT 1** *(garnir) (robe, manches etc)* to edge, to border (**de** with); **les peupliers qui bordent le chemin** the poplars lining the road; **les villes qui bordent la frontière** the towns that border the frontier; *Naut* **navire qui borde les côtes** ship skirting the coast; **b. le lit/les draps** to tuck in the bedclothes/the sheets; **b. qn (dans son lit)** to tuck sb in *or* up **2** *Naut (navire) (de bois)* to plank; *(de fer)* to plate **3** *(avirons)* to ship **4** *(voile)* to haul taut

bordereau, -eaux [bɔrdəro] **NM** *(formulaire)* form; *Com* statement; *(de marchandises)* invoice, account; *(dans un devis)* list, schedule

▸▸ *Com* **b. d'achat** inventory of purchases; *Compta* **b. de caisse** cash statement; *Com* **b. de chargement** cargo list; *Compta* **b. de codification** accounts coding sheet/form; *Compta* **b. de crédit** credit note; **b. de débit** debit note; *Banque* **b. d'encaissement** pay-in slip; *Com* **b. d'escompte** list of bills for discount; *Com* **b. d'expédition** *ou* **d'envoi** dispatch note; *Compta* **b. d'imputation** accounting entry sheet/form; *Com* **b. de livraison** delivery note; **b. de paie** wage slip, salary advice; **b. de(s) prix** price list; *Banque* **b. de remboursement** withdrawal slip; *Banque* **b. de remise (d'espèces** *ou* **de chèques)** pay-in *or* paying-in slip; **b. de réservations** reservation sheet; *Compta* **b. de saisie** accounting input sheet/form, record form; **b. de salaire** wage slip, salary advice; *(liste des salaires payés)* wages sheet; *Banque* **b. de versement** paying-in slip

bordure [bɔrdyr] **NF 1** *(bord)* edge; *(d'un vêtement)* border, edge; *(d'un chapeau)* binding; *(de gant)* welt; *Tricot* band; **la b. du trottoir** the kerb, *Am* the curb; **papier à b. noire** black-edged paper; **la banlieue se développe en b. de la ville** suburbs grow up around the edge of the town; **la maison est en b. de route** the house is by *or* at the roadside; **hôtel en b. de mer** seaside hotel, hotel by the sea **2** *(d'un miroir, d'un tableau etc)* frame, surround **3** *Typ, Ordinat (de paragraphe, de cellule)* border

bordurette [bɔrdyrɛt] **NF** = kerb separating a bus lane from the rest of the roadway

bore [bɔr] **NM** *Chimie* boron

boréal, -ale, -aux, -ales [bɔreal, -o] **ADJ** boreal, north(ern)

borgne [bɔrɲ] **ADJ 1** *(personne)* one-eyed, blind in one eye; *Tech* **trou b.** recessed hole; **mur b.** blind wall; **fenêtre b.** obstructed window **2** *Fig (maison, rue etc)* disreputable, shady

N 1 *(personne)* one-eyed man/woman **2** *Vulg* **étrangler le b.** *(se masturber)* to bang *or Br* bash the bishop

borique [bɔrik] **ADJ** *Chimie (acide)* boric, boracic

boriqué [bɔrike] **ADJ** *Pharm* **pommade boriquée** boracic ointment; **compresse en coton b.** boracic lint compress

bornage [bɔrnaʒ] **NM** *(des limites d'un terrain)* demarcation, marking out; **pierre de b.** boundary stone

borne [bɔrn] **NF 1** *(limite)* boundary marker; *(pierre)* boundary stone; *Fam (kilomètre)* kilometre, *Am* kilometer; **b. kilométrique** kilometre marker, ≃ milestone; *Fig* **il était**

planté là comme une b. he stood there as if he had taken root; *Fam* **il y a 200 bornes entre les deux villes** the two towns are 200 kilometres apart; **bornes** *(d'un royaume, du savoir etc)* boundaries, limits, bounds; **dépasser toutes les bornes** to go too far; **sans bornes** boundless, limitless; **une joie sans bornes** boundless happiness; **il n'y a pas de bornes à la vanité humaine** human vanity knows no bounds **2** *Élec* terminal; **b. de mise à la terre** *ou* **de masse** earth *or Am* ground terminal

▸▸ *Naut* **b. d'amarrage** *(d'un quai)* bollard; **b. d'incendie** (fire) hydrant

borné [bɔrne] **ADJ** *(intelligence)* limited, restricted; *(esprit)* narrow; *(personne)* narrow-minded

borne-fontaine, *pl* **bornes-fontaines NF 1** *(fontaine)* (public) drinking fountain **2** *Can (bouche d'incendie)* (fire) hydrant

borner [bɔrne] **VT** *(terrain)* to mark out, to mark the boundary of, to demarcate; *Fig (vue, pouvoir, ambition, désirs, enquête etc)* to limit, to restrict (**à** to); **b. une route** to set up kilometre markers along a road; **le chemin qui borne la forêt** the path bordering the forest; **les pays qui bornent la France à l'est** the countries that border France in the east *or* that form France's eastern border

VPR se borner 1 *(d'une personne)* to restrict *or* limit oneself (**à** to); **je me borne au strict nécessaire** I restrict *or* limit myself to the absolute essentials; **se b. à faire qch** to limit *or* restrict oneself to doing sth **2** *(des choses)* to be limited, to be restricted, to be confined (**à qch** to sth); **toute leur science se borne à cela** this is the (full) extent of their knowledge; **voici à quoi se borne son raisonnement** this is what his argument comes down to *or* boils down to; **ses visites se bornent à quelques jours** his visits are never any longer than a few days

borsalino [bɔrsalino] **NM** fedora

bortch [bɔrtʃ] **NM** *Culin* borsch(t), bortsch

bosco [bɔsko] **NM** *Naut* bosun, boatswain

bosniaque [bɔsnjak, bɔznjak] **ADJ** Bosnian

N B. Bosnian

Bosnie [bɔsni] **NF** Bosnia; **B.-Herzégovine** Bosnia-Herzegovina

bosnien, -ienne [bɔsnjɛ̃, -jɛn] **ADJ** Bosnian

N B. Bosnian

Bosphore [bɔsfɔr] **NM le B.** the Bosphorus

bosquet [bɔskɛ] **NM** copse, grove, thicket

boss [bɔs] **NM** *Fam* boss; *Fig* **c'est toi le b., après tout** you're the boss *or* you're in charge, after all

bossage [bɔsaʒ] **NM** *Archit* boss

bossa-nova, *pl* **bossas-novas** [bɔsanɔva] **NF** *Mus* bossa nova

bosse [bɔs] **NF 1** *(d'un bossu, d'un chameau etc)* hump; *Fam* **il a roulé sa b. un peu partout** he's knocked about *or* been about a bit **2** *(sur la tête etc)* bump, lump, swelling; *(sur la surface du sol)* bump, unevenness; **se faire une b. en tombant** to fall and get a bump; **la route est pleine de bosses** the road is very bumpy *or* uneven; *Ski* **sauter dans les bosses** to jump moguls; *Fig* **avoir la b. du commerce/des maths** to have a good head for business/maths

bosselage [bɔslaʒ] **NM** embossing

bosseler [bɔsle] **VT** (**je bosselle, n. bosselons; je bossellerai**) **1** *(travailler)* to emboss **2** *(par accident)* to dent, to bash; **casserole toute bosselée** battered saucepan

bosselure [bɔslyr] **NF 1** *(sur l'argenterie)* relief **2** *(de terrain, mur etc)* bumpiness, unevenness

bosser [bɔse] *Fam* **VI** to work

VT *Scol* to bone up on, *Br* to swot up

bossette [bɔsɛt] NF Aut boss

bosseur, -euse [bɔsœr, -øz] N Fam hard worker, slogger

bossoir [bɔswar] NM Naut 1 (pour l'ancre) cathead; (de navire) bow 2 (appareil de levage) davit; **les bras de b.** the davit guys

bossu, -ue [bɔsy] ADJ (personne) hunchbacked; (animal) humped; **tiens-toi droit, tu es complètement b.** straighten up, you're all bent; **tu deviens b.** you're getting a stoop ∎ N hunchback; Fam **rire comme un b.** to laugh one's head off, to split one's sides (laughing)

bossué [bɔsye] ADJ (bouilloire etc) battered; (front) bony

bossuer [bɔsye] VT = **bosseler 2**

boston [bɔstɔ̃] NM 1 Cartes boston 2 (danse) boston

bostonien, -ienne [bɔstɔnjɛ̃, -jɛn] ADJ Bostonian ∎ N **B.** Bostonian

bot [bo] ADJ **pied b.** club foot; (personne) clubfooted person; **main bote** club hand

botanique [bɔtanik] ADJ botanical ∎ NF botany

botaniste [bɔtanist] N botanist

Botswana [bɔtswana] NM Botswana

botte[1] [bɔt] NF (de fleurs) bunch; (de carottes, radis etc) bunch, bundle; (de foin, chanvre) bale, bundle

botte[2] NF (chaussure) (high) boot; **une paire de bottes** a pair of boots; **des bottes en cuir** leather boots; Fig **sous la b. de l'envahisseur/l'ennemi** under the heel of the invader/the enemy; Fig **on entend le bruit des bottes** war is in the air; Géog **la b. de l'Italie** the boot of Italy; Fam **en avoir plein les bottes** to be fed up; Fam **cirer** ou **lécher les bottes de qn** to lick sb's boots; Vulg **il lui a proposé la b.** he asked her straight out to sleep with him
▸▸ **bottes de** ou **en caoutchouc** rubber boots, Br wellingtons, wellington boots, Fam wellies; **bottes de cavalier** ou **de cheval** riding boots; **bottes cuissardes** ou **d'égoutier** waders; **bottes de sept lieues** seven-league boots

botte[3] NF Escrime thrust, lunge, pass; **porter une b.** to thrust, to lunge; Fig **b. secrète** secret weapon

botte[4] NF Scol Fam = students who leave the École Polytechnique with the highest marks; **sortir dans la b.** to be among the best students in one's year

botté [bɔte] NM Can (au football américain) punt

botter [bɔte] VT 1 **b. qn** (le chausser) to put sb's boots on; (le fournir) to supply sb with boots; **être bien botté** to be well shod; **botté de cuir** wearing leather boots; **le Chat botté** Puss in Boots 2 (donner un coup de pied dans) to kick; **b. la balle en touche** (au football) to kick the ball into touch; Fig to dodge the issue; Fam **il lui a botté les fesses** ou **le derrière** he booted him up the backside or gave him a kick up the backside 3 Fam (plaire à) **ça me botte** I like that; **ça m'a vraiment botté de revoir ce film** I really enjoyed seeing that film again; **ça me botte de partir avec vous** I'm really glad or Br Fam chuffed I'm going with you
∎ VI Ftbl Fam to kick the ball
∎ VPR **se botter** to put one's boots on

bottier [bɔtje] NM shoemaker, bootmaker

bottillon [bɔtijɔ̃] NM (de femme) ankle boot

Bottin® [bɔtɛ̃] NM telephone directory, phone book; **être dans le B.** to be in the telephone directory or phone book; **B. mondain** ≃ Who's Who

bottine [bɔtin] NF (de femme) ankle boot; (de bébé) bootee

botulisme [bɔtylism] NM Méd botulism

boubou [bubu] NM bubu, boubou

bouc [buk] NM (billy) goat; (barbe) goatee (beard); **b. émissaire** scapegoat; Fam **puer comme un b., puer le b.** to stink (to high heaven), Br to pong

boucan [bukã] NM Arg row, din, racket; **un b. de tous les diables** the devil of a row; **faire un sacré** ou **du b.** to make or kick up a row or din

boucane [bukan] NF Can smoke

boucané [bukane] ADJ (teint) tanned, weatherbeaten

boucaner [bukane] VT (viande, poisson etc) to smoke, to cure; (la peau de qn) to tan

boucanier [bukanje] NM buccaneer

bouchage [buʃaʒ] NM (d'une conduite etc) blocking (up); (d'une bouteille) corking

bouche [buʃ] NF 1 (de personne) mouth; **avoir/parler la b. pleine** to have/to talk with one's mouth full; **une pipe à la b.** with a pipe in his mouth; **j'ai la b. sèche** my mouth is dry, I've got a dry mouth; **j'ai la b. pâteuse** my tongue is coated; **garder qch pour la bonne b.** to save sth until last; **cela fait venir l'eau à la b.** it makes your mouth water; Fig **faire la fine b.** to be fussy or choosy; **dire qch la b. en cœur** to say sth with a simper; **embrasser qn à pleine b.** to kiss sb passionately; **elle l'embrasse sur la b.** she kisses him on the mouth or lips; **manger à pleine b.** to eat greedily, to gobble one's food; **provisions de b.** food; **dépenses de b.** expenditure on food, money spent on food; **c'est une fine b.** he's a gourmet; **avoir une douzaine de bouches à nourrir** to have a dozen mouths to feed; **les bouches inutiles** unproductive people; **elle n'osait pas ouvrir la b.** she didn't dare open her mouth; **je l'ai appris de sa propre b.** I had it from his own lips; Fig **ôter** ou **enlever le pain de la b. de qn** to take the bread from sb's mouth; **son nom est dans toutes les bouches** everyone's talking about him, his name is on everyone's lips; **elle n'a que ce mot à la b.** that's all she ever says; **demeurer** ou **rester b.** close to remain silent, to hold one's tongue; **b. cousue!** not a word!, mum's the word!, don't breathe a word (of it)!; Arg **ta b.!** shut your mouth!, shut up!; Fam **il en avait la b. pleine** ou **plein la b.** he was full of it, he couldn't talk of anything else; **de b. à oreille** by word of mouth; (officieusement) off the record, unofficially; **la nouvelle est passée de b. en b.** the news went or did the rounds, the news went round or circulated 2 (de cheval, de poisson etc) mouth; **cheval sans b.** ou **fort en b.** hard-mouthed horse; **cheval à la b. chatouilleuse** tender-mouthed horse 3 (d'une rivière, d'un cratère, d'un puits, d'un four etc) mouth; (d'un fusil, d'un canon) muzzle
▸▸ Constr etc **b. d'accès** (d'un égout) manhole; **b. d'aération** air vent; **b. de chaleur** hot air vent; **b. d'eau** hydrant; **b. d'égout** manhole; **b. d'incendie** fire hydrant, Am fireplug; **b. de métro** underground or Am subway entrance

bouché [buʃe] ADJ 1 (conduite etc) blocked; **j'ai le nez b.** my nose is blocked, my nose is stuffed up; **j'ai les oreilles bouchées** my ears are blocked up; Fig **avoir l'esprit b., être b.** to be dense or thick; **être b. à l'émeri** to be a complete moron; **cette voie est bouchée** this is a dead-end job; **temps b.** cloudy or overcast weather 2 **cidre b.** bottled cider

bouche-à-bouche NM INV mouth-to-mouth resuscitation; Br kiss of life; **pratiquer** ou **faire le b. à un blessé** to give an injured person mouth-to-mouth resuscitation or the kiss of life

bouchée [buʃe] NF 1 (quantité) mouthful; **juste une b. pour goûter** just a mouthful to taste; Fig **acheter qch pour une b. de pain** to buy sth for a song or for next to nothing; **ne faire qu'une b. d'un mets** to polish off a dish quickly; Fig **ne faire qu'une b. de qn/qch** to make short work of sb/sth; Fig **mettre les bouchées doubles** to really get a move on, to really get going 2 Culin titbit; **b. (au chocolat)** chocolate; **b. à la reine** chicken vol-au-vent

boucher[1] [buʃe] VT (fente, trou) to fill up or in, to stop (up); (conduite, fenêtre etc) to block (up); (vue) to block; (bouteille) to cork; Fig **cela servira à b. un trou** that will do as a stopgap, that will tide us/them/etc over; **j'ai l'impression d'être là uniquement pour b. un trou** I have the feeling I'm there just as a stopgap or a fill-in; **b. un creux** (à l'estomac) to fill a hole; **b. le passage à qn** to block sb's way, to stand in sb's way; **ta voiture bouche le passage** your car is in the way; **pousse-toi, tu me bouches la vue** move over, you're blocking my view; Fam **elle/ça m'en a bouché un coin** she/that shut me up, she/that took the wind out of my sails
∎ VPR **se boucher** (d'une conduite) to get blocked (up) or clogged (up); **se b. le nez** to hold one's nose; **se b. les oreilles** to put one's fingers in one's ears; Fig to refuse to listen; **se b. les yeux** to put one's hands over one's eyes

boucher[2] NM aussi Fig butcher

bouchère [buʃɛr] NF (woman) butcher; (épouse du boucher) butcher's wife

boucherie [buʃri] NF (boutique) butcher's (shop); (activité) butchery; Fig (massacre) butchery, slaughter; **b. chevaline** horse butcher's (shop); **animaux de b.** animals for slaughter; Fig **ce fut une vraie b.** it was a real slaughter or bloodbath

bouche-trou, pl **bouche-trous** NM Fam stopgap, fill-in, stand-in; Journ, Radio, TV filler; **servir de b.** to act as a stopgap or fill-in or stand-in

bouchon [buʃɔ̃] NM 1 (d'une bouteille de limonade, d'un tube de colle etc) cap, top; (d'un tonneau) stopper, plug, bung; **b. (de liège)** cork; **vin qui sent le b.** corked wine; **b. de verre** glass stopper; **b. à l'émeri** ground(-glass) stopper
2 (embouteillage) (traffic) hold-up, traffic jam; **il y a un b. sur la Nationale 7** there's a hold-up or traffic jam on the N7; **trois kilomètres de b.** a three-kilometre tailback
3 Pêche (d'une ligne) float, bob
4 (de paille) wisp
5 Région (petit restaurant) **b. (lyonnais)** = small restaurant serving specialities of Lyons
6 **tu pousses le b. un peu loin** you're going a bit too far
▸▸ **b. antivol** anti-theft cap; Aut **b. de pressurisation** pressure cap; Aut **b. de radiateur** radiator cap; Aut **b. de remplissage** filler plug or cap; Aut **b. de réservoir** fuel cap; Tech **b. de trop plein** ou **de vidange** drain(ing) plug

bouchonné [buʃɔne] ADJ corked

bouchonner [buʃɔne] VI Aut Fam **ça risque de b. sur l'autoroute** there's a risk of hold-ups or congestion on the motorway; **ça bouchonne à partir d'Évreux** traffic is at a standstill from Évreux onwards
∎ VT (cheval) to rub down

bouchot [buʃo] NM mussel bank or bed or farm

bouclage [buklaʒ] NM 1 Fam (de prisonnier etc) imprisonment, locking up 2 (d'un quartier etc) surrounding, sealing off, cordoning off 3 Ordinat looping; (acoustique) (audio) feedback, howl-round; **b. acoustique** acoustic feedback 4 Typ (d'un journal) putting to bed, edition time

boucle [bukl] NF **1** *(de ceinture, chaussure, harnais etc)* buckle
2 *(de ruban, de ficelle, de cordage, d'une rivière, d'une route), Aviat* loop; **faire une b. pour retourner à …** to loop back to …; **b. à nœud coulant** running loop; **décrire de nombreuses boucles** *(d'une rivière)* to meander; **la Seine fait des boucles avant d'arriver à Rouen** the Seine twists and turns before it gets to Rouen
3 *(anneau)* ring; **b. de rideau** curtain ring
4 *(de cheveux)* curl, ringlet, lock
5 *Sport* lap; **la Grande boucle** the Tour de France
6 *TV, Cin* dialogue loop, film loop
7 *Ordinat* **b. d'attente** wait loop; **b. de bande** tape loop; **b. sans fin** endless loop
▸▸ *TV, Cin* **b. de dialogue** dialogue *or* tape loop; *Tél* **b. locale** local loop; **b. locale radio** wireless local loop; **Boucle d'or** Goldilocks; **b. d'oreille** earring

bouclé [bukle] ADJ *(cheveux)* curly; *(personne)* curly-haired; *Ordinat* **système b.** looped system

bouclement [bukləmɑ̃] NM **1** *(de taureau, porc)* ringing **2** *Suisse (des comptes, d'un budget)* closing

boucler [bukle] VT **1** *(ceinture etc)* to buckle, to fasten; *(chambre, maison etc)* to lock (up); **b. sa valise** to fasten one's suitcase; *(se préparer à partir)* to pack one's bags; *Aut* **b. sa ceinture** to put on *or* fasten one's belt, to belt up; *Fam* **b. une affaire** to finish off *or* settle a matter; *Bourse* **b. une position** to close (out) a position; **il a du mal à b. ses fins de mois** he finds it hard to make ends meet at the end of the month; *Fam* **boucle-la!** belt up!, shut up!; *Typ* **b. une édition** *ou* **un journal** to put a newspaper to bed; *Journ* **b. un sujet** to file a story; **b. les comptes** to close the books
2 b. la boucle *Aviat* to loop the loop; *Fig* to come full circle; **et voilà, la boucle est bouclée** and so we/they/*etc* come full circle
3 *Fam (prisonnier etc)* to lock up, *Fam* to bang up
4 *(quartier etc)* to surround, to seal off, to cordon off
5 *Sport (adversaire)* to lap
VI **1** *(des cheveux)* to curl, to be curly; **ses cheveux bouclent quand il pleut** her hair goes curly when it rains **2** *Ordinat* to get stuck in a loop, to loop round and round
VPR **se boucler 1 se b. chez soi** to shut oneself away **2** *Fam* **se la b.** to keep quiet **3** *Ordinat (lignes)* to wrap

bouclette [buklɛt] NF **1** *(de cheveux)* small curl, ringlet **2** *(de laine, moquette)* curl
ADJ *Tex* **laine b.** bouclé wool

bouclier [buklije] NM **1** *(arme défensive), Constr, Géol* shield; **il lui fit un b. de son corps** he shielded him with his body; *Fig* **on s'attend à une levée de boucliers** an outcry is expected **2** *Aut* bumper; **b. inférieur** undershield
▸▸ **b. atomique** *ou* **nucléaire** nuclear shield; **b. humain** human shield; *Astronaut* **b. thermique** heat shield

Bouddha [buda] N Buddha

bouddhique [budik] ADJ Buddhist

bouddhisme [budism] NM Buddhism

bouddhiste [budist] ADJ, N Buddhist

bouder [bude] VI to sulk; **laisse-le b. dans son coin** leave him to sulk
VT **b. qn/qch** to refuse to have anything to do with sb/sth; **tu me boudes?** aren't you talking to me?; **b. son plaisir** to deny oneself; **il boude la peinture moderne** he's not interested in modern art, he doesn't like modern art; **en été les Parisiens boudent les salles de cinéma** Parisians stay away from *or* don't go to the cinema in summer; **le soleil boudera**

la plus grande partie du pays most of the country won't see any sun
VPR **se bouder** not to talk to each other, to refuse to have anything to do with each other

bouderie [budri] NF *(état)* sulkiness; *(action)* sulk, fit of the sulks; **j'en ai marre de tes bouderies!** I'm fed up with your sulking!

boudeur, -euse [budœr, -øz] ADJ sulky, sullen
N sulky person
NF **boudeuse** *(siège)* courting couch

boudin [budɛ̃] NM **1** *Culin* **b. (noir)** black pudding, *Am* blood sausage; **b. blanc** white pudding; *Fam* **s'en aller en eau de b.** *(d'un projet, d'une démarche etc)* to go to pot *or* down the drain *or* down the tubes **2** *Fam* **boudins** *(doigts)* fat *or* podgy fingers **3** *Fam* **faire du b.** to sulk **4** *Belg (traversin)* bolster **5** *Péj Fam (fille)* fat lump, lump of a girl **6** *Min etc (d'explosif)* sausage; *(de pâte à modeler, terre)* roll; *Naut* **b. gonflable** inflatable fender

boudiné [budine] ADJ **1 b. dans un pantalon trop étroit** bursting *or* bulging out of a tight pair of trousers; **je suis complètement b. dans cette jupe** I'm bursting out all over in this skirt **2** *(doigts)* podgy, fat

boudiner [budine] VT **1** *Tex* to rove, to slub **2** *Tech (fil de fer)* to coil **3** *Fam* **cette robe me boudine** this dress shows all my bulges, I'm bursting out of this dress
VPR **se boudiner se b. dans ses vêtements** to squeeze into one's clothes

boudoir [budwar] NM **1** *(salon)* boudoir **2** *(biscuit)* sponge finger, *Am* ladyfinger

boue [bu] NF **1** *(terre détrempée)* mud; *Fig* **traîner qn dans la b.** to drag sb through the mud; *Fig* **couvrir qn de b.** to throw *or* sling mud at sb **2** *Constr (pisé)* (building) clay **3** *(vase)* sludge, sediment; *(dans une rivière etc)* silt; *(de l'océan)* ooze; **bain de b.** mud bath; **boues activées** radioactive mud; *(épuration des eaux)* activated sludge

bouée [bwe] NF *Naut* buoy; *(pour nager)* rubber ring; **b. sonore** sonobuoy; **b. à sifflet** whistling buoy; **b. à cloche** bell buoy; **b. d'amarrage** *ou* **de corps-mort** mooring buoy; **b. lumineuse** light buoy, floating light; **b. de sauvetage** lifebelt, lifebuoy; *Fig* lifeline; **elle se cramponne à cet espoir comme à une b.** she is clinging to this hope like a lifeline

boueux, -euse [buø, -øz] ADJ *(route, bottes etc)* muddy; *(écriture, impression etc)* smudged, blurred
NM *Fam* dustman, *Am* garbage man *or* collector

bouffant [bufɑ̃] ADJ *(manche)* puff(ed); *(jupe)* full; *(pantalon)* baggy; **cheveux bouffants** bouffant hair
NM *(d'une manche)* puff; *(des cheveux)* body

bouffarde [bufard] NF *Fam (pipe)* pipe

bouffe[1] [buf] ADJ *Mus* **opéra b.** opera bouffe, comic opera

bouffe[2] NF *très Fam (aliments)* grub, *Br* nosh; **faire** *ou* **préparer la b.** to make the grub *or* nosh; **c'est l'heure de la b.!** grub('s) up!; **on pourrait se faire une petite b.** we could have a bite together

bouffée [bufe] NF **1** *(de fumée)* puff; *(de parfum)* whiff; *(d'air)* breath; **le souffle du printemps entrait dans la pièce par bouffées** spring air wafted into the room; **tirer une b. de sa pipe** to take a puff at one's pipe; **avoir une b. délirante** to be/become delirious; **b. de chaleur** blast of hot air; *Méd* hot flush, *Am* hot flash **2** *(de colère etc)* (out)burst, fit; *(d'orgueil)* fit

bouffer [bufe] VI **1** *(d'une manche, d'un corsage etc)* to puff out, to balloon out; *(des cheveux)* to have body; **faire b. ses cheveux** to

give body to one's hair **2** *Fam (manger)* to eat; **j'ai bien bouffé** I've had a really good meal; **quand est-ce qu'on bouffe?** when are we eating?
VT *Fam* **1** *(manger)* to eat; **on n'a rien à b.** there's no grub, there's nothing to eat; *Fig* **il ne va pas te b.** he won't eat you; *Fig* **je l'aurais bouffé** I could have killed him; *Fig* **ça me bouffe!** it really gets me!; **elle se laisse b. par ses enfants/son travail** she has no time for anything but her children/work, all her time is taken up by her children/work; **b. de l'essence** *(d'une voiture)* to be heavy on petrol, to be a gas guzzler; **b. des kilomètres** to drive around; **b. du curé** to be very anti-clerical **2** *(argent, économies)* to blow, to run through
VPR **se bouffer** *Fig Fam* **elles se bouffent le nez constamment** they're always bickering, they're always having a go at each other

bouffetance [buftɑ̃s] NF *Fam* grub, *Br* nosh

bouffeur, -euse [bufœr, -øz] N *Fam* guzzler; **un gros b. de viande** a great meat-eater; **c'est un b. de curé** he's very anti-clerical

bouffi [bufi] ADJ *(yeux, visage)* puffy, puffed up, swollen; **b. d'orgueil** puffed up *or* swollen with pride; *Com* **hareng b.** bloater
NM bloater

bouffir [bufir] VT to swell, to puff up
VI *(des yeux, du visage)* to become swollen, to puff up

bouffissure [bufisyr] NF **1** *(des yeux, du visage)* puffiness, swollenness **2** *(du style)* turgidity

bouffon, -onne [bufɔ̃, -ɔn] NM buffoon, clown, fool; *Hist* jester
ADJ farcical, comical

bouffonner [bufɔne] VI *Vieilli* to play *or* act the buffoon

bouffonnerie [bufɔnri] NF *(caractère)* buffoonery; **faire des bouffonneries** to play *or* act the buffoon

bougainvillée [bugɛ̃vile] NF, **bougainvillier** [bugɛ̃vilje] NM bougainvillea

bouge [buʒ] NM *Péj (maison)* hovel, dump; *(bar)* low dive, sleazy bar

bougeoir [buʒwar] NM *(plat)* candleholder; *(haut)* candlestick

bougeotte [buʒɔt] NF *Fam* **avoir la b.** to be fidgety, to have the fidgets; *(voyager sans cesse)* to have itchy feet

bouger [buʒe] (**je bougeai(s), n. bougeons**)
VI *(remuer, se déplacer)* to move; **rester sans b.** to keep still; **ne bougez pas!** don't move!, keep still!; **ne bouge pas (de là)!** stay where you are!, don't move!; *Phot* **ne bougeons plus!** hold it!; **je ne bougerai pas de la terrasse** I won't move from the terrace, I'll stay on the terrace; **je n'ai pas bougé de chez moi pendant deux jours** I haven't been out *or* I've stayed in for two days; *Fig* **ce chemisier ne bouge pas au lavage** *(ne déteint pas)* this blouse doesn't run in the wash; *(ne rétrécit pas)* this blouse doesn't shrink in the wash; **les prix ne bougent pas** prices are (holding) steady; **les ouvriers/étudiants bougent** the workers/students are restless; *Fam* **ça bouge pas mal, dans cette ville** there's a lot going on *or* happening in this town; **tu la connais, c'est difficile de la faire b.** you know what she's like, it's hard to get her to do anything
VT *Fam* to move, to shift; *Fig* **elle n'a pas bougé le petit doigt** she didn't lift a finger
VPR **se bouger** *Fam* to move; **bouge-toi de là!** shift yourself!; **il ne veut pas se b.** he won't shift himself; **bouge-toi un peu, fais quelque chose!** get up off your backside and do something!; **il faut te b. si tu veux avoir le poste** you'll have to get a move on if you want the job

bougie [buʒi] NF **1** *(en cire)* candle; **à la b., aux bougies** by candlelight; *Fam* **tu as mis de la b. partout sur la nappe!** you've got candle wax all over the tablecloth!; *Arch* **ampoule de 100 bougies** 100 watt bulb **2** *Aut* **b. (d'allumage)** spark plug, *Br* sparking plug **3** *Arg (visage)* mug, *Br* dial

bougnat [buɲa] NM *Vieilli* coal-merchant

bougnoul(e) [buɲul] N *Arg (terme injurieux)* Arab, *Br* ≃ wog

bougon, -onne [bugɔ̃, -ɔn] *Fam* N grumbler, grouch
  ADJ grumpy, grouchy

bougonnement [bugɔnmɑ̃] NM *Fam* grumbling, grousing

bougonner [bugɔne] VI *Fam* to grumble, to grouse

bougre [bugr] NM *Fam* **1** *Vieilli (type)* fellow, *Br* chap, *Br* bloke; **le pauvre b.** the poor devil; **ce n'est pas un mauvais b.** he's not a bad sort **2** *b. d'imbécile* damn(ed) fool, *Br* bloody idiot **3** *Arch* **b.!** blast!, damn it!; **b. que ça fait mal!** heck, that hurts! **4** *Vieilli (sodomite)* bugger

bougrement [bugrəmɑ̃] ADV damn(ed); **il fait b. chaud** it's damn(ed) hot

boui-boui, *pl* **bouis-bouis** [bwibwi] NM *Fam* café, *Péj* dingy café

bouillabaisse [bujabɛs] NF *Culin* bouillabaisse *(Provençal fish soup)*

bouillant [bujɑ̃] ADJ **1** *(qui bout)* boiling; *(très chaud)* boiling hot; **il est b.** *(il a de la fièvre)* he's boiling hot **2** *Fig (ardent)* fiery, hot-headed, impetuous; **b. de colère** seething with anger; **b. d'impatience** bursting with impatience

bouille [buj] NF **1** *Arg (visage)* mug, *Br* dial; **il a une bonne b.** he looks a good sort **2** *(pour la vendange)* grape tub

bouilleur [bujœr] NM **1** *(distillateur)* distiller; **b. de cru** home distiller **2** *(d'une chaudière)* water space

bouilli [buji] *Culin* ADJ boiled
  NM boiled meat, *Can* = beans, cabbage, potatoes, salt pork and ham cooked together for several hours; **b. de bœuf** boiled beef

bouillie [buji] NF **1** *(pour bébés)* baby food; *(à base de céréales)* baby cereal; **préparer la b. du bébé** to prepare the baby's food; **réduire en b.** *(légumes, fruits etc)* to mash, to pulp; **b. de légumes** mashed vegetables; **légumes en b.** mushy vegetables; *Fig* **les voitures ont été réduites en b.** the cars were completely smashed up; *Fam* **s'il me provoque, je vais le mettre** *ou* **réduire en b.!** if he provokes me, I'll beat him to a pulp *or* I'll smash his head in! **2** *(pour le papier)* pulp **3** *Agr* **b. bordelaise** Bordeaux mixture

bouillir [bujir] *(prp* **bouillant;** *pp* **bouilli;** *pr ind* **je bous** [bu], **tu bous, il bout,** n. **bouillons,** v. **bouillez, ils bouillent;** *pr sub* **je bouille,** n. **bouillions;** *imp* **bous, bouillons, bouillez;** *impf* **je bouillais;** *p hist* **je bouillis;** *p sub* **je bouillisse;** *fu* **je bouillirai)** VI to boil; **commencer à b.** to come to the boil; **cesser de b.** to go off the boil; **faire b. qch** to boil sth; **faire b. du linge** to boil laundry; *Fam* **cela fera b. la marmite** that will keep the pot boiling; *Fig* **b. de colère** to seethe with anger; **b. d'impatience** to burst with impatience; **cela me fait b.** that makes my blood boil
  VT *Fam (lait, linge etc)* to boil

bouilloire [bujwar] NF kettle

bouillon [bujɔ̃] NM **1** *(d'un liquide en ébullition)* bubble; *(dans un verre)* (air) bubble; *(dans le métal)* blowhole; *(d'une étoffe)* puff; **bouillir à gros bouillons** to boil fast *or* hard; **au premier b.** as soon as it comes to the boil; **le sang sortait à gros bouillons** the blood was gushing out **2** *Culin (liquide)* stock,

bouillon; **b. gras/maigre** meat/clear stock; **b. de légumes** vegetable stock; **b. cube** stock cube; **boire un b.** *(en nageant)* to get a mouthful; *Fam (professionnellement)* to come to grief, to suffer a heavy loss; **b. de culture** culture medium; *Fig* **b. d'onze heures** poisoned drink **3** *Com* **bouillons** *(de livres, de journaux)* returns, unsold copies

bouillonnant [bujɔnɑ̃] ADJ bubbling; *(torrent)* foaming, seething; *Fig* **b. de vie/d'idées** bubbling over with life/ideas

bouillonnement [bujɔnmɑ̃] NM bubbling; *(de torrent)* foaming, seething; *Fig* **b. de la jeunesse** effervescence *or* impetuousness of youth

bouillonner [bujɔne] VI **1** *(d'eau, de soupe, de bain)* to bubble; *(de torrent)* to foam, to seethe; *Fig* **toutes les idées qui bouillonnent dans sa tête** all the ideas seething in his head; **b. de colère** to seethe with anger; **b. d'impatience** to burst with impatience **2** *Com (d'un journal, d'un magazine)* to remain unsold
  VT *Couture* **b. une manche** to gather a sleeve into a puff

bouillotte [bujɔt] NF hot-water bottle

bouillotter [bujɔte] VI to boil gently, to simmer

boul *abrév* boulevard

boulaie [bulɛ] NF birch plantation

boulange [bulɑ̃ʒ] NF *Fam* bakery trade

boulanger [bulɑ̃ʒe] NM baker
  VT (**je boulangeai(s),** n. **boulangeons)** *(farine)* to work

boulangère [bulɑ̃ʒɛr] NF (woman) baker; *(épouse du boulanger)* baker's wife

boulangerie [bulɑ̃ʒri] NF **1** *(industrie)* bakery trade **2** *(lieu de fabrication)* bakery; *(magasin)* baker's (shop), bakery; **b.-pâtisserie** bread and cake shop

boule [bul] NF **1** *(sphère)* ball; *Fam (tête)* nut, head; **b. de poils** *(régurgité)* hairball; **quelle jolie petite b. de poils** *(chaton)* what a lovely fluffy little thing; **arbre en b.** bushy-topped tree; **se rouler** *ou* **se mettre en b.** *(d'un hérisson etc)* to roll *or* curl (itself) up into a ball; *Fam* **se mettre en b.** *(en colère)* to fly off the handle, to go up the wall; *Fam* **elle/ça me met en b.** she/it gets my back up *or* makes me see red; *Fam* **j'ai les nerfs en b.** I'm a bundle of nerves, my nerves are all on edge; **avoir une b. dans la gorge** to have a lump in one's throat; *Fam* **perdre la b.** to go off one's head, to go round the bend; *Fam* **tu perds la b. ou quoi?** are you off your head?; *Can* **sortir qch des boules à mites** to take sth out of mothballs, to dust sth off
  2 *(pour jouer) (aux boules)* bowl; *(au billard, croquet, hockey)* ball; **jouer aux boules** to play bowls; **lancer la b.** to bowl; **la b.** *(au casino)* boule; *Fam* **avoir les boules** to be pissed off; *(avoir peur)* to be wetting oneself; **ça m'a foutu les boules** it pissed me off VOIR GRAMMAIRE A10
  3 *(de machine à écrire)* golf ball; **imprimante à b.** golf-ball printer
  ► ► **b. de billard** billiard ball; *Ordinat* **b. de commande** trackball; **b. de feu** fireball; **b. de naphtaline** mothball; **b. de neige** snowball; *Fig* **faire b. de neige** to snowball; **histoire qui fait b. de neige** story that snowballs; **b. de nerfs** bundle of nerves; *Ordinat* **b. de pointage** pointer; **b. puante** stink bomb; **b. Quiès®** earplug; *Ordinat* **b. de la souris** mouse ball; **b. à thé** tea ball

bouleau, -eaux [bulo] NM (silver) birch (tree); *(bois)* birch (wood)

boule-de-neige, *pl* **boules-de-neige** NF *(fleur)* guelder rose, snowball tree

bouledogue [buldɔg] NM bulldog

bouler [bule] VI to roll; *Fam* **envoyer b. qn** to send sb packing

VT **b. les cornes d'un taureau** to pad a bull's horns

boulet [bulɛ] NM **1** *Mil* **b. (de canon)** cannonball; *Fig* **tirer à boulet(s) rouge(s) sur qn** to go for sb hammer and tongs; **passer comme un b. (de canon)** to hurtle past *or* by **2** *(de bagnard)* ball and chain; *Fig* **c'est un b. qu'il traînera toute sa vie** it will be a millstone round his neck all his life **3** *Com (de charbon)* (coal) nut **4** *(de cheval)* fetlock (joint)

boulette [bulɛt] NF **1** *(de papier etc)* pellet, small ball **2** *Culin* meatball **3** *Vét* poison ball **4** *Fam (gaffe)* **faire une b.** to put one's foot in it, *Br* to drop a brick *or* a clanger

boulevard [bulvar] NM boulevard; **les grands boulevards** *(à Paris)* the main boulevards; **les boulevards extérieurs** *(à Paris)* the outer boulevards; **b. périphérique** orbital road, ring road; **théâtre de b.** light comedies; *Théâtre* **c'est du bon b.** it's good light comedy; *Fig* **ouvrir un b. à qn/qch** to leave the way open for sb/sth

boulevardier, -ière [bulvardje, -jɛr] ADJ *(humour)* facile

bouleversant [bulvɛrsɑ̃] ADJ profoundly *or* deeply moving, shattering; *(pénible, effrayant)* deeply distressing; **c'était b. de vérité** it was a shattering experience; **elle est bouleversante dans le rôle de ...** she gives a profoundly *or* deeply moving performance as ...

bouleversé [bulvɛrse] ADJ shattered; **j'en suis encore tout b.** I still haven't got over it; **d'une voix bouleversée** in a voice full of emotion, in a very emotional voice; **le visage b. par l'émotion** his/her face twisted with emotion

bouleversement [bulvɛrsəmɑ̃] NM **1** *(de projets, de programmes, des habitudes etc)* disruption; **bouleversements politiques/économiques** political/economic upheavals **2** *(d'une personne)* emotion; **son b. était tel que ...** he was in such an emotional state that ...; he was so emotional that ...; **sa voix trahissait un b. bien plus profond que ...** his/her voice betrayed a far deeper emotion than ...

bouleverser [bulvɛrse] VT **1** *(projets, habitudes etc)* to disrupt; *(la vie de qn)* to turn upside down; *(paysage)* to change radically; **ce changement de majorité a bouleversé la vie du pays** this change of government threw the whole country into confusion **2** *(émouvoir)* to shatter; **la nouvelle l'a complètement bouleversé** he was totally shattered by the news; **son accident l'a profondément bouleversé** his accident was something he found it hard to get over; **voir sur l'écran l'enfant qu'elle portait l'a profondément bouleversée** seeing the child she was carrying on the screen was a deeply *or* profoundly moving experience; **la voix de Piaf me bouleverse** I find listening to Piaf's voice a deeply *or* profoundly moving experience

boulier [bulje] NM **1** **b. (compteur)** abacus, counting frame **2** *Billard* scoring board

boulimie [bulimi] NF *Méd* bulimia; **faire de la b.** to eat compulsively; *Fig* **avoir une b. de connaissance** to have an unquenchable thirst for knowledge

boulimique [bulimik] ADJ, N *Méd* bulimic

boulingrin [bulɛ̃grɛ̃] NM lawn *(bordered by hedges etc)*

bouliste [bulist] N bowls player
  ADJ **club b.** bowling club

boulle [bul] NM boul(l)e, buhl; **cabinet de b.** buhl *or* boul(l)e cabinet

boulocher [bulɔʃe] VI *(d'un pull etc)* to pill

boulodrome [bulɔdrom] NM bowling alley

boulon [bulɔ̃] NM bolt; **b. à écrou** screw bolt; **b. à œil** eyebolt; **b. à oreilles** wing bolt; *Aut* **b.**

de roue wheel bolt; **b. mécanique** machine bolt; *Rail* **b. d'attelage** coupling pin; *Fig* **le gouvernement doit à présent resserrer les boulons** the government must now tighten the screws

boulonnage [bulɔnaʒ] NM bolting

boulonner [bulɔne] VT *Tech etc* to bolt
VI *Fam* to slog *or* slave (away)

boulonnerie [bulɔnri] NF 1 *(fabrique)* nut-and-bolt works; *(industrie)* nut-and-bolt trade 2 *(objets)* nuts and bolts

boulot¹, -otte [bulo, -ɔt] ADJ *Fam* dumpy, plump, tubby
N dumpy *or* tubby person

boulot² NM *(travail)* work; *(emploi)* job; **allez, au b.!** come on, (get) to work!; **refaire les peintures dans une maison, c'est du b.** to repaint a whole house is a lot of work *or* is quite a job; **aller au b.** to go to work; **rentrer du b.** to come back from work; *Fig* **c'est toujours moi qui fais le sale b.** it's always me that does the dirty work
ADJ INV **être b. b.** to be a workaholic, to be work-mad

boulotter [bulɔte] *Fam* VT to eat; **il n'y a rien à b.** there's no grub, there's nothing to eat
VI to eat, *Br* to nosh

boum [bum] INT *(explosion)* bang!, boom!; *(chute)* bang!, crash!; *Enf* **bébé a fait b.** baby's had a tumble
NM 1 *(bruit)* bang; **on a entendu un grand b.** we heard a big bang 2 **en plein b.** in full swing
NF *(fête)* party *(for young people)*

boumer [bume] VI *Arg* **ça boume!** things are great!; **ça boume?** how's things?

bouquet¹ [bukɛ] NM 1 *(fleurs)* bunch of flowers, bouquet; *(petit)* posy; *(d'arbres)* clump; *(de plumes)* plume, tuft; **le b. de la mariée** the bride's bouquet 2 *(d'un vin)* bouquet, nose 3 *(d'un feu d'artifice)* final display; *Fam* **ça, c'est le b.!** that takes the biscuit *or Am* cake!, that's the last straw! 4 *TV* **b. (de programmes)** multichannel package; **b. numérique** digital package; **b. satellitaire, b. satellite** satellite package
▸▸ **b. final** final display; *Culin* **b. garni** bouquet garni, mixed herbs

bouquet² NM 1 *(lièvre)* hare; *(lapin mâle)* buck rabbit 2 *(crevette)* prawn

bouquetière [buktjɛr] NF flower seller

bouquetin [buktɛ̃] NM ibex

bouquin¹ [bukɛ̃] NM *Fam (livre)* book

bouquin² NM *(lièvre)* hare; *(lapin mâle)* buck rabbit

bouquiner [bukine] VI *Fam (lire)* to read

bouquiniste [bukinist] N second-hand bookseller

bourbe [burb] NF mud, mire

bourbeux, -euse [burbø, -øz] ADJ muddy, miry

bourbier [burbje] NM bog, quagmire; *Fig* mess; *Fig* **se tirer d'un b.** to get out of a mess

bourbillon [burbijɔ̃] NM *(d'un abcès, d'un furoncle etc)* core

bourbon [burbɔ̃] NM *(whisky)* bourbon

bourdaine [burdɛn] NF black alder

bourde [burd] NF *Fam* 1 *(baliverne)* tall story; **raconter des bourdes à qn** to have *or Am* to put sb on 2 *(faute)* blunder, *Br* boob, boo-boo; **faire une b.** to put one's foot in it, *Br* to drop a brick *or* a clanger

bourdon¹ [burdɔ̃] NM *(bâton)* pilgrim's staff

bourdon² NM 1 *Mus (de cornemuse)* drone; *(d'un orgue)* bourdon stop; *(note)* drone bass 2 *(cloche)* great bell 3 *(insecte)* bumblebee; **faux b.** drone; *Arg* **avoir le b.** to be down (in the dumps)

bourdon³ NM *Typ* omission

bourdonnement [burdɔnmɑ̃] NM *(d'insectes)* buzz(ing), hum(ming); *(d'un moteur)* hum(ming); *Méd* **b. d'oreilles** buzzing *or* ringing in the ears; **avoir des bourdonnements d'oreilles** to have a buzzing *or* ringing in one's ears

bourdonner [burdɔne] VI *(d'insectes)* to buzz, to hum; *(d'une machine, d'un moteur)* to hum; *(des oreilles)* to buzz, to ring

bourg [bur] NM *(gros village)* small market town

bourgade [burgad] NF village, township

bourge [burʒ] *Fam Péj (abrév* **bourgeois)** ADJ middle-class
N middle-class person

bourgeois, -oise [burʒwa, -waz] ADJ 1 *(personne)* middle-class; **la classe bourgeoise** the middle class, the bourgeoisie; **quartier b.** middle-class area; **cuisine bourgeoise** simple *or* family *or* home cooking; **une belle maison bourgeoise** a grand house 2 *Péj (conventionnel)* middle-class, bourgeois, conventional
N 1 middle-class person; **les grands b.** the upper middle class; **les petits b.** the lower middle class; **en b.** in plain *or* civilian clothes 2 *Péj (béotien)* philistine; **chercher à épater le b.** to try to shock the establishment 3 *(roturier)* commoner 4 *Hist (citoyen)* burgess, burgher, citizen 5 *Suisse (citoyen)* citizen; **les b.** the townspeople
NF *Arg* **bourgeoise** *(épouse)* wife; **la bourgeoise** the old lady, the wife, the missus

bourgeoisement [burʒwazmɑ̃] ADV conventionally; **vivre b.** to live comfortably *or* in a middle-class way; *Admin* **occuper b. un local** to occupy premises for residential purposes

bourgeoisie [burʒwazi] NF 1 middle class(es), bourgeoisie; **la haute/petite b.** the upper/lower middle class; **la moyenne b.** the middle class 2 *Hist (d'une ville)* burgesses, citizens, freemen

bourgeon [burʒɔ̃] NM 1 *Bot* bud; **en bourgeons** in bud 2 *Fam Vieilli (bouton)* spot, pimple 3 *Anat* **b. gustatif** taste bud, *Spéc* gustatory bud

bourgeonnement [burʒɔnmɑ̃] NM 1 *Bot* budding; *(saison)* budding time 2 *Méd* granulation

bourgeonner [burʒɔne] VI 1 *Bot* to bud 2 *Fam (avoir des boutons)* to come out in spots 3 *Méd (d'une blessure)* to granulate

bourgmestre [burgmɛstr] NM burgomaster

Bourgogne [burgɔɲ] NF Burgundy
NM **(vin de) b.** Burgundy (wine)

bourgot [burgo] NM *Can* moose caller

bourguignon, -onne [burgiɲɔ̃, -ɔn] ADJ Burgundian; *Culin* **bœuf b.** bœuf bourguignon *(beef and vegetables cooked in red wine)*
NM *Culin* bœuf bourguignon
N **B.** Burgundian

bourlingue [burlɛ̃g] NF *Fam (errance)* knocking about

bourlinguer [burlɛ̃ge] VI 1 *Naut (d'un navire)* to make heavy weather, to labour, *Am* to labor, to toil 2 *(beaucoup naviguer)* to sail the seven seas; **il a bourlingué dans les mers de Chine** he has sailed the China Seas 3 *Fam (beaucoup voyager)* **b. de par le monde** to knock about the world; **il a beaucoup bourlingué** he's knocked about a lot

bourlingueur, -euse [burlɛ̃gœr, -øz] *Fam* ADJ adventurous
N adventurer, rolling stone; **c'est un grand b.** he's knocked about a bit

bourrache [buraʃ] NF *(plante)* borage

bourrade [burad] NF push, shove; *(dans le dos etc)* thump, slap; *(dans les côtes)* dig, poke, prod

bourrage [buraʒ] NM 1 *(d'une chaise, d'un coussin etc)* stuffing, padding; *(d'un placard, d'un sac etc)* cramming, packing tight; *(d'une pipe avec du tabac)* filling; *(d'une mine, d'une arme à feu etc)* tamping; *(dans une imprimante)* jam; *(répété)* jamming; **b. papier** paper jam, paper blockage 2 *(matériau)* stuffing, filling
▸▸ **b. de crâne** *Fam* eyewash; *surtout Pol (propagande)* brainwashing

bourrasque [burask] NF squall, gust (of wind); **b. de neige** snow flurry; **le vent souffle en b.** the wind is gusting *or* squalling; *Fig* **une b. d'injures** a flurry of insults; *Fig* **elle est passée en b.** she paid a lightning visit; **arriver en b.** to arrive at top speed

bourrasser [burase] VT *Can* to push around, to bully

bourratif, -ive [buratif, -iv] ADJ *Fam (aliment)* stodgy, filling

bourre¹ [bur] NF 1 *(pour rembourrer les chaises etc)* stuffing, padding, filling; *(de coton etc)* waste, fluff; *Bot (des bourgeons)* down, floss; *Tex etc* **b. de soie** floss silk, silk waste 2 *(d'arme à feu)* wad 3 *Arg* **de première b.** first-class, first-rate 4 *Fam* **à la b.** in a rush

bourre² NM *Arg (policier)* cop

bourré [bure] ADJ 1 *(plein)* packed, crammed (**de** with); **b. à craquer** full to bursting; **le coffre est b.** the boot is crammed full; **la tête bourrée de rêves** with his/her head full of dreams; **être b. de complexes** to be one big bundle *or* a mass of complexes; **il est b. d'antibiotiques** he's pumped full of antibiotics; **les kiwis sont bourrés de vitamines** kiwi fruits are packed *or* crammed with vitamins 2 *Arg (ivre)* plastered, smashed; **être complètement b.** to be smashed out of one's mind, to be legless

bourreau, -eaux [buro] NM 1 *(exécuteur)* executioner; *(qui pend)* hangman; *(tortionnaire)* torturer 2 *Fig* tormentor, torturer; **être le b. de qn** to torment *or* torture sb
▸▸ **b. des cœurs** ladykiller; **b. d'enfants** child-beater; **b. de travail** workaholic

bourrée [bure] NF *(danse)* bourrée

bourrelé [burle] ADJ **b. de remords** stricken with remorse

bourrèlement [burɛlmɑ̃] NM *Litt* torment, anguish; *(de remords)* pangs

bourrelet [burlɛ] NM 1 *Fam* **b. (de graisse)** *(au ventre)* spare tyre *or Am* tire, roll of fat 2 *(contre les courants d'air)* weather strip, *Br* draught excluder 3 *(petit coussin)* pad, cushion

bourrelier [burəlje] NM saddler, harness maker

bourrellerie [burɛlri] NF saddlery

bourre-pif, *pl* **bourre-pifs** NM *Fam (coup de poing)* punch on the nose

bourrer [bure] VT 1 *(chaise, coussin etc)* to stuff, to pad; *(placard, sac etc)* to cram, to pack tight; *(pipe)* to fill; **b. une dissertation de références** to stuff *or* cram an essay with references; *Fam* **b. le crâne à qn** to stuff *or* fill sb's head with nonsense; *(d'un professeur)* to stuff *or* fill sb's head with facts; *Pol* to brainwash sb; **on nous bourre le crâne de publicités** we're brainwashed by advertising; *Fam* **b. le mou à qn** to pull the wool over sb's eyes; **b. qn de coups** to beat sb up 2 *(de nourriture)* to fill up; **ne le bourre pas de biscuits** don't fill him up with biscuits 3 *Mil, Min (chargement)* to ram home; *(trou d'explosion, mine)* to stem, to tamp
VI **aliment qui bourre** stodgy *or* filling food; **les bananes, ça bourre** bananas are filling
VPR **se bourrer** 1 *(trop manger)* to stuff oneself, to fill oneself up (**de chocolat** with chocolate)
2 *Fam (se saouler)* to get plastered *or*

smashed; **se b. la gueule** to get smashed out of one's mind, to get legless

bourrette [buʀɛt] NF *Tex* floss (silk)

bourriche [buʀiʃ] NF *(d'huîtres, de gibier etc)* basket, hamper

bourrichon [buʀiʃɔ̃] NM *Fam* **se monter le b.** to get worked up *or* excited, to work oneself up into a state; **monter le b. à qn contre qn** to stir sb up against sb, to set sb against sb

bourricot [buʀiko] NM (small) donkey

bourrin [buʀɛ̃] NM *Fam* **1** *(cheval)* nag **2** *(policier)* cop

bourrique [buʀik] NF *(ânesse)* she ass; *Fam (personne têtue)* pigheaded individual; **faire tourner qn en b.** to drive sb crazy *or* round the bend; **têtu comme une b.** as stubborn as a mule

bourru [buʀy] ADJ surly, gruff, rough

bourse [buʀs] NF **1** *(porte-monnaie)* purse, *Am* coin-purse; **c'est trop cher pour sa b.** it's beyond his means, he can't afford it; **b. bien garnie** well-lined purse; **la b. ou la vie!** your money *or* your life!; **tenir les cordons de la b.** to hold the purse-strings; **sans b. délier** without spending a penny; **faire b. à part** to have separate finances; **faire b. commune** to pool one's money, to share expenses
2 *Anat* **bourses** scrotum; **b. séreuse** bursa
3 *Scol, Univ* **b. (d'études)** grant; **b. de recherche** research grant
4 *Fin* **la B. (des valeurs)** the Stock Exchange, the Stock Market; **la B. monte/est calme** the market is rising/is quiet; **en B.** on the Stock Exchange *or* Stock Market; **valeur cotée en B.** listed *or* quoted share; **jouer à la B.** *ou* **en B.** to play the market, to speculate
▸▸ **b. de commerce** commodities exchange; *Fig* **b. coulisse** unlisted market; **b. de l'emploi** = employment exchange; *Com* **b. de fret** shipping exchange; **b. du travail** *(réunion)* = meeting of local trade unions for the purpose of reaching agreement on how best to defend their interests and provide community services; *(endroit)* = local trade union centre

boursicotage [buʀsikɔtaʒ] NM *Bourse* dabbling on the Stock Market

boursicoter [buʀsikɔte] VI *Bourse* to dabble on the Stock Market

boursicoteur, -euse [buʀsikɔtœʀ, -øz], **boursicotier, -ière** [buʀsikɔtje, -jɛʀ] N *Bourse* small-time speculator

boursier, -ière [buʀsje, -jɛʀ] ADJ **1** *Bourse* **opérations boursières** Stock Exchange *or* Stock Market transactions **2** *Scol, Univ* **étudiant b.** grant holder
N **1** *Scol, Univ* grant holder **2** *Bourse* (Stock Exchange) operator

boursouflage [buʀsuflaʒ] NM *(de la chair, du visage etc)* puffiness; *Fig (du style)* turgidity

boursouflé [buʀsufle] ADJ *(visage, yeux)* swollen, puffy; *(peinture)* blistered; *Fig (style, discours)* turgid

boursouflement [buʀsufləmɑ̃] NM = **boursouflage**

boursoufler [buʀsufle] VT *(visage)* to cause to swell, to puff up; *(peinture)* to blister
VPR **se boursoufler** *(de la peinture)* to blister; *(du visage)* to swell, to puff up

boursouflure [buʀsuflyʀ] NF *(du visage etc)* swelling, puffiness; *(de peinture)* blister, bubbling; *(de pneu)* blister; *Fig (du style, d'un discours)* turgidity

bousculade [buskylad] NF *(agitation)* jostling, pushing and shoving, hustle; *(hâte)* rush; **une b. vers la porte** a rush for the door; **être pris dans la b.** to be caught up in the rush

bousculer [buskyle] VT **1** *(faire tomber)* to knock over; *Fig (habitudes, journée)* to disrupt; **cela va b. vos idées** that'll liven up your ideas **2** *(pousser)* **b. qn** to jostle sb, to bump *or* knock into sb, to knock against sb **3** *(presser)* to rush; **je n'aime pas être bousculé** I don't like being rushed; **il est toujours bousculé** he's always in a rush
VPR **se bousculer** *(d'une foule etc)* to jostle, to push and shove; **les idées se bousculaient dans sa tête** his head was swimming *or* buzzing with ideas; **aux heures de pointe, les voyageurs se bousculent au portillon** in the rush hour, the passengers jostle to get on; **les candidats ne se bousculent pas au portillon** applicants aren't exactly queuing up for the job; *Fig* **ça se bouscule au portillon** he can't get his words out

bouse [buz] NF dung; **b. de vache** cow dung; **une b.** a cowpat

bouseux [buzø] NM *Fam Péj* yokel, bumpkin, *Am* hick

bousier [buzje] NM *(insecte)* dung beetle

bousillage [buzijaʒ] NM **1** *Fam (d'un travail)* botching, bungling; *(résultat)* botch(-up), bungle **2** *Constr* cob, daub

bousiller [buzije] *Fam* VT *(travail)* to botch (up), to bungle; *(voiture, vélo, appareil photo etc)* to wreck; **b. qn** to bump sb off, to do sb in; **b. sa santé** to ruin one's health
VPR **se bousiller se b. la santé** to ruin one's health

bousilleur, -euse [buzijœʀ, -øz] N *Fam* botcher, bungler

boussole [busɔl] NF compass; **b. de marine** mariner's compass; **b. de poche** pocket compass; *Fam* **perdre la b.** to go off one's head

boustifaille [bustifaj] NF *Arg* grub, *Br* nosh

BOUT [bu] NM **1** *(extrémité)* end; **assembler deux planches b. à b.** to join two planks end to end *or* end on; **l'autre b.** *(de la rue, de la ville etc)* the other *or* far end; **de b. en b.** *(reprendre un travail etc)* from start to finish; *Naut* from stem to stern; **d'un b. à l'autre** *(dans l'espace)* from one end to the other; *(dans le temps)* from beginning to end; **lire un livre d'un b. à l'autre** to read a book from cover to cover *or* from start to finish; **d'un b. à l'autre de son œuvre** throughout his works, all through his works; **d'un b. de la semaine/de l'année à l'autre** from one end of the week/year to the next; *Fam* **il n'y a personne à l'autre b.** *(au téléphone)* there's nobody on the other end; *Fig* **je n'en vois pas le b.** I'm nowhere near the end of it; *Fig* **je n'arrive pas à joindre les deux bouts** I can't make ends meet; **au b. du compte** after all, at the end of the day, when all's said and done; **au b. de la rue** at the end/bottom/top of the street; **aller au b. du monde** to go to the ends of the earth; *Fam* **c'est le b. du monde** *(d'un lieu)* it's a godforsaken hole *or* a dump; **Roubaix, ce n'est tout de même pas le b. du monde!** it's not as though Roubaix is miles from anywhere!; **au b. d'une heure/de quelques jours** after an hour/a few days; **au b. d'un moment** after a while; **c'est ce qu'elle répète à tout b. de champ** that's what she keeps saying all the time *or* at every opportunity; **nous ne sommes pas encore au b.** we're not through yet, we're not out of the wood(s) yet; **il n'est pas au b. de ses peines** his troubles aren't over yet; **jusqu'au b.** to the (very) end; **aller jusqu'au b.** to go the whole way *or Fam* hog; *(d'un projet etc)* to see it through; *(avoir des rapports sexuels)* to go the whole way; **aller jusqu'au b. de ses idées** to follow one's ideas through (to their logical conclusion); **il est au b. de sa carrière** he's reached *or* he's at the end of his career; **être à b.** to be exhausted; *Fam* to be all in; **pousser** *ou* **mettre qn à b.** to exasperate sb, *Fam*

to drive sb round the bend; **à b. de patience** at the end of one's patience *or* tether; **être à b. de ressources** *(n'avoir plus rien à dire)* to have run out of ideas *or* suggestions; *(n'avoir plus d'argent)* to have run out of money *or* resources; **être à b. d'arguments** to have run out of arguments; **il est à b. de forces** he has no strength left (in him); **être au b. du rouleau** *(n'en pouvoir plus)* to be at the end of one's tether; *(n'avoir plus d'argent)* to have run out of money; **venir à b. de qch** *(achever)* to get through sth; **venir à b. de la résistance/l'opposition de qn** to break down *or* overcome sb's resistance/opposition; **venir à b. d'une épidémie** to stamp out an epidemic
2 *(pointe)* tip, end; *(de tuyau de pipe)* mouthpiece; *(de fusil)* muzzle; *(d'une canne)* ferrule; **b. du doigt/du nez/de la langue** tip *or* end of the finger/nose/tongue; **avoir un mot sur le b. de la langue** to have a word on the tip of one's tongue; **b. du sein** *(de femme)* nipple; **à b. de bras** at arm's length; *Fig* **porter une entreprise à b. de bras** to carry a firm; **b. de pied, b. renforcé** toecap; **ciseaux à bouts ronds** round-ended scissors; **b. de l'archet** *(d'un violon)* point of the bow; **à b. portant** point-blank, at point-blank range; *Fig* **tenir le bon b.** to be well on the way to success; *Fam* **elle est diplomate jusqu'au b. des ongles** she's a diplomat to her fingertips; **on ne sait jamais par quel b. le prendre** you never know how to approach *or* tackle him; *Arg* **mettre les bouts** to skedaddle, *Br* to hop it
3 *(morceau) (de ficelle, fromage, pain etc)* bit, piece; **b. de papier/tissu** scrap *or* piece *or* bit of paper/material; **b. de cigarette** cigarette end *or* butt *or* stub; **un b. de jardin/terrasse** a bit of garden/terrace; **un b. de ciel bleu** a patch of blue sky; **elle en connaît un b. sur la question** she knows a thing or two about it; **un tout petit b. de femme** a tiny little (slip of a) woman; **un b. de temps** a little while, some while; **un bon b. de temps** quite a while; **nous avons fait un b. de chemin ensemble** we went part of the way together; *Fig (de deux amants)* we were together for a while; *(de deux étudiants)* we studied together for a while; **nous avons fait un bon b. de chemin** we've come/gone a long way; **pour aller à Paris, cela fait un b. de chemin** it's quite a (long) way to Paris
▸▸ *Rel* **(messe du) b. de l'an** Mass, memorial service *(held on the anniversary of sb's death)*; **b. de chou** small child; **quel adorable b. de chou!** what an adorable child!; *Cin, TV* **b. d'essai** screen test; **b. ferré** *(d'une canne)* ferrule; **b. filtre** *(d'une cigarette)* filter tip; *Élec* **b. mort** *(d'une bobine)* dead end; *Cin, TV* **b. de rôle** walk-on *or* bit part

bout-à-bout, *pl* **bouts-à-bouts** [butabu] NM *Cin, TV* rough cut, rough edit

boutade [butad] NF **1** *(trait d'esprit)* joke, jest **2** *(caprice)* whim, caprice

bout-dehors, *pl* **bouts-dehors** NM *Naut* boom; **b. de foc** jib boom

boute-en-train [butɑ̃tʀɛ̃] NM INV live wire; **c'est le b. de la soirée** he's the life and soul of the party; **c'est le b. de la classe** he's the bright spark of the class

bouteille [butɛj] NF bottle; *(contenu)* bottle(ful); **panier à bouteilles** bottle carrier; **nous allons boire une b.** we'll have a bottle (of wine) together; **c'est une bonne b.** it's a good drop (of wine); **mettre du vin en bouteilles** to bottle wine; **mise en bouteilles** bottling; *Fam* **aimer la b.** to like one's drink, to be fond of the bottle; **avoir dix ans de b.** *(d'un vin)* to be ten years old; *Fam* **prendre de la b.** to be getting on a bit, to be getting long in the tooth; **la b. de gaz est vide** the gas cylinder is empty; **acheter une b. de**

gaz/butane to buy a cylinder of gas/butane ▸▸ b. isolante vacuum flask, Thermos® (flask); *Élec* b. de Leyde Leyden jar, electric jar; b. d'oxygène cylinder of oxygen; b. Thermos® vacuum flask,Thermos® (flask)

bouter [bute] VT 1 *Arch* b. l'ennemi hors de France to drive the enemy out of France 2 *Belg, Suisse* b. le feu à qch to set fire to sth, to set sth on fire

bouteur [butœr] NM *Constr* bulldozer

boutiquage [butikaʒ] NM = system of having a range of separate staffed counters within a single retail outlet

boutiquaire [butikɛr] NM shopping area

boutique [butik] NF shop, *surtout Am* store; *Fig Péj (lieu)* dump, hole; b. de mode clothes *or* fashion shop, boutique; b. de vêtements/ de produits diététiques clothes/health food shop; b. de cadeaux gift shop; b. de souvenirs souvenir shop; b. hors taxe duty-free shop, tax-free shop; tenir b. to run a shop; fermer b. to shut up shop; parler b. to talk shop; *Fig* être de la b. to be in the same business; *Fam* j'en ai assez de cette sale b.! I'm sick of this rotten dump *or* hole!; *Fam* il est temps que je change de b. it's time I had a change of job; robe b. designer dress; confection b. boutique-styled

boutiquier, -ière [butikje, -jɛr] NM shopkeeper, *Am* storekeeper

boutoir [butwar] NM *(d'un sanglier etc)* snout; *Fig* coup de b. attack (contre on)

bouton [butɔ̃] NM 1 *(de fleur)* bud; b. de rose rosebud; en b. in bud, budding

2 *(sur un vêtement)* button; b. à queue shank button; b. de plastron de chemise stud; b. de col collar stud

3 *(d'une porte, d'une radio etc)* knob; *Ordinat* push button; *(qu'on pousse)* (push) button; *(d'un fleuret)* button; b. (électrique) switch; appuyer sur le b. to press the button; b. de sonnerie *ou* de sonnette *ou* d'appel bellpush

4 *(sur le visage)* spot, pimple; *(à la suite d'une maladie)* spot; b. d'acné spot caused by acne; avoir des boutons to have spots, to be spotty; *Fig* ça me donne des boutons it brings me out in a rash ▸▸ b. d'arrêt *(d'alimentation électrique)* off switch; *Ordinat (pour interrompre le téléchargement)* stop button; b. de contraste contrast button; b. de contrôle de luminosité brightness control button; *Ordinat* b. de défilement scroll button; boutons de manchette cufflinks; b. de marche on switch; b. marche-arrêt on/off switch, power switch; *Ordinat* b. de navigation navigation button; *Ordinat* b. d'option, b. radio radio button; b. de réglage du contraste contrast control button; b. de réglage (du volume) volume control (knob); *Ordinat* b. de réinitialisation reset button; *Ordinat* b. de souris mouse button; *Ordinat* b. de turbo turbo button

bouton-d'or, *pl* **boutons-d'or** NM *(plante)* buttercup

boutonnage [butɔnaʒ] NM buttoning (up); b. devant/dans le dos front/back fastening; b. à droite/gauche right/left buttoning; veste avec double b. double-buttoning jacket

boutonner [butɔne] VT 1 *(manteau etc)* to button (up), to fasten (up), to do up 2 *Escrime (adversaire)* to button

VPR se boutonner *(d'un manteau etc)* to button (up); *Fam* il a encore du mal à se b. tout seul he still has difficulty doing up his buttons by himself; la robe se boutonne par derrière the dress buttons (up) at the back

boutonneux, -euse [butɔnø, -øz] ADJ *(adolescent, visage etc)* spotty, pimply

boutonnière [butɔnjɛr] NF 1 *(de vêtement)* buttonhole; faire une b. to make a buttonhole; porter une fleur à la b. to wear a buttonhole *or Am* boutonnière; porter une médaille à la b. to wear a medal on one's lapel 2 *Chir* buttonhole; faire une b. à qn to make a buttonhole in sb; *Fig (avec une épée etc)* to pink sb

bouton-poussoir, *pl* **boutons-poussoir** NM push button

bouton-pression, *pl* **boutons-pression** NM press stud, *Am* snap fastener, *Br Fam* popper

bouturage [butyraʒ] NM *(de plantes)* propagation by cuttings

bouture [butyr] NF cutting; faire des boutures to take cuttings

bouturer [butyre] VI *(des plantes)* to make suckers

VT to propagate by cuttings

bouvet [buvɛ] NM grooving plane

bouvier, -ière [buvje, -jɛr] N *(pour les bœufs)* cowherd, cowhand; *(pour les troupeaux)* drover

NM *(chien)* sheepdog

bouvillon [buvijɔ̃] NM steer, young bullock

bouvreuil [buvrœj] NM bullfinch

bovarysme [bɔvarism] NM = tendency to romanticize reality as a way of escaping from the limitations of one's own existence

bovidés [bɔvide] NMPL *Zool* bovids, *Spéc* Bovidae

bovin [bɔvɛ̃] ADJ *(race, regard etc)* bovine; un air b. a bovine look

NMPL bovins bovines, cattle

bovinés [bɔvine] NMPL *Zool* bovines, cattle

bowling [buliŋ] NM 1 *(jeu)* (tenpin) bowling 2 *(endroit)* (tenpin) bowling alley

box[1], *pl* **boxes** [bɔks] NM 1 *(dans un dortoir)* cubicle; *Jur* b. des accusés dock 2 *Aut* lockup (garage) 3 *(dans une étable)* stall, *Br* loose box

box[2], **box-calf** [bɔks(kalf)] NM *(cuir)* box calf

boxe [bɔks] NF boxing; faire de la b. to box; gants/match de b. boxing gloves/match; b. anglaise boxing; b. française kick boxing

boxer[1] [bɔkse] VI to box; b. contre qn to box against *or* fight sb

VT to box against, to fight; *Fam (frapper)* to punch up

boxer[2] [bɔksœr] NM *(chien)* boxer (dog)

boxer[3] [bɔksœr] NM *(short)* shorts

boxer[4] [bɔksɛr] NM *(moteur)* boxer engine

boxeur [bɔksœr] NM boxer

box-office, *pl* **box-offices** [bɔksɔfis] NM box office; *(recettes)* box-office takings; une pièce/un film/un chanteur en tête du b. a box-office hit

boxon [bɔksɔ̃] NM *Fam* brothel; *Fig* quel b.! what a mess!; mettre le b. dans qch to make a mess of sth

boy [bɔj] NM *(domestique)* boy

boyau, -aux [bwajo] NM 1 *(d'animal)* gut, bowel; (corde de) b. (cat)gut; boisson à tordre les boyaux *(fort)* drink that burns the throat; *(de mauvaise qualité)* rotgut 2 *(tuyau)* hose(pipe); *(de vélo)* tubular tyre *or Am* tire 3 *(allée)* narrow alley(way); *Min* narrow gallery; *Mil* communication trench

boycott(age) [bɔjkɔt(aʒ)] NM boycott(ing)

boycotter [bɔjkɔte] VT to boycott

boycotteur, -euse [bɔjkɔtœr, -øz] N boycotter

boy-scout, *pl* **boy-scouts** [bɔjskut] NM *Vieilli* boy scout; *Fig* mentalité de b. boy-scout mentality

BP [bepe] NF *(abrév* boîte postale*)* PO Box; **BP** 5000 = consumer information/protection body

NM *(abrév* brevet professionnel*)* vocational qualification; **BP de barman** vocational qualification in bar work; **BP de cuisinier** vocational qualification in catering

BPA [bepea] NM *Fin (abrév* bénéfice par action*)* EPS

BPF [bepeɛf] *Fin Anciennement (abrév* bon pour francs*) (sur chèque)* = abbreviation printed on cheques and invoices before the amount to be written in figures

bpp [bepepe] NMPL *Ordinat (abrév* bits par pouce*)* bpi

bps [bepeɛs] NMPL *Ordinat (abrév* bits par seconde*)* bps

brabançon, -onne [brabɑ̃sɔ̃, -ɔn] ADJ of/ from Brabant

N B. *(natif)* native of Brabant; *(habitant)* inhabitant of Brabant

NF la Brabançonne the Belgian national anthem

Brabant [brabɑ̃] NM 1 *Géog* Brabant 2 *Agr* b. all-metal wheel plough; charrue à double b. two-furrow plough

bracelet [braslɛ] NM 1 bracelet; *(rigide)* bangle; *(de montre)* strap, bracelet, band; b. de force (leather) wrist-band; b. électronique *ou* de cheville *ou* de détention electronic tag 2 *Fam* bracelets *(menottes)* cuffs, bracelets 3 *(lien)* band

bracelet-montre, *pl* **bracelets-montres** NM wristwatch

brachial, -iale, -iaux, -iales [brakjal, -jo] ADJ *Anat (artère etc)* brachial

brachiopode [brakjɔpɔd] NM *(mollusque)* brachiopod

brachycéphale [brakisefal] ADJ, N brachycephalic

braconnage [brakɔnaʒ] NM poaching

braconner [brakɔne] VI to poach

braconnier [brakɔnje] NM poacher

bractée [brakte] NF *Bot* bract

bradé [brade] ADJ cut-price

brader [brade] VT *(marchandises)* to sell off; *(à prix réduits)* to sell dirt cheap *or* at knockdown prices

braderie [bradri] NF *(foire)* ≃ jumble sale, *Am* ≃ rummage sale; *(magasin)* cut-price *or* discount store; *(liquidation)* clearance sale

braguette [bragɛt] NF *(de pantalon)* flies, fly

brahmane [braman] NM Brahman, Brahmin

brahmanisme [bramanism] NM Brahmanism, Brahminism

brahmine [bramin] NF Brahmani

brai [brɛ] NM pitch, tar

braillard, -arde [brajar, -ard] ADJ *Fam (foule etc)* yelling, noisy; *(enfant)* howling, bawling

N bawler; petit b. noisy brat

braille [braj] NM Braille; lire en b. to read Braille

braillement [brajmɑ̃] NM yelling; *(d'enfant)* howling, bawling; pourquoi ces braillements? *(d'un nourrisson)* what's all the howling about?

brailler [braje] VI to yell; *(d'un enfant)* to howl, to bawl; faire b. sa télévision to have one's television blaring (out)

VT *(chanson)* to bawl (out); *(slogan)* to chant

brailleur, -euse [brajœr, -øz] ADJ, N *Fam* = braillard

braiment [bramɑ̃] NM *(d'un âne)* bray(ing)

brainstorming [brɛnstɔrmiŋ] NM brainstorming; un b. a brainstorming session

brain-trust, *pl* **brain-trusts** [brɛntrœst] NM brains trust

braire [brɛr] VI *(pr ind* il brait, ils braient; *fu* il braira, ils brairont; *cond* il brairait, ils braieraient*)* 1 *(d'un âne)* to bray 2 *Fam* = brailler

braise [brɛz] NF **1** *(charbons)* (glowing) embers; *(charbon de bois)* (live) charcoal; **cuire qch sur/sous la b.** to cook sth over/in the embers (of a fire); **des yeux de b.** glowing or burning eyes; *Fig* **être sur la b.** to be on tenterhooks **2** *Arg Vieilli (argent)* bread, dough

braiser [brɛze] VT *Culin* to braise

braisière [brɛzjɛr] NF *Culin* braising pan

bramement [brammɑ̃] NM *(hurlement)* howl(ing), wail(ing); *(de cerf)* bell(ing)

bramer [brame] VI *(hurler)* to howl, to wail; *(de cerf)* to bell

bran [brɑ̃] NM *(de son)* bran; **b. de scie** sawdust

brancard [brɑ̃kar] NM **1** *(bras) (d'une civière, d'une charrette etc)* shaft, pole; **ruer dans les brancards** *(d'un cheval)* to kick when between the shafts; *Fig* to kick over the traces, to rebel **2** *(civière)* stretcher

brancardier, -ière [brɑ̃kardje, -jɛr] N stretcher bearer

branchage [brɑ̃ʃaʒ] NM *(des arbres)* branches, boughs; **branchages** cut or lopped-off branches

branche [brɑ̃ʃ] NF **1** *(d'un arbre)* branch, bough; *(d'un nerf, d'une rivière etc)* branch; *(de l'industrie etc)* branch, sector; *(d'activité)* line of business; **b. d'activité** area of operations; **la maîtresse b.** the main branch; **céleri en branches** celery; **une b. de céleri** a stick of celery; *Arg* **vieille b.** old mate; *Fig* **avoir de la b.** to look distinguished; **notre b. de la famille** our branch of the family; **la b. maternelle** the mother's side, *Fml* the maternal line; **les branches de la physique** the branches of physics; **c'est une b. très littéraire** it is a very literary discipline; **branches des bois d'un cerf** tines of a stag's antlers **2** *(d'un compas)* leg; *(d'une monture de lunettes)* side; *(d'une fourche)* prong; *(d'une hélice)* blade; *(d'une clé)* shank; *(d'un fer à cheval)* arm; **les branches d'un chandelier** the branches of a candelabra; **b. à coulisse** telescopic leg **3** *Suisse Scol, Univ* subject; **b. principale** main subject, *Am* major; **b. secondaire** secondary subject, *Am* minor **4** *Suisse (chocolat)* = cylindrical bar of chocolate

branché [brɑ̃ʃe] ADJ *Fam* trendy, hip; **être b. sur qch** to be really into sth; **il est b. tennis/techno** he's really into tennis/techno music; **c'est très b. d'avoir des lunettes** wearing glasses is very trendy or is the in thing

branchement [brɑ̃ʃmɑ̃] NM **1** *(d'un appareil électrique, d'un téléphone)* connecting (up), connection; *(à une prise)* plugging in; *(de canalisations, de fils électriques)* branch(ing), junction; **(tube de) b.** branch pipe **2** *Rail* branch line; **b. de voie** junction, points **3** *Ordinat* branch

brancher [brɑ̃ʃe] VT **1** *(appareil électrique, téléphone)* to connect (up); *(à une prise)* to plug in; *Tél* **b. qn** to put sb through, to connect sb; **b. une sonnerie sur le circuit de lumière** to connect a bell up to or run a bell off the light circuit; *Fig* **b. qn sur un sujet** to get sb onto or started on a subject; **il faut que je le branche sur cette affaire** I must get him interested in this business **2** *Fam (plaire à)* **b. qn** to give sb a buzz; **la peinture, ça te branche?** are you into painting?; **on se fait un resto ce soir, ça te branche?** fancy going to a restaurant tonight?; **ta sœur a l'air de le b.** he seems to be interested in your sister

VI *(des oiseaux)* to perch, to roost *(on a branch)*

VPR **se brancher 1** *(des oiseaux)* to perch, to roost; *(d'un appareil électrique)* to plug in;

(canalisation) to connect up to; **se b. sur les grandes ondes** to tune in to long waves **2** *Can Fam (se décider)* to decide, to make up one's mind

branchette [brɑ̃ʃɛt] NF small branch, twig

branchial, -iale, -iaux, -iales [brɑ̃ʃjal, -jo] ADJ *Zool* branchial

branchie [brɑ̃ʃi] NF *(d'un poisson)* branchia, gill

branchitude [brɑ̃ʃityd] NF *Fam* hipness, trendiness; **cette boîte est l'un des hauts lieux de la b. parisienne** this club is one of the trendiest or hippest in Paris

branchu [brɑ̃ʃy] ADJ branchy, branching

brandade [brɑ̃dad] NF *Culin* **b. (de morue)** = salt cod pounded with garlic, oil and cream

brande [brɑ̃d] NF **1** *(bruyère)* heather **2** *(terrain)* heath(land)

Brandebourg [brɑ̃dbur] NM **1** Brandenburg **2** *Couture* **b.** frog; **brandebourgs** frogging; **à brandebourgs** frogged

brandir [brɑ̃dir] VT *(arme)* to brandish, to flourish; *(pour attirer l'attention)* to brandish, to wave; *(la menace de qch)* to hold up

brandon [brɑ̃dɔ̃] NM firebrand; *(flambeau de paille)* torch; *Fig* **c'est un b. de discorde** *(personne)* he's a firebrand; *(sujet, affaire)* it's a bone of contention

brandy [brɑ̃di] NM brandy

branlant [brɑ̃lɑ̃] ADJ shaky; *(dent)* loose; *(chaise, escalier)* rickety; *(immeuble)* ramshackle; *Fig (raison, réputation, vérité)* shaky

branle [brɑ̃l] NM *(mouvement)* swing; *Fig* impulse, impetus; **mettre une cloche en b.** to set a bell swinging or ringing; *Fig* **donner le b. à qch** to get sth going, to give an impetus to sth; **mettre qch en b.** to set sth in motion; **se mettre en b.** to get going

branle-bas [brɑ̃lba] NM INV **1** *Naut* faire le b. de combat to clear the decks for action; **b.!** action stations! **2** *Fig* commotion; **c'était le b. (de combat) dans la ville entière** the whole town was in turmoil; **dans le b. du départ** in the commotion of setting off; **que signifie tout ce b.?** what's all the commotion about?; **il met toute la maison en b.** he's turning the whole house upside down

branlée [brɑ̃le] NF *Fam* thrashing; **prendre ou recevoir une b.** to get a thrashing, to get thrashed

branlement [brɑ̃lmɑ̃] NM *(de la tête)* wagging, shaking

branler [brɑ̃le] VT **1** *(tête)* to wag, to shake **2** *Vulg (masturber)* to jerk off, *Br* to wank off; *Fig* **mais qu'est-ce qu'il branle?** il devrait être là! what the hell's he up to? he should be here!

VI to be shaky; *(de dent)* to be loose; *(de chaise, d'escalier)* to be rickety; *(de maison)* to be ramshackle; **b. dans le manche** *(d'un outil)* to have a loose handle

VPR **se branler** *Vulg (masturber)* to jerk off, *Br* to wank (off); *Fig* **franchement, je m'en branle** to be honest, I don't or couldn't give a fuck or a shit

branlette [brɑ̃lɛt] NF *Vulg* hand-job, *Br* wank; **se faire une b.** to jerk off, *Br* to have a wank

branleur, -euse [brɑ̃lœr, -øz] N *Vulg (bon à rien etc)* nerd, *Br* wanker

branque [brɑ̃k] *Fam* ADJ *(fou)* bonkers, nuts N *(imbécile)* dope, jerk; *(fou)* nutter, headcase, *Am* wacko

braquage [brakaʒ] NM **1** *Aut (des roues)* turning; **(angle de) b.** *(d'une voiture)* steering lock; **rayon ou cercle de b.** turning circle; **b. (au) maximum** full lock **2** *Arg (vol)* hold-up; **faire un b.** to do a hold-up

braque [brak] NM *(chien)* pointer
ADJ *Fam* nutty, crazy

braquemart [brakmar] NM **1** *(épée)* cutlass **2** *Vulg (pénis)* dick, prick, *Br* knob

braquer [brake] VT **1** *(diriger, tourner)* to point; **b. un fusil sur qn/qch** to aim or point a gun at sb/sth; **b. une lunette sur qn/qch** to fix or train a telescope on sb/sth; **il a toujours l'œil braqué sur nous** he's got his eye on us all the time; **b. son attention sur qch** to fix one's attention on sth **2** *Aut (voiture etc)* to turn **3** *(monter) (personne)* to antagonize; **b. qn contre qn/qch** to turn sb against sb/sth; **il est braqué contre le projet** he's dead set against the plan **4** *Arg* **b. une banque** to hold up a bank

VPR **se braquer** to dig one's heels in; **se b. contre qn** to set one's face against sb

VI *Aut* to turn the (steering) wheel; **b. (à fond)** to apply full lock; **b. à gauche** to turn the wheel hard over to the left; **b. au maximum** to apply full lock; **voiture qui braque mal** car that has a poor lock

braquet [brakɛ] NM gear ratio; **changer de b.** to change gear

braqueur, -euse [brakœr, -øz] N armed robber

bras [bra] NM **1** *Anat* arm; **b. droit/gauche** right/left arm; **allonger le b. vers qch** to reach (out) for sth, to stretch out one's arm for sth; **offrir/donner le b. à qn** to offer/give sb one's arm; **prendre le b. de qn** to take sb's arm; **avoir un panier au b.** to have a basket on one's arm; **au b. de qn** on sb's arm; **il est entré, un dossier sous le b.** he came in with a file under his arm; **b. dessus, b. dessous** arm in arm; **les b. m'en tombent** I'm astounded, I'm flabbergasted; **cela m'a coupé b. et jambes** it stunned me; **assis, les b. croisés** sitting with one's arms folded or with folded arms; **rester les b. croisés** *(ne pas travailler)* to twiddle one's thumbs; *(être passif)* to stand idly by; *Fig* **avoir le b. long** to have a lot of influence or *Fam* clout; **accueillir qn à b. ouverts** to welcome sb with open arms; **avoir qn/qch sur les b.** to have sb/sth on one's hands; *Fig* **elle a la responsabilité de l'affaire sur les b.** she carries all the responsibility for the matter; **elle s'est retrouvée avec une famille sur les b.** she found herself with a family to look after or to take care of; *Litt Hum* **être dans les b. de Morphée** to be in the arms of Morpheus; **voiture à b.** handcart; **tenir qch à b. tendus** ou **à bout de b.** to hold sth in one's outstretched arms; **en b. de chemise** in (one's) shirtsleeves; **il m'est tombé dessus à b. raccourcis** he pitched or laid into me; **une partie de b. de fer** an arm-wrestling match; *Fig* a trial of strength; **les syndicats sont engagés dans une partie de b. de fer avec le gouvernement** the unions are at loggerheads with the government; **lancer qch/frapper à tour de b.** to throw sth/strike with all one's might; **faire un b. d'honneur (à qn)** ≃ to stick two fingers up (to sb), *Br* ≃ to give (sb) the V-sign

2 *(homme)* hand, worker; **manquer de b.** to be short handed; **elle c'est la tête, et moi les b.** she's the brains, I'm the brawn

3 *(d'un fauteuil)* arm(rest); *(d'un levier, d'une ancre)* arm; *(d'une grue)* jib; *(d'une croix)* limb; *(d'une pompe)* handle; *Naut (de la vergue)* brace

4 *(de fleuve)* arm

5 *(pouvoir)* arm; **le b. séculier** the secular arm; **le b. de la justice** the arm of the law; **le b. armé d'une organisation** the armed wing of an organization; **le b. politique d'une organisation** the political arm or wing of an organization

6 *(de mollusque)* tentacle

▸ ▸ *Aut* **b. compensateur** compensator arm; *Aut* **b. de contrôle** control arm; *Aut* **b. de direction** steering arm; **b. droit: être le b. droit de qn** to be sb's right hand (man); **b. fisher** *(microphone)* fisher boom; **b. de lecture** pickup arm; **b. de manivelle** crank arm; *Aut* web; *Géog* **b. de mer** arm of the sea; **b. mort** backwater; *Aut* **b. oscillant** radius arm *or* rod; **b. pivotant** *(pour moniteur)* swivel arm; **b. porte-copies** *(pour claviste)* copy-holder; *Aut* **b. de suspension** suspension arm; *Can* **b. de vitesse** *Br* gear lever, *Am* stick shift

brasage [brazaʒ] NM *Métal* brazing

braser [braze] VT *Métal* to braze

brasero [brazero] NM brazier

brasier [brazje] NM *(incendie)* blaze, inferno; **la voiture n'était plus qu'un b.** the car was a ball of flames; *Litt* **le b. du couchant** the fiery glow of the setting sun; **l'ardent b. des passions mortelles** the burning fire of human passion

Brasilia [brazilja] N Brasilia

brasiller [brazije] VI *(de la mer)* to glitter, to sparkle

bras-le-corps (à) [a bralkɔr] ADV **saisir qn à b.** to seize sb round the waist; **prendre un problème à b.** to get to grips with a problem, to tackle a problem head on

brassage [brasaʒ] NM **1** *(de la bière)* brewing **2** *(mélange)* mixing; *Aut* **b. des gaz** mixing; *Fig* **le b. de peuples/cultures** the (inter)mingling *or* (inter)mixing of races/cultures **3** *Naut (de la vergue)* bracing; *Aviat (d'une hélice)* swinging

brassard [brasar] NM armband; **b. de deuil** black armband

brasse [bras] NF **1** *Natation* **b. (coulée)** breaststroke; **nager la b.** to swim breaststroke; **b. papillon** butterfly (stroke); **en quelques brasses, tu es au bout de la piscine** in a few strokes, you'll be at the end of the pool **2** *(ancienne mesure)* fathom

brassée [brase] NF armful; **par brassées** by the armful

brasser [brase] VT **1** *(bière etc)* to brew **2** *(mélanger)* to mix; **b. des affaires** to be doing good business; **b. les cartes** to shuffle the cards; **b. de l'argent** to handle large amounts of money; **b. de l'air** *ou* **du vent** to work without getting anything done **3** *Naut (vergue)* to brace; *Aviat (hélice)* to swing

brasserie [brasri] NF **1** *(fabrique)* brewery; *(industrie)* brewing, beer-making (industry) **2** *(restaurant)* restaurant (with bar), brasserie

brasseur, -euse [brasœr, -øz] N **1** *(fabricant de bière)* brewer **2** *Fig* **b. d'affaires** big businessman, tycoon **3** *Sport* breaststroke swimmer

brassière [brasjer] NF **1** *(de bébé)* (baby's) *Br* vest *or Am* undershirt **2** *Can (soutien-gorge)* bra, *Am* brassière **3 b. de sauvetage** life jacket, life vest

brasure [brazyr] NF **1** *(résultat)* braze, (brazed) seam **2** *(opération)* brazing, hard-soldering **3** *(alliage)* hard solder

Bratislava [bratislava] N Bratislava

bravache [bravaʃ] NM swaggerer, blusterer ADJ swaggering, blustering; **d'un air b.** blusteringly

bravade [bravad] NF bravado; **par b.** out of bravado

brave [brav] ADJ SEE GRAMMAR B10 **1** *(courageux)* brave, courageous **2** *(preceding the noun) (bon)* good; **ce sont de braves gens** they are good *or* decent people; **c'est un b. homme** *ou Fam* **type** he's a good *or* decent man *or* sort; **eh oui, ma b. dame, c'est la vie** well, my dear lady, that's life I suppose **3** *Péj* **il est bien b.** *(pas futé)* he's nice enough, he's OK

NM **1** *(héros)* brave man **2 mon b.** my good man **3** *Péj* **faire le b.** to bluster, to swagger

Il faut noter que l'adjectif anglais **brave** ne signifie jamais **gentil**.

bravement [bravmã] ADV **1** *(courageusement)* bravely, courageously **2** *(avec résolution)* boldly

braver [brave] VT **1** *(affronter) (la mort, le danger)* to brave, to face bravely; **toujours prêt à le danger** always ready to face danger **2** *(défier) (personne)* to defy, to stand up to; **b. les lois/le règlement** to defy *or* flout the law/the rules

bravo [bravo] INT bravo!; *(dans un débat)* hear, hear!; **un grand b. à toute l'équipe technique** a big hand *or* cheer for all the technical crew; **ah b.!** *(tu as encore fait une sottise!)* oh, well done!

NM bravo; **des bravos** applause, cheers

bravoure [bravur] NF **1** *(courage)* bravery, courage **2** *Mus* **chanter son air de b.** to sing one's bravura passage; *Littér* **morceau de b.** purple passage

Brazzaville [brazavil] N Brazzaville

break[1] [brɛk] NM *Aut* estate (car), *Am* station wagon

break[2] NM *Mus, Tennis, Fig* break; *Boxe* **b.!** break!; **balle de b.** break point

brebis [brəbi] NF **1** *Zool* ewe; **lait/fromage de b.** ewe's milk/ewe's-milk cheese **2** *Rel* sheep; **les b.** the flock
▸▸ **b. égarée** lost sheep; *Fig* **b. galeuse** black sheep

brèche [brɛʃ] NF *(dans un mur, une haie etc)* gap, opening; *(dans la coque d'un bateau)* hole; *(dans une lame)* notch; *Mil* breach; *Mil* **monter sur la b.** to stand in the breach; *Fig* **être toujours sur la b.** to be always on the go; **battre qch en b.** to demolish sth

bréchet [breʃɛ] NM *Orn* breastbone

bredouillage [brədujaʒ], **bredouillement** [brədujmã] NM mumbling, muttering

bredouillant [brədujã] ADJ mumbling

bredouille [brəduj] ADJ empty-handed; **rentrer** *ou* **revenir b.** to come back empty-handed

bredouiller [brəduje] VT & VI to mumble, to mutter

bredouilleur, -euse [brədujœr, -øz] ADJ mumbling, muttering
N mumbler, mutterer

bref, brève [brɛf, brɛv] ADJ brief, short; **soyez b.!** be brief!, make it short!; **répondre d'un ton b.** to answer curtly; *Ling* **voyelle brève** short vowel; **dans les plus brefs délais** as soon as possible
ADV in short; **en b.** in brief; **raconter qch en b.** to relate sth in a few words *or* briefly; **b., il accepte** in short *or* in a word *or* to cut a long story short, he accepts; *Fam* **enfin b., elle n'est pas satisfaite** well, in short, she isn't satisfied; **une cousine ou une tante, enfin b., quelqu'un de sa famille** a cousin or an aunt, well anyway, one of his relatives
NM *Rel* (papal) brief

bréhaigne [breɛɲ] ADJ *Vieilli (jument etc)* barren

brelan [brəlã] NM *Cartes* three of a kind, pair royal; **b. d'as** three aces

brêle [brɛl] NF *Fam* cretin, jerk, *Br* tosspot

breloque [brəlɔk] NF **1** *(sur un bracelet etc)* charm; **bracelet à breloques** charm bracelet **2** *Mil* break-off; **battre la b.** to sound the dismiss; *(d'une montre)* to be on the blink; *Fig (intellectuellement)* to wander; **mon cœur bat la b.** *(bat vite)* my heart is racing; *(fonctionne mal)* my heart is playing me up

brème [brɛm] NF *(poisson)* bream

Brême [brɛm] N Bremen

Brésil [brezil] NM Brazil

brésilien, -ienne [breziljɛ̃, -jɛn] ADJ Brazilian; **maillot/slip b.** high-cut swimsuit/briefs
N B. Brazilian

brésiller [brezije] *Tech, Litt* VT to break into small pieces; *(broyer)* to crumble, to pulverize
VI to crumble
VPR **se brésiller** to crumble

Bretagne [brətaɲ] NF Brittany; **Basse-B.** Lower *or* Western Brittany

bretelle [brətɛl] NF **1** *(de soutien-gorge, robe etc)* (shoulder) strap; **(paire de) bretelles** *(de pantalon)* (pair of) braces *or Am* suspenders; *Fam* **se faire remonter les bretelles** to get bawled out **2** *(lanière)* strap; **b. de fusil** rifle sling; **l'arme à la b.** with one's rifle slung over one's shoulder **3** *(route)* access road; *Rail* crossover; **b. d'autoroute** motorway link road, *Br* slip road, ramp; *Aut* **b. d'accès** spur, slip road; *(vers autoroute surélevée)* on-ramp; *Aut* **b. de sortie** exit; *(d'autoroute surélevée)* exit, off-ramp **4** *TV, Radio (magnétophone)* portable tape recorder

breton, -onne [brətɔ̃, -ɔn] ADJ Breton
NM *Ling* Breton
N B. Breton

bretonnant [brətɔnã] ADJ Breton **b.** = Breton-speaking Breton who preserves local traditions; **la Bretagne bretonnante** = Breton-speaking Brittany where local traditions are preserved

brett(el)er [brɛtle, brɛte] VT (**je brettelle** [brɛtɛl], **n. brettelons** [brɛtlɔ̃]) *(pierre etc)* to tool, to tooth; *(bijoux)* to hatch, to chase

bretzel [brɛtzɛl] NM pretzel

breuvage [brœvaʒ] NM **1** *(boisson)* beverage, drink **2** *(potion particulière)* potion; **b. magique** magic potion

brève [brɛv] *voir* **bref**
NF **1** *Journ* short (news) item **2** *Ling (syllabe)* short syllable; *(voyelle)* short vowel

brevet [brəvɛ] NM **1** *(titre)* diploma, certificate; *Naut* **passer son b. de capitaine** to obtain one's master's certificate, *Fam* to get one's ticket; *Jur* **(acte en) b.** contract delivered by a notary in the original **2 b. (d'invention)** patent; **prendre un b.** to take out a patent **3** *Fig (d'honnêteté)* guarantee **4** *Hist (du roi)* (royal) warrant
▸▸ **b. d'apprentissage** indentures, articles; *Scol* **b. (des collèges)** = general exam taken at fifteen, *Br* ≃ GCSE; *Mil* **b. d'état-major** = staff college certificate; *Scol* **b. d'études du premier cycle** *Br* ≃ GCSE, *Am* ≃ high school graduation; **b. d'études professionnelles** = vocational diploma; **b. de pilote** *Aviat* pilot's licence; *Mil* wings; **b. professionnel** vocational qualification; **b. de technicien** = vocational training certificate (for 16-year-olds); **b. de technicien supérieur** = advanced vocational training certificate

brevetable [brəvtabl] ADJ patentable

breveté [brəvte] ADJ **1** *(invention)* patented; **inventeur b.** inventor holding letters patent **2** *(diplômé)* qualified; **officier b. (d'état-major)** = officer who has passed staff college

breveter [brəvte] VT (**je brevette** [brəvɛt], **n. brevetons** [brəvtɔ̃]; **je brevetterai** [brəvɛtre]) *(invention)* to patent; **faire b. une invention** to take out a patent on an invention

bréviaire [brevjɛr] NM *Rel* breviary; *Fig* bible

brévité [brevite] NF *Ling (d'une voyelle etc)* shortness

briard [brijar] NM *(chien)* Briard

bribes [brib] NFPL **b. de conversation** snatches *or* scraps of conversation; **des b. de finlandais** scraps *or* bits of Finnish; **les b. de sa fortune/du repas** the remnants of his fortune/the leftovers of the meal; **apprendre qch par b.** to learn sth piecemeal *or* bit by bit

bric-à-brac [brikabrak] NM INV 1 *(vieux objets)* odds and ends, bric-à-brac, jumble; *Fig* jumble (**de** of); **marchand de b.** second-hand dealer 2 (**boutique de**) **b.** second-hand shop, *Fam* junk shop

bric et de broc (de) [dəbrikedəbrɔk] ADV from one source and another, haphazardly; **maison meublée de b.** house furnished with bits and pieces

bricheton [briʃtɔ̃] NM *Fam (pain)* bread

brick [brik] NM 1 *Naut* brig 2 *Culin* **b. à l'œuf** brik, = egg enclosed in filo pastry and deep fried 3 *(carton)* carton; **b. de lait/de jus d'orange** carton of milk/orange juice; **lait vendu en b.** milk sold in cartons

bricolage [brikɔlaʒ] NM 1 *(travail)* do-it-yourself, *Br* DIY; **faire du b.** to do (some) do-it-yourself *or* DIY; **grande surface de b.** do-it-yourself centre, DIY superstore; **rayon b.** do-it-yourself department; **un mordu du b.** a do-it-yourself enthusiast, a do-it-yourselfer 2 *Péj (réparation)* botch-up; **c'est du b.!** it's a botch-up!

bricole [brikɔl] NF 1 *(babiole)* trifle, little thing; **bricoles** *(objets)* odds and ends; *(travaux)* odd jobs; **offrir une petite b. à qn** to give sb a little something; *Fam* **il va lui arriver des bricoles** he's going to get into a pickle; **s'occuper à des bricoles** to do odd jobs 2 *(pour tirer une charrette etc)* breast strap; *(de cheval)* breast harness

bricoler [brikɔle] VT **b. une affaire** to arrange a piece of business *(often shady)*; **elle a bricolé une table** she's knocked together *or* knocked up a table; **il a bricolé le moteur** he's tinkered with the engine
VI to do do-it-yourself *or Br* DIY; **j'ai passé la matinée à b. dans la maison** I spent the morning doing odd jobs about the house

bricoleur, -euse [brikɔlœr, -øz] N handy-man, *f* handywoman
ADJ **être b.** to be good with one's hands

bride [brid] NF 1 *(du harnais)* bridle; **lâcher la b. à un cheval/à qn** to give free rein to a horse/to sb, to give a horse/sb his head; *Fig* **lâcher la b. à un élève** to allow a pupil more freedom, to give a pupil his head; **laisser à un cheval/à qn la b. sur le cou** to give a horse his head/to give sb a free rein; *Fig* **elle a la b. sur le cou** she has a free rein; **tenir un cheval en b., tenir la b. haute à un cheval** to curb *or* check a horse; *Fig* **tenir qn en b., tenir la b. haute à qn** to keep a tight rein on sb; **tenir ses passions en b.** to keep a tight rein on one's passions; **aller à b. abattue** *ou* **à toute b.** to ride at full speed, to ride full tilt, *Fam* to ride hell for leather; **partir à b. abattue** to set off at top speed; **fureur sans b.** unbridled fury 2 *Couture (de boutonnière)* bar; *(pour un bouton)* loop; *(de bonnet)* string 3 *Tech* strap, tie; *(d'un cylindre, d'un tuyau)* flange, collar; **b. de serrage** clamp, cramp; **tuyau à brides** flanged pipe

bridé, -e [bride] ADJ 1 **yeux bridés** slant(ing) eyes, *Péj* slitty eyes 2 *Aut* **moteur b.** governed engine
N *très Fam* slant-eye, *Am* gook

brider [bride] VT 1 *(cheval)* to bridle; *(personne, colère, passions, déception etc)* to restrain, to curb, to keep in check; **cette contrainte la bride** it's a restraint on him 2 *Culin (volaille)* to truss; *Naut (câble etc)* to lash 3 *Couture (boutonnière)* to bind 4 *(tuyau)* to flange, to clamp

bridge [bridʒ] NM 1 *Cartes* bridge; **b. aux enchères** auction bridge; **b. contrat** contract bridge; **tournoi/club de b.** bridge tournament/club; **faire un b.** to have *or* play a game of bridge 2 *(prothèse dentaire)* bridge

bridger [bridʒe] VI *(je bridgeai(s); n. bridgeons)* to play bridge

bridgeur, -euse [bridʒœr, -øz] N bridge player

bridon [bridɔ̃] NM snaffle (bridle)

brie [bri] NM Brie

briefer [brife] VT to brief; **b. ses collègues sur une affaire** to brief one's colleagues on a matter

briefing [brifiŋ] NM briefing; **faire un b.** to hold a briefing

brièvement [brievmɑ̃] ADV briefly

brièveté [brievte] NF brevity, briefness, shortness; *(de style, d'expression)* brevity

brigade [brigad] NF 1 *Mil* brigade 2 *(de policiers)* squad; *(d'ouvriers)* gang; **chef de b.** foreman
▸▸*Aviat* **b. aérienne** group, *Am* wing; **b. anti-gang** organized crime squad; **b. de gendarmerie** squad of gendarmes; *Hist* **Brigades internationales** International Brigades; **b. de police** police squad; **b. des stupéfiants** *ou Fam* **des stups** drug squad

brigadier [brigadje] NM 1 *Mil* corporal; *(d'artillerie)* bombardier 2 **b. (de police)** (police) sergeant 3 *(d'un groupe d'ouvriers)* foreman 4 *Naut* bowman, bow oar(sman)

brigadier-chef, *pl* **brigadiers-chefs** NM *Mil* rank between corporal and sergeant, lance sergeant

brigand [brigɑ̃] NM *(pillard)* brigand, bandit; *(personne malhonnête)* crook; **le petit b.** the little scoundrel *or* rascal

brigandage [brigɑ̃daʒ] NM (armed) robbery, banditry; **des actes de b.** (armed) robbery

brigantin [brigɑ̃tɛ̃] NM *Hist, Naut* brigantine

brigantine [brigɑ̃tin] NF *Naut* spanker

brigue [brig] NF *Litt* intrigue

briguer [brige] VT *(faveur, amitié, poste etc)* to solicit; **b. des voix** to canvass (for votes)

brillamment [brijamɑ̃] ADV brilliantly

brillance [brijɑ̃s] NF *(d'un bijou, du regard)* brilliance; *Opt* brilliancy; *TV (de l'image etc)* brightness; *Mus* brightness of tone

brillant [brijɑ̃] ADJ *(carrière, élève, orateur etc)* brilliant; *(lumière, couleur)* bright, brilliant; *(pierre précieuse)* sparkling, glittering; *(cheveux, chaussures, cuir)* shiny, glossy; *(conversation)* sparkling; **spectacle b.** splendid sight; **elle avait les yeux brillants de fièvre/joie** her eyes were bright with fever/sparkling with joy; **la situation n'est pas brillante** the situation isn't brilliant; **il est promis à un b. avenir** he has a brilliant future ahead of him
NM 1 *(d'un métal)* brilliance, brightness; *(d'une pierre précieuse)* sparkle, glitter; *(d'un papier, d'un tissu)* shininess, glossiness, sheen; *(de chaussures)* shine, polish; *(de conversation)* sparkle; *(d'esprit, d'intelligence)* brilliance; **et vos cheveux retrouveront leur b. naturel** and your hair will regain its natural shine 2 *(diamant)* brilliant; **monté/taillé en b.** mounted/cut as a brilliant
▸▸**b. à lèvres** lip gloss

brillantine [brijɑ̃tin] NF brilliantine

briller [brije] VI 1 *(du soleil)* to shine; *(de l'acier)* to glint, to gleam; *(d'une bougie)* to glimmer; *(de l'eau)* to shimmer, to glisten; *(des étoiles)* to glitter, to twinkle; *(de la lune)* to gleam, to shine; *(du satin)* to shimmer, to shine; *(des phares)* to glare; *(des braises)* to glow; *(des yeux)* to shine, to gleam; *Prov* **tout ce qui brille n'est pas or** all that glitters is not gold; **faire b. ses chaussures** to shine *or* polish one's shoes; **des yeux qui brillent de colère/de joie** eyes shining *or* gleaming with anger/happiness; **la joie brillait sur son visage** his/her face shone with joy
2 *Fig (exceller)* to shine, to excel, to do well;

il brille en société he shines in company; **b. dans la conversation** to be a brilliant conversationalist; **b. par son savoir/son intelligence** to be extraordinarily knowledgeable/intelligent; **b. par ses dons d'orateur** to be an extraordinarily gifted speaker; **b. par son absence** to be conspicuous by one's absence; **elle ne brille pas par sa ponctualité** she's not noted for her punctuality

brimade [brimad] NF *(tour)* rag; *Scol, Mil* brimades ragging, *Am* hazing; *(plus grave)* bullying, victimization; **faire subir des brimades à qn** to rag *or Am* to haze sb; *(plus gravement)* to bully *or* victimize sb

brimbalement [brɛ̃balmɑ̃] NM *(de voiture, charrette etc)* shaking about; *(de bateau)* swaying, rocking

brimbaler [brɛ̃bale] VT & VI *Fam* = **bringuebaler**

brimborion [brɛ̃bɔrjɔ̃] NM bauble, knick-knack

brimer [brime] VT *(recrue etc)* to rag, *Am* to haze; *(plus gravement)* to bully, to victimize; **il se croyait brimé** he felt he was being picked on *or* got at

brin [brɛ̃] NM 1 *(d'herbe)* blade; *(de myrte, persil, romarin etc)* sprig; *(de mimosa, de muguet)* spray; *(de paille)* wisp; **un beau b. de fille** a fine-looking girl 2 *Fam (petite quantité)* bit (**de** of); **un b. d'air** a breath of air; **un b. d'ironie/de jalousie** a touch *or* hint of irony/jealousy; **sa voix laissait transparaître un b. d'inquiétude** one could detect a note of concern in his voice; **faire un b. de toilette** to have a quick wash (and brush up); **faire un b. de causette** to have a little chat; **il lui a fait un b. de cour** he had a bit of a flirt with her 3 *(de laine, corde, fil etc)* strand 4 **brins d'une antenne** wires of an aerial
ADV **un b.** a bit; **il est un b. ennuyeux** he's a bit of a bore

brindezingue [brɛ̃dzɛ̃g] ADJ *Fam* crazy

brindille [brɛ̃dij] NF twig

bringue [brɛ̃g] NF *Arg* 1 **grande b.** *(fille)* beanpole 2 *(fête)* party; **faire la b.** to party 3 *Suisse Fam (querelle)* row; *(rengaine)* refrain

bringuebaler [brɛ̃g(ə)bale], **brinquebaler** [brɛ̃kbale] VI *Fam (d'une voiture, charrette etc)* to shake about; *(d'un bateau)* to sway, to rock; *(d'une chaîne)* to rattle
VT *Litt* to shake about

bringuer [brɛ̃ge] *Fam* VI 1 *(faire la fête)* to party 2 *Suisse* **arrête de b.!** stop going on about it!
VT *Suisse (harceler)* to go on at
VPR **se bringuer** *Suisse (se disputer)* **ils se bringuaient** they were having a row

brio [brijo] NM **avec b.** with panache, brilliantly; *Mus* **con b.** con brio

brioche [brijɔʃ] NF *Culin* brioche; *Fam* **prendre de la b.** to develop a paunch *or* pot

brioché [brijɔʃe] ADJ **pain b.** = milk bread

brique [brik] NF 1 *(de construction)* brick; **maison de** *ou* **en briques** brick(-built) house; **mur de briques** brick wall; *Fig* **bouffer des briques,** *Fam* **manger des briques à la sauce caillou** to have nothing to eat; **ne t'attends pas à ce que je mange des briques à la sauce caillou** you can't expect me to live on air 2 *(de savon)* bar, cake; *(de béton etc)* block, slab 3 *(de lait, jus de fruit)* carton 4 *Anciennement Arg (dix mille francs)* ten thousand francs
ADJ INV brick-red
▸▸**b. creuse** hollow brick; **b. pleine** solid brick; **b. tubulaire** hollow brick

briquer [brike] VT *(nettoyer)* to scrub down; *Naut (pont)* to holystone

briquet¹ [brikɛ] NM *(appareil)* (cigarette)

lighter; *Arch (à amadou)* tinder box; **b.-tempête** pipe lighter, windproof lighter; **battre le b.** to strike a light

briquet² NM *(chien)* beagle

briquetage [brik(ə)taʒ] NM *(maçonnerie)* brickwork; *(trompe-l'œil)* imitation brickwork

briqueter [brik(ə)te] VT (**je briquette, n. briquetons; je briquetterai**) *(construire)* to brick; *(en trompe-l'œil)* to face with imitation brickwork

briqueterie [brikɛtri] NF brickworks, brickyard

briqueteur [brik(ə)tœr] NM bricklayer

briquetier [brik(ə)tje] NM brick manufacturer

briquette [brikɛt] NF briquette

bris [bri] NM **1** *(de verre, des scellés etc)* breaking **2** *Jur* **b. de prison** prison breakout; **b. de clôture** breaking and entering, *Spéc* breach of close

brisant [brizã] ADJ **explosif b.** high explosive; **obus b.** high-explosive shell
NM **1** *(écueil)* reef, shoal; **brisants** *(vagues)* breakers **2** = **brise-lames**

brise [briz] NF breeze; *Naut* **forte b.** stiff breeze

brisé [brize] ADJ *(détruit)* broken; **ligne brisée** broken line; *Fig* **il est b.** he's a broken man; **b. de fatigue** exhausted, tired out; **b. de chagrin** crushed by grief, brokenhearted

brise-bise NM INV half curtain *(in lower half of window)*

brisées [brize] NFPL *(pour marquer la voie)* broken branches; *(d'un cerf etc)* track; *Fig* **suivre les b. de qn** to follow in sb's footsteps, to follow sb's lead *or* example; *Fig* **aller** *ou* **marcher sur les b. de qn** to poach on sb's territory

brise-fer NM INV clumsy person (who breaks everything)

brise-glace NM INV **1** *(navire)* ice breaker **2** *(d'une pile de pont)* ice breaker; *(d'un navire)* ice beam

brise-jet NM INV tap *or Am* faucet nozzle

brise-lames NM INV **1** *(digue)* breakwater, mole **2** *(le long d'une plage)* groyne

brisement [brizmã] NM *Fig* **b. de cœur** heartbreak

brise-mottes NM INV *Agr* brake harrow

briser [brize] VT *(casser)* to break, to smash; *(mottes de terre, navire)* to break up; *(minerai)* to pound (up), to crush; *(opposition)* to crush, to break down; *(enthousiasme, espérances)* to crush; *(carrière, vie)* to ruin, to wreck; *(grève)* to break; *Vieilli (conversation)* to break off; **b. qn** *(d'une marche etc)* to exhaust sb, to wear *or* tire sb out; *(de difficultés, paroles pessimistes etc)* to wear sb down; **b. une porte** to break open *or* burst open a door; **b. qch en mille morceaux** to smash sth to smithereens *or* into a thousand pieces; **b. qch en éclats** to smash sth to bits *or* to pieces; **porter cette caisse m'a brisé les reins** carrying that box has done my back in; **brisé par la douleur** crushed by grief, heartbroken; **la voix brisée par l'émotion** his voice choked with emotion; **cela me brise le cœur** it breaks my heart; **c'est à vous b. le cœur** it's heartbreaking; *très Fam* **il/ça me les brise** he/it really bugs me *or Br* hacks me off
VI **1 b. avec qn** to break with sb; *Litt Vieilli* **brisons là!** not another word!, enough! **2** *(des vagues)* to break
VPR **se briser 1** *(des vagues, de la porcelaine, du verre etc)* to break; **se b. en mille morceaux** to break *or* smash into a thousand pieces; **cela se brise comme du verre** it's as fragile as glass **2** *Fig (des espoirs)* to be shattered, to be dashed; *(des efforts)* to fail, to come to nothing

brise-tout N INV clumsy person (who breaks everything); **c'est un b.** he's like a bull in a china shop

briseur, -euse [brizœr, -øz] N **b. de grève** strike breaker, *Fam Péj* scab

brise-vent NM INV windbreak

bristol [bristɔl] NM Bristol board, thin cardboard; *(carte de visite)* visiting card

brisure [brizyr] NF **1** *(cassure)* break, crack **2** *(d'un gond)* break; *(d'un volet)* folding joint **3** **brisures** *(petits morceaux)* tiny pieces **4** *Hér* brisure

britannique [britanik] VOIR GRAMMAIRE A18
ADJ British; **les îles Britanniques** the British Isles
N **B.** Briton, *Am* Britisher; **les Britanniques** the British

broc [bro] NM pitcher, (large) jug

brocante [brɔkɑ̃t] NF *(commerce)* bric-à-brac trade; *(magasin)* second-hand shop; *(marché aux puces)* second-hand market

brocanter [brɔkɑ̃te] VI to deal in second-hand goods
VT *(meubles anciens, objets d'occasion etc)* to deal in

brocanteur, -euse [brɔkɑ̃tœr, -øz] N second-hand dealer

brocarder [brɔkarde] VT *Vieilli Litt (personne)* to gibe at

brocart [brɔkar] NM *Tex* brocade; **rideaux de b.** brocade curtains

brochage [brɔʃaʒ] NM **1** *(de livre)* stitching, sewing **2** *Tex* brocading, figuring

broche [brɔʃ] NF **1** *Culin* spit; **faire cuire qch à la b.** to spit-roast sth; **poulet à la b.** chicken on the spit; **b. de boucher** meat skewer **2** *(bijou)* brooch **3** *Tech, Élec* pin; *(d'une serrure)* gudgeon; **b. de charnière** hinge pin; *Élec* **fiche à deux broches** two-pin plug; *Ordinat* **b. de sortie** pinout **4** *Tex* spindle **5** *(de dentiste)* broach; *Chir* pin

broché [brɔʃe] ADJ **1** *Tex* brocaded **2** **livre b.** paperback (book)
NM *Tex (procédé)* brocading; *(tissu)* brocade

brocher [brɔʃe] VT **1** *(livre)* to stitch, to sew **2** *Tex (tissu)* to brocade, to figure; **tissu broché d'or** gold brocade

brochet [brɔʃɛ] NM *(poisson)* pike VOIR GRAMMAIRE A12

brochette [brɔʃɛt] NF **1** *Culin (broche)* skewer; *(plat)* kebab; **b. de fruits de mer** seafood kebab **2** *(de gens)* band, group; **b. de décorations** row of medals *or* decorations; *Iron* **vous faites une belle b.!** you're a fine lot!

brocheur, -euse [brɔʃœr, -øz] N *(de livre)* bookbinder
NF *Typ* **brocheuse** stitching machine; **b. automatique sans couture** perfect binder
NM *Tex* brocade loom

brochure [brɔʃyr] NF **1** *(prospectus etc)* brochure, pamphlet, booklet; **b. publicitaire/touristique** advertising/tourist brochure **2** *(de livres)* stitching, sewing **3** *Tex* brocaded pattern

brocoli [brɔkɔli] NM broccoli; **mange tes brocolis** eat your broccoli

brodequin [brɔdkɛ̃] NM laced boot; *Hist, Théâtre* buskin; *Hist* **appliquer les brodequins à un supplicié** to put the boots on a torture victim

broder [brɔde] VT *Couture* to embroider; *Fig* **b. une histoire** to embroider *or* embellish a story
VI **tu brodes** *(c'est inexact)* you're embroidering; **b. sur des faits** to embroider *or* embellish the facts; **b. sur un sujet** to elaborate on a subject

broderie [brɔdri] NF **1** *(ouvrage)* (piece of) embroidery; **broderies** embroidery **2** *(activité)* embroidery; **faire de la b.** to do embroidery, to embroider; **b. anglaise** broderie anglaise

brodeur, -euse [brɔdœr, -øz] N embroiderer
NF **brodeuse** *(machine)* embroidering machine

broiement [brwamã] NM = **broyage**

brol(l) [brɔl] NM *Belg (tas d'objets, bric-à-brac)* clutter, jumble, bric-à-brac

bromate [brɔmat] NM *Chimie* bromate

brome [brom] NM *Chimie* bromine

bromure [brɔmyr] NM *Chimie* bromide; *Typ* **b. de page** page bromide

bronca [brɔ̃ka] NF *(huées)* booing, jeering; *(protestation collective)* general outcry

bronche [brɔ̃ʃ] NF *Anat* bronchus, *pl* bronchi; **elle est fragile des bronches** she has weak lungs *or* a weak chest; **affection des bronches** bronchial disorder

broncher [brɔ̃ʃe] VI **1** *(de cheval)* to stumble **2** *(réagir)* to react; **sans b.** without batting an eyelid, without turning a hair; **il n'a pas bronché** he didn't bat an eyelid; **le premier qui bronche aura des ennuis!** *(qui bouge)* the first one to move will get it!; *(qui se plaint)* the first one to complain will be in trouble!

bronchiole [brɔ̃ʃjɔl] NF *Anat* bronchiole

bronchique [brɔ̃ʃik] ADJ *Anat* bronchial

bronchite [brɔ̃ʃit] NF *Méd* bronchitis; **faire** *ou* **avoir une b.** to have bronchitis

bronchitique [brɔ̃ʃitik] ADJ, N *Méd* bronchitic

broncho-pneumonie [brɔ̃kɔpnømɔni], *pl* **broncho-pneumonies** NF *Méd* broncho-pneumonia

bronchoscopie [brɔ̃kɔskɔpi] NF *Méd* bronchoscopy

brontosaure [brɔ̃tɔzɔr] NM brontosaurus

bronzage [brɔ̃zaʒ] NM **1** *(de la peau)* tanning; *(hâle)* (sun)tan; **b. intégral** all-over tan **2** *(d'une statue etc)* bronzing; *(d'un canon, de canons de fusil etc)* blueing

bronze [brɔ̃z] NM *(métal, objet d'art)* bronze; **b. à canon** gunmetal; *Fig* **un cœur de b.** a heart of stone; **c'est un homme de b.** he has a heart of stone

bronzé [brɔ̃ze] ADJ **1** *(visage etc)* (sun) tanned, bronzed **2** *(statue etc)* bronze(d)

bronzer [brɔ̃ze] VT **1** *(peau etc)* to tan **2** *(statue etc)* to bronze; *(canon de fusil etc)* to blue
VI to tan, to get a tan; *(de la peau)* to tan; **il bronze vite** he tans quickly
VPR **se bronzer** to sunbathe

bronzette [brɔ̃zɛt] NF *Fam* sunbathing; **faire (de la) b.** to do a bit of sunbathing, to sunbathe

bronzier [brɔ̃zje] NM *Beaux-Arts* maker of bronzes

brook [bruk] NM *Sport* water jump

broquette [brɔkɛt] NF (tin)tack

brossage [brɔsaʒ] NM brushing

brosse [brɔs] NF **1** *(ustensile)* brush; **b. métallique** wire brush; **b. de chiendent** scrubbing brush; **laver le sol à la b.** to give the floor a scrub, to scrub the floor; **donner un coup de b. à qch** to give sth a brush; **donner un coup de b. à qn** to give sb's hair a brush; **enlever la boue d'un coup de b.** to brush off the mud; **cheveux en b.** crew cut; **se faire couper les cheveux en b.** to have a crew cut; **il porte la b.** he has a crew cut; *Fig* **passer** *ou* **manier la b. (à reluire)** to crawl, to bow and scrape; *Can Fam* **partir sur une b. (biture)** to go on a pub crawl, *Am* to go bar-hopping **2** *(pinceau large)* (paint)brush **3** *(d'un renard)* brush
▸▸ **b. à cheveux** hairbrush; **b. à dents** toothbrush; **b. à habits** clothes brush; **b. à ongles** nailbrush

brosser [brɔse] **VT 1** *(tapis, manteau, cheveux etc)* to brush; *(sol)* to scrub; *(cheval)* to brush down; *Belg* **b. un cours** to skip *or* cut a lecture **2** *(peindre)* to paint; **b. les décors d'une pièce** to paint the scenery for a play; **il nous a brossé un rapide tableau de la situation** he gave us a brief outline of the situation; **son article brosse un vaste tableau de la situation** his article paints a broad picture of the situation **3** *Sport (balle, ballon)* to cut, to put spin on
VPR se brosser *(se nettoyer)* to brush oneself down, to brush one's clothes; **se b. les dents** to brush *or* clean one's teeth; **se b. les cheveux** to brush one's hair; *Fam* **tu peux te b.!** you can whistle for it!

brou [bru] **NM 1** *(enveloppe des noix etc)* husk, hull, *Am* shuck **2** *(teinture)* **b. de noix** walnut stain

broue [bru] **NF** *Can Arg* froth; *Fig* **faire** *ou* **péter de la b.** to talk big, to show off

brouet [bruɛ] **NM** gruel, *Br* skilly, *Péj* slop

brouette [bruɛt] **NF 1** *(de jardin)* wheelbarrow **2** *Hist (chaise fermée)* sedan chair *(on two wheels)*

brouettée [bruete] **NF** (wheel)barrowful, barrowload

brouetter [bruete] **VT** to carry in a wheelbarrow, to wheelbarrow

brouhaha [bruaa] **NM** hubbub, brouhaha

brouillage [bruʒaʒ] **NM** *Radio, Électron (accidentel)* interference; *(intentionnel)* jamming; *Tél* scrambling; **b. sonore/visuel** sound/visual interference

brouillard [brujar] **NM 1** *Météo* fog; **il y a du b.** it's foggy; **arrêté par le b., pris dans le b.** fogbound; *Fig* **je suis dans le b.** I'm in a fog; **b. givrant** freezing fog; **voir à travers un b., avoir un b. devant les yeux** to see things through a haze; *Fig* **foncer dans le b.** to push on regardless **2** *Com* day book; *Compta* **b. de caisse** cash book **3** *Phys* aerosol **4** *Aut* **b. carburé** fuel spray

brouillasse [brujas] **NF** = **bruine**

brouillasser [brujase] **V IMPERS** = **bruiner**

brouille [bruj] **NF** quarrel, disagreement; **être en b. avec qn** to be on bad terms with sb, to have fallen out with sb; **c'est une petite b. qui ne durera pas** it's just a tiff, it won't last long

brouillé [bruje] **ADJ 1** *(mélangé)* jumbled (up), mixed (up); *(contours etc)* blurred, fuzzy; *Tél* scrambled; **œufs brouillés** scrambled eggs; **teint b.** blotchy complexion **2 être b. avec qn** to be on bad terms with sb, to have fallen out with sb; **ils sont brouillés** they're on bad terms *or* they've fallen out (with each other); **je suis b. avec les dates/la grammaire** I'm hopeless at dates/grammar

brouille-ménage **NM** *Fam (vin rouge)* red wine, *Br* plonk

brouiller [bruje] **VT 1** *(mélanger) (idées)* to mix up, to jumble (up); **b. des œufs** to scramble eggs; **b. les cartes** to shuffle the cards; *Fig* to confuse the issue, to confuse things; **b. la combinaison d'un coffre** to scramble the combination of a safe; **b. la vue à qn** to blur sb's vision; **l'alcool brouille le teint** alcohol ruins your complexion; **b. les pistes** to cover one's tracks; **cela risquerait de me b. les idées** it might get me into a muddle; **cela a brouillé mes souvenirs** it's confused my memories **2** *(amis etc)* to set against each other, to cause a disagreement between; **je ne voudrais pas vous b. avec elle** I wouldn't want to make you fall out with her **3** *Radio, Électron (émission) (accidentellement)* to cause interference to; *(intentionnellement)* to jam; *Tél* to scramble
VPR se brouiller 1 *(d'idées)* to get mixed up *or* jumbled (up); **tout s'est brouillé dans ma tête** I got all muddled up *or* mixed up; **le temps se brouille** it's clouding over **2** *(de la vue, des yeux)* to get blurred; **yeux brouillés de larmes** eyes blurred with tears **3** *(se disputer)* to quarrel, to fall out (**avec qn** with sb); *Fam* **elle s'est brouillée avec la physique** she's taken a dislike to physics

brouillerie [brujri] **NF** *Fam* tiff

brouilleur [brujœr] **ADJ** *Radio, Électron* **émetteur b.** jamming station; **signal b.** jamming signal
NM *Radio, Électron* jammer, jamming transmitter; *Tél (circuit)* **b.** scrambler

brouillon, -onne [brujɔ̃, -ɔn] **ADJ** muddleheaded; *(au travail)* disorganized, unmethodical; **esprit b.** muddled mind; **travail b.** unmethodical work
N muddler
NM *(ébauche)* (rough) draft; *Scol (notes etc)* rough work; **(papier) b.** scrap *or Am* scratch paper; *Ordinat* **version b.** draft version; **prendre des notes au b.** to take rough notes; **faire un exercice au b.** to do an exercise in rough; **je ne vais pas lire ce b.!** I'm not going to read this scribble!; **(cahier de) b.** rough (note)book; *Fig* **cette présentation n'est qu'un b.** this is only a rough presentation

broum [brum] **INT** brum, brum!

broussaille [brusaj] **NF** *(souvent pl)* scrub, brushwood; **cheveux en b.** tousled *or* unkempt hair; **sourcils en b.** shaggy *or* bushy eyebrows

broussailleux, -euse [brusajø, -øz] **ADJ** *(région)* scrubby, bushy; *(cheveux)* tousled, unkempt; *(sourcils)* bushy, shaggy; **terrain b.** scrubland

broussard [brusar] **NM** bushman

brousse¹ [brus] **NF** **la b.** the bush, *Austr* the outback; *Fam Fig* **the back of beyond, the middle of nowhere; **feux de b.** bush *or* brush fires; *Fam* **son village est perdu en pleine b.** his village is at the back of beyond *or* in the middle of nowhere

brousse² **NF** *Région (fromage)* = cream cheese made from goats' or ewes' milk

broutage [brutaʒ], **broutement** [brutmɑ̃] **NM 1** *(par les bêtes)* grazing, browsing **2** *Tech (des freins, de l'embrayage, d'un outil)* juddering, grabbing

brouter [brute] **VT** *(herbe etc)* to graze, to feed on; *Fig Fam* **elle me les broute, celle-là!** she's a real pain!, she really gets on my nerves!
VI 1 *(des bêtes)* to graze **2** *(des freins, de l'embrayage, d'un outil)* to judder, to grab

broutille [brutij] **NF** trifle, trifling matter; **ils se sont disputés pour une b.** they argued over nothing

brownien [brɔnjɛ̃] **ADJ** *Phys* **mouvement b.** Brownian movement

browning [brɔniŋ] **NM** Browning

broyage [brwajaʒ] **NM** *(d'une pierre, des aliments par les dents etc)* crushing, grinding; *(du charbon)* pulverizing; *Tex (du chanvre etc)* braking

broyer [brwaje] **VT** *(je broie, n. broyons; je broierai)* *(pierre, aliments etc)* to crush, to grind; *(documents)* to shred; *(charbon)* to pulverize; *Tex (chanvre etc)* to brake; **b. des couleurs** to grind colours; **la machine lui a broyé la main** the machine crushed his hand; *Fig* **quand il te serre la main, il te la broie!** he has a crushing handshake!; *Fig* **b. du noir** to be down in the dumps

broyeur, -euse [brwajœr, -øz] **ADJ** *(appareil etc)* crushing, grinding
N *(personne)* crusher, grinder; *Tex* hemp braker *or* dresser
NM *(machine)* crusher, grinder; *(de documents)* shredder; *(de charbon)* pulverizer

► b. d'évier sink disposal unit; **b. d'ordures** waste *or Am* garbage disposal unit

brrr [br] **INT** *Fam* brrr!

bru [bry] **NF** *Vieilli* daughter-in-law

bruant [bryɑ̃] **NM** *(oiseau)* bunting; **b. jaune** yellowhammer

brucelles [brysɛl] **NFPL** tweezers

brucellose [bryseloz] **NF** *Vét, Méd* brucellosis

bruche [bryʃ] **NF** *Entom* **b. des pois** pea beetle, weevil

brugnon [brynɔ̃] **NM** *(fruit)* nectarine

brugnonier [brynɔnje] **NM** nectarine (tree)

bruine [bryin] **NF** drizzle

bruiner [bryine] **V IMPERS** to drizzle; **il bruine** it's drizzling

bruineux, -euse [bryinø, -øz] **ADJ** drizzly

bruire [bryir] **VI** *(prp* **bruissant**; *pr ind* **il bruit, ils bruissent**; *impf* **il bruissait**) *(des feuilles, d'une étoffe)* to rustle; *(d'une machine)* to hum; *(d'un ruisseau, du vent)* to murmur; *(des abeilles)* to buzz

bruissement [bryismɑ̃] **NM** *(des feuilles, d'une étoffe)* rustle, rustling; *(d'une machine)* hum(ming); *(d'un ruisseau, du vent)* murmur(ing); *(des abeilles)* buzzing

bruit [bryi] **NM 1** *(son)* sound, noise; *(vacarme)* noise; *(tapage, scandale)* commotion, fuss; **on n'entend pas les bruits de la rue** you can't hear the noise from the street; **c'est très calme, il n'y a pas un b.** it's very quiet, there's not a sound; **quel b.!** what a row *or* din *or* racket!; **lutte contre le b.** noise abatement campaign; **b. métallique** clang; **b. de vaisselle** clatter of dishes; **b. de marteaux** (sound of) hammering; **b. de pas** (sound of) footsteps; **il y avait des bruits de voix** there was the sound of voices, voices could be heard; **b. sourd** thud; **c'est tombé avec un b. sourd** it fell with a thud; **faire du b.** *(d'un enfant, moteur etc)* to make a noise, to be noisy; **il fait du b. quand il mange** he's a noisy eater; **ça a fait un b. formidable** it made an incredible noise; **enlève tes chaussures, tu feras moins de b.** take off your shoes, you'll make less noise; **ne faites pas de b.!** *(soyez silencieux)* don't make a sound!; *(ne chahutez pas)* don't be noisy!; *Fig* **cette histoire a fait du b. à l'époque** the affair caused a sensation *or* scandal at the time; **beaucoup de b. pour rien** much ado about nothing; **faire grand b. de qch** to make a great to-do *or* a great fuss about sth; **sans b.** without a sound, silently; *Électron etc* **b. parasite** interference, noise **2** *Méd (cardiaque, respiratoire)* murmur **3** *(rumeur)* rumour, *Am* rumor; **répandre** *ou* **faire courir un b.** to spread a rumour; **le b. court que ...** rumour has it that ...; **des bruits courent sur la démission du Premier ministre** there are rumours that the Prime Minister is going to resign; **des bruits circulent** rumours are circulating *or* are going about *or* round; **faux b.** false rumour
► b. d'ambiance background noise; **b. blanc** white noise; **b. de fond** background noise; **b. du moteur** engine noise; **b. de piste** *(d'un enregistrement)* hiss; **b. de roulement** road noise

bruitage [bryitaʒ] **NM** *Théâtre, Cin, TV* sound effects

bruiter [bryite] **VT** *Théâtre, Cin, TV* to add sound effects to

bruiteur, -euse [bryitœr, øz] **N** *Théâtre, Cin, TV* sound-effects man, *f* woman

brûlage [brylaʒ] **NM 1** *(des mauvaises herbes, de l'herbe etc)* burning; *(de la peinture)* burning off; *(des cheveux)* singeing; **se faire faire un b.** to have one's hair singed **2** *(du café)* roasting

brûlant [brylɑ̃] ADJ *(très chaud)* burning (hot); *(café)* boiling (hot), scalding (hot); *(soleil)* burning, scorching, blazing; *Fig (paroles etc)* fiery, passionate; **il a les mains brûlantes** his hands are burning (hot); **désir b.** burning desire; **question brûlante** burning question; **le sujet est d'une actualité brûlante** it's one of the burning issues of the day

brûlé, -ée [bryle] ADJ burnt; *Méd* **il est b. au premier/deuxième/troisième degré** he has first-/second-/third-degree burns; *Culin* **crème brûlée** crème brûlée; **vin b.** mulled wine; *Fam* **tête brûlée** hothead; *Fam* **être b.** *(être compromis)* to be finished
  NM **1 odeur de b.** smell of burning, burnt smell; **goût de b.** burnt taste; **avoir un goût de b.** to taste burnt; **sentir le b.** *(être louche)* to look fishy; *(d'opinions)* to smack of heresy **2** *Can* burnt-out woodland area
  N *(accidenté)* burns victim; *Méd* **les grands brûlés** people with third-degree burns; **crier comme un b.** to scream like a madman

brûle-parfum(s), *pl* **brûle-parfums** [brylparfœ̃] NM perfume burner

brûle-pourpoint (à) [abrylpurpwɛ̃] ADV *(sans détour)* point-blank; *Arch* **tirer sur qn à b.** to fire at sb at point-blank range

brûler [bryle] VT **1** *(papier, bois, objet, les morts etc)* to burn; *(détruire entièrement) (maison etc)* to burn down; *(métal)* to burn away; *(résistance électrique etc)* to burn out; *(peinture)* to burn off; *(blessure)* to cauterize; *(d'un acide)* to corrode; *(d'un consommateur) (électricité, combustible)* to use, to burn; *(bougie)* to burn; **elle fut brûlée vive** *(par accident)* she was burnt to death *or* burnt alive; *(par supplice)* she was burnt at the stake; **b. la cervelle à qn** to blow sb's brains out; *Agr* **b. le terrain** *ou* **la brousse** to burn the ground; **la chaudière brûle beaucoup de charbon** the boiler burns *or* uses a lot of coal; *Fig* **ils ont brûlé leurs dernières cartouches** they've shot their bolt
  2 *(pain, gâteau, rôti etc)* to burn; *(café)* to roast; *(cheveux)* to singe; *(linge)* to scorch; *(personne, peau, yeux etc)* to burn; **le lait est brûlé** the milk has caught; **l'argent lui brûle les doigts** money burns a hole in his pocket; **terre brûlée par le soleil** sun-scorched earth; **le soleil me brûle le dos** the sun is burning *or* scorching my back; *Fam* **b. la route** *ou* **le pavé** to scorch along *or* tear along the road; **la gelée a brûlé les bourgeons** the frost has nipped the buds; **la fumée me brûle les yeux** the smoke made my eyes burn *or* sting *or* smart; *Fig* **b. les planches** to give an inspired performance
  3 *Aut* **b. un feu rouge** to jump the lights, to go through a red light; **b. un stop** to go straight through a stop sign, not to stop at a stop sign; **b. la politesse à qn** to leave sb abruptly, to leave without saying goodbye to sb; *(passer devant qn dans une queue)* to push in front of sb; *Sport* **b. un concurrent** to race past a competitor, to leave a competitor standing; **b. un signal** to overrun a signal
  VI **1** *(flamber) (de bois, charbon etc)* to burn; *(de maison etc)* to burn, to be on fire, to be alight; *(être très chaud)* to be burning (hot); *(de l'eau)* to be boiling (hot), to be scalding (hot); *Méd* to be feverish; *(d'une blessure)* to smart; **j'ai la gorge qui brûle** my throat is burning; **j'ai les yeux qui brûlent** my eyes are burning *or* stinging *or* smarting; **b. lentement** *ou* **sans flamme** to smoulder; **laisser b. la lumière/l'électricité** to leave the light/the lights on *or* burning; **aïe, ça brûle!** ow, that's hot!; *Fam* **tu brûles** *(dans un jeu)* you're getting very warm; **b. de fièvre** to be burning (with fever)
  2 *Fig* **b. de curiosité** to be consumed with

curiosity; **b. d'impatience de faire qch** to be burning (with impatience) *or* bursting (with impatience) to do sth; **b. (du désir) de faire qch** to be burning *or* dying to do sth; *Fam* **les mains lui brûlent** he is dying to be doing things; *Fam* **les pieds lui brûlent** he is itching to be off
  3 *(de la viande)* to burn; *(du lait)* to catch; **j'ai encore fait b. mon repas!** I've burnt my food again!
  4 *Litt, Vieilli* **b. (d'amour) pour qn** to languish for sb
  VPR **se brûler** *(par accident)* to burn oneself *(avec* on); *(exprès)* to set fire to oneself; **se b. les doigts** to burn one's fingers; **se b. la langue** to burn *or* scald one's tongue; **se b. la cervelle** to blow one's brains out

brûleur [brylœr] NM **1** *(d'une cuisinière à gaz etc)* burner **2 b. de café** coffee roaster

brûloir [brylwar] NM *(machine)* coffee roaster

brûlot [brylo] NM **1** *(écrit)* fierce attack **2** *Culin (au sucre)* burnt brandy **3** *Can (moustique)* gnat, midge **4** *Hist, Naut* fire ship

brûlure [brylyr] NF **1** *(blessure)* burn; *Méd* **b. au premier/deuxième/troisième degré** first-/second-/third-degree burn; **des traces de b. de cigarette sur un fauteuil** cigarette burns on an armchair **2 (sensation de) b.** burning (sensation); **brûlures d'estomac** heartburn **3** *Agr* frost nip; *(par le soleil)* scorching; *(du maïs)* blight

brume [brym] NF mist, haze; **un banc de b.** a bank of mist; *Fig* **dans les brumes du sommeil** heavy with sleep; **englué dans les brumes de l'ivresse** in a drunken haze
  ▶▶ **b. de beau temps** heat haze; **b. de chaleur** heat haze

brumeux, -euse [brymø, -øz] ADJ misty, hazy; *Fig (idées, explication etc)* hazy, vague, woolly

brumisateur® [brymizatœr] NM atomizer, spray

brun, brune [brœ̃, bryn] ADJ *(tissu, cheveux etc)* brown; *(peau, personne)* dark, swarthy, dusky; *(teint) (bronzé)* brown, tanned; **tabac b.** dark tobacco; **une bière brune** a brown ale; **il est b. de peau** he's dark-skinned; **elle est naturellement brune** she is a natural brunette
  N *(personne)* dark-haired man, *f* woman; **une belle brune** a lovely brunette
  NM *(couleur)* brown; **b. foncé** dark brown
  NF **brune 1 à la brune** at dusk, at twilight **2** *(bière)* dark beer, *Br* ≃ brown ale

brunante [brynɑ̃t] NF *Can* dusk, twilight

brunâtre [brynɑtr] ADJ brownish

brunch [brœnʃ] NM brunch

brunette [brynɛt] NF brunette

brunir [brynir] VI *(de peau, personne)* to tan, to become tanned; *(de cheveux)* to darken, to go dark; *(de feuillages)* to turn brown; *Culin (de sucre)* to brown; **b. au soleil** to tan
  VT *(peau)* to tan; *(cheveux)* to darken; *Tech (or, métal)* to burnish, to polish

brunissage [brynisaʒ] NM *Tech* burnishing, polishing

brunissement [brynismɑ̃] NM *(de la peau)* tanning; *(résultat)* tan

brunisseur, -euse [brynisœr, -øz] N *Tech* burnisher

brunissoir [bryniswar] NM *Tech* burnisher, polisher

brunissure [brynisyr] NF **1** *(des métaux)* burnish, polish **2** *Agr (potato)* blight *or* rot

Brushing® [brœʃiŋ] NM blow-dry; **se faire un B.** to blow-dry one's hair; **faire un B. à qn** to give sb a blow-dry, to blow-dry sb's hair; **coupe et B.** cut and blow-dry

brusque [brysk] ADJ **1** *(personne, manière,*

ton) abrupt, curt, brusque; *(geste)* abrupt, brusque **2** *(arrêt, changement, départ etc)* sudden, abrupt; *Aut* **tournant b.** sharp bend

brusquement [bryskəmɑ̃] ADV **1** *(soudainement)* suddenly, abruptly; **il a b. changé** he suddenly changed; **la route plonge b./ tourne b. à droite** the road dips sharply/ turns sharply to the right **2** *(sans ménagements)* abruptly, brusquely, curtly

brusquer [bryske] VT **1 b. qn** *(être impoli envers)* to be abrupt *or* curt with sb; *(maltraiter)* to treat sb harshly **2** *(hâter) (décision)* to rush; **b. les choses** to rush things; **il ne faut rien b.** we mustn't rush things; **attaque brusquée** surprise attack; *Fam* **arrête de me b.** stop rushing me

brusquerie [bryskəri] NF abruptness, brusqueness; **avec b.** abruptly, brusquely

brut [bryt] ADJ **1** *(pétrole)* crude; *(sucre)* unrefined; *(diamant)* rough, uncut; *(champagne)* extra-dry, brut; *(cidre)* dry; *(marbre, albâtre)* unpolished; *(bois, peau)* undressed; **toile brute** unbleached cloth; **produit b.** primary product; *Ordinat* **données brutes** raw data; **matières brutes** raw materials; **fonte brute** pig iron; **or b.** gold in nuggets; **b. de décoffrage** *(béton)* unsurfaced exposed; *Fig (non encore peaufiné)* rough around the edges; *(personne)* unrefined; *Métal* **b. de fonte** *ou* **de coulée** rough cast; **à l'état b.** in its raw state; **il nous a exposé le projet à l'état b.** he gave us a general outline of the project; **faire de l'art b.** to produce primitive art; **faits bruts** bald *or* hard facts
  2 *Com (bénéfice, valeur, poids etc)* gross; **salaire b.** gross salary; **marge brute** gross profit margin; **montant b.** gross amount, gross
  NM **1** *(pétrole)* crude (oil) **2** *(champagne)* brut *or* extra-dry champagne
  ADV **le colis pèse b. 20 kilos** *ou* **20 kilos b.** the parcel weighs 20 kilos gross; **elle gagne b. 5000 euros** *ou* **5000 euros b.** she earns 5,000 euros gross, she grosses 5,000 euros

brutal, -ale, -aux, -ales [brytal, -o] ADJ *(violent) (personne, mort)* brutal, violent; *(impoli, brusque) (personne, paroles, révélation, franchise etc)* brutal; **force brutale** brute force; **coup b.** brutal *or* savage blow; **les faits brutaux** the hard *or* brutal facts; **vérité brutale** plain *or* unvarnished truth; **cette vérité était trop brutale pour elle** the truth was too shocking for her; **être b. avec qn** to treat sb roughly *or* harshly; **avec sa manière brutale de dire les choses** with his harsh way of saying things; **arrêt b.** sudden *or* abrupt stop; **frein/embrayage b.** fierce brake/clutch

brutalement [brytalmɑ̃] ADV *(violemment)* brutally, violently; *(rudement)* harshly, roughly; *(sans ambages)* bluntly, plainly; *(soudainement)* abruptly, suddenly; **la route tourne b.** there is a sudden bend in the road, the road bends suddenly; **il a b. changé** he has suddenly changed

brutaliser [brytalize] VT *(femme, enfant, matériel etc)* to ill-treat, to maltreat; *Fam* **il ne faut pas me b.** *(laisse-moi réfléchir)* don't rush me

brutalité [brytalite] NF **1** *(de personne) (violence)* brutality, violence; *(grossièreté)* roughness; **il lui parle avec b.** he has such a rough tone when he speaks to him; **pas de b.!** no violence! **2** *(d'animal)* brutality, savagery **3** *(rapidité)* suddenness, abruptness **4** *(acte violent)* brutal act, brutality; **brutalités de la police** police brutality

brute [bryt] NF **1** *(personne violente)* brute, beast; *(personne grossière)* boor; **sale b.!** filthy beast!; **frapper qn comme une b.** to hit sb brutally *or* violently; **j'ai dû taper dessus comme une b. pour que ça entre** I had to bang at it like mad to get it to go in; **espèce**

de b. épaisse! you great oaf!; **le gangster m'envoya une de ses brutes épaisses** the gangster sent one of his heavies to visit me **2** *Litt (animal)* brute beast

Bruxelles [brysɛl] **N** Brussels

bruyamment [brɥijamɑ̃] **ADV** *(parler, rire)* loudly; *(manger)* noisily

bruyant [brɥijɑ̃] **ADJ** *(rue, voisin)* noisy; *(succès)* resounding; *(rire, applaudissement)* loud; **un quartier peu b.** a quiet neighbourhood

bruyère [brɥijɛr] **NF 1** *(plante)* heather, heath; *(terre)* heath(land), moor(land) **2** **racine de b.** briar root; **pipe en** *ou* **de b.** briar pipe

bryone [brijɔn] **NF** *(plante)* bryony

BSPCE [beɛspeseə] **NM** *Bourse (abrév* **bon de souscription de parts de créateurs d'entreprise)** = stock option in a start-up company with tax privileges

BT [bete] **NM** *abrév* **brevet de technicien**

BTH [beteaʃ] **NM** *abrév* **brevet de technicien hôtelier**

B2B [bitubi] **ADJ** *(abrév* **business to business)** B2B

B2C [bitusi] **ADJ** *(abrév* **business to consumer)** B2C

BTP [betepe] **NM** *(abrév* **bâtiment et travaux publics)** = building and public works sector

BTS [beteɛs] **NM** *(abrév* **brevet de technicien supérieur)** = advanced vocational training certificate; **B. Action Commerciale** professional marketing qualification; **B. Force de Vente** professional sales qualification

buanderie [bɥɑ̃dri] **NF** laundry (room)

Buba [byba] **NF** *(abrév* **Bundesbank)** Bundesbank

bubon [bybɔ̃] **NM** *Méd* bubo

bubonique [bybɔnik] **ADJ** *Méd (peste)* bubonic

Bucarest [bykarɛst] **N** Bucharest

buccal, -ale, -aux, -ales [bykal, -o] **ADJ** *Anat (cavité etc)* buccal; *Méd* **vaccin b.** oral vaccine

buccodentaire [bykodɑ̃tɛr] **ADJ** *(hygiène)* oral

bucco-génital, -ale, -aux, -ales [byko-ʒenital, -o] **ADJ** **rapports bucco-génitaux** oral sex

bûche [byʃ] **NF** *(morceau de bois)* log; *Fam (personne stupide)* blockhead; *Fam* **ramasser une b.** to come a cropper; *Fam* **ne reste pas là comme une b.!** don't just stand/sit there like a dummy!
▸▸ *Culin* **b. de Noël** Yule log

bûcher¹ [byʃe] **NM 1** *(pour le bois)* woodshed **2** *(de supplice)* stake; **monter** *ou* **mourir sur le b.** to be burnt at the stake; **condamné au b.** sentenced to be burnt at the stake **3** *(funéraire)* (funeral) pyre
VT *Can (arbre)* to fell, to cut down

bûcher² *Scol Fam* **VT** *(matière)* to bone up on, *Br* to swot up
VI to slog, to work hard; *(d'un élève, d'un étudiant)* to swot, *Am* to grind

bûcheron [byʃrɔ̃] **NM** woodcutter, woodman, lumberjack

bûchette [byʃɛt] **NF** *(de bois sec)* stick, twig; *(pour apprendre à compter)* stick

bûcheur, -euse [byʃœr, -øz] *Fam* **N** slogger, hard worker; *(élève, étudiant)* swot, *Am* grind
ADJ *(étudiant etc)* hard-working

bucolique [bykɔlik] *Littér* **ADJ** *(poème)* bucolic, pastoral
NF pastoral poem, bucolic

budget [bydʒɛ] **NM** budget; *(dans la publicité, dans le marketing)* account; **b. de l'éducation** education budget; **b. de la marine/de**

la guerre navy/army estimates; **inscrire** *ou* **porter qch au b.** to budget for sth; **boucler le b.** to balance the budget; **vacances/prix pour les petits budgets** budget holidays/prices; **de quel b. disposez-vous pour vos vacances?** what's your holiday budget?, what's the budget for your holiday?
▸▸ **b. des approvisionnements** purchase budget; **b. des charges** overhead budget, cost budget; **b. commercial** sales budget; *UE* **b. communautaire européen** European Community budget; **b. équilibré** balanced budget; **b. de l'État** state budget; **b. d'exploitation** operating budget; **b. de fonctionnement** operating budget; **b. glissant** rolling budget; **b. global** master *or* overall budget; *Compta* **b. des investissements** capital budget; **b. marketing** marketing budget; **b. mensuel** monthly budget; **b. prévisionnel** provisional budget; **b. de production** production budget; *Mktg* **b. de prospection** market exploration budget; **b. publicitaire** advertising budget; **b. des recettes** revenue budget; **b. renouvelable** continuous budget; *Compta* **b. de trésorerie** cashflow, cash budget; **b. des ventes** sales budget

budgétaire [bydʒetɛr] **ADJ** *(dépenses, contrôle)* budgetary; *(année)* financial; **comptabilité b.** budgeting; **contrainte b.** budget constraint; **déficit/excédent b.** budget deficit/surplus

budgétisation [bydʒetizasjɔ̃] **NF** inclusion in the budget; **b. base zéro** zero-base budgeting

budgétiser [bydʒetize] **VT** to include in the budget, to budget for

buée [bɥe] **NF** *(sur les vitres etc)* condensation, steam; *(sur un miroir)* mist; **les vitres sont couvertes de b.** the windows are steamed up *or* covered with condensation; **faire de la b.** *(d'une cuisinière etc)* to make *or* produce steam

buffet [byfɛ] **NM 1** *(meuble)* sideboard; **b. de cuisine** (kitchen) dresser **2** **b. (d'orgue)** organ chest **3** *(repas)* buffet (meal); **b. froid** cold buffet; **b. de salades** salad bar; **b. du petit déjeuner** breakfast buffet; **b. à volonté** unlimited buffet; **b. campagnard** = cold buffet made with country produce; **b. de gare** station buffet, refreshment room **4** *Fam (ventre)* belly; **je n'ai rien dans le b. depuis hier soir** I haven't had a bite to eat since last night; **se mettre quelque chose dans le b.** to get something inside one

buffetier, -ière [byftje, -jɛr] **N** *Vieilli (d'un buffet de gare etc)* buffet manager, *f* buffet manageress

buffle [byfl] **NM** buffalo; **cuir (de) b.** buffalo hide VOIR GRAMMAIRE A12

bufflesse [byflɛs], **bufflonne** [byflɔn] **NF** cow buffalo

bug [bœg] **NM** *Ordinat* bug

bugle¹ [bygl] **NM** *Mus* (key) bugle, flugelhorn

bugle² **NF** *(plante)* bugle

building [bildiŋ] **NM** *(d'appartements, de bureaux)* tower block

buire [bɥir] **NF** ewer, flagon

buis [bɥi] **NM** *(arbre)* box (tree); *(bois)* box(-wood); *Rel* **b. bénit** (blessed) palm

buisson [bɥisɔ̃] **NM** bush; *(plusieurs plantes)* thicket; **un b. de mûres** a bramble thicket
▸▸ *Bible* **b. ardent** burning bush; *Culin* **b. d'écrevisses** = crayfish served piled up on a dish

buissonneux, -euse [bɥisɔnø, -øz] **ADJ** *(terrain etc)* bushy; *(végétation)* scrubby

buissonnière [bɥisɔnjɛr] **ADJ F** **faire l'école buissonnière** to play truant *or Am* hook(e)y

bulbe [bylb] **NM 1** *Bot* bulb, corm **2** *Anat*

bulb; **b. (rachidien)** medulla oblongata **3** *Archit* onion dome

bulbeux, -euse [bylbø, -øz] **ADJ** *Bot* bulbous

bulgare [bylgar] **ADJ** Bulgarian
NM *Ling* Bulgarian
N B. Bulgarian

Bulgarie [bylgari] **NF** Bulgaria

bulldozer [byldozœr] **NM** bulldozer; *Fig Fam* **c'est un b., sa sœur** his sister just bulldozes *or* steamrollers her way through things

bulle [byl] **NF 1** *(d'air etc)* bubble; *Méd (vésicule)* blister; *(enceinte stérile)* bubble; *(de bandes dessinées)* balloon; *Ordinat* **b. d'aide** help pop-up; *Tech* **b. d'air** air-lock; **b. d'encre** *(d'une imprimante)* ink bubble; **b. de savon** soap bubble; **faire des bulles** to blow bubbles; *Méd* **enfant-/bébé-b.** = child/baby kept in sterile surroundings; *Fig Fam* **coincer la b.** to laze *or* lounge around
2 *Bourse* **b. boursière** stock market bubble; **b. Internet** Internet bubble; **b. spéculative** speculative bubble
3 *(lettre du pape)* (papal) bull; **b. d'excommunication** bull of excommunication
4 *Fam (à un devoir)* zero; **prendre une b.** to get a zero
ADJ INV **papier b.** Manila paper
NM *(papier)* Manila paper

buller [byle] **VI** *Fam* to laze about

bulletin [byltɛ̃] **NM 1** *(communiqué)* bulletin; *Scol* **b. (scolaire)** (school) report; *TV* **b. d'actualités** *ou* **d'informations** news bulletin *or* report, news sheet; **b. d'entreprise** newsletter; **b. radiophonique** radio bulletin; *TV, Radio* **b. spécial** newsflash **2** *(papier, certificat)* **b. (d'enregistrement) de bagages** luggage ticket, *Am* baggage check; **b. de consigne** left-luggage *or Am* checkroom ticket
▸▸ **b. d'annulation** cancellation form; **b. blanc** blank ballot paper; *Com* **b. de commande** order form; *Bourse* **b. des cours** (Stock Exchange) price list; *Journ* **b. électronique** electronic news sheet; **b. d'expédition** dispatch note, consignment note; **b. de garantie** guarantee (certificate); **b. d'inscription** registration form; **b. météorologique** weather report; **B. officiel** = official listing of all new laws and decrees; **B. officiel des communautés européennes** = official listing of all new EC directives; **b. de paie** pay (advice) slip, salary advice (note); **b. de participation** entry form; **b. de salaire** pay (advice) slip, salary advice (note); *Méd* **b. de santé** medical bulletin; **b. de souscription d'actions** share subscription form; *Scol* **b. trimestriel** end-of-term report; *UE* **b. de l'Union européenne** Bulletin of the European Union; **b. de vente** sales note; *Suisse* **b. de versement** paying-in slip *or* form; **b. de vote** ballot paper; **b. (de vote) nul** spoiled ballot paper

bulletin-réponse, *pl* **bulletins-réponse** **NM** reply form *or* coupon; *(pour un concours)* entry form

bulleux, -euse [bylø, -øz] **ADJ** *Méd* covered with blisters; *Géol, Méd (pierre, fièvre)* vesicular

bull-terrier, *pl* **bull-terriers** [bulterje] **NM** bull terrier

bumping [bœmpiŋ] **NM** *Aviat* bumping

bungalow [bœgalo] **NM** bungalow

bunker [bunkœr] **NM** *Mil* bunker; *Golf* bunker, *Am* sand trap

buraliste [byralist] **N** *(de bureau de poste)* clerk; *(d'impôts)* receiver of taxes; *(de bureau de tabac)* tobacconist

bure [byr] **NF** *Tex* frieze, rough homespun; *(habit religieux)* frock

bureau, -eaux [byro] **NM 1** *(meuble)* desk;

ordinateur de b. desk-top computer; *Pol* déposer un projet de loi sur le b. to table a bill **2** *(lieu)* office; *(à la maison)* study; **ceci fera d'excellents bureaux** this will be very good office space; **je dois passer au b. à midi** I have to drop by the office at midday; **il y a une bonne ambiance au b.** there's a good atmosphere at *or* in the office; **fournitures de b.** office supplies; **b. central** *(de poste)* main post office; *Tél* exchange; **b. de police** police station; **b. de douane** customs house; **b. informatisé** electronic office, paperless office **3** *(personnel)* office (staff) **4** *(assemblée)* committee; **élire le b.** to elect the committee **5** *(service d'une administration etc)* department, division, bureau; **Deuxième B.** Intelligence Branch *or* Service ▸▸ *Com* **b. d'achat** buying *or* purchase office; *Ordinat* **b. actif** active desktop; **b. d'aide sociale** welfare office; **b. de change** bureau de change; **b. à cylindre** roll-top desk; *Com* **b. de départ** port of departure; *Com* **b. de destination** port of destination; **b. distributeur (des Postes)** main sorting post office; **b. de douane** customs office; *Ordinat* **b. électronique** electronic desktop; *Com* **b. d'enregistrement** registration office; *Com* **b. d'entrée** port of entry; **b. d'études** design *or* planning department *or* office; *(de recherche)* R&D department; *Com* **b. d'expédition** shipping office; **b. d'exportation** export office; **b. des illustrations** picture desk; **b. d'information** information office; **b. d'inscriptions** registration desk; **Bureau international du travail** International Labour Office; **b. de location** box office; **b. des méthodes** organization and methods department, O&M department; **b. ministre** pedestal *or* kneehole desk; **b. d'ordonnancement** scheduling and planning department; *Com* **b. de passage** port of transit; **b. paysager** open-plan office; **b. de perception** tax office; **b. de placement** employment agency *or* bureau; **b. de poste** post office; **b. de publicité** advertising agency; *Journ* bureaux de rédaction newspaper office; **b. de renseignements** enquiry *or* information desk; *(pièce)* information office; **b.-satellite** branch office; *Can* **b. spécial de scrutin** advance poll; **b. de tabac** tobacconist's (shop); **b. de traduction** translation agency; **Bureau de vérification de la publicité** = French advertising standards authority, *Br* ≃ ASA

> Il faut noter que le nom anglais **bureau** est un faux ami. Il ne s'emploie jamais pour désigner une pièce mais pour faire référence à une institution.

bureaucrate [byrokrat] **N** *Péj* bureaucrat

bureaucratie [byrokrasi] **NF** *Péj (système)* bureaucracy; *(ensemble des fonctionnaires)* officialdom

bureaucratique [byrokratik] **ADJ** *Péj* bureaucratic

bureaucratisation [byrokratizasjɔ̃] **NF** *Péj* bureaucratization

bureaucratiser [byrokratize] **VT** *Péj* to bureaucratize

bureautique [byrotik] **NF** office automation

burette [byrɛt] **NF** *(pour l'huile)* oilcan, oiler; *Chimie* burette; *Rel* cruet; *Vulg* **il me casse les burettes** he gets on my tits

burin [byrɛ̃] **NM 1** *(de graveur)* graver, burin; *(gravure)* engraving, print **2** *(ciseau d'acier)* (cold) chisel

burinage [byrinaʒ] **NM** *Tech* chiselling, chipping

buriner [byrine] **VT 1** *(avec un burin)* to engrave; **visage buriné** *(par le vent etc)* seamed face **2** *Tech (metal)* to chisel, to chip

burineur [byrinœr] **NM** *Tech* chipper, chiseller

Burkina [byrkina] **NM** Burkina-Faso

burkinabé, -ée [byrkinabe] **ADJ** of/from Burkina-Faso ◊ **N B.** *(natif)* native of Burkina-Faso; *(habitant)* inhabitant of Burkina-Faso

burlesque [byrlɛsk] **ADJ 1** *(air, situation, projet etc)* ludicrous, ridiculous **2** *Littér (poème, genre etc)* burlesque ◊ **NM** *Littér* **le b.** the burlesque

burlingue [byrlɛ̃g] **NM** *Fam* office

burnes [byrn] **NFPL** *Vulg* balls, nuts, *Br* bollocks; **casser les b. à qn** to piss sb off, *Br* to get on sb's tits, *Am* to break sb's balls

burnous [byrnu(s)] **NM** *(d'Arabe)* burnous(e); *(de bébé)* hooded coat; *Fam* **faire suer le b.** to use sweated labour

bus [bys] **NM 1** *(autobus)* bus **2** *Élec* bus (bar) **3** *Ordinat* bus; **b. d'adresses** address bus; **b. de contrôle** control bus; **b. de données** data bus; **b. entrée/sortie** input/output bus; **b. d'interface** interface bus; **b. local** local bus; **b. multimédia** multimedia bus; **b. rapide** high-speed bus; **b. système** system bus

busard [byzar] **NM** *(oiseau)* harrier

buse[1] [byz] **NF 1** *(oiseau)* buzzard **2** *Fam (idiot)* fool

buse[2] **NF** *(tuyau)* pipe; *Métal* blast pipe; *Aut* **b. de carburateur** carburettor choke tube; *Min* **b. d'injection** injector nozzle; *Aut* **b. de carburateur** carburettor choke tube; *Min* **b. d'aérage** air channel *or* pipe *or* shaft; **b. de ventilation** air vent

buse[3] **NF** *Belg (échec)* failure

business [biznɛs] **NM** *Fam (affaire)* business; **mais qu'est-ce que c'est que ce b.?** what's going on?, what's all this?

businessman [biznɛsman], *pl* **businessmen** [biznɛsmen] *ou* **businessmans** **NM** businessman

businesswoman [biznɛswuman], *pl* **businesswomen** [biznɛswumen] *ou* **businesswomans** **NF** businesswoman

busqué [byske] **ADJ** *(nez)* hook(ed), aquiline, Roman

buste [byst] **NM** *(haut du corps)* chest; *(seins)* bust; *Beaux-Arts* **b. (en hermès)** bust; **peindre qn en b.** to paint a half-length portrait of sb

bustier [bystje] **NM** *(soutien-gorge)* long-line (strapless) bra; *(corsage)* bustier; **robe de bal/maillot à b.** strapless evening gown/swimming costume

but [by(t)] **NM 1** *(objectif)* aim, purpose, object, goal; *(d'un voyage, d'une promenade etc)* destination, goal; **il faut avoir un b. dans la vie** you must have a goal *or* an aim *or* a purpose in life; **il l'a fait avec ce b. en tête** he did it with this aim *or* object in mind; **je vous ai blessé, ce n'était pas mon b.** I've hurt you, it wasn't my intention *or* I didn't mean to; **mesure ayant pour b. d'assurer ...** measure intended to ensure ...; **remplir un b.** to serve a purpose; **un b. personnel** a personal goal; **dans le b. de vous aider** with the object *or* aim *or* intention of helping you; **dans le b. de frauder** with intent to defraud; **dans ce b.** with this aim in view; **se fixer un b.** to set oneself a goal *or* target; **je suis encore loin du b.** I still have a long way to go; **nous sommes tout près du b.** we don't have far to go; **poursuivre son b.** to pursue one's goal *or* aim; **cette loi vise un double b.** this law has a two-fold objective; **il touche au b.** he has nearly reached his goal *or* achieved his aim; **aller droit au b.** to go straight to the point; **errer sans b.** to wander about aimlessly; **c'est le b. recherché** that's what we're aiming for; **c'est le b. de l'opération** that's the (whole) point of the operation; **un coup au b.**

a direct hit; **à b. lucratif** profit-making; **association à b. non lucratif** non-profit-making association, *Am* not-for-profit association **2** *Ftbl etc* goal; **ligne de b.** goal line; **entrée du b.** goal mouth; **marquer un b.** to score a goal; **gagner/perdre (par) 3 buts à 1** to win/lose by 3 goals to 1; **être dans les buts, garder les buts** to be in goal; **b. en or** golden goal **3** **tirer de b. en blanc** to fire point-blank; **faire une offre/répondre de b. en blanc** to make an offer/answer on the spur of the moment; **elle me l'a dit de b. en blanc** she told me point-blank

butane [bytan] **NM** *Chimie* butane; **gaz b.** butane (gas)

butanier [bytanje] **NM** *Naut* butane tanker

buté [byte] **ADJ** stubborn, obstinate; **visage b.** fixed *or* set *or* determined expression

butée [byte] **NF 1** *Tech* thrust; **palier de b.** thrust block *or* bearing; **b. (d'arrêt)** stop **2** *Constr* abutment, buttress **3** *Aut* stop; **en b.** in full lock; **en b. à droite/gauche** in full right/left lock **4** *Typ* **texte en b. gauche/droite** left/right justified text

buter [byte] **VI 1 b. contre qch** *(cogner)* to bump *or* bang into *or* against sth, to knock against sth; *(trébucher)* to stumble *or* trip over sth; **b. contre** *ou* **sur un problème/une difficulté** to come up against a problem/a difficulty **2** *(de poutres etc)* to abut, to rest *(contre* against) ◊ **VT 1** *(braquer)* **b. qn** to put sb's back up **2** *(mur)* to prop up, to buttress, to shore up **3** *Arg (tuer)* to bump off ◊ **VPR se buter** *(s'entêter)* to dig one's heels in, to get stubborn

buteur [bytœr] **NM** *Ftbl* goalscorer; *Rugby* kicker; **le meilleur b.** the top goalscorer

butin [bytɛ̃] **NM** booty; *(de pilleur)* spoils, plunder; *(de voleur)* loot; **le b. des recherches archéologiques** the finds from the archaeological dig

butiner [bytine] **VI** *(des abeilles)* to gather pollen ◊ **VT** *(renseignements etc)* to gather, to collect

butineur, -euse [bytinœr, -øz] **ADJ** pollen-gathering ◊ **NM** *Ordinat* browser

butoir [bytwar] **NM** *Tech* stop, check; *Rail* buffer; **b. d'une porte** door stop(per); *Aut* **b. de pare-chocs** bumper guard, overrider

butor [bytɔr] **NM 1** *(oiseau)* bittern **2** *Fam (lourdaud)* lout, *Br* yob

buttage [bytaʒ] **NM** *(de plantes)* earthing up

butte [byt] **NF 1** *(colline)* hillock, knoll, mound; *Géol* **b. témoin** outlier **2 b. (de tir)** butts; *Fig* **être en b. à qch** to be exposed *or* open to sth

butter [byte] **VT 1** *Agr (sol)* to ridge; *(plantes, un rosier)* to earth up **2** *Arg (tuer)* **b. qn** to bump sb off

buvable [byvabl] **ADJ 1** *(potable)* drinkable; **il est tout à fait b., ce petit vin!** it's a very drinkable little wine, this **2** *Méd* to be taken orally

buvard [byvar] **ADJ papier b.** blotting paper ◊ **NM** *(matière)* blotting paper; *(feuille)* piece *or* sheet of blotting paper; *(sous-main)* blotter

buvette [byvɛt] **NF 1** *(dans une gare etc)* refreshment bar **2** *(dans une station thermale)* pump room

buveur, -euse [byvœr, -øz] **N** drinker; **c'est un grand** *ou* **gros b.** he's a heavy drinker; **une buveuse de bière** a beer-drinker

BVP [bevepe] **NM** *(abrév bureau de vérification de la publicité)* French advertising standards authority, *Br* ≃ ASA

bye(-bye) [baj(baj)] **INT** bye-bye

by-pass [bajpas] NM INV *Chir, Aut* bypass

byronien, -ienne [birɔnjɛ̃, -jɛn] ADJ Byronic

Byzance [bizɑ̃s] N Byzantium; *Fam* **c'est B.** it's the last word in luxury; **c'est pas B.** it's not exactly luxurious

byzantin, -ine [bizɑ̃tɛ̃, -in] ADJ Byzantine; *Fig Péj (querelles etc)* byzantine N B. Byzantine

C¹, c [se] **NM** (lettre) C, c; **c cédille** c cedilla

C² (abrév **Celsius**) C

C++ [seplysplys] **NM** Ordinat C++

c' voir ce

CA [sea] **NM 1** Élec (abrév **courant alternatif**) AC **2** Com (abrév **chiffre d'affaires**) turnover

ÇA [sa] **PRON DÉM** SEE GRAMMAR B15 **1** (cela) it, that; (ceci) it, this; **donne-moi ça** give it to me, give me that; **c'est dégoûtant ça** that's disgusting; **une petite femme haute comme ça** a little woman no taller than that or only so high; **je suis comme ça** I'm like that; Fam **alors comme ça, vous déménagez?** so you're moving, are you?; **allons, pas de ça!** hey! none of that!; **pas de ça chez nous** we don't want any of that here; **ce n'est pas si facile que ça** it isn't as easy as (all) that; **ça oui!** oh yes!, definitely!; **ça non!** oh no!, not on your life!; **il ne manquait plus que ça** that's all we/ I/etc needed; **ça dépend** it or that depends; **à part ça, tout va bien** apart from that, everything's fine; **il y a un peu de ça, effectivement** yes, there's an element of or a bit of that; **ça me fait de la peine de le voir malade** it upsets me to see him ill; **elle n'était pas comme ça avant** she wasn't like that before; **ça va? – comme ci comme ça** how are you? – so-so; **... tout ça quoi ... et cetera, et cetera; qui/quand/où ça?** who/when/where('s that)?; **comment ça?** how's that?; **comment ça, elle est partie?** what do you mean 'she's gone'?; **c'est qui/quoi ça?** who's/what's that?; **ça alors!** goodness (me)!; **ça alors, c'est incroyable!** well I never! or blow me! that's incredible!; **ça y est!** that's it!; **c'est ça!** that's it!, that's right!

2 Fam **ça bavarde là-bas dans le fond de la classe** there's talking going on at the back of the classroom; **regarde-moi ça!** just look at that!; **écoute-moi ça!** just listen to this!; **c'est ça les hommes!** that's men for you!; **ça va, ça vient** (les touristes etc) they come and go; **ça arrive en retard et ça veut qu'on l'attende** he/she/etc arrives late, and then expects me/us/etc to wait for him/her/etc

3 Fam (le sexe) it; **il ne pense qu'à ça** he's got a one-track mind, that's all he thinks about **NM** Psy **le ça** the id

çà [sa] **ADV çà et là** here and there **INT ah çà!** now then!; **ah çà! par exemple!** well, I'm blowed or damned!

cabale [kabal] **NF 1** Rel cab(b)ala **2** (complot) cabal, plot; **monter une c. contre qn** to plot against sb **3** (ligue) cabal, faction

cabaliste [kabalist] **NM** Rel cab(b)alist

cabalistique [kabalistik] **ADJ** cab(b)alistic; Fig **des formules cabalistiques** arcane formulae

caban [kabã] **NM** car coat; Naut peajacket, reefer

cabane [kaban] **NF 1** (bicoque) hut, Péj shack; (en rondins) (log) cabin; (à outils etc) shed; Can **c. à sucre** saphouse **2** Arg (prison) **en c.** in (the) clink, Br in the nick; **trente ans de c.** thirty years in (the) clink or Br in the nick; **faire de la c.** to do time, to be inside

► ► **c. à lapins** (rabbit) hutch; Fig **ils vivent dans des cabanes à lapins** they live in rabbit hutches or shoeboxes

cabanon [kabanɔ̃] **NM 1** (petite cabane) hut, shed **2** (en Provence) (maison de campagne) (country) cottage **3** (chalet de plage) (beach) hut, cabin, chalet **4** (cellule) padded cell; Fam **il est bon pour le c.** he ought to be locked up

cabaret [kabarɛ] **NM 1** (boîte) night club, cabaret **2** Arch (auberge) tavern, inn

cabaretier, -ière [kabartje, -jɛr] **N** Arch innkeeper, tavern keeper

cabas [kaba] **NM 1** (panier) shopping basket; (en tissu) shopping bag **2** (pour les fruits) basket

cabestan [kabɛstã] **NM** Naut capstan; **c. horizontal** windlass; **grand c.** main capstan; **virez au c.!** heave!

cabillaud [kabijo] **NM** (fresh) cod

cabine [kabin] **NF 1** (de bateau, d'avion, vaisseau spatial etc) cabin; Naut **c. de luxe** stateroom, de luxe cabin **2** (de piscine) changing cubicle **3** (de grue) cab, house; (de locomotive, camion) cab; (d'ascenseur) cage, Am car; Aut **c. basculante** tilt cab **4** TV etc **c. du commentateur** commentary booth; **c. de montage** edit suite; **c. de présentation** announcer booth; **c. de projection** projection room; **c. de régie** control room, control cubicle; **c. speak** presentation booth

► ► Rail **c. d'aiguillage** signal box; **c. de bain(s)** (de plage) beach hut; (de piscine) changing cubicle; **c. de douche** shower cubicle; **c. d'essayage** fitting room; **c. Internet** Internet booth; Aviat **c. de pilotage** cockpit, flight deck; **c. téléphonique** (tele)phone or call box, telephone booth

cabinet [kabinɛ] **NM 1** (petite pièce) small room; Fam **les cabinets** the toilet, Br the loo, Am the john

2 (lieu de consultation etc) office; (d'avocat) chambers; (de médecin) consulting room, Br surgery, Am office; (patients, clients etc) practice; **c. conseil** consultancy; **c. de conseil en gestion** management consultancy; **c. d'experts-conseils** consultancy (firm); **c. d'audit** firm of auditors; Mktg **c. d'études** market research firm; **c. d'expertise comptable** accounting firm; **c. immobilier** Br estate agent's or Am realtor's office; **c. juridique** law firm; **c. de recrutement** recruitment agency; **c. de traduction** translation company

3 Pol Vieilli cabinet; (d'un ministre) departmental staff; **question de c.** ministerial question; **homme de c.** adviser; **chef de c.** = principal private secretary

4 (meuble) cabinet

5 (au musée) **c. d'estampes** print room

► ► Hist **c. de lecture** library, reading room; **c. noir** cubbyhole; **c. particulier** (au restaurant) private dining room; **c. de toilette** (small) bathroom or Am washroom

câblage [kablaʒ] **NM 1** Élec (d'une maison, fils) wiring, cabling; Tél **c. en paire torsadée** twisted pair cabling **2** Tex, Élec (de fils etc) twisting together **3** (de message) cabling **4** TV (pose du réseau) cable (TV) installation, cabling; **le c. d'une ville** installing cable (television) in a town

câble [kabl] **NM 1** Élec cable, lead; Tél cable; **poser un c.** to lay a cable; **la télévision par c., le c.** cable television; TV **avoir le c.** to have cable; TV **transmettre par c.** to cablecast **2** (corde) cable; **c. métallique** wire cable; (à brins) stranded wire **3** (message) cable, cablegram; **envoyer un c. à qn** to send sb a cable, to cable sb

► ► **c. d'alimentation** supply or feed or power cable; Naut **c. d'amarrage** mooring cable; Électron **c. coaxial** coaxial cable; Aut **c. de démarrage** jump lead, Am jumper cable; **c. en fibres optiques** fibre-optic or Am fiber-optic cable; **c. en fibre(s) de verre** glass fibre cable; Tech **c. de frein** brake cable; **c. hertzien** radio link; **c. d'imprimante** printer cable; **c. de masse** earth cable, Am ground cable; **c. optique** fibre-optic cable; Tél **c. en paire torsadée** twisted pair cable; Ordinat **c. parallèle** parallel cable; **c. péritel** SCART cable; **c. de raccordement** connecting cable; **c. de remorque** towrope, towline; **c. de retour (à la masse)** return cable; Ordinat **c. série** serial cable; Ordinat **c. de souris** mouse cable; Ordinat **c. USB** USB cable

câblé [kable] **ADJ 1** (ville, région) with cable television; TV cabled; Ordinat, Tél hardwired; **l'immeuble est c.** the building is wired for cable TV; **réseau c.** cable (TV) network **2** Fam (à la page) hip, trendy

câbler [kable] **VT 1** (tordre ensemble) (fils) to twist together **2** (message) to cable **3** TV (ville, quartier) to install cable television in; (émission) to cable

câbleur, -euse [kablœr, -øz] **N** Tech cable-layer

câbliste [kablist] **N** (personne) cable man, cable operator

câblodiffuseur [kablodifyzœr] **NM** cable company

câblodistributeur [kablodistribytœr] **NM** cable company

câblodistribution [kablodistribysjɔ̃] **NF** cable television; Am Admin community antenna television

câblogramme [kablɔgram] **NM** Arch cablegram, cable

câblo-opérateur, pl **câblo-opérateurs** [kablooperatœr] **NM** cable company

cabochard, -arde [kabɔʃar, -ard] *Fam* ADJ pigheaded
N pigheaded person

caboche [kabɔʃ] NF **1** *Fam (tête)* nut; **mets-le toi dans la c.!** get that into your thick skull!; **avoir la c. dure** *(être bête)* to be thick; *(être têtu)* to be pigheaded, to be as stubborn as a mule **2** *(clou)* heavy-headed nail; *(de cordonnier)* hobnail; *(pour les meubles)* stud (nail)

cabochon, -onne [kabɔʃɔ̃, ɔn] NM **1** *(pierre précieuse)* cabochon **2** *(de carafe à liqueur)* (glass) stopper **3** *(pour les meubles)* stud (nail)
N *Can (têtu)* stubborn person; *(incompétent)* bad worker

cabosser [kabɔse] VT *(métal, voiture etc)* to bash up; *(chapeau)* to bash in; **vieux chapeau cabossé** battered old hat; **voiture cabossée** bashed-up or beat-up car

cabot [kabo] *Fam* ADJ = **cabotin** ADJ **1**
NM **1** *(acteur)* = **cabotin** N **1 2** *Péj (chien)* pooch, mutt **3** *Mil* corporal, corp

cabotage [kabɔtaʒ] NM *Naut* coasting, coastal trade, cabotage; *Aviat* cabotage; **grand/ petit c.** offshore/inshore coastal traffic

caboter [kabɔte] VI *Naut* to coast

caboteur [kabɔtœr] NM *Naut* coaster

cabotin, -ine [kabɔtɛ̃, -in] *Fam Péj* ADJ **1** *(acteur)* ham **2** *(personne)* histrionic; **il est c.** he's a show-off
N **1** *(mauvais acteur)* ham (actor, f actress), third-rate actor, f actress **2** *(vantard)* show-off

cabotinage [kabɔtinaʒ] NM *Fam Péj* **1** *Théâtre* ham or third-rate acting **2** *(en politique etc)* histrionics; *(vantardise)* showing off

cabotiner [kabɔtine] VI *Fam Péj* to play to the gallery, to show off

caboulot [kabulo] NM *Arg* seedy pub, dive

cabrage [kabraʒ] NM *(de cheval)* rearing (up); *Aviat* pulling up

cabré [kabre] ADJ *(cheval)* rearing; *(avion)* tail down

cabrer [kabre] VT **1** *(cheval)* to rear up; *(avion)* to nose up **2** *Fig* **c. qn contre qn** to turn or set sb against sb
VI *Aviat* to nose up
VPR **se cabrer** *(d'un cheval)* to rear (up); *Fig* **se c. contre qn/qch** to rebel against sb/sth

cabri [kabri] NM *Zool* kid; *Fig* **sauter comme un c.** to jump for joy

cabriole [kabrijɔl] NF *(saut, bond)* leap, caper; *(en danse)* cabriole; *Équitation* capriole, goat's leap; *(de gymnaste)* somersault; *Fig* clever manoeuvre or *Am* maneuver; **faire des cabrioles** to caper about, to cavort about; **elle s'en est tirée par une c.** she cleverly manoeuvred or *Am* maneuvered her way out of it

cabrioler [kabrijɔle] VI to caper or cavort about

cabriolet [kabrijɔlɛ] NM **1** *Aut* convertible **2** *Hist (voiture à cheval)* cabriolet

CAC [kak] NF *(abrév* **Compagnie des agents de change)** **l'indice C. 40, le C. 40** the CAC 40 (index) *(Paris Stock Exchange Index)*

caca [kaka] NM *Enf, Fam (excrément)* poo, *Am* poop; **as-tu fait c.?** *(à un enfant)* have you done a poo or a number two or a big job?; **jette ça, c'est (du) c.** throw that away, it's nasty or dirty; **c. d'oie** yellowish green; *Fam* **il nous fait un caca nerveux, l'autre!** he's having kittens!, he's having a fit!

cacah(o)uète, cacahouette [kakawɛt] NF peanut; **beurre de c.** peanut butter

cacao [kakao] NM *(boisson, poudre)* cocoa; *Bot* cocoa bean, cacao bean

cacaoté [kakaɔte] ADJ cocoa-flavoured

cacaotier [kakaɔtje] NM *Bot* cacao (tree)

cacaoui [kakawi] NM *Can* long-tailed duck

cacaoyer [kakaɔje] NM *Bot* cacao (tree)

cacatoès [kakatɔɛs] NM cockatoo

cacatois [kakatwa] NM *Naut* royal (sail); **(mât de) c.** royal mast; **c. de perruche** mizzen royal

cachalot [kaʃalo] NM sperm whale, cachalot

cache [kaʃ] NF hiding place, cache; **c. d'armes** arms cache, cache of arms
NM cover; *Phot, Ordinat, Cin (pour tirage)* mask; *(de caméra)* hood; *(pour corriger les bromures)* patch; *(volet)* vignette; **c. d'avant-plan** foreground matte; *TV, Cin* **c. de caméra** camera matte; *TV, Cin* **c./contre c. (électronique)** (electronic) matte; **c. latéral** slide matte; *Ordinat* **c. disque physique** physical disk cache; *Ordinat* **c. du disque dur** hard disk cache; *Ordinat* **c. externe** external cache

caché [kaʃe] ADJ hidden; *(sentiment)* secret

cache-antivol NM INV *Aut etc* security cover

cache-cache NM INV hide-and-seek; **jouer à c.** to play hide-and-seek

cache-col NM INV scarf, muffler

cachectique [kaʃɛktik] ADJ *Méd* cachectic

cache-culbuteur NM INV *Aut* rocker cover

Cachemire [kaʃmir] NM Kashmir

cachemire [kaʃmir] NM *Tex (laine)* cashmere; *(motif)* paisley pattern; **chemise de c.** paisley(-pattern) shirt

cache-misère NM INV **1** *(vêtement)* = coat or wrap hiding shabby appearance **2** *(destiné à cacher des défauts)* **cette mesure n'est qu'un c.** this is just a cosmetic measure designed to distract attention from the real problems

cache-moyeu NM INV *Aut* hub cover

cache-nez NM INV scarf, muffler

cache-pot NM INV flowerpot holder

cache-poussière NM INV dust coat, *Am* duster

cacher [kaʃe] VT *(personne, chose)* to hide, to conceal; *(ses sentiments)* to hide, to conceal, to mask; *Ordinat, Phot* to mask out; **où a-t-il pu c. la clé?** where could he have hidden the key?; **le mur nous cache la vue** the wall blocks or hides our view; **c. qch à qn** to hide or conceal sth from sb; **c. son jeu** to keep one's cards hidden or close to one's chest; *Fig* **il a bien caché son jeu** he kept his cards close to his chest; **il n'y a rien de caché dans cette affaire** everything is open and aboveboard in this transaction; **je ne vous cache pas que je suis déçu** I won't hide or conceal from you that I'm disappointed, I won't hide or conceal my disappointment from you; **c. son âge** to keep one's age a secret; **pour ne rien te c.** to be completely open with you; **il ne cache pas que …** he makes no secret of the fact that …
VPR **se cacher** *(d'une personne)* to hide; *(d'une chose)* to be hidden; **les voleurs se cachent** the thieves are (in) hiding; **le soleil se cache** the sun isn't shining, the sun is behind a cloud; **elle ne se cache pas pour dire qu'elle est communiste** she doesn't hide the fact she's a communist; **se c. de qn** to hide from sb; **sa timidité se cache derrière une certaine rudesse** his shyness is hidden behind a bluff exterior; **je ne m'en cache pas** I make no secret of it; **en se cachant** secretly, *Péj* on the sly; **sans se c.** openly

cache-radiateur NM INV radiator cover

cachère [kaʃɛr] ADJ *Rel* kosher

cache-sexe NM INV G-string; *(d'indigène)* apron

cachet [kaʃɛ] NM **1** *(empreinte)* stamp;

(sceau) seal; *(de fabricant)* (trade)mark; *Hist* **lettre de c.** = order under the King's private seal; *Fig* **c. du génie** the stamp or hallmark of genius; **il a beaucoup de c.** he has a lot of style or a certain cachet; **manteau qui a du c.** stylish coat **2** *(d'artiste, avocat, conseiller etc)* fee; **courir le c.** *(d'un acteur)* to do any job that's going **3** *Pharm* tablet, pill; **un c. d'aspirine** an aspirin (tablet)
► **c. de fabrique** maker's trademark; **c. d'oblitération** postmark; **c. de la poste** postmark

cachetage [kaʃtaʒ] NM *(de lettres etc)* sealing

cache-tampon NM INV hunt-the-thimble or -slipper

cacheter [kaʃte] VT (**je cachette, n. cachetons; je cachetterai**) *(lettre, bouteille etc)* to seal; **cire à c.** sealing wax; **vin cacheté** vintage wine

cacheton [kaʃtɔ̃] NM *Fam (cachet d'artiste)* fee; **courir le c.** = to try to get little jobs here and there

cachetonner [kaʃtɔne] VI *Fam (artiste)* = to try to get little jobs here and there

cachette [kaʃɛt] NF *(pour chose)* hiding place; *(pour personne)* hiding place, hideaway; **en c.** secretly, *Péj* on the sly; **vendre en c.** to sell under the counter; **boire en c. (habituellement)** to be a secret drinker; **il boit en c. de sa famille** he hides his drinking from his family; *Can* **jouer à la c.** to play hide-and-seek

cachexie [kaʃɛksi] NF *Méd* cachexia

cachot [kaʃo] NM **1** *(cellule)* dungeon **2** *(isolement)* solitary confinement

cachotterie [kaʃɔtri] NF mystery; **faire des cachotteries** to be secretive

cachottier, -ière [kaʃɔtje, -jɛr] ADJ *(personne)* secretive
N secretive person; **petit c.!** you secretive little thing!

cachou [kaʃu] NM **1** *(bonbon)* cachou **2** *(teinture)* catechu
ADJ INV reddish-brown

cacique [kasik] NM *(chef)* cacique; *Fam (personne importante)* bigwig, big shot; **les caciques du parti** the party bigwigs

cacochyme [kakɔʃim] ADJ *Hum* doddery

cacophonie [kakɔfɔni] NF cacophony

cacophonique [kakɔfɔnik] ADJ cacophonous

cacou [kaku] NM *Fam* **faire le c.** to act smart, to show off

cactus [kaktys] NM cactus VOIR GRAMMAIRE A14

CAD [seade] NM *(abrév* **Comité d'aide au développement)** DAC

c.-à-d. *(abrév* **c'est-à-dire)** i.e.

cadastrage [kadastraʒ] NM *Admin* land registration

cadastral, -ale, -aux, -ales [kadastral, -o] ADJ *(registre, relevé)* cadastral

cadastre [kadastr] NM *Admin (registre)* cadastre; **employés du c.** survey staff

cadastrer [kadastre] VT *Admin (propriété)* to register in the cadastre

cadavéreux, -euse [kadaverø, -øz] ADJ *(teint)* deathly pale, *Litt* cadaverous

cadavérique [kadaverik] ADJ *(teint)* deathly pale; *Méd* cadaveric; **rigidité c.** rigor mortis; **la rigidité c. s'était déjà installée** rigor mortis had already set in

cadavre [kadavr] NM **1** *(de personne)* corpse, (dead) body, *Fml* cadaver; *(d'animal mort)* carcass, body; *Fam* **c'est un c. ambulant** he's a walking corpse **2** *Arg (bouteille)* empty (bottle), dead man

Caddie® [kadi] NM *(chariot)* trolley, *Am* cart

caddie [kadi] NM *Golf* caddie

cadeau, -eaux [kado] **NM 1** present, gift; **en c.** as a present, as a gift; **faire un c. à qn** to give sb a present *or* gift; **acheter un c. à** *ou* **pour qn** to buy sb a present *or* gift; **je n'en voudrais pas comme c.** I wouldn't have it as a gift; **j'aimerais mieux en faire c.** I'd rather give it away; *Fam* **il ne lui a pas fait de c.** *(il ne l'a pas épargnée)* he didn't spare her; *Fam* **ton frère, ce n'est pas un c.** your brother's a real pain; **partir avec eux, ce n'était pas un c.** going away with them was no picnic **2** *Mktg* free gift, freebie; **c. publicitaire** freebie, giveaway, free gift
▸▸ **c. d'anniversaire** birthday present; **c. de Noël** Christmas present

cadenas [kadna] **NM** padlock; **fermer la porte au c.** to padlock the door

cadenasser [kadnase] **VT** *(porte etc)* to padlock
 VPR se cadenasser 1 *(d'une personne)* to lock oneself away **2** *(d'une porte)* to padlock

cadence [kadɑ̃s] **NF 1** *(d'un vers, mouvement)* cadence, rhythm; **en c.** rhythmically, in time; **taper dans ses mains en c.** to clap (one's hands) in time; **marcher en c.** to march, to walk in time; **forcer la c.** to force the pace; **à la c. de …** at the rate of …; **c. de production** rate of production; *Mil etc* **c. du tir** rate of fire; **prendre la c.** to get in(to) step; **garder la c.** to keep in step **2** *Mus (accords)* cadence; *(de concerto)* cadenza

cadencé [kadɑ̃se] **ADJ 1** rhythmic(al); **pas c., marche!** quick march!; **marcher au pas c.** to march, to walk in time; *(rapidement)* to march *or* walk in quick time **2** *Ordinat* **c. à** running at

cadencer [kadɑ̃se] **VT** (**je cadençai(s)**, n. **cadençons**) *(son style etc)* to give rhythm to; **c. son pas** to walk in time

cadet, -ette [kadɛ, -ɛt] **ADJ la sœur cadette** *(de deux)* the younger sister; *(de plus de deux)* the youngest sister; **avoir trois frères cadets** to have three younger brothers; **la branche cadette** the younger branch
 N 1 *(de deux enfants)* younger (child *or* one); *(de plus de deux enfants)* youngest (child *or* one); **mon c.** my younger brother; **ma cadette** my younger sister; **il est mon c. de deux ans** he's two years younger than I am, he's two years my junior; **c'est le c. de mes soucis** that's the least of my worries **2** *Sport* junior; **épreuve des cadets** junior event **3** *Golf* caddie **4** *Hist, Mil* cadet

Cadix [kadis] **NF** Cadiz

cadmium [kadmjɔm] **NM** *Chimie* cadmium

cadogan [kadɔgɑ̃] **NM** = **catogan**

cador [kadɔr] **NM** *Fam* **1** *(chien)* mutt **2** *(personne influente)* big cheese, big shot

cadrage [kadraʒ] **NM** *Cin, Phot etc (de l'image)* centring, *Am* centering; *(plan)* frame; *(action)* framing; *Ordinat* positioning; *Typ, Ordinat (des dimensions)* cropping; *Typ, Ordinat (des couleurs)* masking

cadran [kadrɑ̃] **NM 1** *(d'horloge, de baromètre etc)* face, dial; *(d'instrument, de téléphone etc)* dial; *Can (réveil)* alarm-clock; **c. solaire** sundial; **faire le tour du c.** *(d'une personne)* to sleep (right) round the clock **2** *Naut* **c. de transmission d'ordres** engine-room telegraph; *Aut* **cadrans (de bord)** display panels

cadrat [kadra] **NM** *Typ* quadrat, quad

cadratin [kadratɛ̃] **NM** *Typ* em space

CADRE [kadr] **NM 1** *(de tableau, porte, miroir etc)* frame; *(de vélo etc)* frame(work); **une photo sous c.** a framed photo
2 *(domaine)* limits, bounds; *(structure)* framework; **sortir du c. de ses fonctions** to exceed (the scope of) one's duties; **ne pas sortir du c. de la légalité** to remain within the bounds of the law; **l'analyse régionale ne**

rentre pas dans le c. de cet article regional analysis is beyond the scope of this article; **s'inscrire dans le c. de** to come within the framework of; **dans le c. de ce programme/ des réformes entreprises par le gouvernement** as part of this programme/the government's programme of reform
3 *(décor)* setting; *(milieu)* environment; **c'est un c. splendide!** it's a splendid setting!; **le manoir et son c. de verdure** the manor and its leafy surroundings; **vivre dans le c. familial** to live in a family environment
4 *Litt (de livre etc)* framework, outline
5 *(dans un formulaire)* space, box; *Ordinat (pour graphique)* box; *(section d'une page)* frame; **c. réservé à l'administration** for official use only
6 *Naut* berth
7 *Radio* frame aerial, loop aerial
8 *(caisse)* **c. d'emballage** packing case
9 *(dans une entreprise)* executive, manager; **les cadres** the managerial staff, the management; *Mil* the (commissioned and non-commissioned) officers; *(d'unité réduite etc)* cadre, staff; **passer c.** *(dans une entreprise)* to become an executive, to be promoted to management; **une femme c.** a female executive *or* manager; **elle est c.** she's an executive, she's in management; **jeune c. dynamique** dynamic young executive, *Fam* whizz kid; **hors c.** seconded, on secondment; **être mis hors c.** to be seconded *or* detached; **rayé des cadres** dismissed; **c. en marketing** marketing executive
▸▸ **c. moyen** middle manager; *Mil* **le C. Noir** = military riding school in Saumur; *Mil* **c. de réserve** reserve list; **c. supérieur** senior executive *or* manager; **c. de vie** environment; **cadres moyens** middle management; **cadres supérieurs** senior management

> **Cadre**
>
> In French companies, employees are divided into two categories, "employés" and "cadres". "Cadres", who are better qualified, tend to occupy more senior posts and consequently enjoy higher salaries, more benefits and more prestige. They are also expected to work longer hours.

cadré [kadre] **ADJ** *TV, Cin* in-frame, on-frame

cadre-adresse, *pl* **cadres-adresses NM** address space

cadre-châssis, *pl* **cadres-châssis NM** *Aut* chassis frame

cadrer [kadre] **VI** to tally (**avec** with)
 VT *Cin, Phot* to centre, *Am* to center; *(plan etc)* to frame; *Ordinat* to position

cadreur, -euse [kadrœr, øz] **N** *TV, Cin* cameraman, *f* woman, camera operator

caduc, -uque [kadyk] **ADJ 1** *Bot (feuille etc)* deciduous **2** *Jur (legs)* null and void; *(accord)* lapsed; *(dette)* statute-barred

caducée [kadyse] **NM** *(symbole de la profession pharmaceutique)* caduceus

caducité [kadysite] **NF** *(d'un système etc)* outmoded nature

cæcum [sekɔm] **NM** *Anat* caecum

CAF [seaɛf] **1** *Com (abrév* **coût, assurance, fret)** cif; **vente C.** sale on cif basis **2** *(abrév* **Caisse d'allocations familiales)** ≃ child benefit office

cafard, -arde [kafar, -ard] **NM 1** *(insecte)* cockroach, *Am* roach **2** *Fam* **avoir le c.** to feel down *or* low, to be down in the dumps; **avoir un coup de c.** to feel a bit down *or* low
 N 1 *Fam (rapporteur)* sneak, telltale **2** *Arch (faux dévot)* hypocrite
 ADJ air c. hypocritical *or* sanctimonious air

cafardage [kafardaʒ] **NM** *Fam* sneaking, telling tales

cafarder [kafarde] *Fam* **VT** to sneak on, to tell tales on, *Am* to snitch
 VI 1 *(rapporter)* to sneak, to tell tales **2** *(avoir le cafard)* to feel down *or* low, to be down in the dumps

cafardeur, -euse [kafardœr, -øz] **N** *Fam* sneak, telltale, *Am* snitch

cafardeux, -euse [kafardø, -øz] **ADJ** *Fam (endroit, soir)* miserable, depressing; **se sentir** *ou* **être c.** to feel down *or* low, to be down in the dumps

caf'conc' [kafkɔ̃s] **NM INV** *Fam abrév* **café-concert**

café [kafe] **NM 1** *(produit, boisson)* coffee; **c. vert/torréfié** unroasted/roasted coffee; **grain de c.** coffee bean; **c. en grains** whole coffee, coffee beans; **c. moulu** ground coffee; **c. en poudre** *ou* **instantané** instant coffee; **un c. (bien) serré** a (very) strong coffee; **un c. léger** a weak coffee; **deux cafés** two coffees; **glace au c.** coffee ice cream **2** *(lieu)* café *(also serving alcoholic drinks)*; **c. tabac** = café cum tobacconist's; **quand on les entend parler, on se croirait au c. du commerce** all they come out with are platitudes **3** *Hist, Littér* coffee-house
 ADJ INV c. (au lait) coffee-coloured
▸▸ **c. complet** = continental breakfast; **c. crème** white coffee, coffee with hot milk; **c. décaféiné** decaffeinated coffee; **c. au lait** white coffee, *Br* coffee with milk; **c. liégeois** = coffee ice cream topped with whipped cream; **c. noir** black coffee; **c. turc** Turkish coffee

> **Café**
>
> In French cafés, a small cup of strong black coffee is called "un (petit) café", "un express" or, colloquially, "un petit noir". This may be served "serré" (extra-strong), "léger" (weak) or "allongé" (diluted with hot water). An "express" with a tiny amount of milk added is called "un noisette". A large cup of black coffee is "un grand café", "un double express" or, colloquially, "un grand noir". Coffee with frothy, steam-heated milk is called "un (grand/petit) crème". The term "café au lait" is almost never used in cafés.

café-concert, *pl* **cafés-concerts NM** = cabaret (club)

caféier [kafeje] **NM** coffee tree

caféière [kafejɛr] **NF** coffee plantation

caféine [kafein] **NF** caffeine; **sans c.** decaffeinated, caffeine-free; **teneur en c.** caffeine content

cafet [kafɛt] **NF** *Fam abrév* **cafétéria**

cafetan [kaftɑ̃] **NM** kaftan, caftan

cafeter [kafte] **VI** = **cafter**

cafétéria [kafeterja] **NF** cafeteria

café-théâtre, *pl* **cafés-théâtres NM** = café where theatrical performances take place

cafetier, -ière [kaftje, -jɛr] **N** café owner
 NF cafetière 1 *(récipient)* coffee pot; *(électrique)* coffee machine *or* maker; **cafetière automatique** *ou* **à pression** percolator **2** *Fam (tête)* nut, *Br* bonce

cafetier-limonadier, *pl* **cafetiers-limonadiers NM** café owner

cafouillage [kafujaʒ] **NM** *Fam* muddle, shambles, mess; *(de moteur de voiture)* missing, misfiring

cafouiller [kafuje] **VI** *Fam* to get into a muddle; *(de projet)* to fall apart *or* to pieces; *(de moteur de voiture)* to miss, to misfire; *(de poste de télévision)* to be on the blink

cafouilleur, -euse [kafujœr, -øz] *Fam* **ADJ** *(personne)* muddle-headed
N muddler

cafouillis [kafuji] **NM** *Fam* shambles, muddle; **c'est un énorme c.** it's a complete shambles; **il y a beaucoup de c. dans la gestion de cette entreprise** the management of this company is really shambolic

caftan [kaftā] **NM** kaftan, caftan

cafter [kafte] **VI** *Fam* to sneak, to tell tales, *Am* to snitch

cafteur, -euse [kaftœr, -øz] **N** *Fam (indicateur)* sneak, *Am* snitch
NM *Ordinat* cookie

cage [kaʒ] **NF 1** *(pour animaux)* cage; *(pour poules)* coop; *(pour lapins)* hutch; *(de puits de mine)* cage; *(de maison)* shell, carcass; *Ftbl* goal; **mettre un oiseau en c.** to cage a bird, to put a bird in a cage; **c. à oiseau/aux lions** bird/lions'cage; *Fig Fam* **c. à lapins** rabbit hutch; *Fig* **être comme un lion en c.** to be like a caged animal; *Fig* **une c. dorée** a gilded cage; *Ftbl* **être dans les cages** to be in goal **2** *(de montre etc)* (protective) cover, case, casing
▸▸ **c. d'ascenseur** lift *or Am* elevator shaft; *Ordinat* scroll box; *Tech* **c. à billes** ball race; **c. d'escalier** stairwell; *Élec* **c. de Faraday** Faraday cage, electrostatic screen; *Anat* **c. thoracique** rib cage

cageot [kaʒo] **NM 1** crate **2** *Fam Péj (fille très laide)* dog

cagette [kaʒɛt] **NF** crate

cagibi [kaʒibi] **NM** *Fam* **1** *(remise)* shed, hut **2** *(débarras etc)* storage room, *Br* boxroom, lumber room

cagna [kaɲa] **NF** *Fam* (small) house

cagnard [kaɲar] **NM** *Fam* blazing sunshine

cagne [kaɲ] **NF** *Scol Fam* = second-year arts class preparing to compete for entrance to the École normale supérieure

cagneux, -euse [kaɲø, -øz] **ADJ** *(personne)* knock-kneed; *(jambes)* crooked; **genoux c.** knock knees
N 1 *Scol Fam* = student in the cagne **2** *(personne qui a les genoux cagneux)* knock-kneed person

cagnotte [kaɲɔt] **NF** *(caisse commune)* kitty; *(de jeux)* pool, kitty, *surtout Am* pot; *Fam (économies)* nest egg

cagot, -ote [kago, -ɔt] *Péj* **N** (sanctimonious) hypocrite
ADJ hypocritical, sanctimonious

cagouille [kaguj] **NF** *(escargot)* snail

cagoule [kagul] **NF 1** *(de moine)* cowl **2** *(de pénitent, cambrioleur)* hood **3** *(passe-montagne)* balaclava (helmet)

cahier [kaje] **NM 1** notebook; *Scol* exercise book **2** *Typ* signature, gathering, section; *(en reliure)* quire **3** *(d'un journal)* section **4** *(revue)* review, journal
▸▸ *Compta* **c. des achats** purchase ledger; **c. de bord** logbook; **c. de brouillon** rough (note)book; *Com, Ind* **c. des charges** *(d'un contrat)* specifications; *(d'une vente)* articles and conditions; *Hist, Fig* **c. de doléances** list of grievances; **c. d'enregistrement** *(de courrier)* mail book; *(d'appels reçus)* telephone log; **c. des prix** price manual; **c. de réclamations** complaints book; **c. de textes** homework book; **c. de travaux pratiques** special notebook for practical work

cahin-caha [kaēkaa] **ADV** *Fam* **aller c.** *(de la santé)* to be so-so; *(d'une personne)* to struggle *or* limp along; **les affaires vont c.** business is slow *or* slack; **la vie continue c.** life goes on (as it must)

cahot [kao] **NM** *(de véhicule)* jolt; *(de route)* bump

cahotage [kaɔtaʒ] **NM** = **cahotement**

cahotant [kaɔtã] **ADJ 1** *(voiture)* jolting, jolty **2** *(route)* bumpy, rough

cahotement [kaɔtmã] **NM** *(mouvement)* jolting, shaking, bumping; *(heurt)* jolt

cahoter [kaɔte] **VT** to jolt, to shake; **vie cahotée** life full of ups and downs; **des enfants cahotés par le divorce** children shaken up by divorce
VI *(d'une voiture, d'une brouette etc)* to jolt along

cahoteux, -euse [kaɔtø, -øz] **ADJ** *(route)* bumpy, rough

CAHT [seaaʃte] **NM** *Com (abrév* **chiffre d'affaires hors taxes)** pre-tax turnover

cahute [kayt] **NF** shack, shanty, hut

caïd [kaid] **NM 1** *(en Afrique du Nord)* kaïd **2** *Arg (chef de bande)* gang leader; **un c. de la drogue** a drug(s) baron; **c'est le gros c. en maths** he's the maths expert; *Fam* **jouer les caïds** *ou* **au c. dans la cour de récréation** to be a playground bully; **il fait le c.** he's acting all high and mighty

caïdat [kaida] **NM 1** *(en Afrique du Nord)* kaïdship **2** *Arg (d'un chef de bande)* gang leadership

caillage [kajaʒ] **NM** = **caillement**

caillant [kajā] **ADJ** *Belg Fam* freezing (cold); **il fait c.** it's freezing (cold)

caillassage [kajasaʒ] **NM** *Fam* throwing *Br* stones *or Am* rocks (**de** at); **il a été assez souvent question du c. des bus dans les banlieues chaudes** the fact that, in the rougher areas, buses often got pelted with *Br* stones *or Am* rocks was much talked about

caillasse [kajas] **NF 1** *Géol* (gravelly) marl **2** *Fam (cailloux etc)* loose stones, scree; **marcher dans la c.** to walk on loose stones *or* scree

caillasser [kajase] **VT** *Fam* to stone

caille [kaj] **NF** quail; **gras comme une c.** (as) plump as a partridge; **elle est chaude comme une c.** she's as snug as a bug in a rug; *Fam* **ma c.** my little dove

caillé [kaje] **NM** curds

caillebotis [kajbɔti] **NM 1** *Naut etc* grating **2** *(treillis, plancher)* duckboard(s)

caillebotte [kajbɔt] **NF** curds

caillebotter [kajbɔte] **VT** *Arch (lait)* to curdle

caillement [kajmã] **NM** *(du lait)* curdling; *(du sang)* clotting, coagulating, coagulation

cailler [kaje] **VT** *(lait)* to curdle; *(sang)* to clot, to coagulate
VI 1 *(du lait)* to curdle; *(du sang)* to clot, to coagulate; **faire c. du lait** to curdle milk **2** *Fam* **ça caille** it's freezing (cold), *Br* it's perishing
VPR **se cailler** *Fam* **on se (les) caille** it's freezing (cold), *Br* it's perishing

caillera [kajra] **NF** *Fam* scum

caillette [kajɛt] **NF** *(des ruminants)* fourth stomach

caillot [kajo] **NM** *(de sang)* clot

caillou, -oux [kaju] **NM 1** *(petite pierre)* stone; **cailloux d'empierrement** (loose) chippings, road metal; **avoir un c. dans sa chaussure** to have a stone in one's shoe; *Fig* **avoir le cœur dur comme un c.** to have a heart of stone **2** *(grosse pierre)* boulder, rock **3** *Fam (pierre précieuse)* stone **4** *Arg (tête)* nut, *Br* bonce; **il n'a plus un poil sur le c.** he's as bald as a coot **5** *Fam* **le C.** *(la Nouvelle-Calédonie)* New Caledonia

cailloutage [kajutaʒ] **NM 1** *(action)* *(de route)* metalling; *(de voie ferrée)* ballasting **2** *(pierres)* *(de route)* road metal; *(de voie ferrée)* ballast

caillouter [kajute] **VT** *(route)* to metal; *(voie ferrée)* to ballast

caillouteux, -euse [kajutø, -øz] **ADJ** *(route etc)* stony; *(plage)* pebbly, shingly

cailloutis [kajuti] **NM** broken stones, chippings, gravel; *(de route)* road metal

caïman [kaimã] **NM** cayman, caiman

Caïn [kaɛ̃] **NM** Cain

Caire (le) [(lə)kɛr] **NM** Cairo

cairn [kɛrn] **NM** cairn

cairote [kerɔt] **ADJ** of/from Cairo
N C. Cairene, person from Cairo

caisse [kɛs] **NF 1** *(pour marchandises)* (packing) case; *(à outils, de rangement)* box, chest; *(à thé etc)* chest; *(de champagne, vin)* case; *(pour plantes)* tub; **c. à savon** soapbox; **c. de melons** crate of melons; **mettre des marchandises en c.** to case goods
2 *(de piano, d'horloge)* case; *(de véhicule)* body(work); **c. de poulie** shell; *Aut* **c. de l'embrayage** clutch casing
3 *Arg (voiture)* car, *Br* motor
4 *Arg (poitrine)* chest; **il s'en va de la c.** his chest is giving out
5 *Mus* drum; **c. claire** side *or* snare drum; **grosse c.** bass drum
6 *Anat* **c. du tympan** middle ear
7 *Com, Fin (coffre)* cash box; *(d'une caisse enregistreuse)* till; *(dans un magasin, un garage etc)* cash desk; *(dans un grand magasin)* cashpoint; *(dans un supermarché)* checkout; **c. (enregistreuse)** cash register; **les caisses de l'État** the coffers of the State; **payez à la c.** pay at the (cash) desk *or* at the till; **tenir la c.** to be in charge of the cash; *(dans un restaurant, un magasin etc)* to be the cashier; **passer à la c.** to go to the cash desk; *(dans un supermarché)* to go through the checkout; *(payer)* to pay; *(se faire payer)* to be paid; *(se faire licencier)* to be paid off
8 *(argent)* cash (in hand); *(recette)* takings; **livre de c.** cashbook; **faire la** *ou* **sa c.** to balance (up) one's cash, to do the takings, *Br* to cash up; **avoir tant d'argent en c.** *(disponible)* to have so much money in hand; **elle est partie avec la c.** she made off with the cash *or* the takings; **'la c.!'** hurla le malfaiteur 'hand over the cash!' shouted the robber
9 *(organisme)* fund; **c. de défense** *(d'une association etc)* fighting fund
10 *Suisse Fam* **prendre une c.** to get plastered; **être (fin) c.** to be (completely) plastered
▸▸ **c. d'allocations familiales** ≃ child benefit office; *Compta* **c. d'amortissement** sinking fund; **c. de chômage** unemployment fund; **c. à claire-voie** crate; **c. de compensation** = equalization fund for payments such as child benefit, sickness benefit, pensions; **c. comptable** cash register; **C. des dépôts et consignations** = administrative department of the French government, in charge of investing and lending public money; *Naut* **c. à eau douce** freshwater tank; **c. électronique** electronic billing machine; **c. enregistreuse** cash register; **c. d'épargne** savings bank; **c. d'épargne-logement** *Br* ≃ building society, *Am* ≃ savings and loan association; **c. de garantie** credit guarantee institution; **c. à laser** laser checkout; **C. nationale d'assurance vieillesse** = French government department dealing with benefit payments relating to old age pensions; *Pol* **c. noire** slush fund; *Can* **c. populaire** credit union; **c. de prévoyance** provident fund; **c. primaire d'assurance maladie** = French government department dealing with health insurance; **c. régionale** ≃ local (bank) branch; **c. de retraite** ≃ pension fund

caissette [kɛsɛt] **NF** small box

caissier, -ière [kɛsje, -jɛr] **N** *(dans un restaurant, un magasin etc)* cashier; *(dans un supermarché)* checkout operator; *Banque* cashier, teller; **c. de nuit** *(dans un hôtel)* night auditor

caisson [kɛsɔ̃] **NM 1** *(caisse)* box, case; *Mil (de munitions etc)* wagon, caisson; *Fam* **se faire sauter le c.** to blow one's brains out **2** *Archit* **plafond à caissons** panelled *or* coffered ceiling **3** *(pour travail sous-marin)* caisson; *Méd* **mal(adie) des caissons** caisson disease, decompression sickness, *Fam* the bends; **c. à air comprimé** decompression chamber **4** *Aut* bay **5** *Cin, TV* **c. de graves** subwoofer; **c. d'insonorisation** blimp

cajoler [kaʒɔle] **VT 1** *(câliner)* to cuddle, to make a fuss of **2** *Vieilli (flatter)* to cajole, to coax, to wheedle

cajolerie [kaʒɔlri] **NF** *(câlin)* cuddle

cajoleur, -euse [kaʒɔlœr, -øz] **ADJ 1** *(câlin)* affectionate **2** *Vieilli (flatteur)* cajoling, wheedling, coaxing
  N *Vieilli (flatteur)* cajoler, wheedler, coaxer

cajou [kaʒu] **NM** cashew (nut)

cake [kɛk] **NM** fruit cake; **mascara en c.** block mascara; *Fam* **être dans le c.** *(avoir la gueule de bois)* to be hung over, to have a hangover; *(être très fatigué)* to be all in

cal, *pl* **cals** [kal] **NM** *Bot, Méd* callus, callosity

calabrais, -aise [kalabrɛ, -ɛz] **ADJ** Calabrian
  NM *Ling* Calabrian dialect
  N C. Calabrian

Calabre [kalabr] **NF** Calabria

calage [kalaʒ] **NM 1** *(de pied de chaise etc)* wedging; *(de roue)* chocking **2** *(fait d'appuyer)* propping (up) **3** *(de manivelle à un axe etc)* wedging, keying; *(de roue à un axe etc)* fixing; *(de valve etc)* jamming, locking **4** *Aut (de moteur)* stalling **5** *(réglage)* adjustment; *(de valve, moteur)* tuning; *Aut* **c. d'allumage** ignition timing **6** *Typ* setting

calamar [kalamar] **NM = calmar**

calamine [kalamin] **NF 1** *Minér* calamine **2** *(dépôt)* carbon deposits

calaminer (se) [səkalamine] **VPR** to get covered with carbon deposits

calamistré [kalamistre] **ADJ** **cheveux calamistrés** brilliantined hair

calamité [kalamite] **NF** *(désastre)* calamity, disaster; *(malheur)* (great) misfortune; **quelle c.!** what a disaster! *Fam* **ce mec, c'est une vraie c.!** this guy is a real *or* a walking disaster!

calamiteux, -euse [kalamitø, -øz] **ADJ** disastrous, *Fml* calamitous

calancher [kalɑ̃ʃe] **VI** *très Fam* to croak, *Br* to snuff it, *Am* to check out

calandrage [kalɑ̃draʒ] **NM** *(dans la fabrication du papier)*, *Tex & Typ* calendering; *(de pneu)* liner

calandre [kalɑ̃dr] **NF 1** *(dans la fabrication du papier)*, *Tex, Typ* calender **2** *Aut* radiator grille

calandrer [kalɑ̃dre] **VT** *Tex, Typ etc* to calender

calandreur, -euse [kalɑ̃drœr, -øz] **N** *(pour les papiers)*, *Tex, Typ* calenderer

calanque [kalɑ̃k] **NF** *(en Méditerranée)* deep narrow creek

calao [kalao] **NM** hornbill

calbar [kalbar] **NM** *Fam (slip)* *Br* scants, *Am* shorts

calcaire [kalkɛr] **ADJ** *(sol, terrain)* chalky; *(roche)* calcareous; *Chimie* **sel c.** calcium salt; **eau c.** hard water
  NM 1 *Géol* limestone **2** *(dans les bouilloires)* fur

calcanéum [kalkaneɔm] **NM** *Anat* heel bone, *Spéc* calcaneum

calcédoine [kalsedwan] **NF** *Minér* chalcedony

calcif [kalsif] **NM** *Fam* **= calecif**

calcination [kalsinasjɔ̃] **NF** calcination

calciner [kalsine] **VT** *(brûler)* to char; *Chimie, Ind* to calcine; **rôti calciné** joint burnt to a cinder; **désert calciné par le soleil** sun-baked desert
  VPR se calciner to burn

calcium [kalsjɔm] **NM** *Chimie* calcium

calcul¹ [kalkyl] **NM 1** *(compte)* calculation, reckoning, computation; **faire un c.** to make a calculation; **faux c., erreur de c.** miscalculation; *Ordinat* **calculs très rapides** number crunching **2** *Scol* **le c.** arithmetic, sums; **faible en c.** bad at sums *or* arithmetic; **enseigner le c.** to teach arithmetic; **apprendre le c.** to learn (how) to count; **règle à c.** slide rule; **problème de c.** arithmetic problem **3** *(prévision)* calculation; **agir par c.** to act from selfish *or* ulterior motives; **ça a été un bon c. de notre part** it was a good move on our part, we did the right thing; **un mauvais c.** a miscalculation; **faire un bon c.** to calculate correctly; **faire un mauvais c.** to miscalculate; **selon nos calculs** according to our calculations
  ▸▸ *Math* **c. différentiel** differential calculus; *Math* **c. intégral** integral calculus; **c. mental** mental arithmetic; **c. des probabilités** theory of probability

calcul² **NM** *Méd (dans la vésicule)* stone, *Spéc* calculus; **avoir des calculs** to have stones in the bladder; *(aux reins)* to have kidney stones; **c. biliaire** gall stone; **c. rénal** kidney stone

calculable [kalkylabl] **ADJ** calculable

calculateur, -trice [kalkylatœr, -tris] **ADJ** *(personne, politique)* calculating
  N *(personne)* **c'est un bon c.** he's good at *or* with figures
  NM 1 *Ordinat* (desktop) calculator; **c. (électronique)** (electronic) computer **2** *(de poche)* (pocket) calculator
  NF calculatrice *(machine)* (desktop) calculator; **calculatrice de bureau** desktop calculator; **calculatrice imprimante** print-out calculator; **calculatrice de poche** pocket calculator

calculé [kalkyle] **ADJ** *(insulte, risque)* calculated; *(méchanceté)* premeditated, calculated; *(insolence)* deliberate; **une bonté calculée** an act of kindness motivated by self-interest

calculer [kalkyle] **VT** *(compter)* *(prix, surface d'un triangle etc)* to work out, to calculate; *(comportement, réflexions etc)* to plan, to calculate; *(conséquences)* to weigh (up); **c. qch de tête** to work sth out *or* calculate sth in one's head; **tout bien calculé** taking everything into account; **c. ses chances de réussite** to calculate *or* to weigh up one's chances of success; **c. ses dépenses au plus juste** to work out *or* calculate one's expenses to the nearest penny
  VI to calculate; *Péj (économiser)* to count every penny; **c. vite et bien** to be quick and accurate at *or* with figures; **machine à c.** adding machine, (desk) calculator

calculette [kalkylɛt] **NF 1** *(appareil)* (pocket) calculator **2** *Fam Hum (personne qui souffre d'acné)* pizza face; **elle sort avec un mec, une vraie c.!** she's going out with this real pizza face guy

caldoche [kaldɔʃ] **ADJ = pertaining to the European community of New Caledonia
  **N C. = New Caledonian of European descent

cale¹ [kal] **NF** *Naut* **1** *(de navire)* hold; **eau de c.** bilge water; **fond de c.** bilge; **à fond de c.** down in the hold; *Fam Fig* **être à fond de c.** to be stony-broke *or* *Am* stone-broke **2** **mettre un navire sur c.** to lay down a ship
  ▸▸ **c. à charbon** bunker; **c. de construction/de lancement** stocks/slip(way); **c. à eau** wa-

ter tank; **c. de radoub** dry dock, graving dock; **c. sèche** dry dock

cale² **NF 1** *(pour mettre un meuble d'aplomb etc)* wedge; *(pour bloquer une roue etc)* chock, block; *Aut (pour augmenter le jeu entre deux pièces)* shim, spacer; **c. de réglage** adjusting shim; **mettre une voiture sur cales** to put a car on blocks; *Aviat* **enlevez les cales!** chocks away! **2** *(support)* prop, strut; *Tech (d'arbre etc)* key

calé [kale] **ADJ 1** *Fam (problème, question, devoir etc)* difficult, tough; **être c. en qch** to be well up in sth, to know all about sth; **ça, c'est c.!** that's cunning!, that's clever! **2** *Belg (prêt)* ready

calebasse [kalbas] **NF** *(fruit, récipient)* calabash, gourd

calèche [kalɛʃ] **NF** *(voiture)* barouche

calecif [kalsif] **NM** *Fam* boxer shorts

caleçon [kalsɔ̃] **NM** boxer shorts; *(de femme)* leggings; *Vieilli* **c. long** long underpants, *Fam* long johns; *Vieilli* **c. de bain** (swimming *or* bathing) trunks

calédonien, -ienne [kaledɔnjɛ̃, -jɛn] **ADJ** Caledonian
  N C. Caledonian

calembour [kalɑ̃bur] **NM** pun, play on words; **faire** *ou* **dire des calembours** to make puns, to pun, to play on words

calembredaine [kalɑ̃brəden] **NF** joke
  NFPL calembredaines nonsense

calendes [kalɑ̃d] **NFPL** *Antiq* calends; **renvoyer qn/qch aux c. grecques** to put sb/sth off indefinitely

calendos [kalɑ̃dos] **NM** *Fam* Camembert (cheese)

calendrier [kalɑ̃drije] **NM 1** *(système, tableau)* calendar; **bloc c.** block calendar; **c. à effeuiller** tear-off calendar; **c. perpétuel** perpetual calendar; **c. grégorien** gregorian calendar **2** *(de voyage, travail etc)* timetable, programme, schedule; **avoir un c. chargé** to have a busy schedule *or* timetable; **le c. de ses visites n'a pas encore été établi** her visits haven't been timetabled *or* scheduled yet; **c. de campagne** media schedule; *Bourse* **c. des émissions** calendar of issues; **c. des remboursements** repayment schedule

cale-pied, *pl* **cale-pieds NM** toe clip

calepin [kalpɛ̃] **NM 1** notebook **2** *Belg (cartable)* briefcase

caler¹ [kale] **VT 1** *(pied de chaise etc)* to wedge; *(roue)* to chock; **c. un chargement** to secure a load (firmly); **c. un malade avec des coussins** to prop up a patient on cushions **2** *(manivelle à un axe etc)* to wedge, to key; *(roue sur un axe etc)* to fix; *(valve etc)* to jam, to lock **3** *Aut (moteur)* to stall **4** *(régler)* *(valve, moteur etc)* to adjust, to tune **5** *Fam (remplir)* **ça vous cale (l'estomac)** it fills you up, it's really filling; **je suis calé** I'm full (up)
  VI *(moteur)* to stall
  VPR se caler 1 *(dans un fauteuil etc)* to settle (oneself) comfortably **2** *Fam* **se c. les joues, se les c.** to stuff oneself, to have a good feed

caler² **VT** *Naut (mât)* to house; *(voile)* to strike
  VI 1 *Naut* **navire qui cale vingt pieds** ship that draws *or* whose draught is twenty feet (of water); **navire qui cale trop** ship that is too deep in the water **2** *Fam (abandonner)* to give up **3** *Can (se dégarnir)* to have a receding hairline

caleter (se) [səkalte] **VPR** *Arg* **= calter**

calfat [kalfa] **NM** *Naut* ca(u)lker

calfatage [kalfataʒ] **NM** *Naut* ca(u)lking

calfater [kalfate] **VT** *Naut* to ca(u)lk

calfeutrage [kalføtraʒ], **calfeutrement** [kalføtrəmɑ̃] **NM 1** *(de brèches)* blocking up, stopping (up), filling (in) **2** *(d'une pièce etc)* draught-proofing

calfeutrer [kalføtre] **VT 1** *(brèches)* to block up, to stop (up), to fill (in) **2** *(pièce etc)* to draught-proof, to make draught-proof
VPR se calfeutrer *(pour avoir chaud)* to make oneself snug; *(pour être seul)* to shut oneself up *or* away

calibrage [kalibraʒ] **NM 1** *(de pièce)* gauging, measuring; *(de thermomètre etc)* calibration; *Com (d'œufs, de fruits etc)* grading **2** *Phot (d'épreuve)* trimming **3** *Typ (de copie)* cast-off

calibre [kalibr] **NM 1** *(d'arme à feu, tuyau etc)* calibre, *Am* caliber, bore; *(de balle etc)* calibre, size; *(d'œufs, de fruits etc)* grade; **fusil de c. 8 mm** *Mil* 8-mm calibre rifle; *Sport* 8-mm gauge gun; **canon de gros c.** heavy gun, large-bore gun; *Fig* **sa sœur est d'un autre c.** his sister is of quite a different calibre, *Fam* his sister is in a different league; **il n'est pas de ce c.-là** he's not a man of that calibre; **j'ai rarement vu une bêtise de ce c.!** I've rarely seen stupidity on such a scale!
2 *(outil)* gauge, *Am* gage; **c. d'épaisseur (à lames)** feeler gauge, set of feelers; **c. de profondeur** depth gauge
3 *(pour la reproduction)* template
4 *(de machine-outil)* jig, former
5 *Arg (revolver)* shooter, *Am* rod; **un gros c.** a heavy pistol

calibrer [kalibre] **VT 1** *(pièce)* to gauge, to measure; *(thermomètre etc)* to calibrate; *Com (œufs, fruits etc)* to grade; *Ordinat (couleurs)* to calibrate **2** *Phot (épreuve)* to trim **3** *Typ (copie)* to cast off

calibreur, -euse [kalibrœr, -øz] **N** calibrator; *Aut* **c. d'air** air bleed jet, air correction jet

calice[1] [kalis] **NM** *Rel* chalice; *Fig* **boire le c. jusqu'à la lie** to drain the cup to the dregs
INT *Can* hell!

calice[2] **NM** *Bot, Anat* calyx

calicot [kaliko] **NM 1** *Tex Br* calico, *Am* unbleached muslin **2** *(portant une publicité etc)* banner **3** *Vieilli (personne)* draper's assistant

califat [kalifa] **NM** caliphate

calife [kalif] **NM** caliph; **vouloir être c. à la place du c.** to want to be top dog

Californie [kaliforni] **NF** California

californien, -ienne [kalifornjɛ̃, -jɛn] **ADJ** Californian
N C. Californian

californium [kalifornjɔm] **NM** *Chimie* californium

califourchon [kalifurʃɔ̃] **ADV à c.** astride; **se mettre à c. sur qch** to sit astride sth, to straddle sth; **monter à c. sur un cheval** to ride a horse astride
NM *Can* bottom, backside, behind

câlin, -ine [kalɛ̃, -in] **ADJ** *(enfant, regard, ton etc)* affectionate
N *(personne)* affectionate person
NM cuddle; **faire un c. à qn** to give sb a cuddle

câliner [kaline] **VT** *(choyer)* *(enfant etc)* to make a fuss of; *(caresser)* to cuddle

câlinerie [kalinri] **NF 1** *(tendresse)* fondness, tenderness **2** *(caresses etc)* caress; *(dans les bras)* cuddle; **faire des câlineries à qn** to cuddle sb

calisson [kalisɔ̃] **NM** = lozenge-shaped sweet made of marzipan

calleux, -euse [kalø, -øz] **ADJ** callous, horny

call-girl, *pl* **call-girls** [kolgœrl] **NF** call girl

calligramme [kaligram] **NM** *Littér* calligramme

calligraphe [kaligraf] **N** calligrapher, calligraphist

calligraphie [kaligrafi] **NF** calligraphy
calligraphier [kaligrafje] **VT** *(impf, pr sub n. calligraphiions, v. calligraphiiez)* *(lettre etc)* to write beautifully (and ornamentally); **nom calligraphié** beautifully (hand)written name

calligraphique [kaligrafik] **ADJ** calligraphic

callosité [kalozite] **NF** callus, callosity

calmant [kalmɑ̃] **ADJ** *(mots etc)* calming, soothing; *Méd (pour les nerfs)* tranquillizing, sedative; *(pour la douleur)* painkilling
NM *Méd (pour les nerfs)* tranquillizer, sedative; *(pour la douleur)* painkiller

calmar [kalmar] **NM** squid

calme [kalm] **NM** *(absence d'agitation)* calm, calmness; *(dans une situation difficile)* coolness, composure; *(de l'air, de la nuit)* stillness; *(du paysage)* peace and quiet, quiet(ness), peacefulness; **je cherche un peu de c.** I'm looking for some peace and quiet; **j'ai besoin d'être au c. pour écrire** I need (to have) peace and quiet in order to write; **moment de c.** lull; **je n'ai pas eu un moment de c. de toute la journée!** I haven't had a minute's peace all day!; **dans le c. de la nuit** in the still of the night; **du c.!** keep cool *or* calm!; **perdre son c.** to lose one's composure *or Fam* cool; **retrouver son c.** to regain one's composure, to calm down; **garder son c.** to keep one's composure, to keep calm *or* cool, *Fam* to keep one's cool; **il est toujours d'un c. incroyable** he is always incredibly calm *or* cool *or* composed; *Naut* **c. plat** dead calm; **les commerçants se plaignent que c'est le c. plat** traders are complaining that business is in the doldrums; **c'est le c. plat dans ma vie sentimentale** my love life is in the doldrums, there's nothing happening in my love life; **calmes équatoriaux** doldrums
ADJ *(nuit etc)* calm, still, quiet; *(personne, air)* calm, cool, composed; *(mer)* calm, smooth; *(ciel)* clear; *Com (marché)* quiet, flat, dull; **elle a des enfants très calmes** she has very placid children; **les affaires sont calmes en août** business is quiet in August; **la Bourse a été c.** the Stock Market has been quiet *or* has had a quiet day

> Attention: ne pas confondre **calm** et **quiet** lorsqu'on traduit **calme**. Le terme **calm** se rapporte généralement à la maîtrise de soi, alors que **quiet** désigne un comportement ou une situation paisible.

calmement [kalməmɑ̃] **ADV** calmly

calmer [kalme] **VT** *(personne)* *(rendre serein)* to calm (down); *(faire taire)* to quieten (down), *Am* to quiet down; *(foule etc)* to calm, to pacify; *(craintes)* to calm, to allay; *(douleur)* to soothe, to ease; *(conscience)* to ease; *(soif)* to quench; *(faim)* to appease; *(ardeur, passion)* to damp, to cool; *(fièvre)* to reduce, to bring down; *Fam* **je vais te le c. en moins de deux!** I'll soon shut him up *or* sort him out!; **c. le jeu** *(dans un jeu de ballon)* to slow down the pace of play; *Fig* to calm things down
VPR se calmer *(de personne)* *(devenir serein)* to calm down; *(se taire)* to quieten down, *Am* to quiet down; *(de tempête)* to abate, to die down, to blow over; *(de vent)* to drop, to subside; *(de mer)* to become calm; *(de pluie)* to ease off; **la douleur se calme** the pain is easing *or* subsiding

calmos [kalmos] **INT** *Fam* chill (out)!, take it easy!

calomel [kalomɛl] **NM** *Pharm* calomel

calomniateur, -trice [kalɔmnjatœr, -tris] **N** *(qui parle)* slanderer; *(qui écrit)* libeller
ADJ *(paroles)* slanderous; *(écrits)* libellous

calomnie [kalɔmni] **NF** *(parlée)* slander, *Fml* calumny; *(écrite, publiée)* libel; **répandre** des calomnies sur qn to cast aspersions on sb; **elle a été en butte à la c.** she has been a victim of slander/libel, she has been slandered/libelled

calomnier [kalɔmnje] **VT** to slander, to malign, *Fml* to calumniate; *(par écrit)* to libel

calomnieusement [kalɔmnjøzmɑ̃] **ADV** slanderously; *(par écrit)* libellously

calomnieux, -ieuse [kalɔmnjø, -jøz] **ADJ** *(paroles)* slanderous; *(écrits)* libellous

caloporteur [kalopɔrtœr] **ADJ** **fluide** *ou* **liquide c.** coolant
NM coolant

calorie [kalɔri] **NF** calorie; **régime basses calories** low-calorie diet; **l'avocat est riche en calories** avocados are high in calories; **ration de calories** calorie intake; **attention aux calories!** watch the calories!

calorifère [kalɔrifɛr] **ADJ** heat-conveying
NM (slow-combustion) stove; *Can* radiator

calorifique [kalɔrifik] **ADJ** *Phys* calorific, thermal; **capacité c.** heat capacity

calorifuge [kalɔrifyʒ] **ADJ** (heat-)insulating; *(vernis etc)* heat-proof; **le bois est c.** wood is a poor conductor of heat
NM heat insulator *or* insulation; *(pour chaudière, tuyau)* lagging

calorifugeage [kalɔrifyʒaʒ] **NM** (heat) insulation; *(de chaudière, tuyau)* lagging

calorifuger [kalɔrifyʒe] **VT** *(je calorifugeai(s); n. calorifugeons)* to insulate; *(chaudière, tuyau)* to lag

calorimètre [kalɔrimɛtr] **NM** *Phys* calorimeter

calorimétrie [kalɔrimetri] **NF** *Phys* calorimetry

calorimétrique [kalɔrimetrik] **ADJ** *Phys (unité etc)* calorimetric(al)

caloriporteur [kalɔripɔrtœr] **ADJ, NM** = **caloporteur**

calorique [kalɔrik] **ADJ** calorific; **ration c.** calorie intake

calorisation [kalɔrizasjɔ̃] **NF** *Tech* calorization, aluminium plating

calorstat [kalɔrsta] **NM** *Aut* thermostat

calot[1] [kalo] **NM 1** *(grosse bille)* (large) marble **2** *Arg (œil)* peeper

calot[2] **NM** *Mil* forage cap, *Am* garrison cap

calotin [kalɔtɛ̃] **NM** *Fam Péj* **1** *(prêtre)* priest **2** *(bigot)* pious churchgoer

calotte [kalɔt] **NF 1** *(chapeau rond)* skullcap; *Rel* calotte; *(de chapeau)* crown; *Arg Péj* **la c.** *(le clergé)* the priests; *Pol* the clerical party **2** *Litt* **la c. des cieux** the vault *or* canopy of heaven **3** *Fam (gifle)* cuff, clout; **flanquer une c. à qn** to give sb a clout, to box sb's ears
► ► *Anat* **c. du crâne, c. crânienne** top part of the skull, skullcap; *Géol* **c. glaciaire** ice cap; *Math* **c. sphérique** portion of a sphere

calotter [kalɔte] **VT** *Fam (personne)* to cuff, to clout

calquage [kalkaʒ] **NM** tracing

calque [kalk] **NM 1** *(copie)* tracing; *(de poème, de portrait etc)* exact copy; **prendre un c. de qch** to make a tracing of sth, to trace sth; **(papier-)c.** tracing paper **2** *Ling* loan translation, calque

calquer [kalke] **VT** *(reproduire)* to trace, to make a tracing of; *Fig* to copy exactly, to imitate; **dessin calqué** tracing; **expression calquée sur l'anglais** expression copied from *or* modelled on the English; **c. sa conduite sur celle de qn que l'on admire** to model one's behaviour on that of sb one admires

calter [kalte] **VI** *Arg (s'enfuir)* to scram, *Br* to scarper

calumet [kalymɛ] **NM** peace pipe, calumet; *Fig* **fumer le c. de la paix avec qn** to smoke the pipe of peace with sb

calva [kalva] NM *Fam abrév* **calvados**

calvados [kalvados] NM calvados, apple brandy

calvaire [kalvɛr] NM *(épreuve pénible)* agony, ordeal; *Rel* calvary; *(croix)* calvary, wayside cross; *Rel* **Le C.** (Mount) Calvary; **c'est un c. de devoir la supporter** it's agony having to put up with her; **sa vie fut un long c.** his life was one long ordeal

calvinisme [kalvinism] NM Calvinism

calviniste [kalvinist] ADJ Calvinistic, Calvinist
 N Calvinist

calvitie [kalvisi] NF baldness; **c. naissante** incipient baldness; **c. précoce** premature baldness

calypso [kalipso] NM *(danse)*, *Mus* calypso

cama [kama] NM *Belg Fam (camarade)* pal, mate, friend

camaïeu, -eux [kamajø] NM *(peinture)* monochrome (painting); *(gravure)* tint drawing

camail [kamaj] NM **1** *Cathol (porté par-dessus le surplis)* cape **2** *Orn (du coq)* neck feathers, hackles

camarade [kamarad] N friend, *Fam* mate, pal; *Pol (terme d'adresse)* comrade, brother; **le c. Gorbatchev** comrade Gorbachev; **c. d'école** *ou* **de collège** school friend; **c. de classe** *ou* **de promotion** classmate; **c. de jeu** playmate; **c. de régiment** old army friend

camaraderie [kamaradri] NF camaraderie, comradeship

camard, -arde [kamar, -ard] ADJ *(nez)* flat; *(personne)* flat-nosed, with a flat nose
 NF **camarde** *Fam* **la camarde** the (Grim) Reaper

camarguais, -aise [kamargɛ, -ɛz] ADJ of/from the Camargue
 N **C.** *(natif)* native of the Camargue; *(habitant)* inhabitant of the Camargue

cambiste [kɑ̃bist] *Fin* N foreign exchange dealer
 ADJ **marché c.** exchange market

Cambodge [kɑ̃bɔdʒ] NM Cambodia

cambodgien, -ienne [kɑ̃bɔdʒjɛ̃, -jɛn] ADJ Cambodian
 N **C.** Cambodian

cambouis [kɑ̃bwi] NM dirty oil, grease

cambrage [kɑ̃braʒ] NM bending; *(du pied, du dos)* arching; *(du bois etc)* cambering, curving

cambré [kɑ̃bre] ADJ bent; *(poutre)* cambered, arched; **pied très c.** foot with a high instep; **taille cambrée** arched *or* curved back; **jambes cambrées** bow legs

cambrement [kɑ̃brəmɑ̃] NM = **cambrage**

cambrer [kɑ̃bre] VT to bend; *(le dos, le pied)* to arch; *(bois etc)* to camber, to curve; **c. la taille** *ou* **les reins** to arch one's back
 VPR **se cambrer** to arch one's back

cambrien, -ienne [kɑ̃brijɛ̃, -jɛn] ADJ, NM *Géol* Cambrian

cambriolage [kɑ̃brijɔlaʒ] NM *(métier)* burglary, housebreaking; *(événement)* burglary, break-in

cambriole [kɑ̃brijɔl] NF *Fam (métier)* burglary, housebreaking

cambrioler [kɑ̃brijɔle] VT *(maison)* to break into, to burgle, *Am* to burglarize; **nous avons été cambriolés pendant les vacances** we were burgled *or* we had a burglary *or* break-in while we were on holiday

cambrioleur, -euse [kɑ̃brijɔlœr, -øz] N burglar, housebreaker

cambrousse [kɑ̃bruz], **cambrousse** [kɑ̃brus] NF *Fam (campagne)* country; **maison à la c.** *ou* **en pleine c.** house in the middle of nowhere *or* (out) in the sticks *or* at the back of beyond

cambrure [kɑ̃bryr] NF *(du bois etc)* camber, curve; *(du pied, du dos)* arch; **chaussures à forte c.** shoes with a high instep; **c. des reins** small of the back

cambuse [kɑ̃byz] NF **1** *Naut* storeroom **2** *(de chantier naval)* canteen **3** *Arg (chambre)* hole, place, room

cambusier [kɑ̃byzje] NM **1** *(à la cantine)* canteen keeper **2** *(de stocks)* storekeeper

came¹ [kam] NF *Tech* cam; **arbre à cames** camshaft; **moteur avec arbre à cames en tête** overhead camshaft engine; **à c. unique** single-cam; **c. de frein** expander

came² *Arg* NF **1** *(drogue)* dope, junk **2** *(diminutif de camelote)(objet de mauvaise qualité)* junk

camé, -ée [kame] N *Arg* junkie, druggie

camée [kame] NM cameo

caméléon [kamelɛ̃] NM *(reptile)*, *Fig* chameleon

camélia [kamelja] NM camellia

camelot [kamlo] NM **1** *Fam (marchand dans la rue)* street vendor *or* seller **2** *Arch (vendeur de journaux)* newsvendor **3** *Hist* **camelots du roi** royalists

camelote [kamlɔt] NF *Fam* **1** *(pacotille)* junk, trash, *Br* rubbish; **n'achète pas cette voiture, c'est de la c.!** don't buy that car, it's a pile of junk *or* an old junk heap! **2** *(toute marchandise)* stuff

camembert [kamɑ̃bɛr] NM **1** *(fromage)* Camembert (cheese) **2** *(diagramme)* pie-chart

camer (se) [səkame] VPR *Arg* to do drugs, to be on drugs; **il se came à l'héroïne** he's on heroin; **elle est complètement camée** she's as high as a kite

caméra [kamera] NF *Cin*, *TV* camera; **il s'est expliqué devant les caméras** he gave an explanation in front of the television cameras; **c. de télévision** television camera; **c. asservie** *ou* **esclave** slave camera; **c. banc-titre** rostrum camera; **c. cachée** hidden camera; **c. d'animation** rostrum camera; **c. fixe** fixed camera; **c. Internet** Web cam, live cam; **c. invisible** hidden camera; **c. de reportage** hand-held camera; **c. en studio** studio (broadcast) camera; **c. grande vitesse** high speed camera; **c. isolée** isolated camera, ISO; **c. légère** lightweight camera, portable single camera; **C. d'or** = important prize awarded at the Cannes Film Festival to a first full-length film; *Mktg* **c. oculaire** eye (movement) camera; **c. portable** portable camera; **c. portative** press camera; **c. sans film** filmless camera; **c. sonore** sound camera; **c. super-8** super 8 camera; **c. vidéo** video camera; **c. vidéo numérique** digital video camera

Il faut noter que le mot anglais **camera** signifie également **appareil photo**.

caméra-film, *pl* **caméras-film** NF film camera, motion picture camera, *surtout Am* movie camera

cameraman [kameraman], *pl* **cameramen** [kameramɛn] NM *Cin*, *TV* cameraman

camérier [kamerje] NM *(du Pape, de cardinal)* chamberlain

cameriste [kamerist] NF *Hist* lady-in-waiting

Cameroun [kamrun] NM **le C.** Cameroon; *Hist* the Cameroons

camerounais, -aise [kamrunɛ, -ɛz] ADJ Cameroonian
 N **C.** Cameroonian

Caméscope® [kameskɔp] NM camcorder; **C. numérique** digital camcorder

camion [kamjɔ̃] NM **1** *Aut* truck, *Br* lorry; **c. de déménagement** removal van; **c. bâché** curtainsider; **c. de dépannage** breakdown truck, *Am* wrecker; **c. pour transport d'auto-** mobiles (car) transporter; **c. réfrigéré** refrigerated lorry; **chauffeur de c.** lorry *or* truck driver; *TV* **c. d'enregistrement (du son)** sound van **2** *(chariot)* dray, wag(g)on

camion-benne, *pl* **camions-bennes** NM dump(er) truck

camion-citerne, *pl* **camions-citernes** NM tanker, *Am* tank truck *or* trailer

camion-magasin, *pl* **camions-magasins** NM mobile shop

camionnage [kamjɔnaʒ] NM *(prix, service)* haulage, *Am* truckage; **une entreprise de c.** a haulage firm, *Am* a trucking business

camionner [kamjɔne] VT *(marchandises)* to transport by *Br* lorry *or* truck, *Am* to truck

camionnette [kamjɔnɛt] NF van, panel van, *Am* delivery truck; **c. de livraison** delivery van

camionneur [kamjɔnœr] NM **1** *(conducteur)* *Br* lorry driver, truck driver, *Am* trucker, teamster; *(de camionnette)* van driver **2** *(transporteur)* haulier, *Am* hauler, *Am* trucker

camisole [kamizɔl] NF **1** *Can, Suisse (tricot de corps)* vest, *Am* undershirt **2** *Arch (chemise de nuit)* nightshirt **3** *(corsage)* camisole
 ▸▸ **c. de force** strait-jacket

camomille [kamɔmij] NF camomile; **tisane de c.** camomile tea; **prendre une c.** to have a cup of camomile tea

camouflage [kamuflaʒ] NM camouflage; *(de la vérité etc)* disguising, hiding; **le c. d'une rentrée d'argent** the concealment of a sum of money received; **le c. d'une faute** the covering up of a mistake

camoufler [kamufle] VT to camouflage; *(vérité, intentions etc)* to disguise, to hide; *(faute)* to cover up; *(rentrée d'argent)* to conceal; **c. un bouton** to cover up *or* camouflage a spot; *Compta* **c. un bilan** to window-dress the accounts; **c. un meurtre en suicide** to make a murder look like suicide
 VPR **se camoufler** to camouflage oneself

camouflet [kamuflɛ] NM affront, snub; **essuyer un c.** to be snubbed

camp [kɑ̃] NM **1** *(campement)* camp; **établir un c.** to pitch camp; **lever le c.** to strike camp; **lit de c.** camp bed; **feu de c.** campfire; **partir faire un c., partir en c.** to go camping; *Fam* **ficher le c.** to clear off, to scram; *Fam* **fous-moi le c.!** clear off!, beat it! **2** *(parti)* camp; **changer de c.** to change sides; **le c. adverse** the opposing camp, the other side; **ils ne sont pas dans le même c.** they're on different sides **3** *(de jeux)* side; **tirer les camps** to pick sides; **faire deux camps** to form two teams
 ▸▸ **c. (de vacances)** (children's) holiday camp, *Am* summer camp; **c. d'adolescents** holiday camp for teenagers, *Am* camp; **c. de concentration** concentration camp; **c. d'internement** internment camp; **c. de loisirs** holiday camp; **c. de la mort** death camp; **c. de prisonniers** prison camp; *Mil* **c. volant** temporary camp

campage-caravanage [kɑ̃paʒkaravanaʒ] NM INV camping-caravanning

campagnard, -arde [kɑ̃paɲar, -ard] ADJ *(allure, accent etc)* country; *(simplicité)* rustic
 N countryman, f countrywoman, *Péj* rustic

campagne [kɑ̃paɲ] NF **1** *(par opposition à la ville)* country(side); **à la c.** in the country; **en pleine c.** deep in the countryside; **vie à la c.** country life; **battre la c.** to scour *or* comb the countryside; *Fig* **son esprit bat la c.** his mind is wandering; **en rase c.** in (the) open country; **maison de c.** country house, place in the country **2** *Mil* **en c.** in the field, on active service; **artillerie de c.** field artillery; **tenue de c.** field dress, combat dress; **entrer** *ou* **se mettre en c.** to begin operations, to take the field; *Fig* to set to work **3** *Mil, Pol etc* campaign; *Mil* **faire c.** to fight a campaign; *Fig* **faire c.** *ou* **se mettre en c. pour qn/contre qch** to campaign on sb's behalf/against sth; **faire c. pour** *ou* **en faveur d'un candidat** to canvass *or* campaign for *or* on behalf of a candidate; *Pol* **entrer en c.** to start to campaign; **partir en c. contre le tabac** to launch an anti-smoking campaign; **c. d'affichage** poster campaign; **c. publicitaire** *ou* **de publicité** advertising *or* publicity campaign, publicity drive; **c. commerciale/de vente** sales campaign; **c. de marketing/de promotion** marketing/promotional campaign; **c. télévisée** television campaign; **c. de presse** press campaign; **c. électorale** election campaign; *Mktg* **c. de dénigrement** countermarketing campaign; **c. de calomnies** *ou* **de diffamation** smear campaign; *Mil* **la c. d'Égypte** the Egyptian campaign

> Attention: ne pas confondre **country** et **countryside** lorsqu'on traduit **campagne**. On utilise **countryside** lorsqu'il risque d'y avoir confusion avec **country** dans le sens de **pays**, ou bien lorsqu'on parle de paysages campagnards.

campagnol [kɑ̃paɲɔl] NM vole

campanile [kɑ̃panil] NM *Archit* campanile, bell tower

campanule [kɑ̃panyl] NF campanula

campé [kɑ̃pe] ADJ **bien c.** *(personne)* well-built; **bien c. sur ses jambes** standing firmly on his feet; **portrait bien c.** well-sketched portrait; **récit bien c.** well-constructed story

campement [kɑ̃pmɑ̃] NM **1** *(action)* camping **2** *(installation)* camp, encampment; *(lieu)* camping ground *or* place; **établir un c.** to camp, to pitch camp; **replier le c.** to strike camp; **matériel de c.** camping equipment

camper [kɑ̃pe] VI **1** *(faire du camping)* to camp; *(dans le jardin etc)* to camp out **2** *(établir un campement)* to camp, to pitch camp, *Mil* to encamp; *Fig (dans un hôtel etc)* to camp out; *Fig* **ils campent ici depuis quinze jours** they've been camping out here for two weeks

▪ VT *(troupes)* to encamp; *(planter)* *(histoire etc)* to put *or* place in context; **il a campé son chapeau sur sa tête** he stuck *or* planted his hat on his head; **un écrivain qui campe bien ses personnages** an author whose characters are well-rounded; *Théâtre* **c. un personnage** to play a part effectively

▪ VPR **se camper se c. devant qn** to plant oneself in front of sb

campeur, -euse [kɑ̃pœr, -øz] N camper

camphre [kɑ̃fr] NM camphor; **essence de c.** camphor oil

camphré [kɑ̃fre] ADJ *(huile etc)* camphorated

camphrier [kɑ̃frije] NM camphor tree

camping [kɑ̃piŋ] NM **1** *(activité)* camping; **faire du c.** to go camping; **c. libre** = non-site camping in suitable spots with permission if required; **c. à la ferme** farm camping; **c. sauvage** unauthorized camping **2** *(lieu)* camp(-ing) site; **c. aménagé** camp site (with facilities)

camping-car [kɑ̃piŋkar], *pl* **camping-cars** NM camper, *Br* Dormobile®, *Am* motor-home, *Am* recreational vehicle

camping-caravaning NM INV camping-caravanning

Camping-Gaz® NM INV camping stove

campos [kɑ̃po] NM *Fam* **donner c. à qn** to give sb a day/an afternoon/*etc* off

campus [kɑ̃pys] NM campus; **vivre sur le c.** to live on campus VOIR GRAMMAIRE A14

camus [kamy] ADJ **1** *(personne)* flat-nosed **2** *(nez)* flat

CAN NM *(abrév* **convertisseur analogue-numérique)** ADC

Canada [kanada] NM Canada; **être/aller au C.** to be in/to go to Canada

Canadair® [kanadɛr] NM fire-fighting plane

canadianisme [kanadjanism] NM *Ling* Canadianism

canadien, -ienne [kanadjɛ̃, -jɛn] ADJ Canadian

▪ N **C.** Canadian; **C. français(e)** French Canadian

▪ NF **canadienne** *(veste)* sheepskin jacket; *(canoë)* Canadian canoe; *(tente)* ridge tent

canaille [kanɑj] NF *(crapule)* scoundrel, rogue; **petite c.!** *(à un enfant)* you little devil *or* rascal!; *Vieilli* **la c.** the rabble, the riff-raff

▪ ADJ *(action)* low, crooked; *(chanson, paroles)* vulgar, coarse; **il a un petit air c.** he has a roguish air about him

canaillerie [kanɑjri] NF **1** *(acte)* low(-down) *or* mean *or* dirty trick **2** *(d'une action)* lowness, crookedness; *(d'une chanson, d'une histoire etc)* vulgarity, coarseness

canal, -aux [kanal, -o] NM **1** *Constr* canal; **c. d'irrigation** irrigation canal; **c. maritime** *ou* **de navigation** ship canal; **c. de dérivation** diversion *or* bypass channel; **le c. de Mozambique** the Mozambique Channel; **le c. de Suez** the Suez Canal; **la zone du c. (de Panama)** the Canal Zone

2 *(de rivière)* channel

3 *(conduite)* conduit, duct, pipe; **c. à air** *ou* **d'aérage** air passage *or* duct; **c. d'amenée** feeder; **c. de fuite** waste pipe; **c. de graissage** oil groove; **c. encreur** *(d'une imprimante)* ink channel

4 *Anat, Bot* canal, duct; **c. alimentaire** alimentary canal; **c. biliaire** bile duct; **c. lymphatique** lymph vessel

5 *Radio, TV, Ordinat* channel; *Can TV* *(chaîne)* (TV) channel; **c. d'accès** access channel; **c. de dialogue en direct** IRC channel; *Radio* **c. de fréquence à large bande** wide-band frequency channel; **c. IRC** IRC channel; *TV* **c. mosaïque** multi-screen channel; *TV* **C. Plus** = French pay television channel; **c. de télévision** television channel; **c. vidéo** video channel

6 *Fig (moyen)* channel; **par le c. de la poste** through the post

7 *Écon, Mktg* channel; **c. de distribution** distribution channel; **c. de distribution court** one-level channel; **c. de distribution long** two-/three-level marketing channel, conventional marketing channel; **c. de communication** promotional *or* communications channel; **c. de communication commerciale** marketing communications channel

> ### Canal+
> Canal+, France's first private television channel, was established in 1982 and started broadcasting in 1984. It broadcasts programmes that have to be unscrambled using a special decoding unit, although for part of the day its programmes can be seen without this device. Canal+ also plays a prominent role in funding international films.

canalisable [kanalizabl] ADJ **eau c.** water which can be channelled *or* canalized; *Fig* **une énergie difficilement c.** energy which is difficult to channel *or* direct

canalisation [kanalizasjɔ̃] NF **1** *(de rivière etc)* canalization **2** *(conduite)* conduit, pipe; *(conduites)* (system of) pipes, piping; *Élec* wiring **3** *(pour pétrole etc)* pipeline **4** *Ordinat* **c. des commandes** command piping

canaliser [kanalize] VT **1** *(région, rivière etc)*

to canalize **2** *(ressources)* to channel, to concentrate **3** *(trafic, foule etc)* to direct

cananéen, -enne [kananeɛ̃, -ɛn] *Bible* ADJ Canaanite

▪ NM *Ling* Canaanite

▪ N **C.** Canaanite

canapé [kanape] NM **1** *(meuble)* sofa, couch, settee; **c. deux places** two-seater sofa, *Am* loveseat; **c. trois places** three-seater sofa; **c. convertible** sofa bed, bed settee **2** *Culin* canapé

canapé-lit, *pl* **canapés-lits** NM sofa bed, bed settee

canaque [kanak] ADJ Kanak

▪ N **C.** Kanak *(indigenous inhabitant of New Caledonia)*

canard [kanar] NM **1** *(oiseau)* duck; *(mâle)* drake; **mare aux canards** duck pond; **chasse aux canards** duck shooting *or* hunting; *Fam* **mon petit c.** my pet, my darling; *Fam* **marcher comme un c.** to waddle; **marcher en c.** to walk with one's feet turned out VOIR GRAMMAIRE A12 **2** *Fam (fausse nouvelle)* false report, *Lit* canard **3** *Fam (journal)* rag **4** *(morceau de sucre)* = sugar lump dipped in coffee, brandy etc **5** *Mus* false note **6** *Can (bouilloire)* kettle

▪▪ **c. de Barbarie** Muscovy duck; *Culin* **c. laqué** Peking duck; *Culin* **c. à l'orange** duck à l'orange; **c. sauvage** wild duck; **c. siffleur** wi(d)geon

canardeau, -eaux [kanardo] NM duckling

canarder [kanarde] VI **1** *(de navire)* to pitch **2** *Mus Fam* to play a false note; *(en chantant)* to sing a false note

▪ VT *Fam* to snipe at, to take pot shots at; **se faire c. à coup de boules de neige** to be pelted with snowballs; *Fig* **il s'est fait c. de questions** he was bombarded with questions

canardière [kanardjɛr] NF **1** *(mare)* duck pond **2** *(lieu) (pour la chasse aux canards)* screen **3** *(fusil)* duck gun, punt gun

canari [kanari] NM canary

▪ ADJ INV *(jaune)* **c.** canary yellow

Canaries [kanari] NFPL **les (îles) C.** the Canary Islands, the Canaries

canasson [kanasɔ̃] NM *Arg (cheval)* nag

canasta [kanasta] NF *Cartes* canasta; **jouer à la c.** to play canasta

cancale [kɑ̃kal] NF Cancale oyster

cancan [kɑ̃kɑ̃] NM **1** *Fam (racontar)* (piece of) gossip; **cancans** tittle-tattle, gossip; **dire** *ou* **faire des cancans** to gossip, to tittle-tattle, to talk (*sur* about) **2** *(danse)* cancan; **danser le c.** to do *or* dance the cancan

cancaner [kɑ̃kane] VI **1** *Fam (médire)* to gossip, to tittle-tattle, to talk (*sur* about) **2** *(d'un canard)* to quack

cancanier, -ière [kɑ̃kanje, -jɛr] *Fam* ADJ gossipy, fond of tittle-tattle

▪ N gossip, scandalmonger

cancer [kɑ̃sɛr] NM **1** *Méd* cancer; **c. du poumon/du sein** lung/breast cancer, cancer of the lung/breast; **c. de la peau** skin cancer; **avoir un c.** to have cancer; **avoir un c. à** *ou* **de l'estomac/au** *ou* **du poumon** to have stomach/lung cancer; **mourir d'un c.** to die of cancer; *Fig* **le chômage est le c. du monde moderne** unemployment is the cancer of the modern world **2** *Astron, Astrol* **le C.** Cancer, the Crab; **être (du signe du) C.** to be (a) Cancer *or* Cancerian **3** *Géog* **le tropique du C.** the tropic of Cancer

cancéreux, -euse [kɑ̃serø, -øz] ADJ *(tumeur etc)* cancerous

▪ N cancer victim *or* sufferer; **les c. en phase terminale** people with terminal cancer, people who are terminally ill with cancer

cancériforme [kɑ̃seriform] ADJ *Méd* cancriform, cancroid

cancérigène [kɑ̃seriʒɛn] ADJ carcinogenic; **produit c.** carcinogen

cancérisation [kɑ̃serizasjɔ̃] NF *Méd* **cela aboutira à la c. de l'organe** that will result in the organ becoming cancerous

cancériser (se) [səkɑ̃serize] VPR *Méd* to become cancerous

cancérogène [kɑ̃serɔʒɛn] ADJ = **cancérigène**

cancérologie [kɑ̃serɔlɔʒi] NF cancerology

cancérologue [kɑ̃serɔlɔg] N cancer specialist

cancre [kɑ̃kr] NM 1 *(crustacé)* crab 2 *Fam (écolier)* dunce, duffer

cancrelat [kɑ̃krəla] NM cockroach, *Am* roach

cancroïde [kɑ̃krɔid] NM *Méd* cancroid

candélabre [kɑ̃delabr] NM 1 *(chandelier)* candelabra, candelabrum, *pl* candelabra 2 *(lampadaire)* lamppost

candeur [kɑ̃dœr] NF ingenuousness, guilelessness, artlessness; **un regard plein de c.** a guileless look

> Il faut noter que le nom anglais **candour** est un faux ami. Il signifie **franchise**.

candi [kɑ̃di] ADJ candied; **fruits candis** crystallized fruit; **sucre c.** sugar candy, rock candy

candidat, -ate [kɑ̃dida, -at] N applicant, candidate (**à une place** for a job); *(à un examen)* candidate; **se porter c. aux élections** to stand *or* run for election

candidature [kɑ̃didatyr] NF *Pol* candidature, candidacy; *(à un poste)* application (**à** for); **poser sa c. à un poste** to apply for a post; **retirer sa c.** *(à un poste)* to withdraw one's application; *Pol* to stand down; **il a retiré sa c. à la présidence** he has stood down as a presidential candidate
> ►► **c. spontanée** unsolicited application

candide [kɑ̃did] ADJ ingenuous, guileless, artless

> Il faut noter que l'adjectif anglais **candid** est un faux ami. Il signifie **franc**.

candidement [kɑ̃didmɑ̃] ADV ingenuously, guilelessly, artlessly

candidose [kɑ̃didoz] NF *Méd* candida

cane [kan] NF (female) duck *(as opposed to drake)*

cané [kane] ADJ *Fam* dead

caner [kane] VI *Arg (avoir peur)* to have the jitters; *(se dégonfler)* to chicken out, *Br* to bottle out; *(mourir)* to snuff it, to kick the bucket

caneton [kantɔ̃] NM (male) duckling

canette¹ [kanɛt] NF *(petite cane)* (female) duckling

canette² NF = **cannette**

canevas [kanva] NM 1 *Tex* canvas; **broderie sur c.** tapestry (work) 2 *Beaux-Arts, Mus, Littér (de dessin, roman etc)* outline

caniche [kaniʃ] NM poodle

caniculaire [kanikylɛr] ADJ *(chaleur, journée etc)* scorching

canicule [kanikyl] NF heatwave; **quelle c.!** what a scorcher!; **la c.** the dog days; **pendant la c. du mois d'août** during the August heatwave

canif [kanif] NM penknife, pocket knife; **donner un coup de c. dans le contrat** *(ne pas respecter ses engagements)* to go back on one's commitments; *(commettre une infidélité)* to have a fling

canin, -ine [kanɛ̃, -in] ADJ canine; **exposition canine** dog show
▪ NF **canine** canine (tooth), eyetooth

caninette [kaninɛt] NF = motorbike used for cleaning dog dirt from the streets

canisse [kanis] NF = **cannisse**

caniveau, -eaux [kanivo] NM 1 *(le long des routes)* gutter 2 *Élec (pour câble)* trough, conduit

cannabis [kanabis] NM cannabis

cannage [kanaʒ] NM 1 *(activité)* caning 2 *(résultat)* canework

canne [kan] NF 1 *(tige)* cane; **sucre de c.** cane sugar 2 *(pour s'appuyer)* (walking) stick, cane 3 *(de souffleur de verre)* blowpipe 4 *Can (de tomates etc)* can, *Br* tin 5 *Arg (jambe)* leg; **avoir de belles cannes** to have a nice pair of legs, to have great legs 6 *Suisse (au hockey sur glace) Br* ice hockey stick, *Am* hockey stick
> ►► *Méd* **c. anglaise** arthritic crutch; **c. blanche** white stick; *Fig* **les cannes blanches** the blind; **c. à pêche** fishing rod; **c. à sucre** sugar cane

canné [kane] ADJ **chaise cannée** cane(-seated) chair

canneberge [kanbɛrʒ] NF cranberry; **sauce aux canneberges** cranberry sauce

canne-épée, *pl* **cannes-épées** NF swordstick

cannelé [kanle] ADJ *(colonne etc)* fluted; *(pneu)* grooved; *(ongle)* ridged

canneler [kanle] VT (**je cannelle, n. cannelons; je cannellerai**) *(colonne)* to flute; *(pneu)* to groove

cannelier [kanəlje] NM cinnamon tree

cannelle¹ [kanɛl] NF *Culin* cinnamon; **bâton de c.** cinnamon stick; **à la c.** cinnamon(-flavoured)

cannelle² NF *(de tonneau)* spigot

cannellonis [kanɛlɔni] NMPL cannelloni

cannelure [kanlyr] NF 1 *(rainure)* groove; *Archit (de colonne)* fluting 2 *(de métal, carton)* corrugation 3 *Bot* **cannelures striae** 4 *Géol* fault fissure

canner [kane] VT *(chaise)* to cane

Cannes [kan] NF *Cin* **le festival de C.** the Cannes Film Festival

cannette [kanɛt] NF 1 *(petite bouteille)* (beer) bottle; **c. de bière** bottle of beer 2 *(boîte contenant une boisson)* can; **la rue était jonchée de cannettes de bière vides** the street was littered with empty beer cans 3 *Tex* spool, cop

canneur, -euse [kanœr, -øz] N cane worker

cannibale [kanibal] N cannibal
▪ ADJ *(pratiques etc)* cannibalistic; **tribu c.** tribe of cannibals

cannibalisation [kanibalizasjɔ̃] NF *(de machine)* cannibalization; *Com* **la c. d'un produit** the erosion of the market share of a product

cannibaliser [kanibalize] VT *(machine)* to cannibalize; *Com (produit)* to eat into the market share of

cannibalisme [kanibalism] NM 1 *(anthropophagie)* cannibalism 2 *Mktg, Tech* cannibalization

cannisse [kanis] NF *Région (pour faire des clôtures etc)* split cane

canoë [kanɔe] NM canoe; **faire du c.** to canoe, to go canoeing; **remonter le fleuve en c.** to canoe up the river

canoéisme [kanɔeism] NM canoeing

canoéiste [kanɔeist] N canoeist

canoë-kayak, *pl* **canoës-kayaks** NM canoeing

canon¹ [kanɔ̃] NM 1 *(pièce d'artillerie)* gun; *Hist* cannon; **c. de 105 mm/de 280 mm** 105 mm/280 mm gun; **poudre à c.** gunpowder; *Fam* **chair à c.** cannon fodder; **le c.** *(artillerie)* the guns; **le gros c.** the heavy guns 2 *(de carabine, montre, stylo)* barrel; *(de clé, serrure)* barrel, pipe; *(d'arrosoir)* spout; *(de seringue)* body; **fusil à deux canons** double-barrelled gun; **c. rayé** rifled barrel 3 *Arch (mesure)* = wine measure equivalent to 0.058 litre; *Fam* **boire un c.** to have a glass of wine
> ►► **c. à âme lisse** smooth-bore gun; **c. anti-aérien** anti-aircraft gun; **c. antichar** anti-tank gun; **c. de bord** naval gun; **c. de char** tank gun; *Naut* **c. de chasse** bow chaser; **c. à électrons** electron gun; **c. lance-harpon** harpoon gun; **c. de marine** naval gun; **c. à neige** snow-blower; **c. paragrêle** cloud seeder; *Naut* **c.²** NM1 **de retraite** sternchaser

canon² NM 1 *Rel (d'un ordre, de la messe etc)* canon 2 *(règle)* canon; **selon les canons de la beauté** according to the canons of beauty 3 *Mus* canon; **c. à deux/trois voix** canon for two/three voices; **reprendre un chant en c.** to sing a round 4 *Fam (personne belle)* babe, knock-out, stunner
▪ ADJ INV 1 **droit c.** canon law 2 *Fam (beau)* gorgeous, *Br* fit

cañon [kanjɔ̃] NM *Géog* canyon, cañon

canonial, -iale, -iaux, -iales [kanɔnjal, -jo] ADJ *Rel* 1 *(heures etc)* canonical 2 *(du chanoine)* canonic(al)

canonique [kanɔnik] ADJ *(livre etc)* canonical; **âge c.** *Rel (de servante de prêtre)* canonical age; *Fam* venerable old age

canonisation [kanɔnizasjɔ̃] NF *Rel* canonization

canoniser [kanɔnize] VT *Rel* to canonize

canon-mitrailleuse, *pl* **canons-mitrailleuses** NM *Mil* pom-pom

canonnade [kanɔnad] NF gunfire; **une c.** a burst of gunfire

canonner [kanɔne] VT to shell, to bombard

canonnier [kanɔnje] NM *Mil* gunner

canonnière [kanɔnjɛr] NF 1 *Naut* gunboat 2 *(ouverture)* loophole

canot [kano] NM *Naut* 1 *(embarcation non pontée)* boat, dinghy; **grand c.** longboat, pinnace; **petit c.** jollyboat 2 *Can (canoë)* canoe
> ►► **c. automobile** motorboat, motor launch; **c. pneumatique** inflatable *or* rubber dinghy; **c. de sauvetage** lifeboat

canotage [kanɔtaʒ] NM *Naut* boating; *(à l'aviron)* rowing; *(à la voile)* sailing; *Can (en canoë)* canoeing; *Can* **faire du c.** to go canoeing

canoter [kanɔte] VI *Naut* to go boating; *(à l'aviron)* to go rowing; *(à la voile)* to go sailing; *Can (en canoë)* to go canoeing

canoteur, -euse [kanɔtœr, øz] N boater; *(à l'aviron)* rower; *Can (canoéiste)* canoeist

canotier [kanɔtje] NM 1 *(rameur)* rower, oarsman 2 *(chapeau)* boater, straw hat

cantal [kɑ̃tal] NM Cantal (cheese)

cantaloup [kɑ̃talu] NM *(fruit)* cantaloup (melon)

cantate [kɑ̃tat] NF *Mus* cantata

cantatrice [kɑ̃tatris] NF *(chanteuse d'opéra)* opera singer; *(de concert)* (concert) singer

cantharide [kɑ̃tarid] NF *(insecte)* cantharis, Spanish fly

cantilène [kɑ̃tilɛn] NF *Mus* cantilena

cantilever [kɑ̃tilevœr] ADJ *Constr* cantilever; **pont c.** cantilever bridge

cantine [kɑ̃tin] NF 1 *(réfectoire)* canteen; *Scol* dining hall; *Univ* refectory; *Scol* **déjeuner à la c.** to have school meals; *Scol* **la c. n'est pas bonne** the food at school is bad; **je les mets à la c. à la rentrée** they're going to start having shool meals next term 2 *(malle)* trunk; *Mil* uniform case, tin trunk; *Mil* **c. médicale** field medical chest

cantique [kɑ̃tik] NM *Rel* hymn; *Bible* **le c. des cantiques** the Song of Songs *or* of Solomon

cantoche [kɑ̃tɔʃ] NF *Fam* canteen

canton [kɑ̃tɔ̃] NM **1** *(en France)* canton (= *administrative division of a department)*; *(en Suisse)* canton; *Can* **les cantons de l'Est** the Eastern Townships **2** *Constr (de route, voie ferrée etc)* section

cantonade [kɑ̃tɔnad] NF **parler à la c.** not to speak to anyone in particular, to speak to all those present; *Théâtre* to speak off; **elle l'a dit à la c.** she said it so that everyone could hear

cantonais, -aise [kɑ̃tɔnɛ, -ɛz] ADJ Cantonese
    NM *Ling* Cantonese
    N **C.** Cantonese

cantonal, -ale, -aux, -ales [kɑ̃tɔnal, -o] ADJ canton, cantonal; **les (élections) cantonales** the cantonal elections

cantonnement [kɑ̃tɔnmɑ̃] NM **1** *Mil (des troupes)* quartering, billeting **2** *(de forêt)* section; *(avec droits de pêche)* stretch of river **3** *Mil (lieu)* quarters, billet

cantonner [kɑ̃tɔne] VT *(isoler, limiter)* to confine (**dans qch** to sth); *(animaux, malades)* to isolate; *Mil (troupes)* to quarter, to billet; **c. les jeunes employés à des tâches dérisoires** to confine *or* restrict *or* limit junior employees to menial tasks
    VI *(troupes)* to be billeted *or* quartered
    VPR **se cantonner** *(dans une pièce etc)* to shut oneself away; *Fig (se limiter)* to confine *or* limit oneself (**dans qch** to sth); **se c. à une tâche** to confine oneself to one task

cantonnier [kɑ̃tɔnje] NM *(sur les routes)* roadmender, roadman; *Rail* lineman

cantonnière [kɑ̃tɔnjɛr] NF *(de lit, de fenêtre)* valance

canular [kanylar] NM *Fam* hoax, *Fam* legpull; **monter un c.** to play a hoax

canule [kanyl] NF *Méd* cannula, canula; *(de seringue)* nozzle

canuler [kanyle] VT **1** *Arg (ennuyer)* **c. qn** to get on sb's nerves *or Br* wick **2** *Scol Fam* to play a practical joke on

canut, -use [kany, -yz] N silk weaver (of Lyons)

canyon [kanjɔn] NM = cañon

canyoning [kanjɔniŋ] NM canyoning

CAO [seao] NF *Ordinat (abrév* **conception assistée par ordinateur)** CAD

caoua [kawa] NM *Fam* coffee

caoutchouc [kautʃu] NM **1** *(substance)* rubber; **c. synthétique** synthetic rubber; **c. Mousse®** foam rubber, sponge rubber; **ballon en c.** rubber ball; *Bourse* **caoutchoucs** rubber shares, rubbers **2** *Vieilli (manteau)* waterproof (coat), raincoat, *Br* mackintosh; *(élastique)* rubber band, elastic band; **caoutchoucs** *(chaussures)* galoshes, overshoes, *Am* rubbers **3** *Bot* rubber plant

caoutchoutage [kautʃutaʒ] NM rubberizing, coating with rubber

caoutchouter [kautʃute] VT to rubberize, to coat with rubber

caoutchouteux, -euse [kautʃutø, -øz] ADJ *Péj* rubbery

CAP [seape] NM *(abrév* **certificat d'aptitude professionnelle)** = vocational training certificate; **C. hébergement** certificate of vocational training in accommodation management

Cap (Le) [ləkap] NM Cape Town

cap [kap] NM **1** *Géog* cape, headland; **le c. Horn** Cape Horn; *Hist* **la Colonie du c.** Cape Colony; **passer** *ou* **franchir** *ou* **doubler un c.** to round a cape; *Fig* to weather *or* overcome

a difficulty; **quand on a franchi le c. de la quarantaine** when you've turned forty; **notre usine va passer le c. des mille employés** our factory will soon top the thousand-employee mark
    2 *Naut, Aviat (direction)* course, direction; **mettre le c. sur ...** to head for ..., to steer for ..., to set course for ...; **mettre le c. au large** to stand out to sea; **c. au vent/au large** head (on) to the wind/to sea; **changement de c.** change of course; *Aviat* **c. de collision** collision course; *Aviat* **conservateur de c.** directional gyro; **c. magnétique** magnetic course *or* heading
    3 de pied en c. from head to foot *or* toe, from top to toe

capable [kapabl] ADJ **1 c. de qch** capable of sth; **être c. de faire qch** to be capable of doing sth, to be able to do sth; **je n'en suis pas c.** I can't do it; **il est c. de tout** he's capable of anything; **c. du meilleur comme du pire** capable of the best as well as the worst; **elle est bien c. d'oublier les clefs!** she's quite capable of forgetting the keys!; **cette maladie est c. de le tuer** this illness might well kill him *or* may be enough to kill him
    2 *(compétent) (personne)* capable, able, competent; **élève très c.** very able pupil
    3 *Jur* competent (**de faire** to do)

capacité [kapasite] NF **1** *(contenance) (de vase, accumulateur etc)* capacity; **c. d'accueil** *(d'un hôtel)* accommodation capacity, available beds; *Élec* **c. (électrostatique)** capacitance
    2 *(aptitude)* ability, capability; **homme de grande** *ou* **de haute c.** very capable *or* able man, man of great ability; **je n'en ai pas les capacités** I don't have the ability *or* skills (to do it); **c. pour les affaires** business ability; **de grandes capacités intellectuelles** great intellectual abilities; **c. de concentration** attention span
    3 *Jur* capacity; **certificat de c. en droit** = certificate entitling holder to practise in some branches of the legal profession; **avoir c. pour faire qch** to be (legally) entitled *or* qualified to do sth; **c. de jouissance** legal right, legal entitlement
    ▸▸ **c. d'achat** purchasing power; *Ordinat* **c. d'adressage** address capability; *Ordinat* **c. de disque/disquette** disk capacity; **c. à emprunter** borrowing capacity; **c. d'endettement** borrowing capacity; **c. de financement** financing capacity; *Fin* **c. d'imposition** ability to pay tax; *Com* **c. linéaire** shelf-space; *Ordinat* **c. de mémoire** memory capacity; **c. de production** production capacity; *Ordinat* **c. de stockage** storage capacity; **c. de traitement** throughput; *Méd* **c. vitale** vital capacity

caparaçon [kaparasɔ̃] NM caparison

caparaçonner [kaparasɔne] VT *(cheval)* to caparison

cape [kap] NF **1** *(vêtement)* cape; *(plus longue)* cloak; **film/roman de c. et d'épée** swashbuckling film/novel; *Fig* **sous c.** secretly, on the quiet; *Fig* **rire sous c.** to laugh up one's sleeve **2** *Naut* **être** *ou* **se tenir à la c.** to lie to, to be hove to; **(se) mettre à la c.** to heave to

capeline [kaplin] NF *(chapeau)* floppy hat

CAPES [kapɛs] NM *Univ (abrév* **certificat d'aptitude au professorat de l'enseignement secondaire)** = postgraduate teaching certificate

---

CAPES

This is a required qualification for state teachers in France. Candidates who pass this competitive exam become "professeurs certifiés" and are entitled to teach in secondary education.

---

capésien, -ienne [kapesjɛ̃, -jɛn] N *Univ* (étudiant) = student preparing to take the CAPES; *(diplômé)* = holder of the CAPES

CAPET [kapɛt] NM *Univ (abrév* **certificat d'aptitude au professorat de l'enseignement technique)** ≃ postgraduate technical teaching certificate

capétien¹, -ienne¹ [kapesjɛ̃, -jɛn] *Hist* ADJ Capetian
    N Capetian

capétien², -ienne² N *Univ (étudiant)* = student preparing to take the CAPET; *(diplômé)* = holder of the CAPET

Capharnaüm [kafarnaɔm] NM *Bible* Capernaum

capharnaüm [kafarnaɔm] NM *Fam (pièce en désordre)* tip, pigsty; *(désordre)* mess

cap-hornier, *pl* **cap-horniers** [kapɔrnje] NM sailing ship/sailor travelling round the Horn

capillaire [kapilɛr] ADJ **1** *(tube, attraction)* capillary; *Anat* **les vaisseaux capillaires** the capillary blood vessels, the capillaries **2 lotion c.** *(pour les cheveux)* hair lotion, hair tonic; **artiste c.** hair stylist
    NM **1** *Bot* maidenhair (fern) **2** *Anat* **les capillaires** the capillaries

capillarité [kapilarite] NF *Phys* capillarity, capillary action

capilliculture [kapilikyltyr] NF hair care

capilotade [kapilɔtad] NF *Fam* **mettre qch en c.** to smash sth to pieces *or* to smithereens; **j'ai le dos en c.** my back's killing me

capitaine [kapitɛn] NM **1** *Mil, Naut* captain; *Naut Fam* skipper **2** *(de bande, gang etc)* leader, head; *Sport* captain, *Fam* skipper; *Mil* **un grand c.** a great (military) leader
    ▸▸ *Mil, Aviat* **c. (d'aviation)** *Br* ≃ flight lieutenant, *Am* ≃ captain; *Naut* **c. de corvette** lieutenant commander; **c. de frégate** commander; **c. de gendarmerie** ≃ police superintendent; **c. d'industrie** captain of industry; **c. au long cours** master mariner; **c. de la marine marchande** captain *or* master (in the merchant navy); **c. des pompiers** ≃ fire chief; **c. de port** harbour *or Am* harbor master; **c. de vaisseau** captain

capitainerie [kapitɛnri] NF harbour master's office

capital, -ale, -aux, -ales [kapital, -o] ADJ **1** *Jur (crime etc)* capital; **la peine capitale** capital punishment, the death penalty
    2 *(essentiel)* essential; **le point c.** the essential *or* main point; **une décision capitale** a major decision; **c'est c.** it's essential; **il est c. qu'il soit présent à la réunion** it is essential for him to be at the meeting; **son défaut c.** his greatest fault; **d'une importance capitale** of capital *or* paramount importance, of the utmost importance; **les sept péchés capitaux** the seven deadly sins
    3 *Typ* **lettre capitale** capital (letter)
    NM **1** *Fin* capital; **détenir 5% du c. d'une société** to have a 5% shareholding in *or* to hold 5% of the shares in a company; **c. et intérêt** principal and interest; **posséder un c.** to have some capital; **les capitaux qui circulent** the capital in circulation; **fuite des capitaux** flight of capital; **association c.-travail** profit-sharing scheme; *Fig* **le c. culturel d'un pays** the cultural wealth of a country; **ces jeunes diplômés représentent un véritable c. pour notre entreprise** these qualified young people are an asset to our company **2** *(capitalistes)* **le c.** capital
    NF **capitale 1** *(ville)* capital (city) **2** *Typ* capital (letter); **(écrire en) capitales d'imprimerie** (write in) block capitals *or* block letters; **petite capitale** small capital
    ▸▸ *Fin* **c. actions** share capital, equity; **c. appelé** called-up capital; **c. autorisé** authorized (share) capital; **c. déclaré** registered

capital; **c. de départ** start-up capital; **c. engagé** capital employed; **c. d'établissement** invested capital; **c. fixe** fixed capital; **c. flottant** floating capital; **c. humain** (d'une entreprise) manpower; **c. improductif** idle capital, unproductive capital; **c. initial** start-up capital; **c.-investissement** investment capital; **c. nominal** nominal capital; **c. non appelé** uncalled capital; **c. réel** capital assets; **c. de réserve** reserve capital; **c. roulant** working capital; **c. de roulement** working capital; **c. social** (issued) share capital; **c. souscrit** subscribed capital; **c. souscrit et appelé** called-up subscribed capital; **c. souscrit et appelé, non versé** subscribed capital called and unpaid; **c. souscrit non appelé** uncalled subscribed capital; **capitaux fébriles** hot money; **capitaux gelés** frozen assets; **capitaux permanents** long-term capital; **capitaux propres** equity, shareholders' equity orfunds

capitalisable [kapitalizabl] **ADJ** (intérêt etc) capitalizable

capitalisation [kapitalizasjɔ̃] **NF** (d'intérêt etc) capitalization

capitaliser [kapitalize] **VT** (intérêt etc) to capitalize
VI 1 Fin to save **2 c. sur qch** (jouer sur) to capitalize on sth

capitalisme [kapitalism] **NM** capitalism; **c. sauvage** ruthless capitalism

capitaliste [kapitalist] **ADJ** capitalist, capitalistic
N capitalist

capitalistique [kapitalistik] **ADJ** (industrie) capital-intensive

capital-risque, pl **capitaux-risques NM** Fin venture capital

capital-risqueur, pl **capital-risqueurs** [kapitalriskœr] **NM** venture capitalist

capitation [kapitasjɔ̃] **NF** Hist, Admin capitation, poll tax

capiteux, -euse [kapitø, -øz] **ADJ** (vin, parfum) heady; (charme) sensuous; (femme) exciting, alluring

Capitole (le) [ləkapitɔl] **NM** (de la Rome ancienne, de Toulouse, de Washington) the Capitol

capiton [kapitɔ̃] **NM** (rembourrage) padding, stuffing; (entre les piqûres) boss

capitonnage [kapitɔnaʒ] **NM** (action, matière) padding, stuffing

capitonné [kapitɔne] **ADJ** (siège, cellule) padded

capitonner [kapitɔne] **VT** (meubles) to pad, to stuff

capitulaire [kapitylɛr] **ADJ** Rel **salle c.** chapter house

capitulation [kapitylasjɔ̃] **NF** capitulation, surrender; **c. sans conditions** unconditional surrender

capituler [kapityle] **VI** to capitulate, to surrender

capon, -onne [kapɔ̃, -ɔn] Fam Vieilli **ADJ** cowardly, Fam yellow
N coward, Br funk

caporal, -aux [kapɔral, -o] **NM 1** Mil lance corporal, Am private first class; **c. d'ordinaire** mess corporal; Hist Fam **le Petit C.** the Little Corporal, Napoleon **2** (tabac) caporal

caporal-chef, pl **caporaux-chefs NM** Mil corporal

caporaliser [kapɔralize] **VT** to militarize, to Prussianize

caporalisme [kapɔralism] **NM** Mil militarism; Fig authoritarianism

capot¹ [kapo] **NM 1** Aut bonnet, Am hood; Aviat (de moteur d'avion) cowl(ing); Naut (bâche) tarpaulin; (de lampe à arc etc) cover,

hood, casing; **c. antibruit** soundproof hood, acoustic hood; Ordinat **c. insonorisant** soundproof lid; **c. d'imprimante** printer hood; Aut **c. de ventilateur** cowl, cowling; Aut **c. moteur** bonnet, Am hood **2** Naut (ouverture) companion hatch

capot² **ADJ INV** Cartes **être c.** not to have taken a single trick

capotage [kapɔtaʒ] **NM** (de bateau) capsizing; Aut, Aviat overturning

capote [kapɔt] **NF 1** Aut (de décapotable) top, Br hood, soft top; **baisser la c.** to put the top orBr hood down **2** Mil (manteau) greatcoat **3** (de dame) bonnet
▸ ▸ Fam **c. (anglaise)** rubber, Br johnny

capoter¹ [kapɔte] **VT** (véhicule) (garnir d'une capote) to put a top orBr hood on; (fermer la capote de) to close the top orBr hood of

capoter² **VI 1** Naut to capsize, to turn turtle; Aut, Aviat to overturn; Fig **notre projet a capoté** our plan fell through or came to nothing **2** Can Fam (divaguer) to talk drivel; **il est complètement capoté** he's completely off his head

cappuccino [kaputʃino] **NM** cappuccino

câpre [kɑpr] **NF** Bot, Culin caper

caprice [kapris] **NM 1** (fantaisie) whim, caprice, fancy; **faire qch par c.** to do sth on a whim or a sudden impulse; **on lui passe tous ses caprices** they indulge his every whim; **par un c. du destin** by a whim of fate; **les caprices de la mode** the vagaries of fashion **2** (crise de colère) tantrum; **faire un c./des caprices** to throw a tantrum/tantrums

capricieusement [kaprisjøzmɑ̃] **ADV** capriciously

capricieux, -ieuse [kaprisjø, -jøz] **ADJ** (personne, courants, vent etc) capricious; (moteur) temperamental; (temps) changeable; (ruisseaux, etc) meandering; **elle est capricieuse** she's always changing her mind; **le vol c. d'un papillon** the flitting of a butterfly
N capricious person; **un petit c.** a child who throws tantrums

capricorne [kaprikɔrn] **NM 1** Astron, Astrol **le C.** Capricorn, the Goat; **être (du signe du) C.** to be (a) Capricorn; Géog **le tropique du C.** the tropic of Capricorn **2** (insecte) capricorn beetle

câprier [kɑprije] **NM** caper bush or plant

caprin [kaprɛ̃] **ADJ** Zool goat, Spéc caprine; Fig goat-like

capsulage [kapsylaʒ] **NM** (de bouteilles etc) capping

capsule [kapsyl] **NF 1** Anat, Bot, Pharm capsule **2** (de bouteille) cap, top **3 c. (spatiale)** (space) capsule **4** (d'armes) (firing) cap, primer; **c. (fulminante)** (de pistolet d'enfant) cap **5** Chimie **c. d'évaporation** evaporating dish **6** Aut **c. à dépression 'avance/retard'** vacuum advance/retard

capsuler [kapsyle] **VT** (bouteille) to seal, to cap, to put a cap on

captage [kaptaʒ] **NM 1** (des eaux) collecting, impounding; Élec (du courant) picking up; **c. d'une émission** picking up or reception of a broadcast **2** (lieu) water catchment

captateur, -trice [kaptatœr, -tris] **N** Jur inveigler; **c. de succession d'héritage** legacy hunter

captation [kaptasjɔ̃] **NF** Jur inveigling of an inheritance

captatoire [kaptatwar] **ADJ** Jur (moyens d'obtenir un héritage) inveigling

capter [kapte] **VT 1** (l'attention de qn) to gain, to capture **2** (courant électrique) to pick up; (eaux) to catch, to impound **3** Radio, Tél (messages) to pick up; (ligne) to tap; **je n'arrive pas à c.** France Inter I can't pick up or

get France Inter **4** Fam (comprendre) to get; **répète, j'ai pas capté** say that again, I didn't get it

capteur [kaptœr] **NM** Phys sensor; **c. solaire** solar panel; **c. de température** temperature sensor; Ordinat **c. photosensible** photosensitive or light-sensitive sensor; Aut **c. de charge** load sensor; **c. de choc/de collision** crash sensor; **c. de pollution** pollution sensor; **c. de vitesse** speed sensor

captieusement [kapsjøzmɑ̃] **ADV** speciously

captieux, -ieuse [kapsjø, -jøz] **ADJ** (argument etc) specious

captif, -ive [kaptif, -iv] **ADJ 1** captive; Fig, Litt **être c. du plaisir** to be a slave to pleasure; **les citoyens captifs des ravisseurs** the members of the public held captive by the kidnappers **2 ballon c.** captive balloon
N captive, prisoner

captivant [kaptivɑ̃] **ADJ** (personne etc) captivating; (livre, film etc) enthralling, gripping

captiver [kaptive] **VT** (personne) to captivate, to enthral; (l'attention de qn) to capture

captivité [kaptivite] **NF** captivity; **être en c.** to be in captivity

capture [kaptyr] **NF 1** (d'un voleur etc) capture, catching; (d'un navire) capture, seizure **2** (proie) catch **3** Ordinat **c. d'écran** screen capture, screen dump, screen shot; **c. vidéo** video capture

capturer [kaptyre] **VT 1** (voleur etc) to capture, to catch; (navire) to capture, to seize **2** Ordinat to capture

capuche [kapyʃ] **NF** hood; (de poche et en plastique) rainhood

capuchon [kapyʃɔ̃] **NM 1** (de manteau etc) hood; (de moine) cowl; (pèlerine) hooded cape; Zool **à c.** hooded **2** (de stylo, tube de dentifrice) cap, top; (de chambre à air) cap; (de cheminée) cowl; Aut **c. anti-poussière** dust cap

capucin [kapysɛ̃] **NM 1** Rel Capuchin (friar) **2** Zool capuchin (monkey); Fam (à la chasse) hare

capucine [kapysin] **NF 1** Rel Capuchin (nun) **2** Bot nasturtium

Cap-Vert [kapvɛr] **NM** le C., les îles du C. Cape Verde

caque [kak] **NF** herring barrel; Prov **la c. sent toujours le hareng** what's bred in the bone will come out in the flesh

caquelon [kaklɔ̃] **NM** fondue dish

caquet [kakɛ] **NM 1** (de poules) cackle, cackling **2** Fam (bavardage) cackle, prattle; **quel c. elle a!** she just prattles on and on!; **elle/ça lui a rabattu** ou **rabaissé le c.** she/that shut him up

caquetage [kaktaʒ], **caquètement** [kakɛtmɑ̃] **NM 1** (de poules) cackle, cackling **2** Fam (bavardage) cackle, cackling, prattling

caqueter [kakte] **VI** (je caquette, n. caquetons; je caquetterai) **1** (de poule) to cackle **2** Fam (bavarder) to cackle, to prattle

caqueteur, -euse [kaktœr, -øz] **N** Fam cackler, prattler

car¹ [kar] **CONJ** for, because SEE GRAMMAR B57

car² **NM 1** bus, Br coach; **prendre le c.** to take the bus or coach, to go by bus or coach; **c. de ramassage scolaire** school bus; **c. de police** police van **2** TV, Radio **c. de reportage** outside broadcast van, OB van; **c. de radio-reportage** outside broadcast van, mobile broadcasting unit; **c. de transmission** transmitter van; **c. régie** outside broadcasting vehicle, OB unit **3** TV **c. monocaméra** single-camera unit; **c. multicaméra** multi-camera unit

Il faut noter que le nom anglais **car** est un faux ami. Il signifie **voiture**.

carabe [karab] NM *(insecte)* ground beetle

carabin [karabɛ̃] NM *Fam* medical student, medic

carabine [karabin] NF rifle; **c. à air comprimé** air gun; **tir à la c.** rifle shooting

carabiné [karabine] ADJ *Fam (vent)* strong, stiff; *(orage)* violent, wild; **rhume c.** stinking or rotten cold; **fièvre carabinée** violent or raging fever; **j'ai une gueule de bois carabinée** I've got one hell of a hangover; **il m'a fait une scène carabinée** he made one hell of a scene

carabinier [karabinje] NM **1** *(en Espagne)* frontier guard **2** *(en Italie)* police officer, carabiniere **3** *Hist* carabineer

Carabosse [karabɔs] NF **la fée C.** the wicked fairy (Carabossa)

Caracas [karakas] N Caracas

caraco [karako] NM camisole

caracole [karakɔl] NF *Équitation* caracole, half turn

caracoler [karakɔle] VI *Équitation* to caracole; *Fam (sautiller)* to prance about, to caper about; *Fig* **c. en tête** to be top dog, to be top of the league

caractère [karakter] NM **1** *(personnalité)* character, nature, disposition; *(détermination)* character; **avoir (un) mauvais** ou **sale c.** to be bad-tempered or *Fml* ill-natured; **avoir (un) bon c.** to be good-tempered or good-natured; **avoir un c. gai/morose** to have a cheerful/morose character or nature, to be of a cheerful/morose disposition; *Fam* **quel fichu c.!** what a bad-tempered so-and-so!; *Fam* **elle a un c. de cochon** she's a bad-tempered so-and-so; **ce n'est pas dans son c. de se mettre en colère** it's not in his nature to get angry; **il est trop jeune de c. pour qu'on lui donne des responsabilités** he's too immature to be given any responsibilities; **avoir du c.** to have character; **manquer de c.** to lack (strength of) character, to have no backbone or spirit, to be spineless; **cette maison a beaucoup de c.** this house has a lot of character; **le c. français** the French character

2 *(attribut)* characteristic, feature; *(aspect)* character, nature; **l'affaire a pris un c. grave** the matter has taken a serious turn; **publication de c. officiel** publication of an official nature; **ce village a un c. rural** this village has a rural character; *Biol* **c. héréditaire/acquis** hereditary/acquired characteristic or feature; **maladie sans c. de gravité** illness not considered to be serious

3 *(signe)* character, letter; *Math etc* symbol; *Typ* **caractères** *(en métal)* type; **écrit en petits caractères** written in small print; **écrivez en caractères d'imprimerie** write in block letters or in (block) capitals, please print; **en petits/gros caractères** in small/large type or print; **c. accentué** accented or accent character; **c. gras** bold character; **caractères gras** bold (type); **en caractères gras** in bold, in bold type; **caractères italiques** italics, italic type; **caractères italiques gras** bold italics, bold italic; **c. majuscule** upper-case character; **c. minuscule** lower-case character; **caractères romains** in roman, in roman type; **c. spécial** special character

4 *Ordinat* character; **le choix** ou **la police de caractères d'une imprimante** the character set of a printer; **caractères par pouce** characters per inch; **caractères par seconde** characters per second; **caractères alphanumériques** alphanumeric characters; **c. de changement de ligne** line feed character; **c. de changement de page** page break character; **c. de commande (d'impression)** (print) command character; **c. de contrôle** control character; **c. d'effacement** delete character; **c. de fin de fichier** end of file character; **c. de fin de ligne** end of line character; **c. flottant** floating character; **c. graphique** graphic character; **c. imprimable** printable character; **c. d'interruption** break character; **c. joker** wildcard; **c. en mode point** bit-mapped character, bitmap character; **c. numérique** numeric(al) character; **c. de retour arrière** backspace character; **c. à sept bits** seven-bit character

caractériel, -ielle [karakterjɛl] ADJ *Psy* **trouble c.** emotional disturbance; **enfant c.** problem child, emotionally disturbed child ▸ N *Psy* emotionally disturbed person; *(enfant)* problem child, emotionally disturbed child; **elle est un peu caractérielle** she's a bit temperamental

caractérisation [karakterizasjɔ̃] NF characterization

caractérisé [karakterize] ADJ **une rougeole caractérisée** a typical or clear or unmistakable case of measles; **c'est de la méchanceté caractérisée** it's downright or sheer spite

caractériser [karakterize] VT to characterize, to be characteristic of, to distinguish; **symptômes qui caractérisent une maladie** characteristic symptoms of an illness; **la bonté qui la caractérise** her characteristic kindness ▸ VPR **se caractériser** to be characterized or distinguished (**par** by)

caractéristique [karakteristik] ADJ characteristic, distinctive, typical; **c. de** characteristic of; **c'est c. de sa façon d'agir** it's typical of his way of doing things ▸ NF *(particularité)* characteristic, feature; **caractéristiques** *(d'une voiture, d'un avion etc)* specifications

caractérologie [karakterɔlɔʒi] NF characterology

carafe [karaf] NF **1** *(récipient) (pour le whisky etc)* decanter; *(pour le vin)* carafe **2** *Fam* **rester en c.** *(d'une personne)* to be (left) stranded; **une voiture restée en c. sur le bord de l'autoroute** a broken-down car on the side of the motorway; **tomber en c.** to break down **3** *Fam (tête)* nut, *Br* bonce

carafon [karafɔ̃] NM *(pour le whisky etc)* small decanter; *(pour le vin)* small carafe; *Fam* **mets-toi ça dans le c.** get that into your thick head or skull

caraïbe [karaib] ADJ Caribbean ▸ NMPL **Caraïbes** Caribs ▸ NFPL **Caraïbes les Caraïbes** the Caribbean; **la mer des Caraïbes** the Caribbean (Sea)

carambolage [karɑ̃bɔlaʒ] NM **1** *Billard* cannon, *Am* carom **2** *(de voitures)* (multiple) pile-up

caramboler [karɑ̃bɔle] VI *Billard* to cannon, *Am* to carom ▸ VT **c. une voiture** to run into a car, to collide with a car ▸ VPR **se caramboler dix voitures se sont carambolées sur l'autoroute** there has been a ten-car pile-up on the motorway

carambouillage [karɑ̃bujaʒ] NM, **carambouille** [karɑ̃buj] NF *Fam Vieilli* = fraudulent reselling of goods being paid for on credit

caramel [karamɛl] NM *Culin* caramel; **bonbons au c., des caramels** *(mous)* caramels; *(durs)* toffees ▸ ADJ INV caramel(-coloured)

caramélisation [karamelizasjɔ̃] NF *Culin* caramelization

caraméliser [karamelize] VT **1** *(sucre)* to caramelize **2** *(moule)* to coat with caramel ▸ VI to caramelize ▸ VPR **se caraméliser** *(rôti)* to brown (well); *(sucre)* to caramelize

carapace [karapas] NF *(de langouste etc)* shell, *Spéc* carapace; *Fig* shell; *Fig* **il est difficile de percer sa c.** it's difficult to get through to him; **la voiture était recouverte d'une c. de boue** the car was encrusted with mud

carapater (se) [səkarapate] VPR *Fam* to beat it, to scram, *Br* to scarper

carat [kara] NM **1** *(de métal, pierre)* carat; or **(à) dix-huit carats** eighteen-carat gold; *Fam* **je te donne jusqu'à trois heures, dernier c.** I'll give you till three o'clock at the latest **2** *(poids)* **c. métrique** carat (weight) *(0.2 g)* **3** *Fam (année)* **il a dépassé les soixante carats** he's over sixty

Caravage (le) [ləkaravaʒ] NM Caravaggio

caravanage [karavanaʒ] NM = **caravaning**

caravane [karavan] NF **1** *(du désert)* caravan; *Fam (de touristes, d'écoliers etc)* conducted party, procession; **la c. du Tour de France** the caravan following the Tour de France cyclists **2** *(remorque)* caravan, *Am* trailer; **c. de tourisme** touring caravan

caravanier, -ière [karavanje, jɛr] N **1** *Aut* caravanner **2** *(dans le désert)* caravaneer ▸ ADJ **chemin c.** caravan route or track

caravaning [karavaniŋ] NM caravanning; **faire du c.** to go caravanning

caravansérail [karavɑ̃seraj] NM caravanserai

caravelle [karavɛl] NF **1** *Naut* car(a)vel **2** *Aviat* Caravelle®

carbochimie [karbɔʃimi] NF *Chimie* organic chemistry

carbonade [karbɔnad] NF = **carbonnade**

carbonate [karbɔnat] NM *Chimie* carbonate; **c. de soude** carbonate of soda, sodium carbonate; *Com* washing soda

carbone [karbɔn] NM *Chimie* carbon; *Journ* black; **c. 14** carbon 14, radiocarbon; **datation au c. 14** radiocarbon dating; **(papier) c.** carbon (paper)

carbonifère [karbɔnifɛr] ADJ, NM *Géol* Carboniferous

carbonique [karbɔnik] ADJ *Chimie* carbonic; **anhydride c., gaz c.** carbon dioxide; **acide c.** carbonic acid; **neige c.** dry ice

carbonisation [karbɔnizasjɔ̃] NF carbonization

carbonisé [karbɔnize] ADJ *(forêt)* burnt to the ground; *(nourriture)* burnt to a cinder; *(corps)* horribly burnt, *Fam* burnt to a cinder

carboniser [karbɔnize] VT *(os, bois etc)* to carbonize; *(forêt)* to burn to the ground; *(viande)* to burn to a cinder

carbonnade [karbɔnad] NF *Culin* **biffteck à la c.** charcoal-grilled steak

carbonyle [karbɔnil] NM *Chimie* carbonyl

carborundum [karbɔrɔ̃dɔm] NM *Chimie* carborundum

carburant [karbyrɑ̃] NM fuel; **c. liquide** liquid fuel; **c. volatil** light-fraction fuel ▸ ADJ containing fuel; **mélange c.** mixture (of petrol or *Am* gas and air)

carburateur [karbyratœr] NM *Aut* carburettor, *Am* carburetor; **c. double corps** twin choke carburettor; **c. à dépression constante** constant-depression carburettor; **c. à venturi variable** variable-venturi carburettor

carburation [karbyrasjɔ̃] NF **1** *Métal* carburization **2** *(de l'essence etc)* carburation

carbure [karbyr] NM *Chimie* carbide; **c. de calcium** calcium carbide

carburé [karbyre] ADJ **1** *Métal* carburized **2** *(air)* carburetted

carburéacteur [karbyreaktœr] NM *Tech* aviation fuel

carburer [karbyre] VT *Métal* to carburize ▸ VI **1 le moteur carbure mal** the mixture is wrong **2** *Fam (travailler)* **ça carbure ici** everyone here's working like mad; **qu'est-ce qu'on a carburé hier!** we worked like mad yesterday! **3** *(fonctionner à)* **il carbure au whisky** whisky keeps him going

carcajou [karkaʒu] NM wolverine, *Am* carcajou

carcan [karkɑ̃] NM *Hist* iron collar; *Fig (contrainte)* yoke, restraint; **le c. des horaires** scheduling constraints

carcasse [karkas] NF **1** *(pour la boucherie)* carcass; *Fam (de personne vivante)* body; *Fam* **promener sa c.** to walk **2** *(de parapluie, capote de voiture, abat-jour etc)* frame(- work); *(de maison, bateau)* shell, skeleton; *(de moteur électrique)* carcass; *(de pneu)* casing, carcass, frame; *(caisse)* bodyshell; **c. diagonale** *(d'un pneu)* diagonal-ply carcass; **c. radiale** *(d'un pneu)* radial-ply carcass; **à c. radiale** *(pneu)* radial-ply

carcéral, -ale, -aux, -ales [karseral, -o] ADJ prison; **vie carcérale** prison life

carcinogène [karsinɔʒɛn] ADJ *Méd* carcinogenic

carcinologie [karsinɔlɔʒi] NF *Méd* oncology, study of cancer

carcinome [karsinom] NM *Méd* carcinoma

cardage [kardaʒ] NM *Tex* **1** *(de la laine etc)* carding, combing **2** *(de tissu)* teaselling

cardan [kardɑ̃] NM *Aut* **c., joint de C.** universal joint, Cardan joint

carde [kard] NF **1** *Culin* chard **2** *Tex* card, carding brush; *(tambour)* teasel

carder [karde] VT *Tex* **1** *(laine etc)* to card **2** *(tissu)* to teasel

cardeur, -euse [kardœr, -øz] *Tex* N carder
  NF **cardeuse** *(machine)* carding machine, carder

cardiaque [kardjak] ADJ *(nerfs, murmure etc)* cardiac; **crise c.** heart attack; **être c.** to have heart trouble *or* a weak heart
  N person with heart disease

cardigan [kardigɑ̃] NM cardigan

cardinal, -ale, -aux, -ales [kardinal, -o] ADJ *(point, nombre, vertu)* cardinal SEE GRAMMAR A76; B58
  NM **1** *Cathol* cardinal **2** *Orn* cardinal (bird)

cardinalat [kardinala] NM *Cathol* cardinalship

cardinalice [kardinalis] ADJ *Cathol* of a cardinal; **revêtir la pourpre c.** to don the scarlet; **élever qn à la dignité c.** to make sb a cardinal

cardiogramme [kardjɔgram] NM *Méd* cardiogram

cardiographe [kardjɔgraf] NM *Méd* cardiograph

cardiographie [kardjɔgrafi] NF *Méd* cardiography

cardiologie [kardjɔlɔʒi] NF *Méd* cardiology

cardiologue [kardjɔlɔg] N *Méd* cardiologist, heart specialist; **chirurgien c.** heart surgeon

cardiorespiratoire [kardjɔrɛspiratwar] ADJ *Méd* cardiorespiratory

cardio-training, *pl* **cardio-trainings** [kardjɔtrɛniŋ] NM cardiovascular fitness training

cardio-vasculaire [kardjɔvaskylɛr] ADJ *Anat, Méd* cardiovascular; *Méd* **accident c.** cardiovascular accident, *Fam* stroke

cardite [kardit] NF *Méd* carditis

cardon [kardɔ̃] NM *Bot, Culin* cardoon

carême [karɛm] NM **1** *(période)* Lent **2** *(jeûne)* (Lenten) fast(ing); **faire (son) c.** to keep Lent, to fast; *Fig* **face de c.** dismal face **3** *Litt (sermons)* (course of) Lenten sermons

carême-prenant, *pl* **carêmes-prenants** NM *Arch* Shrovetide

carénage [karenaʒ] NM **1** *Naut (de bateau)* careening, careenage; *(lieu)* careenage **2** *Aviat, Aut* streamlining

carence [karɑ̃s] NF **1** *Méd* deficiency (**de** in, of); **c. en vitamine E** deficiency in vitamin E, vitamin E deficiency; **maladie de** *ou* **par c.** deficiency disease; **c. alimentaire** nutritional deficiency; **c. affective** emotional deprivation; *Fig* **c. en personnel** staff shortage, shortage of staff **2** *(insuffisance)* shirking of one's obligations; **la c. du père** *(dans l'éducation de son enfant)* the father's non-participation **3** *Jur* insolvency

carencé [karɑ̃se] ADJ *Psy* emotionally deprived

carène [karɛn] NF *(de navire)* bottom, (underwater) hull; **abattre un navire en c.** to careen a ship

caréner [karene] VT **(je carène; je carénerai) 1** *Naut* to careen **2** *Aviat, Aut* to streamline

carentiel, -ielle [karɑ̃sjɛl] ADJ **maladie carentielle** deficiency disease

caressant [karɛsɑ̃] ADJ *(regard, voix)* tender; *(vent)* soft, gentle; *(enfant)* affectionate; **d'une voix caressante** tenderly, affectionately

caresse [karɛs] NF **1** *(d'affection)* caress; **faire des caresses à** *(personne)* to caress; *(animal)* to stroke; *Litt* **la c. du soleil** the sun's caress **2** *Vieilli (flatterie)* flattery

caresser [karese] VT **1** *(par affection) (personne)* to caress; *(animal)* to stroke; **c. qn du regard** to look affectionately *or* tenderly at sb **2** *(espoir, rêve)* to cherish; *(idée)* to toy with; **c. un projet** to nurture a project **3** *Vieilli (flatter)* to flatter; **cette idée caresse son amour-propre** the idea flatters his self-esteem

car-ferry, *pl* **car-ferrys** NM car ferry

cargaison [kargɛzɔ̃] NF **1** *(marchandises)* cargo, freight; **c. de charbon/de marchandises** cargo of coal/merchandise; **c. en vrac** bulk cargo; **c. flottante** cargo afloat; **c. mixte** mixed cargo VOIR GRAMMAIRE A12 **2** *Fam (de passagers, cadeaux etc)* load (**de** of); **toute une c. d'histoires belges** a whole load *or* repertoire of Belgian jokes; **j'avais préparé toute une c. d'excuses** I had all sorts of *or* a whole load of excuses prepared

cargo [kargo] NM *Naut* cargo boat, freighter; **c. mixte** cargo and passenger vessel

> Il faut noter que le nom anglais **cargo** est un faux ami. Il signifie **cargaison**.

cargue [karg] NF *Naut (de voile)* brail

carguer [karge] VT *Naut (voile)* to take in, to brail (up)

cariant [karjɑ̃] ADJ **substance cariante** substance that causes tooth decay

cariatide [karjatid] NF *Archit* caryatid

caribou [karibu] NM *Zool* caribou

caricatural, -ale, -aux, -ales [karikatyral, -o] ADJ *(récit, description etc)* caricatured

caricature [karikatyr] NF *(dessin, description etc)* caricature; **le film est une c. de la vie ouvrière** the film is a caricature of working-class life; *Fam* **quelle c. que cette femme!** what a fright that woman is!

caricaturer [karikatyre] VT to caricature

caricaturiste [karikatyrist] N caricaturist

carie [kari] NF **1** *Méd (d'os)* caries, decay; **c. dentaire** tooth decay, *Spéc* dental caries; **avoir une c.** to have a tooth that needs filling **2** *(d'arbres)* blight; *(de céréales)* smut, bunt

carié [karje] ADJ *Méd (dent)* decayed, bad

carier [karje] *Méd* VT to rot, to decay
  VPR **se carier** to rot, to decay

carillon [karijɔ̃] NM **1** *(sonnerie)* chime(s), *Litt* carillon; *(ensemble de cloches)* peal of bells; *(de porte)* (door) chime(s); *Mus* tubular bells, chimes; **(horloge à) c.** chiming clock

carillonnement [karijɔnmɑ̃] NM *(de cloches)* chiming, ringing

carillonner [karijɔne] VI *(faire sonner les cloches)* to ring the bells; *(des cloches)* to chime, to ring; **c. à la porte** to ring the (door) bell loudly
  VT *(air)* to chime; *(fête religieuse)* to announce with a peal of bells; *Fig* **c. la nouvelle** to spread the news far and wide, to tell the news to all and sundry; **fête carillonnée** high festival

carillonneur, -euse [karijɔnœr, -øz] N bellringer

cariste [karist] N *Tech* fork-lift truck driver

caritatif, -ive [karitatif, -iv] ADJ charitable; **association caritative** charitable organization, charity

carlin [karlɛ̃] NM *(chien)* pug

carlingue [karlɛ̃g] NF **1** *Naut* ke(e)lson **2** *Aviat* cabin

carliste [karlist] N *Hist* Carlist

carmagnole [karmaɲɔl] NF *Hist* **1** *(veste)* jacket *(worn by Revolutionaries in 1793)* **2** *Mus (ronde)* carmagnole

carme [karm] NM *Rel* Carmelite (friar), White Friar

Carmel [karmɛl] NM **1** *Rel* **le C.** the Carmelite order **2** *(couvent) (de carmes)* Carmelite monastery; *(de carmélites)* Carmelite convent

carmélite [karmelit] NF *Rel* Carmelite (nun)

carmin [karmɛ̃] ADJ INV carmine, crimson
  NM carmine

carminé [karmine] ADJ carmine, crimson

carnage [karnaʒ] NM carnage, slaughter; *Fig* **s'il n'arrête pas, je vais faire un c.** if he doesn't stop, I'll kill him

carnassier, -ière [karnasje, -jɛr] ADJ *(animal)* carnivorous, flesh-eating; *Zool (dent)* carnassial; *Fig (cruel) (regard, sourire)* predatory
  NM carnivore; **les carnassiers** carnivores, *Spéc* the Carnivora
  NF **carnassière 1** *Zool* carnassial (tooth) **2** *(sac)* game bag

carnation [karnasjɔ̃] NF **1** *(teint)* complexion; **c. de blonde** fair skin *or* complexion **2** *Beaux-Arts* flesh tint, *Spéc* carnation

carnaval, -als [karnaval] NM *(fête)* carnival; **un masque de c.** a carnival mask; **Sa Majesté C.** King Carnival

carnavalesque [karnavalɛsk] ADJ **tenue c.** carnival costume; *Péj* **un accoutrement c.** a ridiculous get-up

carne [karn] NF **1** *Fam (viande)* tough meat; *(vieux cheval)* old nag **2** *Arg* **quelle c.!** *(cet homme)* what a bastard!; *(cette femme)* what a bitch *or* cow!

carné [karne] ADJ **1** *(rose)* flesh-coloured *or Am* -colored **2** **régime c.** meat diet

carneau, -eaux [karno] NM *Tech* flue

carnet [karnɛ] NM *(cahier)* notebook
  ▸▸ *Scol* **c. (de notes)** = (school) report; **c. d'adresses** address book; *(de publipostage)* address list; *Com* **c. ATA** ATA carnet; *Vieilli* **c. de bal** dance card; **c. blanc** marriages column; *Aut* **c. de bord** logbook, memorandum; **c. de chèques** cheque *or Am* check book; *Com* **c. de commandes** order book; *Com* **c. communautaire** Community carnet; *Aut* **c. de constat amiable** = set of insurance documents to be completed at scene of accident; *Scol* **c. de correspondance** = school report book; *Aut* **c. d'entretien** *(d'une voiture)* servicing booklet; *Belg, Suisse (livret d'épargne)* **c. d'épargne** savings account; *Journ* **c. mondain** society column; *Com* **c. de passage en douanes** carnet; **c. rose** births

column; **c. de route** logbook; **c. de santé** health record; **c. à souche(s)** counterfoil book; **c. de tickets** book of tickets; **c. de timbres** book of stamps; *Aviat* **c. de vol** log(-book); **c. de voyage** travel documents

carnier [karnje] NM game bag

carnivore [karnivɔr] *Zool* ADJ *(animal)* carnivorous, flesh-eating
NM carnivore; **les carnivores** carnivores, *Spéc* the Carnivora

carnotzet [karnɔtset] NM *Suisse* = room set aside for drinking with friends, usually in a cellar

carolingien, -ienne [karɔlɛ̃ʒjɛ̃, -jɛn] *Hist* ADJ Carolingian, Carlovingian
N C. Carolingian, Carlovingian

caroncule [karɔ̃kyl] NF *Anat, Bot, Zool* caruncle; *(de dindon)* wattle

carotène [karɔtɛn] NM carotene

carotide [karɔtid] ADJ *(artère)* carotid

carottage [karɔtaʒ] NM 1 *Fam (vol)* pinching, *Br* nicking; *(escroquerie)* swindling, diddling 2 *Min* taking of cores

carotte [karɔt] NF 1 *(plante)* carrot; *Fam* **Poil de c.** Ginger; *Fam* **les carottes sont cuites** you've/he's/*etc* cooked your/his/*etc* goose, you're/he's/*etc* done for; *Suisse* **c. rouge** beetroot 2 *(promesse)* carrot; **la c. et le bâton** the carrot and stick 3 *Min* core (sample) 4 *(de tabac)* plug; *(enseigne)* tobacconist's sign 5 *Fam* **tirer une c. à qn** to swindle *or* diddle sb 6 *Tennis Fam* drop shot
ADJ INV **cheveux (rouge) c.** ginger *or* red *or Fam* carroty hair

carotter [karɔte] VT 1 *Fam (voler) (chose)* to pinch, *Br* to nick; *(escroquer) (personne)* to swindle, to diddle, *Br* to do; **c. une permission/une signature** to wangle leave/a signature 2 *Min* to take a core (sample) of

carotteur, -euse[1] [karɔtœr, -øz], **carottier, -ière** [karɔtje, -jɛr] N *Fam (voleur)* thief; *(escroc)* swindler

carotteuse[2] NF *Min* core sampler

caroube [karub] NF *Bot* carob (bean)

caroubier [karubje] NM *Bot* carob (tree)

carpaccio [karpatʃjo] NM *Culin* carpaccio

Carpates [karpat] NFPL **les C.** the Carpathian Mountains, the Carpathians

carpe[1] [karp] NM *Anat* carpus

carpe[2] NF *(poisson)* carp; **faire des yeux de c.** to make sheep's eyes; **être muet comme une c.** *(discret)* to be as silent as the grave; **tu es resté muet comme une c. toute la soirée** you didn't open your mouth all evening; **bâiller comme une c.** to yawn one's head off

carpeau, -eaux [karpo] NM *(poisson)* young carp

carpette [karpɛt] NF *(tapis)* rug; *Fam Péj* **s'aplatir comme une c.** to behave like a doormat; *Fam Péj* **c'est une vraie c.** he's a complete doormat

Il faut noter que le nom anglais **carpet** est un faux ami. Il signifie **moquette**.

carpiculture [karpikyltyr] NF carp farming

carpien, -ienne [karpjɛ̃, -jɛn] ADJ *Anat (os etc)* carpal

carquois [karkwa] NM quiver; *Litt* **il a vidé son c.** he has shot his bolt

carrare [karar] NM Carrara marble

carre [kar] NF *(de patin, ski)* edge; *(de livre etc)* corner; *(de planche etc)* cross section; *Ski* **lâcher les carres** to flatten *or* take the edge off the skis

carré, -ée [kare] ADJ 1 *(figure, jardin etc)* square; *(épaules)* square, broad; *Math* **nombre c.** square number; **dix mètres carrés** ten square metres; **partie carrée** ≃ wife-swapping party 2 *(tranché) (réponse)* plain,

straightforward, blunt; *(personne)* straightforward; **être c. en affaires** to be straightforward in one's business dealings
NM 1 *(figure)* square; *Can (place)* (public) square; **c. de papier** slip of paper; **c. de soie** silk square; **c. de choux** cabbage patch; *Naut* **c. (des officiers)** wardroom; *Mil* **former le c.** to get into square formation; *Cartes* **c. de valets** four jacks; **avoir une coupe au c.** *ou* **un c.** to have one's hair in a bob; *Fam* **s'il continue, je vais lui faire une tête au c.!** if he goes on like that, I'm going to punch his face in!
2 *Math (d'un nombre)* square; **élever au c.** to square; *Math* **le c. de six, six au c.** six squared
SEE GRAMMAR B59
3 *Culin* **c. d'agneau** rack of lamb; **c. de l'Est** = type of soft cheese
4 *(élève)* = second-year student *(in certain Grandes Écoles)*
NF **carrée** 1 *Hist, Mus* breve 2 *Fam (chambre)* room
▸▸ *Rail* **c. Jeunes** = reduced-rate rail travel card for young people within France

carreau, -eaux [karo] NM 1 *(motif)* square; *(sur du tissu)* check; **tissu à carreaux** check(ed) material; *Beaux-Arts* **mettre un croquis au c.** to square up a sketch
2 *(de céramique etc)* tile; *(dalle)* flag(stone)
3 *(de fenêtre)* (window) pane; **laveur de carreaux** window cleaner *or Am* washer; **regarder aux carreaux** to look in at the window; **un c. cassé** a broken window
4 *Fam* **carreaux** *(lunettes)* specs, glasses
5 *(sol)* (tiled) floor; **laver le c.** to wash the floor; **coucher qn sur le c.** to lay sb out; **rester sur le c.** *(être tué)* to be killed on the spot; *(être blessé)* to be critically injured; *(être éliminé)* to be out of the running; *(d'un boxeur)* not to get up, to stay on the canvas *or* floor; *Anciennement* **le c. des Halles** *(à Paris)* the (floor of the) market
6 *Cartes* diamond; *Fig* **se tenir à c.** to keep a low profile
▸▸ *Min* **c. de mine** pit head

carreauté [karote] ADJ *Can (chemise)* check(ed)

carrefour [karfur] NM 1 *(de route)* crossroads; **tête de c.** T-junction; **c. décalé** staggered junction; **c. ferroviaire** railway junction; *Fig* **être à un c.** to be at a crossroads; **un c. de nouvelles idées/de tendances** a place for the exchange of new ideas/trends VOIR GRAMMAIRE A13 2 *(réunion)* forum, symposium

carrelage [karlaʒ] NM 1 *(action)* tiling 2 *(carreaux)* tiling, tiles; *(sol)* (tiled) floor; *(mur)* tiled wall

carreler [karle] VT (**je carrelle, n. carrelons; je carrellerai**) 1 *(mettre des carreaux sur)* *(sol, murs)* to tile 2 *(tracer des carreaux sur)* *(feuille de papier etc)* to draw squares on, to square

carrelet [karle] NM 1 *(règle)* square ruler 2 *(aiguille)* large needle 3 *Pêche* square dipping net 4 *(poisson)* plaice

carreleur [karlœr] NM tiler, tile layer; *(d'une cour)* paver

carrément [karemɑ̃] ADV 1 *Géom* square(-ly); **pièce coupée c.** square-cut piece 2 *Fam* **il y est allé c.** he got straight to the point, he didn't beat about the bush, he didn't mess about; **je lui ai dit c. ce que je pensais** I told him straight (out) *or* bluntly *or* in no uncertain terms what I thought; **tu as c. tort** you're simply wrong, you're wrong and that's that

carrer [kare] VT *(planche)*, *Math (nombre etc)* to square
VPR **se carrer** to settle (down) (**dans un fauteuil** in an armchair)

carrier [karje] NM *(ouvrier)* quarryman, quarrier; **(maître) c.** quarry master

carrière[1] [karjɛr] NF 1 *(professionnelle etc)*

career; **faire c.** to make a career for oneself; **suivre une c.** *ou* **faire c. dans le commerce** to make a career in business; **en début/fin de c.** at the start/end of one's career; **c. politique/des armes** political/military career; **militaire de c.** regular (soldier); **diplomate de c.** professional *or* career diplomat; **elle est de la c.** she is in the diplomatic service 2 **donner c. à un cheval** to give free rein to a horse; *Fig* **donner (libre) c. à son imagination** to give free rein *or* free play *or* full scope to one's imagination; **donner c. à ses sentiments, se donner c.** to let oneself go, to give free expression to one's feelings

carrière[2] NF *(lieu)* quarry; **c. à ciel ouvert** open quarry

carriérisme [karjerism] NM *Péj* careerism

carriériste [karjerist] ADJ, N *Péj* careerist

carriole [karjɔl] NF 1 *(petite charrette)* light cart 2 *Can* sleigh, sled

carrossable [karɔsabl] ADJ *(chemin, route)* suitable for motor vehicles

carrossage [karɔsaʒ] NM *Aut* rake, camber

carrosse [karɔs] NM (horse-drawn) coach; **c. d'apparat** state coach; *Fam* **rouler c.** to live in great style; *Can* **c. de bébé** pram, *Am* baby carriage

carrosser [karɔse] VT *Aut (voiture etc)* to fit the body to; *Arg* **elle est bien carrossée** she's got curves in all the right places

carrosserie [karɔsri] NF *Aut* 1 *(construction)* coachbuilding 2 *(caisse) (de voiture etc)* body, coachwork, bodywork

carrossier [karɔsje] NM *Aut* coachbuilder

carroté [karɔte] ADJ *Can (chemise etc)* check(ed), *Am* checkered

carrousel [karuzɛl] NM 1 *Hist (tournoi)* tournament; *(lieu)* tiltyard; *Équitation* carousel; *(manège de chevaux de bois)* roundabout, *Am* carousel 2 *Fig (succession rapide)* **le c. des ministres** the ministerial merry-go-round 3 *(d'une aérogare)* carousel; **c. de livraison des bagages** baggage carousel 4 *Belg, Can, Suisse (manège)* merry-go round, carousel

carrure [karyr] NF 1 *(de personne)* build; *(de manteau)* width across the shoulders; **homme d'une belle c.** well-built man 2 *(de mâchoire etc)* broadness, squareness 3 *Fig* **elle est d'une grande c.** she's a very impressive woman; **il est d'une autre c. que ses concurrents** he is much more impressive than his competitors; **avoir la c. d'un cadre supérieur** to be senior management material

carry [kari] NM = **curry**

cartable [kartabl] NM school bag; *(à bretelles)* satchel

CARTE [kart] NF 1 *(géographique)* map; *Naut* chart; **dresser la c. d'une région** to map (out) an area
2 *(feuille de carton)* card; *Com* business card; *Cartes* (playing) card; **jeu de (52) cartes** pack *or Am* deck of cards; **laisser sa c. chez qn** to leave one's card with sb; **avoir c. au parti** to be a card-carrying member of the party; **jouer aux cartes** to play cards; **une partie de cartes** a game of cards; **donner** *ou* **faire les cartes** to deal (the cards); *Fig* **donner c. blanche à qn** to give sb carte blanche *or* a free hand; **château de cartes** house of cards; **être balayé/s'écrouler comme un château de cartes** to be swept away/collapse like a house of cards; *Fig* **jouer cartes sur table** to put one's cards on the table; *Fig* **jouer la c. des libéraux** to play the liberal card *or* hand; **jouer sa dernière c.** to play one's last card; **abattre ses cartes** to lay one's cards on the table; *Fig* **nous avons encore quelques bonnes cartes en main** we still have several cards up our sleeves; **c. maî-**

tresse *Cartes* master card; *Fig* trump card; *Fig* c'était la c. forcée it was Hobson's choice; *Fig* connaître le dessous des cartes to know the inside story; *Fig* brouiller les cartes to complicate matters, to confuse the issue; femme en c. registered prostitute

3 c. (de restaurant) menu; (*du jour*) today's menu, menu for the day; c. des vins wine list; manger à la c. to eat à la carte; horaires à la c. flexitime; nous vous proposons un vaste choix d'activités à la c. choose from a vast range of activities

4 *Ordinat* card; *(de clavier etc)* map

5 *Com (de boutons etc)* card; c. d'échantillons sample card

▸▸ c. d'abonnement *(pour la bibliothèque etc)* membership card *or* ticket; *(pour les transports, le théâtre etc)* season ticket; *Ordinat* c. accélérateur graphique graphics accelerator card; *Ordinat* c. accélératrice accelerator card; *Aviat* c. d'accès à bord boarding pass, embarkation card; c. accréditive charge card; c. d'adhérent membership card; c. d'affaires business card; *Ordinat* c. d'affichage display card; c. d'alimentation ration book; c. American Express® American Express®(card); c. Amex Amex (card); c. d'animation d'images vidéo video image animation card; c. d'anniversaire birthday card; *Ordinat* c. audio audio card; c. bancaire cash card, cheque card, banker's card; c. bancaire à puce banker's card; c. Bleue® = bank card with which purchases are debited directly from the customer's bank account; *Ordinat* c. bus bus board; c. de chemin de fer season ticket; c. du ciel astronomical map *or* chart; *Ordinat* c. à circuit imprimé *ou* de circuits imprimés printed circuit board, PCB; *Ordinat* c. à circuit(s) intégré(s) integrated circuit card, IC card; c. de circulation (rail/bus) pass; *Admin* c. de commerce trading licence; *Ordinat* c. de communication communication card; *Ordinat* c. de connexion connection card; *Ordinat* c. de contrôle control card; *Ordinat* c. contrôleur de disque disk controller card; c. de crédit credit card; c. de débarquement landing card; c. d'électeur voting card; *Aviat* c. d'embarquement boarding pass, embarkation card; *Ordinat* c. enfichable slot-in card; c. d'entrée pass (card); *Ordinat* c. d'E/S I/O card; c. d'état-major ≃ Ordnance Survey map, *Am* ≃ Geological Survey map; c. d'étudiant student card; c. Eurocard Mastercard® Mastercard®, Access® card; *Ordinat* c. d'extension expansion card *or* board; *Ordinat* c. d'extension mémoire memory expansion card *or* board; *Rail* c. famille nombreuse reduced-rate card for families with three or more children; c. fax fax card; c. de fidélité frequent user card, valued customer card; *Ordinat* c. fille daughterboard; *Biol* c. du génome humain map of the human genome; *Ordinat* c. graphique numérique digital graphics card; *Aut* c. grise ≃ (vehicle) registration document; c. d'identité identity card; c. d'identité bancaire bank card; *Ordinat* c. d'interface interface card; *Ordinat* c. interface réseau network interface card; c. internationale d'étudiant International Student Identity Card; *Rail* c. Inter-rail Inter-Rail Card; c. d'invitation invitation (card); *Rail* c. Jeunes = reduced-rate rail travel card for young people within France; c. à jouer (playing) card; c. de journaliste press card; c. de lecteur library *or* reader's ticket; *Ordinat* c. logique logic card; c. magnétique magnetic card; c. mécanographique punch card; *Ordinat* c. mémoire memory card; c. à mémoire smart card; *Ordinat* c. mère motherboard; c. météorologique meteorological *or* weather map *or* chart; *Ordinat* c. à microcircuit microcircuit card; *Ordinat* c. modem mo-

dem card; c. orange *(à Paris)* = combined monthly pass for the underground, bus and suburban train; c. de paiement payment card; *Tél* c. Pastel phone card *(use of which is debited to one's own phone number)*; *Mktg* c. perceptuelle de marques brand mapping; *Mktg* c. perceptuelle de produits product mapping; c. perforée punch card; *Ordinat* c. à piste magnétique magnetic stripe card; *Ordinat* c. de polices de caractères font card; c. postale (post)card; *Tél* c. à prépaiement phonecard *(with prepaid units)*; c. prépayée prepaid card; c. de presse press card; *Ordinat* c. principale main board; *Ordinat* c. processeur processor card; c. professionnelle professional certificate; c. à puce smart card; c. de réduction discount card; c. de représentant sales representative's official identity card; *Ordinat* c. réseau network card; *Ordinat* c. de réseau sans fil wireless network card; *Ordinat* c. RNIS ISDN card; c. routière road map; *Ordinat* c. SCSI SCSI card; c. de Sécurité sociale National Insurance Card; c. de séjour residence permit; *Ordinat* c. son *ou* sonore sound card; *Ordinat* c. système systems board; c. T reply-paid card; c. de télécopie fax card; c. de téléphone phonecard; c. de train railcard; *(abonnement, forfait)* rail pass; *Ordinat* c. unité centrale CPU board; *Rail* c. Vermeil ≃ Senior Citizen's railcard; *Aut* c. verte green card; *Ordinat* c. vidéo video card; *Ordinat* c. vidéo accélératrice video accelerator card; c. Visa® Visa® card; c. de visite (visiting *or* Am calling) card; *Ordinat* c. vocale voice card; c. de vœux greetings card

carte-adaptateur, *pl* **cartes-adaptateurs** NF *Ordinat* c. réseau network adaptor card

carte-clé, *pl* **cartes-clés** NF key card; c. électronique electronic key card

carte-guide, *pl* **cartes-guides** NF *(pour séparer des fiches)* file separator *or* divider

cartel [kartɛl] NM **1** *Écon* cartel, trust, combine; c. de l'acier/de la drogue steel/drug cartel **2** *Pol* cartel, coalition **3** *(horloge)* wall clock

carte-lettre, *pl* **cartes-lettres** NF letter-card

cartellisation [kartelizasjɔ̃] NF *Écon* cartelization

carter [kartɛr] NM *(d'engrenages)* casing, housing; *(de mécanisme)* cover; *Aut (de vilebrequin)* crankcase; *(d'huile)* engine sump, oil sump; fond de c. sump

carte-réponse, *pl* **cartes-réponses** NF reply card *or* coupon

carterie [kartəri] NF *Com* card shop

cartésianisme [kartezjanism] NM *Phil* Cartesianism

cartésien, -ienne [kartezjɛ̃, -jɛn] ADJ, N *Phil, Math* Cartesian

carte-vue, *pl* **cartes-vues** [kart(ə)vy] NF *Belg* picture postcard

carthaginois, -oise [kartaʒinwa, -waz] *Hist* ADJ Carthaginian

N C. Carthaginian

cartilage [kartilaʒ] NM *Anat* cartilage; *(dans la viande)* gristle

cartilagineux, -euse [kartilaʒinø, -øz] ADJ *Anat* cartilaginous; *(viande)* gristly

cartographe [kartɔgraf] N cartographer

cartographie [kartɔgrafi] NF cartography; c. des gènes gene *or* genetic mapping

cartographier [kartɔgrafje] VT to chart, to make a map of

cartographique [kartɔgrafik] ADJ cartographic(al)

cartomancie [kartɔmɑ̃si] NF fortune telling (by cards), cartomancy

cartomancien, -ienne [kartɔmɑ̃sjɛ̃, -jɛn] N fortune teller *(who uses cards)*

carton [kartɔ̃] NM **1** *(matière)* cardboard; *(feuille, support)* piece of cardboard, (piece of) card; poupée/masque de c. cardboard doll/mask; *Fam* maison de c. jerry-built house; envoyer un c. to send (out) an invitation

2 *(boîte)* (cardboard) box, carton; *(dossier)* (cardboard) file; des cartons de déménagement cardboard boxes for moving (house); faire ses cartons to pack (up) one's things in cardboard boxes; le projet est resté dans les cartons the project never got off the ground; ça dort dans les cartons depuis des mois it's been shelved for months

3 *Beaux-Arts* cartoon, sketch

4 faire un c. *(au tir)* to fill a target; faire un c. *(obtenir un bon résultat)* to make a good score; *Scol Fam* se payer un c. to get a bad *or Fam* rotten mark

5 *Géog* inset (map)

▸▸ *TV* c. aide-mémoire cue card; c. bristol Bristol board; c. à chapeau(x) hatbox; c. de classement file box; c. à dessin portfolio; c. épais millboard; *TV* c. de générique title card; c. d'invitation invitation (card); *Ftbl* c. jaune yellow card; c. ondulé corrugated cardboard; *TV* cartons de prompteur prompt cards; *Ftbl* c. rouge red card; se prendre un c. rouge to get a *or* the red card; *TV* c. volant flip card

cartonnage [kartɔnaʒ] NM **1** *(objets en carton)* cardboard articles; *(fabrication)* making of cardboard articles **2** *(reliure) (action)* board binding; *(couverture)* paper boards; c. pleine toile cloth boards; c. souple limp boards

cartonner [kartɔne] VT *(livre)* to bind in boards, to case; livre cartonné hardback (book)

VI *Fam* to do very well

cartonnerie [kartɔnri] NF **1** *(usine)* cardboard factory **2** *(commerce)* cardboard trade

cartonneux, -euse [kartɔnø, -øz] ADJ like cardboard; neige cartonneuse snow with a crust on top; fromage c. cheese that's gone hard

cartonnier [kartɔnje] NM **1** *(fabricant)* cardboard manufacturer **2** *(meuble)* filing cabinet

carton-paille, *pl* **cartons-pailles** NM strawboard

carton-pâte, *pl* **cartons-pâtes** NM pasteboard; décor de c. cardboard scenery

cartoon [kartun] NM cartoon

cartouche [kartuʃ] NM **1** *Archit etc* cartouche; *(pour titre)* title **2** *Ordinat (sur plan)* box; c. de titre masthead

NF *(de fusil, d'explosif, de stylo, de lecteur de cassettes)* cartridge; *(de machine à écrire)* *Phot* cartridge, cassette; *Mil etc* cent cartouches a hundred rounds (of ammunition)

▸▸ c. à blanc blank cartridge; c. de chasse sporting cartridge; c. de cigarettes carton of cigarettes; c. d'encre *(d'une imprimante etc)* ink cartridge; c. d'encre en poudre *(d'une imprimante)* toner cartridge; *Ordinat* c. de polices font cartridge; c. de rechange *(de stylo)* refill; *Ordinat* c. de stockage amovible removable storage cartridge; c. de toner toner cartridge; c. vidéo video cartridge

cartoucherie [kartuʃri] NF *(fabrique)* cartridge *or* ammunition factory; *(dépôt)* cartridge *or* ammunition store

cartouchière [kartuʃjɛr] NF *(sac)* cartridge pouch; *(ceinture)* cartridge belt

carvi [karvi] NM *(plante)* caraway; (graines de) c. caraway seeds

caryatide [karjatid] NF *Archit* caryatid

caryotype [karjotip] NM *Biol* karyotype

CAS [ka] NM **1** (*situation*) case, situation; (*événement*) occurrence; *Jur, Méd* case; **c. imprévu** unforeseen event; **c. général/particulier** general/particular case; **c. urgent** emergency *or* urgent case; **c'était un c. de légitime défense** it was self-defence; **c. litigieux** dispute; **dans le premier c.** in the first instance; **c'est le c. de le dire** you can say that again; **en pareil c.** in a similar situation, in similar circumstances; **que faire dans un c. de ce genre?** what can one do in a case *or* situation like this?; **c. de rougeole** case of measles; **ce malade est un c. désespéré** this patient is a hopeless case; *Fig* **c'est un c.!** he is a case!; **avez-vous envisagé tous les c.?** have you considered all possibilities *or* eventualities?; **il parle plusieurs langues étrangères, mais ce n'est pas mon c.** he speaks several foreign languages, but I don't; **dans son c., on peut faire une exception** an exception can be made in his case; **dans le c. qui nous occupe** in the case that we are concerned with; **si tel est votre c.** if that's your case

2 **faire (grand) c. de qn/qch** to value sb/sth (highly), to have a high opinion of sb/sth, to set great store by sb/sth; **faire peu de c. de qch** to have a low opinion of sth, to set little store by sth; **je ne fais pas grand c. de votre ami** I don't think much of your friend; **ne faire aucun c. de qch** to take no notice of sth, to pay no attention to sth

3 *Gram* case; **au c. nominatif** in the nominative (case)

4 (*locutions*) **en** *ou* **dans ce c.** in that case, if that's the case, under those circumstances; **en aucun c.** under no circumstances, on no account, not on any account; **en tout c.,** **dans tous les c.** in any case, anyway, in any event; **dans tous les c., il est trop tard** it's too late now anyway *or* anyhow; **dans ce c.-là, auquel c.** in that case; **le c. échéant** if necessary, if need be, should the need arise; **selon le c.** as the case may be; **en c. de nécessité** if need be, if necessary; **en c. de pluie/décès/d'absence** in the event of rain/death/absence; **en c. d'accident** in the event of an accident; **en c. d'urgence** in an emergency; **en c. de besoin, tu peux m'appeler à n'importe quelle heure** if need be, you can call me at any time; **j'ai pris un pull supplémentaire en c. de besoin** I took an extra sweater just in case; **au c. où** *ou* **dans le c. où il viendrait** in case he comes, if he should come; **au c. où ce serait exact** should it prove correct; *Fam* **je te le laisse au c. où** I'll leave it for you just in case

▸▸**c. de conscience** matter of conscience; **c. de divorce** divorce case; (*raisons*) grounds for divorce; **c. d'école** textbook case; **c. d'espèce** special case; **c. de figure** scenario; **c. limite** borderline case; **c. social** person with social problems

casanier, -ière [kazanje, -jɛr] ADJ homeloving, *Péj* stay-at-home
N homebody, *Péj* stay-at-home

casaque [kazak] NF (*de jockey*) blouse, jacket; *Fig* **tourner c.** (*partir*) to turn tail, to flee; (*changer d'opinion*) to turn one's coat

casbah [kazba] NF **1** casbah, kasbah **2** *Fam* (*maison*) place, pad

cascade [kaskad] NF **1** (*chute d'eau*) cascade, waterfall; *Fig* (*de boucles*) cascade; **c. de glace** ice fall; *Fig* **cascades de rires** peals of laughter; **ils ont connu des catastrophes en c.** they experienced a whole string *or* chain of disasters; *Élec* **montage en c.** connection in series; *Ordinat* **menus en c.** pull-down menus **2** *Cin* stunt; **faire de la c.** to do stunts

cascader [kaskade] VI **1** *Litt* (*tomber*) to cascade **2** *Fam Vieilli* (*faire la noce*) to lead a wild life

cascadeur, -euse [kaskadœr, -øz] ADJ *Fam*
Vieilli (*vie etc*) wild, loose
N **1** *Cin* stuntman, *f* stuntwoman; (*de cirque*) acrobat **2** *Fam Vieilli* (*noceur*) person of disorderly habits

cascher [kaʃer] ADJ INV = **kascher**

case [kaz] NF **1** (*hutte*) hut, cabin
2 (*de tiroir etc*) compartment, division; (*pour le courrier*) pigeonhole; (*de formulaire*) box; (*de grille de mots croisés, damier*) square; **cocher la bonne c.** tick the appropriate box; *Fam* **il lui manque une c., il a une c. vide** *ou* **une c. en moins** he's got a screw loose
3 *Radio, TV* slot
4 *Ordinat* button; (*en forme de boîte*) box; **c. d'aide** help button; **c. 'annuler'** cancel button; **c. à cocher** check box; **c. de commande** command button; **c. de contrôle de taille** *ou* **de dimensionnement** size box; **c. de fermeture** close box; **c. 'marche'** walk button; **c. d'option** check box, option button; **c. de pointage** check box; **c. de saisie** input box; **c. zoom** zoom box
5 *Suisse* **c. postale** postbox
▸▸**c. départ** (*dans les jeux*) start; *Fig* **retour à la c. départ** back to square one

caséeux, -euse [kazeø, -øz] ADJ caseous

caséine [kazein] NF *Chimie* casein

casemate [kazmat] NF *Mil* blockhouse, pillbox

caser [kaze] VT **1** (*placer*) to put; **je ne sais pas où c. tous mes livres** I don't know where to put all my books; **j'ai réussi à tout c. dans ma chambre** I managed to find space for everything in *or* to get everything into my room; **c. des papiers** to file papers (away) **2** *Fam* (*établir dans une situation*) to fix up with a job, to find a job for; **elle est bien casée** she's got a good job **3** *Fam* (*marier*) **elle a trois filles à c.** she has three daughters to marry off *or* to find husbands for
VPR **se caser** *Fam* (*se marier*) to (get married and) settle down; (*trouver un emploi*) to get oneself a job, to find a job

caserne [kazern] NF *Mil, Fig, Fam Péj* barracks; **quand j'étais à la c.** when I was in the army; **plaisanteries de c.** locker room jokes, coarse jokes; **c. de pompiers** fire station VOIR
GRAMMAIRE A13

casernement [kazɛrnəma] NM *Mil* **1** (*de troupes*) quartering in barracks, barracking **2** (*lieu*) barrack block

caserner [kazerne] VT *Mil* (*troupes*) to quarter in barracks, to barrack

cash [kaʃ] ADV *Fam* cash; **payer c.** to pay cash (down)

cash and carry [kaʃɛndkari] *Com* NM INV cash-and-carry (store)
ADJ INV cash-and-carry

cash-flow, *pl* **cash-flows** [kaʃflo] NM *Com* cash flow

casier [kazje] NM **1** (*pour le courrier*) (*meuble*) (set of) pigeonholes; (*compartiment*) pigeonhole; (*pour ses vêtements etc*) locker; (*à tiroirs*) filing cabinet, *Am* file cabinet; **c. à bagages** luggage locker; **c. à clés et à courrier** key and mail rack; **c. à skis** ski rack; **c. à bouteilles** bottle rack; **c. à disques** record rack; **c. à musique** music cabinet **2** *Jur* **avoir un c.** to have a record **3** *Pêche* pot; **aller relever ses casiers** to go and lift one's pots
▸▸**c. judiciaire** police *or* criminal record; **avoir un c. judiciaire** to have a record; **avoir un c. judiciaire vierge** to have a clean record

casino [kazino] NM casino

casoar [kazɔar] NM **1** (*oiseau*) cassowary **2** (*plumet*) plume (*worn by cadets of Saint-Cyr*)

Caspienne [kaspjɛn] NF **la mer C.** the Caspian Sea

casque [kask] NM **1** (*de soldat, pompier etc*) helmet; (*de motocycliste*) (crash) helmet; **le**
port du c. est obligatoire helmets must be worn **2** *Radio etc* headphones, headset, earphones; **écouter un disque au c.** to listen to a record on (one's) headphones **3** *Orn* casque; *Bot* helmet **4** (*de salon de coiffure*) (hair) drier
▸▸**c. colonial** pith helmet, topee; *Radio* **c. à écouteurs** headphones, headset, earphones; **c. intégral** crash helmet (*full-faced*); *TV, Radio* **c. interphone** headphone talkback; **Casques blancs** United Nations military observers; **Casques bleus** Blue Berets, United Nations peacekeeping force

casqué [kaske] ADJ helmeted

casquer [kaske] VI *Arg* (*payer*) to fork out, to shell out

casquette [kaskɛt] NF (*chapeau*) cap; *Fig* **avoir plusieurs casquettes** (*responsabilités*) to wear several hats; *Fig Fam* **avoir la c. (de plomb)** to be hungover, to have a hangover

cassable [kasabl] ADJ breakable

Cassandre [kasɑ̃dr] NF Cassandra
N *Fig* prophet of doom, Cassandra; **jouer les C.** to be a Cassandra *or* a prophet of doom and gloom, to prophesy doom and gloom

cassant [kasɑ̃] ADJ **1** (*fragile*) fragile; (*cheveux*) brittle; **c. comme du verre** as fragile as glass **2** *Fig* (*brusque*) (*personne, ton etc*) abrupt, brusque **3** *Arg* (*fatigant*) **c'est pas trop c.** it's not (exactly) back-breaking work

cassate [kasat] NF *Culin* (*glace*) cassata

cassation [kasasjɔ̃] NF **1** *Jur* (*de jugement, testament etc*) annulment, *Spéc* cassation; **Cour de c.** Supreme Court of Appeal; **se pourvoir en c.** to take one's case to the Supreme Court of Appeal **2** *Mil* reduction to the ranks

casse¹ [kas] NF *Typ* (*boîte*) case; **bas/haut de c.** lower-/upper-case letter

casse² NF (*arbre*) cassia

casse³ NF (*action*) breaking, breakage; (*ce qui est cassé*) damage, breakages; **il va y avoir de la c.** something will get broken; *Fam* (*des ennuis*) there'll be trouble; **est-ce qu'il y a eu de la c.?** was anything broken?, were there any breakages?; **payer la c.** to pay for the breakages *or* damage; **vendre qch à la c.** to sell sth for scrap; **envoyer une voiture à la c.** to send a car to the scrapyard; **aller** *ou* **partir à la c.** (*d'une voiture etc*) to go for scrap
NM *Arg* (*cambriolage*) break-in, burglary

cassé [kase] ADJ **1** (*objet, jambe etc*) broken; (*vieillard*) bent, bowed; (*voix*) cracked; *Fam* (*ivre*) smashed, plastered; (*drogué*) stoned; **blanc c.** off-white **2** *Can* (*sans argent*) broke; **c. comme un clou** stony broke

casseau, -eaux [kaso] NM *Typ* half-case

casse-bonbons *Fam* ADJ INV **être c.** to be a pain (in the neck)
N INV pain (in the neck)

casse-cou NM INV **1** (*passage*) danger *or* dangerous spot **2** **crier c. à qn** to warn sb (*of a danger*) **3** (*personne*) daredevil
ADJ INV (*endroit*) dangerous; (*personne*) reckless

casse-couilles *Vulg* ADJ INV **être c.** to be a pain in the arse *or Am* ass
N INV pain in the arse *or Am* ass

casse-croûte NM INV **1** (*repas*) snack, bite **2** *Can* (*snack*) snack bar

casse-cul *Fam* ADJ INV damned annoying
N INV (*personne*) pain (in the arse *or Am* ass)

casse-dalle NM INV *Fam* sandwich

casse-graine NM INV *Fam* snack

casse-gueule *Fam* NM INV (*endroit*) danger *or* dangerous spot; (*entreprise*) risky *or Br Fam* dodgy undertaking
ADJ INV (*endroit*) dangerous; (*entreprise*) risky, *Br* dodgy

cassement [kasmã] NM **1** *Vieilli* c. de tête *(souci)* headache, worry; *(migraine)* splitting headache **2** *Arg, Vieilli (cambriolage)* break-in, burglary

casse-noisettes NM INV (pair of) nutcrackers, *Am* nutcracker

casse-noix NM INV **1** (pair of) nutcrackers, *Am* nutcracker **2** *(oiseau)* nutcracker

casse-pieds *Fam* ADJ INV damned annoying; **ce qu'il est c.** what a pain in the neck (he is)
N INV *(personne)* pain (in the neck)

casse-pierre(s) NM INV *(masse)* stonebreaker's hammer; *Constr (machine)* stonebreaker, stone-crusher

casse-pipes NM INV *Arg* **aller au c.** *Mil* to go (off) to war *or* to the front; *Fig* to be heading for failure

CASSER [kase] VT **1** *(briser) (assiette, jouet, jambe, bras etc)* to break; *(voiture)* to wreck; *(mur)* to break down, to pull down; *(brindille, ficelle)* to break, to snap; *(noix)* to crack; *(pierres)* to break, to crush; **j'ai dû c. le carreau** I had to smash the window; **c. du bois** to chop wood; *Aviat* to crash on landing
2 *(moral)* to break; *(voix)* to strain; *Fam (personne)* to humiliate; *(billet, pièce) (dépenser)* to break; *(chaussures) (pour assouplir)* to break in; *(atmosphère)* to ruin; *(syndicats etc)* to break; **c. une grève** to break a strike; **c. les prix** to slash prices; **c. le marché** to break the market; **cette nouvelle m'a cassé le moral** the news depressed me; *Fig* **c. du sucre sur le dos de qn** to talk about sb behind his/her back; *Théâtre Fam* **c. la baraque** to bring the house down; *Fam* **c. la baraque à qn** to ruin *or* spoil things for sb; *Fig* **c. la croûte** *ou* **la graine, c. une petite graine** to have a snack *or* a bite *or* something to eat; *Fam* **c. sa pipe** to kick the bucket, *Br* to snuff it; *Arg* **c. le morceau** *(avouer)* to spill the beans, to come clean; *(dénoncer)* to grass; *Fam* **ça ne casse rien, ça ne casse pas trois pattes à un canard, ça ne casse pas des briques** it's not up to much, it's nothing to write home about, it's no great shakes; **un spectacle à tout c.** a marvellous *or* fantastic *or* super show; **applaudir à tout c.** to bring the house down; **cela vaut 1000 euros à tout c.** it's worth 1,000 euros at the very most *or* at the outside; **un homme cassé par l'adversité/la douleur/les échecs** a man broken by adversity/pain/failure
3 *(locutions avec parties du corps) Fam* **c. les pieds à qn** to do sb's head in; *Fam* **elle me casse les pieds** *(m'ennuie)* she bores the pants off me; *(m'agace)* she gets on my nerves *or Br* wick; **ça fait deux mois qu'elle me casse les pieds pour que je t'en parle** she's been on at me for two months now to talk to you about it; *Vulg* **il nous casse les bonbons** *ou* **les couilles, il nous les casse** he gets on our tits; *Fam* **c. le cou** *ou* **la figure** *ou Arg* **la gueule à qn** to smash sb's face in; **c. la tête** *ou* **les oreilles à qn** to deafen sb; **c. les reins à qn** to ruin *or* break sb; **c. bras et jambes à qn** to knock sb for six
4 *(dégrader) (officier)* to break, to reduce to the ranks; *(employé)* to demote
5 *Jur (verdict)* to quash, to set aside; **c. un mariage** to annul *or* dissolve a marriage; **c. ses fiançailles** to break off one's engagement
6 *très Fam* **c. de l'arabe** ≃ to go Paki-bashing; **c. du pédé** to go gay-bashing
VI to break; *(de brindille, ficelle)* to break, to snap; **attention, ça casse!** be careful, it's fragile!; **cela casse comme du verre** it's as fragile as glass; *Fig Fam* **ils ont cassé** *(se sont séparés)* they've broken up *or* split up
VPR **se casser 1** *(se briser)* to break; *(de brindille, ficelle)* to break, to snap; **la poutre se**

cassa sous son poids the beam broke under his weight; **elle s'est cassé la jambe** she's broken her leg; *Fam* **il ne s'est pas cassé pour m'aider** he didn't overstrain himself helping me; **le jour où je l'ai rencontré, j'aurais mieux fait de me c. une jambe** I wish I'd never set eyes on him; *Fam* **se c. la figure** *(tomber)* to fall flat on one's face, to come a cropper; *(se blesser)* to smash oneself up; *(rater, faire faillite)* to come a cropper; **se c. la tête** to rack one's brains; *Fam* **ne te casse pas la tête!** don't worry about it!; *Iron* **dis donc, tu ne t'es pas cassé la tête!** well, you didn't exactly strain yourself, did you!; *Fig* **se c. le nez à la porte de qn** to find nobody in *or* at home; *Fig* **il s'est cassé le nez** he's failed, *Fam* he's come a cropper; **se c. les dents** to come a cropper; *Fig* **ne grimpe pas sur cet échafaudage, tu vas te c. le cou!** don't climb up on that scaffolding, you'll break your neck!; *très Fam* **je me suis cassé le cul à lui trouver cette adresse** I really went out of my way *or Arg* bust a gut to find him that address
2 *Arg (partir)* to split, to clear off; **tu viens? on se casse** we're out of here, are you coming?; **casse-toi!** get out of here!, get lost!, beat it!; **elle s'est cassée de chez ses parents** she cleared out of her parents' place

casserole [kasʀɔl] NF **1** *(de cuisine)* (sauce)pan; **veau à la** *ou* **en c.** braised veal; *Arg* **passer à la c.** *(subir des épreuves)* to go through it; *(sexuellement)* to get screwed *or* laid, *Br* to get a good seeing-to; *(être tué)* to get bumped off **2** *Arg (mauvais piano)* tinny piano; **chanter comme une c.** to screech, to sing appallingly **3** *Cin Arg* projector

> Il faut noter que le nom anglais **casserole** est un faux ami. Il signifie **ragoût** ou **cocotte**, selon le contexte.

casse-tête NM INV **1** *(massue)* club; *(matraque)* cosh **2** *(jeu)* puzzle, brainteaser; **c. chinois** Chinese puzzle; *Fig* **c'est un c. chinois** it's baffling **3** *(problème)* headache; **ça a été un c. pour placer tout le monde à table** it was a headache seating everyone at the table

cassetin [kastɛ̃] NM *Typ* box

cassette [kasɛt] NF **1** *(magnétique)* cassette, tape; **écouter/passer une c.** to listen to/to put on *or* play a cassette; **enregistrer qch sur c.** to record sth on (to) cassette, to tape sth; *(vidéo)* to make a video (recording) of sth **2** *(de bijoux)* casket; *Arch* **c. du roi** King's privy purse; **il ne veut jamais puiser dans sa c. personnelle** he never wants to pay for things out of his own pocket
▸ ▸ **c. d'alimentation** *(de copieuse)* paper tray; **c. audio** audio cassette; **c. audionumérique** digital audio tape; *Ordinat* **c. à bande magnétique** mag tape cassette; **c. compacte numérique** digital compact cassette, DCC; **c. de démonstration** demo (tape); *Typ, Ordinat* **c. de fontes** font cassette; **c. numérique** digital audio tape; **c. pirate** pirate tape; *TV etc* **c. prête à diffuser** *ou* **PAD** master tape; **c. de ruban** *(d'une imprimante)* ribbon cassette; **c. de toner** *(d'une imprimante)* toner cassette; **c. vidéo** video (cassette)

cassettothèque [kasetɔtek] NF cassette library

casseur, -euse [kasœʀ, -øz] N **1** c. de pierres stonebreaker **2** *(manifestant)* rioter **3** *(ferrailleur)* scrap (metal) merchant, breaker; **dépôt de c.** breaker's yard; **c. de voitures** (car) breaker **4** *Arg (cambrioleur)* burglar
ADJ **il est c.** he's always breaking things

Cassin [kasɛ̃] NM **le mont C.** Monte Cassino

cassine [kasin] NF *Arch (petite maison)* small house

Cassiopée [kasjɔpe] NF Cassiopeia

cassis[1] [kasis] NM **1** *(baie)* blackcurrant **2** *(arbuste)* blackcurrant bush **3** *(liqueur)* cassis, blackcurrant liqueur; **blanc c.** kir

cassis[2] [kasi(s)] NM *(creux en travers d'une route)* dip

cassis[3] [kasis] NM *Arg (tête)* nut, block

cassolette [kasɔlɛt] NF **1** *(pour parfums)* incense burner **2** *Culin* dish (for one person)

cassonade [kasɔnad] NF brown sugar

cassoulet [kasulɛ] NM *Culin* cassoulet *(stew of beans, pork, goose etc, a speciality of Languedoc)*

cassure [kasyʀ] NF break; *(dans du plâtre etc)* crack; *Fig (dans une amitié etc)* break, rupture; *Géol* fault; *(de tissu)* fold mark, crease; *(d'un pantalon)* crease

castagne [kastaɲ] NF *Fam (coup)* clout, wallop; **va y avoir de la c.** there's going to be a punch-up *or Am* fist fight

castagner [kastaɲe] *Fam* VT to clout, to wallop
VPR **se castagner** to have a *Br* punch-up *or Am* fist fight

castagnette [kastaɲet] NF castanet; **jouer des castagnettes** to play the castanets; *Fig Fam* **j'avais les dents qui jouaient des castagnettes** my teeth were chattering; **ses genoux jouaient des castagnettes** his knees were knocking

caste [kast] NF caste; **la c. des prêtres** the priest caste; **esprit de c.** class consciousness; **avoir l'esprit de c.** to be class conscious; **être hors c.** to be an outcast

castel [kastɛl] NM *(manoir)* manor (house), mansion; *(petit château)* small castle

castillan, -ane [kastijã, -an] ADJ Castilian
NM *Ling* Castilian
N **C.** Castilian

Castille [kastij] NF Castile

casting [kastiŋ] NM *Cin, Théâtre* casting; **passer un c.** to go to a casting

castor [kastɔʀ] NM **1** *(mammifère, fourrure)* beaver; **c. du Chili** *(mammifère)* coypu; *(fourrure)* nutria; **c. du Canada** *(mammifère)* muskrat; *(fourrure)* musquash (fur) **2** *Fig (association)* **(mouvement des) castors** = group of people building their own houses

castrat [kastra] NM eunuch; *Mus* castrato

castrateur, -trice [kastratœʀ, -tris] ADJ *Psy* castrating; *Fig (autoritaire)* repressive

castration [kastrasjɔ̃] NF castration; *(d'un étalon)* gelding; *(d'un chat, d'un chien)* neutering; *(d'une chatte, d'une chienne)* spaying; *Psy* **complexe de c.** castration complex; **c. chimique** chemical castration

castrer [kastre] VT to castrate; *(étalon)* to geld; *(chat, chien)* to neuter; *(chatte, chienne)* to spay

castrisme [kastrism] NM *Pol* Castroism

castriste [kastrist] ADJ, N *Pol* Castroist

casuel, -elle [kazɥɛl] ADJ **1** *(accidentel)* fortuitous **2** *Gram* **flexions casuelles** case endings **3** *Belg (fragile)* fragile
NM *(revenu variable)* perquisites

casuiste [kazɥist] NM *Rel, Fig Péj* casuist

casuistique [kazɥistik] NF *Rel, Fig Péj* casuistry

casus belli [kazysbelli] NM INV casus belli

cata [kata] NF *Fam* **c'est la c.** it's a disaster

cataboliser [katabɔlize] VT *Biol* to catabolize

catabolisme [katabɔlism] NM *Biol* catabolism

catachrèse [katakʀez] NF *Ling* catachresis

cataclysmal, -ale, -aux, -ales [kataklismal, -o] ADJ cataclysmal

cataclysme [kataklism] NM *Géol* cataclysm; *Fig* disaster, cataclysm

cataclysmique [kataklismik] ADJ cataclysmic, cataclysmal; *Fig* disastrous, cataclysmic

catacombes [katakɔ̃b] NFPL catacombs

catadioptre [katadiɔptr] NM *(de véhicule etc)* reflector; *(sur la route)* cat's-eye®

catafalque [katafalk] NM catafalque

cataire [katɛr] NF catmint, catnip

catalan, -ane [katalɑ̃, -an] ADJ Catalan ◾ NM *Ling* Catalan ◾ N **C.** Catalan

catalepsie [katalɛpsi] NF *Méd* catalepsy; **tomber en c.** to have a cataleptic fit

cataleptique [katalɛptik] ADJ, N *Méd* cataleptic

catalogage [katalɔgaʒ] NM *(de livres etc)* cataloguing, *Am* cataloging

Catalogne [katalɔɲ] NF **1** Catalonia **2** *Can Tex* rag rug

catalogue [katalɔg] NM catalogue, *Am* catalog; **c. de vente par correspondance** mail-order catalogue; **je n'achète jamais rien sur c.** I never buy anything from a catalogue; **faire le c. de** to catalogue; **c. de films** film library; **c. méthodique** subject catalogue; **c. de normes** standards catalogue

cataloguer [katalɔge] VT *(livres)* to catalogue, *Am* to catalog; *Fig Péj (étiqueter)* to label; **les médias l'ont cataloguée parmi les révolutionnaires** the media labelled her a revolutionary; **je l'ai catalogué tout de suite** I sized him up immediately

catalpa [katalpa] NM *Bot* catalpa

catalyse [kataliz] NF *Chimie* catalysis; **four à c.** self-cleaning oven

catalyser [katalize] VT *Chimie, Fig* to catalyse

catalyseur [katalizœr] NM *Chimie, Fig* catalyst

catalytique [katalitik] ADJ *Chimie* catalytic; *Aut* **pot c.** catalytic converter

catamaran [katamarɑ̃] NM *Naut* catamaran; *Aviat (d'un hydravion)* floats

Cataphote® [katafɔt] NM = catadioptre

cataplasme [kataplasm] NM *Méd* poultice; **c. sinapisé** mustard poultice or plaster; *Fig* **c'est comme un c. sur une jambe de bois** it's worse than useless

catapultage [katapyltaʒ] NM catapulting; *Aviat* catapult launch(ing); *Fig (dans un poste etc)* catapulting; *Aviat* **crochet de c.** catapulting hook

catapulte [katapylt] NF *Aviat, Mil etc* catapult

catapulter [katapylte] VT to catapult; *Fig (personne)* to catapult (**dans un poste** into a post)

cataracte [katarakt] NF **1** *(d'eau)* cataract, falls; **des cataractes (de pluie)** torrents of rain **2** *Méd* cataract; **se faire opérer de la c.** to have a cataract operation

catarrhal, -ale, -aux, -ales [kataral, -o] ADJ *Méd* catarrhal

catarrhe [katar] NM *Méd* catarrh

catarrheux, -euse [katarø, -øz] *Méd* ADJ *(personne)* catarrhal ◾ N catarrhal person

catastrophe [katastrɔf] NF catastrophe, disaster; **c. ferroviaire/aérienne** rail/air disaster; **c. financière** crash; **c'est la c.!** it's a disaster!; **ce n'est tout de même pas une c.!** it's not the end of the world!; **cet enfant/votre devoir est une c.** this child/your homework is a disaster; **c.! il est déjà là!** panic stations! he's here already!; *Aviat* **atterrir en c.** to make a forced or emergency landing; **je suis passé au bureau en c.** I went to the office in a mad rush or a panic

catastrophé [katastrɔfe] ADJ *Fam* stunned;

il était c. de l'apprendre he was stunned to learn it

catastropher [katastrɔfe] VT *Fam (personne)* to stun, to be a (great) blow to

catastrophique [katastrɔfik] ADJ *(événement, conséquence etc)* catastrophic, disastrous; *Fig (très mauvais)* disastrous, appalling

catastrophisme [katastrɔfism] NM catastrophism; *Fam* **sans vouloir faire du c.** without wishing to be pessimistic

catatonie [katatɔni] NF *Méd* catatonia

catatonique [katatɔnik] ADJ, N *Méd* catatonic

catch [katʃ] NM *Sport* (all-in) wrestling; **faire du c.** to wrestle; **match** *ou* **rencontre de c.** wrestling match

catcher [katʃe] VI *Sport* to wrestle

catcheur, -euse [katʃœr, -øz] N *Sport* (all-in) wrestler

catéchèse [kateʃɛz] NF *Rel* catechism

catéchisation [kateʃizasjɔ̃] NF *Rel* catechization

catéchiser [kateʃize] VT *Rel* to catechize; *Fig (endoctriner)* to indoctrinate; *(sermonner)* to preach at, to lecture

catéchisme [kateʃism] NM *Rel (instruction, livre)* catechism; **aller au c.** to go to catechism class; *Fig* **ce livre est son c.** this book is his bible

catéchiste [kateʃist] N *Rel* catechist

catéchumène [katekymɛn] N *Rel* catechumen; *Fig* novice, tyro

catégorie [kategɔri] NF category; *(d'hôtel, de personnel)* grade; *(de légumes, fruits)* category, grade, class; *(de boxeur)* class; **légumes de première c.** grade one or class one or prime vegetables; **de dernière c.** of poor quality; **morceau de viande de première/ deuxième c.** prime/second cut of meat; **il appartient à cette c. de gens qui …** he belongs to that category or group of people who …; **c. de produit** product category or class; **c. sociale** social category; **c. socioprofessionnelle** socio-professional group, social stratum

catégoriel, -ielle [kategɔrjɛl] ADJ **1** *Ind, Pol* **revendications catégorielles** differential claims **2** *Ling* **symbole c.** category symbol **3** *Phil* categorical

catégorique [kategɔrik] ADJ *(clair) (réponse etc)* categoric(al); *Phil (proposition etc)* categorical; **refus c.** categoric or flat refusal; **elle a été c. sur ce point** she was categorical or quite definite on this point; **il est c., il faut aller à l'hôpital** there's no question about it, you/etc will have to go to hospital; **je suis absolument c., c'est bien l'homme que j'ai vu** I'm absolutely positive that's the man I saw

catégoriquement [kategɔrikmɑ̃] ADV categorically

catégorisation [kategɔrizasjɔ̃] NF categorization; *(de personnel)* grading

catégoriser [kategɔrize] VT to categorize; *(personnel)* to grade

catelle [katɛl] NF *Suisse* ceramic tile

caténaire [katenɛr] ADJ **1** *Rail* **suspension c.** catenary **2** **réaction c.** chain reaction ◾ NF *Rail* catenary

catgut [katgyt] NM *Chir* catgut

cathare [katar] *Hist, Rel* ADJ Cathar ◾ N **C.** Cathar

catharsis [katarsis] NF *Psy, Littér* catharsis

cathartique [katartik] ADJ *Psy, Littér* cathartic

cathédrale [katedral] NF cathedral

cathèdre [katɛdr] NF cathedra

Catherine [katrin] NF **coiffer sainte C.** *(d'une femme)* to be 25 and still unmarried, to be left on the shelf

catherinette [katrinɛt] NF unmarried woman of 25 or over

cathéter [kateter] NM *Méd* catheter

cathétérisme [kateterism] NM *Méd* catheterization

catho [kato] ADJ *Fam* Catholic

cathode [katɔd] NF *Élec* cathode

cathodique [katɔdik] ADJ *Élec* cathodic; **l'univers c.** the world of television; **rayons cathodiques** cathode rays; **tube à rayons cathodiques, tube c.** cathode-ray tube

catholicisme [katɔlisism] NM (Roman) Catholicism

catholicité [katɔlisite] NF **1** **la c.** *(catholiques)* the (Roman) Catholic Church **2** *(orthodoxie)* Catholicity

catholique [katɔlik] ADJ **1** *Rel* (Roman) Catholic; *(universel)* catholic, universal **2** *Fam* **il/ce n'est pas (très) c.** he's/it's a bit fishy; *Hum* **cette façon de faire la soupe n'est pas très c.** this isn't a very orthodox way of making soup ◾ N (Roman) Catholic

catilinaire [katilinɛr] NF lampoon

catimini (en) [ɑ̃katimini] ADV *Fam* stealthily, on the sly or quiet; **entrer/sortir en c.** to steal or *Fam* sneak in/out; **je suis allé l'acheter en c.** I went to buy it on the quiet

catin [katɛ̃] NF **1** *Arg, Vieilli (prostituée)* trollop, whore **2** *Can (poupée)* doll **3** *Can (pansement)* finger bandage

cation [katjɔ̃] NM *Élec* cation

catogan [katɔgɑ̃] NM hair ribbon *(for ponytail)*

Caton [katɔ̃] NM Cato

Caucase (le) [ləkokaz] NM the Caucasus

caucasien, -ienne [kokazjɛ̃, -jɛn] ADJ Caucasian ◾ N **C.** Caucasian

cauchemar [koʃmar] NM *aussi Fig* nightmare; **faire un c.** to have a nightmare; **vision de c.** nightmarish vision; **ça me donne des cauchemars rien que d'y penser** it gives me nightmares just thinking about it; **il me donne des cauchemars** I have nightmares about him; *Fig* **les réceptions officielles étaient son c.** official receptions were a nightmare to or for him

cauchemarder [koʃmarde] VI to have nightmares; *Fig* **cette idée me fait c.** the idea gives me nightmares

cauchemardesque [koʃmardɛsk], **cauchemardeux, -euse** [koʃmardø, -øz] ADJ *(vision etc)* nightmarish; **sommeil cauchemardeux** sleep disturbed by nightmares

caudal, -ale, -aux, -ales [kodal, -o] ADJ *Zool* caudal

cauri(s) [kori] NM cowrie (shell)

causal, -ale, -als *ou* **-aux, -ales** [kozal, -o] ADJ *Gram, Phil* causal

causalité [kozalite] NF *Phil* causality; **rapport/principe de c.** causal relation/principle

causant [kozɑ̃] ADJ *Fam (personne)* chatty, talkative

CAUSE [koz] NF **1** *(origine)* cause; **c. réelle/ apparente** real/apparent cause; **c. de défiance** cause or reason for distrust; *Phil* **c. première/seconde** first/secondary cause; **quelle est la c. de son départ?** what caused him to leave?; **on ne connaît pas la c. de sa mort** the cause of death is unknown; **être (la) c. de qch** to be the cause of sth; **les enfants sont souvent c. de soucis** children are often a cause of worry; **c'est elle qui en est c.** it's her fault, she's to blame; **il s'est fâché, et non sans c.** he got angry, and with good reason; **il s'est mis en colère, et pour c.** he got angry, and for a very good reason; **absent pour c. de santé** absent for health reasons *or* on medical grounds; **fermé pour c. de décès/d'inventaire** closed owing to bereavement/for stocktaking; **à c. de** because of, on account of; **c'est à c. de moi qu'il a manqué le train** it was because of me (that) he missed the train, it was my fault he missed the train; **c'est à c. de toi!** it's all because of you!, it's all your fault!

2 *Jur* cause, (law)suit, action; **c. civile/criminelle** civil/criminal action *or* case; **plaider/gagner une c.** to argue/to win a case; **avocat sans causes** briefless barrister; **confier une c. à un avocat** to brief a barrister; **affaire en c.** case before the court; **entendre une c.** to hear a case; *Fig* **la c. est entendue** there's nothing more to be said; **être en c.** *(d'une personne, d'intérêts etc)* to be involved; **votre probité n'est pas en c.** your honesty is not in question *or* in doubt; **mettre en c. la probité de qn** to question sb's honesty; **mettre qn en c.** *Jur* to summon *or* sue sb; *(impliquer)* to implicate sb; **mettre qn hors de c.** to clear *or* exonerate sb; **il est maintenant hors de c.** he has now been cleared; **en tout état de c.** at all events, in any case; **en connaissance de c.** with full knowledge of the facts

3 *(parti)* cause; **prendre fait et c. pour qn/qch** to take up sb's/sth's cause; **c'est une c. perdue (d'avance)** it's a lost cause; **faire c. commune avec qn** to side with sb, to join forces with sb

▸ ▸ **c. célèbre** famous trial, cause célèbre

causer¹ [koze] VT *(chose)* to cause, to be the cause of; **c. un changement** to bring about a change; **son départ nous a causé beaucoup de chagrin** his departure distressed us greatly *or* caused us great distress; **c. des ennuis à qn** to cause sb problems, to give sb trouble

causer² VI **1** *(parler)* to chat, to talk (**de** about); **c. avec** *ou Fam* **à qn** to have a chat *or* a talk with sb; *Fam* **je ne lui cause plus!** *(je suis fâché avec elle)* I'm not talking to her!; **c. de** to talk about; **c. de la pluie et du beau temps, c. de choses et d'autres** to talk about this and that; **c. affaires/chiffons** to talk business/clothes; **cause toujours, tu m'intéresses!** how interesting!; **faire c. qn** to make sb talk, to get sb to talk **2** *(cancaner)* to talk, to gossip; **on commence à en c.** people are beginning to talk *or* gossip (about it)

causerie [kozri] NF **1** *(discussion)* chat, talk **2** *(conférence)* (informal) talk

causette [kozɛt] NF **1** *Fam* little chat; **faire la c.** *ou* **un brin de c. avec qn** to have a little chat *or Br* a bit of a natter with sb **2** *Ordinat* chat

causeur, -euse [kozœr, -øz] N *(personne)* chatterer
  NF **causeuse** *(siège)* loveseat
  ADJ chatty, talkative

causse [kos] NM *Géog* = limestone plateau in central and southern France

causticité [kostisite] NF *Chimie* causticity; *Fig (d'une personne)* causticity; *(d'une remarque etc)* biting *or* caustic nature

caustique [kostik] ADJ *Chimie* caustic; *Fig (personne, esprit, humour)* caustic; *(remarque etc)* biting, caustic, cutting
  NM *Chimie* caustic
  NF *Opt* caustic

caustiquement [kostikmã] ADV *Fig* caustically, bitingly, cuttingly

cautèle [kotɛl] NF *Litt* wiliness, cunning

cauteleux, -euse [kotlø, -øz] ADJ *Litt* wily, cunning

cautère [kotɛr] NM *Méd* cautery; *Fam* **c'est un c. sur une jambe de bois** it's worse than useless, it won't do any good whatsoever

cautérisation [koterizasjɔ̃] NF *Méd* cauterization

cautériser [koterize] VT *Méd (blessure etc)* to cauterize

caution [kosjɔ̃] NF **1** *(gage),* Com, Fin security, guarantee; *Jur* bail; *Fig (appui)* support, backing; **c. de banque** bank guarantee; *Fin* **c. de bonne fin** performance bond; *Fin* **c. de soumission** bid bond; **il faut verser 1000 euros de c.** you/*etc* must pay a deposit of 1,000 euros; *Jur* **donner** *ou* **fournir c. pour qn** to go *or* stand bail for sb, to bail sb out; *Jur* **mettre qn en liberté sous c.** to release sb on bail; *Fig* **sujet à c.** *(nouvelles etc)* to be treated with caution, unreliable, unconfirmed; *Fig* **le gouvernement a donné sa c. au rachat** the takeover has the government's support *or* backing; *Fin* **c. d'adjudication** bid bond

2 *(personne)* surety, security, guaranty; **se porter c. pour qn** *Jur* to go *or* stand bail for sb; *Com, Fin* to stand surety *or* security for sb

> Il faut noter que le nom anglais **caution** est un faux ami. Il signifie **prudence**.

cautionnement [kosjɔnmã] NM **1** *(contrat)* surety bond **2** *(somme d'argent)* security, guarantee, guaranty; **c. électoral** deposit

cautionner [kosjɔne] VT **1** *(personne)* Com, Fin to stand surety for, to act as guarantor for; *Jur* to go *or* stand bail for, to bail out **2** *Fig (répondre de) (chose)* to answer for, to guarantee; **c. l'honnêteté de qn** to vouch for sb's honesty **3** *Fig (approuver) (idée, action, gouvernement etc)* to support, to back

> Il faut noter que le verbe anglais **to caution** est un faux ami. Il signifie **mettre en garde**.

cavalcade [kavalkad] NF **1** *(défilé)* cavalcade, procession **2** *Fig (bousculade)* swarm, stampede

cavalcader [kavalkade] VI **1** *(d'un groupe de gens etc)* to swarm (about) **2** *Arch* to ride *(in a cavalcade)*

cavale [kaval] NF **1** *Arg (évasion)* escape; **être en c.** to be on the run **2** *Litt (jument)* mare

cavaler [kavale] VI *Arg* to rush around; *(fuir)* to take off, *Br* to scarper, *Br* to do a runner; **c. après qn** *(poursuivre de ses assiduités)* to chase after sb; **je n'ai pas envie de c. le jour de Noël** I don't want to be rushing around on Christmas Day
  VT **c. qn** to get on sb's nerves, to plague *or* pester sb

cavalerie [kavalri] NF **1** *Mil* cavalry; **c. légère** light cavalry, light horse; **c. motorisée** motorized cavalry; **grosse c.** heavy *or* armoured cavalry; *Fig Fam* **Wagner et sa grosse c. de cuivres** Wagner and his heavy brass **2** *(ensemble de chevaux)* stable

cavaleur, -euse [kavalœr, -øz] *Arg* ADJ *(homme)* womanizing; *(femme)* man-chasing
  N *(homme)* skirt chaser, womanizer; *(femme)* man-chaser

cavalier, -ière [kavalje, -jɛr] N **1** *(à cheval)* rider, horseman, *f* horsewoman; **habit de c.** riding costume; *Bible* **les (Quatre) Cavaliers de l'Apocalypse** the (four) Horsemen of the Apocalypse **2** *(qui danse)* partner; *Fig* **faire c. seul** to go it alone, to act alone
  NM **1** *Mil* trooper, cavalryman; *Échecs* knight; *Arch (gentilhomme)* gentleman; *Br Hist* **Cavaliers et Têtes rondes** Cavaliers and Roundheads **2** *(accompagnateur de dame)* escort **3** *Ordinat* jumper **4** *Tech (clou)* staple; *(languette de fichier)* tab
  ADJ **1** **allée** *ou* **piste cavalière** bridle path **2** *(manière, personne)* cavalier, offhand

cavalièrement [kavaljɛrmã] ADV in a cavalier manner, off-handedly

cave¹ [kav] ADJ **1** *(joues, yeux)* hollow, sunken **2** *Anat* **veine c.** vena cava

cave² [kav] NF **1** *(cellier, vins)* cellar; **c. à charbon** coal cellar; **c. à vin** wine cellar; **avoir une bonne c.** to have *or* keep a good cellar; *Fig* **de la c. au grenier** *(ranger, repeindre etc)* from top to bottom, thoroughly **2** *(cabaret)* nightclub **3** **c. à liqueurs** *(meuble)* drinks cabinet

> Il faut noter que le nom anglais **cave** est un faux ami. Il signifie **grotte**.

cave³ NF *Cartes* = stake

cave⁴ NM *Arg* **1** *(personne ne faisant pas partie du milieu)* outsider **2** *(dupe)* sucker, mug
  ADJ **ce qu'il est c.!** what a sucker *or* mug (he is)!

caveau, -eaux [kavo] NM **1** *(petite cave)* small cellar **2** *(cabaret)* nightclub **3** *(funéraire)* burial vault

caver¹ [kave] VT *Arch, Litt* to hollow (out), to dig (out), to excavate
  VPR **se caver** *(des yeux etc)* to become hollow *or* sunken

caver² *Cartes* VT *Arch (miser)* to put up
  VI to put up a stake
  VPR **se caver se c. de deux cents euros** to put up two hundred euros *(as a stake)*

caverne [kavɛrn] NF cave, cavern; *Anat (dans les poumons etc)* cavity; **homme des cavernes** caveman; **la c. d'Ali Baba** Ali Baba's cave; *Fig* **c'est une véritable c. d'Ali Baba** it's a real Aladdin's cave

caverneux, -euse [kavɛrnø, -øz] ADJ **1** *(rocher), Anat (tissu)* cavernous **2** *(voix, grognement)* sepulchral

caviar [kavjar] NM **1** *Culin* caviar; **c. rouge** salmon roe **2** *Fig* blue pencil; **passer au c.** *(article de presse etc)* to blue-pencil, to censor

caviardage [kavjardaʒ] NM *(censure)* blue-pencilling, censoring

caviarder [kavjarde] VT *(article de presse etc)* to blue-pencil, to censor

caviste [kavist] NM cellarman

cavité [kavite] NF cavity, hollow; *Anat, Méd* cavity; **c. articulaire** *(d'un os)* socket; **c. buccale** oral cavity

Cayenne [kajɛn] N *(ville)* Cayenne; **poivre de C.** cayenne (pepper)

CB [sibi] NF *(abrév* **citizens' band, canaux banalisés)** CB

CC [sese] NM *Banque (abrév* **compte courant)** CA

cc [sese] NM *Élec (abrév* **courant continu)** DC

C/C NM *(abrév* **compte (de) chèque)** C/A

CCB [sesebe] NM *(abrév* **compte de chèque bancaire)** C/A

CCI [sesei] NF **1** *(abrév* **Chambre de commerce et de l'industrie)** CCI **2** *(abrév* **Chambre de commerce internationale)** ICC

CCP [sesepe] NM *(abrév* **compte courant postal, compte chèque postal)** ≃ Giro account

CCR [seseɛr] NM *Fin (abrév* **coefficient de capitalisation des résultats)** p/e ratio

CD [sede] NM **1** *(abrév* **corps diplomatique)** CD **2** *(abrév* **compact disc)** CD; **CD audio** audio CD; **CD réinscriptible** CD-RW; **CD vidéo** video CD

CDD [sedede] NM *(abrév* **contrat à durée déterminée)** fixed-term contract

CDI [sedei] NM **1** *(abrév* **centre des impôts)** tax centre, tax office **2** *(abrév* **contrat à durée indéterminée)** permanent contract

CD-I *(abrév* **compact disc-interactif)** CDI

CD-interactif NM interactive CD

CD-Photo NM photo CD

CD-R NM *(abrév* **compact disc recordable)** CD-R

CD-Rom NM INV CD-ROM; **C. d'installation** setup CD-ROM; **C. interactif** interactive CD-ROM

CDV NM (*abrév* **compact disc video**) CDV

CE [seə] NM (*abrév* **Conseil de l'Europe**) Council of Europe
NF (*abrév* **Communauté européenne**) EC

CE¹ [s(ə)] PRON DÉM SEE GRAMMAR B15 (**c'** before parts of **être** *beginning with a vowel*) **1** (*with adj or adv complement*) **c'est exact!** that's right!; **c'est tout à fait possible/fort probable** it's quite possible/highly probable; **ce doit être faux** it's probably untrue; **c'est sur votre bureau** it's on your desk; **le voilà, ce n'est pas trop tôt!** there he is, and about time too!; **est-ce** [es] **assez?** is that enough?; **c'est facile** it's easy; **demain c'est dimanche** tomorrow is Sunday, it's Sunday tomorrow; **c'était inutile de sonner** you needn't have rung; **c'est assez qu'il veuille bien pardonner** it is enough that he is willing to forgive; **c'est à vous de vous en occuper** it's up to you to see to it; **c'est à toi, ce livre? – non, c'est à Paul** is this book yours? – no, it's Paul's SEE GRAMMAR B66

2 (*with noun or pron as complement; with a third person pl complement, the verb should be in the plural but colloquial usage allows the singular*) **c'est moi/c'est nous/ce sont eux** *ou Fam* **c'est eux** it's me/us/them, *Fml* it is I/we/they; **c'est le médecin/c'est Monsieur Pierrot** (*à la porte, au téléphone etc*) it's the doctor/it's Mr Pierrot; **qui a dit ça? – c'est moi/lui/etc** who said that? – me/him/etc or I/he/etc did; **est-ce vous, Jean?** is that you, Jean?; **qui est-ce?** who is it?, who's that?; **c'est un ami que j'avais quand j'étais étudiante** he was a friend of mine when I was a student; **c'est un bon soldat** he's a good soldier; **ce n'est pas un hôtel ici!** this is not a hotel!; **ce n'est pas là mon parapluie** that is not my umbrella; **est-ce que ce sont là vos enfants?** are those your children?; **ce ne sont pas mes chaussures** they *or* these *or* those aren't my shoes; *Fam* **c'est elles qui me l'ont dit** it was them who told me SEE GRAMMAR B66

3 **si ce n'est** except; **personne si ce n'est vos parents** no one except (possibly) your parents

4 (*representing a subject which has been isolated in order to stress it*) **Paris, c'est bien loin!, c'est bien loin, Paris!** it's a long way to Paris!, Paris is a long way away!; **le temps, c'est de l'argent** time is money; **c'est incroyable, ce vent** this wind is incredible

5 (*used with* **que** *or* **qui** *to bring a word into prominence*) **c'est toi qui le dis!** that's what you say!, says you!; **c'est moi qui lui ai écrit** it was I *or Fam* me who wrote to him; **est-ce à moi que vous parlez?** are you speaking to me?; *Litt* **c'est un bon petit garçon que Jean!** what a fine little chap Jean is!; *Litt* **ce serait imprudence que d'y aller** it would be unwise to go (there)

6 (*used with* **que** *to introduce a statement*) **c'est que maman est malade** mother's ill, you see, the point is mother's ill; **c'est qu'il fait froid!** it's cold and no mistake!; **s'il chante, c'est qu'il est de bonne humeur** when *or* if he sings, it means *or* it's because he's in a good mood; **ce n'est pas qu'il n'y tienne pas** it's not that he isn't keen on it, it isn't that he's not keen on it

7 (*used in* **est-ce que** [eskə] *to introduce a question*) **est-ce que je peux entrer?** may I come in?; **est-ce qu'il est là?** is he there? SEE GRAMMAR B64

8 (*locutions*) **pour ce faire** in order to do this; **ce faisant** in so doing, whilst doing so; **ce disant** saying which *or* this, so saying, with these words; **on l'a attaqué et ce** [sə] **en plein jour** he was attacked, and in broad

daylight (too); **sur ce ...** thereupon ..., on that note ...; **sur ce, il sortit son album de photos** whereupon he brought out his photo album; *Arch* **depuis ce ...** since then ...; **tenez-vous beaucoup à ce qu'il vienne?** are you very anxious for him to come?; **je ne m'attendais pas à ce qu'il soit là** I wasn't expecting him to be there; **tu te plains de ce que personne ne te téléphone** you're complaining that no one telephones you; **pour ce qui est de la qualité et du prix** with regard to *or* as regards quality and price; **pour ce qui est de cela** for that matter; **c'est te dire s'il était content** that shows you how happy he was; **c'est tout dire** that says it all; *Litt* **voilà, ce me semble, un avis excellent** that, to my mind, is excellent advice

9 (*with a rel pron*) **ce qui, ce que** what; **je sais ce qui est arrivé** I know what has happened; **c'est ce qui est important** this is what's important; **voilà ce que j'ai répondu** this is what I answered; **je sais ce que c'est que la pauvreté** I know what poverty is; **si vous saviez ce que c'est que de vivre seul** if you knew what it meant *or* what it's like to live alone; **voilà ce que c'est que de mentir** that's what comes of telling lies; **c'est ce qu'il a dit** that's what he said, so he said; **voici ce dont il s'agit** this is the point, this is what it's all about; **ce qu'il y a de plus remarquable, c'est que ...** what is most remarkable is that ..., the most remarkable thing about it is ...; **à ce qu'on dit** according to *or* from what they say; **voici ce à quoi j'avais pensé** this is what I had thought of SEE GRAMMAR A32; A33; B17–18; B23

10 (*referring back to a clause*) **ce qui, ce que** which; **ce qui compte, c'est que tu sois satisfait** what counts is that you're happy; **il faut avoir de l'argent, ce qu'elle n'a pas** you need to have money, which she doesn't have; **il l'a quittée, ce qui est dommage** he has left her, which is a pity; **il est déjà parti, ce que je ne savais pas** he has already gone, which I didn't know SEE GRAMMAR A33; B17–18; B23

11 **tout ce qui, tout ce que** everything, all (that); **voici tout ce que j'ai d'argent** here's all the money I've got; **faites tout ce que vous voudrez** do whatever you like

12 *Fam* **ce que ...!** (*comme*) how ...!; (**qu'est-)ce qu'elle a changé!** how she has changed!; **ce que tu as grandi!** how you've grown!, well, you have grown!; **ce qu'il peut être pénible!** he can be really tiresome!; **ce que j'ai faim!** I'm really hungry!

13 (*with* **à** *+ inf*) **c'est à mourir de rire** it's absolutely hilarious; **c'est à se demander s'il n'est pas fou** one may well wonder if he isn't mad; **c'est à voir** (*ça reste à prouver*) that remains to be seen, we'll have to (wait and) see; (*il faut le voir absolument*) you have to see it; **c'est à refaire** it will have to be done again

CE², **CET, CETTE, CES** [sə, sɛt, se *or* sɛ] ADJ DÉM (*the form* **cet** *is used before a* **n** *or adj beginning with a vowel or* **h** *mute*) **1** (*désigne quelque chose de proche dans l'espace ou dans le temps*) this, that, *pl* these, those; **un de ces jours** one of these days; **tu dois connaître cette histoire, tout le monde la connaît!** you must know this story, everyone does!; **il fera de l'orage cette nuit** there will be a storm tonight; **j'ai mal dormi cette nuit** I slept badly last night; **je l'ai vu/je le verrai ce matin/cet été/cette semaine** I saw him/I'll see him this morning/this summer/this week; **c'est une de ces femmes qui se plaignent tout le temps** she's one of those women who complain *or* she's the sort of woman who complains all the time SEE GRAMMAR A30–1; B14

2 (*par référence à une chose connue*) the; **j'ai encore cette impression que ...** I still have the feeling that ...; **rien de ce genre** nothing of the kind; **je n'ai jamais rien entendu/vu de**

ce genre I've never heard/seen anything of the kind *or* anything like it

3 **ce dernier** the latter

4 **ces** the; **que prendront ces messieurs?** what will you take *or* have, gentlemen?; **ces dames sont au salon** the ladies are in the drawing room

5 **ce ...-ci** this; **ce ...-là** that; **de ce côté-ci/de ce côté-là** on this/that side; **je ne connais pas ce livre-là** I don't know that book; **j'ai vu tous ces films, mais j'ai préféré ce film-ci à tous les autres** I've seen all these films, but I prefer this one to all the others; **prenez cette tasse-ci** take this cup; **je n'oublierai jamais ce jour-là** I'll never forget that day; **je la verrai ces jours-ci** I'll see her in a day or two; **il fait chaud ces jours-ci** it's been warm lately *or* the(se) last couple of days

6 *Fam* (*en intensif*) **eh bien, et cette jambe?** well, how's that leg of yours *or* how's the leg?; **alors, cette lettre, tu me la fais lire?** so, do I get to read that letter of yours?; **et ce café, il arrive?** is that coffee on its way or what?; **et ce vent, qui ne tombe pas!** will that wind ever die down?; **mais laissez-la donc, cette enfant!** do leave that child alone!; **mais c'est qu'elle a grandi, cette petite!** that little girl has really grown!; **cette question!** what an absurd question!; **cette foule!** what a crowd!; **je lui ai écrit une de ces lettres!** I wrote him such a letter!; **j'ai une de ces faims!** I'm ravenous!; **elle a une de ces têtes!** (*elle est fatiguée, malade*) she looks awful!; (*elle est laide*) she's as ugly as sin!; **il a fait une de ces têtes quand je le lui ai montré** you should have seen his face when I showed it to him

CEA [seəa] NM (*abrév* **Commissariat à l'énergie atomique**) = French atomic energy commission

céans [seã] ADV *Arch* (here) within, in this house; *Hum* **le maître de c.** the master of the house

ceci [səsi] PRON DÉM INV this; **et tout c. pour rien, puisqu'il a fallu recommencer** and it was all for nothing, since we/etc had to start again; **c. étant dit, il faut quand même reconnaître qu'il a du talent** having said that, it must be admitted that he's talented; **écoutez bien c.** (now) listen to this; **le cas a c. de particulier que ...** the case is peculiar in that ...; **c. n'explique pas cela** one thing doesn't explain the other SEE GRAMMAR B15

cécité [sesite] NF blindness; **être frappé de c.** to be struck blind; **être atteint de c.** to be blind; **c. verbale** word blindness

cédant, -ante [sedã, -ãt] *Com, Jur* ADJ (*partie*) granting, assigning
N grantor, assignor

céder [sede] (**je cède; je céderai**) VT (*donner*) (*chose*) to give up, to part with (**à** to); (*droit*) to give up, to surrender; *Jur* to transfer, to make over, to assign (**à** to); (*bail*) to dispose of, to sell; **c. qch à bail** to lease sth; **c. sa place à qn** to give up one's seat to sb; **c. le pas à qn** to let sb go first, to give way to sb; **c. du terrain** to give *or* lose ground; *Fig* to back down; **'cédez le passage'** 'give way', *Am* 'yield'; **fonds de commerce à c.** business for sale; **'à c.'** 'for sale'; **je vous le cède pour cent euros** I'll let you have it for a hundred euros; *Vieilli* **ne le c. en rien à qn** to be in no way inferior to sb; **pour l'intelligence, elle ne (le) cède à personne** when it comes to intelligence, she's second to none; **ces artistes russes ne le cédaient en rien à leurs contemporains français** these Russian artists were every bit as good as their French contemporaries
VI (*se soumettre*) (*d'une personne*) to yield, to give in (**à** to); (*s'écrouler*) (*d'une construction, corde etc*) to give way; **le terrain a cédé sous mes pieds** the ground gave way beneath me;

le câble a cédé sous l'effort the rope gave way *or* parted under the strain; **c. sous le poids** to give way *or* break beneath the weight; **c. au sommeil** to succumb to sleep; **c. à la tentation** to give in *or* yield to temptation; *Fig* **leur argumentation cédera à la première analyse** their reasoning will fall apart at the first analysis; **il a cédé à nos revendications** he gave in to our demands; **c. devant les menaces/aux intimidations** to give in *or* yield to threats/to intimidation; **elle a fini par lui c.** *(d'une femme séduite par un homme)* she finally succumbed to *or* gave into him

cédérom [sederɔm] NM *Ordinat* CD-ROM

cédétiste [sedetist] *Pol* ADJ of *or* relating to the CFDT *(French trade union)*
  N member of the CFDT

Cedex [sedɛks] NM *(abrév* **Courrier d'entreprise à distribution exceptionnelle)** = special delivery service for business mail

cédille [sedij] NF *Gram* cedilla; **c c.** c cedilla

cédrat [sedra] NM *(arbre)* citron (tree); *(fruit)* citron; **confiture de cédrats** citron marmalade

cédratier [sedratje] NM citron (tree)

cèdre [sɛdr] NM *(arbre, bois)* cedar; **c. du Liban** cedar of Lebanon; **c. bleu** blue cedar; **table en c.** cedar table

CEE [seəə] NF *(abrév* **Communauté économique européenne)** EEC

CEG [seəʒe] NM *(abrév* **collège d'enseignement général)** = junior secondary school

cégep [seʒep] NM *Can (abrév* **collège d'enseignement général et professionnel)** = college of further education

cégétiste [seʒetist] *Pol* N member of the CGT *(French trade union)*
  ADJ **délégué c.** CGT delegate

CEI [seəi] NM *(abrév* **Communauté des états indépendants)** CIS

ceindre [sɛdr] *(prp* ceignant; *pp* ceint; *pr ind* je ceins, il ceint, n. ceignons; *impf* je ceignais; *p hist* je ceignis; *fu* je ceindrai) *Litt* VT **1** to gird; **c. une épée** to gird on *or* buckle on a sword; **c. l'écharpe municipale** to put on *or* assume one's sash of office; **c. la couronne** *(d'un roi)* to put on *or* assume the crown **2 c. ses reins** to gird up one's loins; **c. ses reins d'une écharpe** to tie a sash round one's waist **3** *(d'une couronne etc) (la tête de qn etc)* to encircle; **tête ceinte d'une couronne de lauriers** head wreathed with laurels **4 c. une ville de murailles** to encircle *or* surround a town with walls
  VPR **se ceindre se c. les reins** to gird (up) one's loins

ceinture [sɛtyr] NF **1** *(en cuir etc)* belt; *(d'une jupe, de pantalon)* waistband; *(du corps)* waist, middle; *(en lutte)* waist lock; **porter une c.** to wear a belt; **une c. de cuir** a leather belt; **élargir la c. d'une jupe** to let out the waistband of a skirt; **l'eau nous arrivait au niveau de la c.** we were up to our waists in water; **porter son écharpe en c.** to tie one's scarf round one's waist; **c. marron/noire** *(arts martiaux)* brown/black belt; **il est c. noire de judo** he's a black belt in judo; **coup au-dessous de la c.** blow beneath *or* below the belt; **desserrer sa c. après un bon repas** to loosen one's belt after a heavy meal; *Fig Fam* **se serrer** *ou* **se mettre la c.** to tighten one's belt; *Fam* **faire c.** to go without; *Fam* **il va tout le temps au restaurant, mais moi, c.!** he goes to restaurants all the time, but I have to go without!
  2 *(marquant une délimitation)* enclosure; *(de murs)* circle; *(de collines)* belt
  3 *Rail* **chemin de fer de c.** *(autour d'une ville)* circle line; **la grande/la petite C.** *(à Paris)* the outer/inner circle railway
  4 *Archit (d'une colonne)* cincture

▸▸ **c. de chasteté** chastity belt; **c. herniaire** (hernia) truss; *Méd* **c. orthopédique** surgical corset; *Anat* **c. pelvienne** pelvic girdle; **c. de sauvetage** lifebelt; *Anat* **c. scapulaire** pectoral *or* scapular arch *or* girdle; *Aut, Aviat* **c. de sécurité** seat belt, safety belt; **c. de sécurité à enrouleur** inertia reel seat belt; *Aut* **c. de sécurité statique** static seat belt; *Aut* **c. de sécurité trois points** lap and shoulder belt, three-point seat belt; *Aut* **c. de sécurité ventrale** lap belt; **c. verte** green belt

ceinturer [sɛtyre] VT **1** *(entourer)* to girdle, to surround; **ville ceinturée de murs** walled town **2** *(personne) (d'un lutteur)* to put a waist lock on; *Rugby, Ftbl* to grab around the waist; **c. un homme dangereux** to collar a dangerous man

ceinturon [sɛtyrɔ̃] NM *Mil etc* belt

CEL [seəɛl] NM *(abrév* **compte d'épargne logement)** savings account *(for purchasing a property)*

CELA [səla, sla] PRON DÉM SEE GRAMMAR B15 **1** *(chose, fait etc)* that; **c., je ne pouvais pas le prévoir** I couldn't have foreseen that; **qu'est-ce que c'est que c.?** what's that?; **il me l'a expliqué très clairement, et c. sans s'énerver le moins du monde** he explained it to me very clearly, and without getting the least bit annoyed; **il y a deux ans de c.** that was two years ago; **c'est pour c. que je viens** that's what I've come for *or* why I've come; **ce n'est quand même pas pour c. que vous vous êtes disputés?** you didn't argue over a little thing like that, did you?; **sans c., je ne serais pas venu** but for that *or* otherwise I wouldn't have come; **à c. près** *ou* **à part c., nous sommes d'accord** we are agreed, with that one exception *or* except on that point; **s'il n'y a que c. de nouveau** if that's all that's new **2** *(* cela *is the pron used as neut subject to all verbs other than* être, *and may be used with* être *as more emphatic than* ce*)* that, it; **c. ne vous regarde pas** that's *or* it's none of your business, that's *or* it's no business of yours; **c. m'est pénible de la voir si malheureuse** its very painful to me to see her *or* seeing her so unhappy **3** *(dans locutions) Fam* **et pourquoi c.?** why is that?; **je trouve que tu exagères – et pourquoi c.?** I think you're exaggerating – why's that *or* how come?; **je l'ai vu – qui c.?/quand c.?/où c.?** I saw him – who (do you mean)?/when (was that)?/where (was that)?; **ce n'est plus c.** it's not what it was, it's not the same any more; **il n'y a que c. pour me tenir éveillé** that's the only thing that will keep me awake; **s'il n'y avait que c.** if that were the only problem; **ah, pour c., oui!** yes, indeed!, yes, of course!; **et avec c., madame?** *(dans un magasin)* anything else, madam?; **elle était très jolie et, avec c., toujours serviable** she was very pretty and, moreover, always willing to help

céladon [seladɔ̃] ADJ INV celadon

célébrant [selebrɑ̃] *Rel* ADJ officiating
  NM celebrant

célébration [selebrasjɔ̃] NF celebration

célèbre [selɛbr] ADJ famous, celebrated (**par** for); **se rendre c. par un acte/une déclaration** to become famous because of something one did/said; **le cas si tristement c. de ...** the notorious case of ...

célébrer [selebre] VT *(je célèbre; je célébrerai)* **1** *(anniversaire, événement, messe etc)* to celebrate; *(rite)* to solemnize, to perform; *(fête religieuse)* to observe, to keep; **c. des funérailles** to hold a funeral **2** *(personne)* to extol; **c. le courage de qn** to praise *or* pay tribute to sb's courage

célébrité [selebrite] NF *(notoriété)* fame, celebrity; *(personne)* celebrity

celer [səle] VT *(je cèle; je cèlerai) Arch, Litt* to conceal, to keep secret (**à** from)

céleri [sɛlri] NM celery; **pied de c.** head of celery; **morceau** *ou* **branche de c.** stick of celery; *Culin* **c. rémoulade** = celeriac in mayonnaise

céleri-rave, *pl* **céleris-raves** NM celeriac

célérité [selerite] NF speed, rapidity; **avec une étonnante c.** with astonishing speed, at an astonishing rate

célesta [selɛsta] NM *Mus* celesta, celeste

céleste [selɛst] ADJ celestial, heavenly; *Fig (divin)* divine; *Litt* **la voûte c.** the vault of heaven; **bleu c.** sky blue; *Fig* **la colère c.** divine wrath; **le C. Empire** the Celestial Empire

célibat [seliba] NM *(vie de célibataire)* single life; *Rel (chasteté)* celibacy; **vivre dans le c.** to remain single; **de plus en plus de femmes choisissent le c.** more and more women are choosing to remain single

célibataire [selibatɛr] ADJ *(non marié)* unmarried, single; **mère c.** unmarried mother
  NM bachelor; **un c. endurci** a confirmed bachelor
  NF single woman; *Admin, Vieilli* spinster

> Il faut noter que l'adjectif anglais **celibate** est un faux ami. Il signifie **chaste**.

celle, celle-ci, celle-là PRON *voir* celui

cellérier, -ière [selerje, -jɛr] N *Rel* cellarer, *f* cellaress

cellier [selje] NM storeroom; *(cave)* cellar

Cellophane® [selɔfan] NM cellophane®; **fromage sous C.** cellophane-wrapped cheese

cellulaire [selylɛr] ADJ **1** *Biol (tissu etc)* cell; *Tél* **téléphone c.** cellular phone, cellphone **2** **convoi c.** *(de la police)* police convoy; **voiture c.** police van; **prison** *ou* **régime c.** solitary confinement **3** *(gestion)* divisional
  NM *Can Tél* mobile (phone), cellphone

cellule [selyl] NF **1** *(d'une prison, d'un couvent etc)* cell; *Fig (section politique)* cell, section; *Fig (élément)* unit; *Mil* **dix jours de c.** ten days in the cells *or Fam* the slammer; **il a passé la nuit en c. de dégrisement** he spent a night in the cells to sober up; **les cellules du parti** the party cells; **réunion de c.** cell meeting; *Com* **c. d'achat** purchasing unit; *Aut* **c. de survie** passenger survival cell; **c. de télévente** telesales unit; *Fig* **la c. de la société** the social unit
  2 *Biol* cell; **c. nerveuse** nerve cell; **c. souche** stem cell; **c. somatique** somatic cell; **différenciation des cellules** cell differentiation
  3 *Aviat* airframe
  4 *Phot etc* **c. photoélectrique** photoelectric cell, photocell; *TV* electric eye
  5 *(de tourne-disque etc)* cartridge

cellulite [selylit] NF *Méd* cellulite; **avoir de la c.** to have cellulite; **traitement anti-c.** anti-cellulite treatment

cellulitique [selylitik] ADJ *Méd* **tissu c.** cellulite tissue

Celluloïd® [selylɔid] NM celluloid®

cellulose [selyloz] NF *Chimie, Com* cellulose

cellulosique [selylozik] ADJ *(vernis etc)* cellulose

celte [sɛlt] ADJ Celtic
  N C. Celt

celtique [sɛltik] ADJ Celtic
  NM *Ling* Celtic

CELUI, CELLE, *pl* **ceux, celles** [səlɥi, sɛl, sø, sɛl]. PRON DÉM SEE GRAMMAR A30–1; B14 **1** *(completed by an adj clause)* the one, *pl* those; **c. dont je t'ai parlé** the one *or* the man I told you about; **celle à qui j'ai écrit** the one *or* the woman I wrote to; **c. qui était parti le dernier** the one who started last; **c. que je t'avais re-**

commandé the one *or* the man I had recommended to you; **tous les plats sont sales, prends c. qui est dans le lave-vaisselle** all the dishes are dirty, take the one in the dishwasher

2 *(quiconque)* he, she, *pl* those; **c. qui mange peu dort bien** he who eats little sleeps well **3** *(followed by* de) **mes livres et ceux de Jean** my books and Jean's; **les hommes d'aujourd'hui et ceux d'autrefois** the men of today and those of former times; **le robinet de la cuisine fuit et c. de la salle de bain aussi** the tap in the kitchen's leaking and so is the one in the bathroom; **c. d'entre vous qui habite à Lyon** whichever one of you lives in Lyons; **ceux d'entre vous qui n'ont pas encore payé leur cotisation** those of you who haven't yet paid your subscription

4 *(suivi d'un participe, d'un adjectif, d'un infinitif)* **tous ceux ayant la même idée** all those with the same idea; **toutes les maisons sont en bois sauf celles voisines de l'église** all the houses are built of wood except those near the church

5 c.-ci, *pl* **ceux-ci** *(en indiquant du doigt)* this (one), *pl* these; *(en se référant à qn ou qch précédemment cité)* the latter; **c.-là,** *pl* **ceux-là** *(en indiquant du doigt)* that (one), *pl* those; *(en se référant à qn ou qch précédemment cité)* the former; **ceux-ci coûtent plus cher que ceux-là** these cost more than those do; **ah, c.-là, quel idiot!** he's such an idiot, that one!; **autre exemple, plus technique c.-là** another example, a more technical one this time

cément [semã] NM cement

cémentation [semãtasjɔ̃] NF *Métal* cementation, case hardening

cémenter [semãte] VT *Métal (acier)* to case-harden

CEN [seɑɛn] NM *(abrév* **Comité européen de normalisation)** European Standards Commission

cénacle [senakl] NM **1** *(coterie)* (literary) club, group, *Litt* coterie **2** *Antiq* cenacle; *surtout Bible* Cenacle, upper room of the Last Supper

cendar [sãdar] NM *Fam* ashtray

cendre [sãdr] NF **1** *(de matières brûlées)* ash(es), cinders; **c. de bois** wood ash; **cendres volcaniques** volcanic ash; *Tech* **cendres volantes** fly ash; **des cendres** *ou* **de la c. (de cigarette)** cigarette ash; **faire cuire des marrons sous la c.** to roast chestnuts in the ashes *or* embers; **mettre** *ou* **réduire une ville en cendres** to reduce a town to ashes; **maison réduite en cendres** house burnt to the ground; *Rel* **le mercredi des Cendres** Ash Wednesday; **visage couleur de c.** ashen face **2** cendres *(mortal)* remains, ashes; **ses cendres seront transportées dans sa ville natale** his ashes will be taken to his home town; *Litt* **les cendres du passé** the embers of the past

cendré [sãdre] ADJ ash-grey, ashen, ashy; **blond c.** ash blond

cendrée [sãdre] NF **1** *Sport etc (piste)* cinder track, dirt track; *(mâchefer)* cinders **2** *(cartouche)* dust shot

cendrer [sãdre] VT *(chemin, piste)* to cinder

cendreux, -euse [sãdrø, -øz] ADJ **1** *(gris, terne)* ashen **2** *(qui contient de la cendre)* full of ashes, ashy, gritty

cendrier [sãdrije] NM *(pour fumeurs)* ashtray; *(d'un poêle)* ashpan; *(d'un fourneau)* ash pit *or* hole

Cendrillon [sãdrijɔ̃] NF **1** Cinderella **2** *Vieilli* **c.** (household) drudge, slavey

cène [sɛn] NF **1** *Bible, Beaux-Arts* **la (Sainte) C.** the Last Supper **2** *Rel (pour l'Église protestante)* Holy Communion, Lord's Supper

cenelle [sənɛl] NF *(baie)* haw

cénobite [senɔbit] NM *(moine)* cenobite

cénotaphe [senɔtaf] NM cenotaph

cénozoïque [senɔzɔik] ADJ, NM *Géol* Cenozoic

cens [sãs] NM **1** *Hist (dans le système féodal)* (quit) rent; **c. électoral** = property qualification *(for the franchise)* **2** *Antiq* census

censé [sãse] ADJ supposed; **je ne veux pas qu'il sache que je suis là, je suis censée rester à la maison aujourd'hui** I don't want him to know I'm here, I was supposed to stay at home today; **je ne suis pas c. le savoir** *(cela est au-dessus de mes compétences)* I can't be expected to know that; *(c'est confidentiel)* I'm not supposed to know about it; **nul n'est c. ignorer la loi** ignorance of the law is no excuse

censément [sãsemã] ADV supposedly

censeur [sãsœr] NM **1** *(de la presse etc)* censor **2** *Scol Anciennement (d'un lycée) (homme)* vice-principal, deputy headmaster; *(femme)* vice-principal, deputy headmistress **3** *(juge)* critic, faultfinder; **c'est un c. juste/impartial** he's a fair/impartial critic **4** *Antiq* censor

censitaire [sãsitɛr] *Hist* ADJ **électeur c.** elector qualified by his tax assessment; **suffrage** *ou* **système c.** voting system based on tax quota

NM eligible voter

censurable [sãsyrabl] ADJ open to censure, censurable

censure [sãsyr] NF **1** *(de la presse etc)* censorship; *Cin etc* (board of) censors; *Psy* censor; **c. de l'actualité** news blackout; **visa de c.** censor's certificate **2** *Pol* **voter une motion de c.** to pass a vote of censure *or* no-confidence **3** *Vieilli* censure, blame; **les censures de l'Église** the censure of the Church

censurer [sãsyre] VT **1** *Cin, Psy etc* to censor; *Cin* **c. une scène** to censor *or* cut a scene **2** *Pol* **c. le gouvernement** to pass a vote of no confidence in the government

---

Il faut noter que le verbe anglais **to censure** est un faux ami. Il signifie **critiquer**.

---

cent¹ [sã] SEE GRAMMAR A12–13; B58 ADJ *(takes a plural* s *when multiplied by a preceding numeral but not when followed by another numeral; does not vary when used as an ordinal)* (a *or* one) hundred; **c. élèves** a hundred pupils, one hundred pupils; **deux cents hommes** two hundred men; **deux c. cinquante hommes** two hundred and fifty men; **page deux c.** page two hundred; **l'an trois c.** the year three hundred; **le numéro trois c. gagne** number three hundred is the winner, the winning number is three hundred; **avoir c. ans** to be a hundred (years old); **avoir c. deux ans** to be a hundred and two; **c. un** [sã ɛ̃] one hundred and one; **je te l'ai dit c. fois** (if I've told you once) I've told you a hundred times; **elle a eu c. fois l'occasion de le faire** she's had every chance to do it; **vous avez c. fois raison** you're absolutely right; **je préférerais c. fois lui dire tout ce de suite plutôt qu'attendre demain** I'd much rather tell him right away than wait until tomorrow; **habiter au c. de la rue Henri Martin** to live at number a hundred *or* to live at one hundred rue Henri Martin; **c. fois mieux** a hundred times better; **c'est la même maison, mais en c. fois plus grand** it's the same house, but a hundred times bigger; *Fam* **je ne vais pas t'attendre (pendant) c. sept ans** I'm not going to wait for you for ever; **faire les c. pas** to pace up and down; *Sport* **le c. mètres** the hundred metres; **courir le quatre cents mètres haies** to run the four hundred metre hurdles; *Fam* **être aux c.**

coups to be frantic *or* in a panic; *Fam* **faire les quatre cents coups** to be up to all sorts of tricks; *Fam* **je vous le donne en c.** I'll give you three guesses!, guess!

NM **1** *(nombre)* a hundred; **je te parie à c. contre un que …** I'll give you a hundred to one that …; **sept pour c.** seven per cent; **une augmentation de deux cents pour c.** an increase of two hundred per cent, a two hundred per cent increase; *Chimie* **solution à trente pour c.** thirty per cent solution; **c. pour c.** a hundred per cent; **il est c. pour c. écossais, c'est un Écossais à c. pour c.** he's a hundred per cent Scottish; **je ne suis pas sûr à c. pour c.** I'm not a hundred per cent sure; *Fam* **elle gagne des mille et des cents** she earns a packet *or* a fortune; *Com Vieilli* **un c. d'œufs** a hundred eggs **2** *Écon (unité divisionnaire de l'euro)* cent

cent² [sɛnt] NM *surtout Can (pièce)* cent

centaine [sãtɛn] NF (about a) hundred; **une c. d'euros** about a hundred euros, a hundred euros or so; **des centaines de livres** hundreds of books; **plusieurs centaines de personnes** several hundred people; **quelques centaines d'euros** a few hundred euros; **atteindre la c.** *(d'éléments, de participants etc)* to be about a hundred; **les gens moururent par centaines/par centaines de mille** people died in (their) hundreds/hundreds of thousands *or* by the hundred/hundred thousand; **ils sont arrivés par centaines** they arrived in their hundreds; *Math* **la colonne/le chiffre des centaines** the hundreds column/figure

centaure [sãtɔr] NM *Myth* centaur

centaurée [sãtɔre] NF *(plante)* centaury

centenaire [sãtnɛr] ADJ *(personne, arbre)* a hundred years old, hundred-year-old; *(tradition etc)* age-old; **ma grand-mère est c.** *(elle a cent ans)* my grandmother is a hundred (years old); *(elle a plus de cent ans)* my grandmother is over a hundred (years old); **plusieurs fois c.** hundreds of years old; **toi, tu finiras c.!** you'll live to be a hundred!; **chêne c.** ancient oak

N centenarian

NM centenary, *Am* centennial

centésimal, -ale, -aux, -ales [sãtezimal, -o] ADJ *(fraction, échelle etc)* centesimal; *Méd* **dilution centésimale** dilution to one part per hundred

centiare [sãtjar] NM centiare, metre

centième [sãtjɛm] ADJ *(anniversaire etc)* hundredth

N hundredth

NM hundredth (part); **je n'ai pas compris le c. de ce qu'il disait** I didn't understand a fraction of what he was saying

NF *Théâtre* hundredth performance

centigrade [sãtigrad] NM centigrade

centigramme [sãtigram] NM centigram(me)

centilitre [sãtilitr] NM centilitre, *Am* centiliter

centime [sãtim] NM centime; *(d'euro)* cent; **je ne lui donnerai pas un c.!** I won't give him a penny!; **ne pas avoir un c.** not to have a penny to one's name; *Admin* **centimes additionnels** special surtax

centimètre [sãtimɛtr] NM **1** *(unité de mesure)* centimetre, *Am* centimeter; *Journ* **c. colonne** column centimetre, ≃ column inch **2** *(ruban)* tape measure

centrafricain, -aine [sãtrafrikɛ̃, -ɛn] ADJ Central African; **République centrafricaine** Central African Republic

N **C.** Central African

Centrafrique [sãtrafrik] NM Central African Republic

centrage [sãtraʒ] NM centring, *Am* centering; *Ordinat* **c. sur tabulation** centre tab

central, -ale, -aux, -ales [sɑ̃tral, -o] ADJ central; *(point etc)* middle, central; *(principal)* central, main; **leur appartement occupe une position centrale dans la ville** their flat is located in the centre of the town *or* is centrally located; **quartier c. de la ville** central area of town, town centre; **Amérique/Asie centrale** Central America/Asia; **(prison) centrale** ≃ county jail; **École centrale** = (university level) State school of engineering; **chauffage c.** central heating; **la maison a le chauffage c.** the house has central heating *or* is centrally heated
NM **1 c. téléphonique** telephone exchange; **c. numérique** digital exchange **2** *Tennis* **le c.** the centre court
NF **centrale 1** *Élec* **centrale (électrique)** power station; **centrale thermique/nucléaire/hydraulique** thermal *or* coal-fired/nuclear/hydroelectric power station; **centrale surgénératrice** fast-breeder power station **2** **centrale (syndicale)** group of affiliated trade unions **3** *Scol Fam* **Centrale** = (university level) State school of engineering; **faire Centrale** to go to the École centrale
▸▸ *Com* **centrale d'achat** (central) purchasing *or* buying group; *(au sein d'une même entreprise)* central purchasing department; **centrale d'alerte** *(d'une voiture etc)* warning system; *Aut* **centrale de commande électronique** electronic control unit, ECU; **centrale de réservations** central reservations unit, central reservations office

centralien, -ienne [sɑ̃traljɛ̃, -jɛn] N student of the École centrale

centralisateur, -trice [sɑ̃tralizatœr, -tris] ADJ *(force etc)* centralizing

centralisation [sɑ̃tralizasjɔ̃] NF centralization, centralizing

centraliser [sɑ̃tralize] VT to centralize

centralisme [sɑ̃tralism] NM *Pol* centralism

centraliste [sɑ̃tralist] NM *Pol* centralist

centre [sɑ̃tr] NM **1** *(base etc)*, *Géom, Pol* centre, *Am* center; **cette question est au c. du débat** this question is at the centre of the debate; **il se croit** *ou* **se prend pour le c. du monde!** he thinks (that) the world revolves round him!; **le c. de la ville** the town centre; **les grands centres urbains** the great urban centres; *Pol* **le c. droit/gauche** the centre right/left **2** *Ftbl etc (passe)* **faire un c.** to make a cross **3** *Rugby* centre; **premier/deuxième c.** inside/outside centre
▸▸ **c. d'accueil** *(pour touristes)* visitor centre; *(pour toxicomanes etc)* centre; **c. d'affaires** business centre; *(dans aéroport, hôtel)* business lounge; *Compta* **c. d'analyse** cost centre; *Compta* **c. (d'analyse) auxiliaire/principal** secondary/main cost centre; *Compta* **c. d'analyse opérationnel** operational cost centre; *Compta* **c. d'analyse de structure** fixed cost centre; **c. d'appels** call centre; **c. d'art dramatique** drama centre; **c. d'artisanat** craft centre; **c. d'attraction** *Phys* centre of attraction; *Fig* centre *or* focus of attention; **c. de chèques postaux** PO cheque account centre; *Com* **c. commercial** shopping precinct, shopping centre *or* mall; *Com, Ordinat* **c. commercial électronique** cybermall; **c. de conférences** conference centre; **c. de coût** cost centre; **c. culturel** arts centre; *Météo* **c. de dépression** storm centre; *TV, Radio* **c. de diffusion** broadcasting centre; *Aut* **c. d'essai** test centre; *Phys* **c. de gravitation** centre of attraction; **c. de gravité** centre of gravity; **c. d'hébergement** rescue centre; **c. hospitalier** hospital (complex); **c. hospitalier spécialisé, CHS** psychiatric hospital; **c. hospitalier universitaire** university teaching hospital; **c. des impôts** tax centre *or* office; **c. industriel** industrial centre; **c. d'information** information centre; **c. d'inté-**

rêt centre of interest; **c. d'intérêt touristique** tourist *or* visitor attraction; **c. de loisirs** leisure *or* recreation centre; **c. médical d'urgence** emergency medical service; **c. national de la recherche scientifique** = Science Research Council; **c. de recherche** research centre; **c. sportif** sports centre; **c. de tri** sorting office; *Rail* **c. de triage** shunting *or* marshalling yard; **c. universitaire** university; **c. de vacances** holiday centre

centré [sɑ̃tre] ADJ *Suisse (magasin, appartement)* central

centrer [sɑ̃tre] VT to centre, *Am* to center (**sur** on); *(roues, outils)* to adjust; *Ftbl etc (ballon)* to centre; *Tennis* **balle mal centrée** mishit; **la balle était bien centrée** the ball came right off the centre of his/her racket; **c. un texte sur une page** to centre a text on a page; **centré sur la production/les ventes** production-/sales-orientated *or* -oriented; **roman centré sur un personnage** novel centred *or* based on one character; **c. une discussion sur un sujet** to base *or* focus a discussion on a subject; **c. l'attention du lecteur sur qch** to focus the reader's attention on sth; **être trop centré sur soi-même** to be too self-centred

centre-répéteur, *pl* **centres-répéteurs** [sɑ̃trərepetœr] NM *TV, Radio* relay station

centre-ville, *pl* **centres-villes** [sɑ̃trəvil] NM town centre; *(d'une grande ville)* city centre, *Am* downtown area; **les boutiques du c.** the shops in the town centre, *Am* the downtown stores; **aller dans le c.** to go into the town centre, *Am* to go downtown

centrifugation [sɑ̃trifygasjɔ̃] NF centrifugation, centrifuging

centrifuge [sɑ̃trifyʒ] ADJ *(force etc)* centrifugal

centrifuger [sɑ̃trifyʒe] VT *(liquide)* to centrifuge

centrifugeur [sɑ̃trifyʒœr] NM, **centrifugeuse** [sɑ̃trifyʒøz] NF centrifuge; *(pour jus de fruits etc)* juice extractor

centripète [sɑ̃tripɛt] ADJ *(force etc)* centripetal

centrisme [sɑ̃trism] NM *Pol* centrism

centriste [sɑ̃trist] *Pol* ADJ (of the) centre
N centrist; **les centristes** the centre

centuple [sɑ̃typl] ADJ hundredfold; **mille est c. de dix** a thousand is a hundred times (as much as) ten
NM a hundred times; **je te le rendrai au c.** I'll repay you a hundred times over

centupler [sɑ̃typle] VT & VI to increase a hundredfold *or* a hundredfold

centurion [sɑ̃tyrjɔ̃] NM *Antiq* centurion

CEP [seəpe] NM *Scol Anciennement abrév* **certificat d'études primaires**

cep [sɛp] NM **1 c. de vigne** vinestock, vine plant **2** *Agr (d'une charrue)* sole

cépage [sepaʒ] NM *(variety of)* vine; **les cépages des vignobles bordelais** grapes from the Bordeaux vineyards

cèpe [sɛp] NM *(champignon)* cepe, boletus

cependant [s(ə)pɑ̃dɑ̃] CONJ however, yet, nevertheless, still, though; **c., je l'aime** but I still love him, I love him nevertheless; **le directeur, c., n'est pas d'accord** the manager, however, does not agree; **vous le saviez depuis longtemps, c., vous ne m'avez pas averti** you'd known about it for a long time but *or* and yet you didn't tell me SEE GRAMMAR B57
ADV *Littt* meanwhile, in the meantime; **c. que** while, whilst

céphalée [sefale] NF *Méd* headache

céphalique [sefalik] ADJ cephalic

céphalopode [sefalɔpɔd] NM cephalopod, *pl* cephalopoda

céramique [seramik] ADJ *(arts etc)* ceramic; **industries céramiques** pottery industry
NF *(art)* ceramics, (art of) pottery; *(matière)* ceramic, pottery; *(objet)* ceramic, piece of pottery; **dalles en c.** ceramic tiles
▸▸ *Méd* **c. dentaire** dental ceramics

céramiste [seramist] N ceramist, ceramicist

Cerbère [sɛrbɛr] NM **1** *Myth* Cerberus **2** *Fig* **c.** ill-tempered hall porter/janitor/concierge

CERC [sɛrk] NM *(abrév* **Centre d'études sur les revenus et les coûts)** = government body carrying out research into salaries and the cost of living

cerceau, -eaux [sɛrso] NM **1** *(cercle)* hoop; **c. de jupon** crinoline hoop; **c. de baril** barrel hoop; **jouer au c.** to play with a hoop; **faire rouler un c.** to bowl a hoop **2** *(au-dessus d'un lit)* cradle

cerclage [sɛrklaʒ] NM **1** *(de tonneaux)* hooping **2** *Méd* **c. (du col de l'utérus)** cervical cerclage

cercle [sɛrkl] NM **1** *Math* circle; **le rayon du c.** the radius of the circle; **quart de c.** quadrant; **(arc de) grand c.** great circle; **entourer la bonne réponse d'un c.** to ring *or* put a circle round the correct answer; **former** *ou* **faire un c. (autour de qn/qch)** to form *or* make a circle (around sb/sth); **en c.** in a circle; **les avions décrivaient des cercles dans le ciel** the planes were circling
2 *(d'amis etc)* circle, set; **le c. de la famille** the family circle; **il m'a introduit dans le c. de ses amis** he introduced me to his circle of friends
3 *(association)* club; **c. littéraire** literary circle *or* society; **c. militaire** *ou* **des officiers** officers' club; **fonder un c.** to set up *or* start a society *or* club
4 *(champ, domaine)* **c. d'activités** circle *or* sphere *or* range of activities; **le c. de ses occupations/responsabilités** the range *or* scope of his work/responsibilities
5 *(objet circulaire)* hoop, ring; **c. d'une roue** (wheel) tyre; **c. d'arpenteur** protractor
▸▸ *Géog* **c. (polaire) arctique** Arctic Circle; *Com* **c. de qualité** quality circle; **c. vertueux** virtuous circle; **c. vicieux** vicious circle; **se retrouver** *ou* **tomber dans un c. vicieux** to be caught in a vicious circle *or* in a catch-22 situation

cerclé [sɛrkle] ADJ **tonneau c.** hooped barrel; **lunettes cerclées d'écaille** horn-rimmed spectacles; **yeux cerclés de bistre** eyes with dark rings round them; **des doigts cerclés d'or** gold-ringed fingers

cercler [sɛrkle] VT *(tonneau)* to hoop; **une main de fer cercla son poignet** a steely grip enclosed *or* encircled his wrist

cercueil [sɛrkœj] NM coffin, *surtout Am* casket; **c. plombé** lead casket

céréale [sereal] NF cereal; **commerce des céréales** corn *or* grain trade; **culture des céréales** cereal-growing; **prendre des céréales au petit déjeuner** to have cereal for breakfast

céréalier, -ière [serealje, -jɛr] ADJ *(production etc)* cereal
N cereal grower

cérébelleux, -euse [serebɛlø, -øz] ADJ *Anat (artère etc)* cerebellar

cérébral, -ale, -aux, -ales [serebral, -o] ADJ *(artère etc)* cerebral; **hémorragie cérébrale** brain haemorrhage; **travail c.** intellectual work; **surmenage c.** mental exhaustion; **elle est trop cérébrale** she's too cerebral *or* intellectual
N intellectual, thinker

cérébro-spinal, -ale, -aux, -ales [serebrospinal, -o] ADJ *Anat, Méd* cerebro-spinal

cérémonial, -iale, -ials *ou Rare* **-iaux, -iales** [seremɔnjal, -jo] ADJ *Arch* ceremonial

NM ceremonial; **c. de cour** court etiquette; **selon le c.** in accordance with protocol

cérémonie [seremɔni] **NF** ceremony; **c'était une c. de mariage très réussie** it was a very nice wedding ceremony; **faire une visite de c.** to make a ceremonial *or* formal visit (**à** to); **tenue** *ou* **habit de c.** dress suit; *Mil* **uniforme de c.** (full) dress uniform; **maître de c.** master of ceremonies; *Hum* **à toi de servir, puisque c'est toi le maître de c.** you can be mother and pour; *Fig* **sans c.** *(réception, repas etc)* informal, casual; *(recevoir qn)* informally; *(renvoyer qn etc)* unceremoniously; **faire des cérémonies** to stand on ceremony; **voilà bien des cérémonies pour peu de choses!** what a performance for such a little thing!; **sans plus de c.** without further ado

cérémonieusement [seremɔnjøzmɑ̃] **ADV** ceremoniously, formally

cérémonieux, -ieuse [seremɔnjø, -jøz] **ADJ** ceremonious, formal

cerf [sɛr] **NM** stag, *Litt* hart; *Culin* venison; **c. commun** (red) deer VOIR GRAMMAIRE A12

cerfeuil [sɛrfœj] **NM** *Culin* chervil

cerf-volant, *pl* **cerfs-volants NM 1** *(jeu)* kite; **lancer** *ou* **faire voler un c.** to fly a kite **2** *(insecte)* stag beetle

cerisaie [s(ə)rizɛ] **NF** cherry orchard

cerise [s(ə)riz] **NF** *(fruit)* cherry; **clafoutis aux cerises** cherry clafoutis, cherries baked in batter; **tarte aux cerises** cherry tart; **confiture de cerises** cherry jam; **rouge comme une c.** as red as a beetroot; *Fig* **la c. sur le gâteau** the icing on the cake

ADJ INV cherry(-red), cerise

cerisier [s(ə)rizje] **NM** *(arbre)* cherry tree; *(bois)* cherrywood

cérium [serjɔm] **NM** *Chimie* cerium

CERN [sɛrn] **NM** *(abrév* **Conseil européen pour la recherche nucléaire)** CERN

cerne [sɛrn] **NM 1** *(autour de la lune etc)* ring, circle; **avoir des cernes (sous les yeux)** to have (dark) shadows *or* circles under one's eyes **2** *(d'un arbre)* age ring

cerné [sɛrne] **ADJ** **avoir les yeux cernés** to have (dark) shadows *or* circles under one's eyes

cerneau, -eaux [sɛrno] **NM** *(fruit)* green walnut

cerner [sɛrne] **VT 1** *(armée, ville etc)* to surround; **rendez-vous, vous êtes cernés!** give yourselves up, you're surrounded! **2** *(identifier)* *(question, vérité etc)* to grasp; **il commence à c. le problème** he's starting to see where the problem lies *or* to identify the problem; **une personne difficile à c.** a difficult person to figure out **3** *(noix)* to shell, to husk; *(arbre)* to ring **4** *(entourer)* to ring, to circle; **des silhouettes cernées d'ombre** shadowy figures

céroplastique [seroplastik] **NF** wax modelling

CERS [seɛrɛs] **NF** *(abrév* **Commission européenne de recherche spatiale)** ESRO

CERTAIN, -AINE [sɛrtɛ̃, -ɛn] **ADJ** SEE GRAMMAR B10 **1** *(preuves, nouvelles etc)* certain, definite; **ils vont à un échec/une mort certain(e)** they're heading for certain failure/death; **s'il est bien une chose certaine** if one thing is sure *or* certain; **il est c. qu'elle viendra** it's certain *or* definite that she'll come, she'll definitely come; **il viendra, c'est c.** he'll definitely come; **il devrait venir, mais ce n'est pas c.** he should come, but it's not certain *or* definite; **il a été déçu, c'est c.** he was disappointed, of course *or* for sure; **tenir qch pour c.** *ou* **pour chose certaine** to look on sth as a certainty, to regard sth as definite; *Fam* **c'est sûr et c.** it's absolutely certain; *Fam* **j'en suis sûr et c.** I'm convinced of it; **il est c. de**

partir he's sure *or* certain to leave; **j'en suis c.** I'm sure *or* certain of it; **moi, je n'en suis pas c.** I'm not so sure myself, I'm not entirely convinced

2 *(avant le nom)* some, certain; **certaines gens affirment que ...** some (people) maintain that ...; **il a un c. charme, c'est indéniable** he has a certain charm, that's undeniable; **après un c. temps** after some *or* a certain time, after a while; **jusqu'à un c. point** up to a (certain) point; **dans un c. sens** in a sense, in a way; **je voudrais vous poser un c. nombre de questions** I'd like to ask you a number of *or* some questions; **on retrouve cette tradition dans certains pays** this tradition can be found in a number of *or* in certain countries; **dans certains cas, on ne peut pas le faire** in certain *or* some cases, it can't be done; **d'un c. âge** middle-aged; **il faut un c. courage pour le faire** you need a certain amount of courage to do it; **cela demande quand même un c. culot** it takes some nerve all the same; **c'est quand même à une certaine distance d'ici** it is quite a distance away; **si un c. M. Martin appelle, dites-lui que ...** if a (certain) Mr Martin calls, tell him ...; **une certaine Martine t'a appelé** there was someone called Martine on the phone for you SEE GRAMMAR A35; B15

PRON certains some (people); **certains pensent le contraire** some people think the opposite *or* take the opposite view; **parmi ces gens, certains n'avaient jamais navigué** some of these people had never sailed; **certains d'entre nous/vous** some of us/you SEE GRAMMAR B16

NM *Bourse* fixed direct rate of exchange

certainement [sɛrtɛnmɑ̃] **ADV** *(probablement)* most probably; **c.!** of course!; **c. pas!** certainly not!

> Il faut noter que l'adverbe anglais **certainly** est un faux ami. Il signifie **sans aucun doute**.

certes [sɛrt] **ADV 1** *(sans doute, bien sûr)* **je n'irais c. pas jusqu'à penser que ...** I certainly wouldn't go as far as believing that ...; **c., tout espoir n'est pas perdu ...** we/I/*etc* haven't given up hope, of course, but ...; **il ne pouvait rien faire d'autre – c., mais il fallait qu'il nous en parle** he couldn't do anything else – granted, but he should have spoken to us about it **2** *Vieilli* most certainly; **oui c.!** yes indeed!

certificat [sɛrtifika] **NM** certificate; **montrer ses certificats** *(d'un ouvrier etc)* to show one's references

▸▸ *Scol* **c. d'aptitude pédagogique à l'enseignement secondaire** = secondary school teaching certificate; **c. d'aptitude professionnelle** = vocational training certificate; **c. d'aptitude au professorat de l'enseignement technique** = specialized teaching certificate for technical subjects; **c. d'arrêt de travail** *(pour cause de maladie)* medical certificate; **c. d'assurance** insurance certificate; **c. de bonne vie et mœurs** character reference; **c. de capacité** *(d'employé)* certificate of proficiency; **c. de concubinage** = official document stating that two people are cohabiting; *Com* **c. de dépôt** *(de marchandises)* warehouse warrant; **c. d'entreposage** warehouse warrant; *Aut etc* **c. d'essai** test certificate; *Scol Anciennement* **c. d'études (primaires)** = certificate given after an examination at the end of an elementary course of studies; *Scol Anciennement* **c. d'études supérieures** *(unité de valeur)* = each of the four examinations for the 'licence'; *(diplôme)* = certificate so obtained; **c. de garantie** certificate of guarantee, guarantee certificate, warranty; **c. d'investissement** investment certificate; *Com* **c. de jaugeage** tonnage cer-

tificate; *Scol Anciennement* **c. de licence** *(unité de valeur)* = each of the four examinations for the 'licence'; *(diplôme)* certificate so obtained; *Méd* **c. médical** medical certificate; **c. de navigabilité** *Naut* certificate of seaworthiness; *Aviat* certificate of airworthiness; **c. nominatif d'actions** registered share certificate; **c. de non-paiement** *(de chèque)* notification of unpaid cheque; *(de lettre de change)* certificate of dishonour; **c. d'origine** *Com* certificate of origin; *(d'un chien etc)* pedigree; *Fin* **c. provisoire** share certificate, (provisional) scrip; **c. provisoire d'assurance** cover note; **c. de qualité** certificate of quality; **c. de résidence** certificate of residence; **c. sanitaire** health certificate; *Scol* **c. de scolarité** school attendance record; *Ordinat* **c. de sécurité** security certificate; *Fin* **c. de titres** share certificate; **c. de travail** *(pour certifier qu'on est employé)* attestation of employment; *(pour certifier qu'on a été employé)* employer's reference; **c. de trésorerie** treasury bond; **c. de vaccination** vaccination certificate; **c. de valeur** certificate of value; *Aut* **c. de vérification du kilométrage** mileage verification certificate

certificateur [sɛrtifikatœr] **NM** *Jur* certifier, guarantor

certification [sɛrtifikasjɔ̃] **NF** *Jur, Com* certification, authentication; **c. d'une signature** witnessing of a signature

certifié, -ée [sɛrtifje] *Scol* **ADJ** **professeur c.** = qualified teacher

N qualified teacher

certifier [sɛrtifje] **VT** *(impf, pr sub* **n. certifiions, v. certifiiez)** *(document)* to certify; **c. une signature** to witness *or* authenticate a signature; *Jur* **copie certifiée conforme** certified true copy *(of an original document)*; **c. une caution** to guarantee a surety; **c. qch à qn** to assure sb of sth; **il m'a certifié que la procédure était légale** he assured me the procedure was legal

certitude [sɛrtityd] **NF** certainty, certitude; **j'en ai la c.** I'm certain *or* sure of it; **dire qch avec c.** to speak with assurance

cérumen [serymɛn] **NM** *Physiol* earwax, *Spéc* cerumen

céruse [seryz] **NF** ceruse, white lead; **blanc de c.** white lead

cerveau, -eaux [sɛrvo] **NM** *Anat* brain; *(esprit)* mind, intellect, brains; *Fam (personne)* brain; *(d'un projet etc)* mastermind; **avoir une tumeur au c.** to have a brain tumour; **rhume de c.** cold in the head, head cold; **vin qui monte au c.** strong wine; **faire travailler son c.** to use one's brain; *Fam* **homme à c. étroit** *ou* **vide** man of limited intelligence, empty-headed man; *Fam* **avoir le c. dérangé** *ou* **fêlé** to be mad *or* cracked *or* nuts; **c'est un c., elle pense à tout** she's a genius, she thinks of everything; **c. électronique** electronic brain

▸▸ **c. antérieur** forebrain; **c. moyen** midbrain; **c. postérieur** hindbrain

cervelas [sɛrvəla] **NM** *Culin* saveloy

cervelet [sɛrvəlɛ] **NM** *Anat* cerebellum

cervelle [sɛrvɛl] **NF** *Anat (substance)* brain; *(esprit)* mind, intellect, brains; *Culin* **c. d'agneau** lamb's brains; **se brûler** *ou* **se faire sauter la c.** to blow one's brains out; **se creuser la c.** to rack one's brains; *Fam* **idée qui me trotte dans la c.** idea running through my head; **sans c.** brainless, dimwitted; **elle n'a rien** *ou* **n'a pas grand-chose dans la c.** she's got nothing between her ears; **avoir une c. de moineau** to be feather-brained *or* scatterbrained *or* empty-headed

cervical, -ale, -aux, -ales [sɛrvikal, -o] **ADJ** *Anat* cervical

cervidé [sɛrvide] NM cervid; **les cervidés** the deer family, *Spéc* Cervidae

Cervin [sɛrvɛ̃] NM **le (mont) C.** the Matterhorn

cervoise [sɛrvwaz] NF *Antiq* barley beer

CES [seɛs] NM **1** *Scol* (*abrév* **collège d'enseignement secondaire**) ≃ secondary school, *Am* ≃ high school **2** *abrév* **contrat emploi-solidarité**

ces *voir* **ce²**

César [sezar] NM **1** *Hist* **Jules C.** Julius Caesar **2** *Cin* = French cinema award

césarien, -ienne [sezarjɛ̃, -jɛn] ADJ *Hist* Caesarean ▪ NF *Méd* **césarienne** Caesarean (section), *Fam* C section; **on lui a fait une césarienne** she had a Caesarean; **elle est née par césarienne** she was born by Caesarean, she was a Caesarean

césium [sezjɔm] NM *Chimie* caesium

cessant [sesɑ̃] ADJ **toute(s) affaire(s)** *ou* **chose(s) cessante(s)** immediately

cessation [sesasjɔ̃] NF cessation; **c. de paiements** suspension of payments; **cette entreprise est en c. de paiements** the company is unable to meet its financial obligations; **c. d'entreprise** ceasing of trading; **après la c. de l'entreprise** after the company ceased trading; **fermé pour cause de c. d'activité** business closed down; **c. des hostilités** ceasefire

cesse [sɛs] NF **1 sans c.** constantly, continually, incessantly; **il est sans c. en train de travailler** he's constantly *or* continually working, he works incessantly; **il a plu sans c. pendant les vacances** it rained non-stop during the holidays; **il parle sans c.** he never stops talking, he talks non-stop **2** *Litt* **il n'aura (pas) de c. qu'il ne réussisse** he won't stop *or* rest until he has succeeded

cesser [sese] VI to cease, to stop; **le vent a cessé** the wind has died down; **faire c. qch** to put a stop to sth; **la douleur devrait bientôt c.** the pain should go away *or* stop soon; **il faudra que ça cesse** this has to stop; **faire c. une rumeur** to scotch a rumour ▪ VT **c. le travail** (*pour grève*) to walk out, to down tools; **c. les affaires** to close down; **c. toutes relations avec qn** to break off all relations with sb; **c. les paiements** to stop *or* suspend *or* discontinue payment(s); **cessez ces cris!** stop that shouting!; *Mil* **cessez le feu!** cease fire!; **c. de faire qch** to stop doing sth; **il n'a pas cessé de neiger pendant plusieurs jours** it didn't stop snowing for several days; **c. de fumer** to give up *or* stop smoking; **il n'a pas cessé de nous observer** he's been watching us all this time; **je n'ai jamais cessé de les voir** I've never stopped seeing them; *Litt* **ne c. de faire qch** to keep doing sth, to persist in doing sth; **il ne cesse de le dire et je pense qu'il a raison** he never stops saying so and I think he's right

cessez-le-feu [seselfø] NM INV ceasefire

cessible [sesibl] ADJ *Jur* transferable, assignable; (*pension etc*) negotiable

cession [sesjɔ̃] NF *Jur* transfer, assignment; **faire c. de qch à qn** to transfer *or* assign *or* surrender sth to sb; **acte de c.** certificate *or* deed of transfer; **c. de bail** leaseback; *Com* **c. de licence** licensing; **c. de licence de marque** corporate licensing; *Mktg* **c. de licence de nom** name licensing; **c. de parts** sale *or* disposal of securities; **c. d'actifs** sale of assets

cession-bail, *pl* **cessions-baux** NF *Fin* leaseback

cessionnaire [sesjɔnɛr] N **1** *Com* transferee, assignee; (*d'un effet de commerce, d'une créance*) holder; *Jur* assignee, cessionary **2** (*d'un chèque*) endorser

c'est-à-dire [setadir] CONJ that is (to say),

i.e.; **un parent, c. son oncle** a relative, that is to say, his uncle; **vous l'avez prévenu? – c. que non** did you let him know? – well, actually, I'm afraid I didn't; **c. que je n'étais pas au courant** the thing is that no one told me; **j'ai raté mon train, c. que je serai en retard** I missed my train so I'll be late; **elle m'en veut – c. qu'elle t'a attendue deux heures** she's annoyed with me – well, you did keep her waiting for two hours; **il m'agace! – c.?** he gets on my nerves! – what do you mean by that?

césure [sezyr] NF caesura; *Ordinat* break, hyphenation; *Ordinat* **c. automatique** soft hyphen; *Ordinat* **c. imposée** hard hyphen; *Ordinat* **c. interactive** interactive *or* prompted hyphenation

CET [seɔte] NM *Scol Anciennement* (*abrév* **collège d'enseignement technique**) ≃ technical college

cet *voir* **ce²**

cétacé [setase] ADJ, NM *Zool* cetacean

cétane [setan] NM cetane

C et F (*abrév* **coût et fret**) C&F

cette *voir* **ce²**

ceux *voir* **celui**

cévenol, -ole [sevnɔl] ADJ (*habitant, natif*) of the Cévennes ▪ N **C.** (*habitant*) inhabitant of the Cévennes; (*natif*) native of the Cévennes

Ceylan [selɑ̃] NM *Anciennement* Ceylon

cézigue [sezig] PRON *Fam* his lordship, *Br* his nibs

cf cf

CFA [seɛfa] (*abrév* **Communauté financière africaine**) **franc C.** CFA franc

CFAO [seɛfao] NF (*abrév* **conception et fabrication assistées par ordinateur**) CADCAM

CFC [seɛfse] NMPL *Chimie* (*abrév* **chlorofluorocarbures**) CFCs

CFDT [seɛfdete] NF (*abrév* **Confédération française démocratique du travail**) = French trade union

CFF [seɛfɛf] NMPL *Suisse Rail* (*abrév* **Chemins de fer fédéraux**) = Swiss railways

CFP [seɛfpe] NM (*abrév* **centre de formation professionnelle**) = training centre

CFTC [seɛftese] NF (*abrév* **Confédération française des travailleurs chrétiens**) = French trade union

CGC [seʒese] NF (*abrév* **Confédération générale des cadres**) = French trade union of managerial staff

CGI [seʒei] NM *Admin* (*abrév* **Code général des impôts**) general tax code ▪ NF *Ordinat* (*abrév* **common gateway interface**) CGI

CGT [seʒete] NF (*abrév* **Confédération générale du travail**) = French trade union

chablon [ʃablɔ̃] NM *Suisse* (*pochoir*) stencil

chabot [ʃabo] NM (*poisson*) (*de mer*) bullhead; (*d'eau douce*) chub

chabrot [ʃabro] NM **faire c.** = to finish one's soup by adding wine to it and drinking it straight from the bowl

chacal, -als [ʃakal] NM *aussi Fig* jackal

cha-cha-cha [tʃatʃatʃa] NM INV *Mus* cha-cha(-cha)

chacon(n)e [ʃakɔn] NF *Mus* chaconne

chacun, -une [ʃakœ̃, -yn] PRON INDÉF **1** (*chaque personne d'un groupe*) each (one), every one; **chacune d'elles a refusé** each (one) *or* every one of them refused; **trois euros c.** three euros each; **ils ont pris c. son** *ou* **leur chapeau** each of them took their *or* *Fml* hat, they each took their hat; **nous avons pris c. notre chapeau** each of us took our *or* *Fml* his hat, we each took our hat; **ils ont c.**

leurs qualités et leurs défauts they each have their good and bad points; **ils sont partis c. de son** *ou* **de leur côté** they (each *or* all) went their separate ways VOIR GRAMMAIRE A35–6 **2** (*tout le monde*) everybody, everyone; **c. pour soi** every man for himself; **c. ses goûts** everyone to their own taste; **c. son tour** each in turn; **on est passé c. son tour** everyone went past in turn; **c. son tour!** wait your turn!; *Fam* **tout un c.** all and sundry, every Tom, Dick and Harry; **c'est à la portée de tout un c.** it's within everyone's reach

chaebol [kebɔl] NM *Écon* chaebol

chafouin [ʃafwɛ̃, -in] ADJ (*air*) foxy, sly; **personne à la mine chafouine** foxy- *or* sly-looking person

chagatte [ʃagat] NF *Vulg* pussy, snatch, *Br* fanny

chagrin¹ [ʃagrɛ̃] ADJ *Litt* chagrined; *Vieilli* sad, downcast; **esprits chagrins** malcontents ▪ NM (*peine*) grief, sorrow, *Fml* affliction; *Vieilli* vexation, chagrin; **avoir du c.** to be sorrowful, to grieve; **il a un gros c.** (*d'un enfant*) he's very upset; **faire du c. à qn** to grieve *or* distress sb; **usé par le c.** careworn; **mourir de c.** to die of grief *or* of a broken heart; **un c. d'amour** an unhappy love affair

chagrin² NM (*cuir*) shagreen

chagrinant [ʃagrinɑ̃] ADJ distressing; *Vieilli* annoying, vexing

chagriner¹ [ʃagrine] VT (*peiner*) to grieve, to distress; *Vieilli* to vex, to annoy; (*chiffonner*) to worry, to bother; **cela me chagrine lorsque je vois que ...** it grieves *or* pains me when I see that ...; **je ne voulais pas vous c. en vous le disant** I didn't want to upset you by telling you ▪ VPR **se chagriner** (*se désoler*) to grieve; (*s'inquiéter*) to fret; *Can* **le temps se chagrine** it's clouding over, it's getting cloudy

chagriner² VT (*cuir*) to shagreen, to grain

chah [ʃa] NM shah

chahut [ʃay] NM *Fam* racket, din; **faire du c.** to make a din, to kick up a din *or* a racket *or* a rumpus, to create an uproar; **les élèves ont fait un c. pour protester contre la décision** the pupils kicked up a racket to show their disapproval of the decision

chahuter [ʃayte] *Fam* VI to make a din, to kick up a din *or* a racket *or* a rumpus, to create an uproar ▪ VT (*orateur*) to heckle, to boo, to barrack; **se faire c.** (*d'orateur*) to be *or* get heckled; **les filles se sont fait c. par les garçons** the boys gave the girls a hard time; **elle se fait c. par ses élèves** she can't control her pupils

chahuteur, -euse [ʃaytœr, -øz] *Fam* ADJ (*étudiant etc*) rowdy, disorderly ▪ N rowdy (person); (*dans un meeting politique*) heckler

chai [ʃɛ] NM wine and spirits store(house)

chaînage [ʃɛnaʒ] NM **1** (*arpentage*) chaining, chain measuring **2** *Constr* (*des murs*) tying, clamping; (*armature*) tie irons, (series of) clamps, ties **3** *Ordinat* chaining; (*de commandes*) piping

chaîne [ʃɛn] NF **1** (*d'acier, d'or etc*) chain; *Naut* cable; **la c. saute facilement** (*sur ma bicyclette*) the chain keeps coming off; **mettre un chien à la c.** to chain up a dog; **briser ses chaînes** to break free from one's chains; *Fig* to throw off one's chains *or* shackles; **faire la c.** (*pour faire passer des seaux etc*) to form a chain; *Ind* **travail/travailleur à la c.** assembly line *or* production line work/worker; **travailler à la c.** to work on the assembly *or* production line; *Naut* **le navire a cassé sa c.** the ship has parted her cable **2** (*série*) (*d'hôtels, de magasins, de petits lacs*) chain; **une grande c. de supermarchés**

a large supermarket chain; *Com* **c. intégrée** corporate-operated group; **c. volontaire** consortium; **c. volontaire de détaillants** voluntary retailer chain; **c. d'idées** train of thought; **réaction en c.** chain reaction **3** *(par correspondance)* chain letter **4** *Chimie, Électron etc* chain **5** *TV* channel; **c. de télévision** television channel; **je regarde la première c.** I'm watching channel one; **changeons de c.** let's change channel; **qu'est-ce qu'il y a sur les autres chaînes?;** what's on the other channels?; **c. publique/à péage** *ou* **payante** public *or* state-owned/subscription *or* pay channel; **c. à la carte** pay-per-view channel; **c. commerciale** commercial channel; **c. d'information continue** news channel; **c. de cinéma** movie channel; **c. de jeux (interactifs)** (interactive) games channel; **c. musicale** music channel; **c. de télé-achat** shopping channel; **c. généraliste** general-interest channel; **c. numérique** digital channel; **c. ouverte** public access channel; **c. par satellite** satellite channel; **c. spécialisée** specialized *or* specialist channel; **c. thématique** thematic *or* theme *or* specialist channel **6** *Tex* warp **7** *Ordinat* string; **c. de caractères** character string; **c. de recherche** search string; **c. à rechercher** search string

▸▸**c. alimentaire** food chain; **c. d'arpenteur** surveying chain, surveyor's chain; *Aviat* **c. de charters** back-to-back; *Aut* **c. de distribution** timing *or* camshaft chain; *Ind* **c. de fabrication** production line; *Ind* **c. du froid** cold chain; **c. (haute-fidélité)** hi-fi; **c. laser** CD system; *Ind* **c. de montage** assembly line; **c. de montagnes** range *or* chain of mountains; **c. de montre** watch chain; *Aut* **chaînes à neige** snow chains; *Ling* **c. parlée** speech chain; *Naut* **c. de port** harbour (chain) boom; **c. de solidarité** network of support; **c. de sûreté** door chain, safety chain; **c. de vélo** bicycle chain

chaîner [ʃene] VT **1** *Constr (murs etc)* to tie **2** *Aut* to put chains on **3** *Ordinat (fichiers)* to join; *(commandes)* to pipe

chaînette [ʃenɛt] NF **1** *(bijou, petite chaîne etc)* small chain; **c. antivol** chain lock **2** *Math* **(arc en) c.** catenary (curve) **3** *Couture* **point de c.** chain stitch

chaînon [ʃenɔ̃] NM **1** *(dans une chaîne)* link; *Fig* **le c. manquant** the missing link **2** *Géog (de montagnes)* secondary chain

chair [ʃɛr] NF **1** *(chez l'homme et les animaux)* flesh; *(de pêche, de melon etc)* flesh, pulp; **en c. et en os** in the flesh, in person; **être (bien) en c.** *(d'un poulet)* to be nice and plump; *(d'une personne)* to be plump *or Fam* tubby; *Fig* **n'être ni c. ni poisson** to be neither fish nor fowl (nor good red herring); **une odeur de c. fraîche** a smell of fresh meat; *Fig* **il aime la c. fraîche** *(d'un séducteur)* he likes them young **2** *Beaux-Arts* **chairs** flesh tints **3** *Rel* body, *Péj* flesh; **la résurrection de la c.** the resurrection of the body; *Bible* **le Verbe s'est fait c.** the Word was made flesh; **c. de sa c.** his own flesh and blood; **souffrir dans sa c.** to suffer in the flesh; **la c. est faible** the flesh is weak; **péché de c.** sin of the flesh; **œuvre de c.** carnal knowledge

ADJ INV **(couleur) c.** flesh-coloured, *Am* flesh-colored

▸▸**c. à canon** cannon fodder; **c. à pâté** sausagemeat; **c. de poule** gooseflesh, goose pimples, *Am* goose bumps; **cela vous donne** *ou* **on en a la c. de poule** it gives you goose pimples, it makes your flesh creep, *Fam* it gives you the creeps; **c. à saucisses** sausagemeat; *Fig Fam* **je vais en faire de la c. à saucisses** I'll make mincemeat of him

chaire [ʃɛr] NF **1** *(dans une église)* pulpit; **monter en c.** to go up into the pulpit **2** *Univ (fonction)* chair, professorship; *(tribune)* chair; **elle a été nommée à la c. d'anglais** she has been appointed to the chair of English; **être titulaire d'une c.** to hold a chair **3** *(trône)* chair, throne; **la c. de saint Pierre, la c. pontificale** the Chair of St Peter, the Holy See; **c. d'un évêque** bishop's throne

chaise [ʃɛz] NF **1** *(siège)* chair, seat; **c. de paille/cannée** straw/cane chair; **prenez donc une c.** have *or* take a seat, *Fig* **être assis ou très Fam avoir le cul entre deux chaises** to be in an awkward position; **porter qn en c., faire la c. à qn** to give sb a chair; **(jeu des) chaises musicales** (game of) musical chairs **2** *Naut etc* rope sling; **nœud de c.** bowline hitch

▸▸**c. à bascule** rocking chair; *Can* **c. berçante/berceuse** rocking chair; **c. de cuisine** kitchen chair; *Jur* **c. électrique** electric chair; **passer à la c. électrique** to go to the (electric) chair; **c. d'enfant** (baby's) high chair; **c. haute** (baby's) high chair; **c. de jardin** garden chair; **c. longue** chaise longue; *(transatlantique)* deckchair; **faire de la c. longue** to have a rest, to put one's feet up; **c. percée** (night) commode; **c. pivotante** swivel chair; **c. à porteurs** sedan chair; **c. de poste** post chaise; **c. roulante** wheelchair

chaisier, -ière [ʃezje, -jɛr] N chairmaker NF *Vieilli* **chaisière** *(dans un jardin public etc)* chair attendant

chaland¹ [ʃalɑ̃] NM *Naut* barge, lighter; **transport par chalands** lighterage

chaland², -ande [-ɑ̃d] N *Vieilli* client; **attirer le c.** to attract customers *or* custom

chalandage [ʃalɑ̃daʒ] NM *Com* shopping

chalazion [ʃalazjɔ̃] NM *Méd* chalazion

chaldaïque [kaldaik] ADJ Chaldean N **C.** Chaldean

Chaldée [kalde] NF *Hist, Géog* Chaldea

chaldéen, -enne [kaldeɛ̃, -ɛn] ADJ Chaldean NM *Ling* Chaldean N **C.** Chaldean

châle [ʃal] NM shawl

chalet [ʃalɛ] NM **1** *(de montagne etc)* chalet **2** *Can* cottage **3** *Arch* **c. de nécessité** public convenience

chaleur [ʃalœr] NF **1** *(température)* heat, warmth; *Fig* warmth; *(d'un plaidoyer etc)* passion; **c. sèche/humide** dry/humid heat; **il fait une c. terrible dans ces dortoirs** it's terribly hot in these dormitories; **tu ne vas pas sortir par cette c.?** you're not going out in this heat, are you?; **vague de c.** heatwave; **il fait une c. lourde/accablante** it's very muggy/it's oppressively hot; **craint la c.** *(sur une étiquette)* store in a cool place; **c. spécifique/latente** specific/latent heat; *Méd* **éprouver des chaleurs, avoir des bouffées de c.** *(d'une femme ménopausée)* to have hot flushes; **sensation de c.** *(après un bain froid etc)* glow; **on a une impression de c. dès qu'on enfile ces gants** you feel warm as soon as you put these gloves on; *Méd* **coup de c.** heatstroke; **les chaleurs** the hot weather; **pendant les grandes chaleurs** during the hot season; **c. de coloris** warmth of colour; **rechercher la c. humaine** to look for human warmth; **parler avec c.** to speak warmly *or* enthusiastically; **il sera accueilli avec c.** he will receive a warm welcome **2** *(des animaux)* heat, rut; **en c.** on heat, *surtout Am* in heat; *Fig Vulg* **il/elle est en c., celui-là/celle-là!** he's/she's randy *or* horny *or* on heat, that one!

▸▸**c. animale** body heat; *Phys* **c. atomique d'un corps** atomic heat of a body

chaleureusement [ʃalørøzmɑ̃] ADV warmly

chaleureux, -euse [ʃalørø, -øz] ADJ *(accueil etc)* warm, cordial, hearty; *(termes, paroles)* glowing; *(applaudissements etc)* enthusiastic; **remercier qn en termes c.** to thank sb warmly

châlit [ʃali] NM bedstead

challenge [ʃalɑ̃ʒ] NM **1** *Sport* challenge match, tournament **2** *Fig (défi)* challenge; **c'est un réel c. que de vouloir changer de travail à son âge** it's a real challenge to want to change jobs at his age

challenger [tʃalɑ̃dʒɛr] NM *Sport etc* challenger

chaloir [ʃalwar] V IMPERS *Arch, Litt (used only in)* **peu me chaut, peu m'en chaut** I don't give a fig, I care not

chaloupe [ʃalup] NF *Naut* launch, longboat, tender; *(à rames)* rowing boat, *Am* rowboat; **c. de sauvetage** lifeboat; **c. à moteur** motor launch; **c. de pêche** fishing boat

chaloupé [ʃalupe] ADJ *(danse, démarche)* swaying

chalumeau, -eaux [ʃalymo] NM **1** *Tech* blowlamp, blowtorch; **faire une soudure au c.** to weld with a blowlamp; **c. oxyacétylénique** oxyacetylene torch **2** *Mus* pipe **3** *Vieilli (paille)* (drinking) straw; **c. de roseau** reed **4** *Can* spout *(for collecting sap of maple tree)*

chalut [ʃaly] NM *Pêche* trawl; **pêcher au c.** to trawl

chalutage [ʃalytaʒ] NM *Pêche* trawling

chalutier [ʃalytje] NM *(bateau)* trawler; *(pêcheur)* trawlerman

chamade [ʃamad] NF **mon cœur battait la c.** my heart was thumping *or* beating wildly

chamailler (se) [səʃamɑje] VPR *Fam* to bicker, to squabble

chamaillerie [ʃamɑjri] NF *Fam (dispute)* squabble, row

chamailleur, -euse [ʃamɑjœr, -øz] ADJ quarrelsome N quarrelsome person, squabbler

chaman [ʃaman] NM *Rel* shaman

chamanisme [ʃamanism] NM *Rel* shamanism

chamarré [ʃamare] ADJ richly- *or* brightly-coloured *or Am* -colored; **c. d'or** with gold brocade

chamarrer [ʃamare] VT *Litt* to bedeck, to adorn

chambard [ʃɑ̃bar] NM *Fam* **1** *(désordre)* disorder, shambles; *(bouleversement)* upset, upheaval **2** *(bruit)* din, racket; **faire du c.** to make *or* kick up a row; *Fig* **ça va faire du c. quand il l'apprendra!** there'll be an unholy row when he finds out *or* hell to pay when he finds out!

chambardement [ʃɑ̃bardəmɑ̃] NM *Fam* upset, upheaval; **un grand c. d'idées** a great shake-up of ideas

chambarder [ʃɑ̃barde] VT *Fam (mettre en désordre) (maison etc)* to turn upside down, to ransack; *(révolutionner) (un ordre établi, la société)* to turn upside down; **tout c.** to turn everything upside down; **c. les plans de qn** to upset sb's applecart

chambellan [ʃɑ̃belɑ̃] NM chamberlain

chambouler [ʃɑ̃bule] VT *Fam (projets, maison etc)* to turn upside down; **il a fallu c. toutes nos vacances à cause de lui** he completely messed up our holiday plans; **tout est chamboulé** everything's all topsy-turvy *or* upside down

chambranle [ʃɑ̃brɑ̃l] NM *(d'une porte, d'une fenêtre)* frame; *(d'une cheminée)* mantelpiece

chambre [ʃɑ̃br] NF **1** *(pièce)* bedroom; *(d'un hôtel etc)* room; **c. à coucher** *(pièce)* bedroom; *(mobilier)* bedroom furniture; **c.**

d'amis spare (bed)room, guest room; **c. d'enfants** children's room; *(pour bébé)* nursery; **c. meublée** furnished room, *Br* bedsit(ter); **c. de bonne** maid's room; *(petit appartement)* attic room; **c. pour deux personnes** *ou* **double** double room; **c. à deux lits** room with twin beds, twin-bedded room; **c. pour une personne** *ou* **à un lit, c. individuelle** single room; **c. à lits jumeaux** twin(-bedded) room; **chambres attenantes** adjoining rooms; **chambres communicantes** connecting rooms; **c. avec petit déjeuner** bed and breakfast; **vous auriez une c. (de) libre?** do you have any vacancies?; **faire c. à part** to sleep in separate rooms; **faire sa c.** to clean (out) *or* tidy (up) one's room; **garder la c.** to keep to one's room; **travailler en c.** to work at home; **ouvrier en c.** homeworker; **sportif/stratège en c.** armchair sportsman/strategist; **musique de c.** chamber music

2 *Admin, Jur* chamber, house, division of a court of justice

3 *Pol* **la C.** the House; **siéger à la C.** to sit in the House

4 *Physiol (de l'œil)* chamber

5 *Tech (d'un fusil, d'une serrure etc)* chamber; **pneu sans c.** tubeless tyre

6 *Belg, Suisse (pièce quelconque)* room; **une maison de six c.** a six-roomed house

▸▸ *Jur* **c. d'accusation** court of criminal appeal; **c. d'agriculture** = farmers' association; **c. à air** *(d'un pneu)* inner tube; *Aut* **c. d'air** air *or* plenum chamber; *Aut* **c. d'alimentation** feed chamber; **c. ardente** ≃ Star Chamber; *Parl* **C. basse** Lower House, Lower Chamber; *Phys* **c. à bulles** bubble chamber; *Aut* **c. de carburation** mixing chamber; *Naut* **c. des cartes** charthouse, chart room; **c. de chauffe** boiler room; *Naut* stokehold; **c. claire** camera lucida; *Fin* **c. de clearing** clearing house; *Tech* **c. de combustion** *ou* **d'explosion** combustion chamber; **C. de commerce (internationale)** (International) Chamber of Commerce; *Fin* **c. de compensation** clearing house; *Fin* **c. de compensation automatisée** automated clearing house; *Jur* **c. correctionnelle** District Court; *Anciennement* **c. des députés** Chamber of Deputies; **c. d'écho** echo chamber; **c. forte** safety vault, strong room; **c. frigorifique** *ou* **froide** cold (storage) room, cold store; **c. à gaz** gas chamber; *Parl* **C. haute** Upper House, Upper Chamber; **c. d'hôte** bed and breakfast; *Nucl* **c. d'ionisation** ionization chamber; *Suisse* **c. à lessive** *(buanderie)* laundry room; **c. des machines** engine room; **c. de mélange** mixing chamber; **c. des métiers** ≃ guild chamber; **c. noire** *Phot* darkroom; *TV, Cin* loading room; *Jur* **c. des requêtes** appeal court; *Aut* **c. de résonance** resonating chamber; *Aut* **c. de turbulence** swirl chamber, turbulence combustion chamber; **c. de vapeur** steam room

chambrée [ʃɑ̃bre] NF **1** *(occupants d'une chambre)* room(ful) **2** *Mil* barrackroom

chambrer [ʃɑ̃bre] VT **1 c. un vin** to bring wine to room temperature; **chambré** at room temperature **2** *Fam (se moquer de)* **c. qn** to pull sb's leg **3** *Vieilli* **c. qn** to confine sb, to lock sb up, to keep sb locked up

chambrette [ʃɑ̃bret] NF little (bed)room

chambrière [ʃɑ̃brijer] NF **1** *Arch* chambermaid **2** *(fouet)* long whip, lunging whip

chameau, -eaux [ʃamo] NM *Zool* camel; **en** *ou* **à dos de c.** on camel (back); **quel c.!** *(d'un homme)* what a bastard!; *(d'une femme)* what a cow *or* bitch!

ADJ *Fam* **ce qu'il/qu'elle est c.!** what a bastard he is/bitch she is!; **ce qu'il peut être c. avec elle!** he can be such a bastard to her!

chamelier [ʃaməlje] NM camel-driver, cameleer

chamelle [ʃamɛl] NF she-camel

chamois [ʃamwa] NM **1** *Zool* chamois; **(peau de) c.** chamois leather, shammy (leather) **2** *Sport* **c. d'or/d'argent/de bronze** = gold/silver/bronze skiing proficiency medal

ADJ INV buff

champ¹ [ʃɑ̃] NM **1** *Agr* field; **c. de blé** field of wheat, wheatfield; **fleur des champs** wild flower; **courir les champs** to wander about the country; **aux champs** in the fields; **prendre** *ou* **couper à travers champs** to go *or* cut across country; **prendre la clef des champs** to run off, to decamp; **en plein(s) champ(s)** in the open (fields); **à tout bout de c.** repeatedly, at every possible opportunity; *Fig* **laisser le c. libre à qn** to leave the field free for sb, to give sb a free hand; **son assistante a le c. libre** his assistant has a free hand *or* rein; **donner le c. libre à qch** to give free rein to sth; *Fig* **le c. est libre** the coast's clear

2 *(espace)* **prendre du c.** to give oneself (plenty of) room *(pour sauter* to jump); **donnez-moi du c.** give me (some) elbow room

3 *Fig (domaine)* field; **ses lectures embrassent un c. très étendu** his reading covers a very wide field *or* a very wide range of subjects; **élargir le c. de son activité** to extend the scope *or* range of one's activities; **le c. de la connaissance** the field of (human) knowledge

4 *Cin etc* shot, picture; *Opt (d'un télescope etc)* field; **c. optique** *ou* **visuel** *ou* **de vision** field of view *or* of vision; *Phot* **profondeur de c.** depth of focus; **hors c.** off camera; **en dehors du c.** out of shot *or* vision; **être dans le c.** to be in shot; **sortir du c.** to go out of shot; **récit hors c.** voice over

5 *Élec, Électron, Radio* field

6 *Ordinat* field; **c. d'action** sensitivity; **c. alphanumérique** alphanumeric(al) field; **c. calculé** calculated field; **c. mémo** memo field; **c. numérique** numeric field; **c. de saisie** form field; **c. de texte** text field; **c. variable** variable field

7 *Beaux-Arts (d'un tableau)* field, ground; *Hér (d'armoiries)* field

8 *Chir* **c. opératoire** field of operation

▸▸ **c. d'aviation** airfield; *Mil* **c. de bataille** battlefield; *Hist* **c. clos** lists; **c. de courses** racecourse, *Am* racetrack; **c. de foire** fairground; **c. de glace** icefield; *Mil* **c. d'honneur** battlefield; **mort** *ou* **tombé au c. d'honneur** killed in action; *Phys* **c. magnétique** magnetic field; **c. de manœuvres** drill *or* exercise *or* parade ground; **c. de mines** minefield; **c. de neige** snowfield; *Ling* **c. sémantique** semantic field; **c. de tir** firing *or* shooting range; *Mil* practice ground; *(d'un fusil)* field of fire

champ² [ʃɑ̃p] NM *Fam (abrév* **champagne)** bubbly, *Br* champers

Champagne [ʃɑ̃paɲ] NF **1** *(région)* Champagne; **C. humide** wet Champagne; **C. pouilleuse** dry Champagne **2** *(eau-de-vie)* **fine c.** liqueur brandy

NM (vin de) C. champagne

champagnisation [ʃɑ̃paɲizasjɔ̃] NF champagnization

champagniser [ʃɑ̃paɲize] VT *(vin)* to champagnize

champenois, -oise [ʃɑ̃pənwa, -waz] ADJ **1** *(de la région)* of Champagne **2 méthode champenoise** (natural) champagnization method, champagne method

N C. *(natif)* native of Champagne; *(habitant)* inhabitant of Champagne

champêtre [ʃɑ̃pɛtr] ADJ rustic, rural; **vie c.** country life; *Admin* **garde c.** country *or* village policeman

champignon [ʃɑ̃piɲɔ̃] NM **1** *Bot* **c. (comestible)** mushroom; **c. vénéneux** poisonous mushroom, toadstool; *Fig* **pousser comme**

un c. to (spring up like a) mushroom; *Fig* **ville c.** mushroom *or* boom town **2** *Méd* fungus, fungoid growth VOIR GRAMMAIRE A14 **3** *(de modiste)* hatstand **4** *Aut Fam* accelerator (pedal); **appuyer sur le c.** to put one's foot down, *Am* to step on the gas

▸▸ **c. atomique** mushroom cloud; **c. de couche** button mushroom; **c. hallucinogène** hallucinogenic mushroom, *Fam* magic mushroom; *Culin* **c. noir** dried mushroom; **c. de Paris** button mushroom

champignonnière [ʃɑ̃piɲɔnjer] NF mushroom bed

champignonniste [ʃɑ̃piɲɔnist] N mushroom grower

champion, -ionne [ʃɑ̃pjɔ̃, -jɔn] N **1** *Sport etc* champion; **le c. du monde d'escrime** the world fencing champion; **un c. de ski** champion; **une championne de gym** a champion gymnast; *Fam* **c'est un c. du bricolage** he's a first-class handyman; **je suis vraiment le c. de la gaffe** I'm a great one for putting my foot in it **2** *(d'une cause etc)* champion, defender; **se poser en** *ou* **se faire le c. de la protection des animaux** to champion the protection of animals

ADJ 1 *Sport* **l'équipe championne du monde** the world champions **2** *Fam* great, *Br Dial* champion; **c'est c.!** it's first-rate!; **elle est championne, ta copine!** your girlfriend is terrific!; **pour les gaffes, il est c.!** he's a great one for putting his foot in it!

championnat [ʃɑ̃pjɔna] NM championship; **c. du monde de course à pied** world running championship

chançard, -arde [ʃɑ̃sar, -ard] *Fam* **ADJ** *(personne)* lucky

N lucky person; **quel c.!** (he's a) lucky devil!

chance [ʃɑ̃s] NF **1** *(possibilité)* chance, likelihood; **vous avez toutes les chances d'être accusé, il y a toutes les chances (pour) que vous soyez accusé** there is every chance *or* likelihood that you will be accused; **il a compris qu'il fallait mettre toutes les chances de son côté** he realized he had to leave nothing to chance; **il a des chances d'être choisi** he stands a good chance of being chosen; **il a peu de chances de réussir** *ou* **de succès** he has little chance of succeeding, he's very unlikely to succeed; **elles ont des chances égales d'être nommées** they have an even chance of being appointed; **donner une** *ou* **sa c. à qn/qch** to give sb/sth a chance; **elle a une c. sur deux de gagner** she has a fifty-fifty chance of winning; **il y a une c. sur cent (pour) qu'elle le voie** there's a chance in a hundred that she'll see him; **il n'a aucune c. (de réussir)** he doesn't stand a chance *or* he has no chance (of succeeding); **calculer** *ou* **évaluer ses chances de succès** to work out one's chances of success; *Fam* **il y a une c.** *ou* **des chances** it's just possible; **il y a très peu de chances qu'elle puisse le faire à temps** there's very little chance that she'll be able to do it on time; **il y a de grandes** *ou* **fortes chances pour qu'on le lui propose** there's every chance that he will be offered it

2 *(sort)* (good) luck, fortune; **la c. lui sourit** fortune smiles on him; **tenter sa c.** to try one's luck, to chance it; **la c. peut tourner à tout moment** our/your/*etc* luck could change at any time; **souhaiter bonne c. à qn** to wish sb luck; **bonne c.!** good luck!; **quelle c.!** what a bit *or* stroke of luck!; **avec un peu de c., on pourra le faire** with a bit of luck, we'll be able to do it; **elle a eu la c. de le rencontrer de son vivant** she was lucky enough to meet him when he was still alive; **avoir de la c.** to be lucky *or* fortunate; **elle n'a pas eu de c.** she was unlucky; **il y a vraiment des gens qui n'ont pas de c.** some people really don't have any luck, *Fam* some people really get all the bad breaks; **porter c. à qn** to bring sb luck; **jour de c.** lucky day; **c'est bien ma c.!** just my luck!; **pas de c.!** hard luck!; **par c.** luckily, fortunately, by a stroke of luck; **la c. est avec nous** our luck's in

> Il faut noter que le nom anglais **chance** ne signifie jamais **bonne fortune.**

chancelant [ʃɑ̃slɑ̃] ADJ unsteady, wavering, shaky; *(courage, détermination)* wavering; *(mémoire)* shaky; **pas chancelants** staggering *or* tottering *or* unsteady footsteps; **une autorité chancelante** shaky *or* wavering authority; **le pouvoir est c.** the government is tottering *or* is on the brink of collapse; **santé chancelante** *(d'un vieillard etc)* delicate *or* poor health

chanceler [ʃɑ̃sle] VI **(je chancelle, n. chancelons; je chancellerai)** *(action)* to stagger, to totter; *(état)* to be unsteady (on one's legs); *(d'une chose)* to wobble; **avancer/reculer/entrer/sortir en chancelant** to stagger *or* totter forward/back/in/out; **l'uppercut le fit c.** the uppercut sent him reeling; **le régime chancelle** the government is tottering; **c. dans sa résolution** to waver *or* falter in one's resolution

chancelier [ʃɑ̃səlje] NM chancellor; *Admin* **c. de l'université** chancellor of the university; **Grand C.** *(en Grande-Bretagne)* Lord Chancellor; **c. de l'Échiquier** Chancellor of the Exchequer

chancelière [ʃɑ̃səljɛr] NF *(pour les pieds)* footmuff

chancellerie [ʃɑ̃sɛlri] NF *Hist (d'une ambassade)* chancery

chanceux, -euse [ʃɑ̃sø, -øz] ADJ *(personne)* lucky, fortunate; **vous voilà bien c.!** you're lucky!, you're in luck!; **Can c.!** (you) lucky devil!

chanci [ʃɑ̃si] ADJ *Vieilli* mouldy, *Am* moldy

chancre [ʃɑ̃kr] NM *Bot, Méd, Vét, Fig* canker; *Méd* **c. syphilitique** chancre; **c. mou** soft chancre; *Arg* **manger comme un c.** to eat like a horse, to make a pig of oneself

chandail [ʃɑ̃daj] NM sweater, jumper

Chandeleur (la) [laʃɑ̃dlœr] NF *Rel* Candlemas

chandelier [ʃɑ̃dəlje] NM *(à une branche)* candlestick; *(à plusieurs branches)* candelabra

> Il faut noter que le nom anglais **chandelier** est un faux ami. Il signifie **lustre.**

chandelle [ʃɑ̃dɛl] NF **1** *(bougie en cire)* candle; *(de suif)* (tallow) candle; **s'éclairer à la c.** to use candlelight; **économies de bouts de c.** cheeseparing; **faire des économies de bouts de c.** to scrimp and save; **travailler/dîner à la c.** to work/dine by candlelight; **un dîner aux chandelles** a candlelit dinner; *Fig* **brûler la c. par les deux bouts** to burn the candle at both ends; *(dépenser trop d'argent)* to be extravagant (with money); *Fig* **le jeu n'en vaut pas la c.** the game is not worth the candle; *Fig* **tenir la c.** to play gooseberry, *Am* to feel like a fifth wheel; *Fig* **en voir trente-six chandelles** to see stars; *Fig* **je vous dois une fière c.** I owe you more than I can repay; **lancer qch en c.** to throw sth straight up in the air
2 *Fam (de morve) (au bout du nez)* snot
3 *Tennis* lob; *Ftbl* high ball; *Rugby* garryowen, up and under; *Gym* shoulder stand; **faire une c.** *Rugby* to do an up and under; *Tennis* to lob the ball; *Gym* **faire la c.** to do a shoulder stand
4 *Aviat* **(montée en) c.** vertical climb; **monter en c.** *(d'un avion)* to climb vertically
5 *Aut* chassis stand
6 *Typ, Journ* full column

chanfrein¹ [ʃɑ̃frɛ̃] NM *(de cheval)* nose, forehead

chanfrein² NM *Archit* chamfered edge, chamfer, bevelled edge

chanfreiner [ʃɑ̃frene] VT *Tech* to chamfer

change [ʃɑ̃ʒ] NM **1** *Fin* exchange; **le c. est avantageux** the exchange rate is good; **au c. du jour** at the current rate of exchange; **c. du dollar** dollar exchange; *Fig* **gagner** *ou* **ne pas perdre au c.** to gain on *or* by the exchange, to lose nothing on the deal; *Fig* **je n'y ai pas perdu au c.** I came out (of it) ahead, I didn't lose by it; **lettre de c.** bill of exchange; **bureau de c.** bureau de change; **opérations de c.** (foreign) exchange transactions; **cours du c.** exchange rate, rate of exchange; **marché des changes** foreign exchange; **agent de c.** stockbroker; **contrôle des changes** exchange control
2 *(chasse)* **donner le c. aux chiens** to put hounds on the wrong scent; *Fig* **donner le c. à qn** to put sb on a false scent *or* trail
3 *(couche-culotte)* **c. (complet)** disposable nappy *or Am* diaper

> Il faut noter que le nom anglais **change** signifie **petite monnaie** quand il se réfère à de l'argent.

changeable [ʃɑ̃ʒabl] ADJ changeable

changeant [ʃɑ̃ʒɑ̃] ADJ changeable, variable; **caractère c.** changeable *or* fickle disposition; **d'humeur changeante** moody; **temps c.** unsettled weather; **soie changeante** shot silk

changement [ʃɑ̃ʒmɑ̃] NM **1** *(d'air, de résidence, de condition etc)* change; *Scol* **c. (de section/de classe)** transfer; **il va y avoir du c.** there are going to be some changes, things are going to change; **ça va te faire un drôle de c. d'avoir un enfant** things will be very different for you when you've got a child; **il vous faudrait un c. d'air** *ou* **d'occupation** you need a change (of scenery); *Théâtre* **c. de décor** scene shift *or* change; *Fig* **un c. de décor peut lui faire du bien** a change of scene *or* scenery may do him good; **il n'y a pas de c.** *(dans son état)* there's (been) no change; **la situation est restée longtemps sans c.** the situation stayed the same *or* remained unchanged for a long time; **son c. est radical, ce n'est plus le même!** he's changed completely, he isn't the same person any more!; **c. de programme** *TV, Cin* change in the (advertised) schedule; *Fig (de projets)* change of plan; **c. de programme, on ne va plus chez Paul** there's been a change of plan, we're not going to Paul's any more; **c. de prix** price change; *Mktg* **c. de marque** brand switching; **'c. de propriétaire'** 'under new ownership'; **'c. de direction'** 'under new management'; **c. de régime** change of government; **c. climatique** *ou* **du climat** climate change, change in the climate; **c. de vent** shift of wind; *Rail* **il y a un c. à Valence** you have to change at Valence; **le voyage est sans c. jusqu'à Paris** the train *etc* goes straight through to Paris
2 *Typ* **c. de page** page break; **c. de page obligatoire** hard page break; **c. de ligne facultatif** soft return; *Ordinat* **c. de ligne** line feed
►► **c. de focale** *(d'une caméra)* zooming; *Cin, TV* **c. de plan** cutaway shot, cutaway; *Aut* **c. de rapports** gear shifting; **c. de vitesse** *(action)* change of gear, (manual) gear change; *(levier)* gear lever; *Théâtre* **c. à vue** transformation scene

CHANGER [ʃɑ̃ʒe] **(je changeai(s), n. changeons)** VT **1** *(remplacer), Fin* to change, to exchange; **c. qch contre qch** to change *or* exchange sth for sth; **elle changerait bien sa place contre** *ou* **pour la tienne** *(situation*

professionnelle, familiale etc) she'd happily swap places with you; **il doit c. sa voiture** he has to change his car, he has to get a new car; **c. les draps** to change the sheets; *Théâtre* **c. le décor** to shift *or* change the scenery; **c. (la couche d')un bébé** to change a baby('s nappy *or Am* diaper); **c. un malade** to put clean clothes on a sick person; **c. un billet de banque** to change a (bank)note; **c. des dollars contre des euros** to change dollars into euros; **c. de l'argent** to change money; **c. un métal en or** to turn *or* change a metal into gold; **la grenouille fut changée en prince** the frog was turned *or* changed into a prince
2 *(modifier)* to change, to alter; *(divertir)* to be a change for; **ils partent vivre en Écosse, ça va les c.!** they're going to live in Scotland, that will be a change for them!; **cela te changera agréablement** *ou* **en bien** that will make a nice change for you; **une promenade me changera les idées** a walk will take my mind off things; **ça nous change du cinéma du coin** that makes a change from the local cinema; **c. sa façon de vivre** to change one's way of life; **ça ne change rien à rien** that doesn't change *or* alter anything, it makes absolutely no difference; **tu n'y changeras rien** there's nothing you can do about it; **elle ne changera pas une virgule au texte** she won't change *or* alter as much as a comma of the text; **cela ne change pas grand-chose** *ou* **rien au fait que …** that doesn't change *or* alter the fact that …; **cela ne change rien** *ou* **pas grand-chose à l'affaire** that makes no difference; **cette robe vous change** that dress makes you look different *or* changes you; **cette expérience l'a beaucoup changée** the experience has changed her a lot; **tu ne le changeras pas!** he'll never change!; *Fam* **ça vous change un homme!** it changes a man!; **voilà qui change les choses du tout au tout** that makes all the difference; **mais cela change tout!** that changes everything!; **c. un livre de place** to move a book; **c. les meubles de place** to change *or* move the furniture around; **c. un fonctionnaire de poste** to transfer a civil servant; **c. l'ordre des mots** to change the word order

VI **1** *(se modifier)* to (undergo a) change, to alter; **cette région a beaucoup changé** this region has changed a lot; **ça n'a pas changé, rien n'a changé** nothing has changed; **le temps va c.** the weather's going to change; **il a changé en mal** *ou* **en pire/en bien** *ou* **en mieux** he's changed for the worse/the better; *Iron* **pour c.** (just) for a change; **et pour c., il était de mauvaise humeur** and just for a change, he was in a bad mood; **tu n'as pas changé** you haven't changed (a bit); *Rail etc* **où dois-je c.?** where do I change?; **je dois c. à Bordeaux** I have to change at Bordeaux; **ça ne pourra pas toujours durer comme ça, il faudra que ça change!** it can't go on like this, things will have to change!
2 c. de to change; **c. de position** to change position; **c. de secrétaire/de train/de travail** to change secretaries/trains/jobs; **c. de gouvernement** to have a change of government, to have a new government; **c. de main** to change hands, to use the other hand; *Fig* **c. de mains** to change hands; **c. de place avec qn** to change seats with sb; **c. d'amis** to change one's friends; **c. de vie** to change one's way of life; **c. de maison** to move (house); **la rue a changé de nom** the name of the street has been changed, the street has changed its name; **le magasin a changé de propriétaire** the shop is under new management; **c. de genre/de coiffure** to change one's style/hairstyle; **c. de vêtements** to change (one's clothes), to get changed; *Fam* **ton chapeau me va mieux, on**

peut c.? *(échanger)* your hat suits me better, can we swap?; **c. de disque** to put another record on, to change the record; *Fig* **change de disque!** change the record!, give it a rest!; **c. de peau** *(d'un serpent)* to change *or* shed *or* slough its skin; **c. d'avis/d'opinion** to change one's mind/opinion; **c. de couleur** to change colour; **elle changea de visage** her expression changed *or* altered; **c. de sujet** to change the subject; **c. de route** to take another road; *Naut* **c. de route** *ou* **de cap** to alter course; *Aut* **c. de vitesse** to change gear; **la rivière a changé de cours** the river has shifted its course; **c. de ton** to change one's tune; **je te prie de c. de ton, ne me parle pas ainsi** please don't talk to me in that tone of voice, don't take that tone of voice with me; **ça change de l'ordinaire** it makes a change
VPR se changer 1 *(mettre d'autres vêtements)* to change (one's clothes)
2 *(se transformer)* **se c. en** to turn into
3 se c. les idées to change one's ideas

changeur, -euse [ʃɑ̃ʒœr, -øz] **N** *(personne)* money changer
NM 1 Radio c. de fréquence frequency changer **2 c. de disques** record changer; **c. de monnaie** change machine

Chang-hai [ʃɑ̃gaj] **NM** Shanghai

chanoine [ʃanwan] **NM** *Rel* canon; *Fam* **gras comme un c.** as round as a barrel; *Fam* **avoir une mine de c.** to be bursting with health; **vie de c.** easy life

chanson [ʃɑ̃sɔ̃] **NF 1** *Mus* song; **c. d'amour** love song; **c. populaire** popular song; **la c. française** French songs; *Fam* **c'est toujours la même c.!** it's always the same old story!; *Fam* **ça, c'est une autre c.!** that's quite another story!; *Fam* **on connaît la c.!** I've heard that one before!; *Vieilli* **chansons (que tout cela)!** nonsense! **2** *Littér* song, lay, verse chronicle; **la c. de Roland** the Song of Roland
▸▸ **c. à boire** drinking song; **c. de geste** chanson de geste, epic poem; **c. de marins** sea shanty; **c. réaliste** cabaret song, music hall song

chansonnette [ʃɑ̃sɔnɛt] **NF** little song, ditty; *Fam* **pousser la c.** to sing a song

chansonnier [ʃɑ̃sɔnje] **NM 1** *(artiste)* = person who sings in cabaret or in clubs **2** *(recueil)* song book

chant¹ [ʃɑ̃] **NM** *Mus* **1** *(d'une personne, d'un animal etc)* singing, song; **le c. du violon/de la mer/du vent** the sound of the violin/of the sea/of the wind; **le c. des oiseaux** the song of the birds, birdsong; **le c. du grillon** chirping of the cricket; *Fig* **c'était son c. du cygne** it was his swan song **2** *(chanson)* song; *(mélodie)* melody, air; **c. de victoire** song of victory; **c. de guerre** battle *or* war song **3** *(art)* singing; **leçon/maître de c.** singing lesson/master; **apprendre le c.** to take singing lessons **4** *Littér* song, lyric; *(d'un poème)* canto
▸▸ **c. choral** choral singing; **c. du coq** crowing of the cock; **au c. du coq** at cockcrow; **c. funèbre** dirge; *Rel* **c. grégorien** Gregorian chant; **c. de Noël** Christmas carol; **c. profane** secular song; **c. sacré** hymn; **c. des sirènes** siren song

chant² **NM** *Constr* edge, side; **pierres (posées) de c.** *ou* **sur c.** stones set on edge *or* edgewise

chantage [ʃɑ̃taʒ] **NM** blackmail; **c. sentimental** *ou* **affectif** emotional blackmail; **faire du c.** to use blackmail; **il lui fait du c. au suicide** he's using suicide threats to blackmail her

chantant [ʃɑ̃tɑ̃] **ADJ** melodious, tuneful; *(vers)* musical; *(accent, voix)* lilting, singsong; **air c.** catchy tune

chantepleure [ʃɑ̃tplœr] **NF** *(de mur)* weephole; *(de gouttière)* spout

chanter [ʃɑ̃te] **VT** *(chanson etc)* to sing; **c. victoire** to exult, *Fam* to crow; **c. les louanges/le courage de qn** to sing sb's praises/praise sb's courage; **poète qui chante la grandeur d'un pays** poet who sings of the greatness of a country; *Rel* **c. la messe** to sing mass; **c. Noël** to celebrate Christmas in song; *Fig* **c. toujours la même chanson** to be always harping on about the same thing; *Fam* **qu'est-ce que vous me chantez là?** what are you talking about?; *Fam* **elle le chante sur tous les tons** she's always going on about it
VI *(d'une personne, d'un oiseau, de la bouilloire)* to sing; *(du coq)* to crow; **c. à pleins poumons** to sing at the top of one's voice; **c. juste/faux** to sing in tune/out of tune; *Fam* **c'est comme si je chantais** I'm wasting my breath; *Fig* **faire c. qn** to blackmail sb; *Fam* **est-ce que cela vous chante?** do you like the idea (of it)?, does that appeal to you?; **viens, si ça te chante** come along, if you fancy the idea; **il vient quand ça lui chante** he comes when he feels like it

Il faut noter que le verbe anglais **to chant** est un faux ami. Il signifie **scander**.

chanterelle¹ [ʃɑ̃trɛl] **NF 1** *Chasse* decoy (bird) **2** *Mus* *(d'un violon etc)* first *or* highest string; *Fam* **appuyer sur la c.** to hammer a point home, to rub it in

chanterelle² **NF** *(champignon)* chanterelle

chanteur, -euse [ʃɑ̃tœr, -øz] **N** singer, vocalist; **c. des rues** street singer, busker; **c. de charme** crooner; **maître c.** *(qui fait du chantage)* blackmailer; *Mus, Hist* mastersinger, Meistersinger
ADJ **oiseau c.** songbird

chantier [ʃɑ̃tje] **NM 1** *(dépôt)* yard, depot; **c. de construction** builder's yard; **c. de bois** timberyard, lumberyard; *Rail* **c. de voies de garage et de triage** shunting yard
2 *(lieu de construction)* (building) site; *(sur la route)* roadworks; **c. de construction** building site; **c. de démolition** demolition site; **chef de c.** site foreman; **travailler au c.** *ou* **sur le c.** to work on (the) site; **'c.'** 'men at work', 'road works'; **'fin de c.'** 'road clear'; **'c. interdit au public'** 'no admittance to the public'; *Min* **c. d'exploitation** working(s); *Naut* **c. naval** *ou* **de construction navale** shipyard; **c. de l'État** naval (dock)yard; **vaisseau sur le c.** vessel on the slips
3 *Fig* **avoir une œuvre en c.** *ou* **sur le c.** to have a piece of work in the pipeline; **il a un film en c.** he's (in the process of) making a film; **il faudra mettre ce travail en c. demain** we must get started on this tomorrow; *Fig* **quel c.!** what a mess!, what a shambles!; *Fig* **la chambre est un vrai c.** *ou* **est en c.** the bedroom is a real tip; *Fam* **ils ont tout laissé en c.** they left the place in a complete mess *or* shambles; **je ne peux pas vous recevoir, la maison est en c.** *(il y a des travaux)* I can't invite you over, we've got workmen in

chantilly [ʃɑ̃tiji] **NF (crème) c.** Chantilly cream, sweetened whipped cream

chantonnement [ʃɑ̃tɔnmɑ̃] **NM** singing softly, crooning; *(fredonnement)* humming

chantonner [ʃɑ̃tɔne] **VT & VI** to sing softly, to croon; *(fredonner)* to hum

chantoung [ʃɑ̃tuŋ] **NM** *Tex* shantung

chantourner [ʃɑ̃turne] **VT** to cut (using a fretsaw/jigsaw); **scie à c.** *(manuelle)* fretsaw; *(machine)* jigsaw, scroll saw

chantre [ʃɑ̃tr] **NM 1** *Litt* *(poète)* poet, bard; **le c. des opprimés** *(qui célèbre leur cause)* the champion of the oppressed; **cet écrivain s'était fait le c. de la toute nouvelle république** this writer had championed the cause of the new republic; **les chantres des bois** the woodland chorus **2** *Rel* cantor; **grand c.** precentor

chanvre [ʃɑ̃vr] **NM** hemp; **cordage de** *ou* **en c.** hemp(en) rope; **c. indien** Indian hemp, hashish; *Fam* **cravate de c.** hangman's noose

chanvrier, -ière [ʃɑ̃vrije, -jɛr] **ADJ** *(industrie etc)* hemp
N *(cultivateur)* hemp grower; *(ouvrier)* hemp worker

chaos [kao] **NM** chaos; **tout est dans un c. épouvantable** everything is in a dreadful state of confusion, everything is dreadfully chaotic, chaos reigns

chaotique [kaɔtik] **ADJ** chaotic, confused

chapardage [ʃapardaʒ] **NM** *Fam* pinching, pilfering

chaparder [ʃaparde] **VT** *Fam* to pinch, to pilfer

chapardeur, -euse [ʃapardœr, -øz] *Fam* **ADJ** pinching, pilfering
N thief, pilferer

chape [ʃap] **NF 1** *(partie couvrante)* screed; *Aut* *(d'un pneu)* tread; *(d'un pont, d'une chaussée)* coping; **ils ont coulé une c. de béton sur la terrasse** they poured a concrete screed onto the terrace; *Fig* **ce ciel gris est une vraie c. de plomb** the grey sky is just like a lead weight; **s'enfermer dans une c. de silence** to retreat behind a wall of silence **2** *Rel* cope **3** *Tech* fork joint, yoke, clevis; *(de poulie)* shell; *(de bielle)* case; **c. de cardan** cardan fork

chapeau, -eaux [ʃapo] **NM 1** *(coiffure)* hat; **carton** *ou* **boîte à c.** hatbox; **ruban de c.** hatband; **porter/mettre un c.** to wear/put on a hat; **saluer qn d'un coup de c.** to raise one's hat to sb; *Can* **donner un coup de c.** *(accepter les exigences de qn)* to give in; *Fig* **un coup de c. à** hats off to; **je vous donne un coup de c.** I take my hat off to you; **ça mérite un coup de c., c'est parfait** that deserves to be praised, it's perfect; **tirer son c. à qn** to take off one's hat to sb; **c.!** bravo!, well done!; **c. bas!** hats off!; **c. bas** hat in hand; **faire passer le c.** to pass the hat round; *Fam* **il travaille du c.** he's got a screw loose; *Fig* **c'est vous qui portez le c. dans cette affaire** you're carrying the can here; **si je me trompe je veux bien manger mon c.!** if I'm wrong I'll eat my hat! **2** *Bot* *(d'un champignon)* cap, *Spéc* pileus **3** *Culin* *(de vol-au-vent, de bouchée à la reine)* lid, top **4** *Typ, Journ* introductory paragraph, lead-in; *Radio, TV* introduction
▸▸ **c. de cardinal** cardinal's hat; **c. chinois** *Mus* crescent; *Zool* limpet; **c. cloche** cloche (hat); **c. à cornes** paper hat; **c. de gendarme** paper hat; **c. haut-de-forme** top hat; **c. de lampe** lampshade; **c. melon** bowler hat; **c. mou** felt hat, trilby, *Am* fedora; **c. de paille** straw hat; **c. de pluie** rain hat; *Aut* **c. de roue** hub cap; *Fam* **prendre un virage sur les chapeaux de roues** to take a corner at top speed; *Fig* **la soirée/notre projet a démarré sur les chapeaux de roues** the evening/our plan got off to a great *or* cracking start; **c. de soleil** sun hat; **c. tyrolien** Tyrolean hat

chapeauter [ʃapote] **VT 1** **elle était bien chapeautée** she was wearing a lovely hat **2** *Typ, Journ* to head **3** *Fig* *(contrôler)* to be in charge of, to head; **elle chapeaute les trois services** she's in charge of *or* heads (up) the three departments

chapelain [ʃaplɛ̃] **NM** *Rel* chaplain

chapelet [ʃaplɛ] **NM** *(de prière)* rosary; *Fig* *(d'invectives, d'insultes)* stream, string; *(de péniches, d'oignons etc)* string; **dire son c.** to say the rosary; **dire une dizaine de c.** to say a decade (of the rosary); *Fam* **débiter** *ou* **dévider** *ou* **défiler son c.** to have one's say, to speak one's mind; **c. de bombes** stick of bombs

chapelier, -ière [ʃapəlje, -jɛr] **ADJ** *(commerce etc)* hat(-making)
N hatter

chapelle [ʃapɛl] **NF 1** *(dans école, hôpital etc)*

chapel; *(d'une église)* (side) chapel; *(d'une paroisse)* chapel of ease; **c. de la (Sainte) Vierge** Lady Chapel; **c. ardente** chapel of rest **2** *Mus, Rel* choir and/or orchestra; **maître de c.** choirmaster **3** *Rel (objets pour la célébration de la messe)* ornaments and plate **4** *Littér, Beaux-Arts* clique, coterie; **esprit de c.** cliquishness, cliquiness **5** *Belg (café)* café

chapellerie [ʃapɛlri] **NF 1** *Com* hat trade; *Ind* hat industry **2** *(magasin)* hatshop

chapelure [ʃaplyr] **NF** *Culin* breadcrumbs

chaperon [ʃaprɔ̃] **NM 1** *(personne)* chaperon(e) **2** *(de faucon)* hood **3** *Littér* **le Petit C. rouge** Little Red Riding Hood **4** *Constr (d'un mur)* coping

chaperonner [ʃaprɔne] **VT 1** *(jeune femme)* to chaperone **2** *Constr (mur)* to cope

chapiteau, -eaux [ʃapito] **NM 1** *Archit (d'une colonne)* capital; *(d'une armoire etc)* cornice **2** *(d'un cirque)* big top; *(le cirque lui-même)* circus; **avoir lieu sous c.** to be held in a marquee **3** *(d'un alambic, d'une fusée)* head

chapitre [ʃapitr] **NM 1** *(d'un livre)*, *Fig* chapter; *(d'un budget etc)* heading, item; **inscrire une somme au c. des recettes/dépenses** to enter a sum under revenue/expenditure; *Fig* **nous aborderons demain ce c.** we will tackle this subject *or* matter tomorrow; **elle est sévère sur le c. de la discipline** she is strict as regards *or* in the matter of discipline; **en voilà assez sur ce c.** that's enough of that, let's drop the subject; **et maintenant, au c. des faits divers …** and now for the news in brief … **2** *Rel (assemblée)* chapter; **salle du c.** chapter house; *Fig* **avoir voix** *ou* **droit au c.** to have a say in the matter

chapitrer [ʃapitre] **VT c. qn** *(réprimander)* to tell sb off; *(faire la morale à)* to lecture sb

chapka [ʃapka] **NF** = fur hat worn in Russia

chaplinesque [ʃaplinɛsk] **ADJ** *(comique, personnage)* Chaplinesque

chapon [ʃapɔ̃] **NM** *Culin* capon

chaptalisation [ʃaptalizasjɔ̃] **NF** chaptalization

chaptaliser [ʃaptalize] **VT** to chaptalize

chaque [ʃak] **ADJ** each, every; **c. femme doit pouvoir travailler et élever ses enfants** every woman should be able to work as well as bring up her children, all women should be able to work as well as bring up their children; **c. chose à sa place** everything in its place; **c. chose en son temps** all in good time; **on fera c. chose en son temps** we'll do it all in good time; **c. fois qu'il vient** whenever *or* every time he comes; **j'y pense à c. instant** I think about it all the time SEE GRAMMAR A35–6; B15

PRON *Fam (chacun)* **ces livres coûtent 100 euros c.** these books cost 100 euros each

char [ʃar] **NM 1** *Mil* tank; **c. léger/moyen/lourd** light/medium/heavy tank; **régiment de chars** tank regiment *or Am* battalion **2** *(agricole)* cart, wagon **3** *Antiq* chariot; *Litt* **le c. de l'État** the Ship of State; *Fam* **arrête ton c.** stop exaggerating **4** *Can Fam (voiture)* car, *Am* automobile

▸▸**c. d'assaut** tank; **c. à bancs** (horse-drawn) charabanc; **c. à bœufs** ox cart; **c. de carnaval** float; **c. de combat** tank; **c. funèbre** hearse; **c. de la mi-carême** float; **c. romain** Roman chariot; *Sport* **c. à voile** sand yacht; **faire du c. à voile** to go sand yachting

charabia [ʃarabja] **NM** *Fam* gibberish, gobbledegook

charade [ʃarad] **NF** riddle, word game *(based on a series of verbal clues, each of which corresponds to a different syllable of the word to be guessed)*

> Il faut noter que le terme anglais **charade** est un faux ami.

charançon [ʃarɑ̃sɔ̃] **NM** *(insecte)* weevil

charançonné [ʃarɑ̃sɔne] **ADJ** weevil(l)ed, weevil(l)y

charbon [ʃarbɔ̃] **NM 1** *(combustible)* coal; *(poussière)* coal dust; **c. (de bois)** charcoal; **grillades au c. de bois** barbecued meat; **poisson grillé sur des charbons** barbecued fish; **marchand de c.** coal merchant, coalman; **soute à c.** coal bunker; **chauffage au c.** coal-fired heating; *Fig Fam* **aller au c.** *(au travail)* to go to work; *(s'y mettre)* to muck in, to get stuck in; **avoir un c. dans l'œil** to have a bit of grit in one's eye; *Fig* **être** *ou* **marcher sur des charbons ardents** to be on tenterhooks, to be like a cat on a hot tin roof **2** *Beaux-Arts* charcoal; **dessin au c.** charcoal drawing **3** *Chimie* carbon; **balai de c.** carbon brush **4** *Méd* charcoal; **c. actif** *ou* **activé** active *or* activated charcoal **5** *(maladie) Agr, Bot* smut, black rust; *Méd, Vét* anthrax

charbonnage [ʃarbɔnaʒ] **NM 1** *(exploitation)* coal mining **2 charbonnages** collieries; **les Charbonnages de France** the (French) National Coal Board

charbonner [ʃarbɔne] **VT 1** *(noircir)* to (blacken with) charcoal **2** *Beaux-Arts (chose)* to make a charcoal sketch of
VPR se charbonner se c. le visage to blacken one's face

charbonneux, -euse [ʃarbɔnø, -øz] **ADJ 1** *(noir)* coal-black; *(yeux)* sooty; **dépôt c.** sooty deposit, carbon deposit **2** *Méd* anthracic, carbuncular; **mouches charbonneuses** anthrax-carrying flies

charbonnier, -ière [ʃarbɔnje, -jɛr] **ADJ** *(industrie etc)* coal (mining); *(commerce etc)* charcoal; **navire c.** collier, coaler
NM 1 *Com (marchand de charbon)* coal merchant, coalman; **noir comme un c.** as black as the ace of spades; *Prov* **c. est maître dans sa maison** *ou* **chez soi** an Englishman's home is his castle; **la foi du c.** simple faith **2** *Naut* coaler, collier
NF charbonnière charcoal kiln

charcuter [ʃarkyte] *Fam* **VT** *(morceau de viande)* to hack up; **c. qn** to hack sb to pieces, to butcher sb; **ce médecin est réputé pour c. ses malades** this doctor has the reputation of being a butcher; **se faire c.** to get hacked to pieces *or* butchered
VPR se charcuter to cut oneself to ribbons; **se c. le menton en se rasant** to nick one's chin shaving

charcuterie [ʃarkytri] **NF 1** *Com (magasin)* ≃ delicatessen **2** *Ind* pork butchery, delicatessen trade **3** *Culin (produits)* **assiette de c.** plate of assorted cooked meats

Charcuterie

A "charcuterie" sells mainly food prepared with pork: sausages, pâtés, ham etc, collectively also known as "charcuterie". Ready-prepared dishes to take away are usually also sold.

charcutier, -ière [ʃarkytje, -jɛr] **N 1** *(commerçant, fabricant)* pork butcher **2** *Fam Péj (chirurgien)* butcher

chardon [ʃardɔ̃] **NM 1** *(plante)* thistle; *Culin* **c. à la liqueur** = coloured chocolate sweet with liqueur centre **2 chardons** *(sur des grilles etc)* (clustered) spikes

chardonneret [ʃardɔnrɛ] **NM** *(oiseau)* goldfinch

charentais, -aise [ʃarɑ̃tɛ, -ɛz] **ADJ** of Charente
N C. *(habitant)* inhabitant of Charente; *(natif)* native of Charente
NF charentaise slipper

CHARGE [ʃarʒ]

> load **1, 5, 6** ▪ cargo **1** ▪ burden **1** ▪ responsibility **2** ▪ charge **4, 6, 7, 9, 10** ▪ exaggeration **12**

NF 1 *(poids)* load, burden; *(sur bateau)* cargo, freight; *(sur camion)* cargo, load; *(du moteur, sur les roues)* load; *(action) (de navire etc)* loading; **en c.** under load; **bête de c.** beast of burden; **je ne veux pas devenir une c. pour eux** I don't want to become a burden to them; *Fig* **la c. affective des paroles de qn** the emotional content of sb's words; **être à c. à qn** to be a burden to sb

2 *(responsabilité)* responsibility; **prendre qn/qch en c.** to take charge of sb/sth, to assume *or* take responsibility for sb/sth; **se prendre en c.** to take care of oneself, to be responsible for oneself; **cela est à votre c.** that's your responsibility; **elle a la c. de réorganiser le service** she's got the job of reorganizing the department; **enfants confiés à ma c.** children entrusted to me *or* in my charge *or* in my care; **avoir c. d'âmes** *Rel* to have a cure of souls; *(d'un père)* to have children in one's care; *Vieilli* **femme de c.** housekeeper **3** *(fonction)* **c. de notaire** notary's office; **c. d'avoué** solicitor's practice

4 *(obligation financière)* charge, expense; **charges incompressibles** necessary expenses; **les réparations sont à la c. du locataire** the tenant is responsible for repairs; **être à la c. de qn** to be dependent on sb, to be supported by sb; *(appel etc)* to be chargeable to sb; **prendre un client en c.** *(d'un taxi)* to pick up a fare; **prise en c.** *(dans un taxi)* minimum fare; *(par la Sécurité sociale)* agreement to pay medical expenses; **être pris en c. à cent pour cent par la Sécurité sociale** to have one's medical expenses fully paid for by Social Security; **charges de famille** dependants; **deux enfants à c.** two dependent children; **charges locatives** maintenance charges; *(de locaux)* rental charges, rental expenses; *(de matériel)* lease charges; **loyer plus les charges** rent plus service charge (and maintenance costs); **charges patronales** employer's contributions

5 *Tech* load; *Aviat* **facteur de c.** load factor **6** *Élec (d'une batterie)* charge; *(d'un circuit etc)* load; **conducteur en c.** live conductor; **mettre une batterie en c.** to put a battery on charge

7 *Phys (d'une particule électrique)* charge **8** **à c. de** on (the) condition that, provided that; **j'accepte, mais à c. de revanche** I accept, but only on condition that you let me return the favour some time; **à c. pour vous de payer** on condition *or* provided that you pay

9 *Mil* charge; **sonner la c.** to sound the charge; **c. de cavalerie** cavalry charge; *Fig* **revenir** *ou* **retourner à la c.** to come back *or* return to the attack

10 *Jur* charge, indictment; **les charges contre lui sont très lourdes** the charges against him are very heavy; **quelles sont les charges contre elle?** what's she being charged with?; **témoin à c.** witness for the prosecution

11 *Fin (d'une dette)* servicing, *Am* service **12** *(d'une histoire)* exaggeration; *Théâtre (d'un rôle)* overacting; *Beaux-Arts, Litt (d'un portrait, d'un personnage)* caricature; **jouer un rôle en c.** to overact a part

▸▸**c. admissible** safe load; *Compta* **c. constatée d'avance** prepayment; *Mil* **c. creuse** hollow(-shaped) charge; **c. d'explosif** *(de fusil etc)* explosive charge; *Compta* **c. fictive** fictitious cost; *Tech* **c. maximum (de rupture)** ultimate *or* breaking load; *Compta* **c. opérationnelle** overhead, operating cost; **c. à payer** sum payable; *Aut* **c. remorquable** towing weight, payload; *Tech* **c. de rupture** breaking *or* shearing stress; **c. de sécurité** safe load; **c. utile** carrying capacity; *(d'un véhicule)* capacity, payload; *(d'un missile)* payload; **c. à vide** empty weight; *Compta* **charges courantes** current expenses; *Compta* **charges d'exploitation** operating costs, running costs; *Compta* **charges financières** interest and other finance charges; **charges fiscales** tax (burden); **charges fixes** fixed costs; *Compta* **charges incorporables** product expenses *or* charges; **charges nettes** net costs; *Compta* **charges patronales** employer contributions; *Compta* **charges à payer** accrued expenses, accruals; **charges publiques** public expenditure; **charges salariales** wage costs; **charges sociales** national insurance contributions, *Am* social security charges *(paid by the employer)*, welfare charges; *Compta* **charges sociales patronales** employer contributions; *Compta* **charges sociales salariales** employee contributions; *Compta* **charges de structure** fixed costs; **charges variables** variable costs

---

Charges

Householders and tenants in blocks of flats are required to pay "charges", a monthly contribution to pay for the general upkeep of the building. In estate agencies, rent is expressed either including this sum ("charges comprises" or "cc") or excluding it ("hors charges" or "charges en sus"). Sometimes, the "charges" include heating costs.

---

chargé, -ée [ʃarʒe] **ADJ 1** *(camion, navire etc)* loaded, laden; *(revolver, appareil photo)* loaded; **bateau lourdement c.** heavily laden ship; **j'étais c. comme un bourricot** *ou* **un baudet** *ou* **un mulet!** I was loaded *or* weighed down!, I felt like a packhorse!; *Fig* **avoir la conscience chargée** to have a guilty conscience; **avoir un passé c.** to have a past; **journée chargée** full *or* busy day; **nous avons un programme c.** we have a full programme; **regard c. de reconnaissance** look full of gratitude; **regard c. de sens** meaningful look; *Litt* **mourir c. d'ans** to die at a ripe old age; **personnage c. d'honneur** a person laden with honours; **le style est très c.** the style is very ornate; **temps c.** overcast weather; **avoir la langue chargée** to have a coated *or* furred tongue; **avoir l'estomac c.** to have an overloaded stomach; *Mil* **obus c.** live shell; *Phys* **particule chargée négativement/positivement** negatively/positively charged particle
2 lettre chargée = registered letter
3 *(responsable)* responsible; **être c. de famille** to have family responsibilities; **être c. d'une mission** to be entrusted with a mission; **il est c. d'enquêter sur elle** he has been assigned to investigate her
4 *Fam (ivre)* loaded, wrecked, wasted
NM c. d'affaires chargé d'affaires; **c. de clientèle** account manager; **c. de comptes** account manager; *Mktg* **c. d'étude** marketing researcher; **c. d'études** project manager; **c. d'étude de marché** market researcher; **c. de mission** *Admin* project leader *or* manager; *Pol* (official) representative; **c. de relations clients** customer relations manager
N *Univ* **c. de cours** = part-time university lecturer; *Can* lecturer

chargeable [ʃarʒabl] **ADJ** *Ordinat* loadable; **c. en résident** memory-loadable

chargement [ʃarʒəmɑ̃] **NM 1** *(action)* *(d'un camion, d'un navire etc)* loading; **machine à laver à c. frontal** front-loading washing machine, *Fam* front-loader; *Rail* **voie de c.** goods siding
2 *Mil (d'une cartouche, d'une bombe, d'un*

obus etc), Phot (d'un appareil photo) loading; *Élec (d'une batterie)* charging; **appareil photo à c. automatique** self-loading camera
3 *(marchandise)* load, cargo, freight; **le c. est arrivé à bon port** the cargo was brought safely to port *or* arrived intact; **c. bien arrimé** well-stowed cargo; **c. partiel** part load
4 *(d'une lettre)* registering; *(lettre)* registered letter; *(colis)* registered parcel

CHARGER [ʃarʒe]

VT to load **1, 4** ▪ to overload **2**
▪ to fill **3, 4** ▪ to charge **4, 7, 8**
▪ to exaggerate **6**
VI to load up **1** ▪ to charge **2**
VPR to weigh oneself down **1** ▪ to take care of *(se charger de)* **3**

VT *(je chargeai(s), n. chargeons)* **1** *(camion, navire etc)* to load; **c. des marchandises** to load *or Naut* to ship goods; **navire chargé de blé** ship laden with wheat; **on charge les bagages dans la soute de l'avion** the luggage is loaded into the aeroplane's hold; *Fam* **c. un client** *(d'un chauffeur de taxi)* to pick up a fare
2 *(alourdir, peser sur)* to overload, to weigh (down); **la voiture est trop chargée** the car is overloaded; **c. une étagère de livres** to overload a shelf with books; **chargé de paquets** weighed down with parcels
3 *(remplir)* to fill; **c. son récit d'anecdotes** to pepper one's story with anecdotes; **table chargée de mets** table laden with food; **pièce chargée de décorations de mauvais goût** room cluttered with tasteless decorations; **mur chargé de tableaux** wall covered in paintings; **mets qui chargent l'estomac** food that lies heavy on the stomach; **le malade ne doit pas c. son estomac** the patient should not overload his stomach; **c. sa mémoire de dates inutiles** to clutter up one's mind with useless dates; **l'air est chargé du parfum des fleurs** the air is heavy with the scent of flowers
4 *(fusil, appareil photo etc)* to load; *(pipe)* to fill; *Élec (batterie)* to charge; *Ordinat* to load (up)
5 c. qn de faire qch to make sb responsible for doing sth, to give sb the responsibility for doing sth; **le patron l'a chargé d'écrire le rapport** the boss made him responsible for writing the report; **je te charge de lui transmettre l'information** I'm entrusting you to give him the information; **j'étais chargé de faire tout le courrier du service** I was in charge of *or* responsible for all the department's mail; **être chargé de l'entretien** to be in charge of *or* responsible for maintenance
6 *(portrait)* to turn into a caricature; *(personne)* to caricature; *(histoire)* to exaggerate, to embroider; *Théâtre (rôle)* to overact; **c. une description** to overdo *or* exaggerate a description, *Fam* to lay it on thick
7 *(attaquer)* to charge (at)
8 *Jur* to charge, to accuse; **c. qn d'un crime** to charge sb with a crime; **on le charge de tous les péchés** he's charged with every sin in the book
9 c. une lettre = to send valuables by post; *(l'affranchir)* to register a letter
VI 1 *Ordinat* to load up **2** *Mil* to charge
VPR se charger 1 *(s'alourdir)* to weigh oneself down
2 *(s'accuser)* to blame oneself
3 se c. de (faire) qch to take care of sth, to look after sth, to take sth on; **je me charge de lui en parler** I'll talk to him about it; **je me charge des enfants de Marie quand elle travaille** I take care of *or* look after Marie's children when she's working; **je m'en chargerai** I'll see to it, I'll take care of it; **ne t'en fais pas, je me charge de lui** don't worry, I'll take care of him

4 se c. automatiquement *Phot* to load automatically; *Ordinat* to load automatically, to autoload

---

chargeur [ʃarʒœr] **NM 1** *(d'arme)* magazine, cartridge clip; *Phot* cartridge; *Élec* (battery) charger; *Ordinat* loader; **c. automatique** self loader; **c. feuille à feuille** *(d'une imprimante)* single sheet feed **2** *(personne)* loader; *(expéditeur)* shipper

chargeuse [ʃarʒøz] **NF** *Tech* loader

charia [ʃarja] **NF** *Rel* sharia

chariot [ʃarjo] **NM** *(petite charrette)* wag(-g)on, cart; *(Caddie® de supermarché)* trolley; *(pour diapositives)* cartridge; *(pour la manutention)* truck, trolley; *(d'hôpital)* trolley, *Am* gurney; *Cin, TV* dolly; *(d'une machine à écrire)* carriage; **c. d'enfant** baby walker; **c. à bagages** luggage trolley; **le c. des desserts/à liqueurs** the dessert/drinks trolley; *Aviat* **c. d'atterrissage** landing gear, undercarriage; **c. à bras** handcart, barrow; **c. élévateur à fourche** fork-lift truck; *TV, Cin* **c. omnidirectionnel** crab(bing) dolly
▶ ▶ *Astron* **le Grand C.** the Great Bear, *Am* the (Big) Dipper; **le Petit C.** the Little Bear, *Am* the Little Dipper

chariot-crabe, *pl* **chariots-crabes NM** *TV, Cin* crab(bing) dolly

charismatique [karismatik] **ADJ** charismatic

charisme [karism] **NM** charisma; **avoir du c.** to have charisma

charitable [ʃaritabl] **ADJ** charitable (**envers** to, towards); **œuvre** *ou* **fondation c.** charity; **vous êtes bien c.** it's very kind of you; **un conseil c.** a friendly piece of advice

charitablement [ʃaritabləmɑ̃] **ADV** charitably

charité [ʃarite] **NF 1** *(amour)* charity, love; **faire qch par c.** to do sth out of charity; *Prov* **c. bien ordonnée commence par soi-même** charity begins at home; *Hist* **dame de c.** district visitor; *Rel* **les Filles** *ou* **les Sœurs de la C.** the Sisters of Charity; **faites-moi** *ou* **ayez la c. de venir/d'écouter mon histoire** please be kind enough to come/to listen to my story **2** *(don)* act of charity; **faire la c. à qn** to give money *or* a donation to sb; **je ne tiens pas à ce qu'on me fasse la c.** I don't want charity; **vivre de charités** to live on charity; **demander la c.** to ask for charity; **la c., messieurs dames** *(dans la rue)* can you spare some change, please?

charivari [ʃarivari] **NM** din, row, racket; **un c. de rires et de pas** noisy laughter and footsteps

charlatan [ʃarlatɑ̃] **NM 1** *(guérisseur)* charlatan; **remède de c.** quack remedy; **tous ces psys sont des charlatans** all these shrinks are quacks **2** *(qui exploite la crédulité publique)* conman, swindler

charlatanerie [ʃarlatanri] **NF** charlatanry, charlatanism

charlatanesque [ʃarlatanɛsk] **ADJ** *(remède etc)* quack

charlatanisme [ʃarlatanism] **NM** charlatanism

Charles [ʃarl] **NM** *Hist* **C. Quint** Charles the Fifth

charleston [ʃarlɛstɔn] **NM** *(danse)* charleston

charlot [ʃarlo] **NM 1** *Fam (personne peu sérieuse)* clown **2** *Cin* **C.** Charlie Chaplin

charlotte [ʃarlɔt] **NF** *Culin* charlotte; **c. aux poires/au chocolat** pear/chocolate charlotte; **moule à c.** charlotte mould

charmant [ʃarmɑ̃] **ADJ** *(personne, chose)* charming, delightful; **une soirée charmante** a delightful evening; **ils se sont disputés devant nous, charmante soirée!** they argued right in front of us, what a delightful *or* charming evening!; **prince c.** Prince Charming; *Fig* **attendre son prince c.** to be waiting for Prince Charming *or* Mr Right to come along; *Iron* **et voilà qu'il pleut, ah, c'est c.!** now it's raining, marvellous!

charme[1] [ʃarm] NM **1** *(attrait)* charm, attraction; **elle a beaucoup de c.** she has great charm, she's very charming; **cela lui donne un certain c.** it gives him a certain charm; **c'est ce qui en fait le c.** that's what makes it so attractive, that's what makes it so charming, that's where its charm lies; **elle n'est pas belle, mais elle a du c.** she's not beautiful, but she is attractive; **faire du c.** to turn on the charm; **elle lui fait du c.** she's turning on the charm with him; **faire son numéro de c. à qn** to use one's charms on sb; **charmes** *(d'une femme)* (physical) attractions, charms; **vivre de ses charmes** to sell one's body for a living; **cette proposition ne manque pas de c.** the suggestion is not without a certain appeal; *Iron* **je suis peu sensible aux charmes des supermarchés** the appeal of supermarkets is lost on me; **chanteur de c.** crooner **2** *(magie)* charm, spell; **être/tomber sous le c.** to be/fall under the spell; **tenir ses auditeurs sous le c.** to hold one's audience spellbound; **rompre le c.** to break the spell; *Fig* **se porter comme un c.** to be in the best of health, to be as fit as a fiddle

charme[2] NM *(arbre)* hornbeam

charmer [ʃarme] VT **1** *(plaire à)* to charm, to delight, to enchant; **elle n'a pas eu de mal à c. son auditoire** she had no difficulty winning over her audience; **être charmé de faire qch** to be delighted to do sth; **j'ai été charmé de vous rencontrer** it's been a pleasure to meet you; **elle est charmée du cadeau** she's delighted *or* enchanted with the gift **2** *(serpent etc)* to charm, to bewitch

charmeur, -euse [ʃarmœr, -øz] ADJ *(regard etc)* charming, appealing; **un sourire c.** a charming *or* winning smile
▸ N charmer
▸▸ **c. de serpents** snake charmer

charmille [ʃarmij] NF **1** *(allée)* walk (bordered by hedges) **2** *(tonnelle)* bower, arbour

charnel, -elle [ʃarnɛl] ADJ *(désirs etc)* carnal; **acte c., union charnelle** carnal act

charnellement [ʃarnɛlmɑ̃] ADV *Litt* carnally; **aimer qn c.** to love sb carnally *or* sexually; **connaître qn c.** to have carnal knowledge of sb

charnier [ʃarnje] NM (open) grave; *Arch, Litt (ossuaire)* charnel (house)

charnière [ʃarnjɛr] NF *(de porte etc)* hinge; *Mil (de deux armées etc)* (point of) junction; *Fam* **nom à c.** double-barrelled name; *Fig* **à la c. de deux grandes périodes** as one great era gives/gave way to another; *Fig* **être à un moment c. de sa vie** to be at a turning point in one's life; *Fig* **un domaine(-)c. (entre deux disciplines)** an area (inter)linking two disciplines; **époque/œuvre c.** transitional period/work

charnu [ʃarny] ADJ fleshy, plump; *(fruit)* pulpy; **des lèvres charnues** fleshy *or* full lips; *Hum* **la partie charnue de son anatomie** his behind *or* posterior

charognard [ʃarɔɲar] NM **1** *Zool* carrion-eater **2** *Arg (exploiteur)* shark, vulture

charogne [ʃarɔɲ] NF **1** *(d'animal)* carrion, decaying carcass **2** *Arg (salaud, crapule)* bastard; *(femme)* bitch

Charon [karɔ̃] NM *Myth* Charon

charpente [ʃarpɑ̃t] NF *(d'un bâtiment etc)* frame(work), skeleton; *(du corps)* frame; *(d'un roman etc)* framework, skeleton, structure; **bois de c.** timber; **avoir une solide c.** *(d'une personne)* to be solidly built

charpenté [ʃarpɑ̃te] ADJ built, constructed; **homme bien** *ou* **solidement c.** well-built man; **pièce de théâtre bien charpentée** well-constructed play

charpenter [ʃarpɑ̃te] VT *(roman etc)* to construct; **c. un discours** to construct *or* frame a speech

charpenterie [ʃarpɑ̃tri] NF **1** *(métier)* carpentry; **faire de la c.** to do carpentry **2** *(atelier)* carpenter's (work)shop; *(chantier)* timberyard

charpentier [ʃarpɑ̃tje] NM carpenter; **c. du bord** shipwright

charpie [ʃarpi] NF **1** viande en c. meat cooked to shreds; **mettre qch en c.** to tear sth to pieces *or* to shreds; **elle a déchiré son livre et en a fait de la c.** she tore her book to shreds; *Fam* **il vous mettra en c.** he'll make mincemeat out of you **2** *(pour faire de pansements)* lint

charretée [ʃarte] NF cartload, cartful; **nous avons eu droit à des charretées d'insultes** we were treated to a heap *or* a pile of insults

charretier, -ière [ʃartje, -jɛr] NM carter, carrier; *Fig* **parler/jurer comme un c.** to talk like a fishwife/swear like a trooper; **langage de c.** coarse language
▸ ADJ **chemin c., voie charretière** cart track

charrette [ʃarɛt] NF cart; **qui va faire partie de la prochaine c. (de licenciements)?** who'll be included in the next round of redundancies?; *Vieilli* **être c.** to be working to a deadline; **faire une c.** to work round the clock; *Suisse Fam* **c. de Paul!** blinking Paul!
▸▸ *Hist* **c. anglaise** dogcart, trap; **c. des condamnés** tumbrel

charriage [ʃarjaʒ] NM **1** *(portage)* haulage, carriage **2** *Géol* thrusting, overthrust

charrier [ʃarje] *(impf, pr sub* **n. charriions, v. charriiez)** VT **1** *(transporter)* to cart, to carry **2** *(entraîner)* to carry along, to wash down; **rivière qui charrie du sable** river that carries *or* brings down sand; **nuages charriés par le vent** wind-driven clouds **3** *Arg (se moquer de)* **c. qn** to wind sb up; **se faire c. par ses amis** to get the wind-up from one's friends
▸ VI *Arg (exagérer)* to go too far *or* over the top; **il charrie vraiment!** he's really having you on!; *Fam* **(il ne) faut pas c.!** come off it!

charroi [ʃarwa] NM cartage, haulage, carriage

charron [ʃarɔ̃] NM cartwright, wheelwright

charroyer [ʃarwaje] VT (*je charroie; je charroierai*) to transport in a cart, to cart

charrue [ʃary] NF **1** *Agr* plough, *Am* plow; **mener la c.** to drive the plough; *Fam* **mettre la c. avant les bœufs** to put the cart before the horse **2** *Can* snowplough, *Am* snowplow

charte [ʃart] NF **1** *(convention)* charter; *Br Hist* **la Grande C.** the Magna Carta; *Pol, Hist* **la c. de l'Atlantique** the Atlantic Charter; **la c. des Nations unies** the United Nations Charter **2** *(document ancien)* (ancient) deed, title; **l'École des chartes** = the School of Palaeography and Librarianship (in Paris)
▸▸ **c. commerciale** commercial charter; *Journ* **c. graphique** *ou* **rédactionnelle** house-style book

charter [ʃartɛr] NM **(avion) c.** charter, chartered aircraft; **vol c.** charter flight; **voyager en c.** to take a charter; **c. partiel** partial charter

chartérisation [ʃarterizasjɔ̃] NF chartering

chartisme [ʃartism] NM *Br Hist* chartism

chartiste [ʃartist] **1** *Univ* = student of the École des chartes **2** *Br Hist* chartist

chartreuse [ʃartrøz] NF **1** *(couvent)* Carthusian monastery, Charterhouse **2** *(alcool)* Chartreuse; **c. jaune/verte** yellow/green Chartreuse

chartreux, -euse [ʃartrø, -øz] N *Rel* Carthusian (monk/nun)

Charybde [karibd] NM Charybdis; **tomber de C. en Scylla** to jump out of the frying pan into the fire

chas [ʃɑ] NM *(d'une aiguille)* eye

chasse [ʃas] NF **1** hunting; *(avec fusil)* shooting; *(événement)* hunt/shoot; **aller à la c.** to go hunting/shooting; **la c. est ouverte/fermée** the shooting season has begun/ended; **c. fermée** close season; **vivre de sa c.** to live off one's catch; **partager la c.** to share the bag; **faire bonne c.** to have good sport, to make a good bag; *Prov* **qui va à la c. perd sa place** if you leave your place, someone will take it; **la c. vient de passer (les chasseurs)** the hunters have just gone by; *(à courre)* the hunt has just gone by; **fusil de c.** shotgun; **chien de c.** retriever; **couteau/habit de c.** hunting knife/coat
2 *(réserve)* **c. gardée** private game preserve; *Fig* **ah non, c. gardée!** private property!, hands off!; **les chasses royales** the royal hunting grounds; **louer une c.** to rent a shoot
3 *(poursuite)* chase; **donner la c. à qn/qch, prendre qn/qch en c.** to chase *or* pursue *or* give chase to sb/sth; **faire la c. à qch** to hunt sth down *or* out; **faire la c. aux abus** to hunt down *or* track down abuse; *Fam* **c. au mari** husband hunting; **faire la c. au mari** to be on the lookout for a husband
4 *Mil, Aviat* **la c.** the fighter aircraft, the fighters; **pilote de c.** fighter pilot
5 **c. (d'eau)** flush; **tirer la c. (d'eau)** to flush the toilet
6 **être en c.** *(d'une chienne, chatte)* to be on heat *or* in season
7 *Typ (épaisseur de la lettre)* width; *(d'une page)* overrun
8 *Aut* caster
▸▸ **c. à la baleine** *(activité)* whaling; *(événement)* whale hunt; **c. au chevreuil** deer hunting *or* stalking; **c. à courre** hunting; **c. au faucon** falconry; **c. au furet** ferreting; **c. au gros gibier** big game hunting; **c. à l'homme** manhunt; **une c. à l'homme a été organisée à travers le pays** a national manhunt has been launched; **c. au lapin** rabbiting; *(avec un fusil)* rabbit shooting; **c. au lévrier** coursing; **c. aux papillons** butterfly catching; **c. aux rats** rat catching; **c. au renard** *(activité)* foxhunting; *(événement)* foxhunt; *Pol* **c. aux sorcières** witch hunt; **c. aux souris** mousing; **c. sous-marine** underwater fishing; **c. au trésor** treasure hunt

Il faut noter que le nom anglais **chase** est un faux ami. Il signifie **poursuite**.

châsse [ʃɑs] NF **1** *Rel* reliquary, shrine **2** *(des lunettes)* mounting, frame **3** *Fam* **châsses** *(yeux)* eyes

chassé [ʃase] NM *(danse)* chassé

chasse-clou, *pl* **chasse-clous** NM nail punch, nail set

chassé-croisé, *pl* **chassés-croisés** NM **1** *(de personnel etc)* rearrangement, reshuffling; **c. de conseillers** reshuffling of advisers; **le c. des vacanciers sur les routes** the busy flow of holidaymakers on the roads; **un c. d'intrigues** a mass of conflicting plots; **un c. de malentendus** a confusion of misunderstandings **2** *(danse)* set to partners

chasse-goupille, *pl* **chasse-goupilles** NM pin punch

chasselas [ʃasla] NM chasselas grape

chasse-marée NM INV *(bateau)* coasting lugger

chasse-mouches NM INV fly swatter

chasse-neige NM INV **1** *(engin)* snowplough, *Am* snowplow **2** *Ski* snowplough, *Am* snowplow; **virage (en) c.** snowplough turn; **descendre une piste en c.** to snow-plough down a ski slope

chasse-pierres NM INV cowcatcher

chasser [ʃase] VT **1** *(animaux)* to hunt; **c. le renard/la perdrix** to go foxhunting/partridge shooting

2 *(personne)* to drive away, to chase out *or* away; *(employé)* to dismiss, *Fam* to sack; *(brouillard etc)* to dispel; **c. qn du pays** to drive sb from the country; **il fut chassé de la classe** he was expelled from the class; **si tu ne paies pas ton loyer, les propriétaires vont te c.** if you don't pay your rent, the owners will evict you; **chasse le chat de la maison!** chase the cat out (of the house)!; **se faire c. de la maison par ses parents** to get thrown out by one's parents; **je ne veux pas vous c., mais il est tard** I'm not trying to get rid of you, but it's getting late; **nous avons été chassés par les moustiques** we were chased away *or* driven away by mosquitoes; **c. une mouche (du revers de la main)** to brush away a fly; **le vent chassait la pluie contre les vitres** the wind was driving the rain against the windowpanes; **le vent va c. les nuages** the wind will blow the clouds away; **c. une mauvaise odeur** to get rid of a bad smell; *Fig* **c. qn/qch de son esprit** to dismiss sb/sth from one's mind *or* thoughts

VI **1** to hunt, to go hunting; *(au fusil)* to shoot, to go shooting; **c. à courre** to hunt, to go hunting; **c. au furet** to ferret; *Fig* **c. sur les terres de qn** to poach on sb's preserve *or* territory

2 *(venir)* to drive; **nuages qui chassent du nord** clouds driving from the north

3 *Naut (d'une ancre)* to drag; **navire qui chasse sur ses ancres** ship dragging her anchors

4 *Aut* to skid

5 *Typ (d'un caractère)* to drive out; *(d'un texte)* to overrun

> Il faut noter que le verbe anglais **to chase** est un faux ami. Il signifie **poursuivre**.

chasseresse [ʃasrɛs] NF *Littér* huntress; **Diane c.** Diana the Huntress

chasseur, -euse [ʃasœr, -øz] N hunter, *f* huntress; *(surtout à courre)* huntsman; **c'est un bon c.** he's a good shot

NM **1** *(dans un hôtel etc)* pageboy, *Am* bellboy, bellhop **2** *Mil, Aviat* fighter; *Naut* **c. de sous-marins** submarine hunter **3** *Mil* rifleman, light infantryman, chasseur; **les chasseurs (à pied)** the light infantry; **les chasseurs alpins** the mountain light infantry ▸▸**c. d'autographes** autograph hunter; **c. d'images** keen photographer; *(professionnel)* professional photographer; **c. de primes** bounty hunter; *aussi Fig* **c. de têtes** headhunter; *Fig* **elle a été recrutée par un c. de têtes** she was headhunted

chasseur-bagagiste, *pl* **chasseurs-bagagistes** NM luggage porter, porter

chasseur-bombardier, *pl* **chasseurs-bombardiers** NM fighter-bomber

chassie [ʃasi] NF *(dans les yeux)* matter, rheum

chassieux, -ieuse [ʃasjø, -jøz] ADJ *(yeux)* rheumy

châssis [ʃasi] NM **1** *(charpente)* frame; *Beaux-Arts* stretcher; **c. de porte/fenêtre** door/window frame; **c. mobile** sash; **c. dormant** sash (frame); **c. à guillotine** sash window **2** *(de jardin)* (cold) frame; **culture sous c.** forcing **3** *Aut* chassis; **c. treillis** box section chassis; **c. tubulaire** box section chassis, space frame chassis; *Fam* **quel beau c.!** *(d'une femme)* she's got a great figure!, *Vieilli* what a chassis! **4** *Typ* chase

chaste [ʃast] ADJ chaste, pure; **un baiser c.** a chaste kiss; *Iron* **oreilles chastes** delicate ears

chastement [ʃastəmā] ADV chastely, innocently

chasteté [ʃastəte] NF chastity, purity

chasuble [ʃazybl] NF **1** **robe c.** pinafore dress, *Am* jumper **2** *Rel* chasuble

chat¹, chatte [ʃa, ʃat] N cat, *m* tom(cat); **le C. botté** Puss in Boots; **petit c.** kitten; *Fam* **mon petit c., ma petite chatte** my dear, my pet, my darling; *Fig* **il n'y avait pas un c. dans la rue** there wasn't a soul in the street; **langues de c.** langues de chat, finger biscuits; *Fig* **appeler un c. un c.** to call a spade a spade; **acheter c. en poche** to buy a pig in a poke; **avoir un c. dans la gorge** to have a frog in one's throat; **faire une toilette de c.** to give oneself a cat('s) lick *or* a lick and a promise; *Prov* **il ne faut pas réveiller le c. qui dort** let sleeping dogs lie; **à bon c. bon rat** tit for tat; **c. échaudé craint l'eau froide** once bitten twice shy; **quand le c. n'est pas là, les souris dansent** when the cat's away the mice will play; **jouer au c. et à la souris avec qn** to play cat and mouse with sb; **la nuit tous les chats sont gris** all cats are grey in the dark

NM *(jeu)* tag, tig; *(celui qui cherche)* it; **jouer à c.** to play tag *or* tig; **c. perché** off-ground tag *or* tig; **c'est toi le c.!** you're it!

▸▸**c. de gouttière** alley cat; **c. à neuf queues** cat-o'-nine-tails; **c. persan** Persian (cat); **c. sauvage** wildcat; **c. siamois** Siamese (cat)

chat² [tʃat] NM *Ordinat (sur Internet)* chat

châtaigne [ʃatɛɲ] NF **1** *(fruit)* (sweet) chestnut **2** *Fam (coup de poing)* smack, clout; **je vais lui flanquer une c.** I'm going to clobber him; **je me suis pris une c.** *(léger choc électrique)* I got a shock ▸▸**c. d'eau** water chestnut

châtaigner [ʃatɛɲe] VT *Fam* to clout, to thump

châtaigneraie [ʃatɛɲrɛ] NF chestnut grove, chestnut plantation

châtaignier [ʃatɛɲe] NM *(arbre, bois)* chestnut

châtain [ʃatɛ̃] ADJ *(féminin rare)* (chestnut-)brown; **une femme c.** *ou* **aux cheveux châtains** a brunette; **cheveux c. clair** (light) brown hair

NM chestnut brown

château, -eaux [ʃato] NM **1** castle; *(manoir)* mansion, manor, hall; *(demeure de famille aristocratique)* stately home; *Hist* (royal) palace; **le c. de Versailles** the palace of Versailles; **les châteaux de la Loire** the Châteaux of the Loire; *Fig* **c'est la vie de c.** it's the life of Riley; *Fig* **elle mène la vie de c.** she leads a life of luxury; *Fig* **bâtir des châteaux en Espagne** to build castles in Spain *or* in the air **2** *(exploitation vinicole)* château; **vin mis en bouteille au c.** château-bottled wine; *Arg* **C.-la-Pompe** (drinking) water, Adam's ale ▸▸*Naut* **c. d'arrière** afterdeck; *Naut* **c. d'avant** forecastle, fo'c'sle; **c. de cartes** house of cards; **c. d'eau** water tower; *Rail* tank; **c. fort** (fortified) castle; *Naut* **c. de poupe** afterdeck; *Naut* **c. de proue** forecastle, fo'c'sle

chateaubriand, châteaubriant [ʃatobrijā] NM *Culin* chateaubriand, porterhouse steak

châtelain [ʃatlɛ̃] NM **1** *Hist* lord of the manor **2** *(propriétaire d'un château)* owner of a/the château

châtelaine [ʃatlɛn] NF **1** *Hist* lady (of the manor) **2** *(propriétaire)* (woman) owner of a/ the château; *(épouse du propriétaire)* wife of an owner of a château/the owner of the chateau **3** *(pour clés etc)* chatelaine

châtelet [ʃatlɛ] NM *Hist* small castle

chat-huant, *pl* **chats-huants** [ʃayā] NM tawny owl, brown owl

châtié [ʃatje] ADJ *(style)* polished; **en langage c.** in refined language

châtier [ʃatje] VT *(impf, pr sub* **n. châtiions, v. châtiiez)* **1** *Littér (enfant etc)* to chastise; **c. son corps** to mortify the flesh; **c. l'audace de qn** to punish sb for his impudence; *Prov* **qui aime bien châtie bien** spare the rod and spoil the child **2** *(style)* to polish

chatière [ʃatjɛr] NF **1** *(pour chat)* cat flap **2** *(pour aération)* ventilation hole **3** *(passage étroit)* narrow underground passage

châtiment [ʃatimā] NM *Litt* punishment, chastisement, castigation; **c. corporel** corporal punishment; **il a reçu un c. sévère** he was severely punished

chatoiement [ʃatwamā] NM shimmer, iridescence, sheen

chaton¹ [ʃatɔ̃] NM **1** *(petit chat)* kitten **2** *Bot* catkin

chaton² NM **1** *(d'une bague)* bezel, setting **2** *(pierre)* stone

chatouille [ʃatuj] NF *Fam* **faire des chatouilles à qn** to tickle sb; **craindre la c.** *ou* **les chatouilles** to be ticklish

chatouillement [ʃatujmā] NM tickling; **éprouver** *ou* **avoir un c. dans la gorge** to have a tickle in one's throat

chatouiller [ʃatuje] VT to tickle; **arrête de c. ta sœur!** stop tickling your sister!; *Fam* **c. les côtes à qn** to give sb a thrashing; **vin qui chatouille le palais** wine that pleases *or* titillates the palate; **de bonnes odeurs de cuisine nous chatouillaient les narines** delicious cooking smells were making our mouths water; **c. la curiosité** to excite *or* arouse curiosity; **c. l'amour-propre de qn** to flatter sb's vanity; **l'envie me chatouille d'aller voir ce qu'ils font** I'm itching to go and see what they're doing; **il ne faut pas le c. sur cette question, il risque de se mettre en colère** don't needle him on the subject, he might get angry

VI to tickle; **ah! ça chatouille!** oh! that tickles!

chatouilleux, -euse [ʃatujø, -øz] ADJ ticklish; *Fig* sensitive, touchy; **elle est très chatouilleuse** she's very ticklish; *Fig* **c. sur le point d'honneur** touchy where honour is concerned, touchy on a point of honour

chatouillis [ʃatuji] NM *Fam* gentle tickling, light tickling; **faire des c. à qn** to tickle sb gently

chatoyant [ʃatwajā] ADJ shimmering, iridescent; *(pierre, imagination etc)* sparkling; **soie chatoyante** shot silk

chatoyer [ʃatwaje] VI *(il chatoie; il chatoiera)* to shimmer; *(d'une pierre)* to sparkle; *Fig* **style qui chatoie** sparkling style

châtré [ʃatre] ADJ *(homme)* castrated; **taureau c.** steer, castrated bull; **étalon c.** gelding, castrated stallion

NM eunuch; *Fam* **voix de c.** high-pitched *or* falsetto voice

châtrer [ʃatre] VT **1** to castrate, to emasculate; *(étalon)* to geld; *(chat)* to neuter **2** *(texte)* to censor, to expurgate

chatte [ʃat] NF **1** *voir* chat **2** *Vulg (sexe féminin)* pussy

chattemite [ʃatmit] NF **faire la c.** to simper

ADJ *(manière)* smooth, ingratiating; *(air)* smooth

chatter [tʃate] VI *Ordinat (sur Internet)* to chat

chatteries [ʃatri] NFPL **1** *(gestes de tendresse etc)* caresses; **se faire des c.** to caress each other **2** *(friandises)* delicacies, dainties

chatterton [ʃatertɔn] NM *Élec* (adhesive) insulating tape, *Am* friction tape

chat-tigre, *pl* **chats-tigres** NM tiger cat

CHAUD [ʃo] ADJ **1** *(modéré)* warm; *(intense)* hot; **un bon pull c.** a good warm jumper; **pendant la chaude saison** during the warm weather; **la soupe est toute chaude** the soup is steaming or piping hot; **repas c.** hot meal; **animal à sang c.** warm-blooded animal; Culin **à mettre dans un four c.** cook in a hot oven; **pleurer à chaudes larmes** to weep bitterly; **il est c., il a de la fièvre** he's very warm or hot, he's running a fever; **le soleil est déjà c.** the sun's already (quite) warm or hot; Prov **il faut battre le fer pendant qu'il est c.** strike while the iron is hot, make hay while the sun shines; Fig **avoir la tête chaude** to be hotheaded; **l'été va être c.** it'll be a hot summer; Fig there will be a lot of unrest this summer; **l'alerte fut chaude** it was a close or near thing; **les points chauds du Proche-Orient** the hot spots or flash points of the Middle East; **chaude discussion** heated discussion; Fig **elle n'est pas chaude pour le projet** she's not keen on or not over-enthusiastic about the project; **c'est un c. partisan/défenseur de ...** he's a keen supporter/defender of ...; **nouvelle toute chaude** hot news, hot gossip; **tout c. de ...** straight from ..., hotfoot from ...; Fig **voix chaude** sultry voice; Beaux-Arts **tons chauds** warm tints

2 Fig **avoir un tempérament c.** to be hottempered; **avoir le sang c.** to be hotblooded; Fam **être c.** to be hot stuff; Fam **c'est un c. lapin** he's a randy devil

ADV **j'aime manger c.** I like my food hot; **le malade doit manger c.** the patient must eat hot food; **il fait très c.** it's hot, it's very warm; **cela ne me fait ni c. ni froid** it makes no difference, it's all the same to me

NM (intense) heat; (modéré) warmth; **garder ou tenir qch au c.** to keep sth hot; **il doit rester au lit, gardez-le bien au c.** he must stay in bed, keep him warm; **je garde ton assiette au c.** I'll keep your plate warm; **chez soi, au c.** at home, in the warmth; **prendre un c. et froid** to catch a chill; **avoir c.** (d'une personne) to be or feel warm/hot; **tu as assez c.?** are you warm enough?; **tu n'as pas trop c.?** you're not too hot?; Fam **il a eu c.** he had a narrow escape; **je crève de c.!** I'm dying of heat!; **travailler un métal à c.** to hot-work a metal; **être opéré à c.** to have an emergency operation; **interroger les spectateurs à c.** to question the audience on the spot; Fig **souffler le c. et le froid** to blow hot and cold

chaudement [ʃodmɑ̃] ADV warmly; **être vêtu c.** to be warmly dressed; **approuver c.** to approve heartily; **il a été c. défendu par elle** he was hotly defended by her

chaude-pisse [ʃodpis] NF INV Arg VD, clap

chaud-froid, pl **chauds-froids** NM Culin **c. de poulet/gibier** chaudfroid of chicken/game

chaudière [ʃodjɛr] NF **1** (de chauffage) boiler; **c. de chauffage central** central heating boiler; **c. à mazout/à gaz** oil-fired/gas boiler; **c. à vapeur** steam boiler or generator **2** Arch (pour la lessive etc) copper **3** Can (seau) bucket; **c. à sucre** = bucket for collecting maple sap

chaudron [ʃodrɔ̃] NM cauldron, Am caldron

chaudronnerie [ʃodrɔnri] NF **1** Ind boilermaking **2** (objets) boilers **3** (atelier) boiler works

chaudronnier, -ière [ʃodrɔnje, -jɛr] N (fabricant) boiler maker

ADJ **industrie chaudronnière** boiler-making

chauffage [ʃofaʒ] NM (d'une pièce etc) heating; (appareils etc) heating system; (dans une voiture) (car) heater; **bois de c.** firewood; **appareil de c.** heater; **c. central** central heating; **c. urbain** district heating; **c. par le sol** underfloor heating; **c. à l'électricité/au gaz/au mazout** electric/gas/oil heating; **installer le c.** to put central heating in; **le c. est détraqué** the boiler or the heat-

ing is out of order; **mettre/arrêter le c.** to turn on/turn off the heating

chauffagiste [ʃofaʒist] N Tech heating engineer

chauffant [ʃofɑ̃] ADJ heating, warming; **couverture chauffante** electric blanket; **plaque chauffante** hotplate

chauffard [ʃofar] NM Fam (mauvais conducteur) roadhog, reckless driver

chauffe [ʃof] NF Tech firing, stoking; **surface de c.** heating surface; **chef de c.** head stoker; Naut **chambre de c.** stokehold; **bleu de c.** boiler suit

chauffe-assiettes NM INV plate warmer

chauffe-bain, pl **chauffe-bains** NM water heater

chauffe-biberon, pl **chauffe-biberons** NM bottle-warmer

chauffe-eau NM INV water heater; (à réservoir) immersion heater

chauffe-pieds NM INV footwarmer

chauffe-plat, pl **chauffe-plats** NM chafing dish, hotplate

chauffer [ʃofe] VT **1** to heat (up), to warm (up); **c. une maison au gaz** to heat a house with gas, to have gas heating; **la chambre n'est pas chauffée** there's no heating in the bedroom, the bedroom's not heated; **c. le fer à blanc/au rouge** to make iron white-/red-hot; **chauffé à blanc/au rouge** white-/red-hot; Aut **c. le moteur** to warm up the engine; **c. une chaudière/une locomotive** to fire/stoke (up) a boiler/an engine

2 Fam **c. qn** to cram or coach sb for an examination; **c. son public** to warm up one's audience; **il faut c. l'affaire** we're going to have to get things moving or hurry things along; **c. qn à blanc** to whip sb into a frenzy

VI **1** (devenir chaud) to get or become hot or warm; **ce radiateur chauffe bien/mal** this radiator gives out/doesn't give out a lot of heat; **la soupe chauffe** the soup's heating or warming up, the soup's on; **mets la soupe à c.** put the soup on (to heat); Fam **faites c. la colle!** that didn't sound very healthy!

2 Fam **ça chauffe, ça va c.** things are beginning to heat up; **je te promets que ça va c. s'il est en retard!** I promise you there'll be trouble if he's late!; **ça chauffe, ce soir!** things are hotting up this evening!; **tu chauffes!** (dans un jeu) you're getting warmer!

3 (d'un roulement à billes etc) to overheat, to run hot; **le moteur a tendance à c.** the engine tends to overheat or to get overheated

VPR **se chauffer** to warm oneself (**au soleil** in the sun); **se c. (les muscles)** to warm up, to limber up; **se c. au mazout** to have oil-fired (central) heating; **nous ne nous chauffions toujours pas** we still hadn't turned the heating on; Fig **je vais lui montrer de quel bois je me chauffe!** I'll show him what I'm made of!

chaufferette [ʃofrɛt] NF (pour les pieds) footwarmer

chaufferie [ʃofri] NF boiler room

chauffeur, -euse[1] [ʃofœr, -øz] N **1** (de voiture, bus, camion) driver; (employé) chauffeur, driver; **c. de camion** truck or Br lorry driver; **c. routier** long-distance truck or Br lorry driver; **elle est chauffeuse de taxi** she's a taxi driver; **les chauffeurs du dimanche** Sunday drivers; **je n'ai pas l'intention de faire le c. toute la journée** I've no intention of chauffeuring people around all day **2** (d'une locomotive à vapeur) stoker

chauffeuse[2] [ʃoføz] NF (chaise) low fireside chair

chaulage [ʃolaʒ] NM (des murs etc) whitewashing; (du sol etc) liming

chauler [ʃole] VT (murs etc) to whitewash; (sol etc) to treat with lime

chaume [ʃom] NM **1** (paille) thatch; **couvrir un toit de** ou **en c.** to thatch a roof; **toit de c.** thatched roof **2** (ce qui reste des céréales) stubble; (champ) stubble field

chaumer [ʃome] VT Agr **c. les champs** to clear fields (of stubble)

chaumière [ʃomjɛr] NF thatched cottage; Fig **un roman à faire pleurer dans les chaumières** a tear-jerking novel; **on en parlera longtemps dans les chaumières** tongues will be wagging about this for a long time

chaussant [ʃosɑ̃] ADJ (chaussure) that fits well

chaussée [ʃose] NF **1** (route) roadway, Am pavement; **'c. glissante'** 'slippery (road) surface'; **'c. déformée'** 'temporary road surface' **2** (digue) dyke, embankment; (dans un endroit marécageux) causeway; **la C. des Géants** the Giant's Causeway **3** (écueil) reef, line of rocks

chausse-pied, pl **chausse-pieds** [ʃospje] NM shoehorn

chausser [ʃose] VT **1** (chaussures, bottes etc) to put on; **chaussé de pantoufles** wearing (his) slippers; **c. les étriers** to put one's feet into the stirrups; **c. ses lunettes** to put one's glasses on

2 (personne) (mettre des chaussures à) to put shoes on; (fournir en chaussures) to supply with footwear, to make footwear for; **se faire c. chez Adrian** to buy or get one's shoes at Adrian's

3 (aller à) to fit; **ce modèle te chausse mieux que l'autre** this style fits you better than the other one

4 Aut (voiture) to put tyres on

5 (arbre) to earth up

VI to fit; **souliers qui chaussent bien** shoes that fit well; **ce soulier chausse étroit** this shoe comes in a narrow fitting; **du combien chaussez-vous?** what size do you take (in shoes)?; **elle chausse du 37** she takes a (size) four

VPR **se chausser** to put one's shoes on; **se c. tout seul** (d'un enfant) to put one's shoes on all by oneself; **se c. chez Simone** to buy one's shoes at Simone's

chausses [ʃos] NFPL Hist breeches; **coller aux c. de qn** to dog sb's footsteps

chausse-trap(p)e, pl **chausse-trap(p)es** [ʃostrap] NF Fig Litt trap

chaussette [ʃosɛt] NF sock; **une paire de chaussettes** a pair of socks; **en chaussettes** in one's socks, in one's stockinged feet; **c. de ski/de sport/de tennis** ski/sports/tennis sock; Arg **un vrai jus de c.** watery coffee; **laisser tomber qn comme une vieille c.** to cast sb aside like an old rag

chausseur [ʃosœr] NM (magasin) shoe shop; (fabricant) shoe manufacturer

chausson [ʃosɔ̃] **1** NM (pantoufle) slipper; (de danse) ballet shoe; (de bébé) (baby's) bootee; **se mettre en chaussons** to put one's slippers on **2** Culin turnover; **c. aux pommes** apple turnover

chaussure [ʃosyr] NF **1** (soulier) shoe; **une paire de chaussures** a pair of shoes; **c. de ville/de sport/habillée** town/sports/dress shoe; **chaussures de marche** ou **de montagne** walking boots; **c. à talon** ou **haute** high-heeled shoe; **c. basse** flat shoe; **c. montante** ankle boot; **chaussures de ski** ski boots; Fam **trouver c. à son pied** to find the right woman/man **2** Ind (boot and) shoe industry or trade **3** (sens large) footwear

chauve [ʃov] ADJ bald; Fig (colline etc) bare; Fam **c. comme un genou** ou **comme un œuf** ou **comme une bille** as bald as a coot

N bald(-headed) person

chauve-souris, pl **chauves-souris** NF bat

chauvin, -ine [ʃovɛ̃, -in] *Péj* **N** jingoist, chauvinist
ADJ jingoistic, chauvinistic

> Il faut noter que le nom anglais **chauvinist** est un faux ami. Il est désormais employé le plus souvent dans le sens de **phallocrate**.

chauvinisme [ʃovinism] **NM** *Péj* jingoism, chauvinism

> Il faut noter que le nom anglais **chauvinism** est un faux ami. Il signifie le plus souvent **phallocratie**.

chauviniste [ʃovinist] **ADJ, N** *Péj* = chauvin

chaux [ʃo] **NF** lime; **c. vive** quicklime; **c. éteinte** slaked lime; **blanchir un mur à la c.** to whitewash a wall; **bâtir à c. et à sable** *ou* **à c. et à ciment** to build firmly *or* solidly; *Fig* **être bâti à c. et à sable** *(d'une personne)* to have an iron constitution

chavirer [ʃavire] **VI 1** *(d'un bateau etc)* to capsize, to overturn, *Fam* to turn turtle; *Fig (sombrer)* to collapse; **faire c.** to capsize; **les plus grands empires chavirent** even the greatest empires collapse *or* fall **2** *(tourner)* to reel, to spin (round); **tout chavire autour de moi** everything's spinning; **ses yeux chaviraient** he was showing the whites of his eyes
VT 1 *(bateau)* to capsize, to overturn **2** *Fam (retourner)* to overwhelm, to bowl over; **il en est tout chaviré** it's knocked him for six

chébran [ʃebrɑ̃] **ADJ INV** *Fam (branché)* trendy

chèche [ʃɛʃ] **NM** North African scarf

chéchia [ʃeʃja] **NF** fez

check-list, *pl* **check-lists** [tʃɛklist] **NF** *Aviat etc Fam* checklist

check-point [tʃɛkpɔint] **NM** **INV** *Mil* checkpoint

check-up [tʃɛkœp] **NM** **INV** *Méd* check-up; **faire un c. à qn** to give sb a check-up; **le médecin me conseille de faire un c.** the doctor is advising me to have a check-up

chef [ʃɛf] **NM 1** *(de famille etc)* head; *(d'une tribu etc)* chief, chieftain; *(d'un parti politique etc)* leader; *(d'une entreprise)* head, manager; *Fam (patron)* boss; *(de jurés)* foreman; *(d'une école de pensée etc)* founder; **c. (cuisinier** *ou* **de cuisine)** (head) chef, chef de cuisine; **le plat du c.** the chef's special; **ingénieur en c.** chief engineer; **rédacteur en c.** chief editor; **Mil commandant en c.** commander-in-chief; **jouer au petit c.** to throw one's weight around; **il se débrouille comme un c.** he's getting on *or* doing very well; **bravo, tu es un c.!** well done, you're a marvel! **2** *Arch, Hum (tête)* head; *Litt* **faire qch de son (propre) c.** to do sth on one's own authority *or Fam* off one's own bat; **au premier c.** first and foremost
▸▸ *Jur* **c. d'accusation** charge, count (of an/ the indictment); **c. d'antenne** programme supervisor; *Ind* **c. d'atelier** (shop) foreman; **c. de bande** ringleader; **c. de bataillon** major; *Admin* **c. de bureau** office manager, *Vieilli* chief *or* senior clerk; *Parl* **c. de cabinet** = (minister's) principal private secretary; **c. chasseur** head porter, *Am* bell captain; **c. comptable** chief accountant; *Cin, TV* **c. costumier** wardrobe supervisor, costume supervisor; **c. de cuisine** head chef, chef de cuisine; **c. de la diplomatie** foreign minister; *Cin, TV* **c. électricien** gaffer; **c. d'équipe** *Sport* captain; *Ind* foreman, charge hand; **c. d'État** head of state; **c. des exploitations** operations manager; **c. de fabrication** production manager, manufacturing manager; **c. de famille** head of the family; **c. de file** leader, lead manager; *(produit)* (market) leader;

Rail **c. de gare** station manager; **c. du gouvernement** head of government; **c. de groupe** group supervisor *or* manager *or* leader; **c. infirmier** charge nurse; **c. des informations** public relations *or* PR manager; **c. de magasin** store manager; **c. de marque** brand manager; *TV, Cin* **c. montage** editor; **c. de musique** bandmaster; **c. de nage** stroke (oar); *TV, Cin* **c. opérateur** cinematographer, head of cameras; **c. opérateur cadreur** lighting-cameraman; **c. d'orchestre** conductor; **c. de partie** chef de partie; **c. de partie boucher** larder chef; **c. de partie poissonnier** fish cook; **c. pâtissier** chef patissier, pastry chef; **c. de patrouille** patrol leader; **c. du personnel** personnel manager, head of personnel; **c. de petit déjeuner** breakfast chef; *TV* **c. de plateau** stage manager, floor boss; *TV etc* **c. de production** production head; *Com* **c. de produit** product manager; **c. de publicité** advertising manager *or* executive; *Naut* **c. de quart** officer of the watch; **c. de rang** head waiter, chef de rang, station waiter, *Am* captain; **c. de rayon** *(dans un magasin)* head of department, department(al) manager, department head; *(dans un hôpital)* consultant; **c. de réception** *(dans un hôtel)* reception manager, front office manager; *Journ* **c. de rubriques** features editor; **c. scout** scout leader; **c. serveur** waiting chef; **c. de service** head of department, departmental manager; *TV etc* **c. de studio** studio supervisor; **c. de train** guard, *Am* conductor; **c. des traitements** data processing *or* DP manager; **c. des ventes** sales manager; *Com* **c. de zone** area manager

chefaillon [ʃɛfajɔ̃] **NM** *Fam* little Hitler

chef-d'œuvre, *pl* **chefs-d'œuvre** [ʃɛdœvr] **NM** masterpiece; **c'est un c. de la littérature/de la peinture** it's a literary/artistic masterpiece

chef-garde, *pl* **chefs-gardes** **NM** *Belg Rail* ticket inspector

chef-lieu, *pl* **chefs-lieux** **NM** chief town *(of department)*, ≃ county town, *Am* ≃ county seat

cheftaine [ʃɛftɛn] **NF** *(des Guides)* captain; *(des jeannettes)* Brown Owl; *(des louveteaux)* cubmistress

cheik(h) [ʃɛk] **NM** sheik(h)

chelem [ʃlɛm] **NM** *Cartes* slam; **grand c.** grand slam; **petit c.** little slam; **faire c. à qn** to make a slam against sb; **elle a fini par me faire c.** I ended up not winning a trick against her; *Tennis etc* **Grand c.** Grand Slam

CHEMIN [ʃ(ə)mɛ̃] **NM 1** *(route)* way, road; *(voie)* path, track; **le c. de la gare** the way to the station; **le c. de la gloire/réussite** the road to glory/success; **le plus court c. d'un point à un autre** the shortest distance between two points; *Fam* **prendre le c. des écoliers** to take a roundabout way *or* the long(est) way round; **demander son c.** to ask one's way; **c'est sur mon c.** it's on my way; *aussi Fig* **nous avons beaucoup de c. à faire** we've a long way to go; *Fig* **il a du c. à faire s'il veut vraiment devenir un concurrent important** he has a long way to go if he wants to become a serious contender; **il faut compter deux ou trois heures de c.** it will take two or three hours to get there; **nous avons fait la moitié du c. ensemble/à pied** we went half the way together/on foot; *Fig* **nous avons déjà fait la moitié du c.** we're already halfway there; **aller son c.**, **aller son petit bonhomme de c.** to jog along; **s'arrêter en c.** to stop on the way; *Fig* **maintenant que tu as fait le plus gros du travail, ce serait bête de t'arrêter en (si bon) c.** now that you've done most of the work, it would be silly to stop; **être en bon c.** to be getting on well; **nous ne pouvons pas nous arrêter en si**

bon c. we can't give up now that we're doing so well; **leur affaire est en bon c.** their business is off to a good start; **elle n'en prend pas le c.** she's not going the right way about it; **le c. faisant** on the way; **faire le c. à pied/en vélo/en voiture** to walk/cycle/drive all the way; **faire un bout de c. avec qn** to go part of the way with sb; *Fig (vivre)* to live with sb for a while; **ils ont fait un bout de c. ensemble** *(dans la vie professionnelle)* their careers followed similar paths for a while; **suivre le droit c.** to stay on the straight and narrow; *aussi Fig* **montrer le c.** to lead *or* show the way; *Fig* **il leur montre le c.** he's showing them the way; **à mi-c.** halfway; **pourquoi s'arrêter à mi-c.?** why stop halfway?; **se mettre en c.** to set out *or* off; **se mettre en c. pour** *ou* **prendre le c. de Paris** to set out *or* off for Paris; **être dans** *ou* **sur le c. de qn** to be or stand in sb's way; **ton vélo est sur le c., pousse-le** your bike is in the way, move it; **il a trouvé un certain nombre de difficultés sur son c.** he found a certain number of difficulties standing in his way; **se mettre dans le c. de qn** to stand in sb's way; **il n'a pas intérêt à se trouver sur mon c.** he'd better keep out of my way; *Fig* **trouver son c. de Damas** to see the light; **ne pas y aller par quatre chemins** *ou* **par trente-six chemins** to go straight to the point; *Fig* **elle fera son c.** she'll get on *or* make her way in life; **il est très ambitieux, il fera du c.** he's very ambitious, he'll go far *or* a long way *or* he'll go places; *Fig* **cette idée fait du c.** the idea is gaining ground; *Arch* **grand c.** highway, high road; **voleur de grand c.** highwayman; *Fam* **être toujours sur les chemins** to be always on the go
2 *Ordinat* path
▸▸ *Ordinat* **c. d'accès** path; *Ordinat* **c. d'accès aux données** data path; *Ordinat* **c. du courrier électronique** mail path; **c. creux** sunken road; **c. critique** critical path; **c. de fer** railway, *Am* railroad; *Ordinat (affichage)* thumbnail; *Journ* page allocation; *Typ* page plan; **aller** *ou* **voyager en** *ou* **par c. de fer** to go *or* travel by rail *or* by train; **c. de fer omnibus/rapide** local/express service; **accident de c. de fer** rail(way) accident; **c. de fer français** French railways; **Chemins de fer nationaux du Canada** Canadian National Railways; **c. de halage** towpath; *Ordinat* **c. du papier** *(d'une imprimante)* paper path; **c. piéton(nier)** footpath; **c. de randonnée** hiking trail; **c. de ronde** covered way; *Tech* **c. de roulement pour billes** ball race; **c. de table** (table) runner; **c. de terre** dirt track; *Can Jur* **c. de tolérance** right of way; **c. de traverse** side road; **c. vicinal** byroad, minor road

chemineau, -eaux [ʃ(ə)mino] **NM** tramp, vagrant

cheminée [ʃ(ə)mine] **NF 1** *(dans une maison)* fireplace; **(manteau de) c.** mantelpiece, chimneypiece; **il y a une c. dans chaque pièce** there's a fireplace in every room; **un feu dans la c.** a fire in the grate; **c'est sur la c.** it's on the mantelpiece; **c. en marbre** marble mantelpiece **2** *(conduit)* chimney (stack); *(de bateau à vapeur)* funnel, smokestack; **c. d'usine** factory chimney; **(conduit de) c.** flue; **le Père Noël passe par la c.** Father Christmas comes down the chimney; **feu de c.** chimney fire; **c. d'aération** air shaft, ventilating shaft **3** *(de lampe à huile)* chimney; **col c.** *(de pull etc)* cowl neck(line) **4** *Géol* chimney; **faire une c.** *(d'un alpiniste)* to chimney
▸▸ *Géol* **c. de fée** fairy chimney; *Géol* **c. volcanique** vent

cheminement [ʃ(ə)minmɑ̃] **NM 1** *(progression)* progression, movement; **le c. des touristes devant les toiles célèbres** the filing past of the tourists in front of the famous paintings; **le c. des eaux** the advance of the water **2** *Mil (vers les positions ennemies)* advance **3 c. de la pensée** advance *or* progress *or* development of thought; *(processus)* thought processes

cheminer [ʃ(ə)mine] **VI 1** *(avancer)* to advance, to move along; **la caravane chemine dans le désert** the caravan makes its way through the desert; **les eaux cheminent dans des canaux souterrains** the water travels through the underground canals **2** *Mil (vers les positions ennemies)* to advance; *Fig* to gain ground; **laisser une idée c.** to let an idea gain ground

cheminot [ʃ(ə)mino] **NM** rail(way) worker, railwayman, *Am* railroader; *(employé)* rail(-way) employee

chemisage [ʃ(ə)mizaʒ] **NM** *(d'une chaudière, d'un cylindre etc)* jacketing, casing; *(d'un fusil, d'un cylindre etc)* lining

chemise [ʃ(ə)miz] **NF 1** *(vêtement)* shirt; **c. à manches longues/courtes** long-/short-sleeved shirt; **en (bras** *ou* **en manches de) c.** in one's shirtsleeves; *Fig* **il change d'avis comme de c.** he changes his mind as often as he changes his shirt; **se moquer de qch comme de sa première c.** not to give a damn *or* two hoots about sth; **il donnerait sa c. au premier venu** he'd give you the shirt off his back **2** *(classeur)* folder; **mettre un livre sous c.** to cover a book **3** *(de chaudière, de cylindre etc)* jacket(ing), casing, sheathing; *(de cylindre, de fourneau etc)* lining; *(de mur)* facing; *Aut* **c. flottante/humide/sèche** slip/wet/dry liner ▸▸ **c. américaine** (woman's) vest, *Am* undershirt; **c. de nuit** (woman's) nightdress; *(d'homme)* nightshirt; *Hist* **Chemises brunes** Brownshirts; *Hist* **Chemises noires** Blackshirts; *Hist* **Chemises rouges** Red Shirts

chemiser [ʃ(ə)mize] **VT** *(chaudière, cylindre etc)* to jacket, to case; *(fusil, cylindre etc)* to line

chemiserie [ʃ(ə)mizri] **NF** *Ind* shirt making; *(ensemble de vêtements)* shirts, underwear and ties; *(fabrique)* shirt factory; *(magasin)* gents' outfitters

chemisette [ʃ(ə)mizɛt] **NF** *(pour hommes)* short-sleeved shirt

chemisier [ʃ(ə)mizje] **NM 1** *(fabricant)* shirtmaker; *(marchand)* men's outfitter **2** *(corsage)* blouse; **robe c.** shirt-waister

chênaie [ʃɛnɛ] **NF** oak grove *or* plantation

chenal, -aux [ʃ(ə)nal, -o] **NM 1** *(d'une rivière, d'un port etc)* channel, fairway; **au milieu du c.** in mid channel **2** *(courant d'eau)* millrace

chenapan [ʃ(ə)napā] **NM** *Hum* rogue, scoundrel

chêne [ʃɛn] **NM** *(arbre)* oak; **c. vert** evergreen oak, holm oak, ilex; **table en c. (massif)** (solid) oak table; *Fig* **être fort comme un c.** to be as strong as an ox

chêneau, -eaux [ʃɛno] **NM** *(d'un toit)* gutter

chêneau, -eaux [ʃɛno] **NM** oak sapling

chêne-liège, *pl* **chênes-lièges NM** cork oak

chenet [ʃ(ə)nɛ] **NM** firedog, andiron

chènevière [ʃɛnvjɛr] **NF** hemp field

chènevis [ʃɛnvi] **NM** hempseed

cheni [ʃni] **NM** *Suisse Fam* **1** *(balayures)* sweepings; *(débris, déchets)* rubbish **2** *(désordre)* mess, shambles **3** *(objets sans valeur)* junk, stuff

chenil [ʃəni(l)] **NM** *(pour chiens)* kennels

chenille [ʃ(ə)nij] **NF 1** *(insecte)* caterpillar; *(d'une autochenille)* band; **c. processionnaire** processionary caterpillar; **véhicule à chenilles** tracked vehicle **2** *Tex* chenille

chenillé [ʃ(ə)nije] **ADJ** *(véhicule)* tracked

chenillette [ʃ(ə)nijɛt] **NF** small tracked vehicle; *Mil* carrier

chenu [ʃəny] **ADJ** *Litt (personne, tête)* hoary; **arbres chenus** old leafless trees

cheptel [ʃɛptɛl] **NM 1** *(troupeaux)* livestock; **c. ovin d'une région** sheep population of a region **2** *Jur* **bail à c.** lease of livestock; **c. (vif)** livestock leased; **c. mort** farm equipment leased

chèque [ʃɛk] **NM** cheque, *Am* check; **c. de 60 euros** cheque for 60 euros; **carnet de chèques** cheque book; **endosser un c.** to endorse a cheque; **faire** *ou* **remplir un c.** to write (out) *or* make out a cheque; **je peux vous faire un c.?** can I give you a cheque?; **à qui dois-je adresser le c.?** who should I make the cheque out to?; **payer qch par c.** to pay for sth by cheque; **toucher un c.** to cash a cheque; **encaisser un c.** *(en espèces)* to cash a cheque; *(le mettre sur son compte)* to pay in a cheque; **déposer** *ou* **mettre un c. à la banque** to pay a cheque into the bank ▸▸ **c. bancaire** (bank) cheque; **c. de banque** banker's draft, *Am* cashier's check; **c. barré** crossed cheque; **c. en blanc** blank cheque; **c. bloqué** stopped cheque; *Fam* **c. en bois** rubber cheque; **c. certifié** certified cheque; **c. compensé** cleared cheque; **c. emploi-service** = special cheque used to pay casual workers such as part-time cleaners, babysitters etc; **c. d'entreprise** company cheque; **c. nominatif** cheque made out to name; **c. non endossable** non-negotiable cheque; **à ordre** cheque to order; **c. ouvert** open cheque; **c. au porteur** bearer cheque; **c. postal** post office cheque; **c. retourné** returned cheque; **c. sans provision** bad cheque, rubber cheque, cheque that bounces; **j'ai fait un c. sans provision** my cheque bounced; **c. stimulation-voyage** = incentive travel cheque issued by companies; **c. de virement** transfer cheque; *Can* **c. visé** certified cheque; **c. de voyage** traveller's cheque

chèque-cadeau, *pl* **chèques-cadeaux NM** gift token *or* voucher; **un c. d'une valeur de 200 euros** a gift token to the value of 200 euros

chèque-dividende, *pl* **chèques-dividendes NM** *Fin* dividend warrant

chèque-livre, *pl* **chèques-livres NM** book token

chèque-repas, *pl* **chèques-repas NM, chèque-restaurant,** *pl* **chèques-restaurant NM** luncheon voucher

chéquier [ʃekje] **NM** cheque *or Am* check book

CHER, CHÈRE¹ [ʃɛr] **ADJ** SEE GRAMMAR B10 **1** *(aimé)* dear, beloved; **être c. à qn** to be dear to sb; **tout ce qui m'est c.** all that I hold dear; **ses espérances les plus chères** his most cherished hopes; **c'est mon vœu le plus c.** it's my dearest wish; **il a retrouvé sa chère maison/son c. bureau** he's back in his beloved house/office; **bien chers frères** dearly beloved brethren; **C. Monsieur** *(dans une lettre)* Dear Mr Smith/*etc*, *(officiel)* Dear Sir; **chers amis de la nature** dear nature lovers; **bonjour, chère Madame** hello, my dear lady; *Iron* **écoutez, chère Madame, c'est tout ce que nous sommes en mesure de vous proposer** I'm sorry, Madam, but that's all we're able to offer you; **cette chère Marie!** dear old Marie!
2 *(coûteux)* dear, expensive; **c'est trop c. pour moi** I can't afford it; **un petit restaurant pas c.** an inexpensive little restaurant; **la vie est chère en ville** it's expensive living in town, the cost of living is high in town(s); **ce n'est pas vendu assez c.** it's underpriced
ADV payer qch c./trop c. to pay a high price/too much for sth; **c'est c. payer (sa liberté)** it's a high price to pay (for one's freedom); **il**

me le payera c. I'll make him pay for it; **coûter c.** to cost a lot, to be expensive; **ça coûte trop c. pour moi** it's too expensive for me, I can't afford it; *Fig* **ça m'a coûté c. de dire ce que je pensais** speaking my mind cost me dearly; *Fig* **ça va vous coûter c.!** you'll pay dearly for this!; *Fam* **je donnerais c. pour savoir ce qu'il lui a dit** I'd give anything *or* a lot to know what he said to him; **je ne donne pas c. de son succès** I don't give much for his chances of success; **cela ne vaut pas c.** it's not worth much; *Fam* **je l'ai eu pour pas c.** I got it cheap
N mon c. my dear (fellow); **ma chère** my dear (girl); **ah, ma chère! quel plaisir de vous voir!** *(avec préciosité)* how nice to see you, my dear!

chérant [ʃerā] **ADJ** *Can* pricey; **un plombier pas c.** a plumber who doesn't charge too much, an inexpensive plumber

CHERCHER [ʃɛrʃe]

VT to look for **1** ▪ to seek **1** ▪ to search for **1** ▪ to fetch **2** ▪ to try to *(chercher à)* **3** ▪ to get at **5**	
VI to look	
VPR to try to find oneself	

VT 1 *(essayer de trouver) (chose, personne)* to look for, to search for, *Fml* to seek; **je l'ai cherché partout** I searched for *or* looked for it high and low, I hunted for it everywhere; **c. une maison à acheter** to look for a house to buy, to be house-hunting; **c. qn du regard** *ou* **des yeux** to look around for sb; **c. un mot dans un dictionnaire** to look up a word in a dictionary; **il cherchait des moyens de s'évader** he looked around for a means of escape; **c. un emploi** to look for a job; **c. son chemin** *ou* **sa voie/une solution** to try to find one's way/a solution; **c. ses mots** to search for words; **je cherche son nom** I'm trying to think of his name; *Fam* **où va-t-il donc c. tout cela?** where on earth does he get that from?; **mais qu'est-ce que tu vas c. là, pourquoi faut-il toujours que tu compliques les choses?** what on earth are you going on about, why do you always have to complicate matters?; **c. sa ruine** to court one's own ruin; **partir c. du secours** to go for help; *Fam* **il l'a bien cherché** he was asking for it
2 aller c. qn/qch to (go and) fetch sb/sth; **envoyer c. qn/qch** to send for sb/sth; **je suis allé le c. à la gare** I went to meet him at the station; **viens me c. à 17 heures** come for me at 5 pm
3 c. à faire qch to try to do sth; **c. à se faire connaître** to try to get oneself known, to try to make a name for oneself; **c. à se faire aimer** to try to make oneself popular; **c. à plaire** to aim to please; *Iron* **il ne faut pas c. à comprendre** don't even try to understand
4 *Fam (atteindre)* **cela va c. dans les 10 000 euros** it will cost about 10,000 euros, you're talking about something like 10,000 euros; **ça va c. dans les deux ans de prison** that will get you about two years in prison; **injures à magistrat, ça peut aller c. loin!** insulting a magistrate can get you into serious trouble!
5 *Fam (provoquer)* to get at, to pick on; **tu me cherches?** are you looking for a fight?; **si tu me cherches, tu vas me trouver** if you want a fight, you'll get one
VI to look, to search; **qui cherche trouve** seek and ye shall find; **il faut c. plus** you'll have to look harder; **cherche!** *(à un chien)* fetch!
VPR se chercher to try to find oneself

chercheur, -euse [ʃɛrʃœr, -øz] **ADJ 1** *(spéculateur)* **esprit c.** enquiring mind **2 tête chercheuse** *(d'un missile)* homing head
N 1 researcher, research worker **2 c. d'or** gold digger

NM 1 Opt *(d'un télescope)* finder **2 c. de fuites** gas leak detector

chère[2] [ʃɛr] **NF** fare, food; **faire maigre c.** to eat frugally; **faire bonne c.** to have a good meal, to eat well; **aimer la bonne c.** to be a lover of good food

chèrement [ʃɛrmɑ̃] **ADV 1** *(affectueusement)* dearly, lovingly **2** *(à haut prix)* dearly, at a high price; **il a payé c. sa liberté** his freedom cost him dearly, he paid a high price for his freedom

chéri, -ie [ʃeri] **ADJ** dear, beloved, darling; **mes enfants chéris** my dearest *or* beloved children; **à notre tante chérie** *(sur une tombe)* to our beloved aunt; **c. des dieux** beloved of the gods

N darling; **mon c., ma chérie** darling, dearest; **c'est le c. de tout le monde** he's everybody's darling *or* favourite

chérif [ʃerif] **NM** *(Mohammedan)* sherif

chérir [ʃerir] **VT** *(être, liberté etc)* to cherish

chérot [ʃero] **ADJ M** *Arg (trop cher)* pricey; **ça lui avait coûté c.** it cost him an arm and a leg

cherra [ʃɛrra] *futur de* **choir**

cherry [ʃeri] **NM** cherry brandy

cherté [ʃɛrte] **NF** high price *or* cost; **c. de la vie** high cost of living

chérubin [ʃerybɛ̃] **NM** *(ange), Fam* cherub; **des chérubins** cherubs; *Rel, Litt* cherubim; *Fam* **potelé et blond comme un c.** as chubby and blond as a cherub

chester [ʃɛstɛr] **NM** Cheshire cheese

chétif, -ive [ʃetif, -iv] **ADJ 1** *(personne)* puny, sickly, scrawny; **arbuste c.** stunted *or* puny shrub **2** *Fig Litt* poor, miserable, wretched; **un repas fort c.** a meagre *or* skimpy *or* scanty meal

chétivement [ʃetivmɑ̃] **ADV 1** *(d'une façon malingre)* punily, weakly **2** *(médiocrement, mal)* poorly, miserably

chevaine [ʃəvɛn] **NM** *(poisson)* chub

cheval, -aux [ʃ(ə)val, -o] **NM 1** *Zool* horse; **homme de c.** horse-lover, born horseman; **à c.** on horseback; **gendarme à c.** mounted policeman; **aller à c.** to ride; **monter sur son c.** to get on one's horse, to mount; **monter à c.** *(faire de l'équitation)* to ride, to go riding; **tu sais monter à c.?** can you ride?; **est-ce que tu montes à c.?** do you ride?; **se tenir bien/mal à c.** to have a good/poor seat, to sit a horse well/badly; **chute de c.** fall off a horse; **être à c. sur qch** to sit astride sth, to straddle sth; **le champ est à c. sur deux communes** the field straddles two villages; *Fig* **être à c. sur l'étiquette** to be a stickler for etiquette; **être à c. sur deux siècles** to straddle two centuries; *Fig* **monter sur ses grands chevaux** to get on one's high horse; **ça ne se trouve pas sous le sabot d'un c.** it doesn't grow on trees; *Fam* **travailler comme un c.** to work like a slave *or* a Trojan; *Fam* **ce n'est pas un mauvais c.** he's not such a bad sort; *Fam* **c'est un vrai c., cette femme** she's a real carthorse that woman; *Fam* **il a mangé** *ou* **bouffé du c.!** he's full of beans!; *Fam* **remède de c.** drastic remedy; *Fam* **fièvre de c.** raging fever; *Fam* **avoir une santé de c.** to be as strong as a horse **2 petits chevaux** = type of board game **3** *Tech, Aut* **une voiture de vingt chevaux,** *Fam* **une vingt chevaux** a twenty-horsepower car

▸▸ *Gym* **c.-d'arçons** (vaulting) horse; **c. d'attelage** carriage horse; **c. à bascule** rocking horse; **c. de bât** packhorse; **c. de bataille** warhorse, charger; *Fig* **c'est son c. de bataille** that's his hobby-horse, he rides the subject to death; **c. de bois** wooden horse; **chevaux de bois** *(manège)* roundabout, merry-go-round; **c. de chasse** hunter; **c. de course** racehorse; **c. fiscal** *(pour taxer les automobiles)* horsepower; **c. de labour** plough

horse; **c. de manège** school horse; **c. marin** seahorse; **c. pur-sang** thoroughbred (horse); *Fam* **c. de retour** *(récidiviste)* repeat offender; **c. de selle** saddle horse; **c. de trait** carthorse, draughthorse; *Myth, Fig* **c. de Troie** Trojan horse

chevaler [ʃ(ə)vale] **VT** *Constr (mur etc)* to shore up

chevaleresque [ʃ(ə)valrɛsk] **ADJ** chivalrous, knightly

chevalerie [ʃ(ə)valri] **NF 1** *(dignité)* knighthood **2** *Hist (institution)* chivalry; **roman de c.** tale of chivalry

chevalet [ʃ(ə)valɛ] **NM 1** *(support)* stand, support, trestle; **c. de scieur** sawbench, sawhorse; **c. de peintre** easel **2** *Mus (de violon)* bridge **3** *Arch* **c. (de torture)** rack

chevalier [ʃ(ə)valje] **NM 1** *(seigneur)* knight; **c. errant** knight errant; **armer** *ou* **faire qn c.** to knight sb, to make sb a knight **2** *(de la Légion d'honneur etc)* chevalier **3** *(oiseau)* sandpiper

▸▸ *Bourse* **c. blanc** white knight; **c. d'industrie** swindler, crook; *Bourse* **c. noir** black knight; **c. servant** faithful admirer; **C. de la Table ronde** Knight of the Round Table

chevalière [ʃ(ə)valjɛr] **NF** signet ring

chevalin [ʃ(ə)valɛ̃] **ADJ** equine; **boucherie chevaline** horse-butcher's (shop); **figure chevaline** horsy face

cheval-vapeur, *pl* **chevaux-vapeur NM** (French) horsepower

chevauchant [ʃ(ə)voʃɑ̃] **ADJ** *(tuiles etc)* overlapping

chevauchée [ʃ(ə)voʃe] **NF 1** *(course à cheval)* ride **2** *(personnes)* cavalcade

chevauchement [ʃ(ə)voʃmɑ̃] **NM** *(des tuiles etc)* overlap(ping); *(des fils électriques etc)* crossing; *(d'os fracturés)* (over)riding; *Typ (de caractères)* falling *or* dropping out of place; *Géol (de couches géologiques)* (over)thrust; *Géol* **faille de c.** overthrust fault; **le c. des horaires ne me permet pas d'assister à ces deux cours** I can't attend both classes because they overlap

chevaucher [ʃ(ə)voʃe] **VI 1** *(l'un sur l'autre)* to overlap; *(de fils électriques etc)* to cross; *Chir (d'os fracturés)* to (over)ride; *Géol* to overthrust; *Typ (de caractères)* to fall *or* drop out of place; *Menuis* **joint chevauché** lapped joint **2** *Litt (aller à cheval)* to ride (a horse)

VT 1 *(vélo etc)* to span **2** *(mur etc)* to straddle, to be astride; *Litt (cheval etc)* to ride; *Vieilli (femme)* to ride; **c. un balai** *(d'une sorcière)* to ride a broomstick

VPR se chevaucher to overlap

chevau-léger, *pl* **chevau-légers** [ʃ(ə)voleʒe] **NM** *Hist* light horseman; **les chevau-légers** the light horse, the light cavalry

chevêche [ʃ(ə)vɛʃ] **NF** *(oiseau)* (sparrow) owl

chevelu, -ue [ʃəvly] **ADJ 1** *(personne)* longhaired **2** *Péj* hairy **3** *Astron* **comète chevelue** bearded comet

N *Fam Péj* **un c.** one of the long-haired brigade

chevelure [ʃəvlyr] **NF 1** (head of) hair; **avoir une belle c.** to have beautiful hair *or* a beautiful head of hair; **femme à la c. rousse/blonde** red-haired/blonde woman; **c. emmêlée** tangled hair; *Fig* **la c. des saules** the verdure of the willows **2** *Astron (d'une comète)* tail

chevenne, chevesne [ʃəvɛn] **NM** *(poisson)* chub

chevet [ʃ(ə)vɛ] **NM 1** *(tête de lit)* bedhead; **lampe de c.** bedside lamp; **table de c.** bedside table, *Am* night table, nightstand; **j'en ai fait mon livre de c.** I've made it my bedside reading *or* book; **rester au c. de qn** to stay at sb's bedside; **les ministres au c. de**

l'agriculture européenne *(titre dans un journal)* ministers concerned about European agriculture **2** *Archit (d'une église)* apse

cheveu, -eux [ʃ(ə)vø] **NM 1** (single) hair; *(ensemble de la chevelure)* hair; **elle a le c. terne** she has dull hair; **avoir le c. rare** to be going thin *or* thinning on top; **un c. blanc** a grey hair; **il ne lui reste pas un c. sur le caillou** he hasn't a hair left on his head; **arriver comme un c. sur la soupe** to arrive at an awkward moment; **il s'en est fallu d'un c. que tout soit à refaire** we/*etc* came within a hair's breadth of having to do it all again; **à un c. près** by a hair's breadth; **à un c. près, je ratais mon train** I caught my train by a hair's breadth; **être à un c. de la ruine** to be within a hair's breadth of ruin; **si vous touchez à un seul c. de sa tête, vous vous en repentirez!** if you lay a finger on him *or* touch a hair on his head, you'll regret it!

2 cheveux hair; **avoir les cheveux longs/courts** to have long/short hair, to wear one's hair long/short; **des cheveux raides/frisés** straight/curly hair; **cheveux gris** grey hair; **j'ai commencé à avoir des cheveux blancs à l'âge de trente ans** I started to go grey when I was thirty; **se faire des cheveux (blancs)** to worry oneself sick; **en cheveux** without a hat (on), bare-headed; **perdre ses cheveux** to lose one's hair; *Fig* **s'arracher les cheveux** to tear one's hair out; *Fig* **couper les cheveux en quatre** to split hairs; **saisir une occasion par les cheveux** to jump at an opportunity; *Fam* **elles se sont prises aux cheveux, elles se sont empoignées par les cheveux** they had a set-to; **argument tiré par les cheveux** far-fetched argument; **cheveux d'ange** *(décorations de Noël)* angel hair; *Culin* angelhair vermicelli

chevillard [ʃ(ə)vijar] **NM** wholesale butcher

cheville [ʃ(ə)vij] **NF 1** *Anat* ankle; **jusqu'à la c.** ankle deep; **se fouler la c.** to sprain one's ankle; *Fig* **il ne vous arrive pas à la c.** he can't hold a candle to you; *Fam Péj* **tu as les chevilles qui enflent** you're getting too big for your boots *or Am* britches

2 *(pour accrocher)* peg, pin; *(pour boucher un trou)* peg, plug; **c. en bois** peg, dowel; **c. en fer** bolt; **c. maîtresse** kingpin; **c. ouvrière** *(d'un véhicule)* kingpin; *Fig* mainspring, kingpin; *Mus* **c. de violon** violin peg; *Com* **vente à la c.** wholesale butchery trade; *Fam* **être en c. avec qn** to be in cahoots with sb **3** *Littér (dans un vers)* padding

cheviller [ʃ(ə)vije] **VT** *(objet)* to pin, to bolt, to peg (together); *Fig* **avoir l'âme chevillée au corps** to be indestructible

cheviotte [ʃəvjɔt] **NF** *Tex* **c. écossaise** tweed

chèvre [ʃɛvr] **NF 1** goat; *(femelle)* she-goat, nanny goat; **fromage/lait de c.** goat's cheese/milk; **barbe de c.** goatee (beard); *Fam* **ménager la c. et le chou** to sit on the fence; *Litt, Prov* to run with the hare and hunt with the hounds; *Fig Fam* **devenir c.** to go up the wall *or* round the bend; **il me rend c.!** he drives me up the wall *or* round the bend! **2** *(chevalet)* carpenter's sawhorse, trestle

NM goat's cheese

chevreau, -eaux [ʃəvro] **NM** kid; **gants de c.** kid gloves

chèvrefeuille [ʃɛvrəfœj] **NM** honeysuckle

chevrette [ʃəvrɛt] **NF 1** *(chevreau)* kid, young (she-)goat **2** *(femelle du chevreuil)* (female) roe deer **3** *(trépied)* tripod

chevreuil [ʃəvrœj] **NM** roe deer, roebuck, *Can* deer; *(gibier)* venison; **peau de c.** buckskin, deerskin

chevrier, -ière [ʃɛvrije, -jɛr] **N** goatherd, *f* goat girl

NM (small green) kidney bean

chevron [ʃəvrɔ̃] NM **1** *Constr (d'un toit)* rafter **2** *Mil etc* (service) stripe, chevron; *Hér* chevron; *Tex* **tissu à chevrons** herringbone pattern(ed) material

chevronné [ʃəvrɔne] ADJ *(qui a de l'expérience)* experienced, seasoned

chevrotain [ʃəvrɔtɛ̃] NM mouse deer, musk deer

chevrotant [ʃəvrɔtɑ̃] ADJ *(voix)* quavering, tremulous

chevrotement [ʃəvrɔtmɑ̃] NM *(de la voix)* quaver(ing), tremor; **avec des chevrotements dans la voix** with a quaver *or* a tremor in one's voice, in a quavering or trembling voice

chevroter [ʃəvrɔte] VI **1** *(d'une personne)* to sing *or* speak in a quavering voice, to quaver; **sa voix chevrote** his voice shakes *or* quavers **2** *(d'une chèvre)* to kid

chevrotine [ʃəvrɔtin] NF buckshot

chewing-gum, *pl* **chewing-gums** [ʃwiŋɡɔm] NM chewing-gum

CHEZ [ʃe] PRÉP **1** *(dans la maison etc de)* **c. qn** at sb's house *or* home; **il n'est pas c. lui** he's not at home, he's not in; **elle est rentrée** *ou* **allée c. elle** she's gone home; **je l'ai reconduit c. lui** I took him home; **je vais c. moi** I'm going home; **je vais c. ma sœur/Nadine** I'm going to my sister's (house)/Nadine's (house); **venez c. nous** come to our house; **il vit c. nous** he lives with us; **vous vivez c. vos parents?** do you live with your parents?; **vous êtes ici c. vous, faites comme c. vous** treat the place as your own, make yourself at home; *Iron* **eh bien, mais faites comme c. vous** that's right, (you) just make yourself at home; **acheter qch c. l'épicier** to buy sth at the grocer's; **il est allé c. le dentiste/le pédicure** he's gone to the dentist('s)/the chiropodist('s); **chacun c. soi, et tout le monde s'en portera mieux** if people minded their own business, there wouldn't be any problems; **on dort mieux c. soi** you always sleep better in your own home; **je ne me sens pas c. moi ici** I don't feel at home here; **c. ...** *(sur une lettre)* care of ..., c/o ...; **un bon vin bien de c. nous** one of our good local wines; **c. nous, c'est mieux** it's better at home; **elle a été à l'école c. les sœurs** she went to a convent school; **derrière c. moi** behind my house; **il habite près de c. son ami** he lives near his friend
2 *(en, dans)* with; **c'est devenu une habitude c. moi** it's become a habit with me; **ce que j'admire c. cet homme, c'est ...** what I admire about *or* in the man is ...; **c'est quand même curieux c. un homme de son âge** it is strange for *or* in a man of his age; **c. Molière** in Molière
3 *(au temps de)* during the time of; **c. les Vikings** during the Viking period
4 *(parmi)* among; **cette expression est courante c. les jeunes** this expression is common among young people; **c. les Américains** among (the) Americans; **c. les animaux** in the animal kingdom, among animals
NM INV **son c.-soi** one's home, one's house

chiader [ʃjade] *Arg* VI to swot
VT *(examen)* to swot (up) for; **il l'a vachement chiadée, sa lettre de candidature** he really took pains over his letter of application; **système chiadé** elaborate system *or* plan

chialer [ʃjale] VI *Arg* to snivel, to blubber; *Can* to whine, to moan

chialeur, -euse [ʃjalœr, -øz] N *Arg* crybaby; *Can* whiner, moaner

chiant [ʃjɑ̃] ADJ *Vulg* bloody annoying *or* irritating; **qu'est-ce qu'elle est chiante, cette fille!** that girl's a pain in the *Br* arse *or Am* ass!; **c. comme la pluie** as boring as hell, dead boring

chianti [kjɑ̃ti] NM chianti

chiard [ʃjar] NM **1** *Fam (enfant)* brat, kid **2** *Suisse Fam (peureux)* chicken, coward

chiasse [ʃjas] NF *Arg* **1** **avoir la c.** *(la diarrhée)* to have the runs *or* the trots; *(avoir peur)* to have the wind up, to be shit-scared **2** *(ennui)* **quelle c.!** what a fucking pain (in the *Br* arse *or Am* ass)!

chiatique [ʃjatik] ADJ *très Fam* **être c.** to be a pain (in the *Br* arse *or Am* ass)

chibre [ʃibr] NM **1** *Vulg (pénis)* cock, prick **2** *Suisse (jeu)* = popular Swiss card game

chic [ʃik] NM **1** *(savoir-faire)* skill, knack; **elle a le c. pour me mettre au rage** she's really got the knack of making me angry, she really knows how to make me angry **2** *(élégance)* smartness, stylishness; **il a du c.** he has style; **femme/chapeau qui a du c.** smart *or* stylish woman/hat **3** *Beaux-Arts* **dessiner de c.** to draw without a model *or* from memory
ADJ INV **1** *(élégant)* smart, stylish, chic; **restaurant c.** fashionable *or* smart *or Fam* posh restaurant; **style c. et décontracté** elegant but relaxed style; **elle est c.** she's got style; **les gens c.** the smart set **2** *Fam* **on a passé une c. soirée** we had a really good evening; **c'est un c. type** he's a good sort, *Am* he's a regular guy; **il a été très c. avec moi** he's been very decent *or* nice to me; **c'est c. de ta part** that's really good *or* decent of you
INT *Fam* **c. (alors)!** great!

chicane [ʃikan] NF **1** *(querelle)* quibbling, wrangling; *Jur* chicanery, pettifoggery; **chercher c. à qn, faire des chicanes à qn** to try to pick a quarrel with sb; *Jur, Vieilli* **gens de c.** pettifoggers **2** *Mil* zigzag trench; *(sur une route etc)* zigzag, chicane **3** *Aut (de silencieux)* baffle

chicaner [ʃikane] VI to quibble (**sur** over, about); *Jur* to chicane, to pettifog; **c. sur les frais** to haggle *or* quibble over the expense
VT **c. qn** to wrangle with sb (**sur** about); **c. qch** to haggle over sth
VPR **se chicaner** to squabble

chicanerie [ʃikanri] NF *surtout Jur* quibbling, chicanery

chicaneur, -euse [ʃikanœr, -øz], **chicanier, -ière** [ʃikanje, -jɛr] N quibbler, haggler
ADJ quibbling, haggling

chiche [ʃiʃ] ADJ *(repas, récolte etc)* scanty, poor; *(personne)* mean, stingy; **être c. de louanges** to be sparing in one's praise; **il est plutôt c. de compliments** he's not very generous with his compliments; *Fam* **être c. de faire qch** to dare to do sth; **tu n'es pas c. d'y aller!** I bet you don't go!; *Fam* **c.!** *(pour défier)* I dare you!; *(pour relever le défi)* you're on!

chiche ADJ **pois c.** chickpea

chiche-kebab, *pl* **chiches-kebabs** [ʃiʃkebab] NM *Culin* shish kebab

chichement [ʃiʃmɑ̃] ADV stingily, meanly

chichi [ʃiʃi] NM *Fam (souvent pl)* chichis affected manners; **pas tant de c.!** don't make so much fuss!; **gens à c.** overpolite *or* gushing people; **faire des chichis** *(se donner des airs)* to put on airs; *(compliquer les choses)* to make a fuss; **repas sans c.** informal meal

chichiteux, -euse [ʃiʃitø, -øz] ADJ *Fam* fussy

chicorée [ʃikɔre] NF **1** *(plante)* **c. (frisée)** endive; **c. sauvage** chicory **2** *(en poudre)* (ground) chicory; **boire de la c.** to drink chicory (coffee)

chicos [ʃikos] ADJ *Fam* classy, smart

chicot [ʃiko] NM *(d'un arbre, d'une dent)* stump

chié [ʃje] ADJ *très Fam* **1** *(formidable)* shithot, *Am* awesome **2** *(qui exagère)* **il est c., lui!** he's got a *Br* bloody *or Am* goddamn nerve!

chiée [ʃje] NF *Vulg* loads, masses; **avoir une c. de livres** to have loads *or* masses of books; **elle a une c. de marmots** she has a swarm of brats *or* kids

chien, chienne [ʃjɛ̃, ʃjɛn] N dog, *f* bitch; **jeune c.** puppy, pup; **'(attention) c. méchant'** 'beware of the dog'; *Natation* **nager à la c.** to dog(gy)-paddle; *Journ* **tenir** *ou* **s'occuper de la rubrique des chiens écrasés** to cover weddings and funerals; *Fig* **ils sont comme c. et chat** they fight like cat and dog; *Fig* **se regarder en chiens de faïence** to glare at one another; **un c. regarde bien un évêque** a cat may look at a king; **rompre les chiens** to call off the hounds; *Fig (dans une conversation)* to change the subject; *Fam* **ce n'est pas fait pour les chiens** it's there to be used; **garder à qn un c. de sa chienne** to have it in for sb; **je lui garde un c. de ma chienne** he won't get away with it; **entre c. et loup** at dusk *or* twilight; *Can* **avec cette femme, mon c. est mort** I don't have a chance with that woman any more; *Prov* **bon c. chasse de race** it runs in the family; **qui veut noyer son c. l'accuse de la rage** give a dog a bad name (and hang him); **c. qui aboie ne mord pas** his/her/*etc* bark is worse than his/her/*etc* bite; **il n'est pas bon à jeter aux chiens** hanging is too good for him; **métier de c.** drudgery; *Fam* **vie de c.** dog's life; *très Fam* **chienne de vie!** life's a bitch!; *Fam* **quel temps de c.!, quel c. de temps!** what awful *or* foul *or* filthy weather!; *Naut* **coup de c.** squall; *Fam* **je ne suis pas ton c.!** don't order me about!; **elle le traite comme un c.** she treats him like a dog; **mourir comme un c.** to die like a dog; *Fam* **nom d'un c.!** oh, hell!
NM **1** *Fam (style)* **avoir du c.** to have charm, to have a certain something **2** **être coiffée à la c.** to wear a fringe **3** *Tech (d'un fusil)* hammer; **se coucher en c. de fusil** to curl up in one's bed; **dormir en c. de fusil** to sleep curled up
ADJ **être c.** *(avare)* to be mean *or* stingy; *(méchant)* to be nasty
▸ ▸ **c. d'appartement** lapdog; **c. d'arrêt** pointer; **c. d'aveugle** guide dog, *Am* seeing-eye dog; **c. bâtard** mongrel; **c. de berger** sheepdog; **c. de chasse** retriever, gundog; **c. couchant** setter; **faire le c. couchant auprès de qn** to fawn on *or* crawl to sb; **c. courant** hound; **c. de garde** guard dog, watchdog; **c. de manchon** lapdog; **c. de mer** dogfish; **c. policier** police dog; **c. de race** pedigree (dog); **c. de salon** lapdog; **c. savant** *(dans un cirque etc)* performing dog; *(enfant etc)* performing monkey; **c. de traîneau** husky

chien-chien, *pl* **chiens-chiens** NM *Fam* doggy

chiendent [ʃjɛ̃dɑ̃] NM **1** *(plante)* couch grass; **pousser comme du c.** to grow like a weed; *Fam* **voilà le c.!** that's the snag *or* the trouble! **2** **brosse en** *ou* **de c.** scrubbing brush

chienlit [ʃjɑ̃li] NF **1** *Fam (pagaïe)* mess, shambles; **c'est la c.!** it's a shambles! **2** *Vieilli (carnaval)* masquerade; *(masque)* carnival mask

chien-loup, *pl* **chiens-loups** NM wolfhound

chiennerie [ʃjɛnri] NF *(avarice)* meanness, tightfistedness

chier [ʃje] VI *Vulg* to shit, to crap; **nul à c.** a load of crap; **ça va c. (des bulles)!** there's going to be one hell of a row *or* stink!; **il n'y a pas à c.!** there are no two bloody *or Vulg* fucking ways about it!; **non mais tu chies dans la colle ou quoi?** what the fuck do you think you're doing?; **tu me fais c.** you're a pain in the arse; **elle me fait c.** she pisses me off; **ça me fait c. de voir qu'il ne prend pas de décision** it really pisses me off to see that he's not making a decision; **qu'est-ce qu'on se fait c. ici!** it's so bloody boring here!; **qu'est-ce que j'ai pu me faire c. à cette soirée!** that party really bored the pants off me!; **je me suis fait c. à l'attendre pour rien** I got pissed off waiting for him and he never showed up; **il ne se fait pas c.** he can't be bothered **VT** *Vulg* **tu vas pas nous c. une pendule!** don't make such a fuss *or Br* a bloody song and dance about it!

chierie [ʃiri] NF *très Fam* **quelle c.!** *Br* what a bloody pain!, what a pain in the *Br* arse *or Am* ass!

chiffe [ʃif] NF **1** *Fam* **mou comme une c.** like a wet rag; **c'est une c. (molle)** he's spineless, he's a drip *or* a weed **2** *Vieilli* rag

chiffon [ʃifɔ̃] NM **1** *(morceau de tissu)* rag; **c. (à épousseter** *ou* **à poussière)** duster; **c. non-peluchaux** lint-free rag; **passez un coup de c. sur l'étagère** give the shelf a dust; **on pourra en faire un c.** keep it for rags; **papier de c.** rag paper; *Fam* **parler chiffons** to talk (about) clothes **2** **mettre ses vêtements en c.** to leave one's clothes in a heap **3** *Péj* **en c. de papier** scrap of paper; *Fam* **tu ne peux pas rendre ce c. à ton professeur!** you can't hand that rubbish in to your teacher!

chiffonnade [ʃifɔnad] NF *Culin* chiffonnade

chiffonnage [ʃifɔnaʒ] NM *(de papier)* creasing, crumpling; *(de vêtement)* creasing, crumpling, rumpling

chiffonné [ʃifɔne] ADJ **1** *(vêtements)* creased, crumpled, rumpled; *(papier etc)* creased; **c'est tout c.** it's all creased **2** *Fig (visage etc)* tired(-looking), drawn; *(air)* worried, bothered

chiffonner [ʃifɔne] VT **1** *(robe etc)* to rumple, to crease, to crumple; *(morceaux de papier etc)* to crumple **2** *Fam (ennuyer)* to worry, to bother; **quelque chose me chiffonne** something's bothering me **VI** to do a bit of sewing **VPR se chiffonner** *(d'un tissu etc)* to crease, to crumple; **ça se chiffonne facilement** it creases easily, it's easily creased

chiffonnier, -ière [ʃifɔnje, -jɛr] N ragman, rag-and-bone man, *Arch* rag picker; **se disputer comme des chiffonniers** to go at it hammer and tongs NM *(meuble)* chiffonier

chiffrable [ʃifrabl] ADJ calculable; **le montant est facilement/difficilement c.** the sum is easy/difficult to calculate; **ce n'est pas c., les sommes sont colossales** it's impossible to calculate, the sums are colossal

chiffrage [ʃifraʒ] NM **1** *(d'une somme etc)* working out, calculating; *(estimation)* quantification **2** *Mus (de la basse)* figuring

chiffre [ʃifr] NM **1** figure, number, numeral; **chiffres arabes/romains** Arabic/Roman numerals; **nombre à trois chiffres** three-figure number; **inflation à deux chiffres** double digit inflation
2 *(total)* amount, total; **en chiffres** *(montant)* in figures; *Fam* **faire du c.** to make a fast turnover
3 *(code)* cipher, code; **(service du) c.** coding *or* cipher department; **officier du c.** cipher officer
4 *(d'un coffre-fort)* combination
5 *(monogramme)* monogram; **mouchoir brodé à son c.** handkerchief embroidered with one's monogram
6 *Mus* figure
▸▸ **c. d'affaires (annuel)** (annual) sales figures, (annual) turnover; **faire un c. d'affaires de 2 millions de euros** to have a turnover of 2 million euros; **c. d'affaires consolidé** group turnover; **c. d'affaires critique** breakeven point; **c. d'affaires global** total sales; **c. d'affaires prévisionnel** projected turnover, projected sales revenue; *Ordinat* **c. ASCII** ASCII number; *Ordinat* **c. binaire** binary

digit; **chiffres bruts** unweighted figures; *Ordinat* **c. de contrôle** check digit; *Ordinat* **chiffres numériques** numerics; **c. de vente** sales figures

chiffrement [ʃifrəmã] NM *(de message)* (en)coding, encryption; *Ordinat* **c. de données** data encryption

chiffrer [ʃifre] VT **1** *(pages d'un livre etc)* to number **2** *(somme etc)* to work out, to calculate; *(évaluer)* to quantify; **les dégâts ne sont pas encore totalement chiffrés** the extent of the damage has not yet been fully assessed; **détails chiffrés** *(d'un projet etc)* figures; **le coût de qch** to quantify the cost of sth **3** *(document, message)* to write in code, to code, to encode; **message chiffré** coded message, message in code **4** *(linge etc)* to mark **5** *Mus (basse)* to figure
VI to add up, to tally; **ça commence à c.** it's starting to add up
VPR se chiffrer se c. à to add up to, to amount to, to total; **à combien cela se chiffre-t-il?** how much does it work out at *or* add up to *or* come to *or* amount to?

chiffreur [ʃifrœr] NM **1** *Com* payments coding clerk **2** *(dans services secrets)* cipher clerk **3** *Ordinat* encoder, encrypter

chignole [ʃiɲɔl] NF **1** *(outil)* hand drill; *(électrique)* electric drill **2** *Fam (mauvaise voiture)* banger

chignon [ʃiɲɔ̃] NM chignon, bun; **se faire un c., coiffer ses cheveux en c.** to put one's hair in a bun; *Fig* **elles se sont crêpé le c.** they had a fight *or* a set-to

chihuahua [ʃiwawa] NM chihuahua

chiite [ʃiit] ADJ, N *Rel* Shiite

Chili [ʃili] NM Chile

chili, chili con carne [ʃili(kɔnkarne)] NM *Culin* chilli (con carne)

chilien, -ienne [ʃiljɛ̃, -jɛn] ADJ Chilean N **C.** Chilean

chimère [ʃimɛr] NF **1** *(monstre)* chimera **2** *Fig (rêve)* pipe dream, *Lit* chimera; **le pays des chimères** the land of fantasy *or* dreams; **se complaire dans des chimères** to live in a dream world; **ce ne sont que des chimères** they are only pipe dreams

chimérique [ʃimerik] ADJ *(esprit)* fanciful; **des monstres chimériques** mythical *or* fabled monsters; **rêve c.** pipe dream; **projet c.** unrealistic *or* fanciful plan; **elle s'est forgé un monde c.** she invented *or* created a dream world

chimie [ʃimi] NF chemistry; **cours de c.** chemistry course *or* class; **c. industrielle** chemical engineering; **c. minérale** inorganic chemistry; **c. nucléaire** nuclear chemistry; **c. organique** organic chemistry

chimiothérapie [ʃimjoterapi] NF *Méd* chemotherapy; **être en c.** to be having *or* undergoing chemo(therapy)

chimique [ʃimik] ADJ chemical; **réaction c.** chemical reaction; **le symbole c. d'un corps** the chemical symbol of a body; **produit c.** chemical; **ces bonbons sont pleins de produits chimiques** these sweets are full of chemicals *or* additives; **société/raffinerie de produits chimiques** chemical company/refinery; *Phys* **rayons chimiques** actinic rays

chimiquement [ʃimikmã] ADV chemically

chimiquier [ʃimikje] NM chemical tanker

chimiste [ʃimist] N chemist; **ingénieur c.** chemical engineer, industrial chemist

> Il faut noter que le sens le plus courant du mot anglais **chemist** est **pharmacien**.

chimpanzé [ʃɛ̃pɑ̃ze] NM chimpanzee, *Fam* chimp

chinchilla [ʃɛ̃ʃila] NM *(mammifère, fourrure)* chinchilla; **veste en c.** chinchilla jacket

Chine [ʃin] NF China

chine [ʃin] NF peddling; **vente à la c.** peddling, hawking
NM **1** *(porcelaine)* (piece of) china **2** *(papier)* rice paper

chiner[1] [ʃine] VT *Tex (tissu)* to mottle; **laine chinée** mottled *or* chiné fabric

chiner[2] VT *Fam* **c. qn** to make fun of sb, to pull sb's leg
VI to hunt for second-hand goods

chinetoque [ʃintɔk] N *Arg Vieilli (terme injurieux)* Chink(y)

chineur, -euse [ʃinœr, -øz] N *(brocanteur)* second-hand dealer; *(amateur)* antique-hunter

chinois, -oise [ʃinwa, -waz] ADJ **1** *(de la Chine)* Chinese **2** *(compliqué)* involved, complicated, over-elaborate
NM **1** *Ling* Chinese; *Fam* **c'est du c.** it's all double Dutch *or* it's all Greek to me **2** *(orange)* = small green orange preserved in brandy **3** *Culin* chinois *(conical strainer)*
N **C.** Chinese (man), *f* Chinese (woman); **les C.** the Chinese

chinoiser [ʃinwaze] VI to quibble (**sur vingt euros** over *or* about twenty euros)

chinoiserie [ʃinwazri] NF **1** *(objet)* chinoiserie, Chinese curio **2** *Fam (complication)* unnecessary complication; **chinoiseries administratives** red tape

chintz [ʃints] NM *Tex* chintz; **des rideaux en c.** chintz curtains

chiot [ʃjo] NM pup(py)

chiotte [ʃjɔt] NF *très Fam* **1** *(voiture)* car, wheels, *Br* motor; *(cyclomoteur)* (motor) scooter, moped **2** *(ennui)* **quelle c.!** what a pain in the *Br* arse *or Am* ass! **3 chiottes** *(W-C) Br* bog, *Am* john; **il a un goût de chiottes** he's got shit taste; **aux chiottes, l'arbitre!** *Br* the referee's a wanker!, *Am* kill the umpire!

chiourme [ʃjurm] NF *Vieilli (galley slaves)*; *(bagnards)* convicts, prisoners

chiper [ʃipe] VT *Fam (voler) (chose)* to pinch, to swipe, to nick; **il s'est fait c. son stylo à l'école** he got his pen pinched *or* swiped *or* nicked at school

chipeur, -euse [ʃipœr, -øz] N *Fam* petty thief

chipie [ʃipi] NF bad-tempered woman; **vieille c.** old cow; **cette petite fille est une vraie c.** she's a real little madam

chipolata [ʃipolata] NF chipolata (sausage)

chipotage [ʃipotaʒ] NM *(fait de contester)* quibbling; *(marchandage)* haggling

chipoter [ʃipote] VI **1** *(picorer)* to nibble, to pick at *or* play with one's food **2** *(contester)* to quibble (**sur** over, about); *(marchander)* to haggle (**sur** over, about)
VT **1** *(nourriture)* to play with, to pick at **2** *(prix)* to haggle over

chipoteur, -euse [ʃipotœr, -øz] ADJ **1** *(avec la nourriture)* picky, fussy; **il est c.** he nibbles *or* picks at his food **2** *(ergoteur)* quibbling; **ils sont chipoteurs** they quibble over everything **3** *(marchandeur)* haggling, quibbling
N **1** *(avec la nourriture)* picky eater **2** *(ergoteur)* quibbler **3** *(marchandeur)* haggler, quibbler

chips [ʃips] NFPL **(pommes) c.** (potato) crisps, *Am* chips

> Il faut noter qu'en anglais britannique **chips** est un faux ami. Il signifie **frites**.

chique [ʃik] NF **1** *(de tabac)* quid; *Arg* **couper la c. à qn** to shut sb up; *Arg* **avaler sa c.** *(mourir)* to snuff it, to kick the bucket **2** *Fam (enflure de la joue)* swollen cheek *(due to toothache)* **3** *Belg (bonbon)* sweet **4** *(insecte)* jigger

chiqué [ʃike] NM *Fam* sham; **c'est du c.** it's all put on *or* a put-up job *or* a fake; **faire du c.** to put on an act, to fake it

chiquement [ʃikmã] ADV *Fam* **1** *(avec élégance)* smartly, stylishly **2** *(avec fair-play etc)* decently; **elle m'a c. invité** she was good *or* kind *or* decent enough to invite me

chiquenaude [ʃiknod] NF flick (of the finger); **donner une c. à qn** to flick sb with one's finger; **d'une c.** with a flick of the finger; **d'une c., il envoya la boulette de papier sur le bureau du prof** he flicked the pellet of paper onto the teacher's desk

chiquer [ʃike] VT *(tabac)* to chew
▪ VI to chew tobacco

chiqueur, -euse [ʃikœr, -øz] N tobacco chewer

chirographaire [kirɔgrafɛr] ADJ *Fin* unsecured

chirographie [kirɔgrafi] NF, **chiromancie** [kirɔmãsi] NF palmistry, *Fml* chiromancy

chiromancien, -ienne [kirɔmãsjẽ, -jɛn] N palmist, *Fml* chiromancer

chiropracteur [kirɔpraktœr] NM chiropractor

chiropractie [kirɔprakti] NF chiropractic

chiropraticien, -ienne [kirɔpratisjẽ, -jɛn] N chiropractor

chiropraxie [kirɔpraksi] NF chiropractic

chiroptères [kirɔptɛr] NMPL *Spéc* Chiroptera

chirurgical, -ale, -aux, -ales [ʃiryrʒikal, -o] ADJ surgical

chirurgie [ʃiryrʒi] NF surgery; **c. plastique/ esthétique/dentaire** plastic/cosmetic/dental surgery; **c. cardiaque** cardiac *or* heart surgery; **c. ambulatoire** day surgery

chirurgien, -ienne [ʃiryrʒjẽ, -jɛn] N surgeon; **c. esthétique** plastic surgeon; **c.-dentiste** dental surgeon; **elle est c.** *ou* **chirurgienne** she's a surgeon

chistera [ʃistera] NM pelota racket, chistera

chiure [ʃjyr] NF flyspeck, insect dirt

ch-l. *abrév* chef-lieu

chlamydia, *pl* **chlamydiae** [klamidja, -dje] NF *Méd* chlamydia

chlâsse [ʃlɑs] ADJ *Arg* knackered; *(ivre)* legless, pissed

chleuh [ʃlø] ADJ, NM *Hist Arg Péj* Jerry

chlinguer [ʃlɛ̃ge] VI *Fam* to stink

chloral, *pl* **chlorals** [klɔral] NM *Chimie* chloral; *Pharm* **c. hydraté, hydrate de c.** chloral (hydrate)

chlorate [klɔrat] NM *Chimie* chlorate

chlore [klɔr] NM *Chimie* chlorine

chlorer [klɔre] VT *Ind* to chlorinate; **eau chlorée** chlorinated water

chlorhydrate [klɔridrat] NM *Chimie* hydrochlorate

chlorhydrique [klɔridrik] ADJ *Chimie (acide)* hydrochloric

chlorique [klɔrik] ADJ *(acide)* chloric

chlorofluorocarbure [klɔrɔflyɔrɔkarbyr] NM *Chimie* chlorofluorocarbon

chloroforme [klɔrɔfɔrm] NM chloroform

chloroformer [klɔrɔfɔrme] VT to chloroform

chlorophylle [klɔrɔfil] NF chlorophyll

chlorophyllien, -ienne [klɔrɔfiljẽ, -jɛn] ADJ chlorophyllous

chloroquine [klɔrɔkin] NF *Pharm* chloroquine

chlorure [klɔryr] NM *Chimie* chloride; **c. de chaux** chloride of lime, bleaching powder; **c. de calcium/sodium** calcium/sodium chloride

chlorurer [klɔryre] VT to chlorinate

choc [ʃɔk] NM **1** *(entre deux corps)* collision, impact, shock; **ça peut se casser au moindre c.** it can break at the slightest impact; **le c. des deux voitures** the collision of the two cars; **sous le c., sous la violence du c.** under the impact; **c. violent** violent collision; **c. arrière/latéral** rear/side impact; **c. frontal** head-on collision, frontal impact; **'résiste aux chocs'** 'shock-proof', 'shock-resistant'; **c. sourd** bump; **c. des verres** clink of glasses **2** *(entre armées etc)* clash; **soutenir le c. de l'ennemi** to withstand the onslaught of the enemy; *Fig* **c. des opinions** clash *or* conflict of opinions **3** *Méd* shock **4** *(émotion brutale)* shock; **ça a été un c. de l'apprendre** it was a shock to hear about it; **ça lui a fait un c. de le revoir** it gave her a shock to see him again; **être en état de c.** to be in a state of shock; **il est encore sous le c.** he's still in shock; **tenir le c.** to stand the shock **5** de c. super-efficient; **troupes/commandos de c.** shock troops; **mesures de c.** shock measures; **personnalité de c.** high-powered *or* dynamic personality

▸▸ **c. boursier** market crisis; **c. culturel** culture shock; **c. électrique** electric shock; **c. opératoire** post-operative shock; *Écon* **c. pétrolier** oil crisis; **c. en retour** *Élec* return shock; *Fig* repercussion, backlash; **c. thermique** thermal shock

-choc [ʃɔk] SUFF drastic, shock; **images-/ photos-c.** images/photos that shock; *Com, Fin* **prix-c.!** drastic reductions!; **programme-c.** crash programme

chochotte [ʃɔʃɔt] *Fam Péj* NF lah-di-dah woman; *(homme)* pouf, fairy; **petite c., va!** you stuck-up so-and-so!; **tu n'oses pas sauter? c., va!** you don't dare jump? go on, you big wimp!; **faire sa c.** to put on airs, to be stuck up
▪ ADJ lah-di-dah, affected, mannered; *(homme) (efféminé)* camp, affected; *(douillet)* oversensitive, squeamish

chocolat [ʃɔkɔla] NM **1** chocolate; **c. aux noisettes/amandes** hazelnut/almond chocolate; **tablette de c.** bar of chocolate; **éclair/gâteau/etc au c.** chocolate éclair/ cake/etc **2** *(boisson)* hot chocolate **3** *(confiserie)* chocolate; **une boîte de chocolats** a box of chocolates
▪ ADJ INV chocolate-coloured; *Fam* **être c.** to have been let down

▸▸ **c. blanc** white chocolate; **c. à croquer** plain *or* dark chocolate; **c. à cuire** cooking chocolate; **c. fondant** chocolate fondant; **c. au lait** milk chocolate; **c. noir** plain *or* dark chocolate

chocolaté [ʃɔkɔlate] ADJ *(boisson etc)* chocolate(-flavoured); **farine chocolatée** chocolate powder

chocolaterie [ʃɔkɔlatri] NF *(fabrique)* chocolate factory; *(magasin)* chocolate shop

chocolatier, -ière [ʃɔkɔlatje, -jɛr] ADJ *(industrie etc)* chocolate
▪ N *(fabricant)* chocolate-maker; *(marchand)* confectioner
▪ NF **chocolatière** chocolate pot

chocottes [ʃɔkɔt] NFPL *Fam* **avoir les c.** to have the jitters; **ça m'a donné** *ou* **filé** *ou* **très** *Fam* **foutu les c.** it gave me the jitters

chœur [kœr] NM choir; *Archit* choir, chancel; *(d'un chanteur de variétés, d'un opéra), Antiq* chorus; **les chœurs** *(d'un opéra, d'un spectacle)* the chorus; **elle est dans les chœurs** she's in the chorus, she's a member of the chorus; **chanter en c.** to sing in chorus; **enfant de c.** altar boy; *(qui chante)* choirboy; *Fam* **son air d'enfant de c.** his angelic *or* choirboy look; **le c. des contestataires** the body of protesters; **en c.** together; **s'informer en c.** to enquire in chorus *or* in unison; **tous en c.!** all together! VOIR GRAMMAIRE A11; A14

choir [ʃwar] VI *(pp* **chu;** *pr ind* **je chois, il choit;** *p hist* **je chus;** *fu* **je choirai, je cherrai;** *the aux is* **être)** *Litt* **1** *(tomber)* **se laisser c. (dans un fauteuil)** to flop, to sink (into an armchair); *Fam* **laisser c. qn/qch** to drop sb/ sth; **tu ne peux pas le laisser c., il faut aller au rendez-vous** you can't let him down, you'll have to keep the appointment **2** *Arch* to fall; **... et la bobinette cherra** ... and the latch will drop

choisi [ʃwazi] ADJ **1** *(sélectionné)* selected; **morceaux choisis de ...** selected passages *or* extracts from ... **2** *(élégant)* select, choice; *(langage)* polished; **parler en termes choisis** to speak in carefully chosen terms, to choose one's words (carefully); **société choisie** select company

choisir [ʃwazir] VT to choose, to pick, to select; **c. ses fréquentations/lectures** to choose *or* pick one's company/reading; **c. entre** *ou* **parmi plusieurs choses** to choose from (among) several things; **il faut c. si oui ou non tu l'achètes** you have to choose *or* decide whether or not to buy it; **à lui de c. quand il veut y aller** it's up to him to decide when he wants to go; **il a bien/mal choisi son moment!** he really picked *or* chose the right/wrong moment!; *Iron* **j'ai choisi mon jour pour aller me promener: il pleut** I really picked a good day to go for a walk: it's raining
▪ VI to choose; **il faudra bien c.** you'll/we'll/ *etc* have to choose *or* decide *or* make a choice; **c. de partir** to choose *or* decide to leave

choix [ʃwa] NM choice; **arrêter** *ou* **fixer son c. sur qch** to decide on sth, to choose sth; **mon c. est fait** I've made my choice; **faire le bon c.** to make the right choice; **l'embarras du c.** the difficulty in choosing; **avoir** *ou* **n'avoir que l'embarras du c.** to be spoiled for choice; **faites votre c.** take your pick; **vous avez le c.** the choice is yours, you have a choice; **je n'ai pas le c.** I don't have a choice; **je n'avais pas le c.** I had no choice; **je vous laisse le c.** you choose; **il nous laisse le c. de la date** he's letting us choose the date; **nous n'avons pas d'autre c. que de ...** we have no option *or* choice but to ...; **vous avez le c. entre ... et ...** you have the choice *or* you can choose between ... and ...; **viande ou poisson au c.** *(sur le menu)* choice of meat or fish; **on a droit à un dessert au c.** there is a choice of dessert; **les matières à option à l'université sont au c. de l'étudiant** optional subjects at university are chosen by the student; **de premier c.** (of the) best quality, first-class; **de second c.** of poor(er) quality; **morceaux de viande de c.** prime cuts; **un grand c. de sous-vêtements** a large *or* wide selection *or* a wide range of underwear; **c. de poésies** a selection of poems; *Admin* **être promu au c.** to be promoted by selection *or* on merit; **questionnaire à c. multiple** multiple-choice questionnaire

choléra [kɔlera] NM *Méd* cholera; **avoir le c.** to have cholera

cholériforme [kɔlerifɔrm] ADJ *Méd* choleriform

cholérique [kɔlerik] *Méd* ADJ choleraic
▪ N cholera patient

cholestérol [kɔlɛsterɔl] NM *Méd* cholesterol; **taux de c.** cholesterol level; *Fam* **j'ai du c.** my cholesterol (level) is too high

cholestérolémie [kɔlɛsterɔlemi] NF *Méd* cholesterol level

chômable [ʃomabl] ADJ **jour c.** public holiday

chômage [ʃomaʒ] NM unemployment; **le c. touche une grande partie de la population**

unemployment affects a high proportion of the population; **le c. des femmes/des jeunes** female/youth unemployment, unemployment among women/young people; **être au c.** to be unemployed or out of work or Fam jobless; **allocation** ou **indemnité de c.** unemployment benefit, Br Fam dole); **toucher le c.** to claim unemployment benefit, to be on unemployment or Br Fam on the dole; **s'inscrire au c.** to sign on; **c. d'une usine** closure of a factory

▸▸ **c. chronique** chronic unemployment; **c. conjoncturel** cyclical unemployment; **c. déguisé** hidden unemployment; **c. frictionnel** frictional unemployment; **c. de longue durée** long-term unemployment; **c. partiel** short-time (working); **être en c. partiel** to be on short time; **c. récurrent** periodic or recurrent unemployment; **c. saisonnier** seasonal unemployment; **c. structurel** structural or long-term unemployment; **c. technique** lay-offs; **être en c. technique** to have been laid off

chôm'du, chômedu [ʃomdy] NM Fam (chômage) **être au c.** to be out of work; **pointer au c.** to be Br on the dole or Am on welfare

chômer [ʃome] VT (jour férié) to keep; **jour chômé** public holiday, Br bank holiday

VI **1** (ne pas travailler) (d'une usine) to be or lie idle; (d'un employé) to be unemployed or out of work; Fig to do nothing; **vous n'avez pas chômé!** you've not been idle or twiddling your thumbs!; **l'an dernier, je n'ai pas eu le temps de c.** I didn't have a spare moment all last year; **laisser c. une terre** to let land lie fallow; **laisser c. son argent** to let one's money lie idle **2** (faire le pont) **c. entre Noël et le jour de l'an** to take time off between Christmas and New Year

chômeur, -euse [ʃomœr, -øz] N unemployed person; **un million de chômeurs** a million unemployed; **les chômeurs** the unemployed; **les chômeurs de longue durée** the long-term unemployed

chope [ʃɔp] NF (récipient) beer mug, tankard; (contenu) mugful

choper [ʃɔpe] VT Arg **1** (voler) to pinch, to nick; **on m'a chopé mon portefeuille** I've had my wallet pinched or nicked, somebody's lifted my wallet **2** (arrêter, prendre) to catch, to nab; **se faire c.** to get caught or nabbed; **je l'ai chopé en train de fouiller dans mes affaires** I caught him rummaging through my things **3** (attraper) (rhume) to catch

chopine [ʃɔpin] NF **1** Fam (contenant) half-litre or Am -liter bottle; **tu viens boire une c.?** (are you) coming for a drink? **2** Can (mesure) pint (0.568 litre)

choquant [ʃɔkã] ADJ (attitude etc) shocking; **un abus c.** a gross or shocking abuse

choqué [ʃɔke] ADJ shocked; **il les regardait d'un air profondément c.** he looked at them, visibly shocked; Can **être c. (contre qn)** to be angry (at sb), Am to be mad (at sb)

choquer [ʃɔke] VT **1** (percuter) to strike, to knock; **nous avons choqué nos verres** we clinked or chinked glasses

2 (contrarier, être désagréable à) to shock, to offend; **ce qui choque le plus dans ces images, c'est que …** the most shocking thing about these pictures is …; **être choqué de qch** to be scandalized or shocked at or by sth; **nous avons été choqués par son manque d'égard** we were shocked or appalled by his lack of consideration; **je suis tout à fait choqué par sa vulgarité** I am deeply shocked by his coarseness; **cela risque de c.** it might cause offence; **sons qui choquent l'oreille** sounds that grate on or offend the ear; **mot qui choque** offensive or rude word; **de telles paroles choquent**

dans la bouche d'une jeune fille such language is shocking in the mouth of or coming from a young girl

3 (blesser moralement) to shock; **j'ai été choqué de le voir tellement changé** I was shocked or it gave me a shock to see such a change in him; **la vue du sang l'a choqué** the sight of blood has shaken him

VPR **se choquer 1** (d'objets) to knock against each other **2** (être scandalisé) to be shocked, to take offence (**de** at); **il n'y a pas de quoi se c.** there's nothing to be shocked at

choral, -ale, -als, -ales [kɔral] ADJ choral; **chant c.** choral singing; **société chorale** choral society

NM choral(e)

NF **chorale** (société) choral society; (chanteurs) choir; **la chorale de l'église** the church choir VOIR GRAMMAIRE A11

chorée [kɔre] NF Méd chorea; Fam Saint Vitus's dance

chorégraphe [kɔregraf] N choreographer

chorégraphie [kɔregrafi] NF choreography; **faire la c. d'un spectacle** to choreograph or do the choreography for a show

chorégraphier [kɔregrafje] VT to choreograph

chorégraphique [kɔregrafik] ADJ choreographic

choria [ʃɔrja] NF Rel (Islam) sharia

choriste [kɔrist] N Mus choir member; (dans une église) chorister; (dans un opéra) chorus singer; (d'une comédie musicale) chorus member; (d'un chanteur) backing singer

chorizo [tʃɔrizo] NM Culin chorizo

chorus [kɔrys] NM **1** **faire c.** to voice one's agreement; **ils ont fait c. avec lui** they voiced their agreement with him **2** (dans le jazz) chorus; **reprendre un c.** to take up the chorus

CHOSE [ʃoz] NF **1** (objet inanimé) thing; **il aime les belles choses** he likes nice things; **les êtres et les choses** living creatures and objects or things, Scol Vieilli **leçon de choses** nature lesson; Fig **être la c. de qn** to belong to sb; **il la considère comme sa c.** he thinks he owns her

2 (abstrait) thing; **j'ai appris une c. incroyable** I've heard something unbelievable; **une c. très grave vient de se passer** something very serious has just happened; **il se passe des choses au ministère** there's something going on in the department; **quelque c. se prépare** something's brewing; **j'ai un tas de choses à faire** I've loads or masses of things to do; **c'est de deux choses l'une, soit il parle, soit …** either he talks, or …; **chaque c. en son temps** everything in its own time; **on m'a dit des tas de choses à son sujet** I've been told heaps of things about him; **dites bien des choses de ma part à …** remember me to …, give my regards to …; **il a dit des choses sur moi?** has he been saying things about me?; **elle dit de ces choses parfois!** the things she comes out with sometimes!; **j'ai bien des choses à vous raconter** I've a lot (of things) to tell you; **ce n'est pas c. aisée de …** it's no easy matter to …; **réaliser cela est une c., l'admettre en est une autre** being aware of it is one thing, admitting it is another; **la c. en question** the case in point; **je vais vous expliquer la c.** I'll explain it or the matter to you; **il a très bien pris la c.** he took it very well; **c'était vraiment la c. à éviter** that was the last thing to do; **cela n'est plus la même c.** that alters the case or things; **nous y sommes retournés, mais ce n'est plus la même c.** we went back (there), but it wasn't the same; Fam **être porté sur la c.** to be obsessed with sex, to have a one-track mind; **je vais te dire une (bonne) c.** I'm

going to or let me tell you something; **c. curieuse, personne n'en savait rien** curiously enough, nobody knew anything about it; **avant toute c.** first of all, above all; **et, c. rare** for once; Jur **c. jugée** res judicata; Pol **la c. publique** the state, Fml res publica

3 **les choses** things; **voici comment se sont passées les choses** here's how things happened; **il a bien/mal pris les choses** he took it well/badly; **prendre les choses à cœur** to take things to heart; **l'état des choses** the state of things; **dans l'état actuel des choses** as things are or stand at the moment; **les choses de ce monde** the things of this world; **par la force des choses** by or through force of circumstance; **il fait bien les choses** he does things in style; **il faut bien voir les choses en face** ou **telles qu'elles sont** you have to face up to things, you have to face facts; **les choses étant ce qu'elles sont** things being as or what they are; **ne pas faire les choses à demi** not to do things by halves; **ce documentaire sur l'alcoolisme va au fond des choses** this documentary on alcoholism gets to the heart of the matter or problem; **n'aie pas peur d'appeler les choses par leur nom** don't be afraid to call a spade a spade or to speak your mind

NM Fam (truc) whatsit, what's-its-name, thingummy; **passe-moi le c.** pass me the whatsit or the what-d'you-call-it; **Monsieur/Madame C.** Mr/Mrs what-d'you-call-him/her, what's-his-name/what's-her-name, Mr/Mrs thingummy; **le petit C.** little what's-his-name

ADJ INV Fam **être** ou **se sentir/avoir l'air tout c.** to feel/look funny or a bit peculiar

chosifier [ʃozifje] VT Phil to reify

chott [ʃɔt] NM Géog saline lake, shott

chou¹, -oux [ʃu] NM **1** (plante) cabbage; Fam **aller planter ses choux** to go and live in the country, to retire to the country; **faire ses choux gras de qch** (s'enrichir) to get rich on sth; **l'opposition a fait ses choux gras de ce scandale** the opposition had a field day with the scandal; **faire c. blanc** to draw a blank; **mon petit c.** darling, dear; **être dans les choux** to be in a fix or a mess; **rentrer dans le c. à qn** to attack or go for sb; **c'est bête comme c.** it's as easy as pie; Fig **feuille de c.** (journal) rag **2** (ruban) bow, rosette **3** Culin **pâte à choux** choux pastry

▸▸ **c. de Bruxelles** Brussels sprout; Culin **c. à la crème** = cream bun; **c. frisé** kale; **c. de Milan** Savoy (cabbage); **c. pommé** round cabbage; **c. rouge** red cabbage

chou², choute [ʃu, ʃut] ADJ Fam **elle est c.** ou **choute!** she's cute!; **c'est d'un c.!** it's so cute!

chouan [ʃwã] NM Hist Chouan

Chouannerie [ʃwanri] NF Hist **la C.** the Chouan revolt

choucas [ʃuka] NM jackdaw

chouchou, -oute [ʃuʃu, -ut] N Fam (préféré) pet, m blue-eyed boy; **le c. du prof** the teacher's pet; **tu es sa chouchoute** you're his favourite or pet

NM (pour mettre dans les cheveux) scrunchy

chouchouter [ʃuʃute] VT Fam to pamper, to spoil; **il aime se faire c.** he enjoys being pampered

choucroute [ʃukrut] NF Culin sauerkraut; **c. garnie** sauerkraut with meat

chouette¹ [ʃwɛt] NF **1** (oiseau) **c. des clochers, c. effraie** screech owl, barn owl; **c. des bois** wood or brown owl; **c. hulotte** tawny owl **2** Fam Péj (femme désagréable) old shrew

chouette² Fam ADJ terrific, marvellous, great; **c'est c.!** that's great or smashing!; **un type vraiment c.** a really great guy; **il a été**

très **c. avec elle** he's been really good to her; *Iron* **tu as l'air c. avec ton chapeau!** you look (like) something else in that hat! **INT c. (alors)!** great!, fantastic!

chou-fleur, *pl* **choux-fleurs NM** cauliflower; **oreille en c.** cauliflower ear

chouïa [ʃuja] **NM** *Fam* **un c. (de)** a tiny bit (of), a smidgen (of); **tu devrais te reposer un c.** you should have a bit of a *or* a little rest

chou-navet, *pl* **choux-navets NM** swede, *Am* rutabaga

chou-palmiste, *pl* **choux-palmistes NM** *Bot* palm cabbage

chou-rave, *pl* **choux-raves NM** kohlrabi

chouraver [ʃurave], **chourer** [ʃure] **VT** *Fam* to pinch, to nick; **on m'a chouravé mon vélo** I've had my bike pinched *or* nicked

chow-chow, *pl* **chows-chows** [ʃoʃo, ʃawʃaw] **NM** chow (dog)

choyer [ʃwaje] **VT** (**je choie; je choierai**) to pamper, to coddle; **c. un espoir** to cherish a hope

chrême [krɛm] **NM** *Rel* chrism, holy oil

chrétien, -ienne [kretjɛ̃, -jɛn] **ADJ** Christian **N** Christian; **un bon c.** a good Christian

chrétiennement [kretjɛnmɑ̃] **ADV** in a Christian manner, like a Christian; **mourir c.** to die a Christian death

chrétienté [kretjɛ̃te] **NF** Christendom

Chris-Craft® [kriskraft] **NM INV** *Naut* Chris-Craft®

Christ [krist] **NM 1 le C.** Christ; **Jésus-C.** [ʒezykri] Jesus Christ **2 c.** crucifix; **un c. d'ivoire/d'ébène** an ivory/ebony crucifix

christiania [kristjanja] **NM** *Ski* christiania, christie (turn)

christianisation [kristjanizasjɔ̃] **NF** christianization

christianiser [kristjanize] **VT** to christianize

christianisme [kristjanism] **NM** Christianity

chromage [kromaʒ] **NM** chromium plating

chromate [kromat] **NM** *Chimie* chromate

chromatique [kromatik] **ADJ 1** *Mus, Opt etc* chromatic **2** *Biol* chromosomal

chromatiquement [kromatikmɑ̃] **ADV** *Mus* chromatically

chromatisme [kromatism] **NM** *Mus* chromaticism; *Beaux-Arts* range of colours

chrome [krom] **NM 1** *Chimie* chromium **2** (*matière*) chrome; (*sur auto etc*) chrome fitting; **jaune de c.** chrome yellow; *Fam* **faire (briller) les chromes** (*de voitures, de bicyclettes etc*) to polish the chrome

chromé [krome] **ADJ** (*métal*) chromium-plated; **acier c.** chrome steel

chromer [krome] **VT 1** (*métal*) to chromium-plate **2** (*acier*) to chrome

chrominance [krominɑ̃s] **TV** chrominance

chromo [kromo] **NM** *Fam* chromo(lithograph), colour print

chromosome [kromozom] **NM** *Biol* chromosome; **c. somatique** autosome, somatic chromosome

chromosomique [kromozomik] **ADJ** *Biol* chromosomal; **maladie c.** chromosomal *or* genetic illness

chronicité [kronisite] **NF** (*d'une maladie, du chômage etc*) chronic nature, *Fml* chronicity

chronique [kronik] **ADJ** (*maladie, chômage etc*) chronic; **mévente c.** slump in sales **NF 1** *Journ* (*financière etc*) news, report, column; **tenir la c. sportive** to write the sports column; *Fig* **défrayer la c.** to be the talk of the neighbourhood *or* town, to be the main topic of conversation; **c. boursière** markets column; **c. financière** financial news; **c. judiciaire** court column; **c. littéraire** book reviews; **c. mondaine** society column; **c. des**

spectacles (entertainments) listings **2** (*annale*) chronicle

chroniquement [kronikmɑ̃] **ADV** chronically

chroniqueur, -euse [kronikœr, -øz] **N 1** *Journ* columnist, editor; **c. boursier** market commentator; **c. judiciaire** court reporter; **c. littéraire** book editor, book reviewer; **c. mondain** gossip columnist **2** (*historien*) chronicler

chrono [krono] **NM** *Fam* stopwatch; **du 220 (km/h) (au) c.** recorded speed of 220 (km/h); **son temps était de 4 minutes 6 secondes, c.** his time by the clock was 4 minutes (and) 6 seconds

chronobiologie [kronobjolɔʒi] **NF** *Biol* chronobiology

chronogramme [kronogram] **NM** planner

chronographe [kronograf] **NM** *Tech* chronograph

chronologie [kronolɔʒi] **NF** chronology; *Cin, TV* chronology, time sequence

chronologique [kronolɔʒik] **ADJ** chronological

chronologiquement [kronolɔʒikmɑ̃] **ADV** chronologically

chronométrage [kronometraʒ] **NM** timekeeping; (*d'une course*) timing

chronomètre [kronomɛtr] **NM 1** (*pour le sport etc*) stopwatch **2** (*montre de précision*) chronometer; *Ordinat* timer

chronométrer [kronometre] **VT** (**je chronomètre; je chronométrerai**) *Sport* to time

chronométreur [kronometrœr] **NM 1** *Sport* timekeeper **2** *Ind* time and motion (study) expert

chronométrique [kronometrik] **ADJ** chronometric(al)

Chronopost [kronopost] **NM** = express mail service in France

chrysalide [krizalid] **NF** *Entom* chrysalis, pupa; *Fig* **sortir de sa c.** to come out of one's shell

chrysanthème [krizɑ̃tɛm] **NM** chrysanthemum

Chrysanthèmes

Chrysanthemums are often associated with funerals in France, and so are never offered as gifts. They are traditionally used to decorate graves, especially on All Saints' Day.

chrysolithe [krizolit] **NF** *Minér* chrysolite, olivine

CHS [seaʃɛs] **NM** (*abrév* **centre hospitalier spécialisé**) psychiatric hospital

chtarbé [ʃtarbe] **ADJ** *Fam* crazy, nuts, off one's rocker

ch'timi [ʃtimi] *Fam* **ADJ** from Northern France **N** person from Northern France

chtouille [ʃtuj] **NF** *très Fam* **la c.** the clap

CHU [seaʃy] **NM INV** (*abrév* **centre hospitalier universitaire**) ≃ teaching hospital

chuchotement [ʃyʃotmɑ̃] **NM** whisper; **chuchotements** whispering, whispers

chuchoter [ʃyʃote] **VI** to whisper; **parler en chuchotant** to speak in a whisper **VT c. qch à l'oreille de qn** to whisper sth in sb's ear

chuchoterie [ʃyʃotri] **NF** whispering, whispered conversation

chuchoteur, -euse [ʃyʃotœr, -øz] **ADJ** whispering **N** whisperer

chuintant, -ante [ʃɥɛ̃tɑ̃, -ɑ̃t] *Ling* **ADJ** **sons chuintants** hushing sounds (*eg* S, Z);

consonne chuintante palato-alveolar fricative **NF chuintante** palato-alveolar fricative

chuintement [ʃɥɛ̃tmɑ̃] **NM 1** *Ling* pronunciation of s as sh **2** (*sifflement*) hissing

chuinter [ʃɥɛ̃te] **VI 1** (*de la chouette*) to hoot **2** *Ling* to pronounce s as sh **3** (*de la vapeur etc*) to hiss

chut [ʃyt] **INT** hush!, sh!

chute [ʃyt] **NF 1** (*fait de tomber*) fall; *Fig* (*d'un ministère etc*) fall, collapse; (*de pression, de température etc*) drop, fall; (*de ventes etc*) slump; **faire une c. (de cheval/moto)** to have a fall *or* a tumble *or* a spill (from one's horse/motorbike), to fall off (one's horse/motorbike); **une c. de 10 mètres** a 10-metre fall; **il a fait une c. de dix mètres** he fell ten metres; **'c. de pierres'** 'danger! falling rocks'; **c. de pluie/neige** rainfall/snowfall; **c. du jour** nightfall; *Litt* **c. des feuilles** autumn, *Am* fall; **la c. des feuilles a eu lieu plus tôt que d'habitude cette année** the trees lost their leaves sooner than usual this year; **c. des cheveux** hair loss; **c. des prix** fall *or* drop in prices; **la c. de l'homme** the Fall; **il m'a entraîné dans sa c.** he has dragged me down with him; *Théâtre* **c. d'une pièce** failure *or Fam* flop of a play; *Cartes* **avoir deux levées de c.** to be two tricks down; **c. d'eau** waterfall; **les chutes Victoria** the Victoria Falls; **c. naturelle** natural waterfall; **hauteur de c.** (*d'eau*) fall, head **3** (*du toit*) pitch; (*de la voix etc*) cadence; (*d'un poème, roman, d'une pièce etc*) end; (*d'histoire drôle*) punchline **4** (*de bois*) off-cut; (*de tissu etc*) scraps, trimmings; (*de métal*) scrap **5** *Cin, TV* waste film; *Journ* last line (*of article*), tag line ▶▶**c. libre** free fall; **descendre en c. libre** to (be in) free fall; *Fig* **ses résultats scolaires descendent en c. libre** his marks are plummeting *or* have taken a nose-dive; **c. des reins** small of the back; *Théâtre* **c. du rideau** fall of the curtain

chuter [ʃyte] **VI** *Fam* (*tomber*) to fall (down); *Fig* to come a cropper, to come to grief; *Théâtre* (*d'une pièce de théâtre*) to be a failure, to flop; *Cartes* **c. de deux levées** to be two tricks down

chyme [ʃim] **NM** *Méd* chyme

Chypre [ʃipr] **NF** (*l'île de*) **C.** Cyprus

chypriote [ʃiprijot] **ADJ** Cypriot **N C.** Cypriot

CI [sei] **NM** *Fin* (*abrév* **certificat d'investissement**) investment certificate

ci¹ [si] **ADV** here; **ce livre-ci** this book; **ces jours-ci** these days; **de-ci, de-là** here and there, on all sides; **par-ci, par-là** here and there; **ci-gît .../-gisent ...** here lies .../lie ...

ci² **PRON DÉM INV** *Fam* **faire ci et ça** to do this and that; **comme ci comme ça** so-so

CIA [seia] **NF** (*abrév* **Central Intelligence Agency**) CIA

ciao [tʃao] **INT** *Fam* ciao

ci-après **ADV** (*dans la suite du texte etc*) later, further on, below; *Jur* here(in)after

cibiche [sibiʃ] **NF** *Fam* fag, ciggie

cibiste [sibist] **N** user of Citizens' Band radio, CB user

ciblage [siblaʒ] **NM** *Mktg* targeting; **c. stratégique** strategic targeting

cible [sibl] **NF** target, mark; (*en publicité*) target; **servir de c. aux railleries de qn** to be the butt *or* the target for sb's jokes; **déterminer/atteindre sa c.** to define/reach the target; **langue c.** target language; *Mktg* **marché c.** (*pour un produit*) target market; **c. commerciale/de communication** marketing/promotional target

ciblé [sible] ADJ *(campagne etc)* targeted (**sur** at)

cibler [sible] VT *Mktg* to target

ciboire [sibwar] NM *Rel* pyx, ciborium

ciboule [sibul] NF *Bot, Culin* spring onion, *Am* scallion

ciboulette [sibulεt] NF *(plante), Culin* chive(s)

ciboulot [sibulo] NM *Arg (tête)* noddle, nut; **se creuser le c.** to rack one's brains; **en avoir dans le c.** to have a lot between one's ears; **elle en a dans le c., cette petite!** she's not just a pretty face, this girl!

cicatrice [sikatris] NF scar; *Fig* **cette séparation a laissé une c. profonde en lui** the separation scarred him deeply *or* left a deep scar on him

cicatriciel, -ielle [sikatrisjεl] ADJ **tissu c.** scar tissue

cicatrisant [sikatrizã] ADJ *(pommade etc)* healing, *Spéc* cicatrizing
▪ NM healing lotion *or* cream

cicatrisation [sikatrizasjɔ̃] NF *(de blessure etc)* healing, closing (up), *Spéc* cicatrization

cicatriser [sikatrize] VT *(blessure etc)* to heal; **le temps cicatrise toutes les blessures** time heals all wounds
▪ VI *(d'une blessure etc)* to heal (up)
▪ VPR **se cicatriser** to heal up; *Fig* to heal

cicéro [sisero] NM *Typ* pica, twelve-point type

ciclée [sikle] NF *Suisse Fam (cri)* shriek

cicler [sikle] VI *Suisse Fam (crier)* to shriek

ciclosporine [siklɔspɔrin] NF *Chimie* cyclosporin A

ci-contre ADV **1** *(en regard)* opposite; *Compta* **porté c.** as per contra **2** *(document etc)* attached

CICR [seiseer] NM *(abrév* **Comité international de la Croix-Rouge)** IRCC

ci-dessous [sid(ə)su] ADV below

ci-dessus [sid(ə)sy] ADV above

ci-devant [sid(ə)vã] ADV previously, formerly
▪ N INV *Hist* aristocrat

CIDEX [sidεks] NM *(abrév* **courrier individuel à distribution exceptionnelle)** = system grouping letter boxes in country areas

CIDJ [seidεʒi] NM *(abrév* **centre d'information et de documentation de la jeunesse)** = library offering careers information and literature to young people

cidre [sidr] NM cider; **c. bouché** bottled cider; **c. doux/brut** sweet/dry cider

cidrerie [sidrəri] NF *(fabrique)* cider house

Cie *(abrév* **Compagnie)** Co

ciel [sjεl] *pl* **ciels, cieux** [sjø] NM **1** *(espace)* sky; **suspendu entre c. et terre** to hang in mid-air; **(couleur) bleu (de) c.** sky-blue; **trouée de c. (bleu)** patch of (blue) sky; **les ciels de l'Italie** the skies of Italy; *Beaux-Arts* **les ciels de Turner** Turner's skies; **carte du c.** map of the heavens; **à c. ouvert** in the open air, out of doors; **sous d'autres cieux** beneath other skies, in other climes; **lever les bras au c.** to raise one's arms to the sky *or* heavenwards; **lever les yeux au c.** to raise one's eyes to heaven; *Fam* **tomber du c.** to be thunderstruck; *Fig* **ça ne va pas te tomber du c.** it won't fall into your lap, you won't get it handed to you on a plate; *Fig* **remuer c. et terre** to move heaven and earth (**pour faire qch** to do sth); **être au septième c.** to be in seventh heaven; *Fig* **élever qn aux cieux** *ou* **jusqu'au c.** to laud sb to the skies
2 *(paradis)* heaven; **il est monté au c.** he's gone to heaven; **notre Père qui es** *ou* **êtes aux cieux** our Father which *or* who art in Heaven; **le royaume des cieux** the Kingdom

of Heaven; **le c. m'en est témoin** (as) Heaven is my witness; **(juste) c.!** (good) heavens!, heavens above!; **aide-toi, le c. t'aidera** God helps those who help themselves; **grâce au c.** thank heavens
3 *pl* **ciels** *Rel (baldaquin)* baldachin, canopy; *(de lit)* canopy; *Min (d'une carrière etc)* roof; **carrière/mine à c. ouvert** opencast quarry/mine

cierge [sjεrʒ] NM *Rel* candle; **brûler un c. à un saint** to burn a candle to a saint

cigale [sigal] NF *(insecte)* cicada; *Fig Fam (dépensier)* spendthrift

cigare [sigar] NM **1** *(à fumer)* cigar **2** *Arg (tête)* nut, bonce; **avoir mal au c.** to have a headache; **mets-toi ça dans le c.** get that into your thick skull

cigarette [sigarεt] NF cigarette; **c. (à) bout filtre** filter-tip cigarette; **la c. du condamné** the condemned man's last cigarette; **c. russe** = long roll-shaped biscuit

cigarettier [sigarεtje] NM cigarette manufacturer

cigarillo [sigarijo] NM cigarillo

cigogne [sigɔɲ] NF **1** *(oiseau)* stork **2** *(levier)* crank lever

ciguë [sigy] NF *(plante), Méd* hemlock

ci-inclus [siε̃kly] ADJ *(inv when it precedes the noun)* **la copie ci-incluse** the enclosed copy
▪ ADV **(vous trouverez) c. copie de votre lettre** please find enclosed a copy of your letter

CIJ [seiʒi] NF *(abrév* **Cour internationale de justice)** ICJ

ci-joint ADJ *(inv when it precedes the noun)* attached, enclosed; **les pièces ci-jointes** the enclosed *or* attached documents
▪ ADV **vous trouverez c. quittance** please find receipt attached *or* enclosed

cil [sil] NM **1** *(eye)*lash; **battre des cils** to flutter one's eyelashes; **faux cils** false eyelashes
2 *Biol* cilium, hair, filament

cilice [silis] NM hair shirt

cillement [sijmã] NM blinking

ciller [sije] VI to blink; *Fig* **il n'a pas cillé** he didn't bat an eyelid

cimaise [simεz] NF ogee moulding; *(à hauteur d'appui)* dado (rail)

cime [sim] NF *(d'une montagne etc)* summit; *(pic)* peak; *(d'un arbre, d'un mât etc)* top; *Fig* **être à la c. de la réussite** to be at the height *or* peak of one's success

ciment [simã] NM cement; **c. à prise rapide** quick-setting cement; **c. armé** reinforced concrete; **c. dentaire** amalgam

cimentation [simãtasjɔ̃] NF cementing

cimenter [simãte] VT to cement; *Fig* **c. une alliance/une amitié/une relation** to cement *or* consolidate an alliance/a friendship/a relationship

cimenterie [simãtri] NF *Ind* cement works

cimeterre [simtεr] NM scimitar

cimetière [simtjεr] NM cemetery, graveyard; *(d'église)* churchyard; **c. de voitures** scrapyard; **c. d'éléphants** elephants' graveyard

cimier [simje] NM **1** *(d'un casque)* crest **2** *(d'un cerf etc)* haunch; *(d'un bœuf)* rump

cinabre [sinabr] NM cinnabar

ciné [sine] NM *Br Fam (spectacle)* pictures, *Am* movies; *(édifice) Br* cinema, *Am* movie theater; **aller au c.** to go to the pictures

cinéaste [sineast] N film maker

ciné-club, *pl* **ciné-clubs** NM film club

cinéma [sinema] NM **1** *(art)* cinema, movies, *Am* motion pictures; **le c. de Pasolini** Pasolini's films; **l'invention du c.** the invention of cinema *or* motion pictures; **studio de c.** film

studio; **faire du c.** *(d'un acteur)* to be a film *or* movie actor, to act in films; *(d'un metteur en scène, technicien etc)* to work in films; **acteur/actrice de c.** film *or* movie actor/actress; **critique de c.** cinema *or* film critic; **industrie du c.** film *or* movie industry, *Am* motion picture industry; *Fam* **c'est du c.** it's all an act, it's all put on; **elle a fait tout un c. pour ne pas y aller** she made a scene so that she didn't have to go; **arrête (un peu) ton c. et va te coucher!** stop making such a fuss and go to bed!
2 *(salle)* cinema, *Am* movie theater, *Br Fam* pictures; **aller au c.** to go to the cinema; **ouvreuse de c.** usherette
▸▸ **c. d'amateurs** amateur film-making, home movies; **c. d'animation** animation; **c. d'art et d'essai** *(genre, bâtiment)* art-house cinema; **c. d'auteur** auteur cinema; **c. direct** direct cinema; **c. à domicile** home cinema; **c. muet** silent films; **c. multi-salle** multi-screen cinema, multiplex; **c. parlant** talking films, *Fam* talkies; **c. permanent** continuous performance; **c. en relief** three-dimensional *or* 3-D films

CinémaScope® [sinemaskɔp] NM CinemaScope®

cinémathèque [sinematεk] NF film library *or* archives; **la C. française** = the French film institute

cinématique [sinematik] ADJ kinematic(al)
▪ NF kinematics

cinématographe [sinematɔgraf] NM cinematograph

cinématographie [sinematɔgrafi] NF cinematography

cinématographier [sinematɔgrafje] VT to film

cinématophotographie [sinematɔfɔtɔgrafi] NF camerawork

cinématographique [sinematɔgrafik] ADJ cinematographic; *(production etc)* cinema, film; **les techniques cinématographiques** cinematic techniques; **une grande carrière c.** a great career in the cinema

cinéma-vérité NM cinéma vérité

cinémomètre [sinemɔmεtr] NM *Tech* speedometer, speed gauge

ciné-parc, *pl* **ciné-parcs** NM *Can* drive-in cinema

cinéphile [sinefil] ADJ film- *or* movie-loving; **public c.** cinema-going public; **ils sont tous très cinéphiles dans cette famille** they're all great film-lovers *or* film buffs *or* movie buffs in that family
▪ N film *or* movie enthusiast *or* buff

cinéraire [sinerεr] ADJ *(urne etc)* cinerary
▪ NF *(plante)* cineraria

Cinérama® [sinerama] NM Cinerama®

ciné-roman, *pl* **ciné-romans** NM = picture book of a film; *Arch (film)* (film) serial

cinétique [sinetik] ADJ *(énergie etc)* kinetic
▪ NF kinetics

cing(h)alais, -aise [sε̃galε, -εz] ADJ Sin(g)halese
▪ NM *Ling* Sin(g)halese
▪ N **C.** Sin(g)halese

cinglant [sε̃glã] ADJ *(pluie etc)* lashing; *(vent etc)* cutting, biting; *(froid)* bitter; *(remarque)* stinging, cutting, scathing

cinglé, -ée [sε̃gle] *Fam* ADJ cracked, crazy; **il est complètement c.** he's off his rocker, he's round the twist
▪ N loony, nutcase

cingler¹ [sε̃gle] VI *Naut* un voilier qui cingle **vers les Canaries** a yacht making for *or* bound for the Canary Islands

cingler² VT *(visage) (du vent)* to sting; *(cheval etc)* to lash, to whip; *(personne)* to lash out at; **une branche m'a cinglé la figure** a branch whipped (against) my face; **la grêle lui cinglait le visage** the hail was stinging his face

cinoche [sinɔʃ] **NM** *Fam* cinema, *Am* movie theater; **aller au c.** to go to the pictures *or* movies; **je me ferais bien un petit c. ce soir** I quite fancy going to the pictures tonight

cinoque [sinɔk] *Arg* **ADJ** batty, crazy ▪ **N** nutcase, headbanger

cinq [sɛk] **ADJ INV 1** five; **à c. heures** at five o' clock **c. (petits) garçons** [sɛ(pti)garsɔ̃] five (little) boys; **c. hommes** [sɛkɔm] five men; **j'en ai c.** [sɛk] I've got five; **c. par c.** five by five, in fives; *Euph* **les c. lettres** ≃ a four-letter word; **je lui ai répondu en c. lettres** I told him where to go; **il était moins c.** it was a near thing *or* a close shave; *Aut* **c. places** five-seater; *Aut* **c. portes** five-door model; *Fig* **faire qch en c. sec** to do sth in five seconds flat; *Radio* **recevoir qn c. sur c.** to receive sb loud and clear; *Journ* **c. colonnes à la une** a banner headline
2 *(dans des séries)* fifth; **page/numéro c.** page/number five; **Henri C.** Henry the Fifth **3** *(pour exprimer les minutes)* **trois heures c.** five past three; **trois heures moins c.** five to three; **attends c. minutes** just give me a minute, *Fam* **hang on a sec**
▪ **NM INV** five; **le c. mars** [sɛ(k)mars] (on) the fifth of March, (on) March the fifth, *Am* (on) March fifth; *Cartes* **un c. de pique** a five of spades; **j'habite au c.** I live at number five

cinquantaine [sɛkɑ̃tɛn] **NF** (about) fifty; **une c. de personnes** about *or* some fifty people, fifty or so people; **approcher la c.** to be getting on for fifty; **passer la c.** to be in one's fifties

cinquante [sɛkɑ̃t] **ADJ INV** fifty; **billet de c. euros** fifty-euro note; **page c.** page fifty; **demeurer au numéro c.** to live at number fifty; **les années c.** the fifties
▪ **NM INV** fifty; **le numéro c.** the number fifty, 50; **c. pour cent ont refusé** fifty per cent refused

cinquantenaire [sɛkɑ̃tnɛr] **NM** fiftieth anniversary
▪ **ADJ** fifty-year-old, fifty years old

cinquantième [sɛkɑ̃tjɛm] **ADJ** fiftieth ▪ **N** fiftieth; **être le c. dans un classement** to be placed *or* come fiftieth in a classification *or* grading
▪ **NM** *(partie)* fiftieth (part)

cinquième [sɛkjɛm] **ADJ** fifth; **loger au c. étage** to live on the fifth *or* Am sixth floor; **être la c. roue de la charrette** *ou* **du carrosse** to feel out of it, *Am* to feel like a fifth wheel ▪ **N** fifth; **elle est arrivée la c.** she came (in) fifth, she came in in fifth place
▪ **NM** *(partie)* fifth (part)
▪ **NF 1** *Scol* **(classe de) c.** ≃ second form *or* year (of secondary school), *Am* ≃ seventh grade **2** *Aut* fifth gear

cinquièmement [sɛkjɛmmɑ̃] **ADV** fifthly, in (the) fifth place

cintrage [sɛtraʒ] **NM** *(action)* bending; *(résultat)* bend

cintre [sɛtr] **NM 1** *(pour les vêtements)* coathanger, clothes hanger; **suspendre sa veste à un c.** to put one's jacket on a (clothes) hanger **2** *(courbure)* curve **3** *Archit (d'un tunnel etc)* arch; *(d'une voûte)* soffit; **arc en plein c.** semicircular arch **4** *Théâtre* **les cintres** the flies; **c. de lumière** lighting batten

cintré [sɛtre] **ADJ 1** *(fenêtre etc)* arched; *(poutre etc)* bent, curved; *(veste etc)* fitted; **taille cintrée** nipped-in waist **2** *Fam* crazy

cintrer [sɛtre] **VT 1** *(tuyau, rail etc)* to bend, to curve **2** *(fenêtre)* to arch **3 c. une veste** to take in a jacket at the waist

CIO [seio] **NM** *(abrév* **Comité international olympique)** IOC

cipaye [sipaj] **NM** sepoy; *Hist* **la révolte des cipayes** the Indian Mutiny

cirage [siraʒ] **NM 1** *(des sols etc)* waxing, polishing; *(des chaussures)* polishing **2** *(substance)* (shoe) polish; **c. de couleur/incolore** coloured/neutral polish; **c. pour cuir/parquet** leather/floor polish; *Fam* **être dans le c.** to be a bit fuzzy, to be confused; *Aviat* to be flying blind

circadien [sirkadjɛ̃] **ADJ** *Biol* **rythme c.** circadian rhythm

circlip [sirklip] **NM** *Tech* circlip

circoncire [sirkɔ̃sir] **VT** *(prp* **circoncisant;** *pp* **conconcis;** *pr ind* **je circoncis;** *pr sub* **je circoncise;** *p hist* **je circoncis;** *fu* **je circoncirai)** to circumcise

circoncis [sirkɔ̃si] **ADJ** circumcised
▪ **NM** circumcised boy/man

circoncision [sirkɔ̃sizjɔ̃] **NF** circumcision

circonférence [sirkɔ̃ferɑ̃s] **NF 1** *Géom* circumference; *(d'un arbre)* circumference, girth; **avoir dix centimètres de c.** to have a circumference of ten centimetres, to be ten centimetres in circumference **2** *(d'une ville etc)* perimeter, boundaries

circonflexe [sirkɔ̃flɛks] **ADJ** *(accent)* circumflex

circonlocution [sirkɔ̃lokysjɔ̃] **NF** circumlocution; **parler par circonlocutions** to speak in a roundabout way, *Fam* to beat about the bush; **après de longues circonlocutions, il finit par nous déclarer que ...** after much beating about the bush, he eventually announced that ...

circonscription [sirkɔ̃skripsjɔ̃] **NF** *Admin etc* division, district, area; **c. électorale** *(au niveau municipal)* ward; *(au niveau national)* constituency, *Can* riding; **c. téléphonique** telephone code area

circonscrire [sirkɔ̃skrir] *(conj like* **écrire)** **VT** *Math* to circumscribe, to draw a line round; *(espace, bloc de maisons)* to surround, to encircle (**par** with, by); *(limiter)* to limit; **c. son sujet** to define the scope of one's subject; **c. un incendie** to bring a fire under control, to contain a fire
▪ **VPR se circonscrire** to be bounded, to be limited; **le débat se circonscrit autour d'une seule idée** the whole debate centres on *or* is centred around one idea

circonspect [sirkɔ̃spe(kt)] **ADJ** circumspect, cautious, wary; **il était c. dans ses propos** he spoke cautiously; **il était c. dans le choix de ses fréquentations** he was careful in his choice of company

circonspection [sirkɔ̃spɛksjɔ̃] **NF** circumspection, caution, wariness; **avec c.** cautiously, warily

circonstance [sirkɔ̃stɑ̃s] **NF 1** *(cas)* circumstance; **dans les circonstances actuelles, il faut se montrer prudent** given the circumstances *or* as things stand, we must tread carefully; **se retrouver dans des circonstances difficiles** to find oneself in difficult circumstances; **en pareille c.** under such circumstances, in such a case; **à la hauteur des circonstances** equal to the occasion; **eu égard aux** *ou* **étant donné les circonstances** all things considered, in *or* given the circumstances; **par un concours de circonstances** by a combination of circumstances; **profiter de la c.** to make the most of the opportunity; **vers de c.** occasional verse; **paroles de c.** words suited to the occasion, appropriate *or* suitable words; **ce ne serait pas de c.** it would not be appropriate
2 *Jur* **circonstances et dépendances** appurtenances; **circonstances atténuantes** extenuating circumstances; **circonstances aggravantes** aggravating circumstances

circonstancié [sirkɔ̃stɑ̃sje] **ADJ** *(rapport)* detailed

circonstanciel, -ielle [sirkɔ̃stɑ̃sjɛl] **ADJ 1** *Litt* circumstantial; **des mesures rigoureusement circonstancielles** measures dictated by exceptional circumstances; **déclaration/mesure circonstancielle** declaration/measure dictated by the circumstances **2** *Gram* **complément c.** *(de temps/de lieu)* adverbial complement of time/place)

circonvenir [sirkɔ̃vnir] **VT** *(conj like* **venir)** *(personne)* to take in

circonvolution [sirkɔ̃volysjɔ̃] **NF** *Anat, Archit* convolution; *Archit (de volutes etc)* circumvolution

circuit [sirkɥi] **NM 1** *Sport* round, lap; *(d'une course de motos etc)* circuit; **c. automobile** racing circuit; **c. de petites voitures** racing track
2 *(itinéraire)* **c. (touristique)** (organized) trip, tour; **c. en car** coach tour; **faire le c. des châteaux de la Loire** to tour the Loire châteaux
3 *(chemin)* way; **refaire tout le c. à pied** to go all the way back on foot; **c. touristique** scenic *or* tourist route; **il faut faire un long c. pour passer d'un côté de l'île à l'autre** you have to make a long detour to get from one side of the island to the other
4 *Élec* circuit; **c. ouvert/fermé** open/closed circuit; **télévision c. fermé** closed circuit television; **c. basse tension** low-tension circuit; **c. haute tension** high-tension circuit; **c. d'induction** inductive circuit; **c. intégré** integrated circuit; **c. de retour à la masse** earth return circuit; **mettre en c.** to connect, to switch on; **couper le c.** to switch off; **rétablir le c.** to switch on (again); **mettre une lampe hors c.** to disconnect a lamp; *Fig* **ils ont tendance à vivre en c. fermé** they tend to lead their own separate existence *or* to live in a closed world; *Fig* **ça fait longtemps que je ne suis plus dans le c.** I've been out of it for ages, I'm hopelessly out of touch; *Fig* **il est complètement hors c.** he's completely out of touch
5 *Tech, Aut* **c. d'allumage** ignition system; **c. d'allumage par bobine** coil-ignition system; **c. de carburant étanche** sealed fuel system; **c. de charge** *(de batterie)* charging system; **c. de démarrage** starting circuit; **c. d'eau** water circuit; **c. de freinage** braking system; **c. de graissage** lubrication circuit; **c. hydraulique** hydraulic circuit; **c. d'injection d'essence** petrol injection system; **c. de lubrification** lubrication system; **c. oléopneumatique** air/hydraulic system; **c. de préchauffage** pre-heating circuit; **c. de refroidissement** cooling system
6 *Ordinat* **c. de commande** command circuit; **c. ET** AND circuit; **c. de liaison** link circuit; **c. logique** logic circuit; **circuits de rafraîchissement** *ou* **de régénération** refresh circuitry
7 *Écon* **c. de commercialisation** marketing network, trade *or* marketing channel; **c. de distribution** distribution channels *or* network; **circuits de vente** commercial channels
▸▸ **c. aventure** adventure holiday; *Radio* **de cryptage** scrambling circuit; *Électron* **c. imprimé** printed circuit

circulaire [sirkylɛr] **ADJ** circular; **billet c.** excursion ticket; **scie c.** circular saw; *Tech* **mouvement c.** rotary motion
▪ **NF** circular

circulairement [sirkylɛrmɑ̃] **ADV** in a circle

circulant [sirkylɑ̃] **ADJ** *Fin (billets, devises)* in circulation; *(capitaux)* circulating

circulation [sirkylasjɔ̃] **NF 1** *(d'autos, d'avions)* traffic; **c. routière** road traffic; **c. aérienne** air traffic; **c. des trains** running of trains; **c. à sens unique/à deux sens** one-/two-way traffic; **c. interdite** no thoroughfare; **les embarras de la c.** traffic congestion; **route à grande c.** trunk road; **accident de la c.** road accident; **la c. est très difficile** the traffic is very heavy; **il y a beaucoup de c. sur les routes** there's a lot of traffic on the roads; *Fig* **disparaître de la c.** to drop out of circulation

2 *(de l'air, du sang, de l'information, des marchandises etc)* circulation; *Méd* **problèmes de c.** circulation *or* circulatory problems; **mettre un livre en c.** to put a book into circulation; **mise en c. de qch** circulation of sth; **retirer un produit de la c.** to take a product off the market

3 *Fin (des billets etc)* circulation; **c. des capitaux/des devises** circulation of capital/currency; **c. monétaire** circulation of money

4 *Pol, Écon* **libre c. des travailleurs/des citoyens** free movement of workers/of citizens

> Il faut noter que le mot anglais **circulation** ne s'emploie jamais pour faire référence à la circulation routière.

circulatoire [siʀkylatwaʀ] **ADJ** *Anat* circulatory

circuler [siʀkyle] **VI 1** *(du sang, de l'air etc)* to circulate, to flow; *(d'une rumeur)* to circulate; **faire c. l'air** to circulate the air; *Fin* **les capitaux qui circulent** capital in circulation, circulating capital; *Fin* **faire c. des effets** to keep bills afloat; **faire c. la bouteille** to pass *or* hand the bottle round; **faire c. une nouvelle** to spread a piece of news; **faire c. une pétition** to circulate a petition

2 *(en voiture)* to travel, to move about; **circulez, il n'y a rien à voir!** move along now, there's nothing to see!; **les autobus circulent jour et nuit** the buses run day and night; **on a du mal à c. en ville** it's not easy to drive in town; **on circule très mal à ce moment de la journée** it's very difficult to get anywhere at this time of day

circumnavigation [siʀkɔmnavigasjɔ̃] **NF** circumnavigation

cire [siʀ] **NF** wax; *(encaustique)* (wax) polish; **bouchon de c.** *(dans l'oreille)* plug of earwax; **c. d'abeille** beeswax; **c. à cacheter** sealing wax; **personnage en c.** waxwork; **c. anti-corrosion** anti-corrosion wax

ciré [siʀe] **ADJ** polished; **parquet c.** polished *or* waxed floor; **chaussures bien cirées** well-polished shoes; **toile cirée** oilcloth
NM oilskin

cirer [siʀe] **VT** *(sols, meubles etc)* to polish, to wax; *(corde etc)* to wax; **c. ses chaussures** to polish one's shoes; *Fam* **c. les bottes à qn** to lick sb's boots; *Arg* **il n'en a rien à c. (de tes histoires)** he doesn't give a damn (about your stories)

cireur, -euse [siʀœʀ, -øz] **N 1** *(de chaussures)* shoeblack, *Am* shoeshine boy; *Fam* **un c. de pompes** a bootlicker **2** *(de sols)* (floor) polisher
NF cireuse *(machine)* (electric) (floor) polisher

cireux, -euse [siʀø, -øz] **ADJ** waxy

cirque [siʀk] **NM 1** circus; **c. forain** *ou* ambulant travelling circus; **aller au c.** to go to the circus; **gens du c.** circus people; **le c. Zavatta** Zavatta's circus **2** *Fam (chambard)* **quel c., ici!** it's like a zoo in here!; **quel c. pour obtenir ces renseignements!** what a performance *or* carry-on just to get this information!; **faire le c.** to rampage around; **faire tout un c.** to make a scene, to kick up a fuss; **arrête de faire ton c.!** stop your silly nonsense! **3** *Géol* cirque, corrie

cirrhose [siʀoz] **NF** *Méd* cirrhosis; **c. du foie** cirrhosis of the liver; **avoir une c. du foie** to have cirrhosis (of the liver)

cirrocumulus [siʀokymylys] **NM INV** *Météo* cirrocumulus

cirrostratus [siʀostratys] **NM INV** *Météo* cirrostratus

cirrus [siʀys] **NM INV** *Météo* cirrus, *Fam* mare's tail

cisaille [sizaj] **NF 1** *(rognures en métal)* parings, cuttings **2** *(massicot)* guillotine **3** **cisailles** shears; *(pour câble)* wirecutters; **c. à haies** hedge clipper(s); **c. à bordures** edging shears VOIR GRAMMAIRE A10

cisaillement [sizajmɑ̃] **NM 1** *(du métal)* cutting, shearing; *(des branches)* pruning **2** *Tech (usure)* shearing, shear

cisailler [sizaje] **VT 1** *(branches)* to prune **2** *(métal)* to cut, to shear **3** *(joue, main etc)* to slash
VPR se cisailler *(d'un métal)* to shear (off)

cisalpin [sizalpɛ̃] **ADJ** *Antiq* on the Roman side of the Alps, Cisalpine; *Hist* **République cisalpine** Cisalpine Republic

ciseau, -eaux [sizo] **NM 1** **(paire de) ciseaux** (pair of) scissors; *(de jardin)* shears, clippers; **ciseaux à bouts ronds** blunt- *or* round-ended scissors; **ciseaux à ongles** nail scissors; **ciseaux de couturière** dressmaking scissors; *Couture* **ciseaux à denteler** pinking shears; **coup de ciseaux** snip (of the scissors); **donner des coups de ciseaux dans qch** to snip away at sth with a pair of scissors; *Fig* **donner des coups de ciseaux dans un texte** to cut down *or* prune a text VOIR GRAMMAIRE A10 **2** *Sport* **c., saut en ciseaux** scissors (jump); *Gym* **faire des ciseaux** to do the scissors **3** *Tech* chisel

ciselage [sizlaʒ] **NM** = **cisellement**

ciseler [sizle] **VT** (**je cisèle; je cisèlerai**) *(or, argent)* to chase, to engrave; *(marbre)* to chisel; *Fig (poème etc)* to polish up, to work on; **c. un bijou** to engrave a design on a piece of jewellery; **visage délicatement ciselé** finely chiselled features

ciseleur [sizlœʀ] **NM** engraver

ciselement [sizɛlmɑ̃] **NM** *(de l'or, de l'argent)* chasing, engraving

ciselure [sizlyʀ] **NF** *(en or, en argent)* chasing, engraving; *(sur le bois)* chiselling, carving; *(sur un bijou, une pièce d'orfèvrerie)* (engraved) design

Cisjordanie [sisʒɔʀdani] **NF** **la C.** the West Bank

cisjordanien, -ienne [sisʒɔʀdanjɛ̃, -jɛn] **ADJ** from the West Bank
N C. = native or inhabitant of the West Bank

cistercien, -ienne [sistɛʀsjɛ̃, -jɛn] *Rel* **ADJ** *(moine, architecture)* Cistercian
NM Cistercian

citadelle [sitadɛl] **NF** citadel, stronghold; *Fig* **une c. du protestantisme** a Protestant stronghold, a stronghold of Protestantism

citadin, -ine [sitadɛ̃, -in] **N** town-dweller, city-dweller
ADJ (belonging to a) town *or* city
NF *Aut* **citadine** supermini

citation [sitasjɔ̃] **NF 1** *(extrait)* quotation; **la référence de la c.** the reference for the quotation, the quotation reference; **fin de c.** end of quotation; *(dans une dictée)* close quotation marks **2** *Jur* (writ of) summons; **c. des témoins** subpoena of witnesses; **notifier une c. à** *(accusé)* to serve a summons on; *(témoin)* to subpoena
▸▸ *Mil* **c. (à l'ordre du jour)** ≃ mention in dispatches; *Jur* **c. à comparaître** *(accusé)* summons; *(témoin)* subpoena

cité [site] **NF 1** *(ville)* city, (large) town; **droit de c.** freedom of the city; *Fig* **ce genre d'original n'a pas droit de c. dans notre entreprise** there is no room for eccentrics like him in my company, our company doesn't take kindly to eccentrics like him; *Fig* **ga-**gner droit de c.** to be accepted **2** *(groupe d'immeubles)* (housing) estate
▸▸ **c.-dortoir** dormitory town; **c.-ghetto** ghetto housing estate; **c.-jardin** garden city; **c. ouvrière** (company-built) housing estate; **c. de transit** temporary settlement; **c. universitaire** = students' hall(s) of residence

Cîteaux [sito] **NM** *Rel* **l'ordre de C.** the Cistercian Order

citer [site] **VT 1** *(rapporter)* to quote, to cite; **c. un auteur** to cite *or* quote (from) an author; **c. qn en exemple** to quote sb as an example, to hold sb up as an example; **c. les paroles de qn** to quote sb's words; **il a dit, et je cite, ...** he said, and I quote, ... **2** *(énumérer)* to name, to list **3** *Jur (qn en justice)* to summon; *(témoin)* to subpoena **4** *Mil* **c. qn (à l'ordre du jour)** ≃ to mention sb in dispatches

citerne [sitɛʀn] **NF** tank, cistern; **c. à mazout** oil tank

cithare [sitaʀ] **NF** *Mus* **1** *(instrument moderne)* zither **2** *Antiq* cithara

citizen band [sitizənbɑ̃d] **NF** Citizens' Band, CB

citoyen, -enne [sitwajɛ̃, -ɛn] **N** citizen; **droits du c.** civic rights; **accomplir son devoir de c.** *(voter)* to do one's civic duty, to vote; **c. d'honneur** = freeman of a city; **elle se déclare citoyenne du monde** she claims that she's a citizen of the world; *Fam* **c'est un drôle de c.!** he's a queer customer!
ADJ *(relatif à la citoyenneté)* civic; **il s'est produit une sorte de rassemblement c. contre l'extrême-droite** there was a sort of citizens' movement against the far right; **il faut encourager l'engagement c. au niveau local pour renforcer le tissu social** civic engagement on a local level should be encouraged as a way of strengthening the fabric of society; **on attend de nos élus un véritable projet c., pas une simple gestion de l'économie** we expect those we elected to come up with a manifesto which truly benefits society, not one which simply manages the economy; **cette société rêve de troquer sa réputation de pollueuse contre celle d'entreprise citoyenne** this company wants to banish its reputation as a polluter and instead to be known for being socially responsible

citoyenneté [sitwajɛnte] **NF** citizenship; **la c. française** French citizenship; **c. d'honneur d'une ville** = freedom of a city

citrate [sitrat] **NM** *Chimie* citrate

citrique [sitrik] **ADJ** *Chimie (acide)* citric

citron [sitrɔ̃] **NM 1** *(fruit)* lemon; **jus de c.** lemon juice; **c. pressé** freshly squeezed lemon juice; **c. givré** = lemon sorbet served inside the skin of a whole lemon; **essence de c.** lemon oil; **écorce de c.** lemon peel; **c. vert** lime **2** *Fam (tête)* nut; **se presser** *ou* **se creuser le c.** to rack *or Am* to cudgel one's brains
ADJ INV lemon-yellow, lemon; **jaune c.** lemon-yellow

citronnade [sitrɔnad] **NF** still lemonade, lemon squash

citronné [sitrɔne] **ADJ** *(par l'odeur)* lemon-scented; *(par le goût)* lemon-flavoured

citronnelle [sitrɔnɛl] **NF 1** *(plante)* citronella **2** *(liqueur)* lemon liqueur

citronnier [sitrɔnje] **NM** *(arbre)* lemon tree

citrouille [sitruj] **NF 1** *(plante)* pumpkin; **tarte à la c.** pumpkin pie; *Fam* **j'ai la tête comme une c.** my head is fit to burst **2** *Arg (tête)* nut

cive [siv] **NF** *Bot, Culin* chives

civelle [sivɛl] **NF** elver

civet [sivɛ] **NM** *Culin (de gibier etc)* stew; **c. de lièvre** jugged hare; **un c. de lapin** (a) rabbit stew

civette¹ [sivɛt] **NF 1** *Zool* civet (cat) **2** *(parfum)* civet (perfume)

civette² NF *Bot, Culin* chives

civière [sivjɛr] NF *(brancard)* stretcher

civil [sivil] ADJ **1** *(de l'État, du citoyen) (droits etc)* civil; **année civile** calendar year; **guerre civile** civil war; *Jur* **droit c.** civil law; *Jur* **se porter partie civile** = to sue for damages someone being tried in a criminal court; **tribunal c.** civil court **2** *(non ecclésiastique)* lay, secular; *(non militaire)* civilian; **mariage c.** civil marriage; **enterrement c.** non-religious burial; **dans la vie civile** in private or civilian life **3** *Arch, Litt (courtois)* polite, courteous ▪ NM **1** *(personne)* **un c.** *(non ecclésiastique)* a layman; *(non militaire)* a civilian **2 dans le c.** in private or civilian life; **en c.** *(police)* in plain clothes; *Mil* in civilian clothes, in mufti, *Fam* in civvies **3** *Jur* **poursuivre qn au c.** to sue sb in the civil courts, to bring a civil action against sb

> Attention: ne pas confondre **civil** et **civilian** lorsque l'on traduit le terme français **civil**. Le terme **civilian** signifie uniquement **non militaire**.

civilement [sivilmɑ̃] ADV **1** *Jur* **se marier c.** to be married at a registry office; **enterré c.** buried without religious ceremony; *Jur* **poursuivre qn c.** to bring a civil action against sb; **c. responsable** liable for damages **2** *Arch, Litt (courtoisement)* politely, courteously, civilly

civilisable [sivilizabl] ADJ civilizable

civilisateur, -trice [sivilizatœr, -tris] ADJ civilizing ▪ N civilizer

civilisation [sivilizasjɔ̃] NF civilization; **la c. pré-colombienne** the pre-Columbian civilization; **les bienfaits de la c.** the benefits of civilization

civilisé [sivilize] ADJ civilized

civiliser [sivilize] VT to civilize; *Fam* **c. qn** to make sb less uncouth or more refined ▪ VPR **se civiliser** to become civilized; *Fam* **il commence à se c.** he's starting to become more civilized or refined

civilité [sivilite] NF **1** **civilités** courtesies, respects; **présenter ses civilités à qn** to pay one's respects to sb **2** *Litt, Vieilli (politesse)* civility, politeness, courtesy

civique [sivik] ADJ *(devoirs etc)* civic; *(droits)* civil; **avoir/développer le sens c.** to have/ foster a sense of civic responsibility; *Scol Anciennement* **instruction c.** civics; *surtout Can* **bibliothèque c.** municipal or public library

civisme [sivism] NM good citizenship, public-spiritedness

clabaudage [klabodaʒ] NM *Litt (médisance)* (spiteful) gossip, backbiting

clabauder [klabode] VI *Litt* **1** *(d'un chien de chasse)* to bark (a lot) **2** *Fig* **c. sur** ou **contre qn** to say nasty things about sb

clabauderie [klabodri] NF = **clabaudage**

clabaudeur, -euse [klabodœr, -øz] ADJ **1** *(chien)* barking **2** *Fig* gossiping, backbiting ▪ N *Fig* gossip, scandalmonger

clac [klak] INT click!; *(d'un fouet)* crack! *(d'un objet qui se casse)* snap!

clafoutis [klafuti] NM *Culin* **c. aux pommes/ limousin** apples/(black) cherries baked in batter

claie [klɛ] NF **1** *(clôture)* fence **2 c. à fruits** (wicker) fruit tray **3** *(crible)* screen, riddle

CLAIR [klɛr]

ADJ clear **1, 4** ▪ bright **2** ▪ light **2, 3, 5** ▪ obvious **4** ▪ thin **5**	
ADV clearly	
NM light **1**	

ADJ **1** *(limpide, transparent) (eau etc)* clear; **teint c.** clear complexion; **ciel c.** clear or cloudless sky; **par temps c.** in clear weather, on a clear day; **voix claire** clear voice; *Mus* **caisse claire** side or snare drum

2 *(pièce etc)* bright, light; **il fait c.** *(jour)* it's (day)light; *(lumière)* there's plenty of light; **dans cette pièce, il fait plus c.** this room is brighter, there's more light in this room; **il ne fait pas très c. ici** there isn't much light here

3 *(couleur)* light, pale; **robe bleu c.** pale blue dress

4 *(sens etc)* clear, obvious, plain; **explication claire** clear or lucid explanation; **ce n'est pas très c., précisez** it's not very clear, be more precise; **il a été très c. là-dessus** he was very clear about it; **je vais être très c.** I'm going to make myself very clear; **il est c. qu'elle a tort** she is obviously or clearly wrong; **voilà qui est c.!** that's clear (enough)!; **c. comme le jour** ou **comme de l'eau de roche** crystal clear, as clear as daylight or crystal; **sa conduite n'est pas claire** his behaviour is suspicious or *Fam* fishy; **avoir l'esprit c.** ou **les idées claires** to be clear in one's mind or in one's ideas; **je n'avais pas les idées très claires ce jour-là** I wasn't thinking very clearly that day; **c'est c. et net** there are no two ways about it; **ils n'ont aucune intention de prolonger notre contrat, c'est c. et net** it's quite obvious that they have absolutely no intention of extending our contract; **je veux une réponse claire et nette** I want a definite answer

5 *(soupe)* thin; *(tissu)* light, thin

ADV plainly, clearly; **voir c.** to see clearly; **il ne voit plus très c.** he can't see too clearly or well; **parler c.** to speak clearly; *Fig* **je commence à (y) voir c.** I'm beginning to see or understand; **son explication est très confuse, je n'y vois pas très c.** his explanation is very confused, I don't quite follow it

NM **1** *(lumière)* light; **c. de lune** moonlight; **au c. de (la) lune** in the moonlight; **les clairs d'une peinture** the (high)lights in a painting

2 en c. in plain language; **message en c.** message in clear; *TV* **émission en c.** *(non crypté)* non-crypted broadcast

3 tirer du vin au c. to decant wine; **sabre au c.** with drawn sword; *Fig* **tirer une affaire au c.** to clear a matter up; **mettre ses idées au c.** to get one's ideas straight; **mettre qch au c. avec qn** to sort sth out with sb, to get sth straight with sb

4 il passe le plus c. de son temps à rêvasser he spends most or the better part of his time daydreaming

clairance [klɛrɑ̃s] NF *Méd (rénale)* clearance

claire [klɛr] NF oyster bed; **fines de c.** = particularly fine variety of fattened oysters, with a green tinge caused by algae

clairement [klɛrmɑ̃] ADV clearly, plainly; **on le voit c. sur le tableau** it's clearly visible on the board; **expliquer c. qch à qn** to explain sth clearly to sb; **je te le dis c.** I'm telling you quite plainly

clairet, -ette [klɛrɛ, -ɛt] ADJ **vin c.** light-red wine; **voix clairette** thin or high-pitched or reedy voice ▪ NM light-red wine ▪ NF **clairette** light sparkling wine

claire-voie, pl **claires-voies** NF **1** *(treillage)* openwork, lattice(work); **porte à c.** (wicket) gate; **clôture à c.** fence, paling; **cloison à c.** grating; **caisse à c.** crate **2** *Archit* clerestory; *Naut* skylight, deadlight

clairière [klɛrjɛr] NF **1** *(dans forêt)* clearing, glade **2** *Tex* thin place

clair-obscur, pl **clairs-obscurs** NM **1** *Beaux-Arts* chiaroscuro, light and shade **2** *(lumière)* twilight

clairon [klɛrɔ̃] NM **1** *(trompette)* bugle; **jouer du c.** to play the bugle; **sonner le c.** to sound the bugle **2** *(joueur)* bugler

claironnant [klɛrɔnɑ̃] ADJ *(son)* loud, brassy; *(voix)* piercing, loud

claironner [klɛrɔne] VI to sound the bugle; *Fig (crier)* to shout loudly ▪ VT **c. une nouvelle** to broadcast or proclaim a piece of news; **il claironna que ...** he proclaimed that ...

clairsemé [klɛrsəme] ADJ *(population etc)* scattered, sparse; *(cheveux)* thin; *(maïs etc)* thinly sown; *(gazon)* sparse; *(arbres)* scattered

clairvoyance [klɛrvwajɑ̃s] NF perceptiveness, clearsightedness; *(pouvoir paranormal)* clairvoyance; **il l'avait analysé avec c.** he had analysed it perceptively

clairvoyant [klɛrvwajɑ̃] ADJ perceptive, clear-sighted; *(paranormal)* clairvoyant; **esprit c.** perceptive mind ▪ NM clairvoyant

clam [klam] NM *(mollusque)* clam

clamecer [klamse] VI *Arg (mourir)* to snuff it, to kick the bucket

clamer [klame] VT to shout out, to proclaim; **c. son innocence** to proclaim or protest one's innocence; **c. son mécontentement** to proclaim one's displeasure

clameur [klamœr] NF clamour; *(du vent, de la tempête)* howling, roaring; **une c. de joie** a shout of joy; **on entendit une c. épouvantable lorsque le bateau coula** there were horrendous screams when the boat went down; **c. publique** hue and cry

clamser [klamse] VI *Arg (mourir)* to kick the bucket, to snuff it

clan [klɑ̃] NM **1** *(tribu)* clan; **c. irlandais/écossais** Irish/Scottish clan; **chef de c.** clan chief **2** *(groupe)* clan, clique

clandestin, -ine [klɑ̃dɛstɛ̃, -in] ADJ *(réunion, atelier)* clandestine, secret; *(travailleur, pari)* illegal; **armée clandestine** underground forces; **mouvement c.** underground movement; **passager c.** stowaway ▪ N *(voyageur)* stowaway; *(immigré)* illegal immigrant; *(travailleur)* illegal worker

clandestinement [klɑ̃dɛstinmɑ̃] ADV *(se réunir)* clandestinely, secretly; *(travailler, transporter, entrer dans un pays)* illegally; **voyager c.** to stow away

clandestinité [klɑ̃dɛstinite] NF clandestineness; **dans la c.** in secret; **entrer dans/sortir de la c.** to go into/come out of hiding; **passer dans la c.** to go underground

clanique [klanik] ADJ clan

clanisme [klanism] NM clannishness

clap [klap] NM *Cin* clapperboard; **c. de fin** tail slate

clapet [klapɛ] NM **1** *Tech* valve; *(de moteur)* poppet valve, mushroom valve; **c. d'admission/d'échappement** inlet/exhaust valve; **c. de dérivation** by-pass valve; **c. de limitation de pression** pressure limiting valve **2** *Élec* rectifier **3** *Arg (bouche)* trap, *Br* gob; **ferme ton c.!** shut your trap!; **il a un de ces clapets!** he never stops (talking)!

clapier [klapje] NM **1** *(terriers)* rabbit warren **2** *(case)* **c. à lapins** rabbit hutch; **(lapin de) c.** tame rabbit; *Fig Fam* **vivre dans un c. à lapins** to live in a rabbit hutch **3** *Géol (dans les Alpes)* scree

clapir [klapir] VI *(d'un lapin)* to squeal ▪ VPR **se clapir** *(d'un lapin)* to hide, to cower

clapotage [klapotaʒ] NM, **clapotement** [klapotmɑ̃] NM *(des vagues)* lapping

clapoter [klapote] VI *(des vagues)* to lap; **mer qui clapote** choppy sea

clapotis [klapoti] NM *(des vagues)* lap(ping)

clappement [klapmɑ̃] NM *(de la langue)* click

clapper [klape] VI **c. de la langue** to click one's tongue

claquage [klakaʒ] NM **1** *(d'un muscle)* strain, pulling; **se faire un c.** to pull *or* strain a muscle **2** *Élec* (electric) breakdown; **c. thermique** thermal breakdown

claquant [klakɑ̃] ADJ *Arg (fatigant)* killing, knackering

claque¹ [klak] NF **1** *(gifle)* slap, smack; **donner** *ou* **mettre** *ou* **très** *Fam* **foutre une c. à qn** to give sb a slap *or* a smack; **recevoir** *ou* **prendre une c.** to get a slap *or* a smack; *Fig* **se prendre une c.** to get a slap in the face; *Fig* **les centristes se sont pris une c. aux dernières élections** the last elections were a slap in the face for the centre party; **il mérite une bonne paire de claques** he deserves a good slap; *Fam* **c'est vraiment une tête à claques!** he's got a face you just want to slap! **2** *Arg* **il (en) a sa c.** *(il est fatigué)* he's knackered *or* shattered; *(il en a assez)* he's fed up with it, he's had enough of it **3** *Théâtre* claque **4** *Can* **claques** *(chaussures)* galoshes, *Am* rubbers

claque² ADJ, NM **(chapeau) c.** opera hat, crush hat

NM *Arg (maison close)* whorehouse, *Br* knocking shop; *(tripot)* gambling den

claqué [klake] ADJ *Fam* knackered, shattered

claquement [klakmɑ̃] NM *(de porte)* slam(ming), bang(ing); *(de dents)* chattering; *(d'un fouet)* crack(ing); *(d'un drapeau)* flap(ping); *(des doigts)* snap(ping); *(des talons, de la langue)* click(ing); *(des sabots)* clatter(ing); *(dans un moteur)* slapping of pistons; **entendre un c. de porte** to hear a door bang, to hear the sound of a door banging; **des claquements de fouets** the cracking of whips

claquemurer [klakmyre] VT **c. qn** to shut sb up

VPR **se claquemurer** to shut oneself up; **se c. dans sa chambre** to shut oneself up in one's room, to stay cooped up in one's room

claquer [klake] VI **1** *(d'une porte)* to slam, to bang; *(d'un drapeau)* to flap; *(des talons)* to click; *(des sabots)* to clatter; *(d'un piston)* to slap; **c. des mains** to clap, to applaud; **elle claque des dents** her teeth are chattering; **c. des doigts** to snap one's fingers; **faire c. sa langue** to click one's tongue; **faire c. la porte en sortant** to slam the door on the way out; *Fam* **c. du bec** to be hungry *or* starving

2 *Arg (d'une personne)* to kick the bucket, to snuff it; *(d'un appareil)* to conk out; *(d'une ampoule électrique)* to go, to blow; *Fam* **l'affaire lui a claqué dans les doigts** *ou* **mains** the deal fell through; **il nous a claqué dans les mains avant que l'ambulance arrive** he died on us before the ambulance arrived

VT **1** *(porte)* to slam, to bang; *(ses doigts)* to snap; *(ses talons)* to click; **c. la langue** to click one's tongue

2 *(gifler)* *(enfant etc)* to slap, to smack

3 *Fam (fatiguer)* *(personne)* to tire *or* wear out

4 *Fam (dépenser)* *(argent)* to squander, to blow; **il claque un fric monstre** he spends money like water; **il claque un fric monstre chez le coiffeur** he spends a fortune at the hairdresser's

VPR **se claquer 1** *Fam (se fatiguer)* to tire *or* wear oneself out **2 se c. un muscle/un ligament** to pull a muscle/tear a ligament

claquette [klaket] NF **1** *Cin* clapperboard **2** *(type de danse)* **(danse à) claquettes** tap dancing, tap dance; **faire des claquettes** to do tap (dancing); **danseur de claquettes**

tap dancer **3 claquettes** *(tongs)* flip-flops, *Am* thongs

claquoir [klakwar] NM clapper; *Cin* clapperboard

clarification [klarifikasjɔ̃] NF *(d'un liquide)* clarifying; *Fig (d'informations)* clarification

clarifier [klarifje] VT to clarify; **c. la situation** to clarify the situation, to clear the matter up

VPR **se clarifier** to (become) clear; **la situation se clarifie** the situation is becoming clear

clarine [klarin] NF cowbell

clarinette [klarinɛt] NF clarinet

clarinettiste [klarinɛtist] N clarinettist

clarisse [klaris] NF *Rel* **(sœur) c.** nun of the order of St Clare

clarté [klarte] NF **1** *(lumière etc)* light, brightness; **une douce/faible c.** a soft/dim light; **à la c. de la lune** by the light of the moon, by moonlight; **la c. de l'aurore** *ou* **de l'aube** the early morning light **2** *(transparence)* clearness, clarity; *(d'un verre etc)* transparency; *(du style)* clarity, lucidity; **la c. de son teint** the clearness of his complexion; **la c. de l'expression** clarity of expression; **parler avec c.** to speak clearly; **c. d'esprit** clear-headedness; **manquer de c.** *(d'une personne)* not to make oneself clear; *(d'un texte, un devoir, un argument)* to be unclear; *Litt* **avoir des clartés sur un sujet** to have some knowledge of a subject

clash [klaʃ] NM *Fam* clash, conflict; **je voudrais éviter tout c. avec elle** I want to avoid clashing with her

classable [klasabl] ADJ classifiable; **une personne difficilement c.** a person who is difficult to classify

CLASSE [klas] NF **1** *(catégorie)* class, division, category; *Admin etc* rank, grade; **c. d'âge** age group; *Aviat etc* **c. touriste/club** tourist/club class; **c. affaires** business class, club class, executive class; **c. économique** economy class; **voyager en c. affaires/club** to travel business/club class; *Rail* **billet de première/deuxième** *ou* **seconde c.** first-/second-class ticket; **différence de c. sociale** difference in *or* of social class; **les hautes classes (de la société)** the upper classes; **la c. moyenne/ouvrière** the middle/working class(es); **c. dirigeante/dominante** ruling/dominant class; **société sans c.** classless society; **conscience de c.** class consciousness

2 *(qualité)* class; **elle n'est pas de la même c. que les autres** she's not in the same class as the others; **un biologiste/sportif de c. internationale** a biologist/sportsman of international rank, a world-class biologist/sportsman; **produits de première c.** top-quality *or* first-class goods; **avoir de la c.** to have class *or* style; **cette robe a beaucoup de c.** that's a very classy *or* stylish dress, that dress has got a lot of class *or* style; **c'est la c.!** what class!

3 *Scol (niveau)* class, form, *Am* grade; *(ensemble des élèves)* class; **c'est un cadeau offert par toute la c.** it's a present from the whole class; **il y a plusieurs classes de sixième au collège** there are several first-year classes at high school; **grandes classes, classes supérieures** upper forms, senior school; **c. de sixième/première/terminale** ≃ first year/lower sixth/upper sixth; **les petites classes** the junior school, the juniors; **il est dans quelle c.?** which *or* what class is he in? VOIR GRAMMAIRE A11

4 *(leçon)* class, lesson; **c. de français** French class; **aller en c.** to go to school; **être en c.** to be in *or* at school; **faire la c.** to teach; **livre de c.** schoolbook

5 (salle de) c. classroom, schoolroom; **en sortant de c.** on coming out of school

6 *Mil (de conscrits)* annual contingent; **la c. 1965** the 1965 class, the 1965 levy; **faire ses classes** to undergo basic training; *Fig* to learn the ropes

7 *Mil (rang)* **(soldat de) deuxième c.** private; *Mil, Aviat* aircraftman, *Am* airman (basic); **(soldat de) première c.** lance-corporal, *Am* private first class; *Mil, Aviat* leading *or* senior aircraftman, *Am* airman first class

8 *Compta* group of accounts

ADJ INV *Fam* classy, stylish; **il s'habille très c.** he is a classy *or* stylish dresser

▸▸ *Scol* **c. de mer** = school study trip to the seaside; **c. de nature** = nature study trip; **c. de neige** = school study and skiing trip to the mountains; **partir en c. de neige** = to go skiing with the school; **c. préparatoire** = preparatory class for the entrance examinations for the grandes écoles; **c. unique** = class where pupils of different levels are taught together by one teacher; **c. verte** = school study trip to the countryside; **partir en c. verte** = to spend time in the countryside with the school

classé [klase] ADJ **1** *Sport* ranked, graded; *Tennis* seeded **2** *(information)* classified; **cette information est classée** that information is classified **3** *(monument etc)* listed

classement [klasmɑ̃] NM **1** *(hiérarchie)* *(dans une classe, une course etc)* position, place; *(des plantes etc)* classification; **c. alphabétique/chronologique** alphabetical/chronological order; *Scol* **c. trimestriel** end of term results; *Scol* **ce trimestre, je suis troisième au c.** I'm third in the class this term; **donner le c.** *(d'un concours)* to give the results; **avoir un bon/mauvais c.** to be well/badly placed; **c. hôtelier** hotel classification; **c. par étoiles** *(d'un hôtel etc)* star rating **2** *(rangement)* *(de documents)* filing; *(d'articles)* sorting out, arranging; **faire du c.** to do some filing; **c. géographique** filing by geographical area; **c. horizontal** horizontal filing; **c. par ordre alphabétique** alphabetical filing

classer [klase] VT **1** *(classifier)* to classify, to class; **les livres sont classés par ordre alphabétique d'auteurs** the books are arranged *or* classified in alphabetical order of author; **monument classé** listed monument; **classés par pays** classified according to country; **ce chanteur, que l'on classe parmi les meilleurs ténors …** this singer, who is ranked among the best tenors …; *Courses de chevaux* **non classés** also ran; *Fam* **je n'ai pas eu de mal à le c.** it didn't take me long to size him up *or* to work out what sort of a person he was **2** *(documents)* to file; *(articles)* to sort out, to arrange; **c. une affaire** to consider a matter closed; **c'est une affaire classée** the matter's closed

VPR se classer to be classified, to rank; **ces faits se classent dans une autre catégorie** these facts fall into another category; **elle se classe parmi les meilleurs de son année** she's among the best in her year; *Sport etc* **se c. troisième** to be placed third, to come in third; *Tennis etc* **il n'a pas réussi à se c.** he failed to get into the rankings

classeur [klasœr] NM *(meuble)* filing cabinet; *(d'écolier etc)* (looseleaf) binder, folder; *Ordinat* filer; **c. à anneaux** ring binder; **c. distributeur** index card box; **c. à levier** lever-arch file

classicisme [klasisism] NM classicism

classieux, -ieuse [klasjø, -jøz] ADJ *Fam* classy

classificateur, -trice [klasifikatœr, -tris] N classifier
   ADJ classifying

classification [klasifikasjɔ̃] NF classification; **c. socioéconomique** socio-economic grouping

classifier [klasifje] VT *(impf, pr sub n.* **classifiions, v. classifiiez)** to classify

classique [klasik] ADJ **1** *Scol* academic, for school use; **faire des études classiques** to study classics; **langues classiques** classical languages; **auteurs classiques** classical authors **2** *(période, musique etc)* classical; *(beauté etc)* classic **3** *(travail etc)* standard; *(exemple, plaisanterie, question etc)* classic; **vêtement/tenue c.** classic garment/outfit; **aimer le style c.** to like the classic style; **guerre c.** conventional warfare; *Fam* **c'est le coup c.!** *(une chose qui se reproduit fréquemment)* that's typical!; *(une ruse connue)* it's the usual trick!; **ça, c'est c.** that's just typical(, that is)
   NM **1** *(auteur)* classical author **2** *(livre)* classic; **les classiques grecs/français** the Greek/French classics; **relire ses classiques** to reread the classics; **c'est un grand c. du jazz/des années soixante** it's a great jazz standard *or* classic/a great sixties classic; **c'est un c. du genre** it's a classic of its kind *or* of the genre **3** *Mus* classical music

> Attention: ne pas confondre **classic** et **classical** lorsque l'on traduit l'adjectif **classique**. Le terme **classic** signifie généralement **typique**, **habituel**, alors que **classical** signifie **traditionnel** et s'oppose à **modern**.

classiquement [klasikmã] ADV classically

claudication [klodikasjɔ̃] NF *Méd, Littl* limp(-ing), *Spéc* claudication

claudiquer [klodike] VI *Litt* to limp

clause [kloz] NF *Jur etc* clause; **c. additionnelle** additional clause, rider; **c. pénale** penalty clause; **c. de style** formal clause; *Fin* **c. au porteur** pay to bearer clause; **c. d'annulation** cancellation clause; **c. d'arbitrage** arbitration clause; **c. compromissoire** arbitration clause; **c. contractuelle** clause of a/the contract; *Com* **c. d'exclusivité** exclusivity clause, exclusive rights clause; **c. d'exonération** exemption clause; *Fin* **c. d'indexation** cost escalation clause, indexation clause; **c. de franchise** excess clause; **c. limitative** limiting clause; **c. de la nation la plus favorisée** most-favoured-nation status; **c. de non-concurrence** non-competition clause; **c. de remboursement** refunding clause; **c. de réserve de propriété** retention of title clause; **c. de résiliation** termination clause, cancellation clause; **c. résolutoire** resolutive clause; **c. de sauvegarde** safeguard clause; *Com* **c. ducroire** del credere clause; **c. dérogatoire** derogatory clause; *Fin* **c. à ordre** clause 'to the order of'; **c. de sortie** escape *or* get-out clause

clausé [kloze] ADJ *Com (connaissement)* dirty

claustra [klostra] NM stone railings

claustral, -ale, -aux, -ales [klostral, -o] ADJ monastic

claustration [klostrasjɔ̃] NF *(isolation)* confinement

claustrer [klostre] VT *(isoler)* to confine, to shut up
   VPR **se claustrer** to shut oneself up; **se c. dans le silence** to retreat into silence

claustrophobe [klostrofɔb] ADJ *Méd* claustrophobic

claustrophobie [klostrofɔbi] NF *Méd* claustrophobia

clavardage [klavardaʒ] NM *Can Ordinat* chat

claveau, -eaux [klavo] NM *Constr, Archit* archstone; **c. droit** keystone

clavecin [klavsɛ̃] NM *Mus* harpsichord

claveciniste [klavsinist] N *Mus* harpsichord player, harpsichordist

claveter [klavte] VT *(je clavette; je clavetterai) Tech* to key, to wedge, to cotter

clavette [klavɛt] NF *Tech* key (bolt), pin, cotter (pin)

clavicorde [klavikɔrd] NM *Mus* clavichord

clavicule [klavikyl] NF *Anat* collarbone, clavicle

clavier [klavje] NM **1** *(de piano, de machine à écrire etc)* keyboard; *(de téléphone)* keypad; *Ordinat* **c. numérique** numerical *or* numeric keypad; **c. AZERTY** AZERTY keyboard; **c. QWERTY** QWERTY keyboard; **c. multifonction(s)** multifunctional keyboard; **c. national** country keyboard; **c. par défaut** default keyboard (layout); **c. à infrarouge** infrared keyboard; **c. sans fil** cordless *or* wireless keyboard **2** *Fig* **la c. des émotions amoureuses** the range *or* gamut of love's emotions

claviste [klavist] N typesetter; *Ordinat* keyboarder

clayette [klɛjɛt] NF **1** *(petite claie)* wire tray *or* rack; *(dans un réfrigérateur)* (wire) shelf **2** *(cageot)* crate

clayon [klɛjɔ̃] NM *(pour les fromages)* wicker tray; *(pour les gâteaux)* cake rack

clé [kle] NF = **clef**

clean [klin] ADJ INV *Fam* straight, clean-living; **elle a un look c.** she has a clean-living *or* straight image

clearing [kliriŋ] NM *Écon* clearing; **accord de c.** clearing agreement

clébard [klebar] NM, **clebs** [klɛps] NM *Arg (chien)* pooch, mutt

CLEF [kle] NF **1** *(d'une porte, d'un code, d'un mystère)* key; **c. de maison** house key; **mes clefs de voiture** my car keys; **fausse c.** skeleton key; **trousseau de clefs** bunch of keys; **fermer une porte à c.** to lock a door; **donner un tour de c. à la porte** to lock the door; **tenir/mettre qch sous c.** to keep/put sth under lock and key; **on l'a mis sous c. depuis hier** he's been under lock and key since yesterday; **la c. est sur la porte** the key is in the lock; **louer une maison clefs en main** to rent a house with immediate *or* vacant possession; **usine clefs en main** turnkey factory *or Am* plant; **prix clefs en main** *(d'une voiture)* on-the-road price; *(d'une maison)* all-inclusive price; **les clefs de la ville** the keys to the city; **la philosophie, c. de la connaissance** philosophy, the key to (all) knowledge; **roman à c.** = novel introducing real characters under fictitious names; **mettre la c. sous la porte** to scarper, to do a runner; **prendre la c. des champs** *(d'un prisonnier etc)* to make a bid for freedom; **position-c.** key position; **industrie-c.** key industry; **un secteur(-)c. de la recherche** a key sector *or* area of research; *Fig* **enquête avec ré-**

compense à la c. an investigation, for the successful conclusion of which there is a reward; **il y a une forte somme d'argent à la c.** there is a large sum of money at stake *or* involved
   2 *Mus* clef; *(armature)* key signature; *(d'un instrument à cordes)* peg; *(d'un instrument à vent)* key; **c. de sol/de fa** treble/bass clef; **jouer avec des dièses à la c.** to play in sharp keys
   3 *Tech* wrench, spanner
   4 *Élec* switch (key); *Tél* **c. Morse** Morse key
   5 *(prise de lutte)* lock
   6 *Ordinat* key; *(du DOS)* switch; **c. d'accès** enter key; **c. de chiffrement** encryption key; **c. de contrôle** control key; **c. électronique** electronic key; **c. gigogne** dongle; **c. d'index** index key; **c. de protection** data protection ► ► **c. allen** allen key; **c. anglaise** adjustable spanner, monkey wrench; **c. à bougie** (spark)plug spanner; **c. à cliquet** ratchet handle; *Aut* **c. de contact** ignition key; *Aut* **c. en croix** wheelbrace, spider; **c. cruciforme** cruciform key; **c. à douille** box spanner; **c. dynamométrique** torque wrench; **c. mixte** combination spanner; **c. à molette** adjustable spanner, *surtout Am* monkey wrench; **c. à œil** ring spanner; **c. ouverte** open-ended spanner; **c. passe-partout** passkey, master key; **c. à pipe** box spanner; **c. plate** (open) end wrench; **c. à puce** computerized key; *Banque* **c. RIB** bank details; **c. des songes** *(livre)* = how to interpret your dreams; *Archit* **c. de voûte** *(d'une arche)* keystone, crown; *Fig* **c'est la c. de voûte de notre entreprise** he's the cornerstone of our firm

clématite [klematit] NF clematis

clémence [klemãs] NF **1** *Fig (de la température)* mildness; **si la c. du temps le permet** if the weather's mild enough **2** *Litt (pardon)* clemency, mercy, leniency (**pour, envers** to(wards))

clément [klemã] ADJ **1** *Fig (température etc)* mild **2** *Litt (indulgent)* clement, merciful, lenient (**pour, envers** to, towards)

clémentine [klemãtin] NF *(fruit)* clementine

clenche [klɑ̃ʃ] NF, **clenchette** [klɑ̃ʃɛt] NF **1** *(d'un loquet)* latch **2** *Belg (poignée)* doorhandle

Cléopâtre [kleopatr] NF *Antiq* Cleopatra

cleptomane [kleptoman] N kleptomaniac

cleptomanie [kleptomani] NF kleptomania

clerc [klɛr] NM **1** *(dans un bureau)* clerk; **c. de notaire** ≃ solicitor's clerk; **petit c.** junior clerk **2** *Rel* cleric **3** *Arch (savant)* learned man, scholar **4** **il n'est pas besoin d'être grand c. pour ...** you don't have to be a genius in order to ...

clergé [klɛrʒe] NM clergy VOIR GRAMMAIRE A11

clérical, -ale, -aux, -ales [klerikal, -o] ADJ, NM *Rel* clerical

cléricalisme [klerikalism] NM *Rel* clericalism

clic [klik] NM **1** *(bruit)* click, clicking; **entendre un c.** to hear a click *or* a clicking sound **2** *Ordinat* click; **double c.** double click; **c. de souris** mouse click
   INT click

clic-clac NM INV *(d'un appareil photo, d'une ceinture de sécurité)* click; *(des talons)* click-clack; *(des sabots)* clatter

cliché [kliʃe] NM **1** *(lieu commun)* cliché **2** *Phot (pellicule)* negative; *(photo)* photograph, shot **3** *Typ* stereotype; *(de caractères)* plate; *(d'illustration)* block; **c. au trait** line block **4** *Ordinat* format, layout; **c. de disque** disk dump; **c. mémoire** dump

clicheton [kliʃtɔ̃] NM *Fam (cliché)* cliché; **l'histoire est d'une banalité affligeante; tous les clichetons sont au rendez-vous** the story is as banal as can be and completely cliché-ridden

clicheur [kliʃœr] NM *Ordinat* screen dump program

client, -ente [klijɑ̃, -ɑ̃t] N *Com* client, customer; *(d'un médecin)* patient; *(d'un chauffeur de taxi)* fare; *(d'un hôtel)* guest; *(dans la publicité)* account; **c'est un bon c.** he's a good customer; **ici, le c. est roi** the customer is always right; **la France est un gros c. du Japon pour la robotique** France is one of Japan's big customers for robotics; **c. actuel** existing customer; *Compta* **c.** douteux doubtful debt, possible bad debt; **c. de passage** passing customer; **clients de passage** passing trade; **c. imprévu** chance customer; *Ordinat* **c. de messagerie électronique** e-mail client, mail reader; **c. potentiel** suspect, potential client, potential customer; **clients potentiels** potential clients, suspect pool; **c. régulier** regular customer; **c. sans réservation** *(dans un hôtel)* chance guest, walk-in; *Fig* **désolé, je ne suis pas c.** sorry, I'm not interested; *Fam* **c'est un drôle de c.** he's a queer customer

clientèle [klijɑ̃tɛl] NF 1 *(d'un magasin)* customers, clientèle; *(d'une entreprise)* customer base; *(d'un médecin, d'un avocat)* practice; **c. actuelle** existing customers; **c. de passage** passing trade 2 *(fait d'acheter)* custom; **obtenir la c. d'un consommateur/d'un pays** to obtain a consumer's/a country's custom *or* business; **accorder sa c. à** to give one's custom to, to patronize

clientélisme [klijɑ̃telism] NM *Péj* (political) patronage, *Spéc* clientelism

clignement [kliɲmɑ̃] NM blink; **faire un c. d'œil** to wink

cligner [kliɲe] VT **c. les yeux** to blink VI **c. des yeux** to blink

clignotant [kliɲɔtɑ̃] ADJ *(yeux)* blinking; *(paupière)* twitching; *(étoile)* twinkling; *(lumière)* flickering, flashing; **feu** *ou* **signal c.** *Naut* intermittent signal; *Aut* flashing light
NM 1 *Aut* indicator, *Am* turn signal; **mettre son c. (à droite/gauche)** to indicate (right/left), *Am* to put on one's turn signal (to turn right/left) 2 *Écon* signal, indicator; **le c. de la hausse des prix/de la crise** the warning light *or* signal that prices are rising/that a recession is on the way

clignotement [kliɲɔtmɑ̃] NM *(des yeux)* blinking; *(des paupières)* twitching; *(d'une étoile)* twinkling; *(d'une lumière)* flickering, flashing

clignoter [kliɲɔte] VI *(des paupières)* to twitch; *(d'une étoile)* to twinkle; *(d'une lumière)* to flicker, to flash; *Ordinat (d'un marqueur etc)* to flash, to blink

clignoteur [kliɲɔtœr] NM *Belg* 1 *Aut (lampe)* indicator, *Am* turn signal; **mettre son c. (à droite/gauche)** to indicate (right/left), *Am* to put on one's turn signal (to turn right/left) 2 *(signal)* warning light

clim [klim] NF *Fam (abrév* climatisation) air-conditioning

climat [klima] NM *aussi Fig* climate; **sous des climats plus ensoleillés** in sunnier climes; **c. de détente** relaxed atmosphere *or* climate; **c. économique** economic climate; **travailler dans un c. d'hostilité** to work in a hostile atmosphere *or* in an atmosphere of hostility

climatique [klimatik] ADJ *(conditions etc)* climatic; **station c.** health resort

climatisation [klimatizasjɔ̃] NF air conditioning; **avoir la c. dans toutes les pièces** to have air conditioning in every room

climatiser [klimatize] VT to air-condition; **chambre climatisée** air-conditioned bedroom

climatiseur [klimatizœr] NM air conditioner; *Aut* climate control system

climatologie [klimatɔlɔʒi] NF climatology

climatologique [klimatɔlɔʒik] ADJ climatological

clin [klɛ̃] NM *Naut* bordé à clin(s) clinker built

clin d'œil [klɛ̃dœj] NM wink; **faire un c. à qn** to wink at sb; **en un c.** in the twinkling of an eye, in a flash; **dans ce film, le réalisateur fait un c. à Bergman** in this film, the director makes passing references to Bergman *or* passing nods to Bergman

clinicien [klinisjɛ̃] ADJ, NM **(médecin) c.** clinician

clinique [klinik] ADJ *(médecine, essais etc)* clinical; **les signes cliniques d'une maladie** the clinical symptoms of an illness
NF 1 *(hôpital privé)* clinic; **chef de c.** senior registrar 2 *(observation des étudiants de médecine)* clinic; *(médecine)* clinical medicine

cliniquement [klinikmɑ̃] ADV clinically

clinquant [klɛ̃kɑ̃] NM tinsel; *(bijoux)* flashy jewellery; **c. du style** flashiness of style; **un journaliste qui donne dans le c. et la vulgarité** a journalist who tends to be flashy and vulgar
ADJ flashy, showy

clip [klip] NM 1 *(broche)* clip; *(boucle d'oreille)* clip-on earring 2 *(pince)* clip 3 *(film)* clip; *(musical)* (music) video; **c. vidéo** video (clip)

clipart [klipart] NM *Ordinat* clip art

clipper¹ [klipœr] NM 1 *Aviat* transport aircraft 2 *Naut* clipper

clipper² [klipe] VT to clip

clique [klik] NF 1 *(gang)* clique, gang; *Fam* **toute la c.** and the rest of the gang, and all the rest of them 2 *Mil (tambours et clairons)* band

cliquer [klike] VI *Ordinat* to click (**sur** on); **c. deux fois** to double-click; **c. avec le bouton gauche/droit de la souris** to left-click/right-click; **c. et glisser** to click and drag

cliques [klik] NFPL *Fam* **prendre ses c. et ses claques** to pack up and leave, to pack one's bags and go

cliquet [klikɛ] NM *Tech etc* catch, pawl, ratchet

cliqueter [klikte] VI (*je cliquette; je cliqueterai*) *(de chaînettes etc)* to rattle; *(de fleurets, d'aiguilles à tricoter)* to click; *(de pièces de monnaie)* to clink, to chink; *(de clés etc)* to jingle, to jangle; *Aut* to knock, to pink

cliquetis [klikti] NM *(de chaînettes)* rattling; *(de pièces de monnaie, de breloques etc)* clink(ing), chinking; *(de clés etc)* jingling, jangling; *(de couverts)* clinking; *(de vaisselle)* clattering; *(de fleurets, d'aiguilles à tricoter)* clicking; *(d'une machine à écrire)* clack; *Aut* knocking, pinking; **j'entendis un léger c.: on essayait de crocheter la serrure** I heard a slight scratching noise: somebody was trying to pick the lock

clisse [klis] NF *(pour bouteilles)* wicker covering; *(pour faire sécher des fromages)* wicker tray

clitoridien, -ienne [klitɔridjɛ̃, -jɛn] ADJ clitoral

clitoris [klitɔris] NM *Anat* clitoris

clivage [klivaʒ] NM 1 *(dans la société)* divide; *(dans un parti politique)* split; **c. social** social divide; **c. idéologique** ideological divide 2 *(de roches etc)* cleavage 3 *(de diamants etc)* cleaving

cliver [klive] VT *(diamants etc)* to cleave, to split
VPR **se cliver** *(de roches etc)* to cleave, to split

cloaque [klɔak] NM 1 *aussi Fig* cesspool; **c. de vices** den of iniquity; **comment peut-il vivre dans ce c.?** how can he live in that pigsty *or* midden? 2 *Anat, Zool* cloaca 3 *Antiq* **le grand C.** the Cloaca Maxima

clochard, -arde [klɔʃar, -ard] N *Fam* tramp, *Am* hobo; **si tu continues comme ça, tu vas finir c.** if you carry on like that, you're going to end up destitute

clochardisation [klɔʃardizasjɔ̃] NF destitution

clochardiser [klɔʃardize] VT to reduce to destitution; *(sans domicile)* to make homeless, to reduce to a state of vagrancy
VPR **se clochardiser** to be reduced to destitution; *(sans domicile)* to be made homeless

cloche [klɔʃ] NF 1 bell; **sonner les cloches** to ring the bells; *Fam* **sonner les cloches à qn** to give sb a good ticking off *or* a good rollicking; **se faire sonner les cloches** to get a good ticking off *or* a good rollicking; **fleurs en c.** bell-shaped flowers; *Fam* **déménager à la c. de bois** to do a moonlight flit; *Fig* **voilà un autre son de c.** that's quite a different version of events 2 *Chimie* bell jar; *(en horticulture)* cloche; *Culin* **c. (de métal)** metal dish cover 3 *(chapeau)* **c.** cloche (hat) 4 *Fam (vagabondage)* **la c.** vagrancy; **être de la c.** to be a vagrant, to be of no fixed abode 5 *Arg* **se taper la c.** to pig out, to stuff oneself 6 *Fam (idiot)* twit, idiot
ADJ *Fam* idiotic, stupid; **avoir l'air c.** to look stupid
► ► *Aut* **c. d'embrayage** clutch bell housing; **c. à fromage(s)** cheese dish cover; **c. à plongeur** diving bell

cloche-pied (à) ADV **sauter à c.** to hop; **s'éloigner à c.** to hop away

clocher¹ [klɔʃe] NM 1 *(d'une église etc)* bell tower, steeple; **course au c.** point-to-point (race) 2 *(paroisse)* home town, home patch; **querelles** *ou* **disputes de c.** petty local quarrels, parish-pump quarrels; **esprit** *ou* **mentalité de c.** small-town mentality, parochialism

clocher² VI 1 *Fam* **il y a quelque chose qui cloche** there's something wrong somewhere; **il y a quelque chose qui cloche dans son histoire** there's something not right about his story; **je ne sais pas ce qu'il y a, mais ça cloche quelque part** I don't know what it is, but something's not right somewhere 2 *Arch (boiter)* to limp, to hobble

clocheton [klɔʃtɔ̃] NM *Archit (d'une église)* (small) steeple; *(ornement)* pinnacle (turret)

clochette [klɔʃɛt] NF 1 *(petite cloche)* small bell, handbell 2 *Bot* bell-flower, bell-shaped flower

clodo [klodo] *Fam* NM tramp, down-and-out, *Am* hobo
ADJ down-and-out

cloison [klwazɔ̃] NF 1 *(entre des pièces)* partition; **mur de c.** dividing wall; **percer une c.** to knock through a (dividing) wall; **coller l'oreille** *ou* **écouter à la c.** to listen through the wall 2 *Naut, Aviat* bulkhead; *Aut* partition, bulkhead; **c. étanche** *Naut* watertight bulkhead; *Aviat* pressure bulkhead; *Fig* watertight compartment; *Fig* **faire tomber les cloisons entre les classes** to bring down class barriers 3 *Biol* septum; *Anat* **c. nasale** nasal septum

cloisonnage [klwazɔnaʒ] NM partitioning

cloisonné [klwazɔne] ADJ 1 *(pièce)* partitioned (off); *Fig* **ces services sont très cloisonnés** these departments are highly compartmentalized 2 *Beaux-Arts (émaux)* cloisonné 3 *Biol* septate(d)
NM cloisonné

cloisonnement [klwazɔnmɑ̃] NM *(d'une pièce etc)* partitioning (off); *Fig* compartmentalization

cloisonner [klwazɔne] VT *(pièce etc)* to partition (off); *Fig* **c. la société** to put up class barriers

cloître [klwatr] NM 1 *(partie d'un monastère*

etc) cloister(s) **2** *(monastère)* monastery, convent; **vie de c.** cloistered life

cloîtrer [klwatre] **VT** *(personne)* to cloister; *Fig* to shut up *or* away; **nonne cloîtrée** enclosed nun

VPR se cloîtrer *(de religieux)* to enter a convent *or* a monastery; *Fig* to shut oneself up *or* away, to live the life of a recluse

clonage [klona3] **NM** *Biol, Ordinat* cloning

clone [klon] **NM** *Biol, Ordinat* clone

cloner [klone] **VT** *Biol, Ordinat* to clone

cloneur [klonœr] **NM** *Mktg* cloner

clope [klɔp] *Arg* **NF OU M** *(cigarette)* fag, ciggie, smoke; **la c. jaunit les doigts** cigarettes make your fingers go yellow; **des clopes!** nothing doing!, no way!

NM *(mégot)* (cigarette-)end *or* butt

cloper [klɔpe] **VI** *Fam* to smoke

clopin-clopant [klɔpɛ̃klɔpɑ̃] **ADV** *Fam* **aller c.** to limp along, to hobble about; *Fig* **commerce qui va c.** business that struggles along

clopiner [klɔpine] **VI** to hobble

clopinettes [klɔpinɛt] **NFPL** *Fam* sweet FA, *surtout Am* zilch; **je ne vais pas travailler pour des c.** I'm not going to work for peanuts

cloporte [klɔpɔrt] **NM** *(insecte)* woodlouse, *Am* sow bug

cloque [klɔk] **NF 1** *(sur la peau, sur la peinture etc)* blister; **faire des cloques** to blister **2** *Agr (des arbres)* blight **3** *Arg* **être en c.** *(enceinte)* to be up the spout, to be knocked up, to be in the club

cloqué [klɔke] **ADJ** *(peinture)* blistered; *Agr (feuille)* blighted, curled; *Tex* **tissu c.** seersucker

NM *Tex* seersucker

cloquer [klɔke] **VI** *(de la peinture)* to blister; *(de la peau)* to blister, to come up in a blister

clore [klɔr] *(pp clos; pr ind je clos, il clôt, ils closent; fu je clorai)* **VT** (= **fermer**, *which has taken its place in most uses)* **1** *(discussion etc)* to end; *(marché)* to conclude; *(compte)* to close; *Bourse (position)* to close out; **l'image qui clôt le livre** the image which ends the book, the image on which the book closes; **c. le débat** to close the meeting, to adjourn; *Ordinat* **c. une session** to log off, to log out **2** *Litt (passage, porte)* to close (off), to shut (up); *(terrain etc)* to enclose

VPR se clore *(d'une réunion etc)* to (come to an) end

clos [klo] **ADJ 1** *(fermé)* closed, shut; **volets c.** closed shutters; **trouver porte close** to find nobody in, to find nobody (at) home; **à la nuit close** after dark; *Jur* **à huis c.** in camera; **réunion à huis c.** closed session; **en vase c.** in isolation; **vivre en vase c.** to live in isolation, to live without any contact with the outside world **2** *(achevé)* finished, concluded; **la discussion est close** the discussion is closed; **l'incident est c.** the matter is closed; **les inscriptions seront closes le 5 mars** the closing date for applications is 5 March; **exercice c. le 31 décembre 2004** year ended 31 Dec 2004 **3** *(entouré) (jardin, monde)* enclosed

NM enclosure; **c. (de vigne)** vineyard

close-combat [klozkɔ̃ba] **NM** *Sport* close combat

closerie [klozri] **NF** small park

clôture [klotyr] **NF 1** *(enceinte)* enclosure, fence; *(en fer)* railing; *Can Sport (au hockey sur glace)* rink; *(au base-ball)* fence; **c. métallique** wire fence; **mur de c.** enclosing wall **2** *(fermeture) (d'une réunion etc)* conclusion, end; *(d'un débat)* closure; **c. des inscriptions le 3 mars** closing date for applications: March 3rd; **discours de c.** closing speech; **prononcer la c. des débats** to pronounce

closure; *Bourse* **cours en c.** closing price; **valeur du mark en c.** closing value of the mark, value of the mark at the close; **c. de la chasse** close of season

3 *Ordinat* close; **c. de session** logging off **4** *Com (d'un compte)* closing; *Bourse (d'une position)* closing (out); *Bourse* **c. par rachat** closure by repurchase; *Compta* **c. annuelle des livres** year-end closing of accounts; *Compta* **c. de l'exercice** end of the financial year **5** *Rel* enclosure; **faire vœu de c.** to take a vow of enclosure

clôturer [klotyre] **VT 1** *(champ etc)* to enclose; *(avec barrière)* to fence in **2** *(session)* to close, to end, to conclude; *Pol* **c. les débats** to close the debate **3** *Com (comptes etc)* to close

VI *Bourse* to close; **le CAC 40 a clôturé en baisse/hausse de 9 points** the CAC 40 closed 9 points down/up; **c. à perte** to close at a loss

clou [klu] **NM 1** nail; **souliers à gros clous** hobnail(ed) boots; **enfoncer un c. avec un marteau** to hammer in a nail; **ceinture à clous** studded belt; *Fam* **ça ne vaut pas un c.** it's not worth a penny *or Am* a red cent; *Fam* **des clous!** nothing doing!, no chance!, *surtout Am* no way!; **pour des clous** for nothing; *Fam* **elle est maigre comme un c.** she's as thin as a rake; *Fam* **mettre qch au c.** to pawn sth

2 *(d'un passage piéton)* stud; **traverser dans les clous** to cross at a pedestrian crossing *or Am* at a crosswalk

3 *Fam (d'un spectacle etc)* star turn, chief attraction; **ça a été le c. de la soirée** it was the high point *or* highlight of the evening

4 *Mil Arg (prison)* cooler, slammer

5 *Méd* boil, carbuncle

6 *(vieux)* **c.** *(voiture)* old banger; *(vélo)* old boneshaker

▸▸c. cavalier staple; **c. à crochet** hook; **c. doré** brass-headed nail, stud; **c. de girofle** clove; **c. sans tête** brad; **c. à souliers** shoe tack; **c. de tapissier** (upholstery *or* carpet) tack

clouer [klue] **VT 1** to nail; **c. une caisse** to nail down a crate; *Fig Fam* **c. le bec à qn** to shut sb up **2** *Fig (chose, personne)* to pin down; **c. qn au sol** to pin sb down; **rester cloué sur place** to be rooted to the spot; **la neige a cloué tous les avions au sol** all planes were grounded due to snow; **être cloué au lit** to be confined to *or Fam* stuck in bed

clouté [klute] **ADJ** *(chaussures etc)* studded; **passage c.** pedestrian crossing, *Am* crosswalk

clouter [klute] **VT** *(chaussures etc)* to stud

clovisse [klɔvis] **NF** *(mollusque)* clam

clown [klun] **NM** clown; **numéro de clowns** clown act; *Fig* **ne fais pas le c.!** stop acting the fool *or* goat!, stop clowning around!; **c'est un vrai c.** he's a real comic *or* clown

clownerie [klunri] **NF** clowning; *Fig* clowning around, playing the fool

clownesque [klunɛsk] **ADJ** clownish

club [klœb] **NM 1** *(association) (sportif, politique)* club; **c. de foot** football club; **c. sportif ou de sport** sports club; **c. de gymnastique** fitness centre, gym; **c. de vacances** holiday club, *Am* vacation center; **c. de compagnie aérienne** airline club; **c. d'investissement** investment club; *Bourse* **c. des amis** fan club **2** *(de golf)* (golf) club **3** *(fauteuil)* **c.** club chair

cluse [klyz] **NF** *Géog* cluse, transverse valley

clystère [klister] **NM** *Méd Arch* clyster, enema

cm *(abrév* **centimètre)** cm

CMJN [seɛmʒiɛn] *Ordinat (abrév* **cyan, magenta, jaune, noir)** CMYK

CMP [seɛmpe] **NM** *Fin (abrév* **coût moyen pondéré)** weighted average cost

CMU [seɛmy] **NF** *(abrév* **couverture maladie universelle)** = law introduced in France to ensure free health care for people on low incomes who have no social security cover

CNA [seɛna] **NM** *(abrév* **convertisseur numérique analogique)** DAC

CNAM [knam] **NM** *(abrév* **Caisse nationale d'assurance maladie)** = French government department dealing with health insurance and sickness benefit

NM *(abrév* **Conservatoire national des arts et métiers)** = school of engineering in Paris

CNCE [seɛnseə] **NM** *(abrév* **Centre national du commerce extérieur)** = national export organization

CNIL [knil] **NF** *(abrév* **Commission nationale de l'informatique et des libertés)** = board which enforces data protection legislation

CNPF [seɛnpeɛf] **NM** *Anciennement (abrév* **Conseil national du patronat français)** = former name of the French employers' association, *Br* ≃ CBI

CNRS [seɛnɛrɛs] **NM** *(abrév* **Centre national de la recherche scientifique)** *Br* ≃ SRC (Science Research Council), *Can* ≃ Science Council of Canada

coaccusé, -ée [koakyze] **N** *Jur* co-defendant

coach [kotʃ] **NM 1** *Aut* two-door car **2** *(entraîneur)* coach

coacquéreur [koakerœr] **NM** joint purchaser

coadjuteur, -trice [koadʒytœr, -tris] **N** *Rel* coadjutor

coadministrateur, -trice [koadministratœr, -tris] **N** co-director; *Jur* co-trustee

coagulable [koagylabl] **ADJ** capable of coagulating, coagulable

coagulant [koagylɑ̃] **ADJ** coagulating, coagulative

NM coagulant

coagulateur, -trice [koagylatœr, -tris] **ADJ** coagulative

coagulation [koagylasʒɔ̃] **NF** coagulation, coagulating

coaguler [koagyle] **VT** *(sang)* to coagulate; *(lait)* to curdle

VI *(du sang)* to coagulate, to clot; *(du lait)* to curdle

VPR se coaguler *(du sang)* to coagulate, to clot; *(du lait)* to curdle

coalescence [koalesɑ̃s] **NF** coalescence

coalisé [koalize] **ADJ** allied

N les coalisés the allies

coaliser [koalize] **VT** *(partis)* to unite into a coalition

VPR se coaliser to unite; *Pol* to form a coalition; *Fig* **ils se sont tous coalisés contre moi** they all ganged up on me *or* joined forces against me

coalition [koalisʒɔ̃] **NF 1** *(alliance)* coalition; **gouvernement de c.** coalition government **2** *Fig Péj* conspiracy; **former une c. contre qn/qch** to join forces against sb/sth

coaltar [koltar] **NM** coal tar; *Fam* **être dans le c.** to be completely out of it, to be in a daze

coassement [koasmɑ̃] **NM** *(de la grenouille)* croak; **des coassements** croaking, croaks

coasser [koase] **VI** *(d'une grenouille)* to croak

coassocié, -ée [koasɔsje] **N** copartner, joint partner

coassurance [koasyrɑ̃s] **NF** mutual assurance

coassurer [koasyre] **VT** to co-insure

coauteur [kootœr] **NM 1** *(d'un livre etc)* joint author, co-author **2** *(d'un crime)* accomplice

coaxial, -iale, -iaux, -iales [kɔaksjal, -jo] **ADJ** coaxial

COB [seɔbe] **NF** Bourse (abrév **Commission des opérations de Bourse**) = Stock Exchange watchdog, Am ≃ SEC

cobalt [kɔbalt] **NM** cobalt; **bleu de c.** cobalt blue; **bombe au c.** cobalt bomb

cobaye [kɔbaj] **NM** (mammifère), Fig guinea pig; Fig **servir de c.** to act as a guinea pig

cobelligérant [kɔbeliʒerɑ̃] **ADJ, NM** cobelligerent

Coblence [kɔblɑ̃s] **NF** Koblenz

cobol [kɔbɔl] **NM** Ordinat COBOL

cobra [kɔbra] **NM** cobra

coca [kɔka] **NM 1** Fam (boisson) Coke®; **prendre un c.** to have a Coke® **2** Bot coca **NF** Pharm coca

cocagne [kɔkaɲ] **NF** mât de **c.** greasy pole; **pays de c.** land of milk and honey, land of plenty

cocaïne [kɔkain] **NF** Pharm cocaine

cocaïnomane [kɔkainɔman] **N** cocaine addict

cocard [kɔkar] **NM** Fam black eye, shiner

cocarde [kɔkard] **NF** rosette; Hist (sur un chapeau) cockade; Aviat roundel, fuselage marking; (dans un avion) company crest; **la c. tricolore** = tricolour cockade, worn on 14 July; **course à la c.** = traditional sport in southern France in which rosettes are snatched from the horns of young cattle

cocardier, -ière [kɔkardje, -jɛr] **ADJ** (chauviniste) chauvinistic, jingoistic **N** chauvinist, jingoist

cocasse [kɔkas] **ADJ** Fam comical, laughable

cocasserie [kɔkasri] **NF** Fam comical nature, ridiculousness

coccinelle [kɔksinɛl] **NF 1** (insecte) ladybird, Spéc coccinella **2** Fam (voiture) (Volkswagen®) beetle

coccyx [kɔksis] **NM** Anat coccyx

coche[1] [kɔʃ] **NM** Arch stagecoach; Fig **faire la mouche du c.** to buzz around self-importantly; Fam **rater** ou **louper** ou **manquer le c.** to miss the boat

coche[2] **NF 1** Vieilli notch, nick; (d'une flèche) nock **2** Ordinat tick, Am checkmark

cochenille [kɔʃnij] **NF** cochineal

cocher[1] [kɔʃe] **NM** coachman, driver; Arch **c. de fiacre** cabman, Fam cabby

cocher[2] **VT 1** (nom etc) to tick (off), Am to check; **c. la case appropriée** tick the appropriate box **2** Vieilli (faire une entaille dans) to nick, to notch

cochère [kɔʃɛr] **ADJ** porte **c.** carriage gateway or entrance

cochet [kɔʃɛ] **NM** cockerel

cocheur [kɔʃœr] **NM** Can (au golf) **c. d'allée** pitching wedge; **c. de sable** sand wedge

Cochinchine [kɔʃɛ̃ʃin] **NF** Hist Cochin-China

cochon, -onne [kɔʃɔ̃, -ɔn] **NM 1** Zool pig; Fig **copains comme cochons** as thick as thieves; Fam **tu es sale comme un c.** you're filthy; **petite cochonne!** you dirty little thing!; **quel c.!** (qui ne nettoie pas après soi) he leaves such a mess behind him!; **gros** ou **gras comme un c.** as round as a barrel; **manger comme un c.** to eat like a pig; **tu écris comme un c.** your writing is appalling; **avoir des yeux de c.** to have piggy eyes; Fig **temps de c.** rotten or stinking weather; Fig Fam **eh ben mon c.!** you old rogue or devil!; **c'est une tête de c.** he's really pig-headed; Fam **un c.** **n'y retrouverait pas ses petits!** what a pigsty!

2 Fam Péj (vicieux) dirty old man; **tu es une petite cochonne!** you've got a filthy mind or a mind like a sewer!; **c'est un c.** (il raconte des histoires immondes) he's got a filthy mind or a mind like a sewer; **quel vieux c.!** what a dirty old man!

3 Arg Péj dirty pig, swine; **jouer un tour de c. à qn** to play a dirty or rotten trick on sb **ADJ** (histoire etc) dirty, smutty, filthy; **film c.** dirty or porn or blue film; **dix mille euros? c'est pas c.** ten thousand euros? that's not bad; **c. qui s'en dédit** it's a deal

▸▸ **c. d'Amérique** peccary; **c. d'Inde** guinea pig; **c. de lait** suck(l)ing pig; **c. de mer** porpoise

cochonceté [kɔʃɔ̃ste] **NF** Fam (propos) filthy talk, foul language; (vacherie) dirty trick; (action obscène) repulsive act; **allez faire vos cochoncetés ailleurs!** go and do that sort of thing somewhere else!; **dire des cochoncetés** to use dirty language, to talk dirty

cochonnaille [kɔʃɔnaj] **NF** Fam foodstuffs made from pork

cochonner [kɔʃɔne] **VT** Fam **1** (mal faire) (travail) to bungle, to botch, to muck up **2** (salir) to dirty, to make a mess of

cochonnerie [kɔʃɔnri] **NF** Arg **1** (saleté) mess; **faire des cochonneries** (des saletés) to make a mess; **dire des cochonneries** to say dirty or smutty things **2** (chose sans valeur) trash, rubbish; (plat) pigswill; **il ne mange que des cochonneries** he only eats junk food

cochonnet [kɔʃɔnɛ] **NM 1** (petit cochon) piglet **2** (aux boules) jack

cocker [kɔkɛr] **NM** cocker spaniel

cockpit [kɔkpit] **NM** (de voitures de courses), Naut, Aviat cockpit

cocktail [kɔktɛl] **NM** (boisson) cocktail; (soirée) cocktail party; Fig (mélange) cocktail, mixture; **c. de fruits** fruit cocktail; **c. Molotov** Molotov cocktail

coco[1] [koko] **NM 1** (plante) noix de **c.** coconut; **huile/beurre de c.** coconut oil/butter **2** Arg (tête) nut, bonce; (estomac) belly; **mets-toi ça dans le c.!** get that into your thick skull! **3** (boisson) = drink made from liquorice, lemon juice and water

coco[2] **NM 1** Enf (œuf) egg **2** Fam (type) fellow, bloke; **drôle de c.** odd bloke, strange guy; **toi, mon c., je t'ai à l'œil** just watch it, mate or chum **3** mon **petit c.** my darling, my pet

coco[3] **NF** Arg (cocaïne) coke, Charlie

coco[4] **ADJ, N** Fam (communiste) commie, red

cocoler [kɔkɔle] **VT** Suisse (dorloter) to cosset

cocon [kɔkɔ̃] **NM** (du vers à soie etc) cocoon; Fig le **c. familial** the family nest; **s'enfermer dans son c.** to retire into one's shell; **il faut sortir de ton c.** you must come out of your shell

cocontractant, -ante [kɔkɔ̃traktɑ̃, -ɑ̃t] **N** Jur contracting partner

cocooning [kɔkuniŋ] **NM** cocooning; **faire du c.** to cocoon

cocorico [kɔkɔriko] **INT** (du coq) cock-a-doodle-doo!

NM 1 (cri du coq) cock-a-doodle-doo **2** (cri) = French victory cheer; **faire c.** to crow

cocoter [kɔkɔte] **VI** Fam to stink; **ça cocote ici** it stinks in here

cocotier [kɔkɔtje] **NM** (arbre) coconut palm; Fig Fam **secouer le c.** to get rid of the dead wood

cocotte [kɔkɔt] **NF 1** Enf (poule) hen, chicken; (en papier) = bird made out of folded paper **2** Fam **ma c.** darling **3** Péj (prostituée) tart **4** Culin (large) stewpan, casserole (dish) **5** Fam **hue, c.!** gee up! **6** Can (pomme de pin) pine cone

Cocotte-Minute®, pl Cocottes-Minute NF pressure cooker

cocréancier, -ière [kɔkreɑ̃sje, -jɛr] **N** Fin joint creditor

cocu, -ue [kɔky] Fam **N** deceived husband, f deceived wife; (homme) Fml cuckold; **faire c. son mari** to cheat on one's husband; **avoir une chance** ou **une veine de c.** to have the luck of the devil; **va donc, eh c.!** get lost, you sucker! **ADJ** deceived, Fml cuckold(ed); **je suis c.** my wife is cheating on me

couage [kɔkɥaʒ] **NM** Arg cuckoldry

cocufier [kɔkyfje] **VT** Fam to be unfaithful to, to cheat on, Fml to cuckold

coda [kɔda] **NF** Mus coda

codage [kɔdaʒ] **NM 1** (chiffrement) coding; **c. de données** data encryption **2** Ling encoding

code [kɔd] **NM 1** (symbole) code; **ils communiquent par c.** they communicate in code; **écrire un message en c.** to write a message in code, to write a coded message; **déchiffrer un c.** to decipher or break or crack a code

2 Ordinat code; **les codes** the codes, the coding; **c. alphanumérique** alphanumeric(al) code; **c. d'erreur** error code; **c. hexadécimal** hexa(decimal) code; **c. abrégé** shortcode; **c. machine** machine code; **c. couleurs** colour coding; **c. d'accès** access code; **c. d'arrêt** stop code; **c. d'autorisation d'accès** access authorization code; **c. d'identification** identification code; **c. d'imprimante** printer code; **c. d'instruction** instruction code; **c. de caractère** character code; **c. de commande** command code; **c. de contrôle** control code; **c. de contrôle de l'imprimante** printer control code; **c. de départ** start code; **c. inhibiteur** inhibit code; **c. natif** source code; **c. objet** object code; **c. source** source code; **c. ASCII** ASCII code

3 (ensemble de règles) law; (livre) (copy of the) code; Jur statute book; Aut passer le **c.** to sit the written part of a driving test; **c. de la morale** moral code; **c. de l'honneur** code of honour

4 Aut **se mettre en code(s)** to dip or Am dim one's headlights; **rouler en code(s)** to drive with dipped headlights; **phares code(s)** dipped headlights

▸▸ **c. assujetti TVA** VAT registration number; **c. civil** civil code, ≃ common law; **c. client** customer code, customer reference number; **c. de commerce** commercial law; **c. confidentiel** security code; (d'une carte bancaire) PIN; **c. général des impôts** general tax code; Biol **c. génétique** genetic code; Banque **c. guichet** bank branch code; **c. de justice militaire** military law; **c. maritime** navigation laws; **c. pénal** penal code; Banque **c. personnel, c. porteur** PIN, personal identity number; **c. postal** postcode, postal code, Am zip code; **C. de la route** Highway Code; **c. secret** secret code; **c. du travail** employment code, employment law, Am labor code, labor laws

---

Code postal

In France, the first two numbers of a given post code correspond to the administrative code number of the relevant "département". Thus all postal codes for Paris begin with 75.

---

codé [kɔde] **ADJ** coded; (pour sécurité) security-coded; (image) scrambled

code-barres, pl codes-barres NM bar code

codébiteur, -trice [kɔdebitœr, -tris] **N** Jur joint debtor

codécision [kɔdesizjɔ̃] **NF** joint decision; UE codecision (procedure)

codéine [kɔdein] **NF** Chimie codeine

codemandeur, -deresse [kɔdəmɑ̃dœr, -drɛs] **N** Jur joint plaintiff

coder [kɔde] VT *(message)* to code

codétenteur, -trice [kɔdetɑ̃tœr, -tris] N *Jur* joint holder

codétenu, -ue [kɔdetny] N fellow prisoner *or* inmate

codeur [kɔdœr] NM *Tech* coder

codéveloppement [kɔdevlɔpmɑ̃] NM co-operative development

CODÉVI [kɔdevi] NM *(abrév* **compte pour le développement industriel)** = savings account, money from which is invested in industrial development

codex [kɔdɛks] NM pharmacopoeia

codicillaire [kɔdisilɛr] ADJ *Jur* codicillary

codicille [kɔdisil] NM *Jur* codicil

codification [kɔdifikasjɔ̃] NF *(des lois etc)* codification, classification; *Ordinat* **c. binaire** binary code; **c. décimale** decimal coding; **c. significative** coding by means of symbols, symbol coding

codifier [kɔdifje] VT *(lois etc)* to codify; *(mettre en système)* to systematize

codirecteur, -trice [kɔdirɛktœr, -tris] N joint manager, f joint manageress; *(d'un PDG etc)* co-director

coédition [kɔedisjɔ̃] NF *(procédé)* joint publishing; *(livre)* joint publication

coefficient [kɔefisjɑ̃] NM **1** *Math* coefficient; *(dans un concours ou examen)* coefficient, weighting factor; **on peut s'attendre à un c. d'erreur** a certain margin of error is to be expected; **c. d'occupation des sols** *(en urbanisme)* plot ratio **2** *Fin* **c. d'activité** activity ratio; **c. de capital** output ratio; **c. de capitalisation des résultats** price-earnings ratio; *Compta* **c. d'exploitation** performance *or* operating ratio; **c. de liquidité** current ratio; **c. de rotation** stock turnover ratio; **c. de solvabilité** risk asset ratio; **c. de trésorerie** cash ratio **3** *Tech* **c. de dilatation** coefficient of expansion; **c. d'écrasement/d'élasticité** modulus of compression/of elasticity; **c. de sécurité** safety factor; **le c. d'augmentation** the rate of increase; *Aut* **c. aérodynamique** *ou* **de pénétration dans l'air** drag coefficient; *Aut* **c. de traînée** drag coefficient, drag factor

cœlacanthe [selakɑ̃t] NM *Zool* coelacanth

cœliaque [seljak] ADJ, N *Méd* coeliac, *Am* celiac

cœliochirurgie [seljɔʃiryrʒi] NF *Méd* laparotomy

cœlioscopie [seljɔskɔpi] NF *Méd* laparoscopy

coentreprise [kɔɑ̃trəpriz] NF joint venture

coéquation [kɔekwasjɔ̃] NF *Admin* proportional assessment

coéquipier, -ière [kɔekipje, -jɛr] N *Sport etc* team-mate

coercible [kɔɛrsibl] ADJ **1** *Phys (gaz etc)* coercible **2** **un bâillement difficilement c.** a yawn that is hard to suppress *or* stifle

coercitif, -ive [kɔɛrsitif, -iv] ADJ coercive; **le pouvoir c. de son discours** the persuasive power of his speech

coercition [kɔɛrsisjɔ̃] NF coercion

CŒUR [kœr] NM **1** *Anat* heart; **maladie de c.** heart disease; **greffe du c.** heart transplant; **c. droit/gauche** right/left side of the heart; **subir une opération à c. ouvert** to have open-heart surgery; **tué d'une balle en plein c.** killed by a bullet in the heart; **en (forme de) c.** heart-shaped; *Fig* **faire la bouche en c.** to simper; **il est arrivé la bouche en c. pour me demander si ...** he came simpering up to me to ask if ...; *Fig* **joli comme un c.** as pretty as a picture; **serrer** *ou* **presser qn contre** *ou* **sur son c.** to hold sb close; *Fam* **faire le joli c.** to put on airs (and graces)
 2 *(ventre)* **avoir mal au c.** to feel sick *or Am*

nauseous; **ça fait mal au c. de voir tout cet argent gaspillé** it makes you sick to see all that money wasted *or* go to waste; **cela soulève le c.** it's nauseating *or* sickening; *Fam* **avoir le c. solide** *ou* **bien accroché** to have a strong stomach
 3 *(siège des sentiments)* heart; **il a l'air dur, mais il a le c. sensible** he looks tough, but he has a tender heart; **avoir** *ou* **garder qch sur le c.** to have sth on one's mind; **tu ne peux pas garder ça sur le c., il faut que tu en parles** you can't keep that to yourself, you'll have to talk about it; **dire ce qu'on a sur le c.** to get it off one's chest; *Fig* **en avoir le c. net** to get to the bottom of it; *Fig* **ouvrir son c. à qn** to open one's heart to sb; **parler à c. ouvert** to speak freely; **avoir la rage au c.** to be seething with anger; **au fond du c.** in one's heart of hearts; **remercier qn de tout (son) c.** *ou* **du fond de son c.** to thank sb wholeheartedly *or* from the bottom of one's heart; **je l'espère de tout mon c.** I sincerely hope so; *Euph* **je sais qu'elle ne me porte pas dans son c.** I know she doesn't like me much *or* isn't very fond of me; **partir le c. léger** to set off with a light heart; **avoir le c. triste** *ou* **lourd** to be heavy-hearted; **avoir le c. gros** *ou* **serré** to have a heavy heart, to be sad at heart; **à c. joie** to one's heart's content; **de gaieté de c.** with a light heart; **ce n'était pas de gaieté de c. que je l'ai fait** I wasn't happy about doing it, I didn't enjoy doing it; **prendre** *ou* **avoir à c. de faire qch** to have one's heart set on doing sth; **la chose qui lui tient** *ou* **qu'il a** *ou* **prend à c. est de donner une éducation à sa fille** he has his heart set on giving his daughter an education; **ce projet lui tient à c.** this project is close to his heart; **ne pas avoir le c. de faire qch** not to have the heart to do sth; **elle n'a plus le c. à rien** she hasn't the heart for anything any more; **avoir le c. à rire** to be in the mood for laughing; **avoir le c. sur la main** to be very generous; **à votre bon c., m'sieurs dames** can you spare a few coins?; **femme de c.** warm-hearted woman; **je serai de c. avec vous** I'll be with you in spirit; **à vous briser** *ou* **fendre le c.** heartbreaking; **histoire d'une tristesse à vous fendre** *ou* **briser le c.** heartbreakingly sad story; **j'en avais le c. brisé** I was broken-hearted; **si le c. vous en dit** if you feel like it; **des gens selon mon c.** people after my own heart; **le c. a ses raisons** the heart has its reasons; **ta proposition lui est allée droit au c.** your offer went straight to his heart
 4 **par c.** by heart; **c'est du par c.** it's been learnt (off) by heart *or* learnt parrot-fashion; **apprendre/savoir qch par c.** to learn/know sth by heart; *Fam* **je la connais par c.** I know her inside out
 5 *(courage)* courage, spirit; **avoir le c. de faire qch** to have the heart to do sth; **donner du c. à qn** to give sb courage; *Fam* **avoir du c. au ventre** to have plenty of guts; **faire contre mauvaise fortune bon c.** to make the best of a bad job, to put a good face on it
 6 *(énergie)* heart, will; **avoir** *ou* **mettre du c. à l'ouvrage** to put one's heart into one's work; **je n'ai pas le c. à l'ouvrage aujourd'hui** I haven't the heart for work today; **il était clair qu'il n'avait pas le c. à l'ouvrage** it was obvious that his heart wasn't in it; **faire qch de bon c.** *ou* **de grand c.** to do sth willingly *or* gladly; **rire de bon c.** to laugh heartily; **y aller de bon c.** to get down to it; **le c. n'y est pas** his/my/*etc* heart isn't in it
 7 *(amour)* **donner son c. à qn** to lose one's heart to sb; **aimer qn de tout son c.** to love sb with all one's heart; *Prov* **loin des yeux, loin du c.** out of sight, out of mind; **des histoires de c.** affairs of the heart; **une affaire de c.** an affair of the heart
 8 *(bonté)* **c'est un** *ou* **il a bon c.** he's kind-hearted, he's a kind-hearted soul; **avoir un c.**

d'or/de pierre to have a heart of gold/of stone; **ne pas avoir de c.** to be heartless
 9 *(centre)* middle, core; *Fig* **le c. du problème** the heart of the matter; **au c. de la ville** in the centre of the town, in the heart of the city; **c. de palmier** heart of palm; **c. d'un chou/d'un artichaut** heart of a cabbage/artichoke heart; *Fam* **avoir un c. d'artichaut** to fall in love with every girl/man one meets, to be always falling in love; **fromage fait à c.** ripe cheese; **au c. de l'hiver** in the depths of winter; **au c. de l'été** at the height of summer
 10 *Cartes* hearts; **dame de c.** queen of hearts; **avez-vous du c.?** have you any hearts?
 11 *(d'imprimante laser)* engine

coexistence [kɔɛgzistɑ̃s] NF coexistence (**avec** with); *Pol* **c. pacifique** peaceful coexistence

coexister [kɔɛgziste] VI to coexist (**avec** with)

COFACE [kɔfas] NF *(abrév* **Compagnie française d'assurances pour le commerce extérieur)** ≃ Export Credit Guarantee Department

coffrage [kɔfraʒ] NM **1** *(pour ouvrages en béton)* formwork, *Br* shuttering **2** *Min (pour galerie etc)* coffering, lining

coffre [kɔfr] NM **1** *(meuble)* chest; *(pour l'argent)* safe; *(à la banque)* safe(ty) deposit box; *Banque* **c. de nuit** night safe; **c. en bois** wooden chest; **c. à jouets** toy box; **c. à linge** linen chest; **percer** *ou* **ouvrir un c.** to break open *or* into a safe; **les coffres de l'État** coffers of State
 2 *Anat Fam* chest; **avoir du c.** *(avoir du souffle)* to have a sound chest, to have a lot of puff; *(avoir de la voix)* to have a powerful voice
 3 *Aut (d'une voiture)* boot, *Am* trunk; *Aut* **c. de toit** car roof box, luggage box; **c. porte-skis** ski box; *Aviat* **c. à bagages** baggage compartment
 4 *(d'une serrure, d'un piano etc)* case
 5 *Naut* **c. d'amarrage** mooring buoy

coffre-fort, *pl* **coffres-forts** NM safe

coffrer [kɔfre] VT **1** *Fam* **c. qn** to put sb behind bars *or* inside *or* away; **faire c. qn** to have *or* get sb put behind bars *or* inside **2** *Min (galerie etc)* to coffer, to line

coffret [kɔfrɛ] NM **1** small box, casket; **c. à bijoux** jewellery box; **c. de disques** boxed set **2** *Ordinat* case; **modèle en c.** cased model **3** *Tél* **c. avec carte prépayée** prepay package

cogénération [koʒenerasjɔ̃] NF *Tech* co-generation

cogérance [koʒerɑ̃s] NF co-management, joint management

cogérant, -ante [koʒerɑ̃, -ɑ̃t] N joint manager

cogérer [koʒere] VT **c. qch** to manage sth jointly

cogestion [koʒɛstjɔ̃] NF joint management, co-management

cogitation [koʒitasjɔ̃] NF *Iron, Vieilli* cogitation, reflection

cogiter [koʒite] VI *Vieilli* to cogitate, to think; **c. sur un problème** to ponder over a problem

cogito [koʒito] NM *Phil* cogito; **le c. de Descartes** the Cartesian cogito, Descartes' cogito

cognac [kɔɲak] NM cognac

cognassier [kɔɲasje] NM quince (tree)

cogne [kɔɲ] NM *Arg (policier)* cop; *(bagarre)* punch-up; **il va y avoir de la c.!** there's going to be trouble *or* a punch-up!

cognée [kɔɲe] NF axe, *Am* ax, hatchet; **jeter le manche après la c.** to throw in one's hand

cognement [kɔɲmɑ̃] NM *(bruit)* thumping,

banging; *(d'un moteur etc)* knocking, combustion knock; **c. (du moteur) diesel** diesel knock

cogner [kɔɲe] **VT** *(heurter)* to knock, to bump; *Fam (épouse, enfants etc)* to knock about; **c. qn en passant** to bump into sb (in passing); *Fam* **se faire c.** to get beaten up *or* knocked about; **il l'a cogné dur** he hit him hard

VI 1 *(frapper, battre)* to bang (**sur** on); **il est tombé de la chaise et sa tête a cogné contre le bureau** he fell off his chair and bumped *or* banged his head on the desk; **c. du poing sur la table** to bang (one's fist) on the table, to thump the table; *Fam* **il cogne dur** he knows how to use his fists; *Fam* **son mari lui cogne dessus chaque fois qu'il est ivre** her husband knocks her about *or* gives her a thumping every time he gets drunk; **c. à une porte** to bang *or* hammer on a door; **j'entends un volet c.** I can hear a shutter banging

2 *(d'un moteur etc)* to knock

3 *Fam (chauffer)* to be scorching; **ça cogne dur dehors** it's absolutely scorching outside, *très Fam* it's bloody hot outside

4 *Fam (puer)* to stink (to high heaven), *Br* to pong

VPR se cogner 1 *(se heurter)* to bump oneself; **se c. à** *ou* **contre qch** to knock against sth; *Fam* **ils se cognent dessus chaque fois qu'ils boivent** they bash each other about whenever they get drunk; *Fig* **se c. la tête contre les murs** to bang one's head against a brick wall **2** *Fam* **se c. qn/qch** to get stuck *or Br* lumbered *or* landed with sb/sth

cogneur [kɔɲœr] **NM** *Boxe etc* hard hitter, bruiser

cogniticien, -ienne [kɔɡnitisjɛ̃, -jɛn] **N** *Ordinat* knowledge engineer

cognitif, -ive [kɔɡnitif, -iv] **ADJ** *Phil* cognitive; **thérapie cognitive** cognitive therapy

cognition [kɔɡnisjɔ̃] **NF** *Phil* cognition

cohabitation [kɔabitasjɔ̃] **NF** cohabitation, living together; *Pol* **sous le régime de la c.** during the period of cohabitation

---

Cohabitation

Originally, this term referred to the period (1986–1988) during which the socialist President (François Mitterrand) had a right-wing Prime Minister (Jacques Chirac), following the victory of the RPR in the legislative elections and Mitterrand's decision not to resign as President. It has since been used to refer to the similar situation which arose following the 1993 elections (with Édouard Balladur as Prime Minister) and more recently the 1997 elections (with the left-wing government of Lionel Jospin co-ruling with the President Jacques Chirac).

---

cohabiter [kɔabite] **VI** to cohabit (**avec** with), to live together; **elle cohabite avec des amies** she lives with friends

cohérence [kɔerɑ̃s] **NF** *(d'un discours)* coherence; *(d'un comportement)* consistency; *(d'une argumentation)* coherence, consistency; **cette explication/ce raisonnement/il manque de c.** that explanation/that line of argument/he is inconsistent; **parler sans aucune c.** to be totally incoherent

cohérent [kɔerɑ̃] **ADJ** *(argumentation)* coherent, consistent; *(comportement)* consistent; *(dans un discours)* coherent

cohéritier, -ière [kɔeritje, -jɛr] **N** coheir, *f* coheiress, joint heir, *f* joint heiress

cohésif, -ive [kɔezif, -iv] **ADJ** cohesive

cohésion [kɔezjɔ̃] **NF** cohesion, cohesiveness

cohorte [kɔɔrt] **NF 1** *Fam (de gens)* horde, band **2** *Hist* cohort

cohue [kɔy] **NF** crowd, mob, throng

coi, coite [kwa, kwat] **ADJ se tenir c.** to keep quiet, to lie low; **en rester c.** to be (left) speechless

coiffage [kwafaʒ] **NM 1** *(de cheveux)* hairdressing, doing someone's hair; *(de ses cheveux)* doing one's hair **2** *(pour recouvrir)* covering

coiffe [kwaf] **NF 1** *(surtout de costume régional)* headdress **2** *(doublure de chapeau)* lining **3** *(pour recouvrir)* cover; *Mil* breech cover; **c. de fusée** fuse cap **4** *(du nouveau-né)* caul

coiffé [kwafe] **ADJ 1 être c. d'un chapeau** to be wearing a hat; **il est né c.** he was born with a caul; *Fig* he was born with a silver spoon in his mouth **2 elle est bien coiffée ce soir** her hair is lovely this evening; **je ne suis pas encore coiffée** I haven't done my hair yet; **il est mal c.** his hair's a mess; **c. en arrière** with one's hair combed back; **il est c. en brosse** he has a crew cut

coiffer [kwafe] **VT 1** *(tête)* to cover; *(bouteille etc)* to cap; **c. un enfant d'un bonnet** to put a bonnet on a child('s head); **ce chapeau vous coiffe bien** that hat suits you; **il était coiffé d'un sombrero** he was wearing a sombrero; **montagne coiffée de neige** snow-capped mountain; **des nuages coiffent presque en permanence le mont Blanc** Mont Blanc is almost permanently covered by clouds *or* has a near permanent cloud-cover; *Fig* **c. sainte Catherine** to be (left) on the shelf, to be 25 and still unmarried

2 *(d'un coiffeur etc)* **c. qn** to do sb's hair; **il coiffe bien** he's a good hairdresser; **se faire c. (les cheveux)** to have one's hair done; **qui vous coiffe?** who does your hair?, who's your hairdresser?; **sur ces photos, les mannequins sont coiffés par Maniatis** in these photos, the models' hair-styling is by Maniatis; **se faire c. chez qn/par qn** to get one's hair done at sb's/by sb **3** *Sport Fam* to overtake; *aussi Fig* **se faire c. (au poteau)** to be pipped at the post **4** *Fam (organisation, service etc)* to head

VPR se coiffer 1 *(mettre)* **se c. d'une casquette** to put on a cap **2** *(se peigner)* to do one's hair; **tu ne t'es pas coiffé aujourd'hui, tes cheveux sont emmêlés** you haven't done your hair today, it's all tangled

coiffeur, -euse [kwafœr, -øz] **N** hairdresser, hair stylist; **c. pour hommes** barber

NF coiffeuse *(meuble)* dressing table

coiffure [kwafyr] **NF 1** *(de cheveux)* hairstyle; **changer de c.** to change one's hairstyle *or* hairdo **2** *(métier)* hairdressing; **salon de c.** hairdresser's, hairdressing salon; *(pour hommes)* barbershop, barber's **3** *(chapeau etc)* headgear; *(de costume régional)* headdress

COIN [kwɛ̃] **NM 1** *(angle)* *(de la bouche, de l'œil etc)* corner; **maison du** *ou* **qui fait le c.** corner house; **à tous les coins de rue** on every street corner; **l'épicier du c.** the grocer on the corner; *(du village etc)* the local *or* corner grocer; *Fam* **je ne voudrais pas le rencontrer au c. d'un bois** I wouldn't like to meet him down a dark alley *or* on a dark night; **mettre un enfant au c.** *(pour le punir)* to make a child stand in the corner; **regard en c.** sidelong glance; **lancer un regard en c. à qn** to look at sb sideways, to give sb a sidelong glance; **sourire en c.** half smile; **regarder qn du c. de l'œil** to look at sb out of the corner of one's eye; *Journ* **le c. du jardinier/santé** the gardener's/health page; **ici, c'est le c. des enfants** this is the children's corner; **c. enfants** *(au restaurant)* children's area; *Rail* **c. fenêtre/couloir** window/aisle

seat; **aux quatre coins du monde** in the four corners of the earth; **elle a visité les quatre coins du monde** she has travelled all over the world; **reliure avec coins** binding with leather corners

2 *(endroit)* spot, place; **un petit c. pas cher** a cheap *or* inexpensive little place; **il habite dans le c.** he lives around here; **je ne suis pas du c.** I'm not local, I'm not from round here, I don't live round here; **les gens du c.** the locals; *Fam* **le petit c.** the smallest room (in the house), *Br* the loo; **coins et recoins** nooks and crannies; **il est resté dans son c. toute la journée** he's been very quiet all day; **c'est quelqu'un qui reste tout le temps dans son c.** he doesn't mix much, he stays in the background; **dans un c. de ma mémoire** in a corner of my memory, in the back of my mind; **mon stylo est introuvable, il a dû tomber dans un c.** I can't find my pen anywhere, it must have got lost somewhere; **j'ai dû le mettre dans un c.** I must have put it somewhere; **chercher qch dans tous les coins** to look everywhere *or* high and low for sth; *Fam* **connaître qch dans les coins** to know sth inside out; **au c. du feu** by the fireside

3 *(parcelle)* patch; **c. des légumes** vegetable patch *or* plot; **c. de ciel bleu** patch of blue sky **4** *(cale)* wedge; **en c.** wedge-shaped; **tranchant du c.** thin end of the wedge **5** *(pour frapper les monnaies)* stamp, die; *Fig* **marqué au c. du génie** bearing the stamp *or* hallmark of genius

---

coinçage [kwɛ̃saʒ] **NM**, **coincement** [kwɛ̃smɑ̃] **NM** wedging, jamming

coincé, -ée [kwɛ̃se] **ADJ** *(bloqué)* *(fermeture, porte, mécanisme)* jammed, stuck; *Psy Fam* uptight (about sex)

N *Fam* **c'est qui, ces deux coincés?** who are those two uptight-looking characters?

coincer [kwɛ̃se] *(je coinça(is), n. coinçons)* **VT 1** *(tiroir etc)* to jam; *(rails etc)* to wedge (up), to chock (up); **j'ai coincé mes cheveux dans ma fermeture Éclair®** I got my hair stuck *or* caught in my zip; **sa main était coincée derrière le radiateur** his hand was trapped *or* caught behind the radiator; **la voiture est coincée entre deux camions** *(en stationnement)* the car is boxed in by two lorries; **je ne peux pas doubler, je suis coincé entre deux camions** I can't overtake, I'm stuck between two lorries; **je suis resté coincé dans un embouteillage** I got snarled up in a traffic jam; **je suis coincé à Prague/dans l'ascenseur** I'm stuck in Prague/in the lift; *Fig* **il est coincé tout le week-end** he's tied up all weekend

2 *(acculer)* to corner; **il m'a coincé** *(je n'ai pas su répondre)* he had me cornered; *Fig* **il faut que je paie, je suis coincé** I'll have to pay, I'm stuck *or* I've no choice; **je vais me retrouver coincé avec deux mensualités à payer** I'll be stuck with two monthly instalments to pay

3 *Fam (arrêter)* to run in, to nick; **il va finir par se faire c.** he'll end up getting nicked

VI 1 *(être bloqué)* to jam, to stick; *Fig* **notre proposition n'a pas été acceptée, ça coince au niveau de la direction** our proposal hasn't been accepted, there's a problem as far as management is concerned

2 *très Fam (sentir mauvais)* to stink, to pong, *Br* to hum

VPR se coincer to jam, to stick; **se c. la tête dans des barreaux** to get one's head stuck in railings; **se c. le doigt dans la porte** to catch one's finger in the door; **évite de te c. le dos!** be careful not to hurt your back!; **il s'est coincé une vertèbre cervicale** he's got a trapped nerve

coïncidence [kɔɛ̃sidɑ̃s] **NF** coincidence; **par une étrange c.** by a strange coincidence

coïncident [kɔɛ̃sidɑ̃] ADJ coincident, coinciding

coïncider [kɔɛ̃side] VI to coincide (avec with); leurs intérêts coïncident they have similar interests; tout coïncide! je connais le coupable it all fits! I know who did it; votre réponse ne coïncide pas avec la question posée there is some discrepancy between your answer and the question that was asked; tous les témoignages coïncident the witnesses all bear each other out or tell the same story; ces deux figures géométriques coïncident the two shapes match each other perfectly

coin-coin NM INV (des canards) quacking; des c. quacks, quacking
INT quack! quack!

coin-cuisine, pl coins-cuisine(s) NM kitchen area, kitchenette

coïnculpé, -ée [kɔɛ̃kylpe] N co-defendant, co-accused

coing [kwɛ̃] NM (fruit) quince

coin-repas, pl coins-repas NM dining area or recess

coït [kɔit] NM coitus, coition

coke [kɔk] NM (combustible) coke
NF Fam (cocaïne) coke

cokéfaction [kɔkefaksjɔ̃] NF coking

cokéfier [kɔkefje] VT to coke

cokerie [kɔkri] NF coking plant

co-koter [kɔkɔte] VI Belg Fam to share a room

co-koteur, -euse [kɔkɔtœr, -øz] N Belg Fam (student) roommate

col [kɔl] NM 1 (d'une robe, d'une chemise etc) collar; faux c. (sur une chemise) detachable collar; (sur un verre de bière) head; c. de fourrure/de dentelle fur/lace collar 2 (d'une bouteille etc) neck 3 Géog col 4 Arch, Litt (de personne) neck; se hausser ou se pousser du c. to push oneself forward 5 Anat (d'un os) neck
▸▸c. blanc white-collar worker; c. bleu blue-collar worker; c. cassé wing collar; c. châle shawl collar; c. cheminée turtleneck; c. Claudine Peter Pan collar; Anat c. du fémur neck of the femur; c. marin sailor's collar; c. rond round neck; c. roulé polo-neck (jumper); Anat c. de l'utérus cervix; cancer du c. de l'utérus cervical cancer; c. en V V-neck

cola [kɔla] NM (plante) cola, kola

colback [kɔlbak] NM Fam attraper/prendre qn par le c. to catch/grab sb by the scruff of the neck

colbertisme [kɔlbɛrtism] NM = economic policy of state intervention and protectionism, from Jean-Baptiste Colbert (1619-1683), finance minister to Louis XIV

col-bleu, pl cols-bleus NM Fam (marin) sailor, bluejacket

colchique [kɔlʃik] NM (plante) meadow saffron, autumn crocus, Spéc colchicum

cold-cream [koldkrim] NM cold cream

col-de-cygne, pl cols-de-cygne NM Tech swan neck

colégataire [kɔlegatɛr] N Jur co-legatee, joint legatee

coléoptère [kɔleɔptɛr] NM beetle; les coléoptères the Coleoptera

colère [kɔlɛr] NF anger, Litt wrath; il s'est mis ou il est entré dans une c. bleue ou noire he flew into a towering rage; piquer ou faire une c. to fly into a rage, to throw a tantrum; être blanc ou blême/rouge de c. to be white/flushed with anger; c. froide cold fury; être en c. to be angry; se mettre en c. to get angry, to lose one's temper (contre qn with sb, Am at sb); je suis en c. contre moi-même I'm

angry with myself; mettre qn en c. to make sb angry, to anger sb; avec c. angrily; il avait des colères terribles he was subject to terrible fits of anger; pas la peine de passer ta c. sur moi there's no point (in) taking your anger out or working your anger off on me; Litt la c. de Dieu the wrath of God
ADJ (voix) irate, angry; (personne) bad-tempered

coléreux, -euse [kɔlerø, -øz], **colérique** [kɔlerik] ADJ (personne) quick-tempered; (disposition) irritable

colibacille [kɔlibasil] NM colon bacillus

colibacillose [kɔlibasiloz] NF Méd colibacillosis

colibri [kɔlibri] NM hummingbird

colifichet [kɔlifiʃɛ] NM trinket, knick-knack

colimaçon [kɔlimasɔ̃] NM snail; escalier en c. spiral staircase

colin [kɔlɛ̃] NM (poisson) hake, Br coley VOIR GRAMMAIRE A12

colinéaire [kɔlineɛr] ADJ Math colinear

colin-maillard [kɔlɛ̃majar] NM (jeu) blind man's buff

colin-tampon NM Fam Hum ou Vieilli se soucier de qch comme de c. not to give two hoots about sth

colique [kɔlik] ADJ Anat (artère etc) colic
NF severe stomach pains; (surtout de bébé) colic; Méd c. néphrétique/hépatique renal/biliary colic; avoir la c. (douleur) to have stomach ache; (diarrhée) to have diarrhoea or Am diarrhea; Fig Fam to have the wind up; Fam cette idée suffit pour me donner la c. the very idea puts the wind up me; Fam quelle c.! what a bore!, what a bind!

colis [kɔli] NM 1 (paquet) parcel, packet, package; par c. postal by parcel post; c. chargé registered and insured parcel; c. exprès special delivery parcel; c. contre remboursement cash on delivery parcel, Am collect on delivery parcel 2 Fam un joli petit c. a knockout, a babe, Br a cracker

Colisée (le) [ləkɔlize] NM the Coliseum

colis-épargne NM INV Com saving stamps scheme

colistier, -ière [kɔlistje, -jɛr] N Pol fellow candidate, Am running mate

colite [kɔlit] NF Méd colitis

collabo [kɔlabo] N Fam = collaborateur 2

collaborateur, -trice [kɔlabɔratœr, -tris] N 1 (associé) fellow worker, associate, Am co-worker; Journ contributor; collaborateurs d'une revue contributors to a magazine 2 Pol, Hist collaborator, collaborationist

collaboration [kɔlabɔrasjɔ̃] NF 1 (aide, soutien) collaboration, co-operation (avec with); travailler en étroite c. to work closely together, to co-operate 2 Pol, Hist collaboration

collaborationniste [kɔlabɔrasjɔnist] N Pol, Hist collaborationist

collaborer [kɔlabɔre] VI 1 (participer) to collaborate, to co-operate (avec with); c. à un journal to contribute to a newspaper; c. à un projet to take part in a project; les deux services collaborent étroitement the two departments work closely together 2 Pol, Hist to collaborate

collage [kɔlaʒ] NM 1 (d'affiches) sticking up, putting up; (de bois etc) gluing, sticking; (de papier etc) pasting; Beaux-Arts collage; Tech sizing; (de produits manufacturés) bonding; Typ c. et endossage forwarding 2 (du vin) fining, clarifying

collagène [kɔlaʒɛn] NM collagen; crème de beauté au c. collagen(-based) cream

collant [kɔlɑ̃] ADJ 1 (adhésif) sticky; (pein-

ture, vernis) tacky; papier c. gummed paper 2 (qui moule) (vêtement) tight- or close-fitting; pantalon c. skintight trousers 3 Fam (personne) qu'est-ce qu'il est c.! you just can't shake him off or get rid of him!; je m'en méfie, il est très c. I'm wary of him, he's very clingy
NM (pair of) tights, Am pantihose; c. uni/fantaisie self-coloured/patterned tights VOIR GRAMMAIRE A10

collante [kɔlɑ̃t] NF Scol Fam = letter giving notice of the date and place of an examination

collapsus [kɔlapsys] NM Méd (d'un malade) collapse; c. cardio-vasculaire circulatory collapse

collatéral, -ale, -aux, -ales [kɔlateral, -o] ADJ collateral; Archit nef collatérale side aisle; Jur parents collatéraux collaterals, relatives; succession collatérale collateral succession
NM 1 Archit side aisle 2 Jur collatéraux collaterals, relatives

collation [kɔlasjɔ̃] NF 1 (repas) light meal, snack 2 (de documents etc) collation 3 (d'un titre etc) granting, conferment

collationnement [kɔlasjɔnmɑ̃] NM (de documents etc) collating, collation

collationner [kɔlasjɔne] VT (deux documents écrits) to collate, to compare

colle [kɔl] NF 1 glue; (pour papier peint) (wallpaper) paste; c. en pot/stick/tube a pot/stick/tube of glue; papier sans c. unsized paper; Fam c'est un vrai pot de c. you just can't get rid of him, he sticks like a leech or like glue 2 Scol etc Fam (question difficile) difficult or sticky question, poser; (examen oral) oral exam; (punition) detention; là, tu me poses une c., je ne sais pas you've got me there, I don't know 3 Arg vivre ou être à la c. to be shacked up together
▸▸c. blanche paste; c. à bois wood glue; c. de bureau (paper) glue; c. au caoutchouc rubber solution; c. forte glue; c. de poisson isinglass

collecte [kɔlɛkt] NF 1 (ramassage) collection; (pour les pauvres etc) collection; la c. des ordures ménagères the rubbish collection; faire ou organiser une c. to make or take a collection; nous faisons une c. au profit des enfants malades we're collecting for sick children or on behalf of sick children; c. de données data collection or gathering; c. de fonds fundraising 2 Rel (prière) collect

collecter [kɔlɛkte] VT to collect

collecteur, -trice [kɔlɛktœr, -tris] N collector; c. d'impôts tax collector
NM Élec (d'une dynamo etc) ring, commutator; Radio c. d'ondes aerial; c. d'échappement exhaust manifold; Aut c. d'admission inlet manifold, throttle line; Aut c. de sortie (turbine) outlet manifold
ADJ égout c. main sewer

collectif, -ive [kɔlɛktif, -iv] ADJ (action, compte-rendu etc) collective, joint; billet (de train) c. group (rail) ticket; une vague de licenciements collectifs a wave of mass redundancies; ferme collective collective (farm); contrat c. collective agreement; l'inconscient c. the collective subconscious; radiographie collective mass radiography; Can Jur recours c. class action suit
NM 1 Gram collective noun SEE GRAMMAR A11; B8 2 Fin c. budgétaire bill of supply 3 (association) co-operative

collection [kɔlɛksjɔ̃] NF 1 (action) collecting, gathering; depuis l'âge de dix ans, il fait la c. des timbres he's been collecting stamps since he was ten; tu n'as jamais fait de c.? have you never collected anything? 2 (de papillons etc) collection; (de livres) series, collection; *Com (d'échantillons)* line; **sa c. de timbres** his stamp collection; **je possède la c. complète des Astérix** I own the complete set of Asterix stories; **pièce de c.** collector's item; **la c. d'hiver** the winter collection; **la nouvelle c. de chez Dior** Dior's new collection; *Beaux-Arts* **c. privée** private collection; *Fam* **j'en ai toute une c.** I've got a whole collection *or* set of them

collectionner [kɔlɛksjɔne] **VT** *(timbres etc)* to collect

collectionneur, -euse [kɔlɛksjɔnœr, -øz] **N** *(de timbres etc)* collector

collectivement [kɔlɛktivmã] **ADV** collectively; **protester/agir c.** to protest/act as a group

collectivisation [kɔlɛktivizasjɔ̃] **NF** *Écon* collectivization

collectiviser [kɔlɛktivize] **VT** *Écon* to collectivize

collectivisme [kɔlɛktivism] **NM** *Écon* collectivism

collectiviste [kɔlɛktivist] **ADJ, N** *Écon* collectivist

collectivité [kɔlɛktivite] **NF 1** *(groupe)* community; **le sens de la c.** community spirit; **vie en c.** community life *or* living; *Admin* **collectivités locales** *(dans un État)* local authorities; *(dans une fédération)* federal authorities; **la c. nationale** the nation, the country; **collectivités professionnelles** professional organizations; **c. publique** government organization; **c. territoriale** = administrative division with a higher degree of autonomy than a *département* **2** *(propriété en commun)* common ownership

collector [kɔlɛktɔr] **NM** *(objet de collection)* collector's item *or* piece

collège [kɔlɛʒ] **NM 1** *Scol* school; **c. d'enseignement secondaire** ≃ secondary (modern) school, *Am* ≃ high school; *Anciennement* **c. d'enseignement technique** technical college; **c. privé** private school; **le brevet des collèges** ≃ school leaving certificate; *Univ* **le C. de France** the College de France *(prestigious higher education institution)* VOIR GRAMMAIRE A6 **2** *Pol* **c. électoral** electoral body *or* constituency, *surtout Am* electoral college **3** *Rel* college; **le Sacré C.** the College of Cardinals

collégial, -iale, -iaux, -iales [kɔleʒjal, -jo] **ADJ** collegial, collegiate
NF collégiale collegiate church

collégialité [kɔleʒjalite] **NF** *(d'une société etc)* collegial structure

collégien, -ienne [kɔleʒjɛ̃, -jɛn] **N 1** *Scol* schoolboy, schoolgirl **2** *Iron* innocent; **je n'aime pas être traité en c.** I don't like being treated like a child; **rougir comme un c.** to blush like a schoolboy; **je me suis fait avoir comme un c.** I fell for it like a fool, I should have known better

collègue [kɔlɛg] **N c. (de travail)** colleague, fellow worker, *surtout Am* co-worker

COLLER [kɔle]

> **VT** to stick **1, 2** ▪ to glue **1** ▪ to paste **1, 6** ▪ to put **2** ▪ to keep in **3** ▪ to fail **3** ▪ to follow closely **4**
> **VI** to stick **1** ▪ to be OK **2**
> **VPR** to stick (together) **1** ▪ to shack up (with) **2**

VT 1 to stick; *(avec de la colle)* to stick, to glue, to paste (**à, sur** to; **on**); **c. le timbre sur l'enveloppe** to stick the stamp on the envelope; **la sueur avait collé ses cheveux** her hair was matted with sweat; **elle avait les paupières collées** her eyelids were stuck together; **c. son visage à** *ou* **contre la vitre** to press one's face to the window; **il est resté**

collé à la télé toute la soirée he was glued to the TV all evening; **il est toujours le nez collé dans ses bouquins** he's always got his nose stuck in a book; **elle a toujours l'oreille collée aux portes** she's always listening at doors; *Fig* **c. qn au mur** to stick sb up against a wall (and shoot him/her)

2 *Fam (mettre)* to stick, to put; **elle a collé le paquet dans un coin** she stuck the parcel in a corner; **ils ont collé le bébé chez la grand-mère** they've dumped the baby on the grandmother; **si tu continues, je te colle en pension** carry on like that and I'll pack you off to boarding school; **on m'a collé ce boulot sans que j'aie dit oui** I got stuck *or* saddled *or Br* lumbered with this job without any say in the matter; **c. une gifle à qn** to slap sb in the face; **si tu continues, je t'en colle une!** if you don't stop, I'll give you one!; **c. une punition à qn** to punish sb; **c. une contravention à qn** to slap a fine on sb

3 c. un élève *(le retenir)* to keep a pupil in; *(lui poser une question difficile)* to catch a pupil out (with a difficult question); **c. un candidat** to fail a candidate

4 *Fam (suivre)* to follow closely; **il me colle!** he sticks to me like glue!; **arrête de me c. au derrière** *ou* **très Fam au cul!** stop following me everywhere!

5 *Ind (papier)* to size; *(produits manufacturés)* to bond; *(vin)* to clarify, to fine

6 *Ordinat* to paste; *TV etc (bande etc)* to splice; **c. et endosser** to forward

VI 1 *(adhérer)* to stick (**à** to); **les pâtes ont collé à la casserole** the pasta has stuck to the pan; **robe qui colle au corps** clinging dress; *Fig* **il faut essayer de c. au style de l'auteur** you must try to stick to the author's style; **la peur qui lui collait à la peau** the fear that was ingrained in him *or* that was part of him

2 *Fam (aller bien)* **ça ne colle pas entre eux** they don't hit it off; **ce qu'elle a dit ne colle pas** what she said doesn't make sense *or* doesn't add up; **leurs témoignages ne collent pas** their testimonies don't tally; **ça colle!** that's OK!; **ça ne va pas c. pour mercredi** it's no go for Wednesday

VPR se coller 1 *(adhérer)* to stick; **les feuilles se sont collées entre elles** the leaves were all stuck together; **elle se colla contre le mur** she flattened herself against the wall; **elle s'est collée contre lui** she clung to him; **c'est toi qui t'y colles** you're landed with it

2 *Arg* **se c. avec qn** to shack up with sb

collerette [kɔlrɛt] **NF 1** *(de vêtement)* collar; *Hist (fraise)* ruff **2** *Bot (de champignon)* annulus **3** *Tech (de tuyau)* flange

collet [kɔlɛ] **NM 1** *(de manteau, robe etc)* collar; **saisir qn au c.** to collar sb, to seize sb by the scruff of the neck; **la police lui mit la main au c.** the police arrested him; **elle est très c. monté** she is very prim (and proper) *or* strait-laced **2** *(cape)* short cape **3** *(de dent, vis, violon etc)* neck; *(de raquette etc)* shoulder; *Bot (de champignon etc)* neck, collar; *Culin* **c. de mouton** neck *or* scrag of mutton **4** *Tech etc (de tuyau etc)* flange, collar, fillet **5** *(pour attraper de petits animaux)* snare, noose; **prendre des lapins au c.** to snare rabbits

colleter [kɔlte] *(* **je collette, n. colletons; je colletterai** *)* **vt** to collar, to seize by the collar
VPR se colleter *Fam* to tussle; **se c. avec qn** to tussle *or* grapple with sb; **se c. avec les difficultés** to struggle *or* grapple with problems

colleur, -euse [kɔlœr, -øz] **N 1** *(personne qui colle)* gluer, paster; **c. d'affiches** billsticker, billposter **2** *Scol Fam* examiner
NF *Cin* **colleuse** (film) splicer, splicing unit

collier [kɔlje] **NM 1** *(bijou)* necklace, necklet; **c. de perles** pearl necklace, string of

pearls; **c. de fleurs** garland of flowers **2** *(de chien, d'esclave etc)* collar; **cheval de c.** draught horse; **cheval franc du c.** a willing *or* hard-working horse; *Fig* **elle a toujours été franche du c.** she's always been very frank and open; *Fig* **donner un coup de c.** to put one's back into it, to make a special effort; *Fig* **reprendre le c.** to get back into harness; **c. de barbe** narrow beard, fringe of beard **3** *Tech* collar, ring; *Tech (de renfort)* clip; *Aut* clamp; **c. de serrage** clamping ring, clamp; **c. de fixation** bracket, clip; **c. de frein** brake band; **c. de palier** bearing collar **4** *Zool (d'oiseau etc)* collar, ring; **pigeon à** *ou* **au c.** ringed *or* ring-necked pigeon **5** *Culin (de bœuf, mouton)* neck

collimateur [kɔlimatœr] **NM** *Astron, Opt* collimator; *Fig* **attention, je vous ai dans mon** *ou* **le c.** careful, I've got my eye on you

colline [kɔlin] **NF** hill

collision [kɔlizjɔ̃] **NF** *(entre véhicules etc)* collision; **entrer en c. avec qch** to collide with *or* run into sth; **c. frontale** head-on collision, frontal collision; **c. latérale** side-on collision, side impact; **c. nucléaire** nuclear collision; *Fig* **c. des intérêts** clash of interests

collocation [kɔlɔkasjɔ̃] **NF 1** *Jur* establishing the order of priority of creditors *(in bankruptcy)* **2** *Ling* collocation

collodion [kɔlɔdjɔ̃] **NM** *Chimie etc* collodion

colloïdal, -ale, -aux, -ales [kɔlɔidal, -o] **ADJ** *Chimie etc* colloidal

colloïde [kɔlɔid] **NM** *Chimie* colloid

colloque [kɔlɔk] **NM 1** *(conférence)* seminar **2** *Fam (conversation)* confab; **avoir un c. avec qn** to have a confab with sb; **être en c.** to be having a confab

collusion [kɔlyzjɔ̃] **NF** *Jur etc* collusion; **c. d'intérêts** merging of interests

collusoire [kɔlyzwar] **ADJ** *Jur* collusive

collutoire [kɔlytwar] **NM** *Pharm* oral medication

collyre [kɔlir] **NM** *Pharm* eyewash, eye lotion

colmatage [kɔlmataʒ] **NM 1** *(de trous dans la route etc)* filling in; *(de trou etc)* plugging (up); *Mil (de position)* consolidation **2** *Agr (de terrain)* warping

colmater [kɔlmate] **VT** *(trous dans la route etc)* to fill in; *(trou etc)* to plug (up); *Mil (position)* to consolidate

colo [kɔlo] **NF** *abrév Fam* colonie de vacances

colocataire [kɔlɔkatɛr] **N** flatmate, *Am* roommate; *Jur* joint tenant, co-tenant

Colomb [kɔlɔ̃] **NM Christophe C.** Christopher Columbus

colombage [kɔlɔ̃baʒ] **NM** *Constr* half-timbering; **maison à colombages** half-timbered house

colombe [kɔlɔ̃b] **NF** *(oiseau), Pol Fig* dove; **c. biset** rock dove *or* pigeon; *Fam* **ma c.** my (little) dove

Colombie [kɔlɔ̃bi] **NF 1** Colombia **2** **la C.-Britannique** British Columbia

colombien, -ienne [kɔlɔ̃bjɛ̃, -jɛn] **ADJ** Colombian
N C. Colombian

colombier [kɔlɔ̃bje] **NM** *(pigeonnier)* dovecot(e), pigeon loft

colombin [kɔlɔ̃bɛ̃] **NM** *Fam (étron)* turd

Colombine [kɔlɔ̃bin] **NF** *Théâtre* Columbine

colombophile [kɔlɔ̃bɔfil] **ADJ** pigeon-fancying, pigeon-fanciers'
N pigeon fancier

colombophilie [kɔlɔ̃bɔfili] **NF** pigeon fancying

colon¹ [kɔlɔ̃] **NM 1** *(pionnier)* settler, colonist **2** *(enfant dans une colonie de vacances)* child (at camp) **3** *Agr* farmer, smallholder

colon² NM *Mil Arg* colonel; **ben, mon c.!** well, I'm damned!

côlon [kolɔ̃] NM *Anat* colon; **c. transverse** transverse colon

colonel [kɔlɔnɛl] NM *Mil* colonel; *Aviat* group captain, *Am* colonel; *Mil* **oui, mon c.** yes, Colonel

colonelle [kɔlɔnɛl] NF *Mil* colonel's wife; *Aviat* group captain's wife, *Am* colonel's wife

colonial, -iale, -iaux, -iales [kɔlɔnjal, -jo] ADJ colonial
  NM *(habitant)* colonial; *(soldat)* soldier of the colonial troops
  NF *Hist, Mil* **la coloniale** the Colonial Army

colonialisme [kɔlɔnjalism] NM *Pol* colonialism

colonialiste [kɔlɔnjalist] ADJ, N *Pol* colonialist

colonie [kɔlɔni] NF **1** *(lieu)* colony, settlement; **vivre aux colonies** to live in the colonies; **administrations des colonies** administration *or* government of the colonies, colonial administration; **c. de vacances** (children's) holiday camp, *Am* summer camp; **envoyer ses enfants en c.** to send one's children to camp; **la c. anglaise de Paris** the English colony in Paris; **c. pénitentiaire** penal settlement *or* colony **2** *(d'animaux)* colony

---

Colonie de vacances

The "colonie de vacances" or "colo" is an integral part of childhood for many French people. The children's parents do not stay with them at the "colonie", the group being supervised by "moniteurs" or "animateurs" (group leaders), who organize games and activities.

---

colonisateur, -trice [kɔlɔnizatœr, -tris] ADJ *(nation etc)* colonizing
  N colonizer

colonisation [kɔlɔnizasjɔ̃] NF colonization, settlement; *Fig* invasion

coloniser [kɔlɔnize] VT *(région)* to colonize, to settle

colonnade [kɔlɔnad] NF *Archit* colonnade

colonnage [kɔlɔnaʒ] NM putting into columns

colonne [kɔlɔn] NF **1** *Archit* column, pillar; **lit à colonnes** four-poster bed **2** *(file de personnes, soldats, choses)* column; **c. par deux/trois/quatre** column of twos/threes/ fours; **c. de secours** relief column; **c. de véhicules en marche** column of moving vehicles; *Pol* **cinquième c.** fifth column **3** *(d'un dictionnaire, journal)* column; **disposé en colonnes** tabular; *Journ* **écrire une c.** to write *or* have a column; **comme je l'écrivais hier dans ces colonnes** as I wrote yesterday in these pages; *Journ* **cinq colonnes à la une** a front-page five-column spread; *Math* **dans la c. des dizaines** in the tens column; **des colonnes de chiffres/de noms** columns of figures/names ►► *Compta* **c. créditrice/débitrice** credit/debit column; *Aut* **c. de direction** steering column; **c. de fumée** column *or* plume of smoke; *Naut* **c. d'habitacle** binnacle; **c. de mercure** column of mercury; **c. montante** *Ind* rising main, riser (pipe); *Élec* service cable, service conductor, riser; **c. Morris =** pillar used to advertise forthcoming events; *Journ* **c. rédactionnelle** editorial column; *Anat* **c. vertébrale** spinal column, spine

colonnette [kɔlɔnɛt] NF *Archit* small column, colonnette

colopathie [kɔlɔpati] NF *Méd* colitis

colophane [kɔlɔfan] NF rosin, colophony

---

coloquinte [kɔlɔkɛ̃t] NF **1** *(plante)* colocynth, bitter apple **2** *Arg (tête)* nut, *Br* bonce

colorant [kɔlɔrɑ̃] ADJ *(matière etc)* colouring, *Am* coloring
  NM **1** *(pour teindre)* colorant, dye **2** *(alimentaire)* colouring, *Am* coloring; **sirop garanti sans c.** syrup guaranteed free from (artificial) colour(s)

coloration [kɔlɔrasjɔ̃] NF **1** *(fait de colorer)* colouring, *Am* coloring; *(de daguerréotype etc)* tinting; **se faire faire une c.** to have one's hair tinted; *Fig Litt* **la tristesse donnait une c. inhabituelle à sa voix** sadness had altered his tone of voice; *Fig* **c. politique** politics, political colour **2** *(de la peau)* colour(ing), *Am* color(ing)

colorature [kɔlɔratyr] NF *Mus* coloratura

coloré [kɔlɔre] ADJ coloured, *Am* colored; **teint c.** florid *or* ruddy complexion; *Fig* **style c.** colourful *or Am* colorful style

colorer [kɔlɔre] VT to colour, *Am* to color; **c. qch en vert** to colour sth green; *Fig* **c. un récit** to lend colour to a tale
  VPR **se colorer** *(de fruit)* to colour, *Am* to color; *(de visage)* to become flushed; **sa voix s'est colorée de tendresse** a note of tenderness crept into his voice

coloriage [kɔlɔrjaʒ] NM *(action)* colouring, *Am* coloring; *(dessin)* coloured *or Am* colored drawing; **album** *ou* **livre de c.** colouring(-in) book

colorier [kɔlɔrje] VT *(impf, pr sub n. coloriions, v. coloriiez)* *(carte, dessin)* to colour *or Am* color (in); **c. qch en rouge/en bleu** to colour sth red/blue

coloris [kɔlɔri] NM shade; *(de tableau, fruit etc)* colours, *Am* colors; *Com* **carte de c.** shade card; **disponible en quatre c.** available in four shades *or* colours; *(combinaison de couleurs)* available in four colourways

colorisation [kɔlɔrizasjɔ̃] NF *Cin* colourization, *Am* colorization

coloriser [kɔlɔrize] VT *Cin* to colourize, *Am* to colorize

coloriste [kɔlɔrist] N **1** *Beaux-Arts* colourist, *Am* colorist **2** *(de cartes postales, jouets etc)* colourer, *Am* colorer, painter **3** *(coiffeur)* colourist, *Am* colorist

colossal, -ale, -aux, -ales [kɔlɔsal, -o] ADJ *(somme)* colossal, huge, gigantic; *(énergie)* colossal, enormous

colossalement [kɔlɔsalmɑ̃] ADV colossally, hugely

colosse [kɔlɔs] NM *(statue)* colossus; *(homme, institution)* giant; **le C. de Rhodes** the Colossus of Rhodes; *Fig* **un c. aux pieds d'argile** a giant with feet of clay

colostomie [kɔlɔstɔmi] NF *Chir* colostomy; **subir une c.** to have a colostomy

colostrum [kɔlɔstrɔm] NM *Physiol* colostrum

colportage [kɔlpɔrtaʒ] NM *(de marchandises)* hawking, peddling; **c. de fausses nouvelles** spreading of rumours

colporter [kɔlpɔrte] VT *(marchandises)* to hawk, to peddle; *(nouvelle, rumeurs)* to spread

colporteur, -euse [kɔlpɔrtœr, -øz] N hawker, pedlar; *Péj* **c. de ragots** gossipmonger

colposcopie [kɔlpɔskɔpi] NF *Méd* colposcopy

colt [kɔlt] NM Colt®

coltinage [kɔltinaʒ] NM *(d'une charge sur le dos)* porterage, carrying

coltiner [kɔltine] VT *(charges)* to carry on one's back
  VPR **se coltiner** *Fam* **se c. qn/qch** to get stuck *or* landed *or Br* lumbered with sb/sth

---

coltineur [kɔltinœr] NM porter *(who carries heavy loads)*; **c. de charbon** coal heaver

columbarium [kɔlɔ̃barjɔm] NM columbarium

colvert [kɔlvɛr] NM *(oiseau)* mallard

colza [kɔlza] NM *(plante)* rape, colza; **huile de c.** rapeseed oil, colza oil

coma [kɔma] NM *Méd* coma; **être dans le c.** to be in a coma; **tomber dans le c.** to go *or* lapse into a coma; **il est dans un c. dépassé** he's brain-dead

comarketing [kɔmarkɛtiŋ] NM comarketing

comateux, -euse [kɔmatø, -øz] *Méd* ADJ comatose
  N patient in a coma

combat [kɔ̃ba] NM **1** *Mil (bataille)* fight, battle; *(activité)* combat; **c. corps à corps** hand-to-hand fight; *(activité)* hand-to-hand fighting; **c. aérien** dog fight; *(activité)* aerial combat; **c. naval** naval engagement *or* action; *(activité)* naval combat; **c. terrestre** land operation; *(activité)* land fighting; **tenue de c.** battledress; **gaz de c.** nerve gas; **c. de rue** street fight; **engager le c.** to go into action (**avec qn** against sb); **mettre hors de c.** to disable, to put out of action; **hors de c.** disabled, out of action; *(régiment)* out of action
  2 *(dispute)* fight; **c. de boxe** boxing match; **c. de coqs** cockfight
  3 *Fig (lutte)* fight; **c. contre la mort** fight against death; **le c. contre l'inflation** the battle *or* fight against inflation; **c'est un c. quotidien** it's a daily struggle; **même c.!** we're fighting for the same thing!; **continuons le c.!** the fight goes on!

combatif, -ive [kɔ̃batif, -iv] ADJ combative, pugnacious; **esprit c.** fighting spirit; **il n'a rien de c.** he's no fighter
  N fighter, battler

combativité [kɔ̃bativite] NF combativeness, pugnacity

combattant [kɔ̃batɑ̃] ADJ fighting, combatant; *Mil* **unité combattante** combatant *or* fighting unit
  NM **1** *(soldat)* combatant, fighter; **anciens combattants** ex-servicemen, *Am* veterans **2** *(dans une dispute)* fighter, brawler **3** *(oiseau)* ruff **4** *Mktg* **c. de front** front-line person

combattre [kɔ̃batr] *(conj like* **battre***)* VT *(ennemi)* to fight (against); *(maladie, théorie)* to fight; *(inflation etc)* to combat, to fight
  VI to fight; **c. pour/contre qn/qch** to fight for/against sb/sth

combe [kɔ̃b] NF *Géog* coomb, anticlinal valley

COMBIEN [kɔ̃bjɛ̃] ADV *(conj when introducing a clause)* **1** *(comme)* how (much); **si tu savais c. je t'aime!** if you knew how (much) I love you!; **j'ai pu constater c. tu avais changé** I could see how much you'd changed; **c. crédules sont tous ces hommes!** how gullible all these men are!
  2 *(en nombre)* how many; **c. de** how many; **c. de fois?** how many times?, how often?; **c. sont-ils?** how many (of them) are there?; **je ne sais pas c. il y en a** I don't know how many (of them) there are; **c'est à c. de kilomètres d'ici?** how many kilometres away is it? how far (away) is it?; **et c. de gens furent tués dans cette guerre!** what a lot of people were killed in that war!
  3 *(en quantité)* how much; **c. de** how much; **c. vous dois-je?** how much do I owe you?; **tu veux c.?** *(d'argent)* how much do you want?; *Fam* **ça fait c.?, c'est c.?** how much (is that)?, how much does that come to?; **depuis c. de temps est-il ici?** how long has he been here?; **il y en a pour c. de temps?** how long will it take?; **tu en as pour c. de temps?** how long will it take you?, how long will you be?; **c. de**

temps vous a-t-il fallu pour venir? how long did it take you to come?; **c'est arrivé il y a je ne sais c. de temps** it happened such a long time ago; **c. y a-t-il d'ici à Londres?** how far is it (from here) to London?; **à c. sommes-nous de Paris?** how far are we from Paris?; **c. pèse-t-elle?** how much does she weigh?; **c. mesure-t-il?** how tall is he?; **elle est enceinte – de c.?** she's pregnant – how far gone is she orhow many months?; **il a fait c. au saut à la perche?** how high did he jump in the pole vault?, what was his height in the pole vault?
NM INV *Fam* **le c. sommes-nous?, on est le c. aujourd'hui?** what's the date (today)?, what's today's date?; **il y a un car tous les c.?** how often is there a bus?; **tu chausses du c.?** what's your shoe size?, what shoe size are you?, what shoe size do you take?

combientième [kɔ̃bjɛ̃tjɛm] *Fam***ADJ tu as été reçu c. à l'examen?** where did you come in the exam?; **tu es c. dans la liste?** where are you on the list?, what position are you in the list?; **c'est la c. fois que tu viens?** how often have you been now?
N elle est arrivée la c.? where did she come in?; **tu veux le c.?** which of them do you want?

combinaison [kɔ̃binɛzɔ̃] **NF 1** *(de lettres, d'idées etc)*, *Math, Chimie* combination; *(de coffre-fort, cadenas)* combination; **c. financière** combine; **la c. gagnante** *(au tiercé)* the winning combination (of numbers); **une heureuse c. de couleurs** a pleasing combination of colours orcolour scheme; *Ordinat* **c. de touches** key combination **2** *(solution)* scheme, plan **3** *(vêtement) (tenue de travail)* boiler suit; *Aviat* flying suit; *(de femme)* slip; **c. de plongée** ou **de planche à voile** wet suit

combinard, -arde [kɔ̃binar, -ard] *Fam* **ADJ** scheming, devious; **il est c.** he's a real schemer
N schemer

combinateur [kɔ̃binatœr] **NM** *Élec* controller, multiple-contact ouselector switch; *Rail* switchgroup

combinatoire [kɔ̃binatwar] **ADJ** combinative; *Math* combinatorial

combine [kɔ̃bin] **NF** *Fam* scheme, trick; **il a une c. pour entrer sans payer** he knows a way of getting in without paying; **il a trouvé la c. pour se faire embaucher** he's found a way of getting taken on; **il faut le mettre dans la c.** we'll have to let orbring him in on it

combiné [kɔ̃bine] **ADJ** *(action etc)* combined, joint
NM 1 *Chimie* compound **2 c. (téléphonique)** receiver, handset **3** *(hi-fi)* radiogram; *Radio etc* **c. micro-casque** headset **4** *Ski* combined downhill and slalom competition **5** *Vieilli (sous-vêtement)* corselet

combiner [kɔ̃bine] **VT 1** *(forces, efforts etc)* to combine, to unite; *(nombres, idées etc)*, *Chimie* to combine **2** *Fam (plan)* to devise, to think up, to concoct; **qu'est-ce que tu as combiné?** what have you come up with?; **elle combine un sale coup** she's plotting something nasty, she's planning a dirty trick
VPR se combiner to combine, to go together **(à, avec** with)

comble [kɔ̃bl] **NM 1** *(maximum) (du bonheur, de l'insolence)* height; *(du désespoir)* depth; *(de la gloire etc)* height, peak, summit; **le c. du ridicule serait de …** it would be the height of absurdity to …; **pour c. de malheur** to cap or crown it all; **ça, c'est le ou un c.!** that's the limit or the last straw!; **elle était au c. de la joie** she was overjoyed, she was beside herself with joy **2** *Archit (en bois)* roof timbers; *(en métal)* roof structure; **c. à deux pans** span roof; **c. brisé** curb roof; **loger sous les combles** to live in an/the attic; **combles aménageables** attic suitable for conversion;

Fig **de fond en c.** from top to bottom; **modifier une organisation de fond en c.** to effect a major shake-up of an organization, to make sweeping changes in an organization
ADJ *(train, autobus, pièce etc)* (jam-)packed; *(mesure)* piled high; *Théâtre* **on a fait salle c.** we had a full or capacity house; *Fig* **la mesure est c.** enough is enough, that's the limit

comblé [kɔ̃ble] **ADJ** *(personne)* happy, contented, satisfied; **il est c.** he has everything he could wish for

combler [kɔ̃ble] **VT 1** *(puits, fossé, trou etc)* to fill in, to fill (up); *(une perte)* to make up, to make good; *(découvert)* to pay off; **c. une lacune** to fill a gap; **c. un besoin** to satisfy a need; **c. un retard** to make up for lost time **2** *(satisfaire) (personne)* to satisfy; **c. les vœux de qn** to fulfil orsatisfy sb's desires; **vous me comblez** you are too kind, I'm overwhelmed; **c. qn de cadeaux** to shower sb with gifts; **elle a été comblée par la nature** she has been blessed by nature

comburant [kɔ̃byrɑ̃] *Chimie etc* **ADJ** combustive
NM combustive agent; *Astronaut* oxidant

combustibilité [kɔ̃bystibilite] **NF** combustibility

combustible [kɔ̃bystibl] **ADJ** combustible; **assemblage d'éléments combustibles** fuel assembly
NM fuel; *(de fusée)* propellant, fuel; **c. nucléaire** nuclear fuel; **c. liquide** liquid fuel

combustion [kɔ̃bystjɔ̃] **NF** combustion; **poêle à c. lente** slow-combustion stove; **c. vive** external combustion; **moteur à c. interne** internal combustion engine; **c. détonante** detonation, combustion knock

Côme [kom] **NF** Como; **le lac de C.** Lake Como

come-back [kɔmbak] **NM INV** *(d'une vedette)* come-back; **faire un c.** to make a come-back

comédie [kɔmedi] **NF 1** *Théâtre (pièce comique, genre)* comedy; **la c. et la tragédie** comedy and tragedy; **jouer la c.** to act; *Fig* to put on an act; **allons! pas de c.!** come on, stop acting!; **c'est une vraie c. quand il faut aller à l'école** it's a real fuss orpalaver when it's time to go to school; **c'est toujours la même c.** it's the same old thing or story every time **2** *Arch (pièce de théâtre)* play
▸▸c. de caractères character comedy; **c. dramatique** drama; **c. de mœurs** comedy of manners; **c. musicale** musical; **c. de situation** situation comedy

comédien, -ienne [kɔmedjɛ̃, -jɛn] **N** *(acteur)* actor, factress; *(acteur comique)* comic actor, f comedienne; *Fig* show-off; **comédiens ambulants** strolling players; *Fig* **c'est une comédienne** she is always putting on an act
ADJ il est très c. he's very theatrical oraffected; **être plus c. que tragédien** to be more of a comic than a tragic actor

Il faut noter que le nom anglais **comedian** est un faux ami. Il signifie **comique**.

comédon [kɔmedɔ̃] **NM** blackhead

comestible [kɔmɛstibl] **ADJ** edible; **denrées comestibles** food, foodstuffs, *Fml* comestibles
NMPL comestibles food, foodstuffs, *Fml* comestibles

comète [kɔmɛt] **NF 1** *Astron* comet; *(feu d'artifice)* **l'année de la C.** the year of the comet *(1811, when Halley's Comet was seen for the first time)*; *Fig* **tirer** ou **faire des plans sur la c.** to build castles in Spain, to indulge in pipe-dreams **2** *(tranchefile)* headband

comice [kɔmis] **NM 1 c. agricole** agricultural association; **comices agricoles** *(foire)* agricultural show **2** *Hist* **comices** electoral meeting

comics [kɔmiks] **NMPL** comic strips, cartoon strips, *surtout Am Fam* funnies

comique [kɔmik] **ADJ 1** *Théâtre (acteur, auteur, rôle etc)* comic; **le genre c.** comedy **2** *(amusant) (histoire, visage etc)* comical, funny
NM 1 *(genre)* comedy; *(acteur)* comic actor; *(auteur)* comic author, writer of comedy; *(boute-en-train)* comic, comedian; **c. de répétition** comedy based on repetition; **c. de situation** situation comedy; **c. troupier** *(genre)* coarse or vulgar comedy **2 le c. de l'histoire, c'est que …** the funny part or the joke is that …

Attention: ne pas confondre **comic** et **comical** lorsqu'on traduit l'adjectif **comique**. Le terme **comic** se rapporte au genre comique, alors que **comical** signifie **amusant**. En outre, l'adjectif **comic** ne s'utilise jamais comme attribut.

comiquement [kɔmikmɑ̃] **ADV** comically

comité [kɔmite] **NM** VOIR GRAMMAIRE A11 committee; **faire partie d'un c.** to sit on a committee; **cette décision sera prise en petit c.** the decision will be made by a select group; **ils se sont mariés en petit c.** they had a quiet wedding; **pour leur anniversaire, ils seront en petit c.** they'll celebrate their anniversary with just a few friends (and relations); **un dîner en petit c.** a small dinner party
▸▸c. consultatif advisory committee or board; **c. de direction** executive ormanagement committee; **c. d'enquête** board of enquiry; **c. d'entreprise** works council or committee; **C. européen de normalisation** European Standards Commission; **c. d'hygiène et de sécurité** health and safety committee; **C. international olympique** International Olympic Committee; **c. de lecture** reading or selection committee; **c. secret** secret session; *Mktg* **c. synectique** idea committee; **c. d'usagers** users' committee

commandant, -ante [kɔmɑ̃dɑ̃, -ɑ̃t] **NM 1** *(officier)* *(d'unité etc)* commander, commanding officer; *(de camp, base etc)* commandant; *Naut (de bateau)* captain *(whatever his rank)*; **c. en chef** commander-in-chief; *Naut* executive officer, first lieutenant; *Aviat* **c. de bord** captain **2** *(rang)*, *Mil* major; *Mil, Aviat* squadron leader, *Am* major; **c. en chef des forces aériennes** ≃ Marshal of the Royal Air Force, *Am* ≃ General of the Air Force

NF commandante commanding officer's wife

commande [kɔmɑ̃d] **NF 1** *Com* order; **faire ou passer une c.** to put in *or* place an order; **livrer une c.** to deliver an order; **fait sur c.** made to order; **ouvrage écrit sur la c. de l'éditeur** work commissioned by the publisher; **payable à la c.** payment with order, cash with order; **c. export** export order; **c. ferme** firm order; **c. renouvelée** repeat order; **c. téléphonique, c. par téléphone** telephone order; *Fig* **sourire de c.** forced smile; **on ne peut pas rire sur c.** you can't laugh to order **2** *Tech (action)* control, operation; *(dispositif)* control; *(mécanisme)* drive, driving (gear); **c. à distance** remote control; **c. manuelle/à pied** hand *or* manual/foot control; **c'est à c. manuelle** it has hand *or* manual controls, it is manually controlled; **levier de c.** control lever; *Aviat* control column; **prendre les commandes** *(d'un avion etc)* to take over the controls; *(d'une société etc)* to take over, to take control; **avion à double c.** dual-control plane; *Élec* **machine à c. électrique** electrically driven machine; *Aut* **c. d'allumage** ignition trigger; *Aut* **c. de démarreur** starter switch; *Aut* **c. de starter** choke control; *Aut* **c. de vitesse de croisière** cruise control; **c. par poignée** *(d'une moto etc)* twist grip; **c. tactile** *(des vitres d'une voiture etc)* one-touch operation; *Aut* **c. électronique du moteur** engine management system; *Aut* **commandes de conduite** driving controls **3** *Ordinat* command; **c. d'annulation** undo command; **c. à bascule** toggle switch; **c. binaire** bit command; **c. de copie** copy command; **c. DOS** DOS command; **c. écran précédent** screen up command; **c. écran suivant** screen down command; **c. d'effacement** delete command; **c. erronée** bad command; **c. de formatage** formatting command; **c. imbriquée** embedded command; **c. d'insertion** insert command; **c. numérique** digital control; **à c. numérique** digitally controlled *or* operated; **c. de recherche** search *or* find command; **c. de recherche et remplacement** search and replace command, find and replace command; **c. de sauvegarde** save command; **c. de soulignage** underline command; **c. du système d'exploitation** operating system command; **à c. vocale** voice-activated

commandement [kɔmɑ̃dmɑ̃] **NM 1** *(ordre)* command, order; *Jur* summons to pay before execution; **dès que je vous en donnerai le c., à mon c.** when I give the command *or* order, on my command; *Rel* **les Dix Commandements** the Ten Commandments **2** *(pouvoir)* command; **avoir/prendre le c.** to be in/take command; **avoir le c. sur ...** to be in command of ..., to have command over ...; *Mil, Naut* **c. en chef** command-in-chief; **c. suprême, haut c.** high command

commander [kɔmɑ̃de] **VT 1** *(diriger)* to command, to be in command of; *(ordonner)* to command, to order; **il commande deux cents hommes** he has two hundred men under his command; **il n'aime pas qu'on le commande** he doesn't like being ordered about; *Fam* **sans vouloir vous c., est-ce que vous pourriez fermer la fenêtre?** I don't want to give orders, but could you close the window? **2** *(marchandises, dîner etc)* to order; *(peinture, ouvrage)* to commission; **c. qch à qn** to order/commission sth from sb; **c. qch par correspondance** to order sth by mail *or Br*

through the post, to mail-order sth; **c. qch par téléphone** to order sth by phone *or* over the phone **3** *(susciter)* to command; **c. le respect/l'attention** to command respect/attention **4** *(dominer) (vallée etc)* to dominate, to command **5** *(maîtriser) (sentiment, réaction etc)* to control **6** *Tech (mouvement, valve etc)* to control; *(machine, arbre etc)* to drive **7** *Ordinat* to drive; **commandé par menu** menu-driven; **commandé à la voix** voice-activated

VI je lui ai commandé de se taire I told *or* ordered him to be quiet; **qui est-ce qui commande ici?** who's in charge here?; **avez-vous déjà commandé?** *(au restaurant)* have you ordered yet?

VPR se commander 1 ces choses-là ne se commandent pas *(sont incontrôlables)* these things are beyond our control; **il faut apprendre à vous c.** you must learn to control yourself **2 les pièces de cet appartement se commandent** the rooms of this flat connect up *or* communicate with each other

commanderie [kɔmɑ̃dri] **NF** *(résidence)* commander's residence

commandeur [kɔmɑ̃dœr] **NM** commander

commanditaire [kɔmɑ̃ditɛr] **ADJ, NM** *Com* **(associé) c.** sleeping *or Am* silent partner; **nous ne savons pas qui sont les commanditaires de l'attentat** we don't know who is behind the attack

commandite [kɔmɑ̃dit] **NF** *Com* **1 (société en) c.** mixed liability company, limited partnership **2** *(fonds)* interest of *or* capital invested by sleeping partner(s)

commandité [kɔmɑ̃dite] **ADJ, NM** *Com* **(associé) c.** active partner, general partner

commanditer [kɔmɑ̃dite] **VT** to finance; *Mktg (tournoi, spectacle)* to sponsor; *(meurtre, attentat etc)* to be behind

commando [kɔmɑ̃do] **NM** *Mil* commando (unit) [VOIR GRAMMAIRE A12]

COMME [kɔm]

[ADV] as **1, 7, 8** ▪ like **1, 6** ▪ alike **1** ▪ as if *(comme si)* **2** ▪ like that *(comme ça)* **4** ▪ such as **6** ▪ in the way of **8** ▪ how *(interjection)* **9**
[CONJ] as **1, 2** ▪ since **1**

ADV 1 *(comparaison)* as; *(de la même manière)* like; **faites c. moi** do as I do; **se conduire c. un fou** to behave like a madman; **il n'est pas c. les autres** he isn't like the others; **tous furent appelés à participer à l'effort de guerre, les femmes c. les hommes** they were all called upon to join in the war effort, men and women alike; **sortir tous les jours, été c. hiver** to go out every day, summer and winter alike; **tout le monde fera la vaisselle, toi c. les autres** everyone will do the washing-up, and that includes *or* goes for you as well as the others; **tout c. un autre** (just) like anyone else; **nous étions c. un seul homme** we were as one man; **c. qui dirait** as one might say; **c. dit l'autre** as they say; **rusé c. un (vieux) renard** (as) sly *or* cunning as a fox; **doux c. un agneau** (as) gentle as a lamb; **haut c. trois pommes** knee-high to a grasshopper; **blanc c. neige** snow-white, white as snow; *Fam* **c. par hasard** as if by chance; **c. prévu** as planned; **il a été puni c. de juste** he's got his just deserts, he's been punished as he deserved; **quelque chose c. deux cents personnes** something like two hundred people; **A c. abricot** A as in apricot; *(en apprenant l'alphabet)* A is for apricot

2 c. (si) (**si** *is expressed only before a finite verb*) as if, as though; **il travaille c. s'il avait vingt ans** he works as if *or* as though he were twenty, he works like a twenty-year-old; **ils faisaient c. si rien ne s'était passé** they acted as if *or* as though nothing had happened; **si de rien n'était** as if *or* as though nothing had happened; **c. si je ne le savais pas!** as if I didn't know!; **tu n'es pas content, mais tu n'as qu'à faire c. si** you're not happy, but you can act as if *or* as though you are; **il leva la main c. pour me frapper** he lifted his hand as if *or* as though to strike me; *Fam* **c'est tout c.** it comes *or* amounts to the same thing

3 c. quoi je ne m'étais pas trompé! which only goes to show I was right!; *Fam* **voici un certificat c. quoi j'ai été malade** here's a certificate to say that I've been ill

4 c. ça like that; *Fam* **c'est c. ça et c'est pas autrement** that's the way it is; **alors c. ça, on fait le mur?** so we're making a run for it, are we?; **(alors) c. ça, vous venez de Paris?** so you come from Paris?; **elle est toujours c. ça?** is she always like that?; **puisque c'est ça, je m'en vais** if that's the way it is *or* things are, I'm going; **elle était grande comment, ta truite? – c. ça!** how big was your trout? – this big!; *Fam* **il me fait c. ça ...** he says to me just like that ...; **comment ça va? – c. ci c. ça** how are you? – so-so

5 drôle c. tout as funny as anything, incredibly funny; **c'est mignon c. tout!** it's as cute as anything! it's so cute!; **c'est facile c. tout!** it's as easy as pie!, it's dead easy!

6 *(tel que)* such as, like; **les bois durs c. le chêne et le noyer** hard woods such as *or* like oak and walnut

7 *(immediately before finite verbs)* as; **faites c. il vous plaira** *ou* **vous voulez** do as you please; **insolent c. il est** insolent as he is; **belle c. elle est, elle n'aura pas de mal à trouver un mari** being as beautiful as she is, she won't have any trouble finding a husband; **c'est arrivé à peu près c. je l'avais prédit** it happened more or less as I predicted; **des montres c. on n'en fait plus maintenant** the kind of watches they don't make any more

8 *(en tant que)* in the way of; **qu'est-ce que vous avez c. légumes?** what have you got in the way of vegetables?, what (kinds of) vegetables do you have?; **avoir qn c. ami** to have sb as a friend; **je l'ai eue c. professeur** I had her as my *or* a teacher; **il a été vendu c. esclave** he was sold as a slave; **ce n'est pas mal c. film** it's not bad as films go

9 *int* how; **c. vous avez grandi!** how you've grown!; **c. elle est bête!** how stupid she is!; **je suis content de vous voir!** how glad I am to see you!, am I glad to see you!; **c. tu as de grandes dents!** what big teeth you have!; **c. de bien entendu, il ne m'a pas appelé** as I might have known, he didn't call me; **c. c'est curieux! j'aurais juré l'avoir laissé là!** how odd! I could have sworn I left it there!; *Fam* **c. tu y vas!** that's a bit much!

10 *Fam (comment)* how; **il y est arrivé Dieu sait c.** he managed it, God (only) knows how; **voilà c. elle est** that's just like her; **elle a fait les carreaux, faut voir c.!** you should see the way she's done the windows!

11 *Fam* **elle a eu c. une hésitation avant de répondre** she seemed to hesitate before answering; **il était c. pantelant** he seemed to be gasping for breath; **à mon avis, on a c. un problème** I think we've got a bit of a problem (here); **j'ai c. l'impression qu'on s'est trompé de route** I have a feeling we're on the wrong road; **il y a là c. un hic!** there seems to be a bit of a catch!; **j'étais c. hypnotisé** it was as if *or* as though I was hypnotized

CONJ [SEE GRAMMAR B58] **1** *(puisque)* as, since, seeing that; **c. vous êtes mon ami, je vous dirai tout** as *or* since *or* seeing that you're my friend, I'll tell you everything

2 *(alors que)* (just) as; **c. il allait frapper, on l'arrêta** (just) as he was about to strike, he was arrested

commémoratif, -ive [kɔmemɔratif, -iv] ADJ commemorative (**de** of); **service c.** memorial service; **monument c.** memorial

commémoration [kɔmemɔrasjɔ̃] NF commemoration; **en c. d'un événement/ d'une personne** in commemoration of an event/a person

commémorer [kɔmemɔre] VT to commemorate

commençant, -ante [kɔmɑ̃sɑ̃, -ɑ̃t] ADJ **une fièvre commençante** the beginnings of a fever; **se lever au jour c.** to get up at daybreak ▪ N beginner; **manuel pour grands commençants** handbook for complete beginners

commencement [kɔmɑ̃smɑ̃] NM beginning, start; **commencements** beginnings, initial stage(s); **au c.** at the beginning *or* start *or* outset; *Bible* **au c. était le verbe** in the beginning was the word; **du c. jusqu'à la fin** from beginning to end, from start to finish; **il faut un c. à tout** you've got to start somewhere; *Fam* **c'est le c. de la fin** it's the beginning of the end

COMMENCER [kɔmɑ̃se] (**je commençai(s), n. commençons**) VT **1** *(entreprendre)* to begin, to start (on), *Fml* to commence; **c. les hostilités** *ou* **la guerre** to commence hostilities, to start a war; **c. un traitement** to go on *or* start a course of treatment; **nous avons mal commencé l'année** we've made a bad start to the year; *Vieilli* **c. un élève en chimie** to give a pupil a grounding in chemistry
  2 *(être au début de)* to begin, to start (**par** with); **le mot qui commence la phrase** the word which starts the sentence
  3 *Typ* **c. en retrait** to indent
  VI to begin, to start, *Fml* to commence; **c. à** *ou* **de faire qch** to begin *or* start to do sth, to begin *or* start doing sth; **l'année commence le 1ᵉʳ janvier** the year begins *or* starts on 1 January; **il commence à pleuvoir** it's beginning *or* starting to rain; **la pluie vient de c.** it's just started raining; **c. par faire qch** to begin *or* start by doing sth; **commençons par votre frère/le commencement** let's start *or* begin with your brother/at the beginning; **pour c., je dois vous dire …** to begin with *or* to start with *or* first of all, I must tell you …; **par où c.?** *(il y a tellement de choses à dire)* where should *or* shall I begin?; **nous allions c. sans vous** we were going to start *or* begin without you; **à c. par …** beginning *or* starting with …; **je commence à en avoir assez!** I've had just about enough!; *Fam* **ça commence à bien faire** it's getting a bit too much, it's getting beyond a joke; *Iron* **ça commence bien!** that's a great start!; *Fam* **tu ne vas pas c.!, ne commence pas!** don't start!; *Enf* **c'est lui qui a commencé!** he started it!

commensal, -ale, -aux, -ales [kɔmɑ̃sal, -o] N **1** *(hôte)* table companion **2** *Biol* commensal

commensurable [kɔmɑ̃syrabl] ADJ commensurable (**avec** with, to)

comment [kɔmɑ̃] ADV **1** *interr* how; **c. allez-vous?** how are you?; **c. (dites-vous)?** I beg your pardon?, what did you say?; **c. faire?** what can *or* should I/we/*etc* do?, what's to be done?; **c. s'appelle-t-il?** what's his name?, what's he called?; **dit-on 'soleil' en japonais?** how do you say 'sun' in Japanese?; **c. est-il, ce garçon?** what's this young man like?, what sort of guy is he?; **c. peut-il me dire des choses pareilles?** how can he talk to me like that *or* say such things to me?; **c. se fait-il que vous soyez toujours en retard?** how *or* why is it that you're always late?

2 *(affirmation)* how, the way; **elle me dira c. faire** she'll tell me how (to do it); **il faut voir c. elle lui parle** you should hear the way *or* how she speaks to him; **faire qch n'importe c.** to do sth in a slapdash manner *or Fam* anyhow *or* any old how

3 *int* what!; **c.! vous n'êtes pas encore parti!** what! haven't you gone yet!; **mais c. donc!** why of course!, by all means!; *Fam* **ça vous a plu? – et c.!** did you like it? – and how! *or* you bet!

▪ NM INV **les pourquoi et les c.** the whys and wherefores

commentaire [kɔmɑ̃tɛr] NM **1** *(remarque)* comment, remark; **faire des commentaires** to make comments *or* remarks; **je te dispense de tes commentaires** I don't need *or* I can do without your comments; **un c. pertinent** a pertinent observation; *Fam* **cela se passe de c.** it speaks for itself, it's obvious; *Fam* **sans c.!, pas de c.!** no comment!; *Fam* **je ne veux pas de c.!** that's final!, don't argue!; *Péj* **les commentaires vont bon train** comment is rife **2** *Radio, TV* commentary; *(lecture d'un texte préparé)* narration; **c. sportif** sports commentary; **c. en direct** live commentary; **c. sur image** voice-over, voice-over narration; **c. en voix off** off-screen narration

▸▸ *Scol* **c. de texte** textual commentary

commentateur, -trice [kɔmɑ̃tatœr, -tris] N *Radio, TV* commentator; **c. sportif** sports commentator

▪ NM *Littér* commentator

commenter [kɔmɑ̃te] VT **1** *(expliquer)* *(texte)* to comment on; *Radio, TV* **c. une course** to do the commentary for *or* to give the commentary on a race; **c. l'actualité** *ou* **les événements** to comment on current events **2** *(donner son avis sur)* to comment on

commérage [kɔmeraʒ] NM *Fam* (piece of) gossip; **commérages** gossip, tittle-tattle

commerçant, -ante [kɔmɛrsɑ̃, -ɑ̃t] ADJ commercial; **quartier c.** shopping area; **rue très commerçante** busy shopping street; **un sourire c.** a PR-type smile; **il n'est pas très c.** he doesn't look after his customers very well ▪ N trader, merchant; *(qui tient un magasin)* shopkeeper; **c. en gros** wholesaler; **c. en détail** retailer; **commerçants** traders, tradespeople; **petits commerçants** small traders *or* shopkeepers

commerce [kɔmɛrs] NM **1 le c.** *(activité)* trade; *(secteur)* trade, commerce; *(affaires)* business, trade; **c. de demi-gros** cash and carry; **c. en** *ou* **de gros/détail** wholesale/retail trade; **le petit c.** shopkeepers, small traders; **c. équitable** fair trade; **c. éthique** ethical trading, ethical trade; **c. intérieur/ extérieur** home/foreign *or* overseas trade; **c. international** world trade, international trade; **il est dans le c.** he's in business; **ça se trouve dans le c.** you can buy it in the shops; **maison de c.** firm; **voyageur de c.** commercial traveller, sales rep(resentative); **école de c.** business school; **port de c.** commercial port; **faire du c.** to trade, to be in business; **faire du c. avec le Japon** to do business with Japan, to have business dealings with Japan; **faire le c. de qch** to trade in sth; **cela fait marcher le c.** it's good for business *or* trade; **hors c.** not for (general) sale; **c. des chevaux** horse dealing; **c. associé** voluntary group, association of distributors; **c. d'exportation/d'importation** export/import trade; **c. d'échange** countertrade; *Ordinat* **c. électronique** electronic commerce, e-commerce, e-business

2 *(magasin)* **(fonds de) c.** business; **commerces** high-street shops; **c. de proximité** local shop *or Am* store; **ouvrir un c.** to open a business

3 *Péj (trafic)* traffic, trade; **faire c. de son honneur/nom** to trade on one's honour/ name; **faire c. de son corps** to sell one's body **4** *Arch, Litt (relations)* intercourse, dealings; **avoir** *ou* **être en c. avec qn** to have dealings with sb; **être d'un c. agréable** to be easy to get on with *or* pleasant to deal with; **fuir le c. des hommes** to flee the company of men **5** *Suisse Fam (ensemble d'objets disparates, affaires)* **range ton c.!** tidy up your stuff *or* things!

commercer [kɔmɛrse] VI (**je commerçai(s); n. commerçons**) to trade, to deal (**avec** with)

commercial, -iale, -iaux, -iales [kɔmɛrsjal, -jo] ADJ *(rapports, pratiques etc)* business, commercial; *(embargo, tribunal)* trade; *(droit)* commercial; *(délégué, direction, service)* sales; *Péj* **film c.** commercial film; **suivre une formation commerciale** to train in business studies

▪ NF **commerciale** *(voiture)* estate car, *Am* station wagon; *(camionnette)* small van ▪ N salesman, representative; **c'est un c.** he's in sales

commercialement [kɔmɛrsjalmɑ̃] ADV commercially

commercialisable [kɔmɛrsjalizabl] ADJ marketable

commercialisation [kɔmɛrsjalizasjɔ̃] NF marketing

commercialiser [kɔmɛrsjalize] VT *(produit)* to market; *(art)* to commercialize; *Fin (effet)* to negotiate

commère [kɔmɛr] NF gossip

commettant [kɔmɛtɑ̃] NM **1** *Com, Jur* principal **2** *Pol* **commettants** constituents

commettre [kɔmɛtr] *(conj like* **mettre***)* VT **1** *(accomplir)* *(crime, péché, injustice)* to commit; **c. une erreur** to make a mistake; *Hum* **il a déjà commis deux pièces de théâtre** he's already to blame for *or* he's already perpetrated two plays **2** *Jur* **c. qn à qch** to appoint sb to sth, to put sb in charge of sth; **c. un avocat d'office à qn** to assign a lawyer to sb **3** *Arch (compromettre)* to expose; **c. sa réputation** to risk one's reputation **4** *Arch (confier)* **c. qch à qn** to commit *or* entrust sth to sb *or* to sb's keeping, to entrust sb with sth

▪ VPR **se commettre** *Litt* to compromise oneself; **se c. avec qn** to compromise oneself by associating with sb

comminatoire [kɔminatwar] ADJ **1** *(lettre)* threatening **2** *Jur (décret etc)* comminatory

commis [kɔmi] NM **1** *(employé)* clerk; *(dans un magasin)* (shop) assistant; *(à la Bourse)* floor trader; *Culin* **c. chef** commis waiter; **c. de banque** bank clerk; **c. aux comptes** government auditor; **c. de cuisine** commis chef; **c. de rang** trainee chef de rang; **c. de salle** waiter; **c. principal** senior clerk; **c. aux écritures** book-keeper; **les grands c.** the senior civil servants **2** *Arch* **c. voyageur** commercial traveller

commisération [kɔmizerasjɔ̃] NF commiseration; **éprouver/avoir de la c.** to feel/ have sympathy; **témoigner de la c. à qn** to show sb sympathy

commis-greffier, *pl* **commis-greffiers** NM assistant to the clerk of court

commissaire [kɔmisɛr] N **1** *Sport* steward; *Sport* **c. des courses** race steward; **c. (de police)** ≃ (police) superintendent, *Am* ≃ (police) captain; **c. principal** ≃ chief superintendent, *Am* ≃ chief of police; *Naut* **c. de la Marine** = supply officer; *Naut* **c. du bord** purser; *Fin* **c. aux comptes** government auditor; **c. d'avaries** average adjuster; *Can* **c. d'école** school commissioner **2** *(membre d'une commission)* commissioner, commission member; *UE* Commissioner, member of the Commission; **c. près du Conseil d'État**

government representative on the Council of State; **c. du gouvernement** government representative; **c. parlementaire** parliamentary commissioner

commissaire-priseur, *pl* **commissaires-priseurs** NM auctioneer

commissariat [kɔmisarja] NM **1 c. (de police)** police station **2** *(fonction)* commissionership; **c. aux comptes** auditorship; *Naut* **c. du bord** pursership **3 c. de la marine** *ou* **maritime** = supply branch **4 C. à l'énergie atomique** = French atomic energy commission

commission [kɔmisjɔ̃] NF **1** *(course)* purchase; **il faut que j'aille faire les commissions** I have to go shopping
  2 *(comité)* commission, committee; *Parl* **renvoi d'un texte en c.** referral of a bill to a committee
  3 *(pourcentage)*, *Com* commission; *Fin* brokerage; **c. de deux pour cent** commission of two per cent; **3% de c.** 3% commission; **être payé à la c.** to be paid on a commission basis; *Com* **maison de c.** firm of commission agents, commission agency; **vente à c.** sale on commission
  4 *(charge)* commission; **avoir la c. de faire qch** to be commissioned *or* empowered to do sth
  5 *(service)* errand; **faire une c.** to run an errand; **on ne m'a pas fait la c.** I wasn't given the message
  6 *Enf* **la petite/grosse c.** a number one/two ▸▸ **c. d'acceptation** acceptance fee; **c. d'affacturage** factoring charges; **c. d'arbitrage** arbitration committee *or* board; **c. d'arrangement** over-riding commission; **c. bancaire** bank commission *or* charge *or* fee; **c. de change** exchange commission; *Banque* **c. de compte** account fee; **c. de confirmation** confirmation fee *or* commission; *(pour crédit)* facility fee; **c. consultative** advisory committee; **c. d'encaissement** collection charge *or* fee; **c. d'endos** endorsement fee; **c. d'engagement** commitment fee; **c. d'enquête** board *or* committee of inquiry; **C. européenne** European Commission; **c. de garantie** guarantee commission; **c. de normalisation** standards commission; **C. des opérations de Bourse** = Stock Exchange watchdog, *Am* ≃ Securities and Exchange Commission; **c. de paiement** collection charge, collection fee; **c. paritaire** joint commission *(with both sides equally represented)*; **c. parlementaire** parliamentary commission; **c. permanente** standing committee; **c. de rachat** redemption fee; **c. de souscription** front load; **c. de tenue de compte** account handling fee; **c. de vente** sales commission

commissionnaire [kɔmisjɔnɛr] NM **1** *(messager)* messenger; *(à l'hôtel, au théâtre)* commissionaire **2** *Com* (commission) agent, broker; **c. exportateur/importateur** export/import agent; **c. de transport** *ou* **de roulage** forwarding agent, carrier; **c. en banque** outside broker; **c. en douane** customs agent *or* broker; **c. agréé en douane** authorized customs broker; **c. en gros** factor; **c. de transport** shipping agent; **c. ducroire** del credere agent; **c. à l'export** export agent

commissionner [kɔmisjɔne] VT to commission

commissure [kɔmisyr] NF *(de la bouche)* corner; *Anat, Bot etc* commissure

commode [kɔmɔd] ADJ **1** *(pratique) (heure, lieu, outil etc)* convenient, suitable; *(outil etc)* handy; *(maison etc)* convenient, comfortable; **c'est très c. pour ranger ses affaires** it's very handy for storing things in **2** *(facile)* easy; **ce que vous me demandez là n'est pas c.** what you

are asking me isn't very easy **3** *(caractère etc)* easy-going, *Fml* accommodating; *Fam* **il n'est pas c.** he's a tough *or* an awkward customer
  NF chest of drawers, commode

commodément [kɔmɔdemɑ̃] ADV *(assis)* comfortably; *(situé)* conveniently

commodité [kɔmɔdite] NF **1** *(facilité)* convenience; **pour plus de c.** for greater convenience; **les commodités de la vie (moderne)** the comforts of (modern) life **2** **commodités** *(toilettes)* toilets, *Am* rest rooms

commodore [kɔmɔdɔr] NM *Mil* commodore

commotion [kɔmosjɔ̃] NF **1 c. politique** political upheaval; *Méd* **c. cérébrale** concussion **2** *(émotion)* shock

commotionner [kɔmosjɔne] VT **1** *Méd* to concuss; **il a été fortement commotionné** he was severely concussed, he had severe concussion **2** *(choquer)* to shake (up), to shock; **cette nouvelle m'a commotionné** this news has given me a shock *or* has shaken me

commuable [kɔmyabl] ADJ *Jur (peine)* commutable

commuer [kɔmye] VT *Jur (peine)* to commute (**en** to)

commun [kɔmœ̃] ADJ **1** *(non exclusif)* common (**à** to); *(travail)* joint; *(ami)* mutual; *Math* **dénominateur c.** common denominator; **jardin c. à deux maisons** garden shared by two houses; **salle commune** common room; *(d'hôpital)* ward; **parties communes** communal areas; **maison commune** town hall; **avoir des intérêts communs** to have interests in common, to have common interests; **faire cause commune avec qn** to make common cause *or* join forces with sb; **il n'y a rien de c. entre eux** they've (got) nothing in common; **c'est sans commune mesure** there's no possible comparison; **vie commune** communal life; *(de couple)* conjugal life; **la vie commune n'est pas facile** living together isn't easy; **rechercher le bien c.** to seek the common good; **d'un c. accord** with one accord; **en c.** in common; **travailler en c.** to work together; **vivre en c.** to live communally; **mettre l'argent/les ressources en c.** to pool money/resources; **on s'est mis en c. pour lui acheter un cadeau** we all clubbed together to buy him a present **2** *(courant)* *(coutume, opinion etc)* common, universal, general; *(événement etc)* common, usual, ordinary, everyday; **sens c.** common sense; *Gram* **nom c.** common noun VOIR GRAMMAIRE A9 ; **lieu c.** commonplace; **il est d'une force peu commune** he's unusually strong **3** *(vulgaire)* common, vulgar
  NM **1** *(de personnes etc)* common run, generality; **le c. des mortels** the ordinary *or* average man; **le c. des spectateurs n'a pas compris** the ordinary *or* average member of the audience didn't understand; **hors du c.** out of the ordinary **2 communs** outhouses, outbuildings

communal, -ale, -aux, -ales [kɔmynal, -o] ADJ **1** *(conjoint) (terrain, propriété)* common, communal **2** *(de la commune) (propriété etc) Br* ≃ council; **école communale** ≃ local primary school
  NMPL **communaux** common land
  NF **communale** ≃ local primary school

communard, -arde [kɔmynar, -ard] ADJ *Hist* of the Commune
  N **1** *Hist* Communard **2** *Péj (communiste)* commie, red

communautaire [kɔmynotɛr] ADJ communal; *Pol (aide, politique)* community; *(surtout UE)* Community; **centre c.** community centre

communautarisme [kɔmynotarism] NM =

emphasis on issues relating to minorities and ethnic communities within society

communauté [kɔmynote] NF **1** *(collectivité)* community; *Rel* community, order; **la c. internationale** the international community; **c. de travail** working community; **c. urbaine** urban community; **C. urbaine de Montréal** Montreal Urban Community; **c. de hippies** hippie commune; **vivre en c.** to live communally; **elle est partie vivre en c.** she's gone off to live in a commune **2** *(d'intérêts, d'idées etc)* similarity, *Fml* community; *Jur* **c. de biens** joint estate *(of husband and wife)*
  ▸▸ **C. économique européenne** European Economic Community

commune [kɔmyn] NF **1** *Admin* commune *(smallest territorial division in France)* **2** *Hist (ville autonome)* free town **3** *Pol* **la Chambre des communes, les Communes** the (House of) Commons **4** *Hist* **la C.** the Commune *(in 1789 and 1871)*

Commune
There are over 36,000 "communes" or administrative districts in France, some with fewer than 25 inhabitants. Each "commune" has an elected mayor and a town council.

---

communément [kɔmynemɑ̃] ADV commonly

communiant, -ante [kɔmynjɑ̃, -ɑ̃t] N *Rel* communicant; **premier c., première communiante** person taking his/her first communion

communicable [kɔmynikabl] ADJ *(impression, idée etc)* that can be communicated; *Jur (droit)* transferable; *(dossier etc)* that can be made available

communicant [kɔmynikɑ̃] ADJ *(chambres etc)* communicating, connecting

communicateur, -trice [kɔmynikatœr, -tris] ADJ *(fil etc)* connecting

communicatif, -ive [kɔmynikatif, -iv] ADJ **1** *(qui parle)* communicative, talkative; **peu c.** uncommunicative **2** *(rire etc)* infectious

communication [kɔmynikasjɔ̃] NF **1** communication; **avoir des problèmes de c.** to have problems *or* difficulties (in) communicating; **c. d'idées** interchange of ideas; **entrer** *ou* **se mettre en c. avec qn** to get in touch *or* in contact with sb; **mettre deux personnes en c.** to put two people in touch *or* in contact with each other; **je n'ai pas eu c. de ce message** the message wasn't passed on to me, I didn't get the message; **voies de c.** lines of communication, communication routes; **portes de c.** communicating doors; **toutes les communications sont coupées** all lines of communication are cut (off); **études de c.** media studies; **travailler dans la c.** to work in the media; *Ordinat* **progiciel de c.** communications *or Fam* comms package; *Mktg* **c. commerciale** marketing communications; **c. de données** data communications, datacomms; *Ordinat* **c. homme-machine** man-machine dialogue; **c. en ligne** on-line communication; **c. de masse** mass communication
  2 *Tél* **c. téléphonique** (telephone) call; **mettez-moi en c. avec M. Martin** put me through to Mr Martin; **je vous passe la c.** I'll put you through; **vous avez la c.** you're through; **la c. est mauvaise** the line is bad; **c. en PCV** reverse charge *or* transferred charge call, *surtout Am* collect call; **c. interurbaine** long-distance call; **c. locale** local call; **c. longue distance** long-distance call; **c. télématique** datacommunications, datacomms
  3 *Mktg (publicité)* promotion; **c. événementielle** event promotion; **c. institutionnelle** corporate promotion, corporate identity; **c.**

produit product promotion; **c. sur le lieu de vente** point-of-sale promotion
4 *(message)* communication, message; *(dans la presse)* statement; **transmettre une c. à qn** to pass on a message to sb; **le président a une importante c. à nous faire** the president has an important message for us *or* has something important to communicate to us; **faire une c. dans un colloque** to read a paper to a conference; *Jur* **donner c. des pièces** to communicate documents

communier [kɔmynje] vi *(impf, pr sub n.* **communiions**, *v.* **communiiez)** *Rel* to receive (Holy) Communion

communion [kɔmynjɔ̃] NF **1** *(communauté)* communion; **être en c. de sentiments avec qn** to be in sympathy with sb; **être en c. avec la nature** to commune with nature **2** *Rel* Communion; **première c., c. privée** first Communion; **faire sa première c.** to make one's first Communion; **c. solennelle** solemn Communion

communiqué [kɔmynike] NM communiqué, official statement; **c. de presse** press release, press hand-out; **c. de sécurité routière** traffic news

communiquer [kɔmynike] vt *(transmettre)* *(information, renseignements etc)* to communicate, to convey (**à qn** to sb); *(joie, peur etc)* to communicate (**à qn** to sb); *(maladie)* to pass on, to give (**à qn** to sb); **c. qch par écrit à qn** to communicate *or* convey sth in writing to sb; **c. ses impressions** to pass on *or* communicate one's impressions
vi **1** *(être en relation)* to communicate (**avec** with); **avoir du mal à c. avec qn** to find it hard *or* difficult to communicate with sb; **refus total de c.** total unwillingness to communicate **2** *(d'une pièce)* to communicate (**avec** with); **toutes les chambres communiquent** all the bedrooms communicate with one another; **porte qui communique au** *ou* **avec le jardin** door that leads into the garden; **canal qui fait c. deux rivières** canal that connects two rivers
vpr **se communiquer 1** *(se transmettre)* to spread; **l'incendie s'est communiqué aux maisons voisines** the fire has spread to the neighbouring houses **2** *Vieilli (être communicatif)* to be communicative

communisant, -ante [kɔmynizɑ̃, -ɑ̃t] ADJ *(personne, journal, parti etc)* with communist sympathies
N communist sympathizer, fellow traveller

communisme [kɔmynism] NM communism

communiste [kɔmynist] ADJ, N communist

commutable [kɔmytabl] ADJ *Tél* switchable

commutateur [kɔmytatœr] NM *Élec* **1** *(de dynamo etc)* commutator **2** *(bouton)* switch; **c. sélecteur** selector switch; **c. téléphonique** exchange; *Ordinat* **c. de données** data switch

commutatif, -ive [kɔmytatif, -iv] ADJ *Jur, Math* commutative

commutation [kɔmytasjɔ̃] NF **1** *Jur (de sentence)* commutation **2** *(changement)* substitution, *Fml* commutation; *(entre documents)* switching; *Gram* replacement, substitution; **le patron a décidé de la c. de deux employés** the boss decided to swap the duties of two employees **3** *Élec* commutation, change-over; *TV etc* **c. de l'image** switching **4** *Ordinat, Tél* switch-over, switching; **c. de bande/de circuits** tape/circuit switching; **c. de message/de paquets** message/packet switching

commutatrice [kɔmytatris] NF *Élec* rotary converter, transformer

commuté [kɔmyte] ADJ *(réseau)* switched

commuter¹ [kɔmyte] vt **1** *Jur (sentence)* to commute **2** *Élec (courant)* to commutate, to

switch over, to change over **3 c. les fonctions** to swap duties
vi *(entre documents, écrans)* to switch; **deux employés qui vont c.** two employees who are going to swap duties
vpr **se commuter** *Ordinat* to switch

commuter² [kɔmytœr] NM *Aviat* commuter plane

Comores [kɔmɔr] NF *Géog* **les îles C.** the Comoro Islands

comorien, -ienne [kɔmɔrjɛ̃, -jɛn] ADJ Comoran
N **C.** Comoran

compacité [kɔ̃pasite] NF *(de la terre etc)* compactness; *(d'un métal)* density; *(de la foule)* denseness

compact [kɔ̃pakt] ADJ **1** *(de petit format)* compact; **voiture compacte** small car, *Am* compact; **disque c.** compact disc **2** *(masse, formation etc)* compact, dense; *(foule)* dense; *(terre)* compact; *(métal)* dense; **majorité compacte** large *or* solid majority; **poudre compacte** pressed (face-)powder
NM compact disc; **disponible en c.** available on CD

Compact Disc® [kɔ̃paktdisk] NM compact disc

compacter [kɔ̃pakte] vt *(fichier, données)* to compress; *(base de données)* to pack

compacteur [kɔ̃paktœr] NM *Ordinat* **c. d'exécutables** execute file compressor; **c. de données** data compressor

compagne [kɔ̃paɲ] NF **1** *(camarade)* (female) companion; **mes compagnes de captivité** my fellow captives **2** *(concubine)* partner; *(épouse)* wife; *(d'un animal)* mate

compagnie [kɔ̃paɲi] NF **1** *(présence)* company, companionship; **n'avoir qu'un vieux chien pour toute c.** to have only an old dog for company; **tenir c. à qn** to keep sb company; **fausser c. à qn** to give sb the slip; **je vais vous fausser c.** this is where I leave you; **dame de c.** (lady's) companion; **être en c. d'amis proches** to be in the company of close friends, to be with close friends; **rechercher la c. de gens simples** to seek the company of simple people; **aller de c. avec ...** to go hand in hand with ...; **être de bonne/mauvaise c.** to be good/poor company; **être de c. agréable** to be pleasant company; **je l'ai trouvé en joyeuse/galante c.** I found him in cheerful company/in the company of a lady; **ils ont voyagé de c.** they travelled together
2 *(groupe)* company, party; **toute la c.** everybody, all of them/us
3 *Com, Théâtre etc* company; *Com* **la maison Thomas et C.** (the firm of) Thomas and Company; *Fam* **ces mecs, c'est arnaqueurs et c.!** those guys are just a bunch of crooks!
4 *Mil* company; **c. de débarquement** landing party
5 *(de perdrix)* covey
▸▸ **c. aérienne** airline; **c. aérienne nationale** flag *or* national airline; **c. d'assurances** insurance company; **c. d'aviation civile** civil airline; *Rel* **la C. de Jésus** the Society of Jesus; **c. maritime** shipping line; **c. mère** parent company; **c. de navigation** shipping company; **c. pétrolière** oil company; **compagnies républicaines de sécurité** riot police; **c. de transports** carrier; **c. de transports nationale** flag carrier

compagnon [kɔ̃paɲɔ̃] NM **1** *(camarade)* companion; *(d'ouvrier)* mate; **c. d'études** fellow student; **c. de voyage** travelling companion; **c'était mon c. de jeu** I used to play with him; *Pol* **c. de route** fellow traveller; **c. d'infortune/de misère** companion in misfortune/in suffering **2** *(ouvrier)* journeyman **3** *Fam (plante)* **c. blanc/rouge** white/red campion **4** *(concubin)* partner; *(époux)* husband

comparable [kɔ̃parabl] ADJ comparable (**à** *ou* **avec qn/qch** to *or* with sb/sth); **ce n'est pas c.** there's no comparison

comparablement [kɔ̃parabləmɑ̃] ADV comparatively

comparaison [kɔ̃parɛzɔ̃] NF **1** comparison; **c. des prix** price comparison; **faire la c. entre deux choses** to compare two things, to make a comparison between two things; **tu peux faire la c. toi-même** you can judge *or* see *or* make the comparison for yourself; **soutenir la c.** to bear *or* stand comparison; **il n'y a pas de c. possible** there's no possible comparison; **c'est sans c. avec ...** it can't be compared with ...; **il est sans c. le plus grand** he is by far *or* he is far and away the tallest; *Prov* **c. n'est pas raison** comparisons are odious; *Gram* **adverbe de c.** adverb of comparison, comparative adverb; **les degrés de c.** the degrees of comparison; **c. par paire** paired comparison
2 *(locutions)* **en c. de ...** compared with, in comparison with ...; **par c.** by comparison; **par c. avec** *ou* **à** compared with
3 *Littér* simile

comparaître [kɔ̃parɛtr] vi *(conj like* **paraître)** *Jur* **c. (en justice)** to appear (before a court); **c. en personne** to appear in person; **c. par avoué** to be represented by counsel; **c. comme témoin** to appear as a witness; **être appelé à c.** to be summoned to appear

comparant, -ante [kɔ̃parɑ̃, -ɑ̃t] *Jur* ADJ appearing in court
N person appearing in court

comparateur [kɔ̃paratœr] NM *Aut etc* dial gauge

comparatif, -ive [kɔ̃paratif, -iv] ADJ comparative; **publicité comparative** comparative advertising
NM *Gram* comparative; **adjectif au c.** comparative adjective; **c. d'infériorité** comparative of lesser degree **SEE GRAMMAR A24–7; B11; B13–14**

comparatiste [kɔ̃paratist] N *Ling* specialist in comparative linguistics; *Littér* specialist in comparative literature

comparativement [kɔ̃parativmɑ̃] ADV comparatively; **il fait bien plus beau aujourd'hui, c. à hier** it's much nicer today compared with *or* to yesterday

comparé [kɔ̃pare] ADJ *(anatomie, histoire, littérature etc)* comparative; **c. à** compared with *or* to

comparer [kɔ̃pare] vt to compare (**à** to; **avec** with); **il compare les étoiles filantes à des cheveux** he compares *or* likens shooting stars to strands of hair; **c. deux objets/textes** to compare two objects/texts; **tu peux c., ma robe est plus large** you can see the difference, my dress is wider
vpr **se comparer je ne peux pas me c. à toi** I can't compare myself with *or* to you; **Haendel ne peut pas se c. à Mozart** Handel can't be compared with *or* to Mozart; **ça ne se compare pas** there's no comparison

comparse [kɔ̃pars] N *Cin* extra; *Théâtre* walk-on, super, *Fml* supernumerary; *Fig Péj* associate; *Théâtre* **rôle de c.** walk-on part

compartiment [kɔ̃partimɑ̃] NM *(de wagon, boîte, tiroir etc)* compartment; *(d'échiquier, de damier)* square; *Rail* **c. de première classe** first-class compartment; **c. fumeurs** smoking compartment, smoker; **c. non-fumeurs** no-smoking compartment, non-smoker; **c. moteur** engine compartment; **c. à bagages** *(d'autocar)* luggage compartment

compartimentage [kɔ̃partimɑ̃taʒ] NM partitioning; *(d'une administration etc)* compartmentalization

compartimenter [kɔ̃partimɑ̃te] vt **1** *(diviser en espaces)* to partition, to divide into compartments **2** *(administration etc)* to compartmentalize

comparution [kɔ̃parysjɔ̃] NF *Jur (au tribunal)* appearance; **défaut de c.** failure to appear

compas [kɔ̃pa] NM **1** *Géom* (pair of) compasses; **c. à pointes sèches** dividers; **c. quart de cercle** wing compasses; *Tech etc* **c. d'épaisseur** callipers; *Fig Fam* **tout faire au c.** to do everything with precision; *Fig* **avoir le c. dans l'œil** to have an accurate eye **2** *Naut* **c. (de mer)** (mariner's) compass; **c. de route** steering compass; **c. gyroscopique** gyrocompass

compassé [kɔ̃pase] ADJ *(personne, manières, ton etc)* stiff, formal

compasser [kɔ̃pase] VT **1** *(distances sur la carte etc)* to measure with compasses; *Naut (carte)* to prick **2** *Litt (ses actes etc)* to control, to regulate

compassion [kɔ̃pasjɔ̃] NF compassion; **avec c.** compassionately

compatibilité [kɔ̃patibilite] NF compatibility

compatible [kɔ̃patibl] ADJ compatible (**avec** with); *Ordinat* **c. abc** abc-compatible; **ces deux applications ne sont pas compatibles** these two applications are incompatible *or* not compatible; **compatible vers le haut/vers le bas** upward/downward compatible; **compatible avec les versions antérieures** backward compatible; **compatible IBM** IBM-compatible; **compatible Mac** Mac-compatible

     NM *Ordinat* **c. (PC)** (PC) compatible

compatir [kɔ̃patir] VI to sympathize; **c. au chagrin de qn** to sympathize with *or* feel for sb in his/her grief

compatissant [kɔ̃patisɑ̃] ADJ compassionate, sympathetic

compatriote [kɔ̃patrijɔt] N compatriot, fellow countryman, *f* countrywoman

compensable [kɔ̃pɑ̃sabl] ADJ that can be compensated for; *(chèque)* clearable; *Fin* **c. à Paris** to be cleared at Paris

compensateur, -trice [kɔ̃pɑ̃satœr, -tris] ADJ *(ressort, aimant etc)* compensating; *Élec (courant)* equalizing; *(dynamo)* balancing; **indemnité compensatrice** compensatory payment, compensation; **pendule c.** compensation pendulum

     NM *(de boussole etc)* compensator, balancer; *Aviat* trimming tab, trimmer; *Aut* **c. de frein** brake compensator

compensation [kɔ̃pɑ̃sasjɔ̃] NF **1** *(de perte)* compensation; **en c. de mes pertes** to compensate for *or* as compensation for my losses; **en c., vous avez droit à deux jours de vacances** to compensate (for it) *or* to make up for it, you can have two days off; **il y a des compensations** there are compensations; *Jur* **c. des dépens** sharing of the costs; *Fin* **chambre de c.** clearing house **2** *Élec (de forces etc)* equalization, balancing; *(de son)* equalization; *Math* **loi de c.** law of large numbers **3** *Naut (de boussole)* adjustment **4** *(de chèque)* clearing; **caisse de c.** = equalization fund for payments such as child benefit, sickness benefit, pensions etc **5** *Psy* compensation

compensatoire [kɔ̃pɑ̃satwar] ADJ compensatory; **droits compensatoires** countervailing duties

compenser [kɔ̃pɑ̃se] VT **1** *(perte)* to compensate for, to make up for, to make good; *(défaut etc)* to compensate for, to make up for, to offset; *Jur etc (dettes)* to set off, to balance (out); *(chèque)* to clear; **talon** *ou* **semelle compensé(e)** built-up heel; **son efficacité compense son mauvais caractère** his efficiency compensates for *or* makes up

for *or* offsets his bad temper; *Jur* **c. les dépens** to divide the costs **2** *Naut (boussole)* to adjust

     VPR **se compenser** to make up for each other, to offset each other

compère [kɔ̃pɛr] NM **1** *(de prestidigitateur etc)* accomplice, associate **2** *Fam Vieilli (camarade)* comrade, crony; **un bon c.** a pleasant companion

compère-loriot, *pl* **compères-loriots** NM **1** *(oiseau)* golden oriole **2** *Méd (sur la paupière)* sty

compète [kɔ̃pɛt] NF *Fam (abrév* **compétition)** competition *(in sport)*; **faire de la c.** to enter competitions

compétence [kɔ̃petɑ̃s] NF **1** *(capacité)* competence, ability, skill (**pour faire qch** to do sth); **avoir toutes les compétences requises pour faire qch** to have all the necessary skills to do sth; **c'est en dehors de mes compétences** it's beyond my capabilities; **faire qch avec beaucoup de c.** to do sth very competently **2** *Jur (de cour de justice etc)* competence, jurisdiction, powers; **cela ne rentre pas dans** *ou* **cela n'est pas de sa c.** that does not come within his province, that is outside his scope; **sortir de sa c.** to exceed one's powers; **c. universelle** universal competence

compétent [kɔ̃petɑ̃] ADJ *Jur etc (tribunal, autorité etc)* competent; **c. en matière de finance** conversant with finance; **je ne suis pas c. en la matière** I am not well up in the subject; **il est très c.** he's very competent; *Com* **adressez-vous au service c.** apply to the appropriate *or* relevant department, apply to the department concerned

compétiteur, -trice [kɔ̃petitœr, -tris] N competitor

compétitif, -ive [kɔ̃petitif, -iv] ADJ *Com (prix etc)* competitive

compétition [kɔ̃petisjɔ̃] NF **1** *(rivalité)* competition, rivalry; **être en c. avec qn** to be in competition with sb, to compete with sb; **c. entre partis politiques** rivalry between political parties; **esprit de c.** competitive spirit **2** *Sport (épreuve)* competition, event; **c. sportive** sports competition, sporting event; **faire de la c.** to go in for competitive sport; **du ski de c.** competitive *or* competition skiing

compétitivité [kɔ̃petitivite] NF competitiveness

compilateur, -trice [kɔ̃pilatœr, -tris] NM *Ordinat* compiler; **c. croisé** cross-compiler

     N **1** *(auteur)* compiler **2** *Péj (plagiaire)* plagiarist

compilation [kɔ̃pilasjɔ̃] NF **1** *Ordinat* compilation **2** *(enregistrement)* compilation **3** *(de documents)* compiling, compilation **4** *Péj (plagiat)* plagiarism

compiler [kɔ̃pile] VT **1** *Ordinat* to compile **2** *(réunir)* to compile **3** *Péj (plagier)* to plagiarize

complainte [kɔ̃plɛ̃t] NF **1** *Arch (plainte)* plaint **2** *Littér, Mus* lament

complaire [kɔ̃plɛr] *(conj like* **plaire)** VI *Litt* **c. à qn** to please sb

     VPR **se complaire** to delight, to revel (**dans qch** in sth; **à faire qch** in doing sth); **elle se complaît dans le malheur** she wallows in her misery

complaisamment [kɔ̃plɛzamɑ̃] ADV **1** *(avec obligeance)* obligingly, kindly **2** *(avec vanité)* complacently, smugly

complaisance [kɔ̃plɛzɑ̃s] NF **1** *(bienveillance)* obligingness, kindness; **avec c.** to do sth out of kindness; **faire qch par c. pour qn** to do sth to oblige sb; **auriez-vous la c. de le faire?** would you be so good *or* so kind as to do it?, would you oblige me by do-

ing it?; **avoir des complaisances pour qn** to be indulgent towards sb; **sourire de c.** polite smile; **sourire d'un air de c.** to smile politely, to give a polite smile; *Com* **billet** *ou* **effet de c.** accommodation bill; **on a fini par lui délivrer un certificat de c.** he was finally issued with a medical certificate *(to which he was not entitled)* **2** *(auto-satisfaction)* complacency, smugness, self-satisfaction; **il s'écoute avec c.** he likes the sound of his own voice; **ton plein de c.** self-satisfied *or* smug tone

complaisant [kɔ̃plɛzɑ̃] ADJ **1** *(bienveillant)* obliging, accommodating, kind (**envers, pour** towards); **prêter une oreille complaisante à qn** to lend sb a sympathetic *or* willing ear **2** *(indulgent) (médecin)* indulgent; *(mari)* complaisant, indulgent **3** *(satisfait)* complacent, smug, self-satisfied

complément [kɔ̃plemɑ̃] NM *(reste)* rest, remainder; *Gram, Biol, Chimie, Math* complement; **il faudra racheter cinq livres de lecture pour faire le c.** we'll have to buy five more readers to make up the numbers; **si on manque de dessert, on fera le c. avec des yaourts** if we're short of desserts, we'll use yoghurts instead; **demander un c. d'information** to ask for more *or* additional information; *Gram* **c. circonstanciel de temps** adverbial phrase of time; *Gram* **c. (d'objet)** object; *Gram* **c. d'objet direct/indirect** direct/ indirect object SEE GRAMMAR A78–9; B52–3 ; *Admin* **c. (de) retraite** supplementary pension

complémentaire [kɔ̃plemɑ̃tɛr] ADJ *(angle, couleur etc)* complementary; **pour tout renseignement c., s'adresser à …** for further *or* additional information, apply to …

complémentarité [kɔ̃plemɑ̃tarite] NF complementarity

COMPLET, -ÈTE [kɔ̃plɛ, -ɛt] ADJ **1** *(entier, intégral) (tenue, service etc)* complete, whole, entire; **rapport très c.** very full *or* comprehensive report; **se faire une idée complète de la situation** to get an overall picture *or* a complete picture *or* an overview of the situation; **deux jours complets** two full *or* whole days; **examen c.** full *or* thorough examination; **voyager dans le plus c. anonymat** to travel completely incognito; **votre devoir est loin d'être c.** your homework is a long way *or* far from being complete; **athlète c.** all-round athlete; **un c. abruti** a complete *or* a total *or* an absolute moron; **échec c.** complete *or* total *or* utter failure; **collection complète d'un auteur** complete works of an author, complete set of an author's works; **formation très complète** thorough training; *Fam* **c'est c.!** that's the last straw!, that's the limit!; **pain c.** wholemeal bread; **pâtes complètes** wholemeal pasta; **riz c.** brown rice **2** *(rempli) (bus), Théâtre (salle etc)* full; **'c.'** 'full (up)'; *(signe devant pension, hôtel etc)* 'no vacancies'

     NM **c. (.-veston)** suit

     2 nous étions au grand c. we turned out in full force; **j'ai invité la famille au c. pour Noël** I've invited the whole family for Christmas; **j'attends que l'assistance soit au c. pour commencer** I'm waiting for everyone to arrive before I begin

complètement [kɔ̃plɛtmɑ̃] ADV completely, totally, wholly; *(ruiné, perdu, idiot)* utterly, completely, totally; **c. nu** stark naked, completely naked; **finir c. un pot de crème** to finish off *or* polish off a pot of cream; **je n'ai pas pu le lire c.** I couldn't read all of it *or* the whole thing

compléter [kɔ̃plete] (**je complète, je complétons; je compléterai**) VT *(collection, garde-robe, formation etc)* to complete; *(formulaire)* to complete, to fill in *or* out; **c. une somme** to make up a sum (of money); **c. une**

gamme de produits to add to a range of products; *Fig* **pour c. le tableau ...** to cap it all ...

VPR se compléter to complement one another; **ils se complètent bien l'un l'autre** they're well-matched, they complement each other well

complétif, -ive [kɔ̃pletif, -iv] ADJ, NF *Gram* **(proposition) complétive** noun clause

complexe [kɔ̃plɛks] ADJ *(caractère, question etc)* complex, complicated; *Gram* **sujet c.** compound subject; *Math* **nombre c.** complex number

NM **1** *Constr, Écon* complex; **vivre dans un grand c.** to live in a complex; **le c. industriel de la vallée du Rhône** the Rhone valley industrial complex; **c. commercial/sportif** shopping/sports centre *or* complex; **c. de loisirs** leisure complex; **c. hôtelier** hotel complex; **c. touristique** holiday *or* tourism complex **2** *Psy* complex; **c. d'infériorité** inferiority complex; **c. d'Œdipe** Oedipus complex; *Fam* **ça me donne des complexes** it gives me a complex, it gives me hang-ups; *Fam* **avoir des complexes** to have a complex *or* a hang-up, to be hung up (**à cause de** about); *Fam* **être sans c.** to have no hang-ups; *Fam* **il est bourré de complexes** he's really hung up, he's full of complexes

complexé [kɔ̃plɛkse] ADJ *Fam* hung up, full of complexes (**par** about)

complexer [kɔ̃plɛkse] VT *Fam* **c. qn** to give sb a complex *or* a hang-up

complexifier [kɔ̃plɛksifje] VT to make (more) complex

VPR se complexifier to become (more) complex

complexion [kɔ̃plɛksjɔ̃] NF constitution; *Vieilli (caractère)* temperament, disposition; **je suis gros de c.** I'm naturally fat, I'm predisposed to be fat

complexité [kɔ̃plɛksite] NF complexity

complication [kɔ̃plikasjɔ̃] NF **1** *(ennui)* complication; **faire des complications** to complicate the issue, to create *or* cause complications *or* problems **2** *(de situation etc)* complexity, intricacy **3** *Méd* **complications** complications

complice [kɔ̃plis] ADJ **être c. de qch** to be party to sth; **des regards complices** knowing glances

N accomplice

complicité [kɔ̃plisite] NF complicity; *Jur* aiding and abetting; *Jur* **agir en c. avec qn** to act in collusion *or* complicity with sb; **accusé de c. de meurtre** accused of being an accessory to murder

complies [kɔ̃pli] NFPL *Rel* compline

compliment [kɔ̃plimɑ̃] NM **1** *(félicitation)* compliment; **avec les compliments de** with the compliments of; **avec les compliments de la maison** with the compliments of the house; **mes compliments au chef** my compliments to the chef; **faire des compliments à qn** to pay sb compliments, to compliment sb; **on lui a fait c. de sa jolie robe** she was complimented on her pretty dress; **(je vous fais) mes compliments** I congratulate you; *Iron* **mes compliments!** congratulations!; **faites-lui mes compliments** (please) give her my regards **2** *(discours)* speech of congratulation, congratulatory speech

complimenter [kɔ̃plimɑ̃te] VT **c. qn pour** *(courage, présence d'esprit)* to congratulate sb on; **c. qn sur** *(toilette, coiffure)* to compliment sb on; **il faut la c. pour son nouveau travail** we must congratulate her on her new job

complimenteur, -euse [kɔ̃plimɑ̃tœr, -øz]

Péj ADJ *(personne)* obsequious; **discours c.** flattering speech

N flatterer

compliqué, -ée [kɔ̃plike] ADJ *(mécanisme, système etc)* complicated, intricate; *(style, texte, théorie etc)* complicated, involved; *(personne)* complicated; **je n'y arrive pas, c'est trop c.** I can't do it, it's too complicated; *Fam* **ce n'est pas c.!** it's quite simple!

N *Fam* complicated individual

compliquer [kɔ̃plike] VT to complicate; **ça risque de c. les choses** that may *or* might well complicate matters

VPR se compliquer *(d'une situation, de la vie, d'un problème)* to get complicated; *Littér, Théâtr (d'une intrigue)* to thicken; **ça se complique!** things are getting a bit complicated!; **il se complique l'existence** he's making life complicated *or* difficult for himself

complot [kɔ̃plo] NM plot, conspiracy; **tramer un c.** to hatch a plot; **mettre qn dans le c.** to let sb in on the plot

comploter [kɔ̃plɔte] VI to plot, to conspire (**contre** against); **c. de faire qch** to plot *or* conspire to do sth

VT to plot; *Fam* **qu'est-ce que vous complotez là?** what are you cooking up *or* plotting now?

VPR se comploter je me demande ce qui se complote par ici I wonder what's being hatched *or* plotted here

comploteur [kɔ̃plɔtœr] NM plotter, conspirator

compo [kɔ̃po] NF *Scol Fam* test; *(plus important)* exam

componction [kɔ̃pɔ̃ksjɔ̃] NF **1** *Rel (contrition)* compunction **2** *Iron* **avec c.** gravely, solemnly

comportement [kɔ̃pɔrtəmɑ̃] NM **1** behaviour, *Am* behavior; **elle a un c. très bizarre avec les enfants** her behaviour towards children is very strange, she behaves very strangely towards children; **psychologie du c.** behaviourism, *Am* behaviorism; **type de c.** behaviour pattern **2** *Mktg* **c. d'achat** buying *or* purchase *or* purchasing behaviour *or Am* behavior; **c. de l'acheteur** buyer *or* purchaser behaviour; **c. du consommateur** consumer behaviour **3** *Bourse, Fin (du marché, des cours, des actions)* performance **4** *Aut* **c. en courbe** *ou* **en virage** cornering (ability); **c. routier** (road) handling; **c. sous-vireur** understeer; **c. survireur** oversteer

comportemental, -ale, -aux, -ales [kɔ̃pɔrtəmɑ̃tal, -o] ADJ behavioural, *Am* behavioral

comporter [kɔ̃pɔrte] VT **1** *(admettre)* to allow, *Fml* to allow of, *Fml* to admit of; **règle qui comporte des exceptions** rule that allows of *or* admits of exceptions **2** *(comprendre)* to comprise; **la fusée comporte quatre étages** the rocket comprises *or* is made up of four stages; **les difficultés que cela comporterait** the difficulties this would involve *or* entail

VPR se comporter to behave (**vis-à-vis de, envers** towards); **mal se c.** to misbehave, to behave badly; **se c. en** *ou* **comme un lâche** to act *or* behave like a coward; **la voiture se comporte aussi bien sur neige que sur terrain sec** the car handles equally well on snow or dry ground; **ses actions se sont bien comportées** his shares have performed well

composant, -ante [kɔ̃pozɑ̃, -ɑ̃t] ADJ *(partie)* component, constituent

NM component, constituent

NF **composante** *(de voltage, force, vitesse etc)* component; **c'est une des composantes de la vie de couple** it's one of the components of married life, it's one of the things that make up married life

composé, -ée [kɔ̃poze] ADJ **1** *(salade)* mixed; *(intérêt, mot etc)* compound; *Chimie* **corps c.** compound; *Gram* **temps c.** compound tense SEE GRAMMAR B26–8 ; **nom c.** compound (noun) VOIR GRAMMAIRE A14 **2** *Bot (fleur)* composite **3** *(compassé) (attitude, comportement etc)* studied

NM *Chimie, Gram etc* compound

NFPL *Bot* **composées** Compositae

composer [kɔ̃poze] VT **1** *(créer) (poème, symphonie etc)* to compose, to write; *(bouquet), Pharm (ordonnance)* to make up **2** *Typ (fonte)* to set, to compose, to typeset; **c. sur ordinateur** to computer-typeset; *Tél* **c. un numéro** to dial a number **3** *(faire partie de)* to make up; **quels sont les ingrédients qui composent ce plat?** which ingredients make up *or* go into this dish?; **les personnes qui composent notre famille** the people who make up our family, all the members of our family; **ce médicament est composé de nombreuses substances** this medicine is made up of *or* is composed of *or* consists of numerous substances **4** **c. son visage** to compose one's features

VI **1** *(s'entendre)* to compromise (**avec** with) **2** *Mus* to compose **3** *Scol* to take *or* sit a test; **les élèves composeront en anglais demain** the pupils will take *or* sit an English test tomorrow

VPR se composer 1 **se c. de** to be made up of, to be composed of, to consist of **2** **se c. un visage de circonstance** to put on a suitable expression

composeur [kɔ̃pozœr] NM *Tél* **c. de numéros** dialler

composeuse [kɔ̃pozøz] NF *Typ* photosetter, typesetting machine

composite [kɔ̃pozit] ADJ composite; **matériau c.** composite (material)

compositeur, -trice [kɔ̃pozitœr, -tris] N **1** *Mus* composer **2** *Typ* compositor, typesetter

composition [kɔ̃pozisjɔ̃] NF **1** *(de sonate, roman, poème etc)* composition, writing; *(d'une ordonnance etc)* making up; *(d'un bouquet)* arrangement; *(d'un portefeuille d'actions)* building up; **un poème de ma c.** a poem I wrote (myself)

2 *(éléments), Chimie, Phys (de l'eau etc)* composition; **la c. d'un repas** the composition of a meal; **la c. des équipes n'est pas encore connue** the teams haven't been announced yet

3 *Mus, Littér etc (œuvre)* composition

4 *Scol (dissertation)* essay; *(examen)* test

5 *(arrangement)* arrangement, compromise; **entrer en c. avec qn** to come to terms with sb

6 **être de bonne c.** to be good-natured

7 *Typ* typesetting, composition; **c. (des caractères)** body setting; **c. informatisée** computer typesetting; **c. programmée** automatic typesetting; *Tél* **c. automatique de numéros** automatic dialling

compost [kɔ̃post] NM *Agr* compost

compostage [kɔ̃pɔstaʒ] NM *(de billet)* (date-)stamping; *(poinçonnage)* punching

composter¹ [kɔ̃pɔste] VT *Agr (terre)* to compost

composter² VT *(billet)* to (date-)stamp; *(poinçonner)* to punch

composteur [kɔ̃pɔstœr] NM **1** *(machine)* date stamp; *(pour poinçonner)* ticket-punching machine **2** *Typ* composing stick

compote [kɔ̃pot] NF *Culin* compote, stewed fruit; **c. de pommes** apple compote, stewed apples; *Fam* **j'ai les jambes en c.** my legs feel like jelly; *Fam* **j'ai la tête en c.** my brain's gone to mush; *Fam* **il lui a mis le visage en c.** he smashed his face to a pulp

compotier [kɔ̃potje] NM fruit dish

compréhensibilité [kɔ̃preãsibilite] NF comprehensibility

compréhensible [kɔ̃preãsibl] ADJ **1** *(clair)* comprehensible, understandable; **c. du** *ou* **par le grand public** understandable by *or* comprehensible to the general public **2** *(justifié)* understandable; **c'est tout à fait c. de sa part** it's altogether understandable on his part

---
Attention: ne pas confondre **comprehensible** et **understandable** lorsqu'on traduit **compréhensible**. Le terme **comprehensible** signifie **intelligible**, alors que **understandable** signifie **concevable, qui se comprend**.
---

compréhensif, -ive [kɔ̃preãsif, -iv] ADJ **1** *(personne)* understanding; **elle s'est montrée très compréhensive là-dessus** she was very understanding about it **2** *(vaste)* comprehensive

---
Il faut noter que l'adjectif anglais **comprehensive** est un faux ami. Il signifie le plus souvent **complet, exhaustif**.
---

compréhension [kɔ̃preãsjɔ̃] NF **1** *(fait de comprendre)* comprehension, understanding; **pour la bonne c. du texte** (in order) to fully understand the text; **cet élève a des problèmes de c.** this pupil has problems understanding *or* problems of comprehension **2** *(bienveillance)* understanding; **il est plein de c.** he is very understanding

COMPRENDRE [kɔ̃prãdr] *(conj like* **prendre***)*

VT to understand **1** ▪ to comprise **2** ▪ to include **3**
VI to understand ▪ to see
VPR to understand each other ▪ to be understandable

VT 1 *(par l'esprit)* to understand, *Fml* to comprehend; **je ne comprends pas ce que vous voulez dire** I don't understand what you mean, *Fam* I don't get you; **difficile à c.** difficult *or* hard to understand; **c. une langue étrangère** to understand a foreign language; **je n'arrive pas à c. cette phrase** I can't make sense of this sentence; **c. la portée d'un acte** to realize *or* understand the consequences of an action; **je ne comprends pas comment/pourquoi il a fait ça** I don't understand *or* see how/why he did it; **dois-je c. que ...?** am I to understand *or* do you mean to say that ...?; **vous m'avez mal compris** you've misunderstood me; **on ne te comprend pas** *(tu parles trop vite)* nobody can understand *or* make out what you say; **je ne le comprends pas** *(il est étrange)* I can't understand him *or* fathom him out, I can't make him out; **il ne comprend rien à rien** he hasn't a clue about anything; **tu peux lui expliquer, il comprend les choses** you can explain to him, he understands about these things; **elle ne comprend pas la plaisanterie** she can't take a joke; **elle n'a pas compris la plaisanterie** she didn't get the joke; **tu comprends ce que je te dis?** do you understand what I'm saying?; **je n'y comprends rien** I can't make head or tail of it, it makes no sense to me; **c'est à n'y rien c.** it's incomprehensible; **ne cherche pas, il n'y a rien à c.** don't even try to understand; **va y c. quelque chose!** you try to make head or tail of it!, *Am* go figure!; **je lui ai fait c. que ... +** *ind* I gave him to understand that ...; *(avec autorité)* I made it clear to him that ...; **se faire c.** to make oneself understood; **me suis-je bien fait c.?** have I made myself clear?; **comment c. ce tableau/ce poème/l'art?** what is one to make of this picture/this poem/art?; **il faut la c.** you have to see things from her point of

view, you have to put yourself in her shoes; **tu n'as pas encore compris qu'il n'en veut qu'à ton argent!** you still haven't realized *or* understood that he's only after your money!; **je n'ai toujours pas compris ce qui s'est passé** I still haven't quite realized *or* grasped *or* understood what has happened; *Fam* **j'ai compris ma douleur** I realized what I had let myself in for

2 *(être composé entièrement de)* to comprise, to be made up of, to consist of; **cet organe comprend trois parties distinctes** this organ is made up of *or* comprises three separate parts

3 *(inclure)* to include; **service non compris** service not included; **le prix comprend tous les frais d'hébergement** the price is fully inclusive of accommodation; **ils ont tous été punis, y compris le plus jeune** they were all punished, including the youngest *or* the youngest included

VI to understand; **ai-je bien compris?** have I understood correctly?; **ah! je comprends!** oh! I see!; **ça va, j'ai compris, ce n'est pas la peine de me faire un dessin!** OK, I understand, you don't need to spell it out to me!; **elle comprend vite** she's quick on the uptake, she catches on quickly; **tu comprends, on ne pouvait pas se le permettre** you see, we just couldn't afford it; **elle finira par c.** she'll understand eventually; **je comprends bien!** I understand!; *Fam* **elle est belle, n'est-ce pas? – je comprends!** she's lovely, isn't she? – and how!

VPR se comprendre *(des gens)* to understand each other; *Fam* **ça se comprend!** it's understandable!, it's not surprising!; **je me comprends!** I know what I'm talking about!

comprenette [kɔ̃prɔnɛt] NF *Fam* **il a la c. un peu dure** he's a bit slow on the uptake

comprenure [kɔ̃prɔnyr] NF *Belg, Can Fam* **être dur de c.** to be slow on the uptake)

compresse [kɔ̃prɛs] NF compress

compresser [kɔ̃prese] VT to compress; *Ordinat (fichier)* to compact, to compress, to zip

compresseur [kɔ̃prescœr] NM **1** *Tech (à air, de gaz, de fluide)* compressor; *(de moteur)* supercharger, impeller, compressor; *(d'air conditionné)* blower, fan; *Aut* **c. Roots** Roots blower; *Aut* **c. centrifuge** centrifugal compressor; *Aut* **c. sur vilebrequin** crankshaft compressor; *Aut* **c. à palettes** vane compressor **2** *Ordinat* **c. de données** data compressor

ADJ M compressing; *Constr* **rouleau c.** road roller, steamroller

compressibilité [kɔ̃presibilite] NF *Phys* compressibility; *(de dépenses, peine de prison etc)* reducibility; **vous êtes assez optimiste quant à la c. des dépenses publiques** you're quite optimistic about the possibility of reducing *or* cutting government spending

compressible [kɔ̃presibl] ADJ **1** *(comprimable)* compressible **2** *(dépenses, peine de prison etc)* reducible

compressif, -ive [kɔ̃presif, -iv] ADJ *(bandage etc)* compressive

compression [kɔ̃mpresjɔ̃] NF **1** *(de gaz, vapeur etc)* compression; **temps de c.** compression stroke **2** *(réduction)* reduction, cutback; *Ordinat (de données)* compression; **c. des dépenses** spending cuts; **c. des dépenses budgétaires** budget cuts; **c. de crédit** credit squeeze; **c. du personnel** reduction of staff, cutback in staff; **mesure de c.** cutback, reduction

comprimable [kɔ̃primabl] ADJ compressible

comprimé [kɔ̃prime] ADJ compressed; **air c.**

compressed air; **outil à air c.** pneumatic tool ▪ NM *Pharm* tablet; **un c. d'aspirine** an aspirin

comprimer [kɔ̃prime] VT **1** *(gaz, artère)*, *Ordinat (fichier)* to compress; **c. la taille** to squeeze the waist in; **c. les dépenses** to cut down *or* reduce expenditure **2** *(sa colère, sa jalousie etc)* to curb, to repress, to restrain; *(larmes)* to repress, to hold back

compris [kɔ̃pri] ADJ **1** *(enregistré)* **bien c.** (fully) understood; **mal c.** misunderstood; **alors, c'est c.?** so, do you understand *or* have you understood?; **la leçon n'a pas été comprise** (the point of) the lesson wasn't understood; **tu fais tes devoirs immédiatement, c.!** you'll do your homework right now, (is that) understood *or* (do you) understand? **2** *(situé)* **la maison est comprise entre deux avancées de la mer** the house lies between *or* is bounded by two arms of the sea; **le passage c. entre les deux dialogues** the passage between the two dialogues

compromettant [kɔ̃prɔmetã] ADJ *(situation)* compromising; *(documents, photos)* incriminating, compromising

compromettre [kɔ̃prɔmetr] *(conj like* **mettre***)* VT **1** *(entacher) (personne, la réputation de qn etc)* to compromise; **être compromis dans un crime** to be implicated in a crime **2** *(mettre en péril) (vie, sécurité, vacances etc)* to jeopardize, to put in jeopardy

VPR se compromettre to compromise oneself; *(s'engager)* to commit oneself; **il s'est compromis dans une affaire de fausses factures** he became implicated in a matter of forged invoices

compromis [kɔ̃prɔmi] NM **1** *(arrangement)* compromise, arrangement; **parvenir à un c.** to reach a compromise, to come to an arrangement; **cette robe est un c. entre l'élégance et la décontraction** this dress is neither too elegant nor too casual **2** *Jur* **mettre une affaire en c.** to submit an affair for arbitration; **c. de vente** provisional *or* preliminary sales agreement **3** *(en assurances)* **c. d'avarie** average bond

compromission [kɔ̃prɔmisjɔ̃] NF *souvent Péj* **1** *(avec sa conscience)* compromising **2** *(résultat)* compromise

compta [kɔ̃ta] NF *Fam* accounting

comptabilisation [kɔ̃tabilizasjɔ̃] NF *Fin* posting, entering in *or* into the accounts; *(dénombrement)* counting; **la c. de l'actif d'une société** recording the assets of a company in the accounts; *Bourse* **c. au prix de marché** marking to market

comptabiliser [kɔ̃tabilize] VT **1** *(dénombrer)* to count **2** *Fin* to post, to enter in the accounts; *Bourse* **c. au prix de marché** to mark to market

comptabilité [kɔ̃tabilite] NF **1** *(livres)* accounts; *(technique)* book-keeping, accounting, accountancy; **c. en partie simple/double** single-/double-entry book-keeping; **livre de c.** account book; **méthode de c.** book-keeping *or* accounting method; **tenir la c. d'une maison** to keep the books *or* the accounts of a firm; *Fin* **c. matières** stock record, stores accounts; **c. analytique** cost accounting; **c. bancaire** bank accounting; **c. budgétaire** budgeting; **c. de caisse** cash basis accounting; **c. commerciale** business accounting; **c. des coûts variables** direct cost accounting; **c. d'exploitation** cost accounting; **c. financière** financial accounting; **c. générale** general accounts; *(système)* financial accounting; **c. de gestion** management accounting; **c.-gestion financière** financial management accounting; **c. informatisée** computerized accounts; **c. de prix de revient** cost accounting; **c. publique** public finance; **c. uniforme** uniform accounting **2** *(service)* accounts department

comptable [kɔ̃tabl] ADJ **1** *Com etc (travail etc)* book-keeping, accounting; **pièce c.** voucher; **machine c.** accounting machine **2** *(responsable)* accountable; **être c. à qn de qch** to be accountable to sb for sth
  N accountant; **c. agréé** chartered accountant, *Am* certified public accountant; **expert c.** chartered accountant; *(vérificateur)* auditor

comptage [kɔ̃taʒ] NM counting

comptant [kɔ̃tɑ̃] ADJ **argent c.** cash; *Fig Fam* **prendre qch pour argent c.** to take sth for gospel truth
  ADV **payer c.** to pay (in) cash
  NM cash; **payer/acheter au c.** to pay (in)/buy for cash; **payable au c.** *(lors d'un achat)* cash *or Am* collect on delivery; *(sur présentation de titre, de connaissement)* payable on presentation; *Com* **c. contre documents** cash against documents, CAD

COMPTE [kɔ̃t] NM **1** *Fin, Banque* account; **tenir les comptes d'une maison** to keep the accounts *or* the books of a firm; **faire ses comptes** to make up *or* do one's accounts; **livre de comptes** account book; **la Cour des comptes** ≃ the Audit Office; **versement à c.** payment on account; **régler son c.** to settle one's account; *Fig Fam* **régler son c. à qn** to settle sb's hash; **avoir un (petit) c. à régler avec qn** to have a bone to pick with sb, to have a score to settle with sb; **on réglera nos comptes plus tard** we'll settle up later; **règlement de comptes** settling of accounts; *Fig Fam* settling of scores *or* accounts; **pour règlement de tout c.** *(sur facture)* in full settlement; **donner** *ou* **régler son c. à un employé** *(le renvoyer)* to dismiss an employee; **avoir un c. chez qn** to have an account with sb; **mettre un montant sur son c.** to pay a sum into one's account; **être/se mettre** *ou* **s'installer à son c.** to be/set up in business on one's own (account); **cela n'entre pas en ligne de c.** that has nothing to do with the matter, that doesn't come into it; **mettre un malheur sur le c. de qn** to lay a misfortune at sb's door, to blame sb for a misfortune; **apprendre qch sur le c. de qn** to learn sth about sb; **faire qch pour le c. de qn** to do sth on sb's behalf; **pour mon c., j'aimerais mieux rester ici** as far as I'm concerned, I'd prefer to stay here; **les bons comptes font les bons amis** pay your debts and keep your friends
  2 *(calcul)* reckoning, calculation; **faire le c. des dépenses** to add up *or* calculate the expenses; **le c. des morts** the death toll *or* tally; **compte à rebours** countdown; **faire le c.** to count backwards; *(avant le lancement d'une fusée)* to count down; **le c. y est** *(somme)* it's the right amount; *(objets, personnes)* they're all here; **ça ne fait pas le c.** it doesn't come to the right amount; **c. rond** round sum; **acheter qch à bon c.** to buy sth cheap; **cela fait mon c.** it's just the thing for me, that suits me; **il y trouve son c.** he gets something out of it, there's something in it for him; **vous êtes loin du c.** you're wide of the mark; *Fig* **au bout du c., en fin de c.** in the end, at the end of the day; **tout c. fait** all things considered, taking everything into account; **à c.-là** in that case; **tenir c. de qch** to take sth into account *or* into consideration; **ne tenir aucun c. de qn/qch** to take no notice of sb/sth, to ignore *or* disregard sb/sth; **c. tenu de son assiduité** considering *or* bearing in mind *or* taking into account his regular attendance; **s'en tirer à bon c.** to get off lightly; *Fam* **il a son c.** *(il en a assez)* he's had enough; *(parce qu'il a bu)* he's had enough (to drink); *Fam* **son c. est bon** he's for it, he's had it
  3 *(explication)* **comptes** explanation; **demander des comptes à qn** to ask sb for an explanation, to call sb to account; **elle ne**

doit de comptes à personne she is answerable to nobody; **rendre des comptes** to explain *or* justify oneself; **je n'ai de comptes à rendre à personne** I don't have to explain *or* justify myself to anyone; **rendre c. de qch** to account for sth; **se rendre c. de qch** to realize sth, to be aware of sth; **se rendre c. que …** to realize that …; **on lui a volé son portefeuille et il ne s'est rendu c. de rien** someone stole his wallet and he didn't notice a thing; *Fam* **tu te rends c.!** would you believe it!; **c. rendu** report; *(littéraire)* (book) review; *(d'une réunion)* minutes; **faire le c. rendu** *(pendant la réunion)* to take the minutes; *(à la réunion suivante)* to read the minutes
  4 *Boxe* count; **rester sur le plancher pour le c.** to be counted out, to be out for the count
  ▸▸ **c. accréditif** charge account; **c. d'achats** purchase account; **c. d'actif** assets account; **comptes analytiques d'exploitation** operational cost accounts; **comptes annuels** annual accounts; **comptes approuvés** certified accounts; **c. d'attente** suspense account; **c. en banque** *ou* **bancaire** bank account; **c. bloqué** escrow *or* frozen *or* blocked account; **c. de caisse** cash account; **c. de capital** capital account; **c. centralisateur** central account; **c. de charges** expense account; **c. chèques** current account, *Am* checking account; **c. chèque postal** ≃ Giro account; **c. client** customer account; *Compta* account receivable; **responsable des comptes-clients** account executive; **c. des clients** *(d'un hôtel etc)* guest folio; **c. collectif** adjustment account, summary account; **c. de compensation** clearing account; **c. conjoint** joint account; **comptes consolidés** consolidated accounts; **c. de contrepartie** contra account; **c. de correspondant** correspondent bank account; **c. courant** current account, *Am* checking account; *Ordinat* **c. de courrier électronique** e-mail account; **c. à crédit** credit account; **c. créditeur** *Compta* account payable; *(à la banque)* account in credit, credit balance; **c. débiteur** *Compta* account receivable; *(à la banque)* account in debit, debit balance; **c. à découvert** overdrawn account; **c. des dépenses et recettes** income and expenditure account; **c. de dépôt** deposit account; **c. en devises étrangères** foreign currency account; **c. divisionnaire** divisional account; **c. d'épargne** savings account, deposit account; **c. d'épargne en actions** share savings account, savings and investment account; **c. d'épargne logement** savings account *(for purchasing a property)*; **c. d'épargne-retraite** retirement savings account; **c. de l'exploitant** owner's capital account; **c. d'exploitation** profit and loss form, P and L; **c. d'exploitation générale** trading account; **comptes fournisseurs** book debts; **comptes de gestion** management accounts; **c. d'immobilisations** fixed asset account; **c. individuel** personal account; **c. Internet** Internet account; **c. joint** joint account; **c. livret** deposit account; **c. de passif** liabilities account; **c. permanent** ≃ charge account, *Br* ≃ credit account; **c. de prêt** loan account; **c. de produits** income account, revenue account; **c. propre** personal account; **c. de régularisation** *(de l'actif)* prepayments and accrued income; *(du passif)* accruals and deferred income; **c. de réserve** reserve account; **c. de résultat** profit and loss account, *Am* income statement; **c. de résultat prévisionnel** interim profit-and-loss statement; **comptes sociaux** company accounts; **c. en souffrance** outstanding account, delinquent account; **c. de stock** inventory account; *Bourse* **c. à terme** forward account; **comptes de tiers** other debtors and creditors

compte-clé, pl **comptes-clés** NM *Com* key-account

compte-gouttes NM INV *Pharm etc* dropper; **mesurer qch au c.** to dole sth out in driblets *or* sparingly; **il donne son argent au c.** he's very sparing with his money

COMPTER [kɔ̃te]

VT	to count **1** ▪ to pay **2** ▪ to ration **3** ▪ to include **4** ▪ to allow **5** ▪ to intend to **5** ▪ to charge for **6**
VI	to count **1, 2, 4** ▪ to matter **2** ▪ to reckon with *(compter avec)* **3** ▪ to rely on *(compter sur)* **4**
VPR	to do a head-count

VT **1** *(dénombrer)* to count; **je vous ai tous comptés?** have I counted you all?; **on ne compte plus les mécontents** we've lost count of the malcontents, we can't keep track of the malcontents; **c. dans ses rangs** to number among one's ranks; **on peut les c. (sur les doigts de la main)** you can count them on the fingers of one hand; **elle compte les jours** she's counting the days; **il y a de cela vingt ans bien comptés** a good twenty years have passed since then; *Fig* **c. les moutons** to count sheep; *Fig* **c. les points** *ou* **les coups** to keep score, to watch from the sidelines
  2 *(donner)* to pay; **c. cent euros à qn** to pay sb a hundred euros
  3 *(donner avec parcimonie)* to ration; **il leur compte leur argent de poche** he rations their pocket money; **marcher à pas comptés** to walk with measured tread; **ses jours sont comptés** his days are numbered
  4 *(inclure)* to include; **ils étaient vingt, sans c. le père et la mère** there were twenty of them, not counting the father and mother; **sans c. que …** not to mention that …, besides the fact that …; **je le compte parmi mes meilleurs amis** I number *or* count *or* consider him among my best friends
  5 *(prévoir)* to allow, to reckon; **j'ai compté deux cents grammes par personne** I've allowed *or* reckoned two hundred grammes per person; **elle compte rentrer à dix heures** she expects *or* intends to be back at ten o'clock; **que comptes-tu faire?** what are you planning *or* intending to do?; **c'était sans c. les embouteillages** that was without allowing for traffic jams
  6 *(facturer)* to charge for; **c. qch à qn** to charge sb for sth; **il a compté 20 euros pour le déplacement** he charged 20 euros for the callout
  7 *Can (marquer)* to score
  VI **1** *(calculer)* to count; **c. de tête/sur ses doigts** to count in one's head/on one's fingers; **c. jusqu'à dix** to count up to ten; **mal c.** to miscount; **apprendre à c.** to learn (how) to count; **dépenser sans c.** to spend money freely *or* like water; **se dépenser sans c.** to give oneself freely; **avec un salaire en moins, ils sont obligés de c.** with one salary less, they have to count the pennies *or* watch every penny; **il compte parmi les meilleurs** he's one of the best, he ranks among the best; *Admin* **à c. du 1er janvier** (with effect) from 1 January, as of 1 January
  2 *(être important)* to count, to matter; **ce qui compte, c'est le travail** work is what matters *or* counts; **ça ne compte pas** that doesn't count *or* matter; **il ne compte plus du tout pour elle** he doesn't mean anything to her any more; **elle ne compte pas,** *Fam* **elle compte pour du beurre** she doesn't count, she counts for nothing; **les heures supplémentaires comptent double** overtime counts double; **à table, il compte pour deux** he eats enough for two
  3 c. avec qn/qch to reckon with sb/sth; **c'est un adversaire avec lequel il faudra c.** he's an opponent who will have to be reckoned with; **il faut c. avec le vent** you have to allow for the wind

4 c. sur qn/qch to count *or* rely *or* depend on sb/sth; **je ne compterais pas trop là-dessus** I wouldn't count on it too much, I wouldn't bank on it; **tu peux c. sur lui pour que tout soit fait à l'envers** you can rely *or* count on him to do everything all wrong; **j'y compte bien!** I should hope so!; *Fam* **compte là-dessus et bois de l'eau!** you'll be lucky!, there's not much hope *or* chance of that!

VPR se compter comptez-vous count yourselves, do a head-count; **ses échecs ne se comptent plus** he has had countless failures; **les maîtresses du roi se comptent par dizaines** the king has dozens of mistresses

compte-titres, *pl* **comptes-titres NM** *Fin* share account

compte-tours NM INV rev *or* revolution counter

compteur [kɔ̃tœr] **NM** meter; *Ordinat* counter; **c. d'électricité/à gaz/d'eau** electricity/gas/water meter; **le c. du taxi** the taximeter, the taxi's meter; **le c. marquait 47 euros** there was 47 euros on the meter; **relever le c.** to read the meter; *Ordinat* **c. d'accès** hit counter; *Aut* **c. de vitesse** speedometer; **c. kilométrique (totaliseur)** ≃ mil(e)ometer; *Am* odometer; *Aut* **c. journalier** trip recorder *or* *Am* odometer; *Nucl* **c. (de) Geiger** Geiger counter; *Mktg* **c. de circulation** traffic counter

comptine [kɔ̃tin] **NF** counting rhyme

comptoir [kɔ̃twar] **NM 1** *Com (table)* counter; *(dans un bar)* bar; **garçon de c.** barman, bartender; **prendre une consommation au c.** to have a drink at the bar; **c. d'enregistrement** check-in desk; **c. d'information** information desk; **c. de réception** reception desk; **c. de vente** sales counter **2** *(cartel)* (marketing) syndicate **3** *Fin* bank; *(de banque)* branch; **c. d'escompte** discount house **4** *(dans un pays éloigné)* trading post **5** *Suisse (foire)* fair *(where items are exhibited and sold)* **6** *Can* **c. de cuisine** worktop, work surface

comptoir-caisse, *pl* **comptoirs-caisses NM** cashier's desk

compulsation [kɔ̃pylsasjɔ̃] **NF** *(d'un ouvrage)* consultation

compulser [kɔ̃pylse] **VT** *(documents, livres etc)* to consult

compulsif, -ive [kɔ̃pylsif, -iv] **ADJ** *(buveur etc)* compulsive; **conduite compulsive** compulsive behaviour

compulsion [kɔ̃pylsjɔ̃] **NF** compulsion

computation [kɔ̃pytasjɔ̃] **NF** computation

comte [kɔ̃t] **NM** count; *(en Grande-Bretagne)* earl

comté [kɔ̃te] **NM 1** *Hist* earldom **2** *Admin* county **3** *Can Pol* riding **4** *(fromage)* = type of Gruyère cheese

comtesse [kɔ̃tɛs] **NF** countess

con, conne [kɔ̃, kɔn] *très Fam* **ADJ** damn stupid, idiotic, *Br* bloody stupid; **elle est trop c. ou conne!** she's too damn stupid for words!; *Fam* **être c. comme la lune** *ou* **un balai** *(d'une personne)* to be as daft as a brush; **c. comme la lune** *(film etc)* damn stupid, *Br* bloody stupid; **c'est pas c.!** that's pretty clever!

N *très Fam* stupid bastard; **faire le c.** to fool *or* mess around; **pauvre c.!** poor bastard *or* *Br* sod!; **t'es vraiment le roi des cons** you really are an utter *or* a complete nerd; **quel c., ce mec!** what a stupid bastard that guy is!; **ce vélo à la c.!** this damn useless bike!

N *Vulg (sexe)* cunt, twat

conard, -arde [kɔnar, -ard] *Vulg* **ADJ** damn stupid, *Br* bloody stupid

N damn fool, *Br* silly bugger

conasse [kɔnas] **NF** *Vulg* silly bitch, stupid cow

concassage [kɔ̃kasaʒ] **NM** *(de pierre etc)* crushing; *(de poivre)* grinding

concasser [kɔ̃kase] **VT** *(pierre etc)* to crush; *(poivre)* to grind

concasseur [kɔ̃kasœr] **NM** crusher
ADJ **rouleau c.** crushing roller

concaténation [kɔ̃katenasjɔ̃] **NF** concatenation

concaténer [kɔ̃katene] **VT** *Ordinat* to concatenate

concave [kɔ̃kav] **ADJ** concave

concavité [kɔ̃kavite] **NF 1** *(fait d'être concave)* concavity **2** *(creux)* hollow, cavity

concédant [kɔ̃sedɑ̃] **NM** *Fin* grantor

concéder [kɔ̃sede] **VT** (**je concède, n. concédons; je concéderai**) **1** *(privilège, droit)* to concede, to grant; *(terrain, concession)* to grant **2** *(reconnaître)* **c. qu'on a tort** to admit that one is wrong; **il fait chaud, je (vous) le concède** it's warm, I grant you **3** *Sport* to give away, to concede; **c. un but** to give away *or* concede a goal

concélébrer [kɔ̃selebre] **VT** *Rel* to concelebrate

concentration [kɔ̃sɑ̃trasjɔ̃] **NF 1** *Phys, Chimie, Nucl* concentration; **grandes concentrations urbaines** conurbations, large urban agglomerations; *Fig* **une grande c. d'oiseaux** a large concentration *or* population of birds; **la c. des intellectuels dans la capitale** the concentration of intellectuals in the capital; **zone à haute c. de population** high-density area; *Typ* **impression à haute c.** high-density printing **2** *(d'entreprises)* integration, merging; *Com* **c. horizontale/verticale** horizontal/vertical integration **3** *(de l'esprit)* concentration; **manquer de c.** to lack concentration; **cela exige une très grande c.** it demands *or* requires great concentration

concentrationnaire [kɔ̃sɑ̃trasjɔnɛr] **ADJ** of concentration camps; **la vie c.** life in a concentration camp
N concentration camp prisoner

concentré [kɔ̃sɑ̃tre] **ADJ 1** *Chimie, Culin etc* concentrated; *(lait)* condensed **2** *(intellectuellement)* concentrating; **il était très c.** he was concentrating hard
NM *Chimie, Culin etc* concentrate; **c. de tomates** tomato purée *or* *Am* paste

concentrer [kɔ̃sɑ̃tre] **VT** to concentrate; *(rayons du soleil)* to focus; **c. son espoir sur une chose** to concentrate *or* focus one's hopes on one thing
VPR se concentrer 1 *(être attentif)* to concentrate (**sur** on); **taisez-vous, je me concentre** be quiet, I'm trying to concentrate **2** *(s'assembler) (d'une foule, d'élèves etc)* to gather; **la population se concentre de plus en plus dans les grandes villes** the population is concentrating more and more in the big cities

concentrique [kɔ̃sɑ̃trik] **ADJ** *Géom etc* concentric

concentriquement [kɔ̃sɑ̃trikmɑ̃] **ADV** concentrically

concept [kɔ̃sɛpt] **NM** concept; **c. d'évocation** advertising concept

concepteur, -trice [kɔ̃sɛptœr, -tris] **N** ideas man, *f* woman; *(de logiciel)* writer, designer; **être c. dans une agence de publicité** to work as an ideas man *or* on the creative side in an advertising agency; **c. graphiste** graphics designer; *Ordinat* **c. de sites Web** web designer

concepteur-projecteur, *pl* **concepteurs-projecteurs NM** ideas man and project manager

concepteur-rédacteur, *pl* **concepteurs-rédacteurs NM** *(d'une agence de publicité)* copywriter

conception [kɔ̃sɛpsjɔ̃] **NF 1** *(d'un enfant, d'une idée)* conception; *Rel* **l'Immaculée C.** the Immaculate Conception **2** *(vue)* concept, idea; **une toute nouvelle c. des mathématiques** a whole new way of looking at mathematics, a completely new approach to mathematics **3** *(création)* design, creation; **c. graphique** graphic design; **c. assistée par ordinateur** computer-aided *or* -assisted design; **c. des produits** product design

conceptualisation [kɔ̃sɛptɥalizasjɔ̃] **NF** conceptualization

conceptualiser [kɔ̃sɛptɥalize] **VT** to conceptualize

conceptuel, -elle [kɔ̃sɛptɥɛl] **ADJ** conceptual

concernant [kɔ̃sɛrnɑ̃] **PRÉP** concerning, with regard to, regarding; **c. votre départ, voici quelques informations** here's some information about your departure

concerner [kɔ̃sɛrne] **VT** to concern, to affect; **pour ou en ce qui concerne cette affaire** with regard to this matter, as far as this matter is concerned; **en ce qui me concerne** as far as I am concerned; **cela vous concerne en rien** that's none of your business, it's no concern of yours; *(vous n'êtes pas en cause)* it doesn't concern *or* affect you at all; **est-ce que cela vous concerne?** is it any business *or* concern of yours?; **ces problèmes vous concernent tous** these problems concern *or* affect you all; **ne pas se sentir concerné** not to feel affected; **prière de vous rendre au bureau pour affaire vous concernant** please come to the office to discuss a matter which concerns *or* involves you

concert [kɔ̃sɛr] **NM 1** *Mus* concert; **salle de c.** concert hall; *Fig* **ce fut un c. d'approbations** there was a chorus of approval **2** *(accord)* **agir de c. avec qn** to act jointly *or* in conjunction *or* *Fml* in concert with sb, to take concerted action with sb; **nous sommes rentrés de c.** we came back together

concertant [kɔ̃sɛrtɑ̃] **ADJ** *Mus* concertante

concertation [kɔ̃sɛrtasjɔ̃] **NF** consultation; **travailler en c.** to work together; **la c. est mise** we must work together *or* co-operate

concerté [kɔ̃sɛrte] **ADJ** *(action)* concerted, united

concerter [kɔ̃sɛrte] **VT** *(plan etc)* to devise together
VPR se concerter to consult (each other), to consult together; **ils se concertèrent sur les moyens d'action** they consulted each other as to how to act

concertina [kɔ̃sɛrtina] **NM** *Mus* concertina

concertiste [kɔ̃sɛrtist] **N** concert performer *or* artiste; *(dans un concerto)* soloist

concerto [kɔ̃sɛrto] **NM** *Mus* concerto

concessif, -ive [kɔ̃sɛsif, -iv] **ADJ** *Gram* concessive

concession [kɔ̃sɛsjɔ̃] **NF 1** *(compromis)* concession; *(de terrain etc)* granting; *(d'un point dans une discussion etc)* yielding; **c. de franchise** grant of franchise; **c. de licence** licensing; **faire des concessions** to make concessions **2** *(terre etc)* concession; *(au cimetière)* plot; **c. à perpétuité** plot held in perpetuity **3** *(d'automobiles)* dealership; *(agence)* agency; *(contrat de franchisage)* franchise; **c. commerciale** agency; **c. exclusive** tied outlet

concessionnaire [kɔ̃sɛsjɔnɛr] **ADJ** *(entreprise etc)* concessionary
N *Com* agent, dealer; *(de licence)* licensee; *(de brevet)* patentee; *(de contrat de franchisage)* franchisee; **votre c. Renault®** your Re-

nault dealer; **c. agréé** approved dealer, authorized dealer; **c. exclusif** sole agent *or* dealer; **c. export** export concessionaire

concevable [kɔ̃s(ə)vabl] **ADJ** conceivable

concevoir [kɔ̃s(ə)vwar] (*prp* **concevant;** *pp* **conçu;** *pr ind* **je conçois,** n. **concevons, ils conçoivent;** *impf* **je concevais;** *p hist* **je conçus;** *fu* **je concevrai) VT 1** (*enfant*) to conceive
2 (*comprendre*) (*concept etc*) to understand; **comment c. de semblables infortunes** it is difficult to imagine such misfortune; **je conçois fort bien que tu sois lasse de la vie à la campagne** I can quite understand that you are tired of living in the country
3 (*imaginer*) (*plan*) to conceive, to devise, to think up; (*idée*) to conceive; **je ne conçois pas de ne jamais le revoir** I can't accept that I'll never see him again; **je ne conçois pas que …** I find it hard to believe that …
4 (*éprouver*) **c. de l'amitié pour qn** to take a liking to sb; **elle en conçut une profonde amertume** it made her very bitter
5 (*uniquement au participe passé*) **télégramme/lettre ainsi conçu(e)** telegram/letter worded as follows *or* that reads as follows
6 (*créer*) (*produit, maquette etc*) to design
VPR se concevoir ça se conçoit that's understandable; **cela se conçoit facilement** that is easy to understand *or* easily understood

conchyliculture [kɔ̃ʃilikyltyr] **NF** shellfish farming

concierge [kɔ̃sjɛrʒ] **N** (*d'immeuble, d'appartements*) caretaker, *Am* janitor, superintendent; (*dans un hôtel*) concierge, house *or* hall porter; *Scol* caretaker, *Am* janitor; *Fam* **c'est une vraie c.** he's/she's a terrible gossip

conciergerie [kɔ̃sjɛrʒəri] **NF 1** (*loge*) caretaker's lodge **2** *Hist* **la C.** the Conciergerie (prison)

concile [kɔ̃sil] **NM** *Rel* council; **c. œcuménique** ecumenical council

conciliable [kɔ̃siljabl] **ADJ** reconcilable

conciliabule [kɔ̃siljabyl] **NM 1** *Fam* (*conversation*) confab; **les enfants étaient en grand c.** the children were having a big confab **2** *Arch* (*réunion*) secret meeting, secret assembly

conciliaire [kɔ̃siljɛr] **ADJ** conciliar

conciliant [kɔ̃siljɑ̃] **ADJ** conciliatory

conciliateur, -trice [kɔ̃siljatœr, -tris] **ADJ** conciliatory
N conciliator

conciliation [kɔ̃siljasjɔ̃] **NF** reconciliation, conciliation; **comité de c.** arbitration committee; **tentative de c.** attempt at reconciliation

conciliatoire [kɔ̃siljatwar] **ADJ** conciliatory

concilier [kɔ̃silje] (*impf, pr sub* n. **conciliions,** v. **conciliiez) VT 1** (*deux choses*) to reconcile; **c. sa vie professionnelle et ses enfants** to combine one's professional life with looking after one's children **2** (*cœurs, estime etc*) to win, to gain; **sa droiture lui a concilié l'admiration de tous les employés** his uprightness won *or* gained him the admiration of all the employees
VPR se concilier 1 (*être compatible*) **se c. avec** to go with; **la prise de ces médicaments se concilie difficilement avec l'alcool** these drugs and alcohol don't go together *or* don't mix very well **2 se c. qn** *ou* **la faveur de qn** to win *or* gain sb's goodwill

Do not confuse with **réconcilier**.

concis [kɔ̃si] **ADJ** concise; **il a exposé la situation en termes c.** he described the situation concisely, he gave a concise description of the situation

concision [kɔ̃sizjɔ̃] **NF** concision, conciseness; **avec c.** concisely, with concision

concitoyen, -enne [kɔ̃sitwajɛ̃, -ɛn] **N** fellow citizen

conclave [kɔ̃klav] **NM** *Rel* conclave

concluant [kɔ̃klyɑ̃] **ADJ** conclusive; **peu c.** inconclusive

conclure [kɔ̃klyr] (*prp* **concluant;** *pp* **conclu;** *pr ind* **je conclus,** n. **concluons, ils concluent;** *impf* **je concluais;** *p hist* **je conclus;** *fu* **je conclurai) VT 1** (*terminer*) (*discours, réunion, repas, roman etc*) to conclude, to end (**par** with) **2** (*signer*) (*accord, traité, contrat*) to enter into, to conclude; **c. une entente** to reach an understanding; **c. un marché** to conclude *or* strike *or* *Fam* clinch a bargain, to make a deal; **marché conclu!** it's a deal!, done!; *Com* **c'est une affaire conclue** it's a bargain, it's a deal; **c. une vente** to close a sale **3** (*déduire*) to conclude; **nous avons conclu que …** we came to the conclusion *or* concluded that …; **que pouvons-nous c. de tout cela?** what conclusions can we draw from all this?; **j'en conclus que …** I conclude that …
VI 1 (*aboutir à la conclusion*) **on a conclu à sa bêtise** we concluded he was stupid; **le jury a conclu au suicide** the jury returned a verdict of suicide; **tout conclut en sa faveur** everything is in his favour **2** (*achever*) **il faut savoir c.** you've got to know when to stop **3** *Fam* (*en matière amoureuse*) to get a result

conclusion [kɔ̃klyzjɔ̃] **NF 1** (*fin*) (*de discours, réunion*) conclusion, end **2** (*action de mener à bien*) (*de traité, d'accord etc*) conclusion, concluding; **c. d'un contrat** signing of a contract **3** (*déduction*) conclusion; *Jur* finding, decision; *Jur* **conclusions** pleas, submissions; **les conclusions d'une enquête** the findings of an enquiry; **en c.** in conclusion; **tirer une c. de qch** to draw a conclusion from sth; *Fam* **c., l'échafaudage s'est écroulé** the result was that the scaffolding collapsed

concocter [kɔ̃kɔkte] **VT** *Fam* (*cocktail*) to concoct; (*histoire, excuse etc*) to concoct, to dream up; **qu'est-ce que tu nous as concocté là?** what's this you've concocted?, what kind of a concoction is this?

concombre [kɔ̃kɔ̃br] **NM** cucumber

concomitance [kɔ̃kɔmitɑ̃s] **NF** concomitance

concomitant [kɔ̃kɔmitɑ̃] **ADJ** (*circonstance, symptômes etc*) concomitant, accompanying

concordance [kɔ̃kɔrdɑ̃s] **NF 1** (*de preuves, témoignages, dates etc*) agreement, *Fml* concordance; **la c. de leurs témoignages ne nous laisse pas de doutes quant à …** the fact that their testimony agrees *or* tallies leaves us in no doubt as to … **2** *Gram* **c. des temps** sequence of tenses **3** (*index*) concordance

concordant [kɔ̃kɔrdɑ̃] **ADJ** (*témoignages, déclarations*) in agreement

concordat [kɔ̃kɔrda] **NM 1** *Rel* concordat **2** *Com* (*document*) (bankrupt's) certificate; (*accord*) composition

concorde [kɔ̃kɔrd] **NF** concord, harmony

concorder [kɔ̃kɔrde] **VI** (*de dates, preuves, témoignages etc*) to agree, to tally (**avec** with); **nos opinions ne concorderont jamais** we'll never be of the same opinion

concourant [kɔ̃kurɑ̃] **ADJ** (*lignes*) concurrent, converging; (*circonstances*) concurrent

concourir [kɔ̃kurir] **VI** (*conj like* **courir) 1** (*de lignes*) to converge **2** (*concorder*) to combine, to unite; **c. à (faire) qch** to work towards (doing) sth; **tout a concouru à ma réussite** everything contributed to my success; **les témoignages concourent à prouver que …** the evidence goes to prove that … **3** *Sport etc* to compete; **c. (avec qn) pour un prix** to compete (with sb) for a prize

concours [kɔ̃kur] **NM 1** (*aide*) aid, assistance, help; **prêter son c. à qn** to help *or* assist sb; **avec le c. de …** with the participation of …; **avec l'aimable c. de Sophie** assisted by Sophie; **c. financier** financial aid; **ce projet a été réalisé avec le c. de plusieurs sociétés** this project was realized with the participation of *or* in association with several companies
2 (*compétition*) competition, contest; *Scol etc* (*examen*) competitive examination; **se présenter à un c.** to go in for *or* enter a competition; *Scol etc* to sit a competitive examination; **recrutement par c.** competitive entry, recruitment by competition; **c. interne/externe** in-house *or* internal/open competition; **c. d'entrée** entrance examination; **c. de vente** sales contest
3 (*d'événements*) coincidence; **par un c. de circonstances** by a combination of circumstances
4 *Arch, Litt* (*de personnes*) concourse, gathering
5 *Banque* loans outstanding, bank lending; **c. bancaire** bank lending
▸▸ **c. agricole/hippique** agricultural/horse show; **c. de beauté** beauty contest; *Scol* **c. général** = competition between all the lycées at baccalauréat level

> ### Concours
> Unlike an ordinary examination, passing a "concours" does not lead to a degree, but rather to a teaching post in the state education system (for example the **CAPES** and **agrégation** (*see boxes at these entries*)), an appointment or promotion in the civil service, or a place in a **grande école** (*see box at this entry*) ("ENA", "Centrale", "ENS", etc). "Concours" are extremely competitive examinations, and the quota of successful candidates is determined in advance. They are usually held over a period of several days, and comprise a series of written and oral examinations requiring a high level of preparation.

concret, -ète [kɔ̃krɛ, -ɛt] **ADJ 1** (*terme etc*) concrete; **cas c.** actual case, concrete example **2 musique concrète** concrete music **3** (*réel*) concrete, tangible, real; **je veux des résultats concrets** I want concrete *or* tangible results
NM le c. (*par opposition à l'abstrait*) the concrete

concrètement [kɔ̃krɛtmɑ̃] **ADV** in concrete terms; **c., qu'est-ce que ça a changé?** what has it changed in real terms?, what concrete changes has it led to?

concrétion [kɔ̃kresjɔ̃] **NF** concretion; *Méd* **concrétions calcaires** chalk stones

concrétiser [kɔ̃kretize] **VT** (*idée, question*) to put in(to) concrete form; (*rêve*) to realize; (*projet, promesse*) to put into effect, to carry out; (*avantage*) to capitalize on; **c. qch en un accord** to firm sth up with an agreement; **ils n'ont pas réussi à c. leur domination** they were unable to capitalize on their domination
VPR se concrétiser to materialize; **nos projets commencent à se c.** our plans are beginning to take shape

concubin, -ine [kɔ̃kybɛ̃, -in] **N 1** *Jur* partner, cohabitee **2** *Péj* (*amant*)

concubinage [kɔ̃kybinaʒ] **NM** cohabitation, *Fml* concubinage; **vivre** *ou* **être en c.** to live together (as man and wife), to cohabit

concupiscence [kɔ̃kypisɑ̃s] **NF** concupiscence

concupiscent [kɔ̃kypisɑ̃] **ADJ** concupiscent

concurremment [kɔ̃kyramɑ̃] ADV **1** (ensemble) jointly; (en même temps) concurrently; **agir c. avec qn** to act jointly or in conjunction with sb **2** (en concurrence) competitively, in competition (**avec** with)

concurrence [kɔ̃kyrɑ̃s] NF **1** Com, Écon etc competition; **faire c. à qn/qch** to compete with sb/sth; **être en c. avec qn** to be in competition with sb; **la libre c.** free or open competition; **c. acharnée** cut-throat competition; **c. déloyale** unfair competition; **c. directe** direct competition; **c. parfaite** perfect competition; **c. pure** pure competition; **c. sauvage** unfair competition; (acharnée) cut-throat competition; **faire jouer la c.** to allow market forces to operate; **prix défiant toute c.** unbeatable price **2 jusqu'à c. de ...** up to ..., not exceeding ..., to the amount of ... **3** Vieilli (d'événements) concurrence, coincidence

concurrencer [kɔ̃kyrɑ̃se] VT (**je concurrençai(s); n. concurrençons**) (dans le commerce etc) to compete with; **leur nouvelle gamme ne peut c. la nôtre** their new line can't compete with ours; **ils nous concurrencent dangereusement** they're very dangerous or serious competitors for us

concurrent, -ente [kɔ̃kyrɑ̃, -ɑ̃t] ADJ **1** (industries, produits etc) competing, rival **2** Vieilli (forces, actions etc) combined

N Com competitor, rival; (pour un prix etc) competitor; (pour un poste etc) candidate; (dans une émission de jeux etc) contestant; Com **c. principal** major competitor; Mktg **c. tardif** late entrant

concurrentiel, -ielle [kɔ̃kyrɑ̃sjɛl] ADJ (entreprises, prix etc) competitive

concussion [kɔ̃kysjɔ̃] NF misappropriation of public funds

condamnable [kɔ̃danabl] ADJ reprehensible, blameworthy

condamnation [kɔ̃danasjɔ̃] NF **1** Jur (jugement) conviction (**pour** for); (peine) sentence; **il a déjà quatre condamnations à son actif** he already has four convictions; **c. à trois mois de prison** three-month prison sentence; **c. à mort** death sentence; **c. à perpétuité** life sentence; Fig **la c. d'un film par la critique** the slating or panning or condemnation of a film by the critics **2** (reproche) condemnation; **la c. de la société de consommation** the condemnation of the consumer society **3** (fermeture) (d'une porte) blocking or sealing up; Aut **c. automatique des portes** automatic door locking; Aut **c. centralisée des portes** central locking

condamné, -ée [kɔ̃dane] N prisoner; **un c. à mort** a prisoner under sentence of death

condamner [kɔ̃dane] VT **1** Jur to sentence; **c. qn à mort/à trois mois de prison** to sentence sb to death/to three months' imprisonment; **c. qn à 10 000 euros d'amende** to fine sb 10,000 euros; Fig **tentative condamnée à l'insuccès** attempt doomed to failure; **le médecin l'a condamné** the doctor has given him up; **être condamné à la solitude** to be condemned to loneliness **2** (obliger à) **cela me condamne à l'attendre** that means I have to wait for him; **pourquoi tant de gens sont-ils condamnés à mourir de faim?** why are so many people condemned to die of hunger? **3** (interdire) to forbid; **la loi condamne la bigamie** bigamy is forbidden by law **4** (murer) (porte, pièce) to block up, to seal up; Fam **as-tu condamné les portes de la voiture?** have you locked the (car) doors?; Fig **c. sa porte** to bar one's door to visitors **5** (blâmer) (personne) to condemn, to blame; (thèse, abus etc) to condemn; **c. l'emploi d'un mot** to object to the use of a word

condé [kɔ̃de] NM Arg (policier) cop

condensateur [kɔ̃dɑ̃satœr] NM Élec condenser, capacitor; Opt condenser

condensation [kɔ̃dɑ̃sasjɔ̃] NF condensation

condensé [kɔ̃dɑ̃se] ADJ condensed; **lait c.** condensed milk; **texte c.** digest
NM digest

condenser [kɔ̃dɑ̃se] VT (gaz, cours etc) to condense (**en** into); (article, récit etc) to condense, to cut down; Ordinat to condense; (base de données) to pack
VPR **se condenser** to condense

condenseur [kɔ̃dɑ̃sœr] NM Phys, Opt condenser

condescendance [kɔ̃desɑ̃dɑ̃s] NF condescension; **parler avec c.** to speak with condescension or condescendingly

condescendant [kɔ̃desɑ̃dɑ̃] ADJ condescending

condescendre [kɔ̃desɑ̃dr] VI **c. à faire qch** to condescend to do sth

condiment [kɔ̃dimɑ̃] NM Culin condiment

condisciple [kɔ̃disipl] N Univ fellow student; Scol schoolmate

CONDITION [kɔ̃disjɔ̃] NF **1** (état) condition; **les conditions de vie/travail** living/working conditions; **en bonne c.** in good condition; **cet athlète n'est pas en c. (pour courir)** this athlete isn't fit or isn't in shape (to run); **pour te mettre en c.** to get you into shape (mentally and physically); **mise en c. physique** getting fit or into shape; **les films de propagande mettaient les foules en c.** the propaganda films conditioned the crowds; **être en bonne/mauvaise c. physique** to be in good/bad (physical) condition or shape; **conditions atmosphériques** atmospheric conditions; **conditions du marché** market conditions; **voyager dans les meilleures conditions** to travel under the most favourable conditions; **attendre que des conditions plus favorables se présentent** to wait until conditions improve or are better; **dans ces conditions, je n'y vais pas** if that's the way it is, I'm not going; **faire une escalade dans de mauvaises conditions (météorologiques)** to climb in bad (weather) conditions; **les conditions n'étaient pas réunies** the conditions weren't quite right

2 (stipulation) condition; **c. nécessaire et suffisante** necessary and sufficient condition; **une c. essentielle** an essential condition; **une c. sine qua non** a prerequisite, a sine qua non; **c'est la c. de votre réussite** that's what will determine your success; **conditions requises** requirements; **faire ses conditions** to name one's (own) terms; **mettre/imposer une c.** to lay down a condition; **il veut bien signer le contrat, mais il y met une c.** he's happy to sign the contract, but on one condition; **avez-vous posé vos conditions?** did you state your terms or conditions?; **offre sans c.** unconditional offer; **se rendre sans c.** to surrender unconditionally; **sous c.** conditionally; **acheter qch sous c.** to buy sth on approval; **d'accord, mais à une c.** OK, but on one condition; **tu peux partir quand tu veux, à c. de me prévenir** ou **à c. que tu me préviennes** you can leave when you like, on condition that or provided (that) or providing (that) you let me know; **tu peux y aller à la c. d'être rentrée à dix heures** you can go, provided (that) or so long as or on condition that you're back by ten o'clock

3 conditions (d'une vente, d'un accord etc) terms; **conditions d'admission** admission requirements; **conditions d'un contrat** terms and conditions of a contract; **conditions de crédit** credit terms; **conditions de discompte** discount terms; **conditions d'entrée** entry requirements; **conditions de faveur** preferential terms; **conditions de**

livraison terms of delivery; **conditions de paiement** terms of payment; **conditions de transport** conditions of carriage, conditions of transport; **conditions générales de vente** general (terms and) conditions of sale; **conditions particulières** (d'un billet etc) restrictions; **conditions particulières de vente** special conditions of sale

4 (sort) condition; **la c. humaine** the human condition; Jur **la c. des étrangers** foreigners' (legal) status; **il faut transformer la c. des ouvriers** the workers' lot needs to be changed

5 (classe sociale) station, status; **se marier avec qn de sa c.** to marry sb of the same social status; **se marier au-dessus/au-dessous de sa c.** to marry above/below one's station; Arch **personne de c.** person of rank

6 Arch **être de** ou **en c. chez qn** to be in service with sb

conditionné [kɔ̃disjɔne] ADJ **1 à air c.** air-conditioned; **il y a l'air c. dans toutes les pièces** there's air-conditioning in every room **2** Com **viande conditionnée** pre-packed meat **3** Phil, Méd, Psy (proposition, réflexe) conditioned

conditionnel, -elle [kɔ̃disjɔnɛl] ADJ conditional
NM Gram conditional (mood) SEE GRAMMAR A40; A52–3; B34

conditionnellement [kɔ̃disjɔnɛlmɑ̃] ADV conditionally

conditionnement [kɔ̃disjɔnmɑ̃] NM **1** (d'air) conditioning **2** Com (fait d'emballer, emballage) packaging; **c. d'expédition** shipping package **3** Psy conditioning

conditionner [kɔ̃disjɔne] VT **1** (air) to condition **2** (être la condition de) to govern; **la météo conditionne l'époque de la récolte** harvest time is determined by the weather conditions; **sa signature conditionne la validité du contrat** his signature is required for the contract to be valid **3** Com (emballer) to package **4** Psy (personne) to condition

conditionneur, -euse [kɔ̃disjɔnœr, -øz] NM **c. d'air** air conditioner
N Com (emballeur) packer

condoléances [kɔ̃dɔleɑ̃s] NFPL condolences; **offrir** ou **présenter ses c.** to offer one's condolences or sympathy; **toutes mes c.** (please accept) my condolences or my deepest sympathy

condom [kɔ̃dɔm] NM condom

condominium [kɔ̃dɔminjɔm] NM Pol condominium

condor [kɔ̃dɔr] NM condor

conductance [kɔ̃dyktɑ̃s] NF Élec conductance

conducteur, -trice [kɔ̃dyktœr, -tris] N Aut driver; (de machine) operator; **c. ivre** drink-driver, drunk driver; **c. de bestiaux** drover; **c. d'autobus** bus driver; **c. de camions** truck or Br lorry driver; Aut **siège (du) c.** driver's seat; **c. de travaux** clerk of works, (works) foreman; **c. d'hommes** leader of men
NM **1** Élec, Phys (de chaleur, d'électricité etc) conductor **2** Élec (fil) lead (wire), main **3** Radio, TV running sheet
ADJ Phys, Élec conductive, conducting

Il faut noter que le nom anglais **conductor** est un faux ami. Il signifie le plus souvent **chef d'orchestre** ou **contrôleur**, suivant le contexte.

conductibilité [kɔ̃dyktibilite] NF Phys, Élec conductivity

conductible [kɔ̃dyktibl] ADJ Phys, Élec conductive

conduction [kɔ̃dyksjɔ̃] NF Phys etc conduction

conductivité [kɔ̃dyktivite] NF *Élec* conductivity

CONDUIRE [kɔ̃dɥir] (*prp* **conduisant;** *pp* **conduit;** *pr ind* **je conduis, n. conduisons, ils conduisent;** *impf* **je conduisais;** *p hist* **je conduisis;** *fu* **je conduirai**) VT **1** (*emmener*) to take; (*en voiture*) to take, to drive; **j'ai dû le c. chez le dentiste de toute urgence** I had to rush him to the dentist; **c. qn à la gare** to take *or* drive sb to the station; **on la conduisit à sa chambre** she was shown *or* taken to her room

2 (*mener*) (*cheval, aveugle etc*) to lead; **c. qn à faire qch** to lead sb to do sth; **ses pas la conduisirent jusqu'à la chapelle** her footsteps led her to the chapel; **les traces de sang nous conduisirent jusqu'au lieu du crime** the bloodstains led us to the scene of the crime; **c. ses hommes au combat** to lead one's men into battle; **cela va nous c. à la catastrophe/ruine** it's going to lead us to disaster/ruin; **c. qn au désespoir/suicide** to drive sb to despair/suicide; **c'est l'appât du gain qui conduit tous ses actes** the thirst for wealth dictates his every action

3 (*piloter*) (*voiture etc*) to drive; (*bateau*) to steer

4 (*l'eau, le gaz etc*) to carry, to convey; **corps qui conduit bien l'électricité** good conductor of electricity

5 (*diriger*) (*entreprise, affaire*) to manage, to run; **un orchestre** to conduct an orchestra
VI **1** *Aut* to drive; **elle conduit bien** she is a good driver

2 (*mener*) to lead; **quel est le chemin qui conduit à la gare?** which is the way to the station?; **cette porte ne conduit nulle part** this door doesn't lead anywhere; **elle se laissa c. comme une enfant jusqu'à la cuisine** she let herself be led like a child into the kitchen
VPR **se conduire 1** (*se diriger*) (*d'un engin*) **ça se conduit comment?** how do you drive it?

2 (*se comporter*) to behave; **se c. mal** (*d'un enfant*) to behave badly, to misbehave; **se c. bien/mal avec qn** to behave well/badly towards sb

conduit [kɔ̃dɥi] NM **1** *Tech* conduit, pipe; *Constr, Tech* **c. d'aération** air duct; **c. de ventilation** ventilation shaft; *Naut* **c. de chaîne** hawse hole; *Aut* **c. d'aspiration** suction pipe; *Aut* **c. de carburant** fuel pipe; *Aut* **conduits d'échappement** exhaust manifold **2** *Anat* **c. auditif** auditory canal, *Spéc* meatus; **c. lacrymal** tear *or* *Spec* lachrymal duct; **c. urinaire** urinary canal

conduite [kɔ̃dɥit] NF **1** (*action d'accompagner*) **les chiens qui assurent la c. du troupeau** the dogs which drive the herd; *Fam* **faire un bout de c. à qn** to go part of the way with sb

2 (*de voiture, charrette etc*) driving; (*de bateau, ballon*) steering; **c. à gauche/droite** (*d'une voiture*) left-/right-hand drive; (*d'un pays*) driving on the left/right; **ma voiture a la c. à gauche** my car is left-hand drive; **leçons de c.** driving lessons; **c. dangereuse** dangerous driving

3 (*d'une entreprise, des affaires, opérations*) management, running; (*d'une armée, flotte etc*) command; (*d'une guerre*) conduct; **être sous la c. de qn** (*suivre des ordres*) to be under sb's leadership; (*suivre des conseils*) to be under sb's guidance; **c. des travaux** supervision of works

4 (*comportement*) behaviour, *Am* behavior, conduct; **je ne sais vraiment plus quelle c. adopter avec elle** I really don't know any more what line to take with her; **c'est ma seule ligne de c.** it's my guiding principle; **mauvaise c.** bad behaviour, misbehaviour, misconduct; **il a été relâché pour bonne c.** he was released for good behaviour; **adop-**

ter une c. différente to start to behave differently; **un écart de c.** a misdemeanour; *Vieilli* **il manque de c.** he has no manners, he doesn't know how to behave; *Hum* **s'acheter une c.** to turn over a new leaf; *Scol* **zéro de c.** no marks for conduct

5 *Tech* pipe, conduit, duct; **c. à air** *ou* **d'air** air duct; **c. d'eau** water pipe *or* main(s); **c. de gaz** gas pipe *or* main(s); **c. souple** hose, flexible pipe; **tuyau de c.** conduit pipe; *Aut* **c. d'arrivée du combustible** supply pipe

▸▸ **c. accompagnée** = learning to drive accompanied by someone holding a full driving licence; *Psy* **c. d'échec** defeatist behaviour; **c. en état d'ivresse** drunk driving; *Tech etc* **c. forcée** (pressure) pipeline; *Aut* **c. fractionnée** stop-go driving; *Aut* **c. de frein** brake line; **c. intérieure** saloon (car), *Am* sedan; **c. montante** flow pipe, rising main; **c. normale** (*de boîte auto*) drive

condyle [kɔ̃dil] NM *Anat* condyle

cône [kon] NM (*objet, forme*) cone; **en forme de c.** cone-shaped; **c. de pin** pine cone; *Géol* **c. de déjection** alluvial cone; *Astron* **c. d'ombre** (*d'une planète etc*) umbra; *Naut* **c. de tempête** storm cone; **c. de signalisation** signal cone; **c. de chantier** traffic cone; *Aut* **c. d'embrayage** clutch cone; *Aut* **c. de friction** friction cone; *Aut* **c. de synchronisation** synchromesh cone, baulking cone

confection [kɔ̃fɛksjɔ̃] NF **1** (*d'un vêtement etc*) making; (*d'un repas*) preparation, making; **elle nous a offert des gâteaux de sa c.** she offered us some of her home-made cakes **2** (*industrie*) (ready-to-wear) clothing industry; **robe/vêtements de c.** ready-made *or* off-the-peg dress/clothes; **maison de c.** (ready-to-wear) clothes company; **travailler dans la c.** to work in the clothing industry *or* *Fam* rag trade

confectionner [kɔ̃fɛksjɔne] VT (*robe*) to make; (*plat*) to prepare, to make

confectionneur, -euse [kɔ̃fɛksjɔnœr, -øz] N clothes manufacturer

confédéral, -ale, -aux, -ales [kɔ̃federal, -o] ADJ confederal; **débat c.** debate within the confederation

confédération [kɔ̃federasjɔ̃] NF confederation, confederacy

confédéré, -e [kɔ̃federe] ADJ (*nations*) confederate; *Ind, Pol* **syndicat non c.** non-affiliated union
NMPL *Hist* **les Confédérés** the Confederates

confédérer [kɔ̃federe] VT (**je confédère, n. confédérons; je confédérerai**) to confederate

confer [kɔ̃fɛr] VT (*impératif*) cf, compare

conférence [kɔ̃ferɑ̃s] NF **1** (*congrès, colloque*) conference, meeting; **tenir c.** to hold a conference; **être en c.** to be in a meeting **2** *Univ etc* (*exposé*) lecture; **maître de conférences** lecturer; **salle de conférences** lecture room; **faire une c. sur l'alcoolisme** to lecture *or* to give a lecture on alcoholism

▸▸ **c. au sommet** summit (conference); *Com, Naut* **c. maritime** shipping conference; **c. de presse** press conference; *Journ* **c. de rédaction** (editors') conference

conférencier, -ière [kɔ̃ferɑ̃sje, -jɛr] N lecturer, speaker; *Univ* lecturer; **c. invité** guest speaker

conférer [kɔ̃fere] VT (**je confère, n. conférons; je conférerai**) VT **1** (*privilèges etc*) to confer, to bestow (à on); **c. le grade de docteur à qn** to confer a doctor's degree on sb; **ils lui ont conféré tous les pouvoirs** they invested him with *or* granted him full authority; **en vertu des pouvoirs qui me sont conférés** by the authority vested in me **2** (*textes*) to compare, to collate
VI to confer (**avec** with); **nous avons conféré**

de l'affaire we talked the matter over, we conferred on the matter

confesse [kɔ̃fɛs] NF **aller/être à c.** to go to/be at confession

confesser [kɔ̃fese] VT **1** (*reconnaître*) to confess, to admit; **je confesse mon ignorance** I confess *or* admit my ignorance; **j'ai menti, je vous le confesse, mais ...** I admit *or* confess I lied, but ..., I lied, I admit it, but ...; **il confesse qu'il s'est trompé** he admits he was mistaken **2** *Rel* (*ses péchés, sa foi*) to confess **3** (*du prêtre*) (*pénitent*) to confess; *Fig Fam* **on trouvera les moyens de le c.** we'll find a way to make him talk
VI **ce prêtre ne confesse pas** this priest doesn't hear confessions
VPR **se confesser** to confess; *Rel* to confess (one's sins); *Rel* **se c. toutes les semaines** to go to confession every week

confesseur [kɔ̃fesœr] NM **1** *Rel, Fig* (father) confessor **2** *Hist* (*de sa religion, foi*) confessor

confession [kɔ̃fesjɔ̃] NF **1** (*aveu*) confession, admission; **faire la c. de qch** to confess to sth, to own up to sth; **je vais vous faire une c.** I've got a confession to make to you **2** *Rel* (*aveu*) confession; *Fam* **on te donnerait le bon Dieu sans c.** you look as though butter wouldn't melt in your mouth **3** *Rel* (*par un prêtre*) hearing of confession; **entendre qn en c.** to hear sb's confession **4** (*croyance*) denomination, faith, religion; **des élèves de toutes confessions** pupils of all denominations; **une école avec des élèves de toutes confessions** a multi-denominational school

confessionnal, -aux [kɔ̃fesjɔnal, -o] NM *Rel* confessional

confessionnel, -elle [kɔ̃fesjɔnɛl] ADJ (*querelles, affaires*) denominational

confetti [kɔ̃feti] NM (piece of) confetti; **confettis** confetti; *Fam* **tu peux en faire des confettis!** you can chuck it out!, you can throw it in the bin! VOIR GRAMMAIRE A14

confiance [kɔ̃fjɑ̃s] NF **1** (*foi*) trust, confidence, faith; **avoir c. en** *ou* **faire c. à qn/qch** to trust sb/sth, to have confidence *or* faith in sb/sth; **il n'a pas c. dans les médecins** he doesn't trust doctors, he has no confidence *or* faith in doctors; **elle a une c. aveugle en toi** she trusts you blindly *or* implicitly; **acheter qch en toute c.** to buy sth with complete confidence; **il me faut un homme de c.** I need a man I can trust *or* rely on; **c'est l'homme de c. du président** he's the one who has the president's confidence; **comment regagner sa c.?** how can I/we/*etc* win back *or* regain his confidence *or* trust?; **abuser de la c. de qn** to abuse sb's trust; **digne de c.** trustworthy, reliable; **maison de c.** reliable firm; **c'est un poste** *ou* **emploi de c.** it's a position of trust; **avec c.** (*avec espoir*) confidently; **je vous parle en toute c.** I know I can trust you (with what I have to say); **tu sais que tu peux me faire c.** you know you can trust me; **faites-moi c.** trust me; *Fam* (*croyez-moi*) believe me; *Pol* **vote de c.** vote of confidence; **un climat de c. économique** a climate of economic confidence

2 (*assurance*) confidence; **manquer de c. en soi** to lack (self-)assurance *or* (self-)confidence

confiant [kɔ̃fjɑ̃] ADJ **1** (*qui fait confiance*) trusting, trustful **2** (*optimiste*) (*nature*) confident (**dans** in) **3** (*qui a confiance en soi*) (*manières etc*) (self-)confident, (self-)assured

confidence [kɔ̃fidɑ̃s] NF confidence; **faire une c. à qn** to confide something to sb, to tell sb a secret; **il ne me fait jamais de c.** he never confides in me; **faire c. de qch à qn** to confide sth to sb; **mettre qn dans la c.** to let sb into the secret; **dire qch en c.** to say sth in confidence *or* confidentially; **confidences sur l'oreiller** pillow talk

Il faut noter que le nom anglais **confidence** signifie également **confiance**.

confident, -ente [kɔ̃fidɑ̃, -ɑ̃t] N confidant, f confidante

confidentialité [kɔ̃fidɑ̃sjalite] NF confidentiality; *Ordinat* **c. des données** data privacy

confidentiel, -ielle [kɔ̃fidɑ̃sjɛl] ADJ confidential; *(mention sur document)* private and confidential; **à titre c.** confidentially, in confidence; *(non officiel)* off-the-record; **succès c.** modest *or* limited success

confidentiellement [kɔ̃fidɑ̃sjɛlmɑ̃] ADV confidentially, in confidence

confier [kɔ̃fje] *(impf, pr sub n. confiions, v. confiiez)* VT 1 *(laisser)* to entrust; **c. qch à qn** to entrust sb with sth, to entrust sth to sb; **c. qch à la garde de qn** to entrust sth to sb's care; **je leur ai confié les enfants** I left the children with them; **je n'oserais pas c. mes économies à cette banque** I wouldn't dare entrust my savings to this bank *or* entrust this bank with my savings 2 *(dire)* to confide; **c. qch à qn** to confide sth to sb, to tell sb sth in confidence; **est-ce que je peux te c. un secret?** can I tell you a secret?, can I share a secret (with you)?
▸ VPR se confier 1 *Fml (s'en remettre)* **se c. à qn/qch** to put one's trust in sb/sth 2 *(s'épancher)* **se c. à qn** to confide in sb; **il ne se confie jamais** he never confides in anyone

configurable [kɔ̃figyrabl] ADJ *Ordinat* configurable

configuration [kɔ̃figyrasjɔ̃] NF 1 configuration; *(de bâtiment)* form, shape; *(du terrain)* lie 2 *Ordinat* configuration; **c. matérielle** hardware configuration

configurer [kɔ̃figyre] VT *Ordinat etc* to configure

confiné [kɔ̃fine] ADJ 1 *(atmosphère etc)* enclosed; *(air)* stale 2 *(enfermé)* shut away *or* up; **vivre c. chez soi** to live shut away *or* up indoors

confinement [kɔ̃finmɑ̃] NM confinement

confiner [kɔ̃fine] VI **c. à** *ou* **avec un pays** *(d'un pays etc)* to border on *or* adjoin a country; *Fig* **courage qui confine à la témérité** courage verging *or* bordering on foolhardiness
▸ VT to confine, to shut away *or* up
▸ VPR se confiner to confine oneself; **se c. chez soi** to shut oneself away *or* up indoors

confins [kɔ̃fɛ̃] NMPL *(de pays, d'État)* confines, borders; **aux c. de la science et de la métaphysique** on the border between science and metaphysics

confiote [kɔ̃fjɔt] NF *Fam (confiture)* jam

confire [kɔ̃fir] VT *(prp confisant; pp confit; pr ind je confis, n. confisons, ils confisent; impf je confisais; p hist je confis; fu je confirai)* *(fruits etc)* to preserve; *(écorce, zeste etc)* to candy; **c. qch au sel/au vinaigre** to salt sth down/pickle sth

confirmatif, -ive [kɔ̃firmatif, -iv] ADJ *(déclaration)* corroborative; *(jugement)* confirmative

confirmation [kɔ̃firmasjɔ̃] NF 1 *(de nouvelle etc)* confirmation, corroboration; **c. écrite** written confirmation; **c. de commande** confirmation of an/the order; **c. de réservation** confirmation of a/the reservation; **c. d'un jugement** confirmation of a sentence; **il m'en a donné c.** he gave me confirmation of it; **c'est la c. de ce que je pensais** that (just) confirms what I thought; **en c. de** in confirmation of 2 *Rel* confirmation; **donner la c. à qn** to confirm sb

confirmer [kɔ̃firme] VT 1 *(nouvelle, juge-*

ment etc) to confirm; **c. un traité** to ratify a treaty; **cela me confirme dans mon opinion** that confirms *or* strengthens me in my opinion; **elle n'a pas été confirmée dans ses fonctions** she was not given the job (which she had been doing temporarily); **l'exception confirme la règle** the exception proves the rule 2 *Rel (personne)* to confirm
▸ VPR se confirmer *(d'un rapport, de doutes etc)* to be confirmed; **le bruit ne s'est pas confirmé** the rumour proved false; **je pensais qu'il était bête et là, ça se confirme** I thought he was stupid and there's the proof of it *or* and I've been proved right

confiscation [kɔ̃fiskasjɔ̃] NF *(de propriété etc)* confiscation, seizure

confiserie [kɔ̃fizri] NF 1 *(de fruits etc)* preserving in sugar 2 *(magasin)* confectioner's (shop), *Br* sweetshop, *Am* candy store 3 *(bonbon)* sweet, *Am* candy; **des confiseries** confectionery, *Br* sweets, *Am* candy

confiseur, -euse [kɔ̃fizœr, -øz] N confectioner

confisquer [kɔ̃fiske] VT *(marchandises, propriété etc)* to confiscate, to seize; **le prof m'a confisqué ma balle** the teacher confiscated my ball; **le président veut c. le pouvoir** the president wants to seize power

confit [kɔ̃fi] ADJ **fruits confits** crystallized *or* candied fruit; *Fig* **être c. en dévotion** to be steeped in piety
▸ NM *Culin* **c. d'oie/de canard** conserve of goose/of duck

confiture [kɔ̃fityr] NF *Culin* jam; **c. de fraises** strawberry jam; **c. d'oranges** (orange) marmalade; *Fig* **ce serait donner de la c. aux cochons** that would be throwing *or* casting pearls before swine

confiturerie [kɔ̃fityrri] NF 1 *(commerce)* jam manufacture 2 *(fabrique)* jam factory

confiturier [kɔ̃fityrje] NM jam maker *or* manufacturer

conflagration [kɔ̃flagrasjɔ̃] NF cataclysm

conflictuel, -elle [kɔ̃fliktɥɛl] ADJ *(témoignages, intérêts etc)* conflicting; **situation conflictuelle** situation of conflict; **ils ont des rapports très conflictuels** they have a very adversarial relationship

conflit [kɔ̃fli] NM 1 *(divergence)* conflict; *(d'intérêts)* conflict, clash; **être en c.** to be at variance *or* *Fam* loggerheads (**avec** with); *(d'intérêts)* to conflict, to clash (**avec** with); **entrer en c. avec qn** to come into conflict with sb, to clash with sb; **le c. des générations** the generation gap; **arbitrage des conflits internationaux** arbitration of international disputes; **conflits sociaux** industrial disputes; **c. du travail** industrial dispute; **c. salarial** pay dispute; *Jur* **tribunal des conflits** = jurisdictional court which decides whether a matter should be dealt with by a civil or other court 2 *(lutte armée)* **c. (armé)** (armed) conflict, war

confluence [kɔ̃flyɑ̃s] NF confluence

confluent [kɔ̃flyɑ̃] NM *(de fleuves, veines etc)* confluence

confluer [kɔ̃flye] VI to meet, to join, to unite; **l'Oise conflue avec la Seine** the Oise flows into the Seine

confondant [kɔ̃fɔ̃dɑ̃] ADJ *(qui met en confusion)* confusing; *(qui trouble)* astounding

confondre [kɔ̃fɔ̃dr] VT 1 *(réunir)* to merge, to mingle, to intermingle; **toutes tendances confondues, les électeurs ont voté en masse pour lui** voters of all political tendencies voted massively for him
2 *(mélanger)* *(noms)* to confuse, to mix up; **je les confonds toujours** I always confuse them *or* mix them up, I always get them confused *or* mixed up
3 *(sidérer)* *(personne)* to astound, to stag-

ger; **son insolence me confond** I'm astounded by his insolence, his insolence astounds me
4 *(démasquer)* *(criminel etc)* to find, to track down; **c. un menteur** to show up a liar
▸ VI to be mistaken; **tu dois c., ce n'est pas ça** you must be mistaken, that's not it at all
▸ VPR se confondre 1 *(de couleurs etc)* to merge, to blend (**en** into)
2 *(de ruisseaux etc)* to merge, to flow into each other; *(d'intérêts etc)* to merge, to be identical; **se c. en excuses/remerciements** to apologize profusely/be profuse in one's thanks; **se c. en excuses/remerciements devant qn** to apologize profusely to sb/thank sb profusely; **leurs voix se confondent au loin** their voices merge *or* mingle in the distance

confondu [kɔ̃fɔ̃dy] ADJ 1 *(décontenancé)* disconcerted; **je suis tout c. de votre bonté** I am overwhelmed by your kindness 2 *(sidéré)* astounded, dumbfounded (**de** at); **en rester c.** to be (left) dumbfounded

conformation [kɔ̃fɔrmasjɔ̃] NF *(de collines, parties du corps etc)* conformation, structure

conforme [kɔ̃fɔrm] ADJ 1 *(identique)* **copie c. à l'original** exact copy; *Admin* **pour copie c.** certified true copy; *Fig* **elle est la copie c. de sa mère** she is the exact *or* very image of her mother 2 *(qui correspond à)* **il mène une vie c. à ses moyens** he lives according to his means; **la réalisation n'est pas c. à ce qui avait été prévu** it is not being carried out in keeping with *or* in accordance with what was agreed; **les sanitaires ne sont pas conformes** the sanitary installations are not standard; **non c.** *(pensée, idée)* unorthodox

conformé [kɔ̃fɔrme] ADJ **bien c.** *(enfant etc)* well-formed; **mal c.** *(membre etc)* misshapen

conformément [kɔ̃fɔrmemɑ̃] ADV **c. à** in accordance with; **c. à la loi** according to *or* in accordance with the law; **c. à vos ordres** in accordance with your orders; **c. à ce qui a été prévu** according to *or* in accordance with what was planned; **tout se passe c. aux plans** everything's going according to plan

conformer [kɔ̃fɔrme] VT to model (**à** on); **sa vie à certains principes** to shape one's life according to certain principles
▸ VPR se conformer **se c. à qch** to conform to sth, to comply with *or* abide by sth; **se c. à la règle** to conform to the rule; *Com* **se c. au modèle** to keep (to) the pattern

conformisme [kɔ̃fɔrmism] NM *(traditionalisme)* conformism, conventionalism; *Rel* conformism, conformity

conformiste [kɔ̃fɔrmist] N *(traditionaliste)* conformist, conventionalist; *Rel (de l'Église anglicane)* conformist
▸ ADJ conformist

conformité [kɔ̃fɔrmite] NF *(ressemblance)* similarity; *Rel* conformity; *(d'un produit aux normes)* compliance; **en c. avec** in accordance with; **être en c. de goûts avec qn** to have similar tastes to sb

confort [kɔ̃fɔr] NM comfort; **hôtel avec tout le c. moderne** hotel with every modern convenience *or Fam* with all mod cons; **manquer de c.** to be lacking in comfort, to be uncomfortable; **une maison sans c.** an uncomfortable house; **elle aime bien son petit c.** she likes her creature comforts *or* her little comforts; **c. d'écoute** *(d'une station de radio)* quality of reception; **c. d'emploi** *(d'un ordinateur etc)* user-friendliness, ease of use; **c. visuel** *(d'un écran)* easiness on the eye; **médicament de c.** = medicine not considered essential and not reimbursed by Social Security

confortable [kɔ̃fɔrtabl] ADJ *(fauteuil,*

maison, chaussures etc), Fig comfortable; *(financièrement)* comfortable, well-off, comfortably off; **des appointements confortables** a comfortable *or* good salary; **une vie c.** a comfortable life(style); *Fig* **il est plus c. de penser que tout va bien** it's easier *or* more comfortable to think that everything is going well

NM *Can (édredon)* quilt, *Am* comforter

confortablement [kɔ̃fɔrtabləmɑ̃] **ADV** comfortably; **installe-toi c.** make yourself comfortable; **être c. rémunéré** to be on a good salary, to be well paid

conforter [kɔ̃fɔrte] **VT** to reinforce, to strengthen, to confirm; *(position, avance)* to consolidate; **cela me conforte dans mon opinion** that reinforces *or* strengthens *or* confirms my opinion

confraternel, -elle [kɔ̃fratɛrnɛl] **ADJ** fraternal, brotherly

confraternité [kɔ̃fratɛrnite] **NF** brotherliness

confrère [kɔ̃frɛr] **NM** *(de profession)* colleague; *(de société)* fellow member

confrérie [kɔ̃freri] **NF** *Rel* brotherhood, confraternity

confrontation [kɔ̃frɔ̃tasjɔ̃] **NF 1** *Jur (d'un accusé avec un témoin)* confrontation, confronting; *Fig (d'opinions, d'idéaux etc)* clash, conflict **2** *(comparaison)* comparison *(à, avec* with); *(de textes)* comparison, collation

confronter [kɔ̃frɔ̃te] **VT 1** to confront; *(prisonnier)* to confront, to bring face to face *(avec, à* with); **être confronté à un problème** to be confronted with a problem **2** *(comparer)* to compare *(avec, à* with); *(textes)* to collate

VPR se confronter se c. à un adversaire to confront an opponent; **nous nous sommes confrontés** we confronted each other *(au sujet de* about)

confucéen, -éenne [kɔ̃fyseɛ̃, -eɛn] **ADJ** Confucian

confucianisme [kɔ̃fysjanism] **NM** Confucianism

confus [kɔ̃fy] **ADJ 1** *(mélangé) (masse etc)* confused, jumbled, chaotic; *(explication)* confused, muddled; *(bruit)* indistinct; *(vision)* dim, blurred; *(style, texte)* obscure, unclear; **une affaire pour le moins confuse** a confused *or* muddled business to say the least **2** *(embarrassé)* embarrassed, abashed; **je suis c.** *(après un faux pas)* I'm so embarrassed, I don't know where to put myself; *(devant votre bonté)* I don't know what to say; **je suis c. de vous déranger** I'm so sorry to disturb you

Il faut noter que l'adjectif anglais **confused** est un faux ami. Il signifie le plus souvent **désorienté, embrouillé**.

confusément [kɔ̃fyzemɑ̃] **ADV** confusedly, vaguely, indistinctly; **j'entrevoyais c. la solution du problème** I was slowly beginning to see a solution to the problem

confusion [kɔ̃fyzjɔ̃] **NF 1** *(désordre)* confusion, disorder, disarray; **il a réussi à s'échapper, profitant de la c. générale** he managed to escape in the general confusion; **mettre la c. dans l'assemblée** to throw the audience into confusion; **jeter la c. dans les esprits** to confuse people; *Méd* **c. mentale** mental aberration; **un moment de c.** a moment of confusion, a moment's confusion **2** *(erreur) (de noms, dates etc)* mix-up, confusion; **il y a eu c. entre deux personnes** they got two people mixed up *or* confused; **c'est une grossière c.** it's a stupid mix-up **3** *(gêne)* embarrassment, confusion; **être rouge de c.** to be red with embarrassment, *Fml* to be cov-

ered in confusion **4** *Jur* **avec c. des peines** the sentences to run concurrently

congé [kɔ̃ʒe] **NM 1** *(vacances)* holiday, *Am* vacation; *Mil* leave; **il ne me reste plus de c. à prendre** I've used up all my holiday (entitlement); **en c.** on holiday, *Am* on vacation; *Mil* on leave; **un après-midi de c.** an afternoon off; **on a c. lundi** we've got Monday off, Monday's a holiday; **prendre c. de qn** to take (one's) leave of sb; **donner c. à qn** to dismiss sb **2** *(avis de renvoi)* notice; **donner son c. à qn** to give sb his notice; **demander son c.** to hand in *or* give one's notice, to give notice; **donner c. à un locataire** to give a tenant notice (to quit) **3** *(autorisation)* authorization, permit; *(de vin en douane)* release; *Naut* **c. de navigation** clearance certificate

▸▸ *Admin* **c. annuel** annual leave, annual holiday, *Am* vacation leave; **c. de longue durée** extended leave; **c. de maladie** sick leave; **c. de maternité** maternity leave; **c. parental d'éducation** = maternity/paternity leave; **c. de paternité** paternity leave; **congés payés** paid holidays *or* leave, *Am* paid vacation; **c. pour convenance personnelle** leave for personal reasons, compassionate leave; **c. sabbatique** sabbatical; **c. sans solde** unpaid leave *or* holidays, *Am* unpaid vacation

congédiable [kɔ̃ʒedjabl] **ADJ** liable to be dismissed at any time; *Mil* due for discharge

congédier [kɔ̃ʒedje] **VT** *(impf, pr sub n. congédiions, v. congédiiez)* **1** *(employé)* to dismiss **2** *(visiteur)* to dismiss; *Mil, Naut (hommes)* to discharge

congelable [kɔ̃ʒlabl] **ADJ** suitable for freezing, freezable; **aliment non c.** foodstuff unsuitable for freezing

congélateur [kɔ̃ʒelatœr] **NM** freezer, deep-freeze

congélation [kɔ̃ʒelasjɔ̃] **NF** *(d'aliments)* (deep-)freezing; *(de l'eau etc)* freezing; *(de l'huile)* congealing; **point de c. de l'eau** freezing point of water; **sac (de) c.** freezer bag

congeler [kɔ̃ʒle] *(il congèle; il congèlera)* **VT** *(aliments)* to (deep-)freeze; *(eau etc)* to freeze; **viande congelée** frozen meat; **ne pas c.** do not freeze

VPR se congeler to freeze

congélo [kɔ̃ʒelo] **NM** *(abrév* **congélateur)** freezer

congénère [kɔ̃ʒenɛr] **ADJ** *Biol* congeneric; *Anat (muscle)* congenerous

N *Biol* congener; *Fam* **lui et ses congénères** him and his sort *or* his like

congénital, -ale, -aux, -ales [kɔ̃ʒenital, -o] **ADJ** congenital; *Méd* **malformation congénitale** congenital malformation; *Fam* **inconscience congénitale** innate *or* congenital thoughtlessness

congère [kɔ̃ʒɛr] **NF** snowdrift

congestif, -ive [kɔ̃ʒɛstif, -iv] **ADJ** *Méd* congestive

congestion [kɔ̃ʒɛstjɔ̃] **NF** *Méd* congestion; **c. cérébrale** stroke; **c. pulmonaire** congestion of the lungs

congestionné [kɔ̃ʒɛstjɔne] **ADJ** *(visage)* flushed, red; *(routes)* congested; **les routes sont très congestionnées** the roads are very congested, there's a lot of congestion on the roads

congestionner [kɔ̃ʒɛstjɔne] **VT 1** *Méd* to congest; *(visage)* to flush **2** *(boucher)* to block, to congest; **les voitures congestionnent la rue** the cars are blocking the street

VPR se congestionner to become congested

conglomérat [kɔ̃glɔmera] **NM** *Écon, Géol* conglomerate

conglomération [kɔ̃glɔmerasjɔ̃] **NF** conglomeration

conglomérer [kɔ̃glɔmere] *(je conglomère, n. conglomérons; je conglomérerai)* **VT** to conglomerate

VPR se conglomérer to conglomerate

Congo [kɔ̃go] **NM le C.** the Congo

congolais, -aise [kɔ̃gɔlɛ, -ɛz] **ADJ** Congolese

N C. Congolese

NM *Culin* coconut cake

congratulations [kɔ̃gratylasjɔ̃] **NFPL** congratulations; **mes c. pour ta réussite** congratulations on your success

congratuler [kɔ̃gratyle] **VT** *(personne)* to congratulate *(pour* on)

VPR se congratuler to congratulate oneself, *Fam* to pat oneself on the back

congre [kɔ̃gr] **NM** conger (eel)

congrégation [kɔ̃gregasjɔ̃] **NF 1** *Rel (communauté)* community *(group of monasteries)*; *(de cardinaux)* congregation **2** *Fig* assembly

congrès [kɔ̃grɛ] **NM** conference, convention; **C. des États-Unis** United States Congress; **membre du C.** congressman, *f* congresswoman; **palais des c.** conference centre; **c. annuel** *(d'un parti politique)* annual conference

congressiste [kɔ̃gresist] **N** conference participant, *Am* conventioneer; *Pol* conference delegate

congru [kɔ̃gry] **ADJ 1 portion congrue** (income providing a) bare living; *Rel (de prêtre)* emolument; **réduire qn à la portion congrue** to put sb on short allowance **2** *Math* congruent **3** *Arch (adéquat)* sufficient, adequate

congruence [kɔ̃gryɑ̃s] **NF** *Math* congruence

congruent [kɔ̃gryɑ̃] **ADJ** *Math* congruent

conifère [kɔnifɛr] **NM** *Bot* conifer

conique [kɔnik, ko-] **ADJ 1** *Géom* conical, cone-shaped; *Math* **section c.** conic section **2** *Tech etc (tige, goupille etc)* coned, tapering; **engrenage c.** bevel gearing

conjectural, -ale, -aux, -ales [kɔ̃ʒɛktyral, -o] **ADJ** conjectural

conjecture [kɔ̃ʒɛktyr] **NF** conjecture, surmise; **se perdre en conjectures** to get lost *or* lose oneself in conjecture(s); **ce n'est que pure c.** it's sheer conjecture

conjecturer [kɔ̃ʒɛktyre] **VT** to conjecture about, to guess at

VI to conjecture, to hypothesize; **il conjecture sur ce qu'il ignore** he conjectures *or* makes guesses about things he knows nothing about

conjoint, -ointe [kɔ̃ʒwɛ̃] **ADJ 1** joint, united; *Fin* **compte c.** joint account; *Jur* **legs c.** joint legacy; **légataires conjoints** co-legatees **2** *Jur (marié)* married

N spouse; **les conjoints** the husband and wife; **féliciter les conjoints** to congratulate the couple; **les conjoints n'ont pas été invités** partners weren't invited

conjointement [kɔ̃ʒwɛ̃tmɑ̃] **ADV** jointly; *Jur* **c. et solidairement** jointly and severally

conjoncteur [kɔ̃ʒɔ̃ktœr] **NM** *Élec* circuit closer

conjoncteur-disjoncteur, *pl* **conjoncteurs-disjoncteurs NM** *Aut* cut-out (valve), *Élec* make-and-break (switch)

conjonctif, -ive [kɔ̃ʒɔ̃ktif, -iv] **ADJ** *(tissu etc)* connective, *Gram* **locution/proposition conjonctive** conjunctive phrase/clause

conjonction [kɔ̃ʒɔ̃ksjɔ̃] **NF 1** *(réunion)* union; **la c. de nos efforts** our combined efforts **2** *Gram* conjunction; **c. de subordination/coordination** subordinating/coordinating conjunction SEE GRAMMAR A73–6; B57–8

conjonctive [kɔ̃ʒɔ̃ktiv] **NF** *(de l'œil)* conjunctiva

conjonctivite [kɔ̃ʒɔ̃ktivit] NF *Méd* conjunctivitis; **faire** *ou* **avoir de la c.** to have conjunctivitis

conjoncture [kɔ̃ʒɔ̃ktyr] NF *(situation)* circumstances, situation; **dans la c. actuelle** at this (present) juncture, under the present circumstances, in the present situation; *Pol, Écon* **c. économique** overall economic situation; **on assiste à une dégradation de la c. économique** the economic situation is deteriorating; **étude de c.** study of the state of the economy

conjoncturel, -elle [kɔ̃ʒɔ̃ktyrɛl] ADJ relating to the current economic climate, economic; *(chômage)* cyclical; **crise conjoncturelle** economic crisis

conjoncturiste [kɔ̃ʒɔ̃ktyrist] NM *Écon* economic analyst

conjugable [kɔ̃ʒygabl] ADJ *Gram* conjugable

conjugaison [kɔ̃ʒygɛzɔ̃] NF *Gram, Biol etc (de verbe, de cellules etc)* conjugation; *Fig Litt* **grâce à la c. de leurs efforts** thanks to their joint efforts SEE GRAMMAR B24

conjugal, -ale, -aux, -ales [kɔ̃ʒygal, -o] ADJ *(devoir)* marital, conjugal; **vie conjugale** married life; **le domicile c.** the marital *or* matrimonial home; **bonheur c.** wedded *or* married bliss; **le lit c.** the marriage bed

conjugalement [kɔ̃ʒygalmɑ̃] ADV conjugally; **vivre c.** to live together as a married couple *or* as man and wife

conjugué [kɔ̃ʒyge] ADJ *(efforts etc)* joint, combined; *Tech* paired, twin; *Math, Opt* conjugate; *Bot* **feuilles conjuguées** conjugate leaves; **machines conjuguées** paired engines

conjuguer [kɔ̃ʒyge] VT **1** *Gram* to conjugate **2** *(unir) (efforts)* to combine
▸ **VPR se conjuguer** *Gram* to be conjugated

conjuration [kɔ̃ʒyrasjɔ̃] NF **1** *(complot)* conspiracy, plot **2** *(charme)* exorcism, conjuration

conjuré, -ée [kɔ̃ʒyre] N conspirator

conjurer [kɔ̃ʒyre] VT **1** *(implorer)* **c. qn de faire qch** to entreat *or* beg *or* beseech *or* implore sb to do sth; **je t'en conjure** I beg *or* beseech *or* implore you **2** *(écarter) (danger, mauvais sort etc)* to avert, to ward off **3** *(démon)* to cast out, to exorcise **4** *Arch (conspirer)* to plot
▸ **VPR se conjurer** to conspire (together) (**contre** against)

connaissable [kɔnɛsabl] ADJ knowable

connaissance [kɔnɛsɑ̃s] NF **1** *(savoir)* knowledge; **prendre c. de qch** to make oneself acquainted with sth, to study *or* examine sth; **avoir c. de qch** to be aware of sth; **donner c. de qch à qn, porter qch à la c. de qn** to inform sb of sth, to make sth known to sb; **il n'a jamais, à ma c., été malade** he has never, to my knowledge *or* as far as I know, had a day's illness; **en (toute) c. de cause** with full knowledge of the facts, advisedly; **je souhaite que vous preniez la décision en toute c. de cause** I hope you're making an informed decision; *Mktg* **c. de la marque** brand familiarity, brand awareness; **connaissances en informatique** computing skills

2 *(contact)* **faire c. avec qn, faire la c. de qn** to make sb's acquaintance, to meet sb; **quand je fis sa c.** when I first knew him; **lier c. avec qn** to strike up an acquaintance with sb; **une figure de c.** a familiar face; **en pays de c.** *(parmi des gens)* among familiar faces; *Fig* on familiar ground; **une personne de ma c.** someone I know, an acquaintance of mine **3** *(personne)* acquaintance; **c'est une de mes connaissances** he is an acquaintance of mine; **je ne la connais pas, c'est une vague**

c. I don't (really) know her, she's just an acquaintance; *Fam* **c'est une vieille c.** I've known him for ages, he's an old acquaintance; *Fam Vieilli* **je l'ai rencontré avec sa c.** I met him with his girlfriend

4 *(maîtrise)* knowledge; *Jur* cognizance; *Phil* cognition; **la c. de soi** self-knowledge; **avoir la c. de plusieurs langues** to know several languages; **ma c. du russe/du droit** my knowledge of Russian/the law; **connaissances** knowledge; **connaissances informatiques** computer literacy; **avoir des connaissances en informatique** to be computer-literate; **avoir de grandes connaissances en mathématiques** to be very knowledgeable about *or* very well versed in mathematics; **elle a des connaissances en maths** she has some knowledge of maths; **avoir des connaissances sommaires sur qch** to have a basic *or* rudimentary knowledge of sth, to know the basics *or* rudiments of sth; **l'acquisition des connaissances** the acquisition of knowledge, the learning process

5 *(conscience)* consciousness; **perdre c.** to lose consciousness; **avoir des pertes de c.** to have blackouts *or* fainting fits; **reprendre c.** to regain consciousness, to come round, to come to; **sans c.** unconscious; **il a toute sa c.** he's fully conscious

connaissement [kɔnɛsmɑ̃] NM *Naut, Com* bill of lading, waybill; **c. aérien** air waybill; **c. clausé** dirty bill; **c. de groupage** groupage bill; **c. de transbordement** transshipment bill; **c. de transport combiné** combined transport bill of lading; **c. direct** through bill; **c. embarqué** shipped bill; **c. fluvial** inland waterway bill of lading; **c. maritime** marine bill of lading; **c. net** clean bill of lading; **c. périmé** stale bill

connaisseur, -euse [kɔnɛsœr, -øz] N connoisseur, expert; **être bon c. en qch** to be an expert judge of sth
▸ ADJ expert, knowledgeable; **je ne suis pas du tout c.** I'm by no means an expert; **regarder qch d'un œil c.** to look at sth with an expert eye

CONNAÎTRE [kɔnɛtr] *(prp* **connaissant;** *pp* **connu;** *pr ind* **je connais, il connaît, n. connaissons;** *impf* **je connaissais;** *p hist* **je connus;** *fu* **je connaîtrai)**

VT to know **1–5** ▪ to be acquainted with **1, 2** ▪ to be familiar with **1, 3** ▪ to meet **2** ▪ to recognize **4**
VPR to know oneself **1** ▪ to know all about **2** ▪ to meet **3**

VT 1 *(détails)* to know, to be aware of, to be acquainted with; *(paroles d'une chanson)* to know; **c. les chemins** to be familiar with the roads; **tu connais la route?** do you know the way?; **je lui connaissais du talent** I knew he had talent; **faire c. qch** to bring sth to light, to make sth known; **faire c. ses intentions** to make one's intentions known; **je vous ferai c. mes intentions** I'll let you know what I intend to do; **il n'a jamais connu l'amour** he has never known *or* experienced love; **il a connu un destin tragique** his was a tragic fate; **elle n'a jamais connu la faim** she's never known hunger *or* what hunger means; **cette région connaît actuellement une famine** this region is now experiencing a famine; **je ne connais pas Milan** I don't know Milan, I'm not familiar with *or* acquainted with Milan; *Fam* **mais bien sûr, je ne connais que ça** it's something I'm totally familiar with, it's a subject I'm quite at home with; **connaissez-vous la nouvelle?** have you heard the news?; **sa bonté ne connaît pas de limites** his goodness knows no bounds; **il est sorti, ni vu ni connu** he went out without anyone noticing; **elle ne connaît que son travail** she's only in-

terested in her work, she lives for her work; *Fam* **elle en connaît un rayon sur la question** she knows a thing or two *or* quite a bit about the matter; **tu ne connais pas ta chance** you don't know how lucky you are, you don't know your luck; *Fam* **je connais la musique** *ou* **la chanson** I've heard it all before, it's the same old story

2 *(personne)* to know, to be acquainted with; *(rencontrer)* to meet, to make the acquaintance of; **c. qn de nom/vue** to know sb by name/sight; **c. qn de réputation** to know sb by reputation, to have heard of sb; **c. son monde** to know the people one has to deal with; **méfie-toi, il connaît du monde** watch out, he knows people; **il est connu comme le loup blanc** everybody knows him *or* has heard of him; **il est connu ici** he's well known around here; **se faire c.** to introduce oneself; *(par le public etc)* to make a name for oneself, to become well known; **je vous le ferai c.** I'll introduce him to you; *Fam* **j'en connais un qui ne va pas être content!** somebody's not going to be happy!; *Fam* **je le connais par cœur/comme ma poche** I know him through and through/can read him like a(n open) book; **ça, c'est un diamant bleu ou je ne m'y connais pas!** that's a blue diamond or I'm a Dutchman *or* I'm very much mistaken!; *Fam* **le foot, ça me connaît** I know all there is to know about football; *Fam* **si tu fais ça, je ne te connais plus** if you do that, I'll have nothing more to do with you *or* I'll disown you

3 *(langue)* to know; *(science, art)* to know about, to be familiar with; **c. à fond** to have a thorough knowledge of, to be thoroughly conversant with; *(une langue)* to have a thorough command of; **elle connaît très bien le russe** she knows Russian very well, she has a very good command of Russian; **je ne connais pas cette théorie** I don't know *or* I'm not familiar with that theory; **il n'y connaît rien** he doesn't know anything about it

4 *(reconnaître)* to know, to recognize; **c. le bien du mal** to know good from evil

5 *Bible (femme)* to know

VI *Jur* **c. de qch** to take cognizance of sth
▸ **VPR se connaître 1 se c. (soi-même)** to know oneself

2 elle s'y connaît en hommes/en œnologie she knows all about men/wine; *Fam* **il s'y connaît** he's an expert

3 *(se rencontrer)* to meet; **ils se sont connus en 1990** they met in 1990

4 il ne se connaît plus he has lost control of himself; **il ne se connaît plus de joie** he's beside himself with joy, he's walking on air

connard, -arde [kɔnar, -ard] ADJ, N = **conard**

connecter [kɔnɛkte] VT *Élec, Électron* to connect; *Ordinat* **connecté** on line; **ne pas être connecté** not to be on line, to be off line; **connecté en anneau/bus/étoile** in a ring/bus/star configuration; **connecté en série** series-connected; **c. en boucle** to daisy-chain
▸ **VPR se connecter** *Élec, Électron* to be connected; *Ordinat* **se c. à un système** to log on to a system

connecteur [kɔnɛktœr] NM *Élec, Électron* connector; *Ordinat* **c. d'extension** expansion slot

connectivité [kɔnɛktivite] NF *Ordinat* connectivity

connement [kɔnmɑ̃] ADV *très Fam* stupidly; **il s'est fait c. piquer sa caisse** the stupid idiot got his car pinched; **et c. j'ai accepté** and like the idiot that I am, I said yes

connerie [kɔnri] NF *très Fam* damned *or Br* bloody stupidity; *(remarque, acte)* damned *or Br* bloody stupid thing; **c'est de la c., ne le crois pas!** it's bullshit *or* crap, don't believe it!; **tu as fait là une c. magistrale** that was bloody stupid of you; **dire** *ou* **raconter des conneries** to talk bullshit *or* crap; **ce sont des conneries** it's a load of crap *or Br* bollocks; **c'est bientôt fini, vos conneries?** will you stop pissing about!; **il a fait quelques conneries dans sa jeunesse** he did some pretty stupid things when he was young

connétable [kɔnetabl] **NM** *Hist* constable

connexe [kɔnɛks] **ADJ** connected, related

connexion [kɔnɛksjɔ̃] **NF 1** *(d'éléments, d'idées etc)* connection **2** *Élec* connection; *Ordinat* **c. directe au réseau** direct network connection; **c. à un autre réseau** *(d'un téléphone portable)* roaming

connivence [kɔnivɑ̃s] **NF** connivance, complicity; **agir/être de c. avec qn** to act/ be in connivance *or* in collusion with sb, to connive with sb; **des regards de c.** conniving looks

connotation [kɔnɔtasjɔ̃] **NF** connotation

connoter [kɔnɔte] **VT** to imply, to connote; *Ling* to connote

connu [kɔny] **ADJ** *(écrivain, chanteur etc)* well-known, famous; **c'est (un fait) bien c.!** that's a well-known fact!, everyone knows that!; **elle est bien connue, celle-là!** that's an old one!, that's an old joke! **NM passer** *ou* **aller du c. à l'inconnu** to go from the known to the unknown

conque [kɔ̃k] **NF 1** *(coquille)* conch **2** *Anat* external ear, *Spéc* concha

conquérant, -ante [kɔ̃kerɑ̃, -ɑ̃t] **ADJ** *(nation etc)* conquering; *Fam* **air c.** swaggering air, swagger **N** conqueror; **Guillaume le C.** William the Conqueror

conquérir [kɔ̃kerir] *(prp* **conquérant;** *pp* **conquis;** *pr ind* **je conquiers, n. conquérons, ils conquièrent;** *impf* **je conquérais;** *p hist* **je conquis;** *fu* **je conquerrai)** **VT** *(pays, peuple)* to conquer; *(personne, animal)* to win over; **ils ont tout de suite été conquis par son charme** they were immediately won over by his charm; **se battre pour c. un marché** to fight (in order) to conquer *or* capture *or* win a market; **c. l'estime de qn** to win *or* gain sb's esteem **VPR se conquérir** to be (hard) won *or* earned

conquête [kɔ̃kɛt] **NF 1** *(action de conquérir)* conquest; **faire la c. d'un pays** to conquer a country; **faire la c. de qn** to make a conquest of sb; **vous avez fait sa c.!** you've made a conquest!; **se lancer à la c. du pouvoir** to make a bid for power; **la c. de nouveaux marchés en Asie est une des priorités de l'entreprise** conquering new Asian markets is one of the company's priorities **2** *(territoire)* conquered territory **3** *Fam (personne)* conquest; **il nous a présenté sa dernière c.** he introduced us to his latest conquest

conquistador [kɔ̃kistadɔr] **NM** conquistador

consacré [kɔ̃sakre] **ADJ 1** *Rel (vaisseau etc)* consecrated, sacred; *(terrain)* hallowed **2** *(coutume etc)* established; **selon l'expression consacrée** as the saying goes; **c. par l'usage** sanctioned by usage

consacrer [kɔ̃sakre] **VT 1** *Rel (autel, le pain et le vin etc)* to consecrate; **c. un évêque/un prêtre** to consecrate a bishop/ordain a priest **2** *(sa vie à Dieu)* to dedicate (à to); *(son temps, énergie à qch)* to devote (à to); **c. sa vie à la lecture et à l'étude** to devote one's life to reading and study; **combien de temps pouvez-vous me c.?** how much time can you spare *or* give me? **3** *(souvenir, endroit etc)* to sanctify, to hallow **4** *(entériner)* to establish

VPR se consacrer se c. à son travail/foyer to devote oneself to one's work/family; **se c. à Dieu** to dedicate oneself to God

consanguin [kɔ̃sɑ̃gɛ̃] **ADJ 1** **frère c./sœur consanguine** half-brother/-sister (on the father's side); **mariage c.** marriage between blood relations, intermarriage **2** *(cheval etc)* inbred

consanguinité [kɔ̃sɑ̃g(ɥ)inite] **NF 1** consanguinity *(through the father)* **2** *(de cheval etc)* inbreeding

consciemment [kɔ̃sjamɑ̃] **ADV** consciously, knowingly, wittingly

conscience [kɔ̃sjɑ̃s] **NF 1** *Physiol, Psy* consciousness; *Phil* (self-)consciousness; **perdre c.** to lose consciousness; **reprendre doucement c.** to slowly regain consciousness *or* come round; **à 80 ans, elle a encore toute sa c.** at the age of 80, she is still very alert; **avoir c. de qch/d'avoir fait qch** to be aware *or* conscious of sth/of having done sth; **avoir c. de ses capacités** to be aware of one's abilities; **prendre c. de qch** to become aware of sth; **il finira par prendre c. de la gravité de la situation** he'll eventually wake up to the seriousness of the situation; **c'est la première fois que j'en ai pris c.** it's the first time that I have been aware of it; **prise de c.** sudden awareness

2 *(morale)* conscience; **mauvaise c.** guilty *or* bad conscience; **j'ai bonne c.** my conscience is clear; **c'est un moyen pour se donner bonne c.** it's a way of easing one's conscience; **c. large** accommodating conscience; **écouter la voix de sa c.** to listen to (the voice of) one's conscience; *Fam* **il a la c. élastique** he is not over-scrupulous; **pour avoir la c. tranquille, je vais vérifier que tout est bien fermé** to set my mind at rest, I'll just make sure everything's locked up; **faire qch par acquit de c.** to do sth for the sake of one's conscience; **dire qch en c.** to say sth in all conscience; **manque de c.** unscrupulousness; **avoir qch sur la c.** to have sth on one's conscience; **ça m'est longtemps resté sur la c.** it was on my conscience *or* preyed on my mind for a long time; **liberté de c.** freedom of conscience; **fais selon ta c.** do as you think right

3 *(dans son travail)* conscientiousness; **faire qch avec c.** to do sth conscientiously ►► **c. de classe** class-consciousness; **c. collective** collective consciousness; **c. professionnelle** professional integrity; **c. de soi** self-awareness

> Attention: ne pas confondre **conscience** et **consciousness** lorsque l'on traduit le terme français **conscience**. Le terme anglais **conscience** se rapporte à la conscience morale, alors que **consciousness** se rapporte à la conscience psychologique et s'oppose à l'inconscience.

consciencieusement [kɔ̃sjɑ̃sjøzmɑ̃] **ADV** conscientiously

consciencieux, -ieuse [kɔ̃sjɑ̃sjø, -jøz] **ADJ** *(personne, travail)* conscientious

conscient [kɔ̃sjɑ̃] **ADJ 1** *(lucide etc)* conscious; *Phil* (self-)conscious; **un être c.** a conscious being; **c'est un choix tout à fait c.** it's an entirely conscious choice; **être c. de qch** to be aware *or* conscious of sth; **être c. de ses devoirs** to be aware of one's duties, to know where one's duty lies; **es-tu c. que tu as failli tous nous tuer?** are you aware *or* do you realize that you nearly killed us all? **2** *Méd* conscious; **le malade n'est plus c.** the patient is no longer conscious *or* has lost consciousness

conscription [kɔ̃skripsjɔ̃] **NF** *Mil* conscription, *Am* draft

conscrit [kɔ̃skri] **NM 1** *Mil (qui a l'âge d'être inscrit)* person liable to conscription; *(qui fait son service)* conscript, recruit, *Am* draftee **2** *Vieilli Fig* novice, greenhorn

consécration [kɔ̃sekrasjɔ̃] **NF 1** *(d'église, d'évêque etc)* consecration; *(de prêtre)* ordination **2** *(du pain et du vin)* consecration **3** *(établissement) (de coutume, réputation)* establishing; **exposer dans cette galerie sera pour lui la c.** exhibiting in that gallery will establish his reputation

consécutif, -ive [kɔ̃sekytif, -iv] **ADJ 1** *(qui se suivent)* consecutive; **pendant trois jours consécutifs** for three days running *or* in a row, for three consecutive days; *Gram* **proposition consécutive** consecutive clause **2** **c. à** following on from; **fatigue consécutive à une longue marche** fatigue resulting from a long walk

consécutivement [kɔ̃sekytivmɑ̃] **ADV** consecutively, in succession; **c. à** following

conseil [kɔ̃sɛj] **NM 1** *(recommandation)* (piece of) advice, *Fml* counsel; *(en marketing, promotion, finance etc)* consultancy; **c'est un homme de bon c.** he gives good *or* sound advice; **c'est un bon c.** that's a good piece of advice, that's good advice; **donner un c. à qn** to advise sb; **demander c. à qn** to ask sb's advice, to ask sb for advice; **j'ai besoin de tes conseils** *ou* **ton c.** I need your advice; **suivre les conseils de qn** to follow *or* heed sb's advice; **j'écoutais les conseils de son expérience** I learned from his experience; **pouvez-vous me donner quelques conseils?** can you give me some hints *or* tips?; *Prov* **la nuit porte c.** sleep on it

2 *(assemblée)* council, committee; *(d'une entreprise)* board; *(réunion)* meeting; **les membres du c.** the members of the board, the board members; **tenir c.** to hold a meeting; *Fig* **tenir un c. de guerre** to hold a council of war; *Mil* **passer en c. de guerre** to be court-martialled

3 *(conseiller) Arch* counsellor, counsel, adviser; *(en marketing, finance etc)* consultant; **avocat-c.** legal consultant; **ingénieur-c.** consulting engineer

4 *Arch, Litt (résolution)* (firm) resolution; **ne savoir quel c. prendre** not to know what decision to make

►► *Com* **c. d'administration** board of directors; **c. d'arbitrage** conciliation *or* arbitration board; **C. des Bourses de Valeurs** regulatory body of the Paris Stock Exchange; *Scol* **c. de classe** = staff meeting, with possible participation of class representatives, to discuss individual pupils and their work, disciplinary matters etc; **c. en communication** media consultant, PR consultant; **C. constitutionnel** = independent body which may be appealed to, to pronounce on the constitutionality of government decisions; *Scol etc* **c. de discipline** disciplinary committee; **passer en c. de discipline** to appear before the disciplinary committee; **c. Ecofin** ECOFIN; **c. économique** economic council; **c. d'entreprise** works committee; **C. d'État** Council of State; **C. de l'Europe** Council of Europe; *Can* **c. exécutif** council of ministers, Cabinet; **c. de famille** *Jur* family council; *Hum* family conference; **c. financier** financial consultant *or* adviser; **c. fiscal** tax consultant; **C. général** regional council; **c. en gestion** management consultant; **c. interministériel** interministerial council; *Jur* **c. judiciaire** guardian, administrator, trustee *(of estate of mentally deficient young person)*; **c. juridique** legal adviser; **c. en mercatique** marketing consultancy; **le c. des ministres** the Cabinet; **c. monétaire** Currency Board; **c. municipal** local council; **C. de la politique monétaire** Monetary Policy Committee; **c. en promotion** advertising consultancy; **c.**

des prud'hommes industrial tribunal, industrial court of arbitration; **c. en publicité** advertising consultant; **c. en recrutement** recruitment consultant; **c. régional** regional council; **C. de sécurité** *(de l'ONU)* Security Council; **c. de surveillance** supervisory board; **c. syndical** trade union council; **C. de l'Union Européenne** Council of the European Union

---

Conseil de classe

The French school year is divided into three terms. In secondary schools, a "conseil de classe", or staff meeting, is held at the end of each term to discuss the progress made by pupils in a given class. A report containing the marks obtained during the term with teachers' comments is filled in for each pupil. The "conseil de classe" is initially held behind closed doors, attended by the teachers of a given class and the head teacher, and then with two elected class representatives present. During the last "conseil de classe" of the year, decisions are taken such as which pupils repeat a year and which should change courses.

---

conseiller[1] [kɔ̃seje] VT **c. qn** to advise sb, to give advice to sb; *(d'un psychiatre etc)* to counsel sb; **c. qch à qn** to recommend sth to sb; **c. un jeune dans ses sorties/lectures/ fréquentations** to advise a youngster as to where he should go/what he should read/ the company he should keep; **je ne vous le conseille pas** I wouldn't if I were you, I wouldn't recommend it; **c. à qn de faire qch** to advise *or* recommend sb to do sth; **l'expérience me conseille d'attendre** experience tells me to wait; **nous avons été très mal conseillés** we were very badly advised, we were given very bad advice; **il est conseillé de ne pas fumer** it is advisable not to smoke

conseiller[2], **-ère** [kɔ̃seje, -ɛr] N *(qui donne son avis)* counsellor, adviser; *(spécialiste)* adviser, consultant; **la jalousie est mauvaise conseillère** do not be guided by jealousy; **c'est un très bon c.** he gives very good advice

▶▶**c. artistique** artistic adviser; **c. de clientèle** customer consultant; **c. commercial** marketing *or* sales consultant; *Jur* **c. à la cour (d'appel)** appeal court judge; **c. économique** economic adviser; **c. financier** financial adviser *or* consultant; **c. financier indépendant** independent financial adviser; **c. fiscal** tax consultant; **c. général** regional councillor; **c. en gestion (d'entreprise)** management consultant; **c. juridique** legal adviser; **c. en mercatique** marketing consultant; *Admin* **c. municipal** local councillor; *Scol* **c. d'orientation** careers adviser; **c. en placements** investment adviser; **c. technique** technical adviser; **c. du travail** personnel consultant

conseilleur, -euse [kɔ̃sejœr, -øz] N *Péj* giver *or* dispenser of (unwanted) advice; *Prov* **les conseilleurs ne sont pas les payeurs** it's easy to give advice when you don't have to pay the price

consensuel, -elle [kɔ̃sɑ̃sɥɛl] ADJ *(accord, décision)* reached by consensus

consensus [kɔ̃sɛ̃sys] NM consensus (of opinion)

consentant [kɔ̃sɑ̃tɑ̃] ADJ **1** *Jur* in agreement; *(partie)* consenting **2 elle est consentante** she's willing

consentement [kɔ̃sɑ̃tmɑ̃] NM consent; **il lui faut le c. de ses parents** he needs his parents' consent; **donner son c. à qch** to give one's consent to sth, to consent to sth; **di-**

vorce par c. mutuel divorce by mutual consent

consentir [kɔ̃sɑ̃tir] *(conj like* **sentir)** VI to consent, to agree; **c. à qch/à faire qch** to consent *or* agree to sth/to do sth; **je consens (à ce) qu'il vienne** I consent *or* agree to his coming; **il a fini par c.** he finally agreed, *Fam* he came round in the end; *Prov* **qui ne dit mot consent** silence means consent
VT **c. un prêt** to grant a loan; **c. une remise à qn** to allow sb a discount

conséquemment [kɔ̃sekamɑ̃] ADV **1 c. à** as a result of, *Fml* in consequence of **2** *Arch, Litt* consequentially

conséquence [kɔ̃sekɑ̃s] NF **1** *(résultat)* consequence, result; **il faut en subir les conséquences** we/you/*etc* must take the consequences; **tu traînes, tu traînes, c. on est encore en retard** you keep dawdling and as a result we're late again; **quelles en seront les conséquences?** what will be the consequences *or* outcome?; **cela ne tire pas à c.** it's of no consequence; **cet événement eut plus d'une heureuse c.** this event had several happy results; **cette erreur n'a pas eu de conséquences graves** this mistake didn't have any serious consequences *or* repercussions; **ton acte sera sans c. sur ton avenir** your action will have no effect on your future; **en c.** *(par conséquent)* consequently, as a result; **agir en c.** to take appropriate action; **en c. de** as a result of, *Fml* in consequence of; *(selon)* according to
2 *(conclusion)* inference, conclusion
3 *(importance)* importance, consequence; **personne sans c.** person of no importance *or Fml* consequence

conséquent [kɔ̃sekɑ̃] ADJ **1** *(cohérent)* consistent; *(esprit)* rational; **il n'est pas c. dans ses actions** he's not consistent in his actions; **être c. avec soi-même** to be consistent **2** *Mus* **partie conséquente d'une fugue** answer of a fugue **3** *Fam* (important) (somme) tidy; *(affaire)* important **4 par c.** consequently, accordingly, therefore
NM *Gram, Math* consequent

conservateur, -trice [kɔ̃sɛrvatœr, -tris] N **1** *(gardien) (de musée)* curator, keeper; **c. de bibliothèque** librarian; **c. des hypothèques** registrar of mortgages; **c. des eaux et forêts** ≃ forestry commissioner **2** *Pol* conservative
NM *(alimentaire)* preservative; **sans c.** preservative-free, free of preservatives
ADJ **1** *Pol* conservative **2** *(procédé etc)* preserving, preservative

conservation [kɔ̃sɛrvasjɔ̃] NF **1** *(de fruits, viande etc)* preserving; **c. par le froid** refrigeration; *(congélation)* freezing **2** *(de bâtiments, santé etc)* preservation; *Biol* **instinct de c.** instinct of self-preservation; **des bâtiments en bon état de c.** well-preserved buildings; **c. des eaux et forêts** ≃ Forestry Commission **3** *(de droits, situation etc)* retention **4** *(d'archives)* keeping **5** *(d'hypothèques)* registration **6** *(état)* (state of) preservation; **des ossements en parfait état de c.** perfectly preserved bones, bones in a perfect state of preservation

conservatisme [kɔ̃sɛrvatism] NM *Pol etc* conservatism

conservatoire [kɔ̃sɛrvatwar] ADJ *Jur (acte etc)* conservatory; **mesures conservatoires** measures of conservation
NM **1** *(musée)* repository, museum; **C. national des arts et métiers** = school of engineering in Paris **2** *(de musique, d'art dramatique)* school, academy, conservatoire, *Am* conservatory; **le C. (de Paris)** the (Paris) Conservatoire

conserve [kɔ̃sɛrv] NF **1** *(alimentaire)* canned *or Br* tinned food; *(en bocal)* preserve; **boîte**

de c. can, *Br* tin; **conserves au vinaigre** pickles; **petits pois en c.** canned *or Br* tinned peas; **mettre en c.** to can, *Br* to tin; **évitez de manger trop de conserves** try not to eat too much canned *or Br* tinned food, *Fam* try not to live out of cans *or Br* tins; *Fam* **tu ne vas pas en faire des conserves!** they're not museum pieces! **2** *Naut* **naviguer de c.** to sail together *(*avec with); *Fig* **de c.** together

conservé [kɔ̃sɛrve] ADJ **femme bien conservée** well-preserved woman

conserver [kɔ̃sɛrve] VT **1** *(fruits, viande etc)* to preserve; *(dans des boîtes)* canned *or Br* tinned food; **c. des tomates en bocaux** to bottle tomatoes; **à c. à l'abri de la lumière** keep away from direct sunlight; **à c. à 6°C** store at 6°C
2 *(bâtiments, meubles, vêtements etc)* to preserve; **cette vie de plein air l'a bien conservé** this outdoor life has kept him well preserved **3** *(droits etc)* to retain, to keep, to maintain; *(emploi)* to keep; **il a conservé précieusement toutes ses lettres d'amour** he carefully kept *or* preserved all her love letters; **je n'en ai pas conservé un bon souvenir** I don't have good memories of it; **c. son sang-froid** *ou* **sa tête** to remain cool, to keep one's head; **elle a réussi à c. ses cheveux malgré le traitement** she has managed to keep *or* not to lose her hair in spite of the treatment; **c. l'allure** to keep up *or* maintain the speed; *Mil* **c. une position** to hold a position
VPR **se conserver** *(d'un aliment)* to keep; **articles qui ne se conservent pas** perishable goods

conserverie [kɔ̃sɛrvəri] NF **1** *(industrie)* canning industry **2** *(fabrique)* cannery, canning factory

considérable [kɔ̃siderabl] ADJ *(nombre, population)* considerable, substantial; *(propriété etc)* considerable, substantial, extensive; *(changement etc)* considerable, significant; **il lui reste un travail c. à faire** he has still got a considerable *or* substantial amount of work to do; **un changement d'une importance c.** a substantial change; **j'ai fait des dépenses considérables** I have been *or* have gone to considerable expense; **l'émotion fut c.** there was quite a stir

considérablement [kɔ̃siderabləmɑ̃] ADV considerably, significantly

considérant [kɔ̃siderɑ̃] NM *Jur* preamble

considération [kɔ̃siderasjɔ̃] NF **1** *(examen attentif)* consideration, attention, thought; **sans c. de prix** without considering the price *or* thinking about the price; **cette offre mérite toute notre c.** this offer deserves our full attention *or* consideration; **après c. de votre demande** having considered *or* studied your application; **prendre en c.** to take into consideration *or* account; *(offre, demande d'emploi etc)* to consider; **en c. de** in consideration of
2 *(constatation)* consideration, factor; **je ne peux pas entrer dans ces considérations** I can't go into that; **poussé par de nombreuses considérations** motivated by a variety of factors *or* considerations
3 *(estime)* regard, esteem, respect; **agir avec/sans c.** to act considerately/inconsiderately; **n'avoir de c. pour personne** to have no consideration for anyone; **tu as agi sans aucune c.** that was most inconsiderate of you; **jouir d'une grande c.** to be highly respected; **veuillez agréer, Monsieur, l'assurance de ma parfaite** *ou* **haute c.** *(dans une lettre)* yours truly; **agréez l'assurance de ma c. distinguée** yours faithfully, *Am* yours truly; **par c. pour** out of consideration *or* regard for
4 considérations *(observations)* observations, reflections, thoughts *(*sur on)

considéré [kɔ̃sidere] ADJ (personne) highly regarded or respected

considérer [kɔ̃sidere] (je **considère**, n. **considérons; je considérerai**) VT **1** (étudier) (problème etc) to consider, to weigh up; **tout bien considéré** taking everything into consideration or account, all things considered, on the whole; **c'est à c.** it's worth bearing in mind; (à étudier) it's worth considering; **considérant que ...** considering that ...
2 (regarder) to consider, to gaze at, to contemplate
3 (respecter) (personne) to respect; **on la considère beaucoup** she is highly thought of or respected, she is held in high regard
4 (juger) **je considère votre lettre comme frivole** I think your letter is flippant, I regard your letter as flippant; **je le considère comme mon meilleur ami** I regard him or consider him or look on him as my best friend; **je considère ce livre comme le meilleur de l'année** I consider this book (to be) the best of the year; **je considère que tu aurais pu te renseigner auparavant** I really think you could have found out beforehand
VPR **se considérer** to consider or regard oneself; **se c. comme responsable** to consider or hold oneself responsible

consignataire [kɔ̃siɲatɛr] NM **1** Jur depositary **2** Com, Naut consignee

consignation [kɔ̃siɲasjɔ̃] NF **1** (d'argent) deposit **2** Com (de marchandises) consignment; **marchandises en c.** goods on consignment **3** **un système pour la c. des bouteilles** a money-back system for bottles

consigne [kɔ̃siɲ] NF **1** (donnée à la sentinelle etc) orders, instructions; **il a pour c. de ne laisser passer personne** his orders are to let nobody pass; **observer la c.** to obey orders; **c'est la c.** those are the orders; **consignes en cas d'incendie** fire notice, fire regulations **2** (punition) Mil confinement to barracks; Scol detention; **deux heures de c.** two hours' detention **3** Rail **c.** (à bagages) left-luggage office, Am checkroom; **c. automatique** lockers, Br left-luggage lockers **4** (de bouteille etc) deposit

consigner [kɔ̃siɲe] VT **1** (argent etc) to deposit; **bouteille consignée** returnable bottle; **c. l'emballage** to charge a refundable deposit on the packaging; **emballage non consigné** non-returnable packing **2** Com (marchandises etc) to consign (à to) **3** (fait etc) to record, to write down; **c. des impressions par écrit** to commit one's impressions to paper **4** Mil (soldat) to confine to barracks; Scol (élève) to keep in; **c. sa porte à qn** to bar one's door to sb **5** Rail **c. ses bagages** to put or deposit one's luggage in the left-luggage office or Am checkroom

consistance [kɔ̃sistɑ̃s] NF **1** (d'un sirop, d'une crème etc) consistency, consistence; **prendre c.** to thicken; Fig **ses projets semblent prendre (de la) c.** his plans seem to be taking shape; **tout cela n'était que rêve sans c.** it was all just a vague dream or Fml a dream without substance; **bruit sans c.** unfounded or groundless rumour; **donner de la c. à qch** to thicken sth; Fig **donner de la c. à un personnage** to flesh out or give substance to a character **2** (de l'esprit, du caractère) firmness, strength; **sans c.** spineless

consistant [kɔ̃sistɑ̃] ADJ (substance) firm, solid; (sauce etc) thick; (repas) substantial; (argument) well-founded, sound

> Il faut noter que l'adjectif anglais **consistent** est un faux ami. Il signifie le plus souvent **cohérent**.

consister [kɔ̃siste] VI **c. en qch** to consist of sth; **le repas consiste en un sandwich et en une pomme** the meal consists of or comprises a sandwich and an apple; **en quoi consiste cette tâche?** what does the task consist of or involve or entail?; **c. dans qch** to consist in sth; **c. à faire qch** to consist in doing sth

consistoire [kɔ̃sistwar] NM Rel consistory

conso [kɔ̃so] NF Fam (abrév **consommation**) drink

consœur [kɔ̃sœr] NF (female) colleague

consolable [kɔ̃sɔlabl] ADJ consolable

consolant [kɔ̃sɔlɑ̃] ADJ consoling, comforting; **ce qui est c., c'est que ...** the comforting thing (about it) is that ...

consolateur, -trice [kɔ̃sɔlatœr, -tris] N Litt comforter, consoler
ADJ consoling, consolatory

consolation [kɔ̃sɔlasjɔ̃] NF (soulagement) consolation, solace, comfort; **chercher une c. dans qch** to seek consolation or solace or comfort in sth; **paroles de c.** words of comfort, comforting or consoling words; **lot** ou **prix de c.** consolation prize; **c'est ma seule c.** it's my only consolation

console [kɔ̃sɔl] NF **1** Ordinat console; Ordinat **c. opérateur** operator console; Aut **c. centrale** central console; **c. de jeux** games console; **c. de visualisation** visual display unit, VDU; TV etc **c. de mixage** sound mixer, mixing desk; TV **c. vidéo** video console, switcher **2** (meuble) console (table) **3** Archit console, corbel, bracket **4** Mus (d'un orgue) console; (d'une harpe) neck

consoler [kɔ̃sɔle] VT to console, to comfort; **c. qn de sa peine** to comfort or console sb in his/her grief; **le temps console** time is a great healer; **si ça peut te c.** if that's any consolation or comfort to you; **ça me console de voir que ça t'est déjà arrivé** it consoles me or is a consolation that it's happened to you too
VPR **se consoler** to console oneself, to find comfort or consolation; **se c. en pensant que ...** to console oneself with the thought that ...; **se c. avec qn** to console oneself with sb; **se c. d'une perte/d'un échec/de la mort de qn** to get over a loss/a failure/sb's death; **elle s'en est vite consolée** she soon got over it; **je ne pourrai jamais m'en c.** I'll never get over it; **elles se sont consolées mutuellement** they consoled or comforted each other

consolidation [kɔ̃sɔlidasjɔ̃] NF **1** (d'un édifice, d'un mur) strengthening, reinforcement; (d'une position, du pouvoir, d'une amitié etc) consolidation, strengthening **2** Méd (d'une blessure) healing; (d'une fracture) knitting, setting **3** Fin (d'une dette flottante) funding; (d'un bilan) consolidation; Mktg **c. de ligne** line filling

consolidé [kɔ̃sɔlide] Fin ADJ **dette consolidée** funded debt; **fonds consolidés** consols; **bilan c.** consolidated balance sheet
NMPL **consolidés** consols

consolider [kɔ̃sɔlide] VT **1** (édifice, mur, coutures) to strengthen, to reinforce; (position, régime, amitié etc) to consolidate, to strengthen **2** Méd (blessure) to heal; (fracture) to knit, to set **3** Fin (dette) to fund; (bilan) to consolidate
VPR **se consolider 1** (se renforcer) (d'un régime) to consolidate its position; (d'une amitié, de liens) to become stronger **2** Méd (d'une blessure) to heal; (d'une fracture) to knit, to set

consommable [kɔ̃sɔmabl] ADJ (solide) edible; (liquide) drinkable; **ce produit n'est c. que cru/cuit** this product must be eaten raw/cooked before eating

consommateur, -trice [kɔ̃sɔmatœr, -tris] N (en général) consumer; (dans un restaurant, un café) customer; **ce pays est un des premiers consommateurs de pétrole** this country is one of the biggest oil consumers; **mes grands-parents sont de grands consommateurs de café** my grandparents are great coffee drinkers; **défense des consommateurs** consumer protection; Mktg **c. cible** target consumer; Mktg **c. final** end-user; **c. moyen** average user
ADJ **pays c.** consuming country

consommation [kɔ̃sɔmasjɔ̃] NF **1** (d'électricité, de pétrole) consumption, use; (de nourriture) consumption, eating; (de boisson) consumption, drinking; (d'une voiture) (petrol or Am gas) consumption; **cette viande est impropre à la c.** this meat is unfit for (human) consumption; **faire une grande c. de papier** to get through or go through or use (up) a lot of paper; **ils font une grande c. de viandes fumées** they get through or consume a lot of smoked meat; **c. quotidienne de vitamines** daily intake of vitamins; **c. intérieure** home consumption; **c. des ménages** household consumption; **c. mondiale** world consumption; **biens de c.** consumer goods; **produits de grande c.** mass market products; **société de c.** consumer society; **crédit à la c.** consumer credit; Aut **c. d'huile** oil consumption; Aut **c. de carburant** fuel consumption; **c. de masse** mass consumption; Aut **c. en ville** urban fuel consumption; Aut **c. en vitesse de croisière** touring consumption; Aut **c. spécifique** specific fuel consumption, sfc; Compta **consommations de l'exercice** total annual expenses **2** (dans un café) drink **3** Litt (d'un travail etc) accomplishment; (d'un crime) perpetration; (du mariage) consummation; **jusqu'à la c. des siècles** until the end of time

consommatique [kɔ̃sɔmatik] NF consumer research

consommé [kɔ̃sɔme] ADJ (habileté etc) consummate; (écrivain, diplomate etc) consummate, accomplished
NM Culin consommé; **c. de poulet** chicken consommé

consommer [kɔ̃sɔme] VT **1** (électricité, pétrole etc) to consume, to use; (nourriture) to consume, to eat; (boisson) to consume, to drink; **'à c. avant fin novembre'** 'best before end November'; **cette voiture consomme trop (d'essence)** this car is heavy on petrol or Am gas **2** (crime) to perpetrate; (mariage) to consummate; Litt (œuvre) to accomplish, to achieve; **la rupture est consommée** they have broken up for good
VI to consume; (dans un café) to drink, to have a drink; **c. au bar** to (have a) drink at the bar; **c. sur place** to eat in
VPR **se consommer** (de la nourriture, de boissons etc) to be consumed; **ce plat se consomme froid** this dish is eaten cold

consomption [kɔ̃sɔ̃psjɔ̃] NF **1** Méd wasting, decline; Arch (tuberculose) consumption **2** Arch, Litt (par le feu) consuming

consonance [kɔ̃sɔnɑ̃s] NF Mus, Ling consonance; **mots aux consonances harmonieuses/bizarres** harmonious/odd-sounding words; **langue à c. germanique** German-sounding language

consonant [kɔ̃sɔnɑ̃] ADJ Mus, Ling consonant

consonantique [kɔ̃sɔnɑ̃tik] ADJ Ling consonant(al)

consonne [kɔ̃sɔn] NF Ling consonant; **c. occlusive/labiale/dentale** plosive/labial/dental (consonant)

consort [kɔ̃sɔr] ADJ **prince c.** prince consort
NMPL Péj **et consorts** and company

consortial, -iale, -iaux, -iales [kɔ̃sɔrsjal, -jo] ADJ Com, Fin consortium, Fml consortial

consortium [kɔ̃sɔrsjɔm] NM Com, Fin

consortium, syndicate; **c. de banques** banking consortium

conspirateur, -trice [kɔ̃spiratœr, -tris] N conspirator; **ils se donnaient des airs de conspirateurs** they had a conspiratorial air about them

   ADJ conspiratorial

conspiration [kɔ̃spirasjɔ̃] NF conspiracy, plot; *Fam* **mais c'est une c.** it's a conspiracy

conspirer [kɔ̃spire] VI **1** *(comploter)* to conspire, to plot (**contre** against) **2** *(contribuer)* to conspire; **tout conspire à me mettre en retard** everything's conspiring to make me late; **tout semble c. à son bonheur/la réussite du projet** everything seems to be conspiring to make him happy/to make the project a success

conspuer [kɔ̃spɥe] VT *(pièce de théâtre, orateur etc)* to boo, to shout down

constamment [kɔ̃stamɑ̃] ADV constantly, continually, continuously

constance [kɔ̃stɑ̃s] NF **1** *(dans une tâche)* persistence, perseverance; *(en amour)* constancy; **manquer de c. en amour** to be fickle; **il a de la c. à t'attendre depuis cinq ans** he's patient to have waited for you for five years; **faire preuve d'une grande c. en amitié** to be unswerving in one's friendships; **travailler avec c.** to work steadily **2** *(de la température, d'un phénomène etc)* constancy, invariability

constant, -ante [kɔ̃stɑ̃, -ɑ̃t] ADJ **1** *(cœur, préoccupation, souci)* constant; *(effort)* persistent; *(amitié, intérêt)* steady, unwavering; **être c. dans la recherche de qch** to be persistent in one's search for sth **2** *Rare (fait)* established **3** *(température)* constant; *(circulation)* continuous, uninterrupted; **à niveau c.** at a constant level **4** *Com* **en euros constants** in real terms

   NF *Math, Phys etc* **constante** constant

constat [kɔ̃sta] NM **1** *Jur* certified *or* official statement *or* report; **dresser un c. d'accident** to write out an accident report; **c. amiable** *(formulaire)* = insurance form to be completed at the scene of an accident; **c. d'huissier** process server's affidavit; **c. de dommages** damages report **2** *(fait)* observation; **c. d'échec** acknowledgement *or* admission of failure; **faire un c. d'échec** to acknowledge *or* admit failure

constatation [kɔ̃statasjɔ̃] NF **1** *(d'un fait etc)* noting, noticing; **procéder aux constatations d'usage** to make the usual *or* routine investigations *or* inquiries **2** *(fait)* observation; **constatations d'une enquête** findings of an enquiry; **la première c. est la suivante** the first point to note is the following; **c'est une simple c.** it's a simple statement of fact **3** *Compta* **c. de stock** stock take **4** *(en assurances)* **c. des dommages** assessment of damages

constaté [kɔ̃state] ADJ *Fin (valeur)* registered; **c. d'avance** *(charge)* prepaid

constater [kɔ̃state] VT **1** *(remarquer)* (fait, amélioration etc) to note, to notice, to observe; **c. une erreur** to discover *or* find a mistake; **je constate que ce que je propose n'est jamais retenu** I notice that what I suggest is never accepted; **vous pouvez c. vous-même qu'elle est partie** you can see for yourself that she's gone; **constate par toi-même!** see for yourself!; **je suis obligé de c. que je me suis trompé** I'm forced to the conclusion *or* to conclude that I've made a mistake **2** *(enregistrer)* to record; **c. un décès** to certify a death; **les experts sont venus c. les dégâts** the experts came to assess the damage

constellation [kɔ̃stelasjɔ̃] NF constellation; **la c. de la Croix du Sud** the Southern Cross;

Fig **une c. de personnes célèbres** a constellation *or* galaxy of famous people

consteller [kɔ̃stele] VT to spangle, to stud; **ciel constellé d'étoiles** star-spangled *or* star-studded sky; **robe constellée de pierreries** dress studded with jewels; **des taches de sang constellent sa chemise** his shirt is spattered with blood

   VPR **se consteller le ciel se constella d'étoiles** the stars came out in the sky; **la neige se mit à tomber et le sol se constella de taches blanches** the snow began to fall and the ground was spotted with white

consternant [kɔ̃sternɑ̃] ADJ *(nouvelles)* alarming, dismaying; **d'une bêtise consternante** alarmingly stupid

consternation [kɔ̃sternasjɔ̃] NF consternation, dismay; **jeter la c. dans un groupe** to fill a group with consternation *or* dismay; **à la c. générale** to everyone's consternation *or* dismay

consterner [kɔ̃sterne] VT *(personne)* to dismay, to fill with consternation *or* dismay; **prendre un air consterné** to look dismayed

constipation [kɔ̃stipasjɔ̃] NF *Méd* constipation

constipé, -ée [kɔ̃stipe] ADJ *Méd* constipated; *Fam (air, manière etc)* ill at ease, stiff, *Fam* constipated; **arrête de prendre cet air c.!** loosen up *or* relax a bit!

   N *Méd* constipated person, sufferer from constipation; *Fig Fam* **quel c.!** what a stuffed shirt!

constiper [kɔ̃stipe] *Méd* VT to constipate

   VI **nourriture qui constipe** constipating food

constituant, -ante [kɔ̃stitɥɑ̃, -ɑ̃t] ADJ **1** *(partie, élément)* constituent, component **2** *Hist* **l'Assemblée constituante** the Constituent Assembly *(of 1789)*

   NM constituent part; *Hist* **les constituants** the members of the Constituent Assembly

   NF *Hist* **la Constituante** the Constituent Assembly *(of 1789)*

constitué [kɔ̃stitɥe] ADJ **1** *(autorité etc)* constituted, organized; **corps constitués** official bodies **2** *Anat* constituted, formed; **enfant bien c.** fine, healthy child; **enfant mal c.** child of poor constitution

constituer [kɔ̃stitɥe] VT **1** *(faire partie de)* to form, to constitute, to make up; **parties qui constituent le tout** parts that form *or* constitute *or* (go to) make up the whole; **ce mobilier constitue tout mon bien** this furniture represents all my worldly goods, this furniture is all I own; **cet acte constitue un outrage aux bonnes mœurs** this action constitutes *or* represents an affront to public decency; **cela devrait c. un délit** that ought to constitute an offence; **être constitué de ...** to be made up of *or* consist of ...; **appartement constitué de six pièces** six-roomed flat

   2 *(créer)* (comité, société commerciale, ministère, équipe etc) to form, to set up; *(bibliothèque, fortune)* to build up

   3 *(par nommer)* to appoint; **c. qn président** to appoint sb president; **c. qn son héritier** to make sb one's heir; **c. une rente/une dot à qn** to settle an annuity/a dowry on sb

   VPR **se constituer 1** *(devenir)* **se c. prisonnier** to give oneself up; **se c. partie civile** to bring a civil suit for damages **2** *(se réunir)* **ils se constituèrent en commission/en association** they formed a committee/an association

constitutif, -ive [kɔ̃stitytif, -iv] ADJ **1** *(composant)* constituent, component; **les éléments constitutifs de l'air** the constituent elements of air **2** *Jur* constitutive; **titre c.** *(d'une propriété)* title deed

constitution [kɔ̃stitysjɔ̃] NF **1** *(physique)* constitution; **avoir une bonne c.** to have a sound constitution, to be fit **2** *(création)* *(de comité)* formation, setting up, constitution; *(de société commerciale)* formation, setting up; *(de ministère)* formation; *(de stocks)* constitution; *(de bibliothèque)* building up **3** *Jur (de rente, dot)* settlement; **c. de partie civile** institution of civil action; **c. d'avoué** briefing *or* instructing of a lawyer **4** *(de l'air, de l'eau)* composition **5** *Pol* constitution; **loi conforme à la c.** law complying with the constitution

constitutionnaliser [kɔ̃stitysjɔnalize] VT *Jur* to constitutionalize

constitutionnalité [kɔ̃stitysjɔnalite] NF constitutionality

constitutionnel, -elle [kɔ̃stitysjɔnɛl] ADJ constitutional

constitutionnellement [kɔ̃stitysjɔnɛlmɑ̃] ADV constitutionally

constricteur [kɔ̃striktœr] ADJ **1** *Anat* muscle **c.** constrictor muscle **2 boa c.** boa constrictor

   NM *Anat* constrictor (muscle)

constriction [kɔ̃striksjɔ̃] NF *(des vaisseaux sanguins)* constriction

constrictor [kɔ̃striktɔr] ADJ, NM **(boa) c.** boa constrictor

constructeur, -trice [kɔ̃stryktœr, -tris] NM *Constr* builder, constructor; **c. automobile ou d'automobiles** car *or* motor manufacturer; **c. naval** shipbuilder

   ADJ *(esprit, démarche)* constructive; *Zool* **animaux constructeurs** home-building animals

constructible [kɔ̃stryktibl] ADJ **terrain c.** building land, land approved for development

constructif, -ive [kɔ̃stryktif, -iv] ADJ constructive

construction [kɔ̃stryksjɔ̃] NF **1** *(d'une maison, d'une route, d'un voilier etc)* construction, building, constructing; *(d'un roman, poème etc)* construction; *(d'une phrase)* structure, construction; **matériaux de c.** building *or* construction materials; **c. aéronautique** aircraft manufacturing; **c. mécanique** (mechanical) engineering; **c. navale** shipbuilding; **maison en c.** house under construction; **il y a plusieurs maisons en c. de l'autre côté de la rue** several houses are being built on the other side of the street; **appareil de c. japonaise** Japanese-built appliance, appliance of Japanese manufacture; **jeu de c.** construction set; *Fig* **c'est une c. de l'esprit** it's purely hypothetical **2** *(bâtiment)* building, construction, structure; **un grand nombre de nouvelles constructions** a large number of new buildings **3** *Géom* figure, construction

constructivisme [kɔ̃stryktivism] NM constructivism

constructiviste [kɔ̃stryktivist] N constructivist

construire [kɔ̃strɥir] *(prp* **construisant***; pp* **construit***; pr ind* **je construis, il construit, n. construisons***; impf* **je construisais***; p hist* **je construisis***; fu* **je construirai***)* VT **1** *(maison, route, etc)* to build, to construct; **pendant qu'on construit la maison** while the house is being built; **région très construite** heavily built-up area; **c. l'Europe** to build a new Europe

   2 *(machine, bateau, avion etc)* to build, to construct; *(roman, poème etc)* to construct; *(théorie)* to construct, to put together; *Gram* **c. une phrase** to construct a sentence

   VPR **se construire** *(d'une résidence etc)* to be built, to be constructed; **la région s'est beaucoup construite** there has been a lot of building in the area, the area has become very built-up; **il s'est construit beaucoup de maisons** a lot of houses have been built; *Gram* **'après que' se construit avec l'indicatif** 'après que' takes the indicative

consubstantiation [kɔ̃sypstɑ̃sjasjɔ̃] NF *Rel* consubstantiation, real presence

consubstantiel, -ielle [kɔ̃sypstɑ̃sjɛl] ADJ *Rel* consubstantial, of one substance (**à**, **avec** with)

consul [kɔ̃syl] NM consul; **le c. de France** the French Consul; **c. général** consul general

consulaire [kɔ̃syler] ADJ consular

consulat [kɔ̃syla] NM *(lieu)* consulate; *(charge)* consulship; *Hist* **le C.** the Consulate (1799)

consultable [kɔ̃syltabl] ADJ *(livre etc)* available for consultation

consultant, -ante [kɔ̃syltɑ̃, -ɑ̃t] ADJ consulting; **médecin c.** consultant
  N consultant; **agence de consultants** consultancy; **c. en gestion** management consultant; **c. médias** media consultant

consultatif, -ive [kɔ̃syltatif, -iv] ADJ consultative, advisory; **à titre c.** in an advisory capacity; **assemblée consultative** consultative assembly

consultation [kɔ̃syltasjɔ̃] NF **1** *(conférence)* consultation, conference; **entrer en c. avec qn** to consult or confer with sb; **c. populaire** consultation of the people
  2 *(chez un avoué, médecin etc)* consultation; **le médecin est en c.** the doctor is with a patient or is seeing a patient; **cabinet de c.** *Méd* consulting room, *Br* surgery, *Am* office; *Jur* chambers; *Méd* **heures de c.** consulting or surgery hours; *Méd* **c. externe** outpatients' department
  3 *(de livre)* consultation, consulting; **encourager la c. des dictionnaires** to encourage the use of dictionaries; **la c. de nos fichiers n'a rien donné** we couldn't find anything in our files; **je pourrai te le dire après c. de mon agenda** I'll be able to tell you after I've checked (in) my diary; **livre de c. facile** book that is easy to consult or use; *Ordinat* **c. de la page** page consultation; *Ordinat* **c. de table** table look-up

consulter [kɔ̃sylte] VT *(personne)* to consult; *(livre, plan etc)* to consult, to refer to; *(site Internet)* to visit; **c. qn du regard** to look questioningly at sb; **c. un médecin/un avocat** to consult a doctor/a lawyer, to take medical/ legal advice; **c. les horaires de départ** to check the departure times; **ouvrage à c.** reference work; **livre facile à c.** book that is easy to consult or use; **c. ses intérêts** to look after one's own interests
  VI *(conférer)* to consult, to hold a consultation; *Méd (d'un docteur)* to see patients, *Br* to take surgery; *(d'un malade)* to go to the doctor('s)
  VPR **se consulter** to consult each other, to confer; **ils se sont consultés avant de venir ici** they put their heads together or conferred before coming here; **se c. du regard** to look questioningly at one another

consumer [kɔ̃syme] VT **1** *(brûler)* to consume; **consumé par le feu** consumed by fire, burnt up; *Fig* **consumé par l'ambition/le remords** consumed or eaten up with ambition/remorse; **les soucis/chagrins le consument** he is sick with worry/grief; **la jalousie le consume** he is consumed or eaten up with jealousy **2** *Litt (fortune, énergie)* to waste
  VPR **se consumer 1 les bûches se consumèrent lentement** the logs burned (away) slowly **2** *(d'une personne)* to waste away, to pine away; **se c. en efforts inutiles** to wear oneself out in useless efforts; **elle se consume d'inquiétude/de chagrin** she's consumed or eaten up with worry/grief

consumérisme [kɔ̃symerism] NM consumerism

consumériste [kɔ̃symerist] ADJ consumer, consumerist

contact [kɔ̃takt] NM **1** *(relation, personne)* contact; **l'espion avoua que son c. travaillait à l'ambassade** the spy admitted that his contact worked at the embassy; **être en c. avec qn/qch** to be in contact with sb/sth; **entrer en c.** *(avec un virus etc)* to come into contact; *(contacter)* to get in contact; **garder/perdre le c. avec qn** to keep in touch/ lose touch with sb; **mettre qn en c. avec qn** to put sb in contact or in touch with sb; **prendre c. ou se mettre en c. avec qn** to get in touch or in contact with sb, to contact sb; **prise de c.** first meeting; **j'ai su qu'il m'était hostile dès le premier c.** I knew that he was hostile towards me from the moment we met; **elle est d'un c. facile/difficile** she's easy/hard to get on with; **il va changer au c. de ces jeunes travailleurs** mixing with these young workers is going to change him; **elle s'est métamorphosée au c. de cette femme** she's completely changed since she met that woman
  2 *(toucher)* contact, touch; **au c. agréable** pleasant to the touch; **je n'ai jamais aimé son c.** I've never liked to be touched by him; **le c. de deux surfaces** the contact between or of two surfaces; **maladies transmises par c.** diseases transmitted by contact, contagious diseases; **au c. de l'eau** on contact with water
  3 *Tech* contact; *Élec* contact, connection; **c. à la terre** contact to earth; **point de c.** contact point; **les fils sont en c.** the wires are in contact; **fiche** *ou* **cheville de c.** contact plug
  4 *Aut* contact, contact breaker point; **contacts** points; **c. coupé** ignition switched off; **c. mis** ignition switched on; **clef de c.** ignition key; **mettre/couper le c.** to switch on/off
  5 *Ordinat* **c. de page** *(sur Internet)* hit

contacter [kɔ̃takte] VT to contact, to get in touch or in contact with

contacteur [kɔ̃taktœr] NM *Élec* contactor; *(du système d'allumage)* switch; **c. d'interdiction** inhibitor switch; **c. de coupure à inertie** inertia cut-off switch; **c. à solénoïde** solenoid switch

contagieux, -ieuse [kɔ̃taʒjø, -jøz] ADJ *(maladie, virus etc)* contagious, infectious; *(personne)* contagious; *(rire, enthousiasme)* infectious
  N contagious patient; **service des c.** isolation ward

contagion [kɔ̃taʒjɔ̃] NF *Méd* contagion; **pour prévenir tout risque de c.** to avoid any risk of contagion; **période de c.** contagious stage; *Fig* **la c. du rire** the infectiousness of laughter

contagiosité [kɔ̃taʒjozite] NF *Méd* contagiousness

container [kɔ̃tɛnɛr] NM *Ind* container

contaminateur, -trice [kɔ̃taminatœr, -tris] *Méd* ADJ contaminating
  N carrier

contamination [kɔ̃taminasjɔ̃] NF *(pollution)* contamination; *Méd* infection

contaminer [kɔ̃tamine] VT *(polluer)* (eau etc) to contaminate; *Méd* to infect; *Ordinat* **disque dur contaminé par un virus** virus-infected hard disk

conte [kɔ̃t] NM **1** *(histoire)* story, tale; **c. de fées** fairy tale or story; **elle vit dans un c. de fées** she's living in a dream world or in a world of her own; **elle vit un c. de fées** her life is a fairy tale; **contes de bonnes femmes** old wives' tales **2** *Vieilli, Litt (histoire invrai-*

semblable) (tall) story, yarn; **c. à dormir debout** cock-and-bull story

contemplateur, -trice [kɔ̃tɑ̃platœr, -tris] N contemplator

contemplatif, -ive [kɔ̃tɑ̃platif, -iv] ADJ contemplative
  N meditator; *Rel* contemplative

contemplation [kɔ̃tɑ̃plasjɔ̃] NF **1** *(d'un tableau etc)* contemplation; **être en c. devant la mer** to gaze (in contemplation) at the sea **2** *(méditation)* contemplation, meditation; **plongé dans la c.** lost in contemplation or meditation **3** *Rel* contemplation

contempler [kɔ̃tɑ̃ple] VT *(nature, tableau etc)* to contemplate, to gaze at
  VPR **se contempler** *(dans un miroir)* to look at or contemplate oneself

contemporain, -aine [kɔ̃tɑ̃pɔrɛ̃, -ɛn] ADJ **1** *(moderne)* contemporary **2** *(du même âge)* contemporary (**de** with); **être c. de qn** to be a contemporary of sb; **ils sont contemporains** they are contemporaries
  N contemporary

contempteur, -trice [kɔ̃tɑ̃ptœr, -tris] N *Litt* despiser

contenance [kɔ̃tnɑ̃s] NF **1** *(d'une bouteille etc)* capacity; *(d'un navire)* burden; **d'une c. de dix litres** capable of holding ten litres, with a capacity of ten litres **2** *(allure)* attitude, bearing; **avoir une c. modeste/fière** to have a modest/proud demeanour or bearing; **faire bonne c.** to put on a bold front; **perdre c.** to lose one's composure; **faire qch pour se donner (une) c.** to do sth to give oneself an air of assurance

contenant [kɔ̃tnɑ̃] NM *(par opposition à contenu)* container

conteneur [kɔ̃tnœr] NM *(pour le transport de marchandises)* container; **c. à bagages** baggage container

conteneur-avion, pl **conteneurs-avions** NM air freight container

conteneurisation [kɔ̃tnœrizasjɔ̃] NF *Com* containerization

conteneuriser [kɔ̃tnœrize] VT *Com* to containerize

contenir [kɔ̃tnir] *(conj like* **tenir***)* VT **1** *(renfermer)* to contain; **le théâtre contient mille places** the theatre holds or seats a thousand; **le dictionnaire contient plus de cinquante mille articles** the dictionary contains or has more than fifty thousand entries; **cette bouteille a contenu du vin** this bottle has had wine in it, this bottle has contained wine; **lettre contenant chèque** letter enclosing cheque **2** *(foule, sentiments etc)* to restrain, to keep or hold in check; *(colère)* to curb, to suppress; *(larmes)* to hold back; **c. l'ennemi** to contain the enemy, to keep the enemy in check
  VPR **se contenir** to contain oneself, to control oneself; **apprendre à se c.** to learn self-control, to learn to control oneself

content [kɔ̃tɑ̃] ADJ *(satisfait)* content, satisfied, pleased, happy (**de** with); *(ravi)* glad; **être c. de son sort** to be content or satisfied with one's lot; **il est très c. ici** he's very happy here; **elle a l'air contente de sa nouvelle voiture** she seems pleased or happy with her new car; **tu n'as pas l'air c.** you don't look very happy or pleased; **je suis c. de vous/moi** I'm pleased with you/myself; **je suis très c. de vous voir** I'm very pleased to see you; **un air trop c. de soi** a smug manner; **tu peux être c. de toi!** tu as vu ce que tu as fait! I hope you're satisfied or happy! just look what you've done!; **non c. de mentir, il vole!** not content or satisfied with lying, he steals as well!; **votre père ne sera pas c.** your father won't be (very) pleased or happy, your father won't like it; **je suis fort c. que vous soyez**

venu I'm so glad you've come; *Fam* **et si tu n'es pas c., c'est pareil** you can like it or lump it

NM manger tout son c. to eat one's fill; **s'amuser tout son c.** to enjoy oneself to one's heart's content; **avoir son c. de qch** to have one's fill of sth

contentement [kɔ̃tɑ̃tmɑ̃] **NM** *(état)* satisfaction, contentment (**de** at, with), *Litt* content; **c. de soi** self-satisfaction; **un sourire de c.** a satisfied *or* contented smile

contenter [kɔ̃tɑ̃te] **VT** *(personne, curiosité)* to satisfy; *(caprice)* to satisfy, to gratify; **un rien le contente** the least thing makes him happy, he's very easily pleased *or* satisfied; **on ne peut pas c. tout le monde** you can't please everyone

VPR se contenter se c. de (faire) qch to be content *or* satisfied *or* happy with (doing) sth, to content oneself with (doing) sth; **il se contente de peu** he's easily satisfied; **il va falloir se c. du strict nécessaire** we shall have to make do with the bare necessities; **je me contenterai de faire remarquer que ...** I will merely point out that ...; **il se contente d'un repas par jour** he only has *or* he is content with one meal a day; **pour tout repas, elle s'est contentée de sandwichs** by way of a meal, she just had sandwiches; **pour toute réponse, il s'est contenté de nous renvoyer la carte, signée** by way of reply, he merely returned the card to us, signed

contentieux, -ieuse [kɔ̃tɑ̃sjø, -jøz] **ADJ** *(affaire)* contentious

NM *Admin* contentious business, matters in dispute; *(querelle grave)* bone of contention; *Jur* litigation; *(service)* legal department; **avoir un c. avec qn** to be in dispute with sb; **le c. franco-espagnol** the Franco-Spanish dispute; **chef du c.** *(d'une société)* head of the legal department

contention¹ [kɔ̃tɑ̃sjɔ̃] **NF** *Litt (des facultés intellectuelles)* application, exertion; **c. d'esprit** intentness of mind

contention² **NF** *Méd (d'une fracture etc)* retention in place, setting; *Psy, (au moyen d'une camisole etc)* restraint, restraining; **collant de c.** support stockings

contenu [kɔ̃tny] **ADJ** *(passion, émotion)* restrained, suppressed, pent-up; *(style)* restrained

NM *(d'un paquet, d'un sachet etc)* contents; *(de lettre, livre etc)* content; *Journ* **c. rédactionnel** editorial content; *Ling* **le c. d'un mot** the content *or* meaning of a word; *Psy* **c. latent/manifeste** latent/manifest content
VOIR GRAMMAIRE A10

conter [kɔ̃te] **VT** *(histoire etc)* to tell, to relate; *Fam* **allez c. ça ailleurs!** (go and) tell that to the marines!; **elle ne s'en laisse pas c.** you can't fool her, she's not easily taken in; **il m'en a conté de belles sur elle!** he told me some fine things about her!; *Hum* **c. fleurette à qn** to whisper *or* murmur sweet nothings to sb

contestable [kɔ̃tɛstabl] **ADJ** questionable, debatable

contestataire [kɔ̃tɛstatɛr] **ADJ** anti-establishment

N protester; **c'est une c.** she's a rebel

contestation [kɔ̃tɛstasjɔ̃] **NF 1** *(controverse)* dispute; **de graves contestations ont surgi au sein du parti** serious dissent has arisen within the party; **être en c. avec qn** to be at variance *or* issue with sb; **élever une c. sur qch** to raise an objection to sth; **il y a matière ou sujet à c.** there are grounds for dispute; **sans c. possible** beyond (all) question, beyond dispute **2** *Pol* protest

conteste [kɔ̃tɛst] **ADV sans c.** indisputably, unquestionably, beyond question

contester [kɔ̃tɛste] **VT** *(argument, droit)* to contest, to dispute, to challenge; *(document, information)* to question, to dispute; **point contesté** controversial point; **c. l'efficacité d'une méthode de travail** to question *or* dispute the effectiveness of a method of working; **je lui conteste le droit de ...** I contest *or* dispute *or* question his right to ...; **il est très contesté** he is very controversial; **je ne conteste pas qu'il ait eu beaucoup à faire** I don't dispute that he had a lot to do **VI** to take issue (**sur** over); *Pol* to protest; **faire qch sans c.** to do sth without protest

conteur, -euse [kɔ̃tœr, -øz] **N 1** *(narrateur)* narrator, storyteller **2** *(écrivain)* story-writer

contexte [kɔ̃tɛkst] **NM** context; **le c. permet de mieux comprendre certains mots** some words are more readily understood in context; **donner un c.** to give a context; **c. historique** *(d'un événement)* historical context; **il faut remettre cet événement dans son c.** we must put this event in its context; **dans le c. de l'économie européenne** (with)in the context of the European economy

contextualiser [kɔ̃tɛkstɥalize] **VT** to contextualize

contextuel, -elle [kɔ̃tɛkstɥɛl] **ADJ** *Ling* contextual

contexture [kɔ̃tɛkstyr] **NF 1** *(des os, des muscles etc)* (con)texture **2** *Vieilli (d'une histoire, d'un poème)* structure, framework

contigu, -uë [kɔ̃tigy] **ADJ** *(mur, maison etc)* adjoining, adjacent, *Fml* contiguous; *(idées, domaine, profession)* related; **c. à ou avec qch** next or adjacent *or Fml* contiguous to sth

contiguïté [kɔ̃tigɥite] **NF** *(d'une maison etc)* adjacency, proximity, *Fml* contiguity; *Fig* **c. des idées/des vues** closeness of ideas/opinions

continence [kɔ̃tinɑ̃s] **NF** continence

continent¹ [kɔ̃tinɑ̃] **ADJ** continent

continent² **NM** *Géog* **1** *(étendue)* continent; **l'Ancien/le Nouveau C.** the Old/the New World **2** *(par rapport à une île)* mainland

continental, -ale, -aux, -ales [kɔ̃tinɑ̃tal, -o] **ADJ** continental; **la France continentale** mainland France
N mainland inhabitant

contingence [kɔ̃tɛ̃ʒɑ̃s] **NF** *Phil* contingency; **les contingences de la vie quotidienne** everyday happenings *or* events; **ignorer les contingences** to ignore the incidentals

contingent [kɔ̃tɛ̃ʒɑ̃] **ADJ** *Phil* contingent; *(peu important)* incidental

NM 1 *Mil* contingent; **le c. annuel d'une classe est de 250 000 hommes** the annual intake *or Br* call-up *or Am* draft totals 250,000 men; **les soldats du c.** the conscripted soldiers **2** *(quota)* quota; *(part)* share, contribution; *(de chambres d'hôtel)* block, allotment; **contingents d'importation/d'exportation** import/export quotas

contingentement [kɔ̃tɛ̃ʒɑ̃tmɑ̃] **NM** *Admin* fixing *or* introduction of quotas; **le c. des importations** the fixing of quotas on imports, the fixing of import quotas

contingenter [kɔ̃tɛ̃ʒɑ̃te] **VT** *Admin* **1** *(importations etc)* to fix quotas on; **des produits contingentés** fixed quota products **2** *(films etc)* to distribute according to a quota

continu [kɔ̃tiny] **ADJ** *(ligne)* continuous, unbroken; *(discussion)* continuous; *(effort)* sustained, continuous; *(souffrance)* constant, endless; *(soin, attention)* constant; *Élec* **courant c.** direct current

NM 1 *Phil, Phys, Math* continuum
2 faire qch en c. to do sth without interruption; **la nouvelle chaîne diffuse des informations en c.** the new channel broadcasts

news bulletins round-the-clock, the new channel provides non-stop *or* round-the-clock news coverage; *Ordinat* **papier en c.** continuous paper

continuateur, -trice [kɔ̃tinɥatœr, -tris] **N** *(de qn)* successor; *(d'une politique)* upholder

continuation [kɔ̃tinɥasjɔ̃] **NF** continuation; **bonne c.!** all the best!

continuel, -elle [kɔ̃tinɥɛl] **ADJ** *(ininterrompu)* continuous; *(qui se répète)* constant, continual; **des plaintes continuelles** constant *or* unending *or* perpetual complaints; **c. devenir** *(de l'individu)* continual evolution *or* development

continuellement [kɔ̃tinɥɛlmɑ̃] **ADV** *(de façon ininterrompue)* continuously; *(de façon répétitive)* constantly, continually

continuer [kɔ̃tinɥe] **VT** *(poursuivre) (études, efforts, politique etc)* to continue (with), to carry on with, to go on with, to keep on with; **continue le repas/la discussion sans moi** go on *or* carry on with the meal/the discussion without me; **c. un trait** to continue *or* extend a line; **c. sa route ou son chemin** to continue on one's way

VI 1 *(dans le temps)* to go on; **c. à ou de faire qch** to go on *or* carry on doing sth, to continue doing sth *or* to do sth; **je continue à ou de me demander si ...** I keep wondering if ...; **continuez!** *(encouragement)* keep it up!, carry on!; *(après une interruption)* go on!, carry on!, continue!; **la guerre continue** the war is still going on; **la vie continue** life goes on; **si tu continues comme ça ...** if you go on *or* carry on like that ...

2 *(dans l'espace)* to continue, to carry on; **jardin qui continue jusqu'à la rivière** garden that extends to the river

3 *Ordinat (dans boîte de dialogue)* to proceed

VPR se continuer 1 *(dans le temps)* to be continued, to be carried on; **une légende qui se continue à travers les siècles** a legend which endures through the centuries; **la fête se continua tard dans la nuit** the party went on late into the night **2** *(dans l'espace)* to continue, to carry on

continuité [kɔ̃tinɥite] **NF** *(d'une action)* continuity; *(d'une tradition, d'une politique etc)* continuation; **assurer la c. d'une tradition** to carry on *or* perpetuate a tradition; *Fin* **c. d'exploitation** going-concern status

continûment [kɔ̃tinymɑ̃] **ADV** continuously

continuum [kɔ̃tinɥɔm] **NM** *Math, Phys etc* continuum; **c. espace-temps** space-time continuum

contondant [kɔ̃tɔ̃dɑ̃] **ADJ** blunt; **objet/instrument c.** blunt object/instrument; **arme contondante** blunt instrument

contorsion [kɔ̃tɔrsjɔ̃] **NF** *(du corps, des membres)* contortion; **faire des contorsions** to contort oneself *or* one's body

contorsionner (se) [səkɔ̃tɔrsjɔne] **VPR** to contort one's body *or* oneself; **ses traits se contorsionnent sous la souffrance** his features are contorted *or* twisted with pain; **la sorcière que l'on brûlait se contorsionnait dans les flammes** the witch they were burning writhed in the flames

contorsionniste [kɔ̃tɔrsjɔnist] **N** contortionist

contour [kɔ̃tur] **NM 1** *(silhouette)* outline, contour; **la route suit les contours de la montagne** the road follows the contours of the mountain **2 contours** *(méandres)* twists and turns **3** *Suisse (virage)* bend

contourné [kɔ̃turne] **ADJ** *(membre, arbre, forme)* twisted, contorted, crooked; *(meuble, pied de chaise etc)* (over)elaborate; *Péj* **style c.** tortuous *or* convoluted style

contournement [kɔ̃turnəmɑ̃] **NM** *(d'une*

montagne, d'un marais etc) skirting; *Rail* (voie de) **c.** loop line

contourner [kɔ̃turne] **VT 1** *(colline, forêt, île etc)* to go round, to skirt (round); *(ville)* to go round, to bypass, to skirt (round); *(obstacle)* to go *or* get round; **c. la loi/une difficulté** to get round *or* circumvent the law/a difficulty **2** *Vieilli (motif, vase etc)* to shape, to trace the outline of

contraceptif, -ive [kɔ̃traseptif, -iv] *Méd* **ADJ** contraceptive; **la pilule contraceptive** the (contraceptive) pill
NM contraceptive; **c. local/oral** barrier/oral contraceptive

contraception [kɔ̃trasepsjɔ̃] **NF** contraception; **méthode de c.** method of contraception, contraceptive method; **changer de c.** to change one's method of contraception; **moyens de c.** contraceptive methods *or* techniques; **c. masculine/féminine** male/female contraception

contractant [kɔ̃traktɑ̃] *Jur* **ADJ** *(partie)* contracting
NM contracting party

contracté [kɔ̃trakte] **ADJ 1** *(muscles, visage etc)* tense, taut; *Fig* **il était très c.** he was very tense **2** *Ling* contracted

contracter¹ [kɔ̃trakte] **VT 1** *(alliance, mariage)* to contract, to enter into; *(dette)* to incur, to contract; **c. des obligations** to enter into commitments; **c. une assurance** to take out an insurance policy **2** *(habitude, goût, manie)* to acquire; *(maladie)* to contract, to catch

contracter² **VT** *(muscles, visage, bouche)* to tense; **visage contracté par la douleur** face drawn with pain
VPR se contracter 1 *(du cœur)* to contract; *(d'un muscle)* to tense (up), to contract; *(d'une personne)* to tense (up), to become tense **2** *Ling (d'un mot, d'un article)* to contract, to be contracted **VOIR GRAMMAIRE A66**

contractile [kɔ̃traktil] **ADJ** *Physiol (muscle etc)* contractile, contractible

contraction [kɔ̃traksjɔ̃] **NF 1** *(d'un corps etc)* contraction; *(d'un muscle)* tensing, contraction; *Physiol* **sentir les premières contractions** *(d'une femme qui va accoucher)* to feel the first contractions **2** *Ling* contraction **3** *Écon (de l'activité, du crédit)* reduction (**de** in); **la c. de la demande** the fall in demand
▸▸**c. de texte** précis, summary; **être bon en c. de texte** to be good at précis

contractuel, -elle [kɔ̃traktɥɛl] **ADJ** *(obligations etc)* contractual; *(droit)* granted by contract; **agent c.** = contractor working for the (local) council
NM *Admin* contract public servant; *(auxiliaire de police)* ≃ traffic warden, *Am* ≃ traffic policeman
NF contractuelle *Admin* contract public servant; *(auxiliaire de police)* ≃ (female) traffic warden, *Am* ≃ traffic policewoman

contracture [kɔ̃traktyr] **NF** *Méd* spasm

contradicteur [kɔ̃tradiktœr] **NM** contradictor

contradiction [kɔ̃tradiksjɔ̃] **NF 1** *(opposition)* contradiction; *Jur* opposition; **porter la c. au sein d'un débat** to bring a dissenting voice into a debate; **esprit de c.** contrariness; **il ne supporte pas la c.** he can't stand being contradicted **2** *(inconséquence)* contradiction, inconsistency; **être en c. avec qch** to contradict sth, to be at variance *or* inconsistent *or* incompatible with sth; **cette théorie est un tissu de contradictions** this theory is a web *or* tissue of contradictions *or* inconsistencies; **être en c. avec soi-même** to contradict oneself

contradictoire [kɔ̃tradiktwar] **ADJ** contra-

dictory (**à** to), inconsistent (**à** with); *(rapports, idées etc)* contradictory, conflicting; *Jur* **jugement c.** judgment after hearing both parties; **débat c.** debate

contradictoirement [kɔ̃tradiktwarmɑ̃] **ADV** *Jur* after hearing both parties

contraignant [kɔ̃trɛɲɑ̃] **ADJ** restricting

contraindre [kɔ̃trɛ̃dr] *(pp contraint; pr ind je contrains, n. contraignons, ils contraignent; impf je contraignais; p hist je contraignis; fu je contraindrai)* **VT 1** *(réprimer) (personne, sentiments, envie etc)* to restrain **2** *(obliger)* **c. qn à faire qch** to force *or* compel *or* oblige sb to do sth; **je fus contraint à ou de quitter mon pays** I was forced *or* compelled *or* obliged to leave my country; *Jur* **c. qn par voie de justice** to bring an action against sb
VPR se contraindre 1 *(se retenir)* to restrain oneself
2 se c. à faire qch to force oneself to do sth, to make oneself do sth

contraint [kɔ̃trɛ̃] **ADJ** *(posture, style etc)* constrained, unnatural; *(sourire)* forced; *(attitude)* stiff, strained; **c. et forcé** under duress

contrainte [kɔ̃trɛ̃t] **NF 1** *(retenue)* constraint, restraint; **parler sans c.** to speak freely *or* without inhibition; **rire sans c.** to laugh without inhibition **2** *(obligation)* constraint; **obtenir qch par la c.** to get sth by force; **faire qch par c.** to be forced to do sth; **agir sous la c.** to act under pressure *or* duress; **c. sociale** social pressure *or* constraint(s); **contraintes du marché** market constraints; **il faut prendre en compte plusieurs contraintes** several constraints *or* limiting factors must be taken into account **3** *Tech* **c. de cisaillement/de traction** shearing/tensile stress *or* strain; **c. en compression** compressive stress; **c. en flambage** bending stress; **c. en torsion** torsional stress
▸▸*Jur* **c. par corps** imprisonment for debt

contraire [kɔ̃trer] **ADJ 1** *(direction)* opposite; *(intérêt, avis etc)* conflicting; **en sens c.** in the opposite direction; **vent c.** adverse *or* contrary wind; **ils sont d'avis contraires** they have conflicting opinions; **sauf avis c.** unless I/you/*etc* hear to the contrary; **c. à la règle** *ou* **aux règlements** against the rules, contrary to the rules; **c. au contrat** contrary to the terms of the contract; **c. aux statuts** contrary to the articles of association **2** *(défavorable)* **le sort lui est c.** fate is against him
NM opposite; **c'est le c.** it's the other way round; **tu connais sa sœur? c'est tout le c. (de lui)** you know his sister? she's the exact opposite (of him); **il ne vous dit pas le c.** he's not denying it; **(bien) au c.** on the contrary; **au c. de ses frères** unlike his brothers; **au c. de ses parents, il est plutôt à gauche** unlike *or* in contrast to his parents, he's a bit left-wing; **il dit toujours le c. de ce qu'on pourrait attendre de lui** he always says the opposite of what you might expect; **tu es en train de dire une chose et son c.** you're saying one thing and then the exact opposite

contrairement [kɔ̃trɛrmɑ̃] **ADV** **c. à** contrary to; *(comparaison)* unlike; **c. à ce que nous avions décidé** contrary to what we had decided; **c. à son habitude, il sortit sans manteau** he went out without a coat, which was unusual for him; **c. à moi, elle aime l'opéra** unlike me, she likes opera

contralto [kɔ̃tralto] **NM** *Mus* contralto, *pl* contraltos

contrariant [kɔ̃trarjɑ̃] **ADJ** *(personne, esprit)* perverse, contrary; *(situation)* annoying, irritating, tiresome; **comme c'est c.!** how annoying!; **elle n'est pas contrariante** she's easy-going, *Péj* she's a bit of a yes-woman

contrarié [kɔ̃trarje] **ADJ** *(personne)* annoyed, bothered; *(projet)* thwarted; **se sentir c. (dans ses projets)** to feel thwarted in one's plans; **un gaucher c.** = a left-handed person forced to write with his/her right hand

contrarier [kɔ̃trarje] **VT** *(impf, pr sub n. contrariions, v. contrariiez)* **1** *(ennuyer)* to annoy, to irritate, to bother; **il cherche à la c.** he's trying to annoy her; **il y a quelque chose qui me contrarie** something's annoying *or* bothering me **2** *(contrecarrer) (projets, desseins)* to thwart, to frustrate; **c. qn dans ses projets** to thwart sb in his/her plans **3** *(alterner) (lignes, formes, couleurs)* to alternate

contrariété [kɔ̃trarjete] **NF 1** *(agacement etc)* annoyance, vexation; **éprouver une vive c.** to be extremely annoyed; **il a dû avoir une grosse/petite c.** something must have upset him a lot/a bit **2** *(d'intérêts, de goûts, de couleurs etc)* clash; **esprit de c.** contrariness

contrastant [kɔ̃trastɑ̃] **ADJ** contrasting

contraste [kɔ̃trast] **NM** contrast; **mettre une chose en c. avec une autre** to contrast one thing with another; **faire c. (avec)** to contrast (with); **en c. avec le rouge** in contrast to the red; **effet de c.** contrasting effect; *TV* **réglage du c.** contrast control *or* adjustment; **le goût du c.** a taste *or* liking for contrast(s); **le c. des idées** the contrast(-ing) of ideas

contrasté [kɔ̃traste] **ADJ 1** contrasted, contrasting; **photo bien/mal contrastée** photo with the right amount of/with not enough contrast **2** *Ordinat* highlighted

contraster [kɔ̃traste] **VI** **c. avec qch** to contrast with sth; **couleurs qui contrastent** contrasting colours
VT to contrast; *(photo)* to add contrast to

contrat [kɔ̃tra] **NM** *(document, convention)* contract, agreement; **un c. de plusieurs milliards de dollars** a contract worth several billion dollars; **un c. de deux ans** a two-year contract; **rupture de c.** breach of contract; **passer un c. (avec qn)** to enter into an agreement (with sb); **décrocher un c.** to win a contract; **notre c. était que ...** our agreement was that ...; *Cartes* **réaliser son c.** to make one's contract
▸▸**c. d'achat** purchase contract; **c. d'affacturage** factoring contract; **c. d'affrètement** contract of affreightment; **c. d'agence** agency contract; **c. d'apprentissage** training contract; **c. d'association** joint venture; **c. d'assurance** contract of insurance; **c. de bail** lease contract; **c. collectif** collective agreement; **c. de concession** licensing contract; *Fin* **c. couverture à terme** forward contract; **c. de crédit-bail** lease-purchase contract; **c. de distribution** distribution contract; **c. à durée déterminée** fixed-term contract; **c. à durée indéterminée** open-ended contract; **c. d'embauche** employment contract, contract of employment, *Am* labor contract; **c. emploi-solidarité** = short-term contract subsidized by the government; **c. exclusif** sole contract; **c. de franchisage** franchise contract; **c. de gestion** management contract; **c. global** blanket contract; **c. hôtelier** = contract between a hotel and a travel agent; **c. de licence** licensing agreement; *Aut* **c. de location** rental agreement; **c. de mariage** marriage contract; **c. de mission d'intérim** temporary contract; **c. notarié** notarized contract; **c. à plein temps** full-time contract; **c. de prêt** loan agreement; *Com* **c. de représentation exclusive** sole agency contract; **c. de service** service contract; **c. social** social contract; *Com* **c. de système** systems contracting; **c. temporaire** temporary contract; **c. à temps partiel** part-time

contract; **c. à temps plein** full-time contract; *Fin* **c. à terme** futures contract; **c. à terme sous option** underlying futures contract; **c. de transport** contract of carriage; **c. de travail** contract of employment, *Am* labor contract; **c. de vente** bill of sale, sales contract

contravention [kɔ̃travɑ̃sjɔ̃] NF *Jur (envers un règlement etc)* contravention, infringement, violation; *(amende)* fine; *(pour stationnement non-autorisé) (amende)* (parking) fine; *(avis)* (parking) ticket; **être en c.** to be in breach of the law; **donner une c. à qn** to book sb, to give sb a (parking) ticket

---

CONTRE [kɔ̃tr]

> **PRÉP** against **1, 2, 5** ▪ with **1** ▪ for **2, 3** ▪ to **4** ▪ contrary to **1, 6** ▪ compared to **8**
> **ADV** against **1** ▪ next to **2**
> **NM** pros and cons *(le pour et le contre)* **1**

PRÉP SEE GRAMMAR A67-8; B55 **1** *(opposition)* against; **nager c. le courant** to swim against the current; **se battre c. qn** to fight against *or* with sb; **se fâcher c. qn** to get angry with sb; **c. son habitude** contrary to his usual practice; **ce serait aller c. sa nature** it would go *or* be against his nature; **l'Irlande c. l'Angleterre** England against *or* versus Ireland; **jouer c. l'Angleterre** to play against England; **la loi c. l'avortement** the anti-abortion law; **lutte c. l'alcoolisme/le cancer** fight against alcoholism/cancer; **je n'ai rien c. lui** I have nothing against him; **tout le monde est c. moi** everyone is against me

2 *(protection)* **sirop c. la toux** cough mixture; **tu es assuré c. le vol?** are you insured against *or* for theft?; **bombe c. les acariens** spray against acarids

3 *(échange)* (in exchange) for; **échanger une chose c. une autre** to exchange one thing for another; **il lui demande de l'argent c. son silence** he's asking him for money in exchange for his silence; **livraison c. remboursement** cash on delivery

4 *(pour)* to; **parier à cinq c. un** to bet five to one; **le projet fut accepté, à dix voix c. deux** the plan was accepted by ten votes to two

5 *(près)* against; **s'appuyer c. le mur** to lean against the wall; **lancer une balle c. un mur** to throw a ball against a wall; **sa maison est tout c. la mienne** his house is right next to mine *or* adjoins mine; **prendre un enfant c. son cœur** to hug a child; **danser joue c. joue** to dance cheek to cheek; **viens un peu c. moi** come and cuddle up to me a bit; **ils dorment l'un c. l'autre** they sleep cuddled up to each other

6 *(en dépit de)* **faire c. mauvaise fortune bon cœur** to put a brave face on things; **c. toute apparence** despite appearances (to the contrary); **c. toute logique** against all logic; **c. toute attente** contrary to all expectation(s)

7 *(comparaison)* compared to; **la livre est à 2 euros c. 1 euro le mois dernier** the pound stands at 2 euros compared to 1 euro *or* as against 1 euro last month

ADV 1 *(opposition)* **parler/voter c.** to speak/vote against; **je n'ai rien c., je ne suis pas c.** I have nothing against it; **beaucoup sont c.** a lot of people are against it; *Fam* **par c.** on the other hand

2 *(proximité)* **le radiateur est allumé, mets-toi tout c.** the heater is on, stand right next to it

NM 1 **disputer le pour et le c.** to argue *or* dispute the pros and cons; **il y a toujours du pour et du c.** there are two sides to everything

2 *Boxe, Escrime* counter

3 *Billard* kiss

---

4 *Cartes* double

contre-accusation, *pl* **contre-accusations** NF countercharge

contre-achat, *pl* **contre-achats** NM counterpurchase

contre-alizé, *pl* **contre-alizés** NM *Météo* anti-trade (wind)

contre-allée, *pl* **contre-allées** NF side road

contre-amiral, *pl* **contre-amiraux** NM rear admiral

contre-analyse, *pl* **contre-analyses** NF second analysis, reanalysis

contre-appel, *pl* **contre-appels** NM *Mil* check roll call, second call

contre-assurance, *pl* **contre-assurances** NF reinsurance

contre-attaque, *pl* **contre-attaques** NF *Mil, Fig* counterattack

contre-attaquer VI to counterattack

contrebalancer [kɔ̃trəbalɑ̃se] *(je contrebalançai(s); n. contrebalançons)* VT *(poids)* to counterbalance; *Fig* to offset, to counterbalance; **les bénéfices ne contrebalancent plus les pertes** profits are no longer balancing losses
▪ **VPR se contrebalancer** *Fam* **se c. de qch** not to give a damn about sth; **il s'en contrebalance** he couldn't give a damn, he couldn't care less; **je me contrebalance de perdre mon boulot** I don't give a damn *or* I couldn't care less about losing my job

contrebande [kɔ̃trəbɑ̃d] NF **1** *(activité)* smuggling, contraband; **faire de la c.** to smuggle goods; **faire entrer des marchandises en c.** to smuggle in goods; **marchandises de c.** smuggled goods; **alcool de c.** bootleg alcohol **2** *(marchandises)* smuggled goods, contraband

contrebandier, -ière [kɔ̃trəbɑ̃dje, -jɛr] N smuggler

contrebas (en) [ɑ̃kɔ̃trəba] ADV lower down, (down) below, on a lower level; **le café est en c. de la rue** the café is below street level

contrebasse [kɔ̃trəbas] NF *Mus (instrument)* (double) bass; *(musicien)* (double) bass player

contrebassiste [kɔ̃trəbasist] N *Mus* (double) bass player

contrebasson [kɔ̃trəbasɔ̃] NM *Mus* double bassoon, contrabassoon

contrebatterie [kɔ̃trəbatri] NF *Mil* counterbattery

contre-bord (à) [akɔ̃trəbɔr] ADV *Naut* courir à c. to sail on opposite tacks *or* on parallel and opposite courses

contrebouter [kɔ̃trəbute] VT *Constr* to buttress, to shore up

contre-braquage, *pl* **contre-braquages** [kɔ̃trəbraka3] NM *Aut* opposite lock

contrebraquer [kɔ̃trəbrake] VI *Aut* to steer into the skid, to apply opposite lock

contrebuter [kɔ̃trəbyte] VT = **contrebouter**

contrecarrer [kɔ̃trəkare] VT *(personne, projets)* to thwart

contrechamp [kɔ̃trəʃɑ̃] NM *Cin* reverse (angle) shot, reverse cut, reaction shot

contre-chant, *pl* **contre-chants** [kɔ̃trəʃɑ̃] NM *Mus* counterpoint

contrechâssis [kɔ̃trəʃasi] NM INV double (window) frame

contrecœur¹ [kɔ̃trəkœr] ADV **à c.** reluctantly, unwillingly; *(donner)* grudgingly

contrecœur² NM **1** *Constr (d'une cheminée)* backplate, fireback **2** *Rail (au centre d'un croisement de voies ferrées)* guardrail, wing-rail, checkrail

contrecoup [kɔ̃trəku] NM *(d'une balle)* rico-

---

chet; *(d'un coup)* jar; *Fig (d'une action, d'un désastre etc)* repercussions, aftereffects; **les contrecoups de la guerre** the repercussions *or* aftereffects of war

contre-courant, *pl* **contre-courants** [kɔ̃trəkurɑ̃] NM **1** countercurrent; **nager à c.** to swim against the current; *Fig* **aller à c. de qch** to go against the current *or* the tide of sth **2** *Aut* contra-flow

contredanse [kɔ̃trədɑ̃s] NF **1** *(danse, air)* quadrille, contredanse **2** *Fam (amende)* fine

contredire [kɔ̃trədir] *(pr ind* **je contredis, n. contredisons, v. contredisez;** *other tenses like* **dire)** VT **1** *(personne)* to contradict **2** *(rapport etc)* to be inconsistent with, to be at variance with, to contradict; *(espérances)* to belie; **les événements contredisent ses prédictions** the events are at variance with his predictions
▪ **VPR se contredire** *(d'une personne)* to contradict oneself; *(de plusieurs personnes)* to contradict each other; **ces deux textes se contredisent** these two texts contradict each other *or* are at variance with each other

contredit [kɔ̃trədi] ADV **sans c.** indisputably, unquestionably, undoubtedly

contrée [kɔ̃tre] NF *Litt (région)* region; *(pays)* country, land; **ils sont partis vers des contrées lointaines** they went off to distant parts *or* lands

contre-écriture, *pl* **contre-écritures** NF *Compta* contra-entry

contre-écrou, *pl* **contre-écrous** NM *Tech* lock nut

contre-emploi, *pl* **contre-emplois** NM *Théâtre, Cin etc* miscasting; **ce rôle est un c. pour lui** he's miscast in that role; **utiliser qn à c.** to miscast sb

contre-enquête, *pl* **contre-enquêtes** NF *Jur* counter-inquiry

contre-épreuve, *pl* **contre-épreuves** NF **1** *(épreuve)* counterproof **2** *Tech (vérification)* check test

contre-espionnage NM counterespionage

contre-essai, *pl* **contre-essais** NM control *or* check test

contre-exemple, *pl* **contre-exemples** NM counter-example

contre-expertise, *pl* **contre-expertises** NF second expert valuation, counterappraisal

contrefaçon [kɔ̃trəfasɔ̃] NF **1** *(pratique)* counterfeiting; *(de signature)* forging **2** *(produit)* fake, imitation; **méfiez-vous des contrefaçons** beware of imitations

contrefacteur [kɔ̃trəfaktœr] NM counterfeiter, forger; *(de signature)* forger

contrefaire [kɔ̃trəfɛr] VT *(conj like* **faire)** **1** *(calquer) (personne, la démarche de qn etc)* to imitate, to mimic; *(déguiser) (voix, écriture etc)* to disguise; *Vieilli (feindre)* to feign; **c. la folie** to feign madness **2** *(pièce, monnaie, produits de marque etc)* to counterfeit, to forge; *(signature)* to forge; *(vidéo, radio-cassette etc)* to pirate **3** *(déformer) (visage)* to distort, to deform

contrefait [kɔ̃trəfɛ] ADJ **1** *(argent etc)* counterfeit, forged; *(signature)* forged **2** *(déformé) (personne, visage)* deformed, misshapen

contre-feu, *pl* **contre-feux** [kɔ̃trəfø] NM **1** *(dans cheminée)* fireback **2** *(feu)* backfire

contrefiche [kɔ̃trəfiʃ] NF *Constr* brace, strut

contreficher (se) [səkɔ̃trəfiʃe] VPR *Arg* **je m'en fiche et m'en contrefiche** I don't give a damn, I couldn't care less; **il se contrefiche de ce que tu penses** he doesn't give a damn *or* couldn't care less about what you think

contre-fil, *pl* **contre-fils** [kɔ̃trəfil] NM *(dans un cours d'eau etc)* opposite direction; *Tech* **travailler le bois à c.** to work wood against the grain

contre-filet, *pl* **contre-filets** [kɔ̃trəfilɛ] NM *Culin* sirloin, tenderloin

contrefort [kɔ̃trəfɔr] NM **1** *Archit* buttress **2** *Géog (de montagne)* spur; **contreforts** foothills **3** *(de chaussure)* stiffener

contrefoutre (se) [səkɔ̃trəfutr] VPR **se c. de** not to give a damn *or Br* a stuff *or Am* a hoot about

contre-haut (en) [ɑ̃kɔ̃trəo] ADV (up) above, higher up, on a higher level

contre-indication, *pl* **contre-indications** NF *Méd* contraindication

contre-indiquer VT *Méd* to contraindicate; *Fig* **c'est contre-indiqué** it's inadvisable *or* unwise

contre-interrogatoire, *pl* **contre-interrogatoires** NM *Jur* cross-examination

contre-jour, *pl* **contre-jours** [kɔ̃trəʒur] NM **1** *(éclairage défavorable) (pour un tableau etc)* light from behind; **tableau pendu à c.** picture hung against the light; **photo prise à c.** photograph taken against the light; **assis à c.** sitting with one's back to the light **2** *Beaux-Arts, Cin, Phot* backlight(ing); **un effet de c.** a backlit *or* contre-jour effect

contre-la-montre [kɔ̃trəlamɔ̃tr] NM INV *Sport* time-trial

contre-lettre, *pl* **contre-lettres** [kɔ̃trəlɛtr] NF *Jur* counter-letter, counter-deed

contremaître, -tresse [kɔ̃trəmɛtr, -trɛs] N foreman, *f* forewoman

contre-manifestant, -ante, *pl* **contre-manifestants, -antes** [kɔ̃trəmanifɛstɑ̃, -ɑ̃t] N *Pol* counter-demonstrator

contre-manifestation, *pl* **contre-manifestations** [kɔ̃trəmanifɛstasjɔ̃] NF *Pol* counter-demonstration

contremarche [kɔ̃trəmarʃ] NF **1** *Mil* countermarch **2** *Constr (d'un escalier)* riser

contremarché [kɔ̃trəmarʃe] NM countermove

contremarketing [kɔ̃trəmarketiŋ] NM countermarketing

contremarque [kɔ̃trəmark] NF **1** *(sur une pièce, une plaque d'or etc)* countermark **2** *Théâtre* passout ticket

contremarquer [kɔ̃trəmarke] VT to countermark

contre-mesure, *pl* **contre-mesures** [kɔ̃trəm(ə)zyr] NF **1** *(mesure)* countermeasure; *Mil* **c. électronique** electronic countermeasure, jamming **2** *Mus* **jouer à c.** to play against the beat *or* out of time

contre-offensive, *pl* **contre-offensives** NF *Mil* counter-offensive

contre-offre, *pl* **contre-offres** NF counter-offer

contre-OPA NF INV counter-bid

contre-ordre, *pl* **contre-ordres** NM = **contrordre**

contrepartie [kɔ̃trəparti] NF **1** *(dans un débat etc)* opposite *or* opposing view; *Com, Fin (dans une transaction)* other party *or* side; *Bourse* **faire la c.** to operate against one's client **2** *(compensation)* compensation; **c. financière** financial compensation; **en c.** in return (**de** for) **3** *(en comptabilité) (d'une inscription)* counterpart; *(d'un registre)* duplicate; **en c.** per contra **4** *Mus* counterpart

contre-passation, *pl* **contre-passations** [kɔ̃trəpasasjɔ̃] NF *Compta* journal entry, contra-entry; *Fin (d'un effet)* return, endorsement, backing

contre-passer [kɔ̃trəpase] VT **1** *Compta (article, entrée)* to reverse, to transfer **2** *Fin (ef-*

fet) to return, to endorse, to back

contre-pente, *pl* **contre-pentes** [kɔ̃trəpɑ̃t] NF counterslope, opposite slope

contre-performance, *pl* **contre-performances** [kɔ̃trəperfɔrmɑ̃s] NF *(d'athlète, d'homme politique etc)* substandard *or* poor performance

contrepèterie [kɔ̃trəpetri] NF spoonerism

contre-pied, *pl* **contre-pieds** [kɔ̃trəpje] NM **1** *(inverse)* opposite; **prendre le c.** *(action)* to do the opposite (**de** from); *(opinion)* to take the opposite view (**de** to); **il prend toujours le c. de ce qu'on lui dit** he always does the opposite of what he's told/says the opposite of what people say **2** *Sport* **prendre son adversaire à c.** to wrong-foot one's opponent; **prendre la balle à c.** to take the ball on the wrong foot **3** *(à la chasse)* back scent

contreplacage [kɔ̃trəplakaʒ] NM *(action)* plywood construction; *(résultat)* plywood surface

contreplaqué [kɔ̃trəplake] NM plywood

contre-plongée, *pl* **contre-plongées** [kɔ̃trəplɔ̃ʒe] NF *Cin, TV* low-angle shot; **vue en c.** low-angle view

contrepoids [kɔ̃trəpwa] NM **1** *Tech* counterweight, counterbalance; *(d'une horloge, d'un monte-charge)* balance weight; *Fig* counterbalance; *Fig* **faire c. à qch** to counterbalance sth, to balance sth out **2** *(d'un funambule)* balancing pole

contre-poil (à) [akɔ̃trəpwal] ADV *(d'un tissu, d'un animal)* the wrong way; *Fam* **prendre qn à c.** to rub sb up the wrong way

contrepoint [kɔ̃trəpwɛ̃] NM *Mus, Fig* counterpoint; **se passer en c.** to happen concurrently

contrepoison [kɔ̃trəpwazɔ̃] NM antidote

contre-porte, *pl* **contre-portes** [kɔ̃trəpɔrt] NF inner door, *Am* screen door

contre-pouvoir, *pl* **contre-pouvoirs** [kɔ̃trəpuvwar] NM anti-establishment force

contre-pression, *pl* **contre-pressions** [kɔ̃trəpresjɔ̃] NF *Aut* back-pressure

contre-projet, *pl* **contre-projets** [kɔ̃trəprɔʒe] NM counterplan

contre-proposition, *pl* **contre-propositions** [kɔ̃trəprɔpozisjɔ̃] NF counterproposal

contre-publicité [kɔ̃trəpyblisite] NF adverse *or* bad publicity; *Fig* **cet article fait de la c. à son auteur** this article is a poor advertisement for its author

contrer [kɔ̃tre] VT **1** *(repousser)* to thwart; *(personne)* to block; **c. un argument** to counter *or* refute an argument; **se faire c.** to come a cropper **2** *Boxe (coup)* to counter **3** *Cartes* to double

contre-rail, *pl* **contre-rails** [kɔ̃trəraj] NM *Rail* guard *or* check rail

Contre-Réforme [kɔ̃trərefɔrm] NF *Hist, Rel* Counter-Reformation

contre-révolution, *pl* **contre-révolutions** [kɔ̃trərevɔlysjɔ̃] NF *Pol* counter-revolution

contre-révolutionnaire, *pl* **contre-révolutionnaires** [kɔ̃trərevɔlysjɔnɛr] ADJ, N counter-revolutionary

contre-segmentation, *pl* **contre-segmentations** [kɔ̃trəsɛgmɑ̃tasjɔ̃] NF *Mktg* countersegmentation

contreseing [kɔ̃trəsɛ̃] NM *Jur* countersignature

contresens [kɔ̃trəsɑ̃s] NM **1** *(de mots etc)* misinterpretation; *(mauvaise traduction)* mistranslation; **comprendre qch à c.** to take sth the wrong way; **faire un c.** to misinterpret; **faire un c. dans une traduction** to make a mistake in a translation; **ce résumé de l'histoire est un c.** this summary of the story is a piece of nonsense **2** *Aut* **à c.** the wrong way, in the wrong direction; **prendre une**

rue à c. to go the wrong way down a street

contresignataire [kɔ̃trəsiɲatɛr] ADJ, N *Jur* countersignatory

contresigner [kɔ̃trəsiɲe] VT to countersign

contretemps [kɔ̃trətɑ̃] NM **1** *(ennui)* hitch, mishap, contretemps; **à moins d'un c.** unless there's a hitch; **voilà un c. bien fâcheux!** that's really made things awkward!; **arriver à c.** to arrive at the wrong moment **2** *Mus* offbeat; **jouer à c.** to play off the beat

contre-terrorisme [kɔ̃trətɛrɔrism] NM counterterrorism

contre-terroriste, *pl* **contre-terroristes** [kɔ̃trətɛrɔrist] ADJ, N counter-terrorist

contre-tirer [kɔ̃trətire] VT *Typ* to run off counter-proofs from, to take a counter-proof of

contre-torpilleur, *pl* **contre-torpilleurs** [kɔ̃trətɔrpijœr] NM *Naut* destroyer

contre-transfert [kɔ̃trətrɑ̃sfɛr] NM *Psy* counter-transference

contretypage [kɔ̃trətipaʒ] NM *TV etc* duping

contretype [kɔ̃trətip] NM *TV etc* dupe, copy tape

contre-ut NM INV *Mus* top C

contre-valeur, *pl* **contre-valeurs** [kɔ̃trəvalœr] NF *Fin* exchange value

contrevenant, -ante [kɔ̃trəv(ə)nɑ̃, -ɑ̃t] ADJ *(partie etc)* offending

N offender; *(à la loi)* contravener, infringer (**à** of)

contrevenir [kɔ̃trəv(ə)nir] VI *(conj like venir)* **c. à** to contravene, to infringe

contrevent [kɔ̃trəvɑ̃] NM **1** *(d'une fenêtre)* (outside) shutter **2** *Constr* brace, strut

contrevérité [kɔ̃trəverite] NF **1** *(affirmation fausse)* untruth, falsehood **2** *Vieilli (destinée à faire entendre le contraire)* ironical statement

contre-verrou, *pl* **contre-verrous** [kɔ̃trəvɛru] NM *Ordinat* lock inhibit

contre-visite, *pl* **contre-visites** [kɔ̃trəvizit] NF = for someone suspected of fraudulently claiming sickness benefit, visit to a specific doctor at Social Security's request; *(par médecin)* = house call made, at the request of an employer, by a doctor (approved by Social Security) to determine whether an employee is genuinely ill

contre-voie (à) [akɔ̃trəvwa] ADV *Rail* monter/descendre à c. to get in/out on the wrong side of the train

contribuable [kɔ̃tribɥabl] N taxpayer; **c. à l'impôt foncier** ≃ ratepayer

contribuer [kɔ̃tribɥe] VI to contribute; **c. à qch** to contribute to(wards) sth; **c. financièrement à qch** to contribute (money) to sth, to make a (financial) contribution to sth; **c. à faire qch** to help (to) do sth; **nous y avons contribué pour une bonne part** we made a handsome contribution to it; **cela contribue pour beaucoup à la rendre heureuse** that goes a long way towards making her happy; **il a beaucoup contribué à …** he has made a great contribution to …, he has played a great part in …

contributif, -ive [kɔ̃tribytif, -iv] ADJ contributory

contribution [kɔ̃tribysjɔ̃] NF **1** *Admin (impôt)* tax; **contributions** *(à l'État)* taxes; *(à la collectivité locale)* rates, *Am* local taxes; **(bureau des) contributions** tax office, *Br* Inland Revenue, *Am* Internal Revenue; **lever** *ou* **percevoir une c.** to collect *or* levy a tax **2** *(part)* contribution, share; *(collaboration)* contribution (**à** to); **mettre qn à c.** to call on sb's services; **mettre qch à c.** to make use of sth

▶▶**c. après remise** discounted contribution; **c. brute** gross contribution; **c. complémentaire** supplementary contribution; **contributions directes** direct taxation; **c. foncière** land tax; **contributions indirectes** indirect taxation; **c. nette** net contribution; **c. sociale généralisée** = income-based tax deducted at source as a contribution to paying off the French social security budget deficit

contrit [kɔ̃tri] ADJ contrite, penitent

contrition [kɔ̃trisjɔ̃] NF *Rel, Litt* contrition, penitence

contrôlable [kɔ̃trolabl] ADJ *(vérifiable)* verifiable, that can be checked *or* verified; *(maîtrisable)* controllable; **des éléments difficilement contrôlables** elements that are hard to control

contrôle [kɔ̃trol] NM **1** *(vérification) (de l'information, de déclarations, de marchandises etc)* checking, verification; *Admin (des services)* inspection, supervision; *Com (des comptes)* auditing, checking; *Sp, Aut* check; *(des pneus)* checking; *Scol* test; *Théâtre etc* **c. des billets** checking of tickets

2 *(surveillance)* control; **exercer un c. sévère sur qn** to maintain strict control over sb, to keep sb under strict supervision; **échapper à tout c.** to get out of control; **(bureau de) c.** ticket office, booking office, *Am* reservation office; *Aviat* **tour de c.** control tower

3 *(maîtrise) (d'un véhicule, d'une machine etc)* control; **avoir le c. de qch** to have control of sth, to be in control of sth; **prendre le c. d'une entreprise** to take over a company; **perdre c. (de la situation)** to lose control (of the situation); **perdre le c. de son véhicule** to lose control of one's vehicle; **c. de soi-même** self-control; **perdre tout c. de soi** to lose all self-control

4 *(marque)* hallmark; *(bureau)* assay office; **poinçon de c.** hallmark stamp

5 *Mil etc* roll, list, register; **c. de service** duty roster; **rayer qn des contrôles de l'armée** to remove sb from the army list

6 *Ordinat* **touche c.** control key

▶▶ *Ordinat* **c. d'accès** access control; *Sport* **c. antidopage** dope test; **c. de bagages** baggage check; **c. bancaire** banking controls; *Compta* **c. du bilan** audit; *Fin* **c. des changes** exchange control; **c. de la comptabilité** accounting control; **c. de comptes** audit; *Univ* **c. continu** continuous assessment; *Ordinat* **c. croisé** cross-check; **faire un c. croisé de** to cross-check; *Ordinat* **c. du curseur** cursor control; **c. à distance** remote control; **c. douanier** customs control; **c. d'efficacité mercatique** marketing efficiency study; **c. des émissions de moteur diesel** diesel emissions test; *Fin* **c. fiscal** tax inspection; **contrôles aux frontières** border controls; **c. d'identité** identity check; **c. de l'immigration** immigration control; **contrôles à l'importation** import controls; *Jur* **c. judiciaire** probation; **placé sous c. judiciaire** put on probation; **c. de luminosité** brightness control; **c. monétaire** monetary control; **c. des naissances** birth control; **c. de parité** parity check; **c. des passeports** passport control; **contrôles phytosanitaires** plant health checks; **c. des points de ventes** store audit; **c. de police** police check; *(lieu)* police checkpoint; **c. des prix** price control; **c. de qualité** quality control; *Com* **c. de la qualité totale** total quality control, TQC; *Aut* **c. radar** radar speed check; **contrôles sanitaires** health checks; *Ordinat* **c. de la souris** mouse control; **c. des stocks** inventory *or* stock control; *Aut* **c. technique** ≃ MOT test

contrôler [kɔ̃trole] VT **1** *(vérifier) (travail)* to supervise, to check; *(comptes)* to check, to audit; *(billets)* to check; *(passeports)* to examine, to check, to inspect; *(information, fait*

etc) to check, to verify; *Compta* **c. les livres** to check the books

2 *(surveiller)* to monitor; *(situation, presse)* to control; **c. les naissances** to control the birth rate; **c. les prix** to control prices; **l'armée contrôle toute cette région** all of this region is under army control, this whole region is controlled by the army; **contrôlé par ordinateur** computer-controlled

3 *(maîtriser) (personne)* to control; **c. ses émotions/réactions** to control one's emotions/reactions; **le parti ne contrôle plus ces éléments indisciplinés** the party can no longer control these unruly elements

4 *(argent, or)* to hallmark, to stamp

5 *Ordinat* **contrôlé par le logiciel** software-controlled; **contrôlé par menu** menu-driven, menu-controlled

VPR **se contrôler** to control oneself

contrôleur, -euse [kɔ̃trolœr, -øz] N **1** *Can* **Bureau du C. Général** Office of the Controller General; **c. des contributions** tax inspector, inspector of taxes; **c. du crédit** credit controller; **c. financier** financial controller; **c. de gestion** management controller; **c. aux liquidations** controller in bankruptcy; *TV etc* **c. de réseau** network controller; **c. (de la) restauration** food and beverage manager

2 *(du travail etc)* supervisor; *(dans un train, bus)* ticket inspector

3 *Aviat* **c. de la circulation aérienne** *ou* **de trafic aérien** air traffic controller

NM **1** *(appareil)* regulator; *Rail* master controller; **c. d'atelier** time recorder, time-clock; *Aut* **c. de vigilance du conducteur** driver alertness monitor

2 *Ordinat* **c. de disque** disk controller; **c. d'unité de disquette** floppy disk controller; **c. d'affichage** display *or* screen controller; **c. de bus** bus controller

contrordre [kɔ̃trɔrdr] NM counterorder, countermand; **il y a c.** the orders have been changed; **sauf c.** unless otherwise directed

controuvé [kɔ̃truve] ADJ false, fabricated, concocted

controversable [kɔ̃trɔvɛrsabl] ADJ controversial, debatable

controverse [kɔ̃trɔvɛrs] NF controversy, debate; **cela prête encore à c.** it is still a controversial topic, it is still surrounded by controversy, it is still a matter of controversy *or* for debate; **donner lieu à c.** to be controversial; **matière à c.** matter for debate

controversé [kɔ̃trɔvɛrse] ADJ controversial

contumace [kɔ̃tymas] NF *Jur* non-appearance (in court); **condamné par c.** sentenced in absentia *or* in one's absence

ADJ *Jur* contumacious, defaulting

contusion [kɔ̃tyzjɔ̃] NF bruise, *Spéc* contusion

contusionner [kɔ̃tyzjɔne] VT to bruise, *Spéc* to contuse

conurbation [kɔnyrbasjɔ̃] NF conurbation

convaincant [kɔ̃vɛ̃kɑ̃] ADJ convincing

convaincre [kɔ̃vɛ̃kr] VT *(conj like* **vaincre***)* **1** *(persuader)* to convince (**de** of, **que** that); **c. qn de faire qch** to persuade *or Am* convince sb to do sth; **j'en suis convaincu** I'm convinced of it; **se laisser c.** to let oneself be persuaded *or* convinced *or* won over; **je l'ai finalement convaincu** I finally convinced him **2** *(prouver la culpabilité de)* **être convaincu de meurtre** to be convicted *or* found guilty of murder

convaincu [kɔ̃vɛ̃ky] ADJ convinced; **parler d'un ton c.** to speak with conviction; **c'est un végétarien c.** he's a committed vegetarian

NMPL **prêcher des convaincus** to preach to the converted

convalescence [kɔ̃valesɑ̃s] NF *Méd* convalescence; **elle est en c.** she's convalescing; **maison de c.** convalescent *or* nursing home **2** *Mil etc* sick leave

convalescent, -ente [kɔ̃valesɑ̃, -ɑ̃t] ADJ, N convalescent

convecteur [kɔ̃vɛktœr] NM convector (heater)

convection [kɔ̃vɛksjɔ̃] NF *Phys* convection

convenable [kɔ̃vnabl] ADJ **1** *(approprié)* appropriate, suitable, fitting; **juger c. de faire qch** to think it appropriate to do sth **2** *(décent) (comportement)* decent, respectable, acceptable; *(tenue)* decent, proper; **ce sont des gens très convenables** they are very decent *or* respectable people; **peu c.** unacceptable; **il n'est pas c. de faire du bruit en mangeant** it is not polite *or* nice *or* proper to make a noise when eating **3** *(acceptable) (salaire, restaurant, pantalon etc)* decent, adequate

convenablement [kɔ̃vnabləmɑ̃] ADV **1** *(d'une façon appropriée)* appropriately, suitably, fittingly **2** *(avec décence)* correctly, properly, decently **3** *(de façon acceptable)* decently; **on peut manger très c. à la cantine** you can eat quite decently in the canteen

convenance [kɔ̃vnɑ̃s] NF **1** *(fait de convenir)* appropriateness, suitability, fitness; **pour (des raisons de) c. personnelle** for personal reasons; **mariage de c.** marriage of convenience; **trouver qch à sa c.** to find sth to one's liking *or* suitable; **il le fera à sa c.** he'll do it at his own convenience **2** *Litt (des goûts)* affinity **3** **les convenances** propriety, the proprieties, etiquette; **comportement contraire aux convenances** unseemly conduct, improper behaviour

convenir [kɔ̃vnir] *(conj like* **venir***)* VI **1** *(conj with* **avoir***)* **c. à** *(aller, plaire)* to suit; **si cela vous convient** if that suits you, if that is convenient *or* all right (for you); **c'est exactement ce qui me convient** it's just what I need; **cet emploi lui convient parfaitement** that job suits him perfectly; **ce climat ne me convient pas** this climate doesn't suit me *or* agree with me; **il est difficile de trouver le mot qui convient** it's difficult to find the appropriate word; **robe qui convient à la circonstance** dress that suits the occasion, dress suitable for *or* befitting the occasion

2 *(conj with* **avoir** *or Lit with* **être***)* **c. de qch** *(être d'accord avec qch)* to agree on sth; *(le reconnaître)* to acknowledge *or* admit sth; **j'ai eu tort, j'en conviens** I was wrong, I admit it, I admit I was wrong; **il convient qu'il a eu tort** he admits that he was wrong

V IMPERS *(conj with* **être***)* **il convient de … ; il est souhaitable de)** it is advisable to …; *(il est de bon ton de)* it is the done thing to …, it is proper to …; **ce qu'il convient de faire, (c')est de …** the right thing to do is to …; **il convient que vous y alliez** you should *or* ought to go; **il fut convenu qu'ils le feraient venir** it was agreed that they would send for him

convention [kɔ̃vɑ̃sjɔ̃] NF **1** *(accord)* agreement; *Jur (d'un contrat etc)* article, clause; **c. écrite/verbale** written/verbal agreement; *Com* **c. d'exclusivité réciproque** mutual exclusivity agreement

2 **les conventions (sociales)** the (social) conventions; **de c.** conventional; *Péj* **amabilité/sourire de c.** superficial courtesy/smile; **par c. nous appellerons x la première inconnue de l'équation** the first unknown of the equation will be called x

3 *Pol (assemblée)* (extraordinary) assembly, *Am* convention; *Hist* **La C. (nationale)** the (National) Convention *(1792)*

▶▶ *Com* **c. d'affrètement** contract of affreightment; **c. cadre** framework convention; **c. collective** collective agreement; **c. de crédit** credit agreement; *Pol* **c. internationale** international convention *or* agreement; *UE* **c. de Lomé** Lomé Convention; **c. monétaire** monetary agreement; *UE* **C. de sauvegarde des droits de l'homme et des libertés fondamentales** European Convention for the Protection of Human Rights and Fundamental Freedoms

conventionné [kɔ̃vɑ̃sjɔne] **ADJ médecin c.** doctor attached to the health system, *Br* ≃ National Health Service doctor; **médecin non c.** ≃ private doctor; **clinique conventionnée** clinic attached to the health system

conventionnel, -elle [kɔ̃vɑ̃sjɔnɛl] **ADJ 1** *(valeur, symbole)*, *Mil (armes etc)* conventional; *Ling* **langage c.** conventional language; **c'est quelqu'un de très c.** he's a very conventional person **2** *Jur (clause etc)* contractual **3** *Péj (peu sincère)* superficial; **affabilité conventionnelle** superficial affability

NM *Hist* member of the National Convention

conventionnellement [kɔ̃vɑ̃sjɔnɛlmɑ̃] **ADV**conventionally; *Jur* by agreement

conventionnement [kɔ̃vɑ̃sjɔnmɑ̃] **NM** *(d'une clinique, d'un médecin)* attachment to the health system

conventionner [kɔ̃vɑ̃sjɔne] **VT** *(clinique, médecin)* to attach to the health system

conventuel, -elle [kɔ̃vɑ̃tɥɛl] **ADJ** *Rel (maison)* conventual; *(vie)* monastic; **bâtiment c.** *(monastère)* monastery; *(couvent)* convent

convenu [kɔ̃vny] **ADJ 1** *(prix, somme)* agreed, stipulated; *(date, moment)* agreed, appointed; **comme c.** as agreed **2** *Péj (langage, style, attitude etc)* conventional

convergence [kɔ̃vɛrʒɑ̃s] **NF** convergence; *Fig* **c. des idées** convergence of ideas, meeting of minds; *UE* **c. économique** economic convergence

convergent [kɔ̃vɛrʒɑ̃] **ADJ** *(lignes, idées, efforts etc)* convergent

converger [kɔ̃vɛrʒe] **VI** (**convergeant; ils convergeaient**) *(de routes, de lignes etc)* to converge; **toutes ces ruelles convergent vers le château** all these lanes meet at *or* converge on the castle; **nos efforts convergent vers le même but** all our efforts are focused on the same objective; **leurs opinions convergent** they are of like mind *or* one mind

convers, -erse [kɔ̃vɛr, -ɛrs] **ADJ** *Rel (frère, sœur)* lay

NF converse converse

conversation [kɔ̃vɛrsasjɔ̃] **NF** conversation, talk; **être en grande c. (avec qn)** to be deep in conversation (with sb); **lier** *ou* **entrer en c.** *ou* **engager une c. avec qn** to get into conversation with sb, to strike up a conversation with sb; **avoir une longue c. avec qn** to have a long *or* lengthy conversation with sb; **faire la c. (à qn)** to chat (with sb); **voilà qui a arrêté net la c.** that stopped the conversation dead, that killed the conversation; **il a fait les frais de la c.** he was the main subject of conversation; **amener un sujet dans une c.** to introduce a topic into a conversation; **c. téléphonique** telephone conversation; **avoir de la c.** to be a good conversationalist; **elle n'a aucune c.** she is a poor conversationalist, she has no conversation; *Tél* **c. 'mains libres'** hands-free conversation

conversationnel, -elle [kɔ̃vɛrsasjɔnɛl] **ADJ** *Ordinat* **mode c.** conversational *or* interactive mode

converser [kɔ̃vɛrse] **VI** to converse, to talk (**avec** with)

conversion [kɔ̃vɛrsjɔ̃] **NF 1** *Fin, Ordinat etc* *(changement)* conversion (**en** into); *Math* **c.**

des fractions conversion of fractions; **c. d'entreprise** change in the line of business; **c. d'un emprunt** conversion of loan notes *or* stock; *Ordinat* **c. de fichier** file conversion; **c. de monnaies** currency conversion **2** *Ski* kick turn; *Mil etc* wheel(ing) **3** *(au catholicisme, au socialisme etc)* conversion (**à** to)

converti, -ie [kɔ̃vɛrti] **ADJ** *(pécheur etc)* converted

N convert

convertibilité [kɔ̃vɛrtibilite] **NF** *Fin* convertibility

convertible [kɔ̃vɛrtibl] **ADJ** convertible (**en** into); **rente c.** convertible interest *(paid by the State on banks securing a national debt)*; **obligations convertibles** convertible bonds; **canapé c.** sofa bed; **fauteuil c.** convertible armchair

NM 1 *Aviat* convertiplane **2** *(canapé)* sofa bed

convertir [kɔ̃vɛrtir] **VT 1** *(changer)* to convert (**en** into); **c. une pièce en bureau** to convert a room into an office; **c. des valeurs en espèces** to convert securities into cash; *Com, Fin* **c. des rentes** to convert stock; **c. un emprunt** to convert loan notes *or* stock **2** *(à une religion, un point de vue etc)* to convert (**à** to) **3** *Ordinat* **c. en mode point par point** to rasterize

VPR se convertir 1 *(à une religion etc)* to convert, to become converted (**à** to) **2 se c. en** *(se transformer)* to change *or* turn into

convertissement [kɔ̃vɛrtismɑ̃] **NM** *Bourse, Fin (de valeurs en espèces)* conversion

convertisseur [kɔ̃vɛrtisœr] **NM 1** *Métal* converter; *Tech, Aut* **c. de couple** torque converter; **c. catalytique à oxydation** oxidization catalytic converter; **c. de couple hydrodynamique** hydraulic (hydro-kinetic) fluid converter; **c. hydraulique** hydraulic converter; **c. multi-étagé** multi-stage converter **2** *Élec, Électron* converter; *TV etc* **c. d'images** image converter; **c. de monnaie** currency converter; *TV etc* **c. numérique de graphiques** graphics digitizer; *Ordinat* **c. analogique numérique** digitizer

convexe [kɔ̃vɛks] **ADJ** convex

convexité [kɔ̃vɛksite] **NF** convexity

convict [kɔ̃vikt] **NM** *Jur* convict

conviction [kɔ̃viksjɔ̃] **NF 1** *(certitude)* conviction; **avoir la c. que ... to** be convinced that ...; **une c. personnelle** a personal conviction; **sans grande c.** without much conviction; **avec/sans c.** with/without conviction **2** *Jur* **pièce à c.** exhibit **3** *convictions (opinions)* convictions, beliefs

convier [kɔ̃vje] **VT** *(impf, pr sub* **n. conviions, v. conviiez)** **1** *(inviter)* to invite; **c. qn à un mariage** to invite sb to a wedding **2 c. qn à faire qch** to urge *or* strongly advise sb to do sth

convive [kɔ̃viv] **N** *(à une table)* guest

convivial, -iale, -iaux, -iales [kɔ̃vivjal, -jo] **ADJ** *(ambiance, soirée)* convivial; *Ordinat* user-friendly

convivialité [kɔ̃vivjalite] **NF** conviviality; *Ordinat* user-friendliness

convocation [kɔ̃vɔkasjɔ̃] **NF 1** *(d'une assemblée etc)* calling together, convening; **recevoir une c.** to receive notice to attend; **c. à l'examen** notification of an examination **2** *Jur* summons

convoi [kɔ̃vwa] **NM 1 c. (funèbre)** funeral procession *or* cortège **2** *Mil* **c. (de troupes)** convoy of troops; **c. administratif** supply column; **c. de prisonniers** convoy of prisoners **3** *(de véhicules)* convoy; **'c. exceptionnel'** 'dangerous/wide load'; **c. automobile** motorcade; *Rail* **c. de marchandises** goods *or* freight train; *Rail* **c. postal** mail train **4** *Naut* convoy

convoiement [kɔ̃vwamɑ̃] **NM** convoying, escorting

convoiter [kɔ̃vwate] **VT** *(poste, richesse)* to covet, to be after; *(rôle)* to be after; *(femme)* to lust after; **c. des yeux** to look lustfully at

convoitise [kɔ̃vwatiz] **NF** covetousness; **regarder qch avec c.** to cast covetous glances *or* look covetously at sth; **exciter les convoitises** to excite envy

convoler [kɔ̃vɔle] **VI** *Hum* **c. (en justes noces)** to marry; **c. en secondes noces** to remarry

convoluté [kɔ̃vɔlyte] **ADJ** *Bot* convolute(d), whorled

convoquer [kɔ̃vɔke] **VT 1** *(assemblée)* to call together, to convene; **c. les actionnaires** to call the shareholders to a meeting; **c. une assemblée générale** to call a general meeting **2** *Admin etc (candidat)* to call in (for an interview); *(témoin)* to summon; **le directeur m'a convoqué (dans son bureau)** the manager called me in (to his office); **c. qn à un examen** to notify sb of an examination

convoyage [kɔ̃vwajaʒ] **NM = convoiement**; *Naut* **faire un c. entre deux ports** to escort ships between two ports

convoyer [kɔ̃vwaje] **VT** (**je convoie, n. convoyons, ils convoient; je convoierai**) *(bateau, troupes etc)* to convoy, to escort; *(des fonds)* to transport by armed guard

convoyeur [kɔ̃vwajœr] **NM 1** *Mil, Naut (personne)* escort; *(navire)* convoy (ship), escort (ship) **2** *Tech, Ind* conveyor **3 c. de fonds** security guard, armed security escort

convulser [kɔ̃vylse] **VT** to convulse; **visage convulsé par la terreur** face convulsed by *or* with terror

VPR se convulser to convulse, to be convulsed; **sa figure se convulsa** his face became contorted

convulsif, -ive [kɔ̃vylsif, -iv] **ADJ** convulsive; **rire c.** convulsive *or* uncontrollable laughter

convulsion [kɔ̃vylsjɔ̃] **NF** convulsion; **être pris de convulsions** to go into convulsions; **se tordre dans des convulsions** to double up *or* writhe in convulsions; *Fig* **c. politique** political upheaval

convulsionner [kɔ̃vylsjɔne] **VT** *Méd* to convulse

convulsivement [kɔ̃vylsivmɑ̃] **ADV** convulsively

coobligé, -ée [kɔɔbliʒe] **N** *Jur* joint obligor, co-obligor

cooccupant, -ante [kɔɔkypɑ̃, -ɑ̃t] **N** co-occupier

cookie [kuki] **NM** *Ordinat* cookie

cool [kul] **ADJ 1** *Fam* cool; **il n'est pas très c., ton père** your father's a bit square *or* a bit of an old fogey **2** *Mus* jazz **c.** cool jazz

coolie [kuli] **NM** coolie

coopé [kɔpe] **NF** *Fam (abrév* **coopération)** *(aide aux PVD)* aid to developing countries; *(service militaire)* = voluntary work overseas, carried out as an alternative to national service

coopérant, -ante [kɔɔperɑ̃, -ɑ̃t] **ADJ** co(-)operative

N *(à l'étranger)* aid worker; *(pendant le service militaire)* = voluntary overseas worker

coopérateur, -trice [kɔɔperatœr, -tris] **N 1** *(collègue)* co-worker, collaborator **2** *(dans une coopérative)* member of a co(-)operative

ADJ agent c. co(-)operating agent

coopératif, -ive [kɔɔperatif, -iv] **ADJ** *(société, personne)* co(-)operative

NF coopérative *(association)* co(-)operative, co-op; *(magasin)* co(-)operative store, co-op; **coopérative de vente/production** sales/production co(-)operative; **coopéra-**

tive d'achat wholesale co(-)operative; **coopérative de crédit** credit union, co(-)operative credit society

coopération [kɔɔperasjɔ̃] NF **1** *(appui)* co(-)operation; **offrir sa c. à qn** to offer to co(-)operate with sb; **travailler en c. avec qn** to work in collaboration with sb **2** *Pol* ≃ Voluntary Service Overseas; **partir en c. en Afrique** to go off to do VSO in Africa **3** *Écon* co(-)operation; **société/mouvement de c.** co(-)operative society/movement

coopératisme [kɔɔperatism] NM *Écon* co(-)operation, co(-)operative system

coopérer [kɔɔpere] VI **(je coopère, n. coopérons; je coopérerai)** to co(-)operate **(à in)**

cooptation [kɔɔptasjɔ̃] NF co-option, co-opting, co-optation; **élu par c.** elected by co-option

coopter [kɔɔpte] VT to co-opt

coordinateur, -trice [kɔɔrdinatœr, -tris] ADJ, N = **coordonnateur**

coordination [kɔɔrdinasjɔ̃] NF *(du travail, d'un projet, des mouvements)* co(-)ordination; *Gram* **conjonction de c.** co(-)ordinating conjunction; *Gram* **avoir une fonction de c.** to act as a co(-)ordinating conjunction SEE GRAMMAR A73–4; B57–8

coordonnateur, -trice [kɔɔrdɔnatœr, -tris] ADJ co(-)ordinating N *(personne)* co(-)ordinator; *Aviat* air-traffic controller

coordonné, -ée [kɔɔrdɔne] ADJ *(mouvement, efforts etc)* co(-)ordinated; *(draps, serviettes etc)* matching; **écharpe et gants coordonnés** scarf and matching or co(-)ordinated gloves; *Gram* **proposition coordonnée** co(-)ordinate clause

NFPL **coordonnées 1** *Math, Géog, Astron* co(-)ordinates **2** *Fam* **donnez-moi vos coordonnées** give me your address and phone number; **je ne connais pas ses coordonnées en ce moment** I don't know where or how to reach him at the moment

coordonner [kɔɔrdɔne] VT to co(-)ordinate **(à, avec** with)

copain, copine [kɔpɛ̃, kɔpin] *Fam* N pal, mate, *Am* buddy; **c. de classe** classmate; **c. de régiment** army mate; **sa nouvelle copine d'école** her new pal at school; **ma (petite) copine** my girlfriend; **mon (petit) c.** my boyfriend; **salut les copains!** *(en arrivant)* hi, gang!; *(en partant)* see you, gang!; **faire profiter les petits copains** to help out one's pals ADJ pally; **ils sont très copains** they're great pals or mates or *Am* buddies; **ils sont très c.-c.** they're very pally or *Am* buddy-buddy

coparental [kɔparɑ̃tal] ADJ coparental

coparentalité [kɔparɑ̃talite] NF coparenthood

copartageant, -ante [kɔpartaʒɑ̃, -ɑ̃t] N *Jur* coparcener, coheir, *f* coheiress

coparticipant, -ante [kɔpartisipɑ̃, -ɑ̃t] N *Jur* copartner

coparticipation [kɔpartisipasjɔ̃] NF *Jur* co-partnership; **c. aux bénéfices** profit-sharing

copeau, -eaux [kɔpo] NM *(de bois, chocolat)* shaving; *(de métal)* cutting; **copeaux de tour** turnings

Copenhague [kɔpɛnag] NF Copenhagen

copiable [kɔpjabl] ADJ copiable

copiage [kɔpjaʒ] NM copying; *Scol* cribbing, copying

copie [kɔpi] NF **1** *(reproduction) (de document, lettre etc)* copy; *Journ, Typ* copy; **faire une c. de qch** to make a copy of sth; *Journ* **être en mal de c.** to be short of copy; *Admin, Jur* **pour c. conforme** certified accurate; **c. certifiée conforme** certified true copy; **c. au carbone** carbon copy; *Com* **c. authentique** certified copy; **c. de lettre** duplicate; **c. pa-**

pier paper copy; **c. stratégie (créative)** *(de publicité)* (creative) copy strategy; **c. de travail** working copy

2 *Scol (d'examen)* paper; **rendre c. blanche** to hand in a blank paper; **c. simple/double** single/double sheet of paper; *Fig* **revoir sa c.** to revise one's proposals

3 *(d'un tableau, d'une statue etc)* copy, reproduction; *(d'un roman, d'un style etc)* imitation; **ce n'est qu'une pâle c. de l'original** it's only a pale imitation of the original

4 *TV, Cin* copy, print; **c. de film** (film) print; **c. antenne** show copy, broadcast master, release print; **c. de montage** cutting copy, workprint; **c. exploitation** show copy; **c. positive** positive print; **c. standard** combined print

5 *Ordinat* **c. sur papier** hard copy, printout; **c. archivée** archive (copy); **c. de bloc** copy block; **c. de disquette** *(commande DOS)* diskcopy; **c. de sauvegarde** *ou* **de secours** backup (copy), security copy; **c. de sûreté** backup (copy)

copier [kɔpje] *(impf, pr sub n.* copiions, *v.* copiiez) VT **1** *(texte, musique etc)* to copy; *(sons)* to dub off; **c. qch au propre** *ou* **au net** to make a fair copy of sth, to copy sth out (neatly); *Ordinat* **c. un document sur le disque dur** to back up *or* copy a document onto hard disk; **c. qch sur disquette** to copy sth to disk **2** *(statue, tableau etc)* to copy, to reproduce; *(personne, style etc)* to imitate; *Scol* to copy, to crib; **elle me copie en tout** she copies everything I do, she copies me in everything VI *Scol* to copy, to crib; **il copie sur son voisin** he's copying *or* cribbing from *or* off the boy next to him

copier-coller NM INV *Ordinat* copy-and-paste

copieur, -ieuse [kɔpjœr, -jøz] ADJ copying, cribbing N *Scol* copier, cribber NM copying machine, (photo)copier NF **copieuse** copier

copieusement [kɔpjøzmɑ̃] ADV *(manger, boire)* copiously; **il s'est servi c.** he took a generous helping; **après un repas c. arrosé** after a meal washed down with a lot of wine; **je me suis fait c. insulter** I got well and truly insulted; **s'ennuyer c.** to be bored to tears

copieux, -ieuse [kɔpjø, -jøz] ADJ *(repas)* copious, hearty, square; *(portion, part, pourboire)* generous

copilote [kɔpilɔt] N *Aviat* copilot

copinage [kɔpinaʒ] NM *Fam* cronyism; **dans ce milieu, tout ne marche que par c.** around here, it's who you know that matters, what counts around here is who you're friendly with; **obtenir un poste par c.** to get a job through one's connections *or* through the people one knows

copine [kɔpin] NF *Fam voir* copain

copiner [kɔpine] VI *Fam* to be pals *or Am* buddies (**avec** with)

copinerie [kɔpinri] NF *Fam* = **copinage**

copiste [kɔpist] N **1** *(clerc etc)* copyist, transcriber; **faute de c.** clerical error **2** *(plagiaire)* copier, imitator

coporteur [kɔpɔrtœr] NM *Fin* joint holder

coposséder [kɔpɔsede] VT *(conj like* posséder*) Jur* to own jointly, to have joint ownership of

copossesseur [kɔpɔsesœr] NM *Jur* joint owner

copossession [kɔpɔsesjɔ̃] NF *Jur* joint ownership, co-ownership

copra(h) [kɔpra] NM copra; **huile de c.** coconut oil

copreneur, -euse [kɔprœnœr, -øz] N *Jur* colessee, co-tenant

coprésentateur, -trice [kɔprezɑ̃tatœr,

-tris] N *TV etc* co-presenter

coprésidence [kɔprezidɑ̃s] NF co-chairmanship, co-presidency

coprésident, -ente [kɔprezidɑ̃, -ɑ̃t] N co-chairperson, co-president

coprocesseur [kɔprɔsesœr] NM *Ordinat* co-processor; **c. arithmétique** maths co-processor

coproducteur, -trice [kɔprɔdyktœr, -tris] N *TV etc* co-producer

coproduction [kɔprɔdyksjɔ̃] NF coproduction, joint production; **ce film est une c. des télévisions française et italienne** this film has been coproduced by French and Italian television

coproduire [kɔprɔdɥir] VT to coproduce

coprophage [kɔprɔfaʒ] ADJ coprophagous

coprophagie [kɔprɔfaʒi] NF coprophagy

copropriétaire [kɔprɔprijetɛr] N *Jur* co-owner, joint owner

copropriété [kɔprɔprijete] NF *Jur* co-ownership, joint ownership; *(propriétaires)* co-owners, joint owners; **acheter/posséder une maison en c.** to buy/own a house jointly; **c. différée** = timeshare taken on a lease basis, converting to ownership after a given period of time

copte [kɔpt] ADJ Coptic NM *Ling* Coptic N **C.** Copt

copulation [kɔpylasjɔ̃] NF copulation

copuler [kɔpyle] VI *(des animaux, humains)* to copulate

copyright [kɔpirajt] NM copyright

coq [kɔk] NM **1** *(oiseau)* cock, *Am* rooster; **jeune c.** cockerel; **le c. gaulois** the French cockerel; **au chant du c.** at cockcrow; **combat(s) de coqs** cockfighting; **un combat de coqs** a cockfight; **c. de combat** fighting cock; *Fam* **rouge comme un c.** as red as a beetroot; *Fam* **fier** *ou* **orgueilleux comme un c.** as proud as a peacock; *Fig* **mollets de c.** wiry *or* spindly legs; *Fig* **être comme un c. en pâte** to be in clover; *Fig* **le c. du village** the local Casanova; **passer** *ou* **sauter du c. à l'âne** to jump from one subject to another; *Boxe* **poids c.** bantamweight **2** *(girouette)* weathercock

▸▸ *Orn* **c. de bruyère** capercaillie, wood grouse; **c. faisan** cock pheasant; *Orn* **c. de roche** cock-of-the-rock; *Culin* **c. au vin** coq au vin

coq² NM *Naut* **(maître-)c.** (ship's) cook

coq-à-l'âne NM INV sudden change of subject

coquard, coquart [kɔkar] NM *Fam* black eye, shiner

coque [kɔk] NF **1** *(d'une noix, d'un fruit)* shell, husk; *(mollusque)* cockle; *Culin* **œuf à la c.** (soft-)boiled egg; *Fig* **c. de noix** flimsy craft **2** *(d'un navire)* hull, bottom; *(d'un avion)* fuselage; *(d'une voiture)* body, shell, bodyshell; *Naut* **double c.** double bottom **3** **chaussures à c.** steel-capped shoes **4** *(de téléphone portable)* fascia

coquelet [kɔklɛ] NM *Culin* cockerel

coquelicot [kɔkliko] NM *Bot* (red) poppy ADJ INV poppy-red

coqueluche [kɔklyʃ] NF *Méd* whooping-cough; **avoir la c.** to have whooping-cough; *Fig* **être la c. des adolescents** to be a teenage idol; *Fig* **être la c. du bureau** to be the darling of the office; *Fig* **il est devenu la c. de ces dames** he has become a heart-throb

coquelucheux, -euse [kɔklyʃø, -øz] ADJ *Méd* **une toux coquelucheuse** a whooping cough

coquerico [kɔk(ə)riko] INT, NM = **cocorico**

coquet, -ette [kɔkɛ, -ɛt] ADJ **1** *(personne)*

particular about one's appearance; *Vieilli (sourire)* coquettish, flirtatious **2** *(ville, jardin, intérieur etc)* charming; *(vêtements)* smart, stylish; *Fam* **coquette somme** tidy sum, nice little sum

NF *Vieilli* **coquette** coquette, flirt

coquetel [kɔktɛl] **NM** *Can* cocktail

coquetier [kɔktje] **NM** egg-cup; *Fam* **gagner le c.** to hit the jackpot; *Iron* **ça y est, j'ai gagné le c.!** that's it, I've really done it now!

coquettement [kɔkɛtmɑ̃] **ADV** *(habillé)* smartly, stylishly; *(meublé)* stylishly, elegantly; *(sourire)* flirtatiously, coquettishly; *Fam (dédommager qn)* handsomely

coquetterie [kɔkɛtri] **NF 1** *(vestimentaire)* consciousness of one's appearance; *Vieilli (désir de plaire)* coquetry, flirtatiousness; **faire des coquetteries** to put on an affected manner; **avec c.** *(habiller, meubler)* stylishly, elegantly **2** *Fam* **avoir une c. dans l'œil** to have a cast in one's eye

coquillage [kɔkijaʒ] **NM 1** *(mollusque)* shellfish; **manger des coquillages** to eat shellfish **2** *(coque vide)* shell

coquillard [kɔkijar] **NM 1** *Hist* ruffian, rogue **2** *Arg* **je m'en tamponne le c.** I don't give a damn or a monkey's

coquille [kɔkij] **NF 1** *(d'escargot, d'huître, d'œuf, de noix etc)* shell; *Fig* **sortir de sa c.** to come out of one's shell; *Fig* **rentrer dans sa c.** to go back or withdraw into one's shell **2** *(plat)* (scallop-shaped) dish **3** *(d'épée)* hand guard or shell **4** *Constr (d'un escalier en colimaçon)* soffit, underpart **5** *Métal* chill, chill mould; *Sport* box, shield; *Méd* **c. (plâtrée)** spinal plaster **6** *Typ* misprint, typo, literal

▸▸ **c. de beurre** (shell-shaped) pat of butter; **c. de noix** walnut shell; *(bateau)* cockleshell; **c. d'œuf** eggshell; **peinture c. d'œuf** eggshell paint; **c. Saint-Jacques** scallop; *(coquillage)* scallop shell

coquillettes [kɔkijɛt] **NFPL** *Culin* pasta shells

coquin, -ine [kɔkɛ̃, -in] **N 1** *(garnement)* rascal, scamp, rogue; **c. de sort!** *(en Provence)* hang it!, damn it!; **petit c.!/petite coquine!** you little rascal! **2** *(canaille)* rogue, scoundrel

ADJ *(sourire)* mischievous; *(sous-vêtement)* naughty; **un air c.** a flirtatious or coquettish look; **des histoires coquines** risqué stories

NF *Arch* **coquine** loose woman, hussy

coquinement [kɔkinmɑ̃] **ADV** *(d'une manière espiègle)* mischievously; *(coquettement)* coquettishly, flirtatiously; **avec un petit bibi c. posé sur l'oreille** with a little hat worn coquettishly over one ear

coquinerie [kɔkinri] **NF** mischievousness, roguishness; *(tour)* mischievous or roguish trick

cor [kɔr] **NM 1** *Mus* horn; **c. (de chasse)** (hunting) horn; **sonner du c.** to sound or blow the horn; **les cors** *(dans un orchestre)* the horns; *Fig* **réclamer qch à c. et à cri** to clamour or *Am* clamor for sth **2** *(sur l'orteil, le pied)* corn; **avoir un c. au pied** to have a corn on one's foot **3** *(d'un andouiller)* tine; **un cerf (de) dix cors** a ten-pointer

▸▸ **c. anglais** cor anglais, English horn; **c. d'harmonie** French horn; **c. à piston** valve horn

corail[1]**, -aux** [kɔraj, -o] **NM** *Zool* coral; **récif de c.** coral reef; *Litt* **lèvres de c.** coral lips

ADJ INV *(couleur)* coral; **des lèvres rouge c.** coral-red lips

corail[2] **NM** *Rail* express (train)

ADJ INV *Rail* **train c.** express (train)

corailleur, -euse [kɔrajœr, -øz] **N** *(pêcheur)* coral gatherer; *(artisan)* coral worker

corallien, -ienne [kɔraljɛ̃, -jɛn] **ADJ** coral-line; **récif c.** coral reef

Coran (le) [lɔkɔrɑ̃] **NM** the Koran

coranique [kɔranik] **ADJ** Koranic

corbeau, -eaux [kɔrbo] **NM 1** *(oiseau)* crow; **grand c.** raven; **c. freux** rook; **noir comme un c.** raven- or crow-black **2** *(auteur de lettres anonymes)* writer of poison-pen letters **3** *Fig Péj (prêtre)* priest; *Vieilli (homme avide)* shark **4** *Archit* corbel, bracket

corbeille [kɔrbɛj] **NF 1** *(panier)* basket **2** *(massif)* (round or oval) flower-bed **3** *Archit (d'un chapiteau corinthien)* bell, corbeil **4** *Bourse* ring, pit **5** *Théâtre* dress circle **6** *Ordinat* wastebasket, *Am* trash; *(dans Windows)* recycle bin; **c. d'arrivée** *(pour courrier électronique)* inbox; **c. de départ** *(pour courrier électronique)* outbox

▸▸ *Bot* **c. d'argent** sweet alyssum; **c. à courrier** desk tray; **c. de fruits** fruit basket; **c. de mariage** wedding presents; **c. des obligations** bond-trading ring; *Bot* **c. d'or** rock alyssum; **c. à ouvrage** work basket; **c. à pain** bread basket; **c. à papier** wastepaper basket

corbillard [kɔrbijar] **NM** hearse

cordage [kɔrdaʒ] **NM 1** *(action) (d'une raquette)* stringing **2** *(corde)* rope; **c. en chanvre** hemp rope; *Naut* **cordages** rigging; **le c.** *(d'une raquette)* the strings

corde [kɔrd] **NF 1** *(lien)* rope; **danseur de c.** tightrope walker; **semelle/échelle de c.** rope sole/ladder; **sauter à la c.** to skip, *Am* to jump rope; *Gym* **grimper à la c.** to climb the rope; *Fig* **tirer sur la c.** to go too far, to push one's luck; *Fig Fam* **il pleut des cordes** it's raining cats and dogs, *Br* it's bucketing down **2** *(d'instrument)* string; **c. (de boyau)** catgut; **c. de violon** violin string; **instrument à cordes** stringed instrument; **les cordes** *(dans un orchestre)* the strings; **orchestre à cordes** string orchestra; **double c.** double stopping; *Fig* **tu as touché ou fait vibrer la c. sensible** you've touched on a subject close to his/her heart; *Fig* **avoir plus d'une c. à son arc** to have more than one string to one's bow **3** *(de pendu)* (hangman's) rope; *Fig Fam* **se mettre la c. au cou** to put one's head in the noose, to put a rope round one's own neck; *Arg (se marier)* to get spliced or hitched; **dire cela, c'était comme parler de c. dans la maison d'un pendu** that was a very tactless thing to say, you/he/*etc* really put your/his/*etc* foot in it; *Fig* **il ne mérite pas la c. pour le pendre** hanging's too good for him **4** *Courses de chevaux* **la c.** the rails; **tenir la c.** *(de coureur)* to be on the inside; *Courses de chevaux* to hug the rails, to be on the inside; *Fig Vieilli* to have the advantage; *Aut* **prendre un virage à la c.** to hug the bend; *Boxe* **les cordes** the ropes; *Boxe* **être dans les cordes** to be on the ropes; **être renvoyé dans les cordes** to be thrown onto the ropes **5** *Tex* thread; **drap/manteau usé jusqu'à la c. ou qui laisse voir la c.** threadbare cloth/coat; *Fig* **plaisanterie/histoire usée jusqu'à la c.** well-worn joke/story, old joke/story **6** *Math (d'un arc)* chord **7** *Fig* **ce n'est pas dans mes cordes** it's not in my line, it's not up my street, it's not my province

▸▸ **c. cervicale** cervical nerve; **c. dorsale** spinal cord; **c. à linge** clothes or washing line; *Gym* **c. lisse** climbing rope; **c. à nœuds** knotted climbing rope; **c. raide** tightrope; *Fig* **être sur la c. raide** to be walking a tightrope; **c. à sauter** skipping rope, *Am* jump-rope; *Anat* **cordes vocales** vocal cords

cordé [kɔrde] **ADJ** *Bot etc* cordate, heart-shaped

cordeau, -eaux [kɔrdo] **NM 1** *(petite corde)* string, line; **un c. de jardinier** garden string or line; *Fig* **tiré au c.** perfectly straight, as straight as a die; *Fig* **lettres tracées au c.** per-

fectly regular letters **2** *Min, Mil (mèche)* fuse, match; **c. Bickford** Bickford or safety fuse **3** *Pêche* paternoster (line)

cordée [kɔrde] **NF 1** *Com* **c. de bois** cord of wood **2** *(d'alpinistes)* rope, roped party; **premier de c.** leader, first on the rope **3** *Pêche* hook length

cordelette [kɔrdəlɛt] **NF** cord, string

cordelier, -ière [kɔrdəlje, -jɛr] **N 1** *Rel (religieux)* Franciscan friar, Cordelier; *(religieuse)* Franciscan nun **2** *Hist* **le Club des Cordeliers** = a left-wing club of the Revolutionary period

NF **cordelière** *(de robe de chambre etc)* cord; *Archit* cable moulding

corder [kɔrde] **VT 1** *(chanvre etc)* to twist into rope **2** *(malle etc)* to rope up **3** *(raquette)* to string **4** *Com (mesurer)* **c. du bois** to cord wood

cordial, -iale, -iaux, -iales [kɔrdjal, -jo] **ADJ 1** *(accueil, atmosphère)* cordial, hearty, warm; *(paroles)* warm **2** *(haine, ennui, mépris etc)* deep(-seated) **3** *Pharm (médicament)* stimulating

NM *Pharm* tonic

cordialement [kɔrdjalmɑ̃] **ADV** cordially, heartily, warmly; **c. vôtre** *(dans une lettre)* yours sincerely; **bien c.** best wishes; *Iron* **elle le déteste c.** she heartily detests him

cordialité [kɔrdjalite] **NF** cordiality, heartiness, warmth; **parler avec c.** to speak warmly

cordier [kɔrdje] **NM 1** *Ind* ropemaker **2** *Mus (d'un violon etc)* tailpiece

cordillère [kɔrdijɛr] **NF** *Géog* cordillera

cordon [kɔrdɔ̃] **NM 1** *(lien)* cord, string; *(d'un câble, d'une corde)* strand, twist; *(d'un ordre)* ribbon; *Électron, Élec* lead; **corde à trois cordons** three-stranded rope; *Arch* **demander le c.** to ask the concierge to open the door; *Fig* **tenir les cordons de la bourse** to hold the purse-strings; *Fig Fam* **il faut couper le c.** you must get away from your mother's apron strings, you must branch out on your own **2** *(d'arbres etc)* row, line; *(de police, de troupes)* cordon; *Archit (dans un mur)* string course, cordon; *(d'une pièce de monnaie)* milled edge

▸▸ *Géog* **c. littoral** offshore bar; *Anat* **c. médullaire** spinal cord; *Anat* **c. ombilical** umbilical cord; *Élec* **c. prolongateur** extension cable or lead; **c. sanitaire** cordon sanitaire; **c. de soie** silk cord; **c. de sonnette** bellpull

cordon-bleu, *pl* **cordons-bleus** **NM** *Fam* cordon bleu (cook)

cordonnerie [kɔrdɔnri] **NF 1** *(métier)* shoe-repairing, shoemending; *(fabrication)* shoe-making **2** *(boutique)* shoe repairer's (shop), shoemender's (shop), cobbler's (shop)

cordonnet [kɔrdɔnɛ] **NM** braid, cord, twist

cordonnier, -ière [kɔrdɔnje, -jɛr] **N 1** *(réparateur)* shoe repairer, shoe-mender, cobbler **2** *(fabricant)* shoemaker; *Prov* **les cordonniers sont les plus mal chaussés** the shoemaker's wife is always the worst shod

Cordoue [kɔrdu] **NF** Cordoba

co-rédiger [korediʒe] **VT** to co-author

Corée [kɔre] **NF** Korea; **C. du Nord/du Sud** North/South Korea

coréen, -enne [kɔreɛ̃, -ɛn] **ADJ** Korean

N C. Korean

coreligionnaire [kɔrəliʒjɔnɛr] **N** co-religionist

Corfou [kɔrfu] **NF** Corfu

coriace [kɔrjas] **ADJ 1** *(viande)* tough, leathery **2** *(personne, adversaire)* tough; **être c. en affaires** to be hard-headed in business

N *Fam* hard-headed or tough customer

coriandre [kɔrjɑ̃dr] **NF** *Bot, Culin* coriander

coricide [kɔrisid] NM *Pharm* corn remover

corindon [kɔrɛ̃dɔ̃] NM *Minér* corundum

Corinthe [kɔrɛ̃t] NF Corinth; *Culin* **raisins de C.** currants

corinthien, -ienne [kɔrɛ̃tjɛ̃, -jɛn] ADJ Corinthian
▸ N **C.** Corinthian

cormoran [kɔrmɔrɑ̃] NM *(oiseau)* cormorant

cornac [kɔrnak] NM elephant keeper, mahout

cornaline [kɔrnalin] NF cornelian

cornaquer [kɔrnake] VT *Fam* to show around

cornard [kɔrnar] NM *Arg* cuckold

corne [kɔrn] NF **1** *(d'animal, d'escargot)* horn; *(d'un insecte)* horn, antenna; **les cornes du diable** the devil's horns; **bêtes à cornes** horned animals; **vipère à cornes** horned viper; **donner un coup de c. à qn** *(d'un taureau)* to gore sb; *(d'un bélier, d'une chèvre)* to butt sb; *Fig Fam* **montrer** *ou* **faire les cornes à qn** to jeer at sb, to mock sb; *Fam* **ouh les cornes!** shame on you/him/etc!; *Fig Fam* **avoir** *ou* **porter des cornes** to be a cuckold; *Fig Fam* **faire (porter) des cornes à qn** to cuckold sb; *Fig* **prendre le taureau par les cornes** to take the bull by the horns **2** *(matériau)* horn; **peigne de c.** horn comb **3** *(cor)* horn **4** *Naut (d'une voile aurique)* gaff **5** *(d'un objet pointu)* tip; *(de la lune)* horn, cusp; *(d'une page)* dog-ear; *(d'un croissant)* end, tip; **chapeau à cornes** cocked hat; **faire une c. à une page** to turn down the corner of a page **6** *(sur les pieds etc)* hard skin; **avoir de la c. au pied** to have hard skin or calluses on one's foot
▸▸ **c. d'abondance** horn of plenty, cornucopia; **la c. de l'Afrique** the Horn of Africa; *Naut* **c. de brume** foghorn; **c. à chaussure** shoehorn; *Culin* **c. de gazelle** = horn-shaped cake

corné [kɔrne] ADJ **1** *(pied, main etc)* horny **2** **page cornée** dog-eared page

corned-beef [kɔrnbif] NM corned beef

cornée [kɔrne] NF *Anat* cornea

cornéen, -enne [kɔrneɛ̃, -ɛn] ADJ *Anat* corneal

corneille [kɔrnɛj] NF crow; **c. noire** carrion crow; **c. mantelée** *ou* **grise** *ou* **cendrée** hooded crow

cornélien, -ienne [kɔrneljɛ̃, -jɛn] ADJ *Littér (tragédie etc)* Cornelian; **situation cornélienne** = situation where there is a conflict between love and duty

cornemuse [kɔrnəmyz] NF *Mus* bagpipes; **joueur de c.** (bag)piper; **c. écossaise/bretonne** Scottish/Breton bagpipes

cornemuseur [kɔrnəmyzœr] NM (bag)piper

corner¹ [kɔrne] VT **1** *(clamer)* to blare out; **c. les ordres à qn** to bawl out *or* yell out orders to sb; **c. qch aux oreilles de qn** to shout sth into sb's ear **2** *(page)* to turn down the corner of
▸ VI **1** *(souffler dans une corne)* to sound a horn; *Aut Vieilli* to sound one's horn, to hoot, to honk **2** *Fam* **la télé nous cornait aux** *ou* **dans les oreilles** the telly was blaring; **les radios leur cornaient dans les oreilles que …** radios were blaring out that … **3** *(des oreilles)* to ring; **les oreilles lui cornent** his ears are ringing

corner² [kɔrnɛr] NM *Ftbl* corner; **tirer un c.** to take a corner

cornet [kɔrnɛ] NM **1** *(de papier)* cone; *(de bonbons, de dragées, de frites)* cornet; **c. de papier** paper cone; **il cria, les deux mains en c. pour mieux se faire entendre** he shouted, cupping his hands to his mouth to make himself heard better; *très Fam* **se mettre quelque chose dans le c.** *(manger)* to get something inside one; **qu'est-ce qu'on s'est mis dans le c.!** we really stuffed ourselves *or* our faces! **2** *Mus (instrument)* cornet; *(d'un orgue)* cornet stop **3** *Arch (petit cor)* small horn **4** *Anat* scroll *or* turbinate bone **5** *Suisse (sac en papier)* paper bag; *(sac en plastique)* plastic bag
▸▸ **c. acoustique** ear trumpet; **c. à dés** dice cup; **c. de glace** ice cream cone *or Br* cornet; *Mus* **c. à pistons** cornet

cornette [kɔrnɛt] NF **1** *(salade)* endive **2** *(coiffe religieuse)* cornet **3** *Mil Arch (de la cavalerie)* pennant, standard
▸ NM *Mil Arch (officier)* cornet, ensign
▸ NFPL *Suisse* **cornettes** *(sorte de pâtes alimentaires)* (elbow) macaroni

cornettiste [kɔrnetist] N *Mus* cornetist, cornet player

corn flakes [kɔrnflɛks] NMPL cornflakes

corniaud [kɔrnjo] NM **1** *(chien)* mongrel **2** *Fam (personne)* idiot, twit

corniche [kɔrniʃ] NF **1** *Archit* cornice **2** *(de rochers)* ledge; *(de glace, de neige)* cornice; **(route en) c.** corniche (road)

cornichon [kɔrniʃɔ̃] NM **1** gherkin **2** *Fam (personne)* idiot, nitwit

cornier, -ière [kɔrnje, -jɛr] ADJ (at the) corner, angle; *Constr* **poteau c.** corner *or* angle post
▸ NF **cornière 1** *Constr (sous les combles)* valley **2** *(pièce en équerre)* angle (iron *or* bar)

cornique [kɔrnik] ADJ Cornish
▸ NM *Ling* Cornish

corniste [kɔrnist] N *Mus* horn player

cornouaillais, -aise [kɔrnwaje, -ɛz] ADJ of *or* from Cornouaille
▸ NM *Ling* Cornouaillais (dialect)
▸ N **C.** *(natif)* native of Cornouaille; *(habitant)* inhabitant of Cornouaille

Cornouaille [kɔrnwaj] NF Cornouaille *(in Britanny)*

Cornouailles [kɔrnwaj] NF Cornwall

cornouille [kɔrnuj] NF *Bot* dogberry, cornel berry

cornouiller [kɔrnuje] NM **1** *Bot* corneltree **2** *(bois)* dogwood

cornu [kɔrny] ADJ *(animal, diable)* horned

cornue [kɔrny] NF **1** *Chimie* retort; **charbon de c.** retort carbon **2** *Métal* steel converter

corollaire [kɔrɔlɛr] NM *(suite)* consequence, corollary; *Math* corollary

corolle [kɔrɔl] NF *Bot* corolla

coron [kɔrɔ̃] NM *(maison)* miner's cottage; *(quartier)* mining village

coronaire [kɔrɔnɛr] ADJ *Anat* coronary

coronarien, -ienne [kɔrɔnarjɛ̃, -jɛn] ADJ *Méd* coronary

corporatif, -ive [kɔrpɔratif, -iv] ADJ corporate, corporative

corporation [kɔrpɔrasjɔ̃] NF *(ordre)* corporate body; *Hist* (trade) guild; **la c. des pharmaciens** the guild of pharmacists, the pharmacists' guild; **c. de droit public** public corporation *or* body

corporatisme [kɔrpɔratism] NM corporatism

corporatiste [kɔrpɔratist] ADJ corporatist

corporel, -elle [kɔrpɔrɛl] ADJ *(être, nature)* corporeal; *(punition)* corporal; *(besoins, exercice)* bodily; *(hygiène)* personal; **expression corporelle** self-expression through movement; **odeur corporelle** body odour, *Fam* BO; *Psy* **schéma c.** body image

corporellement [kɔrpɔrɛlmɑ̃] ADV corporeally, corporally, bodily

CORPS [kɔr] NM **1** *Anat* body; **un c. robuste/lourd** a strong *or* robust/heavy frame *or* body; **soigner son c.** to look after one's body, to take care of oneself; **elle a conservé un c. jeune** she still has a youthful body, she's well-preserved; **entrer dans l'eau à mi-c.** to go into the water up to one's waist; **un petit c. et de grandes jambes** a short body and long legs; **pleurer toutes les larmes de son c.** to cry one's heart out; **frémir/trembler de tout son c.** to quiver/tremble all over; **passer sur le c. de qn** *ou* **à qn** to run over sb; *Fig* to trample sb underfoot; *Fig* **il te passerait sur le c. pour obtenir ce qu'il veut** he'd sell his grandmother to get what he wants; *Fig* **il faudra d'abord qu'il me passe sur le c.!** he'll have to do it over my dead body!; *Fig* **je me demande ce qu'il a dans le c.** I wonder what makes him tick; **il n'a rien dans le c.** *(il n'a rien mangé)* he hasn't eaten anything; *Fig* he has no strength *or* energy; **ça va te tenir au c.** *(tu n'auras plus faim)* that'll fill you up, that'll stick to your ribs; **c'est une nourriture qui tient au c.** it's filling food; *Fam Vieilli* **c'est un drôle de c.** he's a strange character *or Br* bod; *Fig* **faire qch à son c. défendant** to do something reluctantly; *Fig* **se jeter à c. perdu dans un projet/son travail** to throw oneself heart and soul into a project/one's work; **se donner c. et âme à qn/à un travail** to give *or* devote oneself body and soul to sb/to a task; *Jur* **séparation de c.** legal *or* judicial separation; *Jur* **ils ont fait une séparation de c.** they are legally separated; **lutter c. à c.** to fight hand to hand; *Fig* **affronter la réalité c. à c.** to get to grips with reality **2** *(cadavre)* body, corpse; **deux c. ont été retrouvés** two bodies have been recovered; **la levée du c. aura lieu à onze heures** the coffin will leave the house at eleven o'clock **3** *Chimie, Phys* body; **c. simple** simple body; **c. composé** compound (body) **4** *(consistance) (de vin)* body; **avoir du c.** to have body; **vin qui a du c.** full-bodied wine, wine that has body; *Fig* **son projet manque de c.** his plan lacks substance; *Fig* **donner du c. à qch** to give substance to sth; *Fig* **prendre c.** *(d'un projet, d'une idée)* to take shape **5** *(partie principale)* main part; *(d'un texte, d'un article etc)* body; *(d'une robe)* body, bodice; *(d'un cylindre, d'une pompe etc)* barrel; *Typ (de lettre)* body; **faire c. avec qch** to be an integral part of sth; *Naut* **perdu c. et biens** lost with all hands; *Typ* **force de c.** size of type body **6** *(d'ancrage)* dolphin, moorings; **(bouée de) c. mort** (anchor) buoy **7** *(groupe)* **le c. médical/enseignant** the medical/teaching profession; **les grands c. de l'État** = the highest sections of the French administration *(Conseil d'État, Cour des comptes etc)*; **avoir l'esprit de c.** to have esprit de corps **8** *(écrits)* corpus; **c. de lois** body of law(s)
▸▸ *Mil* **c. d'armée** army corps; **c. de ballet** corps de ballet; *Constr* **c. de bâtiment** main (part of a/the) building; *Astron* **c. céleste** celestial *or* heavenly body; *Jur* **c. du délit** corpus delicti; **le c. diplomatique** the diplomatic corps; *Méd* **c. électoral** electorate; *Méd, Chimie* **c. étranger** foreign body; **c. de garde** guardroom; **plaisanterie de c. de garde** barrackroom joke; *Physiol* **c. jaune** yellow body; *Constr* **c. de logis** main (part of a/the) building; **c. de la magistrature** magistrature; **c. de métier** trade; *Hist* corporation, g(u)ild; *Nucl* **c. noir** black body

corps-à-corps NM INV hand-to-hand fight, tussle; *Boxe* clinch

corpulence [kɔrpylɑ̃s] NF stoutness, corpulence; **être d'une forte c.** to be stoutly built *or* of stout build; **un homme d'une faible c.** a slightly built man; **ils n'ont pas la même c.** they are not of the same build

corpulent [kɔrpylɑ̃] **ADJ** stout, corpulent

corpus [kɔrpys] **NM** Jur, Ling corpus

corpusculaire [kɔrpyskylɛr] **ADJ** corpuscular

corpuscule [kɔrpyskyl] **NM** corpuscle

corral, -als [kɔral] **NM** corral, enclosure

correct [kɔrɛkt] **ADJ 1** (sans fautes) (langage, emploi etc) correct; (copie, plan etc) accurate; **il serait plus c. d'employer le subjonctif** it would be more correct to use the subjunctive; **Can Fam il a dit oui? – c.!** did he agree? – correct! or right! **2** (courtois) (personne) correct, proper; **cela n'est pas c. de sa part** that's not right of him; **elle a été correcte avec moi** she behaved correctly towards me; **être c. en affaires** to behave correctly or honestly in one's business dealings **3** Fam (acceptable) (repas, traduction etc) acceptable, decent, reasonable; **son travail est c., sans plus** his work is all right, but nothing special

correctement [kɔrɛktəmɑ̃] **ADV 1** (parler, employer) correctly; **vous n'avez pas répondu c. à la question posée** you didn't answer the question correctly; (sans faire d'erreur) you didn't answer the question accurately **2** (agir, être habillé) correctly, properly; **veux-tu bien répondre c. quand on te parle!** will you talk properly when you're spoken to! **3** (de façon acceptable) reasonably; **elle gagne c. sa vie** she makes a decent or reasonable living

correcteur, -trice [kɔrɛktœr, -tris] **N** (personne) corrector; Scol (de copies d'examen) examiner, marker; Typ proofreader; Journ copy reader; Journ **c. de mise en page** stone sub(-editor)

NM Ordinat checker; Tech corrector; **c. liquide** correcting fluid; Ordinat **c. grammatical** grammar checker; Ordinat **c. d'orthographe** ou **orthographique** spellchecker; Ordinat **c. de style** stylechecker; **c. de tonalité** tone control; TV etc **c. colorimétrique** colour corrector

ADJ (verres etc) correcting, corrective

correctif, -ive [kɔrɛktif, -iv] **ADJ** corrective; Méd **gymnastique corrective** remedial exercises

NM 1 (mise au point) qualifying statement; **apporter des correctifs à une déclaration** to qualify a statement; Com **c. d'ajustement monétaire** currency adjustment factor **2** Méd corrective

correction [kɔrɛksjɔ̃] **NF 1** (d'une faute etc) correction, correcting; Scol (d'un exercice) correcting, marking; Typ (d'épreuves) proofreading, correction, proofing; **faire des corrections dans un texte, apporter des corrections à un texte** to make corrections to a text; **les corrections sont en rouge** the corrections are in red; **maison de c.** reformatory; **je crois, sauf c., qu'il vient demain** unless I'm mistaken, he's coming tomorrow; Ordinat **c. d'orthographe** spellcheck; Aviat, Naut etc **c. de compas** compass adjustment; Aut **c. d'avance** (à l'allumage) ignition advance adjustment

2 (pour punir) beating, thrashing; **tu vas recevoir une bonne c.!** you'll get a good hiding!

3 (d'une robe, d'un discours, d'un style etc) correctness; (d'un comportement) correctness, propriety; **il a été d'une parfaite c. avec moi** he behaved very correctly towards me; **c'est la plus élémentaire des corrections** it's basic good manners; **j'apprécie la c. en affaires** I appreciate honesty in business

correctionnel, -elle [kɔrɛksjɔnɛl] **ADJ** Jur **peine correctionnelle** = penalty of more than five days' (but less than five years') im-

prisonment; **tribunal de police correctionnelle** court of summary jurisdiction

NF Fam **correctionnelle** criminal court; **passer en correctionnelle** to go before the criminal court

corrélatif, -ive [kɔrelatif, -iv] **ADJ, NM** correlative

corrélation [kɔrelasjɔ̃] **NF** correlation; **être en c. étroite** to be closely connected or related

corrélativement [kɔrelativmɑ̃] **ADV** correlatively

correspondance [kɔrɛspɔ̃dɑ̃s] **NF 1** (échange de lettres) correspondence; (lettres) letters, correspondence; **être en** ou **entretenir une c. avec qn** to correspond with sb, to be in correspondence with sb; **enseignement par c.** correspondence courses; **prendre des cours d'anglais par c.** to take a correspondence course in English; **c. commerciale** commercial or business correspondence; **publier la c. d'un auteur** to publish an author's correspondence or (collected) letters

2 (entre les trains) connection; Aviat connecting flight; Can (ticket) transfer; **assurer la c. avec ...** (d'un train, d'un bateau etc) to connect with ...; **j'attends la c.** I'm waiting for my connection

3 (de goûts, entre deux choses etc) correspondence; (d'idées, de principes etc) conformity

correspondant, -ante [kɔrɛspɔ̃dɑ̃, -ɑ̃t] **ADJ 1** (page, illustration), Géom (angle) corresponding (à to) **2 membre c.** (d'un institut etc) corresponding member

N 1 Journ correspondent; **c. de guerre** war correspondent or reporter; **c. permanent** permanent or resident correspondent; **c. sur place** local correspondent; **c. à l'étranger** foreign correspondent

2 (au téléphone) caller; (ami à qui l'on écrit) pen friend; Tél **le numéro de votre c. a changé** the number you have dialled has been changed; **votre c. est en ligne** your party is on the line

3 (agent de voyages) **c. d'agréments** = travel agent (for rail and sea) who has not yet obtained qualifications; **c. de licence** travel agent (for airlines) who has not yet obtained qualifications; **c. local** (pour les voyagistes) resort representative

correspondre [kɔrɛspɔ̃dr] **VI 1 c. à qch** to correspond to sth; **ce qu'il dit ne correspond pas à ses déclarations antérieures** what he is saying doesn't tally with or square with his previous statements; **cela ne correspond pas à votre promesse** that wasn't what you promised; **la théorie ne correspond pas aux faits** the theory does not square with the facts; **son attitude correspond à ce qu'on m'en avait dit** his attitude fits in with or corresponds to what I was told; **j'ai les vis, mais pas les écrous qui correspondent** I have the screws, but I don't have the nuts that go with them or the corresponding nuts

2 (communiquer) (de chambres etc) to communicate; **ces deux pièces correspondent** these two rooms communicate with one another

3 (par lettres) **c. avec qn** to correspond with or write to sb; **ils ont cessé de c.** they have stopped writing or are no longer writing (to each other)

VPR se correspondre (être en relation) to correspond; **leurs goûts se correspondent** they have similar or the same tastes; **ils se correspondent parfaitement** they are perfectly matched or suited

corrida [kɔrida] **NF 1** (de taureaux) bullfight, corrida; **c. pédestre** road race **2** Fam (à l'aéroport, dans les magasins etc) hassle, Br

carry-on; (dispute) ding-dong argument; **quelle c.!** all hell broke loose!; **faire la c. dans sa chambre** to kick up a shindig or racket in one's bedroom

corridor [kɔridɔr] **NM** corridor, passage

corrigé [kɔriʒe] **ADJ** corrected; (press) subbed; **données corrigées des variations saisonnières** seasonally adjusted figures; **en données corrigées des variations saisonnières** seasonally adjusted, adjusted for seasonal variations

NM Scol (d'un exercice) fair copy, correct version; (ouvrage donnant les solutions) key, Fam crib; **le professeur a donné un c. de l'exercice** the teacher gave a model answer to the exercise

corriger [kɔriʒe] (je corrigeai(s), n. corrigeons) **VT 1** (erreur etc) to correct, to put right, to rectify; (mot mal orthographié, les défauts de qn, myopie) to correct; Scol (exercice etc) to correct, to mark; Typ (épreuves) to (proof)read, to correct; Journ (article) to sub-edit, to sub; Naut (compas) to adjust; **je voudrais c. ce que vous avez dit** I'd like to correct what you've said; **c. le tir** Mil to adjust the fire; Fig to adjust one's position; **c. son jugement** to alter one's judgment; **c. qn d'une mauvaise habitude** to cure or break sb of a bad habit **2** (pour punir) **c. qn** to give sb a beating or a thrashing; **se faire c.** to get a beating or a thrashing

VPR se corriger (d'une personne) to mend one's ways, to turn over a new leaf; **se c. de sa gourmandise** to cure oneself of one's greed; **elle ne s'est donc pas corrigée!** she hasn't mended her ways, then!

corrigible [kɔriʒibl] **ADJ** corrigible, rectifiable

corroboration [kɔrɔbɔrasjɔ̃] **NF** corroboration

corroborer [kɔrɔbɔre] **VT** to corroborate

corrodant [kɔrɔdɑ̃] **ADJ, NM** corrosive

corroder [kɔrɔde] **VT** (métal, pierre) to corrode, to eat away

corrompre [kɔrɔ̃pr] **VT 1** (pervertir) (personne, jeunesse, mœurs, goût etc) to corrupt; (air) to pollute; (langage) to debase **2** (soudoyer) to bribe

VPR se corrompre (de vin) to go off; (de goût) to become corrupt(ed)

corrompu [kɔrɔ̃py] **ADJ** (personne, mœurs, goût, texte, disquette) corrupt; (viande) tainted, putrid; (chairs) putrid

corrosif, -ive [kɔrozif, -iv] **ADJ** corrosive; Fig (propos, humour, style) caustic, scathing **NM** corrosive

corrosion [kɔrozjɔ̃] **NF** (d'un métal) corrosion

corroyage [kɔrwajaʒ] **NM** (du cuir) currying; (du métal) welding

corroyer [kɔrwaje] **VT** (pr ind **je corroie**, n. **corroyons**; fu **je corroierai**) (cuir) to curry; (métal) to weld; (bois) to trim, to roughplane

corroyeur [kɔrwajœr] **NM** currier

corrupteur, -trice [kɔryptœr, -tris] **N** (des mœurs) corrupter; (de témoins etc) briber **ADJ** (influence, pouvoir etc) corrupting

corruptible [kɔryptibl] **ADJ** (juge, conscience) corruptible; (matériau) corruptible, perishable

corruption [kɔrypsjɔ̃] **NF** corruption; (de nourriture etc) decomposition; (fait de soudoyer) bribery

corsage [kɔrsaʒ] **NM 1** (chemisier) blouse **2** (d'une robe) bodice, body

corsaire [kɔrsɛr] **NM 1** Hist (navire, homme) corsair, privateer **2** (pantalon) breeches **ADJ** pantalon **c.** breeches

Corse [kɔrs] **NF** Géog Corsica

La Corse

Since the 1970s, the Corsican independence movement has become more radical, with the FLNC (the Corsican Liberation Movement) engaged in a bloody conflict against the French government. In 1982, as part of the law on decentralization, Corsica was attributed a "statut spécial" (special status) allowing for the election of its own assembly, and became a "collectivité locale" in 1991. In 2001 a devolution bill was passed granting Corsica partial control of its own affairs and making the teaching of the Corsican language mandatory in schools.

corse [kɔrs] ADJ Corsican
NM *Ling* Corsican
N **C.** *(personne)* Corsican

corsé [kɔrse] ADJ *(vin)* full-bodied; *(sauce, plat etc)* spicy; *(fromage)* strong, full-flavoured; **café (au goût) c.** full-flavoured coffee; *Fig* **histoire corsée** risqué *or* spicy story; **affaire corsée** tricky business

corselet [kɔrsəlɛ] NM *Entom, Mil etc* corselet

corser [kɔrse] VT *(vin)* to strengthen, to fortify *(by adding spirits)*; *(plat)* to spice up; *(café)* to strengthen; *(récit)* to liven up, to enliven; **c. l'action d'un drame** to intensify the action of a drama
▪ VPR **se corser** to intensify; **l'affaire se corse** *(d'une enquête etc)* the plot thickens; *(dans la vie)* things are getting serious; **ça se corse** things are getting difficult

corset [kɔrsɛ] NM corset; **c. orthopédique** *ou* **médical** (surgical) corset

corseter [kɔrsəte] VT *(pr ind* **je corsète, n. corsetons;** *fu* **je corsèterai)** to corset; *Fig* to restrict, to constrain

corsetier, -ière [kɔrsətje, -jɛr] N corset maker

corso [kɔrso] NM **c. (fleuri)** procession of floral floats

cortège [kɔrtɛʒ] NM **1** *(d'un souverain etc)* retinue, suite, train **2** *(défilé)* procession; **c. funèbre** funeral cortège; **c. nuptial** bridal procession; **défiler en c.** to go past in a procession, to process past; *Fig* **la vie de famille et son c. de problèmes** family life and its accompanying problems

cortex [kɔrtɛks] NM *Anat, Bot* cortex; **c. cérébral** cerebral cortex

cortical, -ale, -aux, -ales [kɔrtikal, -o] ADJ *Anat, Bot* cortical

corticoïde [kɔrtikɔid] NM *Méd* corticoid

corticosurrénal, -ale, -aux, -ales [kɔrtikɔsyrenal, -o] ADJ *Méd* adrenocortical

corticothérapie [kɔrtikɔterapi] NF *Méd* corticotherapy

cortisol [kɔrtisɔl] NM *Méd* hydrocortisone, cortisol

cortisone [kɔrtizɔn] NF *Méd* cortisone

corvée [kɔrve] NF **1** *(obligation pénible)* chore; **les corvées ménagères** the household chores; **je suis de c. de vaisselle ce soir** I'm on washing-up duty tonight; **quelle c.!** what a drag *or* bind!; **c'est une c. que d'aller chez eux** going to see them is a real chore; *Can* **faire une c.** to pitch *or* muck in together (to get a job done) **2** *Mil* fatigue (duty); **(détachement de) c.** fatigue party; **être de c.** to be on fatigue (duty); **c. de cuisine(s)** cookhouse fatigue, *Am* kitchen police; **c. de ravitaillement** supply duty **3** *Hist* corvée

corvette [kɔrvɛt] NF *Naut* corvette

coryphée [kɔrife] NM **1** *(dans un corps de ballet)* ballerina **2** *(d'une secte, d'un parti)* leader, chief

coryza [kɔriza] NM *Méd* head cold, *Spéc* coryza

cosaque [kɔzak] NM cossack

cosécante [kosekãt] NF *Math* cosecant

cosignataire [kosiɲater] ADJ, N cosignatory

cosinus [kɔsinys] NM *Math* cosine

cosmétique [kɔsmetik] ADJ cosmetic
NM **1** *Vieilli* hair cream **2** **les cosmétiques** cosmetics

cosmétologue [kɔsmetɔlɔg] N cosmetics expert, beautician

cosmique [kɔsmik] ADJ *(rayons etc)* cosmic

cosmogonie [kɔsmɔgɔni] NF cosmogony

cosmographie [kɔsmɔgrafi] NF cosmography

cosmologie [kɔsmɔlɔʒi] NF cosmology

cosmonaute [kɔsmɔnot] N cosmonaut

cosmopolite [kɔsmɔpɔlit] ADJ cosmopolitan

cosmopolitisme [kɔsmɔpɔlitism] NM cosmopolitanism

cosmos [kɔsmos] NM *Phil* cosmos; *Astronaut* outer space

cossard, -arde [kɔsar, -ard] *Arg* N lazybones
ADJ lazy

cosse [kɔs] NF **1** *(de petits pois, fèves etc)* pod, husk, hull **2** *Naut (d'un cordage)* thimble, eyelet **3** *Élec (d'un câble)* terminal **4** *Arg* **avoir la c.** to feel lazy

cossin [kɔsɛ̃] NM *Can Fam (truc)* whatsit, thingumabob, thingumajig, thingummy

cossu [kɔsy] ADJ *(personne)* well-to-do, well-off, wealthy; *(maison, intérieur etc)* opulent

costal, -ale, -aux, -ales [kɔstal, -o] ADJ *Anat* costal

costard [kɔstar] NM *Arg* suit

costard-cravate, *pl* **costards-cravates** NM *Fam* suit *(person)*

Costa Rica [kɔstarika] NM Costa Rica

costaud [kɔsto] ADJ *(personne, valise etc)* sturdy; *Fam (alcool, épice)* strong
NM strong *or* sturdy man; *Fam* **tu peux avoir confiance, c'est du c.** trust me, it's sturdy stuff *or* it's sturdily made

costume [kɔstym] NM *(habit)* costume; *(complet)* suit; **c. trois-pièces** three-piece suit; **c. national** national costume *or* dress; **c. ecclésiastique** clerical dress; **c. de cérémonie** *ou* **d'apparat** ceremonial *or* formal dress; *Fam* **c. d'Adam** birthday suit; *Fam* **en c. d'Adam** in one's birthday suit, in the altogether; *Théâtre* **répéter en c.** to have a dress rehearsal; *Can, Suisse* **c. de bain** *(de femme)* swimsuit, *Br* swimming costume; *(d'homme)* swimming trunks, *Am* swimming shorts

costumé [kɔstyme] ADJ **bal c.** fancy-dress ball

costumer [kɔstyme] VT **c. qn** to dress sb up; **il était costumé en Turc** he was dressed (up) as a Turk
▪ VPR **se costumer** to put on fancy dress, to dress up; **se c. en Turc** to dress up as a Turk

costumier, -ière [kɔstymje, -jɛr] N **1** *Com* costum(i)er, dealer in (fancy) costumes **2** *Théâtre* wardrobe master, f mistress; *Cin* costume supervisor

cosy [kɔzi] NM corner divan *(with shelves)*
ADJ *Fam* cosy, *Am* cozy, comfy

cotangente [kɔtãʒãt] NF *Math* cotangent

cotation [kɔtasjɔ̃] NF *Bourse* quotation; **c. à la criée** open-outcry trading; **c. à vue** spot quotation

cote [kɔt] NF **1** *Bourse, Com* quotation; *(liste)* list; **actions inscrites à la c.** listed shares; **retirer de la c.** *(société, action)* to delist; **hors c.** *(actions)* unlisted; *(marché)* unofficial, *Am* over-the-counter; *Courses de chevaux* **c.**

d'un cheval odds on a horse; **c. d'une voiture à l'argus** listed price of a car in the car buyer's guide; *Pol* **pour faire monter sa c. de popularité** *ou* **d'amour** to increase his popularity (rating); *Fam* **avoir la c.** to be popular (**avec, auprès de** with); **alors, tu as la c.?** oh, you're popular!

2 *Com, Jur (d'un document etc)* (classification) mark; *(d'un livre de bibliothèque)* classification *or* shelf mark, pressmark; *Jur (d'un navire)* character, classification

3 *(de dépenses, d'impôts etc)* quota, share **4** *(taille)* (indication of) dimensions; **c. d'origine** standard size

5 *Géog* height; *(au-dessus de la mer)* elevation; *(d'un point dans un diagramme)* altitude; **la c. 304** hill 304; **c. moins/plus 500** 500 below/above sea level

▸▸ **c. d'alerte** *Tech* critical *or* flood level; *Fig* danger point; *Fin* **c. de clôture** closing price; **c. mal taillée** rough and ready settlement; *Admin* **c. mobilière** assessment on income; *Bourse* **c. officielle** official list; **c. des prix** *Bourse* sharelist; *Com* list of prices

côte [kot] NF **1** *Anat* rib; **c. à c.** side by side; *Fam* **se tenir les côtes** to split one's sides laughing; **on lui compterait les côtes, on lui voit les côtes** he's nothing but skin and bone; *Fig Fam* **avoir les côtes en long** to be bone-idle, to be lazy; *Culin* **plat de côtes** dish of spare ribs **2** *(de melon, salade, feuille)* rib; **tissu à côtes** ribbed *or* corded material **3** *(de colline)* slope; *(à monter, à descendre)* hill; *Constr* gradient; **vitesse en c.** speed uphill; *Aut* **démarrage en c.** hill start; **ma voiture a du mal à monter les côtes** my car has problems getting up hills; **à mi-c.** halfway up/down the hill **4** *(rivage)* coast, coastline; **les côtes de (la) France** the coast of France, the French coast; **la C. (d'Azur)** the (French) Riviera; **faire c.** to beach, to run aground; *Naut* **jeter à la c.** to drive ashore, to strand; *Fig Fam* **être à la c.** to be on one's beam ends, to be hard up

▸▸ **c. d'agneau** lamb chop *or* cutlet; **c. de bœuf** rib of beef; *Culin* **côtes découvertes** middle neck; *Anat* **côtes flottantes** floating ribs; *Géog* **la C. d'Ivoire** the Ivory Coast; **c. de porc** pork chop; *Culin* **c. première** loin chop

CÔTÉ [kote]

side 1–4 ▪ aspect 3 ▪ direction 4
▪ way 4 ▪ aside *(de côté)* 6 ▪ nearby *(à côté)* 7 ▪ next to *(à côté de)* 7

NM **1** *(du corps humain)* side; **il a le c. gauche entièrement paralysé** his left side is completely paralysed; **couché sur le c.** lying on one's side; **assis à mes côtés** sitting by my side; **aux côtés de qn** at sb's side; **avoir un point de c.** to have a stitch (in one's side)

2 *(d'une montagne, d'une route, d'une table, d'une feuille etc)* side; **les côtés d'un rectangle** the sides of a rectangle; **les côtés de la médaille** the (two) sides of the medal; **une feuille de papier écrite des deux côtés** a sheet of paper written on on both sides; **de l'autre c. de** on the other side of; **passer de l'autre c. de la rue** to cross the street; *Théâtre* **c. jardin** stage right; **appartement au c. jardin** flat overlooking the garden; **la tour penche d'un c.** the tower leans to one side *or* leans sideways; **ta jupe est plus longue d'un c. que de l'autre** your skirt is longer on one side than (on) the other; *Naut* **présenter le c. à qch** to be broadside on to sth; **navire sur le c.** ship on her beam ends

3 *(aspect)* side, aspect; **le bon/le mauvais c. d'une affaire** the good/bad side *or* aspect of a matter; **le c. recherche m'intéresse plus que le c. enseignement** the research side interests me more than the teaching side; **il a un c. méchant** he has *or* there's a mean streak in him; **il a de bons côtés** he's got a good side to him, he's not all bad; **c'est son c. paternel qui ressort** it's the paternal streak in him coming out; **ça fait partie de ses mauvais côtés** it's one of his bad points; **prendre la vie du bon c.** to look on the bright side of life; **voir le bon/mauvais c. des choses** to see the good/bad side of things

4 *(endroit)* side, direction, way; **cerné de tous côtés** surrounded on all sides; **les gens affluaient de tous côtés** people streamed in from all directions; **se diriger du c. de Paris** to head towards *or* in the direction of Paris; **il habitait du c. de la rivière** he lived near the river; **le vent vient du bon c.** the wind is in the right quarter; **on voit mieux de ce c.-là** you can see better from that side, you can see better from over there; **venez de ce c.** *(par ici)* come over here; *(à droite, à gauche)* come this side; **de ce c.-ci/-là** on this/that side; **ils s'en allèrent chacun de son c.** they went their separate ways; **vivre chacun de son c.** to live separately; **de quel c.?** *(direction)* in which direction?, which way?; *(position)* which side?; **se ranger du c. du plus fort** to side with the strongest; **il a toujours été du c. des opprimés** he's always been on the side of *or* sided with the oppressed; **mettre qn de son c.** to get sb on one's side; **je suis de ton c.** I'm on your side; **sa tante, du c. maternel** his aunt on his mother's side; *Fig* **être né du c. gauche** to be illegitimate; **d'un c. à l'autre** from side to side; **d'un c. …, d'un autre c. …** on the one hand …, on the other hand …; **de mon c., je pense que …** for my part, I think that …; *Fam* **de ce c., il n'y a rien à craindre** there's nothing to worry about on that score

5 *Fam (question)* **c. vitesse, cette voiture est remarquable** as far as speed is concerned *or* speedwise, this car is remarkable; **c. argent** moneywise, as far as money is concerned; **c. repos, ça aurait pu être mieux** on the relaxation side *or* front, it could have been better, it could have been more restful

6 **de c.** *(sauter, se ranger etc)* to one side, aside; **faire un saut de c.** to leap to one side *or* aside, to jump sideways; **avoir une raie de c.** to have a side parting; **regard de c.** sidelong glance; *Fig* **mettre qch de c.** to put sth aside *or* to one side *or* on one side; *Fig* **mettre de l'argent de c.** to put money by *or* aside; *Fig* **j'ai 10 000 euros de c.** I've got 10,000 euros put by; *Fig* **laisser qn/qch de c.** to leave sb/sth out; *Fig* **laisser ses difficultés de c.** to put one's difficulties to one side

7 **à c.** to one side; *(près)* nearby; **la maison est tout à c.** the house is quite near; **il habite à c.** he lives next door; **si vous voulez bien passer à c.** if you'd like to go that way; **les voisins d'à c.** the next-door neighbours; **les gens d'à c.** the people next door; **le salon est à c. de la cuisine** the drawing room is next to the kitchen; **à c. du lit** next to the bed; **il se tenait à c. de moi** he stood at *or* by my side, he stood next to me *or* beside me; **à c. l'un de l'autre** side by side; **tirer à c.** to miss the mark; **vous êtes à c. de la question** you're missing the point; **il est passé à c. de la question** *ou* **du sujet** he missed the point; *Fam* **tu es vraiment à c. de la plaque!** you're really not with it!; **passer à c. d'une difficulté** to avoid a difficulty; **passer à c. des choses importantes/de la vraie vie** to miss out on important things/on real life; **mes ennuis ne sont rien à c. des vôtres** my troubles are nothing compared with *or* beside yours; **il n'est rien à c. de vous** he's nothing compared to you

---

coteau, -eaux [kɔto] NM *(versant)* slope, hillside; *(colline)* hill

côtelé [kotle] ADJ *Tex* ribbed; **velours c.** corduroy

côtelette [kotlɛt, ko-] NF *Culin* chop, cutlet; **c. d'agneau/de porc** lamb/pork chop

coter [kɔte] VT **1** *Com, Bourse (prix, actions etc)* to quote; **des actions cotées en Bourse** shares quoted on the Stock Exchange, listed *or* quoted shares; **être coté à 100 euros** to be trading at 100 euros; *Fam* **ma voiture est vieille, elle n'est plus cotée à l'argus** my car's old, it's not listed in the car buyer's guide any more; **très coté** *Courses de chevaux* well backed, well *or* highly fancied; *Fig* highly rated **2** *Tech etc (dessins etc)* to mark the dimensions on; *(cartes)* to put references on; **point coté** *(de relevé)* reference point, landmark; *(sur une carte)* spot height **3** *Com, Jur (documents etc)* to classify; **coté, daté et paraphé** numbered, dated and signed **4** *Suisse (fermer à clef, verrouiller)* to lock, to bolt

coterie [kɔtri] NF *Péj* set, clique, coterie

côtier, -ière [kotje, -jɛr] ADJ *(fleuve, défense etc)* coastal; *(pêche)* inshore; *(commerce)* coastwise; *(pilote)* coast(ing); **navigation côtière** coastal navigation, coasting NM *(bateau)* coaster, coasting vessel

cotillon [kɔtijõ] NM **1 accessoires de c., cotillons** party novelties **2** *Arch (danse)* cotill(i)on **3** *Arch (jupon)* petticoat; **courir le c.** to chase petticoats, to flirt with the ladies

cotisant, -ante [kɔtizã, -ãt] ADJ *(membre)* paying
N *(à un club etc)* subscriber (**de** to); *(à une caisse)* contributor (**de** to)

cotisation [kɔtizasjõ] NF **1** *(à une caisse etc)* contribution; **c. chômage** unemployment contribution; **c. patronale** employer's contribution; **c. de Sécurité sociale** ≈ National Insurance contribution; **c. syndicale** union dues; **c. vieillesse** pension contribution; **cotisations ouvrières/salariales** employee contributions **2** *(à un club etc)* subscription

cotiser [kɔtize] VI *(à un club)* to subscribe, to pay one's subscription (**à** to); *(à une caisse de retraite, mutuelle etc)* to contribute, to pay one's contributions (**à** to)
VPR **se cotiser** *(pour acheter un cadeau etc)* to club together

côtoiement [kotwamã] NM contact (**de** with); **le c. des personnes célèbres lui monte à la tête** rubbing shoulders *or* mixing with celebrities is going to his head; **le c. quotidien de la mort** the daily contact with death

coton [kɔtõ] NM **1** *(plante, fil, tissu)* cotton; **fil de c.** sewing cotton; **chemise 100% c.** pure *or* 100% cotton shirt; *Fig Fam* **filer un mauvais c.** *(en parlant de la santé, des affaires etc)* to be in a bad way; *(avoir des fréquentations douteuses)* to be going off the rails **2 c. (hydrophile)** cotton wool, *Am* absorbent cotton; **un c.** a piece of cotton wool *or Am* absorbent cotton; *Fig Fam* **j'ai les jambes en c.** my legs feel like cotton wool *or* like jelly; *Fig Fam* **il a du c. dans les oreilles** he's cloth-eared, he's got cloth ears; *Fig* **élever un enfant dans du c.** to (molly)coddle a child **3** *(des plantes)* down
ADJ INV *Fam* tough, tricky; **ça, c'est plutôt c.!** that's a bit tough *or* tricky!
► ► **c. à broder** embroidery thread; **c. à repriser** darning thread *or* cotton

cotonnade [kɔtɔnad] NF cotton fabric; **s'habiller de cotonnades** to wear (clothes made of) cotton *or* cotton clothes

cotonner (se) [səkɔtɔne] VPR **1** *(d'un tissu)* to become fluffy, to fluff up **2 fruit qui se cotonne** fruit that becomes woolly

cotonneux, -euse [kɔtɔnø, -øz] ADJ *(feuille, fruit)* downy; *(nuages)* fluffy, fleecy; *(son)* muffled; *(brouillard)* thick; **style c.** woolly style

cotonnier, -ière [kɔtɔnje, -jɛr] ADJ *(industrie, articles etc)* cotton
N cotton worker, spinner
NM *Bot* cotton plant

coton-poudre, pl **cotons-poudres** NM guncotton, *Am* nitrocotton

Coton-Tige®, pl **Cotons-Tiges** NM cotton bud, *Am* cotton swab

côtoyer [kotwaje] VT *(je côtoie, n. côtoyons; je côtoierai)* *(rivière, forêt etc)* to border on; *(personnes)* to mix with; *Fig* **cela côtoie le ridicule** it's verging on *or* bordering on the ridiculous

cotre [kɔtr] NM *Naut* cutter

cottage [kɔtaʒ] NM *(country)* cottage

cotte [kɔt] NF **1** *Fam (bleu)* overalls; *(sans manches)* dungarees **2** *Mil* **c. d'armes** *(portée sur l'armure)* tunic; **c. de mailles** coat of mail **3** *Arch (jupon)* petticoat

cotutelle [kɔtytɛl] NF *Jur* joint guardianship

cotuteur, -trice [kɔtytœr, -tris] N *Jur* joint guardian

cotylédon [kɔtiledõ] NM *Anat, Bot* cotyledon

cou [ku] NM **1** *(de personne, d'animal, de bouteille etc)* neck; **une chaîne en or autour du c.** (with) a gold chain around his neck; **tendre le c.** to crane one's neck; **se jeter au c. de qn** to throw one's arms round sb's neck; **tordre le c. à une volaille** to wring a bird's neck; *Fig* **je vais lui tordre le c.!** I'll wring his neck (for him)!; *Fig Fam* **endetté jusqu'au c.** up to one's eyes in debt; *Fig* **prendre ses jambes à son c.** to take to one's heels, to show a clean pair of heels; **tu risques de te casser** *ou* **rompre le c.** watch *or* mind you don't break your neck **2** *Suisse (gorge)* throat; **avoir mal au c.** to have a sore throat

couac [kwak] NM **1** *Mus (à la clarinette etc)* squeak, false note; *(de la voix)* false note; **faire un c.** to play a false note; *(d'un chanteur)* to sing a false note **2** *Fig* dissension, disagreement; **il y a des couacs au sein du gouvernement à ce sujet** there is disagreement within the government on this issue

couard, -arde [kwar, -ard] *Littér, Région* ADJ cowardly
N coward

couardise [kwardiz] NF *Vieilli, Littér* cowardice

couchage [kuʃaʒ] NM **1** *(matériel de)* **c.** bedding; **sac de c.** sleeping bag; **et pour le c., comment fait-on?** how about the sleeping arrangements?, who's going to sleep where? **2** *Arg (rapports sexuels)* sleeping around, casual sex

couchant [kuʃã] ADJ **1 le soleil c.** the setting sun; **au soleil c.** at sunset, at sundown **2 chien c.** setter; *Fig* **faire le chien c. auprès de qn** to fawn on sb
NM **1** sunset **2** *(ouest)* west; **dans la direction du c.** westward, in a westerly direction

couche [kuʃ] NF **1** *(de peinture)* coat; *(de beurre, crème solaire, poussière etc)* layer; *Géol* layer, stratum; **les couches de l'atmosphère** the layers *or* strata of the atmosphere; **la c. d'ozone** the ozone layer; **c. de glace** sheet of ice; **c. de fumier** *(au jardin)* hotbed; **champignons de c.** cultivated mushrooms; **couches sociales** social strata, levels of society; **c. d'apprêt** priming coat; **c. de fond** undercoat; **c. anticorrosion** underseal; **c. isolante** underlay; *Arg* **il a** *ou* **il en tient une c.!** he's really stupid *or Br* thick!, what an idiot!

2 *Obst Vieilli* **couches** confinement, labour, *Am* labor; **femme en couches** woman in labour; **couches laborieuses** *ou* **pénibles** difficult (child)birth; **fausse c.** miscarriage; **faire une fausse c.** to have a miscarriage; **mourir en couches** to die in childbirth

3 c. (de bébé) (baby's) nappy, *Am* (baby's) diaper; **mettre une c. au bébé** to put a nappy *or Am* diaper on the baby
4 *Tech* **arbre de c.** engine shaft, main shaft, power shaft
5 *Litt* (lit) bed

couché [kuʃe] ADJ **1** (allongé) lying (down); (au lit) in bed; **(allez) c.!** (à un chien) (lie) down **2** (incliné) **écriture couchée** slanting *or* sloping writing; **blés couchés par le vent** wheat flattened by the wind **3 papier c.** art paper

couche-culotte, *pl* **couches-culottes** NF disposable nappy *or Am* diaper

coucher¹ [kuʃe] NM **1 l'heure du c.** bedtime **2** (gîte) accommodation; **cela va nous assurer le c.** we'll be sure of a bed for the night; **le c. et la nourriture** board and lodging **3** (du soleil) setting; **au c. du soleil** at sunset, at sundown; **un superbe c. de soleil** a magnificent sunset

COUCHER² VT **1** (mettre au lit) to put to bed **2** (offrir un lit à) to put up, to provide with a bed; **je ne peux pas vous c.** I can't put you up **3** (allonger, poser) to lay down; **la pluie a couché les blés** the rain has flattened the wheat; **c. un navire** to throw a ship on her beam ends; **c. un fusil en joue** to aim a gun; **c. qn en joue** to (take) aim at sb; *Fig* **c. qn sur le carreau** to floor sb, to knock sb down **4** (écrire) to set down, to put down, to inscribe; **c. qch par écrit** *ou* **sur le papier** to set *or* put sth down in writing; **c. qn sur son testament** to mention sb in one's will
VI **1** (passer la nuit) to sleep; **c. à l'hôtel/chez des amis** to spend the night *or* to sleep at a hotel/with friends; **c. à la belle étoile/sous la tente** to sleep in the open (air) *or* outside *or* under the stars/in a tent *or* under canvas; **je ne veux pas vous faire c. tard** I don't want to keep you up; *Fig* **c. sous les ponts** to sleep rough
2 *Fam* **c. avec qn** to sleep with sb; **ils couchent ensemble** they're sleeping together; **elle ne couche pas** she doesn't sleep around
VPR **se coucher 1** (au lit) **(aller) se c.** to go to bed; **il est l'heure d'aller se c.** it's bedtime, it's time to go to bed; *Fam* **se c. comme** *ou* **avec les poules** to go to bed early; *Fam* **va te c.!** clear off!, leave me alone!; *Prov* **comme on fait son lit, on se couche** as we make our bed, so must we lie in it
2 (s'allonger) to lie down; **se c. à plat ventre** to lie flat on one's stomach; **ne te couche pas sur ton bureau! tiens-toi droit!** don't slouch over your desk! sit up straight!
3 *Naut* **se c. sur le flanc** to heel over
4 (du soleil, de la lune) to set, to go down

coucherie [kuʃri] NF *Fam* sleeping around, casual sex; **la c., ce n'est pas mon genre** I don't sleep around; **lassée des coucheries de son mari, elle demanda le divorce** fed up with her husband's philandering *or* with her husband's affairs, she sued for divorce

couchette [kuʃɛt] NF *Naut* bunk; *Rail* couchette

coucheur [kuʃœr] NM *Fam* **c'est un mauvais c.** he's an awkward customer

couci-couça [kusikusa] ADV *Fam* so-so

coucou [kuku] NM **1** (oiseau) cuckoo **2** (pendule à) **c.** cuckoo clock **3** (plante) cowslip **4** *Aviat Fam* old crate
INT (pour dire bonjour) cooee!; **c.! (me voilà!)** peek-a-boo!

coude [kud] NM **1** *Anat* elbow; **pull aux coudes usés** pullover with holes in the elbows; **mettre les coudes sur la table** to put one's elbows on the table; **coudes au corps** elbows in; **c. à c.** side by side, close together, shoulder to shoulder; **c. à c. fraternel** friendly jostling; **coup de c.** poke with the elbow,

(pour attirer l'attention) nudge; **donner un coup de c. à qn** to jog sb with one's elbow; (pour attirer l'attention) to nudge sb, to give sb a nudge; *Fig* **se serrer les coudes** to stick together, to help one another; **jouer des coudes** (à travers la foule) to elbow one's way; *Fig* (pour arriver à ses fins) to manoeuvre, *Am* to maneuver; *Fig Fam* **lever le c.** to booze; **huile de c.** elbow grease; **mets-y de l'huile de c.** put some elbow grease into it, use a bit of elbow grease; *Fig* **garder qch sous le c.** to hold on to sth (without doing anything about it); *Fam* **se fourrer le doigt dans l'œil jusqu'au c.** to be barking up the wrong tree, to be completely mistaken
2 (d'une route, rivière etc) (sharp) bend; *Tech* (de barre, tuyau etc) bend, elbow; (d'arbre) crank; **arbre à deux coudes** two-throw crankshaft

coudé [kude] ADJ *Tech* (tuyau) bent, angled, at an angle; (arbre) cranked

coudée [kude] NF **1 avoir les coudées franches** to have plenty of elbow room **2** *Antiq* (mesure) cubit

cou-de-pied, *pl* **cous-de-pied** [kudpje] NM *Anat* instep

couder [kude] VT *Tech* (tuyau etc) to bend (at an angle), to angle; (arbre) to crank

coudoiement [kudwamɑ̃] NM contact, association (de with)

coudoyer [kudwaje] VT (je coudoie, n. coudoyons; je coudoierai) to come into contact with, to rub shoulders with, to mix with; *Fig* **un texte où la vanité de l'auteur coudoie le ridicule** a text in which the author's vanity borders on the ridiculous

coudre [kudr] (*prp* cousant; *pp* cousu; *pr ind* je couds, il coud, n. cousons, ils cousent; *impf* je cousais; *p hist* je cousis; *fu* je coudrai) VT (ourlet etc) to sew, to stitch; (bouton) to sew on, to stitch on; (deux morceaux d'étoffe etc) to sew *or* stitch together; **c. un bouton à une robe** to sew *or* stitch a button on a dress; **c. une jupe** to make (up) *or* sew (up) a skirt; **machine à c.** sewing machine; **c. une plaie** to sew up a wound
VI to sew

coudrier [kudrije] NM hazel (tree)

couenne [kwan] NF **1** (de lard) rind; *Fig Arg* **quelle c.!** what a twerp *or* nerd!; *Fig Arg* **se faire dorer la c.** to expose the body beautiful **2** *Méd* (diphtheric) membrane **3** *Suisse* [kwɛn] (de fromage) rind

couette¹ [kwɛt] NF **1** (dans une housse) duvet, continental quilt **2** *Région, Vieilli* (lit de plumes) feather bed **3** *Tech* bearing **4** *Naut* **couettes courantes** bilge ways

couette² [kwɛt] NF *Fam* (de cheveux) bunch; **elle avait des couettes** she wore her hair in bunches; **se faire des couettes** to put *or* gather one's hair in bunches

couffe [kuf] NF, **couffin** [kufɛ̃] NM (straw) basket; (pour bébé) Moses basket

coug(o)uar [kug(w)ar] NM cougar, puma, mountain lion

couic [kwik] INT eek!, squeak!; *Arg* **faire c.** to croak, *Br* to snuff it

couille [kuj] NF *Vulg* (testicule) ball, *Br* bollock; (problème) balls-up, *Am* ball-up; *Fig* **une c. molle** a drip; *Fig* **avoir des couilles (au cul)** to have balls *or* guts; **notre projet est parti en couilles** our plan has gone down the tubes; **se faire des couilles en or** to make a bundle *or Br* a packet

couillon [kujɔ̃] NM *très Fam* cretin, dope

couillonnade [kujɔnad] NF *très Fam* (discours stupide) **dire des couillonnades** to talk bollocks *or Am* bull **2** (acte stupide) **faire des couillonnades** to cock *or* balls things up, *Am* to ball things up

couillonner [kujɔne] VT *très Fam* (personne) to con; **je me suis fait c.** I've been had *or* done *or* conned

couillu [kujy] ADJ *très Fam* (courageux, audacieux) ballsy, gutsy

couinement [kwinmɑ̃] NM (d'animal) squeak, squeal

couiner [kwine] VI (d'un animal) to squeak, to squeal; (d'un enfant) to whine

coulage [kulaʒ] NM **1** (de statue etc) casting; (de métal fondu, de verre fondu, de savon etc) pouring **2** *Fam* (gaspillage) waste; (chapardage) shrinkage; **c. de stocks** stock shrinkage

coulant [kulɑ̃] ADJ (liquide) running, flowing; (confiture, fromage etc) runny; (vin) smooth; *Fig* (personne) easy-going; **nœud c.** slip *or* running knot; (autour du cou) noose; **style c.** easy *or* flowing style; **il est très c.** he's very easy to get on with *or* very easy-going
NM **1** (anneau) sliding ring; (d'une ceinture) loop **2** (de plante) runner **3** *Fam* (fromage) = very ripe cheese, particularly camembert

coule¹ [kul] NF *Fam* **être à la c.** to know the tricks of the trade, to know the ropes, to know what's what

coule² [kul] NF (de religieux) cowl

coulé [kule] ADJ (mouvement) smooth
NM **1** *Mus* slur **2** (pas de danse) glide **3** *Billard* follow-through

coulée [kule] NF **1** (de liquide) flow; **c. de lave** lava flow; **c. de boue** mudslide **2** *Métal* (de métal fondu) casting; **trou de c.** tap(ping) hole, draw-hole **3** *Natation* glide, push-off

coulemelle [kulmɛl] NF parasol mushroom

COULER [kule] VT **1** (liquide) to pour, to run; (métal fondu) to cast; (cire, ciment) to pour; **c. une pièce/une statue** to cast a piece/a statue; **c. une bielle** to burn out a connecting rod
2 (navire) to sink; *Fig* **c. qn** to bring sb down, to ruin sb, to discredit sb
3 (glisser) **c. un sourire/regard à qn** to steal a smile/look at sb; **c. un mot à l'oreille de qn** to drop *or* whisper a word in sb's ear; *Mus* **c. un passage** to slur a passage
4 c. des jours heureux to have some happy days; *Fam* **se la c. douce** to take things easy
VI **1** (de liquide, rivière etc) to run, to flow; (sable) to trickle; *Fig* (de vers) to flow; (de fromage, maquillage) to run; **faire c. l'eau** to turn the water on; **faire c. un bain** to run a bath; **la sueur coule sur son front** sweat is trickling *or* running down his/her forehead; **le sang a coulé** there was bloodshed; **ce scandale va faire c. de l'encre** this scandal is going to be much written about; *Fig* **ça coule de source** it's obvious; (par voie de conséquence) it follows naturally
2 (de navire) to sink, to go down; (d'une entreprise) to go under; **le nageur a coulé à pic** the swimmer sank like a stone
3 *Litt* (glisser) to slide, to slip; **la martre coula le long du fossé** the marten slithered along the ditch
4 (de tonneau, stylo à plume) to leak; (de nez) to run
VPR **se couler** (se glisser) to slip; **se c. entre les draps** to slip between the sheets, to slip into bed; **se c. dans la foule** to slip *or* disappear into the crowd; **se c. le long du mur** to hug the wall; **elle se laissa c. dans le fauteuil** she slid into the armchair

couleur [kulœr] NF **1** colour, *Am* color; **de quelle c. sont vos yeux?** what colour are your eyes?; **de quelle c. est sa voiture?** what colour car has he got?, what colour is his car?; **en quelle c. vas-tu repeindre la pièce?** what colour are you going to paint the room?; **c. paille/chair** straw-/flesh-coloured; **gens de c.** coloured people, coloureds; **des gens hauts en c.** colourful individuals; **la c., les couleurs** *(linge)* coloureds; **la lessive idéale pour vos couleurs** the ideal soap powder for your coloureds; **photographie/télévision c.** *ou* **en couleur(s)** colour photography/television; *Pol* **la c. d'un journal** the (political) colour *or* (political) complexion of a paper; *Fig* **suivant la c. du temps** it depends on which way the wind is blowing; *Fig* **sous c. de me rendre service** under the pretext *or* guise of doing me a service; *Fig* **style/personnalité sans c.** drab *or* colourless style/personality; *Fig* **immédiatement, ça a pris une autre c.** it immediately started to look different; *Fig Fam* **il en a vu de toutes les couleurs** he's had a hard time, he's been through the mill *or* through a lot; *Fig Fam* **elle nous en fait voir de toutes les couleurs** she gives us a hard time; *Fig Fam* **dépeindre qch sous des couleurs sombres** to paint a gloomy picture of sth, to present a gloomy view of sth; *Fig* **je n'en ai pas encore vu la c.** I've seen no sign of it yet; *Culin* **prendre c.** *(d'un rôti)* to brown SEE GRAMMAR A7; B10 **2** *(de visage)* colour, *Am* color; **perdre ses couleurs** to lose one's colour, to become pale; **sans c.** colourless, pale; *Fam* **quand il l'a su, il a changé de c.** he went pale *or* changed colour *or* blanched when he found out; **tu as repris des couleurs** you're getting your colour back, you're getting some colour (back) in your cheeks; **tu as pris des couleurs** you've caught the sun, you've got a touch of the sun; **tu as des couleurs aujourd'hui** you're looking well today; **le vin lui avait donné des couleurs** his face was flushed from the wine **3** *Mil etc* *(drapeau)* colours, *Am* colors, flag; **envoyer** *or* **hisser les couleurs** to hoist the colours *or* the flag **4** *Sport, Courses de chevaux* **couleurs** *(d'un club, d'une écurie)* colours, *Am* colors; **défendre les couleurs de son club** to play for one's club **5** *(peinture)* paint; **boîte de couleurs** box of paints, paintbox; **des crayons de c.** crayons, coloured pencils; **marchand de couleurs** hardware merchant, *Br* ironmonger **6** *Cartes* suit; **jouer dans la c.** to follow suit; **annoncer la c.** to call (trumps); *Fig Fam* to lay one's cards on the table **7** *(en coiffure)* tint; **se faire faire une c.** to have one's hair tinted ▸▸ **couleurs complémentaires** complementary colours; **couleurs fondamentales** primary colours; *Fig* **c. locale** local colour; *Fig* **ça fait c. locale** it's really ethnic-looking; **couleurs primaires** primary colours; **couleurs primitives** colours of the spectrum; **couleurs spectrales** colours of the spectrum

couleuvre [kulœvr] NF **1** *(serpent)* **c.** (à collier) grass snake; **c. lisse** smooth snake; **paresseux comme une c.** bone-idle; *Fig* **avaler des couleuvres** *(se faire humilier)* to eat humble pie; *(être naïf)* to believe *or* swallow anything **2** *Can (ver)* worm

coulis ¹ [kuli] ADJ **vent c.** draught, *Am* draft

coulis ² NM **1** *Constr* grout **2** *Métal* molten metal **3** *Culin* **c. de tomates/framboises** tomato/raspberry coulis

coulissant [kulisã] ADJ *(porte, panneau etc)* sliding

coulisse [kulis] NF **1** *(glissière)* runner; **fenêtre/porte à c.** sliding window/door; **trombone à c.** slide trombone; **regard en c.** sidelong glance **2** *Couture* hem *(through which to pass tape)* **3** *Théâtre (rainure)* runner, groove; **les coulisses** the wings; **en c.** in the wings; *TV* **behind-the-scenes**; **avoir un laissez-passer pour aller dans les coulisses** to have a backstage pass; *Fig* **les coulisses de la politique** what goes on behind the scenes in politics; *Fig* **rester/être dans les**

coulisses *ou* **en c.** to stay/be in the background **4** *Bourse* outside *or* unlisted market

coulissé [kulise] ADJ **jupe (à ceinture) coulissée** skirt with a drawstring waist

coulisseau, -eaux [kuliso] NM sliding block; *(de pièce de machine)* slide; *(de tiroir)* runner; *Aut etc* slider; *Aut* **c. de sélection** selector rod

coulisser [kulise] VI *Tech etc* to slide
VT **1** *(tiroir)* to provide with runners **2** *Couture (bord)* to run up

coulissier [kulisje] NM *Bourse* outside broker, kerb broker

couloir [kulwar] NM **1** *(dans une maison)* corridor, passage; *(d'un train)* corridor; *Sport (en athlétisme, natation)* lane; *Tennis* tramlines, *Am* alley; **bruits de c.** rumours, whispers **2** *Cin* **c. du film** film channel, track **3** *Géog* gully, gorge ▸▸ *Aviat* **c. aérien** air corridor; **c. d'autobus** bus lane; *Hist* **le c. de Dantzig** the Polish Corridor; *Pol etc* **c. humanitaire** aid corridor; *Naut* **c. de navigation** shipping lane; **c. à vélos** cycle lane

couloiriste [kulwarist] NM *Journ* lobby correspondent

coulon [kulɔ̃] NM *Belg (pigeon voyageur)* carrier pigeon, homing pigeon

coulpe [kulp] NF **battre sa c.** to beat one's breast

COUP [ku]

NM	blow **1**, **2** ▪ knock **1** ▪ shock **1**
	▪ move **2** ▪ attempt **4** ▪ job **5**
	▪ suddenly *(tout à coup)* **6**

NM **1** *(choc)* blow, knock; *(à la porte)* knock, rap; **c. de bâton** blow (with a stick); **c. sur les doigts** rap over the knuckles; *Théâtre* **les trois coups** = the three knocks given just before the curtain rises; **donner de grands coups dans la porte** to pound *or* bang on the door; **enfoncer un clou à coups de marteau** to hammer a nail in; **se donner un c. contre qch** to knock against sth; *Fig* **ça m'a fait un c.!** it gave me such a shock!; *Fig Fam* **tenir le c.** to hold out, to stick it out; *Fig* **il faut que je tienne le c.** I've got to keep going *or* stick it out; **rendre c. pour c.** to return blow for blow, to hit back, to strike back; *Fig* **faire les quatre cents coups** to sow one's wild oats; *Fig Fam* **donner un c. de canif dans le contrat** to have the occasional fling; **faire d'une pierre deux coups, faire c. double** to kill two birds with one stone; **corps couvert de coups** body covered with bruises; *Fig Fam* **faire une traduction à coups de dictionnaire** to do a translation using a dictionary; **c. manqué** miss; **fusil à deux coups** double-barrelled gun; **boire qch à petits coups** to sip sth; *Fam* **un c. de rouge** a glass of red wine; **allons boire un c.** let's go and have a drink; **saluer qn d'un c. de chapeau** to raise *or* tip one's hat to sb; **avoir un bon c. de fourchette** to be a hearty eater; **passer un c. d'éponge sur la table** to wipe over the table with a sponge, to give the table a wipe with a sponge; **donner un c. de frein** to brake; **éviter un obstacle par un c. de volant** to swerve to avoid an obstacle; **c. de cloche** stroke of the bell; **l'horloge sonna trois coups** the clock struck three; **sur le c. de midi** on the stroke of twelve; *Fam* **il va falloir en mettre un c.** we're going to have to pull out (all) the stops **2** *Golf* stroke; *Ftbl* kick; *Boxe* blow, punch; *Échecs etc* move; *Cartes* **finir le c.** to finish the hand **3** *(influence)* **agir sous le c. de la peur** to act through *or* out of fear; **j'ai répondu sous le c. de la colère** I answered in a fit of anger; **il est sous le c. d'une forte émotion** he's in a very

emotional state; **tomber sous le c. de la loi** to come within the provisions of the law; **être sous le c. d'une condamnation** to have a current conviction **4** *(essai)* attempt; **à tous les coups l'on gagne** you win every time; **tu as encore droit à un c.** you've still got another go; **d'un seul c.** at one go; **faire qch du premier c.** to do sth at the first attempt *or* shot; **j'ai deviné du premier c.** I guessed straight off *or* straightaway; **marquer le c.** to mark *or* celebrate the occasion; **accuser le c.** to show that one has been affected; *Fam* **ça vaut le c.** it's worth it, it's worth while; **ça ne vaut pas le c.** it isn't worth it **5** *(affaire)* business, job; **il prépare un mauvais c.** he's up to no good; **être sur un c.** to be on to something good *or* a good thing *or* a winner; *Journ* to have a lead; *Fam* **ça, c'est un sale c.!** what a dirty trick!; **c'est encore un c. de ton ami** it's another of your friend's tricks; **réussir un bon c.** to do well for oneself; **c'est le c. classique** it's the usual thing; *Fam* **il est dans le c.** *(dans le secret)* he knows what's going on; *(impliqué)* he's in on it; *(à la mode)* he's with it; **il faut la mettre dans le c.** we'll have to put her in the picture; *(l'impliquer)* we'll have to get *or* bring her in on it **6** **avoir le c. de main pour faire qch** to have the knack of doing sth; **du (même) c.** *(en même temps)* at the same time; *(donc)* as a result, and so; **il fut tué sur le c.** he was killed outright; **sur le c., je n'ai pas compris** at the time, I didn't understand; **pour le c.** *(en conséquence)* as a result; *(cette fois)* this time; **après c.** after the event; **tout à c., tout d'un c.** suddenly, all of a sudden; **boire trois verres c. sur c.** to drink three glasses one after the other *or* in a row; **encore un c.** once again, once more; **à c. sûr** definitely **7** *Arg (rapports sexuels)* screw, shag; **tirer un c.** to have a screw *or* shag; **c'est un bon c.** he's/she's a good screw *or* a good lay ▸▸ **c. d'aile** stroke *or* flap of the wing; *Boxe* **c. bas** low punch, blow below the belt; *Fig Fam* **il m'a fait un c. bas** he played a lousy trick on me; **c. de bec** peck; *Jur* **coups et blessures** assault and battery; *Fam* **c. de bol** stroke of luck; **c. au but** direct hit; **c. de chance** stroke of luck; **c. de couteau** stab (with a knife); **c. de crayon** pencil stroke; **il a un sacré c. de crayon** he's very good at drawing; **c. de dents** bite; *Tennis* **c. droit** forehand (stroke); **c. d'éclat** distinguished action, glorious deed; *Sport* **c. d'envoi** kickoff; **c. d'épée** (sword) thrust; **c. d'essai** trial shot; **il n'en est pas à son c. d'essai** it's not the first time he's done it; **c. d'État** coup (d'état); **c. de feu** shot; *Fig (dans un restaurant)* lunchtime rush; *Fam* **c. de fil** phone call; **c. de filet** cast; *(prise)* haul; *Sport* **c. franc** free kick; **c. de froid** *Météo* cold snap; *Méd* chill, cold; **c. de fusil** (gun)shot; **il fut tué d'un c. de fusil** he was shot dead; **c. de grisou** firedamp explosion; *Fam* **c. de gueule** shout; **c. de hache** blow *or* stroke (with an axe); *Fig* **faire un c. de Jarnac à qn** to deal sb a cruel and unexpected blow; **c. du lapin** rabbit punch; *(dans un accident de la circulation)* whiplash injury; **c. monté** put-up job; **l'accusé affirmait être victime d'un c. monté** the accused claimed it was a put-up job *or* claimed that he'd been framed; **c. de pied** kick; **c. de poignard** stab (with a dagger); **c. de poing** punch; **il a reçu un c. de poing** he was punched; **c. de queue** flick of the tail; **c. de sifflet** blast of a/the whistle; **c. de soleil** sunburn; **c. de sonnette** ring of the bell; *Base-ball* **c. sûr** strike; **c. de tabac** squall; **c. de téléphone** (tele)phone call; **c. de tête** *Ftbl* header; *Fig* impulsive act; *Fig* **faire qch sur un c. de tête** to do sth impulsively; *Rugby* **c. tombé** drop kick, drop; **c. de tonnerre** *(son)* clap *or* peal of thunder; *Fam* **c. de veine** stroke of luck; **c. de vent** gust of wind; *Fig* **entrer dans une pièce en c. de vent** to burst into a room; *Fig* **partir en c. de vent** to rush off, to dash off; *Fig* **je passe en c. de vent pour te dire …** I've just dropped in to tell you …; *Fam* **il a pris un c. de vieux** he's aged

coupable [kupabl] **ADJ** *(personne)* guilty; **c. de vol** guilty of theft; **s'avouer c.** to admit one's guilt; **elle se sent c.** she feels guilty (about it); *Jur* **plaider c.** to plead guilty; **action c.** culpable act; **faiblesse c.** reprehensible weakness; **des pensées coupables** impure thoughts
N culprit, guilty party; *Fam* **qui est le c.? qui a cassé le vase?** own up! *or* who's the guilty party? who broke the vase?

coupage [kupaʒ] **NM 1** *(de vins)* blending, mixing **2** *(avec de l'eau)* diluting

coupant [kupɑ̃] **ADJ** sharp; **outils coupants** sharp(-edged) tools, edge tools; *Fig* **ton c.** sharp *or* cutting tone

coup-de-poing, *pl* **coups-de-poing** [kudpwɛ̃] **NM 1 c. (américain)** knuckle-duster; *Fig* **opération c.** surprise *or* sudden raid; *Fig* **une opération c. contre l'alcool au volant** a crackdown on drink driving; *Fig* **publicité c.** hard-hitting advertising, advertising that pulls no punches **2** *(silex taillé)* hand axe

coupe[1] [kup] **NF 1** cup, bowl; **c. (à champagne)** (champagne) glass; **c. à fruits** fruit dish *or* bowl; **c. de glace** dish *or* bowl of ice cream; **j'ai bu quatre coupes** I drank four glasses *or* glassfuls; **boire la c. jusqu'à la lie** to drain the cup to the dregs; *Prov* **il y a loin de la c. aux lèvres** there's many a slip 'twixt cup and lip; *Fig* **la c. est pleine** that's the limit **2** *Sport* cup; **la C. de l'America** the America's Cup; *Ftbl* **la C. du monde** the World Cup; *Tennis* **la C. Davis** the Davis Cup; **jouer pour la c.** to play for the cup

coupe[2] **NF 1** *(action)* *(du blé etc)* cutting; *(de tissu)* cutting (out); *(d'arbres)* cutting down, felling; **c. de cheveux** haircut; **une c. et un Brushing®** a cut and blow-dry; **acheter du fromage à la c.** to buy fresh-cut cheese; **mettre un bois en c. réglée** to make periodical cuttings in a wood; *Fam* **mettre qn en c. réglée** to exploit sb systematically; **c. claire** *(d'un secteur de forêt)* clear cut; *(du personnel, des dépenses)* drastic cut; **c. sombre** *(d'un secteur de forêt)* slight thinning; *(du personnel, des dépenses)* drastic cut; **coupes budgétaires** budget cuts
2 *(pièce)* *(de tissu)* length; *(de bois)* piece
3 *(forme)* *(d'un vêtement)* cut; **complet de bonne c.** well-cut suit
4 *Archit* *(plan etc)* section; **c. longitudinale** *ou* **en long** longitudinal section; **c. transversale** *ou* **en travers** cross *or* transverse section; **la machine vue en c.** a section of the machine
5 *Cartes* cut, cutting; **être sous la c. de qn** to lead after sb has cut; *Fig* to be under sb's thumb *or* power; *Fig* **tenir qn sous sa c.** to have sb under one's thumb *or* in one's power
6 *Cin* cut; *(prise)* outtake

coupé [kupe] **ADJ 1** *(taillé)* cut; **costume mal c.** badly cut suit **2 vin c. d'eau** wine and water **3** *Tennis* **balle coupée** cut, slice **4** *(interrompu)* cut off; **la route est coupée** the road is cut off *or* blocked; **être c. du monde** to be cut off from the outside world; **communication téléphonique coupée** cut-off telephone call **5 cheval c.** gelding
NM 1 *Aut* coupé, *Am* two-door sedan; **c. cabriolet** drop-head coupé; **c. sport** sports coupé **2** *(pas de danse)* coupee

coupe-chou, *pl* **coupe-choux NM** *Fam* (cut-throat) razor

coupe-cigare(s), *pl* **coupe-cigares NM** cigar cutter

coupe-circuit NM INV *Élec* cutout, circuit breaker

coupe-coupe NM INV machete

coupée [kupe] **NF** *Naut (ouverture)* gangway; **échelle de c.** accommodation ladder

coupe-faim NM INV appetite suppressant

coupe-feu NM INV firebreak; **porte c.** fire-door

coupe-file, *pl* **coupe-files NM** pass

coupe-frites NM INV chip-cutter *or* -slicer, *Am* French-fry-cutter *or* -slicer

coupe-gorge NM INV dangerous back alley *or* back street

coupe-jarret, *pl* **coupe-jarrets NM** *Vieilli* cut-throat

coupe-légumes NM INV vegetable-cutter *or* -slicer

coupelle [kupɛl] **NF 1** *(petite coupe)* small dish **2** *Chimie* cupel

coupe-ongles NM INV nail clippers

coupe-papier NM INV paper knife, letter opener

COUPER [kupe]

| **VT** to cut **1, 2, 4, 8** ▪ to cut up **1** ▪ to cut down **1** ▪ to cut off **1, 4, 5** ▪ to trump **2** ▪ to cut across **3** ▪ to divide **4** ▪ to switch off **5** |
| **VI** to cut **1, 4** ▪ to get out of *(couper à)* **3** |
| **VPR** to cut oneself **2** ▪ to intersect **3** |

VT 1 *(trancher)* to cut; **c. de la viande en morceaux** to cut up meat (into pieces); **c. une tomate en quartiers** to cut a tomato into quarters, to quarter a tomato; **c. un arbre** to cut down *or* chop down *or* fell a tree; **c. du bois** to cut *or* chop wood; **c. les cheveux à qn** to cut sb's hair; **c. la tête** *ou* **le cou à qn** to cut off sb's head; **c. la gorge à qn** to slit *or* cut sb's throat; *Fig* **c. bras et jambes à qn** to stun sb; **c. les jambes à qn** *(fatiguer)* to do sb in, to wear sb out; **je vais lui c. les oreilles, à ce morveux!** I'm going to tear *or* rip that brat's head off!; *Fig* **c. l'herbe sous le pied de qn** to cut the ground from under sb's feet, to pull the rug out from under sb's feet; **c. un brouillard/un silence/un accent à c. au couteau** a fog/a silence/an accent you could cut with a knife; *Fig* **c. les cheveux en quatre** to split hairs, to nitpick; **j'en donnerais ma tête à c., j'en mettrais ma main à c.** I'd stake my life on it, I'd bet my bottom dollar on it; *Fig* **c. l'aile** *ou* **les ailes à qn** to clip sb's wings; *Couture* **c. un vêtement** to cut out a garment; *Sport* **c. une balle** to cut *or* slice a ball
2 *Cartes* to cut; *(prendre avec l'atout)* to trump
3 *(traverser)* to cut across, to cross; **sentier qui coupe la route** path that cuts across *or* crosses the road; **c. la route** *ou* **le chemin à qn** to cut in in front of sb; **c. la route d'un navire** to cut across the bows of a ship; **la droite AB coupe le plan** the straight line AB cuts the plane
4 *(séparer)* to cut, to divide; **la rivière coupe le département en deux** the river divides *or* cuts the département in two; **la France est coupée en deux:** il y a ceux qui votent à droite, et les autres France is divided: there are those who vote for the right, and the rest; **la proue du navire coupait les vagues** the bow of the ship cut through the waves; **c. l'ennemi de ses bases** to cut off the enemy from its base; **c. la retraite à qn** to cut off sb's retreat
5 *(interrompre)* to cut off; **ces chaussettes sont trop serrées, elles me coupent la circulation** these socks are too tight, they're cutting off my circulation; **c. le souffle à qn** to take sb's breath away; *(d'un coup de poing)* to wind sb; **c. ses effets à qn** to steal sb's

thunder; *(le refroidir)* to take the wind out of sb's sails; **c. les vivres** to cut off supplies; **c. les vivres à qn** to stop sb's allowance; **c. l'appétit à qn** to spoil sb's appetite, to take sb's appetite away; **c. la parole à qn** to interrupt sb; *Fam* **ça te la coupe!** that's floored you!, that's taken the wind out of your sails!; *Arg* **c. le sifflet** *ou* **la musette à qn** *(égorger)* to slit sb's throat; *Fig Fam* **c. le sifflet** *ou* **la chique à qn** to shut sb up; **le rythme monotone de la vie quotidienne était coupé (par) de nombreuses fêtes religieuses** the monotony of daily life was broken *or* relieved by numerous religious festivals; *Tél* **c. la communication** to break off the call; **c. l'eau** to turn off the water; *Élec* **c. le courant** *ou* **l'électricité** to switch off the current; *(de la compagnie d'électricité)* to cut off the power; *Aut* **c. l'allumage** *ou* **le contact** to switch off (the ignition)
6 c. du vin *(en mélangeant)* to blend wine; *(avec de l'eau)* to water down *or* dilute wine
7 *(du vent)* to sting, to lash, to whip
8 *(film, texte)* to cut; *(remarque, séquence)* to cut (out), to edit out; **c. un passage dans un roman** to cut a passage from a novel
VI 1 *(trancher)* to cut; **le couteau coupe bien** the knife cuts well; **ce couteau coupe comme un rasoir** this knife is as sharp as a razor; **attention, ça coupe!** watch out *or* be careful, it's sharp!; *Fig* **c. dans le vif** to take drastic measures, to take strong *or* firm action
2 *Tél* **ne coupez pas!** hold the line!; *Cin* **coupez!** cut!; **c. court à qch** to put a speedy end to sth
3 *Fam (se dérober)* **c. à qch** to get out of doing sth; **c. à une corvée** to get out of *or* dodge *or* shirk a chore; **il n'y coupera pas** he won't get out of it
4 *Cartes* to cut; **c'est à vous de c.** it's your turn to cut; **c. à carreau/à cœur** to trump with a diamond/a heart
5 c. à travers champs to cut across country; **c. par le plus court** to take a short cut
VPR se couper 1 se c. les ongles/les cheveux/etc to cut one's nails/hair/etc
2 *(se blesser)* to cut oneself; **il s'est coupé** *ou* **au doigt** he cut his finger; **elle s'est coupé les veines** she cut *or* slashed her wrists; *Fig* **il se couperait en quatre pour elle** he'd really put himself out for her, he'd bend over backwards for her
3 *(de routes etc)* to intersect, to cross
4 *Fam (se contredire)* to give oneself away
5 se c. de qn to cut oneself off from sb, to sever links with sb

coupe-racines [kuprasin] **NM INV** *Agr* root-slicer *or* -cutter

couper-coller NM INV *Ordinat* cut and paste

couperet [kuprɛ] **NM 1** *(pour la viande)* (meat) chopper, cleaver **2** *(de la guillotine)* blade, knife

couperose [kuproz] **NF 1** *(du visage)* blotchiness, blotches, *Spéc* rosacea **2** *Chimie Vieilli* **c. verte** green vitriol, ferrous sulphate; **c. bleue** blue vitriol, copper sulphate

couperosé [kuproze] **ADJ** *(teint)* blotchy, *Spéc* affected by rosacea

coupeur, -euse [kupœr, -øz] **N** *(de tissu, cuir etc)* cutter; *Fig* **c. de cheveux en quatre** hairsplitter, nitpicker; *Arch* **c. de bourses** pickpocket

coupe-vent NM INV 1 *(dispositif)* windbreak **2** *(blouson)* windcheater, *Am* windbreaker

couplage [kuplaʒ] **NM** *Tech (de roues etc)* coupling, connecting; *(de locomotives)* *Élec, Électron* coupling; *(de publicité)* combination rate

couple [kupl] **NM 1** *(de gens)* couple; *(d'ani-*

maux, d'oiseaux) pair; **c. bien assorti** well-matched couple; **ils font un joli c.** they make a lovely couple; **les invités sont tous venus en couples** the guests all came in couples, the guests all came with (their) partners; **vivre en c.** to live together (as a couple); **c. non cohabitant** = couple who pursue a relationship while maintaining separate living arrangements **2** *Phys* couple; *Tech* **c. (de torsion)** torque; *Phys* **c. thermoélectrique** thermocouple; *Aut* **c. de démarrage** starting *or* cranking torque; *Aut* **c. de pont** final-drive gears; *Aut* **c. moteur** engine torque **3** *Naut* frame, timber; **c. de construction** bulkhead
▪ NF *(pour chiens etc)* leash

couplé [kuple] NM *Courses de chevaux* double; **c. placé** each-way double

coupler [kuple] VT **1** *(bateaux, wagons)* to couple, to attach together; *Élec (prises)* to couple **2** *(chiens)* to leash together

couplet [kuplɛ] NM *(de chanson)* verse; *Fig Fam* tirade, little piece (**sur** about)

coupleur [kuplœr] NM *Électron* coupler; *Ordinat* **c. acoustique** acoustic coupler; *Aut* **c. hydraulique** fluid flywheel *or* coupling

coupoir [kupwar] NM *Tech* cutter

coupole [kupɔl] NF **1** *Archit* dome, cupola; *Fig* **être reçu sous la C.** to be made a member of the Académie française **2** *Mil* cupola

coupon [kupɔ̃] NM **1** *Com (de tissu)* remnant **2** *Fin* **c. d'action** coupon; **c. attaché/détaché ou échu** cum/ex dividend **3** *Rail* **c. d'aller/de retour** outward/return half; **carnet de 10 coupons** book of 10 tickets; **c. de remboursement** redeemable coupon; **c. de vol** flight coupon

couponnage [kupɔnaʒ] NM *Mktg* couponing

coupon-prime, *pl* **coupons-primes** NM gift voucher, gift token

coupon-réponse, *pl* **coupons-réponse** NM reply coupon; **c. international** international reply coupon

coupure [kupyr] NF **1** *(au doigt etc)* cut; **se faire une c.** to cut oneself

2 *(dans une pièce, un livre, un film)* cut; **c. de journal** *ou* **de presse** newspaper cutting *or* clipping, press cutting; **c. radio** radio blackout

3 *Élec* **c. (de courant)** power cut; **il y aura une c. de 5 heures à 7 heures** *(gaz/eau/électricité)* the gas/water/electricity will be cut off between 5 and 7 o'clock

4 *Fig (séparation)* split

5 *Fin* denomination; **c. de 50 euros** 50-euro note; **50 000 euros en petites coupures** 50,000 euros in small notes *or* denominations; **en coupures usagées** in used notes *or Am* bills

6 *Typ* **c. automatique de fin de ligne** automatic line break *or* wrap; **c. de mots** word splits; **c. de page** page break; **faire une c. de page** to do a page break

couque [kuk] NF *Belg* cake

cour [kur] NF **1** *(de souverain)* court; **vivre à la c.** to live at court; **gens de c.** courtiers; **être bien/mal en c.** to be in/out of favour; **elle a une c. de prétendants** she has a circle of suitors

2 *(faite à une femme)* courting, courtship; **faire la c. à une jeune fille/une femme** to court a girl/a woman; **faire la c. à qn** *(flatter)* to curry favour with sb

3 *Jur* court; **messieurs, la C.!** ≃ all rise!; **Haute C.** High Court *(for impeachment of president or ministers)*; **la C. suprême du Canada** the Supreme Court of Canada

4 *Archit* courtyard, yard; **c. de ferme** farmyard; **c. d'honneur** main courtyard; **c. de récréation** *ou* **d'école** schoolyard, *Br* playground; **jouer dans la c.** *(de l'école)* to

play in the playground; *(d'un groupe d'immeubles)* to play in the yard; **c. des grands** playground for the older pupils; *Fig* **jouer dans la c. des grands** to be in the big league, to be in with the big boys; *Mil* **c. de quartier** barrack square; *Théâtre* **côté c.** stage left; **appartement 3 côté c.** flat no 3 overlooking the yard

5 *Belg* toilets; **aller à la c.** to go to the toilet
▪ ▪ **la c. d'appel** the court of appeal; **c. d'Assises** Assize Court; **C. des comptes** ≃ Audit Office; **C. internationale de justice** International Court of Justice; **c. de justice** court of justice; **c. martiale** court martial; **passer devant la c. martiale, passer en c. martiale** to be court-martialled (**pour** for); *Hist* **c. des miracles** = area frequented by beggars and criminals; *Fig* **c'était une vraie c. des miracles** it was a picture of every human misfortune under the sun; **C. pénale internationale** International Criminal Court

courage [kuraʒ] NM courage, bravery; **avoir du c.** to have courage, to be courageous; **perdre c.** to lose heart, to become discouraged; **prendre c.** to take heart; **donner du c. à qn** to give sb courage; **il lui a fallu un certain c. pour le faire** it took a certain amount of courage for him to do it; **se sentir le c. de faire qch** to feel up to doing sth; **prendre son c. à deux mains** to summon up all one's courage, to pluck up courage; **être plein de c.** to be full of energy; **(du) c.!** cheer up!, buck up!; *(pour continuer)* keep it up!, keep going!; **allez, c., les choses vont bien finir par s'arranger!** come on, cheer up *or* don't worry, things'll turn out all right!; **avoir le c. de ses opinions** to have the courage of one's convictions; **vous n'auriez pas le c. de les renvoyer!** you wouldn't have the heart to dismiss them!; **je n'ai pas le c. de faire la vaisselle ce soir** I'm not up to doing the dishes tonight; **se battre avec c.** to fight bravely *or* courageously; **bon c.!** good luck!, all the best!; *Iron* good luck!

courageusement [kuraʒøzmɑ̃] ADV *(bravement)* courageously, bravely; *(résolument)* with a will

courageux, -euse [kuraʒø, -øz] ADJ **1** *(brave)* courageous, brave **2** *(énergique)* energetic; **il n'est pas très c. pour l'étude** he doesn't show much enthusiasm for studying

courailler [kuraje] VI *Can Fam* to chase after women

couailleur [kurajœr] NM *Can Fam* womanizer

couramment [kuramɑ̃] ADV **1** *(facilement)* fluently; **parler c. une langue étrangère** to speak a foreign language fluently **2** *(généralement)* commonly; **ce mot s'emploie c.** this word is in current *or* common use; **on prend l'avion de plus en plus c.** it's becoming more and more common for people to go by plane

courant, -ante [kurɑ̃, -ɑ̃t] ADJ *(eau)* running; *(compte etc)* current; **chien c.** hound; *Typ* **titre c.** running head(line); **dette courante** floating debt; **le mois c.** the current month; **le cinq c.** the fifth inst., the fifth of this month; **fin c.** at the end of this month; **vie courante** everyday life; **mot d'usage c.** word in current *or* common *or* general use, everyday word; **monnaie courante** legal currency; *Fig* **c'est monnaie courante** it's quite usual *or* widespread, it's common practice; **prix c.** current price; *(liste)* price list; *Com* **marque courante** standard make; **de taille courante** of standard size

▪ NM **1** *(dans une rivière etc)* current; **suivre/remonter le c.** to go with/against the current; *Fig* **suivre le c.** to swim *or* go with the tide; **c. d'air** draught, *Am* draft; **c. sous-marin** undercurrent, undertow; **un c. ascendant** a

thermal; *Fig* **c. de population** population movement; **c. de pensée** way of thinking; **c. politique/culturel** political/cultural trend; **écrire au c. de la plume** to write spontaneously *or* off the cuff **2** *Élec* **c. (électrique)** (electric) current, power; **c. continu/alternatif** direct/alternating current; **c. triphasé/biphasé** triphase/biphase current; **c. de repos** quiescent current; *Fig* **le c. ne passe pas entre eux** they're not on the same wavelength; *Fig* **le c. est tout de suite passé entre nous** we clicked right away; *Fig* **faire passer le c. avec son public** to get across to one's audience **3** *(durée)* course; **dans le c. de l'année** in the course of the year; **dans le c. de la semaine** some day this week, in the course of the week **4** **il est au c.** he knows (about it); **mettre qn au c. d'une décision** to tell *or* inform sb of a decision; **elle m'a mis au c.** she told me all about it, she put me in the picture; **je me suis mis très vite au c.** I got the hang of things very quickly; **le professeur est très au c. des nouvelles méthodes** the teacher is very up to date on *or* familiar with the new methods
▪ NF **courante 1** *Mus (danse)* courante **2** *Arg* **la courante** *(diarrhée)* the runs, the trots

> Il faut noter que l'adjectif anglais **current** est un faux ami. Il signifie **actuel**.

courbatu [kurbaty] ADJ *(personne)* aching *or* stiff (all over)

courbature [kurbatyr] NF ache, stiffness; **avoir des courbatures (partout), être plein de courbatures** to be aching *or* stiff (all over)

courbaturé [kurbatyre] ADJ aching (all over); **je me sens tout c.** I'm aching *or* stiff all over

courbe [kurb] ADJ curved, curving; **des lignes courbes** curves
▪ NF curve; *(graphe)* graph; **la route fait une c.** the road curves *or* bends (round); *Math* **c. plane** plane curve; *Géog* **c. de niveau** contour (line); *Méd* **c. de température** temperature curve; **c. des prix/des salaires** price/salary curve; **c. de popularité** popularity curve; *Compta* **c. (d'évolution) des coûts** cost curve; **c. d'apprentissage** *ou* **d'assimilation** learning curve; **c. de croissance** growth curve; *Mktg* **c. (d'évolution) de la demande** demand curve; *Mktg* **c. d'expérience** experience curve; *Mktg* **c. du cycle de vie (d'un produit)** (product) life-cycle curve; **c. d'investissement** investment curve; **c. des ventes** sales chart

courber [kurbe] VT **1** *(tordre)* to bend; **silhouette courbée par l'âge** figure bowed *or* stooped *or* bent with age; **c. la tête** to bow *or* bend one's head; *Fig* **c. l'échine** to submit; *Fig* **c. qn sous son autorité** to bend sb to one's will, to make sb submit to one's will **2** *Suisse Fam* **c. l'école** *(ne pas s'y rendre)* to skip school, *Br* to bunk off
▪ VI to bend; **c. sous le poids** to bend under the weight
▪ VPR **se courber** *(d'une personne)* to bend down, to stoop; **se c. devant qn** to bow to sb; *Fig* to submit to sb; **se c. en deux** to bend double; *Fig* **elle ne se courba jamais devant l'autorité** she never bowed (down) to authority

courbette [kurbɛt] NF *(salut)* bow; *Équitation* curvet; *Fig* **faire des courbettes à** *ou* **devant qn** to bow and scrape to sb

courbure [kurbyr] NF *(de ligne, surface etc)* curvature; *(d'un morceau de bois etc)* bend, curve; *(de poutre)* sagging; *(du dos)* curve; *(de la route)* camber; **c. double** *ou* **en S** S curve

courette [kurɛt] NF small (court)yard

coureur, -euse [kurœr, -øz] N **1** *Sport etc* runner; **c. de fond/de demi-fond** long-distance/middle-distance runner; **c. de vitesse** sprinter; *Can Fig* **laisser la chance au c.** to give somebody a chance; **les coureurs** (*oiseaux*) running birds, *Spéc* Ratitae, ratite birds **2 c'est un c./une coureuse de bals/de cafés** he's/she's always at dances/in cafés

NM **c. (de jupons)** womanizer; **c. de dot** fortune-hunter

NF coureuse (*cavaleuse*) manhunter

ADJ (*homme*) womanizing; (*femme*) manhunting; **il est un peu c.** he's a bit of a womanizer; **elle est un peu coureuse** she's a bit of a manhunter

▸▸ **c. automobile** racing driver; *Can Hist* **c. de(s) bois** trapper; **c. cycliste** racing cyclist

courge [kurʒ] **NF** **1** (*plante*) marrow, *Am* squash **2** *Fam* (*imbécile*) wally, prat, *Br* berk

courgette [kurʒɛt] **NF** courgette, *Am* zucchini

COURIR [kurir] (*prp* **courant**; *pp* **couru**; *pr ind* **je cours, il court, n. courons, ils courent**; *pr sub* **je coure**; *p hist* **je courus**; *fu* **je courrai**; *aux* **avoir**)

VI to run **1, 4, 6** ▪ to race **1** ▪ to chase (*courir après*) **1** ▪ to sail **2** ▪ to go round **3**	
VT to hunt **1** ▪ to run **2** ▪ to roam **3** ▪ to go round **3**	
VPR to be run	
V IMPERS to go round	

VI 1 to run; (*de concurrents etc*) to race, to run (in a race); **monter/descendre la colline en courant** to run up/down the hill; **arriver en courant** to come running (up); *Fig* **faire qch en courant** to do sth in a hurry; *Fig* **cet acteur fait c. tout Paris** the whole of Paris is rushing to see this actor; **j'ai couru toute la journée à la recherche d'un cadeau original** I ran about *or* rushed about all day looking for an original present; **faire c. des chevaux** to race horses; **cours acheter du pain** run out *or Br* nip out and get some bread; **l'assassin court toujours** the murderer is still at large; **c. après qn/qch** to run after sb/sth; **c. après les femmes** to run *or* chase after women; **cet homme me court après depuis plus de cinq ans** that man's been (running) after me *or* chasing me for more than five years; **c. après la gloire/les honneurs/l'argent** to chase after glory/honour/money; **c. après son argent** to chase up one's money; **j'ai couru le prévenir** I ran to warn him; **je cours l'appeler** I'll run and get him; **j'y cours** I'll go at once; **c. à sa perte** to be heading for disaster; **c. à la ruine** to be on the road to ruin; **ses doigts couraient sur les touches du piano** his fingers were running up and down the piano keys; **sa plume courait sur le papier** his pen was racing across the paper; **il laissait c. ses pensées** he let his mind wander; **c. sur ses 60 ans** to be pushing 60; **des frissons glacés couraient le long de son échine** icy shivers were running down his spine; **des nuages couraient dans le ciel** clouds were scurrying across the sky; *Fam* **tu peux toujours c.!** you haven't a hope!, you haven't a snowball's chance!; *Arg* **c. sur le haricot** *ou* **sur le système à qn** to get up sb's nose *or* on sb's nerves *or Br* on sb's wick, to bug sb

2 (*d'un navire*) to sail; **c. au large** to stand out to sea; **c. à terre** to stand in for the land; **c. devant le vent** to run *or* scud before the wind; **c. de l'avant** to forge ahead

3 (*se propager*) (*d'un bruit*) to go round; **le bruit court que …** rumour has it that …, they say that …; **faire c. un bruit** to spread a rumour; **le lierre court le long du mur** the ivy crawls *or* runs along the wall; **les racines courent sous terre** the roots are spreading underground

4 (*du sang, du vin*) to flow; (*de l'eau*) to rush, to run

5 le mois qui court the current month; **par les temps qui courent** nowadays; *Fin* **les intérêts qui courent** the accruing interest; **le bail n'a plus qu'un an à c.** the lease has only one more year to run; *Fam* **laisse c.!** forget it!, drop it!

6 *Sport* (*participer à une course*) to run; **il courra chez Renault l'année prochaine** he'll be driving for Renault next year; **elle court dans l'équipe de France** she runs in the French team *or* is a member of the French running team

VT 1 c. le cerf to hunt the stag, to go stag-hunting; *Fig* **c. deux lièvres à la fois** to have two irons in the fire, to have a finger in more than one pie; **c. un risque** to run a risk; **vous courez un grave danger en restant ici** you're putting yourself in serious danger by staying here; **c. sa chance** to try one's luck

2 c. une course to run a race

3 c. le monde/la campagne to roam the world/the countryside; **c. les magasins** to go round the shops; **c. les théâtres** to go to all the theatres; **c. les filles** *ou* **le jupon** *ou Vieilli* **la prétentaine** *ou Can* **la galipote** to chase after women, to womanize; *Arch* **c. la gueuse** to go philandering; **ça ne court pas les rues** you don't see something like that every day

4 *Fam* (*ennuyer*) **tu commences à me c.!** you're starting to bug me *or Br* do my head in *or Am* give me a pain!

5 *Naut* **c. un bord** to make a tack, to tack

VPR se courir *Sport* **la coupe se courra demain** the cup will be competed for tomorrow; **dans l'épreuve qui se courait aujourd'hui à Auteuil** in the race run at Auteuil today

V IMPERS il court des bruits sur lui there are rumours going round about him

courlieu [kurljø] **NM**, **courlis** [kurli] **NM** *Orn* **c. (cendré), grand c.** curlew

couronne [kurɔn] **NF 1** (*de fleurs, de lauriers etc*) wreath, crown; **c. funéraire** (funeral) wreath; **enterrement sans fleurs ni couronnes** simple burial (with neither flowers nor wreaths); **on a décidé de lui donner la c.** it was decided to declare him the winner *or* champion **2** (*de souverain*) crown; (*de noble*) coronet; **la c.** (*souveraineté*) the Crown; **aspirer** *ou* **prétendre à la c.** to lay claim to the throne; **la triple c.** the (pope's) tiara; *Sport* **the Triple Crown 3** (*pièce de monnaie*) crown; (*en reliure*) crown (size) **4** (*anneau*) (*de nuages etc*) ring; (*pain*) ring-shaped loaf; *Bot, Archit* corona; *Anat* (*de dent*) crown; **se faire poser une c.** to have *or* get a tooth crowned; **en c.** in a ring *or* circle **5** *Tech* (*de poulie, roue*) rim

▸▸ **c. dentée** (*d'un différentiel etc*) crown gear, crown wheel, ring gear; **c. d'embrayage** clutch ring; **c. d'épines** (*du Christ*) the crown of thorns; **c. de pont** crown wheel; *Astron* **c. solaire** solar corona

couronné [kurɔne] **ADJ 1** (*de fleurs etc*) wreathed (**de** with); **lauréat c.** prizewinner; **roman c.** prizewinning novel **2** (*souverain*) crowned; **toutes les têtes couronnées de l'Europe y assistaient** all the crowned heads of Europe were present **3** *Vét* **cheval c.** broken-kneed horse

couronnement [kurɔnmɑ̃] **NM 1** (*de souverain*) coronation, crowning **2** (*de jetée*) capping; (*de bâtiment, colonne*) top; (*de mur*) coping; (*de toit*) ridge **3** *Fig* (*réussite*) crowning achievement **4** (*sur le genou d'un cheval*) scar

couronner [kurɔne] **VT 1** (*auteur, élève etc*) to award a prize to; *Hist* (*vainqueur*) to crown

with a wreath; **un diadème couronne sa tête** a diadem crowns his head; **des pics couronnés de neige** snow-capped peaks; **mes efforts furent couronnés de succès** my efforts were crowned with success; *Fam* **et pour c. le tout …** and to cap *or* crown it all … **2** (*sacrer*) to crown; **c. qn roi** to crown sb king **3 c. une dent** to crown a tooth **4 c. un cheval** to let a horse down on its knees

VPR se couronner 1 to crown oneself **2 se c. le genou** to graze *or* skin one's knee

courre [kur] **VI** *Arch* = **courir**, still used in **chasse à c.** hunting

courriel [kurjɛl] **NM** *Can Ordinat* (*abrév* **courrier électronique**) e-mail

courrier [kurje] **NM 1** (*messager*) courier, messenger; **envoyer un document par c.** to send a document by courier

2 (*lettres*) mail, letters, *Br* post; **par retour du c.** by return (of *Br* post *or Am* mail); **dépouiller son c.** to go through *or* open one's mail; **faire son c.** to write one's letters; **c. interne** internal mail; **c. personnalisé** personalized mail; **c. reçu** (*bac*) in-tray; **c. à expédier** (*bac*) out-tray

3 (*bateau*) mail (boat); (*avion*) mail (plane); *Arch* (*voiture*) mail (coach); *Mil, Aviat* courier, liaison aircraft

4 *Journ* (*titre*) ≃ Mail; (*rubrique*) column; **c. des lecteurs** letters to the Editor, readers' letters; **c. du cœur** advice column, problem page, *Fam* agony column

5 *Ordinat* **c. électronique** electronic mail, e-mail; **envoyer un c. électronique à qn** to e-mail sb; **envoyer qch par c. électronique** to send sth by e-mail; **c. escargot** snail mail

courriériste [kurjerist] **N** *Journ* columnist

courroie [kurwa] **NF 1** strap **2** *Tech* belt; **c. de transmission** driving belt; *Aut* **c. de ventilateur** fan belt; *Aut* **c. d'arbre à cames** cam *or* timing belt; *Aut* **c. d'entraînement** *ou* **de commande** drive belt

courroucé [kuruse] **ADJ** *Litt* (*personne*) incensed, angry

courroucer [kuruse] (**je courrouçai(s); n. courrouçons**) *Litt* **VT** (*personne*) to incense, to anger

VPR se courroucer to become incensed

courroux [kuru] **NM** *Litt* ire, wrath, anger

COURS [kur] **NM 1** (*de rivière*) course; (*du soleil, de la lune etc*) course, path; **descendre le c. de la Tamise** to go down the Thames; **le c. des siècles** the course of the centuries; **suivre le c. de ses idées** to follow one's train of thought; *Fig* **donner libre c. à son imagination/sa colère** to give free rein to one's imagination/one's anger; **la maladie suit son c.** the illness is running its course; **affaires en c.** business in hand; **travaux en c.** work in progress *or* in hand; **année en c.** current year; **en c. de route** during the journey, on the way; **en c. de production** in production; **au c. de la conversation** in the course of *or* during the conversation

2 *Naut* **voyage au long c.** ocean voyage; **capitaine au long c.** captain of an ocean-going vessel

3 (*d'argent*) currency; **avoir c.** (*d'une monnaie*) to be legal tender; (*d'une pratique*) to be current, to be in current use; **donner c. à un bruit** to spread a rumour

4 *Fin, Bourse* price, quotation; (*de devises*) rate; **au c. (du jour)** at the current daily price; **quel est le c. du sucre?** what is the price *or* quotation for sugar?; **dans les c.** in the money; **hors des c.** out of the money

5 (*leçon*) *Univ* lecture; *Scol* lesson; (*ensemble des leçons*) course; **faire un c. d'histoire** to give a history lecture/lesson/course; **elle ne veut plus aller en c.** she doesn't want to go to lectures/school any more; **il ne m'a pas rendu mes c.** he hasn't

given me my notes back; **prendre** *ou* **suivre un c.** to take *or* do a course; **donner des c.** to give classes, to teach
6 *(livre)* textbook, course book
7 *(avenue)* walk, avenue
▸▸ *Fin* **c. d'achat** *ou* **d'acheteur** bid price; **c. des actions** share prices; *Fin* **c. en Bourse** official price; *Fin* **c. des changes** exchange rates; *Fin* **c. de clôture** closing price; *Fin* **c. de compensation** clearing price, settlement price; **c. de conduite** driving lesson; **c. par correspondance** correspondence course; *Fin* **c. demandé** bid price; *Fin* **c. du dont** call price; **c. d'eau** waterway; **c. élémentaire** primary classes; **c. intensif** crash *or* intensive course; *Fin* **c. légal** legal tender; *Fin* **c. de liquidation** settlement price; **c. magistral** lecture; *Fin* **c. du marché** market price; *Fin* **c. moyen** intermediate classes; *Fin* **c. offert** bid price; *Fin* **c. officiel** official exchange rate; *Fin* **c. d'ouverture** opening price; **c. particulier** private lesson; *Fin* **c. pivot** central rate; **c. préparatoire** ≃ first year infants' class, *Am* ≃ nursery school; *Fin* **c. réel de change** real exchange rate; **c. du soir** evening class, night class; *Fin* **c. spot** spot price; *(de devises)* spot rate; *Fin* **c. à terme** forward rate; *Fin* **c. vendeur** offer price; *Fin* **c. à vue** spot rate

course [kurs] NF **1** *(action de courir)* running; **au pas de c.** at a run; *Mil* at *or Am* on the double; **prendre sa c.** to set off; **arrêté en pleine c.** stopped in full flight; *(de qn qui parle)* stopped in mid-stream
2 *Sport (épreuve)* race; *(discipline)* racing; *(à pied)* running; **c. de chevaux** horse race; **les courses** the races; **champ** *ou* **terrain de courses** racecourse; **voiture de c.** racing car; *Fam* **être dans la c.** to be with it, to be in the know, to know what's what; **être encore dans la c.** to be still in the running; **la c. à la Maison-Blanche** the race for the White House; *Fam* **ça va encore être la c. pour être à l'heure** it's going to be another mad rush to be on time
3 *(excursion) (à pied)* hike; *(en montagne)* climb; *(de taxi)* journey; **payer (le prix de) la c.** *(en taxi)* to pay the fare
4 *(achat)* **courses** shopping; **faire des courses** to go shopping, to go shopping; **j'ai encore une c./des courses à faire** I still have some shopping to do; **j'ai oublié mes courses au bureau** I've left my shopping at the office
5 *(pour affaires)* errand; **faire une c.** to run an errand; **garçon de courses** errand boy
6 *(de personne, navire, planète etc)* path, way, course; *(de projectile)* course, flight; **je poursuivis ma c.** I went on my way; *Fig Fam* **être à bout de c.** to be worn out *or* exhausted, to be done in
7 *Tech, Aut (d'outil etc)* movement, travel; *(de piston)* stroke; **à bout de c.** at full stroke; **à mi-c.** at half stroke
8 *Hist, Naut* privateering
9 *Suisse (excursion, voyage organisé)* trip, excursion; *(déplacement en transport en commun)* journey; **aller en c. d'école** to go on a school trip; **un billet simple c., une simple c.** a single ticket
▸▸ **la c. aux armements** the arms race; *Tech* **c. ascendante** upward stroke; *TV, Radio* **c. à l'audience** ratings war; *TV, Radio* **c. à l'Audimat®** ratings war; **c. automobile** motor *or* car race; *(discipline)* motor racing; *Tech* **c. de compression** compression *or* bump stroke; *Sp, Fig* **c. contre la montre** race against the clock; **c. cycliste** cycle race; *(discipline)* cycling; *Sport* **c. d'élan** run-up; *Cyclisme* **c. à étapes** race in stages; **c. de fond** long-distance race; *(sport)* long-distance running; **la c. au nucléaire** the nuclear arms race; **c. d'obstacles** obstacle race; *Courses de che-*

vaux steeplechase; *(en athlétisme)* hurdle race; **c. d'orientation** orienteering race; **c. à pied** race; *(discipline)* running; *Aut* **c. du piston** piston displacement *or* stroke; **c. de plat** flat race; **c. de relais** relay race; **c. en sac** sack race; **c. sur piste/route** track/road racing; **c. de taureaux** *(corrida)* bullfight; *(dans les rues)* bull-running; *Tech* **c. à vide** idle stroke; **c. de vitesse** sprint; *(discipline)* sprinting

courser [kurse] VT *Fam* to chase after, to run after

coursier, -ière [kursje, -jɛr] N messenger, courier; *(à motocyclette)* biker
NM *(cheval)* steed

coursive [kursiv] NF *Naut* gangway

COURT [kur] ADJ short; **avoir les jambes courtes**, *Fam* **être c. sur pattes** to have short legs, to be short in the legs; **avoir la vue courte** to be shortsighted; *Fig* to lack forethought; **avoir l'intelligence courte** to be of limited intelligence; **avoir la respiration** *ou* **le souffle court(e)** to be short-winded, to be short of breath; *Naut* **vague courte** choppy sea; **le chemin le plus c.** the quickest *or* shortest way; *Fam* **il m'a donné 50 euros, c'est un peu c.** he gave me 50 euros, it might not be enough; *Bourse* **prendre une position courte** to go short; **c. intervalle** short *or* brief interval; **à c. terme** in the short term; **de courte durée** short-lived; *(contrat)* short-term; **avoir la mémoire courte** to have a short memory, to be forgetful; **pour faire c.** to cut a long story short
ADV **1** short; **cheveux coupés c.** short hair, hair cut short; *Fig* **s'arrêter c.** to stop short *or* suddenly; **demeurer** *ou* **rester c.** to be at a loss; **tourner c.** *(d'une soirée, d'un concert etc)* to come to a sudden end; **couper c. à qch** to put a speedy end to sth
2 **il est un peu bête – non, il est bête tout c.** he's a bit stupid – no, he's stupid, full stop *or Am* period; **son prénom c'est Charles-Édouard, mais on l'appelle Charles tout c.** his first name is Charles-Édouard, but people just call him Charles (for short)
3 **prendre qn de c.** *(en lui laissant peu de temps)* to give sb short notice; *(sans le prévenir)* to catch sb unawares
4 **à c. de** short of; **à c. d'argent** short of money, hard up; **à c. de personnel** short-staffed; **il n'est jamais à c. d'arguments/d'idées** he's never at a loss for *or* short of an argument/ideas

court² NM **c. (de tennis)** (tennis-)court

courtage [kurtaʒ] NM *Com (profession)* brokerage, broking; *(commission)* brokerage, commission; **c. électronique** e-broking, on-line broking; **vendu par c.** sold on commission; **c. officiel** official brokerage

courtaud, -aude [kurto, -od] ADJ **1** *(chien, cheval)* dock-tailed and crop-eared **2** *(personne)* dumpy, squat, stocky
N **1** *(chien)* dock-tailed and crop-eared dog; *(cheval)* dock-tailed and crop-eared horse **2** *(personne)* dumpy *or* squat *or* stocky person

court-bouillon, *pl* **courts-bouillons** NM *Culin* court-bouillon; **faire cuire qch au c.** to cook sth in a court-bouillon

court-circuit, *pl* **courts-circuits** NM *Élec* short circuit

court-circuitage, *pl* **courts-circuitages** [kursirkɥitaʒ] NM *Élec* short-circuiting

court-circuiter [kursirkɥite] VT *Élec (résistance etc)* to short-circuit; *Fig Fam* to bypass, to short-circuit; *Fig Fam* **c. la filière normale** to bypass the usual channels *or* procedures

court-courrier, *pl* **court-courriers** *Aviat*
ADJ short-haul
NM short-haul plane

courtepointe [kurtəpwɛ̃t] NF (quilted) bedspread

courtier, -ière [kurtje, -jɛr] N *Com, Fin* broker, agent; **c. d'assurances** insurance broker; **c. de commerce** general broker; **c. électronique** e-broker, on-line broker; **c. intermédiaire** inter-dealer broker; **c. de marchandises** commercial broker; **c. maritime** ship broker; **c. en matières premières** commodity broker, commodity dealer; **c. en vins** wine broker; **c. d'affrètement** chartering broker; **c. de change** exchange broker; **c. de fret** freight broker; **c. de l'air** air broker; **c. en valeurs mobilières** stockbroker

courtine [kurtin] NF curtain

courtisan [kurtizɑ̃] NM *Hist* courtier; *Péj (flatteur)* sycophant
ADJ **manières courtisanes** obsequious *or* sycophantic manners

courtisane [kurtizan] NF *Hist, Litt* courtesan

courtiser [kurtize] VT **1** *(flatter)* to pay court to, *Péj* to fawn on **2** *(femme)* to court, to woo, to pay court to

court-jus, *pl* **courts-jus** NM *Fam* short, short circuit

courtois [kurtwa] ADJ *(poli)* courteous (**envers, avec, pour** to, towards); **dire non d'un ton très c.** to say no very courteously; *Littér* **la poésie courtoise** courtly poetry

courtoisement [kurtwazmɑ̃] ADV courteously

courtoisie [kurtwazi] NF **1** *(politesse)* courtesy, courteousness (**envers** to, towards) **2** *(acte)* (act of) courtesy

court-vêtu, *pl* **court-vêtu(e)s** ADJ *(femme)* short-skirted, in a short skirt

couru [kury] ADJ **1** *(recherché) (endroit, opéra etc)* popular **2** *Fam* **c'est c. (d'avance)** it's a sure thing *or Br* a (dead) cert; **c'était c.** it was bound to happen **3** *Courses de chevaux* **18 partants, tous courus** 18 starters, all ran

couscous [kuskus] NM *Culin* couscous

couscoussier [kuskusje] NM couscous steamer

couseuse [kuzøz] NF **1** *(couturière)* sewer, seamstress; *(de reliure)* stitcher **2** *(machine)* stitching machine

cousin¹, -ine [kuzɛ̃, -in] N cousin; **c. germain** first cousin; **cousins au second degré** *ou* **issus de germains** second cousins; *Fam* **c. à la mode de Bretagne** distant relation, sort of relation

cousin² NM *(insecte)* (big) mosquito, *Br Fam* daddy-longlegs

cousinage [kuzinaʒ] NM *Vieilli* **1** *(fait d'être cousin)* cousinship, cousinhood **2** *(famille)* **tout le c.** all the cousins

cousiner [kuzine] VI to be on friendly terms (**avec qn** with sb)

coussin [kusɛ̃] NM **1** *(de siège)* cushion; *Belg, Suisse (oreiller)* pillow; *(de collier de cheval etc)* pad(ding); **c. d'air** air cushion **2** *Sport Arg (au base-ball)* base

coussinet [kusinɛ] NM **1** *(petit coussin)* small cushion **2** *Tech etc* bearing; **c. de tête de bielle** big end bearing; *Tech* **c. de palier** bearing bush; *Rail* **c. de rail** rail chair **3** *Archit (de colonne ionique etc)* coussinet, cushion

cousu [kuzy] ADJ sewn; **c. à la main**, *Fam* **c. main** hand-sewn; *Fig Fam* **c'est du c. main** it's first-rate; *Fig* **rester bouche cousue** to keep one's mouth shut, to keep mum; **bouche cousue!** not a word!, mum's the word!; **c. de fil blanc** obvious, blatant, patent; **mensonge c. de fil blanc** blatant *or* obvious *or* patent lie; **être (tout) c. d'or** to be rolling in money

coût [ku] NM cost; **le c. de la vie** the cost of living; **c. de fonctionnement** operating *or* running cost; **le c. d'une erreur** the price *or* consequences of a mistake; **c. d'achat** purchase cost; *(sur bilan)* cost of goods purchased; **c. d'acquisition** acquisition cost;

coûts administratifs administrative costs; **c. assurance fret** cost insurance freight; **coûts cachés** hidden costs; **c. du capital** capital cost; **c. complet unitaire** total unit cost; **coûts constants** fixed costs or expenses; **coûts constatés** actual costs; **coûts cumulés** cumulative costs; **coûts de développement** development costs; **c. différentiel** differential cost; **c. (total) de distribution** (total) distribution costs; **c. de l'élaboration du produit** product development cost; **c. d'entretien** maintenance cost; **coûts d'exploitation** operational costs; **c. fixe (total)** (total) fixed cost; **coûts fonciers** landed costs; **c. de fret** freight cost; **c. et fret** cost and freight; **coûts hors-médias** below-the-line costs; **coûts indirects** indirect costs; **coûts induits** unavoidable costs; **coûts irrécupérables** sunk costs; **loyaux coûts** (frais de contrat) = costs arising from the execution of a deed; **c. marginal** marginal cost; **c. moyen unitaire** average unit cost; **coûts opérationnels** operational costs; **coûts opératoires** operating costs; **c. pour mille contacts** (d'une publicité) cost per thousand; **c. pour mille contacts utiles** (d'une publicité) cost per thousand of target audience; **c. préétabli** standard cost; **coûts prévisionnels** estimated costs; **c. de production** production cost; **c. réel** real cost; **c. réel d'exploitation** actual operating cost; **c. unitaire (de travail)** unit (labour) cost; **c. unitaire moyen pondéré** weighted average unit cost; **c. variable (unitaire)** variable (unit) cost

coûtant [kutã] ADJ **à prix c.** at cost price

couteau, -eaux [kuto] NM **1** knife; **c. de cuisine** kitchen knife; **c. à pain** bread knife; **c. à fromage** cheese knife; **c. à découper** carving knife; **c. éplucheur** ou **à éplucher** (potato-)peeler; **c. de poche** ou **pliant** pocket knife; (plus grand) clasp knife; **c. à cran d'arrêt** flick knife, Am switchblade (knife); **c. à palette** ou **de peintre** palette knife; **c. à pierre** chisel, stonemason's knife; **c. suisse** Swiss army knife; **c. de chasse** hunting or Am bowie knife; **recevoir un coup de c.** to be or get stabbed or knifed; **planter un c. dans le ventre de qn** to stab or knife sb in the stomach; **jouer du c.** to wield or brandish a knife; Fig **ils sont à couteaux tirés** they're at daggers drawn; Fig **mettre le c. sous** ou **sur la gorge à qn** to hold a gun to sb's head, to point a gun at sb's head; Fig **j'ai le c. sous la gorge** I've got a gun pointed at my head VOIR GRAMMAIRE A12

2 Phys (de fléau de balance) knife edge

3 (mollusque) **(manche de) c.** razor shell, Am razor clam

4 Fig **second c.** (en politique, dans la Mafia etc) minion

couteau-scie, pl **couteaux-scies** NM serrated knife

coutelas [kutla] NM **1** (épée) cutlass **2** (de cuisine) large (kitchen) knife

coutelier, -ière [kutəlje, -jɛr] N cutler

coutellerie [kutɛlri] NF **1** (articles) cutlery; **c. chirurgicale** surgical instruments **2** (industrie) cutlery industry; (magasin) cutlery shop; (usine) cutlery works

coûter [kute] VI to cost; **c. cher/peu** to cost a lot/not to cost much, to be expensive/inexpensive; **cela vous coûtera cher** it'll cost you a lot; Fig you'll pay for that; **coûte que coûte** at all costs, whatever the cost, no matter what; Fam **l'argent ne lui coûte guère** money means nothing to him; **rien ne lui coûte** (parce qu'il peut tout faire) nothing is an effort to him, everything comes easy to him; (il est très énergique) he spares no effort

V IMPERS **je l'ai aidé mais il m'en a coûté** I helped him but I had to force myself to; **il**

m'en coûte de le dire it pains me to have to say this

VT to cost; **combien ça coûte?** how much does it cost?, how much is it?; **ça coûte cent euros** it costs a hundred euros, it's a hundred euros; **ça ne coûte rien** it's free, it doesn't cost anything; **cela coûte les yeux de la tête** it costs an arm and a leg, it costs the earth or a fortune; Fam **ça coûtera ce que ça coûtera!** never mind the cost!, hang the expense!; Fam **ça m'a coûté la peau des fesses** it cost me an arm and a leg, I had to pay through the nose for it; **cela lui a coûté la vie** it cost him his life; **le succès lui a coûté sa vie tranquille** success put an end to his quiet or peaceful life; **ça ne coûte rien d'essayer** there's no harm in trying; **ça me coûte de te quitter** it pains me to leave you; **lui dire tout ça m'a beaucoup coûté** telling him all that was very painful for me

coûteusement [kutøzmã] ADV expensively

coûteux, -euse [kutø, -øz] ADJ costly, expensive, dear; **peu c.** inexpensive

coutil [kuti] NM Tex drill, twill; **c. pour matelas** ticking

co-utilisateur, pl **co-utilisateurs** [koytilizatœr] NM co-user

coutre [kutr] NM (de charrue) coulter

coutume [kutym] NF **1** (tradition) custom; **avoir c. de faire qch** to be in the habit of doing sth, to be accustomed to do sth; **plus aimable que de c.** nicer than usual; **comme de c.** as usual; **je me suis levé plus tard que de c.** I got up later than usual; **une fois n'est pas c.** it doesn't matter or it won't hurt for once **2** Jur (recueil) customary

coutumier, -ière [kutymje, -jɛr] ADJ **1** (habituel) customary, usual; Jur **droit c.** customary law **2** souvent Péj **il est c. du fait** it's not the first time he's done that

NM Jur customary

couture [kutyr] NF **1** (activité) sewing, needlework; **faire de la c.** to sew; **elle est dans la c.** she's in dressmaking; **haute c.** haute couture, high fashion; **maison de haute c.** fashion house **2** (de vêtement) seam; **sans c.** seamless; **c. rabattue** run and fell seam; **c. plate** flat seam; **c. anglaise** French seam; **c. apparente** overstitching, topstitching; **faire une c. à grands points** to tack or baste a seam; Fig **battre qn à plate(s) couture(s)** to beat sb hollow; Fig **examiner qn/qch sur** ou **sous toutes les coutures** to examine sb/sth from every angle

ADJ INV **une veste c.** a designer jacket

couturé [kutyre] ADJ (visage) scarred

couturier, -ière [kutyrje, -jɛr] NM **1** (de haute couture) couturier **2** Anat sartorius

NF **couturière 1** (femme) dressmaker; (ouvrière) seamstress, needlewoman **2** Théâtre = rehearsal preceding the final dress rehearsal

ADJ Anat **muscle c.** sartorial muscle, sartorius

couvage [kuvaʒ] NM = **couvaison**

couvain [kuvɛ̃] NM **1** (amas) nest of insect eggs **2** (rayon) brood comb

couvaison [kuvɛzɔ̃] NF **1** (d'oiseau) brooding or sitting time **2** (d'œufs) incubation, hatching

couvée [kuve] NF **1** (d'œufs) clutch **2** (de poussins), Fam (d'enfants) brood

couvent [kuvã] NM (de femmes) convent; (d'hommes) monastery; (école) convent school; **entrer au c.** to go into a convent

couventine [kuvãtin] NF (religieuse) conventual; (pensionnaire) convent schoolgirl

couver [kuve] VT **1** (œufs) (d'une poule etc) to sit on; (d'un incubateur) to hatch (out), to incubate; **c. quelque chose/une grippe** to be

coming down with or Br sickening for something/flu; **c. qn des yeux** (avec affection) to look fondly at sb; **il est couvé par sa mère** he is mollycoddled by his mother **2** (tramer) **c. des projets de vengeance** to meditate schemes of vengeance; **c. un complot** to hatch a plot

VI (d'une poule etc) to brood, to sit; (du feu, de la passion) to smoulder, Am to smolder; (d'une émeute) to be brewing; **la guerre civile couvait depuis longtemps** civil war had been brewing for a long time

couvercle [kuvɛrkl] NM (de boîte, pot, casserole, bocal etc) lid; (qui se visse) cap, top; Tech (de piston) cover; **c. vissé** screw cap or top; Fig **chaque pot a son c.** everyone will meet their ideal partner some day

couvert[1] [kuvɛr] ADJ **1 c. de** covered with or in; **c. de boue/graffitis** covered with or in mud/graffiti **2** (allée, marché etc) covered; **piscine couverte** indoor swimming pool; Fig **parler à mots couverts** to speak in veiled terms; **ciel c.** overcast sky **3** (avec un chapeau) wearing a hat; **rester c.** to keep one's hat on **4** (habillé) covered up; **c. chaudement, bien c.** warmly dressed, well wrapped up **5** Fig (protégé) covered; (emprunt) secured; **je suis c. par mon assurance** I'm covered by my insurance; **avancer c. vers l'ennemi** to advance on the enemy under cover

couvert[2] NM **1** (de cuisine) knife, fork and spoon; **couverts** cutlery, Am flatware; **une ménagère 24 couverts** a canteen of 24 place settings; **c. à poisson** fish knife and fork

2 (à table) place setting; **mettre le c.** to set or Br lay the table; **mettre trois couverts** to set or Br lay the table for three; Fig **vous trouverez toujours votre c. mis** you can come and have a meal with us any time; **le gîte et le c.** board and lodging; Fam **remettre le c.** (faire qch à nouveau) to do it again; (refaire l'amour) to be at it again

3 (abri) cover, shelter; **être à c.** to be under cover; Com (pour un crédit) to be covered; **se mettre à c.** to take cover; **se mettre à c. de la pluie** to shelter from the rain; **au c. de la nuit** under cover of darkness; **mettre ses intérêts à c.** to safeguard one's interests; **sous le c. de l'amitié** under the cover or cloak or pretence of friendship; **il a agi sous le c. de ses chefs** he acted with the authority of his superiors; **avancer à c. vers l'ennemi** to advance on the enemy under cover; **vendre à c.** to hedge, to sell for futures

4 (prix d'une place au restaurant) cover charge

couverte [kuvɛrt] NF Cér glaze

couverture [kuvɛrtyr] NF **1** (en tissu, laine etc) covering, cover; (sur un lit) blanket; **c. chauffante** electric blanket; **c. de voyage** (travelling) rug; Fig **tirer la c. à soi** to take all the credit; **c. d'un livre** cover of a book; (en papier) dust cover or (dust) jacket of a book; **en c.** on the cover; Fig **sous c. d'amitié** under the cover or cloak of friendship; Fig **servir de c. à qn** to cover up for sb; Mil **troupes de c.** covering troops

2 Constr roofing; **c. en tuiles** tiled roof

3 Agr topping; **engrais en c.** surface or top dressing

4 Fin cover; Bourse margin, hedge; **c. courte/longue** short/long hedge

5 Journ **c. médiatique** media coverage or exposure; **c. d'un événement par un journaliste** coverage of an event by a journalist; **assurer la c. d'un événement** to cover an event, to give coverage to an event

6 Tél (d'un téléphone portable) coverage

▸▸ Aviat **c. aérienne** air cover; **c. d'assurance** insurance cover; **c. maladie universelle** = law introduced in France to ensure free health care for people on low incomes who have no social security cover; **c. santé** health cover; **c. sociale** social security cover; **c. à terme** term insurance cover

couveuse [kuvøz] NF **1** *(poule)* brooder, sitter; **c. artificielle** *(pour œufs)* incubator **2** *(pour nouveau-nés)* incubator; **il a dû être mis en c. à sa naissance** he had to be put in an incubator when he was born

couvrant [kuvrã] ADJ **1** *(qui protège)* covering **2** *(peinture etc)* that covers well

couvrante [kuvrãt] NF *Fam* blanket, cover

couvre-chef, *pl* **couvre-chefs** [kuvrəʃɛf] NM *Fam Hum* headdress, headgear, hat

couvre-feu, *pl* **couvre-feux** [kuvrəfø] NM *Mil* curfew

couvre-lit, *pl* **couvre-lits** [kuvrəli] NM bedspread, coverlet, counterpane; **c. piqué** quilt, *Am* comforter

couvre-livre, *pl* **couvre-livres** [kuvrəlivr] NM (dust) jacket, dust cover

couvre-nuque, *pl* **couvre-nuques** [kuvrənyk] NM *(de casquette)* flap *(to protect back of neck from sun)*

couvre-pied(s), *pl* **couvre-pieds** [kuvrəpje] NM quilt

couvre-plat, *pl* **couvre-plats** [kuvrəpla] NM dish cover

couvreur [kuvrœr] NM roofer; **c. en tuiles/ardoises** tiler/slater; **c. en chaume** thatcher

COUVRIR [kuvrir] *(prp* **couvrant;** *pp* **couvert;** *pr ind* **je couvre, il couvre, n. couvrons;** *pr sub* **je couvre;** *impf* **je couvrais;** *p hist* **je couvris;** *fu* **je couvrirai)** VT **1** *(casserole, meuble, livre), Fin (frais etc)* to cover *(de* with); *(emprunt)* to secure; **il faut c. cet enfant** that child needs to be covered up *or* wrapped up; **être couvert de poussière** to be covered with *or* in dust; **mur couvert de lierre** wall covered *or* overgrown with ivy, ivy-clad wall; **c. qn de cadeaux** to shower sb with gifts; **c. qn de son corps** to shield sb with one's body; **c. qn** *(contre les risques, avec une arme)* to cover sb; **lorsqu'il a agi, il était couvert par ses supérieurs** when he acted, it was with the authority of his superiors; **c. la retraite de l'armée** to cover the army's retreat; **c. les risques** to insure against risks; **le bruit de la cascade couvre les voix** the noise of the waterfall drowns the sound of voices; *Cartes* **c. une carte** to cover a card; **c. cinquante kilomètres en une heure** to cover fifty kilometres in an hour; **c. un défaut/une faiblesse** to hide a fault/a weakness; **prière de nous c. par chèque** kindly remit by cheque; **c. une enchère** to make a higher bid **2** *Journ* **c. un événement** to cover an event **3** *Constr* **c. un toit d'ardoises/de tuiles/de chaume** to slate/tile/thatch a roof **4** *Zool (de mâle) (femelle)* to cover **5** *Bourse (position)* to hedge

VPR **se couvrir 1** *(pour sortir)* to wrap up, to put on warm clothes, to dress warmly; *(pour cacher sa nudité)* to cover oneself up; *(mettre son chapeau)* to put on one's hat; **se c. de gloire** to cover oneself with *or* in glory **2** *Sport* to cover *or* protect oneself; *Escrime* to guard one's body; *Fig (se protéger)* to cover oneself; **se c. d'un alibi** to provide oneself with an alibi **3 le temps** *ou* **ça se couvre** it's clouding over, it's becoming overcast **4 les arbres se couvrent de feuilles** the trees are coming into leaf

covalent [kɔvalã] ADJ *Chimie* covalent

cover-girl, *pl* **cover-girls** [kɔvœrgœrl] NF *Fam* cover girl

covoiturage [kɔvwatyraʒ] NM car-pooling *(for commuting to the workplace)*

cow-boy, *pl* **cow-boys** [kobɔj] NM cowboy

coxal, -ale, -aux, -ales [kɔksal, -o] ADJ *Anat* coxal; **os c.** hip bone

---

coxalgie [kɔksalʒi] NF *Méd* coxalgia

coxarthrose [kɔksartroz] NF *Méd* arthritis of the hip

coyote [kɔjɔt] NM coyote, prairie wolf

CP [sepe] NM *(abrév* **cours préparatoire)** = first year of primary school

CPAM [sepeaɛm] NF *Admin (abrév* **caisse primaire d'assurance maladie)** = French government department dealing with health insurance

CPI [sepei] NF *Jur (abrév* **Cour pénale internationale)** ICC

CPM [sepeɛm] NM *Com (abrév* **coût par mille)** cost per thousand

cpp *Ordinat (abrév* **caractères par pouce)** cpi

cps *Ordinat (abrév* **caractères par seconde)** cps

CQFD [sekyɛfde] *(abrév* **ce qu'il fallait démontrer)** QED

crabe [krab] NM **1** *(crustacé)* crab; **marcher en c.** to walk sideways *or* crabwise **2** *(véhicule)* caterpillar-tracked vehicle

crabot [krabo] NM *Aut* dog clutch

crac [krak] INT *(de bois)* crack!, snap!; *(de tissu)* rip!; *Fam* **et c.!** **il est tombé par terre** and bang! there he was on the floor
NM *(de bois)* crack, snap; *(de tissu)* rip

crac-crac NM *Fam* **faire c.** to do it

crachat [kraʃa] NM **1** *(salive)* spit, spittle; *Méd* sputum; **un c.** a gob of spit **2** *Fam (décoration)* gong

craché [kraʃe] ADJ *Fam* **c'est sa mère tout c.,** **c'est le portrait c. de sa mère** he's the spitting image of his mother; **c'est lui tout c.!** that's just like him!, that's him all over!

crachement [kraʃmã] NM spitting; *(de haut-parleur)* crackling; **c. de sang** spitting of blood; **c. d'étincelles** shower of sparks; **c. de flammes** burst of flames

cracher [kraʃe] VI *(de personne)* to spit; *(de stylo)* to splutter; *(de haut-parleur)* to crackle; *Fam* **il ne crache pas sur le champagne** he doesn't turn up his nose at champagne, he never says no to champagne; *Fig Péj* **c. sur qn** to spit at *or* on sb
VT *(salive etc)* to spit (out); *(d'une cheminée, d'un volcan etc)* (fumée etc) to belch out; **c. du sang** to spit blood; **il va finir par c. ses poumons** he's going to end up coughing his lungs up; **c. des injures** to hurl abuse; *Fam* **j'ai dû c. mille euros** I had to fork out *or* cough up a thousand euros

cracheur, -euse [kraʃœr, -øz] N **c. de feu** fire-eater

crachin [kraʃɛ̃] NM *(fine)* drizzle; **il tombe un petit c.** there's a light drizzle

crachiner [kraʃine] V IMPERS to drizzle

crachoir [kraʃwar] NM spittoon, *Am* cuspidor; *Fig Fam* **tenir le c.** to monopolize the conversation; *Fig Fam* **tenir le c. à qn** to listen to sb rambling on and on

crachotement [kraʃɔtmã] NM *(de personne, feu, moteur)* spluttering, sputtering; *Radio* crackling

crachoter [kraʃɔte] VI *(d'une personne, d'un feu, d'un moteur)* to splutter, to sputter; *Radio* to crackle

crack [krak] NM **1** *(poulain)* crack *or* star horse; *Fam (personne)* genius, ace; **c'est un c. en math** he's a genius at maths **2** *(drogue)* crack

cracker [krakœr] NM **1** *Culin* cracker **2** *(pirate informatique)* cracker

cracking [krakiŋ] NM *Pétr (de pétrole brut)* cracking

Cracovie [krakɔvi] NF Cracow

cracra [krakra] ADJ INV *Fam* dirty

cradingue [kradɛ̃g], **crado** [krado], **crade**

[krad] ADJ *Fam* filthy, *Br* grotty; **la cuisine était vraiment crado** the kitchen was really filthy

craie [krɛ] NF chalk; **falaise de c.** chalk cliff; **c. de tailleur** tailor's *or* French chalk; **bâton de c.** stick of chalk; **inscrire qch à la c.** to chalk sth up

craignos [krɛɲos] ADJ INV **1** *(louche)* shady, *Br* dodgy **2** *(laid)* hideous **3** *(mauvais)* crap, lousy, the pits

CRAINDRE [krɛ̃dr] *(prp* **craignant;** *pp* **craint;** *pr ind* **je crains, il craint, n. craignons, ils craignent;** *pr sub* **je craigne;** *impf* **je craignais;** *p hist* **je craignis;** *fu* **je craindrai)** VT **1** *(redouter)* to fear, to be afraid of; **c. la mort** to fear *or* be afraid of death; **ne craignez rien!** *(n'ayez pas peur)* don't be frightened!; *(ne vous inquiétez pas)* don't worry!; **je crains de le laisser entrer** I am afraid to let him in; **je crains qu'il (ne) soit parti** I'm afraid he's left; **il est à c.** *ou* **il y a lieu de c. que ... (ne) ...** it is to be feared that ...; **il n'y a pas à c. qu'il revienne** there is no fear of his coming back; **elle craint de le revoir** she's frightened *or* afraid of seeing him again; **c. pour qn** to fear for sb, to be anxious about sb **2** *(ne pas supporter)* **ces plantes craignent le gel** these plants don't like *or* can't stand the frost; **je crains le froid** I can't stand *or* bear the cold; **craint l'humidité/le froid** keep in a dry/warm place, keep dry/warm
VI *Fam* **j'ai raté mon exam/mon train,** **ça craint** I've failed my exam/missed my train, what a pain; **du rose et du jaune, ça craint** pink and yellow together, that looks terrible; **pour mon voyage, ça craint** things don't look too good for my trip; **ça craint dans ce pays-là** things are in a real mess over there; **elle craint** she's really awful; **il commence à c.,** **ton copain** that mate of yours is getting beyond a joke

crainte [krɛ̃t] NF fear; **de c. de tomber** for fear of falling; **de c. de se faire mal** for fear of hurting oneself, lest one should hurt oneself; **de c. que ... (ne)** + *sub* lest; **il a parlé plus bas de c. qu'on (ne) l'entende** he spoke more quietly lest he (should) be overheard *or* for fear of being overheard; **il n'a rien dit par c. de ses parents** he said nothing for fear of his parents' reaction; **sans c.** *(employé comme adjectif)* fearless; *(employé comme adverbe)* fearlessly; **soyez sans c., n'ayez c.** have no fear; **la c. du gendarme** the fear of being caught; **un sujet de c.** a matter for concern, a worrying business; **avoir des craintes au sujet de qch** to have some fears *or* worries about sth; **je n'ai aucune c. quant à l'issue de ce projet** I've no fears *or* worries about how this project will turn out

craintif, -ive [krɛ̃tif, -iv] ADJ timid, timorous

craintivement [krɛ̃tivmã] ADV timidly, timorously

cramé [krame] NM *Fam* **ça sent le c.** I can smell burning

cramer [krame] *Fam* VI to burn; **tout a cramé** everything went up in flames *or* in smoke
VT to burn
VPR **se cramer** to burn oneself; **se c. les doigts** to burn one's fingers

cramoisi [kramwazi] ADJ crimson; **devenir c.** *(de honte, de timidité etc)* to flush crimson; *(de colère)* to go purple in the face

crampe [krɑ̃p] NF *Méd* cramp; **avoir une c.** to have cramp; **j'ai une c. au pied** I've got (a) cramp in my foot; **c. de l'écrivain** writer's cramp; **crampes d'estomac** stomach cramps; *Vulg* **tirer sa c.** to get one's leg over

crampon [krɑ̃põ] NM **1** *Constr etc* cramp (iron), staple, clamp, holdfast **2 c. (à glace)** crampon **3** *(pour semelle de botte)* stud; *(de chaussure de course)* spike; *(de fer à cheval)* calk, cog **4** *Bot* tendril **5** *Fam (personne)* **quel c.!** what a leech!

ADJ INV *Fam (personne)* clinging

cramponnement [krɑ̃pɔnmɑ̃] **NM** clinging

cramponner [krɑ̃pɔne] **VT 1** *Constr (pierres etc)* to clamp, to cramp together **2** *Fam* **c. qn** *(s'accrocher à)* to cling to sb; *(importuner)* to pester sb

VPR se cramponner to hold on, to hang on; **cramponne-toi!** hold on!; **se c. à qn/qch** to hold on to *or* to hang on to *or* to cling (on) to sb/sth; *Fig* **se c. à qn** to cling to sb; *Fig* **se c. à la vie/au pouvoir** to cling to *or* hang on to life/power; *Fig* **se c. à un espoir** to clutch at a hope; *Fig* **il se cramponne à cette idée** he clings to this idea

cran [krɑ̃] **NM 1** *(entaille)* notch; *(de roue à rochet)* tooth; *(de ceinture, lanière etc)* hole; *Fig (degré)* rung, step; **c. de l'armé** full cock notch; **c. de sûreté** *ou* **d'arrêt** safety catch; **le c. de sûreté est mis** the safety catch is on; **lâcher une courroie d'un c.** to let a strap out a hole; **resserrer sa ceinture d'un c.** to take one's belt in a notch; **avancer d'un c. dans la hiérarchie** to go up a rung *or* step in the hierarchy; *Fam* **être à c.** to be wound up; *Fam* **avoir du c.** to have guts **2** *(coiffure)* wave; **se faire faire des crans** to have one's hair crimped

crâne [krɑn] **NM** *Anat* skull, *Spéc* cranium; **fracture du c.** fracture of the skull; **défoncer le c. à qn** to smash sb's skull *or* head in, to bash sb's brains in; *Fam* **mets-toi ça dans le c.** get that into your head *or* thick skull

ADJ *Vieilli (air)* gallant

crânement [krɑnmɑ̃] **ADV** *Vieilli* gallantly, bravely

crâner [krɑne] **VI** *Fam* to swagger, to show off

crâneur, -euse [krɑnœr, -øz] *Fam* **N** show-off

ADJ swaggering, showy

crânien, -ienne [krɑnjɛ̃, -jɛn] **ADJ** *Anat* cranial; **la boîte crânienne** the cranium, the skull

craniologie [kranjɔlɔʒi] **NF** craniology

cranter [krɑ̃te] **VT 1** *(roue etc)* to notch **2** *(cheveux)* to crimp

crapahuter [krapayte] **VI** *Fam* **1** *(d'un enfant etc)* to crawl about (all over the place) **2** *Mil (sur un terrain difficile)* to trudge along

crapaud [krapo] **NM 1** *Zool* toad; *Fam (gamin)* kid, child; *Fam* **c'est un vilain c.** he's an ugly little squirt *or* toad **2 c. de mer** angler(-fish) **3** *(défaut)* flaw, blemish **4** *(fauteuil)* tub chair **5** *(piano)* baby grand (piano)

ADJ 1 fauteuil c. tub chair **2 piano c.** baby grand (piano)

crapaudine [krapodin] **NF 1** *Minér* toadstone **2** *Culin* **poulet à la c.** spatchcock (chicken) **3** *Tech (de tuyau d'arrivée d'eau)* grating, strainer **4** *Tech* pivot bearing *or* box *or* hole; *(de gond etc)* socket, gudgeon

crapette [krapɛt] **NF** *Cartes* Russian bank

crapoteux, -euse [krapɔtø, -øz] **ADJ** *Fam (personne)* grubby, dirty; *(endroit)* scuzzy, grimy

crapule [krapyl] **NF** *Fam (canaille)* scoundrel, villain

crapuleusement [krapyløzmɑ̃] **ADV** crookedly, dishonestly

crapuleux, -euse [krapylø, -øz] **ADJ 1** sordid **2** *Arch (débauché)* debauched, dissolute

> Il faut noter que l'adjectif anglais **crapulous** est un faux ami. Il signifie **intempérant**.

craquage [krakaʒ] **NM** *Tech (de pétrole brut)* cracking

craquant [krakɑ̃] **ADJ** *Fam (personne)* irresistible

craque [krak] **NF** *Fam (mensonge)* lie, fib, *Br* porky (pie)

craquelé [krakle] **ADJ** cracked; *Cér* crackled

NM *Cér (faïence, porcelaine, verre)* crackle

craqueler [krakle] (**je craquelle, n. craquelons; je craquellerai**) **VT** to crack; *Cér* to crackle

VPR se craqueler to crack, to become cracked

craquelure [kraklyr] **NF** crack; *Cér* crackle; *Beaux-Arts* craquelure

craquement [krakmɑ̃] **NM** *(de bois qui casse)* crack, snap; *(d'escalier, de plancher etc)* creak(ing); *(de feuilles mortes)* crackling, crackle; *(de neige)* crunching; *(de chaussures)* squeak(ing), creak(ing); **des craquements effrayants** terrifying cracking/creaking noises

craquer [krake] **VI 1** *(faire un bruit sec)* *(de bois qui casse)* to crack, to snap; *(d'escalier, de plancher etc)* to creak; *(de feuilles mortes)* to crackle; *(de neige dure)* to crunch; *(de chaussures)* to squeak, to creak; **faire c. ses doigts** to crack one's fingers

2 *(se déchirer)* to rip, to tear; **les coutures ont craqué** the seams have split; **plein à c.** full to bursting

3 *Fam (échouer)* *(d'une amitié, d'une entente)* to be breaking down

4 *(perdre le contrôle de soi)* to crack up; **elle craque nerveusement** she's cracking up; **j'étais sur le point de c.** I was at breaking point, I was about to crack up; **au bout d'une heure, j'ai craqué et je** ... after an hour I just couldn't take any more and I ...

5 *Fam (être attiré)* **je craque** I can't resist it/them/*etc*; **elle craque toujours devant un éclair en chocolat** she can never say no to *or* resist a chocolate éclair; **ce mec me fait c.** that guy drives me wild; **j'ai fini par c.** I finally cracked *or* gave in *or* succumbed

6 *Can Fam* **riche à c.** really rich; **fou à c.** totally mad

VT 1 c. une allumette to strike a match **2** *Tech (pétrole)* to crack **3** *(déchirer)* to split, to rip

craqueter [krakte] **VI** (**il craquette; il craquettera**) to crackle; *(de grillon)* to chirp; *(de cigogne)* to call, to cry

crash [kraʃ] **NM** *Aviat* crash

crasher (se) [səkraʃe] **VPR** *Fam* **1** *Aviat (s'écraser)* to crash; *(atterrir accidentellement)* to crash-land **2** *(conducteur, véhicule)* to crash; **il s'est crashé contre un arbre** he smashed *or* crashed into a tree; **il s'est crashé en voiture** he crashed his car

crasse [kras] **ADJ** *(ignorance etc)* crass, gross; **être d'une humeur c.** to be in a foul mood

NF 1 *(saleté)* filth, dirt; **vivre dans la c.** to live in squalor **2** *Métal* dross, scum, slag; *(résidus)* scale **3** *Fam (mauvais tour)* dirty trick; **faire une c. à qn** to play a dirty trick on sb, *Br* to do the dirty on sb **4** *Can (personne malhonnête)* crook

crasseux, -euse [krasø, -øz] **ADJ** *(mains, draps etc)* filthy, dirty; *(logement etc)* squalid

crassier [krasje] **NM** slag heap, *Scot* bing

cratère [kratɛr] **NM 1** *Géog (de volcan)* crater **2** *Antiq* crater, (wine) bowl

cravache [kravaʃ] **NF** *(riding)* crop; *Fig* **à la c.** brutally

cravacher [kravaʃe] **VT** *(cheval)* to use the crop on; *(personne)* to horsewhip

VI *Fam (pour finir qch)* to work like mad, *Br* to slog away

cravate [kravat] **NF 1** *(d'homme)* tie, *Am* necktie; **c. blanche** *(sur carton d'invitation)* white tie, tails; **c. noire** *(sur carton d'invitation)* black tie, dinner jacket, *Am* tuxedo; **épingle de c.** tiepin; *Mil* **c. d'un drapeau** bow and tassels of a colour stave; *Fig Fam* **c.**

de chanvre hangman's rope; *Fam* **s'en jeter un derrière la c.** to knock back a drink **2** *(décoration)* insignia, ribbon **3** *(prise de lutte)* headlock **4** *Naut* sling

cravater [kravate] **VT 1** *(mettre une cravate à)* to put a tie on **2** *(attraper par le cou)* to grab round *or* by the neck; *Sport* to get in a headlock **3** *Fam (duper)* to take in, to take for a ride; *(arrêter)* to nick; **je me suis fait c.** *(dupé)* I got taken in *or* taken for a ride; *(arrêté)* I got nicked

VPR se cravater to put a *or* one's tie on

crawl [krol] **NM** *Natation* crawl; **nager le c., faire du c.** to do the crawl

crawler [krole] **VI** *Natation* to do the crawl; **dos crawlé** backstroke, back crawl

crayeux, -euse [krɛjø, -øz] **ADJ** chalky; **d'un blanc c.** chalky-white; **teint c.** chalky *or* chalk-white complexion

crayon [krɛjɔ̃] **NM 1** *(pour écrire)* pencil; **c. de plombagine** *ou* **à mine de plomb** lead pencil; **c. gras** soft lead pencil; *Spéc, TV etc* Chinagraph®; **c. de couleur** coloured pencil, crayon; **c. feutre** felt(-tip) pen; **c. à bille** ballpoint pen; **c. lithographique** litho crayon, *Am* grease pencil; *Ordinat* **c. lumineux** *ou* **optique** light pen; **écrit au c.** written in pencil; **dessin au c.** pencil drawing **2** *(dessin)* pencil drawing *or* sketch **3** *(bâton)* stick; *Méd* pencil; **c. à lèvres** lip pencil; **c. noir** eye pencil, eyeliner; **c. à sourcils** eyebrow pencil

crayonnage [krɛjɔnaʒ] **NM 1** *(action) (gribouillage)* doodling; *(dessin)* sketching; *(traits)* pencil marks **2** *(dessin)* pencil sketch

crayonner [krɛjɔne] **VT 1** *(dessiner)* to draw *or* sketch in pencil, to make a pencil drawing *or* sketch of; *(gribouiller)* to doodle; *Typ* **crayonné** rough **2** *(noter)* to note down *or* write down (in pencil)

CRDS [seɛrdeɛs] **NF** *(abrév* **contribution au remboursement de la dette sociale)** = income-based tax deducted at source as a contribution to paying off the French social security budget deficit

créance [kreɑ̃s] **NF 1** *(foi)* credence, belief; **hors de c.** unbelievable, incredible; **trouver c.** to be believed; **ajouter c. à qch** to give credence to sth

2 *(dette)* debt; *Jur* claim; **mauvaises créances** bad debts; **c. chirographaire** unsecured debt; **c. contestée** contested debt; **c. douteuse** doubtful debt, possible bad debt; **c. exigible** debt due; **c. garantie** secured debt; **c. hypothécaire** debt secured by a mortgage; **c. impayée** unpaid debt *or* unrecovered debt; **c. litigieuse** contested debt; **principale** principal debt; **c. privilégiée** preferred debt; **c. recouvrable** recoverable debt; **créances receivables** receivable, recoverable; **créances clients** accounts receivable, trade debtors; **créances gelées** frozen credits

3 *Arch (confiance)* trust; **lettres de c.** credentials

créancier, -ière [kreɑ̃sje, -jɛr] **N, ADJ** creditor; **c. d'exploitation** trade creditor; **c. hypothécaire** mortgagee; **c. nanti** secured creditor; **c. ordinaire** ordinary *or* unsecured creditor; **c. privilégié** preferred creditor

créateur, -trice [kreatœr, -tris] **ADJ** *(pouvoir, génie)* creative; **une impulsion créatrice** a creative impulse *or* urge; **industrie créatrice d'emplois** job-creating industry

N creator; *Com* creator, designer; *Rel* **le C.** the Creator; **le c. exclusif d'un modèle** the sole *or* exclusive creator *or* designer of a model; **c. d'entreprise(s)** entrepreneur

créatif, -ive [kreatif, -iv] **ADJ** creative

N designer

création [kreasjɔ̃] **NF 1** *(fait de créer)* creation, creating; *(d'institution etc)* creation, founding, establishment; *Com (d'un nouveau produit)* creation, designing; *Théâtre (d'une pièce)* first production; *(d'un rôle)* creation; **les merveilles de la c.** the wonders of creation *or* of the universe; **c. d'emplois** job creation; **il y a eu 3 000 créations d'emplois en mai** 3,000 new jobs were created in May; **la c. (du monde)** the creation (of the world); **je connais cette société depuis sa c.** I have known this firm since it was founded; *Ordinat* **c. de pages Web** web authoring; **c. télévisuelle** television production

2 *(chose créée)* creation; *Com* new product; **une des plus belles créations humaines** one of the finest works of man; **sa robe était une c. de chez Jacques Fath** her dress was a creation by Jacques Fath; **la dernière c. d'un constructeur automobile** a car manufacturer's latest model; **la dernière c. d'un metteur en scène** a director's latest production

créativité [kreativite] NF creativity

créature [kreatyr] NF **1** *(être vivant)* creature; **c. humaine** human being **2** *(personne)* creature; *Fam* **une belle c.** a beautiful creature; **une pauvre c.** a poor *or* wretched creature **3** *Péj (protégé)* creature; *(prostituée)* trollop

crécelle [kresɛl] NF rattle; **quelle c.!** *(bavard)* what a chatterbox!; **voix de c.** rasping voice

crèche [krɛʃ] NF **1** *(garderie)* crèche, day nursery; **mettre ses enfants à la c.** to put one's children in the crèche **2** *Arg (chambre)* pad **3** *(de Noël)* crib, crèche; **c. vivante** ≃ nativity play

Crèche
State-subsidized care for children under three years of age of working families is well established in France, although this is subject to the availability of places.

crécher [kreʃe] VI *Arg (habiter)* to live; *(passer la nuit)* to crash

crédence [kredɑ̃s] NF credence (table), credenza

crédibilité [kredibilite] NF credibility

crédible [kredibl] ADJ credible

crédit [kredi] NM **1** *Fin, Com* credit; **lettre de c.** letter of credit; **carte de c.** credit card; **vendre/acheter qch à c.** to sell/buy sth on credit *or Fam* on tick; **faire c. à qn** to give sb credit; *Fig* to trust sb; **ouvrir un c. chez qn** to open a credit account with sb; **'la maison ne fait pas c.'** 'we do not give credit', 'no credit given', 'please do not ask for credit(, as a refusal often offends)'; **établissement** *ou* **société de c.** loan society, credit establishment; *Journ* **c. photographique** photographer's credit

2 *Litt (influence)* credit, influence, repute; **être en c. auprès de qn** to have credit *or* influence with sb; **avoir du c. auprès de qn** to enjoy sb's confidence *or* trust; **il faut dire à son c. que …** it must be said to his credit that …

3 *(du grand livre, bilan)* credit(or) side; **porter une somme au c. de qn** to credit sb with a sum, to place *or* carry a sum to sb's credit

4 *(subvention)* **crédits** funds, allocation; **voter des crédits** to vote supplies

5 *Can Scol* credit

▸▸ *Fin* **c. back to back** back to back credit; **c. bancaire** bank credit *or* loan; **c. en blanc** blank *or* open credit; **c. bloqué** frozen credit; **c. de campagne** stock financing loan; **c. commercial** trade credit; **c. à la consommation** *ou* **au consommateur** consumer credit; **c. (à) court terme** short-term credit; *Bourse* **c. croisé** cross-currency swap; **c. à découvert** open credit; **crédits de développement**

development loans; **c. documentaire** documentary credit, letter of credit; **c. documentaire révocable/irrévocable/renouvelable** revocable/irrevocable/revolving letter of credit; **c. dos à dos** back to back credit; **c. de droits** delay in payment of indirect taxes; **c. épargne-logement** home purchase loan; **crédits d'équipements** equipment financing; **c. à l'exportation** export credit; **c. foncier** ≃ (government-controlled) building society; **c. gratuit** interest-free credit; **c. immobilier** home loan, mortgage; **c. d'impôt** *(abattement)* tax rebate; *(report)* tax credit; **c. irrévocable** irrevocable letter of credit; **c. (à) long terme** long-term credit; **c. (à) moyen terme** medium-term credit; **c. permanent** revolving credit; **c. personnalisé** individual personal credit arrangement; **c. 'red clause'** red clause credit; **c. renouvelable** revolving *or* revolver credit; **c. à reporter** credit to be carried forward; **c. revolving** revolving credit; **c. de sécurité** swing line; **c. à taux réduit** low-interest loan; **c. à terme** term loan; **c. transférable** transferable letter of credit; **crédits de trésorerie** (short term) credit facilities; **c. de TVA** VAT credit; **c. utilisable à vue** sight letter of credit

crédit-acheteur, *pl* **crédits-acheteurs** NM buyer credit

crédit-bail NM leasing

créditer [kredite] VT **1** *Fin* **c. qn d'une somme** to credit sb *or* sb's account with a sum, to place *or* carry a sum to sb's credit; **c. un compte** to credit an account **2** *Fig* **c. qn de qch** to give sb credit for sth, to credit sb with sth

créditeur, -trice [kreditœr, -tris] N customer in credit

ADJ *(solde etc)* credit; *(qui concerne les créditeurs)* creditor; **être c.** to be in credit; **compte c.** account in credit; **solde c.** credit balance; **nation créditrice** creditor nation

crédit-fournisseur, *pl* **crédits-fournisseurs** NM supplier credit

crédit-relais, *pl* **crédits-relais** NM bridging loan

credo [kredo] NM INV credo, creed; *Rel* **le C.** the (Apostles') Creed; **c. politique** political credo *or* creed

Credoc [kredɔk] NM *(abrév* **crédit documentaire)** = large state-funded market research company in Paris

crédule [kredyl] ADJ credulous

crédulité [kredylite] NF credulity, credulousness

créer [kree] VT to create; **c. des emplois** to create jobs; **c. une chaire** to found *or* establish a chair; **c. une armée** to form an army; **c. l'événement** to be big news; **c. qch de toutes pièces** to create sth out of nothing; **c. une entreprise** to set up a business; **agence récemment créée** recently established agency; **c. une hypothèque** to create a mortgage; **le pouvoir de c.** the power of creation; **cette attitude va lui c. des problèmes** that attitude is going to cause him problems *or* create problems for him; **c. des difficultés à qn** to create *or* cause difficulties for sb; *Théâtre* **c. un rôle** to create a part; **c. un spectacle/une pièce** to produce a show/a play (for the first time); **chemises créées par Dumaine** shirts created *or* designed *or* styled by Dumaine

VPR **se créer 1** *(se former)* to be created **2** *(se faire)* **se c. une clientèle** to build up a clientele; **se c. des problèmes** to create problems for oneself

crémaillère [kremajɛr] NF **1** *(dans la cheminée)* trammel (hook); **pendre la c.** to have a housewarming (party) **2** *Tech etc* (toothed) rack; *Rail* rack rail; **c. (et pignon)** rack and

pinion; **engrenage à c.** rack(-and-pinion) gearing; **chemin de fer à c.** rack *or* cog railway; *Aut* **c. de direction** steering rack

crémant [kremɑ̃] ADJ, NM **(champagne) c.** slightly sparkling champagne

crémation [kremasjɔ̃] NF cremation

crématoire [krematwar] ADJ crematory; **four c.** cremator, *Am* cinerator
NM cremator, *Am* cinerator

crématorium [krematɔrjɔm] NM crematorium

crème [krɛm] NF **1** *Culin* cream; *(sur le lait bouilli)* skin; **fromage à la c.** cream cheese; **fraises à la c.** strawberries and cream; **café c.** white coffee, coffee with milk; *Fig* **c'est la c. des hommes** he's the best of men, he's one of the best; *Fig Fam* **la c.** *(personnes)* the cream **2** **c. pour chaussures** shoe cream *or* polish **3** *(liqueur)* **c. de menthe** crème de menthe, peppermint liqueur; **c. de cassis** (crème de) cassis, blackcurrant liqueur
NM *Fam* **un grand c.** a large (cup of) white coffee

ADJ INV cream(-coloured), *Am* cream(-colored)

▸▸ **c. anglaise** (egg) custard; **c. anti-rides** anti-wrinkle cream; **c. de beauté** skin cream; **c. au beurre** butter cream; **c. brûlée** crème brûlée; **c. (au) caramel** caramel custard, crème caramel; **c. Chantilly** whipped cream; **c. écran** barrier cream; **c. fouettée** whipped cream; **c. fraîche** crème fraîche; **c. fraîche épaisse** double cream; **c. glacée,** *Can* **c. à la glace** ice cream; **c. hydratante** moisturizing cream; **c. de marrons** chestnut purée; **c. pâtissière** confectioner's custard; **c. à raser** shaving cream; **c. renversée** crème caramel *(turned out of its mould)*; *Chimie* **c. de tartre** cream of tartar

crémer[1] [kreme] VT **(je crème, n. crémons; je crémerai)** *(incinérer)* to cremate

crémer[2] VI *(du lait)* to cream

crémerie [krɛmri] NF *(magasin)* dairy, creamery; *Fam* **changer de c.** to go elsewhere

crémeux, -euse [kremø, -øz] ADJ creamy

crémier, -ière [kremje, -jɛr] N dairyman, *f* dairywoman

Crémone [kremɔn] NF Cremona

crémone [kremɔn] NF **1** *(de porte, de fenêtre)* espagnolette **2** *Can (cache-nez)* scarf

crénage [krenaʒ] NM *Typ* kerning

créneau, -eaux [kreno] NM **1** *(de rempart)* crenel, crenelle; *(meurtrière)* loophole, slit; **à créneaux** crenellated; *Fig* **monter au c.** to take a stand **2** *Aut* gap, space; **faire un c.** to reverse into a (parking) space; **stationnement en c.** parallel parking; **elle a raté son c.** she's parked badly *or* made a mess of parking **3** *Com (market)* niche, gap in the market, opening; **c. porteur** potentially lucrative market; **exploiter un nouveau c.** to fill a new gap *or* niche in the market **4** *Radio, TV* slot; **c. horaire** time slot; **c. publicitaire** advertising slot

crénelage [krenlaʒ] NM **1** *(de rempart)* crenellation **2** *(de pièce de monnaie)* milling **3** *Ordinat (en PAO)* aliasing

crénelé [krenle] ADJ **1** *(rempart)* crenellated; *(muni de meurtrières)* loopholed **2** *Bot (feuille etc)* crenate(d) **3** *(pièce de monnaie)* milled; *(écrou)* castellated

créneler [krenle] VT **(je crénelle, n. crénelons; je crénellerai) 1** *(mur etc) (munir de créneaux)* to crenellate; *(munir de meurtrières)* to cut loopholes in, to loophole **2** *(roue etc)* to notch, to tooth; *(pièce de monnaie)* to mill

crénelure [krenlyr] NF crenellation; *Bot (de feuille)* crenelling

créner [krene] VT *Typ* to kern

crénom [krenɔ̃] INT **c. d'un pétard!, c. de nom!** for Pete's sake!

créole [kreɔl] ADJ Creole; **boucles d'oreille créoles** hoop earrings

NM *Ling* Creole

N **C.** Creole

NFPL **créoles** *(boucles d'oreille)* hoop earrings

créosote [kreɔzɔt] NF creosote

créosoter [kreɔzɔte] VT to creosote

crêpage [krepaʒ] NM *(de cheveux)* back-combing; *Fam* **c. de chignon** dust-up, bust-up

crêpe [krep] NF *Culin* pancake; **pâte à c.** pancake batter; **faire sauter des crêpes** to toss pancakes

NM **1** *Tex* crêpe, crape; *(pour le deuil)* black mourning crêpe; **c. de Chine** crêpe de Chine; **c. satin** satin crêpe; **voile de c.** mourning veil **2** *(caoutchouc)* crêpe (rubber); **semelles (de) c.** crêpe(-rubber) soles

crêpelé [kreple] ADJ *(cheveux)* frizzy

crêper [krepe] VT *(cheveux)* to backcomb; *(tissu)* to crimp

VPR **se crêper** *Fig Fam* **se c. (le chignon)** to have a dust-up *or* bust-up

crêperie [krepri] NF creperie, pancake house

crépi [krepi] ADJ, NM *Constr* roughcast

crépier, -ière [krepje, -jɛr] N *(personne)* pancake seller *or* maker

NF **crêpière** pancake griddle

crépine [krepin] NF **1** *(de meubles capitonnés)* fringe **2** *Culin* caul **3** *(de pompe etc)* strainer, filter

crépir [krepir] VT *Constr (mur etc)* to roughcast

crépissage [krepisaʒ] NM *Constr* roughcasting

crépitation [krepitasjɔ̃] NF **1** *(du feu, d'étincelles etc)* crackling **2** *Méd* **c. osseuse** crepitation, crepitus; **c. pulmonaire** crepitations, crepitant rale

crépitement [krepitmɑ̃] NM *(de feu)* crackling; *(de la pluie)* pattering; *(de flamme de bougie)* sputtering, spluttering

crépiter [krepite] VI *(du feu)* to crackle; *(de la pluie)* to patter; *(d'une flamme de bougie, beurre fondu etc)* to sputter, to splutter; **les applaudissements crépitèrent** there was a ripple of applause

crépon [krepɔ̃] NM *Tex* crepon; **papier c.** crêpe paper

crépu [krepy] ADJ *(cheveux)* frizzy, fuzzy, woolly

crépusculaire [krepyskylɛr] ADJ twilight; *Zool* crepuscular; **lumière c.** twilight, half light; **papillon c.** moth; **oiseau c.** night-bird

crépuscule [krepyskyl] NM twilight, dusk; *Fig* twilight; *Fig* **quand on arrive au c. de la vie** when one is in one's twilight years *or* in the twilight of one's life

crescendo [kreʃɛndo] *Mus*ADV crescendo; **aller c.** to grow louder and louder; *Fig (de besoin, plaintes etc)* to get more and more urgent

NM INV crescendo

cresson [kresɔ̃] NM *Bot* cress; **c. de fontaine** watercress

cressonnière [kresɔnjɛr] NF watercress bed *or* pond

Crésus [krezys] NM *Antiq* Croesus; **il est riche comme C.** he's fabulously wealthy

crésyl [krezil] NM *Chimie* cresol, methyl phenol

crétacé [kretase] ADJ, NM *Géol* Cretaceous

Crète [krɛt] NF Crete

crête [krɛt] NF **1** *(d'oiseau)* crest; *(de coq)* comb; *(de crapaud)* horn; **c. de coq** cockscomb; *Fam* **baisser la c.** to look crestfallen **2** *(de montagne)* crest, ridge; *(de vague)* crest;

Constr (de toit) crest, ridge; *(de parapet, mur)* crest, top; *Anat (d'os)* crest; *(de casque)* crest; *Géog* **(ligne de) c.** watershed **3** *Élec* peak

crête-de-coq, *pl* **crêtes-de-coq** NF *Bot* cockscomb

crétin, -ine [kretɛ̃, -in] N *Méd* cretin; *Fam (idiot etc)* cretin, moron, idiot

ADJ *Fam* cretinous, moronic, idiotic; **vous êtes encore plus c. que lui** you're even more of a cretin *or* a moron *or* an idiot than he is

crétinerie [kretinri] NF *(caractère)* imbecility, stupidity, idiocy; **des crétineries** stupid *or* idiotic things

crétinisant [kretinizɑ̃] ADJ mind-numbing

crétiniser [kretinize] VT to turn into a moron *or* an idiot

crétinisme [kretinism] NM *Fam* stupidity, idiocy; *Méd* cretinism

crétois, -oise [kretwa, -waz] ADJ Cretan

N **C.** Cretan

cretonne [krətɔn] NF *Tex* cretonne

cretons [krətɔ̃] NMPL *Can* potted meat *(made from pork)*

creusage [krøzaʒ], **creusement** [krøzmɑ̃] NM *(d'un trou etc)* digging; *(d'un puits)* sinking, digging; *(d'un canal)* cutting, digging

creuser [krøze] VT **1** *(trou, tranchée etc)* to dig; *(puits)* to sink, to dig; *(canal)* to cut, to dig; *Fig (un problème, une question etc)* to examine (closely), to look into (closely); **c. un chemin sous terre** to burrow one's way underground; *Fig* **c. un écart** to widen a gap; *Fig* **c. sa fosse** *ou* **sa tombe** to dig one's own grave; *Fig* **cela a creusé un abîme entre eux** it has created a gulf between them **2** *(faire un trou dans)* to hollow (out); *Agr (sillon)* to plough; **c. la terre** to dig; **front creusé de rides** brow furrowed with wrinkles, deeply lined forehead; **la maladie lui avait creusé les joues** illness had hollowed his cheeks; *Fig* **travail qui creuse l'estomac** work that gives you an appetite

VI to dig; **c. dans le sable** to dig *or* burrow in the sand; **c. très profond** to dig down deep; *Fig* **plus on creuse, plus c'est intéressant** the more (deeply) you go into it, the deeper you go, the more interesting it gets

VPR **se creuser 1** *(de visage)* to grow hollow; **ses joues se creusent** his cheeks are falling in; **l'écart entre eux s'est creusé** the gap between them has widened *or* has got wider **2** *Fig* **se c. (la tête)** to rack *or* cudgel one's brains (**pour faire** to do)

creuset [krøzɛ] NM **1** *Chimie, Ind* crucible, melting pot; *Fig* melting pot **2** *Métal (de haut-fourneau)* crucible **3** *Litt (épreuve de purification)* crucible; **au c. du malheur/de la souffrance** in the crucible of misfortune/suffering

creux, -euse [krø, -øz] ADJ *(arbre, mur, dent)* hollow; *(voix)* hollow, deep; *(chemin)* sunken; **assiette creuse** soup plate; **yeux c.** sunken *or* deep-set eyes; **joues creuses** gaunt *or* hollow cheeks; *Fig* **avoir l'estomac** *ou* **le ventre c.** to be ravenous; **travailler le ventre c.** to work on an empty stomach; *Fig* **avoir la tête creuse** to be empty-headed; *Fig Fam* **avoir le nez c.** to be shrewd *or* far-sighted; **heures creuses** off-peak hours; **période creuse** *(dans l'industrie touristique)* slack season; **l'électricité coûte moins cher en période creuse** electricity costs less offpeak; *Péj* **paroles creuses** empty *or* meaningless words; **spéculations creuses** pointless speculation; *Couture* **pli c.** inverted *or* box pleat; *Fin* **marché c.** sagging market; *Naut* **mer creuse** rough sea

ADV **sonner c.** to sound hollow; *Fig* to sound empty *or* false

NM *(de la main, de l'épaule etc)* hollow; *(d'ar-*

bre, dans un mur) hole, cavity; *(dans le sol, une route)* crevice, cavity; *(d'un rocher)* crevice, cavity; *(de l'estomac)* pit; *(d'une vague, d'une courbe)* trough; *(d'une voile)* belly; **tenir qch dans le c. de la main** to hold sth cupped in one's hand; **c'est si petit que ça tient dans le c. de la main** it's so small you can hold it in the palm of your hand; **succession de c. et de bosses** succession *or* series of bumps and hollows; **le c. des reins** the small of the back; **c. de l'aisselle** armpit; *Fig* **être au c. de la vague** *(d'une personne)* to be in the depths of despair, to have hit rock bottom; *(d'une entreprise)* to have hit rock bottom; *Litt* **dans le c. de, du c. de** in the depths of; *Fam* **avoir un c. dans l'estomac** to be ravenous; **j'ai un petit c.** I'm a bit peckish; **ce chanteur a du c.** *ou* **un bon c.** this singer has a fine bass voice; **une période de c.** a slack period

crevaison [krəvɛzɔ̃] NF *(d'un pneu)* puncture, flat

crevant [krəvɑ̃] ADJ *Fam* **1** *(travail, chaleur)* killing, exhausting, murderous; *(enfant)* exhausting **2** *(histoire etc)* hilarious, priceless, killing

crevard, -arde [krəvar, -ard] *Fam*ADJ **1** *(malingre)* pitifully thin **2** *(affamée)* hungry, starving

N **1** *(personne malingre)* pitifully thin person **2** *(personne affamée)* **c'est un c., celui-là** he's always hungry, he's a bottomless pit

crevasse [krəvas] NF *(dans la peau)* crack; *(dans un mur, le sol)* crack, crevice, fissure; *(dans un glacier)* crevasse; **avoir des crevasses aux mains** to have chapped hands

crevasser [krəvase] VT *(mains)* to chap; *(terre, mur)* to crack, to make cracks *or* fissures in

VPR **se crevasser** *(des mains)* to chap, to get chapped; *(de la terre)* to crack, to fissure

crevé [krəve] ADJ burst; *(pneu)* punctured, flat; *Fam (mort)* dead; *Fam (fatigué)* worn out, fagged out, dead beat; **ça sent le rat c., ici** it smells as if something has died in here

NM *(dans une manche)* slash; **manches à crevés** slashed sleeves

crève [krɛv] NF *Arg (gros rhume)* stinker of a cold, stinking cold; **attraper la c.** to catch one's death of cold

crève-cœur NM INV *(peine profonde)* heartbreak, bitter disappointment; **c'est un vrai c. de devoir te quitter** it's heartbreaking *or* heartrending having to leave you

crève-la-faim NM INV *Fam (miséreux)* down-and-out

crever [krəve] (**je crève, n. crevons; je crèverai**) VI *(éclater)* to burst, to split; *(d'une bête, une plante)* to die; *Arg (d'une personne)* to snuff it, to kick the bucket; **mon pneu a crevé** I've got a puncture *or* a flat; *Fam* **j'ai crevé** I've got a puncture *or* a flat; **c. de jalousie/d'orgueil** to be bursting with jealousy/pride; **il va en c. de jalousie** he's going to be madly jealous; **j'en crève d'envie** I'm dying to; **c. de rire** to split one's sides laughing; *Fam* **c. de faim** *(mourir)* to starve to death; *(avoir faim)* to be starving *or* famished; *très Fam* **je crève la dalle** I'm dying of hunger, I'm absolutely starving; **c. d'ennui** to be bored to death; *Fam* **je crève de froid/de chaleur** I'm freezing/boiling *or* roasting; **il fait une chaleur à c.** it's stifling *or* boiling; *Fam* **qu'il crève!** he can go to hell!; *Fam* **plutôt c.!** I'd rather die!, I'll die first!

VT *(ballon, sac etc)* to burst; *(pneu)* to puncture; *Fig* **c. le cœur à qn** to break sb's heart; *Fig* **ça me crève le cœur de devoir abandonner cette maison** I'm heartbroken about *or* it's heartrending having to leave this house; **c. un œil à qn** to put out *or* gouge out sb's eye; *(accidentellement)* to blind sb in one eye; *Fig Fam* **ça crève les yeux** it stands out *or* sticks out a mile; *Cin Fig* **elle crève l'écran** she fills the screen with her presence; *Fig* **les réservations/inscriptions crèvent le plafond** the floor is sagging under the weight of reservations/registrations; **c. un cheval** to ride *or* work a horse to death

VPR se crever to knock oneself out

crevette [krəvɛt] **NF** *(crustacé)* **c. grise** shrimp; **c. (rose)** prawn; **aller à la pêche à la c.** to go shrimping; *Fam* **cette fille, c'est une vraie c.** she's a real Twiggy

crevettier [krəvɛtje] **NM** *(filet)* shrimping net; *(bateau)* shrimper, shrimp boat

CRF [seɛrɛf] **NF** *(abrév* **Croix-Rouge française)** French Red Cross

cri [kri] **NM** cry, shout, call; *(perçant, aigu) (d'une personne)* scream; *(d'un animal, un oiseau)* cry; *(d'un criquet)* chirp; *(d'une souris)* squeak; **j'ai entendu des cris dans la rue** I heard shouts *or* shouting in the street; **je ne pouvais ignorer le c. de ma conscience** I couldn't ignore the voice of conscience, my conscience was troubling me; **c. d'angoisse/ d'horreur** shriek *or* scream of anguish/horror; **pousser un c. aigu** to scream, to shriek; *Fam* **quand je lui ai dit ça, elle a poussé des cris** she screamed when I told her; **jeter** *ou* **pousser les hauts cris** to shout at the top of one's voice; *Fig* to protest (loudly), to give vent to one's indignation; **réclamer qch à grands cris** to clamour for sth; **appeler qn à grands cris** to shout to sb; *(qui est absent)* to call (loudly) for sb; *Fig Fam* **le dernier c.** the latest fashion *or* style; *Fig* **c'est le dernier c.** it's all the rage, it's the latest thing

▸▸ **c. du cœur** cri de cœur; *Mil* **c. de guerre** war cry

> Attention: ne pas confondre **shout** et **scream** lorsqu'on traduit **cri**. Le terme **scream** désigne le plus souvent un cri inarticulé de douleur ou de frayeur, alors que **shout** se rapporte plutôt à des éclats de voix ou à des paroles prononcées de façon autoritaire ou sous l'effet de la colère.

criailler [kriaje] **VI 1** *(d'un faisan, d'une pintade)* to cry; *(d'une oie)* to honk **2** *(crier)* to bawl, to shout **3** *(se plaindre)* to whine, to complain, *Fam* to grouse, to whinge, to moan

criailleries [kriajri] **NFPL** whining, complaining, *Fam* grousing, whingeing, moaning

criailleur, -euse [kriajœr, -øz] *Fam* **ADJ** whining, complaining; *Fam* whingeing, moaning

N whiner, complainer, *Fam* grouser, moaner, whinger

criant [krijɑ̃] **ADJ** *(erreur)* glaring; *(contraste)* striking; *(abus)* flagrant; **injustice criante** flagrant *or* gross injustice; **c'est la preuve criante de sa mauvaise foi** it's clear proof of his bad faith; **je remarque des différences de traitement criantes** I see signs of glaringly different treatment; **être c. de vérité** *(témoignage, reportage)* to be clearly *or* obviously *or* Fml patently true, to ring true

criard [krijar] **ADJ 1** *(enfant)* whining; **être c.** *(d'un enfant)* to be a whiner; *Fam* **femme criarde** scolding *or* nagging woman **2** *(aigu) (voix)* shrill, high-pitched, piercing; *Fig* **dettes criardes** pressing debts; **couleur criarde** loud *or* gaudy colour; **meublé avec un luxe c.** furnished ostentatiously

criblage [kriblaʒ] **NM** *(du grain etc)* sifting, riddling; *(du charbon, gravier etc)* screening; *(de fruit)* grading

crible [kribl] **NM** sieve, riddle; **c. à gravier/à sable** gravel/sand screen; **passer qch au c.** to sift *or* sieve *or* screen sth; *Fig* to go through sth with a fine-tooth comb

criblé [krible] **ADJ** *(de trous, balles etc)* riddled; **peau criblée de cicatrices** skin covered in scars; *(d'acné, de vérole)* pock-marked skin; *Fig* **être c. de dettes** to be up to one's eyes in debt; **un ciel c. d'étoiles** a sky studded with stars, a star-studded sky

cribler [krible] **VT 1** to sift, to riddle; *(gravier, charbon)* to screen; *(fruit)* to grade **2** *(trouer)* to pierce with holes; **c. qn/qch de balles** to riddle sb/sth with bullets; **c. qn de coups** to strike sb repeatedly; *Fig* **c. qn de reproches/ d'injures/de sarcasme** to heap reproaches/ abuse/sarcasm on sb; **c. qn de questions** to bombard sb with questions

cribleur, -euse [kriblœr, -øz] **N** sifter, riddler, screener

NF cribleuse *(machine)* sifter, sifting machine

cric¹ [krik] **NM** *(lifting)* jack; **c. hydraulique** hydraulic jack; **c. rouleur** trolley jack; **soulever qch au c.** *ou* **à l'aide d'un c.** to jack sth up

cric² [krik] **INT** crack!, snap!; **c.-crac!** *(d'une biscotte)* crunch!; *(d'une clé tournant dans la serrure)* click!

cricket [krikɛt] **NM** *Sport* cricket

cricri [krikri] **NM 1** *(bruit) (de criquet)* chirping **2** *Fam (insecte)* cricket

criée [krije] **NF (vente à la) c.** (sale by) auction; **la c.** *(endroit)* the auction room; *Bourse* **à la c.** by open outcry

crier [krije] *(impf, pr sub* **n. criions, v. criiez)** **VI 1** to cry, to call out, to shout; *(fort)* to scream, to shriek, to yell; **on ne peut pas parler avec lui, il se met tout de suite à c.** you can't talk to him, he just starts yelling *or* shouting; **ne criez pas!** don't shout!; **enfant qui crie** squalling child; **c. de douleur** to cry out *or* scream *or* shriek with pain; **c. comme un sourd** *ou* **un putois** *ou* **un damné** *ou* **comme un cochon qu'on égorge** to shout one's head off; **c. contre** *ou* **après qn** to shout at sb; **c. au secours** to shout for help; **c. au scandale** to protest, to be up in arms; **ils crièrent au miracle** they described it as a miracle

2 *(d'une souris etc)* to squeak; *(d'un criquet)* to chirp; *(d'un oiseau)* to call

3 *(d'une porte, d'un essieu etc)* to squeak, to creak

4 *(de couleurs)* to clash (**avec** with)

VT *(ordre)* to shout (out), to yell (out); **c. des injures à qn** to shout *or* yell abuse at sb; **je lui ai crié de se dépêcher** I called out *or* shouted to him to hurry up; *Fig* **elle le crie sur tous les toits** she's shouting it from the rooftops; **c. la vérité** to proclaim the truth; **c. famine** to cry famine; **c. misère** to complain of hardship *or* distress; **c. vengeance** to cry out *or* call for vengeance; **c. son innocence** to protest one's innocence; **c. une vente** to put goods up for auction; **c. des légumes/des journaux** to sell *or* hawk vegetables/newspapers

> Il faut noter que le verbe anglais **to cry** signifie le plus souvent **pleurer**.

crieur, -ieuse [krijœr, -jøz] **N 1** *(dans la rue)* (street) hawker; **c. de journaux** newspaper seller *or* vendor; *Hist* **c. public** town crier **2** *Théâtre* callboy

crime [krim] **NM 1** crime; *Jur* felony; **c. d'État, c. contre la sûreté de l'État** treason; **commettre un c.** to commit a crime; **être un c. de lèse-majesté** to be lèse-majesté; **le c. ne paie pas** crime doesn't pay; *Fig* **c'est un c. que d'avoir démoli cette maison** it's a crime *or* sin to have pulled down that house; **ce n'est pas un c.!** it's not a crime! **2** *(meurtre)* murder; **l'arme du c.** the murder weapon

▸▸ **c. contre l'humanité** crime against humanity; **c. crapuleux** crime against property; **crimes de guerre** war crimes; **le c. organisé** organized crime

Crimée [krime] **NF la C.** the Crimea

criminaliser [kriminalize] **VT 1** *Jur (affaire)* to refer to a criminal court **2** *(rendre criminel)* to criminalize

criminaliste [kriminalist] **N** *Jur* specialist in criminal law

criminalité [kriminalite] **NF 1** *(d'un acte)* criminal nature **2** *(crimes)* crime, delinquency; **taux de c.** crime rate; **c. informatique** computer crime

criminel, -elle [kriminɛl] **ADJ 1** *Jur (acte, droit, législation, dessein)* criminal; *Litt (âme)* of a criminal; **la police pense que c'est un incendie c.** the police suspect arson **2** *Fam* **ce serait c. de la jeter** it would be criminal *or* a crime to throw it away

N *(malfaiteur)* criminal; *(assassin)* murderer; **c. de guerre** war criminal

NM avocat au **c.** criminal lawyer; **poursuivre qn au c.** to take criminal proceedings against sb

criminellement [kriminɛlmɑ̃] **ADV 1** *(de façon criminelle)* criminally **2** *Jur* before *or* in a court of law; **poursuivre qn c.** to take criminal proceedings against sb

criminologie [kriminɔlɔʒi] **NF** criminology

criminologiste [kriminɔlɔʒist] **N** criminologist

crin [krɛ̃] **NM le c.** *(d'un cheval)* the mane and tail; **matelas de c.** (horse)hair mattress; *Fig* **à tous crins** *(socialiste, féministe, révolutionnaire)* diehard, fanatical, out and out; *(conservateur)* dyed-in-the-wool, diehard; *Vieilli* **être à c.** to be in a bad mood

crincrin [krɛ̃krɛ̃] **NM** *Fam* **1** *(mauvais violon)* squeaky violin, fiddle **2** *(bruit)* squeaking, scraping *(sound)*

crinière [krinjɛr] **NF 1** *(d'un lion, un cheval)* mane; *(d'un casque)* (horsehair) plume **2** *Fam (d'une personne)* mop, mane

crinoline [krinɔlin] **NF** crinoline; **robe à c.** crinoline (dress)

crinquer [krɛ̃ke] **VT** *Can* to wind up; **c. un mécanisme** to wind up a mechanism; *Fig* **il est crinqué** he's hopping mad

crique [krik] **NF** creek, cove, bay

criquet [krikɛ] **NM** *(insecte)* locust; **c. pèlerin** *ou* **migrateur** migratory locust

crise [kriz] **NF 1** *(marasme, période d'instabilité)* crisis; **c. ministérielle** cabinet crisis; **c. du pouvoir** leadership crisis; **c. de l'énergie** energy crisis; *Hist* **la c. de 1929** the Great Depression (of 1929); **vivre une période de c.** to be going through a crisis *or* Fam rough patch; **traverser une c.** to go through a crisis; **il est en pleine c. d'adolescence** he's being a typical teenager; **c. du logement** housing crisis *or* shortage; **c. pétrolière** oil crisis **VOIR GRAMMAIRE A14**

2 *Méd (dans une maladie)* attack, crisis; **elle a été prise d'une c. d'appendicite** she was struck down with appendicitis, she went down with appendicitis; **c. cardiaque** heart attack; **avoir** *ou* **faire une c. cardiaque** to have a heart attack; **c. d'épilepsie** epileptic fit; **c. de foie** bilious attack; **c. de nerfs** attack of nerves, fit of hysterics

3 *Fam (brusque accès)* **piquer une c. (de nerfs)** to have hysterics; *(de colère)* to fly *or* get into a rage; **c. de larmes** fit of crying, *Fam* crying jag; **être pris d'une c. de larmes** to burst into tears; **travailler par crises** to work in fits and starts; **c. de conscience** attack of conscience; *Rel* crisis of conscience; *Fam* **la c.!** what a hoot *or* scream!; **la c. aujourd'hui en classe!** it was a real hoot *or* scream in school today!

crispant [krispɑ̃] **ADJ** *Fam* irritating, annoying; **c'est c., cette situation d'attente** it's irritating *or* annoying having to wait like this; **ce suspense est c.!** the suspense is killing me!; **elle est crispante** she's irritating, she gets on my nerves

crispation [krispasjɔ̃] NF *(des mains)* clenching; *(du visage)* tensing; *(de douleur)* wince; **donner des crispations à qn** to get on sb's nerves

crispé [krispe] ADJ *(personne)* on edge, tense; *(visage)* tense, strained; *(sourire, rire)* forced; **les deux mains crispées sur la serviette** clutching the briefcase with both hands; **c. par le rigor mortis** stiffened by rigor mortis; **visage c. par la douleur** face contorted or screwed up with pain

crisper [krispe] VT **1** *(poings, mains)* to clench; *(muscles)* to contract, to tense; *(corps)* to tense **2** *Fam (irriter)* to irritate, to annoy; **cela me crispe** it irritates me, it gets on my nerves

VPR **se crisper** to contract; **à cette nouvelle, son visage se crispa** his face tensed or froze on hearing the news; **ses mains se crispaient sur le volant** his hands were clutching the wheel; *Fig* **elle se crispe quand elle est en ma compagnie** she tenses up or gets all edgy when she's with me

crispin [krispɛ̃] NM *(de gant)* gauntlet; **gants à c.** *(d'escrimeur, de motocycliste)* gauntlets

criss [kris] NM kris

crissement [krismɑ̃] NM *(de dents)* grating, grinding; *(de la craie sur le tableau)* squeak, squeaking; *(des freins)* squeal, screech, squealing, screeching; *(du gravier, de la neige)* crunch, crunching; **j'ai entendu le c. des pneus sur le gravier** I heard the tyres crunching on the gravel; **le c. des pneus** *(lorsqu'on freine trop brusquement)* the squeal of tyres

crisser [krise] VI *(des freins)* to squeal, to screech; *(de gravier, neige)* to crunch; *(de la craie)* to squeak; **c. des dents** to grind one's teeth

cristal, -aux [kristal, -o] NM **1** *Minér* crystal; **c. de roche** rock crystal **2** *(verre)* crystal; **cristaux** crystal(ware); **boule de c.** crystal ball; **regarder dans sa boule de c.** to look into one's crystal ball, to crystal gaze; **travail du c.** glass cutting and engraving; *Fig* **de c.** *(voix, eau)* crystal-clear; *Ordinat* **affichage à cristaux liquides** liquid crystal display **3** *Litt (eau)* pure water **4** **cristaux de soude** washing soda; **cristaux dessiccatifs de Silicagel®** silica-gel crystals

cristallerie [kristalri] NF *(fabrication)* crystal (glass) manufacture; *(fabrique)* (crystal) glassworks; *(objets)* crystal(ware)

cristallin [kristalɛ̃] ADJ **1** *(roc etc)* crystalline; *(eau, voix etc)* crystal-clear; *(son, note)* ringing **2** *Phys* **réseau c.** crystal lattice

NM *Anat (de l'œil)* crystalline lens

cristallisation [kristalizasjɔ̃] NF *aussi Fig Litt* crystallization; **la neige fait de belles cristallisations** snow produces beautiful crystal formations or structures

cristalliser [kristalize] VT *aussi Fig Litt* to crystallize

VI to crystallize; *Fig Litt* **son idéal a cristallisé autour de ce souvenir** his ideal took shape around that memory

VPR **se cristalliser** to crystallize; *Fig Litt* **son énergie s'est cristallisée dans ce projet** his energy became focused on the project

cristallographie [kristalɔgrafi] NF crystallography

critère [kriter] NM criterion; **critères** criteria; **son seul c., c'est l'avis de son père** his father's opinion is his only criterion; **critères de sélection** selection criteria; *UE* **critères de convergence** convergence criteria; **quel sera votre c. déterminant?** what will be the decisive factor or *Fam* what will swing it as far as you're concerned?; *Fam* **ce n'est pas**

un c. *(on ne peut rien en conclure)* that's no criterion; *Ordinat* **c. de tri** sort criterion

critérium [kriterjɔm] NM **1** *Courses de chevaux* **c. des deux ans** = races to select the best two-year-old **2** *Sport* heat

critiquable [kritikabl] ADJ *(décision, choix, opinion etc)* open to criticism

critique¹ [kritik] ADJ *(qui décide, crucial)* critical, decisive, crucial; *Méd* **phase ou période c.** critical stage or period; *Pol etc* **c'est une phase c. dans les négociations** it's a critical or crucial stage in negotiations; **être ou se trouver dans une situation c.** to be or find oneself in a critical situation; *Méd* **il est dans un état c.** his condition is critical, *Fam* he is critical or on the danger list; **l'heure est c.** we are faced with a crisis, we have a crisis on our hands; **l'âge c.** the menopause; **le moment c.** the decisive moment; *Phys* **point c.** critical point; *Nucl, Fig* **masse c.** critical mass

critique² ADJ *(esprit, personne)* critical; **examiner qch d'un œil c.** to examine sth critically or with a critical eye; **faire une analyse c.** to produce a critique or a critical analysis; **son attitude est trop c.** his attitude is too critical, he's too critical in his attitude

N critic; **c. d'art/de cinéma** art/film critic; **c. de mode** fashion writer; **c. gastronomique** food critic; **c. littéraire** book reviewer, literary critic

NF **1** *(jugement)* (art of) criticism; **c. des textes** textual criticism; **c. dramatique** dramatic criticism; **c. constructive** constructive criticism

2 *(examen)* critical article or paper; *Théâtre, Cin* review; **faire la c. d'une pièce** to review a play; **sa pièce a eu quelques bonnes critiques** his play got a few good reviews

3 *(condamnation)* *(d'une politique, un régime etc)* criticism; **exercer une sévère c. sur soi-même** to be highly self-critical or a stern critic of oneself; **il ne supporte pas ou il n'accepte pas la c.** he can't take criticism; **ce n'est pas une c., mais …** don't take this as a criticism, but …; **formuler une c. ou des critiques** to express criticism, to make a criticism; **être l'objet des critiques du public** to be a target for public criticism

4 la c. *(l'ensemble des critiques)* the critics; **la c. n'a pas aimé** the critics didn't like it

critiquer [kritike] VT **1** *(examiner, juger)* **c. qch** to assess sth, to examine sth critically **2** *(condamner)* *(personne, attitude)* to criticize, to find fault with; **c. qn pour qch/pour ne pas avoir fait qch** to criticize sb for sth/ for not doing sth; **ce n'est pas pour te c., mais …** don't take this as a criticism, but …, I don't mean to criticize (you), but …

VI to criticize; **arrête de c.** stop criticizing

critiqueur, -euse [kritikœr, -øz] N captious or carping critic; **quelle critiqueuse, celle-là!** she's so critical!

croassement [krɔasmɑ̃] NM *(de corneille)* caw(ing); *(de corbeau)* croak(ing)

croasser [krɔase] VI *(de corneille)* to caw; *(de corbeau)* to croak

croate [krɔat] ADJ Croatian

NM *Ling* Croat(ian)

N **C.** Croat(ian)

Croatie [krɔasi] NF Croatia

croc [kro] NM **1** *(crochet)* hook; **c. de boucherie** meat hook; **c. à fumier** muck rake; **c. de marinier** boat-hook **2** *(de loup, chien)* fang; **montrer ses crocs** to show one's teeth; **moustache en c.** handlebar moustache; *Arg* **avoir les crocs** to be famished, to be ravenous

croc-en-jambe, pl **crocs-en-jambe** NM *(pour faire tomber un adversaire)* trip; *Fig* dirty trick; **faire un c. à qn** to trip sb up; *Fig* to pull a fast one on sb

croche [krɔʃ] NF *Mus* quaver, *Am* eighth

note; **double c.** semiquaver, *Am* sixteenth note

croche-pied, pl **croche-pieds** NM = **croc-en-jambe**

crocher [krɔʃe] VT **1** *Naut* **c. qch** to hook (on to) sth, to seize sth with a hook; *Région* **c. sa veste** to hang up one's jacket **2** *Fam (se saisir de)* to grab hold of

VI *Naut (d'une ancre)* to grip, to bite, to hold

crochet [krɔʃɛ] NM **1** hook; **c. à vis** screw hook; **c. de boucherie** meat hook; **c. à boutons** buttonhook; **c. de bureau** spike file; *Tech* **c. d'arrêt** pawl, catch; **c. de sécurité** safety catch; *Fig* **vivre aux crochets de qn** to live off or sponge on sb **2** *(pour l'ouvrage)* crochet hook; **(travail au) c.** crochet work; **faire du c.** to (do) crochet; **faire qch au c.** to crochet sth **3** *(d'un serpent)* (poison) fang **4** *Typ* square bracket **5** *(détour)* faire un c. to make a detour; *(d'une route)* to take a sudden turn; *(d'une voiture, d'un cheval)* to swerve *(to avoid sth)* **6** *Boxe* **c. du gauche/ du droit** left/right hook **7** *Mus (d'une croche)* hook **8** *Radio* **c. radiophonique** talent contest *(on radio)*

crochetable [krɔʃtabl] ADJ *(serrure)* that can be picked, pickable

crochetage [krɔʃtaʒ] NM *(d'une serrure)* picking

crocheter [krɔʃte] VT **(je crochète, n. crochetons; je crochèterai) 1** *(serrure)* to pick **2** *(piquer)* to hook, to pick up with a hook

crocheteur [krɔʃtœr] NM lockpicker, housebreaker

crocheur, -euse [krɔʃœr, -øz] *Suisse* ADJ *(tenace, travailleur)* dedicated and hardworking

N *(personne tenace et travailleuse)* dedicated and hard-working person

crochu [krɔʃy] ADJ *(fil de fer, nez etc)* hooked; *(doigts, mains)* claw-like; *Fig Fam* **avoir les doigts ou les mains crochu(e)s** to be mean or tight-fisted or *Am* a tightwad; *Hist, Phil* **atomes crochus** interlocking atoms; *Fig Fam* **nous nous sommes senti des atomes crochus** we hit it off; *Fig Fam* **je n'ai pas d'atomes crochus avec elle** I don't hit it off with her

croco [krɔko] NM *Fam* crocodile (skin); **sac en c.** crocodile(-skin) handbag

crocodile [krɔkɔdil] NM *(reptile)* crocodile; **sac à main en c.** crocodile(-skin) handbag; *Fig* **larmes de c.** crocodile tears

crocus [krɔkys] NM *(plante)* crocus

CROIRE [krwar] *(prp* **croyant;** *pp* **cru;** *pr ind* **je crois, il croit, n. croyons, ils croient;** *impf* **je croyais;** *p hist* **je crus;** *fu* **je croirai)** VT **1** to believe; **c. qch** to believe sth; **cela, je ne peux pas le c.** I can't believe that, I find that hard to believe; **vous ne sauriez c. combien je suis content** you can't think or imagine how glad I am; **j'aime à c. que …** I hope or trust that …; **il est à c. que …** it would seem that …; **tout porte à ou il faut c. que …** there is every indication that …, it would seem that …; **je ne crois pas que cela suffise** I don't think that will be enough; **je crois que oui/non** I think or believe so/not; **n'en croyez rien!** don't believe (a word of) it!, *Fam* not a bit of it!; *Fam* **d'après ce que je crois …** from what I've heard …; **croyez-le ou non** believe it or not; **je vous croyais anglais/riche** I thought you were English/rich; **on croirait qu'il dort** you'd think he was asleep; **je ne suis pas celle que vous croyez** I'm not that kind of girl; **j'ai cru bien faire** I thought or believed I was doing the right thing; **j'ai cru devoir le prévenir** I thought I ought to warn him; **elle ne croyait pas si bien dire** she didn't know how right she was; **je n'aurais pas cru cela de lui** I wouldn't have or would never have thought it of him; **c. qn** to believe sb, to take sb's word for it; **me croira qui voudra, mais …** you may not believe this, but …; *Fam Iron* **c'est ça, je te crois!** is that so?; **je te crois!** *(bien sûr)* you can say that again!; **croyez-moi, ce n'était pas facile** believe (you) me, it wasn't easy

2 en c. qn to take sb's word for it; *(en suivant son conseil)* to take sb's advice; **vous pouvez m'en c.** (you can) take my word for it, you can take it from me; **s'il faut l'en c. ou** à **l'en c., ce n'est pas difficile** according to him *or* going by what he says, it's not difficult; **je ne pouvais en c. mes yeux/mes oreilles** I couldn't believe my eyes/my ears

VI 1 *(concevoir etc)* to believe (à in); **personne ne croyait** à **la guerre** nobody thought war would break out, nobody thought there would be a war; **le médecin crut** à **une rougeole** the doctor thought it was measles; **franchement, je n'y crois pas** quite frankly, I don't believe it; **c'est** à **ne pas y c.** it's beyond belief, it's unbelievable; *Fam* **faut pas c.!** don't you believe it!; **vous croyez?** do you really think so?; **j'ai cru nécessaire de …** I thought it necessary to …; **veuillez c. ou je vous prie de c.** à **l'expression de mes sentiments distingués** yours sincerely

2 *(adhérer, avoir foi)* to believe; **je ne crois pas** à **ses promesses** I don't believe *or* I have no faith in his promises; **c. en Dieu** to believe in God); **il ne croit plus** he has lost his faith (in God); **je ne peux pas c. sur commande, je dois comprendre** you can't just ask me to believe, I need to understand

VPR se croire *(avec attribut)* to think oneself; **il se croit intelligent** he thinks he's intelligent; **on se serait cru en octobre** it felt like October; **il se croit tout permis** he thinks he can do *or* get away with anything; *Fam* **qu'est-ce qu'il se croit?** who does he think he is?; *Fam* **il se croit sorti de la cuisse de Jupiter** he thinks a lot of himself, he thinks he's the bee's knees; **il s'y croit** he's getting above himself *or* too big for his boots *or Am* britches; **elle s'est toujours crue incapable de réussir** she never thought she would succeed

---

croisade [krwazad] NF **1** *(campagne)* crusade, campaign; **c. contre la drogue** anti-drugs campaign *or* crusade **2** *Hist* crusade; **partir en c.** to go on a crusade

croisé [krwaze] ADJ **1 feu** *ou* **tir c.** crossfire; **mots croisés** crossword; **rimes croisées** alternate rhymes; **race croisée** crossbreed; *Bourse* **participation croisée** cross-holding **2** *(manteau, veste)* double-breasted
NM **1** *Hist* crusader **2** *Tex* twill

croisée [krwaze] NF **1** *(rencontre)* crossing; **c. de chemins** crossroads; *Fig* **être** à **la c. des chemins** to stand at the crossroads, to be at a crossroads **2** *(châssis)* casement; *(fenêtre)* casement window

croisement [krwazmɑ̃] NM **1** *(de véhicules)* passing; *(de lignes, routes etc)* crossing, intersection; **c. de routes** *ou* **de rues** crossroads, junction; **c. dangereux** dangerous crossroads **2** *(des bras, jambes)* crossing **3** *(d'animaux)* crossing, crossbreeding; *(animal)* crossbreed, cross (**entre … et …** between … and …); **faire des croisements de races** to cross breeds; **c. consanguin** interbreeding

croiser [krwaze] VT **1** *(d'une ligne, route)* to cross, to cut across, to intersect; **le pont croise l'autoroute** the bridge goes over *or* crosses the motorway; **c. un châle/une écharpe sur sa poitrine** to wear a shawl/a scarf; **elle a croisé un foulard sur son pull** she wore a scarf crossed over her sweater; **c. les jambes** to cross one's legs; **c. les bras** to fold one's arms; **c. le regard de qn** to meet sb's gaze *or* eyes; **je croise les doigts pour que tu réussisses** I've got my fingers crossed for you; **c. le fer avec qn** to have a sword fight with sb; *Fig* to cross swords with sb

2 *(véhicule, personne)* to pass

3 *(animaux, plantes)* to cross(breed)

VI 1 *(d'un vêtement)* **manteau qui ne croise pas assez** coat that does not have sufficient overlap **2** *Naut* to cruise

VPR se croiser 1 *(de routes)* to cross, to intersect; *(de personnes)* to meet; **ces deux chemins se croisent** these two paths intersect; *Fig* **se c. les bras** to sit back, to sit with arms folded; **leurs vies n'ont fait que se c.** their paths barely crossed; **nous n'avons fait que nous c.** we saw each other only briefly *or* for a moment; **elles ne se sont jamais croisées alors qu'elles étaient dans la même université** their paths never crossed even though they went to the same university; **leurs regards se croisèrent** their eyes met; **nos lettres se sont croisées** our letters have crossed in the post

2 *Hist* to go on a crusade

3 *(s'accoupler)* to mate, to couple; **le cheval peut se c. avec l'âne** the horse can be crossed with the donkey

croiseur [krwazœr] NM *Naut* cruiser; **c. de bataille** battle cruiser; **c. lourd/léger** heavy/light cruiser

croisière [krwazjɛr] NF *Naut etc* **1 vitesse/altitude de c.** cruising speed/altitude; **missile de c.** cruise missile; *Fig* **adopter l'allure de c.** to start ticking over normally; **atteindre le rythme de c.** to reach cruising speed; *Fig* to be working at a comfortable rate *or* tempo **2** *(voyage)* cruise; **faire une c.** *(d'une personne)* to go on *or* take a cruise; *(d'un navire)* to be cruising; **être en c.** to be on a cruise; **navire de c.** cruise ship; **c. fluviale/maritime** river-/sea-cruise

croisillon [krwazijɔ̃] NM **1** *(de croix, fenêtre)* crosspiece, crossbar; *(de chaise etc)* (cross)bar; *Archit* transept; **fenêtre** à **croisillons** lattice window **2** *Aut* trunnion block, spider

croissance [krwasɑ̃s] NF growth; *(d'une banlieue)* growth, spread; **en pleine c.** growing rapidly; **arrêté dans sa c.** *(arbre, enfant)* stunted; **enfant en pleine c.** growing child; **hormone de c.** (human) growth hormone; **finir sa c.** to stop growing; **c. économique** economic growth *or* development; **c. du marché** market growth; **c. par intégration** integrative growth; **c. zéro** zero growth

croissant¹ [krwasɑ̃] ADJ *(plante, tendance etc)* growing; *(richesse, angoisse etc)* growing, increasing; *(ordre)* ascending; *(chaleur, température)* increasing; *Math (nombre, fonction)* monotonic; **les jeunes diplômés arrivent en nombre c.** there's an increasing number of young graduates (on the market)

croissant² NM **1** crescent; **un c. de lune** a crescent moon; **le C.-Rouge** the Red Crescent; **en c.** crescent-shaped **2** *Culin* croissant; **c. aux amandes** almond croissant

croître [krwɑtr] VI *(prp* **croissant;** *pp* **crû,** *f* **crue;** *pr ind* **je croîs, il croît, n. croissons, ils croissent;** *p hist* **je crûs;** *fu* **je croîtrai;** *pr sub* **je croisse;** *p sub* **je crûsse)** to grow, to increase (in size); *(de plantes)* to grow; *(de la lune)* to wax; *(d'une rivière)* to rise, to swell; *(du vent)* to rise; **c. en volume/nombre** to increase in volume/number; **c. en beauté/sagesse** to grow in beauty/wisdom; **les jours croissent** the days are lengthening, the days are getting *or* growing longer; **aller croissant** *(de terreur)* to grow and grow; *(de suspense)* to get worse and worse; *(de bruit)* to get louder and louder; **l'inquiétude de la police va croissant** the police are increasingly anxious *or* concerned; **cela ne fait que c. et embellir** it's getting better and better; *Iron*

it's getting worse and worse; **c. dans l'estime de qn** to rise in sb's esteem; *Prov* **mauvaise herbe croît toujours** ill weeds grow apace

croix [krwa] NF cross; **la sainte C.** the Holy Cross; **mettre en c.** to crucify; **le chemin de (la) C.** the Way of the Cross, the Via Dolorosa; *(les quatorze arrêts)* the stations of the Cross; **faire un chemin de c.** to do the stations of the cross; **le signe de (la) c.** the sign of the cross; **faire le signe de c.** to make the sign of the cross, to cross oneself; **porter une c. au cou** to wear a crucifix; *Fig* **chacun porte sa c.** everyone has their cross to bear; **c. de bois c. de fer, si je mens je vais en enfer** cross my heart (and hope to die); **c'est la c. et la bannière** it's the devil of a job; *Hist* **prendre la c.** to go on a crusade; **la c. (de la Légion d'honneur)** the Cross of the Legion of Honour; **en (forme de) c.** cross-shaped, in the shape of a cross; **mettre des bâtons en c.** to lay sticks crosswise; **mettre les bras en c.** to stretch one's arms out to the sides; **marquer qch d'une c.** to mark sth with a cross; *Fig* **ce jour est** à **marquer d'une c.** it's a red-letter day; **faire une c. en face d'un nom** to tick a name, *or Am* to check off a name; **signer d'une c.** to make one's mark; *Fam* **faire une c. sur qch** to say goodbye to sth, to kiss sth goodbye; *Typ* **c. (mortuaire)** dagger

▸ ▸ **c. gammée** swastika; **c. grecque** Greek cross; **c. de guerre** Military Cross; **c. latine** Latin cross; **c. de Lorraine** cross of Lorraine; **c. de Malte** Maltese cross; **la C.-Rouge** the Red Cross; **c. de Saint-André** St Andrew's cross; *Astron* **la C. du Sud** the Southern Cross

cromlech [krɔmlɛk] NM cromlech

crooner [krunœr] NM *(chanteur)* crooner

croquant¹ [krɔkɑ̃] ADJ *(biscuit, pomme, feuilles de salade etc)* crisp, crunchy

croquant² NM *Péj (paysan)* (country) bumpkin, yokel

croque-au-sel (à la) [alakrɔkosɛl] ADV *Culin* = raw and seasoned only with salt

croque-madame [krɔkmadam] NM INV *Culin* = toasted cheese and ham sandwich, topped with fried egg

croque(-)mitaine, *pl* **croque(-)mitaines** [krɔkmitɛn] NM bogeyman

croque-monsieur [krɔkməsjø] NM INV *Culin* = toasted cheese and ham sandwich

croque-mort, *pl* **croque-morts** [krɔkmɔr] NM *Fam* undertaker; **avoir une figure de c.** to have a long face, to look thoroughly miserable

croquenot [krɔkno] NM *Fam* clodhopper

croquer [krɔke] VI **la salade croque sous la dent** lettuce is crisp *or* crunchy to eat; **c. dans** to bite into

VT 1 to crunch, to munch; *Fig (argent, fortune, héritage)* to squander; **chocolat à c.** plain chocolate; **à sucer ou à c.** may be sucked or chewed; *Fam* **il a croqué son sandwich en deux secondes** he wolfed down his sandwich in two seconds flat; *Fig* **c. la vie à belles dents** to make the most of life, to get the most out of life **2** *(dessiner)* to sketch; *Fam* **elle est jolie** *ou* **mignonne à c.** she's as pretty as a picture **3** *Fam* **c. le marmot** *(attendre)* to cool *or* kick one's heels **4** *Fig* **c. une poulette** *(coucher avec)* to bed a young female

croquet [krɔkɛ] NM **1** *(jeu)* croquet; **faire une partie de c.** to have a game of croquet **2** *Couture* braid **3** *Culin* crisp almond biscuit

croquette [krɔkɛt] NF *Culin (de pomme de terre, poisson etc)* croquette; *(de chocolat)* chocolate drop; **croquettes** *(pour chien, chat)* biscuits, dry food

croqueuse [krɔkøz] N *Fam* **une c. de diamants** a gold-digger; **c. d'hommes** man-eater

croquignole [krɔkiɲɔl] NF = small crisp biscuit

croquignolet, -ette [krɔkiɲɔlɛ, -ɛt] ADJ *Fam* charming, delightful, *Am* cute

croquis [krɔki] NM sketch, rough drawing; *Journ* thumbnail sketch; **faire un c. de qch** to make a (rough) sketch of sth, to sketch sth; *Fig* **faire un c. d'une situation** to sketch or outline a situation; *Fig* **il nous a fait un c. rapide de la situation** he gave us a quick rundown on the situation; *Tech* **c. coté** dimensional sketch

crosne [kron] NM Chinese artichoke *(similar to Jerusalem artichoke)*

cross [krɔs] NM *Fam*, **cross-country** [krɔskuntri] *Sport* cross-country running or racing; *(événement)* cross-country run or race

crosse [krɔs] NF **1** *(de fusil)* butt; *(de pistolet)* grip; *(de violon etc)* scroll; *Bot (de fougère)* crosier; *Culin* **c. de bœuf** knuckle of beef; *Fam* **lever** ou **mettre la c. en l'air** to surrender, to show the white flag, to lay down one's arms **2** *Sport (de hockey)* (hockey) stick; *(de golf)* (golf) club; *Fig Fam* **chercher des crosses à qn** to try to pick a fight with sb **3** *(d'évêque)* (bishop's) crook, crosier

crossman [krɔsman], *pl* **crossmen** [krɔsmen] NM cross-country runner

crotale [krɔtal] NM *(reptile)* rattlesnake, *Am Fam* rattler

crotte [krɔt] NF **1** *(de cheval, mouton, lapin etc)* dung, droppings; **des trottoirs couverts de crottes de chiens** pavements covered in dog dirt; *Fig Fam* **c'est de la c. (de bique)** it's a load of rubbish or crap; *Fam* **elle ne se prend pas pour de la c. (de bique)** she thinks she's the bee's knees or the cat's pyjamas or the best thing since sliced bread; **une c. de** ou **en chocolat** a chocolate; *Fam* **ma petite c.** my dear, (my) darling; *Fam* **c.!** blast!; *Fam* **c. de bique!** blow!, drat! **2** *Vieilli (boue)* mud

crotté [krɔte] ADJ *Fam* dirty, muddy, covered in mud

crotter [krɔte] VT *(chaussures, manteau etc)* to cover in mud
▸ VI *Fam (chien)* to do its business
▸ VPR **se crotter** to get dirty, to get covered in or with mud

crottin [krɔtɛ̃] NM **1** *(excrément) (de cheval)* dung, *Am Fam* road apples; *(de mouton)* droppings **2** *(fromage)* small goat's-milk cheese

crouille [kruj] NM *(terme injurieux)* = racist term used to refer to a North African Arab

croulant [krulɑ̃] ADJ *(bâtiment)* crumbling, tumbledown, ramshackle; *Fig (empire)* crumbling, tottering, ramshackle; *Fam* **un vieux monsieur c.** a doddering old gent
▸ NM *Arg* old fogey, old buffer; **les croulants** the crumblies; **un jour, tu seras un vieux c.** you'll be a crumbly or an old dodderer yourself one day

crouler [krule] VI *(de bâtiment)*, *Fig (empire etc)* to crumble, to be on the point or verge of collapse; *(de la terre)* to give way, to crumble; **c. sous le poids de qch** to give way under the weight of sth; *Fig* **c. sous le poids des ans** *(d'une personne)* to be weighed down with age; *(d'une maison)* to be old and tumbledown; **il croule sous le travail depuis deux mois** he's been staggering under his workload for the last two months; **je croule de sommeil/de fatigue** I'm ready to drop, I'm asleep/dead on my feet; **se laisser c. dans un fauteuil** to slump into an armchair; *Fam* **un projet de c. to ruin a plan**; *Théâtre* **faire c. la salle (sous les applaudissements)** to bring the house down

croup [krup] NM *Méd* croup; **avoir le c.** to have croup

croupade [krupad] NF *Équitation* curvet

croupe [krup] NF **1** *(de cheval)* rump, hindquarters; *Fam (de personne)* behind, rump, backside, *Am* butt; **monter en c.** to ride behind, *Arch* to ride pillion **2** *(de colline, coteau)* brow, crest, top; *(de dune)* top; *Archit (de toit)* hip

croupetons (à) [akruptɔ̃] ADV squatting, crouching; **se tenir à c.** to squat (down); **marcher à c.** to walk crouched down

croupi [krupi] ADJ *(eau)* stagnant, foul

croupier [krupje] NM *(au casino)* croupier

croupière [krupjɛr] NF *(partie de harnais)* crupper; *Fig* **tailler des croupières à qn** *(attaquer)* to tear sb off a strip, to give sb a rocket; *(s'opposer à)* to spike sb's guns, to put a spoke in sb's wheel; *Fig* **se faire tailler des croupières** *(être attaqué)* to get torn off a strip; *(être opposé)* to be foiled or thwarted

croupion [krupjɔ̃] NM *(d'oiseau)* rump; *Fam (d'un poulet cuit, d'une volaille etc)* parson's or *Am* pope's nose; *Fam (d'une personne)* backside, behind, *Am* butt; **se magner le c.** to get a move on

croupir [krupir] VI **1** *(d'une personne)* **c. dans** *(le vice, l'ignorance, l'oisiveté etc)* to wallow in; **c. en prison** to stagnate in prison **2** *(de l'eau)* to stagnate, to grow foul

croupissant [krupisɑ̃] ADJ stagnating; **eaux croupissantes** stagnant water

crousille [kruzij] NF *Suisse (tirelire)* piggybank

croustade [krustad] NF *Culin* croustade

croustillant [krustijɑ̃] ADJ **1** *(biscuit, pâté en croûte etc)* crisp; *(pain)* crisp, crunchy **2** *Fam (histoire, détails etc)* spicy

croustiller [krustije] VI *(d'aliments)* to crunch; **pain qui croustille** crunchy bread

croustilles [krustij] NFPL *Can* crisps, or *Am* chips

croûte [krut] NF **1** *(de pain, tarte etc)* crust; *(du fromage)* rind; *(d'une plaie)* scab; **la c. terrestre** the earth's crust; *Culin* **c. au fromage/à la tomate** = toasted cheese/tomato sandwich; **pâté en c.** = meat pie; *Fam* **casser la c.** to eat; **casser une c.** to have a snack, to have a bite to eat; *Fam* **à la c.!** let's eat!, grub's up!; *Fam* **gagner sa c.** to earn one's daily bread or one's bread and butter; **gratter la c.** to scratch the surface; **c. de rouille** layer of rust; *Méd* **croûtes de lait** cradle cap **2** *Fam (mauvaise peinture)* daub **3** *Fam (imbécile)* idiot, *Br* wally; **quelle c.!** what a wally!; **une vieille c.** an old fossil or buffer

croûter [krute] VI *Fam (manger)* to nosh

croûteux, -euse [krutø, -øz] ADJ scabby, covered with scabs

croûton [krutɔ̃] NM **1** *(de pain)* heel, end; **un c. de pain** the heel of a loaf **2** *Culin (dans la soupe, le potage)* croûton **3** *Arg (vieux)* **c.** old fossil, old stick-in-the-mud

croyable [krwajabl] ADJ believable, credible; **une histoire à peine c.** an unlikely story; **ce n'est pas c.** it's unbelievable or incredible

croyance [krwajɑ̃s] NF *(fait de croire)* belief; *(certitude)* belief, conviction; **c. en Dieu** belief in God; **croyances religieuses** religious beliefs

croyant, -ante [krwajɑ̃, -ɑ̃t] ADJ believing; **il n'est pas c.** he's not a believer
▸ N believer; **les croyants** *(de l'Islam)* the Faithful

CRS [sɛɛrɛs] NM *(abrév* **Compagnie républicaine de sécurité***)* ≃ riot police, state security police; **un C.** a member of the state security police

cru¹ [kry] ADJ **1** *(viande, poisson, légumes)*, *Tex (tissus, soie etc)* raw; *(lait)* unpasteurized; *(cuir)* untreated, raw; *(couleur, lumière)* crude, garish; *Fig (réponse, langage, personne)* blunt; **il mange sa viande crue** he eats his meat raw; *Fig* **dans le jour c.** in the full light of day **2** *(licencieux)* crude, coarse; **cette plaisanterie est un peu crue** that's a rather coarse or crude joke **3** *Belg, Can, Suisse (temps, bâtiment)* damp and cold
▸ ADV **je vous le dis tout c.** I'm not mincing my words, I'm telling you straight (out); **j'ai envie de l'avaler tout c.** I could eat or gobble him (all) up; *(je suis en colère)* I could strangle him; **manger c.** to eat raw food; **être chaussé à c.** to wear shoes without any socks; **monter à c.** to ride bareback

cru² NM vineyard; **les meilleurs crus** *(terroirs)* the best vineyards; *(vins)* the best wines; **un grand c.** a vintage wine; **vin du c.** local wine; **bouilleur de c.** home distiller; **les gens du c.** the locals; **la langue du c.** the local dialect; *Fig* **une histoire de son (propre) c.** a story of his own invention

cruauté [kryote] NF **1** *(dureté)* cruelty *(envers* to*)*; *(de la vie)* cruelty, harshness; **faire preuve de c. mentale envers qn** to be guilty of mental cruelty to sb **2** *(acte)* (act of) cruelty; **les cruautés de son mari** her husband's cruelty

cruche [kryʃ] NF **1** *(récipient)* (earthenware) jug, pitcher; *(contenu)* jugful; *Prov* **tant va la c. à l'eau qu'à la fin elle se casse** the pitcher has gone to the well once too often **2** *Fam (imbécile)* idiot, ass, twit
▸ ADJ *Fam* **être c.** to be thick, to be an idiot; **avoir l'air c.** to look stupid or thick

cruchon [kryʃɔ̃] NM *(récipient)* small jug; *(contenu)* small jugful

crucial, -iale, -iaux, -iales [krysjal, -jo] ADJ **1** *(question, point)* crucial; **être d'une importance cruciale** to be crucially important, to be of crucial importance **2** *(incision etc)* cross-shaped

crucifère [krysifɛr] ADJ cruciferous

crucifiement [krysifimɑ̃] NM *(action)* crucifixion, crucifying; *(martyre)* crucifixion; **c. de la chair** mortifying or mortification of the flesh

crucifier [krysifje] VT *(impf, pr sub* **n. crucifiions, v. crucifiiez***)* *(mettre en croix)* to crucify; *(torturer)* to torture; **c. la chair** to mortify the flesh

crucifix [krysifi] NM INV crucifix

crucifixion [krysifiksjɔ̃] NF crucifixion

cruciforme [krysifɔrm] ADJ cross-shaped, in the shape of a cross; *Fml* cruciform

cruciverbiste [krysivɛrbist] N crossword enthusiast or buff, crossword-puzzler

crudité [krydite] NF **1** *Culin* **crudités** raw vegetables **2** *(d'une couleur)* garishness; *(d'une lumière)* harshness **3** *(d'une expression) (caractère licencieux)* coarseness, crudeness; *(franchise)* bluntness

crue [kry] NF *(d'une rivière etc)* rising, swelling; *(niveau maximum)* flood; **rivière en c.** river in spate; **le Nil est un fleuve à c. périodique** the Nile floods periodically

cruel, -elle [kryɛl] ADJ *(personne)* cruel *(envers, avec* to*)*; *(expérience, alternative, perte)* cruel, bitter; **une femme cruelle** *(en amour)* a cruel or hard-hearted woman

cruellement [kryɛlmɑ̃] ADV cruelly; **c. déçu** bitterly disappointed; **c. éprouvé** sorely tried; **faire c. défaut** to be sorely lacking

cruiser [kruzœr] NM (petit yacht) cruiser

crûment [krymɑ̃] ADV 1 (durement) (parler) (sans détours) bluntly; (ouvertement) openly, unabashedly 2 **éclairé c.** garishly lit

crustacé [krystase] NM **crustacés** shellfish, crustaceans, Spéc Crustacea; **la crevette est un c.** the prawn is a shellfish, prawns are shellfish; Culin **assiette de crustacés** seafood platter

cruzado [kruzado] NM crusado, cruzado

cryobiologie [krijɔbjɔlɔʒi] NF cryobiology

cryochirurgie [krijoʃiryrʒi] NF cryosurgery

cryoconservation [krijokɔ̃sɛrvasjɔ̃] NF cryoconservation

cryogène [krijoʒɛn] ADJ cryogenic; **mélange c.** freezing mixture

cryogénie [krijoʒeni] NF cryogenics

cryothérapie [krijoterapi] NF Méd cryotherapy

cryptage [kriptaʒ] NM encryption, encoding; TV scrambling, encrypting

crypte [kript] NF Archit, Anat crypt

crypté [kripte] ADJ 1 TV (chaîne, film) scrambled 2 (message) coded, in code

crypter [kripte] VT to encode; Tél, TV to encrypt, to scramble

cryptocommuniste [kriptokɔmynist] ADJ, N crypto-communist

cryptogénétique [kriptoʒenetik] ADJ Méd idiopathic

cryptogramme [kriptogram] NM cipher (message)

cryptographie [kriptografi] NF writing in cipher

cryptographique [kriptografik] ADJ cryptographic

cryptologie [kriptolɔʒi] NF cryptology, cryptography

CSA [seɛsa] NM (abrév **Conseil supérieur de l'audiovisuel**) = French broadcasting supervisory body

CSCE [seɛsseə] NF (abrév **Conférence sur la sécurité et la coopération en Europe**) CSCE

CSG [seɛsʒe] NF (abrév **contribution sociale généralisée**) = income-based tax deducted at source as a contribution to paying off the French social security budget deficit

cubage [kybaʒ] NM 1 (action) (d'un tas de bois etc) calculating the cubic content 2 (volume) (d'un réservoir etc) cubic capacity, volume

cubain, -aine [kybɛ̃, -ɛn] ADJ Cuban
N **C.** Cuban

cube [kyb] NM 1 Géom, Math cube; **élever un nombre au c.** to cube a number; **jeu de cubes** building blocks, (wooden) bricks 2 Scol Arg = student repeating a class for the second time 3 Arg (moto) large motorbike (over 500 cc); **les gros cubes** heavy metal
ADJ (mètre, centimètre etc) cubic

cuber [kybe] VT Math (nombre etc) to cube; (évaluer) to calculate the cubic capacity of
VI 1 (contenir) to have a cubic capacity of; **réservoir qui cube vingt litres** tank with a cubic capacity of twenty litres 2 Fam (revenir cher) to mount up, to work out expensive; **ça cube, ça finit par c.** it mounts up

cubique [kybik] ADJ cubic; Math **racine c.** cube root
NF cubic (curve)

cubisme [kybism] NM Beaux-Arts Cubism

cubiste [kybist] ADJ, N Beaux-Arts Cubist

cubitainer [kybitenœr] NM = large cubic plastic container (for bulk purchase of wine etc)

cubital, -ale, -aux, -ales [kybital, -o] ADJ Anat ulnar

cubitus [kybitys] NM Anat ulna

cuchaule [kyʃol] NF Suisse (brioche) brioche

cucu(l) [kyky] ADJ INV Fam **c. (la praline)** (personne, décoration) twee; (film, livre) corny; **elle est gentille, mais un peu c.** she is nice, but she's not really clued up

cueillette [kœjɛt] NF (action) gathering, picking; (fruits, noisettes, baies) crop, harvest; **aller faire la c. de mûres** to go blackberry picking or blackberrying; **une tribu qui vit de la chasse et de la c.** a tribe of hunters and gatherers

cueilleur, -euse [kœjœr, -øz] N (de fruit etc) picker, gatherer

cueillir [kœjir] VT (prp **cueillant**; pp **cueilli**; pr ind **je cueille, il cueille, n. cueillons**; impf **je cueillais**; p hist **je cueillis**; fu **je cueillerai**) (fleurs, fruits etc) to gather, to pick; **c. un baiser** to steal or snatch a kiss; Fig **c. des lauriers** to win laurels; Fig Litt **c. le jour, c. les roses de la vie** to make the most of life; Fig Litt **cueillez le jour** seize the day; Fig Litt **il faut c. les roses de la vie** gather ye rosebuds while ye may; Fig **le crochet du gauche l'a cueilli en plein estomac** the left hook got him right in the stomach; Fig **la mort l'a cueilli en pleine jeunesse** he was cut down in his prime; Fam **c. qn** (passer le chercher) to collect sb, to pick sb up; (l'arrêter) to pick sb up, to nab sb

cuesta [kwɛsta] NF Géog cuesta

cui-cui [kɥikɥi] NM INV cheeping, chirping, chirruping
INT cheep

cuiller, cuillère [kɥijɛr] NF 1 spoon; (contenu) spoon(ful); **c. à dessert** ou **à entremets** dessertspoon; **c. à soupe** soup spoon; (pour mesurer) tablespoon; **c. à café** teaspoon; (plus petite) coffee spoon; **petite c.** teaspoon; **c. à pot** ladle; **avaler une c. de sirop** to swallow a spoonful of medicine; **une c. pour papa, une c. pour maman** (à un enfant) one (spoonful) for Daddy, one (spoonful) for Mummy; **deux cuillers de sucre** two spoons or spoonfuls or spoonsful of sugar; Fig Fam **il n'y va pas avec le dos de la c.** he goes the whole hog, he doesn't go in for half measures, there are no half measures with him; (il est franc) he doesn't pull his punches or mince his words; Fig Fam **en deux** ou **trois** ou **cinq coups de c. à pot** in no time at all, in two shakes (of a lamb's tail); Fig Fam **être à ramasser à la petite c.** (blessé) to be badly hurt or smashed up; (épuisé) to be completely exhausted or all in; (déprimé) to be thoroughly depressed or down in the dumps; Fig Fam **on l'a ramassé à la petite c.** he was scraped off the pavement
2 Pêche spoon (bait), trolling spoon; **pêcher la truite/etc à la c.** to troll or spin for trout/etc **3** (d'une grenade) safety catch **4** Constr (d'une drague) scoop, bucket **5** Arg (main) paw, mitt

cuillerée [kɥijere] NF spoonful; **une c. à soupe de sucre** a tablespoonful of sugar; **deux cuillerées à café de sel** two teaspoons or teaspoonfuls or teaspoonsful of salt; **une c. pour maman** (à un enfant) one (spoonful) for Mummy

cuilleron [kɥijrɔ̃] NM (d'une cuillère) bowl

cuir [kɥir] NM **1** (tanné) leather; (veste) leather jacket; **c. vert** ou **brut** rawhide; **c. en croûte** undressed leather; **c. verni** patent leather; **pantalon en** ou **de c.** leather trousers; **chaussures en c.** leather shoes; **c. à rasoir** razor strop; **cuirs de motocycliste** motorcycle leathers **2** (d'un éléphant), Fam (d'une personne) hide; **c. chevelu** scalp; **tanner le c. à qn** to tan sb's hide, to give sb a good hiding **3** Fam (mauvaise prononciation) incorrect liaison (intrusive t or z); **faire un c.** to make an incorrect or a false liaison (par exemple **cent idées** [sɑ̃zide]; **moi aussi** [mwazosi])

cuirasse [kɥiras] NF **1** (protection) cuirass, breastplate; Fig **trouver le défaut dans la c. de qn** to find sb's weak or vulnerable spot, to find a chink in sb's armour; Fig **une c. de froideur** an air of aloofness **2** (d'un navire de guerre, blindé) armour (plating); **plaque de c.** armour plate

cuirassé [kɥirase] ADJ (armé) armour-plated, Am armor-plated, armoured, Am armored; Naut **croiseur c.** armour-plated cruiser; Fig **être c. contre les attaques** to be hardened to attack
NM Mil, Naut armoured or Am armored ship; **c. (de ligne)** battleship

cuirassement [kɥirasmɑ̃] NM **1** (d'un navire) armouring, Am armoring **2** (cuirasse) armour-plating, Am armor-plating

cuirasser [kɥirase] VT **1** (navire) to armour(-plate), Am to armor(-plate); (machine) to enclose, to protect **2** Arch (soldat) to put a cuirass or breastplate on
VPR **se cuirasser** Arch to put on one's cuirass or breastplate; Fig **se c. contre qch** to arm or steel oneself against or harden oneself to sth

cuirassier [kɥirasje] NM Mil cuirassier

cuire [kɥir] (prp **cuisant**; pp **cuit**; pr ind **je cuis, il cuit, n. cuisons, ils cuisent**; impf **je cuisais**; p hist **je cuisis**; fu **je cuirai**) VT **1** Culin to cook; **c. à l'eau** to boil; **c. des légumes à la vapeur** to steam vegetables; **c. la viande sur le gril** to grill or Am broil the meat; **c. au four** to bake; **un four en terre cuit bien le pain** bread bakes well in a clay oven
2 (briques, poterie etc) to fire, to bake **3** (détruire) (du soleil) to bake; (du gel) to kill (off); **le gel a cuit les géraniums** the frost has nipped the geraniums **4** Suisse (eau, lait) to boil; (vêtements, linge) to boil-wash
VI **1** (des aliments) to cook; **le poulet a cuit trop longtemps** the chicken is overcooked; **pommes à c.** cooking apples; **chocolat à c.** cooking or baking chocolate; **c. à petit feu** ou **à feu doux** to cook slowly, to simmer; Fig Fam **au lieu de me laisser c. à petit feu** instead of keeping me on tenterhooks; Fig Fam **c. (dans son jus)** (avoir très chaud) to be boiling; Fig **laisser c. qn dans son jus** to let sb stew (in their own juice); Fig Fam **on cuit dans cette salle** this room's like an oven; Fam **va te faire c. un œuf!** go to hell!
2 (brûler) (des mains, joues) to burn; (des yeux) to smart
VPR **se cuire se c. au soleil/sur la plage** to bake or roast in the sun/on the beach
V IMPERS **il vous en cuira** you'll be sorry (for it), you'll regret it

cuisant [kɥizɑ̃] ADJ (douleur) smarting, burning; (froid) biting; (remarques) caustic, biting, bitter; **déception cuisante** bitter disappointment; **un échec c.** a stinging defeat

cuiseur [kɥizœr] NM large cooking pot

cuisine [kɥizin] NF **1** (pièce) kitchen; Naut (cook's) galley; **éléments de c.** kitchen units; **ustensiles de c.** cooking utensils; **batterie de c.** (set of) pots and pans; Mil **c. roulante** field kitchen; Ling **latin de c.** dog Latin
2 (préparation) (art of) cooking, cookery, cuisine; **faire la c.** to cook; **c'est lui qui fait la c.** he does the cooking; **il fait de la bonne c., il fait bien la c.** he's a good cook; **c. au beurre/à l'huile** cooking with butter/oil; **c.**

bourgeoise plain *or* home cooking; **livre de c.** cookery *or* recipe book, cookbook **3** *(plats)* food; **restaurant renommé pour sa c.** restaurant famed for its food *or* cuisine; **la nouvelle c.** nouvelle cuisine **4** *Fam (intrigue)* (dirty) tricks; **la c. parlementaire** parliamentary intrigue

cuisiner [kɥizine] **VI** to cook; **elle cuisine bien** she's a good cook ▸ **VT 1** *(dîner)* to make, to cook; **plats cuisinés** ready-cooked dishes, takeaway meals **2** *Fig Fam* **c. qn** to interrogate *or* grill sb

cuisinette [kɥizinɛt] **NF** kitchenette

cuisinier, -ière [kɥizinje, -jɛr] **N** chef, cook; **c. en chef** executive chef ▸ **NF cuisinière** cooker, stove; **cuisinière électrique** electric cooker *or* stove

cuisinier-pâtissier, *pl* **cuisiniers-pâtissiers NM** pastry cook

cuissage [kɥisaʒ] **NM droit de c.** *Fig* sexual harassment *(by a superior)*; *Hist* droit du seigneur

cuissard [kɥisar] **NM 1** *(pour cycliste)* racing shorts **2** *Arch (partie de l'armure)* cuisse, thigh piece

cuissardes [kɥisard] **NFPL** *(bottes de femme)* thigh boots; *(de pêche)* waders

cuisse [kɥis] **NF** *Anat* thigh; *Culin* **c. de poulet** chicken leg, *Fam* drumstick; **cuisses de grenouilles** frogs' legs; *Fig* **avoir la c. légère** to sleep around; *Fam* **se croire sorti de la c. de Jupiter** to have a lot of oneself, to think one is the cat's whiskers

cuisseau, -eaux [kɥiso] **NM** *Culin (de veau)* leg

cuissettes [kɥisɛt] **NFPL** *(pour sportifs)* = short shorts

cuisson [kɥisɔ̃] **NF 1** *(d'aliments)* cooking; **temps de c.** cooking time; **le porc demande une longue c.** pork has to be cooked for a long time; **plaque de c.** hob; **c. au gril** grilling; **c. en bain de friture** deep-fat frying; **c. à la vapeur** steaming **2** *(des briques, de la porcelaine)* burning, firing **3** *(sensation)* **une impression de c.** a burning sensation *or* feeling; **la c. de la fessée qu'elle avait reçue l'empêchait de s'asseoir** she was smarting so much after the spanking that she couldn't sit down

cuissot [kɥiso] **NM** *Culin (de venaison)* haunch

cuistance [kɥistɑ̃s] **NF** *Arg* cooking; *(nourriture)* grub, nosh; **qui est-ce qui fait la c. ce soir?** who's cooking tonight?

cuistot [kɥisto] **NM** *Fam* cook

cuistre [kɥistr] *Péj Litt* **NM 1** *(vaniteux)* pedant **2** *(grossier personnage)* scoundrel ▸ **ADJ** pedantic

cuistrerie [kɥistrəri] **NF** *Péj* **1** *Litt* pedantry **2** *(grossièreté)* scoundrelly behaviour

cuit [kɥi] **ADJ 1** *Culin* cooked; **bien c.** well done; **c. à point** done to a turn; **trop c.** overdone, overcooked; **pas assez c.** underdone, undercooked; **c. au four** baked; **terre cuite** terracotta; **vin c.** = aperitif wine **2** *Fig Fam* **être c.** to be done for, to have had it; **c'est c.!** that's it!, we've had it!; **le cinéma, c'est c. pour ce soir** the cinema's out tonight; **c'est c. pour nos vacances** we've had it as far as a holiday is concerned; **c'est du tout c.** it's a cinch *or* a walkover *or* a doddle **3** *Fam (ivre)* plastered, smashed

cuite [kɥit] **NF 1** *(de briques, poterie)* baking, firing **2** *Fam* **(se) prendre une (bonne) c.** to get plastered *or* tight, *Am* to tie one on

cuiter (se) [səkɥite] **VPR** *Fam* to get tight *or* plastered, *Am* to tie one on

cuivre [kɥivr] **NM 1** *(métal)* **c. (rouge)** copper; **casserole en c.** copper saucepan; **doublé en c.** *(plaqué)* copper-plated; *(par le*

fond) copper-bottomed; *Minér* **minerai de c.** copper ore; **c. jaune** brass; **les cuivres** copper(ware); *(jaunes)* brasses; **faire (briller) les cuivres** to polish the brassware, to do the brasses **2** *Mus* **les cuivres** the brass (section) **3** *(planche)* copperplate

cuivré [kɥivre] **ADJ 1** *(hâlé) (peau, teint) (naturellement)* copper-coloured; *(par le soleil)* bronzed; **cheveux aux reflets cuivrés** auburn hair; **d'un rouge c.** coppery red **2** *(voix)* resonant, ringing; *Mus* **sons cuivrés** brassy tones

cuivrer [kɥivre] **VT 1** *(couvrir de cuivre)* to copper, to coat with copper **2** *(la peau, le teint)* to bronze ▸ **VPR se cuivrer** to turn the colour of copper, to turn coppery

cuivreux, -euse [kɥivrø, -øz] **ADJ** *Chimie (oxyde)* cuprous

cul [ky] **NM 1** *Arg (d'une personne)* arse, *Fam* bum, *Am* ass, *Fam* fanny; **un beau c.** a great bum, a lovely arse, *Am (d'homme)* nice buns; *Vulg* **trou du c.** arsehole, *Am* asshole; **faux c.** bustle; *Fig* **c'est un faux c.** he's two-faced; **renverser qn c. par-dessus tête** to send sb flying *or* head over heels *or* *Vulg* arse over elbow; *Fig* **il en est tombé** *ou* **resté sur le c.** he was flabbergasted; **se taper le c. par terre** to roar with laughter, to split one's sides laughing; **des vacances? mon c.!** holidays? my arse!; *Vulg* **parle à mon c., ma tête est malade!** *(personne ne m'écoute)* I might as well talk to the fucking wall!; *(laisse-moi tranquille)* fuck off!; **avoir le feu au c.** to be in a hell of a rush; *(sexuellement)* to be randy as hell; **être porté sur le c.** to be sex-mad; **revue** *ou* **bouquin de c.** porn magazine; **film de c.** blue *or* porn movie; **être comme c. et chemise** to be as thick as thieves; **ça vaut mieux qu'un coup de pied au c.** it's better than a kick in the pants; **avoir qn dans le c.** to hate sb's guts; **en avoir plein le c.** to be pissed off **(de qch** with sth), to have had a bellyful **(de qch** of sth); **ils l'ont dans le c.** they've had it, that's really screwed them up, that's them buggered; **on a les flics au c.** we've got the cops on our tail; *Mil Arg* **tirer au c.** to swing the lead, to shirk; **c'est un tire-au-c.** he's a shirker *or* skiver; *Can Fam* **n'avoir rien que le c. et les dents** to be at rock-bottom; *Arg* **quel c.!** what a bloody fool *or* prat *or* arsehole *or* *Am* asshole!

2 *Arg (chance)* luck; **avoir du c.** to be lucky *or* jammy; **avoir le c. bordé de nouilles** to be a lucky bastard; **j'ai/elle a gagné le gros lot – quel c.!** I/she won the jackpot – you/the jammy devil!

3 *(d'un animal)* haunches, rump

4 *(d'un sac, tonneau)* bottom; *(d'une bouteille)* bottom, base; **boire c. sec** to down one's drink in one go; **c. sec!** bottoms up!

5 *Naut (d'un navire)* stern

▸ **ADJ INV** silly; **elle est un peu c.** she's a bit of a twerp *or* twit *or* nerd

culasse [kylas] **NF 1** *Mil (de fusil, pistolet)* breech; **c. mobile** *(de carabine)* bolt; **fusil se chargeant par la c.** breech loader; **bloc de c.** breech block **2** *(de moteur)* cylinder head; **joint de c.** cylinder head gasket; *Aut* **c. à flux opposés** cross-flow *or* hemispherical head; *Aut* **c. à flux transversal** cross-flow head

cul-blanc, *pl* **culs-blancs NM** *(oiseau)* wheatear

culbute [kylbyt] **NF 1** *(cabriole)* somersault; **faire la c.** to turn a somersault **2** *(chute)* tumble, heavy fall; **faire une** *ou* **la c.** to fall; **le gamin chuta de son vélo et fit une c.** the kid came off his bike head over heels; *Fig Fam* **faire la c.** *(d'un gouvernement)* to fall; *(d'une entreprise)* to go bust; *Com* **les revendeurs font la c.** the dealers are making a killing *or* a huge profit

culbuter [kylbyte] **VI 1** *(se renverser) (d'un vase, d'un arbre, d'une statue etc)* to topple over; *(de qn)* to take a tumble; **la voiture a culbuté dans le fossé** the car overturned and landed in the ditch **2** *Fam (d'une entreprise)* to go bust *or* *Arg* belly up; *(d'un banquier, homme d'affaires etc)* to come a cropper ▸ **VT 1** *(renverser)* to knock down *or* over; *(gouvernement)* to bring down **2** *très Fam (femme)* to lay

culbuterie [kylbytri] **NF** *Aut* rocker arms

culbuteur [kylbytœr] **NM 1** *(jouet)* tumbler **2** *(de moteur)* rocker (arm) **3** *Tech* tripper device; *(de camion)* tipper

cul-de-basse-fosse, *pl* **culs-de-basse-fosse** [kydbasfos] **NM** dungeon

cul-de-jatte, *pl* **culs-de-jatte** [kydʒat] **NM** legless cripple

cul-de-lampe, *pl* **culs-de-lampe** [kydlɑ̃p] **NM 1** *Archit (ornement)* bracket, corbel **2** *Typ* tailpiece

cul-de-poule [kydpul] **NM** *Arg* **faire la bouche en c.** to purse one's lips

cul-de-sac, *pl* **culs-de-sac** [kydsak] **NM** blind alley, cul-de-sac; *Fig* dead end; **la rue se termine en c.** the street ends in a cul-de-sac *or* is a dead end; *Fig* **être dans un c.** to have reached a dead end

culée [kyle] **NF** *Archit (d'un contrefort)* pier; *Constr (d'un pont)* abutment (pier)

culinaire [kyliner] **ADJ** culinary; **l'art c.** the art of cooking, the culinary art; **les talents culinaires de son mari** her husband's talents as a cook; **recettes culinaires** recipes

culminant [kylminɑ̃] **ADJ point c.** *(d'une chaîne de montagnes)* highest point; *(du pouvoir)* zenith; *(de la renommée, gloire, d'une carrière)* height, peak

culminer [kylmine] **VI 1 le mont Blanc culmine à 4807 mètres** Mont Blanc is 4,807 metres at its highest point **2** *Fig Bourse (de cours)* to reach its highest level, to peak; **sa carrière culmine** it's the crowning point *or* pinnacle of his career; **alors que sa carrière culminait** when his career was reaching its height *or* peak

culot [kylo] **NM 1** *Fam (audace)* cheek, nerve; **tu ne manques pas de c.!, tu as du c.!** you've got a nerve *or* a cheek!; **il a un sacré c.!** he's got a helluva nerve!; **il a tous les culots** he's got a lot of nerve, cheek is his middle name; **y aller au c.** to put a brave face on it, to brazen it out; **vas-y au c. et demande-lui son autographe** just breeze up and ask him for his autograph **2** *(de lampe, bouteille etc)* bottom, base; *Mil (de douille de cartouche, d'obus)* base; *(de cartouche)* head; *Élec (d'ampoule)* base; *Aut (d'une bougie)* body **3** *(dans une pipe)* dottle **4** *Tech (résidu)* residue

culottage [kylotaʒ] **NM** *(d'une pipe)* colouring, seasoning

culotte [kylot] **NF 1** *(pantalon)* **c. courte** short trousers; **c. de cheval** jodhpurs, riding breeches; *Fig Fam* jodhpur thighs; **c. de golf** plus fours; **c. de peau** lederhosen; *Fig Fam* **c'est la femme qui porte la c.** it's the wife who wears the trousers; *Can* **avoir des culottes** to have guts; *Fam* **user ses fonds de c. sur les bancs de l'école** to idle away one's time at school; *Fam* **faire dans sa c.** to be scared stiff, to have the jitters, *Arg* to wet *or* pee oneself **2** *(sous-vêtement) (de femme)* panties, knickers; *(d'enfant)* pants VOIR GRAMMAIRE A10 **3** *Fam* **prendre une c.** *(aux cartes etc)* to lose heavily, *Am* to take a bath **4** *Culin (de bœuf)* rump

culotté [kylote] **ADJ 1** *(pipe)* seasoned; **un plafond c. par la fumée du tabac** a ceiling black with tobacco smoke **2** *Fam (audacieux)* full of cheek *or* nerve, cheeky; **il est**

c. he's got one hell of a nerve (**de faire qch** doing sth)

culotter [kylɔte] **VT** (pipe) to colour, to season

culpabilisation [kylpabilizasjɔ̃] **NF** Psy **1** (action) **la c. de qn** making sb feel guilty **2** (résultat) (feeling of) guilt

culpabiliser [kylpabilize] Psy **VT c. qn** to make sb feel guilty
VI to feel guilty

culpabilité [kylpabilite] **NF** guilt; **nier sa c.** to deny that one is guilty; Jur **verdict de c.** guilty verdict; **sa c. dans cette affaire a été établie** his guilt in the matter has been established; **sentiment de c.** feeling of guilt, guilty feeling

culte [kylt] **ADJ** (livre, film, émission, auteur) cult
NM 1 (vénération) worship; Fig cult; Fig **c. de la personnalité** personality cult, cult of the personality; **avoir le c. de l'argent** to worship money; Fig **avoir un c. pour qn, rendre** ou **vouer un c. à qn** to (hero-)worship sb **2** (religion) form of worship, creed, religion; **liberté du c.** freedom of worship; **changer de c.** to change one's religion **3** (service protestant) (church) service

cul-terreux, pl **culs-terreux NM** Fam Péj country bumpkin, yokel, Am rube, redneck

cultivable [kyltivabl] **ADJ** suitable for cultivation

cultivateur, -trice [kyltivatœr, -tris] **N** farmer; **petits cultivateurs** small farmers, small-holders
NM (machine) cultivator
ADJ agricultural, farming; **les peuples cultivateurs** agricultural people, farming communities

cultivé [kyltive] **ADJ 1** Agr (terre, champs), Biol (virus) cultivated **2** (personne) cultivated, cultured; **gens cultivés** cultivated or educated people

cultiver [kyltive] **VT 1** (sol) to cultivate, to farm **2** Agr (céréales, artichauts) to raise, to grow, to cultivate; (roses) to raise, to grow; Biol (virus), Fig (l'amitié de qn etc) to cultivate; **c. son esprit** to cultivate or improve one's mind; **c. un goût** to cultivate or develop a taste; **il cultive la goujaterie** he makes a point of being boorish, he works hard at being boorish; Fig **il faut c. son jardin** = concentrate on things close to home and don't try to change the world
VPR se cultiver to improve one's mind

cultuel, -elle [kyltɥɛl] **ADJ** of or pertaining to worship; **édifice c.** place of worship

culture [kyltyr] **NF 1** (du sol) cultivation; **c. fruitière** fruit farming; **c. sèche** dry farming; **cultures** land under cultivation **2** (de céréales, artichauts etc) growing, raising; Biol **c. (microbienne/de tissus)** culture (of bacteria/of tissue); **bouillon de c.** culture medium **3** (espèce cultivée) crop **4** (intellectuelle) culture, education; **c. scientifique** scientific knowledge or background; **question de c. générale** question of general knowledge; **avoir une solide c.** to have a sound education; **maison de la c.** ≃ arts centre **5** (civilisation) culture; **la c. gréco-romaine** Graeco-Roman culture or civilization; **c'est une autre c.** it's a different culture or way of life
► ► **c. d'entreprise** corporate culture; **c. physique** physical training, Fam PT

culturel, -elle [kyltyrɛl] **ADJ** (relations, milieu, attaché) cultural; (voyage) educational; **centre c.** community arts centre; **choc c.** culture shock; **subir un choc c.** to suffer (from) culture shock

culturisme [kyltyrism] **NM** body building, Fam pumping iron

culturiste [kyltyrist] **N** body builder

cumin [kymɛ̃] **NM** cumin; **c. des prés** caraway; **munster au c.** Munster (cheese) with caraway seeds

cumul [kymyl] **NM c. des fonctions, c. des mandats** plurality of offices, pluralism; **c. des traitements** drawing of more than one salary

cumulable [kymylabl] **ADJ** des fonctions cumulables offices which can be held simultaneously or concurrently; **des traitements cumulables** salaries which can be drawn concurrently or simultaneously; **ces deux réductions d'impôts ne sont pas cumulables** these two tax reductions may not be claimed at the same time

cumulard, -arde [kymylar, -ard] **N** Fam Péj holder of several official positions (for each of which a salary is drawn)

cumulatif, -ive [kymylatif, -iv] **ADJ** cumulative

cumuler [kymyle] **VT c. des fonctions** to hold more than one office; **c. deux traitements** to draw two (separate) salaries; **il cumule plusieurs emplois** he has several jobs

cumulo-nimbus [kymylonɛ̃bys] **NM INV** Météo cumulo-nimbus

cumulo-stratus [kymylostratys] **NM INV** Météo strato-cumulus, cumulo-stratus

cumulus [kymylys] **NM INV** Météo cumulus

cunéiforme [kyneifɔrm] **ADJ** cuneiform

cupide [kypid] **ADJ** greedy, grasping, moneygrubbing

cupidement [kypidmɑ̃] **ADV** greedily

cupidité [kypidite] **NF** cupidity, greed

Cupidon [kypidɔ̃] **NM** Myth Cupid

cuprifère [kyprifɛr] **ADJ** copper-bearing, Spéc cupriferous

cuprique [kyprik] **ADJ** cupric

curable [kyrabl] **ADJ** (maladie etc) curable; **la lèpre est c.** leprosy can be cured, leprosy is curable

curaçao [kyraso] **NM** curaçao (liqueur)

curage [kyraʒ] **NM** (de canalisation, port) clearing or cleaning out; (de tuyau) flushing

curare [kyrar] **NM** curare

curatelle [kyratɛl] **NF** Jur (d'une succession) trusteeship; (d'un mineur, aliéné) guardianship

curateur, -trice [kyratœr, -tris] **N** Jur (d'une succession etc) trustee; (d'un mineur, aliéné) guardian

curatif, -ive [kyratif, -iv] **ADJ** curative

cure [kyr] **NF 1** Méd (course of) treatment; **c. thermale** hydrotherapy, course of treatment at a spa; **c. d'amaigrissement** diet; **faire une c. de lait/de repos** to go on a milk diet/rest cure; **elle a fait une c. à Vichy** she took the waters at Vichy; **c. de sommeil** sleep cure; **c. de sevrage** detoxification programme **2** (fonction de curé) office of a parish priest; (paroisse) parish; (presbytère) presbytery; **obtenir une c.** to be appointed parish priest **3** n'avoir **c. de qch** not to care about sth; **je n'ai c. de toutes ses médailles** I don't care about all his medals; **tu peux toujours essayer de l'impressionner, elle n'en a c.** she won't take any notice of your attempts to impress her

curé [kyre] **NM** Cathol parish priest; Fam (sans aucune distinction de rang) priest; **monsieur le c.** Father; **il veut se faire c.** he wants to become a priest or to enter the priesthood; Fig Fam **bouffer** ou **manger du c.** to be (violently) anti-clerical

cure-dent(s), pl **cure-dents NM** toothpick

curée [kyre] **NF** = parts of the stag given to the hounds; (mise à mort) kill; Fig **pays livré à la c. des mercenaires étrangers** country handed over to the tender mercies of foreign mercenaries; Fig **ce fut la c. entre les héritiers** the heirs started to fight over the spoils; Fig **les journalistes s'emparèrent de l'affaire et ce fut une véritable c.** the press acted like jackals once they got wind of the story

cure-ongles NM INV nail cleaner

cure-pipe, pl **cure-pipes NM** pipe-cleaner

curer [kyre] **VT** (ses dents) to pick; (une canalisation, un port) to clear or clean out; (une rivière, un canal, un étang) to dredge; (pipe) to scrape, to clean out; **se c. les ongles/les oreilles** to clean one's nails/clean (out) one's ears

curetage [kyrtaʒ] **NM** Chir curetting, curettage

cureter [kyrte] **VT** Chir to curette

cureton [kyrtɔ̃] **NM** Fam Péj priest

curette [kyrɛt] **NF** Tech scraper; Chir curette

curie[1] [kyri] **NF** Antiq, Cathol curia

curie[2] **NM** Phys curie

curieusement [kyrjøzmɑ̃] **ADV** (étrangement) curiously, oddly; **les gens le regardaient c.** people looked at him curiously or gave him curious or funny looks

curieux, -ieuse [kyrjø, -jøz] **ADJ 1** (intéressé) curious, interested; (esprit) inquiring, curious; **être c. de tout/de la vie** to be curious about or interested in everything/life; **elle est curieuse d'archéologie** she's interested in archaeology; **je serais c. de voir cela** I'd be interested in seeing that **2** (indiscret) curious, inquisitive, Fam nos(e)y **3** (étrange) curious, odd, funny, peculiar; **par une curieuse coïncidence** by a strange coincidence; **chose assez curieuse** curiously or funnily enough; **ne me regarde pas comme une bête curieuse** don't look at me as if I had two heads
N inquisitive person, Fam nos(e)y parker, busybody; **méfie-toi, c'est un c.** watch out, he's nos(e)y; **un attroupement de c.** a crowd of onlookers or bystanders; **il était venu en c.** he came just to have a look
NM le plus c. de l'affaire est que ... the strangest or oddest part or thing about it is that ...

curiosité [kyrjozite] **NF 1** (intellectuelle) curiosity, interest; **c. intellectuelle** intellectual curiosity; **pour développer la c. de votre enfant** to arouse your child's sense of curiosity; **satisfaire sa c.** to satisfy one's curiosity; **regarder qn avec c.** to look at sb curiously or enquiringly **2** (indiscrétion) curiosity, inquisitiveness, Fam nosiness; **par c.** out of curiosity; **par simple c., dites-moi ...** just out of curiosity, tell me ...; **la c. est un vilain défaut** curiosity killed the cat **3** (monument) interesting feature or sight; (objet) curio; **curiosités d'une ville** sights of a town

curiste [kyrist] **N** patient taking the waters (at a spa)

curling [kœrliŋ] **NM** Sport curling

curriculum vitae [kyrikylɔmvite] **NM INV** curriculum vitae, CV, Am résumé; **envoyer/établir son c.** to send (off)/draw up one's CV

curry [kyri] **NM** Culin curry; **poulet au c., c. de poulet** curried chicken, chicken curry

curseur [kyrsœr] **NM** Ordinat cursor; Tech (de règle à calcul, compas) cursor, slide, runner; Ordinat **position/déplacement du c.** cursor position/movement

cursif, -ive [kyrsif, -iv] **ADJ 1** (écriture) cursive **2** (rapide) cursory

cursus [kyrsys] **NM** Univ programme, Am program, course of study, curriculum; **établir son c.** to arrange one's course of study; **le c. médical** the medical degree course

curviligne [kyrviliɲ] **ADJ** curvilinear

cuspide [kyspid] **NF** Anat, Bot cusp

custode [kystɔd] NF **1** *Rel (pour hostie)* custodial **2** *(de voiture)* rear quarter panel; *(glace)* quarterlight

cutané [kytane] ADJ skin, *Spéc* cutaneous; **maladie cutanée** skin disease

cuti [kyti] NF *Méd* skin test; *Fam* **virer sa c.** to have a positive reaction to a skin test; *Fig* to have changed radically

cuticule [kytikyl] NF *Anat* epidermis, cuticle

cutiréaction [kytireaksjɔ̃] NF *Méd* = **cuti**

cutter [kœtœr, kytɛr] NM Stanley® knife

cuvage [kyvaʒ] NM, **cuvaison** [kyvɛzɔ̃] NF *(de vin, bière)* fermenting *or* fermentation in vats

cuve [kyv] NF *(storage)* tank, cistern; *(de machine à laver)* tub; *(pour la fermentation des alcools, du vin)* vat, tun; *Vieilli* **c. à lessive** laundry tub; *Phot* **c. à laver/à développement** washing/developing tank

cuvée [kyve] NF **1** *(quantité)* vatful, tunful **2** *(produit)* vintage; *Fig* batch; **vin de première c.** wine of the first growth *or* vintage; **c. de la maison** *ou* **du patron** house wine; *Fig* **être de la même c.** *(d'étudiants)* to be classmates, to be in the same year; *Fig* **la dernière c. du festival de Cannes** the latest batch of films from the Cannes festival

cuver [kyve] VI **1** *(de vin, bière)* to ferment *(in the vats)* **2** *Fam (d'une personne)* to sleep it off VT *Fam* **c. son vin** to sleep it off; **c. sa colère** to simmer down

cuvette [kyvɛt] NF **1** *(wash)*basin, *(wash)*bowl; **c. (de lavabo)** washbasin **2** *(de W.-C.)* bowl, pan; *(de thermomètre)* bulb; *Phot* *(developing)* dish **3** *(dépression)*, *Géog* basin, depression, *Br* punchbowl

CV [seve] NM **1** *Aut (abrév* **cheval-vapeur)** = French administrative unit for car tax purposes **2** *(abrév* **curriculum vitae)** CV, *Am* résumé

CVG [seveʒe] NM *Bourse (abrév* **certificat de valeur garantie)** CVR

cyan [sjã] ADJ INV, NM cyan

cyanhydrique [sjanidrik] ADJ **acide c.** prussic acid

cyanose [sjanoz] NF *Méd* cyanosis

cyanure [sjanyr] NM *Chimie* cyanide; **empoisonnement au c.** cyanide poisoning

cyber [siber] NM cyber

cybercafé [siberkafe] NM cybercafé

cybercommerce [siberkɔmɛrs] NM e-commerce

cybercrime [siberkrim] NM cybercrime

cyberculture [siberkyltyr] NF cyberculture

cyberespace [siberɛspas] NM cyberspace; **dans le c.** in cyberspace

cybermonde [sibermɔ̃d] NM cyberspace; **dans le c.** in cyberspace

cybernaute [sibernot] NM cybernaut

cybernéticien, -ienne [sibernetisjɛ̃, -jɛn] N cybernetics expert, cyberneticist

cybernétique [sibernetik] ADJ cybernetic NF cybernetics

cyberpunk [sibɛrpœnk] NM cyberpunk

cybersexe [sibɛrsɛks] NM cybersex

cyclable [siklabl] ADJ **piste c.** cycle track

cyclamen [siklamɛn] NM cyclamen

cycle [sikl] NM **1** *(d'événements, de poèmes etc)*, *Biol, Chimie* cycle; *(de conférences)* series; *Mktg* **c. commande-livraison-facturation** order-to-remittance cycle; *Mktg* **c. de commercialisation** trade cycle; *Mktg* **c. de la distribution** wheel of retailing; **c. économique** economic cycle; *Com* **c. d'exploitation** operating cycle; *Ordinat* **c. d'exécution** execute cycle; **c. menstruel** menstrual cycle; **c. solaire** solar cycle; *Mktg* **c. de vie** life cycle; *Mktg* **c. de vie du produit** product life cycle, PLC

  2 *Scol* **premier/second c.** junior/senior classes *(in secondary school)*; **elle est prof dans le premier c.** she's a junior school teacher, *Am* she teaches junior school; **élèves du premier c.** junior pupils; **c. primaire/supérieur** primary/higher education

  3 *Aut* **c. d'allumage** ignition cycle; **c. à deux temps** two-stroke cycle; **c. à quatre temps** four-stroke cycle; **c. urbain** urban cycle

  4 *(véhicule)* cycle; **magasin/fabricant de cycles** cycle shop/manufacturer

cyclique [siklik] ADJ cyclical

cyclisme [siklism] NM *Sport* cycling

cycliste [siklist] *Sport* N cyclist ADJ *(course)* cycle; **coureur c.** racing cyclist

cyclo-cross [siklokrɔs] NM *Sport* cyclo-cross

cycloïdal, -ale, -aux, -ales [siklɔidal, -o] ADJ *Math (courbe etc)* cycloidal

cycloïde [siklɔid] NF *Math* cycloid

cyclomoteur [siklomɔtœr] NM moped

cyclomotoriste [siklomɔtɔrist] N moped rider

cyclonal, -ale, -aux, -ales [siklɔnal, -o] ADJ *Météo* cyclonic

cyclone [siklon] NM *Météo (tempête)* cyclone; *(zone de basse pression)* area of low pressure, depression, cyclone; **œil du c.** eye of the storm; *Fig* **elle est entrée comme un c.** she came in like a whirlwind

cyclonique [siklɔnik] ADJ *Météo* cyclonic

cyclope [siklɔp] NM *Myth* Cyclops; *Fig* **travail de c.** colossal undertaking, Herculean task

cyclopéen, -enne [siklɔpeɛ̃, -ɛn] ADJ *Fig* gigantic, colossal; **travail c.** Herculean task

cyclopousse [siklopus] NM trishaw, rickshaw *(drawn by a bicycle)*

cyclorama [siklorama] NM *TV, Cin* cyclorama, cyc

cyclothymie [siklotimi] NF *Psy* manic-depression

cyclothymique [siklotimik] ADJ *Psy* manic-depressive

cyclotourisme [sikloturism] NM bicycle touring, cycling holidays

cyclotron [siklotrɔ̃] NM *Nucl* cyclotron

cygne [siɲ] NM swan; **jeune c.** cygnet; **c. mâle** cob; **c. femelle** pen; **duvet de c.** swansdown; **une robe d'une blancheur de c.** a pure *or* snowy white dress; *Fig* **c'est son chant du c.** it's his swansong; *Tech* **col de c.** swan neck

cylindrage [silɛ̃draʒ] NM *(de route, d'acier etc)* rolling; *Métal* **c. à froid** cold rolling

cylindre [silɛ̃dr] NM **1** *Géom* cylinder **2** *(de moteur)* cylinder; *(de laminoir, essoreuse à rouleaux, calandre etc)* roller; *Aut* **c. de roue** wheel cylinder; **moteur à quatre cylindres** four-cylinder engine; *Aut* **une quatre cylindres** a four-cylinder (car); *Typ* **c. d'impression** printing cylinder, drum; **c. compresseur** road roller; **c. de friction** *(dans une imprimante)* friction cylinder

cylindrée [silɛ̃dre] NF *(de cylindre, moteur)* (cubic) capacity; **petite c.** *(voiture)* small car, *Am* compact; **grosse c.** large car, *Fam* tank

cylindrer [silɛ̃dre] VT *(route, pelouse, métal etc)* to roll

cylindrique [silɛ̃drik] ADJ cylindrical

cymbale [sɛ̃bal] NF *Mus* cymbal

cymbalier, -ière [sɛ̃balje, -jɛr] NM cymbal player, cymbalist

cynégétique [sineʒetik] NF hunting ADJ hunting; **les plaisirs cynégétiques** the pleasures of hunting

cynique [sinik] ADJ **1** *(personne, attitude etc)* cynical **2** *Phil* Cynic NM **1** cynic **2** *Phil* Cynic

cyniquement [sinikmã] ADV cynically

cynisme [sinism] NM **1** cynicism **2** *Phil* Cynicism

cynocéphale [sinosefal] NM dog-faced baboon

cynodrome [sinodrom] NM greyhound (racing) track, *Fam* dog track

cynophile [sinofil] ADJ **équipe c.** (police) dog-handlers, dog-handling team N dog lover

cynor(r)hodon [sinorɔdɔ̃] NM *(fruit)* rosehip; **confiture/tisane de c.** rosehip jam/tea

cyprès [siprɛ] NM cypress (tree)

cypriote [siprijɔt] ADJ Cypriot N **C.** Cypriot

cyrillique [sirilik] ADJ *(alphabet etc)* Cyrillic

cystique [sistik] ADJ *Anat, Méd (conduit, bile, calcul etc)* cystic

cystite [sistit] NF *Méd* cystitis

cytise [sitiz] NM laburnum

cytologie [sitɔlɔʒi] NF *Biol* cytology

cytologique [sitɔlɔʒik] ADJ *Biol* cytological

cytomégalovirus [sitomegalovirys] NM *Méd* cytomegalovirus, CMV

cytoplasme [sitɔplasm] NM *Biol* cytoplasm

cytoplasmique [sitɔplasmik] ADJ *Biol* cytoplasmic

czar [tsar] NM tsar, czar

D, d [de] NM **1** (lettre) D, d; Fig **le système D** (= débrouillardise) resourcefulness; **c'est un champion du système D** he's extremely resourceful; **recourir au système D** to use one's wits; **comment tu as fait pour avoir toutes les places gratuitement? – système D!** how did you manage to get all the tickets for nothing? – I used my wits! **2** Ftbl (abrév **division**) **D1/D2/D3** Div1/Div2/Div3

DAB [deabe] NM Banque (abrév **distributeur automatique de billets**) ATM

dab [dab] NM Arg (père) old man

dac, d'ac [dak] INT Fam (abrév **d'accord**) OK; **si t'es pas d.** (si tu ne veux pas) if you don't want to; **c'est la mieux des trois, si t'es pas d., tu n'as qu'à …** this is the best of the three, if you don't agree, then you should …

Dacron® [dakrɔ̃] NM Tex Terylene®, Am Dacron®

dactyle [daktil] NM Littér dactyl

dactylo [daktilo] N (abrév **dactylographe**) typist
  NF (abrév **dactylographie**) typing; **il est bon en d.** he's good at typing, he's a good typist; **j'ai besoin de la d. dans mon métier** I need typing or I need to be able to type in my job
  NM Can (machine à écrire) typewriter

dactylo-facturière, pl **dactylos-facturières** NF typist invoice clerk

dactylographe [daktilograf] N Vieilli typist
  NM Can (machine à écrire) typewriter

dactylographie [daktilografi] NF typing

dactylographier [daktilografje] VT to type

dactylographique [daktilografik] ADJ (matériel etc) typing

dactyloscopie [daktiloskɔpi] NF fingerprinting, Spéc dactyloscopy

dactyloscopique [daktiloskɔpik] ADJ Spéc dactyloscopic; **examen d.** fingerprint examination

dada [dada] NM **1** Enf (cheval) gee-gee; **aller à d.** to play gee-gees **2** Fam (sujet favori) pet subject; **c'est son nouveau d.** it's his latest hobby-horse; **enfourcher son d.** to get on one's hobby-horse, to get on to one's pet subject **3** Beaux-Arts, Littér **le d.** Dadaism
  ADJ Beaux-Arts, Littér Dadaist; **le mouvement d.** Dadaism

dadais [dadɛ] NM Fam gawk; **un grand d.** a great gawk

dadaïsme [dadaism] NM Beaux-Arts, Littér Dadaism

dadaïste [dadaist] N, ADJ Beaux-Arts, Littér Dadaist

DADS [deades] NF Admin (abrév **déclaration annuelle des données sociales**) PAYE and NIC return

dague [dag] NF (épée) dagger

daguerréotype [dagereɔtip] NM Phot daguerreotype

dahlia [dalja] NM dahlia

dahu [day] NM = imaginary animal figuring in stories told to the gullible

daigner [deɲe] VT to condescend, to deign; **le roi a daigné lui parler** the king condescended to speak to him; **elle n'a même pas daigné me voir** she wouldn't even (condescend to) see me

daim [dɛ̃] NM **1** (animal) (fallow) deer; (mâle) buck **2** (peau) suede; **gants/veste en d.** suede gloves/jacket

daine [dɛn] NF doe

dais [dɛ] NM canopy; **surmonté d'un d.** canopied; Fig **un d. de feuilles** a canopy of leaves

Dakar [dakar] N Dakar

dakin [dakɛ̃] NM Méd (solution de) d. Dakin's solution

dal, dalle [dal] NM Arg **que d.** (rien) zilch, damn all; **j'y vois que d.** I can't see a bloody thing, I can see damn all; **j'ai pigé que d.** I didn't understand a bloody thing, I understood damn all

dalaï-lama, pl **dalaï-lamas** [dalailama] NM Dalai Lama

dallage [dalaʒ] NM **1** (action) paving **2** (revêtement) flagstones

dalle [dal] NF **1** Constr flag(stone), paving stone; (de marbre) slab; **d. de moquette/linoléum** carpet/lino tile; **d. funéraire** gravestone, tombstone **2** Arg = dal **3** Arg **avoir** ou **crever la d.** to be starving; **j'ai une de ces dalles!** I'm starving!, I could eat a horse!

daller [dale] VT (avec dalles) to flag, to pave

dalleur [dalœr] NM paver

dalmatien, -ienne [dalmasjɛ̃, -jɛn] N Dalmatian, f Dalmatian bitch

dalot [dalo] NM Naut scupper (hole)

daltonien, -ienne [daltonjɛ̃, -jɛn] ADJ colour- or Am color-blind
  N colour-blind or Am color-blind man/woman

daltonisme [daltonism] NM colour or Am color blindness

dam [dam] NM **1** au grand d. de qn to the great displeasure of sb **2** Rel **peine du d.** eternal damnation

damage [damaʒ] NM (de la terre) ramming, tamping

damas [damas] NM Tex damask; **nappe en d.** damask tablecloth

damasquinage [damaskinaʒ] NM (de lame) damascening

damasquiner [damaskine] VT (lame etc) to inlay, to damascene

damassé [damase] ADJ **1** Tex damask **2** Métal **acier d.** damask (steel), Damascus steel
  NM Tex damask

damasser [damase] VT Tex, Métal to damask

damassine [damasin] NF Suisse (petite prune) plum; (eau de vie) plum brandy

dame¹ [dam] NF **1** (femme) lady, pl ladies;

Fam (épouse) wife; Arch (femme noble) (noble) lady; **coiffeur/tailleur pour dames** ladies' hairdresser/tailor; **manteau/parapluie de d.** lady's coat/umbrella; **la première d. des États-Unis** the First Lady (of the United States); Fam **elle fait la grande d.** she puts on airs, she's all lah-di-dah; **dames** (pour indiquer les toilettes) ladies; **que prendront ces dames?** what will you take, ladies?; Fam **et pour vous, ma petite d.?** what can I get you, dear?; Fam **ma bonne d., si vous saviez!** my dear, if you only knew!; Fam Vieilli **vous pouvez venir avec votre d.** bring your good lady; Jur **la d. Simon** Mrs Simon; **les dames de France** the royal princesses of France

2 (pièce) (au jeu de dames) king; Échecs, Cartes queen; (au trictrac) piece; **jeu de dames** (game of) draughts, Am checkers; **aller à d.** (au jeu de dames) to make a king; Échecs **to queen** (a pawn); Cartes **la d. de carreau/de trèfle** the queen of diamonds/clubs VOIR GRAMMAIRE A10

3 Tech (paving) beetle; (pour tasser le sol) (earth) rammer
  ▸▸ **d. de compagnie** lady's companion; **d. d'honneur** lady-in-waiting, Vieilli maid of honour; Naut **d. de nage** rowlock, Am oarlock; **D. Nature** Mother Nature; Bot **d. d'onze heures** star of Bethlehem; Hum, Péj **d. patronnesse** Lady Bountiful; Fam **d. pipi** lavatory attendant

dame² INT **d. oui!** well, yes!, why, yes!, rather!; **vous y allez? – d.!** are you going? – what else can I do?

dame-jeanne, pl **dames-jeannes** [damʒan] NF demijohn

damer [dame] VT **1** (au jeu de dames) (pièce) to crown; Fig Fam **d. le pion à qn** to outdo sb **2** Constr (terre) to ram, to tamp

dameuse [damøz] NF Ski piste basher

damier [damje] NM draughtboard, Am checkerboard; **tissu à d.** checked material

damnable [dɑnabl] ADJ Rel deserving of damnation; (relations, idées) to be condemned

damnation [dɑnasjɔ̃] NF damnation; Fam **enfer et d.!** hell and damnation!, damn and blast!

damné, -ée [dɑne] ADJ damned; Fig **c'est son âme damnée** he'd sell his soul for her
  N damned soul; Fig **souffrir comme un d.** to suffer (sheer) torture

damner [dɑne] VT to damn; Fam **faire d. qn** to drive sb crazy
  VPR **se damner** to incur damnation; Fig **il se damnerait pour elle** he would sell his soul to the devil for her

Damoclès [damɔklɛs] NM **l'épée de D.** the sword of Damocles

damoiseau, -eaux [damwazo] NM Arch squire; Hum **alors, jeune d. …** so, young man …

damoiselle [damwazɛl] **NF** *Arch* damsel

damper [dampœr] **NM** *Aut* damper

dan [dan] **NM** *Sport* dan; **il est quatrième d.** he is a fourth dan

dancing [dãsiŋ] **NM** dance hall

dandinement [dãdinmã] **NM** *(de personne)* rolling gait, waddle; *(d'oie)* waddle

dandiner (se) [sədãdine] **VPR** *(d'une personne)* to have a rolling gait, to waddle; *(d'une oie)* to waddle; **se d. d'un pied sur l'autre** to shift from foot to foot; **marcher en se dandinant** to waddle

dandy, *pl* **dandys** [dãdi] **NM** dandy

dandysme [dãdism] **NM** dandyism

Danemark [danmark] **NM** Denmark

danger [dãʒe] **NM** danger; *(cause de danger)* hazard; **il n'y a pas de d.** there's no danger, it's quite safe; **à l'abri du d.** out of danger; **être en d., courir un d.** to be in danger; **mettre en d. la vie de qn** to endanger sb's life; **en d. de mort** in mortal danger; **hors de d.** out of danger; *(d'un malade)* out of danger, off the danger list; **ses jours ne sont plus en d.** *(d'un malade, d'un accidenté)* he's off the danger list *or* out of danger; **sans d.** *(employé adjectivement)* not dangerous, safe; *(employé adverbialement)* without danger, safely; **avec cette voiture, tu es un véritable d. public** you're a proper public menace with that car; *Fam* **pas de d.!** no fear!, not likely!; *Fam* **il n'y a pas de d. qu'il revienne** there's no danger of his coming back

dangereusement [dãʒrøzmã] **ADV** dangerously; **il est d. blessé** he is seriously injured; **vivre d.** to live dangerously

dangereux, -euse [dãʒrø, -øz] **ADJ** dangerous (**pour** to, for); *Mil* **zone dangereuse** danger zone; **produit d.** dangerous *or* hazardous substance; **c'est d. pour la santé** it's bad for *or* harmful to your health; **il est d. de se pencher au dehors** it is dangerous to lean out

dangerosité [dãʒrozite] **NF** dangerousness

danois, -oise [danwa, -waz] **VOIR GRAMMAIRE A19** **ADJ** Danish
NM 1 *Ling* Danish **2 (grand) d.** *(chien)* Great Dane
N D. Dane

DANS [dã]

in **1, 4, 6, 7** ▪ into **2** ▪ out of **3**

PRÉP **VOIR GRAMMAIRE A70-1** **1** *(à l'intérieur de)* in; **d. une boîte** in(side) a box; **il est d. sa chambre** he's in his room; **qu'est-ce que vous avez d. la main?** what have you got in your hand?; **il habite d. Paris même** he lives (right) in Paris; **lire qch d. un journal** to read sth in a newspaper; **tomber d. l'escalier** to fall down the stairs; **d. un rayon de dix kilomètres** within a radius of ten kilometres; **il pleut d. tout le pays** it's raining all over the country; **la main d. la main** hand in hand

2 *(avec mouvement)* into; **mettre qch d. une boîte** to put sth in(to) a box; **il est entré d. leur chambre** he went into their room; **tomber d. l'oubli** to sink into oblivion; **glisser d. l'eau** to slide into the water; **il monta d. le train** he got onto the train; **jette-le d. le vide-ordures** throw it down the chute

3 *(pour faire sortir qch)* out of; **prendre qch d. qch** to take sth out of sth; **boire d. un verre** to drink out of a glass; **copier qch d. un livre** to copy sth out of *or* from a book; **découper un article d. le journal** to cut an article out of the paper; *Culin* **un morceau d. la poitrine** a cut off the breast

4 *(de temps)* in; **d. vingt ans** in twenty years, in twenty years' time; **d. l'après-midi** in *or* during the afternoon; **être d. sa vingt-cinquième année** to be in one's twenty-fifth

year; *Fam* **d. le temps** long ago; **je faisais du vélo d. ma jeunesse** I used to cycle when I was young *or* in my youth; **payer d. les dix jours** to pay within ten days; **je serai prêt à partir d. cinq minutes** I'll be ready to leave in five minutes; **je dois le voir d. le mois/la semaine** I'll be seeing him sometime this month/week; **arriver d. l'heure qui suit** to arrive within the next hour

5 *(environ)* about; **il a d. les quarante ans** he's about forty

6 **être d. le commerce/le bâtiment/l'informatique** to be in trade/construction/computers; **être plongé d. sa réflexion** to be deep in thought; **faire les choses d. les règles** to do things according to the rules; **être d. le secret** to be in on the secret; **travailler d. le bruit/le calme** to work in noisy/calm surroundings; **je ne peux pas travailler d. le bruit/le calme** I can't work when it's noisy/quiet; **d. le doute, abstiens-toi** if in doubt, don't

7 **il est d. mes intentions de l'appeler** I intend to call him, I have the intention of calling him; **d. son excitation/sa hâte/sa peur** in his excitement/hurry/fear; **d. ces circonstances** in *or* under the circumstances; **d. ce cas, faisons autre chose** in that case, let's do something else; **d. ce but** with this in mind, with this aim in view; **d. l'espoir de** in the hope of; **d. ces conditions, je refuse de signer** I refuse to sign under these conditions; **d. l'attente de votre réponse** awaiting your reply

---

dansable [dãsabl] **ADJ** **cet air n'est pas d.** it's not a tune you can dance to; **la musique que les jeunes écoutent maintenant n'est pas d.** you can't dance to the music that young people listen to nowadays

dansant [dãsã] **ADJ 1** *(flamme)* dancing; *(reflet)* shimmering; *(lueur)* flickering **2** *(où l'on danse)* **thé d.** tea dance; **donner une soirée dansante** to give a dance **3** **une musique dansante** music you can dance to

danse [dãs] **NF** *(art)* dance; *(action)* dancing; *(musique)* dance tune; **elle aime la d.** she's fond of dancing; **le tango n'est plus une d. à la mode** the tango is no longer a fashionable dance; *Fig* **entrer dans la d.** to join in; *Vieilli* **mettre une d. à qn** *(réprimander)* to tell sb off; *(frapper)* to beat sb
▸▸ **d. classique** classical dancing, ballet; **d. folklorique** folk dance; *(activité)* folk dancing; *Méd* **d. de Saint-Guy** St Vitus's dance; **d. de salon** ballroom dance; *(activité)* ballroom dancing; **d. du ventre** belly dance; *(activité)* belly dancing

danser [dãse] **VI 1** to dance; **faire d. qn** to dance with sb; *Fig Fam (frapper)* to beat sb up; **le bouchon/le bateau danse sur l'eau** the cork/the boat is bobbing up and down on the water; *Fig* **d. devant le buffet** to go hungry; **vous dansez, mademoiselle?** would you like to dance?; *Fig* **je ne sais sur quel pied d.** *(à cause de ces instructions contradictoires)* I don't know if I'm coming or going **2** *(d'un cheval)* to prance
VT *(valse etc)* to dance
VPR **se danser** *(d'une danse)* to be danced; **c'est un morceau qui se danse** it's a tune you can dance to

danseur, -euse [dãsœr, -øz] **N** dancer; **d. (classique** *ou* **de ballet)** ballet dancer, *f* ballerina; **danseuse de cabaret** cabaret dancer; **d. étoile** lead dancer; **danseuse étoile** prima ballerina; **d. de corde** tightrope walker; **d. mondain** (male) escort; *Péj* **entretenir une danseuse** *(avoir une maîtresse)* to keep a mistress; *(risquer de l'argent)* to take a gamble *or Am* flyer; **il est hors de question que notre entreprise entretienne une danseuse** the company can't afford not to play

it safe; **se mettre en danseuse** to stand up on the pedals; **être en danseuse** to be standing on the pedals

dantesque [dãtɛsk] **ADJ** Dantean, Dantesque

Danube [danyb] **NM** Danube

danubien, -ienne [danybjɛ̃, -jɛn] **ADJ** of the Danube, Danubian

daphnie [dafni] **NF** *Zool* daphnia

dard [dar] **NM 1** *(d'un insecte)* sting; *(d'un serpent)* forked tongue **2** *Pêche* spear, harpoon

darder [darde] **VT** *(lancer)* to hurl; *Fig* **il a dardé sur moi un regard chargé de haine** he shot *or* flashed a glance of hatred at me; **le soleil darde ses rayons sur la plage** the sun is beating *or* blazing down on the beach

dare-dare [dardar] **ADV** *Fam* double-quick, on the double; **rappliquer d.** to come charging up, to come running

darne [darn] **NF** *Culin (de poisson)* steak

dartre [dartr] **NF** *Méd* scurf

dartreux, -euse [dartrø, -øz] **ADJ** *Méd* scabby

darwinien, -ienne [darwinjɛ̃, -jɛn] **ADJ** Darwinian

darwinisme [darwinism] **NM** Darwinism

darwiniste [darwinist] **ADJ, N** Darwinist, Darwinian

DAS¹ [das] **NF** *(abrév* **déclaration d'autorisation de sortie)** export licence

DAS² [deaɛs] **NM** *Com, Mktg (abrév* **domaine d'activité stratégique)** SBU

datable [databl] **ADJ** which can be dated; **ce parchemin est en trop mauvais état pour être d.** the parchment is not in good enough condition to be dated; **ces ossements sont parfaitement datables** it is quite possible to date the bones

datation [datasjɔ̃] **NF** dating

date [dat] **NF** **SEE GRAMMAR A81-2; B60-2** date; **mettre la d. sur une lettre** to date a letter; **sans d.** *(lettre etc)* undated; **erreur de d.** mistake in the date; **la lettre porte la d. du 5 mai** the letter is dated (the) 5th May; **à quelle d. arrivent-ils?** what date do they arrive?; **à cette d.** at that time; **à cette d., j'étais déjà parti** I'd already left by then; **à d. fixe** on a fixed date; *Com, Fin* **à trente jours de d.** thirty days after date; *Fin* **emprunt à longue/à courte d.** long-/short-dated loan; **lettre en d. du 5 mai** letter dated (the) 5th May; *Com* **en d. du 15 courant** dated (the) 15th inst; **être le premier/dernier en d.** to come first/last; **prendre d. pour qch** to fix a date for sth; **faire d.** *(d'un événement)* to be memorable; **une fête qui a fait d.** a memorable *or* momentous party; **amitié de fraîche/de vieille** *ou* **de longue d.** recent/long-standing friendship; **je la connais de longue d.** I've known her (for) a long time; **d. d'achèvement** completion date, date of completion; **d. butoir** deadline, cutoff date; **d. de clôture** closing date; **d. de départ** date of departure, departure date; **d. d'échéance** *(de dû)* maturity date; *(de terme)* expiry date; **d. d'émission** date of issue; **d. d'exigibilité** due date; **d. d'expiration** expiry date; **d. de facturation** date of invoice, invoice date; **d. de jouissance** = date from which interest begins to run; **d. limite** deadline; **d. limite de consommation/de vente/de fraîcheur** use-by/sell-by/best-before date; **d. limite de paiement** deadline for payment; **d. de livraison** delivery date; **d. de naissance/de mariage** date of birth/marriage; **d. d'ouverture de l'exercice** first day of the financial year; **d. de parution** publication date; **d. de péremption** use-by date; *Journ* **d. de rédaction** dateline; **d. de remise** remittance date; **d. de retour** date of return; **d. de valeur** value date; **d. de validité** expiry date

dateline [dɛtlaɪn] NF *Journ* dateline

dater [date] VT (*lettre etc*) to date; **lettre datée du 20** letter dated the 20th; **non daté** undated

VI to date (**de** from); **à d. de ce jour** from today; **à d. du 15** on and after the 15th; **de quand date votre dernier repas?** when did you last eat?; **événement qui date** memorable event; **robe qui date** old-fashioned dress; **cette mode commence à d.** this fashion is becoming dated *or* is beginning to date; **ça ne date pas d'hier** that's nothing new

dateur [datœr] ADJ **tampon** *ou* **timbre d.** date stamp

NM date marker, date stamp; **d. automatique** automatic date stamping machine

datif [datif] NM *Gram* dative (case); **au d.** in the dative

dation [dasjɔ̃] NF *Jur* gift (*made to an heir in the course of one's lifetime to avoid inheritance tax*); **d. en paiement** payment in kind

datte [dat] NF date; **d. fourrée** stuffed date

dattier [datje] NM date palm, date tree

daube [dob] NF **1** *Culin* = meat braised in wine and stock with vegetables; **bœuf en d.** braised beef **2** *Fam* **c'est de la d.** (*ça ne vaut rien*) it's crap

dauber [dobe] VT **1** *Culin* (*viande*) to braise **2** *Arch, Litt* (*personne*) to make fun of

daubière [dobjɛr] NF *Culin* = earthenware pot for braising

dauphin [dofɛ̃] NM **1** *Zool* dolphin **2** *Hist* D. Dauphin **3** *Fig* (*à une position importante*) heir apparent

Dauphine [dofin] NF *Hist* Dauphiness

dauphinois, -oise [dofinwa, -waz] ADJ of/ from the Dauphiné; *Culin* **gratin d.** gratin dauphinois, = sliced potatoes baked with milk and browned on top

N D. (*natif*) native of the Dauphiné; (*habitant*) inhabitant of the Dauphiné

daurade [dɔrad] NF sea bream; **d. (royale)** gilthead (bream)

davantage [davɑ̃taʒ] ADV more; **il m'en faut d.** I need more; **je n'en dis pas d.** I shall say no more; **je ne l'interrogerai pas d.** I won't question him any further; **vous êtes riche, mais il l'est (bien) d.** you're rich, but he's (much) richer; **elle est jolie, mais tu l'es bien d.** she's pretty, but you're much prettier than she is; **nous ne resterons pas d.** we won't stay any longer; **se baisser d.** to stoop lower; **chaque jour d.** more and more every day; **encore** *ou* **même d.** even more; **veux-tu d. de pâtes?** do you want (some) more pasta?

davier [davje] NM **1** *Menuis* cramp **2** (*de dentiste*) forceps

DCA [desea] NF *Mil* (*abrév* **Défense contre avions**) anti-aircraft defence

DD NM *Ordinat* (*abrév* **disque dur**) HD

DDASS [das] NF *Admin* (*abrév* **Direction départementale de l'action sanitaire et sociale**) = local social work department, one of whose tasks is to deal with children who have been abandoned or ill-treated

DDE [dedeə] NF (*abrév* **Direction départementale de l'équipement**) = local offices of the Ministry of the Environment

NM *Ordinat* (*abrév* **dynamic data exchange**) DDE

DDT [dedete] NM *Chimie* (*abrév* **dichloro-diphényl-trichloréthane**) DDT

DE [də] (*before vowels and h mute* d'; *de + le*, **les** *are contracted into* **du, des**)

PRÉP	from **1–3** ▪ by **4, 16** ▪ with **4–6** ▪ in **5, 9, 11** ▪ for **6** ▪ of **9, 11, 12, 16, 18** ▪ on **9, 11, 17** ▪ to **15**
ARTICLE PARTITIF	some, any

PRÉP **1** (*origine*) from; **il vient de Paris** he comes from Paris; **nous sommes de Montpellier** we are from Montpellier; **apprendre qch de source sûre** to hear sth from a reliable source; **l'idée est de vous** the idea is yours *or* comes from you; **je l'ai oublié? c'est bien de moi** did I forget it? that's just like me; **l'express d'Aberdeen** the Aberdeen express; **un vin d'Alsace** an Alsace wine; **sulfate de fer** iron sulphate; **du temps de nos pères** in our fathers' day; **sortir de table** to leave the table; **sortir de chez soi** to leave the house; **de pauvre, il devint riche** he went from rags to riches

2 de … en … from … to …; **de jour en jour** from day to day; **ils sont serruriers de père en fils** they've been locksmiths for generations; **errer de ville en ville** to wander from town to town SEE GRAMMAR A69–71; B55

3 de … à … from … to …; **du matin au soir** from morning till night; **de là à dire oui …** as for saying yes …; **de vous à moi …** between ourselves …; **de vingt à trente personnes** between twenty and thirty people; **passer de la tristesse à la joie** to go from sadness to joy; **de temps à autre** from time to time; **il avait volé des sommes allant de 15 000 à 300 000 euros** he had stolen sums between 15,000 and 300,000 euros

4 (*agent, moyen, instrument*) by; **accompagné de ses amis** accompanied by his friends; **il est détesté de tout le monde** everybody hates him; **apprécié des connaisseurs** appreciated by connoisseurs; **faire qch de soi-même** to do sth of one's own accord; **j'ai fait cela de ma propre main** it's all my own work; **effleurer du doigt** to brush with one's finger; **armé de pierres** armed with stones; **les vautours se nourrissent de cadavres** vultures live on dead animals; **s'amuser d'un rien** to laugh over nothing

5 (*manière*) **il m'a regardé d'un air amusé** he looked at me with an amused expression; **répondre d'une voix douce** to answer in a gentle voice; **d'un ton excédé** in an exasperated voice

6 (*cause*) **sauter de joie** to jump for joy; **ivre de joie** giddy with joy; **je tombe de fatigue** I'm so tired that I'm ready to drop; **de peur de la blesser** for fear of hurting her; **trépigner d'impatience** to stamp one's feet in *or* with impatience; **en rosir d'aise** to go pink with joy; **puni de sa gourmandise** punished for one's greed

7 (*mesure*) **âgé de seize ans** sixteen years old; **un enfant de dix ans** a child of ten, a ten-year-old child; **ma montre retarde de dix minutes** my watch is ten minutes slow; **il est plus grand que moi d'une tête** he's a head taller than I am; **une pièce de 20 centimes** a 20-centime piece; **la terrasse a vingt mètres de long** *ou* **est longue de vingt mètres** the terrace is twenty metres long; **un chèque de 100 euros** a cheque for 100 euros; **une hausse de 10%** a 10% increase; **vingt euros de l'heure** twenty euros an hour; **il a été condamné à deux ans de prison** he was sentenced to two years' imprisonment

8 (*introduisant le complément de l'adjectif*) **digne d'éloges** worthy of praise, praiseworthy; **altéré de sang** thirsting for blood; **large de bassin** wide-hipped; **couvert de puces** covered in fleas; **calme de nature** calm by nature

9 (*propriété*) **le livre de Pierre** Pierre's book; **le toit de la maison** the roof of the house; **le meilleur élève de la classe** the best pupil in the class; **les rues de Paris** the streets of Paris; **la chambre du second** the room on the second *or Am* third floor; **scène de rivière hollandaise** scene on a Dutch river; **la statue est de Rodin** the statue is by Rodin; **une aria de Bach** a Bach aria SEE GRAMMAR B67

10 (*matière*) **un pont de fer** an iron bridge;

une robe de soie a silk dress SEE GRAMMAR B67

11 (*pour différencier, préciser*) **le chien de berger** the sheepdog; **le chien du berger** the shepherd's dog; **la bataille de Culloden** the battle of Culloden; **Notre Dame de Lourdes** Our Lady of Lourdes; **un problème d'algèbre** an algebra problem; **la conférence de Berlin** the Berlin conference; **un hôtel de la rive gauche** a hotel on the left bank; **un conflit de générations** a clash of generations; **le journal d'hier** yesterday's paper; **le mois de mai** (the month of) May; **à quatre heures de l'après-midi** at four (o'clock) in the afternoon; **son devoir de père** his duties as a father; **un don de voyance** a gift of second sight; **la route de Paris** the Paris road; **le professeur de français** the French teacher; **une crème de beauté** a beauty cream; **un conseil d'ami** friendly advice

12 (*partitif*) of; **un verre de vin** a glass of wine; **une livre de café** a pound of coffee; **quelque chose de bon** something good; **la moitié de ses économies** half of his savings; **je ne l'ai pas vu de la soirée** I haven't seen him all evening

13 (*avec une préposition*) **près de la maison** near the house; **autour du jardin** round the garden; **à partir de ce jour-là** from that day (onward); **de par le roi** by royal decree

14 (*pour introduire un complément d'objet*) **nous approchons de Paris** we're getting near *or* approaching Paris; **j'ai changé d'avis** I've changed my mind; **manquer de courage** to lack courage; **convenir d'une erreur** to admit an error

15 (*pour introduire un infinitif*) **il est honteux de mentir** it is shameful to lie; **le mieux était de rire** it was best to laugh; **je crains de n'être en retard** I'm afraid I might be late; **j'aime mieux attendre que de me faire mouiller** I would rather wait than get wet SEE GRAMMAR B33; B36–7

16 (*introduisant une apposition ou un complément du prédicat*) **la ville de Paris** the city of Paris; **il est parti de nuit** he left by night; **je n'ai rien fait de tout le week-end** I haven't done anything all weekend; **on l'a traité de lâche** he was called a coward; **un drôle de type** a funny chap; *Fam* **il y a eu trois hommes de tués** three men were killed; *Fam* **c'est un grand pas de fait** that's a great step forward; *Fam* **la robe est d'un réussi!** the dress is perfect!

17 (*dans titre d'ouvrage, de chapitre*) **de l'amour** (on) love; **des dangers du remords** (on) the dangers of remorse

18 (*dans nom à particule*) **le prince de Condé** the Prince of Condé

19 *Litt* **la musique commença et les enfants de danser** the music began, and the children started to dance

ART PARTITIF (*used also as pl of* **un, une**) **n'avez-vous pas d'amis?** haven't you got any friends?, don't you have any friends?; **sans faire de fautes** without making any mistakes; **je ne veux pas qu'on lui mette de collier** I won't have a collar put on him; **de grands artistes se trouvaient là** there were some distinguished artists there; **elle ne mange plus de viande** she no longer eats meat; **faire de la musique** to make music; **c'est du Bach, n'est-ce pas?** it's Bach, isn't it?; **je bois de l'eau** (*toujours*) I drink water; (*maintenant*) I'm drinking water; **donnez-nous de vos nouvelles** let's hear from you; **avez-vous du pain?** have you any bread?; **donnez-moi de ce vin** give me some of that wine; **donnez-moi du bon vin** give me some good wine; **manger de tous les plats** to have something of everything; **ah ça, des problèmes, tu peux dire qu'elle en a!** she's got problems all right!; **mettre des heures à faire qch** to spend hours doing sth SEE GRAMMAR B5

dé¹ [de] NM **1** *(pour jouer)* die, *plus souvent* dice, *pl* dice; **un coup de dé** a throw of the dice; **jouer aux dés** to play dice; **jeter les dés** to throw the dice; **les dés sont pipés** the dice are loaded; *Fig* **les dés sont jetés** the die is cast; *Culin* **couper en dés** *(légumes etc)* to dice VOIR GRAMMAIRE A10; A13 **2** *Archit (de piédestal etc)* dado, die **3** *Tech* bearing (bush), brass

dé² NM dé *(à coudre)* thimble; *Fig* **un dé à coudre de whisky** a thimbleful of whisky

DEA [deəa] NM *(abrév* **diplôme d'études approfondies)** = post-graduate qualification which is a prerequisite for PhD candidates

deal [dil] NM *Fam* **1** *(de drogue)* (drug) deal; **il a fait de la taule pour d. d'héro** he did time for dealing smack **2** *(accord)* deal

dealer¹ [dilœr] NM *Fam* dealer

dealer² [dile] VT *Fam* to deal; **il deale de la coke** he deals coke

déambulateur [deãbylatœr] NM Zimmer® (frame), walker

déambulatoire [deãbylatwar] NM *Archit* ambulatory

déambuler [deãbyle] VI to stroll (about), to walk up and down, to saunter

deb [deb] *Fam* ADJ *(abrév* **débile)** dumb, *Br* daft
▪ NF *(abrév* **débutante)** deb

débâcher [debaʃe] VT *(terrain de tennis, piscine)* to take the covers off

débâcle [debakl] NF *Mil* debacle, rout; *(de glaces flottantes)* break(ing) up; *Fig (d'une affaire, monnaie etc)* collapse; *(d'une grosse entreprise)* crash; *(d'une équipe de sport)* rout; *Fig* **rien ne laissait supposer une telle d. financière** *(d'une personne, petite entreprise)* financial ruin came quite without warning

débâillonner [debajɔne] VT **d. qn** to remove sb's gag; **d. la presse** to end press censorship

déballage [debalaʒ] NM **1** *(action)* unpacking **2** *(vente au)* **d.** pavement selling **3** *Fam (aveu)* confession, outpouring; *(révélations)* disclosure; **assister au d. public de sa vie privée** to see one's private life being discussed in public

déballer [debale] VT **1** *(produits, caisses)* to unpack **2** *Fam (un secret)* to give away, to disclose; *(sa vie privée)* to talk about, *Fam* to spill the beans about; *(la vérité)* to confess to; **je ne veux pas voir cette affaire déballée devant la presse** I don't want the press to get hold of this

déballonner (se) [sədebalɔne] VPR *Fam* to chicken out, *Br* to bottle out

débandade [debãdad] NF *(d'une armée, d'une équipe etc)* rout; **après le krach, ce fut la d. générale** there was general panic after the Stock Market crash; **c'est la d. dans cette entreprise** the company's in a shambles

débander¹ [debãde] VT *(enlever le bandage de)* to remove a/the bandage from, to unbandage; **il faut lui d. les yeux** we'll have to take the blindfold off him
▪ VI *Vulg* to lose one's erection; *Fig Fam* **travailler pendant des heures sans d.** to work non-stop for hours

débander² (se) [se] VPR **1** *(d'une foule etc)* to disperse; *Mil etc* to scatter **2** *(de qch sous tension)* to relax; *(d'un arc)* to unbend

débaptiser [debatize] VT *(personne, rue etc)* to change the name of, to rename

débarbouillage [debarbujaʒ] NM quick wash

débarbouiller [debarbuje] VT **d. qn** to wash sb's face
▪ VPR **se débarbouiller** to wash one's face

débarbouillette [debarbujɛt] NF *Can* (face) flannel, face cloth, *Am* washrag

débarcadère [debarkadɛr] NM *Naut* landing stage, jetty; *(de marchandises)* wharf

débardage [debardaʒ] NM *Naut (de bois etc)* unloading, unlading

débarder [debarde] VT **1** *Naut (bois etc)* to unload **2** *Rail (bois de charpente, pierres de carrière)* to convey to the railhead

débardeur [debardœr] NM **1** *(tricot)* tank top **2** *(personne)* docker, stevedore, *Am* longshoreman

débarqué, -ée [debarke] ADJ landed
▪ N **un nouveau d.** a new arrival

débarquement [debarkəmã] NM **1** *(de cargaison)* unloading; *(de passagers)* landing, disembarkation; **quai de d.** unloading bay **2** *Mil, Naut* landing; *(d'un train)* detraining; *(d'un bateau)* disembarkation; **troupes de d.** landing force; **d. sur plage** beach landing; *Hist* **le d.** the Normandy landings; *Fig* **quand toute la famille vient à la maison, c'est le d.** it's like the Normandy landings *or* like being invaded when all the family comes; **avec tous les cousins qui arrivent, ça va être un vrai d. ici** we're going to be overrun with all the cousins arriving **3** *Naut (d'un équipage)* paying off, discharge

débarquer [debarke] VT **1** *(cargaison)* to unload; *(marchandises)* to offload; *(passagers d'un bateau)* to disembark, to land; *(passagers d'un bus)* to set down; *(pilote d'un navire)* to drop **2** *Naut (équipage)* to pay off, to discharge; *Fam* **d. qn** to give sb the sack *or* push; *Fam* **se faire d., être débarqué** to get the sack *or* push
▪ VI **1** *(d'un bateau, d'un avion)* to disembark; *surtout Can (d'un train, d'un bus)* to get off, to alight **2** *Fig Fam (arriver)* to turn up, to arrive; **j'ai débarqué dans cette ville hier** I arrived in town yesterday; **je débarque à peine** I've only just got here; **tu débarques!** where have you been?; **à chaque fois qu'on lui demande quelque chose, elle débarque complètement** whenever she's asked a question, she's totally at sea *or* is totally lost; **ce type, il a toujours l'air de d.** that chap never seems to know what's going on

débarras [debara] NM **1** *(endroit)* boxroom, *Br Fam* glory hole **2** **bon d.!** good riddance!

débarrasser [debarase] VT *(table etc)* to clear; **d. qn de qch** to relieve sb of sth; **je vais te d. de ce mauvais rhume/vilain bouton** I'll get rid of that rotten cold/nasty spot for you; **je vais te d. de cette manie de fumer** I'll cure you of the smoking habit; **d. qn de qn** to take sb off sb's hands; *(le tuer)* to get rid of sb for sb; *Fig Fam* **le d. le plancher** to clear out
▪ VPR **se débarrasser se d. de qn/qch** to get rid of sb/sth; **se d. d'une tâche difficile** to get out of a difficult job; **débarrassez-vous!** can I take your things?

débarrer [debare] VT **1** *(porte etc)* to unbar **2** *Can (déverrouiller)* to unlock

débat [deba] NM **1** *(organisé)* debate; **d. télévisé** discussion programme; *(politique)* televised debate; *Pol* **débats (parlementaires)** (parliamentary) debates, proceedings; **le film sera suivi d'un d. (portant) sur …** the film will be followed by a discussion on … **2** *(polémique)* argument, dispute; **trancher un d.** to settle an argument *or* a dispute; **un d. intérieur** an inner debate *or* conflict *or* struggle

débâtir [debatir] VT *(vêtement)* to remove the tacks from

débattement [debatmã] NM *Aut etc* clearance; **d. de roue** wheel deflection

débattre [debatr] *(conj like* **battre)** VT *(discuter)* to debate, to discuss; **prix à d.** price by arrangement; **d. les conditions d'un contrat** to negotiate the conditions of a contract; **je n'ai pas débattu le prix** I didn't argue *or* hag-

gle about the price; **d. d'une question** to discuss a matter
▪ VPR **se débattre** to struggle; **se d. dans l'eau** to flounder, to splash (about) in the water; **se d. comme un forcené** *ou* **comme un beau diable** to struggle like a madman; **se d. contre des agresseurs** to defend oneself against attackers; **se d. contre une difficulté** to struggle with a problem

débauchage [deboʃaʒ] NM *(renvoi)* laying off; *(embauche)* head-hunting

débauche [deboʃ] NF debauchery; **il vit dans la d.** he lives a life of debauchery; **lieu de d.** den of vice; *Jur* **excitation des mineurs à la d.** incitement of minors to vice; *Fig* **le décor de cette pièce est une d. d'imagination** the set is extremely imaginative; **une d. de couleurs** a riot of colour

débauché, -ée [deboʃe] ADJ debauched, profligate
▪ N libertine, rake, *f* debauched woman

débaucher [deboʃe] VT **1** *(inciter à la débauche)* to lead astray; **d. la jeunesse** to corrupt the young; *Fam* **est-ce que je peux te d. et t'inviter au cinéma/restaurant?** can I tempt you with a film/dinner?; *Fam* **c'est lui qui m'a débauché hier soir** he led me astray last night **2** *d. qn (l'inciter à la grève)* to induce sb to strike; *(le renvoyer)* to make sb redundant, to lay sb off; *(l'embaucher)* to head-hunt sb; **on a réussi à le d. de Toshiba avec un très beau salaire** they managed to lure *or* tempt him away from Toshiba with the promise of an excellent salary
▪ VPR **se débaucher** to be corrupted; *Fam* **arrête de travailler et débauche-toi un peu** stop working for a bit and enjoy yourself

débecter [debɛkte] VT *Arg* **d. qn** to turn sb's stomach, to sicken sb

débet [debɛ] NM *Fin* balance due

débile [debil] ADJ *(enfant)* sickly; *(corps)* weak, feeble; *(santé)* poor; *Péj (émission, film, livre etc)* stupid, idiotic; *Péj* **il est complètement d.** he's a complete idiot
▪ N **un(e) d. mental(e)** a mental defective; *Péj* **c'est un d. mental, ce type!** the man's a complete idiot!

débilitant [debilitã] ADJ debilitating, weakening; *Fig* demoralizing; **remède d.** debilitant; **des occupations débilitantes** tiring occupations

débilité [debilite] NF debility, weakness; *Péj* stupidity; **d. mentale** mental deficiency; *Péj* **les films que tu regardes sont d'une d.!** you watch such stupid *or* idiotic films!; *Péj* **je ne supporte pas la d. de son nouveau copain** I can't stand her new boyfriend – he's so stupid

débiliter [debilite] VT to debilitate, to weaken

débinage [debinaʒ] NM *Fam* knocking, running down

débine [debin] NF *Fam* poverty; **être dans la d.** to be (stony) broke

débiner [debine] *Fam* VT to knock, to run down
▪ VPR **se débiner** to scram, to clear off

débineur, -euse [debinœr, -øz] N *Fam* knocker

débit¹ [debi] NM **1** *(ventes)* (retail) sale; **au d. de** to the debit of; **marchandises de bon d.** marketable *or* saleable goods; **la marchandise ne peut pas être fraîche ici, il n'y a aucun d.** the goods here can't be fresh, there's no turnover **2** *Ordinat, Tél* rate; **d. en bauds** baud rate; **d. binaire** bit rate; **d. de données** data throughput; **à haut d.** broadband **3** **d. de tabac** tobacconist's (shop); **d. de boissons** bar **4** *(de bois)* cutting up **5** *Tech (de pompe etc)* discharge, delivery; *(de rivière, de robinet etc)* flow; *Ind* output; *Élec* power supplied; **d. d'air** *(dans un moteur)* air flow **6**

(d'un orateur) delivery; **il a un de ces débits!** he really has the gift of the gab!

débit² NM *Fin* debit; **porter 1 000 euros au d. de qn** to debit sb with 1,000 euros; **d. cumulé** cumulative debit; **d. de caisse** cash debit; **d. immédiat** immediate debit

débitable¹ [debitabl] ADJ *(bois etc)* that can be cut up

débitable² ADJ *(compte)* that can be drawn on

débitant, -ante [debitɑ̃, -ɑ̃t] N **d. de tabac** tobacconist; **d. de boissons** pub owner, *Am* bar owner

débiter¹ [debite] VT **1** *Com (vendre)* to sell retail **2** *(bois)* to cut up, to convert; *(viande)* to cut up **3** *Tech (tant de litres par heure etc)* to discharge; *Ind* to produce; *Ordinat* to output; **les ascenseurs de la tour débitent 500 personnes par heure** the lifts in the tower handle 500 people per hour; **cette usine débite 250 voitures par jour** the output from the factory is 250 cars a day, the factory produces 250 cars a day **4** *(texte, harangue)* to deliver; **l'acteur débite son texte de plus en plus vite** the actor's speaking his lines faster and faster; **ce n'est pas un acteur, il ne fait que d. le texte** he's no actor, he's merely reciting the text; *Péj* **d. des sottises** to talk rubbish; **il m'a débité toutes ces sottises sans s'arrêter** he trotted out all that nonsense to me non-stop; **d. des mensonges** to trot out one lie after another

débiter² VT *Com (inscrire au débit)* to debit; **d. une somme à qn, d. qn d'une somme** to debit sb with an amount; **d. un compte** to debit an account; **d. une somme d'un compte** to debit an account with an amount, to debit an amount to an account

débiteur¹, -euse [debitœr, -øz] N **1** *Péj Vieilli (diseur)* person who holds forth *or* talks rubbish; **d. de calomnies** scandalmonger **2** *Tech* feeding device **3** *(dans un magasin)* shop assistant

débiteur², -trice [debitœr, -tris] N *(qui doit de l'argent)* debtor; *Fig* **je suis votre d.** I am indebted to you, I am in your debt ADJ **1** *Com* **compte d.** debit account; **votre compte est d. de trois mille euros** your account is three thousand euros overdrawn **2** *Cin* **bobine débitrice** top *or* delivery spool ►► **d. concordataire** = bankrupt who has reached a settlement with his debtors; **d. hypothécaire** mortgagor; **d. insolvable** insolvent debtor; **d. principal** primary *or* principal debtor; **d. solidaire** joint and several debtor

débitmètre [debimɛtr] NM *Tech* flowmeter

déblai [deble] NM *Constr, Rail etc* **1** excavation, cut(ting); **route en d.** sunken road **2 déblais** spoil earth

déblaiement [deblɛmɑ̃] NM *(de terrain etc)* clearing

déblatérer [deblatere] (**je déblatère; je déblatérerai**) VT **d. des sottises** to talk nonsense; **d. des injures** to fling abuse (**contre** at); **il ne cesse de d. les pires insultes à ton égard** he's always extremely abusive about you VI **d. contre** *ou* **sur qn/qch** to rail against sb/sth

déblayage [deblɛjaʒ] NM clearing; *(d'une chambre)* clearing out

déblayer [deblɛje] VT (**je déblaye, je déblaie**) **1** *(débris etc)* to clear away, to remove; **d. la neige** to shovel away the snow **2** *(chambre)* to clear out; **d. un terrain** to clear a piece of ground; *Fig* **d. le terrain** *(pour des négociations etc)* to prepare *or* clear the ground *or* the way

déblocage [deblɔkaʒ] NM freeing, releasing; *(de machine)* unjamming; *Fin (des prix etc)* unfreezing; *Psy* **le d. d'inhibitions/de complexes** getting rid of inhibitions/complexes

débloquer [deblɔke] VT **1** *(libérer, mettre en marche)* to free, to release; *(machine)* to unjam; *Tél (téléphone portable)* to unlock; *Fin (prix etc)* to unfreeze; *(compte)* to free, to unfreeze; **d. des fonds** to release funds, to make funds available **2** *Psy* **d. qn** *(ôter les complexes de)* to rid sb of his/her complexes; *(rendre moins timide)* to make sb less inhibited VI *Fam* **1** *(être fou)* to be off one's rocker; *(raconter n'importe quoi)* to talk nonsense; **son grand-père est vieux, il commence à d.** his grandfather is old and going gaga **2** *(ne pas fonctionner correctement)* to be on the blink, *Am* to be on the fritz

débobiner [debɔbine] VT *(rouleau, fil etc)* to unwind

débogage [debɔɡaʒ] NM *Ordinat* debugging

déboguer [debɔɡe] VT *Ordinat* to debug

débogueur [debɔɡœr] NM *Ordinat* debugger

déboires [debwar] NMPL *(déceptions)* disappointments; *(ennuis)* problems, trouble; **essuyer bien des d.** to suffer many disappointments *or* setbacks

déboisement [debwazmɑ̃] NM deforestation

déboiser [debwaze] VT *(région)* to deforest, to clear; *Fam* **se faire d. la colline** to have one's hair cropped

déboîtement [debwatmɑ̃] NM **1** *(d'un membre, d'une articulation)* dislocation **2** *Aut* pulling out

déboîter [debwate] VT **1** *Tech (tuyau etc)* to disconnect, to uncouple **2** *(articulation, membre)* to dislocate **3** *(montre etc)* to remove from its case VI *Aut* to pull out VPR **se déboîter** *(d'une cheville etc)* to become dislocated; **se d. l'épaule/le genou** to dislocate one's shoulder/knee, to put one's shoulder/knee out

débonder [debɔ̃de] VT *(lavabo)* to unblock; *(fût)* to unbung; *Fig Vieilli* **d. son cœur** to pour out one's heart VPR **se débonder** *(d'un lavabo etc)* to unblock; *(d'un fût)* to become unbunged; *Fig Vieilli (d'une personne)* to pour out one's heart

débonnaire [debɔnɛr] ADJ goodnatured, easy-going; **répondre d'un ton d.** to answer goodnaturedly

débordant [debɔrdɑ̃] ADJ **1** *(expansif)* overflowing, brimming over (**de** with); **d. de santé** bursting with health; **avoir une imagination débordante** to be brimful of imagination; **faire preuve d'un enthousiasme/d'une activité débordant(e)** to be brimming *or* bubbling over with enthusiasm/brimful of energy **2** *(qui dépasse)* projecting, protruding; *(en se chevauchant)* overlapping

débordé [debɔrde] ADJ **1** *(de travail etc)* snowed under **2 drap d.** *(pour préparer le lit)* turned-back sheet; *(défait)* untucked sheet; **mon lit est d.** my sheets have come untucked

débordement [debɔrdəmɑ̃] NM **1** *(d'une rivière etc)* overflowing; *Fig (d'enthousiasme, injures etc)* outburst, outpouring **2 débordements** excesses, dissipation, dissolute living **3** *Mil (de l'ennemi)* outflanking

déborder [debɔrde] VI **1** *(du contenu d'un verre etc)* to overflow, to brim over, to run over; **verre plein à d.** glass full to overflowing *or* to the brim; **la rivière a débordé** the river has overflowed its banks; **le lait a dé-**bordé de la casserole the milk has boiled over; **les papiers débordent de la corbeille** the papers are spilling over of the wastepaper basket; **essaie de colorier la maison sans d.** try to colour in the house without going over the edges; **c'est la goutte d'eau qui fait d. le vase** it's the last straw; *TV, Radio etc* **d. sur le temps prévu** to overrun **2** *Fig* **elle déborde de vie** she is bubbling over with *or* brimful of vitality; **d. d'imagination** to be brimful of imagination; **son cœur déborde de reconnaissance** his heart is brimming over with gratitude

VT **1** *(dépasser)* to project *or* extend beyond; *Mil (l'ennemi)* to outflank; **d. son adversaire** *(dans une course)* to overtake one's competitor; **cela déborde le cadre de mes responsabilités/de notre débat** that exceeds my responsibilities/the limits of our discussion **2 d. (les couvertures d')un lit** to untuck a bed; *Naut* **d. une embarcation** to shove off, to sheer off; **d. les avirons** to unship the oars **3** *(enlever les bords de)* to remove the edging from; *Tech* **d. une tôle** to trim the edges of an iron plate

débotté [debɔte] NM **au d.** immediately, *Am* off the bat

débotter [debɔte] VT **d. qn** to take off sb's boots VPR **se débotter** to take off one's boots

débouchage [debuʃaʒ] NM **1** *(d'un tuyau)* unblocking **2** *(d'une bouteille)* uncorking

débouché [debuʃe] NM **1** *(d'un passage etc)* opening; *(d'une vallée)* entrance **2** *(possibilité)* opening, opportunity; *Com, Mktg* outlet, market; **cette formation n'offre aucun d.** the training does not lead to any career openings; **créer de nouveaux débouchés pour un produit** to create new outlets for a product

déboucher [debuʃe] VT **1** *(tuyau bouché etc)* to clear, to unblock **2** *(bouteille)* to uncork, to remove the cork from VI to emerge (**de** from), to come out (**de** of); **cet escalier débouche dans le grenier** the staircase leads to the attic; **cette rue débouche sur la place** this street runs into the square; **voilà sur quoi débouche la guerre** that's what war leads to; **ces études débouchent sur un métier intéressant** this course of study leads to a worthwhile career; **vos expériences ne débouchent sur aucun résultat** your experiments aren't leading anywhere, you're not getting any results with your experiments VPR **se déboucher** *(de tuyau)* to clear, to become unblocked; **la bouteille se débouche facilement** the bottle opens easily, the cork is easily removed from the bottle

déboucheur [debuʃœr] NM drain clearer

débouchoir [debuʃwar] NM *(pour les sanitaires)* (rubber) plunger

déboucler [debukle] VT **1** *(ceinture etc)* to unbuckle **2** *(cheveux)* to take the curl out of

déboulé [debule] NM **tirer un lapin au d.** to shoot a rabbit as it bolts from cover

débouler [debule] VI **1** *(tomber)* to fall head over heels **2** *Fam (arriver)* to turn up, to show up; **ils ont déboulé chez moi sans prévenir** they showed up at my place without any warning **3** *(du gibier)* to start, to bolt (from cover) VT *Fam* **d. l'escalier** to run down the stairs

déboulonnage [debulɔnaʒ] NM, **déboulonnement** [debulɔnmɑ̃] NM **1** *Tech* unriveting, unbolting **2** *Fig (renvoi)* dismissal; **il procéda ensuite au d. systématique de ses anciens collègues** he then proceeded to systematically debunk his former colleagues

déboulonner [debulɔne] VT **1** *Tech* to unrivet, to unbolt **2** *Fig (discréditer)* to debunk; *(de son poste)* to get rid of, to kick out

débourber [deburbe] **VT 1** *(étang, canal)* to clean out; **d. le vin** to draw off *or* decant wine **2** *(voiture etc)* to haul out of the mud

débourrer [debure] **VT 1 d. un cheval** to break in a horse **2 d. sa pipe** to scrape out one's pipe
VI *Fam (ne plus être saoul)* to sober up; **il n'a pas débourré depuis huit jours** he's been drunk for a week; **il ne débourre plus** he's never sober

débours [debur] **NM** expenses; *(pour services aux clients)* visitors paid out, VPO; **faire des d.** to lay out money

déboursement [debursəmɑ̃] **NM** paying out, *Fml* disbursement

débourser [deburse] **VT** *(argent)* to spend, to lay out, to pay, *Fml* to disburse; **sans rien d.** without spending a penny; **je suis toujours en train de d.** I'm always putting my hand in my pocket

déboussoler [debusɔle] **VT** *Fam* to disorientate, *surtout Am* to disorient; **je suis un peu déboussolée dans ce nouveau pays/dans mon nouvel appartement** I'm a bit disoriented *or* lost in this new country/in my new apartment; **cette nouvelle l'a complètement déboussolé** the news completely threw him

debout [dəbu] **ADV 1** *(chose)* upright, on end; *(personne)* standing; **mettre qch d.** to stand sth up *or* on end; **mettre les bouteilles d.** to stand the bottles up(right); **cent ans plus tard, la maison est encore d.** the house is still standing a hundred years later; **elle est d. toute la journée** she's on her feet all day; **rester d.** to stand; **places d. seulement** standing room only; **tenir d.** to be (standing) upright; **c'est si bas qu'on ne peut tenir d.** it's so low that you can't stand up straight; *Fig* **argument qui ne tient pas d.** argument that won't hold water *or* won't stand up; *Fig* **cette institution est** *ou* **tient encore d.** the institution is still in existence; **se tenir d.** to stand; **se tenir d. (sur ses pattes arrières)** *(d'un chien)* to stand on its hind legs; **se (re)mettre d.** to stand up; **conte** *ou* **histoire à dormir d.** silly *or* extravagant *or Fam* cock-and-bull story; **tous les matins je suis d. à six heures** I'm up *or* I get up at six o'clock every morning; **allons, d.!** *(hors du lit)* come on, get up!; **il va mieux, il est déjà d.** he's better, he's up *or* out of bed already
2 *Naut* **d. à la mer** *ou* **à la lame/au vent** head on to the sea/to the wind
ADJ INV 1 *Jur* **magistrature d.** = public prosecutors **2** *Naut* **vent d.** head wind

débouté [debute] **NM**, **déboutement** [debutmɑ̃] **NM** *Jur* nonsuit

débouter [debute] **VT** *Jur* to dismiss; **d. qn (de sa demande/de sa plainte)** to nonsuit sb

déboutonner [debutɔne] **VT** to unbutton; *Vieilli* **rire à ventre déboutonné** to split one's sides laughing
VPR se déboutonner 1 *(d'une personne)* to undo one's buttons; *(d'une robe, d'une chemise etc)* to unbutton; *Fig (se confier)* to get it off one's chest **2** *Can (se montrer généreux)* to splash out

débraillé [debraje] **ADJ** *(personne)* untidy, slovenly; *(tenue)* untidy, sloppy; **manières débraillées** bad manners
NM untidiness, slovenliness; **même au bureau, il est en d.** he's a sloppy dresser even at work

débrailler (se) [sədebraje] **VPR** *Fam* to loosen one's clothing; *Fig* **la conversation se débraille** the conversation is getting a bit out of hand

débranchement [debrɑ̃ʃmɑ̃] **NM** *Élec* disconnection, unplugging

débrancher [debrɑ̃ʃe] **VT** *Élec* to disconnect, to unplug; *Fam* **débranchez-le!** shut him up, will you!

débrayage [debrɛjaʒ] **NM 1** *Aut, Tech* declutching **2** *Fam (grève)* stoppage

débrayer [debrɛje] (**je débraye, je débraie**) **VT** *Tech* to throw out of gear
VI 1 *Aut* to disengage the clutch, to declutch **2** *Fam (se mettre en grève)* to down tools; *(à la fin de la journée)* to down tools, to knock off

débridé [debride] **ADJ** *(passion)* unbridled; *(imagination)* vivid

débridement [debridmɑ̃] **NM 1** *(d'un cheval)* unbridling **2** *Chir (d'une adhérence etc)* incision, slitting up; *(d'un furoncle)* lancing **3** *(déchaînement)* **le d. de son comportement/imagination** his unbridled behaviour/extremely vivid imagination

débrider [debride] **VT 1** *(cheval)* to unbridle **2** *Chir (adhérence etc)* to incise, to slit up; *(furoncle, plaie)* to lance **3** *Culin (volaille)* to untruss
VI *Fig* **travailler dix heures sans d.** to work ten hours at a stretch

débriefer [debrife] **VT** to debrief

débris [debri] **NMPL** *(d'un avion, une voiture)* remains, debris, wreckage; *(de verre, de bois)* splinters, fragments; **d. de métal** scrap (metal); **les d. d'une armée** the remnants of an army; **les d. de sa fortune** the remnants *or* remains of his fortune
NM *Fam* **ce n'est plus qu'un vieux d.** he's just an old wreck!

débronzer [debrɔ̃ze] **VI** to lose one's tan

débrouillard, -arde [debrujar, -ard] **ADJ** resourceful, smart
N resourceful person; **c'est vraiment un d.** he's really resourceful

débrouillardise [debrujardiz] **NF** resourcefulness; **faire preuve de d.** to be resourceful

débrouiller [debruje] **VT 1** *(fil etc)* to unravel, to disentangle; **d. une affaire** to clear up *or* straighten out a situation; **d. une signature** to make out *or* decipher a signature **2** *Fam* **d. qn** to wise sb up; **il faut le d. en anglais/en cuisine** he'll need to be taught some basic English/cooking
VPR se débrouiller to cope, to manage; *Fam* **qu'il se débrouille!** he'll have to manage!, he'll have to sort it out for himself!; **débrouillez-vous!** you'll just have to manage!, you'll just have to sort it out for yourself!; **il a un peu de mal à se d. avec son ordinateur** he's having some trouble coping with his computer; **je me débrouille en russe** I can get by in Russian; **elle s'est débrouillée pour rencontrer le directeur** she worked it so that she got to meet the director

débroussailler [debrusaje] **VT** to clear of undergrowth; *Fig* **d. une question** to clarify a matter

débudgétisation [debydʒetizasjɔ̃] **NF** = transfer from one budget to another

débudgétiser [debydʒetize] **VT** = to transfer from one budget to another; **il faut d. l'État des dépenses de la sécurité sociale** the burden of social security should no longer be borne by the State

débusquer [debyske] **VT** to flush out (of cover)

début [deby] **NM 1** *(commencement)* beginning, start; **au d.** at the start *or* beginning *or* outset; **au d. des hostilités** at the outbreak of hostilities; **au tout d., tout au d.** at the very start *or* beginning; **dès le d.** right at the start, from the outset (**de** of); **je l'ai su dès le d.** I knew from the outset *or* (right) from the beginning; **je le savais depuis le d.** I knew all along *or* from the start; **du d. à la fin** from start to finish; **appointements de**

d. starting salary; **être en d. de carrière** to be at the start of one's career; *Hum* **il faut** *ou* **il y a un d. à tout** there's a first time for everything **2** *(d'un acteur etc)* **débuts** first appearance, début; **faire ses débuts** to make one's first appearance *or* one's début, *Am* to début; **faire ses débuts dans le monde** *(d'une jeune fille)* to come out; **société/entreprise à ses débuts** association/enterprise in its infancy **3** *Ordinat* home; **aller au d.** *(commande)* go top

débutant, -ante [debytɑ̃, -ɑ̃t] **ADJ** novice; **cours pour les skieurs débutants** skiing classes for beginners; **si vous êtes skieur d.** if you're learning (how) to ski; **conducteur d.** newly qualified driver
N 1 *(dans une matière, une discipline etc)* beginner; **cours pour grands débutants** classes for complete beginners **2** *Théâtre* actor/actress making his/her début
NF **débutante** *(dans la haute société)* debutante, *Fam* deb

débuter [debyte] **VI 1** *(commencer)* to begin, to start, to commence; **vous travaillerez ici pour d.** you'll work here to begin with *or* start with; **le film débute par une séquence de meurtre** the film opens with a murder; **le concert a bien/mal débuté** the concert started well/badly, the concert got off to a good/bad start **2** *Cin, Théâtre etc (de personne)* to make one's first appearance *or* one's début, *Am* to début; **mal/bien d. dans la vie** to get off to a bad/good start in life; **je débute dans le métier** I'm new to the business; **d. dans le monde** *(d'une jeune fille)* to come out; **faire d. une jeune fille dans le monde** to bring a girl out; **d. comme professeur** to start off as a teacher

déc [dɛk] **VI** *Fam* **sans d.!** *(je t'assure)* no kidding!, *Br* straight up!; **sans d.?** *(est-ce vrai?)* no kidding?, yeah?

déca [deka] **NM** *Fam (café)* decaf

deçà [dəsa] **PRÉP** **en d. de qch** (on) this side of sth; **rester (très) en d. de la vérité** to be (very) short of the truth
ADV *Arch* on this side; **d. delà** here and there, on all sides

décachetage [dekaʃtaʒ] **NM** *(d'une lettre)* unsealing, opening

décacheter [dekaʃte] **VT** *(conj like* **cacheter** *) (lettre)* to unseal, to open

décade [dekad] **NF** *(période de dix jours)* period of ten days; *(période de dix ans)* decade

> Il faut noter que le nom anglais **decade** est un faux ami. Il signifie uniquement **décennie**.

décadenasser [dekadnase] **VT** to unlock, to take the padlock off

décadence [dekadɑ̃s] **NF** decadence; **la d. d'une civilisation** *(processus)* the decline of a civilization; *(résultat)* the decadence of a civilization; **tomber en d.** to fall into decay; *(d'une personne)* to start to decline

décadent, -ente [dekadɑ̃, -ɑ̃t] **ADJ** decadent
N *Littér, Beaux-Arts* Decadent

décadrage [dekadraʒ] **NM** *Cin* off-centring

décadré [dekadre] **ADJ** *Cin* off-centre

décaèdre [dekaɛdr] *Math* **ADJ** decahedral
NM decahedron

décaféiné [dekafeine] **NM** decaffeinated (coffee); **j'achète toujours du d.** I always buy decaffeinated

décaféiner [dekafeine] **VT** to decaffeinate; **un café décaféiné** a (cup of) decaffeinated coffee

décagonal, -ale, -aux, -ales [dekagɔnal, -o] **ADJ** *Math* decagonal

décagone [dekagon] **NM** *Math* decagon

décaissable [dekɛsabl] ADJ (charge) payable

décaissement [dekɛsmã] NM Com (d'une somme) cash withdrawal or disbursement; **faire un d.** to make an outlay; Compta **décaissements** outgoings

décaisser [dekese] VT **1** (marchandises etc) to unpack **2** (plante, arbuste) to plant out **3** Com (somme) to pay (out); (TVA) to pay

décalage [dekalaʒ] NM **1** (écart) gap; **le d. entre la réalité et les espoirs** the gap between reality and hopes; **d. d'opinions** difference of opinion **2** (d'un instrument) shifting the zero; (quantité) (amount of) shift; **d. vers le haut** upward movement; **d. à droite/gauche** movement to the right/left **3** (retard) time lag; **un d. est prévu pour la date de la réunion** the meeting has been postponed

▸▸ **d. horaire** time difference; **souffrir du d. horaire** to have jet lag

décalaminage [dekalaminaʒ] NM (de moteur) decarbonizing, Fam decoking, decoke

décalaminer [dekalamine] VT (moteur) to decarbonize, Fam to decoke

décalcifiant [dekalsifjã] ADJ Méd decalcifying

décalcification [dekalsifikasjɔ̃] NF Méd decalcification

décalcifier [dekalsifje] Méd VT to decalcify
VPR **se décalcifier** to become decalcified

décalcomanie [dekalkɔmani] NF Cér (procédé) decal(comania); (résultat) decal(-comania), transfer; **faire de la d.** to decal

décalé [dekale] ADJ Fam (personne) out of it, out of touch with reality; (discours, approche) unrealistic

décaler [dekale] VT **1** (meuble) to move, to shift; (instrument) to shift the zero of; **d. l'heure** to alter the time, to change the time or the clock; **d. ses rendez-vous d'une heure** (les avancer) to bring one's meetings forward by an hour; (les reculer) to put one's meetings back by an hour **2** Tech (rivets) to stagger
VPR **se décaler** to move, to shift; **vous pourriez vous d. d'un rang/vers la gauche** you could move up a row/move to the left

décalitre [dekalitr] NM decalitre, Am decaliter

décalogue [dekalɔg] NM Rel Decalogue

décalotter [dekalɔte] VT **1** Fam **d. une bouteille** to open or crack a bottle **2** Méd to pull back the foreskin of

décalquage [dekalkaʒ] NM (de dessin) tracing; (par la chaleur etc) transferring

décalque [dekalk] NM **1** (de dessin) tracing; (par la chaleur etc) transferring; **papier (à) d.** tracing paper **2** (dessin) tracing; (image) transfer; (imitation) copy

décalquer [dekalke] VT (dessin) to trace; (par la chaleur) (plan, image en couleur) to transfer

décamètre [dekamɛtr] NM decametre, Am decameter

décamper [dekãpe] VI Fam to clear out or off; **décampez d'ici!** clear out or off!, get lost!; **tu vas d. et plus vite que ça!** clear off or clear out or get out, on the double!

décan [dekã] NM Astrol decan

décanat [dekana] NM deanship

décanewton [dekanjutɔn] NM decanewton

décaniller [dekanije] VI Fam = **décamper**

décantation [dekãtasjɔ̃] NF decantation, decanting

décanter [dekãte] VT (vin) to decant; Fig **d. ses projets** to mull over one's plans
VPR **se décanter** (de vin) to settle; Fig (de projets) to become clearer; (d'une situation) to settle down, to become clearer; **laisser**

aux choses le temps de se d. to give things time to settle down

décapage [dekapaʒ] NM (d'un meuble etc) stripping; (au papier de verre) sanding (down)

décapant [dekapã] ADJ **1 produit d.** stripper **2** Fig (humour) caustic, vitriolic
NM (pour vernis, peinture) remover, stripper

décaper [dekape] VT (peinture, vernis) to strip, to remove; Tech (métal etc) to scour, to clean; Tech (objets métalliques) to pickle, to dip; **d. un meuble au papier de verre** to sand down a piece of furniture; **d. une surface à peindre** to strip a surface for painting; **d. à la sableuse** to sand-blast
VI Fig Fam **des plaisanteries qui décapent** caustic or vitriolic jokes

décapeuse [dekapøz] NF Tech scraper

décapitation [dekapitasjɔ̃] NF decapitation, beheading

décapiter [dekapite] VT (personne) to decapitate, to behead; (arbre) to pollard; Fig **d. un complot/une association** to root out the ringleaders of a plot/the leaders of a society

décapode [dekapɔd] NM decapod

décapotable [dekapɔtabl] Aut ADJ convertible, open-top; (coupé) drop-head
NF convertible, open-top

décapotage [dekapɔtaʒ] NM lowering the hood

décapoté [dekapɔte] ADJ open

décapoter [dekapɔte] VT Aut to lower the hood of

décapsulage [dekapsylaʒ] NM (de bouteille) opening

décapsuler [dekapsyle] VT (bouteille) to open, to take the top off

décapsuleur [dekapsylœr] NM bottle opener

décapuchonner [dekapyʃɔne] VT to take the top off

décarcasser (se) [sədekarkase] VPR Fam to bust a gut

décarreler [dekarle] VT (surface, pièce) to remove the tiles from

décarrer [dekare] VI Fam to get going, to hit the road

décartellisation [dekartɛlizasjɔ̃] NF Écon, Hist break-up of a cartel

décasyllabe [dekasilab] ADJ decasyllabic
NM decasyllabic verse

décasyllabique [dekasilabik] ADJ decasyllabic

décathlon [dekatlɔ̃] NM Sport decathlon

décathlonien, -ienne [dekatlɔnjɛ̃, -jɛn] N Sport decathlete

décati [dekati] ADJ (visage) wrinkled, that has lost its freshness; (immeuble) shabby, rundown; **vieillard d.** decrepit old man

décatir [dekatir] VT Tex (étoffe) to take the gloss or finish off
VPR **se décatir** to lose one's freshness or one's beauty, to age

décauser [dekoze] VT Belg to malign

décavé [dekave] ADJ **1** Fam (personne riche) ruined; (aux cartes) cleaned out **2** (visage) drawn, pinched

décédé, -ée [desede] ADJ, N surtout Admin deceased

décéder [desede] VI (conj like céder, aux être) surtout Admin to die

décelable [deslabl] ADJ detectable

déceler [desle] VT (je décèle; je décèlerai) **1** (découvrir) to detect; **on a décelé des traces de pneus dans le jardin** tyre marks were found in the garden; **on décèle l'importance qu'a eue sa mère dans tous ses écrits** the importance of his mother can be detected in

all his writings **2** (indiquer) to point to, to indicate; **sa voix décelait la peur** there was (a note of) fear in his voice

décélération [deselerasjɔ̃] NF deceleration, slowing down

décélérer [deselere] VI to decelerate, to slow down

décembre [desãbr] NM December; **en d., au mois de d.** in (the month of) December; **le 25 d.** the 25th of December, December the 25th
SEE GRAMMAR A81–2; B60–2

décemment [desamã] ADV **1** (convenablement) properly, Fml with decorum **2** (correctement) **elle parle anglais d.** her English is reasonable or quite good, she speaks quite decent English **3** (raisonnablement) reasonably; **d., je ne pouvais pas refuser** I couldn't reasonably refuse

décence [desãs] NF **1** (bienséance) (de comportement) propriety, decorum; (d'habillement) decency; **se tenir avec d.** to behave properly or Fml with decorum; **choquer la d.** to offend against decency; **des mots/un comportement qui choque(nt) la d.** offensive words/behaviour **2** (tact) decency; **il aurait dû avoir la d. de s'excuser** he ought to have had the decency to apologize **3** (réserve) decency; **parler avec d.** to speak in restrained terms

décennal, -ale, -aux, -ales [desenal, -o] ADJ decennial

décennie [deseni] NF decade

décent [desã] ADJ **1** decent; (vêtements etc) modest; (comportement, attitude etc) proper; **peu d.** indecent, unseemly **2** (correct) reasonable; **lire d'une manière décente** to read reasonably well

décentrage [desãtraʒ] NM moving off centre or Am center

décentralisateur, -trice [desãtralizatœr, -tris] ADJ decentralizing
N Pol advocate of decentralization, decentralizer

décentralisation [desãtralizasjɔ̃] NF decentralization; **la d. des grandes écoles est devenue nécessaire** it has become necessary to move the grandes écoles out of Paris

décentraliser [desãtralize] VT (administration) to decentralize; (entreprise) to move away from the capital

décentration [desãtrasjɔ̃] NF Opt, Phot decentring, throwing off centre or Am center

décentré [desãtre] ADJ off centre or Am off center

décentrement [desãtrəmã] NM = **décentration**

décentrer [desãtre] VT (table, tableau) to move off centre or Am center; Opt, Tech etc to put out of or off centre, to decentre or Am decenter
VPR **se décentrer** to come or move off centre or Am center

déception [desɛpsjɔ̃] NF disappointment, Fam let-down; **éprouver une d.** to be disappointed; **d. sentimentale** unhappy love affair, disappointment in love

> Il faut noter que le nom anglais **deception** est un faux ami. Il signifie **tromperie**.

décérébrer [deserebre] VT to lobotomize

décernement [desɛrnəmã] NM (d'un prix etc) award

décerner [desɛrne] VT **1** (prix etc) to award; **d. un honneur à qn** to confer an honour on sb **2** Jur **d. un mandat d'arrêt contre qn** to issue a warrant for the arrest of sb

décès [desɛ] NM surtout Admin decease, (natural) death, demise; **acte de d.** death certificate; **fermé pour cause de d.** closed on account of bereavement

décevant [des(ə)vɑ̃] **ADJ 1** (résultat, livre, attitude etc) disappointing **2** Arch (mensonger) (apparence etc) deceptive

décevoir [des(ə)vwar] **VT** (conj like **recevoir**) **1** to disappoint; **il m'a beaucoup déçu** I was very disappointed in him; **ce voyage m'a profondément déçu** I was very disappointed with the trip; **d. l'attente de qn** to disappoint sb, not to live up to sb's expectations; Suisse **d. qn en bien** (le surprendre agréablement) to give sb a pleasant surprise **2** Arch (tromper) to deceive, to delude

> Il faut noter que le verbe anglais **to deceive** est un faux ami. Il signifie **tromper**, **abuser**.

déchaîné [deʃene] **ADJ** (passion) unrestrained, unbridled; (spéculation) wild; **craindre les éléments déchaînés** to fear the fury of the elements; **elle a dû faire face à une presse déchaînée** she had to face a press in full cry; **il est complètement d. à l'idée de la fête** he's hyper or pretty worked up at the thought of the party; **être d. contre qn** to be furious with sb

déchaînement [deʃenmɑ̃] **NM** (des éléments) fury; (des passions) outburst; **d. de rage** outburst of fury, fit of rage; **pourquoi a-t-il fait preuve d'un tel d. contre moi?** why did he fly into a rage with me like that?; **le d. de la tempête** the breaking of the storm; **un d. de l'opinion** a great wave of public opinion

déchaîner [deʃene] **VT** (d'une personne) (passions, colère etc) to arouse, to provoke; **d. l'hilarité** to provoke laughter
VPR **se déchaîner** to break out; **la tempête s'est déchaînée** the storm broke; **se d. contre qn** to fly into a rage with sb

déchanter [deʃɑ̃te] **VI** Fam to become disillusioned

décharge [deʃarʒ] **NF 1** (tirs) discharge, volley; **on lui a envoyé une d. de plombs pour le faire fuir** they fired a few rounds at him to scare him off; **de nombreuses décharges ont été entendues cette nuit** a lot of firing was heard last night; **d. (électrique)** electric shock; **d. d'adrénaline** rush of adrenalin
2 Jur (d'un accusé) release, acquittal; (d'une obligation) discharge; **témoin à d.** witness for the defence; **dire qch à la d. de qn** to say sth in sb's defence
3 Fin (tax) rebate; **porter une somme en d.** to mark a sum as paid; **d. de 50 pour cent** composition of 50p in the pound
4 Tech (sortie etc) discharge, outlet; **tuyau de d.** waste pipe
5 Typ set-off sheet, offset sheet
6 (d'ordures) dumping, tipping; **d. (publique)** rubbish dump, tip; **d. interdite** no dumping, tipping prohibited; **décharges sauvages** fly tipping, Am illegal dumping

déchargement [deʃarʒəmɑ̃] **NM** (de bateau, cargaison etc) unloading; (de marchandises) offloading, unloading

décharger [deʃarʒe] (**je déchargeai(s)**; **n. déchargeons**) **VT 1** (vider) (camion, bateau, cargaison etc) to unload; (marchandises) to offload, to unload; (d'un camion) (gravier) to tip, to dump; (réservoir etc) to empty; (arme à feu) to fire, to discharge; (accumulateur) to discharge; **d. son fusil sur** ou **contre qn** to fire one's gun at sb; Fig **d. sa conscience** to ease one's conscience (**de** of); **d. sa conscience auprès de qn** to unburden oneself to sb; **d. son cœur** to unburden one's heart; **d. sa colère sur qn** to vent one's anger on sb
2 (soulager) (cheval) to relieve, to ease of part of its load; (bateau) to lighten; (poutre) to take the strain off; **d. qn d'une tâche/d'une responsabilité** to relieve sb of a task/a responsibility; Jur **d. qn d'une accusation** to acquit sb of a charge; **d. qn d'une dette** to discharge sb from a debt; **failli déchargé/non déchargé** discharged/undischarged bankrupt
VI 1 Typ encre qui décharge ink that rubs off **2** Vulg (éjaculer) to shoot one's load
VPR **se décharger 1** (d'une personne) **se d. de qn/qch** to get rid of sb/sth; **se d. d'un fardeau** to put down or lay down a load; **se d. de qch sur qn** to shift the responsibility for sth onto sb; **se d. d'une tâche sur qn** to unload a task onto sb **2** (se vider) (d'une arme) to go off; (d'une pile) to run down, to discharge; (d'une colère) to vent itself (**sur** on); **le fleuve se décharge dans un lac** the river flows into a lake

décharné [deʃarne] **ADJ** (corps, membres etc) emaciated; (visage) emaciated, gaunt; (os) stripped of flesh; Fig (arbre) bare; (style) bald

décharner [deʃarne] **VT** (personne) to emaciate; (os) to strip the flesh off

déchaussé [deʃose] **ADJ 1** (sans chaussures) barefoot(ed) **2** avoir les dents déchaussées to have receding gums; **bâtisse aux murs déchaussés** building with unsound foundations

déchaussement [deʃosmɑ̃] **NM** (de murs) laying bare of foundations; **d. de dents** receding gums

déchausser [deʃose] **VT 1** (enlever ses chaussures à) **d. qn** to take off sb's shoes; **d. ses skis** to take off one's skis **2** (arbre) to expose or (lay) bare the roots of; (dent, fondations) to expose
VPR **se déchausser 1** (enlever ses chaussures) to take off one's shoes **2** ses dents se déchaussent he has receding gums, his gums are receding

dèche [dɛʃ] **NF** Fam **être dans la d.** to be stony broke; **c'est la d.** I'm/we're/etc stony broke

déchéance [deʃeɑ̃s] **NF 1** (dégradation, chute) (physique) deterioration, decline; (morale) downfall, ruin; **sa d. a été causée par l'alcool** drink was his downfall; **c'est sa mort de son fils qui est à l'origine de sa d.** it was the death of his son which started him on the downward path
2 Jur, Fin (de droits etc) forfeiture; **action en d. de brevet** action for forfeiture of patent; **d. parentale** loss of parental authority; **d. d'une police** expiry of a policy
3 Pol (d'un monarque) deposition, deposing; (d'un président) removal (after impeachment)
4 Compta **tomber en d.** to lapse

déchet [deʃɛ] **NM 1** déchets waste; **des déchets de tissu** scraps of fabric; **déchets radioactifs/industriels** radioactive/industrial waste; **déchets domestiques** household waste or rubbish; **déchets de métal** scrap (metal); **déchets de viande** scraps of meat **2** Com (de poids, valeur) loss, decrease; **il y a du d.** there is some wastage; **d. de route** loss in transit **3** Péj (personne) down-and-out; **un d. de la société** a social outcast

déchetterie [deʃɛtri] **NF** dump, Br rubbish dump, tip

déchiffonner [deʃifɔne] **VT** to smooth out the creases in

déchiffrable [deʃifrabl] **ADJ** (inscription) decipherable; (écriture) decipherable, legible; **code facilement d.** code that is easy to crack or break

déchiffrage [deʃifraʒ] **NM** Mus sight-reading

déchiffrement [deʃifrəmɑ̃] **NM** deciphering; Ordinat decryption; Ordinat **d. de données** data decryption

déchiffrer [deʃifre] **VT 1** (inscription, écriture etc) to decipher, to make out; (message) to decode; (signaux) to read, to interpret; Ordinat to decrypt; **d. les sentiments d'une personne** to fathom or make out sb's feelings; **d. un mystère** to unravel a mystery **2** (musique) to read, to play at sight, to sight-read; **d. un morceau** to sight-read a piece; **je suis juste en train de d. ce morceau** I'm just learning this piece
VI Mus to sight-read

déchiffreur, -euse [deʃifrœr, -øz] **N** (d'inscription) decipherer; (de message) decoder; (de message secret) code-breaker

déchiqueté [deʃikte] **ADJ 1** (bord) jagged; (littoral) jagged, ragged; **papier à bords déchiquetés** deckle-edge paper **2** (objet) cut to bits or shreds; **une couverture déchiquetée** a tattered blanket

déchiqueter [deʃikte] **VT** (**je déchiquette**; **je déchiquetterai**) (papier) to rip to shreds; (de machine) to shred; (chair) to cut or tear to shreds; (corps, poulet) to hack to pieces

déchiqueteuse [deʃiktøz] **NF** shredder

déchiqueture [deʃiktyr] **NF** slash, long tear

déchirant [deʃirɑ̃] **ADJ** (spectacle) heartrending, harrowing; (douleur) agonizing; **des adieux déchirants** heartrending farewells

déchiré [deʃire] **ADJ 1** (vêtement, couverture, Méd muscle, Fig nation etc) torn; **être d. entre deux personnes** to be torn between two people **2** Fam (ivre) wasted, trashed, Am fried; (drogué) stoned

déchirement [deʃirmɑ̃] **NM** (de tissu, vêtement etc) tearing, Fml rending; Méd (de muscle) tearing; Fig (peine) heartbreak; **cette famille/ce parti connaît des déchirements terribles** the family/party is tearing itself apart

déchirer [deʃire] **VT 1** (tissu, vêtement etc) to tear, Fml to rend; (papier) to tear up; (enveloppe) to tear open; **d. qch en morceaux** to tear sth to pieces or bits or shreds **2** Fig (famille, pays) to tear apart; **d. le cœur à qn** to break sb's heart; **des cris qui déchiraient le cœur** heartrending cries; **un cri aigu déchira le silence** a shrill scream pierced the silence; **des sons qui déchirent le tympan** ear-splitting sounds; **une toux qui déchire la poitrine** a hacking cough; **être déchiré de douleur/remords** to be racked with pain/remorse
VPR **se déchirer 1** (d'un tissu) to tear; **il s'est déchiré un muscle** he's torn a muscle **2** Fig **un couple qui se déchire** a couple who are tearing each other apart; **mon cœur s'est déchiré** I was heartbroken

déchirure [deʃiryr] **NF** (dans un tissu) tear, rip, Fml rent; (blessure) laceration; Fig (peine, chagrin) heartbreak; **le fait de quitter ses parents a été pour lui une véritable d.** it was heartbreaking or heartrending leaving his parents; **une d. musculaire** a torn muscle

déchoir [deʃwar] **VI** (pp **déchu**; pr ind je **déchois**, n. **déchoyons**, ils **déchoient**; p hist je **déchus**; fu je **déchoirai**; aux **être** or **avoir**) **ce quartier a déchu** the area has gone down; **sa popularité déchoit** his popularity is declining; **la maison déchoit de son prestige** the firm is losing its prestige; **par ce mariage/à cause de cet emploi, il déchoit de son rang** he is marrying/the job is beneath him; **ce serait d. (que de s'abaisser à ces tâches vulgaires)** it would be demeaning (to stoop to such common tasks)

déchristianisation [dekristjanizasjɔ̃] **NF** dechristianization

déchristianiser [dekristjanize] **VT** to dechristianize, to turn from Christianity
VPR **se déchristianiser** to turn (away) from Christianity

déchu [deʃy] **ADJ** ange d. fallen angel; roi d.

dethroned king; **police (d'assurance) déchue** expired (insurance) policy; **d. de la nationalité française** deprived or stripped of French nationality; **il est d. de ses droits** he has been stripped of his rights

déci [desi] NM Suisse = decilitre of wine

décibel [desibɛl] NM Phys decibel; **contrôler la puissance en décibels** to monitor the decibel level

décidé [deside] ADJ **1** (fixé) (question etc) settled **2** (caractère, personne, manière) determined; **d'un ton d.** in a decisive tone, decisively; **être d. à faire qch** to be determined or resolved to do sth, to be bent on doing sth; **elle y est bien décidée** she's quite determined or she has quite made up her mind to do it, she's quite bent on doing it; **elle est décidée à tout** she'll do anything

décidément [desidemã] ADV **d. je n'ai pas de chance!** I really haven't any luck!; **d., elle est folle!** she must be mad!; **je n'ai d. pas envie de partir** I really have no desire to go, I have absolutely or positively no desire to go; **on ne peut d. rien faire sans que tu sois dans nos pattes** we can do absolutely nothing without you getting in our way; **je crois qu'il n'est d. bon à rien** in my opinion, he's a positive good-for-nothing

> Il faut noter que l'adverbe anglais **decidedly** est un faux ami. Il signifie le plus souvent **vraiment, franchement**.

DÉCIDER [deside] VT **1** (une question) to decide, to settle; (un voyage, une pause, la guerre etc) to decide on; **voilà qui décide tout!** that settles it!; **d. un déménagement/ une grève** to decide on a move/a strike, to decide to move/to strike; **c'est son manque de sérieux qui a décidé son renvoi** it was his casual attitude that settled the question of whether to sack him
2 d. qn à faire qch to persuade or induce sb to do sth
3 d. que to decide that; **il fut décidé qu'on attendrait sa réponse** it was decided to wait for his reply, it was decided or settled that we/they/etc should wait for his reply
VI **1** (prendre une décision) to decide, to make or take a/the decision; **c'est moi qui décide ici** (tu n'as rien à dire) I'm the one who makes the decisions or who decides here; **je déciderai pour toi** (si tu n'arrives pas à te décider) I'll decide for you; Jur **d. en faveur du plaignant** to find for the plaintiff
2 d. de qch to decide on sth; **c'est le patron qui doit d. de son renvoi** it's the boss who'll have to decide (on) whether or not to sack him; **un événement qui a décidé de sa carrière** an event that determined his career
3 d. de faire qch to decide to do sth; **j'ai décidé de partir demain** I've decided to leave tomorrow
VPR **se décider 1** (prendre une décision) to make up one's mind, to come to a/the decision; **elle n'arrive pas à se d.** she can't make up her mind; **allons, décidez-vous** come on, make up your mind; **se d. à faire qch** to make up one's mind to do sth; **je ne peux pas me d. à le faire/le quitter** I can't bring myself to do it/to leave him; **je ne peux pas me d. au mariage/à la maternité** I can't make up my mind or come to a decision about getting married/having a baby, I can't decide whether to get married/have a baby; **se d. pour qn/qch** to decide on or in favour of sb/sth
2 (de problème, question) to be decided or settled; **leur divorce s'est décidé très rapidement** their decision to get divorced came very quickly, they made their decision very quickly to get divorced
3 Fam **cet engin ne se décide pas à marcher** this machine can't decide or make up its

mind whether to start or not; **il ne se décide pas à faire beau** it can't decide or make up its mind whether to be fine or not

décideur, -euse [desidœr, -øz] N decision-maker

décigramme [desigram] NM tenth of a gram, decigramme

décilitre [desilitr] NM decilitre, Am deciliter

décimal, -ale, -aux, -ales [desimal, -o] SEE GRAMMAR A76; B59 ADJ decimal NF **décimale** decimal place

décimalisation [desimalizasjɔ̃] NF decimalization

décimaliser [desimalize] VT to decimalize

décimation [desimasjɔ̃] NF decimation

décimer [desime] VT to decimate

décimètre [desimɛtr] NM decimetre, Am decimeter

décisif, -ive [desizif, -iv] ADJ **1** (bataille, argument etc) decisive; (preuve) conclusive; **au moment d.** at the critical or crucial moment; **prendre un tournant d.** to take a decisive turn **2** (ton) decisive

décision [desizjɔ̃] NF **1** (choix) decision; Jur ruling, award; **prendre/arriver à une d.** to make or take/come to or reach a decision (**quant à, au sujet de** about); **elle a pris la d. de partir** she has decided to leave; **la d. ne m'appartient pas** it's not up to me to decide, it's not my decision; **forcer une d.** to bring matters to a head; **soumettre une question à la d. de qn** to submit a matter for sb's decision; Sport **faire la d.** (d'un match) to be the decider, to decide matters; **par d. judiciaire** by decision of the court; **d. arbitrale** arbitration ruling, decision by arbitration; **d. autonome** autonomous decision; **d. commune** joint decision; **d. d'achat** buying decision; Jur **d. de justice** court ruling
2 (détermination) resolution, determination; **affirmer qch avec d.** to state sth decisively; **elle ne manque pas d'esprit de d.** she does not lack decisiveness

décisionnaire [desizjɔnɛr] N decision-maker

décisionnel, -elle [desizjɔnɛl] ADJ (responsabilité) decision-making; **avoir un poste d.** to have a job with decision-making responsibilities

déclamateur, -trice [deklamatœr, -tris] N Péj ranter, tub-thumper

déclamation [deklamasjɔ̃] NF **1** (éloquence) oratory, (art of) declamation; **il a une mauvaise d.** he declaims his lines badly **2** Péj (emphase) ranting, spouting; (discours) ranting or bombastic speech

déclamatoire [deklamatwar] ADJ Péj (style) declamatory, high-flown; (discours) ranting, bombastic

déclamer [deklame] VT **1** (discours, vers) to declaim **2** Péj **il déclame tout ce qu'il dit** he makes a performance out of everything he says
VI Péj to rant; Litt **d. contre qn** to rail against sb

déclarable [deklarabl] ADJ (marchandises) liable to duty; (revenu) declarable; **marchandise non d.** duty-free goods

déclarant, -ante [deklarã, -ãt] N Jur, Admin declarant; **d. de TVA** VAT-registered person

déclaration [deklarasjɔ̃] NF declaration, proclamation; (de naissance, décès etc) notification; Compta return; **d. de guerre** declaration of war; **d. de changement de domicile** notification of change of address; **d. d'accident/de vol/d'incendie** accident/theft/fire claim; **d. en douane** customs declaration; **faire une d. à la police** to make a statement to the police; **selon votre d. du ...** according to your statement of the ...; **le chef de l'État**

a une importante **d. à faire** the President has an important announcement to make; **d. d'intention** declaration of intent; **une d. de principe** a statement or declaration of principle; **d. d'amour** declaration of love; **il lui a fait une** ou **sa d.** he declared his love to her
▸▸**d. annuelle de résultats** annual statement of results; **d. annuelle des données sociales** PAYE and NIC return; **d. d'avarie** (ship's) protest; Ordinat **d. de champ** field definition; **d. commune** agreed statement; **d. de décès** = official registration of death (submitted to the Mairie); **d. de dividende** dividend announcement, declaration of dividend; **D. des droits de l'enfant** Declaration of the Rights of the Child; **D. des droits de l'homme** Declaration of Human Rights; **d. d'entrée** declaration or clearance inwards; **d. d'exportation** export declaration; **d. de faillite** declaration of bankruptcy; **d. fiscale** tax return; **d. d'importation** import declaration; **d. d'impôts** tax return; Hist **D. d'indépendance** Declaration of Independence; **d. de patrimoine** = official statement of net personal assets, made by French politicians on being elected to office; Compta **d. de résultats** statement of results, financial statement; **d. de revenus** income tax return; **d. de sinistre** (d'une assurance) damage report; (réclamation) notice of claim, insurance claim; **d. de solvabilité** declaration of solvency; Com **d. de sortie** declaration outwards, clearance outwards; **d. sous serment** affidavit; Com **d. de transit** declaration of goods in transit; **d. de TVA** VAT return; Admin **d. d'utilité publique** = government decision that a large public works project is vital and should therefore go ahead even in the event of public protest; **d. de valeur** declaration of value

Déclaration d'impôts

People in France are required to declare their taxable earnings at the beginning of the year. Thrice-yearly tax payments ("tiers provisionnels") are based on one third of the previous year's total, the final payment being adjusted according to the actual tax owed. It is also possible to pay tax on a monthly basis. This is known as "mensualisation".

déclaré [deklare] ADJ **1** (ennemi, intention etc) declared, avowed; **un partisan d. de la peine de mort** an avowed supporter of the death penalty **2** Admin **d. d'utilité publique** (entreprise, travaux) declared vital by the government (in spite of potential public protest)

déclarer [deklare] VT (ses intentions, désirs etc, à la douane) to declare; Admin (un décès, une naissance, un employé) to register; Ordinat (valeur etc) to define; **d. son incompétence** to admit one's incompetence; Cartes **d. trèfle** to declare or call clubs; **elle a déclaré qu'elle n'en avait jamais eu connaissance** she declared that she had never known anything about it; **je déclare la séance levée** I declare the meeting closed; **d. qn roi** to declare sb king; **déclaré coupable** found guilty; **déclaré coupable de vol** found guilty or convicted of theft; **d. la guerre à qn** to declare war on sb; **avez-vous quelque chose à d.?** have you anything to declare?; **rien à d.** nothing to declare; **d. ses revenus au fisc** to make or Am file one's tax return
VPR **se déclarer 1** (se prononcer) to speak one's mind; **se d. pour** ou **en faveur de/ contre qch** to declare oneself in favour of/ against sth **2** (faire une déclaration d'amour)

to declare one's love **3** *(du feu, d'une maladie, d'une guerre)* to break out **4** *(se dire)* **se d. l'auteur du méfait** to own up to the deed; **elle s'est déclarée satisfaite de l'accord passé** she declared herself satisfied with the agreement that was reached; *Bourse* **se d. acheteur** to call the shares; *Bourse* **se d. vendeur** to put the shares

déclassé [deklase] ADJ **1** *Sport (à une division inférieure etc)* relegated; *(hôtel)* downgraded **2** *Rail Vieilli* reclassed **3** *Péj (personne)* déclassé **4** *Bourse (valeurs)* displaced

déclassement [deklasmɑ̃] NM **1** *Sport (d'équipe de football)* relegation; *(d'hôtel)* downgrading **2** *(de personne)* loss of social position **3** *Bourse (de valeurs)* displacement **4** *Rail Vieilli* reclassification

déclasser [deklase] VT **1** *Sport* to relegate; *(hôtel)* to downgrade **2** *Rail (passagers)* to transfer from one class to another **3** *(socialement)* to lower the social position of **4** *Mil (arme)* to declare obsolete; *(navire de guerre)* to strike off the list **5** *Naut (marin)* to disrate **6** *(déranger) (papiers)* to put out of order

déclassifier [deklasifje] VT *(documents)* declassify

déclenchement [deklɑ̃ʃmɑ̃] NM *(d'un appareil)* starting (up), setting in motion; *(d'un mécanisme)* activation; *Tech (d'une pièce)* releasing, disengaging; *Phot (shutter)* release; **le d. de la sonnerie** the setting off of the alarm; *Fig* **le d. des protestations** the triggering (off) of protests

déclencher [deklɑ̃ʃe] VT *(appareil)* to start (up), to set in motion; *(mécanisme)* to activate, to trip; *(alarme)* to set off, to activate, to trip; *Tech (pièce)* to release, to disconnect, to disengage; *Fig (critiques, questions etc)* to trigger; *Mil* **d. une attaque** to launch an attack

déclencheur [deklɑ̃ʃœr] NM *Phot* shutter release; *Tech* trigger; *Phot* **d. automatique** time release, self-timer

déclic [deklik] NM *(mécanisme) (qui bloque)* pawl, catch; *(qui déclenche)* trigger; *(bruit)* click(ing sound); **chronomètre à d.** stopwatch; **la vue de cette photo a été pour lui un véritable d.** looking at the photo made something go click; **pour qu'il retrouve la mémoire, il suffirait d'un d.** all it would take for him to regain his memory is for something to go click

déclin [deklɛ̃] NM *(du talent, de la santé, de la vigueur, d'une civilisation, d'un art)* decline; *(de la beauté)* fading; *(du jour)* decline, close; *(de la lune)* waning; **être en d.** to be in decline, to decline; **le soleil/la lune est à ou sur son d.** the sun/moon is sinking *or* setting; **une civilisation à son d.** a civilization in decline; **au d. de sa vie** in his declining years

déclinable [deklinabl] ADJ *Gram* declinable

déclinaison [deklinɛzɔ̃] NF **1** *Astron (d'étoile)* declination; **d. magnétique** magnetic variation **2** *Gram* declension

déclinant [deklinɑ̃] ADJ *(lune)* waning; *(beauté, lumière)* fading; *(pouvoirs)* declining; **ses facultés déclinantes** his/her declining faculties

décliner [dekline] VI *(de la lune)* to wane; *(d'une étoile, du talent, de la santé)* to decline; *(du jour)* to draw to a close; *(de la beauté)* to fade; *(de vivacité)* to decrease, to diminish; **une civilisation qui menace de d.** a civilization threatened with decline; **ses sentiments pour elle déclinent de jour en jour** his feelings for her are lessening day by day; **ses facultés déclinent** his/her mind is going

VT **1** *Fml (refuser) (offre, invitation)* to decline; *Com* **d. toute responsabilité** to accept no liability; **d. une juridiction** to refuse to acknowledge a jurisdiction **2** *Gram* to decline **3** *(réciter) (identité)* to state; **d. ses nom et prénoms** to state *or* give one's full name **4** *Com* to produce; **cet imprimé est décliné dans tous les tons** the pattern is available in all shades

VPR **se décliner 1** *Gram* to be declined **2** *Com* to be available

déclive [dekliv] ADJ sloping, inclined
NF **en d.** *(terrain, toit)* sloping

déclivité [deklivite] NF slope, incline, gradient, *Fml* declivity; **angle de d.** angle of gradient

décloisonnement [deklwazɔnmɑ̃] NM decompartmentalization

décloisonner [deklwazɔne] VT to decompartmentalize

déclouer [deklue] VT to take the nails out of

déco [deko] ADJ PL *(abrév* **décoratifs)** **arts d.** art deco
NF *(abrév* **décoration)** decor, decoration; *(métier)* (interior) decorating, interior design; **j'aime beaucoup faire de la d.** I love decorating

décocher [dekɔʃe] VT **1** *(flèche)* to shoot, to let fly; **d. un coup/une ruade** to let fly with a punch/kick; **d. un coup/une ruade à qn** to hit out at/kick sb **2** *Fig* **d. une remarque** to let fly with *or* fire off a comment; **d. une œillade à qn** to flash a glance at sb, to glance fleetingly at sb; **d. un sourire à qn** to flash a smile at sb

décoction [dekɔksjɔ̃] NF decoction

décodage [dekɔdaʒ] NM decoding; *(d'un code)* cracking; *(de chaîne de télévision)* decoding, unscrambling

décoder [dekɔde] VT to decode; *(code)* to crack; *(chaîne de télévision)* to decode, to unscramble

décodeur [dekɔdœr] NM *Ordinat* decoder; *TV, Tél* decoder, unscrambler; *TV* **d. numérique** set-top box

décoiffer [dekwafe] VT **1** *(ôter le chapeau de)* **d. qn** to take off *or* remove sb's hat **2** *(ébouriffer)* **d. qn** to tousle sb's hair
VI *Fig Fam* **c'est un film qui décoiffe** it's an astonishing *or Fam* a mind-blowing film; **ça décoiffe!** it's quite an experience!, *Fam* it's mind-blowing!; **je peux te dire que l'écouter parler, ça décoiffe!** listening to him talk is quite an experience, let me tell you!
VPR **se décoiffer 1** *(se dépeigner)* to mess up one's hair **2** *(ôter son chapeau)* to take off *or* remove one's hat

décoinçage [dekwɛ̃saʒ], **décoincement** [dekwɛ̃smɑ̃] NM *(de pièce coincée)* loosening

décoincer [dekwɛ̃se] *(n.* **décoinçons; je décoinçai(s))** VT *(pièce coincée)* to loosen; *Fam* **d. qn** to loosen sb up
VPR **se décoincer** *Fam* to loosen up

décolérer [dekɔlere] VI *(je* **décolère; je décolérerai)** to calm down; **il ne décolérait pas** he was still fuming; **il n'a pas décoléré depuis huit jours** he's been angry for a week

décollage [dekɔlaʒ] NM **1** *(d'avion, de fusée),* *Fig (d'industrie, d'économie)* takeoff **2** *(de timbre etc)* unsticking, ungluing

décollation [dekɔlasjɔ̃] NF decapitation, beheading

décollé [dekɔle] ADJ **il a les oreilles décollées** his ears stick out

décollement [dekɔlmɑ̃] NM **1** *Méd* **d. de la rétine** detachment of the retina; **d. de racines** body wave **2** *(de timbre etc)* unsticking, ungluing

décoller [dekɔle] VT *(timbre, papier peint, affiche)* to remove; **d. une enveloppe à la va-**

peur to steam open an envelope; *Fig Fam* **d. qn de la télé/du match de foot/de son livre** to prize *or* tear sb away from the TV/the football match/their book
VI **1** *(d'un avion, d'une fusée),* *Fig (d'un pays, d'une économie etc)* to take off **2** *Fam (partir)* to take off, to leave; **bon, on décolle?** shall we get moving?; **il ne décolle pas d'ici** won't budge, he's staying put; **il ne décolle pas de la télé** he's glued to the TV; *Sport* **d. du peloton** to peel away from the pack **3** *Fam (maigrir)* to fade away to nothing
VPR **se décoller** *(d'une enveloppe)* to come unstuck *or* undone; *Méd (de la rétine)* to become detached

décolletage [dekɔltaʒ] NM *(d'une robe) (action)* lowering of the neckline; *(résultat)* neckline

décolleté [dekɔlte] ADJ **robe décolletée** low-necked *or* low-cut dress; **femme décolletée** woman in a low-necked *or* low-cut dress; **tu ne trouves pas que c'est trop d.?** you don't think it's too low?; **robe décolletée dans le dos** dress cut low at the back; *Hum* **elle était décolletée jusqu'au nombril ou aux genoux** she was showing everything she'd got, she was showing a lot of cleavage
NM neck opening, neckline; **d. bateau** boat neck; **d. carré** square neck; **d. en pointe** *ou* **en V** V-neck; **d. rond** round neck; **d. plongeant** plunging neckline; **en grand d.** *en robe de soirée)* in full evening dress; **avoir un beau d.** to have a beautiful neck and shoulders; **il a jeté un œil dans mon d.** he looked down the front of my dress

décolleter [dekɔlte] *(je* **décollette** [dekɔlɛt]*)* VT *(robe)* to cut out the neck of; **il faut te d. beaucoup plus que ça** you'll have to show much more than that; **pour son mariage, on va la d. un peu** for her wedding, we'll give her a slightly lower neckline; **cette robe te décollette trop** the dress is too low(-cut) for you
VPR **se décolleter** to wear a low-necked dress

décolonisation [dekɔlɔnizasjɔ̃] NF decolonization

décoloniser [dekɔlɔnize] VT to decolonize

décolorant [dekɔlɔrɑ̃] ADJ bleaching
NM bleaching agent, bleach

décoloration [dekɔlɔrasjɔ̃] NF *(d'un tissu)* discolo(u)ration, *Am* discoloration, fading; *(des cheveux)* bleaching; **demander une d.** to ask for one's hair to be bleached

décolorer [dekɔlɔre] VT *(tissu)* to discolour, *Am* to discolor, to fade, to take the colour *or Am* color out of; *(cheveux)* to bleach
VPR **se décolorer** to lose its colour *or Am* color, to fade, to bleach; **se d. les cheveux** to bleach one's hair

décombres [dekɔ̃br] NMPL ruins, debris

décommander [dekɔmɑ̃de] VT *(réunion, dîner)* to cancel, to call off; *(invité)* to put off; *(marchandise)* to cancel (the order for)
VPR **se décommander** *(chez le dentiste etc)* to cancel one's appointment; *(à un dîner, une soirée etc)* to cancel

décompacter [dekɔ̃pakte] VT *Ordinat* to uncrunch

décomplexer [dekɔ̃plekse] VT *Fam* to cure of hang-ups; **c'est le sport qui l'a décomplexé** it was sport that cured him of his hang-ups *or* that got rid of his complexes, sport made him feel better about himself

décomposable [dekɔ̃pozabl] ADJ *(texte)* that can be broken up, that can be divided into parts; *(composé)* that can be broken down

décomposé [dekɔ̃poze] ADJ *(viande, feuilles)* decomposed, rotten; *Fig* **il est arrivé complètement d.** *(par l'émotion)* he arrived quite distraught; *(par la peur)* he arrived quite terror-stricken

décomposer [dekɔ̃poze] **VT 1** *Phys, Chimie etc* to decompose; **d. la lumière** to split light; **d. une fraction** to split up a fraction; **d. un pas de deux (en séquences)** to break down a pas de deux into separate sequences **2** *(matière organique)* to decompose, to rot, to decay **3** *(tâches, problème, dépenses)* to break down **4** *Compta (compte, résultats)* to analyse, to break down **5** *(traits)* to contort, to distort; **la souffrance décomposait son visage** his/her face was drawn by suffering

VPR se décomposer 1 *(de corps)* to decompose, to decay; *(de viande)* to decompose, to rot; *(de feuilles)* to decompose, to rot, to decay **2** *(du visage, des traits)* to become distorted with terror

---

Il faut noter que le verbe anglais **to decompose** signifie uniquement **pourrir**.

---

décomposition [dekɔ̃pozisjɔ̃] **NF 1** *Phys, Chimie etc* decomposition; *Compta* **d. des résultats** breakdown of the results **2** *(de viande, feuilles)* decomposition, rotting; *(de corps)* decomposition, decay; *Fig* **la d. d'un empire** the decay of an empire **3** *(de traits)* distortion

décompresser [dekɔ̃prese] **VT** *Tech* to decompress; *Ordinat* to decompress, to unbundle, to uncrunch

VI *Tech* to decompress; *Fig Fam* to unwind

décompresseur [dekɔ̃presœr] **NM** decompressor

décompression [dekɔ̃presjɔ̃] **NF** decompression; *Ordinat* decompression, unbundling; **avoir un accident de d.** *(d'un plongeur)* to get the bends; **robinet de d.** *(dans un moteur)* compression tap; *(dans une machine à vapeur)* petcock

décomprimer [dekɔ̃prime] **VT** to decompress

décompte [dekɔ̃t] **NM 1** *(d'une somme à payer)* deduction; *(calcul)* calculation; **j'ai fait le d. de ce que vous m'avez payé et de ce que vous me devez** I've deducted what you've paid from what you owe me; *Fig Vieilli* **trouver du d.** to be disappointed (**à** in) **2** *Admin, Com (relevé)* detailed account, breakdown

décompter [dekɔ̃te] **VT** *(une somme d'un compte)* to deduct

VI *(d'une horloge)* to miscount *(on striking)*

déconcentration [dekɔ̃sɑ̃trasjɔ̃] **NF 1** *Admin* devolution; *(d'une ville)* decongestion **2** *Chimie* dilution

déconcentrer [dekɔ̃sɑ̃tre] **VT 1** *Admin* to devolve; **d. l'autorité gouvernementale** to decentralize government; **d. une ville** to decongest a city **2 d. qn** to distract sb

VPR se déconcentrer to lose concentration, to be distracted

déconcertant [dekɔ̃sɛrtɑ̃] **ADJ** disconcerting

déconcerté [dekɔ̃sɛrte] **ADJ** disconcerted, taken aback

déconcerter [dekɔ̃sɛrte] **VT 1** *(personne)* to disconcert; **il ne faut pas te laisser d. par ses questions** you mustn't let yourself be disconcerted *or Fam* thrown by his questions **2** *Litt (les plans de qn)* to upset, to confound, to frustrate

VPR se déconcerter to be disconcerted, to lose one's self-assurance; **sans se d.** unabashed

déconditionnement [dekɔ̃disjɔnmɑ̃] **NM** *Psy* aversion therapy

déconditionner [dekɔ̃disjɔne] **VT** *Psy* to treat with aversion therapy; *Fig* **d. l'opinion publique** to shake up public opinion

déconfit [dekɔ̃fi] **ADJ** crestfallen, disheartened; **un air d.** a crestfallen look

déconfiture [dekɔ̃fityr] **NF** *Fam (aux élections, dans un combat etc)* defeat; *(d'une société)* collapse, failure, downfall, ruin; *(faillite)* bankruptcy, insolvency; **tomber en d.** to fail to meet one's liabilities, *Fam* to go under

décongélation [dekɔ̃ʒelasjɔ̃] **NF** defrosting, thawing

décongeler [dekɔ̃ʒle] **VT** (**je décongèle; je décongèlerai**) to defrost, to thaw

décongestif, -ive [dekɔ̃ʒɛstif, -iv] **ADJ, NM** *Méd* decongestant

décongestionner [dekɔ̃ʒɛstjɔne] **VT 1** *Méd (poumons etc)* to relieve congestion in, to clear; **d. un malade** to relieve the congestion in *or* clear a patient's lungs **2** *Fig (rue)* to relieve congestion in; *(aéroport, université)* to relieve congestion at; *(administration)* to decentralize

déconnecter [dekɔnɛkte] **VT** *Élec (fil etc)* to disconnect; *Fig* **les années qu'il a passées en Inde l'ont complètement déconnecté de la vie en Europe** the years he spent in India have put him completely out of touch with what is happening in Europe; **déconnecté de la réalité** out of touch with the real world

VPR se déconnecter *Ordinat* to go off-line

déconner [dekɔne] **VI** *très Fam (en parlant)* to talk rubbish *or* drivel; *(en agissant)* to muck *or* fool around, to act the fool, *très Fam* to bugger around; *(d'une machine)* to act *or* play up; **tu déconnes complètement** you're talking a load of rubbish; **tu sais très bien qu'il a dit ça pour d.** you know very well he said it just as a leg-pull; **allez, déconne pas, viens avec nous!** come on, don't be like that, come with us!; **sans d., c'était super** no fooling, it was great, it was great, I kid you not; **sans d.?** *(est-ce vrai?)* no kidding?, yeah?, *Br* straight up?; **sans d.!** *(en réponse)* you're joking!, no kidding!; **la télé déconne** the TV's acting *or* playing up, the TV's on the blink; **la voiture s'est mise à d.** the car's started to act *or* play up, the car's gone on the blink

déconneur, -euse [dekɔnœr, -øz] **N** *très Fam (en parlant)* person who talks rubbish *or* drivel; *(en agissant)* idiot, clown; **être (un) d. à l'école** to muck *or* fool around at school

déconseiller [dekɔ̃seje] **VT** to advise against; **d. qch à qn** to advise sb against sth; **d. à qn de faire qch** to advise sb against doing sth; **déconseillé à qn** *(livre etc)* unsuitable for sb; **un livre à d. aux jeunes** an unsuitable book for young people; **c'est fortement déconseillé** it's extremely inadvisable *or* unwise; **il est déconseillé de laisser ce produit à la portée des enfants** this product should be kept out of children's reach

déconsidération [dekɔ̃siderasjɔ̃] **NF** disrepute, discredit; **tomber en d.** *ou* **dans la d.** to fall into disrepute

déconsidérer [dekɔ̃sidere] (**je déconsidère; je déconsidérerai**) **VT** to bring into disrepute

VPR se déconsidérer *(d'une entreprise, d'une marque)* to fall into disrepute; *(d'une personne)* to lose respect; **elle s'est définitivement déconsidérée au sein de l'entreprise** she has lost all respect in the company

déconsignation [dekɔ̃siɲasjɔ̃] **NF** *Com* deconsignment

déconsigner [dekɔ̃siɲe] **VT** *(valise)* to collect from the left-luggage office; *(bouteille etc)* to return the deposit on

décontamination [dekɔ̃taminasjɔ̃] **NF** decontamination

décontaminer [dekɔ̃tamine] **VT** to decontaminate

décontenancé [dekɔ̃tnɑ̃se] **ADJ** disconcerted, confused

décontenancer [dekɔ̃tnɑ̃se] (**je décontenançai(s); n. décontenançons**) **VT** to disconcert, to confuse

VPR se décontenancer to become disconcerted *or* confused

décontract [dekɔ̃trakt] **ADJ INV** *Fam* = **décontracté; en (tenue) d.** in casual dress, casually dressed

décontracté [dekɔ̃trakte] **ADJ** *(ambiance)* relaxed; *(attitude, individu)* relaxed, laidback, casual; *(vêtement)* casual; **en tenue décontractée** in casual dress, casually dressed

décontracter [dekɔ̃trakte] **VT** to relax

VPR se décontracter to relax

décontraction [dekɔ̃traksjɔ̃] **NF** relaxation; **sa d. me sidère!** I'm amazed at how relaxed he is *or* laid back he is!; **amener un peu de d. dans les rapports avec ses employés** to make relations with one's employees a little more relaxed *or* less tense

déconvenue [dekɔ̃vny] **NF** mortification, disappointment; **quelle ne fut pas ma d. quand ...** I was mortified when ...; **quelle d.!** how mortifying!

décor [dekɔr] **NM 1** *(d'une maison etc)* decor; **d. de table** table decoration, table centre **2** *Théâtre, Cin, TV* set; *(toile peinte)* backdrop, backcloth; **d. de cinéma** movie *or Br* film set; **d. en extérieur** outdoor set; **décors** sets, scenery; **en d. naturel** on location; *Aut Fam* **rentrer** *ou* **aller/envoyer qn dans le d.** to go/send sb off the road **3** *(environnement)* *(charmant, sordide)* surroundings; *(de montagnes, d'usines)* background, backdrop; *Fig* **il aurait besoin d'un changement** *ou* **de changer de d.** he needs a change (of scene)

décorateur, -trice [dekɔratœr, -tris] **N 1** *(d'intérieur)* (interior) decorator **2** *Théâtre* set *or* stage designer, scenic designer; *(peintre)* scene painter

décoratif, -ive [dekɔratif, -iv] **ADJ** decorative, ornamental; *(arbre)* ornamental; **arts décoratifs** decorative arts; *Péj* **n'avoir qu'un rôle d.** to have a purely decorative role

décoration [dekɔrasjɔ̃] **NF 1** *(d'une maison, d'un appartement)* (interior) decoration, decor; *(d'une église)* ornamentation, embellishment; *TV etc* scenery design; **décorations de Noël** Christmas decorations; **d. florale** floral arrangement; **faire de la d. (d'intérieur)** to do interior decorating **2** *(médaille)* decoration, medal; **porter une d. à la boutonnière** to wear a decoration in one's buttonhole; **remise de décorations** investiture

décorer [dekɔre] **VT 1** *(maison, appartement etc)* to decorate; **cette église est magnifiquement décorée de vitraux anciens** the church has some magnificent old stained glass **2** *(médailler)* to decorate (**de** with)

décorner [dekɔrne] **VT 1** *(bovins etc)* to dehorn, to poll; *Fam* **un vent à d. les bœufs** a howling gale **2** *(page)* to smooth out

décorticage [dekɔrtikaʒ] **NM** *(de crevettes, noisettes)* shelling; *(de riz)* husking; *(d'orge)* hulling; *Fig (d'un texte, d'un auteur)* detailed analysis

décortication [dekɔrtikasjɔ̃] **NF** *(d'un arbre)* barking; *Méd (d'un organe)* decortication

décortiquer [dekɔrtike] **VT** *(crevettes, noisettes)* to shell; *(riz)* to husk; *(orge)* to hull; *(arbre)* to bark; *Méd (organe)* to decorticate; *Fig (texte)* to analyse in detail

décorum [dekɔrɔm] **NM** decorum, propriety; **observer le d.** to observe the proprieties

décote [dekɔt] **NF** *(de devises)* drop, fall (in value); *(d'impôts)* reduction; **d. de TVA** VAT rebate

découcher [dekuʃe] **VI** *(ne pas rentrer)* to stay out all night

découdre [dekudr] (*conj like* **coudre**) VT (*vêtement*) to unpick, to unstitch; (*ourlet*) to rip; (*bouton*) to take off, to remove

VI **en d.** to fight; **être toujours prêt à en d.** to be always ready for a fight

VPR **se découdre** (*d'une poche, d'un ourlet*) to come unstitched *or* undone; (*d'un bouton*) to come off

découler [dekule] VI to follow (**de** from); **il en découle que ...** it follows that ...; **il découle de cette réunion que nous devrons ...** the outcome *or* upshot of the meeting is that we will have to ...; **ces licenciements découlent de la situation de crise** the layoffs are attributable to the crisis, the crisis is the reason for the layoffs

découpage [dekupaʒ] NM **1** (*de gâteau etc*) cutting up; (*de viande*) carving; *Couture (de patrons etc)* cutting out; (*d'une plaque de métal*) punching, stamping, cutting; (*de cuir etc*) punching, pinking; *Ordinat (de fichier, d'image)* splitting; *Pol* **d. électoral** division into constituencies; **matrices pour d.** cutting dies **2** (*résultat*) cutout; **cahier de découpages** scrap book; **faire du d.** *ou* **des découpages** to do some cutting out; **un enfant occupé à ses découpages** a child busy with his/her scraps **3** *Cin (scénario)* **d. (technique)** shooting script

découpe [dekup] NF (*dans un vêtement*), *Typ* cut-out

découpé [dekupe] ADJ **1** (*sommet, montagne*) jagged; (*côte*) jagged, indented **2** *Bot* denticulate

découper [dekupe] VT (*gâteau etc*) to cut up; (*viande*) to carve; (*plan, papier*) to cut out; (*métaux*) to stamp (out), to punch, to cut; (*cuir*) to punch, to pink; *Ordinat (fichier)* to split; (*disque dur*) to partition; **couteau à d.** carving knife; **scie à d.** fretsaw; **d. un article dans un journal** to cut an article out of a newspaper; **d. un texte en plusieurs parties** to divide a text into several parts; *Cin* **d. un scénario** to make a shooting script

VPR **se découper** to stand out, to show up (**sur** on, against); **son ombre se découpait sur le sol** his shadow stood out sharply on the ground; **sa silhouette se découpait dans le soleil** the sunlight threw his silhouette into sharp relief

découpeur, -euse [dekupœr, -øz] N (*personne*) (*de viande*) carver; *Cin* cutter; **d. en cuir** leather cutter

NF **découpeuse** (*machine*) shearing *or* cutting *or* pinking machine

découplé [dekuple] ADJ **bien d.** (*personne*) well-built, muscular

découpler [dekuple] VT (*chiens de meute*) to slip, to uncouple; (*chevaux, wagons*) to uncouple

découpure [dekupyr] NF **1** (*action*) cutting out; (*avec poinçon*) punching, stamping (out); (*avec cisailles*) pinking; (*décoration*) fretwork **2** (*résultat*) (*par poinçonnage*) stamping **3** (*du littoral*) indentation; *Bot (dans une feuille*) denticulation

découragé [dekuraʒe] ADJ discouraged, disheartened

décourageant [dekuraʒɑ̃] ADJ (*nouvelle, situation, travail*) discouraging, disheartening; **vous êtes d.** (*vous n'y arriverez jamais*) you're hopeless; (*vous me découragez*) you're disheartening

découragement [dekuraʒmɑ̃] NM discouragement; **il n'éprouve plus que du d.** he feels totally discouraged *or* disheartened

décourager [dekuraʒe] (**je décourageai(s); n. décourageons**) VT **1** (*démoraliser*) to discourage, to dishearten; **il est découragé au moindre échec** he loses heart *or* becomes discouraged at the slightest setback; **se lais-**

ser d. to (let oneself) be discouraged *or* disheartened **2** (*dissuader*) to discourage, to deter; **d. qn de (faire) qch** to discourage *or* deter sb from (doing) sth, to put sb off (doing) sth; **un ton qui décourage tout humour** a tone that discourages any attempt at humour

VPR **se décourager** to become discouraged *or* disheartened, to lose heart; **ne vous découragez pas!** don't get discouraged!, don't lose heart!; **il se décourage tout de suite** he gives up easily

découronner [dekurɔne] VT (*roi etc*) to dethrone, to depose; *Fig (héros etc)* to debunk; (*arbre*) to pollard

décours [dekur] NM **1** (*de la lune*) waning; **lune à son d.** moon on the wane **2** *Méd (de la fièvre)* abatement; (*d'une maladie*) decline

décousu [dekuzy] ADJ (*ourlet etc*) undone, unstitched; *Fig (mots, idées etc*) disjointed, incoherent; (*remarques, conversation*) rambling, desultory; (*travail*) unmethodical

NM (*de mots, d'idées etc*) disjointedness; (*d'une conversation*) desultoriness

découvert [dekuvɛr] ADJ uncovered; (*région etc*) open; (*ville etc*) exposed, unprotected; **une robe qui laisse les épaules découvertes** a dress that leaves the shoulders bare; **dormir à d.** to sleep without any covers; **la tête découverte** bareheaded; **à visage d.** openly, frankly; **coin de ciel d.** bit of blue sky

NM *Fin* **d. (bancaire)** overdraft; **d. de la balance commerciale** trade gap; **d. en blanc** unsecured overdraft; **demander à bénéficier d'un d.** to apply for an overdraft; **avoir un d. ou être à d. de 1000 euros** (*autorisé*) to have a 1,000 euro overdraft; (*non autorisé*) to be overdrawn by 1,000 euros; *Fin* **être à d.** to be overdrawn; **compte à d.** overdrawn account; **mettre un compte à d.** to overdraw an account; **votre compte est à d. de 2000 euros** your account is overdrawn by 2,000 euros; **crédit à d.** unsecured credit; *Bourse* **vendre à d.** to go a bear, to sell short **2** *agir:* **parler à d.** to act/speak openly; **mettre qch à d.** to expose sth to view; **s'avancer à d.** to move forward without cover

découverte [dekuvɛrt] NF **1** (*d'un pays etc*) discovery; *Mil* scouting, reconnoitring; **aller ou partir à la d.** to explore, to go exploring; **aller à la d. de qch** to go in search of sth; **faire la d. de qch** to discover sth **2** (*scientifique, d'une intrigue etc*) discovery; *Hum* **ce n'est pas une d.!** that's nothing new! **3** *TV, Cin etc* backdrop, backing; **d. photographique** photomural

découvreur, -euse [dekuvrœr, -øz] N discoverer

DÉCOUVRIR [dekuvrir] (*conj like* **couvrir**) VT **1** (*trouver, mettre à jour l'existence de*) (*virus, pénicilline, trésor, coupable etc*) to discover; (*erreur*) to discover, to detect; (*crime*) to discover, to bring to light; (*secret, complot*) to uncover; **il ne parvint pas à d. qui elle était** he couldn't find out who she was; **d. des qualités insoupçonnées en ou chez qn** to discover unsuspected qualities in sb; **de là-haut, on découvrait un paysage magnifique** from the top, we had a magnificent view of the scenery

2 (*apprendre à connaître*) (*la musique classique etc*) to discover; (*personne*) to get to know; **il découvrit alors l'enfer du goulag** he experienced the hell of the gulag camps

3 (*enlever ce qui couvre*) to reveal; (*statue*) to uncover, to unveil; **il m'a découvert ses projets** he disclosed *or* revealed his plans to me; **la mer a découvert des kilomètres de sable blanc en se retirant** the ebbing tide uncovered *or* revealed *or* exposed miles of white sand; **d. un pot** to take the lid off a pot;

d. une maison to take the roof off a house; **un décolleté qui découvre les épaules** a neckline that leaves the shoulders bare; **sa chemise ouverte découvre sa poitrine velue** his open-necked shirt reveals *or* exposes his hairy chest; **d. ses dents** to bare *or* show one's teeth; **d. son cœur** to open one's heart, to bare one's soul; *Échecs* **d. une pièce** to uncover a piece; *Cartes* **d. son jeu** to show one's hand; *Mil* **d. la frontière/ses arrières** to leave the border/the rear exposed *or* open to attack

4 (*apercevoir*) to perceive, to discern; *Naut (terre)* to sight; **craindre d'être découvert** to fear discovery *or* detection

VI (*d'un récif*) to uncover (at low tide)

VPR **se découvrir 1** (*enlever son chapeau*) to take off one's hat; (*se déshabiller*) to take off some of one's clothing; **se d. la tête** to bare one's head; **le malade s'est découvert pendant la nuit** the patient's bedclothes fell off during the night; **en avril, ne te découvre pas d'un fil** ≃ ne'er cast a clout till May be out

2 *Escrime, Mil* to expose oneself

3 (*du ciel*) to clear

4 (*apparaître*) to come into sight

5 (*se révéler*) to come to light; **la vérité se découvre toujours** truth will out

6 (*se trouver*) to discover; **se d. des parents éloignés** to discover some distant relatives; **il s'est découvert une passion pour le jardinage** he discovered (that) he had a passion for gardening

décrassage [dekrasaʒ] NM, **décrassement** [dekrasmɑ̃] NM cleaning, scouring; *Fig* **mon anglais aurait besoin d'un bon d.** my English needs brushing up

décrasser [dekrase] VT to clean, to scour; (*chaudière*) to scale, to clean; (*canon d'une arme*) to remove the fouling from; *Fig Fam* **d. qn** to knock the corners *or* rough edges off sb

VPR **se décrasser** (*se nettoyer*) to clean oneself up; *Fig (en courant etc)* to clean out the system; *Fig Fam (devenir plus sophistiqué)* to lose one's rough edges

décrédibiliser [dekredibilize] VT **toutes ces manœuvres l'ont complètement décrédibilisé auprès du public** he has lost all credibility with the public because of his manoeuvrings

décrément [dekremɑ̃] NM *Ordinat* decrement

décrêpage [dekrɛpaʒ] NM (*de cheveux*) straightening

décrêper [dekrepe] VT (*les cheveux*) to straighten

décrépir [dekrepir] VT (*mur etc*) to strip the plaster *or* roughcast off

VPR **se décrépir** (*de mur etc*) to flake

décrépit [dekrepi] ADJ (*maison, mur*) decrepit, dilapidated, tumbledown; (*personne*) decrepit

décrépitude [dekrepityd] NF decrepitude, decrepit condition; **tomber en d.** (*personne*) to become decrepit

decrescendo [dekreʃɛndo] *Mus* ADV diminuendo, decrescendo; *Fig* **sa carrière va d.** his career's going downhill

NM diminuendo, decrescendo

décret [dekrɛ] NM decree, order; **promulguer un d.** to issue a decree; **d. d'application** = presidential decree affecting the application of a law; **d. ministériel** = order to carry out legislation given by the Prime Minister; **d. présidentiel** *Br* ≃ Order in Council, *Am* ≃ executive order; *Fig* **c'est le d. de la mode** fashion decrees it

décréter [dekrete] VT (**je décrète; je décréterai**) (*état d'urgence, nomination*) to decree, to order; *(loi)* to enact; **il a décrété qu'il n'irait plus jamais sur la Côte d'Azur** he has vowed that he will never go to the French Riviera again; **quand elle décrète quelque chose** when she vows to do something; *Jur* **d. un moratoire** to declare a moratorium

décret-loi, *pl* **décrets-lois** NM *Br* ≃ Order in Council, *Am* ≃ executive order

décrier [dekrije] VT to disparage, to run down; **il a été beaucoup décrié** a lot of people have disparaged him *or* run him down; **ce genre de pratique est assez décrié** a lot of people deplore this kind of thing

décrire [dekrir] VT *(conj like* **écrire***)* **1** *(représenter)* to describe, to depict **2** *Math (courbe, cercle)* to describe, to draw; **la route décrit une courbe** the road bends; **les oiseaux décrivaient de grands cercles** the birds were circling

décrispation [dekrispasjɔ̃] NF *Pol* détente; **climat de d.** atmosphere of détente

décrisper [dekrispe] VT *(personne)* to relax, to make less tense; **d. l'atmosphère** to lighten the atmosphere, to make the atmosphere less tense; **d. la situation** to ease the situation, to make the situation less tense; **la plaisanterie l'a décrispé** the joke made him relax *or* calmed him down
▶ **VPR se décrisper** to relax, *Fam* to lighten up

décrochage [dekrɔʃaʒ] NM *(de wagon)* uncoupling, disconnection; *(d'un tableau)* removal, taking down; *Radio, TV* **diffuser en d.** to broadcast its own programmes; *Radio, TV* **le d. a lieu à 19 h** regional programming begins at 7 pm

décrochement [dekrɔʃmɑ̃] NM *Géol* thrust

décrocher [dekrɔʃe] VT **1** *(détacher) (manteau d'une patère, rideaux, tableau etc)* to take down; *(wagons etc)* to uncouple, to disconnect; *(fermoir)* to undo; *Tél (combiné)* to pick *or* lift up; **d. le téléphone** *(pour ne pas être dérangé)* to take the phone off the hook; *(pour répondre)* to pick up the phone; **décrochez le téléphone** lift the receiver; **le téléphone est décroché** the phone's off the hook
2 *(recevoir) (poste, prix, contrat etc)* to land; **d. la timbale** to hit the jackpot; **d. la croix** to receive a military decoration
▶ VI **1** *Tél* to pick up the phone; *(pour ne pas être dérangé)* to take the phone off the hook **2** *Mil* to beat a retreat, to withdraw
3 *Fig Fam (ne plus se concentrer)* to switch off; **au bout de trois heures de réunion, je décroche** I just switch off after three hours in a meeting; **si cet élève décroche, il est perdu** if this pupil fails to keep up, he won't have a chance; **il commence souvent de nouvelles activités, mais il décroche très vite** he often starts new activities, but loses interest very quickly
4 *Fam (arrêter de se droguer)* to kick the habit; **ça fait trois mois qu'il a décroché** he's been clean for three months
5 *Can Fam (abandonner l'école)* to drop out (of school)
▶ **VPR se décrocher** to come unhooked; **la médaille s'est décrochée** the medal has come unpinned; **se d. la mâchoire** to dislocate one's jaw; *Fam* **bâiller à se d. la mâchoire** to yawn one's head off

décrocheur, -euse [dekrɔʃœr, -øz] N *Can* dropout

décroisement [dekrwazmɑ̃] NM uncrossing

décroiser [dekrwaze] VT *(ses jambes etc)* to uncross

décroissance [dekrwasɑ̃s] NF *(de population)* decrease, decline

décroissant [dekrwasɑ̃] ADJ decreasing; **par ordre d.** in descending order

décroissement [dekrwasmɑ̃] NM *(de la lune)* waning; *(des jours)* shortening

décroît [dekrwa] NM **la lune est sur** *ou* **dans son d.** the moon is in its last quarter

décroître [dekrwatr] VI *(prp* **décroissant***; pp* **décru***; prind* il décroît, ils décroissent; *p hist* il décrut; *fu* il décroîtra) *(de force, population, nombre etc)* to decrease, to decline, to diminish; **les jours commencent à d.** the days are beginning to draw in *or* get shorter; **la lune décroît** the moon is on the wane; **l'intensité de son amour/de la lumière décroît** her love/the light is becoming less intense; **les eaux décroissent** the water level is dropping; **aller (en) décroissant** to be decreasing, to grow gradually less

décrottage [dekrɔtaʒ] NM *(de bottes etc)* cleaning

décrotter [dekrɔte] VT *(bottes etc)* to clean, to remove the mud from; *(semelles)* to scrape; *Fig Fam* **d. qn** to knock the rough edges off sb, to knock sb into shape; **il a vraiment fallu le d.** he had to have the rough edges knocked off him, he had to be knocked into shape

décrottoir [dekrɔtwar] NM shoe scraper; **tapis d.** (wire) doormat

décrue [dekry] NF **1** *(de rivière etc)* fall, drop in level; **la d. des eaux** the drop in the water level **2** *(en nombre etc)* decrease, decline, fall

décryptage [dekriptaʒ] NM deciphering; *(de signaux)* decoding; *Ordinat* decrypting; *Tél, TV* descrambling

décrypter [dekripte] VT to decipher; *(signaux)* to decode; *Ordinat* to decrypt; *Tél, TV* to descramble

DECS [deɔsɛs] NM *(abrév* **diplôme d'études comptables supérieures***)* = postgraduate qualification in accounting

déçu [desy] ADJ disappointed; *Fig Iron* **elle ne va pas être déçue (du voyage)** she's got another think coming; *Fig Iron* **je ne suis pas d. du voyage!** a fine state of affairs!

décuiter [dekɥite] VI *Fam* to sober up

déculottée [dekylɔte] NF *Fam* hammering

déculotter [dekylɔte] VT **d. qn** *(enlever son slip)* to take sb's panties/underpants off; *(enlever son pantalon)* to take sb's trousers off, *Fam Vieilli* to debag sb
▶ **VPR se déculotter** *(enlever son slip)* to take one's panties/underpants off; *(enlever son pantalon)* to let down *or* to drop one's trousers; *Fig Fam* to grovel (**devant, pour** to)

déculpabilisation [dekylpabilizasjɔ̃] NF **la d. de l'avortement** removing the guilt surrounding abortion; **la d. des malades atteints du sida** removing the guilt feelings of AIDS victims

déculpabiliser [dekylpabilize] VT **d. qn** to stop sb feeling guilty (**de qch** about sth); **d. la contraception** to take the guilt out of (using) contraception, to remove the guilt surrounding contraception
▶ **VPR se déculpabiliser** to get rid of one's guilt feelings, to stop feeling guilty

déculturation [dekyltyrasjɔ̃] NF loss of culture

décuple [dekypl] ADJ tenfold; **le prix de leur maison est d. de la nôtre** their house cost ten times as much as ours
▶ NM tenfold increase

décuplement [dekyplømɑ̃] NM multiplication by ten; *Fig* quantum leap

décupler [dekyple] VT to increase *or* multiply tenfold; *Fig* **la peur décuplait mon allure** fear quickened my pace (until I was almost running); **la douleur décupla ses forces** the pain gave him a surge of strength; **sa joie a été décuplée quand il a su que tu venais aussi** he was ecstatic when he found out you were coming too
▶ VI to increase tenfold

dédaignable [dedɛɲabl] ADJ worthy of disdain; **cette somme n'est pas d.** this is a not inconsiderable sum; **cette offre n'est pas d.** it is not an offer to be sniffed at

dédaigner [dedɛɲe] VT *(offre, proposition etc)* to turn up one's nose at, to sniff at, *Fml* to disdain, to scorn; *(injure, conseil)* to disregard; **d. qn** to treat sb with disdain *or* contempt, *Fml* to scorn sb; *Litt* **elle dédaigna de répondre** she disdained to reply; **cette proposition n'est pas à d.** it is not a proposal to be sniffed at; **il ne dédaigne pas un cigare de temps en temps** he is not averse to the occasional cigar, *Fam* he doesn't say no to the odd cigar

dédaigneusement [dedɛɲøzmɑ̃] ADV disdainfully, contemptuously, scornfully

dédaigneux, -euse [dedɛɲø, -øz] ADJ disdainful, contemptuous, scornful (**de** of)

dédain [dedɛ̃] NM disdain, contempt, scorn (**de, pour** for); **avec d.** disdainfully, contemptuously, scornfully, with disdain *or* contempt; **témoigner du d. à qn** to show contempt for sb; **avoir du d. pour qch** to despise sth; **elle n'a que du d. pour lui** she has nothing but contempt for him; **considérer qn avec d.** to look down on sb

Dédale [dedal] NM *Myth* Daedalus

dédale [dedal] NM *(de rues)* labyrinth, maze; **perdu dans le d. de ses réflexions** lost in the maze of one's thoughts

DEDANS [dədɑ̃] ADV inside; **la lettre est d.** the letter is inside; **une voiture nous est rentrée d., nous nous sommes fait rentrer d.** a car smashed into us; *Fam* **je vais lui rentrer d.** I'll smash his face in; *Fig Fam* **mettre** *ou* **ficher qn d.** *(le tromper)* to take sb for a ride; *Fig Fam* **donner d.** to fall into the trap; **marcher les pieds en d.** to be pigeon-toed; **en d.** (on the) inside, within; **il n'était pas si calme en d.** inwardly, he was not so calm; **en d. de** within; **de d.** from within; **il y a vraiment quelqu'un qui vit là-d.?** is somebody actually living there?; *Fam* **c'est un bon film, mais il y a trop de violence d.** it's a good film, but there's too much violence in it
▶ NM *(d'une maison, d'une boîte)* inside, interior; *(d'une personne)* innermost heart; **agir du d.** to act on the *or* from inside; **au-d. et au-dehors** inside and out; **au-d.** (on the) inside, within; **au-d. de** inside, within; **elle le savait au-d. d'elle** inwardly, she knew it

dédicace [dedikas] NF **1** *(de livre etc)* dedication **2** *Rel (d'un édifice etc)* dedication, consecration

dédicacer [dedikase] VT **(je dédicaçai(s); n. dédicaçons)** *(livre)* to write a dedication in; **d. son dernier livre** to sign copies of one's latest book; **livre dédicacé par l'auteur** signed copy of a book

dédicatoire [dedikatwar] ADJ dedicatory

dédié [dedje] ADJ *Ordinat* dedicated

dédier [dedje] VT **1** *(livre, film etc)* to dedicate **2** *Rel (édifice etc)* to dedicate, to consecrate

dédire (se) [sədedir] VPR *(conj like* **dire** *except pr ind* **v. v. dédisez***)* **se d. de** *(déclaration)* to retract, to withdraw; *(accusation)* to withdraw; **se d. d'une promesse** to go back on one's word

dédit [dedi] NM *(de déclaration)* retraction, withdrawal; *(d'accusation)* withdrawal; *(de promesse)* breaking; *(pour rupture de contrat etc)* forfeit, penalty; **en cas de d., vous devrez payer 10% de la somme initiale** in the event of cancellation, you will be required to pay 10% of the initial sum

dédommagement [dedɔmaʒmɑ̃] NM compensation; **50 000 euros de d.** 50,000 euros (in) compensation; **recevoir une**

somme en d. de qch to receive a sum as *or* in compensation for sth; **en d. de la peine que je vous ai causée** to make up for the pain I caused you; **c'est un d. ou pour votre patience** it's in recognition of your patience; **d. de non accès à bord** denied boarding compensation

dédommager [dedɔmaʒe] (**je dédommageai(s); n. dédommageons**) **VT** to compensate, *Fml* to indemnify; **d. qn de qch** to compensate sb for sth; **comment pourrai-je te d.?** how can I ever repay you?; **d. qn d'une perte** to compensate sb for a loss, to make good sb's loss; **pour me d., il m'a invité au restaurant** he took me out to dinner to make up for it; **tiens, dédommage-toi avec ce billet** here, take it out of this

dédoré [dedɔre] **ADJ** tarnished, with the gilt rubbed off

dédorer [dedɔre] **VT** to remove the gilt from

dédouanage [dedwanaʒ] **NM** clearance (through customs)

dédouanement [dedwanmɑ̃] **NM** clearance through customs; *Fig* **le d. de la conscience** salving one's conscience

dédouaner [dedwane] **VT** to clear (through customs), to take out of bond; **d. ses bagages** to clear one's luggage through customs; *Fig* **d. qn** to clear sb
VPR se dédouaner *Fig* to clear one's name

dédoublage [dedublaʒ] **NM 1** (*d'alcool*) diluting **2** (*de manteau etc*) removing the lining

dédoublement [dedubləmɑ̃] **NM 1** (*d'une étoffe pliée etc*) opening out **2** *Psy* dividing *or* splitting into two; **d. de la personnalité** split personality **3** *Rail* **d. d'un train** running an extra train

dédoubler [deduble] **VT 1** (*étoffe pliée etc*) to open out; **d. les rangs** to form single file **2** (*partager*) to divide *or* split into two **3** *Rail* **d. un train** to run an extra train **4** (*vêtement*) to remove the lining of
VPR se dédoubler 1 (*d'une couverture*) to unfold **2** (*se diviser*) to divide, to split; (*cheveux, ongle*) to split; *Psy* to have a split personality; *Fam* **je ne peux pas me d.** I can't be in two places at once

dédramatisation [dedramatizasjɔ̃] **NF le gouvernement travaille à la d. de l'événement** the government is trying hard to play down the significance of the event; **cela a contribué à la d. de la situation** this helped make the situation less tense

dédramatiser [dedramatize] **VT** (*situation*) to take the tension out of; (*événement*) to play down the significance of

déductibilité [dedyktibilite] **NF** deductibility

déductible [dedyktibl] **ADJ** deductible; **d. des impôts** tax deductible

déductif, -ive [dedyktif, -iv] **ADJ** *Phil* deductive

déduction [dedyksjɔ̃] **NF 1** *Com etc* deduction, allowance; **faire d. des sommes payées d'avance** to deduct sums *or* allow for sums paid in advance; **d. fiscale** tax allowance; **d. forfaitaire** (*d'impôts*) standard allowance; **sous d. de 10%** less 10%; **sans d.** terms net cash; **d. faite des frais d'essence** after deduction of petrol costs **2** (*raisonnement*) deduction, inference

déduire [deɥir] (*conj like* **conduire**) **VT 1** (*enlever*) to deduct; **d. 5%** to take off *or* deduct 5%, to allow a deduction of 5%; **tous frais déduits** after deduction of expenses **2** (*conclure*) to deduce, to infer; **de là, on peut d. que ...** from this, it may be deduced that ...

déesse [dees] **NF** goddess

---

défaillance [defajɑ̃s] **NF 1** (*faiblesse*) (*morale*) failing, lapse; (*physique*) deficiency; **cet enfant a de sérieuses défaillances en lecture** the child has serious reading difficulties; **les défaillances des dirigeants de l'entreprise** management's failings; **sans d.** without flinching; **courage sans d.** unflagging *or* unfailing courage; **travailler sans d.** to work tirelessly; **d. de mémoire** memory lapse; **d. cardiaque** heart failure; **d. mécanique** mechanical failure; **la machine a eu une d.** the machine developed a fault; **d. d'entreprise** business failure
2 (*évanouissement*) fainting fit; **avoir une d.** (*s'évanouir*) to faint; (*faiblir*) to flag; **soudain, ce fut la d.** (*il faiblit*) all of a sudden, he flagged
3 *Jur* default(ing)

défaillant, -ante [defajɑ̃, -ɑ̃t] **ADJ 1** (*force, mémoire*) failing; (*santé*) declining; (*cœur*) weak; **de fatigue** exhausted **2** (*qui s'évanouit*) (*voix, personne*) faint; **il avançait d'un pas d.** he walked with a faltering step; **elle était défaillante de bonheur** she was giddy with delight **3** *Jur* defaulting
N *Jur* defaulter, absconder

défaillir [defajir] **VI** (*prp* **défaillant**; *pp* **défailli**; *pr ind* **il défaille, n. défaillons**; *impf* **je défaillais**; *p hist* **je défaillis**; *fu* **je défaillirai ou parfois je défaillerai**) **1** (*faiblir*) to become feeble; **sa mémoire/sa force commence à d.** his/her memory/strength is beginning to fail; **à cette nouvelle, son cœur défaillit** his heart sank at the news; **j'accomplirai le travail sans d.** I'll do the job without flinching **2** (*s'évanouir*) to faint; **d. de faim** to feel faint with hunger

défaire [defɛr] (*conj like* **faire**) **VT 1** (*nœud*) to undo, to untie; (*paquet*) to undo, to unwrap; (*valise*) to unpack; (*ourlet*) to unpick; (*robe etc*) to undo; (*fermeture Éclair®*) to unzip; **d. le lit** (*enlever les draps*) to strip the bed; (*pour se coucher*) to turn down the bed; (*le mettre en désordre*) to rumple the bedclothes; **d. ses cheveux** to let one's hair down
2 (*détruire*) (*puzzle*) to take apart, to take to pieces; (*traité*) to cancel, to annul; (*alliance, mariage*) to break up; *Fam* **d. un marché** to cancel a deal
3 *Ordinat* (*opération*) to undo
4 *Litt* (*battre*) (*armée etc*) to defeat; (*personne*) to get the better of
5 *Litt* **d. qn de qn/qch** to rid sb of sb/sth
6 (*miner*) to devastate; **cette nouvelle l'a complètement défait** he was completely devastated by the news
VPR se défaire 1 (*de vêtements, d'un nœud*) to come undone; (*de cheveux*) to come down; (*de choses jointes les unes aux autres*) to come apart; (*de mariage*) to break up, to fall apart; (*de viande à la cuisson*) to fall apart **2 se d. de qn/qch** to get rid of sb/sth; **se d. de ses marchandises** to get rid of *or* sell off one's stock; **je ne veux pas m'en d.** I don't want to part with it; **se d. d'une mauvaise habitude** to get out of *or* break oneself of a bad habit **3** (*s'altérer*) (*de personne, visage*) to become haggard *or* drawn

défait [defɛ] **ADJ 1** (*traits, visage*) drawn, haggard; **la mine défaite** with a haggard expression; **il est arrivé à l'hôpital, complètement d.** he arrived at the hospital in a state of collapse; **elle était quelque peu défaite après l'échec de son livre** she was somewhat depressed after her book's lack of success **2** (*cheveux, apparence*) dishevelled **3** (*armée etc*) defeated

défaite [defɛt] **NF** defeat; **connaître une d.** to suffer a defeat

défaitisme [defɛtism] **NM** defeatism

défaitiste [defɛtist] **ADJ, N** defeatist

---

défalcation [defalkasjɔ̃] **NF** deduction; **d. faite des frais** after deduction of expenses

défalquer [defalke] **VT** (*une somme d'un total*) to deduct

défatigant [defatigɑ̃] **ADJ** relaxing
NM muscle relaxant

défatiguer [defatige] **VT** to relax; **un bon bain chaud va vous d.** a hot bath will relax you *or* help you (to) unwind
VPR se défatiguer to unwind; **se d. les yeux** to rest one's eyes; **j'ai besoin de me d. la tête** I need to clear my mind

défaufiler [defofile] **VT** *Couture* to remove the tacks from

défausser [defose] **VT** (*clé, tournevis etc*) to straighten (out)
VPR se défausser *Cartes* to discard; **se d. à cœur** to discard one's hearts

défaut [defo] **NM 1** (*imperfection*) (*d'une personne*) fault, shortcoming; (*de pierre précieuse, métal, verre, tissu*) flaw; (*d'une machine*) defect; **chacun a ses défauts** everyone has their faults; **la curiosité est un vilain d.** curiosity killed the cat; **c'est là son moindre d.** that's the least of his faults; **les défauts d'une explication/d'une théorie** the flaws in *or* shortcomings of an explanation/a theory; **avoir un d.** (*d'une machine*) to be defective; **il y a un d. de fonctionnement** it isn't working properly; **cette école n'a qu'un d.** the school has only one drawback; **sans d.** faultless, flawless; **mettre les chiens en d.** to throw the hounds off the scent; *Fig* **mettre qn en d.** to put sb on the spot; **prendre qn en d.** to catch sb napping; **être en d.** to be wrong; **d. de prononciation** speech impediment; **d. de fabrication** manufacturing fault *or* defect; *Com* **défauts apparents** visible defects; *Com* **défauts cachés** hidden defects
2 (*manque*) lack; *Jur* default; **il y a, chez cet enfant, un d. de concentration** the child lacks concentration; **le temps me fait d.** I haven't got the time; **le courage lui a fait d.** his courage failed him; **les provisions font d.** there is a shortage of supplies, supplies are short; **les bonnes places font d.** there is a shortage of good jobs, good jobs are hard to come by; **la place fait d. chez moi** there is a shortage of space *or* space is in short supply at my place; **l'argent fait d. en ce moment** money is tight at the moment; **l'argent lui fait cruellement d.** he is very short of money; **le bon sens lui fait cruellement d.** he is sadly lacking in common sense; **sa ou la mémoire lui fait d.** he can't remember; **si ma mémoire ne me fait pas d.** if I'm not mistaken, if my memory serves me right; **pécher par d.** to sin by omission, to commit a sin of omission; **ou, à d., ...** or, failing that, ...; **à d. de qch** for lack of sth; **à d. de salaire intéressant, elle a au moins l'avantage de travailler près de chez elle** she might not have a very good salary, but at least she works close to home; **le d. de l'épaule** the hollow of the shoulder; *Fig* **j'ai trouvé le d. de la cuirasse ou de l'armure** I've found the chink in his/*etc* armour; **frapper au d. de la cuirasse ou de l'armure** to aim for the chink in his/*etc* armour; *Jur* **faire d.** to fail to appear, to default; *Jur* **jugement par d.** judgment by default; **d. de comparution** failure to appear; **d. de paiement** failure to pay, non-payment, default on payment; **d. de livraison** default on delivery; *Banque* **chèque refusé pour cause de d. de provision** cheque refused by the bank because of insufficient funds; **'d. de provision'** (*tampon sur chèque*) ≃ 'refer to drawer'
3 *Math* **total approché par d.** total rounded down; *Ordinat* **lecteur/clavier par d.** default drive/keyboard

défaveur [defavœr] NF disfavour, *Am* disfavor, discredit; **être en d.** to be in disfavour (**auprès de** with); **il faut vraiment être très désagréable pour s'attirer la d. de mon grand-père** you have to be really unpleasant for my grandfather to take against you

défavorable [defavɔrabl] ADJ unfavourable, *Am* unfavorable (**à** to); **être d. à qn/qch** to be against sb/sth; **les conditions (nous) sont défavorables** conditions are against us

défavorablement [defavɔrabləmɑ̃] ADV unfavourably, *Am* unfavorably

défavorisé [defavɔrize] ADJ *(enfant, pays)* underprivileged; **candidat d.** candidate at a disadvantage; **les milieux les plus défavorisés** the underprivileged classes

défavoriser [defavɔrize] VT to put at a disadvantage, to disadvantage; **cette nouvelle loi défavorisera les couples non mariés** this new law will put unmarried couples at a disadvantage *or* will be unfair to unmarried couples; **d. les candidates** to favour male candidates over female ones; **le climat du désert défavorise les soldats occidentaux** Western soldiers are at a disadvantage in desert climates; **il est défavorisé par sa timidité** his shyness puts him at a disadvantage; **dans son testament, il a défavorisé sa femme par rapport à ses enfants** he favoured his children over his wife in his will

défécation [defekasjɔ̃] NF *Physiol* defecation

défectif, -ive [defɛktif, -iv] ADJ *(verbe etc)* defective

défection [defɛksjɔ̃] NF *Pol* defection; *(de partisan, soldat, allié)* defection, desertion; **je ne m'attendais pas à sa d.** I did not expect him to defect; **au moment de son divorce, il a assisté à la d. de tous ses amis** all his friends deserted him when he got divorced; **elle a été très déçue par les défections qui se sont produites la veille de la réception** she was very disappointed by the number of people who cancelled the day before the party; **à mon mariage, il n'y a eu qu'une seule d.** only one person didn't attend my wedding; **en cas de d.** in the event of cancellation; **faire d.** to desert, to defect, *Fam* to rat

défectueusement [defɛktɥøzmɑ̃] ADV defectively

défectueux, -euse [defɛktɥø, -øz] ADJ defective, faulty

défectuosité [defɛktɥozite] NF **1** *(défaut)* defect, flaw **2** *(mauvaise qualité)* defectiveness

défendable [defɑ̃dabl] ADJ *(position, point de vue, théorie etc)* defensible; **ses théories ne sont absolument pas défendables** his theories are totally indefensible

défendeur, -deresse [defɑ̃dœr, -drɛs] N *Jur* defendant

DÉFENDRE [defɑ̃dr] VT **1** *(lutter pour ou contre, soutenir)* *(théorie, politique, la mémoire de qn)*, *Jur (accusé)* to defend; *(cause)* to champion; *(droit, opinion)* to defend, to uphold; *(ses amis, ses idées)* to defend, to stand up for (**contre** against); **il sait d. ses opinions** he can hold his own; **cette organisation défend les droits de l'homme** this organization defends *or* champions human rights; *Sport* **d. son titre de champion du monde/les couleurs de …** to defend one's world championship title/the colours of …

2 *(protéger)* to defend, to guard (**contre** against, from); *Tennis (service)* to defend; **son pays contre l'envahisseur** to defend one's country against the invader; **la propriété est défendue par deux chiens** the estate is guarded by two dogs; **d. ses intérêts** to protect one's interests; **il a fait cela pour d.**

mes intérêts he did it to defend *or* in defence of my interests; *Fig* **d. son bifteck** to look after number one; **de lourdes tentures défendaient la pièce contre les regards indiscrets** heavy curtains shielded the room from prying eyes; **l'isolation défend la pièce du froid** the insulation shields the room from cold; **les fourrures défendent les Esquimaux du froid** fur clothing protects the Eskimos from the cold; *Ftbl* **Durant défendra les buts de l'équipe d'Aix** Durant will play in goal for Aix

3 *(interdire)* to forbid, to prohibit; **fruit(s) défendu(s)** forbidden fruit; **d. qch à qn** to forbid sb sth; **son père lui a défendu l'entrée de sa maison** his father has forbidden him to set foot over the doorstep; **d. sa porte à qn** to close one's door to sb; **ce médicament est défendu aux enfants** this medicine must not be given to children; **il défend qu'on passe par là** he forbids anyone to go that way; **une herse de fer défendait l'entrée de la crypte** an iron portcullis barred the entrance to the crypt

4 d. à qn de faire qch to forbid sb to do sth; **je te défends d'y aller** I forbid you to go; **son père lui défend de sortir le soir** his father does not allow him to go out at night; **il est défendu de fumer dans les classes** smoking is prohibited in the classrooms; **il m'est défendu de fumer** I'm not allowed *or* I'm forbidden to smoke; **il est défendu de parler au chauffeur** please do not speak to the driver

VPR se **défendre 1** *(se protéger)* to defend oneself; **se d. de** *ou* **contre qch** to defend oneself against sth, to protect *or* shield oneself from *or* against sth; **se d. des agressions** to defend oneself against attack; **se d. avec un couteau** to defend oneself with a knife; **se d. de la pluie** to shelter from the rain; **se d. du froid** to protect oneself from the cold; **se d. contre la critique** to defend oneself against criticism; **se d. des tentations** to steer clear of temptation

2 *Fam (se débrouiller)* **je me défends** I'm holding my own, I'm getting by *or* along; **je me défends en anglais/en tennis** I can hold my own *or* I can get by in English/at tennis; **il se défend bien en affaires** he's a good businessman; **il ne se défend pas mal avec son ordinateur** he's getting on quite well with his computer

3 *(nier)* **se d. de faire/d'avoir fait qch** to deny doing sth

4 *(se justifier)* **cette attitude peut se d.** this attitude is justifiable; **c'est une idée qui se défend** there is something to be said for the idea

5 *(s'empêcher)* *(the pron is the indirect object)* **se d. de faire qch** to refrain from doing sth; **on ne peut se d. de l'aimer** you can't help liking him; **elle ne peut se d. d'un certain sentiment de culpabilité** she can't help feeling guilty; **se d. tout plaisir/toute gourmandise** to deny oneself all pleasure/sweet things

défenestration [defənɛstrasjɔ̃] NF defenestration

défenestrer [defənɛstre] VT to defenestrate

défense¹ [defɑ̃s] NF **1** *(soutien)* *(d'une politique, d'une théorie, d'une opinion etc)*, *Jur* defence, *Am* defense; **prendre la d. de qn** to defend sb; **sans d.** defenceless; **la meilleure d., c'est l'attaque** attack is the best form of defence; *Jur* **la parole est à la d.** the defence may now speak; *Jur* **assurer la d. de qn** to defend sb; **qu'avez-vous à dire pour votre d.?** what do you have to say in your defence?

2 *(protection)*, *Mil, Sp* defence, *Am* defense; **combattre pour la d. de son pays** to fight in defence of one's country; **ligne de d.** line of defence; **moyen de d.** means of defence; **d. nationale** national defence; **d. côtière/aé-**

rienne coastal/air defence; **d. contre avions** anti-aircraft defence; **d. passive** civil defence; *Physiol* **la d. de l'organisme** the organism's defence mechanisms; *Physiol* **défenses immunitaires** immune defences; **d. des consommateurs** consumer protection; *Mktg* **contre-offensive** counter-offensive defence; *Mktg* **d. mobile** mobile defence; *Mktg* **d. préventive** pre-emptive defence; *Jur* **légitime d.** self-defence

3 *(interdiction)* **d. d'entrer/de fumer/de stationner** no entry *or* admittance/smoking/parking; **d. d'afficher** stick no bills; **c'est un secret, d. d'en parler à ton père!** it's a secret so don't go telling your father about it!; *Vieilli* **faire d. à qn de faire qch** to forbid sb to do sth

défense² NF *(d'éléphant, de sanglier etc)* tusk

défenseur [defɑ̃sœr] NM **1** *(d'un enfant, d'une ville etc)* protector, defender; *(d'une cause)* supporter, upholder; *Sport* defender **2** *Jur* counsel for the defence; **qui est son d.?** who's defending him?; **c'est le d. de la veuve et de l'orphelin** he's a champion of the underdog

défensif, -ive [defɑ̃sif, -iv] ADJ defensive ▪ NF **défensive** defensive; **être** *ou* **se tenir sur la défensive** to be on the defensive

défensivement [defɑ̃sivmɑ̃] ADV defensively

déféquer [defeke] VI *(je défèque, n. déféquons; je déféquerai)* *Physiol* to defecate

déférence [deferɑ̃s] NF deference (**pour** for); **par d. pour …** in *or* out of deference to …

déférent [deferɑ̃] ADJ *(manière etc)* deferential

déférer [defere] *(je défère; je déférerai)* VT **1** *Jur (une affaire devant un tribunal)* to submit, to refer; **d. qn à la justice** to hand sb over *or* give sb up to the police **2** *Arch (honneur)* to confer, to bestow (**à** on)

▪ VI **d. à qn** to defer to sb; **d. aux ordres de qn** to comply with sb's orders; **d. à une demande** to accede to a request

déferlant, -ante [defɛrlɑ̃, -ɑ̃t] ADJ, NF *(vague)* **déferlante** breaker, beachcomber; *Fig* surge; **une d. de lettres de protestation** a deluge of letters of complaint; **la d. des jeux électroniques** the sudden influx of video games

déferlement [defɛrləmɑ̃] NM *(de vagues)* breaking; *Fig (d'enthousiasme, de violence, de racisme)* wave; **d. de colère** fit of anger; **d. de touristes/journalistes** invasion of tourists/reporters; **le d. des touristes sur la Côte d'Azur en juillet** the July invasion of the French Riviera by tourists, the descent of tourists on the French Riviera in July

déferler [defɛrle] VT *(drapeau)*, *Naut (voile)* to unfurl

▪ VI *(de vagues)* to break; **la foule déferle dans la rue** the crowd is surging down the street; **la joie/la colère/une rumeur déferlait dans toute la ville** joy/anger/a rumour spread through the entire city; **les vacanciers déferlent sur les routes** holiday-makers are taking to the roads in droves

défet [defɛ] NM *Typ* waste sheet

défi [defi] NM **1** challenge; **lancer** *ou* **jeter un d. à qn** to challenge sb; **relever un d.** to take up a challenge; **la jeunesse a besoin de d.** young people need a challenge **2** *(provocation)* defiance; **mettre qn au d. de faire qch** to defy *or* dare sb to do sth; **avec un sourire de d.** with a smile of defiance, with a defiant smile; **d'un air de d.** defiantly, with a defiant air *or* an air of defiance; **son attitude est un d. à votre autorité** his attitude is a challenge to your authority; **son numéro est un d. aux**

lois de la pesanteur his act defies the laws of gravity

défiance [defjɑ̃s] NF mistrust, distrust, suspicion, wariness; **inspirer** ou **éveiller la d.** to arouse suspicion; **mettre qn en d.** to make sb wary; *Pol* **motion de d.** motion of no confidence; **d. de soi-même** diffidence, lack of self-confidence

défiant [defjɑ̃] ADJ mistrustful, distrustful, cautious, wary

défibrillateur [defibrijatœr] NM *Méd* defibrillator

défibrillation [defibrijasjɔ̃] NF *Méd* defibrillation

déficeler [defisle] *(conj like* ficeler*)* VT *(paquet etc)* to untie, to undo
VPR **se déficeler** to come untied *or* undone

déficience [defisjɑ̃s] NF deficiency; **d. intellectuelle** mental deficiency; **d. (alimentaire)** malnutrition; **d. musculaire** muscle deficiency; **d. immunologique** immune deficiency; **d. en vitamine B** vitamin B deficiency

déficient, -iente [defisjɑ̃, -jɑ̃t] ADJ deficient; *(muscle)* wasted, atrophied, deficient; *(raisonnement, théorie)* weak; **intelligence déficiente** *(insuffisance)* mental deficiency; **enfant d.** *(mentalement)* mentally deficient child; *(physiquement)* physically handicapped *or surtout Am* challenged child
N **d. moteur** person with motor deficiency; **d. mental** mentally deficient person; **les déficients visuels** the visually impaired *or surtout Am* challenged

déficit [defisit] NM *Fin* deficit; **d. de la balance commerciale** trade deficit; **d. budgétaire/commercial** budget/trade deficit; *Pol* **d. démocratique** democratic deficit; **d. extérieur** external deficit, balance of payments deficit; **d. fiscal remboursable** negative income tax; *Compta* **d. reportable** loss carry forward; **d. du secteur public** public sector deficit; **d. social** public spending deficit; **d. de trésorerie** cash deficit; **d. psychologique/mental** psychological/mental deficiency; **être en d.** to be in deficit; **combler un d.** to make good a deficit; **accuser un d.** to show a deficit

déficitaire [defisiter] ADJ *(entreprise)* loss-making, unprofitable; *(compte)* showing a debit balance; *(budget etc)* showing a deficit; *(bilan)* showing a loss; **être d.** *(d'un compte)* to be in debit; *(d'un budget, d'une entreprise)* to be in deficit; *Agr* **récolte d.** short crop

défier [defje] VT **1** *(provoquer)* *(dans une lutte etc)* to challenge; **d. qn au combat/aux échecs** to challenge sb to a fight/to a game of chess **2** *(inciter)* to defy; **je vous défie de faire mieux** I defy you to do better **3** *(braver)* *(danger, mort, balles)* to brave, to face; *(la police)* to taunt; *(la presse)* to confront; **il ne craint pas de d. l'autorité paternelle** he's not afraid to stand up to his father **4** *(résister à)* **d. l'imagination** to defy the imagination; **le spectacle défie toute description** the sight defies *or* is beyond description; **des prix qui défient toute concurrence** unbeatable prices
VPR **se défier** *Fml* **se d. de qn/qch** to mistrust *or* distrust sb/sth; **se d. de soi-même** to be diffident

défigurement [defigyrmɑ̃] NM *(d'une personne)* disfigurement; *(d'une statue)* defacement; *(de la vérité, du sens)* distortion

défigurer [defigyre] VT *(personne, paysage)* to disfigure; *(statue)* to deface; *(la vérité, sens)* to twist, to distort; *(la pensée, les intentions de qn)* to misrepresent; **l'acné la défigure** her acne disfigures her face; **d. un texte** *(d'un acteur)* to ruin a script

défilé [defile] NM **1** *Géog* defile, (mountain) pass **2** *(file)* parade, procession; *Mil* march past; *Aviat* flypast; *(de souvenirs, d'idées)* series; **un d. ininterrompu de touristes** an endless stream of tourists
▸ ▸ *Aviat* **d. aérien** flypast; **d. de mode** fashion show

défilement [defil(ə)mɑ̃] NM **1** *(de bande magnétique, de pellicule)* running **2** *Ordinat* scrolling

> Il faut noter que le nom anglais **defilement** est un faux ami. Il signifie **souillure** ou **profanation**, selon le contexte.

défiler¹ [defile] VT *(perles, collier)* to unstring, to unthread
VPR **se défiler 1** *(de perles etc)* to come unstrung **2** *Mil* **se d. du feu de l'adversaire** to take cover from enemy fire **3** *Fam (se dérober)* to slope off

défiler² VI *(passer en colonne)* to walk in procession; *Mil* to march past, to parade; **les manifestants défilent depuis ce matin** the demonstrators have been marching *or* trooping past since this morning; **des centaines de voitures défilent vers la côte** hundreds of cars are streaming towards the coast; **les images défilaient devant nos yeux** the pictures passed before our eyes; **les souvenirs défilaient dans sa mémoire** the memories came thick and fast; **le paysage défilait à toute vitesse** the countryside sped past *or* flashed past; *Mil* **d. en colonne par deux** to file off in twos; **faire d. une bande/une bobine de film** to run a tape/reel of film; *Ordinat* **faire d. un document** to scroll a document; *Ordinat* **d. vers le bas** to scroll down; *Ordinat* **d. vers le haut** to scroll up

défini [defini] ADJ **1** *(précis)* clearly defined; **mot bien/mal d.** well-defined/badly defined word; **un travail bien d.** a clearly defined piece of work; *Ordinat* **d. par l'utilisateur** user-defined; *Ordinat* **pouvant être d. par l'utilisateur** user-definable **2** *Gram* definite; **passé d.** past definite, preterite, past historic ᴸᴱᴱ SEE GRAMMAR A6–8; B3–4

définir [definir] VT *(conditions, mot etc)* to define; **c'est difficile à d.** it's difficult to define; **il faut d. le poste** we'll have to define what the job entails, we'll have to draw up a job description
VPR **se définir** to describe oneself; **comment vous définissez-vous?** how would you describe yourself?

définissable [definisabl] ADJ definable; *Ordinat* **d. par l'utilisateur** user-definable

définitif, -ive [definitif, -iv] ADJ **1** *(résolution, jugement, version etc)* final, definitive; *(argument)* definitive; **la biographie définitive de Proust** the definitive biography of Proust; **une séparation définitive** a permanent separation; **nommé à titre d.** permanently appointed; **ma décision est définitive** my decision is final; **veuillez noter la fermeture définitive du magasin** please note that the shop has closed down **2** **en définitive** when all is said and done

définition [definisjɔ̃] NF **1** *(d'un mot, de conditions etc)* definition; *(de mots croisés)* clue; **par d.** by definition; **d. de poste** job description **2** *Cin, TV, Phot* definition; **télévision à haute d.** high-definition television

définitivement [definitivmɑ̃] ADV *(décider qch)* definitely; *(partir, s'installer)* for good; *(nommé)* permanently

défiscalisation [defiskalizasjɔ̃] NF removal *or* lifting of taxes

défiscalisé [defiskalize] ADJ tax-free

défiscaliser [defiskalize] VT to remove *or* lift the tax on

déflagration [deflagrasjɔ̃] NF *(explosion)* explosion

déflagrer [deflagre] VI to combust

déflation [deflasjɔ̃] NF *Écon* deflation

déflationniste [deflasjɔnist] *Écon* ADJ deflationary
N deflationist

déflecteur [deflɛktœr] NM *Aut etc (sur vitre)* deflector, quarterlight; **d. de faisceau** beam deflector; **d. de ventilateur** cowl, cowling

défleuraison [deflœrezɔ̃] NF falling of blossom

défleurir [deflœrir] VI *(d'arbre etc)* to lose its blossom
VT *(plante)* to take the flowers off

déflexion [deflɛksjɔ̃] NF deflection

déflocage [deflɔkaʒ] NM **le d. d'un bâtiment** the removal of asbestos insulation from a building

défloraison [deflɔrezɔ̃] NF = **défleuraison**

défloration [deflɔrasjɔ̃] NF *(d'une vierge)* deflowering

déflorer [deflɔre] VT **1** *(vierge)* to deflower **2** *Fig (révéler) (nouvelle)* to announce; *(secret)* to give away

défoliant [defɔljɑ̃] NM *Agr* defoliant

défoliation [defɔljasjɔ̃] NF defoliation

défonçage [defɔ̃saʒ] NM *(d'une boîte, d'une porte etc)* smashing in; *(d'un mur)* knocking down

défonce [defɔ̃s] NF *Fam (par la drogue)* trip; **être en pleine d.** to be on a trip

défoncé [defɔ̃se] ADJ **1** *(détérioré) (porte)* bashed in; *(fauteuil)* battered; **un matelas d.** a mattress with all the stuffing hanging out; **chemin d.** rough *or* bumpy road **2** *Fam (qui a pris de la drogue)* high, stoned

défoncement [defɔ̃smɑ̃] NM = **défonçage**

défoncer [defɔ̃se] (**je défonçai(s); n. défonçons**) VT *(boîte, porte etc)* to smash in, to bash in; *(mur etc)* to knock down; *(tonneau, bateau)* to stave in; *(route)* to break up, to cut up; **il a eu le crâne défoncé dans l'accident** his head was smashed in in the accident; *très Fam* **d. la gueule à qn** to smash sb's face in, to punch sb's lights out, *Am* to punch sb out
VPR **se défoncer** *Fam* **1** *(avec de la drogue)* to get high **2** *(faire un grand effort)* to sweat blood; **il s'est défoncé pour que tu aies ta voiture à temps** he sweated blood *or* bust a gut so you would get your car back in time

déforestation [defɔrɛstasjɔ̃] NF deforestation

déformant [defɔrmɑ̃] ADJ distorting

déformation [defɔrmasjɔ̃] NF *(d'un membre)* deformation; *(d'un visage, de la vérité)*, *Phot (d'une image)* distortion; *(des faits, de la réalité)* distortion, misrepresentation; *(de la pensée)* misrepresentation; *(de vêtement, chaussure)* stretching out of shape; *(de métal)* buckling; *(de bois)*, *Fig (de l'esprit)* warping; **avoir une d. du pied** to have a deformed foot; **à cause de la d. de vos chaussures** because your shoes are all stretched out of shape; **il fume tellement qu'il souffre d'une d. du goût** he smokes so much that he's ruined his palate; **c'est son métier de psychanalyste qui conduit à cette d. de l'esprit chez lui** it's being a psychoanalyst that has warped his mind
▸ ▸ **d. professionnelle** = habits acquired through doing the type of work one does; **elle est professeur, c'est donc par d. professionnelle qu'elle répète tout tout le temps** it must be because she's a teacher that she repeats things all the time; **il fait de la d. professionnelle** he's like that because of his job

déformer [defɔrme] VT *(membre)* to deform; *(vêtement, chaussure)* to stretch out of shape; *(métal)* to buckle; *(bois)* to warp; *(traits, vérité), Phot (image)* to distort; *(réalité, faits)* to distort, to misrepresent; **visage/corps déformé par la douleur/la vieillesse** face/body distorted by *or* with pain/old age; **chaussée déformée** *(sur panneau)* uneven road surface; **d. la pensée de l'auteur** to misrepresent the author's thoughts; **je n'accepte pas que vous déformiez ce que j'ai dit** I won't have you twisting what I said; **il est déformé par son métier** his job has had an effect on him, he's like that because of what he does

  vpr se déformer to get out of shape; *(de bois)* to warp; *(de métal)* to buckle; **ma vision des choses se déforme** I'm not seeing things straight

défoulement [defulmɑ̃] **NM** *Psy Fam* letting off steam; **avoir besoin de d.** to need to let off steam; **laisser aux enfants des moments de d.** to give children time to let off steam

défouler [defule] **VT** *Psy* to liberate; **d. son agressivité sur qn** to vent one's aggressiveness on sb

  vpr se défouler *Fam* to let off steam; **tu n'as pas à te d. sur les enfants** you shouldn't take it out on the children; **elle se défoule dans son travail** she invests all her energies in her job

  vi *Fam* **ça défoule** it helps you let off steam

défourner [defurne] **VT** *(poterie)* to remove from the kiln; *(pain)* to remove from the oven

défragmentation [defragmɑ̃tasjɔ̃] **NF** *Ordinat (de fichiers)* defragmentation

défragmenter [defragmɑ̃te] **VT** *Ordinat* to defragment

défragmenteur [defragmɑ̃tœr] **NM** *Ordinat* defragmenter

défraîchi [defreʃi] **ADJ** *(marchandises)* (shop)soiled; *(fleurs, beauté)* faded; *(vêtement)* shabby, past its best

défraîchir [defreʃir] **VT** *(beauté, couleur, teint)* to fade

  vpr se défraîchir *(de beauté, couleur, teint)* to fade

défraiement [defremɑ̃] **NM** compensation; **je suis en droit d'attendre un d.** I'm entitled to compensation

défrayer [defreje] **VT** (**je défraie, je défraye; je défraierai, je défrayerai**) **1 d. qn** to defray *or* pay sb's expenses; **être défrayé de tout** to have all expenses paid **2 d. la conversation** *(la monopoliser)* to monopolize the conversation; *(en être le sujet)* to be the main topic of conversation; **d. la chronique** to be in the news

défrichage [defriʃaʒ], **défrichement** [defriʃmɑ̃] **NM** *(de terrain)* clearing

défricher [defriʃe] **VT** *(terrain pour la culture)* to clear, to reclaim; *(terrain en friche)* to bring into cultivation; *(terrain vierge)* to break; *Fig* **d. le terrain** to clear the ground; *Fig* **d. un sujet/un nouveau domaine scientifique** to do pioneer work in a subject/pioneer a new field of science

défricheur, -euse [defriʃœr, -øz] **N** *Agr* land clearer, settler; *Fig (dans un domaine)* pioneer

défriper [defripe] **VT** *(vêtement chiffonné)* to smooth out

défriser [defrize] **VT** *(cheveux)* to uncurl, to straighten; *Fig Fam* **ça vous défrise?** have you got a problem with that?; *Fig Fam* **ça me défrise de savoir que c'est lui qui a le poste** it really gets up my nose *or Am* tees me off that he's got the job; *Fam* **qu'on puisse être aussi insolent, ça me défrise** cheek like that gets up my nose *or Am* tees me off

défroisser [defrwase] **VT** *(vêtement)* to take the creases out of

  vpr se défroisser to lose its creases

défroque [defrɔk] **NF** *Fam (vieux habits)* rags

défroqué [defrɔke] **ADJ** *(prêtre)* unfrocked **NM** unfrocked priest

défroquer [defrɔke] **VT** to unfrock **vi** to leave the priesthood

  vpr se défroquer 1 *(abandonner l'état religieux)* to leave the priesthood **2** *Fam (enlever son pantalon)* to take one's trousers *or Am* pants off, *Br* to get one's keks off

défunt, -unte [defœ̃, -œ̃t] **ADJ** deceased; **mon d. mari, mon mari d.** my late husband; *Litt* **des espoirs défunts** lost hopes **N** deceased; **prier pour les défunts** to pray for the dead

dégagé [degaʒe] **ADJ** *(ton, manière)* free and easy; *(mouvements etc)* free; *(ciel, route)* clear; **allure dégagée** swinging stride; **vue dégagée** open view; **je voudrais une coupe avec la nuque très dégagée/les oreilles très dégagées** I'd like a style that's very short at the back/sides *or* that doesn't cover my neck/ears

dégagement [degaʒmɑ̃] **NM 1** *(d'un gage)* redemption, taking out of pawn; *(d'une hypothèque)* redemption **2** *(d'une route, des poumons etc)* clearing; *(du frein)* disengagement, release; *(de verrou)* loosening, slackening; *Pol, Mil* disengagement; *Ftbl* clearance; **escalier de d.** *(privé)* private staircase; *(de secours)* emergency stairs; **porte de d.** *(dans un cinéma etc)* (side) exit **3** *(de vapeur, gaz etc)* escape, release; *(de chaleur)* emission, release; **tuyau de d.** waste pipe; *Fin* **d. de fonds** *ou* **de crédits** release of funds **4** *(devant une maison etc)* open space, clearing; *Aut* clearance; **voie de d.** *Rail* siding; *Aut* slip road; *Aut* **itinéraire de d.** alternative route

dégager [degaʒe] (**je dégageai(s); n. dégageons**) **VT 1** *(gage)* to redeem, to take out of pawn; *(hypothèque)* to redeem; **d. des titres** to release (pledged) securities; **d. des crédits** to release funds; **d. des profits** to show *or* yield a profit; **d. un bénéfice** to show *or* yield a profit; **d. sa parole** to go back on one's word; **d. qn d'une promesse** to release sb from a promise; **d. sa responsabilité d'une affaire** to disclaim responsibility in a matter; **être dégagé des obligations militaires** to have done one's national service

  2 *(libérer)* to free; *(route, pont etc)* to clear; *(verrou)* to loosen, to slacken; **d. le frein** to release the brake; **d. une ville** to relieve a town; **d. les blessés des décombres** to pull the injured clear of the wreckage; *Archit* **d. les vues** to open up vistas; **robe qui dégage les épaules/le cou** dress that leaves the shoulders/the neck bare; *Ftbl* **d. le ballon en touche** to kick the ball over the touchline, to clear the ball; *Fam* **tu vas me d. toutes ces bricoles de tes étagères** I want you to clear all these odds and ends off your shelves

  3 *(laisser échapper) (vapeur, odeur)* to emit, to give off; *(chaleur)* to emit, to give out; **ce tableau dégage une grande sérénité** this painting gives off a feeling of great serenity

  4 *(isoler) (vérité)* to find out; *(impressions)* to get, to gain; *Pol* **d. une majorité** to secure a (working) majority; **d. l'idée principale d'un texte** to identify the main idea of a text; **qu'as-tu dégagé de ta mission?** what did you learn from your mission?; **quels sentiments dégages-tu de ton entretien avec le directeur?** what are your feelings now that you've spoken to the manager?

  vi 1 *Fam (partir)* to clear off; **allez dégage! je t'ai assez vu!** go on, clear off! I've seen enough of you!; **dégagez, s'il vous plaît** move along, please, clear the way, please **2** *très Fam (sentir mauvais)* to stink, *Br* to pong, to hum **3** *Fam (produire un effet puissant) (musique)*

to be mind-blowing, *esp Am* to kick ass; *(plat, épice)* to blow the top of one's head off, to pack a punch

  vpr se dégager 1 *(de ses menottes)* to free oneself (**de** from), to get free (**de** of); *(d'une voiture accidentée, d'une obligation)* to free oneself (**de** from); *(d'une situation difficile)* to extricate oneself (**de** from); **d'un effort violent, il s'est dégagé** he wrenched himself free; **se d. d'une promesse** to get out of a promise; **le ciel se dégage** the sky is clearing; **mon nez commence à se d.** my nose is starting to unblock

  2 *(du gaz, d'une odeur etc)* to be given off (**de** by); **il se dégage de l'oxygène** oxygen is given off; *Fig* **le calme qui se dégage de sa présence** the calm radiated by his presence; **le magnétisme qui se dégage d'elle** the magnetism she radiates

  3 *(ressortir)* to emerge, to come out; **la silhouette du navire s'est dégagée du brouillard** the ship loomed up out of the fog; **la vérité se dégage peu à peu** the truth is gradually coming out; **cette nécessité se dégage de l'étude de la situation** this need becomes apparent after studying the situation

dégaine [degɛn] **NF** *Fam (apparence)* strange appearance; **il a vraiment une d. pas possible avec sa veste à franges** he looks outlandish with his fringed jacket

dégainer [degene] **VT** *(épée)* to unsheathe, to draw; *(pistolet)* to draw **vi** to draw

déganter (se) [sədegɑ̃te] **vpr** to take off one's gloves

dégarni [degarni] **ADJ** *(Frigidaire®, placard etc)* empty; **arbre d.** tree bare of leaves; **front d.** receding hairline; **mon portefeuille est d.** I'm rather low on funds

dégarnir [degarnir] **VT** *(Frigidaire®, placard etc)* to empty; *(chambre, salle etc)* to empty, to clear; *(lit)* to strip; *(compte en banque)* to draw (heavily) on; *Mil (ville etc)* to withdraw troops from; *(robe)* to take the trimmings off; *(arbre)* to thin out

  vpr se dégarnir *(d'un arbre)* to lose its leaves; *(d'une tête)* to go bald; *(d'une salle etc)* to empty; **il commence à se d.** his hair is thinning, he's going bald; **les rayons se sont dégarnis en un rien de temps** the shelves were stripped bare *or* emptied in next to no time

dégât [degɑ] **NM** damage; **il y a eu du** *ou* **un sacré d.** there was a lot of damage; **les gelées ont fait des dégâts dans les vignobles** the frosts have caused a lot of damage in the vineyards; **limiter les dégâts** to limit the damage; *Fig* **il va falloir limiter les dégâts** we'll have to do some damage limitation; **l'alcool fait des dégâts terribles parmi la jeunesse** alcohol is wreaking havoc among young people; **dégâts matériels** material damage; **dégâts des eaux** water damage; **dégâts causés par le feu** fire damage; **dégâts causés par une tempête** storm damage; **dégâts collatéraux** collateral damage

dégauchir [degoʃir] **VT** *(planche etc)* to surface, to rough plane; *(pierre)* to trim

dégauchissage [degoʃisaʒ], **dégauchissement** [degoʃismɑ̃] **NM** *Tech (de planche)* surfacing, rough planing; *(de pierre)* trimming

dégauchisseuse [degoʃisøz] **NF** surfacing machine, surfacer

dégazage [degazaʒ] **NM 1** *Chimie (d'eau etc)* degassing; *(de circuit)* bleeding **2** *(de pétrolier)* cleaning out

dégazer [degaze] **VT 1** *Chimie (eau etc)* to degas; *(freins, chauffage central)* to bleed **2** *(pétrolier)* to clean out

dégel [deʒɛl] NM Météo, Pol thaw; **le d. s'annonce** it's beginning to thaw

dégelée [deʒle] NF Fam thrashing, walloping; **il s'est pris une de ces dégelées** he got an awful thrashing or walloping

dégeler [deʒle] (**il dégèle; il dégèlera**) VT 1 (lac), Fig (personne) to thaw (out); Fig **d. un auditoire** to warm up an audience; **d. l'atmosphère** to make the atmosphere less chilly; **d. les relations entre deux pays** to bring about a thaw in relations between two countries 2 Fin (avoir etc) to unfreeze VI (d'un étang) to thaw; (de pieds) to thaw out VIMPERS **il ou ça dégèle** it's thawing VPR **se dégeler 1** (d'un étang) to thaw; (de pieds) to thaw out 2 Fig (de l'atmosphère) to thaw out; **les relations entre ces deux pays se sont finalement dégelées** there has finally been a thaw in relations between the two countries

dégénératif, -ive [deʒeneratif, -iv] ADJ (trouble, maladie) degenerative

dégénéré, -ée [deʒenere] ADJ 1 degenerate 2 Psy (arriéré) (mentally) defective N Psy mental defective

dégénérer [deʒenere] VI (je dégénère; je dégénérerai) 1 (s'abâtardir) (d'une race) to degenerate (de from; en into); (de qualité) to deteriorate 2 (mal tourner) (d'une conversation, un bal etc) to degenerate (en into); **son rhume a dégénéré en bronchite** his cold developed into bronchitis; **à chaque fois qu'on se voit, ça finit toujours par d.** every time we see each other, it ends up getting out of hand

dégénérescence [deʒeneresãs] NF Méd degeneration; Fig **on observe une nette d. de la moralité chez les jeunes** there has been a distinct decline in moral standards among young people

dégénérescent [deʒeneresã] ADJ Méd degenerating, degenerative

dégingandé [deʒɛ̃gãde] ADJ Fam gangling, lanky

dégivrage [deʒivraʒ] NM Aviat, Aut de-icing; (d'un réfrigérateur) defrosting; (dispositif) defroster

dégivrer [deʒivre] VT Aviat, Aut to de-ice; (réfrigérateur) to defrost

dégivreur [deʒivrœr] NM Aviat, Aut de-icer; (de réfrigérateur) defroster

déglaçage [deglasaʒ] NM, **déglacement** [deglasmã] NM (d'une poêle à frire) deglazing

déglacer [deglase] (conj like glacer) VT Culin (poêle à frire) to deglaze

déglingue [deglɛ̃g] NF Fam decay; **il est en pleine d.** he's completely fallen apart

déglinguer [deglɛ̃ge] Fam VT (appareil, meuble) to smash up, to bust up; **ma moto est toute déglinguée** my motorbike is falling to pieces VPR **se déglinguer** (d'une voiture, d'une moto etc) to fall to pieces

déglutir [deglytir] VT Physiol to swallow

déglutition [deglytisjõ] NF Physiol swallowing

dégobiller [degɔbije] très Fam VI (vomir) to puke, to throw up VT to puke up

dégoiser [degwaze] Fam Péj VT (discours etc) to spout; **qu'est-ce qu'il dégoise?** what's he rattling on or rabbiting on or wittering on about? VI to rattle or witter on

dégommage [degɔmaʒ] NM Fam (renvoi) sacking

dégommer [degɔme] VT Fam 1 (tuer) to blow away, to gun down 2 (tirer sur) to shoot at 3 (évincer) to kick out, to get rid of

dégonflage [degõflaʒ] NM Fam chickening out, Br bottling out; **on a assisté à un d. généralisé** everybody chickened out; **dès qu'il a vu le patron, ça a été le d. total** as soon as he saw the boss, he chickened out or Br lost his bottle

dégonflard, -arde [degõflar, -ard] N Fam chicken (person)

dégonfle [degõfl] NF Fam = **dégonflage**

dégonflé, -ée [degõfle] ADJ 1 (pneu etc) soft 2 Fam (lâche) chicken; **ce que tu peux être d.!** you really are chicken! N Fam chicken; **vous n'êtes qu'une bande de dégonflés** you're all just chicken, Br Arg you've none of you any bottle

dégonflement [degõfləmã] NM (de pneu) deflating, deflation; Com cutback

dégonfler [degõfle] VT 1 (pneu, ballon etc) to deflate, to let the air out of 2 (gonflement) to reduce, to bring down; **d. les prix** to bring prices down 3 (héros) to debunk; **d. la portée d'un événement** to play down or downplay the importance of an event VPR **se dégonfler 1** (de pneu, de ballon) to deflate 2 (de gonflement) to go down 3 Fam (de personne) to chicken out, to get cold feet VI (de gonflement) to go down

dégorgement [degɔrʒmã] NM 1 (d'un égout, d'un évier) unblocking, clearing 2 (de l'eau) release; (de la bile) discharge

dégorger [degɔrʒe] (je dégorgeai(s); n. dégorgeons) VT 1 to discharge; **l'égout dégorge de l'eau sale** the drain is discharging dirty water; **la rue a dégorgé un flot de gens** a crowd of people surged from the street 2 (passage, tuyau) to free, to clear, to unstop; **d. un évier bouché** to clear a blocked sink, to unblock a sink 3 **d. du vin** = to remove sediment from wine prior to its final corking VI 1 (d'un égout, d'un étang) to flow out, to discharge (dans into); (d'une gouttière, d'une rivière) to overflow 2 Culin **faire d. des concombres/etc** = to remove the water from cucumbers/etc by sprinkling them with salt VPR **se dégorger** (d'une rivière, d'un égout) to empty (dans into)

dégot(t)er [degɔte] VT Fam to dig up

dégoulinade [degulinad] NF trickle

dégoulinement [degulinmã] NM trickling

dégouliner [deguline] VI to trickle; **la pluie me dégoulinait dans le cou** the rain was trickling down my neck; **je dégouline** I'm dripping, I'm soaking wet

dégoupiller [degupije] VT (grenade) to pull the pin out of

dégourdi, -ie [degurdi] ADJ bright, sharp, smart; **il n'est pas très d.** he's not very bright, he's not really on the ball; **tu es d. comme un manche de pelle** you're not very smart, Br Fam you're as thick as two short planks N **c'est un d./une dégourdie** he's/she's pretty bright, he's/she's got what it takes

dégourdir [degurdir] VT (membres) to remove the stiffness or numbness from; Vieilli (eau) to take the chill off; **il faut que je dégourdisse ma jambe** I'll have to get the circulation going in my leg again; Fig **d. qn** to teach sb a thing or two, to smarten sb up VPR **se dégourdir** (en marchant) to stretch one's legs; Fig to smarten up; **je vais me d. les jambes** I'm going to stretch my legs a bit

dégourdissement [degurdismã] NM removal of numbness; Fig **il a besoin d'un sacré d.** he really needs wising up

dégoût [degu] NM 1 (répulsion) disgust, distaste, loathing; **il a un véritable d. pour le beurre** he can't stand butter 2 (aversion) dislike; **avoir du d. pour qch** to dislike sth; **j'éprouve beaucoup de d. pour ce genre d'attitude** I really dislike that kind of attitude; **prendre qch en d.** to take a dislike to sth; **il a pris sa vie en d.** he grew weary of

the life he was leading; **le d. de la vie** world-weariness; **le d. de soi** self-loathing

dégoûtant, -ante [degutã, -ãt] ADJ (vue, odeur, personne etc) disgusting, revolting; **c'est d. de mentir/voler** it's disgusting to lie/steal; **elle gagne encore! c'est d.!** she's won again! it's disgusting! N filthy character; **un vieux d.** a dirty old man

dégoûtation [degutasjõ] NF Fam 1 (dégoût) disgust 2 (saleté) filth; **ta chambre est une vraie d.** your room is a pigsty or Br a tip

dégoûté, -ée [degute] ADJ 1 (écœuré) disgusted (de with), Fam sick (de of); **je suis d. de tes mensonges** I'm sick of your lies; **d. de la vie** weary of life; **je suis d. de la viande** I can't face eating meat 2 (difficile) fastidious, squeamish; Iron **vous n'êtes pas d.!** you're not fussy! N **faire le d./la dégoûtée** to turn up one's nose; **quand j'ai fait mon offre, il a fait le d.** when I told him my offer, he turned his nose up at it

dégoûter [degute] VT to disgust; **la viande me dégoûte** meat turns my stomach; **tout cela me dégoûte** I'm sick of it all; **d. qn de qch** to put sb off sth; **c'est à vous d. de l'Espagne/des hommes!** it's enough to put you off Spain/men! VPR **se dégoûter se d. de qn/qch** to take a dislike to sb/sth; **il s'est dégoûté du chocolat** he's put himself right off chocolate

dégoutter [degute] VI to drip, to fall drop by drop (de from); **la pluie dégoutte de son chapeau** the rain is dripping from his hat; **un parapluie dégouttant d'eau** a dripping wet umbrella; **dégouttant de sueur** dripping with sweat

dégradant [degradã] ADJ (travail) degrading; (remarque) derogatory

dégradation [degradasjõ] NF 1 (détérioration) (de monument etc) defacement; (de matériel scolaire, de l'environnement) damage (de to); (de données informatiques) corruption; Fig (de relations internationales) deterioration; **cette maison est dans un état de d. pitoyable** the house is in a shocking state of repair; Phys **d. de l'énergie** dissipation of energy 2 (en rang etc) downgrading; **d. civique** loss of civil rights

dégradé [degrade] NM (de couleurs) gradation; Phot graduated shading; Typ, Ordinat blend; **cheveux coupés en d.** layered hair; **se faire faire un d.** to have a layer cut; Ordinat **d. de couleur** colour scale; Ordinat **d. de gris** grey scale; Typ etc **dégradés de gris** shades of grey

dégrader [degrade] VT 1 (abîmer) (monument) to deface; (matériel, maison) to damage; Ordinat (données) to corrupt 2 Fig (personne) to degrade, to debase; **des conditions de vie qui dégradent la personne** degrading living conditions 3 Mil to downgrade VPR **se dégrader 1** (se détériorer) (de la santé, d'une situation) to deteriorate; (d'un bâtiment etc) to fall into disrepair; **les bâtiments se sont beaucoup dégradés** the buildings have fallen into serious disrepair; **les relations internationales se dégradent** international relations are deteriorating 2 (s'abaisser) to lower or demean oneself 3 Phys (d'énergie) to dissipate

dégrader [degrade] VT (couleurs, lumière) to shade off, to gradate; Phot to vignette

dégrafer [degrafe] VT (robe etc) to unhook, to unfasten, to undo; (bracelet) to unclasp, to unfasten VPR **se dégrafer 1** (d'un vêtement, d'un bracelet) to come undone 2 (d'une femme) to undo one's dress

dégraissage [degresaʒ] NM **1** *Culin* skimming; *Fig* **d. d'une entreprise** removing the fat from *or* downsizing a company; **ils ont fait de sérieux dégraissages dans l'ensemble du secteur** they have cut a substantial number of jobs in the sector **2** *(nettoyage)* drycleaning

dégraisser [degrese] VT **1** *(bouillon)* to skim the fat off; *(animal de boucherie)* to remove the fat from; *Fig* **d. une entreprise** to cut the fat from a company, to downsize a company; **d. les effectifs** to lay off staff **2** *(vêtements etc)* to dry-clean; **donner qch à d.** to hand sth in to the dry-cleaner's
▪ VI *Fig (d'une entreprise)* to cut the fat, to downsize

degré [dəgre] NM **1** *(unité) (de cercle, chaleur, gamme musicale)* degree; *(de boisson alcoolisée)* proof; **angle de 45 degrés** 45-degree angle; **dix degrés au-dessous de zéro** ten degrees below zero; **la température monte d'un d.** the temperature rises by one degree; **à combien de degrés est ce whisky?** what proof is this whisky?; **alcool à 90 degrés** surgical spirit, *Am* rubbing alcohol
2 *(stade, niveau) (de parenté)* degree; **cousins au second d.** cousins once removed, second cousins; *Méd* **brûlure au troisième d.** third-degree burn; *Math* **équation du second/du troisième d.** quadratic/cubic equation; *Scol* **éducation du premier/second d.** primary/secondary education; **les degrés de l'échelle sociale** the rungs of the social ladder; **le plus haut/bas d. de la société** the highest/lowest level of society; **atteindre le plus haut d. de la réussite** to reach the pinnacle of success; **elle est généreuse au plus haut d.** she is generous in the extreme; **je veux bien vous aider, mais seulement jusqu'à un certain d.** I'd be glad to help you, but only up to a point; **prendre une plaisanterie au premier d.** to take a joke seriously; **tu prends tout au premier d.** you take everything literally; **avec lui, il vaut mieux prendre les choses/la plaisanterie au deuxième d.** with him, it's best not to take things/the joke at face value; **par degré(s)** by degrees, gradually; *Fig* **le d. zéro de l'informatique/de la civilisation** the beginnings of computer science/civilization; *Hum* **son bouquin, c'est le d. zéro de la littérature** his book hardly deserves to be classed as literature; **à un d. avancé de civilisation/recherches** at an advanced stage of civilization/research; *Fin* **d. de liquidité** degree of liquidity, liquidity ratio; *Fin* **d. de solvabilité** credit rating
3 *(d'escalier)* step; *(d'échelle)* rung
▸▸ **d. Celsius** degree centigrade *or* Celsius; **d. Engler** degree Engler; **d. Fahrenheit** degree Fahrenheit; **d. Kelvin** degree Kelvin

dégréement [degremã] NM *Naut (d'un mât)* unrigging

dégréer [degree] VT *Naut (mât)* to unrig; *(grue)* to dismantle, to take down

dégressif, -ive [degresif, -iv] ADJ *Com* **tarif d.** tapering rate; **impôt d.** degressive taxation

dégressivité [degresivite] NF *(d'un impôt)* degressive nature

dégrèvement [degrevmã] NM *(d'impôt)* reduction, abatement; **d. fiscal** tax relief

dégrever [degrəve] VT *(je dégrève; je dégrèverai) (impôt)* to reduce, to diminish; *(contribuable)* to grant tax relief to; *(industrie)* to derate; *(édifice)* to reduce the assessment on; *(domaine)* to disencumber

dégriffé [degrife] ADJ **manteau d.** = coat which has had its designer label removed and is sold at a reduced price
▪ NM = item of clothing which has had its designer label removed and is sold at a reduced price

dégringolade [degrɛ̃gɔlad] NF *Fam (chute)* tumble; *Fig (d'un financier)* downfall; *(d'une firme etc)* collapse; *(d'une d. des prix* slump *or* collapse in prices

dégringoler [degrɛ̃gɔle] *Fam* VT to rush *or* tear down, to come rushing *or* tearing down
▪ VI *(d'une personne)* to tumble; *Fig (de prix)* to slump, to collapse; *(d'une entreprise)* to collapse; **d. dans la pente** to tumble down the slope

dégrippant [degripã] NM lubricating *or* penetrating oil

dégripper [degripe] VT *Tech (mécanisme)* to unseize, to free

dégrisement [degrizmã] NM sobering up; *Fig* disillusionment

dégriser [degrize] VT to sober up; *Fig* to bring down to earth
▪ VPR **se dégriser** to sober up; *Fig* to become disillusioned (**au sujet de** about)

dégrossir [degrosir] VT *(bois)* to rough down, to trim; *(pierre)* to rough-hew; *Fig (plan, travail etc)* to rough out; *Fam* **d. qn** to smooth out sb's rough edges; **il est un peu dégrossi depuis qu'il est à Paris** he's become a bit more polished since coming to Paris; **recrues mal dégrossies** raw recruits

dégrossissage [degrosisaʒ], **dégrossissement** [degrosismã] NM *(de bois)* trimming

dégrouiller (se) [sədegruje] VPR *Fam* to get a move on; **allez! dégrouille!** come on! get a move on!; **tu pourrais te d. un peu?** could you get a bit of a move on?; **il n'arrive jamais à se d. assez pour être à l'heure** he never manages to get enough of a move on to be on time

dégroupage [degrupaʒ] NM **1** *Com* deconsolidation **2** *Tél* unbundling

dégroupement [degrupmã] NM dividing into groups; **il va falloir procéder à un d. de la classe** the class will have to be divided into groups

dégrouper [degrupe] VT to divide into groups

déguenillé, -ée [degənije] ADJ ragged, tattered, in rags, in tatters
▪ N **un petit d.** a little ragamuffin

déguerpir [degerpir] VI to clear out *or* off; **d. en vitesse** to bolt; **faire d. l'ennemi** to scatter the enemy

dégueu [degø] ADJ INV *très Fam* = **dégueulasse**

dégueulasse [degœlas] *très Fam* ADJ rotten; *(sale)* filthy; **un repas d.** a disgusting meal; **il fait un temps d.** it's rotten *or* filthy weather; **j'ai passé un week-end d.** I had a rotten weekend; **tu es d. d'avoir fait ça** that was rotten of you; **c'est pas d.** it's bloody good; **il est d. avec elle** he's rotten to her; **se balader en d.** to go around in sloppy old clothes
▪ N **c'est un d.** he's a rotten bastard

dégueulasser [degœlase] VT *très Fam* to muck up, to mess up; **tu vas d. toute la maison** you're going to make the whole house filthy *or* get the whole house into a mess

dégueuler [degœle] VI *très Fam* to spew, to puke

dégueulis [degœli] NM *très Fam* puke, sick

déguiller [degije] *Suisse* VT *(objet dressé)* to knock over; *(pommes, noix, cerises)* to get down; *(arbre)* to cut down
▪ VI to tumble down

déguisé [degize] ADJ **1** *(pour tromper)* disguised; *(pour s'amuser)* dressed up; **être d.** *(pour tromper)* to be disguised *or* in disguise; **je me sens déguisée dans cette robe** I don't feel right in this dress, the dress isn't me **2** *Fig (voix, signature, égoïsme)* disguised; *(impôt, chômage)* hidden; **avec une joie non déguisée** with unconcealed delight; *Culin* **fruits déguisés** = prunes, dates etc stuffed with almond paste

déguisement [degizmã] NM **1** *(pour tromper)* disguise, get-up; *(pour un bal masqué)* fancy dress, costume **2** *Fig* **sans d.** plainly, openly; **livrez-moi votre pensée sans d.** tell me frankly what you think

déguiser [degize] VT **1** *(costumer)* to disguise; **d. un enfant en clown** to dress a child up as a clown **2** *(déformer) (sa voix, son écriture)* to disguise; *(la vérité)* to disguise, to conceal; **parler sans d. sa pensée** to speak plainly *or* openly
▪ VPR **se déguiser** *(pour ne pas être reconnu)* to disguise oneself; *(s'habiller)* to dress up; **se d. en pompier** to dress up as a fireman

dégurgiter [degyrʒite] VT to regurgitate; *Fig* **d. sa leçon** to regurgitate one's lesson

dégustateur, -trice [degystatœr, -tris] N wine taster

dégustation [degystasjõ] NF tasting, sampling; **d. de vin** wine tasting; **ici, d. d'huîtres** oysters served here

déguster [degyste] VT **1** *(tester) (vin etc)* to taste, to sample **2** *(savourer)* to savour, to eat/drink with relish; *Fig (livre etc)* to savour, to appreciate, to enjoy **3** *très Fam* **d. des coups** to get a good hiding; **qu'est-ce qu'on a dégusté!** we didn't half catch it!
▪ VI *très Fam* to suffer; **toute sa vie, elle a dégusté** she's had a rough time of it all her life; **je te préviens, tu vas d.!** you're going to catch it, I can tell you!; **faire d. qn** to give sb a hard time

déhanché [deãʃe] ADJ *(personne)* who walks with a sway of the hips; *Méd* slightly lopsided

déhanchement [deãʃmã] NM swaying of the hips; *(quand on est immobile)* standing with all one's weight on one foot; *Méd* **je remarque un léger d.** I notice a slight lopsidedness; **le d. de la statue** the curve of the statue's hip, the way the statue has all the weight on one foot

déhancher (se) [sədeãʃe] VPR *(en marchant)* to sway one's hips; *(quand on est immobile)* to lean one's weight on one foot

déharnacher [dearnaʃe] VT to unharness

dehors [dəɔr] ADV outside; *Sport* out; **être d.** *(pas chez soi)* to be out; **coucher d.** to sleep out of doors in the open; **dîner d.** *(en plein air)* to dine out of doors *or* in the open; *(au restaurant)* to dine out; *Fam* **mettre** *ou* **ficher** *ou* **foutre qn d.** to kick sb out; *(le renvoyer)* to sack sb; **mettre le nez** *ou* **le pied** *ou* **les pieds d.** to set foot outside (the door); *Naut* **toutes voiles d.** with every sail set; **de d.** from outside; **en d.** (on the) outside; **en d. de la maison** outside the house; **en d. de sa compétence/de cela** apart from his competence/from that; **rester en d. d'une dispute** to keep out of an argument; **je te prie de rester en d. (de cette histoire)** please keep out of this; **en d. du sujet** beside the question; **cela s'est fait en d. de moi** *(sans que je le sache)* it was done without my knowledge; *(sans que j'y participe)* I had no part in it; *Boxe* **compter qn d.** to count sb out
▪ NM **1** *(d'une maison etc)* outside, exterior; **au d.** on the outside; **ne pas se pencher au d.!** do not lean out of the window!; **agir du d.** to act from the outside **2** **les d.** the (outward) appearance; **maison aux d. imposants** house with an imposing exterior; **sous des d. aimables** under a pleasant exterior **3** *(en patinage)* outside edge

déhoussable [deusabl] ADJ *(canapé, siège)* with loose covers

déification [deifikasjõ] NF deification

déifier [deifje] VT to deify, to make a god of

déisme [deism] NM deism

déiste [deist] ADJ, N deist

déité [deite] NF deity

déj [deʒ] NM *Fam* petit d. breakfast

DÉJÀ [deʒa]

already **1** ▪ yet **1** ▪ before **2**

ADV **1** *(dès maintenant)* already; *(si tôt)* yet; faut-il que vous partiez d.? must you go just yet?; vous avez d. trop de travail you have too much work as it is; j'aurais dû le faire il y a d. trois jours I should have done it three days ago as it is; il est d. trois heures it's already three o'clock; tu as d. fini? have you finished already?; elle a d. 20 ans! she's 20 already!; c'est d. vieux that's not exactly news; tu crois qu'il en souffre encore? – ça m'étonnerait, c'est d. vieux do you think he's still suffering? – I'd be surprised if he was, it was all so long ago

2 *(auparavant)* before, previously; je vous ai d. vu I've seen you before; j'avais d. lu ce livre I'd read the book before, I'd already read the book; d. en 1900 as early as 1900; elle avait d. cet air bête quand elle était enfant even as a child she looked stupid; vous avez d. travaillé? have you got work experience?

3 *(intensif)* 10 jours de vacances, c'est d. ça! *ou* c'est d. quelque chose! 10 days' holiday isn't bad at all!; ce n'est d. pas si mal that's not bad at all; *Fam* c'est d. pas mal de gagner 2 000 euros a salary of 2,000 euros isn't that bad; *Fam* une dinde de 4 kg, c'est d. la belle bête! four kilos is not a bad weight at all for a turkey!; il est d. assez gâté comme ça! he's spoiled enough as it is!; *Fam* d. que je n'en ai pas beaucoup, si tu m'en prends la moitié … I haven't got much as it is, so if you take half …

4 *Fam (interrogatif)* qu'est-ce que vous faites, d.? what did you say your job was?; qu'est-ce que tu m'as dit, d.? what did you say?; c'est quoi, d., son nom? what was his name again?

---

déjanté [deʒɑ̃te] ADJ *très Fam* mad, *Br* crackers

déjanter [deʒɑ̃te] VT *(pneu)* to remove from the rim
VI *très Fam* to be mad, to be off one's head *or* rocker; tu déjantes complètement depuis que tu es avec cette fille you haven't been right in the head since you started going with that girl; il a complètement déjanté he's gone right off his rocker
VPR se déjanter *(d'un pneu)* to come off the rim

déjà-vu [deʒavy] NM INV une impression de d. a feeling of déjà vu; leur spectacle n'a rien d'extraordinaire, c'est du d. there's nothing very special about their show, it's all been done before

déjection [deʒɛksjɔ̃] NF **1** *Physiol* evacuation; **déjections** faeces **2** *Géol* ejecta

déjeté [deʒte] ADJ **1** *(position, mur)* crooked, lopsided; il est de plus en plus d. his posture is getting worse and worse; colonne vertébrale déjetée deformed spinal column; elle a la taille déjetée she has one shoulder higher than the other; *Fig* d. à cause de son travail worn out by (his) work **2** *Belg Fam (en désordre)* messy; *(déformé)* deformed

déjeter [deʒte] (il déjette; il déjettera) VT to make lopsided; *(bois)* to warp; *(métal)* to buckle
VPR se déjeter to grow lopsided; *(du bois)* to warp; *(du métal)* to buckle

déjeuner¹ [deʒœne] NM **1** *(repas de midi)* lunch, *Fml* luncheon; prendre son d. to have lunch; un d. d'affaires/de travail a business/working lunch; d. buffet buffet lunch; d. sur l'herbe picnic (lunch); je ne peux pas venir ce midi, j'ai un d. I can't make it at noon, I'm already booked for lunch; il y a des œufs pour le d. it's eggs for lunch VOIR GRAMMAIRE A7 **2** *Suisse, Belg (petit déjeuner)* breakfast **3** *(tasse et soucoupe)* breakfast cup and saucer **4** *Fig* ça a été un d. de soleil *(d'un tissu)* it soon faded; *(d'un sentiment, d'une résolution)* it soon faded, it didn't last long

déjeuner² VI **1** *(le matin)* to (have) breakfast **2** *(à midi)* to (have) lunch; il est resté à d. he stayed for lunch; d. d'un sandwich to have a sandwich for lunch; tu as déjeuné de peu you didn't have much for lunch; d. à l'extérieur to have lunch out; nous avons les Dupont à d. dimanche the Duponts are coming for lunch on Sunday

déjouer [deʒwe] VT *(complot, plans de qn)* to foil; d. la surveillance du professeur to evade the teacher's eye

déjuger (se) [sədeʒyʒe] VPR *(conj like juger)* to reverse one's judgment

DEL [deɛl] NF *(abrév* diode électroluminescente*)* LED

delà [dəla] PRÉP *Arch, Litt* beyond; par d. les mers/monts beyond the seas/the mountains; au d. de beyond; n'allez pas au d. de 300 euros don't go above 300 euros; elle est allée au d. de ses promesses she was better than her word; aller au d. de ses forces/moyens to do more than one is capable of/spend more than one can afford; sa réussite va au d. de tout ce qu'il avait rêvé he has succeeded beyond his wildest dreams; par d. les âges down through the ages; il faut savoir juger les gens par d. les apparences one shouldn't judge by appearances
ADV deçà, d. here and there; au(-)d. beyond; vous voyez ce sommet? au d., c'est l'Autriche do you see that peak? Austria lies beyond that *or* on the other side; avoir droit à 200 cigarettes, pas au d. to be entitled to 200 cigarettes, no more; son savoir ne va pas au d. that's as much as *or* that's all he knows
NM l'au-d. the next world, the hereafter

délabré [delabre] ADJ *(maison, meubles)* dilapidated; complètement d. *(bâtiment)* ramshackle; santé délabrée ruined health

délabrement [delabrəmɑ̃] NM *(de maison, meubles)* dilapidated state; depuis que sa femme est morte, son affaire va au d. since his wife died, his business has been going under; le d. de son entreprise the ruin of his company

délabrer [delabre] VT *(maison)* to dilapidate; *(santé)* to ruin; la mort de sa femme lui a complètement délabré le moral his wife's death has left him in a state of utter depression
VPR se délabrer *(d'une maison etc)* to fall into disrepair, to become dilapidated; sa santé se délabre his health is deteriorating; ses affaires se délabrent his business is going to rack and ruin; son moral se délabre he's becoming more and more depressed

délacer [delase] (je délaçai(s); n. délaçons) VT *(chaussures etc)* to unlace, to undo
VPR se délacer to come unlaced *or* undone

délai [delɛ] NM *(laps de temps)* time allowed, period; *(date limite)* deadline; on vous accordera un d. we will give you more time; dans le d. prescrit *ou* fixé within the required *or* allotted time; d. d'un jour franc one clear day, one whole day; dans un d. de 10 jours within 10 days; il faut compter un d. de 10 jours you must allow 10 days; livrer dans les délais to deliver on time; respecter *ou* tenir les délais to meet the deadline; dernier d. (final) deadline; vous devez me rendre votre dissertation lundi dernier d. you must hand in your dissertation by Monday at the very latest *or* no later than Monday; sans d. without delay, immediately; dans les plus brefs délais as soon as possible; livrable dans un d. de trois jours can be delivered at three days' notice

▸ ▸ d. d'attente waiting period; d. de carence waiting period; *Com* d. de chargement loading time; d. de commercialisation *(d'un produit)* launching period; d. de congé term of notice; d. de crédit credit period; *Com* d. d'embarquement loading time; d. d'exécution deadline; *(de livraison, de production)* lead time; d. garanti de livraison guaranteed delivery period; d. de garantie guarantee period, term of guarantee; d. de grâce period of grace; d. de livraison delivery time *or* period, lead time; d. de livraison: un mois delivery within one month; *Com* d. de paiement *(fixé par contrat)* term of payment, payment period *or* term; demander un d. de paiement to request a postponement of payment; *Jur, Com* d. de préavis term of notice, notice period; d. de production production lead time; d. de réachat repurchase period; d. de récupération du capital investi payback period; d. de réflexion time to think; *Com* cooling-off period; d. de règlement settlement period; d. de remboursement payback period; d. de rigueur strict deadline; avant le 20 février, d. de rigueur by 20 February at the very latest; *Mil etc* d. de route travelling time; d. de validité period of validity

> Il faut noter que le nom anglais **delay** est un faux ami. Il signifie **retard**.

délai-congé, *pl* **délais-congés** NM *Jur, Com (à un employé ou employeur)* term of notice, notice period

délaissement [delɛsmɑ̃] NM **1** *(d'une femme, d'enfants etc) (abandon)* desertion, abandonment; *(négligence)* neglect; *(solitude)* loneliness; être dans un grand d. to be completely abandoned **2** *(d'un droit)* relinquishment, renunciation; *(à l'assureur)* abandonment

délaisser [delɛse] VT **1** *(abandonner)* to desert, to abandon, to forsake; *(négliger)* to neglect; depuis qu'il s'est marié, il délaisse ses amis he has dropped his friends since he got married; cette profession est délaissée par la jeunesse young people are turning their backs on the profession **2** *Jur (droit, succession)* to relinquish, to forgo; *(à l'assureur)* to abandon

délassant [delɑsɑ̃] ADJ *(bain etc)* relaxing; *(lecture)* light, entertaining

délassement [delɑsmɑ̃] NM relaxation, rest; le sport est un d. pour elle sport is a relaxation for her; avoir besoin de d. to need to relax; nous nous sentions dans un état de d. total we felt totally relaxed

délasser [delɑse] VT to relax
VPR se délasser to (take some) rest, to relax

délateur, -trice [delatœr, -tris] N informer, spy

délation [delɑsjɔ̃] NF denouncement

délavage [delavaʒ] NM *(de couleurs etc)* washing out

délavé [delave] ADJ **1** *(couleur etc)* washed out; jean d. *(volontairement)* faded *or* stonewashed jeans; *(à la lessive)* faded jeans **2** terre délavée sodden earth

délaver [delave] VT **1** *(tissu)* to fade **2** *(terre)* to soak (with water)

délayage [delɛjaʒ] NM *(de peinture etc)* thinning out; *Fig Péj* ce devoir n'est que du d. there's far too much padding in this work

délayer [delɛje] VT *(je délaie, je délaye; je délaierai, je délayerai)* **1** *(poudre etc)* to add water to; *(peinture etc)* to thin *(dans with)*; *(liquide)* to water down; d. de la farine dans du lait to mix flour with milk **2** *Fig (discours, texte, théorie)* to pad out

Delco® [dɛlko] NM *Aut* distributor

déléatur [deleatyr] NM INV *Typ* delete (mark), dele

délectable [delɛktabl] ADJ delicious, delightful

délectation [delɛktasjɔ̃] NF delight; *Fml, Hum* delectation

délecter [delɛkte] VT *Litt* to delight
VPR **se délecter** to enjoy oneself; **se d. à (faire) qch** to take delight in (doing) sth

délégant, -ante [delegɑ̃, -ɑ̃t] N *Jur* delegant

délégataire [delegatɛr] N *Jur* delegatee

délégateur, -trice [delegatœr, -tris] N *Jur* delegator

délégation [delegasjɔ̃] NF **1** *(action de déléguer) (de représentants)* delegation, deputing; *(de dette)* assignment, transfer; **agir en vertu d'une ou par d.** to act on the authority invested in one; **d. de pouvoir** delegation of authority; **d. de signature** power of attorney; *Scol* **d. rectorale** (one-year) transfer; **d. de vote** proxy voting **2** *(groupe)* delegation, body of delegates; **envoyer une d. auprès d'un ministre** to send a delegation to a minister; **venir en d.** to come in a delegation

délégué, -ée [delege] ADJ **membre d.** delegate; **ministre d. à l'environnement** Minister for the Environment, Environment Minister
N *(à une réunion)* delegate; *Scol* representative *(at class meetings)*
▸▸ *Scol* **d. de classe** class representative *(at class meetings)*; **d. commercial** sales rep(resentative); **d. des parents** parent representative *(at class meetings)*; **d. du personnel** staff representative; *(syndiqué)* union representative; *Scol* **d. rectoral** = teacher on a one-year placement *(in a job other than the one to which he or she was originally assigned)*; **d. syndical** union representative; *(d'usine)* shop steward

déléguer [delege] (**je délègue; je délégue-rai**) VT **1** *(désigner)* **d. qn pour faire qch** to delegate sb to do sth **2** *(transmettre) (pouvoirs)* to delegate; **c'est un patron qui sait d. ses fonctions** he's a boss who knows how to delegate; **d. une créance** to assign a debt
VI to delegate

délestage [delɛstaʒ] NM *(d'un navire, d'un ballon)* unballasting; *Élec* power cut; **pour assurer le d. des grandes artères** to relieve congestion on the main roads; **itinéraire de d.** alternative route

délester [delɛste] VT *(navire, ballon)* to unballast; *Élec* to cut off the power to; *(voie de communication)* to relieve congestion on; **d. qn d'un fardeau** to relieve sb of a burden; *Fam* **d. qn de son argent** to relieve sb of his/her money
VPR **se délester** *(d'un navire, d'un ballon)* to jettison ballast; **se d. de ses paquets** to set down *or* relieve oneself of one's parcels

délétère [deletɛr] ADJ harmful, *Fml* deleterious; *(gaz)* noxious, poisonous; *(influence etc)* pernicious

délibérant [deliberɑ̃] ADJ *(assemblée)* deliberative

délibératif, -ive [deliberatif, -iv] ADJ *(fonction)* deliberative; **avoir voix délibérative** to be entitled to speak and vote

délibération [deliberasjɔ̃] NF **1** *(examen)* deliberation, debate, discussion; **pendant la d. du jury** during the jury's deliberations, *Fam* while the jury was out; **la question est en d.** the matter is under discussion *or* being deliberated **2** *(réflexion)* consideration, reflection, cogitation; **après mûre d.** after careful consideration **3** *(décision) (d'une assemblée)* resolution, decision, vote

délibéré [delibere] ADJ **1** *(intentionnel)* deliberate, intentional; **agir de propos d.** to act

deliberately *or* intentionally **2** *(résolu) (ton, manière)* deliberate, determined, resolute
NM *Jur (de juges)* consultation, private sitting; **mettre une affaire en d.** = to submit a matter for decision by the Bench, *Am* ≃ to take a matter under advisement

délibérément [deliberemɑ̃] ADV deliberately

délibérer [delibere] VI **1** *(discuter)* to deliberate, to confer; **d. (avec qn) sur qch** to discuss a matter (with sb); **le jury s'est retiré pour d.** the jury retired to consider its verdict **2** *(réfléchir)* to deliberate, to reflect **3** *(décider)* **d. de qch** to decide sth; **le tribunal populaire délibérait de le condamner à mort** the people's tribunal was deciding whether to condemn him to death

délicat, -ate [delika] ADJ **1** *(fragile) (peau)* sensitive, tender; *(fleur etc)* delicate; *(santé)* delicate, frail, weak
2 *(fin) (dentelle, ouvrage)* delicate; *(travail)* fine; *(plat)* fine, refined; **d'une facture très délicate** very delicately made
3 *(raffiné) (goût, personne)* fine, refined, discerning; *(geste)* graceful; *(comportement)* considerate; *(toucher)* delicate, gentle; **avoir les oreilles délicates** to dislike bad language; **avoir le palais d.** to have a discerning palate; **avoir des gestes délicats** to move gracefully; **il est toujours très d. avec les vieilles dames** he's always very considerate towards old ladies; **il a eu une attention délicate pour nous à l'occasion de notre mariage** he was very thoughtful *or* considerate when we got married; **quelle attention délicate!** how thoughtful!, how considerate!
4 *(difficile) (situation, question, opération)* delicate, difficult, tricky; *(problème, travail)* difficult, tricky
5 *(souvent avec négation) (scrupuleux) (personne)* scrupulous; *(conscience)* tender; **peu d.** not very scrupulous, rather unscrupulous
6 *(exigeant)* **d. sur la nourriture** fussy about food; **qu'est-ce qu'il est d.!** isn't he fussy!
N **faire le d.** *(devant un mets)* to be fussy; *(devant le sang)* to be squeamish

délicatement [delikatmɑ̃] ADV delicately; *(s'exprimer)* with delicacy; *(se comporter)* considerately, thoughtfully; **poser d. des verres sur un plateau** to put glasses down gently on a tray; **annoncer d. un décès à qn** to gently break the news of a death to sb; **brodé** finely embroidered; **plat d. préparé** dish prepared with great care

délicatesse [delikatɛs] NF **1** *(fragilité) (de la peau)* tenderness; *(d'une fleur, d'un tissu)* delicacy; *(d'un objet)* fragility; *(de la santé)* frailty
2 *(finesse) (d'une dentelle, d'un ouvrage)* delicacy, fineness; *(d'un tableau)* fineness; *(d'une texture, d'un coloris)* fineness, softness; *(d'un plat)* refinement
3 *(raffinement) (de goût)* refinement; *(d'un geste)* gracefulness; *(de toucher)* delicacy, gentleness; **d'un geste plein de d.** with an extremely graceful movement; **elle posa les verres sur la table avec d.** she gently put the glasses down on the table
4 *(difficulté) (d'une situation)* delicacy, difficulty, awkwardness; *(d'une opération, d'une question, d'un problème, d'un travail)* difficulty; **ce que vous me demandez de lui dire est vraiment d'une d. incroyable** what you're asking me to tell him is extremely difficult *or* awkward; **il est en d. avec la police/le gouvernement** he has to watch his step with the police/the government; **nous sommes en d.** we've had words
5 *(gentillesse)* considerateness, consideration; *(sensibilité)* tact; **agir avec d.** to behave considerately/tactfully; **elle avait des délicatesses pour moi** she treated me very considerately; **c'est une personne pleine de**

d. he's/she's extremely thoughtful *or* considerate

délice [delis] NM delight, extreme pleasure; **cette tarte est un vrai d.** this tart is delicious; **quel d. de se plonger dans un bon bain chaud** what a delight it is to sink into a warm bath

délices [delis] NFPL delight(s), pleasure(s); **faire les d. de qn** to be the delight of sb; **faire ses d. de qch** to delight in sth; **c'est un lieu de d.** this place is heavenly

délicieusement [delisjøzmɑ̃] ADV delightfully; *(en rapport avec le goût)* deliciously; **elle nous a reçus d.** she entertained us delightfully, she was a delightful hostess; **elle réussit d. la paella** she makes a delicious paella; **elle se laissa glisser d. dans l'eau** she slid into the water with delight

délicieux, -ieuse [delisjø, -jøz] ADJ *(nourriture)* delicious; *(personne, robe etc)* delightful, charming

délictuel, -elle [deliktɥɛl] ADJ *Jur* = **délictueux**

délictueux, -euse [deliktɥø, -øz] ADJ *Jur* punishable; **acte d.** misdemeanour, offence, *Am* offense

délié [delje] ADJ slender, fine; *(doigts)* nimble, agile; **taille déliée** slim figure; **avoir la langue déliée** to be talkative; **un esprit d.** a sharp *or* astute mind
NM *Typ etc* thin stroke

délier [delje] VT **1** *(défaire) (corde, rubans etc)* to untie, to undo; *(chaînes)* to undo, to loose; *Fig* **le vin lui a délié la langue** the wine loosened his tongue **2** *(libérer) (prisonnier)* to untie; **d. les mains à qn** to untie sb's hands; **d. qn d'une promesse/d'une responsabilité** to release sb from a promise/a responsibility
VPR **se délier 1** *(se défaire)* to come undone *or* untied, to come loose; *Fig* **sa langue s'est déliée** he began to talk, he found his tongue **2** **se d. d'un serment/d'une promesse** to free oneself from an oath/a promise

délimitation [delimitasjɔ̃] NF *(d'un territoire)* delimitation, demarcation; *(d'une responsabilité, d'un sujet etc)* definition; **poteau de d.** boundary post

délimiter [delimite] VT *(territoire)* to delimit, to demarcate; *(responsabilité, sujet etc)* to define, to set the limits of

délimiteur [delimitœr] NM *Ordinat* delimiter; **d. de bloc** block delimiter, block marker; **d. de champ** field delimiter

délinquance [delɛ̃kɑ̃s] NF delinquency; **d. juvénile** juvenile delinquency; **la petite d. des banlieues** petty crime in the suburbs

délinquant, -ante [delɛ̃kɑ̃, -ɑ̃t] *Jur* ADJ delinquent; **la jeunesse délinquante** juvenile delinquents
N offender; **d. juvénile** juvenile delinquent; **d. primaire** first offender; **d. sexuel** sex offender

déliquescence [delikesɑ̃s] NF **1** *Chimie* deliquescence **2** *Fig Péj (de civilisation, mœurs)* decay, decline; *(de relation, mariage etc)* deterioration; *(d'une personne)* decline; **tomber en d.** *(d'une civilisation)* to fall into decay *or* decline; *(d'un mariage)* to fall apart; *(d'une personne)* to decline

déliquescent, -ente [delikesɑ̃] ADJ **1** *Chimie* deliquescent **2** *Fig Péj (civilisation)* in decay, decaying; *(personne)* declining; *(relation, mariage)* deteriorating; **mœurs ou habitudes déliquescentes** decadent ways

délirant [delirɑ̃] ADJ *Méd (malade, fièvre etc)* delirious; *Fam* **c'est d. de lui demander de tout payer!** it's madness to ask him to pay for everything!; **joie délirante** frenzied joy; **avoir une imagination délirante** to have a wild imagination; **une atmosphère complètement délirante** an atmosphere of total delirium

délire [delir] NM **1** *Méd* delirium; **d. alcoolique** alcoholic dementia; **d. de persécution** persecution mania; **d. de grandeur** delusions of grandeur; **d. hallucinatoire** hallucination; **être victime de délires hallucinatoires** to hallucinate; **d. collectif** mass hysteria; **avoir le d.** to be delirious; **crise** *ou* **accès de d.** attack of delirium; *Fig* **c'est du d.!** it's madness!; **c'est du d. de croire qu'il va divorcer pour toi** you must be off your head if you think that he's going to get a divorce for your sake **2** *(frénésie)* frenzy; **foule en d.** delirious *or* ecstatic crowd; **son amour pour elle va jusqu'au d.** he is madly in love with her; **sa jalousie va jusqu'au d.** he is insanely jealous; *Fam* **cette soirée, c'est le d.!** this is a wild party!; **quand il arrive sur scène, c'est un vrai** *ou* **du d.** the audience goes wild when he appears on stage; *Fam* **on s'est tapé un super d.!** we had a wicked *or* awesome *or* *Br* mental time!

délirer [delire] VI **1** *(de malade)* to be delirious; *(dire n'importe quoi)* to rave; **d. de joie** to be delirious, to be mad with joy; **tu délires!** you're raving! **2** *Fam (s'amuser)* to have a great time, *Am* to have a blast

delirium tremens [delirjɔmtremɛ̃s] NM delirium tremens, *Fam* DTs; **avoir le d.** to have delirium tremens *or Fam* the DTs

délit [deli] NM *Jur* offence, misdemeanour, *Am* misdemeanor; **en flagrant d.** red-handed; *Jur* in flagrante delicto; **prendre qn en flagrant d.** to catch sb red-handed *or* in the act; **pris en flagrant d. d'adultère** caught in flagrante delicto; *Fig* **en flagrant d. de gourmandise/de mensonge/d'ignorance** caught being greedy/lying/showing one's ignorance; **d. politique** political offence; *Fam* **ils l'ont arrêté pour d. de sale gueule** they arrested him because they didn't like the look of him
▸▸**d. d'abus de biens sociaux** misappropriation of corporate funds; **d. civil** tort; **d. de fuite** failure to report an accident; **d. d'initié** insider dealing *or* trading; **d. d'opinion** failure to toe the party line; **d. de presse** violation of the press laws

déliter (se) [sədelite] VPR *(se désintégrer)*, *Fig* to fall apart

délivrance [delivrɑ̃s] NF **1** *(libération)* rescue, release **2** *(soulagement)* relief; **c'est fini! quelle d.!** it's over! what a relief!; **son départ fut une vraie d.** it was a real relief when he left, his departure came as a real relief; **ses aveux lui furent une d.** it was a relief for him to confess; **il attendait la mort comme une d.** he was waiting for death as a release **3** *(de marchandises)* delivery, handing over; *(de certificat, tickets)* issue **4** *(accouchement)* delivery; *(expulsion du placenta)* delivery of the afterbirth; **la d. a été difficile** it was a difficult delivery

délivrer [delivre] VT **1** *(libérer) (captif, otage etc)* to rescue; *(détenu)* to release, to set free; *Fig* to set free *(de* from*)*; **d. qn de ses liens** to free sb from his/her bonds **2** *(soulager)* **d. qn d'un secret trop lourd** to share the burden of a secret with sb; **tu me délivres d'un grand poids** you've taken a weight off my shoulders **3** *(remettre) (marchandises etc)* to deliver, to hand over; *(certificat, ticket)* to issue; *(licence)* to grant **4** *Obst* **d. une femme** *(du placenta)* to deliver a woman of the afterbirth; *(l'accoucher)* to deliver a woman (of a child)
VPR **se délivrer** *(se libérer)* to free oneself; *Fig* **se d. de qn/qch** to get rid of sb/sth; **se d. de ses soucis** to shed one's worries

délocalisation [delɔkalizasjɔ̃] NF *Admin*

(d'entreprise, de production) relocation; *(de capitaux)* expatriation

délocaliser [delɔkalize] VT *Admin* to relocate, to shift; *(capitaux)* to expatriate
VPR **se délocaliser** *(d'une entreprise, d'une usine)* to relocate

délogement [delɔʒmɑ̃] NM *(de locataire)* eviction; *(dans un hôtel)* room change

déloger [delɔʒe] *(conj like* **loger***)* VI **1** to leave (home); **délogez de là!** get out of here! **2** *Belg (découcher)* to sleep out; **il a délogé hier** he didn't come home last night
VT to drive out; *(locataire)* to evict; *(l'ennemi, objet coincé)* to dislodge; **quand il est devant la télé, c'est vraiment difficile de le d.** you just can't shift him when he's in front of the telly

déloquer (se) [sədelɔke] VPR *Fam* to strip off, to get undressed

déloyal, -ale, -aux, -ales [delwajal, -o] ADJ *(ami etc)* disloyal, unfaithful; *(pratique)* unfair; **concurrence déloyale** unfair competition; *Sport* **jeu d.** foul play; *Sport* **coup d.** foul

déloyalement [delwajalmɑ̃] ADV *(agir) (d'un ami)* disloyally; *(d'un concurrent)* unfairly; *(jouer aux cartes)* dishonestly

déloyauté [delwajote] NF *(d'un ami)* disloyalty, treachery; *(d'un concurrent, d'une pratique)* unfairness

Delphes [dɛlf] NFPL Delphi

delta [dɛlta] NM *(lettre grecque)*, *Géog* delta; *Aviat* **aile (en) d.** delta wing

deltaïque [dɛltaik] ADJ *Géog* delta, of a/the delta

deltaplane [dɛltaplan] NM *Sport* hang-glider; **faire du d.** to go hang-gliding

deltoïde [dɛltɔid] ADJ, NM *Anat* deltoid

déluge [delyʒ] NM deluge, flood; *(de pluie)* downpour; *(d'injures)* torrent; *(de larmes)* flood; **elle l'a noyé sous un d. de compliments** she showered *or* overwhelmed him with compliments; *Rel* **le D.** the Flood; **après moi, le d.!** when I'm gone, I don't care what happens!; **cela remonte au d.** it's as old as the hills

déluré [delyre] ADJ *(vif)* sharp, smart; *Péj (provocant)* forward

délurer [delyre] VT *(dégourdir)* **d. qn** to teach sb a thing or two; *Péj* **ses années d'étudiante l'ont un peu trop délurée** she went a bit off the rails when she was a student
VPR **se délurer** *(se dégourdir)* to learn a thing or two; *Péj* to run wild

délustrer [delystre] VT *Tex (étoffe)* to take the shine off

DEM *Anciennement (abrév* **Deutsche Mark***)* DM

démagnétisation [demaɲetizasjɔ̃] NF *Phys* demagnetization

démagnétiser [demaɲetize] VT *Phys* to demagnetize

démago [demago] *Fam* ADJ *(abrév* **démagogique***)* demagogic
N *(abrév* **démagogue***)* demagogue

démagogie [demagɔʒi] NF demagogy, demagoguery

démagogique [demagɔʒik] ADJ demagogic

démagogue [demagɔg] N demagogue
ADJ demagogic, rabble-rousing

démaillage [demɑjaʒ] NM laddering

démailler [demɑje] VT *(tricot)* to unravel; **tes bas sont démaillés** your stockings are laddered, *Am* you have a run in your stockings
VPR **se démailler** *(d'un collant)* to ladder, *Am* to run; **le filet se démaille** the net is torn

démailloter [demajɔte] VT **d. un bébé** to take the swaddling clothes off a baby

demain [dəmɛ̃] ADV tomorrow; **d. soir** to-

morrow evening; **d. en huit** a week tomorrow, *Br* tomorrow week; **à d.!** see you tomorrow!; **remettre un travail à d.** to postpone *or* put off a job till tomorrow; **d'ici d.** between now and tomorrow; **réponds-moi d'ici d.** give me an answer by tomorrow; **le journal de d.** tomorrow's paper; *Fam* **ce n'est pas pour d., ce n'est pas d. la veille** that won't happen for a long time yet; **d. il fera jour** tomorrow is another day; *Fam* **et d. on rase gratis!** pigs might fly!; *Fig* **les parents de d.** tomorrow's parents
NM tomorrow; **tu as d. pour réfléchir** you've got tomorrow to think about it; *Fig* **des demains peu heureux** a not-too-rosy future

démanché [demɑ̃ʃe] ADJ *(outil etc)* without a handle; *(épaule etc)* dislocated
NM *Mus* shift

démanchement [demɑ̃ʃmɑ̃] NM *(d'un outil etc)* removal of the handle; *(de l'épaule etc)* dislocation

démancher [demɑ̃ʃe] VT *(outil etc)* to remove the handle of
VI *Mus* to shift
VPR **se démancher 1** *(d'un outil etc)* to lose its handle **2** *(se déboîter)* **d. l'épaule/le bras** to put one's shoulder/arm out, to dislocate one's shoulder/arm; *Fam* **se d. pour obtenir qch** to move heaven and earth to get sth

demande [dəmɑ̃d] NF **1** *(requête)* request, application, query *(de* for*)*; *Cartes* bid; **faire la d. de qch** to ask for sth; **faire qch à** *ou* **sur la d. de qn** to do sth at sb's request; **faire qch à la** *ou* **sur d.** to do sth on request; **d. (en mariage)** proposal (of marriage), *Vieilli* offer of marriage; **faire sa d. (en mariage)** to propose; **à la d. générale** by popular request; **il faut remplir une d.** you must fill in an application form; **adresser une d.** to apply in writing; **d. d'intervention** request for action; **d. de renseignements** enquiry, request for information
2 *Écon* demand; **l'offre et la d.** supply and demand; **répondre à la d.** to meet demand; **répondre à la d. en qch** to meet the demand for sth; **la d. est en hausse/en baisse** demand is up/down; **d. des consommateurs** consumer demand; **d. déclinante** declining *or* falling demand; **d. dérivée** derived demand; **d. effective** effective demand; **d. élastique** elastic demand; **d. excédentaire** overdemand; **d. globale** global demand, aggregate demand; **d. indésirable** unwholesome demand; **d. du marché** market demand; **d. prévisionnelle** projected demand; **d. soutenue** full demand; **d. surabondante** overfull demand
3 *Jur* **d. en divorce** divorce petition; **d. de dommages-intérêts** claim for damages; **d. principale** main claim; **d. accessoire** related claim; **d. subsidiaire** subsidiary claim; **d. en renvoi** request for referral to another court **4** *(besoin) (de soins, d'affection)* need; **il est perpétuellement dans un état de d. affective** he's always looking for affection **5** *(question)* question, inquiry, enquiry
▸▸**'demandes d'emploi'** *(rubrique)* 'situations wanted'; **d. d'emploi** job application; *(petite annonce)* 'job wanted' advertisement; **faire une d. d'emploi** to apply for a job; **d. de rançon** ransom demand

Il faut noter que le nom anglais **demand** est un faux ami. Il signifie **exigence**.

DEMANDER [dəmɑ̃de]

VT to ask **4** ▪ to ask for **1, 5** ▪ to claim **1** ▪ to apply for **1** ▪ to need **2** ▪ to demand **2, 3** ▪ to want **5**		
VI to ask		
VPR to wonder		

VT **1** *(réclamer, vouloir) (une augmentation,*

l'addition, de l'argent, du travail, des preuves etc) to ask for; **d. qch à qn** to ask sb for sth; **d. un renseignement à qn** to ask sb something, to ask sb for information; **d. à qn de faire qch** to ask sb to do sth; **on nous a demandé nos passeports** we were asked for our passports; **d. à qn son aide/sa protection/un conseil** to ask sb for help/protection/advice; **d. à qn son avis** to ask sb's opinion; **d. la permission/l'autorisation** to ask (for) permission (**de faire qch** to do sth); *Mil* **d. une permission** to ask for or apply for leave; **d. des dommages et intérêts** to claim damages; **d. le divorce** to apply for a divorce; **puis-je vous d. une faveur** ou **un service?** can I ask you a favour?; **d. l'ouverture d'une enquête** to call for an inquiry; **d. un rendez-vous** to request a meeting; *(chez le médecin)* to ask for an appointment; **d. audience** to request an audience; **d. la main de qn** to ask for sb's hand (in marriage); **il a fini par la d. en mariage** he eventually proposed (to her); **combien demandez-vous de l'heure?** how much do you charge an hour?; **combien en demande-t-elle?** how much is she asking for it?; **il ne demande que ça** he'd be only too pleased; *Hum* **que demande le peuple?** what more could I/he/*etc* ask (for)?; **je ne demande qu'une seule chose: qu'on me laisse tranquille** all I ask is to be left alone; **je ne demande qu'une seule chose: qu'il fasse beau** all I ask for is good weather; **je ne demande pas mieux que de vous aider** I'll be only too pleased to help you; **il demande qu'on lui rende justice** he wants justice; **d. la parole** to ask to speak; **je demande la parole!** may I speak!

2 *(nécessiter)* to need, to require; **la situation demande le plus grand tact** the situation needs or requires or calls for tactful handling; **ça demande de gros sacrifices** great sacrifices are called for; **cela demande mûre réflexion** that calls for careful consideration; **le voyage demande trois heures/une semaine** the journey takes three hours/a week; **ce travail demande toute votre attention** the work demands all your attention; **on demande un maçon** builder wanted; **article très demandé** article in great demand

3 *(exiger)* to demand; **d. à qn plus qu'il n'en peut faire** to demand or expect from sb more than he can do; **c'est trop me d.** it's too much to ask of me, it's asking too much; **il ne faut pas lui en d. trop** you mustn't expect too much from him; **d. la lune** to ask for the moon; **d. l'impossible** to ask (for) the impossible

4 *(s'enquérir de)* *(prix, cause, raison)* to ask, to enquire; **d. l'heure, d. l'heure qu'il est** to ask the time; **d. son nom à qn** to ask sb his/her name; **je n'ai pas compris ce qu'il m'a demandé** I didn't understand what he asked me; **d. son chemin à qn** to ask sb the way; **il m'a demandé de tes nouvelles** he asked me how you were; *Fam* **je ne t'ai rien demandé!** I didn't ask for your advice or opinion!; *Fam Hum* **je ne t'ai pas demandé l'heure qu'il est!** mind your own business!; **je vous (le) demande!, je vous demande un peu!** I ask you!

5 *(appeler)* **on vous demande** you're wanted, somebody wants to see you; **on vous demande au téléphone** there is a call for you; **M. Dubois est demandé au téléphone** Mr Dubois is wanted on the telephone; *(annonce)* telephone for Mr Dubois; **un conseiller en peinture est demandé à la caisse no 3** paint consultant to checkout 3, please; **qui demandez-vous?** who do you want to speak to?; **d. un médecin/un prêtre** to ask for a doctor/priest

VI d. à faire qch to ask (permission) to do sth; **il a demandé à sortir** he asked to leave the room; **je demande à parler** may I speak?,

please let me speak; **d. à manger/boire** to ask for something to eat/drink; **je ne demande qu'à rester ici** I would dearly love to stay here; **les suspects ne demandaient qu'à parler** the suspects were only too willing to speak; **il demande à ce qu'on lui rende son argent** he's asking for or he wants his money back; **demande à ce qu'on vienne te chercher** ask someone to come and collect you; **ce vin demande à être bu frais** this wine requires to be drunk chilled; **tu vois, ce n'était pas difficile, il suffisait de d.!** see, it wasn't difficult, you only had to ask!; **il n'y a qu'à d.** you/he/*etc* only have/has to ask; **d. après qn** to ask after or for sb

VPR se demander to wonder, to ask oneself; **c'est ce que je me demande** that's what I'd like to know; **c'est à se d.** ou **on se demande** ou **on peut se d. s'il ne l'a pas fait exprès** it makes you wonder whether he didn't do it on purpose; **je me demande bien pourquoi/ce que/où … ** I really can't think why/what/where …; **des choses comme ça, cela ne se demande pas!** you don't ask that sort of question!

> Il faut noter que le verbe anglais **to demand** est un faux ami. Il signifie **exiger**.

demandeur¹, -deresse [dəmɑ̃dœr, -drɛs] N *Jur* plaintiff; **d. en divorce** petitioner; **d. en appel** appellant

demandeur², -euse [dəmɑ̃dœr, -øz] N **1 d. d'asile** asylum-seeker; **d. d'emploi** job seeker **2** *Com* customer, buyer; **si tu trouves la même robe en solde, je suis demandeuse** if you find the same dress in the sales, I'll take it **3** *Tél* **d. (de la communication)** caller

démangeaison [demɑ̃ʒɛzɔ̃] NF itching; **j'ai une d.** I've got an itch, I'm itching; **j'ai des démangeaisons dans les jambes** my legs itch; *Fig Fam* **une d. de faire qch** a longing or an itching to do sth

démanger [demɑ̃ʒe] VI *(il démangea(it))* to itch; **l'épaule me démange** my shoulder's itching; *Fig* **la main lui** ou **le démangeait** he was itching or dying for a fight; **ça me démange de lui dire ce que je pense** I'm dying or itching to tell him what I think

démantèlement [demɑ̃tɛlmɑ̃] NM *(de fortifications)* demolition, demolishing; *(d'organisation, d'empire)* dismantling, breaking up

démanteler [demɑ̃tle] VT *(je démantèle; je démantèlerai)* *(fortifications etc)* to demolish, to destroy; *(organisation, empire etc)* to dismantle, to break up

démantibuler [demɑ̃tibyle] *Fam* VT *(objet)* to break or smash up; **d. une machine** to smash a machine to pieces

VPR se démantibuler to come to pieces

démaquillage [demakijaʒ] NM removal of make-up; **crème pour le d.** cleansing cream, make-up remover

démaquillant [demakijɑ̃] ADJ lotion/crème **démaquillante** cleansing lotion/cream
NM cleanser

démaquiller [demakije] VT **d. qn** to remove sb's make-up

VPR se démaquiller to remove one's make-up; **se d. les yeux** to remove one's eye make-up

démarcage [demarkaʒ] NM = **démarquage**

démarcatif, -ive [demarkatif, -iv] ADJ **ligne démarcative** line of demarcation

démarcation [demarkasjɔ̃] NF demarcation; **ligne de d.** dividing line, boundary line, demarcation line; *Hist* demarcation line; **c'est sur ce problème que la d. entre les deux partis s'affirme** it is on this problem that the dividing line between the two parties is most evident; **on voit la d. de son fond**

de teint you can see where her foundation stops, *Fam* she's got a tide mark

démarchage [demarʃaʒ] NM *Com (porte-à-porte)* door-to-door selling; *(prospection)* canvassing; **d. à distance** telephone prospecting and selling

démarche [demarʃ] NF **1** *(allure)* gait, step, walk; **d. majestueuse** majestic bearing; **reconnaître qn à sa d.** to recognize sb by his/her walk; **elle avait une d. digne** she moved with dignity **2** *(requête)* step; **faire une d. auprès de qn** to approach sb; **faire les démarches nécessaires pour s'inscrire** to take the necessary steps to enrol; **faire les premières démarches** to take the first steps **3** *Fig (cheminement)* process; **d. intellectuelle** thought process

démarcher [demarʃe] *Com* VI *(faire du porte-à-porte)* to sell door-to-door; **d. pour des calendriers** to sell calendars door-to-door
VT *(prospecter) (clients)* to canvass for

démarcheur, -euse [demarʃœr, -øz] N *Com* **1** *(représentant)* door-to-door salesman/saleswoman **2** *(prospecteur)* canvasser; **d. en publicité** advertisement canvasser

démariage [demarjaʒ] NM *(en horticulture)* thinning out

démarketing [demarketiŋ] NM demarketing

démarquage [demarkaʒ] NM **1** *(de linge, de plat)* removal of the (identification) mark(s) **2** *(plagiat)* copying, plagiarizing **3** *Sport* breaking free from one's opponent

démarque [demark] NF *Com* marking down, markdown; **la d. inconnue** shrinkage

démarqué [demarke] ADJ **1** *Com* marked down **2** *Sport* unmarked

démarquer [demarke] VT **1** *(linge, plat etc)* to remove the identification mark(s) from **2** *Com (marchandises)* to mark down **3** *(livre)* to plagiarize **4** *Sport (partenaire)* to free from a marker
VPR se démarquer *Sport* to break free from one's opponent; *Fig* **un élève qui se démarque des autres** a pupil who stands out or apart from the others

démarrage [demaraʒ] NM **1** *(de moteur etc)* start, starting; *(de voiture etc)* moving off; *Sport (soudain)* spurt; *(d'entreprise)* start-up; *Sport* **faire un d.** to put on a spurt; *Ordinat* **d. automatique** autostart; *Ordinat* **d. à chaud/froid** warm/cold start; **faire un d. en trombe** to shoot off; *Fig* **d. d'une affaire/d'une campagne publicitaire** start of a business/publicity campaign **2** *(d'un navire)* casting off ▸ ▸ *Aut* **d. à l'aide de câbles** jump start; **d. en côte** hill start; **d. à l'embrayage** clutch start; **d. poussé** bump start

démarrer [demare] VI **1** *(d'un train, d'une voiture etc)* to start, to move off; *(d'un conducteur)* to drive away or off; *(d'un coureur)* to put on a spurt; **d. en trombe** *(en voiture)* to shoot off; **d. à froid** to start from cold; *Fig* **son affaire commence à d.** his business is beginning to take off; **j'ai toujours du mal à d. le matin** *(en voiture)* I always have trouble starting in the morning; *Fam Fig* I always have trouble getting started or getting going in the morning **2** *(commencer)* to start; **bien/mal d.** to get off to a good/bad start **3** *(de navire)* to cast off

VT 1 *(voiture, travaux etc)* to start; *Fig (affaire, campagne)* to start (up); *(caméras)* to roll; *Ordinat* to boot (up), to start up; **d. le moteur** *(sens mécanique)* to crank the engine; **d. en remorque** to tow-start; **d. à l'aide des câbles** to jump start **2** *(navire)* to unmoor, to cast off

démarreur [demarœr] NM *Aut* starter (motor); *Ordinat* boot program

démasquer [demaske] VT (enlever le masque de) to unmask; (imposteur, espion) to unmask, to expose; (complot, mensonge) to expose; Fig **d. ses batteries** to show one's hand
VPR **se démasquer** to take off one's mask; Fig to drop the mask

démâtage [demataʒ] NM dismasting

démâter [demate] VI **le voilier a démâté** the yacht lost its mast
VT to dismast

démêlage [demɛlaʒ] NM untangling

démêlant [demɛlɑ̃] ADJ **produit d., crème démêlante** conditioner
NM conditioner

démêlé [demele] NM argument; **avoir un d. avec un collègue** to have an argument or Fml altercation with a colleague; **démêlés (unpleasant) dealings; avoir des démêlés avec la justice** to be in trouble with the law; **il a eu des démêlés avec la police** he's had a few run-ins with the police

démêler [demele] VT (fil, soie etc) to disentangle, to unravel; (cheveux) to untangle, to comb out; Fig **d. un problème/un malentendu** to sort out a problem/clear up a misunderstanding; Fig **avoir qch à d. avec qn** to have sth to clear up or sort out with sb; Fig **on va d. ça ensemble** we'll sort it out together
VPR **se démêler se d. de** to extricate oneself from

démêloir [demɛlwar] NM large-toothed comb

démembrement [demɑ̃brəmɑ̃] NM **1** (d'un empire etc) breaking up, dismemberment; (d'un poulet etc) jointing; (d'une propriété, d'un domaine) dividing up, division **2** Bourse stripping

démembrer [demɑ̃bre] VT (empire) to break up, to dismember; (poulet etc) to cut up, to joint; (royaume, domaine) to divide (up)

déménagement [demenaʒmɑ̃] NM (action) moving (house); (meubles) furniture, things; **c'est pour quand le d.?** when are you/we/etc moving?; **entreprise de d.** removal firm; **camion de d.** furniture orremoval van; **frais de d.** moving expenses orcosts; **votre d. est arrivé** your furniture has arrived; **le d. de ta chambre dans la pièce du fond va prendre du temps** it's going to take some time to move you oryour things into the back room; **le d. de l'entreprise ne s'est pas fait sans mal** the company's move did not go smoothly; **cette entreprise fait une moyenne de six déménagements par semaine** the company does an average of six removals a week; **en sept ans, j'ai fait sept déménagements** I've moved seven times in seven years; **tu veux bien m'aider à faire mon d.?** will you help me move (house)?

déménager [demenaʒe] (je déménageai(s); n. déménageons) VT to move; **qui est-ce qui vous déménage?** who's moving you?, which removal company are you using?; **d. ses meubles** to move house
VI **1** to move; (d'une entreprise) to move, to relocate; (d'un employé) where's he moving to?; Fam **d. à la cloche de bois** to do a moonlight flit; FigFam **il déménage!** he's off his head!, he's round the bend! Fam **allez! déménagez!** scram! get out of here! **2** Fig Fam **moutarde qui déménage** mustard that takes the top of your head off; **musique qui déménage** powerful music

déménageur [demenaʒœr] NM removal man, furniture remover orAm mover

démence [demɑ̃s] NF (folie) insanity, madness, lunacy; Méd **d. précoce** dementia praecox, Fam premature senility; Fam **c'est de la pure d.!** it's sheer madness!, it's insane!

démener (se) [sədemne] VPR (conj like mener) **1** (s'agiter) to thrash about, to throw oneself about, to struggle; **se d. comme un beau diable** (pour échapper) to struggle or fight like a madman; (en dansant) to thrash around; **se d. comme un beau diable pour faire qch** to break one's back to do or doing sth **2** (se dépenser) to exert oneself, to make a great effort; **ils se sont tellement démenés que ...** they exerted themselves to such an extent that ...; **ils avaient beau se d., l'incendie ne s'éteignait pas** despite their tremendous efforts, the fire continued to burn

dément, -ente [demɑ̃, -ɑ̃t] ADJ (fou) mad, insane; Méd demented; Fam **quel monde! c'est d.!** what a crowd! it's unbelievable!; Fam **ce concert était d.** it was a great orterrific concert
N mad or insane person, lunatic; Méd demented person

démenti [demɑ̃ti] NM (flat) denial, contradiction; Journ disclaimer; **donner ou opposer un d. formel à une accusation** to deny an accusation; **publier ou faire paraître un d.** to issue a denial; Journ to publish a disclaimer; **ses actions donnent un d. à ses paroles** his actions belie his words; **ces rumeurs restent sans d.** the rumours have not been denied

démentiel, -ielle [demɑ̃sjɛl] ADJ mad, insane; Fam (idée) mad, insane, crazy; Fam (tenue, prix) wild, wicked

démentir [demɑ̃tir] (conj like mentir) VT to deny; **je démens absolument avoir passé la nuit là-bas** I flatly deny spending the night there; **leur attitude dément complètement leur réputation** their attitude totally belies their reputation; Litt **il a démenti nos espérances** he has not come up to our expectations, he has disappointed us
VPR **se démentir** (cesser) **politesse qui ne se dément jamais** unfailing courtesy; **il a fait preuve d'une attention qui ne s'est jamais démentie** he showed unfailing attention

démerdard, -arde [demɛrdar, -ard] Arg ADJ resourceful; **il n'est vraiment pas d.** he's absolutely hopeless oruseless
N resourceful person; **c'est un d.** he's pretty sharp, he's a smart cookie

démerde [demɛrd] NF Fam **dans ce pays, tout marche à la d.** you have to use your wits to get anything done in this country

démerder (se) [sədemɛrde] VPR très Fam **1** (s'en sortir) to get out of the shit; **tu peux te d.?** can you cope ormanage?
2 (se débrouiller) to cope, to manage, to get by; **elle est assez grande pour se d. seule** she's old enough to take care of orlook after herself; **tu ne voulais pas que je t'aide, maintenant démerde-toi!** you didn't want me to help you, so you can manage on your own now!; **elle se démerde pas mal en cuisine/tennis** she's not a bad cook/tennis player; **elle se démerde pas mal en anglais** she gets by quite well in English; **la prochaine fois, tu te démerderas mieux et tu auras un billet à meilleur prix** you'll manage things better next time, you'll get a cheaper ticket; **se d. pour obtenir qch** to wangle sth; **je sais pas comment il se démerde, il casse tout ce qu'il touche** I don't know how he does it, he breaks everything he lays his hands on
3 (se dépêcher) to get a move on, Am to get it in gear

démerdeur, -euse [demɛrdœr, -øz] ADJ, N Arg = **démerdard**

démérite [demerit] NM Litt **je ne vois pas où est mon d.** I don't see how I'm at fault; **son d. vient du fait qu'elle n'a pas fait ce qu'elle avait promis** she's at fault because she didn't do what she promised; **faire à qn un d. de qch** to reproach sb for sth

démériter [demerite] VI to be at fault; **je ne vois pas en quoi il a démérité** I don't see how he is at fault; **d. auprès de qn** to come down in sb's estimation

démesure [deməzyr] NF disproportion, excessiveness

démesuré [deməzyre] ADJ (mains, jardin) huge, enormous; (orgueil) excessive, Fml inordinate; (ambition) excessive, Fml inordinate, unbounded; **il est d'une taille démesurée** he's enormously tall; **il a des mains démesurées par rapport à ses bras** his hands are out of proportion to his arms

démesurément [deməzyremɑ̃] ADV (haut) enormously, Fml inordinately; (augmenter ses prix) excessively

démettre¹ [demɛtr] (conj like mettre) VT (articulation) to dislocate
VPR **se démettre se d. l'épaule/le genou** to dislocate one's shoulder/knee, to put one's shoulder/knee out

démettre² VT **1** (renvoyer) **d. qn de ses fonctions** to deprive sb of (his/her) office, to remove sb from office or from his/her post **2** Jur (débouter) **d. qn de son appel** to dismiss sb's appeal
VPR **se démettre** (démissionner) to resign; **se d. de ses fonctions** to resign office, to resign from one's job

demeurant (au) [odəmœrɑ̃] ADV **il n'est pas très vif, mais est bien gentil au d.** he's not very bright, but he's very nice all the same orfor all that; **je ne vous donne pas mon avis, au d., je ne suis pas concerné** I'm not telling you what I think, after all, it's none of my business

demeure [dəmœr] NF **1** (résidence) (place of) residence; **une belle d.** a beautiful home, Fml, Litt a fine residence; **dernière d.** last resting place **2** **il est ici à d.** he's here for good or to stay or permanently; Jur **meuble à d.** fixture **3** Jur **mettre qn en d. de payer** to give sb notice to pay; **mise en d.** formal notice, summons; Fig **je vous mets en d. de le faire immédiatement** I'm warning you that I want it done immediately **4** **il y a péril en la d.** you/I/he/etc must act immediately; **il n'y a pas péril en la d.** there's no great rush

demeuré, -ée [dəmœre] ADJ mentally retarded, Péj halfwitted; Fam **il est complètement d., ce mec** the guy's a complete halfwit
N mentally retarded person, Péj halfwit

demeurer [dəmœre] VI **1** (conj with être) (rester) to remain; **je demeure convaincu que ...** I remain convinced that ...; **d. fidèle à qn** to stay faithful to sb; **l'affaire n'en demeurera pas là** the matter won't rest there; **demeurons-en là** let's leave it at that; **il ne pouvait pas d. en place** he couldn't keep still; **elle demeurait assise à nous écouter** she sat listening to us; Litt **je suis demeuré des heures à t'attendre** I waited hours for you; Litt **il est demeuré des mois sans nouvelles** he had no news for months; Fml **l'affaire lui est demeurée de sa famille** he inherited the business from his family **2** (conj with avoir) (habiter) to live, Fml to reside; **d. à la campagne** to live in the country; **il demeure rue de Rivoli** he lives in orAm on the rue de Rivoli

demi, -ie [dəmi] ADJ **1** (après un nom) half; **deux heures et demie** (durée) two and a half hours; (moment) half past two; **un litre/kilo/centimètre et d.** a litre/kilo/centimetre and a half; **il gagne trois fois et demie ce que je gagne** he earns three and a half times as much as I do **2** (avant un nom ou un adjectif) half; **un d.-congé** a half-holiday; **une d.-cuillère de sucre** half a teaspoon of sugar, a half-teaspoon of sugar; **d.-cuit** half cooked
NM **1** (moitié) half; **deux plus un d.** two plus a half **2** (bière) **un d.** ≃ half a pint, a half **3** Ftbl

les demis the halfbacks; *Rugby* **d. de mêlée** scrum half; **d. d'ouverture** stand-off (half), fly half **4** *Suisse* (*vin*) = half a litre of wine
NF demie half hour; **il est la demie** it's half past; **à la demie** at half past
ADV half; **d. plein** half full; **à d.** half; **à d. mort** half dead; **à d. transparent** semi-transparent; **faire les choses à d.** to do things by halves; **croire qn à d.** to half believe sb; **ouvre la fenêtre à d.** open the window half way
NOTE *in the following compounds, unless otherwise stated,* demi *is inv and the second component takes the plural*

demi-arbre NM half-shaft
demiard [dəmjar] NM *Can* half pint
demi-arrière NM *Ftbl* halfback
demi-bas NM knee-length sock; (*pour femmes*) popsock
demi-botte NF half boot
demi-bouteille NF half bottle
demi-canton [dəmikātɔ̃] NM *Suisse* = state of the Swiss confederation which is one half of a divided canton
demi-centre NM *Ftbl* centre half
demi-cercle NM semicircle, half-circle; **en d.** in a semicircle
demi-circulaire ADJ semicircular
demi-clef NF half hitch
demi-deuil NM half mourning
demi-dieu NM demigod
demi-douzaine NF half dozen; **une d. d'œufs** half a dozen eggs, a half-dozen eggs; **une d. de fois** half a dozen times
demi-droite NF *Géom* semi-infinite line, half-line
demi-écrémé ADJ semi-skimmed
demi-fin ADJ **1** (*petits pois, haricots etc*) medium **2** (*or*) twelve-carat
NM twelve-carat gold; **bracelet en d.** twelve-carat bracelet
demi-finale NF *Sport* semifinal
demi-finaliste N *Sport* semifinalist
demi-fond NM INV *Sport* (**course de**) **d.** middle distance race
demi-frère NM half-brother
demi-gros NM retail wholesale; (**commerce de**) **d.** cash and carry
demi-grossiste N cash-and-carry merchant
demi-heure [dəmijœr] NF **une d.** half an hour; **deux demi-heures** two half-hours; **de d. en d., toutes les demi-heures** every half-hour
demi-jour NM half-light; (*crépuscule*) twilight, dusk
demi-journée NF half a day; (*de travail, de congé*) half day; **faire des demi-journées** to work half days; **j'ai pris ma d.** I took a half day
démilitarisation [demilitarizasjɔ̃] NF demilitarization
démilitariser [demilitarize] VT to demilitarize
demi-litre NM half litre *or Am* liter; **un d. de vin** half a litre *or* a half litre of wine
demi-longueur NF *Sport* **une d.** half a length, a half-length
demi-lune NF half-moon; (*fortification*) demi-lune
ADJ INV semicircular
demi-mal, *pl* **demi-maux** NM **il n'y a que** *ou* **ce n'est que d.** it could have been worse
demi-mesure NF **1** (*compromis*) half measure; **avec elle, il n'y a jamais de d.** there are never any half measures with her **2** (*pour chaussures etc*) half-size
demi-mondain, -aine ADJ belonging to the demi-monde *or* fringes of society
NF demi-mondaine demi-mondaine

demi-monde NM demi-monde, fringes of society
demi-mort ADJ half dead
demi-mot (à) [ad(ə)mimo] ADV **comprendre à d.** to (know how to) take a hint; **il a compris à d.** he took the hint; **nous nous comprenons à d.** we don't have to spell everything out (to each other)
déminage [deminaʒ] NM mine clearance; *Naut* minesweeping
déminer [demine] VT to clear of mines
déminéralisation [demineralizasjɔ̃] NF demineralization
déminéraliser [demineralize] VT to demineralize
VPR se déminéraliser to become demineralized
démineur [deminœr] NM (*personne*) bomb disposal expert; (*navire*) minesweeper
demi-pause NF *Mus* minim rest, *Am* half-note rest
demi-pension NF (*à l'hôtel*) half board, *Am* American plan; **sept jours en d.** seven days' half board; *Scol* **mon fils est en d.** my son is a day boarder
demi-pensionnaire N *Scol* day boarder
demi-place NF (*en voyage*) half-fare; (*au théâtre etc*) half-price ticket
demi-pointe NF (*position*) demi-point; (**chausson de**) **d.** demi-point shoe
demi-portion NF *Fam Péj* weed; **eh toi, la d., viens ici!** come here, titch!
demi-produit NM *Écon* semi-finished product
demi-quart NM **1** (*de compas*) half point **2** (*mesure*) ≃ two ounces
demi-queue ADJ, NM (**piano**) **d.** baby grand (piano)
demi-reliure NF quarter-binding; **d. à (petits) coins** half-binding
démis [demi] ADJ (*épaule*) dislocated
demi-saison NF between season, mid season; **vêtements (de) d.** spring/autumn clothes
demi-salaire NM half-pay
demi-sang NM INV halfbred (horse)
demi-sel ADJ INV (*beurre etc*) slightly salted
NM INV 1 (*fromage*) (slightly salted) cream cheese **2** *Fam* (*souteneur*) small-time pimp; (*voyou*) small time gangster
demi-sœur NF half-sister
demi-solde NF *Mil* half-pay; **en d.** on half-pay
NM INV half-pay officer
demi-sommeil NM drowsiness, somnolence
demi-soupir NM *Mus* quaver rest, *Am* eighth-note rest
démission [demisjɔ̃] NF **1** (*au travail*) resignation; **donner sa d.** to hand in *or Fml* tender one's resignation, to resign; *Fig* to give up **2** *Fig* (*abandon*) renunciation; **la d. du père** the father's abdication of his responsibilities
démissionnaire [demisjɔnɛr] ADJ who has resigned; *Fig* **père/mère d.** father/mother who has abdicated his/her responsibilities
démissionner [demisjɔne] VI to resign (**de** from); *Fig* **je démissionne!** I give up!
VT *Fam* to sack
demi-tarif NM half price; **billet d.** (*transports*) half-fare (ticket); *Théâtre, Cin* half-price ticket
demi-teinte NF *Beaux-Arts, Phot* half-tone; **en d.** half-tone; *Fig* **il ne fait pas dans la d.** there are no half measures with him
demi-ton NM *Mus* semitone
demi-tonneau NM *Aviat* half roll

demi-tour NM half-turn; *Mil* about-turn; *Aut* U-turn; *Aut* **d. en trois temps** three-point turn; **un d. de clé** a half-turn of the key; **faire d.** to turn and go back
démiurge [demjyrʒ] NM demiurge
demi-voix (à) [ad(ə)mivwa] ADV in an undertone, under one's breath
demi-volée NF *Tennis* half volley
démo [demo] NF (*abrév* **démonstration**) demo
démobilisateur, -trice [demɔbilizatœr, -tris] ADJ (*paroles, actions*) demotivating, discouraging
démobilisation [demɔbilizasjɔ̃] NF **1** (*de troupes*) demobilization, *Fam* demob **2** (*désintérêt*) apathy, lack of interest
démobiliser [demɔbilize] VT **1** (*troupes*) to demobilize, *Fam* to demob **2** (*décourager*) to demotivate, to discourage; **cette campagne de presse a beaucoup contribué à d. les militants** the press campaign had a very demotivating effect on the militants
VPR se démobiliser to become apathetic *or* discouraged
démocrate [demɔkrat] ADJ democratic
N democrat
démocrate-chrétien, -ienne, *pl* **démocrates-chrétiens, -iennes** ADJ, N *Pol* Christian Democrat
démocratie [demɔkrasi] NF democracy; *Fam* **on est en d., après tout!** it's a free country!; **d. directe** direct democracy; **d. participative** participatory democracy; **d. populaire** people's democracy; **d. représentative** representative democracy
démocratique [demɔkratik] ADJ democratic
démocratiquement [demɔkratikmɑ̃] ADV democratically
démocratisation [demɔkratizasjɔ̃] NF democratization
démocratiser [demɔkratize] VT to democratize
VPR se démocratiser to become (more) democratic
démodé [demɔde] ADJ (*personne, manières*) old-fashioned; (*vêtement*) old-fashioned, out-of-date, out-of-fashion; (*équipement*) old-fashioned, out-of-date; (*idée, théorie*) old-fashioned, out-of-date, outmoded
démoder (se) [sədemɔde] VPR (*de vêtements etc*) to go out of fashion, to become old-fashioned
demodex [demɔdɛks] NM demodex, follicle mite
démodulation [demɔdylasjɔ̃] NF demodulation
démographe [demɔgraf] N demographer
démographie [demɔgrafi] NF demography
démographique [demɔgrafik] ADJ demographic; **statistiques démographiques** demographics; **poussée d.** population growth
demoiselle [dəmwazɛl] NF **1** (*femme célibataire*) single *or* unmarried woman; *Vieilli, Admin* spinster; **les demoiselles Dupin** the Misses Dupin; **c'est une vieille d.** she never married **2** (*jeune fille, employée*) young lady; **les demoiselles du téléphone** the young ladies on the switchboard **3** (*insecte*) dragonfly; **d. (de Numidie)** demoiselle (crane), Numidian crane **4** *Tech* paving beetle
▸▸ **d. de compagnie** lady's companion; **d. d'honneur** (*d'une souveraine*) lady-in-waiting, *Vieilli* maid of honour; (*d'une mariée*) bridesmaid
démolir [demɔlir] VT **1** (*maison, immeuble, quartier etc*) to demolish, to pull down; (*navire*) to break up; (*voiture, jouet etc*) to demo-

lish, to wreck, to smash up; **d. une porte à coups de pied** to kick a door down

2 *Fig (argument, théorie, adversaire, concurrent etc)* to demolish; *(réputation)* to ruin; *(gouvernement, autorité etc)* to undermine; *(auteur, cinéaste, roman, film)* to criticize severely, *Fam* to slate

3 *Fam (battre)* to beat up, to bash about; *(fatiguer)* to tire; **je vais lui d. le portrait!** I'll smash his face in!; **il s'est fait d.** he got beaten up; **cette mauvaise grippe m'a démoli** that bad bout of flu laid me low *or* put me flat on my back; **tout ce travail l'a démolie** she's exhausted *or* shattered after all that work; **d. le foie de qn** *(de l'alcool)* to play havoc with *or* ruin sb's liver; **les piments m'ont démoli l'estomac** those chillis are playing havoc *or* *Fam* merry hell with my stomach

démolissage [demɔlisaʒ] NM *(d'un auteur etc)* severe criticism, *Fam* slating; *(d'une théorie, d'un argument)* demolition

démolisseur, -euse [demɔlisœr, -øz] N **1** *(de bâtiments)* demolition contractor; *(de bateaux)* shipbreaker **2** *Fig (d'un argument etc)* demolisher, destroyer

démolition [demɔlisjɔ̃] NF **1** *(d'une structure)* demolition, pulling down; **chantier de d.** demolition yard **2** *Fig (d'une théorie)* demolition **3 démolitions** *(matériaux)* debris, rubble

démon [demɔ̃] NM **1** demon, devil, fiend; **le d.** *(Satan)* the Devil; **cette femme est un d.** that woman's a (she-)devil; **cet enfant est un petit d.** that child is a little devil; **le d. de la jalousie** the demon of jealousy, the green-eyed monster; **d. de midi** *(d'un homme)* male menopause, midlife crisis; *(d'une femme)* midlife crisis **2** *(génie, esprit etc)* (good/evil) genius; *Myth* daemon **3** *Can* **être en d.** to be furious, to be mad

démonétisation [demɔnetizasjɔ̃] NF **1** *Fin (d'argent)* demonetization, withdrawal from circulation **2** *Fig (d'une personne)* discrediting; **sa d. au sein de l'entreprise a été rapide** he quickly became discredited throughout the company; **pour accélérer sa d.** to speed up the process of discrediting him

démonétiser [demɔnetize] VT **1** *Fin* to demonetize, to withdraw from circulation **2** *Fig (personne)* to discredit

démoniaque [demɔnjak] ADJ demonic, possessed by the devil; *Fig (personne, rire)* fiendish

N person possessed by the devil

démonstrateur, -trice [demɔ̃stratœr, -tris] N demonstrator

démonstratif, -ive [demɔ̃stratif, -iv] ADJ **1** *(convaincant)* (logically) conclusive **2** *(personne)* demonstrative; **peu d.** undemonstrative **3** *Gram* demonstrative

NM *Gram* demonstrative SEE GRAMMAR A30–1; B14–15

démonstration [demɔ̃strasjɔ̃] NF **1** *(preuve)* *(de théorème etc)* demonstration, proof; **d. par l'absurde** reductio ad absurdum; **faire la d. de qch** to demonstrate *or* prove sth **2** *Com (d'article)* demonstration; **je ne peux pas vous vendre cet appareil, il est en d.** I can't sell you this appliance, it's a demonstration model; **d. sur le lieu de vente** instore demonstration; *Boxe* **assaut de d.** sparring match; *Mus* **cassette de d.** demo (tape); **appareil de d.** demonstration model; **est-ce que vous pouvez me faire la d. de cette machine à laver?** could you give me a demonstration of this washing machine? **3** *(manifestation)* *(de tendresse, joie etc)* demonstration; **faire de grandes démonstrations d'amitié** to make a great show of friendship; *Mil* **d. de force** display *or* show of force; **d. navale** naval display

démontable [demɔ̃tabl] ADJ *(machine, armoire etc)* that can be dismantled

démontage [demɔ̃taʒ] NM dismantling, taking to pieces, taking apart

démonté [demɔ̃te] ADJ **1** *(cavalier)* thrown; *Fig (déconcerté)* disconcerted, *Fam* thrown; *(troublé)* upset **2** *(mécanisme etc)* dismantled, taken to pieces, taken apart **3** *(mer)* stormy, raging

démonte-pneu, pl **démonte-pneus** [demɔ̃tpnø] NM tyre *or* Am tire lever

démonter [demɔ̃te] VT **1** *(appareil, moteur, armoire etc)* to dismantle, to take to pieces, to take apart; *(tente)* to dismantle, to take down; *(porte)* to remove from its hinges; *(pneu)* to remove; *(décor)* to strike **2** *(cavalier)* to throw (off), to unseat **3** *(déconcerter)* to disconcert, *Fam* to throw; *(troubler)* to upset; **la nouvelle m'a démonté** I was greatly upset *or* put out by the news; **ça me démonte de le voir dans un tel état** it upsets me to see him in such a state; **elle est complètement démontée depuis qu'elle sait qu'il va partir** she's been in a dreadful state since she found out that he was leaving; **se laisser d.** to get upset *or* flustered, to be thrown **4** *Can (décourager)* to discourage

VPR **se démonter 1** *(d'un mécanisme)* to come apart, to dismantle **2** *Fam* **elle ne se démonte pas pour si peu** she's not so easily put out *or* thrown

démontrable [demɔ̃trabl] ADJ demonstrable, provable

démontrer [demɔ̃tre] VT *(théorème, vérité)* to demonstrate; **d. qu'il est nécessaire de faire qch** to show *or* demonstrate *or* prove that it is necessary to do sth; *Fam* **d. qch par A + B** to prove sth conclusively

démoralisant [demɔralizɑ̃] ADJ demoralizing, disheartening

démoralisateur, -trice [demɔralizatœr, -tris] ADJ demoralizing, disheartening

démoralisation [demɔralizasjɔ̃] NF demoralization

démoralisé [demɔralize] ADJ **il était complètement d.** he was completely demoralized *or* downcast

démoraliser [demɔralize] VT to demoralize, to dishearten

VPR **se démoraliser** to become demoralized, to lose heart

démordre [demɔrdr] VI **ne pas d. de ses opinions** to stand by *or* stick to one's opinions; **elle ne veut pas en d.** she won't give up, she's sticking to her guns; **quand il a une idée, il n'en démord jamais** once he gets an idea in his head, you can't shift him; **ça va être difficile de le faire d. de sa décision** it's going to be difficult to get him to change his mind

démotivation [demɔtivasjɔ̃] NF demotivation; **il ne faut pas laisser s'installer la d. au sein de l'équipe** we mustn't let the team become demotivated

démotiver [demɔtive] VT to demotivate; **ne te laisse pas d. par ses arguments stupides** don't let his stupid arguments put you off

démoulage [demulaʒ] NM *(d'un moulage)* removal from the mould *or* Am mold; *Culin* turning out

démouler [demule] VT *(moulage)* to remove from the mould *or* Am mold; *Culin* to turn out

démoustication [demustikasjɔ̃] NF clearing of mosquitoes; **il faut procéder à la d. de la région** the region must be cleared of mosquitoes

démoustiquer [demustike] VT to clear mosquitoes from

démultiplicateur, -trice [demyltiplikatœr, -tris] *Tech* ADJ *(dispositif)* reducing, reduc-tion

NM reduction system; **d. de vitesse** motor reduction unit

démultiplication [demyltiplikasjɔ̃] NF *Tech* **1** *(de voiture, machine)* gearing down, (gear) reduction **2** *(de vitesses)* reduction ratio

démultiplier [demyltiplije] VT *Tech (voiture, machine)* to gear down; *(de boîte de vitesses)* to reduce the gear ratio of

démuni [demyni] ADJ penniless; **d. de vêtements/papiers d'identité** without any clothes/identification; **d. d'argent** without any money, penniless; **d. de tout** destitute; **d. d'intérêt/d'intelligence/de talent** devoid of interest/intelligence/talent; *Com* **être a. de qch** to be out of sth, to be sold out of sth

démunir [demynir] VT to deprive

VPR **se démunir** to leave oneself short; **se d. de qch** to part with sth

démuseler [demyzle] VT (**je démuselle; je démusellerai**) *(chien)* to unmuzzle; *Fig* **d. la presse** to ungag the press

démystifiant [demistifjɑ̃] ADJ *(histoire, étude etc)* which demystifies; **son film sur Mozart est tout à fait d.** his film gives us an insight into the real Mozart

démystificateur, -trice [demistifikatœr, -tris] ADJ *(histoire, étude etc)* which demystifies

N demystifier

démystification [demistifikasjɔ̃] NF demystification

démystifier [demistifje] VT *(impf, pr sub* NF. **démystifiions, v. démystifiiez**) to demystify

démythification [demitifikasjɔ̃] NF demythologization; **on assiste à la d. de l'ordinateur** computers are no longer regarded with awe *or* are losing their mystique

démythifier [demitifje] VT to demythologize; *(ordinateur)* to remove the mystique surrounding

dénatalité [denatalite] NF fall in the birth rate

dénationalisation [denasjɔnalizasjɔ̃] NF denationalization

dénationaliser [denasjɔnalize] VT to denationalize

dénatter [denate] VT *(cheveux)* to unplait

dénaturalisation [denatyralizasjɔ̃] NF denaturalization

dénaturaliser [denatyralize] VT to denaturalize

dénaturant [denatyrɑ̃] *Chimie* ADJ denaturing

NM denaturant, denaturing agent

dénaturation [denatyrasjɔ̃] NF *Chimie* denaturing

dénaturé [denatyre] ADJ **1** *(dépravé)* *(parents)* unnatural; *(goût)* unnatural, perverted **2** *Chimie (transformé)* denatured

dénaturer [denatyre] VT *(mots)* to misrepresent, to distort; *(actions)* to misrepresent; *Chimie (alcool etc)* to denature; **d. les faits** to distort the facts; **d. les paroles de qn** to misrepresent what sb has said

dénazification [denazifikasjɔ̃] NF denazification

dénazifier [denazifje] VT to denazify

dénégateur, -trice [denegatœr, -tris] N denier

dénégation [denegasjɔ̃] NF denial

déneigement [denɛʒmɑ̃] NM snow clearance *or* removal

déneiger [denɛʒe] VT to clear (away) *or* remove snow from

déneigeuse [denɛʒøz] NF *Can* snowblower

dengue [dɛg] NF *Méd* dengue fever

déni [deni] NM *Jur* denial, refusal; **d. de justice** denial of justice

déniaiser [denjeze] **VT 1** (dégourdir) **d. qn** to teach sb a thing or two, to smarten or Fam wise sb up **2** Fam (faire perdre sa virginité à) **c'est lui qui l'a déniaisée** he was her first **VPR se déniaiser** (se dégourdir) to smarten up, to get smart

dénicher [denife] **VT 1** Fam (trouver) (objet) to find, to unearth; (personne) to find, to track down; **nous avons déniché une maison superbe** we've found a beautiful house; **on a déniché un restaurant très chouette** we've found or Fam sussed out a great restaurant; **elle est allée d. l'homme de sa vie au Canada** she went to Canada to find the man of her dreams **2** (oiseau, œufs) to take out of the nest **3** (animal) to drive out of hiding **VI** (d'un oiseau) to leave the nest

dénicheur, -euse [denifœr, -øz] **N 1** Fig (d'objets) searcher; **d. de curiosités/d'antiquités** curio/antique hunter; **c'est un d. de talents** he's good at spotting talent **2** (d'oiseaux) bird nester

dénicotinisation [denikɔtinizasjɔ̃] **NF** reduction of nicotine

dénicotiniser [denikɔtinize] **VT** to reduce the amount of nicotine in; **du tabac dénicotinisé** low nicotine tobacco

denier [dənje] **NM 1** Antiq denarius; Hist denier; **je l'ai payé de mes deniers** I paid for it with my own money; **payer jusqu'au dernier d.** to pay to the last farthing; **les deniers publics** public money or funds; Cathol **d. du culte** church offering (given privately to parish priest) **2** (de bas) denier; **bas de 30 deniers** 30-denier stockings

dénier [denje] **VT 1** (crime etc) to deny; (responsabilité) to deny, to disclaim **2 d. qch à qn** to refuse or deny sb sth; **d. à qn le droit de faire qch** to deny sb the right to do sth

dénigrant [denigrɑ̃] **ADJ** disparaging, denigrating

dénigrement [denigrəmɑ̃] **NM** disparagement, denigration

dénigrer [denigre] **VT** to disparage, to denigrate

dénivelé [denivle] **ADJ** (surface) uneven **NM** difference or variation in level or height

dénivelée [denivle] **NF** difference or variation in level or height

déniveler [denivle] **VT** (conj like niveler) to make uneven

dénivellation [denivɛlasjɔ̃] **NF**, **dénivellement** [denivɛlmɑ̃] **NM 1** (écart) difference in level or height; **d. d'une route** gradients or ups and downs of a road **2** (action) making uneven

dénombrable [denɔ̃brabl] **ADJ** countable
VOIR GRAMMAIRE A9–12

dénombrement [denɔ̃brəmɑ̃] **NM** counting, Fml enumeration; (de la population) census; Méd **d. des hématies** blood count

dénombrer [denɔ̃bre] **VT** to count, Fml to enumerate; (population) to take a census of

dénominateur [denɔminatœr] **NM** Math denominator; **d. commun** common denominator; **plus petit d. commun** lowest common denominator

dénominatif, -ive [denɔminatif, -iv] **ADJ, NM** Ling denominative

dénomination [denɔminasjɔ̃] **NF** name, denomination, designation; **comment a été décidée la nouvelle d. de certaines régions?** how were the new names for certain regions decided on?; Pharm **d. commune** generic name; **d. commerciale** (de produit) trade name; **d. sociale** company name

dénommer [denɔme] **VT** to name; parfois Péj **un dénommé Charles** someone by the name of Charles; **est-ce que le dénommé Laurent va …?** is that man/boy Laurent going to …?; **le dénommé Jacques Duval est prié de se rendre à la caisse no. 3** would Jacques Duval go to checkout 3; **ci-après dénommé …** hereinafter referred to as …

dénoncer [denɔ̃se] (**je dénonçai(s)**; n. dénonçons) **VT 1** (à la police) (personne) to denounce, to inform against; (crime etc) to expose; **d. qn à la police** to denounce sb to the police; **c'est elle qui a dénoncé son frère à ses parents** it was she who gave her brother away or told on her brother to her parents **2** (protester contre) (traité, abus de pouvoir, la pollution etc) to denounce; **d. un contrat** to terminate a contract, to cancel a contract **3** (révéler) to indicate, to reveal; **son attitude dénonce sa méfiance des autres** his attitude betrays his mistrust of others **VPR se dénoncer** to give oneself up

dénonciateur, -trice [denɔ̃sjatœr, -tris] **N** (d'une personne) informer; **il est le d. de ces crimes** he exposed the crimes **ADJ** (lettre) of denunciation, accusing

dénonciation [denɔ̃sjasjɔ̃] **NF** denunciation

dénotation [denɔtasjɔ̃] **NF** denotation

dénoter [denɔte] **VT** to denote, to show, to indicate

dénouement [denumɑ̃] **NM** (d'un événement) result, outcome; (d'une difficulté) solution; (d'une intrigue, d'une histoire) ending; Théâtre dénouement

dénouer [denwe] **VT** (nœud) to untie, to undo, to loosen; **d. ses cheveux** to undo or let down one's hair; **d. une intrigue** to unravel a plot **VPR se dénouer** (d'un nœud) to come undone; (de cheveux) to come down; (d'un mystère) to be solved; (d'une histoire, d'une enquête) to end; **sa langue se dénoue** he's finding his tongue

dénoyautage [denwajotaʒ] **NM** (d'un fruit) stoning, Am pitting; Fig Écon removal of political appointees from the board

dénoyauter [denwajote] **VT** (fruit) to stone, Am to pit; Fig Écon **d. une entreprise** to remove political appointees from the board of a company

dénoyauteur [denwajotœr] **NM** (machine) stoner

denrée [dɑ̃re] **NF** (pour l'homme) foodstuff; (pour le bétail) feed; **denrées alimentaires** food products, foodstuffs; **denrées périssables** perishable goods; **denrées de consommation courante** staple foods, staples; Fig **la patience est une d. rare** patience is a rare commodity

dense [dɑ̃s] **ADJ 1** Phys dense **2** (foule) dense; (brouillard, forêt) dense, thick; (style) concise, condensed, dense

densité [dɑ̃site] **NF 1** Phys density; **d. moyenne** mean specific weight; **flacon à d.** specific gravity flask **2** (de population etc) density; Ordinat **à double d.** double-density; Ordinat **d. quadruple** quad density; **haute d.** high density **3** Phot (de négatif) density

dent [dɑ̃] **NF 1** Anat tooth; **d. du fond/de devant/du haut/du bas** back/front/top/bottom tooth; **sans dents** toothless; **percer ou faire ses dents** (d'un enfant) to cut one's teeth, to be teething; **se faire les dents sur qch** (d'un chat, d'un enfant) to cut one's teeth on sth; Fig **se faire les dents sur qn** to take it out on sb; **mal ou rage de dents** toothache; **coup de d.** bite; Fig Fam **avoir la d.** to be hungry; **manger/rire à belles dents** to eat hungrily or with relish/laugh heartily; **manger du bout des dents** to pick at one's food; **rire du bout des dents** to force a laugh; **avoir les dents longues** (être ambitieux) to be ambitious, Fam to be hungry; **avoir la d. dure** to have a sharp tongue; **montrer les dents** to show one's teeth; aussi Fig **serrer les dents** to grit one's teeth; **ne pas desserrer les dents** not to open one's mouth; **avoir ou conserver ou garder une d. contre qn** to have a grudge against sb; **ils n'ont rien à se mettre sous la d.** they don't have a bite to eat; **parler entre ses dents** to mumble, to mutter; **être sur les dents** (épuisé) to be worn out; (surmené) to be overworked

2 (de peigne, scie) tooth; (de roue) cog; (de fourchette) prong; (de montagne) (jagged) peak; (de timbre) perforation; **en dents de scie** serrated, jagged; Fig (évolution, progrès) uneven; **roue à dents** cogged wheel **▸▸ d. d'éléphant** elephant's tusk; **d. de lait** milk tooth, first tooth; **d. de sagesse** wisdom tooth

dentaire [dɑ̃tɛr] **ADJ** Anat (hygiène, plaque, pulpe etc) dental; **l'art d.** dentistry

dental, -ale, -aux, -ales [dɑ̃tal, -o] Ling **ADJ** (consonne) dental **NF dentale** dental consonant

dent-de-lion, pl **dents-de-lion** [dɑ̃d(ə)ljɔ̃] **NF** dandelion

dent-de-loup, pl **dents-de-loup** [dɑ̃dlu] **NF** Aut ratchet tooth, catch

denté [dɑ̃te] **ADJ** Tech (couronne, anneau) cogged, toothed; (feuille) jagged, Spéc dentate; **roue dentée** cogwheel

dentelé [dɑ̃tle] **ADJ** (rivage) jagged, indented; (bord) jagged; (feuille) serrated; (timbre) perforated

denteler [dɑ̃tle] **VT** (je dentelle; je dentellerai) to notch, to jag, to indent; (timbre) to perforate

dentelle [dɑ̃tɛl] **NF 1** (tissu) lace; **d. aux fuseaux** pillow lace; **d. à l'aiguille ou au point** point lace; **robe de ou en d.** lace dress; **des dentelles de papier** paper doilies; **crêpe d.** very thin pancake, crêpe; Fig **ne pas faire dans la d.** (y aller carrément) not to mince one's words; (manquer de finesse) to be clumsy; **ça n'est pas de la d.** it's nothing fancy **2** Archit = wrought ironwork that has the appearance of lace, Am ≃ gingerbread

dentellerie [dɑ̃tɛlri] **NF** lacemaking

dentellier, -ière [dɑ̃təlje, -jɛr] **ADJ** (industrie etc) lace(making) **N** lacemaker **NF dentellière** (machine) lacemaking machine

dentelure [dɑ̃tlyr] **NF** (d'un rivage) indentation; (d'une montagne) jagged summit; (d'une feuille) serration; (d'un timbre) perforation

dentier [dɑ̃tje] **NM** set of false teeth, dentures

dentifrice [dɑ̃tifris] **NM** toothpaste, Vieilli toothpowder **ADJ pâte d.** toothpaste; **eau d.** mouthwash; **poudre d.** toothpowder

dentine [dɑ̃tin] **NF** Anat dentine

dentiste [dɑ̃tist] **N** dentist

dentition [dɑ̃tisjɔ̃] **NF 1** (croissance) cutting of teeth, teething; **d. définitive ou permanente** permanent teeth **2** (arrangement) arrangement of the teeth, Spéc dentition

denture [dɑ̃tyr] **NF 1** (dents) set of teeth **2** Tech teeth, cogs, gearing; (du rotor) rotor gear; **à d. hélicoïdale** spiral

Il faut noter que le nom anglais **dentures** est un faux ami. Il signifie **dentier**.

dénucléarisation [denyklearizasjɔ̃] **NF** denuclearization

dénucléariser [denyklearize] **VT** to denuclearize

dénudation [denydasjɔ̃] **NF** Fml stripping, laying bare

dénudé [denyde] ADJ *(campagne, arbre)* bare; *(crâne)* bald; *Élec (fil)* bare

dénuder [denyde] VT *(colline)* to strip, to lay bare; *(arbre)* to strip; *(d'une robe)* to leave bare; **d. un arbre de son écorce** to strip a tree of its bark, to strip the bark off a tree
▸ VPR **se dénuder 1** *(d'une colline)* to grow bare; *(d'un arbre)* to lose its leaves **2** *(se mettre à nu)* to strip (naked); **crâne qui se dénude** balding head

dénué [denɥe] ADJ **d. de** *(raison, intelligence, intérêt etc)* devoid of; **une famille dénuée de tout** a family with absolutely nothing, a destitute family; **d. de tout fondement** totally without foundation

dénuement [denymɑ̃] NM destitution, penury; **être dans le d.** to be destitute *or* poverty-stricken

dénuer (se) [sədenɥe] VPR *Litt* to deprive oneself (**de** of); **se d. de ses biens** to part with all one's possessions

dénutrition [denytrisjɔ̃] NF *Méd* malnutrition

déodorant [deɔdɔrɑ̃] ADJ, NM deodorant

déodoriser [deɔdɔrize] VT to deodorize

déontologie [deɔtɔlɔʒi] NF professional ethics; **code de d.** professional code of ethics; *(écrit)* code of practice

déontologique [deɔtɔlɔʒik] ADJ ethical; **règles déontologiques** rules of ethics

dépannage [depanaʒ] NM **1** *(d'un moteur, d'une voiture en panne etc)* (emergency) repairs; *(remorquage)* recovery; *Ordinat* trouble-shooting; **service de d.** breakdown service **2** *(pour rendre service)* helping out; **elle a eu besoin d'un petit d.** she needed a hand *or* a bit of help

dépanner [depane] VT **1** *(moteur, voiture en panne etc)* to repair, to fix; **il m'a dépanné** he got my car/TV/*etc* going again **2** *Fam (aider)* to help out; *(financièrement)* to tide over, to bail out; **peux-tu me d. de 50 euros?** could you give me 50 euros to bail me out?

dépanneur [depanœr] NM **1** *(de voiture)* breakdown mechanic; *(de téléviseur)* (television) repairman **2** *Can (magasin)* corner shop, *Am* convenience store

dépanneuse [depanøz] NF *Aut* breakdown van *or* lorry, recovery vehicle, *Am* wrecker

dépaquetage [depakta3] NM unpacking

dépaqueter [depakte] VT *(conj like paqueter)* to unpack

déparasiter [deparazite] VT *(poste de radio)* to eliminate the interference in

dépareillé [depareje] ADJ **1** *(gant)* odd; *(service de table)* incomplete; *Com* **articles dépareillés** oddments, job lot **2** *Can (sans pareil)* **c'est un mari d.** he's a husband in a million

dépareiller [depareje] VT *(paire d'objets)* to break up; *(paire de gants, chaussettes)* to lose one of; *(service, collection)* to make incomplete; **en cassant cette assiette, tu as dépareillé mon service de table** my dinner service is incomplete now that you've broken that plate

déparer [depare] VT to spoil, to mar; **d. le paysage** to be a blot on the landscape; **ce tableau ne dépare pas dans le salon** the painting looks very good in the living room

déparier [deparje] VT *(impf, pr sub n. dépariions, v. dépariiez)* to split up, to separate

départ [depar] NM **1** *(d'une personne, d'un véhicule etc)* departure; *(de bateau)* departure, sailing; **quel est le jour de ton d.?** when do you leave?; **dès son d., j'ai rangé sa chambre** I tidied his room as soon as he left; **mon d. de la maison a été douloureux** my leaving home was a painful experience; **le décès de sa mère l'a obligé à un d. précipité** his mother's death forced him to leave hurriedly;

les grands départs (en vacances) the great holiday exodus; **c'était le grand d.** it was the final departure; **le d. de la navette spatiale** the launch of the space shuttle; **le d. du courrier a été retardé** the post has been delayed; **être sur le d.** to be on the point of leaving *or* of departure; **produit de d.** original material; **excursions au d. de Nice** trips (leaving) from Nice; **le train au d. de la voie 9** the train standing at platform 9; **le train à destination de Lille est au d. de la voie 9** the train to Lille will leave from platform 9; **d. anticipé** early departure; **d. différé** delayed departure; **d. matinal** early morning departure; *Com* **d. entrepôt** ex warehouse; *Com* **d. usine** ex works; *Com* **prix d. usine** price ex works; **d. volontaire** *(d'employé)* voluntary redundancy

2 *(du travail)* departure; **exiger le d. d'un employé** to insist on the dismissal of an employee; **il accepte mal son d. en retraite/en préretraite** he's finding it difficult to come to terms with the prospect of retirement/ early retirement

3 *(début)* *(d'un projet, d'une entreprise etc)* start, beginning; **le d. d'une association** the foundation of an association; **point de d.** starting point, point of departure; **prendre qch comme point de d.** to take sth as one's starting point; **langue de d.** *(d'une traduction)* source language; **qui a eu l'idée de d.?** who had the original idea?; **prix de d.** *(à une vente aux enchères)* upset price; **salaire de d.** starting salary; **ça ne ressemble plus du tout au modèle de d.** it doesn't look anything like the original model now; **au d.** at first, to start *or* begin with; **si tu me l'avais dit au d.** if you had told me that at the start *or* the outset; *Banque* **d. d'un compte** opening date of an account

4 *Sport (d'une course etc)* start; **ligne de d.** starting line; *Golf* **(tertre de) d.** tee; **d. arrêté** standing start; **d. lancé** flying start; **faux d.** false start; **donner le d.** to start the race, *Fam* to give the off; *Sp, Fig* **prendre un bon/mauvais d.** to get off to a good/bad start

départager [departaʒe] VT *(conj like partager)* *(candidats, chansons etc)* to decide between; **d. les gagnants** to decide the winners; **d. les votes** to give the casting vote

département [departəmɑ̃] NM *Admin* **1** *(dans un ministère)* **d. (ministériel)** department; **le d. de la peinture moderne** *(dans un musée)* the modern art section **2** *(de la France)* = subdivision administered by a prefect

---

Département

A "département" is the chief administrative division of France. There are 95 "départements" in metropolitan France and 4 overseas and each is administered by a "conseil général" and a "préfet". The number of the "département" corresponds to the first two figures in a postcode and the last two figures in a car registration number.

---

départemental, -ale, -aux, -ales [departəmɑ̃tal, -o] ADJ departmental
▸ NM *Journ* regional (paper)
▸ NF **départementale** secondary *or Br* B road

départir [departir] *(conj like partir, occ like finir)* VT *Litt (faveurs)* to distribute, to dispense, to deal out; *(tâches)* to distribute, to allocate
▸ VPR se **départir il ne se départ jamais de son calme** he never gets excited; **elle ne se départ jamais de sa bonne humeur** her good humour *or Am* humor never deserts her, she is unfailingly good-humoured *or Am* good-humored; **il est connu pour sa bonne**

humeur, dont effectivement il ne se départ jamais he is famous for his good humour, which never fails *or* deserts him

dépassé [depase] ADJ **1** *(démodé)* *(mode, technique, langage)* old-fashioned, out of date; **c'est d.** *(de faire ça)* it's medieval; **se marier à 20 ans, c'est complètement d.** nobody gets married at 20 nowadays **2** *(perdu)* overwhelmed; **je suis d. (par les événements)** things are getting too much for me

dépassement [depasmɑ̃] NM **1** *Aut* overtaking, *Am* passing; **d. interdit** no overtaking, *Am* no passing **2** *Fin* **nous avons un d. de crédit à déplorer** we have failed to keep within our spending limit; **il y a un d. de crédit de plusieurs millions** the budget has been exceeded by several million; **pratiquer le d. d'honoraires** to charge more than will be reimbursed by Social Security; **d. budgétaire** failure to keep within the budget; *Ordinat* **d. de capacité** overflow; *Compta* **d. de coût** cost overrun **3** **d. (de soi-même)** surpassing oneself

DÉPASSER [depase] VT **1** *(aller plus loin que)* *(personne, chose)* to pass, to go past *or* beyond; *(signal)* to overrun; **nous avons dépassé la boulangerie** we have passed *or* gone past the baker's; **cette maison dépasse l'alignement** the house projects beyond the building line; **d. le but** to overshoot the mark

2 *(excéder)* to exceed; **d. la limite de vitesse** to exceed the speed limit; **d. la date limite** to miss the deadline; **ce produit a dépassé la date limite de vente** this product is past its sell-by date; **l'entretien ne dépassera pas un quart d'heure** the interview won't take *or* last more than a quarter of an hour; **d. la durée autorisée de 20 minutes** to take more than the 20 minutes allowed; *Fin* **d. un crédit** to exceed a credit limit; **toutes ces voitures dépassent nos moyens** all these cars are beyond our means; **ne pas d. la dose prescrite** do not exceed the stated dose; **il a dépassé la trentaine** he has turned thirty, he is over thirty

3 *(à la course, en voiture)* to overtake, *Am* to pass

4 *(surpasser)* **d. qch en hauteur** to top sth, to be higher than sth; **d. qn de la tête** to stand a head taller than sb; **d. qn en intelligence/en beauté** to be more intelligent/beautiful than sb; **la beauté des lieux dépasse l'imagination** the scene is beautiful beyond all imagination; **les résultats ont largement dépassé nos espérances** the results far exceeded our expectations *or* were much better than we hoped for

5 *(outrepasser)* **cela dépasse ma compétence** it lies beyond *or* outside my area of responsibility; **les mots ont dépassé ma pensée** I said it in the heat of the moment; **d. les bornes** to overstep the bounds *or* the mark, *Am* to be out of line; **cela dépasse mon entendement, cela me dépasse** *(d'un comportement)* it's beyond me; *(d'une discussion savante)* it's beyond me, it's over my head; **être dépassé par les événements** to be overtaken by events
▸ VI **1** *Aut* to overtake, *Am* to pass; **il est interdit de d. sur ce pont** no overtaking *or Am* passing on this bridge

2 *(être trop long)* **votre jupon dépasse** your underskirt is showing; **son mouchoir dépasse de sa poche** his handkerchief is sticking out of his pocket
▸ VPR se **dépasser** to surpass oneself

---

dépassionner [depasjɔne] VT *(débat, conversation)* to take the heat out of; **il faisait tout ce qu'il pouvait pour d. la conversation** he was doing everything he could to cool *or* calm things down

dépatouiller (se) [sədepatuje] VPR *Fam* to cope, to manage

dépaver [depave] VT *(cour, rue)* to take up the paving from

dépaysé [depeize] ADJ out of one's element; **je me sens d.** I feel like a fish out of water, I don't feel at home; **depuis qu'on l'a changé d'école, il se sent d.** he feels totally lost since changing schools; *Iron* **il pleut autant que chez moi! – eh bien, comme ça tu ne seras pas d.!** it rains as much here as it does at home! – well at least you won't feel homesick!

dépaysement [depeizmɑ̃] NM *(négatif)* disorientation; *(positif)* change of scene; **c'est un grand d. pour lui d'être dans cette ville** he feels really lost in this town; **elle a besoin de d.** she needs a change of scene; **cela te ferait un d.** it would be a change of scene for you

dépayser [depeize] VT *(positivement)* to be a change of scene for; *(négativement)* to disorientate, *surtout Am* to disorient; **mes vacances m'ont beaucoup dépaysé** my holiday provided a great change of scene

dépeçage [depəsaʒ] NM, **dépècement** [depɛsmɑ̃] NM cutting up; *Fig* **le d. du pays fut achevé par les barbares** the barbarians completed the dismemberment of the country

dépecer [depəse] VT (**je dépèce,** n. **dépeçons; je dépècerai**) **1** *(carcasse, volaille)* to cut up; *(baleine)* to flense; **le lion dépèce sa proie** the lion tears its prey; **un corps dépecé** a dismembered body **2** *Fig (territoire)* to dismember

dépeceur, -euse [depəsœr, -øz] N cutter-up; **d. (de baleines)** flenser; **d. d'entreprises** asset-stripper

dépêche [depɛʃ] NF **1** *(lettre officielle)* (official) dispatch, message **2** *(nouvelle)* news item *(sent through an agency);* **d. (télégraphique)** telegram, *Fam* wire; *Journ* **d. d'agence** agency copy; **nous avons appris par d. la démission du président** we have just heard over the wire that the president has resigned

dépêcher [depɛʃe] VT *(un courrier, un messager)* to dispatch

  VPR **se dépêcher** to hurry, to be quick; **dépêchez-vous!** hurry up!; **se d. de faire qch** to hurry to do sth; **dépêche-toi de finir ton travail** hurry up and finish your work; **se d. de rentrer** to hurry home

dépeigner [depeɲe] VT **d. qn** to ruffle sb's hair, to make sb's hair untidy; **elle est toute dépeignée** her hair's all dishevelled

dépeindre [depɛ̃dr] VT *(conj like* **peindre***)* to depict, to picture, to describe

dépenaillé [dep(ə)naje] ADJ *(veste, pantalon etc)* ragged, tattered, in rags, in tatters; *(personne)* in rags, in tatters

dépénalisation [depenalizasjɔ̃] NF decriminalization

dépénaliser [depenalize] VT to decriminalize

dépendance [depɑ̃dɑ̃s] NF **1** *(solidarité)* dependence **2** *(d'un pays)* dependency; *Archit* **dépendances** outbuildings **3** *(asservissement)* dependence, *surtout Am* dependancy; **l'abus de somnifères peut créer une d.** excessive use of sleeping tablets can lead to dependence; **vivre dans la d. complète de qn** to be completely dependent on sb; **être sous la d. de qn** to be under sb's domination *or* control

dépendant [depɑ̃dɑ̃] ADJ dependent; **fonctions dépendantes l'une de l'autre** functions dependent on each other, interdependent functions; **être d. de qn** to be dependent on sb; **être d. de la drogue** to be dependent on drugs

dépendre¹ [depɑ̃dr] VT *(linge etc)* to take down

dépendre² VI to depend; **d. de qn/qch** to depend on sb/sth; **un pays qui dépend d'un autre** a country which is dependent on another; **tout dépend des circonstances** everything depends on the circumstances; **ces événements ne dépendent pas de nous** such events are beyond our control; **cela ne dépend que de toi** that depends on you alone; **il dépend de vous de le faire** it lies *or* rests with you to do it; **cela dépend,** *Fam* **cela dépend des fois** it depends; *Fam* **ça dépend s'il est marié** it depends whether he's married; **il dépend financièrement de ses parents** he is financially dependent on his parents; **je ne dépends pas de lui** I don't take orders from him; **ne d. que de soi(-même)** to be one's own boss; **l'étang dépend aussi de leur domaine** the pond is also part of their estate

dépens [depɑ̃] NMPL **1** **aux d. de** at the expense of; **faire qch aux d. d'autrui** to do sth at other people's expense; **vivre aux d. de qn** to live at sb's expense; **s'amuser aux d. de ses études** to enjoy oneself at the expense of one's studies; **il apprit à ses d. que …** he learnt to his cost that … **2** *Jur* costs; *Com* cost, expenses; *Jur* **être condamné aux d.** to be ordered to pay costs

dépense [depɑ̃s] NF **1** expenditure, expense, outlay; **dépenses** spending; **dépenses du ménage** household expenses; **dépenses courantes** current expenditure *or* expenses; **faire des dépenses** to spend money; **engager une d.** *ou* **des dépenses** to incur expenditure; **nous avons décidé d'engager les dépenses pour les travaux** we decided to go ahead and incur the expenditure of having the work done; **j'ai acheté une voiture, mais je n'arriverai pas à couvrir la d.** I bought a car, but I'll never be able to pay for it; **je n'arriverai pas à couvrir tes dépenses** I won't be able to pay for your extravagance; **je n'aurais pas dû faire cette d.** I shouldn't have spent that money; **pousser à la d.** to encourage people to spend; **c'est une grosse d.** it's a lot of money; **faire trop de dépenses** to spend too much (money); **on ne regardait pas à la d.** there was no stinting, they didn't mind the cost, they spared no expense; **faire de folles dépenses** to spend money extravagantly; **recettes et dépenses** income *or* receipts and expenditure

2 *Tech* **d. à vide** wasted energy; *Fig* **d. de temps/d'énergie** expenditure of time/energy; **d. physique** physical exertion

3 *(d'une communauté religieuse)* bursary

▸▸ *Compta* **dépenses de caisse** cash expenditure; **dépenses en capital** capital expenditure; *Écon* **dépenses des consommateurs** consumer expenditure; *Compta* **dépenses de création** above-the-line costs; *Compta* **dépenses diverses** sundry expenses; **dépenses d'équipement** capital expenditure; *Compta* **dépenses d'exploitation** operating costs; *Compta* **dépenses de fonctionnement** operating costs; *Écon* **dépenses des ménages** household expenditure; *Écon* **d. nationale** national expenditure, government spending; **dépenses publiques** public spending, government spending; **dépenses de santé** *(de l'État)* health spending, health expenditure; **dépenses sociales** spending on social services

dépenser [depɑ̃se] VT **1** *(de l'argent)* to spend; **il dépense peu en livres** he doesn't spend much on books **2** *(temps)* to spend; *(énergie)* to use, to consume; **la voiture dépense très peu d'essence** the car uses *or* consumes very little petrol; **d. toute son énergie/ses forces (à faire qch)** to use up all one's energy/one's strength (in doing

sth; **d. sa salive pour rien** *ou* **inutilement** to waste one's breath

  VI to spend (money); **d. sans compter** to spend lavishly, to be free with one's money; **qu'est-ce que tu peux d. en un mois!** the amount you spend in a month!

  VPR **se dépenser** to use up *or* consume energy; **j'ai besoin de me d.** I need some physical exercise; **se d. pour qn** to spare no trouble on sb's behalf; **il s'est dépensé sans compter pour obtenir ton passeport plus vite** he went to a great deal of trouble to get your passport faster; **se d. en démarches inutiles** to waste one's energies in useless activities

dépensier, -ière [depɑ̃sje, -jɛr] ADJ extravagant

  N **1** *(personne prodigue)* spendthrift **2** *(d'une communauté religieuse)* bursar

déperdition [depɛrdisjɔ̃] NF *(de tissu etc)* waste, wastage; *(de chaleur, d'énergie)* loss

dépérir [deperir] VI *(d'une personne)* to waste away; *(de la santé)* to decline; *(d'une fleur)* to wither; *(d'un arbre)* to decay; *(d'une affaire)* to go downhill

dépérissement [deperismɑ̃] NM *(d'une personne)* wasting away; *(d'une fleur)* withering; *(d'un arbre)* decay; *(d'une affaire, de la santé)* decline

dépersonnalisation [depɛrsɔnalizasjɔ̃] NF depersonalization

dépersonnaliser [depɛrsɔnalize] VT to depersonalize

  VPR **se dépersonnaliser** to lose one's personality *or* character

dépêtrer [depetre] *Fam* VT *(de la boue),* *Fig (d'une situation difficile etc)* to extricate, to free; **d. qn d'une mauvaise affaire** to get sb out of a scrape

  VPR **se dépêtrer** *(de la boue, de racines etc)* to extricate *or* free oneself; *Fig* **se d. de qn** to get rid of sb, to shake sb off

dépeuplé [depœple] ADJ *(pays, région)* depopulated; *(étang)* empty; *(forêt)* cleared, thinned

dépeuplement [depœpləmɑ̃] NM *(d'un pays, d'une région)* depopulation; *(d'un étang)* unstocking; *(d'une forêt)* thinning, clearing

dépeupler [depœple] VT *(pays, région)* to depopulate; *(étang)* to unstock; *(forêt)* to thin, to clear

  VPR **se dépeupler** *(d'un pays, d'une région)* to become depopulated; *(d'une salle)* to empty; *(d'un étang)* to become unstocked; *(d'une forêt)* to thin

déphasage [defazaʒ] NM **1** *Élec* phase displacement; **d. en avant** (phase) lead; **d. en arrière** lag **2** *Fig Fam* **il y a vraiment un d. entre les connaissances qu'on demande à un professeur et la réalité de l'enseignement** there's a big difference between the knowledge demanded of a teacher and the realities of teaching; **le d. est de plus en plus important entre le PDG et le conseil d'administration** the chairman is increasingly out of step with the board

déphasé [defaze] ADJ **1** *Élec, Cin, TV* out-of-phase; **d. en arrière** lagging; **d. en avant** leading **2** *Fig Fam (personne) (désorienté)* disorientated, *surtout Am* disoriented

déphaser [defaze] VT **1** *Élec* to dephase **2** *Fig Fam (personne)* to disorientate, *surtout Am* to disorient

dépiauter [depjote] VT *Fam (lapin etc)* to skin, to flay; *Fig* **d. un texte/un article** to pull a text/an article to pieces

dépigmentation [depigmɑ̃tasjɔ̃] NF *Méd* loss of pigmentation

dépilation [depilasjɔ̃] NF loss of hair

dépilatoire [depilatwar] ADJ depilatory; **crème d.** hair removing cream, depilatory

dépiler [depile] **VT** _Méd_ to cause loss of hair from

dépiquer¹ [depike] **VT** _(pousses)_ to transplant, to prick out

dépiquer² **VT** _Couture_ to unstitch, to unpick

dépistage [depistaʒ] **NM** _(d'un criminel etc)_ tracking down, detection; _(d'une maladie, d'un virus etc)_ (early) detection; **d. obligatoire du sida** compulsory AIDS screening

dépister [depiste] **VT 1** _(gibier, criminel)_ to track down; _(maladie)_ to detect; **d. un traquenard** to spot a trap; **il a été dépisté séropositif** he tested HIV-positive **2** _(chiens de chasse)_ to put off the scent; _(poursuivant)_ to throw off the scent; **il a dépisté la police** he threw the police off the scent, he gave the police the slip

dépit [depi] **NM 1** _(ressentiment)_ spite, resentment; **un accès de d.** a fit of pique; **par d.** out of spite; **elle s'est mariée avec lui par d. amoureux** she married him on the rebound; **il a agi par d. amoureux** he did it because he was disappointed in love; **pleurer de d.** to cry with vexation; **concevoir du d. de qch** to resent sth **2 en d. de** in spite of, despite; **en d. du bon sens** _(illogiquement)_ contrary to common sense

dépité [depite] **ADJ** annoyed; **être tout d.** to be thoroughly annoyed

dépiter [depite] **VT** to spite, to offend

déplacé [deplase] **ADJ 1** _(pas à sa place)_ out of (its) place; **avoir une vertèbre déplacée** to have a slipped disc; _Fig_ **se sentir d.** to feel out of place **2** _(inconvenant)_ _(observation, attitude etc)_ unwarranted, uncalled-for **3** _Pol_ **personne déplacée** displaced person

déplacement [deplasmɑ̃] **NM 1** _(de meubles etc)_ moving, shifting; _(de fonctionnaire, service)_ transfer; _Méd_ **d. de vertèbre** slipped disc; _Ordinat_ **d. du curseur** cursor movement; _Ordinat_ **d. entre fichiers** movement between files; _TV, Cin_ **d. latéral** _(d'une caméra)_ crabbing **2** _(voyage)_ trip, journey; **déplacements** travel; **ces déplacements continuels** this constant travel _or_ travelling; **les déplacements des cadres** executive travel; **être en d.** to be on a (business) trip; **frais de d.** travelling expenses **3** _Naut_ _(d'un navire)_ displacement; **d. en charge** displacement loaded, load displacement; **d. d'air** air displacement

déplacer [deplase] (**je déplaçai(s); n. déplaçons**) **VT 1** _(changer de place)_ _(objet)_ to move, to shift; _(fonctionnaire, service)_ to transfer; _(fonds)_ to move; **il ne peut rien d., il a mal au dos** he can't carry anything, he has a bad back; _Fig_ **d. la question** _ou_ **le problème** to shift the focus of a problem; **vous déplacez le problème** you're dodging the issue; _Hum_ **tout ce qu'il sait faire, c'est de d. de l'air** he just runs around in circles **2 ce navire déplace dix mille tonnes** this ship has a displacement of ten thousand tons
VPR se déplacer 1 _(changer de place)_ to change one's place, to move (around); **il est interdit de se d.** please remain seated; **avoir du mal à se d.** to have difficulty in moving _or_ getting around; **se d. une vertèbre** to slip a disc **2** _(voyager)_ to move about, to travel; **son métier l'oblige à se d.** souvent he does a lot of travelling in his job **3** _(bouger)_ _(d'un bateau, d'un poisson etc)_ to move

déplafonnement [deplafɔnmɑ̃] **NM** removal of the upper limit _or_ ceiling

déplafonner [deplafɔne] **VT** _(prix)_ to remove the upper limit _or_ the ceiling on; _Fin_ **d. un crédit** to raise the ceiling on a credit, to raise a credit limit

déplaire [deplɛr] (_conj like_ **plaire**) **VI d. à qn** _(irriter)_ to displease _or_ offend sb; _(ne pas plaire à)_ to fail to please sb, to be displeasing to sb; **odeur qui déplaît** offensive _or_ disagreeable smell; **tu lui déplais** he dislikes you; **il me déplaît de le faire** I dislike _or_ don't like doing it; **il me déplaît d'avoir à vous le dire, mais …** I hate _or_ I don't like having to tell you this, but …; **il me déplairait vraiment d'avoir à vous faire d'autres remarques** I would be extremely displeased if I had to make any further comment; **cela ne me déplairait pas** I wouldn't mind (it); **il a tout fait pour nous d.** he has been utterly disagreeable; **cela m'a profondément déplu** I was greatly _or_ most displeased by that; _Iron_ **n'en déplaise à la compagnie** with all due respect to those present; **n'en déplaise à votre Altesse!** may it please Your Highness!; **ne vous/leur en déplaise** whether you/they like it or not; **n'en déplaise à mes parents** whether my parents like it or not
VPR se déplaire to be displeased _or_ dissatisfied; **il se déplaît à Paris** he doesn't like Paris; **il ne se déplaît pas à Paris** he quite likes Paris

déplaisant [deplɛzɑ̃] **ADJ** unpleasant, disagreeable

déplaisir [deplezir] **NM** displeasure, annoyance; **à son grand d.** to his great annoyance

déplantage [deplɑ̃taʒ] **NM** digging up, lifting

déplanter [deplɑ̃te] **VT** to take _or_ dig up, to lift

déplantoir [deplɑ̃twar] **NM** hand fork

déplâtrage [deplɑtraʒ] **NM 1 le d. d'un mur** taking _or_ stripping the plaster off a wall **2 le d. d'un bras/d'une jambe** taking an arm/a leg out of plaster

déplâtrer [deplɑtre] **VT 1** _(mur etc)_ to strip the plaster from **2** _(membre)_ to take the plaster off; **on la déplâtre demain** she's having the plaster off tomorrow

dépliage [deplijaʒ] **NM** unfolding, opening out

dépliant [deplijɑ̃] **ADJ** _(qui se déplie)_ folding
NM leaflet; _(plus luxueux)_ brochure; _(feuille pliée)_ fold-out page; **d. promotionnel** promotional leaflet

dépliement [deplimɑ̃] **NM** = **dépliage**

déplier [deplije] (_impf, pr sub_ **n. dépliions, v. dépliiez**) **VT** _(journal, carte)_ to unfold, to open out, to spread out; _(mouchoir)_ to unfold; _(canapé)_ to open out; **d. les jambes** to stretch one's legs
VPR se déplier to unfold, to open out

déplissage [deplisaʒ] **NM** _(d'un tissu etc)_ taking the creases out, smoothing out

déplisser [deplise] **VT** _(tissu etc)_ to take the creases out of, to smooth out
VPR se déplisser _(d'un tissu etc)_ to lose its creases

déploiement [deplwamɑ̃] **NM 1** _(d'ailes etc)_ spreading out, unfolding; _(du drapeau)_ unfurling; _(des troupes, navires etc)_ deployment **2** _(de force, courage)_ display; **un d. d'attentions** a display _or_ show of attention

déplombage [deplɔ̃baʒ] **NM 1** _(d'un compteur d'électricité, d'un paquet etc)_ removal of the seal **2** _(d'une dent)_ removal of the filling **3** _Ordinat_ decoding, decrypting

déplomber [deplɔ̃be] **VT 1** _(compteur d'électricité, paquet etc)_ to remove the seal from **2** _(dent)_ to remove the filling from **3** _Ordinat_ _(logiciel)_ to decode, to decrypt

déplorable [deplɔrabl] **ADJ** _(incident etc)_ deplorable, regrettable; _(comportement, résultats etc)_ disgraceful

déplorablement [deplɔrabləmɑ̃] **ADV** deplorably

déplorer [deplɔre] **VT** to deplore; **vous avez très mal agi et je le déplore** I think it is de-plorable that you behaved so badly; **il est à d. que vous ayez eu cette conduite** it is deplorable that you behaved in such a way; **d. la mort de qn** to grieve over _or_ mourn sb's death

déployer [deplwaje] (**je déploie, n. déployons; je déploierai**) **VT 1** _(journal, carte)_ to unfold, to open out; _(drapeau)_ to unfurl; _(voiles, ailes)_ to spread; _(troupes, police)_ to deploy; **rire à gorge déployée** to roar with laughter **2** _(marchandises, patience etc)_ to display, to show; **il a déployé un énorme effort** he made a tremendous effort; **il va falloir d. des trésors d'ingéniosité** we're/they're/etc going to have to be extremely ingenious
VPR se déployer _(d'une voile, d'un drapeau)_ to unfurl; _(de troupes, de police)_ to deploy; _Mil_ **se d. en éventail** to fan out

déplumé [deplyme] **ADJ** featherless; _Fam (chauve)_ bald

déplumer (se) [sədeplyme] **VPR** _(d'un oiseau)_ to moult; _Fam (d'une personne)_ to go bald

dépoitraillé [depwatraje] **ADJ** _Fam Péj_ with one's shirt/etc all undone (at the front)

dépolarisant [depɔlarizɑ̃] _Phys_ **ADJ** depolarizing
NM depolarizer

dépolarisation [depɔlarizasjɔ̃] **NF** _Phys_ depolarization

dépolariser [depɔlarize] **VT** _Phys_ to depolarize

dépoli [depɔli] **ADJ** _(verre)_ frosted

dépolir [depɔlir] **VT** _(surface)_ to dull, to tarnish; _(verre)_ to frost
VPR se dépolir to become dull, to tarnish

dépolissage [depɔlisaʒ] **NM**, **dépolissement** [depɔlismɑ̃] **NM** _(de surface)_ dulling, tarnishing; _(de verre)_ frosting

dépolitisation [depɔlitizasjɔ̃] **NF** depoliticization

dépolitiser [depɔlitize] **VT** to depoliticize

dépolluer [depɔlɥe] **VT** to clean up

dépollution [depɔlysjɔ̃] **NF** cleaning up

déponent [depɔnɑ̃] **ADJ, NM** _Gram_ deponent

dépopulation [depɔpylasjɔ̃] **NF** depopulation

déportation [depɔrtasjɔ̃] **NF 1** _(d'un prisonnier)_ transportation **2** _(en camp de concentration)_ internment

déporté, -ée [depɔrte] **N 1** _(exilé)_ transported criminal **2** _(de camp de concentration)_ internee, prisoner

déportement [depɔrtəmɑ̃] **NM 1** _Aut_ skidding, swerving **2** _Vieilli_ **déportements** excesses, dissolute life

déporter [depɔrte] **VT 1** _(prisonnier)_ to transport **2** _(en camp de concentration)_ to send to a concentration camp **3** _(navire, avion)_ to carry off course; **voiture déportée par la violence du vent** car blown off the road by the force of the wind

déposant, -ante [depozɑ̃, -ɑ̃t] **N 1** _Fin_ depositor **2** _Jur_ deponent, witness

dépose [depoz] **NF** _(de tapis, moquette)_ lifting, taking up; _(de moteur, radiateur)_ removal

déposer¹ [depoze] **VT** _(enlever)_ _(tapis, moquette)_ to lift, to take up; _(rideaux)_ to take down; _(moteur, radiateur)_ to remove

déposer² **VT 1** _(valise, sac etc)_ to put _or_ set down; **d. une gerbe sur un tombeau** to lay a wreath on a grave; **ma voiture vous déposera à l'hôtel** my car will drop you at the hotel; **puis-je vous d. quelque part?** can I drop you somewhere?; **d. une lettre/un paquet chez qn** to drop off a letter/a parcel at sb's house; **d. la clé à la réception** to leave the key at reception; **défense de d. des ordures** no dumping, *Br* no tipping; **d. les armes** to lay down one's arms, to surrender; *Fml* **d. un baiser sur la joue/le front de qn** to kiss sb on the cheek/forehead; *Fml* **d. ses hommages aux pieds de qn** to pay homage to sb **2** *(confier)* to deposit, to lodge in a safe place; *Com (marque, brevet)* to register; **d. une caution** to leave a deposit; **d. son argent à la banque** to deposit one's money at the bank; *Com* **marque déposée** registered trademark; *Jur* **d. une plainte contre qn** to prefer a charge *or* lodge a complaint against sb; *Com* **d. son bilan** to file one's petition (in bankruptcy); **d. un projet de loi** to table a bill, to bring in a bill **3** *(monarque etc)* to depose **4** *(d'un liquide) (dépôt)* to deposit **VI 1 il faut laisser au liquide le temps de d.** the liquid must be given time to settle **2** *Jur* **d. (en justice)** to give evidence (**contre** against) **VPR se déposer** *(d'une substance)* to settle, to form a deposit

dépositaire [depoziter] N **1** *(de papiers confidentiels)* depositary; *Com* consignee; **d. de valeurs** holder of securities on trust; *Admin* **d. de l'autorité publique** = officer of the State; *Admin* **d. public** = government official with responsibility for the management of public funds **2** *Com (de produits)* agent; **d. agréé/exclusif** authorized/sole agent; **d. de journaux** newsagent

déposition [depozisjɔ̃] NF **1** *Jur* statement, deposition *(made by witness)*; **faire/recueillir une d.** to make/take a statement **2** *(d'un monarque)* deposing **3** *Beaux-Arts* **D. de Croix** Deposition

dépositionner [depozisjɔne] VT *Mktg* to deposition

déposséder [deposede] VT *(je dépossède, n. dépossédons; je déposséderai)* to dispossess, to deprive *(de of)*; **d. qn de sa place** to deprive sb of *or* oust sb from his seat; **d. qn de sa charge** to remove sb from office, to deprive sb of his/her office; **se sentir dépossédé** to feel dispossessed

dépossession [deposesjɔ̃] NF dispossession

dépôt [depo] NM **1** *(action)* deposit, depositing; *(chose confiée)* deposit; **d. d'une gerbe** laying of a wreath; **le d. des manteaux au vestiaire est conseillé** customers are advised to leave their coats in the cloakroom; **faire un d.** *(d'argent)* to make a deposit; **banque de d.** deposit bank; **compte de d.** deposit account; *Com* **d. d'une marque de fabrique** registration of a trademark; *Pol* **d. d'un projet de loi** bringing in *or* tabling of a bill; **avoir** *ou* **détenir qch en d.** to hold sth in trust; **marchandises en d.** *(à la douane)* goods in bond; *Com* **goods on sale or return 2** *(entrepôt)* depot, depository, repository; *Rail* engine shed; *(prison)* prison, jail; **il a passé la nuit au d.** he spent the night in the cells; *Jur* **mandat de d.** warrant of committal *or* commitment *(of prisoner)* **3** *(de précipité, boue etc) (action)* deposition, settling; *(résultat)* deposit, sediment; *(limon)* silt; *(dans une bouilloire)* fur; *(dans un chauffe-eau)* scale; **le d. d'un vin** the sediment in a wine; **il y a du d.** there is a sediment; *Géol* **d. calcaire/sédimentaire** calcareous/sedimentary deposit

▸▸**d. bancaire** bank deposit; *Com* **d. de bilan** (filing of a petition in) bankruptcy; **d. de bois** timber yard; **d. de bouteilles** bottle bank; **d. de distributeur** distribution depot; **d. à échéance fixe** fixed deposit; **d. d'espèces** cash deposit; **d. d'essence** petrol storage depot; **d. d'expédition** sending depot; **d. de fret** freight depot; **d. de garantie** security deposit; **d. interbancaire** interbank deposit;

Jur **d. légal** copyright deposit *(in France, copies of published or recorded documents have to be deposited at the Bibliothèque nationale)*; **d. de(s) marchandises** goods depot; *(entrepôt)* warehouse; *Mil* **d. de munitions** munitions depot; **d. d'ordures** rubbish dump *or Br* tip; **d. de pain** ≃ bread shop *(which does not make its own bread)*; **d. pour conteneurs** container depot; **d. de réception** receiving depot; **d. sacré** sacred trust; *Fin* **d. à terme** term deposit; **d. à terme fixe** fixed deposit; **d. de verre** bottle bank; *Fin* **d. à vue** demand deposit, sight deposit

dépotage [depotaʒ], **dépotement** [depotmɑ̃] NM **1** *(de liquide)* decanting **2** *(de plantes)* repotting; *(de semis)* planting out

dépoter [depote] VT **1** *(liquide)* to decant **2** *(plantes)* to repot; *(semis)* to plant out

dépotoir [depotwar] NM **1** *(dépôt d'ordures)* dump, *Br* rubbish tip; *Fig* **cette chambre est un vrai d.** this room is a real tip *or* dump **2** *Ind* sewage works

dépôt-vente, *pl* **dépôts-ventes** NM sales room

dépouille [depuj] NF **1** *(d'animal)* skin, hide; *(de serpent)* slough; **d. (mortelle)** (mortal) remains **2 dépouilles** *(trésor de guerre)* spoils, booty

dépouillé [depuje] ADJ *(style)* bald; *(arbre)* bare; **vin d.** = wine that has lost its alcohol content; **d. de** lacking in; **ils vivent dans un décor très d.** they live in very spartan surroundings

dépouillement [depujmɑ̃] NM **1 d. volontaire de ses biens** relinquishment *or* renouncement of one's property; **ils vivent dans le d.** they live in utter poverty **2** *(examen)* **d. d'un rapport** examination *or* analysis of a report; **d. des votes** *ou* **du scrutin** counting of the votes; **d. du courrier** going *or* sorting through the mail **3** *TV etc (avant enregistrement)* breakdown

dépouiller [depuje] VT **1** *(priver)* to deprive, to strip (**de** of); **d. qn de ses vêtements** to strip sb; **d. qn de ses droits** to strip sb of his/her rights; **se faire d.** *(dans une affaire)* to lose all one's money; **se faire d. par des voleurs** to be robbed of all one's money; **d. un pays** to plunder a country; **d. un héritier** to rob an heir of his inheritance; **le décor est dépouillé de tout ornement** the surroundings are bare of all ornament; *Fig* **dans le film, le personnage est dépouillé de tout son charme** all the character's charm is lost in the film; *Litt* **la bise a dépouillé les bois** the wind has stripped all the trees bare **2** *(examiner) (le courrier, numéros d'une revue)* to sort, to go through; *(appels d'offres)* to check; **d. un inventaire** to examine *or* analyse an inventory; **d. le scrutin** to count the votes; **pour faire son mémoire, il a dépouillé tout Balzac** he analysed all of Balzac line by line for his thesis **3** *(lapin etc)* to skin **VPR se dépouiller 1** *(d'un insecte, serpent)* to cast (off) its skin; *(d'un arbre)* to shed its leaves; *(du vin)* to lose its strength **2 se d. de qch** to deprive *or* divest *or* rid oneself of sth; **se d. de ses vêtements** to strip off one's clothes, *Fam* to strip; **les arbres se dépouillaient de leurs feuilles** the trees were dropping *or* shedding their leaves

dépourvu [depurvy] ADJ **d. d'intelligence/ d'intérêt** devoid of intelligence/interest; **pays d. d'arbres** treeless country; **être d. (d'argent)** to be penniless **NM être pris au d.** to be caught off (one's) guard, to be taken by surprise

dépoussiérage [depusjeraʒ] NM *Ind* vacuum cleaning, dust removal

dépoussiérant [depusjerɑ̃] NM furniture polish

dépoussiérer [depusjere] VT *Ind* to vacuum-clean, to remove the dust from; *Fig (institution, traduction etc)* to modernize, to bring up to date; *(connaissances)* to brush up

dépravation [depravasjɔ̃] NF (moral) depravity

dépravé, -ée [deprave] ADJ depraved **N** degenerate, depraved person

dépraver [deprave] VT to deprave **VPR se dépraver** to become depraved

dépréciateur, -trice [depresjatœr, -tris] N disparager, belittler

dépréciatif, -ive [depresjatif, -iv] ADJ *(expression, mot etc)* derogatory; **en termes dépréciatifs** in derogatory *or* disparaging terms

dépréciation [depresjasjɔ̃] NF **1** *(dévaluation)* depreciation, fall in value **2** *(mauvaise évaluation)* underrating, undervaluing; *(dénigrement)* disparagement; *Compta* **d. de créances** write-down of accounts receivable

déprécier [depresje] *(impf, pr sub* **n. dépréciions,** v. **dépréciiez)* VT **1** *(biens)* to undervalue; *(mérites, personne, livre)* to underrate **2** *(mal évaluer)* to undervalue **VPR se déprécier 1** *(de valeurs)* to depreciate, to fall; *(de marchandises)* to depreciate, to fall in value **2** *(de personne)* to belittle oneself

déprédateur, -trice [depredatœr, -tris] N **1** pillager **2** *Fin* embezzler **ADJ** pillaging, *Fml* depredatory

déprédation [depredasjɔ̃] NF **1** *(pillage)* pillaging, *Fml* depredation **2** *Fin (de fonds etc)* misappropriation, embezzlement

déprendre (se) [sədeprɑ̃dr] VPR *(conj like* prendre*)* to detach oneself, to get free; **se d. d'une habitude/d'une personne** to get out of a habit/get clear *or* free of a person

dépressif, -ive [depresif, -iv] ADJ depressive

dépression [depresjɔ̃] NF **1** *(affaissement)* depression; *(dans le sol)* hollow, dip; *(dans l'océan)* trough; *Astron (de l'horizon)* dip; *Mil* **angle de d.** *(d'une arme)* angle of depression **2** *(chute) (de valeur)* fall; **d. économique** economic depression, slump; *Météo* **d. (barométrique)** (barometric) depression, low, trough **3** *Psy* (mental) depression; **faire de la d.** to be in a state of depression; *Méd* **d. nerveuse** nervous breakdown; **d. hivernale** seasonal affective disorder, SAD

dépressionnaire [depresjɔner] ADJ **1** *Météo* **zone** *ou* **centre d.** trough, area of low pressure; **système d.** low-pressure system **2** *Écon* slump; **le marché a des tendances dépressionnaires** the market is sliding towards a slump

dépressurisation [depresyrizasjɔ̃] NF depressurization

dépressuriser [depresyrize] VT *(avion, véhicule spatial)* to depressurize

déprimant [deprimɑ̃] ADJ depressing

déprime [deprim] NF *Fam* depression; **la d.** the blues; **c'est la d. dans tous les secteurs de l'économie** all sectors of the economy are depressed; **faire de la d.** to be in a state of depression; **avoir un (petit) coup de d.** to be (a bit) depressed

déprimé [deprime] ADJ **1** *(personne)* depressed **2** *(surface etc)* depressed, low, flat, flattened; **front d.** low forehead **3** *Bourse (marché)* depressed

déprimer [deprime] VT **1** *(personne)* to depress **2** *(surface etc)* to depress, to lower **VI** *Fam* to be depressed

de profundis [deprɔfɔ̃dis] NM *Rel* de profundis

déprogrammation [deprɔgramasjɔ̃] NF *(de rendez-vous, d'émission TV ou radio)* cancellation

déprogrammer [deprɔgrame] **VT** *(rendez-vous, émission TV ou radio)* to cancel; *Ordinat* to remove from a program

déprotection [deprɔteksjɔ̃] **NF** *Ordinat* unprotecting

DEPS [deəpeεs] *Com (abrév* **dernier entré, premier sorti)** LIFO

dépucelage [depyslaʒ] **NM** *Fam* loss of one's virginity; **son d. a eu lieu l'été de ses 15 ans** she had sex for the first time the summer she was 15, the first time for her was the summer she was 15

dépuceler [depysle] **VT** *Fam* to take the virginity of, to deflower; **se faire d.** to lose one's virginity, to have sex for the first time; **il faudrait qu'il se fasse d.** he needs to lose his virginity; **elle a été dépucelée très jeune** she first had sex at a very young age; **c'est lui qui l'a dépucelée** he was her first

DEPUIS [dəpɥi]

PRÉP	since **1** ▪ for **2** ▪ from **2–4**
ADV	since (then) ▪ later
CONJ	since *(depuis que)*

PRÉP **SEE GRAMMAR A72; B31; B55** **1** *(temps)* since; **je ne suis pas sorti d. hier** I haven't been out since yesterday; **en vigueur d. le 1ᵉʳ avril** in force since 1 April; **elle est handicapée d. l'âge de cinq ans** she has been disabled since she was five *or* from the age of five; **ils ne se sont plus quittés d. leur rencontre** they haven't been apart since they first met; **d. ce temps-là, d. lors** since then, since that time; **d. ce jour, tout a changé** everything changed after that, since that day everything has changed; **je suis là d. le déjeuner** I've been here (ever) since lunch; **d. quand êtes-vous ici?** how long have you been here?; **d. quand est-il permis d'entrer sans frapper?** since when can you come in without knocking?

2 *(durée)* for; **je suis ici d. trois jours** I've been here for three days; **d. combien de temps êtes-vous mariés?** how long have you been married (for)?; **il l'aime/vit ici d. toujours** he has always loved her/lived here; **d. le matin jusqu'au soir** from morning till night; **d. le temps que je te le dis** considering how often I've told you; *Fam* **comment vas-tu, d. le temps?** how have you been all this time?; **ça devait casser, d. le temps!** it had to break sometime!, it was bound to break sometime!; **arrivé d. peu** arrived a short while ago; **d. la nuit des temps** since the dawn of time; **d. des siècles** for centuries

3 *(lieu etc)* from; **d. ma chambre, j'entends tout** I can hear everything from my room; **il ne m'a pas parlé d. Rouen** he hasn't spoken to me since (we left) Rouen; *Radio* **concert transmis d. Londres** concert broadcast from London; **un embouteillage d. La Rochelle** a traffic jam all the way from La Rochelle; **téléphoner d. chez soi** to ring from home

4 *(ordre, quantité)* **chemises d. 30 euros (jusqu'à 150 euros)** shirts from 30 (to 150) euros; **des robes d. la taille 34** dresses from size 34 upwards

ADV since (then), since that time; *(par la suite)* afterwards, later; **d., je comprends mieux son attitude** I've understood his attitude better since then *or* since that time; **je l'ai connu d.** I made his acquaintance later

CONJ d. que + *ind* since; **nous ne l'avons pas vu d. qu'il est marié** we haven't seen him since he got married; **d. qu'il sait qu'il va la voir, il ne tient plus en place** he hasn't been able to keep still since he found out he was going to see her; **d. qu'elle couche avec le patron, elle ne nous dit plus bonjour** she hasn't acknowledged us since she's been sleeping with the boss, now that she's sleeping with the boss she doesn't acknowledge us any more; **d. que le monde est monde** since the world began

dépuratif, -ive [depyratif, -iv] **ADJ, NM** *Méd* purgative

dépuration [depyrasjɔ̃] **NF** *(du sang)* cleansing

dépurer [depyre] **VT** *(sang)* to cleanse

députation [depytasjɔ̃] **NF 1** *(action)* delegation, deputing, delegating; *(groupe)* deputation, delegation **2** *Pol (fonction de député)* membership of Parliament; **la d. n'est pas une chose facile** it is not easy being a Member of Parliament; **candidat à la d.** parliamentary candidate; **se présenter à la d.** to stand for Parliament

député [depyte] **NM 1** *(représentant)* deputy, delegate **2** *Pol Br* ≃ Member of Parliament (**de** for), *Am* ≃ Congressman, *f* Congresswoman; **d. du Parlement européen** Member of the European Parliament, MEP; **la Chambre des députés** *Br* ≃ the House of Commons, *Am* ≃ the House of Representatives; **elle a été élue d.** *ou* **députée** she was elected a Member of Parliament *or* to Parliament; **d.-maire** = MP and mayor

députer [depyte] **VT** to appoint as deputy *or* delegate, to depute; **on l'a députe comme ambassadeur au Vatican** he has been appointed ambassador to the Vatican; **c'est lui qui a été député pour les négociations** he's been appointed *or* delegated to take charge of the negotiations

déqualification [dekalifikasjɔ̃] **NF la d. (professionnelle) est de plus en plus fréquente** more and more people are overqualified for their jobs *or* for the work they do; **les jeunes souffrent de la d.** young people are overqualified

déqualifier [dekalifje] **VT** *(de l'automatisation)* *(ouvrier)* to deskill; **on est souvent obligé de d. les gens qu'on embauche** it is frequently necessary to recruit people for jobs they are overqualified for

der [dɛr] **NM** *OU* **NF** *INV Fam (abrév* **dernier)** **la d. des d.** the war to end all wars

déracinable [derasinabl] **ADJ** which can be uprooted; **le racisme n'est guère plus d. aujourd'hui qu'il y a un siècle** it is no easier to uproot *or* eradicate racism now than it was a century ago

déraciné, -ée [derasine] **ADJ** uprooted **N** person who has been uprooted

déracinement [derasinmɑ̃] **NM** *(d'une souche)*, *Fig (d'une personne)* uprooting; *(d'un défaut, d'un abus, d'une idée reçue etc)* eradication

déraciner [derasine] **VT** *(souche, arbre)* to uproot, to tear up by the roots; *Fig (personne)* to uproot; *(défaut, abus, idée reçue)* to eradicate; *(racisme, sexisme)* to uproot, to eradicate

déraidir [derɛdir] **VT** *(membre, tissu etc)* to take the stiffness out of; *Fig (caractère de qn)* to soften **VPR se déraidir** *(d'un membre, tissu etc)* to lose its stiffness; *(d'une personne)* to unbend, to thaw

déraillement [derɑjmɑ̃] **NM** *Rail* derailment

dérailler [derɑje] **VI 1** *(d'un train, d'un tram)* to become derailed, to leave the rails; *(d'une pointe de lecture)* to jump *or* leave the sound groove; **faire d. un train** to derail a train **2** *Fam (d'une machine etc)* to be on the blink; *(d'une personne) (dire une bêtise, se tromper)* to talk nonsense; *(divaguer)* to rave; *(devenir gâteux)* to go gaga

dérailleur [derɑjœr] **NM** *(de bicyclette)* derailleur (gears)

déraison [derεzɔ̃] **NF** *Litt* unreasonableness, folly

déraisonnable [derεzɔnabl] **ADJ** foolish

déraisonnablement [derεzɔnabləmɑ̃] **ADV** foolishly

déraisonner [derεzɔne] **VI** *Litt* to talk nonsense

dérangé [derɑ̃ʒe] **ADJ** *(esprit)* deranged, unbalanced; *(estomac)* upset; *Fam* **tu es complètement d.!** you're off your rocker!

dérangeant [derɑ̃ʒɑ̃] **ADJ** *(film, personnage)* disturbing

dérangement [derɑ̃ʒmɑ̃] **NM 1** *(gêne)* disturbance, trouble; *(perturbation)* disturbed *or* unsettled state; **causer du d. à qn** to put sb to trouble *or* bother; **je ne veux pas te causer de d.** I don't want to put you to any trouble *or* bother; **excusez-moi pour le d.** I'm sorry to disturb *or* trouble you; **il faudrait le dédommager de son d.** we'll have to give him something for his trouble **2** *(désordre)* *(de livres, meubles etc)* disarrangement, disorder; *Élec (dans la ligne etc)* fault; *Tél* **la ligne est en d.** the line is out of order, there's a fault on the line; **d. d'esprit** mental derangement; **d. de l'intestin** upset stomach

déranger [derɑ̃ʒe] **(je dérangeai(s); n. dérangeons) VT 1** *(papiers, livres etc)* to disturb, to put out of order, to disarrange; *(chignon, mise)* to rumple; **il a dérangé ma chambre** he's made my room untidy

2 *(gêner)* *(personne)* to disturb; **ne pas d.** *(sur panneau)* do not disturb; **je ne peux pas travailler, je suis sans arrêt dérangé** I can't work with all these interruptions; **cela vous dérange si j'ouvre la fenêtre?** would you mind if I opened the window?; **je vous dérange?** am I disturbing you?; *Iron* **je ne te dérange pas trop?** am I in your way?; **excusez-moi de vous d.** I'm sorry to disturb *or* trouble you; **si cela ne vous dérange pas** if it's no trouble to you, if that's all right by you, if you don't mind; **je ne voudrais pas vous d. pour rien** I wouldn't want to bring you out for nothing; *Fam Iron* **ça te dérangerait de me laisser tranquille?** would you mind very much leaving me alone?; *Fam* **et alors, ça te dérange?** what business is it of yours?, what's it to you?

3 *(perturber)* *(personne, projets)* to upset; **d. l'esprit de qn** to affect the balance of sb's mind; **avoir le cerveau dérangé** to be deranged; **quelque chose lui a dérangé l'estomac** something has upset his stomach; *Tél* **la ligne est dérangée** the line is out of order; **le temps est complètement dérangé** the weather is all back to front

VPR se déranger **merci de vous être dérangé** thank you for putting yourself out *or* for the trouble you've gone to; **ne vous dérangez pas pour moi** please don't put yourself out *or* go to any trouble on my account; **nous pouvons nous d. à toute heure de la nuit** we can come out at any time of the night; **il ne se dérange jamais, c'est toujours nous qui devons y aller** he never comes to us, we always have to go to him

dérapage [derapaʒ] **NM 1** *Aut* skid; *Aviat, Ski* sideslip; *Pol, Fig (erreur)* bad mistake; *Fig (d'un budget, d'un horaire)* slippage; *(d'une conversation)* deterioration; *Aut* **d. contrôlé** controlled skid; *Fig* **le d. des prix** spiralling prices; **le d. inflationniste** the inflationary spiral; **il y a déjà eu plusieurs dérapages dans cette émission** there have already been several inappropriate outbursts in the programme; **il faudrait éviter tout d. dans les négociations de paix** there must be no hitches in the peace talks, the peace talks must not come unstuck *or* become derailed **2** *Naut (d'ancre)* dragging

déraper [derape] VI **1** *Aut* to skid; *Aviat, Ski* to sideslip; *Fig (des prix)* to be rising uncontrollably, to soar, to rise sharply; *(d'une conversation)* to deteriorate; *Fig* **le budget dérape** there's some slippage in the budget; **il faut éviter que les négociations ne dérapent** the talks must not go wrong *or* come unstuck *or* become derailed; **le débat a rapidement dérapé vers le duel** the discussion rapidly deteriorated into *or* turned into a fight; **les commentaires ont dérapé vers une critique sévère** comment has turned into severe criticism **2** *Naut (d'une ancre)* to drag

dératé [derate] NM *Fam* **courir comme un d.** to run flat out

dératisation [deratizasjɔ̃] NF extermination of rats

dératiser [deratize] VT to clear of rats

dérayage [derɛjaʒ] NM *Cin, TV* polishing out

dérayer [derɛje] VT *Cin, TV* to polish out

derby [dɛrbi] NM **1** *Courses de chevaux* derby; **le D. d'Epsom** the Derby **2** *Ftbl* local derby

derche [dɛrʃ] NM *très Fam* butt, *Br* bum, *Am* fanny; **se magner le d.** to move one's butt *or Br* bum; **un faux d.** a two-faced swine *or Am* stinker

derechef [dərəʃɛf] ADV *Arch, Litt* a second time, yet again, once more

déréférencement [dereferɑ̃smɑ̃] NM *Mktg (d'un produit)* delisting

déréférencer [dereferɑ̃se] VT *(produit)* to delist; **certains produits ont été déréférencés par le distributeur** some products have been delisted by the distributor

déréglé [deregle] ADJ **1** *(machine, horloge etc)* not working properly **2** *(estomac)* upset; *(esprit)* disordered; *(pouls)* irregular; *(temps)* unsettled **3** *(vie)* wild, dissolute; **il a des mœurs complètement déréglées** he is quite dissolute *or* debauched

dérèglement [dereglǝmɑ̃] NM **1** *(d'une machine, d'une horloge)* malfunctioning **2** *(du temps)* unsettled state; *(du pouls)* irregularity; **d. de l'esprit** mental derangement; **j'ai un d. de l'appétit** there is something wrong with my appetite; **d. hormonal** hormone disorder **3** *(de l'imagination)* disordered state; *(de la moralité)* dissoluteness; **il fait montre d'un d. de l'imagination** his imagination is getting out of control; *Vieilli, Hum* **dérèglements** dissolute behaviour

déréglementation [dereglǝmɑ̃tasjɔ̃] NF deregulation

déréglementer [dereglǝmɑ̃te] VT to deregulate

dérégler [deregle] (**je dérègle, n. déréglons; je déréglerai**) VT **1** *(horloge, machine etc)* to cause to malfunction; *Radio, TV* to detune; **tu as déréglé la pendule/le moteur à force de la/le démonter** you've dismantled the clock/the engine so many times that it's gone haywire **2** *(estomac)* to upset; *(personne, esprit, habitudes, temps)* to unsettle; **d. son sommeil** to disrupt one's sleeping pattern; **elle a complètement déréglé son appétit avec tous ses régimes** all these diets have completely disrupted her eating patterns

VPR **se dérégler 1** *(d'horloge, de machine etc)* to go wrong **2** *(de pouls)* to be irregular; *(d'estomac)* to be upset; **son esprit se dérègle** his mind is going; **elle s'est déréglé le système digestif** she's ruined her digestive system **3** *(de moralité)* to become dissolute; *(d'imagination)* to run wild, to get out of control

dérider [deride] VT to cheer up, to brighten up; **c'est impossible de le d.** it's impossible to get a smile out of him

VPR **se dérider** to cheer up, to brighten up

Il faut noter que le verbe anglais **to deride** est un faux ami. Il signifie **ridiculiser**.

---

dérision [derizjɔ̃] NF derision, mockery; **dire qch par d.** to say sth derisively *or* mockingly; **geste de d.** derisive gesture; **tourner qch en d.** to deride sth; **c'est une d.!** *(chose insignifiante)* it's ridiculous *or* laughable!

dérisoire [derizwar] ADJ *(offre, salaire)* derisory, laughable; *(prix)* very low, rock-bottom; **vendre qch à un prix d.** to sell sth at a ridiculously *or* an absurdly low price; **cette objection me paraît d.** that seems an absurd objection to me

dérisoirement [derizwarmɑ̃] ADV laughably, pathetically; **il est payé d.** he's paid a derisory *or* laughable *or* pathetic amount

dérivatif, -ive [derivatif, -iv] ADJ *Ling* derivative

NM distraction (**à, de** from); **c'est un d. à sa douleur** it takes his mind off his grief; **le sport est un excellent d.** sport is an excellent way of taking your mind off things

dérivation [derivasjɔ̃] NF **1** *Aut* diversion; *Tech (d'un cours d'eau)* diversion, tapping; *Élec (du courant)* shunt(ing), branching, tapping; *Tech* by-pass; **canal de d.** headrace, penstock; *Élec* **monté en d.** shunt connected **2** *Ling, Math* derivation **3** *Naut, Aviat* drift

dérive [deriv] NF **1** *Naut* drift, leeway; *Aviat* drift; **(quille de) d.** *Naut* drop keel, centreboard; *Aviat* fin; **angle de d.** angle of drift, drift angle; **à la d., en d.** adrift; **navire en d.** drifting vessel; *Géog* **d. des continents** continental drift **2** *(évolution incontrôlée et dangereuse)* **tout va à la d.** everything has been left to drift; **un mariage/une entreprise qui part à la d.** a failing marriage/business; **des jeunes à la d. dans la grande ville** young people adrift in the big city; **une d. totalitaire est à craindre dans ce pays** this country is in danger of drifting into totalitarianism, there's a danger that this country might be overtaken by totalitarianism

dérivé, -ée [derive] ADJ **1** *(signification etc)* derived, secondary; *Math (fonction, courbe)* derived; **produit d.** *Chimie* by-product; *Bourse* derivative **2** *Élec* **courant d.** shunt current

NM *Ling* derivative; *Chimie, Ind* derivative, by-product; **d. du sang** blood product

NF *Math* **dérivée** derivative

dériver¹ [derive] VT **1** *Tech (cours d'eau)* to divert *or* tap the course of; *Élec (courant)* to shunt, to branch **2** *Ling, Math* to derive

VI *Ling* to be derived (**de** from)

dériver² [derive] VT *Tech* to unrivet

dériver³ [derive] VI **1** *Naut, Aviat* to drift; **d. à vau-l'eau** to drift downstream **2** *Fig (du sujet etc)* to drift away (**de** from)

dériveur [derivœr] NM *Naut* **1** *(bateau)* sailing dinghy *(with centreboard)* **2** *(voile)* storm sail

dérivomètre [derivɔmɛtr] NM *Aviat* drift meter

dermatite [dɛrmatit] NF dermatitis

dermato [dɛrmato] N *Fam (abrév* **dermatologue***)* dermatologist

dermatologie [dɛrmatɔlɔʒi] NF dermatology

dermatologique [dɛrmatɔlɔʒik] ADJ dermatological

dermatologiste [dɛrmatɔlɔʒist], **dermatologue** [dɛrmatɔlɔg] N dermatologist

dermatose [dɛrmatoz] NF *Méd* dermatosis

derme [dɛrm] NM *Anat* derm

dermique [dɛrmik] ADJ *Anat* dermic, dermal

---

dermite [dɛrmit] NF *Méd* = dermatite

DERNIER, -IÈRE [dɛrnje, -jɛr]

ADJ	last **1–6** = final **1** = latest **2**
	= utmost **4** = bottom **3, 5** = worst **5**
N	last **1, 2** = latest **2** = latter **2**
NF	final performance **1** = last edition
	2 = latest **3**
ADV	last (en dernier)

ADJ SEE GRAMMAR B10 **1** *(ultime)* last; *(marquant la fin)* final; **au d. moment** at the last (moment); **à la dernière minute** at the last minute; **des préparatifs de dernière minute** last minute preparations; **les derniers préparatifs** the final preparations; **faire un d. effort** to make a final *or* one last effort; **mettre la dernière main à qch** to give *or* put the finishing *or* final touches to sth; **j'ai dépensé jusqu'à mon d. sou** I've spent my last penny; **la dernière moitié du XVIᵉ siècle** the second half of the 16th century; **les derniers mètres de l'ascension** the final metres of the climb; **d. rappel** *(de facture)* final reminder; **d. paiement** final payment; **c'est mon d. prix** that's my final offer; *Bourse* **d. cours** closing price; *Journ* **dernière heure** copy deadline; *Journ* **dernière page** back page; *Journ* **dernière édition** final edition, late edition; **dernière épreuve** *(dans l'édition)* press proof; **dernière proposition** final offer; **d. délai pour l'inscription** deadline for registration; **il faut libérer la chambre à 9 h, d. délai** *ou Fam* **carat** the room has to be vacated by 9 o'clock at the very latest; **en d. recours** *ou* **ressort** as a last resort; **en dernière analyse** in the final analysis; **en d. lieu** last, lastly; **c'est la dernière personne à qui je demanderais un service** he's the last person I would ask a favour of; **pour la dernière fois** for the last time; **il veut toujours avoir le d. mot** he always has to have the last word; **je n'ai pas dit mon d. mot** I'm not done for yet, there's still fight left in me, you/they/*etc* haven't heard the last of me; **la peste n'a pas dit son d. mot** the plague is still with us, the plague has not been beaten; **c'est ma dernière chance** this is my last chance VOIR GRAMMAIRE A26

2 *(le ou la plus récent(e))* last; **mardi d.** last Tuesday; **le mois d.** last month; **au cours des dernières années** over the past *or* last few years; **la dernière fois, il allait bien** he was well (the) last time I saw him; **je l'ai déjà fait la dernière fois** I did that the last time; **ces derniers temps, ces temps derniers** lately; **dernières nouvelles** latest news; **aux dernières nouvelles, il s'est marié** the last I heard, he had got married; **ce sont les dernières nouvelles que j'ai eues de lui** that's the last I've heard of him; **dernière édition** latest edition; **les derniers développements d'une affaire** the latest developments of an affair; **le d. roman de cet auteur** this author's latest novel; **la dernière mode, le d. cri** the latest fashion, the latest thing; **le d. modèle** the latest model; **mon d. patron était anglais** my last boss was English VOIR GRAMMAIRE A7; A26

3 *(dans l'espace)* last; **la dernière maison du village** the last house in the village; **le d. rang** the back *or* last row; **la dernière marche de l'escalier** *(en haut)* the top step; *(en bas)* the bottom step; **au d. étage** on the top floor; **le d. tiroir de la commode** the bottom drawer of the chest of drawers

4 *Litt (extrême)* utmost; **vérité dernière** ultimate truth; **de la dernière importance** of the utmost *or* greatest importance; **au d. degré** to the utmost *or* highest degree; **le d. degré de la bêtise** the height of stupidity; **atteindre le d. degré de la bêtise** to be the height of *or* the last word in stupidity; **le d. degré de la misère** the depths of poverty; **dans la dernière misère** in utmost poverty; **être du d. bien avec qn** to be extremely friendly with sb, to be great friends with sb; **ils sont du d. bien** they're the best of friends *or* on the best of terms; **être de la dernière insolence avec qn** to be most insolent to *or* with sb; **se débattre avec la dernière énergie** to put up a fierce struggle; **jeter dans le d. désespoir** to cast into the depths of despair; **c'est du d. chic/ridicule** it's the height of elegance/ridiculousness

5 *(le pire)* lowest, worst; **de d. ordre** very inferior; **être le d. élève de la classe** to be last in *or* bottom of the class; **il a été reçu d. au concours** he came in last in the competition; **un hôtel de dernière catégorie** a fourth-rate hotel; **une étoffe de la dernière qualité** *ou* **du d. choix** material of the poorest quality; **c'était la dernière chose à dire/faire** that's the last thing you/he/*etc* should have said/done; *Fml* **ils lui ont fait subir les derniers outrages** they subjected her to the worst outrages

6 *(avec idée de mort)* last; **ils ont bien cru que leur dernière heure était venue** they really thought that their last hour had come; **je m'en souviendrai jusqu'à mon d. jour** *ou* **jusqu'à ma dernière heure** I shall remember it to my dying day; **nous sommes restés avec lui jusqu'à son d. souffle** we stayed with him until the last *or* the end; **rendre le d. soupir** to breathe one's last; **rendre les derniers devoirs à qn** to lay sb out; **recevoir les derniers sacrements** to receive the last rites; **ce sont ses dernières volontés** that was his dying wish; **les dernières dispositions du défunt** the dead man's last will and testament; **accompagner qn à sa dernière demeure** to accompany sb to his/her final resting place

N 1 *(dans classement)* last; *Sport* **il est arrivé le d.** *ou* **bon d.** he came in last; **le d. arrivé** the last to arrive; **il est le d. de sa promotion** he is bottom of his year; **dans les derniers** among the last; **les six derniers** the last six; **c'est le d. de mes soucis** that's the least of my worries; **elle est la dernière à qui je demanderais de l'aide** she's the last person I'd ask for help; **je les arrêterai tous jusqu'au d.** I'll stop each and every last one of them

2 *(dans chronologie)* last, latest; **c'est notre petit d.** he's our youngest (child); **comment va la petite dernière?** how's the little one?; **ce d. répondit …** the latter answered …; **le d. en date** the most recent; **c'est toujours le d. à sortir** he's always last out

3 *Péj* **on la traite comme la dernière des dernières** they treat her like dirt *or* the lowest of the low; **ton frère est vraiment le d. des crétins/des menteurs** your brother is the world's biggest fool/liar; *très Fam* **c'est vraiment la dernière des connes** she really is an utter prat

NF dernière 1 *Théâtre* last night, final performance

2 *Journ (édition)* last edition; *(page)* back page

3 *(nouveauté)* **tu as entendu la dernière de ton frère?** have you heard your brother's latest?

ADV en d. last (of all); **cela vient en d.** that comes last; **il sort toujours en d.** he's always last out; **je mange toujours le meilleur en d.** I always keep the best till last

---

dernièrement [dɛrnjɛrmɑ̃] **ADV** lately, of late, recently

dernier-né, *pl* **-née,** *pl* **derniers-nés, dernières-nées N** youngest child

dérobade [derɔbad] **NF 1** *(de qn, qch)* evasion, avoidance; **c'est le spécialiste de la d.** he's a past master at avoiding the issue; **il pratique beaucoup la d. pour ne pas payer ce qu'il lui doit** he gets out of paying what he owes her as much as he can **2** *(d'un cheval)* swerve, jib

dérobé [derɔbe] **ADJ** *(escalier, porte etc)* hidden, concealed, secret

dérobée (à la) [aladerɔbe] **ADV** stealthily, secretly, on the sly; **regarder qn à la d.** to steal a glance at sb; **sortir à la d.** to steal out

dérober [derɔbe] **VT 1** *(voler)* to steal, to make away with; **d. qch à qn** to steal sth from sb; **d. un baiser** to steal a kiss **2** *(cacher)* to hide, to conceal; **d. qch à qn** to hide sth from sb; **ce mur dérobe la vue** this wall hides the view; **d. qn au danger** to snatch sb from danger

VPR se dérober 1 *(s'échapper)* to escape, to steal away, to slip away (à from); **se d. aux regards** to escape observation, to avoid notice; **se d. à la curiosité de qn** to avoid sb's prying eyes; **se d. à son devoir** to evade *or* shirk one's duty; **je le lui ai demandé, mais il s'est dérobé** I asked him, but he avoided the issue **2** *(manquer)* *(du sol, des genoux, des jambes)* to give way (**sous** beneath) **3** *(de cheval)* to swerve, to jib

dérogation [derɔgasjɔ̃] **NF** *(pour passer un examen)* waiver, exemption; *Jur* waiver; *(à une loi)* derogation, impairment (à of); **d. à qch** departure from sth, exception to sth; **par** *ou* **en d. à cette règle** this rule notwithstanding, as an exception to this rule; **je n'admettrai aucune d.** I will allow no exceptions

dérogatoire [derɔgatwar] **ADJ** *Jur* **clause d.** waiver, *Spéc* derogatory clause

déroger [derɔʒe] **VI (je dérogeai(s); n. dérogeons) d. à l'usage/à la loi** to depart from custom/the law; **d. à un principe** to waive a principle; *Hist* **d. (à noblesse)** to lose rank; **d. à son rang** to lower *or* demean oneself

dérougir [deruʒir] **VI 1** *Vieilli (perdre de sa rougeur)* to stop blushing **2** *Can Fam* **ne pas d.** *(du travail)* not to let up; *(être bondé)* to be jam packed; *(être en colère)* to be always raging; *(être soûl)* to be permanently pissed

dérouillée [deruje] **NF** *très Fam* beating, belting

dérouiller [deruje] **VT 1** *(enlever la rouille de)* to take *or* get the rust off **2** *très Fam (battre)* to beat up

VI *très Fam* **1** *(être battu)* to get beaten up, to catch it; **qu'est-ce qu'il a dérouillé!** he really took a beating! **2** *(souffrir)* to suffer, to have a hard time; **depuis qu'il a cette otite, qu'est-ce qu'il dérouille** he's suffered agonies with that earache

VPR se dérouiller se d. les jambes to stretch one's legs; **se d. la mémoire** to refresh one's memory

déroulement [derulmɑ̃] **NM 1** *(d'une intrigue, des événements)* unfolding, development, progress; **nous avons besoin de connaître le d. de votre journée** we need to know how you spent the day; **le d. des travaux s'est passé normalement** the work went smoothly; **pendant tout le d. de la cérémonie** throughout the ceremony; **il a surveillé tout le d. des opérations** he monitored operations from start to finish **2** *(d'une bobine etc)* unwinding

dérouler [derule] **VT** *(rouleau)* to unroll; *(store)* to let down; *(câble etc)* to unwind, to uncoil; **le serpent a déroulé ses anneaux** the snake uncoiled itself; *Ordinat* **d. un menu** to pull down a menu; *Fig Litt* **il a déroulé le fil de sa vie** he recounted *or* unfolded the story of his life

VPR se dérouler 1 *(d'un rouleau)* to come unrolled, to unroll; *(d'un store)* to come down; *(d'un câble etc)* to come unwound; *(d'un serpent)* to uncoil **2** *Fig* to unfold; **le paysage se déroule devant nous** the landscape unfolds *or* stretches out before us; **les événements qui se déroulent à Paris** the events (that are) unfolding *or* taking place in Paris; **la manifestation s'est déroulée dans le calme** the demonstration went off peacefully *or*

was peaceful; **son existence se déroule dans la plus grande monotonie** he leads the most monotonous of existences

dérouleur [derulœr] **NM** *Ordinat* tape drive, streamer; **d. de bandes** tape streamer

déroutage [deruta3] **NM d. de marchandises** rerouting of goods

déroutant [derutɑ̃] **ADJ** disconcerting

déroute [derut] **NF** *(débandade)* rout, disorderly retreat; **l'ennemi fut mis en d.** the enemy was put to flight *or* was routed

déroutement [derutmɑ̃] **NM** *Naut, Aviat* rerouting, diversion

dérouter [derute] **VT 1** *(confondre)* to nonplus, *Fam* to throw **2** *(tromper)* to lead astray; **d. la police** to throw the police off the scent; **d. les soupçons** to divert suspicion **3** *(navire, avion etc)* to divert, to reroute

derrick [derik] **NM** *Pétr* derrick

DERRIÈRE [dɛrjɛr] **PRÉP 1** *(au dos de)* behind, *Am* in back of; **il s'est caché d. le rideau** he hid behind the curtain; **les uns d. les autres** one behind the other; *aussi Fig* **les autres sont loin d. moi** the others are way behind me; **il faut toujours être d. elle** *ou* **son dos** you always have to be at her back; **il a laissé une femme et deux enfants d. lui** he left a wife and two children; **d. des abords chaleureux** behind a cordial façade; **faire qch d. (le dos de) qn** to do sth behind sb's back; **dire du mal d. (le dos de) qn** to say nasty things about sb behind his/her back; **c'est lui qui est d. tout ça** he's the one behind all this

2 de d. from behind; **sortir de d. un buisson** to come out from behind a bush

ADV 1 *(en arrière)* behind, at the back, in the rear; **laisser qn d.** to leave sb behind; **regarder d.** to look back; **ton parapluie est d.** your umbrella is at the back; **enfiler un pull sens devant d.** to put on a pullover back to front; **ça se ferme d.** it fastens (up) at the back; *Aut* **aller** *ou* **monter d.** to sit in the back *or Am* in back; **taisez-vous, d.!** *(en voiture)* be quiet back there!; *(dans une pièce)* be quiet at the back!

2 par d. from behind; **attaquer qn par d.** to attack sb from behind *or* from the rear; **cette robe s'attache par d.** the dress does up at the back; **il a dû passer par d.** he had to go round the back; *Fig* **elle le critique par d.** she criticizes him behind his back

NM 1 *(d'édifice etc)* back, rear; **le d. de la tête** the back of the head; **porte de d.** back door; **pattes de d.** hind legs

2 *(postérieur)* behind, backside, bottom, *Am* butt; *(d'un animal)* hindquarters; *Fig Fam* **il en est tombé sur le d.** it knocked him for six, he nearly fainted (with surprise); **recevoir des coups de pied dans le** *ou* **au d.** to get kicked in the behind *or* up the backside

déruralisation [deryralizasjɔ̃] **NF** rural depopulation

dérushage [derœʃa3] **NM** *TV, Cin* first view

dérusher [deryʃe] **VT** *Cin, TV* to edit

derviche [dɛrviʃ] **NM** dervish; **d. tourneur** dancing *or* whirling dervish

des [de] *voir* **de**

dès [dɛ] **PRÉP** since, from, as early as, as long ago as; **d. sa jeunesse** from childhood; **d. l'abord** from the outset, from the (very) first; **d. maintenant,** *Fml* **d. à présent** from now on, *Fml* henceforth; **j'ai décidé de commencer le projet d. maintenant** I've decided to start on the project now *or* immediately; **d. 1840** as far back as 1840; **d. le matin** first thing in the morning; **d. son arrivée** the minute *or* the moment he arrives/arrived, as soon as he arrives/arrived; **d. mon retour** immediately on my return; **je te téléphonerai d. mon retour** I'll call you as soon as *or* immediately *or* the minute I get back; **d. sa première remarque, j'ai senti que ...** as soon as he spoke *or* from the moment he spoke, I felt that ...; **d. les premiers froids** as soon as it starts to get cold; **elle est ivre d. le premier verre** she's tipsy after one drink, one drink and she's tipsy; **d. la porte, il commença à crier** he had no sooner reached the door than he began to shout; **d. l'autoroute, on sentait la différence de température** as soon as we reached the motorway, we could feel the difference in temperature; **d. Paris, la pluie tombait** it rained all the way from Paris; **d. que** + *ind* as soon as, the moment that; **d. lors** *(dans le temps)* then; *(par conséquent)* consequently, therefore; **ils vendirent leur maison et d. lors, partirent habiter à Paris** as soon as they sold their house, they went off to live in Paris; **d. lors que vous refusez** seeing that *or* since you refuse SEE GRAMMAR B31–2

désabonnement [dezabɔnmɑ̃] NM cancellation (of subscription)

désabonner [dezabɔne] VT **d. qn à une revue** to cancel sb's subscription to a magazine
▪ VPR **se désabonner** to stop subscribing, to cancel one's subscription (**à** to)

désabusé [dezabyze] ADJ disillusioned, disenchanted

désabusement [dezabyzmɑ̃] NM disillusionment, disenchantment

désabuser [dezabyze] VT *Litt* **d. qn** to disillusion sb, to open sb's eyes; **c'est un esprit désabusé** he's disillusioned

désacclimater [dezaklimate] VT **d. qn/qch** to remove sb/sth from their/its natural habitat

désaccord [dezakɔr] NM *(mésentente)* disagreement; *(d'intérêts etc)* clash; **les désaccords entre les États-Unis et Cuba** the disagreements *or* the dissension between the United States and Cuba; **c'est un de leurs désaccords** it's one of the things they disagree about; **être** *ou* **se trouver en d. avec qn sur qch** to disagree *or* be at odds with sb about sth; **sujet de d.** bone of contention; **d. entre la théorie et la pratique** discrepancy between theory and practice; **il y a d. entre ses paroles et sa conduite** his words are inconsistent *or* not in keeping with his conduct; **vivre en d. avec son époque** to be out of step with one's time

désaccordé [dezakɔrde] ADJ *Mus* out of tune

désaccorder [dezakɔrde] *Mus* VT *(instrument)* to put out of tune
▪ VPR **se désaccorder** to go out of tune

désaccoupler [dezakuple] VT **1** *Tech (wagons)* to uncouple; *Élec* to disconnect **2** *(chiens de meute)* to slip, to uncouple

désaccoutumance [dezakutymɑ̃s] NF **d. de** *ou* **à la drogue** breaking the habit of taking drugs; **la d. à la drogue est quelque chose de pénible** overcoming drug addiction is a painful process; *Fig* **j'étais tellement bien avec toi que la d. va être longue et douloureuse** being with you was so good that learning to live without you will be a long and painful process

désaccoutumer [dezakutyme] VT **d. qn à (faire) qch** to get sb out of the habit of (doing) sth
▪ VPR **se désaccoutumer** to lose the habit; **se d. de (faire) qch** to get out of the habit of (doing) sth

désacralisation [desakralizasjɔ̃] NF *(de la famille etc)* desanctification

désacraliser [desakralize] VT *(famille etc)* to desanctify

désactivation [dezaktivasjɔ̃] NF *Nucl (d'un site)* cleaning up; *Ordinat* deactivation

désactiver [dezaktive] VT *Nucl (site)* to clean up; *Ordinat* to deactivate, to disable

désadaptation [dezadaptasjɔ̃] NF unsuitability; **il montre une d. au milieu scolaire** he shows signs of not being suited to school life

désadapter [dezadapte] VT **d. qn de qch** to wean sb away from sth; **le risque de les d. à** *ou* **de leur vie quotidienne** the danger of creating a gulf between them and their everyday life

désaffectation [dezafɛktasjɔ̃] NF *(fermeture) (d'un bâtiment)* closing down; *(d'une église)* deconsecration

désaffecté [dezafɛkte] ADJ disused; **église désaffectée** deconsecrated church

désaffecter [dezafɛkte] VT *(bâtiment public etc)* to put to another purpose; *(fermer) (bâtiment)* to close down

désaffection [dezafɛksjɔ̃] NF disaffection (**pour** with)

désagrafer [dezagrafe] VT *(vêtement)* to unfasten, to undo
▪ VPR **se désagrafer** to unfasten *or* undo one's dress/*etc*

désagréable [dezagreabl] ADJ *(personne, remarque)* unpleasant, disagreeable (**à** to); *(odeur)* unpleasant, nasty; *Euph* **ce n'est pas d.** that's (a bit of) all right

désagréablement [dezagreabləmɑ̃] ADV unpleasantly, disagreeably

désagrégation [dezagregasjɔ̃] NF disintegration, breaking up

désagréger [dezagreʒe] (**je désagrège, n. désagrégeons; je désagrégeai(s); je désagrégerai**) VT to cause to disintegrate; **la bombe a complètement désagrégé l'immeuble** the bomb completely destroyed the building, *Fam* the bomb smashed the building to smithereens; **la météorite a désagrégé la navette spatiale** the space shuttle disintegrated when the meteorite hit it
▪ VPR **se désagréger** to disintegrate, to break up

désagrément [dezagremɑ̃] NM trouble; **causer du d.** *ou* **des désagréments à qn** *(d'une personne)* to cause unpleasantness for sb; **sa voiture lui cause beaucoup de désagréments** his car gives him lots of problems; **il a beaucoup de désagréments avec sa voiture** he's got a lot of problems with his car; **les désagréments de la situation** the unpleasantness of the situation; **l'éloignement et la solitude font partie des désagréments de la situation** distance and loneliness are two of the things that make this a difficult situation

désaimantation [dezɛmɑ̃tasjɔ̃] NF demagnetization

désaimanter [dezɛmɑ̃te] VT to demagnetize

désaisonnalisé [desezɔnalize] ADJ seasonally adjusted

désaligné [dezaliɲe] ADJ out of alignment, out of line

désaltérant [dezalterɑ̃] ADJ thirst-quenching

désaltérer [dezaltere] (**je désaltère, n. désaltérons; je désaltérerai**) VT **d. qn** to quench sb's thirst
▪ VI **le thé désaltère mieux qu'une boisson glacée** tea is more thirst-quenching than an ice-cold drink
▪ VPR **se désaltérer** to quench one's thirst

désambiguïsation [dezɑ̃biɡɥizasjɔ̃] NF clarification

désambiguïser [dezɑ̃biɡɥize] VT *(situation)* to clarify, to clear up; **il faut absolument d. ta relation avec lui vis-à-vis de ta famille** you really must make your relationship with

him crystal-clear to your family; **un mot est souvent désambiguïsé par un contexte** a word in context is rarely ambiguous

désâmer (se) [sədezame] VPR *Can* to work oneself to death

désamiantage [dezamjɑ̃taʒ] NM removal of asbestos fireproofing

désamorçage [dezamɔrsaʒ] NM *(d'une bombe, d'un obus etc)*, *Fig (d'un conflit)* defusing

désamorcer [dezamɔrse] (**je désamorçai(s); n. désamorçons**) VT *(bombe, obus etc)*, *Fig (conflit, querelle)* to defuse; *Fig (neutraliser) (complot)* to render harmless

désamour [dezamur] NM **1** *(cessation de l'amour)* falling out of love **2** *(désillusion)* disenchantment, disillusionment

désanamorphoser [dezanamɔrfoze] VT *(image)* to unsqueeze

désannoncer [dezanɔse] VT *Radio (morceau de musique, émission)* to back-announce

désaper (se) [sədezape] VPR *Fam* to strip off

désapparier [dezaparje] VT *(objets)* to remove one of a pair of, to spoil a pair of; *(couple d'oiseaux, d'animaux)* to separate; **j'ai un tas de gants désappariés** I've got piles of odd gloves

désappointement [dezapwɛ̃tmɑ̃] NM *Litt* disappointment

désappointer [dezapwɛ̃te] VT *Litt* to disappoint

désapprendre [dezaprɑ̃dr] VT *Fml* to forget; *(exprès)* to unlearn

désapprobateur, -trice [dezaprɔbatœr, -tris] ADJ disapproving; **regard d.** disapproving look, look of disapproval

désapprobation [dezaprɔbasjɔ̃] NF disapproval (**de** of); **regard de d.** disapproving look, look of disapproval; **murmure de d.** murmur of disapproval

désapprouver [dezapruve] VT to disapprove of; **elle désapprouve mon projet** she disapproves *or* doesn't approve of my plan; **il désapprouve que je vienne** he disapproves of my coming; **je le désapprouve de ne pas avoir travaillé** I disapprove of the fact that he didn't work

désapprovisionné [dezaprɔvizjɔne] ADJ *(compte)* overdrawn

désarçonner [dezarsɔne] VT *(de cheval)* to unseat, to throw; *Fig (d'un adversaire, d'une question, d'une situation)* to floor, to throw

désargenté [dezarʒɑ̃te] ADJ **1** *(fourchette, cuillère etc)* tarnished **2** *Fam (personne)* broke

désarmant [dezarmɑ̃] ADJ *(sourire etc)* disarming

désarmé [dezarme] ADJ **1** *(personne) (qui n'a plus d'arme)* disarmed; *(qui n'a jamais eu d'arme)* unarmed, defenceless **2** *(arme)* unloaded **3** *(navire)* laid up, out of commission

désarmement [dezarməmɑ̃] NM **1** *(d'une personne)* disarming; *Mil, Pol* disarmament; *Mil, Pol* **d. nucléaire** nuclear disarmament; **d. progressif/multilatéral/unilatéral** progressive/multilateral/unilateral disarmament **2** *Naut (de navire)* laying up

désarmer [dezarme] VT **1** *(une personne, un pays)* to disarm; *Fig* **il montrait une franchise qui vous désarmait** he was disarmingly frank **2** *(arme) (enlever les balles de)* to unload; *(placer le cran de sûreté de)* to uncock **3** *Naut (navire)* to lay up
▪ VI *(cesser) (always neg)* **haine/désir de vengeance qui ne désarme pas** unrelenting *or* relentless hatred/desire for vengeance; **sa colère ne désarme pas** he is still angry

désarrimage [dezarimaʒ] NM *Naut etc (d'une cargaison)* shifting

désarrimer [dezarime] VT *Naut etc (cargaison)* to shift

désarroi [dezarwa] NM disarray, confusion; **jeter qn dans le d.** to throw sb into disarray; **il est en plein** *ou* **dans un grand d.** he's in a state of utter disarray *or* confusion

désarticulation [dezartikylasjɔ̃] NF *Méd* dislocation

désarticuler [dezartikyle] VT *Méd* to dislocate; *Fig* **d. un échafaudage** to dismantle scaffolding
▪ VPR **se désarticuler** to be double-jointed

désassemblage [dezasɑ̃blaʒ] NM dismantling

désassembler [dezasɑ̃ble] VT to dismantle, to take apart

désassembleur [dezasɑ̃blœr] NM *Ordinat* disassembler

désassortir [dezasɔrtir] VT *(conj like assortir)* **1** *(série, collection etc)* to spoil, to break up; **service de table désassorti** dinner service made up of odd pieces **2** *(magasin)* to clear (of stock)

désastre [dezastr] NM disaster, calamity; **d. financier** financial disaster, crash; **la soirée fut un vrai d.** the party was a disaster; **courir au d.** to court disaster

désastreusement [dezastrøzmɑ̃] ADV disastrously

désastreux, -euse [dezastrø, -øz] ADJ disastrous; **un travail d.** a dreadful *or* an appalling piece of work

désatellisation [dezatelizasjɔ̃] NF **la d. d'un pays** making a country more autonomous

désatomisation [dezatɔmizasjɔ̃] NF nuclear disarmament

désatomiser [dezatɔmize] VT to undertake the nuclear disarmament of

désavantage [dezavɑ̃taʒ] NM disadvantage, drawback; **avoir un d. par rapport à qn** to be at a disadvantage compared with sb; **tourner au d. de qn** to go against sb; **cette solution a le d. d'être trop coûteuse** the drawback to *or* disadvantage of this solution is its expense; **c'est un d. de taille** it's a sizeable drawback; **il vous a été présenté à son d.** you saw him in a disadvantageous *or* an unfavourable light

désavantagé [dezavɑ̃taʒe] ADJ at a disadvantage, disadvantaged (**par** by); **être désavantagé par rapport à qn** to be at a disadvantage compared with sb; **être très désavantagé par sa taille** to be greatly handicapped by one's size, to be at a great disadvantage because of one's size

désavantager [dezavɑ̃taʒe] VT (**je désavantageai(s)**; **n. désavantageons**) to put at a disadvantage, to disadvantage; **il désavantage toujours son fils par rapport à sa fille** he always favours his daughter over his son

désavantageusement [dezavɑ̃taʒøzmɑ̃] ADV disadvantageously, unfavorably, *Am* unfavorably

désavantageux, -euse [dezavɑ̃taʒø, -øz] ADJ disadvantageous, unfavourable, *Am* unfavorable

désaveu [dezavø] NM **1** *(reniement) (d'une action, d'une œuvre, d'une opinion)* disowning; *(d'une promesse, d'une parole)* retraction; *Jur* **d. de paternité** repudiation of paternity; **faire un d. public** to make a public retraction **2** *(condamnation)* disapproval; **encourir le d. de ses supérieurs** to incur the disapproval of one's superiors; **il a été l'objet du d. de toute la population** he was universally condemned

désavouer [dezavwe] VT **1** *(renier) (action, œuvre, enfant, opinion etc)* to disown; *(promesse, parole)* to go back on, to retract; *(paternité)* to disclaim, to deny; **d. un man-**

---

dataire to withdraw recognition from an agent **2** *(condamner) (le comportement, les propos, l'attitude etc de qn)* to deplore
▪ VPR **se désavouer** to go back on one's word

désaxé, -ée [dezakse] ADJ **1** *Tech (came etc)* eccentric; **roue désaxée** wheel out of true **2** *(esprit)* unbalanced
▪ N unbalanced person

désaxer [dezakse] VT **1** *Tech (cylindre etc)* to set over; *(roue)* to put out of true **2** *(esprit)* to unbalance

descellement [desɛlmɑ̃] NM *(d'un cachet)* breaking; *(d'un document)* breaking the seal; *(d'une pierre)* loosening

desceller [desele] VT *(cachet)* to break; *(document)* to unseal, to break the seal of; *(pierre)* to loosen

descendance [desɑ̃dɑ̃s] NF **1** *(origine)* descent, *Fml* lineage **2** *(postérité)* descendants

descendant, -ante [desɑ̃dɑ̃, -ɑ̃t] ADJ *(mouvement)* downward; **marée descendante** ebbing tide; *Mil* **garde descendante** old guard; **ligne descendante** (genealogical) line of descent; *Mus* **gamme descendante** descending scale
▪ N descendant

descendeur, -euse [desɑ̃dœr, -øz] N *Ski* downhill specialist *or* skier; *Cyclisme* downhill racer

---

DESCENDRE [desɑ̃dr]

VI to come down **1, 2, 4–6** ▪ to go down **1, 2, 8, 9** ▪ to get off **3** ▪ to fall **4, 5, 9** ▪ to stay **7** ▪ to raid **10**	
VT to go down **1** ▪ to take down **2** ▪ to bring down **2, 5** ▪ to lower **3** ▪ to put away **4** ▪ to shoot down **5**	

VI *(aux* **être**, *occ* **avoir**) **1** *(allant vers le point de référence fixé)* to come down, *Fml* to descend; *(s'éloignant du point de référence fixé)* to go down, *Fml* to descend; **tu descends par l'escalier ou par l'ascenseur?** are you going to walk down or take the lift?; **d. d'un arbre/d'une échelle** to come down *or* get down from a tree/a ladder; **d. d'une colline** to come down a hill; **peux-tu faire d. les enfants de cet arbre?** can you get the children down out of *or* down from that tree?; **peux-tu m'aider à d.?** can you help me down?; **d. en glissant/en courant/en boitant** to slide/run/limp down; *Aviat* **d. en vol plané** to glide down; **d. en parachute** to parachute down; **d. en rappel** to abseil down; **d. (de Paris) en province** to go to the provinces (from Paris); **d. (du nord) en voiture/en train** to travel down (from the north) by car/train; **d. dans le midi en voiture/en train** to travel to the south by car/train; **d. en ville** to go into town; **il faut d. par ce chemin** you have to go down by this path *or* take this path down; **on peut d. en une nuit?** can we do the journey down in one night?; *Fig* **d. dans la rue** to take to the streets; *Fig* **d. dans l'arène** to enter the fray; **d. du trône** to leave the throne; *Fig* **descends de ton nuage!** come down to earth!; **les scaphandriers sont descendus à 150 m de profondeur** the divers reached a depth of 150 m; **le premier nageur à d. en dessous des 23 secondes au 50 m nage libre** the first swimmer to break 23 seconds in the 50 m freestyle; *Sport* **d. en seconde division** to move down to the second division; *Fig* **d. plus avant** *ou* **plus à fond dans une question** to consider a question at a deeper level; *Fig* **d. en soi-même** to take a close look at oneself

2 *(par l'escalier etc) (allant vers le point de référence fixé)* to come downstairs; *(s'éloignant du point de référence fixé)* to go downstairs; **tu peux d.?** **j'ai besoin de toi à la cuisine** can you come down(stairs)? I need

---

you in the kitchen; **il est descendu à la cave** he's gone down(stairs) to the cellar; **il n'est pas encore descendu** he isn't down yet; **faites-le d.** *(en l'envoyant chercher)* send him down; *(en l'appelant)* call him down

3 *(d'un véhicule)* to get off, *Fml* to alight; **je descends à Lille/à la prochaine** I'm getting off at Lille/at the next stop; **'aucun voyageur ne descend dans cette gare'** 'the train does not stop here'; **c'est ici que je descends** this is where I get off; **tout le monde descend!** *(au terminus)* all change!; **d. du train** to get off the train; **d. de cheval/de vélo/de moto** to dismount; **d. à terre** *(d'un bateau)* to go ashore, to land

4 *(baisser) (de prix)* to come down, to fall; *(de température)* to drop, to fall; *(de marée)* to fall, to go out; **le baromètre descend** the glass is falling; **il faut faire d. la fièvre** we must bring his temperature down; **sa voix ne descend pas plus bas** his voice won't go any lower

5 *(tomber) (de brouillard)* to come down; *(des ombres)* to fall; **le fleuve descend vers la mer** the river flows down to the sea; **le soleil descend sur l'horizon** the sun is sinking below the horizon; **la nuit** *ou* **le soir va d.** it will soon be nightfall *or* dark; **le précipité descend au fond de l'éprouvette** the precipitate drops to the bottom of the test-tube; **une grande paix était descendue en lui** a great sense of peace came over him

6 *(s'étendre)* to extend downwards; *(de route, rue)* to go downhill; **les cheveux lui descendent jusqu'à la taille** her hair comes down to her waist; **une robe qui descend jusqu'aux chevilles/genoux** an ankle-/knee-length dress, a dress that comes down to the ankles/knees; **ce chemin descend au village** this path goes down to the village; **la colline descend (en pente douce) jusqu'à la mer** the hill slopes (gently) down to the sea; **la route descend en lacets** the road winds down

7 *(loger)* **d. chez des amis** to stay with friends; **d. à l'hôtel** to put up *or* stay at a hotel

8 *Fam* **mon dîner ne descend pas** my dinner won't go down; **un petit verre pour faire d. mon repas** a drop of something to wash down my meal; **qu'est-ce qu'il descend dans les soirées!** he can really put it away at parties!

9 *Fig (s'abaisser)* to lower oneself; **il est descendu bien bas** he has fallen very low; *Péj* **jusqu'au mensonge** to stoop to lying; **d. dans l'estime de qn** to go down in sb's estimation **10** *(faire irruption)* **la police est descendue dans la boîte de nuit** the police raided the nightclub

11 *Fig (venir de)* to be descended (**de** from); **ces gens-là descendent d'une ancienne famille** these people are descended from an ancient family

12 *TV (image)* to slip

VT *(aux* **avoir**) **1** *(dévaler)* **d. les marches/la rue** to go down the steps/the street; **d. la rivière** to go downriver; **d. la rivière en nageant/en canoë/en radeau** to swim/canoe/raft downriver; **d. un escalier quatre à quatre** to race downstairs; *Mus* **d. la gamme** to run down the scale

2 *(porter vers le bas) (allant vers le point de référence fixé)* to bring down; *(s'éloignant du point de référence fixé)* to take down; *Fam (déposer)* to drop, to put down; **d. la poubelle** to take the rubbish down; **peux-tu me d. mon pull?** will you bring me down my sweater?; **je vous descendrai à votre porte** I'll drop you at your door

3 *(abaisser) (store, étagère)* to lower; **descends le tableau un peu plus vers la droite** move the picture down a bit on the right

4 *Fam (repas, boisson)* to put away, to knock

back, to sink; **il a descendu toutes les bières** he's guzzled all the beer
5 *Fam (animal, homme, avion)* to bring down, to shoot down; **la police l'a descendu, il s'est fait d. par la police** he was shot down *or* shot dead by the police; *Fig* **d. qn en flammes** to shoot sb down in flames; *Fig* **ils l'ont descendu en beauté** they crucified him

descente [desãt] **NF 1** *(action de descendre)* descent; *Ski (course)* downhill (race); *Ski* **faire de la d.** to do downhill (skiing); **j'ai fait une d. en rappel** I abseiled down; **la d. en rappel est dangereuse** abseiling is dangerous; *Cyclisme* **être bon en d.** to be good downhill *or* on the downhill sections; **c'était une d. difficile** *(en alpinisme)* it was a difficult descent; **d. de cheval** dismounting; *Aviat* **d. en vol plané** glide; **d. en parachute** parachute jump; **accueillir qn à la d. du train** to meet sb off the train; **d. interdite** *(sur panneau)* up only
2 *(incursion)* raid; **d. de police** police raid; *Jur* **d. sur les lieux** visit to the scene *(of a crime etc)*; *Fig* **faire une d. en boîte (de nuit)** to go to a nightclub; *Ftbl* **d. des avants** attack by the forwards
3 *Méd (d'un organe)* prolapse
4 *(pente)* slope, incline; **une d. rapide** a steep slope; **d. dangereuse** dangerous hill; **ralentir dans la d.** to slow down when going downhill
5 *(tuyau)* downpipe, rainwater pipe
6 *Fam* **il a une bonne d.** he can really put it away
▸▸ *Beaux-Arts* **D. de Croix** Deposition; **d. de lit** bedside rug

déscolarisation [deskɔlarizasjɔ̃] **NF** *(action)* removal from school; *(résultat)* lack of schooling *or* education; **les impératifs des travaux agricoles conduisent à la d. des enfants en milieu rural** children in rural areas are taken out of school because of the demands of farm work; **on assiste à une d. massive des jeunes gitans** the level of school attendance among young gipsies is falling drastically

déscolariser [deskɔlarize] **VT** to remove from *or* take out of school

descripteur [dɛskriptœr] **NM** *Ordinat* descriptor

descriptible [dɛskriptibl] **ADJ** describable

descriptif, -ive [dɛskriptif, -iv] **ADJ** descriptive
NM *(d'une maison)* description; *(d'une machine, d'un appareil)* instructions, explanatory leaflet; *Constr* specification; **un d. de vos souhaits** a list of what you would like, your wish list

description [dɛskripsjɔ̃] **NF** description; **d. orale/écrite** verbal/written description; **faire la d. de qn/qch** to give a description of sb/sth, to describe sb/sth; *Tech* **conforme à la d.** as described *or* represented; **d. de brevet** patent specification; **d. commerciale** trade description; **d. de poste** job description

désectorisation [desɛktɔrizasjɔ̃] **NF** freedom of choice *(by virtue of the fact that parents no longer need to send their children to the school designated for their area)*; **la d. de l'école primaire se fera plus vite que celle de l'école secondaire** freedom of choice will come about in primary schools sooner than in secondary schools

désectoriser [desɛktɔrize] **VT d. le primaire/secondaire** = to allow parents to choose which primary/secondary school they send their children to, regardless of where they live

désembourber [dezãburbe] **VT** *(véhicule etc)* to extricate from the mud

désembourgeoiser [dezãburʒwaze] **VT** *(personne)* to make less conventional *or* less middle-class; *(profession, activité etc)* to make less middle-class, to remove the middle-class aura surrounding
VPR se désembourgeoiser to become less conventional *or* less middle-class; **les facs de droit ont beaucoup de mal à se d.** law faculties are finding it very difficult to attract students from outside the middle classes

désembouteiller [dezãbuteje] **VT** *(route)* to unblock; *(ligne téléphonique)* to unjam

désembrouiller [dezãbruje] **VT** *(signaux, données)* to unscramble

désembrouilleur [dezãbrujœr] **NM** *(de signaux etc)* descrambler

désembuage [dezãbɥaʒ] **NM** demisting; **d. arrière** rear demister

désembuer [dezãbɥe] **VT** to demist

désembueur [dezãbɥœr] **NM** demister

désemparé [dezãpare] **ADJ 1** *(personne)* at a loss; **il reste d.** he's quite at a loss; **très d.** very much at a loss **2** *(navire, avion)* disabled

désemparer [dezãpare] **VT** *Naut (navire)* to disable
VI sans d. without stopping; **ils travaillent des heures sans d.** they work for hours on end

désemplir [dezãplir] **VT** *(bouteille etc)* to partially empty
VI son magasin ne désemplit pas his shop is always full *(of customers)*
VPR se désemplir to empty

désencadrement [dezãkadrəmã] **NM** *Écon (des crédits)* unblocking

désenchaîner [dezãʃene] **VT d. qn** to unchain sb, to remove sb's chains

désenchanté [dezãʃãte] **ADJ** *(personne)* disillusioned; *(sourire)* wistful

désenchantement [dezãʃãtmã] **NM 1** *(déception)* disillusion **2** *Vieilli (désensorcellement)* removal of a/the spell

désenchanter [dezãʃãte] **VT 1** *(décevoir)* to disillusion **2** *Vieilli (désensorceler)* to remove a/the spell from

désenclavement [dezãklavmã] **NM** opening up

désenclaver [dezãklave] **VT** to open up

désencombrement [dezãkɔ̃brəmã] **NM** *(d'un passage etc)* clearing, freeing

désencombrer [dezãkɔ̃bre] **VT** *(passage etc)* to clear, to free **(de** of)

désencrasser [dezãkrase] **VT** to clean

désencroûter [dezãkrute] **VT d. qn** to get sb out of his/her rut
VPR se désencroûter to get out of the *or* one's rut; **j'ai besoin de me d.** I need to get out of this rut I'm in *or* out of my rut

désendettement [dezãdɛtmã] **NM** debt reduction, reduction in borrowings; **il faut aboutir au d. des ménages** household debt must be reduced; **le d. des pays de l'Est se fera progressivement** Eastern countries will gradually be relieved of their debt burden

désendetter (se) [sədezãdete] **VPR** to get out of debt, to clear one's debts

désenfiler [dezãfile] **VT** *(aiguille)* to unthread; *(perles etc)* to unstring
VPR se désenfiler *(d'une aiguille)* to come unthreaded; *(de perles)* to come unstrung

désenflammer [dezãflame] **VT** *Méd (plaie etc)* to reduce the inflammation in

désenfler [dezãfle] **VI** to become less swollen; **ma joue/cheville désenfle** the swelling in my cheek/ankle is going down, my cheek/ankle is less swollen
VPR se désenfler = **VI**

désenfumer [dezãfyme] **VT** to get rid of the smoke in

désengagement [dezãgaʒmã] **NM** disengagement

désengager [dezãgaʒe] **(je désengageai(s); n. désengageons) VT d. qn** to release sb from an obligation; **d. sa parole** to go back on one's word
VPR se désengager to free oneself of an obligation; **je ne peux pas me d.** I can't get out of it

désengorgement [dezãgɔrʒəmã] **NM** *(d'un tuyau etc)* unblocking

désengorger [dezãgɔrʒe] **VT** *(je désengorgeai(s); n. désengorgeons) (tuyau etc)* to unblock

désenivrer [dezãnivre] **VT d. qn** to sober sb up
VI to sober up, to become sober; **il ne désenivre pas** he's never sober

désennuyer [dezãnɥije] **(je désennuie, n. désennuyons; je désennuierai) VT d. qn** to keep sb amused
VPR se désennuyer to amuse oneself, to keep oneself amused

désensabler [dezãsable] **VT 1** *(bateau)* to get off the sand; *(voiture etc)* to dig out of the sand **2** *(chenal etc)* to dredge of sand

désensevelir [dezãsəvlir] **VT** *(objet)* to dig up; *(cadavre)* to disinter, to exhume

désensibilisateur [desãsibilizatœr] **NM** *Phot* desensitizer

désensibilisation [desãsibilizasjɔ̃] **NF** *Méd, Phot* desensitization

désensibiliser [desãsibilize] **VT** *Méd, Phot* to desensitize; *Fig* **de telles images ont désensibilisé l'opinion** people have become hardened as a result of pictures such as these

désensorceler [dezãsɔrsəle] **VT** *(je désensorcelle, n. désensorcelons; je désensorcellerai)* to free from a/the spell

désensorcellement [dezãsɔrsɛlmã] **NM** removal of a/the spell

désentortiller [dezãtɔrtije] **VT** *(fil etc)* to untwist; *(laine etc)* to disentangle

désentraver [dezãtrave] **VT** *(personne)* to unshackle; *(animal)* to unhobble

désenvaser [dezãvaze] **VT 1** *(égout)* to clear out, to remove the sludge from; *(port)* to remove the silt from **2** *(voiture)* to get out of the mud, to extract from the mud

désenvoûtement [dezãvutmã] **NM** removal of a/the spell; **procéder au d. de qn** to remove a/the spell from sb

désenvoûter [dezãvute] **VT** to remove a/the spell from

désépaissir [dezepesir] **VT** *(sauce, cheveux)* to thin

déséquilibrant [dezekilibrã] **ADJ** *(effet)* unbalancing; **être d.** to have an unbalancing effect *(pour* on)

déséquilibre [dezekilibr] **NM** imbalance; **la chaise était en d.** the chair wasn't balanced properly; *Psy* **d. émotif** emotional maladjustment; *Méd* **d. nutritionnel** nutritional imbalance; **d. financier** financial imbalance; **d. de la balance commerciale** unfavourable trade balance

déséquilibré, -ée [dezekilibre] **ADJ** unbalanced
N unbalanced person

déséquilibrer [dezekilibre] **VT** *(personne)* *(mentalement, physiquement)* to unbalance; *(déconcerter)* to throw off balance; *(objet)* to unbalance, to throw out of balance

désert [dezɛr] **ADJ** *(lieu)* deserted; *(pays, région)* uninhabited; **une île déserte** a desert island
NM desert; **d. de sable** sandy desert; **un d. de glace** an icy waste; *Fig* **prêcher dans le d.** to be a voice crying in the wilderness; *Fig* **en-**

tamer sa traversée du d. to go into the wilderness; **après cinq années de traversée du d.** after five years in the wilderness

Do not confuse with the adjective **désertique**.

déserter [dezɛrte] VT to desert; *Fig (cause)* to desert, to abandon; *(idéal)* to abandon; *Mil* **d. son poste** to desert one's post; **d. l'armée** to desert (from the army); **nos amis désertent notre maison depuis quelque temps** we've been deserted by our friends recently, our friends have been staying away recently ▸ VI to desert

déserteur [dezɛrtœr] NM deserter

désertification [dezɛrtifikasjɔ̃] NF *Géog* desertification; *Fig* **la d. du Massif central** the desertion of the Massif Central

désertion [dezɛrsjɔ̃] NF *(de l'armée, d'un parti)* desertion

désertique [dezɛrtik] ADJ *Géog* desert, of the desert; **région d.** desert region

Do not confuse with the adjective **désert**.

désertisation [dezɛrtizasjɔ̃] NF = **désertification**

désescalade [dezɛskalad] NF *Pol, Mil* de-escalation

désespérance [dezɛsperɑ̃s] NF *Litt* loss of hope, despair

désespérant [dezɛsperɑ̃] ADJ **1 c'est d.** it's enough to drive you to despair; **cet enfant est d.** that child will drive me to despair; **il fait un temps vraiment d.** the weather's really appalling; **tu es vraiment d'une stupidité désespérante** you really are incredibly stupid, you're so stupid you'll drive me to despair; **tu es vraiment d'une nullité désespérante** you really are absolutely hopeless **2** *Litt (image, vision)* heartbreaking

désespéré, -ée [dezɛspere] ADJ *(sans espoir) (regard, discours)* desperate, of despair, despairing; *(situation)* desperate; *(extrême) (mesure, solution)* desperate; *(après décès, accident)* in despair, distressed; **être dans un état d.** to be in a hopeless or desperate state; **il est d. depuis la mort de sa femme** he has been in despair since his wife died; **sa voix était désespérée** he sounded desperate ▸ N **1** desperate person; **agir en d.** to act out of desperation, to commit an act of despair **2** *(suicidé)* suicide (victim)

désespérément [dezɛsperemɑ̃] ADV *(avec désespoir)* despairingly, hopelessly; *(avec acharnement)* desperately

désespérer [dezɛspere] *(je désespère, n. désespérons; je désespérerai)* VI to despair, to lose hope; **je ne désespère pas d'y arriver un jour** I still hope to get or I haven't given up hope of getting there one day; **d. de qn** to despair of sb; **il désespère de pouvoir rentrer chez lui** he despairs of ever getting home; **il désespère de sa situation** he's in despair about the situation he's in ▸ VT to drive or reduce to despair; **il désespère sa femme par son attitude** he drives his wife to despair with his attitude ▸ VPR **se désespérer** to be in despair, to give way to despair

désespoir [dezɛspwar] NM **1** despair; **être au d.** to be in despair; **elle était au d. de ne pouvoir vous aider** she was distressed or extremely upset that she wasn't able to help you; **enfant qui fait** *ou* **est le d. de sa famille** child who is the despair of his family; **cette cuisine fait mon d.** this kitchen will drive me to despair; **réduire qn au d.** to drive sb to desperation or to despair; **en d. de cause** in desperation, as a last resort **2** *(plante)* **d. des peintres** London pride

désétatisation [dezetatizasjɔ̃] NF denationalization

désétatiser [dezetatize] VT *Écon, Pol (industrie)* to denationalize

désexualiser [desɛksɥalize] VT to desexualize, to desex

déshabillage [dezabijaʒ] NM undressing

déshabillé [dezabije] NM négligé

déshabiller [dezabije] VT to undress; **d. qn du regard** to undress sb with one's eyes, to mentally undress sb ▸ VPR **se déshabiller** to undress (oneself), to take off one's clothes; *(enlever son manteau etc)* to take off one's coat/etc

déshabituer [dezabitɥe] VT **d. qn de (faire) qch** to get sb out of or break sb of the habit of (doing) sth ▸ VPR **se déshabituer** to get out of or lose the habit (**de** of)

désherbage [dezɛrbaʒ] NM weeding

désherbant [dezɛrbɑ̃] NM weedkiller

désherber [dezɛrbe] VT *(jardin, champ)* to weed

déshérence [dezerɑ̃s] NF *Jur* default of heirs, escheat; **tomber en d.** to escheat

déshérité [dezerite] ADJ *(sans héritage)* disinherited; *(démuni)* deprived ▸ NMPL **les déshérités** the underprivileged

déshéritement [dezeritmɑ̃] NM disinheritance

déshériter [dezerite] VT to disinherit; *Fig Hum* **être déshérité par la nature** *(d'une personne inintelligente)* to be not very bright; *(d'une personne laide)* to be no oil painting

déshonnête [dezɔnɛt] ADJ *Arch* improper, immodest, unseemly

déshonnêtement [dezɔnɛtmɑ̃] ADV *Arch* improperly, immodestly

déshonnêteté [dezɔnɛt(ə)te] NF *Arch, Litt* impropriety, immodesty, unseemliness

déshonneur [dezɔnœr] NM dishonour, *Am* dishonor

déshonorant [dezɔnɔrɑ̃] ADJ *(comportement, métier)* dishonourable, *Am* dishonorable; **des paroles déshonorantes pour notre famille/la profession** remarks that bring dishonour on or discredit the family/the profession

déshonorer [dezɔnɔre] VT **1** *(discréditer)* to disgrace, to bring disgrace or dishonour or *Am* dishonor on, to dishonour; **il se croirait déshonoré de serrer la main à des étrangers** he would feel it reflected on his honour or he would think it beneath him to shake hands with a foreigner; **être déshonoré par un jeune blanc-bec** to be put to shame by a complete beginner; *Vieilli* **d. une jeune fille/une femme** to seduce a girl/a woman **2** *Fig (abîmer) (paysage, édifice etc)* to disfigure, to spoil ▸ VPR **se déshonorer** to disgrace oneself

déshuiler [dezɥile] VT to extract or separate or remove oil from

déshumaniser [dezymanize] VT to dehumanize

déshumidification [dezymidifikasjɔ̃] NF dehumidification

déshydratation [dezidratasjɔ̃] NF dehydration

déshydrater [dezidrate] VT to dehydrate; **je suis déshydraté** I'm dehydrated; **noix de coco déshydratée** desiccated coconut ▸ VPR **se déshydrater** to become dehydrated; **on se déshydrate beaucoup en avion** you get very dehydrated when you fly

déshydrateur [dezidratœr] NM dehydrator

déshydrogénation [dezidrɔʒenasjɔ̃] NF *Chimie* dehydrogenation

déshydrogéner [dezidrɔʒene] VT *(je dés-*

hydrogène, n. déshydrogénons; je déshydrogénerai) *Chimie* to dehydrogenate

déshypothéquer [dezipɔteke] VT *(conj like* **hypothéquer**) *(domaine)* to free from mortgage

desiderata [deziderata] NMPL desiderata; **quels sont vos d.?** what can I do for you?

design [dizajn] NM design; **ils sont entièrement meublés en d.** they have nothing but designer furniture; **société de d.** design company; **il fait du d. (industriel)** he's a(n industrial) designer, he's in (industrial) design ▸ ADJ INV designer; **un intérieur très d.** a designer interior

désignation [dezinasjɔ̃] NF **1** *(appellation)* designation; *(de marchandises etc)* description **2** *(choix)* appointment; **d. de qn pour un poste** appointment of sb to a position

designer [dizajnœr] NM designer; **d. graphiste** graphics designer; **d. presse** newspaper designer

désigner [dezine] VT **1** *(signaler)* to point out, to indicate; **est-ce que tu peux le d.?** can you point him out?; **d. qch du doigt** to point sth out, to point at sth; **il a pris le siège qu'on lui avait désigné** he took the seat they pointed to or indicated; **d. qch à l'attention de qn** to call or draw sb's attention to sth; **je désigne à votre attention que …** I would call or draw your attention to the fact that … **2** *(choisir)* to appoint; **d. un jour** to appoint or set or fix a day; **d. qn à** *ou* **pour un poste** to appoint sb to a position; **il est tout désigné pour le faire** he's just the man to do it, he's cut out for it; **sa compétence la désigne à cet emploi** her ability makes her the right person for the job; **il a été désigné pour nous représenter** he was chosen to represent us **3** *(nommer)* to refer to; **d. qn par son nom** to refer to sb by name; **d. qn par un surnom** to call sb by a nickname; **on désigne, sous ce nom, tous les gaz de cette famille** this name is applied to all the gases in the family ▸ VPR **se désigner se d. volontaire** to volunteer

désillusion [dezilyzjɔ̃] NF disillusion

désillusionnement [dezilyzjɔnmɑ̃] NM disillusionment

désillusionner [dezilyzjɔne] VT to disillusion

désincarcération [dezɛ̃karserasjɔ̃] NF *(de débris d'une voiture etc)* release, freeing

désincarcérer [dezɛ̃karsere] VT *(des débris d'une voiture etc)* to free

désincarné [dezɛ̃karne] ADJ disembodied; *souvent Iron* **il paraît totalement d.** he seems above it all

désincarner (se) [sədezɛ̃karne] VPR to become disembodied

désincrustant [dezɛ̃krystɑ̃] ADJ *Tech (substance)* scaling; **masque d.** *(cosmétique)* face pack ▸ NM *Tech* scale preventive

désincrustation [dezɛ̃krystasjɔ̃] NF *Tech (d'une chaudière etc)* scaling

désincruster [dezɛ̃kryste] VT *Tech (chaudière etc)* to scale; **un masque pour d. la peau** a mask for removing impurities from the skin

désindexation [dezɛ̃dɛksasjɔ̃] NF de-indexing

désindexer [dezɛ̃dɛkse] VT to de-index

désindustrialisation [dezɛ̃dystrijalizasjɔ̃] NF de-industrialization

désindustrialiser [dezɛ̃dystrijalize] VT to de-industrialize

désinence [dezinɑ̃s] NF *Gram* (flexional) ending

désinfectant [dezɛ̃fɛktɑ̃] **ADJ, NM** disinfectant

désinfecter [dezɛ̃fɛkte] **VT** to disinfect

désinfection [dezɛ̃fɛksjɔ̃] **NF** disinfection

désinflation [dezɛ̃flasjɔ̃] **NF** Écon disinflation

désinformation [dezɛ̃fɔrmasjɔ̃] **NF** disinformation

désinformer [dezɛ̃fɔrme] **VT** to disinform

désinscrire (se) [sədezɛ̃skrir] **VPR** Ordinat to unsubscribe

désinsectisation [dezɛ̃sɛktizasjɔ̃] **NF** pest control

désinsectiser [dezɛ̃sɛktize] **VT** to clear of insects, to remove the insects from

désinstallateur [dezɛ̃stalatœr] **NM** Ordinat deinstaller

désinstallation [dezɛ̃stalasjɔ̃] **NF** Ordinat deinstallation

désinstaller [dezɛ̃stale] **VT** Ordinat to deinstall

désintégration [dezɛ̃tegrasjɔ̃] **NF** (des roches) weathering; Nucl (nuclear) disintegration; (de l'atome) splitting; Fig (d'un groupe) break-up; (de la famille, de la société) disintegration

désintégrer [dezɛ̃tegre] (**je désintègre, n. désintégrons; je désintégrerai**) **VT** (roches) to weather; Nucl (matière) to disintegrate; (atome) to split; Fig (groupe, famille etc) to break up
▪ **VPR se désintégrer** (de roches) to weather; Nucl (de matière) to disintegrate; (d'atome) to split; Fig (d'un groupe, d'une famille) to break up; (d'un mariage) to break up, to fall apart; (de la société, de la famille) to disintegrate

désintéressé [dezɛ̃terese] **ADJ** (opinion, avis etc) disinterested, impartial; (motif) disinterested, unselfish; (personne) disinterested, selfless; **il agit de manière tout à fait désintéressée** he is being quite impartial

désintéressement [dezɛ̃teresmɑ̃] **NM 1** (d'opinion, d'avis) disinterestedness, impartiality; (de motif) disinterestedness, unselfishness; (de personne) disinterestedness, selflessness **2** Com (de partenaire) buying out; (de créditeur) paying off

> Do not confuse with **désintérêt**.

désintéresser [dezɛ̃terese] **VT** Com (partenaire) to buy out; (créditeur) to pay off
▪ **VPR se désintéresser se d. de qn/qch** to take no further interest in sb/sth

désintérêt [dezɛ̃tere] **NM** disinterest

> Do not confuse with **désintéressement**.

désintermédiation [dezɛ̃termedjasjɔ̃] **NF** disintermediation

désintoxication [dezɛ̃tɔksikasjɔ̃] **NF** Méd detoxification; **faire une cure de d.** to undergo treatment for alcoholism/drug addiction, Am Fam to be in detox

désintoxiquer [dezɛ̃tɔksike] Méd **VT** to treat for alcoholism/drug addiction; Fig **il ne fait que regarder la télévision, il faut le d.!** all he does is watch television, we'll have to break him of the habit!
▪ **VPR se désintoxiquer** to come off alcohol/drugs; Fig **je cours tous les jours pour me d.** I run every day to clean out my system; Fig **aller à la campagne pour se d.** to go to the countryside to clean out one's system or to get the city air out of one's lungs

désinvestir [dezɛ̃vɛstir] **VI** Fin to disinvest (**dans** in)
▪ **VPR se désinvestir depuis qu'il sait qu'il va être licencié, il s'est désinvesti de son travail** since finding out that he's going to be made

redundant, he has ceased to take an interest in his job or he no longer makes any effort at work

désinvestissement [dezɛ̃vɛstismɑ̃] **NM** Fin divestment

désinvolte [dezɛ̃vɔlt] **ADJ** (manière) casual, airy, unselfconscious; (mouvements) easy, free; **d. à l'égard de qn** casual or offhand with sb; **il a quand même été très d. en ne venant pas à mon anniversaire** it was very offhand of him not to come to my birthday party

désinvolture [dezɛ̃vɔltyr] **NF** (naturel) (de manières) unselfconsciousness; (de mouvement) ease; (sans-gêne) casualness; **avec d.** casually; **sa d. devient insupportable** his casualness or his offhand or airy manner is becoming unbearable; **il travaille avec une d. qui commence à agacer au bureau** his casual approach to work is beginning to irritate people in the office

désir [dezir] **NM 1** (souhait) desire; **avoir un d. de qch** to have a desire for something; **d. de plaire** desire to please; **d. ardent** craving, longing; **ardent d. de réussir** ardent desire to succeed; **selon le d. de son père** in accordance with his father's wishes; **éprouver le d. de faire qch** to want to do sth; **prendre ses désirs pour des réalités** to indulge in wishful thinking; **tes désirs sont des ordres** your wish is my command **2 d. (sexuel)** (sexual) desire

désirabilité [dezirabilite] **NF** desirability

désirable [dezirabl] **ADJ** desirable; **peu d.** undesirable

désirer [dezire] **VT 1** (souhaiter) to want, to desire; **d. ardemment qch** to crave sth, to yearn or long for sth; **d. qch de qn** to want sth of or from sb; **je désire le voir** I want or wish to see him; **je désire qu'il vienne** I want him to come; **cela laisse à d.** it leaves a lot to be desired; **elle se fait d.** (elle n'arrive pas) she's keeping us waiting; **elle aime se faire d.** (ce n'est pas une femme facile) she plays hard to get; **je n'avais plus rien à d.** I had nothing left to wish for; **que désirez-vous?**, Fam **vous désirez?** (dans un magasin) can I help you?; (qu'est-ce que je vous sers?) what would you like? **2** (sexuellement) to desire; **je te désire** I want you

désireux, -euse [dezirø, -øz] **ADJ** desirous (**de** of); **d. de plaire** anxious to please; **je serais très d. de la connaître** I would very much like to meet her

désistement [dezistəmɑ̃] **NM 1** cancellation; Jur (de réclamation) waiver; (de procès) withdrawal **2** Pol withdrawal of one's candidature, standing down

désister (se) [sədeziste] **VPR 1** Jur **se d. d'une poursuite** to withdraw an action; **se d. d'une demande** to waive a claim **2** Pol to withdraw (one's candidacy), to stand down

desk [dɛsk] **NM** Journ desk

deskman, pl **deskmen, deskmans** [dɛskman, mɛn] **NM** Journ deskman

désobéir [dezɔbeir] **VI** to be disobedient; **d. à qn/un ordre** to disobey sb/an order; **d. à une règle** to break a rule

désobéissance [dezɔbeisɑ̃s] **NF** disobedience (à of); **d. à une règle** disregard for or breaking of a rule; **d. civile** civil disobedience

désobéissant [dezɔbeisɑ̃] **ADJ** disobedient

désobligeance [dezɔbliʒɑ̃s] **NF** disagreeableness (**envers** to)

désobligeant [dezɔbliʒɑ̃] **ADJ** (personne, manière, mots etc) disagreeable, ungracious (**envers** to)

désobliger [dezɔbliʒe] **VT** (**je désobligeai(s); n. désobligeons**) to offend

désobstruer [dezɔpstrye] **VT** (tuyau, passage, tunnel etc) to clear (of an obstruction)

désodé [desɔde] **ADJ** salt-free

désodorisant [dezɔdɔrizɑ̃] **ADJ** deodorant
▪ **NM** (pour le corps) deodorant; (pour la maison) air freshener

désodoriser [dezɔdɔrize] **VT** to deodorize

désœuvré [dezœvre] **ADJ** unoccupied, idle; **me trouvant d.** finding myself with nothing to do, Fam being or finding myself at a loose end; **je ne supporte pas de rester d. plus de cinq minutes** I can't bear to be idle for more than five minutes
▪ **NMPL les désœuvrés** people with nothing to do

désœuvrement [dezœvrəmɑ̃] **NM** idleness; **par d.** to kill time, for want of something to do

désolant [dezɔlɑ̃] **ADJ** (nouvelle etc) distressing; **tu es vraiment d.** you drive me to despair; **ce temps est d.** this weather is very depressing

désolation [dezɔlasjɔ̃] **NF 1** (dévastation) desolation, devastation, laying waste **2** (affliction) grief, sorrow; **être plongé dans la d.** to be grief-stricken; **sa fille ne fait plus de danse et c'est sa grande d.** she is heartbroken that her daughter has given up dancing

désolé [dezɔle] **ADJ 1** (région etc) desolate, dreary **2** (navré) sorry; **je suis (terriblement) d. de vous avoir fait attendre** I'm (so or very) sorry to have kept you waiting; **d., je n'ai pas le temps** sorry, I haven't got the time; **je suis d. mais ce n'est pas la meilleure candidate** I'm sorry but she isn't the best candidate **3** (affligé) upset

désoler [dezɔle] **VT 1** (affliger) to distress, to grieve; **son échec à l'examen le désole** he's very upset about failing the exam **2** Vieilli, Litt (pays etc) to devastate, to ravage, to lay waste
▪ **VPR se désoler** to be distressed, to be upset

désolidariser (se) [sədesɔlidarize] **VPR** (d'une personne) to break away, to break ranks; **se d. de ou d'avec ses collègues** to break with one's colleagues; **se d. d'une cause** to withdraw one's support from a cause; **se d. d'un projet** to withdraw from a project

désopilant [dezɔpilɑ̃] **ADJ** screamingly funny, hilarious

désordonné [dezɔrdɔne] **ADJ 1** (chambre, bureau etc) untidy; (personne) (qui n'est pas organisé) disorganized; (qui ne range pas) untidy; (mouvements) uncoordinated; **une fuite désordonnée** a disorderly flight; **il a un esprit trop d.** he's too scatterbrained **2** Litt (vie etc) disorderly; (dépenses) reckless

désordre [dezɔrdr] **NM 1** (manque d'organisation) disorder, confusion; (manque d'ordre) untidiness; **quel d.!** what a mess!; **il règne dans leur maison un d. incroyable** their house is incredibly untidy; **tu as mis du d. dans toute la maison, tu as mis toute la maison en d.** you've made the entire house untidy; **c'est un peu le d. dans ses papiers** his papers are not altogether in order; **c'est le d. dans sa dissertation** his thesis lacks organization or is not clearly thought out; **être en d.** (d'une pièce etc) to be untidy; **cheveux en d.** tangled or untidy hair; Fig **ça fait d.!** (ça ne se fait pas) it's just not done!; (ce n'est pas sérieux) that's a laugh!
2 (agitation) **mettre le d. dans les rangs** to cause confusion in the ranks; **il arrive toujours à mettre un d. infernal dans la classe** he always manages to cause an uproar in the classroom; Fam **il a fait du d. dans la rue** he caused a disturbance in the street; **le d. qui règne à l'Assemblée nationale ces jours-ci** the present commotion in the Natio-

nal Assembly; **d. de la pensée** confused thinking

3 désordres *(émeutes)* disturbances, riots; **de graves désordres ont éclaté** serious disturbances have broken out

4 *Litt (licence)* licentiousness; **vivre dans le d.** to lead a life of licentiousness

5 *Méd* disorder; **d. nerveux/fonctionnel/hormonal** nervous/functional/hormone disorder; **d. affectif saisonnier** seasonal affective disorder, SAD

désorganisation [dezɔrganizasjɔ̃] NF disorganization

désorganisé [dezɔrganize] ADJ disorganized

désorganiser [dezɔrganize] VT *(système etc)* to disrupt; *(plans etc)* to upset
VPR se désorganiser to become disorganized

désorientation [dezɔrjɑ̃tasjɔ̃] NF disorientation; *(déconcertation)* confusion, bewilderment

désorienté [dezɔrjɑ̃te] ADJ *(perdu)* disorientated, *surtout Am* disoriented; *(déconcerté)* confused, bewildered; **après l'anesthésie, il était complètement d.** he was completely disorientated *or* totally confused after the anaesthetic

désorienter [dezɔrjɑ̃te] VT **1** *(égarer) (personne)* to disorientate, *surtout Am* to disorient; *(compas, instrument)* to throw out (of adjustment) **2** *(déconcerter)* to confuse, to bewilder; **l'anesthésie l'a désorienté** he is disorientated *or* confused because of the anaesthetic

désormais [dezɔrmɛ] ADV from now on(wards), in future, *Litt* henceforth

désorption [dezɔrpsjɔ̃] NF *Chimie* desorption

désossé [dezɔse] ADJ *(viande, poisson)* boned; *(gigot, jambon)* off the bone; *Fig (personne)* supple; *Péj (style etc)* flabby, flaccid

désossement [dezɔsmɑ̃] NM *(de viande, poisson)* boning

désosser [dezɔse] VT *(viande, poisson)* to bone; *Fig (phrase, livre)* to dissect
VPR se désosser to contort oneself

désoxydant [dezɔksidɑ̃] *Chimie* ADJ deoxidizing
NM deoxidizer

désoxyder [dezɔkside] VT *Chimie, Métal* to deoxidize

desperado [dɛsperado] NM desperado

despote [dɛspɔt] NM despot; *Fam* **sa fille est un d.!** her daughter is a regular tyrant!
ADJ mari/femme d. despotic husband/wife

despotique [dɛspɔtik] ADJ *(pouvoir etc)* despotic

despotiquement [dɛspɔtikmɑ̃] ADV despotically

despotisme [dɛspɔtism] NM despotism

desquamation [dɛskwamasjɔ̃] NF peeling, *Spéc* exfoliation; *Méd (pathologique)* desquamation

desquamer [dɛskwame] VT to exfoliate
VI to peel (off); *Méd* to desquamate
VPR se desquamer to peel

desquels, desquelles [dekɛl] *voir* **lequel**

DESS [deəɛsɛs] NM *(abrév* **diplôme d'études supérieures spécialisées)** = postgraduate diploma

dessaisir [desezir] VT *Jur* **d. un tribunal d'une affaire** to remove a case from a court
VPR se dessaisir se d. de qch to relinquish sth, to part with sth, to give sth up

dessaisissement [desezismɑ̃] NM **1** *Jur* **d. d'un tribunal d'une affaire** removal of a case from a court **2** *(abandon)* **d. de qch** relinquishment of sth

dessalage [desalaʒ] NM *(du poisson, de la viande etc)* soaking *(to remove salt)*

dessalaison [desalɛzɔ̃] NF **1** *(du poisson, de la viande etc)* soaking *(to remove salt)* **2** *(de l'eau de mer)* desalination

dessalé [desale] ADJ **1** *(viande, poisson etc)* soaked *(to remove salt)* **2** *Fam (personne)* wide awake, sharp

dessalement [desalmɑ̃] NM *(de l'eau de mer)* desalination

dessaler [desale] VT **1** *(viande, poisson)* to remove the salt from *(by soaking)*; *(eau de mer)* to desalinate **2** *Fam* **d. qn** to sharpen sb's wits
VI *Naut* to capsize
VPR se dessaler 1 *(devenir moins salé)* to become less salty **2** *Fam (d'une personne)* to learn a thing or two

dessangler [desɑ̃gle] VT *(horse)* to ungirth, to take the girths off

dessaouler [desule] VT & VI *Fam* = **dessoûler**

desséchant [deseʃɑ̃] ADJ *(vent)* drying

desséché [deseʃe] ADJ *(étang, rivière)* dry, dried-up; *(sol, bouche)* dry, parched; *(peau)* dry; *(bois)* seasoned, dried; *(plante)* dry, withered; *Fig (personne) (maigre)* shrunken; *(insensible)* without feelings, without emotions, dried-up; **il est d.** *(insensible)* he's dead inside, he's got no feelings left

dessèchement [deseʃmɑ̃] NM *(d'un étang, d'une rivière)* drying up; *(d'un sol)* drying; *(du bois)* seasoning, drying; *(d'une plante)* withering; *Vieilli Fig (du corps)* shrunkenness; *Fig (dureté) (d'une personne)* lack of feeling

dessécher [deseʃe] *(je dessèche, n. desséchons; je dessécherai)* VT *(sol, étang, rivière)* to dry up; *(bois)* to season; *(denrées alimentaires)* to dry; *(noix de coco)* to desiccate; *(du vent, de la chaleur etc) (plante)* to wither; *(peau)* to dry; *(bouche)* to dry, to parch; *(de maladie, l'âge etc) (corps)* to shrink; *Fig* **d. le cœur de qn** to harden sb's heart
VPR se dessécher *(du sol)* to dry up, to become dry; *(d'un étang, d'une rivière etc)* to dry up, to go dry; *(d'une plante)* to wither; *(d'une personne) (maigrir)* to waste away; *Fig (devenir insensible)* to become insensitive

dessein [desɛ̃] NM intention, purpose, *Litt* design; **avoir le d. de faire qch** to intend to do sth; **former le d. de faire qch** to plan to do sth; **dans ce d.** with this intention, with this in mind; **à d.** on purpose, purposely, intentionally; **c'est à d. que je n'ai pas répondu** I deliberately didn't answer; **à d.** *ou* **dans le d. de vous revoir** in order to see you again

desseller [desele] VT *(cheval)* to unsaddle

desserrage [deseraʒ] NM *(d'une vis)* loosening; *(d'une ceinture, d'un nœud)* slackening, loosening

desserrement [desɛrmɑ̃] NM loosening

desserrer [desere] VT *(vis)* to loosen; *(ceinture, nœud)* to loosen, to slacken; *(poing, dents)* to unclench; *(frein à main)* to release, to take off; **je n'ai pas desserré les dents** I didn't open my mouth, I didn't utter a word; **peux-tu d. les livres sur l'étagère?** can you move the books on the shelf so they're a bit less tightly packed?
VPR se desserrer *(d'une vis)* to work loose; *(d'une ceinture, d'un nœud)* to come loose; *(d'étreinte)* to relax

dessert [desɛr] NM dessert, *Br* pudding, *Br* sweet; **venez pour le d.** come for dessert; **être privé de d.** to go without dessert; **qu'est-ce qu'il y a comme** *ou* **au d.?** what's for dessert?; **carte des desserts** dessert menu

desserte [desɛrt] NF **1** *(service)* service; **d.**

d'un port par voie ferrée rail service to a port; **chemin de d.** service road **2** *Rel* ministry

desserte [desɛrt] NF *(meuble)* sideboard; **d. (roulante)** trolley

dessertir [desɛrtir] VT *(pierre précieuse)* to remove from its setting

desservant [desɛrvɑ̃] NM *Rel* incumbent

desservir [desɛrvir] VT *(conj like* **servir)** **1** *(de chemins de fer etc)* to serve; *(de porte)* to lead into; **ce train ne dessert pas toutes les gares** this train does not stop at every station; **ville bien desservie** town with efficient public transport **2** *Rel (paroisse etc)* to minister to

desservir [desɛrvir] *(conj like* **servir)** VT **1** *(table)* to clear **2** *(nuire à)* to do harm to; **d. qn** to do sb a disservice; **cela risque de vous d.** that may be to your disadvantage; **cela desservirait mes intérêts** it would be detrimental to my interests; **son perfectionnisme la dessert** her perfectionism isn't doing her any good
VI to clear away
VPR se desservir to do oneself a disservice; **il se dessert par sa malhonnêteté** he's not doing himself any good by being dishonest

dessiccatif, -ive [desikatif, -iv] *Méd* ADJ *(produit)* drying
NM drying agent

dessiccation [desikasjɔ̃] NF desiccation

dessiller [desije] VT *(yeux)* to open; *Fig* **d. les yeux à** *ou* **de qn** to open sb's eyes (to the facts)
VPR se dessiller *(des yeux)* to open; *Fig* **ses yeux se dessillèrent** his eyes were opened

dessin [desɛ̃] NM **1** *(art)* (art of) drawing, sketching; *(croquis etc)* drawing; **être bon en d.** to be good at drawing, to be a good drawer; **d. à la plume** pen-and-ink sketch; **d. au trait** line drawing; **d. à main levée** free-hand drawing; **un d. d'enfant** a child's drawing; **les dessins de Degas** Degas' drawings; **faire du d. publicitaire** to be a commercial artist; *Fam* **faut-il que je te fasse un d.?** do I have to draw a picture *or* spell it out for you?; *Tech* **planche à d.** drawing board; **d. d'ensemble** general assembly drawing; **d. de profil** profile drawing
2 *(motif)* design, pattern; **tissu à dessins** patterned fabric; **une robe avec de jolis dessins** a pretty patterned dress
3 *(contour) (d'un visage etc)* outline
▸▸ *Cin* **dessin(s) animé(s)** cartoon(s); **d. assisté par ordinateur** computer-assisted design; **d. humoristique** cartoon; **d. industriel** industrial drawing; **d. de mode** fashion design

dessinateur, -trice [desinatœr, -tris] N **1** *(artiste)* sketcher, drawer; **d. humoristique** cartoonist **2** *(de papier peint)* designer; *(de mode)* fashion artist **3** *Tech* draughtsman, *f* draughtswoman, *Am* draftsman, *f* draftswoman; **d. industriel** draughtsman; **d. cartographe** cartographer; **d. concepteur** *(de mobilier etc)* designer

dessiner [desine] VT **1** to draw, to sketch; **d. qch d'après nature** to draw sth from nature; **d. à l'encre/à la craie** to draw in ink/chalk **2** *(papier peint, tissu, plan etc)* to design **3** *Fig (tracer)* to show, to outline; **les montagnes dessinent leur courbe sur le ciel** the line of the mountains stands out against the sky; **vêtement qui dessine bien la taille** garment that shows off the waist; **visage bien dessiné** finely chiselled face
VPR se dessiner 1 *(se voir)* to stand out, to be outlined; **les arbres se dessinent à l'horizon** the trees stand out *or* are outlined on the horizon; **parfois, un sourire se dessinait sur ses lèvres** a smile occasionally played *or* hovered on her lips **2** *(se préciser)* to take

shape; **nos projets de vacances se dessinent vaguement** our holiday plans are beginning to take shape; **on voit se d. un virage à gauche de l'opinion** we can see the beginnings of a shift to the left in public opinion

dessouder [desude] **VT 1** *Tech* to unsolder **2** *Arg (tuer)* to waste, *Br* to do in
▸ **se dessouder le tuyau s'est dessoudé** the pipe has come unsoldered

dessoûler [desule] *Fam* **VT** to sober up, to make sober
VI to become sober, to sober up; **il ne dessoûle pas depuis son mariage** he hasn't been sober since he got married

dessous [dəsu] **ADV** underneath; **passez (par-)d.** go underneath (it); **prendre/porter qch par (en) d.** to take hold of/carry sth from underneath; *Fig* **il fait des choses par (en) d.** he does things in an underhand way; **en d.** underneath; **l'appartement d'en d.** the downstairs flat, the flat downstairs; **regarder qn (par) en d.** to look at sb furtively *or* stealthily; **rire en d.** to laugh up one's sleeve; **agir en d.** to act in an underhand way; **ci-d.** below; **dans la note ci-d.** in the note below; **là-d.** under there; *Fig* **il y a quelque chose de bizarre là-d.** there's something funny about it; **au-d.** below; **son bureau est au-d.** his office is on the next floor down; **une maison avec un garage au-d.** a house with a garage underneath (it); *Fig* **pour vingt euros et au-d., vous ne trouverez rien de bien** you won't find anything decent for less than twenty euros
PRÉP 1 de d. from under(neath) *or* beneath **2 par-d.** underneath **3 au-d. de** under; **au-d. de 100 euros, on ne trouve rien** you won't find anything under 100 euros; **un peu au-d. de Paris** slightly to the south of Paris; *Fig* **elle est bien au-d. de toi** she's not nearly as good as you; **il est au-d. de sa tâche** he's not up to the job; **être au-d. de tout** to be beneath contempt **4 en d. de** under(neath); **tu es très en d. de la vérité** you're not even close
NM les gens du d. the people on the floor below, the downstairs neighbours; **d. d'une assiette** underside of a plate; **d. de robe** slip, *Vieilli* petticoat; *Fig* **avoir le d.** to get the worst of it, to be defeated; **être dans le troisième** *ou* **trente-sixième d.** to be in the depths of despair; **les d. de la politique** the shady side of politics; **je voudrais bien connaître le d. de toute cette histoire** I'd really like to know what they're not telling us (in this whole affair); *Fig* **connaître le d. des cartes** to be in the know, to know what's going on
NMPL *(sous-vêtements)* (ladies') underwear, *Fam* undies; *(raffiné)* lingerie

dessous-de-bouteille [d(ə)sudbutɛj] **NM INV** coaster

dessous-de-bras [d(ə)sudbra] **NM INV** dress shield

dessous-de-plat [d(ə)sudpla] **NM INV** table mat

dessous-de-table [d(ə)sudtabl] **NM INV** backhander; *Fig* **verser un d. à qn** to pay sb a bribe, to give *or* slip sb a backhander

dessous-de-tasse [d(ə)sud(ə)tas] **NM INV** saucer

dessous-de-verre [d(ə)sudvɛr] **NM INV** coaster

dessus [dəsy] **ADV** (up)on (it/them); **il a marché d.** he trod on it; **mais il n'y a pas l'adresse d.** but the address isn't on it, but it doesn't have the address on (it); **avec du chocolat d.** with chocolate on top; **j'ai failli lui tirer d.** I nearly shot him; **vous avez mis le doigt d.** you've put your finger on it, you've hit the nail on the head; *Fig Fam* **il m'est tombé d. dans le métro** he buttonholed me *or*

grabbed hold of me in the underground; **la police finira bien par lui mettre la main d.** the police will track him down eventually; **impossible de mettre la main d.!** *(d'une chose)* I just can't/couldn't lay my hands on it!; **marcher bras d. bras dessous** to walk arm in arm; **au-d.** at the top, on top, above; **mettre les meilleures pommes (au-)d.** to put the best apples on top *or* at the top; **l'appartement au-d.** the flat upstairs, the upstairs flat; **avec de la crème au-d.** with cream on top; **vous ne trouverez rien au-d.** you'll find nothing better; **voir ci-d.** see above; **là-d.** up there; **il y a beaucoup à dire là-d.** a lot could be said on that score; *Fam* **ne compte pas là-d.!** don't count on it!; **là-d., elle partit** and with that, she left
PRÉP 1 de d. from, off; **elle ne leva pas les yeux de d. son ouvrage** she didn't lift her eyes from *or* look up from *or* take her eyes off her work
2 au-d. de above; **au-d. de 15 ans** over 15, more than 15 (years old); **au-d. de Lyon** *(au nord de)* north of Lyons; **nous volons au-d. de l'Alsace** we are flying over Alsace; *Fig* **il est bien au-d. de toi** he's much better than you are; **je suis au-d. de tout cela** I'm above all that; **au-d. de tout soupçon** above suspicion; **c'est au-d. de mes forces** I'm not strong enough (to do it); **c'est au-d. de mes capacités/moyens** I can't do/afford it; **rien n'est au-d. de sa foi** his faith can move mountains
3 par-d. above, over; *Fam* **j'en ai par-d. la tête** I've had it up to here
NM *(de table etc)* top; **l'étage du d.** the top floor; *Théâtre* **les d.** the flies; **avoir le d.** to have the upper hand, to be on top; **(re)prendre le d.** to get over it

dessus-de-cheminée [d(ə)sydʃəmine] **NM INV** mantelshelf runner

dessus-de-lit [d(ə)sydli] **NM INV** coverlet, bedspread

déstabilisant [destabilizɑ̃], **déstabilisateur, -trice** [destabilizatœr, -tris] **ADJ** unsettling; *Pol, Fin* destabilizing; **cet incident a été très d. pour les élèves** the incident was very unsettling for *or* had a very unsettling effect on the pupils; **cela a été très d. pour le gouvernement** it has had an extremely destabilizing effect on the government

déstabilisation [destabilizasjɔ̃] **NF** unsettling; *Pol, Fin* destabilization

déstabiliser [destabilize] **VT** to unsettle; *Pol, Fin* to destabilize

déstalinisation [destalinizasjɔ̃] **NF** *Pol* destalinization

déstaliniser [destalinize] **VT** *Pol* to destalinize

destin [dɛstɛ̃] **NM** fate, destiny; **avoir un d. tragique** to be ill-fated; **qui aurait pu prévoir son d.?** who could have predicted his fate *or* what would become of him?; **le d. a voulu que …** fate decreed that …; **le d. nous a réunis** fate brought us together; **accepter son d.** to accept one's fate *or* destiny; **se mettre dans les mains du d.** to trust to fate; **nous nous souviendrons du d. tragique qui fut le sien** we shall remember his tragic fate

destinataire [dɛstinatɛr] **N** *(de lettre etc)* addressee, recipient; *(de marchandises)* consignee; *(de mandat postal)* payee

destination [dɛstinasjɔ̃] **NF 1** *(direction)* destination; **quelle est votre d.?** where are you going (to) *or* heading (for) *or* bound (for)?; **d. touristique** tourist destination; **trains/vols à d. de Paris** trains/flights to Paris; **articles à d. de la province et de l'étranger** goods for the provinces and for export; **arriver à d.** to arrive at one's destination **2** *(d'un édifice, d'une somme d'argent etc)* purpose

destinée [dɛstine] **NF 1** *(vie)* destiny; **unir sa**

d. à celle de qn to marry sb; *Litt* **il était promis à de si grandes destinées** he was destined for such great things **2** = **destin**

destiner [dɛstine] **VT 1 d. qch à qn** to mean *or* intend sth for sb; **le sort qui nous est destiné** what fate holds in store for us; **cette remarque t'était personnellement destinée** that remark was meant for *or* aimed at you; **ce paquet vous est destiné** this parcel is meant for *or* addressed to you; **d. une somme d'argent à un achat** to allot *or* assign a sum of money to a purchase; **la recette du concert est destinée à la recherche contre le sida** the money from the concert will go to *or* towards AIDS research; **des marchandises destinées à l'exportation** goods intended for export; **il avait destiné son fils au barreau** he had intended his son for the bar; **on la destinait au fils du maire** they intended that she should marry the mayor's son; **cette salle est destinée aux répétitions** this room is used for rehearsals
2 *Vieilli (prédestiner)* to destine; **nous étions destinés à nous rencontrer** we were destined *or* fated to meet
▸ **VPR se destiner se d. à qch** to intend to take up sth (as a profession); **il se destine à la médecine** he intends to be a doctor

destituable [dɛstituabl] **ADJ** *(fonctionnaire)* dismissible; *(souverain)* deposable; **il n'est pas destituable** *(fonctionnaire)* he cannot be dismissed (from his post); *(officier)* he cannot be stripped of his rank

destituer [dɛstitɥe] **VT** *(renvoyer)* to dismiss, to discharge; *Mil* to discharge; *(fonctionnaire)* to remove from office; *(souverain)* to depose; **d. un général de son commandement** to relieve a general of his command

destitution [dɛstitysjɔ̃] **NF** dismissal; *Mil* discharge; *(d'un souverain)* deposition

déstockage [destɔkaʒ] **NM** *Com* destocking, reduction in stocks; *Compta* **d. de production** *(poste de bilan)* decrease in stocks

déstocker [destɔke] **VT** *Com* to destock, to reduce stocks of

destrier [dɛstrije] **NM** *Arch* charger, war horse

destroy [dɛstrɔj] **ADJ INV** *Fam (musique)* = loud, fast and aggressive; *(personne)* self-destructive; *(jean)* ripped; *(voiture)* beat up, wrecked, *Br* knackered; **avoir une allure complètement d.** to look wasted

destroyer [dɛstrɔjœr, dɛstrwaje] **NM** *Naut, Mil* destroyer

destructeur, -trice [dɛstryktœr, -tris] **ADJ** *(enfant, guerre etc)* destructive
N destroyer
NM *(appareil)* **d. de documents** shredder

destructible [dɛstryktibl] **ADJ** destructible

destructif, -ive [dɛstryktif, -iv] **ADJ** destructive

destruction [dɛstryksjɔ̃] **NF** *(de preuves, papiers, ville etc)* destruction; *(de rats etc)*, *Fig (d'une race)* extermination

déstructuration [destryktyrasjɔ̃] **NF** *(de la société)* breakdown, disintegration

déstructuré [destryktyre] **ADJ 1** *(vêtement)* unstructured, deconstructed **2 une société déstructurée** a society in which traditional structures have broken down

déstructurer [destryktyre] **VT 1** *(vêtement)* to deconstruct **2** *(société)* **le chômage a déstructuré la société** society has been undermined by unemployment; **des populations déstructurées par le chômage/la guerre** people whose lives have been destroyed *or* shattered by unemployment/war

désuet, -uète [desɥɛ, -ɥɛt] **ADJ** *(mot)* obsolete; *(théorie)* obsolete, antiquated, out-of-date; *(vêtement)* out-of-date, old-fashioned; *(charme)* old-fashioned

désuétude [desyetyd] NF disuse; **tomber en d.** to fall into disuse; *(d'un mot)* to become obsolete; *Jur (d'un droit etc)* to lapse; *(d'une loi)* to fall into abeyance; **d. calculée** planned *or* built-in obsolescence

désuni [dezyni] ADJ *(personnes)* divided, disunited; *(manœuvre)* uncoordinated; **des amis désunis par la guerre** friends divided by war

désunion [dezynjɔ̃] NF *(de personnes)* lack of unity; *(dans la famille etc)* dissension

désunir [dezynir] VT *(personnes, famille etc)* to divide; **questions qu'on ne peut pas d.** questions that cannot be treated separately (from each other), indissolubly linked questions; **des amants que le temps a désunis** lovers who grew apart with the passage of time
▶ VPR **se désunir** *(d'un athlète)* to lose one's stride

désynchronisé [desɛ̃krɔnize] ADJ out of synch

désyndicalisation [desɛ̃dikalizasjɔ̃] NF *(de la classe ouvrière)* decline in union membership (**de** among)

désyndicaliser [desɛ̃dikalize] VT *(entreprise)* to de-unionize

détachable [detaʃabl] ADJ detachable

détachage [detaʃaʒ] NM *(de vêtements etc)* stain *or* spot removal

détachant [detaʃɑ̃] ADJ stain- *or* spot-removing
NM stain *or* spot remover

détaché [detaʃe] ADJ **1** loose, detached; *(animal)* untethered; **pièces détachées** spare parts **2** *(délégué)* seconded *(to another department)*; *Mil* detached **3** *Fig (manière etc)* detached; **d. des biens de ce monde** detached from the world, unworldly

détachement [detaʃmɑ̃] NM **1** *(d'un employé)* secondment; **il est en d. à l'université de Cambridge** he has been seconded *or* is on secondment to the University of Cambridge **2** *Mil (de troupes)* detachment, draft, *Am* detail; **d. de corvée** fatigue party **3** *(indifférence)* detachment (**de** from); **d. des biens de ce monde** detachment from the world, unworldliness

détacher[1] [detaʃe] VT **1** *(défaire)* to detach; *(rideau)* to take down; *(chaîne)* to undo; *(animal)* to unether; *Rail (wagon à plate-forme)* to uncouple; **je ne peux pas en d. mes yeux** I can't take my eyes off it; **d. un chèque du carnet** to tear out a cheque; **d. les pétales d'une fleur** to pick *or* pluck the petals off a flower **2** *Fig* **d. qn de qch** to turn sb away from sth; **son indiscrétion a détaché de lui tous ses amis** his lack of discretion cost him all his friends *or* caused all his friends to turn away from him; **ses parents ont réussi à le d. de ce chien** his parents managed to free him *or* get him away from the dog **3** *(déléguer)* to attach, to second; *Mil* to detach; *Mil* **d. un officier auprès de qn** to detach an officer to serve with sb; **fonctionnaire détaché à un autre service** official temporarily attached *or* seconded to another department; **se faire d.** to be seconded; *Mil* to be detached **4** *(découper)* **d. une figure dans un tableau** to make a figure stand out in a picture; **d. les syllabes d'un mot** to pronounce each syllable of a word separately; *Mus* **d. les notes** to detach the notes
▶ VPR **se détacher 1** *(de nœud etc)* to come undone; *(d'animal)* to break loose; *(de poignée)* to break *or* come off, to become detached; *(de bouton)* to come off; *(de pièces)* to come apart; *(de peinture)* to flake *or* come away *or* off; **l'écorce se détache** the bark is peeling off *or* coming away

2 *Fig* **se d. de sa famille/qn** to separate *or* break away from one's family/sb; *(se désintéresser)* to grow apart from one's family/sb; **il s'est complètement détaché de toutes ces choses qui autrefois l'intéressaient** he has completely cut himself off from everything that used to interest him; **ils se sont beaucoup détachés l'un de l'autre** they've grown wide apart; **il s'est détaché peu à peu de la maison où il avait passé son enfance** he has gradually detached himself from his childhood home

3 *(se séparer)* **un petit groupe de coureurs se détacha en avant** a small group of runners broke away (from the field) *or* pulled ahead (of the field)

4 *(ressortir)* **se d. sur un fond/l'horizon** to stand out against a background/the horizon

détacher[2] VT *(nettoyer)* *(vêtements etc)* to remove stains *or* spots from

détacheur, -euse [detaʃœr, -øz] ADJ **flacon d.** (bottle of) stain remover
NM stain remover

détail [detaj] NM **1** *(élément)* detail; **donner tous les détails** to enter into *or* go into all the details, to give full details; **elle n'a pas donné de détails** she didn't go into detail, she didn't give any details; **raconter qch en d.** *ou* **dans les détails** to give a detailed account of sth; **décrire qch en d.** to describe sth in detail, to give a detailed description of sth; **elle va encore me faire le d. de ses vacances** she's going to give me yet another detailed account of her holiday; *Fig Fam* **ne pas faire de détails** not to make any exceptions; **sans faire de détails** without exception; **demander plus de détails** to ask for more details (**sur, à propos de** about, of); **nous n'avons pas encore de détails** there are no details as yet; **pour plus de détails** for more details; **c'est un d.** it's not important, it's a detail; **se perdre dans les détails** to get bogged down in detail; *Com* **le d. d'un compte** the items of an account; **le d. d'une facture** the breakdown of an invoice; **faire le d. de ses dépenses** to itemize one's expenses

2 *Com* retail; **vendre au d.** to sell (goods) retail; **magasin de vente au d.** retail store; **marchand au d.** retailer; **prix de d.** retail price; **commerce de d.** retailing; **être dans le commerce de d.** to be in retailing

3 *Admin, Mil* **service de d.** executive duties; **officier de d.** ≃ quartermaster officer

détaillant, -ante [detajɑ̃, -ɑ̃t] N *Com* retailer; **d. indépendant** independent retailer; **d. spécialisé** specialist retailer

détaillé [detaje] ADJ **1** *(récit, description etc)* detailed **2** *Com* **état d. de compte** detailed *or* itemized statement of account

détailler [detaje] VT **1** *Com (marchandises)* to retail, to sell retail **2** *(énumérer) (raisons)* to list; *Com (facture)* to itemize **3 d. qn (de la tête aux pieds)** to scrutinize sb, to look sb up and down

détaler [detale] VI *Fam (d'une personne)* to bolt, to take off; *(d'un cheval etc)* to bolt; **la souris détala vers son trou** the mouse bolted *or* scuttled off to *or* scurried off to its hole

détartrage [detartraʒ] NM *(de chaudière)* descaling; *(de dents)* tartar removal, scaling

détartrant [detartrɑ̃] NM *(pour chaudière)* scaler
ADJ **dentifrice d.** toothpaste for tartar removal

détartrer [detartre] VT *(chaudière)* to (de)scale; *(dents) (d'un dentiste)* to scale, to remove the tartar from; *(d'un dentifrice)* to remove the tartar from

détartreur [detartrœr] NM *(pour chaudière)* scaler

détaxation [detaksasjɔ̃] NF removal of tax

détaxe [detaks] NF **1** *(levée)* **la d. des tabacs** *(réduction)* the reduction of duty *or* tax on tobacco; *(suppression)* the lifting of tax or duty on tobacco; **vendu en d.** duty-free; **la d. des marchandises à l'exportation** the lifting of duty on exports **2** *(remboursement)* refund; **cela m'a fait cent euros de d.** I got a hundred euros in duty refunded

détaxé [detakse] ADJ *(produits, articles)* duty-free

détaxer [detakse] VT to take the tax off, to remove the tax on; **marchandises détaxées** duty-free goods

détectable [detɛktabl] ADJ detectable

détecter [detɛkte] VT to detect

détecteur, -trice [detɛktœr, -tris] ADJ *Tech* detecting, sensing; *Électron* **lampe détectrice** detector valve
NM *Tech* detector; *Électron* detector, sensor
▶▶ *Aut* **d. d'anomalie** fault warning sensor; *Aut* **d. anti-pincement** anti-pinch sensor; *Aut* **d. de choc** crash sensor; *Aut* **d. de cognement** knock sensor; *Aut* **d. de collision** crash sensor; *Com* **d. de faux billets** forged banknote detector; **d. de fumée** smoke detector *or* alarm; **d. de mensonges** lie detector, *Spéc* polygraph; **d. de mines** mine detector; *Électron* **d. d'ondes** wave detector; *Électron* **d. de particules** particle detector; **d. de radar** radar detector; *TV etc* **d. transistorisé** solid-state sensor; *Ordinat* **d. de virus** virus detector

détection [detɛksjɔ̃] NF detection, location; **d. électromagnétique** radio location; **d. sous-marine** underwater detection; *Mil, Naut* **d. des mines** mine detection; **d. à ultrasons** ultrasound detection; *Ordinat* **d. d'erreurs** error detection; *Ordinat* **d. virale** virus detection

détective [detɛktiv] NM detective; **d. privé** private detective; **d. d'hôtel** house detective, hotel detective

déteindre [detɛ̃dr] *(conj like* **teindre**) VT to take the colour out of
VI *(d'un tissu)* to fade, to lose colour; **d. au lavage** to run in the wash; **le ruban a déteint sur ma robe** the colour of the ribbon has come off on my dress; *Fig* **cela déteint sur eux** it rubs off on them; *Fig* **j'espère que leur politesse déteindra sur elle** I hope some of their politeness rubs off on her

dételage [detlaʒ] NM **1** *(de chevaux)* unharnessing, unhitching **2** *Rail (de wagons)* uncoupling

dételer [detle] (je **dételle**, n. **dételons**; je **détellerai**) VT **1** *(chevaux)* to unharness, to unhitch; *(bœufs)* to unyoke **2** *Rail (wagons)* to uncouple
VI *Fam* to ease off, to stop working; **travailler dix heures sans d.** to work for ten hours without letting up, to work non-stop for ten hours; **on dételle à six heures** we stop (work) at six o'clock

détendeur [detɑ̃dœr] NM *Tech* pressure reducer, relief valve

détendre [detɑ̃dr] VT *(cordage de raquette, cordes de guitare)* to slacken, to loosen; *(arc)* to unbend; **d. un ressort** to release a spring; **d. des relations/l'atmosphère** to make relations/the atmosphere less strained; **d. les nerfs** to steady the nerves
▶ VPR **se détendre** *(de tissu)* to stretch; *(de ressort)* to uncoil; *(de vapeur)* to be reduced in pressure; *(d'un gaz, de l'air chaud)* to expand; *(se relaxer)* to relax; **se d. pendant une heure** to relax for an hour; **son visage se détendit dans un sourire** his face relaxed into a smile; **la situation se détend** the situation is easing *or* is becoming less tense

détendu [detɑ̃dy] ADJ *(lâche)* slack; *(conversation etc)* relaxed

détenir [detnir] **VT** *(conj like* **tenir***)* **1** *(passeport, titres etc)* to hold, to be in possession of; *(le pouvoir, Sport coupe, record du monde)* to hold; **d. un objet volé** to be in possession of a stolen object; **d. un secret** to have a secret; **ils détiennent 30% des parts de la société/des parts de marché** they have a 30% shareholding in the company/a 30% market share **2** *(personne)* to detain, to keep *or* hold prisoner

détente [detɑ̃t] **NF 1** *(relaxation)* recreation; **dans ses rares moments de d.** in the little time he has to relax; **j'ai besoin de quelques instants de d.** I need to relax for a few moments, I need a few moments' relaxation **2** *(de qch de tendu)* loosening, slackening; *(de relations etc)* easing; *Pol* détente; *(d'un athlète)* spring; **avoir une belle d.** to jump well, to be a good jumper; **d'une d. de la jambe droite, il envoya le ballon dans le but anglais** stretching out his right leg, he sent the ball into the England goal; **travaillant tout en d., il parvint à sauter les 2 mètres** with a powerful spring, he managed to clear the 2-metre mark **3** *(d'une arme)* trigger; *Fam* **il est dur à la d.** *(pingre)* he's tight-fisted *or* stingy; *(il ne comprend pas vite)* he's slow on the uptake **4** *Tech (de la vapeur, des gaz)* expansion; *(dans un moteur)* explosion *or* power stroke; **soupape de d.** expansion valve **5** *Écon (des taux d'intérêt)* lowering, easing

détenteur, -trice [detɑ̃tœr, -tris] **N** *(de droits d'auteur, titres, coupe etc)* holder; **d. de titres** stockholder, shareholder; **d. d'obligations** bondholder; **d. du record du monde** world record holder

détention [detɑ̃sjɔ̃] **NF 1** *(de titres etc)* holding; *(d'armes à feu etc)* possession **2** *(captivité)* detention, imprisonment; **d. provisoire** detention pending trial

détenu, -ue [detny] **N** prisoner, inmate

détergence [detɛrʒɑ̃s] **NF** detergency

détergent [detɛrʒɑ̃] **ADJ, NM** detergent

déterger [detɛrʒe] **VT** *Tech (taches d'huile etc)* to clean, to remove

détérioration [deterjɔrasjɔ̃] **NF** deterioration

détériorer [deterjɔre] **VT** *(matériel, santé)* to damage; *(marchandises)* to spoil; **la radio m'est revenue complètement détériorée** the radio came back absolutely ruined; **détérioré en cours de transport** damaged in transit
VPR se détériorer to deteriorate

déterminable [detɛrminabl] **ADJ** determinable, which can be determined

déterminant [detɛrminɑ̃] **ADJ** *(facteur, cause etc)* deciding, decisive; **sa présence a été déterminante pour la signature du contrat** his presence was the determining factor in the decision to sign the contract
NM *Ling* determiner; *Math* determinant

déterminatif, -ive [detɛrminatif, -iv] VOIR GRAMMAIRE A32 *Ling, Gram* **ADJ** *(mot etc)* determinative, defining; **phrase déterminative** defining clause
NM determiner, determinative

détermination [detɛrminasjɔ̃] **NF 1** *(fermeté)* determination, resolution; **avec d.** with determination, determinedly, resolutely **2** *(résolution)* resolve, determination; **rien ne pourra faire flancher ma d.** nothing will make me any less determined, nothing will shake my resolve **3** *(d'une espèce, d'une date, d'une zone etc)* determination; *(du sang, d'une bactérie)* typing; **d. des prix** price setting

déterminé [detɛrmine] **ADJ 1** *(domaine, objectif etc)* specific, particular; *(durée)* specific, set, definite; **dans un sens d.** in a given

direction; **il faut arriver au but/à l'objectif d.** we have to achieve the goal/the objective that was set; **il l'a fait dans un but d.** he did it for a specific reason **2** *(personne, manière etc)* determined, resolute; **être d. à faire qch** to be determined to do sth

déterminer [detɛrmine] **VT 1** *(définir)* *(date, fait, nom, valeur etc)* to determine, to establish; *(espèce)* to determine; *(sang, bactérie)* to type; **d. un lieu de rendez-vous** to fix *or* decide on a meeting place **2** *(causer)* *(changement)* to cause, to give rise to; *(action, décision)* to determine, to dictate **3** *(décider)* **d. qn à faire qch** to induce *or* move *or* impel sb to do sth; **qu'est-ce qui vous a déterminé à partir?** what made you (decide to) leave? **4** *Gram* to determine
VPR se déterminer to make up one's mind (**à faire qch** to do sth)

déterminisme [detɛrminism] **NM** *Phil* determinism

déterministe [detɛrminist] *Phil* **N** determinist
ADJ determinist(ic)

déterré, -ée [detere] **N** *Fam* **il a un air *ou* une mine *ou* une tête de d.** he looks like death warmed up

déterrer [detere] **VT** *(trésor enfoui etc)* to dig up, to unearth; *(arbre)* to uproot; *(cadavre)* to exhume; *Fig (vieux livre etc)* to dig up

détersif, -ive [detɛrsif, -iv] **ADJ, NM** detergent

détersion [detɛrsjɔ̃] **NF** *(nettoyage)* cleaning with a detergent; *Méd (d'une plaie etc)* cleansing

détestable [detɛstabl] **ADJ** *(personne)* detestable, hateful; *(travail etc)* *(de mauvaise qualité)* awful, dreadful, very bad; *(inintéressant)* awful, ghastly; *(temps, humeur)* foul, ghastly

détestablement [detɛstabləmɑ̃] **ADV** *(se conduire, chanter, parler)* extremely badly, appallingly; **faire la cuisine d.** to be an extremely bad *or* an appalling cook; **il parle anglais/travaille d.** his English/work is extremely bad *or* is appalling

détester [detɛste] **VT** to detest, to hate; **je déteste être dérangé** I hate to be *or* I hate *or* detest being disturbed; **elle ne déteste pas (de) courir** she's quite fond of running; **il ne déteste pas les bonbons** he rather likes sweets

déthéiné [deteine] **ADJ** *(thé)* decaffeinated

détonant [detɔnɑ̃] **ADJ** *(substance)* explosive; **explosif d.** high explosive; *Tech, Fig* **mélange d.** explosive mixture
NM explosive

détonateur [detɔnatœr] **NM** detonator; *Fig* **être le d. de qch** to spark sth off

détonation [detɔnasjɔ̃] **NF** *(explosion)* detonation; *(bruit)* explosion; *(bruit d'arme à feu)* report, bang; *Aut* knocking, detonation

détoner [detɔne] **VI** *(de dynamite etc)* to detonate, to explode; *(de carburant)* to knock; **faire d. qch** to detonate sth

Do not confuse with **détonner**.

détonner [detɔne] **VI** *(d'un instrument)* to be out of tune; *(d'un chanteur)* to sing out of tune *or* off-key; *(d'un pianiste etc)* to play out of tune; *(de couleurs)* to clash; **ses bijoux détonnent dans ce milieu** her jewels are out of place *or* out of keeping in these circles; **il détonne dans cet entourage** he looks out of place in that circle; **la remarque détonne dans ce texte** the remark jumps out in this text *or* looks really out of place in this text

Do not confuse with **détoner**.

détordre [detɔrdr] **VT** *(fil etc)* to untwist

VPR se détordre *(de fil etc)* to come untwisted, to untwist

détortiller [detɔrtije] **VT** *(fil etc)* to untwist; *(cheveux etc)* to disentangle

détour [detur] **NM 1** *(tracé)* *(d'une route, d'une rivière)* turn, curve, bend; **la route fait un brusque d.** the road makes a sharp turn *or* bends sharply; **je l'ai aperçue au d. du chemin** I spotted her at the bend in the path; *Fig* **au d. de la conversation** in the course of the conversation
2 *(dans un parcours)* detour; **faire un long d.** to make a long detour; **d. obligatoire de 5 km** (mandatory) 5 kilometre diversion; **ça vaut le d.** it's worth the trip; *Fig* **tu verrais son nouveau copain, il vaut le d.** her new boyfriend is really something
3 *Fig (biais)* **user de détours pour arriver à un but** to achieve one's end in a roundabout way; **répondre sans d.** to give a plain *or* straightforward answer; **vous pouvez me parler sans d.** you can speak frankly to me

détourage [detura3] **NM** *Cin* cropping

détourné [deturne] **ADJ** *(route, itinéraire)* indirect, roundabout; **chemin d.** by-road; *Fig* **par des voies détournées, de façon détournée** indirectly, in a roundabout way; **ce n'est pas la peine de prendre des chemins détournés pour me le dire** you might as well tell me straight out, why go all around the houses to tell me?

détournement [deturnəmɑ̃] **NM** *(d'une rivière etc)* diversion, diverting; *(du trafic)* diversion, rerouting
▸▸ *Fin* **d. d'actif** embezzlement of assets; **d. d'avion** hijacking; *Fin* **d. de fonds** misappropriation of funds, embezzlement; *Jur* **d. de mineur** corruption of a minor; **d. de pouvoir** takeover (of power)

détourner [deturne] **VT 1** *(trafic, rivière etc)* to divert; **d. un avion** to hijack a plane; **d. l'attention de qn** to divert *or* distract sb's attention; **d. qn de** *(son travail, mauvaises fréquentations)* to get sb away from; **d. qn de sa route** to take sb out of his/her way; **comment as-tu pu te laisser d. de ton devoir?** how could you have let yourself be distracted from your duty?; **d. qn du droit chemin** to lead sb astray; **il faut absolument le d. de ce projet** we really must get him to drop the idea; **d. la conversation** to change the subject; **d. les soupçons** to avert suspicion **2** *(fonds)* to misappropriate, to embezzle **3** **d. la tête pour éviter de voir qn** to look the other way *or* to turn one's head away so as not to see sb; **d. les yeux** to avert one's gaze, to look away, to turn one's eyes away
VPR se détourner to turn away *or* aside (**de** from); *Fig* **se d. de ses études/amis** to neglect one's studies/friends

détoxication [detɔksikasjɔ̃] **NF** detoxication

détoxiquer [detɔksike] **VT** to detoxicate

détracter [detrakte] **VT** *Litt* to denigrate, to disparage

détracteur, -trice [detraktœr, -tris] **N** detractor, disparager

détraqué, -ée [detrake] **ADJ** *(appareil)* out of order; *(digestion, estomac)* upset; *(santé)* ruined; *Fam (personne)* *(psychologiquement)* unhinged; **ma radio est toute détraquée** there is something very wrong with my radio; **il a le cerveau d.** his mind is unhinged; **avoir les nerfs détraqués** to be a nervous wreck; **le temps est d.** the weather is unsettled
N *Fam* psycho

détraquement [detrakmɑ̃] **NM** *(d'un appareil, de la santé etc)* breakdown

détraquer [detrake] **VT** *(appareil)* to put out

of order; *(mécanisme)* to throw out of gear; *Fam* **cette déception lui a détraqué le cerveau** the disappointment has unhinged his mind; **ça va te d. l'estomac** that'll upset your stomach

VPR se détraquer *(d'un appareil, de la santé etc)* to break down; *(de l'estomac)* to be upset; *(du temps)* to become unsettled; **se d. l'estomac/les nerfs** to upset one's stomach/ruin one's nerves

détrempe¹ [detrɑ̃p] NF *(de mur)* distemper; *Beaux-Arts* tempera

détremper² NF *(d'acier)* annealing

détremper¹ [detrɑ̃pe] VT *(gorger d'eau)* to soak; **champ/terre détrempé(e)** sodden *or* waterlogged field/earth

détremper² VT *(acier)* to anneal

détresse [detrɛs] NF **1** *(angoisse)* distress, grief, anguish; **elle est dans une grande d.** she is extremely distressed *or* heartbroken **2** *(dénuement)* financial straits *or* difficulties; **être en d.** to be in financial difficulties, to have money problems **3** *(perdition)* **en d.** *(navire)* in distress; *(voiture, avion)* in difficulties; **signal de d.** distress signal, SOS; *Aut* **feux de d.** hazard warning lights, *Fam* hazards; *Méd* **d. respiratoire** respiratory distress syndrome

détriment [detrimɑ̃] NM **au d. de qn/qch** to the detriment of sb/sth; **je l'ai appris à mon d.** I found it out to my cost

détritus [detritys] NM rubbish, refuse

détroit [detrwa] NM *Géog* strait(s), sound

détromper [detrɔ̃pe] VT **d. qn** to put sb right **VPR se détromper** to realize that one was wrong; **il a fini par se d.** he finally realized his mistake *or* that he was wrong *or* mistaken; **je ne demande pas mieux que de me d.** I'll be quite happy to admit that I was mistaken; **détrompez-vous!** open your eyes!

détrôner [detrone] VT **1** *(monarque)*, *Sport (champion)* to dethrone **2** *(supplanter) (ancienne méthode etc)* to supersede

détrousser [detruse] VT **d. qn** *Hum* to relieve sb of his/her valuables; *Arch* to rob sb

détrousseur [detrusœr] NM *Arch* highwayman, footpad

détruire [detrɥir] *(prp* **détruisant;** *pp* **détruit;** *pr ind* **je détruis, je détruisons;** *impf* **je détruisais;** *p hist* **je détruisis;** *fu* **je détruirai)** VT **1** *(démolir) (édifice, ville etc)* to destroy; *(empire etc)* to destroy, to overthrow; *(bateau etc)* to break up, to scrap; *(voiture, avion etc)* to destroy, *Fam* to demolish, to write off **2** *(anéantir) (maison, village)* to destroy; *(mariage)* to destroy, to wreck; *(moisson, alibi)* to ruin, to destroy; *(santé)* to ruin; **d. les espérances de qn** to destroy *or* dash sb's hopes; **il a détruit sa fortune au jeu** he spent all his money gambling **3** *(tuer)* to kill; **l'épidémie va d. 200 000 personnes** the epidemic is likely to kill 200,000 people **VPR se détruire** *(se suicider)* to kill oneself

dette [dɛt] NF *Fin, Fig* debt; **faire des dettes** to run into debt; **avoir des dettes** to be in debt, to have debts; **avoir 10 000 euros de dettes** to be 10,000 euros in debt; **être criblé de dettes** to be crippled with debt; **avoir une d. de reconnaissance envers qn** to owe sb a debt of gratitude, to be under an obligation to sb; **être en d. envers qn** to be indebted to sb, to be under an obligation to sb; **payer sa d. à la justice** *ou* **à la société** to pay one's debt to society

▸▸*Compta* **dettes actives** accounts receivable, assets; **dettes bancaires** bank debts; **d. caduque** debt barred by the Statute of Limitations; **dettes compte** book debts; **d. consolidée** consolidated debt; **d. à court terme** short-term debt; *Compta* **dettes à court terme** current liabilities; **la d. de l'État**

the national debt; **d. exigible** debt due for (re)payment; **d. d'exploitation** trade debt; **d. extérieure** foreign debt; **d. flottante** floating debt; **d. foncière** property charge; *Compta* **dettes fournisseurs** accounts payable; **d. d'honneur** debt of honour; *(hypothécaire)* mortgage debt; **d. inexigible** unrecoverable debt; **d. inscrite** consolidated debt; **d. de jeu** gambling debt; **d. liquide** liquid debt; *Compta* **dettes à long terme** long-term liabilities; *Compta* **dettes à moyen terme** medium-term liabilities; *Compta* **dettes passives** accounts payable, liabilities; **d. privilégiée** preferred debt; **la d. publique** the national debt; **d. sociale** social debt; **d. véreuse** bad debt

deuche [dœʃ], **deudeuche** [dœdœʃ] NF *Fam* Citroën 2CV

DEUG [dœg] NM *(abrév* **diplôme d'études universitaires générales)** = university degree awarded after a two-year course of study

> **DEUG**
> In French universities, students take the "DEUG" or the "DEUST" ("diplôme d'études universitaires scientifiques et techniques") after two years of courses. They may then take further courses leading to the "licence" (the equivalent of a bachelor's degree). Most students who obtain the "DEUG" choose to do this, while the majority of students who obtain the "DEUST" leave university and go straight into employment.

deuil [dœj] NM **1** *(perte)* bereavement; **fermé pour cause de d.** *(annonce)* closed owing to bereavement; **il y a eu plusieurs deuils dans leur famille** there have been several deaths in their family **2** *(manifestation)* mourning; **porter le d., être en d.** to be in mourning; **porter le d. de qn** to be in mourning for sb; *Fig* **elle porte le d. de sa jeunesse/de sa fortune** she is mourning the loss of her youth/her fortune; **se mettre en d., prendre le d.** to go into mourning; **quitter le d.** to come out of mourning; *Fig* **la montagne est en d.** the mountain looks desolate; *Fig Fam* **il avait toujours les ongles en d.** his fingernails were always dirty; **grand d.** deep mourning; **semaine de d.** week of mourning; **décréter une journée de d. national** to order a day of national mourning, ≃ to order the flags to be flown at half mast *or Am* half-staff; *Vieilli* **conduire le d.** to be chief mourner; *Fam* **faire son d. de qch** to give sth up as *or* for lost

DEUST [døst] NM *(abrév* **diplôme d'études universitaires scientifiques et techniques)** = university degree awarded after a two-year course of study in science and/or technical subjects

deutérium [døterjɔm] NM *Chimie* deuterium

Deutéronome [døterɔnɔm] NM *Bible* Deuteronomy

deutsche Mark [dɔjtʃmark, døtʃmark] NM *Anciennement* Deutschmark

deux [dø, *before a vowel sound in the same word group* døz] ADJ INV **1** two; **d. enfants** [døzɑ̃fɑ̃] two children; **j'en ai d.** [dø] I have two (of them); **d. ou trois** [døzutrwa] two or three; **d. fois** twice; **on a dû lui enlever les d. yeux** they had to remove both his eyes; **des d. côtés du fleuve** on either side *or* on both sides of the river; **tous (les) d.** both; **tous les d. jours** every other day, every two days, every second day; **nous/vous/eux d.** *(sujet)* we/you/those two, the two of *or* both of us/you/them; *(complément)* us/you/

those two, the two of *or* both of us/you/them; **entre d. âges** middle-aged; **être pris entre d. feux** to be caught in the middle; **être assis** *ou* **avoir le derrière** *ou très Fam* **le cul entre d. chaises** to be in an awkward position; **vivre à d.** to live together; **à d. tranchants** *(lame)* double-edged; *Fig* two-edged; *Fig* **une économie/une Europe à d. vitesses** a two-speed economy/Europe; **faire d. poids d. mesures** to apply double standards; **de d. choses l'une, il viendra seul ou il ne viendra pas** he'll either come on his own or he won't come at all; **de d. choses l'une, soit tu pars en vacances avec nous, soit tu restes à la maison** either you come on holiday with us or you stay at home – take your pick *or* it's up to you; **en d. temps, trois mouvements** in two ticks, in no time at all, in next to no time; **les mathématiques/les ordinateurs et moi, ça fait d.** I just don't get on with mathematics/computers; **ma sœur et moi, ça fait d.** *(ne nous confondez pas)* my sister and I are two different people; *(nous sommes fâchés)* my sister and I just don't get along; *Vulg* **cette voiture de mes d.** that fucking car

2 *(peu de)* **j'ai d. mots à lui dire** I've a bone to pick with him; **c'est à d. pas** *ou* **d. minutes d'ici** it's only a short distance away, it's two minutes away; **je reviens dans d. minutes** I'll be back in a minute *or Fam* a tick; **tu peux venir? – d. secondes!** can you come here? – just a minute!; **ça va te prendre d. secondes** it will only take you a minute; *Fam* **être à d. doigts de faire qch** to be on the verge of *or* within an inch of doing sth; **je suis à d. doigts de terminer** *ou* **d'avoir terminé** I've very nearly finished

3 *(deuxième)* **Charles D.** Charles the Second; **chapitre d.** chapter two; *Fam* **il est arrivé d. ou troisième** he came in second or third; **est numéro d. dans mes pensées** he takes second place *or* comes second in my thoughts; **c'est le numéro d. des fabricants de produits textiles** it's the second largest textile manufacturer

NM INV two; *Cartes* two, deuce; *Cartes* **le d. de cœur** the two of hearts; **la table de d.** the two times table; **d. fois d. font quatre** two times two *or* twice two is four; *Fig* **c'est clair comme d. et d. font quatre** it's as clear as day; **aujourd'hui nous sommes le d.** today is the second, it's the second today; **casser qch en d.** to break sth in two; **diviser** *ou* **couper une ligne en d.** to bisect a line; **marcher par d.** to walk in pairs *or* twos; *(dans une procession)* to march two abreast; **entrer d. par d.** to come in two by two *or* in twos; **à nous d.** *(entre amis)* let's get on with it (together); *(à un adversaire)* let's fight it out; *Fam* **il fera ça en moins de d.** he'll do it in two ticks *or* in no time at all *or* in next to no time; *Fam* **comme pas d.** as anything; **pas de d.** *(danse)* pas de deux; *Fig* **entre les d.** average, OK; **tu as froid ou chaud? – entre les d.** are you hot or cold? – I'm just right; **tu as réussi ton examen? – entre les d.** how did your exam go? – so-so; **alors, tu l'aimes ou tu ne l'aimes pas? – entre les d.** well, do you like it or not? – I'm not sure one way or the other; **tu as envie de venir? – je ne sais pas, entre les d.** do you want to come? – I don't know, I do and I don't; **jamais d. sans trois** it never rains but it pours; *Fam* **je n'ai fait ni une ni d.** I didn't think twice

deux-chevaux [døʃ(ə)vo] NF INV *Aut* deux-chevaux, 2CV

deux-deux (à) ADJ *Mus* in two-two time

deux-huit (à) ADJ *Mus* in two-eight time

deuxième [døzjɛm] ADJ second; **appartement au d. étage** second-floor flat, *Am* third-floor apartment; **le d. exportateur/annonceur du monde** the world's second largest exporter/advertiser; *Math* **équation du d. degré** quadratic equation; **d. classe** second class, standard class; **d. épreuve** *(dans l'édition)* revise; *Rugby* **d. temps** second phase

N second; **elle est née la d.** she is the second child

NM *(étage)* **habiter au d.** to live on the second *or Am* third floor

NF *Journ* **d. de couverture** inside front cover, IFC

deuxièmement [døzjɛmmɑ̃] **ADV** secondly, in the second place

deux-mâts [døma] **NM INV** *Naut* two-master

deux-pattes [døpat] **NF INV** *Fam* Citroën 2CV

deux-pièces [døpjɛs] **NM INV 1** *(maillot de bain)* two-piece (swimsuit); *(ensemble, tailleur)* two-piece **2** *(appartement)* two-roomed flat *or Am* apartment

deux-points [døpwɛ̃] **NM INV** *Typ* colon

deux-ponts [døpɔ̃] **NM INV** *Naut* two-decked ship; *Aviat* double-decker (aircraft)

deux-quatre **NM INV** *Mus* two-four time

deux-roues [døru] **NM INV** two-wheeled vehicle, two-wheeler; **je circule en d.** I get around on two wheels

deux-temps **NM INV 1** *Mus* two-two time **2** *(moteur)* two-stroke (engine); **(mélange) d.** two-stroke mixture

deuzio [døzjo] **ADV** *Fam* second(ly)

dévaler [devale] **VI** to go down, to descend; *(de cours d'eau)* to rush down; **le jardin dévale jusqu'à la rivière** the garden slopes down *or* extends down to the river

VT d. l'escalier to rush down the stairs; **d. la rue à toute vitesse** to race down the street

dévaliser [devalize] **VT** *(banque)* to rob; *(maison)* to burgle; *Fam (frigo, placard etc)* to raid; *Fig* **j'ai dévalisé la boutique** I bought up the shop; **on a été dévalisé en manteaux rouges** all the red coats have been snatched up

dévalorisation [devalɔrizasjɔ̃] **NF 1** *(action)* *(de la monnaie)* devaluation; *Com (de marchandises)* marking down; *(résultat)* *(de la monnaie)* fall in value, depreciation; *Com (de marchandises)* mark-down **2** *Fig (d'une personne, d'une politique)* discrediting

dévaloriser [devalɔrize] **VT** *(monnaie)* to devalue; *Com (marchandises)* to mark down

VPR se dévaloriser *(de monnaie)* to depreciate; *Com (de marchandises)* to lose value; *(d'une personne)* to put oneself down; **se d. dans l'esprit du public** to discredit oneself in the eyes of the public

dévaluation [devalɥasjɔ̃] **NF** *Écon (de la monnaie)* devaluation

dévaluer [devalɥe] **VT** *(monnaie)* to devalue

VPR se dévaluer to lose value

devancement [dəvɑ̃smɑ̃] **NM** *Mil* **d. d'appel** enlistment before call-up; *Fin* **d. d'une échéance** payment before the due date, pre-payment

devancer [dəvɑ̃se] **VT** (**je devançai(s); n. devançons**) **1** *(dans un classement)* to come ahead of; **d. ses concurrents** to be ahead of the competition **2** *(distancer)* to leave behind, to out-distance, to outstrip; **je vous ai devancé** I got here before you **3** *(prévenir)* *(personne, critiques)* to forestall; *(demande, désirs de qn)* to anticipate; **d. son époque** to be ahead of one's time; *Mil* **d. l'appel** to enlist before call-up; *Fin* **d. une échéance** to settle an account early, to pay a bill before the due date

devancier, -ière [dəvɑ̃sje, -jɛr] **N** predecessor

DEVANT [dəvɑ̃] SEE GRAMMAR B55

PRÉP in front of **1, 2** ▪ ahead of **1** ▪ in the face of **3**
ADV in front **1, 2** ▪ past **1** ▪ ahead **2**
NM front **1**

PRÉP 1 *(en face de, en avant de)* in front of; **assis d. moi** sitting in front of me; **il est loin d. nous** he is a long way in front of *or* ahead of us; **marchez tout droit d. vous** carry straight on; **regardez d. vous** look where you're going; **je passe d. elle tous les jours** I pass her every day; **elle est passée d. moi dans la queue** she went in front of *or* ahead of me in the queue; **avoir du temps/de l'argent d. soi** to have time/money to spare; **tu as la vie d. toi** you've got your whole life ahead of you; **assis d. un verre de vin** sitting over a glass of wine; **navire d. Calais** ship off Calais **2** *(en présence de)* in front of; **il l'a frappée d. les enfants** he hit her in front of the children; **éprouver de la gêne d. qn** to feel ill at ease with sb *or* in sb's presence; **je n'ai su que faire d. cette petite fille en pleurs** I didn't know what to do when faced *or* confronted with this little girl in tears; **s'incliner d. qn** to bow to sb; **paraître d. ses pairs** to appear before one's peers **3** *(face à)* **être courageux d. le danger** to show courage in the face of danger; **égaux d. la loi** equal in the eyes of the law; **sa position d. ce problème** his position on the problem; **il ne sait quelle attitude adopter d. de tels problèmes/mon malheur** he doesn't know what attitude to adopt when faced with *or* in the face of such problems/my unhappiness; **d. cet état de choses/votre silence** in view of *or* given this state of affairs/your silence

ADV 1 *(en face)* in front; **tu cherches la bibliothèque? tu es (juste) d.** you're looking for the library? you're right in front of it; **son magasin? je passe d. tous les jours** his shop? I pass *or* go past it every day; **il est passé d. et il ne l'a même pas vu** he went right past it and didn't even see it; **passer (par) d.** to come in the front way; **porter qch sens d. derrière** to wear sth back to front; **sa robe se ferme d.** her dress closes at the front *or Am* in front **2** *(en avant)* **aller d.** to go in front, to lead the way; **marcher/courir d.** to walk on/run on ahead; **partir d. pour arriver le premier** to go on ahead so as to get there first; **envoyer qn d.** to send sb on (in front); **passe d.** go ahead of *or* in front of me/us/*etc*; **s'asseoir d.** *(en voiture)* to sit in the front *or Am* in front; **ils sont d. sur la photo** they're at the front in the photograph; **tu n'as pas vu Martin? – je crois qu'il est d.** have you seen Martin? – he's up ahead, I think; **les voleurs sont loin d. maintenant** the thieves are far ahead of us by now; **avoir des places d.** to have seats at the front; **vous pouvez passer des verres d.?** will you pass some glasses to the front? **3** *Arch, Litt* **comme d.** as before

NM 1 front (part); **d. (de chemise)** (shirt) front; *Tricot* **d. gauche/droit** left/right front; **chambre sur le d.** front room; **dents de d.** front teeth; **pattes de d.** forelegs; *Com* **d. de caisse** checkout display; **prendre les devants** to go on ahead; *Fig* to make the first move; **gagner les devants** to take the lead **2** **aller au-d. de qn** to meet sb on the way; **aller au-d. des vœux de qn** to anticipate sb's wishes; **courir au-d. du danger** to court danger, to go to meet danger; **tu vas au-d. de gros ennuis** you're looking for trouble

devanture [dəvɑ̃tyr] **NF** *(d'un édifice)* façade, front; **d. de magasin** *(façade)* shop-front; *(vitrine)* shop window

dévastateur, -trice [devastatœr, -tris] **ADJ** devastating

dévastation [devastasjɔ̃] **NF** devastation, destruction, havoc

dévaster [devaste] **VT** *(pays)* to devastate, to lay waste, *Fml* to ravage; *(cultures)* to devastate, to destroy, to ruin

déveine [devɛn] **NF** *Fam* (run of) bad luck; **être dans la d.** to be down on one's luck; **quelle d.!** (what) hard luck!

développé [devlɔpe] **NM 1** *Sport (en haltérophilie)* press **2** *(en danse)* développé

développement [devlɔpmɑ̃] **NM 1** *(du corps)* development, growth; *(des muscles, des fleurs, des facultés etc)* development; **d. d'une entreprise** growth of a business; **d. durable** sustained development; **mon entreprise est en plein d.** my business is growing fast; **d. de produit** product development; **d. régional** regional development; *Écon* **un pays en voie de d.** a developing country; **personne n'aurait pu s'attendre à de tels développements** no one could have expected such developments; **suivre les développements d'une affaire** to follow the developments of an affair; **un des développements possibles de l'affaire** one of the possible consequences of the scandal **2** *Phot (traitement complet)* processing, developing; *(étape du traitement)* developing **3** *(des ailes)* spreading out, opening out; *(des branches d'un arbre etc)* spread; *Math (d'une expression contractée etc)* expansion, development **4** *Cyclisme* roll out, development, = distance covered by a bicycle in one revolution of the pedals; **bicyclette avec un d. de six mètres** ≃ bicycle with a six-metre gear *or* geared to six metres **5** *Mus, Beaux-Arts (d'un thème, d'une dissertation)* development; *Fig* **se lancer dans de grands développements** to go into detailed explanations *or* great detail

développer [devlɔpe] **VT 1** *(muscles, facultés, commerce etc)* to develop **2** *(ailes)* to spread out, to open out; *Math (expression contractée etc)* to expand, to develop **3** *Phot (traiter)* to process; *(révéler)* to develop; **faire d. une pellicule** to have a film developed *or* processed; **faire d. des photos** to have photos developed **4** *(élargir) (sujet, idée, sa pensée)* to develop **5** *Aut (chevaux)* to deliver; *Cyclisme* **bicyclette qui développe six mètres** bicycle that has a gear of six metres *or* that is geared to six metres

VPR se développer 1 *(d'un enfant, d'un pays, de fleurs, de l'intelligence etc)* to develop; **l'affaire ne va pas tarder à se d. et se transformer en un véritable scandale** the affair will soon develop into a real scandal **2** *(s'étendre)* to spread out, to expand, to extend; **la plaine se développe à perte de vue** the plain extends *or* stretches out as far as the eye can see

développeur [devlɔpœr] **NM** *(société de logiciels)* developer

développeuse [devlɔpøz] **NF** *(pour imprimante laser)* developer

devenir [dəvnir] **NM** gradual change, development; **la langue est dans un perpétuel d.** the language is in a constant state of flux

VI *(conj like* venir, *the aux is* être*)* to become; **il devint général** he became a general; **il était devenu (un) homme** he had grown into a man; **il devient vraiment indiscret** he's becoming *or* getting really indiscreet; **que devenez-vous ces temps-ci?** what are you up to these days?; **que devient votre cousin?** how is your cousin getting on?; **qu'est-il devenu?** what has become of him?; **que vais-je d. sans toi?** what will become of me without you?, what will I do without you?, where will I be without you?; **qu'est devenu mon livre?** what's happened to my book?; **d. grand** *(en taille)* to grow tall; *(en âge)* to grow up; **d. vieux** to grow old, to get old; **c'est à d. fou!** it's enough to drive you mad!; **d. tout rouge** to go all red, to blush; **quand je lui ai dit ça, il est devenu tout heureux/tout dépité** he was delighted/extremely annoyed when I told him

dévergondage [devɛrgɔ̃daʒ] NM **1** *(d'attitude, de personne)* shamelessness **2** *(de style, d'imagination)* extravagance

dévergondé, -ée [devɛrgɔ̃de] ADJ **1** *(attitude, personne)* shameless **2** *(style, imagination)* extravagant ◆ N shameless person; **cette petite dévergondée** the little hussy

dévergonder (se) [sədevɛrgɔ̃de] VPR to become (quite) shameless

dévernir [devɛrnir] VT *(meubles etc)* to take the varnish *or* the polish off

déverrouillage [devɛrujaʒ] NM *(de porte etc)* unbolting, unlocking; *Ordinat* unlocking; *Aut* **d. du capot par l'intérieur** internal bonnet release; *Aut* **d. du hayon par l'intérieur** internal hatchback release

déverrouiller [devɛruje] VT *(porte etc)* to unbolt, to unlock; *(arme)* to release the bolt of; *Ordinat* to unlock; *(majuscules)* to lock off; *Ordinat* **d. en écriture** *(fichier)* to unlock, to remove the read-only lock on

dévers [devɛr] NM **1** *(d'un mur etc)* inclination, slope; *(d'une route dans un virage)* banking; *Rail* vertical slant, cant *(of outer rail at curve)* **2** *(dans le bois etc)* warp, twist

déversement [devɛrsəmɑ̃] NM *(liquide)* discharge, overflow; *(action)* pouring out

déverser[1] [devɛrse] VT *(eau)* to pour; *(trop-plein d'un canal etc)* to discharge; *(détritus etc)* to tip, to dump; *(déchets)* to dump; **le train déversa des centaines de vacanciers sur le quai** the train deposited hundreds of holiday-makers on the platform; *Fig* **il a déversé des torrents d'injures sur sa femme** he showered his wife with abuse, he heaped abuse on his wife; **d. sa colère sur qn** to take one's anger out on sb
◆ VPR **se déverser** *(d'une rivière etc)* to empty, to flow *(dans* into)

déverser[2] VT **1** *(mur etc)* to slope; *(route)* to bank; *(voie ferrée)* to raise the outer rail of **2** *(planche de bois)* to warp
◆ VI **1** *(d'un mur etc)* to incline, to lean **2** *(du bois)* to warp

déversoir [devɛrswar] NM **1** *(de citerne, bassin etc)* overflow; *Tech (de barrage)* spillway **2** *Fig (exutoire)* outlet, safety valve

dévêtir [devɛtir] *(conj like* **vêtir**) VT to undress, to strip
◆ VPR **se dévêtir** *(complètement)* to undress, to strip, to take off one's clothes; *(partiellement)* to take off some of one's clothing

déviance [devjɑ̃s] NF *Psy* deviance

déviant [devjɑ̃] ADJ *Psy* deviant

déviation [devjasjɔ̃] NF deviation; *Aut* detour, *Br* diversion; *(d'un compas)* variation; *(de la colonne vertébrale)* curvature; *(de l'utérus)* displacement

> Il faut noter que le nom anglais **deviation** ne s'utilise jamais dans un contexte routier.

déviationnisme [devjasjɔnism] NM *Pol* deviationism

déviationniste [devjasjɔnist] ADJ, N *Pol* deviationist

dévidage [devidaʒ] NM *Tex etc (de bobine)* unwinding; *(pour faire une bobine)* reeling, spooling

dévider [devide] VT *Tex etc (dérouler)* to unwind; *(pour faire une bobine)* to reel, to spool; **d. son rosaire** to reel off the rosary;

Fam **il m'a dévidé son chapelet** he reeled off his whole story to me

dévideur [devidœr] NM *Ordinat* streamer

dévidoir [devidwar] NM *Tex* reeling machine, reel; *(pour tuyaux)* hose reel; *(pour câbles)* drum

dévier [devje] *(impf, pr sub* n. **déviions,** v. **déviiez)** VI **1** to deviate, to swerve; *Tech* to run out of true; *(de la colonne vertébrale)* to be out of alignment, not to be straight; **faire d. une balle** to deflect a bullet; *Naut, Aviat* **d. de sa route** *(par accident)* to go *or* stray off course; *(volontairement)* to turn off *or* deviate from course **2** *Fig* to deviate *(de* from); **elle ne dévie jamais de ses principes** she never deviates *or* departs from her principles; **cette conversation dévie** this conversation is getting out of hand
◆ VT *(coup, balle)* to turn aside, to deflect; *Phys (rayon)* to deflect; *(circulation)* to divert

devin, devineresse [dəvɛ̃, dəvinrɛs] N diviner; *(prophète)* soothsayer, *Fam* fortune teller; *Fam* **je ne suis pas d.** I can't tell *or* predict the future

devinable [davinabl] ADJ foreseeable

deviner [dəvine] VT *(énigme, secret etc)* to guess; *(futur)* to predict; *(la pensée de qn)* to read; **vous ne devinez pas?** can't you guess?; **devine qui j'ai vu/pourquoi il est là/comment il est venu** guess who I saw/why he's here/how he came; *Fam* **je ne pouvais pas d.!** how was I supposed to know!

devineresse *voir* **devin**

devinette [dəvinɛt] NF riddle, conundrum; *(jeu)* guessing game; **poser une d. à qn** to ask sb a riddle

devis [dəvi] NM *(descriptif)* estimate; *Tech* specification; **d. estimatif** estimate, quote, quotation; **ils m'ont fait un d. de 5 000 euros** they quoted me *or* they gave me a quote of 5,000 euros; **je voudrais qu'on me fasse un d.** I'd like an estimate *or* quote *(pour* for)

dévisager [devizaʒe] VT **(je dévisageai(s); n. dévisageons)** to stare *or* look hard at

devise [dəviz] NF **1** *Fin* currency; **devises étrangères** foreign currency; **d. internationale** international currency; **d. forte** strong *or* hard currency; **d. faible** soft *or* weak currency; **d. contrôlée** managed currency; **d. convertible** convertible currency; **d. non convertible** non-convertible currency; **marché des devises** currency market **2** *Hér* device; *(d'une personne)* motto; *Fig* **telle est ma d.** that's my motto VOIR GRAMMAIRE A12

deviser [dəvize] VI to converse

devise-titre, *pl* **devises-titres** NF *Fin* foreign security, exchange currency

dévissage [devisaʒ] NM **1** *(d'un écrou)* unscrewing **2** *(en montagne)* fall

dévisser [devise] VT *(boulon, écrou etc)* to unscrew
◆ VI *(d'alpiniste)* to fall
◆ VPR **se dévisser** to unscrew; *(par accident)* to come unscrewed; *Fig* **se d. la tête** *ou* **le cou** to screw one's head round

de visu [dəvizy] ADV with my/his/*etc* own eyes; **je préférerais me rendre compte d.** I'd rather see it with my own eyes, I'd rather see for myself; **je veux m'assurer d. que tu as fait le travail** I want to see for myself that you've done the work

dévitalisation [devitalizasjɔ̃] NF *(d'une dent)* root canal treatment, *Spéc* devitalization; **subir plusieurs dévitalisations** to have root canal treatment on several teeth

dévitaliser [devitalize] VT *(dent)* to carry out root canal treatment on, *Spéc* to devitalize

dévitaminé [devitamine] ADJ lacking in vitamins

dévoiement [devwamɑ̃] NM *(d'un conduit etc)* canting, tilting

dévoilement [devwalmɑ̃] NM *(de visage, statue, plaque etc)* unveiling; *Fig (d'un nom, un secret etc)* disclosure, revelation; *(d'une conspiration)* unmasking; *(d'une fraude)* uncovering

dévoiler [devwale] VT *(visage, statue, plaque etc)* to unveil; *Fig (nom, secret etc)* to reveal, to disclose; *(conspiration)* to unmask; *(fraude etc)* to uncover; **d. ses charmes** to show *or* reveal all
◆ VPR **se dévoiler** *(de secret etc)* to come to light

DEVOIR[1] [dəvwar] NM **1** *(obligation morale ou sociale)* duty; **je l'ai fait par d.** I did it from a sense of duty; **avoir le sens** *ou* **le sentiment du d.** to have a sense of duty; **un homme/une femme de d.** a man/woman with a sense of duty; **manquer à son d.** to fail in one's duty; **faire** *ou* **remplir son d. (envers qn/la patrie)** to do one's duty (by sb/one's country); **se faire un d. de faire qch** to make a point of doing sth; **se mettre en d. de faire qch** to make it one's duty *or* responsibility to do sth; **il est de mon d. de vous le dire** it is my duty *or* my responsibility to tell you; **je sais ce qui est de mon d.** I know my duty, I know where my duty lies; **mes devoirs de citoyen/de père** my duties *or* obligations as a citizen/as a father; **avoir un d. de réserve** to be bound by professional secrecy; *Pol* **d. d'ingérence** duty to intervene
2 *Scol (en classe)* test; *(à la maison)* homework; **un d. de latin** a Latin test; **faire ses devoirs** to do one's homework; **d. sur table** class test; **d. à rendre** take-home (exam); **devoirs de vacances** holiday homework
3 *Vieilli (hommage)* **devoirs** respects; **rendre ses devoirs à qn** to pay one's respects to sb; **rendre à qn les derniers devoirs** to pay one's last respects to sb

DEVOIR[2] *(prp* **devant;** *pp* **dû,** *f* **due;** *pr ind* **je dois, n. devons, ils doivent;** *pr sub* **je doive, n. devons, ils doivent;** *impf* **je devais;** *p hist* **je dus;** *fu* **je devrai)**

> VT to owe
> V AUX must **1, 2, 4** ◾ to be obliged to **2**
> ◾ to be bound to **2** ◾ to have to **1–3** ◾ to
> be supposed to **3** ◾ to be due to **3**

VT *(être redevable de)* **d. qch à qn** to owe sb sth, to owe sth to sb; **il me doit mille euros** he owes me a thousand euros; **il ne veut rien d. à personne** he doesn't want to owe anyone anything, he doesn't want to be indebted to anyone for anything; **d. du respect à son père** to owe respect to one's father; **je lui dois d'être en vie, je lui dois la vie** I owe my life to him, I owe him my life; **je lui dois bien cela** it's the least I can do for him, I owe him that at least; **il doit sa réussite à ses parents, sa réussite est due à ses parents** he owes his success to his parents; **je te dois une fière chandelle** I'm forever in your debt

V AUX SEE GRAMMAR A60–1; B39 **1** *(obligation)* **vous devez** *ou* **devrez vous trouver à votre poste à trois heures** you must *or* you have to be at your post at three o'clock; **elle a cru d. refuser** she thought it advisable to refuse; **tu dois honorer tes parents** you must honour your parents; **fais ce que dois, vienne que pourra** do your duty, come what may; **les commandes doivent être adressées à … orders should be sent to …; je ne savais pas ce que je devais faire** I didn't know what (I ought) to do; **il aurait dû m'avertir** he should have warned me, he ought to have warned me
2 *(nécessité)* **tous les hommes doivent mourir** all men must die; **finalement, j'ai dû céder**

I had to *or* I was obliged to give way in the end; **tu dois absolument lui en parler** you really must talk to him about it; **il ne devait plus les revoir** he was (destined) never to see them again; **cela devait arriver!** it was bound to *or* it had to happen!; **dût-il m'en coûter la vie** were I to die for it

3 *(intention)* **je dois partir demain** I am (supposed) to *or* I have to leave tomorrow; **je devais la rencontrer à Paris** I was (supposed) to meet her in Paris; **je ne devais pas être là, mais j'ai changé d'avis** I hadn't planned on being there, but I changed my mind; **le train doit arriver à midi** the train is due (to arrive) at twelve o'clock

4 *(supposition)* **vous devez avoir faim** you must be hungry; **il doit être trois heures** it must be three o'clock; **il ne doit pas avoir plus de 40 ans** he can't be more than 40; **il a** *ou* **avait dû me prendre pour un autre** he must have taken me for someone else; **elle devait avoir cinq ans quand elle a eu son accident** she must have been five when she had the accident; **la pollution devrait s'accroître d'ici à la fin du siècle** pollution is expected to increase by the end of the century

VPR se devoir 1 *(être obligé de se consacrer à)* **je me dois à ma famille/mon travail** I must devote myself to my family/my work; **je me dois de le faire** it's my duty to do it

2 comme il se doit as is (only) right and proper

dévoisé [devwaze] **ADJ** *Ling* devoiced

dévoisement [devwazmɑ̃] **NM** *Ling* devoicing

dévoltage [devɔltaʒ] **NM** reduction of voltage

dévolter [devɔlte] **VT** *Élec (courant)* to reduce the voltage of

dévolu [devɔly] **ADJ** *Jur (héritage etc)* devolving (**à** to, upon); **part dévolue à la ligne paternelle** share that falls to the heirs on the father's side; **c'est le terrain qui lui a été d.** the land went to him; **être d. à qn de faire qch** to fall to sb's lot to do sth; **voilà la tâche qui vous a été dévolue** that is the task which has been assigned to you

NM jeter son d. sur qn/qch to set one's heart on sb/sth, to be determined to have sb/sth, *Hum Péj* to have designs on sb/sth

dévolution [devɔlysjɔ̃] **NF** *Jur* devolution; **d. d'un héritage à l'État** escheat

dévorant [devɔrɑ̃] **ADJ 1** *(envie, besoin)* overwhelming; **avoir une faim dévorante** to be ravenous; **j'ai une envie dévorante de le voir** I've got a burning desire to see him **2** *(maladie)* wasting; *(passion)* devouring

dévorer [devɔre] **VT 1** *(manger) (proie)* to devour; *(nourriture)* to devour, *Fam* to gobble up, to wolf down; **pour ne pas être dévoré par les moustiques** so as not to be eaten alive by mosquitoes; **d. qn des yeux** *ou* **du regard/de baisers** to devour sb with one's eyes/with kisses; *Fig* **d. un livre** to devour *or* gobble up a book; *Fig* **d. la route** to tear along, to eat up the miles; **d. sa fortune** to squander one's fortune **2** *(consumer) (de flammes)* to devour; *Fig* **l'ambition/la jalousie la dévore** she is consumed by *or* devoured by *or* eaten up with ambition/jealousy; **il ne faut pas que cela dévore tout votre temps** don't let it take up all your time; **l'angoisse le dévore** he's sick with worry; **dévoré de remords** eaten up *or* stricken with remorse

dévoreur, -euse [devɔrœr, -øz] **N** devourer; *Fig* **d. de livres** avid reader, bookworm; **d. de films** avid cinemagoer; **d. de pellicule** *Cin* avid *or* keen cinemagoer; *Phot* avid *or* keen photographer

dévot, -ote [devo, -ɔt] **ADJ** *(fervent)* devout,

religious, pious, *Péj* sanctimonious; *Rel* **être d. à un saint** to be a votary of a saint

N devout person, *Péj* bigot; *Arch* **faux d.** hypocrite

dévotement [devɔtmɑ̃] **ADV** devoutly

dévotion [devosjɔ̃] **NF 1** *(ferveur)* devoutness, piety; **faire ses dévotions** to make one's devotions, to say one's prayers; *Péj* **être confit en d.** to be sanctimonious; **fausse d.** hypocrisy **2** *(adoration)* devotion; **avoir une grande d. pour qn/qch** to be devoted *or* extremely attached to sb/sth; **avoir une grande d. pour un acteur/écrivain** to be a great admirer *or* a devotee of an actor/a writer; **être à la d. de qn** to be fanatically attached to sb

> Do not confuse with **dévouement**.

dévoué [devwe] **ADJ** *(ami etc)* devoted, staunch, loyal; **votre (tout) d.** *(dans une lettre)* yours sincerely; **être très/entièrement d. à qn** to be very attached/utterly devoted to sb

dévouement [devumɑ̃] **NM 1** *(devoir)* self-sacrifice, dedication to duty; *(d'un scientifique etc)* dedication **2** *(amour)* devotion, devotedness; **soigner qn avec d.** to nurse *or* look after sb devotedly *or* with devotion

> Do not confuse with **dévotion**.

dévouer (se) [sədevwe] **VPR 1** *(se consacrer)* to sacrifice oneself (**pour qn** for sb); **il faut que quelqu'un se dévoue** somebody has to do it **2** *Vieilli* **se d. à** to devote oneself to, to dedicate oneself

dévoyé, -ée [devwaje] **ADJ** astray

N delinquent

dévoyer [devwaje] *(***je dévoie, n. dévoyons; je dévoierai***)* **VT** *Litt* to lead astray

VPR se dévoyer to go astray, to leave the straight and narrow

dextérité [dɛksterite] **NF** dexterity, skill; **conduire ses affaires avec d.** to manage one's business cleverly *or* skilfully

dextre [dɛkstr] **NF** *Vieilli, Hum* right hand; **veux-tu t'asseoir à ma d.?** will you sit on my right?

dextrine [dɛkstrin] **NF** *Chimie, Ind* dextrin

dézinguer [dezɛ̃ge] **VT** *Fam* **1** *(détruire)* to wreck **2** *(critiquer)* to pull to pieces, to slam **3** *(tuer)* to bump off

dézipper [dezipe] **VT** *Ordinat (fichier)* to unzip

DG [deʒe] **NM** *(abrév* **directeur général***)* GM, *Am* CEO

NF *(abrév* **direction générale***)* general management, senior management

DGA [deʒea] **NM** *(abrév* **directeur général adjoint***)* assistant general manager

NF *(abrév* **Délégation générale pour l'armement***)* = section of the French armed forces responsible for building and testing armaments

DGSE [deʒeɛsə] **NF** *(abrév* **Direction générale de la sécurité extérieure***)* = French military intelligence service, *Br* ≃ MI6

DHEA [deaʃəa] **NF** *(abrév* **déhydroépiandrostérone***)* DHEA

DI [dei] **NF** *(abrév* **déclaration d'importation***)* import declaration

diabète [djabɛt] **NM** *Méd* diabetes; **d. sucré** (sugar) diabetes, *Spéc* diabetes mellitus; **avoir du d.** to have diabetes

diabétique [djabetik] *Méd* **ADJ** diabetic; **être d.** to be (a) diabetic, to have diabetes

N diabetic; **chocolat/confiture pour diabétiques** diabetic chocolate/jam

diable [djabl] **NM 1** devil; **le d.** *(Satan)* the Devil, Satan, *Fam* Old Nick; *Fam* **s'agiter** *ou*

se démener comme un beau d. *ou* **comme un d. dans un bénitier** to struggle *or* fight like mad; *Fam* **il s'est défendu comme un beau d.** he put up quite a fight; **faire le d. (à quatre)** to kick up a row; **avoir le d. au corps** to be possessed; **tirer le d. par la queue** to be hard up; *Can* **parler au d.** to be psychic; **que le d. l'emporte!** the devil take him!; **(que) le d. m'emporte si j'y comprends quelque chose!** I'll be hanged *or* damned if I understand (it)!; **c'est le d. pour lui faire entendre raison** it's damned hard to make *or* it's the devil of a job making him see reason; **c'est bien le d. si ...** it would be surprising if ...; **ce n'est pas le d.** *(c'est facile)* it's not that difficult; **d. de mer** devil fish, (manta) ray

2 d.! (good) heavens!, goodness!; **où d. est-il allé?** where the devil has he gone?; **que d. cherche-t-il?** what the devil is he looking for?; **pourquoi d. m'a-t-il demandé cela?** why the devil did he ask me that?; **du d. si je peux te répondre!** I'm damned if I can tell you!; **que d.!** for heaven's *or* goodness' sake!

3 en d. extremely, *Fml* in the extreme; **têtu en d.** extremely stubborn, obstinate in the extreme; **il demeure au d.** he lives miles away; **au d. vauvert** a long way (away); **allez au d.!** go to hell!, *Vieilli* go to the devil!; **tu peux aller au d. avec tes belles promesses** you and your promises can go to hell!; **envoyer qn au d.** to tell sb to go to hell; **au d. l'avarice/le régime!** to hell with the expense/the diet!; **à la d.** anyhow; *Culin* in a spicy sauce; **c'est fait à la d.** it's been done any old how; *Culin* **steak à la d.** devilled steak; **ce d. de parapluie** that wretched umbrella; **un d. de temps, un temps du d.** wretched *or* dreadful weather; **j'ai une faim du d.** *ou* **de tous les diables** I'm ravenous; **il fait un froid/une chaleur du d.** it's dreadfully cold/hot; **un bruit de tous les diables** a hell of a din

4 un petit d. *(enfant)* a little devil; **pauvre d.!** poor devil *or* beggar!; **un drôle de petit d.** a funny little chap *or* beggar; **un grand d.** a big fellow; **c'est un bon d.** he's not a bad sort

5 *(chariot)* (two-wheeled) trolley; *Rail* (railway porter's) barrow, luggage truck

6 *(jouet)* jack-in-the-box

diablement [djablǝmɑ̃] **ADV** *Fam (fort, bon, amusant etc)* damn, damned, *Vieilli* devilish(ly); **il y a d. longtemps que je ne l'ai pas vu** I haven't seen him for a hell of a long time; **il faisait d. froid** it was hellish(ly) cold

diablerie [djablǝri] **NF 1** *Fam (espièglerie)* devilry, devilment **2** *Arch (sorcellerie)* devilry, sorcery **3** *(intrigue)* machination, intrigue

diablesse [djablɛs] **NF** *(diable femelle, méchante femme)* she-devil; *(jeune fille)* devil

diablotin [djablɔtɛ̃] **NM 1** *(petit diable, enfant coquin)* little devil, imp **2** *(pétard)* (Christmas) cracker

diabolique [djabɔlik] **ADJ** diabolic(al), fiendish

diaboliquement [djabɔlikmɑ̃] **ADV** diabolically, fiendishly

diabolisation [djabɔlizasjɔ̃] **NF** demonization

diaboliser [djabɔlize] **VT** to demonize

diabolo [djabɔlo] **NM 1** *(jouet)* diabolo **2** *(boisson)* lemonade (drink) with syrup; **d. menthe** mint and lemonade syrup

diachromie [djakrɔmi] **NF** *Phot* screenplate colour photography

diachronie [djakrɔni] **NF** *Ling* diachrony

diachronique [djakrɔnik] **ADJ** *Ling* diachronic

diaconesse [djakɔnɛs] **NF** *Rel* deaconess

diacre [djakr] **NM** *Rel* deacon

diacritique [djakritik] ADJ Ling diacritic(al); **signe d.** diacritic(al)

diadème [djadɛm] NM tiara

diagnostic [djagnɔstik] NM Méd (de maladie) diagnosis; **porter** ou **faire un d.** to make a diagnosis; **le d. de la maladie doit être porté le plus tôt possible** the disease must be diagnosed as soon as possible; **ce médecin a un d. très sûr** this doctor makes very reliable diagnoses; **quel est votre d.?** what's your diagnosis?; Ordinat **d. d'autotest** self-test diagnosis; **d. financier** financial health-check, diagnostic audit

diagnostique [djagnɔstik] ADJ Méd (aptitude, signe etc) diagnostic

diagnostiquer [djagnɔstike] VT Méd, Fig to diagnose; **on a diagnostiqué un diabète** the illness has been diagnosed as diabetes

diagnostiqueur [djagnɔstikœr] NM Méd diagnostician; **elle n'est pas bon d.** she's not a good diagnostician, diagnosis is not her strong point

diagonal, -ale, -aux, -ales [djagɔnal, -o] ADJ Math etc diagonal
NF diagonale diagonal (line); **en diagonale** diagonally; Fig **lire qch en diagonale** to skim sth

diagonalement [djagɔnalmɑ̃] ADV diagonally

diagramme [djagram] NM diagram; **d. circulaire** ou **à secteurs** pie chart; **d. en bâtons** ou **à barres** bar chart; **d. de circulation** flow chart; **d. de relations fonctionnelles** functional relations diagram; **d. des flux** flowchart

dialectal, -ale, -aux, -ales [djalɛktal, -o] ADJ Ling dialectal

dialecte [djalɛkt] NM dialect; **en d.** in dialect

dialecticien, -ienne [djalɛktisjɛ̃, -jɛn] N dialectician

dialectique [djalɛktik] ADJ (argument) dialectic(al)
NF dialectics

dialectiquement [djalɛktikmɑ̃] ADV dialectically

dialogue [djalɔg] NM dialogue, Am dialog; Pol dialogue, talks; **d. Nord-Sud** dialogue or talks between North and South; **écrire les dialogues d'un film** to write the dialogue for a movie or Br film; **le d. est de Valérie Devaux** dialogue by Valérie Devaux; Ordinat **mode de d.** interactive mode; Ordinat **d. d'établissement de liaison** handshake, handshaking; Ordinat **d. en direct** Internet Relay Chat, IRC; **c'est un d. de sourds** it's a dialogue of the deaf

dialoguer [djalɔge] VI to hold a dialogue or Am dialog, to converse; Ordinat to communicate; **d. avec son ordinateur** to interact with one's computer
VT Littér to write in dialogue or Am dialog form

dialoguiste [djalɔgist] N Cin dialogue or Am dialog writer

dialyse [djaliz] NF Méd, Chimie dialysis; Méd **il faut qu'on lui fasse une d. tous les mois** he has to have dialysis once a month

dialyser [djalize] VT Chimie to dialyse

dialyseur [djalizœr] NM Méd dialysis machine

diam [djam] NM Fam (abrév **diamant**) sparkler, rock

diamant [djamɑ̃] NM diamond; Typ gem; **d. de première eau** diamond of the first water; **d. brut** rough diamond; **d. de vitrier** glass cutter, Spéc glazier's diamond, diamond point

diamantaire [djamɑ̃tɛr] ADJ Tech (pierre) diamond-like, sparkling
NM (tailleur) diamond cutter; (vendeur) diamond merchant

diamantifère [djamɑ̃tifɛr] ADJ Géol etc (région) diamantiferous; (gravier etc) diamond-yielding or-bearing

diamétral, -ale, -aux, -ales [djametral, -o] ADJ diametric(al), diametral

diamétralement [djametralmɑ̃] ADV diametrically; **opinions d. opposées** diametrically opposed views

diamètre [djametr] NM diameter; **la roue a 60 cm de d.** the wheel is 60 cm in diameter or 60 cm across; Aut **d. de braquage hors tout** overall turning circle

diane [djan] NF Mil Arch, Litt reveille; **battre** ou **sonner la d.** to sound reveille

diantre [djɑ̃tr] INT Arch, Litt **que d. désirez-vous?** what the devil do you want?; **d., c'est cher!** it's devilishly expensive!; **d., comme vous y allez!** good heavens! that's going a bit far!

diapason [djapazɔ̃] NM Mus **1** (ton) pitch, diapason; Fig **se mettre au d. de la compagnie** to adapt oneself to the company, to fall in with the mood of the company **2** (appareil) tuning fork; (à vent) pitch pipe **3** (registre) compass, range

diaphane [djafan] ADJ diaphanous

diaphonie [djafɔni] NF Radio etc crosstalk

diaphragme [djafragm] NM **1** Anat diaphragm **2** Tech (d'un télescope, d'une cellule électrique etc), Cin, TV diaphragm; Phot (d'un objectif) diaphragm, T-stop, iris; Mus (d'une enceinte) soundbox; Méd (contraceptif) diaphragm, Fam (Dutch) cap; Phot **d. iris** iris diaphragm

diaphragmer [djafragme] VT, VI Phot to stop down; **diaphragmez à 11** stop down to 11, use stop number 11

diaphyse [djafiz] NF shaft, diaphysis

diapo [djapo] NF Fam (abrév **diapositive**) slide, transparency

diaporama [djapɔrama] NM slide show

diapositive [djapozitiv] NF Phot slide, transparency; **d. en couleurs** colour slide

diapré [djapre] ADJ variegated, mottled, speckled

diaprer [djapre] VT to variegate, to mottle, to speckle

diaprure [djapryr] NF Litt iridescence; **elle portait une robe dont le satin faisait des diaprures** she wore a gown of iridescent or shimmering satin

diariste [djarist] N diarist

diarrhée [djare] NF Méd diarrhoea, Am diarrhea; **avoir la d.** to have diarrhoea; **d. du voyageur** holiday tummy; Fig Péj **ce type fait de la d. verbale** that guy suffers from verbal diarrhoea

diarrhéique [djareik] ADJ Méd diarrhoeic, Am diarrheic; diarrhoeal, Am diarrheal
N person subject to diarrhoea or Am diarrhea

diaspora [djaspɔra] NF Rel, Pol diaspora

diastole [djastɔl] NF Physiol diastole

diatomée [djatɔme] NF (algue) diatom

diatomique [djatɔmik] ADJ Chimie diatomic

diatonique [djatɔnik] ADJ Mus (échelle, intervalle) diatonic

diatoniquement [djatɔnikmɑ̃] ADV Mus diatonically

diatribe [djatrib] NF diatribe (**contre** against)

dichotomie [dikɔtɔmi] NF dichotomy

dichotomique [dikɔtɔmik] ADJ dichotomous; Psy **test d.** yes/no test, true/false test

dichromatique [dikrɔmatik] ADJ dichromatic

dico [diko] NM Fam (abrév **dictionnaire**) dictionary

dicotylédone [dikɔtiledɔn] Bot ADJ dicotyledonous
NF dicotyledon

Dictaphone® [diktafɔn] NM Dictaphone®

dictateur [diktatœr] NM dictator; **ton de d.** dictatorial tone

dictatorial, -iale, -iaux, -iales [diktatɔrjal, -jo] ADJ dictatorial

dictatorialement [diktatɔrjalmɑ̃] ADV dictatorially

dictature [diktatyr] NF Pol, Fig dictatorship; **d. militaire** military dictatorship; **d. du prolétariat** dictatorship of the proletariat; Fig **il fait de la d. intellectuelle** he tells people what to think

dictée [dikte] NF dictation; Scol dictation (exercise); **d. musicale** musical dictation; **prendre qch sous la d.** (d'une secrétaire) to take sth down in shorthand; **écrire qch sous la d. de qn** to write sth at sb's dictation; **agir sous la d. de son cœur/de sa conscience** to follow the dictates of one's heart/one's conscience

dicter [dikte] VT (lettre etc) to dictate; **d. ses conditions** to dictate or lay down one's conditions; **votre conscience vous dictera votre devoir** you must follow the dictates of your conscience; **d. sa volonté à qn** to impose one's will on sb; **je ne veux pas qu'on me dicte ma conduite!** I won't be dictated to!; **ces mesures ont été dictées par la conjoncture économique** these measures were dictated by the economic situation

diction [diksjɔ̃] NF diction; **professeur de d.** elocution teacher

dictionnaire [diksjɔnɛr] NM dictionary; **d. de langue** dictionary; **d. anglais-français** English-French dictionary; **le d. d'un enfant de 10 ans** the vocabulary of a 10-year-old child; **c'est un d. ambulant** he's a walking encyclopaedia; **elle parle comme un d.** she talks as if she's swallowed a dictionary
▸▸**d. analogique** thesaurus; **d. de césure** hyphenation dictionary; **d. électronique** electronic dictionary; **d. encyclopédique** encyclopaedic dictionary; **d. géographique** gazetteer; **d. de poche** pocket dictionary; **d. de synonymes** thesaurus

dicton [diktɔ̃] NM (common) saying

didacthèque [didaktɛk] NF Ordinat set of educational software, Am set of teachware

didacticiel [didaktisjɛl] NM Ordinat tutorial (program); (à l'école) courseware, educational software, Am teachware

didactique [didaktik] ADJ **1** (ouvrage, voyage) educational **2** (mot, langage) technical
NF didactics

didactiquement [didaktikmɑ̃] ADV educationally

didactyle [didaktil] ADJ Zool didactyl(e)

dièdre [djɛdr] Math ADJ (angle) dihedral
NM dihedron

diélectrique [dielɛktrik] Élec ADJ dielectric; (milieu) insulating, non-conducting
NM dielectric

diérèse [djerɛz] NF Ling, Chir diaeresis

dies academicus [djesakademikys] NM INV Suisse = annual public ceremony in universities marking the start of the new academic year and the conferment of honorary doctorates

dièse [djɛz] Mus NM sharp; **double d.** double sharp
ADJ sharp; **fa d.** F sharp

diesel [djezɛl] NM (carburant) diesel; **moteur d.** diesel engine
NF (voiture) diesel

diéséliste [djezelist] N Tech diesel fitter

diéser [djeze] VT (**je dièse, n. diésons; je diéserai**) *Mus* (*note*) to sharpen, *Am* to sharp

diète¹ [djɛt] NF diet; (*jeûne*) fast; **d. lactée** milk diet; **être à la d.** (*régime*) to be on a diet; (*jeûne*) to be fasting; **mettre qn à la d.** to put sb on a diet

diète² NF *Hist, Pol* diet

diététicien, -ienne [djetetisjɛ̃, -jɛn] N dietitian, dietician

diététique [djetetik] *Méd* ADJ (*menu, repas*) diet; (*supplément*) dietary; **magasin/restaurant d.** health food shop/restaurant
NF dietetics

DIEU, pl **dieux** [djø] NM **1** god; **les dieux de l'Égypte ancienne** the gods of ancient Egypt; **beau comme un d. (grec)** like a Greek god; **il danse comme un d.** he's a wonderful dancer, *Vieilli* he dances divinely; **être aimé** *ou* **béni des dieux** to be blessed with good fortune, to be a favourite of the gods; **jurer ses grands dieux** to swear (by all that's holy) **2** D. God; **D. le père** God the Father; *Fig* **ce n'est pas D. le père** he's not God Almighty; **la voix de D.** the voice of God; **croire en D.** to believe in God; **un homme de D.** a holy man; **s'il plaît à D., si D. (le) veut** please God, God willing; **D. merci!, D. soit loué!** thank God!; **le bon D.** God; **recevoir le bon D.** to receive the Holy Sacrament; **on lui donnerait le bon D. sans confession** he looks as though butter wouldn't melt in his mouth; **mais qu'est-ce que j'ai fait au bon D. pour mériter ça/avoir un mari aussi stupide!** what in heaven's *or* God's name have I ever done to deserve this/ to deserve such a stupid husband!; *Fam* **y a pas de bon D.** there's no justice in the world; **pour l'amour de D.** for goodness' *or* God's sake; **devant D. et devant les hommes** by Almighty God; **D. vous bénisse** God bless you; **D. vous garde** God keep you; **D. m'en garde, à D. ne plaise** God forbid; **D. vous entende** may your prayers be answered; **D. sait si j'ai travaillé** goodness *or* heaven *or* God knows I've worked hard enough; **D. sait quoi** God knows what; **D. seul le sait** God only knows; *Fam* **il va y aller D. sait comment** he's going, God knows how (he'll get there); **D. m'est témoin que je n'ai pas dit cela** as God is my witness, I never said that; **chaque jour** *ou* **tous les jours que D. fait** every day that God sends; *Vieilli* **à D. vat!** it's in God's hands now!
INT **1** (*admis*) **mon D.!, grand D.!** God!, my God!, good God!; **grands dieux!** heavens!; **mon D. oui!** God, yes!; **mon D. je veux bien!** well, I don't mind!; **D. qu'elle est petite!** goodness *or* God she's small!; *Fam* **c'est pas D. possible!** it's just not possible!, I refuse to believe it!; **c'est pas D. possible d'être aussi bête!** it's just not heavenly possible to be that stupid!
2 (*profane*) **bon D.!, D. de D.!, bon D. de bon D.!, (sacré) nom de D.!** for Christ's sake!, God almighty!, hell!

diffamant [difamɑ̃] ADJ (*paroles*) slanderous, defamatory; (*écrits*) libellous, defamatory

diffamateur, -trice [difamatœr, -tris] N (*en paroles*) slanderer; (*par écrit*) libeller

diffamation [difamasjɔ̃] NF defamation (of character); (*paroles*) slander; (*écrits*) libel; **campagne de d.** smear campaign; **poursuivre qn en d.** to sue sb for defamation of character; **procès en d.** slander/libel trial

diffamatoire [difamatwar] ADJ defamatory; (*paroles*) slanderous; (*écrits*) libellous

diffamer [difame] VT to defame; (*en paroles*) to slander; (*par écrit*) to libel

différé [difere] ADJ **1** (*paiement, rente*) deferred **2** *Radio, TV* prerecorded; *Élec* **coupe-circuit à action différée** time-lag cut-out;
Phot **obturateur à action différée** delayed action shutter; *Ordinat* **traitement d.** off-line processing
NM *Radio, TV* (*émission*) prerecording, prerecorded programme; **émission en d.** (pre-)recorded broadcast

différemment [diferamɑ̃] ADV differently (**de** from)

différence [diferɑ̃s] NF difference; **d. de goûts** difference of taste; **la d. de A à B** *ou* **entre A et B** the difference between A and B; **d. d'âges** age difference; **d. d'opinions** difference of opinion; *Élec* **d. de potentiel** potential difference, pd; **d. de prix** price difference; **quelle d. avec …!** what a difference from …!; **il n'y a pas de d. entre eux** there's nothing to choose between them; **cela ne fait pas de d.** it makes no difference *or Br Fam* no odds; **il ne faut pas faire de d. entre ses enfants** you shouldn't treat your children differently, you should not discriminate between your children; **il y a trop de d. d'âge entre eux** there's too much of *or* too big an age gap *or* age difference between them; **faire la d. d'une chose avec une autre** *ou* **entre une chose et une autre** to distinguish *or* discriminate between one thing and another; **c'est ça qui a fait la d.** that's what made the difference; **je vous dois la d.** I'll owe you the difference; **à la d. de …** unlike …; **à la d. que …** except that …

différenciateur, -trice [diferɑ̃sjatœr, -tris] ADJ differentiating
NM **d. sémantique** semantic differential

différenciation [diferɑ̃sjasjɔ̃] NF differentiation; *Mktg* **d. de ligne** line featuring

différencier [diferɑ̃sje] (*impf, pr sub n.* **différenciions**) VT to differentiate (**de, d'avec** from); *Math* (*équation etc*) to obtain the differential (coefficient) of; **rien ne les différencie** there's nothing to differentiate them
VPR **se différencier 1** (*de deux personnes*) to be different (from each other), to differ; **ils se différencient par leurs écharpes de couleurs différentes** you can tell them apart by their different-coloured scarves **2** (*d'une personne*) **se d. de** to differentiate oneself from

différend [diferɑ̃] NM dispute, difference of opinion, disagreement (**entre** between); *Jur* dispute; **avoir un d. avec qn** to disagree *or* have a disagreement with sb (**sur** about); **ils ont un d. sur l'éducation des enfants** they disagree *or* differ on how the children should be educated; **il a un d. avec son voisin à propos de la clôture du jardin** he is at odds with his neighbour over the garden fence; **il a un d. avec son père qui empoisonne leurs relations depuis de nombreuses années** a long-standing difference of opinion between him and his father has poisoned their relationship

différent [diferɑ̃] ADJ **1** (*distinct*) different (**de** from, *Am* than); **un avis d. du premier** a different opinion from the first, an opinion that differs from the first; **elle utilise une recette différente de la tienne** her recipe is different from yours VOIR GRAMMAIRE A70 **2** (*divers*) (*toujours au pl*) **différents** various; **différentes personnes l'ont vu** different people *or* various people *or* a number of people saw him; **à différentes reprises** at various times, off and on

différentiation [diferɑ̃sjasjɔ̃] NF *Math* differentiation

différentiel, -ielle [diferɑ̃sjɛl] ADJ differential
NM *Aut etc* differential; *Com* **d. de prix** price differential; *Ling* **d. sémantique** semantic differential; **d. de taux d'intérêt** interest rate differential
NF *Math* **différentielle** differential

différer [difere] (**je diffère, n. différons; je différerai**) VT (*retarder*) (*jugement*) to defer, to postpone; (*paiement*) to defer; (*décision, départ*) to postpone, to put off; *Fml* **d. de faire qch** to defer doing sth
VI (*être différent*) to differ; **nos origines diffèrent complètement** our backgrounds are completely different; **ils diffèrent de race et de langue** they differ in race and speech; **nous différons d'opinion** our opinions differ; **nous différons en tout** we differ on everything; **ils diffèrent par la taille** they differ in height, they are of different heights; **nous différons sur le choix de l'école des enfants** we differ on *or* do not agree on which school the children should go to

difficile [difisil] ADJ **1** (*ardu*) (*travail, situation etc*) difficult, hard; **d'accès d.** difficult to get to; **le plus d. est fait** the hardest *or* most difficult part is over; **il est très d. de le joindre** it is very difficult to contact him, he is very difficult to contact
2 (*délicat*) difficult; **circonstances difficiles** difficult *or* trying circumstances; **les temps sont difficiles** times are hard; **il m'est d. d'accepter** it is difficult for me to accept, I can't very well accept; **les fins de mois sont difficiles** things are difficult at the end of the month
3 (*personne*) difficult to get on with, hard to please; **enfant d.** difficult *or* problem child; **elle est d. à vivre** she is difficult to get on with; **il est d. sur la nourriture** he's difficult *or* fussy about his food; **elle est très d. sur la ponctualité/l'orthographe** she is very fussy about punctuality/spelling; **si la maison ne te plaît pas, c'est que tu es vraiment d.** you must be really hard to please *or* fussy if you don't like the house
N **faire le/la d.** to be hard to please; **ne faites pas le d.** don't be difficult, stop fussing
ADV *Belg* **avoir d. à** *ou* **de faire qch** to have problems *or* difficulty doing sth

difficilement [difisilmɑ̃] ADV with difficulty, not easily; **il apprend d.** he is a slow learner; **on peut d. lui dire une chose pareille** you can hardly *or* you can't possibly tell him something like that; **c'est d. faisable** it's virtually impossible

difficulté [difikylte] NF difficulty; **être en d.** to be in difficulties *or* trouble; **cela ne présente aucune d.** that doesn't present any difficulty; **c'est sans d.** it's easy, it's not difficult; **aimer la d.** to like to make things difficult for oneself; **tourner la d.** to get round a difficulty; **faire** *ou* **soulever des difficultés** to create obstacles, to raise objections, to make difficulties; **cela ne fera pas de d., que je sache** there won't be any difficulty as far as I know; **se heurter à de graves difficultés** to come up against serious difficulties; **avoir de la d. à faire qch** to have difficulty doing sth, to find it hard *or* difficult to do sth; **avoir des difficultés matérielles** to be in financial difficulties; **créer des difficultés à qn** to put difficulties in sb's way, to make difficulties for sb; **difficultés de trésorerie** cashflow problems

difforme [difɔrm] ADJ (*personne*) deformed; (*membre*) malformed, misshapen, twisted; **troncs d'arbres difformes** gnarled treetrunks

difformité [difɔrmite] NF (*d'une personne*) deformity; (*d'un membre*) malformation; **la d. de son bras n'est pas irrémédiable** his malformed arm *or* the malformation in his arm is not incurable

diffracter [difrakte] VT *Opt* to diffract

diffraction [difraksjɔ̃] NF *Opt* diffraction

diffus [dify] ADJ (*lumière*) diffused; (*matière*) diffuse; (*pensée, idées*) vague; **éclairs d.** sheet lightning; **style d.** diffuse *or Fml* prolix style; **écrivain d.** verbose *or Fml* prolix writer

diffusément [difyzemã] **ADV** *(penser)* vaguely; *(écrire)* in a diffuse style; **la musique/la conversation nous parvenait d.** we couldn't hear the music/the conversation very clearly

diffuser [difyze] **VT** *(lumière, chaleur)* to diffuse, to spread; *Radio, TV (émission etc)* to broadcast, to air; *(idées, nouvelles)* to spread; *(livres, journaux)* to distribute; *(rapport)* to circulate; **une émission diffusée en direct/différé** a live/prerecorded broadcast; **d. qch sur Internet** to webcast sth; **leurs produits sont diffusés sur une grande échelle** they are widely-available products **VPR se diffuser** *(d'idées, de nouvelles, de lumière), Phys (des ondes)* to spread

diffuseur [difyzœr] **NM 1** *(de lumière, de sèche-cheveux)* diffuser; *(dans un moteur)* mixer, diffuser; *TV, Radio* broadcaster; *(écran diffuseur)* diffuser, scrim; *(compresseur)* diffuser; *(d'un chauffage)* air vent; **d. de parfum** room scenter; *Aut* **à d. fixe** fixed-choke **2** *(de livres, journaux)* distributor **3** *Ordinat* **d. en ligne** webcaster

diffusion [difyzjõ] **NF 1** *(de lumière, chaleur)* diffusion **2** *(de nouvelles, d'idées)* spread, spreading; *Radio, TV (d'émission)* broadcasting, airing; *Cin* screening; *(de livres)* distribution; *(de journal)* circulation; **en deuxième d., en seconde d.** repeated, repeat; *TV etc* **d.** audionumérique digital audio broadcasting; *TV etc* **d. de données par satellite** satellite data broadcasting; **d. de masse** *(d'un journal etc)* mass circulation; **d. directe par satellite** direct satellite broadcasting, DSB; **d. hertzienne** terrestrial broadcasting; **d. numérique** *Com* stock holding distribution; *TV etc* digital broadcasting; *TV, Radio* **d. terrestre** terrestrial broadcasting

digérer [diʒere] *(je digère, n. digérons; je digérerai)* **VT 1** *(nourriture)* to digest; **je ne digère pas le porc** pork does not agree with me, I find pork difficult to digest **2** *Fig (ce qu'on lit, ce qu'on apprend)* to digest, to take in, to assimilate; *Fam (accepter)* *(insultes etc)* to swallow; **je n'ai toujours pas digéré le coup qu'il m'a fait à Noël** I still haven't got over what he did to me at Christmas; **des vérités dures à d.** unpalatable truths **VI je digère mal** my digestion is bad, I have bad digestion

digest [daiʒɛst, diʒɛst] **NM** *Journ* digest

digeste [diʒɛst] **ADJ** *Fam (aliment)* easily digestible; **ce livre est vraiment peu d.** the book is indigestible

digestibilité [diʒɛstibilite] **NF** digestibility

digestible [diʒɛstibl] **ADJ** digestible

digestif, -ive [diʒɛstif, -iv] **ADJ** *(de la digestion)* digestive; *(substance)* which aids digestion; **le tube d.** the digestive tract; **avoir des troubles digestifs** to have digestive problems, to have problems with one's digestion **NM** liqueur, after-dinner drink

digestion [diʒɛstjõ] **NF** digestion; **elle a une d. difficile** she has problems with her digestion *or* digestive problems

Digicode® [diʒikɔd] **NM** door code *(for entrance to a building)*

digit [diʒit] **NM** *Ordinat* **1** *(chiffre)* digit **2** *(caractère)* character

digital¹, **-ale, -aux, -ales** [diʒital, -o] **ADJ** *Ordinat* digital; **code d.** digital code; **affichage d.** digital display; **horloge/montre à affichage d.** digital watch/clock

digital², **-ale, -aux, -ales** **ADJ** *(nerf etc)* digital; **empreinte digitale** fingerprint; **prendre les empreintes digitales de qn** to take sb's fingerprints, to fingerprint sb

NF *Bot, Méd* **digitale** digitalis; *Bot* **digitale pourprée** foxglove

digitaline [diʒitalin] **NF** *Chimie, Pharm* digitalin

digitaliser [diʒitalize] **VT** *Ordinat* to digitize

digitaliseur [diʒitalizœr] **NM** *Ordinat* digitizer

digne [diɲ] **ADJ 1** *(méritant)* deserving, worthy (**de** of); **cela est d. de récompense** that deserves a reward; **d. d'éloges** praiseworthy; **d. de foi** reliable; **d. d'être remarqué** noteworthy; **il est d. d'être remercié** he deserves thanks *or* to be thanked; **il n'est pas d. d'être notre représentant** he does not deserve *or* he is not fit to be our representative; **il n'est pas d. de vivre** he is not fit to live; **ce film est d. d'être vu** it's a film worth seeing; **je ne suis pas d. de toi** I am not worthy of you, you're too good for me; **une mère d.** a fit mother **2** *(à la hauteur)* **d. de** worthy of; **une attitude peu d. d'un chef d'État** an attitude that is hardly worthy of a head of state; **d. d'une mère** of a mother, motherly; **son attitude n'est pas d. d'une mère** her attitude is not motherly *or* not that of a mother; **il est d'une gentillesse avec toi d. d'une mère** he is almost motherly towards you; **d. de ce nom** worthy of the name; **prouver qu'on est une mère d. de ce nom** to prove that one is a fit mother; *Hum* **tu es bien le d. fils de ton père** you're your father's son all right; **un adversaire d. de soi** a worthy opponent; **un roman d. de la grande tradition française** a novel in the great French tradition; **tâchez de vous montrer d. de (représenter) la France** try to show that you're worthy to represent France **3** *(honorable, décent)* *(air, personne etc)* dignified; **il est incapable de rester d. après trois verres de vin** after three glasses of wine, he is incapable of acting in a dignified fashion, he loses all dignity after three glasses of wine

dignement [diɲ(ə)mã] **ADV 1** *(avec dignité)* with dignity, in a dignified fashion; **il a réagi très d.** he reacted with great dignity **2** *(légitimement)* **être d. récompensé** to be justly rewarded

dignitaire [diɲiter] **NM** *(de l'Église)* dignitary

dignité [diɲite] **NF 1** *(grandeur)* dignity; **elle manque de d.** she's undignified; **elle fit une entrée pleine de d.** she came in with great dignity; **toute personne a droit à la d.** everyone is entitled to their dignity **2** *(haute fonction)* high office *or* position, *Fml* dignity; **installer qn dans une d.** to install sb in an office

digramme [digram] **NM** *Ling* digraph

digraphie [digrafi] **NF** *Com* double-entry bookkeeping

digression [digrɛsjõ] **NF** digression; **faire une d.** to digress, to stray *or* wander from the point

digue [dig] **NF** *Tech* dyke; *(d'une voie navigable etc)* embankment; *(en pierre)* breakwater; *(contre l'érosion)* sea wall; *Fig (aux passions etc)* barrier

diktat [diktat] **NM** diktat, dictate

dilapidateur, -trice [dilapidatœr, -tris] **ADJ** spendthrift **N** *(de fortune)* spendthrift, wastrel; *(de fonds publics, de biens)* embezzler

dilapidation [dilapidasjõ] **NF** *(de fortune)* wasting, squandering; *(de fonds publics, de biens)* embezzlement, misappropriation

dilapider [dilapide] **VT** *(fortune)* to waste, to squander; *(fonds publics)* to misappropriate, to embezzle

dilatation [dilatasjõ] **NF** *(des pupilles)* dilation; *(de l'estomac)* distension; *(des gaz)* expansion; *Constr* **joint de d.** expansion joint

dilater [dilate] **VT** *(agrandir)* *(pupilles)* to dilate; *(estomac)* to distend; *(gaz)* to expand; **il a les pupilles dilatées** his pupils are dilated; *Fig* **d. le cœur** to cheer *or* gladden the heart **VPR se dilater** *(de pupilles)* to dilate; *(de l'estomac)* to become distended; *(d'un gaz)* to expand

dilatoire [dilatwar] **ADJ** *(tactique etc)* delaying; *Jur* dilatory; **faire des réponses dilatoires** to stall for time

dilemme [dilɛm] **NM** dilemma; **être devant un d.** to be in a dilemma; *Mktg (produit)* wildcat

dilettante [diletãt] **N** dilettante, amateur; **faire des sciences en d.** to dabble in science

dilettantisme [diletãtism] **NM** dilettantism, amateurism

diligemment [diliʒamã] **ADV** *Litt* **1** *(avec soin)* diligently **2** *(avec rapidité)* promptly, quickly

diligence [diliʒãs] **NF 1** *Litt (soin)* diligence, industry, application **2** *Litt (rapidité)* haste, dispatch; **faire d.** to hurry, to make haste **3** *(véhicule)* (stage)coach **4** *Jur* proceedings

diligent [diliʒã] **ADJ** *Litt* **1** *(appliqué)* diligent, industrious; **soins diligents** assiduous care **2** *(rapide)* speedy, prompt

diluant [diluã] **NM** thinner

diluer [dilɥe] **VT** *(boisson)* to dilute, to water down (**de** with); *(peinture)* to thin down (**de** with); *(pouvoir)* to weaken; *(discours, dissertation)* to pad

dilution [dilysjõ] **NF** *(de peinture)* thinning down; *(de boisson)* dilution, watering down; *(de pouvoir)* weakening; *(de discours, dissertation)* padding; **d. de capital** dilution of capital

diluvien, -ienne [dilyvjɛ̃, -jɛn] **ADJ 1** *(fossiles etc)* diluvian; *(dépôt, argile etc)* diluvial **2** *Fig* **pluie diluvienne** torrential rain

dimanche [dimãʃ] **NM** Sunday; **d. des Rameaux/de Pâques** Palm/Easter Sunday; **ses habits du d.** one's Sunday clothes *or* best; *Fam* **un chauffeur du d.** a weekend *or* Sunday driver; **un peintre du d.** a weekend painter; **la promenade du d.** the (usual) Sunday stroll; **on passe tous les dimanches en famille** we spend every Sunday with the family; **je hais les dimanches** I hate Sundays (*voir aussi samedi*) SEE GRAMMAR A81–2; B61–2

dîme [dim] **NF** *Hist* tithe; *Fig* **l'État prélève sa d. sur le tabac** the government takes its cut on tobacco

dimension [dimãsjõ] **NF 1** *(grandeur)* dimension, size; **à deux/trois dimensions** two-/three-dimensional; **quelles sont les dimensions de la pièce?** how large is the room?, what is the size of the room?; **prendre les dimensions de qch** to take the measurements of sth, to measure sth; **taillé à la d.** cut to size; **coupé dans sa plus grande/petite d.** cut lengthways/crossways SEE GRAMMAR B59 **2** *(importance)* *(d'une faute)* magnitude, enormity; **te rends-tu compte de la d. de ta gaffe?** do you realize what an enormous blunder you made?; *Fig* **prendre les dimensions d'une expédition/d'une révolution** to take on the dimensions of an expedition/a revolution; **le suspens est une d. prépondérante de son œuvre** suspense is a significant feature of his work; **ce travail n'est pas à la d. de son talent** the work is not equal to his talent; **il n'a pas la d. d'un homme d'État** he is not the stuff that statesmen are made of; **cette découverte prend enfin ses vraies dimensions** people are finally realizing the true importance of this discovery

dimensionner [dimãsjɔne] **VT** *Ordinat (figure)* to size

diminué [diminɥe] **ADJ 1** *Tex (tricot)* fully-fashioned; *Mus (intervalle)* diminished; *Archit* **colonne diminuée** tapering column **2** *(affaibli)* weakened, diminished; **c'est un homme d.** he is not the man he was; **il est très d. physiquement/mentalement** he is physically/mentally a lot weaker

diminuer [diminɥe] **VT** *(prix)* to reduce, to lower; *(dépenses)* to reduce, to decrease, to cut down; *(salaire)* to reduce, to decrease, to cut; *(autorité, pouvoir, crédibilité etc)* to lessen, to diminish; *(son capital, l'importance de qch)* to diminish; **d. les chances de succès** to diminish *or* lessen *or* reduce the chances of success; **d. sa consommation d'alcool** to reduce *or* cut down one's alcohol consumption; **d. l'ardeur des foules** to decrease the fervour *or Am* fervor of the crowds; **la maladie l'a considérablement diminuée** the illness has weakened her considerably; *Fig* **cela vous diminuerait aux yeux du public** it would lower *or* diminish you in the eyes of the public; **d. le son** to turn down the volume; **d. la semaine de travail** to reduce *or* cut the working week; **d. la longueur de qch** to make sth shorter, to shorten sth; **d. la hauteur de qch** to lower the height of sth; **d. la largeur de qch** to make sth narrower; *Tricot* **d. l'encolure de quatre mailles** to decrease four stitches at the neck

VI to diminish, to decrease, to lessen; *(de profits)* to decrease, to fall off, to decline; *(de prix)* to decrease, to fall; *(de fièvre)* to abate; *(de douleur)* to decrease, to diminish; **d. de vitesse** to slow down, to reduce speed; **les jours diminuent** the days are drawing in *or* are growing shorter; **ses forces ont diminué** his strength has declined; **sa toux a diminué** he is not coughing as much; *Naut* **d. de toile** to shorten sail

VPR se diminuer to lower *or* demean oneself

diminutif, -ive [diminytif, -iv] **ADJ** diminutive

NM *(d'un nom commun)* diminutive; *(d'un nom propre)* pet name, nickname; **'jupette' est le d. de 'jupe'** 'jupette' is the diminutive (form) of 'jupe'

diminution [diminysjɔ̃] **NF** *(de nombre)* decrease, decline; *(de prix)* reduction, decrease, lowering; *(de dépenses)* cutting down; *(de salaire)* decrease; *(de vitesse)* slackening; *(du son)* fading; *(de fièvre)* abatement; *(de douleur)* decrease, lessening; *Tricot* **commencer les diminutions** to begin decreasing; *Tricot* **faire trois diminutions** decrease three stitches

dimorphe [dimɔrf] **ADJ** *Biol* dimorphic, dimorphous

dimorphisme [dimɔrfism] **NM** *Biol* dimorphism

dinanderie [dinɑ̃dri] **NF** brassware; *(de cuisine)* brass kitchen utensils

dinar [dinar] **NM** dinar

dînatoire [dinatwar] **ADJ** *Fml, Hum (apéritif, goûter)* copious, *Hum* mammoth

dinde [dɛ̃d] **NF 1** *(volaille)* turkey hen; *Culin* turkey **2** *Fam (femme sotte)* stupid woman

dindon [dɛ̃dɔ̃] **NM** turkey (cock); *Fig* **être le d. de la farce** to be fooled *or* duped, to be made a fool of; **c'est le fisc qui est le d. de la farce** it's the tax man who's been conned

dindonneau, -eaux [dɛ̃dɔno] **NM** young turkey, turkey poult

dîner¹ [dine] **NM** VOIR GRAMMAIRE A7 **1** *(repas du soir)* dinner; **prendre son d.** to have one's dinner; **je donne un d. ce soir** I'm having a dinner party tonight; **je ne peux pas venir ce soir, j'ai un d.** I can't come this evening, I'm already booked for dinner; **il y a des pâtes pour le ou au ou à d.** it's pasta for dinner; **d. dansant** dinner-dance; **d.-débat/-con-**cert/-spectacle dinner-debate/-concert/-show; **d. de gala** gala dinner; **d. de famille** family dinner **2** *Belg, Can, Suisse (déjeuner)* lunch

dîner² **VI 1** *(prendre le repas du soir)* to dine, to have dinner; **d. en ville** *ou* **à l'extérieur** to dine out; **d. dehors** to eat out; **d. chez des amis** to dine *or* have dinner with friends; **à quelle heure dînez-vous?** what time do you have dinner?; **il est resté à d.** he stayed for dinner; **avoir/inviter qn à d.** to have/invite sb for *or* to dinner; **nous avons les Dupont à d.** the Duponts are coming for dinner; **elle dîne de peu** she doesn't eat very much at dinner; **elle a dîné de peu** she didn't have much dinner, she didn't eat very much at dinner; **il a dîné d'une tranche de jambon** he had a slice of ham for dinner; *Prov* **qui dort dîne** he who sleeps forgets his hunger **2** *Belg, Can, Suisse (déjeuner)* to (have) lunch; **elle est partie à d.** she's gone to lunch

dînette [dinɛt] **NF** *Fam (service)* doll's teaset; *(repas)* dolls' tea party; **jouer à la d.** to have a dolls' tea party

dîneur, -euse [dinœr, -øz] **N** diner

ding [diŋ] **INT** ting-a-ling

dingo¹ [dɛ̃go] **NM** *(animal)* dingo

dingo² **ADJ, N** *Fam* = **dingue**

dingue [dɛ̃g] *Fam* **ADJ 1** *(fou)* crazy, nuts (**de qn/qch** about sb/sth; **de faire qch** to do sth); **c'est complètement d. de croire qu'on va s'en sortir** it's absolutely crazy to think we're going to get out of this **2** *(incroyable) (fête, fringues, bouquin)* great, terrific; **c'est d. ce que la ville a changé** it's incredible how much the town has changed; **c'est d. ce que la vie est chère** the cost of living is terrible; **c'est d., la pluie qui tombe ici** it's terrible how much it rains here, it rains a terrific lot here; **il a fait un orage d.** there was a terrific storm

N nutcase, crackpot, loony; **ce d. est arrivé chez moi sans prévenir** the nutcase turned up on my doorstep without warning; **envoyer qn chez les dingues** to send sb to the loony bin *or* funny farm; **c'est un d. de la moto** he's crazy *or* nuts about motorbikes; **d. d'informatique** computer freak

dinguer [dɛ̃ge] **VI** *Fam* **s'en aller d.** *(d'une personne)* to go flying; **sa voiture est allée d. contre un mur** his car went flying *or* headlong into a wall; **envoyer d. qn** *(le pousser)* to send sb flying (**contre** into); *(l'éconduire)* to send sb packing; **envoyer d. qch** to send sth flying; **je vais tout envoyer d.** I'm going to pack it all in

dinguerie [dɛ̃gri] **NF** *Fam* stupidity; **ce film est d'une d.!** it's an incredibly stupid film!; **voilà sa dernière d.: s'acheter une moto!** you know what his latest mad *or* crazy idea is? to buy a motorbike!; **ils ne savent faire que les dingueries** they get up to all sorts of nonsense; **il est capable des pires dingueries** he's capable of doing the most idiotic things

dinosaure [dinozɔr] **NM** *(animal)*, *Fig* dinosaur; *Fig* **dinosaures de la politique** political dinosaurs

diocésain, -aine [djɔsezɛ̃, -ɛn] **ADJ, N** *Rel* diocesan

diocèse [djɔsɛz] **NM** *Rel* diocese

diode [djɔd] **NF** *Radio* diode; *Ordinat* **d. électroluminescente** light-emitting diode

dionysiaque [djɔnizjak] **ADJ** Dionysiac
NFPL **les dionysiaques** the Dionysia

diorama [djɔrama] **NM** diorama

dioxine [djɔksin] **NF** dioxin

dioxyde [djɔksid] **NM** *Chimie* dioxide

diphasé [difaze] **ADJ** *Élec (système etc)* two-phase

diphtérie [difteri] **NF** *Méd* diphtheria; **avoir la d.** to have diphtheria

diphtérique [difterik] **ADJ** *Méd* diphther(i-t)ic, diphtherial

diphtongue [diftɔ̃g] **NF** *Ling* diphthong

diphtonguer [diftɔ̃ge] **VT** *Ling* to diphthongize

diplodocus [diplɔdɔkys] **NM** diplodocus

diplomate [diplɔmat] **N** *(fonctionnaire, négociateur)* diplomat
NM *Culin* ≃ trifle
ADJ diplomatic

diplomatie [diplɔmasi] **NF** *(tact)*, *Pol* diplomacy; **entrer dans la d.** to enter the diplomatic service; **user de d.** to be diplomatic

diplomatique [diplɔmatik] **ADJ 1** *(service, corps, immunité etc)* diplomatic; **valise d.** diplomatic bag, *Fam* bag, *Am* (diplomatic) pouch **2** *(habile)* diplomatic, tactful; **ce n'était pas très d. de sa part** that wasn't very diplomatic *or* tactful of him; **maladie d.** diplomatic flu

diplomatiquement [diplɔmatikmɑ̃] **ADV** diplomatically

diplôme [diplom] **NM** *(d'enseignant, de docteur etc)* diploma; *Univ* degree; **elle a des diplômes** she has qualifications
  ▸▸ **d. d'études approfondies** = postgraduate qualification which is a prerequisite for PhD candidates; **d. d'études supérieures spécialisées** = postgraduate diploma; **d. d'études universitaires générales** = university degree awarded after a two-year course of study; **d. d'études universitaires scientifiques et techniques** = university degree awarded after a two-year course of study in science and/or technical subjects; **d. universitaire de technologie** = post-baccalauréat technical qualification awarded after two-years

diplômé, -ée [diplome] **ADJ** *Univ* graduate; *(architecte, infirmière)* qualified, certified; **un ingénieur d. de l'École polytechnique** an engineering graduate of the École polytechnique
N holder of a diploma; *Univ* graduate

diplômer [diplome] **VT** to confer a diploma on; *Univ* to confer a degree on, *Am* to graduate

diplopie [diplɔpi] **NF** *Méd* double vision, diplopia

dipode [dipɔd] **ADJ, NM** *Zool* biped

dipsomane [dipsɔman], **dipsomaniaque** [dipsɔmanjak] **ADJ, N** dipsomaniac

dipsomanie [dipsɔmani] **NF** dipsomania

diptère [diptɛr] *Entom* **ADJ** two-winged, *Spéc* dipterous
NM dipter(an); **les diptères** the Diptera

diptyque [diptik] **NM** diptych; *Littér* two-part literary work

dirco [dirko] **NM** *(abrév* **directeur commercial***)* marketing manager; *(en chef)* marketing director

dircom [dirkɔm] **NM** *(abrév* **directeur de la communication***)* communications manager; *(en chef)* communications director

dire¹ [dir] **NM** statement, assertion; *Jur* allegation; **on ne peut pas se fier à leurs dires** you can't trust what they say; **au d. de l'expert** according to expert opinion *or* the expert; **selon son d., à son d., à ses dires** according to him, by his own account; **maintenir son d.** to stand by one's statement *or* what one said

DIRE² *(prp* **disant**; *pp* **dit**; *pr ind* **je dis, n. disons, v. dites, ils disent**; *impf* **je disais**; *p hist* **je dis**; *fu* **je dirai***)*

VT	to say **1–5, 7, 8, 11** ▪ to tell **1–4, 7, 9, 11** ▪ to think **6** ▪ to look/sound/*etc* like *(on dirait...)* **6** ▪ to show **9** ▪ to suit *(dire à)* **10** ▪ to recite **11** ▪ to mean *(vouloir dire)* **13**
VPR to say **1, 3, 5, 6** ▪ to think **2, 4**

vt 1 *(exprimer)* to say; **il ne savait plus quoi d.** he didn't know what to say; **dites 33** *(chez le médecin)* say 'Ah'; **elle a dit 'rénumération' au lieu de rémunération'** she said 'rénumération' instead of 'rémunération'; **c'est justement ce que j'allais d.!** that's just what I was about to say!; **alors, qu'est-ce qu'il t'a dit?** well, what did he say to you?; **vous ne m'en avez jamais rien dit** you never mentioned it *or* said a thing about it; **mettez que je n'ai rien dit** forget I said that; **il n'y a pas à d., c'est vraiment le meilleur** there are no two ways about it, it's really the best; **je ne sais que d. pour vous remercier** I don't know how to thank you; **je ne sais que d. pour vous consoler** I don't know what to say to comfort you; **elle n'a plus dit un mot** she didn't say another word; **ce ne sont pas des choses à d.** you don't say that kind of thing; **tu ne sais plus ce que tu dis!** *(tes mots dépassent ta pensée)* you don't know what you're saying!; **arrête de d. n'importe quoi** stop talking nonsense; **j'ai un mot à te d.** *(pour mettre au courant)* I've got something to tell you; *(d'un ton menaçant)* I've something to say to you; **d. ce qu'on pense** to say what one thinks, to speak one's mind; **j'ai dit ce que j'avais à d.** I've said what I had to say; **ce disant ..., ceci dit ...** with these words ..., having said that ...; **un ami, que dis-je! un frère** a friend, no, a brother!; **c'est facile à d., c'est plus facile à d. qu'à faire** (it's) easier said than done; **d. bonjour à qn** to say hello to sb; **d. bonjour de la main** to wave hello; **d. bonsoir à qn** to say goodnight to sb, to wish sb goodnight; **comme on dit** as the saying goes, as they say; **comment dites-vous cela en français?** how do you say that in French?, what is the French for that?; **d. du mal de qn** to speak ill of sb; **je vous dis que non** no, I said; **je t'ai déjà dit que oui!** I've already said yes!; **là je ne dis pas non** I wouldn't say no; **sans mot d.** without (saying) a word; *Prov* **qui ne dit mot consent** silence is tantamount to consent; **pour ainsi d.** so to speak, as it were; *Fam* **on a comme qui dirait des ennuis** we have what you might call a few problems; **faire des stocks de sucre lorsqu'on habite à Moscou, je ne dis pas, mais à Paris!** stocking up on sugar when you live in Moscow, that's fair enough *or* that's one thing, but in Paris!; **ou, pour mieux d. ...** or, to be more specific ...; **il est un peu lent, pour ne pas d. complètement idiot** he's a little slow or, to put it bluntly, he's a complete idiot; **autrement dit** in other words; **cela va sans d.** that goes without saying, of course, naturally; **il va sans d. que vous venez avec votre épouse** needless to say *or* naturally, your wife is invited as well, your wife is invited as well, of course; **comment dirais-je?** how shall I put it?; **je ne sais comment d.** I don't know how to put it; **qui dit mieux?** *(à une vente aux enchères)* any advance?; **dites toujours!** go on, say it!, *Fam* **fire away!**; **il faut le d. vite!** it's easy to say!; **c'est vite dit** it's easier said than done; *Enf* **c'est celui qui dit, qui l'est!** it takes one to know one!

2 *(informer)* to tell; **qui te l'a dit?** *(comment le sais-tu?)* who told you?; **elle m'a dit que tu étais à Paris** she told me (that) you were in Paris; **qui t'a dit ça?** *(ce n'est pas vrai)* who told you that?; **c'est Sophie qui me l'a dit** it was Sophie who told me; **elle a dit qu'elle arriverait en retard** she said she'd be late; **envoyer d. à qn que ...** to send word to sb that ...; **d. un secret** to tell a secret; **il faudra bien que tu le lui dises un jour** you'll have to tell him some day; **ne me dis rien, tu as gagné!** don't tell me *or* let me guess, you've won!; **ne me dis pas que tu as gagné!** don't tell me *or* don't say you've won!; **il dit dans sa lettre que ..., sa lettre dit que ...** he says in his let-

ter that ...; **faire d. qch à qn** *(en le forçant)* to make sb say sth; *(pour prévenir)* to send word of sth to sb; **je lui ai fait d. de venir** I sent for him; **elle ne se le fit pas d. deux fois** she didn't wait to be told twice; *Fam* **je ne te le fais pas d.!** tell me something I don't know!; **faire d. qch par qn** to send word of sth through sb; **il a fait d. à son patron qu'il ne viendrait pas** he sent word to his boss that he wouldn't be coming in

3 *(affirmer)* to tell; **moi, je vous dis qu'il ne viendra pas** I say he won't come; **je le dis et je le répète** let me make myself perfectly clear; **qui vous dit qu'elle est vraiment aveugle?** who says she's really blind?; **quand je vous le disais!, je vous l'avais bien dit!** I told you so!, didn't I say so?; *(puisque)* **je vous le dis!** take my word for it!; **il est vraiment parti avec elle?** – *(puisque)* **je vous le dis** has he really gone off with her? – you can take it from me (he has) *or* take my word for it; **je peux reprendre du gâteau?** – *(puisque)* **je vous le dis!** can I have some more cake? – of course you can!; *Fam* **c'est lui, je te dis** it's him, I tell you; **c'est moi qui vous le dis** let me tell you, believe me; **c'est toi qui le dis!,** *Fam* **que tu dis!** if you say so!; **je sais ce que je dis!** I know what I'm talking about!; *Fam* **à qui le dites-vous?** you're telling me!; **tu ne crois pas si bien d.!** you're telling me!, how right you are!, *Am* you've said a mouthful!; **on peut d. qu'il a eu de la chance** he was lucky, you might say; *Fam* **tu l'as dit (bouffi)!** you('ve) said it!; **c'est beaucoup d.** that's saying (quite) a lot, that's going rather far; **c'est peu d.** that's putting it mildly; **c'est peu d. de d. qu'il est petit!** he's small, and that's putting it mildly!, he's small, to put it mildly!, *Br* he isn't half small!; *Fam* **je ne te dis pas la fête démente que c'était!** the party was so wild, it was unreal!; *Fam* **je ne te dis que ça** say no more, enough said; **vous m'en direz tant!** you don't say!; *Enf Fam* **on dit qu'on est des astronautes** let's be astronauts; **vous m'avez dit adorer la musique** you told me you loved music; **on le dit mort** they say he is dead, he is said *or* reported to be dead; **enfin, ça c'est ce qu'elle dit!** well, that's what she says!

4 to say; *Enf* **je vais le d. à ma mère** I'm going to tell mum on you; **je vais le d.!** I'm going to tell!; *Fam* **je vais te d.** let me tell you; *Fam* **je te dis pas la surprise quand ils sont arrivés!** I can't tell you what a surprise it was when they arrived!; **il a fait une tête quand il m'a vue, je te dis pas!** I can't describe the expression on his face when he saw me!; **à vrai d., à d. vrai** to tell the truth, to be truthful; **pour tout (vous) d.** to be honest (with you), to be truthful, to tell (you) the truth; **c'est (tout) d.** need I say more?; **c'est d. s'il t'aime** that shows how much he loves you; **à ce qu'elle dit** according to her; **entre nous soit dit, soit dit entre nous** between ourselves, between you and me and the gatepost; **soit dit en passant** *ou* **entre parenthèses** by the by, by the way, incidentally

5 *(décider)* **aussitôt dit, aussitôt fait** no sooner said than done; **alors c'est dit, voilà qui est dit** (well then,) that's settled *or* that's decided; **disons à quatre heures** let's say four o'clock, four o'clock, say; **ce qui est dit est dit** a promise is a promise; **tenez-vous cela pour dit** don't let me have to tell you again, that's my last word; **mais tout n'est pas dit** but that's not the last of it; **tant que tout n'est pas dit** while things are still up in the air, until things are definite one way or the other; **tant que tout n'est pas dit pour le mariage** until the wedding is definitely going to take place; **il est dit que je resterai célibataire** I'm destined to stay single

6 *(penser)* to think *(de* of); **alors, qu'est-ce**

que tu en dis? well, what do you think?; **qu'en dira-t-on?, qu'est-ce que les gens vont d.?** what will people say *or* think?; **qu'est-ce que tu dirais d'aller au cinéma?** how about going to see a film?; **on aurait dit qu'elle était hypnotisée/que c'était la fin du monde** you would have thought she was hypnotized/it was the end of the world; **avec sa canne, on aurait dit Charlot** he looked like Charlie Chaplin with his cane; **qui eût dit qu'elle se marierait?** who would have thought she'd get married?; **et d. qu'elle n'a que vingt ans!** and to think (that) she's only twenty!; **on dirait qu'il va pleuvoir** it looks like rain; **on dirait qu'il pleut** it looks as if it is raining; **on dirait du Mozart** it sounds like Mozart; **on dirait du gin** it tastes like gin

7 *(ordonner)* **d. à qn de faire qch** to tell sb to do sth; **faites ce qu'on vous dit** do as you're told; **dites-lui d'entrer** tell *or* ask him to come in; **dites qu'on le fasse entrer** tell *or* ask them to show him in; **le prof a dit de lire le premier chapitre** the teacher said to read the first chapter; **taisez-vous, j'ai dit!** be quiet, I said!; **je ne le dirai pas deux fois!** I won't tell you twice *or* again!

8 *(protester)* to say; **il est trop tard, je ne peux plus rien d.** it's too late, I can't say anything now; **j'ai eu une augmentation conséquente, je n'ai rien à d.** I got a decent rise, I can't complain; **tu as quelque chose à d. à ça?** have you got any objection?; **très bon travail, rien à d.** this is very good work, I have no complaints; **il y a beaucoup à d. sur ton travail** there's quite a lot I'd like to say about your work; **tu n'as rien à d.!** I don't want to hear a word out of you!; **je n'ai rien à d. contre lui** I have no objection to him; **il n'y a pas à d.** there's no denying it, there's no doubt about it; **il n'y a pas à d.** *ou* **on a beau d., c'est utile d'avoir un homme chez soi** there's no denying that it's useful to have a man about the house; **vous avez beau d. (le contraire)** you can say what you like; **tu as beau d. qu'elle ne ment pas** you can say she doesn't lie until you're blue in the face; **j'ai beau d. (tout ce que je veux), il ne m'écoute jamais** I can talk until I'm blue in the face, he never listens to me; **ce n'est pas pour d., mais ...** I hate to tell you this, but ...; **ne pas avoir son mot à d.** not to have any say; **tu n'as pas ton mot à d. sur cette question** you don't have any say in the matter

9 *(indiquer)* to show, to express; **horloge qui dit l'heure exacte** clock that tells the right time; **cela en dit long sur son courage** it speaks volumes for his courage; *Litt* **sa démarche/son visage disait son désespoir** his despair was evident in his gait/face; **qu'est-ce qui vous dit qu'il viendra?** how do you know he will come?; **ce nom/cette musique ne me dit rien** the name/the music means *or* conveys nothing to me; **quelque chose me dit que ...** something tells me that ...

10 *(plaire)* **d. à** to suit, to appeal to; **ça te dit?** what about it?, how about it?; **ça te dit de partir en vacances avec nous?** how about coming on holiday with us?; **si cela te dit, si le cœur t'en dit** if you feel like it; **cela ne me dit (trop) rien, cela ne me dit pas** I don't feel like it; **cela ne me dit trop rien de manger chinois ce soir** I don't feel like eating Chinese this evening; **en hiver, rien ne me dit** I don't feel like doing anything in winter; *Fam* **alors, ton tricot, qu'est-ce que ça dit?** how did your sweater turn out?; **pour l'instant, il ne dit pas grand-chose** it doesn't look like much at the moment; **cela ne me disait rien de bon** *ou* **rien qui vaille** I didn't like the look of it; **le fait qu'il soit si hésitant ne me dit rien de bon** *ou* **rien qui vaille** I don't like the fact *or* I'm a bit concerned that he's hesitating so much

11 *(réciter)* *(ses prières, la messe)* to say; **d.**

des vers *ou* de la **poésie** to recite poetry; **d. son chapelet** to tell one's beads

12 *(nommer)* **Jacques, dit Jacko** Jacques, also known as *or* alias *or Fam* aka Jacko; *(en le présentant)* Jacques, or Jacko to us

13 *(signifier)* **vouloir d.** to mean; **je veux d. … that is to say …**, I mean …; **que voulez-vous d. par là?** what do you mean by that?; **que veut d. ce mot?** what does this word mean?; *Fam* **ça dit bien ce que ça veut d.** it means what it says; **qu'est-ce à d.?** what does this mean?; **est-ce à d. qu'il ne viendra pas?** does this mean he won't come?; **qui dit bordeaux dit bon vin** Bordeaux is synonymous with good wine

14 laisse-les d., ils sont stupides! let them talk, they're stupid!; **je me suis laissé d. que … I** hear that …

15 dis donc, je viens de penser qu'on pourrait se voir ce week-end by the way *or Fam* hey, I've just had a thought, we could see each other this weekend; **tu as grandi, dis donc!** goodness *or* my word, you've grown!; **non mais dis donc, tu ne vas pas recommencer!** you're not going to start up again!; **dis donc, tu te fiches de moi!** you don't give a damn about me, do you?; **ben dis donc!** well I'm damned!; **tu m'emmènes, dis, sur ta moto?** take me for a ride on your motorbike; **non mais, dis donc!** do you mind!

VPR se dire 1 *(réciproque)* **on se dit bonjour de temps en temps** we say hello from time to time

2 *(penser)* **je me disais que tout était fini** I thought it was all over; **dis-toi bien que ça aurait pu être plus grave** tell yourself it could have been worse; **je me disais bien que je l'avais déjà vu quelque part** I knew I'd seen him before

3 *(être correct)* **ça se dit en français?** can you say that in French?; **cela ne se dit pas** that isn't said; **des choses pareilles ne se disent pas** you don't say things like that; **cela se dit d'une personne mais certainement pas d'un objet** you can say that about *or* of a person but definitely not about *or* of a thing

4 *(se croire)* **on se dirait en Suisse** you would think you were in Switzerland; **on se dirait en été** you would think it was summer

5 *(se prétendre)* **elle se dit écossaise/à Londres** she says she is Scottish/in London

6 comment ça se dit en français? how do you say that in French?

> Attention: ne pas confondre **to say** et **to tell** lorsqu'on traduit **dire**. Le verbe **to tell** est toujours suivi d'un complément d'objet désignant la personne à qui l'on s'adresse.

direct [dirɛkt] **ADJ 1** *(sans détour) (question, chemin)* direct, straight; *(personne)* direct, straightforward; **quel est le chemin le plus d. pour aller à la mairie?** what's the most direct way to get to the town hall?; **d'ici, la route est directe** it's a straight road from here; **tu ne peux pas te tromper, c'est d.** you can't go wrong, it's a straight road; **il y a fait une allusion directe** he made a direct reference to it, he referred to it directly

2 *(sans intermédiaire) (impôts)*, *Tél (ligne)* direct; **descendre de qn en ligne directe** to be a direct descendant of sb; *Gram* **complément d'objet d.** direct object; SEE GRAMMAR B18–19; B52–3 **mon supérieur d.** my immediate superior; **il y a des ventes directes au grand public dans leur entrepôt** they sell direct to the public from their warehouse; **être en rapport** *ou* **contact d.** *ou* **en relations directes avec qn** to be in direct contact with sb; **d. sur cassette** live on tape

3 *(sans arrêt)* **train d.** through train, fast train; *Aviat* **vol d.** direct flight

NM 1 *Radio, TV* live broadcasting; **ce n'est jamais du d.** it's never broadcast live; **il préfère le d. au playback** he prefers performing live to miming; **émission en d.** live broadcast; **vous allez entendre ce concert en d. de l'Opéra de Paris** you will hear this concert live from the Paris Opera House

2 *Boxe* straight; **d. du droit/du gauche** straight right/left; **s'il continue de m'énerver, je lui mets un d. au menton** if he keeps on annoying me, I'll punch him on the jaw

3 *Rail* through *or* fast train (**pour** to)

4 *Ordinat* **en d.** in direct mode

ADV *Fam* directly; **je pars d. vers Grenoble** I'm going to Grenoble direct; **s'il recommence, je vais d. chez le proviseur** if he starts again, I'm going straight to the headmaster

directement [dirɛktəmɑ̃] **ADV 1** *(sans détour)* straight, directly; **en arrivant, je vais d. au lit** I'm going straight to bed when I arrive; **si tu prends ce chemin, tu arrives d. à la rivière** this road will take you straight to the river; **se précipiter d. sur un endroit/qch** to head straight for a place/sth; **elle est venue d. vers nous** she came straight towards us; **se diriger d. au nord** to go due north; **répondre d. à la question** to give a direct *or* straight answer to the question; **dis-moi d. combien tu veux** tell me straight out how much you want **2** *(sans intermédiaire)* directly; **expédier des marchandises d. à qn** to send goods direct to sb; **d. du producteur au consommateur** direct *or* straight from the producer to the consumer

directeur, -trice [dirɛktœr, -tris] **N** *Com (qui fait partie du conseil d'administration)* director; *(d'un magasin, d'un service)* manager; *Scol* head(teacher), *Am* principal; *Univ (d'une UER)* head; *(de prison)* governor; *(de journal)* editor; *(d'expédition etc)* leader; *Cin, Radio, TV* director

ADJ *(équipe, instances)* management, executive; *(force)* directing, managing, controlling; *(principe)* guiding; **comité d.** steering committee; **roue directrice** front wheel; **lignes directrices** guidelines; **l'idée directrice d'un livre** the central theme of a book

▸ ▸ **d. des achats** purchasing director/manager; **d. adjoint** deputy director/manager; **d. administratif** executive director; **d. administratif et financier** administrative and financial manager; **d. d'agence** branch manager; *Radio* **d. d'antenne** station director; **d. artistique** artistic director, production designer; *Journ* art editor, art director; **d. de banque** bank manager; *Pol* **d. de cabinet** *(d'un ministre)* ≃ principal private secretary; *TV, Cin etc* **d. de casting** casting director; *TV, Radio* **d. de chaîne** network controller; **d. de la clientèle** customer relations manager; **d. commercial** sales director/manager; **d. de la communication** communications director/manager; **d. des comptes-clients** accounts director/manager; *Rel* **d. de conscience** spiritual adviser; **d. de la création** creative director; **d. du crédit** credit manager; **d. de division** *(au siège)* divisional director; **d. d'exploitation** operations director/manager; **d. export** export director/manager; *Journ* **d. de la fabrication** production director/manager; **d. financier** financial manager; *(en chef)* financial *or* finance director; **d. général** *(d'un ministère)* ≃ permanent under-secretary; *Com* chief executive officer, managing director; *(d'organisation internationale, EDF etc)* director general; **d. gérant** executive director; **d. (de l')informatique** computer manager; **d. intérimaire** temporary director/manager, interim manager, acting manager; **d. de marché**

market manager; **d. du marketing** marketing director/manager; **d. de marque** brand manager; **d. de mercatique-vente** sales and marketing director/manager; **d. du personnel** personnel director/manager; **d. de la photographie** *Cin* director of photography, cinematographer; *Journ* picture editor; **d. de production** production director; **d. de produit** product manager, brand manager; **d. des programmes** director of programming, programme controller; **d. de projet** project director/manager; **d. de la publicité** advertising director/manager; **d. de recherche et développement** director of research and development, R&D director; **d. de recherche marketing** marketing research director/manager; **d. de (la) rédaction** managing editor; **d. régional** regional director/manager, area director/manager, district manager; **d. régional des ventes** regional sales manager; **d. des relations publiques** public relations director/manager; **d. des ressources humaines** human resources manager; **d. de service** head of department, unit manager; **d. des services techniques** technical director; *Rel* **d. spirituel** spiritual adviser; *TV, Radio* **d. de station** station manager; *TV, Radio* **d. de studio** studio manager; **d. de succursale** branch manager; **d. technique** technical manager; **d. de télévision** television director; *Univ* **d. de thèse** thesis director; **d. des ventes** sales director/manager; **d. des ventes et du marketing** sales and marketing director/manager

directif, -ive [dirɛktif, -iv] **ADJ** *Psy (entretien, questionnaire)* directive; *(question)* leading, directive; *Péj (personne, attitude)* managing; **ces instructions sont purement directives** these instructions are for guidance only; **c'est un chef très d.** he's the kind of manager who takes all the decisions himself; **il a des méthodes très directives** he's very managerial *or Fam* bossy

direction [dirɛksjɔ̃] **NF 1** *(d'une affaire, d'une usine, d'un théâtre, d'une école)* management, running; *(d'un parti, d'un pays)* leadership; *(d'un procès, d'une enquête)* conduct; *(d'une équipe, de travaux, d'opérations)* management, supervision; **elle a été promue à la d. du journal/du lycée** she's been promoted to editor/headmistress; **orchestre (placé) sous la d. de Karajan** orchestra conducted by Karajan *or Am* under the baton of Karajan; **projet mené sous la d. du Pr. Lacroix** *(qui y a travaillé activement)* project carried out under the leadership of Prof. Lacroix; *(qui l'a supervisé)* project carried out under the supervision of Prof. Lacroix; **c'est lui qui a pris la d. des opérations** he was in charge of operations; **on lui a confié la d. d'une nouvelle équipe de recherches** he was put in charge of a new research team

2 *(personnes) (d'une administration)* management; **une décision prise au niveau de la d.** a management decision; **j'irai me plaindre à la d.** I'll complain to the management

3 *(lieux) (d'un conseil)* offices; *(d'une firme etc)* head office

4 *Aut, Naut (mécanisme)* steering; *Aut* **la d. est un peu raide** the steering's a bit stiff

5 *(orientation)* direction; *Naut* bearing, course; **changer de d.** to change direction; *Naut* to alter course; **toutes/autres directions** *(sur panneau)* all/all other directions; **ton devoir part dans toutes les directions** your homework goes off in all directions; **quelle d. ont-ils prise?** which way did they go?; **ce train va en d. de Paris** this train is going to Paris; **ses recherches prennent une nouvelle d.** his research is taking a new direction; **chercher la solution dans une autre d.** to look elsewhere for the solution

6 *Cin, TV* directing, direction

▸▸*Aut* **d. assistée** power steering; **d. collégiale** collegiate management; **d. commerciale** sales management; **d. du contentieux** legal department; **d. des crédits** credit management; *Aut* **d. à crémaillère** rack and pinion steering; **D. départementale de l'action sanitaire et sociale** = office administering health and social services at regional level; **d. des entreprises** business management; **d. de l'exploitation** operations management; *(service)* operations department; **d. financière** financial management; *(service)* finance department; **d. générale** general management, senior management; **D. générale des Impôts** ≃ Inland Revenue, *Am* ≃ IRS; *Admin* **D. générale de la santé** = central administrative body for health and social services; *Admin* **D. des hôpitaux** = central government office for hospital administration; *Aut* **d. mécanique** manual steering; **d. mercatique** marketing department; **d. par objectifs** management by objectives; **d. du personnel** personnel management; *(service)* personnel department; **d. de la production** production control; **d. de la rédaction** editorial department; **D. de la surveillance du territoire** = French secret service; **d. du trésor** finance department; **d. des ventes** sales management; *Ordinat* **d. systématisée** systems management

directionnel, -elle [dirɛksjɔnɛl] ADJ *(antenne etc)* directional

directive [dirɛktiv] NF directive, order, instruction; *Pol* guideline

directoire [dirɛktwar] NM 1 *Hist* **le D.** the Directoire *(1795)*; **chaise D.** Directoire chair 2 *Admin, Com* executive board

directorial¹, -iale, -iaux, -iales [dirɛktɔrjal, -jo] ADJ *Com etc* directorial, managerial

directorial², -iale, -iaux, -iales ADJ *Hist (constitution, gouvernement)* of the Directoire

directrice [dirɛktris] NF, ADJ *voir* **directeur**

dirham [diram] NM dirham

dirigé [diriʒe] ADJ controlled, managed; **économie dirigée** planned economy; *Scol* **activités dirigées** extra-curricular activities; *Univ* **travaux dirigés** classwork; *(en laboratoire)* lab work, practicals

dirigeable [diriʒabl] ADJ dirigible NM *Aviat* dirigible (balloon), airship

dirigeant, -ante [diriʒɑ̃, -ɑ̃t] ADJ *(principe, philosophie etc)* guiding; **classes dirigeantes** ruling classes; *Pol* **le rôle d. du parti Communiste** the leading role of the Communist Party N *(d'un parti etc)* leader; *(d'un pays)* leader, ruler; **d. d'entreprise** company manager; **d. syndical** union leader

DIRIGER [diriʒe] *(je dirigeai(s); n. dirigeons)* VT 1 *(être à la tête de) (entreprise, affaire, usine, théâtre, école etc)* to manage, to run; *(pays)* to lead, to run; *(orchestre)* to conduct; *(journal)* to edit; *(expédition, débat)* to lead; *(procès, enquête, séance etc)* to conduct; *(travaux, équipe)* to manage, to supervise; *(circulation)* Cin, TV to direct; **d. la production** to control production

2 *(orienter) (fusil, arme, télescope)* to aim, to level, to point (**sur** at); *(personne)* to direct; *(navire)* to steer, to navigate; **d. un colis sur Paris** to send a parcel off to Paris; **d. ses pas vers ...** to go *or* move towards ...; to direct one's steps towards ...; **peux-tu d. ta lampe vers le plafond?** can you move your lamp so it's pointing towards the ceiling?; **d. son regard vers** *ou* **sur qn/qch** to look at sb/sth; **d. son attention sur qch** to turn one's attention to sth; **d. ses accusations contre qn** to level

or aim accusations at sb; **vers qui sont dirigées tes critiques?** who is your criticism aimed at?; **les filles sont souvent dirigées vers des études littéraires** girls are often steered towards arts subjects

VPR **se diriger** 1 *(aller)* **se d. vers un endroit** to make for *or* head for a place, to make one's way towards a place; **le navire se dirigea vers le port** the ship steered *or* headed for the harbour; **se d. vers qn** to go up to sb; **nous nous dirigeons vers une crise encore plus profonde** we are heading for an even greater crisis; **de plus en plus de femmes se dirigent vers l'informatique** more and more women are going into computers

2 *(s'orienter)* **se d. à l'aide d'une boussole/du soleil** to use a compass/the sun to guide oneself; **je n'arrive jamais à me d. dans le noir** I can never find my way around in the dark

dirigisme [diriʒism] NM *Écon* state control, dirigisme

dirigiste [diriʒist] *Écon* ADJ **système d.** state-controlled economy N advocate of a state-controlled economy

dirlo [dirlo] N *Fam (abrév* **directeur**) head (teacher), *Am* principal

discal, -ale, -aux, -ales [diskal, -o] ADJ *Méd* **hernie discale** slipped disc

discernable [disɛrnabl] ADJ discernible, visible

discernement [disɛrnəmɑ̃] NM 1 *(distinction)* discrimination (**de ... et de ...** between ... and ...) 2 *(jugement)* judgment, discernment; **agir sans d.** to act rashly

discerner [disɛrne] VT 1 *(distinguer)* to discern, to distinguish; **on discernait une maison dans le lointain** we could (just) see *or* make out a house in the distance 2 *(différencier)* **d. qch de qch** to distinguish sth from sth, to discriminate between sth and sth; **d. le bien du mal** to tell right from wrong 3 *(sentir)* to detect, to discern; **d. de la tristesse dans la voix de qn** to detect a note of sadness in sb's voice

disciple [disipl] N disciple, follower

disciplinable [disiplinabl] ADJ that can be disciplined

disciplinaire [disiplinɛr] ADJ *(mesure, sanction etc)* disciplinary

discipline [disiplin] NF 1 *(règlement)* discipline; **maintenir la d.** to maintain discipline *or* order; **un prof qui ne sait pas maintenir la d.** a teacher who cannot keep discipline 2 *Scol (matière)* subject, discipline, branch of learning; **quelles sont les disciplines enseignées ici?** what subjects are taught here? 3 *(fouet)* scourge

discipliné [disipline] ADJ disciplined

discipliner [disipline] VT *(élèves)* to control, to maintain discipline over; **d. ses cheveux avec de la laque** to control one's hair with lacquer; *Fig* **d. ses instincts** to curb one's instincts VPR **se discipliner** to discipline oneself, to exercise self-control

disc-jockey, *pl* **disc-jockeys** [diskʒɔkɛ] NM disc jockey

disco [disko] NF *Fam (abrév* **discothèque**) disco ADJ, NM **(musique) d.** disco (music)

discobole [diskɔbɔl] NM *Sport* discus thrower

discographie [diskɔgrafi] NF discography

discographique [diskɔgrafik] ADJ *(rubrique, production)* record

discoïde [diskɔid], **discoïdal, -ale, -aux, -ales** [diskɔidal, -o] ADJ disc-shaped, *Spéc* discoid(al)

discompte [diskɔ̃t] NM discount

discontinu [diskɔ̃tiny] ADJ discontinuous; *(ligne)* broken NM discontinuity

discontinuer [diskɔ̃tinɥe] VI to stop, to discontinue; **parler pendant des heures sans d.** to talk for hours on end without stopping *or* without a break VT *Litt* to stop, to discontinue

discontinuité [diskɔ̃tinɥite] NF discontinuity

disconvenir [diskɔ̃vnir] VI *(conj like* **venir**, *the aux is* **avoir**) **je n'en disconviens pas** I admit it, I don't deny it

discophile [diskɔfil] N record enthusiast

discordance [diskɔrdɑ̃s] NF *(de sons)* discordance, dissonance; *(d'opinions)* difference; *(de personnalités, couleurs)* clash

discordant [diskɔrdɑ̃] ADJ *(son)* discordant, dissonant; *(bruit)* grating, jarring; *(couleurs, personnalités)* clashing; *(preuves, opinions etc)* conflicting

discorde [diskɔrd] NF discord, dissension, strife; **semer la d.** to make trouble, to sow discord

discorder [diskɔrde] VI *(de couleurs, témoignages)* to clash (**avec** with); **sa voix discorde dans l'orchestre** her voice clashes with the orchestra

discothèque [diskɔtɛk] NF 1 *(organisme)* record library; *(collection)* record collection *or* library; *(meuble)* record cabinet 2 *(boîte de nuit)* discothèque, *Fam* disco

discount [diskunt] NM 1 *(rabais)* discount 2 *(magasin)* discount shop *or* store

discounter¹ [diskunte] VT to reduce the price of; **tout est discounté** there's a discount on everything, everything's reduced

discounter², discounteur [diskuntœr] NM discount shop *or* store; *(personne)* discount trader

discoureur, -euse [diskurœr, -øz] N *Péj* speechifier

discourir [diskurir] VI *(conj like* **courir**) to discourse, *Péj* to air one's opinions (**sur** on)

discours [diskur] NM 1 *(allocution)* speech; **prononcer** *ou* **faire un d.** to make a speech; **d. de clôture** closing speech; *Pol* **d. sur l'état de l'Union** *(du président des États-Unis)* State of the Union Speech; **d. d'ouverture** opening speech; *Pol* **d.-programme** policy statement; **d. de réception** acceptance speech; **d. du trône** Speech from the Throne

2 *(exposé)* discourse, dissertation, treatise; *Littér* **le D. de la méthode** the Discourse on Method

3 *(langage)* speech; *Gram* **parties du d.** parts of speech; **d. indirect/direct** indirect *or* reported/direct speech; **d. rapporté** reported speech VOIR GRAMMAIRE A63; A78

4 *(paroles)* talk; **tenir un d.** to talk to sb at length; **se perdre en longs d.** to talk endlessly; **elle a** *ou* **tient un d. très clair** she speaks very clearly; **tous ces beaux d. ne nous avancent à rien** all this talk isn't getting us anywhere

discourtois [diskurtwa] ADJ discourteous

discourtoisement [diskurtwazmɑ̃] ADV discourteously

discourtoisie [diskurtwazi] NF *Arch* discourtesy

discrédit [diskredi] NM discredit, loss of credit; **être en d. auprès de qn** to be in disfavour with sb; **jeter le d. sur qn** to bring discredit on sb

discréditer [diskredite] VT *(théorie etc)* to discredit VPR **se discréditer** *(d'une idée, d'une théorie)* to become discredited *(auprès* ou *aux yeux de qn* in sb's eyes); *(d'une personne)* to discredit oneself *(auprès* ou *aux yeux de qn* with sb)

discret, -ète [diskrɛ, -ɛt] ADJ 1 *(plein de re-*

tenue) (personne, comportement etc) discreet; **sous pli d.** under plain cover; **tu sauras rester d.?** you'll keep it to yourself, won't you?; *Iron* **il m'énerve avec ses allusions discrètes** those subtle hints of his are getting on my nerves; **sois d., il ne faut pas qu'elle l'apprenne** don't go repeating this, she mustn't find out **2** *(modeste) (personne)* quiet, unobtrusive, unassuming; *(vêtements)* sober, simple, plain; *(apparence)* inconspicuous; *(endroit)* quiet, secluded; **une discrète touche de bleu** a discreet touch of blue **3** *Math (quantité)* discrete; *Phys (fonction)* discontinuous

discrètement [diskrɛtmɑ̃] **ADV 1** *(avec retenue)* discreetly, with discretion; **il lui a parlé d.** he had a quiet word with him **2** *(modestement)* quietly, modestly, simply; **maquillé d.** discreetly made up

discrétion [diskresjɔ̃] **NF 1** *(retenue)* discretion; **avoir de la d.** to be discreet; **d. assurée** discretion guaranteed; **la d. d'une intervention** the discreetness of an intervention; **user de qch avec d.** to use sth in moderation **2** *(sobriété)* **la d. avec laquelle elle se conduit** her unassuming behaviour; **s'habiller avec d.** to dress simply *or* plainly; **elle se maquille avec d.** she is always discreetly made up **3** **être à la d. de qn** to be in sb's hands; **pain à d.** unlimited bread, as much bread as one wants

discrétionnaire [diskresjɔnɛr] **ADJ** *(pouvoirs etc)* discretionary

discrètos [diskrɛtɔs] **ADV** *Fam* on the quiet

discriminant [diskriminɑ̃] **ADJ** discriminating
  NM *Math* discriminant

discrimination [diskriminasjɔ̃] **NF** discrimination; **ils étaient victimes de d.** they were victims of discrimination, they were discriminated against; **d. raciale/sexuelle** racial/sexual discrimination; **sans d. de race ni de sexe** regardless of race or sex, without discrimination on the grounds of race or sex; **d. positive** positive discrimination, *Am* affirmative action

discriminatoire [diskriminatwar] **ADJ** discriminatory, discriminating

discriminer [diskrimine] **VT** *Litt* to discriminate, to distinguish

disculpation [diskylpasjɔ̃] **NF** exoneration; **sa d. n'a pas été facile à obtenir** it was not easy to clear him *or* to prove him innocent

disculper [diskylpe] **VT d. qn** to clear sb, to prove sb innocent, to exonerate sb (**de** of)
  VPR se disculper to clear oneself, to prove oneself innocent (**de** of)

discursif, -ive [diskyrsif, -iv] **ADJ** discursive

discussion [diskysjɔ̃] **NF** discussion; *(plus passionnée)* argument; *(émission)* discussion programme; **avoir une d.** to have a discussion/an argument (**sur, à propos de** about); **la question est en d.** the question is under discussion; **sans d. possible** indisputably; **il s'exécuta sans d.** he complied without arguing (the point); **pas de d., au travail!** don't argue, get to work!

discutable [diskytabl] **ADJ** debatable, questionable; **tu as agi d'une manière qui est tout à fait d.** your behaviour was altogether questionable

discutailler [diskytaje] **VI** *Fam Péj (chicaner)* to quibble

discuté [diskyte] **ADJ** *(question)* disputed; *(livre, sujet)* much discussed; **être très d.** to be hotly disputed *or* the subject of much discussion

discuter [diskyte] **VT** *(examiner)* to discuss, to debate; *(contester)* to question, to dispute; **d. un droit** to dispute a right; **d. un problème** to discuss a problem; **discutons la chose** let's

discuss it, let's talk it over; *Fam* **d. le coup** *ou* **le bout de gras** to have a natter *or* a chat; **prix à d.** negotiable
  VI 1 *(parler)* to discuss; *(débattre)* to debate; **d. avec qn sur qch** to debate sth with sb; **d. de politique** to discuss *or* talk politics, to argue about politics; **il faut qu'on en discute** we must discuss it; **d. du prix de qch** to haggle over the price of sth; **on ne peut pas d. avec toi** it's impossible to have a discussion with you; **on pourrait peut-être d. avant de se battre?** could we discuss it first before we start fighting? **2** *(protester)* to argue (**avec** with); **ne discutez pas** no arguing, don't argue; **il n'y a pas à d.** I don't want any arguments *or* arguing; **suis-moi sans d.** follow me without any arguments, follow me and don't argue; **on ne discute pas avec la loi** the law's the law
  VPR se discuter to be discussed *or* debated; **ça se discute** that's debatable

disert [dizɛr] **ADJ** *Litt* eloquent, fluent

disette [dizɛt] **NF** scarcity, *Fml* dearth; **d. d'eau** drought; **vivre dans la d.** to live in poverty

diseur, -euse [dizœr, -øz] **N 1 d./diseuse de bonne aventure** fortune teller **2** *(qui déclame)* orator

disgrâce [disgrɑs] **NF** disfavour, disgrace; **encourir la d. de qn** to incur sb's displeasure; **tomber en d. (auprès de qn)** to fall into disfavour (with sb)

disgracié [disgrasje] **ADJ** out of favour, in disgrace

disgracier [disgrasje] **VT** *(impf, pr subj* **n. disgraciions, v. disgraciiez)** *(ministre)* to dismiss

disgracieux, -ieuse [disgrasjø, -jøz] **ADJ** *(personne, mouvement, geste)* awkward, ungraceful; *(visage etc)* ugly

> Il faut noter que l'adjectif anglais **disgraceful** est un faux ami. Il signifie **honteux, scandaleux.**

disjoindre [disʒwɛdr] *(conj like* **joindre)** **VT** to separate, to take apart; *Jur* **d. deux causes** to treat two cases separately
  VPR se disjoindre to come apart, to separate

disjoint [disʒwɛ̃] **ADJ** *(pièces)* separated; *(problèmes)* unconnected, separate

disjoncter [disʒɔ̃kte] *Élec* **VT** *(circuit)* to break
  VI to fuse; *Aut* to cut out; *Fig Fam* to crack up

disjoncteur [disʒɔ̃ktœr] **NM** *Élec* circuit breaker, cut-out

disjonctif, -ive [disʒɔ̃ktif, -iv] **ADJ** disjunctive SEE GRAMMAR B20

disjonction [disʒɔ̃ksjɔ̃] **NF** *(de tuyaux, lames de parquet)* separation

dislocation [dislɔkasjɔ̃] **NF** *(d'une articulation)* dislocation; *(d'une machine etc)* taking to pieces, dismantling; *(d'un empire, d'un État etc)* dismemberment; *Géol* fault; *Mil etc (des troupes etc)* dispersal, breaking up

disloqué [dislɔke] **ADJ** *(épaule, genou)* dislocated; *(machine)* dismantled; *(empire, État etc)* dismembered, broken up

disloquer [dislɔke] **VT** *(épaule, genou)* to dislocate; *(machine)* to take to pieces, to dismantle; *(troupes)* to break up, to disperse; *(empire, État)* to break up, to dismember
  VPR se disloquer *(d'un empire)* to break up, to fall to pieces; **son bras s'est disloqué** he's dislocated his arm

disparaître [disparɛtr] **VI** *(conj like* **paraître)** **1** *(s'en aller)* to disappear, to vanish; **elle a disparu sans laisser de traces** she has disappeared *or* vanished without trace; **la petite fille a disparu il y a une semaine** the little girl disappeared *or* went missing a week ago; *Fam* **disparais, je t'ai assez vu** clear off, I've had enough of you

2 *(devenir invisible)* to disappear, to vanish; **d. dans la foule** to disappear *or* vanish into the crowd; *Fam* **d. de la circulation** to vanish from *or* drop out of circulation; **d. aux regards** to vanish from sight, to disappear from view; *Cin, TV* **d. en fondu** to fade out **3** *(mourir)* to die; **tous ses amis ont disparu** all his friends have died *or* are dead; *Naut* **disparu en mer** lost at sea; **faire d. qn** to get rid of sb
4 *(finir) (d'un bouton)* to disappear, to vanish, to go away; *(d'une mode, d'une tradition)* to die out; **faire d. une tache/une difficulté** to get rid of *or* remove a stain/a difficulty; **faire d. la douleur** to make the pain disappear *or* go; **j'ai pris un cachet pour faire d. la douleur** I took a pill to relieve *or* get rid of the pain; **sa timidité disparaît peu à peu** his shyness is wearing off

disparate [disparat] **ADJ** *(différent)* dissimilar, *Fml* disparate; *(qui ne s'accorde pas)* ill-matched, ill-assorted; **couleurs disparates** clashing colours; **ils ont un mobilier très d.** no two pieces of their furniture are alike *or* the same

disparité [disparite] **NF** disparity

disparition [disparisjɔ̃] **NF 1** *(départ, absence)* disappearance; **remarquer la d. de qch** to notice that sth has disappeared; **j'ai remarqué la d. de ma carte de crédit deux jours plus tard** I first missed my credit card two days later; **sa d. date de six mois** he disappeared *or* vanished six months ago, he has been missing for six months; *Cin, TV* **d. en fondu** fade **2** *(mort)* death; **depuis la d. de son mari** since the death of her husband, since her husband died; **la d. des dinosaures ne s'est pas faite en un jour** dinosaurs did not disappear *or* vanish *or* die out overnight

disparu, -ue [dispary] **ADJ 1** *Mil* missing (in action); **être porté d.** to be reported missing; **marin d. en mer** sailor lost at sea **2** *(race, espèce etc)* extinct; *(monde, époque etc)* vanished, bygone **3** *(invisible)* **la cicatrice une fois disparue** once the scar has/ had disappeared; **aussitôt le soleil d., elle rentra** she went home as soon as the sun had disappeared
  N 1 *(défunt)* deceased; **nos chers disparus** our dear departed **2** *Mil* missing soldier *(believed dead)*, *Am* MIA (= missing in action)

dispatcher¹ [dispatʃœr] **NM** dispatcher

dispatcher² [dispatʃe] **VT** to dispatch

dispatching [dispatʃiŋ] **NM** dispatching; *Journ* assignment list

dispendieusement [dispɑ̃djøzmɑ̃] **ADV** *Litt* expensively

dispendieux, -ieuse [dispɑ̃djø, -jøz] **ADJ** *Litt (goûts, procédure etc)* expensive

dispensaire [dispɑ̃sɛr] **NM** free clinic, free health centre

dispensateur, -trice [dispɑ̃satœr, -tris] **N** *(de charité, justice etc)* dispenser

dispense [dispɑ̃s] **NF 1** *(du service militaire etc)* exemption; *Rel* dispensation; **d. d'âge** age dispensation; **une d. d'âge peut être accordée dans les cas où …** the age limit may be waived in cases where … **2** *(certificat)* (certificate of) exemption

dispenser [dispɑ̃se] **VT 1 d. qn de (faire) qch** to excuse *or* exempt sb from (doing) sth; **d. qn du service militaire** to exempt sb from military service; **dispensez-moi de ce voyage** spare me this journey; **se faire d. de sport** to be excused *or* let off sport, to get off sport; *Rel* **d. qn d'un vœu** to release sb from a vow; **je vous dispense de vos commentaires** you can keep your remarks to yourself **2** *(charité, faveurs etc)* to dispense, to distribute; *Méd* **d. des soins** to dispense care

VPR se dispenser se d. de (faire) qch to get out of (doing) sth; **on peut s'en d.** we can do without it; *Hum* **il se dispense toujours de dire bonjour** he never says hello; **c'est un élève qui peut se d. de travailler en français** he can afford not to work at his French

dispersal [dispersal] NM *Aviat* apron

dispersant [dispersɑ̃] NM *Chimie* dispersant, dispersal agent

dispersé [disperse] ADJ *(feuilles, famille etc)* scattered, dispersed; *(travail etc)* lacking in order, disorganized

disperser [disperse] VT *(foule, famille)* to disperse, to scatter, to break up; *(feuilles)* to disperse, to scatter, to spread (far and wide); **une armée** to rout an army; *Fig* **d. son attention sur plusieurs choses** to divide one's attention among several things

VPR se disperser *(de nuages)* to disperse, to break up; *(de foule, de famille)* to disperse, to scatter, to break up; *Fig* **tu as tendance à trop te d.** you tend to spread yourself too thin(ly)

dispersion [dispersjɔ̃] NF 1 *(des gens, des feuilles)* scattering, dispersal; *(de la foule, des nuages)* dispersal, breaking up; *(de l'armée)* rout; *Fig* **la d. d'un esprit** an unfocused mind 2 *Opt (de la lumière)* dispersion, decomposition 3 *Suisse (peinture)* emulsion (paint)

disponibilité [dispɔnibilite] NF *(de personne, de sièges, de capital etc)* availability; **il a une grande d. d'esprit** he has a very receptive mind; *Mil* **la d.** the reserve; **mettre qn en d.** *Ind (en chômage)* to lay sb off; *Mil* to release sb temporarily from duty; **prendre une d.** to take a sabbatical, to take leave of absence; **demander une mise en d.** to ask for (a) leave of absence; *Com* **d. numérique** stock holding distribution; *Fin* **disponibilités** available funds, liquid assets; **disponibilités monétaires** money supply; **disponibilités du stock** items available in stock

disponible [dispɔnibl] ADJ available; *(actif)* liquid; **places disponibles** vacant *or* unoccupied seats; **il n'y avait plus un siège d.** there weren't any seats left, no seats were available; **êtes-vous d. ce soir?** are you free tonight?; *Mil* **officier d.** unattached officer, half-pay officer

NM 1 *Com* **marché du d.** spot market 2 *Fin* **le d.** liquid assets 3 *Mil* reservist

dispos [dispo] ADJ fit and well, in good form; **frais et d.** raring to go, bright-eyed and bushy-tailed; **esprit d.** alert mind; **je n'ai pas l'esprit d. aujourd'hui** I don't feel very alert today

disposé [dispoze] ADJ 1 *(personne)* **être bien/mal d.** to be in a good/bad mood; **être bien d. pour** *ou* **envers qn** to be well disposed towards sb; **être** *ou* **se sentir d. à faire qch** to feel disposed *or* willing *or* in the mood to do sth; **je suis tout d. à pardonner** I am quite willing *or* fully prepared to forgive 2 *(arrangé)* arranged, set out; **fleurs disposées avec goût** tastefully arranged flowers

disposer [dispoze] VT 1 *(objets)* to set out, to arrange; *(table)* to lay, to set; **il faudra d. le salon autrement** the living room will have to be rearranged; **comment vas-tu d. les invités?** what are the seating arrangements for the guests? 2 **d. qn à (faire) qch** to dispose *or* incline sb to (do) sth

VI 1 **d. de qn/qch** to have sb/sth at one's disposal; **disposez de moi** I am at your service; **de combien de temps disposons-nous?** how much time do we have?; **les renseignements dont je dispose** the information at my disposal; **vous pouvez en d.** you may use it; **d. de ses biens en faveur de qn** to dispose of *or* make over one's property to sb; **le droit des peuples à d. d'eux-mêmes** the right of peo-

ple to self-determination 2 *Fml (partir)* **vous pouvez d.** that will be all, you may go 3 *(décider)* *Prov* **l'homme propose, Dieu dispose** man proposes, God disposes

VPR se disposer se d. à faire qch to get ready to do sth; **se d. à partir** to get ready to leave

Il faut noter que le verbe anglais **to dispose of** est un faux ami. Il signifie **se débarrasser de**.

dispositif [dispozitif] NM 1 *Tech* device; **d. de commande/de manœuvre** driving/controlling gear *or* mechanism; **d. de sûreté** safety device 2 *(ensemble de moyens)* system, machinery; *Mil* plan of action; *(des troupes dans une bataille etc)* disposition, deployment; **d. d'attaque** attack force; **d. de défense** defence system; **un important d. policier sera mis en place** there will be a large police presence; **il s'agit d'un d. gouvernemental pour favoriser l'emploi des jeunes** it's a government plan to stimulate youth employment

▸▸ *Ordinat* **d. d'alimentation** power unit; *(pour papier)* sheet feed; **d. d'alimentation feuille à feuille** *(d'une imprimante)* cut sheet feed, stacker; **d. d'alimentation papier** *(d'une imprimante)* sheet feed, paper feed; *Aut* **d. antidémarrage** engine immobilizer; *Aut* **d. d'avance centrifuge** centrifugal advance mechanism; *TV etc* **d. de balayage** scanner; *TV etc* **d. de colorisation** colourizer; **d. de coupure** cut-out (device); **d. d'entraînement à traction** *(d'une imprimante)* tractor feed; *Ordinat* **d. externe** external device; *Ordinat* **d. de pointage à boule** trackball; *Aut* **d. de préchauffage** pre-heater; *Tél* **d. de redirection d'appel** call-forwarding device; *Ordinat* **d. de sortie** output device; *Ordinat* **d. de stockage** storage device; *Aut* **d. de verrouillage 'sécurité enfant'** child lock; *Ordinat* **d. de visualisation** display unit

disposition [dispozisjɔ̃] NF 1 *(arrangement)* *(d'une maison, d'un jardin etc)* layout; **réfléchir à la d. des sièges** to think about the seating plan; **d. du terrain** lie of the land; **comment est la d. des lieux?** what's the layout of the place?; *Ordinat* **d. de texte/de clavier** text/keyboard layout

2 *(disponibilité)* disposal; **avoir la libre d. de son bien** to be free to dispose of one's property; **libre d. de soi-même** self-determination; **d. fiscale** tax provision; *Fin* **d. à vue** sight clause; **avoir qch à sa d.** to have sth at one's disposal; **mettre qch à la d. de qn** to put *or* place sth at sb's disposal, to make sth available to sb; **je suis à votre (entière) d.** I am at your disposal *or* (entirely) at your service

3 *(humeur)* **être dans de bonnes/mauvaises dispositions** to be in a good/bad mood; **être dans de bonnes dispositions à l'égard de qn** to be favourably disposed towards sb; **choisis un jour où il sera dans les meilleures dispositions pour t'écouter/te voir** choose a day when he'll be most likely to give you a favourable hearing/see you; **dans quelles dispositions est-il?** what kind of mood is he in?; **être en bonne d. pour faire qch** to be disposed *or* inclined *or* in the mood to do sth

4 *(dons)* **avoir des dispositions pour qch** to have a natural ability *or* an aptitude for sth; **dispositions naturelles pour la musique** aptitude *or* natural bent for music; **cet enfant a des dispositions** he is a (naturally) gifted child

5 *(tendance)* tendency, predisposition; **avoir une d. au rhumatisme** to have a tendency *or* to be predisposed to rheumatism; **d. à pleurer souvent** tendency to cry a lot

6 **dispositions** *(préparatifs)* arrangements; **prendre des dispositions pour faire qch** to

make the necessary arrangements to do sth; **prends tes dispositions pour être libre ce jour-là** make arrangements *or* arrange to be free that day; **vous n'avez qu'à prendre vos dispositions** you'll just have to make arrangements

7 *Jur* **dispositions** *(d'un testament)* provisions, conditions; *(d'une loi)* clauses, provisions, conditions; **les dispositions contenues dans l'article 34** the provisions of article 34

disproportion [disprɔpɔrsjɔ̃] NF lack of proportion, disproportion (**entre** between)

disproportionné [disprɔpɔrsjɔne] ADJ out of proportion, disproportionate (**par rapport à, avec** to)

dispute [dispyt] NF 1 *(querelle)* dispute, quarrel, *Fml* altercation; **c'est un sujet de d. entre eux** it is a subject of dispute *or* bone of contention between them 2 *Arch (débat)* debate; **sujet en d.** subject under discussion

disputé [dispyte] ADJ **une question très disputée** a very controversial *or* hotly disputed matter; **un match très d.** a very hard-fought match; **ce poste sera très d.** there will be a lot of competition for the position; **c'est un héritage d. par tous les membres de la famille** the entire family is quarrelling over the inheritance

disputer [dispyte] VT 1 *(contester)* **d. qch à qn** to contend with sb for sth; *Fml* **je ne peux imaginer palais qui puisse le d. en splendeur à celui-ci** I cannot imagine a palace to rival this one in splendour 2 *Sport* **d. un match** to play a match; **d. une course (sur mille mètres)** to run a (thousand-metre) race; *Fig* **d. le terrain** to fight every inch of the way 3 *Fam* **d. qn** to tick *or* tell sb off; **il s'est fait d. par son père** he got ticked off *or* told off by his father, he got a ticking off *or* telling off from his father

VI 1 *(discuter)* to quarrel, to argue (**avec** with); **d. d'un sujet avec qn** to quarrel *or* argue with sb about *or* over a subject 2 *Fml (rivaliser)* **d. de zèle/d'élégance avec qn** to vie with sb in zeal/elegance

VPR se disputer 1 *(se quereller)* to quarrel, to argue, to wrangle (**pour** over, about; **avec** with) 2 *(se battre pour)* to fight for; **deux chiens qui se disputent un os** two dogs fighting over a bone; **ils se disputent à qui aura le plus gros morceau** they are arguing about who should get the biggest piece 3 *(se jouer)* **le match se disputera à Wimbledon** the match will be played *or* will take place at Wimbledon; **la finale devrait se d. entre les USA et l'Australie** the final is expected to be between the USA and Australia

disquaire [diskɛr] N record dealer; **en vente chez tous les disquaires** on sale in all record shops

disqualification [diskalifikasjɔ̃] NF *Sport* disqualification

disqualifier [diskalifje] *(impf, pr sub* n. **disqualifiions**, v. **disqualifiiez**) VT 1 *Sport* to disqualify 2 *Litt (discréditer)* to discredit

VPR se disqualifier *Litt* to disgrace oneself

disque [disk] NM 1 disc, *Am* disk; *Rail* disc signal; *Aut* **frein à d.** disc brake; **appareil photo à disques** disc camera 2 *Mus* record, disc; **mettre un d.** to play a record; *Fig Fam* **changer de d.** to change the record *or* subject 3 *Ordinat* disk; **station de travail sans d.** diskless workstation 4 *Sport* discus; **lanceur de d.** discus thrower; **arriver deuxième au lancer de d.** to come second in the discus

▸▸ *Ordinat* **d. amovible** removable disk; **d. audionumérique** compact disc; *Ordinat* **d. cible** target disk; **d. compact** compact disc, CD; **d. compact interactif** interactive CD, CD-I; **d. compact vidéo** video compact disc; *Ordinat* **d. de démarrage** boot disk; **d. de dé-**

monstration demo (record); *Ordinat* **d. de destination** destination disk; *Ordinat* **d. dur** hard disk; *Ordinat* **d. dur externe** external hard disk; *Aut* **d. d'embrayage** clutch plate *or* disc; *Ordinat* **d. fixe** fixed disk; *Anat* **d. intervertébral** (intervertebral) disc; **d. laser** laser disc; **d. magnétique** magnetic disk; *Ordinat* **d. magnéto-optique** optical disk, optomagnetic disk; **d. maître** master disk; **d. microsillon** long-playing record, LP; *Ordinat* **d. optique** optical disk; *Ordinat* **d. optique compact** CD-ROM; *Ordinat* **d. souple** floppy disk; *Ordinat* **d. source** source disk; *Admin, Aut* **d. de stationnement** parking disc; *Ordinat* **d. système** system disk; **d. vidéo** videodisc; **d. vidéo numérique** digital versatile disk, digital video disk; **d. en vinyle** vinyl disc

disquette [disket] NF *Ordinat* diskette, disk; *Fam* floppy (disk); **sur d.** on diskette, *Fam* on floppy; **d. de copie** copy disk; **d. de démarrage** boot disk, start-up disk; **d. de démonstration,** *Fam* **d. démo** demo disk; **d. de destination** destination disk; **d. de diagnostic** diagnostic disk; **d. de distribution** master disk; **d. (à) double densité** double density disk; **d. haute densité** high-density disk; **d. d'installation** installation disk, installer; **d. magnétique** magnetic disk, **d. optique** optical disk, floptical disk; **d. d'origine** source disk; **d. programme** program disk; **d. (à) simple densité** single density disk; **d. source** source disk; **d. système** system disk, systems disk; **d. de travail** working disk, work disk; **d. vierge** blank unformatted disk

disruptif, -ive [disryptif, -iv] ADJ *(force, décharge électrique etc)* disruptive

dissection [diseksjɔ̃] NF *(d'un corps, d'une œuvre littéraire etc)* dissection

dissemblable [disɑ̃blabl] ADJ dissimilar, unlike; **d. à qch** unlike sth, different from *or Am* than sth

dissemblance [disɑ̃blɑ̃s] NF dissimilarity, difference (**entre** between)

dissémination [diseminasjɔ̃] NF *(de graines, de peuple, d'amis etc)* scattering; *(de germes)* spreading; *Mil (de troupes)* deployment; *(d'idées)* spread, dissemination; *(de nouvelles)* spread; **la d. de notre famille date de deux siècles** our family has been scattered for two centuries; **depuis la d. de mon groupe d'amis** since my group of friends scattered *or* broke up; **le territoire est si étendu que cela favorise la d. des entreprises** the vastness of the area means that companies tend to be spread rather thinly

disséminer [disemine] VT *(graines, groupe d'amis, peuple etc)* to scatter; *(germes)* to spread; *Mil (troupes)* to deploy; *(idées)* to spread, to disseminate; *(nouvelles)* to spread; **les écoles sont très disséminées** the schools are very thin on the ground
 VPR **se disséminer** *(de personnes)* to scatter; *(de germes, idées)* to spread

dissension [disɑ̃sjɔ̃] NF dissension, discord

dissentiment [disɑ̃timɑ̃] NM disagreement

disséquer [diseke] VT (**je dissèque; je disséquerai**) *(cadavre, œuvre littéraire etc)* to dissect

dissert [disert] NF *Fam (abrév* **dissertation***)* essay

dissertation [disertasjɔ̃] NF **1** *Scol* essay **2** *Vieilli (étude)* dissertation (**sur** (up)on)

disserter [diserte] VI **1 d. sur un sujet** to discourse on a subject **2** *Péj (parler beaucoup)* to talk at length, *Fam* to hold forth; **d. pendant des heures** to hold forth for hours

dissidence [disidɑ̃s] NF *Rel, Pol* dissidence, dissent; **la d.** *(dissidents)* the dissidents, the dissident movement

dissident, -ente [disidɑ̃, -ɑ̃t] ADJ *Pol* dissident; *Rel* dissenting
 N *Pol* dissident; *Rel* dissenter, nonconformist

dissimilation [disimilasjɔ̃] NF *Ling* dissimilation

dissimilitude [disimilityd] NF dissimilarity

dissimulateur, -trice [disimylatœr, -tris] ADJ dissembling
 N dissembler, deceiver

dissimulation [disimylasjɔ̃] NF **1** *(hypocrisie)* dissembling, deceit; **agir avec d.** to act in an underhand way **2** *(de la vérité, de ses sentiments)* concealment; *(d'une faute)* covering up; *Jur* **d. d'actif** (fraudulent) concealment of assets

dissimulé [disimyle] ADJ **1** *(caché) (sentiments, défauts, rides etc)* hidden, concealed; **avec un plaisir non d.** with unconcealed delight **2** *(secret) (homme, caractère)* secretive

dissimuler [disimyle] VT *(sentiments, vérité)* to hide, to conceal; *(faute)* to cover up; **d. qch à qn** to hide sth *or* keep sth (back) from sb; **il se dissimule la vérité** he's deceiving himself; **le rideau dissimule le siège des W.-C.** the curtain screens off the lavatory; **d. ses revenus** to conceal one's income; **je ne (vous) dissimule pas que je souhaite partir** I cannot hide the fact that I want to leave
 VPR **se dissimuler** to be hidden, to hide; **sa jalousie ne peut se d.** he cannot hide his jealousy; **parmi tant de qualités se dissimule un défaut** a weakness lies hidden *or* lurks among so many qualities

dissipateur, -trice [disipatœr, -tris] N spendthrift, squanderer, waster
 ADJ *(personne)* spendthrift; *(gestion)* wasteful

dissipation [disipasjɔ̃] NF **1** *(d'argent)* squandering, wasting; *(de temps, d'énergie)* wasting; *(de nuages)* dispersal; *(de craintes, soupçons)* dispelling; *(de malentendu)* clearing up; **après d. des brouillards matinaux** after the morning mist lifts/lifted *or* clears/cleared; **d. calorique** heat dissipation **2** *(débauche)* dissipation, dissolute living; **une vie de d.** a dissolute life, a life of dissipation **3** *(à l'école)* inattentiveness, lack of attention

dissipé [disipe] ADJ **1** *(débauché)* dissipated, dissolute; **mener une vie dissipée** to lead a riotous life **2** *Scol (élève)* inattentive

dissiper [disipe] VT **1** *(argent)* to squander, to waste; *(temps, énergie)* to waste; *(nuages)* to disperse, to scatter, to dispel; *(brouillard)* to disperse, to clear away, to dispel; *(malentendu)* to clear up; *(craintes, soupçons)* to dispel **2** *(distraire)* to distract; **il se laisse facilement d.** he is easily distracted
 VPR **se dissiper 1** *(de soupçons, malentendu)* to vanish, to disappear; **le brouillard se dissipe** the fog is lifting *or* clearing (away); **ses doutes se sont dissipés** his doubts faded **2** *(se laisser distraire) (à l'école etc)* to be inattentive; **il se dissipe vite** his attention soon wanders

dissociable [disɔsjabl] ADJ separable

dissociation [disɔsjasjɔ̃] NF separation; *Chimie* decomposition, dissociation; **la d. nécessaire entre la vie privée et la vie professionnelle** the need to keep one's private life separate from one's work

dissocier [disɔsje] VT *(idées etc)* to separate; *Chimie (composé)* to dissociate
 VPR **se dissocier de d. d'un groupe** to dissociate oneself from a group

dissolu [disɔly] ADJ *(personne, vie)* dissolute

dissolubilité [disɔlybilite] NF dissolubility

dissoluble [disɔlybl] ADJ **1** *Pol (assemblée etc)* which can be dissolved, dissoluble **2** *Arch (substance)* soluble

dissolution [disɔlysjɔ̃] NF **1** *(d'un parlement, d'un mariage)* dissolution; *(d'un contrat)* dissolution, termination **2** *Chimie (d'une substance dans un liquide)* dissolving; *(colle)* rubber solution **3** *(d'un corps)* decomposition; *(d'une matière)* decomposition, breakdown **4** *Litt (débauche)* dissoluteness, licentiousness, profligacy

dissolvant [disɔlvɑ̃] ADJ **1** *(qui dissout)* solvent **2** *Vieilli (climat)* debilitating; *(doctrine)* corrupt
 NM solvent; *(pour ongles)* nail varnish remover

dissonance [disɔnɑ̃s] NF *Mus* discord; *Fig* clash

dissonant [disɔnɑ̃] ADJ *Mus* dissonant, discordant; *Fig* clashing

dissoudre [disudr] *(prp* **dissolvant;** *pp* **dissous,** *f* **dissoute;** *pr ind* **je dissous, il dissout, n. dissolvons;** *impf* **je dissolvais;** *p hist & p sub are lacking; fu* **je dissoudrai**) VT **1** *(substance)* to dissolve **2** *(parlement, mariage)* to dissolve; *(association)* to dissolve, to break (up); *(entreprise)* to wind up
 VPR **se dissoudre** to dissolve; **se d. dans l'eau** to dissolve in water; *Fig* **colère qui se dissout en larmes** anger that dissolves into tears

dissuader [disɥade] VT **d. qn de faire qch** to dissuade sb from doing sth, to talk sb out of doing sth; **d. qn de partir** to persuade sb not to leave, to dissuade sb from leaving, to talk sb out of leaving

dissuasif, -ive [disɥazif, -iv] ADJ dissuasive; **ils pratiquent vraiment des prix dissuasifs** their prices are enough to put you off

dissuasion [disɥazjɔ̃] NF dissuasion (**de** from); *Mktg* demarketing; **d. nucléaire** nuclear deterrence; *Mil, Pol* **force de d.** deterrent

dissyllabe [disilab] ADJ di(s)syllabic
 NM di(s)syllable

dissyllabique [disilabik] ADJ di(s)syllabic

dissymétrie [disimetri] NF asymmetry

dissymétrique [disimetrik] ADJ asymmetric(al)

distance [distɑ̃s] NF SEE GRAMMAR B59 distance; **une faible d.** a short way *or* distance; **il y a une d. de cinq km entre ces deux points** there is a distance of five km between these two points, these two points are five km apart; **on ne voyait rien à cette d.** you couldn't see anything at that distance; **suivre qn à d./à peu de d.** to follow sb at a distance/at a short distance; **à quelle d. sommes-nous de la ville?** how far are we from the town?; **à une courte d.** a short distance away (**de** from), within easy reach (**de** of); **c'est à une grande d.** it's a long way away *or* off (**de** from); *Mil etc* **à petite** *ou* **faible d.** at short range; *Ordinat etc* **à d.** remote; *Tech* **commande à d.** remote control; **à d.** *(juger, influencer qn)* at *or* from a distance; **tenir qn à d.** to keep sb at a distance; **il me tient à d. de tous les projets intéressants** he keeps me away from all the interesting projects; **conserver** *ou* **garder ses distances, se tenir à d.** to keep at a distance, to remain aloof; *Fig* **il conserve** *ou* **garde ses distances par rapport à la gauche/aux intellectuels/à sa famille** he keeps at a distance *or* holds himself aloof from the left/intellectuals/his family; **se tenir à une d. respectueuse** to remain at a respectful distance; **je vous prie de vous tenir à une d. respectueuse de ma fille** please keep away from my daughter; **de d. en d.** at intervals; **prendre ses distances** *Mil* to dress; *Gym* to space out; *Fig* **prendre de la d.** to stand back (**par rapport à** from); *Sp, Fig* **tenir la d.** to go the distance, to stay *or* last the course
 ►► *Aut* **d. d'arrêt** stopping distance; *Opt* **d.**

focale focal distance, focal length; **d. de freinage** braking distance; *Phot* **d. hyperfocale** hyperfocal distance; *Phot* **d. de mise au point minimale** minimum focusing distance, MFD; *Aut* **d. de sécurité** thinking distance; **d. tarifaire** *(dans un taxi)* chargeable distance

distancement [distɑ̃smɑ̃] **NM** *(de cheval)* disqualification

distancer [distɑ̃se] **VT** (je **distançai(s); n. distançons**) **1** *Sp, Fig (devancer)* to outdistance, to outrun, to outstrip; **se laisser d.** to drop away, to fall *or* lag behind; **il se laisse d. par les autres** he is letting the others outdistance him *or* pull ahead; **le parti socialiste distance la droite de deux points** the socialists are two points ahead of the conservatives; **ce périodique distance tous les autres par sa qualité** this periodical surpasses all the others in quality **2** *(disqualifier) (cheval)* to disqualify

distanciation [distɑ̃sjasjɔ̃] **NF** detachment; *Théâtre* **l'effet de d.** the alienation effect

distancier (se) [sədistɑ̃sje] **VPR se d. de qn/qch** to distance oneself from sb/sth

distant [distɑ̃] **ADJ 1** *(éloigné)* distant; *(PC, modem)* remote; **nos deux maisons sont distantes d'un kilomètre l'une de l'autre** our two houses are a kilometre apart **2** *Fig (froid)* distant, standoffish, aloof; **elle est très distante avec moi** she's being very distant towards me

distendre [distɑ̃dr] **VT** *(estomac)* to distend; *(muscle)* to strain, to pull; *(corde, fil etc)* to stretch to breaking point; *Fig* **le temps a distendu notre amitié** we've drifted apart with time

VPR se distendre *(se relâcher) (d'une corde, d'un élastique, d'un vêtement, de la peau)* to stretch; *(de l'estomac)* to become distended, to swell; **il s'est distendu un muscle** he has pulled *or* strained a muscle; *Fig* **notre relation se distend** we're drifting apart

distension [distɑ̃sjɔ̃] **NF** *(de l'estomac)* distension; *(d'un muscle)* straining, pulling; *(d'une corde, d'un fil etc)* slackening, loosening; *(de la peau, d'un élastique)* stretching

distillat [distila] **NM** *Chimie* distillate

distillateur [distilatœr] **NM** distiller

distillation [distilasjɔ̃] **NF** *(du whisky), Pétr* distillation, distilling; *Pétr* **d. fractionnée** fractional distillation

distiller [distile] **VT 1** *(alcool, pétrole etc)* to distil, *Am* to distill; *Litt (ses pensées)* to refine; **eau distillée** distilled water **2** *(poison)* to distil, to exude; *Fig (colère, ennui etc)* to exude

VI *Chimie* to distil, to exude (**de** from)

distillerie [distilri] **NF** *(lieu)* distillery; *(procédé)* distilling

distinct [distɛ̃(kt)] **ADJ 1** *(séparé)* distinct, separate; **une organisation distincte de la nôtre** an organization that is distinct from ours, a different organization from ours; **mon poste est d. du sien en cela que je …** my job differs from his in that I … **2** *(clair) (silhouette, voix etc)* distinct, clear

distinctement [distɛ̃ktəmɑ̃] **ADV** distinctly, clearly

distinctif, -ive [distɛ̃ktif, -iv] **ADJ** *(signe, trait etc)* distinctive, characteristic, distinguishing

distinction [distɛ̃ksjɔ̃] **NF 1** *(différence)* distinction; **faire une d. entre deux choses** to make a distinction *or* differentiate *or* distinguish between two things; **sans d.** without distinction, indiscriminately; **sans d. de race ou de couleur** irrespective *or* regardless of race or colour; **d. sociale** social *or* class distinction **2** *(dignité)* distinction, honour, *Am* honor; *(décoration)* decoration **3** *(éminence)*

distinction, eminence; **un personnage de haute d.** a highly distinguished person **4** *(élégance)* air of distinction, elegance; **avoir de la d.** to be distinguished

distinguable [distɛ̃gabl] **ADJ** distinguishable

distingué [distɛ̃ge] **ADJ 1** *(remarqué) (écrivain, politicien etc)* distinguished, eminent, noted **2** *(élégant) (personne, maintien)* distinguished; *(goût)* refined; *(vêtement)* smart; **avoir un air d.** to look distinguished **3 je vous prie d'agréer l'expression de mes sentiments distingués** *(dans une lettre)* Yours sincerely

distinguer [distɛ̃ge] **VT 1** *(particulariser)* to distinguish, to mark, to characterize; **sa mise soignée le distinguait de la foule** his impeccable appearance made him stand out from *or* set him apart from the crowd **2** *(pour honorer)* to honour, *Am* to honor; **il a été distingué pour son premier roman** he received an award for his first novel **3** *(différencier)* to distinguish; **il a appris à d. les champignons** he has learnt how to tell the various kinds of mushroom apart *or* to distinguish between the various kinds of mushroom; **d. qch de qch** *ou* **d'avec qch** to distinguish *or* tell sth from sth; **on peut à peine les d. l'un de l'autre** you can hardly tell them apart; **à quoi les distingues-tu?** how do you tell them apart? **4** *(discerner)* to discern, to perceive; **je ne peux pas d. ses traits** I cannot make out his features; **je l'ai distinguée dans la foule** I spotted her in the crowd; **d. une nuance d'amertume dans la voix de qn** to detect a trace of bitterness in sb's voice

VPR se distinguer 1 *(s'illustrer)* to distinguish oneself (**par** by); **il s'est surtout distingué par ses articles en neurobiologie** he was particularly noted for his articles on neurobiology; **on ne peut vraiment pas dire qu'il se distingue par son intelligence** he hardly stands out as being very intelligent; **il ne se distingue ni par son physique ni par ses qualités intellectuelles** neither his physical nor his intellectual qualities are anything out of the ordinary **2** *(se différencier) (dans une foule etc)* to be noticeable *or* conspicuous, to stand out; **se d. des autres** to be distinguishable from others (**par** by); **il se distingue de son frère par son grand nez** you can tell him from his brother by his big nose; **leur maison se distingue des autres à cause de ses volets bleus** their house stands out from the others because of its blue shutters; **comment la reine se distingue-t-elle des autres abeilles?** in what way does the queen differ from the other bees? **3** *(être perçu)* **au loin se distinguait la côte** the coastline could be seen in the distance

distinguo [distɛ̃go] **NM** difference; **il y a un d. à faire entre l'élégance et le raffinement** elegance and refinement are not quite the same thing *or* are not one and the same; **faire des distinguos entre les mots** to bring out the shades of meaning between words

distique [distik] **NM 1** *(vers français)* couplet **2** *Antiq* distich

distordre [distɔrdr] **VT** *(traits, bouche)* to distort

distorsion [distɔrsjɔ̃] **NF** *(d'un visage, d'une image optique, d'une impulsion électrique etc)* distortion; *(entre deux facteurs, deux salaires)* imbalance; *Radio* **d. de phase** phase distortion; *Radio etc* **d. de crête** peak distortion; *Radio etc* **d. de fréquence** frequency distortion; *Radio etc* **d. harmonique** harmonic distortion; *TV etc* **d. de l'image** image distortion; *TV* **d. géométrique** geometric distortion

distraction [distraksjɔ̃] **NF 1** *(inattention)*

absentmindedness, lack of attention, abstraction; **par d.** inadvertently, absentmindedly; **avoir des moments de d.** to have moments of absentmindedness; **c'est une d. que nous ne pouvons te pardonner** we cannot forgive such absentmindedness on your part **2** *(loisir)* amusement, recreation; **distractions** entertainment; **ce bled manque de d.** there's nothing to do around here; **la lecture et le cinéma sont mes distractions préférées** reading and going to the cinema are my favourite forms of recreation *or* what I like doing best in my spare time; **depuis que ses enfants sont partis, elle n'a plus aucune d.** she's got nothing to occupy her mind now that her children have left home; **distractions en vol** in-flight entertainment

distraire [distrɛr] *(conj like* **traire**) **VT 1** *(l'attention de qn)* to distract, to divert; **d. qn de ses travaux** to distract sb from his/her work **2** *(divertir)* to divert, to entertain, to amuse; **j'aime bien que tu viennes me voir, ça me distrait** I like you to visit me, it gives me something else to think about

VPR se distraire to amuse oneself; **elle a besoin de se d.** she needs to relax a bit *or* to enjoy herself

distrait [distrɛ] **ADJ** absentminded; **air d.** absentminded *or* abstracted *or* distracted look; **d'une oreille distraite** with only half an ear; **vous êtes d.** you're not paying attention; **élève d.** inattentive pupil

> Il faut noter que l'adjectif anglais **distracted** est un faux ami. Il signifie **préoccupé**.

distraitement [distrɛtmɑ̃] **ADV** absentmindedly, abstractedly

distrayant [distrejɑ̃] **ADJ** *(livre, spectacle)* diverting, entertaining

distribanque [distribɑ̃k] **NF** cash dispenser

distribuer [distribɥe] **VT 1** *(donner) (prix, bonbons etc)* to distribute, to hand out; *(provisions, vivres etc)* to distribute, to issue; *(ordres)* to hand out, to give out; *(cartes)* to deal; *(du facteur)* to deliver; **il a commencé à d. des coups** he started to lash out with his fists; **d. des sourires à tout le monde** to bestow smiles on everybody **2** *(répartir)* **d. les fleurs en plusieurs classes** to classify flowers; *Cin, Théâtre* **d. les rôles** to cast the parts (in a/the play), to cast a/the play; **d. un dividende** to pay a dividend; **appartement bien/mal distribué** well/badly laid out flat; **d. son temps de la façon la plus logique** to allocate *or* apportion one's time in the most logical fashion possible; **conduites qui distribuent l'eau dans la ville** pipes that supply water to the city; **expliquez de quelle manière le sang est distribué dans notre corps** explain how blood circulates through our body **3** *(commercialiser) (produit, film, livres etc)* to distribute

distributaire [distribytɛr] **N** *Jur* distributee

distributeur, -trice [distribytœr, -tris] **N** *Com* distributor, dealer

NM 1 *Cin* (film) distributor **2** *Tech, Aut* distributor

▸▸ **d. agréé** authorized dealer, authorized distributor; **d. automatique** automatic vending machine, slot machine; **d. (automatique) de billets** cashpoint, *Am* ATM; *Rail etc* ticket machine; **d. (automatique) de boissons** drinks machine, drinks dispenser, drinks vending machine; **d. automatique de titres de transport** automatic ticket dispenser; **d. de cigarettes** cigarette machine; *Élec* **d. de courant** distributor; **d. d'engrais** fertilizer spreader; **d. de presse** press distributor; *Tech* **d. de vapeur** steam distributor *or* regulator, steam valve

distributif, -ive [distribytif, -iv] ADJ *Gram (terme, pronom etc)* distributive

distribution [distribysjɔ̃] NF **1** *(don)* distribution; *(de fonctions, de tâches etc)* allocation, allotment; *(de rations, vivres)* issue; *(de lettres, marchandises)* delivery; *Scol* **d. des prix** prizegiving, speech day; **il va y avoir une d. gratuite de saucissons au rayon charcuterie** sausages will be given away at the meat counter **2** *(répartition)* *(d'une maison, d'un appartement)* layout; *Aut* distribution; *Bot* **d. des plantes** classification of plants; *Écon* **d. des richesses** distribution of wealth; *Théâtre* **d. des rôles** *(choix)* casting; *(liste)* cast; **une brillante d.** an all-star cast; *Théâtre, Cin* **d. par ordre d'entrée en scène** characters *or* cast in order of appearance; **d. des eaux** water supply; **d. d'une maladie selon les classes d'âge** incidence of a disease by age group; **d. d'un bénéfice** distribution of profits; **d. de dividende** payment of a/the dividend; **d. par câble** cable distribution **3** *Com* distribution; **réseau de d.** distribution network; **droits de d.** distribution rights; **grande d.** large-scale distribution; **d. à flux tendus** just-in-time distribution; **d. de masse** mass distribution; **d. exclusive** exclusive distribution; **d. numérique** stock holding distribution

distributionnel, -elle [distribysjɔnɛl] ADJ *Ling (analyse, linguistique)* distributive

distributivement [distribytivmɑ̃] ADV distributively

distributivité [distribytivite] NF *Math* distributive law

district [distrikt] NM district, region

dit [di] ADJ **1** *(décidé)* settled, fixed; **à l'heure dite** *(à l'heure convenue)* at the appointed *or* agreed time; *(à l'heure fixée)* at the time indicated; **au jour d.** on the appointed *or* agreed day **2** *(appelé)* called; **la zone dite tempérée** the temperate zone as it is called ▸ NM *Littér* traditional story *(usually in verse)*; **le d. des trois larrons** the story of the three thieves

dithyrambe [ditirɑ̃b] NM *(panégyrique)* eulogy; *Littér* dithyramb; **se lancer dans un d. sur qch** to go into raptures about sth

dithyrambique [ditirɑ̃bik] ADJ *(mots etc)* eulogistic; *Littér* dithyrambic

dito [dito] ADV ditto

diurèse [djyrez] NF *Méd* diuresis

diurétique [djyretik] ADJ, NM *Méd* diuretic

diurne [djyrn] ADJ *Bot, Zool* diurnal

diva [diva] NF **1** *Mus* diva **2** *(célébrité)* star

divagation [divagasjɔ̃] NF **1** *(propos)* divagations d'un fou ravings *or* ramblings of a madman **2** *(de rivière)* shifting from its course; *Jur (du bétail etc)* straying

divaguer [divage] VI **1** *(dans un discours)* to digress, to stray from the point; **malade qui divague** patient whose mind is wandering *or* who is rambling; **vous divaguez!** you're raving! **2** *(de rivière)* to shift its course; *Jur (de bétail etc)* to stray

divan [divɑ̃] NM **1** *(meuble)* divan, couch; **d.-lit** divan (bed) **2** *Hist* divan

divergence [divɛrʒɑ̃s] NF *(de lignes, de rayons etc)* divergence; *(d'opinions)* difference

divergent [divɛrʒɑ̃] ADJ *(lignes)* divergent; *(opinions)* differing, different

diverger [divɛrʒe] VI *(il divergea(it); n. divergeons)* *(de lignes, de rayons)* to diverge *(de* from); *(d'opinion)* to differ, to diverge *(de* from); **nos opinions divergent sur certains points** our opinions differ on certain points

divers [divɛr] ADJ **1** *(différent)* different, varied; *(rubrique)* miscellaneous; **le dessert consistait en fruits d.** there was a variety of fruit for dessert, there were various kinds of fruit for dessert; **à des heures diverses** at different times; **ils ont eu des fortunes diverses** they had varying fortunes; **des opinions très diverses** very varied opinions, a wide range of opinions; **une clientèle très diverse** a wide clientele, a wide range of customers; **frais d.** sundry expenses, sundries; *Journ* **faits d.** news items; **un fait d.** a minor incident **2** *(always preceding the noun)* *(plusieurs)* various, a number of **3** *Arch (nature etc)* changing, varying

diversement [divɛrsəmɑ̃] ADV in various *or* different ways; **les participants ont d. compris la question** the contestants understood the question in different ways; **mes élèves ont d. réussi l'examen** my pupils had varying degrees of success in the exam

diversification [divɛrsifikasjɔ̃] NF diversification; *Bourse* **d. de portefeuille** portfolio diversification

diversifier [divɛrsifje] *(impf, pr sub n. diversifiions, v. diversifiiez)* VT *(économie, cultures, produits, placements)* to diversify; *(activités, intérêts, couleurs etc)* to vary ▸ VPR **se diversifier** *(de compagnie)* to diversify

diversion [divɛrsjɔ̃] NF diversion; *(changement)* change, distraction; **faire d.** to create a diversion; **faire d. à la tristesse de qn** to cheer sb up; **cela fera une d. à tes ennuis** it will take your mind off your troubles

diversité [divɛrsite] NF *(variété)* variety, diversity; *(différence)* difference; **une grande d. de races/de milieux sociaux** a wide variety of races/classes; **étant donné la d. de leurs intérêts** given that they have such different *or* varying interests; **j'admire la d. de ses talents** I admire the variety of talents that he has; **d. biologique** biological diversity, biodiversity

divertir [divɛrtir] VT **1** *(amuser)* to entertain, to amuse **2** *Vieilli (coup etc)* to divert, to ward off; *(personne)* *(d'un projet, d'une intention etc)* to turn *(away)*; *(attention)* to divert; *(somme d'argent)* to misappropriate ▸ VPR **se divertir** to enjoy oneself; **se d. de la stupidité/de la balourdise de qn** to laugh at sb's stupidity/clumsiness; **se d. l'esprit** to amuse *or* entertain oneself

divertissant [divɛrtisɑ̃] ADJ amusing, entertaining

divertissement [divɛrtismɑ̃] NM **1** *(amusement)* entertainment, amusement, diversion; **on manque de d. dans ce bled** there's nothing to do in this place; **il faut trouver des divertissements pour les enfants** we have to find something to amuse the children *or* for the children to do **2** *Mus* divertimento **3** *Jur* **d. de fonds** misappropriation of funds

dividende [dividɑ̃d] NM *Math, Fin* dividend; **d. anticipé** advance dividend; **d. brut** gross dividend; **d. cumulatif** cumulative dividend; **d. d'action** share dividend; **d. définitif** final dividend; **d. en espèces** cash dividend; **d. final** final dividend; **d. majoré** grossed-up dividend; **d. net** net dividend; **dividendes accrus** accrued dividends; **sans d.** ex dividend, *Am* dividend off

divin [divɛ̃] ADJ *(volonté etc)* divine; *Fam (musique, climat etc)* heavenly; **le d. Enfant** [divinɑ̃fɑ̃] the Holy Child ▸ NM **le d.** the divine

divinateur, -trice [divinatœr, -tris] N *Arch* diviner, soothsayer ▸ ADJ *(don, pouvoir etc)* of prophecy

divination [divinasjɔ̃] NF **1** *(occultisme)* divination, soothsaying; **l'astrologie et autres méthodes de d.** astrology and other methods of telling the future **2** *(intuition)* intuition; **faire preuve d'un peu de d.** to do a bit of guesswork

divinatoire [divinatwar] ADJ *(science, art, don)* of divination; **baguette d.** divining rod, dowsing rod

divinement [divinmɑ̃] ADV divinely

divinisation [divinizasjɔ̃] NF deification

diviniser [divinize] VT to deify

divinité [divinite] NF **1** *(nature de Dieu)* divinity, divine nature; *(du Christ)* godhead **2** *(dieu)* deity, god, divinity, f goddess

diviser [divize] VT **1** *(partager)* to divide; *(travail, gains, héritage)* to divide, to share out *(entre* among); **divise le gâteau en trois** divide the cake in *or* into three; **ce pays est divisé en plusieurs provinces** the country is divided into several provinces; **la semaine est divisée en jours** the week is divided *or* split up into days; **d. une question en plusieurs points** to break down a question into several points; *Math* **d. un nombre par un autre** to divide one number by another **2** *(opposer)* to divide; **les questions déontologiques divisent les scientifiques** scientists are divided on questions of ethics; **l'opinion est divisée au sujet de cette affaire** opinion on the matter is divided; **d. pour (mieux) régner** divide and rule **3** *Arch (délimiter)* **les Pyrénées divisent la France d'avec l'Espagne** the Pyrenees divide *or* separate France from Spain ▸ VPR **se diviser** to divide *(en* into); **l'examen se divise en trois parties** the examination is divided into three parts; **l'équipe s'est divisée en deux** the team divided itself *or* split up into two groups; **le chemin se divise en deux** the road divides *or* forks

diviseur [divizœr] NM **1** *Math* divisor; **plus grand commun d.** highest common factor; **nombre/fraction d.** divisor number/fraction **2** *Tech* divider; *Élec* **d. de courant** current divider

divisibilité [divizibilite] NF divisibility

divisible [divizibl] ADJ divisible

division [divizjɔ̃] NF **1** *(d'un tout en parties)*, *Math* division *(en* into); **j'ai des divisions à faire** I've got some division to do; **je déteste les divisions** *ou* **faire des divisions** I hate division; **d. du marché** market division SEE GRAMMAR A77; B59

2 *(partie)* *(d'un tout)* part, portion, section; *Admin* division, department, branch; *Scol* group, section; *Mil, Naut* division; **les divisions d'un livre** the sections of a book; **d. de formation professionnelle** training division; **d. des exportations** export division; **d. internationale** international division

3 *(désaccord)* discord, dissension, disagreement; **semer la d. au sein d'une famille** to cause dissent in a family; **depuis le dernier congrès, c'est la d. qui règne dans le parti** division has reigned in the party since the last congress

4 *Typ* hyphen ▸▸ *Mil* **d. blindée** armoured division; *Biol* **d. cellulaire** cell division; **d. du travail** division of labour

divisionnaire [divizjɔnɛr] ADJ *Mil* divisional; *Admin* **commissaire d.** ≃ (police) superintendent ▸ NM ≃ (police) superintendent; *Mil* major general

divorce [divɔrs] NM *Jur* divorce; **les enfants sont ceux qui pâtissent le plus du d.** divorce is hardest on the children; **demander le d.** to ask for a divorce; *Jur* to sue for divorce, to file a petition for divorce; **obtenir le d.** to get a divorce; **être en instance de d.** to be getting a divorce, to have started divorce proceedings; **se solder par un d.** to end in divorce; *Fig* **le d. de la langue écrite d'avec la langue parlée** the gulf between the written and the spoken language

▶▶**d. à l'amiable** no-fault divorce; **d. par consentement mutuel** divorce by mutual consent

divorcé, -ée [divɔrse] ADJ divorced ▸ N divorced man, f woman, divorcee

divorcer [divɔrse] VI (**je divorçai(s); n. divorçons**) **d. (d')avec qn** to divorce sb; **il veut d.** he wants a divorce; **ils ont divorcé l'année dernière** they got divorced *or* they got a divorce last year; **pourquoi est-ce que tu ne lui demandes pas de d.?** why don't you ask him for a divorce?; **un couple sur trois divorce** one marriage in three ends in divorce

divulgateur, -trice [divylgatœr, -tris] N (police) informer; (de secrets) betrayer

divulgation [divylgasjɔ̃] NF disclosure (**de** of)

divulguer [divylge] VT (secret) to divulge, to reveal, to disclose; (nouvelle) to reveal; **il a divulgué qu'il y aurait des licenciements** he revealed *or* disclosed that there would be layoffs

dix [dis] ADJ INV (at the end of the word group [dis]; before n or adj beginning with a vowel sound [diz]; before n or adj beginning with a consonant [di]) **1 il est d. heures** [dizœr] it's ten o'clock; **j'en ai d.** [dis] I have ten; **les d. commandements** the Ten Commandments; Scol **devoir noté sur d.** homework marked out of ten; **avoir d. sur d. à sa dictée** to get ten out of ten for dictation; **avoir d. sur d. à chaque œil** to have twenty-twenty vision **2** (ordinal uses etc) **le d. mai** [lədime] the tenth of May; **Charles D.** Charles the Tenth; **le numéro d.** number ten

▸ NM INV (souvent [dis]) **d. et demi** [disedmi] ten and a half; **j'habite au d.** I live at number 10; Cartes **le d. de trèfle** the ten of clubs; **le X est le signe du d. romain** X is ten in Roman numerals

dix-huit [dizɥi(t)] ADJ INV eighteen; **le d. mai** the eighteenth of May

▸ NM INV eighteen; **j'ai eu un d. en maths** I got 90% in maths

dix-huitième [dizɥitjɛm] ADJ, N eighteenth

dixième [dizjɛm] ADJ, N tenth

dixièmement [dizjɛmmɑ̃] ADV tenthly, in tenth place

dixit [diksit] **il faut couper tous les arbres, Papa d.** all the trees have to be cut down, Dad says *or* or so Dad says

dix-neuf [diznœf] ADJ INV nineteen; **le d. mai** the nineteenth of May

▸ NM INV nineteen

dix-neuvième [diznœvjɛm] ADJ, N nineteenth

dix-sept [dis(s)ɛt] ADJ INV seventeen; **le d. mai** the seventeenth of May

▸ NM INV seventeen

dix-septième [dis(s)ɛtjɛm] ADJ, N seventeenth

dizain [dizɛ̃] NM Littér ten-line stanza

dizaine [dizɛn] NF Math ten; **une d.** (environ dix) about ten, ten or so; Math **compter par dizaines** to count in tens; **une d. de personnes** ten or so people, about ten people; **il y a une d. d'années** about ten years ago, ten or so years ago

dizygote [dizigɔt] Biol ADJ fraternal ▸ N fraternal twin

DJ [didʒe] NM DJ

djebel [dʒebɛl] NM jebel, mountain

djellaba [dʒelaba] NF djellaba

djembé [dʒɛmbe] NM djembe (drum)

Djibouti [dʒibuti] N Djibouti

djihad [dʒiad] NM jihad

djinn [dʒin] NM djin(n), jinn

DLC [deɛlse] NF (abrév **date limite de consommation**) best-before date

DNS [deɛnɛs] NM Ordinat (abrév **Domain Name System**) DNS

do [do] NM Mus (note) C; (solfège) doh

doberman [dɔbɛrman] NM Doberman

doc [dɔk] NF Fam abrév **documentation**

docile [dɔsil] ADJ (enfant, animal) docile; (cheveux) manageable

docilement [dɔsilmɑ̃] ADV docilely

docilité [dɔsilite] NF docility

dock [dɔk] NM Naut **1** (bassin) dock; **les docks** the dock(s), the dockyard; **d. de carénage/flottant** dry/floating dock **2** Com warehouse; **d. entrepôt** dock-warehouse; **d. frigorifique** cold storage dock

docker [dɔker] NM docker, dock worker, Am longshoreman

docte [dɔkt] ADJ Litt, Iron (when it precedes noun) learned

doctement [dɔktəmɑ̃] ADV Litt, Iron in a learned manner, learnedly

docteur [dɔktœr] NM **1 d. (en médecine)** doctor (of medicine); **leur fille est d.** their daughter is a doctor; **le d. Thomas** Dr Thomas; **bonjour, d.** good morning, doctor **2** Univ **d. ès lettres** ≃ PhD; **Mlle Laurent est d. ès sciences** Miss Laurent is a doctor of science; **d. en droit** doctor of law **3** Rel **les docteurs de l'Église** the Doctors of the Church

doctoral, -ale, -aux, -ales [dɔktɔral, -o] ADJ Péj (air, ton) pompous

doctoralement [dɔktɔralmɑ̃] ADV Péj pompously

doctorat [dɔktɔra] NM Univ doctorate; **d. d'État** ≃ D Litt/DSc/etc, **d. de 3ᵉ cycle** ≃ PhD

doctoresse [dɔktɔrɛs] NF Vieilli woman doctor

doctrinaire [dɔktriner] ADJ doctrinaire

doctrinal, -ale, -aux, -ales [dɔktrinal, -o] ADJ doctrinal

doctrine [dɔktrin] NF doctrine, tenet

docudrame [dɔkydram] NM TV docudrama

document [dɔkymɑ̃] NM document ▸▶Com **documents contre acceptation** documents against acceptance; Com **d. administratif unique** unique data folder; TV, Cin **d. d'archives** library document; Aut **documents de bord** vehicle documents; **d.-canevas** (de publipostage) form document; Com **documents d'embarquement** shipping documents; Typ **d. d'exécution** artwork; Com **d. d'expédition** shipping document; **d. interne à l'entreprise** internal company document; **d. maître** master document; Com **documents maritimes** shipping documents; Com **d. d'offre** tender document; Com **documents contre paiement** documents against payment; **d. source** source document; Compta **d. de synthèse** financial statements; **d. transmissible** transferable document; Com **d. de transport combiné** combined transport document; **d. de travail** working document; **d.-type** (de publipostage) form document; **documents de voyage** travel documents

documentaire [dɔkymɑ̃tɛr] ADJ (intérêt, valeur etc) documentary; **à titre d.** for (your) information; Cin **film d.** documentary

▸ NM **1** Cin documentary **2 d. touristique** travelogue

documentaliste [dɔkymɑ̃talist] N **1** (d'archives) documentalist, archivist; Admin information officer **2** TV etc researcher

documentariste [dɔkymɑ̃tarist] N Cin, TV documentarist

documentation [dɔkymɑ̃tasjɔ̃] NF **1** (informations, documents) documentation; **la bibliothèque n'a aucune d. sur le sujet** the library has no documentation on the subject; **ils ont réuni une d. très riche pour leur film** they gathered a wide range of documentary evidence for their film; **d. iconographique** pictorial *or* iconographic documentation; **service de la d.** research department **2** (publicités) literature, information, documentation; **voulez-vous recevoir notre d.?** would you like us to send you our brochure?; **système de d. automatique** automated information service; **d. de presse** press kit; **d. touristique** travel literature, tourist literature **3** (technique) documentation (technique)

documenter [dɔkymɑ̃te] VT (sujet) to document; (déclaration etc) to support with documentary evidence; **d. qn sur une question** to brief sb on a question; **elle est bien documentée** she is well informed on the subject; **son étude n'était pas solidement documentée** his study was not well documented

▸ VPR **se documenter** to gather documentation *or* information *or* material

dodécaèdre [dodekaɛdr] NM Math dodecahedron

dodécagonal, -ale, -aux, -ales [dodekagonal, -o] ADJ Math twelve-sided, dodecagonal

dodécagone [dodekagon] NM Math dodecagon

dodécaphonique [dodekafɔnik] ADJ Mus twelve-tone, dodecaphonic

dodécaphonisme [dodekafɔnism] NM Mus twelve-tone system, dodecaphony

dodelinement [dɔdlinmɑ̃] NM (de la tête) nodding

dodeliner [dɔdline] VI **il dodelinait de la tête** his head kept falling forward *or* nodding

dodo¹ [dodo] NM Enf (sommeil) sleep, byebyes; (lit) bed; **faire d.** to sleep; **aller au d.** to go to bed *or* to bye-byes; **qui c'est qui faire un gros d.?** who's a sleepy boy/girl then?; **d.!** go to sleep!; **allez, au d.!** bed!

dodo² NM (oiseau) dodo

dodu [dɔdy] ADJ Fam plump, chubby

doge [dɔʒ] NM Hist doge

dogmatique [dɔgmatik] ADJ dogmatic

dogmatiquement [dɔgmatikmɑ̃] ADV dogmatically

dogmatiser [dɔgmatize] VI to be dogmatic

dogmatisme [dɔgmatism] NM dogmatism

dogme [dɔgm] NM dogma

dogue [dɔg] NM mastiff; Fig **être d'une humeur de d.** to be like a bear with a sore head

doigt [dwa] NM **1** finger; Anat, Zool digit; **d. de pied** toe; Fig **mettre les doigts de pied en éventail** to relax thoroughly, to do absolutely nothing; **le petit d.** the little finger; Fam **mon petit d. me l'a dit** a little bird told me; **lever le d.** (en classe etc) to put one's hand up; Fig **ne pas lever** *or* **remuer le petit d.** not to lift a finger; **compter sur ses doigts** to count on one's fingers; **je peux compter mes amis sur les doigts de la main** I can count my friends on the fingers of one hand; **je ne sais rien faire de mes dix doigts** I'm not good with my hands; **porter une bague au d.** to wear a ring on one's finger; **promener ses doigts sur qch** to run one's fingers over sth; **elle a des doigts de fée** she's good with her hands; **il a les doigts verts** he has green fingers *or* Am a green thumb; **se faire taper sur les doigts** to be rapped over the knuckles, to get a rap on the knuckles; Mus **avoir un morceau dans les doigts** to have mastered a piece; **savoir qch sur le bout des doigts** to know sth inside out, to have sth at one's fingertips; **elle est élégante/spirituelle/méchante jusqu'au bout des doigts** she is elegant/witty/nasty through and through;

elle est française jusqu'au bout des doigts she is French to her fingertips; **menacer qn du d.** to shake *or* wag one's finger at sb; **elle lui fit signe du d. (de venir)** she beckoned to him (to come over); **désigner** *ou* **montrer qn/qch du d.** to point at sb/sth; *Fam* **faire un d. d'honneur à qn** to give sb the finger, *Am* to flip sb the bird; *Fig* **mettre le d. dans l'engrenage** to get involved; **il a mis le d. dans l'engrenage de la drogue** he got involved *or* mixed up in drugs; **vous avez mis le d. dessus** you've put your finger on it, you've hit the nail on the head; **je crois que je touche le problème du d.** I think I see what the problem is; **nous touchons le but/la vérité du d.** we're very close to *or* within an inch of our goal/the truth; *Fam* **se mettre** *ou* **se fourrer le d. dans l'œil (jusqu'au coude)** to be completely wrong; **fourrer ses doigts partout** to be into everything; **croiser les doigts** to cross one's fingers; **je croise les doigts** I've got my fingers crossed; **croisons les doigts pour que ça marche** let's cross our fingers that it works; *Fam* **mener qn au d. et à l'œil** to keep a tight rein on sb; **elle se laisse mener au d. et à l'œil par son mari** her husband only has to raise a finger and she jumps; **obéir au d. et à l'œil** to obey immediately; **filer** *ou* **glisser entre les doigts de qn** to slip through sb's fingers; **s'en mordre les doigts** to regret it; **j'ai voulu lui tenir tête et je m'en mords les doigts** I tried standing up to her and I regret it *or* I'm sorry I did; **ils sont ensemble comme les (deux) doigts de la main** they are very close; *Fam* **gagner les doigts dans le nez** to win hands down; **faire qch les doigts dans le nez** to do sth as easy as winking; **être le petit d. sur la couture du pantalon** to be a lackey

2 *(mesure)* finger's breadth; **la robe est trop courte d'un d.** the dress is a fraction too short; **un d. de cognac** a nip *or* drop *or* spot of brandy; **être à deux doigts de la mort** to be within an inch of death; **il était à un d.** *ou* **à deux doigts de refuser** he was within an ace of refusing

3 *(objet)* **doigts d'un gant** fingers of a glove; *Aut* **d. de distribution** rotor arm

doigté [dwate] NM **1** *Mus (d'un morceau de musique)* fingering; **exercices de d.** five-finger exercises **2** *(de dactylo)* touch; *(d'un chirurgien)* skill **3** *Fig* tact, diplomacy; **manquer de d.** to be tactless

doigter [dwate] VT **1** *(d'un musicien)* to finger **2** *(d'un compositeur)* to mark with the proper fingering
VI to finger; **elle doigte bien/mal** her fingering is good/bad

doigtier [dwatje] NM fingerstall

doit [dwa] NM *Com* debit, liability; **d. et avoir** debits and credits; *(personnes)* debtors and creditors

dol [dɔl] NM *Jur* fraud, wilful misrepresentation

Dolby® [dɔlbi] NM Dolby®; **en D. stéréo** in Dolby stereo

dôle [dol] NF *Suisse* = red wine from the canton of Valais

doléances [dɔleɑ̃s] NFPL complaints; **faire ses d.** to air one's grievances

dolent [dɔlɑ̃] ADJ *(voix, personne etc)* doleful, plaintive

doline [dɔlin] NF *Géol* sink-hole, *Spéc* doline

dollar [dɔlar] NM dollar; **la zone d.** the dollar area; **d.-titre** dollar security; **d. américain** US dollar; **dollars constants** dollars in real terms; **dollars courants** actual dollars

dollarisation [dɔlarizasjɔ̃] NF *Écon* dollarization

dolman [dɔlmɑ̃] NM dolman; *(de hussard)* short-skirted jacket

dolmen [dɔlmɛn] NM dolmen

dolomie [dɔlɔmi], **dolomite** [dɔlɔmit] NF *Minér* dolomite; *Géog* **les Dolomites** the Dolomites

dolomitique [dɔlɔmitik] ADJ *Géol* dolomitic

dolosif, -ive [dɔlɔzif, -iv] ADJ *Jur* fraudulent

domaine [dɔmɛn] NM **1** *(propriété)* estate, property; *Jur* demesne; **il est interdit de chasser sur leur d.** hunting is forbidden on their land; **ils ont plusieurs domaines dans le vignoble bordelais** they own several pieces of land in the Bordeaux wine-growing area; **domaines de la Couronne** Crown lands; **D. (de l'État)** State(-administered) property; **d. public** public property; **cet ouvrage est tombé dans le d. public** this work is out of copyright *or* has come into the public domain, the copyright on this work has run out *or* lapsed; **le d. forestier** the national forests; **d. skiable** skiing area; **cette pièce est mon d.** this room is my domain

2 *(rayon)* field; **d. d'une science** field *or* scope of a science; **d. des affaires** business domain; **d. de compétence** area of expertise, area of competence; **cela n'entre pas dans le d. de mes connaissances** that's not my field *or* domain; **ce n'est pas de mon d.** that's not my field *or* my line; **une intervention aussi délicate est du d. de la microchirurgie** such a delicate operation calls for microsurgery; **c'est du d. du possible** it is within the realm of possibility, it is not beyond the bounds of possibility; **il est bon dans tous les domaines** he is good in all fields *or* areas; **c'est son d. réservé** it's his private domain; *Mktg* **d. concurrentiel** competitive scope; *Mktg* **d. d'activité stratégique** strategic business area

3 *Ordinat (partie d'une adresse Internet)* domain

domanial, -iale, -iaux, -iales [dɔmanjal, -jo] ADJ *(domaines, forêts etc)* national, (belonging to the) State

dôme [dom] NM **1** *Archit* dome, cupola **2** *Litt (du ciel, des arbres)* vault, canopy; *Géog* dome

domestication [dɔmɛstikasjɔ̃] NF domestication

domesticité [dɔmɛstisite] NF **1** *(service)* domestic service **2** *(personnel)* domestic staff, household **3** *(d'un animal)* domesticity; **la d. est impossible chez certaines races** some breeds are impossible to tame *or* domesticate

domestique [dɔmɛstik] ADJ **1** *(vie, soucis)* domestic; *(occupations, tâches, déchets)* household; *(querelle)* family, domestic; **économie d.** home economics; **accidents domestiques** accidents in the home **2 animal d.** domestic animal; *(qu'on a chez soi)* pet; **éléphant d.** tame *or* domesticated elephant
N servant, *Fml, Am* domestic

domestiquer [dɔmɛstike] VT *(animal)* to domesticate; *(personne)* to subjugate, to bring to a state of subjection; *(énergie atomique etc)* to harness

domicile [dɔmisil] NM (place of) residence, home, *Jur* domicile; **sans d. fixe** of no fixed abode *or* address; **élire d. au 3, rue Hoche** to take up residence at no 3, rue Hoche; **dernier d. connu** last known address; **à d.** in one's home, at home; **travailler à d.** to work from home; **notre épicier livre à d.** our grocer has a (home) delivery service; **vous préférez être livré à d. ou au bureau?** do you want it delivered to your home or your office?; **franco à d.** carriage paid; *Jur* **d. conjugal** marital *or* matrimonial home; *Jur* **abandon du d. conjugal** desertion; **d. fiscal** tax domicile; *Sport* **match à d.** home game *or* match; **jouer à d.** to play *or* be at home;

le PSG joue à d. contre Lille PSG is at home to Lille

domiciliaire [dɔmisiljɛr] ADJ *(visite etc)* home

domiciliataire [dɔmisiljatɛr] N *(de chèque)* paying bank; *(d'effet)* paying agent

domiciliation [dɔmisiljasjɔ̃] NF *Com* domiciliation; **d. bancaire** payment by banker's order

domicilié [dɔmisilje] ADJ resident, domiciled (**à** at); *Com* domiciled

domicilier [dɔmisilje] VT *(impf, pr sub* **n. domiciliions, v. domiciliiez)** *Com* to domicile

domien, -ienne [dɔmjɛ̃, -jɛn] ADJ of/from the French overseas departments
N D. *(natif)* native of the French overseas departments; *(habitant)* inhabitant of the French overseas departments

dominance [dɔminɑ̃s] NF *Biol* dominance

dominant, -ante [dɔminɑ̃, -ɑ̃t] ADJ *(couleur, opinion etc)* predominating, prevailing; *(trait, idée etc)* dominant, outstanding; *Biol* **caractère d.** dominant (characteristic)
NF **dominante 1** *(ce qui domine)* chief characteristic; **un ameublement avec une dominante moderne** furniture which is predominantly *or* primarily modern; **la dominante de son programme politique est la protection de l'environnement** environmental protection is the main plank of his platform; **elle avait une tenue très pâle, avec une dominante rose** she was wearing a very pale outfit, in which pink predominated *or* was the main colour; **une classe à dominante scientifique** a class where the emphasis is on scientific subjects **2** *Mus* dominant (note)

dominateur, -trice [dɔminatœr, -tris] N *Litt* ruler
ADJ *(pays, caractère)* dominating; *Péj (personne, ton, attitude etc)* domineering, overbearing

domination [dɔminasjɔ̃] NF domination; **la d. de l'URSS sur les autres pays de l'Est** the USSR's domination of the other Eastern bloc countries; **d. morale** dominance, domination; **il exerce sur elle une telle d. morale que ...** he dominates her so completely that ..., he has such sway over her that ...; **d. de soi-même** self-control; **être sous la d. de qn** to be under sb's thumb

dominer [dɔmine] VT **1** *(assujettir)* *(personne)* to dominate; *(empire)* to rule over; **l'ambition le domine** he is dominated by ambition; **se laisser d. par un collègue autoritaire** to let oneself be dominated by an authoritarian colleague; **d. une classe** *(d'un professeur)* to control a class

2 *(surpasser)* *(adversaire, concurrent)* to surpass, *Fam* to be streets ahead of; **sa voix dominait toutes les autres** his voice rose *or* was heard above all the others; **dans son domaine, il domine absolument tous les savants** he stands head and shoulders above all the other scientists in his field

3 *(prédominer dans)* *(travail, caractère, humeur)* to be the dominant feature of; **c'est la question du chômage qui domine les préoccupations du gouvernement** unemployment is predominant among the government's concerns; **le rouge domine toute sa garde-robe** red is the dominant colour in her wardrobe; **le sapin domine dans les forêts allemandes** fir is the predominant species of tree in German forests

4 *(maîtriser)* *(timidité, passions)* to master, to overcome; *(larmes, Fig (son sujet)* to master; *(paresse, envie de faire qch)* to overcome; **d. la situation** to be master of the situation, to have the situation under control; *Sport* **d. la partie** to dominate the game

5 *(surplomber)* to dominate; **le château do-**

mine la vallée the castle dominates the valley; **il domine les enfants de son âge d'une tête au moins** he stands at least a head above other children of his age; **de sa terrasse, on domine la mer** you overlook the sea from his balcony

VI 1 (*l'emporter*) to dominate; **notre équipe a dominé tout le long du match** our team dominated the entire match *or* was in control throughout the match; **ce sont ses arguments qui dominent** his arguments carry the day; **leur entreprise domine dans le secteur du prêt-à-porter féminin** their company dominates the women's ready-to-wear sector; **notre entreprise domine largement dans ce secteur** our company is by far the largest in the sector; **elle domine de très loin sur ses collègues** she is *or* stands head and shoulders above her colleagues, she is far better than *or Fam* streets ahead of her colleagues; **il domine en taille sur les autres enfants de son âge** he is taller than the other children in his age group

2 (*prédominer*) to be predominant; **c'est la couleur bleue qui domine** blue is the predominant *or* predominating colour; **les jeunes de moins de 15 ans dominent dans le club** young people under 15 are in the majority in the club; **chez lui, c'est l'égoïsme/la gentillesse qui domine** selfishness/kindness is his dominant characteristic; **parmi mes préoccupations, c'est l'avenir de mes enfants qui domine** my children's future is my main concern

VPR se dominer to be self-controlled, to control one's feelings; **il ne pouvait plus se d.** he couldn't control himself any longer; **dès qu'il boit deux verres, il n'arrive plus à se d.** two drinks and he loses all self-control

dominicain, -aine [dɔminikɛ̃, -ɛn] **ADJ 1** *Rel* (*moine, religieuse*) Dominican **2** *Géog* Dominican; (*natif, habitant*) of Santo Domingo; **la République Dominicaine** the Dominican Republic, Santo Domingo

N 1 *Rel* Dominican **2** *Géog* **D.** Dominican

dominical, -ale, -aux, -ales [dɔminikal, -o] **ADJ** **l'oraison dominicale** the Lord's prayer; **repos d.** day of rest; *Rel* Sabbath; **dans la religion chrétienne, le repos d. est une coutume** in Christianity, it is traditional for Sunday to be a day of rest; **ouverture dominicale des magasins** Sunday opening *or* shopping

dominion [dɔminjɔn] **NM** *Pol* dominion

Dominique [dɔminik] **NF** *Géog* **la D.** Dominica

domino [dɔmino] **NM** domino; **jouer aux dominos** to play dominoes VOIR GRAMMAIRE A12

dommage [dɔmaʒ] **NM 1** (*préjudice*) damage, injury; **causer un d. à qn** to do sb harm *or* an injury; **il s'en est tiré sans d.** he came out of it unscathed **2** (*dégâts matériels*) dommages damage; **aucun d. n'est à déplorer** no damage is reported; **les dommages causés par l'explosion sont énormes** the explosion caused tremendous damage; **dommages collatéraux** collateral damage **3** (*quel*) **d.!** what a pity!, what a shame!; **c'est (bien) d. qu'elle ne soit pas venue** it's a (great) pity that she didn't come; **le plus d. c'est que tu ne l'aies jamais rencontré** it's a great pity that you never met him; **d. que tu n'aies pas le temps** it's a pity you haven't the time

ADJ INV *Suisse* (*que l'on ne veut pas endommager*) **il ne faut pas mettre des habits d. pour faire le ménage** you shouldn't wear your good clothes to do the housework

▸▸ *Jur* **d. causé avec intention de nuire** malicious damage; **d. corporel** personal *or* physical injury; **dommages de guerre** war damages; **dommages et intérêts, dommages-intérêts** damages; **poursuivre qn en**

dommages-intérêts to sue sb for damages, to bring an action for damages against sb; **verser/obtenir des dommages-intérêts** to pay/to be awarded damages; **dommages-intérêts compensatoires** compensation; **d. matériel** damage to property; **d. moral** psychological damage; **dommages punitifs** punitive damages

dommageable [dɔmaʒabl] **ADJ** detrimental, injurious; *Jur* prejudicial; *Jur* **acte d.** tort

domotique [dɔmɔtik] **NF** home automation

domptable [dɔ̃(p)tabl] **ADJ** capable of being tamed *or* subdued, tamable

domptage [dɔ̃(p)taʒ] **NM** (*d'animal*) (*apprivoisement*) taming; (*dressage*) training; (*de cheval*) breaking in; (*de fleuve, de la nature*) taming; **le d. du criminel n'a pas été facile** it was not easy to subdue the criminal

dompter [dɔ̃(p)te] **VT** (*animal*) (*apprivoiser*) to tame; (*dresser*) to train; (*cheval*) to break in; (*ses sentiments, passions etc*) to subdue, to overcome; (*fleuve, la nature*) to tame; (*personne*) to subdue

dompteur, -euse [dɔ̃(p)tœr, -øz] **N** (*d'animaux*) tamer, trainer; **d. de chevaux** horsebreaker

DOM-TOM [dɔmtɔm] **NMPL** (*abrév départements et territoires d'outre-mer*) = French overseas departments and territories

DON [deɔen] **NM** *Ordinat* (*abrév disque optique numérique*) CD-ROM

don [dɔ̃] **NM 1** (*cadeau*) gift, present; (*à un musée, une œuvre*) donation; **d. de M. Roland** (*dans un musée*) gift of Mr Roland, donated by Mr Roland; **un d. en nature/espèces** a donation in kind/cash; **faire d. à qn de qch** to make a present *or* a donation of sth to sb; *Fig* **les dons de la terre** the fruits of the earth; **cet enfant est un d. du ciel** that child is a gift from heaven; **le d. de soi** self-sacrifice; **faire d. de sa vie à Dieu** to give one's life to God **2** (*aptitude*) gift, talent; **le d. des langues** a gift *or* talent for languages; *aussi Iron* **avoir le d. de faire qch** to have a gift *or* talent *or* genius for doing sth

▸▸ **d. d'organes** organ donation; **d. du sang** blood donation; **d. de sperme** sperm donation

donataire [dɔnatɛr] **N** *Jur* donee

donateur, -trice [dɔnatœr, -tris] **N** donor

donation [dɔnasjɔ̃] **NF** donation, gift; *Jur* **d. entre vifs** gift (*made to avoid inheritance tax*); **donations parents-enfants** donations from parents to children

donation-partage, *pl* **donations-partages** **NF** *Jur* = distribution of estate during one's lifetime to avoid inheritance tax

donc [dɔ̃k] **CONJ** (*marque la conséquence*) so; **il répond exactement à mes besoins, j'en suis d. très satisfait** it's exactly what I need, so I'm very satisfied with it; **je pense, d. je suis** I think, therefore I am

ADV 1 (*emphatique*) **vous voilà d. de retour** so you're back (again); **tu le savais d. depuis le début?** so you knew from the start?, you knew from the start then?; **que voulez-vous d.?** what(ever) do you want?; **mais taisez-vous d.!** do be quiet!, *Fam* do shut up!; **allons d.!** nonsense!, come on!, come now!; **comment d.?** how do you mean?; **pensez d.!** that's what you think!, that'll be the day!; **tu as d. oublié?** have you forgotten?; **où vas-tu d.?** [dɔ̃] where are you going?; **cela vous plaît d.?** you like it, then?, so you like it? **2** (*après interruption ou digression*) **d. pour en revenir à notre sujet** so *or* well, to come back to our subject; **je disais d. que ...** I was saying, then, that ..., as I was saying, ...

dondon [dɔ̃dɔ̃] **NF** *Fam* fat woman/girl; **grosse d.** great lump of a woman/girl

donjon [dɔ̃ʒɔ̃] **NM** (*d'un château*) keep, donjon

don Juan [dɔ̃ʒɥɑ̃] **NM** Don Juan

donjuanesque [dɔ̃ʒɥanɛsk] **ADJ** Don Juan

donjuanisme [dɔ̃ʒɥanism] **NM** Don Juanism

donnant-donnant [dɔnɑ̃dɔnɑ̃] **ADJ** **c'est d., je te prête ma voiture et tu me prêtes ton aspirateur** it's only fair, I lend you my car and you lend me your vacuum cleaner; **avec elle, c'est toujours d.** she always expects something in return; **désormais, ce sera d.** from now on, things are going to be a bit fairer around here, from now on, it's going to be a two-way street around here

donne [dɔn] **NF** *Cartes* deal; **à vous la d.!** your deal!; **faire la d.** to deal; **fausse d.** misdeal; *Fig* **il y a fausse d.** there's been a mistake; *Fig* **nouvelle d.** new state of affairs; **il y a une nouvelle d. des pays de l'Est** the situation in the Eastern bloc has changed; **le partage du travail sera une nouvelle d. dans la situation économique** job-sharing will be a new factor in the economic situation

donné [dɔne] **ADJ 1** given; **propriété donnée en dot** property given as a dowry; *Fam* **c'est d.** it's dirt cheap, it's a gift, I'm/he's/*etc* giving it away **2** (*défini*) given; **à un point d./une distance donnée** at a given *or* certain point/distance; **des quantités données** given quantities; **à un moment d.** then; **à un moment d., tu seras bien obligé de le lui dire** you'll have to tell him sometime *or* sooner or later **3** **étant d. deux triangles** given two triangles; **étant d. l'heure tardive** since it's so late; **étant d. qu'il était mineur** since *or* as he was a minor

donnée [dɔne] **NF** (*d'un problème etc*) given information; (*d'un roman etc*) fundamental idea *or* subject; **données** data; VOIR GRAMMAIRE A11 **si je n'ai pas toutes les données du problème** if I don't have all the data *or* information on the problem; **données brutes** raw data; *Écon* **en données corrigées des variations saisonnières** with adjustments for seasonal variations, seasonally adjusted; **traitement des données** data processing; *Ordinat* **support de données** data carrier; *Ordinat* **commutateur de données** data switch; **données nominatives** personal data; *Ordinat* **données numériques** digital data; *Ordinat* **données à sept bits** seven-bit data; *Ordinat* **banque de données** data bank; *Ordinat* **base de données** database

DONNER [dɔne]

VT to give **1–13** ▪ to donate **1, 2** ▪ to hand in **4** ▪ to leave **4** ▪ to cause **7** ▪ to yield **8** ▪ to produce **8**		
VI to give **1** ▪ to stretch **7** ▪ to deal **8**		
VPR to devote oneself **1** ▪ to give oneself **2, 3, 6** ▪ to choose **7** ▪ to be on **9**		

VT 1 (*offrir*) (*quelque chose de concret, siège, livre, travail etc*) to give; **d. son sang** to give blood; **d. un cadeau à qn** to give a present to sb, to give sb a present; **il m'a donné 100 euros** he gave me 100 euros; **d. son corps à la science** to donate one's body to science; **d. sa place à une vieille dame** to give (up) one's seat to an old lady; **d. à boire à qn** to give sb something to drink; **c'est toi qui nous donnes à manger?** are you giving us lunch/*etc*?; **d. c'est d.** a gift is a gift

2 (*faire don de*) (*temps, amour, hospitalité etc*) to give; **d. sa vie pour qn** to give one's life for sb; **d. son temps pour une cause** to give *or* donate one's time to a cause; **d. le jour** *ou* **la vie à un enfant** to give birth to a child; **d. la mort à qn** to kill sb

3 (*céder, vendre*) to give; **je vous en donne dix euros** I'll give you ten euros for it; **je lui**

donne 20 euros de l'heure I pay him 20 euros an hour; **je te donne mon pull contre ta jupe** I'll give you my sweater (in exchange) for your skirt, I'll swap my sweater for your skirt; **en d. à qn pour son argent** to give sb their money's worth; *Fig* **ah, il veut avoir plus de responsabilités, et bien, on va lui en d. pour son argent** if he wants more responsibility, we'll give him it and then some more *or* we'll give him as much as he wants and more; **elle donnerait n'importe quoi** *ou* **tout ce qu'elle a au monde pour que cela se réalise** she'd give anything for that to happen; **je donnerais beaucoup pour le savoir** I'd give a lot to know

4 (*confier*) to give; **d. à qn qch à garder** to give sb sth to look after, *Fml* to entrust sb with sth; **d. ses chaussures à ressemeler** to leave one's shoes to be resoled; **d. un vêtement à nettoyer** *ou* **au teinturier** to hand in a piece of clothing to be dry-cleaned; **d. ses enfants à garder** to leave one's children to be looked after

5 (*dire, communiquer*) (*avis, détails, description, ordres, conseils etc*) to give; **d. l'heure** to tell the time; **vous pourriez me d. l'heure?** could you give me the time?; **le journal donne des nouvelles alarmantes sur la crise** the newspaper gives alarming news of the crisis; **tu lui donneras le bonjour de ma part** say hello to him for me; **tu pourrais d. des nouvelles de temps en temps!** you could let me/us/*etc* hear from you occasionally!; **je vous le donne en cent** *ou* **en mille** you'll never guess; **donnez-moi le jour et l'heure de votre arrivée** give me your date and time of arrival; *Péj* **il faudrait qu'on lui donne du 'Maître' pour qu'il soit satisfait** he won't be happy unless he's addressed as 'Maître'; **il lui a donné du 'Madame la Comtesse' toute la soirée** he 'Countess'd her this and 'Countess'd her that all evening

6 (*octroyer*) (*sa parole, son accord, du temps, une chance, délai, occasion, pourboire etc*) to give; **j'y reviendrai plus tard, si l'occasion m'en est donnée** I'll give you there again later if I get the chance; **d. sa fille en mariage à qn** to give one's daughter to sb in marriage; **d. sa confiance à qn** to put one's trust in sb

7 (*causer*) (*de l'énergie, de l'appétit, des coliques etc*) to give; **cette odeur me donne mal à la tête** this smell is giving me a headache; **d. du souci à qn** to cause sb worry; **d. sujet** *ou* **matière à discussion** to be a subject for discussion *or* debate; **cela m'a donné l'idée de …** that gave me the idea to …; **son histoire donne plus à rire qu'à pleurer** his story is funny rather than sad, his story makes you want to laugh rather than cry; **toute cette histoire m'a donné à réfléchir** the entire business made me think/laugh; **d. envie de rire** to be laughable *or* comical; **ça me donne envie de rire** that makes me want to laugh; **d. faim/soif/sommeil/chaud/le vertige à qn** to make sb hungry/thirsty/sleepy/hot/dizzy; **cette fenêtre donne de la lumière dans la pièce** that window makes the room brighter; **je lui ai donné à entendre que …** I gave him to understand that …; **cela me donne à croire que …** it leads me to believe that …

8 (*produire*) to give; (*récoltes*) to yield; **arbre qui donne de beaux fruits** tree that gives *or* yields *or* bears fine fruit; **les arbres donnent de l'ombre** the trees give shade; **elle a donné trois beaux enfants à son mari** she gave *or* bore her husband three beautiful children; **d. le la avec un diapason** to give an A with a tuning fork; **d. de l'électricité** to produce electricity; **essai qui ne donne rien** fruitless *or* unsuccessful attempt; **une méthode qui ne donne rien** a method that doesn't work; *Fam* **ça n'a rien donné** nothing came of it, it didn't work out; **je me demande ce que cela**

va d. I wonder what will come of it *or* what the result of it will be; *Fam* **qu'est-ce que ça donne?** how does it look?

9 (*mettre*) to give; **d. un baiser/une caresse/une gifle/une fessée à qn** to give sb a kiss/a caress/a slap in the face/a spanking; **d. un coup de peigne à ses cheveux** to give one's hair a quick comb; **il faudrait d. une couche de peinture supplémentaire** we'll have to put on an extra coat of paint; **tu peux d. un coup de balai dans la cuisine?** can you give the kitchen a sweep?; *Fig* **tu donnes ta langue au chat?** do you give up *or* in?

10 (*organiser*) (*bal, dîner, conférence etc*) to give; (*pièce*) to put on *or* perform a play; **qu'est-ce qu'on donne au cinéma aujourd'hui?** what's on at the cinema today?

11 (*attribuer*) **on donne ses théories pour révolutionnaires** they say his theories are revolutionary, his theories are said to be revolutionary; **je lui donne vingt ans** I reckon he's about twenty; **les médecins lui donnent deux jours (à vivre)** the doctors give him two days (to live); **d. tort/raison à qn** to disagree/agree with sb

12 (*conférer*) (*impression*) to give; (*poids, valeur*) to give, to lend; **d. un sens à sa vie** to give (a) meaning to one's life; **ta nouvelle coiffure te donne un air jeune** your new hairdo makes you look younger

13 (*passer*) **tu peux me d. le livre qui est dans le tiroir/sur la table?** can you give me the book out of the drawer/off the table?; **il m'a donné son rhume** he gave me his cold, I caught his cold

14 (*accorder*) **il n'est pas donné à tout le monde d'être (un) écrivain** not everybody can be a writer

15 *Arg* (*vendre*) to grass on (**à** to)

VI 1 (*faire un don*) to give; **aimer d.** to like to give, to like giving; **2** (*cogner*) **le navire a donné sur les rochers** the ship ran onto *or* struck the rocks; **d. de la tête contre qch** to knock *or* strike *or* bump one's head against sth; *Fig Fam* **ne pas savoir où d. de la tête** not to know which way to turn; **sa tête alla d. dans le ventre de son adversaire** his head went straight into his opponent's stomach; **le soleil donne dans la pièce** the sun is streaming into the room **3** (*tomber*) **d. dans le piège** *ou Fam* **le panneau** to fall into the trap; **d. dans** (*avoir un penchant pour*) to be given to; **il donne dans la bigoterie** he is rather bigoted; **il donne dans les petites minettes en ce moment** he really goes for young babes at the moment; **d. dans le genre théâtral** to lapse into the melodramatic

4 (*produire*) **si les blés donnent cette année** if there is a good crop of wheat this year; *Fam* **ça donne!** it's something else!, it's wicked *or Br* mental!; *Fam* **s'ils se disputent, ça va d.** if they argue, there'll be trouble; **leur chaîne/sa musique a donné à fond toute la soirée** their stereo/the music was blaring all evening

5 (*charger*) **faire d. un bataillon** to send a battalion into action

6 (*déboucher*) **la fenêtre donne sur la cour** the window looks onto the yard; **cette porte donne sur** *ou* **dans le jardin** this door leads (out) into the garden

7 (*s'allonger*) (*d'une corde, d'une jupe*) to stretch

8 *Cartes* to deal; **mal d.** to misdeal; **c'est à qui de d.?** whose deal is it?

VPR se donner 1 (*se consacrer*) to devote oneself (**à** to); **elle s'est donnée entièrement** she gave fully of herself

2 (*s'offrir*) **se d. en spectacle** to make an exhibition of oneself; **se d. des airs** to put on airs, to give oneself airs; **se d. un genre** to make out one is something one is not; **c'est**

un genre qu'elle se donne it's just a front; *Fam* **se la d.** to show off, to pose

3 (*s'accorder*) **se d. toutes les chances de réussir** to give oneself every chance of succeeding; **se d. le temps de réfléchir** to give oneself *or* take time to think; **s'en d. (à cœur joie)** to enjoy oneself (to the full), to have a good time, to have a field day; **se d. du bon temps** to have a good time, to enjoy oneself; **se d. bonne conscience** to salve one's conscience; **se d. pour tâche de …** to set oneself the task of …; **se d. pour mission de …** to make it one's mission to …

4 se d. un coup de peigne/brosse to give one's hair a quick comb/brush; **se d. un coup de marteau sur le pouce** to hit one's thumb with a hammer; **se d. du tourment** to torment oneself

5 (*se prétendre*) **il se donne pour un grand musicien** he says he is *or* claims he is *or* claims to be a great musician

6 (*sexuellement*) to give oneself

7 (*choisir*) (*chef, président etc*) to choose, to select

8 (*échanger*) **se d. des coups** to exchange blows, to hit each other; **se d. des baisers** to kiss each other; **se d. l'accolade** to embrace each other; **se d. une poignée de main** to shake hands

9 *Cin* to be on, to be showing; **hier soir se donnait chez Maxim's la soirée d'adieu du Comte Orloff** Count Orloff's farewell party took place at Maxim's last night

V IMPERS c'est le spectacle le plus épouvantable qu'il m'a (jamais) été donné de voir it was the most horrifying sight I'd ever been unfortunate enough to witness

donneur, -euse [dɔnœr, -øz] **N 1** *Méd* donor; **d. de sang/sperme** blood/sperm donor; *Méd* **d. universel** universal donor; *Com* **d. d'ordre** principal; *Péj* **d. d'avis** *ou* **de conseils** know-all; **d. de caution** guarantor **2** *Cartes* dealer **3** *Arg* (*délateur*) grass

don-quichottisme [dɔ̃kiʃɔtism] **NM** quixotism

DONT [dɔ̃] **PRON REL** SEE GRAMMAR A33; B23; B62

1 (*exprimant le complément du verbe et indiquant la provenance*) **la pièce d. elle sort** the room she is coming out of; **la ville d. je viens** the town I come from; **la famille d. je descends** the family I am descended from *or* from which I am descended

2 (*exprimant le complément du verbe et indiquant le moyen, la manière etc*) **la façon d. il me regardait/est habillé** the way (in which) he looked at me/is dressed

3 (*au sujet de qui, de quoi*) **une fille d. on ne sait rien** a girl we know nothing about, *Fml* a girl about whom we know nothing; **un film d. on parle beaucoup** a film that is being talked about a lot; **un incident d. on se souviendra** an incident that will be remembered

4 (*exprimant l'objet du verbe*) **le livre d. j'ai besoin** the book (that) I need; **voici ce d. il s'agit** this is what it's all about; **l'homme d. il s'agit** the man in question; **l'homme d. elle se moque** the man she's making fun of, *Fml* the man of whom she is making fun

5 (*exprimant l'objet de l'adjectif*) **la femme d. il est amoureux** the woman he is in love with; **le groupe d'enfants d. vous êtes responsable** the group of children you are responsible for; **le souvenir d. elle est si honteuse** the memory she is so ashamed of

6 (*exprimant le complément de nom et indiquant la possession, la qualité, la matière*) **la dame d. je connais le fils** the lady whose son I know; **la dame d. le fils vous connaît** the lady whose son knows you; **la chambre d. la porte est fermée** the room with the closed door; **cet objet d. le nom m'échappe**

this object, the name of which escapes me **7** (*exprimant le complément de nom et indiquant une partie d'un tout*) **quelques-uns étaient là, d. votre frère** there were a few people there, including your brother; **un rêve d. il ne me reste que cette image** a dream of which I remember nothing but this image, a dream I remember nothing about except this image; **un film d. voici le résumé** a film of which the following is a summary; **la maison d. on voit le toit** the house whose roof can be seen; **le parti d. le chef vient de mourir** the party whose leader has just died

donzelle [dɔzɛl] **NF** *Fam Péj* woman who puts on airs

dopage [dɔpaʒ] **NM** doping; (*en athlétisme, cyclisme etc*) drug-taking; *Fig* (*de l'économie*) boosting

dopant [dɔpã] **ADJ produit d.** drug
NM drug

dope [dɔp] **NF** *Fam* (*drogue*) dope

doper [dɔpe] **VT** *Sport etc* to dope; *Fig* (*économie, monnaie etc*) to boost, to give a boost or fillip to
VPR se doper to take stimulants, to dope oneself

dope sheet [dopʃit] **NM** *TV* dope sheet

doping [dɔpiŋ] **NM** doping

Doppler [dɔplɛr] **ADJ** *Phys* **effet D.** Doppler effect
NM *Méd* = use of Doppler's method to determine speed at which the blood is circulating

dorade [dɔrad] **NF** (*poisson*) gilthead bream, sea bream

doré [dɔre] **ADJ 1** (*recouvert d'or*) gilded, gilt; **d. sur tranche** gilt-edged; **papier d.** gold-coloured paper **2** (*couleur d'or*) (*blé, lumière*) golden, honey-coloured, *Am* honey-colored; (*yeux*) golden (brown); (*peau*) golden (brown), honey-coloured; *Culin* (*gâteau passé au jaune d'œuf*) glazed; (*viande, pommes de terre, gâteau cuit*) browned, golden; **cheveux blond d.** golden hair
NM *Can* (*poisson*) wall-eyed pike, yellow pike

dorée [dɔre] **NF** (*poisson*) (John) Dory

dorénavant [dɔrenavã] **ADV** from now on, *Fml* henceforth

dorer [dɔre] **VT 1** (*recouvrir d'or*) to gild; *Fig* **d. la pilule à qn** to sugar the pill for sb **2** (*donner une couleur dorée à*) (*peau*) to turn golden; *Culin* (*gâteau*) to glaze; (*viande, pommes de terre*) to brown; **le soleil dorait les cimes** the sun shed a golden light on the hilltops or turned the hilltops golden
VI *Culin* to brown
VPR se dorer to turn a golden colour or *Am* color; **elle se dore** ou *Fam* **se dore la pilule au soleil** she's sunbathing, she's getting a suntan

doreur, -euse [dɔrœr, -øz] **N** gilder

dorique [dɔrik] **ADJ** *Archit* Doric

dorlotement [dɔrlɔtmã] **NM** coddling, pampering

dorloter [dɔrlɔte] **VT** to coddle, to pamper; **se laisser/se faire d.** to let oneself be/to be coddled or pampered
VPR se dorloter to coddle or pamper oneself

dormance [dɔrmãs] **NF** *Biol* dormancy

dormant [dɔrmã] **ADJ 1** (*eau*) still, stagnant **2** *Tech* **serrure dormante** dead lock **3** *Fig Fml* (*passions, instincts, sensualité*) dormant **4** *Fin* (*capitaux, compte*) dormant
NM (*d'une porte, d'une fenêtre*) frame, casing

dormeur, -euse [dɔrmœr, -øz] **ADJ poupée dormeuse** doll with eyes that close
N (*personne endormie*) sleeper; **ne réveille pas les dormeurs** don't wake the people who're sleeping; **c'est un grand** ou **gros d.**

he sleeps a lot; **en vacances, je redeviens un gros d.** I sleep a lot when I'm on holiday; **je ne partirai plus en week-end avec ces dormeurs** I'm not going away with them for the weekend again, all they do is sleep
NM (*crustacé*) edible crab
NF dormeuse (*boucle d'oreille*) sleeper

DORMIR [dɔrmir] **VI** (*prp dormant; pp dormi; pr ind je dors, n. dormons; impf je dormais; p hist je dormis*) **1** to sleep; **il dort** he's sleeping, he's asleep; **d. profondément** ou **d'un profond sommeil** to be fast asleep, to be in a deep sleep; **bien/mal d.** to sleep well/badly; **elle dort d'un sommeil léger** she's a light sleeper; **d. du sommeil du juste** to sleep the sleep of the just; **je n'ai pas dormi de la nuit** I haven't slept a wink, I didn't sleep a wink or get a wink's sleep (all night), I didn't sleep all night; **il n'en dort pas** he can't (get to) sleep for thinking of it; **parler/pleurer/crier en dormant** to talk/cry/shout in one's sleep; **le café m'empêche de d.** coffee keeps me awake; *Fam* **ce n'est pas ça qui va m'empêcher de d.** I won't lose any sleep over it; **d. trop longtemps** to oversleep; **d. à poings fermés** ou **comme une souche** ou **comme un loir** ou **comme une marmotte** ou **comme une brute** ou **comme un sonneur** to sleep soundly or like a log; **ne d. que d'un œil** to sleep with one eye open; **vous pouvez d. tranquille** ou **sur les** ou **vos deux oreilles** you can rest easy; **avoir envie de d.** to be or feel sleepy or drowsy; **il dort debout** he's asleep on his feet, he can't keep his eyes open; **une histoire** ou **un conte à d. debout** a tall or cock-and-bull story; **il dort sur son travail** he's falling asleep over his work; *Fam* **ce n'est vraiment pas le moment de d.** there's no time for sleeping now

2 *Fig* (*d'une ville, d'une forêt*) to be sleeping, to be asleep; **une espèce de génie dort en lui** he has a kind of latent genius; **elle a laissé ses projets d. trop longtemps** she waited too long to carry out her plans; **ce serait dommage de laisser d. tes talents de couturier** it would be a pity not to make use of your dressmaking talents or a pity to let your dressmaking talents go to waste; **un roman qui dort dans un tiroir** a novel languishing in a drawer; **c'est idiot d'avoir des capitaux qui dorment** it's stupid to have capital lying idle, it's stupid not to make your capital work for you; **eau qui dort** stagnant or still water; *Prov* **il n'est pire eau que l'eau qui dort** still waters run deep

dormitif, -ive [dɔrmitif, -iv] **ADJ** *Méd* soporific

dorsal, -ale, -aux, -ales [dɔrsal, -o] **ADJ** dorsal; **région dorsale de la main** back of the hand; *Aviat* **parachute d.** back-type parachute
NF dorsale 1 *Ling* dorsal consonant **2** *Géog* ridge; *Météo* **dorsale barométrique** ridge of high pressure

dort-en-chiant, *pl* **dorts-en-chiant** [dɔrãʃjã] **N** *Fam* slowcoach, *Am* slowpoke

dortoir [dɔrtwar] **NM** dormitory; **ville-d., cité-d.** dormitory town

dorure [dɔryr] **NF 1** (*couche d'or*) gilding **2** *Culin* (*d'un gâteau*) glazing (with egg yolk) **3** (*ornement doré*) gilt, gilding; **uniforme couvert de dorures** gold-braided uniform

doryphore [dɔrifɔr] **NM** Colorado beetle

DOS [dɔs] **NM** *Ordinat* DOS; **depuis le D., à partir du D.** through (the) DOS

DOS [do] **NM 1** *Anat* back; **avoir le d. voûté** to be round-shouldered; *Fig* **il a bon d.** he's got a broad back or shoulders; **elle a bon d. la grève des postes, dis plutôt que tu n'as pas écrit** why don't you admit that you haven't written instead of blaming it on the postal

strike?; *Fam* **j'en ai plein le d.** I'm sick of it, I'm fed up with it; **faire le gros d.** (*d'un chat*) to arch its back; *Fig* (*faire des difficultés*) to dig one's heels in, *Br Fam* to turn bolshie; **mon fils fait toujours le gros d. pour aller se coucher** my son always kicks up a fuss at bedtime; **tourner le d. à qn** to turn one's back on sb; (*quand on est debout/assis*) to stand/sit with one's back to sb; **ils tous mes amis m'ont tourné le d.** all my friends have turned their back on me; **avoir le d. tourné à qn/qch** to have one's back to sb/sth; **dès qu'il a le d. tourné** the moment or as soon as his back is turned; **en d. d'âne** ridged, razor-backed; **pont en d. d'âne** humpbacked bridge; **attention, d. d'âne** beware uneven road surface; **voyager à d. d'âne** to ride or travel on a donkey; **d. à d.** back to back; *Fig* **leur mère les a renvoyés d. à d.** their mother couldn't decide which of them was the guilty party; **je les renvoie d. à d.** I think they're equally guilty or as bad as each other; **on peut les renvoyer d. à d.** they're equally guilty; *Fam* **se mettre tout le monde à d.** to set everybody against you; **partir sac au d.** to set off with one's pack on one's back; **faire qch derrière** ou **dans le d. de qn** to do sth behind sb's back; **robe décolletée dans le d.** low-backed dress; **elle porte ses cheveux dans le d.** she wears her hair loose or down; **ça fait froid dans le d.** it's scary or creepy, it gives you the shivers; **j'en ai un frisson dans le d.** it sends a shiver down my spine; *Fig Fam* **la maison, on l'a dans le d.** we can kiss the house goodbye; *Fig Fam* **faire un enfant dans le d. à qn** to stab sb in the back; **je ne l'ai vu que de d.** I only saw him from the back, I only got a back view of him; **dormir sur le d.** to sleep on one's back; *Fig Fam* **depuis un mois, j'ai mon patron/le fisc sur le d.** I've had my boss/the tax man on my back for a month; *Fam* **il me tombe toujours sur le d.** (*il m'attaque*) he's always on my back; (*il arrive à l'improviste*) he's always just turning up; **le fisc va te tomber sur le d.** you're going to have the tax man on your back, you're going to bring the tax man down on you; **le repassage, c'est toujours sur son d. que ça tombe** he always gets landed with the ironing; **quand mes frères font des bêtises, c'est toujours sur mon d. que ça tombe** I always get the blame when my brothers do something stupid; **mettre qch sur le d. de qn** to saddle sb with sth; **quand il a été interrogé, il a tout mis sur mon d.** when he was questioned, he put all the blame on me; **il a tout mis sur le d. des petits copains et est parti tranquillement en vacances** he offloaded everything onto his friends and blithely went off on holiday; **il s'est mis une sale histoire sur le d.** he's landed himself in real trouble; **gagner de l'argent** ou **s'enrichir sur le d. de qn** to get rich off sb, to make money on sb's back; **je n'ai rien à me mettre sur le d.** I haven't a thing to wear; *Fam Vieilli* **faire la bête à deux d.** to have it off; *Fam Vieilli* **faire la bête à deux d. avec qn** to sleep with or have it off with sb

2 (*d'une chaise, d'une page, d'un couteau etc*) back; (*du nez*) bridge; (*d'un livre*) spine; **signer au d. d'un chèque** to endorse a cheque; **voir au d.** see over or overleaf; *Fin* **d. d'un effet** back of a bill

3 (*nage*) **d. (crawlé)** backstroke; **nager le** ou **faire du d. (crawlé)** to do the backstroke

dosage [dozaʒ] **NM** *Chimie etc* (*d'ingrédients*) proportioning; *Méd* (*de médicaments*) dosage; *Méd* **d. hormonal** test to determine hormone levels

dos-d'âne [dodan] **NM INV** bump; **pont en d.** humpbacked bridge

dose [doz] **NF** *Chimie etc* (*d'un élément dans un mélange*) proportion, amount; (*de médi-*

cament) dose; **d. mortelle** lethal dose; **ne pas dépasser la d. prescrite** do not exceed the stated dose; *Fig* **par** *ou* **à petites doses, à d. homéopathique** in small doses; **une légère d. d'ironie** a tinge of irony; *Fam* **il faut une sacrée d. de culot/d'humour pour faire cela** it takes a helluva nerve/a great sense of humour to do that; **forcer la d.** to overdo it; *Fam* **avoir sa d.** to have had more than enough; **avoir sa d. de lecture/de ménage/de cinéma américain** to have had one's fill of reading/housework/American films; *Fam* **en avoir sa d.** to have had one's fill, to have had more than enough; **la pluie, je t'assure que j'en ai ma d.** I've had my fill of rain *or* more than enough rain, let me tell you

doser [doze] VT *Chimie etc (pour évaluer)* to determine the quantity of; *(pour constituer)* to proportion; *(médicament)* to measure out; **je n'arrive jamais à d. la farine dans mes gâteaux** I never manage to get the right amount of flour in my cakes; *Fig* **il faut savoir d. l'ironie** you have to get the amount of irony just right

doseur [dozœr] NM measure; **verre d.** *Culin* measuring jug; *(pour l'alcool)* measure

doseur-distributeur, *pl* **doseurs-distributeurs** NM *(de carburant)* fuel distributor

dossard [dosar] NM *Sport* number

dossier [dosje] NM **1** *(d'un siège)* back, backrest; **chaise à d. droit** straight-backed chair; **d. réglable** adjustable back; **d. rabattable** folding seatback; **d. repliable** folding seatback

2 *(pièces, documents)* file, dossier; *(d'un prisonnier, d'un malade)* record; *(chemise)* folder, file; *Ordinat* file; **verser une pièce au d.** to file a document; **constituer un d. sur qn/qch** to build up a file on sb/sth; **d. d'appel d'offres** tender documents; **d. client** client file; **d. crédit** credit file; **d. de demande d'introduction en Bourse** listing agreement; **d. de demande de prêt** loan application form; **d. 'divers'** miscellaneous file; **d. de domiciliation** domiciliation papers, domiciliation file; **d. de douane** customs papers *or* file; **d. d'information** information pack; **d. de lancement** *(d'un produit)* product launch file; **d. médical** medical record; *Fam* **d. offre** tender documents; **d. de presse** book of press cuttings, scrap book; **d. scolaire** school records; **d. suspendu** suspension file; *Ordinat* **d. système** system folder; **d. de voyage** travel documents

3 *(sujet)* question, matter; **le d. de la couche d'ozone est assez important** the ozone layer is a fairly important question *or* matter; **le d. du GATT** the GATT question, GATT matters; **s'occuper du d. de l'environnement** to be responsible for environmental matters; **avoir un d. brûlant à traiter** to have a controversial issue to deal with; **je pense qu'il est temps de fermer le d. Staline** I think it's time to draw a line under the Stalin question

dot [dɔt] NF **1** *(pour un mariage)* dowry, marriage settlement; **il l'a épousée pour sa d.** he married her for her dowry; **coureur de d.** fortune hunter **2** *(pour une religieuse)* dowry

dotal, -ale, -aux, -ales [dɔtal, -o] ADJ *(propriété)* dotal; *Jur* **régime d.** (marriage) settlement in trust

dotation [dɔtasjɔ̃] NF **1** *(fonds)* *(d'hôpital, de collège etc)* endowment, foundation; *(à la famille royale, à un chef d'État)* allowance **2** *Can Admin* **agent de d.** staffing officer; **d. en effectifs** staff increase **3** *Compta* provision; **d. aux amortissements** depreciation provision, allowance for depreciation, charge for depreciation; **d. aux provisions** charge to provisions; **d. en capital** capital contribution

doter [dɔte] VT *(hôpital, collège etc)* to en-

dow; *Vieilli (mariée)* to dower; **être doté de toutes les vertus** to be endowed with every virtue; **d. une usine d'un matériel neuf** to equip a factory with new plant; **la nature l'a dotée d'une intelligence remarquable** nature has bestowed exceptional intelligence on her *or* has endowed her with exceptional intelligence; **d. une provision** to make a provision

douaire [dwɛr] NM dower

douairière [dwɛrjɛr] ADJ, NF dowager

douane [dwan] NF *Admin* customs; **(droits de) d.** (customs) duty; **passer à la d.** *ou* **au bureau de d.** to go through customs; **passer qch (en fraude) à la d.** to smuggle sth through customs; **formalités de d.** customs formalities; **à l'aéroport, les formalités de d. sont vraiment simplifiées** it's really easy to go through customs at the airport; **agent des douanes** customs officer; **marchandises en d.** bonded goods; **franc de d.** duty paid; **d. volante** mobile customs and excise unit

douanier, -ière [dwanje, -jɛr] ADJ customs; **tarif d.** customs tariff; **union douanière** customs union; **barrières douanières** tariff barriers

N customs officer

doublage [dublaʒ] NM **1** *(d'une feuille de papier, d'une couverture, d'un fil etc)* doubling, folding in half **2** *(d'une quantité, d'un salaire etc)* doubling **3** *(d'un manteau)* lining **4** *Cin (de voix)* dubbing; *(dans une scène)* doubling *(de* for); **d. du film en anglais** English dubbing of the film; **d. du dialogue (en boucle)** dialogue looping **5** *Aut* **d. d'aile** wing valance

DOUBLE [dubl] ADJ **1** *(mesure, quantité, consonne, lit, chambre etc)* double; *Scol* **copie d.** double sheet of paper; **valise à d. fond** suitcase with a false bottom; **faire qch en d. exemplaire** to do sth in duplicate; **coup d.** *(au tir)* right and left; **mot qui fait d. emploi (avec un autre)** redundant word; **'vends micro-ondes, cause d. emploi'** *(de petite annonce)* 'microwave for sale, duplicate item'; **sa canne à pêche a une longueur d. de la mienne** his fishing rod is twice the length of *or* twice as long as mine; **fermer une porte à d. tour** to double-lock a door; **enfermer qn à d. tour** to lock sb in; **à d. effet** dual- *or* double-action; **outil à d. usage** dual-purpose tool; **à d. tranchant** *(couteau)* double-edged; *Fig* two-edged; **comptabilité en partie d.** double-entry bookkeeping; **d. allumage** *(de moteur)* dual ignition; **avoir une d. nationalité** to have dual nationality; **foyer à d. revenu** two-income household; **d. whisky** double *or* large whisky; *Mus* **d. croche** semiquaver, *Am* sixteenth note; **d. mètre rule** *(which measures two metres)*; **d. nœud** double knot; **doubles rideaux** curtains, *Am* drapes; *Fig* **faire coup d.** to kill two birds with one stone; **test en d. aveugle** double blind test; *Fig* **mettre les bouchées doubles** to work twice as hard; **d. vitrage** double glazing; **d. arbre à cames** twin cam, twin camshaft; *Tél* **(à) d. bande** dual-band; **d. carburateur** twin carburettor; *UE* **d. circulation** *(de monnaies)* dual circulation; *Journ* **d. colonne** double column; *Ordinat* **d. densité** double density; *Aut* **d. ligne blanche** double white line; *Journ* **d. page** (double-page) spread; **l'article prend une d. page** it's a two-page spread; *Jur* **d. peine** double punishment *(consisting of a prison sentence followed by expulsion from the country)*; *Typ, TV, Cin* **d. prise** double-take; **d. interligne** double spacing; **en d. interligne** double-spaced; *Typ* **d. soulignement** double underlining; *Typ* **d. souligné** double underline **2** *(ambigu)* **d. personnalité** dual personality; **mener une d. vie** to lead a double

life; **mot à d. sens** ambiguous word; **agent d.** double agent; **jouer un d. jeu avec qn** to play a double game with sb; **je n'ai pas le don de d. vue** I'm not endowed with ESP, I'm not psychic, I don't have second sight

ADV **voir d.** to see double

NM **1** *(quantité)* double; **j'ai le d. de votre âge** I'm twice your age; **ça m'a coûté le d.** it cost me twice as much *or* double; **mettre qch en d.** to double sth, to fold sth in two *or* half; *Tennis* **d. messieurs/dames/mixte** men's/ladies'/mixed doubles; **faire un d.** *(dans un jeu)* to throw a double

2 *(exemplaire)* duplicate, copy; *Ordinat* backup; **faire qch en d.** *(lettre, devoir, clé)* to make two copies of sth; **je dois tricoter le pull en d.** I'll have to make two pullovers of the same pattern; **avoir un d. des clefs** to have duplicate keys *or* a spare set of keys; **avoir un d. de tous les papiers importants** to have duplicates of all the important papers; **prends-le, je l'ai en d.** take it, I have two of them; **j'ai un timbre en d. dans ma collection** I have two copies of a stamp in my collection; **j'ai tous mes papiers en d. au cas où** I have duplicates *or* copies of all my papers just in case

3 *(personne)* double

doublé [duble] ADJ **1** doubled **2** *(veste, gants)* lined *(* **de** with) **3** *Cin* dubbed, re-voiced

NM **1 d. (or)** gold plate, rolled gold; *(bijouterie)* gold-plated jewellery *or Am* jewelry; **d. argent** silver plate; *(bijouterie)* silver-plated jewellery **2** *(à la chasse), Sport* double

double-bande, *pl* **doubles-bandes** [dublabãd] NF *TV* double head

double-blanc, *pl* **doubles-blancs** [dublablã] NM *(aux dominos)* double blank

double-clic, *pl* **doubles-clics** [dublaklik] NM *Ordinat* double-click; **faire un d.** to double-click

double-cliquer [dublaklike] VI *Ordinat* to double-click

double-commande, *pl* **doubles-commandes** [dublakɔmãd] NF *Aviat, Aut* dual controls

double-corde, *pl* **doubles-cordes** [dublakɔrd] NF *Mus (sur un violon etc)* double-stopping

double-crème, *pl* **doubles-crèmes** [dublakrɛm] NM (type of) cream cheese

double-débrayage [dubladebrejaʒ] NM *Aut* double-declutching; **faire un d.** to double-declutch

double-décimètre, *pl* **doubles-décimètres** [dubladesimɛtr] NM ruler

double-fenêtre, *pl* **doubles-fenêtres** [dublaf(ə)nɛtr] NF sash window, double-hung window

doublement[1] [dubləmã] ADV doubly

doublement[2] NM **1** *(d'un nombre, d'une somme, d'une lettre etc)* doubling; *(d'une feuille de papier)* folding in two *or* in half; *(d'une couverture, d'un fil)* folding in two *or* in half, doubling; *Ordinat* **d. de vitesse d'horloge** clock speed doubling **2** *Aut* overtaking, *Am* passing; **tenter un d.** to try to overtake; **d. interdit** no overtaking

doubler [duble] VT **1** *(montant, taille etc)* to double; **d. le pas** to quicken one's pace

2 *(feuille de papier)* to fold in two *or* in half; *(couverture, fil)* to fold in two *or* in half, to double; *Mus* **d. une partie** to double a part

3 *(manteau, gant etc)* to line

4 *Belg, Can, Suisse Scol (redoubler)* to repeat *(a school year)*

5 *Cin (voix)* to dub; *Cin (acteur)* to stand in for; *Théâtre (rôle, acteur)* to understudy; **il se fait d. pour les cascades** he's got a stand-in for his stunts; *Cin* **d. une prise** to do a double-take

6 *(passer)* **d. les gens dans une queue** to jump a queue, to sneak past the people in a queue; **d. une voiture** to overtake *or Am* pass a car; *Naut* **d. un cap** to double *or* make *or* weather a cape
7 *Fam (trahir)* to double-cross; **on s'est fait d.** we've been double-crossed
VI 1 *(de population etc)* to double, to increase twofold **2** *Aut* to overtake, *Am* to pass; **défense de d.** no overtaking, *Am* no passing **3** *Belg,Can, Suisse Scol (redoubler)* to repeat a year
VPR se doubler une haine qui se double de mépris hatred coupled with contempt

doublet [dublɛ] **NM** *(pierre précieuse), Ling* doublet

doubleur [dublœr] **NM** *Ordinat* **d. de fréquence** clock speed doubler

doublon¹ [dublɔ̃] **NM** *Typ* double, word keyed twice

doublon² **NM** *Hist (monnaie)* doubloon

doublonner [dublɔne] **VI notre nouvelle imprimante doublonne avec l'ancienne** our new printer makes the old one redundant, our new printer means that we no longer need the old one

doublure [dublyr] **NF 1** *(d'un vêtement, d'un sac de couchage etc)* lining **2** *Théâtre* understudy; *Cin* stand-in, body double; *(cascadeur)* stunt man/woman

douce [dus] *voir* **doux**

douce-amère, *pl* **douces-amères** [dusamɛr] **NF** woody nightshade, bittersweet

douceâtre [dusɑtr] **ADJ** sweetish, *Péj* sickly sweet

doucement [dusmɑ̃] **ADV** *(délicatement)* gently; *(bas)* softly; *(en faisant attention)* gently, carefully, slowly; **allez-y d.!** gently does it!, easy does it!; **les affaires vont d.** business is so-so; *Fam* **(allez-y) d. avec le vin** go easy on the wine, *Arg* **ça m'a fait d. rigoler** I had a good laugh over it; *Fam* **d. les basses!** take it easy!

doucereux, -euse [dusrø, -øz] **ADJ 1** *(goût etc)* sweetish, *Péj* sickly (sweet) **2** *(personne)* smooth, smooth-tongued; *(voix, ton)* smooth, sugary

doucet, -ette [dusɛ, -ɛt] **ADJ** *Arch (personne)* meek, mild
NF doucette *(plante)* corn salad, lamb's lettuce

douceur [dusœr] **NF 1** *(d'un son, d'une matière etc)* softness; *(d'un climat)* mildness; *(d'une atmosphère)* pleasantness; **d. de vivre** easy *or* relaxed way of life; **les douceurs de l'amitié** the comforts *or* pleasures of friendship **2** *(de caractère)* gentleness; *(d'un sourire)* sweetness; **traiter qn avec d.** to treat sb gently *or* with kindness; **employer la d. avec un enfant/un animal** to be gentle with a child/an animal; **en d.** gently; **la voiture a démarré en d.** the car started smoothly; **allez-y en d.!** gently does it!, easy does it!; **poser un avion en d.** to land an aircraft smoothly, to make a smooth landing **3** *(sucreries)* **douceurs** sweets, sweet things; **aimer les douceurs** to have a sweet tooth; *Fig* **dire des douceurs à une femme** to whisper sweet nothings to a woman **4** *(du miel, d'un parfum etc)* sweetness

douche [duʃ] **NF 1** shower; *(installation)* shower (unit); **prendre une d.** to take a shower; **être sous la d.** to be in the shower; **préférer la d. au bain** to prefer a shower to a bath; **passer à la d.** to take a shower; **les douches** the shower room(s), the showers **2** *Fam (de pluie)* **on s'est pris une de ces douches!** we got soaked! **3** *Fig* disappointment; **plus jamais je ne voudrais me prendre une d. pareille** I don't want another disappointment like that ever again

▶▶ d. écossaise (alternately) hot and cold shower; *Fig* **il a un caractère tellement changeant qu'avec lui, c'est toujours la d. écossaise** he's so unpredictable that you never know where you are with him; *Fig* **ça m'a fait l'effet d'une d. écossaise** it came as a bit of a shock; *Fig* **d. froide** terrible disappointment, let-down

doucher [duʃe] **VT 1** *(pour laver)* **d. qn** to give sb a shower **2** *Fam (d'une averse)* to soak; **se faire d. par l'orage** to get soaked in the storm **3** *Fam (fustiger)* to tell off; *(décevoir)* to shock; **il s'est fait d. par le patron** he got a telling-off from the boss; **ça m'a vraiment douché** it came as a real shock
VPR se doucher to take a shower, to shower

douchette [duʃɛt] **NF 1** *(pomme)* shower head **2** *(pour codes-barres)* bar code reader

doudou [dudu] **NF** *(aux Antilles)* girlfriend

doudoune¹ [dudun] **NF** *(anorak)* down jacket

doudounes² **NFPL** *Fam (seins)* boobs

doué [dwe] **ADJ** *(acteur, musicien etc)* gifted, talented; **il n'est guère d. pour les langues** he has no gift for languages, he's no linguist; *Hum* **tu es vraiment d.!** that was really intelligent *or* clever!

douer [dwe] **VT** to endow *(de* with); **il est doué d'une bonne mémoire** he has a good memory

douille [duj] **NF** *(d'un outil etc)* socket; *(d'une ampoule électrique)* lamp socket; *(d'une cartouche etc)* case; *Culin* piping nozzle; **d. à (pas de) vis** screw lamp holder

douiller [duje] **VI** *Fam (coûter cher)* to cost an arm and a leg; **la prochaine facture de téléphone, ça va d.** the next phone bill is going to be sky-high; **c'est un restau qui douille** the prices are sky-high in that restaurant, it costs an arm and a leg to eat in that restaurant

douillet, -ette [dujɛ, -ɛt] **ADJ 1** *(coussin)* soft, downy; *(lit)* cosy **2** *(trop délicat)* **ne sois pas si d.!** don't be such a baby *or Fam* wimp!
NF douillette 1 *(robe de chambre)* quilted housecoat *or Am* robe; *(de curé)* overcoat **2** *Can (couvre-lit)* quilted bedspread

douillettement [dujɛtmɑ̃] **ADV** *(confortablement)* cosily; **quand il fait froid, je m'installe d. sous la couette** when it's cold, I snuggle down under the quilt; **j'étais d. enroulée dans mon châle** I was all snug and cosy *or* I was wrapped up warmly in my shawl; **élever un enfant d.** to coddle a child; **il a été élevé trop d.** he was coddled too much as a child; **sa mère le traite toujours d.** his mother still coddles him

douleur [dulœr] **NF 1** *(physique)* pain; *(diffuse)* ache; **d. aiguë** sharp pain; **pousser un cri/des cris de d.** to cry out with *or* in pain; **j'ai une d. persistante dans le genou** I have a persistent ache in my knee; **se sentir des douleurs par** *ou* **dans tout le corps** to ache all over; **j'ai des douleurs dans le ventre** I've got pains in my stomach; **sans d.** *(accouchement)* painless **2** *(morale)* sorrow, grief; **il a eu la d. de perdre sa mère** he had the painful experience of losing his mother; **partager la d. de qn** to share sb's sorrow *or* grief, to feel for sb; **nous avons la d. de vous faire part du décès de …** we regret to inform you of the death of …; *Fam* **si je le chope, il va comprendre sa d.!** if I catch him, he'll get what's coming to him *or* his worst nightmares will come true!

douloureusement [dulurøzmɑ̃] **ADV** painfully; *(regarder qn)* sorrowfully; **il s'est cogné le genou d.** he gave himself a painful knock on the knee; **c'est une perte qu'elle ressent d.** she feels the loss deeply; **il a été d. atteint par la mort de sa grand-mère** his grandmo-

ther's death upset him very much *or* affected him deeply

douloureux, -euse [dulurø, -øz] **ADJ 1** *(coup, maladie, opération etc)* painful; *(au contact)* sore, tender; **mon dos est d. aujourd'hui** my back hurts *or* aches today, my back is hurting today **2** *(perte, événement etc)* sad, distressing; *(séparation)* painful; *(circonstances)* painful, distressing; *(regard)* pained, sorrowful; **des cris d.** heart-rending *or* mournful cries
NF *Fam* **la douloureuse** the bill; **apportez-moi la douloureuse** let's see what the damage is

DOUTE [dut] **NM 1** *(incertitude)* doubt, uncertainty; **être dans le d.** to be in doubt, to be doubtful *(au sujet de qch* about sth); **mettre qch en d.** to question sth, to cast doubt on sth; **mettre en d. la parole de qn** to doubt sb's word; **il n'y a pas de** *ou* **aucun d.** there's no doubt about it, it is beyond doubt *or* beyond (all) question; **laisser qn dans le d. est cruel** it's cruel to leave sb in doubt *or* in a state of uncertainty; **je ne lui ai laissé aucun d. quant à mes sentiments pour lui** I left him in no doubt about my feelings for him; **cela ne fait plus aucun d.** there is no longer any doubt about it; **nul d. qu'il (ne) soit mort** there is no doubt that he is dead; **sans d.** no doubt, probably; **sans aucun d.** without (any) doubt; **vous ne me reconnaissez pas, sans d.** I don't suppose you recognize me; **sans d. viendra-t-il, sans d. qu'il viendra** I expect he'll come, he'll probably come; *Prov* **dans le d., abstiens-toi** when in doubt, don't **2** *(soupçon)* doubt, misgiving, suspicion; **avoir des doutes sur** *ou* **au sujet de qn/qch** to have doubts *or* misgivings *or* suspicions about sb/sth; **avoir un d. (sur qch)** to have misgivings *or* doubts (about sth); **j'ai un d. sur la vérité de ce qu'il dit** I have doubts about whether he's telling the truth; **il y a quand même un d. sur son passé** there is still some doubt about his past

DOUTER [dute] **VI** to doubt; **il était à n'en point d. courageux** his courage was beyond all question; **d. de qn/qch** to doubt sb/sth; **je n'ai jamais douté de vos compétences** I have never doubted your ability; **je n'ai jamais douté de ta venue** I never doubted that you would come; **je n'ai jamais douté de te voir** I never doubted that I would see you; **d. du zèle de qn** to doubt *or* question sb's enthusiasm, to have doubts about sb's enthusiasm; **elle doute de vous avoir rencontré** she's not sure whether she's met you; **il ne doute de rien** he is full of self-confidence; **j'en doute** I doubt it, I have my doubts (about it); **j'en doute fort** I doubt it very much, I have very strong doubts
VT je doute qu'il soit assez fort I doubt whether he is strong enough; **je n'ai jamais douté que tu viennes** I never doubted that you would come; **je ne doute pas qu'il (ne) vous vienne en aide** I am confident that he will help you
VPR se douter se d. de qch to suspect sth; **il ne se doute de rien** he doesn't suspect anything; **je m'en doutais (bien)** I guessed *or* thought as much; **elle est surprise, je m'en doute** she is surprised, I'm sure *or* I dare say; **je ne me doutais pas qu'il fût là** I had no idea that he was there; **je me doute bien que c'est un peu difficile** I rather suspect *or* think it's going to be difficult; **j'étais loin de me d. que cela arriverait** I never thought for a moment that that would happen; *Fam* **on s'en serait douté!** I might have known *or* guessed!

douteux, -euse [dutø, -øz] **ADJ 1** *(incertain)* doubtful; *(origine, authenticité)* doubtful, questionable; **il est d. qu'il vienne** it is doubtful whether he will come; **il n'est pas**

d. que ... (ne) + *sub ou plus souvent* que + *ind* there is no doubt that ...; **créance douteuse** bad debt **2** *(honneur, compagnie, fraîcheur, mœurs etc)* dubious; **jour d.** dubious *or* uncertain light; **des vêtements d.** *ou* **d'une propreté douteuse** dubious clothes; **d'un blanc d.** of a dubious white; **d'un goût d.** *(plaisanteries, vêtements, pièce)* in dubious taste; **il a des petites copines d'un goût d.** he has some rather dubious girlfriends

douve [duv] **NF 1** *Agr* trench, ditch; *Courses de chevaux* water jump; **douves** *(d'un château)* moat **2** *(planche)* stave

Douvres [duvr] **N** Dover

doux, douce [du, dus] **ADJ 1** *(au toucher)* smooth, soft; *(au goût)* mild; **eau douce** fresh water; *(non calcaire)* soft water; **poisson d'eau douce** freshwater fish; *Fam* **marin d'eau douce** landlubber; **peau douce** smooth *or* soft skin

2 *(air, ton etc)* pleasant, agreeable; **d. souvenir** pleasant memory; **mener une vie douce** to lead a calm *or* peaceful life; *Fam* **se la couler douce** to take it easy; **faire les yeux d. à qn** to make sheep's eyes at sb; *Iron* **douce perspective!** charming prospect!

3 *(mouvement, voix, pente)* gentle; *(couleur, son)* soft, subdued; *(lumière)* mellow, soft, subdued; *(climat, hiver)* mild; *(moteur, suspension)* sweet; **chaleur douce** moderate heat; *Culin* **faire cuire à feu d.** to cook on a low heat *or* in a low oven; **lime douce** smooth file; **drogue douce** soft drug; **des médecines douces** alternative forms of medicine; **consonne douce** soft consonant

4 *(nature, regard)* mild, gentle; **être d. avec les enfants** to be kind to children; *(d'un animal)* to be good *or* gentle with children; **être d. avec les animaux** to be kind to animals; **il est très d. avec son petit garçon** he's very gentle with his little boy; **d. comme un agneau** as gentle as a lamb

5 *Fam* **c'est de la folie douce!** it's sheer madness!

ADV *Fam* **filer d.** to tread warily, to watch one's step; **là, tout d.!** steady, steady!

NM préférer le sec au d. to prefer dry (wine) to sweet

NF douce 1 *Fam (petite amie)* girlfriend; **allez, viens, ma d.** come on, sweetheart **2 en d.** discreetly, quietly, *Fam* on the QT

N *Fam* **c'est un d./une douce** he's/she's a gentle creature

douzain [duzɛ̃] **NM** *Littér* twelve-line poem

douzaine [duzɛn] **NF** dozen; **trois douzaines d'œufs** three dozen eggs; **une d. de personnes** about a dozen people, a dozen or so people; **il y a une d. d'années** about twelve years ago, a dozen or so years ago; **quand nous avions une d. d'années** when we were about twelve; **à la d.** by the dozen; *Fig* **il y en a à la d.** there are dozens *or* lots of them SEE
GRAMMAR A12–13; B60

douze [duz] **ADJ INV** twelve; **le d. mai** the twelfth of May; **Louis D.** Louis the Twelfth; **d. heures** twelve o'clock (noon)
NM INV twelve

douzième [duzjɛm] **ADJ, N** twelfth

douzièmement [duzjɛmmɑ̃] **ADV** twelfthly, in the twelfth place

doyen, -enne [dwajɛ̃, -ɛn] **N 1** *(d'un chapitre, d'une faculté)* dean; *(d'un corps, d'une association etc)* doyen **2** *(personne la plus âgée)* senior; **elle est la doyenne de notre groupe** she's the oldest in *or* the oldest member of our group; **d. d'âge** oldest

doyenné [dwajɛne] **NM** *Rel (dignité, résidence)* deanery

NF d. (du comice) comice (pear)

dpi [depei] *(abrév* **dots per inch***)* dpi

drache [draʃ] **NF** *Région* downpour; **on s'est pris une de ces draches!** we got soaked *or* drenched!

dracher [draʃe] **V IMPERS** *Région* to pour

drachme [drakm] **NF** *Anciennement* drachma

draconien, -ienne [drakɔnjɛ̃, -jɛn] **ADJ** *(règlement)* draconian; **régime d.** very strict diet

dragage [dragaʒ] **NM 1** *(nettoyage)* *(d'une rivière, d'un port etc)* dredging **2** *(d'une rivière pour retrouver un corps etc)* dragging; **d. des mines** mine-sweeping

dragée [draʒe] **NF 1** *(confiserie)* sugar(ed) almond; *Pharm* sugar-coated pill; **tenir la d. haute à qn** to make sb dance to one's tune **2** *(petit plomb)* small shot; *Arg (balle)* bullet

dragéifier [draʒeifje] **VT** *Pharm (pilule)* to coat with sugar, to sugar; **comprimé dragéifié** sugar-coated tablet

drageon [draʒɔ̃] **NM** *Bot* sucker

dragon [dragɔ̃] **NM 1** *Myth, Fig* dragon; *Fig* **c'est un d. de vertu** she pretends to be such a paragon of virtue; **d. volant** *(reptile)* flying lizard **2** *Mil* dragoon; **dragons portés** ≃ motorized cavalry

dragonne [dragɔn] **NF** *(d'une épée, d'un sabre)* sword knot; *(d'un parapluie)* strap

drague [drag] **NF 1** *Tech* dredger; *(grappin)* drag, grappling hook; *Pêche* dredge, dragnet; **d. suceuse** pump dredger; **d. à godets** bucket dredger **2** *Fam (pour séduire)* chatting up men/women, *Am* hitting on men/women; **il y a de la d. dans l'air** someone's getting the come-on; **un champion** *ou* **professionnel de la d.** an expert at chatting up women; **c'est un lieu de d. idéal** it's an ideal place for chatting people up

draguer [drage] **VT 1** *(nettoyer) (rivière, port etc)* to dredge **2** *(pour retrouver qch) (étang etc)* to drag; *(bras de mer)* to sweep; *Pêche (huîtres etc)* to dredge for **3** *Fam (hommes, femmes)* to chat up, to try to pick up, *Am* to hit on; **il m'a draguée** he tried to pick me up
VI *Fam* to chat up men/women, *Am* to hit on men/women; **ça drague sec** *ou* **dur ici** there's a lot of chatting up going on here

dragueur, -euse [dragœr, -øz] **NM 1** *(bateau)* dredger; **d. de mines** minesweeper **2** *(ouvrier), Tech* dredgerman; *(avec grappin)* dragman
N *Fam* **c'est un d.** he's always on the pull *or* *Am* on the make; **c'est une sacrée dragueuse** she's always chatting up the men

drain [drɛ̃] **NM 1** *(conduit)* drain(pipe) **2** *Chir* drainage tube

drainage [drɛnaʒ] **NM 1** *(d'un champ, d'une plaie etc)* drainage, draining **2** *(d'argent, de capital)* drain

drainer [drene] **VT 1** *(sol, abcès)* to drain **2** *(commerce, capital, talent, ouvriers etc)* to draw, to attract

Dralon® [dralɔ̃] **NM** Dralon®

DRAM [dram] **NF** *Ordinat (abrév* **dynamic random access memory***)* DRAM

dramatique [dramatik] **ADJ** *Théâtre* dramatic; **l'art d.** drama; **école d'art d.** drama school; **auteur d.** playwright; *Fig* **il est arrivé quelque chose de d.** something dreadful *or* terrible has happened; **mais c'est d.!** that's dreadful *or* terrible!; **je ne considère pas son départ comme d.** I don't think his leaving is a tragedy; *Fam* **c'est pas d.** it's not a tragedy, it's not the end of the world
NF *TV* television play *or* drama; *Radio* radio play *or* drama

Il faut noter que l'adjectif anglais **dramatic** ne signifie jamais **terrible** ni **tragique**.

dramatiquement [dramatikmɑ̃] **ADV** tragically

Il faut noter que l'adverbe anglais **dramatically** est un faux ami. Il signifie le plus souvent **radicalement**.

dramatisation [dramatizasjɔ̃] **NF** dramatization

dramatiser [dramatize] **VT 1** *(événement etc)* to dramatize **2** *(roman)* to dramatize, to adapt for the stage

dramaturge [dramatyrʒ] **NM** dramatist, playwright

dramaturgie [dramatyrʒi] **NF** dramatic art

drame [dram] **NM 1** *(genre littéraire)* drama; *Arch (pièce)* play; **d. lyrique** *(opéra)* opera; *(oratorio)* oratorio; **d. psychologique** psychological drama **2** *Fig* drama, tragedy; **la scène a tourné au d.** the scene took a tragic turn; **il ne faut pas en faire un d.** there's no need to make a drama out of it *or* to dramatize it; **ce n'est pas un d.** it's not the end of the world, it's nothing to get upset about; **il nous a fait tout un d. parce que son stylo avait disparu** he made quite a scene because his pen had disappeared **3** *Cin, Radio, TV* drama; **d. judiciaire** courtroom drama; **d. reconstitué** drama documentary, dramadoc; **d. télévisé** television drama

drap [dra] **NM 1** *Tex* cloth; **d. fin** broadcloth; **d. d'or/de soie** gold/silk brocade; *Hist* **le camp du D. d'or** the Field of the Cloth of Gold **2 d. (de lit)** sheet; **d. de dessous/dessus** bottom/top sheet; **se mettre dans** *ou* **entre les draps** to go to bed; *Fig* **être dans de beaux** *ou* **mauvais** *ou* **vilains draps** to be in a fine mess *or* in a pickle *or* in a predicament **3** *Belg (serviette)* towel; **d. de maison** table cloth
▸▸ **d. de bain** bath sheet; **d. mortuaire** pall; **d. de plage** beach towel

drapé [drape] **ADJ 1** *(couvert d'un drap)* covered with a sheet *or* a cloth **2** *(à plis)* draped; **robe drapée sur les épaules** dress draped at the shoulders
NM *(d'un vêtement)* drape

drapeau, -eaux [drapo] **NM** flag; *Mil (regimental)* colour; *Cin, TV (sur lumière)* flag, gobo; **arborer** *ou* **hisser un d.** to hoist a flag; *Mil* **présentation du d.** ≃ trooping the colour; *Fig* **être sous les drapeaux** to serve in the (armed) forces; **mourir pour le d.** to die for the flag *or* one's country; *Fig* **se ranger sous les drapeaux de la Serbie/des verts** to join the Serbian/greens' camp; *Arg* **planter un d.** to leave without paying (the bill); *Aviat* **mettre une hélice en d.** to feather a propeller; *Sport* **abaisser le d. à l'arrivée du premier concurrent** to flag in the winner
▸▸ **d. blanc** white flag; **d. noir** black flag; **d. rouge** red flag

drapement [drapmɑ̃] **NM** *(de tissu)* draping

draper [drape] **VT 1** *Tex (laine)* to process **2** *(étoffe)* to drape
VPR se draper to wrap oneself up, to drape oneself *(dans, de* in); *Fig* **se d. dans sa dignité** to stand on one's dignity

draperie [drapri] **NF 1** *(usine)* cloth factory; *(commerce)* drapery (trade) **2** *Beaux-Arts* drapery **3** *(tenture)* curtains, *Am* drapes

drap-housse, *pl* **draps-housses NM** fitted sheet

drapier, -ière [drapje, -jɛr] **N** *(marchand)* draper; *(fabricant)* cloth manufacturer
ADJ *(industrie)* cloth(-making); *(ouvrier, marchand)* cloth

DRASS [dras] **NF** *Admin (abrév* **Direction régionale des affaires sanitaires et sociales***)* = office administering health and social services at regional level

drastique [drastik] **ADJ** drastic

NM *Méd* drastic purgative

drave [drav] **NF** *Can (de rondins)* drive

draver [drave] **VT** *Can (rondins)* to float, to drive

draveur [dravœr] **NM** *Can* driver, raftsman

draw-back, *pl* **draw-backs** [drobak] **NM** *Com* drawback

dreadlocks [drɛdlɔks] **NFPL** dreadlocks

drelin [drəlɛ̃] **INT** *Vieilli* ting-a-ling, tinkle

Dresde [drɛzd] **N** Dresden

dressage [dresaʒ] **NM 1** *(d'un mât, d'un monument, d'un échafaudage etc)* erection, raising; *(d'une tente)* pitching **2** *Tech (d'un morceau de bois etc)* trimming, dressing; *(d'une tige, d'une barre)* straightening **3** *(d'un animal)* training; *Fam (d'un enfant)* strict upbringing; *Équitation* **d. (élémentaire)** breaking in; *Équitation* **d. (supérieur)** dressage; **ce n'est pas une éducation qu'ils donnent à cet enfant, c'est un d.** that child isn't being brought up, he's being trained

dresser [drese] **VT 1** *(ériger) (mât, monument, échafaudage etc)* to erect, to put up, to raise; *(échelle, lit)* to put up; *(tente)* to pitch, to put up; *(bûcher)* to erect; **d. la tête** to hold up *or* lift one's head; *(pour regarder)* to look up; **d. les oreilles** *(d'un animal)* to prick up *or* cock its ears; *Fig* **d. l'oreille** to prick up one's ears; **une histoire à faire d. les poils** *ou* **les cheveux (sur la tête)** a hair-raising story, a story to make your hair stand on end **2** *Tech (morceau de bois)* to trim, to dress; *(fil)* to straighten out **3** *(établir) (plan, rapport, estimation etc)* to prepare, to draw up; *(liste, inventaire)* to prepare, to draw up, to make out; **d. un contrat** to draw up a contract; **d. une carte** to make a map; **pourriez-vous me d. la liste de ce dont vous avez besoin?** could you make a list for me of what you need? **4** *(préparer) (piège)* to set; *Fig* **d. ses batteries** to draw up a battle plan *or* a plan of action *or Litt* one's batteries; **d. la table** *ou* **le couvert** to lay *or* set the table; **d. un plat** to put food on a plate, to arrange a dish **5** *(animal), Fam (enfant)* to train (**à faire qch** to do sth); *(cheval)* to break in; *Arch, Péj (recrue)* to train, to drill; *Fam* **ça le dressera!** that'll teach him!, that'll put him in his place!; *Fig* **d. une personne contre une autre** to set one person against another

VPR **se dresser 1** *(se lever)* to stand up, to rise; *(sur une chaise, dans un lit)* to sit up; *(se tenir droit)* to hold oneself erect *or* straight; *(d'un cheval)* to rear (up); *(d'un chien)* to stand up; **se d. sur la pointe des pieds** to stand on tiptoe; **ses cheveux se dressaient (sur sa tête)** his hair stood on end; *Fig* **quand je le vois, j'ai les poils qui se dressent** my hackles rise whenever I see him; **les obstacles qui se dressent sur notre chemin** the obstacles that stand *or* lie in our way; *Fig* **se d. contre qch** to rise up *(in protest)* **2** *(s'apprivoiser)* to be tamed; **les hérissons ne se dressent pas** hedgehogs can't be tamed

dresseur, -euse [drɛsœr, -øz] **N** *(d'animaux)* trainer; **d. de chevaux** horse-breaker; **d. de fauves** wild animal tamer

dressing(-room), *pl* **dressings** *ou* **dressing-rooms** [drɛsiŋ(rum)] **NM** dressing room

dressoir [drɛswar] **NM** dresser, sideboard

dreyfusard, -arde [drɛfyzar, -ard] **N** *Hist* supporter *or* defender of Dreyfus

DRH [deɛraʃ] **NM** *(abrév* **directeur des ressources humaines)** HRD, human resources manager

NF *(abrév* **direction des ressources humaines)** HRM, human resources management

dribble [dribl] **NM** *Ftbl etc* dribble

dribbler [drible] *Ftbl etc* **VI** to dribble

VT *(ballon)* to dribble; **d. un joueur** to dribble round a player

dribbleur [driblœr] **NM** *Ftbl etc* dribbler

dribbling [dribliŋ] **NM** *Rugby* forward ruck

drill[1] [drij] **NM** *(singe)* drill

drill[2] [dril] **NM** *Mil etc* drill

drille[1] [drij] **NM** *Fam Vieilli* **c'est un bon** *ou* **joyeux d.** he's always good for a laugh

drille[2] **NF** *Tech* hand drill

driller [drije] **VT** *Tech* to drill, to bore

dring [driŋ] **INT** ting-a-ling

drink [driŋk] **NM** *Fam* drink

drisse [dris] **NF** *Naut* halyard

drive [drajv] **NM** *Tennis, Golf* drive

drive-in [drajvin] **NM INV** drive-in

driver[1] [drajvœr] **NM 1** *Sport (dans les courses de trot)* driver **2** *Golf (club)* driver

driver[2] [drajve] **VI** *Tennis, Golf* to drive

VT 1 *Tennis, Golf (balle)* to drive **2** *(dans les courses de trot)* to drive

drogman [drɔgmɑ̃] **NM** *Vieilli* dragoman

drogue [drɔg] **NF 1** *(stupéfiant)* drug, narcotic; **d. dure/douce** hard/soft drug; **prendre de la d.** to take *or* be on drugs; **trafic de d.** drug trafficking; **l'argent de la d.** drug money; **il faut lutter contre la d. dans les lycées** we have to fight against drugs in high schools; *Hum* **moi, ma d., c'est le chocolat** chocolate is what I'm hooked on, I'm a chocaholic; *Fig* **la télévision est une d. pour beaucoup de gens** lots of people are television addicts *or* are hooked on television **2** *Vieilli (médicament)* remedy, medicine; *Péj* nostrum, quack remedy

drogué, -ée [drɔge] **N** drug addict; *Fig* **les drogués de l'information** information addicts; **les drogués de la cigarette** people hooked on cigarettes

droguer [drɔge] **VT 1** *(malade)* to dose (with medicine); **je déteste les médecins qui vous droguent** I hate doctors who force medicine on you **2** *(victime)* to drug; *(cheval de course etc)* to dope, *Arg* to nobble

VPR **se droguer 1** *(prendre des stupéfiants)* to take drugs; **il se drogue** he's taking drugs, he's on drugs; **il se drogue à l'héro** he's on heroin **2** *Pharm* to be always taking drugs; **elle est obligée de se d. pour dormir** she has to take drugs in order to be able to sleep

droguerie [drɔgri] **NF** *(magasin)* ≃ hardware store, *Br* ironmonger's *(selling paint, cleaning materials etc)*; *(commerce)* ≃ hardware trade

droguet [drɔgɛ] **NM** *Tex Vieilli* drugget

droguiste [drɔgist] **NM** ≃ hardware dealer, *Br* ironmonger *(dealing in paints, cleaning materials etc)*; **épicier d.** grocer and general storekeeper

droit[1]**, droite** [drwa, drwat] **ADJ 1** *(vertical)* straight; **se tenir d.** to hold oneself erect, to stand up straight; **d. comme un i** *ou* **un piquet** as straight *or* stiff as a poker; **col d.** stand-up collar; **jupe droite** straight skirt; **veste droite** boxy jacket; *(non croisée)* single-breasted jacket; *Math* **angle d.** right angle; **section droite** cross section **2** *(non courbe) (route, ligne)* straight; **coup d.** *Escrime* straight thrust; *Tennis* forehand drive; **en ligne droite** in a straight line, as the crow flies; *Fig* **ces boucles d'oreille me viennent en droite ligne de ma grand-mère** I inherited these earrings from my grandmother; **ses idées viennent en droite ligne de celles de son père** he gets his ideas from his father; *Fig* **ne pas s'écarter du d. chemin** not to leave the straight and narrow; **ramener qn dans le d. chemin** to bring sb back to the straight and narrow; *Couture* **dans le d. fil** on the straight; *Fig* **son étude est dans le d. fil des conceptions freudiennes** his study

is in line with Freudian concepts; *Naut* **mettre la barre droite** to right the helm; *Naut* **d. la barre!** helm amidships!

3 *(honnête) (personne, conduite)* upright, honest

ADV 1 c'est d. devant vous *ou* **tout d.** it's straight ahead of you; **marcher d.** to walk straight *or* in a straight line; *Fig* **to toe the line; aller d. au fait** to get straight to the point; **aller** *ou* **courir d. à qch** to be heading straight for sth; **votre cadeau/proposition m'est allé(e) d. au cœur** I am deeply touched *or* moved by your gift/suggestion; **écrire d.** to write straight *or* in a straight line; *Naut* **d. devant, d. debout** right ahead

2 *Suisse (tout à fait, exactement)* **c'est d. son père** he's the spitting image of his father; **elle est d. arrivée** *(tout juste)* she's just arrived

NF droite straight line; **tracer une droite reliant A à B** to draw a line connecting A and B

droit[2]**, droite** **ADJ** *(main, jambe, gant etc)* right; **être le bras d. de qn** to be sb's right-hand man; **du côté d.** on the right-hand side

NF droite 1 *(côté droit)* right (hand), right-hand side; **tourner à droite** to turn (to the) right; **rouler à droite** to drive on the right; **tenir** *ou* **garder sa droite** to keep to the right; **à ma droite, le château** to *or* on my right is the castle; **sur la droite, il y a un feu** on the right there is a traffic light; **reconnaître sa droite de sa gauche** to know one's left from one's right; **le placard de droite** the right-hand cupboard, the cupboard on the right; **à droite du placard** to *or* on the right of the cupboard; **regarder de droite à gauche** to look from right to left; **courir à droite et à gauche** to run about all over the place; **j'entends dire à droite et à gauche** *ou* **de droite et de gauche que …** I hear from all quarters *or* on all sides that …; *Naut* **(la barre) à droite!** starboard!

2 *Pol* **la droite** the right (wing); **candidat/idées/journal de droite** right-wing candidate/ideas/newspaper; **voter à droite** to vote for the right; **droite dure** hard right; **droite modérée** soft right

NM *Boxe* right; **crochet du d.** right hook; **direct du d.** straight right

right **1**	▪ fee **2**	▪ tax **2** ▪ duty **2**
▪ law **3**		

NM 1 *(prérogative)* right; **d. de chasse/pêche** hunting/fishing rights; **le d. du plus fort** the law of the jungle; **avoir d. de vie et de mort sur qn** to have the power of life and death over sb; **avoir d. de regard sur qch** to have the right to approve sth, *Fam* to have a say on sth; **avoir le d. de savoir** to have the right to know; **tous droits réservés** all rights reserved; **faire valoir ses droits** to assert one's rights; **avoir d. à qch** to have a right to sth, to be entitled to sth; **il a d. à mes excuses** I owe him an apology; *Fam Iron* **il a eu d. aux inévitables recommandations** he was treated to the inevitable good advice; *Fam* **ce soir, on va encore y avoir d.** the same treat is in store for us again this evening; *Fam* **ils parlent de licencier 300 personnes, je sens que je vais y avoir d.** they're talking about laying off 300 people and I think that's going to include me; *Fam* **s'il pleut dans tout le pays, il n'y a pas de raison qu'on n'y ait pas d.** if it's raining all over the country, there's no reason why here should be any exception *or* why we should escape; **ce coupon (vous) donne d. à …** this coupon entitles you to …; **avoir le** *ou* **être en d. de faire qch** to have a right to do sth, to be justified in doing sth, to be entitled to do sth; **je n'ai pas le d. de le faire** I'm not allowed to do it; **tu n'as pas le d. de me reprocher cela** you've no right to hold that

against me; **avoir des droits sur qn/qch** to have rights over sb/sth; **tu n'as aucun d. sur les décisions de tes enfants** you have no say in your children's decisions; **à bon d.** (d'une façon justifiée) with good reason; (selon la loi) legitimately; **de d. et de fait** de facto and de jure; **à qui de d.** to whom it may concern; **s'adresser à qui de d.** to apply to the proper quarter or to an authorized person; **être dans son (bon) d.** to be within one's rights; **tu serais dans ton d. si tu lui demandais une compensation** you'd be within your rights asking him for compensation; **de quel d. me critiques-tu?** by what right do you criticize me?, what gives you the right to criticize me?, what right have you to criticize me?; **de quel d. êtes-vous entré?** what right had you or what gave you the right to come in?; **faire d. à une demande** to comply with or accede to a request; **les droits de l'amitié** the claims of friendship; **Commission européenne des droits de l'homme** European Commission of Human Rights; **Convention relative aux droits de l'enfant** Convention on the Rights of the Child

2 (en argent) fee, due; (imposition) duty; (taxe) tax; Compta **d. fixe** fixed rate of duty; **exempt de droits** duty-free; **allocation de fin de droits** = reduced amount of unemployment benefit (paid to people whose benefit period has almost expired); **(chômeur en) fin de droits** = unemployed person whose benefit period is running out

3 Jur law; **le d.** the law; **d. administratif** administrative law; **d. aérien** aviation law; **d. bancaire** banking law; **d. de brevet** patent law; **d. civil** civil law; **d. commercial** commercial law; **d. communautaire** Community law; **d. de la consommation** consumer law; **d. constitutionnel** constitutional law; **d. coutumier** common law; **d. commun** common law; **d. des contrats** contract law; **d. criminel** criminal law; **d. douanier** customs legislation; **d. écrit** statute law; **d. fiscal** tax law; **d. hôtelier** hotel law; **d. international** international law; **d. de marque** trademark law; **d. des obligations** ≃ law of contract; **d. pénal** criminal law; **d. public** public law; **d. privé** private law; **d. romain** Roman law; **d. des sociétés** corporate law; **d. du travail** labour laws; **faire son d.** to study or read law; **étudiant en d.** law student

▸▸ **d. d'accès** right of access; **droits acquis** vested rights; Com **droits acquittés** duty paid; **d. d'admission** (prérogative) right of entry; (imposition) import duty; Fin, Com **droits ad valorem** ad valorem duty; **d. d'aînesse** birthright; TV **droits d'antenne** broadcasting rights; **d. d'asile** right of asylum; **droits d'auteur** royalties; **d. au bail** (bien incorporel) leasehold; (comme bien incorporel) right to a lease; Aviat, Naut **droits de cabotage** cabotage rights; **d. canon** canon law; **d. de cité** freedom of a/the city; Fig **il n'a pas d. de cité dans cette maison** he is not welcome in this house; **droits civils** civil rights; **droits du consommateur** consumer rights; Com **d. de courtage** brokerage (fee); **droits de diffusion** broadcasting rights; **monarchie de d. divin** kingship by divine right; **droits de douane** (customs) duty; **d. d'entrée** (coût) admission fee; (prérogative) right of entry; (imposition) import duty; Com **droits exclusifs** sole rights; **droits d'exclusivité** exclusive rights; **droits d'exécution en public** performing rights; **droits d'exploitation d'un feuilleton** serial rights; **droits d'exploitation pour le monde entier** world (wide) rights; **droits d'exploitation à la télévision** TV rights; **droits d'exploitation vidéo** video rights; **d. d'exportation** export duty; **d. de grève** right to strike; **d. d'importation** import duty; **droits d'inscription** registration fee; **droits internationaux** international

rights; **droits d'interprète** performing rights; **d. de licenciement** right to dismiss (employees); **d. de passage** right of way; **droits de port** harbour dues; Jur **d. de rachat** repurchase right, buyback right; Journ **d. de rectification** right of reply; Journ **d. de réponse** right of reply; **d. de reproduction** reproduction rights; **avoir le d. du sang** to have the nationality of one's parents; **avoir le d. du sol** to have the nationality of the country where one was born; Fin, Com **droits de sortie** export duty; **d. de souscription (d'actions)** subscription right; **droits statutaires** statutory rights; **droits de succession** death duties; Admin **d. de timbre** stamp duty; Fin **droits de tirage** drawing rights; **droits de tirage spéciaux** special drawing rights; **droits de trafic** (des compagnies aériennes) traffic rights; **d. d'usage** right of use; **d. aux vacances** holiday entitlement; **droits de vote** voting rights

droitement [drwatmã] ADV **faire son travail d.** to do an honest day's work; **il juge les gens d.** he judges people fairly

droitier, -ière [drwatje, -jɛr] ADJ **1** right-handed **2** Pol Fam right-wing ▸ N right-handed person

droiture [drwatyr] NF rectitude, honesty

drolatique [drolatik] ADJ Litt comic, humorous, droll

drôle [drol] ADJ **1** (amusant) funny, amusing; **je ne trouve pas ça très d.** I don't think that's very funny; **ça ne va pas être d.** it's not going to be much fun; Fam **vous êtes d.! qu'auriez-vous fait à ma place?** come on! what would you have done in my place?

2 (étrange) funny, odd, strange; **je l'ai trouvé d. hier** he was behaving rather oddly or strangely yesterday; **c'est d. que je ne t'aie pas reconnu tout de suite** it's funny or odd that I didn't recognize you immediately; **une d. d'odeur** a funny or a strange or an odd smell; **quelle d. d'idée!** what a funny or a strange or an odd idea!; **j'ai dû faire une d. de tête** I must have looked a bit taken aback; Fam **un d. de type** a queer fish, an odd sort; Fam **la d. de guerre** the phoney war

3 Fam (sacré) **il faut une d. de patience** it needs an awful lot or surtout Am a heck of a lot of patience; **il a une d. de force** he's awfully strong; **en voir de drôles** (avoir des ennuis) to have an awful time (of it); **ils en ont vu de drôles pendant leur voyage au Maroc** they had an incredible time on their trip to Morocco; **en faire voir de drôles à qn** to give sb an awful time (of it)

ADV Fam **ça m'a fait tout d. de te voir là** it gave me a funny or a strange or an odd feeling to see you there

NM **1** Arch (mauvais sujet) rascal, knave, scamp **2** Région (jeune garçon) lad

drôlement [drolmã] ADV **1** funnily, strangely, oddly **2** Fam (sacrément) awfully, awful; **les prix ont d. augmenté** prices have gone up an awful lot; **je me suis d. amusé** I had a great time, I had an awful(ly) good time or an awful lot of fun; **elle est d. bien** (remarquable) she's a terrific person; (belle) she's gorgeous, she's great-looking

drôlerie [drolri] NF (caractère amusant) funniness; (action) joke; (parole) joke, funny remark

drôlesse [droles] NF **1** Vieilli (femme effrontée) bitch **2** Région (jeune fille) lass

dromadaire [dromadɛr] NM dromedary

drop (goal) [drop(gol)] NM Rugby drop goal

droppage [dropaʒ] NM Aviat (parachute) drop; **zone de d.** drop zone

drosophile [drozofil] NF fruit fly

drosser [drose] VT Naut (du vent, courant) to drive

dru [dry] ADJ (herbe, blé etc) thick, dense; (cheveux, barbe) thick; (pluie) heavy ▸ ADV **tomber d.** to fall thick and fast; **pousser d.** (de l'herbe etc) to grow thickly

drugstore [drægstor] NM drugstore

druide, druidesse [drɥid, drɥidɛs] N druid, f druidess

druidique [drɥidik] ADJ druidic(al)

druidisme [drɥidism] NM druidism

drummer [drœmœr] NM Mus drummer

drupe [dryp] NF Bot drupe

dry [draj] ADJ INV dry; **champagne d.** dry champagne; **whisky d.** neat or straight whisky ▸ NM INV dry Martini®

dryade [drijad] NF (nymphe) dryad, wood nymph

DST [deɛste] NF (abrév Direction de la surveillance du territoire) = French Secret Service

DTP [detepe] NM (abrév diphtérie, tétanos, polio) diphtheria, tetanus and polio vaccination

DTS [deteɛs] NMPL (abrév droits de tirage spéciaux) special drawing rights

du [dy] voir **de**

dû, due [dy] ADJ **1** (que l'on doit) due, owing, owed; Com **en port dû** carriage forward **2** (causé) **ce retard est dû à ...** this delay is due to ...; **son licenciement est dû aux difficultés économiques de l'entreprise** he was made redundant because of or due to the company's economic difficulties; **sa maladresse est due à sa timidité** his clumsiness is caused by or is due to his shyness **3** (approprié) **en temps dû** in due course; **contrat rédigé en bonne et due forme** contract drawn up in due form, formal contract ▸ NM due; **chacun sera rétribué selon son dû** everyone will be paid according to his due

dualisme [dɥalism] NM dualism

dualiste [dɥalist] ADJ dualistic ▸ N dualist

dualité [dɥalite] NF duality

dubitatif, -ive [dybitatif, -iv] ADJ doubtful, dubious

dubitativement [dybitativmã] ADV doubtfully, dubiously

Dublin [dyblɛ̃] N Dublin

dublinois, -oise [dyblinwa, -waz] ADJ of/from Dublin ▸ N **D.** Dubliner

duc [dyk] NM **1** duke **2** (oiseau) horned owl; **grand d.** eagle owl

ducal, -ale, -aux, -ales [dykal, -o] ADJ ducal

duché [dyʃe] NM duchy, dukedom

duchesse [dyʃɛs] NF **1** duchess; Péj **elle fait la d.** she puts on airs **2** (fruit) (poire) **d.** duchess pear **3** Culin **pommes (de terre) d.** duchesse potatoes

Duchnoque [dyʃnɔk] NM Fam pal, matey, Am bud, buddy

Ducon [dykɔ̃], **Ducon-la-joie** [dykɔ̃laʒwa] NM très Fam shit-for-brains, Br dick features

ducroire [dykrwar] NM Com del credere; (agent) del credere agent

ductile [dyktil] ADJ ductile, tensile

ductilité [dyktilite] NF ductility

duègne [dɥɛɲ] NF Arch duenna, chaperon

duel¹ [dɥɛl] NM duel; **se battre en d.** to fight a duel; **provoquer qn en d.** to challenge sb to a duel; **d. oratoire** battle of words

duel² NM Gram dual (number)

duelliste [dɥelist] NM duellist

duettiste [dɥetist] N Mus duettist

duffel-coat, duffle-coat, pl **duffel-coats, duffle-coats** [dœfœlkot] NM duffel coat, duffle coat

dulcinée [dylsine] NF *Hum* love of one's life

dum-dum, *pl* **dum-dums** [dumdum] NF dumdum bullet

dûment [dymã] ADV duly, in due form

dumping [dœmpiŋ] NM *Com* dumping; **faire du d.** to dump; **être accusé de faire du d.** to be accused of dumping; **d. social** social dumping

dune [dyn] NF dune, sandhill

dunette [dynɛt] NF *Naut* poop (deck)

Dunkerque [dœkɛrk] NF Dunkirk

duo [dɥo] NM *Mus* duet; *Théâtre* duo; *Fam* **d. d'injures** slanging match

duodécimal, -ale, -aux, -ales [dɥodesimal, -o] ADJ duodecimal

duodénal, -ale, -aux, -ales [dɥodenal, -o] ADJ *Anat* duodenal

duodénite [dɥodenit] NF *Méd* duodenitis

duodénum [dɥodenɔm] NM *Anat* duodenum

duopole [dɥɔpɔl] NM *Com* duopoly

dupe [dyp] NF dupe, *Fam* sucker; **prendre qn pour d.** to fool sb, to take sb in; **c'est un marché de dupes** I've/he's/*etc* been had *or* taken in *or* swindled
▪ ADJ naive, gullible, easily deceived; **je ne suis pas d.** I'm not fooled *or* taken in; **il me ment, mais je ne suis pas d.** I'm well aware that he's lying to me

duper [dype] VT to dupe, to deceive, to fool, to take in
▪ VPR **se duper** to deceive oneself

duperie [dypri] NF *(tromperie)* deception; **victime d'une d.** victim of deception; **une vaste d.** one vast deception

dupeur, -euse [dypœr, -øz] N *Litt* trickster, deceiver

duplex [dyplɛks] ADJ INV *Tél* duplex; *TV, Radio* link-up
▪ NM INV 1 *Tél, TV* duplex, diplex; **(émission en) d.** link-up 2 *(appartement)* maison(-n)ette, *Am* duplex

duplexer [dyplɛkse] VT *Tél* to duplex

duplicata [dyplikata] NM INV duplicate (copy)

duplicateur [dyplikatœr] NM duplicator, duplicating machine

duplication [dyplikasjɔ̃] NF 1 *Math* duplication; *Biol* doubling 2 *Tél* duplexing; *Ordinat* **d. de logiciel** software copying

duplicité [dyplisite] NF duplicity, double dealing

dupliquer [dyplike] VT *Tél* to duplex

DUR, DURE [dyr]

ADJ hard **1–5** ▪ tough **1** ▪ difficult **2–4** ▪ severe **4**	
ADV hard	
N tough guy ▪ hard liner	

ADJ **1** *(rigide) (substance)* hard; *(viande)* tough; **œuf d.** hard-boiled egg; **pain d.** stale bread; **être d. à cuire** *(de viande)* to take a lot of cooking; *Fam (de personne)* to be a tough nut; **eau dure** hard water
2 *(qui résiste à l'effort)* hard, difficult; **cette porte est dure (à ouvrir)** this door is stiff, this door is hard *or* difficult to open; *Aut etc* **commande dure** stiff control; **être d. à la peine** to be a tireless worker; **avoir l'oreille dure, être d. d'oreille** *ou Fam* **de la feuille** to be hard of hearing; **avoir la tête dure** to be obstinate *or* pig-headed; **avoir la vie dure** *(d'une personne, d'un animal)* to be hard to kill; *Fig* **les idées reçues ont la vie dure** preconceived ideas die hard; *Fam* **être d. à la détente** *(lent à comprendre)* to be slow on the uptake
3 *(difficile) (travail etc)* hard, difficult; **c'est**

d. à croire it's hard *or* difficult to believe; **enfant d.** difficult *or* problem child
4 *(pénible)* hard, difficult; **hiver d.** hard *or* severe winter; **des scènes très dures** distressing *or* painful sights; **rendre la vie dure à qn** to make sb's life a misery; **la vie est dure** it's a hard life; **les temps sont durs** times are hard; **avoir un coup d.** to be dealt a severe blow; **une dure épreuve** a severe trial, a sore test; **être à dure école** to have a hard time of it
5 *(sévère, cruel)* hard; **avoir le cœur d.** to be hard-hearted *or* callous; **être d. envers** *ou* **pour** *ou* **avec qn** to be hard *or* rough on sb; **c'est un tendre sous ses dehors très durs** he's quite soft-hearted under that tough exterior of his
▪ ADV *Fam (travailler, cogner)* hard; **le soleil tape d. ce matin** the sun is really beating down this morning; **croire qch d. comme fer** to be quite convinced of sth; **il croit d. comme fer que ...** he is quite convinced *or* really believes that ...; **d. d.!** (what a) bummer!; **d. d. la rentrée dans mon nouveau bahut!** what a bummer having to go to a new school next term!
▪ NM **1** *Constr* **bâtiment en d.** permanent building
2 *Arg (train)* train
▪ N *Fam (personne)* **un d.** a tough guy, a hard nut; *Pol* a hardliner; **un d./une dure à cuire** a hard-boiled man/woman; **il aime bien jouer les durs** he likes to act tough
▪ NF **coucher sur la dure** *(sur le sol)* to sleep on the floor; *(dehors)* to sleep rough; **vivre à la dure** to rough it; **il a été élevé à la dure** he's had a hard upbringing, he was brought up in the school of hard knocks; *Fam* **en dire de dures à qn** to tell sb where to get off; *Fam* **elle en a vu de dures** she's had a hard *or* tough time (of it)

durabilité [dyrabilite] NF durability

durable [dyrabl] ADJ durable, lasting, long-lasting

durablement [dyrabləmã] ADV durably

duraille [dyraj] ADJ *Fam* hard; **il était d., le problème de maths** the maths question was a real pig; **se faire piquer son mec par sa meilleure copine, c'est plutôt d.** it's a bit of a bummer *or* downer when your best friend steals your man

Duralumin® [dyralymɛ̃] NM Duralumin®

durant [dyrã] PRÉP during; **d. toute sa vie, sa vie d.** during his whole life, throughout his life; **parler des heures d.** to talk for hours on end *or* for hours at a time; **d. quelques instants** for a few moments

durcir [dyrsir] VT to harden, to make hard; *Fig* **d. la ligne du parti** to harden *or* stiffen the party line; **il a durci son opinion** his opinion has stiffened; **la France a décidé de d. ses positions au sujet du GATT** France has decided to take a tougher position *or* a harder line on GATT
▪ VI *(de pain, sol)* to harden, to become hard; *(du ciment etc)* to set, to harden
▪ VPR **se durcir** to harden; *Fig (d'opposition)* to stiffen; **ses traits se sont durcis** his features have hardened

durcissement [dyrsismã] NM *(de pain, du sol)* hardening; *(du ciment etc)* setting, hardening; *Fig (d'opposition, d'opinion)* stiffening; *(d'une attitude)* hardening

durée [dyre] NF *(d'un règne, de la guerre etc)* duration; *(d'un tissu, d'édifice etc)* lasting quality, wear; *(d'une ampoule)* life; *Mus (d'une note)* length, value; *(d'un film, d'une émission)* running time, screen time; **bonheur de courte/longue d.** short-lived/lasting happiness; **d. d'un bail** duration *or* term of a lease; **contrat à d. illimitée** *ou* **indéterminée** permanent contract; **quelle est la d.**

de votre congé? how long is your leave?, how long does your leave last?; **disque longue d.** long-playing record, LP; *Cin* **d. de projection** running time; **d. de crédit** term of loan; **d. de séjour** length of stay; **d. de validité** period of validity; **d. de vie** lifespan; *(d'une pile etc)* life; *(d'une machine etc)* useful life; *(d'un produit)* shelf-life, life expectancy; **d. de vol** flight time; **d. de voyage** journey time; **d. du travail** working hours; *Compta* **d. d'amortissement** depreciation period; *Radio* **d. d'écoute** listening time; *Ordinat* **d. de connexion** on-line time

durement [dyrmã] ADV **1** *(avec vigueur) (se battre)* hard **2** *(péniblement)* **d. éprouvé** sorely tried **3** *(sévèrement, cruellement) (répondre, parler)* harshly, roughly; *(touché)* severely; **on l'a élevée d.** she had a harsh *or* hard upbringing; **très d. touché par qch** very hard hit by sth; **d. secoué dans un accident/par une nouvelle** severely *or* badly shaken up in an accident/by a piece of news

durer [dyre] VI **1** *(avoir une durée) (d'un congé, d'une opération etc)* to last; **voilà trois ans que cela dure** it's been going on for three years; **votre congé dure combien de temps?** how long does your leave last *or* is your leave?
2 *(continuer, perdurer)* to last; **cela ne durera pas** it can't *or* won't last; **pourvu que ça dure!** long may it last *or* continue!; **ça va d. longtemps, cette plaisanterie?** hasn't this gone on long enough?; **ça ne peut pas d.** this can't go on; *Fam* **ça durera ce que ça durera** it'll last as long as it's meant to last; **cette réparation n'est pas très solide, mais ça durera ce que ça durera** it's not a brilliant repair job, but it'll do for the moment *or* for the time being; **faire d. qch** *(une réunion, une conversation téléphonique, un repas)* to drag sth out; *(un manteau, un livre etc)* to make sth last; *Hum* **faire d. le plaisir** to prolong the agony; **tissu qui durera** material which will wear well; *Péj* **elle dure la mémé** the old woman is hanging on
3 *Fam Région* **il ne peut pas d. en place** he can't stay put *or* keep still

dureté [dyrte] NF **1** *(d'une substance, de l'eau)* hardness; *(de la viande)* toughness **2** *(d'une personne, d'une voix)* harshness; *(d'un hiver, d'un climat)* severity; *(de traits)* hardness; **d. de cœur** hard-heartedness; **parler avec d.** to speak harshly

durillon [dyrijɔ̃] NM *(sur la main)* callus; *(sur le pied)* corn, callus

Durit® [dyrit] NF *Aut, Aviat etc* hose (connection), flexible pipe; *Fam* **péter une D.** *(se mettre en colère)* to hit the roof *or Am* ceiling

DUT [deyte] NM *(abrév* **diplôme universitaire de technologie***)* = post-baccalauréat technical qualification awarded after two years

duvet [dyvɛ] NM **1** *(sur le menton, un oisillon, une pêche etc)* down; **d. de l'eider** eiderdown; **d. du cygne** swan's down **2** *(sac de couchage)* sleeping bag **3** *Belg, Suisse (couette)* duvet, continental quilt

duveté [dyvte] ADJ downy

duveter (se) [sədyvte] VPR to become downy

duveteux, -euse [dyvtø, -øz] ADJ downy

DVD [devede] NM *(abrév* **Digital Video Disc** *ou* **Digital Versatile Disc***)* DVD

DVD-R [devedeɛr] NM *Ordinat (abrév* **Digital Video Disc-Recordable***)* DVD-R

DVD-ROM [devederɔm] NM *Ordinat (abrév* **Digital Video Disc-Read Only Memory***)* DVD-ROM

DVD-RW [devedeɛrdubləve] NM *Ordinat (abrév* **Digital Video Disc-Rewritable***)* DVD-RW

dwell [dwɛl] NM *Aut* dwell

dynamique [dinamik] ADJ dynamic; *Fam* c'est un type d. he's lively *or* dynamic *or* go-ahead
▮ NF dynamics; **d. de groupe** group dynamics; **d. du marché** market dynamics

dynamiquement [dinamikmɑ̃] ADV dynamically

dynamisant [dinamizɑ̃] ADJ motivating, stimulating

dynamisation [dinamizasjɔ̃] NF motivation, stimulation

dynamiser [dinamize] VT to motivate, to stimulate

dynamisme [dinamism] NM dynamism; *Fam (vitalité)* dynamism, vitality, drive

dynamiste [dinamist] N *Phil* dynamist

dynamitage [dinamitaʒ] NM dynamiting

dynamite [dinamit] NF dynamite

dynamiter [dinamite] VT *(édifice etc)* to dynamite, to blow up; *Fig (idée, certitude, conception)* to explode

dynamiteur, -euse [dinamitœr, -øz] N dynamiter

dynamo [dinamo] NF *Élec* dynamo

dynamoélectrique [dinamoelɛktrik] ADJ *Elec* dynamoelectric(al)

dynamogène [dinamɔʒɛn] ADJ *Physiol* energy-giving

dynastie [dinasti] NF dynasty

dynastique [dinastik] ADJ dynastic

dyne [din] NF *Phys* dyne

dysenterie [disɑ̃tri] NF *Méd* dysentery

dysentérique [disɑ̃terik] ADJ *Méd* dysenteric

dysfonctionnement [disfɔ̃ksjɔnmɑ̃] NM *(d'un organe)* dysfunction, malfunction; *(d'une institution, d'un service)* failure

dyslexie [dislɛksi] NF *Méd* dyslexia

dyslexique [dislɛksik] ADJ dyslexic ▮ N dyslexic

dysménorrhée [dismenɔre] NF *Méd* dysmenorrhoea, *Am* dysmenorrhea

dyspepsie [dispɛpsi] NF *Méd* dyspepsia

dyspepsique [dispɛpsik], **dyspeptique** [dispɛptik] ADJ, N *Méd* dyspeptic

E¹, e [ə] **NM** *(lettre)* E, e

E² *(abrév Est)* E

EAO [əao] **NM** *Ordinat (abrév enseignement assisté par ordinateur)* CAL

EARL [əaɛrɛl] **NF** *abrév* **Exploitation agricole à responsabilité limitée**

eau, *pl* **eaux** [o] **NF 1** *(liquide naturel)* water; **e. potable** drinking water; **e. non potable** water unfit for drinking; *(sur panneau)* not drinking water; **e. du robinet** tap water; **e. courante** running water; **faire installer l'e. courante** to have water laid on; **e. en bouteille** bottled water; **laver le plancher à grande e.** to swab down the floor; **passer à l'e.** to rinse; **cuire à l'e.** to boil; **pommes de terre à l'e.** boiled potatoes; **whisky sans e.** neat whisky; **se mettre à l'e.** to go on the wagon; **service des eaux** water supply; **e. de la ville** main(s) water; **château d'e.** water tower; **conduite d'e.** water main(s); **il est tombé beaucoup d'e.** a lot of rain fell; **chaussures qui prennent l'e.** shoes that let in water; **faire de l'e.** *(d'une locomotive, d'un bateau)* to water, to take on water; *Vieilli* **être comme l'e. et le feu** to be as different as or to be like chalk and cheese; *Fam* **compte là-dessus et bois de l'e.!** don't count on it!; *Fig* **mettre de l'e. dans son vin** to tone it down a bit; *Fam* **s'en aller en e. de boudin** to go down the tubes *or* up the spout; *Fam* **il y a de l'e. dans le gaz** there's trouble brewing

2 ville d'eau(x) spa; **prendre les eaux** to take *or* drink the waters

3 *(étendue, masse)* water; **au bord de l'e.** by the water's side *or* edge; **restaurant au bord de l'e.** waterside restaurant; **sur l'e.** afloat; **tomber à l'e.** to fall into the water; *Fig (d'un plan)* to fall through; *Fig Fam* **mes vacances sont à l'e.** my holiday is up the spout *or* down the tubes; **mettre un navire à l'e.** to launch a ship; **se mettre à l'e.** to go in (for a swim); *Fig* **se lancer** *ou* **se jeter à l'e.** to take the plunge; *Fig* **apporter de l'e. au moulin de qn** to strengthen sb's case, to provide sb with ammunition; *Fig* **porter de l'e. à la rivière** *ou* **à la mer** to take coals to Newcastle; **il passera de l'e. sous les ponts avant que** *ou* **d'ici à ce que ...** it will be a long time before ...; **mais depuis, bien de l'e. est passée sous les ponts** a lot of water has flowed under the bridge since then, that was a long time ago; *Fig* **pêcher en e. trouble** to fish in troubled waters; *Fig* **nager** *ou* **naviguer en e. trouble** to sail close to the wind; **faire e.** *(d'un bateau)* to leak, to spring a leak; **cours d'e.** *(rivière, fleuve)* river; *(ruisseau)* stream; **jet d'e.** fountain; **pièce d'e.** (ornamental) lake; *(petite)* pond, pool, water feature; **eaux internationales/françaises** international/French waters; **dimanche: grandes eaux à Versailles** the fountains will play at Versailles on Sunday; *Fig Fam* **c'était les grandes eaux** the waterworks started, he/she turned on the waterworks; *Fig Fam* **on va avoir droit aux grandes eaux** we'll be in for waterworks *or* floods of tears; *Fig* **dans ces eaux-là** *or* thereabouts; **mortes-eaux** neap tides; **vives-eaux** spring tides; **hautes/basses eaux** high/low water; *Fig* **nager entre deux eaux** *(ne pas s'engager)* to sit on the fence; **être dans les eaux d'un navire** to be in the wake of a ship; *Fig* **être** *ou* **naviguer dans les eaux de qn** *(rallier ses opinions)* to take the same line as sb; **il navigue dans les eaux de plusieurs peintres en vue** he hangs around several well known painters

4 *(sécrétions du corps humain)* **être tout en e.** to be dripping with perspiration; **cela me fait venir** *ou* **me met l'e. à la bouche** it makes my mouth water; **j'ai l'e. à la bouche rien que d'y penser** my mouth is watering just thinking about it; **j'en ai l'e. à la bouche!** my mouth is watering (already)!; **cloque pleine d'e.** water blister; **poche des eaux** amniotic sac, bag of waters; **elle a perdu les eaux** her waters have broken

5 *(d'un melon)* juice; **les concombres rendent beaucoup d'e.** cucumbers give off *or* out a lot of water

6 *(pureté)* **de la plus belle e.** *(diamant)*, *Fig (charlatan etc)* of the first water; **ces deux-là sont de la même e.** they're two of a kind, they're tarred with the same brush

▶▶ **e. bénite** holy water; **e. de Cologne** eau de Cologne; **e. déminéralisée** deionized water; **e. dentifrice** mouthwash; **e. distillée** distilled water; **e. douce** *(non salée)* fresh water; *(sans calcaire)* soft water; *Fam* **marin d'e. douce** landlubber; **e. dure** hard water; **e. de fleurs d'oranger** orange flower water; **e. gazeuse** carbonated *or* sparkling water; **e. grasse** washing-up water; **e. de Javel** bleach; **e. de lavande** lavender water; *Nucl* **e. lourde** heavy water; **e. de mélisse** = liqueur made from lemon balm; **e. minérale** (natural) mineral water; **e. oxygénée** hydrogen peroxide; **e. de parfum** eau de parfum; **e. plate** still water; **e. de pluie** rainwater; **e. de refroidissement** cooling water; **e. régale** aqua regia; **e. de roche** spring water; **e. de rose** rose water; *Fig* **roman/film à l'e. de rose** soppy *or* slushy novel/film; **e. rougie** = water with a drop of wine in it; **eaux de ruissellement** runoff; **e. de Seltz** soda water, Seltzer (water); **e. de source** spring water; **eaux territoriales** territorial waters; **eaux thermales** thermal *or* hot springs; **e. de toilette** toilet water, eau de toilette; **eaux usées** waste water; **traitement des eaux usées** waste water treatment; **e. de vaisselle** washing-up water

eau-de-vie, *pl* **eaux-de-vie** [odvi] **NF** *(de prune etc)* brandy

eau-forte, *pl* **eaux-fortes NF 1** *Chimie* aqua fortis, nitric acid **2** *Beaux-Arts* etching, etched engraving

eaux-vannes [ovan] **NFPL** sewage (water)

ébahi [ebai] **ADJ** astounded, *Fam* flabbergasted, staggered; **un regard é.** a look of blank astonishment

ébahir [ebair] **VT** to astound, *Fam* to flabbergast, to stagger

VPR s'ébahir to be dumbfounded (**de** by)

ébahissement [ebaismã] **NM** astonishment

ébarbage [ebarbaʒ] **NM** *(d'un livre)* trimming the pages; *(d'une feuille de papier)* trimming the edges; *(d'une haie, pelouse)* clipping; *(d'une surface métallique)* removal of the burrs

ébarber [ebarbe] **VT** *(feuille de papier)* to trim (the edges of); *(livre)* to trim the pages of; *(haie, pelouse)* to clip; *(surface métallique)* to remove the burrs from

ébarbure [ebarbyr] **NF** *(de métal etc)* burr, paring; *(de papier)* trimming

ébats [eba] **NMPL** playing (about); **é. (amoureux)** lovemaking; **au milieu de leurs é. (amoureux)** in the middle of their lovemaking, while they were making love

ébattre (s') [sebatr] **VPR** *(conj like* **battre***)* to frolic, to play (about); *(des animaux)* to gambol

ébaubi [ebobi] **ADJ** *Fam* flabbergasted

ébauchage [ebofaʒ] **NM** *(d'un tableau)* roughing out, sketching out; *(d'un roman etc)* roughing out, outlining

ébauche [ebof] **NF** *(d'un tableau)* rough sketch; *(d'un roman, poème etc)* outline, rough draft; *(d'une lettre, traduction)* draft; *(d'un projet)* outline; **faire l'é. de** *(roman, lettre, traduction)* to draft; *(tableau)* to make a rough sketch of, to sketch out; *(projet)* to outline; **ce projet n'est qu'à l'état d'é.** the plan is still sketchy; **l'architecte n'en est qu'à l'é. du plan** the architect is still only at the planning stage; **il semble qu'il y ait une é. de réconciliation entre l'OLP et Israël** there seem to be the first tentative signs of a reconciliation between the PLO and Israel; **il n'y a qu'une é. de relations entre eux** relations between them are very tentative; **je n'ai réussi à avoir avec lui qu'une é. de conversation** I managed only a rather stilted conversation with him; **il a marmonné l'é. d'un remerciement** he grudgingly muttered a few words of thanks; **é. d'un sourire** suspicion *or* ghost of a smile; **é. d'un espoir** glimmer of hope

ébaucher [ebofe] **VT** *(tableau, roman)* to rough out; *(projet, mise en scène)* to sketch out, to outline; *(lettre)* to draft, to make a draft of; *(réconciliation, amitié)* to take the first tentative steps towards; *(statue)* to rough-hew; **é. une traduction** to make a draft *or* rough translation, to draft a translation; **é. un sourire** to give a faint smile, to smile faintly; **é. un geste** to make a vague gesture; **les négociations étaient à peine ébauchées et déjà ...** talks had barely been mooted before ...; **é. des hypothèses** to put forward tentative hypotheses; **é. une conversation avec qn** to have a stilted conversation with sb

ébène [ebɛn] NF ebony; **(d'un noir) d'é., (noir) é.** jet black; *Hist* **(bois d')é.** slaves; **marchand d'é.** slave-trader

ébénier [ebenje] NM *(arbre)* ebony tree; **faux é.** laburnum

ébéniste [ebenist] NM cabinetmaker

ébénisterie [ebenistəri] NF *(métier)* cabinetmaking

éberlué [ebɛrlɥe] ADJ *Fam* flabbergasted

éblouir [ebluir] VT *aussi Fig* to dazzle; *Fig* **il a préparé ce plat pour vous é.** this dish to impress you

éblouissant [ebluisɑ̃] ADJ dazzling, blinding; *Fig* dazzling; **d'une beauté éblouissante** dazzlingly beautiful

éblouissement [ebluismɑ̃] NM dazzle, glare; *Fig (émerveillement)* amazement; *Fig* **quand on arrive chez eux, c'est un véritable é.** their place is dazzling; *Fig* **l'é. qu'il ressentit lorsqu'il la vit** his sense of dazzlement when he saw her; *Méd* **avoir des éblouissements** to have fits of dizziness

ébonite [ebɔnit] NF vulcanite, ebonite

éborgner [ebɔrɲe] VT **1 é. qn** to blind sb in one eye, to put sb's eye out; **j'ai failli m'é.** I nearly put my eye out **2** *(arbre fruitier)* to disbud

éboueur [ebwœr] NM dustman, *Am* garbage man

ébouillanter [ebujɑ̃te] VT to scald
VPR **s'ébouillanter** to scald oneself

éboulement [ebulmɑ̃] NM **1** *(écroulement) (de falaise, côte, remblai)* collapse; **l'é. de la falaise/carrière a fait deux morts** two people were killed when the cliff collapsed/the quarry fell in; **il y a eu un é. dans la mine** there has been a cave-in at the mine; **si vous allez vers la carrière, méfiez-vous des éboulements** if you're going in the direction of the quarry, watch out for falling rocks **2** *(tas)* landslide, landslip

> Do not confuse with **éboulis**.

ébouler (s') [sebule] VPR *(d'une falaise, une côte)* to collapse, to slip; *(d'une mine)* to cave in; *(d'un remblai)* to collapse

éboulis [ebuli] NM mass of fallen earth; *(en montagne)* scree

> Do not confuse with **éboulement**.

ébourgeonnage [eburʒɔnaʒ] NM, **ébourgeonnement** [eburʒɔnmɑ̃] NM disbudding

ébourgeonner [eburʒɔne] VT *(arbre fruitier)* to disbud

ébouriffant [eburifɑ̃] ADJ *Fam* breathtaking, hair-raising

ébouriffé [eburife] ADJ **1** *(cheveux, personne)* dishevelled **2** *Fam* amazed

ébouriffer [eburife] VT **1** *(les cheveux de qn)* to ruffle, to tousle; **é. qn** to ruffle *or* tousle sb's hair **2** *Fam* **e. qn** *(époustoufler)* to take sb's breath away

ébranchage [ebrɑ̃ʃaʒ] NM, **ébranchement** [ebrɑ̃ʃmɑ̃] NM *(d'un arbre)* stripping *or* lopping the branches

ébrancher [ebrɑ̃ʃe] VT *(arbre)* to lop off *or* strip the branches from

ébranchoir [ebrɑ̃ʃwar] NM billhook

ébranlement [ebrɑ̃lmɑ̃] NM **1** *(tremblement) (de vitres, mur, édifice)* shaking; **l'é. des murs a été si violent qu'ils se sont lézardés** the walls shook so violently that they cracked; *Fig* **ce scandale a provoqué l'é. du gouvernement** the scandal caused the government to totter, the scandal rocked the government **2** *(choc nerveux)* shock; **la mort**

de son ami a provoqué un véritable é. chez elle she went to pieces after her friend's death **3** *(départ, mise en route) (d'un train, une procession, un convoi)* departure

ébranler [ebrɑ̃le] VT **1** *(édifice, mur)* to shake, to rock; *(vitres)* to shake **2** *Fig (personne)* to shake (up), to upset; *(confiance, nerfs, régime, dictature, économie)* to shake; **il ne faut pas te laisser é. par ses critiques** don't let his criticism get to you; **il a été très é. par l'annonce de cet accident** he was very shaken *or* upset by the news of the accident; **la nouvelle a ébranlé le pays tout entier** the entire country was rocked by the news
VPR **s'ébranler** *(d'un train)* to start, to move off; *(d'une procession, un convoi, une caravane)* to move *or* set off

Èbre [ɛbr] NM **l'È.** the Ebro

ébréché [ebreʃe] ADJ chipped

ébrécher [ebreʃe] VT **(j'ébrèche; j'ébrécherai)** *(assiette, tasse, verre, lame etc)* to chip; *Fig Fam (réputation)* to damage; *Fig Fam (son capital)* to make a hole in

ébréchure [ebreʃyr] NF chip

ébriété [ebrijete] NF (state of) drunkenness *or* intoxication *or* inebriation; **en état d'é.** in a state of inebriation

ébrouement [ebrumɑ̃] NM **1** *(d'un cheval)* snorting, snort **2** *(d'ailes)* flap(ping); *(dans l'eau)* splashing about

ébrouer (s') [sebrue] VPR **1** *(d'un cheval)* to snort **2** *(d'ailes)* to flap; *(dans l'eau)* to splash about

ébruitement [ebrɥitmɑ̃] NM spreading

ébruiter [ebrɥite] VT *(secret)* to give away; *(accord, pourparlers)* to leak; *(nouvelle)* to spread
VPR **s'ébruiter** *(d'une nouvelle)* to spread, *Fam* to get (a)round

EBS [əbeɛs] NM *(abrév* **encéphalite bovine spongiforme)** BSE

ébullition [ebylisjɔ̃] NF boiling point; **l'é. de l'eau se fait à 100°C** the boiling point of water is 100°C, water boils at 100°C; **arriver à é.** to come to the boil; **amener à é.** bring to the boil; **maintenir en é. pendant cinq minutes** boil for five minutes; *Fig* **en é.** *(village, maison)* in turmoil; *(personne)* very excited, worked up

écaillage [ekajaʒ] NM **1** *(d'un poisson)* scaling; *(des huîtres)* opening **2** *(de peinture)* flaking off, peeling off; *(d'émail)* scaling off, chipping

écaille [ekaj] NF *(d'un poisson)* scale; *(d'une tortue)* shell; *(de peinture)* flake; *(d'émail)* chip; *Litt Fig* **les écailles lui tombèrent des yeux** the scales fell from his eyes; **lunettes à monture d'é.** tortoiseshell-rimmed spectacles; **peigne en é.** tortoiseshell comb

écailler¹ [ekaje] VT **1** *(poisson)* to scale; *(huître)* to open **2** *(chaudière)* to scale
VPR **s'écailler** *(de l'émail)* to chip (off); *(de la peinture)* to peel (off), to flake (off)

écailler², -ère [ekaje, -ɛr] N *(marchand)* oyster seller; *(dans un bar, un restaurant)* oyster opener
NF **écaillère** oyster knife

écailleux, -euse [ekajø, -øz] ADJ *(poisson)* scaly; *(ardoise)* flaky

écale [ekal] NF *(d'une noix)* hull, husk; *(d'une châtaigne)* shuck

écaler [ekale] VT *(noix)* to hull, to husk; *(châtaignes)* to shuck

écarlate [ekarlat] ADJ scarlet; **devenir é.** to blush, to go *or* turn scarlet
NF scarlet

écarquiller [ekarkije] VT **é. les yeux** to open one's eyes wide, to stare, *Fam* to goggle

écart¹ [ekar] NM **1** *(entre deux chiffres, deux températures)* difference (**de** in); *Compta*

spread, variance; *Bourse* spread; *Mktg* gap; *(stratégie d'attaque)* bypass attack; **é. d'opinions/de points de vue** difference of opinions/points of view; **on constate de grands écarts dans ses résultats** his results are very uneven; **il y a des écarts de niveau trop importants dans cette classe** ability differs *or* varies too much in the class; **il y a un é. important entre ma sœur et moi** there's a big (age) gap *or* a big difference in age between my sister and me; **il y a un é. de trois ans entre eux** there's a three-year gap *or* three years between them, they're three years apart; **l'é. entre les deux équipes s'est beaucoup réduit** the gap between the two teams has narrowed considerably; **é. de prix/de salaires** price/wage differential; **réduire l'é. entre deux salaires** to narrow the gap between two wages; *Com* **é. entre le prix de vente et le coût** margin between cost and selling price; *Bourse* **é. vertical** vertical spread; *Bourse* **écarts de cours** price spreads; *Tech* **é. admissible** tolerance

2 *(distance) (entre étagères, tableaux etc)* distance, space; **l'é. entre chaque soldat doit être de …** there must be a (distance of) … between each soldier, soldiers must be … apart; **faire le grand é.** to do the splits

3 *(déviation) Tech (de l'aiguille d'une boussole)* deflection; **faire un é.** *(d'un piéton)* to step aside, to swerve; *(d'un cheval)* to shy; *(d'une voiture, un vélo)* to swerve; **il ne fait jamais d'écarts de régime** he never breaks his diet, he always keeps to *or Fam* sticks to his diet

4 à. l'é.: j'ai mis mes verres en cristal à l'é. I've put my crystal glasses out of the way; **je mets sa suggestion à l'é.** for l'instant I'm putting *or* setting his suggestion aside for the moment; **se sentir à l'é.** to feel isolated *or* out of things; **se tenir à l'é.** to keep *or* stay in the background; *(du monde, de la foule etc)* to keep oneself apart, to hold oneself aloof; **se tenir à l'é. de la politique** to keep out of *or* away from politics; **mettre *ou* tenir qn à l'é.** to keep sb at a distance; **les autres enfants le mettent *ou* tiennent à l'é.** the other children don't let him join in; **tenir qn à l'é.** to keep sb away (**de qch** from sth); **il tient sa femme à l'é. de ses affaires** he keeps his wife out of his business, he doesn't involve his wife in his business; **un terrain à l'é. de la ville** a piece of land outside the town; **habiter à l'é.** to live in a remote *or* lonely spot

▸▸ *Bourse* **é. d'acquisition** goodwill; **é. budgétaire** budgetary variance; **écarts de conduite** transgressions, misbehaviour; **ses écarts de conduite ont fini par lasser sa femme** his wife finally got tired of his behaviour *or Fam* carryings-on; **elle a cessé ses écarts de conduite** she's stopped misbehaving, she's settled down; *Fin* **écarts de conversion** exchange adjustments; **é. des coûts** cost variance; **écarts de jeunesse** youthful indiscretions; **écarts de langage** bad language; **faire des écarts de langage** to use bad language; *Compta* **é. net** net variance; **é. de prime** option spread; *Tech* **é. type** standard deviation

écart² [ekar] NM *Cartes* **1** *(action)* discarding **2** *(carte)* discard

écartant [ekartɑ̃] ADJ *Can* disorienting

écarté¹ [ekarte] ADJ **1** *(maison, endroit)* isolated, lonely, remote **2** *(distant) (bras, pieds)* apart; *(yeux)* widely spaced; **avoir les dents écartées** to have gaps between one's teeth **3** *Can (personne)* lost

écarté² [ekarte] NM *Cartes* (game of) écarté

écartelé [ekartəle] ADJ *Hér* quartered, quarterly

écarteler [ekartəle] VT **(j'écartèle; j'écartèle-**

rai) **1** *(criminel)*, *Hér (écu)* to quarter **2** *Fig* **se sentir écartelé** to be torn (**entre** between)

écartement [ekartəmɑ̃] **NM 1** *(séparation)* separation; **l'é. des volets** the opening of the shutters; *Tech* **pièce d'é.** spacer **2** *(d'un obstacle)* setting aside; **depuis l'é. des gêneurs, la société va beaucoup mieux** things have been much better in the company since it got rid of the trouble-makers **3** *(distance) (entre des barres etc)* space, gap, clearance; *Rail (de la voie)* gauge; *Aut* **é. des essieux** wheelbase; *Aut* **é. des roues** track; *Aut* **é. des électrodes** spark *or* plug *or* electrode gap

écarter[1] [ekarte] **VT 1** *(séparer) (doigts)* to spread out; *(branches)* to part; *(rideaux)* to draw back, to open; *(ses bras)* to open; *(ses jambes)* to spread, to open; *(ses coudes)* to square; *(personnes, objets)* to move *or* push aside; **le service d'ordre devait é. les fans sur son passage** the marshals had to push a way for him through the crowd of fans; *Fig* **le temps nous écarte l'un de l'autre** we are drifting apart with time

2 *(éliminer, exclure) (candidat, réclamation, solution, proposition)* to turn down; *(soupçon)* to divert; *(coup, danger)* to ward off, to avert; **é. les obstacles de son chemin** to brush aside the obstacles in one's path; **é. qn de son chemin** to push sb out of one's way; **ses interventions nous ont écartés de notre sujet** his interruptions caused us to stray *or* wander from the subject *or* to digress; **être écarté de son but** to be deflected from one's goal

VPR s'écarter 1 *(se séparer) (de personnes)* to move apart; *(de routes)* to diverge; **plus on avance vers le nord, plus les maisons s'écartent les unes des autres** the further north you go, the further apart the houses become; **la foule s'est écartée sur le passage des pompiers** the crowd parted *or* drew aside to let the firemen through; *Fig* **nos chemins s'écartent de plus en plus** we are drifting further and further apart; *Fig* **nos aspirations/nos vies s'écartent de plus en plus** our aims in life/our lives are increasingly different

2 *(s'éloigner) (de piéton)* to move *or* step aside; *(de voiture, de vélo)* to swerve; *(dévier)* to deviate, to stray (**de** from); **s'é. du sujet** to digress, to deviate *or* wander from the subject; **s'é. des règles** to depart from the rules; **ne vous écartez pas de la route** keep to the road; **s'é. du droit chemin** to stray from the straight and narrow

3 *Can (s'égarer)* to get lost, to go astray

écarter[2] **VT** *Cartes* to discard

écarteur [ekartœr] **NM** *Aut* **é. de mâchoire** shoe expander

ecchymose [ekimoz] **NF** bruise, *Spéc* ecchymosis

Ecclésiaste (l') [leklezjast] **NM** *Bible* (the book of) Ecclesiastes

ecclésiastique [eklezjastik] **ADJ** ecclesiastical
NM ecclesiastic, cleric, clergyman

écervelé, -ée [eservəle] **ADJ** harebrained, scatterbrained
N scatterbrain

ECG [əseʒe] **NM** *Méd (abrév électrocardiogramme)* ECG

échafaud [eʃafo] **NM 1** scaffold; **monter sur** *ou* **à l'é.** to go to the scaffold, to mount the scaffold; **finir sur l'é.** to die on the scaffold, *Hum* **tu vas finir sur l'é.** you'll end up hanged **2** *Vieilli (estrade)* stand, platform

échafaudage [eʃafodaʒ] **NM 1** *(passerelles etc)* scaffolding; *(d'objets)* pile; *Fig (d'une argumentation, théorie)* structure, fabric; **é. pour caméra** (camera) tower **2** *(procédé)* erection of scaffolding; *Fig (d'une fortune)*

building up; *(d'une argumentation, théorie)* construction; *(de projets)* devising, putting together

échafauder [eʃafode] **VI** to erect (a) scaffolding
VT *Fig (projet, système)* to put together, to devise; *(argumentation)* to put together, to construct

échalas [eʃala] **NM** *(pour soutenir une plante)* cane, stake; *Fig* **grand é.** beanpole; **il est sec comme un é.** he's a real beanpole

échalier [eʃalje] **NM 1** *(clôture)* barrier, hurdle *(closing gap)* **2** *(échelle)* stile

échalote [eʃalɔt] **NF** *(plante)* shallot, *Can* scallion; *Can* **é. française** shallot

échancré [eʃɑ̃kre] **ADJ** low-cut; **robe échancrée dans le dos** dress cut low in the back, dress with a low back

échancrer [eʃɑ̃kre] **VT** *(robe etc)* to cut out the neckline of; *(planche)* to notch; **littoral échancré** indented coastline

échancrure [eʃɑ̃kryr] **NF** *(décolleté)* low neckline; *(découpe de veste)* vent, slit; *(d'une planche)* notch; *(d'un littoral)* indentation

échange [eʃɑ̃ʒ] **NM 1** *(de prisonniers, d'idées, de coups etc)* exchange; **faire l'é. de qch pour** *ou* **contre qch** to exchange sth for sth; **recevoir/donner qch en é.** to receive/give sth in exchange *or* in return (**de qch** for sth); **est-il possible de faire l'é.?** is it possible to exchange it?, can it be exchanged?; *Fam* **on fait é.?** want to swap?; **é. d'appartement** flat swap; **de violents échanges entre la police et les manifestants** *(physique)* violent clashes between the police and demonstrators; *(verbal)* violent exchanges between the police and demonstrators; **échanges culturels** cultural exchanges; **c'est un é. de bons procédés** one good turn deserves another, I'm/he's/*etc* returning a favour *or Am* favor; **nous faisons des échanges de bons procédés** we do favours for each other, we help each other out

2 *Fin* exchange; *(commerce)* trade; **échanges commerciaux** trade; **échanges internationaux** international trade; **échanges intracommunautaires** intra-Community trade; **le volume des échanges** the volume of trade; **les échanges entre la France et l'Allemagne** trade between France and Germany **3** *Bourse* **é. d'actions** share swap; **é. cambiste** treasury swap; **é. de créances** debt swap; **é. de créances contre actifs** debt equity swap; **é. de devises** currency swap; **é. financier** swap; **é. de taux d'intérêt** interest rate swap

4 *Tennis* rally; **on va faire quelques échanges?** shall we knock a few balls about?
▸▸ *Ordinat* **é. de données** data exchange *or* swap; *Ordinat* **é. de données dynamique** dynamic data exchange; *Ordinat* **é. de données informatisé** electronic data interchange; **é. linguistique** language exchange holiday; *Tech* **é. standard** standard replacement; **é. à terme** forward swap; *Pol* **é. de voix** vote-trading

échangeable [eʃɑ̃ʒabl] **ADJ** exchangeable

échanger [eʃɑ̃ʒe] **VT** (**j'échangeai(s); n. échangeons**) *(coups, idées, injures, lettres)* to exchange; *(objets, articles)* to exchange, to trade, *Fam* to swap, *Vieilli* to barter (**contre** for); **les articles soldés ne sont ni repris ni échangés** sales goods may not be returned or exchanged; **il m'a échangé un timbre espagnol contre un anglais** he traded *or Fam* swapped me a Spanish stamp for an English one; **é. des impressions** to exchange *or* compare impressions

échangeur [eʃɑ̃ʒœr] **NM 1** *(sur une autoroute)* interchange; *(sur une route)* (cloverleaf) intersection **2** *Phys* (heat) exchanger; *Aut* **é. air/air** air-to-air exchanger

échangisme [eʃɑ̃ʒism] **NM** partner swapping

échangiste [eʃɑ̃ʒist] **N** partner swapper
ADJ partner-swapping

échanson [eʃɑ̃sɔ̃] **NM** *Hist* cup-bearer

échantillon [eʃɑ̃tijɔ̃] **NM 1** *(de tissu)* sample; *(d'un travail)* sample, specimen; *(pour un sondage)* population sample; *Méd* specimen; **prendre** *ou* **prélever des échantillons de qch** to take samples of sth, to sample sth; **catalogue d'échantillons** sample *or* pattern book; *Mktg* **non conforme à l'é.** not up to sample **2** *Vieilli* **brique/tuile d'é.** standard brick/tile
▸▸ *Mktg* **é. aléatoire** random sample; **é. aréolaire** cluster (area) sample; **é. gratuit** free sample; **é. gratuit, ne peut être vendu** free sample, not for resale; **é. par quotas** quota sample; **é. probabiliste** probability sample; **é. publicitaire** free sample; **é représentatif** representative sample

échantillonnage [eʃɑ̃tijɔnaʒ] **NM 1** *(vérification)* sampling, testing; *(groupe de personnes)* sample; **l'é. se fait sur un produit sur cent** one product in a hundred is sampled *or* tested; **un é. est effectué systématiquement** sampling is done systematically **2** *Com* making up of samples; *(d'un tissu etc)* making up of patterns; **un é. de ce que je sais faire/de mes capacités** a sample of what I can do/of my ability; **voici un é. de sa bêtise** here's an example of how stupid he is
▸▸ *Mktg* **é. aléatoire** random sampling; **é. empirique** purposive *or* non-random sampling; **é. non probabiliste** non-random *or* non-probability sampling; **é. par zone** area sampling

échantillonner [eʃɑ̃tijɔne] **VT 1** *(vin)* to sample, to taste; *(population)* to sample **2** *Com (préparer des échantillons de)* to prepare samples of; *(tissues etc)* to prepare patterns of **3** *(étalonner) (articles)* to make according to sample

échantillonneur, -euse [eʃɑ̃tijɔnœr, -øz] **N** *Com (personne)* tester, sampler

échappatoire [eʃapatwar] **NF** way out; **le sommeil est mon é.** sleep is my escape mechanism; **é. fiscale** tax loophole
ADJ **clause é.** escape clause

échappé [eʃape] **NM** *Sport* breakaway; **les trois échappés** the three breakaway riders

échappée [eʃape] **NF 1** *Sport (dans une course)* breakaway; **être dans l'é.** to be part of the breakaway group **2** *(espace libre)* space, gap, interval; **é. (de vue)** vista (**sur** over); **é. de lumière** shaft of light; **é. de ciel** patch of sky; **é. de soleil** burst of sunshine; **é. de beau temps** short spell of fine weather; *Fig* **faire qch par échappées** to do sth in fits and starts **3** *(pour véhicules)* turning space **4** *(d'un escalier)* headroom

échappement [eʃapmɑ̃] **NM 1** *(de vapeur)* exhaust, release; *Aut (mouvement)* exhaust stroke; **(tuyau d')é.** waste-steam pipe; *Aut* exhaust (pipe); *Aut* **pot d'é.** silencer, *Am* muffler; *Aut* **(soupape d')é. libre** cut-out; **gaz d'é.** exhaust fumes; **clapet d'é.** exhaust cut-out **2** *(d'une montre)* escapement; **montre à é.** lever watch **3** *Ordinat* escape

échapper [eʃape] **VI é. à** *(quelqu'un)* to escape from; *(grippe, punition)* to escape *or Fam* dodge; *(corvées)* to get out of, to dodge; **é. à la mort** to escape death; **é. à un coup** to dodge a blow; **é. aux recherches** *(d'un criminel, un animal)* to evade capture; **cette édition a échappé à mes recherches** I missed this edition in my research; **é. à l'impôt** to avoid tax; **le prisonnier nous a échappé** the prisoner got away from us *or* escaped; **le vase m'a échappé des mains** the vase slipped out of my hands; **é. à tout contrôle** to be out of control; **cet enfant/ce chien**

échappe à notre contrôle this child/dog has got out of hand *or* is beyond our control; **il n'y a pas moyen d'y é.** there is no escaping it *or* getting away from it; **je n'échapperai pas à une leçon de morale** I'm in for a sermon; **peux-tu é. quelques heures à ton patron?** can you get away from work for a few hours?; **on ne m'échappe pas comme ça** you don't get away *or* escape that easily; **é. à toute définition** to defy definition; **é. à la règle** to be an exception to the rule; **tu n'échappes pas à la règle** you're no exception to the rule; **leurs baisers n'ont pas échappé à mes regards** it did not escape my notice that they were kissing; **l'enfant a échappé à la vue de sa mère cinq minutes seulement** the child was out of his mother's sight for only five minutes; **ce fait a échappé à mon attention, ce fait m'a échappé** this fact escaped *or* slipped my attention, this fact escaped me; **rien ne lui échappe** he doesn't miss a thing; **son nom m'échappe** his name escapes *or* eludes me, his name has slipped my mind; *Fam* **vous l'avez échappé belle** you've had a narrow escape

2 laisser é. *(personne, animal)* to let escape; *(de l'air d'un ballon)* to let out; *(vapeur)* to let off; *(larme)* to let fall; *(secret, soupir, cri, grossièreté)* to let out; *(faute d'orthographe, détail)* to overlook; **laisser é. son stylo** to let one's pen slip from one's fingers; **laisser é. l'occasion** to let the opportunity slip

3 *(parole, cri etc)* **pas un mot ne lui a échappé** he didn't let anything slip, he didn't say a word; **je n'aurais pas dû le dire mais ça m'a échappé** I shouldn't have said it but it just slipped out; **un sanglot/une injure lui échappa** he let out a sob/an oath

VPR **s'échapper** *(s'évader)* to escape (**de** from); **s'é. de prison** to escape from prison, to break out of prison; **je n'arriverai jamais à m'é. de cette réunion de famille** I'll never manage to get out of this family reunion; *Fam* **il faut que je m'échappe pendant quelques minutes** I've got to go somewhere (else) for a few minutes, I must be off; **le gaz s'échappe** the gas is leaking; **un cri s'échappa de ses lèvres** a cry burst from his lips; **de hautes flammes s'échappaient de tous côtés** great flames were shooting from every side

VT *Can (laisser échapper)* to drop

écharde [eʃard] NF splinter

écharpe [eʃarp] NF scarf VOIR GRAMMAIRE A12; *(de cérémonie)* sash; *(au bras)* sling; **porter le bras en é.** to have one's arm in a sling; **en é.** diagonally, crosswise; **prendre une voiture en é.** to hit a car sideways on; **se prendre en é.** *(de voitures)* to collide at an angle; *(de trains)* to collide at the points

écharper [eʃarpe] VT *(membre, personne)* to slash; *(viande)* to hack (up); *(troupes)* to cut to pieces; **vous allez vous faire é.!** you'll get torn to pieces!

échasse [eʃas] NF **1** stilt; **être monté sur des échasses** to be on stilts; *Fam (avoir de longues jambes)* to have long legs, to be long in the leg **2** *Orn* stilt

échassier [eʃasje] NM *Orn* wader

échauder [eʃode] VT *(théière)* to warm; *Fig* **se faire é., être échaudé** to get one's fingers burnt, to burn one's fingers; **elle hésite à se remarier car son premier mariage l'a échaudée** she's reluctant to get married again because she got her fingers burnt the first time

échauffant [eʃofɑ̃] ADJ *Arch (aliment)* that causes constipation

échauffement [eʃofmɑ̃] NM **1** *(d'une pièce, d'un moteur)* overheating; *(d'une céréale, du foin)* fermenting; *(d'une corde)* chafing **2** *(excitation)* overexcitement; **le débat a provoqué l'é. des esprits**

the discussion got people worked up, people got rather worked up *or* tempers got rather heated during the discussion; **dans l'é. de la discussion** in the heat of the argument; **l'é. de l'économie** the overheating of the economy **3** *(d'un athlète)* warm(ing)-up; **exercices d'é.** warm-up *or* limbering-up exercises **4** *Arch (constipation)* constipation

échauffer [eʃofe] VT **1** *(chauffer)* *(pièce, moteur)* to overheat; *(céréales, foin)* to cause fermentation in; **frottement qui échauffe les roues** friction that overheats the wheels **2** *(exciter)* **discussion qui échauffe les esprits** discussion that gets people worked up; *Fam* **é. la bile** *ou* **les oreilles** *ou* **les sangs à qn** to get up sb's nose, to get on sb's nerves **3** *(athlète)* to warm up

VPR **s'échauffer** to become *or* get overheated; *(d'un athlète etc)* to warm *or* limber up; *Tech* to run hot, to heat; *(de céréales, du foin)* to ferment; **ne vous échauffez pas** don't get excited

échauffourée [eʃofure] NF scuffle, skirmish; *(entre bandes)* clash; *Mil* skirmish

échéance [eʃeɑ̃s] NF date of payment; *(terme d'un effet)* falling due, maturity; *(de contrat)* expiry date; **venir à é.** to fall due; **payable à l'é.** payable at maturity; **à trois mois d'é.** at three months' date; **billet à longue/courte é.** long-/short-dated bill; **politique à longue/courte é.** long-/short-term policy; **emprunter/prêter à courte é.** to borrow/lend short; **faire face à une é.** to meet a bill; **avoir de lourdes échéances** to have a lot of bills to pay each month, to have a lot of monthly payments to make

▸▸ *Fin* **é. commune** equation of payment; *Fin* **é. à court terme** short-term maturity; **l'é. électorale** election day, the elections; *Fin* **é. emprunt** loan maturity; *Fin* **é. fixe** fixed maturity; *Compta* **échéances de fin de mois** end of month payments; *Fin* **é. à long terme** long-term maturity; *Fin* **é. proche** short maturity, near month; *Fin* **é. à vue** sight bill *or* maturity

échéancier [eʃeɑ̃sje] NM **1** *Fin* bill book; *Compta* due date file, aged debtor schedule; *Com* **é. de paiement** payment schedule **2** *(calendrier pour les travaux etc)* timetable, schedule

échéant [eʃeɑ̃] ADJ **1** *Fin* falling due **2** **le cas é.** if necessary, if need be

échec [eʃɛk] NM **1** *(défaite)* failure; *(revers)* check, setback; **l'é. des discussions** the failure *or* breakdown of the negotiations; **l'é. scolaire** doing badly at school, poor performance at school; **les problèmes familiaux sont très souvent à l'origine de l'é. scolaire** family problems are often the reason why children do badly at school; **voué à l'é.** bound to fail, doomed to failure; **reconnaître son é.** to admit defeat *or* failure; **cela va se solder par un é.** it will end in failure; **subir un é.** to suffer a setback; *Can* **mettre en é.** *(au hockey)* to check; *Fig* **tenir l'ennemi en é.** to hold the enemy in check; **faire é. à** *(activités, agissements etc)* to put a stop to; **faire é. à qn/aux projets de qn** to foil *or* frustrate sb/sb's plans

2 *(jeu)* **é.!** check!; **é. et mat** checkmate; **faire é. au roi** to check the king; **échecs** chess; **une partie d'échecs** a game of chess; **joueur d'échecs** chess player

échelle [eʃɛl] NF **1** ladder; **é. d'incendie** *ou* **de pompiers** fireman's ladder; **é. double** stepladder; **é. de corde** rope ladder; **é. coulissante** extension *or* extending ladder; **faire la courte é. à qn** to give sb a leg up *or Am* a boost; *Fam* **vous voulez me faire monter à l'é.** you're having *or Am* putting me on, you're pulling my leg

2 *Fig* **l'é. sociale** the social ladder; **être en**

haut *ou* **au sommet de l'é.** to be at the top of the tree *or* the ladder

3 *(d'une carte, maquette etc)* scale; **l'é. est de 1/10 000** the scale is 1/10,000; **ton train électrique est à quelle é.?** what scale is your electric train?; **carte à petite/grande é.** small-/large-scale map; *Fig* **faire les choses sur une grande é.** to do things on a large scale; **à l'é. mondiale/nationale** on a world/national scale; **à l'é. de l'homme** on a human scale; **à l'é. de temps humain** on a human time scale; *Ordinat* **intégration à grande/petite é.** large-/small-scale integration

4 *Hist* **les échelles du Levant** the (commercial) ports of the Levant; **les échelles de Barbarie** the Barbary ports

5 *(dans un collant)* ladder, *Am* run; **j'ai fait une é. à mon collant** I've laddered my tights, *Am* I have a run in my tights

6 *(dans les cheveux)* **elle me fait des échelles** she cuts my hair in steps; **dommage qu'il y ait toutes ces échelles** it's a pity that it's all so uneven *or* all so up and down

▸▸ *Mktg* **é. d'attitudes** attitude scale; **é. de Beaufort** Beaufort scale; *Mus* **é. chromatique/diatonique/harmonique** chromatic/diatonic/harmonic scale; *Mktg* **é. de classement** rating scale; *Naut* **é. de commandement** *ou* **d'honneur** companion ladder; **é. des êtres** evolutionary ladder; **dans l'é. des êtres** on the evolutionary ladder; *Typ, Ordinat* **é. des gris** levels of grey; *Mktg* **é. d'importance** importance scale; *Rel* **é. de Jacob** Jacob's ladder; **é. de marée** tide gauge; **é. de meunier** open staircase; **é. mobile** *(des prix etc)* sliding scale; *Naut* **é. de revers** Jacob's ladder; **é. de Richter** Richter scale; **sur l'é. de Richter** on the Richter scale; **é. à saumons** salmon ladder; *Mus* **é. des sons** scale; *Naut* **é. de tirant d'eau** water *or* draught marks, *Am* immersion scale; **é. des traitements** *ou* **des salaires** salary scale; **é. des valeurs** scale of values

échelon [eʃlɔ̃] NM **1** *(d'une échelle)* rung **2** *(degré d'une hiérarchie, organisation)* step, grade, *Fml* echelon; **monter par échelons** to rise by degrees *or* by successive stages; **les échelons de l'administration** the grades of the civil service; **le dernier/premier é.** the bottom/top grade *or* step; **il a gravi rapidement tous les échelons** he climbed the ladder rapidly; **j'en suis au dernier é.** I'm at *or* I've reached the top of my grade **3** *(niveau)* level; **à l'é. ministériel/directoriel** at ministerial/managerial level; **à l'é. régional/national** on a regional/national level; **à tous les échelons** at all levels, at every level; *Bourse* **é. de cotation** tick size

échelonnement [eʃ(ə)lɔnmɑ̃] NM **1** *(des paiements)* spreading out; *(des vacances)* staggering; **l'é. des travaux se fera sur plusieurs mois** the work will be spread out over several months; **le cours suit un é. bien précis** the course timetable is laid out very precisely **2** *(de poteaux, maisons)* row

échelonner [eʃ(ə)lɔne] VT **1** *(objets)* to space out, to place at intervals; *(paiements)* to spread (out), to stagger; **congés échelonnés** staggered holidays **2** *Mil (troupes)* to dispose in echelon *or* in depth

VPR **s'échelonner** *(d'objets)* to be spaced out; **les paiements s'échelonnent sur deux ans** the payments are spread (out) over two years; **les arbres s'échelonnent sur plusieurs kilomètres** the trees stretch for several kilometres; **le cours s'échelonne sur dix niveaux** there are ten levels of difficulty in the course; **le remboursement de la dette s'échelonnera sur dix ans** the repayment of the debt will be spread out *or* staggered over a ten year period

écheniller [eʃ(ə)nije] VT *(arbres fruitiers)* to clear of caterpillars

écheveau, -eaux [eʃ(ə)vo] NM *(de fil etc)* hank, skein; *Fig* **é. de rues** maze of streets; **l'é. d'une intrigue** the intricacies *or* complexities of a plot; **un é. de mensonges/problèmes** a tissue of lies/a host of problems

échevelé [eʃəvle] ADJ **1** *(personne)* dishevelled **2** *Fig (danse, fête)* wild; *(course)* mad

échevin [eʃ(ə)vɛ̃] NM **1** *Arch* municipal magistrate **2** *Belg* deputy mayor

échine [eʃin] NF **1** *Anat* spine, backbone; *Fig* **courber** *ou* **plier l'é.** to submit, to kowtow (**devant qn** to sb); *Fig* **avoir l'é. souple** *ou* **flexible** to bow and scrape **2** *Culin* loin (of pork); **une côte de porc dans l'é.** a pork loin chop

échiné [eʃine] ADJ *Can* tired out, exhausted

échiner (s') [seʃine] VPR *(se fatiguer)* to exhaust oneself, to tire oneself out (**à faire qch** doing sth); *(se donner du mal)* to go to great lengths, to make a great effort (**à faire qch** to do sth)

échiquier [eʃikje] NM **1** *(damier)* chessboard; **en é.** in a chequered *or Am* checkered pattern; *Pol Fig* **l'é. mondial/européen** the world/European stage *or* arena **2** *Br Pol* **l'É.** the Exchequer

écho [eko] NM **1** echo; **faire é.** to echo (back); **il y a de l'é.** there's an echo; *Fig* **se faire l'é. des opinions de qn** to echo *or* repeat sb's opinions; *Fig* **je n'ai eu aucun é. de leur discussion** I've heard nothing about their discussion; *Fig* **ma proposition/mon offre est restée sans é.** I got no feedback on my suggestion/offer, I never heard any more about my suggestion/offer; *Fig* **trouver un é.** to get a response VOIR GRAMMAIRE A12 **2** *Ordinat* echo; *Électron* **éliminateur** *ou* **suppresseur d'é.** echo suppressor; **échos parasites** clutter; **é. local** local echo **3** *TV* ghost(ing); *Radio* echo **4** *Journ* **échos** news in brief; **échos mondains** gossip column

échocardiographie [ekokardjografi] NF echocardiography

échographie [ekografi] NF *(ultrasound)* scan; **passer une é.** to have a scan

échoir [eʃwar] VI *(prp* **échéant;** *pp* **échu;** *pr ind* **il échoit, ils échoient;** *impf* **il échoyait;** *p hist* **il échut;** *fu* **il échoira;** *aux souvent* **être**) **1** *Litt* **é. à qn** to fall to sb; **le devoir m'échut de lui apprendre la nouvelle** it fell to me to break the news to him **2** *Fin (d'une dette etc)* to fall due; *(d'un investissement etc)* to mature; **abonnement échu** expired subscription; **billets échus** bills (over)due; **intérêts échus** outstanding interest, interest due; **intérêts à é.** accruing interest; **le terme échoit le 20 de ce mois** the date for payment is the 20th of this month; **le délai est échu** the deadline has expired

échoppe [eʃɔp] NF *Com* booth, stall; *(de cordonnier)* (cobbler's) small (work)shop

écho-sondeur, *pl* **écho-sondeurs** NM *Naut* echo sounder, sonic depth finder

échotier, -ière [ekɔtje, -jɛr] N *Journ* gossip columnist

échouage [eʃwaʒ], **échouement** [eʃumɑ̃] NM running aground; *(sur la plage)* beaching

échouer [eʃwe] VI **1** *Naut* to run aground, to be stranded, to ground; *(d'une baleine)* to beach; **navire échoué** ship aground, stranded vessel *or* ship; **échoué à sec** high and dry; *Fig* **é. dans** *(pays hostile, bar mal famé etc)* to end *or* land up in **2** *(ne pas réussir)* *(d'un plan etc)* to fail, to come to nothing; *(d'une personne)* to fail; **é. à un examen** to fail an examination; **faire é.** *(projet)* to wreck; *(complot)* to foil
VT *Naut (bateau)* to beach, to run aground
VPR **s'échouer** *Naut* to run aground, to be driven ashore; *(d'une baleine)* to beach

écimage [esimaʒ] NM *(d'un arbre)* topping, pollarding

écimer [esime] VT *(arbre)* to top, to pollard

éclaboussement [eklabusmɑ̃] NM splashing, spattering

éclabousser [eklabuse] VT *(avec un liquide)* to splash, to spatter (**de** with); *Fig* **é. qn** *(salir)* to damage sb's reputation, to sully sb's (good) name

éclaboussure [eklabusyr] NF *(de boue etc)* splash, spatter; *Fig (à la réputation)* blemish, blot, smirch; **le président n'a reçu aucune é. dans cette histoire** the president came out of the business with his reputation intact, none of the mud stuck to the president

éclair [eklɛr] NM **1** *Météo* flash of lightning; **éclairs** lightning; **éclairs de chaleur** heat lightning; **il y a des éclairs** there's lightning; **rapide comme l'é.** quick as lightning *or* as a flash; *Fig* **en un é.** in a flash, quick as a flash; **la voiture passa comme un é.** the car flashed by; **cette pensée traversa mon esprit comme un é.** the thought flashed through my mind **2** *(d'une arme etc)*, *Fig (de lucidité, génie)* flash; **lancer des éclairs** *(d'un diamant, des yeux etc)* to flash **3** *Culin* éclair
ADJ INV *(visite, attaque)* lightning; **guerre é.** blitzkrieg; **il a fait un passage é. au sein de la rédaction** he had a very brief spell on the editorial team

éclairage [eklɛraʒ] NM **1** *(fait d'éclairer)* lighting, illumination; *Cin, Théâtre* lighting; *(par projecteurs)* floodlighting; *Phot* light; **é. doux** soft lighting **2** *Fig* light; **sous cet é.** (seen) in this light; **montrer qch sous un autre é.** to show sth in a different light **3** *Mil, Naut* scouting
▸ ▸ **é. d'ambiance** background light; **é. d'appoint** fill light; **é. sur batterie** sungun; **é. clair-obscur** Rembrandt *or* chiaroscuro lighting; **é. en contre-jour** backlighting; **é. de cyclorama** cyclorama light; **é. direct/indirect** direct/indirect lighting; **é. à l'électricité/au gaz** electric/gas lighting; **é. de faible intensité** low-key lighting; **é. frisant** rimming; *Aut* **é. intérieur automatique** courtesy light; **é. de plateau** stage lighting; **é. aux projecteurs** floodlighting; **é. public** street lighting; **é. à la Rembrandt** Rembrandt lighting; *Aut* **é. de route** full-beam headlights; **é. de sécurité** emergency lighting; **é. en trois points** three-point lighting; *Aut* **é. de ville** dipped headlights

éclairagiste [eklɛraʒist] N *Cin, Théâtre* lighting technician *or* engineer

éclairant [eklɛrɑ̃] ADJ *(pouvoir etc)* lighting, illuminating; **fusée éclairante** flare; *Fig* **une explication éclairante** an enlightening *or* illuminating explanation

éclaircie [eklɛrsi] NF **1** *(dans les nuages etc)* break, opening, rift; *Météo* bright interval; *Fig* improvement **2** *(dans une forêt)* clearing, glade

éclaircir [eklɛrsir] VT **1** *(rendre plus clair)* *(couleur, teinte, les cheveux etc)* to lighten; **é. le teint** to clear the complexion **2** *Fig (élucider) (mystère)* to throw light on, to clear up; *(situation)* to clarify **3** *(rendre moins épais)* *(forêt, sauce)* to thin; *(jeunes plants etc)* to thin out
VPR **s'éclaircir 1** *(du temps)* to clear (up), to become bright(er); *(du ciel)* to clear, to brighten; *(du teint, de la voix)* to clear, to become clear(er); **s'é. la voix** to clear one's throat; *Fig* **l'avenir semble s'é.** the future seems to be getting brighter; **son visage s'éclaircit** his/her face brightened up *or* lit up; **mes idées se sont peu à peu éclaircies** my ideas gradually became clearer **2** *(se dissiper) (d'un mystère, de doutes)* to be cleared up; *(de brouillard)* to clear (up) **3** *(des cheveux)* to grow thin, to be thinning; **enfin**

les arbres s'éclaircirent at length the trees thinned out

éclaircissage [eklɛrsisaʒ] NM **1** *(du verre)* polishing **2** *(de plantes)* thinning out

éclaircissant [eklɛrsisɑ̃] ADJ lightening, highlighting

éclaircissement [eklɛrsismɑ̃] NM **1** *(élucidation)* clarification, *Fml* elucidation; *(explication)* explanation; **l'é. de ce mystère a pris des mois** it was months before the mystery was cleared up; **demander des éclaircissements sur qch** to ask for an explanation of sth; **s'ils me demandent des éclaircissements sur mon rapport** if they ask me for clarification on my report **2** *(de cheveux)* lightening; **je me suis fait faire un é.** I had my hair lightened

éclairé [eklere] ADJ lit; *Fig (personne, esprit, public)* enlightened

éclairement [eklermɑ̃] NM illumination, lighting

éclairer [eklere] VT **1** *(pièce, vitrine)* to light, to illuminate; *(personne)* to light the way for; *Cin, Phot, TV* to light; **é. un angle sombre** to light up a dark corner; **cafés éclairés au néon** cafés with neon lights, neon-lit cafés; **une pièce bien/mal éclairée** a well-lit/badly lit room; **éclaire-moi, que j'ouvre la serrure** give me some light so that I can open the lock; *Fig* **un sourire éclaira son visage** a smile lit up his/her face **2** *(expliquer) (sujet)* to shed *or* throw light on; **é. qch d'un jour nouveau** to shed *or* throw new light on sth **3** *(informer)* to enlighten; **éclairez-moi sur ce sujet** tell me what it's all about; *Fam* **si tu pouvais é. ma lanterne sur cette affaire** if you could put me in the picture about this matter **4** *Mil* **é. le terrain** *ou* **la marche** to reconnoitre the ground, to scout
VI *(donner de la lumière)* **cette lampe éclaire mal** this lamp doesn't give a very good light
VPR **s'éclairer 1** *(pour avoir de la lumière)* **il s'éclaire toujours au pétrole/gaz** he still has *or* uses oil lamps/gaslight; **s'é. à la bougie/avec une lampe de poche** *(pour voir le chemin)* to light one's way with a candle/torch, to use a candle/torch to see by **2** *(devenir lumineux) (d'un bâtiment etc)* to light up; **son visage s'est éclairé** his/her face lit up *or* brightened **3** *Fig (devenir compréhensible) (d'une situation etc)* to become clear(er); **tout s'éclaire!** things are *or* everything is becoming clear(er)!

éclaireur, -euse [eklɛrœr, -øz] NM **1** *Mil* scout; *Naut* scouting vessel, scout; *Aviat* **avion é.** reconnaissance aircraft; *Mil, Fig* **partir en é.** to go off for a scout around; *Fig* **il est parti en é. pour voir s'il y avait de la place au restaurant** he's gone to check the seat situation in the restaurant; **il part un mois avant, en é.** he's leaving a month in advance to check things out **2** *Aut* **é. de coffre** boot *or Am* trunk light
N (boy) scout, *f* (girl) guide; **chef é.** scoutmaster, *f* guide captain

éclampsie [eklɑ̃psi] NF *Méd* eclampsia

éclat [ekla] NM **1** *(fragment)* *(de bois)* splinter; *(de pierre)* chip; *(de mica)* flake; **é. d'obus** piece of shrapnel; **éclats d'obus** shrapnel; **voler en éclats** to fly *or* burst into pieces; **un é. de verre** a fragment *or* splinter of glass; **éclats de verre** *(bris)* broken glass; *(projeté)* flying glass **2** *(son) (de rire)* burst; **é. de colère** outburst of anger; **de grands éclats de voix** loud voices; **partir d'un grand é. de rire** to burst out laughing; **rire aux éclats** to roar with laughter **3** *Fig (scandale)* scandal, stir, fuss; **elle fait**

des éclats à chaque fois qu'elle sort she causes commotion wherever she goes; **j'espère qu'il n'y aura pas d'é. pendant la réunion** I hope the meeting passes off quietly, I hope nobody makes a fuss at the meeting; **il adore provoquer des éclats dans les soirées mondaines** he loves creating a commotion at parties; **sans é.** quietly, without any fuss

4 *(du soleil)* glare; *(d'un diamant)* glitter, lustre; *(du regard)* sparkle; *(de couleurs)* brilliance, vividness; **l'é. de ses yeux** the sparkle in his/her eyes; **l'é. de la jeunesse** the bloom *or* freshness of youth; **le soleil brille de son plus vif é.** the sun is (shining) at its brightest *or* most brilliant

5 *(de style etc)* brilliance; *(d'une cérémonie, période, de la gloire etc)* splendour, *Am* splendor; **action** *ou* **coup d'é.** brilliant feat; **il aime faire les choses avec é.** he likes to do things with style

éclatant [eklatã] **ADJ 1** *(son, rire)* loud, ringing **2** *(lumière, couleur, succès)* dazzling, brilliant; *(bijoux)* sparkling, glittering; **teint é.** glowing *or* blooming complexion; **être dans une forme éclatante** to be on brilliant *or* dazzling form; **é. de santé** glowing *or* blooming with health

éclate [eklat] **NF** *Fam* **c'est l'é.** it's a laugh *or* a hoot; **c'est pas l'é.** it's not exactly a barrel of laughs

éclaté [eklate] **ADJ** *(groupe)* scattered, dispersed; *(programme, mesures)* fragmented, fragmentary; **paysage politique é.** fragmented political landscape; **avoir une vision éclatée des choses** to have a fragmented view of things
NM *Tech* exploded view

éclatement [eklatmã] **NM** *(d'un obus)* bursting, explosion; *(d'une arme)* explosion; *(d'un pneu)* bursting, blow-out; *(d'un tuyau)* bursting; *(d'un verre)* shattering; *(du foie, de la rate)* rupture; *(d'un convoi, un groupe)* dispersal; *Pol (d'un parti)* splitting (up), fragmentation; *Aut* **é. de l'étincelle** spark

éclater [eklate] **VI 1** *(d'un obus)* to burst, to explode; *(d'une arme)* to explode; *(d'une mine)* to blow up; *(d'un pneu, un ballon)* to burst; *(d'un verre)* to shatter; **faire é. qch** to burst/explode/shatter sth; **faire é. un pétard** to set off a firework; *Fig* **le groupe a fini par é.** the group finally split up
2 *(de la guerre, un incendie, une épidémie, un conflit)* to break out; *(d'un orage, un scandale)* to break; *(de la colère)* to burst out; **quand la guerre éclata** at the outbreak of the war, when war broke out; **le tonnerre éclata** there was a clap of thunder; **l'hymne national éclata dans la salle** the people in the room broke into the national anthem
3 *Fig (de personne)* **é. de rire** to burst out laughing; **é. en applaudissements** to burst into applause; **é. en sanglots** to burst into tears; **é. de colère** to fly into a rage
4 *(être manifeste)* to be obvious *or* evident, to stand out; **les préjugés de l'auteur éclatent à chaque page** the author's prejudices stand out on every page; **l'indignation éclatait dans ses yeux** his eyes were blazing with indignation
VPR s'éclater *Fam* to have a wild *or* a really good time; **s'é. comme une bête** to freak out
VT *Fam (pneu)* to burst; *Fig Fam* **je vais l'é., je vais lui é. la tête** *ou* **la gueule** I'll smash his head in

éclateur [eklatœr] **NM** *Aut* spark gap

éclectique [eklektik] **ADJ, N** eclectic

éclectisme [eklektism] **NM** eclecticism

éclipse [eklips] **NF** *(de soleil, lune)* eclipse; *Fig* **é. totale de la raison/mémoire** total loss of reason/memory; *Fig* **après une longue é.** after a long absence

éclipser [eklipse] **VT 1** *Astron (soleil, lune)* to

eclipse **2** *Fig (surpasser) (personne)* to eclipse, to outshine, to overshadow, *Fam* to put in the shade; *(événement, exploit etc)* to eclipse, to overshadow
VPR s'éclipser 1 *Fam (s'esquiver)* to make off, to make oneself scarce **2** *Astron* to be eclipsed; *(être voilé)* to be obscured

écliptique [ekliptik] **ADJ, NM** *Astron* ecliptic

éclisse [eklis] **NF 1** *(plaque de bois)* (wooden) wedge **2** *(éclat)* piece of split wood **3** *Méd* splint **4** *Rail* fishplate

éclisser [eklise] **VT** *Méd (membre)* to put in splints, to splint

éclopé, -ée [eklope] **ADJ** lame, limping
NM *Mil* temporarily disabled soldier
N *Hum* person with a limp

éclore [eklɔr] **VI** *(pp éclos; pr ind il éclôt, ils éclosent; impf il éclosait; no p hist; fu il éclora; aux souvent être, parfois avoir)* **1** *(d'œufs, de poussins)* to hatch (out), to be hatched; **faire é. un œuf** to hatch (out) an egg **2** *(de fleurs, bourgeons)* to open; *Fig (d'un talent)* to be born, to appear; **roses fraîches écloses** roses that have just opened; *Litt* **le jour est près d'é.** dawn is near; *Fig* **faire é. un talent** to nurture *or* develop a talent

éclosion [eklozjɔ̃] **NF 1** *(d'œufs, de poussins)* hatching **2** *(de fleurs)* opening, blooming; *Fig (d'un talent)* birth

écluse [eklyz] **NF 1** *(de canal)* lock; **droit d'é.** lock fee, lockage; **(porte d')é.** lock gate, sluice (gate); **é. de moulin** mill dam; *Fam Fig* **lâcher** *ou* **ouvrir les écluses** to turn on the waterworks **2** *(d'un dock)* tide gate **3** *Ordinat* firewall

éclusée [eklyze] **NF** *Tech* lock water

écluser [eklyze] **VT 1** *(canal)* to equip with locks **2** *(péniche)* to pass through a lock **3** *Fam (boire)* to knock back
VI *Fam* **qu'est-ce qu'elle écluse!** she doesn't half knock it back!

éclusier, -ière [eklyzje, -jɛr] **N** lock keeper

éco- [eko, eko] **PRÉF** eco-

écobilan [ekobilã] **NM** life-cycle analysis

écœurant [ekœrã] **ADJ 1** *(dégoûtant) (nourriture)* nauseating, sickening; *(personne)* disgusting, sickening; **c'est un peu é. si on en mange trop** it's a bit sickly if you eat too much of it; **il a une manière de manger vraiment écœurante** it's quite sickening *or* disgusting *or Fam* sick-making watching him eat, it really turns the stomach watching him eat **2** *(décourageant)* disheartening, discouraging, demoralizing; **c'est é., elle a encore eu une augmentation!** it's sickening, she's got another rise!; **tu as une chance écœurante!** what disgusting luck!; **c'est é. ce que tu peux avoir de la chance** you're so lucky it makes me sick; *Can* **Steven est é. dans le rôle de Jake** Steven is unreal in the role of Jake
NM *Can* disgusting *or* loathsome man

écœuranterie [ekœrãtri] **NF** *Can Fam* **1** *(saleté)* filth **2** *(coup bas)* dirty trick; **elle m'a fait une é.** she played a dirty trick on me

écœurement [ekœrmã] **NM 1** *(physique)* nausea; *(dégoût)* disgust, loathing; **manger du chocolat jusqu'à é.** to eat chocolate until you feel sick *or* to the point of nausea; *Fig* **j'ai jardiné jusqu'à é.** I've done so much gardening I'm sick (and tired) of it *or* I'm fed up; **sa cruauté a provoqué l'é.** de tout le monde everyone was disgusted *or* nauseated by his/her cruelty, his/her cruelty turned everyone's stomach; **on ne peut le regarder agir sans é.** it's impossible to watch him at work without feeling disgust **2** *(découragement)* discouragement, dejection; **maintenant c'est l'é.** now I've/he's/*etc* become discouraged *or* lost heart; **ça a été l'é. dans toute la classe** the entire class lost heart

écœurer [ekœre] **VT 1** *(physiquement)* **e. qn** to nauseate sb, to make sb feel sick *or Am* nauseous; *(dégoûter)* to disgust sb, to make sb feel sick; *(révolter)* to disgust sb **2** *(décourager)* to dishearten, to discourage; **son attitude l'écœure tellement que …** he finds his/her attitude so disheartening *or* discouraging that …; *Fam* **elle est écœurée de son job** she is sick of *or* fed up with her job; **ça m'écœure que …** it sickens me *or* makes me sick that … **3** *Can Fam (donner envie)* **e. qn** to make sb green with envy

écoinçon [ekwɛ̃sɔ̃] **NM** *Constr* corner piece *or* stone

écolabel [ekolabɛl] **NM** ecolabel

écolage [ekolaʒ] **NM 1** *Suisse (frais de scolarité)* school fees **2** *Belg (formation)* training

école [ekɔl] **NF** VOIR GRAMMAIRE A6-7 **1** *(établissement)* school; **maîtresse/maître d'é.** (primary) school teacher; **les grandes écoles** = prestigious university-level colleges which prepare students for senior posts in public administration, engineering and business
2 *(enseignement)* school; **aller à l'é. jusqu'à 16 ans** to go to school until the age of 16; **faire l'é.** to teach; **faire l'é. buissonnière** to play truant *or Am Fam* hooky; **reprendre l'é.** to go back to school; *Fam* **je n'ai pas é. aujourd'hui** there's no school today; *Fig Hum* **tu peux retourner à l'é.** what did they teach you at school?; *Fig* **vous êtes à bonne é.** you're in good hands; *Fig* **à l'é. de la vie** in the university of life
3 *(mouvement)* *(de pensée, d'art, de littérature)* school; **faire é.** *(d'une théorie, d'un penseur)* to win a following
4 *Mil (exercice)* drill, training; **é. du soldat** drill; **é. de tir** rifle drill, knotting and splicing; *Aviat* **appareil d'é.** training aircraft
▶ ▶ **é. de l'air** flying school; **École des Arts et Métiers** = engineering college *(of university level)*; **é. des Beaux-Arts** art school; **é. de cinéma** film school; **é. de commerce** business school; **é. de conduite** driving school; **é. confessionnelle** ≃ independent *or* private school; **é. de danse** dance *or* dancing school; **é. de dessin** art school; *Suisse* **é. enfantine** nursery school; **é. d'équitation** riding school; **é. hôtelière** hotel school; **é. de journalisme** school of journalism; **é. libre** ≃ independent *or* private school; **é. maternelle** nursery school, kindergarten; **é. militaire** military academy; **é. de musique** music school; **É. nationale d'administration** = prestigious university-level college preparing students for senior posts in the civil service and public management; **É. nationale supérieure d'ingénieurs** = university-level college for the continuing education of qualified engineers; *Anciennement* **é. normale** ≃ teacher training college; **É. normale supérieure** = university-level college that prepares students for senior posts in teaching and other professions; **é. de police** police college *or Am* academy; **é. primaire** primary school; **é. privée** ≃ independent *or* private school; **é. publique** state *or Am* public school; *Suisse* **é. de recrues** *(instruction militaire obligatoire)* compulsory military training; **é. secondaire** secondary school, *Am* high school; **é. de secrétariat** secretarial college; **É. supérieure des sciences économiques et commerciales** = grande école for management and business studies

écolier, -ière [ekɔlje, -jɛr] **N** *(du primaire)* (primary) schoolboy, *f* (primary) schoolgirl; **écoliers** schoolchildren; *Fig* **le chemin des écoliers** the longest way round; **papier é.** exercise paper

écolo [ekɔlo] **ADJ, N** *Fam (abrév* **écologiste)** green

écologie [ekɔlɔʒi] **NF** ecology

écologique [ekɔlɔʒik] ADJ ecological, environmental

écologisme [ekɔlɔʒism] NM concern for the environment, environmental awareness

écologiste [ekɔlɔʒist] N ecologist; *Pol* ecologist, environmentalist
ADJ *(parti)* green, ecology; *(politique)* green, environmentalist

e-commerce [ikɔmɛrs] NM e-commerce

écomusée [ekɔmyze] NM ecomuseum

éconduire [ekɔ̃dɥir] VT *(conj like* **conduire***)* **1** *(congédier)* **é. qn** to get rid of sb, to show sb the door; **j'ai eu beaucoup de mal à les é.** I had a lot of trouble getting rid of them **2** *(refuser) (prétendant)* to reject, to turn down; *(suppliant, requérant) (en personne)* to turn away; *(par lettre)* to turn down

éconocroques [ekɔnɔkrɔk] NFPL *Arg* savings

économat [ekɔnɔma] NM **1** *(fonction)* stewardship, bursarship **2** *(bureau)* steward's *or* bursar's office **3** *(magasin)* staff (discount) store; *Com (coopérative)* multiple *or* chain store

économe [ekɔnɔm] N *(d'un collège, d'une institution etc)* steward, bursar
ADJ economical, thrifty; **é. de paroles/de son temps** sparing with words/of one's time
NM potato peeler

Note that **économe** means **thrifty** and cannot be used to translate **economic**, for which the correct translation is always **économique**.

économètre [ekɔnɔmɛtr] N econometrician, econometrist

économétrie [ekɔnɔmetri] NF econometrics

économétrique [ekɔnɔmetrik] ADJ econometric

économie [ekɔnɔmi] NF **1** *(système)* economy; **é. de troc** barter economy; **nouvelle é.** new economy; **la fermeture de l'usine a eu des conséquences désastreuses sur l'é. de la région** the closure of the factory has had disastrous consequences for the region's economy
2 *(gain)* economy, saving; *(vertu)* economy, thrift; **avoir le sens de l'é.** to be thrifty, to be good with money; **elle n'a aucun sens de l'é.** she's no good at managing money, she's got no idea about money; **é. de temps** time saving; **faire une é. de temps/d'énergie/de vingt pour cent** to save time/energy/twenty per cent; **ça représentera une énorme é. de temps** it will be an enormous saving of time *or* an enormous time saver, it will save an enormous amount of time; **je vais faire l'é. d'un coup de fil** I'll save myself a phone call; **je pense qu'on ne pourra pas faire l'é. d'une réunion** I don't think we can do without a meeting, I think a meeting is essential; **ce mariage a vraiment été fait à l'é.** the wedding was really done on the cheap
3 *(discipline)* economics
4 économies savings; **j'ai quelques économies** I have a few *or* some savings; **faire des économies** to save money; **je n'arrive pas à faire d'économies** I can't manage to save; **réaliser d'importantes économies** to save a lot of money, to make major savings; **faire des économies de chauffage** to save money *or* economize on heating; **prendre sur ses économies** to break into *or* draw on one's savings; **il n'y a pas de petites économies** every little helps
5 *(organisation) (d'une œuvre littéraire, loi etc)* arrangement, structure
▸▸**é. du bien-être** welfare economy; *Fam* **économies de bouts de chandelles** cheeseparing (economy); **é. capitaliste** capitalist

economy; **é. classique** classical economics; **é. de la demande** demand-side economics; **é. à deux vitesses** two-speed economy; **é. dirigée** planned economy; **économies d'échelle** economies of scale; **é. d'entreprise** business management *or* studies; **é. de l'environnement** environmental economics; **é. éthique** caring economy; **é. immergée** underground economy; **é. industrielle** industrial economics; **é. informelle** informal economy; **é. libérale** open market economy; **é. de libre entreprise** free-enterprise economy; **é. de marché** market economy; **é. mixte** mixed economy; **é. mondiale** world economy; **é. noire** black economy; **é. de l'offre** supply-side economics; **é. ouverte** open economy; **é. parallèle** black economy; **é. planifiée** planned economy; **é. politique** political economy, economics; **é. sociale** social economy; **é. solidaire** economy of solidarity, socially responsible economy; **é. souterraine** black economy, underground economy; **é. de subsistance** subsistence economy; **é. de transition** transition economy; **é. de troc** barter economy

économique [ekɔnɔmik] ADJ **1** *(problème, doctrine)* economic; **science é.** economics **2** *(bon marché, avantageux)* economical; **vitesse é.** *(d'une voiture etc)* economical speed; **cycle é.** *(d'un lave-vaisselle etc)* economy cycle; *Aviat* **classe é.** economy class; **bouteille/voiture é.** economy (size) bottle/ economy car

Attention: ne pas confondre **economic** et **economical** lorsque l'on traduit **économique**. **Economic** signifie **qui se rapporte à l'économie** alors que **economical** signifie **qui permet d'économiser**.

économiquement [ekɔnɔmikmɑ̃] ADV *(à peu de frais)*, *Écon* economically, inexpensively; **les é. faibles** people on low incomes

économiser [ekɔnɔmize] VT *(argent)* to economize, to save; *(temps, énergie)* to save; *(électricité, gaz)* to economize on, to save on; *(ressources etc)* to conserve; **économisez 100 euros** 100 euros off, save 100 euros; **é. ses paroles** to be sparing of one's words; **é. ses forces** to conserve one's strength; **é. sa salive** to save one's breath
VI to economize, to save *(sur on)*

économiseur [ekɔnɔmizœr] NM *Aut* fuel-saving device, economizer; *Ordinat* **é. d'écran** screen saver

économiste [ekɔnɔmist] N economist

écope [ekɔp] NF *Naut* bailer, scoop

écoper [ekɔpe] VT **1** *(barque)* to bail (out); **é. l'eau d'une embarcation** to bail out a boat *or* the water out of a boat **2** *Fam (recevoir comme punition)* **c'est encore moi qui ai écopé de la punition** it was me that caught it again; **é. (de) cinq ans de prison** to cop *or* get five years' prison
VI to get the blame, to catch *or* cop it; **j'en ai marre é. pour les autres** I'm sick of getting the blame for what other people do

écoproduit [ekɔprɔdɥi] NM eco-friendly product, environmentally-friendly product

écorçage [ekɔrsaʒ] NM *(d'arbres)* barking; *(d'oranges)* peeling; *(de riz)* husking

écorce [ekɔrs] NF **1** *(d'un arbre)* bark; *(d'une orange)* rind, peel; *(de riz)* husk; *(de châtaigne)* skin **2** *Géog* **l'é. terrestre** the earth's crust **3** *Bot* cortex **4** *Fig (apparence)* outward appearance

écorcer [ekɔrse] VT *(j'écorçai(s); n. écorçons)* *(arbre)* to bark; *(orange)* to peel; *(riz)* to husk

écorché, -ée [ekɔrʃe] NM **1** *Beaux-Arts* anatomical model, écorché **2** *Tech* sectional *or* cutaway view
N *Fig* **é. vif** tortured soul

écorchement [ekɔrʃəmɑ̃] NM *(d'un animal)*, skinning

écorcher [ekɔrʃe] VT **1** *(animal)* to skin; *(criminel)* to flay; *Fig Fam* **é. les clients** to fleece the customers **2** *(érafler) (jambe, peau etc)* to graze, to scrape; *(la gorge) (de l'alcool)* to burn, to rasp; *(d'un plat pimenté)* to burn; *(d'un bonbon)* to scratch; *Fig Fam* **é. une langue/un nom** to murder a language/ name; **son qui écorche l'oreille** sound that grates on the ear
VPR **s'écorcher** to graze oneself; **s'é. le genou** to graze *or* scrape one's knee; **s'é. le tibia** to graze *or* bark one's shin

écorcheur, -euse [ekɔrʃœr, -øz] N **1** *(d'animal)* skinner **2** *Fig Fam (voleur)* extortionist; **ce sont de véritables écorcheurs** they rob you blind

écorchure [ekɔrʃyr] NF graze, scratch

éco-recharge, *pl* **éco-recharges** NF eco-refill

écorner [ekɔrne] VT **1** *(meuble, statue etc)* to chip *or* damage the corner(s) of; **é. (les pages d')un livre** to dog-ear (the pages of) a book **2** *Fig* **é. son capital/ses économies** to break into one's capital/savings **3** *Can (animal)* to dehorn; *Fig* **un vent à é. les bœufs** a fierce gale

écornifler [ekɔrnifle] VT *Fam Vieilli (repas, argent)* to cadge, to scrounge *(à qn off sb)*
VI *Can (être indiscret)* to snoop (around), to pry

écornifleur, -euse [ekɔrniflœr, -øz] N **1** *Fam Vieilli* sponger, cadger, scrounger **2** *Can Fam (personne indiscrète)* snooper
ADJ *Can Fam* snooping, prying

écossais, -aise [ekɔsɛ, -ɛz] VOIR GRAMMAIRE A19 ADJ *(paysage, personne etc)* Scottish; *(whisky)* Scotch; **tissu é.** tartan, plaid
N **É.** Scot, Scotsman, *f* Scotswoman
NM **1** *(tissu)* tartan, plaid **2** *Ling (dialecte de l'anglais)* Scots; *(langue celtique)* (Scots) Gaelic

Écosse [ekɔs] NF Scotland

écosser [ekɔse] VT *(pois)* to shell, to pod; *(haricots)* to shell

écosystème [ekɔsistɛm] NM *Biol* ecosystem

écot [eko] NM **payer son é.** to pay one's share

écotaxe [ekotaks] NF ecotax

écotourisme [ekoturism] NM ecotourism

écoulement [ekulmɑ̃] NM **1** *(d'un liquide)* flow, discharge; *Constr (du toit etc)* run-off; **fossé d'é.** drain; *(tube d')é.* *(d'une baignoire)* waste pipe; **l'é. se fait mal** it's not flowing very well; *Aviat* **é. (des filets) d'air** air flow
2 *Méd* discharge
3 *(de la circulation)* flow; **l'é. de la foule dans le métro** the streams of people moving through the metro
4 *Com (de marchandises)* sale; **marchandises d'é. facile** goods that sell easily *or* fast, goods with a ready sale; **l'é. de ces vieux parapluies sera plus facile** it will be easier to sell *or* dispose of these old umbrellas
5 *(du temps)* passage, passing; **vous n'avez pas le droit de répondre après é. du temps** you must answer before the time is up

écouler [ekule] VT *(marchandises)* to sell (off), to dispose of, to move; **é. des faux billets** to put forged notes into circulation; *Com* **é. à perte** to sell at a loss
VPR **s'écouler 1** *(d'un liquide)* to flow out, to run out *(de* of); *(de la circulation)* to flow; **le public s'écoulait sagement du théâtre** the audience was leaving the theatre quietly; **faire s'é. l'eau** to run off *or* drain off the water; **mon argent s'écoule à une vitesse!** I just don't know where my money goes to! **2** *(de marchandises)* to sell, to move **3** *(du temps)* to pass, to elapse

écourter [ekurte] VT *(robe, texte, citation)* to

shorten; (visite, discours) to curtail, to cut short; (barbe, moustache) to trim; (queue de chien) to dock

écoute¹ [ekut] **NF 1** Vieilli **être** ou **se tenir aux écoutes** to listen, to eavesdrop; Fig to keep one's ears open; **être aux écoutes derrière la porte** to be listening at the door; Mil **poste d'é.** listening post

2 Radio (fait d'écouter) listening; (audience) listeners; **é. de contrôle** monitoring; **se mettre** ou **se porter à l'é., prendre l'é.** to listen in, to tune in; Mil, Radio **être à l'é.** to be listening (**de** to); Radio **ne quittez pas l'é.!, restez à l'é.!** stay tuned (in)!, keep listening!; **heure de grande é.** Radio peak listening time; TV peak viewing time; **aux heures de grande é.** during prime time; **émission programmée à une heure de grande é.** prime-time programme; **cette émission bénéficie d'une grande é.** the programme has a large audience or stands high in the ratings; **dès la première é. ...** (d'un disque, d'un morceau) the first time you hear it ...; **indice d'é.** ratings; Tél **table d'é.** tapping equipment; **elle est sur (table d')é.** her phone is being tapped; **écoutes téléphoniques** telephone tapping

3 être à l'é. de (électeurs, opinion publique) to be in touch with; (enfants) to be attentive to the needs of; **être toujours à l'é. des autres** to be always willing to lend a sympathetic ear to others

4 (d'un sanglier) **écoutes** ears

écoute² NF Naut (d'une voile) sheet; **nœud d'é.** sheet bend; **point d'é.** clew

écouter [ekute] **VT 1** to listen to; Radio **vous écoutez France Inter** you are listening or tuned to France Inter; **savoir é.** to be a good listener; **je vais te faire é. un morceau** I'll play you some music; **é. qn jusqu'au bout** to hear sb out; **é. aux portes** to listen at doors, to eavesdrop; **écoutez!** listen!, look (here)! **2** (suivre) (personne, avis) to listen to, to pay attention to; **ne les écoutez pas!** don't listen to them, don't pay them any attention!; **é. sa conscience** to listen to or be guided by one's conscience; **savoir se faire é.** to know how to command respect; **il faudrait quand même que tu te fasses é. par tes enfants/élèves** even so, your children/pupils ought to listen to you or obey you or be obedient; **il est très écouté au sein du gouvernement** the government listens closely to him or to what he has to say, he has the ear of the government

VPR s'écouter il s'écoute trop he coddles himself; **elle a tendance à s'é. parler** she likes the sound of her own voice; **si je m'écoutais** if I did what I wanted

écouteur [ekutœr] **NM** Tél receiver; **prendre l'é.** to listen in; Radio **écouteurs** earphones, headphones; TV, Radio **é. auriculaire** earpiece

écoutille [ekutij] **NF** Naut hatchway

écouvillon [ekuvijɔ̃] **NM** (pour bouteille, biberon) (bottle) brush; Méd swab

écouvillonner [ekuvijɔne] **VT** (bouteille) to clean out; Méd (cavité) to swab

écrabouillage [ekrabujaʒ] **NM**, **écrabouillement** [ekrabujmã] **NM** Fam squashing, crushing

écrabouiller [ekrabuje] **VT** Fam to squash, to crush; **se faire é. par une voiture** to get flattened by a car

écran [ekrã] **NM 1** (pour protéger) screen; **elle fit un é. de sa main** she shielded or shaded her eyes with her hand; **on ne peut pas voir le lac car les arbres font é.** you can't see the lake because it's screened by the trees; **elle se cachait derrière l'é. de ses cheveux** she was using her hair as a screen to hide behind; **il m'a fait é. de son corps pour me**

protéger he shielded me with his body **2** TV, Cin, Phot screen; **porter une pièce à l'é.** to adapt a play for the screen; **la technique de l'é.** film technique; **Delon crève l'é. dans ce film** Delon gives a riveting performance in this film; **vedette de l'é.** film star; **sur les écrans, cette semaine** what's on this week (at the movies or Br cinema); **prochainement sur vos écrans** coming to a cinema or Am movie theater near you; **le petit é.** the small screen, television; **le grand é.** the big screen, cinema; **téléviseur à é. plat** flat-screen television **3** Ordinat screen, display; **à l'é.** on screen; **plein é.** full screen

▸▸ Ordinat **é. d'accueil** logo screen; TV, Radio **é. acoustique** acoustic screen; Ordinat **é. à affichage accéléré** accelerated display screen; Ordinat **é. d'aide** help screen; **é. antibruit** noise barrier; **é. antireflets** antiglare screen; **é. basse radiation** low radiation screen; **é. cathodique** cathode ray tube screen; **é. de cheminée** fire screen; **é. de cinéma** cinema or movie screen, motion picture screen; TV **é. de contrôle** control monitor; TV **é. de contrôle de l'image** picture monitor (screen); TV **é. de contrôle studio** studio monitor; Ordinat **é. couleur** colour screen or display; Ordinat **é. à cristaux liquides** liquid crystal screen; Ordinat **é. de dialogue** dialog(ue) screen; Ordinat **é. divisé** split screen; Ordinat **é. à fenêtres** split screen; **é. de fumée** smoke screen; **é. haute résolution** high resolution screen; **é. à matrice active/passive** active/passive matrix screen; **é. monochrome** monochrome screen; TV **é.-mosaïque,** pl **écrans-mosaïques** multi-screen, multi-split screen; Cin **é. panoramique** wide screen; Ordinat **é. (à) plasma** (gas) plasma screen; Ordinat, TV **é. plat** flat screen; Ordinat **é. pleine page** A4 screen; **é. de prévisualisation** preview monitor; Cin **é. de projection** projection screen; Ordinat **é. protecteur** ou **de protection** shield; **é. publicitaire** commercial break; Ordinat **é. rétro-éclairé** back-lit screen; Ordinat **é. de saisie** input screen; **é. solaire** sun block; Cin **é. de sûreté** (de projecteur) cut-off; Ordinat **é. tactile** touch or touch-sensitive screen; **é. de télévision** TV screen; TV **é.-témoin,** pl **écrans-témoins** monitor; **é. TFT** TFT screen; **é. total** sun block; Ordinat **é. de travail** working or work screen; TV **é. de vision** review screen; TV **é. de visualisation** display screen

écrasant [ekrazã] **ADJ** (poids, défaite, impôts, responsabilité etc) crushing; (preuve, majorité, victoire) overwhelming; (travail) back-breaking; (chaleur) overpowering

écrasé [ekraze] **ADJ nez é.** flat nose

écrasement [ekrazmã] **NM** (d'un fruit) crushing; (accidentellement) squashing; (d'une personne, un animal) (par une voiture) running over; Fig (d'un peuple) oppression; (d'une armée, une équipe) crushing defeat; Ordinat (de données, d'un fichier) zapping; Aviat **é. (au sol)** crash

écrase-merde [ekrazmɛrd] **NMPL** Fam clodhoppers

écraser [ekraze] **VT 1** (fruit) to crush; (accidentellement) to squash; (boîte, membre, ail) to crush; (carton) to flatten; (cafard) to squash; (mouche) to swat; (cigarette) to stub out; (piéton, chien, hérisson) to run over or down; **é. des œufs durs pour un plat** to mash up hard boiled eggs for a dish; **il s'est fait é. par une voiture** he was or got run down or over by a car; Fam **é. l'accélérateur** ou **le champignon** to step on the gas; **é. le frein** to jam on the brakes; Fig Fam **je compte sur toi pour é. le coup** I'm relying on you to keep quiet or not to say anything

2 Fig (assommer) **é. d'impôts** to overburden with taxes; **écrasé d'impôts** crushed by

taxation, staggering under the burden of taxation; **écrasé de travail** overwhelmed with or Fam snowed under with work; Fam **é. le marché** to glut or flood the market; **être écrasé de chaleur** to be dropping with the heat; **il écrase les gens de sa richesse** he uses his wealth to put other people down

3 (vaincre) (adversaire, troupes etc) to crush; **il écrase tout le monde en latin** he is much better than everyone else at Latin

4 Ordinat (fichier) to zap

5 Arg **en é.** to sleep like a log

VI Arg **écrase!** shut up!, drop dead!, put a sock in it!

VPR s'écraser s'é. au sol (d'une personne) to crash to the ground; (d'un avion) to crash; **la neige s'écrasait sous nos pieds** the snow crunched under our feet; Fig **on s'écrase devant le cinéma** there's a tremendous crush outside the cinema; Fig Fam **à sa place, je m'écraserais** if I were him I'd keep my head down or keep a low profile; Arg **écrase-toi!** shut it!, button it!

écraseur, -euse [ekrazœr, -øz] **N** Fam road hog

écrémage [ekremaʒ] **NM 1** (du lait) creaming, skimming **2** Fig **ce lycée n'aurait pas de si bons résultats sans un sévère é. des élèves** the school wouldn't get such good results if it didn't choose only the very best pupils or if it didn't pick and choose its pupils; **le recrutement de leurs élèves passe par un sacré é.** they only take the crème de la crème; Mktg **é. du marché** market skimming

écrémer [ekreme] **VT** (j'écrème; j'écrémerai) (lait) to cream, to skim; Mktg (marché) to skim; Fig to take the best or the cream of, to cream off; **lait écrémé** skim(med) milk

écrémeuse [ekremøz] **NF** (cream) separator, creamer

écrêter [ekrete] **VT 1** (coq) to remove the comb of **2** Fig (revenus, prix etc) to even out

écrevisse [ekrəvis] **NF** (crustacé) (freshwater) crayfish; Fam **rouge comme une é.** as red as a lobster; Fam **marcher comme une é.** to walk backwards

écrier (s') [sekrije] **VPR** to cry (out), to exclaim

écrin [ekrɛ̃] **NM** (jewel) case

écrire [ekrir] (prp **écrivant;** pp **écrit;** pr ind **j'écris,** n. **écrivons,** ils **écrivent;** p hist **j'écrivis;** fu **j'écrirai**) **VT** (lettre, livre, chanson, mémoires) to write; (noter) to write down; **é. qch à** ou **avec de l'encre** to write sth in ink; **machine à é.** typewriter; **é. une lettre à la main** longhand, handwritten; **é. une lettre à la machine** to type a letter; **é. un mot à la hâte** to scribble a note; **é. un mot à qn** to drop sb a line; **é. à qn** to write to sb; **je lui ai écrit de venir** I've written asking him to come; Ordinat **é. qch sur un disque** to write sth to disk; **il est écrit que je n'irai jamais** I'm fated not to get there; **c'est écrit** it is bound to happen; **c'est écrit sur ta figure** you can tell from his/her face, it's written all over his/her face; **é. qch noir sur blanc** ou **en toutes lettres** to put sth in black and white; **tant que je ne verrai pas mon nom écrit noir sur blanc** until I see my name in black and white

VI to write; **il écrit bien** his (hand)writing is good, he has good handwriting; (d'un écrivain) he's a good writer, he writes well; **ce stylo écrit très bien** this pen writes very well; **é. dans les journaux** to write for the papers; **é. à l'encre** to use ink

VPR s'écrire 1 (s'orthographier) to be spelled; **comment ça s'écrit?** how do you spell it? **2** (correspondre) **ils s'écrivent** they write to each other

écrit [ekri] **NM 1** consigner ou coucher qch par é. to put or set sth down in writing; **convention par é.** written agreement

2 *(texte)* (written) document; **faire/signer un é.** to draw up/to sign a document; **les écrits de Bossuet** the writings *or* works of Bossuet; *Journ* **é. diffamatoire** libel **3** *Scol* **échouer à l'é.** to fail in the written examination

écriteau, -eaux [ekrito] NM notice

écritoire [ekritwar] NF *(coffret)* writing case

écriture [ekrityr] NF **1** *(système, caractères)* writing, script; *Typ* script; *Ordinat* write **2** *(main)* (hand)writing; **elle a une belle é.** her handwriting is good, she has good handwriting; **elle a une vilaine é.** her handwriting is dreadful **3** *Compta* entry, item **4** *Com* **écritures** accounts; **tenir les écritures** to keep the accounts; **employé aux écritures** accounts *or* ledger clerk **5** *Rel* **l'É. sainte, les saintes Écritures** Holy Scripture, Holy Writ **6** *Littér* writing; *TV, Cin* **é. de scénarios** scriptwriting, screenwriting ▸▸ **é. abrégée** speedwriting; **é. d'ajustement** corrected entry; **é. automatique** automatic writing; *Compta* **é. de clôture** closing entry; *Compta* **écritures comptables** accounting entries; *Compta* **é. conforme** corresponding entry; *Typ* **é. cursive** cursive; *Typ* **é. droite** upright script; *Typ* **é. grasse** bold typeface, boldface; *Compta* **é. d'inventaire** closing entries; *Typ* **é. en italique** italic script; *Compta* **écritures en partie double** double entry bookkeeping; *Compta* **écritures en partie simple** single-entry bookkeeping; **é. phonétique** phonetic script; *Compta* **é. regroupement** consolidated entry; *Compta* **é. de régularisation** adjusting entry; *Cin, TV* **é. de scénarios** scriptwriting, screenwriting; *Compta* **é. de virement** transfer entry

écrivailler [ekrivaje] VI *Péj* to be a hack (writer), to scribble

écrivailleur, -euse [ekrivajœr, -øz] N, **écrivaillon** [ekrivajɔ̃] NM *Péj* hack (writer), scribbler

écrivain [ekrivɛ̃] NM **1** *(auteur)* author, writer; **femme é.** woman writer **2** *Arch* **é. public** (public) letter writer

écrivasser [ekrivase] VI *Péj* = **écrivailler**

écrivassier, -ière [ekrivasje, -jɛr] N *Péj* hack (writer), scribbler

écrou¹ [ekru] NM *Jur* committal (to prison); **sous é.** detained, in detention; **levée d'é.** release, discharge (from prison)

écrou² NM *Tech* nut; **é. à ailettes** *ou* **à oreilles** thumb *or* wing *or* butterfly nut; **é. crénelé** *ou* **à créneaux** *ou* **à encoches** castellated nut; **é. de réglage** adjusting *or* adjuster nut

écrouelles [ekruɛl] NFPL *Arch* scrofula, king's evil

écrouer [ekrue] VT *Jur* to imprison, to commit to prison

écroulement [ekrulmɑ̃] NM *(d'un édifice, un pont, une personne, de prix etc)* collapse; *(de terre, roche)* fall; *(d'un empire)* fall, collapse

écrouler (s') [sekrule] VPR **1** *(d'un édifice, un pont, une personne, de prix)* to collapse; *(d'espoirs)* to crumble away; **empire près de s'é.** empire on the verge of collapse **2** *s'é.* **sur une chaise** to drop *or* flop onto a chair; **s'é. de fatigue** to collapse *or* drop with exhaustion; **écroulé dans un fauteuil** slumped in an armchair; *Fam* **écroulé (de rire)** doubled up with laughter

écru [ekry] ADJ *(tissu)* unbleached, ecru, natural-coloured; **soie écrue** raw silk; **toile écrue** holland

ecsta [eksta] NF *Fam (abrév ecstasy)* E

ecstasy [ɛkstasi] NF ecstasy

ectoplasme [ɛktɔplasm] NM *Biol* ectoplasm

ECU [eky] NM INV *Anciennement (abrév European Currency Unit)* ECU

écu [eky] NM **1** *(monnaie)* ECU; *Arch Fin* crown **2** *(bouclier)* shield; *Hér* escutcheon, coat of arms

écubier [ekybje] NM *Naut* hawsehole

écueil [ekœj] NM *Naut* reef, shelf; *Fig (danger)* pitfall; **donner sur les écueils** *(d'un bateau)* to strike the rocks; *Fig* **se heurter à un é.** to hit a snag

écuelle [ekɥɛl] NF *(assiette large)* bowl; **une é. de soupe** a bowl(ful) of soup; **é. du chien/chat** dog's/cat's bowl *or* dish

éculé [ekyle] ADJ *(chaussure)* down-at-heel; *Fig (tour, plaisanterie, argument)* well-worn, hackneyed

écumage [ekymaʒ] NM *(de la soupe, la confiture, du métal fondu)* skimming

écume [ekym] NF *(dans la bouche, sur la bière)* froth, foam; *(sur la mer)* foam; *(sur la soupe, la confiture, le métal fondu)* scum; **il avait l'é. à la bouche** he was foaming at the mouth; **cheval couvert d'é.** foam-covered horse; *Minér* **é. (de mer)** *(magnésite)* meerschaum

écumer [ekyme] VT **1** *(soupe, confiture, métal fondu etc)* to skim **2** *(piller)* to scour, to pillage; **é. les mers** *(des pirates)* to scour the seas, to buccaneer; *Fig* **j'ai écumé tous les magasins pour le trouver** I scoured the shops looking for it ▪ VI *(du vin, de la bouche etc)* to foam, to froth; *(de la mer)* to foam; *(de la soupe, la confiture, du métal fondu etc)* to form a scum; **cheval qui écume** foaming horse; **é. (de rage)** to foam (with rage)

écumeur [ekymœr] NM **é. (de mer)** buccaneer, pirate

écumeux, -euse [ekymø, -øz] ADJ *(mer, vagues)* foaming; *(bière)* foamy, frothy; *(confiture etc)* scummy

écumoire [ekymwar] NF skimmer, perforated spoon; **é. à friture** slotted spoon; *Fig* **troué comme une é.** riddled with holes

écureuil [ekyrœj] NM squirrel; **é. volant** flying squirrel

écurie [ekyri] NF stable; **é. (de courses)** *(de chevaux, voitures)* (racing) stable; **mettre les chevaux à l'é.** to stable the horses; *Fam* **quelle é.!** what a pigsty!; *Myth* **les écuries d'Augias** the Augean stables

écusson [ekysɔ̃] NM **1** *(de serrure)* key-plate, keyhole scutcheon **2** *Hér* escutcheon, shield, coat of arms **3** *(emblème d'étoffe)* badge; *Mil* tab, badge, (collar) patch

écuyer, -ère [ekɥije, -ɛr] NM **1** *(instructeur)* riding master **2** *Arch (gentilhomme)* squire, armour-bearer; *(servant la famille royale)* equerry; *Hist* **grand é.** Master of the Horse ▪ N rider, horseman, f horsewoman; **é. de cirque** circus rider, equestrian, f equestrienne; **bottes à l'écuyère** riding boots

eczéma [egzema] NM *Méd* eczema; **avoir** *ou* **faire de l'é.** to have eczema

eczémateux, -euse [egzematø, -øz] ADJ *Méd* eczematous

édam [edam] NM Edam

edelweiss [edɛlvɛs, -vajs] NF *(plante)* edelweiss

Éden [edɛn] NM *Bible* **l'É., le jardin d'É.** Eden, the Garden of Eden; *Fig* **un é.** a paradise, a Garden of Eden

édénique [edenik] ADJ *Litt* idyllic

édenté [edɑ̃te] ADJ *(personne, peigne)* toothless; *(animal)* toothless, *Spéc* edentate

édenter [edɑ̃te] VT *(peigne, scie, lame)* to break the teeth of

EDF [ədeɛf, edeɛf] NF *(abrév* **Électricité de France***)* (French) Electricity Board

EDI [ədei] NM *Ordinat (abrév* **échange de données informatisé***)* EDI

édicter [edikte] VT *(loi)* to enact, to decree; *(peine)* to decree, to prescribe

édicule [edikyl] NM *(urinoir)* public convenience

édifiant [edifjɑ̃] ADJ edifying

édification [edifikasjɔ̃] NF **1** *(d'un monument, d'un bâtiment)* erecting, erection, building; *Fig (d'un empire, d'une fortune)* building up **2** *(instruction morale)* edification, moral improvement; **pour votre é.** for your edification

édifice [edifis] NM building, *Fml* edifice; **édifices publics** public buildings; *Fig* **apporter sa pierre à l'é.** to make a contribution, to do one's bit; *Fig* **tout l'é. social** the whole fabric *or* structure of society

édifier [edifje] VT **1** *(bâtiment)* to build; *Fig (empire, fortune etc)* to build up; *(système)* to develop, to put together **2** *(d'un sermon)* to edify; *Iron* **ces dernières révélations nous ont tous édifiés** these latest revelations were an education for us all; **c'est sans doute pour nous é. qu'il a tenu ce discours** he probably made the speech for our edification

édile [edil] NM **1** *Antiq* aedile, *Am* edile **2** *(magistrat officiel)* municipal official, town councillor

Édimbourg [edɛ̃bur] N Edinburgh

édimbourgeois, -e [edɛ̃burʒwa, -az] ADJ of Edinburgh ▪ N **É.** person from Edinburgh

édit [edi] NM *Hist* edict

éditer [edite] VT **1** *(publier)* *(livre etc)* to publish; *(disque)* to produce **2** *(commenter)* *(texte)* to edit **3** *Ordinat* to edit; **pouvant être édité** editable

> Il faut noter que le verbe anglais **to edit** ne s'emploie jamais pour dire **publier**.

éditeur, -trice [editœr, -tris] N **1** *(d'une maison d'édition)* publisher **2** *(commentateur)* editor ▪ NM *Ordinat (de programme)* editor ▸▸ **é. de disques** record producer; *Cin* **é. de film** film releasing company; *Ordinat* **é. d'icônes** icon editor; *Ordinat* **é. HTML** HTML editor; *Ordinat* **é. d'images** image editing program, image editor; *Ordinat* **é. de liens** linker, link editor; *Ordinat* **é. de logiciels** software company; *Ordinat* **é. orienté en lignes** line editor; **é. de presse** newspaper publisher; **é. de texte** text editor; **é. de vidéo** video publisher

édition [edisjɔ̃] NF **1** *(activité, métier)* publishing; **maison d'é.** publishing house *or* firm; **é. de disques** record production; **é. électronique** e-publishing; **é. musicale** music publishing; **travailler dans l'é.** to work in publishing; **le monde de l'é.** the publishing world; **é. sur le Web** Web publishing **2** *(texte commenté)* edition; *(exemplaire)* edition, issue, impression; **é. de luxe** library edition; **é. scolaire** school edition; **é. originale** first edition; **é. (entièrement) revue et corrigée** major new edition; *Hum* **où est le sucre? – dans le placard, troisième é.!** where's the sugar? – for the third time, it's in the cupboard! **3** *Journ (de journaux)* edition; **dernière é.** final edition; **l'é. du matin/soir** the morning/evening edition; *TV* **l'é. du journal télévisé** the (television) news bulletin; **é. spéciale** *(de journal)* special edition; *(de revue)* special issue; **é. exceptionelle** extra; **é. locale** local edition **4** *(action de commenter)* editing **5** *Ordinat* editing; **é. de liens** linking; **é. pleine page** full page editing; **é. électronique** electronic publishing

> Il faut noter que le terme anglais **edition** est un faux ami. Il ne désigne jamais **l'industrie du livre**.

éditique [editik] NF Ordinat desktop publishing

édito [edito] NM Journ (abrév **éditorial**) leading article, leader, editorial

éditorial, -iale, -iaux, -iales [editɔrjal, -jo] Journ ADJ editorial
 NM leading article, leader, editorial

éditorialiste [editɔrjalist] N Journ leader writer, editorialist, editorial writer

édouardien, -ienne [edwardjɛ̃, -jɛn] ADJ Hist Edwardian

édredon [edrədɔ̃] NM eiderdown, quilt

éducable [edykabl] ADJ teachable, Fml educable

éducateur, -trice [edykatœr, -tris] N (enseignant) educator, instructor; (spécialiste) educationalist; **é. spécialisé** special education teacher
 ADJ educational

éducatif, -ive [edykatif, -iv] ADJ educational

éducation [edykasjɔ̃] NF **1** (enseignement) education; **faire l'é. de qn** to educate sb; Hum **toute ton é. est à (re)faire!** your education has been sadly neglected!; **en rock, toute mon é. est à faire** I know absolutely nothing or I'm totally ignorant about rock music; **l'é. politique de la jeunesse** the political education of young people **2** (par les parents) upbringing; **sans é.** ill-bred, uncouth; **avoir de l'é.** to be well-bred, to have good manners; **il manque d'é.** he has no manners, he is ill-mannered or ill-bred; **quel manque d'é.!** what manners! **3** Fig (de la volonté, de l'esprit) training
 ▸▸ **é. manuelle et technique** handicraft classes; **l'É. nationale** Br ≃ Department for Education and Employment, Am ≃ Department of Education; **é. permanente** continuing education; **é. physique** physical training or education; **é. professionnelle** vocational training; **é. religieuse** religious instruction; **é. sexuelle** sex education

> Il faut noter que le nom anglais **education** ne fait référence qu'à l'instruction scolaire et à l'enseignement et non à la façon dont on est élevé.

édulcorant [edylkɔrɑ̃] ADJ sweetening
 NM sweetener; **é. de synthèse** artificial sweetener

édulcorer [edylkɔre] VT **1** (médicament, boisson etc) to sweeten **2** Fig (théorie, compte rendu) to water down; (roman pornographique) to tone down

éduquer [edyke] VT **1** (donner un enseignement à) (enfant, peuple etc) to educate **2** (élever) to bring up; **mal éduqué** ill-bred, ill-mannered **3** Fig (volonté, esprit etc) to train; **le goût est quelque chose qui s'éduque** taste has to be learnt

EED [əəde] NM Pol (abrév **échange électronique de données**) EDI

EEE [əəə] NM (abrév **Espace économique européen**) EEA

EEG NM (abrév **électroencéphalogramme**) EEG

effaçable [efasabl] ADJ **1** (encre, crayon, inscription) erasable **2** Ordinat (mémoire) erasable

effaçage [efasaʒ] NM erasing

efface [efas] NF Can Fam Br rubber, Am eraser

effacé [efase] ADJ (personne, manières) self-effacing, retiring; (rôle) small, insignificant; (menton) receding; **mener une vie très effacée** to live very quietly

effacement [efasmɑ̃] NM **1** (d'un mot) (en gommant) erasure; (de message) erasing; (d'une bande magnétique) blanking, erasing;

Ordinat deletion; (d'une tache) removal; (par le temps, les éléments) (d'une inscription) wearing away; (des souvenirs) fading **2** (d'une personne) self-effacement

effacer [efase] (**j'effaçai(s); n. effaçons**) VT **1** (enlever) (mot) to erase, to rub out; (enregistrement, bande) to wipe, to erase; Ordinat to erase, to delete; **e. le tableau** to clean the blackboard; Ordinat **e. l'écran** to clear the screen; **e. une tache** to remove a stain; (en lavant) to wash out a stain; (avec un chiffon) to wipe off a stain; **e. des imperfections** to smooth out imperfections; **sculptures effacées par le temps** carvings worn away by time; **e. toutes traces de son passage** to remove or eliminate all traces of one's presence
 2 Fig (faire oublier) **e. un mauvais souvenir** to erase or wipe out or blot out an unhappy memory; **e. qch de sa mémoire** to blot sth out of or erase sth from one's memory; **il a réussi à e. toutes mes craintes** he made my fears vanish; **on efface tout et on recommence** we'll wipe the slate clean and make a fresh start
 3 (éclipser) Fig to put in the shade
 4 e. le corps to stand sideways; **e. les épaules** to throw back one's shoulders
 VPR **s'effacer 1** (disparaître) (d'une inscription) to wear away; Fig (d'un sentiment, un souvenir) to fade (away); **la tache s'effacera à l'eau** it will wash off; **la tache ne s'est pas effacée au lavage** the stain didn't come out in the wash; **cette encre ne s'efface pas bien** anything written in this ink doesn't rub out very well; Fig **avec le temps, tout s'efface** everything fades with time; **ton chagrin s'effacera** you'll get over it
 2 (s'écarter) to stand or move aside, to move to one side; Fig **depuis quelque temps il s'était effacé** for some time he had kept in the background; **il s'est effacé devant moi pour me laisser passer** he stood aside to let me pass; **il a tendance à s'e. derrière elle** he tends to hide behind her

effaceur [efasœr] NM **e. (d'encre)** ink eraser or Br rubber

effarant [efarɑ̃] ADJ frightening, alarming; **ils pratiquent des prix effarants** their prices are frightening or shocking; **il y avait un monde e. sur les plages** there were an awful lot of people on the beach; **d'une naïveté effarante** alarmingly or shockingly naive

effaré [efare] ADJ alarmed

effarement [efarmɑ̃] NM alarm

effarer [efare] VT to alarm, to scare; **son hypocrisie m'effare!** his/her hypocrisy astounds me!; **je suis effaré par les prix!** the prices are frightening or shocking!, I'm astounded at the prices!

effarouchement [efaruʃmɑ̃] NM startling, frightening (away)

effaroucher [efaruʃe] VT **1** (effrayer) to scare, to alarm; (faire reculer) to scare away, to frighten away **2** (choquer) to shock
 VPR **s'effaroucher 1** (s'effrayer) to be scared or alarmed (de by); **elle s'effarouche pour un rien** she gets frightened at the least little thing, the least little thing frightens her; **il ne risque pas de s'e. pour si peu** he's unlikely to let a little thing like that frighten him **2** (s'offusquer) to be shocked (de by, at)

effectif, -ive [efɛktif, -iv] ADJ **1** (efficace) (traitement etc) effective, efficacious **2** (réel) (travail, rendement etc) effective, actual; Fin (circulation) active; (valeur) real
 NM (employés) manpower, (number of) employees, staff; (d'un club, bataillon) strength, numbers; Naut complement; **à e. réduit** under or below strength; Scol **réduire l'e. des classes à 25** to reduce the size of classes or reduce class numbers to 25; **l'e. est au**

complet we are at full strength or up to strength; Mil **les effectifs** the total strength; **crise d'effectifs** manpower crisis; **e. budgétaire** budgetary strength, Am authorized strength

effectivement [efɛktivmɑ̃] ADV **1** (réellement, de manière effective) actually, in reality, really; **contribuer e. au processus de paix** to make a real contribution to the peace process **2** (en effet) actually, in (actual) fact; **c'est pratique, hein? – e.!** it's practical, isn't it? – (yes) indeed! or indeed it is!; **e., on aurait pu prévoir un parapluie** we should have thought about bringing an umbrella, Fam we should have brought an umbrella right enough; **il a e. travaillé sur ce projet** he did actually work on the project

> Il faut noter que l'adverbe anglais **effectively** est un faux ami. Il signifie **efficacement**.

effectuer [efɛktɥe] VT (réforme, mesure etc) to carry out, to bring into effect; (mouvement, opération) to execute; (paiement) to make, Fml to effect; (voyage, calcul, Mil (retraite) to make; (réconciliation) to bring about; **e. des démarches** to take steps; Com **e. une commande** to place an order; **e. une réservation** to make a reservation
 VPR **s'effectuer** (d'une réforme etc) to be carried out, to be brought into effect; (d'un mouvement, d'une opération) to be executed; (d'un paiement, voyage) to be made; (d'une réconciliation) to be brought about

efféminé [efemine] ADJ effeminate

efféminer [efemine] VT to make effeminate; (pensée) to emasculate

effervescence [efɛrvesɑ̃s] NF (bouillonnement) effervescence; Fig (agitation) agitation, turmoil; (excitation) excitement; **ville en e.** town seething with excitement or in (a) turmoil; **il avait l'esprit en e.** his mind was in a ferment

effervescent [efɛrvesɑ̃] ADJ (comprimé, aspirine) effervescent; Fig (tempérament) excitable, exuberant; (foule) excited

effet [efɛ] NM **1** (résultat, conséquence) effect (sur on); **les mesures du gouvernement n'ont eu aucun e.** the government's measures have had no effect; **cela a eu pour e. de le mettre en colère** this had the effect of making him angry; **sa fréquentation a un e. désastreux sur ma fille** going out with him has had a disastrous effect on my daughter; **ce poison a pour e. de paralyser le système nerveux** this poison results in the paralysis of the nervous system; **faire de l'e.** to have an effect, to be effective; **son départ précipité a fait de l'e.** his hurried departure caused a stir; **faire de l'e. sur** to have an effect on; **ma remarque a fait son petit e.** my remark caused a stir; **faire e.** to take effect; **produire l'e. voulu** to produce the desired effect; **une relation de cause à e.** a cause and effect relationship; **à cet e.** with that in mind, Fml to that end, with this end in view; **cet appareil n'a pas été conçu à cet e.** the machine was not designed for that purpose; **sans e.** ineffective, ineffectual; **mes conseils sont restés ou demeurés sans e.** my advice had no effect or was ineffective; **sous l'e. de l'alcool/la drogue** under the influence of alcohol/drugs; **il t'a injurié sous l'e. de la colère** he insulted you because he was angry; **je suis encore sous l'e. de la colère** I'm still angry, I still haven't calmed down; **les feuilles sont tombées sous l'e. de la chaleur** the leaves dropped off with the heat; **ce n'est qu'un e. de sa timidité** it's only because he is shy; **à quel e.?** to what end?; **e. secondaire** side effect; **ce n'était que l'e. du hasard** it was only by pure or sheer chance; **créer un**

e. de surprise to cause a stir; **nous ne gagnerons cette bataille qu'en créant un e. de surprise** we won't win this battle unless we can take the enemy by surprise

2 *(impression)* impression; **c'est l'e. que cela m'a fait** that's how it impressed orstruck me; **quel e. ça te fait qu'elle revienne?** how do you feel about her coming back?; **les pleurs de sa femme ne lui firent aucun e.** his wife's tears had no effect on him; **elle me fait l'e. d'une fille plutôt équilibrée** she strikes me as being a fairly well-balanced girl; **sa réponse a fait l'e. d'une bombe** his answer came as or was a bombshell; *Fam* **et c'est tout l'e. que ça te fait?** is that all it means to you?; **à chaque fois qu'il me parle, ça me fait un drôle d'e.** I feel all funny inside whenever he talks to me; **ça m'a fait un drôle d'e.** it gave me a funny or strange feeling, it made me feel all funny or strange; **ça fait un drôle d'e. de penser que ...** it's funny or strange to think that ...; **il fit une pause pour mieux juger de l'e. de ses paroles** he paused to see what effect his words were having; **cela fait mauvais e. de le faire attendre** it looks bad to keep him waiting; **ça a fait bon e. que tu aies mis une jupe** your wearing a skirt made a good impression; **faire bon/mauvais e. à qn** to make a good/bad impression on sb; **faire de l'e.** to make a show, to attract attention; **dès que je l'ai vu, il m'a fait de l'e.** I fancied him the minute I saw him; **eh bien! elle te fait de l'e.!** she's got quite an effect on you, I see!; *Fam* **ça m'a fait de l'e. de la voir si pâle** it gave me quite a turn to see her so pale

3 *(but recherché, force artistique)* **manquer son e.** *(d'un discours)* not to have the desired effect; *(d'une plaisanterie)* to misfire, to fall flat; **il voulait faire une entrée triomphale mais il a manqué son e.** he wanted to make a triumphant entry but it fell flat; **soigner ses effets** to work hard to make the right impression; **rechercher les effets** to try to make an impression; **ménager ses effets** to have a sense of the dramatic; **un e. de contraste** contrasting effect; **e. de style** stylistic effect; *Litt* **phrases à e.** words used for effect; **un orateur qui fait des effets de voix** a speaker who makes striking use of his voice; **faire des effets de jambes** to show off one's legs, to draw attention to one's legs; **faire des effets de manches** *(d'un avocat)* to have a dramatic courtroom style; *Beaux-Arts* **e. de lune** moonlight effect

4 *(application)* effect; **mettre un projet à e.** to put a plan into action or into effect; **prendre e.** *(d'une loi etc)* to take effect, to come into effect or force; **e. rétroactif d'une loi/d'un accord** retroactive effect of a law/an argument; **augmentation avec e. rétroactif au 1ᵉʳ avril** rise retroactive or backdated to April 1st

5 *Tennis* spin; **balle qui a de l'e.** ball that has spin; **donner de l'e. à sa balle** to put spin on one's ball; *Billard* **e. de côté** side (screw); **mettre trop d'e.** to put on too much spin

6 *Tech* **e. utile** efficiency; **à simple e.** single-action, single-acting; **à double e.** double-action, double-acting; **e. Edison** Edison effect; **e. photoélectrique** photoelectric effect

7 *Fin* bill; **e. accepté** accepted bill; **e. bancable** eligible list; **e. bancaire** bill, draft; **e. de commerce** bill, draft; **e. de complaisance** accommodation bill; **e. à courte échéance** short, short-dated bill; **e. à date fixe** fixed-term bill; **e. domicilié** domiciled bill; **e. à l'encaissement** bill for collection; **effets à encaisser** accounts receivable; **e. endossé** endorsed bill; **e. escompté** discounted bill; **e. libre** clean bill; **e. à longue échéance** long, long-dated bill; *Bourse* **effets nominatifs** registered stock; **e. à ordre** promissory note; **effets à payer** bills payable; **e. au porteur**

bearer bill, bill made out to bearer; **effets publics** government stock or securities; **effets à recevoir** bills receivable; **e. en souffrance** overdue bill; **e. à taux flottant** floating rate note, FRN; **e. à terme** period or term bill; **e. à usance** usance bill; **e. à vue** sight bill or draft

8 **effets** *(affaires)* possessions, belongings; **effets personnels** personal effects; *Jur* goods and chattels

9 **en e.** *(réellement)* actually, in (actual) fact; **oui, je m'en souviens, en e.** yes, I do remember; **en e., c'est ce que je me suis dit** that's just what I thought; **mais c'est monstrueux! – en e.!** it's abominable! – isn't it just!

▸▸ *Fin* **e. balançoire** see-saw effect; **e. boomerang** boomerang effect; **avoir un e. boomerang** to boomerang; **e. boule de neige** snowball effect; *Aut* **e. de chasse** caster action; **e. Doppler** Doppler effect; *Cin, TV* **effets d'éclairage** lighting effects; *Typ* **e. d'escalier** jagged appearance, jaggy; *TV, Radio* **e. Larsen** audio or acoustic feedback, howl-round; **e. d'optique** visual effect; *Cin, TV* **effets optiques** camera effects; **e. pervers** undesired effect; *Méd* side effect; **e. de serre** greenhouse effect; **des gaz à e. de serre** greenhouse gases; *Cin etc* **effets sonores** sound effects; *Cin etc* **effets spéciaux** special effects; *Ordinat, TV* **e. de transition** melt; *Phys* **e. tunnel** tunnel effect; **effets vidéo** video effects; *Cin, TV* **effets visuels** visual effects

effeuillage [efœjaʒ] NM **1** *(d'arbres fruitiers etc)* thinning out of leaves **2** *Fam* striptease, strip

effeuillaison [efœjɛzɔ̃] NF, **effeuillement** [efœjmɑ̃] NM leaf fall

effeuiller [efœje] VT *(d'une personne) (arbre fruitier)* to thin out the leaves of; *(fleur)* to pluck the petals of; *(du vent) (arbre)* to blow off the leaves of; **e. la marguerite** to play 'he/she loves me, he/she loves me not'

effeuilleuse [efœjøz] NF *Fam* stripper, striptease artist

efficace [efikas] ADJ *(action, remède)* effective, *Fml* efficacious; *(machine)* efficient; *(personne)* efficient, capable; **prêter à qn un appui e.** to give sb useful or helpful support

> Attention: ne pas confondre **effective** et **efficient** lorsqu'on traduit **efficace**. **Effective** signifie **qui fait de l'effet** alors que **efficient** signifie **compétent**.

efficacement [efikasmɑ̃] ADV effectively; *(avec le minimum d'effort)* efficiently

efficacité [efikasite] NF *(d'un remède, d'une prière etc)* effectiveness, *Fml* efficacy; *(d'une machine etc)* efficiency; *Écon* **e. économique** economic efficiency

efficience [efisjɑ̃s] NF efficiency

efficient [efisjɑ̃] ADJ efficient

effigie [efiʒi] NF **1** *(portrait)* effigy; **pendre qn en e.** to hang sb in effigy **2** *(sur une pièce etc)* effigy, head

effilage [efilaʒ] NM *(d'un tissu)* fraying, ravelling out

effilé [efile] ADJ **1** *(tissu)* frayed; **une frange effilée** a ragged fringe **2** *(allongé) (outil)* tapered, pointed; *(doigts)* tapering; *(silhouette)* rangy; **amandes effilées** slivered almonds **3** *(poulet)* dressed, drawn

NM *Tex* fringe

effilement [efilmɑ̃] NM **1** *(des doigts)* tapering **2** *(de tissu)* fraying

effiler [efile] VT **1** *Tex* to fray **2** **e. les cheveux** to taper hair

VPR **s'effiler 1** *(d'un tissu)* to fray **2** *(d'un visage)* to taper, to come to a point

effilochage [efilɔʃaʒ] NM *Tex (en peignant)* teasing out

effiloche [efilɔʃ] NF *(de fils laissés libres)* fringe

effilocher [efilɔʃe] VT *Tex (avec un peigne)* to tease out

VPR **s'effilocher** *(d'un tissu)* to fray

efflanqué [eflɑ̃ke] ADJ *(animal)* lean, rawboned; *(personne)* skinny, lanky

effleurement [eflœrmɑ̃] NM *(frôlement)* (light gentle) touch; *(de l'eau)* skimming; **touche à e.** touch-sensitive key

effleurer [eflœre] VT **1** *(frôler)* to touch lightly; *(accidentellement)* to brush (against); *(surface de l'eau)* to skim; *Fig* **e. un sujet** to touch on a topic; *Fig* **quelques soupçons l'avaient effleuré** some misgivings had crossed his mind; *Fig* **cette idée ne m'a jamais effleuré** the idea never crossed or entered my mind **2** *(égratigner) (peau)* to graze

efflorescence [eflɔresɑ̃s] NF **1** *Chimie* efflorescence **2** *(sur les fruits)* bloom **3** *Litt* **être en pleine e.** to be flourishing

efflorescent [eflɔresɑ̃] ADJ *Chimie* efflorescent

effluent [eflyɑ̃] ADJ effluent

NM effluent; **e. urbain** (sewage) effluent; **effluents radioactifs** radioactive waste

effluve [eflyv] NM *(émanation)* emanation; **de riches effluves** rich fragrance; *Fig Litt* **les effluves du passé** the ghosts of the past

effondré [efɔ̃dre] ADJ *(personne)* griefstricken

effondrement [efɔ̃drəmɑ̃] NM *(d'un pont, un mur, un bâtiment etc)* collapse; *(d'un toit)* collapse, falling in; *(d'une mine)* caving in; *Géol* subsidence; *Fig (d'un plan)* falling through; *(d'une personne, une fortune, une monnaie)* collapse; *(d'un gouvernement, empire)* collapse, downfall; *Com (des prix, marchés)* slump (**de** in), collapse; **il est dans un état d'e. complet** he is in a state of total collapse

effondrer [efɔ̃dre] VT *(briser) (toit)* to bring down; *(mur)* to break down

VPR **s'effondrer** *(d'un pont, un mur, un bâtiment)* to collapse; *(d'un toit)* to collapse, to fall in, to cave in; *(d'une mine)* to cave in; *Fig (d'un projet)* to fall through; *(des prix)* to slump; *(d'une monnaie, de cours)* to collapse; *(d'une personne, d'un gouvernement, d'un empire)* to collapse; **toute son histoire s'effondre** his whole story is collapsing or falling to pieces; **s'e. en larmes** to break down and cry, to dissolve into tears; **s'e. dans un fauteuil** to collapse or sink or flop into an armchair; **le marché s'est effondré** the bottom has fallen out of the market

efforcer (s') [sefɔrse] VPR (**je m'efforçai(s); n. n. efforçons**) to strive, to endeavour, *Am* to endeavor; **s'e. de faire qch** to do one's utmost or one's best to do sth, to make every effort to do sth; **je m'y efforce** I'm doing my best or utmost

effort [efɔr] NM **1** effort; **allons, encore un (petit) e.** come on, try again or a bit more effort; **son médecin lui a interdit tout e.** his doctor has forbidden any exertion; **cela va te demander un certain e.** you'll need to exert yourself a lot; **après bien des efforts** after a great deal of effort; *Fam* **après l'e., le réconfort** I/you/etc deserve this; *Fam* **appliquer la loi du moindre e.** to take the line of least resistance; *Fam* **il est partisan du moindre e.** he doesn't believe in exerting himself; *Péj* **son travail sent l'e.** his work reeks of effort; **il a progressé mais doit encore faire des efforts** he's made progress but still needs to make an effort; **sans e.** effortlessly, without effort; **elle parle anglais sans e.** she speaks English effortlessly; **je suis prêt à faire un e. pour ton projet** I'm willing to help with your project; **faire un e.**

pour faire qch to make an effort to do sth; **faire un violent e. pour se lever** to make a great effort to get up; **faire un e. d'adaptation** to make an effort to adapt; **faire un e. d'imagination** to use one's imagination; **fais un petit e. d'imagination!** use a bit of imagination!; **cela demande un sacré e. d'imagination** it takes an awful lot of imagination, it puts quite a strain on the imagination; **faire un e. de mémoire** to rack one's brains; **faire un e. sur soi-même** to exercise self-control; **faire tous ses efforts pour réussir** to make every effort *or* do one's utmost to succeed; **faire l'e. de faire qch** to make the effort to do sth; **e. de volonté** effort of (the) will; **ce travail demande un e. intellectuel immense** this is a very demanding job intellectually
2 *Méd Vieilli* strain, rick; **se donner** *ou* **attraper un e.** to rick one's back
3 *Tech* strain, stress
▸▸ *Tech* **e. de cisaillement** shearing stress; *Mktg* **e. de commercialisation** *ou* **de marketing** marketing effort; **e. financier** financial outlay; **e. de guerre** war effort; *Tech* **e. de rupture** breaking strain; *Tech* **e. de tension** tensile stress; *Tech* **e. de torsion** torque; *Aut* **e. de traction** tractive effort, pull; *Aut* **efforts en virage** cornering force

effraction [efraksjɔ̃] NF *Jur* breaking and entering; **entrer par e.** to break in; **vol avec e.** burglary; **il n'y a pas eu e.** there was no sign of a burglary

effraie [efrɛ] NF *(oiseau)* barn owl, screech owl

effranger [efrãʒe] *(j'effrangeai(s); n. effrangeons)* VT *(bords d'un tissu)* to fray
VPR **s'effranger** to fray, to become frayed

effrayant [efrɛjã] ADJ frightening; *Fig (chaleur, appétit, charme)* tremendous; *(prix, bêtise, laideur)* frightening

effrayer [efrɛje] *(j'effraie, j'effraye, n. effrayons; j'effraierai, j'effrayerai)* VT *(faire peur à)* to frighten, to scare; *(inquiéter)* to alarm; **l'énormité de la besogne nous effraie** the magnitude of the task appals *or* alarms us
VPR **s'effrayer** to be frightened *(de* at); **elle s'effraie pour un rien** the least little thing frightens her, she takes fright at the least little thing; **je m'effraie de la lenteur avec laquelle elle travaille** I'm alarmed by how slowly she works; **d'après lui, il n'y a aucune raison de s'e.** according to him there's no need to be frightened *or* alarmed *or* there's no need for alarm

effréné [efrene] ADJ *(passion, curiosité)* unbridled, unrestrained; *(efforts)* frantic; *(galop)* frantic, mad

effritement [efritmã] NM *(du plâtre, d'un revêtement)* crumbling (into dust); *(de la roche)* weathering; *Fig (d'une autorité, une majorité, de fonds)* erosion

effriter [efrite] VT to cause to crumble *or* disintegrate; *(du vent) (roche)* to weather
VPR **s'effriter** *(de plâtre, d'un revêtement)* to crumble, to disintegrate; *(de la roche)* to weather; *Fig (d'une autorité, une majorité, de fonds)* to be eroded

effroi [efrwa] NM *Litt* terror, fear, dread; **je fus saisi d'e.** I was seized by terror, I was terror-stricken

effronté [efrɔ̃te] ADJ *(personne, manières)* impudent, insolent; *(mensonge, menteur)* barefaced, brazen

effrontément [efrɔ̃temã] ADV impudently, insolently; *(mentir)* brazenly

effronterie [efrɔ̃tri] NF *(d'une personne, de manières)* effrontery, insolence, impudence; *(d'un mensonge)* brazenness

effroyable [efrwajabl] ADJ *(qui fait peur)*

dreadful, appalling, horrifying; *Fam (énorme) (dépense, foule, erreur)* dreadful, terrible

effroyablement [efrwajabləmã] ADV *Fam* dreadfully, terribly

effusion [efyzjɔ̃] NF **1 e. de sang** bloodshed **2** *(exubérance)* effusiveness; **avec e.** effusively, gushingly; **une e. de tendresse** an outpouring of affection

égaiement [egemã] NM cheering up

égailler (s') [segaje] VPR to disperse, to scatter

égal, -ale, -aux, -ales [egal, -o] ADJ **1** *(équivalent) (part, poids etc)* equal; **être é. à** to be equal to, to equal; **toutes choses égales (d'ailleurs)** all (other) things being equal; **à travail é., salaire é.** equal pay for equal work; **la partie n'est pas égale** they/we/you are not evenly matched; **ils sont de force/ d'intelligence égale** they are equally strong/intelligent; **à surface égale, je préfère mon appartement au sien** square foot for square foot, I prefer my flat to his/hers; **à expérience égale, ils préfèrent recruter un homme qu'une femme** if they have two candidates with identical experience, they prefer to hire a man rather than a woman
2 *(constant) (respiration, son)* even, regular; *(allure, pouls)* steady; *(sol)* level, even; *(climat)* equable; **homme d'humeur égale** even-tempered man; **fournir un effort é.** to work steadily; **il reste é. à lui-même** he's still his same old self
3 **cela m'est (bien) é.** it's all the same *or* all one to me; *(cela ne m'intéresse pas)* I don't care; **c'est é., elle aurait pu venir!** all the same, she could have come!
N equal; **s'associer avec ses égaux** to associate with one's equals; **elle est mon égale** she is my equal; **traiter qn d'é. à é., traiter qn en é.** to treat sb as an equal; **nous avons eu une discussion d'é. à é.** we had a discussion as equals *or* on equal terms *or* on an equal footing; **sans é.** unequalled, matchless; **elle est d'une malhonnêteté sans é.** she is incredibly dishonest; **il me chérit à l'é. d'un fils** he loves me like a son; **sa beauté n'a d'é. que sa bêtise** her beauty is only equalled by her stupidity

égalable [egalabl] ADJ which can be equalled *or* matched; **c'est un exploit difficilement é.** it's a achievement that will be difficult to match, it'll be a hard act to follow

également [egalmã] ADV **1** *(de la même manière)* equally; **é. bon** equally good; **servir tout le monde é.** to give everyone an equal serving; **j'aime é. sa mère et son père** I like his/her mother as much as I do his/her father **2** *(aussi)* also, as well, too; **j'en veux é.** I want some too *or* as well

égaler [egale] VT **1** *(être égal à) (personne, score)* to match (up to) *(en* for); **deux et deux égalent quatre** two and two equal *or* make four; **é. un record** to equal a record; **rien n'égale sa beauté** her beauty is unequalled **2** *Arch (rendre égal)* to make equal; **la douleur égale les hommes** grief makes all men equal; **peut-on é. Mozart à Bach?** can Mozart be considered the equal of Bach?

égalisateur, -trice [egalizatœr, -tris] ADJ *(système, effet etc)* equalizing, levelling; *Sport* **but/point é.** equalizer

égalisation [egalizasjɔ̃] NF **1** *(équilibrage)* equalization, equalizing; *Math* **é. à zéro** equating to zero; *Sport* **(but/point d')é.** equalizer; **réussir l'é.** to score the equalizer **2** *(nivellement) (du sol)* levelling, evening out

égaliser [egalize] VT **1** *(salaires, pression etc)* to equalize, to make equal; **é. les cheveux de qn** to trim sb's hair; *Math* **é. une expression à**

zéro to equate an expression to zero; *Sport* **é. la marque** to equalize, to draw level **2** *(sol)* to level, to even out
VI *Sport* to equalize

égaliseur [egalizœr] NM *Électron* equalizer; **é. graphique** graphic equalizer

égalitaire [egaliter] ADJ, N egalitarian

égalitarisme [egalitarism] NM egalitarianism

égalitariste [egalitarist] ADJ, N egalitarian

égalité [egalite] NF **1** *(équivalence)*, *Pol* equality; *Tennis* deuce; **être sur un pied d'é. avec qn** to be on an equal footing *or* on equal terms with sb; **é. des chances** equal opportunities; **é. des salaires** equal pay; *Sport* **à é.** *(équipes)* level; *(résultat)* drawn, tied; *Golf* all square; *Fig* **maintenant, nous sommes à é.** now we're even; *Sport* **course à é.** dead heat, tie; *Courses de chevaux* **parier à é. sur un cheval** to lay evens on a horse **2** *(constance) (de la respiration, d'un son etc)* evenness, regularity; *(d'une allure, du pouls)* steadiness; *(du sol)* evenness; *(de l'esprit)* equanimity; **é. d'humeur** even-temperedness

égard [egar] NM **1** *(attention)* consideration; **avoir é. à qch** to take sth into consideration *or* into account, to make allowance(s) *or* to allow for sth; **eu é. aux circonstances** in view of *or* considering the circumstances; **eu é. à son âge** in view of *or* given his age; **sans é. à** regardless of, irrespective of
2 à tous (les) égards in all respects, in every respect; **à certains égards** in some respects; **n'ayez aucune crainte à cet é.** don't worry about that, don't have any worries on that score; **être injuste à l'é. de qn** to be unjust to(wards) sb; **il a été très gentil à mon é.** he has been very kind to me
3 *(respect)* consideration, respect, regard; **faire qch par é. pour qn** to do sth out of respect *or* consideration for sb; **être sans é.** *ou* **n'avoir aucun é. pour qn** to have no consideration for sb; **avoir des égards pour qn** to be considerate towards sb, to show sb consideration; **elle est toujours accueillie avec les égards dus à son rang** she is always greeted with the respect due to her rank; **il nous a reçus avec beaucoup d'égards** he received us very warmly

égaré [egare] ADJ **1** *(personne)* lost; *(animal)* stray, lost **2** *(hagard) (regard)* distraught; *(yeux)* wild

égarement [egarmã] NM **1** *(délire, distraction)* **é. (d'esprit)** (mental) aberration; **il a parfois des moments d'é.** sometimes what he says/does doesn't make much sense, *Fam* there are times when he's not all there **2 égarements** *(dérèglements de conduite)* wild behaviour, wildness; **il est revenu de ses égarements** he has seen the error of his ways

égarer [egare] VT *(perdre) (personne)* to lose; *(en donnant de mauvaises indications)* to mislead; *(objet)* to mislay, to lose; **il jouait à é. les nouveaux arrivants** it amused him to get the newcomers lost; *Fig* **égaré par tant de malheurs** distraught by so many misfortunes; **la douleur/colère vous égare** you don't know what you're saying because of the pain/because you're so angry; **il faut à tout prix é. ses soupçons** we have to avert his/her suspicions at all costs
VPR **s'égarer 1** *(se perdre) (personne)* to lose one's way, to get lost; **colis qui s'est égaré** parcel that has got lost *or* gone astray **2** *(dévier)* **s'é. du droit chemin** to wander from the straight and narrow **3** *(sortir du sujet)* to stray *or* wander from the point; **son esprit s'égare** his mind is wandering

égayer [egeje] *(j'égaie, j'égaye, n. égayons; j'égaierai, j'égayerai)* VT *(malade, personne*

déprimée) to cheer up; *(invités)* to amuse; *(conversation)* to liven up; *(pièce, robe, la vie de quelqu'un)* to brighten (up)
VPR s'égayer *(s'amuser)* to have fun, to enjoy oneself; *(s'animer)* to cheer up; **s'é. aux dépens de qn** to have fun at sb's expense, to make fun of sb

Égée [eʒe] **ADJ la mer É.** the Aegean (Sea)

égéen, -éenne [eʒeɛ̃, -eɛn] **ADJ** Aegean

égérie [eʒeri] **NF** muse

égide [eʒid] **NF** aegis, shield; *Fig* **sous l'é. de** under the aegis *or* care of; *Fig* **se mettre sous l'é. des lois** to take refuge in the law

églantier [eglɑ̃tje] **NM** wild rose *or* dog rose (bush)

églantine [eglɑ̃tin] **NF** *(fleur)* wild *or* dog rose

églefin [egləfɛ̃] **NM** haddock

église [egliz] VOIR GRAMMAIRE A6–7 **1 l'É. (catholique romaine)** the (Roman) Catholic Church; **l'É. anglicane** the Church of England, the Anglican Church; **l'É. et l'État** Church and State; **gens d'É.** churchmen **2** *(bâtiment)* church; **l'é. Saint-Pierre** St. Peter's (church); **aller à l'é.** to go to church; **se marier à l'é.** to get married in (a) church, to have a church wedding

églogue [eglɔg] **NF** *Littér* eclogue

ego [ego] **NM INV** ego

égocentrique [egosɑ̃trik] **ADJ** self-centred, egocentric
N self-centred *or* egocentric person

égocentrisme [egosɑ̃trism] **NM** egocentricity, self-centredness; *Psy* egocentrism

égoïne [egɔin] **NF** *(scie)* **é.** handsaw

égoïsme [egɔism] **NM** selfishness, egoism

égoïste [egɔist] **N** egoist, selfish person
ADJ selfish, self-centred, egoistic

égoïstement [egɔistəmɑ̃] **ADV** selfishly, egoistically

égorgement [egɔrʒəmɑ̃] **NM** *(d'un cochon, d'une personne)* cutting the throat

égorger [egɔrʒe] *(j'égorgeai(s); n. égorgeons)* **VT 1** *(animal, personne)* to cut the throat of **2** *Vieilli (ruiner)* to bleed white *or* dry
VPR s'égorger *Fig* to kill each other

égorgeur, -euse [egɔrʒœr, -øz] **N** *(assassin)* cut-throat

égosiller (s') [segozije] **VPR** *(en parlant)* to bawl, to shout (oneself hoarse); *(en chantant)* to sing at the top of one's voice, *Fam* to sing one's head off; **mais je m'égosille à vous le dire!** I've told you so till I'm blue in the face *or* I'm hoarse!

égotisme [egɔtism] **NM** egotism

égotiste [egɔtist] **N** egotist
ADJ egotistic(al)

égout [egu] **NM** *(canalisation souterraine)* sewer; **eaux d'é.** sewage; **é. collecteur** main sewer; **bouche d'é.** manhole; **rat d'é.** sewer rat

égoutier [egutje] **NM** sewerman

égouttage [egutaʒ] **NM** *(de la vaisselle, d'un fromage frais etc)* draining

égouttement [egutmɑ̃] **NM 1** *(de l'eau)* dripping **2** *(égouttage)* draining

égoutter [egute] **VT** *(fromage frais, pâtes etc)* to drain
VPR s'égoutter *(d'un fromage frais, de vaisselle etc)* to drain
VI to drain; **laisser é. la vaisselle** to leave the dishes to drain

égouttoir [egutwar] **NM 1** *(dans l'évier)* draining board; *(mobile)* drainer, draining rack **2** *(passoire)* colander; **panier é.** *(d'une friteuse)* basket

égrappage [egrapaʒ] **NM** *(de raisins)* picking off

égrapper [egrape] **VT** *(raisins, baies)* to pick off from the bunch

égratigner [egratiɲe] **VT** *(écorcher)* to scratch; *Fig* to have *or* take a dig at
VPR s'égratigner to scratch oneself

égratignure [egratiɲyr] **NF** *(écorchure)* scratch; *Fig* dig, gibe; **je m'en suis sorti sans une é.** I escaped without a scratch

égrenage [egrənaʒ] **NM, égrènement** [egrɛnmɑ̃] **NM** *(de pois, maïs etc)* shelling; *(de raisins, baies)* picking off

égrener [egrəne] (**j'égrène, n. égrenons; j'égrènerai**) **VT 1** *(maïs, pois etc)* to shell; *(raisins, baies)* to pick off **2** *Fig* **é. son chapelet** to tell one's beads; **la pendule égrenne les heures** the clock ticks away; **é. ses souvenirs** to call up one's memories one by one
VPR s'égrener 1 *(de raisins, baies)* to fall *or* drop from the bunch; *(du blé)* to become strung out **2** *Fig (d'un cortège)* to become strung out; **des lumières s'égrenaient le long du quai** a string of lights stretched along the quay

égrillard [egrijar] **ADJ** *(personne, chanson, histoire etc)* bawdy, ribald; **en société, il a des manières égrillardes** he tends to be bawdy in company

Égypte [eʒipt] **NF** Egypt

égyptien, -ienne [eʒipsjɛ̃, -jɛn] **ADJ** Egyptian
N É. Egyptian
NM *Hist, Ling* Egyptian

égyptologie [eʒiptɔlɔʒi] **NF** Egyptology

égyptologue [eʒiptɔlɔg] **N** Egyptologist

eh [e] **INT** hey!; **eh bien!** well!, now then!; **eh bien, comment ça va aujourd'hui?** so how are you today?; **eh bien, je ne sais pas** well I don't know; **eh bien, je vais m'en occuper** oh well, I'll deal with it; **eh oui!** that's right!; **eh! que voulez-vous que j'y fasse?** well what do you want me to do about it?

éhonté [eɔ̃te] **ADJ** *(mensonge, menteur)* shameless, barefaced, brazen

eider [edɛr] **NM** *(oiseau)* eider (duck)

einsteinien, -ienne [ajnʃtajnjɛ̃, -jɛn] **ADJ** of/typical of Einstein

éjaculateur [eʒakylatœr] **NM** *Physiol* **é. précoce** premature ejaculator

éjaculation [eʒakylasjɔ̃] **NF** *Physiol* ejaculation; **é. précoce** premature ejaculation

éjaculer [eʒakyle] **VI** *Physiol* to ejaculate

éjectable [eʒɛktabl] **ADJ** *Aviat* **siège é.** ejector seat

éjecter [eʒɛkte] **VT** *(cartouche, pilote etc)* to eject; *Fam (expulser)* to throw *or* kick out (**de** of); **elle s'est fait é.** she was *or* got thrown *or* kicked out

éjection [eʒɛksjɔ̃] **NF** *(d'une cartouche, d'un pilote etc)* ejection; *Fam (expulsion)* throwing out, kicking out; **éjections volcaniques** ejecta

élaboration [elabɔrasjɔ̃] **NF** *(d'un plan, d'une idée)* working out, development; *(d'une constitution, une loi etc)* drawing up; **é. de concept** concept development; *Mktg* **é. de produit** product development

élaboré [elabɔre] **ADJ** *(technique, machine)* sophisticated; *(plan)* elaborate

élaborer [elabɔre] **VT** *(plan, idée)* to work out, to develop; *(constitution, loi etc)* to draw up; **é. le profil de qn** to profile sb

élagage [elagaʒ] **NM** *(d'un arbre),* *Fig (d'un film, un roman etc)* pruning; *Mktg* **é. de la ligne** line pruning

élaguer [elage] **VT** *(arbre),* *Fig (film, roman etc)* to prune

élagueur, -euse [elagœr, -øz] **N** pruner

élan¹ [elɑ̃] **NM 1** *Sport etc (action de s'élancer)* *(avec les jambes)* run-up; *(avec les bras)* swing; *Sport* **prendre de l'é. ou son é.** to take

a run (-up); **saut sans/avec é.** standing/running jump; **mal calculer son é.** to misjudge one's run-up; **d'un seul é.** *(en sautant)* at one bound; *(en courant)* in one burst; *Fig* **elle courut chez sa mère d'un seul é.** she ran all the way to her mother's without stopping
2 *Fig (impulsion)* **donner de l'é. à l'industrie** to give a boost to industry
3 *(vitesse)* momentum, impetus; **emporté par son é., il trébucha** carried away by his own momentum, he tripped; **emportée par son é., la voiture alla au fossé** gathering momentum, the car went into the ditch; **perdre de l'é.** to lose momentum; *Fig* **le général Dupont brisa l'é. des forces ennemies** General Dupont broke the momentum of the enemy forces; **impossible de les arrêter dans leur é.** it's impossible to stop them once they've got going *or* started
4 *(transport)* *(d'enthousiasme)* burst, outburst; *(de tendresse, passion)* surge; **un é. créatif** a creative outburst; **dans un é. amoureux** in a surge of love; **il ne connaissait plus aucun des élans de sa jeunesse** he no longer felt the impulses of his youth; **éprouver un é. (naturel) vers qn** to feel (naturally) drawn to sb; **rien n'a jamais pu briser l'é. qui me portait vers elle** nothing could ever break the force which drew me towards her; **contenir ou maîtriser ses élans** to keep one's impulses in check
5 *(ferveur)* fervour, *Am* fervor; **parler avec é.** to speak with fervour *or* fervently
6 *(accent)* **sa voix avait des élans lyriques** her voice had a lyrical ring; **le violon avait des élans plaintifs** the violin had plaintive tones
7 *Phil* **é.** vital life force

élan² **NM** *(animal)* (Scandinavian) elk; **é. du Canada** moose

élancé [elɑ̃se] **ADJ** *(silhouette, personne, arbre)* slim, slender; **aux formes élancées** *(bateau, voiture)* streamlined

élancement [elɑ̃smɑ̃] **NM** *(douleur)* shooting pain

élancer [elɑ̃se] *(j'élançai(s); n. élançons)* **VI ma jambe m'élance, ça m'élance dans la jambe** I've got shooting pains in my leg
VPR s'élancer *(en courant)* to rush, to dash; *Sport (prendre son élan)* to take a run-up; **s'é. dans une course effrénée** to break into a mad dash; **s'é. sur qn** to rush *or* make a rush at sb; **le chat s'élança sur moi** the cat flew at me; **s'é. à l'assaut des vagues** *(d'un navire, un surfeur)* to take to the water, *Litt* to brave the seas; **s'é. à l'assaut d'un sommet** to attack *or* tackle a peak; **s'é. vers le ciel** to soar skywards
VT la cathédrale élance ses flèches vers le ciel the cathedral's spires soar skywards

élargir [elarʒir] **VT 1** *(route, rue)* to widen, to broaden; *(robe)* to let out; *(chaussures)* to stretch; *(tube)* to expand; *(trou)* to enlarge; *(propriété)* to enlarge, to extend, to add to; **robe qui élargit les épaules** dress which makes the shoulders look broader
2 *Fig (groupe, gamme de produits)* to expand; *(connaissance, débat)* to broaden, to widen, to expand; *(horizon)* to broaden; **é. un marché** to broaden a market
3 *Jur (prisonnier)* to release, to set free
VPR s'élargir 1 *(d'une route, une rue)* to widen (out), to broaden (out); *(de hanches, d'épaules)* to broaden (out); *(de chaussures, d'un jean etc)* to stretch
2 *Fig (d'un groupe)* to expand; *(de son horizon)* to broaden; *(d'un débat)* to broaden, to widen; **ses idées se sont élargies au contact des jeunes** he became more broadminded through being in contact with young people

élargissement [elarʒismɑ̃] **NM 1** *(d'une route, d'une rue etc)* widening, broadening;

(d'une robe) letting out; *(de chaussures)* stretching; *(d'une propriété)* extension, enlargement **2** *Fig (d'un groupe, des connaissances)* expansion; *(de son horizon)* broadening; *(d'un débat)* broadening, widening, expansion; **l'é. de l'Union européenne** the enlargement of the EU; *Mktg* **é. du marché** market rollout **3** *Jur (d'un prisonnier)* release

élasticité [elastisite] **NF** *(d'un corps, de la peau, d'une matière)* elasticity; *(d'un pas)* springiness (**de** of), spring (**de** in); *Fig (de principes etc)* flexibility; *Com* **é. de l'offre/ de la demande** elasticity of supply/demand; *Com* **é. des prix** price elasticity

élastine [elastin] **NF** elastin

élastique [elastik] **ADJ 1** *(corps, matière etc)* elastic; **gomme é.** india rubber; **balle é.** rubber ball; **d'un pas é.** with a springy *or* buoyant step **2** *Fig (règlement, principes)* flexible; **conscience é.** accommodating conscience
   NM 1 *Couture etc* elastic; **en é.** elastic **2** *(de bureau)* elastic *or Br* rubber band; *Fig Fam* **les lâcher avec un é.** to have moths in one's wallet **3** *(jeu)* **jouer à l'é.** to play at elastics; **saut à l'é.** bungee jumping

élastiqué [elastike] **ADJ** elasticated

élastomère [elastɔmɛr] **NM** *Chimie, Ind* elastomer

Elbe [ɛlb] **NF** (**l'île d')E.** (the island of) Elba **NM** (river) Elbe

eldorado [ɛldorado] **NM** eldorado; **il veut faire de son pays un véritable e. pour les investisseurs étrangers** he wants to turn his country into a land of opportunity for foreign investors

électeur, -trice [elɛktœr, -tris] **N 1** *Pol* elector, voter; **mes électeurs** the people who voted for me; **carte d'é.** voting *or* polling card **2** *Hist* É. Elector; **Électrice** Electress

électif, -ive [elɛktif, -iv] **ADJ** elective

élection [elɛksjɔ̃] **NF 1** *(d'un député, un pape, une reine de beauté etc)* election; **é. partielle** by-election; **jour des élections** polling *or* election day; **annuler l'é. de qn** to unseat sb; **se présenter aux élections** to stand as a candidate (**in** the elections), to stand for election; **remporter les élections** to win the election **2** *(choix)* election, choice; **mon pays d'é.** the country of my choice; *Jur* **faire é. de domicile** to elect domicile; *Rel* **le peuple d'é.** the chosen people
   ▸▸ **élections européennes** European elections; **élections législatives** (parliamentary) election(s), general election; **élections municipales** = local (council) elections; **é. présidentielle** presidential election

---

Élections

All French citizens of eighteen or over are entitled to vote in elections, which take place on a Sunday. Polling stations are often set up in local schools. Voters collect leaflets (each corresponding to the different political parties or candidates), go to a booth and put their chosen leaflet into the envelope provided. It is then placed in the ballot box ("l'urne") supervised by the "assesseur", who utters the words "a voté!". Unlike Britain with its first-past-the-post system, the French electoral system is based on a type of proportional representation. As from 2002 presidential elections take place every five years. General elections are also held every five years.

électoral, -ale, -aux, -ales [elɛktoral, -o] **ADJ** *(campagne, comité, promesses)* election;

circonscription électorale constituency, *Can* riding; **liste électorale** electoral register *or* roll; **corps é.** electorate

électoralisme [elɛktoralism] **NM** *Péj* electioneering

électoraliste [elɛktoralist] **ADJ** electioneering, vote-catching

électorat [elɛktora] **NM 1** *Pol* voters, electorate; **consulter l'é.** to go to the country; **l'é. communiste/féminin** the communist/female vote, communist/female voters **2** *(droit de vote)* franchise **3** *Hist* É. electorate

Électre [elɛktr] **N** Electra

électricien, -ienne [elɛktrisjɛ̃, -jɛn] **N** electrician; **ingénieur é.** electrical engineer

électricité [elɛktrisite] **NF** electricity; **panne d'é.** power cut *or* failure; **faire poser** *ou* **installer l'é.** to have electricity put in *or* installed; **il faut refaire l'é. de la cuisine** we're going to have to rewire the kitchen; *Fig Fam* **il y a de l'é. dans l'air** the atmosphere is electric
   ▸▸ **é. atmosphérique** atmospherics; **é. statique** static (electricity)

électrification [elɛktrifikasjɔ̃] **NF** electrification

électrifier [elɛktrifje] **VT** *(chemin de fer)* to electrify; *(village)* to bring electricity to, to electrify

électrique [elɛktrik] **ADJ 1** *(courant, train etc)*, *Fig (atmosphère)* electric **2** *(ingénierie)* electrical

électriquement [elɛktrikmã] **ADV** electrically

électrisant [elɛktrizã] **ADJ** *Fig* electrifying

électrisation [elɛktrizasjɔ̃] **NF** *Élec* electrification; **à é. positive** positively charged, charged with positive electricity

électriser [elɛktrize] **VT** *Élec*, *Fig (audience)* to electrify; *Élec* **fil électrisé** live wire

électro- [elɛktro] **PRÉF** electro-

électro-acousticien, -ienne **N** electro-acoustics expert
   ADJ electroacoustics

électro-aimant, *pl* **électro-aimants** **NM** electromagnet

électrocardiogramme [elɛktrokardjogram] **NM** *Méd* electrocardiogram

électrocardiographe [elɛtrokardjograf] **NM** *Méd* electrocardiograph

électrocardiographie [elɛktrokardjografi] **NF** *Méd* electrocardiography

électrochimie [elɛktroʃimi] **NF** electrochemistry

électrochimique [elɛktroʃimik] **ADJ** electrochemical

électrochoc [elɛktroʃɔk] **NM** *Méd*, *Fig* electric shock; **traitement par électrochocs** electric shock treatment; **on lui a fait des électrochocs** he was given electric shock treatment

électrocopie [elɛktrokɔpi] **NF** xerography

électrocuter [elɛktrokyte] **VT** to electrocute; **se faire é.** to be electrocuted

électrocution [elɛktrokysjɔ̃] **NF** electrocution

électrode [elɛktrɔd] **NF** electrode; **é. de masse** earth electrode

électrodomestique [elɛktrodɔmɛstik] **ADJ** **appareils électrodomestiques** household electrical appliances *or Am* electricals **NM** **l'é.** electrical goods *or Am* electricals

électrodynamique [elɛktrodinamik] **ADJ** electrodynamic
   NF electrodynamics

électro-encéphalogramme, *pl* **électro-encéphalogrammes** **NM** *Méd* electroencephalogram

électro-encéphalographie **NF** *Méd* electroencephalography

électrogène [elɛktroʒɛn] **ADJ** **groupe é.** generator; **appareil é.** *(d'un poisson)* electric organ

électroluminescent [elɛktrolyminesã] **ADJ** light-emitting

électrolyse [elɛktroliz] **NF** electrolysis

électrolyser [elɛktrolize] **VT** to electrolyse

électrolyte [elɛktrolit] **NM** electrolyte

électrolytique [elɛktrolitik] **ADJ** electrolytic

électromagnétique [elɛktromaɲetik] **ADJ** electromagnetic

électromagnétisme [elɛktromaɲetism] **NM** electromagnetism

électromécanicien, -ienne [elɛktromekanisjɛ̃, -jɛn] **N** electrical engineer

électromécanique [elɛktromekanik] **ADJ** electromechanical
   NF electromechanics

électroménager [elɛktromenaʒe] **ADJ** **appareils électroménagers** household appliances *or Am* electricals
   NM household appliances *or Am* electricals

électrométallurgie [elɛktrometalyrʒi] **NF** electrometallurgy

électrométallurgique [elɛtrometalyrʒik] **ADJ** electrometallurgical

électromètre [elɛktrometr] **NM** electrometer

électromoteur, -trice [elɛktromotœr, -tris] **ADJ** electromotive
   NM electromotor

électron [elɛktrɔ̃] **NM** *Phys* electron

électronégatif, -ive [elɛktronegatif, -iv] **ADJ** electronegative

électronicien, -ienne [elɛktronisjɛ̃, -jɛn] **N** electronics specialist; **ingénieur é.** electronics engineer

électronique [elɛktronik] **ADJ** *(équipement, musique, point de vente, argent, réservation)* electronic; *(faisceau, flux, microscope, télescope)* electron; **l'industrie é.** the electronics industry
   NF electronics; **é. aérospatiale** avionics

électroniquement [elɛktronikmã] **ADV** electronically

électronucléaire [elɛktronykleɛr] **ADJ** *(industrie, centrale)* nuclear power; **énergie é.** nuclear power
   NM nuclear power

électronvolt [elɛktrɔ̃volt] **NM** electronvolt

électrophone [elɛktrofɔn] **NM** record player

électropositif, -ive [elɛktropozitif, -iv] **ADJ** electropositive

électroscope [elɛktroskɔp] **NM** electroscope

électrosensible [elɛktrosãsibl] **ADJ** electrosensitive

électrostatique [elɛktrostatik] **ADJ** electrostatic
   NF electrostatics

électrotechnique [elɛktroteknik] **ADJ** electrotechnical
   NF electrical engineering

électrothérapie [elɛktroterapi] **NF** *Méd* *(pratique)* electrotherapy; *(étude)* electrotherapeutics

électrovalve [elɛktrovalv] **NF** *Aut* solenoid; **é. de starter** starter solenoid

électrovanne [elɛktrovan] **NF** solenoid valve

élégamment [elegamã] **ADV** *(vêtu)* elegantly, smartly; *(maquillée)* smartly; *(agir)* courteously; **coiffée é.** with an elegant *or* smart hairstyle

élégance [elegɑ̃s] NF elegance; *(d'un geste, d'un comportement)* courtesy; *(d'une méthode, d'une solution)* neatness; **l'é. du chat siamois** the elegance *or* grace of a Siamese cat; **habillé avec é.** elegantly *or* smartly dressed; **savoir perdre avec é.** to be a good loser; **elle a eu l'é. de ne pas protester** she had the courtesy not to protest

élégant, -ante [elegɑ̃, -ɑ̃t] ADJ *(vêtements, restaurant, style etc)* elegant; *(méthode, solution)* neat; *(geste, comportement)* courteous; **c'était une façon élégante de me dire que ...** it was a polite *or* diplomatic way of telling me that ...; **il use de procédés peu élégants** he uses rather callous measures
▸ NM *Arch* dandy
▸ NF **élégante** well- *or* smartly *or* fashionably dressed woman

élégiaque [eleʒjak] ADJ elegiac

élégie [eleʒi] NF elegy

élément [elemɑ̃] NM **1** *(naturel)* element; **les quatre éléments** the four elements; *Fig* **être dans son é.** to be in one's element; *Fig* **je ne me sens pas dans mon é. ici** I'm not in my element here, I'm like a fish out of water here
2 *Chimie* element; *Phys* **é. radioactif** radioactive element
3 *(partie)* *(d'une structure, un problème etc)* element, component, constituent; *(d'un médicament)* ingredient; *(d'un compte)* item; **les éléments d'un ensemble** the elements *or* parts of a whole; *Tech* **é. chauffant** heating unit *or* element; *Aut* **é. filtrant en papier** paper filtering element; *Ordinat* **é. de menu** menu item; *Tech* **é. mobile** working part; *Électron* **é. de calculateur** *ou* **de calculatrice** *ou* **électronique** computer unit; **éléments préfabriqués** prefabricated *or* ready-made units; **mobilier formé d'éléments** modular furniture
4 *(personne)* element; **les éléments indésirables de la population** the undesirable elements of the population; **l'é. féminin** the female element *or* contingent; **l'é. féminin est faiblement représenté dans cette société** there are few women in the company; **j'ai de bons éléments dans ma classe** I've got some good material in my class; **avec lui, nous avons perdu un très bon é.** we've lost a good man in him
5 *Élec (d'une batterie, d'un accumulateur)* cell; **batterie de cinq éléments** five-cell battery
6 *(rudiment) (de science etc)* **éléments** elements, rudiments; **avoir quelques éléments en espagnol** to have elementary *or* rudimentary Spanish; **Éléments de chimie** *(livre)* Elementary Chemistry
7 *(donnée)* **éléments** data, information; **l'é. décisif** the deciding factor; **aucun é. nouveau à signaler** nothing new to report
8 *Mil* **éléments blindés/motorisés** armoured/motorized units

élémentaire [elemɑ̃tɛr] ADJ **1** *Chimie, Phys (analyse chimique, particule d'atome etc)* elementary **2** *(de base) (connaissance)* elementary, rudimentary; *(cours, problème etc)* elementary; *(minimal) (habitation)* basic, rudimentary; *Scol* **cours é.** = second and third years of primary school; **cours é. de ski/danse** skiing/dance classes for beginners; **c'est é.!** *(évident)* it's elementary!, it's simple!; *(le minimum)* it's the least I/you/*etc* could do!; **c'est la politesse la plus é.** it's only common courtesy

éléphant [elefɑ̃] NM elephant; **é. mâle/femelle** bull/cow elephant; **é. d'Afrique/d'Asie** African/Indian elephant; **é. marin** *ou* **de mer** elephant seal, sea elephant; **comme un é. dans un magasin de porcelaine** like a bull in a china shop

éléphanteau, -eaux [elefɑ̃to] NM elephant calf; *(très jeune)* baby elephant

éléphantesque [elefɑ̃tɛsk] ADJ *Fam* phantine, gigantic, colossal; **elle est d'une bêtise é.** she is colossally stupid

éléphantiasis [elefɑ̃tjazis] NM *Méd* elephantiasis

élevage [elvaʒ] NM **1** *(de bovins, chevaux, moutons etc)* breeding, rearing; **l'é.** stock breeding; **é. intensif/en batterie** intensive/battery farming; **é. des animaux à fourrure** fur farming; **faire de l'é.** to breed *or* rear cattle, to be a stock breeder; **région d'é.** breeding area; **poulet d'é.** battery-reared chicken **2** *(ferme)* (stock) farm, *Am* ranch, *Austr* station

élévateur, -trice [elevatœr, -tris] ADJ **chariot é. à fourche** fork-lift truck
▸ NM **1** *(appareil)* elevator, lift, hoist; **é. à bascule** tip; **é. à augets** *ou* **à godets** bucket elevator; **é. (à fourche)** fork-lift truck **2** *Élec* **é. de tension** step-up transformer

élévation [elevasjɔ̃] NF **1** *(action d'élever) (d'un mur, de la voix etc)* raising; *(de la température, des prix etc)* raising, increasing; *(d'une statue etc)* erection, setting up; *Rel (de l'hostie)* elevation; *Math* **é. d'un nombre au carré/à la puissance 10** raising a number to the square root/to the power of 10
2 *(action de s'élever) (de température, prix etc)* rise, increase; **é. du niveau des eaux** rise in water level; **é. du pouls** quickening of the pulse
3 *Fig* **lire Platon contribue à l'é. de l'esprit** reading Plato improves the mind; **é. des sentiments/du caractère** nobility of sentiments/character
4 *Archit (projection)* elevation
5 *(tertre)* rise (in the ground), mound

élévatoire [elevatwar] ADJ *(appareil)* lifting, hoisting

élevé [elve] ADJ **1** *(montagne, prix)* high; *Fig (style, esprit)* noble, elevated; *(rang, position)* high, exalted; **l'officier ayant le grade le plus é.** the senior *or* highest-ranking officer; **il occupe un rang é. dans ce parti** he ranks high in the party; **de rang é.** high-ranking; **pouls é.** rapid pulse **2** *(éduqué)* **bien é.** well brought up, well-bred, well-mannered; **mal é.** badly brought up, ill-bred, ill-mannered; *Fam* **c'est très mal é. de parler la bouche pleine** it's very rude *or* very bad manners to speak with your mouth full; **c'est un mal é., ce garçon** he has bad manners, that boy

élève [elev] N *Scol* pupil, student; *(d'un peintre, un musicien etc)* pupil
▸ NF **1** *(animal)* young stock animal **2** *(plante)* seedling
▸▸ **é. infirmière** student nurse; *Mil* **é. officier** cadet; **é. pilote** trainee *or* student pilot

élever [elve] *(j'élève, n. élevons; j'élèverai)* VT **1** *(faire monter) (niveau d'eau, voix etc)* to raise; *(prix, température etc)* to increase, to raise; *(charge)* to lift up, to raise; **é. un nombre au carré/au cube** to square/cube a number; **é. un nombre à la puissance 4** to raise a number to the power 4; **é. une perpendiculaire** to raise a perpendicular
2 *(dresser) (monument, statue, mur etc)* to erect, to put up; *(les bras, le poing, les yeux)* to raise; *Fig (objection, difficultés)* to raise; *Fig* **quelqu'un a-t-il une critique à é.?** does anyone have any criticism to make?; *Fig* **é. des autels à qn** to praise sb to the skies
3 *(rehausser) (immeuble, mur etc)* to raise, to make higher; *(plafond, plancher)* to raise; **é. un mur de 20 cm** to raise a wall by 20 cm, to make a wall 20 cm higher
4 *(porter à un rang supérieur)* to promote (**au rang de** to)

5 *(édifier) (esprit)* to improve; **é. le débat** to raise the tone of the proceedings
6 *(éduquer) (enfant)* to bring up, to raise; **bébé élevé au sein/au biberon** breast-/bottle-fed baby; *Fam* **é. qn dans du coton** to raise sb in cotton wool, to coddle sb
7 *(faire l'élevage de) (bovins, chevaux etc)* to rear, to breed; *(lapins)* to breed; *(abeilles, volaille)* to keep
▸ VPR **s'élever 1** *(avec mouvement)* to rise (up); **l'hélicoptère s'élevait doucement dans les airs** the helicopter rose smoothly into the air; **un cri s'éleva** a shout went up
2 *(sans mouvement)* to stand; **le château s'élève sur la colline** the castle stands on the hill; **la maison s'élevait dans le soleil couchant** the house stood silhouetted against the setting sun
3 *(monter) (de la température, des prix etc)* to rise, to increase, to go up
4 *(paraître) (de doutes, difficultés)* to arise
5 *(protester)* **s'é. contre qch/qn** to rise up against sth/sb; **je m'élève contre la validité de ce testament** I contest the validity of this will
6 *Fig* **s'é. à force de travail** to work one's way up; **s'é. socialement** to climb up the social ladder; **s'é. au-dessus des préjugés** to rise above prejudice; **ses pensées ne s'élèvent jamais au-delà de sa petite personne** his thoughts never rise above himself; **des lectures qui permettent à l'âme de s'é.** spiritually uplifting reading matter
7 *(atteindre)* **s'é.** à to come to, to amount to; **la note s'élève à 1000 euros** the bill comes to *or* adds up to *or* totals 1,000 euros

éleveur, -euse [elvœr, -øz] N *(de bovins)* stock breeder, cattle farmer; **é. de chevaux/chiens** horse/dog breeder; **é. de moutons/poulets** sheep/poultry farmer
▸ NF **éleveuse** *(pour poussins)* brooder

elfe [ɛlf] NM elf VOIR GRAMMAIRE A12

élider [elide] *Ling* VT *(voyelle)* to elide
▸ VPR **s'élider** to be elided, to elide

éligibilité [eliʒibilite] NF *Pol* eligibility

éligible [eliʒibl] ADJ *Pol* eligible

élimé [elime] ADJ *(tissu, vêtement)* worn, threadbare

élimer [elime] VT *(tissu, vêtement)* to wear thin
▸ VPR **s'élimer** to wear thin

élimination [eliminasjɔ̃] NF *aussi Physiol* elimination; **procéder par é.** to use a process of elimination; **en procédant par é.** by a process of elimination; *Ind etc* **é. des déchets** waste disposal; *Radio* **é. des parasites** suppression of noise *or* interference

éliminatoire [eliminatwar] ADJ *(examen)* qualifying; **5 est une note é.** five counts as a fail; **il a eu une note é.** he didn't get a pass mark; **épreuve é.** qualifying heat *or* round, qualifier
▸ NF qualifying *or* eliminating heat *or* round, qualifier

éliminer [elimine] VT **1** *(candidat, suspect)* to eliminate; *(possibilité, théorie)* to rule out, to exclude; *Physiol (déchets)* to get rid of, to eliminate; **être éliminé** *(d'un candidat)* to be knocked out *or* eliminated; **ils ont tous été éliminés pour dopage** they were all disqualified for drug-taking **2** *(tuer)* to liquidate
▸ VI *Physiol* to get rid of *or* eliminate body wastes

élire [elir] VT *(conj like lire)* **1** *(candidat, représentant etc)* to elect; **é. un député** ≃ to elect *or* return a Member of Parliament; **é. qn président** to elect sb president, to vote sb in as president **2 é. domicile** to take up residence (**à** in); *Jur* to elect domicile (**à** in); **une souris a élu domicile dans notre grenier** a mouse has moved into *or* taken up residence in our attic

élisabéthain, -aine [elizabetɛ̃, -ɛn] ADJ Elizabethan
▪ N **É.** Elizabethan

élision [elizjɔ̃] NF *Ling* elision SEE GRAMMAR B2

élite [elit] NF élite, elite; **les élites** the élite; **l'é. de …** the cream *or* élite of …; **personnel d'é.** select *or* hand-picked personnel; **régiment/tireur d'é.** crack regiment/shot

élitisme [elitism] NM elitism

élitiste [elitist] ADJ, N elitist

élixir [eliksir] NM elixir; **l'é. de longue vie** the elixir of life; **é. parégorique** = medicine for treating diarrhoea, *Spéc* paregoric (elixir)

elle, *pl* **elles** [ɛl] PRON PERS F SEE GRAMMAR A27; B18; B66 **1** *(sujet) (personne)* she; *(chose)* it; *(bébé, animal, nation, navire)* it, she; **elles** they; **e. chante** she sings; **elles dansent** they dance; **e. arrivée, la fête a pu commencer** once she had arrived the party was able to start; **e., dégoûtée, a fait la grimace** she grimaced in disgust; **e., e. n'aurait même pas levé le petit doigt** she wouldn't have raised a finger; **e., se marier? tu ne la connais pas!** her get married? you don't know *her*!; **qui a fait ça? – c'est e.** who did that? – she did *or* her!; **e. est bien bonne, celle-là!** that's a good one! **2** *(objet) (personne)* her; *(chose)* it; *(bébé, animal etc)* it, her; **elles** them; **et e., tu l'oublies?** and are you forgetting *her*?; **tu la connais, e.?** do you know her?; **tu les imagines, e. et lui, sur des skis!** imagine the pair of them on skis! **3** *(avec qui, que)* **c'est e. qui est partie la première** she left first; **c'est e. que j'ai rencontrée dans la rue** it was her I met in the street; **son père est déjà là et e. qui n'arrive pas** her father's here already and she hasn't arrived yet; **c'est à e. qu'il veut avoir affaire** it's her he wants to talk to **4** *(avec préposition)* **je suis content d'e./d'elles** I am pleased with her/them; **e. ne pense qu'à e.** she thinks only of herself; **dis-le-lui, à e.** tell *her*, **ce n'est pas à moi, c'est à e.** it's not mine, it's hers; **c'est à e. de dire si e. veut venir** it's up to her to say if she wants to come *or* not; **e. possède une entreprise à e.** she has her own company; **je l'ai entendu dire par une relation à e.** I heard it from a relation of hers; **un portrait d'e.** *(qu'elle a fait)* a portrait by her; *(où elle est représentée)* a portrait of her; **il aimait sa patrie et mourut pour e.** he loved his country and died for it **5** *(dans comparaisons)* **il est mieux qu'e.** he is better than she is *or* than her; **il boit plus qu'e.** he drinks more than she does *or* than her; **je fais mon travail aussi bien qu'e.** I work as well as she does, my work is as good as hers; **je fais comme e.** I do what she does **6** *(interrogatif, emphatique)* **viendra-t-e.?** will she come?; **ta directrice est-e. toujours en activité?** is your boss still working?; **la télévision est-e. toujours en panne?** is the television still not working?; **qu'e. est jolie, cette broche!** how pretty that brooch is!; **eh bien, ta cousine, e. n'est pas près de me revoir** well, your cousin isn't likely to see me again in a hurry

ellébore [ɛlebɔr] NM *(plante)* hellebore

elle-même [ɛlmɛm] PRON PERS *(d'une personne)* herself; *(d'une chose)* itself; *(d'un bébé, d'un animal, d'une nation)* itself, herself; **elles-mêmes** themselves; **mais e. n'est pas sans défauts** but she's no paragon herself; **c'est e. qui me l'a dit** she told me so herself, she herself told me so

ellipse [elips] NF **1** *Gram* ellipsis **2** *Géom* ellipse

ellipsoïdal, -ale, -aux, -ales [elipsɔidal, -o] ADJ *Géom* ellipsoidal
▪ NM **ellipsoïde** [elipsɔid] *Géom* ADJ ellipsoidal
▪ NM ellipsoid

elliptique [eliptik] ADJ *Gram, Géom* elliptical; **style e.** elliptical style

elliptiquement [eliptikmɑ̃] ADV *Gram* elliptically

élocution [elɔkysjɔ̃] NF **1** *(diction)* elocution; *(débit)* delivery; **avoir une é. trop rapide** to speak too quickly; **avoir une é. claire** to speak *or* enunciate clearly; **défaut d'é.** speech impediment *or* defect **2** *Belg Scol (exposé)* talk, presentation

éloge [elɔʒ] NM **1** *(discours)* eulogy; **é. funèbre** eulogy, funeral oration **2** *(louange)* praise; **faire l'é. de qn/qch** to speak very highly of *or* in praise of sb/sth; **faire son propre é.** to sing one's own praises, *Br* to blow one's own trumpet; **digne d'éloges** praiseworthy; **c'est tout à votre é. d'avoir accepté** it's to your credit that you accepted; **il fait du bénévolat et c'est tout à son é.** to his credit, he does volunteer work

élogieusement [elɔʒjøzmɑ̃] ADV **parler é. de** to speak very highly of

élogieux, -ieuse [elɔʒjø, -jøz] ADJ *(discours, article)* of praise, *Fml* eulogistic, laudatory; **parler de qn/qch en termes é.** to speak very highly of sb/sth; **les critiques ont été é. avec son dernier film** the critics praised his last film

éloigné [elwaɲe] ADJ *(endroit, passé, futur etc)* distant, remote; *(parent)* distant; **la ville est très éloignée** the town is a long way away *or* off, the town is very far away; **la ville est éloignée de cinq kilomètres** the town is five kilometres away; **ils sont éloignés d'un kilomètre** they are one kilometre apart, there is a kilometre between them; **maison éloignée de la gare** house a long way from the station; **notre mariage est encore à une date éloignée** our wedding is still a long way off; **la date en est trop éloignée pour que je puisse savoir si je serai libre** it's too far away for me to say whether I'll be free or not; **dans un avenir peu é.** in the near *or* not-too-distant future; **rien n'est plus é. de ma pensée** nothing is further from my thoughts; **se tenir é. de qch** to keep away from sth, to steer clear of sth; *Fig* **je ne suis plus é. de croire que …** I'm coming round to believe that *or* to the belief that …

éloignement [elwaɲ(ə)mɑ̃] NM **1** *(action) (d'une personne indésirable)* removal; **l'é. de sa famille est nécessaire à sa guérison** his family must be kept away if he is to recover **2** *(fait d'être éloigné)* absence; **je ne supporte plus notre é.** I can't bear us to be apart any longer; **plus l'é. dure, plus il renforce notre amour** the longer we are apart *or* the longer the separation lasts, the stronger our love grows; **l'é. est difficile à vivre** it is difficult to be apart *or* separated **3** *(distance) (dans l'espace)* distance, remoteness; *(dans le temps)* remoteness; **l'é. de nos deux bureaux ne favorise pas la communication** distance between our two offices does not help communication; **avec l'é. on arrive mieux à comprendre ce qui s'est passé** with the benefit of hindsight *or* the passage of time it is easier to understand what happened

éloigner [elwaɲe] VT **1** *(écarter dans l'espace) (personne, objet)* to move away, to take away, to remove; **é. qch de qch** to move sth away from sth; **é. qn du feu/de la voiture** to move sb away from the fire/car; **ce trajet nous éloigne du centre ville** this route takes us away from the centre of town; **é. les loups/les moustiques** to keep the wolves/mosquitoes away *or* at bay; **tes parents cherchent à m'é. de toi** your parents are trying to keep me away from you; **mon travail m'éloigne de toute vie sociale** my work makes it impossible to socialize **2** *(dans le temps)* **chaque jour m'éloigne un** peu plus de cette époque that time recedes with each day that passes **3** *(distraire, détourner)* **é. une crainte/une pensée/des soupçons** to banish a fear/dismiss a thought/avert suspicion; **é. qn de son travail** to keep sb away from his work
▪ VPR **s'éloigner 1** *(s'écarter dans l'espace) (d'une personne)* to move away; *(d'un objet)* to move away *or* off; **voudriez-vous vous é. un peu?** would you please stand further away *or* back, would you please move back *or* away a little; **ne vous éloignez pas!** don't go too far away!; **l'orage s'éloigne** the storm is passing; *Fig* **avec le temps, ce souvenir s'éloignera** the memory will fade with time **2** *(se distraire, se détourner)* **s'é. de la vérité** to stray *or* wander from the truth; **s'é. de son devoir** to neglect one's duty; **s'é. du sujet** to wander from the subject; **s'é. de tout le monde** to distance oneself from everybody; **je sens bien que tu t'éloignes (de moi)** I feel you're growing away from me; **le temps a fait qu'ils se sont éloignés l'un de l'autre** they drifted apart with time

élongation [elɔ̃gasjɔ̃] NF *Méd* pulled muscle; **se faire une é.** to pull a muscle

éloquemment [elɔkamɑ̃] ADV eloquently

éloquence [elɔkɑ̃s] NF **1** *(loquacité) (d'une personne)*, *Fig (d'un tableau, de l'expression du visage)* eloquence **2** *(rhétorique)* oratory

éloquent [elɔkɑ̃] ADJ *(personne, discours)* eloquent; *Fig (silence, geste etc)* eloquent, expressive; **ces chiffres sont éloquents** the figures speak volumes *or* speak for themselves; **52 à 0, le score est é.** 52-nil: the score speaks for itself; **son expression dégoûtée était éloquente** his expression of disgust said it all

élu, -ue [ely] ADJ *Pol* elected; **président é.** president elect; *Bible* **le peuple é.** the chosen people
▪ N **1** *Rel* **les élus** the elect **2** *Pol (député, conseiller)* elected representative; **les élus du peuple** the people's representatives; **les élus locaux** local *or* town councillors **3** *Hum* **qui est l'heureuse élue?** who's the lucky girl *or* lady?; **l'é. de son cœur** the man of her choice

élucidation [elysidasjɔ̃] NF elucidation

élucider [elyside] VT *(mystère)* to clear up; *(question, problème)* to clarify

élucubrations [elykybrasjɔ̃] NFPL *Péj* flights of fancy, wild imaginings

élucubrer [elykybre] VT *Péj* to dream up

éluder [elyde] VT to evade, to elude; **é. le paiement de l'impôt** to evade payment of tax

élusif, -ive [elyzif, -iv] ADJ *(réponse, attitude)* evasive

Élysée [elize] NM **1** *Myth* **L'É.** Elysium **2** *Pol* **(le palais de) l'É.** the Élysée palace *(the residence of the President of the French Republic)*
▪ ADJ **les champs Élysées** *Myth* the Elysian Fields; **les Champs-Élysées** *(à Paris)* the Champs Élysées

> **Élysée**
> This eighteenth-century palace near the Champs-Élysées in Paris is the official residence of the French President. The name is often used to refer to the presidency itself.

élyséen, -enne [elizeɛ̃, -ɛn] ADJ **1** *Myth* Elysian **2** *Pol* of the Élysée palace

em [ɛm] NM *Typ* em

émaciation [emasjasjɔ̃] NF emaciation

émacié [emasje] ADJ *(silhouette, visage etc)* emaciated

émacier (s') [semasje] VPR to become emaciated

émail, -aux [emaj, -o] NM enamel; *Cér* glaze; **en é.** *(casserole etc)* enamel(led)

e-mail, email [imɛl] NM e-mail

émaillage [emajaʒ] NM **1** *(des métaux précieux etc)* enamelling **2** *Cér* glazing

émailler [emaje] VT **1** *(métal etc)* to enamel; **émaillé au four** stove-enamelled **2** *Cér (porcelaine)* to glaze **3** *Fig (des fleurs, étoiles etc) (champs, ciel etc)* to stud, to spangle; **texte émaillé de métaphores** text littered with *or* full of metaphors

émailleur, -euse [emajœr, -øz] N enameller

émaillure [emajyr] NF enamelling, enamel work

émanation [emanasjɔ̃] NF emanation; **é. fétide** foul odour; *Fig* **cet ordre, é. de sa volonté ...** this order, an expression *or* a product of his will ...; **être l'é. de qch** to emanate from sth

émancipateur, -trice [emɑ̃sipatœr, -tris] ADJ liberating, emancipating
N emancipator

émancipation [emɑ̃sipasjɔ̃] NF emancipation; *Fig (de l'esprit, de la pensée etc)* liberation, freeing

émancipé [emɑ̃sipe] ADJ *(femme, populations)* emancipated

émanciper [emɑ̃sipe] VT *(peuple, esclave)* to emancipate; *(femme)* to emancipate, to liberate; *Jur (mineur)* to emancipate
VPR **s'émanciper** to become emancipated; *Fig* to become liberated; *Fig* **elle n'a jamais réussi à s'é. de l'éducation stricte qu'elle a reçue** she never managed to break free from her strict upbringing; **elle s'est drôlement émancipée** she's become very liberated

émaner [emane] VI **é. de qch** *(de fumée etc)*, *Fig (d'un ordre, du pouvoir, du charme)* to emanate from sth

émargement [emarʒəmɑ̃] NM **1** *(initiales)* initialling (in the margin); *(signature)* signature; **feuille d'é.** *(de présence)* attendance sheet; *(de paie)* pay sheet; **é. du courrier** signing for the mail **2** *(annotation)* marginal note **3** *Typ (de pages)* trimming

émarger [emarʒe] **(j'émargeai(s); n. émargeons)** VT **1** *Admin (document, compte etc)* to initial (in the margin); *(signer)* to sign; *(courrier)* to sign for **2** *(annoter) (livre etc)* to make marginal notes in **3** *Typ (pages etc)* to cut down *or* trim the margins of
VI to draw one's salary; **il émarge aux fonds secrets** he's paid out of the secret funds

émasculation [emaskylasjɔ̃] NF emasculation

émasculer [emaskyle] VT to emasculate

embâcle [ɑ̃bakl] NM *(obstruction dans un cours d'eau)* blockage; *(par un bloc de glace)* ice block *or* jam

emballage [ɑ̃balaʒ] NM **1** *(action)* packing; *(dans du papier)* wrapping; **papier d'e.** wrapping paper **2** *(boîte etc)* packaging, packing (material); *(papier)* wrapping; **emballages vides** (returned) empties **3** *Cyclisme* (final) spurt
► ► **e. bulle** blister pack; **e. consigné** returnable *or* refundable packaging; **e. gratuit** packaging free of charge; **e. perdu** nonreturnable *or* throwaway *or* disposable packaging; *Com* **e. récupérable** recoverable packaging; **e. sous vide** vacuum-packed

emballé [ɑ̃bale] ADJ *Fam* (mad) keen, enthusiastic

emballement [ɑ̃balmɑ̃] NM **1** *(de moteur)* racing; *(de cheval)* bolting; **l'e. du cheval a provoqué la mort du cavalier** the rider was killed when the horse bolted **2** *(enthousiasme soudain)* burst of enthusiasm; *(colère)* surge of anger; **prompt aux emballements** easily carried away; **pas d'e.** *(par en-*

thousiasme) let's not get carried away!; *(par colère)* let's not get worked up! **3** *Bourse* boom (**de** in); **cela aboutirait certainement à l'e. de l'économie** that would definitely lead to the economy spiralling out of control

emballer [ɑ̃bale] VT **1** *(empaqueter)* to pack; *(dans du papier)* to wrap; *(marchandises)* to package; **emballé sous vide** vacuum-packed; *Arg* **e. qn** *(arrêter)* to nick sb; *Arg* **e. une fille** *(draguer)* to pull a girl **2** *(moteur)* to race, to rev **3** *Fam (enthousiasmer)* to excite, to thrill; **ça ne m'emballe pas vraiment de les voir** I'm not exactly thrilled about seeing them *or* mad keen to see them; **être emballé par qn/qch** to be (mad) keen on sb/sth
VPR **s'emballer 1** *(d'un moteur)* to race; *(d'un cheval)* to bolt, to run away **2** *Fam (se laisser emporter) (par enthousiasme)* to get carried away, to get excited; *(par colère)* to get worked up **3** *Bourse (des cours, d'une monnaie)* to spiral out of control

emballeur, -euse [ɑ̃balœr, -øz] N packer

embarbouiller [ɑ̃barbuje] VT *(personne)* to muddle, to confuse
VPR **s'embarbouiller** to get muddled up

embarcadère [ɑ̃barkader] NM landing stage, jetty

embarcation [ɑ̃barkasjɔ̃] NF (small) boat, small craft

embardée [ɑ̃barde] NF *Aut* swerve; *Naut* yaw; **faire une e.** *(d'une voiture)* to swerve; *(d'un bateau)* to yaw

embargo [ɑ̃bargo] NM embargo; **mettre l'e. sur** to put an embargo on, to embargo; **lever l'e. sur** to raise *or* lift the embargo on; **e. économique** economic embargo

embarqué [ɑ̃barke] ADJ **1** *Aut, Aviat etc* onboard **2** *(journaliste)* embedded

embarquement [ɑ̃barkəmɑ̃] NM **1** *(action d'embarquer) Naut (de passagers)* embarkation; *(de marchandises)* shipping; *(dans un train, avion, car) (de passagers)* boarding; *(de marchandises)* loading; *Rail, Mil (de troupes)* entrainment; *Rail* **quai d'e.** departure platform; *(de chargement)* loading platform **2** *(action de s'embarquer) Naut* embarkation, boarding; *Rail, Aviat, Aut* boarding; **le vol 123 est prêt pour l'e.** flight 123 is ready for boarding *or* is now boarding; **e. immédiat porte 5** now boarding at gate 5; **carte d'e.** boarding card

embarquer [ɑ̃barke] VT **1** *Naut (passagers)* to embark; *(marchandises)* to ship; *(dans un train, avion, car) (passagers)* to take on board; *(marchandises)* to load; *Rail, Mil (troupes)* to entrain
2 *Naut* **e. de l'eau** to take in *or* ship water
3 *Fam (emmener)* to take (with one); *(voler)* to pinch, to nick; *(arrêter)* to nick
4 *Fam (entraîner) (en week-end, au cinéma)* to take *or* carry off; **son divorce l'a embarqué dans un procès sans fin** his divorce got him involved *or* embroiled in an endless lawsuit; **elle embarque toujours sa copine dans ses escapades** she always involves her friend in her escapades; **une entreprise mal embarquée** an undertaking that has got off to a bad start
VI **1** *Naut (partir)* to embark (**pour** for); **e. (sur un navire)** to go on board, to board (a ship); **e. (dans un train/un autobus)** to board *or* get on (a train/bus); **une personne supplémentaire peut e. dans ma voiture** there's room for one more in my car; **on embarque à 7h demain matin** we're leaving at 7 o'clock tomorrow morning
2 *Naut* **le bateau embarque** the boat is taking in water
VPR **s'embarquer 1** *(partir)* to embark (**pour** for); **s'e. sur un navire** to go on board *or* to board a ship

2 *Fig* **s'e. dans** to get mixed up *or* involved in; *(une entreprise, une discussion)* to embark on; **dans quoi est-ce que je me suis embarqué?** what have I got myself into?

embarras [ɑ̃bara] NM **1** *(situation difficile)* difficulty, trouble, *Fam* fix; **tirer qn d'e.** to help sb out of trouble *or* a difficulty *or Fam* a fix; **n'avoir que l'e. du choix** to be spoiled for choice; **je suis dans l'e.** I'm in trouble *or Fam* in a fix *or* a bind

2 *(difficulté financière)* **se trouver** *ou* **être dans l'e.** to be in (financial) difficulties

3 *(gêne)* embarrassment; **répondre avec e.** to reply with embarrassment, to reply embarrassedly *or* in confusion; **plonger qn dans l'e.** to embarrass sb

4 *(obstacle)* **je vous donne beaucoup d'e.** I'm putting you to a lot of bother *or* trouble; **faire des** *ou* **de l'e.** to make a fuss, to make a song and dance (**au sujet de** about); **être un e. pour les autres** to be a bother to other people

5 *Aut* **e. de voitures, e. de la circulation** traffic hold-up

6 *Méd* **e. gastrique** upset stomach

embarrassant [ɑ̃barasɑ̃] ADJ **1** *(qui encombre) (colis, valise etc)* cumbersome **2** *(qui gêne) (question, situation)* embarrassing, awkward

embarrassé [ɑ̃barase] ADJ **1** *(encombré) (table, pièce etc)* cluttered; **avoir les mains embarrassées** to have one's hands full

2 *(confus) (gestes)* hampered; *(style)* awkward; **prononciation embarrassée** unclear *or* garbled pronunciation; **explications embarrassées** involved *or* confused explanations; **dès qu'il met un costume, ses gestes sont embarrassés** he feels hampered in a suit

3 *(gêné) (personne, sourire, manière etc)* embarrassed; **je suis très e. de devoir lui dire** I am very embarrassed about having to tell him; **me voilà bien e.** I'm in a really awkward situation, I'm really embarrassed

4 *Méd* **avoir l'estomac e.** to have an upset stomach; **avoir la langue embarrassée** to have a coated *or* furred tongue

embarrasser [ɑ̃barase] VT **1** *(encombrer) (personne)* to hamper; *(table, pièce etc)* to clutter up (**de** with); **cette valise t'embarrasse, laisse-moi la porter** that suitcase is cumbersome for you, let me carry it; **je peux poser mon manteau?** il m'embarrasse can I put my coat down? it's a bit of a nuisance **2** *(gêner)* to embarrass; **tu m'embarrasses beaucoup en me demandant ce service** you're really embarrassing me *or* putting me in a very awkward situation by asking me this favour
VPR **s'embarrasser 1** *(s'encombrer)* to burden oneself (**de** with) **2** *(s'inquiéter) (toujours négativement)* to trouble *or* bother oneself (**de** with), to be concerned (**de** about); **elle ne s'embarrasse pas de scrupules** she doesn't let scruples get in her way, she's not overscrupulous **3** *(s'embrouiller)* **s'e. dans** *(vêtements)*, *Fig (mensonges etc)* to get tangled up in

embastiller [ɑ̃bastije] VT *Hist, Hum* to put in jail

embauchage [ɑ̃boʃaʒ] NM *(de travailleurs etc)* taking on, hiring, engaging

embauche [ɑ̃boʃ] NF **1** *(action)* taking on, hiring, engaging **2** *(emploi)* employment; **chercher de l'e.** to look for a job *or* for employment; **il n'y a pas d'e.** there are no jobs *or* vacancies, *Am* we're/they're/*etc* not hiring at the moment

embaucher [ɑ̃boʃe] VT *(travailleur)* to take on, to hire, to engage; **e. qn pour le poste de** *ou* **comme** to engage *or* recruit sb as; *Fam* **je**

me suis encore fait e. pour faire la vaisselle I got hired again to do the washing-up

VI to recruit, to take on *or* hire *or* engage people

embaucheur, -euse [ãboʃœr, -øz] **N** employer; **les embaucheurs ne sont pas légion de nos jours** not many companies are recruiting people *or* taking people on these days

embauchoir [ãboʃwar] **NM** shoe tree; *(pour bottes)* boot tree

embaumement [ãbommã] **NM** *(de corps)* embalming

embaumer [ãbome] **VT 1** *(corps)* to embalm **2** *(parfumer)* to perfume, to scent; *(répandre une odeur de)* to be fragrant with; **air embaumé** fragrant *or* balmy air; **l'église embaume l'encens** the church is heavy with (the scent of) incense; **l'encens embaume l'église** the scent of incense fills the church **VI** to be fragrant

embaumeur [ãbomœr] **NM** *(de corps)* embalmer

embéguiner (s') [sãbegine] **VPR** *Vieilli* **s'e. de qn** to become infatuated with sb

embellie [ãbɛli] **NF** *(éclaircie)* bright spell; *Naut* calm spell, lull; *Fig (de l'économie, d'une situation etc)* improvement; **courte e.** bright interval

embellir [ãbɛlir] **VT** *(pièce, parc etc)* to make (more) attractive; *(personne)* to make look (more) beautiful, to improve the looks of; *Fig (histoire, vérité etc)* to improve on, to embellish; **le mariage/la maternité l'embellit** married life/motherhood suits her **VI** to grow (more) beautiful

embellissement [ãbɛlismã] **NM 1** *(fait de rendre plus beau) (d'une pièce, d'un parc)* improvement; *Fig (d'une histoire, de la vérité etc)* embellishment; **e. de qn** improving sb's looks **2** *(décoration)* embellishment, embellishing touch; **il faudra apporter des embellissements à l'appartement** the flat needs improving *or* needs a few embellishing touches

emberlificoter [ãbɛrlifikɔte] *Fam* **VT 1** *(empêtrer)* to tangle up, to entangle **2** *(duper)* to take in **VPR s'emberlificoter s'e. dans** *(vêtements), Fig (mensonges etc)* to get tangled up in

embêtant [ãbɛtã] **ADJ** *Fam (personne, problème etc)* annoying; *(situation)* awkward; **c'est drôlement e.!** it's really annoying!

embêtement [ãbɛtmã] **NM** *Fam (agacement)* annoyance; *(souci)* worry, trouble; **faire des embêtements à qn** to cause *or* make trouble for sb

embêter [ãbete] *Fam* **VT** *(agacer)* to annoy; *(ennuyer)* to bore; **ça m'embête d'y aller** *(ça m'ennuie)* I can't be bothered going *or* to go; *(ça me gêne)* I wish I didn't have to go; **ça m'embête d'arriver en retard** I don't like being late; **je suis drôlement embêté avec ma fille** I'm having a lot of trouble with my daughter **VPR s'embêter** to be/get bored (stiff); *Iron* **je vois que tu ne t'embêtes pas!** I see you don't do badly for yourself!; **s'e. avec** *(des histoires d'argent, des scrupules, sa belle-mère etc)* to bother oneself about *or* with

emblée (d') [dãble] **ADV** directly, right away, straight off; *(réussir)* at the first attempt

emblématique [ãblematik] **ADJ** emblematic(al); *Fig* symbolic

emblème [ãblɛm] **NM** *(insigne)* emblem, device; *Fig (symbole)* symbol; *Mktg* **e. de marque** brand mark

embobiner [ãbɔbine] **VT** *Fam (duper)* to take in; *(enjôler)* to get round; **ne vous laissez pas e.** don't let yourself be had *or* taken in

---

emboîtable [ãbwatabl] **ADJ** *(chaise)* stacking, stackable; *(boîte, table etc)* that fits into a nest

emboîtage [ãbwataʒ] **NM 1** *(action d'emboîter) (de chaises)* stacking; *Constr (de tuyaux, poutres etc)* jointing **2** *(d'un livre)* casing; *(étui d'un livre)* slipcase

emboîtement [ãbwatmã] **NM** *(de chaises)* stacking; *Constr (de tuyaux, poutres etc)* jointing

emboîter [ãbwate] **VT 1** *(assembler) (morceaux, pièces etc)* to fit together *or* into each other; *(boîtes, tables etc)* to nest; *(chaises)* to stack; *Constr (tuyaux, poutres etc)* to joint; **e. le pas à qn** to follow close on sb's heels; *Fig* to follow suit, to follow sb's lead **2** *(envelopper)* **e. un livre** to case a book **VPR s'emboîter** *(de pièces, morceaux etc)* to fit together *or* into each other; *(de boîtes, tables etc)* to nest; *(de chaises)* to stack

embolie [ãbɔli] **NF** *Méd* embolism; **e. gazeuse/pulmonaire** air/pulmonary embolism; **e. cérébrale** clot on the brain, *Spéc* cerebral embolism

embonpoint [ãbɔ̃pwɛ̃] **NM** stoutness, corpulence; **avoir de l'e.** to be stout *or* corpulent

embouché [ãbuʃe] **ADJ** *Fam* **mal e.** *(grossier)* foul-mouthed; *(de mauvaise humeur)* in a foul mood

emboucher [ãbuʃe] **VT 1** *(trompette etc)* to put to one's mouth; *Fig Vieilli* **e. la trompette** to trumpet the news **2 e. un cheval** to put the bit in a horse's mouth

embouchure [ãbuʃyr] **NF 1** *(d'une trompette, sarbacane etc)* mouthpiece **2** *(d'un sac, vase)* opening, mouth **3** *(d'un fleuve)* mouth

embourber (s') [sãburbe] **VPR 1** *(d'une voiture)* to get stuck (in the mud) **2** *Fig Péj* to flounder, to get bogged down; **il s'est embourbé dans des explications compliquées** he got bogged down in complicated explanations

embourgeoisement [ãburʒwazmã] **NM** attainment of middle-class respectability; *(d'un quartier)* gentrification

embourgeoiser (s') [sãburʒwaze] **VPR** to become bourgeois *or* middle-class; *(d'un quartier)* to become gentrified

embout [ãbu] **NM** *(d'un parapluie, d'une canne etc)* ferrule, tip; *(d'un câble)* terminal; *(d'un tuyau)* nozzle; *(d'un tirant, fil etc)* connector

embouteillage [ãbutɛjaʒ] **NM 1** *(encombrement)* (traffic) hold-up, traffic jam, *Fam* snarl-up; **tomber dans les embouteillages** to get caught in traffic **2** *(de navires)* bottling up

embouteiller [ãbutɛje] **VT 1** *(rue, autoroute etc)* to block (up), to jam (up); *(circulation)* to tie up, to hold up, *Fam* to snarl up; **circulation embouteillée** congested traffic; **route embouteillée** road blocked with traffic **2** *(navires)* to bottle up

emboutir [ãbutir] **VT 1** *(véhicule)* to bash in; **tout l'arrière de ma voiture est embouti** the entire rear end of my car is bashed in; **je me suis fait e. par mon voisin** my neighbour crashed into me **2** *(métal)* to stamp, to press; **châssis en tôle emboutie** pressed steel frame **3** *(arrondir)* to emboss

emboutissage [ãbutisaʒ] **NM 1** *(de voitures)* collision; **l'e. d'une voiture par un autobus** the collision between a bus and a car **2** *(de métaux)* stamping, pressing **3** *(fait d'arrondir)* embossing

embranchement [ãbrãʃmã] **NM 1** *(croisement) (d'une route, d'un rail, d'une conduite etc)* junction; *(bifurcation) (sur une route)* fork **2** *Rail* branch line **3** *Biol* sub-kingdom, *Spéc* phylum

---

embrancher [ãbrãʃe] **VT** *(route, conduite etc)* to connect up, to join up (**à** to) **VPR s'embrancher** to join (up) (**sur** with)

embrasement [ãbrazmã] **NM 1** *Arch (incendie)* conflagration **2** *Litt* **l'e. des cieux au soleil couchant** the blazing sunset **3** *Litt (agitation)* agitation, turmoil; **il ne pouvait pas lutter contre l'e. de son cœur** he could not fight against the love that flared up in his heart

embraser [ãbraze] **VT** *Litt* **1** *(maison, champs etc)* to set ablaze **2** *(d'un coucher de soleil)* to set aglow **3** *Fig (imagination)* to fire; *(foule)* to fire, to set aglow, *Péj* to inflame **VPR s'embraser 1** *(prendre feu)* to blaze up **2** *(rougeoyer)* to glow **3** *Fig Litt* **dès que je l'ai vu, mon cœur s'est embrasé** the mere sight of him kindled a flame; **l'imagination des jeunes romantiques s'embrase trop vite** young romantics have an imagination that is too readily inflamed; **quand j'entendais des histoires sur l'Afrique, mon imagination s'embrasait** hearing stories about Africa fired my imagination; **les esprits s'embrasaient dans ces réunions** the meetings had an inflammatory effect on those present

embrassade [ãbrasad] **NF** embrace, hug; **ce furent des embrassades à n'en pas finir lorsqu'ils se retrouvèrent** they hugged and kissed for ages when they met again

embrasse [ãbras] **NF** *(d'un rideau)* tieback

embrasser [ãbrase] **VT 1** *(donner un baiser à)* to kiss; **je t'embrasse de tout mon cœur** *(dans une lettre)* with fondest love; **e. qn sur la bouche/la joue** to kiss sb on the mouth/cheek
2 *Vieilli (étreindre)* to embrace
3 *(adopter) (croyance, religion, doctrine, théorie)* to embrace; *(carrière)* to take up; *(cause)* to embrace, to take up; **e. la carrière diplomatique** to enter the diplomatic service
4 *(contenir) (sujet, période, cas de figure)* to embrace, to cover, to take in; **il faut e. tous les problèmes** we have to look at all the problems; **le cours embrassera l'ensemble du moyen âge** the course will cover the whole of the Middle Ages; **e. qch du regard** to take sth in at a glance; **il embrassa toute sa famille d'un regard satisfait** he cast a satisfied eye over his family
VPR s'embrasser to kiss (each other)

> Il faut noter que le verbe anglais **to embrace** ne signifie jamais **donner un baiser**.

embrasure [ãbrazyr] **NF 1** *Constr* embrasure; **l'e. de la porte/fenêtre** the door/window recess **2** *Mil (dans un mur)* embrasure; *Naut* gun port

embrayage [ãbrɛjaʒ] **NM 1** *(action) Aut* letting in *or* engaging the clutch; *Tech (de pièces de moteur)* coupling, engaging **2** *(pièce) Aut* clutch; *Tech* coupling (gear); **pédale d'e.** clutch pedal
▸▸ **e. à cônes** cone clutch; **e. à crabot** dog clutch; **e. à diaphragme** diaphragm spring *or* DS clutch; **e. électromagnétique** magnetic clutch; **e. à friction** friction clutch; **e. hydrodynamique** fluid clutch; **e. monodisque** single-plate *or* disc clutch; **e. multidisque** multi-disc clutch pack; **e. de prise directe** lock-up clutch

embrayer [ãbrɛje] (**j'embraie, j'embraye, n. embrayons; j'embraierai, j'embrayerai**) **VT** *Tech (pièces de moteur)* to couple, to engage
VI 1 *Aut* to let in *or* engage the clutch **2** *Fam (commencer à parler de)* **e. sur** to get going *or* started on; **on pourrait peut-être e. sur un autre sujet** maybe we could change the subject **3** *Can Fam (se dépêcher)* **embraye!** get a move on!, hurry up!

embrigadement [ɑ̃brigadmɑ̃] NM *(de supporters etc)* recruitment (**dans** to, into)

embrigader [ɑ̃brigade] VT *(supporter etc)* to recruit (**dans** to, into)

embringuer [ɑ̃brɛ̃ge] *Fam* VT **e. qn dans qch** to get sb mixed up in sth; **il ne veut pas se laisser e. dans cette histoire** he doesn't want to get mixed up in it

VPR **s'embringuer** to get mixed up (**dans** in)

embrocation [ɑ̃brɔkasjɔ̃] NF *Méd* embrocation

embrocher [ɑ̃brɔʃe] VT **1** *Culin (viande etc)* to put on a/the spit **2** *Fam* **e. qn** *(d'un coup d'épée)* to skewer sb

embrouillage [ɑ̃bruja ʒ] NM = **embrouillement**

embrouillamini [ɑ̃brujamini] NM *Fam* confusion, muddle; **sa vie sentimentale est un tel e. que ...** his love life is so complicated *or* involved that ...; **comment veux-tu que je m'y retrouve dans cet e. de papiers?** how can I be expected to know what I'm doing when these papers are in such a muddle?

embrouillé [ɑ̃bruje] ADJ **1** *(fils)* tangled **2** *Fig (papiers, lettres etc)* mixed up, in a mess; *(situation, idées, arguments etc)* confused, muddled; *(style, affaire)* complicated, involved

embrouillement [ɑ̃brujmɑ̃] NM **1** *(de fils) (action)* tangling; *(état)* tangle **2** *Fig (d'une situation, d'idées etc) (action)* muddling, confusing; *(état)* muddle, confusion; **l'e. de la situation est tel que ...** the situation is so confused that ...; **cela a provoqué un tel e. dans son esprit que ...** this confused him so much that ...

embrouiller [ɑ̃bruje] VT **1** *(fils)* to tangle (up) **2** *Fig (personne, situation, idées etc)* to confuse, to muddle (up); **il a embrouillé la situation encore plus** he confused the situation even further, he made the situation even more confused; **il a réussi à m'e. ou à e. mes idées** he managed to confuse me; *Fam* **ni vu ni connu je t'embrouille** hey presto; *Fam* **... alors qu'il était avec une autre: ni vu ni connu je t'embrouille** ... while all the time he was with another woman – talk about a con artist *or* about being conned!

VPR **s'embrouiller** *(d'une personne, d'une situation, d'idées etc)* to get muddled (up) *or* confused; **je me suis embrouillé dans mes rendez-vous** I got my appointments muddled, I got into a muddle with my appointments

embroussaillé [ɑ̃brusaje] ADJ *(sentier, jardin, dunes etc)* covered with *or* in bushes; **cheveux embroussaillés** tousled hair; **le jardin est complètement e.** the garden is completely overgrown

embrumé [ɑ̃bryme] ADJ *(temps)* misty; *(horizon)* hazy; *Fig (esprit) (par l'alcool)* fuddled, fogged; **il avait l'esprit e. par toutes ces paroles** all that talking had left him feeling less than clear-headed

embrumer [ɑ̃bryme] VT *(paysage, ville etc)* to cover with mist *or* haze; *Fig (de l'alcool) (esprit)* to fuddle, to fog; **tous ces discours lui ont embrumé l'esprit** his/her mind is less than clear after all those speeches

VPR **s'embrumer** *(du ciel)* to become misty *or* hazy; *(du paysage, d'une ville, une île)* to become covered with mist *or* haze; *Fig (des idées)* to become foggy *or* cloudy; **avec chaque verre, mon esprit s'embrumait un peu plus** with each glass, my brain became a little more fogged

embruns [ɑ̃brœ̃] NMPL spray, spindrift

embryologie [ɑ̃brijɔlɔʒi] NF *Biol* embryology

embryologique [ɑ̃brijɔlɔʒik] ADJ *Biol* embryologic(al)

embryologiste [ɑ̃brijɔlɔʒist] N *Biol* embryologist

embryon [ɑ̃brijɔ̃] NM embryo; *Fig* **un e. de roman/dissertation** an embryonic novel/ dissertation; **ne nous emballons pas, ce n'est encore qu'un e. de projet** don't let's get carried away, it's still just a vague plan

embryonnaire [ɑ̃brijɔnɛr] ADJ *Biol* embryonic; **sac e.** embryo sac; *Fig* **à l'état e.** in an embryonic state, in embryo; **le projet en est encore à un stade e.** the project is still at a very early stage *or* in its very early stages

embryotomie [ɑ̃brijɔtɔmi] NF *Obst* embryotomy

embu [ɑ̃by] *Beaux-Arts* ADJ *(couleur, tableau)* flat, dull

NM *(d'une couleur)* flatness, dullness

embûches [ɑ̃byʃ] NFPL traps; **tendre** *ou* **dresser des e. à qn** to set traps for sb; **sujet plein d'e.** tricky subject; **la vie est semée d'e.** life is full of pitfalls

embuer [ɑ̃bɥe] VT *(de la vapeur etc) (verre etc)* to mist up, to cloud; **yeux embués de larmes** eyes dimmed *or* clouded with tears; **pare-brise embué** misted(-up) windscreen

embuscade [ɑ̃byskad] NF ambush; **dresser** *ou* **tendre une e. à qn** to lay *or* set an ambush for sb; **attirer qn dans une e.** to ambush *or* waylay sb; **se tenir en e.** to lie in ambush *or* in wait; **tomber dans une e.** to be ambushed *or* waylaid

embusqué [ɑ̃byske] NM **1** *Mil* shirker, dodger **2** *Rugby* **les embusqués** the back row of forwards

embusquer [ɑ̃byske] *Mil* VT **1** *(placer en embuscade)* to place in ambush **2** *(affecter loin du front)* to find a cushy posting for

VPR **s'embusquer 1** *(se mettre en embuscade)* to lie in ambush **2** *(se faire affecter loin du front)* to get a cushy posting

éméché [emeʃe] ADJ *Fam* slightly the worse for wear *or* drink, tipsy

émeraude [emrod] NF *Minér* emerald

NM *(couleur)* emerald green

ADJ INV emerald green

émergence [emɛrʒɑ̃s] NF emergence; **c'est là que se trouve le point d'é. de la source** the spring emerges here; **on assistait à l'é. de nouvelles théories politiques** new political theories were emerging *or* were coming to the fore

émergent [emɛrʒɑ̃] ADJ emergent, emerging

émerger [emɛrʒe] VI **(j'émergeai(s); n. émergeons) 1** to emerge (**de** from) **2** *Fig (de la vérité, d'un fait etc)* to emerge, to come to light; *(d'un nouvel écrivain etc)* to emerge; *Fam (d'une personne)* to come to; *Fam* **le dimanche, il n'émerge jamais avant midi** he never surfaces before noon on Sundays

émeri [emri] NM emery; **papier** *ou* **toile (d')é.** emery paper; **bouchon à l'é.** (ground glass) stopper; **bouché à l'é.** *(flasque)* stoppered; *Fam (personne)* bone-headed

émerillon [emrijɔ̃] NM *(oiseau)* merlin

émeriser [emrize] VT to coat with emery

émérite [emerit] ADJ **1** *(expérimenté) (artisan, ouvrier, médecin etc)* skilled, experienced **2** *(professeur)* emeritus

émerveillement [emɛrvɛjmɑ̃] NM **1** *(enchantement)* wonder, amazement **2** *(chose)* amazing *or* wonderful thing; **c'était un é.** it was amazing *or* wonderful; **un é. perpétuel** a constant source of amazement

émerveiller [emɛrvɛje] VT *(enchanter)* to fill with wonder, to amaze; **être émerveillé par** to marvel at, to be filled with wonder by

VPR **s'émerveiller s'é. de** *ou* **devant** *(s'étonner de)* to be amazed by; *(s'enchanter de)* to marvel at; **la jeunesse s'émerveille de pas grand-**

chose it doesn't take much to amaze young people

émétique [emetik] ADJ, NM emetic

émetteur, -trice [emetœr, -tris] ADJ **1** *Fin (banque, organisme)* issuing; **é. de cartes** card issuer **2** *Radio* transmitting; **poste é.** transmitter; **station émettrice** transmitting *or* broadcasting station

N *(de billets, d'actions etc)* issuer; *(d'un chèque)* drawer

NM **1** *TV, Radio* transmitter; **é. monophonique/stéréo** monoaural/stereo transmitter; **é. terrestre** ground transmitter **2** *Phys (de radiation, son etc)* emitter

émetteur-récepteur, *pl* **émetteurs-récepteurs** NM *Radio* transmitter-receiver, transceiver; **é. (portatif)** walkie-talkie; **é. additionnel** transverter

émettre [emɛtr] *(conj like* **mettre***)* VT **1** *(cri)* to give, to utter, to emit; *(rot, soupir)* to give; *(son)* to make, to emit; *(fumée)* to give off, to emit; *(chaleur)* to give out *or* off, *(lumière)* to give (out); **la seiche émet de l'encre** the cuttlefish ejects ink; **mon ordinateur émet un bruit bizarre** my computer is making a funny noise

2 *Fig (opinion, avis)* to voice, to express; *(objection)* to voice, to raise, to put forward; *(idée)* to voice, to put forward

3 *Radio, TV (programme)* to transmit, to broadcast; *(onde, signal)* to send out

4 *Fin (chèque, nouveau billet etc)* to issue; *(prêt)* to float; *Jur (fausse monnaie)* to utter; *Fin* **é. un emprunt** to issue loan stock, to make a bond issue; *Fin* **é. une lettre de crédit** to open a letter of credit

VI *Radio, TV* to transmit, to broadcast

émeu, *pl* **émeus** [emø] NM *(oiseau)* emu

émeute [emøt] NF riot, outbreak, disturbance; **tourner à l'é.** to turn into a riot; **de terribles émeutes ont éclaté dans tout le pays** dreadful riots *or* rioting broke out throughout the country

émeutier, -ière [emøtje, -jɛr] N rioter

émietter [emjete] VT **1** *(pain, fromage, roche etc)* to crumble (up) **2** *Fig (domaine, empire etc)* to break up; *(pouvoir)* to erode, to eat away at; *(fortune)* to fritter away, to squander; *(énergie, forces)* to waste

VPR **s'émietter 1** *(du pain, fromage, d'une roche etc)* to crumble **2** *Fig (d'un domaine, un empire, un pouvoir etc)* to crumble away; **sa fortune s'émiettait au fil des années** his fortune disappeared little by little over the years

émigrant, -ante [emigrɑ̃, -ɑ̃t] ADJ migrant

N emigrant

émigration [emigrasjɔ̃] NF **1** emigration; **pays à forte/faible é.** country with high/ low emigration **2** *Zool* migration

émigré, -ée [emigre] N *Pol, Écon* migrant; *Hist* (political) exile, émigré; **travailleurs émigrés** migrant workers

émigrer [emigre] VI **1** to emigrate **2** *Zool* to migrate

émincé [emɛ̃se] NM *Culin (plat)* = thinly sliced meat or poultry in sauce; *(tranche)* thin slice *(of meat)*

émincer [emɛ̃se] VT **(j'éminçai(s); n. émin- çons)** *(de la viande, des légumes etc)* to slice thinly

éminemment [eminamɑ̃] ADV eminently

éminence [eminɑ̃s] NF **1** *(géographique)* hill, *Litt* eminence **2** *Anat* eminence; **l'é. du pouce** the ball of the thumb **3** *Rel* **son É. le cardinal** his Eminence the Cardinal; *Fig* **l'É. grise** the power behind the throne, the eminence grise **4** *Arch (excellence)* eminence

éminent [eminɑ̃] ADJ *(personne)* eminent, distinguished; **il nous a rendu d'éminents services** he rendered us outstanding service

émir [emir] NM emir

émirat [emira] NM emirate; **les Émirats arabes unis** the United Arab Emirates

émissaire [emisɛr] ADJ **bouc é.** scapegoat
NM **1** (envoyé) emissary **2** (d'un lac) outlet, drainage channel

émission [emisjɔ̃] NF **1** (de son, fluide etc) emission; (de sons, cris etc) utterance; (de chaleur, lumière) emission, giving out; **tuyau d'é.** discharge pipe
2 Radio, TV (action) transmission, broadcasting; (programme) programme, Am program, broadcast, show; **poste d'é.** transmitter; **station d'é.** transmitting or broadcasting station; **une é. pour les enfants** a children's programme or broadcast
3 Électron é. **électronique** electron emission; Nucl é. **de particules** particle emission
4 Fin (de billets de banque, timbres-poste etc) issue; Bourse é. **boursière** ou **d'actions** share issue; Bourse é. **de conversion** conversion issue; Bourse é. **d'actions gratuites** scrip issue; Banque é. **fiduciaire** fiduciary or note issue; Bourse é. **obligataire** ou **d'obligations** bond issue; é. **par séries** block issues
5 Jur uttering
▸▸ Radio, TV é. **en différé** recorded broadcast; é. **diffusée simultanément** simultaneous broadcast; é. **en direct** live broadcast; é. **éducative** educational programme; é. **pour enfants** children's television; é. **pour enfants d'âge pré-scolaire** pre-school programme; é. **d'expression directe** live debate programme; é. **d'expression directe (de formation politique)** party political broadcast; é. **en extérieur** outside broadcast, Spéc OB; é. **d'informations** news programme; é. **de jeux (télévisés)** (TV) game(s) show; é. **magazine** magazine programme; é. **payante** premium programme; é. **pilote** pilot; é. **en public** audience show; é. **de radio** radio programme; é. **radiotélévisée** simulcast; é. **relayée** relay; é. **de reportage** feature programme; **émissions scolaires** schools broadcasting; **émissions de service public** public-service broadcasting; é. **sportive** sports programme; é. **de télévision** television programme; é. **tout public** family programme; é. **de variétés** variety programme or show

emmagasinage [ɑ̃magazinaʒ] NM (de marchandises) storage, warehousing; (d'électricité, de chaleur) storing up, accumulation

emmagasiner [ɑ̃magazine] VT (marchandises) to store, to warehouse; (électricité, chaleur) to store up, to accumulate; Fig (souvenirs, connaissances) to store up

emmailloter [ɑ̃majɔte] VT **1** (membre etc) to wrap (up), to swathe; **l'infirmière m'a emmailloté la cheville dans un bandage** the nurse wrapped a bandage round my ankle; **bien emmailloté dans des couvertures** well wrapped up in blankets **2** (langer) (nourisson) to swaddle

emmanchement [ɑ̃mɑ̃ʃmɑ̃] NM **1** fitting or fixing of a handle (**d'un outil** (on) to a tool) **2** (d'une pièce à une autre) fitting; **cela rendait l'e. des deux pièces impossible** it made it impossible to fit the two parts together

emmancher [ɑ̃mɑ̃ʃe] VT **1** (outil) to fit or fix a handle to **2** (tuyaux) to fit together, to joint; (pièce dans une autre) to fit (**dans** to) **3** Fig Fam (travail, affaire etc) to get started on
VPR **s'emmancher** (de deux pièces) to fit together; Fig Fam **bien/mal s'e.** to get off to a good/bad start

emmanchure [ɑ̃mɑ̃ʃyr] NF **1** armhole; **la veste me serre aux emmanchures** the jacket's too tight at the armpits **2** Belg (combine) scheme, trick

emmêlement [ɑ̃mɛlmɑ̃] NM (de fils, laine etc) tangling; (état) tangle; Fig (de faits, d'une histoire) mixing up, muddling; (état) mix-up, muddle

emmêler [ɑ̃mɛle] VT (fil, cheveux etc) to tangle; Fig (faits, histoire) to mix up, to muddle
VPR **s'emmêler** (de fils, cheveux etc) to become tangled, to get in a tangle; Fig (de faits, d'une histoire) to become mixed up or muddled, to get into a muddle; Fam **s'e. les pédales** to get all mixed up or confused

emménagement [ɑ̃menaʒmɑ̃] NM moving in; **nous avons dû remettre notre e. à plus tard** we had to put off moving in or we had to put our move off to later; **comment s'est passé ton e.?** how did the move go?

emménager [ɑ̃menaʒe] (**j'emménageai(s)**) VI to move in; **e. dans** to move into
VT (meubles, personne) to move in; **e. qn/ qch dans** to move sb/sth into

emmener [ɑ̃mne] VT (**j'emmène; j'emmènerai**) **1** (prendre avec soi) (enfant etc) to take (with one); (prisonnier etc) to lead or take away; Fam (objet) to bring; **je vous emmène avec moi** I'm taking you with me; **je t'emmène passer le week-end à Florence** I'm taking you (off) to Florence for the weekend; **cette année nous emmenons les enfants** we're taking the children away this year; **il m'a emmené à l'aéroport en voiture** he drove me to the airport; **e. promener qn** to take sb for a walk
2 (entraîner) (soldats, équipe de sport, peloton etc) to lead; (sprint) to lead (in); **les co-équipiers se sont relayés pour e. leur leader** the other members of the team took turns acting as pacemaker for their leader
3 (transporter) (d'un bateau, d'un avion etc) (passagers) to take, to carry

emment(h)al [emɛtal] NM (fromage) Emment(h)al (cheese)

emmerdant [ɑ̃mɛrdɑ̃] ADJ Arg (qui contrarie) damned or Br bloody annoying; (qui ennuie) damned or Br bloody boring; **ce que tu peux être e.!** you can be a real pain (in the bum or neck or Am butt)!

emmerde [ɑ̃mɛrd] NF Arg = **emmerdement**

emmerdement [ɑ̃mɛrd(ə)mɑ̃] NM Arg **emmerdements** (damned) bother, trouble; **depuis le début de l'année, je ne lui arrive que des emmerdements** he's had a helluva time of it since the beginning of the year; **pour les emmerdements, j'ai été servi aujourd'hui!** I've had a bloody awful day!; **un e.** a damned or Br bloody nuisance; **j'ai encore eu un e. avec la bagnole/les flics** I had trouble with the car/the police again; **tu parles d'un e.!** what an absolute pain (in the neck or bum or Am butt)!

emmerder [ɑ̃mɛrde] Arg VT **1 e. qn** (contrarier) to get up sb's nose or on sb's nerves; (ennuyer) to bore sb stiff or silly or rigid; **ça m'emmerde mais il va vraiment falloir que j'y aille** it's a real pain (in the neck or bum or Am butt), but I'm going to have to go; **arrête d'e. ta sœur!** stop annoying your sister! **2** (comme défi) **dis-lui que je l'emmerde!** tell him from me he can (go and) get stuffed!; **toi je t'emmerde!** get stuffed!, Vulg fuck you!; **moi, les gens, je les emmerde!** I don't give a shit or Vulg a fuck what people think!
VPR **s'emmerder 1** (s'ennuyer) to be bored stiff or silly or rigid; **qu'est-ce qu'on s'emmerde en colonie de vacances/avec eux** holiday camp is/they're bloody boring!; Iron **tu ne t'emmerdes pas!** you're not doing badly for yourself!; (tu as du culot) you've got some or a helluva nerve! **2** (se donner du mal) **je me suis vraiment emmerdé à monter ces étagères** it was a real pain putting up those shelves; **je ne me suis pas emmerdée à faire le ménage pour que …** I didn't go to all the

bother or trouble of doing the housework just so that …; **tu t'emmerdes beaucoup pour pas grand-chose** you're putting yourself to a lot of trouble for nothing

emmerdeur, -euse [ɑ̃mɛrdœr, -øz] N Arg (qui contrarie) damned or Br bloody nuisance, pain (in the neck or bum or Am butt); (qui ennuie) helluva or Br bloody bore

emmitoufler [ɑ̃mitufle] VT to wrap or muffle up (**dans, de** in)
VPR **s'emmitoufler** to get muffled up (**dans, de** in); **tâche de bien t'e.** try to wrap up well

emmurer [ɑ̃myre] VT (victime) to immure, to wall in or up; (d'une chute de pierres) (mineurs) to trap

émoi [emwa] NM (trouble) emotion, agitation; (plaisir) excitement; (anxiété) anxiety; **être (tout) en é.** (troublé) to be all excited or all in a flutter; **toute la ville était en é.** the whole town was in a commotion; **non sans é.** in some agitation

émollient [emɔljɑ̃] ADJ, NM emollient

émoluments [emɔlymɑ̃] NMPL emoluments, remuneration; **percevoir des é.** to receive payment

émondage [emɔ̃daʒ] NM **1** (d'un arbre) pruning, trimming **2** (de graines) cleaning

émonder [emɔ̃de] VT (arbre), Fig (livre, texte) to prune, to trim

émondeur, -euse [emɔ̃dœr, -øz] N pruner

émondoir [emɔ̃dwar] NM pruning hook

émoticon [emɔtikɔ̃] NM Ordinat smiley, emoticon

émotif, -ive [emɔtif, -iv] ADJ (personne, réaction etc) emotional
N emotional person

émotion [emɔsjɔ̃] NF emotion; Fam (inquiétude) fright, shock; **vive é.** strong emotion; (exaltation) excitement, thrill; **le meurtre de l'enfant a provoqué une vive é.** people were shocked by the child's murder; **l'atterrissage mouvementé a provoqué une vive é. parmi les passagers** the bumpy landing frightened the passengers; **ressentir une vive é.** (attendrissement) to be greatly moved; (exaltation) to be thrilled; (peur) to be very frightened; **parler avec é.** to speak emotionally; Fam **j'ai eu une é.** I've had a fright or shock; Fam **tu nous as vraiment donné des émotions** you gave us a real fright, you really frightened us

émotionnel, -elle [emɔsjɔnɛl] ADJ Psy (réaction etc) emotional

émotionner [emɔsjɔne] VT Fam to affect

émotivité [emɔtivite] NF emotionalism; **être d'une trop grande é.** to be too emotional

émoulu [emuly] ADJ Fam **jeune homme frais é. du collège/de son université** young man fresh from school/university

émoussé [emuse] ADJ (pointe, lame) blunt; Fig (sentiment, qualité etc) diminished; **une patience émoussée par le temps** patience diminished or worn thin by time; **il a l'appétit é. par la maladie** illness has blunted or taken the edge off his appetite

émousser [emuse] VT (lame, pointe, crayon, angle) to blunt; Fig (sens, passions etc) to dull, to blunt; (appétit) to take the edge off; **le temps a émoussé sa résistance** time has lessened or worn away his resistance
VPR **s'émousser** (d'une lame, pointe) to get blunt; Fig (des sens, passions) to become blunted or dulled; **mon appétit s'est émoussé depuis que je suis malade** I've not had much appetite or I haven't felt much like eating since I fell ill

émoustillant [emustijɑ̃] ADJ arousing, titillating

émoustiller [emustije] VT to arouse, to titillate

émouvant [emuvã] ADJ *(attendrissant)* moving, touching; *(bouleversant)* stirring, thrilling

émouvoir [emuvwar] *(pp* **ému***; otherwise conj like* **mouvoir)** VT *(toucher)* to move, to touch; *(inquiéter)* to upset; **é. qn (jusqu')aux larmes** to move sb to tears; **cela ne m'émeut pas le moins du monde** that doesn't upset me in the least; **encore tout ému de la rencontre** still very upset by the meeting; **facile à é.** emotional, easily moved *or* upset; **ça n'a pas eu l'air de l'é.** he seemed quite unsympathetic
▪ VPR **s'émouvoir** *(se troubler)* to be touched *or* moved; **rester sans s'é. à la vue de leur malheur** to remain unmoved by their plight; **ce qu'il me déclara sans s'é. le moins du monde** which he announced to me with perfect composure; *Fam* **pas de quoi s'é.** it's nothing to get worked up about

empaffé [ãpafe] NM *Vulg* dickhead, prick, *Br* wanker

empaillage [ãpajaʒ] NM **1** *(d'animaux morts)* stuffing **2** *(de plantes)* mulching with straw **3** *(de chaises)* bottoming with straw

empaillé, -ée [ãpaje] ADJ *(oiseau, renard etc)* stuffed; *Fam* **avoir l'air e.** to be self-conscious *or* awkward

empailler [ãpaje] VT **1** *(animal mort)* to stuff **2** *(plantes)* to mulch with straw **3** *(chaise)* to bottom with straw
▪ VPR **s'empailler** *Fam (se quereller violemment)* to lay into each other

empailleur, -euse [ãpajœr, -øz] N *(d'animaux)* taxidermist

empalement [ãpalmã] NM impalement

empaler [ãpale] VT to impale
▪ VPR **s'empaler** to impale oneself

empanaché [ãpanaʃe] ADJ plumed, decorated with plumes; *Fig* **style e.** pompous *or* flowery style

empannage [ãpanaʒ] NM *Naut* gybe

empanner [ãpane] VI *Naut* to gybe

empapaouter [ãpapaute] VT *Vulg* to bugger; **va te faire e.!** go to hell!, *Br* bugger off!, sod off!

empaquetage [ãpaktaʒ] NM packing (up)

empaqueter [ãpakte] VT (**j'empaquette; j'empaquetterai**) to pack up, to package

empaqueteur, -euse [ãpaktœr, -øz] N packer

emparer (s') [sãpare] VPR **s'emparer de** *(ville, otage, butin, pouvoir)* to seize; *(téléphone, porte-monnaie etc)* to grab (hold of), to seize; *Sport (ballon)* to take possession of, to get hold of; *(d'un doute, une obsession, de la jalousie etc) (personne)* to take hold of; **depuis que cette idée s'est emparée de mon esprit** since the idea took hold of me; **la presse s'est emparée de cette histoire** the press got hold of the story; **il s'est emparé de ce prétexte pour partir** he used it as a pretext to leave

empâté [ãpate] ADJ *(visage)* fleshy, bloated

empâtement [ãpatmã] NM **1** *(de la volaille)* fattening (up) **2** *(d'une personne, d'un visage)* bloating; *(d'un corps)* bloating, thickening **3** *Beaux-Arts* impasto

empâter [ãpate] VT **1** *(engraisser) (volaille)* to fatten (up) **2** *(épaissir) (corps)* to bloat, to thicken; *(visage)* to bloat, to coarsen; **la vie à la campagne l'a empâtée** she has put on weight in the country **3** *(couvrir d'une pâte) (langue)* to coat, to fur up; *Beaux-Arts* to impaste
▪ VPR **s'empâter 1** *(d'une personne, d'un corps)* to become bloated; *(d'un visage)* to coarsen; **elle s'est empâtée depuis quelque temps** she has put on weight recently **2** *(de la langue)* to become coated, to fur up

empattement [ãpatmã] NM **1** *(d'une voiture)* wheelbase **2** *Typ* serif; **sans e.** sans serif **3** *(d'un mur)* footing

empatter [ãpate] VT *(mur)* to give footing to

empaumer [ãpome] VT **1** *(au jeu de paume) (attraper)* to catch in the palm of the hand; *(frapper)* to strike with the palm of the hand **2** *Fam Vieilli* **se laisser** *ou* **se faire e.** to be tricked *or* taken in **3** *(d'un magicien etc) (carte, pièce etc)* to palm

empêché [ãpeʃe] ADJ *(retenu)* held up, detained

empêchement [ãpeʃmã] NM **1** *(contretemps)* **j'ai eu un e.** I got held up *or* detained, something came up at the last minute; **en cas d'e., veuillez prévenir 24 heures à l'avance** please give us 24 hours notice if you cannot keep the appointment; **en cas d'e., nous remettrons la réunion à la semaine suivante** if anybody can't make the meeting, we'll postpone it to the following week **2** *Jur* **e. de mariage** impediment to marriage

empêcher [ãpeʃe] VT **1** *(action, événement etc)* to prevent; *(mouvement, progrès etc)* to obstruct, to impede; **ce vent empêchera la pluie** this wind will keep the rain off
2 e. qn de faire qch to stop *or* prevent *or* keep sb from doing sth; **rien ne m'empêchera de te rejoindre** nothing will stop me (from) joining you; **il sera difficile de l'en e.** it will be difficult to stop *or* prevent him/her; **tu ne m'empêcheras pas de penser que j'ai raison** I still think I'm right, you won't convince me that I'm wrong; *Fam* **ce n'est pas ça qui m'empêchera de dormir** I won't lose any sleep over it; **la pluie empêche que nous (ne) sortions** the rain is preventing *or* stopping us from going out; **il n'y a rien qui t'empêche de lui téléphoner** there's nothing to stop you telephoning him/her; **je ne vous empêche pas de partir/dîner, au moins?** I hope I'm not keeping you from going/your dinner!
3 il n'empêche que cela nous a coûté cher all the same *or* nevertheless it has cost us dear; **cela n'empêche pas qu'il aurait pu s'excuser** all the same *or* nevertheless, he could have apologized; *Fam* **n'empêche** all the same; *Fam* **qu'est-ce que ça empêche?** what does that matter?, what odds *or* difference does that make?; *Fam* **ça n'empêche rien!** that doesn't matter!, it makes no odds *or* difference!
▪ VPR **s'empêcher** *(souvent nég)* **s'e. de faire qch** to stop oneself *or* prevent oneself *or* refrain from doing sth; **je ne pouvais m'e. de rire** I couldn't help laughing, I had to laugh; **je ne peux pas m'e. de la taquiner** I can't help teasing her; **elle ne peut jamais s'e. de dire ce qu'il ne faut pas** she can never stop herself from saying what she shouldn't; **je ne peux pas m'en e.** I can't help it, I can't stop myself

empêcheur, -euse [ãpeʃœr, -øz] N *Fam* **e. de danser** *ou* **de tourner en rond** spoilsport, wet blanket

empeigne [ãpeɲ] NF *(de chaussure)* upper, vamp; *Arg* **gueule d'e.** ugly mug

empennage [ãpenaʒ] NM *(d'une flèche)* feathering, feathers; *(d'une bombe)* fins, vanes; *(d'une torpille)* fins; *(d'un avion)* empennage, tail

empenner [ãpene] VT *(flèche)* to feather

empereur [ãprœr] NM emperor

emperlousé [ãperluze] ADJ *Fam* dripping with pearls

empesage [ãpzaʒ] NM *(d'un col, d'une chemise etc)* starching

empesé [ãpze] ADJ **1** *(col, chemise etc)* starched **2** *Fig (manière)* stiff, starchy, unbending; *(style)* stiff

empeser [ãpze] VT (**j'empèse; j'empèserai**) *(col, chemise etc)* to starch

empester [ãpeste] VT **e. l'alcool/le parfum** to reek *or* stink of alcohol/perfume; **le frigo empeste le fromage** the fridge stinks of cheese; **le fromage empeste le frigo** the cheese is stinking out the fridge; **e. qn (avec sa fumée)** to stink sb out (with one's smoke)
▪ VI to stink, to smell to high heaven

empêtrer (s') [sãpetre] VPR to become entangled; **s'e. les pieds dans les broussailles** to get one's feet caught in the undergrowth; *Fig* **s'e. dans** *(explications, discours, mensonges)* to get tangled up in; *Fig* **s'e. dans une sale affaire** to get involved *or* mixed up in a bad business

emphase [ãfaz] NF pompousness, pomposity; **avec e.** pompously; **solennel mais sans e.** solemn but not pompous; **parler sans e.** to speak simply

emphatique [ãfatik] ADJ pompous

> Il faut noter que l'adjectif anglais **emphatic** est un faux ami. Il signifie **énergique** ou **catégorique**.

emphatiquement [ãfatikmã] ADV pompously

> Il faut noter que l'adverbe anglais **emphatically** est un faux ami. Il signifie **énergiquement** ou **catégoriquement**.

emphysémateux, -euse [ãfizematø, -øz] N *Méd* emphysema sufferer

emphysème [ãfizɛm] NM *Méd* emphysema

empiècement [ãpjɛsmã] NM *(d'un vêtement)* yoke

empierrement [ãpjɛrmã] NM **1** *(action) (d'une route)* metalling, macadamization; *Rail* ballasting **2** *(couche de pierres) (d'une route)* macadam, (road) metal; *Rail* ballast

empierrer [ãpjere] VT *(route)* to metal, to macadamize; *Rail* to ballast

empiétement [ãpjetmã] NM encroachment *(sur* on); **c'est un e. sur ma vie privée** it's an encroachment on my private life; **cette barrière est un e. sur mon terrain** that fence encroaches on my land; **e. sur les droits de qn** infringement of sb's rights

empiéter [ãpjete] VI (**j'empiète; j'empiéterai**) **e. sur** *(le terrain, le temps, la vie privée de quelqu'un)* to encroach on; **cette affiche empiète sur l'autre** this poster overlaps the other; **son collègue essaie d'e. sur ses attributions** his colleague is trying to trespass on his/her territory; **e. sur les droits de qn** to infringe sb's rights

empiffrer (s') [sãpifre] VPR *Fam* to stuff *or* gorge oneself (**de** with)

empilable [ãpilabl] ADJ *(chaise, boîte etc)* stacking

empilage [ãpilaʒ] NM, **empilement** [ãpilmã] NM **1** *(action) (de livres, bois etc)* stacking, piling (up) **2** *(pile)* pile, stack

empiler [ãpile] VT **1** *(livres, bois)* to stack, to pile (up) **2** *(passagers dans un véhicule)* to cram **3** *Fam (duper)* to do; **se faire e.** to be done *or* had; **se faire e. par qn** to be done by sb
▪ VPR **s'empiler 1** *(de livres, dossiers etc)* to pile up; *(former une pile)* to be piled up **2** *(de passagers)* **s'e. dans** to cram into

empire [ãpir] NM **1** *(domination)* authority, dominion; *(contrôle)* influence, control; **sous l'e. d'un tyran** ruled by a tyrant, under the rule *or Litt* sway of a tyrant; **avoir de l'e. sur qn** to have influence over sb; **user de** *ou* **exercer son e. sur qn** to use one's power over sb; **la religion exerce un véritable e. sur lui** religion has a real hold on him; **avoir de l'e. sur soi-même** to be self-controlled; **avoir**

peu d'e. sur soi-même to have little self-control; avoir beaucoup d'e. sur soi-même to be very self-controlled, to have a lot of self-control; quand j'ai bu, je n'ai plus aucun e. sur moi-même I lose all self-control when I drink; faire qch sous l'e. de la boisson/de la colère to do sth under the influence of drink/ in a fit of anger; elle s'est enfuie sous l'e. de la peur she fled in fear 2 *Hist, Pol* empire; le Saint E. romain germanique the Holy Roman Empire; le premier E., l'E. the First Empire; le second E. the Second Empire; style/ meubles E. Empire style/furniture; je ne changerais pas de travail pour un e. I wouldn't change my job for all the tea in China *or* if you paid me 3 *(groupe commercial)* empire

▸▸ le Céleste E. the Middle Kingdom, the Celestial Empire; l'E. du Milieu the Middle Kingdom, the Celestial Empire; l'E. du Soleil-Levant the Land of the Rising Sun

empirer [ãpire] **VI** to worsen, to get *or* to grow worse, to deteriorate; est-ce que les choses s'arrangent avec ton mari? – non, elles empirent are things any better with your husband? – no, they're (getting) worse **VT** to worsen, to make worse, to aggravate

empirique [ãpirik] **ADJ** empiric(al)

empirisme [ãpirism] **NM** empiricism

empiriste [ãpirist] **ADJ, N** *Phil* empiricist

emplacement [ãplasmã] **NM 1** *(d'une tente, d'un édifice etc)* site, location; *(sur un marché, dans un parking)* space; à l'e. d'un ancien tombeau on the site of an old tomb; e. publicitaire *(sur un mur, dans un journal)* advertising space; *Naut* e. de chargement loading berth 2 *Ordinat* slot; e. pour carte d'extension expansion slot; e. (pour) périphériques extension slot; e. d'évolutivité upgrade slot; e. pour carte card slot

emplafonner [ãplafɔne] **VT** *Fam* to crash into; elle s'est fait e. par mon voisin my neighbour crashed into her

emplâtre [ãplatr] **NM 1** *Pharm (pansement)* (sticking *or* adhesive) plaster; e. contre *ou* pour les cors corn plaster; *Fig* c'est un e. sur une jambe de bois it's (of) no earthly use; *Fam* cette purée, quel e.! this mashed potato is really stodgy 2 *Fam (personne)* wimp

emplette [ãplɛt] **NF 1** *(achat)* purchase; aller faire ses emplettes to go shopping; faire l'e. de qch to buy *or* purchase sth 2 *(choses achetées)* emplettes shopping, purchases; mes dernières emplettes my latest purchases, the latest things I've bought

emplir [ãplir] **VT** to fill (de with); la foule emplissait les rues the crowd filled the streets; cette nouvelle m'emplit de joie the news fills me with delight; les enfants emplissaient la cour de rires the playground was full of children's laughter

▪ **VPR s'emplir** to fill (up) (de with)

emploi [ãplwa] **NM 1** *(utilisation)* use; l'e. du béton est de plus en plus courant concrete is being used increasingly; ce mot est d'un e. rare the word is rarely used; je n'en aurais pas l'e. I wouldn't have any use for it *or* get any use out of it; quel e. vas-tu faire de tout cet argent/ce temps? what are you going to do with all that money/time?; je me demande quel e. il peut bien faire de ce vieux meuble? I wonder what use he has for that old piece of furniture; faire bon/mauvais e. de qch to make good/bad use of sth, to put sth to good/bad use; mode d'e. directions *or* instructions for use; prêt à l'e. ready to use 2 *(situation)* job; *(travail)* employment, work; être sans e. to be out of work *or* out of a job, to be unemployed; chercher un e. to be looking for work *or* a job; avoir un e. to have a job, to be in work; la crise/situation de l'e. the employment crisis/situation; il

faut faire quelque chose pour l'e. something has to be done about employment; agence nationale pour l'e. = (French state) employment agency, *Br* ≃ Jobcentre®; *Journ* demandes d'e. situations wanted; j'ai adressé plusieurs demandes d'e. I sent off several job applications; *Journ* offres d'e. situations vacant; création d'emplois job creation; sécurité de l'e. job security; partage de l'e. job-sharing; *Écon, Pol* plein e. full employment; les sans e. the jobless; e. à plein temps full-time job; e. à temps partiel part-time job

3 *Théâtre* c'est elle qui tient l'e. de la fille de la star she is cast as the star's daughter, she plays (the part of) the star's daughter; on le cantonne dans des emplois de grand amoureux he is typecast as the great lover; *Fig* il a le physique *ou* la tête *ou* *Fam* la gueule de l'e. he looks the part

▸▸ emplois-jeunes = jobs created for young people, particularly in the public sector and in education, as part of a programme to combat unemployment; emplois de proximité = employment in the community *(as a way of reducing unemployment)*; e. saisonnier seasonal employment; e. du temps timetable, schedule; elle a un e. du temps très chargé she has a very busy *or* full timetable *or* schedule; e. vacant vacancy

employabilité **NF** employability

employé, -ée [ãplwaje] **N** employee; e. (de bureau) office worker; e. de banque bank clerk; e. d'une administration government employee, civil servant; l'e. du gaz vient demain the gas man's coming tomorrow; e. aux écritures accounts *or* ledger clerk; e. des postes post office clerk; e. de mairie town hall employee; e. occasionnel casual worker; e. à plein temps/à temps partiel full-time/part-time employee; être e. des postes/de mairie to work for the Post Office/at the town hall; e. de chemin de fer railway employee; e. à l'enregistrement des bagages check-in clerk; être e. de maison to do domestic work

employer [ãplwaje] (j'emploie; j'emploierai) **VT 1** *(utiliser) (outil, mot, technique, force etc)* to use; e. son énergie à faire qch to devote all one's energies to doing sth; j'emploierai tous les moyens I'll use whatever means I have to; e. les grands moyens to go to great lengths; e. son temps à nettoyer/ étudier to spend one's time cleaning/studying; il ne sait à quoi e. son temps he doesn't know what to do with his time; bien e. son temps to use one's time well, to make good use of one's time, to put one's time to good use; elle ne sait pas e. son argent she doesn't know how to use her money; à quoi vas-tu e. cette somme? what are you going to spend the money on?; cet ordinateur n'emploie que des disquettes de double densité the computer only takes double-density disks

2 *Com* e. une somme en recette to put *or* enter an amount in the receipts

3 *(faire travailler) (ouvrier, personnel etc)* to employ; e. qn comme secrétaire to employ sb as secretary; e. qn à des corvées/des petits travaux to employ sb to do the chores/ odd jobs; je suis employé par plusieurs sociétés I am employed by *or* work for several companies

▪ **VPR s'employer 1** *(d'une personne)* s'e. à faire qch to work on doing sth; je m'y emploie I'm working on it 2 *(être utilisé)* to be used 3 *Vieilli* s'e. pour qn to exert oneself on sb's behalf

employeur, -euse [ãplwajœr, -øz] **N** employer

emplumé [ãplyme] **ADJ** feathered

empocher [ãpɔʃe] **VT 1** *(toucher) (argent,*

chèque etc) to pocket, to receive 2 *(mettre dans sa poche)* to pocket

empoignade [ãpwaɲad] **NF** *Fam* brawl, punch-up

empoigne [ãpwaɲ] **NF** *Fam* c'était la foire d'e. dans les magasins it was bedlam in the shops, the shops were full of people pushing and shoving; c'est la foire d'e. pour se faire servir it's a real scrum getting served; quelle foire d'e. ici! what a scrum!; la vie n'est qu'une foire d'e. life's just a rat race *or* a free-for-all

empoigner [ãpwaɲe] **VT** *(attraper) (objet)* to grab (hold of), to grasp, to seize; *(personne)* to seize, to grab (hold of), *Fam* to collar

▪ **VPR s'empoigner** to brawl, to have a punch-up

empois [ãpwa] **NM** (laundry) starch; *Tex* dressing

empoisonnant [ãpwazɔnã] **ADJ** *Fam (irritant)* annoying, irritating; *(ennuyeux)* boring; c'est vraiment e., ces retards continuels these constant delays are an absolute pain

empoisonné **ADJ** *Fig (trait, paroles)* poisonous, vicious; *Fig* calice empoisonné poisoned chalice; il m'a fait un cadeau empoisonné en me nommant à ce poste he wasn't exactly doing me a favour by appointing me to that job

empoisonnement [ãpwazɔnmã] **NM 1** *(intoxication) (d'une personne, de la nourriture)* poisoning 2 *Fam (souci, ennui)* problem; je n'ai que des empoisonnements I've got nothing but problems; la vie avec lui est un e. continuel life with him is just one thing after another; quel e.! what a pain (in the neck)!

empoisonner [ãpwazɔne] **VT 1** *(intoxiquer) (personne, nourriture, animal, flèche, étang)* to poison

2 *(empester)* du poisson pourri empoisonnait la pièce there was a smell of rotten fish in the room, the room smelled of rotten fish; des odeurs de cuisine empoisonnaient la pièce the room was full of cooking smells; odeur qui empoisonne l'air smell that taints the air

3 *Fig (altérer) (existence, mariage)* to poison; *Fam (irriter)* to annoy, to irritate; *(ennuyer)* to bore; la vie de qn to make sb's life a misery; vraiment, ça m'empoisonne de devoir y aller I'm really fed up about having to go; il m'empoisonne à toujours me téléphoner I'm fed up with his constant telephoning

▪ **VPR s'empoisonner 1** *(se tuer)* to poison oneself

2 *Fig (s'ennuyer)* to be bored; qu'est-ce qu'on s'empoisonne dans cette soirée! this is a really boring party!; s'e. l'existence to make one's life a misery; essaie de trouver ce livre mais ne t'empoisonne pas l'existence avec ça try to find the book but don't go to too much trouble over it

empoisonneur, -euse [ãpwazɔnœr, -øz] **N 1** *(criminel)* poisoner 2 *Fam (personne qui ennuie)* bore; *(personne qui irrite)* nuisance, pest

empoissonner [ãpwasɔne] **VT** to stock with fish

emporté, -ée [ãpɔrte] **ADJ** *(personne)* irascible, quick-tempered; avoir un caractère e. to be irascible *or* quick-tempered, to be quick to lose one's temper; d'un ton e. irascibly

N irascible *or* quick-tempered person

emportement [ãpɔrtəmã] **NM 1** *(colère)* (fit of) anger; répondre avec e. to reply angrily 2 *Litt, Vieilli (élan) (d'enthousiasme, d'excitation etc)* burst, surge; dans l'e. de la discussion in the heat of the debate

emporte-pièce [ãpɔrtəpjɛs] **NM INV** *Tech*

punch; *Culin* pastry cutter; **découper qch à l'e.** to stamp *or* punch sth out; *Culin* to cut out (with a pastry cutter); *Fig* **style à l'e.** incisive style; *Fig* **mots à l'e.** biting *or* cutting words; *Fig* **répondre à l'e.** to reply incisively *or* trenchantly

emporter [ɑ̃pɔʀte] **vt 1** *(partir et prendre avec soi)* to take (with one); *(enlever d'un lieu)* to take away; *(emmener)* to carry *or* take away; **e. un blessé sur un brancard** to carry off *or* take away a wounded man on a stretcher; **ils ont emporté de quoi manger** they took some food with them; **plats à e.** take-away food; *Fam* **il ne l'emportera pas au paradis** he'll live to regret it; **(que) le diable l'emporte!** to hell with him!; **le train qui m'emporte vers le nord** the train which is carrying *or* taking me northwards; **il a emporté son secret dans la tombe** he took his secret to the grave (with him)
2 *(entraîner, arracher) (du courant, de la lave)* to sweep *or* carry away; **le choléra l'emporta** cholera carried him off; **il a eu une jambe emportée par un obus** a shell took *or* blew one of his legs off; **le vent emporta son chapeau** the wind blew his/her hat off *or* away; **la tempête a emporté le toit** the roof came off in the storm; *Fig* **autant en emporte le vent** promises are cheap, talk is easy; **cette moutarde vous emporte la bouche** *ou Arg* **la gueule** this mustard takes the roof off your mouth; *Fig* **se laisser e. par** *(la colère, l'enthousiasme, l'imagination, les sentiments)* to get *or* let oneself be carried away by
3 *(conquérir) (fort, ville etc)* to take (by assault); **e. la victoire** to be victorious, to be the victor (**contre** over); **e. la décision** to win out, to carry the day; *Fam* **e. le morceau** to win one's case; **l'équipe nantaise l'a emporté par deux buts à zéro** the Nantes team won (by) two goals to nil; **le coureur hollandais l'emporte haut la main** the Dutch runner is winning hands down; **avec lui, c'est toujours l'amitié qui l'emporte** friendship is always the most important consideration *or* outweighs everything else as far as he's concerned; **considérations qui l'emportent sur toutes les autres** considerations that override *or* outweigh all others; **ce dossier/ce candidat/ce prototype l'emporte sur tous les autres** this file/candidate/prototype stands head and shoulders above the others *or* is streets ahead of the others; **en ce qui concerne le culot, elle l'emporte vraiment sur tout le monde** she's streets ahead of everybody when it comes to cheek; **ici, la pluie l'emporte sur le soleil** there's much more rain than sunshine here; **ici, le rugby l'emporte sur le foot** rugby is more important *or* popular than football here
vpr s'emporter 1 to lose one's temper, to fly into a rage (**contre qn** with sb)
2 *(d'un cheval)* to bolt

empoté, -ée [ɑ̃pɔte] *Fam* **adj** cack-handed **n** cack-handed idiot

empoter [ɑ̃pɔte] **vt** *(plantes)* to pot

empourprer [ɑ̃puʀpʀe] **vt** to tinge with crimson
vpr s'empourprer *(d'un visage)* to flush, to go crimson; *(du ciel)* to turn crimson

empoussiéré [ɑ̃pusjeʀe] **adj** covered with dust, dusty

empreindre [ɑ̃pʀɛ̃dʀ] *(prp* **empreignant;** *pp* **empreint;** *pr ind* **j'empreins, il empreint, n. empreignons, ils empreignent;** *impf* **j'empreignais;** *p hist* **j'empreignis;** *fu* **j'empreindrai)** **vt** *(dans la cire)* to impress, to imprint, to stamp; *Fig* **visage empreint de mélancolie/de terreur** face marked *or* stamped with sadness/full of terror; *Fig* **article empreint d'un certain sérieux** article with serious overtones; *Fig* **des histoires empreintes**

d'onirisme stories with a dreamlike quality
vpr s'empreindre *(d'un visage, d'une expression etc)* to be marked *or* stamped (**de** with)

empreinte [ɑ̃pʀɛ̃t] **nf 1** *(trace, impression)* impression, (im)print; *Typ* mould, *Am* mold; *(de satellite)* footprint; **prendre l'e. de qch** to take an impression of sth; **les loups ont laissé des empreintes dans la neige** the wolves left tracks *or* footprints in the snow; **e. des roues** tyre tracks; **e. de pas** footprint; **e. de doigt** fingermark; **prendre** *ou* **relever les empreintes de qn** to take sb's fingerprints, to fingerprint sb; **relever les empreintes sur un revolver** to fingerprint a revolver **2** *Fig (du génie, du passé, de l'éducation etc)* stamp, (hall)mark; **mettre son e. sur qch** to put one's stamp *or* mark on sth; **marquer qn/qch de son e.** to put one's stamp *or* mark on sb/sth; **être marqué de l'e. de qn** to bear sb's stamp *or* mark
▸ ▸ **e. digitale** fingerprint; **e. génétique** genetic fingerprint; **e. en plâtre** plaster cast; **e. vocale** voice print

empressé, -ée [ɑ̃pʀese] **adj 1** *(prévenant) (vendeur)* eager, willing; *(serviteur, docteur, admirateur etc)* attentive; **des soins empressés** assiduous attentions; **ils m'ont entouré de soins empressés** they gave me every care and consideration; **il lui fait une cour empressée** he is courting her assiduously **2** *Litt (pressé)* **il est e. à vous revoir** he is eager to see you again
n *Péj* **faire l'e. auprès de qn** to dance attendance on sb

empressement [ɑ̃pʀesmɑ̃] **nm 1** *(prévenance) (d'un vendeur)* eagerness, willingness (**à faire qch** to do sth); *(d'un serviteur, docteur, admirateur etc)* attentiveness; **témoigner de l'e. auprès de qn** to pay marked attention(s) to sb; **son e. auprès des femmes est presque gênant** he is almost embarrassingly attentive to women **2** *(hâte)* eagerness; **il montre peu d'e. à faire les travaux** he doesn't seem to be very eager *or* keen to do the work; **avec e.** eagerly; **tous les soirs il rentre chez lui avec e.** he hurries home every evening, he is eager to get home every evening; **mettre beaucoup d'e. à faire qch** to hasten to do sth

empresser (s') [ɑ̃pʀese] **vpr 1** *(se dépêcher)* **s'e. de faire qch** to hurry to do sth; **il s'empressa de répondre à ma lettre** he lost no time in answering my letter **2** *(être prévenant)* **s'e. à faire qch** to do sth eagerly, to hasten to do sth; **s'e. auprès de qn** to pay marked attention(s) to sb; **s'e. autour d'un accidenté de la route** to be busy attending to the victim of a road accident; **tout le monde s'empresse autour d'elle** everyone crowds *or* flocks round her

emprise [ɑ̃pʀiz] **nf 1** *(domination)* hold; **avoir de l'e. sur qn** to have a hold over sb; **sous l'e. de l'alcool** under the influence of alcohol; **sous l'e. de son amour pour elle** swayed by his love for her; **c'est sous l'e. de la colère qu'il l'a mise à la porte** he fired her in a fit of anger **2** *Jur (de terres etc à des fins publiques)* expropriation, acquisition

emprisonnement [ɑ̃pʀizɔnmɑ̃] **nm** imprisonment; **e. à perpétuité** life imprisonment; **peine d'e.** prison sentence; **il a été condamné à une peine d'e. de cinq ans** he was sentenced to five years in prison *or Fml* to a five-year term of imprisonment, he was given a five-year prison sentence

emprisonner [ɑ̃pʀizɔne] **vt 1** *(mettre en prison)* to imprison, to put in prison **2** *Fig (serrer) (esprit)* to imprison; **e. le buste dans un corset** to squeeze into a corset; **col qui emprisonne le cou** collar that is too tight

emprunt [ɑ̃pʀœ̃] **nm 1** *(action)* borrowing; **ce n'est pas à moi, c'est un e.** it's not mine, it's

borrowed; **nom d'e.** assumed name; **son nom de scène est un nom d'e.** he acts under an assumed name
2 *(somme)* loan; **faire un e. à qn** to borrow (money) from sb; **faire un e.** *(auprès d'une banque etc)* to take out a loan; **contracter un e.** to raise a loan; **couvrir un e.** to cover a loan; **e. public** public loan; **e. d'État** government loan; *Bourse* state bond; **e. à court/long terme** short-/long-term loan; **procéder à un nouvel e.** to make a new loan issue; **faire un e. de plusieurs millions à la banque** to borrow several million from the bank, to take out a bank loan of several million; **e. conversion** conversion loan; **e. à découvert** unsecured loan; **e. en devises** currency loan; **e. garanti** secured loan; **e. indexé** indexed loan; **e. obligataire** bond issue, loan stock; *(titre)* debenture bond; **e. obligataire convertible** convertible loan stock; **e. perpétuel** perpetual loan; **e. remboursable sur demande** call loan, loan repayable on demand; **e. de remboursement** refunding loan; **emprunts à taux fixe** fixed-rate borrowing; **e. à terme** term loan; **e. sur titres** loan on securities *or* stock
3 *Ling* borrowing (**à l'anglais** from English)

emprunté [ɑ̃pʀœ̃te] **adj** *(manière, personne)* self-conscious, stiff, awkward; **il était tellement impressionné par elle qu'il en devenait e.** he was so impressed by her that it made him self-conscious; **dit-elle d'un ton e.** she said self-consciously *or* awkwardly

emprunter [ɑ̃pʀœ̃te] **vt 1** *(objet, argent)* to borrow (**à** from); **est-ce que je peux t'e. ton fiancé pour cette danse?** can I borrow your fiancé for this dance?; **elle a emprunté ses manières à sa mère** she copies her mother's ways **2** *(route, chemin)* to take; **le cortège emprunta la rue de Rivoli** the procession took *or* went down the Rue de Rivoli
vi to take out a loan, to borrow; **e. à long/à court terme** to borrow long/short; **e. à intérêt** to borrow at interest

emprunteur, -euse [ɑ̃pʀœ̃tœʀ, -øz] **n** borrower

empuantir [ɑ̃pɥɑ̃tiʀ] **vt** to make stink; *(pièce)* to stink out, to make stink

EMS [ɛɛmɛs] **nm** *Ordinat (abrév* **enhanced messaging service)** EMS

ému [emy] **adj** *(touché)* moved, touched; *(passionné)* roused; **voix émue** voice filled with emotion; **garder un souvenir é. de qch** to retain a touching memory of sth; **j'en suis encore tout é.** I still haven't got over it; **être é. (jusqu')aux larmes par qch** to be moved to tears by sth; **il était trop é. pour s'asseoir/lui parler** he was too nervous to sit down/talk to her

émulateur [emylatœʀ] **nm** *Ordinat* emulator; **é. de terminal** terminal emulator; **é. graphique** graphics emulator

émulation [emylasjɔ̃] **nf 1** *(concurrence)* competitiveness **2** *Ordinat* emulation; **é. de terminal** terminal emulation

émule [emyl] **n** *(imitateur)* emulator; *(concurrent)* competitor; **j'ai fait des émules** people followed my lead *or* example

émuler [emyle] **vt** *Ordinat* to emulate

émulseur [emylsœʀ] **nm** *(appareil)* emulsifier

émulsif, -ive [emylsif, -iv] **adj** *Pharm* emulsive; *Chimie* emulsifying

émulsifiable [emylsifjabl] **adj** *Chimie* emulsifiable

émulsifiant [emylsifjɑ̃] **adj** emulsifying **nm** emulsifier

émulsifier [emylsifje] **vt** to emulsify

émulsion [emylsjɔ̃] **nf** emulsion

émulsionner [emylsjɔne] **vt** to emulsify

EN [əɛn] **NF** *Anciennement abrév* **École normale**

EN¹ [ã]

| in **1–4, 6, 8, 9** ▪ to **1, 7, 8** ▪ at **1, 4, 6** ▪ on **1, 4, 11** ▪ about **2** ▪ within **2** ▪ made of **5** ▪ into **7** ▪ by **9** ▪ as **10, 11** ▪ like **10** ▪ + ing **11** |

PRÉP SEE GRAMMAR B55–6 **1** *(lieu)* in; *(avec mouvement)* to; **être/aller en ville/montagne** to be in/to go (in)to town/the mountains; **en province** in the country, in the provinces; **il est parti en mer** he's gone to sea; **une promenade en mer** a boat trip; **en tête/queue** at the head/in the rear; **la suite en page quatre** continued on page four; **aller en France/Amérique** to go to France/America; **être en Avignon/Arles** to be in Avignon/Arles; **être en Saône-et-Loire** to be in Saône-et-Loire; **regarder en l'air** to look up at the sky; **le mariage aura lieu en l'église Saint-Jean** the marriage will be celebrated *or* held at St. John's (Church); **c'était comment en classe aujourd'hui?** how was school today?; **le Christ en croix** Jesus on the cross; **garde ça en mémoire** keep that in mind; **de branche en branche** from branch to branch **2** *(avec pron pers)* **il y a quelque chose en lui que j'admire** there is something I admire about him; **un homme en qui** *ou* **en lequel j'ai confiance** a man whom I trust; **c'est en nous-mêmes que nous devons chercher la réponse** we must look for the answer within ourselves; **en chaque être** in every being **3** *(temps)* in; **en été/automne/hiver** in (the) summer/autumn/winter; **né en 1967** born in 1967; **en avril** in April; **aujourd'hui en huit** a week today; **on peut y aller en cinq heures** you can get there in five hours; **en l'an 1800** in (the year) 1800; **en ce temps-là** in those days, at that time; **d'année en année** from year to year, year by year; **son état s'aggravait de jour en jour** he was getting worse by the day; **fermé en semaine** closed weekdays; **il a été guéri en deux semaines** he was cured (with)in two weeks **4** *(état)* in; **être en deuil/en loques/en tenue de sport** to be in mourning/in rags/in sports clothes; **lait en poudre** powdered milk; **en vers/prose** in verse/prose; **en direct** live; **laisser les choses en l'état** to leave everything as it is; **en l'absence du chef** in the absence of the boss; **en présence de mon avocat** in the presence of my lawyer; **arbres en fleur** trees in blossom *or* flower; **être en guerre** to be at war; **en vacances** on holiday **5** *(composition)* made of; **montre en or** gold watch; **c'est en or** it's made of gold; **table en marbre** marble table; **évier en inox**® stainless-steel sink; **pull en laine** woollen sweater **6** *(description)* **escalier en spirale** spiral staircase; **chemin en pente** sloping road; **docteur en médecine** doctor of medicine; **peintre en bâtiment** house painter; **fort/faible en mathématiques** good/bad at mathematics; **parler en français/anglais** to speak in French/English; **marcher en silence** to walk in silence; **en votre honneur** in your honour **7** *(annonce un changement)* into; **changé en serpent** changed into a serpent; **traduire une lettre en français** to translate a letter into French; **peindre qch en bleu** to paint sth blue; **de mal en pis** from bad to worse; **tomber en admiration devant qn/qch** to be filled with admiration for sb/sth **8** *(indique une division)* **briser qch en morceaux** to break sth (in)to bits; **casser qch en deux** to break sth in two; **pièce en trois actes** play in three acts; **vendre en paquets/feuilles** to sell in packets/sheets **9** *(manière)* **s'épuiser en d'inutiles efforts** to exhaust oneself in useless efforts; **venir en taxi/avion** to come by taxi/by plane *or* air; **en trois bonds** in three jumps **10** *(comme)* **envoyer qch en cadeau** to send sth as a present; **donner qch à qn en compensation** to give sb sth by way of *or* as compensation; **il mourut en brave** he died like the brave man that he was; **agir en honnête homme** to act like an honest man; **prendre la chose en philosophe** to take it philosophically **11** *(avec gérondif)* **il marchait en lisant son journal** he walked along reading his paper; **il répondit en riant** he answered with a laugh; **elle entra/sortit en dansant** she danced in/out; **on apprend en vieillissant** we learn as we grow older; **il s'est aigri en vieillissant** he has become embittered with age; **en faisant cela vous l'offenserez** you'll offend him by doing that; **en arrivant à Paris** on arriving in Paris; **en vous écrivant hier j'ai oublié de vous le dire** I forgot to mention it when writing to you yesterday; **en attendant** while waiting, in the meantime; **tout en tricotant, elle nous racontait des histoires** as she knitted she told us stories; **s'enrhumer en marchant sous la pluie** to catch a cold (through *or* from) walking in the rain; **tout en étant riche, il vit très simplement** whilst (he is) rich, he leads a very simple life SEE GRAMMAR B38

EN²

| from there **1** ▪ it **2–7** ▪ some/any **6–8** |

PRON SEE GRAMMAR B19–20 **1** *(de cet endroit)* from there; **il en revient** he's just come back from there; **où en étions-nous?** *(dans un livre, travail etc)* where were we?; **j'en sors à l'instant** I'm just leaving **2** *(de ce fait)* **si vous étiez riche, en seriez-vous plus heureux?** if you were rich, would you be happier for it *or* any the happier?; **je n'en dors plus la nuit** it keeps me awake at night, I can't sleep at night for it; **j'en ris encore** I still laugh about it; **en tirer une conclusion** to draw a conclusion from it; **j'en suis encore toute retournée** I'm still all of a flutter **3** *(remplaçant un nom régi par* **de**) **j'aime mieux ne pas en parler** I would rather not speak about it; **combien en demande-t-il** *ou* **en veut-il?** how much does he want for it?; **qu'en pensez-vous?** what do you think of *or* about it?; **les rues en sont pleines** the streets are full of it/them; **il reçut une blessure et en mourut** he received a wound and died of *or* from it; **il en devint amoureux** he fell in love with her; **il faut en faire un film!** they should make a film of it *or* turn it into a film!; **que vais-je en faire, de cette table?** what am I going to do with this table?; *Fam* **en être** *(être homosexuel)* to be one of them **4** *(de choses, remplaçant le possessif)* **j'ai la valise mais je n'en ai pas la clef** I have the suitcase but I haven't (got) the key (for it); **prends la boîte mais n'en perds pas le couvercle** take the box, but don't lose the lid (to it); **je ne savais rien de cet endroit, je n'en connaissais que le nom** I didn't know anything about the place, I only knew the name **5** *(remplaçant une proposition)* **il ne l'a pas fait, mais il en est capable** he didn't do it but he's (quite) capable of it **6** *(nombre, quantité)* **j'en ai un/trois/plusieurs** I have one/three/several (of them); **combien en voulez-vous?** *(quantité)* how much do you want?; *(nombre)* how many do you want?; **elle en a déjà vu beaucoup pour son âge** she has already seen a lot for her age; **j'en ai** I have some; **je n'en ai pas** I don't have any, I have none; **en avez-vous?** do you have any, have you (got) any?; **parmi ses livres il y en a d'excellents** some of his books are excellent; **il en a mangé deux cuillerées** he ate two spoonfuls (of it) **7** *(locutions)* **je n'en ai pas encore fini avec lui** I haven't or finished with him yet; **si le cœur vous en dit** if you feel so inclined, if you feel like it; **en venir aux mains** to come to blows; **est-ce à ça que tu en es réduit?** have you been reduced to that?; **ne t'en fais pas!** don't worry!; **il en va de même pour toi** it's the same for you; **il en est ainsi** that's the way it is; **je n'en puis plus** I can't bear it any longer; **elle en aime un autre** she loves someone else; **à en croire les racontars** if we are able to believe the tales; **il y en a qui ... some people ...** **8** *(après un impératif)* **prenez-en** take some; **prenez-en dix** take ten (of them); **va-t'en, allez-vous-en** go away; **va en chercher** go and get some; **donne-m'en!**, *Fam* **donne-moi-z-en!** give me some!; **souvenez-vous-en!** remember! **9** *(après la forme pronominale de certains verbes)* **s'en aller** to go away; **il s'en est allé** he went away; **s'en retourner** to go back, to return

en³ [ɛn] **NM** *Typ* en

ENA [ena] **NF** *abrév* **École nationale d'administration**

enamouré [ãnamure], **énamouré** [enamure] **ADJ** *(regard, sourire etc)* amorous; **être e.** *ou* **é. de qn** to be enamoured *or Am* enamored of sb

enamourer (s') [sãnamure], **énamourer (s')** [senamure] **VPR** to become enamoured *or Am* enamored (**de** of)

énarchie [enarʃi] **NF** *Fam* = elite system dominated by the graduates of the École nationale d'administration

énarque [enark] **N** = graduate of the École nationale d'administration

en-arrière [ãnarjer] **NM INV** *(au patinage)* backward glide

énarthrose [enartroz] **NF** *Anat* ball-and-socket joint, *Spéc* enarthrosis

en-avant [ãnavã] **NM INV 1** *Rugby* forward pass; *(dans les mains)* knock-on **2** *(au patinage)* forward glide

en-but [ãby(t)] **NM INV** *Rugby* in-goal

encabaner (s') [sãkabane] **VPR** *Can* to shut oneself up *or* away

encablure [ãkablyr] **NF** *Arch (mesure)* cable (length) *(approx 200 m)*; **je n'habite qu'à quelques encablures du bureau** I live a stone's throw from the office

encadré [ãkadre] **NM** *Journ, Typ (dans un texte)* box; *(presse écrite)* boxed article; *(petites annonces)* display advertisement; *Ordinat* **e. graphique** graphics box; *Ordinat* **e. texte** text box
   ADJ panelled-in, boxed

encadrement [ãkadrəmã] **NM 1** *(d'un tableau, d'une fenêtre etc) (action)* framing; *(cadre)* frame; **dans l'e. de la porte** in the doorway; *Tech* **e. en caoutchouc** rubber seal **2** *Admin, Ind, Sport etc (action d'encadrer) (du personnel, d'une équipe sportive)* management; *(d'un groupe d'enfants, de handicapés, d'étudiants)* supervision; *Mil (d'une unité)* officering; *(personnes qui encadrent) (du personnel, d'une équipe sportive)* management, managers; *Mil* officers; *(cadres)* executives; **fonctions d'e.** executive functions; **personnel d'e.** management, managerial staff; **e. d'une colonie de vacances** supervisory staff of a holiday camp **3** *Écon* **e. du crédit** restriction on credit, credit restriction(s) *or* squeeze; **diminuer l'e. du crédit** to reduce credit restrictions, to loosen the credit squeeze; **e. des loyers** rent control; **e. des prix** price control(s)

encadrer [ākadre] **VT 1** *(tableau, photo, porte etc)* to frame

2 *(entourer) (des mots, une phrase)* to circle; *(le visage)* to frame; **jardin encadré de haies** garden enclosed by hedges; **encadré par deux gendarmes** flanked by two policemen; **encadré de ses gardes du corps/de jolies filles** surrounded by his bodyguards/by pretty girls

3 *Admin, Ind, Sport etc (personnel, équipe)* to manage; *(groupe d'enfants, de handicapés, d'étudiants)* to supervise; *Mil (unité)* to officer; **nous sommes bien encadrés** our management is good

4 *Écon (prix, loyers, crédits)* to control
5 *Fam (supporter)* **je ne peux pas l'e.** I can't stand *or* abide him
6 *Fam (entrer dans)* **il a encadré un arbre** he wrapped his vehicle round a tree

encadreur, -euse [ākadrœr, -øz] **N** picture framer

encager [ākaʒe] **VT** (**j'encageai(s); n. encageons**) *(oiseau, animal)* to cage; **tenir qn encagé** to keep sb caged up; **tenir un oiseau/un animal encagé** to keep a bird/an animal in a cage *or* caged up

encagoulé [ākagule] **ADJ** hooded

encaissable [ākɛsabl] **ADJ** cashable, *Br* encashable

encaisse [ākɛs] **NF** *Com* cash (in hand); **e. de 1000 euros** cash balance of 1,000 euros; **e. or et argent** *ou* **e. métallique d'un pays** gold and silver holding of a country; *Banque* **pas d'e.** no funds

encaissé [ākese] **ADJ** *(vallée)* deep; *(rivière)* deeply embanked; *(route)* sunken

encaissement [ākɛsmā] **NM 1** *(d'un chèque)* cashing, paying in, *Br* encashment; *(d'argent)* receipt, collection; *(d'une traite)* collection; **donner un chèque à l'e.** to cash a cheque; **encaissements et décaissements** cash inflows and outflows **2** *(d'une vallée)* depth; *(d'une rivière)* deep embankment; **dans l'e. de la route** in the deep cutting made by the road

encaisser [ākese] **VT 1** *(chèque)* to cash, *Br* to encash; *(argent)* to receive, to collect; *(traite)* to collect; **e. de l'argent** *(sur son compte)* to pay in cash; *Bourse* **e. un premium** to receive a premium **2** *Fam (supporter) (des coups, des remarques, des critiques)* to take; **je ne sais comment il fait pour e. les coups aussi bien** I don't know how he stands up to being hit; **je n'arrive plus à e. ma belle-mère** I can't take my mother-in-law any more; **je ne peux pas l'e.** I can't stand him/her **3** *(resserrer) (de collines)* to hem in; *Tech (rivière etc)* to embank **4** *Com* **e. des marchandises** to pack goods

VPR s'encaisser *(d'une rivière, route etc)* to be hemmed in; **la route s'encaisse profondément entre les montagnes** mountains tower above the road on both sides

VI *Fam* **il sait e.** he can take it; **qu'est-ce qu'il a encaissé!** he took a lot of punishment; **elle a plutôt bien encaissé** she took it rather well; **e. sans broncher** to grin and bear it

encaisseur [ākɛsœr] **NM** *(de loyer, dettes etc)* collector

encan [ākā] **NM vendre qch à l'e.** to sell sth by *or* at auction; *aussi Fig* **mettre qch à l'e.** to put sth up for auction; *Fig* **la loi semble mettre la justice à l'e.** the law seems to put a low price on justice

encanaillement [ākanajmā] **NM** slumming it

encanailler (s') [sākanaje] **VPR** to like slumming it, to hang around with doubtful characters; **il faudrait qu'elle s'encanaille un peu** she ought to break out *or* loosen up a bit and live

encapuchonner [ākapyʃɔne] **VT** *(personne, la tête de quelqu'un)* to put a hood on; *(machine)* to put a hood on, to cover (with a hood); *(stylo)* to put the top on; **encapuchonné** hooded

VPR s'encapuchonner to put on a *or* one's hood

encart [ākar] **NM** *Journ* slip sheet; *(attaché)* inset; *(mobile)* (loose) insert; **e. dépliant** gatefold; **e. publicitaire** *Journ* advertising supplement; *TV, Radio* commercial break

encartage [ākartaʒ] **NM** *Typ* inserting, insetting

encarté [ākarte] **ADJ** *(membre)* card-carrying; **il est e. au PC** he's a card-carrying *or* paid-up member of the communist party

encarter [ākarte] **VT 1** *Typ (pages)* to inset; *(notice dans un livre)* to insert **2** *(épingles, boutons etc)* to card

en-cas [ākɑ] **NM INV** snack (meal)

encaserner [ākazɛrne] **VT** *Mil* to put in barracks; **être encaserné à** to be barracked at

encastrable [ākastrabl] **ADJ** *(machine à laver, cuisinière etc)* that can be built in *or* fitted

encastré [ākastre] **ADJ** *(machine à laver, cuisinière)* built-in, fitted; *(four, baignoire)* built-in; *(interrupteur)* flush-fitting, set-in

encastrement [ākastrəmā] **NM 1** *(action)* *(d'une machine à laver, cuisinière)* fitting, building in; *(d'un interrupteur)* flush-fitting, setting in **2** *(espace prévu)* recess

encastrer [ākastre] **VT** *(machine à laver, cuisinière)* to build in, to fit; *(four, baignoire)* to build in; *(interrupteur)* to flush fit, to set in
VPR s'encastrer *(de deux éléments)* to fit together; **s'e. dans** *(d'une machine à laver, une cuisinière)* to fit into; **la voiture s'est encastrée sous un camion** the car embedded itself under a lorry

encaustiquage [ākɔstika ʒ, āko-] **NM** *(d'un parquet, de meubles)* waxing, wax-polishing

encaustique [ākɔstik, āko-] **NF** *(pour les meubles)* wax, polish

encaustiquer [ākɔstike, āko-] **VT** *(parquet, meubles)* to wax, to polish

encavage [ākavaʒ] **NM** *Suisse (de vin)* cellarage, cellaring; *(de fromage, légumes, fruits)* storage in a cellar

encavement [ākavmā] **NM** *(du vin)* cellaring

encaver [ākave] **VT** *(vin etc)* to cellar

encaveur [ākavœr] **NM 1** *(ouvrier)* cellarman **2** *Suisse (négociant)* wine-maker, wine producer

enceindre [āsɛ̃dr] **VT** *(conj like* **ceindre***)* to surround (**de** with)

enceinte¹ [āsɛ̃t] **NF 1** *(mur)* (surrounding) wall; *(palissade)* fence **2** *(espace)* enclosure; *(d'église, de couvent)* precinct(s); *Courses de chevaux* ring; **dans l'e. du parc** within *or* inside (the confines of) the park; **il est interdit de pénétrer en voiture dans l'e. du parc** cars may not enter the park, cars are not allowed into the park; **dans l'e. de l'école** on school premises; **en dehors de l'e. de l'école** outside school **3** *(sonore)* **e. (acoustique)** speaker

enceinte² **ADJ F** pregnant, *Fam* expecting, *Litt* with child; **femme e.** pregnant woman, expectant mother; **e. de cinq mois** five months pregnant; **être e. d'un petit garçon/de jumeaux** to be expecting a little boy/twins; **elle est e. de Paul** she's pregnant by Paul, she's expecting Paul's child; **mettre qn e.** to make *or* get sb pregnant

encens [āsā] **NM** incense

encensement [āsāsmā] **NM 1** *Rel* censing **2** *Fig* flattery, toadying

encenser [āsāse] **VT 1** *Rel* to cense **2** *Fig* **e. qn** to flatter sb outrageously
VI *(d'un cheval)* to toss its head up and down

Attention: le verbe anglais **to incense** est un faux ami. Il signifie **rendre furieux**.

encenseur, -euse [āsāsœr, -øz] **N 1** *Rel* thurifer, censer bearer **2** *Fig Vieilli* sycophant

encensoir [āsāswar] **NM** *Rel* censer; *Fig Péj* **donner des coups d'e.** to butter people up; **donner des coups d'e. à qui il faut** to butter up the right people

encéphale [āsefal] **NM** brain, encephalon

encéphalite [āsefalit] **NF** *Méd* encephalitis; **e. léthargique** sleeping sickness; *Vét* **e. bovine spongiforme** bovine spongiform encephalopathy, BSE

encéphalogramme [āsefalɔgram] **NM** *Méd* (electro)encephalogram

encéphalographie [āsefalɔgrafi] **NF** *Méd* (electro)encephalography

encéphalomyélite [āsefalɔmjelit] **NF** *Méd* encephalomyelitis

encerclement [āserkləmā] **NM** encircling, surrounding; **après l'e. de l'ennemi** after the enemy was surrounded *or* encircled

encercler [āserkle] **VT 1** *(ennemi, manifestants etc)* to encircle, to surround **2** *(mot)* to circle, to ring

enchaîné [āʃene] **NM** *TV, Cin* dissolve, mix

enchaînement [āʃɛnmā] **NM 1** *(série)* *(d'événements)* series, chain, train; *(d'idées, de mesures)* series **2** *(liaison)* *(d'idées, de séquences etc)* linking, connection; *TV, Cin (entre deux vues)* melt; **l'e. des paragraphes est très important** the way in which the paragraphs follow on from each other *or* the paragraphs are linked is very important **3** *(en danse)* sequence (of steps); *(en ballet)* enchaînement **4** *(dans un spectacle)* filler **5** *Ordinat* concatenation

enchaîner [āʃene] **VT 1** *(animal)* to chain up; *(prisonnier)* to chain up, to put in chains; *Fig (la presse, les passions)* to curb; **e. à un poteau** to chain (up) to a post **2** *(lier) (idées, faits, mots etc)* to link (up), to connect; **il est incapable d'e. deux phrases** he can't string *or* put two sentences together; **ils enchaînaient les sujets très vite** they moved very quickly from one subject to another; **e. le tournage de plusieurs épisodes** to shoot several episodes one after the other; **pour la répétition de ce soir, on enchaîne toutes les scènes/chansons** at this evening's rehearsal we'll run through all the scenes/songs one after the other without a break **3** *Cin, TV* to dissolve

VI 1 *(continuer)* to move on, to go on, to carry on; **e. sur un sujet** to move on to a subject; **on enchaîne avec les nouvelles internationales** we'll move on to the international news **2** *Cin* to dissolve, to fade *(into next scene)*; *Théâtre* to carry straight on
VPR s'enchaîner *(de faits, d'épisodes etc)* to be linked together; **on voit comme les choses s'enchaînent** you can see how things hang together *or* are linked together; **les événements se sont enchaînés très vite** things moved *or* happened very quickly

enchanté [āʃāte] **ADJ 1** *(magique etc) (personne, objet, endroit)* enchanted; **la Flûte enchantée** the Magic Flute **2** *(ravi)* enchanted, delighted; **être e. de qch** to be enchanted by *or* delighted with sth; **e. (de faire votre connaissance)** pleased to meet you, how do you do?

enchantement [āʃātmā] **NM 1** *(magie)* enchantment, magic; *(effet)* (magic) spell; **rompre un e.** to break a spell; **comme par e.** as if by magic; **c'est par e. qu'elle s'est transformée en princesse** she was magically turned into a princess **2** *(ravissement)* enchant-ment, delight; *(merveille)* delight; **être dans l'e.** to be enchanted *or* delighted (**de** by)

enchanter [ɑ̃ʃɑ̃te] **VT 1** *(ensorceler)* to en-chant, to bewitch, to cast a spell on **2** *(ravir, plaire à)* to enchant, to delight; **cette idée ne l'enchante pas** he's not taken with the idea *or* keen on the idea

enchanteur, -eresse [ɑ̃ʃɑ̃tœr, -rɛs] **NM 1** *(sorcier)* enchanter **2** *Fig (charmeur)* char-mer

NF enchanteresse enchantress
ADJ *(sourire)* bewitching, captivating; *(dis-cours, endroit etc)* enchanting, delightful, charming

enchâssement [ɑ̃ʃɑsmɑ̃] **NM** *(d'un bijou)* setting, mounting

enchâsser [ɑ̃ʃase] **VT 1** *Rel (relique)* to en-shrine **2** *(bijou)* to set, to mount **3** *Fig (dans un texte)* to insert, to slot in
VPR s'enchâsser to fit perfectly (**dans** into)

enchâssure [ɑ̃ʃasyr] **NF** *(support)* (d'un bi-jou) setting, mount

enchère [ɑ̃ʃɛr] **NF** bid; **les enchères, l'e.** the bidding; **commencer les enchères à 2000 eu-ros** to start the bidding at 2,000 euros; **faire** *ou* **porter une e.** to make a bid; **vente aux en-chères** (sale by) auction; **enchères publiques** public auction; **couvrir une e.** to make a higher bid, to bid higher; **couvrir l'e. de qn** to bid higher than sb, to outbid sb; **pousser** *ou* **faire monter les enchères** to raise *or* push up the bidding; *Fig* to increase the stakes; **vendre/acheter qch aux enchères** to sell/buy sth at auction; **mettre qch aux enchères** to put sth up for auction, to auction sth (off); *Fig* **il l'a pour ainsi dire mise aux enchères** he auctioned her off *or* sold her to the highest bidder, so to speak; *Cartes* **manille aux en-chères** auction bridge; **système des enchè-res** *(au bridge)* bidding system

enchérir [ɑ̃ʃerir] **VI 1** *(dépasser)* to make a higher bid; **e. de dix euros** to bid another ten euros; **e. sur qn** to outbid sb, to make a higher bid than sb; *Fig* to go one better than sb; **e. sur le prix des marchandises** to make a higher bid for the goods **2** *Vieilli (devenir plus cher)* to rise *or* go up in price

enchérissement [ɑ̃ʃerismɑ̃] **NM** *Vieilli (de prix)* rise, increase

enchérisseur, -euse [ɑ̃ʃerisœr, -øz] **N** bid-der; **au plus offrant et dernier e.** to the highest bidder

enchevaucher [ɑ̃ʃ(ə)voʃe] **VT** *(tuiles etc)* to fix *or* lay with an overlap

enchevêtré [ɑ̃ʃ(ə)vetre] **ADJ** *(écheveau, fils)* tangled, in a tangle; *(style, idées)* confused; *(affaires, revues)* in a mess; **un amas de bran-ches enchevêtrées** a tangle of branches

enchevêtrement [ɑ̃ʃ(ə)vetrəmɑ̃] **NM** *(de fils, branches)* tangle; *(d'objets, d'idées)* confusion, muddle; **l'e. de ses idées est tel que …** he is so confused that …; **comment s'y retrouver dans cet e. d'événements?** how on earth are you supposed to make sense of these events when they're all so confused?

enchevêtrer [ɑ̃ʃ(ə)vetre] **VT** *(fils, branches etc)* to tangle (up); *(situation)* to confuse, to muddle
VPR s'enchevêtrer *(de fils, branches etc)* to get tangled *or* in a tangle; *(d'objets)* to get muddled (up) *or* mixed up; *(d'une situation)* to get confused *or* muddled

enchifrené [ɑ̃ʃifrəne] **ADJ** *Vieilli* **il est e.** his nose is blocked

enclave [ɑ̃klav] **NF** *(terrain)*, *Fig* enclave; **l'es-calier fait e. dans la pièce** the staircase leads directly *or* into the room

enclaver [ɑ̃klave] **VT 1** *(poutres etc)* to wedge in, to fit in **2** *(territoire)* to enclose, to make

an enclave of; **domaine qui enclave deux pe-tites terres** estate which encloses two small properties **3** *(une pièce dans une autre)* to fit (**dans** into); **e. deux anneaux l'un dans l'au-tre** to interlock two rings, to fit two rings together

enclenchement [ɑ̃klɑ̃ʃmɑ̃] **NM** *Tech (d'une vitesse, d'un mécanisme etc)* engaging; *(de pièces)* interlocking

enclencher [ɑ̃klɑ̃ʃe] **VT** *(vitesse, mécanisme etc)* to engage; *(pièces)* to interlock; *Fig (en-treprise, projet etc)* to set in motion, to get under way; *Fig* **maintenant que le processus est enclenché, ça va être difficile de faire marche arrière** now that things have been set in motion *or* are under way, there's no going back
VPR s'enclencher *(d'une vitesse, d'un méca-nisme etc)* to engage; *(de pièces)* to interlock; *Fig* **bien/mal s'e.** to get off to a good/bad start

enclin [ɑ̃klɛ̃] **ADJ** inclined, disposed (**à faire qch** to do sth); **elle est encline à la paresse/à la panique** she is inclined *or* tends to be lazy/to panic; **il est e. à l'alcoolisme** he is in-clined to drink, he has alcoholic tendencies

enclitique [ɑ̃klitik] **NM** *Ling* enclitic

enclore [ɑ̃klɔr] **VT** *(conj like* **clore***)* to en-close; *(d'une palissade)* to fence in; *(d'un mur)* to wall in

enclos [ɑ̃klo] **NM 1** *(espace)* enclosure; *(pour chevaux)* paddock **2** *(clôture)* enclosure; *(mur)* (enclosing) wall

enclume [ɑ̃klym] **NF 1** anvil; **e. de cordon-nier** (shoemender's) last; *Fig* **être entre le marteau et l'e.** to be between the devil and the deep (blue) sea **2** *Anat (de l'oreille in-terne)* anvil

encoche [ɑ̃kɔʃ] **NF** *(dans un morceau de bois)* notch (**à, sur** in); *(d'une flèche)* nock; *(pour répertoire à onglets)* notch; *Ordinat* **e. de protection contre l'écriture** write-protect notch; *Élec* **armature à encoches** slotted armature

encochement [ɑ̃kɔʃmɑ̃] **NM** notching

encocher [ɑ̃kɔʃe] **VT** *(morceau de bois)* to notch; *(livre)* to thumb-index

encodage [ɑ̃kɔdaʒ] **NM** *Ling, Ordinat* encoding

encoder [ɑ̃kɔde] **VT** *Ling, Ordinat* to encode

encodeur [ɑ̃kɔdœr] **NM** *Ordinat* encoder

encoignure [ɑ̃kwaɲyr] **NF 1** *(d'une pièce)* corner, angle **2** *(petit meuble)* corner cupboard

encollage [ɑ̃kɔlaʒ] **NM** *(à l'aide de colle) (de papier)* pasting; *(de bois)* glueing; *(à l'aide d'apprêt) (de papier, tissu, plâtre etc)* sizing; *Typ* perfect binding

encoller [ɑ̃kɔle] **VT** *(à l'aide de colle) (papier)* to paste; *(bois etc)* to glue, to apply glue to; *(à l'aide d'apprêt) (papier, tissu, plâtre etc)* to size

encolure [ɑ̃kɔlyr] **NF 1** *(de chameau, d'au-truche etc)* neck; *Courses de chevaux* **gagner d'une e.** to win by a neck **2** *(tour de cou)* neck size; **homme de forte e.** thickset *or* stocky man **3** *(échancrure) (d'un vêtement)* neck (opening); **e. carrée** square neck

encombrant [ɑ̃kɔ̃brɑ̃] **ADJ** *(meuble, valise etc)* cumbersome, bulky; *(colis)* bulky; **ce ca-napé est e.** the sofa is too big, the sofa takes up too much space *or* is in the way; **ils l'ont liquidé car il devenait trop e.** they bumped him off because he was becoming too much of a liability; **un témoin e.** an unwanted wit-ness

NMPL *Région* **les encombrants passent de-main** the bulk refuse disposal people are coming tomorrow; **mettre qch aux encom-brants** to put sth out for collection; **j'ai**

trouvé cette table aux encombrants I found this table in among rubbish put out for collection

encombre [ɑ̃kɔ̃br] **NM sans e.** without mis-hap, safely; **il a obtenu son diplôme sans e.** he got his degree without any problem

encombrement [ɑ̃kɔ̃brəmɑ̃] **NM 1** *(état) (de la circulation)* congestion; *(des rues, de l'es-pace aérien)* overcrowding; *(de lignes télé-phoniques)* jamming, blocking; *(de texte)* depth **2** *(amas)* clutter, litter; **il y a un tel e. de livres dans son bureau** his/her office is so cluttered up with books **3** *(espace, volume) (d'une voiture, d'un meuble etc)* (overall) di-mensions **4** *Ordinat* footprint; **faible e. sur le disque dur** low use of hard disk space

encombrer [ɑ̃kɔ̃bre] **VT** *(pièce)* to clutter (up); *(passage, route etc)* to obstruct, to block; *(lignes téléphoniques)* to jam, to block; **e. les rues** to congest the streets; **table encombrée de papiers** table littered with papers; **sentier encombré de ronces** path overgrown with brambles; **les lignes té-léphoniques sont vraiment encombrées** the telephone lines are really busy; **e. le marché** to glut *or* saturate the market; **j'ai les mains encombrées** my hands are full; **je ne veux pas de ce divan, il m'encombrerait** I don't want this sofa, it would just clutter my place up; **tu m'encombres, sors d'ici!** you're get-ting under my feet, get out!
VPR s'encombrer s'e. de *(colis, équipement etc)* to load oneself down with; *Fig (obliga-tions, enfants etc)* to burden oneself *or* saddle oneself with; **je ne vais pas m'e. de scrupules** I'm not going to be over-scrupulous

encontre (à l') [alɑ̃kɔ̃tr] **ADV** in opposition; **cela va à l'e. de la loi** that's against the law; **tu n'as pas le droit d'aller à l'e. du projet** you have no right to try to stop *or* go against the project; **cela va à l'e. de ce qu'il proposait la semaine dernière** that's the opposite of *or* contradicts what he was saying last week; **ces nouvelles méthodes vont à l'e. de tout ce qu'on m'a toujours appris** these new methods go against *or* are contrary to *or* run counter to everything I've been taught; **cela va à l'e. du bon sens** it goes against common sense

encorbellement [ɑ̃kɔrbɛlmɑ̃] **NM** *Archit (d'un mur etc)* corbelling; *(d'un étage supé-rieur)* overhang; **fenêtre en e.** oriel window

encorder (s') [sɑ̃kɔrde] **VPR** *(en alpinisme)* to rope up

ENCORE [ɑ̃kɔr]

still **1–3** ▪ not yet *(pas encore)* **2** ▪ more **3** ▪ another **3, 4** ▪ again **4** ▪ even more/less *(encore plus/moins)* **3** ▪ moreover **5** ▪ if that *(et encore)* **6** ▪ although *(encore que)* **7** ▪ only **9**

ADV 1 *(toujours)* still; **je cherche e. une expli-cation** I am still looking for an explanation; **je ne suis e. qu'étudiant** I'm still only a stu-dent, I'm only a student as yet

2 pas e. not yet; **elle n'est pas e. mariée** she isn't married yet, she's still not married; **elle n'est e. jamais** *ou* **e. pas venue me voir** she hasn't come to see me yet, she still hasn't come to see me; **un homme que je n'avais e. jamais vu** a man I'd never seen before

3 *(davantage)* more; **e. un mot** (just) one word more; **en voulez-vous e.?** would you like some more?; **e. du vin, s'il vous plaît!** some more wine please!; **e. une tasse de café** another cup of coffee; **pendant trois mois e., pendant e. trois mois** for three months longer, for another three months; **il est e. plus beau que je ne le pensais** he's even better looking than I thought; **il y a e.**

moins de relief que dans mon pays it's even flatter than where I come from; **réduire e. le prix** to reduce the price still or even further or more; **c'est e. pire** it's even worse, it's worse still

4 (de nouveau) again; **voilà e. la pluie!** here's the rain again!; **nous l'avons e. vu hier** we saw him again yesterday; **qu'est-ce qu'il a e. fait?** now what's he done?, what's he done now or this time?; **il y a e. eu un meurtre d'enfant** another child has been murdered; **quoi e.?** now what?; **e. une fois** once more, once again; **e. autant** as much again; **e. vous!** (what) you again?

5 (en plus) moreover, furthermore; **non seulement stupide, mais e. têtu** not only stupid, but also pigheaded or Fam but pigheaded to boot; **que faut-il que je prenne e.?** what else do I need to take?

6 (restrictif) **e. s'il était reconnaissant!** if only he was at least grateful!; **si e. je savais où il se cache** if I only knew or if only I knew where he was hiding; **il aura peut-être une chance là-bas, et e.!** perhaps he'll have a chance over there, but only just or but not much of one!; **il vous en donnera dix euros et e.!** he'll give you ten euros for it, if that!; Fam **il faudrait e. que je trouve une voiture!** for a start or first I would have to find a car!; **(mais) il faudrait-il qu'elle accepte!** she has to agree first!

7 e. que + sub (al)though, even though; **e. qu'il ne me soit rien** (al)though he is nothing to me; **temps agréable e. qu'un peu froid** pleasant if or though rather cold weather

8 il a dit qu'il avait bien aimé – mais e.? he said he liked it – but what exactly did he say?; **elle est sympa – mais e.?** she's nice – yes, go on!

9 (pas plus tard que) **hier e. je lui ai parlé** I spoke to him only yesterday, I just spoke to him yesterday; **c'est ce que nous nous disions e. hier soir** ou **hier soir e.** that's what we were saying only or just last night

---

encorné [ãkɔrne] ADJ (animal) horned

encorner [ãkɔrne] VT (d'un taureau) to gore

encornet [ãkɔrnɛ] NM (mollusque) squid

encoubler (s') [sãkuble] VPR Suisse to trip over

encourageant [ãkuraʒã] ADJ (personne) encouraging; (nouvelles, résultat, événement etc) encouraging, heartening

encouragement [ãkuraʒmã] NM encouragement; **prime d'e.** incentive; **e. à la vertu/au crime** incentive to virtue/to crime; **recevoir peu d'encouragements à faire qch** to receive little encouragement or little inducement to do sth

encourager [ãkuraʒe] VT (j'encourageai(s)) **1** (personne) to encourage, to cheer on; **ils m'ont beaucoup encouragé** they encouraged me a lot, they gave me a lot of encouragement; **être encouragé par qn** to be encouraged by sb, to receive or get encouragement from sb; **encouragé par les premiers résultats** encouraged or heartened by the first results; **elle l'a encouragé d'un sourire** she gave him an encouraging smile, she smiled at him encouragingly; **e. qn à faire qch** to encourage sb to do sth **2** (arts) to encourage, to foster, to promote; (plan) to promote; **la presse encourage l'utilisation de certaines drogues** the press encourages the use of certain drugs; **l'oisiveté encourage le vice** idleness encourages or promotes vice

encourir [ãkurir] VT (conj like courir) (dépense) to incur; (punition, reproches, sanctions) to incur, to bring (up)on oneself; **e. des risques** to run risks; **il sait qu'il encourt une lourde punition** he knows he risks being severely punished

en(-)cours [ãkur] NM INV **1** Banque loans outstanding, exposure; **e. de crédit** exposure; **e. débiteur autorisé** authorized overdraft facility **2** Compta **e. de production de biens** work-in-progress

encrage [ãkraʒ] NM Typ inking (up)

encrassé [ãkrase] ADJ (tuyau) clogged-up; (bougie) sooted-up; (chaudière) scaled-up

encrassement [ãkrasmã] NM (des vêtements, mains etc) dirtying; Aut (d'une bougie) fouling, sooting (up); (d'une machine etc) clogging, choking

encrasser [ãkrase] VT (ses vêtements, mains etc) to dirty; Aut (bougie) to soot up; (machine etc) to clog, to choke
▪ **VPR s'encrasser** to get dirty; Aut (d'une bougie) to soot up; (d'une machine) to get clogged or choked

encre [ãkr] NF **1** ink; **écrit à l'e.** written in ink; **cela a fait couler beaucoup d'e.** a lot has been written about it; **doigts couverts d'e.** inky fingers, fingers covered in ink; **noir comme de l'e.** inky black, black as ink; Fig **nuit d'e.** inky black night; Fam **c'est la bouteille à l'e.** it's got everyone scratching their head or stumped; Psy **test de la tache d'e.** inkblot or Rorschach test **2** Zool (de seiche) ink
▸ ▪ **e. de Chine** Indian ink; **e. d'impression** printing ink; **e. d'imprimerie** printing ink, printer's ink; **e. en poudre** toner; **e. sympathique** invisible ink

encrer [ãkre] VT Typ to ink (up)

encreur [ãkrœr] ADJ **ruban e.** (typewriter) ribbon; Typ **rouleau e.** inker

encrier [ãkrije] NM inkwell, inkpot, inkstand

encroûté [ãkrute] ADJ Fam (personne) (stuck) in a rut, set in one's ways; **qu'est-ce que tu peux être e.!** what a stick-in-the-mud you are!; **vieux bonhomme e.** old fogey or stick-in-the-mud; **il mène une vie très encroûtée** he is very set in his ways

encroûtement [ãkrutmã] NM **1** (d'une tuyauterie) encrustation **2** Fam (d'une personne) sinking into a rut; **sortir ou tirer qn de son e.** to get sb out of his/her rut

encroûter [ãkrute] VT **1** (tuyauterie) to encrust **2** Fam (personne) **la retraite l'a encroûté** retirement has made him set in his ways or got him into a rut
▪ **VPR s'encroûter 1** (d'une tuyauterie) to become encrusted (**de** with) **2** Fam (d'une personne) to get into a or stuck in a rut, to become set in one's way

enculé, -ée [ãkyle] N Vulg bugger, arsehole, Am asshole

enculer [ãkyle] VT Vulg to bugger; **va te faire e.!** bugger off!, sod off!; Fig **e. les mouches** to nit-pick

encuver [ãkyve] VT (peaux, raisins) to vat

encyclique [ãsiklik] NF Rel encyclical

encyclopédie [ãsiklɔpedi] NF encyclop(a)edia; Fam **une e. vivante** a walking encyclop(a)edia

encyclopédique [ãsiklɔpedik] ADJ encyclop(a)edic

encyclopédiste [ãsiklɔpedist] N encyclop(a)edist

endéans [ãdeã] PRÉP Belg within

endémie [ãdemi] NF endemic (disease)

endémique [ãdemik] ADJ Méd, Fig endemic (à to)

endenter [ãdãte] VT **1** (roue etc) to tooth, to cog, to ratchet **2** (assembler) (roues) to mesh

endetté [ãdete] ADJ in debt; Fig in debt, indebted (**envers** to); **très e.** deep(ly) or heavily in debt

endettement [ãdɛtmã] NM (action) running or getting into debt; (état) debt; Compta indebtedness, gearing; **e. des consommateurs** consumer debt; **e. extérieur** foreign debt; **e. intérieur** internal debt; **e. public** public debt; **l'e. des pays du Tiers Monde** the debt burden of Third World countries; **cela a provoqué l'e. du pays** this caused the country to get into debt; **ratio d'e.** debt ratio; **facilité d'e.** borrowing capacity

endetter [ãdete] VT to get into debt; **l'acquisition de nouvelles machines a endetté la société** the purchase of new machinery has got the company into debt
▪ **VPR s'endetter** to run or get into debt; **s'e. trop lourdement** to take on too many debts

endeuiller [ãdœje] VT (famille, nation etc) to plunge into mourning; (événement) to cast gloom over; **maison endeuillée** house in mourning

endêver [ãdeve] VT & VI Can Fam **il m'endêve, il me fait e.** he infuriates me

endiablé [ãdjable] ADJ (personne) lively, full of life; (musique, rythme etc) wild, frenzied

endiguement [ãdigmã] NM **1** (action) (d'un cours d'eau) embanking, dyking (up) **2** (digue) embankment, dyke **3** Fig (de l'inflation) containment, holding in check; (de la violence, la pauvreté, du chômage) containment; **tenter l'e. de la violence/de la hausse des prix** to attempt to contain violence/price increases

endiguer [ãdige] VT **1** (cours d'eau) to embank, to dyke (up) **2** Fig (foule, colère, hausse des prix) to hold back, to contain; (inflation, pauvreté, chômage, violence) to contain

endimanché [ãdimãʃe] ADJ all dressed up, in one's Sunday best

endimancher (s') [sãdimãʃe] VPR to put on one's best clothes or one's Sunday best, to get all dressed up

endive [ãdiv] NF endive; (chicorée) chicory; Fam **pâle comme une e.** as white or pale as a sheet

endocarde [ãdɔkard] NM Anat endocardium

endocardite [ãdɔkardit] NF Méd endocarditis

endocarpe [ãdɔkarp] NM Bot endocarp

endocrine [ãdɔkrin] ADJ F Physiol (glande) endocrine

endocrinien, -ienne [ãdɔkrinjɛ̃, -jɛn] ADJ Physiol (glande etc) endocrine, endocrinal

endocrinologie [ãdɔkrinɔlɔʒi] NF endocrinology

endoctrinement [ãdɔktrinmã] NM indoctrination

endoctriner [ãdɔktrine] VT to indoctrinate, Fam to brainwash

endogame [ãdɔgam] ADJ endogamous

endogamie [ãdɔgami] NF endogamy

endogène [ãdɔʒɛn] ADJ endogenous

endolori [ãdɔlɔri] ADJ (bras etc) sore, painful

endolorir [ãdɔlɔrir] VT (bras etc) to make sore or painful
▪ **VPR s'endolorir** to become sore or painful

endolorissement [ãdɔlɔrismã] NM Litt pain, soreness

endommagement [ãdɔmaʒmã] NM (action) damaging (**de** of); (résultat) damage (**de** to)

endommager [ãdɔmaʒe] (j'endommageai(s)) VT **1** to damage, to do damage to **2** Ordinat to corrupt; **fichier endommagé** damaged or corrupt file

endomorphine [ãdɔmɔrfin] NF Physiol endorphin

endormant [ãdɔrmã] ADJ (ennuyeux) (dis-

cours, réunion etc) boring, wearisome; *(tâche)* boring, humdrum

endormi, -ie [ɑ̃dɔrmi] ADJ **1** *(personne)* asleep, sleeping; *(voix, village)* sleepy; **avoir l'air e.** to look sleepy; **j'ai la jambe endormie** my leg has gone to sleep *or* is numb **2** *Fam (inerte, lent) (personne)* inattentive, half-asleep **3** *Fig (passion, intérêt etc)* dormant **N** *(personne inerte, lente)* slowcoach

Attention: le terme **asleep** n'est jamais utilisé comme épithète.

endormir [ɑ̃dɔrmir] *(conj like* **dormir***)* VT **1** *(d'une drogue, un hypnotiseur etc)* to put *or* send to sleep; *(d'une mère) (enfant)* to send *or* lull to sleep **2** *(ennuyer)* to send *or* put to sleep **3** *(apaiser) (douleur)* to deaden; **e. les soupçons** to allay suspicion
VPR **s'endormir 1** to fall asleep, to go to sleep, *Fam* to drop off (to sleep) **2** *Fig (d'une douleur)* to die away; *(de soupçons)* to be allayed

endormissement [ɑ̃dɔrmismɑ̃] NM **1** falling asleep, *Fam* dropping off (to sleep) **2** *Ordinat* hibernation, sleep mode

endorphine [ɑ̃dɔrfin] NF *Physiol* endorphin

endos [ɑ̃do] NM *(sur chèque)* endorsement

endoscope [ɑ̃dɔskɔp] NM *Méd* endoscope

endoscopie [ɑ̃dɔskɔpi] NF *Méd* endoscopy

endossable [ɑ̃dosabl] ADJ *(chèque)* endorsable

endossataire [ɑ̃dosatɛr] N endorsee

endossement [ɑ̃dosmɑ̃] NM *(d'un chèque)* endorsement; **e. en blanc** blank endorsement

endosser [ɑ̃dose] VT **1** *(veste etc)* to put on **2** *(responsabilité)* to assume, to shoulder; **je ne vais pas encore e. tes erreurs** I'm not going to take the responsibility *or* shoulder the blame for your mistakes again **3** *(chèque)* to endorse; **e. en blanc** to blank endorse **4** *(en reliure) (livre)* to back

endosseur, -euse [ɑ̃dosœr, -øz] N *(d'un chèque)* endorser

endroit [ɑ̃drwa] NM **1** *(lieu)* place, spot; **c'est l'e. idéal pour un magasin** it's the ideal place *or* spot for a shop; **je ne sais plus à quel e. j'ai rangé mes lunettes** I don't know where I put my glasses; **je me suis arrêté à cet e. du livre, j'ai arrêté ma lecture à cet e.** this is where I stopped reading, I stopped reading here; **ça me fait mal à cet e.** it hurts me (just) here; **c'est à cet e. que ça vous fait mal?** is this where it hurts?; **par endroits** here and there, in places; **en plusieurs/certains endroits** in several/certain places; **rire au bon e.** to laugh in the right place; *Fam* **le petit e.** *Br* the loo, *Am* the john
2 *(bon sens)* right side; **ton pull n'est pas à l'e.** your sweater's on the wrong way round; *(les coutures ne sont pas à l'intérieur)* your sweater's on inside out; **remets la bouteille à l'e.** turn the bottle the right way up; *Tricot* **maille à l'e.** plain stitch; **deux à l'e., deux à l'envers** knit two, purl two

enduire [ɑ̃dɥir] *(prp* **enduisant;** *pp* **enduit;** *pr ind* **j'enduis, il enduit;** *impf* **j'enduisais;** *p hist* **j'enduisis;** *fut* **j'enduirai)** VT **e. de** *(peinture, ciment, colle etc)* to coat *or* cover with; *(crème, boue etc)* to smear with
VPR **s'enduire s'e. de crème à bronzer** to smear *or* rub *or* cover oneself with suntan cream

enduit [ɑ̃dɥi] NM **1** *(de goudron, peinture etc)* coat, application **2** *Constr (plâtre)* plastering, coat of plaster; **e. de ciment** cement rendering; **e. imperméable** proofing **3** *Cér* glaze, glazing

endurable [ɑ̃dyrabl] ADJ endurable

endurance [ɑ̃dyrɑ̃s] NF **1** *(physique)* stamina, staying power, endurance **2** *(morale)* endurance, powers of resistance; **il n'a pas eu l'e. nécessaire pour résister à la pression** he wasn't tough enough to stand up to the pressure **3** *Aut etc* **épreuve/course d'e.** endurance trial/run

endurant [ɑ̃dyrɑ̃] ADJ **1** *(résistant)* tough; **elle n'était pas assez endurante** she wasn't tough enough *or* didn't have enough stamina **2** *Vieilli (patient)* enduring, long-suffering

endurci [ɑ̃dyrsi] ADJ **1** *(dur) (personne)* hard, callous; *(cœur)* hard **2** *(invétéré) (criminel)* hardened; *(célibataire)* confirmed; *(haine)* inveterate

endurcir [ɑ̃dyrsir] VT **1** *(cuirasser) (quelqu'un, le cœur de qn)* to harden; **son séjour dans l'armée l'a endurci** his time in the army toughened him up **2** *(rendre résistant)* to harden, to toughen (up); **être endurci à la fatigue** to be inured *or* hardened to fatigue
VPR **s'endurcir 1** *(moralement)* to become hard; **il s'est beaucoup endurci** he has become very hard **2** *(physiquement)* to toughen up, to become hardened

endurcissement [ɑ̃dyrsismɑ̃] NM **1** *(action) (moral)* hardening; *(physique)* hardening, toughening (up) **2** *(état) (moral)* hardness, callousness; *(physique)* hardness, toughness

endurer [ɑ̃dyre] VT *(épreuve, mauvais traitements)* to endure, to bear; **je ne vois pas pourquoi je devrais e. cela** I can't see why I should put up with that

enduro [ɑ̃dyro] NM *Sport* enduro

Énée [ene] N Aeneas

Énéide (l') [leneid] NF *Littér* the Aeneid

énergétique [enɛrʒetik] ADJ **1** *(médicament, nourriture etc)* energizing, energy-giving; **dépense é.** expenditure of energy **2** *Écon (ressources, besoins etc)* energy
NF energetics

Note that **énergétique** means **energy-giving**: it should not be confused with **énergique** which means **energetic**.

énergie [enɛrʒi] NF **1** *(force)* energy; **apporter** *ou* **appliquer** *ou* **mettre toute son é. à une tâche/à faire qch** to devote *or* direct all one's energies to a task/to doing sth; **je n'ai pas assez d'é. pour sortir ce soir** I haven't got the energy to go out this evening; **je ne me sens pas beaucoup d'é.** I'm not feeling very energetic; **avec é.** energetically; *(refuser, répondre)* forcefully, vigorously; **elle conduit avec é.** she's an aggressive driver; **il a fait face à la situation avec é.** she faced up to the situation with spirit; **l'é. d'un passage/d'un style** the vigour of a passage/style; **sans é.** *(adjectivement)* listless; *(adverbialement)* listlessly; **il agit avec l'é. du désespoir** to do sth with the strength born of desperation **2** *Ind* energy, power; **faire des économies d'é.** to save energy; **la crise de l'é.** the energy crisis
▸▸ **é. atomique** atomic energy, nuclear power; **é. cinétique** kinetic energy; **é. électrique** electrical power; **é. éolienne** wind power; **é. hydraulique** hydraulic power; **é. nucléaire** nuclear power; **é. potentielle** potential energy; **é. solaire** solar power *or* energy; **é. thermique** thermal power

énergique [enɛrʒik] ADJ **1** *(personne)* energetic, dynamic; *(vendeur)* aggressive; *(personnalité)* forceful; **une jeune femme é.** a young woman with plenty of spirit *or* drive; **un visage é.** a strong face **2** *(mesures)* strong, drastic; *(langage)* strong, forceful; *(geste)* emphatic, forceful; *(coup de pied, coup)* forceful; *(médicament, remède)* powerful

Note that **énergique** means **energetic**: it should not be confused with **énergétique** which means **energy-giving**.

énergiquement [enɛrʒikmɑ̃] ADV *(nier)* energetically, forcefully; *(agir, parler)* forcefully; *(refuser, répondre)* forcefully, vigorously; *(conduire)* aggressively; **s'y mettre é.** to put one's back into it

énergisant [enɛrʒizɑ̃] ADJ *(médicament, nourriture etc)* energizing, energy-giving
NM *Méd* antidepressant

énergumène [enɛrgymɛn] N *Fam* maniac; **c'est un drôle d'é.** he's a queer fish

énervant [enɛrvɑ̃] ADJ **1** *(personne, habitude etc)* irritating; *(bruit)* nerve-racking **2** *Vieilli (climat)* enervating

énervé [enɛrve] ADJ *(agacé)* irritated; *(excité) (personne)* on edge, edgy, agitated; *(rire)* nervous

énervement [enɛrvəmɑ̃] NM *(agacement)* irritation; *(excitation)* edginess

énerver [enɛrve] VT **1 é. qn** *(agacer)* to get on sb's nerves, to irritate sb; *(exciter)* to get sb worked up, to agitate sb **2** *Vieilli (débiliter)* to enervate, to weaken
VPR **s'énerver** to get excited *or* agitated *or* (all) worked up

Il faut noter que le verbe anglais **to unnerve** est un faux ami. Il signifie **troubler**.

enfaîteau, -eaux [ɑ̃feto] NM *Constr* ridge tile

enfaîtement [ɑ̃fetmɑ̃] NM *Constr* ridge tiling, ridging

enfaîter [ɑ̃fete] VT *Constr (toit)* to ridge

enfance [ɑ̃fɑ̃s] NF **1** *(jeunesse)* childhood; *(de garçon)* boyhood; *(de fille)* girlhood; **elle a eu une e. heureuse/difficile** she had a happy/difficult childhood; **dans mon e.** in my childhood, when I was a child; **depuis mon e.** ever since I was a child; **souvenir/camarade d'e.** childhood memory/friend; **petite e.** infancy, early childhood; **des souvenirs datant de la petite e.** memories of when one was very small, early childhood memories; **l'e. d'une civilisation** the dawn *or* beginning of a civilization; *Fam* **c'est l'e. de l'art** it's (mere) child's play; **industrie encore dans son e.** industry still in its infancy; **retomber en e.** to sink into one's second childhood *or* one's dotage **2** *(enfants)* **l'e.** children

enfant [ɑ̃fɑ̃] N **1** *(jeune)* child, *pl* children; *Jur (mineur)* infant; **c'est une belle e.** she's a beautiful child; **e. en bas âge** infant; **éducation des enfants** children's education; **babil d'e.** childish prattle; **elle me parle comme à un e.** she talks to me as if I was a child; **les droits de l'e.** children's rights; **menu e.** children's menu; **l'e. qui est en chacun de nous** the child in all of us; **je l'ai connu e.** I have known him since he was a child; *Fam* **c'est un jeu d'e.** it's child's play; *Fam* **il n'y a plus d'enfants** honestly, kids nowadays!; **se conduire en e., faire l'e.** to act *or* behave childishly *or* like a child, to be childish; **e. surdoué** exceptionally gifted child
2 *(fils, fille)* child; **elle attend un e.** she's expecting a child *or* baby; *Fam* **il lui a fait un e.** she had a child by him; **être en mal d'e.** *(d'une femme)* to be broody; *Fam* **c'est son e.** *(création)* it's his baby *or* his brainchild; **couple sans e.** childless couple; **mourir sans enfants** to die childless *or Jur* without issue
3 *(descendant)* **un e. du peuple** a child of the people; **un e. de Paris** a native of Paris
4 *(terme d'affection) Fam* **salut, les enfants!** *(à des adultes)* hello people!, hi guys *or* gang!
▸▸ **e. de l'amour** love child; **e. de la balle** child who follows in his father's footsteps; **c'est un e. de la balle** he was born in a trunk;

Méd **e. bleu** blue baby; **e. bulle** = child who has to be kept in a sterile environment because of an immune deficiency; **e. de chœur** *Rel* altar boy; *Fig* naive person; *Fig* **je ne suis pas un e. de chœur** I'm no saint *or* no angel; **e. gâté** spoilt child; **les enfants d'Israël** the children of Israel; *Rel* **l'E. Jésus** the Christ Child, *Enf* Baby Jesus; *Rel* **les enfants de Marie** the Legion of Mary; *Fig* **c'est une e. de Marie** she's an innocent; **cela fait bien longtemps que ce n'est plus une e. de Marie** it's a long time since she was as pure as the driven snow; **e. martyr** battered baby/child; **e. naturel** illegitimate child; *Jur* natural child; **e. prodige** child prodigy; *Rel*, *Fig* **e. prodigue** prodigal son; **e. terrible** enfant terrible; **e. de troupe** army child *or Fam* brat; **e. trouvé** foundling; **e. unique** only child

enfantement [ãfãtmã] NM childbirth; *Fig (d'une œuvre littéraire)* production

enfanter [ãfãte] VT *(enfant)* to bear, to give birth to; *Fig (œuvre littéraire)* to produce, to give birth to; **la discorde enfante le crime** discord begets crime

enfantillage [ãfãtijaʒ] NM **enfantillage(s)** childishness, infantile behaviour; **de l'e. pur et simple** sheer childishness; **ne fais pas d'enfantillages!** don't be childish *or* infantile!

enfantin [ãfãtɛ̃] ADJ **1** *(voix)* child's; *(jeu, littérature)* children's; *Péj (remarque, action etc)* childish, infantile; **des voix enfantines** children's voices; **babil e.** childish prattle **2** *(élémentaire)* elementary; **c'est e.** it's child's play; **c'est d'une simplicité enfantine** it's childishly simple

enfarger [ãfarʒe] *Can* VI to trip
  VPR **s'enfarger** to trip over

enfariné [ãfarine] ADJ *(visage, cheveux etc) (de farine)* covered with flour; *(de poudre)* smothered in powder; *Fam* **je suis arrivée, la gueule enfarinée, demander mon augmentation** I arrived in all innocence *or* quite unsuspecting to ask for my rise; **à chaque fois qu'il casse quelque chose, il vient la gueule enfarinée** whenever he breaks something he turns up looking all innocent *or* as if butter wouldn't melt in his mouth

enfer [ãfɛr] NM **1** *Rel etc* l'e. hell; **les enfers** the underworld; *Myth* Hades; **l'E. de Dante** Dante's Inferno; *Fig* **aller en e.** to go to hell; **il fait de ma vie un e.** he's making my life hell; **elle a vécu un véritable e.** she's been through sheer *or* a living hell; **c'est vraiment l'e. à la maison** it's sheer hell at home; **quelquefois c'est l'e. pour se garer ici** it can be hell trying to park here; **l'e. de la drogue/de la prostitution/du chômage** the living hell of drug addiction/of prostitution/of unemployment; **descente aux enfers** ou **en e.** descent into hell; **une vision d'e.** a vision of hell; **aller un train d'e.** to go at top speed *or Fam* hell for leather; **bruit d'e.** hellish noise; *Fam* **une soirée d'e.** *(excellent)* a great *or* terrific party; **cette fille est d'e.!** she's a great *or* terrific girl

  2 *(dans une bibliothèque)* = library department containing books not available to the public

enfermement [ãfɛrməmã] NM imprisonment

enfermer [ãfɛrme] VT **1** *(personne, objet)* to shut up; **e. qch/qn (à clef)** to lock sth/sb up; **tenir qn enfermé** to keep sb shut up *or* locked up; **e. qn dehors** to shut *or* lock sb out; **j'ai été enfermé dans une pièce toute la journée** I've been shut up *or* cooped up in a room all day; **vivre trop enfermé** to stay at home too much; *Fam* **il est bon à e.** he ought to be locked up; *Fig* **e. un mot dans une définition trop étroite/qn dans un rôle inadéquat** to confine a word in an excessively

narrow definition/sb in an inadequate role; **e. qn dans ses contradictions** to trap sb in his own contradictions; **e. le savoir dans les bibliothèques** to lock away *or* shut away knowledge in libraries; **être enfermé dans ses pensées** to be wrapped up in one's thoughts

  2 *(entourer) (jardin, terrain, bâtiment)* to enclose, to surround; *Sport (concurrent)* to hem *or* box in

  VPR **s'enfermer** to shut oneself up; *(à clef)* to lock oneself in; **s'e. dehors** to lock oneself out; *Fig* **s'e. dans le silence/un rôle** to retreat into silence/to confine oneself to a role; **depuis qu'il est prof, il s'est enfermé dans le rôle de M. je sais tout** he's turned into a real know-it-all since he became a teacher; **Johnny Weissmuller s'est enfermé dans le rôle de Tarzan** Johnny Weissmuller never tried to be anybody but Tarzan

enferrer (s') [sãfere] VPR **s'e.** to impale oneself (**sur** on); *Fig (dans une explication, ses mensonges etc)* to get tangled up *or* bogged down

enfichable [ãfiʃabl] ADJ *Élec* that can be plugged in; *Ordinat* slot-in

enficher [ãfiʃe] VT *Élec* to plug in

enfiévré [ãfjevre] ADJ *(front)*, *Fig (imagination)* fevered; *Fig (atmosphère)* feverish; *(foule)* in a fever (of excitement), at fever pitch

enfièvrement [ãfjevrəmã] NM fever (of excitement)

enfiévrer [ãfjevre] (**j'enfièvre; j'enfiéverai**) VT **1** *(énerver) (personne, imagination)* to excite, to fire, to stir **2** *Méd Vieilli* to make feverish
  VPR **s'enfiévrer 1** *(se passionner)* to get excited *or* all worked up; **s'e. pour une cause** to become passionate about a cause **2** *Méd Vieilli* to grow feverish

enfilade [ãfilad] NF **1** *(de portes, maisons, colonnes, couloirs etc)* succession, series; *(de pièces etc)* series, suite; **nos deux chambres sont en e.** we have adjoining rooms; **la cuisine et la buanderie sont en e.** the kitchen and the laundry room are next to *or* adjoin each other; **maisons en e.** row of houses; **je me suis perdue dans l'e. des couloirs** I got lost in the maze of corridors *or* the endless corridors **2** *Mil* enfilade; **tir d'e.** raking *or* enfilading fire

enfiler [ãfile] VT **1** *(aiguille)* to thread; *(perles)* to string **2** *(rue, couloir etc)* to take, to go along **3** *(vêtements)* to slip on, to pull on; *(pantalon, bas)* to pull on **4** *Vulg (sexuellement)* to screw, to lay; **ce que je cherche, moi, le samedi soir, c'est une fille à e.** I'm out to get laid on a Saturday night **5** *(troupes etc)* to enfilade, to rake
  VPR **s'enfiler 1** *(s'engager)* **s'e. dans un couloir/une rue** to go along a corridor/street **2** *Fam (consommer) (boisson)* to down, to knock back; *(nourriture)* to put away, to guzzle; **s'e. un bon dîner** to have a slap-up meal; **je me suis enfilé un sandwich en vitesse** I grabbed a sandwich, I had a quick sandwich **3** *Fam (avoir à supporter) (tâche)* to get stuck *or* landed with **4** *(de gants, bottes)* to pull on, to go on; *(d'un étui)* to slide on

enfin [ãfɛ̃] ADV **1** *(en dernier lieu)* last, finally, lastly; **e. et surtout** last but not least

  2 *(plutôt)* **blonde, e. châtain clair** blond, well, light brown; **elle n'est pas mal, e. pour son âge** she's not bad – for her age, that is; **c'était une soirée géniale, e. je veux dire qu'on ne s'est pas ennuyé** it was a good party – we weren't bored, I mean

  3 *(finalement)* at last, finally, at length; **e. vous voilà!, vous voilà e.!** here you are at last!; **j'y suis e. arrivée** I finally managed, I managed it at last

  4 *(résignation)* that's that!; **e. c'est la vie** well, that's life!; **mais e., si elle est heureuse!** but as long as she's happy!; **mais e. bon, c'est son problème** oh well, that's *his* problem!; **e., n'en parlons plus!** let's forget it; **e.! ce qui est fait est fait** what's done is done

  5 *(exaspération)* **e. quoi, tu n'as plus 10 ans!** after all, you're not 10 any more!; **on est en République e., quoi!** it's a free country after all!; **mais e. je te l'avais déjà dit!** I'd already told you!; **mais e., c'est pas vrai!** I don't believe it!; **e., lâche-moi un peu!** give me some peace!, give it a rest!

  6 *(hésitation, pour résumer)* well; **e. je ne dis pas non, mais …** well, I'm not saying no, but …; **mais e., s'il acceptait!** but still, if he did accept!; **e. (bref) c'était la panique!** in short *or* in a word *or* to cut a long story short, it was panic!; **c'est un homme, e.! il a sa dignité!** he's a man after all! he has his dignity!

enfirouâper [ãfirwape] VT **1** *Fam (tromper)* to fool, to hoodwink; **se faire e. (se faire avoir)** to get taken for a ride, to be had; *(être enjôlé)* to be taken in; *(se faire mettre enceinte)* to get knocked up **2** *Fam (nourriture)* to gulp down, to wolf down

enflammé [ãflame] ADJ **1** *(bois, brindille, torche)* burning, blazing; *(allumette)* burning; *(soleil, coucher de soleil)* fiery **2** *(joues) (de froid)* glowing; *(de fièvre, gêne, chaleur)* burning **3** *Méd (plaie, gorge etc)* inflamed **4** *Fig (discours, caractère etc)* fiery, passionate; **faire une déclaration enflammée à une femme** to make a passionate declaration to a woman

enflammer [ãflame] VT **1** *(mettre en flammes)* to set light to, to set ablaze; **e. une allumette** to strike a match **2** *Méd (plaie, gorge etc)* to inflame **3** *Fig (personne, imagination de qn)* to excite, to fire, to stir up; **la colère enflamme son regard** his/her eyes are blazing with anger; **l'urgence de la situation enflamme ses talents d'orateur** the urgency of the situation is arousing his talents as a speaker
  VPR **s'enflammer 1** *(prendre feu)* to catch fire, to burst into flames, to blaze up **2** *(d'une plaie, de la gorge)* to become inflamed **3** *(d'une personne, de l'imagination)* to be stirred; **chaque jour, il s'enflamme pour une cause nouvelle/un auteur nouveau** he develops a passion for a new cause/a different author every day; **s'e. de colère** *(d'une personne)* to flare up

enfle [ãfl] ADJ *Suisse (cheville, joue)* swollen

enflé [ãfle] ADJ *(rivière, membre etc)* swollen; *(prix)* inflated; *(style)* inflated, turgid, bombastic
  NM *Fam* idiot

enfléchure [ãfleʃyr] NF *Naut* ratline

enfler [ãfle] VT **1** *(membre, rivière, paupières etc)* to swell, to cause to swell; *(prix)* to inflate; **e. les joues** to puff out *or* blow out one's cheeks; **e. les voiles** *(du vent)* to fill the sails; **e. la voix** to raise one's voice; **des paupières enflées** swollen eyelids; *Vieilli* **e. le nombre/la dépense** to swell *or* add to the number/the expense **2** *Fig (exagérer) (histoire, son succès etc)* to exaggerate; **e. son style** to inflate one's style
  VI *(d'un membre, des paupières, des joues etc)* to swell (up)
  VPR **s'enfler 1** *(d'un membre, des paupières, des joues etc)* to swell (up); *(d'une voix)* to rise **2** *(d'une rivière etc)* to swell, to rise **3** *(d'un style)* to become inflated *or* turgid

enflure [ãflyr] NF **1** *(d'un membre etc)* swelling **2** *(d'un style)* turgidity **3** *Fam (imbécile)* jerk

enfoiré, -ée [ãfware] N *Vulg* bugger, bastard

enfoncé [ãfɔ̃se] ADJ *(yeux)* deep-set; *(ca-*

vité, ravin etc) sunken, deep; *(sol, village)* low-lying

enfoncement [ɑ̃fɔ̃smɑ̃] NM **1** *(action d'enfoncer) (d'un pieu, clou etc)* driving in; *(d'une aiguille etc)* sticking in, pushing in; *(d'une porte etc)* forcing, breaking open **2** *(action de s'enfoncer) (du sol)* giving way **3** *(creux) (dans le sol)* hollow, depression; *(dans le mur)* alcove, recess; *Naut* bay, bight; **dans l'e. de la porte** in the doorway

enfoncer [ɑ̃fɔ̃se] (**j'enfonçai(s)**) VT **1** *(pieu, clou)* to drive in; *(aiguille, épingle)* to stick in, to push in; **e. un clou dans une planche** to drive a nail into a plank; **e. un couteau dans** to thrust *or* plunge *or* stick a knife into; **e. au marteau** to hammer in; **e. la main dans sa poche** to thrust one's hand into one's pocket; **e. son chapeau sur sa tête** to jam *or* cram one's hat on one's head; **e. la clef dans la serrure** to insert the key in the lock; *Fig* **e. qn dans la misère** to plunge sb into poverty; *Fig Fam* **je ne peux pas lui e. cela dans la tête** I can't get it into his head; *Fig Fam* **tu n'étais pas obligé de l'e. comme ça!** you didn't have to be so hard on him/her!

2 *(défoncer) (porte)* to break down *or* open; *(fût)* to stave in; *(voiture)* to smash into; **e. une porte à coups de pied** to kick a door in *or* down; *Fig* **e. une porte ouverte** *ou* **des portes ouvertes** to state the obvious **3** *Fam (battre) (personne, équipe)* to hammer, to wipe the floor with

VI *(dans la boue, mer)* to sink; **nous enfoncions jusqu'aux genoux** we sank into it up to our knees

VPR **s'enfoncer** *(d'un clou, couteau etc)* to sink *or* go in; *(d'un bateau)* to sink; *(du sol)* to subside, to give way; **la balle s'enfonça dans le mur** the bullet embedded itself in the wall; **s'e. dans son fauteuil** to sink into one's armchair; **s'e. dans l'ombre** to disappear in *or* be swallowed up by the darkness; **s'e. dans une rue/dans un bois** to go down a street/to plunge into a wood; **il s'est enfoncé trop loin dans la rue** he went too far along the street; **s'e. dans l'étude/dans la rêverie** to bury oneself in study/to sink into reverie; **s'e. dans le crime** to sink deep(er) into crime; **s'e. dans son opinion** to become entrenched in one's opinion

enfonceur, -euse [ɑ̃fɔ̃sœr, -øz] NM **c'est un e. de portes ouvertes** he's got a gift for stating the obvious

enfonçure [ɑ̃fɔ̃syr] NF depression, hollow

enfouir [ɑ̃fwir] VT to bury *(* **dans** in; **sous** beneath, under); *Agr (fumier)* to plough in; **les mains enfouies dans ses poches** with his hands buried in his pockets

VPR **s'enfouir** to bury oneself

enfouissement [ɑ̃fwismɑ̃] NM burying; *Agr (de fumier)* ploughing in

enfourcher [ɑ̃furʃe] VT *(cheval, vélo)* to get on, to mount; *Fig* **e. son dada** to get on one's hobbyhorse

enfourchure [ɑ̃furʃyr] NF *Vieilli (d'arbre, de jambes)* fork

enfournage [ɑ̃furnaʒ], **enfournement** [ɑ̃furnəmɑ̃] NM *(de pain etc)* putting in the oven; *(de poteries, briques etc)* putting in the kiln

enfourner [ɑ̃furne] VT *(pain etc)* to put in the oven; *(poteries, briques etc)* to put in the kiln; *Fam (avaler)* to put away; **e. les passagers dans un autobus** to pack *or* cram passengers into a bus

VPR **s'enfourner** *Fam* to pile, to pack (**dans** into)

enfourneur [ɑ̃furnœr] NM oven man; *Cér* kiln man

enfreindre [ɑ̃frɛ̃dr] VT *(prp* **enfreignant;** *pp* **enfreint;** *pr ind* **j'enfreins, il enfreint, ils en-**

freignent; *impf* **j'enfreignais;** *p hist* **j'enfreignis;** *fu* **j'enfreindrai**) *(loi)* to infringe, to break; *(règlements)* to contravene, to act contrary to; *(ordres)* to disobey; *(vœu)* to break; **e. les dispositions d'un traité** to violate a treaty; **e. un contrat** to violate a contract

enfuir (s') [sɑ̃fɥir] VPR *(conj like* **fuir**) to run away, *Litt* to flee, to fly; *(d'un escroc)* to abscond; *(d'amoureux)* to elope; **s'e. de prison** to escape from prison; **à mesure que les jours s'enfuyaient** as the days flew by; *Litt* **mon bonheur menace de s'e.** my happiness is in danger of evaporating

enfumé [ɑ̃fyme] ADJ **1** *(pièce, atmosphère)* smoky **2** *(murs etc)* smoke-blackened

enfumer [ɑ̃fyme] VT **1** *(pièce)* to fill with smoke **2** *(murs etc)* to blacken with smoke **3** *(personne, abeilles etc)* to smoke out

enfûtage [ɑ̃fytaʒ] NM *(d'un vin)* putting in barrels *or* casks

enfutailler [ɑ̃fytaje], **enfûter** [ɑ̃fyte] VT *(vin)* to put in barrels *or* casks

engagé [ɑ̃gaʒe] ADJ **1** *Littér, Pol etc (littérature, artiste etc)* committed **2** *Archit (colonne etc)* engaged **3** *navire e.* ship on her beam-ends **4** *Mil* **soldat e.** volunteer

NM *Mil* **e. (volontaire)** volunteer; *Courses de chevaux, Cyclisme* **la liste des engagés** the list of starters

> Il faut noter que l'adjectif anglais **engaged** est un faux ami. Il ne s'utilise jamais dans un contexte politique.

engageant [ɑ̃gaʒɑ̃] ADJ *(manière etc)* engaging, prepossessing; *(sourire)* winning, engaging; **il a écouté ma proposition d'un air e.** he listened to my suggestion sympathetically

engagement [ɑ̃gaʒmɑ̃] NM **1** *(promesse etc)* promise, undertaking, commitment; **faire honneur à** *ou* **tenir** *ou* **respecter ses engagements** to honour *or Am* honor *or* fulfil *or Am* fulfill one's commitments; **e. écrit** written undertaking; *Fin* **e. à court terme** short-term undertaking; **contracter** *ou* **prendre un e.** to enter into an undertaking; **elle a pris l'e. de le faire** she undertook to do it; **sans e. (de votre part)** without obligation (on your part), without any commitment (on your part) **2** *Fin (d'un capital)* tying up, locking up; *(de dépenses)* incurring; **e. à court terme** short-term undertaking **3** *(mise en gage) (de bijoux)* pawning, pledging; *(d'un domaine)* mortgaging **4** *(embauche) (d'un employé)* engagement, appointment, hiring; *(d'un pianiste etc)* booking; *Mil* (voluntary) enlistment; **se trouver sans e.** to be out of work; *Théâtre* to be resting **5** *Sport (pour un événement sportif)* entering, entry **6** *(commencement) (de conversation, négociations)* beginning, start, opening; *(d'entreprise, de projet etc)* setting in motion; *Jur (poursuites)* institution; *Mil, Naut (bataille)* engagement, action; *(coup d'envoi) Ftbl* kick-off; *(au hockey)* bully-off; *Escrime* engagement; **l'e. des négociations ne pourra se faire avant le mois prochain** negotiations cannot begin *or* start before next month; **pour que l'e. du projet soit possible** in order to get the project under way *or* to set the project in motion **7** *(à une cause etc)* commitment (**à** to) **8** *(encouragement)* encouragement; **c'est un e. à poursuivre votre effort** it's an encouragement to continue your effort **9** *(introduction) (du pied)* putting; *(d'une clé)* fitting, inserting; *(d'un véhicule)* driving (**dans** into)

10 *Physiol* **e. du fœtus** engagement of the foetus

ENGAGER [ɑ̃gaʒe] (**j'engageai(s)**)

VT	to commit **1**	▪	to tie up **2**	▪	to pawn
3	▪ to hire **4**	▪	to begin **5**	▪	to involve
6	▪ to urge **7**	▪	to engage **11**		
VPR	to commit oneself **1, 2**	▪	to promise		
1, 2	▪ to get involved in (**s'engager dans**)				
3	▪ to enlist **5**	▪	to fit into (**s'engager**		
dans) **6**	▪ to enter **7**	▪	to begin **8**		

VT **1** *(lier par une obligation ou une promesse)* to commit, to bind; **e. sa parole** to pledge *or* give one's word; *(dans une affaire)* to commit oneself; **cette lettre ne vous engage pas** this letter does not bind *or* commit you; **cela vous engage à vie** it's a lifetime commitment; **cela ne vous engage à rien** it doesn't commit you to anything; **votre responsabilité est engagée dans cette affaire** you have certain responsibilities in this matter; **c'est ce que je crois, mais ça n'engage que moi** it's what I think, but it's just my way of looking at things

2 *Fin (argent)* to lock up, to tie up; *(dépenses)* to incur; **e. sa fortune/des capitaux dans une affaire** to lock up *or* tie up one's fortune/capital in a deal

3 *(mettre en gage) (au mont-de-piété)* to pawn; *(auprès de créanciers)* to pledge; *(propriété)* to mortgage

4 *(embaucher) (employé)* to hire, to take on; *(pianiste)* to book; *Mil (recrue)* to enlist; *(mercenaire)* to hire

5 *(commencer) (conversation, négociations)* to begin, to start, to open; *(entreprise, projet etc)* to get under way, to set in motion; *Jur (poursuites)* to institute, to start; **e. la partie** to begin the match *or* game; **la partie est maintenant bien engagée** the match is now well under way; **e. le jeu** *Ftbl* to kick off; *(au hockey)* to bully off; **e. le combat** to join battle, to engage; **e. les hostilités** to open hostilities; **e. des troupes** to bring troops into action, to engage troops

6 *(entraîner)* to involve (**dans** in); **le pays tout entier se voit engagé dans ce conflit** the whole country finds itself involved *or* caught up in this conflict; **e. qn dans une querelle** to involve sb in *or* draw sb into a quarrel

7 *(inciter)* **e. qn à faire qch** *(d'une personne)* to urge *or* encourage sb to do sth; *(d'une situation, d'un événement)* to encourage sb to do sth

8 *(introduire)* **e. le pied dans l'étrier** to put one's foot in the stirrup; **e. la clef dans la serrure** to fit *or* insert the key in the lock; **e. un véhicule dans une allée** to drive a vehicle into a lane

9 *Sport (inscrire sur liste des concurrents)* to enter; **cet entraîneur a deux chevaux engagés dans cette course** this trainer has two horses entered in the race

10 *(entraver) (corde etc)* to catch, to foul, to entangle; *(machinerie)* to jam; **e. une ancre** to foul an anchor; **e. un aviron** to catch a crab; **e. un vaisseau** to run a ship aground

11 *Tech (engrenage)* to engage, to put into gear; *Aut* **e. la première** to change into first (gear)

VPR **s'engager 1** *(promettre)* **s'e. à faire qch** to promise to do sth, to commit oneself to do sth, *Fml* to undertake to do sth; **s'e. par traité à faire qch** to contract to do sth; **je m'engage à vous payer dans les 30 jours** I promise to pay you within 30 days; **je me suis trop engagé pour reculer** I have gone too far *or* I'm too far in to pull out now; **s'e. vis-à-vis de qn** to commit oneself to sb; **je ne veux pas m'e.** *(sentimentalement)* I don't want to get involved

2 *(prendre position) (écrivain, intellectuel)* to commit oneself

3 *(se lancer)* **s'e. dans une aventure/un combat/une affaire** to get involved in an adventure/a fight/a deal
4 *(se faire embaucher)* **s'e. chez qn** to be *or* get taken on by sb; **s'e. comme cuisinier** to get (oneself) a job as *or* get taken on as a cook
5 *Mil* to enlist, to join up
6 *(se loger)* to fit; **un tube s'engage dans l'ouverture** a pipe fits into the opening
7 *(pénétrer)* **s'e. dans une rue/forêt** to turn into a street/to enter a forest; **il s'engagea dans le passage pour piétons sans regarder à droite ni à gauche** he stepped out onto the pedestrian crossing without looking left or right; **la voiture s'engagea dans le rond-point** the car pulled out onto the roundabout; **nous nous engageâmes dans un étroit boyau** we moved into a narrow passageway
8 *(commencer)* *(d'une bataille, conversation etc)* to begin
9 *Sport* **s'e. pour une course** to enter for a race
10 *(d'une corde, hélice etc)* to foul, to become fouled; *(d'une machine)* to jam

engazonnement [ãgazɔnmã] NM *(fait de semer)* sowing with grass seed
engazonner [ãgazɔne] VT *(semer)* to sow with grass seed
engeance [ãʒãs] NF *Fam* **quelle e.!** what a crew!
engelure [ãʒlyr] NF chilblain
engendrement [ãʒãdrəmã] NM **1** *(d'enfant)* fathering, *Bible* begetting **2** *(de chaleur etc)* generation; *(de maladie, pauvreté)* breeding
engendrer [ãʒãdre] VT **1** *(enfant)* to father, *Bible* to beget; *(d'un étalon etc)* to sire **2** *Fig (conflit)* to engender, to give rise to; *(maladie, pauvreté)* to breed; *(chaleur etc)* to generate, to develop
engin [ãʒɛ̃] NM *(machine)* machine; *(outil)* device, contrivance; *Mil (missile)* missile; *Fam (objet)* thing; **engins de pêche** fishing tackle; **passage d'engins** heavy plant crossing; **engins de guerre** engines of war; **e. amphibie** amphibious craft *or* vehicle; **e. blindé** armoured vehicle; **e. blindé de reconnaissance** armoured car; **e. de mort** deadly weapon; **e. prohibé** illegal hunting/fishing device; **e. spatial** spacecraft; **e. de terrassement** earthmoving machine; **e. de manutention** machine for handling goods

Il faut noter que le nom anglais **engine** est un faux ami. Il signifie **moteur**.

engineering [ɛndʒiniriŋ] NM engineering
englober [ãglɔbe] VT **1** *(inclure)* to include (**dans** in); **e. les innocents parmi les coupables** to include the innocent with the guilty **2** *(annexer)* to merge (**dans** into); **ces états furent englobés dans l'Empire** these states were merged into the Empire
engloutir [ãglutir] VT **1** *(avaler) (boisson)* to gulp down; *(nourriture)* to wolf down **2** *(submerger) (bateau, village etc)* to engulf, to swallow up **3** *(son capital etc) (d'une entreprise, projet etc)* to swallow up; *(d'une personne)* to sink (**dans** in)
VPR s'engloutir *(d'un bateau)* to sink
engloutissement [ãglutismã] NM **1** *(d'une boisson)* gulping down; *(de la nourriture)* wolfing down **2** *(d'un village etc)* engulfing, swallowing up; *(d'un bateau)* sinking **3** *(d'une fortune etc)* swallowing up
engluage [ãglyaʒ], **engluement** [ãglymã] NM **1** *(de brindilles, d'un oiseau)* liming **2** *(enduit)* (bird)lime
engluer [ãglye] VT *(brindilles, oiseau)* to lime
VPR s'engluer *(d'un oiseau)* to get caught in

lime; **s'e. les doigts** to get sticky fingers; *Fig* **s'e. dans une situation difficile/des problèmes/des dettes** to get bogged down in a difficult situation/problems/debts
engoncer [ãgõse] VT *(d'un vêtement)* **e. qn** to make sb look hunched up; **être engoncé dans sa veste** to be hunched up in one's jacket
engorgement [ãgɔrʒəmã] NM **1** *(action) (d'un passage, tuyau etc)* choking, blocking, clogging; **e. des marchés** glutting of the markets **2** *(bouchon)* obstruction, stoppage; *Méd* engorgement, congestion
engorger [ãgɔrʒe] (**j'engorgeai(s)**) VT **1** *(passage, tuyau etc)* to choke (up), to block, to clog **2** *(marché)* to glut **3** *Méd (organe)* to engorge, congest
VPR s'engorger 1 *(d'un tuyau etc)* to become choked (up) *or* blocked (up) *or* clogged **2** *Méd (d'un organe)* to become engorged *or* congested **3** *(d'une route, d'un carrefour)* to become blocked up *or* congested
engouement [ãgumã] NM **1** *(admiration)* infatuation, craze (**pour qn/qch** for sb/sth) **2** *Méd (d'une hernie)* obstruction
engouer (s') [sãgwe] VPR **1** *Méd (d'une hernie)* to become obstructed **2** **s'e. de qn/qch** to become infatuated with *or* go crazy over sb/sth
engouffrement [ãgufrəmã] NM *(d'un vaisseau par la mer etc)* engulfment, engulfing, swallowing up
engouffrer [ãgufre] VT *(bateau etc)* to engulf, to swallow up; **e. une fortune** to swallow up a fortune; *Fam* **e. sa nourriture** to devour *or* gulp down *or* wolf down one's food; *Fam* **qu'est-ce que j'ai engouffré!** I really wolfed *or* gulped it down!
VPR s'engouffrer *(d'un bateau etc)* to be engulfed *or* swallowed up; **il s'engouffra dans la gare** he plunged *or* dived into the station; **le vent s'engouffra par la porte** the wind swept in through the door
engoulevent [ãgulvã] NM *(oiseau)* nightjar
engourdir [ãgurdi] ADJ **1** *(membre, corps etc)* numb; **j'ai le pied e.** my foot has gone to sleep *or* is numb **2** *Fig (esprit)* dull, sluggish
engourdir [ãgurdir] VT **1** *(membre, corps etc)* to numb **2** *(endormir) (esprit, douleur)* to dull
VPR s'engourdir 1 *(d'un membre etc)* to grow numb, to go to sleep **2** *Fig (de l'esprit)* to become dull *or* sluggish **3** *(d'un animal qui hiberne)* to become dormant
engourdissement [ãgurdismã] NM **1** *(état) (d'un membre etc)* numbness; *(de l'esprit)* dullness, sluggishness; *(d'un animal qui hiberne)* torpor **2** *(action) (d'un membre etc)* numbing; *(de l'esprit, d'une douleur)* dulling
engrais [ãgrɛ] NM **1** *(pour l'élevage)* **mettre des bœufs à l'e.** to put cattle to fatten **2** *(fertilisant)* fertilizer; **e. (animal)** manure; **e. chimiques** chemical fertilizers; **e. verts** green fertilizers
engraissage [ãgrɛsaʒ], **engraissement** [ãgrɛsmã] NM *(des animaux)* fattening
engraisser [ãgrɛse] VT **1** *(animaux)* to fatten **2** *(personne)* to make fat **3** *(terre)* to fertilize
VI *(d'une personne, d'un animal)* to get fat
VPR s'engraisser *(s'enrichir)* to grow fat; **l'État s'engraisse sur le dos des travailleurs** the State grows fat at the workers' expense
engrangement [ãgrãʒmã] NM *(des céréales)* getting in, *Litt* garnering
engranger [ãgrãʒe] VT (**j'engrangeai(s)**; n. **engrangeons**) *(céréales)* to get in, *Litt* to garner
engrenage [ãgrənaʒ] NM **1** *Tech (roues dentées)* gears; *(disposition du système)* gearing; **e. hélicoïdal** helical *or* screw gear; **système ou jeu d'engrenages** train *or* set of gears;

Aut **e. de démarrage** starter gear; **e. à train planétaire** planetary gearing; **engrenage(s) de transmission** driving gear; **e. en prise constante** constant-mesh gear; **e. à variations progressives** gradually variable gear; **e. à vis sans fin** worm gears **2** *Fig (des événements)* chain, mesh, web; **être pris dans l'e.** to be *or* get caught (up) in the system; **l'e. de la violence/de l'agressivité** the spiral of violence/aggression; **mettre le doigt dans l'e.** to get caught up in it
engrènement [ãgrɛnmã] NM **1** *Agr (d'un moulin etc)* feeding with grain **2** *Tech* engaging, meshing
engrener [ãgrəne] (**j'engrène; j'engrènerai**) VT **1** *Agr (moulin, batteuse)* to feed grain into **2** *Tech (pignons)* to engage, to mesh; **e. dans** to engage into, to mesh with; *Fam* **e. une affaire** to set a thing going
VPR s'engrener *Tech* to engage (**dans** into), to mesh (**dans** with)
engrenure [ãgrənyr] NF *Tech (disposition de roues)* gearing
engrosser [ãgrose] VT *Arg (femme)* to make pregnant, to knock up; **se faire e.** to get knocked up (**par** by)
engueulade [ãgœlad] NF *Fam (réprimande)* bawling out; *(querelle)* row, *Br* slanging match; **passer une e. à qn** to give sb a bawling out; **e. à qn** to bawl sb out; **recevoir une e.** to get a bawling out
engueuler [ãgœle] *Fam* VT **e. qn** *(réprimander)* to give sb hell, to give sb a roasting; **se faire e.** to be given a roasting; **e. qn comme du poisson pourri** to call sb every name under the sun
VPR s'engueuler to have a row *or Br* slanging match
enguirlander [ãgirlãde] VT **1** *(décorer)* to garland (**de** with) **2** *Fam* = **engueuler**
enhardir [ãardir] VT to embolden, to put courage into, to give courage to
VPR s'enhardir to become bold(er); **s'e. à faire qch** to pluck up the courage to do sth
enharmonie [ãnarmɔni] NF *Mus* enharmonic change
enharmonique [ãnarmɔnik] ADJ *Mus* enharmonic
enharnacher [ãarnaʃe] VT *(cheval)* to harness
énième [enjɛm] ADJ nth; **pour la é. fois** for the nth *or* umpteenth time
N nth
énigmatique [enigmatik] ADJ enigmatic
énigmatiquement [enigmatikmã] ADV enigmatically
énigme [enigm] NF *(problème, mystère)* enigma, riddle; *(devinette)* riddle; **proposer une é. à qn** to ask sb a riddle; **trouver le mot ou la clé de l'é.** to find the answer to the riddle, to guess *or* solve the riddle; **parler par énigmes** to speak in riddles; **ce garçon est une é. pour moi** I can't make the boy out; **ça, c'est une é. pour moi** it's a mystery to me
enivrant [ãnivrã] ADJ *(parfum)* intoxicating, heady; *(vitesse)* exhilarating, dizzying; **vivre dans un luxe e.** to live in fabulous luxury
enivrement [ãnivrəmã] NM **1** *(par l'alcool)* intoxication, inebriation **2** *Fig* exhilaration; **dans l'e. de** intoxicated *or* exhilarated by
enivrer [ãnivre] VT **1** *(avec de l'alcool)* to intoxicate, to inebriate, to make drunk **2** *Fig (exalter)* to intoxicate, to exhilarate; **enivré par le succès** intoxicated *or* exhilarated by success
VPR s'enivrer 1 *(devenir ivre)* to become intoxicated *or* inebriated (**de** with), to get drunk (**de** on) **2** *Fig* **s'e. de mots** to get drunk on words

enjambée [ãʒãbe] **NF** stride; **marcher à grandes enjambées** to stride along

enjambement [ãʒãbmã] **NM** *Littér* enjamb(e)ment

enjamber [ãʒãbe] **VT** *(obstacle, fossé etc)* to step over *or* across; *(d'un pont) (rivière etc)* to span

enjeu [ãʒø] **NM 1** *(au jeu)* stake **2** *Mil, Pol etc* stakes; **quel est l'e.?** what is at stake?, what are the stakes?

enjoindre [ãʒwɛ̃dr] **VT** *(conj like* **joindre)** *Littér* **e. à qn de faire qch** to enjoin *or* call upon *or* charge sb to do sth

enjôlement [ãʒolmã] **NM 1** *(action)* cajoling, wheedling, coaxing **2** *(paroles etc)* cajolery, blandishment

enjôler [ãʒole] **VT** to cajole, to wheedle, to coax

enjôleur, -euse [ãʒolœr, -øz] **N** coaxer, cajoler, wheedler
ADJ coaxing, cajoling, wheedling

enjolivement [ãʒolivmã] **NM** *(ornement)* embellishment, ornament; *(dans un récit)* embellishment

enjoliver [ãʒolive] **VT** *(pièce, robe etc)* to embellish, to ornament; *(faits, histoire etc)* to embellish, to embroider

enjoliveur, -euse [ãʒolivœr, -øz] **N** c'est un e. he likes to embellish *or* embroider his stories
NM *Aut* hubcap, wheel trim; **e. de phare** headlamp rim

enjolivure [ãʒolivyr] **NF** *(ornement)*, *Fig* embellishment

enjoué [ãʒwe] **ADJ** vivacious, lively, playful

enjouement [ãʒumã] **NM** vivaciousness, liveliness, playfulness

enkystement [ãkistemã] **NM** *Méd* encystation, encystment

enkyster (s') [sãkiste] **VPR** *Méd (d'une tumeur)* to become encysted, to encyst

enlacement [ãlasmã] **NM 1** *(de rubans, branches)* intertwining, interlacing **2** *(en entourant)* enlacing, entwining

enlacer [ãlase] *(j'enlaçais)* **VT 1** *(rubans, branches)* to intertwine, to interlace; *(entourer)* to entwine, to enlace, to twine round; *(papiers)* to tie up **2** *(étreindre)* to clasp in one's arms, to hug, to embrace
VPR s'enlacer 1 *(s'étreindre)* to hug, to embrace (each other); **amants enlacés** lovers (clasped) in an embrace **2** *(s'entrelacer)* to intertwine, to interlace

enlaidir [ãlɛdir] **VT** *(personne)* to make ugly, to disfigure; *(paysage, ville etc)* to disfigure; **cette robe l'enlaidit** that dress makes her look ugly
VI to grow ugly *or* plain
VPR s'enlaidir to make oneself look ugly *or* plain

enlaidissement [ãlɛdismã] **NM** *(de personne) (par accident)* disfigurement; *(naturel)* growing ugly *or* plain, loss of good looks; *(de paysage, ville etc)* disfigurement

enlevage [ãlvaʒ] **NM** *(dans une course d'aviron)* spurt

enlevé [ãlve] **ADJ** *(représentation, style etc)* lively, spirited; *(danse, sonate etc)* performed in a lively *or* spirited fashion

enlèvement [ãlɛvmã] **NM 1** *(de meubles, d'une étiquette, d'une tache, de peinture)* removal, removing; *(des bagages, ordures)* collection; **e. des ordures** garbage disposal; *Com* **e. et livraison** collection and delivery **2** *(kidnapping)* kidnapping, abduction; *Jur* **e. de mineur** abduction of a minor; **e. d'enfant** baby-snatching **3** *Mil (d'une position)* taking, storming, carrying
▸▸ *Hist* **l'e. des Sabines** the rape of the Sabine women

enlever [ãlve] *(j'enlève; j'enlèverai)* **VT 1** *(vêtements, étiquette, bouton, couvercle etc)* to remove, to take off; *(meubles etc)* to move, to take away; *(tapis)* to take up; *(rideaux)* to take down; *(pelure, peinture etc)* to peel off, to remove; *(tache)* to remove, to take out; **le couvert** to clear away, to clear the table; *Fam* **il a fallu lui e. les végétations** he had to have his adenoids removed *or* taken out; *Litt* **enlevé par la mer** carried away *or* washed away by the sea; **la mort l'enleva à vingt ans** death carried him off at twenty; **e. qch à qn** to take sth away from sb; **enlève-lui ces allumettes des mains** take those matches off him; **enlève-toi de là!** get off there!; **il m'a enlevé mes cors** he removed my corns; **cette erreur n'enlève rien à votre valeur** this mistake takes nothing away from *or* in no way detracts from your merit; **cela m'a enlevé tout mon courage/toute ma bonne humeur** it has drained me of all courage/of my good humour; **e. à qn la garde d'un enfant** to remove *or* take a child from sb's care *or* custody; **e. à qn le goût de qch** to take away sb's taste for sth
2 *(kidnapper)* to kidnap, to abduct; **se faire e. par son amant** to elope (with one's lover)
3 *(remporter)* *Mil (position)* to take, to carry, to storm; *Sport etc (course, victoire, prix)* to win; *(commande, contrat)* to win, to secure; **e. la décision** to win *or* carry the day, to win through; **e. les suffrages** *Pol* to win *or* capture votes; *Fig* to be liked by everyone, to be universally liked
4 *(soulever) (poids, couvercle)* to raise, to lift (up); *(ballon)* to send up; **le vent enlève la poussière** the wind raises the dust; **e. son cheval** *(le faire bondir)* to lift one's horse; *(le faire partir)* to set one's horse at full gallop; *Fig* **la foule fut enlevée par ces paroles** the crowd was carried away by these words
5 e. un morceau (de musique) to play a piece (of music) in a lively *or* spirited fashion
VPR s'enlever 1 *(d'un couvercle)* to come off; *(de la peinture, peau etc)* to come *or* peel off; *(d'une tache)* to come out **2** *(de marchandises)* to sell quickly, to be snapped up **3** *(d'un ballon etc)* to rise **4** *(d'un cheval)* to take off

enlisement [ãlizmã] **NM** *(dans les sables mouvants etc)* sinking

enliser [ãlize] **VT** *(voiture, roue etc) (dans la boue, le sable etc)* to get stuck
VPR s'enliser *(d'une personne) (dans un marécage etc)* to sink, to be sucked down; *(d'une voiture etc) (dans la boue, le sable etc)* to sink, to get stuck; *Fig* **s'e. dans ses explications/habitudes** to get bogged down in one's explanations/habits

enluminer [ãlymine] **VT 1** *(illustrer) (manuscrit, livre etc)* to illuminate **2** *(colorer) (gravure, carte etc)* to colour, *Am* to color **3** *Fig* **visage enluminé** flushed *or* glowing face

enlumineur, -euse [ãlyminœr, -øz] **N** *(artiste)* illuminator

enluminure [ãlyminyr] **NF 1** *(action d'illustrer) (d'un manuscrit etc)* illumination, illuminating **2** *(action de colorer) (de gravures etc)* colouring, *Am* coloring **3** *Fig (d'un visage)* colour, *Am* color **4** *(lettre, dessin)* illumination

enneigé [ãnɛʒe] **ADJ** *(montagne, champ etc)* snow-covered; *(route, village etc)* snowbound, snowed-up

enneigement [ãnɛʒmã] **NM** *(action)* snowing up; *(état)* snow cover; **bulletin d'e.** snow report

ennemi, -ie [ɛnmi] **N** enemy; **se faire un e. de qn** to make an enemy of sb, to turn sb against one; **passer à l'e.** to go over to the enemy; **e. public numéro un** public enemy number one; **les ennemis de la liberté** the enemies of freedom; *Prov* **le mieux est l'e. du bien** leave well alone   VOIR GRAMMAIRE A11
ADJ enemy; **le camp e.** the enemy('s) camp; **en pays e.** in enemy country

ennoblir [ãnoblir] **VT 1** *(esprit etc)* to ennoble, to elevate **2** *Tex (tissu etc)* to improve (the quality of)

> Do not confuse with **anoblir**, which means **to raise to the peerage**.

ennui [ãnɥi] **NM 1** *(souci)* worry, anxiety; *(problème)* problem; **avoir des ennuis *(soucis)*** to be worried *or* anxious; *(problèmes)* to have problems; **avoir des ennuis de santé/d'argent/de voiture** to have health/money/car problems; **avoir des ennuis avec la police** to be in trouble with the police; **avoir des ennuis avec ses voisins** to have trouble *or* problems with one's neighbours; **si tu continues, tu vas avoir des ennuis** if you carry on, you'll be in trouble; **petits ennuis** minor worries, *Péj* petty worries; **créer** *ou* **susciter** *ou* **faire des ennuis à qn** to make trouble for sb, to create problems for sb; **je ne voudrais pas vous attirer d'ennuis** I wouldn't want to get you into trouble; **quel e.!** what a nuisance *or* bother *or* *Fam* bind!; **l'e., c'est que je ne lui ai rien expliqué** the trouble is that I haven't explained anything to him
2 *(lassitude)* boredom, *Litt* ennui; **ils me font mourir d'e.** they bore me to death *or* stiff; **sa conversation est d'un e.!** his/her conversation is so boring!

ennuyant [ãnɥijã] **ADJ** *Belg, Can* **1** *(lassant) (travail, conférencier, collègue)* boring, dull; **e. à mourir** *ou* **à périr** *ou* **comme la pluie** *ou* **comme la mort** (as) dull as ditchwater *or Am* dishwater, deadly boring **2** *(fâcheux)* annoying, tiresome; **c'est e. qu'il ne puisse pas venir** *(regrettable)* it's a pity (that) he can't come; *(contrariant)* it's annoying *or* a nuisance that he can't come

ennuyé [ãnɥije] **ADJ 1** *(contrarié)* annoyed, bothered (**de** about) **2** *(las)* bored (**de** with)

ennuyer [ãnɥije] *(j'ennuie; j'ennuierai)* **VT 1** *(contrarier)* to annoy, to bother; **cela vous ennuierait-il d'attendre?** would you mind waiting?; **je ne voudrais pas vous e.** I don't want to bother you; **cela m'ennuie de ne pouvoir le lui expliquer** it annoys me that I can't explain it to him; **je suis très ennuyé de la savoir fâchée** it bothers *or* upsets me a lot to know that she is angry
2 *(agacer)* to annoy, to irritate; **qu'est-ce qu'elle m'ennuie avec ses chichis!** I'm really getting tired of the fuss she makes!
3 *(lasser)* to bore; **il m'ennuie à mourir** he bores me to death
VPR s'ennuyer to be/get bored; **je m'ennuie à ne rien faire** *(maintenant)* I'm bored *or Fam* fed up with doing nothing; *(en général)* I get bored if I have nothing to do; **s'e. de faire qch** to get tired of doing sth

> Il faut noter que le verbe anglais **to annoy** signifie **importuner** ou **irriter** et non **lasser**.

ennuyeux, -euse [ãnɥijø, -øz] **ADJ 1** *(contrariant)* annoying, irritating; **comme c'est e.!** what a nuisance! **2** *(lassant)* boring, tedious, dull; **mortellement e.** deadly boring *or* dull

énoncé [enõse] **NM 1** *(des faits)* statement; *(d'un problème)* term, *Jur (d'une sentence)* terms; *(d'un contrat, d'une loi etc)* text, wording; *(d'une question)* wording **2** *Ling* utterance

énoncer [enõse] *(j'énonçai(s))* **VT** *(opinion, fait, conditions etc)* to state
VPR s'énoncer *(d'une opinion)* to be stated

énonciation [enɔ̃sjasjɔ̃] NF *(d'un fait etc)* stating, statement

enorgueillir [ɑ̃nɔrgœjir] VT to make proud VPR **s'enorgueillir s'e. de qch/d'avoir fait qch** to be proud of *or* pride oneself on sth/having done sth

énorme [enɔrm] ADJ *(personne, édifice, succès, quantité, perte etc)* enormous, huge; **il a été élu à une é. majorité** he was elected by a huge *or* overwhelming majority; **mensonge é.** whopping lie, whopper; **raconter des choses énormes** to say outrageous things; **il n'est pas mort, c'est déjà é.** he's still alive, which is incredible

énormément [enɔrmemɑ̃] ADV enormously, hugely, tremendously; **je le regrette é.** I'm extremely *or Fam* awfully sorry; **elle a é. changé** she has changed enormously *or* a great deal; **é. de bien/d'argent** an enormous amount *or* a great deal of good/money; **é. de gens** a great many *or Fam* lots of people

énormité [enɔrmite] NF **1** *(d'une demande, d'un péché, d'un crime etc)* enormity, outrageousness **2** *(taille démesurée) (d'une personne, d'un édifice)* enormousness, hugeness; **l'é. du gaspillage** the huge *or* enormous amount wasted **3** *(bévue)* (dreadful) blunder; **commettre une é.** to put one's foot right in it, to make a (dreadful) blunder; **ce traité est plein d'énormités** this treaty is full of (written) mistakes *or Fam* howlers **4 dire des énormités** to say the most outrageous things

enquérir (s') [sɑ̃kerir] VPR *(conj like* **acquérir***)* to inquire, to make inquiries (**de** about); **s'e. du prix** to ask the price; **il s'est enquis de vous/de votre santé** he inquired *or* asked after *or* about you/your health

enquête [ɑ̃kɛt] NF *Jur, Parl etc* inquiry; *(policière)* investigation(s), inquiries; *(sondage)* survey, opinion poll; *Journ* (investigative) report, exposé; *Mktg* market probe; **l'inspecteur mène l'e.** the inspector is leading the investigation(s) *or* inquiries; **ouvrir une e.** to set up *or* open an inquiry; **faire** *ou* **procéder à une e. sur qch** *Jur etc* to hold *or* conduct an inquiry into sth; *(de la police)* to carry out *or* conduct an investigation into sth; **commission d'e.** court of inquiry; *Br Parl* select committee; **elle a décidé de faire sa petite e.** she decided to investigate; *Com* **e. sur les prix** price survey; **e. auprès des consommateurs** consumer survey
▸▸ *Jur* **e. administrative** public inquiry; **e. omnibus** omnibus survey; **e. postale** postal survey; **e. par questionnaire** questionnaire survey; **e. scientifique** scientific investigation; **e. sociologique** sociological survey; **e. par sondage** sample survey; **e. téléphonique** telephone interview *or* survey

enquête-pilote, *pl* **enquêtes-pilotes** NF *Mktg* pilot survey

enquêter [ɑ̃kete] VI *Jur* to hold an inquiry; *(de la police)* to make investigations; *(faire un sondage)* to conduct a survey (**sur** into); **e. sur une affaire** to inquire into a matter, to investigate a matter

enquêteur, -euse [ɑ̃ketœr, -øz] ADJ *Jur* **commissaire e.** investigating commissioner
N investigator; *(qui fait un sondage)* researcher; *Journ* interviewer; *Mktg* pollster

enquêtrice [ɑ̃kɛtris] NF investigator; *(qui fait un sondage)* researcher; *Journ* interviewer; *Mktg* pollster

enquiquinant [ɑ̃kikinɑ̃] ADJ *Fam (agaçant)* irritating, annoying; *(lassant)* boring

enquiquinement [ɑ̃kikinmɑ̃] NM *Fam (souci, problème)* nuisance; **enquiquinements** trouble; **mon patron me fait des enquiquinements** my boss is giving me trouble; **je n'ai que des enquiquinements**

avec ma voiture I have nothing but trouble with my car, my car gives me nothing but trouble

enquiquiner [ɑ̃kikine] VT *Fam (agacer)* to irritate, to annoy; *(lasser)* to bore (stiff)

enquiquineur, -euse [ɑ̃kikinœr, -øz] N *Fam* nuisance, pest; *(raseur)* (crashing) bore

enraciné [ɑ̃rasine] ADJ *(habitude, haine etc)* deep-rooted, deep-seated; **elle est enracinée dans cette région/ses habitudes** she is firmly rooted in this region/her habits

enracinement [ɑ̃rasinmɑ̃] NM **1** *(action d'enraciner) (d'un jeune arbre)* digging in **2** *(action de s'enraciner) (d'un arbre), Fig (d'une idée etc)* taking root; *(d'une personne)* putting down of roots

enraciner [ɑ̃rasine] VT **1** *(arbre etc)* to dig in, to root **2** *Fig (principes etc)* to establish, to implant
VPR **s'enraciner** *(d'un arbre)* to take root; *Fig (d'une personne)* to put down roots; *Fig (de sentiments, d'habitudes, d'une coutume etc)* to take root, to become established *or* deeply rooted

enrageant [ɑ̃raʒɑ̃] ADJ infuriating, maddening

enragé, -ée [ɑ̃raʒe] ADJ **1** *(chien etc)* rabid **2** *Fam (partisan etc)* rabid, out-and-out; *(sportif etc)* keen
N *Fam* fanatic; **un e. de golf** a golf fanatic *or* enthusiast, a keen golfer

enrager [ɑ̃raʒe] VI *(j'enrageai(s); n.* **enrageons***)* to be furious; **elle enrage de ne pas pouvoir le faire** she's furious at not being able to do it; **faire e. qn** to infuriate *or* madden sb; *(taquiner)* to tease sb

enrayage [ɑ̃rejaʒ] NM **1** *(blocage) (d'une roue)* locking; *(d'un mécanisme, d'une arme etc)* jamming **2** *(montage des rayons) (d'une roue)* spoking

enrayer [ɑ̃reje] VT **1** *(bloquer) (arme à feu, machine etc)* to jam; *(roue)* to lock; *Fig* **e. une maladie/un fléau** to arrest *or* check a disease/scourge **2** *(équiper de rayons) (roue)* to spoke
VPR **s'enrayer 1** *(d'une arme à feu, machine etc)* to jam **2** *(d'une épidémie)* to abate

enrayure [ɑ̃rejyr] NF *(rayons) (d'une roue)* spokes

enrégimenter [ɑ̃reʒimɑ̃te] VT **1** *(dans un parti, une organisation etc)* to enrol **2** *Mil* to form into regiments

enregistrable [ɑ̃r(ə)ʒistrabl] ADJ *(musique, émission etc)* recordable

enregistrement [ɑ̃r(ə)ʒistrəmɑ̃] NM **1** *(action d'inscrire) (de faits etc)* recording; *Jur (de la naissance, d'un acte etc)* registration; *(d'une commande)* booking, entering (up); *(de bagages)* check-in; **guichet d'e.** *(à l'aéroport etc)* check-in (desk); **e. anticipé** advanced check-in; **e. d'une compagnie** incorporation of a company; *Admin* **droit d'e.** stamp duty; *Admin* **l'E.** the Registration department
2 *Tech (action, disque etc)* recording; *Ordinat (de données)* logging, recording; **e. comptable** accounting entry; *Ordinat* **e. de transactions** transaction logging; **e. haute fidélité** hi-fi recording; **e. laser** *(procédé)* laser recording; *(disque)* laser disc; **e. sur magnétoscope** video recording; **e. numérique** digital recording; **e. vidéo** video recording; **e. sur bande/cassette** tape/cassette recording; **studio d'e.** recording studio; *TV, Radio* **e. son** *ou* **sonore** audio *or* sound recording; **e. vocal** voice recording; *TV* **camion d'e. (du son)** sound van; **passer un e.** to play a recording
3 *Ordinat (article de base de données)* record

enregistrer [ɑ̃r(ə)ʒistre] VT **1** *(inscrire) (faits*

etc)* to record; *Jur (naissance, acte etc)* to register; *(commande)* to book, to enter (up); *(bagages)* to check in; **société enregistrée** incorporated company; **les meilleures ventes enregistrées depuis des mois** the best recorded sales for months; **e. le courrier** to log the mail **2** *Fam (mémoriser)* to note, to memorize **3** *Tech (musique, émission)* to record, to tape; *(cassette vidéo)* to record; *(CD-ROM)* to write; *(données)* to store; **e. un disque** to make a record; **e. sur bande** to tape, to record on tape; **e. au magnétoscope** to video, to record on video; **musique enregistrée** recorded music; *Ordinat* **programme enregistré** stored programme
VPR **s'enregistrer** *(d'une cassette etc)* to record

enregistreur, -euse [ɑ̃r(ə)ʒistrœr, -øz] ADJ *(appareil, mécanisme)* recording; **caisse enregistreuse** cash register
NM *(appareil)* recorder
▸▸ **e. à bande** (strip) chart recorder; **e. de pression** pressure recorder; **e. de son** *ou* **sonore** sound recorder; **e. à tambour** drum recorder; *Ind* **e. de temps** time clock *or* recorder; *Aviat* **e. de vol** flight recorder, black box

enrhumer [ɑ̃ryme] VT **e. qn** to give sb a cold; **être enrhumé** to have a cold
VPR **s'enrhumer** to catch a cold

enrichi [ɑ̃riʃi] ADJ **1** *(personne)* wealthy, *Péj* nouveau riche; *Fig* **il est sorti e. de ses voyages** his travelling has enriched his mind; **céréales enrichies en vitamines** cereals with added vitamins, vitamin-enriched cereals; **liquide vaisselle e. en lanoline** washing-up liquid with added lanolin *or* enriched with lanolin **2** *Typ (texte)* enhanced **3** *Phys (uranium)* enriched

enrichir [ɑ̃riʃir] VT **1** *(personne, pays)* to enrich, to make rich(er) **2** *Fig (art, collection, esprit etc)* to enrich; **e. la langue française** to enrich the French language **3** *Phys (uranium etc)* to enrich; **e. la terre** to enrich the soil **4** *Typ (texte)* to enhance
VPR **s'enrichir 1** *(d'une personne, d'un pays)* to grow rich(er) **2** *Fig (d'une langue etc)* to grow *or* become richer (**de** with; **en** in); **s'é. à force de lectures/de voyages** to enrich one's mind through reading/travel

enrichissant [ɑ̃riʃisɑ̃] ADJ *(expérience etc)* enriching

enrichissement [ɑ̃riʃismɑ̃] NM **1** *(de l'esprit, d'une collection etc)* enriching, enrichment; *(d'entreprise)* increase in capital; **e. personnel** personal enrichment **2** *Phys (de l'uranium etc)* enrichment **3** *Typ (attribut)* enhancement, special typographical feature **4** *TV, Radio* **e. audio** audio sweetening

enrobage [ɑ̃rɔbaʒ], **enrobement** [ɑ̃rɔbmɑ̃] NM *(action, enveloppe)* coating; **e. de sucre/chocolat** sugar/chocolate coating

enrobé [ɑ̃rɔbe] ADJ *Fam* chubby, plump

enrober [ɑ̃rɔbe] VT *(bonbon, pilule etc)* to coat (**de** with); *Fig* **e. une nouvelle peu agréable dans un flot de paroles** to wrap up a piece of unpleasant news in a mass of words

enrôlé [ɑ̃role] NM *Mil* enlisted man

enrôlement [ɑ̃rolmɑ̃] NM enrolment; *Mil* enlistment

enrôler [ɑ̃role] VT *(membres, travailleurs)* to enrol, to recruit; *Mil* to enlist; *Hist* **e. de force** to press-gang, to impress
VPR **s'enrôler** to enrol; *Mil* to enlist

enroué [ɑ̃rwe] ADJ *(personne, voix)* hoarse, husky

enrouement [ɑ̃rumɑ̃] NM hoarseness, huskiness

enrouer [ɑ̃rwe] VT *(voix, personne)* to make hoarse *or* husky

VPR s'enrouer to get hoarse; **s'e. à force de crier** to shout oneself hoarse

enroulable [ɑ̃rulabl] ADJ winding; *Aut* **ceinture de sécurité e.** inertia-reel seat belt

enroulement [ɑ̃rulmɑ̃] NM **1** *(de tissu, tapis etc)* rolling up; *(de câble, ruban etc)* winding up **2** *Élec (fil)* coil, winding; **e. du champ d'excitation** field winding; **e. en série** series winding **3** *(ornement)* scroll, volute

enrouler [ɑ̃rule] VT **1** *(rouler) (carte, tapis etc)* to roll up; *(câble, ruban etc)* to wind up **2** *(envelopper)* to wrap up (**dans** in)
VPR s'enrouler *(d'un serpent etc)* to coil (up); *(d'un film, fil etc)* to wind; **s'e. dans une couverture** to wrap oneself up in a blanket

enrouleur [ɑ̃rulœr] NM *Aut* **e. (de ceinture de sécurité)** inertia reel, seat-belt retractor; **ceinture de sécurité à e.** inertia-reel seat belt

enrubanner [ɑ̃rybane] VT to decorate with a ribbon/ribbons

ENS [ɛnɛs] NF *(abrév* **École normale supérieure)** = university-level college that prepares students for senior posts in teaching and other professions

ENSA [ɛnsa] NF *(abrév* **École nationale supérieure agronomique)** = one of five competitive-entry agricultural engineering schools

ensablement [ɑ̃sabləmɑ̃] NM **1** *(d'un bateau)* running aground, stranding **2** *(d'un port)* silting up; *(de tuyaux)* choking up (with sand) **3** *(amené) (amené par l'eau)* sandbank, sand bar; *(amené par le vent)* sand dune

ensabler [ɑ̃sable] VT **1** *(sur le sable) (bateau)* to strand, to run aground; *(véhicule)* to get stuck in the sand **2** *(d'une inondation) (terre)* to cover with sand; *(port, rivière)* to silt up, to sand up
VPR s'ensabler 1 *(d'un bateau, véhicule, poisson)* to get stuck in the sand **2** *(d'un port, d'une rivière)* to silt up; *(de tuyaux)* to get choked up (with sand)

ensachage [ɑ̃saʃaʒ] NM *(de bonbons etc)* bagging; *(de céréales etc)* sacking

ensacher [ɑ̃saʃe] VT *(bonbons etc)* to put into bags, to bag; *(céréales etc)* to put into sacks, to sack

ensanglanter [ɑ̃sɑ̃glɑ̃te] VT *(chemise, corps etc)* to stain with blood; **e. une nation** to plunge a nation into a bloodbath; **mains ensanglantées** bloodstained *or* bloody hands; **événement ensanglanté par un attentat** event marred by the bloody violence of an assassination attempt

ENSBA NF *(abrév* **École nationale supérieure des Beaux-Arts)** = leading art school in Paris

enseignant, -ante [ɑ̃sɛɲɑ̃, -ɑ̃t] ADJ teaching; **corps e.** teaching profession
N teacher

enseigne [ɑ̃sɛɲ] NF **1** *(panonceau) (d'un magasin, cinéma etc)* sign; **e. au néon** neon sign; **à l'e. du Lion d'or** at the (sign of the) Golden Lion; **e. bancaire** big bank; *Fig Fam* **nous sommes tous logés à la même e.** we are all in the same boat; *Prov* **à bon vin point d'e.** good wine needs no bush **2** *Mktg* brand name **3** *Litt* **à telle e. que ...** so much so that ... **4** *Hist, Mil (drapeau etc)* ensign
NM **1** *Hist, Mil (soldat)* standard-bearer, ensign **2** *Naut* **e. (de vaisseau)** sub-lieutenant, *Am* ensign

enseignement [ɑ̃sɛɲmɑ̃] NM **1** *(instruction)* teaching; **l'e. de l'anglais** the teaching of English; **méthode d'e.** teaching method; **il est dans l'e.** he is a teacher, he teaches **2** *(éducation, formation)* education; **e. des ou pour adultes** adult education; **e. du premier/second degré, e. primaire/secondaire** primary/secondary education; **e. supérieur** higher education **3** *(leçon tirée de l'expérience)* lesson; **tirer un e. de qch** to learn a lesson from sth

▸▸**e. assisté par ordinateur** computer-aided *or* -assisted learning; **e. par correspondance** teaching by correspondence courses; **e. à distance** distance learning; **e. en groupe** group teaching; **e. libre** private education; **e. mixte** coeducation; **e. technique** technical education

enseigner [ɑ̃sɛɲe] VT **1** *(apprendre)* to teach; **e. la grammaire à qn** to teach sb grammar; **e. à qn à faire qch** to teach sb (how) to do sth; **e. l'anglais** to teach English; **l'expérience nous enseigne que ...** experience teaches *or* shows us that ... **2** *Vieilli (indiquer)* to show, to point out; **e. à qn son devoir** to point out his/her duty to sb
VI to be a teacher, to teach

ensemble [ɑ̃sɑ̃bl] ADV together; **vivre e.** to live together; **ils se marièrent e.** they married (each other); **aller (bien) e.** *(de personnes)* to be well-matched; *(de choses)* to go together; **ils vont mal e.** *(de personnes)* they're ill-matched; **on pourrait partir tous e.** we could all go together *or* in a group; **ne répondez pas tous e.** don't all answer at once *or* at the same time; **vendre tous ses meubles e.** to sell all one's furniture at once
NM **1** *(totalité)* whole, entirety; **l'e. du travail est bon** the work as a whole is good; **l'e. d'un tableau** the general effect of a picture; **vue d'e.** comprehensive *or* general view, overall picture; **idée d'e.** *(d'un sujet)* broad *or* general idea; **dans l'e.** on the whole, taken all round, by and large; **la classe, prise dans son e., a un bon niveau** the class, (taken) as a whole, is of a good standard
2 *(unité)* cohesion, unity; **mouvement d'e.** combined movement; **l'exécution manque d'e.** the execution lacks cohesion *or* is ragged; **avec e.** all together, in unison, as one
3 *(groupe) (de gens)* group; *(d'objets, de faits, de conditions)* set; *(de meubles)* suite; *(de services etc)* package; **e. vocal** (small) choir; **e. de couleurs** harmonious (group of) colours; **e. de données** set of data; *Mktg* **e. de besoins** need set; *Mktg* **e. de considérations** consideration *or* product (choice) set
4 *(vêtements)* ensemble, outfit; **e. pantalon** trouser suit, *Am* pant suit
5 *(d'habitations)* block; **grand e.** residential estate
6 *Math* set; **e. vide** empty set
7 *Aut* **e. moteur-boîte** power unit

ensemblier [ɑ̃sɑ̃blije] NM interior decorator; *Cin, TV* assistant set designer

ensemencement [ɑ̃s(ə)mɑ̃smɑ̃] NM **1** *Agr* sowing **2** *Biol* seeding

ensemencer [ɑ̃s(ə)mɑ̃se] VT *(j'ensemençai(s))* **1** *Agr (champ)* to sow **2** *Biol (milieu de culture)* to seed

enserrer [ɑ̃sere] VT *(objet, partie du corps)* to encircle tightly; **e. qn dans ses bras** to clasp sb in one's arms, to embrace *or* hug sb

ensevelir [ɑ̃s(ə)vlir] VT **1** *Litt (enterrer) (corps)* to bury, to entomb; *Fig (secret)* to hide away; **l'avalanche a enseveli le village sous la neige** the avalanche buried the village in snow; *Fig* **il a été enseveli sous des tonnes de lettres** he was snowed under with letters **2** *(mettre dans un linceul) (corps)* to shroud
VPR s'ensevelir *(dans un livre, à la campagne etc)* to bury oneself

ensevelissement [ɑ̃s(ə)vlismɑ̃] NM *(de mort)* burial; *(dans un linceul)* shrouding; *(sous la neige, des décombres etc)* burying; *Fig (de secret)* hiding away

ENSI [ɛnsi] NF *(abrév* **École nationale supérieure d'ingénieurs)** = competitive-entry engineering institute

ensilage [ɑ̃silaʒ] NM *(de récoltes)* ensilage

ensiler [ɑ̃sile] VT *(récoltes)* to ensile

ensoleillé [ɑ̃sɔleje] ADJ *(lieu, jour etc)* sunny

ensoleillement [ɑ̃sɔlɛjmɑ̃] NM **1** *(état)* sunniness **2** *(période)* sunny period; **cinq journées d'e.** five days of sun(shine)

ensoleiller [ɑ̃sɔleje] VT **1** *(pièce, mur etc)* to bathe in sunlight **2** *Fig (la vie de qn etc)* to brighten (up), to light up

ensommeillé [ɑ̃sɔmeje] ADJ *(personne)* sleepy, drowsy; *(yeux, visage)* sleepy

ensorcelant [ɑ̃sɔrsəlɑ̃] ADJ *(sourire etc)* bewitching

ensorcelé [ɑ̃sɔrsəle] ADJ bewitched, under a spell

ensorceler [ɑ̃sɔrsəle] VT *(j'ensorcelle; j'ensorcellerai)* **1** *(envoûter)* to bewitch, to cast *or* put a spell (up) on **2** *Fig (personne)* to bewitch, to captivate

ensorceleur, -euse [ɑ̃sɔrsəlœr, -øz] ADJ bewitching
NM sorcerer; *Fig* charmer
NF **ensorceleuse** sorceress; *Fig* enchantress

ensorcellement [ɑ̃sɔrsɛlmɑ̃] NM **1** *(action)* bewitching; *(état)* bewitchment; *(sorcellerie)* sorcery **2** *Fig (charme)* charm, spell

ensuite [ɑ̃sɥit] ADV *(plus tard)* after(wards), later; *(puis)* then, next, after that; **et e.?** what then?, what next?; *Fam* **e. de quoi/de cela, il s'est mis en colère** after which/after that he lost his temper; **les pompiers marchaient en tête, e. venait la musique** the firemen led the procession, next came the band; **d'abord, c'est très cher, et e. ça ne te va pas du tout** for one thing it's very expensive and for another it doesn't at all suit you

ensuivre (s') [sɑ̃sɥivr] VPR *(conj like* **suivre)** to follow, to ensue, to result; **jusqu'à ce que mort s'ensuive** *(battre qn etc)* to death; **les résultats qui s'ensuivent** the results which ensue *or* follow; **il s'ensuit qu'il est sans emploi** the consequence is he's out of a job; *Fam* **et tout ce qui s'ensuit** and all the rest of it, and all that goes with it; *Litt* **vos erreurs s'ensuivront de graves sanctions** your errors will result in grave punishment

ensuqué [ɑ̃syke] ADJ *Région, Fam* dazed, in a daze

entablement [ɑ̃tabləmɑ̃] NM *Archit (au-dessus d'une colonnade)* entablature; *Constr (support de toit)* coping

entacher [ɑ̃taʃe] VT **1** *(l'honneur de qn)* to sully, to besmirch, to cast a slur on **2** *Jur (contrat etc)* to vitiate; **entaché de nullité** voidable

entaille [ɑ̃taj] NF **1** *(dans un morceau de bois etc)* notch; *(longue)* groove; **à entailles** notched; *(longues)* grooved **2** *(blessure)* gash, cut; *(superficielle)* nick, cut; **se faire une e. au menton** to cut one's chin

entailler [ɑ̃taje] VT **1** *(morceau de bois etc)* to notch; *(d'une longue encoche)* to groove **2** *(blesser)* to gash, to cut; *(superficiellement)* to nick, to cut
VPR s'entailler **s'e. le doigt** to cut one's finger

entame [ɑ̃tam] NF **1** *(de pain, jambon etc)* first slice **2** *Cartes (d'une couleur)* opening (card)

entamer [ɑ̃tame] VT **1** *(pain, jambon etc)* to start on, to cut into; *(fût)* to broach; *(bouteille, pot de confiture etc)* to start on, to open; *(défense)* to penetrate, to breach; *(chair)* to cut into; **e. la peau** to break the skin; **doutes qui entament la foi/les convictions de qn** doubts that undermine *or* shake sb's faith/convictions; **e. l'honneur de qn** to damage sb's honour; **e. son capital** to break into one's capital
2 *(commencer à entreprendre) (travail, recherche etc)* to begin, to commence, to start (on); *(négociations)* to start, to open; **e. une conversation** to strike up a conversation; **e. des démarches** to begin to take steps, to ini-

tiate steps; **e. des relations avec qn** to enter into relations with sb; *Jur* **e. des poursuites contre qn** to initiate *or* institute proceedings against sb; **e. un sujet** to broach a subject; *Com* **e. une vente** to open a sale

3 *Cartes* **e. trèfle** to open clubs

entartrage [ɑ̃tartraʒ] NM *(d'une chaudière etc)* furring (up), scaling

entartrer [ɑ̃tartre] VT *(chaudière etc)* to fur (up), to scale

  VPR **s'entartrer** *(d'une chaudière)* to fur (up), to become furred; *(des dents)* to scale up

entassement [ɑ̃tasmɑ̃] NM **1** *(de pierres etc)* piling (up), heaping (up); *(de caisses etc)* stacking **2** *(de passagers, bétail etc)* crowding *or* packing together

entasser [ɑ̃tase] VT **1** *(pierres, livres, vêtements etc)* to pile (up), to heap (up); *(caisses etc)* to stack (up); *(argent)* to amass, to pile up **2** *(serrer) (passagers, bétail etc)* to pack *or* crowd *or* cram together

  VPR **s'entasser 1** *(d'objets)* to pile up **2** *(de personnes)* to crowd *or* huddle together

ente [ɑ̃t] NF **1** *Agr etc (greffe)* scion, graft; *(porte-greffe)* stock **2** *(de pinceau)* handle

entendement [ɑ̃tɑ̃dmɑ̃] NM understanding; **dépasser l'e.** to be beyond all understanding

entendeur [ɑ̃tɑ̃dœr] NM **à bon e. salut!** a word to the wise (is enough)

ENTENDRE [ɑ̃tɑ̃dr]

  VT to hear **1, 2** ▪ to listen to **2** ▪ to understand **3** ▪ to insinuate *(laisser entendre)* **3** ▪ to mean **4** ▪ to intend **5**
  VI to hear
  VPR to get on **1** ▪ to agree **2** ▪ to be heard **3** ▪ to be understood **4** ▪ to know about *(s'y entendre à)* **5**

VT **1** *(ouïr)* to hear; **j'entendis un cri** I heard a cry; **je n'entends rien (de ce que tu dis)** I can't hear a thing (you're saying); **on l'entend à peine** you can hardly hear him/it, he/it is scarcely audible; **je pouvais à peine me faire e.** I could hardly make myself heard; **parlez plus fort, je ne vous entends pas bien** speak up, I can't hear you very well; **je l'entendis rire** I heard him laugh *or* laughing; **tu n'as pas entendu quelque chose?** didn't you hear anything?; **on n'entend que toi, ici! c'est lassant à la fin!** yours is the only voice we can hear, it's so annoying!; **e. qch de ses propres oreilles** to hear sth with one's own ears; **je ne veux plus e. parler de lui** I don't want to hear him mentioned again *or* to hear another word about him; **e. dire que ...** to hear (it said) that ...; **on a entendu dire que sa femme l'a quitté** it is rumoured *or* said that his wife has left him; **je le sais parce que je l'ai entendu dire** I know it by *or* from hearsay; **e. qn dire qch** to hear sb say sth; **e. parler de** *(connaître l'existence de)* to hear of; *(être au courant de)* to hear about; **je ne veux pas en e. parler!** I don't want to hear (a word) about it!; **celui-là, il va e. parler de moi** *ou* **du pays!** he'll get a piece of my mind *or* a good ear-bashing!; **celui-là, il va m'e.!** he'll hear me!; **je ne veux pas en e. plus!** I don't want to hear any more *or* another word about it!; **il répétait, à qui voulait l'e., que ...** he'd tell anyone who would listen that ...; **je l'entends d'avance** *ou* **d'ici!** I can hear it already!; **e. des voix** to hear voices; *Fam* **ce qu'il ne faut pas e.!** I've heard it all now!; *Fam* **qu'entends-je, qu'ouïs-je, qu'acoustiqué-je?** *ou* **qu'entends-je, qu'ouïs-je, rêvé-je** *ou* **dors-je?** ≃ I can't believe my ears! SEE GRAMMAR A39; B35

2 *(écouter) (suppliant etc)* to hear, to listen to; **on le congédia sans l'e.** he was dismissed without a hearing *or* without being heard; **e.**

la messe to hear a mass; **e. qn en confession** to hear sb's confession; **aller e. un concert** to go to a concert; **à vous e., il a eu tort** judging from *or* going by what you say, he was in the wrong; **refuser d'e. une requête** to turn a deaf ear to a request; **e. raison** to listen to reason; **il n'a rien voulu e.** he would not listen; *Jur* **l'affaire sera entendue demain** the case will be heard *or* comes up (for hearing) tomorrow; **le juge a entendu les témoins** the judge heard the witnesses; **que Dieu entende nos prières** may our prayers be answered

3 *(comprendre) (langue, passage d'un texte etc)* to understand; **ce n'est pas ainsi qu'il l'entend** he doesn't see it that way *or* like that; **donner à e. à qn que ...** *(faire croire)* to lead sb to believe that ...; *(faire comprendre)* to give sb to understand that ...; **laisser e. qch** to insinuate *or* imply sth; **il n'entend pas la plaisanterie** he can't take a joke; **je n'y entends rien** I don't know the first thing about it

4 *(vouloir dire)* to mean; **qu'entendez-vous par là?** what do you mean by that?

5 *(vouloir)* **e. faire qch** to intend *or* mean to do sth; **il n'y entend pas malice** he means *or* intends no harm; **faites comme vous l'entendez** do as you think best, do as you please; **j'entends que vous veniez** I expect you to come; **je n'entends pas qu'on le vende** I won't hear of it being sold; **elle voulait trouver du travail, mais lui ne l'entendait pas ainsi** she wanted to get a job, but he wouldn't hear of it

VI *(par l'ouïe)* to hear; **il entend mal** he is hard of hearing; **il est impossible de se faire e. ici!** it's impossible to make youself heard here!; **un bruit se fit e.** a noise was heard; **attends, j'ai mal entendu!** hold on, I don't think I heard you right!; **tu entends!** *(menace)* do you hear (me)!

VPR **s'entendre 1** *(sympathiser)* to get on; **ils s'entendent bien** they get on (well); **je ne m'entends pas du tout avec elle** I don't get on at all with her; **je crois que nous sommes faits pour nous e.** I think we were made to get on well together; **nous n'étions pas faits pour nous e.** we weren't suited to each other; **ils s'entendent comme larrons en foire** they are as thick as thieves

2 *(se mettre d'accord)* to agree; **s'e. directement avec qn** to come to a direct understanding with sb; **s'e. pour commettre un crime** to conspire to commit a crime; **il faudrait vous e., il est venu ou il n'est pas venu?** get your story straight, did he come or not?; **entendons-nous bien!** *(mettons les choses au clair)* let's get things straight!

3 *(être perçu par l'ouïe)* to be heard; **sa voix ne s'entend guère** his/her voice is hardly audible *or* can hardly be heard; **on ne s'entend plus ici** you can't hear yourself speak *or* think here

4 *(être compris)* to be understood; **cela s'entend** of course, that goes without saying

5 **s'e. à, s'y e. à** *(être habile à) (chevaux, voitures etc)* to know (all) about, to understand; **s'e. aux affaires** to have a good head for business; **elle s'y entend à mettre de l'huile sur le feu** she has a knack for adding fuel to the fire

entendu, -ue [ɑ̃tɑ̃dy] ADJ **1** *(complice, informé) (regard, sourire)* knowing; **d'un air e.** knowingly; **intérêt bien e.** enlightened self-interest **2** *(décidé)* **très bien, (c'est) e.** fine, agreed *or* all right!; **c'est une affaire entendue** that's agreed *or* settled; **et bien e., vous toucherez la moitié du bénéfice** and of course, you'll get half the profit

N *Vieilli* **faire l'e.** to pretend to know all about it

enténébrer [ɑ̃tenebre] VT *(il enténèbre; il*

enténébrera) *Litt* to envelop *or* plunge in darkness *or* gloom

entente [ɑ̃tɑ̃t] NF **1** *(entre personnes) (accord)* agreement, understanding *(entre* between); *(relation)* harmony; **arriver à une e.** to reach an agreement *or* understanding; **terrain d'e.** common ground; **après e. avec les autorités** after consultation with the authorities; **il faut vivre en bonne e. avec ses voisins** one must live in harmony with one's neighbours; **la bonne/mauvaise e. qui règne dans la famille** the good/bad feeling that prevails in the family **2** *(compréhension)* **mot à double e.** word with a double meaning

  ▶▶ *Hist* **E. cordiale** Entente Cordiale; **e. industrielle** *(cartel)* combine

enter [ɑ̃te] VT *(arbre)* to graft

entérinement [ɑ̃terinmɑ̃] NM *Jur* ratification, confirmation; *Fig* endorsement

entériner [ɑ̃terine] VT *Jur* to ratify, to confirm; *Fig (approuver) (action, nouveau mot etc)* to endorse

entérique [ɑ̃terik] ADJ *Méd* enteric, intestinal

entérite [ɑ̃terit] NF *Méd* enteritis

enterrement [ɑ̃tɛrmɑ̃] NM **1** *(sous la terre)* burial, *Fml* interment; *Fig* **c'est l'e. de tous mes projets/espoirs** that has killed off all my plans/hopes; *Hum* **c'était vraiment un e. de première classe** it really got the thumbs down; *Hum* **faire un e. de première classe à un projet** to give a plan the thumbs down, to shelve a plan for good **2** *(cérémonie)* funeral; *Fam* **figure** *ou* **tête d'e.** long face; **faire une tête d'e.** to look sombre **3** *(cortège)* funeral procession

enterrer [ɑ̃tere] VT **1** *(enfouir) (chose)* to bury, to put in the earth; *(bulbes)* to plant **2** *(inhumer) (corps)* to bury, *Fml* to inter; *Fam* **il nous enterrera tous** he will outlive us all; *Fig* **e. un projet** to scrap a plan; *Fig* **e. un désaccord/une querelle** to bury a disagreement/a quarrel; *Fig* **elle désire e. toute cette affaire** she wants the whole thing buried and forgotten; *Fig* **e. sa vie de garçon** to have a stag party *or Am* bachelor party

  VPR **s'enterrer** *Fig* **il s'est enterré au fin fond de la campagne normande** he buried himself in the depths of the Normandy countryside

entêtant [ɑ̃tetɑ̃] ADJ *(vin, parfum, musique etc)* heady

en-tête, *pl* **en-têtes** [ɑ̃tɛt] NM *(d'une lettre, d'un document)* heading; *Com* letterhead; *Typ (d'une page etc)* headline; *Ordinat* header; **e. de facture** billhead; *Journ* **e. de colonne** column header; **papier à e.** headed paper

entêté, -ée [ɑ̃tete] ADJ obstinate, stubborn

  N obstinate *or* stubborn person

entêtement [ɑ̃tetmɑ̃] NM obstinacy, stubbornness; **e. à faire qch** persistence in doing sth

entêter [ɑ̃tete] VT **e. qn** *(d'un vin, d'une odeur, de la musique etc)* to go to sb's head, to make sb giddy

  VPR **s'entêter** to persist, to be persistent; **s'e. dans une opinion** to persist in an opinion; **s'e. à faire qch** to persist in doing sth

enthousiasmant [ɑ̃tuzjasmɑ̃] ADJ *(plan, idée etc)* exciting

enthousiasme [ɑ̃tuzjasm] NM enthusiasm *(pour* for); **avec e.** enthusiastically, with enthusiasm; **faire qch sans e.** to do sth half-heartedly *or* without enthusiasm

enthousiasmer [ɑ̃tuzjasme] VT *(personne)* to fire *or* fill with enthusiasm; **il est revenu enthousiasmé** he came back full of *or* fired with enthusiasm

  VPR **s'enthousiasmer** to be/become enthusiastic, to enthuse *(pour* about)

enthousiaste [ɑ̃tuzjast] **N** enthusiast **ADJ** enthusiastic

entiché [ɑ̃tiʃe] **ADJ** infatuated (**de** with), *Fam* crazy (**de** about)

enticher (s') [sɑ̃tiʃe] **VPR s'e. de qn/qch** to become infatuated with *or Fam* crazy about sb/sth

entier, -ière [ɑ̃tje, -jɛr] **ADJ 1** *(sans division, sans diminution) (ville, boîte, quantité etc)* whole, entire; *(pas cassé, pas entamé) (assiette, gâteau etc)* intact, whole; *(boîte, bouteille etc)* full; **lait e.** whole milk, *Br* full-cream milk; **la France entière** the whole of France; **il a mangé le gâteau tout e.** he ate the whole (of the) cake; **pendant des heures entières** for hours on end; **conserver sa réputation entière** to keep one's reputation intact; **le problème reste e.** the problem is no nearer solution *or* remains unsolved; *Math* **nombre e.** integer, whole number; **cheval e.** stallion; **payer place entière** *Rail* to pay full fare; *Théâtre* to pay full price **2** *(absolu) (autorité, confiance etc)* complete, full; **l'entière direction de qch** the entire *or* sole management of sth; **se donner tout e. à son travail** to devote oneself entirely to one's work; **elle est tout(e) entière à ce qu'elle fait** she is engrossed in *or* intent on what she is doing; **jouir d'une entière liberté** to enjoy complete *or* total freedom; **donner entière satisfaction** to give complete *or* total satisfaction **3** *(sans compromis) (personne)* unyielding, uncompromising **NM 1** *(totalité)* entirety; **raconter une histoire dans son e.** to relate a story in its entirety; **en e.** wholly, entirely, totally; **il a lu le livre en e.** he read the whole (of the) book *or* the entire book; **il a fait ses devoirs en e.** he has done all (of) his homework; **nom en e.** name in full, full name **2** *Math (nombre)* integer, whole number

entièrement [ɑ̃tjɛrmɑ̃] **ADV** entirely, wholly, completely; **il n'est pas e. mauvais** he's not all bad

entièreté [ɑ̃tjɛrte] **NF** entirety

entité [ɑ̃tite] **NF** entity; *Compta* item

entoilage [ɑ̃twalaʒ] **NM 1** *(action) (de carte etc)* mounting on canvas; *Couture* stiffening with canvas **2** *(toile)* canvas mount

entoiler [ɑ̃twale] **VT** *(carte etc)* to mount on canvas; *Couture* to stiffen with canvas; **carte entoilée** canvas-mounted map

entôler [ɑ̃tole] **VT** *Arg (en particulier d'une prostituée) (client etc)* to fleece, to rob

entomologie [ɑ̃tɔmɔlɔʒi] **NF** entomology

entomologique [ɑ̃tɔmɔlɔʒik] **ADJ** entomological

entomologiste [ɑ̃tɔmɔlɔʒist] **N** entomologist

entonner [ɑ̃tɔne] **VT** *(vin etc)* to barrel, to cask

entonner [ɑ̃tɔne] **VT** *(commencer à chanter) (chanson)* to strike up, to start; *Vieilli* **e. les louanges de qn** to sing sb's praises

entonnoir [ɑ̃tɔnwar] **NM 1** *(ustensile)* funnel; **en (forme d')e.** funnel-shaped **2** *(cavité)* funnel; *(produit par une bombe etc)* crater

entorse [ɑ̃tɔrs] **NF 1** *Méd* sprain, wrench; **se faire une e. à la cheville/au poignet** to sprain *or* twist *or* wrench one's ankle/wrist **2** *Fig* **faire une e. à la loi/au règlement** to bend *or* stretch the law/the rules; **faire une e. à la vérité** to twist *or* distort the truth; **faire une e. à son régime** to break one's diet; **tu peux bien faire une petite e. à tes habitudes** you can surely make an exception

entortillement [ɑ̃tɔrtijmɑ̃] **NM 1** *(action) (d'un fil, papier etc)* twisting, wrapping; *(d'un serpent, du lierre etc)* twisting, twining, coiling **2** *(état)* entwinement

entortiller [ɑ̃tɔrtije] **VT 1** *(envelopper) (bonbon etc)* to wrap (up) (**dans** in); *(enrouler) (fil, papier etc)* to twist, to wrap (**autour de** round) **2** *(circonvenir) (personne)* to get round **3** *(embrouiller) (phrases, réponses etc)* to make convoluted; **e. une demande dans des explications fumeuses** to wrap up a request in woolly explanations
VPR s'entortiller 1 *(d'un serpent, du lierre etc)* to twist, to twine, to coil (**autour de** round) **2** *(s'empêtrer)* to get entangled, to get tangled (up) (**dans** in); **il s'est entortillé les pieds dans le tapis** he got his feet entangled *or* tangled (up) in the carpet; *Fig* **elle s'entortillait dans des explications compliquées** she tied herself in knots with complicated explanations **3** *(s'enrouler) (dans une couette etc)* to wrap oneself up (**dans** in)

entour [ɑ̃tur] **NM à l'e. de** *(ville etc)* round (about); *Litt* **les entours de** the environs *or* surroundings of

entourage [ɑ̃turaʒ] **NM 1** *(bordure) (d'une ouverture, d'un parterre de fleurs etc)* border; *(d'un bijou)* setting; **miniature avec un e. de perles** miniature set in pearls **2** *(amis, relations)* circle (of friends/acquaintances); *(collègues)* associates; *(de ministre etc)* attendants; *(de souverain)* entourage, suite; **dans son e. proche** in his/her close circle

entourer [ɑ̃ture] **VT 1** *(border, enceindre)* to surround (**de** with); **e. un champ d'une clôture** to fence in a field; **veuillez e. la bonne réponse en rouge** please circle *or* ring the correct answer in red; **e. qn de ses bras** to put one's arms round sb, to hold *or* take sb in one's arms; **cheminée entourée de marbre** fireplace enclosed in marble **2** *(être autour de)* to surround; *(armée)* to encircle, to surround; **les gens qui vous entourent** the people around *or* about you; **le monde qui nous entoure** the world around us; **entouré d'amis** surrounded by friends; **un rang de perles entourait son cou** a string of pearls encircled her neck, she had a string of pearls round her neck; **entouré de mystère** wrapped *or* shrouded in mystery **3** *(s'occuper de) (personne)* to rally round; **il est très entouré (d'amis)** he is surrounded by friends; **e. qn de soins/respect** to lavish attention on sb/to show respect to sb; **au moment de son divorce, sa famille l'a beaucoup entouré** his family rallied round *or* supported him at the time of his divorce
VPR s'entourer s'e. d'amis/de belles choses to surround oneself with friends/fine things

entourloupe [ɑ̃turlup], **entourloupette** [ɑ̃turlupɛt] **NF** *Fam* dirty trick; **faire une e. à qn** to play a dirty trick on sb

entourlouper [ɑ̃turlupe] **VT** *Fam* **e. qn** to play a dirty trick on sb, *Br* to do the dirty on sb, *Am* to do sb dirt

entourloupette [ɑ̃turlupɛt] **NF** nasty *or* dirty trick; **faire une e. à qn** to play a dirty trick on sb

entournure [ɑ̃turnyr] **NF** *(de vêtement)* armhole; *Fam* **être gêné aux entournures** *(mal à l'aise)* to feel awkward *or* ill at ease; *(financièrement)* to feel the pinch

entracte [ɑ̃trakt] **NM 1** *Théâtre, Cin (intervalle)* intermission, *Br* interval; **à l'e.** in the intermission *or Br* interval **2** *Théâtre (pièce)* entr'acte, interlude

entraide [ɑ̃trɛd] **NF** mutual aid

entraider (s') [sɑ̃trede] **VPR** to help one another *or* each other

entrailles [ɑ̃traj] **NFPL** *(du corps)* entrails, intestines, bowels; *Litt (de la mère)* womb; *Fig* **les e. de la terre** the bowels of the earth; *Fig* **ce reportage m'a remué les e.** this report made a deep and painful impression on me; *Fig* **ne pas avoir d'e.** to be heartless

entrain [ɑ̃trɛ̃] **NM** *(d'une fête, musique, conversation etc)* liveliness, spirit; *(d'une personne)* high spirits, spirit, liveliness; **être plein d'e., avoir de l'e.** *(d'une personne)* to be full of life *or* of go; **musique pleine d'e.** lively music; **manger avec e.** to eat with gusto; **travailler avec e.** to work with a will; **donner plus d'e. à la conversation** to liven up the conversation; **ça manque d'e., tout ça** that's all a bit half-hearted; **faire qch sans e.** to do sth half-heartedly

entraînant [ɑ̃trɛnɑ̃] **ADJ** *(air, rythme, style)* lively; *(éloquence)* stirring

entraînement [ɑ̃trɛnmɑ̃] **NM 1** *(d'un élève etc), Sport, Courses de chevaux* training; **un e.** a training session, a work-out; **suivre un e.** to follow a training programme; **à l'e.** in training; **il s'est blessé à l'e.** he hurt himself training; **il a marqué un but comme à l'e.** he scored a text-book goal; **match d'e.** practice game; **terrain d'e.** training *or* practice ground; **avoir de l'e.** to be well trained; *Fig Fam* **toi qui as de l'e., fais-le** you've had a lot of practice at this type of thing, you do it; **manquer d'e.** to be out of training **2** *Tech* drive; **arbre d'e.** drive shaft; *Aut* **e. par chaîne** chain drive; **e. à friction** *(d'une imprimante)* friction feed; *Ordinat* **e. du papier** *(d'une imprimante)* paper advance; **e. à picots** *ou* **à traction** *(d'une imprimante)* tractor drive *or* feed **3** *Litt (des passions)* force

entraîner [ɑ̃trene] **VT 1** *(d'une rivière etc)* to sweep along, to carry away; *(d'une locomotive etc)* to pull, to draw (along); **e. qn quelque part** to drag *or* take sb off somewhere; **il m'a entraîné chez lui** he took me along to his house; **il vous entraînera dans sa chute** he will drag you down with him **2** *Tech (partie de machine etc)* to drive; *Tech* **entraîné par courroie** belt-driven **3** *(exercer une influence sur)* **e. qn à faire qch** to lead *or* induce sb to do sth; **être entraîné dans un piège** to be lured *or* led into a trap; **cela nous entraînera dans des problèmes** that will lead *or* get us into problems; **entraîné par l'éloquence de l'orateur** carried away by the speaker's eloquence; **se faire e.** to be *or* get led astray; **se laisser e.** to allow oneself to be led astray; **se laisser e. à faire qch** to be drawn into doing sth **4** *(causer) (accident, malheur etc)* to result in, to bring about; *(problème, dépense etc)* to entail, to involve; **cela entraînera un retard** it will involve *or* lead to delay; **décision qui peut e. des inconvénients** decision that may give rise to difficulties **5** *(former) (élève etc)* to train; *Sport (athlète, équipe)* to coach, to train; *(cheval de course etc)* to train; *(cycliste)* to pace; **e. qn à faire qch** to train sb to do sth
VPR s'entraîner *(d'un élève etc)* to train oneself; *Sport* to train; **s'e. à faire qch** to train oneself to do sth

entraîneur [ɑ̃trɛnœr] **NM 1** *Sport (d'un athlète, d'une équipe)* coach, trainer; *(d'un cheval etc)* trainer; *(d'un cycliste)* pacemaker, pacer **2** *(chef)* **e. d'hommes** leader of men

entraîneuse [ɑ̃trɛnøz] **NF 1** *(dans une boîte de nuit etc)* hostess **2** *Sport (d'une athlète, d'une équipe)* coach, trainer; *(d'un cheval etc)* trainer

entrant [ɑ̃trɑ̃] **ADJ** *(fonctionnaire)* newly appointed; *(représentant parlementaire)* newly elected; **les élèves entrants** the new pupils
N les entrants et les sortants those entering and those leaving

entrapercevoir [ɑ̃trapɛrsəvwar] **VT** *(conj like* **apercevoir***)* to catch a fleeting glimpse of

entrave [ɑ̃trav] **NF 1** *(d'un cheval etc)* hobble; **entraves** *(d'un forçat etc)* fetters, shackles **2** *Fig* hindrance, impediment (**à** to); **e. à la cir-**

culation hindrance to traffic; **e. à la liberté/à la bonne marche de la justice** interference with freedom/with the due process of the law

entravé [ɑ̃trave] ADJ **jupe entravée** hobble skirt

entraver [ɑ̃trave] VT **1** *(cheval etc)* to hobble; *(forçat etc)* to put in fetters or shackles **2** *Fig (action, carrière etc)* to hinder, to hamper, to impede; **e. la circulation** to hold up or block the traffic **3** *Fam (comprendre)* to get; **je n'y entrave rien** ou **que dalle** I don't get it (at all)

ENTRE [ɑ̃tr]

> between **1, 4, 5** ▪ among **2, 4, 5** ▪ in **2, 3** ▪ of **2** ▪ through **5**

PRÉP SEE GRAMMAR A69; B56 **1** *(deux choses, personnes, dates etc)* between; **choisir e. deux choses** to choose between two things; **distance de 10 kilomètres e. deux villes** distance of 10 kilometres between two towns; **e. deux et trois (heures)** between two and three (o'clock); *Fig* **e. les deux** *(ni l'un ni l'autre)* between the two; *(comme ci comme ça)* so-so; **être e. la vie et la mort** to be between life and death; **être e. deux âges** to be middle-aged; *Fig* **voir qn/faire qch e. deux portes** to see sb/to do sth for a brief moment **2** *(parmi)* among(st); **un homme dangereux e. tous** a most dangerous man; **un homme qu'il admirait e. tous** a man he admired above all others; **un jour e. mille** a day in a thousand; **il y avait e. autres, un Dürer et un Rembrandt** there were, among(st) other things or others, a Dürer and a Rembrandt; **ce jour e. tous** this day of all days; **d'e.** (from) among; **plusieurs d'e. nous** several of us; **l'un d'e. vous** one of you; **hésiter e. plusieurs solutions/routes/robes** to hesitate between several solutions/roads/dresses; **elle l'a choisi e. tous les hommes présents** she chose him from among all the men present **3** *(dans)* **tomber e. les mains de l'ennemi** to fall into the enemy's hands; **tenir qch e. les mains** to hold sth in one's hands; **serrer qn e. ses bras** to clasp sb in one's arms, to hug sb; **parler e. ses dents** to mumble, to mutter; **e. ces murs** within these walls **4** *(rapport réciproque) (deux personnes)* between; *(plus de deux personnes)* among(st); **ils se sont mis d'accord e. eux** they agreed among(st) themselves; **qu'est-ce qu'il y a de semblable e. lui et moi?** what similarities are there between him and me?; **mais qu'y a-t-il e. eux, exactement?** but what's (going on) between them exactly?; **soit dit e. nous** between ourselves; **nous dînerons e. nous** we'll have dinner alone or by ourselves; **nous sommes e. amis** we are among(st) friends; **se marier e. cousins** to intermarry with cousins; **discuter e. connaisseurs** to talk as one expert to another; *Fam* **il faut que je te parle e. quat'z'yeux** I've got to talk to you in private **5** *(à travers)* through; **se faufiler e. les arbres** to thread one's way through or between or among(st) the trees; **passer e. les mailles** to slip through the net; **lire e. les lignes** to read between the lines

entrebâillement [ɑ̃trəbɑjmɑ̃] NM **l'e. de la porte/fenêtre** the half-open door/window

entrebâiller [ɑ̃trəbɑje] VT *(porte, fenêtre)* to half-open; **la porte était entrebâillée** the door was ajar or half open

entrebâilleur [ɑ̃trəbɑjœr] NM door chain

entrechat [ɑ̃trəʃa] NM **1** *(saut de danse)* entrechat **2** *(gambade)* leap; **faire des entrechats** to prance (about), to cavort

entrechoquer [ɑ̃trəʃɔke] VT to knock or bang together; **e. des verres** to chink glasses
VPR **s'entrechoquer** to knock or bang

against one another; *(de verres)* to chink; *Fig (de personnalités, d'idées etc)* to clash; **elle parle tellement vite que les mots s'entrechoquent** the words come tumbling out when she speaks

entrecôte [ɑ̃trəkot] NF *Culin* rib steak, entrecôte

entrecoupé [ɑ̃trəkupe] ADJ *(discours, sommeil, voyage etc)* interrupted, broken; *(représentation, lecture etc)* interrupted; **d'une voix entrecoupée** with a catch in one's voice

entrecouper [ɑ̃trəkupe] VT *(discours, voyage, représentation etc)* to interrupt (**de** with)

entrecroisement [ɑ̃trəkrwazmɑ̃] NM *(de lignes etc)* intersection, crisscross; *(de fils etc)* interlacing

entrecroiser [ɑ̃trəkrwaze] VT *(lignes etc)* to intersect, to (criss)cross; *(fils etc)* to interlace
VPR **s'entrecroiser** *(de lignes, routes etc)* to intersect, to (criss)cross; *(de fils etc)* to interlace

entre-déchirer (s') [sɑ̃trədeʃire] VPR to tear each other to pieces

entre-deux [ɑ̃trədø] NM INV **1 il est arrivé dans l'e.** he arrived in the intervening period **2** *Couture (bande)* insertion

entre-deux-guerres [ɑ̃trədøgɛr] NM INV inter-war years *(1918-1939)*

entre-dévorer (s') [sɑ̃trədevɔre] VPR to devour one another or each other

ENTRÉE [ɑ̃tre] NF **1** *(action d'entrer)* entry, entrance; **e. (en scène) d'un acteur** an actor's entrance (on to the stage); **à leur e., tous se levèrent** as they entered, everybody stood up; **faire son e.** to make one's entrance; **faire une e. triomphale/discrète** to make a triumphant/discreet entrance; **faire son e. dans le monde** *(d'une fille)* to come out (into society); **l'e. en gare du train** the entry of the train into the station; **l'e. du Japon dans la seconde guerre mondiale** the entry of Japan into the Second World War; **depuis l'e. en guerre du pays** since the country entered the war; **mon e. dans cette société date de six mois** I joined this company six months ago; **e. en fonction** assumption or taking up of one's duties; **l'e. en fonction du nouveau directeur est prévue pour …** the new director is scheduled to take up his post on …; **e. en fusion** beginning to melt; **e. en ébullition** coming to the boil; *Fig* **à l'e. de l'hiver** at the beginning of winter; *Fig* **d'e. (de jeu)** from the outset, from the very beginning

2 *(accès)* admission, admittance **(dans un** ou **d'un lieu** to a place); **se voir refuser l'e. d'un lieu** to find oneself refused admission or entry to a place; **avoir ses entrées dans un lieu** to have the run of a place; **avoir ses entrées chez** ou **auprès de qn** to have free access to sb; **e. interdite** no admittance, no entry; **e. interdite au public/aux moins de 12 ans** public/under 12s not admitted, no admittance to the public/to under 12s; **e. interdite à tout véhicule** vehicles prohibited; **payer son e.** to pay one's admission fee or entrance fee; **prendre une e. au musée/théâtre** to buy a museum/theatre ticket; **film qui fait des records d'e.** film that breaks box-office records; **on a fait mille entrées le premier soir** a thousand people came on the first night; **e. à l'hôpital** admission into hospital

3 *(action de devenir membre)* **e. dans l'armée/le club/le parti** joining the army/club/party; **e. dans l'enseignement/la finance** going into or taking up teaching/finance; **e. à l'université** going to university; **e. au couvent** going into a convent, taking the veil; **l'e. de la Norvège dans la CEE** Norway's en-

try into the EEC; **mon e. dans cette famille ne s'est pas vraiment bien passée** I didn't fit into the family very well

4 *Com* entry; *(de marchandises importées)* importation; **droit d'e.** import duty; **e. en douane** inward customs clearance

5 *(voie d'accès)* way in, entrance, entry (**e** to); *(d'un tunnel, port etc)* entrance, mouth; *(vestibule)* entrance hall; **e. réservée au personnel** staff entrance; **e. des fournisseurs** tradesmen's entrance; **e. principale** main entrance

6 *(ouverture)* **e. de clef** keyhole; **e. d'air** intake; *Radio* **e. de poste** lead-in

7 *Ordinat (processus)* input, entry; *(information)* entry; *(touche)* enter (key); *(de caractère etc)* entering; **données d'e.** input (data); **e. (par le) clavier** keyboard input; **e. (à partir du) scanneur** scanned input; **e. de données** data input or entry; **e. de données à distance** remote data input or entry; **e. de gamme** entry level; **e. de papier** paper input; **e. opérateur** operator input; **e./sortie** input/output; **e./sortie parallèles** parallel input/output

8 *Culin* starter

9 *(de dictionnaire, livre de comptes etc)* entry

10 *Compta (dans un livre de comptes)* entry; **e. d'argent** cash received

▸▸ **e. des artistes** stage door; **e. libre** *(dans un musée)* admission free, free admission; *(dans une boutique)* no obligation to buy; **e. en matière: après cette e. en matière** after this introduction; *Radio* **e. de poste** lead-in; **e. de service** service entrance; **e. en vigueur** coming into force or effect or operation

entre-égorger (s') [sɑ̃tregɔrʒe] VPR to cut one another's or each other's throats

entrefaites [ɑ̃trəfɛt] NFPL **sur ces e.** at that moment

entrefilet [ɑ̃trəfilɛ] NM *Journ* paragraph, short item; **l'affaire a eu droit à un e.** there was a paragraph or there were a few lines in the newspaper about it

entregent [ɑ̃trəʒɑ̃] NM social sense, savoir-faire; **elle a de l'e.** she knows how to get on with people

entrejambe [ɑ̃trəʒɑ̃b] NM *Couture* crotch, crutch; **hauteur de l'e.** inside leg measurement

entrelacement [ɑ̃trəlasmɑ̃] NM *(de rubans, fils, branches)* intertwining, interlacing, interweaving

entrelacer [ɑ̃trəlase] *(conj like* lacer*)* VT *(rubans, fils, branches)* to intertwine, to interlace, to interweave; **les mains entrelacées** with one's/their/etc fingers entwined; *Ordinat* **écran entrelacé** interlaced screen
VPR **s'entrelacer** to intertwine, to interlace, to interweave

entrelacs [ɑ̃trəla] NM interlaced design, tracery

entrelarder [ɑ̃trəlarde] VT *Culin (viande)* to lard; *Fig* **e. un discours de citations** to interlard a speech with quotations

entremêlement [ɑ̃trəmɛlmɑ̃] NM **1** *(action)* (inter)mingling **2** *(résultat)* (inter)mixture

entremêler [ɑ̃trəmele] VT to (inter)mix, to (inter)mingle; **e. des couleurs** to mix or blend colours; **ordres entremêlés de jurons** orders interspersed with oaths
VPR **s'entremêler** to (inter)mix, to (inter)mingle

entremets [ɑ̃trəmɛ] NM *Culin* dessert, *Br* sweet

entremetteur, -euse [ɑ̃trəmɛtœr, -øz] NM *(dans une querelle)* intermediary, mediator; *(dans une liaison amoureuse)* go-between

entremettre (s') [sɑ̃trəmɛtr] VPR *(conj like* mettre*)* *(dans une querelle)* to intervene, to mediate; *(dans une liaison amoureuse)* to act as go-between

entremise [ɑ̃trəmiz] **NF** intervention, mediation; **par l'e. de qn** through sb

entrepont [ɑ̃trəpɔ̃] **NM** *Naut* 'tween decks; **passager d'e.** steerage passenger

entreposage [ɑ̃trəpozaʒ] **NM** storing; *(en douane)* bonding

entreposer [ɑ̃trəpoze] **VT** to store; *(en douane)* to bond, to put in bond; **e. des marchandises** to warehouse goods, to put goods in a warehouse

entrepositaire [ɑ̃trəpoziter] **NM** *(employé)* warehouseman

entrepôt [ɑ̃trəpo] **NM** warehouse, store; **e. (de la douane)** bonded warehouse; **e. frigorifique** cold store; **e. de stockage** warehouse; **marchandises en e.** goods in store; *(en douane)* goods in bond; **e. privé/public** private/public bonded warehouse

entreprenant [ɑ̃trəprənɑ̃] **ADJ** enterprising, go-ahead; *(auprès des femmes)* forward

entreprenariat [ɑ̃trəprənarja] **NM** entrepreneurship

entreprendre [ɑ̃trəprɑ̃dr] **VT** *(conj like* **prendre)** *(commencer) (tâche, étude, voyage etc)* to undertake; **e. des démarches** to take steps; **e. de faire qch** to undertake to do sth **2 e. une femme** to make advances to(-wards) a woman **3** *(entretenir)* **elle m'a entrepris sur son sujet favori** she engaged me in conversation about *or* started talking to me about her favourite subject

entrepreneur, -euse [ɑ̃trəprənœr, -øz] **N 1** *Constr* contractor; **e. (en bâtiment)** building contractor; **e. de transports** carrier, *Br* haulier, *Am* hauler; **e. de pompes funèbres** undertaker, funeral director, *Am* mortician **2** *(patron)* businessman

entreprise [ɑ̃trəpriz] **NF 1** *(action, initiative)* enterprise, undertaking, venture; *Écon* **la libre e.** free enterprise; **l'e. privée** private enterprise

2 *(firme)* company, firm; **chef d'e.** company head; **e. commerciale** business enterprise *or* operation; *Mktg* **e. dauphin** runner-up company; *Mktg* **e. dominante/défendable/à la traîne** dominant/tenable/trailing firm; **e. exportatrice** export company; **e. familiale** family business; **e. industrielle** manufacturing concern *or* company; *Mktg* **e. innovatrice** innovator, market pioneer company; **e. d'investissement** investment company; **e. de messageries** parcel delivery company; **e. multinationale** multinational (company); **e. en participation** joint venture; **e. de pompes funèbres** undertaker's, funeral director's; **e. prestataire de services** service company; **e. privée** private company; **e. publique** public corporation; **e. de transports** haulage *or* carrying company; **e. de travail intérimaire** temp agency; **e. unipersonnelle** one-man business, sole trader; **e. unipersonnelle à responsabilité limitée** sole trader with limited liability

3 *Jur (louage)* contracting; **travail à l'e.** contract work, work by *or* on contract; **mettre qch à l'e.** to put sth out to contract

4 *Vieilli* **entreprises** *(tentatives de séduction)* advances

ENTRER [ɑ̃tre]

> **VI** to come in **1, 4** ▪ to go in **1, 4** ▪ to enter **1, 2, 4, 7** ▪ to go to **3** ▪ to fit **5** ▪ to log in **6** ▪ to go into *(entrer dans)* **9–11** ▪ to join *(entrer dans)* **2, 10** **VT** to bring in **1** ▪ to take in **1** ▪ to enter **3** ▪ to input **3**

VI *(aux* **être)** **1** *(aller)* to go in, to enter; *(venir)* to come in, to enter; *(réussir à pénétrer)* to get in; **e. dans une salle** to enter *or* go into/

come into a room; **entrez!** come/go in!; **entre dans la voiture/l'ascenseur** get into the car/lift; **défense d'e.** no admittance, private; **il a réussi à e. sans payer** he managed to get in without paying; **je n'aime pas les gens qui entrent sans frapper** I don't like people who come in *or* enter without knocking; **faire e. qn** *(en l'appelant)* to call sb in; **faites e.** send *or* show him/her/them in, have him/her/them come in; **fais-le e.!** *(chez soi)* let him in; *(au bureau)* send *or* show him in; **laisser e. qn/qch** to let sb/sth in; **e. en passant** to drop in, to look in (**chez qn** on sb); **je n'ai fait qu'e. et sortir** I just dropped in for a moment; **empêcher qn d'e.** to keep sb out, to stop sb entering *or* getting in; **le voleur est entré par la fenêtre** the thief got in through the window; **il n'a pas pu e.** he couldn't get in; **le train entre en gare** the train is pulling into the station; **le navire entre au port** the ship is coming into harbour; **e. en courant/en dansant** to run/dance in; **e. furtivement** to sneak in, to steal in; **e. dans un pays** to enter a country; *Théâtre* **Hamlet entre (en scène)** enter Hamlet; **vous qui entrez ici, abandonnez toute espérance** abandon hope, all ye who enter here

2 *(devenir membre)* **e. dans l'armée/la police** to join the army/the police; *Mil* **e. dans la carrière** to become an officer; **e. en religion** to take (holy) orders; **il est entré à l'hôpital comme infirmier** he joined *or* started working at the hospital as a nurse; **e. aux PTT** to start working for the Post Office; **e. au service de qn** to enter sb's service; **e. dans la Communauté européenne** to join the European Community

3 *(être admis)* **e. à l'université** to go to university; **j'entre à l'hôpital demain** I'm going into hospital *or Am* the hospital tomorrow; **e. en maternelle** to start nursery school

4 *(pénétrer, s'infiltrer) (de l'eau, de l'air etc)* to go/come in; **le clou est entré dans le mur** the nail went into the wall; **nous constatons que la balle est entrée dans le crâne et l'a traversé de part en part** we can see that the bullet entered the skull and came through the other side; **la clef n'entre pas dans la serrure** the key won't *or* doesn't go *or* fit in the lock; **les liens étaient tellement serrés qu'ils lui sont entrés dans les chairs** the straps were so tight that they cut into his flesh; **une pareille idée ne lui serait jamais entrée dans la tête** such an idea never entered his head; **faire e. une idée dans la tête de qn** to put an idea in sb's head; *Fig* **le doute/la peur entra dans son esprit** his mind filled with doubts/fear

5 *(tenir)* **on n'entrera jamais à vingt dans cette petite pièce** we'll never get twenty people into that small room; **la télévision n'entre pas dans le carton** the television won't *or* doesn't go *or* fit in the box; *Fam* **ça ne veut pas e.** it won't go in; **faire e. qch dans qch** to insert *or* put sth in sth; **je ne peux pas faire e. toutes mes affaires dans une seule valise** I can't get *or* fit all my things in one suitcase

6 *Ordinat* to log in *or* on

7 *Com (de marchandises importées)* to be imported; **ces marchandises sont entrées en fraude sur le territoire** these goods were smuggled into the country

8 *(marque le début de)* **e. dans une colère terrible** to get extremely angry; **la Roumanie entre en démocratie** Romania is embracing democracy; **elle entre tout juste en convalescence** she's just beginning to convalesce; **e. en ébullition** to begin to boil, to come to the boil; **e. en effervescence** to begin to effervesce; **e. en fonction** to take up one's duties; **e. dans la vie active** to start one's working life; **e. en vigueur** to come into force *or* effect *or* operation; **e. dans sa ving-**

tième **année** to turn nineteen; **e. dans une ère nouvelle** to enter a new era; *Mil* **e. en campagne** to take the field; *Mil* **e. en guerre** to enter the war; **e. en méditation** to begin to meditate; **on entre en hiver** winter is just beginning; *Com* **e. en liquidation** to go into liquidation

9 *(faire partie de)* **e. dans une catégorie** to fall into a category; **cela ne peut pas e. en ligne de compte** that cannot be taken into account *or* consideration; **cela entre dans ses projets** that is part of his plans; **il est entré dans ma vie tout d'un coup** he came into my life all of a sudden; **dans tout ceci l'imagination entre pour beaucoup** in all this imagination plays a large part; **e. dans la légende** to become a legend; **e. dans l'histoire** to go down in history; **aucun produit chimique n'entre dans la composition de ce dessert** no chemical product goes into the making of this dessert; *Com* **e. dans un marché** to enter a market

10 e. dans *(danse, débat etc)* to join in; *(les idées, les vues, les sentiments de qn etc)* to share, to go along with sb; **e. dans les détails/de longues explications** to go into the details *or* into detail/long explanations; *TV, Cin* **e. dans le champ** to come into shot

11 e. dans *(heurter) (arbre, mur etc)* to go into, to run into; *Fam* **on est entrés dans le décor** we went off the road

VT *(aux* **avoir)** **1** *(introduire)* to bring in; *(vu de l'extérieur)* to take in; **e. des marchandises en fraude** to smuggle in goods

2 *(enfoncer)* **elle a failli m'e. son parapluie dans l'œil** she nearly poked me in the eye with her umbrella; **il m'a entré ses dents/ongles dans le cou** he sank his teeth/nails into my neck

3 *Ordinat (données)* to enter, to input; *(au clavier aussi)* to key up *or* in

V IMPERS il entre beaucoup de calculs dans sa générosité there's a lot of calculation behind his/her generosity; **il n'entre pas dans mes projets de me marier tout de suite** getting married right away is not part of my plans

entre-rail, *pl* **entre-rails** [ɑ̃trəraj] **NM** *Rail (d'une voie)* gauge

entresol [ɑ̃trəsɔl] **NM** entresol, mezzanine (floor)

entre-temps [ɑ̃trətɑ̃] **ADV** meanwhile, in the meantime

▪ **NM INV** *Arch* **dans l'e.** in the meantime

entretenir [ɑ̃trət(ə)nir] *(conj like* **tenir)** **VT 1** *(soigner) (maison, jardin, routes etc)* to maintain, to keep up; *(machine)* to maintain; *(d'un fournisseur) (appareil)* to service; **e. qch en bon état** to keep sth in good condition *or* repair; **une moquette facile à e.** a carpet which is easily looked after; **j'entretiens la voiture moi-même** I look after the car myself; **e. sa santé/sa beauté** to look after *or* take care of one's health/beauty; **e. sa forme** to keep fit; **e. son français** to keep up one's French; **e. le feu** to keep the fire going

2 *(pourvoir à la subsistance de) (famille, maîtresse, flotte etc)* to maintain, to support, to keep; **je ne veux pas me faire e.** I don't want to be a kept man/woman

3 *(nourrir)* **e. des soupçons/des craintes** to entertain *or* harbour suspicions/fears; **e. une correspondance avec qn** to keep up a correspondence with sb; **e. l'espoir de qn** to keep sb's hopes alive; **e. qn dans l'ignorance** to keep sb in ignorance; **e. qn dans l'erreur** to allow sb to continue to labour under a misapprehension; **il faut e. l'idée que la paix va revenir** we must keep alive the idea that peace will return; **e. de bonnes relations avec** *(personne)* to remain on good terms with; *(pays)* to maintain good relations with

4 *(parler à)* **e. qn de qch** to converse *or* talk with sb about sth, to discuss sth with sb **5** *Compta (comptes)* to keep in order ▶ **VPR s'entretenir 1 s'e. avec qn (de qch)** to converse *or* talk with sb (about sth) **2** *(se maintenir en forme)* to keep fit

> Il faut noter que le verbe anglais **to entertain** est un faux ami. Il signifie le plus souvent **divertir**.

entretenu [ɑ̃trətny] ADJ **1 femme entretenue** kept woman **2 bien/mal e.** *(maison, jardin etc)* well-kept/badly kept **3** *Radio (oscillations)* sustained; *(ondes)* undamped, continuous

entretien [ɑ̃trətjɛ̃] NM **1** *(soins)* (d'une maison, d'un jardin, des routes etc)* upkeep, maintenance; *(d'une machine)* maintenance; *(par le fournisseur)* (d'un appareil)* servicing, service; **facile/difficile à l'e., d'e. facile/difficile** easy/difficult to maintain; **cher à l'e.** expensive to maintain; **e. des chambres** *(d'hôtel)* room servicing; **personnel d'e.** maintenance staff; **manuel d'e.** service manual; **produits d'e.** (household) cleaning materials **2** *(subsistance)* (d'une famille, armée etc)* support, maintenance **3** *(conversation)* conversation, talk; *(audience)* interview; **j'ai eu un e. avec lui** I had a talk *or* conversation with him; **j'ai réussi à décrocher un e.** *(pour une embauche)* I managed to get myself an interview; **e. téléphonique** telephone conversation; **avoir des entretiens avec le patronat** to hold talks *or* discussions with the employers **4** *Mktg* **e. assisté par ordinateur** computer-assisted interviewing; **e. centré** structured interview; **e. de groupe** group interview; *(activité)* group interviewing; **e. libre** *ou* **non structuré** unstructured interview; **e. organisé** arranged interview; **e. spontané** intercept interview; **e. structuré** structured interview; **e. par téléphone** telephone interview; *(activité)* telephone interviewing

entretoile [ɑ̃trətwal] NF *Couture* (lace) insertion

entretoise [ɑ̃trətwaz] NF *Aut* spacer; *(étai)* strut; **e. de réglage** distance piece

entre-tuer (s') [sɑ̃trətɥe] VPR to kill one another *or* each other

entre-voie, *pl* **entre-voies** [ɑ̃trəvwa] NF *Rail* space between tracks

entrevoir [ɑ̃trəvwar] VT *(conj like voir)* to catch sight *or* a glimpse of; *(indistinctement)* to make out; **je n'ai fait que l'e.** I caught only a glimpse of him; **il entrevoyait la vérité** he had an inkling of the truth; **j'entrevois des difficultés** I foresee difficulties

entrevue [ɑ̃trəvy] NF interview; *(entre hommes politiques, hommes d'affaires etc)* meeting; **avoir/fixer une e. avec qn** to have/arrange an interview *or* a meeting with sb

entrisme [ɑ̃trism] NM *Pol* entryism

entriste [ɑ̃trist] N, ADJ *Pol* entryist

entropie [ɑ̃trɔpi] NF *Phys* entropy

entrouvert [ɑ̃truvɛr] ADJ *(fenêtre, fleur etc)* half-open; *(gouffre)* gaping, yawning; **laissez la porte entrouverte** leave the door ajar; **la bouche entrouverte** with one's mouth half-open

entrouvrir [ɑ̃truvrir] *(conj like ouvrir)* VT *(porte, yeux, bouche etc)* to half-open ▶ **VPR s'entrouvrir** to half-open; *(d'un gouffre)* to open up, to gape, to yawn

entuber [ɑ̃tybe] VT *très Fam (duper)* to con, to have; **il s'est fait e.** he was conned *or* had

enturbanné [ɑ̃tyrbane] ADJ turbaned, wearing a turban

énucléation [enykleasjɔ̃] NF *Chir* enucleation

énucléer [enyklee] VT *Chir (tumeur, œil)* to enucleate

énumératif, -ive [enymeratif, -iv] ADJ enumerative

énumération [enymerasjɔ̃] NF enumeration, listing

énumérer [enymere] VT **(j'énumère, n. énumérons; j'énumérerai)** to enumerate, to list

énuquer (s') [senyke] VPR *Suisse* to break one's neck

énurésie [enyrezi] NF *Méd* enuresis

énurétique [enyretik] N, ADJ *Méd* enuretic

envahir [ɑ̃vair] VT *(pays etc)* to invade, to overrun; *Com* **e. le marché** to flood the market; **envahi par les mauvaises herbes** overgrown with weeds; **envahi par l'eau** flooded; **quand le doute/le sommeil nous envahit** when we are overcome with doubt/sleep; **la politique envahit tout** politics gets into everything; *Fig Fam* **je ne voulais pas les e.** *(déranger)* I didn't want to intrude (upon them)

envahissant [ɑ̃vaisɑ̃] ADJ *(voisins)* intrusive; *(plantes)* invasive; *Fig (désir, soupçon, odeur etc)* overwhelming

envahissement [ɑ̃vaismɑ̃] NM invasion

envahisseur [ɑ̃vaisœr] NM invader

envapé [ɑ̃vape] ADJ *Fam* out of it, ripped, *Br* off one's face

envasement [ɑ̃vazmɑ̃] NM *(d'un port etc)* silting up

envaser [ɑ̃vaze] VT *(port etc)* to silt up; *(bateau)* to run on the mud ▶ **VPR s'envaser** *(d'un port etc)* to silt up; *(d'un bateau, d'une personne)* to get stuck in the mud

enveloppant [ɑ̃vlɔpɑ̃] ADJ **1** *(couvrant)* **ce manteau est bien e.** this coat covers well; **regard e.** look that takes everything in; *Aut* **pare-chocs e.** wraparound bumper **2** *Fig (séduisant)* (personne, mots, manières etc)* captivating

enveloppe [ɑ̃vlɔp] NF **1** *(d'un colis etc)* wrapper, wrapping **2** *(pour lettre)* envelope; **envoyer qch sous e.** to send sth under cover; **e. timbrée** stamped envelope; **e. timbrée avec nom et adresse** stamped addressed envelope, SAE **3** *(apparence)* **un bon cœur sous une rude e.** a rough diamond; *Litt* **l'e. mortelle** *ou* **charnelle** this mortal coil **4** *(somme d'argent)* **l'e. de la recherche** the research budget; **de combien est l'e. du service/du projet?** how high is the departmental budget/the budget for the project?; **e. budgétaire** (allotted) budget, budget allocation; **e. fiscale** savings scheme with tax advantages; **e. salariale** wages bill; *Fam* **recevoir une e.** *(pot-de-vin)* to receive a bribe *(revêtement)* *(d'une chaudière)* sheathing, casing, jacket; *Aut (d'un pneu)* outer cover, casing **6** *(des graines etc)* husk, hull
  ▶ ▶ **e. autocollante** self-seal envelope; **e. calorifuge** lagging; **e. à fenêtre** window envelope; **e. matelassée** padded envelope, Jiffy bag®; *Philat* **e. premier jour** first-day cover; **e. T** ≃ business reply *or* reply-paid envelope

enveloppé [ɑ̃vlɔpe] ADJ *Fam* **bien e.** *(personne)* well-padded, plump

enveloppement [ɑ̃vlɔpmɑ̃] NM **1** *(action)* (d'un colis etc)* wrapping (up); *Mil* **manœuvre d'e.** pincer movement, envelopment **2** *Méd (linges)* pack; **e. froid** cold pack

envelopper [ɑ̃vlɔpe] VT **1** *(marchandises, bébé etc)* to wrap (up); **e. un paquet** to wrap up *or* do up a parcel; **enveloppé de bandages** swathed in bandages; **e. des remarques désagréables dans des phrases gentilles** to wrap up unpleasant remarks in kind words

2 *(entourer)* *(personne)* to surround, to encircle, to close in on; **la nuit nous enveloppa** darkness closed in on us; **enveloppé de mystère/brume** shrouded in mystery/in mist; **e. qch du regard** to take sth in with one's gaze ▶ **VPR s'envelopper s'e. dans une couverture** to wrap oneself up in a blanket; *Fig* **s'e. dans son silence** to immure oneself in silence

enveloppe-réponse, *pl* **enveloppes-réponses** NF reply-paid envelope

envenimé [ɑ̃v(ə)nime] ADJ *(plaie)* poisoned, septic; *Fig* **discussion envenimée** acrimonious discussion

envenimement [ɑ̃v(ə)nimmɑ̃] NM *(d'une plaie)* poisoning; *Fig (d'une querelle, discussion)* embittering; *(d'une situation)* aggravation

envenimer [ɑ̃v(ə)nime] VT *(plaie)* to poison, to make septic; *Fig (querelle, discussion)* to envenom, to embitter; *(situation)* to aggravate ▶ **VPR s'envenimer** *(d'une plaie)* to fester, to turn septic; *Fig (d'une querelle, discussion)* to grow acrimonious; *(d'une situation)* to become aggravated

envergure [ɑ̃vɛrgyr] NF **1** *(d'un oiseau, avion)* wingspread, wingspan **2** *Fig (ampleur)* scope; **de grande e., d'e.** *(réforme, rapport, question)* far-reaching, wide-ranging; *(opération, firme)* large-scale; **esprit de grande e.** wide-ranging mind; **leur affaire commence à prendre de l'e.** their business is beginning to expand *or* grow **3** *(de personne)* calibre, *Am* caliber; **homme d'e./de cette e.** man of calibre/of this calibre; **cet homme manque d'e.** this man is of a low calibre

envers[1] [ɑ̃vɛr] NM *(d'un document, d'une assiette etc)* reverse, back; *(d'une médaille, pièce)* reverse; **l'endroit et l'e. d'un tissu** the right and the wrong side of a material; **l'e. de la vie** the seamy side of life; *Fig* **l'e. du décor** the other side of the picture; **à l'e.** *(du mauvais côté)* inside out; *(avec le haut en bas)* the wrong way up, upside down; *(dans le mauvais sens)* the wrong way round, back to front; *(en désordre)* upside down; **le monde à l'e.** the world turned upside down; *Hum* **il travaille? c'est le monde à l'e.!** he's working? wonders will never cease!; **j'ai la tête à l'e.** my brain is in a whirl; *Tricot* **une maille à l'endroit, une maille à l'e.** knit one, purl one

envers[2] PRÉP toward(s); **juste e. tous** just to(wards) *or* with everyone; **leur devoir e. leur patrie** their duty to(wards) their country; **avoir une dette e. qn** to be indebted to sb; **e. et contre tous** in spite of everyone, in the face of all opposition

enviable [ɑ̃vjabl] ADJ enviable

envi (à l') [alɑ̃vi] ADV **faire qch à l'e.** to vie with one another in doing sth, to try to outdo each other doing sth

envie [ɑ̃vi] NF **1** *(désir)* desire **(de qch** for sth; **de faire** to do); **avoir e. de qch/de faire qch** to want sth/to do sth; **j'ai des envies de fraises** I have cravings for strawberries; *Fam* **j'ai une de ces envies de champagne!** I've got a real craving for champagne!, I could really do with some champagne!; **ce gâteau plein de crème me fait e.** I like the look of *or Br* fancy that cake filled with cream; **j'avais e. de dormir/boire/manger** I felt sleepy/thirsty/hungry; **avoir e. de rire/de vomir** to feel like laughing/being sick, to want to laugh/be sick; **être pris d'une terrible e. de rire** to have a terrible urge to laugh; *Fam* **ça m'a pris comme une e. de pisser** it was a sudden urge; **avoir bien** *ou* **très e. de faire qch** to really want to do sth; **brûler d'e. de faire qch** to be burning *or* dying to do sth; **donner**

à qn l'**e. de faire qch** to make sb want to do sth; **il a e. que je fasse cela** he wants me to do that; **je n'ai pas e. que ça se sache** I don't want it to be known; **c'est une e. qui te passera** you'll get over your craving; *Fam* **ça va lui passer son e.** it'll be just what he wants; **je vais lui ôter l'e. de s'amuser** I'll stop his messing around; **avoir e. de qn** *(sexuellement)* to want sb; *Fam* **avoir e.** *(avoir besoin d'uriner)* to want or have to go; *(de sexe)* to want it

2 *(jalousie)* envy; **être dévoré d'e.** to be consumed or green with envy; **faire e. à qn** to make sb envious; **regarder qch avec e.** to look enviously at sth; **cette situation confortable, ça fait e.** a good job like that makes people envious; **porter e. à qn** to envy sb

3 *(au doigt)* hangnail; *(sur la peau)* birthmark

envier [ɑ̃vje] **VT** *(impf, pr sub n. enviions)* to envy, to be envious of; **e. qch à qn** to envy sb sth; **je t'envie de ne jamais avoir faim!** I envy your never being hungry!; **elle n'a rien à e. à personne** she has no cause to be envious of anyone

envieux, -ieuse [ɑ̃vjø, -jøz] **ADJ** envious *(de* of)
N envious person; **faire des e.** to make people envious

environ [ɑ̃virɔ̃] **ADV** *(à peu près)* about, around; **il a e. quarante ans** he's about or around forty **VOIR GRAMMAIRE A67**
NMPL environs *(d'une ville etc)* surroundings, surrounding area; **habiter aux** *ou* **dans les environs de Paris** to live in the vicinity of or near Paris; **aux environs de Pâques/cinq heures** around Easter/five o'clock; **aux environs de cent euros** in the region or vicinity of a hundred euros, about or around a hundred euros

environnant [ɑ̃virɔnɑ̃] **ADJ** *(campagne etc)* surrounding

environnement [ɑ̃virɔnmɑ̃] **NM 1** *(naturel, personnel)* environment; **protection de l'e.** environmental protection, protection of the environment; **qui ne nuit pas à l'e.** environment-friendly; **e. commercial** business environment; **e. du marché** market environment; *Com* **e. institutionnel/marketing** corporate/marketing environment **2** *Ordinat* environment; **e. partagé** shared environment

environnemental, -ale, -aux, -ales [ɑ̃virɔnmɑ̃tal, -o] **ADJ** environmental

environnementaliste [ɑ̃virɔnmɑ̃talist] **N** environmentalist

environner [ɑ̃virɔne] **VT** to surround; **environné de** surrounded by
VPR s'environner s'e. d'intellectuels to surround oneself with intellectuals

envisageable [ɑ̃vizaʒabl] **ADJ** conceivable, imaginable; **ce n'est pas e.** it's inconceivable *or* unimaginable

envisager [ɑ̃vizaʒe] **VT** *(j'envisageai(s))* *(considérer)* *(question, situation, remède etc)* to consider; *(imaginer comme possible, projeter)* *(conséquence, événement etc)* to envisage; **e. l'avenir** to look to the future; **le cas que nous envisageons** the case under consideration; **cas non envisagé** unforeseen case; **comment envisagez-vous la question?** what are your views on or how do you see the matter?; **il n'envisageait pas de partir** he wasn't thinking of leaving, he wasn't considering leaving; **e. un chiffre d'affaires** to forecast turnover

envoi [ɑ̃vwa] **NM 1** *(action)* *(d'un représentant, de troupes etc)* sending; *(d'une lettre, d'un colis etc)* sending, dispatch(ing); *(d'argent, de fonds)* sending, remittance; *(de marchandises)* sending, dispatch(ing), for-

warding; **e. par mer** shipment; **faire un e. tous les mois** to send *or* dispatch goods every month; **e. exprès** express delivery; **e. groupé** grouped consignment; **e. postal** postal delivery; **e. recommandé** recorded delivery; **faire un e. de fonds à qn** to send *or* remit funds to sb; **e. contre paiement** cash with order

2 coup d'e. *Ftbl* kickoff; *(d'un événement, festival, projet etc)* start, *Fam* kickoff

3 *(ce qui est envoyé)* *(colis)* parcel; *(lettre)* letter; *(marchandises)* consignment (**de** of); **e. de l'auteur** presentation copy; **j'ai bien reçu votre e. du 10 octobre** I acknowledge receipt of your consignment of 10 October

4 *Ordinat* **e. multiple** crossposting; **faire un e. multiple de qch** to cross-post sth

5 *Littér (d'un poème)* envoi

envol [ɑ̃vɔl] **NM** *(d'oiseaux)* taking flight or wing; *(d'un avion)* takeoff; **piste d'e.** (take-off) runway; *Naut* **pont d'e.** flight deck

envolée [ɑ̃vɔle] **NF 1** *(action)* *(d'oiseaux)* flight **2** *Fig* **e. lyrique/oratoire** flight of lyricism/oratory **3** *Fin (hausse rapide)* **l'e. du dollar** rapid rise in the dollar

envoler (s') [sɑ̃vɔle] **VPR 1** *(d'un oiseau)* to fly away, to fly off; *(d'un avion)* to take off; **faire s'e. des oiseaux** to put birds to flight; **mon avion s'envole** *ou* **je m'envole dans une heure** my plane takes off *or* my flight leaves in an hour **2** *Fig* **l'euro s'envole** the euro is rising rapidly; **s'e. dans les sondages** to rise rapidly in the opinion polls **3** *(emporté par le vent)* *(d'un chapeau etc)* to blow off; *(de papiers etc)* to blow away; **le temps s'envole** time flies **4** *Fam (disparaître soudainement)* *(d'une personne, d'un sac à main etc)* to vanish, to disappear

envoûtant [ɑ̃vutɑ̃] **ADJ** *(fascinant)* bewitching, captivating

envoûtement [ɑ̃vutmɑ̃] **NM 1** *(maléfice)* bewitchment **2** *Fig (fascination)* bewitchment, captivation; **cette région me fait l'effet d'un e.** this region has a bewitching or captivating effect on me

envoûter [ɑ̃vute] **VT** *(en employant la magie)* to bewitch; *Fig (fasciner)* to bewitch, to captivate

envoûteur, -euse [ɑ̃vutœr, -øz] **N** sorcerer, *f* sorceress

envoyé, -ée [ɑ̃vwaje] **ADJ** **bien e.** *Sport (balle)*, *Fig Fam (remarque)* well-aimed; *Fam* **c'est e.!** *(bien dit)* well said!; *(bien exécuté)* well done!
N *(messager)* messenger; *(d'un parti etc)* representative; *(d'un gouvernement)* envoy; *Journ* **e. spécial** special correspondent; *Journ* **e. de la rédaction** staff correspondent

envoyer [ɑ̃vwaje] **VT** *(j'envoie, n. envoyons; j'enverrai)* *(personne)* to send; *(lettre, colis etc)* to send, to dispatch; *(argent)* to send, to remit; *(marchandises)* to send, to dispatch, to ship; *(des excuses, condoléances etc)* to send; **e. par courrier** to mail, *Br* to post; **e. qn à Paris** to send sb to Paris; **e. une lettre à qn** to send sb a letter, to send a letter to sb; **e. un publipostage à** to mailshot; **je lui ai envoyé mes félicitations** I sent him my congratulations; **envoyez-moi un petit mot** drop me a line; **e. sa démission** to send in *or Fml* to tender one's resignation; **elle lui a envoyé un regard noir/une gifle** she gave him a black look/slap (in the face); **e. un baiser à qn** to blow sb a kiss; **e. chercher qn** to send for sb; **j'ai envoyé Paul prendre de ses nouvelles** I sent Paul to ask after him; *Fam* **je ne lui ai pas envoyé dire** I told him straight *or* to his face; *Fam* **e. promener** *ou* **balader** *ou* **paître qn, e. qn sur les roses** to send sb packing; *Fam* **j'en ai assez, je vais tout e. promener** *ou* **valser** *ou* **dinguer** I've had enough,

I'm going to chuck it all in or throw in the towel; *Naut* **e. les couleurs/une vergue** to hoist the colours/send up a yard
VI *Naut* **envoyez!** about ship!

VPR s'envoyer 1 *(par courrier etc)* **ils s'envoient des cartes postales régulièrement** they regularly send postcards to each other **2** *Fam* **s'e. un verre de vin** to knock back a glass of wine; *Fam* **s'e. une corvée** to get landed *or* stuck with a tedious job; *Arg* **il ne pense qu'à s'e.** en l'air all he thinks about is having sex *or Br* having it off *or* away; *Arg* **s'e. une fille/un mec** to have sex *or Br* have it off *or* away with a girl/guy

envoyeur, -euse [ɑ̃vwajœr, -øz] **N** sender; **retour à l'e.** return to sender

enzyme [ɑ̃zim] **N** enzyme; **produit de lavage aux enzymes** cleaning product with biological action

éocène [eɔsɛn] *Géol* **ADJ** *(période)* Eocene
NM Eocene

éolien, -ienne [eɔljɛ̃, -jɛn] **ADJ** **harpe éolienne** aeolian harp; **érosion éolienne** wind erosion; **énergie éolienne** wind energy; **moteur é.** wind-powered engine
NF éolienne wind turbine

épagneul [epaɲœl] **NM** spaniel

épais, -aisse [epɛ, -ɛs] **ADJ** *(cheveux, doigt, mur, tranche, sauce etc)* thick; *(feuillage, brouillard)* dense, thick; *(foule, buisson)* dense; *(livre)* thick, fat; *(ombre, nuit)* deep, dark; *(silence)* deep; **é. de deux mètres** two metres thick; **avoir la taille épaisse** to be thickset; *Fam* **avoir l'esprit é.** to be dense or thick; **peu é.** thin
ADV 1 *(pousser, semer)* thick(ly) **2** *Fam (beaucoup)* **il n'y en a pas é.** there's not much of it
NM **couper dans l'é.** to cut into the thick part; **au plus é. de la foule/forêt** in the heart of the crowd/forest

épaisseur [epɛsœr] **NF 1** *(de cheveux, d'un mur, d'une sauce etc)* thickness; *(d'un feuillage, du brouillard)* density, thickness; *(d'une foule)* density; *(d'une ombre, de la nuit)* darkness; **le mur a deux pieds d'é.** the wall is two feet thick; **courroie en trois épaisseurs** three-ply belt; **une é. de tissu** a layer of material; **le peu d'é. d'une planche** the thinness of a board **2** *(d'un esprit)* dullness **3** *(profondeur)* *(d'une personne, d'un personnage de roman etc)* depth

épaissir [epesir] **VT** *(sauce, peinture etc)* to thicken; *(ombre, mystère)* to deepen
VI *(d'une sauce etc)* to thicken, to get thick(er); *(d'une personne)* to fill out
VPR s'épaissir *(de cheveux, du brouillard, d'une sauce etc)* to thicken, to get thick(er); *(d'une personne)* to fill out; *(d'une ombre, d'un mystère)* to deepen

épaississant [epesisɑ̃] **NM** *(substance)* thickener

épaississement [epesismɑ̃] **NM** *(du brouillard, d'une sauce etc)* thickening; *(d'une personne)* filling out

épanchement [epɑ̃ʃmɑ̃] **NM 1** *Arch, Litt (d'un liquide)* pouring out, discharge; *Méd* **é. de synovie** synovial extravasation **2** *Fig (de sentiments)* outpouring, *Litt* effusion; *(de pensées)* outpouring

épancher [epɑ̃ʃe] **VT 1** *Arch, Litt (liquide)* to pour out, to discharge; *Fig* **é. sa bile** to vent one's spleen **2** *Fig (son amour, ses soucis etc)* to pour out; **é. son cœur** to pour out one's heart, to unbosom oneself
VPR s'épancher 1 *Arch, Litt (d'un liquide)* to pour out; *Méd (du sang etc)* to extravasate **2** *Fig (d'une personne)* to pour out one's heart, to unbosom oneself

épandage [epɑ̃daʒ] **NM** *(de fumier etc)* spreading; **champs d'é.** sewage farm

épandeur, -euse [epɑ̃dœr, -øz] N *(machine) (de fumier, d'asphalte etc)* spreader

épandre [epɑ̃dr] VT *(fumier etc)* to spread
  VPR s'épandre *Litt* to spread (**sur** over)

épanoui [epanwi] ADJ *(fleur)* in full bloom, full-blown; *(visage, sourire)* beaming; **une jeune femme épanouie** a young woman in full bloom

épanouir [epanwir] VT *(fleur, pétales)* to open out; *(voiles, plumes)* to spread; **un large sourire lui épanouit le visage** his face broadened into a grin
  VPR s'épanouir 1 *(d'une fleur)* to open out, to bloom **2** *(d'un visage)* to beam, to light up; *(d'une personne heureuse)* to beam **3** *(d'une jeune fille, personnalité, civilisation etc)* to blossom

épanouissant [epanwisɑ̃] ADJ *(travail, vie etc)* fulfilling

épanouissement [epanwismɑ̃] NM **1** *(action) (d'une fleur)* opening out, blooming; *(d'un visage)* lighting up; *(d'une jeune fille, personnalité, civilisation etc)* blossoming **2** *(plénitude)* (full) bloom; **elle a trouvé l'é. physique et moral** she is at her physical and mental peak

épargnant, -ante [eparɲɑ̃, -ɑ̃t] N saver, investor; **les petits épargnants** small savers *or* investors

épargne [eparɲ] NF **1** *(action, vertu)* saving, economy; *Fig (de temps, forces)* saving; **caisse d'é.** savings bank; **plan d'é.-logement** *Br* ≃ building society (savings) account, *Am* ≃ savings and loan association account; **é. des entreprises** company reserves; **é. liquide** on-hand savings; **é. mobilière** fixed savings; **é. privée** private investors; **é. productive** re-invested savings; **é. salariale** save as you earn, SAYE **2** *(sommes)* savings **3** *(épargnants)* **la petite é.** small savers *or* investors; **l'é. privée** private investors

épargne-retraite NF retirement savings scheme; **plan d'é.-retraite** personal pension scheme *or* plan

épargner [eparɲe] VT **1** *(argent, provisions)* to save (up), to put by; *(beurre, sel etc)* to be sparing with **2** *(énergie, temps)* to save; **é. ses forces** to save one's strength; **épargne-moi tes explications/tes jérémiades/les détails!** spare me your explanations/your complaining/the details!; **é. à qn la peine de faire qch** to save sb the trouble of doing sth **3** *(prisonnier etc)* to spare, to have mercy on; **elle a toujours tenté d'é. ses enfants** she has always tried to shield her children; **l'incendie a épargné notre village** the fire spared our village
  VT to save (**sur qch** on sth)

éparpillement [eparpijmɑ̃] NM **1** *(action) (d'objets, de foin etc)* scattering; *(d'une foule, de troupes etc)* scattering, dispersal; *Fig (des efforts, de l'attention etc)* dissipation **2** *(état)* scattered state

éparpiller [eparpije] VT *(objets, foin etc)* to scatter, to strew about; *(foule, troupes etc)* to scatter, to disperse; *Fig (efforts, attention etc)* to dissipate
  VPR s'éparpiller *(d'objets etc)* to scatter; *(d'une foule, de troupes etc)* to scatter, to disperse; *Fig (d'une personne)* to dissipate one's energies

épars [epar] ADJ *(maisons, moutons etc)* scattered; *(végétation, population, informations)* sparse; *(cheveux)* thin

éparvin [eparvɛ̃] NM *Vét (d'un cheval)* spavin

épatant [epatɑ̃] ADJ *Fam* splendid, wonderful

épate [epat] NF *Fam* swank, swagger; **faire de l'é.** to show off, to swank; **on l'a fait à l'é.** it was done to show off

épaté [epate] ADJ **1** *(table etc)* splay-footed;

(nez) flat **2** *Fam (étonné)* dumbfounded, flabbergasted

épatement [epatmɑ̃] NM **1** *(d'un nez)* flatness **2** *Fam (étonnement)* astonishment, amazement

épater [epate] VT **1** *(rendre plat)* to flatten out the base of **2** *Fam (étonner)* to astound, to amaze; **rien ne l'épate, il ne se laisse pas é.** nothing surprises him, he isn't easily impressed

épaulard [epolar] NM killer whale, grampus, orc

épaule [epol] NF shoulder; **large d'épaules** broad-shouldered; **hausser les épaules** to shrug (one's shoulders); *Culin* **é. d'agneau** shoulder of lamb; **donner un coup d'é. à qn** to shoulder sb; *Fig* to give sb a push in the right direction; **charger un fardeau sur son é.** to shoulder a burden; *Mil* **l'arme sur l'é.** with rifle at the slope; **rouler les épaules** *(en marchant)* to swagger

épaulé-jeté, *pl* **épaulés-jetés** [epoleʒ(ə)te] NM *(en haltérophilie)* clean-and-jerk

épaulement [epolmɑ̃] NM **1** *(mur)* revetment, retaining wall **2** *(rempart)* breastwork **3** *(d'une colline)* shoulder

épauler [epole] VT **1** *(fusil)* to bring to one's shoulder **2 é. qn** *(aider)* to back sb up **3** *(mur)* to retain, to support **4** *Couture* to attach shoulder pads to
  VT to take aim

épaulette [epolɛt] NF **1** *(bretelle) (d'une combinaison)* shoulder-strap **2** *Mil* epaulette **3** *(rembourrage)* shoulder pad

épave [epav] NF *(navire, voiture)* wreck; *Fig (loque humaine)* (human) wreck; *Fig* **les épaves de la société** the flotsam of society; **épaves flottantes** flotsam; **épaves rejetées** jetsam

épeautre [epotr] NM spelt

épée [epe] NF sword; *Escrime* épée; **coup d'é.** swordthrust; *Fig* **coup d'é. dans l'eau** wasted effort; **Marc est une bonne é.** Marc is a good swordsman; *Fig* **é. de Damoclès** Sword of Damocles

épeiche [epɛʃ] NF *Orn* great spotted woodpecker

épeichette [epɛʃɛt] NF *Orn* lesser spotted woodpecker

épéiste [epeist] N *Escrime* épéeist

épeler [eple] (**j'épelle; j'épellerai**) VT **1** *(mot, nom etc)* to spell; **mot mal épelé** misspelt word **2** *(lire avec difficulté) (texte)* to spell out
  VT to spell

épépiner [epepine] VT *(raisins, tomates etc)* to remove the seeds *or* pips from, to deseed; *(pommes)* to core

éperdu [epɛrdy] ADJ *(regard)* distraught, frantic; *(amour, besoin etc)* violent; *(résistance)* desperate; **é. de joie/douleur** frantic with joy/grief

éperdument [epɛrdymɑ̃] ADV *(aimer)* madly, to distraction; *(travailler)* desperately, frantically; **é. amoureux** head over heels in love, madly in love; *Fam* **je m'en fiche é. I** couldn't care less, I don't give a damn

éperlan [epɛrlɑ̃] NM *(poisson)* smelt, sparling

éperon [eprɔ̃] NM **1** *(d'un cavalier)* spur; **donner de l'é. à son cheval, piquer de l'é.** to spur (on) one's horse; **gagner ses éperons** to win one's spurs **2** *(d'une violette, d'une montagne, d'un coq)* spur **3** *Hist (d'un vaisseau de guerre)* ram **4** *(d'un pont)* cutwater

éperonner [eprɔne] VT **1** *(cheval)* to spur (on), to put spurs to; *Fig* **é. qn** to spur *or* urge sb on **2** *Hist (vaisseau ennemi)* to ram **3** *(bottes etc)* to spur, to put spurs on

épervier [epɛrvje] NM **1** *(oiseau)* sparrowhawk; *Pol Fig* hawk **2** *Pêche* castnet

éphèbe [efɛb] NM *Iron (beau jeune homme)* Adonis

éphélide [efelid] NF freckle

éphémère [efemɛr] ADJ *(bonheur etc)* ephemeral, short-lived, fleeting; **ce chanteur n'a connu qu'un succès é.** this singer enjoyed only a short-lived *or* brief success
  NM *Entom* mayfly, ephemera

éphéméride [efemerid] NF **1** *(calendrier)* tear-off *or* block calendar **2** *Astron (publication annuelle)* ephemeris; **éphémérides** *(tables)* ephemerides

Éphèse [efɛz] N Ephesus

épi [epi] NM **1** *(de grain)* ear; *(de fleur)* spike; **blés en é.** wheat in the ear; **monter en é.** *(de céréales)* to ear; **é. de maïs** *Agr* corncob; *Culin* corn on the cob **2** *(mèche de cheveux)* tuft of hair; **ses cheveux font des épis** his/her hair sticks up in tufts **3** *(jetée)* spur, groyne; *Rail (de voie)* spur; *Aut* **stationnement en é.** angle parking; *Constr* **appareil en é.** herringbone bond
  ▸▸*Archit* **é. de faîtage** finial

épicarpe [epikarp] NM *Bot* epicarp

épice [epis] NF spice; **pain d'é.** ≃ gingerbread; **quatre épices** allspice

épicé [epise] ADJ *(nourriture, plat etc)* highly spiced, spicy, hot; *(assaisonnement)* spicy, hot; *Fam* **conte é.** spicy story

épicéa [episea] NM *(arbre)* spruce

épicentre [episɑ̃tr] NM *(d'un tremblement de terre)* epicentre

épicer [epise] VT (**j'épiçai(s)**) *(nourriture, plat etc)* to spice; *Fam (histoire etc)* to spice up, to add a bit of spice to

épicerie [episri] NF **1** *(produits)* groceries; **é. fine** delicatessen; **être dans l'é.** to be in the grocery business **2** *(magasin)* grocer's (shop) **3** *Can Fig* **liste d'é.** *(de griefs etc)* shopping list

épicier, -ière [episje, -jɛr] N grocer; *Fig Péj* **d'é.** *(idées, littéraire etc)* common-or-garden; *(encre, savon etc)* cheap, ordinary; *Fig Péj* **mentalité d'é.** small-town mentality

épicurien, -ienne [epikyrjɛ̃, -jɛn] ADJ epicurean; *Phil* Epicurean
  N epicure; *Phil* Epicurean

épicurisme [epikyrism] NM **1** *Phil* Epicureanism **2** *(recherche du plaisir)* epicur(ean)ism

épicycloïdal, -ale, -aux, -ales [episiklɔidal] ADJ *Tech (engrenage)* epicyclic

épidémie [epidemi] NF *Méd, Fig* epidemic

épidémiologie [epidemjɔlɔʒi] NF epidemiology

épidémiologique [epidemjɔlɔʒik] ADJ epidemiological

épidémiologiste [epidemjɔlɔʒist] N epidemiologist

épidémique [epidemik] ADJ *Méd* epidemic; *Fig* contagious

épiderme [epidɛrm] NM *Anat, Bot* epidermis, skin; *Fig* **avoir l'é. sensible** *ou* **délicat** to be thin-skinned *or* touchy

épidermique [epidɛrmik] ADJ *(tissu etc)* epidermal, epidermic; *Fig* **une réaction é.** a kneejerk reaction

épier [epje] VT *(impf, pr sub n. épiions, v. épiiez) (espionner) (personne, les activités de qn etc)* to spy on, to keep a watch on; *(observer pour découvrir) (signe, occasion etc)* to watch out for; *(la réaction de qn)* to watch for

épigastre [epigastr] NM *Anat* epigastrium

épigastrique [epigastrik] ADJ *Anat* epigastric

épiglotte [epiglɔt] NF *Anat* epiglottis

épigone [epigon] NM *Litt (successeur)* epigone

épigramme [epigram] NF epigram

épigraphe [epigraf] NF epigraph

épigraphie [epigrafi] NF epigraphy

épilation [epilɑsjɔ̃] NF removal of unwanted hair (**de** from); (des sourcils) plucking

épilatoire [epilatwar] ADJ (crème etc) hair-removing, depilatory

épilepsie [epilɛpsi] NF Méd epilepsy; **crise d'é.** epileptic fit

épileptique [epilɛptik] ADJ, N Méd epileptic

épiler [epile] VT to remove unwanted hair from; (sourcils) to pluck
   VPR s'épiler **s'é. les jambes à la cire** to wax one's legs

épilogue [epilɔg] NM epilogue; Fig **j'attends l'é. de cette histoire** I'm waiting for the rest of the story

épiloguer [epilɔge] VT Arch to pass censure on
   VI to go on (and on), to hold forth (**sur** about)

épinard [epinar] NM (plante) spinach; Culin **épinards** spinach; **épinards en branches** leaf spinach

épine [epin] NF **1** (arbre) thornbush **2** (piquant) Bot thorn, prickle; Zool spine, prickle; **tirer une é. du pied à qn** (tirer d'embarras) to get sb out of a mess; (soulager) to relieve sb's mind
   ▸▸**é. blanche** hawthorn; Anat, Ordinat **é. dorsale** backbone; **é. noire** blackthorn; **é. de rat** butcher's broom

épinette [epinɛt] NF **1** Can Bot spruce **2** Mus spinet **3** (cage) hen coop

épinettière [epinɛtjer] NF Can spruce grove

épineux, -euse [epinø, -øz] ADJ **1** (arbuste, tige) thorny, prickly, spiky; (poisson) spiny; Fig (question, problème) thorny, tricky; Fig **être dans une situation épineuse** to be in a tricky or ticklish situation **2** Anat (excroissance) spinous
   NM thornbush

épinglage [epɛ̃glaʒ] NM pinning

épingle [epɛ̃gl] NF pin; **attacher avec des épingles** (cheveux, poster) to pin up; (morceau de tissu, feuilles) to pin together; Fig **tiré à quatre épingles** dressed up to the nines; Fig **tirer son é. du jeu** to extricate oneself; Fig **chercher une é. dans une botte de foin** to look for a needle in a haystack; Fig **monter qch en é.** (exagérer) to make too much of sth
   ▸▸**é. à chapeau** hatpin; **é. à cheveux** hairpin; **virage en é. à cheveux** hairpin bend or Am turn; **é. de cravate** tiepin; **é. à linge** clothes peg or Am pin; **é. de ou à nourrice** safety pin; **é. de signalisation** (d'une fiche) marker tag; **e. de sûreté** safety pin

épingler [epɛ̃gle] VT **1** (attacher) to pin, to fasten with a pin/pins (**à** to; **sur** on); **é. ses cheveux** to pin up one's hair **2** Fam (arrêter) to nab, to collar

épinière [epinjer] ADJ Anat **moelle é.** spinal cord

épinoche [epinɔʃ] NF stickleback

Épiphanie [epifani] NF Rel Epiphany

épiphénomène [epifenɔmɛn] NM epiphenomenon

épiphyse [epifiz] NF Anat epiphysis

épique [epik] ADJ epic; **poème é.** epic (poem)

épiscopal, -ale, -aux, -ales [episkɔpal, -o] ADJ Rel episcopal

épiscopat [episkɔpa] NM (fonction, ensemble des évêques) episcopate

épiscope [episkɔp] NM episcope

épisiotomie [epizjɔtɔmi] NF Chir episiotomy

épisode [epizɔd] NM episode; **feuilleton ou film à épisodes** serial; **feuilleton en six épi-**

sodes six-part serial; **la suite au prochain é.** tune in again to find out what happens next; Fig watch this space; Fig **ce n'est qu'un é. malheureux** it's just an unfortunate episode

épisodique [epizɔdik] ADJ (intermittent) episodic; (accessoire) minor

épisodiquement [epizɔdikmɑ̃] ADV occasionally, now and again

épisser [epise] VT (corde, câble) to splice

épissure [episyr] NF splice

épistémologie [epistemɔlɔʒi] NF epistemology

épistémologique [epistemɔlɔʒik] ADJ epistemological

épistolaire [epistɔler] ADJ epistolary; **être en relation é. avec qn** to correspond with sb; **nous n'avons que des relations épistolaires** our only contact is by letter

épistolier, -ière [epistɔlje, -jer] N letter writer

épitaphe [epitaf] NF epitaph

épithélium [epiteljɔm] NM Biol epithelium

épithète [epitɛt] NF epithet; Gram attribute
VOIR GRAMMAIRE A17

épitoge [epitɔʒ] NF **1** Univ (bande d'étoffe) ≃ (graduate's) hood **2** Antiq (vêtement) cloak

épitomé [epitɔme] NM (abrégé d'un ouvrage) epitome

épître [epitr] NF epistle; (partie de la messe) Epistle; **côté de l'é.** (de l'autel) Epistle side

éploré [eplɔre] ADJ (personne) tearful, weeping; (expression, voix) tearful

épluchage [eplyʃaʒ] NM (de fruits, pommes de terre etc) peeling; (d'une salade) cleaning; (de crevettes) peeling, shelling; (de noisettes, pois) shelling; Fig (d'un texte, journal etc) detailed examination

épluche-légumes [eplyʃlegym] NM INV vegetable or potato peeler

éplucher [eplyʃe] VT (fruits, pommes de terre etc) to peel; (salade) to clean; (crevettes) to peel, to shell; (noisettes, pois) to shell; Fig (texte, journal, publicités etc) to go through or examine in detail; Fig **ma mère épluche mon emploi du temps** my mother checks up on how I spend my time

épluchette [eplyʃɛt] NF Can **é. de blé d'Inde** corn-husking party

éplucheur, -euse [eplyʃœr, -øz] N (instrument, personne) peeler; **é. de pommes de terre** potato peeler

épluchure [eplyʃyr] NF (pelure) peeling

EPO [epeo] NF (abrév **érythropoïétine**) EPO

épointage [epwɛ̃taʒ] NM (en cassant) (d'un crayon) breaking the point; (en usant) (d'une aiguille, d'un crayon, d'un outil etc) blunting

épointé [epwɛ̃te] ADJ (aiguille, crayon, outil etc) blunt

épointer [epwɛ̃te] VT (en cassant) (crayon) to break the point of; (en usant) (aiguille, crayon, outil etc) to blunt

éponge [epɔ̃ʒ] NF **1** (naturelle) sponge **2** Com sponge; **donner un coup d'é. à qch** to wipe sth with a sponge; **effacer une tache d'un coup d'é.** to sponge out a stain; Fig **passons l'é.** let's forget it; Boxe **jeter l'é.** to throw in the sponge or towel; Fig **l'industrie française jette l'é. dans le domaine de la construction automobile** French industry is throwing in the sponge or towel as regards the building of cars; Tex **tissu é.** (terry) towelling; **serviette é.** terry towel; Fam **il boit comme une é., c'est une véritable é.** he drinks like a fish
   ▸▸**é. métallique** (pan) scourer, scouring pad; **é. végétale** vegetable sponge, loofah

épongeage [epɔ̃ʒaʒ] NM (d'un liquide) sponging up, mopping up; (d'une surface) sponging (down)

éponger [epɔ̃ʒe] (**j'épongeai(s); n. épongeons**) VT **1** (liquide) to sponge up, to mop up **2** (surface) to sponge (down), to mop; (cheval, voiture etc) to sponge down; (le front de qn) to mop **3** Fin (déficit etc) to mop up, to absorb
   VPR s'éponger **s'é. le front** to mop one's brow

épontille [epɔ̃tij] NF Naut shore, prop

épontiller [epɔ̃tije] VT Naut to prop, to shore (up)

éponyme [epɔnim] ADJ eponymous

épopée [epɔpe] NF Littér, Fig epic

époque [epɔk] NF **1** (historique) epoch, era, age; Géol age, period; **l'é. glaciaire** the ice age; **la Belle É.** the Belle Epoque; **quelle é. (nous vivons)!** what times we live in!; **il n'est plus de son é.** he's out of step or tune with the times; **meubles d'é.** period furniture, (genuine) antique furniture; **à l'é., elle était très reconnue** at the time she was highly regarded; **faire é.** (d'une invention, déclaration etc) to leave its mark on history; **découverte qui fait é.** epoch-making discovery **2** (moment précis) time; **à l'é. de sa naissance** at the time of his birth; **à cette é. de l'année** at this time of year; **à l'é., je faisais le grand écart** I was doing the splits at the time

épouillage [epujaʒ] NM delousing

épouiller [epuje] VT to delouse

époumoner (s') [sepumɔne] VPR (en criant) to shout oneself hoarse; (en chantant) to sing oneself hoarse; **c'est ce que je m'époumone à te dire!** I've told you so until I'm hoarse

épousailles [epuzaj] NFPL Arch nuptials, wedding

épouse [epuz] NF wife; Admin spouse VOIR GRAMMAIRE A12

épousée [epuze] NF Vieilli bride

épouser [epuze] VT **1** to marry, Vieilli to wed; **é. une grosse dot** to marry (into) money **2** Fig (cause, doctrine etc) to espouse, to take up, to adopt; **les Français ont épousé le golf** the French have taken up golf; **é. la forme de qch** to take on the exact shape of sth; **sa robe épousait les courbes de son corps** her dress hugged the curves of her body; **la route épouse la colline** the road follows the hill round

époussetage [epusetaʒ] NM (de meubles etc) dusting

épousseter [epuste] VT (conj like **jeter**) (meubles etc) to dust; (vêtements etc) to brush (the dust from); (cheval) to rub down

époustouflant [epustuflɑ̃] ADJ Fam amazing, astounding

époustoufler [epustufle] VT Fam to amaze, to astound

épouvantable [epuvɑ̃tabl] ADJ dreadful, appalling

épouvantablement [epuvɑ̃tabləmɑ̃] ADV dreadfully, appallingly

épouvantail [epuvɑ̃taj] NM (dans un jardin) scarecrow; Péj (personne laide ou bizarrement habillée) fright; (personne terrifiante) bogey; (chose terrifiante) bugbear, bogey

épouvante [epuvɑ̃t] NF terror, fright; **jeter ou porter l'é. dans un pays** to spread terror in a country; **saisi d'é.** terror-stricken, frightened to death; **film d'é.** horror film; **elle pense à cette rencontre avec é.** she is dreading the meeting

épouvanté [epuvɑ̃te] ADJ terror-stricken

épouvanter [epuvɑ̃te] VT to terrify, to scare
   VPR s'épouvanter to take fright (**de** at)

époux [epu] NM husband; Admin spouse; **les é.** the married couple, the husband and wife; **les é. Thomas** Mr and Mrs Thomas

éprendre (s') [seprɑ̃dr] **VPR** (conj like **prendre**) **s'é. de** (personne) to fall in love with; (son travail, une idée etc) to become passionate about

épreuve [eprœv] **NF 1** (essai) test, trial; **faire l'é. de qch** to test sth; **mettre qch/qn à l'é.** to put sth/sb to the test; **à l'é. du feu/de l'eau** fireproof/waterproof; **à l'é. des balles** bulletproof; **l'é. de vérité pour …** the critical test for …; **mécanisme à toute é.** foolproof mechanism; **bonté/courage à toute é.** unfailing kindness/courage; **être mis à rude é.** (d'une personne, de la patience, de l'honneur etc) to be severely tested; (de jouets etc) to be roughly treated or handled; **les bateaux/arbres ont été mis à rude é. par la tempête** the boats/trees took a battering from the storm **2** Scol, Univ (écrite) (examination) paper; (orale) test **3** Sport (d'une rencontre d'athlétisme) event **4** (adversité) trial, ordeal; **dans l'é.** in adversity; **passer par de rudes épreuves** to go through a bad or hard time **5** Typ proof; **corriger les épreuves d'un livre** to proofread a book; **première é.** first proof; **dernière é.** final proof **6** Phot print; Cin **épreuves (de tournage)** rushes

▸▸ Typ **é. bonne à filmer** camera-ready copy, CRC; Typ **é. de calage** machine proof; Sport **é. contre la montre** time trial; Sport **é. éliminatoire** (preliminary) heat; Sport **é. d'endurance** endurance test; Hist **é. du feu** ordeal by fire; Sport **é. finale** final; **é. de force** trial of strength, showdown; Typ **épreuves d'imprimerie** printer's proofs; **épreuves d'initiation** initiation rites; **é. d'outrance** resistance test; Typ **é. ozalide** ozalid; Typ **é. de page** page proof; Sport **é.-phare** major event; Typ **é. en placard** galley (proof); Sport **épreuves sur piste** track events; **é. de résistance** resistance test

épris [epri] **ADJ 1 é. de qn** in love with sb **2 é. de qch** passionate about sth

éprouvant [epruvɑ̃] **ADJ** (pénible) trying, tiring

éprouvé [epruve] **ADJ 1** (testé) (remède) proven, well-tried; (spécialiste, loyauté etc) proven; (allié) trusty, staunch; (matériaux) tested **2** (famille) stricken; (région) hard-hit; **troupes très éprouvées** troops that have suffered a great deal

éprouver [epruve] **VT 1** (tester) (machine, matériaux, méthode etc) to test; (personne, courage etc) to put to the test, to test **2** (ressentir) (sensation, douleur etc) to feel, to experience; **les sentiments qu'il éprouve pour moi** the feelings that he has for me **3** (subir) (perte) to sustain, to suffer; (difficultés) to meet with

éprouvette [epruvɛt] **NF** test tube
ADJ bébé é. test-tube baby

EPS [əpeɛs] **NF** (abrév **éducation physique et sportive**) PE

epsilon [ɛpsilɔn] **NM** (lettre grecque) epsilon

épucer [epyse] **VT** (j'épuçai(s); n. épuçons) (chien etc) to rid of fleas

épuisant [epɥizɑ̃] **ADJ** exhausting

épuisé [epɥize] **ADJ 1** (très fatigué) exhausted, tired out, worn out **2** (sol, mine) exhausted, worked out; Élec **pile épuisée** dead battery; Nucl **uranium é.** depleted or impoverished uranium **3** Com (livre, édition) out of print; (marchandises) sold out, out of stock; **tous nos stocks sont épuisés** all our stocks are exhausted

épuisement [epɥizmɑ̃] **NM 1** (fatigue) exhaustion; **danser/marcher jusqu'à é.** to dance/walk till one drops; **rouler/nager jusqu'à é.** to drive/swim until one is exhausted; **mort d'é.** dead with exhaustion **2** (de provisions, de munitions, d'une mine, d'un sol, d'un stock etc) exhaustion; (de ressources) depletion; (d'une citerne) draining, emptying; Nucl (de l'uranium) depletion, impoverishment; Com **jusqu'à. é. des stocks** while stocks last

épuiser [epɥize] **VT 1** (fatiguer) to exhaust, to wear or tire out **2** (provisions, munitions etc) to use up, to exhaust; (mine, sol) to exhaust, to work out; (ressources) to deplete; (citerne) to drain, to empty; (stock) to exhaust, to run low on; (marchandises) to sell out; **é. un sujet** to exhaust a subject; **cette marche a épuisé toute mon énergie** that walking has used up all my energy **3** (lettre de crédit) to use up
VPR s'épuiser 1 (se fatiguer) to exhaust oneself, to tire or wear oneself out; **je m'épuise à vous le dire** I've told you so until I'm blue in the face **2** (d'une source etc) to dry up, to run dry; (d'un stock, de l'argent, de provisions etc) to run out, to give out

épuisette [epɥizɛt] **NF 1** Pêche landing net **2** Naut (pelle) scoop, bailer

épurateur [epyratœr] **NM** Tech purifier; **é. de gaz** gas purifier, (gas) scrubber

épuration [epyrasjɔ̃] **NF** (de l'eau) purification; (du gaz) purification, scrubbing; (du pétrole, d'un minerai) refining; Fig (d'une langue, d'un style) refining; Pol purge, purging

épure [epyr] **NF** working drawing; (dessin fini) (d'un édifice, moteur etc) finished plan

épurer [epyre] **VT** (eau) to purify; (gaz) to purify, to scrub; (pétrole, minerai) to refine; Fig (langue, style) to refine; Pol (parti, personnel etc) to purge

équarrir [ekarir] **VT 1** (bois, pierre) to square **2** (animal) to quarter, to cut up

équarrissage [ekarisaʒ] **NM 1** (du bois, de la pierre) squaring **2** (de carcasses d'animaux) quartering, cutting up; **chantier d'é.** knacker's yard

équarrisseur [ekarisœr] **NM** knacker

équarrissoir [ekariswar] **NM 1** (couteau) knacker's knife **2** (abattoir) knacker's yard

Équateur [ekwatœr] **NM** Ecuador

équateur [ekwatœr] **NM** equator; **sous l'é.** at or on the equator; **é. magnétique** magnetic equator; Astron **é. céleste** celestial equator

équation [ekwasjɔ̃] **NF** equation; Math **é. du premier/du deuxième degré** simple/quadratic equation; Compta **é. de bénéfice** profit equation; Compta **é. de coût** cost equation; Mktg **é. de la demande** demand equation; Mktg **é. de réponse de marché** sales-response function; Mktg **é. de vente** sales equation

équatorial, -iale, -iaux, -iales [ekwatɔrjal, -jo] **ADJ** equatorial
NM Astron equatorial (telescope)

équatorien, -ienne [ekwatɔrjɛ̃, -jɛn] **ADJ** Ecuadorian
N É. Ecuadorian

équerre [ekɛr] **NF 1** (instrument) **é. (à dessin)** set square; **é. à coulisse** (sliding) calliper gauge; **fausse é.** bevel square; **é. à onglet** mitre square; **é. d'arpenteur** cross-staff **2 en é., à l'é.** at right angles; **d'é.** square, straight; **mettre qch d'é.** to square sth **3** (pièce métallique) corner plate

équestre [ekɛstr] **ADJ** (statue, sports etc) equestrian; (exercices etc) (horse)riding

équeuter [ekøte] **VT** (fruit) to remove the stalk(s) from

équiangle [ekɥiɑ̃gl] **ADJ** Géom equiangular

équidés [ek(ɥ)ide] **NMPL** Zool Equidae

équidistance [ekɥidistɑ̃s] **NF** equidistance

équidistant [ekɥidistɑ̃] **ADJ** equidistant (de from)

équilatéral, -ale, -aux, -ales [ekɥilateral, -o] **ADJ** Géom equilateral

équilibrage [ekilibraʒ] **NM** balancing

équilibrant [ekilibrɑ̃] **ADJ** (élément) balancing; **poids é.** counterweight; Psy **c'est un facteur é. dans la vie d'un enfant** it's a stabilizing factor in a child's life

équilibre [ekilibr] **NM 1** (d'un corps, objet) balance, equilibrium; (d'un avion) stability; **avoir le sens de l'é.** to have a sense of balance; **mettre qch en é.** to balance sth; **tenir qch en é. sur son nez** to balance sth on one's nose; **perdre l'é.** to lose one's balance; **faire perdre l'é. à qn** to throw sb off (his/her) balance; **cet acrobate fait de l'é. ou des tours d'é.** this acrobat does balancing tricks; **la chaise est en é. instable** the chair is precariously balanced **2** (mental) (mental) balance or equilibrium; **elle manque d'é.** she is unbalanced **3** Pol **budget en é.** balanced budget; **é. budgétaire** balanced budget; **é. européen** balance of power in Europe; **l'é. des rapports/des forces** (entre deux pays) the balance of relations/power; **l'é. de la terreur** the balance of terror **4** (des éléments d'un ensemble) balance, harmony; TV, Cin **é. des couleurs** colour balance

équilibré [ekilibre] **ADJ** (chargement, repas etc) balanced; (personne) well-balanced, stable; (vie) regular, stable; **mal é., non é.** unbalanced; **vie peu équilibrée** irregular or unstable life

équilibrer [ekilibre] **VT** (charge, éléments d'une composition etc) to balance; (bateau, avion) to trim; **é. qch par un contrepoids** to counterbalance sth; **é. un budget** to balance a budget, to break even; Aut **é. les roues** to balance the wheels; **cette expérience dans le monde du travail l'a équilibré** this work experience has stabilized him
VPR s'équilibrer to balance each other (out); (budget) to balance

équilibreur [ekilibrœr] **NM** Aviat stabilizer

équilibriste [ekilibrist] **N** (acrobate) equilibrist; (funambule) tightrope walker

équille [ekij] **NF** (poisson) launce, sand eel

équin [ekɛ̃] **ADJ** equine; **pied é.** club foot

équinisme [ekinism] **NM** Méd (difformité) club foot

équinoxe [ekinɔks] **NM** equinox; **é. de printemps/d'automne** spring/autumn(al) equinox; **vent d'é.** equinoctial gale

équinoxial, -iale, -iaux, -iales [ekinɔksjal, -jo] **ADJ** equinoctial

équipage [ekipaʒ] **NM 1** (d'un navire, avion) crew; Naut **maître d'é.** boatswain; Naut **les hommes de l'é. the crew** VOIR GRAMMAIRE A11 **2** (suite) equipage, retinue; **arriver en grand é.** to arrive in state **3** Hist (voiture, chevaux etc) equipage **4** Vieilli (tenue) attire **5** (équipement) Mil train, equipment; Tech equipment, gear; **é. de construction** builder's or construction equipment or gear

équipe [ekip] **NF** VOIR GRAMMAIRE A11 **1** Sport team; (d'un canot à rames) crew; **sport d'é.** team sport **2** (personnes qui travaillent ensemble) (de chercheurs, médecins etc) team; (d'ouvriers) gang; Mil working party; **travailler par équipes** to work in shifts; **chef d'é.** (gang) foreman; **encourager le travail d'é.** to encourage teamwork; **esprit d'é.** team spirit; **faire é. avec qn** to team up with sb; Fam **nous étions une é. de joyeux lurons** we were a cheerful crew or lot; Fam **en voilà une fine é.!** what a crew! **3** Mktg **é. commando** venture team; **é. commerciale** marketing team

▸▸ TV, Cin **é. caméra** camera crew; Cin **é. de cinéma** film crew; Sport **é. de cricket** cricket team or eleven; Rail **é. de conduite** ou de locomotive engine crew; **é. de création** creative team; **é. de dactylos** typing pool; *Com* **é. dirigeante** management team; *Journ* **é. d'investigation** investigative team; **é. de jour** day shift; **é. de nuit** night shift; *Journ* back-bench; *TV, Cin* **é. de prise de vue** camera crew; *TV, Cin* **é. de production** production team; **é. de secours** rescue team; **é. du son** sound crew; *Journ* **é. de soutien** back-bench; **é. de télévision** television crew; *TV, Cin* **é. de tournage** camera crew, film crew; *Com* **é. de vente** sales team or force

équipée [ekipe] NF *(frasque)* escapade, lark; *(promenade, voyage)* jaunt

équipement [ekipmɑ̃] NM **1** *(action)* *(d'un atelier, d'une cuisine)* equipping, equipment, fitting out (**de** with); **é. en hommes** manning; **plan d'é.** national national development plan **2** *(matériel)* equipment; *(d'un soldat)* kit; *(de camping, ski etc)* gear, equipment **3** *(installations)* facilities
▸ ▸ **é. acoustique** audio equipment; **é. audiovisuel** audiovisual equipment; **é. automobile** car accessories; **équipements collectifs** public facilities or amenities; **é. électrique** electrical fittings; **é. industriel** industrial plant; *Ordinat* **é. informatique** computer equipment; *Aut* **é. intérieur** internal fittings; **é. routier** road signs; *Aut* **équipements spéciaux** *(chaînes)* chains; *(pneus cloutés)* studded tyres; **e. de survie** survival kit

équipementier [ekipmɑ̃tje] NM *Aut* parts manufacturer

équiper [ekipe] VT *(atelier, cuisine etc)* to equip, to fit out (**de** with); *(sportif, armée etc)* to equip, *Br* to kit out (**de** with); **é. un navire** *(d'appareils etc)* to equip or fit out a ship; *(en hommes)* to man a ship; **é. une voiture pour la neige** to equip a car for the snow; **é. une ville en terrains de sport** to provide a town with sports grounds; **appartement avec cuisine équipée** flat with cooking facilities; *Fam* **comme vous voilà équipé!** what a get-up!
VPR **s'équiper** to equip oneself

équipier, -ière [ekipje, -jɛr] N *Sport* team member; *Naut* crew member; *Naut* **mené par 14 équipiers** manned by a crew of 14, with a 14-man crew

équitable [ekitabl] ADJ **1** *(marché, partage etc)* equitable, fair, just **2** *(personne)* impartial, fair-minded, fair

équitablement [ekitabləmɑ̃] ADV equitably, fairly

équitation [ekitasjɔ̃] NF (horse)riding, *Fml* equitation; **faire de l'é.** to go riding; **école d'é.** riding school

équité [ekite] NF equity, equitableness, fairness

équivalence [ekivalɑ̃s] NF equivalence; *Univ* **avoir/obtenir une é.** to have/get an equivalent diploma; **ce diplôme est une é. du bac** this diploma is the equivalent of the baccalauréat

équivalent [ekivalɑ̃] ADJ equivalent (**à** to)
NM equivalent; **sans é.** without equal, unequalled

équivaloir [ekivalwar] VI *(conj like* **valoir***)* to be equivalent or equal (**à** to); **cela équivaut à un refus** that amounts to a refusal

équivoque [ekivɔk] ADJ **1** *(ambigu)* *(mots, faits, attitude etc)* equivocal, ambiguous **2** *(douteux)* *(conduite, honnêteté, passé etc)* questionable, doubtful, dubious
NF **1** *(ambiguïté)* ambiguity; **sans é.** *(adj)* unequivocal; *(adv)* unequivocally **2** *(malentendu)* misunderstanding (**sur** about)

érable [erabl] NM *(arbre, bois)* maple; **é. à sucre** sugar maple; **sirop/sucre d'é.** maple syrup/sugar

érablière [erablijɛr] NF *Can* maple grove

éradication [eradikasjɔ̃] NF eradication

éradiquer [eradike] VT to eradicate

érafler [erafle] VT *(genou etc)* to scratch, to graze; *(cuir etc)* to scuff; *(bois, meuble)* to scratch
VPR **s'érafler s'é. le coude** to graze or scrape one's elbow

éraflure [eraflyr] NF *(au genou etc)* scratch, graze; *(sur cuir etc)* scuff (mark); *(sur bois, meuble)* scratch (mark)

éraillé [eraje] ADJ **1** *(tissu)* frayed; *(surface)* scratched; *(corde)* fretted **2 yeux éraillés** bloodshot eyes **3** *(voix)* hoarse

éraillement [erajmɑ̃] NM **1** *(d'un tissu)* fraying; *(d'une corde)* fretting; *(d'une surface)* scratching **2** *(éraflure)* scratch **3** *(de voix)* hoarseness

érailler [eraje] VT **1** *(tissu)* to fray; *(ourlet etc)* to unravel; *(corde)* to fret **2** *(peau, surface etc)* to scratch **3** *(voix)* to make hoarse
VPR **s'érailler 1** *(d'un ourlet etc)* to unravel, to come unravelled; *(d'un tissu)* to fray; *(d'une corde)* to fret **2** *(d'une voix)* to become hoarse

éraillure [erajyr] NF *(marque)* scratch

erbium [ɛrbjɔm] NM *Chimie* erbium

ère [ɛr] NF era; **en l'an 1150 de notre è.** in (the year) 1150 AD; **avant notre è.** BC; **è. de prospérité** period of prosperity

érecteur, -trice [erɛktœr, -tris] ADJ *Physiol* erector

érectile [erɛktil] ADJ erectile

érection [erɛksjɔ̃] NF **1** *(d'une statue, d'un mât etc)* erection, setting up, raising **2** *Physiol* erection; **être en é.** to have an erection

éreintage [erɛ̃taʒ] NM = **éreintement 2**

éreintant [erɛ̃tɑ̃] ADJ *Fam (travail etc)* back-breaking, exhausting

éreinté [erɛ̃te] ADJ *Fam* exhausted, worn out

éreintement [erɛ̃tmɑ̃] NM **1** *(fatigue)* exhaustion **2** *(critique sévère)* savage criticism, *Br* slating

éreinter [erɛ̃te] VT **1** *(fatiguer)* *(personne, animal)* to exhaust, to wear or tire out **2** *Fam (critiquer)* *(livre, représentation, auteur etc)* to criticize savagely, *Br* to slate
VPR **s'éreinter** to exhaust oneself, to wear or tire oneself out (**à faire** doing)

éreinteur, -euse [erɛ̃tœr, øz] N savage critic

érémiste [eremist] N *Fam* = person receiving the RMI benefit

Erevan [erevan] N Yerevan

erg[1] [ɛrg] NM *Phys (unité)* erg

erg[2] NM *Géog* erg

ergol [ɛrgɔl] NM *Astronaut* propellant

ergonome [ɛrgɔnɔm] N ergonomist

ergonomie [ɛrgɔnɔmi] NF ergonomics

ergonomique [ɛrgɔnɔmik] ADJ ergonomic

ergot [ɛrgo] NM **1** *(d'un coq etc)* spur; *Fam* **monter ou se dresser sur ses ergots** *(se montrer menaçant)* to show one's teeth **2** *(d'un chien etc)* dewclaw **3** *Agr, Pharm* ergot **4** *Tech* lug; **é. d'arrêt** stop lug; **é. de tracteur** *(d'imprimante)* tractor pin

ergotage [ɛrgotaʒ] NM quibbling, cavilling

ergoté [ɛrgote] ADJ **1** *(oiseau)* spurred; *(chien)* dewclawed **2** *Agr (seigle, blé)* affected with ergot

ergoter [ɛrgote] VI to quibble, to cavil (**sur** about)

ergoteur, -euse [ɛrgotœr, -øz] ADJ cavilling, quibbling
N quibbler, caviller

ergothérapeute [ɛrgoterapøt] N occupational therapist

ergothérapie [ɛrgoterapi] NF occupational therapy

Érié [erje] NM **le Lac É.** Lake Erie

ériger [eriʒe] *(j'érigeai(s))* VT **1** *(dresser)* *(statue, temple, mât etc)* to erect, to set up, to raise **2** *(créer)* *(bureau, tribunal etc)* to establish, to set up **3** *Fig* **é. qn en** to set sb up as, to elevate sb to the status of; **é. qch en** to elevate sth to the status of, to present sth as; **é. une église en cathédrale** to raise a church to (the dignity of) a cathedral
VPR **s'ériger s'é. en spécialiste** to set oneself up as a specialist

ermitage [ɛrmitaʒ] NM hermitage

ermite [ɛrmit] NM hermit; **vivre en e.** to live the life of a recluse

éroder [erɔde] VT *(côte, rochers etc)* to erode, to wear away; *(métaux etc)* to corrode, to eat away

érogène [erɔʒɛn] ADJ erogenous

éros [eros] NM **1** *Psy* **l'é.** Eros **2** *Myth* **É.** Eros

érosif, -ive [erozif, -iv] ADJ erosive

érosion [erozjɔ̃] NF erosion, wearing away; *Fig* erosion; **é. dentaire** dental erosion; *Fig* **é. monétaire** depreciation of money

érotique [erotik] ADJ erotic

érotiquement [erotikmɑ̃] ADV erotically

érotisation [erotizasjɔ̃] NF eroticization

erotiser [erotize] VT to eroticize

érotisme [erotism] NM *(caractère érotique)* eroticism; *(goût pour le plaisir sexuel)* erotism

érotologue [erotolog] N sexologist

érotomane [erotoman] N erotomaniac

errance [ɛrɑ̃s] NF *Litt* roving, wandering; **vie d'e.** roving or wandering life

errant [ɛrɑ̃] ADJ *(personne, vie etc)* roving, wandering; **chevalier e.** knight errant; **le Juif e.** the Wandering Jew; **chien e.** stray dog; **pensées errantes** wandering thoughts

errata [ɛrata] NM INV *Typ* errata; **feuille d'e.** errata slip

erratique [ɛratik] ADJ erratic

erratum, pl errata [ɛratom, -ta] NM *Typ* erratum, pl errata

erre [ɛr] NF **1** *Naut (lancée)* way; **e. pour gouverner** steerage way; **avoir de l'e.** to have way on; **perdre de l'e.** ou **son e.** to lose way **2 erres** *(d'un cerf etc)* track, spoor, slot; *Fig* **suivre les erres de qn** to follow in sb's footsteps

errement [ɛrmɑ̃] NM *Fin* **é. du marché** market fluctuation
NMPL **errements** erring or bad ways; **retomber dans** ou **revenir à ses anciens errements** to fall back into one's bad old ways

errer [ɛre] VI **1** *(d'un marcheur etc)* to wander (about), to roam, to rove; **e. par les rues** to wander about or roam the streets; **e. comme une âme en peine** to wander about like a lost soul; **laisser e. ses pensées** to let one's thoughts wander or stray **2** *Litt (se tromper)* to err, to be mistaken

erreur [ɛrœr] NF **1** *(faute, inexactitude)* error, mistake; **e. de plume** slip of the pen; **e. de date** mistake in the date; **e. de jugement** error of judgment; **e. de sens** wrong meaning; **faire** ou **commettre une e.** to make a mistake; **faire e.** to be mistaken; **par e.** by mistake; **sauf e.** if I am not mistaken; **sauf e. ou omission** errors and omissions excepted; **il y a e. sur la personne** you've/they've/etc got the wrong person; **il n'y a pas d'e. (possible)** there's no doubt about it; *Fam* **c'est un malin, pas d'e.** he's a smart one and no mistake; **e.!** wrong!, not so!
2 *(opinion fausse)* error; **être dans l'e.** to be under a misapprehension, to be mistaken; **induire qn en e.** to mislead sb
3 *(action regrettable ou blâmable)* error; **revenir de ses erreurs** to turn over a new leaf

4 *Ordinat* error; **message d'e.** error message; **correction des erreurs** error correction

▸▸ *Ordinat* **e. aléatoire** random error; *Ordinat* **e. d'analyse (syntaxique)** parse error; *Ordinat* **e. d'arrondi** rounding error; **e. de calcul** miscalculation; *Ordinat* **e. de codage** coding error; **e. d'échantillonnage** sampling error; *Ordinat* **e. d'écriture** write error; *Ordinat* **e. d'entrée** input error; *Ordinat* **e. disque** disk error; **e. de jeunesse** youthful error; **e. judiciaire** miscarriage of justice; *Ordinat* **e. de lecture** read error; *Ordinat* **e. de logiciel** software *or* system error; *Ordinat* **e. de parité** parity error; *Ordinat* **e. de programmation** program *or* programming error; *Ordinat* **e. de saisie** keyboarding error; *Ordinat* **e. de syntaxe** syntax error; **e. système** system error; **e. typographique** printing error; *(coquille)* misprint

erroné [ɛrɔne] **ADJ** *(déclaration etc)* erroneous

erronément [ɛrɔnemã] **ADV** erroneously

ersatz [ɛrzats] **NM INV** ersatz, substitute; **e. de café/littérature** ersatz coffee/literature

erse¹ [ɛrs] **ADJ, NM** *Ling* Erse

erse² **NF** *Naut* grummet, grommet

éructation [eryktasjɔ̃] **NF** belch

éructer [erykte] **VI** to belch
     VT *Fig* **é. des injures** to hurl abuse

érudit, -ite [erydi, -it] **ADJ** erudite, scholarly, learned
     N scholar

érudition [erydisjɔ̃] **NF** erudition, learning, scholarship; **discourir avec é.** to talk learnedly

éruptif, -ive [eryptif, -iv] **ADJ** *(maladie, roche etc)* eruptive

éruption [erypsjɔ̃] **NF 1** *(d'un volcan)* eruption; **faire é., entrer en é.** to erupt **2 é. dentaire** *ou* **des dents** cutting of teeth **3** *Méd* rash, eruption **4** *Fig (de colère, joie etc)* eruption, outburst

> Do not confuse with **irruption**.

érysipèle [erizipɛl] **NM** *Méd* erysipelas

érythème [eritɛm] **NM** *Méd* rash, *Spéc* erythema; **é. fessier** nappy *or* *Am* diaper rash; **é. solaire** sunburn

Érythrée [eritre] **NF** Eritrea

érythréen, -enne [eritreɛ̃, -ɛn] **ADJ** Eritrean
     N É. Eritrean

E/S *Ordinat (abrév* **entrée/sortie)** I/O

ès [ɛs] **PRÉP docteur ès lettres/sciences** ≃ PhD, DPhil; **licencié(e) ès lettres/sciences** ≃ Bachelor of Arts/Science, BA/BSc; *Admin, Jur* **ès qualités** ex officio

ESB [œsbe] **NF** *Vét (abrév* **encéphalite spongiforme bovine)** BSE

esbigner (s') [sɛsbiɲe] **VPR** *Fam* to clear off, to take off, *Am* to book it, to fade

esbroufe [ɛzbruf] **NF** *Fam* bluff(ing); **faire de l'e.** to show off, to overdo it; **avoir qn à l'e.** to bluff sb

esbroufeur, -euse [ɛzbrufœr, -øz] **N** *Fam* swaggerer

escabeau, -eaux [ɛskabo] **NM 1** *(tabouret)* (wooden) stool **2** *(marchepied)* stepladder, *Br* (pair of) steps; **e. de bibliothèque** library steps

escadre [ɛskadr] **NF** *Naut* squadron; *Aviat* **e. aérienne** wing; **chef d'e.** *Naut* squadron commander; *Aviat* wing commander

escadrille [ɛskadrij] **NF 1** *Naut* flotilla **2** *Aviat (unité)* flight

escadron [ɛskadrɔ̃] **NM 1** *Mil* squadron; **e. de chars** armoured squadron; **chef d'escadron(s)** major **2** *Aviat* squadron; **e. de**

chasse/bombardement fighter/bomber squadron **3** *Fig (groupe)* *(de touristes, journalistes etc)* troop, band

escagasser [ɛskagase] *Région* **VT 1** *(rouer de coups)* to beat up **2** *(irriter)* to annoy, to irritate
     VPR s'escagasser *(s'épuiser)* to wear oneself out (**à faire qch** doing sth); *(se donner du mal)* to go to a lot of trouble (**à faire qch** to do sth)

escalade [ɛskalad] **NF 1** *(action)* *(d'un mur, d'une falaise etc)* climbing, scaling; *Sport* (rock)climbing; **faire de l'e.** to go (rock)-climbing **2** *(parcours)* climb **3** *(d'une guerre, des prix, de la violence etc)* escalation; **les charges locatives n'ont pas cessé leur e.** service charges are still escalating; **on a remarqué son e. verbale** it was noted that he got more and more carried away as he spoke
     ▸▸ *Sport* **e. libre** free climbing

escalader [ɛskalade] **VT** to climb, to scale; *Hist, Mil (forteresse)* to escalade

escalator [ɛskalatɔr] **NM** escalator

escale [ɛskal] **NF 1** *(temps d'arrêt)* *Naut* call; *Aviat* stop(over), layover; **faire e.** *Naut* to put into port; *Aviat* to touch down; **faire e. à Londres** *Naut* to put in *or* call at London; *Aviat* to stop over at London; *Aviat* **escales prévues** scheduled stops; **vol sans e.** nonstop flight; **une e. de quatre heures** *Naut* a four-hour call; *Aviat* a four-hour stop(over) **2** *(lieu)* *Naut* port *or* place of call; *Aviat* stop(over)

escalier [ɛskalje] **NM 1** *(marches)* (flight of) stairs; *(cage)* staircase; **rencontrer qn dans l'e.** *ou* **dans les escaliers** to meet sb on the stairs; *Fig* **j'ai l'esprit de l'e.** I always think of an answer when it's too late; *Ski* **monter en e.** to sidestep; *Fig Fam* **avoir des escaliers dans les cheveux** to have unevenly cut hair **2** *Tech* step; **en e.** stepped **3** *Typ (de titres)* step effect; **courbe en e.** jaggy
     ▸▸ *Naut* **e. des cabines** companionway; **e. en colimaçon** spiral staircase; **e. d'honneur** main *or* grand staircase; **e. mécanique** escalator, *Can* **e. mobile** escalator; **e. roulant** escalator; **e. de secours** fire escape; **e. de service** backstairs; **e. à vis** spiral staircase

escalope [ɛskalɔp] **NF** *Culin* escalope

escamotable [ɛskamɔtabl] **ADJ** *(antenne)*, *Aviat (train d'atterrissage)* retractable; *(meuble)* foldaway, collapsible; *Aut (phares)* retractable

escamotage [ɛskamɔtaʒ] **NM 1** *(par un illusionniste)* conjuring away, vanishing; **tour d'é.** vanishing trick **2** *Fig (d'une tâche)* skipping; *(d'un problème, d'une question)* dodging **3** *Aviat (d'un train d'atterrissage)* retraction **4** *(vol)* stealing

escamoter [ɛskamɔte] **VT 1** *(d'un illusionniste)* to conjure away, to make vanish **2** *Fig (éviter) (tâche)* to skip; *(problème, question)* to dodge **3** *Aviat (train d'atterrissage)* to retract **4** *(voler)* to sneak off with, to steal; **on m'a escamoté ma montre** someone's sneaked off with *or* stolen my watch

escamoteur, -euse [ɛskamɔtœr, -øz] **N 1** *(illusionniste)* conjuror **2** *(voleur)* sneak thief

escampette [ɛskãpɛt] **NF** *Fam* **prendre la poudre d'e.** *(s'enfuir)* to make off, *Br* to do a bunk

escapade [ɛskapad] **NF** *(excursion)* jaunt; *(fugue)* running off *or* away; **faire une e.** to run off *or* away

escarbille [ɛskarbij] **NF** cinder

escarboucle [ɛskarbukl] **NF** *(pierre précieuse)* carbuncle

escarcelle [ɛskarsɛl] **NF** **tomber dans l'e. de qn** *(de l'argent, d'une collection de tableaux*

etc) to come sb's way; *(de la direction d'une entreprise etc)* to end up *or* wind up in sb's hands; **tout le département est tombé dans l'e. des socialistes** the whole department ended up *or* wound up in the hands of the socialists

escargot [ɛskargo] **NM** snail; **allure d'e.** snail's pace; *Fam* **il marche comme un e.** he's walking at a snail's pace; **nous avancions à la vitesse d'un e.** we were moving at a snail's pace; *Fig* **opération e.** slowing down of the traffic *(by protesting truck drivers)*

escargotière [ɛskargɔtjɛr] **NF 1** *(parc)* snailery **2** *(plat)* snail dish

escarmouche [ɛskarmuʃ] **NF** skirmish

escarpé [ɛskarpe] **ADJ** *(route, montagne, pente)* steep; *(falaise)* sheer

escarpement [ɛskarpəmã] **NM** *(versant)* steep slope; *Géog* escarpment; *Géog* **e. de faille** fault scarp

escarpin [ɛskarpɛ̃] **NM** pump, *Br* court shoe; *(pour danser)* pump

escarpolette [ɛskarpɔlɛt] **NF** *Vieilli (balançoire)* swing

escarre, eschare [ɛskar] **NF** *Méd* scab; *(dû aux draps etc)* bedsore

Escaut (l') [lɛsko] **NM** the Scheldt

eschatologie [ɛskatɔlɔʒi] **NF** eschatology

Eschyle [eʃil] **N** Aeschylus

escient [ɛsjã] **NM** **à bon e.** wisely, judiciously; **à mauvais e.** unwisely

esclaffer (s') [sɛsklafe] **VPR** to burst out laughing, to roar with laughter, to guffaw

esclandre [ɛsklãdr] **NM** *(scandale, tapage)* (noisy) scene; **faire** *ou* **causer un e., faire de l'e.** to make a scene

esclavage [ɛsklavaʒ] **NM** *(état)* slavery; *(action)* enslavement; **réduire qn en e.** to enslave sb, to reduce sb to slavery; *Fig* **l'e. du bureau** the drudgery of the office; *Fam* **mais c'est de l'e.!** *(exploitation)* but it's slave labour!

esclavagisme [ɛsklavaʒism] **NM** slavery; *(doctrine)* pro-slavery

esclavagiste [ɛsklavaʒist] **N** pro-slaver
     ADJ état e. slave state

esclave [ɛsklav] **N** slave; **marchand d'esclaves** slave trader; **il fut vendu comme e.** he was sold into slavery; *Fig* **elle est l'e. de sa famille** she is a slave to her family; *Fig* **être l'e. de la mode/de son travail** to be a slave to fashion/one's work
     ADJ être e. de ses habitudes to be a slave to *or* the slave of one's habits

escogriffe [ɛskɔgrif] **NM (grand) e.** *(homme grand)* beanpole

escomptable [ɛskɔ̃tabl] **ADJ** *Compta* discountable

escompte [ɛskɔ̃t] **NM 1** *Com* discount; **accorder** *ou* **faire un e. sur les prix** to allow *or* give a discount on the prices; **maison d'e.** cutprice *or* discount store; **e. à** a discount; *Can* **50% d'e. sur toute la marchandise** 50% discount on all goods; **e. professionnel** *(au détaillant)* trade discount; **e. sur les achats en gros** *ou* **en quantité** volume purchase discount, quantity *or* bulk discount; **e. à forfait** forfaiting

     2 *Fin* **e. (de banque)** discount; **e. officiel, taux d'e.** (bank) discount rate; **e. de caisse** *ou* **au comptant** cash discount; **e. commercial** trade discount; **e. de règlement** discount for early payment, settlement discount; **prendre à l'e. un effet de commerce** to discount a bill of exchange

     3 *Can (remise)* discount; **50% d'e. sur toute la marchandise** 50% discount on all goods

escompter [ɛskɔ̃te] **VT 1** *Fin (traite)* to discount **2** *(s'attendre à)* to expect, to anticipate (**que** that); **e. une hausse** to anticipate an increase; **e. faire** to expect to do, to anticipate doing; **le succès escompté** the expected or anticipated success

escorte [ɛskɔrt] NF *Mil, Naut etc* escort; **faire e. à qn** to escort sb; **sous (bonne) e.** under escort; **conduire un prisonnier sous (bonne) e.** to escort a prisoner; *Naut* **sous l'e. d'une corvette** convoyed or escorted by a corvette

escorter [ɛskɔrte] VT to escort; *Naut* to convoy, to escort

escorteur [ɛskɔrtœr] NM *Naut* escort (vessel)

escouade [ɛskwad] NF 1 *(d'ouvriers)* squad, gang; *(de touristes, jeunes gens etc)* group 2 *Hist, Mil* squad

ESCP [aɛssepe] NF *(abrév* **École supérieure de commerce de Paris)** = prestigious business and management school

escrime [ɛskrim] NF *Sport* fencing; **faire de l'e.** to fence

escrimer (s') [sɛskrime] VPR to fight; **s'e. à faire qch** to do all one can to do sth, to try very hard to do sth

escrimeur, -euse [ɛskrimœr, -øz] N *Sport* fencer

escroc [ɛskro] NM swindler, crook

escroquer [ɛskrɔke] VT *(personne)* to swindle, to cheat, to trick; **e. qch à qn, e. qn de qch** to swindle or to cheat or to trick sb out of sth

escroquerie [ɛskrɔkri] NF *(action)* swindling; *(résultat)* swindle; *Jur (délit)* fraud; **mais c'est de l'e.!** it's a swindle, *Br* it's daylight robbery!

escudo [ɛskydo] NM *Anciennement* escudo

esgourde [ɛsgurd] NF *Arg* ear, *Br* lughole

eskimo [ɛskimo] ADJ INV Eskimo, Inuit; **les coutumes e.** Eskimo or Inuit customs ▪ NM *Ling* Eskimo, Inuit ▪ N **E.** Eskimo, Inuit

Ésope [ezɔp] N Aesop

ésotérique [ezɔterik] ADJ esoteric

ésotérisme [ezɔterism] NM esotericism

espace [ɛspas] NM 1 *(étendue, distance)* space; **laisser de l'e.** to leave space or room; **un e. de dix mètres entre deux choses** a distance or space or gap of ten metres between two things; **laisser un e. entre deux mots** to leave a space between two words; **l'e. parcouru** the distance covered
2 *(durée)* **pendant le même e. de temps** in the same space of time; **en l'e. d'une semaine** within a week
3 *(vide), Astron* space; **regarder dans l'e.** to stare into space; **e. extra-atmosphérique** outer space; **vol ou voyage dans l'e.** space flight
4 *Géom* space; **e. à trois/quatre dimensions** three-/four-dimensional space
5 *Ordinat* **e. disque** disk space; **e. insécable** hard space; **e. mémoire** memory space; **e. ressort** soft space; **e. de stockage** storage space; **e. Web** Web space
6 *Mktg* **e. d'exposition** display area; **e. de PLV** in-store advertising space ▪ NF *Typ* space; **e. fine/moyenne/forte** hair/medium-sized/thick space
▸▸ **e. aérien** airspace; *Typ* **e. blanc** space; *Com* **e. cargo** cargo space; *TV, Cin* **e. filmique** filmic space; *Admin* **e. judiciaire européen** common European legal framework; **e. mort** dead space; *Aut* clearance volume; **e. publicitaire** advertising space; **e. de rangement** storage space; **e. de rayonnage** shelf space; **e. social européen** common European social legislation; **e. vital** living space; **espaces verts** green spaces

espacement [ɛspasmã] NM 1 *(action)* spacing out; *(résultat)* spacing; *(distance)* space, distance; *Ordinat* **e. arrière** backspace; *Aut*

e. des sièges seat pitch; **barre d'e.** *(d'une machine à écrire etc)* space bar 2 *Typ (entre deux lettres)* space; *(interligne)* space (between the lines), spacing; **e. des caractères/lignes** character/line spacing; **e. fixe/proportionnel** fixed/proportional spacing

espacer [ɛspase] *(j'espaçai(s))* VT *(objets, lignes, paiements, visites etc)* to space out; *Ordinat, Typ* to interspace; **e. des choses d'un mètre** to space things out a metre apart; **il faut e. nos rencontres** we must meet less often
▪ VPR **s'espacer** 1 *(de visites, lettres, cris etc)* to become less frequent 2 *(de personnes)* **espacez-vous** space yourselves out

espace-temps NM INV *Math, Phys* space-time (continuum)

espadon [ɛspadɔ̃] NM swordfish

espadrille [ɛspadrij] NF espadrille, rope-soled sandal

Espagne [ɛspaɲ] NF Spain

espagnol, -ole [ɛspaɲɔl] VOIR GRAMMAIRE A19 ADJ Spanish ▪ NM *Ling* Spanish ▪ N **E.** Spaniard; **les E.** the Spanish, the Spaniards

espagnolette [ɛspaɲɔlɛt] NF *(window)* fastener *(long vertical bar with pivoting central catch)*

espalier [ɛspalje] NM 1 *(mur)* wall *(for espaliers)*; **(arbre en) e.** espalier 2 *Gym* wall bars

espar [ɛspar] NM *Naut* spar

espèce [ɛspɛs] NF 1 *(sorte)* kind, sort; **gens/livres de toute e.** people/books of all kinds or of every description; **il portait une e. de chemise à fleurs** he wore a kind or a sort of flowery shirt; **cela n'a aucune e. d'importance** that's of no importance whatsoever, that's not at all important; *Fam* **cette e. d'idiot** that stupid idiot, that silly fool; *Fam* **e. d'idiot!** you idiot!; *Fam* **une e. de mec bizarre** a strange sort of guy; *Péj* **l'e. de blonde qui lui sert de femme** that blonde he calls his wife; **des gens de son e.** people like him, people of his kind or sort; **un escroc/menteur/avare de la pire e.** a crook/liar/miser of the worst sort or kind, the worst sort or kind of crook/liar/miser
2 *Jur* **cas d'e.** specific case; **loi applicable en l'e.** law applicable to the case in point; *Fig Fam* **je suis un cas d'e.** I'm a special case
3 **espèces** *(argent)* cash; *Hist (monnaie métallique)* coin; **payer en espèces** to pay in cash; **espèces sonnantes et trébuchantes** hard cash; *Compta* **espèces en caisse** cash in hand
4 *Bot, Zool* species; **l'e. humaine** the human race, mankind; **e. en voie de disparition** endangered species VOIR GRAMMAIRE A13
5 *Rel* (Eucharistic) species

espérance [ɛsperɑ̃s] NF hope; **vivre dans l'e.** to live in hope; **dans l'e. de faire** in the hope of doing; **dans l'e. que** in the hope that; **contre toute e.** against or contrary to all expectation; **au-delà de nos espérances** beyond our expectations, beyond expectation; **fonder son e. sur qn/qch** to found one's hopes on sb/sth; **mettre ses espérances en qch** to pin one's hopes on sth; **l'affaire n'a pas répondu à nos espérances** the business did not come up or live up to our expectations; **cet enfant donne de grandes espérances** this child shows great promise or is very promising; *Hum* **avoir des espérances** to have expectations *(of an inheritance)*; **tu es toute mon e.** you are my only hope
▸▸ **e. de vie** *(d'une personne)* life expectancy; *(d'un produit)* life expectancy, shelf life

espérantiste [ɛsperɑ̃tist] *Ling* N Esperantist ▪ ADJ *(société etc)* Esperanto

espéranto [ɛsperɑ̃to] NM *Ling* Esperanto

espérer [ɛspere] *(j'espère; j'espérerai)* VT *(quelque chose)* to hope for; *(s'attendre à) (personne, chose)* to expect; **j'espère vous revoir** I hope to see or I'll see you again; **j'espère qu'il viendra** I hope that he comes or will come; **je n'espère pas qu'il vienne** I don't expect him to come; **je ne vous espérais plus** I had given you up, I wasn't expecting you to come any more
▪ VI 1 **e. en Dieu** to trust in God 2 **j'espère bien** I hope so; **espérons!** let's hope so!

esperluète, esperluette [ɛsperlɥɛt] NF ampersand

espiègle [ɛspjɛgl] ADJ *(enfant, réponse etc)* mischievous ▪ N *(enfant)* imp; **petit(e) e.** little monkey

espièglerie [ɛspjɛgləri] NF 1 *(caractère)* mischievousness; **par pure e.** out of pure mischief 2 *(tour)* prank

espingouin [ɛspɛ̃gwɛ̃] *Arg* ADJ Dago ▪ NM **E.** Dago

espion, -ionne [ɛspjɔ̃, -jɔn] N *(d'une puissance étrangère)* spy, secret agent; *(de police), Fig* spy; **avion-/satellite-e.** spy plane/satellite

espionnage [ɛspjɔnaʒ] NM espionage, spying; **faire de l'e.** to spy; **réseau/roman d'e.** spy network/novel; **l'e. industriel** industrial espionage

espionner [ɛspjɔne] VT *(quelqu'un, les mouvements de qn etc)* to spy on ▪ VI to spy

espionnite [ɛspjɔnit] NF *Fam Hum* spy fever

esplanade [ɛsplanad] NF esplanade

espoir [ɛspwar] NM 1 *(espérance)* hope; **avoir l'e. de faire qch** to have hopes of or to be hopeful of doing sth; **avoir de l'e.** to have hope(s); **dans l'e. de vous revoir** in the hope of seeing you again; **avoir bon e.** to be full of hope; **reprendre e.** to be or become hopeful again; **mettre son e. en qch/qn** to put one's hopes in or to pin one's hopes on sth/sb; **nourrir l'e. de faire qch** to live in hope of doing sth; **c'est sans e.** it's hopeless; **il n'y a plus d'e.** there's no hope any more, all hope is gone or lost; **tous les espoirs sont permis** things look hopeful; *Prov Iron* **l'e. fait vivre** hope springs eternal
2 *(personne, chose)* hope; **vous êtes/ce plan est leur seul e.** you are/this plan is their only hope; **un e. du tennis français/de la chanson française** one of the most promising French tennis players/French singers; **ce sont les espoirs du patinage artistique** they are the most promising figure skaters around

ESPRIT [ɛspri]

| mind **1** ▪ spirit **2, 5–7** ▪ wit **1, 3** |
| ▪ person **4** |

NM 1 *(intellectuel)* mind; **d'e. lent** slow-witted; **d'e. vif** quick-witted; **avoir l'e. large/étroit** to be broad-/narrow-minded; **avoir l'e. tranquille** to be easy in one's mind; **avoir l'e. libre** to have a clear mind; **avoir l'e. mal tourné** to have a dirty mind; **perdre l'e.** to go out of one's mind; **elle avait l'e. ailleurs** her thoughts were or her mind was elsewhere; **où aviez-vous l'e.?** what were you thinking of?; **c'est une vue de l'e.** that's theoretical or all theory; **présence d'e.** presence of mind; **ça m'est sorti de l'e.** it slipped my mind, it went clean out of my head; **qu'avez-vous à l'e.?** what are you thinking of?; **elle n'avait pas l'e. à ce qu'elle faisait** her mind wasn't on or she didn't have her mind on what she was doing; **je n'ai pas l'e. à plaisanter ce matin** I'm not in the mood for joking or in a joking mood this morning; *Hum* **l'e. est fort mais la chair est faible** the spirit is willing but the flesh is weak; **une pareille idée ne me serait jamais venue à l'e.**

such an idea would never have occurred to me *or* crossed my mind *or* entered my head; **dans mon e.**, ça ne veut pas dire la **même chose** to my mind that doesn't mean the same thing; **dans mon e., ils arrivaient demain** I thought they were coming tomorrow; **avoir l'e. de se taire** to have the (good) sense to be silent; **perdre/reprendre ses esprits** to lose/regain consciousness

2 *(attitude, qualité)* spirit; **e. de compétition** competitive spirit; **e. d'entreprise** enterprise spirit, spirit of enterprise; **avoir bon e.** to be good-natured; **faire du mauvais e.** to be negative; **je n'ai pas l'e. de sacrifice** I'm not the sort to make sacrifices; **avoir l'e. d'analyse/scientifique** to have an analytical/a scientific (turn of) mind

3 *(humour)* wit; **avoir de l'e.** to be witty; **mots** *ou* **traits d'e.** witticisms, witty remarks; **faire de l'e.** to display one's wit

4 *(personne)* person; **un e. dangereux** a dangerous person *or* man/woman; **un e. fort** a freethinker; **les grands esprits de notre siècle** the great minds of our century; *Prov* **les grands esprits se rencontrent** great minds think alike

5 *(sens)* spirit; **s'attacher à l'e. de la loi plutôt qu'à la lettre** to go by the spirit of the law rather than the letter; **c'est dans cet e. qu'a été conçue cette organisation** it is in this spirit that the organization was conceived

6 *(désincarné)* spirit; *(fantôme)* spirit (of the dead), ghost; **le Saint-E., l'E. saint** the Holy Ghost, the Holy Spirit; *Hum* **je ne suis pas un pur e., il faut bien que je mange** I'm flesh and blood, I do have to eat; **l'e. malin** the Evil One; **e., es-tu là?** *(dans une séance de spiritisme)* is there anybody there?

7 *Chimie etc* (volatile) spirit

8 *Méd Arch* **esprits animaux** animal spirits

▸ ▸ **e.-de-bois** wood alcohol; **e. brut** raw spirits; **e. de caste** class consciousness; **e. de chapelle** cliquishness; **e. de clan** clannishness; **e. de clocher** parochialism; **e. de corps** esprit de corps; **e. d'équipe** team spirit; **e. de famille** family feeling; **e. frappeur** spirit-rapper; **e.-de-sel** spirits of salt; **e.-de-vin** spirits of wine

esquif [ɛskif] **NM** *Litt (embarcation)* skiff; **frêle e.** frail barque *or* vessel

esquille [ɛskij] **NF** splinter (of bone)

esquimau, -aude, -aux [ɛskimo, -od, -o] **ADJ** *(occ inv in feminine)* Eskimo, Inuit; **chien e.** husky

N E. Eskimo, Inuit

NM 1 *(glace)* **e.®** ≃ choc-ice *(on a stick)*, *Am* ≃ ice-cream bar, Eskimo Pie® **2** *Ling* Eskimo, Inuit

esquimautage [ɛskimotaʒ] **NM** *Sport* Eskimo roll

esquintant [ɛskɛ̃tɑ̃] **ADJ** *Fam (travail, voyage etc)* exhausting, tiring; *(personne)* tiresome

esquinter [ɛskɛ̃te] *Fam* **VT 1** *(fatiguer)* to do in, to wear out **2** *(abîmer)* (montre, outil etc) to do in, to ruin; *(voiture etc)* to bash up, *Br* to prang; *(blesser)* to do in; **il a eu le bras esquinté dans sa chute** he did his arm in when he fell **3** *(critiquer)* (auteur, film etc) to slam, *Br* to slate

VPR s'esquinter 1 *(se fatiguer)* to do oneself in, to wear oneself out **(à faire doing) 2** *(s'abîmer)* **s'e. la santé/les yeux** to ruin one's health/eyes **(à faire doing)**; **je me suis esquinté la jambe en tombant** I did my leg in when I fell

esquisse [ɛskis] **NF** *Beaux-Arts* (rough) sketch; *Typ (de page)* rough layout; *Fig (d'un projet, d'un roman etc)* sketch, outline; *Fig* **l'e. d'un sourire** the ghost *or* suggestion of a smile; *Fig* **l'e. d'une aide de la part du gouvernement** the tiniest amount of aid from the government

esquisser [ɛskise] **VT** *(portrait etc)* to sketch; *Fig (plan, roman, personnage etc)* to sketch, to outline; *Fig* **e. un sourire** to give a slight smile; *Fig* **e. un geste** to make a slight gesture; *Fig* **e. un geste de la main** to give a slight wave, to sketch a wave

VPR s'esquisser un sourire s'esquissa sur son visage he gave a slight smile; *Fig* **un plan commençait à s'e. dans mon esprit** a plan started to take shape in my mind

esquive [ɛskiv] **NF** *Sport etc (mouvement)* dodge; *Fig (d'une question, d'un problème etc)* dodging, evasion; *Boxe etc* **e. de la tête** dodge

esquiver [ɛskive] **VT** *(coup)*, *Fig (question, problème, devoir, créancier etc)* to avoid, to dodge, to evade

VI e. (de la tête) to dodge

VPR s'esquiver to slip away *or* off, to make oneself scarce

essai [ɛsɛ] **NM 1** *(test, épreuve) (d'un produit, d'une machine, d'une voiture etc)* test, trial; *TV, Cin* audition; *Com* **à l'e.** on a trial basis; **faire l'e. de qch** to test sth, to try sth out; **faites un e. avant de vous décider** try it out before you decide; *TV, Cin* **faire faire un e. à qn** to audition sb; **mettre qn/qch à l'e.** to put sb/sth to the test; **essais comparatifs** comparative tests; **prendre qch/qn à l'e.** to take sth/sb on trial, to take sth on approval/sb on probation; **pilote d'e.** test pilot; *Cin* **bout d'e.** screen test

2 *(tentative)* attempt, try; **faire un e.** to have a try, to make an attempt; **elle fait des essais de jardinage plutôt infructueux** she makes rather fruitless attempts at gardening; **au premier e.** at the first attempt *or* try; **coup d'e.** trial go *or* attempt; **à titre d'e.** subject to approval

3 *Littér* essay

4 *Métal (de l'or, de l'argent)* assay(ing); **fourneau d'e.** assay furnace

5 *Rugby* try; **marquer un e.** to score a try; **transformer un e. (en but)** to convert a try

▸ ▸ *Ordinat* **e. approfondi** beta test; **e. à banc** bench test; *TV, Cin* **e. de caméra** screen test; *Aut* **e. de chute** drop test; *Aut* **e. de collision frontale** frontal impact test; *Tech* **e. en endurance** endurance test; *Mktg* **e. gratuit** free trial; *TV, Cin* **e. image** test shot; **e. nucléaire** nuclear test; *Ordinat* **e. de performance** benchmark; *Ordinat* **e. préliminaire** alphatest; **essais de produit** product testing; *Aut* **e. routier** *ou* **sur route** road test; *TV, Radio* **e. de voix** voice test; *Aviat* **essais en vol** test flights

essaim [ɛsɛ̃] **NM** *(d'abeilles, d'étudiants etc)* swarm; *(de filles)* bevy

essaimage [ɛsɛmaʒ] **NM 1** *(d'abeilles)* swarming; *Fig (de la population, d'une famille)* spreading; *Fig* **l'e. de notre entreprise** the expansion of our firm's branch network **2** *(époque)* swarming time

essaimer [ɛseme] **VI** *(des abeilles)* to swarm; *Fig (d'une population, d'une famille)* to spread; *(d'une firme)* to expand

VT *(d'une firme) (usines, filiales etc)* spread

essayage [ɛsɛjaʒ] **NM** *(de vêtements, chaussures etc)* trying on, fitting; **on fera les rectifications après la deuxième e.** adjustments will be made after the second fitting; **cabine** *ou* **salon d'e.** fitting room

essayer [ɛseje] **(j'essaie, j'essaye, n. essayons; j'essaierai, j'essayerai) VT 1** *(tester) (machine, produit etc)* to test, to try out; *(pour la première fois, avant d'acheter etc) (nouveau gadget, restaurant, coiffeur etc)* to try (out); *(voiture)* to test-drive, to try out; *(vin, plat etc)* to try, to taste; *(vêtements, chaussures etc)* to try on; *(utiliser) (remède, politesse, sa force etc)* to try

2 *(tenter)* **e. de faire qch** to try *or* attempt to do sth; **n'essaie pas de me mentir** don't try

lying *or* to lie to me; **essayez de l'attraper** try to *or* and catch it; **laissez-moi e.** let me (have a) try; **sois courageux! – on va e.!** be brave! – I'll try!; **e. les maths/les agences matrimoniales** to try maths/the marriage bureaux VOIR GRAMMAIRE A43–4

3 *Métal (minerai)* to assay

VPR s'essayer s'e. à qch/à faire qch to try one's hand *or* one's skill at sth/at doing sth

essayeur, -euse [ɛsɛjœr, -øz] **N 1** *(de vêtements)* fitter **2** *(d'une machine, d'un produit etc)* tester **3** *(d'or, d'argent)* assayer

essayiste [ɛsɛjist] **N** essayist

esse [ɛs] **NF 1** *(crochet)* S-hook **2** *(cheville d'essieu)* linchpin **3** *(de violon etc)* f-hole, sound hole

ESSEC [ɛsɛk] **NF** *(abrév* École supérieure des sciences économiques et commerciales*)* = university-level business school

essence [ɛsɑ̃s] **NF 1** *Aut* petrol, *Am* gas, gasoline; **à e.** petrol-powered; **poste d'e.** filling station, petrol *or Am* gas station; *Fam* **faire de l'e.** to fill up **2** *(extrait) (de plante, café, viande etc)* essence; **e. de citron** lemon oil; **e. de roses** rose oil, attar of roses **3** *(caractère fondamental)*, *Phil* essence; **par e.** essentially **4** *(espèce) (d'arbre)* species; **essences résineuses** resinous trees, conifers

▸ ▸ **e. à faible indice d'octane** low-octane petrol; **e. à indice d'octane élevé** high-octane petrol; **e. ordinaire** two-star petrol, *Am* regular gas; **e. sans plomb** unleaded (petrol *or Am* gas), lead-free petrol *or Am* gas; **e. de térébenthine** oil *or* spirits of turpentine

essentiel, -ielle [ɛsɑ̃sjɛl] **ADJ 1** *(fondamental) (vérité, caractère etc)* essential; *(raison)* basic, main **2** *(nécessaire)* essential, necessary **(à, pour** for); **il est e. d'avoir compris ce point** it is essential *or* necessary to have understood this point **3** *(très important)* essential; **il est e. d'avoir lu ce livre** it is essential to have read this book

NM l'e. *(le point central)* the main point; *(les points centraux)* the main points; *(la majeure partie)* the main *or* greater part (**de** of); **l'e. des effectifs est resté à la base** the greater part *or* most of the men stayed at base; **n'apportez que l'e.** bring only the (bare) essentials *or* the basics; **l'e. est d'agir/que tu lui parles** the main *or* important thing is to act/that you talk to him; **vous avez la santé, c'est l'e.** you're healthy, that's the main *or* important thing

essentiellement [ɛsɑ̃sjɛlmɑ̃] **ADV 1** *(par nature)* essentially, fundamentally **2** *(principalement)* essentially, mainly; *(avant tout)* above all

esseulé [ɛseœle] **ADJ** *(abandonné)* alone; *(solitaire)* lonely

essieu, -ieux [ɛsjø] **NM** axle; *(de chariot)* axle tree; **e. avant/arrière** front/rear axle; **e. fixe** dead axle

essor [ɛsɔr] **NM 1** *(d'un oiseau)* flight; **prendre son e.** to fly off *or* away **2** *Fig (d'une industrie, d'une économie, d'un pays etc)* (rapid) growth, expansion; **e. économique** economic expansion; **prendre son e.** to take off; **prendre un grand e.** to grow *or* expand very rapidly; **industrie en plein e.** booming *or* fast-growing industry; **donner un nouvel e. à qch** to give a lift *or* boost to sth; **l'économie connaît un nouvel e.** the economy is experiencing a new boom *or* is expanding rapidly again

essorage [ɛsɔraʒ] **NM** *(de linge)* spin-drying; *(à la main, avec une essoreuse à rouleaux)* wringing

essorer [ɛsɔre] **VT** *(vêtements)* to spin(-dry); *(à la main, avec une essoreuse à rouleaux)* to wring; *(salade)* to spin

essoreuse [esɔʀøz] NF spin-dryer; **e. à rouleau** wringer, mangle; **e. à salade** salad spinner

essoufflé [esufle] ADJ out of breath, short of breath, winded

essoufflement [esuflǝmɑ̃] NM shortness of breath, breathlessness; *Fig* **en raison de l'e. de l'économie** because the economy is running out of steam

essouffler [esufle] VT *(personne, cheval)* to wind, to make out of breath
▸ **VPR s'essouffler** to get out of breath *or Fam* puff; *Fig (d'un roman, d'une personne créative, de l'économie etc)* to run out of steam; *Fig* **s'e. à faire qch** to struggle to do sth

essuie [esɥi] NM *Belg (essuie-mains)* hand towel; *(torchon)* cloth, tea towel; *(serviette de bain)* bath towel

essuie-glace, *pl* **essuie-glaces** [esɥiglas] NM *Aut* windscreen *or Am* windshield wiper; **e. arrière** rear wiper; **e. deux vitesses** two-speed wiper

essuie-mains [esɥimɛ̃] NM INV hand towel

essuie-meubles [esɥimœbl] NM INV duster

essuie-phare, *pl* **essuie-phares** [esɥifaʀ] NM headlamp wiper

essuie-pieds [esɥipje] NM INV doormat

essuie-tout [esɥitu] NM INV kitchen paper

essuie-verres [esɥivɛʀ] NM INV glass cloth

essuyage [esɥijaʒ] NM *(de vaisselle)* wiping, drying; *(d'une surface mouillée)* wiping (down); *(d'eau etc)* wiping up, mopping up; *(nettoyage)* wiping (clean); *(époussetage)* dusting

essuyer [esɥije] (**j'essuie; j'essuierai**) VT **1** *(sécher) (assiettes etc)* to wipe, to dry; *(surface)* to wipe (down); *(nettoyer)* to wipe (clean); *(épousseter)* to dust; *(éponger) (liquide)* to wipe up, to mop up; *(larmes)* to wipe away; **e. la vaisselle** to dry the dishes, to dry up; **e. ses pieds avant d'entrer** to wipe one's feet before going/coming in **2** *(subir) (défaite, perte)* to suffer; *(insultes, reproches etc)* to suffer, to endure, to be subjected to; **e. un refus** to meet with a refusal; **e. le feu de l'ennemi** to come under enemy fire; **e. une tempête** to weather a storm
▸ **VPR s'essuyer** to wipe oneself, to dry oneself; **s'e. les pieds/la bouche/les yeux** to wipe one's feet/mouth/eyes

est¹ [ɛ] *voir* **être²**

est² [ɛst] NM INV **1** *(point cardinal)* east; **à l'e., dans l'e.** in the east; **où est l'e.?** which way is east?; **la partie la plus à l'e. de l'île** the easternmost part of the island; **le vent vient de l'e.** it's an east *or* easterly wind, the wind is coming from the east; **un vent d'e.** an easterly wind; **le vent d'e.** the east wind; **aller au** *ou* **vers l'e.** to go east *or* eastwards; **les trains qui vont vers l'e.** trains going east, eastbound trains; **rouler vers l'e.** to drive east *or* eastwards; **aller droit vers l'e.** to head due east; **la cuisine est plein e.** *ou* **exposée à l'e.** the kitchen faces due east; **le soleil se lève à l'e.** the sun rises in the east
2 *(partie d'un pays, d'un continent)* east, eastern area *or* regions; *(partie d'une ville)* east; **l'e. de l'Italie** eastern Italy, the east of Italy; **dans l'e. de l'Espagne** in eastern Spain, in the east of Spain; **elle habite dans l'e.** she lives in the East; **il habite dans l'e. de Paris** he lives in the east of Paris; **elle est de l'e.** she's from the east; **les gens de l'e.** people who live in the east
▸ ADJ INV *(côte, face)* east; *(banlieue, partie, région)* eastern; **la façade e. d'un immeuble** the east-facing wall of a building; **la chambre est côté e.** the bedroom faces east; **dans la partie e. de la France** in the East of France, in eastern France; **la côte e. des États-Unis** the East coast *or* Eastern seaboard of the

United States; **suivre la direction e.** to head *or* to go eastwards; *Pol, Hist* **l'E.** Eastern Europe, Eastern European countries; **les pays de l'E.** the countries of Eastern Europe, Eastern European countries; *Hist* **le bloc de l'E.** the Eastern bloc

establishment [ɛstablɪʃmɛnt] NM *Pol* establishment

estacade [ɛstakad] NF *Naut (pieux)* stockade; *(jetée)* pier (on piles)

estafette [ɛstafɛt] NF **1** *Hist (courrier)* courier **2** *Mil (agent de liaison)* liaison officer **3** *(camionnette)* van

estafilade [ɛstafilad] NF *(d'un rasoir, d'une épée)* gash

est-allemand, -ande [ɛstalmɑ̃, -ɑ̃d] *Anciennement* ADJ East German
▸ N **E.-A.** East German

estaminet [ɛstaminɛ] NM *(small)* café, bar *(esp in N France and Belgium)*

estampage [ɛstɑ̃paʒ] NM **1** *Tech (d'un métal, d'une pièce, du cuir etc)* stamping **2** *Fam (action d'escroquer)* swindling, fleecing; *(résultat)* swindle

estampe [ɛstɑ̃p] NF **1** *(image)* print; **cabinet des estampes** *(d'une bibliothèque)* print room; *Hum* **tu es allée voir ses estampes japonaises?** did he show you his etchings? **2** *(outil)* stamp

estamper [ɛstɑ̃pe] VT **1** *Tech (métal, pièce, cuir etc)* to stamp **2** *Fam (escroquer)* to swindle, to fleece

estampeur, -euse [ɛstɑ̃pœʀ, -øz] N **1** *Tech (personne, outil)* stamper **2** *Fam (escroc)* swindler

estampillage [ɛstɑ̃pijaʒ] NM *(d'un document etc)* stamping; *(de marchandises)* marking

estampille [ɛstɑ̃pij] NF *(sur un document etc)* stamp; *(sur un produit)* mark

estampiller [ɛstɑ̃pije] VT *(document etc)* to stamp; *(marchandises)* to mark

este [ɛst] ADJ Estonian
▸ NM *Ling* Estonian
▸ N **E.** Estonian

ester [ɛstɛʀ] NM *Chimie* ester

esthète [ɛstɛt] N aesthete, *Am* esthete

esthéticien, -ienne [ɛstetisjɛ̃, -jɛn] N **1** *(spécialiste des soins de beauté)* beautician, beauty therapist **2** *(artiste, poète etc)* aesthetician, *Am* esthetician

esthétique [ɛstetik] ADJ aesthetic, *Am* esthetic; *(beau)* aesthetically *or Am* esthetically pleasing; **chirurgie e.** plastic surgery
▸ NF *(science)* aesthetics, *Am* esthetics; *(beauté)* aesthetic *or Am* esthetic quality; **ça manque d'e.** it's not very aesthetically *or Am* esthetically pleasing

esthétiquement [ɛstetikmɑ̃] ADV aesthetically, *Am* esthetically

esthétisme [ɛstetism] NM aestheticism, *Am* estheticism

estimable [ɛstimabl] ADJ **1** *(honorable) (personne, qualité)* estimable **2** *(assez bon) (travail, artiste etc)* fairly good **3** *(calculable) (frais, perte)* assessable

estimatif, -ive [ɛstimatif, -iv] ADJ *(coût etc)* estimated; **devis e.** estimate, quotation

estimation [ɛstimasjɔ̃] NF **1** *(détermination de la valeur) (d'un prix, d'une distance, d'un poids etc)* estimation; *(de marchandises)* valuation, appraising; *(de dommages, besoins)* assessment, estimation; **faire une e.** to give an estimation/a valuation/an assessment; **e. approximative** rough estimate; *Mktg* **des besoins** needs assessment; *Compta* **e. des frais** estimate of costs **2** *(valeur, quantité estimée)* estimate

estime [ɛstim] NF **1** *(respect)* esteem, regard;

avoir de l'e. pour qn/qch to esteem sb/sth; **avoir beaucoup d'e. pour qn/qch** to have great regard for sb/sth, to hold sb/sth in high regard; **tu as baissé dans mon e.** you have gone down in my estimation; **tenir qn en grande/en médiocre e.** to think highly/little of sb, to hold sb in high/low regard; **avoir un succès d'e.** to be a critical (though not a popular) success **2** *Naut* reckoning; **à l'e.** by dead reckoning; *Fig* by guesswork; **navigation à l'e.** dead reckoning

estimer [ɛstime] VT **1** *(déterminer la valeur de) (prix, distance, poids etc)* to estimate; *(marchandises)* to value, to appraise; *(dommages)* to assess; *Naut* to reckon; **faire e. une maison** to have a house valued; **les experts estiment que les pertes s'élèvent à plusieurs milliards** the experts estimate *or* that the losses total several hundred million; *Naut* **longitude estimée** longitude by dead reckoning
2 *(considérer)* to consider, to think (**que** that); **j'estime qu'il est de mon devoir de parler** I consider *or* think it (is) my duty *or* that it is my duty to speak; **je n'estime pas que vous ayez besoin d'y aller** I don't consider *or* think it (is) necessary for you to go, I don't think you need to go; **il n'a pas estimé nécessaire de me prévenir** he didn't consider *or* think it (was) necessary to warn me
3 *(respecter) (personne)* to have a high opinion of, to think highly of, to esteem; *(les qualités de qn, la musique etc)* to value, to have a high opinion of; **elle est estimée de tous** she is highly thought of *or* is esteemed by everyone; **j'estime son dévouement à sa juste valeur** I value his dedication at its true worth
▸ **VPR s'estimer s'e. satisfait/heureux** to consider oneself satisfied/lucky

estivage [ɛstivaʒ] NM *Agr (du bétail etc)* summering on mountain pastures

estival, -ale, -aux, -ales [ɛstival, -o] ADJ *(résidence, vêtements, travail etc)* summer; **station estivale** summer resort

estivant, -ante [ɛstivɑ̃, -ɑ̃t] N *(summer)* holiday-maker *or Am* vacationer

estiver [ɛstive] VT *Agr (bétail etc)* to summer on mountain pastures

estoc [ɛstɔk] NM **frapper d'e. et de taille** to cut and thrust

estocade [ɛstɔkad] NF *(en tauromachie)* deathblow; **donner l'e. à** *(taureau), Fig (adversaire)* to deal the deathblow to

estomac [ɛstɔma] NM stomach; **avoir l'e. vide** *ou* **creux/plein** to have an empty stomach/be full (up); **creux de l'e.** pit of the stomach; **mal d'e.** stomach ache; **avoir un e. d'autruche** to have a cast-iron stomach; **avoir e. dans les talons** to be ravenous *or* starving; *Fig Fam* **avoir de l'e.** *(courage)* to have plenty of guts; *(culot)* to have plenty of cheek; *Fig Fam* **la faire à l'e.** to try it on (**à qn** with sb)

estomaqué [ɛstɔmake] ADJ *Fam* staggered, astounded, flabbergasted

estomaquer [ɛstɔmake] VT *Fam* to stagger, to astound, to flabbergast

estompage [ɛstɔ̃paʒ] NM *Beaux-Arts* stumping, shading off (with a stump)

estompe [ɛstɔ̃p] NF *Beaux-Arts* stump; **dessin à l'e.** stump drawing

estompé [ɛstɔ̃pe] ADJ *(contour, image, couleurs etc)* indistinct, blurred; *(souvenirs)* blurred, dim; *Ordinat* dimmed

estomper [ɛstɔ̃pe] VT *Beaux-Arts (dessin)* to stump, to shade off (with a stump); *Fig (paysage, contour, souvenir etc)* to blur, to dim; *(contraste)* to tone down; *(rides)* to smooth out; **le temps estompera la douleur** time will ease the pain

VPR s'estomper *(d'un souvenir)* to become blurred; *(de la douleur)* to ease; *(des rides)* to be smoothed out; *(des couleurs)* to fade; *(des contours)* to fade, to blur

Estonie [ɛstɔni] **NF** Estonia

estonien, -ienne [ɛstɔnjɛ̃, jɛn] **ADJ** Estonian
 NM *Ling* Estonian
 N E. Estonian

estoquer [ɛstɔke] **VT** *(d'un matador) (taureau)* to kill

estouffade [ɛstufad] **NF** *Culin* e. de bœuf beef stew

estourbir [ɛsturbir] **VT** *Fam* **1** *(tuer)* to do in **2** *(étonner)* to astound, to knock sideways; **je suis encore tout estourbi de la chance que j'ai eue** I'm still quite astounded how lucky I was

estrade [ɛstrad] **NF** dais, rostrum, platform; **e. réservée à la presse** press box

estragon [ɛstragɔ̃] **NM** *Bot, Culin* tarragon

estran [ɛstrɑ̃] **NM** strand, foreshore

estrapade [ɛstrapad] **NF** *Hist (supplice)* strappado; *Naut* dipping from the yard arm

estrogène [ɛstrɔʒɛn] **NM** *Physiol* oestrogen, *Am* estrogen

estropié, -ée [ɛstrɔpje] **ADJ** crippled, maimed
 N cripple

estropier [ɛstrɔpje] **VT** *(impf, pr sub* n. estropiions)* **1** *(personne)* to cripple, to maim **2** *Fig (valse, langue étrangère etc)* to murder; *(mot, nom)* to mispronounce; *(texte)* to mutilate

estuaire [ɛstɥɛr] **NM** estuary

estudiantin [ɛstydjɑ̃tɛ̃] **ADJ** *(vie, univers etc)* student

esturgeon [ɛstyrʒɔ̃] **NM** sturgeon

et [e] **CONJ** *(note there is no liaison with* **et**: j'ai écrit et écrit [ʒeekrieekri]) **1** and; **toi et moi partirons demain** you and I will leave tomorrow; **c'est un homme d'une grande énergie, et qui arrivera** he is a man of great energy, who will succeed; **et son frère et sa sœur** both his brother and his sister; **je ne peux pas et répondre au téléphone et ouvrir la porte** I can't answer the phone *and* open the door; **et d'un, il pleut et de deux, je n'ai pas envie d'y aller** first(ly) it's raining, and second(ly) I don't want to go; **j'aime le café, et vous?** I like coffee, do you?; **et les dix euros que je vous ai prêtés?** and (what about) the ten euros I lent you?; **et le garçon de se sauver** at this the boy ran off; **et elle de rire!** and she burst out laughing!

 2 *(dans les nombres etc)* **vingt/trente/etc et un** twenty/thirty/*etc*-one; **soixante et onze** seventy-one; **il est quatre heures et demie** it's half past four
 NM **1** *Ordinat* **et commercial** ampersand **2** *Ordinat* **ET** AND; **circuit ET** AND gate

ETA [ɔtea] **NF** *(abrév* Euskadi ta Askatasuna) ETA

étable [etabl] **NF** cowshed

Il faut noter que le nom anglais **stable** est un faux ami. Il signifie **écurie**.

établi[1] [etabli] **NM** (work)bench

établi[2] **ADJ** *(gouvernement, réputation etc)* established; **l'Église établie** the Established Church; **considérer qch comme chose établie** to take sth for granted; **l'ordre é.** the established order

établir [etablir] **VT** **1** *(créer) (forme de gouvernement, affaire, paix, relations, contact etc)* to establish; *(agence)* to set up; *(édifice)* to put up, to erect; *(barrage, voie ferrée)* to construct; *(lieu de résidence)* to settle, to fix; *(machinerie)* to install, *Am* to instal; *(voile)* to set; *(camp)* to pitch; *(prix)* to fix, to set; *(taxe, tribunal etc)* to institute, to create;

(plan, proposition etc) to draw up; *(règlement)* to prescribe, to lay down; *(principe)* to lay down; *(devis, facture, bilan, budget)* to draw up; **é. un chèque** to make out *or* write a cheque; **é. un chèque à l'ordre de** to make a cheque payable to; **é. une balance** to strike a balance; **é. une moyenne** to work out an average; **é. un record** to set a record
 2 *(démontrer) (fait, l'innocence de qn)* to establish, to prove; **é. une accusation** to establish *or* substantiate a charge; **é. un parallèle entre** to establish *or* draw a parallel between
 3 *(asseoir) (autorité, droits, réputation etc)* to establish; *(fortune)* to establish, to build up *(*sur on*)*; **é. le silence** to establish silence; **é. une démonstration sur des arguments solides** to base a proof on sound arguments **4** *(pourvoir d'une situation)* to set up *(*dans in; comme as*)*; **il a établi tous ses enfants** he has settled all his children, he has set all his children up in life; *Vieilli* **il lui reste une fille à é.** *(à marier)* he still has a daughter at home
 VPR s'établir **1** *(dans une ville, un pays etc)* to settle *(*à, dans, en in*)* **2** *(pour exercer un métier)* s'é. épicier to set (oneself) up as a grocer; **elle s'est établie à son compte** she set up (in) business on her own **3** *(se poser en)* s'é. chef/juge to set oneself up as a leader/ judge **4** *(d'une coutume, d'une idée, de rapports etc)* to become established; **le silence s'est enfin établi** silence was established at last

établissement [etablismɑ̃] **NM** **1** *(création) (de forme de gouvernement, affaire, paix etc)* establishment; *(d'agence)* setting up; *(d'édifice)* putting up, erection; *(d'un lieu de résidence)* settling, fixing; *(de machinerie)* installation; *(de voile)* setting; *(de camp)* pitching; *(de prix)* fixing; *(de taxe, tribunal)* institution, creation; *(de plan, proposition etc)* drawing up; *(de règlement)* prescribing, laying down; *(de principe)* laying down; *Tél* **é. d'appel** call connection; *Fin* **é. d'un compte** opening an account, setting up an account; **é. des menus** *(dans un restaurant)* menu planning; *Com* **é. des prix** pricing
 2 *(démonstration) (de fait, innocence de qn)* establishment, proving
 3 *(d'autorité, de droits, réputation etc)* establishment
 4 *(de ses enfants)* settling
 5 *(institution)* establishment, institution; **é. thermal** hydropathic establishment, spa; **é. hospitalier** hospital; **é. scolaire** educational establishment; **é. pénitentiaire** prison, penal establishment; **é. bancaire** bank; **é. de crédit** credit institution; *Compta* **é. déclarant** company making the return; **é. dépositaire** = financial institution holding securities on trust; **é. financier** financial institution; *Fin* **é. payeur** paying bank
 6 *Hist* **établissements** *(colonies)* settlements, colonies
 7 *Com* business, firm; **les établissements Martin** Martin & Co; **é. principal** main branch *or* office; **é. industriel** factory

étage [etaʒ] **NM** **1** *(d'un bâtiment)* floor, storey, *Am* story; **à deux étages** two-storeyed, *Am* two-storied; **au troisième é.** on the third floor, *Am* on the fourth floor; **monter à l'é.** to go upstairs; **dévaler les étages** to race down the stairs; **elle est dans les étages** she's somewhere upstairs
 2 *(d'une construction, d'un terrain)* level; *(d'un jardin)* terrace; *(d'un gâteau)* tier; **gâteau à quatre étages** four-tiered cake
 3 *Géol* stage, formation
 4 *Tech* stage; **compression par étages** compression by stages; **fusée à trois étages** three-stage rocket
 5 *Péj* **de bas é.** *(esprit, histoire etc)* mediocre,

second-rate; **individu de bas é.** worthless individual
 6 *Can Sport* **le deuxième é.** the (club) management

étagement [etaʒmɑ̃] **NM** *(de plantations, vignes)* terracing

étager [etaʒe] *(j'étageai(s))* **VT** **1** *(sièges, livres, groupe de personnes etc)* to arrange in tiers; **jardin étagé** terraced garden; **vignes étagées** vines arranged in terraces; **poulie étagée** cone pulley **2** *Tech* compression étagée compression by stages, staged compression
 VPR s'étager *(des maisons, vignes etc)* to rise in tiers

étagère [etaʒɛr] **NF** *(meuble)* (set of) shelves; *(planche)* shelf VOIR GRAMMAIRE A12

étai[1] [etɛ] **NM** *Naut (cordage)* stay; **voile d'é.** staysail

étai[2] **NM** *Constr etc* stay, prop, strut; **é. de mine** pit prop

étaiement [etɛmɑ̃] **NM** *Constr etc* shoring (up), propping (up)

étain [etɛ̃] **NM** **1** *(métal)* tin; **é. battu, é. en feuilles** thin sheet tin; **papier d'é.** tinfoil, silver paper **2** *(pour la vaisselle, les bijoux)* pewter; **vaisselle d'é.** pewter (plate); **une très belle collection d'étains** a very fine collection of pewter (pieces)

étal, -als [etal] **NM** **1** *(de boucher)* (butcher's) stall, meat stall **2** *(au marché)* (market) stall

étalage [etalaʒ] **NM** **1** *Com (des marchandises)* display, show; *(vitrine)* (display) window; *(impôt)* = tax paid by street trader; **faire l'é.** to set out one's goods; *(vitrine)* to dress the window(s); **mettre qch à l'é.** to display sth for sale; **article qui a fait l'é.** shopsoiled *or Am* shopworn article; *Journ* **é. publicitaire** display advertising **2** *Fig (de richesse, des connaissances etc)* display, show, parading; **faire é. de ses bijoux/son savoir/ sa richesse** to show off *or* parade one's jewels/knowledge/wealth; **faire é. de sa force** to show one's strength; **elle fait é. de sa vie privée** she flaunts her private life

étalager [etalaʒe] **VT** *(j'étalageai(s))* *Com (marchandises)* to display for sale

étalagiste [etalaʒist] **N** window dresser

étale [etal] *Naut* **ADJ** *(mer, marée)* slack; *(brise)* steady
 NM OU NF é. du flot slack water

étalement [etalmɑ̃] **NM** **1** *(du linge à sécher, de papiers sur la table etc)* spreading out; *(d'une nappe, du beurre etc)* spreading; *(de la peinture etc)* application; *(des marchandises)* displaying **2** *(des vacances)* staggering *(*sur over*)*; *(des travaux, d'un cours etc)* spreading (out) *(*sur over*)*; *(de paiements)* spreading, staggering *(*sur over*)*

étaler [etale] **VT** **1** *(étendre) (linge à sécher, papiers etc)* to spread out, to lay out; *(nappe, beurre etc)* to spread; *(peinture, onguent)* to apply *(*sur to*)*; *(marchandises)* to display (for sale); *(ses cartes)* to lay down
 2 *Fig (montrer) (sa richesse, ses connaissances)* to display, to show off, to parade; *(ses malheurs)* to parade, to draw attention to; **é. sa vie** to tell one's life story; **é. une affaire au grand jour** to make a matter public; **l'affaire était étalée à la une des journaux** the story was splashed across the front page; *Hum* **la culture, c'est comme la confiture: moins on en a, plus on l'étale** = people who don't have much culture have to make the most of it
 3 *(échelonner) (vacances, paiements, envoi du courrier etc)* to stagger *(*sur over*)*; *(travaux, cours, opération etc)* to spread *(*sur over*)*; **é. les remboursements sur plusieurs exercices** to spread (out) the repayments over several financial years

4 *Naut (courant, vent)* to stem **5** *Fam (faire tomber) (personne)* to lay out, to floor

VPR s'étaler 1 *(d'un village, parc etc)* to spread out; **arbre à cime étalée** large-crowned tree; **cette peinture s'étale mal** this paint goes on badly **2** *(parader) (des gens riches etc)* to flaunt oneself; **son succès s'étale à la une des journaux** his success is splashed across the front pages **3** *(se vautrer)* to sprawl **4** *Fam (tomber)* **s'é. par terre** to fall flat on the ground; **s'é. de tout son long** to go *or* measure one's length **5** *(des vacances, paiements etc)* to be spread (**sur** over)

étalon¹ [etalɔ̃] NM *(cheval)* stallion

étalon² NM *(modèle de mesure)* standard; *Fig (modèle)* standard, yardstick; **mètre é.** standard metre; *Écon* **l'é.-or** the gold standard; **é.-or lingot** gold bullion standard; **é. monétaire** monetary standard

étalonnage [etalɔnaʒ] NM, **étalonnement** [etalɔnmɑ̃] NM **1** *(action de vérifier) (d'un poids, d'une mesure)* standardization; *(d'un instrument)* gauging, testing **2** *(action de graduer) (d'un thermomètre etc)* calibration; *Cin, TV* calibration, grading **3** *Psy (d'un test)* standardization

étalonner [etalɔne] VT **1** *(vérifier) (poids, mesure)* to standardize; *(instrument)* to gauge, to test **2** *(graduer) (thermomètre, baromètre etc)* to calibrate; *Cin, TV* to calibrate, to grade **3** *Psy (test)* to standardize

étamage [etamaʒ] NM **1** *(de cuivre etc)* tinning; *(d'une tôle de fer)* tinplating **2** *(d'un miroir)* silvering

étambot [etɑ̃bo] NM *Naut* sternpost

étamer [etame] VT **1** *(cuivre etc)* to tin; *(tôle de fer)* to tinplate **2** *(miroir)* to silver

étameur [etamœr] NM tinner, tinsmith

étamine¹ [etamin] NF *Tex* muslin; *(pour filtrer, cribler)* butter muslin, cheesecloth; **passer à l'é.** *(liquide)* to filter; *(farine etc)* to sift

étamine² NF *Bot* stamen

étanche [etɑ̃ʃ] ADJ *(bateau, toit etc)* watertight; *(montre, bottes etc)* waterproof; **é. à l'eau/à l'air/à la poussière** watertight/air-tight/dustproof; **cloison é.** *Naut* watertight bulkhead; *Fig (entre services, disciplines etc)* impenetrable barrier, *esp Am Fam* Great Wall of China

étanchéité [etɑ̃ʃeite] NF *(d'un bateau, toit etc)* watertightness; *(d'une montre, de bottes etc)* waterproofness; **é. à l'eau/à l'air** water-tightness/airtightness; **vérifier l'é.** to check for leaks (**de** in)

étancher [etɑ̃ʃe] VT **1** *(liquide)* to check the flow of; *(sang)* to staunch; *(les larmes de qn)* to dry; *Naut* **é. une voie d'eau** to stop a leak **2** *(sa soif)* to quench, to slake **3** *(rendre étanche)* to make watertight

étançon [etɑ̃sɔ̃] NM *Constr, Naut (étai)* shore, stanchion

étançonnement [etɑ̃sɔnmɑ̃] NM shoring up

étançonner [etɑ̃sɔne] VT to shore up

étang [etɑ̃] NM pond, pool

étant [etɑ̃] *voir* **être²**

étape [etap] NF **1** *(lieu)* stop(over), stopping place; **faire é.** to stop; **nous avons fait é. à Bordeaux** we stopped over(night) at Bordeaux; **brûler une é.** *(d'un train, un autobus)* to go past *or* miss a stop, to fail to stop (at a scheduled stop); **comme nous étions pressés, nous avons brûlé l'é. de Strasbourg** since we were in a hurry, we missed out Strasbourg *or* we didn't stop in Strasbourg;

brûlons la prochaine é. et continuons jusqu'à Lyon let's press on to Lyons without stopping; *Fig* **brûler les étapes** *(dans une entreprise, un métier)* to move up the ladder very quickly; *(dans une tâche)* to cut corners **2** *(distance à parcourir) (d'un voyage, d'une course etc)* stage, leg; **à** *ou* **par petites étapes** by *or* in easy stages; **nous avons fait hier une é. de 500 kilomètres** we covered *or* did 500 kilometres yesterday **3** *Fig (phase) (d'une vie, d'un processus etc)* stage; **une procédure en deux étapes** a two-stage *or* -step procedure; **l'é. suivante consiste à …** the next step is to …; **é. par é.** stage by stage, step by step, one stage *or* step at a time; **par étapes** by *or* in stages *or* steps

ÉTAT [eta]

state **1, 5, 6, 8** ▪ condition **1** ▪ position **1** ▪ profession **3** ▪ form **7** ▪ list **7**

NM **1** *(façon d'être)* state, condition; *Phys* state; **à l'é. solide/liquide/naturel** in its solid/liquid/naturel state; **é. du ciel** weather conditions; **é. de la mer** conditions at sea; **l'é. des routes** road conditions; **é. du marché** state of the market; **à l'é. neuf** *(dans une petite annonce)* as new; **à l'é. pur** *(métal)* unalloyed; *Fig* **c'est de la bêtise/de l'incompétence à l'é. pur** it is sheer *or* downright stupidity/incompetence; **retourner à l'é. sauvage** to revert to the wild; **une plante qui pousse à l'é. sauvage** a plant which grows in the wild; **dans l'é. actuel des choses** given the current state of affairs; **dans l'é. actuel de nos connaissances** given what we know at the moment; **être dans un triste/piteux é.** to be in a sorry/pitiful state; *Hum* **elle est dans un é. intéressant** *(enceinte)* she's in the family way; **tu ne devrais pas porter cette valise dans ton é.** you shouldn't be carrying that case in your condition; *Fam* **être dans tous ses états** to be in a real *or* terrible *or* dreadful state; **il n'y a pas de quoi se mettre dans un é. pareil!** there's no point getting into such a state (about it)!; **te voilà dans un bel é.!** that's some state you're in!; **tu as vu dans quel é. tu t'es mis?** have you seen the state you've got yourself into?; **on a retrouvé des ossements en parfait é. de conservation** we found some perfectly preserved bones; **en (bon) é.** *(machine, voiture, maison etc)* in good condition *or* repair; **navire en bon é. (de navigabilité)** seaworthy ship; **en mauvais é.** in bad condition; **en é. de rouler** *(voiture)* roadworthy; **en é. de voler** *(avion)* airworthy; **être en é. de marche** to be in working order; *Aut* to be roadworthy, to be in a roadworthy condition; *Méd* **être en é. de manque** to have withdrawal symptoms; *Psy* **en é. de veille** in a waking state; **remettre en é.** *(maison etc)* to renovate, to repair; *(moteur)* to overhaul, to recondition; **tenir qch en é.** to look after sth, to keep sth in good repair; **laisser les choses en l'é.** to leave things as they are *or* stand; **vendre qch en l'é.** to sell sth as it is; **être/se sentir en é. de faire qch** to be/feel up to doing sth; **elle n'est plus en é. de travailler** she's not up to working any more; **tu n'es pas en é. de conduire** you're in no condition *or* in no fit state to drive; **le blessé n'est pas encore en é. de parler** the injured man is still not in a condition to talk; **je ne suis pas en é. de vous répondre** I am not in a position to give you an answer; **êtes-vous en é. de le recevoir?** *(décemment habillé)* are you presentable?, are you fit to be seen?; *(assez bien portant)* do you feel up to seeing him?, are you up to seeing him?; **nous sommes maintenant en é. d'affirmer que les otages ont tous été libérés** we are now in a position to confirm that the hostages have all been released; **être hors**

d'é. to have broken down; **il faut mettre ces terroristes hors d'é. de nuire** these terrorists must be prevented from doing harm **2** **faire é. de** to refer to, to mention **3** *(profession)* **militaire/épicier de son é.** soldier by profession/grocer by trade **4** *Hist (groupe social)* **le Tiers É.** the Third Estate **5** *(nation, autorité centrale)* **l'É.** the state *or* State; **coup d'É.** coup (d'état); **le budget de l'É.** the state budget; **homme d'é.** statesman; **femme d'É.** stateswoman; **pour des raisons d'É.** for reasons of state; **un É. dans l'É.** a state within a state; **É. croupion** rump state; **É. de droit** legitimate state; **É. fédéral** federal state; **É. membre** member state; **É. neutre** neutral state; **É. paria** rogue state; **É. paternaliste** nanny state; **É. providence** welfare state; **servir d'É. tampon** to serve as a buffer state; **É. voyou** rogue state **6** *(territoire aux États-Unis)* state **7** *(rapport) (imprimé)* form; *(des dépenses, ventes)* statement, list; *(des paiements, marchandises)* schedule, list; **rayer qn des états** to strike sb off the rolls **8** *Ordinat* **en é. de veille** in standby mode; **é. d'attente** wait state; **sans é. d'attente** with zero wait states

▸ ▸ **é. d'alerte** state of alert; **être en é. d'alerte** to be on the alert; *Mil* to be in a state of alert; **états d'âmes: avoir des états d'âme** to engage in soul-searching; **je n'ai pas eu d'états d'âme avant de le virer** I didn't engage in too much soul-searching before I fired him; **tu nous embêtes avec tes états d'âme** you're getting on our nerves with your constant soul-searching; *Compta* **é. de caisse** cash statement; **é. de choc: en é. de choc** in a state of shock; **é. de choses** state of affairs, situation; *Admin* **é. civil** *(d'une personne)* (civil) status; *(à la mairie)* register *or* *Br* registry office; **actes de l'é. civil** = birth, marriage and death certificates; **informer l'é. civil d'un décès** to register a death; *Compta* **états comptables** accounting records; *Compta* **états comptables et commerciaux** internal company records; **é. de compte** *Can* bank statement, statement of account; *Compta* **position on an account**; *Pol* **é. d'ébriété: en é. d'ébriété** in a state of intoxication; **é. d'esprit** state *or* frame of mind; *Pol* **é. d'exception** state of emergency; **é. de fait: c'est un é. de fait** it's an undeniable *or* established fact; *Jur* **é. de frais** bill of costs; **les États généraux** the States General; **é. de grâce** *Rel* state of grace; *Pol* honeymoon period; **é. de guerre** state of war; **l'é. de guerre a été déclaré** a state of war has been declared; **é. d'impression** report form; *Fin* **é. imprimé** printed statement *or* form; **é. d'ivresse: en é. d'ivresse** in a state of intoxication; **é. des lieux** inventory of fixtures *(in rented premises)*; **le propriétaire est tenu de faire l'é. des lieux avec son locataire** the landlord is obliged to agree an inventory of fixtures with the tenant; **é. néant** nil return; **é. nominatif** list of names, (nominal) roll; *Compta* **é. de rapprochement** reconciliation statement; *Compta* **é. récapitulatif** final assessment, adjustment account; **é. de santé** state of health; **é. second** (state of) trance; *Admin, Mil* **états de service** service record; **é. de siège** state of siege; **é. de situation** status *or* state-of-play report; *Compta* **é. TVA** VAT statement *or* return; **é. d'urgence** state of emergency

étatique [etatik] ADJ *Pol* (of the) state; **l'appareil é.** the machinery of state

étatisation [etatizasjɔ̃] NF *(action)* establishment of state control (**de** over); *(doctrine)* state control

étatisé [etatize] ADJ state-controlled, state-run

étatiser [etatize] VT *(firme etc)* to bring under state control

étatisme [etatism] NM state control

étatiste [etatist] ADJ **système é.** system of state control
   N partisan of state control

état-major, *pl* **états-majors** NM **1** *Mil (officiers)* (general) staff; *(lieu)* headquarters; **officier d'é.** staff officer; **carte d'é.** Br ≃ Ordnance Survey map, *Am* ≃ Geological Survey map **2** *(d'une firme)* senior staff, management; *(d'un parti politique)* leadership

États-Unis [etazyni] NMPL **les É. (d'Amérique)** the United States (of America), *Fam* the States VOIR GRAMMAIRE A12

étau, -aux [eto] NM **1** *Tech* vice, *Am* vise; **é. d'établi** bench vice **2** *Fig (restrictions)* stranglehold; **les kidnappeurs sentaient l'é. se resserrer autour d'eux** the kidnappers could feel the net closing around them; **je suis prise là-dedans comme dans un é.** I can't get out of it, they've/he's/*etc* got me in a stranglehold

étayage [eteja ʒ] NM *Constr etc* shoring, propping (up)

étayer [eteje] (**j'étaie, j'étaye; j'étaierai, j'étayerai**) VT **1** *Constr etc (mur etc)* to prop (up), to shore (up) **2** *Fig (argumentation)* to buttress; *(déclaration, théorie etc)* to support, to back up; **pour é. ses allégations** in support of his/her allegations
   VPR **s'étayer s'é. sur** *(d'une théorie, de la défense etc)* to be based *or* founded on

etc [ɛtsetera] ADV etc

et c(a)etera [ɛtsetera] ADV etcetera

été¹ [ete] NM VOIR GRAMMAIRE A7 summer; **é. comme hiver il se rend à son travail à vélo** he cycles to work winter and summer alike; **en é.** in (the) summer *or* summertime; **pendant l'é.** 2004 in the summer of 2004; **l'é. prochain** next summer; **un jour d'é.** a summer('s) day; **heure d'é.** summer time, *Am* daylight (saving) time; **temps/vêtements d'é.** summer weather/clothes
   ▸▸ **é. indien** Indian summer; **é. de la Saint-Martin** Indian summer

été² *voir* **être²**

éteignoir [etɛɲwar] NM (candle) snuffer; **en é.** conical

éteindre [etɛ̃dr] (*conj like* **teindre**) VT **1** *(incendie, bougie, cigarette etc)* to extinguish, to put out; *(gaz)* to turn off; *(lumière, radio, radiateur etc)* to switch off, to turn off; *Fam (pièce)* to switch off (the lights) in **2** *Tech (chaux)* to slake, to slack; *(fer chauffé au rouge etc)* to quench **3** *Fig (mettre fin à) (dette)* to pay off; *(querelle)* to put an end to; **é. le feu de l'ennemi** to silence the enemy's guns **4** *Fig (affaiblir) (couleur)* to fade, to soften; **les couleurs ont été éteintes par le temps** the colours have faded with time; **le temps éteint les passions** passions fade with time
   VPR **s'éteindre 1** *(d'un incendie, d'une cigarette, d'une lampe etc)* to go out **2** *Fig (s'affaiblir) (d'une couleur, une passion)* to fade; *(d'un son, de rires)* to die away, to subside; *(d'une voix)* to die away; **le jour s'éteint** daylight is failing *or* fading **3** *Fig (disparaître) (d'une personne)* to pass away, to die; *(d'une race, famille)* to become extinct, to die out
   VI **1** to switch off (the lights) (**dans** in) **2** laisser **é. le feu** to let the fire go out

éteint [etɛ̃] ADJ **1** être é. *(d'un incendie, d'une cigarette, d'une lampe etc)* to be out; *(de l'électricité, d'une radio etc)* to be off; *Aut* rouler tous feux éteints to drive without (any) lights **2** *(race, famille, volcan)* extinct **3** *Fig (couleur)* dull; *(yeux)* dull, lacklustre, *Am* lackluster; *(voix)* faint, lifeless; **depuis qu'elle l'a quitté, il a l'air tout é.** all the life

seems to have gone out of him *or* all of the stuffing seems to have been knocked out of him since she left him; **je l'ai trouvée éteinte hier soir** I found her rather subdued last night

étendard [etɑ̃dar] NM **1** *Mil (drapeau)* standard **2** *Fig (symbole)* banner; **lever l'é. de la révolte** to raise the standard of revolt; **se ranger sous l'é. de qn** to join sb's camp

étendoir [etɑ̃dwar] NM **1** *(cordes)* clotheslines **2** *(cour)* drying yard; *(salle)* drying room

étendre [etɑ̃dr] VT **1** *(déployer) (carte, nappe etc)* to spread (out); *(linge)* to hang up; *(beurre, onguent, fumier etc)* to spread; *(peinture)* to apply (**sur** to), to spread (**sur** on, over); **é. qn** to stretch sb out; **é. le bras** to stretch out *or* reach out (one's arm); **é. les bras** to open one's arms wide, to spread out one's arms; **é. ses ailes** to spread its wings; **é. qn (par terre) d'un coup de poing** to knock sb down *or* Fam flat, Fam to deck sb; *Boxe etc* **se faire é.** to go down, Fam to get decked; Fam **se faire é. à un examen** to fail an exam
   2 *(développer) (influence, pouvoir, connaissances etc)* to extend, to widen, to expand; *(limites, propriété)* to extend; **é. une peau** to stretch a skin; **é. la pâte** to roll out the dough; **é. les termes d'une loi** to widen *or* broaden the terms of a law; **é. sa connaissance des langues étrangères au chinois** to expand *or* extend one's knowledge of foreign languages to include Chinese
   3 *(diluer) (vin, lait etc)* to dilute; **é. d'eau une boisson** to water down a drink
   4 *Ordinat (mémoire)* to upgrade
   VPR **s'étendre 1** *(s'allonger)* to lie down, to stretch out; Fig **s'é. sur un sujet** to dwell on a subject; Fig **il ne s'est pas étendu sur les raisons de son absence** he didn't enlarge *or* expand on the reasons for his/her absence
   2 *(aller)* to stretch, to extend; **la ligne s'étend depuis Ivry jusqu'à Charenton** the line stretches *or* extends *or* runs from Ivry to Charenton; **aussi loin que le regard peut s'é.** as far as the eye can see; **notre parc s'étend sur plusieurs hectares** our grounds spread over several acres
   3 *(se développer) (d'un incendie, d'une épidémie, d'une grève etc)* to spread; *(d'une fortune, d'une affaire, d'un empire etc)* to expand, to grow larger; *(d'un pouvoir)* to widen, to increase; *(d'une influence)* to spread, to widen, to increase; *(des connaissances, du vocabulaire)* to widen, to broaden

étendu, -ue [etɑ̃dy] ADJ **1** *(plaine, forêt)*, Fig *(connaissances, vocabulaire)* wide, extensive; Fig *(influence)* far-reaching, widespread **2** *(bras, jambes)* outstretched; **é. sur un divan** stretched out *or* lying on a couch *(dilué)* diluted (**de** with)
   NF **étendue** *(d'un champ, d'une région etc)* area, extent; *(d'une calamité, grève, épidémie)* scale, extent; *(d'eau, de sable etc)* expanse, stretch; *(de terre etc)* expanse, tract; *(d'une voix, d'un instrument)* range, compass; *(des connaissances, du vocabulaire, du pouvoir de qn etc)* extent, scope; **sur une grande étendue** over a wide area; **sur toute l'étendue du champ** over the entire field; **te rends-tu compte de l'étendue de ton erreur?** do you realize the extent *or* the magnitude of your error?

éternel, -elle [etɛrnɛl] ADJ **1** *(être, Dieu etc)* eternal; **le père é.** the everlasting Father **2** *(vie, joie etc)* eternal, everlasting; **neiges éternelles** eternal snow **3** Fig *(regrets)* eternal, endless; *(amour)* eternal, undying; *(discussion, conversations, bavardages)* endless, never-ending; **vous aurez droit à ma reconnaissance éternelle** I shall be eternally grateful to you; **un é. causeur** an inve-

terate chatterer; **tu es un é. mécontent** you're never satisfied; **fumant son éternelle cigarette** smoking the inevitable cigarette
   NM **1 l'É.** *(Dieu)* the Eternal; *Hum* **c'est un grand fumeur/grand paresseux devant l'É.** he's an incurable smoker/incurably lazy **2 l'é. féminin** the archetypal female

éternellement [etɛrnɛlmɑ̃] ADV **1** *(durer, attendre, rester etc)* for ever; **é. reconnaissant** eternally grateful **2** *(continuellement)* constantly, for ever; **il est é. mécontent** he's never satisfied; **elle a é. raison** she's always right; **il est é. en retard** he's constantly *or* always late

éterniser [etɛrnize] VT **1** *Litt* **é. le nom/la mémoire de qn** to immortalize sb's name/memory; **si nous pouvions é. cette heure** if only we could make this hour last for ever **2** *(prolonger) (discussion, crise, procès etc)* to drag out (for ever)
   VPR **s'éterniser** *(d'une discussion, d'une crise, d'un procès etc)* to drag on (for ever); **j'ai horreur que les adieux s'éternisent** I hate long drawn-out goodbyes; **s'é. chez qn** to outstay one's welcome

éternité [etɛrnite] NF eternity; **de toute é.** from time immemorial; **il y a une é. ou des éternités que je ne vous ai vu** it's ages since I saw you, I haven't seen you for ages; **j'aimerais autant que notre visite ne dure pas une é.** I really don't want to stay longer than necessary; **j'ai attendu pendant une é.** I waited an eternity, I waited for ages

éternuement [etɛrnymɑ̃] NM sneeze

éternuer [etɛrnɥe] VI to sneeze

êtes [ɛt] *voir* **être²**

étêtage [etɛtaʒ], **étêtement** [etɛtmɑ̃] NM *(d'un arbre)* pollarding, topping

étêter [etɛte] VT *(poisson, clou etc)* to remove the head from; *(arbre)* to pollard, to top

éthane [etan] NM *Chimie* ethane

éthanol [etanɔl] NM ethanol

éther [etɛr] NM ether; *Litt (air, ciel)* ether

éthéré [etere] ADJ ethereal

Ethernet® [etɛrnɛt] NM *Ordinat* Ethernet®

éthéromane [eterɔman] N ether addict

Éthiopie [etjɔpi] NF Ethiopia

éthiopien, -ienne [etjɔpjɛ̃, -jɛn] ADJ Ethiopian
   N **É.** Ethiopian

éthique [etik] ADJ **1** *(problème etc)* ethical **2** *Gram* **datif é.** ethical dative
   NF *(science, règles de conduite)* ethics; **l'é. puritaine** the Puritan ethic

ethnie [ɛtni] NF ethnic group

ethnique [ɛtnik] ADJ *(groupe etc)* ethnic

ethnocentrisme [ɛtnosɑ̃trism] NM ethnocentrism

ethnographe [ɛtnɔgraf] N ethnographer

ethnographie [ɛtnɔgrafi] NF ethnography

ethnographique [ɛtnɔgrafik] ADJ ethnographic(al)

ethnolinguistique [ɛtnolɛ̃gɥistik] NF ethnolinguistics

ethnologie [ɛtnɔlɔʒi] NF ethnology

ethnologique [ɛtnɔlɔʒik] ADJ ethnological

ethnologue [ɛtnɔlɔg] N ethnologist

éthologie [etɔlɔʒi] NF ethology

éthologique [etɔlɔʒik] ADJ ethological

éthologiste [etɔlɔʒist] N ethologist

éthyle [etil] NM *Chimie* ethyl

éthylène [etilɛn] NM *Chimie* ethylene

éthylène-glycol NM INV ethylene glycol

éthylique [etilik] ADJ *Chimie* ethylic; **alcool é.** ethyl alcohol
   N *Méd* alcoholic

éthylisme [etilism] NM *Méd* alcoholism

éthylomètre [etilɔmɛtr], **éthylotest** [etilo-test] NM Breathalyzer®

étiage [etjaʒ] NM (baisse d'eaux) low water; (niveau le plus bas) lowest water level; **échelle d'é.** water gauge

étincelage [etɛ̃slaʒ] NM 1 Tech **soudure par é.** flash welding 2 Méd electrotherapy

étincelant [etɛ̃slɑ̃] ADJ (diamant, métal, lac etc) sparkling, glittering; (étoile) twinkling, glittering; (yeux), Fig (esprit, conversation, livre etc) sparkling; **un diamant plus é. que celui-là** a diamond that sparkles more than that one; **le lac était é. sous le soleil** the lake sparkled in the sunlight; **elle avait les yeux étincelants de colère/de convoitise/de joie** her eyes glinted or flashed with anger/gleamed with envy/sparkled with joy

étinceler [etɛ̃sle] VI (**il étincelle; il étincelait; il étincellera**) (d'un diamant, métal, lac etc) to sparkle, to glitter; (d'une étoile) to twinkle, to glitter; (des yeux), Fig (de l'esprit, la conversation, un livre etc) to sparkle; **ses yeux étincelaient de joie/de colère/de convoitise** his eyes sparkled with joy/glinted or flashed with anger/gleamed with envy; **é. de propreté** to be sparkling clean

étincelle [etɛ̃sɛl] NF 1 (du feu, d'allumage etc) spark; **lancer des étincelles** to throw out sparks; (d'un diamant, des yeux) to sparkle, to flash; Fig **elle a fait des étincelles à ses derniers examens** she was brilliant or she shone in her last exams; Fig Fam **ça va faire des étincelles, il va y avoir des étincelles** sparks will fly 2 Fig (de vie, génie) spark; (de bon sens) spark, glimmer; **il a eu une é. de génie** he had a stroke of genius, he had a brilliant idea; **une é. de courage** a fleeting moment of courage

étincellement [etɛ̃sɛlmɑ̃] NM (d'un diamant, métal, lac etc) sparkle, glitter; (d'une étoile) twinkle, glitter; (des yeux) sparkle

étiolement [etjɔlmɑ̃] NM 1 (d'une plante) legginess, straggliness; Agr (intentionnel) blanching; **pour empêcher l'é. de vos plantes** to stop your plants going leggy or straggly 2 Méd etiolation 3 Fig (de l'esprit, la mémoire etc) deterioration

étioler [etjɔle] VT 1 (plante) to make leggy; Agr (intentionnellement) to blanch; **une plante étiolée** a leggy or straggly plant 2 **é. qn** (d'un manque d'air) to weaken sb, to make sb sickly; (de la maladie) to leave sb in a weakened condition or sickly; **une intelligence étiolée** an intellect in decline

▶ VPR **s'étioler 1** (d'une plante) to go leggy 2 (d'une personne) to grow sickly, to go into a decline 3 (de l'esprit, de la mémoire etc) to deteriorate

étiologie [etjɔlɔʒi] NF Méd (étude, causes) aetiology, Am etiology

étique [etik] ADJ emaciated

étiquetage [etiktaʒ] NM (de bagages, colis etc) labelling; (de marchandises) labelling, ticketing; **é. de l'apport nutritionnel** nutritional labelling; **é. de la composition** ingredient labelling; **é. des pourcentages** (des principaux ingrédients) percentage labelling; **é. du prix** price marking

étiqueter [etikte] VT (**j'étiquète; j'étiquèterai**) 1 (bagage, colis etc) to label; (marchandises) to label, to ticket 2 Fig (personne) to label (**comme** as)

étiqueteur, -euse [etiktœr, -øz] N (personne) labeller

NF **étiqueteuse** (machine) labelling machine, labeller

étiquette [etikɛt] NF 1 (d'une valise, d'un colis etc) label; (indiquant le prix) (price) label, ticket; **coller une é. sur un paquet** to label a parcel, to stick a label on a parcel 2 Fig (désignation) (d'une personne) label; **coller une é.**

à qn to stick a label on sb, to label sb; **é. politique** political affiliation; **quelle est son é. politique?** what are his/her politics? 3 (protocole) etiquette; **l'é. de la cour** Court etiquette or ceremonial

▶ ▶ **é. d'adresse** address label; **é. autocollante** self-adhesive or sticky label; Com **é. de calibrage** (d'un produit) grade label; Com **é. descriptive** descriptive label; **é. 'fabriqué en'** 'made-in' label; **é. gommée** sticky label; **é. d'identification** (d'un produit) identification label; Com **é. magnétique** security tag; Com **é. porte-prix** price label; Com **é. promotionnelle** promotional label

étirable [etirabl] ADJ **film é.** cling film

étirage [etiraʒ] NM (d'un métal, du verre etc) drawing (out); **é. à chaud/froid** hot/cold drawing; **é. du fil** wire drawing

étirement [etirmɑ̃] NM (des membres, du corps) stretching; **faire des étirements** to do stretching exercises

étirer [etire] VT (métal, verre etc) to draw (out); (fil, textiles) to draw

▶ VPR **s'étirer 1** (se détendre) (d'une personne) to stretch 2 (s'allonger) (d'un tissu, vêtement) to stretch 3 (se prolonger) (d'une journée, d'une réunion etc) to drag on (for ever)

étoffe [etɔf] NF 1 Tex material, fabric; **étoffes de soie** silk fabrics 2 Fig **avoir l'é. d'un chef d'état/d'un écrivain/d'un héros** to have the makings of a statesman/writer/hero; **elle a de l'é.** she's got character, there's a lot to her; **manquer d'é.** (d'un film, un roman) to lack substance, to be thin or insubstantial

étoffé [etɔfe] ADJ (voix) rich, full; **homme é.** stout or thickset man; **discours é.** pithy speech

étoffer [etɔfe] VT Fig (discours, livre, personnage) to flesh out; (effectifs, équipe) to beef up

▶ VPR **s'étoffer** (d'une personne) to fill out

étoile [etwal] NF 1 Astron star; **à la clarté des étoiles** in the starlight; **un ciel sans étoiles** a starless sky; **un ciel (par)semé d'étoiles** a starry or star-studded sky; **coucher** ou **dormir à la belle é.** to sleep in the open or out of doors; **né sous une bonne/mauvaise é.** born under a lucky/an unlucky star; **croire** ou **avoir foi en son é.** to believe in or trust to luck; Fam **voir des étoiles (en plein midi)** to see stars

2 (ornement, objet etc) star; Typ asterisk, star; **é. à cinq branches** five-pointed star; **les graviers ont fait des étoiles sur le pare-brise** the gravel starred the windscreen; **hôtel cinq étoiles** five-star hotel; **c'est un deux étoiles** it has a two-star rating

3 Aut roundabout, Am traffic circle

4 Cin, Théâtre (vedette) star; **une grande é. de la chanson** a big singing star; **é. montante** rising star

5 Ordinat **connecté en é.** in a star configuration

▶ ▶ Astron **é. du berger** evening star; **é. de David** Star of David; Astron **é. filante** shooting star; Zool **é. de mer** starfish; Astron **é. polaire** Pole Star; Astron **é. triple** triple star

étoilé [etwale] ADJ 1 (ciel) starry, star-studded; (nuit) starry, starlit 2 (fêlé) (pare-brise) starred

étoiler [etwale] VT 1 (parsemer d'étoiles) to stud with stars; Fig (parsemer) to stud (**de** with); **la nuit étoile le ciel** the night sky is studded with stars 2 (pare-brise, verre etc) to star, to make a star-shaped crack in

▶ VPR **s'étoiler** (du ciel) to fill with stars

étole [etɔl] NF (fourrure), Rel stole

étonnamment [etɔnamɑ̃] ADV astonishingly, amazingly, surprisingly

étonnant [etɔnɑ̃] ADJ astonishing, amazing; **rien d'é. à cela** that's not surprising,

no wonder; **ce n'est pas é. qu'il soit malade** it's not surprising or it's no wonder that he's ill; **comme c'est é., il m'avait dit le contraire** how strange or odd, he had told me the opposite; **c'est é. mais personne n'a été blessé** it's amazing or astonishing that no one was hurt; **chose étonnante, il est arrivé** astonishingly or amazingly or surprisingly (enough), he arrived; **vous êtes é.!** you amaze me sometimes!

NM **l'é. est qu'il soit venu** the astonishing or amazing or surprising thing is that he came

étonné [etɔne] ADJ surprised; (plus fort) astonished, amazed (**de qch** at sth; **de voir** to see); **un regard é.** a surprised look; (plus fort) a look of astonishment or amazement, an astonished look; **je suis très é. qu'on ne m'ait rien dit** I'm amazed or astonished or extremely surprised that nobody said anything to me

étonnement [etɔnmɑ̃] NM astonishment, amazement, surprise; **frappé** ou **saisi d'é.** taken aback; **à mon grand é.** to my great surprise, much to my surprise, to my amazement; **imaginez (quel a été) mon é. quand …** imagine my surprise or astonishment when …; **faire l'é. de tout le monde** to astonish or surprise everybody

étonner [etɔne] VT to astonish, to amaze, to surprise; **cela ne m'étonnerait pas** it wouldn't surprise me, I wouldn't be the least bit surprised; **ça ne m'étonne pas du tout** it doesn't surprise me in the least, I'm not the least bit surprised; **ce qui m'étonne, c'est qu'il a menti** what surprises or astonishes me is that he lied; **cela m'étonne qu'elle soit venue** I'm surprised or astonished or amazed that she came; **il n'est pas venu? ça m'étonne** ou **voilà qui m'étonne** he didn't come? that's surprising; Fam **alors ça, ça m'étonnerait** that'll be the day; **ça m'étonne de toi, tu m'étonnes** I'm surprised at you; Fam **tu m'étonnes!** you don't say!, tell me something I don't know!; **tu m'étonneras toujours!** you never cease to astonish me!

▶ VPR **s'étonner** to be astonished, to be surprised, to wonder (**de** at); **je m'étonne de vous voir** I'm astonished or surprised to see you; **je m'étonne qu'il ne voie pas le danger** it amazes me or I am astonished that he does not see the danger; **comment s'é. qu'il ait refusé?** can you wonder or is it any wonder that he refused?; **je ne m'étonne plus de rien** nothing surprises me any more; **essaie, tu pourrais t'é. toi-même** try, you might surprise yourself

étouffant [etufɑ̃] ADJ (air, chaleur), Fig (atmosphère) stifling, suffocating; (temps) oppressive, sultry; **une journée étouffante** a stifling hot day

étouffe-chrétien [etufkretjɛ̃] NM INV Fam **sa tarte est un é., c'est de l'é., sa tarte** his/her tart is pure stodge; **c'est un peu é.** it's a bit stodgy

étouffée [etufe] NF Culin **cuire à l'é.** to braise

étouffement [etufmɑ̃] NM 1 (asphyxie) suffocation; **sensation d'é.** feeling of breathlessness, stifling feeling; **la victime a été tuée par é.** the victim was suffocated (to death); **mourir d'é.** to die of or from suffocation 2 Fig (d'un scandale) hushing up; (de rumeurs, d'un complot, d'une révolte) suppression

étouffer [etufe] VT 1 (personne) (avec un oreiller etc) to suffocate, to smother; (en serrant) to suffocate, to choke; (de plantes) to choke; **la chaleur m'étouffe** the heat is stifling (me); Iron **ce ne sont pas les scrupules qui l'étouffent** he's/she's not overscrupulous; **ça t'étoufferait de dire merci?** would it choke you to say thank you?; **ça t'étouffe-**

rait d'être poli? it wouldn't kill you to be polite!

2 *Fig (cri, passion, créativité)* to stifle; *(bâillement, rire)* to stifle, to smother, to suppress; *(feu)* to smother; *(révolte)* to quell, to suppress; *(scandale, affaire)* to hush up; *(son)* to muffle; *Mus* to damp; *Élec (étincelle)* to quench; **é. un sanglot** to stifle a sob, to choke back a sob; **é. un scandale dans l'œuf** to nip a scandal in the bud

VI to suffocate; **é. de rire/colère** to choke with laughter/anger; *Fig* **dans cette ville, j'étouffais** I was suffocating in that town; **on étouffe ici** it's stifling here

VPR s'étouffer to suffocate; *(en mangeant)* to choke; **je me suis étouffé avec une bouchée de pain** I choked on a piece of bread; **plantes qui s'étouffent** plants that choke one another

étouffoir [etufwar] NM *(d'un piano)* damper

étourderie [eturdəri] NF **1** *(caractère)* carelessness, thoughtlessness, *Fam* scattiness; **faute d'é.** careless mistake; **par é.** inadvertently, in an unthinking moment; **il est d'une é. incroyable** he is incredibly scatterbrained *or Fam* scatty **2** *(action)* foolish mistake

étourdi, -ie [eturdi] ADJ *(irréfléchi)* thoughtless, careless; *(écervelé) (personne)* scatterbrained, featherbrained, *Fam* scatty

N *(écervelé)* scatterbrain, featherbrain

NF *Arch* **à l'étourdie** thoughtlessly, heedlessly

étourdiment [eturdimã] ADV without thinking

étourdir [eturdir] VT *(personne) (d'un coup, choc etc)* to stun, to daze; *Fig (d'un vin, d'éloges etc)* to make dizzy *or* giddy; *Fig* **je suis tout étourdie** my head's spinning

VPR s'étourdir to let one's hair down, to live it up; **s'é. dans la boisson** to drown one's sorrows (in drink)

étourdissant [eturdisã] ADJ **1** *(bruit)* deafening, ear-splitting **2** *(nouvelles, succès etc)* staggering, stunning, astounding; **e. de beauté** astoundingly *or* staggeringly *or* stunningly beautiful, stunning; **e. de bêtise** astoundingly *or* staggeringly stupid

étourdissement [eturdismã] NM **1** *(vertige)* giddiness, dizziness; **avoir un é.** to feel giddy *or* dizzy; **cela me donne des étourdissements** it makes me feel giddy *or* dizzy, it makes my head spin *or* swim **2** *Litt (griserie)* (feeling of) euphoria

étourneau, -eaux [eturno] NM **1** *(oiseau)* starling **2** *Fam (personne)* scatterbrain

étrange [etrãʒ] ADJ strange, peculiar, odd; **chose é., il est revenu** strange to say *or* strangely enough *or* oddly enough, he came back

étrangement [etrãʒmã] ADV strangely, oddly, peculiarly; **cela ressemble é. à la rougeole** it looks suspiciously like measles

étranger, -ère [etrãʒe, -ɛr] ADJ **1** *(d'un autre pays)* foreign **2** *(inconnu)* strange, unfamiliar (à to); **sa voix ne m'est pas étrangère** his voice is not unfamiliar; **la haine lui est étrangère** he doesn't know what hatred is; **la musique lui est étrangère** he has no knowledge of music, *Fam* music is a closed book to him **3** *(extérieur)* foreign (à to); *Méd, Fig* **corps é.** foreign body; **entrée interdite à toute personne étrangère** no entry to unauthorized personnel; **des éléments étrangers se sont introduits dans l'enceinte de l'école** outsiders entered the school premises; **elle est étrangère à cette firme/au projet** she isn't a member of this firm/involved in the plan; **il est é. à tout ce qui s'est passé ici** he doesn't have anything to do with what happened here

N **1** *(d'un autre pays)* foreigner; *Admin* alien **2** *(d'un autre groupe)* stranger, outsider; **ce**

club est fermé aux étrangers the club is for members only; **je suis un é. ici** I'm a stranger here, *Fam* I'm a foreigner in these parts

NM **l'é.** *(pays étrangers)* foreign countries *or* parts; **aller/vivre à l'é.** to go/live abroad; **correspondant à l'é.** foreign correspondent; **voyages à l'é.** foreign travel; **investissement à l'é.** foreign *or* outward investment

---

Attention: ne pas confondre **foreigner** et **stranger** lorsqu'on traduit le nom **étranger**. **Foreigner** s'applique uniquement à quelqu'un venant d'un autre pays, alors que **stranger** désigne quelqu'un d'extérieur à un groupe donné.

étrangeté [etrãʒte] NF *(d'une conduite, d'une robe etc)* strangeness, oddness, peculiarity

étranglé [etrãgle] ADJ *(passage, vallée etc)* narrow; *(taille)* nipped-in; *(voix)* strangled, choked, choking; *Méd (hernie)* strangulated

étranglement [etrãgləmã] NM **1** *(d'une personne)* strangling, strangulation; *(en lutte)* stranglehold; *Fig (de la liberté, la presse)* stifling; **il est mort par é.** he died of strangulation, he was strangled; **ce n'est pas l'é. qui a provoqué la mort** strangulation was not the cause of death **2** *(action de resserrer) (de la taille)* narrowing; *(d'un tube etc)* constriction, narrowing; *Aut, Tech* throttling; **soupape d'é.** throttle valve; *Méd* **é. herniaire** strangulated hernia **3** *(partie resserrée) (d'une rivière)* narrow part, narrows; *(d'une route)* bottleneck; **la route présente un é.** the road bottlenecks *or* forms a bottleneck

étrangler [etrãgle] VT **1** *(personne)* to strangle, to throttle; *Fig (liberté, la presse)* to stifle; **sa cravate l'étrangle** his tie is choking *or* strangling him; **la colère l'étrangle** he/she is choking with rage; *Fig* **les impôts m'étranglent** taxes are killing me **2** *(resserrer) (taille, tube etc)* to constrict; *Tech (vapeur etc)* to throttle; *Méd (vaisseau sanguin)* to strangulate; *Aut* **é. le moteur** to throttle (down) the engine

VPR s'étrangler 1 *(en mangeant)* to choke (**avec** on); **s'é. (de colère/d'indignation/de rire)** to choke (with anger/indignation/laughter) **2** *(de voix)* to choke; *(de paroles)* to stick in one's throat; **j'entendis un sanglot s'é.** I heard a choked sob; **mais les mots se sont étranglés** but the words died on his lips, but he couldn't get the words out **3** *(se resserrer) (d'une rivière)* to narrow; *(d'une rue)* to narrow, to (form a) bottleneck

étrangleur, -euse [etrãglœr, -øz] N *(personne)* strangler

NM *Aut, Tech* throttle

étrave [etrav] NF *Naut* stem; **de l'é. à l'étambot** from stem to stern; **lame d'é.** bow wave

être¹ [etr] NM **1** *Phil (existence)* being; **l'ê. et le néant** being and nothingness

2 *(âme)* being; **tout mon ê. se révolte à cette idée** my entire being rebels at the idea; **du fond de son ê.** from the depths of his/her being

3 *(personne)* being; *Biol, Litt* being, creature; **je ne veux partager ce secret qu'avec un ê. cher** I want to share this secret only with someone close to me; **elle pensait aux êtres chers qui étaient si loin** she thought of her loved ones so far away; **l'ê. aimé** the beloved; **pauvres petits êtres!** poor little things!; **c'est un ê. hors du commun** he/she is someone out of the ordinary *or* is no common mortal; **c'est un ê. méprisable** he's a despicable creature; **un ê. supérieur** a higher *or* superior being; **nul ê. au monde ne t'a aimé plus que moi** no one in the world loved you more than I; **ê. fantastique/mythique/surnaturel** fantastic/mythical/supernatural creature; *Litt* **un ê. de feu/lumière/ténèbres** a creature of fire/light/darkness

▸▸ **ê. humain** human being; **l'Ê. suprême** the Supreme Being; **ê. vivant** living creature; **on n'a trouvé aucun ê. vivant sur cette planète** we found no living creature on the planet

ÊTRE²

to be **1–8, 10, 11**	▪ impersonal verb **9**
▪ to belong to **12**	▪ auxiliary verb **13, 14**
▪ passive form **15**	▪ to go **16**

VI *(prp* étant; *pp* été; *pr ind* je suis, tu es, il est, n. sommes, v. êtes, ils sont; *pr sub* je sois, tu sois, il soit, n. soyons, v. soyez, ils soient; *imp* sois, soyons, soyez; *impf* j'étais; *p hist* je fus, tu fus, il fut, n. fûmes, v. fûtes, ils furent; *p sub* je fusse; *fu* je serai) **1** *(exister)* to be; **je pense, donc je suis** I think, therefore I am; *Rel* **je suis celui qui est** I am that I am; **le temps n'est plus où ...** the days are gone when ...; **l'ancien projet n'est plus** the old plan is a thing of the past; *Fml* **elle n'est plus** she is no longer with us; **quand on pense que tout cela aurait pu ne pas ê.** to think that all that may never have happened; **si cela était** if that were the case; **(et) quand cela serait** even if it were the case; **cela étant** that being so *or* the case; **la plus belle voiture qui soit** the finest car there is; **eh bien, soit!** very well then!; **ainsi soit-il** so be it, amen; *Rel* amen; **maudit soit-il!** damn him to hell!; *Prov* **on ne peut pas ê. et avoir été** you can't stay young for ever; **nous sommes le dix** it's the tenth (today); **la vérité est entre ces extrêmes** the truth lies between these extremes

2 *(copule)* to be; **c'est ma mère** this is my mother; *(au téléphone)* it's my mother; **c'est le chef de gare** he's the stationmaster; **c'est un ou il est chef de gare** he's a stationmaster; **soit AB la base d'un triangle** let AB be the base of a triangle; **soit un triangle ABC** given a triangle ABC; **l'homme est mortel** man is mortal; **nous étions deux/plusieurs** there were two/several of us; **vous êtes tout pour moi** you mean everything to me; **c'est quelqu'un!** he/she's somebody!; *Fam* **est-il drôle!** he's *so* funny!

3 *(+ adv)* to be; **vous êtes ici chez vous** treat this place like your own; **elle est très mal/beaucoup mieux** she is very ill/much better; **ê. bien avec qn** to be on good terms with sb **4** *(locutions avec 'à' + nom)* **ê. au travail/à son bureau** to be at work/at one's desk; **ê. à l'agonie** to be dying; **vous n'êtes pas à ce que je dis** you're not paying attention to what I'm saying; **il est tout à son travail** he is entirely engrossed in his work; **il est à Paris** he is in Paris; **le temps est au beau** the weather's set fair; **le temps est à l'orage** there's a storm brewing; **les prix sont à la baisse** prices are on the decrease, prices are coming down

5 *(locutions avec 'de' + nom)* **ce tableau est de Gauguin** this picture is by Gauguin; **il est de Londres** he is from London; **il était de la CIA** he was a member of the CIA; **il n'est pas des nôtres** he isn't one of us, he isn't with us; **serez-vous des nôtres, ce soir?** will you be joining us this evening?; **il est de mes amis** he's a friend of mine, he's one of my friends; **ê. de service** to be on duty; **ils sont de la même promotion** they're in the same year *or Am* class; **cet enfant est d'un caractère étrange** this child has a strange character *or* nature; **l'enfant est-il de lui?** is the child his?; **c'était d'un simple!** it was so simple!; **je suis de noce samedi prochain** I've got a wedding next Saturday

6 *(+ à + inf)* **j'étais là à l'attendre** I was there waiting for him; **la maison est à louer** the house is to let; **elle est tout le temps à se plaindre** she's always *or* forever complaining; **elles étaient encore à médire** they were running people down again; **c'était à pré-**

voir it was to be expected; **c'est à craindre** I fear so

7 (+ à + inf avec idée d'obligation) **cette idée est à creuser** this idea will have to be thoroughly looked into; **c'est à prendre ou à laisser** take it or leave it; **lui seul est à blâmer** he alone is to blame

8 (avec 'ce') **je sais ce qui est arrivé** I know what happened; **savez-vous ce que c'est?** do you know what it is?; **est-ce vrai?** is it true?; **serait-ce vrai?** can it be or could it (possibly) be true?; **ce n'est pas qu'il soit ingrat, mais …** it's not that he's ungrateful, but …; **ne fût-ce que, ne serait-ce que** if only; **vous venez, n'est-ce pas?** you're coming, aren't you?; **vous ne venez pas, n'est-ce pas?** you're not coming, are you?; **n'est-ce pas qu'il a de la chance?** isn't he lucky?; Litt **je le ferais (si ce) n'était que je dois partir** I would do it if I didn't have to leave; **n'était mon rhumatisme** if it weren't or wasn't for my rheumatism; **il l'aurait bien épousée, n'eût été qu'il la trouvait trop orgueilleuse** he would gladly have married her, were it not for the fact that he found her too proud SEE GRAMMAR B64

9 (impers) **il est midi** it is twelve o'clock; **il est temps de partir** it is time to go; **il est de mon devoir de rester** it is my duty to stay; Litt **il n'est que de comparer les deux pour se rendre compte de leur différence** one need only compare the two to become aware of the difference between them; **il n'est point d'amours sans larmes** there is no love without tears; **comme si de rien n'était** as if nothing had happened; **soit dit sans offense** if you don't mind my saying so; **il était une fois une fée** once upon a time there was a fairy; **un héros, s'il en fut (jamais)** a hero, if ever there was one; **il est à craindre/prévoir que …** it's feared/expected that …; **il est à croire/espérer que …** it's to be believed/hoped that …; **il fut un temps où …** there was a time when …; **il m'est très douloureux de vous annoncer …** it is with great sorrow that I inform you …; **il m'est impossible de vous répondre** it's impossible for me to give you an answer; **il est probable qu'ils sont déjà mariés** they're probably already married SEE GRAMMAR B29

10 (avec 'en' indéterminé) **où en sommes-nous?** how far have we got?, where are we?; **où en êtes-vous de vos travaux?** how far have you got with your work?; **l'affaire en est là** that is how things stand; **j'en étais là de mes suppositions quand …** I'd reached that point or I'd got that far in my assumptions when …; **si vous m'aviez écouté, on n'en serait pas là** if you had listened to me, we wouldn't be where we are now; **vous n'en êtes pas encore là!** you haven't come to that (point or stage) yet!; **il n'en est pas à son coup d'essai** this is not his first attempt; **je ne sais plus où j'en suis** I don't know where I am or what I'm doing; **j'en suis à me demander si …** I'm beginning to wonder whether …; **nous n'en sommes pas à le renvoyer** we haven't reached the point of sacking him yet; **on n'en est pas à un euro près** we're not going to quibble over a euro; **j'en suis pour mon argent** I've spent my money to no purpose, I've thrown my money away; **j'en suis pour mille euros** I'm a thousand euros the poorer; **c'en est trop!** it's too much!, this is past bearing!; **c'en est assez!** enough!; **il en est de l'homme comme de la nature** it's the same with man as with nature; **puisqu'il en est ainsi** since that's how things are; **il n'en est rien!** nothing of the kind!; **comment pourrait-il en ê. autrement?** how could it be any other way?, how could things be any different?; **il en est** (d'un complot, d'une société secrète etc) he's one of them; (est homosexuel) he's one of them, he's the other way in-

clined; **nous allons faire une partie de golf, vous en êtes?** we're going to have a round of golf, can we count you in? or are you game? or are you up for it?

11 (avec 'y' indéterminé) **il y est pour quelque chose** he's got something to do with it; **j'y suis pour un tiers** I'm in for a third share; **ça y est!** that's it!; **ça y est? tu as fini?** is that it? have you finished?; **vous y êtes?** (vous comprenez?) are you with me?, have you got it?; (vous avez trouvé?) have you got it?

12 (appartenir) **ê. à qn** to belong to sb; **à qui sont ces livres?** whose books are these?, who do these books belong to?; **la victoire est à nous** victory is ours; **je suis à vous dans un moment** I'll be with you in a moment; **sois à moi!** be mine!; **c'est à vous de jouer** it's your turn to play; **c'est à vous de veiller sur l'enfant** it's your job or it's up to you to look after the child

13 (avec aller, rester, tomber etc aux temps composés) **il est déjà arrivé** he has already arrived; **il est arrivé hier** he arrived yesterday; **elle est née en 1974** she was born in 1974 SEE GRAMMAR B27–8; B38–9

14 (avec vpr aux temps composés) **nous nous sommes trompés** we (have) made a mistake; **ils se sont aimés** they loved each other; **elle s'est fait mal** she (has) hurt herself SEE GRAMMAR B38–9

15 (pour indiquer le passif) to be; **il fut puni par son père** he was punished by his father; **il est aimé de tout le monde** he is loved by everyone; **j'entends ê. obéi** I mean to be obeyed SEE GRAMMAR A54–5; B38–9

16 Fam (= aller, aux temps composés et au passé simple) **j'avais été à Paris** I had been to Paris; **j'ai été voir Martin** I've been or I went to see Martin; **vous avez été trop loin** you went too far, you've gone too far; **ça a été** (ça a marché) it went OK

17 (= s'en aller, au passé simple) **il s'en fut ouvrir la porte** he went off to open the door

18 **quand il fut pour partir** just as he was about to leave

étreindre [etrɛ̃dr] vt (prp **étreignant**; pp **étreint**; pr ind **j'étreins, il étreint**, n. **étreignons**; impf **j'étreignais**; p hist **j'étreignis**; fu **j'étreindrai**) (personne) to embrace, to clasp in one's arms; **spectacle qui nous étreint le cœur** sight that wrings one's heart, heart-rending sight; **la peur/la douleur l'étreignait** fear/pain gripped him; **la douleur l'étreignait trop fort** the pain had too strong a grip or hold (on him); Prov **qui trop embrasse mal étreint** = that's what comes of trying to do too much at once

étreinte [etrɛ̃t] NF **1** (entre personnes) embrace; **ils ne pouvaient cesser leurs étreintes** they couldn't stop embracing or hugging **2** (en lutte) lock **3** Fig (pression) grip; **tu ne peux imaginer ce qu'est l'é. de la misère** you cannot imagine what it's like to be in the grip of poverty; **l'é. de la douleur se faisait sentir de plus en plus** the pain was strengthening its grip or hold

étrenne [etrɛn] NF **1** (cadeau) **étrennes** New Year's gift; **les étrennes du facteur/de l'éboueur** ≃ the postman's/dustman's Christmas box **2** (premier usage) **avoir l'é. de qch** to have the first use of sth, to be the first person to use sth, Fam to christen sth; **pour une fois, tu auras l'é. d'un manteau** you'll have a new coat for once

étrenner [etrene] vt (objet) to use for the first time, Fam to christen; (vêtement) to wear for the first time; **c'est moi qui vais é. les nouveaux bureaux** I'll be the first person to use the new offices

vi Arg **tu vas é.!** (être puni) you're going to catch or get it!

êtres [etr] NMPL Arch **connaître les ê. d'une maison** to know one's way about a house

étrette [etrɛt] Can Fam ADJ narrow; (personne) narrow-minded

NF (personne d'esprit étroit) narrow-minded person

étrier [etrije] NM **1** Équitation stirrup; **vider les étriers** to be thrown; Fig to be thrown or disconcerted; Fig **avoir le pied à l'é.** to be on the point of leaving; (être en bonne voie pour réussir) to be off to a good start; Fig **il a eu du mal à mettre le pied à l'é.** he had trouble getting started or getting off the ground; Fig **mettre le pied à l'é. à qn** to give sb a helping hand; **boire** ou **prendre le coup de l'é.** to have one for the road **2** Méd **é. (de soutien)** stirrup, leg rest; **é. (de traction** ou **de réduction)** calliper **3** Anat (de l'oreille) stirrup bone **4** Aut stirrup, shackle; (de frein) caliper

étrille [etrij] NF **1** (brosse) currycomb **2** Zool small edible crab

étriller [etrije] vt **1** (cheval) to curry **2** Fam (réprimander) **é. qn** to give sb a dressing-down or a telling-off **3** Fam (faire payer trop cher) to fleece, to sting

étripage [etripaʒ] NM (d'un poisson, d'un lièvre) gutting; (d'un poulet etc) drawing; Fam (tuerie) bloodbath, slaughter

étriper [etripe] vt (poisson, lièvre) to gut; (poulet etc) to draw; Fig Fam **je vais l'é.** I'll murder or slaughter him, I'll have his guts for garters

VPR **s'étriper** Fam (se battre) to make mincemeat of each other

étriqué [etrike] ADJ **1** (vêtement) skimpy, tight **2** Fig (perspective, vie) narrow; (avenir) limited

étriquer [etrike] vt Couture (vêtement) to make too tight; **cette robe vous étrique** that dress is too tight on you

étriver [etrive] Can vt to irritate, to annoy

vi **faire é.** to drive mad

étrivière [etrivjer] NF stirrup leather

étroit [etrwa] ADJ **1** (peu large) (ruban, sentier, épaules), Fig (esprit, vue) narrow; (espace, pièce etc) narrow, confined, cramped; Fig (idées) hidebound; Fig **la voie étroite** the straight and narrow; Fig **avoir l'esprit é.** to be narrow-minded

2 (serré) (nœud) tight; (manteau etc) tight(-fitting); Fig (amitié, lien etc) close; **je suis en rapport é. avec sa sœur** I am in close contact or touch with his sister; **être en étroite collaboration avec** to work closely or in close co-operation with; **règlements étroits** strict rules; **sous étroite surveillance** under close surveillance; **le sens é. d'un mot** the strict meaning of a word

3 **être à l'é.** (dans son logement etc) to be cramped for room; (financièrement) to be in straitened circumstances

étroitement [etrwatmɑ̃] ADV **1** (nouer, tenir) tightly; Fig (lier, collaborer) closely **2** (observer une règle) strictly; **surveiller qn é.** to watch sb closely, to keep a close watch on sb

étroitesse [etrwatɛs] NF (d'un ruban, d'un sentier, des épaules etc) narrowness; Fig **é. d'esprit** narrow-mindedness; **l'é. de ce bureau** the lack of space in this office

étron [etrɔ̃] NM piece of excrement, Vulg turd

étrusque [etrysk] ADJ Etruscan

N **É.** Etruscan

Ets Com (abrév **établissements**) **E. Legrand** Legrand

étude [etyd] NF **1** Scol, Univ etc (action) (d'un sujet, texte, auteur etc) study, survey; **voyage d'études** educational or study tour; **aimer l'é.** to like studying; **faire des études de français/de droit** to study or Br read French/law; **il a fait ses études à Eton/Oxford** he was educated at Eton/he went to or studied at

Oxford; **payer les études de qn** to pay for sb's education; **faire de brillantes études** to do extremely well at university; **j'ai arrêté mes études à 16 ans** I left school when I was 16; **négliger ses études** to neglect one's studies; **achever ses études** to finish one's studies *or* education; *Péj* **cela sent l'é.** it reeks of effort **2** *Scol (heure)* (private) study period, *Br* prep; **(salle d')é.** (private) study room, *Br* prep room; **je laisse mes enfants à l'é. jusqu'à 5 heures** = I leave the children in homework class until 5 o'clock **3** *(action de considérer) (d'une question, d'un plan etc)* study, investigation, survey; *Constr* survey; **bureau d'études** research department; **ingénieur d'études** design engineer; **voyage d'études** study *or* field trip; **procéder à l'é. d'une question, mettre une question à l'é.** to study *or* investigate *or* go into a question **4** *(texte, musique, peinture etc)* study; *Mus* **é. pour violon** violin study; *Beaux-Arts* **é. de tête** study of a head **5** *(bureau)* office; *(d'un avocat)* office, *Br* chambers; *(charge) (d'un juriste)* practice ▸▸ *Mktg, Com* **é. AIO** AIO research; *Mktg, Com* **é. d'audience** audience research; *Mktg, Com* **é. des besoins** needs study *or* analysis; **é. de cas** case study; **é. client** customer survey; *Mktg, Com* **é. commerciale** marketing study; **études commerciales** *Mktg* marketing research; *(dans école de commerce etc)* business studies; **é. de communication** communications study; **études de communication** media studies; **é. comparative** comparative study; **é. du comportement** behavioural study *or* analysis; *Mktg, Com* **é. du comportement du consommateur** consumer behaviour study; *Mktg, Com* **é. auprès des consommateurs** consumer *or* customer survey; *Mktg, Com* **é. auprès des consommateurs finaux** end-user survey; **é. documentaire** desk research; **é. de faisabilité** feasibility study; **é. du lectorat** readership survey; *Mktg, Com* **é. de marché** market research; *Mktg, Com* **une é. de marché** a market study; **faire une é. de marché** to do market research; **ce cabinet est spécialisé dans les études de marché** the company specializes in market research; *Mktg, Com* **é. de marché standard** omnibus survey; **é. marketing** marketing study; **é. des performances** *(d'un employé)* performance appraisal; **é. préliminaire** preliminary study; *Mktg, Com* **é. de produit** product analysis; **études qualitatives** qualitative research; **études quantitatives** quantitative research; *Mktg, Com* **é. de satisfaction de la clientèle** customer satisfaction survey; **é. sur le terrain** field study; **études sur le terrain** field research; *Mktg, Com* **études sur les ventes** sales research

étudiant, -ante [etydjɑ̃, -ɑ̃t] **N** student; **é. en médecine/en droit/en lettres** medical/law/arts student; **é. de première/seconde année** first/second-year student, *Am* freshman/sophomore
ADJ *(vie, mouvement etc)* student

étudié [etydje] **ADJ 1** *(soigneusement préparé) (effet, discours etc)* carefully prepared; **prix très étudiés** very fair prices **2** *Péj (affecté) (politesse, geste)* affected, studied; *(manières, sourires)* affected

étudier [etydje] *(impf, pr sub* **n. étudiions)** **VT 1** *Scol, Univ etc (sujet, texte, auteur etc)* to study; *Scol (leçon)* to prepare; *Mus, Théâtre (instrument, rôle etc)* to study; **é. une matière en vue d'un examen** to read up a subject for an examination **2** *Péj (son apparence etc)* to study; **elle étudie ses poses** she strikes poses **3** *(considérer) (question, plan, théorie etc)* to study, to examine; **sa demande mérite d'être étudiée** his application merits examination

4 *(observer) (société, personne, visage etc)* to study
VI to study
VPR s'étudier 1 *(se regarder, s'analyser)* to study *or* examine oneself, to take stock of oneself; *Péj (manquer de naturel)* to be affected **2** *(s'observer l'un l'autre)* to study each other, to take stock of each other; **ils se sont longuement étudiés** they took careful stock of each other **3** *Arch* **s'é. à faire qch** to take pains to do sth, to make a point of doing sth; **il s'étudiait à m'éviter** he studiously avoided me

étui [etɥi] **NM** case; **é. (de revolver)** holster; **é. de cartouche** cartridge case; **é. de cassette** cassette case; **é. à lunettes** glasses case; *Naut* **é. de voile** sail cover

étuvage [etyvaʒ] **NM** *Chimie, Ind (séchage)* drying; *(stérilisation)* sterilization

étuve [etyv] **NF 1** *(aux thermes)* steam room; **é. sèche** hot-air steam cabinet; **é. humide** steam *or* vapour bath **2** *Chimie, Ind etc (pour sécher)* drying oven; *(pour stériliser)* sterilizer; **é. à incubation** *ou* **à cultures** incubator **3** *Fam (lieu où il fait trop chaud)* oven

étuvée [etyve] **NF** *Culin* **à l'é.** braised

étuver [etyve] **VT 1** *(sécher) (fruit etc)* to dry; *(stériliser) (vêtements contaminés etc)* to sterilize **2** *Culin* to braise

étymologie [etimɔlɔʒi] **NF** etymology
étymologique [etimɔlɔʒik] **ADJ** etymological
étymologiquement [etimɔlɔʒikmɑ̃] **ADV** etymologically
étymologiste [etimɔlɔʒist] **N** etymologist
étymon [etimɔ̃] **NM** etymon

eu [y] *voir* avoir[1]

eucalyptus [økaliptys] **NM** eucalyptus; **essence d'e.** eucalyptus oil
Eucharistie (l') [løkaristi] **NF** *Rel* the Eucharist
eucharistique [økaristik] **ADJ** *Rel* Eucharistic(al)
Euclide [øklid] **N** Euclid
euclidien, -ienne [øklidjɛ̃, -jɛn] **ADJ** *Math* Euclidean
eugénique [øʒenik] **NF**, **eugénisme** [øʒenism] **NM** eugenics
euh [ø] **INT** er
eunuque [ønyk] **NM** eunuch
euphémique [øfemik] **ADJ** euphemistic
euphémiquement [øfemikmɑ̃] **ADV** euphemistically
euphémisme [øfemism] **NM** euphemism
euphonie [øfɔni] **NF** euphony
euphonique [øfɔnik] **ADJ** euphonious, euphonic
euphorbe [øfɔrb] **NF** *Bot* euphorbia
euphorie [øfɔri] **NF** euphoria
euphorique [øfɔrik] **ADJ** euphoric
euphorisant [øfɔrizɑ̃] **ADJ** *(effet, atmosphère etc)* exhilarating; *Méd (drogue)* antidepressant, *Spéc* euphoriant
NM anti-depressant drug, *Spéc* euphoriant
Euphrate (l') [løfrat] **NM** the Euphrates
eurafricain, -aine [ørafrikɛ̃, -ɛn] **ADJ** Eurafrican
N E. Eurafrican
Eurasie [ørazi] **NF** Eurasia
eurasien, -ienne [ørazjɛ̃, -jɛn] **ADJ** Eurasian
N E. Eurasian
eurêka [øreka] **INT** eureka
eurent [yr] *voir* avoir[1]
Euripide [øripid] **N** Euripides
EURL [øyɛrɛl] **NF** *Com (abrév* **entreprise unipersonnelle à responsabilité limitée)** trader with limited liability

euro [øro] **NM** *(monnaie)* euro
euro- **PRÉF** Euro-
eurobanque [ørobɑ̃k] **NF** Eurobank
eurobudget [ørobydʒe] **NM** Eurobudget
euro-certificat **NM** *Bourse* euro-certificate
eurochèque [ørofɛk] **NM** Eurocheque
eurocommunisme [ørokɔmynism] **NM** Eurocommunism
Eurocorps [ørokɔr] **NM** *Mil* Eurocorps
eurocrate [ørokrat] **N** Eurocrat
eurocrédit [ørokredi] **NM** Euroloan
eurodéputé [ørodepyte] **NM** *Pol* Euro MP
eurodevise [ørodəviz] **NF** *Fin* Eurocurrency
eurodollar [ørodɔlar] **NM** Eurodollar
eurofranc [ørofrɑ̃] **NM** eurofranc
Euroland(e) [ørolɑ̃d] **NF** Euroland
euromarché [øromarfe] **NM** *Fin* Euromarket
euromissile [øromisil] **NM** Euromissile
euromonnaie [øromɔnɛ] **NF** *Fin* Eurocurrency
euro-obligation **NF** *Fin* Eurobond
Europe [ørɔp] **NF** Europe; **l'E. verte** (European) Community agriculture *or* farming; **l'E. des quinze** the European Union *(comprising fifteen member states)*; **l'E. sociale** social Europe *(a united Europe committed to a progressive social and welfare policy)*
européanisation [øropeanizasjɔ̃] **NF** Europeanization
européaniser [øropeanize] **VT** to Europeanize
VPR s'européaniser to become Europeanized
européen, -enne [øropeɛ̃, -ɛn] **ADJ** European
N E. European
euroscepticisme [øroseptisism] **N** *Pol* Euroscepticism
eurosceptique [øroseptik] **N** *Pol* Eurosceptic
Euro Stoxx [ørostɔks] **NM** Euro Stoxx; **l'E. 50** the Euro Stoxx 50 index
eurostratégique [ørostrateʒik] **ADJ** *Mil* Eurostrategic
Eurotunnel [ørotynɛl] **NM** Channel tunnel
Eurovision [ørovizjɔ̃] **NF** Eurovision
eut [y] *voir* avoir[1]
euthanasie [øtanazi] **NF** euthanasia
eutrophe [øtrɔf], **eutrophique** [øtrɔfik] **ADJ** eutrophic
eutrophisation [øtrɔfizasjɔ̃] **NF** eutrophication
eux [ø] *voir* lui[2]
eux-mêmes [ømɛm] **PRON PERS** themselves
évacuateur, -trice [evakɥatœr, -tris] **ADJ** *(tuyau etc)* drainage
évacuation [evakɥasjɔ̃] **NF 1** *(de matières du corps)* evacuation, voiding, discharge; *(d'eau, de pus etc)* draining (off); **course d'é.** *(d'un moteur)* exhaust stroke **2** *(de population, troupes, blessés etc)* evacuation; *(d'une salle etc)* evacuation, clearing; *Naut (d'un bateau)* abandoning; *Mil* **hôpital d'é.** clearing hospital
évacué, -ée [evakɥe] **N** evacuee
évacuer [evakɥe] **VT 1** *(matières du corps)* to evacuate, to discharge, to void; *(vapeur)* to vent; *(eau, pus etc)* to drain (off) **2** *(faire partir)* to evacuate; **faire é. tous les habitants** to evacuate all the inhabitants **3** *(quitter) (forteresse, ville etc)* to evacuate, to vacate; **faire é. une salle** to evacuate *or* clear a hall; *Naut* **é. le bâtiment** to abandon ship **4** *Fig (problème)* to get rid of, to solve; **c'est une question que je préférerais é. le plus vite**

possible it's a matter I'd like to dispose of as soon as possible

évadé, -ée [evade] **N** escaped prisoner, fugitive

évader (s') [sevade] **VPR** *(de prison, de la réalité etc)* to escape (**de** from)

> Il faut noter que le verbe anglais **to evade** est un faux ami. Il signifie **éviter**.

évaluateur, -trice [evalɥatœr, -tris] **N** *Can* valuer, appraiser

évaluation [evalɥasjɔ̃] **NF 1** *(action) (d'une propriété, d'un bien etc)* valuation, appraisal; *(des dommages)* assessment; *(d'un poids, d'un nombre etc)* estimation; *Com* **é. du coût** cost assessment; **é. des coûts** cost analysis; **é. financière** financial appraisal; **é. des risques** risk assessment **2** *(quantité, valeur) (d'une propriété, d'un bien etc)* valuation; *(des dommages)* assessment; *(d'un poids, d'un nombre etc)* estimate

évaluer [evalɥe] **VT** to evaluate; *(propriété, bien etc)* to value, to appraise; *(dommages)* to assess (**à** at); *(poids, nombre, risques etc)* to estimate; *Fin* **é. le(s) coût(s) de** to cost

évanescent [evanesɑ̃] **ADJ** evanescent

évangélique [evɑ̃ʒelik] **ADJ** *Rel* evangelical

évangélisateur, -trice [evɑ̃ʒelizatœr, -tris] *Rel* **ADJ** evangelistic **N** evangelist

évangélisation [evɑ̃ʒelizasjɔ̃] **NF** *Rel* evangelization

évangéliser [evɑ̃ʒelize] **VT** *Rel* to evangelize

évangélisme [evɑ̃ʒelism] **NM** *Rel* evangelism

évangéliste [evɑ̃ʒelist] **NM** *Rel* evangelist; *(auteur de l'un des Évangiles)* Evangelist

évangile [evɑ̃ʒil] **NM 1** *Rel* **l'É.** the Gospel; **l'É. selon saint Jean** the Gospel according to St. John; **l'é. du jour** the gospel for the day; *Fig* **prendre qch pour parole d'é.** to take sth for gospel (truth); *Fig* **ce n'est pas l'é.** it's not Holy Writ **2** *Fig (livre important)* bible

évanoui [evanwi] **ADJ** unconscious; **tomber é.** to fall down in a faint; **on l'a trouvé é.** he was found unconscious *or* in a (dead) faint

évanouir (s') [sevanwir] **VPR 1** *(disparaître) (d'une silhouette, apparition, ombre)* to vanish, to disappear; *(d'un souvenir, rêve)* to fade (away); *(d'un son)* to die away, to fade away **2** *(perdre conscience)* to faint

évanouissement [evanwismɑ̃] **NM 1** *(disparition) (d'un fantôme, d'une personne etc)* vanishing, disappearance; *(d'un souvenir, rêve)* fading; *(d'un son)* dying away, fading away; *Radio* fade-away **2** *(syncope)* faint(ing fit); **avoir un é.** to faint **3** *Aut (de freins)* fade

évaporation [evaporasjɔ̃] **NF** evaporation

évaporé, -ée [evapore] *Péj* **ADJ** featherbrained, scatterbrained **N** featherbrain, scatterbrain

évaporer [evapore] **VI faire é. un liquide** to evaporate a liquid **VT** *Arch* **é. un liquide** to evaporate a liquid **VPR s'évaporer 1** *(d'un liquide, parfum etc)* to evaporate **2** *Fam (disparaître)* to vanish (into thin air)

évasé [evaze] **ADJ** *(vase, tuyau etc)* wide-mouthed; *(vêtement)* flared

évasement [evazmɑ̃] **NM** *(d'un vase, tuyau etc)* wide mouth; *(d'un vêtement)* flare

évaser [evaze] **VT** *(vase, verre etc)* to widen (out) the opening of; *(tuyau, conduite etc)* to open out; *(ouverture)* to widen; *Couture (vêtement)* to flare **VPR s'évaser** to widen, to open out; *Couture* to flare

évasif, -ive [evazif, -iv] **ADJ** evasive

évasion [evazjɔ̃] **NF 1** *(de prison etc)* escape

(**de** from); **réussir son é.** to succeed in escaping; **le roi de l'é.** the master escaper **2** *Fig (distraction)* escape; *(hors de la réalité)* escapism; **avoir besoin d'é.** to need to escape; **littérature d'é.** escapist literature

▸▸ **é. de capitaux** flight *or* exodus of capital; **é. fiscale** tax evasion

> Il faut noter que le nom anglais **evasion** est un faux ami. Il signifie le plus souvent **dérobade**.

évasivement [evazivmɑ̃] **ADV** evasively

Ève [ɛv] **N** Eve; *Fam* **je ne le connais ni d'È. ni d'Adam** I don't know him from Adam

évêché [eveʃe] **NM** *(diocèse)* bishopric, see; *(palais)* bishop's palace; *(dignité)* bishopric

éveil [evɛj] **NM 1** *(action) (de la nature, la curiosité, la nation etc)* awakening; **être en é.** *(d'une personne)* to be on the alert; *(de l'esprit)* to be alert **2** *(alerte)* **donner l'é.** to raise the alarm; **donner l'é. à qn** to alert sb, to put sb on his/her guard

éveillé [eveje] **ADJ 1** *(non endormi)* awake; **rêve é.** waking dream; **tenir qn é.** to keep sb awake; **é. ou endormi** waking or sleeping **2** *(vif) (personne)* wide-awake, alert, bright; **garçon (à l'esprit) é.** bright boy

éveiller [eveje] **VT** *Litt (personne)* to awake(n); *Fig (curiosité, soupçons, jalousie etc)* to arouse, to awaken; *(intelligence, imagination etc)* to bring out, to develop **VPR s'éveiller** *(d'une personne)* to awake(n); *Fig (de la curiosité, des soupçons etc)* to be aroused; *(de l'intelligence, de l'imagination etc)* to show itself, to develop; *Litt* **elle s'éveille à l'amour** she is awakening to love

événement [evɛnmɑ̃] **NM** event, occurrence; *Fig (livre, spectacle etc important)* event; **attendre la suite des événements** to await the course of events; **créer l'é.** to make big news; **semaine fertile en événements** eventful week; **é. médiatique** media event; **les événements (de mai 68)** the events of May 1968; *Hum* **quand il fait la vaisselle, c'est (tout) un é.** it's a real event when he does the dishes

événementiel, -elle [evɛnmɑ̃sjɛl] **ADJ** *(information, histoire, programme télévisé etc)* factual

évent [evɑ̃] **NM 1** *(de la nourriture, d'un vin, d'un parfum)* mustiness; *(de la bière)* flatness, staleness **2** *(d'une baleine)* blowhole, spout **3** *Tech* vent(hole)

éventail [evɑ̃taj] **NM 1** *(instrument)* fan; **en é.** fan-shaped; *Fig Fam* **elle est restée les doigts de pied en é. toute la matinée** she lazed around all morning; **voûte en é.** fan vaulting **2** *(choix) (de marchandises, salaires, possibilités etc)* range, mix, set; **é. de produits** product *or* sales mix; **é. des prix** price range

éventaire [evɑ̃tɛr] **NM 1** *(d'un marchand ambulant etc)* tray **2** *(étal)* (street) stall

éventé [evɑ̃te] **ADJ** *(nourriture, vin, parfum etc)* musty; *(bière)* flat, stale; *Fig (secret)* well-known

éventer [evɑ̃te] **VT 1** *(vêtements)* to air; *(grain)* to expose to the air; *(mine, mèche)* to ventilate **2** *(avec un éventail etc)* to fan **3** *Fig (découvrir) (secret, complot)* to find out, to discover; **é. la mèche** to discover *or* find out the secret; **le secret est éventé** the secret is out **VPR s'éventer 1** *(de la nourriture, d'un vin, d'un parfum)* to go musty; *(de la bière)* to go flat *or* stale **2** *(avec un éventail etc)* to fan oneself

éventration [evɑ̃trasjɔ̃] **NF** *Méd* rupture, hernia

éventrer [evɑ̃tre] **VT** *(personne, animal)* to disembowel, to eviscerate; *(poisson)* to gut;

(volaille) to draw; *(colis)* to rip *or* tear open; *(fût, boîte)* to break *or* smash open; *(porte)* to burst open; *(sac, matelas)* to slit open

éventreur [evɑ̃trœr] **NM** disemboweller; **Jack l'É.** Jack the Ripper

éventualité [evɑ̃tɥalite] **NF 1** *(circonstance)* eventuality, contingency, possibility; **parer à toute é.** to provide for all eventualities *or* contingencies; **dans l'é. d'un changement de date** in the event of a change of date; **dans cette é.** if that happens *or* should happen **2** *(possibilité) (de guerre etc)* possibility

éventuel, -elle [evɑ̃tɥɛl] **ADJ** *(successeur, profits, guerre etc)* possible, potential; **client é.** potential *or* prospective customer

> Il faut noter que l'adjectif anglais **eventual** est un faux ami. Il signifie **final**.

éventuellement [evɑ̃tɥɛlmɑ̃] **ADV** possibly; **il viendra avec sa cousine et é. avec sa tante** he'll come with his cousin and possibly with his aunt; **faites cet exercice en vous servant é. d'un dictionnaire** do this exercise using a dictionary if necessary; **j'aurais é. besoin de votre concours** I may need your help (later); **tu veux venir avec nous? – é.!** do you want to come with us? – possibly!

> Il faut noter que l'adverbe anglais **eventually** est un faux ami. Il signifie **finalement**.

évêque [evɛk] **NM** *Rel* bishop; *Prov* **un chien regarde bien un é.** a cat may look at a king; **bonnet d'é.** bishop's mitre; *Fam (d'une volaille)* parson's nose

évertuer (s') [severtɥe] **VPR s'é. à faire qch** to do one's utmost *or* make every effort to do sth; **je m'évertue à lui répéter que c'est impossible** I'm tired of telling him that it's impossible; **s'é. sur qch** to struggle with sth

éviction [eviksjɔ̃] **NF** *(d'un rival, d'une tête de parti etc)* ousting, supplanting; *(d'un locataire)* eviction; **depuis son é. du parti** since his/her ousting *or* since being ousted from the party

évidage [evidaʒ] **NM** *(d'une pierre, du bois etc)* hollowing out, scooping out

évidement [evidmɑ̃] **NM** *(action) (d'une pierre, du bois etc)* hollowing out, scooping out; *Chir* scraping out

évidemment [evidamɑ̃] **ADV 1** *(bien sûr)* of course **2** *Arch (manifestement)* obviously, clearly

> Il faut noter que l'adverbe anglais **evidently** est un faux ami. Il signifie **manifestement, à l'évidence**.

évidence [evidɑ̃s] **NF 1** *(d'un fait, de la vérité etc)* obviousness, clearness; **se rendre à l'é.** to yield to *or* face the facts; **nier** *ou* **refuser l'é.** to deny the obvious *or* what is obvious; **de toute é., à l'é.** clearly, obviously; **mais c'est une é.!, mais c'est l'é.** même but it's obvious *or* self-evident! **2** **être en é.** *(d'un objet)* to be in a prominent position, to be conspicuous; **mettre en é.** *(marchandises)* to display prominently; *(idée)* to give prominence to, to underline; **je vais les laisser bien en é. sur la table** I'll leave them in a prominent position on the table; **se mettre en é.** to try to get oneself noticed

> Il faut noter que le nom anglais **evidence** est un faux ami. Il signifie le plus souvent **preuve**.

évident [evidɑ̃] **ADJ** *(erreur, vérité, preuve, raisonnement)* obvious, clear, plain; **il est é. qu'elle se trompe** it is obvious *or* clear that she is mistaken; **il était d'une évidente mauvaise foi** he was obviously *or* clearly insincere; **tu crois qu'on va réussir? – c'est é.!** do you think we'll succeed? – of course (we will)!; *Fam* **c'est pas é.!** *(pas facile)* it's not easy

évider [evide] VT *(pierre, bois etc)* to hollow out, to scoop out; *Culin (tomate, pomme etc)* to scoop out

évier [evje] NM sink

évincer [evɛ̃se] VT (**j'évinçai(s)**) *(rival, tête de parti etc)* to oust (**de** from), to supplant; *(locataire)* to evict

> Il faut noter que le verbe anglais **to evince** est un faux ami. Il signifie **faire preuve de, manifester**.

éviscération [eviserasjɔ̃] NF *Chir* evisceration

éviscérer [evisere] VT (**j'éviscère, n. éviscérons**) to eviscerate

évitable [evitabl] ADJ avoidable

évitage [evitaʒ] NM *Naut* **1** *(mouvement) (d'un bateau)* swinging; **bassin d'é.** turning basin **2** *(espace)* room to swing, sea room

évitement [evitmã] NM **1** *(action d'éviter)* avoidance; **faire une manœuvre d'é.** to take evasive action; *Biol* **réaction d'é.** avoiding reaction **2** *Rail* **voie** *ou* **gare d'é.** siding; **ligne d'é.** loop line

éviter [evite] VT **1** *(ne pas heurter)* to avoid, to miss; *(ne pas subir)* to avoid, to steer clear of; *(ne pas rencontrer) (personne)* to avoid, to keep clear of; *(regard)* to avoid; **é. l'alcool/le sucre** to avoid *or* keep off alcohol/sugar; **é. un coup** to avoid *or* dodge a blow; **é. la question** to avoid *or* dodge the issue; **é. de faire qch** to avoid doing sth; **évite de recommencer!** don't start again!; **j'essaie d'é. qu'il ne le découvre** I'm trying to avoid his discovering it; **é. que le vent n'entre dans la maison** to prevent the wind getting into the house, to keep the wind out of the house; **évite que ça se sache** don't let it get out, prevent it getting out **2** *(épargner)* **é. des ennuis/une corvée à qn** to save *or* spare sb trouble/a chore; **ça m'évitera d'avoir à le faire** it will save me having to do it

VI *Naut* **é. sur l'ancre** to swing at anchor; **évité au vent** riding the wind

VPR **s'éviter 1** **s'é. qch** to avoid sth **2** *(se fuir)* to avoid each other

évocable [evɔkabl] ADJ *Jur* **cause é.** = case that may be transferred to a higher court

évocateur, -trice [evɔkatœr, -tris] ADJ evocative, suggestive (**de** of)

évocation [evɔkasjɔ̃] NF **1** *(par la magie) (d'un esprit etc)* evocation, calling forth, conjuring up **2** *(d'un souvenir, du passé etc)* evocation, conjuring up, recalling; **à l'é. de son premier amour** when she recalled her first love; *(mentionné par un tiers)* when reference was made to her first love; **le pouvoir d'é. d'un lieu/mot** the evocative power of a place/word

évolué [evɔlɥe] ADJ *(race, pays, société)* (highly) developed, advanced; *(personne)* mature, broadminded; *Ordinat (langage)* high-level

évoluer [evɔlɥe] VI **1** *(se déplacer) (d'un bateau, de troupes etc)* to manœuvre, *Am* to maneuver; *(d'un danseur, d'un cerf-volant, d'un poisson etc)* to move around; *Fig* **é. dans la haute société** to move in high society; **j'ignore dans quel milieu elle évolue maintenant** I don't know what circles she moves in now **2** *(se développer) (d'une théorie, d'une science, d'une ville, d'une entreprise etc)* to evolve, to develop; *(d'une personne, d'une maladie)* to develop **3** *Ordinat* **faire é.** to upgrade

évolutif, -ive [evɔlytif, -iv] ADJ evolutionary; *Méd (maladie)* progressive; *Ordinat* up-

gradeable; **méthode évolutive, ski é.** short-ski method; **poste é.** position with promotion prospects

évolution [evɔlysjɔ̃] NF **1** *(déplacement) (d'un bateau, de troupes etc)*; **évolutions** manœuvres, *Am* maneuvers; *(d'un danseur, d'un patineur etc)* movements **2** *(développement) (d'une théorie, d'une science, d'un peuple, d'un conflit etc)* evolution, development; *(d'une personne, d'une maladie)* development; *Biol* evolution; **être contre toute é.** to be against any development; **suivre une lente é.** to evolve *or* develop slowly

évolutionnisme [evɔlysjɔnism] NM *Biol* evolutionism

évolutionniste [evɔlysjɔnist] *Biol* ADJ evolutionist(ic)
N evolutionist

évolutivité [evɔlytivite] NF *Ordinat* upgradeability

évoquer [evɔke] VT **1** *(se remémorer) (souvenir, passé etc)* to recall, to conjure up, to evoke **2** *(faire penser à)* to be reminiscent of; **qu'est-ce que cela vous évoque?** what does that remind you of *or* conjure up for you?; **son nom/ce visage ne m'évoque rien** his name/this face means nothing to me *or* doesn't ring a bell with me **3** *(aborder)* to touch on, to mention; **nous n'avons fait qu'é. le sujet** we've only touched on the subject **4** *(par la magie) (esprit, démon, mort etc)* to evoke, to call forth, to conjure up

ex [eks] N *Fam* ex; **un de mes ex** one of my exes

ex- [eks] PRÉF ex-; **ex-femme/-champion** ex-wife/-champion

ex abrupto [eksabrypto] ADV straight off

exacerbation [ɛgzasɛrbasjɔ̃] NF exacerbation

exacerber [ɛgzasɛrbe] VT *(douleur, irritation etc)* to exacerbate, to aggravate; **susceptibilité exacerbée** exaggerated sensitivity; **nationalisme exacerbé** extreme nationalism
VPR **s'exacerber** to become acute

exact [ɛgza(kt)] ADJ **1** *(précis) (quantité, poids, nombre, calcul etc)* exact, precise; *(fidèle) (rapport, description, copie etc)* exact, accurate; *(juste) (solution, mot, réponse etc)* right, correct; **l'heure/la date exacte** the right *or* correct *or* exact time/date; **une montre exacte** a precise *or* accurate watch; **e. à un millimètre près** correct *or* accurate to within a millimetre; **c'est e.** *(vrai)* it's quite true, it's a fact; **il est e. que j'ai dit cela** it's quite true that I said that; **vous vous appelez bien Martin? – e.!** your name is Martin? – correct! **2** *(ponctuel)* punctual, on time; **il est e. à payer son loyer** he is punctual in paying his rent, he pays his rent on time; **je n'ai pu être e. au rendez-vous** I couldn't be on time for the appointment **3** *Litt (strict) (discipline, obéissance etc)* strict, rigorous

exactement [ɛgzaktəmã] ADV *(précisément) (calculer, placer etc)* exactly, precisely; *(fidèlement) (rapporter, reproduire etc)* exactly, accurately; *(avec justesse) (répondre, raisonner etc)* correctly; **il est e. deux heures** it is exactly *or* precisely two o'clock; **c'est très e. ce que je veux dire** that's exactly *or* precisely what I mean; **e. le même** exactly the same; **je sais e. combien** I know exactly *or* precisely how much; **un effet e. contraire** a directly opposite effect

exaction [ɛgzaksjɔ̃] NF **1** *(d'impôt etc)* exaction; *(vol)* extortion **2** **exactions** *(actes cruels)* atrocities

exactitude [ɛgzaktityd] NF **1** *(précision) (d'une quantité, d'un calcul etc)* exactness, precision; *(fidélité) (d'un rapport, d'une copie etc)* exactness, accuracy; *(justesse) (d'une solution, réponse etc)* correctness; **calculer/**

mesurer avec e. to calculate/measure exactly *or* precisely **2** *(ponctualité)* punctuality; **avec e.** punctually; *Prov* **l'e. est la politesse des rois** punctuality is the politeness of kings

ex æquo [ɛgzeko] ADV *Scol, Sport etc* **être (classés) e.** to tie, to be equally placed; **être troisième e.** to tie for third place, to be placed equal third; **être e. avec qn** to tie with sb, to be placed equal with sb
N INV **il y avait trois e. pour la première place** three people tied for first place; **départager les e.** to break the tie

exagération [ɛgzaʒerasjɔ̃] NF exaggeration; **sans e.** *(faire un récit)* without exaggerating; *(boire, aimer le chocolat etc)* in moderation; **on peut dire sans e. que ...** it is no exaggeration to say *or* one can say without exaggeration that ...; **se montrer ferme sans e.** to be firm without overdoing it *or* going to extremes

exagéré [ɛgzaʒere] ADJ *(commentaire, récit, geste)* exaggerated; *(prix, salaire)* exorbitant, excessive; *(pessimisme, nationalisme)* excessive; **confiance exagérée** overconfidence; **il n'est pas e. de dire que ...** it is no exaggeration to say that ...; **dire qu'il est bête, c'est un peu e.** it's a bit much *or* a bit excessive to say that he's stupid

exagérément [ɛgzaʒeremã] ADV excessively; **il lui fait e. confiance** he trusts him/her far too much; **elle a e. tardé avant de répondre** she delayed for far too long before replying

exagérer [ɛgzaʒere] VT *(faits, vérité, danger, qualités de qn etc)* to exaggerate, to overstate; *(forme, proportions etc)* to exaggerate; **il ne faut rien e., n'exagérons rien** things should be kept in proportion, let's not exaggerate
VI *(en parlant)* to exaggerate; *(abuser)* to go too far, to overstep the mark; **il faut toujours que tu exagères!** you always exaggerate!; **il ne faut pas e.!** that's a bit excessive *or* much!; *Fam* **faut pas e., mon vieux** don't exaggerate!; **sans e., il y en avait bien soixante** without exaggeration there were sixty of them
VPR **s'exagérer** **s'e. qch** to overestimate sth

exaltant [ɛgzaltã] ADJ *(discours, musique, expérience etc)* exciting

exaltation [ɛgzaltasjɔ̃] NF **1** *(excitation)* (great) excitement; *Méd* overexcitement; **e. mystique** exaltation; **il a préparé son départ dans l'e.** he got ready to leave in (a state of) great excitement **2** *(action de louer) (de la vertu, d'une personne etc)* exalting, extolling **3** *Rel* **E. de la Sainte Croix** Exaltation of the Cross

exalté, -ée [ɛgzalte] ADJ *Péj (discours, sentiment)* wild, impassioned; *(imagination, esprit)* wild; *(personne)* fanatical, hotheaded
N *Péj* fanatic, hothead

exalter [ɛgzalte] VT **1** *(exciter) (imagination, esprit)* to stir, to fire; *(ressentiment, orgueil etc)* to intensify; **ses voyages/lectures/expériences l'ont exalté** his travels/reading/experiences fired his imagination **2** *(louer) (personne, les qualités de qn)* to exalt, to extol, to glorify
VPR **s'exalter** to get excited

exam [ɛgzam] NM *Fam* exam

examen [ɛgzamɛ̃] NM **1** *(observation, analyse) (d'un document, d'un spécimen, de faits etc)* examination; *(des comptes)* inspection; **après un e. attentif de la situation/du problème** after a careful examination of the situation/problem; **cette assertion ne supporte pas l'e.** this assertion will not bear examination; **mettre une question à l'e.** to examine *or* look into *or* go into a matter;

après e., **e. fait** (up)on examination **2** *Méd* **e. (médical)** (medical) examination, medical, checkup; **e. de la vue** sight *or* eye test; **e. médical complet** complete checkup **3** *Scol, Univ etc* exam, examination; **passer un e.** to sit *or* take an exam; **faire passer un e. à qn** to examine sb; **être reçu/refusé à un e.** to pass/fail an exam; **jury d'e.** examining body, examiners

▸▸**e. blanc** mock exam; **e. de conscience** soul-searching; *Jur* **e. contradictoire** examination made in the presence of both parties to a contract; **e. d'entrée** entrance exam; **e. financier** financial review; **e. partiel** *(d'année)* half-year exam; *(de semestre, trimestre)* half-term exam; **e. de passage** end-of-year exam, *Am* final exam; **e. prénuptial** premarital checkup

examinateur, -trice [ɛgzaminatœr, -tris] N examiner

examiner [ɛgzamine] VT **1** *(étudier, analyser)* *(document, spécimen, faits etc)* to examine; *(comptes)* to inspect, to go through; *(machinerie)* to check; **e. une question** to examine *or* look into *or* go into a matter; **e. une demande** to consider a request; **e. les lieux** to inspect the premises **2** *(regarder, observer)* **e. l'horizon** to scan *or* survey the horizon; *Fig* **elle m'a examiné de la tête aux pieds** she eyed me from head to toe *or* up and down **3** *Méd (patient)* to examine; **se faire e. par un médecin** to have oneself *or* be examined by a doctor **4** *Scol, Univ etc Arch* to examine; **e. qn en algèbre** to examine sb in algebra

VPR **s'examiner 1** *(dans une glace etc)* to examine oneself **2** *(de plusieurs personnes)* *(s'observer)* to examine each other

exanthème [ɛgzātɛm] NM *Méd* exanthema

exaspérant [ɛgzasperā] ADJ exasperating, irritating, aggravating

exaspération [ɛgzasperasjō] NF **1** *(énervement)* exasperation, irritation, aggravation **2** *Vieilli (d'une douleur, d'un sentiment)* aggravation

exaspérer [ɛgzaspere] *(j'exaspère; j'exaspérerai)* VT **1** *(énerver)* *(personne)* to exasperate, to irritate, to aggravate **2** *(douleur, sentiment)* to aggravate

VPR **s'exaspérer** *(d'une douleur, d'un sentiment)* to become acute

exaucement [ɛgzosmā] NM *(d'un souhait, désir)* granting, fulfilment

exaucer [ɛgzose] VT *(j'exauçai(s), n. exauçons)* **1** *(souhait, désir)* to grant, to fulfil, *Am* to fulfill; **exauce ma prière!** hear my prayer! **2 e. qn** to grant sb's wish, to hear *or* answer sb's prayer; **te voilà exaucé** your prayer is answered

ex cathedra [ɛkskatedra] ADV *Rel, Fig* ex cathedra

excavateur, -trice [ɛkskavatœr, -tris] N *Constr* excavator, (mechanical) digger

excavation [ɛkskavasjō] NF **1** *(trou)* excavation; *(creusée par une bombe)* crater **2** *(action)* excavation, excavating

excaver [ɛkskave] VT to excavate

excédant [ɛksedā] ADJ exasperating, tiresome

excédent [ɛksedā] NM *(de nourriture, de sucre dans le sang etc)* surplus, excess; *(d'un budget, d'une balance)* surplus; **somme en e.** sum in excess; **dégager un e.** to show a surplus; **budget en e.** surplus budget; **e. budgétaire** budget(ary) surplus; **vous garderez l'e.** you will keep what is left over; **e. de poids** excess weight; **e. de dépenses** deficit; **e. de bagages** excess luggage *or* baggage; **e. de blé** wheat surplus; **la balance commerciale est en e.** the trade balance shows a surplus,

there is a trade surplus; *Compta* **e. de caisse** cash overs; **e. commercial** trade surplus; **e. d'exploitation** operating profit; **excédents et déficits** overs and shorts

excédentaire [ɛksedātɛr] ADJ *(production)* excess, surplus; *(poids)* excess; *(budget)* surplus; **balance commerciale e.** trade surplus

excéder [ɛksede] VT *(j'excède, n. excédons; j'excéderai)* **1** *(dépasser)* *(quantité, somme, période)*, *Fig (limite etc)* to exceed; **e. les moyens de qn** to be beyond sb's means; **nos pertes excèdent nos bénéfices** our losses are greater than our profits **2** *(outrepasser)* *(forces, compétences)* to be beyond; **e. ses pouvoirs** to exceed *or* overstep one's powers **3** *(irriter)* to exasperate; **j'étais excédé** I was exasperated, I had lost all patience **4** *Vieilli (épuiser)* to tire *or* wear out; **excédé de fatigue** worn out, tired out

excellemment [ɛksɛlamā] ADV *Litt* excellently

excellence [ɛksɛlās] NF **1** excellence; *Scol* **prix d'e.** class prize *(for all-round standard)*; **c'est le chercheur/l'homme à femmes par e.** he's the researcher/ladies' man par excellence; **c'est un têtu/paresseux par e.** he's stubbornness/laziness itself **2** *(titre)* **Son/Votre E.** His/Her/Your Excellency

excellent [ɛksɛlā] ADJ excellent, first-rate **(en** at, in); **en excellente santé** in the best of health, in excellent health

exceller [ɛksele] VI to excel **(en** at, in; **à faire qch** in doing sth)

excentré [ɛksātre] ADJ **1** *(quartier, maison etc)* far from the centre, remote **2** *Tech* off centre

excentricité [ɛksātrisite] NF **1** *(caractère, acte bizarre)* eccentricity **2** *(d'un quartier, d'une maison etc)* remoteness **3** *Math etc (d'un cercle, d'une orbite etc)* eccentricity

excentrique [ɛksātrik] ADJ **1** *(bizarre)* *(personne, comportement, idée etc)* eccentric, odd **2** *(loin du centre)* *(faubourg, quartier etc)* remote, far from the centre **3** *Math etc (cercle, orbite etc)* eccentric

N *(personne)* eccentric

NM *(mécanisme)* eccentric

excentriquement [ɛksātrikmā] ADV eccentrically

excepté [ɛksɛpte] PRÉP except, apart from, with the exception of; **tous les jours e. quand il pleut** every day except *or* apart from *or* with the exception of when it rains; **la maison nous convient e. qu'il n'y a pas de garage** the house suits us except for (the fact) that there's no garage

ADJ **les femmes exceptées** except for *or* apart from the women; **j'aime tous leurs meubles, le bahut e.** I like all their furniture except for *or* apart from the sideboard

excepter [ɛksɛpte] VT to exclude, to except **(de** from), to make an exception of; **si l'on excepte une seule rue** with the exception of *or* apart from one street; **sans e. les enfants** without excluding the children, including the children

exception [ɛksɛpsjō] NF **1** exception **(à** to); **faire une e.** to make an exception **(pour** for); **faire une e. à une règle** to make an exception to a rule; **faire e. à une règle** to be an exception to a rule; **c'est l'e. qui confirme la règle** it's the exception that proves the rule; **à quelques exceptions près** with a few exceptions; **à quelques rares exceptions près** with very few exceptions; **à une e. près** with one exception; **sans e.** without exception; **tous, à l'e. du docteur** *ou* **e. faite du docteur** all, except (for) *or* with the exception of the doctor; **c'est un être d'e.** he's an exceptional person; **l'e. culturelle** the cultural exception **2** *Jur* objection, plea *(by the defence)*

exceptionnel, -elle [ɛksɛpsjɔnɛl] ADJ **1** *(qui fait exception)* *(circonstances, situation etc)* exceptional; **congé e.** special leave **2** *(remarquable)* exceptional, outstanding; **sa femme/sa voiture/son livre n'a rien d'e.** his wife/his car/his book is nothing special

exceptionnellement [ɛksɛpsjɔnɛlmā] ADV exceptionally; **e. tu peux partir maintenant** just this once you can leave now; **nous ouvrirons e. le soir de Noël** we will open specially on Christmas Eve

excès [ɛksɛ] NM **1** *(excédent, démesure)* excess; **e. de l'offre sur la demande** excess of supply over demand; **pécher par e. de zèle, faire de l'e. de zèle** to be overzealous; **l'e. de ses prétentions** his/her excessive claims, the excessive nature of his/her claims; **c'est un peu un e. de précautions** these are rather excessive precautions; **avec e.** *(boire, fumer, travailler etc)* excessively, to excess; **manger avec e.** to overeat, to eat excessively *or* to excess; **dépenser avec e.** to overspend; **réagir avec e.** to overreact *(à qch** to sth); **sans e.** *(manger, utiliser etc)* in moderation; **(jusqu')à l'e.** to excess, excessively; **se dépenser à l'e.** to overexert oneself; **gentil/scrupuleux à l'e.** kind/scrupulous to a fault, overkind/overscrupulous; **tomber dans l'e.** to overdo it, *Fam* to go over the top; **tomber dans l'e. inverse** to go to the other extreme

2 *(abus)* excess; **commettre** *ou* **se laisser aller à des e.** to overdo things, to go too far; **des e. (de table)** overeating, overindulgence; **faire des e. (de table)** to overeat, to overindulge; **évitez tout e.** avoid overdoing things; *(alimentaire)* avoid overeating

▸▸**des e. de conduite** loose living; **des e. de langage** immoderate language; *Jur* **e. de pouvoir** action ultra vires; *Aut* **e. de vitesse** speeding, exceeding the speed limit; **faire un e. de vitesse** to speed, to exceed the speed limit

excessif, -ive [ɛksɛsif, -iv] ADJ *(longueur, chaleur, quantité etc)* excessive; *(opinion, idée)* extreme; *(optimisme, idéalisme)* excessive, unwarranted; *(prix)* exorbitant, excessive; *(langage)* immoderate; *(orgueil)* inordinate; **des mois de travail e. l'a rendu malade** he has become ill through months of overwork; **il est e.** he goes to extremes; **il fait un vent e. pour sortir le bébé** it's far too windy to take the baby out

excessivement [ɛksɛsivmā] ADV **1** *(trop)* excessively; **manger e.** to overeat, to eat excessively *or* to excess; **il avait bu e.** he had been drinking to excess **2** *(extrêmement)* extremely

exciper [ɛksipe] VI *Jur* to put in a plea; *Litt* **e. de son ignorance/sa bonne foi** to plead ignorance/one's good faith

excipient [ɛksipjã] **NM** *Pharm* excipient

exciser [ɛksize] **VT** *Chir* to excise, to cut out

exciseur, -euse [ɛksizœr, -øz] **N** *Chir* excisor, excisionist

excision [ɛksizjɔ̃] **NF** *Chir* excision

excitabilité [ɛksitabilite] **NF** excitability

excitable [ɛksitabl] **ADJ** excitable

excitant [ɛksitã] **ADJ** *(nouvelles, débat, film, perspective, sexuellement etc)* exciting; *(effet)* stimulating
  NM stimulant

excitation [ɛksitasjɔ̃] **NF 1** *(action)* *(à la violence, au racisme etc)* incitement (**à** to); **e. à la révolte** incitement to rebellion **2** *(résultat)* excitement; **e. (sexuelle)** (sexual) arousal *or* excitement; **dans l'e. du moment** in the excitement of the moment **3** *Élec, Physiol* excitation
  ►► *Jur* **e. des mineurs à la débauche** incitement of minors to commit immoral acts

excité, -ée [ɛksite] **ADJ 1** *(énervé)* worked-up; *(plein d'anticipation)* excited **2** *(sexuellement)* excited
  N *(personne)* hothead

exciter [ɛksite] **VT 1** *(attiser)* *(curiosité, jalousie etc)* to excite, to arouse; *(pitié)* to arouse; *(appétit)* to whet; *(rire)* to provoke; **e. l'envie de tout le monde** to make everybody envious; **e. la pitié de qn** to move sb to pity, to arouse sb's pity
  2 *(encourager)* to urge on; **e. qn à la révolte** *ou* **à se révolter** to incite sb to revolt; **e. qn contre qn** to set sb against sb; **e. la meute contre le gibier** to urge on the pack to hunt their quarry
  3 *(énerver)* *(intellectuellement)* to excite, to thrill; *(physiquement)* to excite; *(sexuellement)* to arouse, to excite; **excité à l'idée de partir en vacances** excited *or* thrilled at the idea of going on holiday; **trop e. qn** to overexcite sb; **le café/le tabac excite** coffee/tobacco acts as a stimulant
  4 *Fam (irriter)* to irritate, to annoy
  5 *Physiol (nerf, muscle)* to excite, to stimulate; *Élec (dynamo)* to excite
  VPR s'exciter *Fam* to get excited, to get worked up; *(sexuellement)* to get aroused *or* excited; **t'excite pas, je vais te le rendre, ton fric!** calm down *or* don't get worked up, I'll give you your money back!

exclamatif, -ive [ɛksklamatif, -iv] **ADJ** exclamatory; *Gram* **proposition exclamative** exclamation, interjection

exclamation [ɛksklamasjɔ̃] **NF** exclamation; **pousser des exclamations** to exclaim

exclamer (s') [sɛksklame] **VPR** *(de joie, de surprise, d'admiration)* to exclaim, to shout out; *(de douleur, colère)* to cry out, to shout out (**de** in, with); **'toi ici!' s'exclama-t-il** 'you here!' he exclaimed; **s'e. sur la montée du chômage/de la violence** to make a lot of noise about rising unemployment/violence

exclu, -ue [ɛkskly] **ADJ 1** *(non compris)* **le prix des travaux, TVA exclue** the cost of the work, excluding VAT; **le mois d'août jusqu'au 31 e.** the month of August excluding the 31st **2** *(impensable)* out of the question, impossible; **il est e. que +** *sub* it's out of the question *or* impossible that; **il est e. qu'il vienne avec nous** it's out of the question for him to come with us, *Fam* there's no way he's coming with us; **il n'est pas e. que ...** it's not out of the question that ...
  N outcast; **les exclus de la société** social outcasts, the outcasts of society; **les exclus du progrès** those whom progress has ignored *or* passed by

exclure [ɛksklyr] *(prp* **excluant;** *pp* **exclu;** *pr ind* **j'exclus, n. excluons;** *impf* **j'excluais;** *p hist* **j'exclus;** *fu* **j'exclurai) VT 1** *(expulser)* *(d'un parti, d'une école etc)* to expel; *(d'une fonc-*

tion publique) to remove; *(d'une salle, réunion)* to eject (**de** from)
  2 *(ne pas permettre ou admettre)* to exclude (**de** from); **e. le pain de son régime** to exclude *or* cut out bread from one's diet; **e. l'alcool de sa table** not to allow alcohol in the house; **elle a exclu le rouge dans ses vêtements** she doesn't wear anything with red in it; **e. la TVA de la somme** to exclude the VAT from *or* leave the VAT out of the sum; **l'alcool est exclu de la vente le dimanche** alcohol is not allowed to be sold on Sundays
  3 *(ne pas considérer)* to rule out; **e. la possibilité d'un accord** to rule out the possibility of an agreement; **cette hypothèse est à e.** this possibility is out of the question; **cela n'exclut pas que vous puissiez enseigner** that doesn't rule out the possibility of your teaching
  VPR s'exclure *(de théories etc)* to be mutually exclusive

exclusif, -ive [ɛksklyzif, -iv] **ADJ 1** *(non partagé)* *(occupation, intérêt etc)* exclusive; *(but, mission)* sole; *Com (droit, agent etc)* exclusive, sole; *(article, modèle, reportage, interview etc)* exclusive; **une interview exclusive** an exclusive (interview); **il a un intérêt e. pour les papillons** he is solely interested in butterflies; **pendant les vacances, son occupation exclusive a été de courir** during the holidays, running was his sole activity **2** *(sélectif)* *(dans ses opinions)* self-opinionated; *(dans ses goûts)* selective; **elle est très exclusive dans ses amitiés** she is very selective in her choice of friends; **il est e. en amour** he's a one-woman man
  NF exclusive *(mesure d'exclusion)* bar; **prononcer l'exclusive contre, frapper d'exclusive** to bar, to debar; **sans exclusive** without exception

exclusion [ɛksklyzjɔ̃] **NF 1** *(expulsion)* *(d'un parti, d'une école etc)* expulsion; *(d'une fonction publique)* removal; *(d'une salle, réunion)* ejection (**de** from); **e. temporaire** suspension **2 e. (sociale)** social exclusion **3 à l'e. de** to the exclusion of; *(à l'exception de)* with the exception of

exclusivement [ɛksklyzivmã] **ADV** exclusively, solely; **parking e. réservé aux clients de l'hôtel** customer parking only; **il aime e. les opéras de Verdi** he likes Verdi's operas to the exclusion of all others; **de lundi jusqu'à vendredi e.** from Monday to Friday exclusive

exclusivisme [ɛksklyzivism] **NM** exclusivism

exclusiviste [ɛksklyzivist] **N** exclusivist

exclusivité [ɛksklyzivite] **NF 1** *Com (droit)* sole *or* exclusive rights (**de** in); *TV, Cin (de film)* first run; **en e.** exclusively; **avoir un contrat d'e.** to have an exclusive contract (**chez** with); **ce modèle se trouve en e. chez ...** this model is exclusive to *or* can only be found at ...; **nous avons l'e. de la vente de ce produit** we have the (sole) rights for this product; **c'est notre journal qui a eu l'e. de son interview** our paper had an exclusive with him; **en e. dans le Figaro** a Figaro exclusive; **film en e.** exclusive film; **film en première e.** movie *or Br* film receiving its first showing; *Fig* **ne pas avoir l'e. de l'intelligence/de la beauté** not to have a monopoly on intelligence/beauty **2** *Com (article)* exclusive article; *(film)* movie *or Br* film on general release; *Journ (article)* exclusive, scoop; **c'est une e. Mercedes** it's exclusive to Mercedes **3** *(des sentiments)* selectiveness

excommunication [ɛkskɔmynikasjɔ̃] **NF** excommunication

excommunier [ɛkskɔmynje] **VT** *(impf, sub* **n. excommuniions)** to excommunicate

excoriation [ɛkskɔrjasjɔ̃] **NF** *(éraflure)* graze, *Spéc* excoriation

excorier [ɛkskɔrje] **VT** *(peau)* to graze, *Spéc* to excoriate

ex-coupon [ɛkskupɔ̃] **ADV** *Bourse* ex coupon

excrément [ɛkskremã] **NM** **excrément(s)** excrement

excrémentiel, -elle [ɛkskremãsjɛl] **ADJ** excremental

excréter [ɛkskrete] **VT** (**j'excrète; j'excréterai**) to excrete

excréteur, -trice [ɛkskretœr, -tris] **ADJ** excretory

excrétion [ɛkskresjɔ̃] **NF 1** *(action)* excretion, excreting **2** *(déchet)* **excrétions** excreta

excrétoire [ɛkskretwar] **ADJ** excretory

excroissance [ɛkskrwasãs] **NF** excrescence

excursion [ɛkskyrsjɔ̃] **NF** *(en car, voiture etc)* excursion, trip; *(d'une journée)* day trip, day tour; *(de plusieurs jours)* tour; *(lors d'une escale)* shore excursion, trip ashore; *(à pied)* hike, long walk; **faire une e., partir en e.** to go on an excursion *or* a trip/a tour/a hike *or* a walk; **e. en car** coach trip

excursionner [ɛkskyrsjɔne] **VI** *Vieilli (en car, voiture etc)* to go on excursions *or* trips; *(pendant plusieurs jours)* to go touring; *(à pied)* to go hiking *or* walking

excursionniste [ɛkskyrsjɔnist] **N** *(en car, voiture etc)* tourist, excursionist, *Br* tripper; *(à pied)* hiker, walker

excusable [ɛkskyzabl] **ADJ** excusable, forgivable; **ce n'est absolument pas e.** it's absolutely inexcusable *or* unforgivable

excuse [ɛkskyz] **NF 1** *(raison)* excuse; **une bonne e.** a good excuse; **ce n'est pas une e.!** that's no excuse!; **trouver une e. à qch/pour faire qch** to find an excuse for sth/for doing sth; **je prends mon travail comme e. pour ne pas partir** I'm making my work the excuse for not going; **tu lui trouves toujours des excuses** you're always finding excuses for him; **tu n'as aucune e. de ne pas avoir prévenu** you have no excuse for not letting us know; **c'est sans e.** it's inexcusable *or* unforgivable
  2 excuses *(regrets)* apology; **faire** *ou* **présenter ses excuses à qn** to make one's apologies *or* to apologize to sb; **je vous fais mes plus plates excuses** *ou* **mes excuses les plus plates** you have my humble apologies; **il exige des excuses** he is demanding an apology; **je vous dois des excuses** I owe you an apology; **lettre d'excuses** letter of apology
  3 *Fam* **faites e.!** sorry!
  4 *(au tarot)* excuse

excuser [ɛkskyze] **VT 1** *(justifier)* *(personne, action)* to excuse, to make excuses for, to apologize for; **e. qn auprès de qn** to apologize for sb to sb; **l'ignorance n'excuse rien** ignorance is no excuse
  2 *(pardonner)* *(personne, erreur, colère etc)* to excuse; **excusez-moi, veuillez m'e.** excuse me, pardon me, I'm sorry; **excuse-moi de te déranger** I'm sorry to disturb you, excuse me for disturbing you; **excuse-moi de ne pas t'avoir téléphoné** I'm sorry I didn't phone you; **excusez-moi de vous le faire remarquer** excuse me for saying so, I hope you don't mind my mentioning it; *Fml* **je vous prie de m'e.** I do beg your pardon; **excusez ma curiosité mais ...** excuse *or* forgive my curiosity but ...; **tu es tout excusé** there's no need to apologize, that's quite all right; *Hum* **excusez du peu!** would you believe!, if you please!
  3 *(dispenser)* to excuse; **se faire e.** to ask to be excused; **peux-tu m'e. auprès de lui?** can you ask him to excuse me?; **liste des présents, absents, excusés** list of those present, those absent and those from whom apologies have been received; **e. un juré** to excuse a juror (from attendance)

VPR s'excuser to apologize; *Iron* **surtout ne t'excuse pas!** an apology wouldn't go amiss!; **s'e. auprès de qn** to apologize to sb; **s'e. de qch/de faire qch** to apologize for sth/ doing sth; *Fam* **je m'excuse!** sorry!, excuse me!; *Prov* **qui s'excuse s'accuse** he who excuses himself accuses himself

ex-dividende [ɛksdividɑ̃d] ADV *Fin* ex dividend

ex-droit [ɛksdrwa] ADV *Bourse* ex rights

exécrable [ɛgzekrabl] ADJ atrocious, abominable, execrable

exécrablement [ɛgzekrabləmɑ̃] ADV atrociously, abominably, execrably

exécration [ɛgzekrasjɔ̃] NF *Litt (du crime etc)* execration, detestation; **avoir qn/qch en e.** to loathe sb/sth

exécrer [ɛgzekre] VT (**j'exècre; j'exécrerai**) *Litt* to execrate, to loathe, to detest

exécutable [ɛgzekytabl] ADJ feasible; *Ordinat (programme)* executable

exécutant, -ante [ɛgzekytɑ̃, -ɑ̃t] N *Mus* performer, executant; **il n'a été qu'un simple e.** he was just doing what he was told or carrying out orders

exécuter [ɛgzekyte] VT **1** *(effectuer) (travail, plan)* to execute, to carry out; *(ordres, décision)* to carry out, to act upon; *(promesse)* to carry out, to fulfil; *(danse, morceau de musique, contrat)* to perform, to execute **2** *(confectionner) (peinture, décor etc)* to produce, to execute **3** *Ordinat (programme)* to execute, to run; *(commande)* to execute, to carry out **4** *Jur (débiteur)* to distrain upon; *(décret, loi etc)* to enforce, to give effect to **5** *(mettre à mort) (criminel etc)* to execute, to put to death; *Sport Fam (battre) (adversaire)* to slaughter; *Fam (critiquer) (travail, auteur etc)* to savage **6** *Bourse (spéculateur)* to hammer; *(client)* to sell out against

VPR s'exécuter to comply; **il faudra bien vous e.** you'll have to bring yourself to do it

exécuteur, -trice [ɛgzekytœr, -tris] N **1** *Jur* **e. testamentaire** executor; **exécutrice testamentaire** executrix **2** *Arch (d'un plan, d'une tâche)* executant

NM *(bourreau)* **e. (des hautes œuvres)** executioner

exécutif, -ive [ɛgzekytif, -iv] *Pol* ADJ *(pouvoir etc)* executive

NM **l'e.** the executive

exécution [ɛgzekysjɔ̃] NF **1** *(d'un plan, travail)* execution, carrying out; *(d'ordres, d'une décision)* carrying out; *(d'une promesse)* fulfilment; *(d'une danse, d'un morceau de musique)* performance, execution; *(d'une peinture, d'un roman etc)* execution; *Mil, Hum* **e.!** jump to it! at the double!; **droit d'e.** performing rights; **difficultés d'e. d'un morceau de musique** difficulties in the execution of a piece of music; **mettre un projet à e.** to put a plan into execution or operation, to carry out a plan; **travaux en voie d'e.** work in progress **2** *Ordinat* running, execution **3** *Jur (d'un débiteur)* distraint (**de** upon); *(d'une loi, d'un décret etc)* enforcement **4** *(mise à mort)* **e. (capitale)** execution; **ordre d'e.** death warrant; *Mil* **peloton d'e.** firing squad or party **5** *Bourse* **e. au prix du marché** execution at market

exécutoire [ɛgzekytwar] ADJ *Jur* **1** **jugement (de force) e.** enforceable decision *(of the court)* **2** *(formule)* executory

exégèse [ɛgzeʒɛz] NF exegesis

exégète [ɛgzeʒɛt] N exegete

exemplaire¹ [ɛgzɑ̃plɛr] ADJ **1** *(comportement, courage)* exemplary **2** **c'était une puni-**

tion e. the punishment was intended as an example

exemplaire² NM **1** *(livre, gravure etc)* copy; **en deux/trois exemplaires** in duplicate/triplicate; **photocopier un texte en 20 exemplaires** to make 20 photocopies of a text; **le livre a été tiré à 10 000 exemplaires** 10,000 copies of the book were published; **le journal tire à 150 000 exemplaires** the newspaper has a circulation of 150,000; **e. gratuit** presentation copy; **e. de lancement** advance copy; **exemplaires de passe** overs; **e. de service de presse** press copy **2** *(spécimen) (de plante, d'animal etc)* example

exemplairement [ɛgzɑ̃plɛrmɑ̃] ADV exemplarily; **elle a vécu e.** she led an exemplary life; **il a été puni e.** he was punished as an example to others

exemple [ɛgzɑ̃pl] NM **1** *(modèle)* example, model *(**pour** for)*; **donner l'e.** to set an example *(**à** to)*; **suivre l'e. de qn, prendre e. sur qn** to follow sb's example; **suivre le mauvais e. de qn** to follow sb's bad example; **prendre qn pour ou comme e.** to take sb as one's model, to model oneself on sb; **citer qn/qch en e.** to quote sb/sth as an example; **prêcher d'e.** to practise what one preaches; **faire un e.** *(en punissant qn)* to set an example; **servir d'e. à qn** *(d'une réussite etc)* to be an example to sb; *(d'une punition etc)* to be a lesson or a warning to sb; **infliger une punition à qn pour l'e.** to punish sb as an example or a warning to others **2** *(cas)* example, instance; *(mot, phrase)* example; **il est l'e. même du type qui ne sait pas ce qu'il veut** he's the perfect example of someone who doesn't know what he wants; **sans e.** without parallel, unparalleled; **être d'une gentillesse/d'un égoïsme sans e.** to be of unparalleled kindness/egoism; **j'en connais plein: e., ma mère** I know lots: my mother, for example or for instance **3** **par e.** for example, for instance; **un de ces jours, par e. dimanche** one of these days, say or for example or for instance on Sunday; *Fam* **ah ça par e.!** *(étonnement)* well really!; *Fam* **ah non, par e.!** I should think not!

exemplification [ɛgzɑ̃plifikasjɔ̃] NF exemplification

exemplifier [ɛgzɑ̃plifje] VT to exemplify

exempt, -te [ɛgzɑ̃, -ɑ̃t] ADJ **e. de** *(service militaire etc)* exempt from; *(anxiété, danger, maladie etc)* free from; **e. de soucis** free from care, carefree; **e. de droits (de douane)** free of duty, duty-free, non-dutiable; **e. d'impôts** tax-exempt, exempt from tax; **e. de TVA** zero-rated; **e. de port** carriage free; **elle a eu une vie dont tout souci était e.** she has had a life free from all care; **sa remarque n'était pas exempte d'une certaine amertume** his remark was not without a trace of bitterness

N *(personne)* exempt *(**de** from)*

exempter [ɛgzɑ̃te] VT *(d'impôt, de service militaire etc)* to exempt *(**de** from)*; *(d'anxiété, de risques etc)* to safeguard *(**de** against)*; **e. qn de faire qch** to exempt or excuse sb from doing sth

VPR s'exempter **s'e. de qch/de faire qch** to get out of sth/doing sth

exemption [ɛgzɑ̃psjɔ̃] NF exemption *(**de** from)*; **liste d'exemptions** *(de la douane)* free list; **e. d'impôts** tax exemption

exerçable [ɛgzɛrsabl] ADJ *Bourse* exerciseable

exercé [ɛgzɛrse] ADJ *(œil, oreille)* trained; *(main)* practised; **avoir l'œil/l'oreille exercé(e) à qch ou à faire qch** to have a trained eye/ear for doing sth

exercer [ɛgzɛrse] (**j'exerçai(s)**) VT **1** *(former) (son corps, esprit)* to exercise; *(mémoire)* to train; *Mil (soldats)* to drill; **e. qn à qch/à faire**

qch to train sb in sth/to do sth; **e. son esprit à l'art de la rhétorique** to train one's mind in the art of rhetoric **2** *(user de) (autorité, talent etc)* to exercise; **e. son influence sur qn** to exert or exercise one's influence on sb, to bring one's influence to bear on sb; **e. une pression sur qch/qn** to exert pressure on sth/sb; **e. ses droits** to exercise one's rights; **e. un contrôle sur** to exercise control over **3** *(profession)* to practise; **e. des fonctions** to carry out duties; **j'exerce le métier de journaliste** I'm a journalist by profession **4** *Bourse (option)* to exercise; **e. par anticipation** to exercise in advance

VI *(d'un médecin, juriste etc)* to practise, to be in practice

VPR s'exercer 1 *(d'un chanteur, sportif etc)* to practise; **s'e. à qch/à faire qch** to practise sth/doing sth; **s'e. au piano** to practise the piano **2** *(se manifester) (autorité, pouvoir)* to make itself felt; **sa mauvaise foi s'exerce aussi contre ses proches** his/her close relations also feel the effects of his/her dishonesty

exercice [ɛgzɛrsis] NM **1** *(physique)* exercise; **faire des exercices** to do (some) exercises; **prendre ou faire de l'e.** to (take) exercise; **manquer d'e.** to lack exercise; **e. physique** physical exercise **2** *Mil* drill(ing); **être à l'e.** to be on parade; **faire l'e.** to drill **3** *Sport, Mus, Scol etc (mouvement, tâche)* exercise; **exercices de grammaire** grammar exercises; **faire ses exercices** to do one's exercises; **faire des exercices au piano** to do (some) piano exercises; **e. d'évacuation en cas d'incendie** fire drill **4** *(du pouvoir, d'un droit)* exercise; *(d'une profession)* practice; **dans l'e. de ses fonctions** in the exercise or discharge of one's duties; **être en e.** *(d'un avocat etc)* to be in practice, to be practising; **avocat en e.** practising lawyer; **le président en e.** the president in office; **être condamné pour e. illégal de la médecine** to be sentenced for the illegal practice of medicine or for practising medicine illegally **5** *Rel* **l'e. du culte** public worship **6** *(en comptabilité)* financial year, *Am* fiscal year; **bilan en fin d'e.** end-of-year balance sheet; **e. bénéficiaire** profitable year ▸▸ *Compta* **e. budgétaire** financial or *Am* fiscal year; **e. comptable** financial or accounting or *Am* fiscal year; **e. en cours** current financial year, *Am* current fiscal year; **e. écoulé** last financial or *Am* fiscal year; **e. financier** financial or *Am* fiscal year; **e. fiscal** tax year

exerciseur [ɛgzɛrsizœr] NM *(appareil de gymnastique)* exerciser; *(pour poitrine)* chest expander

exergue [ɛgzɛrg] NM *(d'une médaille)* inscription, *Spéc* exergue; *(d'une illustration)* inscription; *(d'un texte)* epigraph; *Fig* **mettre une idée en e.** to highlight an idea, to point up an idea

exfoliant [ɛksfɔljɑ̃] ADJ exfoliating

NM face/body scrub, *Spéc* exfoliant

exfoliation [ɛksfɔljasjɔ̃] NF exfoliation

exfolier (s') [sɛksfɔlje] VPR to exfoliate, to scale off

exhalaison [ɛgzalɛzɔ̃] NF *(odeur, vapeur)* exhalation

exhalation [ɛgzalasjɔ̃] NF *(action)* exhalation, exhaling

exhaler [ɛgzale] VT *(odeur, vapeur etc)* to give off; *(soupir)* to breathe; *Fig (joie, colère etc)* to give vent to, to vent; *Fig* **cette maison exhale la tristesse** sadness pervades this house

VPR s'exhaler *(d'une odeur, de la vapeur etc)* to be given off

exhaussement [ɛgzosmɑ̃] NM *(d'un mur, édifice etc)* increase in the height

exhausser [ɛgzose] VT *(mur, édifice etc)* to heighten, to increase the height of; **e. une maison d'un étage** to add a storey to a house

exhaustif, -ive [ɛgzostif, -iv] ADJ exhaustive

exhaustivement [ɛgzostivmɑ̃] ADV exhaustively

exhaustivité [ɛgzostivite] NF exhaustiveness

exhiber [ɛgzibe] VT **1** *(documents etc)* to produce; *(passeport, carte d'identité etc)* to present, to show **2** *(animaux)* to exhibit, to show **3** *Péj (ses connaissances, richesses, vêtements)* to show off, to flaunt; *(photos etc)* to show off; **e. ses muscles** to show off or display one's muscles
▶ VPR **s'exhiber** to flaunt oneself

exhibition [ɛgzibisjɔ̃] NF **1** *Jur (de documents)* production **2** *(présentation) (d'animaux)* show **3** *Péj (étalage) (de connaissances, richesses)* flaunting, showing off; *(de muscles)* display

> Il faut noter que le nom anglais **exhibition** est un faux ami. Il signifie le plus souvent **exposition**.

exhibitionnisme [ɛgzibisjɔnism] NM exhibitionism

exhibitionniste [ɛgzibisjɔnist] N exhibitionist

exhibo [ɛgzibo] N *Fam (abrév* **exhibitionniste***)* exhibitionist

exhortation [ɛgzɔrtasjɔ̃] NF exhortation (**à qch** to sth; **à faire qch** to do sth)

exhorter [ɛgzɔrte] VT to exhort (**à qch** to sth; **à faire qch** to do sth), to urge (**à faire qch** to do sth)

exhumation [ɛgzymasjɔ̃] NF *(d'un corps)* exhumation; *(d'un trésor, des vestiges d'une ville etc)* digging up, excavation; *Fig (de vieux documents etc)* unearthing; *(de vieilles rancunes, souvenirs etc)* digging up; *(d'une ancienne loi, coutume etc)* exhumation

exhumer [ɛgzyme] VT *(corps)* to exhume; *(trésor, vestiges d'une ville etc)* to dig up, to excavate; *Fig (vieux documents etc)* to unearth; *(vieilles rancunes, souvenirs etc)* to dig up; *(ancienne loi, coutume etc)* to exhume

exigeant [ɛgziʒɑ̃] ADJ *(personne, travail etc)* demanding, exacting; **être trop e.** *(d'une personne)* to expect too much, to be too demanding; *Iron* **je ne suis pas e., je demande juste la fortune et la célébrité!** I don't want much, just fame and fortune!

exigence [ɛgziʒɑ̃s] NF **1** *(caractère)* **elle est d'une e. insupportable** she's intolerably demanding **2** *(condition) (d'un client etc)* demand, requirement; *(d'un métier, milieu)* demand; **l'e. ou les exigences de l'étiquette** the demands or requirements of etiquette

exiger [ɛgziʒe] VT *(j'exigeai(s))* **1** *(demander en insistant) (action, paiement, silence etc)* to demand, to require, to insist on (**de** from); *(rançon)* to demand; **trop e. des forces de qn** to overtax sb's strength; **e. qu'une chose soit faite** to insist on a thing being done, to demand that a thing be done; **j'exige des excuses/que vous vous excusiez** I demand an apology/that you apologize; **j'exige réparation** I demand redress; **j'exige d'être payé immédiatement** I demand to be paid or I insist on being paid immediately, I demand or insist on immediate payment; **le port de la cravate est exigé** ties must be worn
2 *(nécessiter) (soin, action etc)* to require, to necessitate, to call for; **prendre les mesures qu'exigent les circonstances** to take the ne-

cessary measures; **ces plantes exigent des engrais particuliers** these plants require or need special fertilizer; **aucune qualification particulière n'est exigée pour ce poste** no special qualification is required or needed for this post

exigibilité [ɛgziʒibilite] NF *Fin* **date d'e.** due date; **e. de taxe** tax liability; **e. immédiate** immediately due

exigible [ɛgziʒibl] ADJ *(dette, impôt)* payable, due (for payment); **le paiement est e. dès réception de la facture** payment is due upon receipt of the invoice; **e. à vue** payable at sight

exigu, -uë [ɛgzigy] ADJ *(lieu)* cramped, tiny; *Vieilli (somme)* meagre, slender

exiguïté [ɛgziguite] NF *(d'un lieu)* crampedness, tininess; *Vieilli (d'une somme)* meagreness

exil [ɛgzil] NM *(expulsion)* exile; **envoyer qn en e.** to send sb into exile, to exile sb; **vivre en e.** to live in exile; **se sentir en e.** to feel like an exile

exilé, -ée [ɛgzile] N *(personne)* exile

exiler [ɛgzile] VT *(d'un pays)* to exile (**de** from); *(d'une ville, de la cour etc)* to banish (**de** from); *Fig* **on l'a exilé à l'autre bout de la classe** he was banished or exiled to the other end of the classroom
▶ VPR **s'exiler** *Pol* to go into (voluntary) exile; *Fig* to cut oneself off or withdraw (from the world); **il s'est exilé à la campagne pour terminer son livre** he withdrew to the country to finish his book; **s'e. à l'autre bout du monde** to go into self-imposed exile on the other side of the world; **s'e. de la ville** to cut oneself off from the town

existant [ɛgzistɑ̃] ADJ existing; **lois existantes** existing laws, laws in force
NM *Com* **e. en caisse/en magasin** cash/stock in hand

existence [ɛgzistɑ̃s] NF **1** *Phil (être)* existence, (state of) being **2** *(vie)* existence, life; **changer d'e.** to change one's (way of) life; **mener une e. tranquille** to lead a quiet existence or life; **dans l'e.** in life **3** *(présence, réalité)* existence (**de** of) **4** *(durée) (d'une institution etc)* life; **il est improbable que ce gouvernement puisse dépasser un an d'e.** it's unlikely that this government can stay in existence for longer than a year **5** *Compta* **existences en caisse** cash on hand

existentialisme [ɛgzistɑ̃sjalism] NM *Phil* existentialism

existentialiste [ɛgzistɑ̃sjalist] ADJ, N *Phil* existentialist

existentiel, -elle [ɛgzistɑ̃sjɛl] ADJ existential

exister [ɛgziste] VI *(vivre, être réel, se trouver)* to exist; *Com* to be available; **il existe** *(il y a)* there is, *pl* there are; **existe-t-il une vie sur Mars?** does life exist on Mars?, is there life on Mars?; **la maison existe toujours** the house still exists or is still standing; *Com* the firm still exists or is still in existence; **je n'arrive pas à croire qu'un autre monde puisse e.** I just can't believe that there is another world or that another world exists; **les roses noires, ça n'existe pas** there is no such thing as a black rose, black roses don't exist; **rien n'existe pour lui que l'art** nothing but art matters to him; **pour elle, l'amour/le bonheur/le danger n'existe pas** love/happiness/danger doesn't exist for her; **et l'amitié, cela existe, non?** there is such a thing as friendship, isn't there?; **je ne veux pas vous déranger, faites comme si je n'existais pas** I don't want to disturb you, pretend I'm not here or I don't exist; *Hum* **si ta sœur/le vélo n'existait pas, il faudrait l'inventer** if your sister/the bicycle didn't exist, we would have to invent her/it

exit [ɛgzit] ADV *Théâtre* exit, *Fml* exeunt; **e. les gardes** exit or esp *Fml* exeunt the guards; *Fig Fam* **le ministre des affaires étrangères** out goes or exit the foreign minister

ex-libris [ɛkslibris] NM *(vignette)* bookplate, ex-libris

ex navire [ɛksnavir] ADJ, ADV *Com* ex ship

ex nihilo [ɛksniilo] ADV, ADJ INV out of or from nothing, ex nihilo

exo [ɛgzo] NM *(abrév* **exercice***) Fam* exercise

exocet [ɛgzose(t)] NM **1** *(poisson)* flying fish **2** **Exocet®** *(missile)* Exocet

exocrine [ɛgzɔkrin] ADJ *Physiol* exocrine

exode [ɛgzɔd] NM **1** *(émigration)* exodus; *Hist* **l'e.** = the flight of the French civilian population during the 1940 German invasion **2** *Bible* **l'E.** *(livre)* Exodus; *(émigration des Hébreux)* the Exodus
▶▶ **e. des capitaux** flight of capital; **l'e. des cerveaux** the brain drain; **e. rural** rural depopulation

exogame [ɛgzogam] ADJ *(tribu etc)* exogamous

exogamie [ɛgzogami] NF exogamy

exogène [ɛgzoʒɛn] ADJ exogenous

exonération [ɛgzonerasjɔ̃] NF exemption; **e. d'impôts** or **fiscale** tax exemption; **e. de TVA** exemption from VAT; **e. de responsabilité** exemption from liability

exonérer [ɛgzonere] VT *(j'exonère; j'exonérerai)* *(personne)* to exempt; *(marchandises)* to exempt from import duty; **être exonéré d'impôts** to be exempt from tax; **exonéré de TVA** VAT-exempt, zero-rated

exophtalmie [ɛgzɔftalmi] NF *Méd* exophthalmus, exophthalmos

exophtalmique [ɛgzɔftalmik] ADJ *Méd (goitre)* exophthalmic

exoplanète [ɛgzoplanɛt] NF *Astron* exoplanet

exorbitant [ɛgzɔrbitɑ̃] ADJ *(prix, demande etc)* exorbitant

exorbité [ɛgzɔrbite] ADJ *(yeux)* protruding; *Fig* **ils regardaient, les yeux exorbités** they were watching with their eyes bulging (out of their heads)

exorciser [ɛgzɔrsize] VT *(démon, possédé)* to exorcize; *(démon)* to cast out; *(fantôme)* to lay; *Fig (ses peurs, les démons de sa jeunesse etc)* to exorcize

exorcisme [ɛgzɔrsism] NM exorcism

exorciste [ɛgzɔrsist] N exorcist

exorde [ɛgzɔrd] NM exordium

exosmose [ɛgzɔsmoz] NF *Phys* exosmosis

exotique [ɛgzɔtik] ADJ exotic; **une collection d'objets exotiques** a collection of exotica; **poisson e.** tropical fish

exotisme [ɛgzɔtism] NM exoticism

expansé [ɛkspɑ̃se] ADJ *(polystyrène)* expanded

expansibilité [ɛkspɑ̃sibilite] NF *(d'un gaz, de l'eau)* expansibility

expansible [ɛkspɑ̃sibl] ADJ *(gaz, eau)* expansible

expansif, -ive [ɛkspɑ̃sif, -iv] ADJ **1** *(exubérant) (personne)* expansive, outgoing **2** *Phys (force etc)* expansive

expansion [ɛkspɑ̃sjɔ̃] NF **1** *Phys (des gaz, de l'univers etc)* expansion; **l'univers en e.** the expanding universe **2** *(développement) (d'une ville, industrie etc)* expansion; *(d'idées, d'une culture etc)* spread(ing); **e. coloniale** colonial expansion; **taux d'e. économique** economic growth rate; **être en pleine e.** *(d'une économie, entreprise)* to be booming **3** *(exubérance)* expansiveness; **avec e.** expansively **4** *Ordinat* **carte d'e.** expansion card

expansionnisme [ɛkspɑ̃sjɔnism] **NM** expansionism

expansioniste [ɛkspɑ̃sjɔnist] **ADJ, N** expansionist

expansivité [ɛkspɑ̃sivite] **NF** expansiveness

expatriation [ɛkspatrijasjɔ̃] **NF** expatriation; *Fin* **e. de capitaux** movement of capital abroad

expatrié, -ée [ɛkspatrije] **ADJ** expatriate, *Fam* expat; *(réseau de vente etc)* overseas **N** expatriate, *Fam* expat

expatrier [ɛkspatrije] *(impf, pr sub* **n. expatriions)** **VT** *(personne)* to expatriate; *(capitaux)* to move abroad
VPR s'expatrier to settle abroad

expectative [ɛkspɛktativ] **NF** *(attente)* expectation (**de** of); **nous vivons dans l'e.** we are living in hope; **rester dans l'e.** to wait and see

expectorant [ɛkspɛktɔrɑ̃] **ADJ, NM** *Méd* expectorant

expectoration [ɛkspɛktɔrasjɔ̃] **NF** *(action, crachat)* expectoration

expectorer [ɛkspɛktɔre] **VT** to expectorate

expédient [ɛkspedjɑ̃] **ADJ** *Fml* expedient **NM** expedient, makeshift; **vivre d'expédients** to live by one's wits; **user d'expédients** to resort to evasion

expédier [ɛkspedje] **VT** *(impf, pr sub* **n. expédiions)** **1** *(envoyer)* to dispatch, to send off; *Com* to dispatch, to ship; **e. des marchandises par navire** to send goods by sea, to ship goods; **e. un colis par chemin de fer** to dispatch *or* send *or* ship a parcel by rail; **e. par fret aérien** to airfreight; *Fam* **expédiez-le-moi!** *(personne)* send him along (to me)!; *Fam* **e. qn dans l'autre monde** *ou* **au cimetière** to dispatch sb to the next world **2** *(se débarrasser de)* to get rid of, to dispose of; **elle a expédié ses enfants chez sa belle-mère/en colonie de vacances/au lit** she sent *or* packed her children off to her mother-in-law's/to camp/to bed; **il a tendance à e. ses patients un peu vite** *(d'un médecin)* he tends to pack his patients out of the surgery rather quickly **3** *(faire rapidement) (tâche etc)* to deal promptly with; *(ses devoirs, sa dissertation)* to dash off; **e. son déjeuner** to make short work of one's lunch; **e. les affaires courantes** to deal with *or* get rid of the day-to-day matters **4** *Jur (contrat, acte etc)* to draw up

expéditeur, -trice [ɛkspeditœr, -tris] **N 1** *(d'une lettre, d'un colis etc)* sender; **e./expéditrice J. Martin** from *or* sender J. Martin **2** *Com (de marchandises)* shipper, consigner; *(par bateau)* shipper **ADJ** *(bureau, compagnie, gare etc)* shipping, dispatching

expéditif, -ive [ɛkspeditif, -iv] **ADJ** speedy, expeditious; **il est toujours très e. avec ses patients** he spends very little time with his patients; **je n'aime pas beaucoup ces méthodes expéditives** I don't appreciate this hasty way of doing things

expédition [ɛkspedisjɔ̃] **NF 1** *(envoi)* dispatch, sending; *Com* shipping, shipment; **e. par mer** shipping, shipment; *Com* **bulletin d'e.** waybill; *Com* **e. de détail** retail shipment; **e. exclusive** exclusive shipment; **e. maritime** maritime shipment; **e. par avion** airfreighting; **e. par bateau** shipping; **e. par chemin de fer** sending by rail, railfreighting; **e. par courrier** mailing; **e. par la poste** mailing; *Com* **e. partielle** part shipment *or* consignment; *Com* **e. port à port** port-to-port shipment; *Com* **expéditions** *(service)* dispatch (department), shipping (department) **2** *(marchandises)* consignment, shipment **3** *(voyage, opération militaire)*, *Fig* expedi-

tion; **partir en e.** to go (off) on an expedition; *Fig* **dis donc, pour venir chez toi, quelle e.!** it's quite an expedition *or* a trek getting to your place! **4** *Admin* **il est chargé de l'e. des affaires courantes** he is in charge of day-to-day matters; **je préfère m'occuper d'abord de l'e. des affaires courantes** I prefer to deal with *or* get rid of the day-to-day matters first **5** *Jur (d'un contrat etc)* *(authentic)* copy

expéditionnaire [ɛkspedisjɔnɛr] **ADJ** *Mil* expeditionary **N** *Com* shipping clerk

expérience [ɛksperjɑ̃s] **NF 1** *(pratique)* experience; **avec l'e., tu sauras que …** you'll find out with experience that …; **il a de l'e.** he's got experience, he's experienced; **elle a deux ans d'e.** she has two years' experience; **il nous faut quelqu'un qui a de l'e.** we need someone with experience; **avoir l'e. de qch** to have experience of sth, to be experienced in sth; **il a l'e. des enfants/de ce genre de voitures** he is used to children/this kind of car; **savoir qch par e.** to know sth from experience; **sans e.** inexperienced (**de** in), with no experience (**de** of); **il est sans e. de la vie** he has no experience of life **2** *(essai)* experiment; **faire l'e. de** *(mauvaise humeur, douleur)* to experience; *(la vie à deux)* to experience, to try; *(machine)* to try out; **j'ai fait l'e. de la douleur** I've experienced pain, I've had experience of pain; **j'en ai malheureusement fait l'e.** that has been my experience unfortunately *or* as I've discovered to my cost; **nous avons décidé de tenter l'e.** we've decided to give it a try *or* a go; **tu pourrais tenter l'e. des clubs de rencontre** you could give dating agencies a try **3** *(test scientifique)* experiment; **e. en laboratoire** laboratory experiment; **e. sur le terrain** field experiment; **faire une e.** to carry out *or* do an experiment (**sur** on)

Attention: ne pas confondre **experience** et **experiment** lorsque l'on traduit **expérience**. **Experience** s'applique à la pratique que l'on a d'une chose, alors que **experiment** ne s'utilise que pour l'essai d'une chose nouvelle.

---

expérimental, -ale, -aux, -ales [ɛksperimɑ̃tal, -o] **ADJ** experimental

expérimentalement [ɛksperimɑ̃talmɑ̃] **ADV** experimentally

expérimentateur, -trice [ɛksperimɑ̃tatœr, -tris] **N** experimenter; *(scientifique)* (scientific) research worker

expérimentation [ɛksperimɑ̃tasjɔ̃] **NF** experimentation; **l'e. de ce produit n'a pas encore été faite** the product has not yet been tested; **e. sur l'homme** *(d'un vaccin etc)* human experiments, tests on humans

expérimenté [ɛksperimɑ̃te] **ADJ** experienced; **il a un œil e. pour repérer les bonnes affaires** she's got a good eye for a bargain

expérimenter [ɛksperimɑ̃te] **VT** *(tester)* *(remède, modèle, vaccin etc)* to test, to try out (**sur** on); **cette machine a été longuement expérimentée** the machine has been thoroughly tested
VI to experiment, to carry out experiments

expert [ɛkspɛr] **ADJ** expert, skilled (**en, dans** in; **à faire qch** in doing sth); **elle est experte à vous faire douter de vous-même** she is an expert at making you doubt yourself; **être e. en la matière** to be an expert in the matter **NM** expert; *(d'assurance, d'objets d'art)* valuer, appraiser; *Naut* surveyor; **e. financier/fiscal** financial/tax expert

expert-comptable, *pl* **experts-comptables NM** *Br* ≃ chartered accountant, *Am* ≃ certified public accountant

expert-conseil, *pl* **experts-conseils NM** consultant

expertise [ɛkspɛrtiz] **NF 1** *(évaluation) (d'une œuvre d'art etc)* *(expert)* valuation, appraisal; *(dans les assurances) (de dommages)* (expert) assessment; *Jur* expert opinion *or* testimony; *(dans les assurances)* **rapport d'e.** assessor's report, claims adjuster's report; *Naut* **e. d'avarie** damage survey; **e. médico-légale** forensic examination; *Jur* **e. contradictoire** valuation made in the presence of both parties to a contract **2** *(rapport)* expert's report **3** *(compétence)* expertise

expertiser [ɛkspɛrtize] **VT** *(œuvre d'art etc)* to value, to appraise; *(dommages)* to assess

expert-répétiteur, *pl* **experts-répétiteurs NM** *Fin* loss *or* average adjuster

expiable [ɛkspjabl] **ADJ** which can be atoned for; **tu as commis une faute, certes, mais elle est e.** yes, you made a mistake but you can make up for it

expiation [ɛkspjasjɔ̃] **NF** atonement (**de** for), expiation (**de** of)

expiatoire [ɛkspjatwar] **ADJ** expiatory

expier [ɛkspje] **VT** *(impf, pr sub* **n. expiions)** *(péché, crime)* to atone for, to pay the penalty for, *Fml* to expiate; *(erreur)* to atone for, to make up for

expirant [ɛkspirɑ̃] **ADJ** *Litt (personne)* dying; *(flamme)* dying, guttering; **voix expirante** faint *or* barely audible voice

expiration [ɛkspirasjɔ̃] **NF 1** *(respiration)* breathing out, exhalation, *Spéc* expiration; **pendant** *ou* **sur l'e.** on exhalation, as you/he/etc exhale(s) *or* breathes out **2** *(d'un contrat, un bail etc)* expiry, *Am* expiration; **venir** *ou* **arriver à e.** to expire, to run out

expirer [ɛkspire] **VI 1** *Litt (mourir)* to die, *Fml* to expire; *Fig (d'une flamme, d'une vague)* to die; *(d'un feu)* to go out; *(d'un son)* to die *or* fade away **2** *(d'un contrat, un bail etc)* to expire, to run out; **mon congé est expiré** my leave is up *or* has expired **3** *(respirer)* to breathe out, to exhale, *Spéc* to expire
VT *(air)* to breathe out, to exhale, *Spéc* to expire

explétif, -ive [ɛkspletif, -iv] **ADJ, NM** *Gram* expletive

explicable [ɛksplikabl] **ADJ** explicable, explainable; **ces phénomènes ne sont explicables que par le paranormal** such phenomena can only be explained *or* accounted for in terms of the paranormal; **sa conduite est difficilement e.** his behaviour is difficult to explain, it is difficult to account for his behaviour

explicatif, -ive [ɛksplikatif, -iv] **ADJ** explanatory; *Com* **notice explicative** directions for use; *Gram* **proposition relative explicative** non-defining relative clause

explication [ɛksplikasjɔ̃] **NF** explanation (**à** for); **je ne comprends pas les explications de la machine** I don't understand the instructions for the machine; **il a quitté la réunion sans aucune e.** he left the meeting without (giving) any explanation; **donner l'e. de qch** to account for *or* explain sth; **j'exige des explications!** I demand an explanation!; **avoir une e. avec qn** *(discuter)* to talk things over with sb; *(se disputer)* to have it out with sb; **je crois qu'il va falloir que nous ayons une petite e. tous les deux** I think we're going to have to have a little talk, you and I; **il y a eu une violente e. entre les deux équipes** there was a violent altercation between the two teams
▸▸ *Scol, Univ* **e. de textes** critical analysis

explicite [ɛksplisit] **ADJ** explicit (**sur** about)

explicitement [ɛksplisitmɑ̃] **ADV** explicitly;

formuler e. une demande to make an explicit request

expliciter [εksplisite] VT *(texte, pensées, clause d'un contrat etc)* to clarify; **il n'a pas voulu e. ses intentions** he did not want to be explicit about what he meant to do

expliquer [εksplike] VT **1** *(communiquer) (ses idées, plans etc)* to explain (**à qn** to sb); **ce serait trop long à e.** it would take too long to explain; *Fam* **on s'est pris un de ces savons, je t'explique pas...** you wouldn't have believed the telling-off we got... **2** *(élucider) (doctrine, théorème etc)* to explain, to expound, to elucidate; *(mystère, signification)* to explain **3** *(indiquer la raison de) (action, fait, attitude etc)* to explain, to account for

VPR s'expliquer 1 *(communiquer ses idées)* to explain oneself; *(se justifier)* to justify one's behaviour, to explain oneself; **me serais-je mal expliqué?** perhaps I didn't make myself clear *or* wasn't plain enough; **je m'explique** this is what I mean, let me explain; **elle s'est expliquée sur différents reproches qu'on lui faisait** she justified herself with regard to the things they reproached her with **2** *(comprendre)* **je ne m'explique pas pourquoi** I can't understand why **3** *(être explicable)* **cela s'explique facilement** that's easily understandable *or* explainable; **il y a des choses qui ne s'expliquent pas** some things can't be explained; **c'est bizarre mais ça s'explique** it's strange but it can be explained *or* there's an explanation for it; **sa mort ne s'explique que par un suicide** his death can only be put down to suicide, suicide is the only explanation for his death; **le mauvais temps s'explique par la présence d'une dépression** the presence of a depression explains the bad weather; **et bien voilà, tout s'explique!** so you see, there's a reason for everything! **4** *(de plusieurs personnes)* to talk things over; **s'e. avec qn** *(discuter)* to talk things over with sb; *(se disputer)* to have it out with sb; **expliquez-vous une bonne fois pour toutes** get it sorted out once and for all; **viens un peu, on va s'e. dehors** come on, we'll settle this outside; **ils se sont expliqués au couteau** they settled it with knives

exploit [εksplwa] NM **1** *(sportif, oratoire etc)* feat, achievement; *(militaire, amoureux)* exploit; **il est arrivé à l'heure, tu te rends compte d'un e.!** he arrived on time, which was quite an achievement for him! **2** *Jur* **e. (d'huissier)** writ

exploitable [εksplwatabl] ADJ *(terre)* farmable; *(mine, forêt)* workable; *(ressources naturelles)*, *Fig, Péj* exploitable; **tes documents ne sont pas exploitables dans l'optique de mes recherches** I can't make use of your documentation for my research; **e. par ordinateur** machine readable; **corpus e. par ordinateur** computerized corpus; *Fig Péj* **elles sont facilement exploitables** they are easily exploited *or* easy to exploit

exploitant [εksplwatɑ̃] N **1** *Com, Ind (de mine)* operator; **les exploitants de l'entreprise** the people running the company; **e. (agricole)** farmer; **petits exploitants** small farmers **2** *Cin (propriétaire)* owner; *(directeur)* manager, *Am* exhibitor

exploitation [εksplwatasjɔ̃] NF **1** *(action) (d'une mine, forêt etc)* working; *(d'une ligne de chemin de fer, ligne aérienne, ferme etc)* running, operation; *(d'une terre)* farming; *(des ressources naturelles)*, *Fig, Péj* exploitation; *Com (d'un brevet)* commercialization; *Ordinat* **système d'e.** operating system; **société d'e.** development company; **mettre une terre en e.** to bring a piece of land into cultivation; **faire l'e. industrielle de qch** to produce sth on an industrial scale; **e. capita-**

liste capitalist exploitation; **l'e. de l'homme par l'homme** the exploitation of man by man; *Fig Péj* **c'est de l'e.!** it's exploitation! **2** *(entreprise)* concern; **e. agricole** farm; **petite e. agricole** small farm, smallholding; **e. forestière** forestry concern *or* operation; **e. minière** mine; **e. à ciel ouvert** open cast mine; **e. industrielle** industrial concern; **e. commerciale** business (concern); **e. familiale** family business

exploiter [εksplwate] VT **1** *(mine)* to work; *(forêt)* to work, to exploit; *(ressources naturelles, brevet)* to exploit; *(invention)* to use; *(chemin de fer, ferme, journal etc)* to run, to operate; *(terre)* to farm; *Fig (situation, talent, idée etc)* to exploit, to make the most of, to capitalize on **2** *Péj (abuser de) (personne, l'ignorance de qn etc)* to exploit, to take (unfair) advantage of

exploiteur, -euse [εksplwatœr, -øz] N *(de main-d'œuvre, de l'ignorance de qn etc)* exploiter

explorateur, -trice [εksplɔratœr, -tris] N *(personne)* explorer

exploration [εksplɔrasjɔ̃] NF **1** *(d'un pays, d'une maison)*, *Fig (d'un sujet etc)* exploration; **voyage d'e.** voyage of discovery; **partir en e.** to go off exploring *or* on an exploration **2** *Méd* exploration

exploratoire [εksplɔratwar] ADJ exploratory

explorer [εksplɔre] VT **1** *(pays, maison)*, *Fig (sujet, possibilité etc)* to explore **2** *Méd (blessure, cavité)* to explore, to probe

exploser [εksploze] VI **1** *(d'une bombe)* to explode, to go off; *(d'un avion, d'une chaudière etc)* to explode, to blow up; *(d'un gaz)* to explode; **faire e. une bombe** to explode a bomb **2** *Fig (se mettre en colère)* **e. (de colère)** to explode, *Fam* to blow one's top **3** *Fam (apparaître)* **ils ont explosé sur la scène rock il y a vingt ans** they burst onto the rock scene twenty years ago **4** *Fam (augmenter de façon spectaculaire)* to soar, to (sky) rocket

VT *Fam* **1** *(battre)* **e. qn** to kick sb's head in, to smash sb's face in **2** **être explosé (de rire)** to be killing oneself (laughing), to be cracking up, to be in stitches

explosible [εksplozibl] ADJ *(gaz etc)* explosive

explosif, -ive [εksplozif, -iv] ADJ *(obus, force etc)*, *Fig situation, question, tempérament etc)* explosive; *Ling (consonne)* plosive; **il est d'un tempérament e.** he tends to explode *or* erupt *or Fam* blow his top

NM explosive

explosion [εksplozjɔ̃] NF *aussi Fig* explosion; **e. atomique** atomic explosion; **e. volcanique** volcanic explosion *or* eruption; **faire e.** to explode; **e. de fureur/rires** explosion *or* (out)burst of fury/laughter; **e. démographique** population explosion; **e. des naissances** baby boom

expo [εkspo] NF *Fam (abrév* **exposition)** exhibition

exponentiel, -ielle [εksponɑ̃sjεl] ADJ, N *Math* exponential

export [εkspɔr] NM export; **l'e., le service e.** the export branch; *Ordinat* **e. de données** data export

exportable [εkspɔrtabl] ADJ exportable

exportateur, -trice [εkspɔrtatœr, -tris] N exporter

ADJ exporting; **pays e. de vin** wine-exporting country

exportation [εkspɔrtasjɔ̃] NF *(action)* export(ation), exporting; *(produit)* export; *Ordinat (d'un fichier)* exporting; *Ordinat (données exportées)* exported data; **le montant des exportations a augmenté de 10%**

cette année exports have risen by 10% this year; **ce produit marche très fort à l'e.** this product is doing very well on the export market, we export a lot of this product; **l'e. de nos produits a rencontré un vif succès** our products have been very successful on the export market; **réservé à l'e.** reserved for export, for export only; **articles d'e.** exports; **faire de l'e.** to export; **exportations visibles/invisibles** visible/invisible exports; **e. de capitaux** export of capital; **commerce d'e.** export trade; **e. kangourou** piggybacking

exporter [εkspɔrte] VT *Com, Ordinat* to export (**vers** to); **ces articles s'exportent mal** these items are difficult to export; *Fig* **ce genre de coutume s'exporte mal** this type of custom does not export *or* travel well; **cette mode a été** *ou* **s'est exportée dans le monde entier** the fashion has spread throughout the world

exposant, -ante [εkspozɑ̃, -ɑ̃t] N *(artiste, firme etc)* exhibitor

NM **1** *Math* exponent, (power) index **2** *Typ (chiffre, lettre)* superscript, superior **3 en exposant** superscript **3**

exposé [εkspoze] NM **1** *(de faits, d'une situation etc)* statement, account, report; *Scol, Univ* presentation; **faire un e. des faits** to give an account of the facts; **après avoir fait un bref e. de la situation** after outlining the situation; **faire l'e. d'un projet** to sketch out a plan; **e. verbal (de mission)** briefing; *Compta* **e. de la situation de l'entreprise** statement of the company's position **2** *(discours)* (short) talk; **faire un e.** to give a (short) talk **3** *Jur* **e. des motifs** *(d'un projet de loi)* preamble

exposer [εkspoze] VT **1** *(montrer) (marchandises, œuvres d'art etc)* to exhibit, to show, to display; **objet exposé** exhibit; **ça fait très longtemps qu'il n'a pas exposé** he hasn't exhibited anything for a very long time; **être exposé (sur un lit de parade)** to lie in state; **e. des marchandises en vitrine** to display goods for sale **2** *(expliquer) (plans, raisons, problème etc)* to set out, to unfold, to expound; *(ses griefs, problèmes, son point de vue)* to air; **je leur ai exposé ma situation** I explained my situation to them **3** *(présenter) (à la chaleur, lumière etc)* to expose (**à** to); *(à la critique, un danger etc)* to expose, to lay open (**à** to); *Hist (nouveau-né)* to expose; **il faut e. cette plante à la lumière le plus possible** the plant must receive *or* get as much light as possible; **parce que la plante n'était pas du tout exposée** because the plant wasn't getting any light at all; **exposé à tous les vents** exposed *or* open to the four winds; **maison exposée au nord** house facing north *or* with a northern outlook; *Phot* **e. un film à la lumière** to expose a film **4** *(risquer) (sa vie, son honneur etc)* to risk, to take chances with; **e. qn** to put sb in danger **5** *Mus* to introduce; *Littér* to set out

VPR s'exposer to put oneself in danger; **s'e. à des critiques** to lay oneself open *or* expose oneself to criticism; **il s'expose à des poursuites** he is laying himself open to prosecution; **s'e. au soleil** to expose oneself to the sun; **si tu t'exposes trop longtemps** if you stay in the sun too long

exposition [εkspozisjɔ̃] NF **1** *(action de montrer) (de marchandises, d'œuvres d'art, de fleurs etc)* display; *(d'un corps)* lying in state **2** *(dans un musée, une galerie)* exhibition **3** *(salon, foire)* exhibition, show; **salle d'e.** exhibition room, *Can* showroom; **e. interprofessionnelle** trade exhibition *or* show; **e. commerciale** trade exhibition; **E. universelle** world fair; *Mktg* **e. sur le lieu de vente** point of sale display; *Mktg* **e. sur le marché** market exposure

4 *(de faits, raisons etc)* exposition

5 *(au froid, danger etc)* exposure (**à** to); *(d'une maison)* aspect, exposure; *Phot* exposure; **e. solaire** exposure to the sun; **il lui faut au minimum une heure d'e.** (**à la lumière**) **par jour** it needs at least an hour of light a day; *Fin* **e. aux risques** exposure

6 *Littér, Mus* exposition, introduction; *Mus* **d'e.** introductory, expository; *Littér* **scène d'e.** prologue, *Am* prolog

7 *Typ* **e. directe des plaques** computer to plate, CTP

exposition-vente, *pl* **expositions-ventes** NF *Com* show, exhibition *(where the items are for sale)*

exprès¹, -esse [ɛksprɛs] ADJ *(explicite)* *(ordre, mise en garde etc)* express, distinct, explicit; **vous avez l'interdiction expresse de jouer dans la rue** you are expressly forbidden to play in the street; **défense expresse de fumer** smoking strictly prohibited

ADJ INV, NM *Arch* **(lettre/paquet) e.** special delivery *or Br* express letter/parcel; **par** *ou* **en e.** (by) special *or Br* express delivery

exprès² [ɛksprɛ] ADV *(à dessein)* on purpose, intentionally, deliberately; *(spécialement)* specially, especially; **elle est sortie e. pour l'acheter** she went out specially *or* expressly to buy it; **je ne l'ai pas fait e.** I didn't mean to do it, I didn't do it on purpose *or* intentionally *or* deliberately; **je n'ai pas fait e. d'être méchante avec elle** I didn't mean to *or* set out to be nasty to her, I wasn't nasty to her on purpose; **j'ai déclenché l'alarme sans le faire e.** I set off the alarm without meaning to; **il fait de vous contredire** he makes a point of contradicting you; **j'aurais voulu le faire e., je n'y serais pas arrivé** I couldn't have done it if I'd tried *or* if I'd wanted to; **c'est fait e.** it's (quite) intentional *or* deliberate; **c'est fait e. pour ranger des crayons** it's designed *or* meant for holding pencils; **elle est trop grande, ta robe – c'est fait e.** your dress is too big for you – it's meant to be (that way *or* like that); **on dirait un fait e.** you'd think it was done on purpose *or* was intentional; *Iron* **comme (par) un fait e., il pleuvait** and of course *or* wouldn't you know it, it was raining

express [ɛksprɛs] ADJ **1** *(train)* fast, express **2** *(coffee)* espresso

NM **1** *(train)* fast train **2** *(café)* espresso (coffee)

expressément [ɛksprɛsemɑ̃] ADV **1** *(catégoriquement)* expressly **2** *(spécialement)* expressly, specially

expressif, -ive [ɛksprɛsif, -iv] ADJ *(langage, musique, regard, visage etc)* expressive

expression [ɛksprɛsjɔ̃] NF **1** *(d'un sentiment, d'une pensée, d'une opinion, d'une douleur etc)* expression; *(du visage)* expression, look; **il faudrait que tu soignes l'e.** you'll have to express yourself better; **l'e. de nos idées doit se faire par le biais d'un journal** we must express our ideas in a newspaper; **au-delà de toute e.** *(employé comme adjectif)* inexpressible; *(employé comme adverbe)* inexpressibly; **veuillez recevoir l'e. de mes sentiments distingués** *(en fin de lettre)* *(quand le destinataire n'est pas nommé dans l'introduction)* yours faithfully; *(quand le destinataire est nommé)* yours sincerely; **l'e. de son visage ne changea pas** his expression didn't change; **un visage plein d'e.** a very expressive face, a face full of expression; **auteur de l'e. anglaise** author writing in English; **sans e.** expressionless; *Mus* **jouer avec e.** to play with expression *or* feeling

2 *(locution)* expression, phrase; **e. familière** colloquialism, colloquial expression;

e. figée, e. toute faite set *or* fixed expression

3 *Math* expression; *Fig* **la famille, réduite à sa plus simple e.** the family, reduced to its simplest expression; *Hum* **une jupe réduite à sa plus simple e.** a skirt that leaves little to the imagination; *Fig* **un meublé dont le mobilier était réduit à sa plus simple e.** a furnished room that hardly merited the term

▸▸ **e. algébrique** algebraic expression; **e. corporelle** self-expression, music and movement; *Ordinat* **e. logique** logical expression; *Ordinat* **e. de sélection** selection command; *Ordinat* **e. de tri** sort command

expressionnisme [ɛksprɛsjɔnism] NM *Beaux-Arts* expressionism

expressionniste [ɛksprɛsjɔnist] ADJ, N *Beaux-Arts* expressionist

expressivement [ɛksprɛsivmɑ̃] ADV expressively

expressivité [ɛksprɛsivite] NF expressiveness

exprimable [ɛksprimabl] ADJ which can be expressed, expressible; **sa douleur/joie n'était pas e.** his pain/happiness was inexpressible

exprimer [ɛksprime] VT **1** *(par des mots)* *(sentiment, pensée, opinion, douleur etc)* to express (**à qn** to sb); *(d'un regard, geste etc)* *(douleur, plaisir etc)* to express, to show **2** *Math (quantité, valeur etc)* to express **3** *(extraire en pressant) (jus)* to squeeze out (**de** from)

VPR **s'exprimer** *(en parlant, en agissant etc)* to express oneself; **si l'on peut s'e. ainsi** if one may put it this way *or* like this; **le président ne s'est pas encore exprimé sur ce sujet** the president has yet to voice an opinion on the matter; **s'e. par gestes** to use sign language

expropriation [ɛksprɔprijasjɔ̃] NF *Jur (de propriété, propriétaire)* expropriation

exproprier [ɛksprɔprije] VT *(impf, pr sub n.* **expropriions)** *Jur* to expropriate

expulser [ɛkspylse] VT **1** *(étranger)* to deport, to expel; *(locataire)* to evict; *(perturbateur etc)* to eject; *(élève, étudiant, membre de parti etc)* to expel (**de** from); *Sport (joueur)* to send off **2** *Physiol* to expel

expulsif, -ive [ɛkspylsif, -iv] ADJ *Méd* expulsive

expulsion [ɛkspylsjɔ̃] NF **1** *(d'un étranger)* deportation; *(d'un locataire)* eviction; *(d'un perturbateur etc)* ejection; *(d'un élève, d'un membre de parti etc)* expulsion; *Sport (d'un joueur)* sending off **2** *Physiol* expulsion

expurgation [ɛkspyrgasjɔ̃] NF *(d'un livre etc)* expurgation

expurger [ɛkspyrʒe] VT *(j'expurgeai(s))* *(livre etc)* to expurgate; **un récit très expurgé de cette histoire** an expurgated *or* sanitized version of the matter

exquis [ɛkski] ADJ **1** *(manières, goût, nourriture etc)* exquisite; *(personne, sourire, temps)* delightful **2** *(douleur)* exquisite

exsangue [ɛksɑ̃g, ɛgzɑ̃g] ADJ *(patient, organe, visage etc)* anaemic, *Am* anemic; *Fig (œuvre d'art etc)* anaemic, bloodless; *(pays)* bled white; *(entreprise, région)* on its knees; *Fig* **elle est devenue e.** she turned deathly pale, the blood drained from her face; *Fig* **il est sorti e. de cette épreuve** he was drained by the ordeal

exsanguino-transfusion, *pl* **exsanguino-transfusions** [ɛksɑ̃g(ɥ)inɔtrɑ̃sfyzjɔ̃] NF *Méd* exchange transfusion

exsudation [ɛksydasjɔ̃] NF exudation

exsuder [ɛksyde] VT & VI to exude

exta [ɛksta] NF *Fam (abrév* **ecstasy)** E

extase [ɛkstɑz] NF **1** *Rel, Psy* ecstasy, trance

2 *(admiration)* rapture, ecstasy; **être en e. devant qch/qn** to be in raptures *or* ecstasies over sth/sb, to be rapturous about sth/sb; **tomber en e. devant qn/qch** to go into raptures over sb/sth

extasié [ɛkstɑzje] ADJ *(personne, regard)* ecstatic, enraptured

extasier (s') [ɛkstɑzje] VPR *(impf, pr sub n.* **n. extasiions)** to be in *or* go into ecstasies *or* raptures (**sur** about; **devant** over); **elle s'est longuement extasiée sur ses enfants/devant mes géraniums** she went into great raptures about her children/my geraniums

extatique [ɛkstatik] ADJ *(personne, regard)* ecstatic, enraptured; *(état, vision)* ecstatic

extenseur [ɛkstɑ̃sœr] ADJ *Anat (muscle)* extensor

NM **1** *Gym* (chest) expander **2** *Anat* extensor

extensibilité [ɛkstɑ̃sibilite] NF *(de fibres)* ability to stretch, stretchability; *(d'un métal)* tensile nature

extensible [ɛkstɑ̃sibl] ADJ **1** *(métal)* tensile; *(vêtement, tissu)* stretch; *Fig (idée, définition etc)* flexible; *Fig* **ma fortune n'est malheureusement pas e.** unfortunately my funds are not limitless *or Fam* I'm not made of money **2** *Ordinat* upgradeable; *(mémoire)* expandable, upgradeable

extensif, -ive [ɛkstɑ̃sif, -iv] ADJ **1** *Agr* **culture extensive** extensive farming **2** *sens* **e.** *(d'un mot)* extended meaning

extension [ɛkstɑ̃sjɔ̃] NF **1** *(d'un muscle, bras, ressort etc)* stretching, extension; **être en e.** *(d'un ressort)* to be released; *(d'un gymnaste etc)* to be stretched out

2 *Fig (d'un territoire, d'une firme etc)* enlargement, expansion; *(d'un contrat)* extension; *(d'une maladie, d'une langue, d'un incendie etc)* spread; **leur but est l'e. du territoire** territorial expansion is their aim; **il veut l'e. de ses pouvoirs** he wants to extend his powers; **il faut éviter l'e. de l'épidémie/ de l'incendie** the epidemic/fire must be prevented from spreading; **cette langue a forcément une e. restreinte** the language is necessarily restricted to a fairly small area; **donner de l'e. à une loi** to extend a law; **e. du commerce** business expansion; **prendre de l'e.** *(d'une entreprise etc)* to expand, to grow; *(d'une maladie, d'un incendie)* to spread

3 *(d'un mot)* extended meaning; **par e.** by extension

4 *Ordinat* expansion; **e. du nom de fichier** filename extension; **e. mémoire** memory expansion *or* upgrade; **carte d'e.** expansion board

5 *Mktg* **e. de la gamme** range stretching; **e. de la marque** brand extension; **e. de ligne** line extension; **e. de marché** market expansion

exténuant [ɛkstenɥɑ̃] ADJ exhausting

exténuation [ɛkstenɥasjɔ̃] NF *(du corps, de l'esprit)* exhaustion

exténuer [ɛkstenɥe] VT to exhaust; **être exténué (de fatigue)** to be exhausted *or* worn out

VPR **s'exténuer** to exhaust oneself, to tire oneself out (**à faire** doing); **je m'exténue à lui dire de ne pas y aller** I'm tired of telling him not to go

> Il faut noter que le verbe anglais **to extenuate** est un faux ami. Il signifie **atténuer**.

extérieur [ɛksterjœr] ADJ **1** *(surface, partie etc)* exterior, outer, external; *(escalier, éclairage, poche, intérêts etc)* outside; *(port, boulevards)* outer; *(signe, apparence etc)* outward; *(facteur, cause)* external; *Péj (gentillesse, pitié etc)* superficial; *(fragilité, assurance)* outward; **il habite dans un quartier e. à la ville** he lives outside the city;

pour des raisons qui te sont complètement extérieures for reasons that have absolutely nothing to do with you; **elle est extérieure à cette entreprise/ce service** she doesn't work for this company/this department; **avoir des activités extérieures** to have outside interests; *Péj* **sa fragilité est toute extérieure** her fragility is all on the surface; **le côté e. de qch** the outer side *or* outside of sth; **le monde e.** the outside world; **fonds extérieurs** external financing; **sans aide extérieure** without outside help, *Fam* under one's own steam

2 *(étranger) (commerce, politique etc)* external, foreign

NM 1 *(d'un bâtiment, d'une boîte etc)* exterior, outside; **vu de l'e.** seen from the outside; **vue de l'e.,** cette entreprise a l'air de bien marcher judging by appearances, the company seems to be doing well; **à l'e.** *(d'un bâtiment)* outside; *(d'une boîte etc)* on the outside; **à l'intérieur et à l'e.** inside and out; **juger de l'e.** to judge by appearances; *Sport* **match à l'e.** away match; **à l'e. de la gare/ville** outside the station/town; **cette peinture est prévue pour l'e.** the paint is intended for outside use

2 l'e. *(pays étrangers)* foreign countries; **à l'e.** abroad; **de l'e.** from abroad; **les relations avec l'e.** foreign relations

3 *Cin* location shot; **il tourne en e.** he's on location; **extérieurs tournés à Rueil** shot on location in Rueil; **émission en e.** outside broadcast, OB

extérieurement [ɛksterjœrmɑ̃] **ADV 1** *(dehors)* externally, on the outside **2** *(en apparence)* on the surface

extériorisation [ɛksterjɔrizasjɔ̃] **NF** *(d'un sentiment)* manifestation, display; *Psy* exteriorization, externalization

extérioriser [ɛksterjɔrize] **VT** *(sentiment)* to show, to express; *Psy* to exteriorize, to externalize

VPR s'extérioriser *(d'un sentiment)* to show *or* manifest itself; *(d'une personne)* to express oneself, to externalize; **il s'extériorise très peu** he shows little of what he's feeling

extériorité [ɛksterjɔrite] **NF** exteriority

exterminateur, -trice [ɛkstɛrminatœr, -tris] **ADJ** *(rage)* destructive **N** exterminator, destroyer

extermination [ɛkstɛrminasjɔ̃] **NF** *(d'une race, d'une armée etc)* extermination, destruction

exterminer [ɛkstɛrmine] **VT** *(race, armée etc)* to exterminate, to destroy, to wipe out

externalisation [ɛkstɛrnalizasjɔ̃] **NF** outsourcing

externaliser [ɛkstɛrnalize] **VT** to outsource

externat [ɛkstɛrna] **NM 1** *(école)* day school **2** *(élèves)* day pupils **3** *Méd* non-resident (medical) studentship

externe [ɛkstɛrn] **ADJ 1** *(surface, partie etc)* external, outside, outer; *(cause)* external; **côté e.** outside; **angle e.** exterior angle; *Ordinat* **dispositif e.** external device; *Pharm* **à usage e.** for external use only **2 élève e.** day pupil

N 1 *(élève)* day pupil **2** *Méd* **e. (des hôpitaux)** non-resident (medical) student, *Am* extern

exterritorialité [ɛksteritɔrjalite] **NF** ex(tra)territoriality

extincteur, -trice [ɛkstɛ̃ktœr, -tris] **ADJ** *(matériel etc)* extinguishing **NM** fire extinguisher

extinction [ɛkstɛ̃ksjɔ̃] **NF 1** *(d'un incendie etc)* extinguishing, putting out; *Mil* **e. des feux** lights out; **l'e. des feux** *ou* **des lumières se fait à 22h** lights out at 10 pm; *Aut* **e. retardée** *(d'une lumière)* delayed cut-off **2** *Jur (d'un droit etc)* extinguishment; *(d'un con-*

trat) termination; *(d'une hypothèque)* redemption; *Compta* **e. d'une dette** discharge of a debt **3** *(d'une race, espèce)* extinction; **espèce menacée** *ou* **en voie d'e.** endangered species; **depuis l'e. des dinosaures** since dinosaurs became extinct **4 e. de voix** loss of one's voice; **avoir une e. de voix** to have lost one's voice

extirpateur [ɛkstirpatœr] **NM** *Agr (instrument)* weeder

extirpation [ɛkstirpasjɔ̃] **NF** *(d'une plante, de mauvaises herbes)* uprooting; *Chir (d'une tumeur etc)* extirpation

extirper [ɛkstirpe] **VT** *(plante)* to root out *or* up; *Fig (vices)* to eradicate, to root out; *Fam* **e. qn de son lit** to drag sb out of bed; **e. qn d'une situation impossible/un piège** to extricate sb from an impossible situation/a trap; **je n'ai pas réussi à lui e. un mot** I couldn't drag *or* get a word out of him

VPR s'extirper s'e. de son lit/de dessous la couette to drag oneself out of bed/from beneath the quilt; **s'e. de son pull/d'un enchevêtrement de racines** to extricate oneself from one's pullover/a tangle of roots

extorquer [ɛkstɔrke] **VT** *(argent, promesse etc)* to extort, to wring (**à qn** from sb)

extorqueur, -euse [ɛkstɔrkœr, -øz] **N** extortioner

extorsion [ɛkstɔrsjɔ̃] **NF** extortion; **e. de fonds** extortion of funds

extra [ɛkstra] **NM INV 1** *aussi Culin* (special) treat; **faire/s'offrir un e.** to do/treat oneself to something special; **on s'est fait un petit e. en achetant du homard** we treated ourselves a little and bought lobster **2** *(serviteur)* extra help *or* hand; **faire des e. chez qn** to do occasional work for sb; **pour la soirée, on prendra deux e.** we'll take on two extra people for the party

ADJ INV 1 *(de qualité supérieure) (vin, repas, vêtement etc)* first-class, first-rate; *Fam (remarquable) (personne, roman, vacances etc)* terrific, fantastic, fabulous; **tu viens passer le week-end avec nous? c'est e.!** you're spending the weekend with us? (that's) fantastic *or* terrific! **2** *Can Fam (en supplément)* extra; **la taxe est e.** the tax is extra *or* on top

extra- [ɛkstra] **PRÉF** extra-

extra-comptable **ADJ** *Compta (ajustement)* off-balance sheet

extraconjugal, -ale, -aux, -ales [ɛkstrakɔ̃ʒygal, -o] **ADJ** extramarital

extracteur [ɛkstraktœr] **NM** *(appareil, instrument)* extractor

extractible [ɛkstraktibl] **ADJ** *(autoradio)* removable

extractif, -ive [ɛkstraktif, -iv] **ADJ** extractive

extraction [ɛkstraksjɔ̃] **NF 1** *(de dents)* extraction, *Fam* pulling; *(de charbon, minerai)* extraction, mining; *(de pierres)* quarrying; *(de pétrole, de gaz etc)* extraction; *Chir (d'une balle etc)* removal **2** *Math (d'une racine carrée* ou *cubique)* extraction **3** *Fig* **de haute/basse e.** of noble/humble extraction *or* birth

extrader [ɛkstrade] **VT** to extradite

extradition [ɛkstradisjɔ̃] **NF** extradition

extra-dry **ADJ INV** *(boisson alcoolisée)* extra dry

extra-fin **ADJ 1** *(petit, fin) (pois, aiguille etc)* extra-fine **2** *Com (de qualité supérieure) (chocolat)* superfine, top-quality; *(beurre)* top quality

extra-fort **ADJ** extra-strong **NM** *Couture* bias binding

extra(-)galactique **ADJ** *Astron* extra-galactic

extraire [ɛkstrɛr] *(conj like* **traire**) **VT** *(épingle, clou etc)* to pull out, to draw out; *(dent)*

to extract, to take out, to pull (out); *(charbon, minerai)* to extract, to mine; *(pierre)* to quarry; *(pétrole, gaz, jus etc)* to extract; *(citation, passage etc)* to extract, to excerpt; *(balle, chose de son portefeuille etc)* to take out, to remove; *(blessés, corps) (d'une voiture, des décombres)* to free; **cette citation est extraite du Roman de la rose** this quotation is taken from the Roman de la rose; **des plants** to lift seedlings; *Math* **e. une racine** to extract a root

VPR s'extraire s'e. de sa voiture to free oneself from *or* wriggle out of *or* squeeze out of one's car

extrait [ɛkstrɛ] **NM 1** *(produit)* extract, essence; **e. de viande** meat extract; **e. de lavande** lavender essence; **e. de café** coffee extract **2** *(d'un livre, discours, auteur etc)* extract, excerpt; *(de film)* extract, clip; *Jur, Fin (d'un acte, compte rendu)* abstract; **e. de presse** press cutting; *TV* **extraits pré-enregistrés** recorded highlights

▸▸ **extraits d'archives** archive footage; **e. de baptême** certificate of baptism, baptismal certificate; **e. de casier judiciaire** = documentary evidence that one does not have a criminal record; **e. de compte** *Compta* statement of account; *Banque* bank statement; **e. de film** film clip; **e. de naissance** birth certificate

extrajudiciaire [ɛkstraʒydisjɛr] **ADJ** extrajudicial

extra-légal, -ale, -aux, -ales **ADJ** bordering on the illegal; **ils ont employé des méthodes extra-légales** they used methods that bordered on the illegal *or Fam* that were legally a bit iffy; **les procédés extra-légaux ne lui font pas peur** he's not bothered about sailing a bit close to the wind *or* doing things that are not altogether above board

extralinguistique [ɛkstralɛ̃gɥistik] **ADJ** extralinguistic

extralucide [ɛkstralysid] **ADJ, N (voyante) e.** clairvoyant

extra-muros [ɛkstramyros] **ADJ INV** *(quartier)* suburban, outside town **ADV** *(habiter)* outside town, in the suburbs; **se promener e.** to go for a stroll in the suburbs

extranet [ɛkstranɛt] **NM** *Ordinat* extranet

extraordinaire [ɛkstraɔrdinɛr] **ADJ 1** *(spécial) (réunion, mesures etc)* extraordinary, special; *(messager, mission)* special; **assemblée générale e.** extraordinary general meeting; **frais** *ou* **dépenses extraordinaires** *(non prévues)* extras; *(uniques)* non-recurring expenditure

2 *(étonnant) (nouvelles, événement etc)* extraordinary, astonishing; **cela n'a rien d'e.** that's nothing out of the ordinary; **cela n'a rien d'e. après ce que tu lui as dit** that's not surprising given what you said to him

3 *(remarquable) (personne, beauté, succès)* extraordinary, outstanding; *(chaleur, prix)* extraordinary; *Fam (très bon) (livre, vin etc)* really good; **elle est vraiment e. dans cette robe** she looks quite extraordinary in that dress; **elle a fait un travail e.** she did outstanding work; **par e.** by a *or* some remote chance; **si par e. tu la voyais** if by some remote chance you should see her; **quand par e. nous nous rencontrons** when we meet, which we rarely do

extraordinairement [ɛkstraɔrdinɛrmɑ̃] **ADV** extraordinarily

extra-parlementaire **ADJ** extra-parliamentary

extraplat [ɛkstrapla] **ADJ** *(montre, calculette etc)* slimline

extrapolation [ɛkstrapɔlasjɔ̃] **NF** extrapolation

extrapoler [εkstrapɔle] vi to extrapolate (à **partir de** from)

extrascolaire [εkstraskɔlεr] ADJ *(activités etc)* extra-curricular

extrasensible [εkstrasɑ̃sibl] ADJ *(phéno-mène)* extrasensory

extra(-)sensoriel, extra(-)sensorielle ADJ *Psy (perception etc)* extrasensory

extrasystole [εkstrasistɔl] NF *Physiol* extra-systole

extra(-)terrestre, *pl* **extra(-)terrestres** ADJ, N extraterrestrial

extraterritorial, -ale, -aux, -ales [εkstratεritɔrjal, -o] ADJ extraterritorial

extraterritorialité [εkstratεritɔrjalite] NF extraterritoriality

extra-utérin ADJ *Méd* **grossesse extra-utérine** ectopic pregnancy

extravagance [εkstravagɑ̃s] NF **1** *(d'une idée, d'un comportement, de vêtements etc)* extravagance; *(d'une personne)* eccentrici-ty; *(de dépenses)* exorbitance; *(d'un désir)* immoderateness; **des idées d'une telle e.** such extravagant ideas **2** *(action, remarque)* piece of nonsense; **il a dit un tas d'extrava-gances** he talked a lot of nonsense

> Il faut noter que le nom anglais **extrava-gance** signifie également **gaspillage, dé-pense inconsidérée**.

extravagant, -ante [εkstravagɑ̃, -ɑ̃t] ADJ *(idée, comportement, vêtements etc)* extrava-gant; *(personne)* eccentric; *(prix, demande)* exorbitant; *(désir)* immoderate N eccentric (person)

> Il faut noter que l'adjectif anglais **extrava-gant** signifie également **dépensier**.

extraversion [εkstravεrsjɔ̃] NF *Psy* extro-version

extraverti, -ie [εkstravεrti] ADJ, N *Psy* ex-trovert

extrême [εkstrεm] ADJ **1** *(point, limite etc)* far, extreme, farthest; *(jeunesse, vieillesse)* extreme; *(froid, plaisir etc)* extreme, in-tense; **à l'e. limite, j'accepterai d'attendre une semaine de plus** I'll agree to wait ano-ther week at the most *or* at the outside; **il pousse la pingrerie jusqu'à son point e.** he takes meanness to extremes; **tu ne m'appel-les qu'en cas d'e. urgence** only call me in cases of extreme urgency *or* if it's extremely urgent; **d'une maigreur e.** extremely thin; **j'ai l'e. regret de vous annoncer que ...** I am extremely sorry to tell you that ...; *Pol* **e. droite/gauche** far *or* extreme right/left

2 *(excessif) (mesure, solution)* extreme, drastic, severe; *(cas, situation, opinion)* ex-treme; **elle est e. en tout** she is extreme in everything; **être e. dans ses opinions** to hold extreme opinions

NM extreme; **les extrêmes** *(de chaleur et froid)*, *Math (d'une proportion)* the extremes; **il passe d'un e. à l'autre** he goes from one extreme to the other; **prudent à l'e.** cautious in the extreme *or* to a fault; **pousser les cho-ses à l'e.** to take *or* carry matters to extre-mes; **elle a réagi à l'e.** her reaction was rather extreme; **il la déteste à l'e.** he cordial-ly detests her; **les extrêmes se touchent** ex-tremes meet

extrêmement [εkstrεmmɑ̃] ADV extremely, exceedingly

extrême-onction NF *Rel* extreme unction

Extrême-Orient (l') NM the Far East

extrême-oriental, -ale, -aux, -ales ADJ Far East, Far Eastern N E. Oriental

extrémisme [εkstremism] NM extremism

extrémiste [εkstremist] ADJ, N extremist

extrémité [εkstremite] NF **1** *(bout) (d'un lac,* *d'une route, d'une jambe, d'une corde etc)* end; *(d'un doigt, d'une aile etc)* tip; *(d'une ai-guille, une épée etc)* point; **les extrémités** *(pieds et mains)* the extremities, the hands and feet; **j'ai les extrémités glacées** my hands and feet are frozen

2 *(excès)* **extrémité(s)** extremes; **pousser qch à l'e.** to carry *or* take sth to extremes; **pousser qn à une e.** *ou* **à des extrémités** to drive sb to extremes; **en venir à des extrémi-tés** to resort to extreme measures; *(à la vio-lence)* to resort to violence

3 *(situation désespérée)* extremity; **dans cette e.** in this extremity; **réduit à l'e.** in dire distress *or* straits, reduced to extremity; **être à la dernière** *ou* **à toute e.** to be at the point of death, to be close to death

extrinsèque [εkstrε̃sεk] ADJ extrinsic; **va-leur e.** *(de monnaie)* face value

extroversion [εkstrɔvεrsjɔ̃] NF *Psy* extro-version, extraversion

extroverti, -ie [εkstrɔvεrti] ADJ, N *Psy* extro-vert, extravert

extrusion [εkstryzjɔ̃] NF *Tech* extrusion

exubérance [εgzyberɑ̃s] NF *(d'une per-sonne, de la végétation, d'un style etc)* exuberance; **avec e.** with exuberance, exuberantly

exubérant [εgzyberɑ̃] ADJ *(personne, végé-tation, joie, style etc)* exuberant

exultation [εgzyltasjɔ̃] NF exultation

exulter [εgzylte] vi to exult, to rejoice (**de faire** in doing)

exutoire [εgzytwar] NM outlet (**à sa colère** for one's anger)

ex-voto [εksvɔto] NM INV *Rel* ex-voto, votive offering

eye-liner, *pl* **eye-liners** [ajlajnœr] NM eyeliner

ezine, e-zine [izin] NM e-zine, ezine

F¹ 1 (*abrév* **franc(s)**) F, fr **2** (*abrév* **Fahrenheit**) F

F², **f¹** [ɛf] **NM INV** (*lettre*) F f; **un F2/3/***etc* (*appartement*) a two-/three-/*etc* roomed flat *or Am* apartment

f² (*abrév* **féminin**) f

fa [fa] **NM INV** *Mus* (*note*) F; (*quand on chante la gamme*) fa; **clef de fa** bass clef, F clef

FAB [ɛfabe] *Com* (*abrév* **franco à bord**) FOB

fable [fɑbl] **NF 1** (*légende*) fable; **célèbre dans la f.** famous in fable **2** (*invention*) story, tale; **c'est pure f.** it's pure invention; **être la f. de la ville** to be the laughing stock of the whole town

fabliau, -aux [fɑblijo] **NM** *Littér* fabliau

fablier [fɑblije] **NM** book of fables

fabricant, -ante [fabrikɑ̃, -ɑ̃t] **N** maker, manufacturer; **f. de chapeaux** hat maker *or* manufacturer; **f. d'automobiles** car maker *or* manufacturer; **gros/petit f.** large/small manufacturer

fabricateur, -trice [fabrikatœr, -tris] **N f. de fausse monnaie** counterfeiter, forger; **f. de faux papiers** forger of documents; **f. de fausses nouvelles** scandalmonger

fabrication [fabrikasjɔ̃] **NF 1** (*à la main*) making; *Ind* manufacture, manufacturing; **f. artisanale** production by craftsmen; **produits de f. artisanale** handmade products; **f. industrielle** industrial manufacture; **f. par lots** batch production; **f. assistée par ordinateur** computer-aided manufacture; **f. intégrée par ordinateur** computer-integrated manufacturing; **f. sous contrat** contract manufacturing; **défaut de f.** manufacturing defect; **secret de f.** trade secret; **f. en série** mass production; **elle a amené une tarte de sa f.** she brought along a tart she had made herself; **n'employer que la meilleure f.** to employ only the best workmanship; **article de f. française** article made in France **2** (*de fausses nouvelles*) fabrication; (*de document, fausse monnaie*) forging **3** *Typ* production

fabrique [fabrik] **NF 1** (*fabrication*) manufacture; **prix de f.** manufacturer's *or* factory price; **marque de f.** trademark **2** (*établissement*) factory; **f. de papier** paper mill **3** *Rel* (**conseil de) f.** = (parochial) church council, vestry

> Il faut noter que le nom anglais **fabric** est un faux ami. Il signifie le plus souvent **tissu**.

fabriquer [fabrike] **VT 1** *Ind* (*étoffes, bicyclettes etc*) to manufacture; **f. des véhicules en série** to mass-produce vehicles; **fabriqué en série** mass-produced

2 (*artisanalement*) to make; **nous fabriquons nos produits à la main** we make our products by hand; **fabriqué sur mesure** made to measure; *Fig* **l'entraîneur qui a fa-**briqué le champion de ski the coach who created *or* made the ski champion; **cela a contribué à f. son personnage médiatique** that helped to turn him/her into a media figure *or* to make a media figure out of him/her **3** (*pour tromper*) (*mensonge, histoire*) to make up, to fabricate; (*faux papiers*) to forge; **f. de la fausse monnaie** to counterfeit *or* forge money; **histoire fabriquée de toutes pièces** completely made-up *or* fabricated story

4 *Fam* (*faire*) to do; **qu'est-ce qu'il fabrique?** what's he up to?, what's he doing?; **qu'est-ce que j'ai pu f. avec mon briquet?** what can I have done with my lighter?; **je me suis tout à coup demandé ce que je fabriquais là** I suddenly wondered what I was doing there

fabulateur, -trice [fabylatœr, -tris] **ADJ** *aussi Psy* fantasizing

N compulsive liar

fabulation [fabylasjɔ̃] **NF** fantasizing; (*pathologique*) compulsive lying

fabuler [fabyle] **VI** to fantasize; (*pathologique*) to make things up, to fabricate

fabuleusement [fabyløzmɑ̃] **ADV** fabulously

fabuleux, -euse [fabylø, -øz] **ADJ 1** (*qui appartient à la légende*) (*bête*) fabulous, mythical; (*caractère, exploits*) mythical, legendary **2** *Fig* (*incroyable*) (*aventure, temps, somme d'argent, film etc*) fabulous, fantastic

fabuliste [fabylist] **NM** fabulist

FAC [ɛfase] **NM** *Admin abrév* **fonds d'aide et de coopération**

fac [fak] **NF** *Fam* university; **f. de droit/de lettres** faculty of law/arts; **à la f., en f.** at university, *Fam* at uni

façade [fasad] **NF 1** (*de bâtiment*) façade; **hôtel en f. sur la place** hotel facing the square **2** (*apparence*) pretence, façade, show (**de** of); **elle a l'air méprisant – non, ce n'est qu'une f.** she looks scornful – no, it's just a pretence *or* a front; **ne faire qch que pour la f.** to do sth just for show; **générosité/patriotisme de f.** sham generosity/patriotism **3** *Fam* (*visage*) **se ravaler la f.** (*se maquiller*) to put one's face on; **démolir la f. à qn** to smash sb's face in **4** (*d'un modem etc*) front panel **5** (*en assurances*) fronting

face [fas] **NF 1** (*visage*) face; **jeter des accusations à la f. de qn** to throw accusations in sb's face; **elle n'a pas hésité à lui jeter à la f. qu'il était hypocrite** she told him straight to his face that he was a hypocrite; **les blessés de la f.** those with facial injuries; **sauver la f.** to save (one's) face; **perdre la f.** to lose face; **tomber f. contre terre** to fall flat on one's face; **f. de carême** long face; *Péj* **f. de rat** rat-face; *Fig* **la f. du monde** the face of the world; **crier à la f. du monde** to shout to the whole world

2 *Litt* (*surface*) **la f. des eaux/de la terre** the face of the waters/of the earth

3 (*côté*) (*d'une lame d'épée*) flat; (*d'une lentille, d'un disque*) side; (*d'une médaille*) ob-verse; (*d'une pièce*) head (side); **f.!** (*en jouant à pile ou face*) heads!; **f. avant** front; **f. arrière** back; **polyèdre à douze faces** twelve-sided polyhedron; **à deux faces** (*disquette*) double-sided; **tissu (à) double f.** reversible fabric; **ruban adhésif à double f.** double-sided adhesive tape; **la f. cachée de la lune** the hidden side of the moon; **considérer qch sous toutes ses faces** to consider sth from all sides *or* from every angle; **c'est une des nombreuses faces du problème** it's one of the many aspects of the problem; **change le disque de f.!** turn the record over!; **dans son nouveau disque, je préfère la f. A à la f. B** on his new record I prefer the A side to the B side *or* I prefer side A to side B

4 **faire f. à** to face, to be facing *or* opposite; *Fig* (*responsabilités, dépenses, besoins*) to meet; (*situation, difficultés*) to face up to; **faire f. à ses créanciers** to face up to one's creditors; **les deux maisons se font f.** the two houses face *or* are facing *or* are opposite each other

5 **portrait de f.** full-face portrait; **vue de f.** front view; *Théâtre* **place de f.** front-facing seat; **se présenter de f.** to be face on; **il l'a attaquée de f.** he attacked her from the front; *Fig* he attacked her openly; **la maison (d')en f.** the house opposite; **regarder qn (bien) en f.** to look sb (full *or* straight) in the face; **si elle l'apprend, je n'oserais plus la garder en f.** if she found out, I wouldn't be able to look her in the face again; **il n'ose pas le lui dire en f.** he daren't tell him/her to his/her face; **regarder les choses/la mort en f.** to face facts/death; **en f. de** opposite, facing; **les maisons en f. de l'école** the houses opposite *or* facing the school; **en f. l'un de l'autre, en f. l'un de l'autre** opposite each other, facing each other; **si tu les mets l'un en f. de l'autre** if you put them face to face *or* opposite each other; **en f. du professeur, il change d'attitude** in front of the teacher his attitude changes; **on est en f. d'un problème difficile** we are faced with a difficult problem

6 f. à facing; **la chambre f. à la mienne** the room facing mine; **f. à cette situation, on n'avait pas le choix** faced with that situation we had no choice; **f. à f.** face to face (**avec** with); **mettre deux témoins f. à f.** to bring two witnesses face to face; **on s'est retrouvé f. à f.** we found ourselves face to face

face-à-face **NM INV** face-to-face encounter/debate

face-à-main, *pl* **faces-à-main NM** lorgnette

face-texte, *pl* **faces-textes NM** *Journ* facing matter

facétie [fasesi] **NF** joke; **dire des facéties** to crack jokes; **faire des facéties** to play jokes *or* pranks

facétieux, -ieuse [fasesjø, -jøz] **ADJ** (*petit garçon, regard*) mischievous

facette [fasɛt] NF *(d'un diamant, de l'œil d'un insecte, Fig d'une personnalité, d'un problème etc)* facet; **(taillé) à facettes** (cut) in facets, facetted; **une personnalité/une histoire/une réalité à facettes** a multi- *or* many-facetted personality/story/reality; **examiner un problème sous toutes ses facettes** to examine a problem from every angle

facetter [fasete] VT to facet

fâché [faʃe] ADJ **1** *(mécontent)* angry, annoyed; **être f. contre qn** to be angry *or* annoyed with sb; **être f. avec qn** to have fallen out with sb; **ils sont fâchés** they've fallen out *or* they're on bad terms (with each other); **tu n'es pas f., au moins?** you're not angry, are you?; **elle est fâchée avec les maths** she can't get on with maths, she has problems *or* trouble with maths; *Hum* **tu es f. avec l'ordre/ton rasoir?** being tidy/shaving doesn't come naturally to you, does it? **2** *(désolé)* sorry; **être f. de qch/pour qn** to be sorry about sth/for sb; *Iron* **je ne suis pas f. que ça soit terminé** I'm not exactly sorry *or* sad that it has finished; **je ne suis pas f. de m'asseoir** I'm glad to get the weight off my feet

fâcher [faʃe] VT **1** *(rendre mécontent)* to annoy, to make angry, to anger; **ton attitude me fâche beaucoup** your attitude annoys me a lot *or* makes me very angry **2** *(affliger)* to grieve
▶ VPR **se fâcher 1** *(se mettre en colère)* to get angry *or* annoyed, to lose one's temper; **attention! je vais me f.!** be careful or I'll get angry!; **se f. contre qn** to get annoyed *or* angry with sb; *Fam* **se f. tout rouge** to blow one's top, to go up the wall **2** *(se brouiller)* to fall out, to quarrel (**avec qn** with sb)

fâcherie [faʃri] NF quarrel, disagreement

fâcheusement [faʃøzmɑ̃] ADV **1** *(malheureusement)* unfortunately **2** *(surpris)* unpleasantly; *(impressionné)* unfavourably, *Am* unfavourably

fâcheux, -euse [faʃø, -øz] ADJ *(événement, question, complication, changement etc)* unfortunate, annoying; *(position, situation)* awkward, unfortunate; *(nouvelles)* annoying; *(exemple)* unfortunate; **j'ai eu la fâcheuse idée de lui en parler** I had the unfortunate idea of talking to him/her about it; **il serait f. que tu arrives en retard** it would be a pity if you arrived late; **c'est f.!** what a nuisance!, how annoying!
▶ N *(importun)* nuisance

facho [faʃo] ADJ, N *Fam Péj* fascist

facial, -ale, -iaux, -ales [fasjal, -jo] ADJ *(muscle, angle etc)* facial; **massage f.** facial *or* face massage

faciès [fasjɛs] NM **1** *(aspect du visage)* features; *Méd* facies **2** *Bot, Géol* facies

facile [fasil] ADJ **1** *(travail, problème, vie etc)* easy; **c'est f. à faire** it's easy to do *or* easily done; **c'est f. à dire** that's easily said; **c'est plus f. à dire qu'à faire** it's easier said than done; **avoir la vie f.** to have an easy life; **c'est f. comme bonjour** it's as easy as pie, it's child's play; **il lui est f. de le faire** it's easy for him (to do it); **f. d'emploi** easy to use; **d'une mise en place f., f. à installer** easily installed; **besognes faciles** light *or* easy tasks
2 *(caractère)* easy-going; **homme f. à vivre** man easy to get along with *or* to get on with; **il n'a pas l'air f. en affaires** he doesn't seem an easy man to do business with; **f. à émouvoir** easily moved; **cet enfant est f.** this child is no problem; *Péj* **femme f.** woman of easy virtue, loose woman
3 *(superficiel)* *(plaisanterie, littérature, style etc)* facile
4 *(qui vient facilement)* **il n'a pas la parole f.** words don't come easily to him; **il n'a pas l'argent f.** he's a bit tight-fisted; **un milieu où**

l'argent est f. an environment where there's plenty of money around; **elle a les larmes faciles** she is easily moved to tears; **avoir la gâchette f.** to be trigger-happy; **elle a la plume f.** she is a fluent writer, writing comes easily to her
▶ ADV **1** *(au moins)* easily, at least; **on met trois jours f. pour traverser l'île** it takes easily *or* at least three days to cross the island; **en trois jours, j'aurai lu f. deux livres** I'll easily read two books in three days
2 *Belg* **avoir f. à** *ou* **de qch** to find it easy to do sth, to have no problem doing sth

facilement [fasilmɑ̃] ADV easily; **il rit f.** it's easy to make him laugh; **je mettrai f. deux jours pour le faire** it'll take me easily *or* at least two days to do it

facilité [fasilite] NF **1** *(d'une tâche, d'un problème etc)* easiness; *(à faire qch)* ease; **avec f.** easily, with ease; **les enfants comprennent l'informatique avec une f. déconcertante** children understand computers with disconcerting ease; *Péj* **elle choisit toujours la f.** she always chooses the easy option *or* the easy way out; **c'est une solution de f.** it's the easy solution *or* way out **2** *(moyen, occasion)* **avoir toutes facilités pour faire qch** to have every opportunity of doing sth **3** *(aptitude)* aptitude, talent (**pour qch** for sth); **écrire avec f.** to write fluently *or* with ease; **f. à faire qch** aptitude for doing sth; **f. de parole** fluency; **elle a beaucoup de facilités pour les/en maths** she has great aptitude for maths
▶ ▶ **f. d'accès pour fauteuils roulants** wheelchair access; **f. d'accès pour personnes handicapées** disabled access; *Banque* **f. de caisse** overdraft *or* cash facility; *Banque* **facilités de crédit** credit facilities; **f. d'écoulement** *(d'un produit)* saleability; **f. d'emploi** *(d'un ordinateur etc)* user-friendliness; *Fin* **facilités d'endettement** borrowing capacity; *Fin* **facilités de paiement** credit *or* payment facilities; *Com* **f. de reprise** trade-in facility; **facilités de transport** transport facilities

faciliter [fasilite] VT to make easier; **f. qch à qn** to make sth easier for sb; **cela ne va pas f. les choses** it won't make things (any) easier

facob [fakɔb] NM *(abrév* **traité facultatif obligatoire)** open cover

FAÇON [fasɔ̃]

way **1**	▪ manner **1**	▪ so as to *(de façon à)* **3**
▪ so that *(de façon que)* **4**		
▪ behaviour *(façons)* **5**	▪ making **7**	

NF **1** *(manière de faire qch)* way, manner; **ils vivent encore à la f. de leurs ancêtres** they still live in the manner of their ancestors *or* as their ancestors did; **il n'y a pour toi qu'une seule f. de t'en sortir** there's only one way for you to come through all right; **il n'y a pas trente-six façons de le faire** there are no two ways of doing it; **avoir une f. à soi de faire qch** to have one's own way of doing sth; **je le ferai à ma f.** I shall do it (in) my own way; **ce n'est qu'une f. de parler** it's just a manner of speaking; **ce n'est pas une f. de parler à son père** that's no way to speak to one's father; **ce n'est pas une f. de parler pour un petit garçon** that's no way for a little boy to speak; **je ne tolérerai pas ces façons de parler** I won't tolerate that sort of language; **tu pars en vacances? – oui, f. de parler, je vais garder mes neveux** are you going on holiday? – yes, I suppose you could say that *or* in a manner of speaking *or* sort of, I'm looking after my nephews; **ce n'est pas ma f. de faire** it's not my way of doing things; **ils agissent tous de la même f.** they all act alike *or* in the same way; **elle a une curieuse f. de voir les choses** she has a strange way of

looking at things; **de la bonne f.** properly, in the right way; **la f. dont l'anglais est enseigné** the way (in which) English is taught; *Suisse* **avoir bonne/mauvaise f.** to look good/bad, to create a good/bad impression
2 de cette f. (in) this way, *Fml* thus; **venez avec nous, de cette f. cela ne vous coûtera rien** come with us, that way it won't cost you anything; **d'une ou de f. générale, on peut dire que …** generally speaking, one can say that …; **d'une f. ou d'une autre** one way or another, somehow or other; **de toute f. j'irai** anyhow *or* anyway *or* in any case I shall go; **en aucune f.!** not at all!, by no means!; **cela ne me dérange en aucune f.** it doesn't disturb me in any way
3 de f. à so as to; **parlez de f. à vous faire comprendre** speak so that you can be understood; **elle parle de f. à ce que tout le monde l'entende** she speaks so that *or* in such a way that everyone can hear her SEE GRAMMAR B33
4 de (telle) f. que so that; **parlez de f. qu'on vous comprenne** speak so that you can be understood; **il pleuvait de telle f. que je fus obligé de rentrer** it was raining so hard that I had to go home; *Vieilli* **il pleuvait, de f. que je fus obligé de rentrer** it was raining, (and) so I had to go home SEE GRAMMAR B33
5 façons *(comportement)* manners, behaviour; **en voilà des façons!** what a way to behave!; **ce ne sont pas des façons!** that's no way to behave!
6 sans façon(s) *(personne)* unaffected, straightforward; **traiter qn sans f.** to treat sb in an offhand manner; **un repas sans f.** an unpretentious *or* a simple meal; **non merci, sans f.** no thanks, really (not); **sans plus de façons** without further *or* any more ado; **faire des façons** to make a fuss; **on est entre nous, on ne va pas faire de façons** we're all friends here, we won't stand on ceremony
7 *(exécution)* making, fashioning; *(style)* style; **f. d'un manteau** making (up) of a coat; *(coupe)* cut of a coat; **matière et f.** material and labour; **compter 50 euros de f.** to charge 50 euros for labour; **on travaille à f.** *(dans une annonce)* customers' own materials made up; **un poème de sa f.** a poem of his own composition; **robe qui a bonne f.** well-cut dress; *Agr* **donner une f. à la terre** to cultivate the soil; **cuir f. porc** imitation pigskin; **sac f. cuir** imitation leather bag

faconde [fakɔ̃d] NF *(de l'élocution)* fluency, volubility, *Péj* garrulousness; **avoir de la f.** to be fluent *or* voluble, *Péj* to be garrulous; **quelle f.!** he/she talks so much!, *Fam* what a bletherer!

façonnage [fasonaʒ] NM **1** *(action de travailler)* *(du bois)* working, shaping; *(sur un tour)* turning; *(de l'argile)* fashioning **2** *(fabrication)* *(à la main)* making, fashioning; *Couture* making (up); *Ind* manufacturing **3** *(dans l'édition)* forwarding **4** *Fig (d'une personne)* shaping

façonné [fasone] ADJ *Tex (tissu)* figured

façonnement [fasonmɑ̃] NM = **façonnage**

façonner [fasone] VT **1** *(travailler)* *(bois, métal, pierre etc)* to work, to shape; *(sur un tour)* to turn; *(argile)* to fashion; *Agr* **f. la terre** to work the soil **2** *(fabriquer)* *(à la main)* to make, to fashion; *Couture* to make (up); *Ind* to manufacture **3** *(dans l'édition)* to forward **4** *Fig (personne, caractère)* to mould, *Am* to mold, to shape; **f. qn à son image** to mould sb in one's own image

façonnier, -ière [fasonje, -jɛr] ADJ *(personne)* affected, mannered
▶ NM *Ordinat* computer bureau

fac-similé, *pl* **fac-similés** [faksimile] NM facsimile

factage [faktaʒ] NM **1** *(de marchandises)* carriage (and delivery); **payer le f.** to pay the carriage **2** *(de lettres etc)* delivery

facteur [faktœr] **NM 1** *(de la poste)* postman, *Am* mailman **2** *(élément)* factor; **le f. chance/ humain/temps** the chance/human/time factor; **f. coût** cost factor; **f. économique** economic factor; *Méd* **f. de risque** risk factor; *Mktg* **f. de situation** situational factor; **f. déterminant** determining factor, determinant; *Méd* **f. rhésus** rhesus factor **3** *Math* factor; **f. premier/commun** prime/common factor; **mettre un nombre en facteurs** to factorize a number **4** *Mus (fabricant)* maker; **f. d'orgues** organ builder; **f. de pianos** piano maker

factice [faktis] **ADJ 1** *(objet)* false, artificial; *(articles en vitrine)* dummy; *(moustache, barbe)* false; **cuir/diamant f.** imitation leather/diamond; **les bouteilles de parfum en vitrine sont factices** the bottles of perfume in the window are dummies **2** *Fig (joie, pitié etc)* false, feigned; *(sourire)* forced; *(beauté)* artificial

factieux, -ieuse [faksjø, -jøz] **ADJ** factious, seditious
▪ **N** agitator, troublemaker

faction [faksjɔ̃] **NF 1** *Mil* sentry duty, guard; **être de** *ou* **en f.** to be on guard *or* on sentry duty; **mettre qn en f.** to put sb on guard; *Fig* **j'ai dû me mettre en f. devant sa porte** I had to wait around outside his/her door **2** *(groupe)* faction

factionnaire [faksjɔnɛr] **NM** *(sentinelle)* sentry, guard; **poser/relever un f.** to post/relieve a sentry *or* guard

factitif, -ive [faktitif, -iv] **ADJ** *Gram* causative, factitive

factoriel, -ielle [faktɔrjɛl] **ADJ, NF** *Math* factorial

factoring [faktɔriŋ] **NM** *Com* factoring

factorisation [faktɔrizasjɔ̃] **NF** *Math* factorization

factotum [faktɔtɔm] **NM** factotum

factrice [faktris] **NF** postwoman, *Am* mailwoman

factuel, -elle [faktɥɛl] **ADJ** factual

facturation [faktyrasjɔ̃] **NF** invoicing, billing; **(service de) f.** invoice department; *Ordinat* **f. à la durée** pay-as-you-go

facture¹ [faktyr] **NF 1** *(style)* *(d'un morceau de musique, d'un poème, d'un tableau etc)* construction; *(d'un artiste etc)* style, technique **2** *Mus (fabrication)* making; *(d'orgues)* building

facture² **NF** *Com* invoice, bill (of sale); **faire** *ou* **dresser** *ou* **établir une f.** to make out an invoice; **f. d'électricité/de gaz** electricity/gas bill; **selon** *ou* **suivant f.** as per invoice; *Écon* **la f. pétrolière de la France** France's oil bill
▪ ▪ **f. d'achat** purchase invoice; **f. d'avoir** credit note; **f. certifiée** certified invoice; **f. client** guest bill; **f. commerciale** commercial invoice; **f. de confirmation** confirmation invoice; **f. consulaire** consular invoice; **f. de débit** debit note; **f. détaillée** itemized invoice; **f. de doit** debit note; **f. douanière** customs invoice; **f. à l'exportation** export invoice; **f. originale** invoice of origin; **f. pro forma** pro forma invoice; **f. provisoire** pro forma invoice; **f. rectificative** amended invoice; **f. de transitaire** forwarding agent's invoice; **f. de vente** sales invoice

facturer [faktyre] **VT** *(marchandises)* to invoice; **le papier nous a été facturé 50 euros** we were invoiced 50 euros for the paper

facturette [faktyrɛt] **NF** credit card sales slip

facturier, -ière [faktyrje, -jɛr] **NM** *(livre)* sales book; **f. d'entrée** purchase ledger; **f. de sortie** sales ledger

N *(employé)* invoice clerk; **f. d'entrée** purchase ledger clerk; **f. de sortie** sales ledger clerk

facultatif, -ive [fakyltatif, -iv] **ADJ** optional; **arrêt f.** request stop

facultativement [fakyltativmɑ̃] **ADV** optionally

faculté [fakylte] **NF 1** *(don, capacité)* faculty, ability, power; **facultés de l'esprit** *ou* **intellectuelles** intellectual faculties; **ne pas avoir la f. de marcher** to be unable to walk; **jouir de toutes ses facultés** to be in possession of all one's faculties; **elle n'a plus toutes ses facultés** she no longer has all her faculties; **homme doué de grandes facultés** man of great abilities
2 *(droit)* right; *(possibilité)* option; **avoir la f. de faire qch** *(droit)* to have the right to do sth; *(possibilité)* to have the option of doing sth; **f. de rachat** buy-back option
3 *Vieilli* **facultés** *(ressources)* resources, means; **elle dépense au-dessus de ses facultés** she spends beyond her means
4 *Univ* faculty; **professeur de f.** = (university) professor; *Vieilli* **la F.** the Faculty of Medicine; *(les médecins)* the medical profession; *Hum* **la F. m'interdit de boire** I'm forbidden to drink, doctor's orders; **à la f., en f.** at university; **entrer en f.** to go to university
▪ ▪ *Com* **facultés assurées** insured cargo

fada [fada] *Fam* **ADJ** *(fou)* crazy
▪ **N** crackpot

fadaise [fadɛz] **NF** silly remark; *(chose insignifiante)* trifle; **débiter des fadaises** to talk nonsense

fadasse [fadas] **ADJ** *Fam (goût, boisson, nourriture etc)* insipid, bland; *(couleur)* pale, washed-out; *(livre, style etc)* dreary, dull

fade [fad] **ADJ** *(plat, boisson, goût etc)* insipid, bland; *(plaisanterie)* tame; *(compliments)* banal, bland; *(couleur)* drab, washed-out; *(odeur)* stale; *(livre, conversation, style etc)* dull, dreary; *(beauté)* insipid

fadé [fade] **ADJ** *Fam* **être f.** *(remarquable)* to beat them all, to take the biscuit *or Am* the cake

fader (se) [səfade] **VPR** *Fam* **se f. qn/qch** to get landed with sb/sth

fadeur [fadœr] **NF 1** *(d'un plat, d'une boisson, de goût etc)* insipidness, blandness; *(d'une plaisanterie)* tameness; *(de compliments)* banality; *(d'une couleur)* drabness; *(d'une odeur)* staleness; *(d'un livre, style etc)* dullness, dreariness; *(d'une beauté)* insipidness
2 fadeurs *(compliments)* banal *or* bland compliments; **dire des fadeurs à qn** to pay sb banal *or* bland compliments

fading [fadiŋ] **NM** *Radio* fading; *Aut* (brake) fade

faf [faf] **N** *Fam* fascist

fafiot [fafjo] **NM** *Arg* banknote, *Am* bill

fafouin, -ouine [fafwɛ̃, -win] *Can Fam* **ADJ** scatter-brained, *Br* scatty
▪ **N** scatterbrain; **arrête de faire le f., tu vas avoir un accident!** stop acting the fool *or* clowning around, you'll have an accident!

fagot [fago] **NM** bundle of firewood; *Fig* **sentir le f.** to smack of heresy; *Fam* **bouteille de vin de derrière les fagots** bottle of wine from the hidden store *or* kept for special occasions; **un repas de derrière les fagots** an extra-special meal; **une idée de derrière les fagots** a remarkable idea

fagotage [fagɔtaʒ] **NM 1** *(du bois)* tying up in bundles **2** *Péj (accoutrement)* ridiculous get-up *or* rig-out

fagoter [fagɔte] **VT 1** *(bois)* to tie up in bundles **2** *Péj (accoutrer)* to rig *or* deck out; **mal/ bizarrement fagoté** badly/oddly dressed
▪ **VPR se fagoter** *Péj* to rig *or* deck oneself out

FAI [ɛfai] **NM** *Ordinat (abrév* **fournisseur d'accès à l'Internet)** IAP

faiblard [fɛblar] **ADJ** *Fam* (a bit) weak, weakish

faible [fɛbl] **ADJ 1** *(physiquement)* *(personne, membres etc)* weak, feeble; *(cœur, yeux, constitution)* weak; *(arche, branche etc)* weak, unstable; *(pays, armée etc)* weak; **avoir la vue f.** to have weak *or* poor eyesight; **le sexe f.** the weaker sex; **une f. femme** a helpless woman
2 *(intellectuellement)* *(personne, idée, style, film etc)* weak, poor; *(intelligence)* low; **élève f. en chimie** pupil weak *or* poor in *or* at chemistry; **f. d'esprit** feeble-minded; **côté/point f.** weak side/point; **et le terme est f.!** and that's putting it mildly!
3 *(moralement)* *(personne)* weak, soft; *(caractère)* weak; **être f. avec qn** to be weak *or* soft with sb; **f. de caractère** weak-willed
4 *(léger)* *(café, vin etc)* weak; *(son, voix)* faint, quiet; *(odeur)* faint, slight; *(lumière)* faint, dim; *(vent)* light; *Mus* **temps f.** weak *or* unaccented beat; **boisson f. en alcool** low-alcohol drink; **f. en calories** low-calorie
5 *(petit)* *(quantité, majorité etc)* small; *(avantage, différence, réaction, chance, espoir)* slight; *(prix, revenu, loyer etc)* low; *(récolte, rendement)* poor; *(vitesse)* low, slow; **à une f. hauteur/profondeur** not very high up/deep down; **cela ne vous en donne qu'une f. idée** that gives you only a vague idea of it; *Naut* **f. tirant d'eau** shallow draught; **à f. émission** low-emission
6 *Gram (verbe, conjugaison)* weak
▪ **N** *(personne sans force morale)* weakling, weak person; **les faibles** the weak; **les faibles d'esprit** the feeble-minded; **défendre le f. et l'opprimé** to defend the weak and oppressed
▪ **NM 1** *(défaut)* weak point, weakness; **le f. chez moi, c'est …** my weak point *or* weakness is …
2 *(penchant)* weakness; **avoir un f. pour qch/qn** to have a weakness for sth/a soft spot for sb; **prendre qn par son f.** to take advantage of sb's weakness

faiblement [fɛbləmɑ̃] **ADV** *(résister, insister, protester)* weakly, feebly; *(éclairer)* faintly, dimly; *(parler, crier)* quietly, faintly; *(entendre)* faintly; **f. attiré/parfumé** slightly attracted/flavoured

faiblesse [fɛblɛs] **NF 1** *(physique)* *(d'une personne, des membres etc)* weakness, feebleness; *(du cœur, de la vue, d'une constitution etc)* weakness; *(d'une arche, d'une branche, d'un gouvernement, d'une armée etc)* weakness; *(syncope)* (sudden) faintness; **elle eut une f.** she (suddenly) felt faint; **je tombais de f.** I was ready to drop (with exhaustion); **donner des signes de f.** *(d'une machine)* to be showing signs of wear and tear; *Vieilli* **tomber en f.** to swoon, to faint
2 *(intellectuelle)* *(d'un élève, argument, style etc)* weakness, poorness; **f. d'esprit** feeble-mindedness
3 *(morale)* weakness (**envers qn** towards sb); **f. de caractère** weakness of character; **la f. humaine** human weakness *or* frailty; **f. d'une mère** a mother's indulgence; **avoir la f. de faire qch** to be weak enough to do sth; **dans un moment de f. je lui ai dit oui** in a moment of weakness I said yes to him; **avoir des faiblesses pour qn** to have a soft spot for sb
4 *(manque d'intensité)* *(d'un son, d'une odeur, d'une lumière)* faintness; *(du vent)* lightness
5 *(petitesse)* *(d'une quantité, majorité etc)* smallness; *(d'une différence, réaction etc)* slightness; **la f. de leurs revenus** their low income
6 *(défaut)* *(d'une personne)* weakness, fail-

ing; *(d'une œuvre d'art, d'une théorie etc)* weakness

faiblir [fεblir] VI to weaken; *(de la vue, du cœur, de la lumière)* to fail; *(de la voix)* to lose its strength, to fail; *(du vent)* to abate, to drop; *(du courage)* to fail, to flag; **sa force faiblit** he's not as strong as he was; **le film faiblit vers la fin** the film falls off *or* tails off towards the end

faïence [fajɑ̃s] NF **1** *(matière)* earthenware **2** *(objet)* piece of earthenware; **faïences** crockery, earthenware

faïencerie [fajɑ̃sri] NF **1** *(articles)* crockery, earthenware **2** *(fabrique)* pottery (works) **3** *(commerce)* pottery (trade)

faïencier, -ière [fajɑ̃sje, -jer] N *(fabricant)* crockery *or* earthenware maker; *(marchand)* crockery *or* earthenware dealer

faignant, -ante [fεɲɑ̃, -ɑ̃t] ADJ, N *Fam* = **fainéant**

faille [faj] NF **1** *Géol* fault; **ligne de f.** fault line **2** *Fig (dans un argument)* flaw; *(dans une amitié)* rift, breach; **sans f.** *(raisonnement)* flawless; *(dévotion)* unfailing; *(fidélité)* unwavering; **faire preuve d'une volonté sans f.** to be iron-willed, to have a will of iron

failli, -ie [faji] ADJ, N *Jur* bankrupt; **f. concordataire** = bankrupt who has reached a settlement with his debtors; **f. non déchargé** undischarged bankrupt; **f. réhabilité** discharged bankrupt

faillibilité [fajibilite] NF fallibility

faillible [fajibl] ADJ fallible; **tout le monde est f.** anybody can make a mistake

faillir [fajir] VI *(prp* **faillant;** *pp* **failli;** *pr ind* je **faux, il faut, n. faillons;** *p hist* je **faillis;** *fu* je **faillirai;** *used mostly in inf, p hist and compound tenses)* **1** *(manquer)* **f. à son devoir** to fail in *or* fall short of one's duty; **f. à une promesse/sa parole** to fail to keep a promise/one's word; **sans f.** unfailingly; **dont la loyauté n'avait jamais failli** whose loyalty had never wavered or faltered; **ne pas f. à sa réputation** to live up to one's reputation; **la mémoire me faut** my memory fails me **2** **j'ai failli manquer le train/le croire** I nearly *or* almost missed the train/believed him; **il faillit être écrasé** he narrowly missed being run over; **j'ai bien failli me noyer** I (was) very nearly drowned; **j'ai failli lui en parler** I nearly spoke to him about it; *Iron* **j'ai failli attendre** so you decided to show up, did you?

faillite [fajit] NF **1** *Com* bankruptcy, insolvency; **être en (état de) f.** to be bankrupt *or* insolvent; **f. simple** bankruptcy; **f. frauduleuse** fraudulent bankruptcy; **faire f.** to go bankrupt; **déclarer** *ou* **mettre qn en f.** to declare sb bankrupt **2** *(échec) (d'un projet, d'espoirs etc)* failure; **la mort de l'acteur principal, c'était la f. du film** the death of the main actor meant the collapse of the film

faim [fɛ̃] NF hunger; **avoir f.** to be *or* feel hungry; **avoir très** *ou* **grand f., avoir une grosse f.** to be *or* feel very hungry; **avoir un peu f.** *ou Fam* **une petite f.** to be *or* feel a bit hungry; **je n'ai plus f. du tout** I'm not at all hungry any more; **avoir une f. de loup** to be ravenous; **mourir de f.** to die of hunger *or* starvation, to starve to death; *(avoir très faim)* to be starving; **j'ai une de ces faims,** *Fam* **je crève de f.** I'm starving; **manger à sa f.** to eat one's fill; **rester sur sa f.** to remain hungry; *Fig* to be left unsatisfied; **tromper sa f.** to take the edge off one's appetite; *Fig* **avoir f. de gloire/d'absolus** to hunger *or* thirst after glory/absolutes

faîne [fɛn] NF beechnut

fainéant, -ante [fεneɑ̃, -ɑ̃t] ADJ lazy, idle N lazybones

fainéanter [fεneɑ̃te] VI to idle about, to loaf about; **f. au lit** to laze in bed

fainéantise [fεneɑ̃tiz] NF laziness, idleness

faire¹ [fεr] NM **1 il y a loin du dire au f.** saying is one thing, doing another **2** *Beaux-Arts, Littér* technique

FAIRE² *(prp* **faisant** [fəzɑ̃]; *pp* **fait** [fε]; *pr ind* je **fais, il fait, n. faisons** [fəzɔ̃], v. **faites** [fεt], ils **font;** *pr sub* je **fasse;** *imp* **fais, faisons, faites;** *p hist* je **fis;** *fu* je **ferai)**

VT to make **1–3, 18**	■ to do **5–7, 9, 19**
■ to say **6**	■ to have **10** ■ to go **11** ■ to
cause **12**	■ to amount to **13** ■ to clean
19	■ to look (+ *adjective*) **20** ■ to play
21	
VI to relieve oneself	
V IMPERS to be **1, 2**	
V AUX to make **2, 3**	■ to have /to get **4,**
5	
VPR to become **2**	■ to get used to (*se*
faire à) **3**	■ to make **4, 8** ■ to happen **6**

VT **1** *(façonner)* to make; **f. un gâteau/du cidre** to make a cake/cider; **statue faite en** *ou* **de marbre** statue made (out) of marble; **vêtements tout faits** ready-made clothes; **expressions toutes faites** ready-made *or* set phrases; **f. un poème/un tableau** to write a poem/paint a picture; **f. un chèque de 100 euros** to make out *or* write (out) a cheque for 100 euros; **je vais lui f. un chèque** I'll make him out *or* write him (out) a cheque; **f. la guerre** to wage war; **faites l'amour pas la guerre** make love not war; **f. des provisions** to lay in provisions; **f. de l'eau/du charbon** to take in water/coal; **f. un miracle** to work *or* perform a miracle; **ferme où on fait de la betterave** farm that grows beet

2 *(créer)* to make; **Dieu a fait l'homme à son image** God made *or* created man in his own image; **ils ne veulent pas f. d'enfants** they don't want to have (any) children; *Fam* **f. un enfant à qn** to make *or* get sb pregnant; **ma femme m'a fait deux merveilleuses petites filles** my wife has given me two wonderful little girls; **f. ses petits** *(d'une chienne, chatte)* to have her litter, to have her pups/kittens; **les vieilles gens sont ainsi faits** old people are like that, that's how old people are; **comment est-il fait?** *(à quoi ressemble-t-il?)* what does he look like?; **il n'est pas fait pour cela** he is not the man *or* is not cut out for that; **jambe bien faite** shapely leg

3 f. un geste to make a gesture; **elle lui fit un signe de la main** she waved to him/her; *Fam* **f. de l'œil à qn** to make eyes at sb, to give sb the eye

4 *Arg* **tu es fait, mon vieux!** you've had it, chum!; **on m'a fait ma montre** *(volé)* someone's pinched my watch

5 *(se livrer à une activité)* to do; **qu'est-ce que vous faites?** what are you doing?; **qu'est-ce que vous faites toute seule dans votre grande maison?** what do you do all alone in your big house?; **qu'est-ce qu'il y a à f.?** what is there to do?; **il n'y a rien à f.** *(pour résoudre le problème)* there is nothing to be done, there's no help for it; **je n'ai rien à f.** I've nothing to do; **je n'ai rien à f. avec eux** I have nothing to do with them; **il n'a rien à f. ici** he has no business here; **que f.?** what is/was to be done?, what can/could he/we/*etc* do?; **je ne sais que f.** I don't know what to do; **qu'allez-vous f. de votre fils?** what are you going to do with your son?; **qu'avez-vous fait de mon parapluie?** what have you done with my umbrella?; **n'avoir que f. de qch** to have no need of sth; **autant que f. se peut** as far as (is) possible; **c'est la dernière chose à f.** it's the last thing that ought to be done; **je le regardais f.** I watched him doing it; **est-ce que je peux ouvrir la fenêtre? – faites donc!** may I open the window? – do!, by all means!; **fai-**

tes vite! be quick about it!, look sharp!; **nous avons fort à f. avec nos quatre garçons** we've got our work cut out *or* our hands full with our four boys; **il n'a pas le temps de vous voir aujourd'hui, il a fort à f.** he doesn't have time to see you today, he's extremely busy; **homme à tout f.** odd-job man; **grand bien vous fasse!** much good may it do you!; **c'est bien fait (pour toi)!** it serves you right!; **c'est toujours ça de fait** it's something done (at least); *Fam* **traverser la Manche à la nage, faut le f.!** swimming the Channel is no easy matter, not everybody can swim the Channel; *Fam* **mettre du sel à la place du sucre, faut le f. quand même!** putting salt in instead of sugar, how stupid can you get!, you really have to be stupid to put salt in instead of sugar!; **voilà qui est fait** that's done

6 *(dire)* to say; **'vous partez demain!' fit-il** 'you leave tomorrow!' he said *or* exclaimed; **il fit un petit 'oh' de surprise** he gave a little 'oh' of surprise

7 *(accomplir)* **f. son devoir** to do one's duty; **f. la ronde** to go *or* do one's rounds; *Fam* **f. ses besoins** to relieve oneself; *(d'un chien, d'un chat)* to do its business

8 f. un métier to practise a trade; **f. les cuirs/la laine** to deal in leather/wool; **nous ne faisons que le gros** we are wholesalers only, **quel article faites-vous?** what's your line?; **nous ne faisons plus les pulls en laine** we don't do *or* stock woollen sweaters any more

9 *(pratiquer, étudier)* **f. du sport** to do sport; **f. de la politique** to be involved in politics; **on ne va pas f. de politique, mais c'est quand même un problème grave, non?** we don't want to bring politics into it, but it's a serious problem all the same, isn't it?; **j'ai fait de l'anglais à l'école** I did English at school; **il fait sa médecine/son droit** he is reading *or* studying medicine/law; *Fam* **elle veut f. Polytechnique** she wants to go *or* study at the Polytechnique; *Fam* **il veut f. médecin/pompier** he wants to be a doctor/fireman; **f. son apprentissage** to serve *or* do one's apprenticeship

10 *Fam (maladie)* to have; **il doit f. une crise de foie** he must have liver trouble; **tu ne vas quand même pas f. une maladie!** there's no need to get so upset about it *or* to take it that way!; *Fam* **tu ne vas pas nous f. une crise!** you're not going to have one of your tantrums!

11 *(déplacement)* **f. quelques pas sur le trottoir/dans la rue** to go *or* take a few steps along the pavement/along the street; **f. les magasins** to go round *or* do the shops; **f. une promenade** to go for a walk; **ce représentant fait la province** this representative does *or* covers the provinces; *Fam* **on a fait l'Inde l'année dernière** we did India last year; *Fam* **f. du cent à l'heure** to go *or* do a hundred kilometres an hour

12 *(causer)* to cause; **f. pitié/peur** to arouse pity/fear; **ça fait peur!** it's frightening!; **f. peur à qn** to frighten sb, to scare sb; **cela me fait de la peine que tu partes** it makes me sad *or* upsets me that you're going

13 *(mesure)* to amount to, to come to; **combien cela fait-il?, ça fait combien?** how much does that come to?, what does that make?; **deux fois deux font quatre** two twos are four, twice two is four; **je vous fais les deux cadres pour 200 euros** I can let you have both frames for 200 euros; **ça fait trois jours qu'il est parti** it's three days since he left; **ça fait bien deux ans (que je ne l'ai pas revu)** it's a good two years (since I last saw him); **ce poulet fait trois kilos** this chicken weighs three kilos; **combien faites-vous la livre de chocolat?** how much do you charge for a pound of chocolate?

14 'cheval' fait 'chevaux' au pluriel 'cheval' becomes 'chevaux' in the plural

15 *(être)* to be; **f. l'admiration de tous** to be admired by everyone; **cela fera mon affaire** that will suit me; **quel taquin vous faites!** what a tease you are!

16 *(importer)* **qu'est-ce que ça fait?** what does it matter?, who cares?; **ça fait qu'on va le déranger encore une fois** it means we'll have to disturb him again; **qu'est-ce que cela vous fait?** what's that to you?; **si cela ne vous fait rien** if you don't mind; **cela ne fait rien** never mind, it doesn't matter; *Fam* **qu'est-ce que ça peut bien te f.?** what has that got to do with you?; *Fam* **ça me fait que je dois encore t'attendre** it means I have to wait for you again

17 *(remplaçant le verbe qui précède)* **pourquoi agir comme vous le faites?** why do you act as you do?; **il m'a traité comme il aurait fait d'un** *ou* **pour un animal** he treated me as he would an animal

18 *(former)* **je ferai de toi un homme** I'll make a man of you; **cette solution a fait beaucoup d'heureux** this solution made a lot of people happy; **elle en a fait un paresseux** she's made him lazy; **elle en a fait un vaurien** she's turned him into a good-for-nothing; **f. des chaussures à son pied** to break in a pair of shoes; *Prov* **l'habit ne fait pas le moine** appearances are deceptive

19 *(arranger)* **f. la chambre/ses chaussures** to clean *or* do the room/one's shoes; **f. le ménage/la vaisselle** to do the housework/the washing-up; **f. les vitres** to do *or* clean the windows; **f. la poussière** to do the dusting; **f. du rangement dans ses affaires** to put one's things in order, to tidy up one's things; **f. sa valise** to pack one's (suit)case; **f. ses ongles** to do one's nails; *Cartes* **à qui de f.?** whose call is it?

20 *Fam* **ça fait riche** it looks expensive; *Fam* **ça fait jeune** it makes you look young; **vases qui font bien sur la cheminée** vases that look good on the mantelpiece; **ça fera très bien avec ton tailleur vert** that'll go very well with your green suit; **il ne fait pas quarante ans** he doesn't look forty; **ça fait bizarre de savoir qu'elle ne vit plus ici** it's funny to think she doesn't live here any more

21 *Théâtre, Cin (jouer le rôle de)* to play; **moi je fais le gendarme et toi le voleur** I'll be the cop and you can be the robber; **f. celui qui sait tout** to be a know-all; **un des invités faisait le croupier** one of the guests acted as croupier; **elle ne va pas f. la reine ici** she isn't going to queen it here; **le mort** to pretend to be dead; *Fig* to play dead; *(au bridge etc)* to be dummy; **f. l'imbécile, f. l'idiot** to play *or* act the fool

22 *(locutions avec 'en')* **ne t'en fais pas** don't worry; **il n'en fait qu'à sa tête** he does what he likes; **n'en faites rien** don't do any such thing; **c'en est fait de lui** it's all over for him, he's done for

23 *(locutions avec 'y')* **rien n'y fit** it was no use; **que voulez-vous que j'y fasse?** what do you expect me to do about it?; **il sait y f.** he knows how to go about things; **il sait y f. avec les enfants** he's good with children, he knows how to handle children

24 *Fam (faire croire)* **la f. à qn** to take sb in; **on ne me la fait pas!** nothing doing!, I'm not going to be had!

25 *Fam* **ça le fait** it's well cool *or* awesome; **ça le fait pas de se pointer avec une heure de retard le premier jour** it's so crap to show up an hour late on your first day

VI *Fam (faire ses besoins)* to relieve oneself; **un chien a fait sur la pelouse** a dog has made a mess *or* done its business on the lawn

V IMPERS SEE GRAMMAR B29; B66 **1 il fait beau (temps)** it's fine (weather); **il fait froid/**chaud it's cold/hot; **il fait du soleil/de la neige** it's sunny/snowing; **par le froid qu'il fait** in this cold weather

2 il fait bon près de la cheminée it's nice by the fireside; **il fait mauvais voyager par ces routes** it is hard travelling on these roads; **il fait bon parler à ses amis** it's nice *or* good to talk to one's friends; **il faisait mauvais paraître avec ces gens-là** it was bad to be seen with people like that

V AUX 1 *(avec 'que')* **il ne fait que lire toute la journée** he does nothing but read all day; **je n'ai fait que le toucher** I only touched it; **je ne fais que d'arriver** I have only just arrived; **je n'ai que f. de vos problèmes** your problems are of no concern to me; **c'est ce qui fait que je suis venu si vite** that is why *or* this is how it happens that I came so quickly; **les événements qui font que les choses sont comme elles sont** the events that make things what they are; **faites qu'il vienne demain** see to it *or* make sure that he comes tomorrow

2 *(le nom ou le pronom objet est sujet de l'infinitif)* **le soleil fait fondre la neige** the sun makes the snow melt *or* melts the snow; **nous l'avons fait sortir par la porte de derrière** we made him leave by the back door; **on le fit chanter** he was made to sing; **il nous a fait venir** he sent for us; **faites-le entrer** show him in; **f. attendre qn** to keep sb waiting SEE GRAMMAR A56; B37

3 *(avec verbe pronominal)* **f. asseoir qn** to make sb sit down; **f. coucher un enfant** to put a child to bed; **je le fis s'arrêter** I made him stop SEE GRAMMAR A56; B37

4 *(le nom ou le pronom est objet de l'infinitif)* **f. bâtir une maison** to have *or* get a house built; **f. deux exemplaires** to have *or* get two copies made; **faites-le réparer** get *or* have it mended SEE GRAMMAR A56; B37

5 f. f. qch à qn to get sb to do sth, to have sb do sth; **il lui a fait f. son repassage** he got her to do his ironing, he had her do his ironing; **il fit lâcher prise à son adversaire** he made his opponent let go, he got his opponent to let go; **faites-lui lire cette lettre** get him to read *or* make him read this letter; **je lui ai fait observer qu'il se faisait tard** I pointed out to him that it was getting late; **faites-lui comprendre qu'il n'est pas le bienvenu** make him understand that he is not welcome; **je le ferai examiner par un médecin** I shall have *or* get him examined by a doctor VOIR GRAMMAIRE A41

VPR se faire 1 *(devenir meilleur) (fromage)* to ripen; *(vin)* to mature; **il s'est fait seul** he's a self-made man

2 *(devenir)* to become; **se f. vieux** to become *or* grow *or* get old; **si ça continue, je vais me f. bonne sœur** I'm going to become a nun if things go on like this

3 *(s'adapter)* **se f. à qch** to get used *or* accustomed to sth; **se f. à la fatigue** to become resistant *or* inured to tiredness; **tes chaussures vont finir par se f.** your shoes will eventually get worn in; **permettre aux engrenages de se f.** to run in the gears

4 se f. des amis/relations to make friends/contacts; **cette couleur de vernis ne se fait plus** they've stopped making that shade of varnish, that shade of varnish has been discontinued; **ces choses-là ne se font pas** these things are not done; **cela se fait beaucoup dans cette partie du monde** it's very common in this part of the world; **les robes en lamé se font beaucoup cette année** lamé dresses are very popular *or* are in this year; **se f. une opinion/une idée sur qch** to form an opinion/get some idea about sth; *Fam* **se f. tant par mois** to make *or* earn so much a month; **(ne) t'en fais pas** don't worry

5 *(impers)* **il se fait tard** it's getting late; **il se fit un long silence** a long silence followed, there was a long silence; **comment se fait-il que vous soyez en retard?** how is it that you're late?

6 *(s'accomplir)* to happen; **il pourrait bien se f. que je ne revienne pas** I might very well not come back; **le miracle s'est fait tout seul** the miracle came about *or* happened by itself; **le mariage ne se fera pas** the marriage will not take place *or* will not happen

7 *(+ inf)* **se f. photographier** to have *or* get oneself photographed, to have one's photograph taken; **un bruit se fit entendre** a noise was heard; **ne vous faites pas tant prier** don't take so much asking; **elle adore se f. attendre** she loves making people wait for her; **il ne se le fit pas dire deux fois** he didn't need to be told twice; **il s'est fait punir** he's got himself punished; *Vulg* **il peut aller se f. foutre** he can fuck off; **va te f.!** get out of here!, *Br* sling your hook!, eff off!, *Am* bug off! SEE GRAMMAR A54–5; B39

8 il se fait plus pauvre qu'il ne l'est makes himself out to be poorer than he is

9 *très Fam* **se f. qn** *(avoir des rapports sexuels avec)* to screw *or Br* shag sb; *(battre)* to beat the shit out of sb; *Fam* **on se fait un film/un resto chinois** do you fancy going to see a film/going for a Chinese?

10 *Fam (supporter)* **celui-là, il faut se le f.!** he's a total pain (in the neck)!

faire-part NM INV *(d'un mariage, d'une naissance, d'un décès etc)* announcement; **le présent avis tiendra lieu de f.** friends please accept this intimation

faire-valoir NM INV **1** *Agr* farming; **exploitation en f. direct** farm run by the owner **2** *(personne)* foil; *(de comique)* stooge

fair-play [fɛrplɛ] ADJ INV **être f.** to be fair, to play fair
NM INV fair play; **faire preuve de f.** to play fair

faisabilité [fəzabilite] NF feasibility; **étude de f.** feasibility study

faisable [fəzabl] ADJ feasible

faisan [fəzɑ̃] NM **1** *(coq)* **f.** *(cock)* pheasant; **f. doré** golden pheasant VOIR GRAMMAIRE A12 **2** *Arg (escroc)* crook

faisandage [fəzɑ̃daʒ] NM *Culin (du gibier)* hanging

faisandé [fəzɑ̃de] ADJ **1** *Culin (viande)* high, gamy **2** *Fam (corrompu) (littérature, personne, société etc)* decadent; *(milieu politique)* corrupt

faisandeau, -eaux [fəzɑ̃do] NM young pheasant

faisander [fəzɑ̃de] VT *Culin (gibier)* to hang

faisanderie [fəzɑ̃dri] NF pheasantry

faisane [fəzan] NF *(poule)* **f.** hen pheasant

faisceau, -eaux [fɛso] NM **1** *(rayons)* beam; **f. lumineux** *ou* **de lumière** beam of light, *Spéc* pencil of rays; **f. laser** laser beam; **f. de particules** particle beam **2** *Électron* **f. d'électrons** *ou* **électronique** electron beam; **f. hertzien** electromagnetic wave; *TV* **f. cathodique explorateur** scanning electron beam; **f. radar** radar beam; *Aut* **f. convergent** converging beam; *Aut* **f. divergent** diverging beam; *Aut* **f. parallèle** parallel beam **3** *(de branches etc)* bundle; *Anat (de fibres)* fasciculus, fascicle; *(d'ampoules électriques)* cluster; *Rail (de voies de garage)* group; *Aut* **f. du radiateur** radiator core; *Fig* **un f. d'habitudes/de preuves** a body of customs/proof; **un f. d'amitiés** a network of friendships; *Antiq* **les faisceaux** the fasces; *Archit* **colonne en f.** clustered column; *Mil* **former/rompre les faisceaux** to pile/unpile arms

faiseur, -euse [fəzœr, -øz] N **1** *(qui fabrique qch)* maker; *Prov* **les grands diseurs ne sont pas les grands faiseurs** the greatest talkers are the least doers; **f. de dentelles** lacemaker; **f. de ponts** bridge builder; *Vieilli* **costume du meilleur f.** suit from the best tailor; **f. de miracles** miracle worker; **f. de tours** conjurer; **f. d'embarras** fusspot, *Am* fussbudget; **f. de projets** schemer; *TV, Radio* **f. d'audimat** = television *or* radio personality guaranteed to boost the ratings; **f. de mariages** matchmaker; **faiseuse d'anges** backstreet abortionist **2** *Péj* (*poseur*) pushy type

faisselle [fɛsɛl] NF (*fromage*) type of fromage frais; (*récipient*) = basket *or* pot for draining cheese

fait¹ [fɛ] ADJ **1** (*mûr*) (*fromage*) ripe; **fromage f. à cœur** fully ripe cheese; **une expression toute faite** a cliché; **j'ai f. la vaisselle, vite f., bien f.** that's the washing up done; **être bien f. de sa personne** to be good-looking; *Culin* **f. maison** home-made
2 avoir les ongles/yeux faits to have nail polish/eye make-up on
3 être f. pour qch/qn to be made for sth/sb; **cette voiture est faite pour la ville** this car is made *or* designed for town driving; **ils sont faits l'un pour l'autre** they're made for each other; **il est f. pour faire du cinéma/pour être avocat** he's cut out to act in films/to be a lawyer; *Fam* **on peut mettre un chapeau dans cette boîte – oui, c'est f. pour** you can put a hat in this box – yes, that's what it's for; **ça f. joli – c'est f. pour** that looks pretty – it's supposed *or* meant to; **sers-toi, c'est f. pour** help yourself, that's what it's there for
4 *Fam* (*ivre*) blitzed, wasted, gassed

FAIT²

| act **1** ▪ fact **2** ▪ event **3** |

NM **1** (*acte*) act; **le f. de boire** (the act of) drinking; **observer les (moindres) faits et gestes de qn** to watch sb's every move; **rendre compte de ses faits et gestes** to give an account of oneself; (*surtout à la police*) to give an account of one's movements; **f. d'armes** feat of arms; **f. de guerre** feat; **cela est du f. de Martin** this is Martin's doing; **prendre qn sur le f.** to catch sb in the act *or* redhanded; **quels sont les faits?** (*dans un procès*) what are the facts?; **quels sont les faits reprochés à mon client?** what is my client being accused of *or* charged with?; **où étiez-vous au moment des faits?** where were you at the time in question?; **parler n'était pas son f.** he was no talker; **dire son f. à qn** to tell sb what one thinks, to give sb a piece of one's mind
2 (*réalité*) fact; **f. accompli** fait accompli; **prendre f. et cause pour qn** to stand up for sb; **ceci est un f.** this is a (matter of) fact; **roi de nom plutôt que de f.** king in name rather than in fact; **possession de f.** actual possession; **il est de f. que c'était un traître** it is a fact that he was a traitor; **aller droit au f.** to go *or* get straight to the point; **en venir au f.** to come to the point; **être au f.** to be au fait; **mettre qn au f.** to acquaint sb *or* make acquainted with the facts; **mettre qn au f. de qch** to inform sb about sth, to acquaint sb with sth; **être le f. de** to be characteristic of; **c'est le f. de tous les incapables que de se chercher des excuses** incompetents always try to find excuses for themselves; **la renaissance du judo français est le f. de quelques champions** the renaissance of judo in France is entirely due to a few champions; **je suis au f.** I know all about it; **être sûr de son f.** to be sure of one's facts; **au f.!** get to the point!; **au f., que venez-vous faire ici?** by the way, what have you come here for?; **en f., de f.** as a matter of fact, in point of fact, in actual fact, actually; **de f., cela est un refus** that is in effect a refusal; **de ce f.** for that reason, on that account; **du f. ou par le f. qu'il boite** owing to the fact that

or because he limps; **par le seul f. d'y être** by the mere fact of *or* simply by being there; **expert en f. de vins** expert as regards wine *or* when it comes to wine; **en f. de soupe, c'était du bouillon clair** it wasn't so much soup as stock
3 (*événement*) occurrence, event; **un f. nouveau s'est produit** there was a new development; *Journ* **'faits divers'** 'news in brief' (*dealing with local and human interest stories*); **f. divers** news item; **tenir la rubrique des faits divers** = to cover weddings and funerals

faîtage [fɛtaʒ] NM *Constr* **1** (*poutre*) rooftree, ridgepole **2** (*couverture*) ridge sheathing; (*tuiles*) ridge tiling

faîte [fɛt] NM *Constr* (*d'un toit*) ridge **2** *Géog* **ligne de f.** watershed, crest line **3** (*d'une maison, d'un arbre etc*) top; **le f. de la gloire** the height *or* pinnacle of glory

faîtière [fɛtjɛr] ADJ, NF *Constr* (tuile) **f.** ridge tile; (lucarne) **f.** skylight

faitout NM, **fait-tout** NM INV [fɛtu] stewpot

faix [fɛ] NM **1** (*poids*) burden, load; **le f. des années** the weight of years; **le f. des impôts** the burden of taxation **2** *Obst* foetus and placenta

fakir [fakir] NM fakir

falaise [falɛz] NF cliff

falbalas [falbala] NMPL *Couture* furbelows, flounces; *Fig* (*de l'architecture, la poésie baroque*) frills and furbelows, extravagances

fallacieusement [falasjøzmɑ̃] ADV fallaciously; (*promettre*) misleadingly

fallacieux, -ieuse [falasjø, -jøz] ADJ (*argument, raisonnement etc*) specious; (*espoir*) false; (*promesse, apparence*) misleading; **sous un f. prétexte** on false pretexts

FALLOIR [falwar] (*no prp; pp* **fallu**; *pr ind* **il faut**; *pr sub* **il faille**; *impf* **il fallait**; *p hist* **il fallut**; *fu* **il faudra**) V IMPERS SEE GRAMMAR A60; B29; B40 **1** (*être nécessaire*) **il lui faut un nouveau pardessus** he needs a new overcoat; **avez-vous tout ce qu'il (vous) faut?** have you got all you want *or* require *or* need?; **faut-il tout cela?** is all that necessary?; **c'est juste ce qu'il (me) faut** that's the very thing (I want), that's just the (right) thing; **nous en avions plus qu'il ne nous en fallait** we had more than enough *or* than we needed; **il m'a fallu trois jours pour le faire** it took me three days to do it; **il faut compter deux heures pour y aller** you'll have to allow two hours to get there; **il va bien f. que le lui dises** you're going to have to tell him; **je l'ai fait parce qu'il le fallait** I did it because I had to; **elle fera ce qu'il faut** she will do what is necessary *or* what needs *or* has to be done; **il a tout ce qu'il faut pour réussir** he has everything he needs *or* *Fam* he's got what it takes to succeed; **je lui ai tout donné, qu'est-ce qu'il lui faut de plus!** I've given him everything, what more does he want!; *Fam* **il faut ce qu'il faut!** you might as well do things in style!; **il me faudrait une livre de beurre** I need a pound of butter
2 comme il faut properly; **se conduire comme il faut** to behave properly *or* in a civilized manner *or* in the right way; **il/elle est très comme il faut** he's very gentlemanly/she's very ladylike; **ce sont des gens très comme il faut** they're very decent *or* respectable people; **votre toilette est tout à fait comme il faut** your dress is just right
3 (*devoir*) **il faut partir** I/we/you/*etc* must go *or* have to go; **il faut dire qu'il s'est bien comporté** it must be said *or* I am bound to say he behaved well; **il nous faut le voir, il faut que nous le voyions** we must see him, we have to see him; **il lui faut se dépêcher** he must hurry; **il faudra marcher plus vite** we

shall have to walk faster; **il fallait porter plainte** you should have *or* ought to have made a complaint; **il fallait le dire!** you should have said so!, why didn't you say so?; **il n'aurait pas fallu attendre** you shouldn't have *or* ought not to have waited; **comme il fallait s'y attendre** as was (only) to be expected; **il faut qu'il ait été fâché pour dire cela** he must have been angry to have said that; **c'est ce qu'il faudra voir!** we must see about that!; **la police a arrêté l'homme qu'il ne fallait pas** the police have arrested the wrong man; **elle fera mieux la prochaine fois – oui, faut voir** she'll do better next time – well, we'll see (about that); **elle est habillée/lui a répondu, faut voir comment!** you wouldn't believe the way she's dressed/she answered him; *Fam* **tu vas le lui dire? – faut bien!** are you going to tell him? – I've got to, I've got no choice!; **je vous en prie, il ne fallait pas!** you shouldn't have!; **c'est simple, mais il fallait y penser** it's simple once you've thought of it; **il a fallu qu'elle apprenne cet accident!** of course, she would have to hear about the accident!; **encore faut-il que ce soit vrai** even so, it still must be true; **il ne faudrait pas que je les rencontre** it would never do for me to meet them; **il ne faudrait pas qu'il le dise deux fois** he'd better not say it again; **il ne faudrait pas que je vous mette en retard** I'd better not make you late; **il ne faut pas y aller** you mustn't go there
4 (*with 'le' = noun clause*) **il viendra s'il le faut** he will come if need be *or* if necessary *or* if he has to; **vous êtes revenu à pied? – il l'a ou il a bien fallu** you walked back? – there was nothing else for it, I had no choice
VPR **s'en falloir il s'en faut de deux euros** it is two euros short; **je ne suis pas satisfait, il s'en faut de beaucoup** *ou* **tant s'en faut** I am not satisfied, far from it *or* not by a long way; **il s'en faut de beaucoup que l'autobus (ne) soit plein** the bus is far from being full; **il s'en est fallu de peu** *ou* **peu s'en est fallu qu'il ne mourût** he very nearly died, it was touch and go whether he died; **cinq livres ou peu s'en faut** the best part of five pounds, very nearly five pounds; **il s'en est fallu de rien qu'il (ne) fût écrasé** he was within an ace *or* an inch *or* a hair's breadth of being run over; **il s'en faut de peu qu'il accepte** he is more than half inclined to accept; **il s'en faudrait de peu pour que le projet démarre** it wouldn't take much for the plan to get off the ground; **vous êtes satisfait? – peu s'en faut!** are you satisfied? – not at all!

falot¹ [falo] NM **1** (*lanterne*) (hand) lantern **2** *Mil Fam* court martial

falot², -ote [falo, -ɔt] ADJ (*terne*) (*personne*) dreary, drab

falsificateur, -trice [falsifikatœr, -tris] N (*de documents, de comptes*) falsifier; (*d'une signature*) forger; (*de la nourriture, d'un vin etc*) adulterator

falsification [falsifikasjɔ̃] NF (*de documents, de comptes etc*) falsification; (*d'une signature*) forging; (*de la nourriture, d'un vin etc*) adulteration; *Fig* (*de la pensée de qn, de la vérité*) misrepresentation

falsifier [falsifje] VT (*impf, pr sub n.* **falsifiions, v. falsifiiez**) (*document*) to falsify; (*signature*) to forge; (*nourriture, vin etc*) to adulterate; (*élections*) to rig; **f. les comptes ou écritures** to falsify *or* doctor the accounts; **f. la pensée de l'auteur** to misrepresent the author's thinking

falzar [falzar] NM *très Fam* (pair of) trousers, *Am* (pair of) pants

famé [fame] ADJ **mal f.** disreputable, seedy, *Fml* of ill repute

famélique [famelik] ADJ (*personne, chien*)

half-starved; **les ventres faméliques de l'Afrique** the starving of Africa

fameusement [famøzmã] ADV *Fam (très)* incredibly, really; **on s'est f. bien amusé** we had a whale of a time; **il a f. réussi son coup** he really pulled it off

fameux, -euse [famø, -øz] ADJ **1** *(ayant bonne réputation)* famous; *(ayant mauvaise réputation)* notorious (**par, for** for); **c'est un f. coquin, celui-là** he's quite a lad!; **c'est donc ça, ton f. régime miracle!** so this is your famous miracle diet! **2** *Fam (très bon)* splendid, marvellous, tremendous; *(très mauvais)* terrible, awful; **vous commettez une fameuse erreur** you're making a terrible *or* an awful *or* a (mighty) big mistake; **ce n'est pas f. ton boulot/son dernier roman** your job/his latest novel isn't up to much *or* isn't anything special; **c'est pas f.** it's not brilliant

familial, -iale, -iaux, -iales [familjal, -jo] ADJ *(vie, conflits etc)* family; *(pension, hôtel)* family-run, owner-managed; *Com (paquet, pot etc)* family-size; **entreprise familiale** family firm; **l'ambiance est familiale** there is a family atmosphere; **allocations familiales** child benefit, *Am* dependent's allowance
  NF *Aut* **familiale** (family) estate car, *Am* station wagon

familiarisation [familjarizasjõ] NF familiarization

familiariser [familjarize] VT **f. qn avec qch** to familiarize sb with sth, to get sb used to sth; **je ne suis pas encore familiarisé avec les lieux** I don't know my way around yet
  VPR **se familiariser se f. avec qch** *(en le pratiquant)* to familiarize oneself with sth, to get to know sth; *(en s'y habituant)* to get accustomed *or* used to sth; **se f. avec un lieu** to get to know a place, to get to know one's way around; **peu familiarisé avec** unfamiliar *or* unacquainted with; **il n'est pas encore très familiarisé avec cet ordinateur/avec les animaux** he hasn't really got used to this computer/to animals yet

familiarité [familjarite] NF **1** *(intimité)* familiarity; **être d'une grande f. avec qn** to be on very familiar terms with sb; **être d'une trop grande f. avec qn** to be too familiar *or* overfamiliar with sb **2** *(comportement amical)* informality, friendliness; **se permettre trop de familiarités avec qn** to be too familiar *or* to take liberties with sb; **pas de f., je vous prie** please don't be familiar

familier, -ière [familje, -jɛr] ADJ **1** *(avec qn)* familiar; *(amical)* friendly; **être f. avec qn** to be on familiar terms with sb; **il s'est montré trop f.** he was too familiar, he was overfamiliar; **expression familière** colloquial *or* familiar expression, colloquialism; **le langage f.** colloquial *or* familiar language; **animal f.** pet **2** *(habituel)* familiar; **visage qui lui est f.** face which is familiar *or* well-known to him; **ta voix ne lui est pas familière** he doesn't know *or* recognize your voice; **mon cadre f.** my usual surroundings; **cette question lui est familière** he is familiar with the subject; **le mensonge lui est f.** he is a habitual liar **3** *(de la maison)* **dieux familiers** household gods
  N *(d'un café, club etc)* regular visitor (**de** to), regular (**de** of); *(d'une sorcière)* familiar; **un f. de la maison** a regular visitor to the house, an intimate friend of the household

familièrement [familjɛrmã] ADV familiarly; *(amicalement)* informally; **ces insectes que l'on nomme f. ...** these insects, which are commonly *or* familiarly known as ...; **il lui donna f. une petite tape sur la joue** he gave her a friendly little pat on the cheek

familistère [familistɛr] NM workers' co-operative association

famille [famij] NF **1** *(mère, père, enfants)* fa-

mily; *(ensemble des parents)* family, relatives, relations; **il faut que je vous présente à ma f.** *(parents)* I must introduce you to my parents; *(conjoint, enfants)* I must introduce you to my family; **f. nombreuse** large family; **réduction f. nombreuse** family reduction *or* discount; **f. monoparentale** one-parent *or* single-parent family; **f. patchwork, f. tuyau de poêle** patchwork family, extended family *(consisting of children, parents etc of divorced parent's new spouse)*; **charges de f.** dependants; **chef de f.** head of the family; *Admin* householder, head of the household; **soutien de f.** (main) wage earner, breadwinner; **fils de f.** young man of good social standing; **il a épousé une jeune fille de bonne f.** he married a girl from a good family *or* a well-bred girl; **avoir l'esprit de f.** to have family feeling; **dîner/passer le week-end en f.** to dine/spend the weekend at home with one's family; **avec eux je me sens en f.** I feel quite at home with them; **nous réglons toujours nos problèmes en f.** we always settle our problems within the family; **c'est de f.** it runs in the family; **pension de f.** (small) boarding house; *Jur* **prévenir la f.** to inform the next of kin; *Cartes* **le jeu des sept familles** happy families; *Fam* **on va se faire un repas des familles** we'll make ourselves a nice little meal; *Fam* **on s'est fait une petite soirée des familles** we had a cosy little *or* nice little evening together; *Fig* **ils appartiennent à la même f. politique/littéraire** they belong to the same political/literary grouping; **f. de produits** product family; **f. de caractères** typeface VOIR GRAMMAIRE A11
  2 *Ling, Bot, Zool* family

famine [famin] NF famine; **crier f.** to plead poverty, to complain of hard times; **salaire de f.** starvation wages; **prendre une ville par la f.** to starve a city into submission

Famtour [famtur] NM *(tourisme)* familiarization tour, fam trip

fan [fan] NM *Fam (admirateur)* fan

fana [fana] *Fam* ADJ *(enthousiaste)* dead keen (**de** on), mad (**de** about, on)
  N **f. du football/de la moto** football/motorbike fanatic *or* freak

fanage [fanaʒ] NM *(du foin)* tedding, tossing

fanal, -aux [fanal, -o] NM lantern; *Rail (de locomotive)* headlight; *Naut (sur les côtes)* beacon, lantern; *(sur un bateau)* (ship's) lantern

fanatique [fanatik] ADJ fanatical; **être f. de qn/qch** to be mad about *or* on sb/sth
  N *(enthousiaste)* fanatic; *Pol, Rel* fanatic, zealot; **f. du football** football fanatic; **fanatiques de Pavarotti** Pavarotti fans; **je ne suis pas un f. du poisson** I'm not mad *or* crazy about fish

fanatiquement [fanatikmã] ADV fanatically

fanatisation [fanatizasjõ] NF fanaticization; **la f. des foules était due à une propagande très bien menée** extremely skilful propaganda turned the crowds into fanatics *or* made the crowds fanatical

fanatiser [fanatize] VT to turn into fanatics, to make fanatical; **des religieux fanatisés** religious fanatics

fanatisme [fanatism] NM *(enthousiasme)* fanaticism (**pour** for); *Pol, Rel* fanaticism, zealotry

fanchon [fãʃõ] NF kerchief, headscarf

fandango [fãdãgo] NM fandango

faner [fane] VT **1** *(foin)* to ted, to toss **2** *(couleur, étoffe etc)* to fade; *(fleur, plante)* to fade, to wither, to wilt
  VPR **se faner** *(d'une fleur, plante)* to fade, to wither, to wilt; *(d'une couleur, étoffe, Fig (de la beauté, la santé, un souvenir etc)* to fade;

une odeur de parfum fané a smell of stale perfume

fanes [fan] NFPL *(de carottes)* tops; *(de radis)* stalks

faneur, -euse [fanœr, -øz] *Agr* N *(ouvrier)* haymaker
  NF **faneuse** *(machine)* tedder, tedding machine

fanfare [fãfar] NF **1** *(air) (de cuivres)* flourish, fanfare; *Fig* **réveil en f.** brutal awakening **2** *(orchestre)* brass band; *Mil* military band; **la f. du village** the village band

fanfaron, -onne [fãfarõ, -ɔn] ADJ boastful
  N braggart, boaster; **faire le f.** to brag, to boast; **alors, on ne fait plus le f. maintenant, hein?** we're not so high and mighty now, are we!

fanfaronnade [fãfarɔnad] NF **1** *(caractère)* bragging, boasting **2 fanfaronnades** *(actes, propos)* bragging, boasting

fanfaronner [fãfarɔne] VI to brag, to boast

fanfreluche [fãfrəlyʃ] NF *(sur une robe, un rideau etc)* trimming, *Péj* frill

fange [fãʒ] NF *Litt* mire, mud; *Fig* **élevé dans la f.** brought up in the gutter; *Fig* **croupir dans la f.** to be living surrounded by filth; *Fig* **traîner qn dans la f.** to drag sb *or* sb's name through the mud

fangeux, -euse [fãʒø, -øz] ADJ *Litt* miry, muddy; *Fig* murky

fanion [fanjõ] NM *(de club, bateau, corps d'armée etc)* pennant, pennon; *Ski (de balisage)* flag

fanon [fanõ] NM **1** *(de baleine)* whalebone, baleen **2** *(de bœuf)* dewlap; *(d'oiseau)* wattle; *(de cheval)* fetlock **3** *Rel (de mitre)* lappet

fantaisie [fãtezi] NF **1** *(envie)* **il a eu** *ou* **il lui a pris la f. de se baigner** he took it into his head to go swimming, he had a sudden idea *or* notion to go swimming; **chacun s'amusait à sa f.** everyone amused themselves as the fancy took them *or* as they pleased; **qu'est-ce que c'est que cette f.?** what's come over you?; **il lui passe toutes ses fantaisies** he gives in to her every whim; **nous ne pouvons nous permettre aucune f.** we can't afford to indulge ourselves
  2 articles (de) f. fancy goods; **pain (de) f.** fancy bread *(not sold by weight)*; **bijoux (de) f.** costume jewellery; **du rhum f.** = inexpensive rum of less than usual strength and quality
  3 *(imagination)* imagination; **sa vie manque de f.** his life is very dull *or* unexciting; **donner un peu de f. à sa vie** to add a bit of excitement to one's life; **elle était d'une f. rafraîchissante** she was refreshingly imaginative
  4 *(œuvre)*, *Mus* fantasia; *Littér* fantasy

Il faut noter que le nom anglais **fantasy** est un faux ami. Il signifie **rêve, fantasme**.

fantaisiste [fãtezist] ADJ **1** *(original, peu orthodoxe) (personne)* unconventional, unorthodox, different; *(procédés)* unorthodox; **elle a brisé des horaires fantaisistes** she keeps strange *or* odd hours; **je ne veux pas d'employé f.** I don't want any oddballs working for me **2** *(inventé, sans fondement) (interprétation, histoire etc)* fanciful, far-fetched; **les déclarations fantaisistes que vous avez faites à la presse** your extremely fanciful statements to the press
  N **1** *(original)* eccentric; *(qui manque de sérieux)* unreliable person **2** *Théâtre* variety artist

fantasmagorie [fãtasmagɔri] NF phantasmagoria; **des histoires pleines de fantasmagories** fantasies

fantasmagorique [fɑ̃tasmagɔrik] ADJ phantasmagoric(al)

fantasme [fɑ̃tasm] NM (situation imaginée) fantasy; **tu vis dans tes fantasmes** you're living in a fantasy world

fantasmer [fɑ̃tasme] VI to fantasize (**sur** about)

fantasque [fɑ̃task] ADJ (personne, manières etc) whimsical; (histoire, forme etc) odd, weird

fantassin [fɑ̃tasɛ̃] NM foot soldier, infantryman

fantastique [fɑ̃tastik] ADJ 1 (imaginaire) (être, animal etc) imaginary 2 (surnaturel) (lumière, atmosphère etc) weird, eerie 3 (incroyable) (idée, histoire etc) fantastic 4 (formidable) (succès, plan, somme etc) fantastic; **paysage d'une beauté f.** fantastically beautiful scenery 5 Beaux-Arts, Cin, Littér fantastic
▪ NM **le f.** the fantastic; (art) fantasy art; (littérature) fantasy literature

fantastiquement [fɑ̃tastikmɑ̃] ADV fantastically; (d'une manière surnaturelle) weirdly, eerily

fantoche [fɑ̃tɔʃ] NM (marionnette), Fig (personne) puppet
▪ ADJ **gouvernement f.** puppet government

fantomatique [fɑ̃tɔmatik] ADJ ghostly

fantôme [fɑ̃tom] NM ghost, phantom; Cin, TV ghost, ghosting; **train f.** ghost train; Mus **le Vaisseau F.** the Flying Dutchman; **ville f.** ghost town; **membre(-) f.** phantom limb; Fig **ce n'est plus qu'un f.** (très maigre) he's just a skeleton, he's nothing but skin and bone; Pol **gouvernement/cabinet f.** shadow government/cabinet

fanzine [fɑ̃zin] NM fanzine

FAO NF Ordinat (abrév **fabrication assistée par ordinateur**) CAM

faon [fɑ̃] NM fawn, calf

FAQ [efɑky] Ordinat (abrév **frequently asked questions, foire aux questions**) FAQ

faquin [fakɛ̃] NM Arch, Péj varlet

FAR [far] NF Mil (abrév **force d'action rapide**) = (French) strike force, Am ≃ RDF

far [far] NM **f. breton** custard flan (with prunes)

farad [farad] NM Élec (unité) farad

faramineux, -euse [faraminø, -øz] ADJ Fam phenomenal, staggering; **il lui a fait des compliments pour le moins f.** his compliments were slightly over the top

farandole [farɑ̃dɔl] NF farandole

faraud, -aude [faro, -od] Fam Vieilli ADJ swanky, swaggering
▪ N swaggerer; **faire le f.** to swagger

farce [fars] NF 1 Culin stuffing 2 (tour) (practical) joke, prank, trick; **faire des farces à qn** to play tricks or (practical) jokes on sb; Com **farces et attrapes** tricks and jokes; **magasin de farces et attrapes** joke shop; Can Fam **f. plate** sick or tasteless joke 3 Théâtre, Fig farce; **la situation va tourner à la f.** the situation is becoming farcical or is turning into a farce
▪ ADJ Fam Vieilli funny, comical

farceur, -euse [farsœr, -øz] ADJ (rire, œil) roguish, mischievous
▪ N 1 (qui fait des tours) (practical) joker, prankster; **je me demande qui est le petit f. qui m'a fait ça** I wonder who the joker is that I have to blame for this 2 (blagueur) joker, wag; **c'est un f. qui vous aura dit cela** somebody's been pulling your leg

farcir [farsir] VT 1 Culin (volaille, légume etc) to stuff 2 Fig (bourrer) to cram, to stuff (**de** with); **arrête de lui f. le crâne avec tes histoires** stop filling his/her head with your non-

sense; Fam **j'ai la tête farcie** my head's fit to burst
▪ VPR **se farcir 1 se f. la tête d'idées romantiques** to fill one's head with romantic ideas 2 Fam (travail, lessive etc) to get landed or stuck or Br lumbered with; **on va encore devoir se f. ta mère tout le week-end** we're going to have to put up with your mother again all weekend; **il faut se le f.** he's impossible or really hard to get on with; **tu as lu son livre? il faut se le f.** have you read his book? it's really hard going 3 Vulg (posséder sexuellement) to screw, Br to have it off with, Am to ball

fard [far] NM make-up; **f. à joues** blusher; **f. à paupières** eye shadow; **la vérité sans f.** the plain unvarnished truth; **parler sans f.** to speak candidly or openly; Fam **piquer un f.** to go red, to blush

fardage [fardaʒ] NM Com (de marchandises inférieures) camouflaging

farde [fard] NF Belg 1 (cahier) exercise book 2 (chemise) folder 3 (cartouche de cigarettes) carton (of cigarettes)

fardeau, -eaux [fardo] NM burden, load; Fig burden; **le f. des impôts** the burden of taxation; Fig **c'est un lourd f. qu'il traîne** it's a millstone round his neck

farder [farde] VT 1 (maquiller) (personne, son visage) to make up; **trop fardé** over made-up; **f. la vérité/les faits** to gloss over or disguise the truth/facts; **le film présente une version fardée de cet événement** the film presents a dressed-up or cosmetic version of the event 2 Com (marchandises inférieures) to camouflage
▪ VPR **se farder** to make up one's face, to put on one's make-up; **se f. les yeux** to put eye shadow on

farfadet [farfadɛ] NM (hob)goblin, sprite

farfelu, -ue [farfəly] Fam ADJ (personne, idée etc) weird, strange
▪ N weirdo

farfouiller [farfuje] VI Fam to rummage (about)

faribole [faribɔl] NF (propos) piece of nonsense; **dire des faribotes** to talk nonsense

farinacé [farinase] ADJ farinaceous

farine [farin] NF 1 flour; **folle f.** flour dust, mill dust; **f. d'avoine** oatmeal; **f. de maïs** cornflour, Am cornstarch; **f. de moutarde** mustard powder; **f. de poisson** fish meal; **farines animales** bone meal; Fam **de la même f.** of the same kind; **ce sont gens de (la) même f.** they are birds of a feather; Fam **rouler qn dans la f.** to take sb for a ride 2 Tech **f. de forage** bore dust

fariner [farine] VT Culin to coat with flour, to flour

farineux, -euse [farinø, -øz] ADJ 1 (qui est recouvert de farine) floury, covered with flour; Péj (au goût) floury 2 (contenant de la fécule) (nourriture) starchy, Spéc farinaceous
▪ NMPL starchy food, Spéc farinaceous food

farlouse [farluz] NF Orn meadow pipit

farniente [farnjɛnte] NM (pleasurable) idleness, dolce farniente

farouche [faruʃ] ADJ 1 (pas apprivoisé) (animal, oiseau) timid, shy; **leurs chats ne sont pas farouches** their cats are quite tame 2 (timide) (personne) shy 3 (acharné, violent) (ennemi, résistance, regard etc) fierce; **volonté f.** iron or unshakeable will 4 (peu civilisé) (gens, pays etc) wild, uncivilized

farouchement [faruʃmɑ̃] ADV fiercely

fart [far(t)] NM (ski) wax

fartage [fartaʒ] NM (de skis) waxing

farter [farte] VT (skis) to wax

fascicule [fasikyl] NM 1 (d'une publication) instalment, part, section; (brochure) bro-

chure, leaflet; **publier un livre par fascicules** to publish a book in parts or instalments 2 Mil **f. de mobilisation** call-up instructions

fasciculé [fasikyle] ADJ Bot fascicular, fasciculate

fascinant [fasinɑ̃] ADJ (personne) fascinating; (beauté, yeux, sourire etc) captivating, bewitching

fascinateur, -trice [fasinatœr, -tris] ADJ Litt captivating, bewitching

fascination [fasinasjɔ̃] NF fascination

fascine [fasin] NF (de brindilles) faggot; Constr fascine

fasciner[1] [fasine] VT 1 (d'un serpent) (proie) to fascinate, to hypnotize 2 (attirer l'attention de) to fascinate; (charmer) to captivate, to bewitch; **elle est fascinée par l'argent** she is very impressed by money

fasciner[2] VT Constr (rive etc) to line with fascines; **route fascinée** corduroy road

fascisant [faʃizɑ̃] ADJ Pol fascistic

fasciser [faʃize] VT Pol to make fascist

fascisme [faʃism] NM Pol fascism

fasciste [faʃist] ADJ, N Pol fascist

faste[1] [fast] NM INV (d'une cérémonie) pomp, splendour, Am splendor; (d'une demeure) sumptuousness, splendour; **mariage sans f.** quiet wedding; **la cérémonie aura lieu sans f.** the ceremony will be a simple affair

faste[2] ADJ Antiq **jour f.** lawful day; (jour favorable) lucky day; **période f.** good period; **je paie la note, je suis dans une période f.!** I'll pay the bill, I'm in the money, I'm flush

fast-food, pl **fast-foods** [fastfud] NM 1 (restauration) fast food 2 (lieu) fast-food restaurant, fast-food bar

fastidieusement [fastidjøzmɑ̃] ADV tiresomely, tediously

fastidieux, -ieuse [fastidjø, -jøz] ADJ dull, tiresome, tedious; **besognes fastidieuses** drudgery

> Il faut noter que l'adjectif anglais **fastidious** est un faux ami. Il signifie **pointilleux, difficile**.

fastoche [fastɔʃ] ADJ Fam dead easy

fastueusement [fastyøzmɑ̃] ADV sumptuously, lavishly

fastueux, -euse [fastyø, -øz] ADJ (personne, vie) lavish; (ameublement, dîner etc) sumptuous

FAT [fat] NF Ordinat (abrév **File Allocation Table**) FAT

fat [fa(t)] ADJ (personne) conceited, self-satisfied
▪ NM conceited or self-satisfied person

fatal, -als [fatal] ADJ 1 (mortel) (accident, résultat etc) fatal; **heure fatale** fatal hour, hour of death; **coup f.** deadly or fatal blow; **le choc lui a été f.** the shock killed him 2 (nuisible) (beauté, oubli) fatal; **f. à qn** fatal or disastrous for sb; **erreur fatale** fatal mistake; Ordinat **f. error** fatal error; **femme fatale** femme fatale 3 (inévitable) inevitable; **c'est f.** it's bound or sure to happen, it's inevitable; **on ne peut pas échapper au cours f. des choses** you can't avoid the inevitable

fatalement [fatalmɑ̃] ADV inevitably; **ils devaient f. se fâcher** they were bound to fall out

> Il faut noter que l'adverbe anglais **fatally** est un faux ami. Il signifie **mortellement ou irrémédiablement**.

fatalisme [fatalism] NM fatalism

fataliste [fatalist] N fatalist
▪ ADJ fatalistic

fatalité [fatalite] NF 1 (destin) fate; **poursuivi**

par la f. pursued by fate; **c'est la f.!** it's just bad luck!; **c'est (comme) une f.** it's an awful coincidence **2** (*malédiction*) misfortune **3** (*inévitabilité*) inevitability

> Il faut noter que le nom anglais **fatality** signifie également **victime**.

fatidique [fatidik] ADJ fateful

fatigabilité [fatigabilite] NF tendency to get tired; **il est d'une grande f.** he gets tired very easily

fatigable [fatigabl] ADJ easily tired

fatigant [fatigɑ̃] ADJ **1** (*épuisant*) tiring, exhausting; **c'est f. pour le cœur** it strains the heart; **c'est f. pour les yeux** it's tiring on the eyes, it's a strain on the eyes **2** (*lassant*) annoying, tiresome, wearisome; **c'est f. de ne jamais réussir** it's annoying or tiresome or wearisome never to be successful

> Attention: ne pas confondre **tiring** et **tiresome** lorsqu'on traduit **fatigant**. **Tiring** s'applique à la fatigue physique alors que **tiresome** exprime la lassitude.

fatigue [fatig] NF **1** (*d'une personne, des membres etc*) tiredness, weariness, fatigue; **tomber** *ou* **être mort de f.** to be dead tired, to be ready to drop; **ressentir une grande/légère f.** to feel very/a bit tired or weary; **f. nerveuse** nervous exhaustion; **f. intellectuelle** mental strain; **f. oculaire** eyestrain; **état de f. générale** general fatigue **2** *Tech* (*d'un métal, d'une pièce etc*) fatigue **3** (*effort pénible*) strain, effort; **épargner** *ou* **éviter à qn la f. de qch/de faire qch** to save sb the strain or effort of sth/of doing sth

fatigué [fatige] ADJ **1** (*épuisé*) (*personne, membres etc*) tired (out), weary; (*traits, regard, voix etc*) tired; (*yeux, cœur*) strained; (*cerveau*) tired, overworked; **f. par le voyage** travel-worn, travel-weary **2** *Fig* **f. de qch/qn** tired or weary of sth/sb; **f. de faire qch** tired or weary of doing sth **3** *Méd* (*dérangé*) (*estomac, foie etc*) upset **4** (*usé*) (*vêtements, chaussures etc*) worn (out), shabby; (*moteur*) worn out

fatiguer [fatige] VT **1** (*épuiser*) (*personne*) to tire (out), to make tired or weary; (*cheval*) to tire; (*surmener*) to overwork; **f. le cœur/les yeux** to strain the heart/the eyes; *Iron* **si ça ne te fatigue pas trop évidemment** not if it's too tiring for you or it's not too much of an effort of course **2** (*soumettre à un long usage etc*) (*machine, moteur, solive etc*) to strain; (*vêtements, chaussures etc*) to wear out; (*champ, sol*) to exhaust, to impoverish; **f. un livre** to give a book a lot of hard wear **3** (*remuer*) (*salade*) to mix, to toss **4** (*importuner*) to annoy, to irritate; (*lasser*) to weary, to wear down

VI (*d'une personne*) to tire, to get tired (out); (*d'un bateau, moteur*) to labour, *Am* to labor; (*d'une solive etc*) to show strain; **je commence à f. sérieusement** I'm beginning to get really tired

VPR se fatiguer (*d'une personne*) to get tired (out), to tire; (*en travaillant beaucoup*) to tire oneself out (**à faire qch** doing sth); **se f. les yeux/le cœur** to strain one's eyes/heart; *Iron* **il ne s'est pas (trop) fatigué** he didn't exactly exert himself; **ne te fatigue pas, je m'en occupe** don't bother, I'll see to it; **c'était bien la peine que je me fatigue à préparer le repas** a fat lot of use it was me wearing myself out getting the meal ready; **ne vous fatiguez pas, je suis au courant** don't waste your breath, I know all about it; **se f. de qch/qn** to get tired or to tire of sth/sb; **se f. de faire qch** to get tired or to tire of doing sth

fatras [fatra] NM (*d'idées, de papiers etc*) jumble, muddle, hotchpotch

fatuité [fatɥite] NF (self-)conceit, self-satisfaction

fatwa [fatwa] NF *Rel* fatwa; **prononcer une f. contre qn** to declare or issue a fatwa against sb

fauber(t) [fobɛr] NM *Naut* (deck) swab, mop

faubourg [fobur] NM **1** (*quartier périphérique*) suburb; **accent des faubourgs** (Parisian) working-class accent **2** (*quartier de grande ville*) district

faubourien, -ienne [foburjɛ̃, -jɛn] ADJ (*accent etc*) (Parisian) working-class N working-class Parisian

fauchage [foʃaʒ] NM **1** (*du blé, d'un champ de blé etc*) reaping; (*de l'herbe, d'une prairie etc*) mowing, cutting **2** *Mil* (*de troupes*) mowing down; (*procédé de tir*) sweeping of the ground (with machine-gun fire)

fauchaison [foʃɛzɔ̃] NF **1** (*saison*) reaping time; (*où l'on fauche l'herbe*) mowing time **2** (*action*) = **fauchage 1**

fauchard [foʃar] NM *Agr* double-edged slasher

fauche [foʃ] NF *Fam* **1** (*vol*) pinching, thieving; **méfie-toi, il y a de la f. au lycée** watch out, there's a lot of thieving going on at school **2** (*manque d'argent*) penniless ness; **c'est vraiment la f. en ce moment** I'm really broke just now

fauché [foʃe] ADJ *Fam* **f. (comme les blés)** (flat) broke, stony-broke, *Am* stone-broke

faucher [foʃe] VT **1** (*blé, champ de blé etc*) to reap; (*herbe, prairie etc*) to mow, to cut; *Fam* **f. l'herbe sous le pied de qn** to cut the ground from under sb's feet **2** (*abattre*) (*d'une voiture, une mitraillette*) (*piétons, troupes etc*) to mow down; (*d'une guerre, une maladie*) to wipe out; *Rugby, Ftbl etc* **f. son homme** to bring down one's man **3** *Fam* (*voler*) to swipe, to pinch; **elle m'a fauché ma montre/mon mari** she has swiped or pinched my watch/husband

VI 1 *Fam* **ça fauche par ici** things get swiped or nicked round here **2** *Mil* to sweep the ground (with machine-gun fire)

faucheur, -euse [foʃœr, -øz] N (*personne*) reaper; (*qui fauche les herbes*) mower NM (*insecte*) harvestman, *Am* daddy-long-legs

NF **faucheuse** (*machine*) reaper; (*pour herbes*) mower; **la Faucheuse** (*la Mort*) the Grim Reaper

faucheux [foʃø] NM (*insecte*) harvestman, *Am* daddy-long-legs

faucille [fosij] NF sickle, (reaping) hook; **la f. et le marteau** the hammer and sickle

faucon [fokɔ̃] NM **1** (*oiseau*) falcon, hawk; **f. mâle** tercel, tiercel; **f. pèlerin** peregrine falcon; **chasser au f.** to hawk; **chasse au f.** hawking, falconry **2** *Pol* hawk

fauconneau, -eaux [fokono] NM *Orn* young falcon

fauconnerie [fokɔnri] NF **1** (*lieu*) hawk house, falcon house **2** (*chasse*) falconry, hawking

fauconnier [fokɔnje] NM falconer

faufil [fofil] NM *Couture* basting or *Br* tacking thread

faufilage [fofilaʒ] NM *Couture* basting, *Br* tacking

faufiler [fofile] VT *Couture* to baste, *Br* to tack **VPR se faufiler** (*se glisser*) to thread one's way (**dans, entre, parmi** through); (*entrer*) to slip in, to sneak in; **il s'est faufilé jusqu'au premier rang** he worked his way to the front; **il s'était faufilé parmi les invités** he had slipped in or sneaked in with the guests; **se f. entre les voitures** to nip in and out of the traffic, to thread one's way through the traffic

faufilure [fofilyr] NF *Couture* **1** (*résultat*) basted or *Br* tacked seam **2** (*action*) basting, *Br* tacking

faune¹ [fon] NM *Myth* faun

faune² NF (*animaux*) fauna, animal life; *Fig Péj* **la f. des boîtes de nuit** the nightclub set; **il fréquente une f. bizarre** he associates with a funny crowd

faunesque [fonɛsk] ADJ faun-like

faussaire [fosɛr] N forger

fausse [fos] ADJ *voir* **faux¹**

faussement [fosmɑ̃] ADV wrongly, falsely; **un sourire f. aimable** a deceptively pleasant smile

fausser [fose] VT **1** (*sens, réalité, résultat, faits etc*) to distort; (*informations, chiffres*) to distort, to skew; (*l'esprit, le jugement de qn*) to warp **2** (*clé, serrure, axe etc*) to buckle, to bend, to twist **3 f. compagnie à qn** to give sb the slip

VPR **se fausser 1** (*d'une voix*) to become forced or strained **2** (*d'une clé, d'une serrure, d'un axe etc*) to buckle, to bend

fausset¹ [fosɛ] NM *Mus* falsetto; **chanter f.** to sing falsetto; *Fig* **voix de f.** falsetto or high-pitched voice

fausset² NM (*d'un tonneau*) spigot, vent peg; **trou de f.** vent hole

fausseté [foste] NF **1** (*d'une déclaration, idée etc*) falseness, falsity **2** (*de caractère*) duplicity

faustien [fostjɛ̃] ADJ Faustian

faut [fo] *voir* **falloir**

faute [fot] NF **1** (*erreur*) mistake, error; **f. d'étourderie** *ou* **d'inattention** careless mistake; **f. de français** = grammatical mistake or error; *Ordinat* **f. de frappe** miskey, keying error, typo; **f. d'impression** misprint; **f. de jugement** error of judgment; **f. d'orthographe** spelling mistake; **faire une f.** to make a mistake or an error

2 (*responsabilité*) fault; **être en f.** to be at fault; **trouver** *ou* **prendre qn en f.** to catch sb out; **c'est la f. de** *ou Fam* **à Pierre** it's Pierre's fault, Pierre's to blame; *Fam* **ce n'est quand même pas ma f. s'il pleut!** it's hardly my fault if it rains!, you can hardly blame me if it rains!; *Fam* **ce n'est pas (de) ma f.** it's not my fault, I'm not to blame; **à qui la f.?** whose fault is it?, who's to blame?; **c'est un peu (de) ma f.** I'm partly to blame; **il a été puni par ma f.** it's my fault he was punished; *Fam* **c'est la f. de personne** it's nobody's fault, nobody's to blame; **c'est la f. à pas de chance** it's just bad luck

3 (*manque*) **le courage lui a fait f.** his courage failed him; **la main-d'œuvre nous fait f.** we're short of labour; **votre jovialité nous a fait f.** we missed your joviality; **et pourtant ce n'est pas l'envie qui lui faisait f.** and yet it's not because he didn't want to; **ne faire f. de rien** to deny oneself nothing; **nous ne nous faisons jamais f. de lui écrire** we never fail to write to him; **il n'est pas fait f. de le lui dire devant tout le monde** he made sure he told him in front of everybody; **sans f.** without fail; **f. d'argent/de temps** for lack or want of money/time; **f. d'essayer** for want of trying; **f. de preuves** for lack of evidence; **f. d'ordres précis** in the absence of definite instructions; **f. de paiement** for non-payment; *Compta* **f. de provision** for lack of funds; **f. de quoi** failing which, otherwise; **f. de réponse satisfaisante** failing a satisfactory reply; **f. de paiement sous quinzaine, nous serons dans l'obligation de majorer notre facture de 10%** should payment not be made within fourteen days, we shall be obliged to add a 10% surcharge to your bill

4 (*délit*) offence, *Am* offense; (*mauvaise action*) misdemeanour, *Am* misdemeanor;

(*péché*) sin, transgression; (*mauvaise conduite*) misconduct; **f. professionnelle** professional misconduct

5 *Ftbl* foul; *Tennis* fault; *Ftbl* **commettre une f. sur qn** to foul sb; *Tennis* **double f.** double fault; *Tennis* **f. de pied** foot fault; *Tennis* **faire une double f.** double fault; *Tennis* **f. de pied** to double-fault/foot-fault; *Ftbl* **f. de main** hand ball; **faire une f. de main** to handle the ball

> Il faut noter que le nom anglais **faute** signifie également **défaut**.

fauter [fote] vi *Fam Vieilli (d'une femme)* to go astray

fauteuil [fotœj] NM **1** armchair, easy chair; **f. à oreillettes** wing chair; **f. à bascule** rocking chair; **f. pliant** folding chair; **f. de dentiste** dentist's chair; **f. roulant** wheelchair; *Théâtre* **f. d'orchestre** seat in the stalls *or Am* orchestra; *Théâtre* **f. de (premier) balcon** dress-circle seat, *Am* balcony seat; *Fig* **arriver dans un f.** (*sans peine*) to win hands down, *Br* to walk it; **il a remporté la course/les élections dans un f.** he won the race/election hands down **2** (*d'une assemblée*) chair; **occuper le f.** to be in the chair; **le f. de président** the chairmanship **3 f. (d'académicien)** seat (in the Académie française)

fauteur [fotœr] NM **f. de troubles** *ou* **de désordre** agitator, troublemaker; **f. de guerre** warmonger

fautif, -ive [fotif, -iv] ADJ **1** (*incorrect*) faulty, incorrect; **calcul f.** miscalculation; **mémoire fautive** defective memory **2** (*coupable*) at fault, in the wrong

N person at fault *or* in the wrong; **va savoir qui est le f. dans cette histoire!** who knows who's at fault *or* to blame in this business!

fautivement [fotivmã] ADV incorrectly; **j'avais f. éteint mes phares** I had switched off my headlights by mistake

fauve [fov] ADJ **1** (*couleur*) fawn, tawny **2** **bête f.** (*grand félin*) big cat; *Arch* (*cerf, daim*) deer **3 odeur f.** musky smell **4** *Beaux-Arts* Fauve, Fauvist

NM **1** (*grand félin*) big cat; **chasse aux (grands) fauves** big-game hunting; **cette chambre sent le f.** it smells sweaty *or* of sweat in this room; **tu sens le f.** you smell sweaty *or* sweat **2** (*couleur*) fawn **3** *Beaux-Arts* Fauve, Fauvist

fauverie [fovri] NF (*dans un zoo*) big-cat house

fauvette [fovɛt] NF *Orn* warbler; **f. d'hiver** *ou* **des haies** hedge sparrow, dunnock; **f. des roseaux** reed warbler

fauvisme [fovism] NM *Beaux-Arts* Fauvism

FAUX¹, FAUSSE [fo, fos]

ADJ	false **1–4** ▪ untrue **1** ▪ fake **2**
	▪ bogus **2** ▪ deceitful **3** ▪ wrong **4**
ADV	out of tune **1** ▪ wrong **1**
NM	false **1** ▪ imitation **2** ▪ forgery **3**

ADJ **1** (*qui n'est pas vrai*) false, untrue; **il est f. qu'elle soit …** it's false *or* untrue that she is …; **fausse nouvelle** false report; **f. témoin** perjurer; **f. témoignage** false evidence; (*délit*) perjury; **faire un f. témoignage** to give false evidence, to commit perjury; **donner de f. espoirs à qn** to give sb false hope

2 (*qui n'est pas d'origine*) (*cheveux, dents, cils etc*) false; (*bijoux etc*) imitation, fake; (*docteur*) bogus; **f. bilan** fraudulent balance sheet; **fausse écriture** false entry; **fausse facture** fake invoice; **fausse monnaie** fake *or* counterfeit money; **fabriquer de la fausse monnaie** to counterfeit money; **f. seins** false breasts, *Fam* falsies; **j'ai eu une fausse joie** I got excited about nothing; **elle m'a fait une fausse joie en me le faisant croire** she built up my hopes by making me believe it;

fausse clef skeleton key; **fausse cartouche** dummy cartridge; **f. plafond** false ceiling; **fausse fenêtre** blind window; *Ling* **f. ami** false friend; **faire un f. sens** to give an inaccurate translation/definition; **un f. Monet** a forged *or* fake Monet; *Anat* **fausses côtes** floating ribs; *TV, Cin* **f. raccord** jump cut; *Typ* **f. titre** half title; **fausse sortie** *Mil* feint sortie; *Théâtre* fake *or* sham exit; *Fig* **il a fait une fausse sortie** he pretended to leave

3 *Péj* (*hypocrite*) (*personne*) false, deceitful; (*honte, pudeur, modestie*) false; **c'est un f.** *Fam* **jeton** *ou* **très** *Fam* **cul** he's a hypocrite *or Fam* a phoney; **un f. frère** a false friend

4 (*incorrect*) wrong; **fausse date** wrong date; **vous avez fait un f. numéro** you've got *or* dialled *or Am* dialed the wrong number; **raisonnement f.** unsound *or* faulty reasoning; **présenter qch sous un f. jour** to present sth in a false light, to misrepresent sth; **situation fausse** awkward situation; **balance fausse** inaccurate scales; *Aut* **f. alignement** misalignment; **f. poids** false weight; **faire un f. mouvement** to make an awkward movement; **f. pas** slip, stumble; *Fig* faux pas, (social) blunder; **faire un f. pas** (*en marchant*) to stumble, to trip; *Fig* to put one's foot in it, to make a faux pas; (*faire un écart de conduite*) to make a faux pas; **un f. pas en montagne peut vous coûter la vie** one false step in the mountains can cost you your life; *Méd* **fausse couche** miscarriage; **faire fausse route** to take the wrong road; *Fig* to be on the wrong track; **f. calcul** miscalculation; **faire un f. calcul** to miscalculate; *Mus* **fausse note** wrong note; *Fig* false note; *Fig* **il n'y a eu aucune fausse note** there were no hitches, everything went smoothly

ADV **1 chanter f.** to sing out of tune, to sing off key; **cela sonne f.** that doesn't sound right; **ses paroles sonnent f.** his words have a hollow ring (to them); **rire qui sonne f.** hollow laugh(ter); *Fam* **avoir tout f.** to have it all wrong

2 poser le pied à f. to miss one's footing; **accuser qn à f.** to wrongly *or* falsely accuse sb; **porter à f.** to be out of true

NM **1** (*ce qui n'est pas vrai*) **le f.** the false; **distinguer le vrai du f.** to distinguish truth from falsehood

2 (*imitation*) (*œuvre d'art*) forgery, fake; **(bijouterie en) f.** costume *or* imitation jewellery

3 (*contrefaçon*) forgery; *Jur* **usage de f.** use of forgeries; **inculpé pour f. et usage de f.** charged with forgery and use of forgeries; **s'inscrire en f. contre qch** to dispute the validity of sth; *Compta* **f. en écritures** forgery

faux² NF **1** *Agr* scythe **2** *Anat* falx

faux-bourdon, *pl* **faux-bourdons** NM **1** *Mus* fauxbourdon **2** *Entom* drone

faux-cul, *pl* **faux-culs, faux-derche**, *pl* **faux-derches** NM *Fam* two-faced *Br* swine *or Am* stinker

faux-facturier, *pl* **faux-facturiers** NM = person using fake invoices to commit fraud

faux-filet, *pl* **faux-filets** NM *Culin* sirloin, tenderloin

faux-fuyant, *pl* **faux-fuyants** NM **1** (*prétexte*) subterfuge, evasion, dodge; **chercher des faux-fuyants** to hedge, to prevaricate; **une réponse claire et nette, sans f.** a straight answer with no hedging *or* without any ifs and buts **2** *Arch* (*sentier*) bypath

faux-monnayeur, *pl* **faux-monnayeurs** NM forger, counterfeiter

faux-rond, *pl* **faux-ronds** NM *Aut* run-out

faux-semblant, *pl* **faux-semblants** NM pretence, sham

faux-titre, *pl* **faux-titres** NM *Typ* half-title

faveur [favœr] NF **1** (*aide, considération*) favour, *Am* favor; **gagner** *ou* **obtenir la f. de qn** to gain sb's favour; **recevoir des marques de f. de qn** to receive signs of favour from sb; **avoir la f. de qn** to be in favour with sb; **être en (grande) f. auprès de qn** to be in (high) favour with sb; **perdre la f. de qn** to fall out of favour with sb; **prix/traitement de f.** preferential *or* special price/treatment; **billet de f.** complimentary ticket; *Jur, Fin* **en f. de** in favour of

2 (*bienfait*) favour, *Am* favor; **faire une f. à qn** to do sb a favour; **nous feriez-nous la f. de venir dîner chez nous** would you do us the favour of coming to have dinner with us; **par f. spéciale** as a special favour; **elle lui accorde ses faveurs** she bestows her favours on him

3 plaider en f. de qn to plead in sb's favour *or Am* favor; *Vieilli* **on lui fit grâce en f. de sa jeunesse** he was let off in consideration of his youth; **quête en f. de qn/qch** collection in aid of sb/sth

4 à la f. de qch with the help of sth; **à la f. de la nuit** under cover of darkness

5 (*ruban*) ribbon

favorable [favɔrabl] ADJ **1** (*bienveillant*) (*opinion*) favourable, *Am* favorable (**à** to); **il est f. à cette idée** he is in favour *or Am* favor of this idea; **elle vous est f.** she is favourably *or Am* favorably disposed towards you; **elle a présenté les choses sous un jour f.** she presented things in a favourable light *or* favourably **2** (*convenable*) favourable, *Am* favorable; (*situation, occasion, circonstances*) auspicious; (*vent*) favourable, fair; **le moment était f. pour lui parler** it was a good moment to speak to him; **recevoir un accueil f.** to be given a favourable reception; **peu f.** unfavourable, *Am* unfavorable

favorablement [favɔrabləmã] ADV favourably, *Am* favorably

favori, -ite [favɔri, -it] ADJ (*personne, objet, cheval de course etc*) favourite, *Am* favorite
N (*personne*) favourite, *Am* favorite
NF **favorite** (*maîtresse du roi*) favourite *or Am* favorite (mistress)
NM **1** *Courses de chevaux* favourite, *Am* favorite; **le grand f.** the odds-on *or* clear favourite **2** *Ordinat* **favoris** favorites

favoris [favɔri] NMPL sideburns, (side) whiskers

favorisé [favɔrize] ADJ (*milieu, famille*) privileged

favoriser [favɔrize] VT **1** (*avantager*) (*personne*) to favour, *Am* to favor; **le fait qu'elle soit une femme peut la f.** the fact that she's a woman may work in her favour; **les événements l'ont/ne l'ont pas favorisé** events were in his favour *or* on his side/not in his favour *or* against him; **favorisé par le destin** blessed by fate **2** (*encourager*) (*commerce, arts, crime, maladie, croissance etc*) to encourage, to promote **3** (*faciliter*) (*entreprise, fuite etc*) to assist, to further

favorite [favɔrit] ADJ, NF *voir* **favori**

favoritisme [favɔritism] NM favouritism, *Am* favoritism; **essayez de ne pas faire de f.** try not to show favouritism

fax [faks] NM (*appareil*) fax (machine); (*message*) fax; **envoyer qch par f.** to send sth by fax, to fax sth; **numéro de f.** fax number; *Ordinat* **f. modem** fax modem; **f. sur papier ordinaire** plain paper fax

faxer [fakse] VT to fax; **je vous faxe les chiffres** I'll fax the figures to you

fayot, -ote [fajo] *Arg* NM (*haricot sec*) bean N *Péj* crawler, creep

fayotage [fajotaʒ] NM *Arg Péj* crawling

fayoter [fajote] VI *Arg Péj* to crawl, to creep

FB NM *Anciennement abrév* franc belge

fco ADV *Com abrév* **franco**

FCP [εfsepe] NM *Fin* (*abrév* **fonds commun de placement**) investment trust, mutual fund

FCPE [εfsepeə] NM *Fin* (*abrév* **fonds commun de placement d'entreprise**) company investment fund

FCPR [εfsepeεr] NM *Fin* (*abrév* **fonds commun de placements à risques**) VCT

f. c(t). (*abrév* **fin courant**) at the end of this month

FDM (*abrév* **fin de mois**) end of month

FDR [εfdeεr] NM (*abrév* **fonds de roulement**) working capital

féal, -ale, -aux, -ales [feal, -o] ADJ *Arch* (*vassal etc*) feal, faithful, trusty

fébrifuge [febrifyʒ] ADJ, NM *Méd* febrifuge; *Pharm* antifebrile, antipyretic

fébrile [febril] ADJ (*pouls, patient etc*) feverish, febrile; *Fig* (*activité, conversation etc*) feverish; **tout le village était f.** the entire village was in a state of excitement

fébrilement [febrilmɑ̃] ADV feverishly; (*parler, préparer qch*) excitedly, hurriedly

fébrilité [febrilite] NF feverishness

fécal, -ale, -aux, -ales [fekal, -o] ADJ faecal, *Am* fecal; **matières fécales** faeces, *Am* feces

fèces [fεs] NFPL **1** faeces, *Am* feces **2** *Chimie* sediment, precipitate

FECOM [fekɔm] NM (*abrév* **Fonds européen de coopération monétaire**) EMCF

fécond [fekɔ̃] ADJ (*femme, animal, œuf, esprit*) fertile; (*terre*) fruitful; (*travail, idée*) fruitful, productive; (*sol, imagination*) fertile, rich; (*auteur, peintre, sculpteur etc*) prolific, productive; **ses films sont féconds en … his/her films are full of …**

fécondabilité [fekɔ̃dabilite] NF *Physiol* fertilizability; **taux de f.** fertility rate

fécondable [fekɔ̃dabl] ADJ fertilizable

fécondateur, -trice [fekɔ̃datœr, -tris] ADJ fertilizing

fécondation [fekɔ̃dasjɔ̃] NF *Biol* (*d'un œuf, ovule*) fertilization; (*d'une femme, d'un animal femelle*) impregnation; (*d'une fleur, plante*) pollination; **f. in vitro** in vitro fertilization; **f. artificielle** (*d'une femme*) artificial insemination; (*d'une fleur, plante*) artificial pollination

féconder [fekɔ̃de] VT *Biol* (*œuf, ovule*) to fertilize; (*femme, animal femelle*) to impregnate; (*fleur, plante*) to pollinate

fécondité [fekɔ̃dite] NF **1** *Physiol* fertility, *Fml* fecundity; **taux de f.** reproduction rate **2** *Fig* (*d'un sol, de l'imagination etc*) fertility; (*d'une idée*) fruitfulness, productiveness; (*d'un écrivain*) productiveness

fécule [fekyl] NF starch; *Culin* **f. de pommes de terre** potato starch *or* flour

féculent [fekylɑ̃] ADJ (*aliment*) starchy
    NM starchy food; **tu manges trop de féculents** you eat too much starchy food *or* starch

FED [εfəde] NM (*abrév* **Fonds européen de développement**) EDF

FEDER [fedεr] NM (*abrév* **Fonds européen de développement régional**) ERDF

fédéral, -ale, -aux, -ales [federal, -o] ADJ **1** federal **2** *Suisse* federal (*relative to the Swiss Confederation*)
    NM *Hist Am* Federal; **les fédéraux** (*le FBI*) the Feds

fédéraliser [federalize] VT to federalize

fédéralisme [federalism] NM federalism

fédéraliste [federalist] ADJ, N federalist

fédérateur, -trice [federatœr, -tris] ADJ (*politique*) federative; **élément/principe f.** unifying element/principle
    N unifier

fédératif, -ive [federatif, -iv] ADJ federative

fédération [federasjɔ̃] NF (*d'états*) federation; **f. de syndicats (ouvriers)** amalgamated (trade) unions; **f. sportive** sports federation

fédéré [federe] ADJ (*états*) federate
    NM *Hist* federate

fédérer [federe] (**je fédère; je fédérai**) VT (*états*) to federate, to federalize
    VPR **se fédérer** to federate

fée [fe] NF fairy; **pays des fées** fairyland; *Fig* **doigts de f.** nimble fingers; **une f. du logis** an ideal homemaker; *Suisse* **f. verte** absinthe

feed-back [fidbak] NM INV *Électron, Physiol etc* feedback

feeder [fidœr] NM **1** *Élec* feeder (cable) **2** (*de gaz*) (gas) pipeline

feeling [filiŋ] NM (*sensibilité*) feeling; **avoir un bon f. pour qch** to have a good feeling about sth; **faire qch au f.** to do sth by feel

féerie [fe(e)ri] NF **1** *Théâtre, Cin* fantasy, extravaganza **2** (*spectacle merveilleux*) enchantment; **une f. de lumières** an enchanting display of lights **3** *Vieilli* (*pouvoir des fées*) (power of) enchantment; (*monde des fées*) fairyland

féerique [fe(e)rik] ADJ **1** (*château, monde etc*) fairy, magic **2** *Fig* (*d'une beauté irréelle*) (*vue, paysage etc*) magical, enchanting

feignant, -ante [fεɲɑ̃, -ɑ̃t] ADJ, N *Fam* = **fainéant**

feignasse [fεɲas] NF *Arg* lazy so-and-so

feignasser [fεɲase] VI *Arg* to lounge *or* laze around

feindre [fɛ̃dr] (*prp* **feignant**; *pp* **feint**; *pr ind* **je feins, n. feignons**; *pr sub* **je feigne**; *impf* **je feignais**; *p hist* **je feignis**; *fu* **je feindrai**) VT (*maladie, surprise etc*) to feign, to simulate, to sham; **f. de faire qch** to pretend to do sth, to make a pretence of doing sth
    VI *Litt* to dissemble; **inutile de f.** it's no use pretending

feint [fɛ̃] ADJ **1** (*simulé*) (*maladie, joie etc*) feigned, assumed, sham **2** *Archit* (*porte, fenêtre*) blind, dummy

feinte [fɛ̃t] NF **1** *Boxe, Escrime, Mil* feint; *Ftbl, Rugby etc* **faire une f. (de passe)** to (sell a) dummy **2** (*ruse*) ruse, trick, dodge; *Vieilli* (*dissimulation*) sham, pretence, *Am* pretense; **sans f.** frankly, without pretence

feinter [fɛ̃te] VI *Boxe, Escrime* to feint, to make a feint; *Ftbl, Rugby etc* to (sell a) dummy
    VT *Fam* (*duper*) to take in

feldspath [fεldspat] NM *Minér* fel(d)spar

fêlé, -ée [fele] ADJ **1** (*verre, voix etc*) cracked **2** *Fig Fam* **il a le cerveau f.** *ou* **la tête fêlée, il est f.** he's a bit cracked *or* crazy; **tu es complètement f. de le lui avoir dit!** you're absolutely crazy to have told him!
    N *Fam* maniac; **f. du jazz/des chocolats** jazz/chocolate freak

fêler [fele] VT (*verre, porcelaine etc*) to crack
    VPR **se fêler** (*du verre, de la porcelaine, de la voix etc*) to crack

félicitations [felisitasjɔ̃] NFPL congratulations; **adresser des f. à qn** to congratulate sb (**pour qch** on sth); **(toutes mes) f.!** (many) congratulations!; **il a eu les f. du jury** he was congratulated by the jury, he received the jury's congratulations

félicité [felisite] NF bliss, felicity, happiness

féliciter [felisite] VT to congratulate; **f. qn pour** *ou* **sur qch/d'avoir fait qch** to congratulate sb on sth/on having done sth; **je ne vous félicite pas!** you'll get no praise from me!
    VPR **se féliciter** (*être content*) to be pleased *or* satisfied (**de qch** with sth); (*se louer*) to congratulate oneself (**de qch** on sth; **d'avoir**

fait qch on having done sth); **félicitons-nous de ce que nous avons la vie sauve** let us be thankful we came out alive

félidé [felide] NM *Zool* feline; **les f.** the cat family, *Spéc* the Felidae

félin, -ine [felɛ̃, -in] ADJ (*race*) feline; *Fig* (*grâce, souplesse etc*) feline, cat-like
    NM **1** feline; **les grands félins** the big cats; *Spéc* the great felines **2** *Bourse* stripped bond

fellah [fella] NM fellah, Arab peasant

fellation [felasjɔ̃] NF fellatio

félon, -onne [felɔ̃, -ɔn] *Hist, Litt* ADJ treacherous, disloyal
    N traitor

félonie [feloni] NF *Hist, Litt* (*déloyauté*) treachery, disloyalty; (*acte*) act of treachery

felouque [fəluk] NF (*bateau*) felucca

fêlure [felyr] NF crack; **f. du crâne** fracture of the skull; *Fig* **une f. dans notre amitié/leur couple** a rift between us/them

femelle [fəmεl] ADJ **1** (*sexe*) female; (*animal*) she-, female; (*éléphant, baleine*) cow; (*oiseau*) hen **2** *Tech* (*vis*) female; *Élec* **prise f.** socket **3** *Bot* female, *Spéc* pistillate
    NF (*animal*) female; *très Fam Péj* (*femme*) female

féminin, -ine [feminɛ̃, -in] ADJ (*personne, charme etc*) feminine; (*hormone, population*) female; (*équipe, groupe, magazine, mode etc*) women's; **le sexe f.** the female sex; **vêtements féminins** women's clothes, clothes for women; **les conquêtes féminines d'un homme** a man's female conquests
    NM *Gram* feminine; **ce mot est du f.** this word is feminine; **au f.** in the feminine SEE GRAMMAR A16–17; B5–8

> Attention: ne pas confondre **female** et **feminine** lorsque l'on traduit **féminin**. On utilise **feminine** pour décrire les qualités que la société associe traditionnellement aux femmes, alors que **female** s'utilise pour qualifier ce qui est propre au sexe féminin.

féminisant [feminizɑ̃] ADJ (*gène*) feminizing

féminiser [feminize] VT **1** (*donner le caractère féminin à*) to make feminine; (*rendre efféminé*) to make effeminate; **f. une profession** to bring *or* introduce more women into a profession; **profession très féminisée** largely female profession, female-dominated profession **2** *Biol* (*animal mâle*) to feminize **3** *Gram* (*mot*) to make feminine
    VPR **se féminiser 1** (*d'une femme*) to become more feminine; (*devenir efféminé*) to become effeminate; **la profession se féminise** the profession is attracting more and more women **2** *Biol* (*d'un animal mâle*) to feminize

féminisme [feminism] NM feminism

féministe [feminist] ADJ, N feminist

féminité [feminite] NF femininity

femme [fam] NF **1** (*personne*) woman, *pl* women; **les femmes, la f.** (*le sexe féminin*) women, womankind; **l'émancipation de la f.** the emancipation of women; **cherchez la f.** there's got to be a woman behind it; **elle est très f.** she's very feminine; **la f. de ma vie** the woman of my dreams, the only woman for me; **être très f. du monde** to be a wonderful hostess; **f. auteur** woman author, authoress; **f. ministre** female minister; **f. metteur en scène** woman *or* female director; **f. de tête** woman with a good head on her shoulders; **f. médecin** woman *or* lady doctor; **parapluie de f.** lady's umbrella; **elle n'est pas f. à se plaindre** she's not the sort (of woman) to complain; **une bonne f.** a simple *or* good-natured woman; *Fam* (*femme*) a woman; **sa bonne f. de mère** his old mother; *Fam Péj* **ma bonne f.** *(épouse)* my or the missus, my old woman; *Péj* **une vieille bonne f.** a little old woman; **contes/remèdes de bonne f.** old wives' tales/remedies

2 *(épouse)* wife; *Vieilli* **chercher f.** to look for a wife; **prendre f.** to take a wife; **il l'a prise pour f.** he took her as his wife; *Jur* **la f. Dupont** the wife of Dupont VOIR GRAMMAIRE A12

▸▸ **f. de chambre** housemaid; *(dans un hôtel)* maid, *Br* chambermaid, room attendant; **f. de charge** housekeeper; **une f. fatale** a femme fatale; **f. au foyer** housewife, *Am* home-maker; **f. d'intérieur** houseproud housewife; **je ne suis vraiment pas une f. d'intérieur** I'm not really keen on housework, I'm not houseproud; **f. de ménage** cleaning lady, domestic help; **une f. du monde** a society woman, a woman who moves in the best social circles; **une f.-objet** a sex object; **f. de service** cleaner, *Br* charwoman; **f. soldat** woman soldier

femmelette [famlɛt] NF *Péj (femme)* weak woman, weakling; *(homme)* weakling

fémoral, -ale, -aux, -ales [femɔral, -o] ADJ *Anat* femoral

fémur [femyr] NM *Anat* femur, thighbone

FEN [fɛn] NF *abrév* **Fédération de l'éducation nationale**

fenaison [fənɛzɔ̃] NF **1** *(action)* haymaking, hay harvest **2** *(saison)* haymaking season

fendage [fɑ̃daʒ] NM *Tech (d'ardoises, du bois)* splitting, cleaving

fendant, -ante [fɑ̃dɑ̃, -ɑ̃t] ADJ *Arg* hysterically funny
▪ NM **1** *Arg (pantalon)* trousers, keks, *Am* pants **2** *Suisse (vin)* = white wine from the Valais canton made from the fendant grape variety
▪ NF *Arg* **fendante: quelle f.!, la f.!** what a scream or a hoot!

fendard [fɑ̃dar] *Arg* ADJ *(amusant)* **c'est f.** it's hysterical or side-splitting
▪ NM *(pantalon) Br* trousers, keks, *Am* pants

fendeur [fɑ̃dœr] NM *Tech (d'ardoises, de bois etc)* splitter

fendillé [fɑ̃dije] ADJ *(pierre, bois, peau, peinture etc)* cracked; *(vernis, porcelaine)* crazed

fendillement [fɑ̃dijmɑ̃] NM *(du bois, de la peau, de la peinture etc)* cracking; *(du vernis, de la porcelaine)* crazing

fendiller [fɑ̃dije] VT *(pierre, bois, peau, peinture etc)* to crack; *(vernis, porcelaine)* to craze
▪ VPR **se fendiller** *(du bois, de la peau, de la peinture etc)* to crack; *(du vernis, de la porcelaine)* to craze

fendre [fɑ̃dr] VT *(bois, ardoise, diamant etc)* to split, to cleave; *(sol, mur, plâtre etc)* to crack, to fissure; **f. le crâne/la lèvre à qn** to split (open) sb's skull/lip; **f. les eaux** to plough through the waters; **f. l'air** to cleave the air; *(d'un son)* to rend the air; **f. la foule** to force or push one's way through the crowd; **il gèle à pierre f.** it's freezing hard, there's a hard frost; **c'était à f. l'âme** ou **le cœur** it was heartbreaking or heartrending; **la vue de cet enfant abandonné lui fendit le cœur** the sight of the abandoned child broke his heart or made his heart bleed; **bruit à f. la tête** ou **à vous f. les oreilles** ear-splitting noise
▪ VPR **se fendre 1** *(du bois)* to split, to crack; **se f. le crâne/la lèvre** to split (open) one's skull/lip; *Fam* **se f. la pipe** ou **la gueule** ou **la poire** *(rire)* to split one's sides (laughing); *(s'amuser)* to have a good laugh **2** *Escrime* to lunge **3** *Arg* **se f. de 200 euros** to fork out or shell out 200 euros; **il s'est fendu d'un bouquet**

de fleurs he forked out or shelled out for a bunch of flowers; **tu ne t'es pas fendu** it didn't break you or the bank; *(pas fatigué)* you didn't bust a gut

fendu [fɑ̃dy] ADJ *(jupe)* slit; *(crâne, lèvre)* split; *(assiette)* cracked; *(sabot)* cloven; **né avec le palais f.** born with a cleft palate; **sourire f. jusqu'aux oreilles** broad grin, grin like a Cheshire cat; **yeux bien fendus** large or wide-open eyes; **des yeux fendus en amandes** almond-shaped eyes; **vis à tête fendue** slotted screw

fenestrage [fənɛstraʒ], **fenêtrage** [fənɛtraʒ] NM *(d'un bâtiment)* windows, *Spéc* fenestration; *Ordinat* windowing

fenêtre [f(ə)nɛtr] NF **1** *Archit* window; **f. à guillotine** sash window; **f. croisée** ou **à battants** casement window; **f. à coulisse** sliding window; **f. en saillie** bay window; *(courbe)* bow window; *Rail, Aviat* **siège côté f.** window seat; *TV* **f. d'observation** observation window; **regarder par la f.** to look out of the window; *Fig* **une f. sur le monde/l'actualité** a window on the world/on current events
2 *(dans un document)* blank, space; *(dans une enveloppe)* window; **enveloppe à f.** window envelope
3 *Astronaut* **f. de lancement** (launch) window
4 *Ordinat* window; **f. d'aide** help window; **f. d'édition** editing or edit window; **f. de dialogue** dialog(ue) window; **f. déroulante** pull-down window; **f. flottante** floating window; **f. graphique** graphics window; **f. activée** active window; **f. de saisie** text box

fenêtrer [fənɛtre] VT *(bâtiment)* to put windows in; *(bandage)* to fenestrate

fenil [fəni(l)] NM hayloft

fennec [fenɛk] NM *Zool* fennec

fenouil [fənuj] NM *Bot, Culin* fennel

fente [fɑ̃t] NF **1** *(fissure) (dans le bois)* split, crack; *(dans le sol, un mur etc)* crack **2** *(ouverture) (d'une tirelire, boîte aux lettres etc)* slot, slit; *(dans un volet)* slit, gap; *(dans un mur)* crack; *(dans une tête de vis)* slot, groove; *(de jupe, manche, poche)* slit; *(de veste)* vent **3** *Escrime* lunge

fenugrec [fenygrɛk] NM *Bot* fenugreek

féodal, -ale, -aux, -ales [feɔdal, -o] ADJ feudal

féodalisme [feɔdalism] NM feudalism

féodalité [feɔdalite] NF *Hist* feudalism, feudal system

fer [fɛr] NM **1** *(métal)* iron; **minerai de f.** iron ore; **f. coulé** ou **de fonte** cast iron; **f. en saumon** ou **en gueuse** pig iron; **f. forgé** wrought iron; **fil de f.** wire; *Fig* **discipline de f.** iron discipline; **homme de f.** man of iron or steel; **dur comme (le) f.** as hard as iron; **j'y crois dur comme f.** I believe in it very firmly; **une santé de f.** an iron constitution; **avoir une volonté de f.** to have an iron will or a will of iron
2 *(partie métallique) (d'une hache, flèche)* head; *(d'une pelle)* blade; *(d'un lacet)* tag; **f. de lance** spearhead; *Fig* **le f. de lance du libéralisme** the spearhead of liberalism; **le f. de lance de l'industrie française** the flagship of French industry
3 *(arme)* sword; **croiser** ou **engager** ou **battre le f. avec qn** to cross swords with sb; **par le f. et par le feu** by force of arms
4 *(instrument)* **f. (à repasser)** *(pour le linge)* iron; **f. électrique/à vapeur** electric/steam iron; **donner un coup de f. à qch** to iron or press sth; **f. à friser** curling tongs or iron; *Obst Vieilli* **fers** forceps; **f. à souder** soldering iron; **marquer au f. rouge** to brand
5 *Golf* iron; **grand f.** driving iron; **f. droit** putter; **un f. 6** a (number) 6 iron
6 fers *(chaînes)* irons, chains, fetters; **être**

aux fers to be in irons or chains; *Fig* **mettre aux fers** to fetter; *Fig* **briser les fers** to throw off one's chains
7 f. (à cheval) horseshoe; **en f. à cheval** horseshoe-shaped; **tables disposées en f. à cheval** tables arranged in a horseshoe pattern; **mettre un f. à un cheval** to shoe a horse; **perdre un f.** to cast a shoe; *Fam* **tomber les quatre fers en l'air** *(d'une personne)* to fall flat on one's back
8 *Typ* **au f.** full-out; **f. de reliure** tool
9 *Méd* **(sels de) f.** iron

fer-blanc, *pl* **fers-blancs** NM tin(plate); **boîte en f.** tin can; **articles en f.** tinware

ferblanterie [fɛrblɑ̃tri] NF **1** *(industrie)* tinplate industry; *(commerce)* tinplate trade **2** *(boutique)* hardware store, *Br* ironmonger's (shop) **3** *(articles en fer-blanc)* tinware; *(quincaillerie)* hardware, *Br* ironmongery

ferblantier [fɛrblɑ̃tje] NM **1** *(ouvrier)* tinsmith **2** *(marchand)* hardware dealer, *Br* ironmonger

féria [ferja] NF (annual) festival *(in Spain and Southern France)*

férié [ferje] ADJ **jour f.** (public) holiday, *Br* bank holiday, *Am* legal holiday; **lundi prochain est f.** next Monday is a (public) holiday

férir [ferir] VT **sans coup f.** without any difficulty

ferler [fɛrle] VT *(voile)* to furl

fermage [fɛrmaʒ] NM **1** *(mode d'exploitation)* (tenant) farming **2** *(loyer)* (farm) rent

fermail, -aux [fɛrmaj, -o] NM *Arch* (ornamental) clasp

ferme¹ [fɛrm] ADJ **1** *(chair, fruit, beurre etc)* firm; *(pâte)* stiff; *(terre)* firm, solid; *Fig (personne, action, décision etc)* firm; *(écriture)* firm, steady; **poutre f.** firm or rigid beam; **la terre f.** dry land, terra firma; **fromage à pâte f.** hard cheese; **le malade n'est pas encore f. sur ses jambes** the patient is not yet steady on his legs; **il répondit d'une voix f.** he replied in a firm or steady voice; **d'un pas f.** with a firm step; **le marché reste très f.** the market continues very steady; **il faut être f. avec elle** you must be firm with her; **j'ai la f. intention de le lui dire** I firmly intend telling him; **être f. dans ses desseins/sa décision** to be firm or steadfast in one's intentions/decision; **attendre qn/qch de pied f.** to be more than ready for sb/sth
2 *(date)* firm, definite; *(prix)* firm; **prendre un engagement f.** to enter into a firm undertaking; **vente/offre f.** firm or definite sale/offer
▪ ADV *(frapper, pousser etc)* hard; *(parler etc)* firmly; *(travailler, boire)* hard; *(discuter)* keenly; **s'ennuyer f.** to be bored stiff or rigid; **batailler f.** to fight hard; **tenir f.** *(d'une personne)* to stand fast or firm, to hold one's own *(contre* against); *(d'un clou etc)* to hold fast; **j'y travaille f.** I'm working hard on it; **croire fort et f. aux esprits** to be a firm believer in spirits; **vendre f.** to make a firm sale; **acheter f.** to make a firm purchase

ferme² NF **1** *(exploitation agricole)* farm; *(maison)* farmhouse; *(bâtiments)* farm buildings; **petite f.** small farm, *Br* smallholding; **f. d'élevage** cattle farm; **produits de la f.** farm produce **2** *(mode d'exploitation)* **bail à f.** farming lease; **prendre une terre à f.** to take a lease of or to lease a piece of land; **donner une terre à f.** to farm out or lease out a piece of land **3** *Hist, Admin (de taxes)* farming (out) **4** *Constr (d'un toit, pont)* truss **5** *Théâtre* flat

fermé [fɛrme] ADJ **1** *(magasin, boîte, etc)* closed, shut; *(route)* closed; *(vêtement)* fastened, done up; *(mer)* landlocked; **bout f.** *(d'un tuyau)* dead end; **c'est f. à clé** it's

locked; **dormir à poings fermés** to sleep soundly *or* like a log; **je pouvais y aller les yeux fermés** I could go there blindfold *or* with my eyes closed *or* shut; **être f. à qch** *(d'une personne)* to have no feeling for *or* no appreciation of sth; **il a l'esprit f. aux mathématiques** mathematics is a closed book to him; **il a une attitude plutôt fermée face aux jeunes** he is an old fogey; *Ling* **voyelle fermée** closed vowel; *Tech* **position fermée** off position
2 *(impénétrable) (expression, visage)* impassive, inscrutable
3 *(sélect) (société, club, milieu)* exclusive, select
4 *Élec (circuit)* closed

fermement [fɛrməmɑ̃] **ADV** firmly

ferment [fɛrmɑ̃] **NM** *(de vin)*, *Fig (de mécontentement)* ferment; **f. lactique** bacillus used in yoghurt-making

fermentation [fɛrmɑ̃tasjɔ̃] **NF** *(du vin)* fermentation; *Fig* agitation, unrest, ferment

fermenter [fɛrmɑ̃te] **VI 1** *(du vin, de la bière)* to ferment, to work; *(de la pâte)* to rise **2** *Fig (de l'esprit, de passions)* to be in a ferment

FERMER [fɛrme] **VT 1** *(porte, fenêtre, boîte, parapluie, livre etc)* to close, to shut; *(vêtement)* to fasten, to do up; *(usine, entreprise)* to close down; *Ordinat (fichier, fenêtre)* to close; *(commande)* to end; **f. violemment la porte** to slam *or* bang the door (shut); **f. sa porte à qn** to close one's door to sb; *Fig* **f. la porte à qch** to close the door on sth; **f. ses portes** to close down; **f. la porte à clef/au verrou** to lock/bolt the door; **f. les rideaux** to draw *or* close the curtains; **f. une maison** to shut up a house; **f. boutique** to shut up shop; **f. une liste/un débat** to close a list/a debate; **fermez la parenthèse** close brackets; *Fig* **fermons la parenthèse et revenons à notre sujet** let's leave that now and get back to the subject; **f. la frontière** to close (off) the frontier; **f. une carrière à qn** to close a career to sb; **f. un robinet/l'eau/le gaz** to turn off a tap/the water/the gas; **f. l'électricité/la radio** to turn off *or* switch off the light/the radio; *Élec* **f. un circuit** to close a circuit; *TV, Cin* **f. par un volet** to wipe off; *Fin* **f. un compte** to close an account; *Rail* **f. la voie** to close (off) the line; **f. les yeux** to close *or* shut one's eyes; **manger la bouche fermée** to eat with one's mouth closed *or* shut; *Fam* **je n'ai pas pu f. l'œil de la nuit** I couldn't sleep a wink all night; *Fig* **il faut f. les yeux sur ses erreurs** one has to turn a blind eye *or* close *or* shut one's eyes to his mistakes; **très** *Fam* **ferme ta gueule!**, **ferme-la!**, **la ferme!** shut up!, shut it!, shut your mouth *or* trap!
2 f. la marche to bring up the rear
VI 1 *(d'une porte, boîte, d'un magasin etc)* to close, to shut; *(d'un vêtement)* to fasten, to do up; *(d'une usine, d'une entreprise) (temporairement)* to close, to shut; *(définitivement)* to close down; **le couvercle ferme mal** the lid doesn't shut *or* close properly; **on ferme le lundi** we close *or* shut on Mondays, we are closed *or* shut on Mondays; **on ferme!** we're closing!, it's closing time!
2 *Bourse (actions)* to close; **les actions ont fermé à six euros** shares closed at six euros
VPR se fermer *(d'une porte, boîte, des yeux etc)* to close, to shut; *(d'un vêtement)* to fasten, to do up; *(d'une plaie)* to heal, to close up; **à cette demande, son visage se ferma** at this request his face froze; **tu te fermes toujours quand on te parle de tes parents** you always clam up when people talk to you about your parents; *TV, Cin* **se f. en fondu** to fade out

fermeté [fɛrməte] **NF 1** *(de la chair, d'un fruit, du sol, de l'écriture etc)* firmness; *(d'une pâte)* stiffness; *Bourse* **f. des cours** steadiness of

prices **2** *(résolution)* firmness; *(dans l'adversité)* steadfastness; **f. d'esprit/de caractère** strength of mind/of character; **agir avec f.** to act firmly; **faire preuve de f. envers qn** to be firm with sb

fermette [fɛrmɛt] **NF** *(petite ferme)* small farm; *(maison de campagne)* (small) farmhouse

fermeture [fɛrmətyr] **NF 1** *(action) (des grilles, d'une porte etc)* closing, shutting; *(d'une route, frontière, liste, d'un débat)* closing; *Ordinat (de fichier, fenêtre)* closing; *(de commande)* ending; *(cessation d'activité) (d'un magasin, d'une entreprise)* closure, closing-down, *Am* closing-out; *TV, Cin* fade; *TV, Cin* **f. en fondu** fade out; *TV, Cin* **f. au noir** fade out, fade-to-black; **f. automatique des portières** *(annonce)* doors close *or* shut automatically; *Aut* remote control locking; *Aut* **f. centralisée** central locking; **f. à clef** locking; **f. des ateliers** *(définitive)* closing down of the workshops; **heure de f.** *(d'un magasin)* closing time; *(d'une usine, d'un bureau)* finishing time; **il faut qu'on se dépêche si on veut arriver avant la f. du magasin** we'll have to hurry if we want to get there before the shop shuts *or* closes; **faire la f. d'un magasin** to shut up a shop; **f. pour cause de réparations** *(sur une pancarte)* closed for repairs; **il venait me chercher à la f. du bureau** he came for me after work; **l'entreprise a annoncé la f. définitive de toutes ses succursales en France** the company has announced the closing down *or* the closure of all its branches in France; **f. de la pêche/chasse** close of the fishing/hunting season; **f. d'un compte** closing of an account; *Élec* **f. du circuit** closing of the circuit
2 f. d'esprit narrow-mindedness
3 *(dispositif) (de vêtement, sac etc)* fastener; **f. éclair®**, **f. à glissière** zip (fastener), *Am* zipper; **f. à rouleau** *(d'un magasin)* revolving shutter

fermier, -ière [fɛrmje, -jɛr] **NM 1** *Agr* farmer; *(locataire)* (tenant) farmer **2** *Hist, Admin* **f. général** farmer general
NF fermière (woman) farmer; *(épouse)* farmer's wife
ADJ beurre f. dairy butter; **poulet f.** farm *or* free-range chicken

fermoir [fɛrmwar] **NM 1** *(agrafe) (d'un bracelet, sac, livre etc)* clasp; *(bouton-pression)* (snap) fastener **2** *Can (fermeture à glissière)* *Br* zip *or* *Am* zipper

féroce [ferɔs] **ADJ** *(animal, personne)* ferocious, savage, fierce; *(regard, attaque, critique)* fierce, ferocious; *(joie, moquerie etc)* savage, cruel; *(appétit)* ravenous; *(désir)* raging, wild; **bête f.** wild animal *or* beast

férocement [ferɔsmɑ̃] **ADV** ferociously, savagely, fiercely

férocité [ferɔsite] **NF** ferocity, ferociousness; **avec f.** fiercely

Féroé [ferɔe] **NM les îles F.** the Faroe Islands, the Faroes

ferrage [fɛraʒ] **NM** *(d'un cheval)* shoeing; *(d'une roue)* rimming (in metal)

ferraillage [fɛrajaʒ] **NM** *Constr (d'un bâtiment en béton armé)* (steel) framework

ferraille [fɛraj] **NF 1** *(métaux)* old iron, scrap (iron); **tas de f.** scrap heap; *Fam (vieille auto)* heap of scrap iron; **mettre qch à la f.** to put sth on the scrap heap; **faire un bruit de f.** to rattle, to clank; **marchand de f.** scrap merchant **2** *Fam (petite monnaie)* loose *or* small change

ferraillement [fɛrajmɑ̃] **NM 1** *Péj (combat à l'épée)* sword rattling **2** *(bruit) (d'une voiture etc)* rattling, clanking

ferrailler [fɛraje] **VI 1** *Péj (se battre à l'épée)* to clash swords; *Fig* **f. avec qn** to cross

swords with sb, to clash with sb; **j'ai longtemps ferraillé avec l'ordinateur avant de comprendre comment il marchait** I had a long battle with the computer before I understood how it worked **2** *(faire un bruit de ferraille)* to clank, to rattle

ferrailleur [fɛrajœr] **NM 1** *Péj (bretteur)* sword rattler **2** *(revendeur)* scrap merchant

ferrate [fɛrat] **NM** *Chimie* ferrate

ferré [fɛre] **ADJ 1** *(canne)* metal-tipped; *(chaussure)* hobnailed; *(roue)* metal-rimmed; *(cheval)* shod; *(lacet)* tagged; **cheval f. à glace** roughshod horse; *Rail* **voie ferrée** *(rails)* track; *(route)* railway, *Am* railroad (line); **les utilisateurs de la voie ferrée** railway *or* *Am* railroad users; **par voie ferrée** by rail; *Rail* **réseau f.** railway *or* *Am* railroad system *or* network **2** *Fam (calé)* **être f. sur** *(sujet, chimie etc)* to be well up in *or* on

ferrer [fɛre] **VT 1** *(canne)* to tip with metal; *(chaussure)* to nail; *(roue)* to rim with metal; *(cheval)* to shoe; *(lacet)* to tag **2** *Pêche (poisson)* to strike

ferret [fɛrɛ] **NM** *(de lacet)* tag

ferreur [fɛrœr] **NM f. de chevaux** shoeing smith, *Br* farrier

ferreux, -euse [fɛrø, -øz] **ADJ** *Chimie, Minér* ferrous; **alliages f.** iron alloys, ferro-alloys

ferricyanure [fɛrisjanyr] **NM** *Chimie* ferricyanide

ferrique [fɛrik] **ADJ** *Chimie (sel etc)* ferric

ferrite [fɛrit] **NF** ferrite; *Ordinat* **mémoire à f.** ferrite core memory

ferro- [fɛrɔ] **PRÉF** ferro-

ferrochrome [fɛrɔkrom] **NM** *Métal* ferrochrome, ferrochromium

ferrocyanure [fɛrɔsjanyr] **NM** *Chimie* ferrocyanide

ferroélectricité [fɛrɔelɛktrisite] **NF** ferroelectricity

ferroélectrique [fɛrɔelɛktrik] **ADJ** ferroelectric

ferromagnétique [fɛrɔmaɲetik] **ADJ** ferromagnetic

ferromagnétisme [fɛrɔmaɲetism] **NM** ferromagnetism

ferronnerie [fɛrɔnri] **NF 1** *(objets)* **f. (d'art)** (decorative) ironwork, wrought ironwork; **grille en f.** wrought-iron gate **2** *(métier)* ironwork **3** *(atelier)* ironworks

ferronnier, -ière [fɛrɔnje, -jɛr] **N 1** *(artisan)* **f. (d'art)** worker in wrought iron **2** *(commerçant)* ironware dealer

ferrotypie [fɛrɔtipi] **NF** *Phot* ferrotype

ferroutage [fɛrutaʒ] **NM** combined rail and road transport

ferroviaire [fɛrɔvjɛr] **ADJ** *(réseau, compagnie, trafic etc)* railway, *Am* railroad; **transports ferroviaires** rail transport; **les grandes lignes ferroviaires** the main railway *or* *Am* railroad lines

ferrugineux, -euse [fɛryʒinø, -øz] **ADJ** ferruginous; **source ferrugineuse** chalybeate spring

ferrure [fɛryr] **NF 1** *(garniture)* (iron) fitting; **ferrures de porte** door fittings; **ferrures en cuivre** brass fittings **2** *(d'un cheval)* shoeing

ferry, pl ferries [fɛri] **NM** ferry; **f. roulier** roll-on roll-off ferry; **f. trans-Manche** cross-Channel ferry

ferry-boat, pl ferry-boats [fɛribot] **NM** *(pour voitures)* (car) ferry; *(pour trains)* (train) ferry

fertile [fɛrtil] **ADJ** *(sol, champ etc)* fertile; *Fig (esprit, imagination)* fertile, inventive; *(compositeur, écrivain etc)* inventive; **semaine f. en événements** eventful week; **la semaine fut f. en discussions** the week was packed with discussions

fertilisable [fɛrtilizabl] **ADJ** fertilizable

fertilisant [fɛrtilizɑ̃] **ADJ** fertilizing **NM** fertilizer

fertilisation [fɛrtilizasjɔ̃] **NF** fertilization

fertiliser [fɛrtilize] **VT** to fertilize

fertilité [fɛrtilite] **NF** (du sol, de l'imagination etc) fertility

féru [fery] **ADJ** f. d'un sujet passionately interested in a subject; **être f. d'une idée** to be set on an idea; Arch **f. de qn** smitten with sb

férule [feryl] **NF** Hist, Scol ferule (ruler for punishment on the hands); Fig **être sous la f. de qn** to be under sb's sway or domination or rule

fervent, -ente [fɛrvɑ̃, -ɑ̃t] **ADJ** (dévotion, admirateur, chrétien etc) fervent, ardent, keen; (amour) ardent; (prière) fervent; (approbation) enthusiastic **N** devotee (**de** of)

ferveur [fɛrvœr] **NF** fervour, Am fervor; **avec f.** (prier) fervently, earnestly; (travailler) with enthusiasm; (aimer) ardently; (écouter) eagerly

fesse [fɛs] **NF 1** Anat buttock; **fesses** buttocks, behind, bottom; Fam **donner à qn un coup de pied aux fesses** to give sb a kick in the pants or up the backside; Fam **poser ses fesses** ou **une f.** (s'asseoir) to park one's backside; très Fam **attraper qn par la peau des fesses** to grab hold of sb just in time; très Fam **serrer les fesses** (avoir peur) to have the wind up, to have the jitters; (être courageux) to sit tight; très Fam **occupe-toi de tes fesses!** mind your own damn business!; très Fam **avoir qn aux fesses** to have sb on one's tail; très Fam **coller aux fesses de qn** to stick to sb like glue; (d'un camion etc) to sit on sb's tail; très Fam **film/revue de fesses** porn or dirty film/magazine, tit and bum magazine; très Fam **histoire de fesses** dirty story; (aventure) purely sexual affair **2** (de navire) tuck

fessée [fese] **NF 1** (coups) spanking; **donner une f. à qn** to give sb a spanking, to spank sb **2** Fig (défaite) drubbing

fesse-mathieu, pl **fesse-mathieux** [fɛsmatjø] **NM** Vieilli skinflint, Scrooge

fesser [fese] **VT f. qn** to spank sb, to smack sb's bottom

fessier, -ière [fesje, -jɛr] **ADJ** Anat (muscle etc) buttock, Spéc gluteal; **poche fessière** (de pantalon etc) hip pocket **NM 1** Anat gluteal muscle **2** Fam (fesses) backside, behind

festif, -ive [fɛstif, -iv] **ADJ** festive

festin [fɛstɛ̃] **NM** feast, banquet; **quel f.!** what a feast!, what a spread!; **faire (un) f.** to feast

festival, -als [fɛstival] **NM** festival; **f. du film** film festival; **f. culturel** arts festival

festivalier, -ière [fɛstivalje, -jɛr] **ADJ** festival **N** (participant) festival participant; (visiteur) festival-goer

festivités [fɛstivite] **NFPL** festivities, celebrations

fest-noz [fɛstnoz] **NM** = traditional Breton village festival

feston [fɛstɔ̃] **NM 1** (de fleurs) festoon **2** Couture scallop; **à festons** scalloped; **point de f.** buttonhole stitch

festonner [fɛstɔne] **VT 1** (de guirlandes) to festoon **2** Couture to scallop

festoyer [fɛstwaje] **VI** (je festoie; je festoierai) to feast

feta [feta] **NF** feta (cheese)

fêtard, -arde [fɛtar, -ard] **N** Fam reveller

fête [fɛt] **NF 1** (de village) fete, fête, fair; (de ville) festival; **f. champêtre** ou **de village** village fete or fair; **f. de la bière** beer festival

2 (soirée) party; **donner une f.** to give a party; **faire une f.** to have a party; **une petite f.** a party **3** (gaieté) air de f. festive air; **le village était en f.** the village was in a festive mood; **faire la f.** to have a wild time, to live it up; **faire f. à qn** to welcome sb with open arms; **mon chien me fait f. quand je rentre le soir** my dog is all over me when I come back in the evening; **être de la f.** to be one of the party; **se faire une f. de (faire) qch** to look forward to (doing) sth; **il ne s'était jamais vu à pareille f.** he had never had such a good time; Iron **il n'était pas à la f.** it wasn't much fun for him **4** (du saint dont on porte le nom) saint's or name day; **souhaiter une bonne f. à qn** to wish sb a happy saint's day; Iron **ça va être ta f.!** you're in for it!; Iron **on va lui faire sa f.!** he'll get what's coming to him! **5** (célébration) Rel feast, festival; (civile) holiday; **jour de f.** Rel feast day; (jour férié) public holiday; **les fêtes (de fin d'année)** the Christmas and New Year holidays; **c'est f. demain** tomorrow is a holiday; Fig **ce n'est pas tous les jours f.** Christmas comes but once a year; Fam **elle est de bonne humeur?, c'est la f.!** she's in a good mood?, put the flags out! ▶ ▶ **f. foraine** funfair; Beaux-Arts **f. galante** fête galante; **f. légale** bank holiday, Am legal holiday; **f. des mères** Mother's Day; **f. mobile** mov(e)able feast; **la f. des Morts** All Souls' Day; **f. nationale** national holiday; **la f. nationale du 14 juillet** Bastille Day; **f. des pères** Father's Day; **f. du travail** Labour Day

Fête de la musique

This annual event takes place throughout France on 21 June, the summer solstice. Both amateur and professional musicians take to the streets and there are many impromptu live performances, with bars and restaurants as well as museums and hospitals serving as free venues for jazz, classical, rock and many other styles of music. The festival was originally launched in 1982 by the minister of culture, Jack Lang, following the election of François Mitterand's socialist government. Such has been its success and popularity in France that the event has now spread to many other European countries.

Fête-Dieu, pl **Fêtes-Dieu NF** Rel Corpus Christi

fêter [fete] **VT 1** (victoire, événement, Noël etc) to celebrate; **f. la naissance de qn** to celebrate sb's birthday; **f. ses soixante ans** to celebrate one's sixtieth birthday; **f. un saint** to keep a saint's day; **le projet est fini? il faut f. cela!** the project's finished? let's celebrate! or that calls for a celebration! **2** (accueillir chaleureusement) to fete

fétiche [fetiʃ] **NM** (objet de culte) fetish; (mascotte) mascot; **couleur/nombre f.** lucky colour/number

fétichisme [fetiʃism] **NM** fetishism

fétichiste [fetiʃist] **ADJ** fetishistic **N** fetishist

fétide [fetid] **ADJ** fetid, rank, stinking, foul

fétidité [fetidite] **NF** fetidness

fétu [fety] **NM f. (de paille)** (wisp of) straw; **être emporté comme un f.** to be blown along like a straw in the wind

fétuque [fetyk] **NF** Bot fescue (grass)

feu¹, pl **feux** [fø] **NM 1** (élément, flammes, incendie) fire; **le f. et l'eau** fire and water; **mettre le f. à qch** to set fire to sth, to set sth on fire; Fam **flanquer** ou très Fam **foutre le f. à qch** to put a match to sth; **mettre une ville à**

f. et à sang to put a town to fire and sword; **prendre f.** to catch fire; **faire du f.** to make a fire; **allumer/faire un f.** to light/make a fire; Fig **jouer avec le f.** to play with fire; **faire f. des quatre fers** (d'un cheval) to make the sparks fly; Fig (d'une personne) to go all out; **il fait f. de tout bois** he makes the most of his opportunities, he turns everything to account; Fam **avoir le f. au derrière** ou très Fam **au cul** to be in a tearing hurry; **enlever de la peinture au f.** to burn paint off; **en f.** on fire; **joues en f.** burning cheeks; **visage en f.** flushed face; **j'avais la gorge en f.** my throat was burning or on fire; **soleil de f.** fiery sun; **f. de forêt** forest fire; **il y a le f. à la grange!** the barn's on fire!; **au f.!** fire!; Fig **faire la part du f.** to cut one's losses; Fam **il n'y a pas le f. (au lac)** there's no particular hurry; **il n'y a pas de quoi crier au f.** there's nothing to get excited about; **jeter f. et flamme (contre qn)** to be in a rage (with sb), to rage (at sb); **est-ce que vous avez du f.?** have you got a light?

2 (passion) ardour, Am ardor, passion; Arch (amour) love; **tout f. tout flamme** burning with enthusiasm; **parler avec f.** to speak passionately; **dans le f. de la discussion/l'action** in the heat of the debate/the action; **avoir le f. sacré** to burn with enthusiasm; **il a un tempérament de f.** he has a fiery temperament

3 (matières allumées) fire; **f. nu** open fire; **garniture de f.** fire irons; **au coin du f.** by the fire(side)

4 mettre une chaudière en f. to fire up a boiler

5 (supplice) **condamner qn au f.** to condemn sb to be burnt at the stake; **j'en mettrais la main au f.** I would swear to it; **épreuve du f.** ordeal by fire; **faire mourir qn à petit f.** to kill sb slowly, to make sb die a lingering death; Fig to keep sb on tenterhooks

6 Culin (de cuisinière) burner; **faire cuire à f. doux** ou **à petit f.** to cook gently or over a low heat; (au four) to cook in a slow oven; **à grand f., à f. vif** over a high heat; (au four) in a hot oven; **ustensiles qui vont au f.** fireproof utensils; **cuisinière à quatre feux** four-burner cooker; **j'ai du lait sur le f.** I've got some milk on the stove; **coup de f.** (slight) burning; Fig busiest time; **nous sommes arrivés en plein coup de f.** we arrived right at the busiest time

7 (maison) hameau de 50 feux hamlet of 50 houses; **n'avoir ni f. ni lieu** to be homeless, to have neither hearth nor home

8 Mil etc (tir) fire; (combat) action; **arme à f.** firearm; **bouche à f.** piece of ordnance or artillery; **faire f. (sur qn)** to fire or shoot (at sb); **commencer** ou **déclencher** ou **ouvrir le f.** to open fire; **f.!** fire!; **sous le f.** under fire; **faire long f.** (d'un pistolet), Fig (d'un plan etc) to hang fire; Fig **leur amitié ne fera pas long f.** their friendship won't last long; **aller au f.** to go into action; **coup de f.** (gun)shot; **tirer des coups de f.** to fire shots; **nous avons reçu des coups de f.** we were fired on or shot at; **il n'a jamais vu le f.** he has never seen action; Fig **être entre deux feux** to be caught in the middle, to be in the crossfire

9 Naut (lumière) light; **feux (d'entrée) de port** harbour lights; **droits de feux** light dues; **f. à occultations** ou **à éclipses** occulting light; **feux de route** navigation lights; **feux de mouillage** (d'un navire) anchor lights; **f. de tribord** starboard light

10 Aviat (lumière) light; **feux de balisage** boundary lights; **feux de piste** runway lights; **feux de bord** ou **de navigation** navigation lights

11 Aut (de signalisation) light; **f. rouge** (lumière) red light; (objet) (traffic) lights, Am traffic light; **f. orange/vert** amber/green light; **feux tricolores** traffic lights; **feux (de signalisation)** (traffic) lights; **attendre au(x)**

feu(x) to wait at the lights; *Fig* **donner le f. vert** to give the green light *or* the go-ahead (à to)

12 *Aut (de véhicule)* light; **tous feux éteints** without lights; **f. de brouillard** *ou* **antibrouillard** fog lamp; **feux de croisement** dipped headlights, *Am* low beams; **feux de détresse** hazard (warning) lights, *Fam* hazards; **feux de position** sidelights; **feux de recul** reversing lights; **feux de route** driving lights, headlights on full beam *or Am* high beam; **en feux de route** on full beam; **feux arrière** rear lamps, tail lights; **feux blancs** driving lights, headlights and side lights; **feux de freinage** brake lights; **feux de stationnement** parking lights; **f. de gabarit** side lamp; **f. de plaque** number plate light; **f. de stop** brake light

13 *Rail* **f. d'avant** *(d'une locomotive)* headlight; **f. d'arrière** *(d'un train)* tail *or* rear light

14 **feux d'un diamant** fire *or* sparkle of a diamond; **une pierre qui brille de mille feux** a stone that sparkles brilliantly; **yeux pleins de f.** flashing eyes; **les feux de la rampe** the footlights; **être sous les feux des projecteurs** to be in the glare of the spotlights; *Fig* to be in the limelight; **il est sous les feux de l'actualité** he is very much in the news at the moment

15 **mettre une fusée à f.** to fire a rocket; **mise à f.** blastoff, launch

ADJ INV rouge f. flame-coloured; **chien noir et f.** black-and-tan dog

▸▸ **f. d'artifice** fireworks; *(spectacle)* firework display; **ça a été un véritable f. d'artifice, ce débat** there were real fireworks at the debate; **f. de Bengale** Bengal light; **f. de camp** campfire; **f. de cheminée** fire in the hearth; **f. de joie** bonfire; **f. roulant** running fire, drumfire; *Fig* **un f. roulant de questions** a barrage of questions

feu² **ADJ** *(inv if preceding article or poss adj)* late; **la feue reine, f. la reine** the late queen; **f. mon père** my late father; **fils de feue Berthe Dupont** son of the late Berthe Dupont, son of Berthe Dupont deceased

feudataire [fødatɛr] **NM** *Hist* feudatory

feuillage [fœjaʒ] **NM** leaves, foliage

feuillaison [fœjɛzɔ̃] **NF** leafing, coming into leaf

feuille [fœj] **NF 1** *(de plante, d'arbre)* leaf; **f. morte** dead leaf; *Aviat* **descente en f. morte** dead-leaf dive; *Fam* **il est dur de la f.** he's hard of hearing VOIR GRAMMAIRE A12 **2 f. de métal** sheet of metal; **fer en feuilles** sheet iron; **f. d'or** gold leaf; **f. d'étain** tinfoil; **f. de bois** thin board **3** *(de papier)* sheet; **f. volante** *ou* **mobile** loose sheet; **feuilles d'un livre** leaves of a book; *Typ* **bonnes feuilles** advance proofs **4** *(journal)* paper

▸▸ **f. d'accompagnement** covering document; **f. des arrivées et des départs** *(d'un hôtel etc)* arrival and departure list, A&D list; *Compta* **f. d'avancement** flow sheet; *Ordinat* **f. de calcul** spreadsheet; **f. de chou** cabbage leaf; *Fam Péj (journal)* rag; **oreilles en f. de chou** cauliflower ears; *TV etc* **f. de conducteur** cue sheet; *TV, Cin* **f. d'exposition** exposure sheet; **f. de garde** *(d'un livre)* fly leaf; **f. d'impôt** tax return; *Compta* **f. de liquidation** settlement note; **f. de maladie** = form given by doctor to patient for claiming reimbursement from Social Security; *TV etc* **f. de mixage** cue sheet; **f. des mouvements** *(d'un hôtel etc)* arrival and departure list, A&D list; **f. d'occupation journalière** *(d'un hôtel)* daily density chart, daily forecast chart; *TV, Radio* **f. d'ordre de passage à l'antenne** rundown sheet; **f. de paie** *ou* **paye** payslip; **f. de présence** attendance sheet; *(d'un employé)* time sheet; **f. de réservation** reservation form, booking form; **f. des réveils** *(d'un hôtel etc)* call sheet; **f. de route** *Com* waybill; *Mil* travel warrant; *(dans un processus)* road map; **f. de service** (duty) roster; **f. de soins** medical expense claim form; **f. de style** style sheet; **f. de température** temperature chart; **f. de travail** worksheet; **f. de versement** paying-in slip; **f. de vigne** *(sur sculpture)* vine leaf, fig leaf; *Culin* stuffed vine leaf; *Aviat* **f. de vol** flight plan

feuille-à-feuille **ADJ** *Ordinat (imprimante)* sheet-fed

feuillée [fœje] **NF** *Litt* greenery, branches **NFPL** *Mil* **feuillées** *(dans un camp)* latrines

feuille-morte **ADJ INV, NM INV** *(couleur)* russet

feuilleret [fœjrɛ] **NM** *Tech* rabbet plane, grooving plane

feuillet [fœjɛ] **NM 1** *(d'un livre)* leaf; **à feuillets rechargeables** loose-leaf **2** *(de bois)* thin sheet

feuilletage [fœjtaʒ] **NM** *Culin* **1** *(action)* *(d'une pâte)* rolling and folding **2** *(de la pâte)* flakiness **3** *(pâte)* flaky pastry

feuilleté [fœjte] **ADJ** *(roche)* foliated, laminated, lamellar; *(verre)* laminated; **parebrise (en verre) f.** laminated windscreen *or Am* windshield; *Culin* **pâte feuilletée** flaky pastry, puff pastry, *Am* puff paste **NM** *Culin* pastry *(made from flaky pastry)*; **un f. au jambon/au fromage** a ham/cheese pastry

feuilleter [fœjte] **VT** (**je feuillette; je feuilletterai**) **1** *Culin (pâte)* to roll and fold **2 f. un livre** to turn over the pages of a book; *(sommairement)* to leaf through *or* flip through a book **3** *Ordinat* to scroll; **f. en arrière** to page up, to scroll up; **f. en avant** to page down, to scroll down

feuilleton [fœjtɔ̃] **NM 1** *Journ (chronique)* (regular) feature **2** *Journ, Radio, TV (histoire)* serial, serial drama; *(populaire)* soap (opera); **publier un roman en feuilletons** to serialize a novel; **f. télévisé** *(sur plusieurs semaines)* TV serial; *(sur plusieurs années)* soap opera

feuilletoniste [fœjtɔnist] **N** *Journ (auteur de romans-feuilletons)* serial writer; *(chroniqueur)* feature writer

feuillu [fœjy] **ADJ** *(ayant beaucoup de feuilles)* leafy; *(à feuilles)* broad-leaved **NM** broad-leaved tree

feuillure [fœjyr] **NF** *Menuis* rabbet, groove

feulement [følmɑ̃] **NM** *(de tigre)* snarl, growl; *(de chat)* growl

feuler [føle] **VI** *(d'un tigre)* to snarl, to growl; *(d'un chat)* to growl

feutrage [føtraʒ] **NM 1** *Tech (du poil, de la laine, d'un tissu)* felting **2** *(d'une surface, d'un objet)* felting, covering with felt **3** *(d'un vêtement de laine)* matting, felting

feutre [føtr] **NM 1** *Tex* felt; **chaussons de f.** felt slippers **2** *(chapeau)* felt hat, fedora **3** **(crayon) f.** felt(-tip) pen, felt-tip; **stylo f.** felt-tip (pen)

feutré [føtre] **ADJ 1** *(garni de feutre)* felt(-covered); **porte feutrée** baize door **2** *(son)* muffled; **à pas feutrés** silently; **s'éloigner à pas feutrés** to steal away, to slip quietly away; **traverser la pièce à pas feutrés** to pad across the room **3** *(après le lavage)* *(lainage)* matted

feutrer [føtre] **VT 1** *Tech (poil, laine)* to felt, to make into felt **2** *(garnir de feutre)* to cover with felt, to felt **3** *Fig (son)* to muffle **VI** *(d'un vêtement en laine)* to become matted, to felt **VPR se feutrer** *(d'un vêtement en laine)* to become matted, to felt

feutrine [føtrin] **NF** felt; *(sur table de billard)* baize

fève [fɛv] **NF 1** *(plante, graine)* broad bean; *(dans la galette des Rois)* charm **2** *Can (haricot)* bean; **f. verte** string bean; **f. jaune** wax bean **3 f. de cacao** cocoa bean

février [fevrije] **NM** February; **en f.** in February; **au mois de f.** in (the month of) February; **le sept f.** (on) the seventh of February, (on) February the seventh, *Am* (on) February seventh SEE GRAMMAR A81–2; B60–2

fez [fɛz] **NM** fez

FF **NM** *Anciennement abrév* **franc(s) français**

FFI [ɛfɛfi] **NFPL** *Hist (abrév* **Forces françaises de l'intérieur** *)* = French Resistance forces in France during World War Two

FFL [ɛfɛfɛl] **NFPL** *Hist (abrév* **Forces françaises libres** *)* = Free French Army

fi [fi] **INT** *Vieilli, Hum* **1** fie!, for shame! **2 faire fi de qch** to scorn sth; **je fais fi de toutes vos remarques** I don't give a fig for what you have to say

fiabilité [fjabilite] **NF** reliability, dependability

fiable [fjabl] **ADJ** reliable, dependable

fiacre [fjakr] **NM** *(voiture à cheval)* hackney (carriage *or* cab)

fiançailles [fjɑ̃saj] **NFPL** engagement; **pendant leurs f.** while they were engaged, during their engagement

fiancé, -ée [fjɑ̃se] **ADJ** engaged (**à** *ou* **avec qn** to sb) **NM** fiancé; **les fiancés** *(couple)* the engaged couple **NF fiancée** fiancée

fiancer [fjɑ̃se] **VT** *Vieilli* to betroth (**à** *ou* **avec qn** to sb) **VPR se fiancer** to become *or* get engaged (**à** *ou* **avec qn** to sb)

fiasco [fjasko] **NM** fiasco; *(spectacle)* flop; **faire f.** *(d'un projet)* to come to nothing; *(d'un spectacle)* to be a flop, to flop

fiasque [fjask] **NF** (Italian) flask

fibranne [fibran] **NF** *Tex* staple fibre *or Am* fiber

fibre [fibr] **NF 1** fibre, *Am* fiber; **riche en fibres (alimentaires)** rich in (dietary) fibre; **panneau de fibres agglomérées** fibreboard, *Am* fiberboard; **coton à fibres longues** long-staple cotton; **fibres synthétiques** synthetic fibres; **la f. optique** fibre optics; **fibres optiques** optical fibres; **câble en fibres optiques** fibre optic cable; **f. de verre** glass fibre, fibreglass, *Am* fiberglass; **f. de carbone** carbon fibre **2** *Fig* **faire jouer la f. paternelle/patriotique** to play on paternal/patriotic feelings; **elle n'a pas la f. maternelle** she's not the maternal sort

fibreux, -euse [fibrø, -øz] **ADJ** *(tissu)* fibrous; *(viande)* stringy

fibrillation [fibrijasjɔ̃] **NF** *Méd* fibrillation

fibrille [fibrij] **NF** small fibre *or Am* fiber; *Physiol, Bot* fibril(la)

fibrine [fibrin] **NF** *Physiol* fibrin

fibrineux, -euse [fibrinø, -øz] **ADJ** *Physiol* fibrinous

fibrinogène [fibrinɔʒɛn] **NM** *Physiol* fibrinogen

fibrociment® [fibrosimɑ̃] **NM** fibrocement

fibromateux, -euse [fibrɔmatø, -øz] **ADJ** *Méd* fibromatous

fibrome [fibrom] **NM** *Méd* fibroma, fibroid

fibroscope [fibrɔskɔp] **NM** *Méd* fibroscope, *Am* fiberscope

fibroscopie [fibrɔskɔpi] **NF** *Méd* fibreoptic endoscopy

fibule [fibyl] **NF** *(agrafe)* fibula

ficaire [fikɛr] **NF** *Bot* lesser celandine, pilewort

ficelage [fis(ə)laʒ] **NM 1** *(action)* tying up **2** *(liens)* string(s)

ficelé [fis(ə)le] ADJ **1** *(lié) (colis, prisonnier etc)* tied up **2** *Fam (habillé)* got up; **être f. comme l'as de pique** to be dressed like a scarecrow **3** *Fam* **c'est bien/mal f.** *(d'un texte, d'une histoire, d'un film)* it hangs/doesn't hang together well; **un scénario bien f.** a well-crafted screenplay

ficeler [fis(ə)le] VT **(je ficelle; je ficellerai)** *(colis, prisonnier)* to tie up

ficelle [fisɛl] NF **1** *(mince corde)* string; **les ficelles de la marionnette** the puppet's strings **2** *Fig* **c'est lui qui tire les ficelles** he's the one who pulls the strings; **les ficelles du métier** the tricks of the trade; **connaître les ficelles (du métier)** to know the ropes, to know the tricks of the trade; **la f. est un peu grosse** that won't fool anybody **3** *(pain)* small French stick
▪ ADJ *Vieilli* crafty, wily

fiche¹ [fiʃ] NF **1** *Élec (prise)* plug; *(broche)* pin; *Tél (patch)* plug; *(électrique)* jack plug **2** *(morceau de papier)* slip (of paper); *(formulaire)* form; *(dépliant)* leaflet; **remplir une f.** to fill in *or* fill out a form; **faire des fiches de lecture** to write a book report; **fiches-cuisine/-tricot/-santé** *(dans un magazine)* cookery/knitting/health cards **3** *(carte)* (index) card; **jeu de fiches** card index; **mettre des informations en** *ou* **sur fiche(s)** to card-index data **4** *(cheville) (en fer, bois etc)* peg, pin
▸▸ **f. d'accueil** registration form; *Admin* **f. anthropométrique** = (criminal) dossier; **f. d'appréciation** customer satisfaction questionnaire; **f. d'arrivée** registration form; **f. de blocage** *(d'un hôtel etc)* block card, reservation rack card, room rack card; **f. cartonnée** index card; **f. client** customer record; *(d'un hôtel etc)* room rack card; *(sur ordinateur)* guest folio, guest file; **f. de compte** accounts card; **f.-contact** contacts file; *Ind* **f. de contrôle** checking form, *Br* docket; **f. courrier** mail checklist *or* file; **f. dentaire** dental chart; **f. d'entretien** service record; *Ordinat* **f. d'état** report form; **f. d'état civil** = record of civil status *(birth details and marital status)*; **f. explicative** information sheet; **f. de facture** account card; **f. fournisseur** supplier file; *Ordinat* **f. gigogne** dongle; **f. d'hôtel** *(clé)* key card; *Compta* **f. d'imputation** data entry form; **f. d'inscription** registration form; **f. Kardex** *(d'un hôtel etc)* guest history card; **f. médicale** medical record (card); **f.-message** message form; **f. d'observations** *(questionnaire d'évaluation)* comment card; **f. d'occupation** *(d'un hôtel etc)* room rack card; **f. de paie** payslip; **f. à perforations marginales** edge punched card; **f. perforée** perforated card; *Com* **f. de pointage** clocking-in card; **f. de police** = registration card to be filled in by hotel guests from non-EU countries; *(au débarquement)* landing card; **f. de poste** *(descriptif des tâches à accomplir)* task sheet; **f. de présence** *(de salarié)* attendance sheet; **f.-prospect** potential-customer file; **f. signalétique** personal details card; **f. de stock** stock sheet; **f. en T** T-card; **f. technique** specifications sheet; **f. téléphonique** telephone jack plug; *(broche)* telephone jack; *(pour message)* telephone memo; **f. verticale suspendue** vertical suspension file; **f. à visibilité** visible card record; **f. voyageur** *(d'un hôtel etc)* = registration card for foreign guests; **f. Whitney** *(d'un hôtel etc)* Whitney card

fiche² VT, VPR *Fam* = **ficher²**

ficher¹ [fiʃe] VT **1** *(enfoncer) (clou, pieu etc)* to drive in; *(lame)* to plunge; *(épingle)* to stick in; **f. une épingle dans qch** to stick a pin into sth **2** *(mettre sur fiche)* *(informations)* to file (away); to put on file; *(personne)* to put on file; **il est fiché aux stups** the drugs squad have got him on their files
▪ VPR **se ficher** to stick **(dans** in); **la flèche se**

ficha en plein milieu de la cible the arrow hit the middle of the target; **la balle se ficha dans le mur** the bullet became embedded in the wall

ficher² *(inf souvent* **fiche;** *pp* **fichu)** *Fam* VT **1** *(mettre)* to stick, to shove, *Br* to bung; **f. par terre** *(chapeau etc)* to chuck on the ground; *Fig (gouvernement)* to bring down, to overthrow; *(projet)* to mess up, to put paid to; **t'as tout fichu par terre** you've messed everything up; *Fig* **f. qn à la porte** to chuck sb out; **f. qn dedans** *Br* drop sb in it **2** *(faire)* to do; **il n'a rien fichu de la journée** he's done damn all all day, he hasn't done a thing all day **3** *(donner)* **f. une gifle à qn** to give sb a slap in the face; **fiche-moi la paix!** leave me alone!, clear off!; **je t'en fiche!** no way!, you must be joking!; **je t'en ficherai, tiens, moi, des petits copains à ton âge!** boyfriends at your age – what are you thinking of!; **ça la fiche mal** *(fait mauvais effet)* it looks really bad (**de faire** to do) **4** **f. le camp** to shove off, to clear off; **fiche-moi le camp!** shove off!, clear off!; **va te faire fiche!** get lost!, go to hell!
▪ VPR **se ficher 1** *(se mettre)* **se f. par terre** *(tomber)* to fall flat; **se f. dedans** *(se tromper)* to make a boo-boo *or* a blunder; **soyons attentifs pour ne pas nous f. dedans cette fois** let's take care we don't land ourselves in it this time **2** **se f. de qn/qch** *(tourner en ridicule)* to make fun of sb/sth; *(mépriser)* not to give a damn about sb/sth; **vous vous fichez de moi!** what do you take me for?; **ça, c'est se f. du monde!** well, what a damned cheek!, that's just not taking things seriously!; **je m'en fiche (pas mal)** I don't give a damn, I couldn't care less; **elle s'en fiche que son père ne soit pas d'accord** she doesn't give a damn *or* couldn't care less if her father doesn't agree

fichet [fiʃɛ] NM *(utilisé au trictrac)* peg

fichette [fiʃɛt] NF **f. client** *(d'un hôtel etc)* reservation card; **f. d'arrivée** arrival form

fichier [fiʃje] NM **1** *(ensemble de fiches)* card index, card-index system; **2** *(boîte)* card-index box; *(meuble)* card-index cabinet; *(à tiroirs)* card-index filing cabinet **3** *Ordinat* **volume du f.** file size
▸▸ **f. à accès aléatoire** random access file; **f. à accès limité** restricted file; **f. actif** active file; **f. d'adresses** address file; **f. d'application** application file; **f. ASCII** ASCII file; **f. de base de données** database file; **f. BAT** batch file; **f. binaire** binary file; **f. (des) clients** client *or* customer file; **f. de commande** command file; **f. compte-rendu** log file; *Journ* **f. de coupures** cuttings file; **f. en cours** current file; **f. de destination** target file; **f. disque** disk file; **f. document** document file; **f. d'entrée** input file; **f. exécutable** executable *or* execute file; **f. FAQ** FAQ file; **f. historique** history file; **f. à imprimer** print(er) file; **f. indexé** indexed file; **f. d'intendance** control file; **f. journal** logging file; **f. Kardex** *(d'un hôtel etc)* guest history file; **f. en lecture seule** read-only file; **f. lisez-moi** read-me file; **f. maître** master file; **f. MP3** MP3 file; **f. non structuré** flat file; **f. par points** bitmap file; **f. principal** master file; **f. rotatif** rotating card index, rotary (card) file; **f. des salariés** personnel files; **f. de sauvegarde** backup file; **f. de secours** backup file; **f. séquentiel** batch *or* sequential file; **f. signature** signature file; **f. de sortie** output file; **f. source** source file; **f. système** system file; **f. (de) texte** text file; **f. de travail** working *or* work file; **f. de tri temporaire** temporary sort file

fichtre [fiʃtr] INT *Vieilli, Fam* **1** *(étonnement)* golly!, good gracious! **2** *(admiration)* my!, *Br* I say! **3** *(contrariété)* blow!, blast! **4** *(intensif)*

f. oui! I should say so!, rather!; **f. non!** not likely!, no fear!

fichtrement [fiʃtrəmã] ADV *Vieilli (extrêmement)* awfully, frightfully; **je n'en sais f. rien!** how the heck should I know?

fichu¹ [fiʃy] ADJ *Fam* **1** *(maudit)* rotten, awful; **quel f. pays!** what a godforsaken country!; **quel f. temps!** what filthy *or* awful weather!; **tu as vraiment un f. caractère!** nobody can say a word to you; **cette fichue machine** this damn *or* bloody machine **2** *(en mauvais état, perdu)* **il est f.** he's done for, it's all up with him, he's had it; **c'est f.!** *(sans espoir)* (we can) forget it!; **c'est f. pour dimanche** Sunday's out, we can forget Sunday; **ma robe/voiture est fichue** my dress/car has had it **3** *(habillé)* **être bien/mal f.** to be well/badly turned out *or* dressed **4** *(bâti, conçu)* **elle est vraiment bien fichue, cette fille** that girl's got a great body on her; **c'est bien/mal f.** it's well/badly designed **5** **être mal f.** *(un peu malade)* to be out of sorts, *Br* to be off colour **6** *(capable)* **elle serait fichue d'oublier le rendez-vous** she'd be quite capable of forgetting the appointment, I wouldn't put it past her to forget the appointment; **il n'est pas f. de faire cuire des pâtes** he's not even capable of cooking pasta, even cooking pasta is beyond him

fichu² NM headscarf; *(couvrant les épaules)* fichu, (small) shawl

fictif, -ive [fiktif, -iv] ADJ **1** *(imaginaire)* fictitious, imaginary **2** *(faux) (promesse)* false; *(nom, adresse etc)* false, fictitious; *(lutte)* sham **3** *Fin* **valeur fictive** *(de billets)* face value

fiction [fiksjɔ̃] NF *(fait imaginé)*, *Littér* fiction; **film de f.** fictional film; **livre de f.** work of fiction; **la réalité dépasse la f.** truth is stranger than fiction; **la politique-f.** political pie in the sky; **roman de politique-f.** political novel

fictivement [fiktivmã] ADV **1** *(par la pensée)* in one's imagination *or* mind **2** *Littér* fictitiously

ficus [fikys] NM *Bot* ficus

fidéicommis [fideikɔmi] NM *Jur* trust

fidéicommissaire [fideikɔmisɛr] NM *Jur* trustee

fidèle [fidɛl] ADJ **1** *(loyal) (ami, supporter, serviteur etc)* faithful, loyal; *(époux, chien)* faithful; **lecteur/client f.** regular *or* loyal reader/customer; **rester f. à une promesse** to stand by *or* keep a promise; **rester f. à la mémoire de qn** to remain true *or* faithful to sb's memory; **être f. à ses engagements** to stand by one's commitments; **rester f. à ses idées** to remain true to one's ideas; **peu f.** unfaithful; *Iron* **f. à lui-même, il a oublié mon anniversaire** true to character *or* true to form, he forgot my birthday; **comment l'as-tu trouvé? – f. à lui-même** how did you find him? – his usual self; **elle est toujours f. au poste** she never misses a day; *Mktg* **f. à la marque** brand-loyal **2** *(exact) (copie, traduction, récit etc)* faithful, accurate; *(traducteur, historien, témoin)* accurate; *(mémoire, souvenir)* reliable; **la traduction n'est pas f. au texte** the translation is not faithful to the original; **le document est peu f. aux événements** the document is not a faithful *or* an accurate account of what happened
▪ N *(partisan)* (loyal) supporter; *Com* regular *or* loyal customer; *(lecteur de journal)* regular *or* loyal reader; *TV* regular *or* loyal viewer; **je suis un f. de votre émission** I always watch *or* I never miss your programme; *Rel* **les fidèles** the faithful; *(à l'église)* the congregation

fidèlement [fidɛlmɑ̃] ADV 1 *(servir)* faithfully, loyally; *Com* loyally 2 *(traduire, reproduire etc)* accurately, faithfully

fidélisation [fidelizasjɔ̃] NF f. de la clientèle building of customer loyalty; f. à la marque creation of brand loyalty

fidéliser [fidelize] VT *(clients, lecteurs, spectateurs etc)* to win the loyalty of; f. la clientèle to create customer loyalty; f. une équipe to keep a team together

fidélité [fidelite] NF 1 *(loyauté) (d'un ami, chien etc)* faithfulness; *(d'un époux)* faithfulness, fidelity; *Com (d'un client, lecteur, spectateur etc)* loyalty; **serment de f.** oath of allegiance; **f. conjugale** marital fidelity; **f. à ses engagements** standing by one's commitments; *Mktg* **f. du consommateur** consumer loyalty; *Mktg* **f. à la marque** brand loyalty; **f. à ou de la couleur** colour fidelity 2 *(exactitude) (d'une traduction, copie etc)* faithfulness, accuracy; *(de la mémoire)* reliability; **haute f.** high fidelity, hi-fi

Fidji [fidʒi] NFPL **les îles F.** Fiji, the Fiji Islands

fidjien, -ienne [fidʒjɛ̃, -jɛn] ADJ Fijian
  NM *Ling* Fijian
  N **F.** Fijian

fiduciaire [fidysjɛr] ADJ *(prêt, devise etc)* fiduciary; **monnaie f.** paper money; **avoirs en monnaie f.** *(d'une banque)* cash holdings; **société f.** trust company; *Jur* **en dépôt f.** in trust
  NM *Jur* fiduciary, trustee

fiduciairement [fidysjɛrmɑ̃] ADV *Jur* in trust

fief [fjɛf] NM 1 *Hist* fief 2 *Fig (spécialité)* domain 3 **f. électoral** loyal constituency; **un f. socialiste** a socialist stronghold

fieffé [fjefe] ADJ *(menteur, ivrogne)* inveterate

fiel [fjɛl] NM 1 *(de bœuf, volaille etc)* gall 2 *Fig (venin)* bitterness, venom, malice; **plein de f.** venomous; **épancher son f.** to vent one's spleen

fielleux, -euse [fjelø, -øz] ADJ bitter

fiente [fjɑ̃t] NF *(d'oiseaux)* droppings

fienter [fjɑ̃te] VI *(d'un oiseau)* to leave droppings

fier¹, -ère [fjɛr] ADJ 1 *(digne)* proud; **courage f.** noble courage; **être trop f. pour mendier** to be too proud to beg; **être f. de ses enfants** to be proud of one's children; **je n'étais pas f. de moi** I wasn't proud of myself; **être f. de qch/d'avoir fait qch** to be proud of sth/of having done sth; **il n'y a pas de quoi être f.** that's nothing to boast about *or* to be proud of; **f. comme Artaban** as proud as a peacock
  2 *(hautain)* proud, haughty; **alors, on est moins f., n'est-ce pas?** not quite so high and mighty now, are we?; *Fam* **c'est une fille pas fière** she's not a stuck-up girl; *Fam* **il n'est pas f. pour deux sous** he's not at all stuck-up
  3 *(extrême)* **f. imbécile** first-rate *or* real idiot; **tu m'as fait une fière peur** you gave me a fine *or* real fright; **vous avez eu une fière idée** you've had a great idea
  N **faire le f.** to show off; **il fait le f. avec sa nouvelle voiture** he's showing off with his new car; **inutile de faire le f., ça sera pareil pour toi** it's no good giving yourself airs (and graces), it'll be the same for you

fier² (se) [səfje] VPR *(impf & pr sub* **n. n. fiions)** **se f. à qn/qch** *(avoir confiance en)* to trust sb/sth; *(compter sur)* to rely on *or* count on sb/sth; **fiez-vous à moi** *(action)* leave it to me; *(renseignement)* take my word for it; **ne te fie pas aux apparences** don't trust *or* go by *or* go on appearances; **se f. à la parole de qn** to take sb's word for it, to believe sb; **ne vous y fiez pas** beware!; *(n'y croyez pas)* don't count on it

fier-à-bras, *pl* **fiers-à-bras** NM swaggerer, braggart

fièrement [fjɛrmɑ̃] ADV 1 *(dignement)* proudly 2 *Arch (d'une manière hautaine)* haughtily 3 *Vieilli (extrêmement)* famously

fiérot, -ote [fjero, -ɔt] *Fam* ADJ *(personne)* cocky
  N **faire le f.** to swagger (around)

fierté [fjɛrte] NF 1 *(satisfaction)* pride; **tirer f. de qch** to take pride in sth; **ma fille/maison est ma f.** my daughter/house is my pride and joy; **la réussite de l'entreprise est notre f.** we pride ourselves on the success of the venture; **c'est avec f. que je vous présente …** I take pride in presenting to you …, I proudly present to you … 2 *(arrogance)* pride, haughtiness 3 *(amour-propre)* pride, self-respect

fiesta [fjɛsta] NF *Fam (fête)* binge, fling; **faire une ou la f.** to live it up, to have a wild time; **c'est la f.!** it's party time!

fièvre [fjevr] NF 1 *Méd (maladie)* fever; *(température)* temperature; **elle a 40 de f.** her temperature's at 40, she has a temperature of 40 degrees; **avoir beaucoup de f.** to have a high temperature; **avoir (de) la f.** to be feverish, to have a (high) temperature; *Fam* **avoir une f. de cheval** to have a raging fever 2 *(excitation)* excitement, frenzy; **sans f.** calmly; **dans la f. de la campagne électorale** in the heat *or* excitement of the electoral campaign; **dans la f. de l'action/des débats** in the heat of the action/debates; **travailler avec f.** to work feverishly; **elle en parle avec f.** she speaks of it excitedly 3 *(désir)* passion **(de qch** for sth); *(rage)* urge **(de faire qch** to do sth)
  ▸▸ **f. amarile ou jaune** yellow fever; **f. de Malte** Malta fever; **f. paludéenne** malaria; **f. quarte** quartan fever; **f. typhoïde** typhoid (fever)

fiévreusement [fjevrøzmɑ̃] ADV feverishly, frantically

fiévreux, -euse [fjevrø, -øz] ADJ 1 *Méd (pouls, personne etc)* feverish 2 *Fig (activité, préparations etc)* feverish, frantic; *(imagination)* feverish; *(attente)* anxious

fifille [fifij] NF *Fam* little girl, daughter; **f. à son papa** daddy's little girl

fifre [fifr] NM 1 *(instrument)* fife 2 *(joueur)* fife (player)

fifrelin [fifrəlɛ̃] NM *Vieilli* **ce ne vaut pas un f.** it's not worth a penny

fifty-fifty [fiftififti] ADV **faire f., partager f.** to go halves *or* fifty-fifty; **partager qch f.** to share sth fifty-fifty *or* half and half

figé [fiʒe] ADJ *(sauce, huile)* congealed; *(sourire)* fixed; *(style)* stilted; *(société)* fossilized; **locution figée** set phrase; **elle est figée dans cette situation** she is stuck in this situation

figer [fiʒe] *(figeant; il figeait)* VT *(sang)* to coagulate, to congeal; *(huile, sauce)* to congeal; **des cris à vous f. le sang** blood-curdling cries; **ce spectacle lui a figé le sang** the sight made his blood run cold; **figé sur place** rooted to the spot
  VPR **se figer** *(du sang)* to coagulate, to congeal; *(de l'huile, d'une sauce)* to congeal; *Fig (d'un regard, de traits)* to freeze; **elle se fige si on lui en parle** she justs stares past you if you talk to her about it; **se f. dans une attitude/un point de vue** to persist in an attitude/a point of view; **son sang se figea (dans ses veines)** his/her blood ran cold; **son sourire se figea quand il entendit la nouvelle** his smile froze when he heard the news

fignolage [fiɲɔlaʒ] NM *Fam (d'un travail, dessin etc)* touching up

fignoler [fiɲɔle] *Fam* VT *(travail, dessin etc)* to put the finishing touches to, to touch up
  VI to be meticulous

fignoleur, -euse [fiɲɔlœr, -øz] ADJ meticulous
  N perfectionist, meticulous worker

figue [fig] NF *(fruit)* fig; **f. de Barbarie** prickly pear

figuier [figje] NM fig (tree); **f. de Barbarie** prickly pear

figurant, -ante [figyrɑ̃, -ɑ̃t] N *Théâtre* walk-on, extra; *Cin* extra; **rôle de f.** *Théâtre* walk-on (part), bit part; *Cin* bit part; *Fig* **avoir un rôle de f. dans qch, n'être qu'un f. dans qch** to take no active part *or* be just an onlooker in sth

figuratif, -ive [figyratif, -iv] ADJ *(plan)* figurative; *(art, artiste)* figurative, representational
  N figurative *or* representational artist

figuration [figyrasjɔ̃] NF 1 *(représentation)* figuration, representation 2 *Théâtre (acteurs)* walk-on actors, *Fam* supers; *(rôle)* walk-on (part), bit part; **faire de la f.** to do walk-on parts, to play bit parts 3 *Cin (acteurs)* extras; *(rôle)* bit part; **faire de la f.** to play bit parts

figurativement [figyrativmɑ̃] ADV figuratively

figure [figyr] NF 1 *(visage)* face; **jeter qch à la f. de qn** to throw sth in sb's face; *Fam* **casser la f. à qn** to smash sb's face in; *Fam* **casser la f.** to fall flat on one's face; *Fig (échouer)* to come a cropper; **je me suis cassé la f. en vélo/dans les escaliers** I fell off my bike/down the stairs
  2 *(mine)* face, *Fml* countenance; **faire bonne f. à qn** to act pleasantly towards sb; **faire bonne f.** to make a good impression; **faire une drôle de f.** to pull a face, to give a funny look; **faire triste f.** to pull a long face; **ne plus avoir f. humaine** to be totally disfigured; *Hum* **mes vieilles chaussures n'ont plus f. humaine** my old shoes are falling to pieces
  3 *(représentation, image)* figure; **figures de cire** waxworks, waxwork figures; *Cartes* **les figures** *Br* the court cards, the face cards; **figures géométriques** geometrical figures; **figure de proue** *(d'un bateau)*, *Fig (d'un parti politique etc)* figurehead; **livre avec figures dans le texte** book with figures *or* diagrams in the text; **prendre f.** to take shape; **faire f. de riche** to give an impression of wealth; **elle fait f. d'intellectuelle dans ce milieu** she gives the impression of *or* has the appearance of an intellectual amongst these people; **faire pauvre ou piètre f.** to cut a sorry figure
  4 *(personnage)* figure; **les grandes figures de la Guerre** the great figures of the War
  5 *(de danseur, patineur etc)* figure; **figures libres** freestyle; **figures imposées** compulsory figures
  6 *Ling* figure; **f. de mots ou de rhétorique** figure of speech; **f. de style** stylistic device

---

Il faut remarquer que lorsqu'il s'applique à une personne, le nom anglais **figure** signifie **silhouette**.

---

figuré [figyre] ADJ 1 *(plan)* diagrammatic 2 *Ling* **sens f.** figurative meaning
  NM *Ling* **au f.** in the figurative sense, figuratively; **au propre comme au f.** literally and figuratively

figurément [figyremɑ̃] ADV figuratively

figurer [figyre] VT to represent; **une croix figure une église sur le plan** a cross stands for *or* represents *or* indicates a church on the map; **la scène figure le camp des brigands** the scene shows *or* represents the brigands' camp
  VI 1 *(se trouver)* to appear, to figure; **je ne**

veux pas que mon nom figure dans l'affaire/le livre I don't want my name to appear *or* figure in the matter/the book; **f. dans un catalogue/une bibliographie** to be listed *or* appear in a catalogue/a bibliography; **voici les chevaux qui figurent à l'arrivée** here are the names of the winning horses **2** *Théâtre* to have a walk-on (part); *Cin* to have a bit part

VPR se figurer to imagine (**que** that); **se f. qch** to imagine sth; **figurez-vous la situation** imagine the situation, picture the situation (to yourself); **ne vous figurez pas que je sois satisfait** don't get the idea that I'm satisfied; **si tu te figures que je vais te pardonner, tu te trompes** if you imagine I'm going to forgive you, you're mistaken; **je suis à sec, figure-toi** believe it or not, I'm broke; **figure-toi que, nous aussi, on a loué une maison dans ce village** would you believe it, we've rented a house in that village as well

figurine [figyrin] NF figurine, statuette

fil [fil] NM **1** *Tex (brin)* thread, yarn; *(de toile d'araignée)* thread; *(tissu)* linen; **f. de coton/nylon** cotton/nylon thread *or* yarn; **f. de lin** linen yarn *or* thread; **des draps pur f.** (pure) linen sheets; **gants de f.** cotton gloves; **laine trois/quatre fils** three-/four-ply wool; *Fig* **astuce cousue de f. blanc** obvious *or* blatant trick; *Fig* **c'est cousu de f. blanc** you can see right through it, it won't fool anybody; *Fig* **de f. en aiguille** little by little, bit by bit, gradually; **démêler les fils d'une intrigue** to unravel the threads of a plot; *Fig* **trouver le f. d'Ariane** *ou* **le f. conducteur** to find the clue (to the mystery); **le f. rouge** recurrent theme; **il n'y a pas de f. conducteur dans ce roman** there's no unifying thread in this novel; **mince comme un f.** as thin as a rake **2** *(de câble, corde etc)* strand; *(de marionnette)* string; *Fig* **c'est lui qui tient les fils** he's the one who holds (all) the strings; *Fig* **être dans le droit f. de qch** to be in line with sth; **le droit f. du parti n'a pas changé depuis dix ans** the party line hasn't changed in ten years; *Fig* **sa vie ne tenait qu'à un f.** his life hung by a thread; **il ne tenait qu'à un f. qu'il soit renvoyé** it was touch and go whether he would be dismissed; *Fam* **avoir un f. à la patte** *(être tenu par un engagement)* to be tied down; *Fam* **se mettre un f. à la patte** to tie oneself down; *Sport* **être coiffé sur le f.** to be pipped at the post, to be beaten at the wire **3** *(métallique)* wire; *Fam* **donner du f. à retordre à qn** to give sb trouble **4** *Élec* **f. (électrique)** (electric) wire; **f. (souple)** lead, cord, *Br* flex; **f. téléphonique** telephone wire; *Tél* **donner** *ou* **passer un coup de f. à qn** to give sb a call, to call sb (up), *Br* to give sb a ring, *Br* to ring sb (up); **recevoir** *ou* **avoir un coup de f. de qn** to get a (phone) call from sb; **être au bout du f.** to be on the line *or* phone; **je viens d'avoir Martin au bout du f.** I've just had Martin on the line *or* phone; **télégraphie/téléphonie sans f.** wireless telegraphy/telephony; **téléphone sans f.** cordless telephone **5** *(de bois, viande)* grain; **les haricots verts ont des fils** *ou* **sont pleins de fils** the green beans are stringy; **haricots sans fils** stringless beans; **contre le f., à contre-f.** against *or* across the grain; **dans le sens du f.** with the grain; **couper dans le droit f.** *(bois)* to cut along the grain; *(tissu)* to cut on the straight **6** *Fig (cours)* **au f. de l'eau** with the current, downstream; **se laisser aller au f. de l'eau** to let oneself drift (with the current); **au f. des jours/semaines/heures** as the days/weeks/hours go by, with the passing days/weeks/hours; **le f. des événements** the chain of events; **perdre/reprendre le f. de la conver-**

sation to lose/pick up the thread of the conversation; **j'ai perdu le f., je ne sais plus où j'en suis** I've lost the thread, I don't know where I am any more; **suivre le f. des idées de qn** to follow the thread of sb's ideas **7** *(d'un couteau, d'une épée etc)* edge; **donner le f. à un rasoir** to put an edge on a razor; *Fig* **le président est sur le f. du rasoir** the president is on a knife edge; *Litt* **passer des prisonniers au f. de l'épée** to put prisoners to the sword

▸▸ **f. à bâtir** basting thread; **f. de bougie** (spark) plug lead; **f. à coudre** (sewing) thread, cotton; **f. à couper le beurre** cheesewire; *Fig* **il n'a pas inventé le f. à couper le beurre** he'll never set the Thames on fire; **f. dentaire** dental floss; **f. d'Écosse** lisle thread; **chaussettes en f. d'Écosse** lisle socks; **f. de fer** wire; **fil(s) de fer barbelé(s)** barbed wire; **f. de masse** *ou* **de terre** earth (wire), *Am* ground (wire); **f. de la vierge** gossamer

filage [fila3] NM *Tex* spinning

filaire [filɛr] *Tél* ADJ corded, plug-in NM corded *or* plug-in phone

filament [filamɑ̃] NM **1** *(de viande)* fibre, *Am* fiber; *(de lampe électrique)* filament; **ça a trop de filaments pour être mangé** it's too stringy to eat **2** *Biol* filament

filamenteux, -euse [filamɑ̃tø, -øz] ADJ filamentous

filandière [filɑ̃djɛr] NF *Tex Arch* (hand-)spinner

filandreux, -euse [filɑ̃drø, -øz] ADJ **1** *(viande, légumes)* stringy **2** *Fig Péj (explication, phrase etc)* involved, confused

filant [filɑ̃] ADJ **1** *(qui coule)* fluid **2** **étoile filante** shooting star, falling star

filasse [filas] NF *(matière)* tow; **f. de chanvre** hemp

ADJ INV **cheveux (blond) f.** tow-coloured hair; **aux cheveux (blond) f.** tow-headed, tow-haired

filateur [filatœr] NM (spinning) mill owner

filature [filatyr] NF **1** *Tex (action)* spinning **2** *(fabrique)* (spinning) mill; **f. de coton** cotton mill **3** *(par un détective etc)* shadowing, tailing; **il a été pris en f.** he was shadowed *or* tailed

fil-de-fériste, *pl* **fil-de-féristes** [fildəferist] N high-wire artist

file [fil] NF **1** *(de gens, voitures etc)* line; **f. (d'attente)** queue, *Am* line; *Aviat* stacking; **se mettre** *ou* **se ranger en f.** to line up; **prendre la f., se mettre à la f.** to join the queue *or Am* line; *Ordinat* **f. d'attente** print queue *or* list; **mettre en f. d'attente** to spool, to queue; **marcher à la f.** *ou* **en f.** to walk in single file *or* one behind another; **à la** *ou* **en f. indienne** in single *or* Indian file; **entrer/sortir en f.** *ou* **à la f.** to file in/out; **cinq bières à la f.** five beers in a row *or* in succession *or* one after another; **trois jours à la f.** *ou* **de f.** three days in a row *or* in succession; *Aut* **stationner en double f.** to double-park **2** *Aut (couloir)* lane; **ne changez pas de f.** keep in lane; **rouler dans** *ou* **sur la f. de droite** to drive in the right-hand lane

filé [file] ADJ **1** *(bas, collant)* with a run, *Br* laddered **2** **verre f.** spun glass
NM *Tex, Tech* thread; **f. d'or** gold thread

filer [file] VT **1** *(coton, verre etc)* to spin; *Fig* **f. des jours heureux** to live very happily; *Fam* **ils filent le parfait amour** they are living love's dream
2 *Naut (câble)* to pay out, to run out; *(amarres)* to slip
3 *(métaphore)* to spin out, to draw out; *Mus (note)* to draw out, to sustain; *(huile)* to pour out in a trickle; *Cartes* **f. les cartes** to lay the cards down slowly; **il m'a filé entre les doigts** he slipped between my fingers

4 *(d'un détective etc) (suspect)* to shadow, to tail
5 *Fam (donner)* **f. qch à qn** to give sb sth; **lui ai filé ma voiture/un conseil** I gave him my car/a piece of advice; **f. un coup de pied/une gifle à qn** to give sb a kick/a slap; **f. de l'aide** *ou* **un coup de main à qn** to give sb a hand
6 *(démailler) (bas, collant)* to put a run in, *Br* to ladder

VI **1** *(passer très vite)* **le temps file** time flies; **laisser f. un câble** to pay out a cable; **l'argent lui file entre les mains** *ou* **les doigts** money runs through his hands *or* fingers like water; **train qui file à toute vitesse** train rushing along at full speed; **les voitures filaient sur la route** cars were speeding along the road; *Naut* **f. (à) vingt nœuds** to proceed at twenty knots
2 *Fam (partir en vitesse)* to dash *or* rush off; **f. (en douce)** to slip away *or* off; **allez, filez!** clear off!, scram!; *(dépêchez-vous)* off you go!; **f. à l'anglaise** to sneak off, to take French leave
3 *Fam* **f. doux** to toe the line, to behave oneself
4 *(de bas, collant)* to run, *Br* to ladder; **j'ai un bas qui file** I've got a run *or Br* ladder
5 **la lampe file** the lamp is smoking
6 *(de l'huile etc)* to run

filet¹ [filɛ] NM **1** *(de lumière)* thin streak; *(d'air)* thin stream; *(d'eau, de bave)* trickle, dribble; *(de sang)* trickle; *(de fumée etc)* thread, wisp; **f. de voix** thin *or* weak voice; *Culin* **ajoutez-y un f. de citron/vinaigre** add a dash of lemon/vinegar; **f. d'une vis** thread *or Spéc* worm of a screw **2** *Anat (de la langue)* frenum, string **3** *Bot (d'étamine)* filament **4** *(de reliure)*, *Archit* fillet **5** *Typ* rule; **f. maigre** hairline (rule)

filet² NM *Culin* fillet; **f. mignon** filet mignon *(small fillet steak)*

filet³ NM **1** *(ouvrage à mailles)* net; *(au cirque)* (safety) net; **f. de pêche** fishing net; **f. à papillons** butterfly net; **être pris au f.** to be caught with a net; *Fig* **faire tomber** *ou* **attirer qn dans ses filets** to ensnare sb; **un beau coup de f. pour la police** a good haul for the police; **travailler sans f.** *(d'un trapéziste)* to work without a net; *Fig* to go out on a limb, to take risks; **f. à provisions** string *or* net bag; **f. pour cheveux** hairnet; *Rail* **f. à bagages** luggage rack **2** *Tennis, Ftbl etc* net; *Tennis* **monter au f.** to go up to the net; **balle de f.** let (ball); **juge de f.** net-cord judge

filetage [filta3] NM *Tech* **1** *(action)* threading, screw cutting **2** *(filets) (de vis)* thread, *Spéc* worm; *Tech* **f. Acmé** Acme thread; **f. Whitworth** Whitworth thread

fileter [filte] VT *(je filète; je filèterai)* *Tech* **1** *(métal)* to wiredraw; *(fil)* to draw **2** *(boulon, tige etc)* to thread, to screw

fileur, -euse [filœr, -øz] N *Tex (de métier à tisser)* spinner

filial, -ale, -aux, -ales [filjal] ADJ filial
NF *Com* **filiale** subsidiary (company); **filiale consolidée** consolidated subsidiary; **filiale de distribution** marketing subsidiary; **filiale de vente** sales subsidiary

filialement [filjalmɑ̃] ADV filially

filiation [filjasjɔ̃] NF **1** *(lien de parenté)* filiation; **en f. directe** in direct line; **un descendant en f. directe** a direct descendant **2** *Litt (famille)* descendants **3** *Fig (de mots, d'événements etc)* relationship (**de** between); **des théories en f. directe avec ce texte** theories directly related to this text

filière [filjɛr] NF **1** *Admin* channels; **la f. administrative** the (usual) official channels; **passer par** *ou* **suivre la f.** *(pour obtenir qch)* to go through official channels; *(comme employé)* to work one's way up; **choisir la f. nu-**

cléaire to go down the nuclear road, to choose the nuclear path; *Scol* **suivre une f.** **scientifique/commerciale** to study scientific/business subjects **2** *(de trafiquants, terroristes etc)* network; **remonter la f.** to go back along the network (to the person at the top); **démanteler une f.** to break up a ring **3** *Tech (pour fileter une vis)* screw plate; *(pour étirer)* draw(ing) plate; **travailler un métal à la f.** to draw a metal **4** *Zool (d'une araignée, d'un ver à soie)* spinneret **5** *Fin* **f. électronique** electronic transfer

filiforme [filiform] ADJ **1** *Zool* filiform, threadlike **2** *Fam (très mince) (personne, jambes etc)* spindly

filigrane [filigran] NM **1** *(ouvrage d'orfèvrerie)* filigree; **broche en f.** filigree brooch **2** *(de papier, billet de banque etc)* watermark; **à f.** watermarked; *Fig* **lire en f.** to read between the lines; **apparaître en f. dans qch** to be implicit in sth

filigrané [filigrane] ADJ **1** *(broche)* filigreed **2** *(papier)* watermarked

filin [filɛ̃] NM rope

fille [fij] NF **1** *(descendante directe)* daughter; *Fig* **la superstition est (la) f. de l'ignorance** superstition is born of ignorance **2** *(enfant)* girl; **petite f.** little girl; **jeune f.** girl, young woman; **faire la jeune f. de la maison** *(à un cocktail)* to pass or hand round the snacks; **ma pauvre f.!** my poor child or dear!; **nom de jeune f.** maiden name; **école de filles** girls' school; *Fig* **jouer la f. de l'air** to escape, to get out **3** *(femme)* woman; **vieille f.** old maid, spinster; **habitudes de vieille f.** old-maidish habits; *Vieilli* **rester f.** to remain single or unmarried **4** *Rel* **les filles de Port-Royal** the sisters or nuns of Port-Royal

▶▶ **f. de cuisine** kitchenmaid; **f. de ferme** farm girl; **f. d'honneur** maid of honour; *surtout Vieilli* **f. de joie** fille de joie, prostitute; **f. à matelots** prostitute *(whose customers are primarily sailors)*; **f. publique** prostitute; **f. des rues** streetwalker; **f. de salle** *(dans un hôtel)* waitress; *(dans un hôpital)* nursing auxiliary; **f. de service** maidservant; *Vieilli* **f. à soldats** prostitute *(whose customers are primarily soldiers)*

fille-mère, *pl* **filles-mères** NF *Péj, Vieilli* unmarried mother

fillette [fijɛt] NF **1** *(petite fille)* little girl **2** *Arg (bouteille) (de vin)* half-bottle

filleul, -eule [fijœl] N godson, *f* goddaughter; **f. de guerre** = soldier in action 'adopted' by a woman, who sends letters, parcels etc

film [film] NM **1** *Phot* film **2** *Cin (pellicule)* film; *(œuvre)* film, picture, movie, *Am* motion picture; **le f.** *(art)* film, cinema; **tourner un f.** to make a film; *Fam* **il n'a rien compris au f.** he hasn't taken anything in; *Fam* **se faire un f.** to be living in a dream world; **f. en noir et blanc/en couleur** black and white/colour film **3** *Fig (déroulement) (d'événements)* sequence; **revoir le f. de sa vie** to look back over one's life **4** *(couche)* film; **f. alimentaire** cling film; **f. dentaire** (dental) plaque; **sous f. plastique** shrink-wrapped; **recouvert d'un f. protecteur** covered with a protective film

▶▶ **f. d'action** action film, action movie; **f. d'actualité** newsreel, news film; **f. d'animation** animated film, cartoon; **f. d'archives** library film; **f. d'art et d'essai** arthouse film; **f. d'auteur** film d'auteur; **f. d'aventures** adventure film; **f. catastrophe** disaster film; **f. documentaire** documentary film; **f. dramatique** drama; **f. d'entreprise** corporate film, corporate video; **f. d'épouvante** horror film or movie, thriller; **f. d'espionnage** spy film; **f. à faible budget** low-budget movie; **f.**

fantastique science fiction film; **f. de genre** genre film; **f. à gros succès** blockbuster movie; **f. de guerre** war film; **f. d'horreur** horror film or movie; **f. institutionnel** corporate video; **f. long métrage** feature film; **f. muet** silent film, silent movie; **f. noir** film noir; **f. parlant** talkie; **f. plat** two-dimensional film; **f. policier** detective film; **f. pornographique** pornographic film, blue movie; **f. publicitaire** *(à la télévision)* commercial; *(au cinéma)* cinema advertisement; **f. en relief** 3D film; **f. de science-fiction** science fiction film; **f. semi-documentaire** semi-documentary; **f. de série B** B-movie, B-feature; **f. sonore** sound film; **f. à succès** box-office hit; **f. de suspense** thriller; **f. télévisé** television film; **f. en 3D** 3D film; **f. vidéo** video film; **f. classé X** adults-only movie or Br film, Br X-rated movie or film

filmage [filmaʒ] NM *Cin* filming

filmer [filme] VT **1** *Tech (enduire)* to cover with a film **2** *Cin* to film; *(scène)* to film, to shoot
VI *Cin* to film

filmique [filmik] ADJ cinematic, filmic

filmographie [filmɔgrafi] NF *Cin* filmography

filmologie [filmɔlɔʒi] NF film studies

filmothèque [filmɔtɛk] NF microfilm library

filoche [filɔʃ] NF *Fam* shadowing, tailing

filoguidé [filogide] ADJ wire-guided

filon [filɔ̃] NM **1** *Min* vein, seam, lode **2** *Fam (situation lucrative)* cushy job; **il tient le f., il a déniché** ou **trouvé le (bon) f.** he's struck it rich; *Fig* **trouver un f.** to find a goldmine; **j'ai un bon f. pour avoir des vidéos gratuites** I know where I can get free videos easily

filou [filu] NM **1** *(escroc)* rogue, swindler, crook **2** *(enfant)* rascal, rogue

filoutage [filutaʒ] NM swindling, cheating

filouter [filute] VT **1** *Vieilli* **f. qch à qn** to steal sth from sb **2** **f. qn** to swindle or cheat sb

filouterie [filutri] NF **1** *(action)* swindling, cheating **2** *(manœuvre)* swindle, fraud

fils [fis] NM son; **elle et ses deux f.** she and her two boys or sons; **c'est bien le f. de son père** he's a chip off the old block; **être le f. de ses œuvres** to be a self-made man; **c'est le f. spirituel de René Char** he's the spiritual son of René Char; **M. Duval f.** Mr Duval junior; **le f. Duval** young Duval; *Rel* **le F. de Dieu/de l'homme** the Son of God/of Man

▶▶ **f. de famille** young man of good social standing; *Péj* **à papa** daddy's boy; *Vulg* **f. de pute** son of a bitch

filtrage [filtraʒ] NM **1** *(d'un liquide, gaz, son etc)* filtering **2** *Fig (contrôle) (des informations, visiteurs etc)* screening

filtrant [filtrɑ̃] ADJ filtering; **verre f.** filter glass; **lunettes à verres filtrants** glasses with filter lenses

filtration [filtrasjɔ̃] NF filtration, filtering

filtre [filtr] NM *Tech, Phot, Élec, Ordinat etc* filter; **(bout) f.** filter (tip); **je fume des (cigarettes) f.** I smoke filter-tipped cigarettes or filter tips; **(café) f.** filter coffee; **papier f.** filter paper

▶▶ **f. à air** air filter; *Radio, TV* **f. anti-parasites** interference filter or suppressor; *Ordinat* **f. anti-reflet** glare screen; **f. audio** audio filter; **f. à brouillard** *(pour une caméra)* fog filter; **f. à café** coffee filter; **f. à carburant** fuel filter; **f. au charbon** carbon filter; **f. à combustible** fuel filter; **f. correcteur** corrective filter; **f. couleur** colour medium; *Phot* **f. de couleur** ou **coloré** colour filter; *Ordinat* **f. écran** screen filter; **f. à essence** petrol filter; **f. à huile** oil filter; *Ordinat* **f. d'importation/exportation** import/export filter; **f. à parti-**

cules dust filter; **f. à pollen** pollen filter; *TV, Cin* **f. pour objectif de caméra** camera lens filter

filtrer [filtre] VT **1** *(eau, café, gaz, son, lumière etc)* to filter **2** *Fig (contrôler) (informations, visiteurs etc)* to screen
VI *(d'un liquide)* to filter, to percolate, to seep *(à travers* through); *(d'une nouvelle)* to leak out, to filter out; **la lumière filtrait à travers** ou **par les branches** the light filtered through the branches; **ils n'ont rien laissé f. de ses déclarations** they have said nothing about his statement, *Fam* they're keeping a very tight lid on what he said

─────

FIN¹ [fɛ̃]

─────

end **1, 2** ▪ expiry **1** ▪ death **1** ▪ back **1** ▪ purpose **2** ▪ aim **2**

─────

NF **1** *(dernier moment) (de film, réunion, travail etc)* end, conclusion; *(de contrat, de bail etc)* expiry, expiration; *(d'empire, de régime etc)* end, fall; *(d'un espoir, de malheurs etc)* end; *(mort)* end, death; *Cin* **'f.'** 'The End'; **le cinquième en partant de la f.** the fifth from the end, the last but four; **f. du jour** close of day; **f. du mois** end of the month; *Com* **f. de mois** monthly statement; **de f. de mois** end-of-month; **assurer ses fins de mois** to make sure one has enough money at the end of the month; **avoir des fins de mois difficiles** to be always short of money at the end of the month; **f. de l'exercice** end of the financial year; **de f. d'exercice** year-end; **en f. d'exercice** at the end of the financial year; **payable f. courant/prochain** payable at the end of this/next month; **on se reverra f. mars** ou **à la f. de mars** we'll meet again at the end of March; **en f. de soirée** towards the end of the evening; **il a faibli en f. de trimestre** his work fell off towards the end of the term; **il est venu vers la f. de l'après-midi** he came late in or towards the end of the afternoon; **en f. d'année** at the end of the year; **jusqu'à la f. des temps** ou **des siècles** till the end of time; **le vocabulaire est à la f. du livre** the vocabulary is at the back of the book; **à la f. de la liste, en f. de liste** at the end of the list; **sans f.** *(emploi adjectival)* endless; *(plaintes, interrogatoire)* endless, never-ending; *(emploi adverbial)* endlessly; **vis sans f.** endless screw; **il parle sans f.** he never stops talking, he talks endlessly; **f. prématurée** untimely death or end; **il a eu une belle f./une f. affreuse** he had a good/terrible end or death; **on sent bien que la f. n'est pas loin** we've a feeling the end is not far away or it can't be long now; **vers la f., il n'était plus le même** he wasn't the same towards the end; **le lave-vaisselle est sur sa f.** the dishwasher is on its last legs; **toucher** ou **tirer à sa f.** *(d'un projet, d'une union)* to come or draw to an end or a close; **l'année touche** ou **tire à sa f.** the year is drawing to an end or a close; **votre participation touche à sa f.** your participation will soon be over or at an end; **le contrat touche à sa f.** the contract will expire soon; **être en f. de course** *(d'une vis)* to be screwed fully home; *(d'un piston)* to have reached the end of its stroke; *Fig (d'une personne)* to have come to the end of the road; **chômeur en f. de droits** unemployed person who is coming to the end of his benefit; **mettre f. à qch** to put an end or a stop to sth; **mettre f. à sa vie** ou **ses jours** to put an end to one's life; **elle se marie pour faire une f.** she's getting married in order to settle down; **prendre f., avoir une f.** to come to an end; **mener une affaire à bonne f.** to bring a matter to a successful conclusion, to deal successfully with a matter; **c'est la f.** this is the end; **la f. du monde** the end of the world; **ce n'est pas la f. du monde** it's not the end of the world; *Fam* **c'est la f. de tout** that's the (absolute) end; **c'est Patrick qui a dit** *ou* **eu le mot de la f.** it was Patrick who had the last *or* final word; **à la f. il répondit** in the end *or* finally *or* at last he answered; *Fam* **tu es stupide à la f.!** you're really very stupid; **tu m'ennuies à la f.!** you're really annoying me!; **en f. de compte** *(après tout)* in the end, after all; *(tout bien considéré)* all things considered, taking everything into account; *(pour conclure)* finally, to conclude; *Fam* **à la f. des fins** when all's said and done, at the end of the day

2 *(but)* end, aim, purpose; **la f. justifie les moyens** the end justifies the means; **arriver** *ou* **parvenir** *ou* **en venir à ses fins** to achieve one's ends *or* aims *or* purpose, to get what one wants; **une f. en soi** an end in itself; **à cette f. il faut avoir beaucoup de patience** to this end *or* in order to achieve this one must have a lot of patience; **à quelle f.?** for what purpose?, to what end?, with what end in view?; **je vous le fais parvenir à toutes fins utiles** I'm sending it to you should you need it; **aux fins de faire qch** with a view to doing sth; **à seule(s) fin(s) de l'aider** for the sole purpose of helping him; *Jur* **aux fins de débauche** for immoral purposes

3 *Jur* **renvoyé des fins de la plainte** discharged, acquitted

► ► *Ordinat* **f. de ligne** line end; *Ordinat* **f. de page** pagebreak; *Ordinat* **f. de page obligatoire** hard page break; *Ordinat* **f. de paragraphe** paragraph break; **f. de race:** **comportement f. de race** degenerate behaviour; *Com* **f. de série** discontinued line; *Ordinat* **f. de session** logoff; **f. de siècle: style/mœurs f. de siècle** f. de siècle *or* decadent style/morals

---

FIN²,-INE [fɛ̃, fin]

ADJ	thin **1** ▪ fine **1–3** ▪ first-class **2** ▪ subtle **4**
NM	the ultimate *(le fin du fin)*
ADV	absolutely **1** ▪ finely **2**

ADJ 1 *(mince)* *(papier, tranche)* thin; *(étoffe)* fine, thin; *(cheveux, pluie, grains, sable, aiguille, pointe)* fine; *(traits)* fine, delicate; *(silhouette)* slender; *(cheville)* neat

2 *(de première qualité)* fine, first-class; **vins fins** choice *or* fine wines; **or f.** pure *or* fine gold; **lingerie fine** fine lingerie; **des souliers fins** elegant shoes; **un repas f.** a choice *or* exquisite meal; **fines herbes** mixed herbs, fines herbes; **épicerie fine** delicatessen

3 *(expert)* fine; **f. connaisseur de vins** fine judge of wine; **f. tireur** crack shot; **fine lame** fine swordsman; **f. stratège** fine *or* expert strategist; **fine cuisinière** gourmet cook; **avoir l'ouïe fine** to have sharp ears *or* an acute ear *or* a keen ear; **avoir le nez f.** to have a keen sense of smell; *Fig* **elle a le nez f.** she's sharp

4 *(subtil)* subtle; **une fine mouche** a sharp customer; **fine ironie** subtle irony; **il est trop f. pour vous** he's too clever for you; **elle n'est pas très fine, cette jeune femme** that young woman isn't very bright; **bien f. qui le prendra** it would take a smart man to catch him; *Iron* **qu'est-ce que c'est f.!** oh, very funny!

5 **dans le f. fond du hangar/du panier** right at the back of the shed/the bottom of the basket; **au f. fond de la Sibérie** in deepest Siberia; **au f. fond de moi** in my heart of hearts; **le f. mot de l'histoire** the truth of the matter

NM 1 le f. du f. the ultimate **2 jouer au (plus) f.** to have a battle of wits

ADV 1 tout était f. prêt everything was absolutely ready; **être f. soûl** to be blind drunk **2** *(finement)* finely; **café moulu f.** finely ground coffee; **des crayons taillés f.** sharp-pointed pencils

final, -ale, -als, -ales [final] **ADJ 1** final; **point f.** full stop, *Am* period; *Fig* **mettre un point f. à une affaire** to put a stop *or* an end to a matter; **va te coucher, point f.!** bed time! and that's final! **2** *Phil, Gram (cause, proposition)* final

NM 1 *Mus (d'opéra etc)* finale **2 au f.** in the end

finale [final] **NF 1** *Sport* final; **f. de coupe** cup final; **aller/être en f.** to go *or* get through to/to be in the finals **2** *Ling (de mot)* final *or* end syllable

NM *Mus (d'opéra etc)* finale

finalement [finalmɑ̃] **ADV** in the end, finally

finaliser [finalize] **VT** to finalize

finaliste [finalist] **ADJ, N** finalist

finalité [finalite] **NF** *(objectif)* aim, objective; *Phil* finality; *Biol* adaptation

finance [finɑ̃s] **NF 1** finance; **monde de la f.** financial world, world of finance; **la haute f.** high finance; *(le milieu)* the financiers, the bankers; **être dans la f.** to be in finance; **f. d'entreprise** corporate finance; *Fam* **faire qch moyennant f.** to do sth for a consideration *or* for a fee **2 finances** finances; **nos finances sont mal en point** our finances are in bad shape; **lois de finances** financial laws; **ministre des Finances** minister of Finance, *Br* ≃ Chancellor of the Exchequer, *Am* ≃ Secretary of the Treasury; **le Ministère des Finances** the Treasury

financement [finɑ̃smɑ̃] **NM** financing, funding; *(surtout d'un mécène)* (financial) backing; **f. à court terme** short-term financing; **f. par endettement** debt financing; **f. initial** start-up capital; **f. à long terme** long-term financing; **f. à moyen terme** medium-term financing

financement-relais, *pl* **financements-relais NM** *Fin* bridge financing

financer [finɑ̃se] **VT** (**je finançai(s), n. finançons**) to finance, to fund; *(surtout d'un mécène)* to back, to put up the money for; **BP financera le projet à 50%** BP will put up half of the funding for the project; **l'opération a été entièrement financée par emprunt** the transaction was 100% financed through borrowing

financier, -ière [finɑ̃sje, -jɛr] **ADJ** financial; **avoir des problèmes financiers** to be in financial *or Fml* pecuniary difficulties; **crise financière** financial crisis; **le marché f.** the money market; *Culin* **sauce financière** = white sauce containing small pieces of sweetbread, dumplings and mushrooms

NM financier; **f. d'entreprise** corporate finance manager

financièrement [finɑ̃sjɛrmɑ̃] **ADV** financially

finasser [finase] **VI** to resort to trickery

finasserie [finasri] **NF** trick

finasseur, -euse [finasœr, -øz], **finassier, -ière** [finasje, -jɛr] **N** *Vieilli* trickster

finaud, -aude [fino, -od] **ADJ** wily, cunning **N** crafty devil

finauderie [finodri] **NF** trickery

fine [fin] **NF** liqueur brandy; **une f. à l'eau** = a brandy and soda

finement [finmɑ̃] **ADV 1** *(délicatement)* finely, delicately **2** *(subtilement)* *(analyser, apprécier)* subtly; **elle avait f. prévu ce coup-là** she had shrewdly *or* cleverly foreseen that that would happen

finesse [fines] **NF 1** *(d'un tissu)* fineness; *(d'exécution)* delicacy; *(du sable)* fineness; *(de taille)* slenderness, slimness **2** *(subtilité)* subtlety; **f. d'ouïe/de l'odorat** keenness *or* acuteness of hearing/of smell; **f. de goût** good taste; **f. d'esprit** shrewdness; **discours plein de f.** speech full of subtlety *or* finesse;

elle a beaucoup de f. she's very shrewd; **parodie pleine de f.** clever *or* subtle parody; **finesses d'un métier** niceties *or* subtleties *or* fine points of a craft; **il connaît toutes les finesses du métier** he knows all the tricks of the trade **3** *(d'une pointe, d'une image optique ou d'une lame)* keenness

finette [finɛt] **NF** *Tex* brushed cotton

fini [fini] **ADJ 1** *(terminé)* finished, over; **c'est f. (tout cela), tout est f.** that's all over (and done with); **c'est f. entre nous** we're finished, it's all over between us; **(c'est) f. de rire** the fun's over; **c'en est un homme f.** he's finished, he's done for **2** *(ouvrage)* well finished; **cette robe est mal finie** this dress is badly finished; *Péj* **un idiot f.** a complete idiot; **un alcoolo/voleur f.** an out-and-out drunkard/thief **3** *(espace, temps, nombre)* finite

NM 1 *(d'un produit manufacturé)* finish **2 le f. et l'infini** the finite and the infinite

finir [finir] **VT** *(tâche, études, conversation etc)* to finish; *(vie)* to end; **f. un tableau/une sculpture** to finish (off) a picture/sculpture; **tu as fini ton assiette?** have you finished what's on your plate?; **ils ont fini la soirée au poste** the evening ended with them in the police station; **je vais f. ces chaussures** I'll wear these shoes out

VI to end, to finish; **quand est-ce que ça finit?** when does it end *or* finish?; **comment est-ce que ça a fini?** how did it end?; **à quelle heure tu finis?** what time do you finish?; **f. en pointe** to end *or* terminate in a point; **une histoire qui finit bien/mal** a story with a happy/sad ending; **tout est bien qui finit bien** all's well that ends well; **il finira mal** he'll come to a bad end; **ça va mal f. tout ça!** no good will come of all that!, it will all end in disaster!; **l'histoire ne finit pas là** that's not the end of the story; **f. à l'hôpital/dans un fossé** to end up *or* finish up in hospital/a ditch; **en f. avec qn/qch** to be *or* have done with sb/sth; **il faut en f. avec ces idées reçues** we must break with *or* shake off these preconceived ideas; **je voudrais en f.** I want to get it over (with); **il voulait en f. (avec la vie)** he wanted to put an end to it all *or* to end it all; **vous n'avez pas encore fini tous les deux!** are you two still at it!; *Fam* **c'est pas bientôt fini, ce bordel?** is this racket going to stop soon?; **cela n'en finit pas** there's no end to it; **il n'en finit plus de se préparer dans la salle de bain** he takes ages in the bathroom getting ready; **pour f.** to cut a long story short; **histoires/ennuis à n'en plus f.** endless *or* interminable stories/problems; **et pour f., voici le dessert** and to finish (with), here's dessert; **cette route n'en finit pas** this road seems to go on (and on) for ever; **elle a des jambes à n'en plus f.** she has incredibly long legs; **f. de faire qch** to finish doing sth; **f. par faire qch** to end up (by) doing sth; **tu vas f. par le faire pleurer** you'll end up (by) making him cry; **elle finira par t'oublier/s'y habituer** she'll forget you/get used to it in the end *or* eventually; **la justice finit par triompher** justice triumphs in the end *or* in the long run *or* eventually; **tout finit toujours par arriver** everything comes to those who wait

finish [finiʃ] **NM** *Sport (fin)* finish; *(impulsion finale)* finish, final burst; **il a un bon f.** he has a strong finish; *Fig* **on l'a eu au f.** we got him in the end

finissage [finisaʒ] **NM** *Ind* finishing (off)

finissant [finisɑ̃] **ADJ** finishing; *(société)* in decline; **le jour f.** dusk, twilight

finisseur, -euse [finisœr, -øz] **N** *Ind, Sport* finisher

finition [finisjɔ̃] **NF** finishing; *(résultat)* finish; **les finitions** the finishing touches; *Cou-*

ture **les finitions sont très soignées** it's very well finished; *Tricot* **je déteste faire les finitions** I hate the sewing up

finlandais, -aise [fɛ̃lɑ̃dɛ, -ɛz] VOIR GRAMMAIRE A19 ADJ Finnish
  N F. Finn

Finlande [fɛ̃lɑ̃d] NF Finland

finnois [finwa] VOIR GRAMMAIRE A19 ADJ Finnish
  NM *Ling* Finnish

finno-ougrien, -ienne [finougrijɛ̃, -jɛn] *Ling* ADJ Finno-Ugric
  NM Finno-Ugric

fiole [fjɔl] NF **1** *(flacon)* phial, flask **2** *Arg (tête)* nut, *Br* bonce; *(visage)* mug; **se payer la f. de qn** to make a fool of sb

fion [fjɔ̃] NM **1** *Arg Vulg* arse, *Am* ass **2** *Can, Suisse* **lancer des fions à qn** to taunt sb

fiord [fjɔr] NM *Géog* fjord, fiord

fioriture [fjɔrityr] NF *(d'une écriture)* flourish; *(du style)* embellishment; *Mus* fioritura, ornament, embellishment; **une lettre pleine de fioritures** a flowery letter

fiotte [fjɔt] NF *Vulg* queer, *Br* poof, *Am* fag

fioul [fjul] NM fuel oil

FIP [fip] *(abrév* **France Inter Paris)** = French radio station broadcasting mainly light music

firmament [firmamɑ̃] NM *Litt* firmament

firme [firm] NF firm VOIR GRAMMAIRE A11

firmware [fœrmwɛr] NM *Ordinat* firmware

FIS [fis] NM *(abrév* **Front islamique du salut)** **le F.** the FIS, the Islamique Salvation Front

fisc [fisc] NM *Admin* tax department ≃ Inland Revenue, *Am* ≃ Internal Revenue; **avoir des ennuis avec le f.** to have problems with the taxman

fiscal, -ale, -aux, -ales [fiskal, -o] ADJ fiscal; **l'administration fiscale** the tax(ation) authorities; **timbre f.** revenue stamp; **fraude/évasion fiscale** tax evasion/avoidance; **paradis f.** tax haven; **abri f.** tax shelter

fiscalement [fiskalmɑ̃] ADV from a tax point of view, fiscally

fiscalisation [fiskalizasjɔ̃] NF taxing, taxation

fiscaliser [fiskalize] VT to tax

fiscaliste [fiskalist] N tax specialist

fiscalité [fiskalite] NF tax system; **f. directe** direct taxation; **f. écologique** green taxation; **f. indirecte** indirect taxation; **f. locale** local taxation; **f. des entreprises** corporate taxation; **optimiser la f. de qch** to improve the tax efficiency of sth, to make sth more tax efficient

fissa [fisa] ADV *Fam* **faire f.** to get a move on, to get one's skates on

fissible [fisibl] ADJ *Phys* fissionable, fissile

fissile [fisil] ADJ **1** = fissible **2** *(roche)* fissile, tending to split

fission [fisjɔ̃] NF *Nucl* fission; **f. de l'atome** atomic fission, splitting of the atom

fissuration [fisyrasjɔ̃] NF cracking, fissuring

fissure [fisyr] NF crack, fissure; *Fig (entre amis)* split; **les fissures du mur** the cracks in the wall; **cette dispute provoqua une f. dans notre amitié** this quarrel caused a rift in our friendship

fissurer [fisyre] VT to crack, to fissure; *Fig* to split (up)
  VPR **se fissurer** to crack, to fissure; *Fig* to split (up)

fiston [fistɔ̃] NM *Fam* son, lad; **allons (mon) f.!** now then, young fellow *or* my lad *or* sonny!

fistule [fistyl] NF *Méd* fistula

fistuleux, -euse [fistylø, -øz] ADJ *Méd* fistulous

FIV [ɛfive] NF *Biol (abrév* **fécondation in vitro)** IVF

fivète [fivɛt] NF *Biol* in vitro fertilization

fixage [fiksaʒ] NM **1** *Phot* fixing; **bain de f.** fixing bath **2** *Bourse* fixing

fixateur, -trice [fiksatœr, -tris] NM *(de teintures)* fixer; *Phot* fixer, fixing solution *or* bath; *Biol* fixative; *(pour cheveux)* hair spray, lacquer
  ADJ **bactéries fixatrices d'azote** nitrogen-fixing bacteria

fixatif [fiksatif] NM *(pour dessins)* fixative

fixation [fiksasjɔ̃] NF **1** *(de date)* fixing; **f. de prix** price setting *ou* fixing, pricing; **f. d'un prix d'appel** loss-leader pricing; **f. d'un prix de soumission** sealed-bid pricing; **f. de l'impôt** tax assessment; **f. du prix en fonction du coût** cost-plus pricing; **f. du prix en fonction du taux de rentabilité souhaité** target-return pricing; **f. du prix optimal** optimal pricing; **f. du prix unitaire** unit pricing **2** *(d'étagère etc)* fixing; *(de sables mouvants), Chimie (d'azote)* fixation; **f. par bride** *ou* **par collier** clamping; **vis de f.** fixing screw, set screw; **patte de f.** anchor(ing) clip **3** *Tech* attachment, anchor; *Ski* (ski) binding **4** *Psy* fixation (**à qn** on sb); **faire une f. sur qch/qn** to become obsessed with *or* fixated on sth/sb

fixe [fiks] ADJ **1** *(immobile)* fixed; **idée f.** obsession, idée fixe; **regard f.** fixed *or* steady gaze; **grue f.** fixed *or* stationary crane; **essieu f.** dead axle; *Mil* **f.!** attention! **2** *(arrêté)* fixed; **prix f.** fixed *or* set price; **à prix f.** at fixed prices; **frais fixes** fixed costs; **traitement f.** fixed salary; **adresse f.** permanent address; **sans domicile f.** of no fixed abode; **prendre ses repas à heure f.** to eat at fixed *or* set times; *Ordinat* **disque f.** fixed disk; **beau (temps) f.** set fair (weather); **arrêt f.** compulsory stop
  NM **1** *(salaire)* fixed salary; **toucher un f.** to be on a fixed salary **2** *Fam (de drogue)* fix

fixé [fikse] ADJ **1** *(date, heure, jour)* agreed, appointed; **à la date fixée** on the agreed *or* appointed day **2** **être f. sur qch** to have made up one's mind about sth; **je ne suis pas f.** I haven't made my mind up yet; **eh bien, maintenant, tu es f.** well, now you know

fixe-chaussettes [fiks(ə)ʃosɛt] NM INV suspender, *Am* garter

fixement [fiksəmɑ̃] ADV fixedly; **regarder f. qch** to stare at sth

fixer [fikse] VT **1** *(immobiliser)* to fix; **les vis qui fixent la serrure** the screws that hold the lock; *Fig* **f. qch dans sa mémoire** to implant sth in one's memory; **f. l'attention de qn** to hold *or* engage sb's attention; **f. son attention sur qch** to fix *or* focus one's attention on sth; **f. les yeux sur qch/qn** to fix one's eyes on sth/sb, to gaze *or* stare at sth/sb; *(scruter)* to look hard *or* intently at sth/sb; **f. qn (du regard)** to stare at sb; **ça va le f.** that will make him settle down
  2 *Chimie, Phot* to fix
  3 *(déterminer) (date, heure, jour)* to fix, to set, to arrange; *(rendez-vous)* to fix, to arrange; *(dommages, taxes)* to fix, to set; *(conditions, règlements)* to fix, to lay down; **f. un salaire** to fix a salary; **f. le prix de** to price; **f. un prix** to set a price, to fix a price; *Bourse* **f. un cours** to make a price
  4 **f. qn sur qch** to put sb in the picture about sth
  VPR **se fixer 1** *(s'installer)* to settle down **2** *(s'arrêter)* to become fixed; **l'orthographe du mot se fixa au XVIIIᵉ siècle** the spelling of the word became fixed in the 18th century; **se f. un objectif** to set oneself a target; **elle s'est fixée sur cette idée** she's got the idea

in her head (and nothing will shift it); **il s'est fixé sur ce type d'écran** he has gone for *or* decided on this type of screen

fixette [fikset] NF *Fam* **faire une f. sur qn/qch** to be obsessed with sb/sth, *Br* to have sb/sth on the brain

fixeur [fiksœr] NM *Bourse* **f. de prix** price maker

fixisme [fiksism] NM *Biol* creationism

fixité [fiksite] NF *(du regard)* fixity, steadiness

fjord [fjɔr(d)] NM *Géog* fjord, fiord

flac [flak] NM, INT plop; **faire f.** to plop

flaccidité [flaksidite] NF flabbiness, flaccidity

flacon [flakɔ̃] NM small (stoppered) bottle; *(de laboratoire)* flask; **f. à parfum** perfume bottle; **f. à liqueur** liqueur decanter

fla-fla [flafla] NM *Fam* show, ostentation; **faire du f.** to show off

flagada [flagada] ADJ INV *Fam* washed out, all in, dead beat

flagellation [flaʒelasjɔ̃] NF flogging, whipping; *(sur soi-même)* flagellation

flagelle [flaʒɛl] NM *Biol* flagellum

flagellé [flaʒele] ADJ, NM *Biol* flagellate

flageller [flaʒele] VT to flog, to whip
  VPR **se flageller** to scourge oneself

flageolant [flaʒɔlɑ̃] ADJ shaking, trembling; **j'ai les jambes flageolantes** my legs are shaking *or* trembling

flageoler [flaʒɔle] VI *(des jambes)* to shake, to tremble; **elle flageole sur ses jambes** *(de peur)* she is shaking at the knees; *(de fatigue)* she's dead on her feet

flageolet¹ [flaʒɔle] NM *Mus* flageolet

flageolet² NM *Bot, Culin* flageolet (bean)

flagorner [flagɔrne] VT *Péj* to fawn on, to toady to

flagornerie [flagɔrnəri] NF *Péj* fawning, toadying

flagorneur, -euse [flagɔrnœr, -øz] N *Péj* toady, sycophant

flagrant [flagrɑ̃] ADJ *(injustice, mensonge etc)* flagrant, blatant; **pris en f. délit** caught in the act, caught red-handed; **pris en f. délit de mensonge** caught (out) lying; *Fam* **c'est f.!** it's (glaringly) obvious!

flair [flɛr] NM **1** *(des chiens)* scent, (sense of) smell, nose **2** *(d'une personne)* intuition; **avoir du f.** to have good intuition

flairer [flere] VT **1** *(d'un chien) (gibier)* to scent, to smell (out), to nose out; *Fig* **f. le danger** to scent *or* smell *or* sense danger; **f. le mensonge** to detect a lie; **f. que** to sense that **2** *(sentir)* to smell **3** *Belg Fam Péj (empester)* to stink *or* to reek of

flamand, -ande [flamɑ̃, -ɑ̃d] ADJ Flemish
  NM *Ling* Flemish
  N F. Fleming

flamant [flamɑ̃] NM flamingo; **f. rose** pink flamingo VOIR GRAMMAIRE A12

flambage [flɑ̃baʒ] NM **1** *(des cheveux, d'un poulet etc)* singeing; *(d'une aiguille)* sterilization; *(d'un bûcher)* charring **2** *(d'une plaque de métal)* buckling, collapse

flambant [flɑ̃bɑ̃] ADV **1 f. neuf** brand new *Can Fam (complètement)* completely, totally; **f. nu** stark naked, starkers
  ADJ **1** *(bûche, soleil)* blazing, flaming **2** **houille flambante** bituminous *or* soft coal
  NM bituminous *or* soft coal

flambard [flɑ̃bar] NM *Fam* **faire le f.** to show off

flambé [flɑ̃be] ADJ **1** *Culin* flambé(ed) **2** *Fam* **il est f.** he's done for, his goose is cooked

flambeau, -eaux [flɑ̃bo] NM **1** *(torche)* torch; **descente/retraite aux flambeaux**

torch-lit descent/procession; **à la lueur des flambeaux, aux flambeaux** by torchlight; *Fig* **reprendre le f.** to take up the torch; *Fig* **passer le f. aux futures générations** to hand on the torch to future generations **2** (*chandelier*) candlestick

flambée [flɑbe] NF **1** (*feu*) blaze, blazing fire; **faire une f. dans la cheminée** to light a fire in the hearth **2** *Fig* (*de violence*) flare-up, outbreak; (*des prix*) upsurge, escalation; (*de colère*) outburst

flambement [flɑbmɑ] NM (*d'une plaque de métal*) buckling, collapse

flamber [flɑbe] VI **1** (*brûler*) to blaze; **f. comme une allumette** to burn like matchwood **2** (*prix*) to escalate **3** (*d'une barre de métal etc*) to buckle, to collapse

▸ VT (*cheveux, volaille etc*) to singe; *Culin* flambé; **f. une aiguille** to sterilize a needle (in a flame); *Fig* **elle a flambé l'argent du ménage au jeu** she gambled away *or* blew the housekeeping money; **c'est fou ce qu'elle flambe comme argent** it's crazy the amount of money she throws away!

flambeur [flɑbœr] NM *Arg* big-time gambler

flamboiement [flɑbwamɑ] NM blazing, blaze

flamboyant [flɑbwajɑ] ADJ **1** (*feu*) blazing; (*yeux*) blazing, flashing **2** *Archit* flamboyant

flamboyer [flɑbwaje] VI (*il flamboie*) (*du feu*) to blaze; **f. de colère** (*des yeux*) to blaze *or* flash with anger

flamingant, -ante [flamɛgɑ, -ɑt] ADJ (*ville, personne*) Flemish-speaking
▸ N *Pol* Flemish nationalist

flamme [flam] NF **1** (*de feu*) flame; **en flammes** on fire, ablaze; **dévoré par les flammes** consumed by flames; **retour de f.** (*d'une arme*) back flash; *Tech* backfire, backfiring; *Fig* backlash; **passer à la f.** to singe **2** *Litt* (*amour*) passion, love; **déclarer à une femme** to declare one's love for a woman **3** (*enthousiasme*) fire, enthusiasm; **discours plein de f.** fiery speech **4** (*drapeau*) pennant, streamer **5** (*sur lettre*) (*marque postale*) slogan

flammèche [flamɛʃ] NF spark

flan [flɑ] NM **1** *Culin* (baked) custard; (*tarte*) custard pie; **f. chimique** *ou* **en poudre** custard powder **2** (*d'une pièce, d'un disque etc*) blank **3** *Typ* flong, mould, *Am* mold **4** *Fig* **en rester** *ou* **en être comme deux ronds de f.** to be flabbergasted; *Fam* **c'est du f.** it's rubbish!; *Fam* **j'ai dit ça au f.** I said it just for the sake of it *or* just for something to say; *Fam* **y aller au f.** to try it on, to bluff

flanc [flɑ] NM (*d'un animal*) side, flank; (*d'une personne*) side; (*d'un pneu*) wall, profile, side wall; **route à f. de coteau** road following the hillside; **être sur le f.** (*malade*) to be laid up; (*épuisé*) to be quite worn out; **ces difficultés l'ont mise sur le f.** these problems really took it out of her; **battre des flancs** (*d'un cheval*) to heave, to pant; *Mil* **par le f. droit!** by the right!; **attaquer de f.** to attack on the flank; **le navire se présentait de f.** the ship was broadside on; **prêter le f. à la critique** to lay oneself open to criticism; *Fam* **tirer au f.** to shirk, *Br* to skive

flancher [flɑʃe] VI *Fam* (*faiblir*) to give in, to weaken; **ce n'est pas le moment de f.!** don't give in now!; **son cœur a flanché** his heart gave out; **sans f.** without flinching

flanchet [flɑʃe] NM *Culin* flank

Flandre [flɑdr] NF Flanders

flandrin [flɑdrɛ] NM *Arch Fam* **grand f.** gangling *or* gangly fellow

flanelle [flanɛl] NF *Tex* flannel; **f. (de) coton** flannelette; **pantalon de f. grise** grey flannels; *Fam* **il devrait mettre sa f.** he ought to wear his jacket

flâner [flɑne, flane] VI **1** (*se promener*) to stroll, to saunter **2** (*perdre son temps*) to hang about; **perdre son temps à f.** to idle away one's time

flânerie [flɑnri, flanri] NF (*balade*) strolling; (*oisiveté*) idling

flâneur, -euse [flɑnœr, flanœr, -øz] ADJ idle
▸ N **1** (*promeneur*) stroller **2** (*oisif*) idler, loafer

flanquer[1] [flɑke] VT (*bâtiment*), *Mil* (*colonne, ennemi*) to flank; **flanqué de deux agents** flanked by two policemen

flanquer[2] *Fam* VT (*jeter*) to chuck, to fling, to throw; **f. une gifle/un coup de pied à qn** to give sb a slap/kick; **f. qn à la porte** *ou* **dehors** to throw sb out; (*licencier*) to fire sb, *Br* to sack sb; **f. la trouille** *ou* **les jetons à qn** to give sb the jitters, to put the wind up sb
▸ VPR **se flanquer se f. par terre** to come a cropper, to take a tumble; **elle s'est flanquée dans le ravin** she plunged into the ravine

flapi [flapi] ADJ *Fam* dead beat, fagged out

flaque [flak] NF puddle; **f. de sang** pool of blood

flash, *pl* **flashes** [flaʃ] NM **1** *Phot* flash(light); **prendre une photo au f.** to take a picture using a flash **2** *Cin* flash; **f. publicitaire** commercial **3** *TV, Radio* newsflash; **f. d'informations** newsflash; *TV, Radio* **f. spécial** (special) newsflash

flashant [flaʃɑ] ADJ *Fam* flashy

flash-back [flaʃbak] NM INV flashback; **faire un f.** to flash back

flasher [flaʃe] VI *Fam* **f. sur qch/qn** to really fall for sth/sb

flasque[1] [flask] ADJ (*chair*) flabby, flaccid; (*style*) limp; (*chapeau*) floppy

flasque[2] NF flask

flasque[3] NM *Mil* (*d'un affût de canon*) cheek; *Aut* hubcap, wheel disc; (*d'une roue*) flange

flatter [flate] VT **1** (*complimenter*) to flatter; **f. qn sur son bel esprit** to flatter sb on his wit; **je suis flatté de votre proposition** I am flattered by your proposal

2 (*avantager*) **cette coupe ne la flatte pas** that style doesn't flatter her; **peintre qui flatte ses modèles** painter who flatters his sitters

3 (*plaire*) (*l'oreille*) to delight, to be pleasing to, to please; **spectacle qui flatte les yeux** sight that is pleasing to the eye; **plat/vin qui flatte le palais** dish/wine that delights the taste buds *or* the palate; **f. les caprices de qn** to pander to *or* humour *or* indulge sb's whims

4 (*tromper*) to delude; **f. qn de l'espoir de qch** to hold out false hopes of sth to sb

5 (*animal*) to stroke, to caress; **f. un cheval** to pat a horse

▸ VPR **se flatter** to flatter oneself, to delude oneself; **elle se flattait de réussir** she flattered herself *or* felt sure that she would succeed; **il se flatte qu'on a** *ou* **ait besoin de lui** he flatters himself that he is indispensable; **se flatte de son habileté** to congratulate oneself on one's cleverness; **se f. d'avoir fait qch** to pride oneself on having done sth; **à ta place, je ne m'en flatterais pas** if I was in your place it's not something I'd be proud of

flatterie [flatri] NF flattery; **ce ne sont que de viles flatteries** it's just base flattery

flatteur, -euse [flatœr, -øz] ADJ (*remarque, portrait, couleur*) flattering; (*personne*) full of flattery; **peu f.** unflattering; **il a fait un tableau f. de la situation** he painted a rosy picture of the situation
▸ N flatterer

flatulence [flatylɑs] NF *Méd* flatulence; **avoir des flatulences** to suffer from flatulence

flatulent [flatylɑ] ADJ *Méd* flatulent

flatuosité [flatɥozite] NF wind; *Méd* flatus

FLE [flə] NM (*abrév* **français langue étrangère**) French as a foreign language

fléau, -aux [fleo] NM **1** (*calamité*) scourge, curse; *Fig* plague, pest, bane; *Fam* **c'est un vrai f.!** he's/it's a real pain! **2** (*à céréales*) flail **3** (*d'une balance*) beam, arm

fléchage [fleʃaʒ] NM (*de direction*) signposting

flèche[1] [flɛʃ] NF **1** (*projectile*) arrow; **pistolet à flèches** dart gun; **fer de f.** arrowhead; **faire f. de tout bois** to use all available means, to use all means at one's disposal; **partir en** *ou* **comme une f.** (*d'une personne*) to shoot off; **monter en f.** (*d'un avion*) to shoot (straight) up; (*des prix*) to shoot up, to rocket; *Fig* **elle lui a décoché des flèches méchantes** she let fly a few barbed remarks in his direction; **je ne supporte plus ses petites flèches** I can't stand his digs at me any longer

2 (*de direction*) arrow; **suivre les flèches** to follow the arrows; **f. lumineuse** pointer; (*de sortie de secours etc*) luminous arrow; *Aut* **f. de direction** trafficator

3 **chevaux attelés en f.** horses driven tandem; **cheval de f.** leader, leading horse

4 (*d'une église*) spire

5 (*d'une grue*) jib, boom

6 *Naut* (*d'un mât*) pole; (*d'un cutter*) topsail

7 *Archit* (*d'une arche*) rise; *Aviat* (*d'un plan à profil d'aile*) camber

8 (*d'un câble*) sag, dip

9 *Ordinat* **f. de défilement** scroll arrow; **f. vers la droite** right arrow; **f. vers la gauche** left arrow; **f. vers le bas** down arrow; **f. vers le haut** up arrow; **flèches verticales** up and down arrow keys

flèche[2] NF (*de lard*) flitch

flèche[3] NM *Fam* **j'ai pas un f.** I'm totally broke

flécher [fleʃe] VT (*route, direction*) to arrow; **itinéraire fléché** arrowed *or* signposted route

fléchette [fleʃɛt] NF dart; **jouer aux fléchettes** to play darts VOIR GRAMMAIRE A10

fléchi [fleʃi] ADJ *Ling* **forme fléchie** inflected form

fléchir [fleʃir] VT **1** (*bras, jambe*) to bend, to flex; **f. le genou devant qn** to bend *or* bow the knee to sb **2** (*émouvoir*) to sway; **se laisser f.** to let oneself be swayed

▸ VI **1** (*se ployer*) to bend; (*des jambes, troupes etc*) to give way; (*d'un câble, d'une poutre*) to sag **2** (*diminuer*) (*de prix*) to fall; **les prix fléchissent** prices are falling, prices are coming down; **le dollar fléchit** the dollar is weakening *or* falling; **son autorité fléchit** his authority is weakening; **elle n'a pas fléchi** she didn't give in *or* yield

fléchissement [fleʃismɑ] NM **1** (*du genou etc*) bending; (*d'une poutre etc*) yielding, bending; (*d'un câble etc*) sagging **2** (*des prix*) falling, drop; (*des devises*) weakening; *Bourse* **f. des cours** fall *or* drop in share prices

fléchisseur [fleʃisœr] ADJ, NM *Anat* (muscle) **f.** flexor

flegmatique [flɛgmatik] ADJ phlegmatic, imperturbable

flegmatiquement [flɛgmatikmɑ] ADV phlegmatically, imperturbably

flegme [flɛgm] NM **1** (*imperturbabilité*) phlegm, imperturbability; **faire perdre son f. à qn** to make sb lose their composure *or* *Fam* cool; **le f. britannique** British phlegm **2** *Méd* phlegm

flémingite [flemɛʒit] NF *Fam* total laziness; **il fait de la f. aiguë** he's being bone idle

flemmard, -arde [flɛmar, -rd] N *Fam* lazy sod *or* so-and-so

flemmarder [flemarde] VI *Fam* to lounge about; **f. au lit** to laze in bed

flemmardise [flemardiz] NF *Fam* laziness, idleness

flemme [flɛm] NF *Fam* laziness, idleness, slacking; **j'ai la f. de le faire** I can't be bothered to do it; **tirer sa f.** to lounge about

flet [flɛ] NM flounder

flétan [fletɑ̃] NM halibut

flétri [fletri] ADJ withered

flétrir[1] [fletrir] VT *(peau)* to wither; *(couleurs etc)* to fade; *(plantes)* to wither (up), to wilt ▶ **VPR se flétrir** *(des plantes)* to wither, to wilt; *(de la peau)* to wither

flétrir[2] VT 1 *(crime)* to stigmatize; *Hist (criminel)* to brand 2 *(la réputation de qn)* to blacken, to sully, to stain

flétrissure[1] [fletrisyr] NF withering

flétrissure[2] NF *(déshonneur)* stain, blemish

fleur [flœr] NF 1 *Bot* flower; *(d'arbre)* blossom, bloom; **arbre en fleur(s)** tree in blossom *or* in flower *or* in bloom; **fleurs des champs** wild flowers; **fleurs en pot** flowering pot plant; **ni fleurs, ni couronnes** ≃ no flowers by request; **envoyer des fleurs à qn** to send sb flowers; *Fig* to pat sb on the back; **f. artificielle/en papier** artificial/paper flower; **tissu à fleurs** flowered *or* flowery material; *Fig* **faire une f. à qn** to do sb a favour; *Fig* **elle le couvre de fleurs** she heaps praise (up)on him; **être f. bleue** to be (naively) romantic; *Fam* **elle y est arrivée comme une f.** she managed it without a hitch *or* a problem 2 *Fig Litt* **dans** *ou* **à la f. de l'âge** in the prime of life; **dans la première f. de la jeunesse** in the first flush *or* flower of youth; **la fine f. de la société** the cream of society 3 *(d'antimoine, de vin etc)* fleurs flowers 4 **à f. de** on the surface of; **à f. d'eau** just above (the surface of) the water; **voler à f. d'eau** to skim the water; **émotions à f. de peau** skin-deep emotions; **avoir les nerfs à f. de peau** to be all on edge 5 *(d'une peau)* hair side, grain side 6 **f. de farine** top-quality flour

fleurage [flœraʒ] NM *(sur un tissu, tapis)* floral pattern

fleurdelisé [flœrdəlize] ADJ decorated with fleurs-de-lis; *Hér* fleury ▶ NM *Can (drapeau du Québec)* flag of Quebec

fleurer [flœre] VT *Litt* to smell of; **f. la violette** to smell of violets; *Fig* **ça fleure l'intrigue/les pots-de-vin** it smacks of a plot/of bribery, I/he/etc can smell a plot/bribery

fleuret [flœrɛ] NM *(épée)* foil; *Min* borer

fleurette [flœrɛt] NF 1 **conter f. à qn** to whisper sweet nothings to sb 2 **crème f.** ≃ single cream

fleuri [flœri] ADJ 1 *(en fleurs)* in bloom, in flower, in blossom; *(orné de fleurs) (tissu, robe)* flowered, flowery; *(vaisselle)* flower-patterned; **village f.** ≃ village taking part in a flower competition; **avoir la boutonnière fleurie** to have a flower in one's buttonhole; *(décoré)* to wear a decoration 2 *(sentier etc)* flowery; *(teint)* florid; *(style)* flowery, florid

fleurir [flœrir] *(prp* **fleurissant**, *Litt* **florissant**; *impf* **il fleurissait**, *Litt* **il florissait)** VI 1 *(des plantes)* to flower, to bloom, to blossom 2 *(l'art, du commerce etc)* *(usu* **florissant**, **florissait)** to blossom, to flourish, to prosper ▶ VT *(table)* to decorate with flowers; *(boutonnière)* to put a flower in; *(tombe)* to lay flowers on

fleuriste [flœrist] N 1 *(commerçant)* florist, flower seller 2 *(horticulteur)* flower grower 3 *(de fleurs artificielles)* artificial flower maker

fleuron [flœrɔ̃] NM 1 *(ornement)* flower, fleuron; *Archit* finial; **c'est le plus beau f. de no-**

tre collection it's the jewel in our collection 2 *Bot* floret

fleuve [flœv] NM river *(as opposed to tributary)*; **f. (côtier)** short coastal river; *Fig* **un f. de sang/de larmes** a river of blood/a flood of tears; **des fleuves de boue** rivers of mud ▶ ADJ INV **roman-f.** saga; **discours-f.** lengthy speech

flexibilité [flɛksibilite] NF flexibility; *(de matériaux)* pliability; *(du corps)* flexibility, suppleness, litheness; *Fin (d'une entreprise, de la main-d'œuvre)* flexibility

flexible [flɛksibl] ADJ 1 *(souple)* flexible, supple; *(matériaux)* pliable; **tuyau f.** hose(-pipe) 2 *(adaptable) (personne)* flexible; *(disposition)* accommodating; *(malléable)* pliable, pliant; **avoir des horaires flexibles** to work flexible hours, to be on flexitime ▶ NM *(tuyau)* hose(pipe); *Élec* flexible lead, *Br* flex; *Aut* **f. de frein** brake hose

flexion [flɛksjɔ̃] NF 1 *(fléchissement)* flexion, bending; *Gym* **f. du corps** trunk exercise; *Tech* **effort de f.** bending stress 2 *(d'une tige)* buckling, collapse 3 *Ling (de mot)* inflexion; **langue à flexions** inflected language

flexionnel, -elle [flɛksjɔnɛl] ADJ *Ling* inflected; **langue flexionnelle** inflected language

flibuste [flibyst] NF *Hist (piraterie)* buccaneering, freebooting; *(pirates)* buccaneers, freebooters

flibustier [flibystje] NM 1 *Hist* buccaneer, freebooter 2 *Arch Fam (escroc)* cheat, crook

flic [flik] NM *Fam (policier)* cop, copper; **voilà les flics!** it's the cops!

flicage [flikaʒ] NM *Fam (par la police)* heavy policing; *Fig* heavy-handed supervision

flicaille [flikaj] NF *Fam* **la f.** the pigs

flic flac NM splish splash; *(d'un fouet)* crack

flingue [flɛ̃g] NM *Fam (arme)* shooter, piece

flinguer [flɛ̃ge] *Fam* VT 1 *(tuer avec une arme à feu)* to gun down 2 *(abîmer)* to wreck, to bust, *Br* to knacker 3 *(critiquer sévèrement)* to shoot down, to savage ▶ VPR **se flinguer** to blow one's brains out; **il n'y a pas de quoi se f.** it's not the end of the world; **c'est à se f.!** it's enough to make you chuck yourself under a train!

flip [flip] NM *Fam* 1 *(déprime)* **être en plein f.** to be on a real downer; **c'est le f.!** what a downer! 2 *(après l'absorption de drogue)* depression, downer *(as the after-effect of taking cocaine or amphetamines)*

flip-flap, *pl* **flips-flaps** [flipflap] NM *Gym* back(ward) flip

flippant [flipɑ̃] ADJ *Fam (déprimant)* grim; *(effrayant)* creepy

flipper[1] [flipœr] NM *(appareil)* pinball (machine); *(jeu)* pinball; **jouer au f.** to play pinball

flipper[2] [flipe] VI *Fam* 1 *(d'un drogué)* to be spaced out 2 *(s'angoisser)* to freak out; **ça me fait f.** that freaks me out; **elle flippe à cause de son travail** her work is freaking her out

fliquer [flike] VT *Fam* to police heavily; **fliqué** overrun with cops; *Fig* **au bureau, on a vraiment l'impression d'être fliqués** in the office we really feel we're being watched like criminals; **il flique complètement sa femme** he watches his wife like a hawk

flirt [flœrt] NM 1 *(amourette)* flirtation, flirting; **ce n'est qu'un f.** I/he/etc was only flirting 2 *Vieilli* **mon f.** my boyfriend/girlfriend; **un de mes anciens flirts** an old flame of mine

flirter [flœrte] VI to flirt; *Fam* **f. avec le danger** to flirt with danger; *Fig* **il flirte avec la police/l'opposition** he's flirting with the police/the opposition

FLN [ɛfɛlɛn] NM *Hist (abrév* **Front de libération nationale)** = national liberation front in Algeria

FLNC [ɛfɛlɛnse] NM *(abrév* **Front de libération national de la Corse)** = Corsican liberation front

FLNKS [ɛfɛlɛnkaɛs] NM *Can (abrév* **Front de libération nationale kanak et socialiste)** = Kanak national liberation front in New Caledonia

flo [flo] N *Can Fam* teenager, *Am* teen

floc [flɔk] INT, NM splash

flocage [flɔkaʒ] NM *Tex* flocking

floche [flɔʃ] ADJ flossy; **soie f.** floss silk

flocon [flɔkɔ̃] NM 1 *(de neige, céréale)* flake; **flocons d'avoine** oat flakes; *Can* **flocons de maïs** cornflakes; **purée en flocons** instant mashed potato 2 *(de laine, coton)* tuft, flock

floconneux, -euse [flɔkɔnø, -øz] ADJ fleecy, fluffy

floculation [flɔkylasjɔ̃] NF *Chimie* flocculation

flonflons [flɔ̃flɔ̃] NMPL tiddly-om-pom-pom

flop [flɔp] NM *Fam* flop; **faire un f.** to be a flop

flopée [flɔpe] NF *Fam* **une f., des flopées** *(d'enfants, de gens)* loads, masses

floquer [flɔke] VT *Tex* to flock

floraison [flɔrɛzɔ̃] NF 1 *(d'arbre)* flowering, blossoming; **l'arbre est en pleine f.** the tree is in full flower *or* blossom 2 *Fig* upsurge (**de** in)

floral, -ale, -aux, -ales [flɔral, -o] ADJ floral; **exposition florale** flower show

floralies [flɔrali] NFPL flower show

flore [flɔr] NF *Bot* flora; *Physiol* **f. intestinale** intestinal flora

floréal [flɔreal] NM *Hist* = eighth month of the French Republican calendar *(April-May)*

florès [flɔrɛs] NM *Litt Vieilli* **faire f.** to prosper

Floride [flɔrid] NF Florida

florifère [flɔrifɛr] ADJ flower-bearing, *Spéc* floriferous; **plante très f.** prolific flowerer

florilège [flɔrilɛʒ] NM anthology

florin [flɔrɛ̃] NM *Anciennement* florin

florissant [flɔrisɑ̃] ADJ *(affaire, pays, peuple)* flourishing, prosperous; *(santé, mine)* blooming; **d'une santé florissante** in the best of health

flot [flo] NM 1 *(marée)* flood (tide); *Litt* **les flots bleus** the ocean blue; **elle s'endormit, bercée par le bruit des flots** she fell asleep, lulled by the sound of the waves 2 *(de larmes)* flood; *(de sang, d'injures)* torrent, stream; *(de gens, voitures)* stream; **un f. de paroles** a torrent *or* flood of words; **entrer à flots** *(de gens, du soleil)* to flood in, to stream in; **f. de dentelle/rubans** cascade of lace/ribbons; **couler à flots** to pour out 3 **être à f.** *(d'un bateau)* to be afloat; *Fig (d'une personne)* to have one's head above water; **mettre un navire à f.** to launch a ship; **remettre un navire à f.** to refloat a ship; **mon compte en banque est à f.** my bank account is in the black *or* in credit; **remettre qn à f.** to put sb back in the black; **ce cours vous permettra de vous remettre à f. en russe** this course will get you going in Russian again *or* will bring your Russian back up to scratch again

flottabilité [flɔtabilite] NF buoyancy; **caisson** *ou* **réservoir de f.** buoyancy tank

flottable [flɔtabl] ADJ 1 *(d'un cours d'eau)* floatable *(for rafts of wood)* 2 *(du bois)* floatable, buoyant

flottage [flɔtaʒ] NM *(de bois)* floating; **bois de f.** raft wood; **train de f.** timber raft

flottaison [flɔtɛzɔ̃] NF floating; *Naut* **(ligne de) f.** waterline; **f. en charge** load line; **f. lège** light waterline

flottant [flɔtã] ADJ **1** (dette, moteur etc) floating; (chiffre) fluctuating; Ordinat **virgule flottante** floating point **2** (toge, cheveux) flowing, loose; **filet f.** drift net **3** (électorat, opinion) undecided, wavering; **électeur f.** floating voter
    NM Bourse float

flotte [flɔt] NF **1** (bateaux) fleet; **f. de ligne ou de combat** battle fleet; **f. de commerce** merchant fleet; **être dans la f.** to be in the navy; **f. aérienne** air fleet; **f. marchande** merchant marine **2** Fam (pluie) (eau) water; **il tombe de la f.** it's pouring with rain; **c'est de la f., ce café!** this coffee's like water!

flottement [flɔtmã] NM **1** (d'une ligne de troupes etc) wavering, swaying; (d'un drapeau) flapping, fluttering; (d'une chaîne, roue) wobble; (d'une devise) fluctuation **2** (hésitation) wavering, hesitation; **il y eut un moment de f.** there was a moment's hesitation; **il y a toujours des flottements dans ses exposés** there are always some uneven patches in his talks

flotter [flɔte] VI **1** (sur l'eau) to float **2** (au vent) to float, to stream; (des cheveux) to stream **3** (hésiter) to waver, to hesitate; (des pensées) to wander; **un sourire flottait sur ses lèvres** a smile played or hovered on his/her lips **4** (des devises) to fluctuate; **faire f.** to float **5** (des vêtements) to hang loosely; **il flotte dans ses vêtements** his clothes are far too big for him, Fam his clothes drown him
    VT **f. du bois** to float timber (down a stream); **bois flotté** driftwood
    V IMPERS Fam **il flotte** it's raining

flotteur [flɔtœr] NM **1** (ouvrier) raftsman (in charge of timber raft) **2** (d'une canne à pêche, d'un hydravion, carburateur etc) float **3** (d'un robinet) ball; **robinet à f.** ballcock

flottille [flɔtij] NF (de bateaux) flotilla; (d'avions) squadron; **f. de pêche** fishing fleet

flou [flu] ADJ (contour, peinture) blurred; (image) blurred, fuzzy, out of focus; (son) muffled, indistinct; (horizon) hazy; (idée) hazy, vague; (cheveux) soft, fluffy; (robe) loose (-fitting)
    NM (d'un contour, d'une image) blur, fuzziness; (d'un son) indistinctness; (de l'horizon) haziness; (d'une idée) haziness, vagueness; (des cheveux) softness, fluffiness; (d'une robe) looseness; **le f. revient à la mode** loose-fitting clothes are back in fashion; **f. artistique** Phot soft-focus effect; Fig deliberate vagueness; **elle a préféré rester dans un f. artistique** she preferred to remain deliberately vague

flouche [fluʃ] N Can Fam teenager

flouer [flue] VT Fam to swindle; **se faire f.** to be swindled, to be done

flouse, flouze [fluz] NM Arg (argent) bread, dough, cash

FLQ [ɛfɛlky] (abrév **franco long du quai**) FAS

fluctuant [flyktɥã] ADJ fluctuating; **un esprit f.** a weathercock; **elle est fluctuante dans ses projets** her plans are liable to change

fluctuation [flyktɥasjɔ̃] NF **1** (changement) fluctuation; **f. des prix** price fluctuation; **f. saisonnière** seasonal fluctuation; Écon **bande ou marge de f.** fluctuation band or margin **2** Élec **fluctuations de tension** voltage fluctuations

fluctuer [flyktɥe] VI to fluctuate

fluent [flɥã] ADJ (sol) flowing, loose; Méd **hémorroïdes fluentes** bleeding piles

fluet, -ette [flyɛ, -ɛt] ADJ (personne) thin, slender; (voix) thin, reedy

fluide [flɥid] ADJ (huile, situation) fluid; (style, pensée) fluid, flowing; **la circulation était f.** the traffic was flowing steadily; **les**

---

accords fluides de la sonate the fluid chords of the sonata
    NM **1** fluid; **f. de nettoyage** cleaning fluid; Aut **f. de frein** brake fluid; **f. aéré** aerated fluid; **f. d'embrayage** clutch fluid; **f. glacial** = ice-cold liquid used by children for pranks; **f. de refroidissement** coolant; **f. moteur** engine fluid; Phys **la mécanique des fluides** fluid mechanics **2** **avoir du f.** (d'un médium) to have strange powers

fluidifier [flɥidifje] VT to thin, to fluidify

fluidité [flɥidite] NF fluidity; **f. de la circulation** steady flow of traffic

fluo [flyo] ADJ INV Fam fluorescent

fluor [flyɔr] NM Chimie fluorine; **dentifrice au f.** fluoride toothpaste; Minér **spath f.** fluorspar

fluoration [flyɔrasjɔ̃] NF (de l'eau) fluoridation

fluoré [flyɔre] ADJ **dentifrice f.** fluoride toothpaste

fluorescence [flyɔresɑ̃s] NF fluorescence

fluorescent [flyɔresɑ̃] ADJ fluorescent; **rose/vert f.** fluorescent pink/green

fluorine [flyɔrin] NF Minér fluorspar

fluorure [flyɔryr] NM Chimie fluoride

flûte [flyt] NF **1** (instrument) flute; **f. à bec** recorder; **f. de Pan** panpipes; **f. traversière, grande f.** concert flute; **petite f.** piccolo **2** (musicien) flautist, flute (player), Am flutist **3** (pain) small French stick; Suisse (biscuit) breadstick **4** (verre) flute; **f. à champagne** champagne flute **5** Fam **flûtes** (jambes) pins; **jouer ou se tirer des flûtes** to show a clean pair of heels
    INT Fam blow!, drat!; **f. alors, il est déjà parti!** blow it or drat it, he's gone already!

flûté [flyte] ADJ **voix flûtée** flute-like or piping voice

flûtiau, -aux [flytjo] NM penny whistle

flûtiste [flytist] N flautist, flute player, Am flutist

fluvial, -iale, -iaux, -iales [flyvjal, -jo] ADJ river attrib fluvial; **police fluviale** river police; **pêche fluviale** river fishing, angling; **alluvions fluviales** fluvial deposits; **port f.** river port

fluviatile [flyvjatil] ADJ **mollusques fluviatiles** river or freshwater molluscs

flux [fly] NM **1** (de mots) flow, stream **2** (marée montante) flow, flood; **le f. et le reflux** the ebb and flow; Pol Fam the swing of the pendulum; Fig **le f. et le reflux des visiteurs** the coming and going of visitors; **f. de fonds** flow of funds; **f. de trésorerie** cashflow; **f. monétaire** cashflow **3** Méd flow, flux; **f. menstruel** menstrual flow **4** Chimie, Métal flux **5** Phys, Élec **f. magnétique** magnetic flux; **f. lumineux** luminous or light flux; **f. électronique** electron flow or stream

fluxion [flyksjɔ̃] NF Méd inflammation; **f. à la joue** swollen cheek; **f. de la gencive** gumboil; **f. de poitrine** pneumonia

FM [ɛfɛm] NF (abrév **modulation de fréquence**) FM

FME [ɛfɛmə] NM (abrév **Fonds monétaire européen**) EMF

FMI [ɛfɛmi] NM (abrév **Fonds monétaire international**) IMF

FN [ɛfɛn] NM (abrév **Front national**) = French extreme right-wing party

FNAC [fnak] NF (abrév **Fédération nationale d'achat des cadres**) = chain of stores selling books, hi-fis, photographic equipment etc

FNE [ɛfɛnə] NM (abrév **Fonds national de l'emploi**) = state fund providing aid to jobseekers and workers who accept lower-paid work to avoid redundancy

---

FNGS [ɛfɛnʒeɛs] NM (abrév **Fonds national de garantie des salaires**) = national guarantee fund for the payment of salaries

FNI [ɛfɛni] NFPL Mil (abrév **forces nucléaires intermédiaires**) INF

FNSEA [ɛfɛnɛsɑa] NF (abrév **Fédération nationale des syndicats d'exploitants agricoles**) farmers' union, Br ≃ NFU

FO [ɛfo] NF (abrév **Force ouvrière**) = French trade union

FOB, fob [ɛfɔbe] ADJ INV, ADV FOB; **vente f.** FOB sale

foc [fɔk] NM Naut jib; **grand f.** main or outer jib; **petit f.** fore staysail; **f. d'artimon** mizzen-topmast staysail

focal, -ale, -aux, -ales [fɔkal, -o] ADJ Math, Opt focal

focalisation [fɔkalizasjɔ̃] NF Opt, Électron focusing; Mktg targeting; Mktg **f. stratégique** strategic targeting

focaliser [fɔkalize] VT Opt, Électron to focus; Mktg to target Fig **f. son attention/l'attention de qn sur qch** to focus one's/sb's attention on sth
    VPR **se focaliser** to focus (**sur** on)

fœhn [føn] NM **1** (vent) foehn **2** Suisse (sèche-cheveux) hair-dryer

fœhner [føne] VT Suisse (sécher au sèche-cheveux électrique) to dry with a/the hair-dryer

fœtal, -ale, -aux, -ales [fetal, -o] ADJ f(o)etal

fœtus [fetys] NM f(o)etus

fofolle [fɔfɔl] Fam ADJ F nutty, daft
    NF nutty or daft woman

foi [fwa] NF **1** **bonne f.** sincerity, honesty; **mauvaise f.** insincerity, dishonesty; Phil bad faith; **il est de bonne/mauvaise f.** he is sincere/insincere; **je le lui ai dit en toute bonne f.** I told him that in good faith; **témoin de bonne/mauvaise f.** truthful/untruthful witness; **témoin digne de f.** trustworthy or reliable or credible witness; **ma f., oui!** yes indeed!; **c'est ma f. vrai** that is certainly or definitely true; Arch **f. d'honnête homme** on my word as a gentleman; **sur la f. de sa lettre** on the strength of his letter
    2 (confiance) belief, trust, confidence; **avoir f. en qn/qch** to have faith in or to believe in sb/sth; **avoir f. en l'avenir** to have confidence in the future; **ajouter ou attacher f. à une nouvelle** to give credence to or to credit or to believe (in) a piece of news; **texte qui fait f.** authentic text; **la lettre doit partir avant le 29, le cachet de la poste faisant f.** the letter must be postmarked no later than the 28th; Jur **en f. de quoi** in witness whereof; **ligne de f.** Opt zero alignment; Naut, Aviat lubber line
    3 Rel faith, belief; **avoir la f.** to have faith; Fig **il faut vraiment avoir la f.** you have to be really dedicated; Iron **il n'y a que la f. qui sauve** faith is a wonderful thing; **acte/article de f.** act/article of faith; **profession de f.** profession of faith; Cathol confirmation; Pol (d'un candidat) mission statement; **répandre la f.** to spread the Word; **la f. démocratique** faith or belief in democracy; **il n'a ni f. ni loi, il est sans f. ni loi** he fears neither God nor man

foie [fwa] NM liver; Culin **f. de veau/volaille** calf's/chicken liver; **huile de f. de morue** cod-liver oil; Fig Fam **se ronger ou se manger les foies** to be climbing the walls, to go beserk; très Fam **avoir les foies** to be scared out of one's wits; **ça m'a foutu les foies** it scared me out of my wits
    ▸▸ **f. gras** foie gras

foie-de-bœuf, pl **foies-de-bœuf** NM beefsteak fungus

foin [fwɛ̃] NM **1** (fourrage) hay; **faire les foins**

to make hay; **tas de f.** haycock; **meule de f.** haystack; **rhume des foins** hay fever; *Fam* **faire du f.** *(scandale)* to kick up *or* make a fuss; *(bruit)* to kick up *or* make a din; **ce scandale a fait du f. dans le milieu politique local** this scandal made waves in local political circles **2** *(d'artichaut)* choke **3** *Arch* **f. de …** the devil take …

foire [fwar] NF fair; **f. commerciale** trade show; **f. internationale** international (trade) fair; **f. professionnelle** trade fair; **f. commerciale de Marseille** Marseilles trade fair; *Ordinat* **f. aux questions** frequently asked questions, FAQ; **champ de f.** fairground; *Fam* **c'est la f. ici** *(désordre)* it's chaos in here; *(bruit)* it's bedlam in here; **faire la f.** to have a good time, to have fun

foire-exposition, *Fam* **foire-expo,** *pl* **foires-expositions, foires-expos** NF trade fair *or* exhibition

foirer [fware] *très Fam* VI *(rater)* **la mission/ le plan/la soirée a complètement foiré** the mission/the plan/the evening was a complete balls-up *or Am* ballup *or* cockup; **ses prévisions ont complètement foiré** his predictions were a mile out; **il a tout fait f.** he cocked everything up; *Mil* **fusée qui foire** shell that doesn't go off
▶ VT to cock up, to mess up

foireux, -euse [fwarø, -øz] ADJ **1** *très Fam* *(qui échoue)* hopeless; **c'est un plan f.** that plan is going to be a cock up **2** *Fam (lâche)* chicken, yellow **3** *Vulg (qui a la diarrhée)* suffering from the runs *or* the trots

fois [fwa] NF **1** *(occasion)* time; **une f.** once; *Belg* **venez une f. voir** *(donc)* just come and see; **une f. et une seule** just the once, once and once only; **il était une f. un roi** once upon a time there was a king; **deux f.** twice; **par deux f.** not once but twice; **combien de f.?** how many times?, how often?; **trois f. quatre font douze** three times four is twelve; **trois f. plus grand** three times as big; **je l'ai acheté pour trois f. rien** I bought it for next to nothing; **il faut du beurre? – oui, mais trois f. rien** do you need some butter? – yes, but the smallest amount *or* but hardly any; **tu t'es fait mal? – non, c'est trois f. rien** have you hurt yourself? – no, it's nothing at all; **encore une f.** once more, once again; **y regarder à deux f. (pour faire qch)** to think twice (before doing sth); **une (bonne) f. pour toutes** once and for all; **la première/deuxième f.** the first/second time; **c'est la première f. que j'en fais** it's my first time, it's the first time I've done it; **une dernière f., arrête!** for the last time, stop it!; **cette f.** this time; **pour cette f.** this once; **une autre f.** another time, on another occasion; **d'autres f.** at other times; **bien des f.** many times, often; **deux f. par jour** twice daily *or* a day; **il faut le boire en une f.** you must drink it at *or* in one go *or Fam* in a oner; **toutes les f. ou chaque f. que j'y pense** every time *or* whenever I think about it; **pour une f. tu as raison** you're right for once; **pour une f. que je peux y aller, il faut qu'il vienne aussi!** it's the one time I can go *or* for once I can go and he has to come as well!; **c'est la seule f. où j'ai regretté** that's the only time when *or* that I had regrets; **il y a des f. où je me demande à quoi tu penses** there are times when I wonder what you're thinking about; **une f. que vous aurez des informations** once you have *or* as soon as you have some information; **à la f.** at the same time, at once; **à la f. utile et pas cher** both useful and inexpensive; **pas trop vite, une chose à la f.!** slow down, one thing at a time; **pas tous à la f.!** one at a time!, not all at once!, not all at the same time!; **je n'arrive pas à écouter de la musique et lire à la f.** I can't listen to music and read at the same time; *Fig* **tu ne peux**

pas courir deux lièvres à la f. you can't do two things at once *or* at the same time
2 *Fam* **des f.** *(parfois)* sometimes; **vous n'auriez pas un câble de remorque, des f.?** you haven't by any chance got a towrope?; **des f. qu'il viendrait** in case he should come; **non, mais des f.!** really now!

foison [fwazɔ̃] NF **1** *Arch* abundance, plenty **2 à f.** in abundance; **il y en a à f.** there are plenty of them, they are abundant; **des pommes à f.** apples in abundance, apples galore

foisonnant [fwazonɑ̃] ADJ abundant, plentiful

foisonnement [fwazonmɑ̃] NM **1** *(abondance)* abundance; **un f. de détails** an abundance of details; **le f. des idées** the proliferation of ideas **2** *(multiplication)* multiplying **3** *(augmentation de volume)* swelling, expansion

foisonner [fwazone] VI **1** to abound (**de, en** in, with); **le gibier foisonne ici** game is plentiful here; **il foisonne de bonnes idées** he's bursting with good ideas; **une école d'art où les jeunes talents foisonnent** an art school bursting with young talent **2** *(d'animaux)* to multiply **3** *(augmenter de volume)* to swell, to expand

fol [fɔl] ADJ *voir* **fou**

folâtre [fɔlɑtr] ADJ *(personne)* playful, lively; *(agneau, poulain)* frisky

folâtrer [fɔlɑtre] VI *(d'une personne)* to romp, to frolic; *(d'un agneau etc)* to gambol, to frisk about

folâtrerie [fɔlɑtrəri] NF *Arch* **1** *(d'un agneau)* friskiness; *(d'un chaton)* playfulness **2** *(blague)* frolic, romp

foldingue [fɔldɛ̃g] *Fam* ADJ crazy, nutty
▶ N nutter

folerie [fɔlri] NF *Can Fam* **elle a fait une f. en épousant cet homme** she was crazy *or* mad to marry that man; **faire des f.** *(faire le clown)* to clown about; *(dépenser beaucoup)* to be extravagant

foliacé [fɔljase] ADJ *Bot* foliaceous

foliaire [fɔljɛr] ADJ *Bot* foliar

foliation [fɔljasjɔ̃] NF *Bot* foliation

folichon, -onne [fɔliʃɔ̃, -ɔn] ADJ playful, lighthearted; *Fam* **ce n'est pas f.** it's not much fun

folichonner [fɔliʃone] VI *Arch* to play *or* romp about

folie [fɔli] NF **1** *Méd* madness, lunacy; **accès de f.** fit of madness; **être pris de f.** to go mad; **avoir un grain de f.** to be a bit touched; **aimer qn à la f.** to be madly in love with sb, to love sb to distraction; **aimer qch à la f.** to be mad on sth, to be crazy about sth; *Fam* **c'est de la f., tout ce monde!** all these people, it's crazy *or* madness! **2** *(inconscience)* folly; **c'est de la f.!** it's madness!, it's crazy!; **c'est de la f. douce** it's sheer madness!, it's absolutely crazy!; **il a eu la f. de céder** he was mad enough to give in; **dire des folies** to talk wildly, to say crazy things; **faire des folies** to do crazy things; *(faire des achats extravagants)* to go mad; *Hum* **faire des folies de son corps** to put oneself about **3** *Archit* folly
▶ **f. furieuse** raving madness; **f. des grandeurs** delusions of grandeur, megalomania

folio [fɔljo] NM folio

foliole [fɔljɔl] NF *Bot* leaflet

folioter [fɔljɔte] VT to folio; *(par page)* to paginate

folk [fɔlk] ADJ, NM *Mus* folk

folkeux, -euse [fɔlkø, -øz] N *Fam (amateur de musique folklorique)* folkie

folklo [fɔlklo] ADJ *Fam (bizarre)* weird; **il est f.** he's a weirdo *or* an oddball

folklore [fɔlklɔr] NM folklore; *Fam* **c'est du**

f., ce n'est pas sérieux it's a load of nonsense, you can't take it seriously

folklorique [fɔlklɔrik] ADJ *(costume)* traditional; **danses folkloriques** folk *or* country dances; *Fam* **c'était f.** it was bizarre

folkloriste [fɔlklɔrist] N folklorist, specialist in folklore

folle [fɔl] ADJ *voir* **fou**

follement [fɔlmɑ̃] ADV **1** *(avec excès)* madly, foolishly, rashly; **être f. amoureux** to be madly in love **2** *(au plus haut point)* madly, wildly; **s'amuser f.** to have a wonderful time

follet, -ette [fɔlɛ, -ɛt] ADJ **1** *Arch* **esprit f.** elfish spirit, sprite, (hob)goblin; **feu f.** will-o'-the-wisp, Jack-o'-lantern; *Fig* **c'est un vrai feu f.** he's here today and gone tomorrow **2 poil f.** *(d'un oiseau, visage)* down; **cheveux follets** stray lock(s)

folliculaire [fɔlikylɛr] ADJ follicular

follicule [fɔlikyl] NM *Bot, Anat* follicle

folliculine [fɔlikylin] NF *Anat* folliculin

fomentateur, -trice [fɔmɑ̃tatœr, -tris] N agitator, troublemaker

fomentation [fɔmɑ̃tasjɔ̃] NF fomentation

fomenter [fɔmɑ̃te] VT to stir up, *Fml* to foment

fonçage [fɔ̃saʒ] NM **1** *(de tonneau)* bottoming, heading **2** *(de puits)* boring, sinking

foncé [fɔ̃se] ADJ *(couleur)* dark; **bleu f.** dark blue

foncer [fɔ̃se] *(je fonçai(s), n. fonçons)* VT **1** *(teinte)* to darken **2** *Culin (moule)* to line **3** *(tonneau)* to bottom, to head **4** *(pieu)* to sink, to drive (in); *(puits)* to sink, to bore
▶ VI **1 f. sur qn** to rush at *or* swoop (down) on sb; *(d'un taureau, joueur de football)* to charge (at) sb **2** *Fam (se déplacer très vite)* to speed along; *(se hâter)* to get a move on; **la voiture a foncé dans la foule** the car ploughed into the crowd; *Fam* **f. dans le tas** to charge in with fists flying; *Fig Fam* **ne te pose pas de questions, fonce!** don't ask any questions, just do it! **3** *(s'assombrir)* to darken

fonceur, -euse [fɔ̃sœr, -øz] *Fam* N dynamic *or* go-ahead type
▶ ADJ dynamic, go-ahead

foncier, -ière [fɔ̃sje, -jɛr] ADJ **1** of land; **propriété foncière** landed property; **le propriétaire f.** the landowner; **rente foncière** ground rent; **impôt f.** land tax; **crédit f.** land bank **2** *Fig (fondamental) (honnêteté)* fundamental, basic
▶ NM land tax; **f. bâti** landed property; **f. non bâti** land for development

foncièrement [fɔ̃sjɛrmɑ̃] ADV fundamentally, basically

fonction [fɔ̃ksjɔ̃] NF **1** *(poste)* office; **la f. publique** the public *or* civil service; **entrer en fonction(s), prendre ses fonctions** to take up one's duties; **être en f.** to be in office; **cela ne fait pas partie de mes fonctions** that's not part of my duties, that doesn't come within my remit; **voiture/appartement de f.** company car/flat; *(de fonctionnaire)* car/flat that goes with the job
2 *(rôle)* function; **faire f. de gérant** to act as manager; **cette table fait f. de table à café** this table acts *or* serves as a coffee table; **adjectif qui fait f. d'adverbe** adjective that is used *or* functions as an adverb; *Anat* **fonctions de l'estomac/du cœur** functions of the stomach/heart; **c'est la f. qui crée l'organe** necessity is the mother of invention
3 *Math* function; **f. inverse** inverse function; **être f. de** to be a function of; *Mktg* **f. de la demande** demand function, market demand function
4 en f. de *(résultats etc)* according to; **exprimer une quantité en f. d'une autre** to ex-

press one quantity in terms of *or* as a function of another; **les prix varient en f. de la demande** prices vary in accordance with *or* according to demand

5 *Ordinat* **f. booléenne** Boolean function; **f. de comptage de mots** word count facility; **f. de contrôle** control function; **f. 'couper-coller'** cut-and-paste facility; **f. d'éditeur de texte** text editing feature; **f. multimédia** multimedia facility; **f. multitâche** multitasking facility; **f. recherche et remplacement** search and replace function; **f. de recopie** copy function; **f. de répétition** repeat function; **f. de réponse automatique** autoresponder, mailbox; **f. de sauvegarde** save function; **f. de vérité** truth function

fonctionnaire [fɔ̃ksjɔnɛr] N state employee; *(dans l'administration)* civil servant; **haut/petit f.** high-/low-ranking official *or* civil servant; *Péj* **mentalité de f.** bureaucratic mentality

---

Fonctionnaire

This term covers a broader range of public service employees than the term "civil servant", from high-ranking members of the state administration to public-sector teachers and post office workers. "Fonctionnaires", of whom there are more than four and a half million in France, are normally recruited through competitive state examination and enjoy greater job security and other privileges to which private sector employees are not automatically entitled.

---

fonctionnalisme [fɔ̃ksjɔnalism] NM functionalism

fonctionnaliste [fɔ̃ksjɔnalist] ADJ functionalist

fonctionnalité [fɔ̃ksjɔnalite] NF functionality

fonctionnariat [fɔ̃ksjɔnarja] NM employment by the state

fonctionnariser [fɔ̃ksjɔnarize] VT *(employés, profession)* to make part of the public *or* civil service

fonctionnarisme [fɔ̃ksjɔnarism] NM *Péj* officialdom, bureaucracy, *Fam* red tape

fonctionnel, -elle [fɔ̃ksjɔnɛl] ADJ functional

fonctionnellement [fɔ̃ksjɔnɛlmɑ̃] ADV functionally

fonctionnement [fɔ̃ksjɔnmɑ̃] NM **1** *(du gouvernement, d'un plan etc)* functioning, working; **pour le bon f. du service, il est préférable que tous les employés aient les mêmes horaires** if the department is to run efficiently it is preferable that all staff have the same working hours **2** *(d'une machine etc)* functioning, operation, running, working; **en (bon) état de f.** in (good) working order; **mauvais f.** malfunction, fault; **panne due à un mauvais f. du carburateur** breakdown due to a malfunction in the *or* a malfunctioning carburettor; **cycle de f.** operating cycle; *Ordinat* **f. en réseau** networking

fonctionner [fɔ̃ksjɔne] VI *(d'une machine, d'un mécanisme)* to function, to work; *(d'une personne)* to function, to operate; *Ordinat* to run; **les trains ne fonctionnent plus** the trains are no longer running; **les freins n'ont pas fonctionné** the brakes failed, the brakes didn't work; **faire f. une machine** to operate *or* work a machine; *Élec* **f. sur courant continu** to operate *or* run on direct current; **f. sur piles** to run on batteries, to be battery-operated; **dans cette atmosphère mon cerveau ne peut pas f.** my brain can't function in this atmosphere

---

FOND [fɔ̃]

bottom **1**, **2** ▪ back **1** ▪ content **3** ▪ basically *(au fond)* **1** ▪ thoroughly *(à fond)* **1** ▪ background **4** ▪ long-distance running **5** ▪ cross-country skiing **5**

NM **1** *(partie la plus profonde)* bottom; *(de chapeau)* crown; *(de chaise, de pantalon)* seat; *(de tonneau)* bottom, head; *(de la gorge)* back; *(de l'abîme sans f.* bottomless chasm; **boîte à double f.** box with a false bottom; **bateau à f. plat** flat-bottomed boat; **f. de cylindre/chaudière** cylinder/boiler head; **f. de bouteille** dregs; **il n'en reste qu'un f.** there's only a drop left; **râcler ses fonds de tiroir** to scrape around *(for money)*; **du f. du cœur** from the bottom of one's heart; **tu connais le f. de ma pensée** you know what my thoughts *or* feelings really are; *Fig* **au f., dans le f.** basically; **dans le f. elle n'est pas méchante** she's not a bad sort at heart *or* deep down *or* she's basically not a bad sort; **au f., c'est ce qu'il voulait** (deep down) that's what he really wanted; **au f. il était très flatté** in his heart of hearts he was extremely flattered; **aller au f. d'une affaire/d'un problème** to get to the bottom *or* root of a matter/problem; **à f.** *(étudier)* thoroughly; **enfoncer un clou à f.** to hammer a nail home, to drive a nail all the way in; **respire à f.** breathe deeply; **on a fait le ménage à f. dans la cuisine** we cleaned the kitchen thoroughly; **se consacrer** *ou* **se donner à f. à qch** to devote oneself totally to sth; **il s'est engagé à f. dans le combat écologique** he committed himself wholeheartedly *or* body and soul to the struggle for the environment; **connaître un sujet à f.** to have a thorough knowledge of a subject; **à f. (de train)** (at) full tilt; *Fig* **elle a touché le f.** she's hit rock bottom

2 *(de l'océan)* bottom, bed; **il n'y a pas assez de f. pour plonger/jeter l'ancre** the water isn't deep enough for diving/for dropping anchor; **f. de sable** sandy bottom; **prendre f.** *(d'une ancre)* to bite, to grip; **envoyer un navire par le f.** to send a ship to the bottom; **grands fonds** ocean depths *or* deeps; **courant de f.** undertow; **lame de f.** groundswell

3 *(fondement)* **rebâtir une maison de f. en comble** to rebuild a house from top to bottom; *Fig* **il a un bon f.** he's good at heart *or* basically good; **faire f. sur qn/qch** to rely *or* depend on sb/sth; **le f. et la forme** the form and the content *or* substance; **le f. de cette politique** the essential features of this policy; **question de f.** fundamental question; *Journ* **article de f.** feature (article); *Mus* **jeu de f.** *(d'un orgue)* pipe stop; **f. sonore** *ou* **musical** background music *or* sound

4 *(partie la plus éloignée)* *(d'une peinture)* background; *(d'un espace clos)* far end; **la salle du f.** the room at the end, the far room; *Fam* **fonds de boutique** oddments, old stock; **au (fin) f. du désert/de l'Australie** in the heart of the desert/Australia; **au fin f. de la campagne** in the depths of the country; *Théâtre* **toile de f.** backdrop, backcloth; *Fig* **avec la guerre en toile de f.** against a backdrop of war; *Tennis* **ligne de f.** baseline; **bruit de f.** background noise; **sur un f. de musique tzigane** with gipsy music in the background

5 *Sport* **le f.** long-distance running; **course de (grand) f.** long-distance race; *Ski* cross-country race; **coureur de f.** long-distance runner; **ski de f.** cross-country skiing, langlauf; **cheval qui a du f.** horse with staying power

6 *Typ* **f. perdu** bleed; **à f. perdu** bleeding; **(blanc de) petit f.** back margin, gutter; **(blanc de) grand f.** fore-edge, gutter

---

▸▸ **f. d'artichaut** artichoke heart; **f. de cale** bilge; **tous les mutins furent enfermés à f. de cale** the mutineers were all locked away in the bottom of the hold; **f. musical** background music; *Méd* **f. d'œil** examination of the retina; **f. de robe** (full-length) slip; **f. scénique** scenic background; **f. sonore** background music; **f. de teint** foundation (cream)

fondamental, -ale, -aux, -ales [fɔ̃damɑ̃tal, -o] ADJ *(principe, postulat, différence, erreur, contradiction)* basic, fundamental; **il est f. que tout soit prêt à temps** it is (absolutely) essential that everything is ready in time; **le vocabulaire f. d'une langue** the basic *or* base vocabulary of a language; **pierre fondamentale** foundation stone; **couleurs fondamentales** primary colours; *Mus* **son f.** *(d'une corde)* root, generator; *Univ* **recherche fondamentale** basic research

NMPL **fondamentaux les fondamentaux de qch** the basics *or* fundamentals of sth

fondamentalement [fɔ̃damɑ̃talmɑ̃] ADV fundamentally, basically

fondamentalisme [fɔ̃damɑ̃talism] NM *Rel* fundamentalism

fondamentaliste [fɔ̃damɑ̃talist] ADJ fundamentalist

N **1** *(scientifique)* scientist engaged in basic research **2** *Rel* fundamentalist

fondant [fɔ̃dɑ̃] ADJ melting; **poire fondante** pear that melts in the mouth; **un chocolat f.** a fondant chocolate; **viande fondante** very tender meat; **tons fondants** blended shades (of colour)

NM **1** *(bonbon)* fondant; **un f. au chocolat** a chocolate fondant **2** *Tech* flux

fondateur, -trice [fɔ̃datœr, -tris] ADJ **membre f.** founder *or* founding member; **les mythes fondateurs d'une culture** the underlying myths of a culture

N *(d'une ville, société etc)* founder

fondation [fɔ̃dasjɔ̃] NF **1** *(d'une ville, d'un hôpital etc)* founding, foundation; **f. d'une entreprise** setting up of a business **2** *(fonds)* endowment (fund), foundation **3** *(établissement)* foundation **4** *Constr* **fondations** foundations

fondé [fɔ̃de] ADJ *(doutes, peurs)* well-founded, justified; **vos craintes ne sont pas fondées** your fears are groundless *or* unfounded *or* unjustified; **mal f.** *(soupçons)* groundless, ill-founded; **établissement f. en 1850** established 1850; **être f. à croire** to have good reason(s) to believe; **qu'est-ce qu'il y a de f. dans ces bruits?** is there any justification for anything in these reports?, is anything in these reports justified?

NM *Jur* **f. de pouvoir** agent *(holding power of attorney)*; *(mandant)* proxy; *(directeur de banque)* manager with signing authority

fondement [fɔ̃dmɑ̃] NM **1** *(base)* foundation, base; **soupçons sans f.** groundless *or* unfounded suspicions **2** *Fam (derrière)* behind, backside; *(anus)* back passage

fonder [fɔ̃de] VT *(ville)* to found; *(société, journal)* to start, to set up; **f. une famille** to start a family; **f. un hôpital** *(en donnant un legs)* to found a hospital; **f. ses espérances sur qch** to base *or* build one's hopes on sth; **document fondé sur des témoignages réels** document based on authentic accounts; **théorie fondée sur des textes scientifiques** theory based on scientific texts

VPR **se fonder se f. sur qch** *(d'une personne)* to go by sth, to base oneself on sth; *(d'une remarque, théorie)* to be based on sth; **sur quoi se fonde-t-il pour le nier?** what are his grounds for denying it?; **un espoir qui se fondait sur une information fausse** a hope that was based on misinformation

fonderie [fɔ̃dri] NF **1** *(extraction) (de minerai)* smelting; *(fusion) (de métaux)* founding, casting **2** *(usine) (d'extraction)* smelting works; *(de fusion)* foundry

fondeur [fɔ̃dœr] NM *(maître de forges)* ironmaster; *(ouvrier) (d'extraction)* smelter; *(de fusion) (metal)* founder; **f. en cuivre** brass founder; **f. en caractères, f. typographe** type founder

fondeur², **-euse** [fɔ̃dœr, -øz] N *Ski* cross-country skier

fondre [fɔ̃dr] VT **1** *(liquéfier) (minerai)* to smelt; *(métal)* to melt down; *(sucre)* to dissolve; *(neige, cire etc)* to melt; **f. deux fils ensemble** to fuse two wires together **2** *(fabriquer) (cloche, arme etc)* to cast, to found **3** *TV etc* to fade; **f. des teintes** to blend colours **4** *Com (compagnies)* to amalgamate, to merge

VI **1** *(se liquéfier)* to melt; *(de la neige)* to melt, to thaw; *(du sucre)* to dissolve; **le beurre fond au soleil** butter melts in the sun; **faire f. le beurre dans une casserole** melt the butter in a saucepan; *Élec* **faire f. un fusible** to blow a fuse; *Fig* **mon cœur fondit (de pitié)** my heart melted (with pity); **je fonds** my heart melts; **f. en larmes** to dissolve in(to) tears; **l'argent lui fond entre les doigts** money runs through his fingers; **il fond à vue d'œil** he's visibly wasting away **2** **f. sur sa proie** to pounce upon *or* to swoop (down) upon one's prey

VPR **se fondre** to merge; *(de compagnies)* to amalgamate, to merge; **se f. dans la brume** to disappear into the mist; **se f. dans la foule** to merge *or* blend into the crowd; **leur maison se fond dans le paysage** their house merges into the landscape; **se f. dans l'anonymat** to hide under the cloak of anonymity

fondrière [fɔ̃drijɛr] NF pothole *(full of water)*; **une f. marécageuse** a bog; *Can* **f. de mousse** muskeg

fonds [fɔ̃] NM **VOIR GRAMMAIRE A10** **1** *(organisme)* fund; **F. européen de coopération monétaire** European Monetary Cooperation Fund; **F. monétaire européen** European Monetary Fund; **F. monétaire international** International Monetary Fund; **F. national de garantie des salaires** national guarantee fund for the payment of salaries; **F. européen de développement** European Development Fund; **F. européen de développement régional** European Regional Development Fund; **F. national de l'emploi** = French national employment fund; **F. social européen** European Social Fund; **F. de stabilisation des changes** exchange equalization account

2 *(dans un musée)* collection; *Fig* **c'est un f. inestimable pour les chercheurs** it is an invaluable resource for researchers; **le f. commun de toutes les langues indo-européennes** the common stock of all Indo-European languages

NMPL **1** *(argent)* fund

2 *(ressources)* funds; **réunir des f.** to raise funds; **je n'ai pas les f. suffisants pour ouvrir un magasin** I don't have the (necessary) funds *or* capital to open a shop; **mise de f.** paid-in capital; **mouvement de f.** flow of capital; **rentrer dans ses f.** to recoup one's losses; **être en f.** to be in funds; **appel de f.** call upon shareholders; **ne pas toucher à ses f.** not to touch one's capital; **placer son argent à f. perdu** to purchase an annuity; **je l'ai aidé, mais je savais que c'était à f. perdu** I helped him, but I knew I wouldn't get my money back; **prêt à f. perdu** loan without security

3 *Bourse* **des fonds** stocks, securities; **f. d'État, f. publics** Government stock(s)

▸▸ **f. de caisse** float; **f. de chômage** unemployment fund; **f. de clientèle** customer

base; **f. de commerce** business; **f. de commerce à vendre** business for sale (as a going concern); **f. commercial** goodwill; **f. commun** common fund, pool; **f. commun de placement** investment trust, mutual fund; **f. de dotation** endowment fund; **f. d'épargne-retraite** retirement savings fund; **f. disponibles** liquid assets, available funds; **f. de garantie** guarantee fund; **f. de grève** strike fund; **f. d'investissement** investment fund; **f. liquides** available funds; **f. de pension** pension fund; **f. de prévoyance** contingency fund; **f. propres** equity; **f. publics** government funds, *(valeurs)* government stocks; **f. de réserve** reserve funds; **f. de roulement** working capital; **f. de secours** emergency fund; **f. social** company funds; **f. de terre** (piece of) land

fondu, -ue [fɔ̃dy] ADJ *(beurre)* melted; *(plomb, lave)* molten; **neige fondue** *(qui tombe)* sleet; *(par terre)* slush

NM **1** *(de couleurs)* blending **2** *Cin* dissolve, fade; **faire un f.** to fade; **faire un f. au noir** to fade to black; **s'ouvrir en f.** to fade in; **ouverture en f.** fade-in; **fermeture en f.** fade-out; **f. enchaîné** mix, lap dissolve, dissolve; **faire un f. enchaîné** to fade in-fade out; **f. par ondulation** ripple dissolve; **f. par passage au flou** defocus dissolve

NF *Culin* **fondue (savoyarde)** (cheese) fondue; **fondue bourguignonne** fondue bourguignonne, beef fondue

N *Fam* **1** *(fou)* round the bend, out to lunch, off one's rocker *or* trolley **2** *(enthousiaste)* fanatic, freak; **un f. d'informatique/de skateboard** he's a computer/skateboard freak

fongible [fɔ̃ʒibl] ADJ fungible

fongicide [fɔ̃ʒisid] ADJ fungicidal
NM fungicide

fongueux, -euse [fɔ̃gø, -øz] ADJ *Méd* fungous

fontaine [fɔ̃tɛn] NF **1** *(source)* spring; **F. de Jouvence** Fountain of Youth; *Prov* **il ne faut pas dire 'f., je ne boirai pas de ton eau'** never say never **2** *(construite)* fountain **3** *(petit réservoir)* cistern; **f. filtrante** *ou* **de ménage** (household) filter

fontainier [fɔ̃tenje] NM **1** water engineer **2** *(qui cherche de l'eau)* well borer *or* sinker

fontanelle [fɔ̃tanɛl] NF *Anat* fontanel(le)

fonte¹ [fɔ̃t] NF **1** *(de neige)* melting, thawing; *(d'or, d'argent etc)* melting down; *(de minerai)* smelting; *Métal* casting, founding; **pièces de f.** castings; *(fer de)* **f., f. de fer** cast iron; **f. d'acier** cast steel; **poêle en f.** cast-iron stove; *Méd* **f. musculaire** wasting of muscle **2** *Typ* font; **f. bitmap** bitmap font; **f. de caractère** character font; **f. écran** screen font; **f. imprimante** printer font; **f. reconnue optiquement** OCR-font; **f. vectorielle** outline font

fonte² NF *(d'une selle)* holster

fonts [fɔ̃] NMPL **f. baptismaux** (baptismal) font; **tenir un enfant sur les f. baptismaux** to be godfather/godmother to a child

foot [fut] NM *Fam* soccer, *Br* football; **jouer au f.** to play soccer *or Br* football

football [futbol] NM soccer, *Br* football

footballeur, -euse [futbolœr, -øz] N soccer player *or Br* football player

footballistique [futbolistik] ADJ *Hum (qui a trait au football)* soccer, *Br* football; **à la veille de la coupe du monde, la frénésie f. s'est à nouveau emparée du pays** on the eve of the World Cup, football fever has taken over the country again

footeux [futø] NM *Fam (joueur)* soccer player, *Br* football player; *(supporter)* soccer fan, *Br* football fan

footing [futiŋ] NM jogging; **faire son f.** to go jogging, to jog

for [fɔr] NM **le f. intérieur** the conscience;

dans *ou* **en son f. intérieur** in one's heart of hearts, deep (down) inside

forage [fɔraʒ] NM **1** *(action) (de puits)* drilling, boring, sinking; **f. pétrolier** drilling oilwells **2** *(trou)* borehole, drill hole

forain, -aine [fɔrɛ̃, -ɛn] ADJ **1** *(itinérant)* itinerant; **spectacle f.** travelling show; **hercule f.** strongman *(at a fair)*; **baraque foraine** fairground stall; **fête foraine** funfair; **marchand f.** stallholder **2** *Naut* **mouillage f.** open berth
N fair stallholder

forban [fɔrbɑ̃] NM pirate, buccaneer; *Fig* rogue, crook

forçage [fɔrsaʒ] NM **1** *(de plantes)* forcing **2** = **forcement 3** *Tech* **introduction d'air par f.** ram air induction

forçat [fɔrsa] NM *(prisonnier)* convict; *(galérien)* galley slave; *Fig* **mener une vie de f.** to slave away, to work like a slave; **la maçonnerie est un métier de f.** building work is really backbreaking; **je ne supporte plus cette vie de f.** I can't stand this slavery any more

FORCE [fɔrs]

| **NF** strength **1** ▪ force **4, 5** ▪ by (dint of) *(à force de)* **6** |
| **ADJ INV** many |

NF **1** *(vigueur)* strength; **être à bout de force(s)** to have no strength left; **je n'ai pas beaucoup de f.** I've not got much strength, I'm not very strong; **donner des forces** to give strength; **(re)prendre des forces** to (re)gain strength; **ménager ses forces** to save *or* conserve *or Fml* husband one's strength; **la maladie le laissa sans f.** the illness left him (feeling) weak, the illness sapped his strength; **ne pas sentir sa f.** not to know one's own strength; **cette épreuve est au-dessus de ses forces** this test is beyond him *or* is too much for him; **lui parler fut au-dessus de mes forces** it was too much for me to speak to him; **il le frappa avec f.** he hit him hard *or* forcefully; **mon doute revint avec f.** my doubts returned with renewed force; **de toutes ses forces** *(pousser, frapper etc)* with all one's strength *or* might; **j'essaie de toutes mes forces de le convaincre** I'm trying as hard as I can to convince him; **elle le veut de toutes ses forces** she wants it with all her heart; **vouloir à toute f. faire qch** to be determined to do sth, to want to do sth at all costs; **il veut à toute f. qu'on soit rentré à minuit** he wants us to be back at midnight at all costs; **elle n'avait plus la f. de répondre** she didn't have the strength (left) to answer, she had no strength left to answer; **je ne me sens pas/ne suis pas de f. à faire cela** I don't feel/I'm not up to *or* equal to doing it; **elle ne se sentait pas la f. de lui en parler** she didn't feel up to talking to him about it; **de f. égale, de même f.** equally matched, well matched; **ce qui fait votre f., c'est ...** your strength is ...; **être bâti en f.** to be stocky, to be strongly built; **dans la f. de l'âge** in the prime of life

2 *(courage)* **f. d'âme** moral strength, fortitude; **elle a une sacrée f. de caractère** she has incredible strength of character

3 tour de f. tour de force; *Constr* **(jambe de) f. force** piece, strut; **f. de résistance à la tension** tensile strength

4 *(violence)* force; **faire appel à** *ou* **avoir recours à la f.** to resort to force; **céder à la f.** to give in *or* yield to force; **faire qch de vive f.** to do sth by sheer force; **entrer** *ou* **pénétrer de f. dans une maison** to force one's way into a house; **faire entrer qch de f. dans qch** to force sth into sth; **f. lui fut d'obéir** he was obliged to obey, he had no option but to obey; *Jur* **un cas de f. majeure** *(en assurance)* an act of God; **c'était un cas de f. majeur** there was no other option, circumstances were beyond my/our/your/*etc* control; *Naut* **faire f. de voiles** to crowd on (all) sail; **faire f. de rames** to row *or* pull hard; *Prov* **la f. prime le droit, f. passe droit** might is right; **il devra le faire, de gré ou de f.** he'll have to do it whether he wants to or not, he'll have to do it willy-nilly

5 *(d'un coup, du vent, d'un argument)* force; **vent de f. 8** force 8 gale; **les forces de la nature** the forces of nature; **f. vitale** life force; **c'est une f. de la nature** he's a mighty force; **par la f. des choses** through force of circumstance; **la f. de l'habitude** force of habit; **dans toute la f. du mot** in the strongest sense of the word, in every sense of the word

6 **à f. de** by (dint of); **à f. d'y penser** by (dint of) thinking about it; **à f. de travailler** by (dint of) hard work; **à f. d'explications** by (dint of) explanation; **à f. de volonté** by sheer force of will; **à f. de répéter** by constant repetition; **il s'est enroué à f. de crier** he shouted himself hoarse; **à f. de jouer dehors le soir, tu vas t'enrhumer** by playing outside in the evening you'll end up with a cold; **il va se lasser, à f.** he'll get tired of it in the long run

7 *Phys* **f. motrice** motive power; *Fig* driving force; **f. d'inertie** inertia; **f. vive** kinetic energy, momentum; *Élec* **f. (électrique)** (electric) power; **prise de f.** power point; **f. centrifuge** centrifugal force; **f. centripète** centripetal force; **f. de traction** traction *or* tractive force; **forces d'inertie** inertia forces; **forces de cisaillement** shear forces; *Aut* **forces en virage** cornering force

8 **les forces armées** the armed forces, the services; **f. de dissuasion** deterrence; **f. de frappe** strike force; **f. d'interposition** interposition force; **f. de paix** peacekeeping force; **f. tactique** *ou* **d'intervention** task force; **la f. publique, les forces de police** *ou* **de l'ordre** the police (force), the forces of law and order; **les forces vives du pays** the country's resources; **nous étions là en force(s)** we were there in (full) force; **ils sont arrivés en f.** they arrived in force; *Écon* **les forces du marché** market forces; *Mktg* **forces, faiblesses, opportunités et menaces** strengths, weaknesses, opportunities and threats, SWOT; **f. de travail** workforce; **f. de vente** sales force; **forces nucléaires intermédiaires** intermediate-range nuclear forces

ADJ INV *Arch, Litt* **f. gens/anecdotes** a great number of *or* (very) many people/anecdotes; **f. bière** copious amounts of beer

forcé [fɔrse] **ADJ 1** *(obligé)* forced; *Aviat* **atterrissage f.** forced *or* emergency landing; *Jur* **travaux forcés** hard labour; *Fam* **mariage f.** shotgun wedding, forced marriage; **la comparaison est un peu forcée** the comparison is a bit forced; **exemple f.** far-fetched example **2** *(affecté)* **rire/sourire f.** forced laugh/smile **3** *(involontaire)* **prendre un bain f.** to fall in (the water) **4** *Fam* **c'est f.!** it's inevitable!

forcement [fɔrsəma] **NM** forcing (open); **f. de blocus** blockade running

forcément [fɔrsema] **ADV** inevitably; **nous étions f. en retard** inevitably *or* of course, we were late; **elle le sait f. déjà** she's bound to *or* she must know already; **elle sera f. déçue** she's bound to be disappointed; **f.!** of course; **pas f.** not necessarily; **l'herbe est verte, f., il a plu tous les jours** the grass is green but it's not surprising, it has been raining every day

forcené, -ée [fɔrsəne] **ADJ 1** *Arch (personne)* lunatic, mad **2** *(extrême) (marche, imagination)* frenzied; *(amateur de bons vins etc)* passionate; *(individualisme)* fanatical, rabid; **un goût f. du travail** a fanatical liking for work

N maniac, madman, *f* madwoman; **crier comme un f.** to scream like a madman/madwoman

forceps [fɔrsɛps] **NM** *Obst* forceps; **accouchement au f.** forceps delivery

forcer [fɔrse] (**je forçai(s)**) **VT 1** *(obliger)* to force, to compel; **f. qn à faire qch** to force *or* compel sb to do sth, to make sb do sth; **sans vouloir te f.** il faudrait faire la vaisselle I don't want to force you, but the washing-up has to be done; **personne ne t'y force** no one is forcing you; **f. la main à qn** to force sb's hand; **f. le respect/l'admiration (de qn)** to command sb's respect/admiration; **être forcé de faire qch** to be forced to do sth; **f. une femme** to violate *or* rape a woman; *Mil* **f. un poste** to take a post by storm *or* by force; **f. une serrure/un coffre** to force (open) a lock/a safe; **f. la caisse** to force open the till, to break into the till; **f. une porte** to force (open) *or* break open a door; **f. la porte de qn** to force one's way into sb's place; **f. le destin** to force the hand of destiny

2 *(voix)* to force; *(mât)* to strain; *(plaque)* to buckle; *Fam* **f. la note** to overdo it; **f. l'allure** *ou* **le pas** to force the pace; **f. le sens** to strain *or* distort the meaning; **f. un cheval** to override a horse; **f. des fleurs** to force flowers; **f. un cerf** to run down a stag, to bring a stag to bay; **f. la dose d'un médicament** to take/give too large a dose of a medicine

3 *Ordinat (justification, coupure de page)* to force

VI *Naut* **f. de voiles** to crowd on sail; **f. sur les avirons** to strain at the oars; **le vent force** the wind is rising; *Cartes* **f. sur l'annonce de qn** to overcall *or* overbid sb; **tu y arriveras sans f.** you'll get there without straining yourself *or* without too much effort; **essayez de garder les jambes raides, mais ne forcez pas** try to keep your legs straight, but don't strain yourself; **ne force pas, ça doit se fermer tout seul!** don't force it, it has to close by itself!; *Fam* **f. sur la bouteille** to overdo the drinking; **je crains d'avoir forcé sur le poivre** I'm afraid I've overdone it (with) the pepper

VPR se forcer *(s'obliger)* to force oneself; **se f. à faire qch** to force oneself to do sth

forcing [fɔrsiŋ] **NM** *Sport* sustained pressure; *Fig Fam* **il a fallu faire le f. pour qu'il accepte** we had to put on a lot of pressure to get him to accept; **avoir qn au f.** to pressurize sb, to put pressure on sb

forcir [fɔrsir] **VI 1** *(d'une personne)* to fill out, to get bigger **2** *(des éléments)* **le vent/la tempête forcit** the wind is picking up/the storm is getting stronger

forclore [fɔrklɔr] **VT** *Jur* to debar

forclusion [fɔrklyzjɔ̃] **NF** *Jur* debarment; *Fin* foreclosure

forer [fɔre] **VT** *(roche)* to drill, to bore; *(puits)* to drill, to bore, to sink

forestier, -ière [fɔrɛstje, -jɛr] **ADJ** *(zone)* forest(ed); **chemin f.** forest road; **essences forestières** forest trees; **une exploitation forestière** a forestry development; **garde f.** forester, forest warden, *Am* ranger

NM forester

foret [fɔrɛ] **NM 1** *(vrille)* drill **2 f. à bois** gimlet; **f. de charpentier** auger **3** *(vilebrequin)* (brace) bit

forêt [fɔrɛ] **NF** forest; **f. vierge** virgin forest; **région couverte de forêts** forest(ed) region; *Admin* **le service des Eaux et Forêts** *Br* ≃ the Forestry Commission, *Am* ≃ the Forest Service; *Fig* **une f. de mâts** a forest of masts; *Prov* **les arbres vous cachent la f.** you can't see the wood *or Am* forest for the trees; **F.noire** Black Forest; *Culin* Black forest gateau

foreur [fɔrœr] **NM** borer, driller; *Pétr* **f. d'ex-**

ploration oil prospector, *Am Fam* wildcatter

foreuse [fɔrøz] **NF** *(outil)* drill; *Min etc* rock drill; **f. à main** hand drill

forfaire [fɔrfɛr] **VI** *(conj like* **faire**) *Arch, Litt* **f. à son devoir** to fail in one's duty; **f. à l'honneur** to forfeit one's honour; **f. à sa parole** to break one's word

forfait¹ [fɔrfɛ] **NM** *(crime)* heinous crime

forfait² **NM** *(contrat)* fixed-price contract; *Fin* lump sum; **le f. comprend les frais de location et d'entretien du matériel** the set *or* fixed price includes the cost of hire and maintenance of the equipment; **f. (-voyage)** package (deal); **travail à f.** fixed-price work; **travailler au f.** to do fixed-price work; **prix à f.** all-in price; **et pour un f. de 500 euros** and for an all-in price of 500 euros, and for 500 euros all in; **vente à f.** outright sale; **f. avion + location de voiture** fly drive; **f. de remontées mécaniques** ski *or* lift pass; **f. de ski** ski pass; **forfait-vacances** holiday package; **f. week-end** weekend package; *Com* **f. de port** carriage forward

forfait³ **NM** *Courses de chevaux* fine, forfeit *(paid for scratching a horse)*; **déclarer f. pour un cheval** to scratch a horse; **déclarer f.** *(d'un athlète, concurrent)* to scratch; *Fig* to throw in the towel; **l'équipe a déclaré f.** the team withdrew

forfaitage [fɔrfɛtaʒ] **NM** forfaiting

forfaitaire [fɔrfɛtɛr] **ADJ** **marché f.** fixed-price contract; **paiement f.** lump sum; **indemnités forfaitaires** basic allocation; **prix f.** all-in price; **voyage à prix f.** package tour

forfaitairement [fɔrfɛtɛrma] **ADV** *Fin* in a lump sum; *(facturer)* in a lump sum, in one amount

forfaiture [fɔrfɛtyr] **NF** *(abus de pouvoir)* abuse of authority; **f. au devoir/à l'honneur** breach of duty/honour

forfanterie [fɔrfɑ̃tri] **NF** bragging, boasting

forge [fɔrʒ] **NF** forge; **f. (de maréchal-ferrant)** smithy; **mener un cheval à la f.** to take a horse to the blacksmith's; **f. de serrurier** locksmith's workshop; **maître de forges** ironmaster; **pièce de f.** forging

forgeable [fɔrʒabl] **ADJ** *(métal)* forgeable

forgeage [fɔrʒaʒ] **NM** forging

forger [fɔrʒe] (**je forgeai(s)**) **VT 1** *(métal)* to forge; **fer forgé** wrought iron; **cela forge le caractère** it forms *or* moulds the character, it is character-forming; **f. un homme** to form a man's character; *Prov* **c'est en forgeant qu'on devient forgeron** practice makes perfect **2** *(inventer) (histoire, excuse)* to fabricate, to make up; *(mot)* to coin; *(accusation)* to trump up; *(vision)* to conjure up; **histoire forgée de toutes pièces** completely fabricated *or* made-up story

VPR se forger **se f. une réputation** to carve out a reputation for oneself; **se f. un idéal de vie** to create an ideal lifestyle for oneself

> Il faut noter que le verbe anglais **to forge** signifie également **contrefaire**.

forgeron [fɔrʒərɔ̃] **NM** (black)smith

forgeur, -euse [fɔrʒœr, -øz] **N** *(de nouvelles, mensonges)* inventor, fabricator; *(de mots)* coiner

NM *Litt (forgeron)* metal worker

formage [fɔrmaʒ] **NM** *Tech* forming

formaldéhyde [fɔrmaldeid] **NM** *Chimie* formaldehyde

formalisation [fɔrmalizasjɔ̃] **NF** formalization

formaliser [fɔrmalize] **VT** to formalize; **logique formalisée** formal logic

VPR se formaliser to take offence (**de** at), to take exception (**de** to)

formalisme [fɔrmalism] NM **1** formality; **f. administratif** bureaucracy, *Fam* red tape; **f. intransigeant** rigid obsession with formalities **2** *Beaux-Arts* formalism

formaliste [fɔrmalist] ADJ **1** formalistic **2** *Beaux-Arts* formalist
N formalist

formalité [fɔrmalite] NF **1** *(procédure)* formality; **c'est une pure f., ce n'est qu'une f.** it's just a formality; **formalités douanières** customs formalities; **formalités d'entrée** entry requirements; **sans autre f.** without further ado **2** *(cérémonie)* formality; **sans formalité(s)** informal

format [fɔrma] NM *(de livre)*, *Ordinat* format; *(de papier)*, *Phot* size, format; **f. de poche** pocket size; **papier f. A4/A3** A4/A3 paper format; *Typ* **f. paysage** landscape format; *Typ* **f. portrait** portrait format; **f. tabloïd** tabloid format; **f. de page** page format *or* layout; *Ordinat* **f. ASCII** ASCII format; **f. carte de crédit** credit card format; **f. d'impression** print format; **f. d'écran** screen format; **f. de fichier** file format; **f. de papier** paper format; **f. de paragraphe** paragraph format; *TV etc* **f. de présentation** show format

formatage [fɔrmataʒ] NM *Ordinat* formatting; **f. de bas niveau** low-level format(ting); **f. de haut niveau** high-level format(ting); **f. logiciel** soft sectoring

formater [fɔrmate] VT *Ordinat* to format

formateur, -trice [fɔrmatœr, -tris] ADJ formative; **expérience formatrice** formative experience
N trainer

formation [fɔrmasjɔ̃] NF **1** *(constitution)* formation; *(de caractère)* forming, development; **la f. du goût/de la personnalité** the development of taste/the personality; **volcan en voie** *ou* **en cours de f.** volcano in the process of formation; **mot de f. savante** word of learned origin; **la f. du pluriel en anglais** the formation of the plural in English **2** *(éducation)* training; **avoir une excellente f.** to have an excellent training; **elle a reçu une f. littéraire/scientifique** she received a literary education/a scientific training; **suivre une f.** to do *or* take a training course; **il lui faut une f.** he needs (some) training; **il est technicien de f.** he trained as a technician; **f. en alternance** *ou* **alternée** = training given partly in an educational institution and partly in the workplace; **f. continue** *ou* **permanente** continuing education, continuous training; **f. professionnelle** vocational training; **f. courte** *ou* **accélérée** intensive training; **être en f.** to be undergoing training; **stage de f.** training course; **f. sur le tas** *ou* **par la pratique** on-the-job training; **f. dans l'entreprise** in-house training **3** *(de roche)* formation; *Mil* **f. serrée** close formation **4** *(groupe)*, *Mil* unit; *Mus* group; **une petite f. de jazz** a small jazz band; **f. aérienne** aerial unit; **f. politique** political group

forme [fɔrm] NF **1** *(configuration)* form, shape; **formes** *(d'un bateau)* lines; *(d'une personne)* figure; *(d'une femme)* curves; **les formes d'un tableau/paysage** the lines of a picture/shapes of a landscape; **vêtement qui épouse les formes** close-fitting *or* figure-hugging garment; **en f. d'œuf** egg-shaped; **gomme en f. de voiture** eraser in the shape *or* form of a car, car-shaped eraser; **yeux en f. de billes** eyes like marbles; **sous la f. d'une nymphe** in the form *or* shape of a nymph; **c'est une différente f. d'esprit** it is a different way of thinking; **l'histoire racontée sous une nouvelle f.** history told in a new way; **présenter les choses sous une autre f.** to present things in a different *or* in

another way; **statistiques sous f. de tableau** statistics in tabular form; **le produit existe aussi sous f. de bombe aérosol** the product also comes as an aerosol spray; **sous toutes ses formes** in all its forms *or* guises; **sans f.** shapeless; **prendre f.** to take shape; **mettre en f.** *(texte)* to format **2** *(procédure)* form; **arrêt cassé pour vice de f.** judgment quashed on a technical point; **renvoyer qn sans autre f. de procès** to dismiss sb without further ado; **avertir qn dans les formes** to give sb formal *or* due warning; **il faut y mettre les formes** it must be done tactfully; **faire qch dans les formes** to do sth in the accepted way; **en bonne et due f.** in due form, according to the proper form; **faire une réclamation en bonne et due f.** to use the correct procedure in making a complaint; **de pure f.** purely formal; **vérification de pure f.** routine check; **pour la f.** as a matter of form **3** **être en f.** to be on form *or* in good form; **être très en f.** *ou* **en pleine f.** *ou* **en grande f.** to be in great form; *Fam* **tenir** *ou* **péter la f.** to be in cracking form; **ne pas être en f., être en mauvaise f.**, *Fam* **ne pas avoir la f.** not to be on form, to be in poor form; **c'est bon pour la f.** it's good for you, it'll do you good; *Fam* **alors, c'est la f.?** how are you doing? **4** *Ind* former, forming block; *(pour fromage etc)* mould, *Am* mold; *(de cordonnier)* last; *(pour élargir)* shoe tree; *(de chapelier)* block; **chapeau haut de f.** top hat **5** *Naut* dock **6** *Typ* forme, *Am* form **7** *Com* **f. sociale** type of company

formé [fɔrme] ADJ fully formed, fully developed; **jeune fille formée** fully-developed girl; **un personnel bien f.** well-trained staff

formel, -elle [fɔrmɛl] ADJ **1** *(ordre)* express; *(démenti)* flat, categorical; *(veto)* absolute; **défense formelle** strict prohibition; **il a été tout à fait f. sur ce point** he was quite adamant *or* definite on this point; **je suis f.** I'm (absolutely) positive **2** *(de principe)* (distinction, attitude) formal **3** *Phil* (cause) formal

formellement [fɔrmɛlmɑ̃] ADV **1** *(interdit)* strictly; **promettre f.** to promise faithfully; **s'engager f. à régler ses dettes** to vow to pay off one's debts; **accuser f. qn** to specifically accuse sb; **l'homme a été f. reconnu** the man was positively identified **2** *(en considérant la forme)* formally; **une argumentation f. inattaquable** an argument that cannot be attacked on formal grounds

Il faut noter que l'adverbe anglais **formally** signifie le plus souvent **officiellement** ou **de façon cérémonieuse**, selon le contexte.

former [fɔrme] VT **1** *(créer) (gouvernement, collection etc)* to form; *Rail (train)* to make up; **f. un projet/des idées** to form a plan/ideas; **les murs forment un carré** the walls form a square; **ils forment une famille unie** they are a united family; **ils forment une bonne équipe/un beau couple** they make a good team/a lovely couple **2** *(pilote, cheval etc)* to train; *(caractère)* to form, to mould, *Am* to mold; **f. son esprit/son goût** to develop one's mind/taste; **f. l'oreille/l'œil** to train the ear/eye; **cela forme le caractère** it forms *or* moulds the character, it is character-forming; **cette université a formé des hommes remarquables** this university has turned out *or* produced some remarkable men; *Tech* **f. par roulage** to roll **3** **nous avons formé des vœux pour sa réussite** we wished him every success

VPR **se former 1** *(se développer)* to form, to develop; *(apparaître) (d'un fruit)* to form; *(d'un plan)* to take shape; **des cristaux se forment dans la roche** crystals form in rock;

une jeune fille qui se forme a girl who is developing; **se f. en cortège/en carré** to form (into) a procession/(into) a square **2** *(apprendre son métier)* to train oneself; *(s'instruire)* to educate oneself; **se f. aux affaires** to acquire a business training; **se f. sur le tas** to learn on the job

formica® [fɔrmika] NM formica®; **en f.** formica

formidable [fɔrmidabl] ADJ **1** *(extraordinaire)* tremendous **2** *(bon)* great, fantastic; *Iron Fam* **tu es/c'est f.!** you're/it's incredible! **3** *Vieilli (effrayant)* fearsome, formidable

Il faut noter que l'adjectif anglais **formidable** est un faux ami. Il signifie le plus souvent **redoutable**.

formidablement [fɔrmidabləmɑ̃] ADV **1** *(énormément)* tremendously, fantastically; **nous avons été f. accueillis** we were given a tremendous *or* fantastic welcome **2** *Arch (de manière effrayante)* formidably, fearsomely

formique [fɔrmik] ADJ *Chimie (acide)* formic

formol [fɔrmɔl] NM *Chimie* formalin, formol

formulable [fɔrmylabl] ADJ **une opinion difficilement f.** an opinion that is difficult to formulate; **une théorie f. en termes clairs** a theory that can be clearly formulated

formulaire [fɔrmylɛr] NM **1** *(imprimé)* form; **remplir un f.** to fill in *or* out a form; **f. E111** form E111; **f. d'appréciation** customer satisfaction questionnaire; **f. d'assurance** insurance form; **f. de candidature** (job) application form; **f. de détaxe** tax free shopping form; *Ordinat* **f. de saisie** input form **2** *(recueil)* formulary; *(de pharmaciens)* formulary, pharmacopoeia

formulation [fɔrmylasjɔ̃] NF formulation, wording

formule [fɔrmyl] NF **1** *Math, Chimie etc* formula VOIR GRAMMAIRE A14
2 *(paroles)* expression, phrase; **f. magique** magic formula; *Suisse Pol* = name given to the coalition that forms the executive body of the Swiss government; **f. de début** *(d'une lettre)* opening; **f. de politesse** *(au début d'une lettre)* standard opening; *(à la fin)* standard closure, letter ending; **f. finale** standard closure, letter ending; **selon la f. consacrée** as the expression goes; **trouver la f. juste** to find the right phrase **3** *(méthode)* formula; **c'est la f. idéale pour les vacances en famille** it's the ideal formula for a family holiday; **nous vous proposons différentes formules de crédit/de remboursement** we offer you various credit/repayment options *or* methods *or* formulae; **nous avons aussi une f. à 1000 euros** we also have a 1000-euro option **4** *Aut* **f. un/deux** Formula One/Two **5** *Admin (formulaire)* form; **f. de chèque** *Br* cheque form, *Am* blank cheque; **f. de demande de crédit** credit application form; **f. de réponse** reply form; *Com* **f. de soumission** tender form; **f. de télégramme** telegram form

formule-hôtel, *pl* **formules-hôtel** NF hotel package

formuler [fɔrmyle] VT *(doctrine)* to formulate; *(document)* to draw up; *(souhait)* to express; *(proposition)* to formulate, to put into words; *(plainte)* to lodge; *(règlement)* to formulate, to lay down

fornication [fɔrnikasjɔ̃] NF fornication

forniquer [fɔrnike] VI to fornicate

FORPRONU [fɔrprɔny] NF *(abrév* **Forces de protection des Nations unies)** UNPROFOR

fors [fɔr] PRÉP *Litt* except, save; **tout est perdu f. l'honneur** all is lost save honour

forsythia [fɔrsisja] NM *Bot* forsythia

FORT [fɔr]

ADJ	strong **1, 2** ▪ intense **2** ▪ loud **2** ▪ large **5** ▪ big **5**
ADV	loud **1** ▪ hard **1** ▪ very **2**
NM	forte **1** ▪ fort **2**

ADJ 1 *(vigoureux)* strong; **f. comme un Turc** *ou* **un bœuf** as strong as an ox; **utiliser la manière forte** to use strong-arm tactics, to use force; **trouver plus f. que soi** to meet one's match; **s'attaquer à plus f. que soi** to take on more than one can handle; **courage, il faut être f.** cheer up! you/we/*etc* must be strong; **f. de son expérience** with a wealth of experience behind one; **f. de son récent succès** bolstered by one's recent success; **f. de ses certitudes** secure in the strength of one's convictions; **f. de son bon droit** in the knowledge that right is on one's side; **il est une forte tête** he's/she's very strong-minded; **un esprit f.** a freethinker; **avoir affaire à forte partie** to be up against a strong opponent; **être f. en mathématiques/en ski/aux échecs** to be good at mathematics/skiing/chess; **elle est forte sur la question** she is well up in *or* knowledgeable about the matter; **il est f. pour critiquer, mais quand il faut travailler ...** he's good at criticizing, but when it comes to working ...
2 *(corde, boisson, sauce, haleine etc)* strong; *(fièvre, vent)* high; *(chaleur)* intense, great; *(lumière)* strong, bright, intense; *(pluie, mer)* heavy; *(voix)* loud; **moutarde forte** strong mustard; *Fig* **elle a fait (une) forte impression** she made a strong impression; **avoir une forte odeur** to have a strong smell; **c'est plus f. que moi!** I can't help it!; **j'avais une forte envie de rire/de lui casser la figure** I was very tempted to laugh/to smash his face in; *Fam* **c'est trop f.!**, **c'est un peu f. (de café)!** that's a bit much!; **ce qu'il y a de plus f.,** **c'est qu'on n'y peut rien** the worst of it is that nothing can be done about it; **à plus forte raison** all the more so (**que** since)
3 place/ville forte fortress/fortified town
4 se faire f. de faire qch to be sure *or* convinced one can do sth; **elles se font f. de le retrouver** they are sure *or* convinced they can find it
5 *(gros)* *(personne)* large, stout; *(lèvres)* thick, full; *(poitrine)* large; **homme à la forte charpente** solidly built man; **elle est forte des hanches** she's big round the hips, she has large hips; **forte somme** large sum of money; **forte différence** big *or* great difference; **forte baisse** *(de prix)* slump; **forte hausse des prix** sharp *or* big rise in prices; **forte pente** steep slope; **armée forte de cinq mille hommes** five-thousand-strong army, army five thousand strong; *Com* **prix f.** full price; **acheter qch au prix f.** to buy sth at *or* for the full price, to pay (the) full price for sth
ADV 1 *(parler, crier, chanter)* loudly, loud; *(tirer)* hard; **frapper f.** to strike *or* hit hard; *Fam* **y aller f.** to overdo it, to go over the top; **sentir f.** to smell strong; *Fam* **faire (très) f.** to do brilliantly, to do really well
2 *(très)* very, extremely; **il a été f. mécontent** he was very *or* extremely annoyed; **j'en suis f. aise** I'm very pleased; **c'est f. dommage** it's a great *or* real pity; **f. bien** very well; **f. heureusement, il était là** he was there, which was very fortunate
3 *(beaucoup)* **j'ai f. à faire** I have a great deal *or* a lot to do; **nous avons eu f. à faire avec cette jeune fille/ce radiateur électrique** we had our work cut out with that girl/that electric heater; **j'en doute f.** I very much doubt it
NM 1 *(spécialité)* strong point, forte; **la politesse n'est pas son f.** politeness is not his

strong point *or* his forte; **le f. et le faible de l'affaire** the strong and weak points of the matter; **le f. d'un bois** the heart of a wood; **au plus f. de l'hiver** in the depths of winter; **au f. de l'été/de l'épidémie** at the height of summer/of the epidemic; **au (plus) f. du combat** in the thick of the fight; **le plus f., c'est que je lui avais déjà dit** the best of it is, I'd already told him; *Prov* **la raison du plus f. est toujours la meilleure** might is right
2 *(citadelle)* fort, stronghold
▸▸ *Fam* **f. en gueule** loud-mouthed; **c'est un f. en gueule** he's a loudmouth; *Péj* **f. en thème** swot, *Am* grind; **forts des Halles** market porters

fortement [fɔrtəmɑ̃] ADV *(désirer, souhaiter, influencé)* strongly, greatly; *(tirer, pousser)* hard; *(impressionner)* greatly; **insister f. sur qch** to insist firmly *or* strongly on sth; **j'espère f. qu'il viendra** I very much *or* I sincerely hope he'll come; **f. épicé** highly spiced; **f. critiqué** strongly *or* highly criticized; **f. irrité** greatly *or* extremely irritated; **c'est f. conseillé** it's strongly advised; **f. charpenté** solidly built

forteresse [fɔrtərɛs] NF fortress, stronghold; **f. volante** flying fortress

fortiche [fɔrtiʃ] *Fam* ADJ clever, smart
N **1** clever *or* smart cookie; **c'est un f. en chimie** he's really good at chemistry **2** *Vieilli* *(personne robuste)* brawny person

fortifiant [fɔrtifjɑ̃] ADJ *(nourriture, boisson)* fortifying; *(air)* bracing, invigorating
NM *Méd* tonic

fortification [fɔrtifikasjɔ̃] NF *(action, ouvrages)* fortification

fortifier [fɔrtifje] *(impf & pr sub* n. **fortifiions)* VT **1** *(ville)* to fortify; *(mur, corps)* to fortify, to strengthen; *(muscles)* to tone up, to strengthen **2** *(sentiment, impression)* to strengthen; **cela m'a fortifié dans ma décision** that strengthened me in my decision
VPR **se fortifier 1** *(devenir plus fort)* to get *or* become stronger; **il faut qu'il se fortifie le dos** he has to strengthen his back **2** *Mil* to raise a line of defences; *(en creusant des tranchées)* to dig oneself in

Fortifs [fɔrtif] NFPL *Arg* **les F.** = the old defence works around Paris, once a favourite area for criminals

fortin [fɔrtɛ̃] NM small fort

Fortran [fɔrtrɑ̃] NM *Ordinat* FORTRAN

fortuit [fɔrtɥi] ADJ *(rencontre, événement)* chance, fortuitous; **dans cette affaire, rien n'est f.** nothing is fortuitous *or* nothing can be put down to chance in this matter; **toute ressemblance avec des personnes existantes ou ayant existé serait purement fortuite** any resemblance to persons living or dead is entirely coincidental; *Jur* **cas f.** act of God

fortuitement [fɔrtɥitmɑ̃] ADV by chance, fortuitously

fortune [fɔrtyn] NF **1** *(chance)* fortune, chance, luck; **chercher f.** to try one's luck; **revers de f.** reversal of fortune, setback in one's fortunes; **mauvaise f.** misfortune; **avoir la bonne/la mauvaise f. de rencontrer qn** to have the good fortune/misfortune to meet sb, to be fortunate/unfortunate enough to meet sb; **faire contre mauvaise f. bon cœur** to make the best of a bad job; **connaître des fortunes diverses** to have varying (degrees of) success; **la f. d'une théorie/d'une œuvre d'art** the fortunes of a theory/a work of art; **dîner à la f. du pot** to take pot luck; **inviter qn à la f. du pot** to invite sb to come and take pot luck; *Prov* **la f. sourit aux audacieux** fortune favours the brave; **installation de f.** temporary *or* makeshift installation; **lit de f.** makeshift bed; **réparations de f.** makeshift *or* emergency

repairs; **moyens de f.** makeshift means; *Naut* **mât de f.** jury mast; **(voile de) f.** crossjack (foresail); **f. de mer** perils of the sea
2 *(richesse)* fortune, wealth; **faire f.** to make one's fortune *or* a fortune; **avoir de la f.** to be well off; **sa f. est importante** he has a considerable fortune *or* considerable wealth; **c'est une grosse f.** he's a very wealthy man; **être l'artisan de sa f.** to be a self-made man; **valoir une f.** to be worth a fortune; **voilà toute ma f.** that's all I've got

fortuné [fɔrtyne] ADJ **1** *(riche)* rich, wealthy, well-off **2** *Arch, Litt* *(chanceux)* fortunate, happy

Il faut noter que l'adjectif anglais **fortunate** signifie uniquement **qui a de la chance.**

forum [fɔrɔm] NM forum; *Ordinat* **f. de discussion** discussion group, forum; **f. Internet** Web forum; **f. en ligne** online forum; **f. sur l'éducation** forum *or* symposium on education; *Radio etc* **f. populaire** vox pop; **F. social mondial** World Social Forum

fosse [fos] NF **1** *(creux)* pit, hole; *(abyssale)* trough; *Sport* (sand) pit; *Anat* fossa; *Min* pit; **les animaux des grandes fosses** animals living on the ocean bed **2** *(tombe)* grave; **f. commune** common grave; *Fam* **avoir un pied dans la f.** to have one foot in the grave; **creuser sa f. avec ses dents** to eat oneself into an early grave
▸▸ **f. d'aisances** cesspool; **f. aux lions** lions' den; *Théâtre* **f. d'orchestre** orchestra pit; **f. à purin** liquid manure pit; *Aut* **f. (de réparation)** inspection pit; **f. septique** septic tank

Do not confuse with **fossé.**

fossé [fose] NM **1** *(tranchée, au bord de la route)* ditch; *(douve)* moat; *Géol* trough **2** *Fig (entre personnes)* gulf; **le f. ne cesse de se creuser entre eux** there is an ever-widening gulf between them; **le f. des générations** the generation gap
▸▸ *Géol* **f. d'effondrement** rift valley; *Aut* **f. d'inspection** inspection pit

Do not confuse with **fosse.**

fossette [fosɛt] NF dimple

fossile [fosil] NM fossil; *Fam* **un vieux f.** an old fossil
ADJ fossil

fossilifère [fosilifɛr] ADJ fossiliferous

fossilisation [fosilizasjɔ̃] NF fossilization

fossiliser [fosilize] VT to fossilize
VPR **se fossiliser** to fossilize, to become fossilized; *Fig* **les mentalités se sont fossilisées** attitudes have become fossilized

fossoyeur [foswajœr] NM gravedigger; *Fig* destroyer

fou [fu], **fol**, **folle** [fɔl] *(the form* **fol** *is used in the masculine before a vowel or h mute)* ADJ
1 *(dément)* mad, insane; **devenir f.** to go mad *or* insane; **f. à lier** raving mad, out of one's mind; **cette musique/situation me rend f.** the music/situation is driving me mad; **il y a de quoi devenir f.** it's enough to drive you mad; **f. de joie/de terreur/de rage/d'inquiétude** beside oneself with joy/fear/rage/worry; **être f. de qn** to be mad *or* crazy about sb; **être f. d'amour pour qn** *ou* **f. amoureux de qn** to be madly in love with sb; **entre eux, c'est l'amour f.** they're madly in love, they're crazy about each other; **vivre l'amour f.** to be madly in love; **f. de peinture/ski** mad *or* crazy about painting/skiing, dead keen on painting/skiing; **des diamants? mais tu es f.!** diamonds? you're crazy!; **tu serais f. de ne pas accepter** you'd be mad *or* crazy not to accept; *Fam* **pas folle, la guêpe!** there are no flies on her!, she's not stupid!; **il n'est pas f.** he's no fool

2 folles illusions wild delusions; *Bible* **les vierges folles** the foolish virgins; **les années folles** the Roaring Twenties; **un fol espoir** a foolish *or* mad hope

3 *(énorme)* tremendous; **succès f.** tremendous *or* wild success; **mettre un temps f. à faire qch** to take absolutely ages to do sth; **il gagne un argent f.** he makes pots of money, he rakes it in; **à une allure folle** at breakneck speed; **il y avait un monde f.** there was an enormous *or* a tremendous crowd; **un prix f.** an exorbitant price; *Fam* **c'est f. ce que c'est grand!** it's incredible how big it is!; **d'une gaieté folle** wildly happy

4 *(incontrôlé)* *(mèche de cheveux)* stray, loose; *(camion)* runaway; *(boussole, aiguille)* crazy; *(roue)* idle, free; *(poulie)* loose; **f. rire** (uncontrollable) giggling; **avoir un f. rire** to have (a fit of) the giggles; *Fam* **avoir une patte folle** to have a gammy *or* Am gimpy leg; **herbes folles** rank weeds; *Bot* **folle avoine** wild oats

N lunatic, madman, f madwoman; **f. furieux** raving lunatic, maniac; **espèce de vieille folle!** crazy old woman!; *Fam* **il travaille comme un f.** he works like mad; **c'est une histoire de fous** I can't make head (n)or tail of it; *Fam* **maison de fous** madhouse; **f. du volant** reckless driver; *Litt* **la folle du logis** (wild *or* fevered) imagination; **faire le f.** to play *or* act the fool; **plus on est de fous plus on rit** the more the merrier

NM **1** *Échecs* bishop **2** *Hist (bouffon)* jester, fool **3** *Orn* **f. de Bassan** gannet

NF *Péj Fam* **folle** *(homosexuel)* queen; **grande folle** raving queen

fouace [fwas] NF *Culin* = **fougasse**

foucade [fukad] NF *Litt* caprice, passing whim

foudre[1] [fudr] NF lightning, *surtout Bible* thunderbolt; **la f. est tombée sur la maison** the house was struck by lightning; **maison frappée par la f.** house struck by lightning; *Fig* **coup de f.** love at first sight; **avoir le coup de f. pour qn** to fall in love at first sight; **j'ai eu le coup de f. pour cette maison** I fell in love with this house at first sight

NFPL **foudres** *(colère)* wrath

NM **un f. de guerre** a great warrior; *Fig* **ce n'est pas un f. de guerre** he wouldn't say boo to a goose; **f. d'éloquence** powerful orator

foudre[2] NM *(tonneau)* tun, large cask

foudroyant [fudrwajã] ADJ *(attaque, nouvelles)* devastating; *(regard)* withering; *(succès)* stunning, staggering; **progrès foudroyants** lightning progress; **une mort foudroyante** a sudden death; **poison f.** devastatingly lethal poison

foudroyer [fudrwaje] VT (**je foudroie; je foudroierai**) to strike; **être foudroyé** to be struck by lightning; **arbre foudroyé** tree struck by lightning; *Fig* **l'apoplexie l'a foudroyé** he was struck down by apoplexy; **la mort l'a foudroyé alors qu'il n'avait que 30 ans** he was struck down when he was only 30; **elle le foudroya du regard** she gave him a withering look; **cette nouvelle m'a foudroyé** I was thunderstruck *or* devastated by the news; **la division fut foudroyée par la puissance de feu de l'ennemi** the division was decimated by enemy fire power

fouet [fwɛ] NM **1** whip; **donner le f. à qn** to whip *or* flog sb; **faire claquer son f.** to crack one's whip; **coup de f.** lash, stroke; *Fig* fillip, stimulus; **l'air de la mer lui a donné un coup de f.** the sea air has perked him up *or* given him a lift; **donner un coup de f. à l'économie** to give a fillip to the economy, to stimulate *or* boost the economy; **être frappé de plein f.** *(d'une cible)* to receive a direct hit; **frapper la balle de plein f.** to connect well with the

ball; **il a reçu le ballon de plein f.** the ball came straight at him; **collision de plein f.** head-on collision **2** *(de cuisine)* whisk **3** *(de l'aile d'un oiseau, de la queue d'un chien)* tip; *Naut (d'une poulie)* tail

fouettard [fwɛtar] ADJ **le Père F.** the Bogeyman

fouettement [fwɛtmã] NM *(d'une voile)* flapping; *(d'une corde, de la pluie etc)* lashing

fouetter [fwete] VT **1** *(personne)* to whip, to flog; *(cheval)* to whip; *(œufs)* to beat, to whisk; *(crème)* to whip; **ils l'ont fouetté jusqu'au sang** they whipped *or* flogged him until he bled; **la pluie fouette les vitres** the rain is lashing (against) the panes; *Fam* **il n'y a pas de quoi f. un chat** there's nothing to make a fuss about; *Fam* **avoir d'autres chats à f.** to have other fish to fry **2** *Fig (exciter)* to excite, to stimulate; **vent qui fouette le sang** wind that makes the blood tingle; **le sang fouetté par le désir** spurred on *or* stimulated by desire

VI **1** *(d'un câble)* to lash, to whip; *(d'une voile)* to flap; **la pluie fouette contre les vitres** the rain is lashing (against) the panes **2** *Fam (sentir mauvais)* to stink, to pong **3** *Arg (avoir peur)* to be scared stiff

foufou [fufu] *Fam* ADJ M nutty, daft
NM nutter

foufoune [fufun], **foufounette** [fufunɛt] NF *Vulg (sexe de femme)* pussy, *Br* fanny

fougasse [fugas] NF *Culin* flat bread *(sometimes stuffed with anchovies, olives etc)*

fougeraie [fuʒrɛ] NF patch of ferns

fougère [fuʒɛr] NF fern; **f. aigle** bracken; **f. arborescente** tree fern

fougue [fug] NF fire, spirit, passion; **la f. de la jeunesse** youthful high spirits; **cheval plein de f.** spirited horse

fougueusement [fugøzmã] ADV fierily; *(embrasser)* passionately

fougueux, -euse [fugø, -øz] ADJ *(personne)* fiery, ardent, spirited; *(cheval)* spirited; **tempérament f.** fiery temperament

fouille [fuj] NF **1** *(fosse)* excavation, pit; **f. à ciel ouvert** open pit **2** *Archéol* **fouilles** dig, excavations; **faire des fouilles** to carry out excavations *or* a dig **3** *(d'un suspect, voyageur)* search(ing), frisking; *(d'un lieu)* search(ing); **passer à la f.** to be searched *or* frisked; **la police a fait une f. complète de ses bureaux** the police made a thorough search of his offices **4** *très Fam (poche)* pocket; *Fig* **se remplir les fouilles, s'en mettre plein les fouilles** to line one's pockets **5** *Can (chute)* fall; **prendre une f.** to fall, to tumble

fouillé [fuje] ADJ detailed

fouille-merde, *pl* **fouille-merdes** N *très Fam* muckraker

fouiller [fuje] VT *(maison)* to search; *(personne)* to search, to frisk; *(tiroir)* to search (through), to go through; *(valise)* to go through; *(bois)* to scour, to comb; *(terre)* to dig; *Archéol (emplacement d'un ancien site)* to excavate; **f. toutes ses poches** to go through *or* look in all one's pockets; **ses yeux fouillaient la salle** his eyes *or* he scanned the room; **f. un problème** to go thoroughly into a problem, to explore a problem thoroughly

VI **1** *(d'un lapin)* to burrow; *(d'un cochon)* to root **2 f. dans une armoire/sa poche** to search *or* rummage in a cupboard/in one's pocket; **j'ai fouillé dans toutes les poches sans rien trouver** I've gone through *or* searched all the pockets without finding anything; **f. dans les papiers de qn** to search *or* go through sb's papers; **f. dans les librairies pour trouver un livre** to search around in bookshops for a book; **quand je**

n'ai rien à faire, je vais f. dans les librairies when I've nothing to do, I go and rummage around *or* poke around in bookshops; **f. dans le passé** to delve into the past; **f. dans sa mémoire** to search one's memory

VPR **se fouiller** to go through one's pockets; *Arg* **tu peux te f.!** nothing doing!; **il peut se f. s'il croit qu'on lui en donnera!** if he thinks we're going to give him some, he's got another think coming!

fouilleur, -euse [fujœr, -øz] N **1** *Archéol* excavator, digger **2** *(à la douane)* officer who carries out body-searches **3** *(fouineur)* rummager, searcher; **f. de brocantes/de bibliothèques** an avid frequenter of second-hand shops/libraries

NF *Agr* **fouilleuse** subsoil plough *or* Am plow

fouillis [fuji] NM *(de papiers, jouets etc)* jumble, muddle; *(de lianes)* tangle; **range ton f.** put away your mess; **c'est le f. ici** it's a mess in here

fouinard, -arde [fwinar, -ard] *Fam* ADJ nosy, prying, inquisitive
N nosy parker, pryer

fouine [fwin] NF *Zool* stone marten; *Fam* **tête de f.** weasel-faced, ferret-faced

fouiner [fwine] VI *Fam* to ferret about, to nose about; **f. dans les affaires d'autrui** to poke one's nose into other people's business

fouineur, -euse [fwinœr, -øz] ADJ, N *Fam* = **fouinard**

fouir [fwir] VT to dig; *(d'animaux)* to burrow, to dig

fouisseur, -euse [fwisœr, -øz] ADJ *(animal)* burrowing
N burrower

foulage [fulaʒ] NM **1** *(de raisins)* pressing, crushing **2** *(du cuir)* tanning; *(de tissu)* fulling **3** *Typ* impression

foulant [fulã] ADJ pressing, crushing; **pompe foulante** force pump; *Fam* **ce n'est pas bien f.** it won't kill you/her/*etc*

foulard [fular] NM **1** scarf **2** *Tex* foulard

foule [ful] NF **1** *(de gens)* crowd, *Litt* throng; *(d'idées, de souvenirs)* host; **j'ai une f. de choses à te raconter/à faire** I've got lots of things to tell you/to do; **il y a f.** there are crowds of people (there); **il n'y a pas f.** there's hardly anyone around; **psychologie des foules** crowd psychology; **mouvement de foule(s)** movement in the crowd; **entrer en f.** to crowd in; **les réfugiés arrivent en f. à la frontière** the refugees are flocking to the border; **faire f. autour de qn** to crowd round sb, to mob sb; **fuir la f.** to flee the crowds; **quelle f. dans les rues!** how crowded the streets are!; *Vieilli* **on en trouve en f.** there are loads of them **2** *Can (du caribou)* migration

foulée [fule] NF **1** *Sport, Équitation* stride; **parcourir les champs à longues foulées** to stride over the fields; **courir à petites foulées** to trot along; *Sport* **courir** *ou* **rester dans la f. d'un concurrent** to follow close behind a competitor, to slip-stream; **avoir une bonne f.** to have a good stride; *Fig* **dans la f., j'ai aussi vérifié les comptes** while I was at it, I also checked the accounts **2** **foulées** *(d'animaux sauvages)* track(s), spoor

fouler [fule] VT **1** *(herbe)* to trample (down), to tread down; *(raisins)* to press, to crush; **f. qch aux pieds** to trample sth underfoot; *Fig* **les droits de l'homme sont foulés aux pieds!** human rights have been trampled underfoot!; **nous foulions pour la première fois le sol de Grèce** we were setting foot for the first time on Greek soil **2** *Tex (tissu)* to full; *(cuir)* to tan

VPR **se fouler 1 se f. la cheville** to sprain *or* twist one's ankle **2** *Fam* **se f. (la rate)** to strain oneself, to overexert oneself; **tu ne t'es pas foulé!** you didn't (exactly) strain *or* overexert yourself!

fouleur, -euse [fulœr, -øz] N **1** *(de raisins) (personne)* winepresser **2** *Tex (personne) (de tissu)* fuller; *(de cuir)* tanner

fouloir [fulwar] NM *(pour le raisin)* wine press

foulon [fulɔ̃] NM *Tex (de tissu)* fuller; **chardon à f.** fuller's teasel; **terre à f.** fuller's earth; **(moulin à) f.** fulling mill

foulonnier [fulɔnje] NM = **fouleur 2**

foulque [fulk] NF *Orn* coot

foultitude [fultityd] NF *Fam* **une f.** loads, masses (**de** of)

foulure [fulyr] NF sprain; **f. du poignet/de la cheville** sprained wrist/ankle

four [fur] NM **1** *(de cuisine)* oven; **f. à gaz** gas oven; **f. électrique** electric oven; **f. de boulanger** baker's oven; **f. à micro-ondes** microwave (oven); **faire cuire au f.** *(pain)* to bake; *(viande)* to roast; **il fait noir comme dans un f.** it's pitch black; **vaisselle allant au f.** ovenware; **plat allant au f.** ovenproof dish; *Fam* **ouvrir une bouche (grande) comme un f.** to open one's mouth really wide; **on ne peut être à la fois au f. et au moulin** you can't be in two places at the same time; *Culin* **petits fours** petits fours

2 *Ind* kiln; *(avec combustion du contenu)* furnace; **f. à chaux** lime kiln; **f. à briques** brick kiln; **f. à émaux** enamelling kiln; **f. solaire** solar furnace

3 *Fam (fiasco)* flop; **la pièce/l'exposition a fait un f.** the play/exhibition was a flop; **il a fait un f. avec son discours** his speech was a flop

fourbe [furb] ADJ cheating, double-dealing, two-faced

N cheat, rogue, double-dealer

fourberie [furbəri] NF **1** *(hypocrisie)* deceit, cheating, double-dealing **2** *(action)* underhand trick

fourbi [furbi] NM *Fam* **1** *(attirail)* gear, tackle, *Br* clobber; *(de soldat)* kit; **tout le f.** the whole (kit and) caboodle; *Fig* **quel f., je ne retrouve rien!** what a muddle *or* mess, I can't find anything! **2** *(truc)* thingummy, thingy

fourbir [furbir] VT *(métal)* to polish up, to shine up, to furbish; *Fig* **f. ses armes** to prepare for battle

fourbissage [furbisaʒ] NM *(du métal)* polishing, furbishing

fourbu [furby] ADJ exhausted, tired out

fourche [furʃ] NF **1** *Agr* fork; **f. à foin** hayfork, pitchfork; **remuer le sol à la f.** to fork the ground; **chariot (élévateur) à f.** forklift (truck); *Aut* **f. d'attelage** trailer hitch **2** *(de bicyclette, d'arbre, de route, de rivière)* fork; *(de pantalon)* crotch, *Br* crutch; *Aut* Y junction; **mes cheveux ont des fourches** my hair has split ends; **en forme de f.** forked; **la route fait une f.** the road forks **3** *Hist* **les Fourches Caudines** the Caudine Forks; *Fig* **passer sous les fourches caudines** to suffer torments

fourchée [furʃe] NF *(de foin)* pitchforkful

fourcher [furʃe] VI **1** **sa langue a fourché** he made a slip of the tongue **2** *Arch* to fork, to divide

VT *(sol)* to fork

fourchet [furʃɛ] NM *Vét* foot rot

fourchette [furʃɛt] NF **1** *(ustensile)* fork; **f. à poisson/à dessert** fish/dessert fork; *Fam* **il a un joli *ou* bon coup de f., c'est une bonne f.** he's a hearty eater, he has a healthy *or* hearty appetite; **manger avec la f. du père Adam** to eat with one's fingers

2 *Mil, Fin* bracket; **prendre une cible en f.** *ou*

à la f. to bracket a target; **f. de salaire** wage bracket; **f. de prix** price bracket *or* range; *Bourse* **f. de cotation** trading range; **f. de cours de clôture** closing range; **f. de cours d'ouverture** opening range; **f. d'imposition** tax bracket; **f. de taux** rate band

3 *Cartes* tenace

4 *(d'un volatile)* wishbone; *(d'un sabot de cheval)* frog

5 *(de balance)* beam support

6 *Tech* belt guide, shifter; **f. de débrayage** clutch throw-out fork; **f. d'embrayage** clutch fork

fourchu [furʃy] ADJ forked; *(bâton, menton)* cleft; **pied f.** cloven hoof; **avoir les cheveux fourchus** to have split ends; **avoir la langue fourchue** to speak with a forked tongue

fourgon¹ [furgɔ̃] NM *(de cheminée)* poker; *(de four)* (fire) rake

fourgon² [furgɔ̃] NM *Aut* van; **f. automobile** (motor) van; **f. blindé** armoured van **2** *Rail* **f. de queue** rear (brake) van, guard's van, *Am* caboose

▸▸ **f. à bagages** luggage van, *Am* baggage car; **f. à bétail** cattle truck; **f. cellulaire** police van *or* *Am* wagon; **f. funèbre, f. funéraire, f. mortuaire** hearse

fourgonner [furgɔne] VT *(feu)* to poke, to rake

VI to poke the fire; *Fam* **f. dans un tiroir** to poke about *or* rummage about in a drawer

fourgonnette [furgɔnɛt] NF (small *or* light) van

fourguer [furge] VT *Fam (vendre)* to flog; *(donner)* to unload; **f. qch à qn** *(vendre)* to flog sb sth; *(donner)* to unload sth onto sb

fourmi [furmi] NF ant; *Fig* **c'est une vraie f.** he's/she's a busy bee, he's/she's always beavering away (at something); **avoir des fourmis dans les jambes** to have pins and needles in one's legs

fourmilier [furmilje] NM anteater

fourmilière [furmiljer] NF anthill, ants' nest; *Fig* **cette banlieue est une véritable f. (humaine)** this suburb is swarming *or* teeming with people; **donner des coups de pied dans la f.** to stir things up

fourmi-lion, *pl* **fourmis-lions** NM *Entom* ant-lion

fourmillement [furmijmɑ̃] NM **1** *(d'insectes)* swarming; **un f. de détails/d'idées** a welter of details/ideas **2** *(dans les membres)* pins and needles

fourmiller [furmije] VI to swarm, to teem; **les vers fourmillaient dans ce fromage** the cheese was alive with maggots; *Fig* **la ville fourmille d'ingénieurs** the town is swarming *or* teeming with engineers; **ouvrage qui fourmille de fautes** work teeming *or* riddled with mistakes; **f. d'idées** to be bursting with ideas; **f. d'impressions** to be full of impressions

fournaise [furnɛz] NF **cette chambre est une (vraie) f.** this room's like an oven

fourneau, -eaux [furno] NM **1** *(de chaudière)* furnace; **f. d'une pipe** bowl of a pipe **2 f. de cuisine** (kitchen) range; **f. à gaz** gas stove *or* *Br* cooker; **c'est David qui est aux fourneaux ce soir** David is the chef this evening **3** *Métal* furnace; **haut f.** blast furnace **4** *Min* **f. de mine** mine chamber, blast hole

fournée [furne] NF *(de pains)* batch; *Fig Fam* batch, contingent

fourni [furni] ADJ **1** *(magasin, bibliothèque etc)* **(bien) f.** well-stocked **2** *(cheveux)* thick; *(barbe)* bushy, thick; **barbe peu fournie** sparse *or* thin beard

fournil [furni] NM bakehouse

fourniment [furnimɑ̃] NM *Fam* gear, *Br* clobber

fournir [furnir] VT **1** *(approvisionner)* to supply; **f. qch à qn, f. qn en qch** to supply sb with sth; **qui fournit la famille royale?** who is the Royal Family's supplier?, who supplies the Royal Family?

2 *(produire)* to supply, to provide; *(documents)* to produce, to furnish; *(idées)* to provide; **f. une caution** to give a guarantee, to provide security; **vignoble qui fournit un bon vin** vineyard that yields *or* produces a good wine; **l'ENA fournit de futurs hauts fonctionnaires** the ENA produces *or* turns out the senior civil servants of the future; **f. un effort considérable** to make a considerable effort; **f. des renseignements à qn** to supply *or* provide *or* furnish sb with information; **vous devez f. votre carte d'identité** you must present *or* show your identity card; **il pourra peut-être te f. du travail** he might be able to give you some work; **f. le gîte et le couvert** to provide board and lodging; **cela te fournira l'occasion de le rencontrer** it will provide you with *or* give you the opportunity of meeting him; **f. une bonne raison à qn** to provide sb with *or* give sb a good reason; **pièces à f.** required documents; *Cartes* **f. du trèfle** to follow a club lead; *Sport* **f. un jeu remarquable** to play an outstanding game

VI *Vieilli* **f. aux dépenses** to defray the expenses; **f. aux besoins de qn** to supply sb's wants

VPR **se fournir 1 se f. en qch** to get in supplies of sth; **ils se fournissent (en vin) chez ce négociant** they get their supplies (of wine) from this merchant

2 *(d'une barbe etc)* to grow thick

fournissement [furnismɑ̃] NM *Fin* contribution *(in shares)*

fournisseur, -euse [furnisœr, -øz] N **1** *Com* supplier; **l'entrée des fournisseurs** the tradesman's entrance; **f. de navires** *ou* **de la marine** ships' chandler; **le plus grand f. français en meubles** the biggest French supplier of furniture; **f. attitré** approved *or* official supplier; *(habituel)* regular supplier; **f. exclusif** sole supplier; **f. principal** prime supplier; **f. secondaire** secondary supplier **2** *Ordinat* **f. d'accès** (Internet) access provider; **f. de contenu** content provider

ADJ **les pays fournisseurs de la France** the countries that supply France (with goods), France's suppliers

fourniture [furnityr] NF **1** *(approvisionnement)* supplying, provision **2 fournitures** supplies; **façon et fournitures** making-up and materials; **fournitures et services** supplies and services

▸▸ **fournitures de bureau** office supplies; **fournitures de navires** ships' chandlery; **fournitures scolaires** educational stationery

---

Il faut noter que le mot anglais **furniture** est un faux ami. Il signifie **meubles**.

---

fourrage [furaʒ] NM fodder, forage; **f. sec/ vert** hay/silage; **rentrer du f.** to harvest forage

fourrager¹ [furaʒe] (**n. fourrageons; je fourrageai(s)**) VI *(pour s'alimenter)* to forage; *Fam (fouiller)* to rummage, to forage

VT **1** *Fam (papiers)* to rummage through **2** *Arch (pays)* to pillage, to ravage

fourrager², -ère [furaʒe, -ɛr] ADJ **plantes fourragères** fodder crops; **betterave fourragère** mangel-wurzel

NF **fourragère 1** *(champ)* field sown with fodder crop **2** *Mil* fourragère, shoulder braid

fourre [fur] NF *Suisse (d'un oreiller)* pillowcase; *(d'un édredon)* quilt cover; *(d'un livre)* jacket; *(d'un disque)* sleeve; *(dossier, chemise)* file, folder

fourré [fure] ADJ **1** *(manteau, gants etc)* (fur-)lined; *(bois)* thick, dense; **chocolats fourrés à la crème** chocolate creams; **bonbon f.** sweet with a soft centre, *Am* candy with a soft center **2** *Escrime* **coup f.** exchanged hit, double hit; *Fig* **méfie-toi, c'est un coup f.** look out, it's a trap; **faire un coup f. à qn** to trick sb; *Vieilli* **paix fourrée** hollow *or* mock peace
▪ NM thicket; *(à la chasse)* cover

fourreau, -eaux [furo] NM *(d'épée)* sheath, scabbard; *(de parapluie)* cover; *(robe)* sheath dress; **remettre l'épée au f.** to sheathe one's sword; *Tech* **soupapes à fourreaux** sleeve valves
▪ ADJ **jupe/robe f.** pencil skirt/sheath dress

fourrer [fure] VT **1** *Fam (mettre)* to stick; **je les avais fourrés dans le coin** I'd stuck them in the corner; **f. ses mains dans ses poches** to stick *or* stuff *or* shove one's hands in one's pockets; **mais où ai-je bien pu f. ça?** where on earth have I stuck it?; **f. son nez partout** to poke *or* stick one's nose into everything; **f. qn au trou** to stick *or* chuck sb in jail; **il est toujours fourré dans mes pattes** he's always under my feet; **il est toujours fourré au bistrot** he's always stuck in the pub
2 *(avec de la fourrure)* to line (with fur)
3 *Tech (jointure)* to pack
4 **f. un chocolat/une crêpe de liqueur** to fill a chocolate/a pancake with liqueur; **f. une dinde de marrons** to stuff a turkey with chestnuts
▪ VPR **se fourrer** *Fam* **il s'est fourré dans le coin/sous le lit** he got into the corner/under the bed; **où est-il allé se f.?** wherever has he got to? wherever has he hidden himself?; **je ne savais plus où me f.** I didn't know where to put myself; **se f. dans une sale affaire** to get involved in a nasty business; *Fam* **il se fourre les doigts dans le nez** he picks his nose; *Fig Fam* **si tu crois que je vais l'attendre, tu te fourres le doigt dans l'œil** if you think I'm going to wait for him, you've got another think coming

fourre-tout [furtu] NM INV **1** *(pièce)* junk room; *(placard)* junk cupboard **2** *(sac)* holdall, *Am* carryall; *Aut* storage pocket
▪ ADJ INV **sac f.** holdall, *Am* carryall; **placard f.** junk cupboard; *Péj* **une loi f.** a mishmash *or* ragbag of a law

fourreur [furœr] NM furrier

fourrier [furje] NM *Mil* quartermaster sergeant

fourrière [furjɛr] NF *(pour animaux, voitures)* pound; **mettre un chien/une voiture en f.** *ou* à la f. to impound a dog/a car

fourrure [furyr] NF **1** *(peau préparée, vêtement)* fur; **manteau de f.** fur coat **2** *(pelage)* fur, coat **3** *(de jointure)* packing; *Aut* **f. de frein** brake lining

fourvoiement [furvwamã] NM *Litt* going astray

fourvoyer [furvwaje] *(je fourvoie; je fourvoierai)* *Litt* VT to mislead, to lead astray
▪ VPR **se fourvoyer** to lose one's way; *Fig* to make a mistake, to go astray

foutage [futaʒ] NM *Fam* **c'est du f. de gueule** you/they/*etc* gotta be kidding!, *Br* that's just taking the piss!

foutaise [futɛz] NF *très Fam* bullshit, crap; **c'est de la f.!** that's (a load of) bullshit *or* crap!

fouteur, -euse [futœr, -øz] N *Fam* **f. de merde** shit-stirrer

foutimasser [futimase] VI *Suisse Fam (perdre son temps)* to mess about

foutoir [futwar] NM *très Fam* dump, tip

foutraque [futrak] ADJ *Fam* nuts, *Br* crackers

foutre¹ [futr] *(pp* **foutu***; pr ind* **je fous, n.**

foutons) ADV *Fam Vieilli* damned; **je n'en sais f. rien** I know damn all about it
▪ VT *très Fam* **1** *(mettre)* **je me demande où elle a pu le f.** where the hell has she put it?; **f. qch par terre** to chuck *or* fling sth on the ground; **f. qn à la porte** to chuck sb out; **f. le bordel** to create havoc *or* chaos; **f. qn en rogne** *ou* **en pétard** to make sb hopping mad; **ça la fout mal** that won't look too good; **ça a tout foutu en l'air** that screwed *or Vulg* fucked everything up
2 *(faire)* to do; **il ne fout rien** he does damn all *or Br* bugger all; **il n'a pas l'air de f. grand-chose** he doesn't seem to do much at all; **qu'est-ce que tu fous dans mon bureau?** what the hell are you doing in my office?; **ça fait deux heures que je t'attends, qu'est-ce que tu fous?** I've been waiting for you for two hours, what (the hell) are you playing at?; **je ne sais pas quoi f. de lui/de cette vieille table** I don't know what the hell to do with him/this old table; **je n'en ai rien à f.** I couldn't give a damn, I couldn't care less; **qu'est-ce que ça peut f.?** so what?, what the hell does it matter?; **qu'est-ce que ça peut f. qu'on soit en retard?** so what if we're late, what the hell does it matter if we're late?; **qu'est-ce que ça peut te/lui f.?** what the hell is it to you/him?, what the hell does it matter to you/him?; **f. le camp** to piss off, *Br* to bugger off; **qu'il aille se faire f.** he can piss off *or Vulg* fuck off; **va te faire f.!** piss off!, *Vulg* fuck off!
3 *(donner)* **je vais lui f. une bonne raclée** I'll give him a good hiding; **elle m'a foutu la honte** *(d'elle)* I was ashamed of her; *(de moi)* she made me ashamed of myself; **f. la trouille à qn** to put the wind up sb, to scare sb stiff; **ça nous a foutu un coup** it gave us a nasty shock; **qu'est-ce qui m'a foutu un empoté pareil!** what an absolute oaf you are!; **je t'en fous!** some chance!, you'll be lucky!; **je t'en foutrais, du champagne!** champagne, you'll be lucky! *or* I should coco!
4 *Vieilli Vulg (posséder sexuellement)* to fuck
5 *Suisse* **f. qch bas** *(démolir)* to knock sth down; **f. qn bas** *(tuer)* to kill sb *or Br* to do sb in
▪ VPR **se foutre** *très Fam* **1** *(se mettre)* **il s'est encore foutu dans une affaire louche** he's got (himself) mixed up in some shady business again; **se f. par terre** to fall flat on one's face; **se f. sur la gueule** to beat the living daylights out of each other; **se f. en l'air** to top oneself; **il s'est foutu dedans!** he got it wrong!
2 se f. de qn/qch *(se moquer de)* to make fun of sb/sth, to take the piss *or Br* the mickey out of sb/sth; *(être indifférent à)* not to give a damn about sb/sth; **se f. de la gueule de qn** to take the piss *or Br* the mickey out of sb; **tu te fous du monde ou quoi?** who the hell do you think you are?; **c'est vraiment se f. (de la gueule) du monde!** he/they/*etc* must think we're absolute idiots!; **elle se fout complètement de ce que j'en pense** she doesn't give a damn (about) what I think of it; **je m'en fous** I don't give a damn
3 *Suisse* **se f. bas** *(se suicider)* to commit suicide *or Br* to top oneself; **se f. en bas** *(tomber)* to fall

foutre² NM *Vulg (sperme)* come, *Br* spunk

foutrement [futrəmã] ADV *Fam* damn, *Br* bloody; **f. bien** damn well, *Br* bloody well; **je n'en sais f. rien** I know damn all *or Br* bugger all about it

foutriquet [futrikɛ] NM *Péj Vieilli* little runt *or* squirt

foutu [futy] ADJ *Vulg* **1** *(maudit)* damn (awful), *Br* bloody (awful) **2** *(en mauvais état, perdu)* ruined; **il est f.** he's had it, he's done for; **ma bagnole/robe est foutue** my car/dress has had it; **c'est f.!** forget it!; **pour la**

fête de demain, c'est f. you can forget the party tomorrow; **c'est f. pour mon augmentation** I can forget *or* it's goodbye to my pay rise **3** *(bâti, conçu)* **elle est plutôt bien foutue** she's got a great body; **c'est bien/mal f.** it's well/badly designed **4** *(malade)* **je suis mal f.** I feel really *or Br* bloody awful **5** *(capable)* **elle n'est même pas foutue de le faire** she's not up to doing it; **elle serait foutue de le lui dire** she's quite likely to tell him

fox(-terrier), *pl* **fox(-terriers)** [fɔks(terje)] NM fox terrier

fox-trot [fɔkstrɔt] NM INV foxtrot

foyer [fwaje] NM **1** *(domicile)* home, household; *surtout Mktg* household unit; **le f. familial** (the) family home; **le f. conjugal** the marital home; **rentrer dans ses foyers** to return home; **mère** *ou* **femme au f.** housewife; **homme au f.** househusband; **fonder un f.** to start a family; *Fin* **f. fiscal** household *(as a tax unit)*
2 f. d'étudiants student residence; **f. de jeunes travailleurs** young workers' hostel; **f. d'accueil et d'hébergement** *(pour les gens à la rue)* hostel for the homeless
3 *Scol* common room; *Théâtre* foyer; **f. des artistes** green room
4 *(de chaleur, d'infection)* source; *(d'incendie, d'érudition, de conflits)* seat, centre, *Am* center; **f. d'intrigue** hotbed of intrigue
5 *(âtre)* fireplace, hearth; *(de locomotive)* firebox; **f. de chaudière** boiler furnace
6 *(de lentille, courbe etc)* focus; **verres à double f.** bifocal lenses, bifocals

frac [frak] NM tail coat, tails

fracas [fraka] NM *(de verre cassé, du tonnerre)* crash; *(de l'orage)* din; *(des armes)* clash; *(vacarme)* racket, din; **faire du f.** *(d'un événement)* to create a sensation; **à grand f.** with a lot of fuss, with a great to-do; **elle sortit avec f.** she stormed out

fracassant [frakasã] ADJ *(bruit)* deafening; *Fig* **c'est une nouvelle/révélation fracassante** it's a shattering *or* staggering piece of news/revelation; **succès f.** resounding success

fracasser [frakase] VT to smash (to pieces), to shatter; **il aurait eu la tête fracassée** he would have smashed his head in
▪ VPR **se fracasser** to crash, to smash; **tu vas te f. la tête!** you'll smash your head in!

fractal, -ale, -aux, -ales [fraktal] ADJ fractal
▪ NF **fractale** fractal

fraction [fraksjɔ̃] NF **1** *Math* fraction; **f. ordinaire** vulgar fraction; **f. décimale** decimal fraction; **f. périodique** recurring decimal SEE GRAMMAR A76; B59 **2** *(partie)* part, portion; *Pol* splinter group; **ça a duré une f. de seconde** it lasted a fraction of a second *or* a split second; *Compta* **f. imposable** part subject to tax; **f. d'intérêt** interest accrued **3** *Rel (du pain)* breaking

fractionnaire [fraksjɔnɛr] ADJ fractional; **nombre f.** improper fraction

fractionnel, -elle [fraksjɔnɛl] ADJ *(tactique)* divisive

fractionnement [fraksjɔnmã] NM **1** *(d'une propriété, d'un groupe)* dividing up, splitting up; *(de paiements)* spreading (out); *(d'actions)* splitting **2** *Chimie* fractional distillation; *(d'huiles minérales)* cracking **3** *Com* breaking bulk

fractionner [fraksjɔne] VT **1** *(diviser)* to divide up, to split up; *Math* to fractionize; **f. le paiement** to pay in instalments; **nous allons devoir f. l'opération en plusieurs phases** we'll have to break down *or* split the operation into several stages **2** *Chimie (distillation)* to fractionate; *(huiles minérales)* to crack

VPR se fractionner *(de gens, d'objets)* to split up, to divide up; **le groupe se fractionne en deux** the group splits *or* divides in two

fractionnisme [fraksjɔnism] **NM** *Pol (tactique)* divisive tactics; *(caractère)* factionalism

fractionniste [fraksjɔnist] **N** *Pol* factionalist

fracture [fraktyr] **NF 1** *(d'une serrure, porte)* breaking open, forcing **2** *Méd, Géol* fracture; **f. du crâne** fractured skull; **f. simple** simple *or* closed fracture; **f. multiple** multiple fracture; **f. ouverte** open fracture **3** *Pol* **f. Nord-Sud** North-South divide; **la f. sociale** the gap between the haves and have-nots in society

fracturer [fraktyre] **VT 1** *(serrure, porte, coffre-fort)* to break open, to force **2** *(os)* to fracture

VPR se fracturer to fracture, to break; **se f. le tibia** to fracture one's tibia

fragile [fraʒil] **ADJ** *(construction)* fragile, flimsy; *(verre)* brittle; *(personne, santé)* fragile, frail, delicate; *(estomac)* weak, delicate; *(autorité)* weak, unstable; *(bonheur)* precarious, fragile; *(équilibre)* delicate; *(hypothèse)* shaky; **elle est f. des poumons/de la gorge** she has delicate lungs/a delicate throat; **ne la brutalise pas, elle est encore f.** *(psychologiquement)* don't treat her roughly, she's still (feeling) fragile

fragilisation [fraʒilizasjɔ̃] **NF** weakening

fragiliser [fraʒilize] **VT** to weaken

fragilité [fraʒilite] **NF** *(d'une construction)* fragility; *(du verre)* brittleness; *(d'une personne)* frailty, weakness, fragility; *(d'une hypothèse)* shakiness; *(d'un équilibre)* delicacy

fragment [fragmã] **NM** *(de pierre)* fragment, piece; *(d'os)* fragment, splinter; *(de chanson, conversation)* fragment, snatch; *(d'un livre)* extract

fragmentaire [fragmãtɛr] **ADJ** fragmentary; *(connaissances)* sketchy, patchy, fragmentary

fragmentation [fragmãtasjɔ̃] **NF** fragmentation

fragmenter [fragmãte] **VT** to fragment, to split up; *(travail)* to divide up, to split up; **f. la publication d'un ouvrage** to publish a work in parts

frai [frɛ] **NM 1** *(action, période)* spawning *(of fish)* **2** *(œufs)* spawn; *(poissons)* fry **3** *(de pièces de monnaie)* abrasion, wear

fraîche [frɛʃ] **ADJ** *voir* **frais[1]**

fraîchement [frɛʃmã] **ADV 1** *(recevoir)* coolly; **accueillir qn f.** to give sb a cool reception; *Fam* **ça va f. ce matin** it's a bit chilly this morning **2** *(récemment)* **f. marié/divorcé/arrivé** newly *or* recently married/divorced/arrived; **fleurs f. cueillies** freshly picked flowers

fraîcheur [frɛʃœr] **NF 1** *(température)* freshness, coolness; **dans la f. du soir** in the cool of the evening; **une sensation de f.** a feeling of freshness; **rechercher un peu de f.** to seek out a cool spot **2** *(de fleurs, nourriture, couleurs, d'idées, de film etc)* freshness; *(de la jeunesse)* freshness, bloom; **elle a perdu sa f. d'esprit** she has lost her freshness of mind

fraîchir [frɛʃir] **VI** *Météo* **1** *(devenir frais)* to freshen, to grow colder *or* cooler **2** *(du vent)* to freshen

frais[1], fraîche [frɛ, frɛʃ] **ADJ 1** *(froid)* *(vent)* fresh, cool; *Fig (réception)* cool; *(rafraîchi)* chilled; **un accueil plutôt f.** a rather cool welcome

2 *(récent)* *(pain, fruits, fleurs, traces)* fresh; *(souvenir)* recent, fresh; **air f.** fresh air; **œufs f.** fresh *or* new-laid eggs; **les croissants sont tout f. de ce matin** the croissants are fresh this morning; **de fraîche date** not long ago,

recently; **amis de fraîche date** recent friends; **l'encre est encore fraîche** the ink is still wet; **peinture fraîche** wet paint

3 teint f. fresh complexion; **avoir l'haleine fraîche** to have fresh breath; **cette robe n'est plus très fraîche, mais elle fera l'affaire** this dress isn't very fresh any more, but it will do; **f. et dispos** hale and hearty; **être f. comme un gardon** to be bright-eyed and bushy-tailed; **être fraîche comme une rose** to be as fresh as a daisy; *Fam* **me voilà f.!** I'm in a nice mess *or* a pretty fix!

4 avoir de l'argent f. to have new money
ADV il fait f. it's cool *or* fresh; **servir/boire f.** serve/drink chilled *or* cool; **roses toutes fraîches ou f. cueillies** freshly picked roses; **herbe f. ou fraîche coupée** freshly *or* newly cut grass; **il est f. débarqué de sa province** he is fresh from the country; **f. émoulu de l'université** fresh out of *or* from university; **rasé de f.** freshly shaven; **peint de f.** freshly painted
NM prendre le f. to take some *or* a breath of (fresh) air; **à mettre** *ou* **à conserver au f.** to be kept cool *or* in a cool place; **mettre le vin au f.** to put the wine to cool; *Fig Fam* **ils l'ont mis au f.** they've put him in the cooler, they've locked him up *or* put him inside; *Météo, Naut* **avis de grand f.** gale warning
NF fraîche 1 *Arg (argent)* cash, dough **2 à la fraîche** in the cool part of the day

frais[2] **NMPL** expenses, costs; **f. d'un procès** costs of a lawsuit; **j'ai eu beaucoup de f. ce mois-ci** I've had a lot of expense(s) this month; **faire de gros f.** to go to great expense; **faux f.** incidental expenses; **note de f.** expense account; **tous f. payés** all expenses paid; *Jur* **être condamné aux f.** to be ordered to pay costs; **rentrer dans ses f.** to cover one's expenses; *Fig* **j'ai fait les f. de la plaisanterie** the joke was at my expense; *Fig* **faire les f. de la conversation** to keep the conversation going; *(à ses dépens)* to be the subject of the conversation; **faire les f. d'une politique** to pay the price for a policy; **faire qch à ses f.** to do sth at one's own expense; **à grands/à bas f.** at great/little cost; **se mettre en f.** to go to great expense, *Fam* to put oneself out of pocket; **se mettre en f. de politesse** to go out of one's way to be polite; **j'en suis pour mes f.** it's been a lot of trouble for nothing, I've been wasting my time; **exempt de f., sans f.** free of charge; *(sur une lettre de change)* no expenses; *Fam* **aux f. de la princesse** at the expense of the government/firm/*etc*; **f. accessoires** incidental costs *or* expenses; **f. d'achat** purchase costs; **f. d'adhésion** membership charge; **f. administratifs** administrative costs; **f. d'administration** administrative costs; *(en échange d'un service)* handling charge; **f. d'administration générale** general overheads, general administration costs, *Am* general overhead; **f. d'agence** agency fee; **f. d'amortissement** amortization *or* depreciation charges; **f. d'annulation** cancellation charge; **f. de banque** bank charges; **f. de Bourse** transaction costs; **f. de camionnage** haulage; **f. de commercialisation** marketing costs; **f. de constitution** *(de société)* startup costs; *(de compte)* set-up fee; **f. consulaires** consular fees; *Bourse* **f. de courtage** brokerage, commission; **f. de déplacement** travelling *or* travel expenses; **f. différés** deferred charges; **f. de distribution** distribution costs; **f. de douane** customs duties; **f. d'encaissement** collection charges *or* fees; **f. d'entrée** *(d'une sicav)* front-end *or* front-load fees; **f. d'envoi** carriage costs; **f. d'établissement** startup costs; **f. d'exploitation** operating costs, operational costs; **f. extraordinaires** extraordinary expenses; **f. financiers** interest charges, financial costs;

f. fixes fixed charges; **f. de fonctionnement** operating costs; *Com* **f. généraux** overheads, *Am* overhead; **f. de gestion** administration costs; **f. inclus** inclusive of costs; **f. d'inscription** membership fee; **f. d'installation** initial expenses; **f. de lancement** set-up *or* start-up costs; **f. de liquidation** closing-down costs; **f. de livraison** delivery charges; **f. de main-d'œuvre** labour costs; **f. de manutention** handling charges; **f. de pilotage** pilotage; **f. de port** carriage; **f. de port et d'emballage** postage and packing; **f. portuaires** port charges; **f. de publicité** advertising costs; **f. de représentation** expense account, entertainment allowance *or* expenses; **f. de réservation** booking fee, reservation charge; **f. de scolarité** school fees; **f. de sortie** exit charges, back-end load; **f. de tenue de compte** account charges; *(de compte bancaire)* bank charges; **f. de transport** carriage; **f. de trésorerie** finance costs; **f. variables** variable costs

fraisage [frɛzaʒ] **NM 1** *Métal (de surface)* milling; *(de trou)* reaming; *(de trou de vis)* countersinking **2** *(par le dentiste)* drilling

fraise[1] [frɛz] **NF 1** *(fruit)* strawberry; **f. des bois** wild *or Am* field strawberry; **tarte aux fraises** strawberry tart; **confiture de fraises** strawberry jam; **sirop de f.** strawberry cordial; *Fig* **sucrer les fraises** to have the shakes; *Arg* **un coup en pleine f.** a punch in the kisser; *Arg* **amène ta f.!** get yourself over here!; *Arg* **il est tout le temps à ramener sa f.** he's always sticking his oar in **2** *Méd* strawberry (mark)
ADJ INV *(couleur)* strawberry-pink; **f. écrasée** crushed strawberry; **écharpe f.** strawberry-pink scarf

fraise[2] **NF 1** *Culin (de veau, d'agneau)* caul **2** *Hist (col)* ruff **3** *(de dinde)* wattle **4** *Tech* milling cutter, mill; **f. (conique)** countersink **5** *(de dentiste)* drill

fraiser [frɛze] **VT 1** *(dent)* to drill **2** *Tech (surface)* to mill; *(trou)* to ream; *(trou de vis)* to countersink

fraiseraie [frɛzrɛ] **NF** strawberry field

fraiseuse [frɛzøz] **NF** *Tech* milling machine

fraisier [frɛzje] **NM 1** *Bot* strawberry plant **2** *Culin* strawberry cream cake

fraisil [frɛzi(l)] **NM** coal cinders

fraisure [frɛzyr] **NF** countersink, countersunk hole

framboise [frɑ̃bwaz] **NF** *(fruit)* raspberry; *(liqueur)* raspberry liqueur; **tarte aux framboises** raspberry tart
ADJ INV raspberry

framboisé [frɑ̃bwaze] **ADJ** raspberry-flavoured, *Am* raspberry-flavored

framboisier [frɑ̃bwazje] **NM 1** *Bot* raspberry bush *or* cane **2** *Culin* raspberry cream cake

franc[1] [frɑ̃] **NM** *(monnaie)* franc; **f. suisse** Swiss franc; **f. or** gold value of the franc; **ancien/nouveau f.** old/new franc; **f. constant** inflation-adjusted franc, franc in real terms; **francs courants** actual francs; **je l'ai eu pour trois francs six sous** I got it for next to nothing; **f. symbolique** nominal sum; **un f. symbolique de dommages et intérêts** token damages

franc[2], franche [frɑ̃, frɑ̃ʃ] **ADJ 1** *(sincère)* *(personne)* frank, open, candid; *(réponse, conversation)* frank, candid; **je serai f. (avec vous)** I'll be frank *or* candid *or* honest (with you); **pour être f.** to be frank *or* candid; **sa réponse a au moins le mérite d'être franche** at least he answered frankly *or* candidly; **un regard f.** an open look; **un oui f. et massif** a clear and overwhelming yes; **être f. comme l'or** to be totally frank; **être f. du collier** to be completely open; *(serviable)* to be compliant

2 *(libre)* free; **f. de tout droit** duty-free; **f. d'avarie particulière** free of particular average; **f. d'impôts** tax free, free of tax; **f. de casse** free of breakage; **f. de toute avarie** free of average; **f. de port** carriage paid, carriage free; **zone/ville franche** free zone/city; **port f.** free port; *Ftbl* **coup f.** free kick; *Mil* **corps f.** commando (unit)

3 *(net) (couleur, vin)* pure; *(rupture)* clean; *(escroc)* downright, out-and-out; **situation franche** clear *or* unequivocal position; **c'est un f.** Breton he's a true Breton; **vin f. de goût** wine clean to the taste; **terre franche** loam; **ça a été une franche rigolade** it was an absolute scream; **huit jours francs** eight clear days

ADV **pour parler f.** frankly *or* candidly speaking; **parlons f.** let's be frank (with each other)

franc³, franque [frã, frãk] *Hist* ADJ Frankish

N **F.** Frank

français, -aise [frãsɛ, -ɛz] ADJ French; **impossible n'est pas f.** impossible? there's no such word (in the language); **c'est bien f. cette attitude** that's a typically French attitude

ADV **acheter f.** to buy French; **rouler/boire/ manger f.** to drive French cars/drink French wine/eat French food

NM *Ling* French; **parler f.** to speak French; *(correctement)* to speak properly; *Fam* **tu ne comprends pas le f.?** ≃ don't you understand (plain) English?

N **F.** Frenchman, f Frenchwoman

NF *Ordinat* **imprimer à la française** to print portrait

franc-bord, *pl* **francs-bords** NM *Naut* freeboard; **bordé à f.** carvel built

franc-bourgeois, *pl* **francs-bourgeois** NM *Hist* freeman

France [frãs] NF France; **vivre/aller en F.** to live in/go to France; **les vins de F.** French wines; **être** *ou* **faire (très) vieille F.** to be rather old-fashioned; **F. 2** = French state-owned TV channel; **F.3** = French state-owned TV channel; **F. Info** = French state-owned news radio station; **F. Inter** = French state-owned radio station; **F. Télécom** = state-owned company which runs all telecommunications services, until 1991 part of the PTT

Francfort [frãkfɔr] N Frankfurt; **saucisse de F.** frankfurter

franchement [frãʃmã] ADV **1** *(ouvertement)* frankly, candidly, openly; **(très) f., je ne sais pas quoi dire à ça** (quite) frankly, I don't know what to say to that; **je vais te parler f.** I'll be frank with you; **il me l'a dit f.** he told me openly; **y aller f.** to go right ahead with it; **vas-y f., appuie sur la manette** go on, push the joystick hard **2** *(tout à fait, vraiment)* really; **c'était f. stupide/mauvais** it was really *or* downright stupid/bad; **j'en suis f. dégoûté** I'm absolutely sick of it; **f., tu comprends ça, toi?** honestly (now), do you understand that?; **non, mais f.!** no, honestly *or* really!; **tu as de ces idées, f.!** the ideas you have, honestly *or* really!

franchir [frãʃir] VT *(obstacle, difficulté)* to get over, to clear; *(fossé)* to jump (over), to clear; *(rapides)* to shoot; *(limite)* to exceed; *(porte)* to pass *or* walk through; *(rivière, frontière)* to cross; **la panthère franchit le mur d'un seul bond** the panther cleared *or* jumped over the wall in one bound; **f. la ligne d'arrivée** to cross the finishing line; **f. le Rubicon** to cross the Rubicon; **f. le pas** to take the plunge; **f. le seuil** to step over *or* to cross the threshold; **f. le mur du son** to break

(through) the sound barrier; **si l'on franchit un certain cap** if a certain point is passed; **f. la barre des 3 millions** to pass the 3 million mark

franchisage [frãʃizaʒ] NM *Com* franchising

franchise [frãʃiz] NF **1** *(sincérité)* frankness, openness, candour, *Am* candor; *(franc-parler)* plain speaking, outspokenness; **en toute f.** quite frankly; **parler avec f.** to speak frankly *or* candidly **2** *(exonération)* exemption; **faire entrer qch en f.** to import sth duty-free; **entrée en f.** free import; **bagages en f.** baggage allowance **3** *(d'assurance)* excess, *Am* deductible **4** *Hist* **charte de f.** charter (of freedom) *(of city)* **5** *Com* franchise

▸▸ **f. (de) bagages** baggage allowance; **f. douanière** exemption from customs duties; **f. fiscale** tax exemption; **f. postale** = official paid; **f. de TVA** VAT exemption, zero-rating; **en f. de TVA** VAT-exempt, zero-rated

> Il faut noter que le nom anglais **franchise** ne signifie jamais **sincérité**.

franchisé, -ée [frãʃize] N *Com* franchisee
ADJ **magasin f.** franchise

franchiser [frãʃize] VT to franchise

franchiseur, -euse [frãʃizœr, -øz] N *Com* franchisor

franchissable [frãʃisabl] ADJ *(route)* passable; *(col de montagne)* negotiable; *(obstacle)* surmountable

franchissement [frãʃismã] NM *(d'obstacle)* clearing; *(de fossé)* jumping; *(de rivière)* crossing

franchouillard, -arde [frãʃujar, -ard] *Fam Péj* ADJ archetypally French
N archetypal Frenchman, f Frenchwoman

francilien, -ienne [frãsiljɛ̃, -jɛn] ADJ of *or* from the Île-de-France *(the greater Paris region)*
N **F.** inhabitant of the Île-de-France *(the greater Paris region)*

francisant, -ante [frãsizã, -ãt] N French specialist

francisation [frãsizasjõ] NF **1** *(d'un mot étranger)* gallicizing, *Fam* Frenchifying **2** *Naut* registry as a French ship

franciscain, -aine [frãsiskɛ̃, -ɛn] ADJ, N *Rel* Franciscan

franciser [frãsize] VT **1** *(mot étranger)* to gallicize, *Fam* to Frenchify **2** *Naut (bateau)* to register as French

francisque [frãsisk] NF = emblem of the Vichy government

francité [frãsite] NF Frenchness

franc-maçon, *pl* **francs-maçons** NM freemason

franc-maçonnerie NF freemasonry

franc-maçonnique ADJ masonic

franco [frãko] ADV **1** *Com* **f. (de port)** post(age) paid, carriage free, carriage paid; **f. allège** free over side; **f. de port et d'emballage** post(age) and packing paid; **f. d'emballage** free of packing charges; **livré f.** delivered free *or* post(age) paid; **f. (à) bord** free on board, FOB; **f. de douane** free of customs duty; **f. frontière** free at frontier; **f. gare de réception** free on rail; **f. de tous frais** free of all charges; **f. le long du navire** free alongside ship; **f. long du bord** free alongside ship; **f. long du quai** free alongside ship; **f. rendu** free at; **f. transporteur** free carrier; **f. wagon** free on rail **2** *Fam* **vas-y f.!** go right ahead!

franco-allemand ADJ Franco-German

franco-américain ADJ Franco-American

franco-britannique ADJ Anglo-French

franco-canadien, -ienne ADJ French Canadian
NM *Ling* Canadian French

franco-français ADJ pure French; **une entreprise franco-française** a 100% French-owned company

francophile [frãkɔfil] ADJ, N francophile

francophilie [frãkɔfili] NF love of all things French

francophobe [frãkɔfɔb] N francophobe
ADJ francophobe, francophobic

francophobie [frãkɔfɔbi] NF francophobia

francophone [frãkɔfɔn] ADJ French-speaking
N French speaker

francophonie [frãkɔfɔni] NF French-speaking world

franc-parler NM plain speaking, outspokenness; **avoir son f.** to speak one's mind, to be outspoken, not to mince one's words

franc-tireur, *pl* **francs-tireurs** NM *Mil* franc-tireur, irregular (soldier); *Fig* maverick

frange [frãʒ] NF *(de carpette, cheveux etc)*, *Fig* fringe

franger [frãʒe] VT (**je frangeai(s)**) to fringe, to border

frangin [frãʒɛ̃] NM *Fam* brother

frangine [frãʒin] NF *Fam* sister

frangipane [frãʒipan] NF *Culin* almond paste, frangipane

frangipanier [frãʒipanje] NM *Bot* frangipani (tree)

franglais [frãglɛ] NM Franglais

franquette [frãkɛt] NF **à la bonne f.** simply, without ceremony; **on mangera à la bonne f.** we will eat simply; **un repas à la bonne f.** a simple meal; **c'est à la bonne f. chez eux** they don't stand on ceremony at home

franquisme [frãkism] NM Francoism

franquiste [frãkist] ADJ pro-Franco
N supporter of Franco

frappadingue [frapadɛ̃g] ADJ *Fam* crazy, bonkers, *Br* mental

frappant [frapã] ADJ *(image, ressemblance etc)* striking

frappe [frap] NF **1** *(dactylographie)* typing; *Ordinat* keying; **elle a une f. rapide** she can type/key fast; **la lettre est à la f.** the letter is being typed/keyed; **faute de f.** typing/keying error; **vitesse de f.** typing/keying speed; *Ordinat* **f. au kilomètre** continuous input; *Ordinat* **f. en continu** type-ahead **2** *(de pièces de monnaie)* striking, minting **3** *(au base-ball)* hit; *Boxe* punch; *Ftbl* strike, kick **4** *Mil* **force de f.** strike force; **des frappes aériennes** airstrikes **5** *Arg* **petite f.** hoodlum

frappé [frape] ADJ **1** iced, well chilled; **café f.** iced coffee; **champagne f.** chilled champagne, champagne frappé **2** *Fam (fou)* crazy

frappement [frapmã] NM striking; *(bruit)* knocking

frapper [frape] VT **1** to hit, to strike; **f. légèrement** to tap; **être frappé à mort** to be fatally *or* mortally wounded; **la balle l'a frappé en plein cœur** the bullet hit him right in the heart; **f. des marchandises d'une taxe** to impose a duty on goods; **être frappé par une maladie** to be struck down by a disease; **être frappé par un deuil** to be suffering from bereavement; **être frappé de mutisme** to be struck dumb; **f. qn d'étonnement** to strike sb with amazement; **cela a frappé son imagination** that caught his/her imagination; **ce qui m'a frappé le plus, c'était son sang-froid** what struck *or* impressed me most was his coolness; **je fus frappé par leur ressemblance** I was struck by their resemblance; **je suis frappé de le retrouver dans cette situation** I'm surprised to find him in this situation; *Théâtre* **f. les trois coups** to give the three knocks *(at the start of a play)*; *Fig* **f. un**

grand coup to strike a decisive blow; *Fig* **f. à la tête** to strike at the top **2** *(médaille)* to strike; *(pièces de monnaie)* to strike, to mint; *(papier peint)* to emboss; *(motif)* to punch (out), to cut out; *(cuir)* to block **3** *(lettre)* to type; *Ordinat* to key; *Ordinat* **f. au kilomètre** to input continuously **4** *(refroidir)* to ice; *(boisson)* to chill; **f. le champagne** to put the champagne on ice **VI 1** to strike, to hit; **f. du poing sur la table** to bang (on) the table; **f. à la porte** to knock on *or* at the door; **f. doucement à la porte** to tap on *or* at the door; **la prochaine fois vous pourrez entrer sans f.** next time you can come in without knocking; **entrez sans f.** *(notice)* come *or* go straight in; **on frappe** there's someone (knocking) at the door; *Fig* **vous frappez à la bonne/mauvaise porte** you've come to the right/wrong place; **il va falloir f. à toutes les portes** we will have to ask for help from all quarters **2 f. des mains** *ou* **dans ses mains** to clap (one's hands); **f. du pied** to stamp (one's foot) **3** *Fam (agir)* to strike; **le gang a encore frappé** the gang has struck again; **la grippe va f. durement** the flu will hit everyone hard **VPR se frapper 1 se f. les cuisses** to slap one's thighs; **se f. le front** to slap one's forehead; **se f. la poitrine** to beat one's chest **2** *Fam* to get oneself worked up, to get oneself into a flap *or* panic; **ne vous frappez pas** don't panic, don't flap

frappeur, -euse [fʀapœʀ, -øz] **N** *Métal* striker; *(de papier peint)* embosser **ADJ esprit f.** spirit-rapper

frasque [fʀask] **NF** escapade, prank; **frasques** carryings-on, misbehaviour; **faire des frasques** to get up to mischief *or* to no good; **ses frasques de jeunesse** his youthful indiscretions

fraternel, -elle [fʀatɛʀnɛl] **ADJ** fraternal, brotherly; **geste f.** friendly gesture

fraternellement [fʀatɛʀnɛlmɑ̃] **ADV** fraternally, in a fraternal manner; **nous nous embrassâmes f.** we kissed like brothers

fraternisation [fʀatɛʀnizasjɔ̃] **NF** fraternization

fraterniser [fʀatɛʀnize] **VI** to fraternize

fraternité [fʀatɛʀnite] **NF** fraternity, brotherhood; **on trouve une certaine f. d'esprit entre eux** you can see a certain kinship of spirit between them

fratricide [fʀatʀisid] **ADJ** fratricidal **NM** *(crime)* fratricide **N** *(personne)* fratricide

fraude [fʀod] **NF** fraud; *(à un examen)* cheating; **f. électorale** electoral fraud, vote rigging; **f. fiscale** tax evasion; **en f.** fraudulently, unlawfully; **passer qch en f.** to smuggle sth in/out; **il entra en f. dans le pays** he entered the country illegally *or* unlawfully

frauder [fʀode] **VT** to defraud, to cheat, to swindle; **f. le fisc** to evade tax; **f. la douane** to defraud customs, to smuggle; **vin fraudé** adulterated wine **VI** to cheat (**sur** on); **f. sur la marchandise** to cheat the customer; **il a l'habitude de f. dans le métro** he always avoids buying a ticket for the underground, he's a fare-dodger

fraudeur, -euse [fʀodœʀ, -øz] **N** defrauder, cheat; *(trafiquant)* smuggler; **le nombre de fraudeurs dans les transports en commun a diminué** the number of fare-dodgers on public transport has decreased

frauduleusement [fʀodyløzmɑ̃] **ADV** fraudulently; **je le vis se glisser f. dans le cinéma** I saw him slipping into the cinema without paying

frauduleux, -euse [fʀodylø, -øz] **ADJ** frau-

dulent; **édition frauduleuse** pirated edition

frayer [fʀeje] (**je fraye** *ou* **fraie, n. frayons; je frayerai** *ou* **fraierai**) **VT 1 f. un chemin** to clear a path; *Fig* to blaze a trail; **f. la voie à qn** to pave the way for sb **2** *(d'un cerf)* to scrape, to rub; *Vét (d'un cheval)* to gall **VI 1** *(d'un poisson)* to spawn **2** *Fig* **f. avec qn** to mix *or* associate with sb; **je ne fraye pas avec des gens de cette espèce** I don't mix with that sort of people; **elle fraye peu** she doesn't mix much, she's not much of a mixer **VPR se frayer se f. un passage** to clear a way (for oneself); **se f. un chemin à travers la foule** to force *or* push *or* elbow one's way through the crowd; *Fig* **se f. un chemin dans …** to make one's way in …

frayère [fʀejɛʀ] **NF** spawning ground *(of fish)*

frayeur [fʀejœʀ] **NF** fright *(de* of*)*; **tu m'as fait une de ces frayeurs!** you really frightened me!, you gave me such a fright!; **j'ai eu une f., j'ai cru que j'avais oublié mes clés** I had *or* got a fright, I thought I had forgotten my keys; **vous me donnez des frayeurs** you're getting me worried; **se remettre de ses frayeurs** to recover from one's fright

FRBG [ɛfɛʀbeʒe] **NM** *(abrév* **fonds pour risques bancaires généraux)** FGBR

fredaine [fʀədɛn] **NF** prank, escapade; **faire des fredaines** to get into *or* up to mischief; *(amoureuses)* to carry on

fredonnement [fʀədɔnmɑ̃] **NM** *(d'un air)* humming

fredonner [fʀədɔne] **VT, VI** to hum

free-jazz [fʀidʒaz] **NM** *Mus* free jazz, freeform jazz

free-lance [fʀilɑ̃s] **ADJ INV** freelance **NM INV travailler en f., faire du f.** to work freelance, to do freelance work, to freelance **N INV** freelance, freelancer

freesia [fʀezja] **NM** *Bot* freesia

freeware [fʀiwɛʀ] **NM** *Ordinat* freeware; **freewares** freeware programs

freezer [fʀizœʀ] **NM** freezer compartment

frégate [fʀegat] **NF 1** *Naut* frigate; **capitaine de f.** commander **2** *Orn* frigate bird

frein [fʀɛ̃] **NM 1** *Aut* brake; **il a fallu donner un coup de f. très rapide** we had to brake very suddenly; *Fig* **donner un coup de f. à une entreprise** to put a brake on an undertaking; **un coup de f. à la création d'entreprises** a check to reduce the number of new firms; **mettre un f. à qch** to curb *or* check sth; **mettre un f. aux désirs de qn** to curb *or* bridle sb's desires; **mettre un f. à la montée de la colère** to stem *or* curb *or* check the rising tide of anger; **curiosité/imagination sans f.** unbridled curiosity/imagination; **f. à l'expansion** brake on growth **2** *(mors)* bit; **ronger son f.** *(d'un cheval)*, *Fig (d'une personne)* to champ at the bit **3** *Anat (de la langue)* fr(a)enum

▸ ▸ f. à air (comprimé) airbrake; **freins arrière** rear brakes; **freins assistés** power brakes; **freins avant** front brakes; **freins à bande** band brakes; *Can* **f. à bras** handbrake, *Am* parking brake; **f. à disque** disc brake; **f. sur échappement** exhaust brake; **f. d'embrayage** clutch stop; **f. à main** handbrake, *Am* parking brake; **f. moteur** engine brake; **utilisez votre f. moteur** *(sur panneau)* engage low gear; **f. à pédale** foot brake; **f. au pied** foot brake; **f. secondaire** emergency brake; **f. de stationnement** handbrake, *Am* parking brake; **f. à tambour** drum brake; **f. sur transmission** transmission brake; **f. à vide** vacuum brake

freinage [fʀɛnaʒ] **NM 1** *(action)* braking; *Fig (de l'inflation)* curbing; *(de la production)* cutting back; *(des importations, des salaires)* reduction; **distance de f.** braking distance; **traces de f.** skid marks; *Aviat* **parachute de**

f. brake parachute **2** *(système)* brake system, brakes

freiner [fʀene, fʀɛne] **VT 1** *(véhicule)* to brake **2** *(ralentir)* to slow down; **des arbres ont freiné sa chute** trees broke his fall **3** *(inflation, production etc)* to curb, to check; **f. qn** to keep sb in check, to restrain sb **VI** to brake; **f. à bloc** to jam on *or* slam on the brakes; *Fig* **ce sont les patrons qui freinent** it's the bosses who are back-pedalling; **il voudrait moderniser l'usine mais son père freine des quatre fers** he'd like to modernize the factory, but his father is putting a brake on that idea

VPR se freiner *Fig* to keep oneself in check, to restrain oneself

freinte [fʀɛ̃t] **NF** *Com* wastage, loss in volume/weight *(during transit or manufacture)*

frelatage [fʀəlataʒ] **NM** *(du vin, de la nourriture etc)* adulteration

frelater [fʀəlate] **VT** *(alcool, nourriture)* to adulterate

frêle [fʀɛl] **ADJ** *(personne, enfant, voix)* frail, weak; *(silhouette)* frail; *(embarcation, cabane)* flimsy, frail

frelon [fʀəlɔ̃] **NM** hornet

freluquet [fʀəlykɛ] **NM** *Fam* (young) whippersnapper

frémir [fʀemir] **VI 1** *(vibrer)* to quiver; *(des vitres)* to shake, to rattle; *(des feuilles)* to rustle; *(du vent)* to sigh; *(de l'eau chaude)* to simmer; **l'air frémissait encore des échos d'une flûte lointaine** the air was still vibrating to the echoes of a distant flute **2** *(d'une personne)* *(de peur)* to shake, to tremble, to shudder, to quake; *(de froid)* to shiver, to shudder; *(de plaisir, joie, d'impatience)* to tremble, to quiver; *(de colère, d'inquiétude)* to shake, to tremble, to quiver (**de** with); **il m'a fait si peur, j'en frémis encore** he scared me so much I'm still shaking *or* trembling

frémissant [fʀemisɑ̃] **ADJ** *(eau)* simmering; *(voix)* trembling, shaky; *(feuillage, chair)* quivering, trembling; **sensibilité frémissante** quivering sensitivity

frémissement [fʀemismɑ̃] **NM 1** *(des feuilles)* rustle; *(de l'eau chaude)* simmering; *(du vent)* sighing; **le f. des champs de blé sous la brise** the wheatfields quivering in the breeze **2** *(frisson)* *(de peur)* shudder; **f. de plaisir/joie** thrill of pleasure/joy; **un f. de colère/d'impatience/d'inquiétude** a quiver of anger/impatience/anxiety; **avec un f. de crainte** shaking *or* quaking with fear; **avec un f. dans la voix** with a trembling *or* shaky voice; **des frémissements parcouraient son corps** he was shaking *or* trembling all over; **un léger f. parcourut tous les auditeurs** a slight shudder went through the audience

frênaie [fʀɛnɛ] **NF** ash plantation

french-cancan [fʀɛnʃkɑ̃kɑ̃] **NM** cancan

frêne [fʀɛn] **NM** *(arbre)* ash (tree); *(bois)* ash

frénésie [fʀenezi] **NF** frenzy; **applaudir avec f.** to applaud frantically; **travailler/parler avec f.** to work/talk frenziedly; **f. d'achat** buying spree

frénétique [fʀenetik] **ADJ** *(activité)* frenzied, frantic; *(rythme)* frenetic, frenzied; *(passion)* wild

frénétiquement [fʀenetikmɑ̃] **ADV** frenziedly, frenetically

Fréon® [fʀeɔ̃] **NM** Freon®

fréquemment [fʀekamɑ̃] **ADV** frequently

fréquence [fʀekɑ̃s] **NF 1** *(occurrence)* frequency; **la f. d'un mot dans un texte** the frequency of a word in a text; **f. du pouls** pulse rate; **f. d'achat** purchase frequency **2** *Phys, Radio etc* frequency; *(de son)* tone; **basse/haute f.** low/high frequency; **très haute f.** very high frequency; **bande de fréquences**

frequency band; **modulation de f.** frequency modulation; **f. absolue** absolute frequency; **f. cumulée** cumulative frequency; *Ordinat* **f. d'horloge** clock speed *or* frequency; **f. d'horloge du microprocesseur** microprocessor clock frequency; **f. porteuse** carrier; **f. radio** radio frequency; **f. de rafraîchissement** refresh rate; **f. réglée** adjusted frequency; **f. relative** relative frequency; **f. sonore** audio frequency

fréquent [frekɑ̃] ADJ frequent; **il est f. de voir des jeunes couples divorcer** you frequently *or* often see young couples getting divorced; **il est peu f. que ...** it is not very often that ...

fréquentable [frekɑ̃tabl] ADJ **des gens peu fréquentables** people you wouldn't want to associate with; **il redeviendra peut-être f. s'il paye des dettes** people will perhaps want to know him again if he pays his debts; *Hum* **tôt le matin, il n'est pas f.** he's not in the best of moods *or* he's not nice to know early in the morning

fréquentatif, -ive [frekɑ̃tatif, -iv] ADJ *Gram* frequentative

fréquentation [frekɑ̃tasjɔ̃] NF **1** *(fait d'aller à)* frequenting (**de** of); **f. des théâtres** theatre-going; **la f. des cinémas a baissé** cinema-going has decreased; **cela demande une f. assidue** it requires regular attendance; **f. des grands auteurs** acquaintance with the great writers **2 fréquentations** company; **mauvaises fréquentations** bad company; **elle a de mauvaises fréquentations** she keeps bad company; **surveillez ses fréquentations** keep a watch on the company he keeps; **ce ne sont pas des fréquentations pour une jeune fille** these are not the sort of people a young girl should be associating with

fréquenté [frekɑ̃te] ADJ *(endroit, route)* busy; **bar f. par les étudiants** bar frequented by students, student bar; **hôtel bien f.** hotel with a good clientele; **endroit mal f.** place with a bad reputation

fréquenter [frekɑ̃te] VT **1** *(endroit)* to frequent **2 f. qn** to see sb regularly; *(comme petite amie, petit ami)* to go out with sb; **nous ne nous fréquentons plus beaucoup** we don't see much of each other any more; **je fréquente peu ce genre de personnes** I don't associate much with that type of person; **quels gens fréquente-t-il?** who does he go around with?, what company does he keep?; **je t'interdis de f. les voisins** I forbid you to speak to the neighbours; **parmi tous ceux que je fréquente** amongst all my acquaintances

▸ VPR **se fréquenter** to see each other regularly; *(d'un couple)* to go out with each other

frère [frɛr] NM **1** brother; **ils s'aiment comme des frères** they love each other like brothers; **on va partager en frères** we'll share it amicably; *Fam* **tu es un f. (pour moi)** you're a real friend; **faux f.** false friend; **alors, vieux f., quoi de neuf?** well, old chum *or* pal, what's new?; **les hommes sont tous frères** all men are brothers; **pays/peuples frères** sister countries/nations **2** *Rel* friar; **mes bien chers frères** dearly beloved brethren VOIR GRAMMAIRE A13 ; **j'ai fait mes études chez les frères** I studied with the brothers

▸ ▸ **f. lai** lay brother; **f. de lait** foster brother; *Fam* **f. trois-points** freemason; **frères d'armes** brothers-in-arms

frérot [frero] NM *Fam* kid *or* little brother

fresque [frɛsk] NF fresco; **ce roman est une f.** painting in fresco; **ce roman est une f. historique** this novel is a historical epic; **le film est une f. sociale sur l'Italie des années 50** the film is a social portrait of Italy in the 50s

fresquiste [frɛskist] ADJ, N (peintre) f. fresco painter

fressure [fresyr] NF *(d'un veau, mouton etc)* pluck; *Culin* fry

fret [frɛ(t)] NM **1** *(prix) (de navire etc)* freight, freightage; **payer le f.** to pay the freight **2** *(louage)* chartering; **prendre un navire à f.** to charter a ship; **donner un navire à f.** to freight (out) a ship; **avion de f.** charter aircraft **3** *(cargaison) (d'un bateau, avion)* cargo, freight; *(d'un camion)* load, freight; **f. aérien** air freight; **expédier par f. aérien** to airfreight; **f. express** express freight; **f. intérieur** inland freight; **f. maritime** sea *or* ocean freight; **f. par conteneur** containerized freight; **f. à forfait** through freight

fréter [frete] VT (**je frète; je fréterai**) *(donner en location) (bateau)* to freight (out), to charter; *(avion)* to charter; *(prendre en location) (voiture)* to hire

fréteur [fretœr] NM ship charterer, freight forwarder; *(armateur)* shipowner; **f. et affréteur** owner and charterer

frétillant [fretijɑ̃] ADJ *(poisson)* wriggling, wriggly; *Fig (personne)* lively; **elle était toute frétillante à l'idée de le revoir** she couldn't keep still at the thought of seeing him again

frétillement [fretijmɑ̃] NM *(d'un poisson)* wriggling; *(d'une queue)* wagging; *Fig* fidgeting

frétiller [fretije] VI *(d'un poisson)* to wriggle; **le chien frétille de la queue** the dog is wagging its tail; **l'enfant frétille d'impatience** the child is fidgeting with impatience; **f. de joie** to quiver with joy

fretin [frɔtɛ̃] NM *Pêche, Fig* **(menu) f.** small fry

frette[1] [frɛt] NF *Tech* (binding) hoop, collar, ferrule; *(d'axe)* band; **f. de moyeu** *(de roue)* nave ring

frette[2] NF *Archit, Hér* fret

freudien, -ienne [frødjɛ̃, -jɛn] ADJ *Psy* Freudian

freudisme [frødism] NM *Psy* Freudianism

freux [frø] NM rook; **colonie de f.** rookery

friabilité [frijabilite] NF crumbliness, *Spéc* friability

friable [frijabl] ADJ crumbly, *Spéc* friable

friand [frijɑ̃] ADJ fond of delicacies; **être f. de qch** to be fond of sth; **être f. de sucreries** to have a sweet tooth; *Fig* **f. de louanges** fond of praise

▪ NM *Culin (feuilleté)* small savoury pastry; *(gâteau)* small almond cake

friandise [frijɑ̃diz] NF titbit, delicacy

Fribourg [fribur] N *(en Allemagne)* Freiburg; *(en Suisse)* Fribourg

fric [frik] NM *Fam (argent)* dough, *Br* dosh; **j'ai plus de f.!** I'm out of dough!, I'm skint!

fricassée [frikase] NF *Culin* fricassee; *Belg* bacon omelette; *Fam* **f. de museaux** hugging and kissing

fricasser [frikase] VT *Culin* to fricassee

fricatif, -ive [frikatif, -iv] ADJ, NF *Ling* fricative

fric-frac, pl **fric-frac(s)** NM *Arg* burglary, break-in

friche [friʃ] NF fallow land; **f. industrielle** industrial wasteland; **rester** *ou* **être en f.** to lie fallow, to remain uncultivated; *Fig* **une idée/un projet qui est** *ou* **reste en f.** an idea/a plan which has not yet been taken up; **elle laisse son talent/son génie en f.** she's letting her talent/genius go to waste

frichti [friʃti] NM *Fam* grub, *Br* nosh

fricot [friko] NM *Fam* grub, *Br* nosh; **faire le f.** to do the cooking

fricotage [frikɔtaʒ] NM *Fam* fiddling

fricoter [frikɔte] *Fam* VT *Culin* to cook; *Fig (manigancer)* to scheme, to plot; **je me demande ce qu'il fricote** I wonder what he's up to *or* what he's cooking up

▪ VI **1** *(trafiquer)* to be on the fiddle **2** *(avoir des relations sexuelles)* **ils fricotent ensemble** they're sleeping together

fricoteur, -euse [frikɔtœr, -øz] N *Fam (trafiquant)* wide boy

friction [friksjɔ̃] NF **1** *(massage)* rubdown; *(du cuir chevelu)* scalp massage **2** *Phys, Tech* friction; **embrayage à f.** friction clutch; **réduire les frictions** to reduce friction; **entraînement par f.** *(d'une imprimante)* friction feed **3** *Fig (heurt)* friction; **cause de f.** cause of friction; **cela reste un point de f.** that remains a bone of contention

frictionnel, -elle [friksjɔnɛl] ADJ *(chômage)* temporary

frictionner [friksjɔne] VT *(membre)* to rub; **f. qn** to rub sb down, to give sb a rubdown; **f. la tête de qn** to massage sb's scalp, to give sb a scalp massage

▸ VPR **se frictionner** to rub oneself down

fridolin [fridɔlɛ̃] NM *Fam (terme injurieux)* Kraut, Fritz; **les fridolins** Jerry, the Jerries

frigidaire® [friʒidɛr] NM refrigerator, fridge; *Fam* **mettre un projet au f.** to put a plan into cold storage *or* on ice

frigide [friʒid] ADJ *(femme)* frigid; *Litt (cœur, caractère)* cold, icy

frigidité [friʒidite] NF frigidity, frigidness

frigo [frigo] NM *Fam* fridge, refrigerator; *Fam* **mettre un projet au f.** to put a plan into cold storage *or* on ice

frigorification [frigɔrifikasjɔ̃] NF *(de viande)* refrigerating, refrigeration

frigorifié [frigɔrifje] ADJ frozen; *Fam* **être f.** *(d'une personne)* to be frozen stiff

frigorifier [frigɔrifje] VT *(viande)* to refrigerate

frigorifique [frigɔrifik] ADJ refrigerating, *Am* frigorific; **appareil f.** refrigerator; **mélange f.** freezing mixture; **wagon f.** refrigerator van; **entrepôt f.** cold store

frigoriste [frigɔrist] NM refrigerating engineer

frileusement [friløzmɑ̃] ADV with a shiver

frileux, -euse [frilø, -øz] ADJ *(personne)* sensitive to the cold; **je suis très f.** I really feel the cold, I'm very sensitive to cold, I'm a chilly sort of person; **une attitude/réponse frileuse** a timid attitude/answer

frilosité [frilozite] NF *Litt* sensitivity to the cold; *Fig* nervousness, hesitancy

frimaire [frimɛr] NM *Hist* = third month of the French Republican calendar *(Nov-Dec)*

frimas [frima] NM *Litt* (hoar)frost, rime

frime [frim] NF *Fam* show, pretence; **tout ça, c'est de la f.** that's all show *or* all put on; **il le fait pour la f.** he does it for show

frimer [frime] VI *Fam* to show off

frimeur, -euse [frimœr, -øz] N *Fam* show-off

frimousse [frimus] NF **1** *Fam* sweet *or* pretty little face **2** *Ordinat (smiley)* smiley

fringale [frɛ̃gal] NF *Fam* hunger; **avoir la f.** to be ravenous *or* starving *or* famished; *Fig* **une f. de qch** a craving for sth; **avoir une f. de voyage** to have itchy feet, to have an urge to travel

fringant [frɛ̃gɑ̃] ADJ *(cheval)* spirited, lively, frisky; *(personne)* dashing

fringuer [frɛ̃ge] VT *Fam* to dress; **bien fringué** well turned out, well dressed

▪ VI *Arch* ou *Can Fam* to prance about, to skip about

▸ VPR **se fringuer** to get dressed; **il ne sait pas se f.** *(il n'a aucun goût)* he's got no dress sense

fringues [frɛ̃g] NFPL *Fam (vêtements)* gear, togs, clothes; **elle est folle de f.** she's clothes-mad, she's mad about clothes

fripé [fripe] ADJ *Can Fam* exhausted, beat, *Br* knackered

friper [fripe] VT *(vêtement)* to crumple, to crush; **visage fripé** crumpled face
VPR **se friper** *(d'un vêtement)* to get crushed *or* crumpled

friperie [fripri] NF *(magasin)* second-hand clothes shop; *(vêtements)* second-hand clothes

fripes [frip] NFPL second-hand clothes

fripier, -ière [fripje, -jɛr] N second-hand clothes dealer

fripon, -onne [fripɔ̃, -ɔn] N *Vieilli (caractère)* rogue, knave; *Fig* **petit f./petite friponne!** you little rascal *or* devil!
ADJ *(sourire, regard, air)* mischievous, roguish

friponnerie [fripɔnri] NF *Vieilli (caractère)* roguery, knavery; *(action)* mischievous prank

fripouille [fripuj] NF **1** *Fam* rogue, scoundrel **2** *Arch (racaille)* rabble, riff-raff

friqué [frike] ADJ *Fam* loaded, rolling in it

friquet [frikɛ] NM tree sparrow

frire [frir] *(pp* **frit;** *pr ind* **je fris, tu fris, il frit;** *no pl;* **fu je frirai)** VT to fry; **je fris du poisson** I'm frying fish
VI to fry; **faire f. qch** to fry sth; **le poisson frit** the fish is frying

frisant [frizɑ̃] ADJ **lumière frisante** oblique light

frisbee® [frizbi] NM Frisbee®

Frise [friz] NF Friesland

frise [friz] NF *Archit* frieze; *Théâtre* **frises** border

frisé, -ée [frize] ADJ *(cheveux)* curly; *(personne)* curly-haired; **salade frisée** curly lettuce; **velours f.** uncut velvet, terry; **elle est frisée comme un mouton** she's got frizzy hair
NF **frisée** *(chicorée)* curly endive
N *Fam* **1** *(enfant)* curly-haired child **2** *Fam (terme injurieux)* Kraut, Fritz, *Br* Jerry

friselis [frizli] NM *Litt (des feuilles)* rustling

friser [frize] VT **1** *(cheveux)* to curl; **f. (les cheveux de) qn** to curl sb's hair; **fer à f.** curling tongs **2** *(approcher)* **f. l'accident** to have a narrow escape; **on a frisé la catastrophe** we came within a hair's-breadth *or* an inch of disaster; **on frise la dispute** we're close to arguing *or* to an argument; **cela frise l'impertinence** it's verging on the impertinent; **il frisait la soixantaine** he was close on sixty
VI *(d'une personne)* to have curly hair

frisette [frizɛt] NF *(de cheveux)* ringlet, small curl

frison¹ [frizɔ̃] NM *(de cheveux)* curl; *(de bois, papier etc)* shaving

frison², -onne [frizɔ̃, -ɔn] ADJ Friesian; **vache frisonne** Friesian cow
NM *Ling* Friesian
N **F.** Friesian

frisotter [frizɔte] VT **f. (les cheveux de) qn** to crimp sb's hair
VI to curl, to be frizzy

frisquet, -ette [friskɛ, -ɛt] ADJ *Fam (vent)* chill(y); **il fait f.** it's a bit chilly *or Br Fam* parky

frisson [frisɔ̃] NM *(de froid, peur)* shiver, shudder; *(de plaisir)* thrill; **avoir des frissons** to shiver, *Fam* to have the shivers; **j'en ai des frissons** it makes me shudder; **ça me donne des frissons rien que d'y penser** it makes me shudder just thinking of it; *Fig* **le f. de l'eau/des arbres** the rippling of the water/quivering of the trees

frissonnement [frisɔnmɑ̃] NM *(action)* shivering, shuddering; *(tremblement)* shudder, shiver; **un f. de plaisir** a thrill of pleasure

frissonner [frisɔne] VI **1** *(de froid, de peur)* to shiver, to shudder; **f. de joie** to be thrilled **2** *(du feuillage)* to quiver; *(de l'eau)* to ripple

frisure [frizyr] NF *(des cheveux)* curliness; **frisures** curls, curly hair; **se faire faire des frisures** to have one's hair curled

frit, -ite [fri, frit] ADJ **1** *Culin* fried; **pommes de terre frites** French fried potatoes, (French) fries, *Br* chips **2** *Arg* **il est f.** he's had it
NF **1** *Culin* **frites** (French) fries, *Br* chips; **un steak frites, s'il vous plaît!** steak and chips, please **2** *Fam* **avoir la frite** to be on form; **ça va te donner la frite** that'll perk you up **3** *Fam (tape sur les fesses)* **faire une frite à qn** to flick sb on the bottom

friter [frite] *Fam* VT *(battre)* **f. qn** to beat sb up, to kick sb's head in
VPR **se friter** to have a punch-up *or Am* fist fight

friterie [fritri] NF chip stall

friteuse [fritøz] NF deep fryer, *Br* chip pan; **f. électrique** electric fryer

fritillaire [fritilɛr] NF *Bot* fritillary

fritter [frite] VT *(métal)* to sinter

friture [frityr] NF **1** *(action)* (de la nourriture) frying; *(huile)* (deep) fat, oil *(for frying)*; *(aliments)* fried food; **f. (de poissons)** fried fish **2** *Radio, Tél* **(bruits de) f.** crackling (noise), interference **3** *Belg (friterie)* chip stall

Fritz [frits] NM INV *Fam (terme injurieux)* Fritz, *Br* Jerry

frivole [frivol] ADJ frivolous

frivolement [frivolmɑ̃] ADV frivolously

frivolité [frivolite] NF **1** *(caractère)* frivolity, frivolousness; *(vétille)* trifle **2** *Couture* **frivolités** (fancy) trimmings

froc [frɔk] NM **1** *(de moine)* habit, frock, gown; **prendre le f.** to become a monk; **jeter le f. aux orties** to leave the priesthood **2** *Fam (pantalon)* trousers, *Am* pants; **très Fam faire dans son f.** to shit oneself

froid [frwa] ADJ **1** *(vent, temps, bain, radiateur etc)* cold; **à table!, ça va être f.!** come and eat, it's getting cold!; **repas f.** cold meal; **buffet f.** cold buffet; **viandes froides** cold meat(s)
2 *Fig (personne)* cold; *(manière, accueil)* cold, chilly; *(style)* cold, unemotional; **se montrer** *ou* **être f. avec** *ou* **envers qn** to be cold towards sb, to treat sb coldly *or* coolly; **garder la tête froide** to remain cool (and collected), to keep one's composure; **cela me laisse f.** it leaves me cold; **colère froide** controlled *or* suppressed anger; **la guerre froide** the cold war
ADV **soluble à f.** soluble when cold; *Aut* **démarrer à f.** to start from cold; **parler à f. d'une catastrophe** to speak calmly *or* unemotionally about a catastrophe; *Méd* **opérer à f.** to perform non-emergency surgery; **prendre** *ou* **cueillir un adversaire à f.** to catch an opponent unawares *or* off guard *or Br* on the hop
NM **1** cold; **il fait f.** it's cold; *Fam* **il fait un f. de canard** *ou* **de loup** it's freezing (cold); *Météo* **coup de f.** cold snap; **prendre (un coup de) f.** to catch a chill *or* a cold; **les grands froids** the coldest part of the winter; **une vague de f.** a cold spell; **avoir f.** to be *or* feel cold; **j'ai f. aux mains** my hands are cold, I've got cold hands; *Fig* **cela m'a fait** *ou* **donné f. (dans le dos)** it sent (cold) shivers down my spine; *Fig* **elle n'a pas f. aux yeux** she's very determined, she's got plenty of nerve; **battre f. à qn** to cold-shoulder sb
2 *Fig* coolness; **ils sont en f.** there's a coolness between them; **je suis en f. avec lui** there's a coolness between me and him; **jeter un f.** to cast a chill
3 **l'industrie du f.** the refrigerating industry; **le f. industriel** refrigeration; **la chaîne du f.** the refrigeration chain

froidement [frwadmɑ̃] ADV **1** *(avec réserve)* coldly, coolly; **être f. accueilli** to be given a cold welcome *or* cool reception; **il les a abattus f.** he shot them in cold blood *or* cold-bloodedly **2** *(calmement)* calmly; **il faut étudier f. le problème** we must consider the problem calmly

froideur [frwadœr] NF **1** *(de manière)* coldness, chilliness; **sa f. me met mal à l'aise** his coldness makes me ill at ease; **il est toujours d'une très grande f. avec moi** he is always very cold towards me; **avec f.** coldly **2** *(indifférence)* coldness, indifference; **contempler le spectacle avec f.** to look coldly on; **analysons le problème avec f.** let us analyse the problem calmly **3** *(manque de sensualité)* coldness, iciness

froidure [frwadyr] NF *Litt* cold; **par ces temps de f.** in this cold weather

froissant [frwasɑ̃] ADJ hurtful, wounding

froissement [frwasmɑ̃] NM **1** *(action)* (de muscle) bruising; *(de papier, tissu etc)* crumpling, creasing **2** *(bruit)* (du papier, de la soie etc) rustle, rustling **3** *Fig Vieilli (d'intérêts)* conflict, clash **4** *(vexation)* **un f. d'amour-propre** a blow to one's pride; **éviter tous froissements** to avoid ruffling any feathers *or* hurting anyone's feelings; **il risque d'y avoir des froissements entre elles** there's a chance of some hurt feelings between them

froisser [frwase] VT **1** *(muscle)* to bruise; *(tissu, papier)* to crumple, to crease **2** **f. qn** to offend sb, to give offence to sb, to hurt *or* wound sb's feelings
VPR **se froisser 1** *(d'un tissu)* to crease, to crumple **2** *(d'une personne)* to take offence *or* umbrage *(de* at), to take exception *(de* to)

frôlement [frolmɑ̃] NM *(contact)* brushing *(contre* against); *(son)* rustle

frôler [frole] VT *(effleurer)* to brush, to touch lightly; **l'avion a frôlé la cime des arbres** the plane skimmed the treetops; **f. les murs** to hug the walls; **il a frôlé la mort** he came close to death *or* had a brush with death; **on a frôlé la catastrophe/la dispute** we came close to disaster/to arguing; **ton attitude frôle le ridicule** your attitude verges on *or* borders on the ridiculous
VPR **se frôler** to touch one another lightly, to brush each other; **les deux voitures se sont frôlées** the two cars brushed past each other

fromage [frɔmaʒ] NM cheese; **f. bien fait** ripe cheese; **omelette/soufflé au f.** cheese omelette/soufflé; *Fig Fam* **pas la peine d'en faire un f.** it's not worth making a fuss about; *Fam* **un gentil petit f.** a nice little earner
► ► **f. blanc** fromage blanc; **f. fermenté** fermented cheese; **f. fondu** cheese spread; **f. frais** fromage frais; **f. à pâte molle/dure** soft/hard cheese; **f. à pâte persillée** blue(-veined) cheese; *Culin* **f. de tête** brawn, *Am* headcheese

fromager, -ère [frɔmaʒe, -ɛr] ADJ cheese; **industrie fromagère** cheese industry
N *(commerçant)* cheese merchant, *Br* cheesemonger; *(fabricant)* cheesemaker

fromagerie [frɔmaʒri] NF *(lieu de fabrication)* cheese dairy; *(magasin)* cheese shop

froment [frɔmɑ̃] NM wheat; **pain de f.** wheaten bread; **farine de f.** wheat flour

fronce [frɔ̃s] NF *Couture* gather; **jupe à fronces** gathered skirt

froncement [frɔ̃smɑ̃] NM wrinkling, puckering; **f. de(s) sourcils** frown

froncer [fʀɔ̃se] **VT** (**je fronçai(s)**) **1** *(plisser)* to wrinkle, to pucker; **f. les sourcils** to frown, *Litt* to knit one's brows **2** *Couture* to gather

frondaison [fʀɔ̃dɛzɔ̃] **NF** *(apparition des feuilles)* foliation; *(feuillage)* foliage

fronde¹ [fʀɔ̃d] **NF** *Bot* frond

fronde² **NF 1** *(arme)* sling; *(jouet)* catapult, *Am* slingshot **2** *Hist* **la F.** the Fronde; *Fig* **esprit de f.** spirit of revolt *or* rebellion

fronder [fʀɔ̃de] **VT** *Vieilli (critiquer)* to lampoon
VI 1 *Hist* to belong to the Fronde; *Fig* to rebel **2** *Arch* to use one's sling

frondeur, -euse [fʀɔ̃dœʀ, -øz] **N 1** *Hist* member of the Fronde **2** *(rebelle)* rebel
ADJ rebellious, anti-authority

front [fʀɔ̃] **NM 1** *(de personne)* forehead, *surtout Litt* brow; **marcher le f. haut** to walk with one's head (held) high; **relever le f.** to hold one's head high; **courber** *ou* **baisser le f.** to submit; **faire f. à qn/qch** to face up to *or* stand up to sb/sth; **faire f.** to face up to things; **et vous avez le f. de me dire cela!** you have the nerve to tell me that!
2 *(de bâtiment)* front, face; *(de colline)* brow; *Pol* front; **f. de bataille** battle front; *Mil* **le f.** the front (line); **partir sur le** *ou* **au f.** to go (up) to the front; **nouvelles du f.** news from the front; *Météo* **f. chaud/froid** warm/cold front; *Pol* **f. commun** united *or* common front; **faire f. commun contre qn/qch** to join forces against sb/sth
3 de f. *(côte à côte)* side by side, one next to the other; **marcher à trois de f.** to walk three abreast; **mener plusieurs choses de f.** to have several things on the go at once; *Mil* **marche de f.** march in line; *Naut* **en ligne de f.** line abreast
4 vue de f. front view; **attaque de f.** frontal attack; **attaquer qn de f.** to attack sb from the front; *Fig* to attack sb head-on; **aborder un problème de f.** to tackle a problem head-on; **heurter qn/qch de f.** to run head-on into sb/sth
▸▸ **f. de mer** (sea)front; **le F. populaire** = French left-wing coalition in power 1936-38; *Min* **f. de taille** working face, coal face

frontal, -ale, -aux, -ales [fʀɔ̃tal] **ADJ** frontal; *(collision)* head-on; *Ordinat* front-end; **ordinateur f.** front end; **os f.** frontal bone; **chargement f.** front loading; *Min* **lampe frontale** cap lamp
NM *Anat* frontal bone; *Com* facing; **f. de rayonnage** shelf facing
NF *Com* **frontale** shelf facing

frontalier, -ière [fʀɔ̃talje, -jɛʀ] **ADJ** **régions frontalières** frontier *or* border regions
N inhabitant of the frontier zone; *(travailleur)* cross-border commuter

fronteau, -eaux [fʀɔ̃to] **NM 1** *Archit* small pediment **2** *Rel (de nonne)* frontlet

frontière [fʀɔ̃tjɛʀ] **NF** *Pol* border; *Fig* boundary; **f. naturelle** natural border; **f. linguistique** linguistic boundary; **incident de f.** border incident; *Fig* **ma liberté ne connaît pas de f.** my freedom knows no bounds; **faire reculer les frontières du savoir** to roll back the frontiers of knowledge; **aux frontières de la vie et de la mort** between life and death; **se situer à la f. du possible** to stretch the bounds of what is possible; **dépasser les frontières du possible** to go beyond the bounds of what is possible
ADJ *(ville)* frontier, border; **poste f.** border *or* frontier post

Attention: ne pas confondre **frontier** et **border** lorsque l'on traduit **frontière**. On ne peut utiliser que **border** pour décrire la limite qui sépare deux États.

frontispice [fʀɔ̃tispis] **NM** frontispiece

frontiste [fʀɔ̃tist] **ADJ** of the (French) National Front
N member of the (French) National Front

front-office, *pl* **front-offices** [fʀɔ̃tɔfis] **NM** *Banque* front office

fronton [fʀɔ̃tɔ̃] **NM** *Archit* pediment; *(à la pelote basque)* fronton

frottage [fʀɔtaʒ] **NM** *(d'un membre etc)* rubbing, chafing; *(des sols etc)* polishing

frottée [fʀɔte] **NF** *Vieilli* **1** *(volée)* beating, thrashing **2 f. (d'ail)** = bread which has been toasted then rubbed with a clove of garlic

frotte-manche, *pl* **frotte-manches** [fʀɔtmɑ̃ʃ] **N** *Belg Fam* bootlicker

frottement [fʀɔtmɑ̃] **NM 1** *(friction)* rubbing; *Méd* **f. pleural** pleural rub; *Phot* **marques de f.** stress marks; *Fig* **il y a quelques frottements entre eux** there is some friction between them **2** *Tech* friction; *(de freins)* binding; **f. de glissement** sliding friction; **usure par f.** abrasion

frotter [fʀɔte] **VT** *(membre)* to rub; *(sol)* to rub; *(avec une brosse)* to brush; *(cuivre)* to polish; **je vais te f. le dos pour te réchauffer** I'll rub your back to warm you up; **si je t'y reprends, je te frotterai les oreilles!** I catch you at it again, I'll give you what for!; **f. une allumette** to strike a match; *Vieilli* **être frotté de latin** to have a smattering of Latin
VI to rub; **la roue frotte (contre le frein)** the wheel is rubbing (against the brake)
VPR **se frotter 1 se f. les mains** to rub one's hands (together); *Fig* to rub one's hands; **se f. les yeux** to rub one's eyes; **se f. contre qch/qn** to rub (up) against sth/sb **2** *Fig* **se f. aux artistes** to rub shoulders with artists; **se f. au monde professionnel** to be in contact with the professional world; **des gens auxquels il vaut mieux ne pas se f.** people it's best to keep away from *or* not to get involved with; **ne vous y frottez pas!** don't get involved!, don't meddle!; *Fig* **qui s'y frotte s'y pique** if you meddle, you'll get your fingers burnt

frotteur, -euse [fʀɔtœʀ, -øz] **N** *(personne)* floor polisher
NM *(de train électrique)* sliding contact, (collecting) shoe; *Aut* slipper

frotti-frotta [fʀɔtifʀɔta] **NM** *Fam* **faire du f.** to rub up against each other

frottis [fʀɔti] **NM 1** *Beaux-Arts* scumble **2** *Biol (pour examen au microscope)* smear; **f. vaginal** cervical smear

frottoir [fʀɔtwaʀ] **NM** *(ustensile)* rubber; *(brosse)* scrubbing brush; *(de boîte d'allumettes)* friction strip; *(de dynamo)* brush

frou(-)frou, *pl* **frou(-)frous** [fʀufʀu] **NM** *(bruit)* *(d'une robe en soie, de feuilles)* rustle, rustling; *(vêtement féminin)* frill

froufroutant [fʀufʀutɑ̃] **ADJ** frilly

froufrouter [fʀufʀute] **VI** to rustle

froussard, -arde [fʀusaʀ, -aʀd] *Fam* **ADJ** yellow, chicken
N chicken, coward

frousse [fʀus] **NF** *Fam* fear, fright; **avoir la f.** to be scared, to have the wind up; **avoir la f. de faire qch** to be scared to do *or* of doing sth; **ça m'a donné** *ou* **foutu la f.** that scared me to death *or* put the wind up me

fructidor [fʀyktidɔʀ] **NM** *Hist* = twelfth month of the French Republican calendar *(August-September)*

fructifère [fʀyktifɛʀ] **ADJ** fruitbearing

fructification [fʀyktifikasjɔ̃] **NF** *(d'un arbre)* fruition, fructification; *(d'un investissement)* yield; *Fig (d'une idée, d'un projet)* fruition

fructifier [fʀyktifje] **VI** *(d'arbres)* to bear fruit, *Spéc* to fructify; *Fig* **ses placements commencent à f.** his investments are beginning to show *or* yield a profit; **il sait faire**

f. son argent he knows how to get a return on his money

fructose [fʀyktoz] **NM** fructose

fructueusement [fʀyktɥøzmɑ̃] **ADV** fruitfully, profitably

fructueux, -euse [fʀyktɥø, -øz] **ADJ** fruitful, profitable

frugal, -ale, -aux, -ales [fʀygal, -o] **ADJ** *(personne, repas)* frugal

frugalement [fʀygalmɑ̃] **ADV** frugally

frugalité [fʀygalite] **NF** frugality

frugivore [fʀyʒivɔʀ] **ADJ** *(animal)* fruit-eating
N fruit-eater

fruit¹ [fʀɥi] **NM** fruit; **manger des fruits** to eat (some) fruit; **manger un f.** to eat some fruit *or* a piece of fruit; **producteur de fruits** fruit grower; **f. vert** unripe fruit; **le f. d'un mariage** the offspring of a marriage; **le f. de plusieurs années de travail** the fruit of several years' work; **porter des fruits** *(d'un arbre)* to bear fruit; *Fig* **porter ses fruits** *(d'une action, d'un investissement etc)* to bear fruit; **avec f.** to good purpose
▸▸ **fruits des bois,** *Suisse* **petits fruits** fruits of the forest; **fruits confits** crystallized fruit; *Culin, Rel* **f. défendu** forbidden fruit; **fruits déguisés** = dates, prunes etc stuffed with almond paste; **fruits de mer** seafood; **f. de la passion** passion fruit; **fruits rafraîchis** fruit salad soaked in alcohol; **fruits rouges** red berries and currants; *Fig* **f. sec** failure; **fruits secs** dried fruit

fruit² **NM** *Constr (d'un mur, contrefort etc)* batter

fruité [fʀɥite] **ADJ** fruity

fruiterie [fʀɥitʀi] **NF** *(magasin)* fruiterer's *or* greengrocer's shop, *Am* fruit store; *(local)* fruit storeroom

fruiticulteur, -trice [fʀɥitikyltœʀ, -tʀis] **N** fruit grower

fruitier, -ière [fʀɥitje, -jɛʀ] **ADJ** **arbre f.** fruit tree
N fruit dealer, *Br* fruiterer, greengrocer
NM 1 *(local)* fruit storeroom; *(étagère)* stand of fruit trays **2** *(verger)* orchard

frusques [fʀysk] **NFPL** *Fam (vêtements)* gear, togs, *Br* clobber

fruste [fʀyst] **ADJ** *(style, personne)* rough, unpolished; *(pièce, statue)* worn

frustrant [fʀystʀɑ̃] **ADJ** frustrating

frustration [fʀystʀasjɔ̃] **N 1** *Psy* frustration **2** *(d'un légataire)* cheating, defrauding

frustré, -ée [fʀystʀe] **ADJ** frustrated
N frustrated person; **c'est un f.** he's so frustrated

frustrer [fʀystʀe] **VT 1** *Psy* to frustrate **2** *(priver)* **f. qn de qch** to deprive sb of sth; **vous l'avez frustré de sa victoire/réussite** you robbed *or* deprived him of his victory/success; **on m'a frustré de mes biens** I have been cheated out of *or* defrauded of my property

FS [ɛfɛs] *abrév* franc suisse

FSE [ɛfɛsə] **NM** *(abrév* **Fonds social européen)** ESF

FSM [ɛfɛsɛm] **NM** *(abrév* **Forum social mondial)** WSF

FTP [ɛftepe] **NMPL** *(abrév* **Francs-tireurs et partisans)** = French Communist resistance group in the Second World War

fuchsia [fyʃja] **NM** *Bot* fuchsia
ADJ INV fuchsia

fucus [fykys] **NM** fucus, sea wrack

fuel [fjul] **NM** fuel oil

fufute [fyfyt] **ADJ** *Fam* **il n'est pas très f.** he's a bit thick

fugace [fygas] **ADJ** fleeting, transient; **impression f.** fleeting impression

fugacité [fygasite] NF *Litt* fleetingness, transience

fugitif, -ive [fyʒitif, -iv] ADJ **1** *(personne)* fugitive, runaway **2** *(fugace) (désir, émotion)* transitory, fleeting, ephemeral, short-lived; **ombre fugitive** fleeting shadow
  N fugitive, runaway

fugitivement [fyʒitivmã] ADV fleetingly

fugue [fyg] NF **1** *Mus* fugue **2 faire une f.** to run away

fuguer [fyge] VI *Fam* to run away

fugueur, -euse [fygœr, -øz] ADJ who runs away a lot
  N runaway

fuir [fɥir] *(prp* fuyant; *pp* fui; *pr ind* je fuis, n. fuyons, ils fuient*)* VI **1** *(s'enfuir)* to run away, to flee *(devant* from*)*; **f. de son pays** to flee one's country; **faire f.** to put to flight; **bête à faire f.** as stupid as can be; **le temps fuit** time flies, time is slipping by; **f. devant les responsabilités** to shirk one's responsibilities; *Naut* **f. devant le vent** to scud or run before the wind; **il a le regard qui fuit** he has shifty eyes; **f. à toutes jambes** to run off at top speed or as fast as one can **2** *(de l'horizon)* to recede **3** *(d'un robinet, tonneau etc)* to leak; *(de gaz, d'eau)* to leak, to escape
  VT **1** *(éviter) (responsabilité, amis, journalistes)* to shun, to avoid; *(question)* to evade, to avoid; **f. sa famille** to shun one's family; *Litt* **f. le monde** to flee society; **le sommeil me fuit** I cannot sleep **2** *(abandonner)* to flee, to run away from; **f. son pays** to flee one's country
  VPR se fuir *(s'éviter)* to avoid each other

fuite [fɥit] NF **1** flight **(devant** from*)*; **prendre la f.** to take flight; **être en f.** to be on the run; **mettre l'ennemi en f.** to put the enemy to flight; *Fam* **la f. des cerveaux** the brain drain; **la f. des capitaux** the flight of capital; **renversé par une voiture qui a pris la f.** run over by a hit-and-run driver; *Fig* **la f. en avant de la consommation** the headlong rush of consumerism; **la course aux armements est une f. en avant** the arms race is being blindly pursued by all governments; **à partir de là, c'était la f. en avant** from then on there was no turning back; **la seule solution possible était la f. en avant** the only possible solution was to keep on going, the only way out was forward
  2 *(de liquide, gaz, d'information)* leak; **f. de gaz** gas leak; **il y a eu des fuites en histoire** some of the history questions leaked out
  3 *(devant des difficultés, des problèmes)* evasion, avoidance
  4 la f. du temps the passage or passing of time
  5 *Beaux-Arts* **point de f.** vanishing point

fulgurant [fylgyrã] ADJ *(lumière)* flashing; *(attaque, changement)* lightning; *Méd (douleurs)* stabbing, searing; **une découverte fulgurante** a dazzling discovery; **une idée fulgurante** a sudden and brilliant idea; **lancer un regard f. à qn** to look daggers at sb; **elle a connu un succès f.** she was brilliantly successful; **une explication d'une clarté fulgurante** a brilliantly clear explanation

fulguration [fylgyrasjõ] NF lightning; *Méd* fulguration

fulgurer [fylgyre] VI to flash

fuligineux, -euse [fyliʒinø, -øz] ADJ *(couleur)* smoky, sooty; *(ciel)* murky

fulmicoton [fylmikɔtõ] NM guncotton

fulminant [fylminã] ADJ *(ton)* exceedingly angry, furious; *(poudre)* fulminating; *Spéc (douleur)* fulminant

fulminer [fylmine] VT *(accusations)* to thunder, to roar
  VI **f. contre qn/qch** to fulminate or inveigh against sb/sth

fumage¹ [fymaʒ] NM, **fumaison** [fymɛzõ] NF *(d'une terre)* manuring, dressing, dunging

fumage² NM, **fumaison** NF *(de poisson, viande)* smoking, smoke-curing

fumant [fymã] ADJ **1** *(âtre, cendres)* smoking **2** *(soupe, cheval etc)* steaming; *Fam* **f. de colère** fuming **3** *Fam (remarquable)* terrific, sensational; **faire un coup f.** to pull off a masterstroke

fumasse [fymas] ADJ *Fam* fuming

fumé [fyme] ADJ **1** *(poisson, viande etc)* smoked, smoke-cured **2 verre f.** smoked glass; **verres fumés** dark lenses; *(lunettes)* dark glasses, sunglasses

fume-cigare [fymsigar] NM INV cigar holder

fume-cigarette [fymsigaret] NM INV cigarette holder

fumée [fyme] NF **1** *(de feu, cigarette etc)* smoke; **rideau de f.** smokescreen; **noir de f.** lampblack; **la f. (du tabac) vous gêne-t-elle?** do you mind my smoking?; *Fig* **partir** ou **s'en aller en f.** to go up in smoke; *Prov* **il n'y a pas de f. sans feu** there's no smoke without fire **2** *(de la soupe etc)* steam; *(du charbon de bois)* fumes; *(d'alcool)* vapours, *Am* vapors

fumer¹ [fyme] VT *(terre)* to manure, to dress, to dung

fumer² VI **1** *(d'un âtre, d'une lampe, d'un moteur)* to smoke **2** *(d'un fumeur)* to smoke; **défense de f.** no smoking; **f. comme un pompier** ou **un sapeur** to smoke like a chimney; **f. tranquillement** to have a quiet smoke; **il est allé en f. une dans la cour** he went for a smoke or to have a smoke in the yard **3** *(de la soupe etc)* to steam **4** *Fam (de colère)* to fume
  VT **1** *(poisson, viande)* to smoke(-cure) **2** *(pipe, tabac etc)* to smoke; **il fumait cigarette sur cigarette** he was chainsmoking **3** *Arg (battre)* to clobber, to thump; *(tuer)* to kill, *Br* to do in

> Il faut noter que le verbe anglais **to fume** est un faux ami. Il signifie **fulminer**.

fumerie [fymri] NF **f. d'opium** opium den

fumerolle [fymrɔl] NF *(de volcan)* smoke and gas

fumet [fymɛ] NM **1** *(de la nourriture qui cuit)* aroma, *(pleasant)* smell; *(du vin)* bouquet **2** *(à la chasse)* scent

fumeterre [fymtɛr] NF *Bot* fumitory

fumette [fymɛt] NF *Fam* getting stoned; **c'est un habitué de la f.** he gets stoned regularly; **il y a que la f. qui l'intéresse** all he's interested in is getting stoned

fumeur, -euse [fymœr, -øz] N smoker; **f. de pipe/cigares** pipe/cigar smoker; **f. d'opium** opium smoker; *Rail* **compartiment fumeurs/non fumeurs** smoking/non-smoking compartment, *Fam* smoker/non-smoker

fumeux, -euse [fymø, -øz] ADJ *(lampe)* smoky, smoking; *(ciel, idées, explications, projets)* hazy; **quel esprit f.!** what a woolly mind!

fumier [fymje] NM **1** *(engrais)* manure, dung; **fosse à f.** slurry pit **2** *(tas)* dunghill, manure heap **3** *Vulg (salaud)* bastard; **espèce de f.!** you bastard!; **le f.!, il m'a menti!** he lied to me, the bastard!

fumigation [fymigasjõ] NF fumigation; *Méd* inhalation

fumigène [fymiʒɛn] NM *(en horticulture)*, *Mil* smoke-producing device
  ADJ *Mil* **grenade f.** smoke grenade

fumiger [fymiʒe] VT *(je fumigeai(s))* to fumigate

fumiste [fymist] NM **1** *Fam (sur qui on ne peut compter)* shirker, *Br* layabout; **c'est un f.** he doesn't exactly kill himself working **2**

(installateur) heating engineer **3** *Vieilli (farceur)* practical joker
  ADJ *Fam* unreliable, irresponsible

fumisterie [fymistəri] NF **1** *(métier)* heating engineering **2** *Fam (farce)* con, farce; **c'est une vaste f.** it's a huge con, it's an absolute farce

fumivore [fymivɔr] ADJ smoke-absorbing

fumoir [fymwar] NM smoking room; *(pour la viande, le poisson etc)* smokehouse

fumure [fymyr] NF *(de champ)* manuring, dressing, dunging

fun [fœn] *Fam* ADJ *(amusant, divertissant)* fun; **c'est pas très f.** it's not much fun
  NM fun; **faire qch pour le f.** to do sth for fun

funambule [fynãbyl] N tightrope walker, *Spéc* funambulist

funambulesque [fynãbylɛsk] ADJ **1 l'art f.** the art of tightrope walking; **acrobatie f.** high-wire acrobatics **2** *Fig (idées, projet etc) (original)* fantastic, bizarre; *(casse-cou)* reckless

funboard [fœnbɔrd] NM funboard

funèbre [fynɛbr] ADJ **1** *(cérémonie)* funeral; **hymne** ou **chant f.** dirge; **marche f.** funeral or dead march **2** *(lugubre)* funereal, gloomy

funérailles [fyneraj] NFPL funeral; **f. nationales** state funeral

funéraire [fynerɛr] ADJ *(dépenses)* funeral; *(urne)* funeral, funerary; **pierre f.** tombstone, gravestone; **drap f.** pall

funérarium [fynerarjɔm] NM funereal home, *Br* funeral parlour, *Am* funeral parlor

funeste [fynɛst] ADJ **1** *Litt (accident)* deadly, fatal **2** *(erreur, conséquences)* fatal, disastrous, catastrophic; **influence f.** disastrous influence; **être f. à qch** to be fatal to sth **3** *Arch (triste)* funereal, gloomy

funiculaire [fynikylɛr] ADJ funicular
  NM funicular (railway)

funk [fœnk] ADJ INV, NM INV *Mus* funk

funky [fœnki] *Mus* ADJ INV funky
  NM INV funky music

fur [fyr] NM **au f. et à mesure** as one goes along, bit by bit; **au f. et à mesure, j'ai compris comment ça fonctionnait** I understood how it worked as I went along or bit by bit; **au f. et à mesure des besoins** as and when required, as needed; **au f. et à mesure de la progression des travaux** as work progresses; **au f. et à mesure de ses recherches** as he progressed with his research; **au f. et à mesure que tu en as besoin** as and when you need it; **je repasse mon linge au f. et à mesure que je le lave** I iron my clothes as soon as I've washed them

furax [fyraks] ADJ *Fam* livid, *Am* fit to be tied

furet [fyrɛ] NM **1** *(animal)* ferret; **chasse au f.** chasser au f. to go ferreting; **jeu du f.** ≃ hunt-the-slipper **2** *Fig Arch* nosy parker

furetage [fyrtaʒ] NM **1** *(pour lapins)* ferreting **2** *Fig* prying, nosing around; *(dans l'armoire)* rummaging (about), ferreting (about)

fureter [fyrte] VI *(je furette; je furetterai)* **1** *(chasser)* to ferret, to go ferreting **2** *(chercher)* to pry, to nose around; **f. dans les armoires** to ferret (about) or rummage (about) in the cupboards

fureteur, -euse [fyrtœr, -øz] N **1** *(chasseur)* ferreter **2** *Fam Péj* nosy parker
  NM *Can Ordinat* browser
  ADJ prying, *Fam* nosy; **regard f.** inquisitive look

fureur [fyrœr] NF **1** *(colère)* fury, rage; **être en f.** to be in a rage or fury, to be furious; **tu vas le mettre en f.** you'll infuriate or enrage him, you'll make him furious; **se mettre dans une f. (noire)** to fly into a (towering) rage; **la f. des combats dans le Golfe** the battle raging in the Gulf; **la f. des flots** the fury of the waves **2** *(passion)* passion; **aimer qn/qch avec f.** to be passionately fond of sb/ sth; **avoir la f. de bâtir** to be mad on building; **la f. du jeu** a passion for gambling; **faire f.** to be all the rage

furia [fyrja] **NF** *Fam (d'une foule)* frenzy; **ils n'ont pas pu résister à la f. bordelaise** they had no answer to the Bordeaux team's furious onslaught

furibard [fyribar] **ADJ** *Fam* livid, *Am* fit to be tied

furibond [fyribɔ̃] **ADJ** furious; **elle lui a lancé un regard f.** she glared at him

furie [fyri] **NF 1** *(passion)* fury; **critiquer qn/ se battre avec f.** to criticize sb/fight furiously; **applaudir/crier avec f.** to applaud/shout frantically; **la f. du jeu** a passion for gambling; **en f.** infuriated, enraged; **se mettre en f.** to fly into a rage **2** *Myth* **les Furies** the Furies; *Fig* **c'est une f.** she's a shrew; **comme une f.** like a wild thing

furieusement [fyrjøzmɑ̃] **ADV 1** furiously **2** *Vieilli, Hum (très)* extremely, really; **on s'est f. amusé** we had a great time

furieux, -ieuse [fyrjø, -jøz] **ADJ 1** *(en colère)* furious; **être f. contre qn** to be furious with sb; **elle est furieuse qu'on ne l'ait pas prévenue** she's furious that nobody told her; **il est f. contre lui-même** he's furious with himself; **être f. de qch** to be furious with *or* at sth; **je suis f. de constater que vous n'avez fait aucun effort** I'm furious to see that you've made no effort at all; **rendre qn f.** to enrage *or* infuriate sb; **taureau f.** mad *or* raging bull; **tempête furieuse** raging *or* howling storm; **il a un f. appétit** he has a tremendous appetite; **un f. désir de vivre** a tremendous desire to live; **pousser des cris f.** to shout furiously **2** *(forcené)* mad; **c'est un fou f.** he's a raving lunatic

N c'est un f. he's a raving lunatic

furoncle [fyrɔ̃kl] **NM** *Méd* boil, *Spéc* furuncle

furonculose [fyrɔ̃kyloz] **NF** *Méd* furunculosis

furtif, -ive [fyrtif, -iv] **ADJ** furtive, stealthy

furtivement [fyrtivmɑ̃] **ADV** furtively, stealthily; **entrer/sortir f.** to steal in/out, to enter/leave furtively

fusain [fyzɛ̃] **NM 1** *(arbre)* spindle tree **2** *Beaux-Arts (crayon)* charcoal (pencil); *(dessin)* charcoal (drawing)

fusant [fyzɑ̃] **ADJ** fusing; **obus f.** time shell

fuseau, -eaux [fyzo] **NM 1** *Tex* spindle; *(pour dentelle)* bobbin; **f. de quenouille** distaff; **en f.** tapered, tapering; **jambes en f.** slender legs **2 f. horaire** time zone **3 fuseaux** *(pantalon)* ski pants; **la mode du f. *ou* des fuseaux revient** ski pants are coming back into fashion

fusée [fyze] **NF 1** *(projectile)* rocket; **lancer une f.** to launch a rocket; **avion-f.** rocket-propelled aircraft; **il est parti comme une f.** he shot off like a rocket **2** *(de bombe etc)*

fuse, *Am* fuze **3** *(d'arbre, d'axe)* spindle; *Aut* stub axle, hub carrier

▸▸ **f. air-air** air-to-air missile; **f. d'appoint** booster; **f. de détresse** distress rocket; **f. de direction** stub axle; **f. éclairante** flare; **f.-engin** missile; **f. à étages** multistage rocket; **f. à un étage** one-stage rocket; *Astronaut* **f. interplanétaire** space rocket; **f. percutante** percussion fuse; **f. à pétard** maroon; *Naut* **f. porte-amarre** life(-saving) rocket; **f. porteuse** carrier rocket; **f. de signalisation** signal rocket; **f. sonde** probe; **f. à temps** time fuse; **f. volante** sky rocket

fuselage [fyzlaʒ] **NM** *Aviat* fuselage

fuselé [fyzle] **ADJ** *(colonne, doigts)* tapering; *Aut* streamlined

fuseler [fyzle] **VT** (**je fuselle; je fusellerai**) to taper; *Aut* to streamline

fuser [fyze] **VI 1** *(de cire chaude)* to run, to melt; *Fig* **des rires fusèrent de toutes parts** there were bursts of laughter from all sides, laughter erupted from all sides; **des cris/des remarques fusèrent de toutes parts** cries/ comments were suddenly heard from all sides **2** *Chimie (de sel)* to crackle **3** *(de fusible)* to burn slowly

fusibilité [fyzibilite] **NF** fusibility

fusible [fyzibl] **ADJ** fusible

NM *Élec* fuse, *Am* fuze; *(fil métallique)* fuse wire; **f. de sûreté** safety fuse, cut-out

fusiforme [fyzifɔrm] **ADJ** spindle-shaped

fusil [fyzi] **NM 1** *(arme)* gun, rifle; *Fig* **changer son f. d'épaule** to change (one's) tack; **entendre un coup de f.** to hear a shot; **c'est un de nos meilleurs fusils** he's one of our best shots; **coup de f.** gunshot, rifle shot; *Fam (dans un hôtel)* overcharging, fleecing; *Fam* **c'est le coup de f., dans ce restaurant** the prices in this restaurant are extortionate; *Fam* **quel coup de f.!** what a rip-off! **2** *(d'un briquet à amadou)* steel; *(pour aiguiser)* (sharpening) steel

▸▸ **f. à air comprimé** air gun; **f. automatique** automatic gun *or* rifle; **f. à chargeur** magazine rifle; **f. de chasse** shotgun, sporting gun; **f. à deux coups** double-barrelled gun; **f. harpon** harpoon gun; **f. rayé** rifle

fusilier [fyzilje] **N** fusilier; **f. marin** marine

fusillade [fyzijad] **NF** *(tir)* fusillade, rifle fire

fusiller [fyzije] **VT 1** *(par un peloton d'exécution)* to shoot; *Fig* **f. qn du regard** to look daggers at sb **2** *Fam Vieilli (abîmer)* to wreck, to ruin

fusil-mitrailleur, *pl* **fusils-mitrailleurs NM** light machinegun

fusion [fyzjɔ̃] **NF 1** *(par la chaleur)* melting; *Spéc* fusion; *Métal* smelting; **point de f.** melting point; **fer en f.** molten iron **2** *Nucl* fusion **3** *Fig (d'idées, de philosophies etc)* merging, combining **4** *(de compagnies, partis politiques etc)* merger; **fusions-rachats** mergers and acquisitions; *Ordinat* **f. de fichiers** file merge

fusion-acquisition, *pl* **fusions-acquisitions NF** merger acquisition

fusionnement [fyzjɔnmɑ̃] **NM** *Com (de compagnies)* merger, amalgamation

fusionner [fyzjɔne] **VI** *(de sociétés, communes, partis politiques)* to merge, to amalgamate

VT *(sociétés, communes, partis politiques)* to merge, to amalgamate; *Ordinat* to merge

fustigation [fystigasjɔ̃] **NF** *Litt* castigation

fustiger [fystiʒe] **VT** (**je fustigeai(s)**) *Arch (battre)* to thrash, to beat; *Fig Litt (critiquer)* to castigate

fût [fy] **NM 1** *(de fusil)* stock; *(de scie, de raquette etc)* handle **2** *(de colonne, cheminée)* shaft; *(de candélabre)* stem; *(de rivet)* shank; *(d'arbre)* bole **3** *(baril)* cask, barrel; *(pour l'huile)* drum; **tirer de la bière du f.** to draw beer from the wood *or* cask *or* barrel

futaie [fytɛ] **NF** forest *(producing timber from full-grown trees)*; **arbre de haute f.** full-grown tree

futaille [fytaj] **NF** *(baril)* cask, barrel

futaine [fytɛn] **NF** *Tex* fustian

futal [fytal], **fute** [fyt] **NM** *Fam* trousers, *Am* pants

futé, -ée [fyte] **ADJ** cunning, wily, crafty

N c'est un petit f. he's a cunning *or* crafty devil

futile [fytil] **ADJ** *(argument, occupation)* trivial, trifling; *(prétexte)* idle; *(personne)* frivolous

futilement [fytilmɑ̃] **ADV** frivolously

futilité [fytilite] **NF** triviality; **s'occuper à des futilités** to fritter away one's time; **une conversation pleine de futilités** a conversation full of trivialities

futon [fytɔ̃] **NM** futon

futur, -ure [fytyr] **ADJ** future; **la vie future** the life to come; **les générations futures** future *or* coming generations; **f. acheteur** prospective buyer; **un f. artiste** a budding artist; **f. client** prospective client; **mon f. emploi/appartement** my next job/flat; **mon f. mari** my future husband, my husband-to-be

N *Hum* **mon f./ma future** my fiancé/fiancée, my intended

NM 1 *(avenir)* future; **le f. m'inquiète** I am worried about the future; **quel f. pour l'Europe?** what will Europe's future be? **2** *Gram* future (tense); **au f.** in the future (tense) SEE GRAMMAR A50–2; B24; B31

futurisme [fytyrism] **NM** *Beaux-Arts, Archit* futurism

futuriste [fytyrist] *Beaux-Arts, Archit* **ADJ** futuristic

N futurist

fuyant [fɥijɑ̃] **ADJ 1** *(ligne, menton)* receding; *Beaux-Arts* **lignes fuyantes** perspective lines **2** *(personne, attitude)* evasive; *(yeux)* shifty

fuyard, -arde [fɥijar, -ard] **ADJ** *Arch* shy, timid

N fugitive, runaway

FV NF *(abrév* **fréquence vocale**) VF

G, g [ʒe] NM **1** *(lettre)* G, g; **une force égale à plusieurs G** a force of several G **2** *Belg Fam* (*abbr* **GSM**) *(téléphone portable)* mobile, *Am* cell(phone)

g. 1 *abrév* **gauche 2** *abrév* **gramme(s)**

G7 [ʒesɛt] NM *(abrév* **Groupe des Sept**) G7

G8 [ʒeɥit] NM *(abrév* **Groupe des Huit**) G8

gabardine [gabardin] NF **1** *Tex* gabardine **2** *(imperméable)* gabardine (raincoat)

gabare [gabar] NF **1** *Naut* sailing barge; *(pour charger, décharger un navire)* lighter; *(chaland)* transport vessel, store ship, scow **2** *Pêche* dragnet

gabarit [gabari] NM **1** *Naut (d'un bateau)* model; *(d'une pièce de bateau)* mould, *Am* mold; *Constr (d'un bâtiment)* outline **2** *Tech* template, templet; *Ordinat* template; **g. d'assemblage** assembly jig, assembling gauge; **g. de mise en page** master page; **tour à g.** copying lathe **3** *Rail (sous un pont)* clearance; **g. de chargement** loading gauge; **g. d'écartement (des voies)** rail *or* track gauge **4** *Fam* **un grand/petit g.** a huge/tiny man, *f* woman; **des gens de son g.** people of his calibre

gabegie [gabʒi] NF *(mauvaise gestion)* mismanagement; *(désordre)* muddle, chaos

gabelle [gabɛl] NF *Hist* salt tax

gabelou [gablu] NM *Péj* customs officer

gabier [gabje] NM *Naut* topman; **g. breveté** able(-bodied) seaman

gable [gabl], **gâble** [gabl] NM *Archit* gable; *(charpente)* (triangular) window canopy

Gabon [gabɔ̃] NM Gabon

gabonais, -aise [gabɔnɛ, -ɛz] ADJ Gabonese

  N **G.** Gabonese

gâchage [gɑʃaʒ] NM **1** *(du mortier, du plâtre)* mixing **2** *(gaspillage)* waste, wasting **3 g. des prix** price undercutting

gâche¹ [gɑʃ] NF **1** *(pour le plâtre)* trowel **2** *(de pâtissier)* spatula

gâche² [gɑʃ] NF **1** *(d'une serrure)* (box) staple, keeper; *(d'une fenêtre)* (latch) catch; *(d'un pêne)* striking box *or* plate, strike box; *Aut* **g. de porte** striker plate **2** *Tech (pour cliquet)* notch

gâchée [gɑʃe] NF *Constr (de ciment etc)* batch

gâcher [gɑʃe] VT **1** *(gâter)* to spoil; *(bâcler)* *(travail)* to bungle, to botch, to mess up; *(gaspiller)* *(nourriture, pellicule etc)* to waste; *(fortune)* to waste, to squander; **il a gâché notre plaisir/la soirée** he spoiled our pleasure/the evening; **tu as tout gâché en lui racontant ça** you've spoilt *or* ruined everything by telling him that; **g. ses chances de succès** to spoil one's chances; **g. sa vie** to waste one's life; **g. le métier** to spoil it for others *(by undercutting them)*; **g. le marché** to spoil the trade **2** *(mélanger) (mortier, plâtre)* to mix; **g. la chaux** to slack lime

gâchette [gaʃɛt, gaʃɛt] NF **1** *(d'une arme)* trigger; *Fam* **avoir la g. facile** to be trigger-happy **2** *(d'une serrure)* spring catch **3** *Tech* pawl **4** *Électron* gate

gâcheur, -euse [gɑʃœr, -øz] ADJ wasteful
  N waster
  NM *Constr* plasterer's mate

gâchis [gɑʃi] NM **1** *(mortier)* wet mortar **2** *(désordre)* mess; *(gaspillage)* waste; **vous avez fait un beau g. dans la cuisine!** you've made a right mess in the kitchen!; **je ne supporte pas le g.** I can't stand waste *or* wastefulness; **quel g.!** what a waste!

gadelle [gadɛl] NF *Can Bot* redcurrant

gadget [gadʒɛt] NM gadget, *Fam* gizmo; **des mesures-gadgets** gimmicky measures

gadgétisation [gadʒetizasjɔ̃] NF **la g. des voitures/ordinateurs** the adding of gadgets to cars/computers; **la g. de la société** the increasing use of gadgets in society

gadgétiser [gadʒetize] VT to add gadgets to; **g. la société** to increase the use of gadgets in society; **g. une voiture** to customize a car (with gadgets)

gadgétomanie [gadʒetɔmani] NF *Fam* mania for gadgets

gadin [gadɛ̃] NM *Fam* **prendre** *ou* **ramasser un g.** to fall flat on one's face, *Br* to come a cropper

gaditan, -ane [gaditɑ̃, -an] ADJ of *or* from Cadiz
  N **G.** *(natif)* native of Cadiz; *(habitant)* inhabitant of Cadiz

gadoue [gadu] NF *(boue)* mud, slush; *(engrais)* sewage sludge

Gaël [gaɛl] NM Gael

gaélique [gaelik] ADJ, NM *Ling* Gaelic

gaffe [gaf] NF **1** *Fam (maladresse)* blunder, booboo; **faire une g.** to put one's foot in it, to make a blunder **2** *(perche)* boathook; *Pêche* gaff; *Arg* **avaler sa g.** to croak, *Br* to kick the bucket **3** *Fam* **faire g.** to pay attention; **fais g.!** look out!, watch it! **4** *Arg* prison warder, screw

gaffer¹ [gafe] VT **1** *(objet flottant etc)* to hook; *Pêche (saumon etc)* to gaff **2** *Fam* **gaffe un peu la nana!** get a look at that chick!
  VI *Fam* **1** *(commettre une bévue)* to put one's foot in it, to make a blunder **2** *Fam (regarder)* to look; **gaffe un peu!** have a look!
  VPR **se gaffer** *Suisse Fam* to watch out

gaffer² [gafœr] NM *TV, Cin* gaffer

gaffeur¹, -euse [gafœr, -øz] N *Fam* blunderer, blundering fool; **c'est un g.** he's always putting his foot in it

gaffeur² NM *Cin, TV* **g. grip** alligator clip

gag [gag] NM *Théâtre, Cin etc* gag; **tu es renvoyé – c'est un g.!** you're fired – you're kidding *or* joking?; **son pantalon a craqué au milieu de la réunion, le g.!** his trousers split during the meeting, what a scream!

gaga [gaga] *Fam* N old dodderer
  ADJ gaga

gage [gaʒ] NM **1** *Com, Jur* security; *(chez le prêteur sur gages)* pledge; *Fig (garantie)* guarantee; **laisser qch en g.** to leave sth as security; **mettre qch en g.** to pawn sth; **mise en g.** pawning; **prêteur sur gages** pawnbroker; **ma montre est en g.** my watch is in pawn; **lettre de g.** debenture bond; *(pour hypothèque)* mortgage bond; *Jur* **g. mobilier** mortgage over assets, mortgage over property; **rester en g.** to remain as surety; **votre parole sera le meilleur des gages** your word will be the best guarantee

  2 *(preuve)* token; **les ambassadeurs nous ont apporté des gages de bonne volonté** the ambassadors brought us tokens of goodwill *or* goodwill tokens; **g. d'amour** token of love, love token; **je t'offre ce livre en g. de notre amitié** I offer you this book as a token of our friendship

  3 *(aux jeux)* forfeit

  4 *(salaire)* **gages** wages, pay; *Péj* **être aux gages de qn** to be in the pay of sb; **tueur à gages** hired assassin *or* killer

gagé [gaʒe] ADJ *(montre, bijoux etc)* pawned; *Jur (emprunt)* secured; **meubles gagés** furniture under distraint; **recettes non gagées** unassigned *or* unpledged revenue

gager [gaʒe] VT (**je gageai(s); n. gageons**) **1** *Litt* **je gagerais que …** I would wager *or* bet that … **2** *(emprunt)* to guarantee, to secure; **g. qch** to deposit sth as security, to pledge sth as security

gageur [gaʒœr] NM *Jur* pledgor

gageure [gaʒyr] NF **1** *(action difficile)* difficult undertaking, challenge; **réussir la g. de faire qch** to succeed in the difficult task of doing sth **2** *(pari) Litt* wager, bet

gagiste [gaʒist] NM *Jur* pledgee

gagnant, -ante [gaɲɑ̃, -ɑ̃t] ADJ *(billet, numéro, combinaison etc)* winning; **jouer un cheval g.** to back a winner *or* a winning horse
  N winner; **partir g.** *(à une course)* to start favourite *or* *Am* favorite; *Fig* to be bound to succeed; **il joue g.** he can't lose

gagne-pain [gaɲpɛ̃] NM INV livelihood; **trouver un g.** to find a job; **il n'aime pas ce qu'il fait, c'est juste un g.** he doesn't like what he does, it's just a way of earning a living *or* of making his bread and butter

gagne-petit [gaɲpəti] NM INV low wage earner; *Péj (personne qui n'a aucune ambition)* small-timer

GAGNER [gaɲe]

| **VT** to earn **1** ▪ to gain **2, 3** ▪ to win **3,** |
| **4** ▪ to win over **2** ▪ to get to **5** ▪ to |
| spread to **6** |
| **VI** to win **1** ▪ to increase **3** |

VT 1 *(comme rémunération)* to earn; **g. cinq**

mille euros par mois to earn five thousand euros a month; **g. gros** to earn or make big money; (d'une société) to make large profits; **g. sa vie** to earn one's living; **g. bien/mal sa vie** to earn or make/not to earn or make a good living; **g. de quoi vivre** to earn a living, to earn enough to live on; Fam **g. sa croûte** ou **son bifteck** to earn one's crust; Fam **g. des mille et des cents** to earn or make a fortune or a packet; **ce que je gagne suffit à nos besoins** I earn enough to keep us; Fam **il l'a bien gagné** he's earned it; Fam **j'ai gagné ma journée!** it's just not my day!

2 (obtenir) (réputation, fortune, avantages) to gain; (se concilier) (partisan, mari) to win over; (profiter) to gain (à by); **g. du temps** to save time; (sur un délai serré) to gain time; **g. des parts de marché** to gain share; **chercher à g. du temps** to play for time; **g. de l'espace** to save space; **j'ai gagné trois places dans la queue** I've moved up three places in the queue; **c'est autant de gagné, c'est toujours ça de gagné** that's something, anyway; **nous ne gagnerons rien à attendre** there is nothing to be gained or we'll gain nothing by waiting; **nous n'y avons gagné que des problèmes** all it brought us was problems; **et moi, qu'est-ce que j'y gagne?** and what do I get out of it?, what's in this for me?, and where do I come in?; **tu as tout à g.** you've everything to gain; **il n'y a rien à y g.** there's nothing to be gained by it, it won't get you anywhere

3 (victoire) to win, to gain; (bataille, guerre) to win; Fig **la partie n'est pas gagnée** we haven't won yet; **je vais essayer de faire le travail que vous me demandez mais ce n'est pas gagné!** I'll try to do the work you want me to do, but I can't promise anything!; **si elle dit oui, c'est gagné** if she says yes, then everything's OK or all right

4 (jeu, course, prix, somme) to win; **g. qn à une cause** to win sb over to a cause; **g. qn à une idée** to sell sb an idea; **g. la confiance/l'estime/l'amitié de qn** to win or gain sb's confidence/respect/friendship

5 (atteindre) (ville, sortie, porte) to reach, to get to; **g. le haut** to reach or get to the top; Naut **g. le port** to reach port, Spéc to fetch into port

6 (de maladie, d'infection) to spread to; **l'enflure a gagné la gorge** the swelling has spread to the throat; **le rire gagna l'assemblée tout entière** the laughter spread through the whole audience

7 (rattraper) **g. un navire** to gain on or overhaul a ship; **g. le devant** to forge ahead, to take the lead; **la nuit nous gagna** darkness overtook us; **le feu/l'épidémie gagne** the fire/the epidemic is spreading; **g. du terrain** to gain ground; (sur la mer etc) to reclaim land; **la mer gagne du terrain** the sea is encroaching on the land; **la faim nous gagnait** we were getting hungry; **le doute/la peur/la joie les gagne** doubt/fear/joy overcomes them or sweeps over them; **gagné par le sommeil/la peur/les larmes** overcome by sleep/by fear/with tears; Naut **g. le vent** to make or fetch to windward; **g. le vent d'une pointe** to weather a headland; **g. de l'avant** to forge ahead

VI 1 (être vainqueur) to win; **g. dans un fauteuil** to walk it, to win by a walkover; **g. haut la main** to win hands down

2 (profiter) **g. à qch/à faire qch** to benefit from sth/from doing sth; **tu gagnerais à partir** it would be in your (best) interest or to your advantage to leave; **il ne gagne pas à se montrer trop empressé envers elle** it isn't to his advantage to be too attentive to her, he won't get anything out of being too attentive to her; **g. à être connu** to improve with acquaintance; **j'ai gagné au change** I got the best of the bargain or deal

3 (croître) to increase; **g. en intensité** to increase or gain in intensity; **g. en profondeur/beauté** to increase in depth/beauty, to become deeper/more beautiful; **g. en vigueur** to become stronger; **le mécontentement gagne en force** there is increasing discontent

4 Naut **g. au vent** to make or fetch to windward

gagneur, -euse [gaɲœr, -øz] N winner; **avoir un tempérament** ou **un caractère de g.** to be a winner

NF Arg **gagneuse** (prostituée) pro

gai [gɛ, ge] ADJ (chanson) cheerful, merry, lively; (personne) cheerful, merry, lively, in good spirits; (voix) cheerful, cheery; (chambre, couleur etc) bright, cheerful; **g. comme un pinson** happy as a lark or a sandboy; **avoir un naturel g.** to be of a cheerful disposition; Fam **être un peu g.** (ivre) to be tipsy or tight; **avoir le vin g.** to get merry when one drinks; Iron **ça va être g.!** that will be nice!; Iron **il vérifie en permanence ce que je fais, c'est g.** he's continually checking what I'm doing, it's charming or really nice; **tout cela n'est pas très g.** it's all a bit depressing

gaiement [gemɑ̃, gemɑ̃] ADV cheerfully, merrily, gaily; Iron **allons-y g.!** let's get on with it!

gaieté [gete] NF cheerfulness, gaiety; **vous n'êtes pas/cela n'est pas g.d'une g. folle!** you're/it's hardly a bundle of fun or laughs!; **déborder de g.** to be bubbling over with high spirits; **retrouver sa g.** to recover one's spirits, to perk up, to buck up; **je ne le fais pas de g. de cœur** I don't enjoy doing it, it's not something I do willingly

gaillard, -arde [gajar, -ard] ADJ **1** (vigoureux) (personne) strong, vigorous; **un petit vent g.** a good stiff breeze, a lively breeze; **frais et g.** hale and hearty; **il se sentait g.** he felt in good form; **mon grand-père est encore très g. pour son âge** my grandfather is still very sprightly for his age **2** Vieilli (jovial) (humeur) merry, lively, cheerful; (grivois) (histoire, commentaire) bawdy, Am off-color

N (homme) hearty or vigorous type; **un grand et solide g.** a great strapping man; **tu ne vas pas pleurer, un grand g. comme toi!** you're not going to cry, a big guy like you!; **toi mon g., tu ne perds rien pour attendre!** just you wait, chum or Br mate or Am fella; **c'est un sacré g.!** (vigueur sexuelle) he's quite a lad or stud!; **une grande gaillarde** a strapping woman; (légère) a bit of a girl; Arch **un vert g.** a rip

NM Naut **g. d'avant** forecastle; **g. d'arrière** poop; **haut de g.** deep-waisted

NF **gaillarde** (danse) galliard

gaillardement [gajardəmɑ̃] ADV **1** (gaiement) cheerfully, good-humouredly **2** (sans faiblir) boldly, bravely, gallantly

gaillardise [gajardiz] NF **conter des gaillardises** to tell risqué or off-colour stories or jokes

gaillette [gajɛt] NF (de charbon) lump

gaîment [gemɑ̃, gemɑ̃] ADV = **gaiement**

gain [gɛ̃] NM **1** (d'une compétition, d'une guerre etc) winning; Jur **avoir** ou **obtenir g. de cause** to win one's case; **donner g. de cause à qn** to decide in favour of sb; **il y a chances égales de g. et de perte** it's an even chance, there's a fifty-fifty chance

2 (profit) gain, profit; (salaire) earnings; (au jeu) winnings; **g. d'argent** financial gain; **avoir l'amour du g.** to love making money; **un g. de temps/place** a saving of time/space; **ça nous fait un sacré g. de temps/de place** that saves us an awful lot of time/space; **g. retiré d'une lecture/d'une expérience** benefit or profit acquired from read-ing/from an experience; **gains de productivité** productivity gains

3 Élec etc gain; **g. en courant** current gain; **g. en tension** voltage magnification; Électron **g. d'étage** stage gain; Nucl **g. de régénération** breeding gain

▸▸ Compta **g. latent** unrealized gain; TV etc **g. vidéo** video gain

gainage [gɛnaʒ] NM Tech, Constr etc casing, sheathing, sleeving; Nucl (du combustible etc) canning, casing, cladding

gaine [gɛn] NF **1** (cache) case, casing; **g. en cuir** leather case; **g. métallique** metallic sheath or sleeve; **câble sous g.** sheathed cable; **g. souple** flexible sheath; Nucl **g. d'électrons/d'ions** electron/ion sheath **2** Anat, Bot sheath **3** (sous-vêtement) girdle, corset, foundation (garment) **4** Géol gangue, matrix **5** Constr, Min etc shaft, duct

▸▸ **g. d'aération** ventilation shaft

gaine-combinaison, pl **gaines-combinaisons** NF corselet

gaine-culotte, pl **gaines-culottes** NF panty girdle

gainer [gene] VT (de cuir, de soie, de nylon etc) to sheath, to cover (de in)

Gal Mil (abrév **Général**) Gen

gal [gal] NM Phys gal

gala [gala] NM gala; **en habit** ou **tenue de g.** in gala dress, in full dress; Fig in one's best clothes, in one's Sunday best; **inutile de mettre ton habit de g.** don't bother putting on your best clothes or getting dressed up; **dîner en grand g.** to dine in state, to dine with great ceremony; **g. de bienfaisance** ou **de charité** charity gala

Galaad [galaad] NM Littér Galahad

galactique [galaktik] ADJ galactic

galactogène [galaktɔʒɛn] ADJ, NM Physiol galactagogue

galamment [galamɑ̃] ADV (avec politesse) politely, courteously; (d'un homme) gallantly, like a gentleman; Litt (noblement) honourably, Am honorably; **se tirer g. d'une affaire** to come out of an affair with honour or Am honor

galandage [galɑ̃daʒ] NM Constr brick partition

galant [galɑ̃] ADJ (homme) gallant, chivalrous, gentlemanly; Arch (élégant) gay, elegant; **homme g.** ladies' man; **vers galants** love poems; **femme galante** woman of loose morals; Hum **être en galante compagnie** to be in the company of the opposite sex; **rendez-vous g.** romantic rendezvous; **g. homme** gentleman, man of honour; **se conduire en g. homme** to behave like a gentleman

NM Vieilli, Litt gallant; (coureur de jupons) philanderer; **faire le g. auprès d'une dame** to court or pay court to a lady; (flirter) to flirt with a lady

galanterie [galɑ̃tri] NF **1** (envers les femmes) gallantry, chivalry, courteousness; **dire des galanteries à qn** to pay sb compliments **2** (intrigue) love affair, intrigue

galantine [galɑ̃tin] NF Culin galantine

Galapagos [galapagos] NFPL **les (îles) G.** the Galapagos (Islands)

Galatée [galate] N Myth Galatea

Galatie [galasi] NF Galatia

galaxie [galaksi] NF Astron galaxy

galbe [galb] NM (d'un meuble, d'un balustre etc) curve; (des jambes, hanches etc) curve(s), contour; (d'une voiture) sweep, lines

galbé [galbe] ADJ (jambe etc) shapely

galber [galbe] VT (vase, commode etc) to give curves to; Tech (feuille de métal) to curve, to bend (lightly)

gale [gal] **NF 1** *Méd* scabies; *Méd* **g. bédouine** prickly heat; *Fig* **je n'ai pas la g.!** I haven't got the plague! **2** *Fam (personne)* nasty person; *Fam* **être mauvais comme la g.** to be a nasty character *or Br* nasty piece of work **3** *Vét (de mouton)* scab; *(de chien, chat)* mange **4** *Bot* scab

galée [gale] **NF** *Typ* composing galley

galéjade [galeʒad] **NF** *Région* tall story; **débiter** *ou* **dire des galéjades à qn** to pull sb's leg

galéjer [galeʒe] **VI** *Région* to tell tall stories

galène [galɛn] **NF** *Minér* galena, sulphide of lead

galéopithèque [galeɔpitɛk] **NM** *Zool* flying lemur

galère [galɛr] **NF 1** *Hist (navire)* galley; *Naut* **avirons en g.!** rest on your oars!; **être condamné aux galères** to be sentenced to the galleys **2** *(locutions) Fam* **après plusieurs mois de g.** after several months of hassle; **je me suis mis dans une g. pas possible** I got myself into an incredible mess *or* pickle; **c'est une vraie g.** it's a real pain *or* drag; **il lui arrive g. sur g.** it's just one disaster after another for him; **c'est la g. pour se garer le samedi** it's a (real) hassle *or* pain to find a parking space on Saturdays; **et vogue la g.!** let's see what happens!; *Hum* **mais que diable allait-il faire dans cette g.?** but what the hell was he doing mixed up in that?; **dans quelle galère est-ce que je me suis embarqué?** what have I let myself in for?
    ADJ *Fam (plans)* crazy, madcap; *(vacances)* hassle-filled; **c'est g. de trouver une cabine téléphonique dans cette ville** it's a (real) hassle to find a phone box in this town

galérer [galere] **VI** *Fam* to have a hard time (of it)

galerie [galri] **NF 1** *(passage, salle)* gallery; *Can (véranda)* porch **2** *Théâtre* balcony, gallery; **première g.** dress circle; **seconde g.** upper circle; **la troisième g.** the gallery, *Fam* the gods; **tout ce qu'il fait, c'est pour (épater) la g.** everything he does is just showing off *or* playing to the gallery **3** *Min* gallery, level, drift; **g. d'avancement** heading **4** *Aut (sur toit)* roof rack, roof rail **5** *(sur meuble)* cornice **6** *(d'une digue)* run
    ▸▸ **g. d'art** art gallery; *Élec* **g. des câbles** cable tunnel; **g. marchande** shopping arcade; **g. de portraits** portrait gallery

galérien [galerjɛ̃] **NM** galley slave; **travailler comme un g.** to work like a (galley) slave; *Fam* **mener une vie de g.** to lead a dog's life

galeriste [galrist] **N** gallery owner

galet [galɛ] **NM 1** *(caillou)* pebble; **galets** shingle, pebbles; **plage de galets** shingly *or* shingle beach **2** *Tech* roller, runner, wheel; **g. de roulement** travelling *or* running wheel; *Aut* **g. de direction** roller **3** *Pêche (d'un filet)* float **4** *Ordinat (dans souris)* roller

galetas [galta] **NM** *(sous les toits)* garret, attic; *Péj (taudis)* hovel

galetouse [galtuz] **NF** *Arg* mess tin, dixie

galette [galɛt] **NF 1** *(crêpe de blé noir)* buckwheat pancake **2** *(biscuit rond sablé)* butter biscuit; *Naut* (ship's) biscuit; *Fam* **plate comme une g.** flat as a pancake **3** *Fam (argent)* dough, bread; **il a de la g.** he's loaded, he's rolling in it **4** *Fam (disque, CD)* disc
    ▸▸ **galette des Rois** Twelfth Night cake; **g. de fioul** *ou* **de mazout** *ou* **de pétrole** patch of oil

galetteux, -euse [galetø, -øz] **ADJ** *Vieilli* loaded, rolling in it

galeux, -euse [galø, -øz] **ADJ** *(chien)* mangy; *(arbre)* scabby; *(pelouse)* patchy; *Méd* **plaie galeuse** sore caused by scabies; **murs g.** peeling *or* flaking walls; *Fig* **des mauvais garçons g.** some evil-looking types

galgal, -als [galgal] **NM** *Archéol* cairn, barrow

galibot [galibo] **NM** *Min* pit boy

Galice [galis] **NF** *(en Espagne)* Galicia

Galicie [galisi] **NF** *(en Pologne)* Galicia

galicien, -ienne [galisjɛ̃, -jɛn] **ADJ** Galician *(in Spain or Poland)*
    N G. Galician *(in Spain or in Poland)*

Galien [galjɛ̃] **NM** Galen

Galilée[1] [galile] **NF** *Bible* Galilee

Galilée[2] **N** *Hist* Galileo

galiléen, -enne [galileɛ̃, -ɛn] **ADJ** Galilean
    N G. Galilean

galimatias [galimatja] **NM** gibberish

galion [galjɔ̃] **NM** *Naut* galleon

galipette [galipɛt] **NF** *Fam* somersault; **faire des galipettes** to do somersaults; *(ébats amoureux)* to have it off, to bonk

galipot [galipo] **NM 1** *Com (résine)* galipot, white resin **2** *Can* **courir le g.** to chase women

galle [gal] **NF** *Bot* gall; **g. de chêne** oak apple

Galles [gal] **NF** **le pays de G.** Wales; **Prince de G.** Prince of Wales; *Tex* Prince of Wales check

gallican, -ane [galikã, -an] **ADJ, N** *Rel* Gallican

gallicanisme [galikanism] **NM** *Rel* Gallicanism

gallicisme [galisism] **NM** Gallicism

gallinacé [galinase] *Orn* **ADJ** gallinaceous
    NMPL gallinacés Gallinaceae

gallique[1] [galik] **ADJ** *Hist* Gallic

gallique[2] **ADJ** *Chimie (acide)* gallic

gallium [galjɔm] **NM** *Chimie* gallium

gallois, -oise [galwa, -waz] **ADJ** Welsh
    NM *Ling* Welsh
    N G. Welshman, *f* Welshwoman; **les G.** the Welsh

gallomanie [galɔmani] **NF** Gallomania

gallon [galɔ̃] **NM** gallon

gallo-romain, pl gallo-romains [galorɔmɛ̃] **ADJ** Gallo-Roman

gallup [galœp] **N** **sondage g.** Gallup poll

galoche [galɔʃ] **NF 1** *(chaussure)* clog *(with leather upper)*; *Fam* **menton en g.** jutting chin **2** *très Fam* **rouler une g. à qn** to French-kiss sb, *Br* to snog sb

galon [galɔ̃] **NM 1** *Couture* braid; **g. de finition** upholstery binding **2** *Mil* **galons** *(de sous-officier)* stripes; *(d'officier)* bands, gold braid; *Naut (d'officier)* stripes; *(dans la marine marchande)* bands; **priver qn de ses galons** to reduce sb to the ranks; **gagner ses galons** to win *or* get *or* earn one's stripes; *Fam* **prendre du g.** to be promoted; *Fam* **arroser ses galons** to celebrate one's promotion

galonné [galɔne] **NM** *Arg (officier)* officer; *(sous-officier)* NCO

galonner [galɔne] **VT** *Couture* to (trim with) braid; **habit galonné d'or** gold-trimmed coat

galop [galo] **NM** *Équitation* gallop; **prendre le g.** to break into a gallop; **au g.** at a gallop; **grand g., triple g.** full gallop; **g. de manège** hand gallop; **petit g.** canter; **partir au (grand** *ou* **triple) g.** to gallop away; *Fig* **arriver au (grand** *ou* **triple) g.** to come like a shot; *Fig* **faire qch au g.** to do sth double-quick *or* at top speed; **allez, au travail! et au g.!** come on, to work!, and be quick about it! *or* and make it snappy!; *Scol* **g. d'essai** mock exam; *Fig* **ce séminaire ne constitue qu'un g. d'essai** this seminar is just a trial run

galopade [galɔpad] **NF 1** *Équitation* gallop; **le bruit d'une g.** the sound of galloping **2** *(bruit)* stampede

galopant [galɔpɑ̃] **ADJ** *(chevaux etc)* galloping; *(inflation etc)* galloping, runaway; **démographie galopante** rapid population growth; **phtisie galopante** galloping consumption; **le flot g. des vagues** the rushing waves

galoper [galɔpe] **VI 1** *Équitation* to gallop; **se mettre à g.** to break into a gallop **2** *Fig (courir)* to charge along; *(çà et là)* to gallop *or* rush around; **g. après qn/qch** to run after sb/sth; **il galopa jusqu'au bourg** he charged off to the village; **les enfants galopaient dans le salon** the children were charging around in the living room
    VT *Rare (cheval)* to gallop

galopeur, -euse [galɔpœr, -øz] **N** *(cheval)* galloper

galopin [galɔpɛ̃] **NM** *Fam* urchin, ragamuffin; **espèce de petit g.!** you little rascal *or* devil!

galure [galyr], **galurin** [galyrɛ̃] **NM** *Fam* hat, *Br* titfer

galvanique [galvanik] **ADJ** *(cellule etc)* galvanic; **plaqué g.** electroplate; **dorure g.** electrogilding

galvanisation [galvanizasjɔ̃] **NF** *(métallisation)* galvanization, galvanizing; *Élec* galvanism

galvaniser [galvanize] **VT 1** *(entreprise)* to give new life to, to inject new life into; *(foule, corps, organe)* to galvanize **2** *Métal* to galvanize; *(de zinc)* to zinc; *Élec* to (electro)plate; **tôle galvanisée** galvanized (sheet) iron

galvanisme [galvanism] **NM** *Méd* galvanism

galvano [galvano] **NM** *Typ Fam* electro

galvanomètre [galvanɔmɛtr] **NM** *Élec* galvanometer

galvanoplastie [galvanɔplasti] **NF** galvanoplasty, electrodeposition; *Ind* electroplating; *Typ* electrotyping

galvanoplastique [galvanɔplastik] **ADJ** galvanoplastic

galvanoscope [galvanɔskɔp] **NM** galvanoscope; *Tél* (linesman's) detector

galvanotype [galvanotip] **NM** *Typ* electrotype

galvanotypie [galvanotipi] **NF** *Typ* electrotyping

galvaudage [galvodaʒ] **NM** *(de talent, capacités)* prostituting

galvauder [galvode] **VT** *(nom, réputation)* to bring into disrepute; *(talents, dons)* to prostitute; **g. un mot** to overuse a word
    VPR se galvauder to damage one's reputation

gambade [gɑ̃bad] **NF** leap, gambol, caper; *Équitation* gambade; **gambades** capers; **faire des gambades** to leap about, to gambol, to caper

gambader [gɑ̃bade] **VI** to leap *or* frisk about, to gambol, to caper

gambas [gɑ̃bas] **NFPL** large prawns

gamberge [gɑ̃bɛrʒ] **NF** *Arg* **ton plan manque de g.** your plan shows a lack of thought; **il va falloir une bonne g. pour s'en sortir** we'll need to have a good think to get out of this one; **être en pleine g.** to be deep in thought; *(rêver)* to be daydreaming

gamberger [gɑ̃bɛrʒe] *Fam* **VI** to think deeply; **tu gamberges trop pour être heureux** you spend too much time thinking to be happy; **tu ne vas pas te mettre à g. pour si peu** you're not going to start brooding over such a small thing
    VT to work out, to figure out; *Fam* **c'est lui qui a gambergé le coup de la banque** he's the one who masterminded the bank job

gambette[1] [gɑ̃bɛt] **NM** *(oiseau)* redshank

gambette[2] **NF** *Arg (jambe)* pin, leg; **jouer** *ou* **tricoter des gambettes** to beat it, to leg it

Gambie [gɑ̃bi] **NF** **la G.** the Gambia

gambiller [gɑ̃bije] **VI** *Arg Vieilli (danser)* to jig about

gambit [gãbi] NM *Échecs* gambit; **(pion de) g.** gambit pawn

gamelle [gamɛl] NF **1** *(de soldat)* dixie, mess tin; *(d'ouvrier)* billy(can); *Hum (assiette)* plate; **préparer la g. du chien** to prepare the dog's food **2** *Fam* **(se) ramasser** *ou* **(se) prendre une g.** to fall flat on one's face **3** *très Fam (baiser)* French kiss; **rouler une g. à qn** to French-kiss sb, *Br* to snog sb

gamète [gamɛt] NM *Biol* gamete

gamétocide [gametɔsid] NM *Méd* gametocide

gamétogénèse [gametoʒenɛz] NF *Biol* gametogenesis

gamin, -ine [gamɛ̃, -in] N *(enfant)* kid, child; **une gamine de dix ans** a girl of ten; **ce n'est qu'un grand g.** *(d'un adulte)* he's just a big kid **ADJ 1** *(espiègle)* lively, mischievous **2 elle est encore gamine** she's still just a child **3** *(puéril)* childish

gaminerie [gaminri] NF *(acte)* childish prank *or* trick; *(comportement)* childishness, childish behaviour; **il a passé l'âge de ces gamineries** he's too old to behave so childishly *or* in such a childish way

gamma [gama] NM *(lettre)*, *Phot* gamma; *Nucl* **rayons g.** gamma rays

gammaglobuline [gamaglɔbylin] NF *Biol* gamma globulin

gamme [gam] NF **1** *(de couleurs, de services, d'articles etc)* range; **une vaste g. de produits** a vast range of products; **g. de prix** price range; **toute la g. des sensations** the whole gamut *or* range of sensations; **produit bas/haut de g.** bottom-of-the-range *or* downmarket/top-of-the-range *or* up-market product; **milieu de g.** middle-of-the-range; **un ordinateur d'entrée de g.** an entry level computer **2** *Mus* scale; **g. montante/descendante** rising/falling scale; **faire des gammes** to do *or* practise scales; *Fig* **faire ses gammes** to learn the ropes
▸▸*Aut* **g. moyenne** mid-range; *Aut* **g. de transmission** driving range

gammée [game] ADJ F **croix g.** swastika

gamopétale [gamopetal] ADJ *Bot* gamopetalous

ganache [ganaʃ] NF **1** *Culin* ganache, = filling for cakes made from chocolate, butter and cream **2** *Fam (imbécile)* fool, idiot; **vieille g.** old codger, *Am* geezer **3** *(d'un cheval)* lower jaw, jowl

Gand [gã] N Ghent

gang¹ [gãg] NM gang; **guerre des gangs** gang warfare VOIR GRAMMAIRE A11

gang² [gɛ̃g] NF *Can (bande)* band, group; **une g. de bandits** a gang

ganga [gãga] NM pintailed (sand) grouse

Gange [gãʒ] NM **le G.** the Ganges

ganglion [gãglijɔ̃] NM **1** *Anat* ganglion; **g. nerveux** ganglion cell; **ganglions lymphatiques** lymph nodes *or* glands; **j'ai des ganglions** my glands are swollen, I have swollen glands **2** *Vét* spavin

ganglionnaire [gãglijɔnɛr] ADJ *Anat* ganglionic; **fièvre g.** glandular fever

gangrené [gãgrəne] ADJ **1** *Méd* gangrenous, gangrened **2** *Fig* corrupt

gangrène [gãgrɛn] NF **1** *Méd* gangrene; **avoir la g.** to have gangrene; **g. gazeuse** gas gangrene; **g. des os** necrosis **2** *Fig* canker

gangrener [gãgrəne] **(il gangrène; il gangrènera)** VT **1** *Méd* to gangrene **2** *Fig* to corrupt
VPR **se gangrener 1** *Méd* to become *or* go gangrenous **2** *Fig* to become corrupt

gangreneux, -euse [gãgrənø, -øz] ADJ *Méd* gangrenous

gangster [gãgstɛr] NM gangster

gangstérisme [gãgsterism] NM gangsterism

gangue [gãg] NF *(de pierre précieuse, de minerai)* gang(ue), matrix; *Fig (couche) (de boue, de glace etc)* layer; *Fig* **il n'a jamais pu sortir de la g. de son éducation/de la religion** he was never able to free himself from the straitjacket of his education/of religion

ganse [gãs] NF *(cordon)* braid, (plaited) cord, edging, piping

gansé [gãse] ADJ *(vêtement)* braided

ganser [gãse] VT *(vêtement)* to braid, to trim

gant [gã] NM glove; *(armure)* gauntlet; **mettre ses gants** to put one's gloves on; **gants en daim/tissu** suede/fabric gloves; **gants fourrés** lined gloves; **gants de caoutchouc** rubber gloves; *Fig* **cela vous va comme un g.** *(de vêtement)* it fits you like a glove; *(de couleur)* it suits you down to the ground *or* to aT; **ce métier lui va comme un g.** the job suits her down to the ground, the job is tailor-made for her; *Fig* **il faut prendre** *ou* **mettre des gants pour l'approcher** *ou* **avec lui** you have to handle him with kid gloves (on); **tu as intérêt à prendre** *ou* **mettre des gants pour le lui dire** you'd do well to tell him gently; **jeter le g. à qn** to throw down the gauntlet to sb; **relever le g.** to take up the gauntlet, to accept the challenge; *Fig* **souple comme un g.** easygoing
▸▸**g. de boxe** boxing glove; **g. de crin** massage glove; **g. de Neptune** glove sponge; **g. de toilette** ≃ facecloth, (face) flannel, *Am* washcloth

gantelé [gãtle] ADJ gauntleted; **la main gantelée** the mailed fist

gantelet [gãtlɛ] NM gauntlet

ganter [gãte] VT to glove
VI **g. du sept** to take a (size) seven in gloves
VPR **se ganter** to put one's gloves on

ganterie [gãtri] NF **1** *(industrie)* glove-making; *(commerce)* glove trade **2** *(fabrique)* glove factory; *(magasin)* glove shop; *(rayon)* glove counter *or* department

gantier, -ière [gãtje, -jɛr] N glover

gantois, -oise [gãtwa, -waz] ADJ of/from Ghent
▸ N **G.** *(natif)* native of Ghent; *(habitant)* inhabitant of Ghent

gapette [gapɛt] NF *Fam* (flat) cap

garage [garaʒ] NM **1** *(de voiture)* garage; **g. à plusieurs étages** multi-storey car park, *Am* tiered parking lot; **g. de** *ou* **à bicyclettes** bicycle *or* bike shed; **g. de canots** boathouse, boat shed; **g. d'autobus** bus depot; **g. d'avions** (aircraft) hangar; *Rail* **g. de machines** engine shed; **j'ai mis la voiture au g.** I've put the car in the garage; *Can* **vente de g.** garage sale **2** *(atelier)* garage; **ma voiture est au g. jusqu'à la semaine prochaine** my car is at the garage until next week **3** *Rail* shunting, sidetracking

garagiste [garaʒist] NM *Aut (propriétaire)* garage owner; *(mécanicien)* garage mechanic; **j'emmène la voiture chez le g.** I'm taking the car to the garage

garance [garãs] NF **1** *Bot* madder(wort); *Fam* **petite g., g. de chien** squinancy wort **2** *(teinture)* madder (dye)
ADJ INV madder

garant, -ante [garã, -ãt] N guarantor; **se rendre** *ou* **se porter g. de qn** to answer for sb; *(devant la justice)* to go bail for sb; *(à la banque)* to stand guarantor for sb; **g. solidaire** joint and several guarantor; **tout sera fini en temps voulu, je m'en porte g.** everything will be finished on time, I can vouch for *or* guarantee it; **ça va marcher, j'en suis garante** it will work, I give you my word; **être g. de ses faits** to be answerable *or* accountable for one's actions; **les pays seront ga-**

rants du respect de l'accord the countries will be guarantors of the agreement

garantie [garãti] NF **1** *(précaution)* guarantee, safeguard **(contre** against); *(gage)* guarantee; **prendre des garanties contre le vol/les risques d'incendie** to take precautions against theft/fire risk
2 *(de l'exécution d'un contrat)* guarantee, pledge; *(d'un paiement)* security, guaranty; **fonds déposés** *ou* **détenus en g.** funds lodged *or* held as security for sb; **elle m'a donné toutes les garanties que...** she gave me every guarantee that ...
3 *Com (de qualité etc)* guarantee, warranty; **vendu avec g.** sold with a guarantee; **la voiture est encore sous g.** the car is still under guarantee; **il va essayer, mais c'est sans g.** he'll try, but there's no guarantee (that he'll succeed); **lettre de g. d'indemnité** letter of indemnity
4 *Fin* underwriting; **syndicat de g.** underwriters' syndicate
▸▸*Fin* **g. accessoire** collateral security; **g. bancaire** bank guarantee; *Fin* **g. de bonne exécution** *ou* **de bonne fin** performance bond; **g. contractuelle** contractual guarantee; **g. conventionnelle** contractual cover; *Bourse* **g. de cours** hedging; *Com* **g. de crédit acheteur** buyer credit guarantee; **g. de crédit à l'exportation** export credit guarantee; **g. d'exécution** contract bond; *Com* **g. illimitée** unlimited warranty; *Com* **g. légale** legal guarantee; *Com* **g. limitée** limited warranty; *Fin* **g. offre** bid bond; *Jur* **g. parlementaire** *(d'un député)* parliamentary privilege; *Com* **g. pièces et main d'œuvre** parts and labour warranty; *Com* **g. prolongée** extended warranty; *Com* **g. de remboursement** money-back guarantee; *Com* **g. retour atelier** return-to-base warranty *or* guarantee; *Com* **g. sur site** on-site warranty *or* guarantee; *Com* **g. totale** full warranty

garantir [garãtir] VT **1** *(dette, montre etc)* to guarantee; **créance garantie** secured debt; **pendule garantie (pour) deux ans** clock guaranteed for two years; **nous garantissons un délai de livraison d'une semaine** we guarantee delivery within seven days; **g. un fait** to vouch for a fact; **je vous en garantis le succès** I guarantee (you) success, I guarantee that you'll be successful; **je vous garantis qu'il viendra** I guarantee that he'll come; **je te garantis que je l'ai aperçu dans la foule** I can vouch for the fact that I spotted him in the crowd; **je peux te g. qu'il ne reviendra pas** I can guarantee you he won't come back, he won't come back, I warrant you; **elle m'a garanti qu'elle serait à l'heure** she gave me a guarantee that she'd be on time; **je te le garantis** I can vouch for it
2 *Fin (émission d'actions etc)* to underwrite; **g. un emprunt** to secure a loan
3 *(protéger)* to protect **(de** against, from); **ce double vitrage va vous g. du froid** this double-glazing will protect *or* shield you from the cold
4 *Jur* **g. qn contre qch** to indemnify sb from *or* against sth; **son assurance le garantit contre le vol** his insurance covers him against theft
VPR **se garantir se g. contre le froid/le vent** to protect oneself from the cold/the wind

garce [gars] NF **1** *Fam Péj* bitch, cow; **g. de vie!** what a bitch of a life! **2** *Vieilli (prostituée)* whore, tart

garçon [garsɔ̃] NM **1** *(enfant mâle)* boy; **école de garçons** boys' school; **petit g.** small *or* little boy; **se sentir un petit g. à côté de qn** to feel like a child beside sb, to feel dwarfed by sb; **tu es un grand g. maintenant** you're a big boy now
2 *(fils)* boy, son
3 *(jeune homme)* young man; **un g. d'une**

vingtaine d'années a young man of about twenty; **un bon** ou **brave g.** a good lad; **un beau** ou **joli g.** a handsome young man; **il est assez beau g.** he's quite a good-looking or handsome young man; **un mauvais g.** a bad sort **4** (serveur) waiter **5** Vieilli (célibataire) bachelor; **il est encore g.** he's still single or still a bachelor; **vieux g.** confirmed bachelor; **des habitudes de vieux g.** bachelor habits or ways
►► **g. d'ascenseur** liftboy, lift attendant, Am elevator operator; **g. boucher** butcher's boy; **g. de bureau** office boy; Naut **g. de cabine** (cabin) steward; **g. de café** ou **de restaurant** waiter; **g. coiffeur** hairdresser's assistant; **g. de courses** errand or message boy; **g. d'écurie** groom; **g. d'étage** floor waiter; **g. de ferme** farm hand; **g. d'honneur** best man; **g. manqué** tomboy; **g. de pont** deck steward; **g. de recette** bank messenger

garçonne [garsɔn] **NF 1 être coiffée à la g.** (d'une femme) to have an urchin cut; **style/ vêtements à la g.** boyish style/clothes **2** Vieilli bachelor girl

garçonnet [garsɔnɛ] **NM** (petit garçon) little boy; Com **taille g.** small boy's size

garçonnier, -ière [garsɔnje, -jɛr] **ADJ** boyish

garçonnière [garsɔnjɛr] **NF** Vieilli bachelor flat or Am apartment

GARDE¹ [gard]

| care **1** ▪ guarding **2** ▪ guard **3, 5, 6** |
| ▪ to watch out (prendre garde) **3** |

NF 1 (protection) (d'une personne, chose) care; **confier qch/qn à la g. de qn**, **confier la g. de qch/qn à qn** to entrust sb with (the care of) sth/sb; **c'est son oncle qui en a la g.** he's in the care of his uncle; **être sous bonne g.** to be in safekeeping; **avoir qch en g.** to have charge of sth; **que Dieu nous ait en g.** may God protect us; **je vous laisse les enfants en g.** I'm leaving the children in your care or safekeeping or charge; **droit de g.** (right of) custody **2** (surveillance) (d'une frontière, d'une machine etc) guarding; **soldat de g. à la porte** soldier on guard at the door; **être de g.** to be on guard or Naut on duty; **monter la g.** to mount guard; **la police assurera la g. du tribunal** the police will guard the court, the court will be under police guard; **à la g.!** guard turn out!; **assurer la g. de nuit** to be on night call or duty; Mil **poste de g.** guardroom; **chien de g.** guard dog, watchdog; **sentinelle de g.** duty sentry; **médecin de g.** doctor on duty; **pharmacie de g.** emergency or duty chemist **3** (méfiance) **mettre qn en g. contre qch/qn** to put sb on his guard against sth/sb; **être** ou **se tenir sur ses gardes** to be on one's guard; **prendre g. à qn/qch** to watch out for sth/sb, to beware of sb/sth; **prenez g. aux orties!** mind or watch the nettles!; **prenez g.!** watch out!, look out!, take care!; (menace) watch out! **4** (attention) **prendre g. à qch/qn** to attend to or pay attention to sth/sb; **un fait auquel on n'a pas pris g.** a fact that has been left out of consideration; **faire qch sans y prendre g.** to do sth without realizing it; **je n'y ai pas pris g.** I didn't notice anything; **prendre g. que ... (ne)** + sub to be careful or to take care that ...; **prenez g. qu'il (ne) vous voie** be careful or take care (that) he doesn't see you; **prendre g. à** ou **de ne pas faire qch** to be careful or take care not to do sth; **prenez g. à** ou **de ne pas vous perdre** mind you don't get lost, be careful or take care not to get lost; Vieilli **prendre g. de faire qch** to be careful or take care to do

sth; **prenez g. de tomber** mind you don't fall **5** (groupe de soldats) **le corps de g.**, **la g.** the guard; **relever la g.** to change the guard; **la g. à cheval** the Horseguards; **la g. à pied** the Footguards **6** Boxe, Escrime (position d'attente) guard; **se mettre en g.** to take one's guard, to square up; Escrime **en g.!** en garde!; Boxe, Fig **baisser sa g.** to lower or drop one's guard **7** Aut **g. au sol** ground clearance **8** Tech (partie d'une épée) hilt; **gardes** (d'une serrure) wards **9** Cartes covering card; **avoir une g. à cœur** to have a covering card in hearts
►► Fin **g. en dépôt de titres** safe custody; Mil **g. descendante** old guard; Mil **g. du peau** colour or Am color guard; **g. d'enfants** child-minding; Jur **g. des enfants** (après un divorce) custody of the children; **g. d'honneur** guard of honour or Am honor; Hist **la G. impériale** the Imperial Guard (of Napoleon); **la G. mobile** the security police; Mil **g. montante** new or relieving guard; **la G. républicaine** the Republican Guard (of Paris); Jur **g. à vue** police custody; **il a été mis/est resté en g. à vue** he was put/was kept in police custody

garde² **NM 1** (sentinelle) guard **2** (soldat d'une garde) guardsman
NF (pour les malades) nurse; (pour les enfants) nanny
►► **G. des Archives** Br ≃ Master of the Rolls; **g. champêtre** rural policeman; **g. du corps** bodyguard; Mil **gardes du corps** lifeguards; **g. forestier** forester, forest warden, Am ranger; **g. mobile** = member of the security police; **g. de nuit** (pour un malade) night nurse (privately employed); Mil night watchman; Hist, Admin **G. des Sceaux** = Minister of Justice

gardé [garde] **ADJ 1** Cartes **roi g.** guarded king; **dame gardée** guarded queen **2 toute(s) proportion(s) gardée(s)** all things considered, making all due allowance

garde-à-vous **NM INV** Mil (position of) attention; **se mettre** ou **être** ou **se tenir au g.** to stand to attention; **au g.** at attention; **g.!** attention!

garde-barrière, pl **gardes-barrière(s)** [gard(ə)barjɛr] **N** level-crossing, Am grade-crossing keeper
NF Ordinat firewall

garde-boue [gardəbu] **NM INV** (d'une bicyclette etc) mudguard

garde-chasse, pl **gardes-chasse(s)** [gardə ʃas] **NM** gamekeeper

garde-chiourme, pl **garde(s)-chiourme(s)** [gardəʃjurm] **NM** Hist (de galériens) warder; Fig (personne autoritaire et brutale) martinet, tyrant

garde-corps [gardəkɔr] **NM INV** (mur) parapet, balustrade; Naut (corde) guard rope; Naut **g. arrière** stern rail

garde-côte, pl **gardes-côte(s)** [gardəkot] **NM** (bateau) coastguard vessel; Vieilli (soldat) coastguard

garde-feu [gardəfø] **NM INV 1** fireguard **2** Can (personne) forest warden

garde-fou, pl **garde-fous** [gardəfu] **NM** (mur) parapet, balustrade; (en fer) (d'un pont etc) railing, guardrail; Fig safeguard

garde-frein, pl **gardes-frein(s)** [gardəfrɛ̃] **NM** Rail brakesman, Am brakeman

garde-frontière, pl **gardes-frontière(s)** [gardəfrɔ̃tjɛr] **NM** border guard

garde-ligne, pl **gardes-ligne(s)** [gard(ə)liɲ] **NM** Rail track watchman

garde-magasin, pl **gardes-magasin(s)** [gardəmagazɛ̃] **NM** warehouseman; Mil quartermaster

garde-malade, pl **gardes-malade(s)** [gard(ə)malad] **N** nurse

garde-manger [gardəmɑ̃ʒe] **NM INV** meat safe

garde-meuble, pl **garde-meuble(s)** [gardəmœbl] **NM** furniture repository, warehouse; **mettre une table au g.** to put a table into storage or store

gardénal® [gardenal] **NM** Méd ≃ Luminal®

gardénia [gardenja] **NM** gardenia

garde-pêche, pl **gardes-pêche** [gardəpɛʃ] **NM** (personne) water bailiff, Am fish warden **NM INV** (bateau) fisheries protection vessel

garde-place, pl **garde-place(s)** [gardəplas] **NM** Rail reservation ticket holder; (ticket) reservation ticket

garde-port, pl **gardes-port(s)** [gardəpɔr] **NM** wharfmaster (on river)

GARDER [garde]

| **VT** to look after **1** ▪ to guard **1** ▪ to |
| protect **2** ▪ to save **2, 6** ▪ to keep **3, 4,** |
| **6, 7** ▪ to stay in **5** |
| **VPR** to beware of (se garder de) **1** ▪ to |
| take care not to do (se garder de faire) **2** |
| ▪ to keep **4, 5** |

VT 1 (surveiller) (maison, boutique, sac, enfants) to look after, to mind; (prisonnier) to guard, to watch over; **g. un troupeau** to tend a flock; Fam **nous n'avons pas gardé les cochons ensemble!** don't take liberties!; **comment peut-il me parler ainsi, nous n'avons pas gardé les cochons ensemble!** how can he talk to me like that, what a liberty!; Jur **g. qn à vue** to keep or hold sb in custody **2** (protéger) to protect (**de** from); **si au moins cela pouvait te g. de faire des bêtises** if that could at least stop you (from) acting stupidly; **que Dieu nous garde de la souffrance!** may God protect or save or deliver us from suffering! **3** (conserver) to keep; **g. un vêtement (sur soi)** to keep a garment on; **g. qn à dîner/ pour le week-end** to get sb to stay for dinner/for the weekend; **g. qn en otage** to keep or hold sb hostage; **par cette chaleur il vaut mieux g. le lait au réfrigérateur** it's better to keep the milk in the fridge in this heat; **g. une pièce intacte** to keep a room as it was left or in its original state; Journ **g. la Une** to hold the front page **4** (continuer d'avoir) to keep; (somme d'argent) to keep, to put by; **g. ses illusions/son innocence** to keep one's illusions/innocence; **g. son sang-froid** to keep cool (and collected); **g. rancune à qn** to harbour or Am to harbor resentment against sb, to bear a grudge against sb; **g. les yeux fermés** to keep one's eyes closed; **g. le sourire** to keep (on) smiling; **g. son sérieux** to keep a straight face; **g. la ligne** to keep or maintain one's figure; **je garde un bon/mauvais souvenir de mon séjour en Italie** I have (kept) a good/bad memory of my stay in Italy **5** (rester dans) **g. la chambre** to keep to or stay in one's room; **être obligé de g. le lit** to have to stay in bed, to be laid up **6** (réserver) to keep, to save; **garde-moi une place à côté de toi!** save or keep me a place next to you!; **je vous ai gardé du café** I've kept or saved you some coffee; Fig **g. une dent contre qn**, **g. un chien de sa chienne à qn** to hold a grudge against sb, to have it in for sb; Fig **g. une poire pour la soif** to keep something for a rainy day; Fig **g. qch pour la bonne bouche** to save sth up as a treat; **g. le meilleur pour la fin** to save or keep the best till last **7** (respecter) **g. ses distances/son rang** to keep one's distance/one's rank; **g. un secret**

to keep a secret; **garde ça pour toi** *(je ne veux pas qu'on l'apprenne)* keep that to yourself

VPR se garder 1 *(se méfier de)* **se g. de qn/qch** to beware of sb/sth

2 *(s'abstenir de)* **se g. de faire qch** to take care *or* be careful not to do sth; **gardez-vous (bien) de le perdre** mind you don't lose it!, take care *or* be careful not to lose it!; **je m'en garderai bien!** there's no chance of me doing that!, I'll do no such thing!, *Fam* no fear!

3 *Cartes* **se g. à trèfle** to keep a covering card in clubs

4 *Fam (conserver)* **tes réflexions, tu peux les g.!** you can keep your opinion(s) *or* thoughts *or* comments to yourself!; **ses amis/ses soirées, elle peut se les g.!** she can keep *or* stick her friends/parties!

5 *(se conserver) (denrées)* to keep; **viande qui ne se garde pas bien** meat that does not keep well

---

garderie [gard(ə)ri] NF **1** *(pour enfants en bas âge)* day nursery, *Am* daycare center; *(dans magasin, université etc)* crèche, *Am* baby-sitting service; *(le soir, après l'école)* child-minding service **2** *(de garde forestier)* beat, domain

garde-rivière, *pl* **gardes-rivière(s)** [gard(ə)rivjɛr] NM river policeman

garde-robe, *pl* **garde-robes** [gard(ə)rɔb] NF wardrobe; **renouveler sa g.** to renew *or* replenish one's wardrobe

gardeur, -euse [gardœr, -øz] N *(d'animaux)* keeper; **g. de cochons** pig keeper, *Vieilli* swineherd; **g. de vaches** cowherd; **g. de moutons** shepherd

garde-voie, *pl* **gardes-voie** [gard(ə)vwa] NM *Rail* track watchman

gardian [gardjɑ̃] NM *(en Camargue)* herdsman

gardien, -ienne [gardjɛ̃, -jɛn] N *(concierge)* caretaker, *Am* janitor; *(de musée, de parking)* attendant; *Fig (de libertés, traditions etc)* guardian; **g. des intérêts publics** guardian *or* protector of the public interest; **se poser en g. de l'ordre** to set oneself up as a guardian *or* an upholder of public order

▸▸*Sport* **g. (de but)** goalkeeper; **g. d'immeuble** caretaker, porter, *Am* janitor; **g. de nuit** night watchman; **g. de la paix** policeman; **g. de phare** lighthouse keeper; **g. de prison** prison warder *or* *Am* guard

gardiennage [gardjɛnaʒ] NM *(de ponts)* guarding; *(d'un bâtiment)* caretaking; *(d'un port)* security; **société de g.** security firm

gardon [gardɔ̃] NM roach; *Fig* **frais comme un g.** fresh as a daisy, bright-eyed and bushy-tailed

gare¹ [gar] NF *Rail* (railway *or* *Am* railroad) station, train station; **(colis à prendre) en g.** (parcel) to be (left till) called for; **chef de g.** stationmaster, station manager; **g. d'arrivée/de départ** station of arrival/departure; **quelle est la g. d'arrivée à Londres?** what station does the train arrive in at London?; **entrer** *ou* **arriver en g.** *(d'un train)* to arrive in *or* come into the station; **quai numéro 3, le train entre en g.** the train is now approaching platform 3; **café/hôtel de la g.** station café/hotel

▸▸**g. aérienne** air terminal; *Naut* **g. (fluviale)** dock; **g. de fret** cargo terminal; **g. de marchandises** goods *or* freight station; **g. maritime** harbour *or* *Am* harbor station; **g. routière** bus *or* coach station, bus depot; **g. routière (de marchandises)** road haulage depot; **g. de triage** marshalling yard; **g. de voyageurs** passenger station

gare² INT **1** *(menace)* **g. à toi si on l'apprend** woe betide you if anyone finds out!; *Fam* **si je te reprends à voler du gâteau, g. à tes fes-**

---

ses! if I catch you stealing cake again, you've had it *or* *Br* you're for it! **2** *(attention)* **g. à la casse!** mind you don't break it!; **g. à la peinture!** mind the paint!; *Vieilli* **g. les coups de fusil des chasseurs!** watch out *or* mind out for the hunters and their guns; **sans crier g.** without warning

garenne [garɛn] NF **1** *(rabbit)* warren; **lapin de g.** wild rabbit **2** *(réserve)* fishing preserve

garer [gare] VT *(voiture)* to park; *(train)* to shunt on to a siding; *(bateau)* to dock; **g. un avion** to park a plane; *(mettre à l'abri)* to put a plane in the hangar

VPR se garer 1 *Aut* to park; **la voiture s'est garée le long du trottoir** the car parked beside *or* drew in beside the pavement; **j'ai eu de la peine à me g.** I had trouble parking; **se g. facilement** to have no trouble parking; **tu trouveras à te g. dans le quartier** you'll find somewhere to park in the area **2 se g. de qch/qn** to avoid *or* steer clear of sth/sb

Gargantua [gargɑ̃tɥa] NM glutton, guzzler

gargantuesque [gargɑ̃tɥɛsk] ADJ gargantuan; **un appétit/repas g.** a gargantuan appetite/meal

gargariser (se) [səgargarize] VPR to gargle; *Péj* **se g. de formules pédantes** to delight *or* revel in pedantic expressions

gargarisme [gargarism] NM *(produit)* gargle; *(action de se gargariser)* gargling; **il doit (se) faire un g. par jour** he has to gargle once a day

gargote [gargɔt] NF *Péj* cheap restaurant

gargotier, -ière [gargɔtje, -jɛr] N *Péj* **1** *(patron d'une gargote)* owner of a cheap restaurant; **je vais aller dire deux mots au g.** I'm going to give the guy who runs this cheap place a piece of my mind **2** *(mauvais cuisinier)* poor cook

gargouille [garguj] NF **1** *Archit* gargoyle **2** *(d'un gouttière, d'une pompe)* (water)spout

gargouillement [gargujmɑ̃] NM **1** *(de l'eau)* gurgling **2** *(de l'estomac)* rumbling, gurgling; **j'ai eu des gargouillements pendant toute la réunion** my stomach rumbled *or* gurgled all through the meeting

gargouiller [garguje] VI **1** *(de l'eau)* to gurgle **2** *(de l'estomac)* to rumble, to gurgle **3 sol qui gargouille sous les pas** squelchy *or* squishy ground

gargouillis [garguji] NM = **gargouillement**

garnement [garnəmɑ̃] NM *(enfant)* scamp, rascal, imp

garni [garni] ADJ **1 bien g.** *(bourse)* well-lined; *(magasin)* well-stocked; *(maison)* well-appointed; **panier g.** food hamper, hamper of food **2** *Culin* garnished; *(plat, viande)* with vegetables; **choucroute garnie** sauerkraut with sausages **3** *Vieilli (meublé) (chambre)* furnished

NM *Vieilli (meublé)* furnished room(s)

garnir [garnir] VT **1** *(munir de ce qui protège, renforce etc)* to fit out **(de** with); *(commode, tiroir)* to line; *(fauteuil)* to stuff; **garni de feutre** felt-lined; **g. un mur de plaques de polystyrène** to cover *or* line a wall with polystyrene tiles

2 *(embellir, compléter) (robe, chapeau etc)* to trim **(de** with); **une robe garnie de dentelle** a dress trimmed with lace, a lace-trimmed dress; **la passementerie qui garnit cette veste est très colorée** the braid trimming on that jacket is very colourful

3 *Culin (plat)* to garnish; **une entrecôte garnie de pommes frites et de salade** a rib steak (served) with chips and salad

4 *(remplir)* to fill; *(cave)* to stock; **g. une étagère de disques** to fill a shelf with records

VPR se garnir la salle se garnit the hall *or* *Théâtre* the house is beginning to fill up *or* is filling up

---

garnison [garnizɔ̃] NF *Mil* garrison; **mettre une g. dans une ville** to garrison a town; **ville de g.** garrison town; **être en g.** *ou* **tenir g. dans une ville** to be garrisoned *or* stationed in a town

garnissage [garnisaʒ] NM **1** *(remplissage) (d'un coussin, d'une couette etc)* stuffing; *(décoration) (d'un manteau)* trimming; *Aut* **g. de plafond** headliner, headlining; *Aut* **g. de siège** seat trim **2** *Tech (d'un piston)* packing; *(d'une chaudière)* lagging **3** *(matériau)* packing, stuffing; *Métal (d'un fourneau)* lining **4** *Tex (d'un tissu)* napping, raising

garniture [garnityr] NF **1** *(d'un fusil)* mountings; *(d'un navire)* rigging; *(d'une commode)* (metal) furnishings; **garnitures d'une serrure** wards of a lock; **g. d'une pompe à incendie** hose of a fire engine; **g. intérieure d'une voiture** upholstery *or* interior trim of a car

2 *(ornement) (d'un chapeau, d'une robe etc)* trimming, decoration

3 *Culin (d'un plat)* garnish; *(légumes)* vegetables; *(d'un vol-au-vent)* filling; **pour la g., vous avez le choix entre des haricots verts ou des frites** to go with it, you have a choice of green beans or chips

4 *Tech (de joint)* packing; *(de piston)* stuffing *(piece)*; *(de chaudière)* lagging; *Typ* furniture

▸▸**g. de bureau** desk set; **g. de cheminée** mantelpiece ornaments; **g. d'embrayage** clutch lining; **g. de feu** *ou* **de foyer** (set of) fire irons; *Aut etc* **g. de frein** brake lining; *(de disque de frein)* brake pad; **g. de lit** bedding; **g. de toilette** toilet set

Garonne [garɔn] NF **la G.** the Garonne

garrigue [garig] NF *Géog* garrigue

garrocher [garɔʃe] VT *Can Arg (pierres etc)* to throw

garrot¹ [garo] NM **1** *Méd* tourniquet; **appliquer un g. (à qn)** to put a tourniquet on (sb) **2** *Hist* **(supplice du) g.** gar(r)otting, gar(r)otte

garrot² NM *Zool (de cheval, de vache etc)* withers

garrottage [garɔtaʒ] NM **g. d'une blessure** putting a tourniquet on a wound

garrotte [garɔt] NF *Hist* gar(r)otte, gar(r)otting

garrotter [garɔte] VT *(prisonnier etc)* to tie up; *Fig* **g. les opposants au régime/l'opinion publique** to muzzle *or* silence the régime's opponents/public opinion

gars [gɑ] NM *Fam (jeune homme)* lad, young man; *(homme)* guy, *Br* bloke; **un petit g.** a little boy; **un beau g.** a good-looking *or* handsome young man; **un brave g.** a good lad; **un drôle de g.** an odd guy *or* *Br* bloke; **allons-y, les g.!** come on, lads *or* boys!; **bonjour, mon petit g.!** *(à un enfant)* hello, young man!

Gascogne [gaskɔɲ] NF Gascony; **le golfe de G.** the Bay of Biscay

gascon, -onne [gaskɔ̃, -ɔn] ADJ Gascon

NM *Ling* Gascon

N **G.** Gascon; **offre** *ou* **promesse de G.** hollow *or* empty promise

gasconnade [gaskɔnad] NF boasting, bragging

gas(-)oil [gazɔjl, gazwal] NM diesel oil *or* fuel, *Am* gas oil, *Br* derv

gaspacho [gaspatʃo] NM gazpacho

gaspard [gaspar] NM *Arg* rat

gaspillage [gaspijaʒ] NM *(d'argent)* wasting, squandering; *(de nourriture, temps)* wasting; **je n'admets pas le g. de nourriture** I won't allow food to be wasted; **c'est du g.** it's a waste, it's wasteful; **pas de g.!** don't be wasteful!; **quel g.!** what a waste!; **c'est un vrai g. de temps/d'argent** it's a real waste of time/money

gaspiller [gaspije] VT *(argent, son talent, ses dons)* to waste, to squander; *(eau, papier, son énergie)* to waste, to waste, to squander; **g. son temps** to waste one's time (**à faire qch** doing sth)

gaspilleur, -euse [gaspijœr, -øz] N spendthrift
ADJ wasteful

gastéropode [gasterɔpɔd] NM *Zool* gast(e)ropod

gastralgie [gastralʒi] NF *Méd* stomach pains, *Spéc* gastralgia

gastralgique [gastralʒik] ADJ *Méd* gastralgic

gastrectomie [gastrɛktɔmi] NF *Chir* gastrectomy

gastrique [gastrik] ADJ gastric; **embarras g.** stomach upset, upset stomach

gastrite [gastrit] NF *Méd* gastritis

gastro-entérite, *pl* **gastro-entérites** [gastroɑ̃terit] NF *Méd* gastroenteritis

gastro-entérologie [gastroɑ̃terɔlɔʒi] NF *Méd* gastroenterology

gastro-entérologue, *pl* **gastro-entérologues** [gastroɑ̃terɔlɔg] N *Méd* gastroenterologist

gastro-intestinal, -ale, -aux, -ales [gastroɛ̃tɛstinal, -o] ADJ *Méd* gastrointestinal

gastronome [gastrɔnɔm] NM gastronome, gourmet

gastronomie [gastrɔnɔmi] NF gastronomy

gastronomique [gastrɔnɔmik] ADJ gastronomic(al)

gastropode [gastrɔpɔd] NM *Zool* gast(e)ropod

gâté [gate] ADJ 1 *(pourri) (fruit)* damaged, spoilt; *(dents)* rotten, decayed; **viande gâtée** meat that has gone off or is bad, bad meat 2 *Fig* **enfant g.** spoilt or pampered child; **l'enfant g. de la famille/de la littérature russe** the blue-eyed boy of the family/of Russian literature

gâteau, -eaux [gato] NM 1 cake; **faire un g.** to make or bake a cake; **g. d'anniversaire** birthday cake; *Fam* **c'est du g.** it's a piece of cake, it's child's play; *Fam* **ce n'est pas du g. de la convaincre** it's no easy matter convincing her; *Fam* **avoir sa part du g.** to have one's slice or share of the cake; *Fam* **se partager le g.** to share out the cake 2 *(masse compacte, plate)* cake; *(de fulmicoton etc)* disc 3 *Suisse* tart
ADJ INV *Fam* **papa g.** *(qui cède tout à ses enfants)* indulgent father; **c'est un vrai papa g.** he's a real soft touch with his children; *Fam* **marraine g.** fairy godmother
▸ ▸ **g. de cire** honeycomb; **g. marbré** marble cake; **g. de miel** honeycomb; **g. de riz** ≃ rice pudding; **g. sec** biscuit, *Am* cookie; **g. de semoule** ≃ semolina pudding

gâter [gate] VT 1 *(paysage, plaisir)* to spoil, to ruin; **la grêle gâte le blé** hail damages wheat; **les mouches gâtent la viande** flies infect meat; **ce qui ne gâte rien** which is no bad thing 2 *(choyer) (enfant, mari)* to spoil, to pamper, to overindulge; **il a été très gâté à Noël** he was really spoilt at Christmas; **on n'est (vraiment) pas gâtés: de la pluie, du vent, le froid!** marvellous, isn't it: rain, wind, cold!; **la vie ne les avait pas gâtés** life hadn't treated them kindly; **il n'est pas gâté par la nature** nature hasn't been very kind to him
VPR **se gâter** *(affaires, temps)* to take a turn for the worse, to deteriorate; **le poisson se gâte facilement** fish quickly goes bad or off

gâterie [gatri] NF 1 *(petit cadeau)* treat, small present 2 *(friandise) (pour enfants)* treat, goody 3 *Euph Hum* **faire une petite g. à qn** to go down on sb

gâte-sauce [gatsos] NM kitchen boy; *Péj Vieilli (cuisinier)* bad cook

gâteux, -euse [gatø, -øz] *Fam* N doddering old man, f woman, old dodderer
ADJ *(sénile)* senile; *Fam* **avec leurs petits-enfants, ils sont complètement g.** they're totally besotted with their grandchildren, they absolutely dote on their grandchildren

gâtifier [gatifje] VI *Fam* to go gaga; **il commence à g. sérieusement, le grand-père** grandad's going gaga or soft in the head

gâtisme [gatism] NM *Méd* senility, senile decay; *Fig* **leurs épanchements sentimentaux ne sont rien moins que du g.** the way they bill and coo you'd think they were going soft in the head

GATT [gat] NM *Écon (abrév* **General Agreement on Tariffs and Trade**) GATT

gatter [gate] VT *Suisse Fam (cours)* to skip, to cut; **g. l'école** to play truant or *Am* hook(e)y

gauche [goʃ] ADJ 1 *(maladroit) (personne, attitude, démarche, style etc)* awkward, clumsy; *(tentative)* clumsy, bungling; **attraper un objet d'un geste g.** to catch an object awkwardly or clumsily
2 *Tech (déformé) (surface etc)* warped, crooked, out of true
3 *(par opposition à droit)* left; **main g.** left hand; *Fig* **mariage de la main g.** living together; *Fig* **se lever du pied g.** to get out of bed on the wrong side; **rive g.** left bank; **côté g.** *Aut (quand on conduit à gauche)* nearside; *(quand on conduit à droite)* offside; *Équitation* nearside
NF 1 *(côté)* left; **assis à ma g.** seated on my left; **mon voisin de g.** my left-hand neighbour; **le tiroir de g.** the left-hand drawer; **le magasin de g.** the shop on the left; **à g.** on the left(-hand side), to the left; **tournez à g.** turn left; **la première rue à g.** the first street on the left; **sur votre g., vous pouvez voir la tour Eiffel** on your left(-hand side) you can see the Eiffel Tower; **à g. de la porte d'entrée/de Marie** on or to the left of the entrance/of Marie; **en France, on double à g.** in France, you overtake on the left; **conduire à g.** to drive on the left; **lire de g. à droite** to read from left to right; **Fam mettre de l'argent à g.** to put some money aside or away; **heureusement, elle avait de l'argent à g.** fortunately she had some money put aside or tucked away; *Fam* **passer l'arme à g.** to kick the bucket; **vis/hélice à pas de g.** left-handed screw/left-hand propeller; *Fam* **jusqu'à la g.** to the end, to the last; **ils nous ont eus jusqu'à la g.** they cheated us left, right and centre
2 *Pol* **la g.** the left; **politique/gouvernement/etc de g.** left-wing politics/government/etc; **homme de g.** man of the left; **l'extrême g.** the far or extreme left; **être à g.** to be on the left, to be left-wing; **voter à g.** to vote for the left; **la g. plurielle** = the rainbow coalition of socialists, communists and ecologists in the government of Lionel Jospin *(elected in 1997)*; *Fam* **la g. caviar** champagne socialists
NM *Boxe etc (poing gauche)* left; **feinter du g.** to feint with the left; **un crochet du g.** a left hook

gauchement [goʃmɑ̃] ADV awkwardly, clumsily

gaucher, -ère [goʃe, -ɛr] ADJ left-handed
N left-hander; *Boxe* southpaw; **g. contrarié** = natural left-hander brought up to be right-handed

gaucherie [goʃri] NF awkwardness, clumsiness

gauchi [goʃi] ADJ *Tech* = **gauche 2**

gauchir [goʃir] VI *(du bois etc)* to warp; *(du fer)* to buckle
VT 1 *(déformer)* to warp; *(fer)* to buckle 2 *Aviat* **g. l'aileron** to bank 3 *Fig (idée, événe-*

-ment, témoignage, réalité) to distort, to misrepresent
VPR **se gauchir** *(de bois)* to warp; *(de fer)* to buckle

gauchisant, -ante [goʃizɑ̃, -ɑ̃t] ADJ **écrivain g.** writer with left-wing sympathies
N **c'est un g.** he has left-wing sympathies, *Fam* he's a bit of a lefty

gauchisme [goʃism] NM *Pol* leftism

gauchissement [goʃismɑ̃] NM 1 *(de bois etc)* warping; *(de fer)* buckling 2 *Aviat* banking

gauchiste [goʃist] ADJ *Pol* left-wing, leftist
N left-winger, leftist, *Fam* lefty

gaucho [goʃo] NM *(gardien de troupeaux)* gaucho
N *Pol Fam* lefty

gaudriole [godrijɔl] NF *Fam Vieilli* 1 *(plaisanterie grivoise)* dirty or saucy or broad joke 2 **il/elle ne pense qu'à la g.** he's/she's only interested in one thing, he's/she's got a one-track mind

gaufrage [gofraʒ] NM *(du cuir, papier)* embossing; *(du lin)* goffering, fluting; *(d'une couverture)* blocking; **g. à froid** blind embossing

gaufre [gofr] NF 1 *Culin* waffle; **moule à gaufres** waffle iron 2 **g. de miel** honeycomb

gaufrer [gofre] VT *(cuir, velours, papier)* to emboss, to figure; *(lin)* to goffer, to flute; *(fer)* to corrugate; *(couverture)* to block

gaufrette [gofrɛt] NF wafer (biscuit)

gaufrier [gofrije] NM waffle iron

gaufrure [gofryr] NF *(sur cuir)* stamped design; *(sur lin)* goffering

Gaule [gol] NF *Antiq* Gaul

gaule [gol] NF 1 *(perche)* pole; *Pêche* fishing rod 2 *Vulg* **avoir la g.** to have a hard-on

gaulé [gole] ADJ *Fam* **être bien/mal g.** to have/not to have a great bod

gauler [gole] VT 1 *(arbre fruitier, noyer)* to beat, to thrash; *(fruits, noix)* to bring down *(using a pole)* 2 *Fam (attraper)* **se faire g.** to get caught

gaullien, -ienne [goljɛ̃, -jɛn] ADJ de Gaulle-like

gaullisme [golism] NM *Pol* Gaullism

> **Gaullisme**
> The political ideology inspired by the ideas of General de Gaulle includes nationalism, independence from foreign powers, and a strong executive. Gaullists are strongly committed to the defence of France's prestige on the international scene.

gaulliste [golist] ADJ, N *Pol* Gaullist

gaulois, -oise [golwa, -waz] ADJ Gallic; **esprit g.** (broad) Gallic humour; **contes g.** saucy or spicy stories
NM *Ling* Gaulish
N **G.** Gaul
NF **Gauloise®** Gauloise *(popular brand of cigarette)*

gauloiserie [golwazri] NF *(plaisanterie)* broad or saucy joke; *(caractère)* sauciness

gausser (se) [səgose] VPR *Litt* **se g. de qn** to laugh at or make fun of or sneer at sb; **vous vous gaussez!** you jest!

gavage [gavaʒ] NM *(engraissement) (de la volaille)* force-feeding, cramming; *Méd* tube-feeding

gave [gav] NM *Géog* (mountain) torrent *(in the Pyrenees)*

gaver [gave] VT *(engraisser) (volaille)* to force-feed, to cram; *(personne) (de nourriture)* to fill up, to stuff (**de** with); *Méd* to force-feed; *Fig* **g. qn de qch** to cram or stuff sb with sth; **j'ai été gavée de littérature classique** I had classical literature crammed into me; **la télévision gave les enfants de dessins animés** television feeds children a constant diet of cartoons

VPR se gaver *Fam (de chocolat, cacahuètes etc)* to gorge oneself (**de** on), to stuff oneself (**de** with); *Fig* **se g. de romans policiers/jeux vidéo** to read detective novels/play video games till they're coming out of one's ears

gavotte [gavɔt] NF *Mus* gavotte

gay [gɛ, ge] ADJ, NM *Fam (homosexuel)* gay

gaz [gaz] NM **1** gas; **gisement de g.** gas field; **faire la cuisine au g.** to cook by gas; **cuisinière à g.** gas cooker; *Culin* **sur le g.** on the gas; **allumer/couper le g.** to light/turn off the gas; **réchaud à g.** gas stove *(for camping)*; **usine à g.** gasworks; **chambre à g.** gas chamber; *Fam* **il y a de l'eau dans le g.** things aren't going too well, things are looking bad; *Fam* **être dans le g.** to be out of it **2** *Aut Fam* **mettre les g.** to put one's foot down, *Am* to step on the gas; *Aviat* to open up the throttle; **à pleins g.** *(rouler)* flat out; *(partir)* with the throttle full open **3** *Méd* **avoir des g.** to have wind *or Am* gas; **lâcher un g.** to break wind, *Am* to pass gas

▸▸ **g. ammoniac** ammonia gas; **g. asphyxiant** poison gas; **g. carbonique** carbon dioxide; **g. de combat** poison gas; **g. comprimé** compressed gas; **g. domestique** domestic gas; **g. d'échappement** exhaust fumes *ou* gas; **g. d'éclairage** town gas; **g. hilarant** laughing gas; **g. inerte** inert gas; **g. lacrymogène** tear gas; **g. des marais** marsh gas; **g. naturel** natural gas; **g. de pétrole liquéfié** liquefied petroleum gas; **g. rare** rare gas; **g. toxique** poison gas; **g. de ville** town gas; **la cuisinière est-elle branchée sur le g. de ville?** is the kitchen connected to the mains gas?

Gaza [gaza] N **la bande de G.** the Gaza Strip

gazage [gazaʒ] NM *Mil* gassing

gaze [gaz] NF **1** gauze; *Méd* **g. oxygénée** antiseptic *or* sterilized gauze **2** *Vieilli (voile)* thin veil

gazé, -ée [gaze] ADJ gassed; **soldats gazés** soldiers killed by (poison) gas

N (poison) gas victim

gazéification [gazeifikasjɔ̃] NF *Chimie* gasification; *(des boissons)* carbonation

gazéifier [gazeifje] VT *(pr sub, impf n.* **gazéifiions, v. gazéifiiez)** *Chimie* to gasify; *(boissons)* to carbonate

gazelle [gazɛl] NF gazelle; **avoir des yeux de g.** to be doe-eyed

gazer [gaze] VT *Mil (troupes)* to gas

VI *Fam (aller vite)* to zoom along; **ça gaze!** everything's OK *or* fine!; **ça gaze?** all right?, everything OK?; **ça ne gaze pas très fort pour lui** things aren't going too well for him

gazetier [gaztje] NM *Arch* journalist

gazette [gazɛt] NF *Vieilli (journal)* gazette, newspaper; *Fam* **c'est une vraie g.** he/she knows all the local gossip; *Fam* **cette femme est la g. de l'immeuble** that woman can tell you *or* knows everything that goes on in the building

gazeux, -euse [gazø, -øz] ADJ **1** *Chimie* gaseous **2** *(eau)* carbonated, fizzy; *(boisson)* fizzy, sparkling

gazier, -ière [gazje, -jɛr] ADJ **l'industrie gazière** the gas industry

NM **1** *(dans une usine à gaz)* gas works employee; *(chargé des installations dans les immeubles etc)* gas fitter, gasman **2** *Arg (individu)* guy, *Br* bloke

gazinière [gazinjɛr] NF gas cooker

gazoduc [gazɔdyk, gaz-] NM gas pipeline, gas main

gazogène [gazoʒɛn, gaz-] NM gas producer, gas generator; **gaz de g.** producer gas

gazole [gazɔl] NM **= gasoil**

gazoline [gazɔlin] NF gasoline, gasolene

gazomètre [gazɔmɛtr] NM gasometer, gas holder

gazon [gazɔ̃] NM **1** *(herbe)* grass, turf **2** *(surface)* lawn; **défense de marcher sur le g.** keep off the grass **3** *(motte de terre)* turf, sod **4** *Bot* **g. mousse** mossy saxifrage

gazonnage [gazɔnaʒ] NM turfing, planting with turf

gazonné [gazɔne] ADJ grass-covered, turfed

gazonnement [gazɔnmɑ̃] NM **= gazonnage**

gazonner [gazɔne] VT to cover with turf, to turf

VI *(d'un terrain)* to become covered with grass

gazouillant [gazujɑ̃] ADJ *(oiseau)* twittering, warbling, chirping; *(bébé)* babbling, gurgling; *(enfant)* prattling; **ruisseau g.** babbling brook

gazouillement [gazujmɑ̃] NM *(des oiseaux)* twittering, warbling, chirping; *(d'un bébé)* babbling, gurgling; *(des enfants)* prattle, prattling; *(de l'eau qui coule)* babbling, murmuring

gazouiller [gazuje] VI *(d'un oiseau)* to twitter, to warble, to chirp; *(d'un bébé)* to babble, to gurgle; *(d'un enfant)* to prattle; *(d'eau)* to babble, to murmur

gazouilleur, -euse [gazujœr, -øz] ADJ *(oiseau)* twittering, warbling, chirping; *(bébé)* babbling, gurgling; *(enfant)* prattling; **ruisseau g.** babbling brook

gazouillis [gazuji] NM **= gazouillement**

GB [ʒebe] NF *(abrév* **Grande-Bretagne)** GB

G-C [ʒese] *abrév* **grand-croix**

GDB [ʒedebe] NF *Fam (abrév* **gueule de bois)** hangover

GDF [ʒedeɛf] NM *abrév* **Gaz de France**

geai [ʒɛ] NM *Orn* jay

géant, -ante [ʒeɑ̃, -ɑ̃t] N **1** *Myth* giant, *f* giantess **2** *(personne anormalement grande)* giant; *Gym* **pas de g.** giant stride; *Fig* **avancer** *ou* **aller à pas de g.** to make great strides, to make spectacular progress; **la Chaussée des Géants** the Giant's Causeway **3** *(personne exceptionnelle)* giant; **les géants de la politique** the giants of politics, the political giants; **les géants de l'art** the great masters; **les géants du football** the football(ing) greats

ADJ **1** *(arbre, écran etc)* giant, gigantic; *Com* **carton g.** giant (-size) packet **2** *Fam (super)* **c'est g.** fantastic!, wicked!

gecko [ʒeko] NM gecko

gégène [ʒeʒɛn] NF *Fam* **= torture by electric shock**

géhenne [ʒeɛn] NF *Bible* Gehenna, Hell

geignard, -arde [ʒɛɲar, -ard] *Fam* ADJ *(personne, voix)* whining, *Br* whingeing

N whiner

geignement [ʒɛɲmɑ̃] NM *(action)* whining; *(résultat)* whine

geindre [ʒɛ̃dr] VI *(prp* **geignant;** *pp* **geint;** *pr ind* **je geins, il geint,** *n.* **geignons, ils geignent;** *impf* **je geignais;** *p hist* **je geignis;** *fu* **je geindrai)** **1** *(gémir)* to moan, to groan; **g. de douleur** to moan *or* groan with pain **2** *Fam (se plaindre constamment)* to whine, *Br* to whinge

geisha [gɛʃa] NF geisha

gel [ʒɛl] NM **1** *Météo* frost; *Fig* **g. des négociations** suspension of negotiations; **g. des subventions** freezing of subsidies; **g. des armements/des crédits** the arms/credit freeze **2** *(dans les produits cosmétiques) (pour les cheveux)* gel; **dentifrice en g.** gel toothpaste; **se mettre du g.** to put gel on one's hair **3** *Chimie* gel

▸▸ **g. douche** shower gel; *UE* **g. des terres** set-aside

gélatine [ʒelatin] NF gelatin(e); *Culin* **feuille de g.** sheet of gelatine

gélatiné [ʒelatine] ADJ gelatinized

gélatineux, -euse [ʒelatinø, -øz] ADJ gelatinous

gelé [ʒ(ə)le] ADJ *(lac, rivière)* frozen; *(nez, main etc)* frostbitten; *(plante)* frost-nipped; *Fig (assistance)* cold, indifferent; *Fin (bloqué) (fonds)* frozen; **mourir g.** to freeze to death; *Fam* **je suis complètement g.** I'm absolutely frozen *or* freezing; *Fam* **être g. jusqu'aux os** to be chilled to the marrow *or* bone; **ils ont eu les pieds gelés** they had frostbite in their feet

gelée [ʒ(ə)le] NF **1** *(gel)* frost; **forte g.** hard frost **2** *Culin* jelly; *(à base de fruits)* jelly, *Am* jello; **g. de veau/poulet** veal/chicken jelly; **œufs en g.** eggs in jelly; **g. de cassis** blackcurrant jelly *or Am* jello

▸▸ **g. blanche** hoar (frost), white frost; **g. royale** royal jelly

geler [ʒ(ə)le] *(je* **gèle,** *n.* **gelons; je gèlerai)** VT **1** to freeze; *(lac, rivière)* to freeze (over); *(route)* to make icy; **froid qui gèle les conduites d'eau** cold that freezes the water pipes; **fleurs gelées par le froid** flowers nipped by the frost **2** *Fin (bloquer) (crédits, capital)* to freeze

VI *(d'un lac, d'une rivière)* to freeze (over); **l'étang a gelé d'un bout à l'autre** the pond has *or* is completely frozen over; **plantes qui gèlent facilement** plants easily damaged by frost; **on gèle dans cette salle** it's freezing in this room; **tu ne gèles pas, toi?** aren't you freezing *or* frozen?

V IMPERS **il gèle** it is freezing; **il gèle à pierre fendre** it's freezing hard; **il a gelé blanc cette nuit** there was a white frost last night

VPR **se geler** *(personne)* to freeze; *très Fam* **on se les gèle aujourd'hui** it's damned cold, *Br* it's brass monkey weather

gélifiant [ʒelifjɑ̃] NM gelling agent

gélifier [ʒelifje] *Chimie* VT *(transformer en gel)* to gel

VPR **se gélifier** to gel

gélinotte [ʒelinɔt] NF **g. (des bois)** hazel grouse; **g. des prairies** prairie chicken

gélose [ʒeloz] NF *Chimie* agar-agar

gélule [ʒelyl] NF *Pharm* capsule

gelure [ʒ(ə)lyr] NF frostbite

Gémeaux (les) [leʒemo] NMPL *Astron, Astrol* Gemini; **être (du signe des) G.** to be (a) Gemini

gémellaire [ʒemelɛr] ADJ twin

gémellité [ʒemelite] NF **taux de g.** incidence of twin births

gémination [ʒeminasjɔ̃] NF *Biol etc* gemination

géminé [ʒemine] ADJ **1** *Biol (feuilles)* geminate, twin; *Chimie* geminate; *Archit* **colonnes géminées** twin columns **2** *Ling* **consonnes géminées** doubled *or* geminate consonants

gémir [ʒemir] VI **1** *(d'une personne)* to groan, to moan; *(d'une porte)* to creak; *(du vent)* to moan; **g. de douleur** to groan *or* moan with pain; **g. sous le joug de la tyrannie** to groan under the yoke of tyranny **2** *(d'une colombe, tourterelle)* to coo

gémissant [ʒemisɑ̃] ADJ *(personne)* moaning, groaning; **voix gémissante** wailing voice; **essieu g.** creaking axle

gémissement [ʒemismɑ̃] NM **1** *(d'une personne)* groan, moan; *(de porte)* creaking; *(de vent)* moaning; **je ne supporte plus tes**

gémissements I can't bear your moaning *or* groaning any longer **2** *(d'une colombe etc)* cooing

gemmage [ʒɛmaʒ] **NM** tapping *(of trees for resin)*

gemme [ʒɛm] **NF 1** *Minér* gem (stone), precious stone **2** *(sève)* pine resin **3** *Bot Arch* (leaf) bud
▪ **ADJ pierre g.** gem stone; **sel g.** rock salt

gemmé [ʒeme, ʒɛme] **ADJ** *Litt* gemmed, jewelled

gemmer [ʒeme, ʒɛme] **VT** to tap

gemmeur [ʒɛmœr] **NM** tapper

gémonies [ʒemɔni] **NFPL** *Litt* **traîner** *ou* **vouer qn aux g.** to hold sb up to public obloquy

gênant [ʒɛnɑ̃] **ADJ 1** *(embarrassant) (personne)* embarrassing; *(situation, silence)* embarrassing, awkward; *(témoin)* awkward; **j'ai trouvé extrêmement g. que tu abordes ce sujet** it was extremely embarrassing of you to mention the subject **2** *(encombrant) (objet)* cumbersome; **votre fils n'est pas g.** your son is no trouble *or* no bother; **il peut être très g. quand il nous interrompt** he can be a real nuisance when he interrupts us; **les jupes longues sont gênantes** long skirts are awkward *or* are a nuisance

gencive [ʒɑ̃siv] **NF 1** *Anat* gum; **abcès à la g.** abscess on the gum, gumboil **2** *Fam* **un coup dans les gencives** a punch on the jaw; *Fig* **prends ça dans les gencives!** take that!; **elle lui a envoyé des gencives tout ce qu'elle avait contre lui** she told him to his face everything she didn't like about him

gendarme [ʒɑ̃darm] **NM 1** gendarme, policeman, *Br* ≃ police constable; **gendarmes à cheval** mounted police; **gendarmes motocyclistes** motorcycle police; *Fig* **sa mère est un vrai g.** his mother is a real battle-axe; **jouer aux gendarmes et aux voleurs** to play (at) cops and robbers; *Fam* **faire le g.** to boss people about; *Fam* **la peur du g.** the fear of being caught; **chapeau de g.** paper hat **2** *(d'une pierre précieuse)* flaw **3** *Géol* rock pinnacle, gendarme **4** *Culin Fam (hareng saur)* red herring; *(saucisson)* = flat, dry sausage
▸ ▸ *Aut Fam* **g. couché** sleeping policeman

gendarmer (se) [səʒɑ̃darme] **VPR** *(contre qn, une proposition etc)* to kick up *or* create a fuss **(contre** about); **il n'y a pas de quoi se g.** there's nothing to get worked up about

gendarmerie [ʒɑ̃darməri] **NF 1** *(corps) (en France)* gendarmerie, police force; **g. nationale** = national police force, gendarmerie; **la G. royale du Canada** the Royal Canadian Mounted Police **2** *(lieu)* gendarmes' headquarters

gendre [ʒɑ̃dr] **NM** son-in-law

gène [ʒɛn] **NM** *Biol* gene; **g. terminator** terminator gene; **structure du g.** gene structure; **banque/famille de gènes** gene bank/family

gêne [ʒɛn] **NF 1** *(confusion)* embarrassment; **éprouver une certaine g. à parler en public** to feel rather ill at ease *or* embarrassed when speaking in public; **ressentir de la g. en présence de qn** to feel ill at ease *or* embarrassed in sb's presence; **elle a ressenti une certaine g. à le lui demander** she felt rather embarrassed *or* awkward about asking him; **je n'aurais aucune g. à le faire** I wouldn't be at all embarrassed about doing it; **où (il) y a de la g., (il n')y a pas de plaisir** there's no point in standing on ceremony **2** *(dérangement)* inconvenience; **nous prions nos clients de bien vouloir excuser la g. occasionnée par les travaux** we apologize to customers for the inconvenience caused by the work; **vous ne me causerez aucune g.** you won't inconvenience me in the least, you won't cause me any inconvenience

3 *(difficulté physique)* discomfort; **sentir une g. respiratoire** *ou* **pour respirer** to have difficulty (in) breathing; **elle éprouve une g. intense à avaler** she has great difficulty swallowing
4 *(manque d'argent)* **être dans la g.** to be short of money, to be in financial difficulties
5 *Arch (physique, morale)* torture

gêné [ʒene] **ADJ 1** *(embarrassé)* embarrassed, ill at ease; **je suis tellement gênée de tous ces cadeaux que vous me faites** I'm so embarrassed by all these presents you're giving me; *Fam* **il n'est pas g., lui!** he's got a nerve!; **elle avait l'air g. d'arriver si tard** she seemed embarrassed at arriving so late; **je serais trop g. de le lui dire** I'd be too embarrassed to tell him; **silence g.** embarrassed *or* awkward *or* uneasy silence; *Fam* **être g. aux entournures** to be ill at ease; **être g. par un vêtement** to be hampered by a garment **2** *(qui manque d'argent)* short of money, in financial difficulties; *Fam* **être g. aux entournures** to be short of money

généalogie [ʒenealɔʒi] **NF 1** *(ascendance)* genealogy, descent; *(d'un cheval, d'un chien etc)* pedigree **2** *(science)* genealogy

généalogique [ʒenealɔʒik] **ADJ** genealogical; **livre g.** *(de chevaux)* stud book; *(du bétail)* herd book

généalogiquement [ʒenealɔʒikmɑ̃] **ADV** genealogically

généalogiste [ʒenealɔʒist] **N** genealogist

gêner [ʒene] **VT 1** *(perturber, empêcher) (activité)* to interfere with; **g. la circulation** to hold up *or* block the traffic; **g. le passage** to be in the way; **g. la vue** to obstruct *or* block the view; **ma valise vous gêne-t-elle?** is my case in your way?; **pousse-toi, tu vois bien que tu gênes** move along, you can see you're in the way!; **je veux bien venir avec vous mais je ne veux pas vous g.** I'd love to come with you but I don't want to be in the *or* your way; **les enfants me gênent quand je dois me concentrer** the children disturb *or* bother me when I have to concentrate; **ça me gêne dans mon travail** it disturbs me when I'm trying to work; **une bonne nous gênerait dans notre intimité** a maid would intrude on our privacy; **ce point de côté me gêne pour marcher** this stitch in my side makes it difficult for me to walk; **recule-toi, tu me gênes pour passer** move back, you're in my way *or* you're stopping me from getting past; **si tu pouvais te pousser, tu me gênes pour passer les vitesses** could you move over, I can't change gear with you there; **j'ai été gêné par le manque de temps/ma méconnaissance du milieu** I was hindered *or* hampered by the lack of time/my ignorance of the milieu; **j'ai été gêné par le bruit/la lumière/le monde** I was disturbed by the noise/the light/the people; **ça te gêne si je mets la musique plus fort?** do you mind if I turn up the music?; **cela vous gênerait-il que je revienne demain?** would it disturb you *or* bother you *or* put you out if I come back tomorrow?; **cela ne te gênerait pas de me prêter ta voiture?** would you mind lending me your car?; **ce qui me gêne, c'est que …** what bothers me is that …; **le froid ne me gêne pas** I don't mind the cold; **la fumée vous gêne-t-elle?** do you mind my smoking?
2 *(serrer)* **mes souliers me gênent** my shoes pinch *or* are too tight; **cette ceinture/ce col me gêne** this belt/this collar is too tight; **cette jupe trop étroite me gêne pour marcher** I find it hard to walk in this tight skirt
3 *(mettre mal à l'aise)* to embarrass; **cela me gênait de le rencontrer** it would be awkward for me to meet him, I would feel uncomfortable meeting him; **sa présence me gêne** I feel awkward *or* embarrassed in his presence, his presence makes me feel ill at

ease; **ça me gêne qu'il écoute** I feel uneasy with him listening; *Fam* **et alors, ça te gêne?** what's it to you?, any objections?
▪ **VPR se gêner 1 je ne me suis pas gêné pour le lui dire** I didn't hesitate to tell him so, I made no bones about telling him so; **ne te gêne pas pour le lui faire remarquer** go right ahead and point it out to him; **il trouve que le café ne vient pas assez vite? qu'il ne se gêne surtout pas pour le faire!** he thinks the coffee's taking too long? he can always make it himself!; **il ne se gêne pas avec nous** he doesn't stand on ceremony with us; **elle aurait tort de se g.** she has no need to feel embarrassed; *Iron* **il ne se gêne pas!** he's not backward in coming forward!; *Iron* **ne vous gênez pas!** make yourself at home!; *Iron* **faut pas se g.!** don't mind me!
2 *(dans un lieu)* to be in each other's way; **il y a beaucoup de place, nous ne nous gênerons pas** there's a lot of room, we won't be in each other's way
3 *Suisse (être intimidé)* to be shy

général, -ale, -aux, -ales [ʒeneral, -o] **ADJ** general; **assemblée/amnistie générale** general assembly/amnesty; **appeler à une grève générale** to call a general strike; **dans l'intérêt g.** in the general interest; **à la surprise générale** to everyone's surprise; **à la demande générale, nous allons rechanter la dernière chanson** by popular request we are going to sing the last song again; **satisfaire à la demande générale** to satisfy popular *or* general demand; *Théâtre* **répétition générale** dress rehearsal; **état g.** general *or* overall condition; **médecine générale** general medicine; **inspecteur g.** inspector general; **quartier g.** headquarters; *Hist* **états généraux** States General; **officier g.** *Mil etc* general officer; *Naut* flag officer; **le consentement g.** common consent; **d'une façon générale** generally speaking; **en règle générale** as a general rule, generally; **en g.** *(globalement)* in general; *(habituellement)* as a rule, generally; **la nature humaine en g.** human nature in general; **en g., elle se couche tôt** she goes to bed early as a rule, she generally goes to bed early
▪ **NM 1** *(ce qui est universel)* **le g.** the general; **passer du g. au particulier** to go from the general to the particular **2** *Mil* general
▪ **NF générale 1** *Théâtre* dress rehearsal **2** *Mil (alerte)* alarm call; **battre la générale** to call to arms, to sound the alarm; *Naut* to beat to quarters **3** **bonjour, madame la générale** *(qui s'appelle Leclerc)* hello, Mrs Leclerc
▸ ▸ **g. d'armée** (army) general; **g. d'armée aérienne** air chief marshal, *Am* major general; **g. de brigade** brigadier, *Am* brigadier general; **g. de brigade aérienne** air commodore, *Am* brigadier general; **g. de corps d'armée** lieutenant general; **g. de corps d'armée aérienne** air marshal, *Am* lieutenant general; **g. de division** major general; **g. de division aérienne** air vice-marshal, *Am* major general

généralement [ʒeneralmɑ̃] **ADV** generally; **il y a g. une trentaine d'élèves par classe** there are generally *or* usually about thirty pupils in a class

généralisable [ʒeneralizabl] **ADJ** that can be generalized

généralisateur, -trice [ʒeneralizatœr, -tris] **ADJ** *(esprit, méthode)* generalizing

généralisation [ʒeneralizasjɔ̃] **NF 1** *(extension)* generalization; **craindre la g. d'un conflit** to fear that a conflict will spread; *Méd* **g. d'un cancer** spread of a cancer **2** *(de propos)* generalization; **une g. hâtive** a sweeping generalization; **faire des généralisations** to make generalizations, to generalize; **tomber dans les généralisations** to lapse into generalization(s)

généraliser [ʒeneralize] **VT** to generalize; **g. une loi** to extend a law; **il a tendance à tout g.** he tends to generalize; *Méd* **un cancer généralisé** a generalized cancer

VI to generalize; **on ne peut pas g.** you can't generalize

VPR se généraliser *(d'une utilisation)* to become widespread; *(d'un usage, un conflit, une grève)* to spread; **la crise économique s'est généralisée** the economic crisis has spread

généralissime [ʒeneralisim] **NM** generalissimo, commander-in-chief

généraliste [ʒeneralist] **N** *Méd* general practitioner, GP, *Am* family practitioner

ADJ médecin g. general practitioner, GP, *Am* family practitioner; **radio/télévision g.** general-interest radio/television

généralité [ʒeneralite] **NF 1** *(majorité)* **dans la g. des cas** in the majority *or* generality of cases, in most cases **2** *(notion générale)* generality; **s'en tenir à des généralités** to confine oneself to generalities *or* to general remarks; **exposer quelques généralités dans un cours d'introduction** to present some general ideas in an introductory course

générateur, -trice [ʒeneratœr, -tris] **ADJ** *(machine etc)* generating; *(force, organe)* generative; **g. de** productive of; **un colorant alimentaire g. de troubles gastriques** a food colouring *or Am* coloring which causes gastric problems; *Fig* **une situation génératrice de conflits/d'idées** a situation that generates *or* produces conflict/ideas; **une situation peu génératrice d'emplois** a situation that generates *or* produces few jobs; **son discours a été g. de nombreuses questions** his speech threw up *or* raised a great many questions; *Élec* **station ou usine génératrice** generating station *or* plant; **chaudière génératrice** steam boiler

NM generator

NF génératrice generator, generating set; *Nucl* **génératrice nucléaire** nuclear power reactor

▸▸ *Ordinat* **g. de caractères** character generator; *TV* caption generator; *TV, Cin* **g. de couleur** colour synthesizer; *Ordinat* **g. d'écrans** screen generator; *Ordinat* **g. d'effets numériques** digital effects generator; *Ordinat* **g. d'effets spéciaux** (special) effects generator, SEG; *Élec* **g. d'électricité** electricity generator; *Ordinat* **g. d'états** report generator; *Ordinat* **g. graphique** graphics generator; *Électron* **g. d'impulsions** pulse generator; *Ordinat* **g. de menus** menu builder; **g. de signaux** *Électron* signal(ling) generator; *TV* colour coder; *Ordinat* **g. de son** sound generator; *TV etc* **g. de synchro** synchronizing generator, sync pulse generator, SPG; *TV, Cin* **g. de titres graphiques** graphic titler; **g. de vapeur** (steam) boiler, steam generator

génératif, -ive [ʒeneratif, -iv] **ADJ** generative

génération [ʒenerasjɔ̃] **NF 1** *(classe d'âge, degrés de filiation)* generation; **la g. actuelle** the present generation; **la jeune g.** the younger generation; **ils ne sont pas de la même g.** they are not (of) the same generation; **les gens de ma g.** the people of my generation; **de g. en g.** from generation to generation, through the generations; **immigrés de la deuxième g.** second-generation immigrants; **la g. pub/vidéo/***etc* the advertising/video/*etc* generation; **la nouvelle g. d'ordinateurs/de machines à laver** the new generation of computers/washing machines VOIR GRAMMAIRE A11 **2** *(action de générer, produire)* generation; *(de vapeur etc)* generation, production; *(de métaux)* formation

▸▸ *Ordinat* **g. automatique de textes** automatic generation of texts; *Ordinat* **g. d'écrans** screen generation; *Biol* **g. spontanée** spontaneous generation

générer [ʒenere] **VT** (**je génère, n. générons; je générerai**) **1** *(faire naître)* *(idées, images, profits)* to generate; *Ordinat* **généré par ordinateur** computer-generated **2** *(produire)* *(électricité, vapeur etc)* to generate, to produce

généreusement [ʒenerøzmɑ̃] **ADV** generously; **il nous a servi g. à manger** he gave us a generous meal; **il nous a g. versé à boire** he gave us a generous amount to drink

généreux, -euse [ʒenerø, -øz] **ADJ** *(charitable)* generous; *Vieilli Fam* *(noble)* *(âme)* noble, generous; **il est très g. avec les enfants** he is very generous with (the) children; **un don g.** a generous gift; **terre généreuse** fertile soil; **vin g.** generous wine, wine with a fine bouquet; **elle a des formes généreuses** she has generous curves, she is a buxom woman

N generous person

générique [ʒenerik] **ADJ** generic; **produit g.** no-name *or* generic product; **médicament g.** generic drug

NM *TV, Cin* credits, titles; **faire le g.** to do the captions; **son nom ne figure pas au g.** his name doesn't appear in the credits, he doesn't get a credit; **g. de début** opening credits; **g. de fin** closing credits, end titles; **g. déroulant** rolling credits, rolling titles

générosité [ʒenerozite] **NF** *(libéralité)* generosity; **avec g.** generously; **g. de cœur** kindness of heart; **dans un élan de g.** in a sudden fit of generosity; **n'abuse pas de ma g.** don't abuse my generosity; **générosités** acts of generosity

Gênes [ʒɛn] **N** Genoa

genèse [ʒənɛz] **NF** genesis; *Bible* **la G.** (the Book of) Genesis

genet [ʒ(ə)nɛ] **NM** jennet

genêt [ʒ(ə)nɛ] **NM** *Bot* broom

généticien, -ienne [ʒenetisjɛ̃, -jɛn] **N** geneticist

génétique [ʒenetik] **ADJ** genetic; **code/empreinte/manipulation g.** genetic code/fingerprint/engineering; **fond g. commun** gene pool

NF genetics

génétiquement [ʒenetikmɑ̃] **ADV** genetically; **g. modifié** genetically modified

genette [ʒ(ə)nɛt] **NF** genet

gêneur, -euse [ʒɛnœr, -øz] **N** nuisance

Genève [ʒ(ə)nɛv] **N** Geneva

genevois, -oise [ʒənvwa, -waz] **ADJ** Genevan

N G. Genevan

genévrier [ʒənevrije] **NM** juniper

génial, -ale, -aux, -ales [ʒenjal, -o] **ADJ 1** *(inspiré par le génie)* *(invention, livre, tableau etc)* brilliant; **œuvre géniale** work of genius, brilliant work; **compositeur g.** composer of genius, brilliant composer **2** *Fam (extraordinaire)* *(idée, film, soirée etc)* brilliant, great; **c'est g.!** that's brilliant *or* great!; **un mec g.** a great guy; **tu es g.!** you're a genius!, you're brilliant!

> Il faut noter que l'adjectif anglais **genial** est un faux ami. Il signifie **cordial**.

génialement [ʒenjalmɑ̃] **ADV** brilliantly

génie [ʒeni] **NM 1** *(qualité, personne)* genius; **homme de g.** man of genius; **une idée/invention de g.** a brilliant idea/invention; **un trait de g.** a stroke of genius; **avoir le g. de qch/pour faire qch** to have a genius *or* gift for sth/for doing sth; *Iron* **tu as vraiment le g. pour te faire des ennemis** you have a real genius *or* a real gift for making enemies VOIR GRAMMAIRE A14 **2** *(allégorie)* spirit; **g. d'une langue** genius *or* spirit of a language **3** *(être mythique)* genie; **son mauvais g.** his evil genius; **le petit g. de la forêt** the forest sprite; **les génies des contes arabes** the genies *or* the jinn of the Arabian Nights **4** *Tech* engineering; *Mil* **le (Corps du) G.** *Br* ≃ the Royal Engineers, the Engineers, *Am* ≃ the Corps of Engineers, the Engineer Corps; *Mil* **officier du g.** engineer officer; *Mil* **soldat du g.** engineer, *Br* sapper

▸▸ **g. aéroporté** airborne engineers; **g. de l'air** aviation engineers; **g. atomique** atomic *or* nuclear engineering; *(corps)* atomic *or* nuclear engineers; **g. civil** civil engineering; *(corps)* civil engineers; **g. électronique** electronic engineering; *Méd* **g. génétique** genetic engineering; **g. industriel** industrial engineering; **g. logiciel** systems engineering; *Tech* **g. maritime** marine *or* naval architecture; *(corps)* marine *or* naval architects

genièvre [ʒənjɛvr] **NM 1** *(fruit)* juniper berry; *(arbre)* juniper (tree); *Pharm* **essence de g.** juniper oil **2** *(alcool)* gin

génique [ʒenik] **ADJ** *Méd* **thérapie g.** gene therapy

génisse [ʒenis] **NF** heifer

génital, -ale, -aux, -ales [ʒenital, -o] **ADJ** genital; **les organes génitaux** the genitals, the genital organs; **appareil g.** genitalia

géniteur, -trice [ʒenitœr, -tris] **NM** *Zool* sire **N** *Hum* father, *f* mother; **nos géniteurs** our parents

génitif [ʒenitif] **NM** *Gram* genitive (case); **au g.** in the genitive VOIR GRAMMAIRE A15–16

génito-urinaire, *pl* **génito-urinaires** [ʒenitoyriner] **ADJ** *Anat* genito-urinary

génocide [ʒenɔsid] **NM** genocide

génois, -oise [ʒenwa, -waz] **ADJ** Genoese **N G.** Genoese

génoise [ʒenwaz] **NF** sponge cake

génome [ʒenom] **NM** *Biol* genome

génomique [ʒenomik] **NF** genomics VOIR GRAMMAIRE A10

génotype [ʒenotip] **NM** *Biol* genotype

genou, *pl* **genoux** [ʒ(ə)nu] **NM 1** *Anat* knee; **sa robe lui arrivait au-dessus du g./aux genoux** her dress came down to just above the knee/to her knees; **enfoncé jusqu'aux genoux dans la boue** knee-deep in mud, up to one's knees in mud; **avoir les genoux en dedans** to be knock-kneed; **à genoux** kneeling, on one's knees; **se mettre à genoux** to kneel (down), to go down on one's knees; *Fig* **être à genoux devant qn** to worship sb; *Fig* **se mettre à genoux devant qn** to go down on one's knees to sb; *Fig* **demander qch à genoux** to ask for sth on bended knee; **plier** *ou* **ployer** *ou* **fléchir le g. devant qn** to bend the knee to sb; *Fig* **être sur les genoux** to be on one's last legs, to be about to drop; **ce projet m'a mis sur les genoux** this project has worn *or* tired me out; **tenir un enfant sur ses genoux** to hold a child on one's knee *or* in one's lap; **sur les genoux des dieux** in the lap of the gods; **faire du g. à qn** to play footsie with sb

2 *Tech* **joint à g.** ball-and-socket joint

genouillère [ʒ(ə)nujɛr] **NF 1** *(protection du genou)* kneepad, knee guard; *Méd* knee bandage **2** *Tech* **articulation à g.** toggle joint

genre [ʒãr] **NM 1** *(sorte)* kind, sort, type; **quel g. de voitures/de livres?** what kind *or* sort *or* type of cars/books?; **quel g. de vie mène-t-il?** what kind *or* sort of (a) life does he lead?; **toutes les tentatives de ce g. ont échoué** all attempts of this kind *or* sort have failed; **c'est plus dans son g.** that's more in his line; **dans son g., c'est un artiste** he is

an artist in his way; **très bon dans son g.** very good of its kind; **décorations en tout g.** ou en tous genres decorations of all kinds; **c'est ce qu'on fait de mieux dans le g.** it's the best of its kind; **c'est dans le g. de ...** it's like ...; **un peu dans le g. de ...** rather or a bit like ...; **elle est unique en son g.** she is one of a kind; **un voyage vraiment unique en son g.** a journey unique of its kind; **ce n'est pas mon g.** it's not my style; **coucher à droite et à gauche, ce n'est pas mon g.** I'm not into sleeping around, sleeping around's not my thing; **c'est tout à fait mon g.** (cette robe) it's just my style; (ce mec) he's just my type; **c'est tout à fait son g. d'arriver en retard** it's just like her to be late; **ce n'est pas son g.** that's not like him; **ce n'est pas le g. (de femme) à se plaindre** she's not the sort (of woman) to complain; **sa nouvelle copine est du g. pot de colle** his new girlfriend's the clinging sort or kind; **tu vois le g.?** you know the sort?; **vin blanc g. sauternes** white wine of the Sauternes type; **étui g. maroquin** case in imitation morocco VOIR GRAMMAIRE A13
2 Beaux-Arts, Littér genre; **le roman policier est un g. littéraire très populaire** the detective novel is a very popular literary genre; **le g. comique** comedy; **le g. tragique** tragedy; **peinture de g.** genre painting; **tableau de g.** genre painting or picture
3 (race) race; Bot, Zool etc genus, pl genera; **le g. humain** the human race, mankind
4 (goût) **c'est bon/mauvais g.** it is good/bad form or in good/bad taste
5 Gram gender; **s'accorder en g. et en nombre** to agree in gender and number SEE GRAMMAR B5–8

gens [ʒɑ̃] NMPL **1** (individus) people; **il y avait peu de g. dans la salle** there were not many people in the hall; Théâtre **there was a poor house; de braves g.** good people; **de petites g.** people of modest means; **des g. sans histoires** nice, ordinary people; **beaucoup de g.** ou **bien des g.** l'ont vu lots of or many people have seen it; **que vont dire les g.?** what will people say?; Fam **un tas de g. pense(nt) que ...** loads of people think that ...; **qui sont ces gens-là?** who are these people?; **il y a des g. qui ...** there are (some) people who ..., some people ...
2 (individus de même profession, état etc) **les g. du pays** ou Fam **du coin** the locals, the local people; **jeunes g.** (garçons et filles) young people; (jeunes hommes) young men
3 (nation) **le droit des g.** the law of nations
4 Vieilli (domestiques) servants, domestics; (de roi etc) retinue
▸▸ **g. d'affaires** business people, Vieilli **g. d'Église** clergy; **g. de lettres** men of letters; **g. de maison** domestic servants; **g. du monde** society people; **g. de théâtre** theatre or theatrical people; **g. du voyage** (gitans) travellers

gent [ʒɑ̃] NF Arch, Hum race, tribe; **la g. moutonnière** the ovine race; **la g. masculine** the male sex

gentiane [ʒɑ̃sjan] NF **1** Bot gentian **2** (liqueur) gentian bitters

gentil¹, -ille [ʒɑ̃ti, -ij] ADJ **1** (aimable) kind, nice; **tu es bien gentil de m'aider** it's very nice or kind or good of you to help me; **elle a été très gentille pour** ou **avec moi** she was very nice or kind to me; Iron **elle est bien gentille** she's harmless enough; **c'est gentil de votre part (de m'écrire)** it is kind or good of you (to write to me); **dire un mot gentil à qn** to say a kind word to sb; **sois gentil(le)** (à un enfant) be a good boy/girl; (à un adulte) be an angel; **tu veux bien être gentil et aller me chercher des cigarettes** would you be an angel and fetch me some cigarettes; **tu n'as pas été gentil, tu n'auras pas de bonbon** you haven't been good or you've been naughty, you won't get a sweet

2 (agréable) nice; **un gentil petit village** a nice or pretty little village; **c'est gentil chez eux** it's nice at their place, they've got a nice place
3 (considérable) **une gentille somme** a nice little sum

> Il faut noter que les adjectifs anglais **genteel** et **gentle** sont des faux amis. **Genteel** signifie **respectable** ou **affecté**, selon le contexte, et **gentle** signifie **doux**.

gentil² NM Hist, Rel Gentile

gentilhomme [ʒɑ̃tijɔm], pl **gentilshommes** [ʒɑ̃tizɔm] NM gentleman; Hist **g. de la Chambre du Roi** gentleman of the Privy Chamber

gentilhommière [ʒɑ̃tijɔmjɛr] NF **1** country seat, manor house **2** (en Belgique) boarding house for men

gentilité [ʒɑ̃tilite] NF Hist, Rel Gentiles

gentillesse [ʒɑ̃tijɛs] NF (bonté) kindness; **elle a fait cela par g.** she did that out of kindness; **auriez-vous la g. de ...** would you be so kind as to ...; **elle a eu la g. de venir elle-même** she was kind enough to come herself; **dire des gentillesses à qn** to say nice or kind things to sb

gentillet, -ette [ʒɑ̃tijɛ, -ɛt] ADJ rather or quite nice; **roman g.** silly or Fam soppy novel

gentiment [ʒɑ̃timɑ̃] ADV **1** (aimablement) kindly; (sagement) nicely; **elle m'a g. proposé de venir avec moi** she kindly offered to come with me; **elle m'a g. tenu compagnie** she was kind enough to keep me company, she kindly kept me company **2** Suisse (sans précipitation) **fais-le g., tu as tout le temps** take your time, there's no hurry

gentleman, pl **gentlemen** [dʒɛntləman] NM gentleman; Courses de chevaux amateur jockey

gentleman-farmer, pl **gentlemen-farmers** [dʒɛntləmanfarmœr] NM gentleman farmer

génuflexion [ʒenyflɛksjɔ̃] NF genuflexion; **faire une g.** to genuflect

géo [ʒeo] NF Scol Fam geography, geog

géocentrique [ʒeosɑ̃trik] ADJ Astron geocentric

géocentrisme [ʒeosɑ̃trism] NM geocentrism

géochimie [ʒeoʃimi] NF geochemistry

géocroiseur [ʒeokrwazœr] NM Astron near-earth asteroid

géode [ʒeɔd] NF **1** Géol, Méd geode **2** (à Paris) **la G.** the Géode (the spherical building housing a cinema at the Cité des Sciences in Paris)

géodésie [ʒeodezi] NF geodesy, geodetics

géodésique [ʒeodezik] ADJ geodesic, geodetic; **point g.** triangulation point

géodynamique [ʒeodinamik] ADJ geodynamic
NF geodynamics

géographe [ʒeograf] N geographer

géographie [ʒeografi] NF **1** (science) geography; **g. économique** economic geography; **g. humaine** human geography **2** (livre) geography book

géographique [ʒeografik] ADJ geographic(al); **carte g.** map; **dictionnaire g.** gazetteer; **Institut g. national** Br ≃ Royal Geographical Society

géographiquement [ʒeografikmɑ̃] ADV geographically

geôle [ʒol] NF Littér jail, Br gaol

geôlier, -ière [ʒolje, -jɛr] N Littér jailer, Br gaoler

géologie [ʒeolɔʒi] NF geology

géologique [ʒeolɔʒik] ADJ geological

géologiquement [ʒeolɔʒikmɑ̃] ADV geologically

géologue [ʒeolɔg] N geologist

géomagnétique [ʒeomaɲetik] ADJ geomagnetic

géomagnétisme [ʒeomaɲetism] NM geomagnetism

géomancie [ʒeomɑ̃si] NF geomancy

géométral, -ale, -aux, -ales [ʒeometral, -o] ADJ (projection, élévation) flat (as opposed to perspective view) NM flat projection

géomètre [ʒeometr] NM **1** geometer, geometrician; (arpenteur) **g.** (land) surveyor **2** Entom geometer (moth)

géométrie [ʒeometri] NF geometry; **g. plane** plane geometry; **g. analytique** analytical or co-ordinate geometry; **g. dans l'espace** ou **à trois dimensions** solid or three-dimensional geometry; Aviat **avion à g. fixe/variable** fixed-/variable-geometry or fixed-/swing-wing aircraft; Fig **à g. variable** that varies according to circumstances

géométrique [ʒeometrik] ADJ geometric(al); **progression g.** geometrical progression; **esprit g.** orderly mind

géométriquement [ʒeometrikmɑ̃] ADV geometrically

géomorphologie [ʒeomɔrfɔlɔʒi] NF geomorphology

géophone [ʒeofɔn] NM geophone, sound detector

géophysicien, -ienne [ʒeofizisjɛ̃, -jɛn] N geophysicist

géophysique [ʒeofizik] ADJ geophysical NF geophysics

géophyte [ʒeofit] NM Bot geophyte

géopolitique [ʒeopolitik] NF geopolitics

georgette [ʒɔrʒɛt] NF Tex **crêpe g.** georgette (crepe)

Géorgie [ʒeɔrʒi] NF Georgia; **G. du Sud** South Georgia

géorgien, -ienne [ʒeɔrʒjɛ̃, -jɛn] ADJ Georgian
N **G.** Georgian

Géorgiques (les) [leʒeɔrʒik] NFPL Littér (de Virgile) the Georgics

géostationnaire [ʒeostasjɔnɛr] ADJ Astronaut **satellite g.** geostationary satellite

géostratégique [ʒeostrateʒik] ADJ geostrategic

géosynchrone [ʒeosɛ̃krɔn, ʒeosɛ̃kron] ADJ geosynchronous

géosynclinal, -aux [ʒeosɛ̃klinal, -o] NM Géol geosyncline

géothermie [ʒeotɛrmi] NF geothermics

géothermique [ʒeotɛrmik] ADJ geothermal

gérance [ʒerɑ̃s] NF (action) (d'une entreprise) management; (fonction, période) managership; **mettre un commerce en g.** to appoint a manager for a business; **prendre un commerce en g.** to take over the management of a business; **donner la g. d'un commerce à qn** to appoint sb manager of a business; **une g. de cinq ans** a five-year managership; **g. libre** tenant management; (entreprise) rented business; **g. de portefeuille** portfolio management

géranium [ʒeranjɔm] NM (sauvage) geranium, crane's bill; (plante d'ornement) pelargonium, Fam geranium

gérant, -ante [ʒerɑ̃, -ɑ̃t] N manager, f manageress; (d'un journal) managing editor; **g. d'affaires** business manager; **g. de fonds** fund manager; **g. majoritaire** manager with a controlling interest; **g. minoritaire** manager with a minority interest; **g. non associé** salaried manager, manager with no holding in a business; **g. de portefeuille** portfolio manager

gerbage [ʒɛrbaʒ] **NM 1** *(des céréales)* binding, sheaving **2** *(action d'empiler) (de tonneaux, de ballots)* stacking, piling

gerbe [ʒɛrb] **NF 1** *(de blé)* sheaf; **mettre le blé en gerbes** to bind the wheat into sheaves, to sheave *or* sheaf the wheat; **g. de fleurs** spray of flowers; **g. d'étincelles** shower of sparks; **g. de feu** burst of flame; **g. d'eau** spray *or* shower of water VOIR GRAMMAIRE A12 **2** *Mil* cone of fire **3** *Vulg* **avoir la g.** *(avoir envie de vomir)* to feel like throwing up *or* puking; *(vomir)* to throw up, to puke; **foutre la g. à qn** to make sb want to throw up *or* puke

gerber [ʒɛrbe] **VT 1** *(mettre en gerbes) (céréales)* to bind, to sheave, to sheaf **2** *Tech (empiler) (tonneaux, cageots, caisses)* to stack, to pile
VI *Vulg (vomir)* to throw up, to puke; **ça me fait g. de voir que ...** it makes me puke to see that ...

gerbera [ʒɛrbera] **NM** *Bot* gerbera

gerbeuse [ʒɛrbøz] **NF** *(pour tonneaux etc)* stacker, stacking machine

gerbier [ʒɛrbje] **NM** *(de céréales)* stack

gerbille [ʒɛrbij] **NF** gerbil

gerboise [ʒɛrbwaz] **NF** jerboa

gerce [ʒɛrs] **NF 1** *(fente) (dans le bois)* crack, fissure **2** *Entom* clothes moth

gercé [ʒɛrse] **ADJ** cracked; *(mains, lèvres)* chapped

gercer [ʒɛrse] *(il gerçait; il gerça)* **VT** *(mains, lèvres)* to chap; *(bois, terre)* to crack
VI *(des lèvres, mains)* to chap
VPR se gercer *(des lèvres, mains)* to chap

gerçure [ʒɛrsyr] **NF** *(sur la peau)* chap; *(dans le sol)* crack, fissure; *Tech (dans le bois)* shake, flaw; *(dans le métal)* hair crack, hairline; **avoir des gerçures aux mains/lèvres** to have chapped hands/lips; **pour éviter d'avoir des gerçures** to avoid chapped hands/lips

gérer [ʒere] *(je gère, n. gérons; je gérerai)* **VT** *(journal, hôtel etc)* to manage, to run; *(région, état etc)* to manage, to administer; *(finances, conflit, situation difficile)* to manage; *(temps)* to organize, to manage; **mal g. ses finances** to mismanage one's finances; **g. la crise** to see the crisis through, to manage the crisis; **g. une affaire** to handle a matter

gerfaut [ʒɛrfo] **NM** gyrfalcon, gerfalcon

gériatre [ʒerjatr] **N** *Méd* geriatrician

gériatrie [ʒerjatri] **NF** *Méd* geriatrics

gériatrique [ʒerjatrik] **ADJ** *Méd* geriatric

germain¹, -aine [ʒɛrmɛ̃, -ɛn] *Hist* **ADJ** Germanic, Teutonic
N G. German, Teuton

germain² **ADJ** *Jur* **frère g.** full brother; **sœur germaine** full sister; **cousin g.** first cousin; **cousins issus de germains** second cousins

germandrée [ʒɛrmɑ̃dre] **NF** *Bot* germander

germanique [ʒɛrmanik] **ADJ 1** *Hist (relatif aux Germains)* Germanic, Teutonic **2** *(relatif aux Allemands et à l'Allemagne)* German
NM *Ling* Germanic

germanisant, -ante [ʒɛrmanizɑ̃, -ɑ̃t] **N** Germanophile

germanisation [ʒɛrmanizajɔ̃] **NF** Germanization

germaniser [ʒɛrmanize] **VT** to Germanize

germanisme [ʒɛrmanism] **NM** Germanism

germaniste [ʒɛrmanist] **N** *Ling* Germanist, student of German

germanium [ʒɛrmanjɔm] **NM** *Chimie* germanium

germanophile [ʒɛrmanɔfil] **ADJ, N** Germanophile

germanophobe [ʒɛrmanɔfɔb] **ADJ** Germanophobic
N Germanophobe

germanophobie [ʒɛrmanɔfɔbi] **NF** Germanophobia

germanophone [ʒɛrmanɔfɔn] **ADJ** German-speaking
N German speaker

germanopratin, -ine [ʒɛrmanopratɛ̃, -in] **ADJ** of/from Saint-Germain-des-Prés
N = person from Saint-Germain-des-Prés

germe [ʒɛrm] **NM 1** *(embryon, plantule etc)*, *Biol* germ; *(de pomme de terre)* eye; **germes de soja** bean sprouts **2** *(virus)* germ; **germes pathogènes** pathogenic bacteria; *Fig* **les germes d'une révolution/de la corruption** the seeds of a revolution/of corruption; **contenir qch en g.** to contain the seeds of sth

germer [ʒɛrme] **VI** *(d'une plante)* to germinate; *(des pommes de terre)* to sprout; *Fig (d'une idée, d'un plan)* to germinate

germicide [ʒɛrmisid] **NM** germicide
ADJ germicidal

germinal, -aux, -ale, -aux, -ales [ʒɛrminal, -o] **ADJ** *Biol* germinal
NM *Hist* = the seventh month of the French Republican calendar *(March-April)*

germinateur, -trice [ʒɛrminatœr, -tris] **ADJ** germinative

germinatif, -ive [ʒɛrminatif, -iv] **ADJ** *Biol* germinative, germinal; **plasma g.** germ plasm

germination [ʒɛrminasjɔ̃] **NF** *Biol* germination

germoir [ʒɛrmwar] **NM 1** *(pour les plantes)* seed tray **2** *(d'une brasserie)* malt house, malting

gérondif [ʒerɔ̃dif] **NM** *Gram* **1** gerund VOIR GRAMMAIRE A43-4 **2** *(cas latin)* gerundive; **au g.** in the gerundive

gérontocratie [ʒerɔ̃tɔkrasi] **NF** *Pol* gerontocracy

gérontologie [ʒerɔ̃tɔlɔʒi] **NF** *Méd* gerontology

gérontologue [ʒerɔ̃tɔlɔg] **N** *Méd* gerontologist

gérontophile [ʒerɔ̃tɔfil] **N** gerontophile

gérontophilie [ʒerɔ̃tɔfili] **NF** gerontophilia

gésier [ʒezje] **NM** *Orn* gizzard; *Arg (estomac)* guts

gésir [ʒezir] **VI** *(used only in the following forms:* prp **gisant;** *pr ind* **il gît,** *n.* **gisons, vous gisez, ils gisent;** *impf* **je gisais** *etc) Litt* to lie; **il gisait dans son sang** he was lying *or* weltering in his blood; **ci-gît/-gisent ...** *(sur une tombe)* here lies/lie ...; **des papiers froissés gisaient çà et là** crumpled papers were lying here and there; *Fig* **c'est là que gît le lièvre** that's the crux of the matter

gesse [ʒɛs] **NF** *Bot* vetch, everlasting pea; **g. odorante** sweet pea

gestaltisme [gɛstaltism] **NM** *Psy* Gestalt (psychology)

gestapo [ʒɛstapo] **NF** *Hist* Gestapo; **un officier de la g.** a Gestapo officer

gestation [ʒɛstasjɔ̃] **NF** *Physiol* gestation; *Fig* **projet/livre/etc en g.** plan/book/etc in preparation

geste¹ [ʒɛst] **NM 1** *(mouvement)* gesture; **faire un g.** to make a gesture; **pas un g. ou je tire** one move and I'll shoot; **le moindre g., et toute la classe est punie!** one move out of any of you and the entire class will be punished; **d'un g., il nous a fait entrer** he waved us in, he gestured to us to go/ come in; **saluer qn d'un g.** to wave to sb; **il lui montra la porte d'un g.** he gestured him towards the door; **il me le fit comprendre d'un g.** he indicated it to me with a gesture;

d'un g., elle m'indiqua où se trouvait le coffre-fort she gestured to where the safe was; **d'un g. de la main** with a wave of the hand; **je te l'indiquerai d'un g. de la main** I'll indicate it to you; **faire un g. (de la main)** *(pour dire au revoir)* to give a wave (of one's hand), to wave; **sans faire un g.** without moving; **écarter qn d'un g.** to wave sb aside; **g. de résignation** shrug of resignation; **joindre le g. à la parole** to suit the action to the word
2 *(action)* gesture; **un beau g.** a fine *or* handsome gesture; **un g. de générosité** a generous gesture; **faire un g.** to make a gesture; **tu pourrais faire un g. pour les aider** you could do something to help them; **faire un g. pour les sans-abri** to do something for the homeless, to do something to help the homeless; **elle n'a pas fait un g. (pour l'aider)** she didn't do a thing *or* lift a finger (to help him); **avoir le g. large** to be generous

geste² **NF** *Littér* **(chanson de) g.** chanson de geste *(medieval verse chronicle of heroic exploits)*

gesticulation [ʒɛstikylasjɔ̃] **NF** gesticulation, gesticulating

gesticuler [ʒɛstikyle] **VI** to gesticulate

gestion [ʒɛstjɔ̃] **NF** *Fin (d'une entreprise, de travaux, des comptes etc)* management; *(d'affaires)* conduct; **mauvaise g.** bad management, mismanagement
► ► **g. actif-passif** assets and liabilities management; **g. administrative** administration; **g. de bases de données** database management; **g. budgétaire** budgetary control; **g. de capital** asset management; *Ordinat* **g. des césures** hyphenation control; **g. de la communication** communications management; **g. de comptes-clés** key-account management; **g. par consensus** consensus management; *Ordinat* **g. des couleurs** colour management; **g. des coûts** cost management; *Ordinat* **g. des disquettes** disk management; **g. de la distribution** distribution management; **g. de la distribution physique** physical distribution management; *Ordinat* **g. de données** data management; **g. des effectifs** manpower management; **g. d'entreprise** business management; *Ordinat* **g. de fichiers** file management; **g. financière** financial management; **g. de fonds** fund management; **g. hôtelière** hotel administration *or* management, hospitality management; **g. indicielle** indexed portfolio; **g. des investissements** investment management; *Com* **g. logistique** logistics management; **g. marketing** marketing management; **g. de marque** brand management; *Com* **g. des matières** materials management; *Ordinat* **g. de mémoire** memory management; **g. multifeuille** *(de tableur)* multi-spreadsheet handling; **g. par objectifs** management by objectives; *Ordinat* **g. du papier** paper handling; *Ordinat* **g. de parc réseau** network management; *Ind* **g. de la production** production control; **g. de produits** product management; **g. qualité** quality control, quality management; **g. de la qualité totale** total quality management, TQM; **g. de portefeuille** portfolio management; **g. des ressources humaines** human resources management; **g. des sociétés** business management; *Ordinat* **g. sonore** sound handling, sound management; **g. des stocks** inventory *or* stock control; **g. stratégique** strategic management; **g. des systèmes d'information** informations systems management

gestionnaire [ʒɛstjɔnɛr] **ADJ** administrative
N 1 administrator; *(d'un service)* manager; **g. de fonds** fund manager; **g. de portefeuille** portfolio manager **2** *Ordinat* manager, dri-

ver; **g. de fichiers** file manager; **g. de fichiers et de répertoires** filer; **g. de la souris** mouse driver; **g. de mémoire** memory manager; **g. de projets** project management package; **g. de périphérique** device manager; **g. de réseau** network manager

gestuel, -elle [ʒɛstɥɛl] ADJ gestural
NF **gestuelle** body language

Gethsémani [ʒɛtsemani] N *Bible* Gethsemane

geyser [ʒɛzɛr] NM geyser

Ghana [gana] NM Ghana

ghanéen, -éenne [ganeɛ̃, -ɛɛn] ADJ Ghanaian
N **G.** Ghanaian

ghetto [geto] NM ghetto

ghettoïsation [getoizasjɔ̃] NF ghettoization

GIA [ʒeia] NM (*abrév* **Groupes islamiques armés**) GIA

gibbeux, -euse [ʒibø, -øz] ADJ gibbous

gibbon [ʒibɔ̃] NM gibbon

gibbosité [ʒibozite] NF hump

gibecière [ʒibsjɛr] NF (*de chasseur*) game bag

gibelotte [ʒiblɔt] NF *Culin* **g. (de lapin)** fricassee of rabbit cooked in white wine

giberne [ʒibɛrn] NF *Hist* cartridge pouch; *Prov* **tout soldat a un bâton de maréchal dans sa g.** every private has the makings of a general

gibet [ʒibɛ] NM gibbet, gallows

gibier [ʒibje] NM game; **menu g.** small game; **gros g.** big game; *Fig* big game, big fish; **manger du g.** to eat game; *Fig* **beau g.** attractive women
▸▸ **g. d'eau** waterfowl; **g. à plumes** game birds; **g. à poil** game animals; *Fig* **g. de potence** gallows bird

giboulée [ʒibule] NF sudden shower *or* downpour; **giboulées de mars** ≃ April showers

giboyeux, -euse [ʒibwajø, -øz] ADJ abounding in game, well stocked with game

Gibraltar [ʒibraltar] N Gibraltar

gibus [ʒibys] NM opera hat, crush hat

giclée [ʒikle] NF (*d'eau, de sang*) spurt

giclement [ʒiklǝmɑ̃] NM (*de boue*) splashing up; (*de sang*) spurting

gicler [ʒikle] VI 1 (*du sang*) to spurt; (*de l'eau*) to spurt out, to squirt out; (*de la boue*) to splash up; **faire g. de l'eau avec un pistolet à eau** to squirt water out of a water pistol; **et ça m'a giclé à la figure** and it splashed into my face 2 *Fam* (*partir*) to be off, to push off, *Am* to split 3 *Fam* (*être mis à la porte*) to get fired, *Br* to get the sack 4 *Suisse* (*être projeté*) **g. en l'air** to be thrown into the air

gicleur [ʒiklœr] NM *Aut* jet; **g. de ralenti** idling jet

GIE [ʒeiǝ] NM (*abrév* **groupement d'intérêt économique**) economic interest group

GIF [geief] NM (*abrév* **Graphics Interchange Format**) GIF; **GIF animé** animated GIF

gifle [ʒifl] NF slap (in the face); *Fig* slap in the face; **donner** *ou Fam* **flanquer une g. à qn** to slap sb (in the face), to give sb a slap (in the face); **prendre** *ou* **recevoir une g.** to get a slap (in the face)

gifler [ʒifle] VT **g. qn** to slap sb (in the face), to give sb a slap (in the face); **visage giflé par le vent** face lashed by the wind; *Fig* **mots qui giflent** stinging words

GIG [ʒig *or* ʒeiʒe] NM *abrév* **grand invalide de guerre**

giga [ʒiga] ADJ INV *Fam* mega

gigahertz [ʒigaɛrts] NM *Phys* gigahertz

gigantesque [ʒigɑ̃tɛsk] ADJ gigantic; **d'une taille g.** gigantic, of a gigantic size

gigantesquement [ʒigɑ̃tɛskǝmɑ̃] ADV gigantically

gigantisme [ʒigɑ̃tism] NM *Méd* gi(g)antism; *Fig* **le g. des villes** the gigantic size of the cities

gigaoctet [ʒigaɔktɛ] NM *Ordinat* gigabyte

GIGN [ʒeiʒeɛn] NM (*abrév* **groupe d'intervention de la gendarmerie nationale**) = special task force of the gendarmerie

gigogne [ʒigɔɲ] ADJ **la mère G.** ≃ the old woman who lived in a shoe; **une mère G.** = the mother of a large and ever-increasing family; **tables gigognes** nest of tables; **lits gigognes** beds that fit one inside the other; **poupées gigognes** set of (Russian) dolls; *Mil* **fusées gigognes** multistage rocket

gigolette [ʒigɔlɛt] NF *Culin* leg of turkey

gigolo [ʒigɔlo] NM *Fam* gigolo

gigot [ʒigo] NM 1 *Culin* (*d'agneau, de mouton*) leg 2 (*d'un cheval*) hind leg; *Fam Hum* (*d'une personne*) leg, thigh

gigoter [ʒigɔte] VI 1 *Fam* (*se trémousser*) to wriggle, to fidget 2 (*d'un animal à l'agonie*) to give a convulsive jerk

gigue¹ [ʒig] NF (*danse*) jig

gigue² NF 1 *Culin* (*de chevreuil*) haunch 2 *Arch Fam* **gigues** (*jambes*) stumps, pins 3 *Fam* **une grande g.** (*fille grande et maigre*) a beanpole (of a girl)

gilde [gild] NF *Hist* guild

gilet [ʒilɛ] NM (*sans manches*) waistcoat, *Am* vest; (*veste en laine*) cardigan; *Fig Fam* **venir pleurer dans le g. de qn** to come crying to sb
▸▸ **g. d'armes** fencing jacket; **g. pare-balles** bulletproof jacket; **g. de sauvetage** life jacket

gin [dʒin] NM gin; **g. tonic** gin and tonic, G and T

gindre [ʒɛ̃dr] NM baker's assistant

gingembre [ʒɛ̃ʒɑ̃br] NM ginger; **racine de g.** root ginger, fresh ginger; **biscuits au g.** ginger biscuits

gingival, -ale, -aux, -ales [ʒɛ̃ʒival, -o] ADJ *Anat* gingival

gingivite [ʒɛ̃ʒivit] NF *Méd* gingivitis

ginkgo [ʒɛ̃ko] NM ginkgo, gingko

ginseng [ʒɛ̃sɑ̃, ʒinsɑ̃g] NM *Bot* ginseng

girafe [ʒiraf] NF 1 (*animal*) giraffe; *Fig* (*personne*) beanpole; *Fam* **peigner la g.** to waste one's time; (*ne rien faire*) to do damn all; *Fig* **avoir un cou de g.** to have a long neck VOIR GRAMMAIRE A12 2 *Cin Arg* (*de micro*) boom; **g. avec plate-forme d'opérateur** perambulator

girafeau, -eaux [ʒirafo], **girafon** [ʒirafɔ̃] NM baby giraffe

girandole [ʒirɑ̃dɔl] NF 1 (*chandelier*) girandole, candelabra; (*feux d'artifice*) girandole 2 (*grappe*) (*de fleurs*) cluster; (*de bijoux*) girandole

girasol [ʒirasɔl] NM *Minér* fire opal, girasol

giration [ʒirasjɔ̃] NF gyration; *Naut* **cercle de g.** turning circle

giratoire [ʒiratwar] ADJ (*mouvement*) gyratory; **sens g.** roundabout, *Am* traffic circle
NM *Suisse* (*rond-point*) roundabout, *Am* traffic circle

giravion [ʒiravjɔ̃] NM *Aviat* rotary wing aircraft, rotorcraft

girelle [ʒirɛl] NF *Zool* rainbow wrasse

girl [gœrl] NF chorus girl, showgirl

girofle [ʒirɔfl] NM *Bot* clove; **un clou de g.** a clove; **huile de g.** oil of cloves

giroflée [ʒirɔfle] NF *Bot* stock; **g. jaune** *ou* **des murailles** wallflower; *Fig Fam* **une g. (à cinq feuilles)** a slap in the face

giroflier [ʒirɔflije] NM *Bot* clove tree

girolle [ʒirɔl] NF chanterelle (mushroom)

giron [ʒirɔ̃] NM 1 (*partie du corps*) lap; **tenir un enfant dans son g.** to hold a child in *or* on one's lap; *Fig* **garder un enfant dans son g.** to wrap in cotton wool, to mollycoddle a child; **se réfugier dans le g. familial** to take refuge in the bosom of one's family; **le g. de l'Église** the bosom of the Church 2 *Constr* (*d'une marche*) tread

girond, -e [ʒirɔ̃, -ɔ̃d] ADJ *Fam* (*souvent au sujet d'une femme*) curvy; *Péj* on the plump side

girondin, -ine [ʒirɔ̃dɛ̃, -in] ADJ 1 *Hist* Girondist 2 **le vignoble g.** the vineyards of the Gironde
N **G.** (*natif*) native of the Gironde; (*habitant*) inhabitant of the Gironde
NM *Hist* Girondist

girouette [ʒirwɛt] NF weathercock, (weather)vane; *Fig* (*personne*) weathercock

gisant [ʒizɑ̃] ADJ *Litt* (*personne*) lifeless
NM *Beaux-Arts* (*sur une tombe*) recumbent figure

gisement [ʒizmɑ̃] NM 1 *Minér* deposit; *Min* lode, vein; **g. pétrolifère** oilfield; **gisements houillers** coal deposits 2 *Aviat, Naut* bearing; **g. à la boussole** compass bearing
▸▸ *Com* **g. de clientèle** pool of customers, potential customers; *Archéol* **g. préhistorique** prehistoric site

gitan, -ane [ʒitɑ̃, -an] ADJ gipsy; **la culture gitane** gipsy *or* Romany culture
N gipsy
NF **Gitane**® Gitane® (*popular brand of cigarette*)

gîte¹ [ʒit] NM 1 (*logement*) lodging, resting place; (*d'un cerf*) lair; (*d'un lièvre*) form; **ne pas avoir de g.** to be homeless; **revenir au g.** to return to one's home; **offrir le g. et le couvert à qn** to offer sb board and lodging; **trouver un lièvre au g.** to find a hare sitting 2 *Min* stratum, bed, deposit; **gîtes houillers** coal deposits
▸▸ **g. 'camping-caravaning' à la ferme** campsite in close proximity to a farm; **g. 'chambre d'hôte'** bed and breakfast; *Culin* **g. de derrière** shank; *Culin* **g. de devant** shin, *Am* shank; **g. d'enfants** holiday placements for children with a rural family; **g. équestre** rural gîte with horses for hire; **g. d'étape** = transit accommodation for hikers, cyclists etc; *Culin* **g. à la noix** silverside; **g. rural** gîte, self-catering holiday cottage/apartment; **g. rural communal** gîte communally owned by a village or group of villages

gîte² NF *Naut* list(ing); **avoir** *ou* **prendre de la g.** to list, to heel; **donner de la g. sur tribord** to list to starboard

gîter [ʒite] VI 1 *Naut* to list, to heel 2 *Vieilli* (*loger*) to lodge; (*d'un animal*) to find shelter; (*d'un oiseau*) to perch

giton [ʒitɔ̃] NM catamite

givrage [ʒivraʒ] NM *Aviat* icing

givrant [ʒivrɑ̃] ADJ *Météo* **brouillard g.** freezing fog

givre [ʒivr] NM 1 *Météo* frost, hoar frost, rime 2 (*dans un réfrigérateur, sur un pare-brise etc*) frost

givré, -e [ʒivre] ADJ 1 (*couvert de givre*) (*arbre, gazon*) covered with frost; *Aviat* iced up 2 *Culin* **orange givrée** = orange sorbet served in an orange skin; **un verre g. avec du sucre** a glass frosted with sugar 3 *Fam* (*fou*) nuts, crazy; **il est complètement g.** he's completely off his rocker

givrer [ʒivre] VT *Météo* to cover with frost
VI *Aviat* to ice up
VPR **se givrer** *Aviat* to ice up

givreux, -euse [ʒivrø, -øz] ADJ (*diamants*) with icy flecks

givrure [ʒivryr] NF (*sur un diamant*) icy fleck

glabre [glɑbr] ADJ *Biol* glabrous, smooth; **visage g.** *(rasé)* clean-shaven face; *(imberbe)* hairless face

glaçage [glasaʒ] NM **1** *Culin (d'un gâteau)* icing, *Am* frosting; *(de la pâte à tarte)* glazing **2** *Tech* glazing

glaçant [glasɑ̃] ADJ *Fig (manière, accueil)* frosty, icy; *Vieilli (froideur, vent)* icy

glace [glas] NF **1** *(eau à l'état solide)* ice; **patiner sur la g.** to skate on the ice; **cube de g.** ice cube; *Can* **sur g.** *(boisson)* on the rocks; **vous voulez de la g.?** do you want ice (in it)?; **avec g. ou sans g.?** with or without ice?; **g. pilée** crushed ice; **un pain de g.** a block of ice; **glaces de fond** bottom ice, anchor ice; **g. flottante** floating ice, drift ice; **navire retenu** *ou* **pris par les glaces** ice-bound ship; *Fig* **rester de g.** to remain impassive; *Fig* **un accueil de g.** a frosty *or* icy reception; *Fig* **rompre la g.** to break the ice **2** *(vitre)* (pane of) glass; *(miroir)* mirror; **se regarder dans la g.** to look at oneself in the mirror; *Fig* **il ne peut plus se regarder dans la g.** he can't look himself in the face; **Galerie des Glaces** *(à Versailles)* Hall of Mirrors **3** *(crème congelée)* ice cream; **une g.** an ice cream; **g. à la vanille/à la fraise** vanilla/strawberry ice cream; **g. à l'italienne** soft ice cream; **un cornet de g.** a(n ice-cream) cone *or Br* cornet; **marchand de glaces** ice-cream man *or* seller **4** *Culin (sur gâteau)* icing, *Am* frosting; *(sur pâte à tarte)* glaze **5** *(défaut) (d'un diamant)* flaw
▸▸ *Aut* **g. de custode** quarterlight, quarter-window; **g. à main** hand mirror; **g. sans tain** two-way mirror

glacé [glase] ADJ **1** *(rivière, lac)* frozen; *(pièce)* freezing (cold), icy (cold); *(avec des glaçons) (café)* iced; **l'eau est glacée** the water is icy cold *or* freezing (cold); **j'ai les pieds glacés** my feet are freezing *or* frozen, my feet are (as) cold as ice; **g. jusqu'aux os** chilled to the bone *or* marrow; *Fig* **accueil/politesse glacé(e)** frosty *or* icy reception/politeness; **regard g.** cold stare **2** *(brillant) (papier)*, *Phot (épreuve)* glossy; **gants glacés** glacé kid gloves; **soie glacée** watered silk, glazed thread; *Culin* **cerises glacées** glacé cherries

glacer [glase] *(je glaçai(s); n. glaçons)* VT **1** *(congeler)* to freeze; *(refroidir)* to chill; *Fig* **cela me glace (le sang)** it makes my blood run cold; **des hurlements/des propos à vous g. le sang** spine-chilling words *or* blood-curdling screams; **il me glace** he gives me the creeps; **g. qn d'effroi/de terreur** to paralyse *or* freeze sb with fear/terror **2** *Culin (gâteau)* to ice, *Am* to frost; *(pâte à tarte)* to glaze **3** *Tech* to glaze
VPR **se glacer** *(de l'eau)* to freeze; **son sang se glaça** his blood ran cold

glacerie [glasri] NF *(fabrique)* glass works; *(commerce)* glass trade

glaceur [glasœr] NM glazer

glaceux, -euse [glasø, -øz] ADJ *(diamant)* flawed

glaciaire [glasjɛr] ADJ *Géol (vallée)* glacial; **période g.** ice age
NM ice age

glacial, -ale, -als *ou* **-aux, -ales** [glasjal, -o] ADJ *(pl rarely used)* **1** *(température, froid, temps, air)* freezing, icy; **vent g.** icy *or* cutting *or* bitter wind; **zone glaciale** arctic region **2** *Fig (ton, manière, accueil, ambiance, politesse)* frosty, icy; *(sourire)* frosty; **elle est vraiment glaciale, cette femme** that woman is a real cold fish

glacialement [glasjalmɑ̃] ADV frostily, icily

glaciation [glasjasjɔ̃] NF glaciation

glacier¹ [glasje] NM *Géol* glacier

glacier² NM *(fabricant)* ice-cream maker; *(vendeur)* ice-cream seller; **pâtissier-g., g.-confiseur** confectioner and ice-cream seller

glacière [glasjɛr] NF **1** *(de pique-nique)* cool bag *or* box, *Austr Fam* Esky® **2** *Fam (de frigidaire)* freezer compartment, icebox; **cette chambre est une vraie g.!** this room's like an icebox! **3** *Arch (local)* ice room

glaciérisme [glasjerism] NM glacier climbing

glaciériste [glasjerist] NM glacier climber

glaciologue [glasjɔlɔg] N glaciologist

glacis [glasi] NM **1** *Mil, Géol* glacis **2** *Constr* ramp **3** *Beaux-Arts* glaze

glaçon [glasɔ̃] NM *(pendant)* icicle; *(pour rafraîchir une boisson)* ice cube; *(sur une rivière)* **glaçons** drift *or* broken ice; **vous prendrez votre whisky avec ou sans glaçons?** would you like ice in your whisky?; **avec ou sans glaçons?** with or without ice?; **un whisky avec des glaçons** a whisky on the rocks; *Fig Fam* **c'est un g.!** he's a cold fish!; **j'ai les pieds comme des glaçons** my feet are like blocks of ice

glaçure [glasyr] NF *Cér* glaze

gladiateur [gladjatœr] NM gladiator; **combat de gladiateurs** gladiatorial combat

glaïeul [glajœl] NM gladiolus, *pl* gladioli; **g. des marais** (sword) flag

glaire [glɛr] NF **1** *Vieilli (d'œuf)* white **2** *Méd* mucus, phlegm; **g. cervicale** cervical mucus

glaireux, -euse [glɛrø, -øz] ADJ glairy, glaireous

glaise [glɛz] NF **(terre) g.** clay

glaiser [gleze] VT **1** *(amender avec de la glaise) (sol)* to clay, to dress with clay **2** *(enduire de glaise)* to line with clay

glaiseux, -euse [glezø, -øz] ADJ clayey

glaisière [glezjɛr] NF clay pit

glaive [glɛv] NM *Arch, Litt* blade, sword; *Fig Litt* **le g. de la justice** the sword of justice

glamour [glamur] *Fam* ADJ *(personne, allure)* glamorous
NM glamour, *Am* glamor

glanage [glanaʒ] NM gleaning

gland [glɑ̃] NM **1** *(passementerie)* tassel **2** *Bot* acorn; **glands** *(pour les cochons)* mast **3** *Anat* glans; *Fig très Fam* **tu es un vrai g.** you're a stupid prick

glande [glɑ̃d] NF *Anat, Bot* gland; **g. surrénale** suprarenal gland; **glandes sexuelles** sexual glands; *Vulg* **foutre les glandes à qn** *(énerver)* to piss sb off; *(mettre mal à l'aise)* to put the wind up sb; *Vulg* **avoir les glandes** *(être énervé)* to be pissed off; *(être mal à l'aise)* to have the wind up

glander [glɑ̃de] VI *très Fam (ne rien faire)* to loaf around; *(attendre)* to hang around; **mais qu'est-ce qu'il glande, il devait arriver à trois heures** where the hell is he, he was supposed to be here at three; **ça fait deux ans qu'il glande** that's two years now he's been loafing around *or* doing sweet FA; **je me demande ce qu'il glande toute la journée** I wonder what the hell he gets up to all day; **j'en ai rien à g.** I don't give a shit

glandeur, -euse [glɑ̃dœr, -øz] N *très Fam* layabout; **c'est un vrai g., ce mec-là** the guy does sweet FA

glandouiller [glɑ̃duje] VI *très Fam (ne rien faire)* to loaf around; **arrête de g. et fais quelque chose d'utile** *(ne rien faire)* get off your backside and do something useful; *(ne rien faire d'utile)* stop mucking around and do something useful

glandu [glɑ̃dy] NM *très Fam* halfwit, dope

glandulaire [glɑ̃dylɛr], **glanduleux, -euse** [glɑ̃dylø, -øz] ADJ glandular; **infection glanduleuse** glandular infection

glane [glan] NF *Agr* **1** *(action)* gleaning; **glanes** gleanings **2** *(d'oignons)* string, rope

glaner [glane] VT *Agr* to glean; *Fig* **g. des renseignements** to glean information

glaneur, -euse [glanœr, -øz] N *Agr* gleaner

glaouis [glawi] NMPL *Vulg* balls, nuts, *Br* bollocks

glapir [glapir] VI *(d'un chien)* to yelp, to yap; *(d'un renard)* to bark; *(d'une personne, d'une radio, d'un saxophone)* to shriek
VT to shriek

glapissant [glapisɑ̃] ADJ *(chien)* yapping, yelping; **voix glapissante** shrill voice

glapissement [glapismɑ̃] NM *(de chiots)* yapping, yelping; *(de renards)* barking; *(de personne, tempête, vent)* shrieking; **on entendait les glapissements de la concierge dans l'escalier** the concierge could be heard shrieking on the stairs

glas [glɑ] NM knell; **sonner le g.** to toll the knell; *Fig* **sonner le g. de qch** to sound the death knell for sth

glasnost [glasnɔst] NF glasnost

glaucome [glokom] NM *Méd* glaucoma

glauque [glok] ADJ **1** *(couleur)* blue-green, *Litt* glaucous **2** *(trouble) (eau)* murky; *Fam (film, plaisanteries)* tasteless, in bad taste; **je suis partie très vite, l'ambiance était g.** I left very quickly since the atmosphere was pretty heavy; **il est un peu g., son copain** his friend's a bit creepy

glaviot [glavjo] NM *très Fam* gob of spit

glavioter [glavjɔte] VI *très Fam* to spit, *Br* to gob

glèbe [glɛb] NF **1** *Arch (motte de terre)* clod; *(terre lourde et grasse)* heavy soil **2** *Arch, Litt (sol cultivé)* glebe, soil, land

glène¹ [glɛn] NF *Anat* socket

glène² NF *Naut* coil of rope

glissade [glisad] NF sliding; *(pas de danse)* glissade; **faire une g.** *ou* **des glissades** to slide; *Aviat* **g. sur l'aile** side slip; *Aviat* **g. sur la queue** tail slide

glissage [glisaʒ] NM sliding down *(of cut timber in the mountains)*

glissant [glisɑ̃] ADJ **1** *(anguille, trottoir etc)* slippery; *Fig* **c'est un terrain g.** it's a delicate *or* tricky subject; **elle est sur un terrain g.** she is on dangerous ground **2** *Tech* **joint g.** sliding joint, slip joint

glisse [glis] NF **1** *Ski (aptitude à glisser)* glide **2** **les sports de g.** = sports involving sliding motion, e.g. skiing, surfing, windsurfing, snowboarding

glissé [glise] ADJ, NM *(de danseur)* **(pas) g.** glissé

glissement [glismɑ̃] NM *(action)* sliding; *Aviat* sideslipping; *Pol* **g. à gauche** *ou* **vers la gauche** swing to the left
▸▸ *Électron* **g. de fréquence** frequency variation; *Ling* **g. de sens** shift in meaning; *Géol* **g. de terrain** landslide; *(moins important)* landslip

glisser [glise] VI **1** *(par accident)* to slip; *(d'une roue)* to skid; **le couteau lui a glissé des mains** the knife slipped from his hands; **son pied a glissé** his foot slipped; *Fig* **g. entre les mains** *ou* **les doigts de qn** to slip through sb's fingers; *Aviat* **g. sur l'aile** to sideslip **2** *(volontairement) (sur la glace, la neige etc)* to slide; **faire g.** *(pièce d'une machine)* to slide; **se laisser g. le long d'une corde** to slide down a rope; *Ordinat* **faire g.** *(pointeur etc)* to drag; **g.-lâcher** to drag and drop **3** *(avancer comme en glissant) (sur l'eau)* to glide; *Fig* **un sourire ironique glissa sur ses lèvres** an ironic smile stole over his face **4** **g. sur** *(sujet)* to touch lightly on, to skip over; **l'épée lui glissa sur les côtes** the sword glanced off his ribs; *Fig* **mes reproches ont**

glissé sur lui comme l'eau sur les plumes d'un canard I took him to task but it was like water off a duck's back; **rien ne l'émeut, tout glisse sur lui** nothing bothers him, it's all water off a duck's back; **glissons (là-dessus)** let's not dwell on that, let's skip over that

5 *(avoir une surface glissante)* to be slippery; **fais attention, ça glisse ce matin** watch out, it's slippery this morning; **la chaussée glisse beaucoup** the road is very slippery

VT *(introduire, passer etc)* to slip; **g. une lettre sous la porte** to slip a letter under the door; **g. qch dans la poche de qn** to slip sth into sb's pocket; **essaie de g. quelques citations dans ta dissertation** try to slip a few quotations into your essay; **g. un mot à l'oreille de qn** to drop a word in sb's ear; **g. un mot à qn** to have a quick word with sb; **j'ai glissé votre nom pendant le débat** I dropped your name into the debate

VPR se glisser to slip **(dans** into); **il s'est glissé discrètement dans la salle de conférence** he slipped discreetly into the lecture theatre; **se g. dans son lit** to slip or creep into bed; **retrouvez les erreurs qui se sont glissées dans le texte** locate the errors that have crept or slipped into the text

NM *Ordinat* **g. d'icônes** icon drag

glisser-lâcher, *pl* **glissers-lâchers NM** *Ordinat* drag and drop; **g. d'icônes** icon drag and drop

glissière [glisjɛr] **NF 1** *Tech* runner, slide; *Com* shelf strip; **à g.** sliding; **fermeture à g.** zip (fastener), *Am* zipper; **porte à glissières** sliding door; **banc à glissières** *(en aviron)* sliding seat **2 g. (de sécurité)** crash barrier **3** *Ind (pour le charbon)* chute

glissoir [gliswar] **NM 1** *(d'une machine)* slide, sliding block **2** *(pour le bois)* timber slide or chute

glissoire [gliswar] **NF** slide *(on ice or snow)*

global, -ale, -aux, -ales [glɔbal, -o] **ADJ** *(somme)* total, inclusive, global; *(paiement)* lump; **une vision globale des problèmes** an overall or a global view of the problems; *Scol* **méthode globale** word recognition method

globalement [glɔbalmã] **ADV** overall, all in all; **on peut g. s'estimer gagnant** overall or all in all we've come out on top

globalisation [glɔbalizasjõ] **NF** globalization

globaliser [glɔbalize] **VT 1** *(problèmes)* to lump together; **essayez de g. vos réponses** try to give a general answer **2** *(mondialiser)* to globalize

VPR se globaliser *(phénomène, problème)* to become global

globalité [glɔbalite] **NF** **prendre un problème dans sa g.** to tackle a problem as a whole; **répondre à la g. des questions** to give an answer to cover all questions

globe [glɔb] **NM 1** *(sphère)* globe, sphere **2** *(terre)* globe; *(des insignes royaux)* orb; **la surface du g.** the surface of the globe; **une partie inhabitée du g.** an uninhibited part of the globe; **faire le tour du g.** to go round the world; **le g. du soleil** the orb of the sun **3** *(en verre) (d'une pendule)* glass dome or cover; **g. électrique** electric light globe; **statuette sous g.** statuette under glass; **c'est à conserver sous g.** it ought to be kept under glass; *Fig* **conserver qn/qch sous g.** to keep sb/sth under wraps **4** *Météo* **g. de feu** fireball, globe lightning

▸▸**g. oculaire** *ou* **de l'œil** eyeball; **g. terrestre** *(la terre)* earth; *(objet)* globe

globe-trotter, *pl* **globe-trotters** [glɔbtrɔtœr] **NM** globetrotter

globine [glɔbin] **NF** *Biol* globin

globulaire [glɔbylɛr] **ADJ** globular; *Méd* **numération g.** blood count

globule [glɔbyl] **NM** *(d'air, d'eau)* globule; *Physiol* (blood) corpuscle, blood cell; *Pharm* small pill; **globules blancs/rouges** white/red corpuscles or blood cells

globuleux, -euse [glɔbylø, -øz] **ADJ** globular; **yeux g.** protruding eyes

globuline [glɔbylin] **NF** *Biol, Chimie* globulin

glockenspiel [glɔkɛnʃpil] **NM** *Mus* glockenspiel

gloire [glwar] **NF 1** *(renom)* glory, fame; **se couvrir de g.** to cover oneself in glory; **être au sommet de la g.** to be at the height of one's fame; **elle a eu son heure de g.** she has had her hour of glory; **il est mort en pleine g.** he died at the height of his fame; **se faire** *ou* **tirer g. de qch** to glory in sth, to pride oneself on sth; **travailler pour la g.** to work for the glory (of it) or for nothing; **ce n'est pas la g.** it's not exactly brilliant

2 *(personne célèbre)* celebrity; **une g. oubliée** a forgotten celebrity; **il est la g. de notre école** he is the pride of our school

3 *(splendeur)* **la g. de Dieu** the glory of God; **la famille royale dans toute sa g.** the royal family in all its splendour

4 *(manifestation de respect)* glory, praise; **rendre g. à Dieu/qn** to glorify God/sb; **g. à Dieu!** glory (be) to God!; **g. aux soldats morts pour la France!** glory to the soldiers who died for France!; **à la g. de qn** in praise of sb

5 *Beaux-Arts (auréole)* glory, nimbus

glomérule [glɔmeryl] **NM** *Anat* glomerulus

gloria [glɔrja] **NM 1** *Rel* Gloria **2** *Fam Arch (café)* = coffee served with spirits

glorieusement [glɔrjøzmã] **ADV** gloriously

glorieux, -euse [glɔrjø, -øz] **ADJ 1** *(mémorable)* glorious; **ce n'est pas très g.** it's not exactly brilliant **2** *(illustre)* glorious; **porter un nom g.** to have an illustrious name; **il est promis à un avenir g.** he has a glorious future ahead of him; **un soldat g.** a renowned soldier **3** *Arch, Litt (fier)* proud **(de** of); *Péj* **g. de qch** vain or conceited about sth

NMPL les g. the saints in glory

glorification [glɔrifikasjõ] **NF** glorification

glorifier [glɔrifje] *(impf, pr sub* **n. glorifiions, v. glorifiiez)* **VT** to glorify, to praise

VPR se glorifier to boast; **se g. de (faire) qch** to glory in (doing) sth, to boast of (doing) sth

gloriole [glɔrjɔl] **NF pour la g.** for the kudos of it; **faire qch par g.** to do sth in order to show off; **c'est une attitude de g.** he's just showing off

glose [gloz] **NF** *(explication)* gloss; *Péj* **gloses** gossip; **g. marginale** marginal note; **dire la vérité sans g.** to speak the plain or unvarnished truth

gloser [gloze] **VT** *(expliquer) (texte)* to gloss, to expound

VI to comment **(sur** on), *Péj* to gossip **(sur** about); *Vieilli* **g. sur qch/qn** *(critiquer)* to find fault with sth/sb

glossaire [glɔsɛr] **NM 1** *(pour termes spécifiques)* glossary **2** *(d'une langue)* vocabulary

glossine [glɔsin] **NF** tsetse fly

glossolalie [glɔsɔlali] **NF** glossolalia

glottal, -ale, -aux, -ales [glɔtal, -o] **ADJ** *Ling, Anat* glottal

glotte [glɔt] **NF** *Anat* glottis; *Ling* **coup de g.** glottal stop

glouglou [gluglu] **NM 1** *(bruit d'un liquide)* glug-glug, gurgle; **faire g.** to gurgle **2** *(cri de la dinde)* gobble

glouglouter [gluglute] **VI** *(de la dinde)* to gobble

gloussement [glusmã] **NM** *(de la poule)* clucking, cluck; *(de la dinde)* gobbling, gobble; *Fam (d'une personne)* chuckling, chuckle, chortle

glousser [gluse] **VI** *(d'une poule)* to cluck; *(d'une dinde)* to gobble; *Fam (d'une personne)* to chuckle, to chortle

glouteron [glutrõ] **NM** *Bot* burdock, burr

glouton, -onne [glutõ, -ɔn] **ADJ** greedy, gluttonous

N glutton
NM *Zool* wolverine

gloutonnement [glutɔnmã] **ADV** gluttonously, greedily

gloutonnerie [glutɔnri] **NF** gluttony, greed

glu [gly] **NF** *(pour prendre les oiseaux)* bird lime; *(colle)* glue; **prendre des oiseaux à la g.** to lime birds; *Fig Fam* **c'est une vraie g., ce type!** the guy clings like a limpet or sticks like glue

gluant [glyã] **ADJ** *(collant)* sticky; *(paroi, limace)* slimy

gluau, -aux [glyo] **NM** lime twig *(for catching birds)*

glucide [glysid] **NM** *Biol, Chimie* carbohydrate; **riche en glucides** *(aliment)* high or rich in carbohydrates

glucose [glykoz] **NM** glucose; **g. sanguin** blood sugar

glucosé [glykoze] **ADJ** containing glucose; **une solution glucosée** a glucose solution

glutamate [glytamat] **NM** glutamate

gluten [glytɛn] **NM** gluten; **sans g.** gluten-free

glutineux, -euse [glytinø, -øz] **ADJ** glutinous

glycémie [glisemi] **NF** *Méd* glycaemia

glycérine [gliserin] **NF** *Chimie* glycerin(e), glycerol

glycériner [gliserine] **VT** to put glycerin(e) on

glycérol [gliserɔl] **NM** *Chimie* glycerol, glycerin(e)

glycine¹ [glisin] **NF** wisteria, wistaria

glycine² **NF** *Biol, Chimie* glycine

glycogène [glikɔʒɛn] **NM** *Chimie* glycogen

glycol [glikɔl] **NM** *Chimie* glycol

glyphe [glif] **NM** *Archéol* glyph, groove, channel

glyptique [gliptik] **NF** glyptics

GM [ʒeɛm] **NM** *(abrév* **gentil membre)** = holidaymaker (at the Club Med)

GMS [ʒeɛmɛs] **NFPL** *(abrév* **grandes et moyennes surfaces)** = large and medium-sized commercial outlets

gnangnan [ɲãɲã] *Fam* **ADJ INV** drippy; *(livre)* soppy; **elle est g.** she's a real drip

N drip

gnaule [ɲol] **NF** *Fam* rotgut

gneiss [gnɛs] **NM** *Géol* gneiss

gniac [ɲjak] **NF** *Fam* fighting spirit, drive; **avoir la g., être plein de g.** to have plenty of drive

gniole [ɲol] **NF** *Fam* rotgut

gnocchi [ɲɔki] **NMPL** *Culin* gnocchi

gnognote, gnognotte [ɲɔɲɔt] **NF** *Fam* **c'est de la g.** *(mauvaise qualité)* it's a load of rubbish; **c'est pas de la g., cette voiture** that car is quite something

gnole, gnôle [ɲol] **NF** *Fam* rotgut

gnome [gnom] **NM** gnome; *Fig Péj (homme)* dwarf, midget

gnomique [gnomik] **ADJ** gnomic

gnon [ɲõ] **NM** *Fam (coup de poing)* thump, wallop; **se prendre un g.** to get thumped or walloped; **on lui a filé un g. dans le pif** he got a thump or he got thumped on the nose

gnose [gnoz] **NF 1** *Hist, Rel* gnosticism **2** *Vieilli* gnosis

gnosticisme [gnɔstisism] **NM** *Hist, Rel* gnosticism

gnostique [gnɔstik] ADJ, N *Rel* gnostic

gnou [gnu] NM gnu, wildebeest

gnouf [nuf] NM *Mil Arg* glasshouse

GO [ʒeo] NFPL *Radio* (*abrév* **grandes ondes**) LW

NM (*abrév* **gentil organisateur**) = activity organizer (at the Club Med)

go (tout de) [tud(ə)go] ADV straight away; **répondre tout de go** to answer straight off *or* straight out

Go NM *Ordinat* (*gigaoctet*) GB

goal [gol] NM *Sport* goalkeeper, *Fam* goalie

gobelet [gɔblɛ] NM (*en argent, étain, cristal*) tumbler; (**verre**) **g.** tumbler; **g. en plastique/ carton** plastic/paper cup; **tour de g.** conjuring trick (*with tumblers*); *Vieilli Fig* trick

gobeletier [gɔblətje] NM (*fabricant*) glassware manufacturer; (*vendeur*) glassware dealer

gobe-mouches [gɔbmuʃ] NM INV **1** *Orn* flycatcher **2** *Bot* **dionée g.** Venus's fly trap, Venus flytrap **3** *Fam* (*personne*) simpleton, dope

gober [gɔbe] VT (*nourriture*) to gulp down; *Fig* **g. le morceau** *ou* **l'hameçon** to swallow *or* rise to the bait; *Fam* **g. des mouches** to stand gaping; *Fig* **il gobe tout ce qu'on lui dit** he believes everything he's told, he'll swallow anything; *Fam* **je ne peux pas la g.** I can't stand her

VPR **se gober** *Fam* to think a lot of oneself, to fancy oneself

goberger (se) [sɔgɔbɛrʒe] VPR (**je me gobergeai(s); n. n. gobergeons**) *Fam* (*prendre ses aises*) to take things easy, to look after oneself; (*faire bombance*) to live it up, to have a ball

gobeur, -euse [gɔbœr, -øz] N gulper, swallower; *Fig Fam* **c'est un g.** he's very gullible, he'll swallow anything

gobie [gɔbi] NM goby

godailler [gɔdaje] VI = **goder**

godasse [gɔdas] NF *Fam* shoe

godelureau, -eaux [gɔdlyro] NM *Péj Vieilli* popinjay

godemiché [gɔdmiʃe] NM dildo

goder [gɔde] VI (*d'un vêtement*) to pucker (up), to ruck (up); **g. aux genoux** to bag at the knees

godet [gɔdɛ] NM **1** (*récipient*) pot; **g. à couleur** saucer for mixing watercolours; **g. à huile** (*d'une machine*) waste oil cup; **g. d'une pipe** bowl of a pipe; *Fam* **viens boire un g.** come and have a jar **2** (*de noria*) scoop; (*d'un dragueur, d'un excavateur, d'une roue à eau*) bucket; *Tech* (*au pied d'une machine*) socket; *Min* skip; **roue à godets** overshot wheel **3** *Couture* (*ondulation*) flare; (*lé*) gore; **à godets** flared; (*à lés*) gored

godiche [gɔdiʃ] *Fam* ADJ (*empoté*) clumsy, hamfisted

NF **quelle g., cette fille!** what a lump (of a girl)!

godille [gɔdij] NF **1** *Naut* scull; **aller à la g.** to (single-)scull **2** *Ski* wedeln; **faire de la g.** to wedeln

godiller [gɔdije] VI **1** *Naut* to (single-)scull **2** *Ski* to wedeln

godilleur [gɔdijœr] NM *Naut* sculler

godillot [gɔdijo] NM *Mil* boot; *Fam* (*gros soulier*) clodhopper

goéland [gɔelɑ̃] NM gull; **g. argenté** herring gull

goélette [gɔelɛt] NF *Naut* (*navire*) schooner; (**voile**) **g.** trysail

goémon [gɔemɔ̃] NM wrack

goglu [gɔgly] NM *Can* (*oiseau*) bobolink

gogo [gogo] ADV *Fam* **à g.** galore; **avoir de l'argent à g.** to have money galore *or* to burn

gogo [gogo] NM *Fam* sucker, mug

goguenard [gɔgnar] ADJ mocking

goguenardise [gɔgnardiz] NF mockery

goguenot [gɔgno] *Arg* NM *Vieilli* (*pot de chambre*) po, jerry

NMPL **goguenots** bog, *Am* john

gogues [gɔg] NMPL *Arg* = **goguenots**

goguette [gɔgɛt] NF *Fam* **être en g.** to be (a bit) tight *or* merry; (*faire la noce*) to be out for a good time

goï, *pl* **goïm** [gɔj, gɔjim] NM *Rel* goy, *pl* goyim

goinfre [gwɛ̃fr] *Fam* N greedyguts, pig

ADJ greedy, piggish

goinfrerie [gwɛ̃frəri] NF gluttony, guzzling

goinfrer (se) [sɔgwɛ̃fre] VPR *Fam* to guzzle, to gorge oneself; **se g. de qch** to gorge oneself on sth, to guzzle sth

goitre [gwatr] NM *Méd* goitre, *Am* goiter

goitreux, -euse [gwatrø, -øz] *Méd* ADJ (*cou, gonflement, personne*) goitrous

N goitrous person

golden [gɔldɛn] NF INV Golden Delicious (apple)

goldo [gɔldo] NF *Fam* = Gauloise® cigarette

golem [gɔlɛm] NM (*dans le folklore juif*) golem

golf [gɔlf] NM *Sport* golf; **on fait un g. demain?** how about a game of golf tomorrow?; (**terrain de**) **g.** golf course; **g. miniature** miniature golf; **jouer au g.** to play golf; **pantalon de g.** plus fours

golfe [gɔlf] NM gulf, bay; **le G. Persique** the Persian Gulf; **les États** *ou* **les pays du G.** the Gulf States; **la guerre du G.** the Gulf War

golfer [gɔlfe] VI *Can* to play golf

golfeur, -euse [gɔlfœr, -øz] N golfer

gomina® [gɔmina] NF hair cream, brilliantine

gominer (se) [sɔgɔmine] VPR to plaster down one's hair (*with brilliantine etc*); **cheveux gominés** plastered-down hair

gommage [gɔmaʒ] NM **1** (*action d'enduire de gomme*) gumming **2** *Tech* (*des valves, des pistons*) sticking, gumming **3** (*pour effacer*) erasing, *Br* rubbing out **4** (*produit de beauté*) facial scrub; **se faire un g.** to give oneself a facial scrub; **g. pour le corps** body scrub

gommant [gɔmɑ̃] ADJ **crème gommante, soin g.** face scrub

gomme [gɔm] NF **1** (*substance*) gum; **boule de g.** gum **2** (*pour effacer*) eraser, *Br* rubber; *Fam* **histoire à la g.** pointless story; **idée/soirée à la g.** pathetic idea/party; **individu à la g.** useless individual **3** *Fam* **mettre (toute) la g.** to get a move on, to get one's skates on; *Aut* to put one's foot down

▸ ▸ **g. arabique** gum arabic; **g. à crayon** eraser, *Br* rubber; **g. à encre** ink eraser; **g. laque** shellac; **g. à mâcher** chewing gum; **g. pour machine à écrire** typewriter eraser *or Br* rubber

gomme-gutte, *pl* **gommes-guttes** [gɔmgyt] NF gamboge

gomme-laque, *pl* **gommes-laques** NF shellac, lac

gommer [gɔme] VT **1** (*enduire de gomme*) to gum **2** (*effacer*) to erase, *Br* to rub out; *Fig* **g. une partie de son passé/un souvenir pénible** to erase part of one's past/a painful memory **3 g. les cellules mortes de la peau** to remove dead skin **4** *Tech* to stick, to gum; **piston gommé** gummed piston

gomme-résine, *pl* **gommes-résines** NF gum resin

gommette [gɔmɛt] NF coloured *or Am* colored sticker

gommeux, -euse [gɔmø, -øz] ADJ gummy, sticky; **plante gommeuse** gum-yielding plant

NM *Fam Vieilli* dandy, fop, *Am* dude

gommier [gɔmje] NM gum tree

gonade [gɔnad] NF *Biol* gonad

gond [gɔ̃] NM (*de porte*) hinge; **mettre une porte dans ses gonds** to hang a door; **sortir de ses gonds** (*d'une porte*) to come off its hinges; *Fig Fam* to fly off the handle, to lose one's temper

gondolage [gɔ̃dɔlaʒ] NM (*du bois*) warping; (*du papier*) curling; (*d'une plaque de fer*) buckling

gondolant [gɔ̃dɔlɑ̃] ADJ *Fam* (*histoire*) side-splitting, hilarious

gondole [gɔ̃dɔl] NF **1** (*barque*) gondola **2** (*présentoir*) island, gondola

gondolement [gɔ̃dɔlmɑ̃] NM = **gondolage**

gondoler [gɔ̃dɔle] VI (*du bois*) to warp; (*du papier*) to curl; (*d'une plaque de fer*) to buckle

VPR **se gondoler 1** (*du bois*) to warp; (*du papier*) to curl; (*d'une plaque de fer*) to buckle; **mon disque s'est gondolé à la chaleur** my record's warped in the sun, the sun's warped my record **2** *Fam* (*rire*) to fall about laughing, to split one's sides laughing

gondolier, -ière [gɔ̃dɔlje, -jɛr] N gondolier

gonfalon [gɔ̃falɔ̃], **gonfanon** [gɔ̃fanɔ̃] NM *Hist* gonfalon, gonfanon

gonflable [gɔ̃flabl] ADJ inflatable

gonflage [gɔ̃flaʒ] NM **1** inflation; **vérifier le g. (des pneus)** to check the tyre *or Am* tire pressure **2** *Cin* blow-up printing

gonflant [gɔ̃flɑ̃] ADJ **1** (*coiffure*) bouffant **2** *très Fam* (*énervant*) maddening, irritating

NM (*d'une coiffure*) bouffant; **mousse qui donne du g. à vos cheveux** mousse which gives body to your hair

gonfle [gɔ̃fl] *Suisse* NF (*congère*) snowdrift

ADJ (*enflé, gonflé*) swollen, puffy; (*ballonné*) bloated

gonflé [gɔ̃fle] ADJ **1** (*boursouflé*) (*yeux*) swollen, puffy; (*visage*) bloated, swollen, puffy; (*estomac*) bloated, swollen; (*pieds, chevilles*) swollen; *Fig* **g. d'orgueil** puffed up with pride; **avoir le cœur g. de chagrin** to be heart-broken; **elle avait les yeux gonflés de larmes** her eyes were swollen with tears **2** *Naut* (*voile*) full **3** *Fam* **tu es g.** (*culotté*) you've got a nerve; **c'est g. ce qu'il a fait là** what he did took some nerve; **g. à bloc** keyed up; (*en pleine forme physique*) full of beans; (*sûr de soi*) sure of oneself; *Aut Fam* **moteur g.** hotted-up *or* souped-up engine **4** (*exagéré*) **prix gonflés** excessive prices

gonflement [gɔ̃fləmɑ̃] NM **1** (*des pneus, d'un ballon*) inflating, inflation; (*de l'estomac*) swelling **2** (*exagération*) (*de prix*) excessive increase; (*de résultats, statistiques*) exaggeration

gonfler [gɔ̃fle] VT **1** (*pneu*) to blow up, to pump up, to inflate; (*ses joues*) to puff out, to blow out; **g. un ballon/un matelas pneumatique** to inflate *or* blow up a balloon/an airbed; **le vent gonfle les voiles** the wind fills the sails; **les bons résultats de son fils la gonflent d'orgueil** her son's good results make her as proud as a peacock; **cette bonne nouvelle gonfla son cœur de joie** the good news filled his heart with joy

2 (*faire augmenter de volume*) to swell; **torrent gonflé par les pluies** torrent swollen by the rains

3 *Fig* (*grossir*) (*résultats, conséquences*) to exaggerate; **g. les chiffres d'un sondage** to inflate *or* exaggerate the figures from a poll; **g. l'importance de qch/qn** to exaggerate *or* overstress the importance of sth/sb; **le prof a gonflé les notes** the teacher bumped up the marks; **g. un événement** to hype an event

4 *Cin* to blow up, to enlarge

5 *Aut Fam (un moteur)* to hot up, to soup up

6 *très Fam (énerver)* **g. qn** to get on sb's nerves, to irritate sb; **il nous les gonfle avec ses matchs de foot** he really gets on our nerves *or* he's a real pain in the neck with his football matches

VI to swell; **le bois a gonflé** the wood has swollen; **laisser g. les haricots toute une nuit** to leave the beans to soak all night; **laisser de la pâte g.** to let dough rise

VPR se gonfler to swell; **les poumons se gonflent** the lungs fill; *Fig* **se g. d'orgueil** to swell up with pride; **se g. de colère** to be bursting with rage; **mon cœur s'est gonflé de joie à cette nouvelle** my heart filled with joy at the news

gonflette [gɔ̃flɛt] **NF** *Fam Péj* pumping iron; **faire de la g.** to pump iron

gonfleur [gɔ̃flœr] **NM** (air) pump

gong [gɔ̃(g)] **NM 1** *Mus* gong **2** *Boxe* bell; *Fig* **sauvé par le g.** saved by the bell

goniomètre [gɔnjɔmɛtr] **NM** *Radio* goniometer, position finder, direction finder; *Mil* dial sight

goniométrie [gɔnjɔmetri] **NF** goniometry, position finding, direction finding

gonococcie [gɔnɔkɔksi] **NF** *Méd* gonorrhoea, *Am* gonorrhea

gonocoque [gɔnɔkɔk] **NM** *Méd* gonococcus

gonze [gɔ̃z] **NM** *Arg Vieilli (homme)* fellow, *Br* chap

gonzesse [gɔ̃zɛs] **NF** *très Fam (femme)* chick, *Br* bird, *Am* broad

gordien [gɔrdjɛ̃] **ADJ M** *Fig* **trancher le nœud g.** to cut the Gordian knot

gore [gɔr] *Fam* **ADJ INV** *(sanglant)* gory **NM** *(genre)* gore (cinema); *(film)* gore film

goret [gɔrɛ] **NM** piglet; *Fam (enfant malpropre)* little pig; **manger comme un g.** to eat like a pig

goretex® [gɔrtɛks] **NM** *Tex* Gore-Tex

gorge [gɔrʒ] **NF 1** *(gosier, cou)* throat; **avoir mal à la g., avoir un mal de g.** to have a sore throat; **un serrement de g.** a lump in one's throat; **avoir la g. serrée** to have a lump in one's throat; **parler avec la g. serrée par la peine/l'angoisse** to speak in a voice trembling with sorrow/anguish; **crier à pleine g. ou à g. déployée** to shout at the top of one's voice; **rire à pleine g. ou à g. déployée** to roar with laughter; *Fig* **faire des gorges chaudes de qch** to laugh sth to scorn; **trancher la g. à qn** to cut sb's throat; *Fig* **s'il s'en rend compte, il va me trancher la g.** if he finds out, he'll kill me; **le chien lui a sauté à la g.** the dog leapt at his throat; **ce n'est pas une raison pour me sauter à la g.** that's no reason to jump down my throat; *Fig* **avoir le couteau sous la g.** to have a gun at one's head; *Fig* **je le tiens à la g.** I've got him by the throat, I've got a stranglehold on him; *Fig* **prendre qn à la g.** to get sb in a stranglehold; **nous étions pris à la g., nous ne pouvions rien faire d'autre** we were in a stranglehold *or* we had a gun at our heads, we couldn't do anything else; **pris à la g. par ses créanciers, il …** with his creditors holding a gun to his head, he …; **faire rentrer à qn ses mots dans la g.** to make sb eat his/her words; *Fig* **cela m'est resté en travers de la g.** that stuck in my throat *or* gullet; *Fig* **rendre g.** to make restitution; **je lui ferai rendre g.** I'll make him pay it back

2 *(poitrine) (d'une femme)* bosom, breast; *(d'un pigeon)* breast

3 *Géog* gorge

4 *Tech* groove; *Archit* quirk, gorge; *(d'un écrou)* furrow; *(d'un pistolet, d'un étui à car-*

touches) neck; *(d'un verrou)* tumbler; *Archit* **moulure à g.** grooved moulding

gorgé [gɔrʒe] **ADJ** **une éponge gorgée d'eau** a sponge full of water; **sol g. d'eau** sodden soil; **champs gorgés d'eau** waterlogged fields; **des fruits gorgés de soleil** sun-kissed fruit; **g. de sang** gorged with blood

gorge-de-pigeon **ADJ INV** dove-coloured, *Am* dove-colored

gorgée [gɔrʒe] **NF** *(de vin)* mouthful; **petite g.** sip; **boire qch à petites gorgées** to sip sth; **avaler qch/finir son verre d'une g.** to swallow sth/finish one's glass in one (gulp)

gorgeon [gɔrʒɔ̃] **NM** *Fam* drink

gorger [gɔrʒe] (je gorgeai(s), n. gorgeons) **VT** *(oies)* to cram

VPR se gorger to stuff oneself (**de** with), to gorge oneself (**de** on, with); **la terre se gorgea d'eau** the ground became waterlogged; *Fig* **elle semblait se g. de sa présence** it seemed as if she couldn't see enough of him

Gorgone [gɔrgɔn] **NF** *Myth* Gorgon

gorgonzola [gɔrgɔ̃zɔla] **NM** Gorgonzola (cheese)

gorille [gɔrij] **NM 1** *(mammifère)* gorilla **2** *Fig Fam* gorilla, bodyguard

gosier [gozje] **NM** *(pharynx)* throat, gullet; **avoir une arête dans le g.** to have a fishbone stuck in one's throat; *Fam* **avoir le g. sec** to be dry *or* thirsty; **rire à plein g.** to laugh loudly *or* heartily; *Fam* **avoir le g. en pente** to have a permanent thirst, to like one's drink

gospel [gɔspɛl] **NM** gospel (music)

gosse [gɔs] **N 1** *Fam (enfant)* kid; **c'est encore une g.** she's just a kid; **elle est venue avec ses deux gosses** she came along with her two kids **2** *Fam (jeune)* **c'est une belle g.** she's a smashing girl; **il est plutôt beau g.** he's quite good-looking **3** *Can Arg* **gosses** balls ▸▸ **g. de riches** spoilt rich kid

gosser [gɔse] **VT** *Can Fam* to whittle

Goth [gɔt] **N** *Hist* Goth

gotha [gɔta] **NM** **le g. du show-business/de la finance** the show-business/financial elite; **le G. (almanach)** ≃ Burke's Peerage

gothique [gɔtik] **ADJ** Gothic
NM *Archit, Ling* Gothic
NF *Typ* Gothic, *Br* black letter; **écrire en g.** to write in Gothic script

gotique [gɔtik] **NM** *Ling* Gothic

gouache [gwaʃ] **NF** *Beaux-Arts* gouache; **peindre à la g.** to paint in gouache

gouailler [gwaje] **VI** *Vieilli* to joke

gouailleur, -euse [gwajœr, -øz] *Vieilli* **ADJ** *(ton)* joking, mocking, bantering
N joker

goualante [gwalɑ̃t] **NF** *Fam Vieilli* popular song

gouape [gwap] **NF** *Arg* lout

gouda [guda] **NM** *Culin* Gouda

goudron [gudrɔ̃] **NM** tar; **g. (de gaz** *ou* **de houille)** coal tar; **g. de bois** wood tar; **g. minéral** asphalt, bitumen

goudronnage [gudrɔnaʒ] **NM** tarring

goudronner [gudrɔne] **VT** to tar; **route goudronnée** tarred road; **toile goudronnée** tarpaulin; **papier goudronné** tar-lined paper

goudronneur [gudrɔnœr] **NM** tar sprayer *or* spreader

goudronneuse[1] [gudrɔnøz] **NF** *(machine)* tar sprayer; *(pour l'asphalte)* asphalt spreader

goudronneux, -euse[2] [gudrɔnø, -øz] **ADJ** tarry; *(huile)* gummy

gouffre [gufr] **NM** gulf, abyss, chasm; *(tourbillon)* whirlpool, vortex; *Géol* sinkhole, *Br* swallow hole; **g. béant** yawning gulf *or* chasm; **g. sous-marin** oceanic abyss; *Fig Litt*

le g. de l'oubli/du désespoir the depths of oblivion/despair; *Fig* **être au bord du g.** to be on the edge of the abyss; *Fig* **c'est un g. d'ignorance** the depths of his ignorance are unfathomable; *Fig* **cette voiture est un g.** this car just swallows up money, with this car it's like pouring money into a bottomless pit; *Mktg* **g. financier** *(produit)* financial disaster, dog

gouge [guʒ] **NF** *Tech* gouge, hollow chisel

gougère [guʒɛr] **NF** *Culin* gougère *(choux pastry with cheese)*

gougnafier [guɲafje] **NM** *Fam* nerd

gouille [guj] **NF** *Suisse (flaque d'eau)* puddle; *(étang, mare)* pond

gouine [gwin] **NF** *Arg (lesbienne)* dyke, les

goujat [guʒa] **NM** boor, churl

goujaterie [guʒatri] **NF** boorishness, churlishness

goujon[1] [guʒɔ̃] **NM** gudgeon; *Fam* **taquiner le g.** to do a bit of fishing

goujon[2] **NM** *Constr (en maçonnerie)* gudgeon; *Menuis* tenon; *Tech* bolt, stud; *Menuis* **g. perdu, g. prisonnier** dowel (pin); *Tech* **g. de jonction** assembling pin, bolt; **g. de charnière** hinge pin; **g. d'arbre** shaft gudgeon

goujonner [guʒɔne] **VT** *Menuis* to dowel; *Constr* to joggle; *Tech* to pin, to bolt

goulache, goulasch [gulaʃ] **NF OU NM** *Culin* goulash

goulafre [gulafr] *Belg* **ADJ** *(glouton)* greedy
N *(glouton)* greedy person

goulag [gulag] **NM** Gulag

goulée [gule] **NF** *Fam* big mouthful, gulp; **j'ai besoin d'une bonne g. d'air pur** I need a good lungful of fresh air; **il tira sur son havane, et aspira une grosse g.** he drew deeply on his cigar

goulet [gulɛ] **NM 1** *Géog (défilé)* gully; **g. d'étranglement** bottleneck **2** *Naut (chenal) (d'un port)* gut, bottleneck, narrows; **le G. de Brest** the Brest Channel

gouleyant [gulɛjɑ̃] **ADJ** *(vin)* pleasant, easy-drinking

goulot [gulo] **NM** *(d'une bouteille)* neck; **boire au g.** to drink (straight) from the bottle; *Fig* **g. d'étranglement** bottleneck; *Fig Vulg* **refouler du g.** to have foul breath

goulotte [gulɔt] **NF** *Tech* chute; *(d'un wagonnet à charbon)* spout

goulu, -ue [guly] **ADJ 1** *(glouton)* greedy, gluttonous; *(regards)* hungry, greedy **2 pois g.** sugar pea
N *(personne)* glutton

goulûment [gulymɑ̃] **ADV** greedily, voraciously; *(regarder)* hungrily, greedily

goupil [gupi] **NM** *Arch* fox

goupille [gupij] **NF** *Tech* pin; **g. fendue** split pin, cotter; **g. d'arrêt** stop bolt

goupiller [gupije] **VT 1** *Tech* to pin; *(boulon)* to cotter **2** *Fam (arranger)* to fix (up); **bien/mal goupillé** well/badly organized; **je me demande ce qu'il est en train de g.** I wonder what he's up to
VPR se goupiller *Fam (d'une montre, un mécanisme)* to work; *Fig* **ça s'est bien goupillé** it worked out well; **ça s'est mal goupillé** it didn't work out

goupillon [gupijɔ̃] **NM 1** *Rel (pour eau bénite)* sprinkler, aspergillum **2** *(pour biberons, bouteilles)* bottle brush

gourance [gurɑ̃s] **NF** *Fam* boob, bloomer, *Am* goof; **faire une g.** to (make a) boob, to make a bloomer, *Am* to goof

gourbi [gurbi] **NM 1** *(cabane)* hut, shack **2** *Fam (taudis)* hovel

gourd [gur] **ADJ** numb (with cold); **avoir les doigts gourds** to have numb fingers

gourde[1] [gurd] **NF 1** *Bot* gourd **2** *(récipient)* *pour boissons)* flask; *(coloquinte)* gourd **3** *Fam (personne stupide)* dope, dimwit

ADJ *Fam* dopey, dimwitted

gourde² NF *Fin (monnaie de Haïti)* gourde

gourdin [gurdɛ̃] NM club, cudgel, bludgeon

gourer (se) [səgure] VPR *Fam* to boob, to make a boob *or* bloomer, *Am* to goof; **se g. de route** to lose one's way; **se g. d'adresse** to get the wrong address

gourgandine [gurgɑ̃din] NF *Vieilli* loose woman

gourgane [gurgan] NF *Can* broad bean

gourmand, -ande [gurmɑ̃, -ɑ̃d] ADJ *(personne)* greedy; **être g. de** *(sucreries)* to be fond of; *Fig* to be greedy for; **ma voiture est vraiment gourmande en essence** my car really gobbles up the *Br* petrol *or Am* gas; **cet appareil est très g. d'électricité** this appliance gobbles up *or* consumes a lot of electricity; **pois g.** sugar pea, mangetout, *Am* snowpea

N *(personne)* gourmand

NM *(branche parasite)* sucker

gourmander [gurmɑ̃de] VT *Litt* to rebuke, to chide

gourmandise [gurmɑ̃diz] NF **1** greediness; **avec g.** greedily **2 gourmandises** delicacies, *Fam* goodies

gourme [gurm] NF **1** *Méd Vieilli* impetigo **2** *Vét* strangles **3** *Fig Vieilli* **jeter sa g.** to sow one's wild oats

gourmé [gurme] ADJ *Litt Péj* stiff, starchy, affected

gourmet [gurmɛ] NM gourmet; *Fig (connaisseur)* connoisseur; **un fin g.** a discerning gourmet

gourmette [gurmɛt] NF **1** *(d'une montre)* chain; *(bracelet)* chain (bracelet) **2** *(pour les chevaux)* curb (chain)

gourou [guru] NM *Rel, Fig* guru

gousse [gus] NF *(de légumineuses)* pod; **g. d'ail** clove of garlic; **g. de vanille** vanilla pod

gousset [gusɛ] NM **1** *(poche)* fob (pocket); **il a le g. bien garni** his pockets are well lined; **montre de g.** fob watch **2** *Tech* (shoulder) bracket, stay plate, gusset (plate)

GOÛT [gu]

taste **1–5**	▪ flavour **2**	▪ liking **4**
▪ style **6**		

NM **1** *(sens)* taste; *Fam* **faire passer le g. du pain à qn** *(le tuer)* to do away with sb; *(ôter l'envie de recommencer)* to put a stop to sb's little games

2 *(saveur)* taste, flavour, *Am* flavor; *(du vin)* bouquet; **g. amer/épicé** bitter/spicy taste; **avoir un g. de terroir** *(de pain)* to have a taste of the country; *(d'un accent)* to have a rural twang; **cela a le g. de la banane/du gin** it tastes like banana/gin; **donner du g. à un mets** to give a dish flavour; **manquer de g., ne pas avoir de g.** *(d'un plat)* to be tasteless, to have no taste; **sans g.** *(adjectif)* tasteless; *(adverbe)* tastelessly

3 *(préférence)*, *Culin* **ajouter du sucre et du citron selon son g.** add sugar and lemon to taste; **chacun ses goûts, des goûts et des couleurs on ne discute pas, tous les goûts sont dans la nature** everyone to his (own) taste, there's no accounting for taste; **affaire de g.** matter of taste

4 *(prédilection, convenance)* taste, liking; **avoir des goûts de luxe** to have expensive tastes; **il a des goûts bizarres** he has strange tastes; **une maison/un homme à mon g.** a house/a man to my taste *or* liking; **elle n'est pas à mon g.** I don't care for her, she's not to my taste *or* liking; **trouver qch/qn à son g.** to find sth/sb to one's taste *or* liking; **le g. des affaires** a taste *or* liking for business; **g. pas-**

sager passing fancy; **avoir du g. pour** *ou* **le g. de qch** to have a taste *or* liking for sth; **faire qch par g.** to do sth from inclination, to do sth because one likes to; **je n'habite pas ici par g.** I don't live here from choice; **je le fais par g. du travail bien fait** I do it because I like to see work well done; **prendre g. à qch** to acquire a taste *or* develop a liking for sth; **avec le temps elle y a pris g.** it grew on her, she developed a liking for it; **elle n'a plus (de) g. à rien** she no longer wants to do anything; **reprendre g. à la lecture/à la musique** to regain one's taste for reading/music; **reprendre g. à la vie** to regain one's zest for living, to find life worth living again

5 *(discernement, jugement)* taste; **g. parfait** perfect taste; **il a du g.** he has (good) taste; **une femme de g.** a woman of taste; **remarque d'un g. douteux** remark in doubtful taste; **une plaisanterie/image de mauvais g.** a joke/picture in bad taste; **une robe de mauvais g.** a tasteless dress; **décoration de bon g.** tasteful decoration; **elle s'habille avec g.** she has (a) good dress sense, she has good taste in clothes

6 *Litt (style)* style, manner; **peint dans le g. de Watteau** painted in the style *or* manner of Watteau; **quelque chose dans ce g.-là** something like that, something of that sort

---

goûter [gute] NM snack; *(à quatre heures)* (afternoon) tea; **l'heure du g.** teatime; **elle est invitée pour le g.** *ou* **à un g.** she has been invited to tea

VT **1** *(savourer)* *(nourriture)* to taste; *(pour la première fois)* *(nourriture, boisson)* to taste, to try **2** *Fig (aimer, apprécier)* *(la musique, la beauté de la nature etc)* to enjoy, to appreciate; **g. le silence de la nuit** to savour *or* relish the silence of night **3** *Belg, Can (avoir un goût de)* to taste; **ce fruit goûte le pourri** this fruit tastes rotten

VI **1 g. à quatre heures** to have tea *or* a snack at four o'clock **2 g. de qch** to taste sth; *Fig* **elle a goûté de tous les petits boulots** she's had a go at all sorts of jobs; **g. à qch** to taste sth, to try sth **3** *Belg (avoir bon goût)* to taste nice

goûteur, -euse [gutœr, -øz] N taster

goutte [gut] NF **1** *(d'un liquide)* drop; **g. à g.** drop by drop; **tomber g. à g.** *(d'un liquide)* to drip; *Fig* **c'est la g. d'eau qui fait déborder le vase** it's the last straw, it's the straw that breaks/broke the camel's back; **se ressembler comme deux gouttes d'eau** to be as alike as two peas in a pod; *Fig* **c'est une g. d'eau dans la mer** it's a drop in the ocean; **il suait à grosses gouttes** the sweat was pouring off him; **il n'y a pas eu une g. de pluie depuis trois mois** there hasn't been a drop of rain for three months; **il tombait quelques gouttes** it was spitting with rain; *Fam* **avoir la g. au nez** to have a runny *or* dripping nose; **g. d'eau** drop of water; *(bijou)* drop

2 *(petite quantité)* drop; **g. de cognac** *(dans une sauce)* dash *or* drop of brandy; **boire une g. de cognac après le repas** to have a drop *or* nip of brandy after one's meal; **encore une g. de café?** a drop more coffee?; *Fam* **boire la g.** to have a nip

3 *Pharm* **gouttes** drops; **prendre des gouttes** to take drops; **gouttes pour le nez** nose *or* nasal drops; **gouttes auriculaires** ear drops

4 *Méd* gout; **avoir la g.** to suffer from *or* have gout, to be gouty

ADV *Arch, Hum* **je n'entends g. à ce que vous dites** I don't understand a word of what you're saying; *Litt* **je n'y vois g.** I can't see a thing

goutte-à-goutte NM INV *Méd* drip; **g. intraveineux** intravenous drip; **on lui fait un g.** he's on a drip; **on a dû lui faire** *ou* **mettre un g.** he had to be put on a drip

gouttelette [gutlɛt] NF droplet, tiny drop

---

goutter [gute] VI to drip

goutteux, -euse [gutø, -øz] *Méd* ADJ *(personne)* gouty

N gout sufferer

gouttière [gutjɛr] NF **1** *(le long du toit)* gutter, guttering **2** *(le long du mur)* drainpipe, downpipe, *Am* downspout **3** *Anat (d'un os)* groove **4** *Méd* cradle, (cradle-like) splint **5** *Typ (de page)* gutter

gouvernable [guvɛrnabl] ADJ *(bateau, entreprise, équipe)* manageable; *(pays)* governable; **peu g.** *(entreprise, équipe)* unmanageable; *(pays)* ungovernable

gouvernail [guvɛrnaj] NM *Naut* rudder; **roue du g.** (steering) wheel; **tenir le g.** to be at the wheel *or* at the helm, to steer; *Fig* **tenir le g. de l'État/d'une affaire** to be at the helm of the state/of a business

  ▸▸ *Aviat* **g. de direction** rudder; *Naut* **g. de plongée** *(d'un sous-marin)* horizontal rudder; **g. de profondeur** *Naut* diving rudder, plane, hydroplane; *Aviat* elevator

gouvernance [guvɛrnɑ̃s] NF **1** *(action de gouverner)* government **2** *(manière de gérer)* governance, government; **g. mondiale** global governance

gouvernant, -ante¹ [guvɛrnɑ̃, -ɑ̃t] ADJ *(classe, parti)* governing, ruling

NMPL **les gouvernants** those in power

gouvernante² [guvɛrnɑ̃t] NF *(qui garde les enfants)* governess; *(qui s'occupe d'une personne, d'un hôtel)* housekeeper; **g. d'étage** *(d'un hôtel)* floor housekeeper; **g. du soir** *(d'un hôtel)* turndown housekeeper; **g. générale** *(d'un hôtel)* executive *or* head housekeeper

gouverne [guvɛrn] NF **1** *Naut* steering; *Fig* **pour votre g.** for your guidance **2** *Aviat* **gouvernes** control surfaces; **g. compensée** balanced surface; **g. de direction** rudder; **g. de profondeur** elevator

gouvernement [guvɛrnəmɑ̃] NM *Pol* government; **le g. français/britannique** the French/British government; **sous le g. Jospin** during Jospin's term of office, during Jospin's administration; **le chef du g.** the head of (the) government; **former un nouveau g.** to form a new government; **g. républicain/parlementaire** republican/parliamentary government; **g. central** central government; **g. de coalition** coalition government; **g. de cohabitation** = government in which the President and the parliamentary majority are from different parties; **g. fantoche** puppet government; **g. fédéral** federal government; **g. majoritaire** majority government; **g. minoritaire** minority government; **g. provisoire** provisional government; **g. représentatif** representative government; **g. de transition** interim government VOIR GRAMMAIRE A11

gouvernemental, -ale, -aux, -ales [guvɛrnəmɑ̃tal, -o] ADJ governmental; **politique gouvernementale** government(al) policy; **le parti g.** the governing *or* ruling party, the party in government; **un journal g.** a government newspaper

gouverner [guvɛrne] VT **1** *(diriger)* *(un pays)* to govern, to rule; *(dominer)* to control; **Dieu gouverne l'univers** God is the ruler of the universe; **g. ses passions/sa colère/sa jalousie** to control *or* govern one's passions/anger/jealousy; *Tech* **mouvement gouverné par un pendule** movement regulated *or* governed *or* controlled by a pendulum

2 *Naut (bateau)* to steer; **faire g.** to con; **g. sur un port** to steer *or* stand *or* head for a port, to bear in with a port; **g. à la lame** to steer by the sea; **gouvernez droit!** steady!

3 *Gram* **verbe qui gouverne l'accusatif** verb that governs *or* takes the accusative

4 *Vieilli* to manage, to administer; **bien g.**

ses ressources to husband one's resources **vi1** *Pol* to govern; **un parti qui gouverne depuis des années** a party which has governed or has been in government for years **2** *Naut* navire qui ne gouverne plus ship that no longer answers to her helm; **bateau qui gouverne bien** boat that steers well

vpr se gouverner 1 *Pol* to govern oneself, to be self-governing; **droit des peuples à se g. eux-mêmes** right of peoples to self-government **2** *(se maîtriser)* to control oneself

gouverneur [guvɛʀnœʀ] nm *(d'une province, d'une banque etc, d'un État des États-Unis)* governor; *Mil (d'une position fortifiée)* commanding officer; *Can* **G. Général** Governor General; *Can* **Lieutenant-G.** Lieutenant-Governor

goy, *pl* **goyim** [gɔj, gɔjim] nm *Rel* = **goï**

goyave [gɔjav] nf guava

goyavier [gɔjavje] nm *Bot* guava (tree)

GPAO [ʒepeao] nf *Ordinat (abrév* **gestion de production assistée par ordinateur)** computer-aided production management

GPL [ʒepeɛl] nm *(abrév* **gaz de pétrole liquéfié)** LPG

GPO [ʒepeo] nf *(abrév* **gestion par objectifs)** MBO

GPS [ʒepeɛs] nm *Tél (abrév* **global positioning system)** GPS

GQG [ʒekyʒe] nm *Mil (abrév* **grand quartier général)** GHQ

GR [ʒeɛʀ] nm *(abrév* **sentier de) grande randonnée)** official hiking trail, long-distance footpath

Graal (le) [lagʀal] nm *Littér* the (Holy) Grail; **la quête du G.** the quest for the (Holy) Grail

grabat [gʀaba] nm *(de paille, de chiffons)* pallet

grabataire [gʀabatɛʀ] adj bedridden ◾ n bedridden invalid

grabuge [gʀabyʒ] nm *Fam* rumpus; **il y aura du g.** there'll be a rumpus or *Br* ructions; **ça va faire du g. s'il l'apprend!** there's going to be a stink if he finds out!

Grâce [gʀas] nf *Myth* **les trois Grâces** the three Graces

grâce [gʀas] nf **1** *(charme)* grace, gracefulness, charm; **avoir de la g.** to be graceful; **avec g.** gracefully; **se déplacer avec g.** to move gracefully; **il fait des grâces devant le miroir** he's preening himself in front of the mirror **2** *(bienveillance, faveur)* favour, *Am* favor; **obtenir/accorder une g.** to obtain/to grant a favour; **faire une g. à qn** to do sb a favour or a kindness; **faites-moi la g. d'oublier cette histoire** do me the favour or kindness of forgetting this matter; **c'est trop de grâces que vous me faites!** you really are too kind!; **demander une g. à qn** to ask a favour of sb; **trouver g. devant qn** ou **auprès de qn** ou **aux yeux de qn** to find favour in sb's eyes; **se mettre dans** ou **entrer dans** ou **obtenir les bonnes grâces de qn** to obtain the good graces of sb, *Fam* to get into sb's good books; **de g.!** for pity's sake!; **les grâces de Dieu** God's blessings; *Com* **jours** ou **terme de g.** days of grace; *Rel* **en état de g.** in a state of grace; *Fig* **le président a joui d'une période d'état de g. après son élection** the president could do no wrong after he was elected, the president enjoyed a honeymoon with the voters after he was elected; *Fig* **être en g. auprès de qn** to be in sb's good books; **l'an de g. 1802** the year of grace 1802; **coup de g.** coup de grâce; **donner le coup de g. à un animal** to put an animal out of its misery or pain **3** *(volonté)* **de bonne g.** willingly, readily; **de mauvaise g.** unwillingly, grudgingly; **il aurait mauvaise g. à nous laisser ici** *(après ce que nous avons fait pour lui)* it would be ungracious of him to leave us here

4 g. à qn/qch *(avec l'aide de)* thanks to sb/sth; **g. à votre aide** thanks to your help; **g. à Dieu** with God's help, by God's grace **5** *(remerciements)* **rendre g. à Dieu** to give thanks to God; **(rendons) g. à Dieu!** thanks be to God!; **action de grâce(s)** thanksgiving; *Can* **Jour de l'action de g.** Thanksgiving Day **6** *Jur* pardon; **lettre(s) de g.** reprieve; **demander** ou **crier g.** to beg or plead for mercy; **g.!** mercy!; **droit de g.** right of reprieve; **accorder sa g. à qn** to pardon sb; **je vous fais g. cette fois-ci** I'll let you off this time; **je vous fais g. du reste** I'll spare you the rest; *(ne m'en dites ou n'en faites pas plus)* you needn't do or say any more; **je vous fais g. des détails** I'll spare you the details; **je vous fais g. des 50 euros qui manquaient** I'll let you off or overlook the missing fifty euros **7** *(titre honorifique)* **sa G. le duc** His Grace the Duke
▸▸**g. présidentielle** presidential pardon

gracier [gʀasje] vt *(impf, pr sub* **n. graciions, v. graciiez)** to reprieve

gracieusement [gʀasjøzmã] adv **1** *(avec grâce)* gracefully; **se déplacer g.** to move gracefully **2** *(aimablement)* graciously, kindly **3** *(gratuitement)* free of charge, gratis; **la maison est heureuse de vous remettre g. ce stylo** the company is pleased to offer you this pen with its compliments

gracieuseté [gʀasjøzte] nf graciousness, kindness; **faire une g. à qn** to do sb a kindness or a favour

gracieux, -euse [gʀasjø, -øz] adj **1** *(qui a de la grâce, du charme) (figure, style etc)* graceful **2** *(aimable)* charming **3** *(gratuit)* free (of charge); **à titre g.** gratis, free of charge; **exemplaire envoyé à titre g.** complimentary or presentation copy **4** *(pour exprimer le respect)* **notre g. souverain** our gracious Sovereign

gracile [gʀasil] adj *(tige, cou)* slender; *(personne)* slim, slender

gracilité [gʀasilite] nf slenderness, slimness

Gracques (les) [legʀak] nmpl *Antiq* the Gracchi

gradation [gʀadasjõ] nf gradation

grade [gʀad] nm **1** *Mil, Admin* rank; **avoir le g. de caporal/sergent** to have the rank of corporal/sergeant; **monter en g.** to be promoted; **ça va le faire monter en g.** that will get him promoted; *Fam* **en prendre pour son g.** to be hauled over the coals, to be given a ticking off **2** *Univ* **g. universitaire** (university) degree **3** *Math* grade **4** *Tech (de l'huile de voiture)* grade

gradé [gʀade] nm **1** *Mil* non-commissioned officer, NCO; **tous les gradés** all ranks *(commissioned and non-commissioned)* **2** *Naut* **les gradés** the petty officers

grader [gʀade] vi *Suisse (accéder à une fonction supérieure dans l'armée, une profession, un sport)* to be promoted

gradient [gʀadjã] nm gradient

gradin [gʀadɛ̃] nm **1** *(d'amphithéâtre, de stade)* row or tier of seats; *Sport* **être assis dans les gradins** to be sitting on the terraces, *Am* to be sitting in the bleachers **2** *Tech* **poulie à gradins** cone pulley, stepped pulley; *Élec* **disposer les balais en gradins** to stagger the brushes *(of a dynamo)*

graduation [gʀaduasjõ] nf **1** *(d'une échelle)* graduation **2** *(ensemble des divisions)* graduation, scale

gradué [gʀadue] adj **1** *(qui porte une graduation)* graduated; **verre g.** measuring glass **2** *(progressif) (exercices, problèmes etc)* graded, progressive

graduel, -elle [gʀaduɛl] adj gradual

graduellement [gʀaduɛlmã] adv gradually

graduer [gʀadue] vt **1** *(thermomètre, verre etc)* to graduate **2** *(doses)* to increase gradually

graffiter [gʀafite] vt to cover with graffiti

graffiteur, -euse [gʀafitœʀ, -øz] n graffiti artist, graffitist

graffiti [gʀafiti] nm a piece of graffiti; **des g.** graffiti VOIR GRAMMAIRE A11

graillé [gʀaje] adj *Can (pour faire qch)* well-equipped; *Arg (bien monté)* well-hung

grailler [gʀaje] vi1 *(parler)* to speak hoarsely or huskily; *(d'une corneille)* to caw **2** *Arg (manger)* to eat

graillon [gʀajõ] nm **sentir le g.** to smell of burnt fat; **avoir un goût de g.** to taste greasy

graillonner [gʀajɔne] vi *(parler)* to speak hoarsely or huskily

grain [gʀɛ̃] nm **1** *(graine, fruit de petite taille)* grain; **poivre en grains** peppercorns; **donner du g. à moudre à qn** to give sb food for thought **2** *(céréales, pour volaille)* grain; **entrepôt de g.** granary; **alcool de g.** grain alcohol; **poulet de g.** corn-fed chicken **3** *(granule) (de sable, de poudre)* grain; *(de poussière)* speck; **g. de chapelet** rosary bead; *Fig* **g. de coquetterie/d'originalité** touch or hint of coquetry/originality; **un g. de folie** a touch of madness; **pas un g. de bon sens/de vérité** not a grain or not an ounce of common sense/of truth; *Fig Fam* **il a un g.** he's not quite right in the head, he's not all there **4** *Tex (d'un tissu)* grain, texture; *(d'une peau)* rough side; **côté g. du cuir** grain side of leather; **contre le g.** against the grain; **à gros grains** coarse-grained; **à grains fins/serrés** fine-/close-grained; **ruban gros g.** petersham **5** *Pharm* pellet **6** *Phot* grain; **la photo a du g.** the photo looks grainy **7** *Naut* squall; **essuyer un g.** to meet with a squall; **veiller au g.** to look out for squalls; *Fig* to keep a weather eye open
▸▸**g. de beauté** beauty spot, mole; **g. de blé** grain of wheat; **g. de café** coffee bean; **g. de grenade** pomegranate seed; **g. de moutarde** mustard seed; **g. d'orge** barleycorn, grain of barley; **g. de poivre** peppercorn; **g. de raisin** grape; **g. de sel: mettre son g. de sel** to put or stick one's oar in, *Am* to put in one's ten cents' worth

> Do not confuse with **graine**.

graine [gʀɛn] nf *Bot* seed; **monter en g.** *(d'une plante)* to run or bolt to seed; *Fig (d'une femme)* to be (left) on the shelf; *(d'une personne)* to shoot up; *Fam* **regarde un peu ce qu'a fait ton cousin, et prends-en de la g.!** just look at what your cousin's done and take a leaf out of his book!; **c'est une mauvaise g.** he's a bad lot; *Péj* **g. de voyou/voleur!** you little lout/thief!; *Fam* **casser la g.** to have a bite to eat, to have a snack
▸▸**g. d'anis** aniseed; **g. de lin** linseed; **g. de moutarde** mustard seed; **g. d'orge** barleycorn, grain of barley; *Menuis* barleycorn

> Do not confuse with **grain**.

grainer [gʀene] vt *(poudre à canon)* to granulate; *(cire)* to shred; *(sel)* to grain

graineterie [gʀɛntri] nf *(commerce)* seed trade; *(boutique)* seed shop

grainetier, -ière [gʀɛntje, -jɛʀ] n corn chandler

graissage [gʀɛsaʒ] nm **1** *Tech* greasing, oiling, lubrication; **huile de g.** lubricating oil; **circuit de g.** lubrication system; **faire faire un g.** to have one's car lubricated **2** *Typ* emboldening

graisse [gʀɛs] nf **1** *(d'animal, de personne)* fat; *Tech* grease; **g. animale/végétale** animal/vegetable fat; **pistolet** ou **pompe** ou **injecteur à g.** grease gun **2** *Typ* thickness of type; *(de caractère)* weight **3** *(altération)* **tourner à la g.** *(d'un vin)* to become ropy ▸▸**g. de baleine** blubber; **g. pour engrenages** gear lubricant; **g. pour essieux** axle grease; **g. lubrifiante** lubricant; *Tech* **g. minérale** crude paraffin, mineral jelly; **g. de phoque** seal blubber; **g. de porc** lard; **g. au silicone** silicone grease

graisser [grese] VT **1** *(enduire de graisse)*, *Tech* to grease, to oil, to lubricate; *(bottes)* to oil, *Br* to dubbin; **g. ses vêtements** *(par accident)* to get grease on one's clothes, to make one's clothes greasy; **g. la patte à qn** to grease sb's palm, to bribe sb **2** *Typ* to embolden VI **1** *(d'un vin)* to become ropy **2 onguent qui ne graisse pas** non-greasy ointment

graisseur, -euse [grescer, -øz] *Tech* ADJ **godet g.** grease box; **pistolet g.** grease gun N *(ouvrier)* greaser, oiler

NM *(appareil)* greaser, lubricator; *(point de graissage)* grease *or* lubrication nipple, nipple

graisseux, -euse [grescø, -øz] ADJ **1** *(taché de graisse)* greasy **2** *(tumeur, tissu)* fatty; **bourrelet g.** roll of fat **3** *(altéré) (vin)* ropy

graminacées [graminase] NFPL *Bot* Graminaceae

graminé, -ée [gramine] *Bot* ADJ graminaceous NFPL **graminées** grasses, *Spéc* Graminaceae

grammage [grama3] NM *(du papier)* grammage, gms

grammaire [gramer] NF **1** *(science, règles)* grammar; **faute/règle de g.** grammatical error/rule **2** *(livre)* grammar (book)

grammairien, -ienne [gramεrjε̃, -jεn] N grammarian

grammatical, -ale, -aux, -ales [gramatikal, -o] ADJ grammatical

grammaticalement [gramatikalmã] ADV grammatically

gramme [gram] NM gram(me); **ne pas perdre/prendre un g.** not to lose/not to put on an ounce; *Fig Fam* **il n'a pas un g. de fantaisie/bon sens** he hasn't an ounce of imagination/common sense

gramophone [gramɔfɔn] NM gramophone

GRAND, -ANDE [grã, grãd]

ADJ ▪ big **1, 4, 8** ▪ large **1, 7** ▪ long **1**
▪ great **1, 6–8** ▪ tall **2** ▪ high **2, 3, 6**
▪ main **3**
ADV ▪ big ▪ on a large scale *(en grand)*
▪ wide ▪ much, many
N ▪ grown-up ▪ big boy

ADJ SEE GRAMMAR B10 **1** *(de taille)* big, large; **grande ville/maison** large *or* big town/house; **grands bras/grandes jambes** long arms/legs; **grande distance** great distance; **c'est à une grande distance d'ici** it's a long way away from here; **plus g. que nature** larger than life; **un g. lit** a big *or* large bed; *(à deux personnes)* a double bed; **la grande échelle** *(des pompiers)* the (firemen's) tall *or* long ladder; **faire de grands pas** to take big *or* large strides; *Fig* **marcher à grands pas vers la gloire/la sagesse** to stride towards glory/wisdom; **la démocratie avance à grands pas** democracy is making great strides, democracy is advancing by leaps and bounds; **avancer à grands pas vers la paix/la réussite** to make great strides towards peace/success; **avancer à grands pas vers la catastrophe/la guerre** to advance rapidly towards disaster/war; *Opt* **(objectif) g. angle** wide-angle lens; **un g. A** a capital A; **le G. Montréal** Greater Montreal; **une grande société** a big *or* large company; **les grandes sociétés pétrolières** the big *or* large *or* major oil companies

2 *(en hauteur)* tall; **homme g.** tall man; **un g. homme blond** a tall fair man; **un g. palmier** a tall palm tree; **cet enfant est très g. pour son âge** that child is very tall for his age; **pas plus g. que ça** only so high

3 *(principal)* chief, main; **la g.-rue** the high street, *Am* the main street; **la g.-messe** high mass; **le g. salon** the main drawing room; **grande ligne** inter-city line

4 *(qui n'est plus enfant)* **quand tu seras g.** when you're big *or* grown up, when you're old enough; **elle n'est pas assez grande pour comprendre** she's not old enough to understand; **je suis assez g. pour me débrouiller tout seul** I'm big *or* old enough to fend for myself; **un g. garçon** a big boy; **son g. frère** his big brother

5 *(en quantité, intense)* **g. bruit** loud noise; **g. froid** severe *or* intense cold; **g. vent** high wind; **g. désordre** great disorder; **g. buveur** big *or* heavy *or* hard drinker; **grandes pluies** heavy rain; **laver** *ou* **nettoyer à grande eau** *(sol, cour etc)* to wash down (with large quantities of water); **le g. air leur fera du bien** the fresh air will do them good; **vivre au g. air** to live in the open air; **il fait g. jour** it's broad daylight; **étaler sa vie privée au g. jour** to expose one's private life to the public gaze; **sa malhonnêteté/le scandale est apparu(e) au g. jour** his dishonesty/the scandal has been exposed

6 *(pour insister)* **une grande heure/journée** a full *or* good hour/day; **il est g. temps que tu le lui dises** it's high time you told him; **avec le plus g. plaisir** with the greatest (of) pleasure; **ils sont grands amis** they are great friends

7 *(important, puissant)* great; **une grande découverte** a great discovery; **un g. nombre** a large number; **le g. nombre n'apprécierait pas ce genre de films** the majority (of people) wouldn't appreciate this type of film; **grande diffusion** *(de journaux etc)* mass circulation; **grande distribution** mass distribution; **dans le plus g. détail** in the greatest *or* fullest detail; **en grande partie** largely, to a great extent; **un g. jour** a big *or* great day; **grandes dates de l'histoire** great dates in history; **g. changement** big *or* major *or* great change; **un g. amour** a great love; **le g. amour** true love; **nous étions au g. complet** we were all there; **l'équipe/la famille au g. complet** the whole team/family; **un acteur sans g. talent** an actor with little talent, an undistinguished actor; **un homme de g. talent** a very talented man, a man with great talent; **grands vins** great *or* vintage wines; **un g. cru de bordeaux** a great Bordeaux vintage; **un g. savant/écrivain** a great scientist/writer; **une grande dame** a great lady, a grand lady; **une grande dame de la littérature** a great literary lady; **grands hommes** great men; **un g. seigneur** a nobleman; **se donner des grands airs** to give oneself airs (and graces)

8 *(fastueux, ambitieux)* **un g. projet** a great *or* grand plan; **un g. mariage** a big wedding

9 *(dans un titre, un grade)* **g. officier de la Légion d'honneur** Grand Officer of the Legion of Honour

ADV **faire g.** to do things in a big way *or* on a large *or* grand scale; **voir g.** *(avoir de vastes projets)* to have big ideas, to think big; **ils avaient vu g. pour le banquet** they didn't do things by halves for the banquet; **ouvrir la fenêtre tout g.** to open the window wide; **faire les choses en g.** to do things in a big way *or* on a large *or* grand scale; **ils voient toujours tout en g.** they always see everything on a grand scale; **statue en g.** life-size statue; **reproduction en g.** enlarged copy; **je veux la même photo en g.** I want the same photo but enlarged; **le même poupée, mais en g.** the same doll, but bigger *or* larger; **yeux grand(s) ouverts** wide open eyes; **il était assis là, la bouche grande ouverte** he was sitting there with his mouth wide open; **ouvrir toutes les fenêtres en g.** to open all the windows wide; **il n'y avait pas g. monde** there weren't many people there; **il n'y a pas g.**

vent there's not much wind, it's not very windy N *(personne de grande taille, adulte)* **grands et petits** *(en taille)* big and small; *(en âge)* old and young, grown-ups and children; *Scol* **les grands** the senior boys (and girls), the seniors; **mon g.** my friend; **ma grande** my dear; *Scol* **la cour des grands** the older children's playground; *Fig* **jouer dans la cour des grands** to be like the big boys

NM *(homme, État puissant)* **g.** **(d'Espagne)** grandee; **les grands** the great men; **les grands de ce monde** those in high places; **Alexandre le G.** Alexander the Great; *Pol* **les Grands** the Great Powers, the Superpowers; **les Quatre Grands** the Big Four; **les grands du pétrole** the oil giants ▸▸**g. blessé** seriously wounded person; **les grands blessés** the seriously wounded; **la grande bourgeoisie** the upper middle class; **g. brûlé** seriously burned person; *(d'un point de vue médical)* serious burns case; *Scol* **les grandes classes** the upper forms, *Am* the higher grades; *Pol* **g. corps de l'État** = senior civil servants recruited through the École nationale d'administration; **les grands départs** the holiday rush; **grande école** = prestigious university-level institute with competitive entrance examination; **g. écran** wide screen; **le g. écran** *(le cinéma)* the big screen, the silver screen; *Pol* **les grands électeurs** = body electing members of the (French) Senate; **g. ensemble** housing estate; **vivre dans un g. ensemble** to live on a housing estate; *Journ* **g. format** broadsheet; *Compta* **g. livre des achats** purchase ledger; *Compta* **g. livre des comptes** accounts ledger; *Compta* **g. livre général** nominal ledger, general ledger; *Compta* **g. livre de paie** wages ledger; *Compta* **g. livre des ventes** sales ledger; **g. magasin** department store; **le G. Marché (européen)** the European Market; **grandes marées** spring tides; *Naut* **le g. mât** the mainmast; **le g. monde** (high) society; **le g. Nord** the far North; *Radio* **grandes ondes** long wave; *Ordinat* **g. ordinateur** mainframe; **grande personne** grown-up; **le g. public** the general public, the public at large; **un film/une émission pour le g. public** a film/a programme *or Am* program designed to appeal to a wide audience; **les grandes puissances** the great *or* major powers; *Mil* **g. quartier général** general headquarters; **g. reporter** senior reporter, chief reporter; *Ordinat* **g. réseau** wide area network; **grande surface** superstore; **grande surface spécialisée** specialist superstore; **les grandes vacances** the summer holidays *or Am* vacation; *Univ* the long vacation

Grandes écoles

These are highly selective establishments which exist in parallel to the universities. Admission is usually only possible after two years of intensive preparatory studies ("écoles préparatoires") and a competitive examination (concours – see box at this entry). Graduates from these institutions typically go on to work in senior and executive posts in the civil service or the private sector. The "grandes écoles" include HEC (management), Polytechnique, Centrale, the École des Mines and the École des Ponts et Chaussées (engineering), the ENA (senior civil service) and the École normale supérieure (humanities or science). Having been to a "grande école" is comparable in prestige to having an Oxbridge degree in Britain or a degree from Harvard or Yale in the US.

grand-angle [grãtãgl], *pl* **grands-angles**

[grɑ̃zɑ̃gl], **grand-angulaire** [grɑ̃tɑ̃gylɛr], *pl* **grands-angulaires** [grɑ̃zɑ̃gylɛr] *Opt* **ADJ** wide-angle

NM wide-angle lens

grand-chose PRON INDÉF *(souvent employé avec pas) (peu de choses)* **pas g.** not much; **elle ne fait pas g.** she doesn't do much; **il n'y a pas g. qui le fasse rire** there's not much that makes him laugh; **il ne sera** *ou* **ne fera jamais g.** he'll never amount to much; **cela ne fait pas g.** it's of no great importance, it doesn't matter much; **il prend des médicaments mais ça ne fait pas g.** he takes medicine, but it doesn't help much; **la mort de son chien ne lui a pas fait g.** his dog's death didn't bother him much; **cela ne vaut pas g.** it's not worth much; **ça n'a pas servi à g.** it wasn't much use; **ce ne sont que quelques fleurs, ce n'est pas g.** it's just a few flowers, nothing much

N *Fam (personne)* **un/une pas g.** a dead loss

grand-croix, *pl* **grands-croix NF INV** Grand Cross *(of the Legion of Honour)*
NM Knight Grand Cross

grand-duc, *pl* **grands-ducs NM 1** *(noble)* grand duke; *Fam* **faire la tournée des grands-ducs** to go out on the town **2** *(oiseau)* great horned owl, eagle owl

grand-ducal, -ale, -aux, -ales ADJ grand-ducal

grand-duché, *pl* **grands-duchés NM** grand duchy

Grande-Bretagne [grɑ̃dbrətaɲ] **NF** Great Britain

grande-duchesse, *pl* **grandes-duchesses NF** grand duchess

grandelet, -ette [grɑ̃dlɛ, -ɛt] **ADJ** *Fam Vieilli* tallish

grandement [grɑ̃dmɑ̃] **ADV 1** *(noblement)* grandly, nobly **2** *(généreusement)* **faire les choses g.** to do things lavishly *or* on a lavish *or* grand scale **3** *(largement)* greatly; **se tromper g.** to be greatly mistaken; **avoir g. raison/tort** to be completely *or* absolutely right/wrong; **avoir g. le temps** to have ample time; **il est g. temps de/que …** it is high time to/that …; **avoir g. de quoi vivre** to have plenty to live on

grandeur [grɑ̃dœr] **NF 1** *(taille)* size; *(d'un arbre)* height, size; **échelle de grandeurs** scale of sizes; **g. nature** full-size(d), life-size(d); **une poupée de la g. d'un enfant de deux ans** a doll the size of *or* as big as a two-year-old child; **deux vases de la même g.** two vases (of) the same size; **nous sommes de la même g.** we are the same height *or* size; *Fig* **regarder qn du haut de sa g.** to look down on sb

2 *(importance, ampleur)* importance; *(d'un amour, d'un sentiment, d'une folie)* greatness; *(d'une conception)* grandeur; *Math* magnitude; *Astron* **étoile de première g.** star of the first magnitude

3 *(importance dans la société)* **se donner des airs de g.** to give oneself airs (and graces); **avoir la folie des grandeurs** to have delusions of grandeur

4 *(gloire)* greatness, grandeur; **une chanteuse d'opéra très admirée au temps de sa g.** an opera singer greatly admired when she was at her peak; **g. et décadence d'un empire** rise and fall of an empire; **la g. de Rome** the grandeur *or* greatness of Rome

5 *(dignité, noblesse)* nobility; **g. d'âme** magnanimity, nobility of soul

6 *(titre honorifique)* **sa G. l'archevêque** His Grace the Archbishop; **votre G.** *(à un duc, une duchesse, un archevêque)* Your Grace

grand-guignol NM INV *Péj* **c'est du g.** it's all blood and thunder

grand-guignolesque [grɑ̃giɲɔlɛsk] **ADJ**
Péj (personne) blood-and-thunder; *(pièce de théâtre, film etc)* gruesome

grandiloquence [grɑ̃dilɔkɑ̃s] **NF** grandiloquence

grandiloquent [grɑ̃dilɔkɑ̃] **ADJ** grandiloquent

grandiose [grɑ̃djoz] **ADJ** *(cérémonie, proportions)* imposing, grandiose; *(spectacle, vue)* imposing, awe-inspiring; **sa gaffe a quand même été g.** his blunder was a real beauty

grandir [grɑ̃dir] **VI** *(en taille)* to grow; *(en âge)* to grow up; **elle a grandi** she has grown, she is taller; **il a grandi en un rien de temps** he shot up really quickly; **un arbre qui grandit vite** a tree which grows quickly, a fast-growing tree; **il comprendra en grandissant** he'll understand as he grows up *or* grows older; *Fig* **g. en sagesse/beauté** to increase *or* grow in wisdom/beauty; **son influence/son importance/sa compréhension grandit** his influence/importance/understanding is increasing *or* growing; **sa faim allait grandissant** he grew more and more hungry

VT g. l'importance de qch to exaggerate *or* overstate the importance of sth; **ses talons la grandissent** her heels make her look taller; *Fig* **ses malheurs l'ont grandi** his misfortunes have made him stronger; *(aux yeux des autres)* his misfortunes have increased his stature; **il est sorti grandi de ce conflit/de cette épreuve** he came out of this conflict/the ordeal a stronger person; **cela ne la grandit pas à mes yeux** that does not improve her standing in my eyes

VPR se grandir se g. en se haussant sur la pointe des pieds to make oneself taller by standing on tiptoe

grandissant [grɑ̃disɑ̃] **ADJ** *(influence, peur, torpeur etc)* growing, increasing

grandissement [grɑ̃dismɑ̃] **NM 1** *Opt* magnification **2** *Vieilli* growth, increase

grandissime [grɑ̃disim] **ADJ** *Fam* marvellous, tremendous; **g. favori** firm favourite

grand(-)livre, *pl* **grands(-)livres NM** *Com* ledger; **g. de ventes** sales ledger

grand-maman, *pl* **grand(s)-mamans NF** *Can, Suisse Enf* grandma, granny

grand-mère, *pl* **grand(s)-mères NF** grandmother; *Fam (vieille femme)* old granny

grand-messe, *pl* **grand(s)-messes NF** *Rel* high mass; *Fig* ritual; *(de parti politique)* jamboree

grand-monde [grɑ̃mɔ̃d] **NM** *Can (adultes)* **le g.** grown-ups

grand-oncle [grɑ̃tɔ̃kl], *pl* **grands-oncles** [grɑ̃zɔ̃kl] **NM** great-uncle

grand-papa, *pl* **grand(s)-papas NM** *Can, Suisse Enf* grandpa, grandad

grand-peine (à) ADV with great difficulty

grand-père, *pl* **grands-pères NM** grandfather; *Fam (vieil homme)* grandad, grandpa

grand-prêtre, *pl* **grands-prêtres NM** high priest

grand-route, *pl* **grand-routes NF** main road

grand-rue, *pl* **grand-rues NF** high street, main street

grands-parents NMPL grandparents

grand-tante, *pl* **grand(s)-tantes NF** great aunt

grand-vergue, *pl* **grand(s)-vergues NF** *Naut* main yard

grand-voile, *pl* **grand(s)-voiles NF** *Naut* mainsail

grange [grɑ̃ʒ] **NF** barn

granit(e) [granit] **NM** granite; *Fig Litt* **cœur de g.** heart of stone

granité [granite] **ADJ** granite-like

NM 1 *Tex* pebble weave **2** *Culin (glace)* = water ice

graniteux, -euse [granitø, -øz] **ADJ** *Minér* granitic

granitique [granitik] **ADJ** granitic

granivore [granivɔr] **ADJ** granivorous
N granivore

granulaire [granylɛr] **ADJ** granular

granulation [granylasjɔ̃] **NF** *Tech* granulation

granule [granyl] **NM** granule; *Pharm* small pill

granulé [granyle] **ADJ** granulated
NM *Pharm* granule; **médicaments en granulés** granulated medicine

granuler [granyle] **VT** to granulate

granuleux, -euse [granylø, -øz] **ADJ** granular; *Biol* **cellule granuleuse** granule cell

grape(-)fruit, *pl* **grape(-)fruits** [grɛpfrut] **NM** grapefruit

graphe [graf] **NM** graph; **g. en ligne** line chart

grapheur [grafœr] **NM** *Ordinat* graphics package

graphie [grafi] **NF** *Ling* written form

graphique [grafik] **ADJ** *(signe, méthode etc)* graphic; **arts graphiques** graphic arts; *Ordinat* **palette g.** graphics palette

NM diagram; *(sur un axe)* graph; *Ordinat* graphic; *Ordinat* **g. de gestion** management chart; **g. de type camembert** pie chart; **g. de type lignes** line chart; **g. financier** financial chart; **g. à secteurs** pie chart; **g. à tuyaux d'orgue** bar chart; **g. à** *ou* **en barres** bar chart; **g. en colonnes** bar chart

---

Il faut noter que l'adjectif anglais **graphic** signifie également **détaillé** ou **cru**, selon le contexte.

---

graphiquement [grafikmɑ̃] **ADV** graphically

graphisme [grafism] **NM 1** *(écriture)* hand(writing) **2** *Beaux-Arts* **le g. élégant de Degas** Degas' elegant style of drawing *or* handling of line; *Ordinat* **graphismes** graphics

graphiste [grafist] **N** graphic designer, graphic(s) artist

graphitage [grafitaʒ] **NM** *Tech* graphitization

graphite [grafit] **NM** graphite

graphité [grafite] **ADJ** **huile graphitée** graphite oil

graphiteux, -euse [grafitø, -øz], **graphitique** [grafitik] **ADJ** graphite

graphologie [grafɔlɔʒi] **NF** graphology

graphologique [grafɔlɔʒik] **ADJ** graphological

graphologue [grafɔlɔg] **N** graphologist

grappe [grap] **NF 1** *(de raisin)* bunch; *(de lilas, de glycine)* cluster; *Fig (de gens)* cluster, group; *Vulg* **lâche-moi la g.** piss off **2** *Bot* raceme **3** *Ordinat (de terminaux)* cluster

---

Il faut noter que le nom anglais **grape** est un faux ami. Il signifie **grain de raisin**.

---

grappillage [grapijaʒ] **NM 1** *(de raisin)* gleaning **2** *Fig (d'argent)* making something on the side; *(petits vols)* pilfering

grappiller [grapije] **VI** *(dans un vignoble)* to glean

VT 1 *Fig (recueillir au hasard)* to pick up; **g. des renseignements** to glean information **2** *Fig (détourner)* to make on the side; *(piquer, voler)* to pilfer

grappin [grapɛ̃] **NM 1** *Naut* grapnel, grappling (hook *or* iron); *Fig Fam* **mettre le g. sur qch/qn** to get one's hands on *or* get hold of sth/sb **2** *(benne) (d'un dragueur)* grab; *(d'une grue)* clutch

GRAS, GRASSE [grɑ, grɑs]

ADJ fatty **1** ▪ fat **2** ▪ greasy **3** ▪ heavy **4** ▪ thick **4** ▪ throaty **4** ▪ bold **5** ▪ smutty **7**	
ADV much **1** ▪ coarsely **2**	
NM fleshy part **1** ▪ fat **2** ▪ bold **3**	

ADJ 1 *(viande, nourriture, tissu)* fatty; **matières grasses** fats; **yaourt à 0% de matière grasse** fat-free yoghurt; *Chimie* **acide g.** fatty acid; **mardi g.** Shrove Tuesday

2 *(gros) (personne, animal)* fat; *(poulet)* plump; **g. comme un porc** *ou* **un cochon** as fat as a pig; *très Fam* **être g. du bide** to be flabby round the stomach; *Fig* **tuer le veau g.** to kill the fatted calf; **plante grasse** succulent (plant)

3 *(graisseux) (chiffon, cheveux etc)* greasy; **eaux grasses** swill; **crème pour peaux grasses** cream for greasy skin

4 *(épais) (terre)* heavy, clayey; *(boue)* thick, slimy; **crayon g.** soft lead pencil; **vin g.** ropy wine; **toux grasse** loose *or* phlegmy cough; **voix grasse** throaty voice; **rire g.** throaty laugh

5 *Typ* bold; **caractères g.** bold(-faced) type

6 *Fig* **offrir une grasse récompense** to offer a handsome reward; **faire la grasse matinée** to have a lie-in

7 *(graveleux) (histoire)* smutty, dirty

ADV 1 **faire g., manger g.** to eat meat *(esp on a fast day)*; *Arg* **il n'y en a pas g.** *(non comptable)* there's not much of it; *(comptable)* there aren't many of them; **des gens comme lui, il n'y en a pas g.!** there aren't many people like him!; **il n'y a pas g. à manger** there's not much to eat

2 **rire g.** to laugh coarsely

NM 1 *Anat* **le g. de la jambe/du bras/du ventre** the fleshy part of the leg/arm/stomach

2 *(du jambon, de la viande)* fat; *Fam* **discuter le bout de g.** to chew the fat *or* the rag

3 *Typ* bold; **en g.** in bold, in bold(-faced) type

gras-double, *pl* **gras-doubles NM** *Culin* tripe

grassement [grɑsmɑ̃] **ADV 1** *(confortablement)* **vivre g.** to live off the fat of the land **2** *(d'une façon peu élégante)* **rire g.** to laugh coarsely **3** *(largement)* **récompenser qn g.** to reward sb handsomely *or* generously; **g. payé, g. rétribué** very well paid

grasseyement [grɑsɛjmɑ̃] **NM** pronunciation of one's r's from the back of the throat

grasseyer [grɑsɛje] **VI** to pronounce one's r's from the back of the throat

grassouillet, -ette [grɑsuje, -ɛt] **ADJ** *(personne)* plump, chubby

grateron [gratrɔ̃] **NM** *Bot* goose-grass, cleavers

graticiel [gratisjɛl], **gratuiciel** [gratɥisjɛl] **NM** *Ordinat* freeware

gratifiant [gratifjɑ̃] **ADJ** rewarding, gratifying

gratification [gratifikasjɔ̃] **NF 1** *(prime)* bonus; **g. de fin d'année** end of year bonus **2** *Psy* gratification

Il faut noter que le nom anglais **gratification** ne signifie jamais **prime**.

gratifier [gratifje] **VT** *(impf, pr sub n.* **gratifiions, v. gratifiiez)* **1 g. qn de qch** to present sb with sth; **il a été gratifié d'une grosse récompense** he was presented with a large reward; *Iron* **être gratifié d'une amende** to be landed with a fine; **et je fus gratifié d'une paire de gifles** and my reward was a slap in the face **2** *Psy (personne)* to gratify

gratin [gratɛ̃] **NM 1** *Culin* gratin; **un g. de pâtes/de poisson** a pasta/fish gratin; **au g.** au gratin, (cooked) with (breadcrumbs and) grated cheese; **chou-fleur au g.** = cauliflower cheese **2** *Fig Fam* **le g.** *(le beau monde)* the upper crust

▸▸ **g. dauphinois** gratin dauphinois, = sliced potatoes baked with milk and browned on top

gratiné, -ée [gratine] **ADJ 1** *Culin* sprinkled with (breadcrumbs and) cheese, au gratin **2** *Fig Fam* **une addition gratinée** an enormous bill; **c'est g.!** that's a bit much!; **une histoire gratinée** an incredible story; **il était g., l'exam de ce matin!** this morning's exam was a real killer *or* was really stiff!; **son mari, il est g.** her husband's a prize idiot

NF *Culin* **gratinée** onion soup au gratin

gratiner [gratine] **VT** to cook au gratin

VI **un plat qui gratine au four** a dish browning in the oven

gratis [gratis] **ADV** gratis, for nothing, free of charge

ADJ *(billet)* free

gratitude [gratityd] **NF** gratitude

gratos [gratos] **ADV** *Fam* free (of charge), for nothing

grattage [gratɑʒ] **NM 1** *(d'un mur)* scraping; *Chir (d'un os)* scraping **2** *Tex* teaseling, napping, raising

gratte [grat] **NF 1** *Fam (profits illicites)* pickings, profits on the side; **faire de la g.** to make a bit on the side **2** *Fam (guitare)* guitar; **jouer de la g.** to play the guitar **3** *Can* snowplough, *Am* snowplow **4** *Belg (griffure)* scratch; *(éraflure)* scratch, scrape

gratte-ciel NM INV skyscraper

gratte-cul, *pl* **gratte-culs NM** rosehip

gratte-dos NM INV backscratcher

grattement [gratmɑ̃] **NM** scratching

gratte-papier NM INV *Péj* pen-pusher

gratte-pieds NM INV (metal) doormat

gratter [grate] **VT 1** *(avec les ongles)* to scratch; *(avec qch de dur)* to scrape; *(effacer)* *(mot, inscription)* to scratch out; *(tache)* to scrape off; **g. (la terre) du pied** *(d'un cheval)* to paw the ground; **g. le dos de qn** to scratch sb's back; *Fam* **ça me gratte terriblement** it makes me itch like mad; **poil à g.** itching powder; **vin qui gratte le gosier** wine that is harsh *or* rough on the throat; *Fig* **g. les fonds de tiroir** to scrape around for money; **c'est une affaire où il n'y a pas grand-chose à g.** you can't make much out of that

2 *Fam (dépasser) (un coureur, une autre voiture)* to overtake, to pass; *Fig* to overtake

3 *Tex* **laine grattée** brushed wool

VI 1 **pull qui gratte** scratchy pullover; **g. à la porte** to tap at the door; *Fig* **il a l'air très cultivé, mais si tu grattes un peu ...** he has a very cultured air, but if you scratch away his veneer a bit ...; **pas besoin de g. beaucoup pour s'apercevoir qu'il est bête** it soon becomes pretty obvious that he's stupid

2 g. du violon/de la guitare to scrape away on the fiddle/to strum away on the guitar

3 *(ne pas glisser)* **plume qui gratte** scratchy nib

4 *Fam* **j'ai gratté toute la nuit** *(travaillé)* I slaved away all night; *(écrit)* I scribbled away all night

VPR se gratter 1 to scratch oneself; **se g. jusqu'au sang** to scratch oneself raw; **se g. la tête/l'oreille** to scratch one's head/ear **2** *très Fam* **tu peux toujours te g.!** you can whistle for it!, nothing doing!

gratteron [gratrɔ̃] **NM** *Bot* goose grass, cleavers

gratteux, -euse [gratø, -øz] *Can* **ADJ** stingy, mean

N miser

grattoir [gratwar] **NM** scraper; *Typ* slice; **g. de bureau** erasing knife, scraper eraser

grattons [gratɔ̃] **NMPL** pork scratchings

grat(t)ouiller [gratuje] **VT** *Fam* **1** *(démanger)* **ça me g.** it makes me itch **2** *(guitare)* to strum away on

gratuit [gratɥi] **ADJ 1** free (of charge); **à titre g.** gratis, free of charge; **prêt à titre g.** free loan **2** *Fig (acte, insulte, violence etc)* gratuitous

gratuité [gratɥite] **NF 1** **la g. de l'enseignement/des soins hospitaliers** free education/hospital care **2** *Fig (d'une insulte, de la violence etc)* gratuitousness

Il faut noter que le nom anglais **gratuity** est un faux ami. Il signifie **pourboire**.

gratuitement [gratɥitmɑ̃] **ADV 1** for nothing, free (of charge) **2** *Fig (sans motif)* gratuitously, without provocation

gravats [grava] **NMPL 1** *(après criblage de plâtre) (du plâtre)* screenings **2** *(après démolition)* rubble

grave [grav] **ADJ 1** *(digne, solennel) (visage)* grave, serious; *(ton)* grave, solemn; *(expression)* sober, solemn; *(très important) (affaires)* important, weighty; *(qui a des conséquences fâcheuses) (blessure)* serious; **elle ne s'absente de son travail que pour raison g.** she never stays away from work except for serious reasons; **faire** *ou* **commettre une g. erreur** to make a serious mistake; **subir une g. opération** to undergo a serious operation; **accident qui a fait un mort et deux blessés graves** accident in which one person died and two were seriously injured; **hélas!, il y avait plus g.** alas! there was worse to come

2 *Mus (note, voix)* low, deep; **sons graves** bass tones

3 *Gram* **accent g.** grave (accent)

4 *Fam (dérangé)* **il est g.** he's not all there, he's off his rocker *or Br* head

5 *Arch (lourd)* heavy; *Phys* **corps g.** heavy body

NM *Mus* bass; **sa voix n'est belle que dans le g.** *ou* **les graves** his voice is attractive only in the low registers

ADV *Fam* in a bad way; **il me prend la tête g.** he really *or Br* seriously bugs me

gravé [grave] **ADJ** **pierre gravée** engraved stone; **image gravée** graven image

graveleux, -euse [gravlø, -øz] **ADJ 1** *(terre)* gravelly **2** *(histoire, chanson)* smutty, dirty

gravelle [gravɛl] **NF** *Méd Arch* gravel

gravement [gravmɑ̃] **ADV 1** *(avec dignité)* gravely, solemnly **2** *(d'une manière importante, dangereuse)* **g. malade/blessé** seriously ill/injured; **il s'est g. trompé** he was seriously *or* greatly mistaken; **il est g. menacé** he faces a serious threat

graver [grave] **VT** *(matériau, motif)* to engrave; *(disque compact)* to burn; *Mus* **g. un disque** to make *or* cut a record; **g. à l'eau-forte** to etch; *Fig* **cela reste gravé dans ma mémoire** *ou* **en moi** it is engraved on my memory; *Fig* **ce n'est pas gravé sur son front** you can't tell from looking at him

graveur [gravœr] **NM 1** *(personne)* engraver; **g. à l'eau-forte** etcher; **g. sur bois** wood engraver **2** *(instrument)* **g. de CD** CD burner, CD writer; **g. de CD-ROM** CD-ROM burner, CD-ROM writer; **g. de CD réinscriptible** CD rewriter; **g. de disque compact** compact disc recorder

ADJ **bain g.** etching bath

gravide [gravid] **ADJ** *Méd* gravid

gravier [gravje] **NM** gravel; **couvrir un chemin de g.** to cover a path with gravel, to gravel a path

gravillon [gravijɔ̃] NM (fine) gravel, grit; **gravillons** Br loose chippings, Am gravel

gravillonnage [gravijɔnaʒ] NM (fine-)gravelling

gravillonner [gravijɔne] VT to (fine-)gravel

gravimétrie [gravimetri] NF Phys gravimetry

gravimétrique [gravimetrik] ADJ Phys gravimetric

gravir [gravir] VT (montagne, escalier) to climb; (échelle) to climb, to mount; Fig **g. les échelons** to climb the ladder

gravissime [gravisim] ADJ extremely serious

gravitation [gravitasjɔ̃] NF Phys gravitation

gravitationnel [gravitasjɔnɛl] ADJ Phys gravitational; **force gravitationnelle** force of gravity

gravité [gravite] NF 1 Phys gravity; **g. spécifique** specific gravity; **centre de g.** centre of gravity; **alimentation par g.** gravity feed 2 (réserve, sérieux) gravity, seriousness 3 (danger) (d'une maladie, d'une opération) seriousness; **blessure sans g.** slight or minor wound; **accident/chute sans g.** minor accident/fall 4 (importance) (d'un problème) gravity, seriousness

graviter [gravite] VI 1 to revolve (**autour de** round); **g. autour de la terre** to orbit the earth; Fig **g. autour de qn** to hover around sb; **les flatteurs qui gravitent dans les hautes sphères du pouvoir** the flatterers who move in the higher echelons of power 2 Vieilli to gravitate (**vers** towards)

gravois [gravwa] NMPL Vieilli = gravats

gravure [gravyr] NF 1 (action) engraving; **g. à l'eau-forte** etching; **g. en creux** intaglio engraving; **g. en taille-douce** copperplate engraving; **g. sur bois** woodcutting, wood engraving 2 (ouvrage) engraving; **g. à l'eau-forte** etching; **g. en taille-douce**, **g. sur cuivre** copperplate (engraving); **g. sur bois** woodcut, wood engraving; **g. en couleurs** colour print; **g. hors texte** full-page plate; **g. avant la lettre** proof before letters; **g. de mode** fashion plate; Fig **cette fille est une g. de mode** that girl's a real fashion plate

grayé [greje] ADJ Can (pour faire qch) well-equipped; Arg (bien monté) well-hung

gré [gre] NM 1 (goût) **à mon g.**, **selon mon g.** to my liking, to my taste; (à ma guise) as I please or like; **elle va et vient à son (bon) g.** she comes and goes as she pleases or likes; **je m'habille à mon g.** I dress to please myself; **trouver qch à son g.** to find sth to one's liking; **une chambre à mon g.** a room that I like or that suits me, a room to my liking 2 (volonté) **se marier contre le g. de son père** to get married against one's father's wishes; **elle a dû accepter contre son g.** she had to accept against her will; **bail renouvelable au g. du locataire** lease renewable at the option of the tenant; **de mon propre g.**, **de mon plein g.** of my own free will, of my own accord; **de bon g.** willingly, gladly; **de mauvais g.** reluctantly; **bon g. mal g.** whether we/you/etc like it or not, willy-nilly; **il faut qu'il vienne de g. ou de force** he has to come whether he wants to or not, he has to come willy-nilly; **au g. des flots** at the mercy of the waves; **de g. à g.** by (mutual) agreement; **vendre de g. à g.** to sell by private contract, to sell privately; Fig **au g. des événements/circonstances** (agir, changer d'avis etc) according to how events turn out/to circumstances 3 Fml (gratitude) **savoir g. à qn de (faire) qch** to be grateful to sb for (doing) sth; **nous vous saurions g. de bien vouloir …** we would be grateful if you would kindly …; Vieilli **savoir mauvais g. à qn de qch** to be annoyed with sb about sth

grèbe [grɛb] NM grebe

grébiche [grebiʃ], **grébige** [grebiʒ] NF 1 Typ (d'un manuscrit etc) file number 2 (classeur) loose-leaf binder

grec, grecque [grɛk] ADJ Greek; **les orateurs grecs** the Greek orators; **tragédie grecque** Greek tragedy; **profil g.** Grecian profile
▪ NM Ling Greek; **g. ancien/moderne** Ancient/Modern Greek
▪ N **G.** Greek
▪ NF **grecque 1** Culin **à la grecque** stewed with olive oil and herbs 2 Archit, Beaux-Arts Greek key pattern, Greek border

Grèce [grɛs] NF Greece

gréciser [gresize] VT to Hellenize; **g. un mot** to give a Greek form to a word

gréco-latin, pl **gréco-latins** [grekolatɛ̃] ADJ Ling Gr(a)eco-Latin

gréco-romain, pl **gréco-romains** [grekorɔmɛ̃] ADJ Gr(a)eco-Roman

gredin, -ine [grədɛ̃, -in] N Vieilli (vaurien) rascal, wretch; Fam **petit g.!** you little rascal or horror!

gredinerie [grədinri] NF Vieilli (acte) mean or underhand action; (conduite) mean or underhand behaviour

gréement [gremɑ̃] NM Naut 1 (ensemble des voiles) rigging; (équipement) gear 2 (disposition des mâts et des voiles) (d'un bateau) rig; **g. Marconi** Bermuda rig

gréer [gree] VT Naut (mât, bateau etc) to rig; (hamac, filets etc) to sling; **gréé en carré** square-rigged; **g. une vergue** to send up a yard

gréeur [greœr] NM Naut rigger

greffage [grefaʒ] NM Chir, Bot grafting

greffe¹ [grɛf] NF 1 Chir (de peau, de tissu) graft; (d'organe) transplant; Bot graft, slip; **g. du cœur/du rein** heart/kidney transplant; **g. hépatique** liver transplant 2 Bot (action) **g. par œil détaché** budding; **g. en écusson** shield grafting or budding

greffe² NM 1 Jur clerk of the court's office 2 Fin (de société par actions) registry

greffé, -ée [grefe] N Méd **g. cardiaque** ou **du cœur** heart transplant patient

greffer [grefe] VT Chir, Bot (peau, tissu, bouture) to graft; Chir (organe) to transplant

greffeur [grefœr] NM Bot grafter, budder

greffier [grefje] NM 1 Jur clerk (of the court) 2 Admin, Fin registrar 3 Arg (chat) pussy(-cat), moggy

greffoir [grefwar] NM grafting knife

greffon [grefɔ̃] NM Chir (de tissu, de peau) graft; (d'organe) transplant; Bot graft, slip

grégaire [greger] ADJ gregarious; **l'instinct g.** the herd instinct

> Il faut noter que lorsque l'adjectif anglais **gregarious** s'emploie à propos de personnes, il signifie **sociable**.

grégarisme [gregarism] NM gregariousness

grège [grɛʒ] ADJ 1 **soie g.** raw silk 2 (couleur) whitish-beige

grégeois [greʒwa] ADJ Antiq, Mil **feu g.** Greek fire

grégorien, -ienne [gregɔrjɛ̃, -jɛn] ADJ (rite, réforme) Gregorian; **chant g.** Gregorian chant
▪ NM Gregorian chant

grêle¹ [grɛl] ADJ (jambe, membres, main) skinny; (tige, silhouette) slender; (voix, son) shrill; Anat **intestin g.** small intestine

grêle² NF hail; **orage de g.** hailstorm; Fig **g. de coups/balles** hail or shower of blows/bullets

grêlé [grele] ADJ (peau) pockmarked

grêler [grele] V IMPERS **il grêle** it's hailing
▪ VT (cultures etc) to damage by hail; **la région a été complètement grêlée** the whole region has been hit by hail

grelin [grəlɛ̃] NM Naut hawser

grêlon [grelɔ̃] NM hailstone

grelot [grəlo] NM (small) bell; (de traîneau) sleigh bell; Fam **avoir les grelots** (avoir peur) to have the wind up

grelottement [grəlɔtmɑ̃] NM 1 (tremblement) shivering 2 (tintement) jingling, tinkling

grelotter [grəlɔte] VI 1 (trembler) **g. de froid/de peur** to shiver or tremble or shake with cold/fear 2 (tinter) to jingle, to tinkle

greluche [grəlyʃ] NF Péj très Fam chick, Br bird

Grenade [grənad] NF 1 (en Espagne) Granada 2 (aux îles du Vent) **la G.** Grenada

grenade [grənad] NF 1 Mil (projectile) grenade; **g. à main** hand grenade; **g. fumigène** smoke grenade; **g. lacrymogène** tear-gas grenade; Naut **g. sous-marine** depth charge 2 (fruit) pomegranate

grenadier¹ [grənadje] NM (arbre) pomegranate (tree)

grenadier² NM Mil grenadier; Fig tall and masculine woman; **boire comme un g.** to drink like a fish

grenadière [grənadjer] NF Mil (d'un fusil) band

grenadine [grənadin] NF 1 Culin grenadine 2 Tex grenadine

grenaillage [grənajaʒ] NM Tech shot blasting

grenaille [grənaj] NF 1 (en métal) shot; **g. de plomb** lead shot 2 (pour la volaille) refuse grain, tailings 3 Belg **grenailles errantes** (sur panneau) loose chippings, Am gravel

grenailler [grənaje] VT (métal) to granulate

grenat [grəna] NM garnet
▪ ADJ INV garnet-red

grené [grəne] ADJ (dessin) stippled; (cuir) grainy
▪ NM (de dessin) stipple; (de cuir) grain

greneler [grənle] VT (je grenelle, n. grenelons; je grenellerai) (papier, cuir) to grain

grener [grəne] (je grène, n. grenons; je grènerai) VI (des céréales etc) to seed
▪ VT 1 (réduire en grains) (poudre à canon) to granulate; (cire) to shred; (sel) to grain 2 (donner un aspect grené à) (papier, cuir) to grain

grènetis [grɛnti] NM (d'une pièce) milled edge

grenier [grənje] NM 1 (pour grain, fourrage) granary; **g. à foin** hayloft; **g. à blé** corn loft, Am wheat loft; Fig **l'Égypte était le g. du monde ancien** Egypt was the granary of the ancient world 2 (sous les combles) attic, garret; **chercher qch de la cave au g.** to hunt high and low for sth, to search the house from top to bottom for sth; **ranger la maison de la cave au g.** to tidy up the house from top to bottom

grenouillage [grənujaʒ] NM Fam Péj shady dealing, scheming

grenouille [grənuj] NF 1 (animal) frog 2 Fam (tirelire) ≃ piggy bank; **manger la g.** to make off with the cash
▸▸ Fig **g. de bénitier** Holy Joe; **g. taureau** ou **mugissante** bullfrog

grenouiller [grənuje] VI Fam Péj to go in for shady dealing, to scheme

grenouillère [grənujer] NF 1 (marécage) frog-pond 2 (pour bébé) sleepsuit

grenu [grəny] ADJ 1 (blé etc) grainy, full of grain 2 (cuir, peau etc) grained; (sel) coarse-grained, crystalline
▪ NM graininess, granularity

grenure [grənyr] NF **1** *Beaux-Arts* stippling, stipple **2** *(du cuir)* grain(ing)

grès [grɛ] NM **1** *Géol* sandstone **2** *(céramique)* poterie de g., **g. cérame** stoneware; **cruche en g.** stoneware jug

gréseux, -euse [grezø, -øz] ADJ gritty, sandy; **roches gréseuses** sandstone rocks, sandstones

grésil [grezi(l)] NM fine hail

grésillement [grezijmã] NM *(du feu)* crackling; *(de la flamme)* sputtering; *(d'une poêle à frire)* sizzling

grésiller [grezije] V IMPERS to hail

grésiller [grezije] VI *(du feu)* to crackle; *(de la flamme)* to sputter; *(d'une poêle à frire)* to sizzle

gressin [gresɛ̃] NM *Culin* bread stick

greubons [grøbõ] NMPL *Suisse Culin* = leftover fat from cooked pork, fried and used as an ingredient in certain Swiss dishes

grève [grɛv] NF **1** *(arrêt du travail)* strike; **se mettre en g.** to go on *or* come out on strike, to strike, to take strike action *or* industrial action; **être en g., faire g.** to be on strike; **g. des trains/de la poste** train/postal strike; **briseur de g.** strike breaker; **piquet de g.** (strike) picket; **droit de g.** right to strike; **lancer un ordre de g.** to issue a strike order **2** *(le long de la mer)* (sea)shore, *Litt* strand; *(d'un fleuve)* (river) bank, *Litt* strand; **les grèves de la Loire** the sandbanks of the Loire; *Hist* **la (place de) G.** = open space on the banks of the Seine where dissatisfied workmen used to assemble
▸ ▸ **g. de la faim** hunger strike; **faire une g. de la faim** to be/go on hunger strike; **g. générale** general strike; **g. partielle** partial strike; **g. perlée** go-slow (strike), *Am* slowdown; **g. avec préavis** official strike; **g. de protestation** protest strike; **g. sauvage** wildcat strike; **g. de solidarité** sympathy strike; **g. surprise** lightning strike; **g. sur le tas** sit-down strike; **g. tournante** staggered strike; **g. du zèle** work-to-rule, go-slow; **faire la g. du zèle** to work to rule

grever [grəve] VT *(je grève, n. grevons; je grèverai)* **1** *(alourdir)* *(succession)* to burden, to encumber; *(pouvoir d'achat)* to restrict; **grevé d'impôts** weighed down *or* burdened with tax; **ce week-end aux sports d'hiver a grevé notre budget** this winter sports weekend has put a strain on our budget **2** *Jur (propriété)* to mortgage

gréviste [grevist] N striker; **g. de la faim** hunger striker
ADJ **mouvement g.** strike movement

GRH NF *(abrév* **gestion des ressources humaines)** HRM

gribiche [gribiʃ] ADJ **sauce g.** = flavoured mayonnaise with chopped hard-boiled egg and capers
NF *Can (femme acariâtre)* shrew

gribouillage [gribujaʒ] NM *(écriture)* scrawl, scribble; *(dessin)* doodle

gribouille [gribuj] NM *Vieilli* simpleton, nitwit, *Br* clot
NF *Can (dispute)* quarrel, fight

gribouiller [gribuje] VT & VI *(écrire)* to scribble, to scrawl; *(dessiner)* to doodle

gribouilleur, -euse [gribujœr, -øz] N scribbler

gribouillis [gribuji] NM = **gribouillage**

grief [grijɛf] NM grievance, ground for complaint; **faire g. à qn de qch** to hold sth against sb; **on lui a fait g. de ne pas se mêler aux autres** it was held against him that he didn't mix with the others

> Il faut noter que le nom anglais **grief** est un faux ami. Il signifie **chagrin**.

grièvement [grijɛvmã] ADV seriously, severely, badly

griffe [grif] NF **1** *(d'animal)* claw; *(d'un faucon)* claw, talon; **faire ses griffes** *(d'un chat)* to sharpen its claws; *Fig* to cut one's teeth; **coup de g.** scratch; **donner un coup de g. à qn** to claw *or* scratch sb; *Fig* to have a dig at sb; *Fig* **montrer les griffes** to show one's claws; *Fig* **arracher qn des griffes de qn** to snatch sb out of sb's clutches; *Fig* **tomber/être sous** *ou* **entre les griffes de qn** to fall into/be in sb's clutches
2 *Tech etc* claw, clip, clamp; *(outil)* dog; *(sur un bijou)* claw; **accouplement/embrayage à griffes** claw coupling/clutch; **griffes de monteur** climbing irons
3 *Bot (de la vigne)* tendril; *(d'asperge)* crown
4 *(empreinte)* stamped signature; *(ce qui sert à faire cette empreinte)* (signature) stamp; *(sur vêtements)* label; *Fig* stamp; **g. de grande marque** designer label; **g. de réception** received stamp; **on reconnaît la g. de Zola dans ce roman** the novel bears Zola's stamp; **on reconnaît la g. de Saint-Laurent** you can recognize the Saint-Laurent style

griffé [grife] ADJ designer; **foulard g.** designer scarf

griffer [grife] VT **1** *(d'un animal)* to scratch, to claw **2** *(signer)* *(vêtement)* to put one's label on; **Chanel a griffé cette veste** this jacket bears the Chanel label

griffon [grifõ] NM **1** *Myth* griffon, gryphon, griffin **2** *(chien)* griffon (terrier) **3** *(oiseau)* griffon (vulture)

griffonnage [grifɔnaʒ] NM *(écriture)* scrawl, scribble; *(dessin)* quick sketch

griffonnement [grifɔnmã] NM *Beaux-Arts (en cire)* wax model; *(en terre)* clay model

griffonner [grifɔne] VT *(écrire)* to scrawl, to scribble; *(dessiner)* to sketch quickly

griffu [grify] ADJ **patte griffue** clawed foot; **main griffue** claw-like hand

griffure [grifyr] NF scratch

grigner [griɲe] VI *Tex* to pucker, to crinkle up

grignotage [griɲɔtaʒ] NM nibbling; *Fig (de libertés)* erosion

grignotement [griɲɔtmã] NM nibbling

grignoter [griɲɔte] VT to nibble (at); *Fig (libertés)* to erode; *Fig* **g. son capital/ses économies** to eat into one's capital/one's savings; **les zones industrielles grignotent nos campagnes** industrial estates are gradually disfiguring our countryside
VI to nibble

grignoteur, -euse [griɲɔtœr, -øz] N nibbler

grigou [grigu] NM *Fam* skinflint, miser

gri-gri [grigri] NM amulet; *(porte-bonheur)* charm

gril [gril] NM **1** *(de cuisine)* grill, *Am* broiler; **faire cuire qch sur le g.** to grill sth, *Am* to broil sth; *Fig Fam* **être/mettre qn sur le g.** to be/keep sb on tenterhooks **2** *Tech* grating *(protecting sluice gate)*; *Rail, Naut* gridiron; *Théâtre* grid, gridiron **3** *Anat* **g. costal** rib cage

grill [gril] NM **1** *TV etc (pour l'éclairage)* pipe grid **2** *Culin* steakhouse, grill

grillade [grijad] NF *Culin* grilled *or Am* broiled meat; **faire des grillades** to have a barbecue

grillage¹ [grijaʒ] NM **1** *(de noix, de café etc)* roasting **2** *Métal (de minerais)* calcining, roasting **3** *Tex* singeing

grillage² NM **1** (metal) grating, grill(e); **g. en fil de fer** wire netting; **poser un g. électrifié** to put up an electrified fence **2** *Élec (de plaque d'accumulateur)* grid, frame

grillager [grijaʒe] VT *(je grillageai(s); n. grillageons)* **1** *(garnir d'un grillage)* to fit a grill(e) to; **fenêtre grillagée** window covered with wire mesh; **verre grillagé** wired glass **2** *(entourer d'un grillage)* to surround with wire netting

grille [grij] NF **1** *(à l'entrée d'un parc, jardin etc)* (entrance) gate; *(clôture basse) (autour d'un monument etc)* railings; **séparé de la rue par une g.** separated from the road by railings **2** *(pour l'écoulement) (d'un évier, d'un égout etc)* grating, grate **3** *(à mailles fines)* screen, netting; *(du parloir d'un couvent)* grill(e) **4** *Élec (d'un accumulateur, d'un tube à électrons)* grid; **courant de g.** grid current **5** *(tableau quadrillé) (de mots croisés)* grid
▸ ▸ **g. d'analyse par fonction** functional analysis chart; **g. d'avancement** career structure; **g. d'entrée d'air** air vent; **g. de gestion** managerial grid; **g. d'horaires** timetable, schedule; *Compta* **g. d'imputation** table of account codes; **g. indiciaire** salary structure *or* scale; **g. produit/marché** product/market grid; *Radio, TV* **g. des programmes** programme schedule *or* grid; *Aut* **g. de radiateur** radiator grille; **g. de réchauffeur** heater matrix; **g. de rémunération** salary scale; *Ordinat* **g. de saisie** input grid; **g. des salaires** salary scale

grille-calandre, *pl* **grilles-calandres** NF *Aut* grille

grille-pain NM INV toaster

griller¹ [grije] VT **1** *(rôtir, passer au gril) (viande)* to grill, *Am* to broil; *(pain)* to toast; *(café, marrons)* to roast **2** *Métal (minerai)* to roast, to calcine **3** *Tex* to singe **4** *(brûler)* to scorch, to burn; *Élec Fam (ampoule, fusible, moteur etc)* to burn out; **végétation grillée par le soleil** vegetation scorched by the sun; *Fam* **g. une cigarette** to smoke *or* have a cigarette; *Arg* **il est grillé** *(dévoilé)* his game's up; *(rayé)* he's had it; **g. un concurrent** to leave a competitor standing; *Fam* **g. un feu rouge** to jump the lights; *Fam* **g. les étapes** *(dans sa carrière)* to shoot up the ladder; *(dans un travail)* to cut corners
VI **1** *Culin (d'un morceau de viande)* to grill, *Am* to broil; *(d'un morceau de pain)* to toast; *(de marrons)* to roast; *Fig* **g. d'impatience** to be burning with impatience; *Fig* **g. d'envie de faire qch** to be bursting *or* itching to do sth **2** *Élec (sauter)* to burn out
VPR **se griller** **se g. au soleil** to roast in the sun; *Fam* **se g. auprès de qn** to blot one's copybook with sb

griller² VT *(fenêtre)* to cover with wire mesh

grilloir [grijwar] NM grill

grillon [grijõ] NM cricket

grill(-room), *pl* **grill(-rooms)** [grilrum] NM grill (room)

grimaçant [grimasã] ADJ grimacing

grimace [grimas] NF grimace; **faire une g.** to make *or* pull a face, to grimace; **arrête de faire des grimaces au professeur** stop making faces at the teacher; **faire la g.** *(avec dégoût)* to pull a long face; **faire une g. de douleur** to wince; **faire des grimaces** *(être maniéré)* to put on airs; *Prov* **on n'apprend pas à un vieux singe à faire des grimaces** ≃ don't teach your grandmother to suck eggs

grimacer [grimase] *(je grimaçai(s), n. grimaçons)* VI **1** to grimace, to make *or* pull a face; **g. de douleur** to grimace *or* wince with pain
VT **g. un sourire** to force a smile, to give a wry smile

grimacier, -ière [grimasje, -jer] ADJ grimacing; *Vieilli (maniéré)* affected

grimage [grimaʒ] NM *Théâtre (action)* making up; *(résultat)* make-up

grimer [grime] *Théâtre* VT *(un acteur, son visage)* to make up
VPR **se grimer** *(d'un acteur)* to make up

grimoire [grimwar] NM **1** *(de sorcier)* book of spells **2** *(ouvrage confus et illisible)* piece of gibberish *or* mumbo-jumbo

grimpant [grɛ̃pɑ̃] ADJ *(animal)* climbing; **plante grimpante** climbing plant, climber; **rosier g.** climbing rose
▪ NM *Arg (pantalon)* trousers, *Am* pants

grimpe [grɛ̃p] NF rock-climbing; **faire de la g.** to go rock-climbing

grimpée [grɛ̃pe] NF *(stiff)* climb

grimper [grɛ̃pe] VI **1** *(monter)* to climb (up); *(faire de l'escalade)* to climb; **il a grimpé sur la muraille** he climbed (up) on to the wall; **la route grimpe jusqu'au col** the road climbs (up) to the pass; **ça grimpe** it's steep **2** *(de plantes)* to climb **3** *Fig (des prix)* to climb
▪ VT **1** *(montagne, échelons)* to climb (up); **g. l'escalier** to climb (up) *or* go up the stairs **2** *Vulg (posséder sexuellement)* to ride, to shaft, *Br* to shag

grimpette [grɛ̃pɛt] NF *Fam (chemin)* short, steep climb

grimpeur, -euse [grɛ̃pœr, -øz] ADJ *(oiseau)* climbing
▪ NM climber; *(de rocher)* rock-climber; *(en cyclisme)* hill climber; **c'est un bon/mauvais g.** *(d'un cycliste)* he's good/bad on hills

grinçant [grɛ̃sɑ̃] ADJ **1** *(qui grince)* creaking **2** *(caustique) (remarque)* caustic; **elle a un humour g.** she has a caustic wit

grincement [grɛ̃smɑ̃] NM *(d'une porte, de roues etc)* creaking; **g. de dents** grinding *or* gnashing of teeth; *Fig* **il y a eu des grincements de dents** there was much gnashing of teeth

grincer [grɛ̃se] VI *(je grinçai(s); n. grinçons)* *(d'une porte, de roues etc)* to creak; *(d'une chauve-souris)* to squeak; **g. des dents** to grind *or* gnash one's teeth; **cela fait g. des dents** it sets your teeth on edge; **porte qui grince sur ses gonds** creaking door

grinche [grɛ̃ʃ] ADJ *Suisse (grincheux)* grumpy, grouchy

grincheux, -euse [grɛ̃ʃø, -øz] ADJ grumpy, bad-tempered
▪ N grump, grumpy *or* bad-tempered person

gringalet [grɛ̃galɛ] NM *(homme, garçon)* (little) shrimp, weakling
▪ ADJ M puny

gringue [grɛ̃g] NM *Fam* **faire du g. à qn** to chat sb up, *Am* to sweet-talk sb

griotte [grijɔt] NF **1** *Bot* morello (cherry); **chocolats aux griottes** cherry liqueur chocolates **2** *Minér* griotte (marble)

grip [grip] NM *Sport* **1** *(position de la main au golf, au tennis)* grip **2** *(revêtement)* grip

grippage [gripaʒ], **grippement** [gripmɑ̃] NM *Tech (d'un palier, d'un piston etc)* seizing, jamming, binding

grippal, -ale, -aux, -ales [gripal, -o] ADJ *Méd* flu; **soulage les états grippaux** relieves flu symptoms; **virus g.** flu virus

grippe [grip] NF **1** *Méd* flu, *Fml* influenza; **se faire vacciner contre la g.** to be vaccinated against flu; **attraper/avoir la g.** to catch *or* get/have (the) flu; **g. intestinale** gastric flu **2** **prendre qn/qch en g.** to take a dislike to sb/sth

grippé [gripe] ADJ **1** *Méd* **être g.** to have (the) flu **2** *Tech (moteur, mécanisme etc)* seized(-up) **3** *Méd (visage)* pinched, drawn

gripper [gripe] VT *Tech (mécanisme)* to seize up, to jam
▪ VI **1** *(d'une étoffe)* to crinkle (up), to wrinkle, to pucker **2** *(de paliers)* to seize (up), to bind, to jam
▪ VPR **se gripper** = VI **2**

grippe-sou, *pl* **grippe-sou(s)** NM skinflint, miser, Scrooge

gris [gri] ADJ **1** *(couleur)* grey, *Am* gray; *(temps)* cloudy, dull, overcast; **il fait g. ce matin** it's cloudy *or* dull *or* overcast this morning, it's a grey *or* dull morning; **g. de poussière** grey with dust; **robe g. clair** light grey dress; **aux cheveux g.** grey-haired; *Anat* **substance grise** grey matter; *Fam* **faire fonctionner sa matière grise** to get one's grey matter working; **vin g.** rosé wine; **faire grise mine** to look anything but pleased; **faire grise mine à qn** to give sb a cool welcome **2** *(ivre)* tipsy
▪ NM **1** *(couleur)* grey, *Am* gray; *Ordinat* **tons de g.** shades of grey; **s'habiller en g.** to dress in *or* wear grey **2** *(cheval)* grey, *Am* gray **3** *(tabac gris)* shag
▪▪ **g. acier** steel grey; **g. anthracite** charcoal grey; **g. ardoise** slate grey; **g.-bleu** blue-grey; **g. perle** pearl grey; **g. pommelé** *(cheval)* dapple-grey; **g. souris** soft grey; **g.-vert** greenish-grey

grisaille [grizaj] NF **1** *(caractère morne)* greyness, dreariness, *Am* grayness **2** *Beaux-Arts* grisaille; **peindre en g.** to paint in grisaille

grisailler [grizaje] VT *Beaux-Arts* **g. qch** to paint sth in grisaille
▪ VI to turn *or* go grey *or Am* gray

grisant [grizɑ̃] ADJ *Fig (succès, atmosphère)* intoxicating, exhilarating, heady; *(aventure, soirée)* exhilarating; **à une vitesse grisante** at (an) exhilarating speed

grisâtre [grizatr] ADJ greyish, *Am* grayish

grisbi [grizbi] NM *Arg (argent)* dosh, *Br* lolly

grisé [grize] NM *Ordinat* grey *or Am* gray tone; **en g.** *(article)* dimmed

griser [grize] VT **1** *(rendre gris)* to make grey *or Am* gray; *Ordinat* to shade **2** *(enivrer)* to make drunk *or* tipsy; *Fig* **grisé par le succès** carried away *or* intoxicated by *or* with success
▪ VPR **se griser** **se g. d'air pur** to get drunk on fresh air; **se g. des paroles de qn/de musique** to get carried away by sb's words/by music

griserie [grizri] NF **1** *(ivresse)* tipsiness **2** *Fig (exaltation)* exhilaration, excitement

grisette [grizɛt] NF *Arch* = young dressmaker, milliner, florist etc, usually of easy virtue

gris-gris NM amulet; *(porte-bonheur)* lucky charm

grisonnant [grizɔnɑ̃] ADJ *(cheveux)* greying, *Am* graying, touched with grey *or Am* gray; **avoir les tempes grisonnantes** to be greying at the temples; **un cinquantenaire g.** a greying fifty-year-old

grisonner [grizɔne] VI *(de cheveux, personne)* to go grey *or Am* gray

grisou [grizu] NM *Min* firedamp; **coup de g.** firedamp explosion

grive [griv] NF *(oiseau)* thrush; **soûl comme une g.** drunk as a lord; *Prov* **faute de grives on mange des merles** beggars can't be choosers, half a loaf is better than none

grivelé [grivle] ADJ *(plumage)* speckled

grivèlerie [grivɛlri] NF *Jur* = offence consisting of ordering a meal in a restaurant without having the money to pay for it

griveton [grivtɔ̃] NM *Fam* private (soldier), *Br* squaddie

grivois, -oise [grivwa, -waz] ADJ *(histoire, chanson, plaisanterie)* risqué, saucy, bawdy

grivoiserie [grivwazri] NF *(plaisanterie)* risqué *or* saucy joke; *(histoire)* risqué *or* saucy story; *(acte)* rude gesture

grizzli [grizli], **grizzly** [grizli] NM grizzly (bear)

Groenland [grɔenlɑ̃(d)] NM Greenland

groenlandais, -aise [grɔenlɑ̃dɛ, -ɛz] ADJ of *or* from Greenland
▪ NM *Ling* Greenlandic
▪ N **G.** Greenlander

grog [grɔg] NM grog, toddy

groggy [grɔgi] ADJ INV *Fam* groggy

grognard [grɔɲar] NM **1** *Hist* = soldier of Napoleon's Old Guard **2** *(militant traditionnaliste)* member of the old guard **3** *Vieilli (grincheux)* grumbler

grognasse [grɔɲas] NF *Vulg Péj* old bag, old cow

grognasser [grɔɲase] VI *Fam* to grumble, to grouse, *Br* to whinge

grogne [grɔɲ] NF *Fam* grumbling; **c'est la g. chez les ouvriers/dans le milieu étudiant** the workers/the students are grumbling

grognement [grɔɲmɑ̃] NM **1** *(d'un cochon)* grunt(ing); *(d'un chien, ours)* growl(ing); **pousser des grognements** *(d'un cochon)* to grunt **2** *(d'une personne)* growl; **pousser un g.** to growl

grogner [grɔɲe] VI **1** *(d'un cochon)* to grunt; *(d'un chien)* to growl **2** *(d'une personne)* to grumble, to grouse, to moan; **g. contre qn** to grumble *or* complain about sb
▪ VT **g. un refus/une réponse** to growl out a refusal/an answer

grognon, -onne [grɔɲɔ̃, -ɔn] N grumbler, grouser, moaner
▪ ADJ *(f* **grognon** *or* **grognonne***)* grumpy, grumbling; **c'est une femme g.** *ou* **grognonne** she's always grumbling *or* moaning, she's a grumpy woman; **qu'est-ce que tu peux être g.!** what a grumbler *or* grouser *or* moaner you are!

grognonner [grɔɲɔne] VI *Fam* to grouse, to grumble, to moan

groin [grwɛ̃] NM *(d'un cochon)* snout; *Fig Péj (de personne)* ugly face

grole, grolle [grɔl] NF *très Fam (chaussure)* shoe

grommeler [grɔmle] *(je grommelle, n. grommelons; je grommellerai)* VI to mutter; *(d'un sanglier)* to snort, to grunt
▪ VT **g. un juron** to mutter an oath

grommellement [grɔmɛlmɑ̃] NM muttering

grondement [grɔ̃dmɑ̃] NM **1** *(d'un chien)* growl(ing), snarl(ing) **2** *(du tonnerre)* rumble, rumbling; *(d'un torrent de montagne, des vagues, d'un moteur)* roar(ing); *(des canons)* booming

gronder [grɔ̃de] VI **1** *(d'un chien)* to growl, to snarl **2** *(du tonnerre)* to rumble; *(des canons)* to boom; *(des vagues)* to roar; **la révolte/le mécontentement gronde** there are rumblings of rebellion/discontent
▪ VT *(réprimander)* to scold, to tell off; **attention, tu vas te faire g.!** watch out, or you'll get into trouble!

gronderie [grɔ̃dri] NF scolding

grondeur, -euse [grɔ̃dœr, -øz] ADJ **1** *(voix)* scolding, nagging; *(humeur, tempérament)* peevish **2** *(orage, torrent etc)* rumbling

grondin [grɔ̃dɛ̃] NM gurnard, gurnet

groom [grum] NM **1** *(dans un hôtel)* page, *Am* bellhop **2** *Équitation Arch* groom

---

GROS, GROSSE¹ [gro, gros]

ADJ	big **1, 2, 5** ▪ large **1, 5** ▪ thick **1** ▪ heavy **1, 3, 6** ▪ stout **1, 2** ▪ fat **2** ▪ coarse **3, 4** ▪ serious **5**
ADV	a lot
N	fat man/woman
NM	bulk **1** ▪ wholesale **2, 3**

ADJ 1 *(grand)* big, large; **g. morceau** big *or* large piece, lump; *Fig* **l'examen de statistiques, voilà le g. morceau** the statistics exam is the big one; **grosse corde** thick *or* stout rope; **g. pullover** thick *or* heavy *or* chunky sweater; **g. souliers** strong *or* stout shoes; **grosses chaussettes** thick *or* heavy socks;

g. moteur high-powered engine; **g. doigt de pied** big toe; **de grosses lèvres** thick lips; **avoir un g. ventre** *(être bien en chair)* to have a paunch, to have a pot(belly); **avoir une grosse tête** to have a large head; *Fig* **avoir la grosse tête** to be big-headed, to be swollen-headed; **prendre** *ou* **attraper la grosse tête** to get big-headed; **une orange grosse comme le poing** an orange the size of *or* as big as your fist; *Fig* **un mensonge g. comme une maison** *ou* **comme ça** a whopping lie, a whopper of a lie; *Fig* **faire les g. yeux** to glare, to glower; **yeux g. de larmes** eyes swollen with tears; **avoir le cœur g.** to have a heavy heart, to be sad at heart; **je suis parti le cœur g.** I left with a heavy heart; *Fig* **elle a un cœur g. comme ça** she's so big-hearted; *Péj* **g. nigaud** *ou* **bêta!** you big *or* great ninny *or Br* twit!; **écrire qch en g. caractères** to write sth in big *or* large letters; **g. utilisateur** heavy user; **g. mangeur** *or* hearty eater; **g. buveur** heavy *or* big drinker; **g. appétit** big *or* hearty appetite; **g. rhume** heavy cold; **grosse fièvre** high fever; **un g. kilo** a good kilo; **avoir un g. chagrin** to be very upset; **une grosse récolte** a bumper harvest; *Naut* **grosse mer** heavy *or* rough sea; **g. temps** stormy *or* rough weather; **grosse averse/pluie** heavy shower/rain; **g. vent** high wind; **grosse cavalerie** heavy cavalry

2 *(corpulent)* big, fat, stout; **un g. bébé** a big *or* fat baby; **un g. bonhomme** a fat gentleman

3 *(pas fin)* **grosse toile** coarse linen; **grosse voix** gruff voice; **faire la grosse besogne** to do the heavy work

4 *(grossier)* **un peu g.** not very subtle, a bit too obvious; **c'est un peu g.!** that's a bit much!; **g. rire** coarse laugh; **grosse indélicatesse** gross impropriety

5 *(important)* **grosse somme** large sum (of money); **ce n'est pas une grosse affaire** *(entreprise)* it's not a big company; *(préoccupation)* it's no big deal; **grosse commande** bulk order; **la plus grosse partie de nos affaires/notre personnel** the bulk of our business/our staff; **grosse faute** serious *or* gross mistake; **g. propriétaire (terrien)** big landowner; **grosse héritière** wealthy heiress

6 être g. de conséquences/menaces/etc to be heavy with consequences/threats/*etc*

ADV *(beaucoup)* **gagner g.** to earn a lot, to make big money; **ça peut rapporter g.** it can bring in a lot; **je donnerais g. pour savoir qui a fait ça** I'd give a lot to know who did that; **il y a g. à parier qu'il ne viendra pas** a hundred to one he won't come!; **il risque g.** he's taking a big risk, he's risking a lot; **jouer g.** *Cartes* to play for high stakes; *Fig* to take a big risk, to risk a lot

N *(personne corpulente)* large *or* fat man/woman; **eh bien, mon g.!** well, old boy *or Br* old man!; *(à un enfant)* well, my boy!, well, son!; *Fam* **un g./une grosse plein(e) de soupe** a tub of lard

NM 1 *(partie la plus importante)* bulk; **le g. de la cargaison/du personnel** the bulk of the cargo/the staff; **le g. de l'armée** the main body *or* the bulk of the army; **le g. du peuple** the mass *or* bulk of the people; **le g. d'une mission** the main part of a mission; **le plus g. est fait** the biggest part of the job is done; **le plus g. du courrier** the bulk of the mail; **le g. de l'été/l'hiver** the height of summer/depths of winter; **g. d'un mât** thick end of a mast

2 *Com* wholesale (trade); **marchand de g.** wholesaler; **vente de g.** wholesale; **ils ne vendent/font que du g.** they only sell/deal wholesale; **commerce de g.** wholesale business; **boucher de g.** wholesale butcher

3 écrire en g. to write in big *or* large letters; **raconter ce qui s'est passé en g.** to tell roughly what happened; **il y avait en g.**

---

quinze personnes there were roughly *or* about fifteen people there; **acheter en g.** to buy wholesale; *(en grosse quantité)* to buy in bulk; **vendre en g.** to sell wholesale

▸▸ *Fam* **g. bonnet** big shot, bigwig; *Typ* **g. corps** headings type, headline type; **g. gibier** big game; *Fam* **grosse légume** big shot, bigwig; **g. mot** swearword; *TV, Cin* **g. plan** tight shot; *TV, Cin* **en g. plan** in close-up; *TV, Cin* **en très g. plan** very close up; *TV, Cin* **g. plan d'objet/de tête** insert/head shot; **g. porteur** jumbo jet; **g. porteur polyvalent** multi-purpose large-capacity jet; **g. rouge** cheap red wine, *Br* plonk; **g. sel** cooking salt; *Ordinat* **g. système** mainframe; *Typ* **g. tirage** best-seller; *Journ* **g. titre** banner headline; **en g. titres** in banner headlines; *Journ* **g. titre de deuxième ordre** second lead, half lead

---

gros-bec, *pl* **gros-becs** NM hawfinch, grosbeak

gros-cul, *pl* **gros-culs** NM *Fam* lorry, *Am* truck

groseille [grozɛj] NF **g. (rouge)** redcurrant; **g. (blanche)** white currant; **g. à maquereau** gooseberry; **gelée de groseille(s)** redcurrant jelly

groseillier [grozeje] NM (red)currant bush; **g. à maquereau** gooseberry bush

gros-grain, *pl* **gros-grains** NM *Tex* grosgrain

Gros-jean [groʒɑ̃] NM *Prov* **se retrouver G. comme devant** to be back where one started

grosse[2] [gros] NF **1** *Com* gross **2** *Jur* engrossment **3** *Arch (écriture)* roundhand (writing)

grossesse [grosɛs] NF pregnancy; **interruption volontaire de g.** termination *(of pregnancy)*; **robe de g.** maternity dress; **pendant sa g.** during her pregnancy, while *or* when she was pregnant

▸▸ **g. extra-utérine** *or* **ectopique** ectopic pregnancy; **g. gémellaire** twin pregnancy; **g. nerveuse** false *or* phantom pregnancy; **g. à risque** high-risk pregnancy

grosseur [grosœr] NF **1** *(taille, volume)* size; *(des lèvres)* thickness; **un objet de la g. d'un œuf** an object the size of an egg **2** *Méd* lump, growth

grossier, -ière [grosje, -jɛr] ADJ **1** *(impoli)* *(personne)* rude (**envers** to); *(vulgaire)* *(personne, air)* uncouth, coarse; *(langage, plaisanterie)* coarse, crude; **un g. personnage** an uncouth individual; **il a été on ne peut plus g.** he was extremely rude; **parler d'un ton g.** to speak coarsely *or* crudely **2** *(commun, rudimentaire)* *(nourriture, tissu, vaisselle etc)* coarse, rough; *(méthode)* crude; *(dessin)* crude, rough; *(goûts, traits du visage)* unrefined, coarse; **c'est un esprit g.** he's ignorant, he's a Philistine **3** *(de taille)* **stupidité grossière** crass stupidity; **ignorance grossière** gross *or* crass ignorance; **faute grossière** gross mistake, blunder; **une ruse grossière** a very obvious trick

grossièrement [grosjɛrmɑ̃] ADV **1** *(imparfaitement)* roughly, crudely; **table g. façonnée** roughly *or* crudely made table **2** *(approximativement)* roughly; **calculer g. un prix/le nombre de personnes** to roughly calculate a price/the number of people **3** *(de façon importante)* **se tromper g.** to be grossly mistaken **4** *(de façon impolie)* *(parler, répondre)* rudely

grossièreté [grosjɛrte] NF **1** *(caractère rudimentaire)* *(d'un objet fabriqué)* coarseness, roughness **2** *(incorrection)* *(de manières, personne)* coarseness **3** *(parole grossière)* **dire des grossièretés à qn** to say crude *or* coarse things to sb

grossir [grosir] VT **objet grossi trois fois** object magnified three times; **torrent grossi**

---

par les pluies torrent swollen by the rain; **ce pantalon le grossit** those trousers make him look fatter; **g. les rangs des mécontents** to swell the ranks of the discontented; **g. sa voix** to raise one's voice; *Fig* **g. les faits/une histoire/une affaire** to exaggerate the facts/a story/a matter; **g. l'importance de qch/le rôle de qn dans une action** to exaggerate the importance of sth/sb's part in an action

VI *(d'animaux, de fruits)* to get bigger *or* larger; *(de personne)* to put on weight, to get fatter; *(de mer)* to get rough, to rise; *(de rivière)* to swell; **elle a grossi de deux kilos** she has put on two kilos; **elle a beaucoup grossi** she has put on a lot of weight *or* has got fatter

grossissant [grosisɑ̃] ADJ **1** *(qui devient plus gros)* *(foule, bruit)* growing, swelling **2** *(qui rend plus gros)* enlarging; **verre g.** magnifying glass

grossissement [grosismɑ̃] NM **1** *(augmentation de taille)* increase in size **2** *(action de rendre plus gros)* *(d'un objet à travers un verre)* magnification, enlargement **3** *(capacité d'un instrument d'optique)* *(d'un verre)* magnification, magnifying power

grossiste [grosist] N wholesaler, wholesale dealer; **g. généraliste** general wholesaler; **g. importateur** import wholesaler

grosso modo [grosomodo] ADV roughly; **il y avait g. cinquante personnes** there were roughly fifty people; **g. c'est une comédie** roughly speaking *or* broadly speaking it's a comedy; **raconter l'affaire g.** to give a general account of the matter

grossoyer [groswaje] VT (**je grossoie, n. grossoyons; je grossoierai**) *Jur (document)* to engross

grotesque [grotɛsk] ADJ *(personne, allure, idée)* ludicrous, ridiculous; *Beaux-Arts (personnage)* grotesque

NM *Littér, Beaux-Arts* **le g.** the grotesque; **cet homme/cette situation est d'un g.!** the man's/the situation's ludicrous *or* ridiculous!

NFPL *Beaux-Arts* **grotesques** grotesques

grotesquement [grotɛskəmɑ̃] ADV ludicrously, ridiculously

grotte [grot] NF cave; **g. naturelle/préhistorique** natural/prehistoric cave; **g. artificielle** grotto

grouillant [grujɑ̃] ADJ swarming, crawling, alive (**de** with); **rue grouillante de monde** street swarming with people; **foule grouillante** teeming crowd

grouillement [grujmɑ̃] NM swarming; **le g. des asticots dans la viande avariée** the maggots swarming around in the rotten meat; **son esprit torturé n'était plus qu'un g. sans nom de pensées incohérentes** his tortured mind was nothing but a teeming mass of incoherent thoughts

grouiller [gruje] VI **1** *Vieilli (bouger)* to move **2** *(de touristes, clients etc)* to swarm around; **la foule grouillait dans la rue** the street was teeming *or* swarming with people; **g. de** to swarm *or* crawl with; **fromage qui grouille de vers** cheese-swarming *or* crawling *or* alive with maggots; **ce bouquin grouille de bonnes idées** this book is teeming with good ideas

VPR se grouiller *Arg* to get a move on, to get one's skates on; **grouille(-toi)!** get a move on!, get your skates on!

grouillot [grujo] NM *Bourse* messenger (boy); *TV, Cin* runner, best boy

groupage [grupaʒ] NM **1** *Com* groupage, consolidation; *(de paquets)* bulking **2** *Méd* (blood) grouping

groupe [grup] NM **1** *(de gens, choses)* group; *(d'arbres)* group, clump; *(musiciens)* group, band; *(d'étoiles)* group, cluster; **marcher en g.** to walk in a group; **un g. de touristes descendit du car** a party *or* group of tourists got out of the coach; **travailler/acheter qch en g.** to work/buy sth as *or* in a group; **se mettre en groupes de trois** to get into *or* form groups of three; **ils arrivaient par groupes de deux ou trois** they arrived in twos and threes; **faire partie d'un g. de rock** to be in a rock group *or* band VOIR GRAMMAIRE A11

2 *Ling* **g. verbal/nominal/de mots** verbal/nominal/word group; **g. consonantique** consonant cluster

3 *Mil* **g. de combat** squad; **demi-groupe** section, *Am* half squad; **g. d'artillerie** battery, *Am* battalion; **g. d'intervention** task force; **g. d'aviation** squadron *(of transport aircraft)*

▸▸ **g. d'âge** age group; *Mktg* **g.-cible**, *pl* **groupes-cibles** target group; **g. de consommateurs** consumer group, customer group; *Pol* **g. de contact** contact group; *Ordinat* **g. de discussion** discussion group; *Élec* **g. électrogène** generating set, generator; **g. ethnique** ethnic group; **g. d'étude** study group; **g. financier** financial group; **g. hospitalier** hospital complex; **g. hôtelier** hotel group; **le G. des Sept/des Huit** the Group of Seven/Eight; **g. industriel** industrial group; **g. d'intérêt** interest group; **g. d'intérêt commun** common-interest group; **g. d'intervention de la gendarmerie nationale** = special task force of the gendarmerie; **g. linguistique** language group; *Aut* **g. moto-propulseur** powerplant; **g. multimédia** communications conglomerate, multimedia group; *Ordinat* **g. de nouvelles** newsgroup; *Pol* **g. parlementaire** parliamentary group; **g. de presse** press group, newspaper group; *Pol* **g. de pression** pressure group; **g. de prix** price bracket; *Mktg* **g. de prospects** prospect pool; **g. de protection de l'environnement** environmental protection group; *Méd* **g. à risque** risk group; *Méd* **g. sanguin** blood group; **quel est votre g. sanguin?** what's your blood group?, what blood group are you?; **g. scolaire** *(bâtiments)* school complex; *(élèves)* school party; **g. socio-économique** socio-economic group; *Mktg* **g. stratégique** strategic group; *Mktg* **g. suivi** *(panel)* control group; *Mktg* **g.-témoin**, *pl* **groupes-témoin** focus group; **g. test de consommateurs** consumer group focus; **g. de travail** working party, work group; *Com* **g. volontaire** voluntary group

groupé ADJ **1** *Com* consolidated **2** *Ordinat* blocked

groupement [grupmɑ̃] NM **1** *(action)* grouping; *Ind, Com (d'intérêts)* pooling; **g. des enfants d'après l'âge** classification of children by age groups **2** *(association)* group; **g. de consommateurs** consumer(s') group; **g. de détaillants** retailers' group **3** *Mil* group, formation; **g. d'infanterie** brigade group, *Am* battle group; **g. tactique** task force

▸▸ **g. d'achat** purchasing cooperative, purchasing group; *Com* **g. à l'export** consolidation for export; **g. d'intérêt économique** economic interest group, intercompany partnership; **g. professionnel** trade association

grouper [grupe] VT to group (together); *(moyens, ressources)* to pool; *Com* to consolidate, to group; *(paquets)* to bulk; **si nous groupons nos informations, nous aurons plus vite un résultat** if we pool our information, we'll get a result more quickly

VPR **se grouper** *(dans une association)* to join together, to form a group; *(dans un lieu)* to gather; **se g. autour du feu** to gather round the fire; **se g. autour d'un chef** to gather *or* rally round a leader; **essayons de rester groupés** let's try to stay in a group

groupeur [grupœr] NM *Com* consolidator; **g. de fret aérien** air freight consolidator; **g. maritime** maritime freight consolidator; **g. routier** road haulage consolidator

groupie [grupi] NF *Fam* groupie

groupusculaire [grupyskylɛr] ADJ *(qui tient du groupuscule)* small-scale; **la gauche g.** *(formée de groupuscules)* the small groups of the left

groupuscule [grupyskyl] NM *Pol Péj* small group; **des groupuscules néo-nazis** small neo-Nazi groups

grouse [gruz] NF *Zool* grouse

gruau [gryo] NM **1 (farine de) g.** (fine) wheat flour; **pain de g.** fine wheaten bread **2 g. (d'avoine)** groats **3** *Can* porridge

grue [gry] NF **1** *(oiseau)* crane; *Fam* **faire le pied de g. (en attendant qn)** to hang about (waiting for sb), to kick *or* cool one's heels (waiting for sb); **cou de g.** long scraggy neck **2** *Tech* crane; *TV, Cin* cherry picker; **g. volée** *ou* **à flèche** jib crane; **g. à pivot** revolving crane; **g. à flotteur** pontoon crane; *Rail* **g. d'alimentation** (water) crane; *TV, Cin* **g. de prise de vue** camera crane; *TV, Cin* **g. hydraulique** simon crane **3** *Arg (prostituée)* tart

gruger [gryʒe] VT (je **grugeai(s)**; n. **grugeons**) **1** to swindle; **se faire g.** to be swindled **2** *Can* **g. l'avance de qn** *(dans un sondage etc)* to eat into sb's lead

grume [grym] NF **1** *(écorce)* bark; **bois en g.** rough timber, undressed timber **2** *(bûche)* log

grumeau, -eaux [grymo] NM **1** *(dans une sauce etc)* lump; **pâte à crêpes pleine de grumeaux** lumpy pancake mixture **2 grumeaux de sel** specks of salt

grumeler (se) [səgrymle] VPR (il **se grumelle**; il **se grumellera**) **1** *(d'une sauce)* to go lumpy **2** *(du lait)* to curdle, to clot

grumeleux, -euse [grymlø, -øz] ADJ **1** *(sauce)* lumpy **2** *(lait)* curdled **3** *(d'aspect granuleux)* *(poire)* gritty

grumier [grymje] NM timber lorry

grutier [grytje] NM crane driver *or* operator

gruyère [gryjɛr] NM Gruyère (cheese); **crème de g.** = processed Gruyère (cheese)

GSM [ʒeɛsɛm] NM **1** *Tél (abrév* global system for mobile communications*)* GSM; **réseau G.** GSM network **2** *Belg (téléphone portable)* mobile (phone), *Am* cellphone

GSS [ʒeɛsɛs] NF *(abrév* grande surface spécialisée*)* specialist superstore

guacamole [gwakamɔle] NM *Culin* guacamole

Guadeloupe [gwadlup] NF Guadeloupe

guadeloupéen, -enne [gwadlupeẽ, -ɛn] ADJ of Guadeloupe
N **G.** person from Guadeloupe

guano [gwano] NM guano

Guatemala [gwatemala] NM Guatemala

guatémaltèque [gwatemaltɛk] ADJ Guatemalan
N **G.** Guatemalan

gué [ge] NM ford; **passer une rivière à g.** to ford a river

guéable [geabl] ADJ *(rivière)* fordable

guède [gɛd] NF *Bot* woad, pastel

guéer [gee] VT *(cours d'eau)* to ford

guéguerre [gegɛr] NF *Fam* squabble; **c'est la g. entre les différents chefs de service** the different heads of department are squabbling (amongst themselves)

guelfe [gɛlf] NM *Hist* Guelph

guelte [gɛlt] NF *Com Vieilli* commission, percentage *(on sales)*

guenille [gənij] NF **1** (old) rag; **en guenilles** in rags (and tatters) **2** *(chose sans intérêt)* worthless object

guenon [gənɔ̃] NF **1** *Zool* female monkey **2** *Fam (femme)* ugly woman, fright

guépard [gepar] NM cheetah

guêpe [gɛp] NF **1** *(insecte)* wasp; **nid de guêpes** wasps' nest; **piqûre de g.** wasp sting; *Fig* **taille de g.** wasp waist **2** *(femme rusée)* **une fine g.** an artful *or* crafty woman; *Fam* **pas folle, la g.!** she's nobody's fool!

guêpier [gepje] NM **1** *(nid)* wasps' nest; *Fig (situation)* sticky *or* tricky situation; **se fourrer** *ou* **tomber dans un g.** to get oneself into a sticky *or* tricky situation **2** *(oiseau)* bee eater

guêpière [gepjɛr] NF basque

guère [gɛr] ADV SEE GRAMMAR B62–3 *(always with neg expressed or understood)* hardly (any), not much, not many, very little, very few; **je ne l'aime g.** I don't care much for him; **je n'ai g. dormi** I didn't get much sleep, I hardly slept, I didn't sleep much; **cette histoire n'a g. eu de conséquences** this business had hardly any *or* very few consequences; **il n'a g. d'argent/temps** he hasn't much money/time, he has hardly any money/time; **vous n'en avez g. non plus** *(non comptable)* you haven't much either; *(comptable)* you haven't many either; **je n'en sais g. plus** I hardly know anything more about it, I don't know much more about it; **il ne nous en parle g.** he hardly *or* scarcely talks to us about it; **je ne suis g. invitée à ces soirées** I'm hardly ever *or* scarcely ever invited to these parties; **il n'est g. plus grand que toi** he's hardly *or* scarcely taller than you; **il ne tardera g. à venir** he'll not be long in coming, he'll be here before long; **on ne tarda g. à entendre parler de lui dans les journaux** it wasn't long before he was mentioned in the newspapers; **tout cela n'a g. duré longtemps** all that didn't last very long; **il n'y a g. qu'elle qui soit au courant** she's about the only one (who's) in the picture; **il ne mange g. que du pain** he eats hardly anything but bread; **cela ne se dit plus g.** you don't hear that much now, hardly anybody says that now; **je n'y tiens plus g.** I'm not as keen (on it) as I used to be; **il n'en reste plus g.** *(non comptable)* there's hardly any left; *(comptable)* there are hardly any left; **il n'y a g. plus de six ans** it's barely more than six years ago; **la voyez-vous? – g.!** do you see her? – hardly ever!; **et celui-là, comment le trouvez-vous? – g. mieux!** and that one, what do you think of it? – hardly better *or* not much better!; **tu as mieux dormi qu'hier? – oh, g. mieux!** did you sleep better than yesterday? – hardly!

guéret [gerɛ] NM fallow land

guéri [geri] ADJ cured; *(rétabli)* better, recovered; *Fig* **être g. d'une peur/d'un préjugé** to be cured of a fear/a prejudice; **je ne pense plus à lui, je suis guérie** I don't think of him any more, I've got over him

guéridon [geridɔ̃] NM pedestal table, gueridon, dumb waiter

guérilla [gerija] NF **1** *(guerre)* guer(r)illa warfare **2** *Vieilli (groupe)* band *or* troop of guer(r)illas

> Il faut noter que le nom anglais **guerrilla** est un faux ami. Il signifie **guérillero**.

guérillero [gerijero] NM guer(r)illa

guérir [gerir] VT *(personne, une maladie)* to cure; *(une blessure)* to heal; *Fig* **g. qn d'une habitude** to cure *or* break sb of a habit
VI *(d'une personne)* to get better, to be cured, to recover; *(d'une blessure)* to heal; *(d'une maladie)* to get better, to be cured; **il n'en guérira pas** *Méd* he won't recover from it; *Fig* he won't get over it; *Fig* **un chagrin qui ne guérit pas** an incurable grief, a grief that cannot be cured

VPR se guérir to get better, to be cured; **se g. de sa timidité** to get over *or* overcome one's shyness; *Fig* **se g. de ses préjugés** to overcome one's prejudices, to cure oneself of one's prejudices

guérison [geriz5] NF **1** (*rétablissement*) recovery; **en voie de g.** on the way *or* road to recovery; **attends la g. complète avant de sortir** wait until you are completely recovered before going out **2** (*action de guérir*) (*d'une maladie*) cure; (*d'une blessure*) healing; *Fig* **la g. d'une peine** the healing of a sorrow

guérissable [gerisabl] ADJ curable; (*blessure*) that can be healed

guérisseur, -euse [gerisœr, -øz] N healer, *Péj* quack (doctor)
    NM (*d'une tribu*) medicine man

guérite [gerit] NF **1** *Mil* sentry box **2** (*petit abri*) (*pour gardien*) cabin, shelter

guerre [ger] NF**1** (*conflit armé*) war; (*technique*) warfare; **la g. a éclaté entre …** war has broken out between …; **déclarer la g. à un pays** to declare war on a country; **pays en g.** country at war; **se mettre en g.** to go to war; **en temps de g.** in wartime, in time of war; **état de g.** state of war; **crime/criminel de g.** war crime/criminal; *Mil, Fig* **ruses de g.** tactics; **invalide de g.** war invalid, disabled ex-serviceman; **nom de g.** nom de guerre; *Fig* pseudonym, nom de guerre; **on entre dans une logique de g.** war is the only logical outcome; **faire la g. à** *ou* **contre un pays** to wage war on *or* against a country; **nous avons fait la g. ensemble contre la Prusse** we fought *or* served together against Prussia; *Arch* **le Ministère de la G.,** *Fam* **la G.** the Ministry of War, the War Department; *Hist* **la Grande G.** the Great War; **la première/la seconde g. mondiale** the First/Second World War, World War One/Two

2 *Fig* **partir en g. contre la drogue/l'injustice** to declare war on drugs/injustice; **elle fait la g. à son fils pour qu'il ne fume pas** she's fighting a running battle with her son about smoking; **faire la g. aux inégalités/concurrents** to wage war on inequality/competitors; **entre Jean et lui, c'est la petite g.** Jean and he are always trying to score off each other; **c'est la g. entre elle et son mari** it's war between her and her husband; **être en g. ouverte avec** *ou* **contre qn** to be openly at war with sb; **de g. lasse j'y consentis** I gave in for the sake of peace and quiet; **il est sur le pied de g. depuis 8 heures ce matin** he's been on the go since 8 o'clock this morning; **à la g. comme à la g.** we'll/you'll/*etc* have to do the best we/you/*etc* can, we'll/you'll/*etc* have to make the best of what we've/you've/*etc* got; (*tous les moyens sont justifiés*) if that's the way he wants it (that's the way he'll/*etc* get it); **c'est de bonne g.** it's fair enough, all's fair in love and war

▸▸**g. de 70** Franco-Prussian War; **g. aérienne** air war; **g. atomique** atomic war; (*technique*) atomic warfare; **g. bactériologique** germ warfare; **g. de Cent Ans** Hundred Years' War; **g. chimique** chemical warfare; **g. civile** civil war; **g. conventionnelle** conventional warfare; **g. des Deux-Roses** War of the Roses; **g. éclair** blitzkrieg; **g. économique** economic warfare; **g. d'embuscade** guerilla warfare; **g. des étoiles** star wars; **g. froide** cold war; **g. idéologique** ideological war; **g. de libération** war of liberation; **g. des nerfs** war of nerves; **g. planétaire** global war; **g. de positions** static warfare; *Com* **g. des prix** *ou* **des tarifs** price war; **guerres de religion** wars of religion; **g. sainte** holy war; **g. terrestre** land war; **g. totale** total war; **g. de tranchées** trench warfare; **g. de Trente Ans** Thirty Years' War; **g. d'usure** war of attrition

guerrier, -ière [gerje, -jer] ADJ warlike, martial; **danse guerrière** war dance; **il est d'humeur guerrière** he is in a belligerent mood
    NM warrior

guerroyer [gerwaje] VI (**je guerroie, n. guerroyons; je guerroierai**) to war, to wage war (**contre** against); *Fig* **g. contre l'inégalité/l'hypocrisie** to struggle against *or* wage war on inequality/hypocrisy

guet [ge] NM **1** (*action*) watch; *Mil* **poste de g.** lookout post; **faire le g.** to be on watch *or* on the lookout **2** *Hist* (*patrouille*) watch

guet-apens, *pl* **guets-apens** [getapã] NM (*piège*) ambush, trap; *Fig* trap; **attirer qn dans un g.** to ambush sb; **tomber dans un g.** to fall into an ambush *or* a trap, to be ambushed

guêtre [getr] NF gaiter; *Fam* **traîner ses guêtres** to wander about *or* around

guetter [gete] VT (*une occasion*) to watch out for; **le guépard guettait sa proie** the cheetah was lying in wait for its prey; **g. l'arrivée/la sortie/le passage de qn** to watch out for sb arriving/leaving/going past; **je guette les petites annonces** I keep an eye on the small ads *or Am* the classifieds; **le surmenage/la dépression le guette** overwork/depression will get him in the end; **ce qui te guette, toi, c'est une bonne indigestion** you're heading for a nasty attack of indigestion

guetteur [getœr] NM *Mil, Naut* lookout (man); **poste de guetteurs** lookout post

gueulante [gœlãt] NF *Arg* uproar, din; **elle a poussé une g.** she raised the roof, she kicked up a stink

gueulard¹, -arde [gœlar, -ard] ADJ **1** *très Fam* (*qui crie*) loudmouthed **2** *Fam* (*gourmand*) greedy
    N **1** *très Fam* (*personne qui crie*) loudmouth **2** *Fam* (*gourmand*) greedy guts

gueulard² [gœlar] NM **1** *Métal* (*d'un four*) mouth **2** *Naut* loudhailer

gueule [gœl] NF**1** (*d'un animal, d'un poisson*) mouth; *Fig* **se jeter dans la g. du loup** to put one's head in the lion's mouth

2 *très Fam* (*bouche*) mouth; *Vulg* **il pue de la g.** his breath stinks; **ça emporte** *ou* **arrache la g.** it takes the roof of your mouth off; **c'est un fort en g.** *ou* **une grande g.** he's a loudmouth; **avec sa grande g., il fallait qu'il parle** he's such a blabbermouth *or* he's got such a big mouth it's no wonder he gave the game away; **coups de g.** shouting session; **(ferme) ta g.!** shut your mouth *or* face!, shut it!; **s'en mettre plein la g.** to stuff oneself; **se bourrer la g.** to get plastered *or* sloshed; **une fine g.** a gourmet; **crever la g. ouverte** to die like a dog

3 *très Fam* (*visage*) mug, face; **il est arrivé, la g. enfarinée, pour …** he turned up, innocence itself, to …; **se fendre la g.** to laugh one's head off, to split one's sides laughing; **avoir une sale g.** (*être moche*) to have an ugly mug; (*avoir mauvaise mine*) to look rotten; (*avoir l'air déprimé*) to look down in the mouth; **faire une sale g.** to pull a long face; **faire une drôle de g.** to pull *or* make a strange face; **il a été arrêté pour délit de sale g.** he was arrested because they didn't like the look of his face; **il/ce fromage a une bonne g.** I like the look of him/this cheese; **avoir une belle g.** to have a pretty face; **faire la g.** to sulk; **faire la g. à qn** to be in a huff *or* a bad mood with sb; **faire une g. d'enterrement** to look thoroughly depressed; **casser la g. à qn** to smash sb's face in; **se casser la g.** to fall flat on one's face, to come a cropper; *Fig* (*d'une entreprise*) to come a cropper; **se foutre de** *ou* **se payer la g. de qn** to take the piss out of sb; **(s')en prendre plein la g.** (*se faire insulter*) to get a right mouthful (of abuse); (*se faire frapper*) to get one's face

smashed in; **sa g. ne me revient pas** I don't like the look of him

4 *Fam* (*allure*) **elle a de la g. cette fille** she's quite a girl, that girl's really got something (about her); **ce tableau a de la g.** that's some picture; **ce chapeau a une drôle de g.** that hat looks odd

5 (*ouverture*) (*d'un sac, d'un puits, d'un tunnel etc*) mouth; (*d'un fusil*) muzzle

▸▸**g. de bois** hangover; **se réveiller avec / avoir la g. de bois** to wake up with/have a hangover; *Hist, Mil* **gueules cassées** = soldiers with serious facial injuries; **g. noire** coal-miner

gueule-de-loup, *pl* **gueules-de-loup** NF **1** *Bot* snap-dragon **2** *Constr* (chimney) cowl, chimney jack **3** (*de machine*) (exhaust) muffler

gueulement [gœlmã] NM *Fam* (*cri*) yell; (*cris*) yelling, yells; **pousser des gueulements** to yell

gueuler [gœle] *très Fam* VI to yell, to bawl; **si je suis en retard, ça va g. à la maison** if I'm late I'll get bawled out at home; **faire g. la radio/sa télévision** to turn the radio/one's television up full blast
    VT (*chanson, ordres etc*) to bawl out, to yell out

gueules [gœl] *Hér* gules

gueuleton [gœlt5] NM *Fam* blowout; **faire un bon petit g. entre amis** to have a good blowout with some friends

gueuletonner [gœltone] VI *Fam* to have a blowout

gueuse¹ [gøz] NF **g. (de fonte), fer en g.** pig

gueuserie [gøzri] NF **1** *Arch, Litt* (*condition*) beggary **2** *Vieilli* (*action*) foul deed

gueux, gueuse² [gø, gøz] N**1** *Fam* **courir la gueuse** to chase women; (*de façon générale*) to be a woman-chaser **2** *Arch, Litt* (*mendiant*) beggar **3** *Vieilli* (*fripon*) rascal, rogue

gueuze, gueuse³ [gøz] NF (*bière*) = type of Belgian beer

gugusse [gygys] NM clown; *Fam* **faire le g.** to clown *or* fool around, to act the fool; *Fam* **quel g., ce type!** what a clown this guy is!

gui¹ [gi] NM *Bot* mistletoe; **boules de g.** clumps of mistletoe

gui² NM *Naut* **1** (*espar*) boom **2** (*corde*) guy(rope)

guibol(l)e [gibɔl] NF *Fam* (*jambe*) pin, leg; **j'en ai plein les guiboles** my legs have had it; *Vieilli* **jouer des guibolles** to stir one's stumps

guiches [giʃ] NFPL kiss curls

guichet [giʃɛ] NM**1** ticket desk, ticket office; *Banque* position, window, *Am* wicket; *Théâtre* box office; **g. automatique** (*pour billets*) automatic ticket machine; *Banque* **g. automatique (de banque)** cash dispenser, *Am* ATM; **g. fermé** (*sur panneau*) position closed; *Théâtre etc* **on joue à guichets fermés** the performance is sold out **2** (*dans une porte*) grille, grating; (*dans une prison etc*) wicket (gate) **3** (*au cricket*) wicket; **gardien de g.** wicketkeeper

guichetier, -ière [giʃtje, -jer] N (*de banque*) (counter) clerk, assistant, teller

guidage [gidaʒ] NM **1** *Électron* (*d'un avion*) guidance; **tête de g.** homing head; *Aviat* **g. par radio-maillage** *ou* **par radio-mailles** grid guidance **2** *Tech* (*d'une pièce mobile*) guiding; (*sur un tour de forage*) centring, *Am* centering; *Aut* steering

guide [gid] NM**1** (*personne*) guide; **g. dans un musée** museum guide; **g. local** local guide; **n'oubliez pas le g.** don't forget the guide; **la loyauté a toujours été son g.** loyalty has always guided him

2 (*manuel*) guide (book); **g. touristique/des rues de Londres** tourist/London street guide; **g. de conversation** phrase book; **g.**

gastronomique restaurant guide, good food guide; **g. de voyages** travel directory; *Ordinat* **g. de l'utilisateur** instruction manual

3 *Tech* **g. de courroie** belt guide; *Aut* **g. chaîne** chain guide; **g.-classement** file divider; *Électron* **g. d'ondes** wave guide; **g.-papier** *(d'une imprimante)* paper guide; **g.-ruban** *(d'une imprimante)* ribbon guide; **g.-sortie** *(d'une fiche)* file extraction marker

4 *Typ* **g. de caractères** type book; **g. du style maison** house-style book

5 *Belg (indicateur de chemin de fer)* railway timetable; *(annuaire)* telephone book

NF 1 *Équitation* rein; *Fig* **mener la vie à grandes guides** to live in lavish style **2** *(fille faisant du scoutisme)* (girl) guide, *Am* girl scout; **g. aînée** ranger

▸▸ **g.-conférencier**, *pl* **g.-conférenciers** guide; **g. de haute montagne** mountain guide; **g.-interprète**, *pl* **g.-interprètes** bilingual tour guide

guide-âne, *pl* **guide-âne(s)** NM *Vieilli* beginner's handbook

guide-fil NM INV thread guide

guider [gide] VT *(personne, cheval)* to guide; *Tech* **guidé par radio** radio-controlled; **g. un enfant dans le choix d'une carrière** to guide a child in the choice of a career; **se laisser g. par son intuition** to be guided by one's intuition

guidon [gidɔ̃] NM **1** *(de vélo)* handlebars; *Fig* **avoir la tête** *ou* **le nez dans le g.** to have one's nose to the ground; *Fig Fam* **moustaches en g. de bicyclette** handlebar moustache **2** *Mil (étendard)* guidon, pennant; *Naut (pavillon)* burgee **3** *(viseur) (d'une arme à feu)* foresight, bead

guignard, -arde [giɲar, -ard] N *Fam Vieilli (malchanceux)* unlucky person

NM *(oiseau)* **pluvier g.** dotterel

guigne[1] [giɲ] NF *Bot* sweet cherry; *Fam* **se soucier de qch/qn comme d'une g.** not to give *or* care a damn *or* a fig about sth/sb

guigne[2] NF *Fam (malchance)* bad luck; **porter la g. à qn** to bring sb bad luck; **avoir la g.** to be out of luck

guigner [giɲe] VT *(personne, chose)* to sneak a look at, to give a surreptitious *or* sidelong glance at; *Fig (avoir des vues sur)* to have one's eye on; *Cartes* **g. le jeu du voisin** to sneak a look at one's opponent's hand

guignol [giɲɔl] NM **1** *(personnage)* ≃ Punch; *Fam Péj (personne)* clown, joker; *Fam* **faire le g.** to clown around, to play *or* act the fool **2** *(spectacle)* ≃ Punch and Judy show; **aller au g.** ≃ to go to see the Punch and Judy show; *Fig Fam* **c'est du g.!** it's a farce *or* joke!

guignolades [giɲɔlad] NFPL fooling around

guignolet [giɲɔlɛ] NM cherry brandy; **un g. kirsch** a cherry brandy with kirsch

guignon [giɲɔ̃] NM *Fam Vieilli* bad luck

guilde [gild] NF **1** *(club) (pour disques, livres etc)* club **2** *Hist* guild; **g. de commerçants** merchant guild

guili-guili [giligili] NM INV *Fam* tickle; **faire g. à qn** to tickle sb

Guillaume [gijom] N William; **G. le Conquérant** William the Conqueror

guillaume [gijom] NM *Menuis* rabbet(ing) plane; **g. à onglet** mitre plane, *Am* miter plane

guilledou [gijdu] NM *Fam Vieilli* **courir le g.** to chase after women; *(d'une façon générale)* to be a woman-chaser

guillemets [gijmɛ] NMPL inverted commas,

quotation marks, *Fam* quotes; **mot entre g.** word in inverted commas *or* quotation marks; **mettez ce mot entre g.** put this word in inverted commas *or* quotation marks; **ouvrez/fermez les g.** *(en dictant)* quote/unquote, open/close inverted commas *or* quotation marks; **c'est un artiste entre g.** he's an artist, in inverted commas *or* quote unquote; *Typ* **g. fermants** closing quote marks; *Typ* **g. ouvrants** opening quote marks; *Typ* **g. simples** single quotes

guillemot [gijmo] NM guillemot

guilleret, -ette [gijrɛ, -ɛt] ADJ **1** *(gai) (personne, ton, pas)* jaunty, lively **2** *(léger) (plaisanterie)* risqué

guillotine [gijɔtin] NF guillotine; **fenêtre à g.** sash window; **cisailles à g.** guillotine shears; **aller à la g.** to go to the guillotine

guillotiner [gijɔtine] VT to guillotine

guimauve [gimov] NF *Bot* marsh mallow; *Culin (pâte de)* **g.** marshmallow; *Bot* **g. rose** hollyhock; *Fig Péj* **c'est de la g.** it's pure sentimentality, *Fam* it's soppy *or* slushy; **des romans à la g.** sentimental *or Fam* soppy *or* slushy novels

guimbarde [gɛ̃bard] NF **1** *Mus* Jew's harp **2** *Fam (vieille voiture)* (old) jalopy, *Br* old banger **3** *(outil)* router plane, grooving plane

guimpe [gɛ̃p] NF **1** *(de religieuse)* wimple **2** *(chemisette)* chemisette

guincher [gɛ̃ʃe] VI *Fam* to dance

guindage [gɛ̃daʒ] NM hoisting

guindaille [gɛ̃daj] NF *Belg Fam* student party; **il adore faire la g.** he loves to party

guindé [gɛ̃de] ADJ *(personne, air)* stiff, starchy; *(atmosphère)* strained; *(langage)* affected; *(style)* stilted, stiff; *(réception)* posh

guindeau, -eaux [gɛ̃do] NM *Naut* windlass

guinder [gɛ̃de] VT *Tech* to hoist, to windlass; *Naut (mât)* to send up, to sway up

VPR **se guinder** *(d'une personne, d'une ambiance)* to become stiff; *(d'un style)* to become stilted *or* stiff; *(d'une ambiance)* to become strained

Guinée [gine] NF Guinea

guinée [gine] NF *Arch (monnaie)* guinea

Guinée-Bissau [ginebiso] NF Guinea-Bissau

guinéen, -enne [ginéɛ̃, -ɛn] ADJ Guinean

N **G.** Guinean

guingois [gɛ̃gwa] ADV **de g.** askew, lopsided; **il se tenait un peu de g.** he was standing a bit lopsided; *Fig* **tout va de g.** everything's going wrong

guinguette [gɛ̃gɛt] NF café *(with music and dancing, often in the open)*

guipure [gipyr] NF guipure (lace)

guirlande [girlɑ̃d] NF *(de fleurs etc)* garland; **g. de Noël** piece of tinsel; **g. de papier** paper chain; **g. de perles** string of pearls; **g. lumineuse** string of lights; *Ordinat* **connecté en g.** in a token ring configuration

guise [giz] NF **faire qch à sa g.** to do sth as one pleases *or* likes; **faire** *ou* **agir à sa g.** to do as one pleases *or* likes; **il n'en fait qu'à sa g.** he just does as he pleases *or* likes; **à ta g.!** as you please *or* like!; **en g. de** by way of

guitare [gitar] NF guitar; **g. électrique** electric guitar; **g. hawaïenne** Hawaiian guitar; **g. sèche** acoustic guitar; **g. classique** classical guitar

guitariste [gitarist] N guitarist, guitar player

guitoune [gitun] NF **1** *Fam (tente)* tent **2** *Mil Arg* dugout, shelter

gulden [guldɛn] NM *Fin Anciennement (florin)* guilder

guppy [gypi] NM guppy

guru [guru] NM *Rel, Fig* guru

gus [gys] NM *Fam* guy

gustatif, -ive [gystatif, -iv] ADJ gustative, gustatory; **papilles gustatives** taste buds

gustation [gystasjɔ̃] NF tasting, *Spéc* gustation

gutta-percha, *pl* **guttas-perchas** [gytapɛrka] NF gutta-percha

guttural, -ale, -aux, -ales [gytyral, -o] ADJ *(son)* guttural; *(voix)* throaty, guttural; *Anat* **artère gutturale** carotid artery

NF *Ling* **gutturale** guttural

Guyana [gɥijana] NM Guyana

guyanais, -aise [gɥijanɛ, -ɛz] ADJ Guianese, Guianan

N **G.** Guianese, Guianan

Guyane [gɥijan] N Guiana; **G. française** French Guiana; *Hist* **G. britannique** British Guiana

guyot [gɥijo] NF guyot (pear)

gym [ʒim] NF *Fam* gym; **faire de la g.** to do gym; **un cours de g.** a gym class

gymkhana [ʒimkana] NM *Sport* rally

gymnase [ʒimnaz] NM **1** *Sport* gymnasium **2** *Suisse (lycée)* = state school attended by pupils between the ages of 15 and 19, *Br* ≃ secondary school, *Am* ≃ high school

gymnaste [ʒimnast] N gymnast

gymnastique [ʒimnastik] ADJ gymnastic; **partir au pas g.** to set off at a jog trot

NF gymnastics; *Fig* **g. de l'esprit** mental gymnastics; *Fig* **il faut faire toute une g. pour sortir de cette auto** you have to be a contortionist to get out of this car

▸▸ **g. corrective** remedial gymnastics; **g. matinale** morning exercises; **g. respiratoire** breathing exercises; **g. rythmique** eurhythmics

gymnote [ʒimnɔt] NM electric eel

gynécée [ʒinese] NM *Antiq, Bot* gynaeceum, *Am* gyneceum

gynécologie [ʒinekɔlɔʒi] NF gynaecology, *Am* gynecology

gynécologique [ʒinekɔlɔʒik] ADJ *(examen)* gynaecological, *Am* gynecological

gynécologue [ʒinekɔlɔg] N gynaecologist, *Am* gynecologist

gypaète [ʒipaɛt] NM bearded vulture, lammergeyer

gypse [ʒips] NM *Minér* gypsum, plasterstone

gypseux, -euse [ʒipsø, -øz] ADJ *Minér* gypseous

gypsophile [ʒipsɔfil] NF *Bot* gypsophila

gyrocompas [ʒirokɔ̃pa] NM *Naut* gyrocompass

gyromètre [ʒirɔmɛtr] NM *Aviat* gyrometer

gyrophare [ʒirofar] NM flashing *or* rotating light

gyropilote [ʒiropilɔt] NM *Aviat* gyropilot, automatic pilot

gyroscope [ʒirɔskɔp] NM gyroscope; *Aviat* **g. directionnel** directional gyroscope

gyroscopique [ʒirɔskɔpik] ADJ gyroscopic; **compas g.** gyrocompass

gyrostat [ʒirɔsta] NM gyrostat

H, h [aʃ] **NM** SEE GRAMMAR A5; B3 **1** *(lettre)* H, h; **h muet** mute h; **h aspiré** aspirate h; *Mil etc* **l'heure H** zero hour; **bombe H** H bomb **2** *Fam* **H** *(haschisch)* hash, *Br* blow; **trois grammes de H** three grams of hash

*ha [ɑ] **INT** ah!; **ha, ha!** *(rire)* ha!, ha!

*habanera [abanera] **NF** habanera

habeas corpus [abeaskɔrpys] **NM** *Jur* habeas corpus

habile [abil] **ADJ 1** clever, skilful, *Am* skillful; *(rusé)* cunning; *(film, roman)* clever; **il faut être h. pour faire cette réparation** it takes skill to do this kind of repair; **elle n'est pas h. de ses mains** she's not good with her hands; **mains habiles** skilled hands; **façonner qch d'une main h.** to make sth skilfully; **h. à faire qch** clever at doing sth; **il est h. en affaires** he's a good businessman; **ce n'était pas très h. de ta part** that wasn't very clever *or* bright of you **2** *Jur* **h. à succéder** able *or* competent to inherit

habilement [abilmɑ̃] **ADV** *(avec adresse)* cleverly, skilfully, *Am* skillfully; *(avec ruse)* cunningly

habileté [abilte] **NF 1** *(adresse)* ability, skill **2** *(intelligence)* cleverness; **texte commenté avec h.** cleverly analysed text **2** *Jur* ability, title; **avoir h. à hériter** to be entitled to succeed

habilitation [abilitasjɔ̃] **NF** *Jur* **h. de qn à faire qch** enabling (of) sb to do sth

habilité [abilite] **NF** *Jur* ability, title; **avoir h. à hériter** to be entitled to succeed

habiliter [abilite] **VT** *Jur* **h. qn à faire qch** to enable *or* entitle sb to do sth; **habilité à signer** *(employé de banque)* authorized to sign

habillage [abijaʒ] **NM 1** *(d'un enfant etc)* dressing; **l'h. des petits prend beaucoup de temps** dressing the children takes ages
2 *Culin (de la viande, du gibier à plumes)* dressing; *(de la volaille)* drawing and trussing; *(d'un poisson)* cleaning
3 *(des arbres)* pruning, trimming
4 *(d'une montre etc)* assembly, putting together
5 *Tech (d'une chaudière etc)* lagging
6 *Com (de marchandises)* packaging; **h. transparent** blister pack
7 *Aut* **h. intérieur** trim
8 *(de page)* design, presentation
9 *Ordinat* text wrap, runaround
10 *TV, Radio* **h. chaîne** station identification *(including on-air promos, transitions and titles)*; **les téléspectateurs ont mal accueilli le nouvel h. de la chaîne** the TV channel's new look did not go down well with the viewers
11 *Compta* **h. de bilan** window-dressing of a balance-sheet

habillé [abije] **ADJ 1** dressed; **être bien/mal h.** to be well/badly dressed; **h. en femme/cosmonaute** dressed up as a woman/spaceman; **h. de bleu/d'un complet** dressed in

blue/in a suit; **h. chaudement** warmly clad *or* dressed; **h. légèrement** lightly clad *or* dressed; **s'endormir tout h.** to go to sleep with one's clothes on **2** *(élégant)* smart; **soirée habillée** reception, formal *or Fam* dressy occasion; **trop h.** *(robe)* too dressy; *(personne)* over-dressed; **cette robe est très habillée** this dress is very smart; **ce n'est pas très h.** it isn't very dressy

habillement [abijmɑ̃] **NM 1** *(action)* clothing, dressing **2** *(vêtements)* clothes, dress **3** *(industrie)* clothing industry

habiller [abije] **VT 1** *(de vêtements)* to dress; **h. un enfant en soldat** to dress a child up as a soldier; *Fig Vieilli* **h. qn pour l'hiver** to tell sb off
2 *Culin (viande, gibier à plumes)* to dress; *(volaille)* to draw and truss; *(poisson)* to clean
3 *(arbre)* to prune, to trim
4 *(montre etc)* to put *or* piece together; *(pièces)* to assemble; *Typ* **h. une gravure** to run type round a block
5 *(fournir en vêtements)* to clothe; **elle se fait h. par Lacroix** she has clothes made for her by Lacroix, she buys *or* gets her clothes at Lacroix; **qui habille la princesse?** who makes the princess's clothes?, where does the princess get her clothes?; **ma mère nous habillait** my mother made all our clothes; *Fam* **h. qn** *(en dire du mal)* to bad-mouth sb, *Br* to slag sb off
6 *(garnir)* to cover (up), to wrap up; *(chaudière etc)* to lag; *Com (marchandises)* to label, to package; **h. une pièce** to decorate a room; **tableau de bord habillé de cuir** leather-padded dash(board); **h. des meubles de housses** to put loose covers on furniture; *TV etc* **h. le décor** to dress set
7 *(aller)* to suit; **un rien t'habille** you look good in anything; **il suffit d'un rien pour l'h.** he/she looks good in anything, she can wear anything; **ce tissu l'habille bien/mal** this material suits/does not suit him/her *or* flatters/does not flatter him/her
8 *Compta (bilan)* to window-dress
VPR **s'habiller 1** to dress (oneself), to get dressed; *(d'un prêtre etc)* to robe; **il ne sait pas encore s'h. tout seul** he can't get dressed by himself yet, he can't dress himself yet; **elle s'habille n'importe comment** she wears any old thing; **elle ne sait pas s'h.** she has no dress sense; **comment vous habillez-vous pour la soirée?** what are you wearing to the party?; **s'h. chaudement/légèrement** to dress warmly/lightly; **s'h. long/court/jeune** to wear long/short/young clothes; **s'h. en femme** to dress up as a woman
2 **s'h. sur mesure** to have one's clothes made to measure; **elle s'habille chez Dior** she buys her clothes from Dior; **s'h. de neuf** to put on one's new clothes *or* one's new outfit

3 *(pour le dîner etc)* to dress; **faut-il s'h.?** do we have to get dressed up?

habilleur, -euse [abijœr, -øz] **N** *Théâtre* dresser

habit [abi] **NM 1** dress, costume; **habits** clothes; **mettre ses habits** to put on one's clothes; **il faut l'aider à mettre ses habits/enlever ses habits** he has to be helped on/off with his clothes; *Vieilli* **marchand d'habits** *(fripier)* dealer in second-hand clothes; **h. de travail** working clothes; **le costume et la cravate, ce sont mes habits de travail** I wear a suit and tie to work **2** **h. (de soirée)** evening dress, tails; **l'h. est de rigueur** formal *or* evening dress must be worn **3** *(d'une sœur, d'un moine)* habit; **prendre l'h.** *(d'un homme)* to become a monk *or* priest, to take holy orders; *(d'une femme)* to become a nun; *Prov* **l'h. ne fait pas le moine** appearances can be deceptive
▶▶ **h. de cheval** riding habit *or* clothes; **h. de cour** court dress; **habits du dimanche** Sunday best; **ils arrivèrent en habits du dimanche** they came in their Sunday best; **h. ecclésiastique** clerical dress; **h. vert** = green coat worn by members of the Académie française; **il rêvait de revêtir l'h. vert** he dreamed of becoming a member of the Académie française

habitabilité [abitabilite] **NF 1** *(d'une maison)* habitability, fitness for habitation **2** *(capacité)* capacity; **une h. de cinq personnes** space for five people

habitable [abitabl] **ADJ** (in)habitable, fit for habitation; **l'appartement est immédiatement h./n'est pas h.** the apartment is ready to move into/is uninhabitable

habitacle [abitakl] **NM** *Aviat* cockpit; *Naut* binnacle; *Aut* passenger compartment, cabin

habitant, -ante [abitɑ̃, -ɑ̃t] **N 1** *(d'une ville)* inhabitant, resident; *(d'une maison)* occupier, occupant; **ville de 10 000 habitants** town of 10,000 inhabitants; **nombre d'habitants au kilomètre carré** number of inhabitants per square kilometre; **loger chez l'h.** *Mil* to be billeted with the locals; *(en voyage)* to rent a room in sb's house; **par h.** *(dans les statistiques)* per capita **2** *Litt* **les habitants des bois** the denizens *or* creatures of the woods **3** *Can (fermier)* small-scale farmer, *Can* habitant [abitɑ̃]
ADJ *Can Péj* **il est un peu h.** he's a bit of a country bumpkin

habitat [abita] **NM 1** *(d'un animal, d'une plante)* habitat **2** *Géog* settlement; **h. dispersé** open settlement; **c'est un type d'h. propre à ce pays** this type of dwelling *or* housing is unique to this country; **h. nomade/sédentaire** nomadic/sedentary settlement **3** *(logement)* **h. rural/urbain** rural/urban housing; **l'amélioration de l'h. est l'une des priorités du nouveau maire** improving housing conditions is one of the new mayor's priorities

habitation [abitasjɔ̃] NF **1** habitation; **impropre à l'h.** unsuitable *or* unfit for human habitation; **locaux à usage d'h.** premises for residential use **2** *(lieu)* dwelling (place), residence, abode; **une h. bien aménagée/située/chauffée** a well-equipped/well-situated/well-heated house; **changer d'h.** to change one's residence; **groupe (d'habitations)** *(lotissement)* housing estate
▸▸**h. à loyer modéré** *Br* ≃ council flat/house, *Am* public housing unit

habiter [abite] VT *(maison, lieu)* to live in; **la région n'est pas habitée** the area is uninhabited; **c'est très peu habité par ici** very few people live around here; **cette pièce n'a jamais été habitée** this room has never been used; **Vénus est-elle habitée?** is there life on Venus?; **une planète habitée** an inhabited planet; *Fig* **la certitude qui m'habite** my personal conviction; **le calme qui l'habite depuis peu** the inner calm which he has recently acquired; **elle est habitée par la haine** she is full of hatred
VI to live (à in, at); **h. (à) Paris/la campagne** to live in Paris/in the country; **j'habite au 3, place des Cardeurs** I live at number 3, place des Cardeurs; **h. en Italie** to live in Italy; **vous habitez chez vos parents?** do you live with your parents?; **elle habite avec son frère/cet homme** she lives with her brother/this man

habitude [abityd] NF **1** habit, custom; **bonne/mauvaise h.** good/bad habit; **faire qch par h.** to do sth from *or* out of habit, to do sth from force of habit; **prendre l'h. de faire qch** to get into the habit of doing sth; **se faire une h. d'arriver en retard** to have a habit of being late; **avoir l'h.** *ou* **avoir une h. de faire qch** to be in the habit of doing sth; **ça ne la gênera pas, elle a l'h.** that won't bother her *or* she won't mind, she's used to it; **je n'ai pas l'h. de mentir** I'm not in the habit of lying; **prendre de mauvaises habitudes** to get into bad habits, to pick up bad habits; **c'est une question d'h.** it's a question of habit; **avoir une longue h. du travail en commun** to have long experience of working together; **nous avons une longue h. de l'édition** we have long experience in the field of publishing; **ce n'est pas une h. chez moi, ce n'est pas dans mes habitudes** I don't make a habit of it; **à** *ou* **selon** *ou* **suivant son h.** as he usually does/did, as is/was his custom *or Fml* wont; **se défaire d'une h., perdre une h.** to get out of a habit, to break a habit; **faire perdre une h. à qn** to break sb of a habit; **d'h.** usually, ordinarily, normally; **meilleur que d'h.** better than usual; **comme d'h.** as usual; **plus tôt que d'h.** earlier than usual; **habitudes d'achat** shopping habits, buying habits; **habitudes d'écoute** listening habits; *TV* viewing habits
2 *(dextérité)* knack; **je n'en ai plus l'h.** I'm out of practice
3 habitudes ways, customs; **les habitudes du pays** the customs of the country

habitué, -ée [abitɥe] N *(d'une maison)* frequent *or* regular visitor; *(d'un restaurant, d'un magasin)* regular customer, regular; **c'est un h. de la maison** *(client)* he's a regular (customer)

habituel, -elle [abitɥɛl] ADJ usual, customary, regular; **cette attitude ne lui est pas habituelle** this is not his/her usual attitude, he/she doesn't usually take this attitude; **c'est le problème h. avec elle** it's the usual problem with her; *Fam* **c'est le coup h.** it's the same old story, it's par for the course; **elle nous a fait le coup h.** she's played the usual *or* the same old trick on us

habituellement [abitɥɛlmɑ̃] ADV usually, habitually, regularly; **elle arrive h. vers 18 heures 30** she usually arrives around half past six

habituer [abitɥe] VT to accustom, *Fml* to habituate; **h. qn à qch** to get sb used to sth, to accustom sb to sth; **il faut h. les enfants au rythme de l'école** you have to get the children used *or* accustomed to the pace of school; **h. des enfants à la politesse** to get children into the habit of being polite; **h. qn à la fatigue** to accustom sb to fatigue; **il faut h. son esprit à la concentration** you have to get used to concentrating; **maintenant j'y suis habitué** I'm used to it now; **elle est habituée à rester seule** she's used to being alone; **h. qn à faire qch** to get sb into the habit of doing sth, to get sb used to doing sth; **il faut les h. à manger peu de sucre** you must get them into the habit of *or* get them used to not eating much sugar
VPR **s'habituer** to get used, to get *or* grow accustomed (à to); **tu verras, tu vas t'y h.** you'll get used to it, you'll see; **s'h. à travailler très tôt le matin** to get used to working very early in the morning; **je n'arrive pas à m'y h.** I just can't get used to it; **je ne m'habituerai jamais à …** I'll never get used to …; **je ne m'y suis toujours pas habitué** I still haven't got used to it; **s'h. à une idée** to get used to an idea

*****hâblerie** [ablǝri] NF **1** *(attitude)* bragging, boasting **2** *(propos)* boast

*****hâbleur, -euse** [ablœr, -øz] ADJ bragging, boasting, boastful
N boaster, braggart

*****Habsbourg** [apsbur] N *Hist* **la maison de H.** the House of Hapsburg

*****hachage** [aʃaʒ] NM *(de viande etc)* chopping (up), mincing; *(de la paille etc)* cutting

*****hache** [aʃ] NF axe, *Am* ax; **h. à main** hatchet; **fait** *ou* **taillé à coups de h.** rough-hewn, hacked out; **visage taillé à coups de h.** angular face; **exécuter qn à la h.** to chop sb's head off; *Vieilli* **porter la h. dans les dépenses publiques** to axe *or* cut public spending
▸▸*Arch* **h. d'abordage** scuttling axe; *Arch* **h. d'armes** battleaxe; **h. de guerre** tomahawk; *Fig* **enterrer la h. de guerre** to bury the hatchet

*****haché** [aʃe] ADJ **1** minced, chopped; **bifteck h.** minced beef, mince, *Am* ground beef; **steak h.** steak mince **2** *(style etc)* staccato, jerky; **un film h. par des publicités** a film interspersed with adverts **3** *(dessin)* (cross)hatched; *(carte)* hachured
NM = **hachis**

*****hache-légumes** NM INV *Culin* vegetable cutter

*****hachement** [aʃmɑ̃] NM = **hachage**

*****hache-paille** NM INV *Agr* chaffcutter

*****hacher** [aʃe] VT **1** to chop (up); *(viande)* to mince, *Am* to grind; **la grêle a haché les récoltes** the crops have been cut to shreds by the hail; **h. menu** to mince finely, to chop up small; *Fig* **h. qn menu comme chair à pâté** to make mincemeat of sb; *Fig* **se faire h.** *(se faire battre)* to be cut to pieces; **elle est prête à se faire h. pour lui** she'd do anything for him; **si tu reviens à cette heure, tu vas te faire h. menu** if you come home at this hour, you'll have your head in your hands!; *Fig* **plutôt me faire h. (menu) que de dire oui** I'd rather die than say yes **2** = **hachurer**

*****hachette** [aʃɛt] NF hatchet

*****hache-viande** NM INV *Culin* mincer

*****hachis** [aʃi] NM *Culin (à la viande)* minced *or Am* ground meat, mince; *(au poisson)* chopped fish; **h. de veau** minced veal; **h. Parmentier** *(au bœuf)* ≃ cottage pie; *(avec viande blanche)* ≃ dish similar to cottage

pie, made with white meat; *(au mouton)* ≃ shepherd's pie; **h. d'herbes** chopped herbs

*****hachisch** [aʃiʃ] NM hashish; **fumer du h.** to smoke hash

*****hachoir** [aʃwar] NM *Culin* **1** *(couteau)* chopper **2** *(planche)* chopping board **3** *(électrique)* mincing machine, mincer

*****hachurage** [aʃyraʒ] NM *Ordinat* hatching

*****hachurer** [aʃyre] VT to (cross)hatch; *(carte)* to hachure

*****hachures** [aʃyr] NFPL (cross)hatching; *(sur une carte)* hachures; **carte en h.** hachured map

*****hacienda** [asjɛnda] NF hacienda

*****hacker** [akœr] NM *Ordinat* hacker

*****haddock** [adɔk] NM *Culin* smoked haddock

Hadrien [adrijɛ̃] N Hadrian; **le mur d'H.** Hadrian's wall

*****Haendel** [ɛndɛl] N Handel

*****hagard** [agar] ADJ *(visage)* haggard, drawn; *(expression, regard, yeux)* wild, distraught

hagiographe [aʒjɔgraf] N hagiographer

hagiographie [aʒjɔgrafi] NF hagiography

hagiographique [aʒjɔgrafik] ADJ hagiographic(al)

*****haie** [ɛ] NF **1** *(clôture)* hedge(row) **2** *Sport* hurdle; *Équitation* fence; *Sport* **course de haies** hurdle race, *Fam* hurdles; **400 mètres haies** 400 metre hurdles **3** *(d'arbres, de pieux, de curieux etc)* line, row; **faire** *ou* **former une h.** to line up
▸▸**h. d'honneur** guard of honour *or Am* honor; **h. vive** quickset hedge

*****haïku** [aiku] NM haiku

*****haillon** [ajɔ̃] NM *(vêtements)* rag; **être en haillons** to be in rags (and tatters); **des enfants en haillons** children dressed in rags (and tatters)

*****haine** [ɛn] NF hatred (**pour** of, for), hate; **avoir de la h. pour qn/qch** to hate *or* detest sb/sth; **éprouver de la h. pour qn/qch** to feel hatred for sb/sth; **prendre qch/qn en h.** to take a strong aversion to sth/sb; **en haine** *ou* **par h. de qch** out of hatred of *or* for sth; *très Fam* **j'ai la h.!** I'm bloody furious; *très Fam* **les jeunes de la cité ont la h.** young people on the estate are full of rage

*****haineusement** [ɛnøzmɑ̃] ADV with (bitter) hatred

*****haineux, -euse** [ɛnø, -øz] ADJ full of hatred *or* hate; **regard h.** a look full of hatred; **d'un ton h.** with hate in his/her/*etc* voice; **une femme haineuse** a woman full of hatred

> Il faut noter que l'adjectif anglais **heinous** est un faux ami. Il signifie **atroce, abominable**.

*****haïr** [air] *(je hais* [ɛ]*, tu hais, il hait, n. haïssons; imp* **hais***; otherwise regular)* VT to hate, to detest, to loathe; **c'est ce que je hais le plus au monde** I hate *or* detest *or* loathe that more than anything else in the world; **h. qn d'avoir fait qch** to hate sb for doing *or* having done sth; *Can Fam* **h. qn à s'en confesser** to hate sb's guts
VPR **se haïr** *(soi-même)* to hate oneself; *(de deux personnes)* to hate each other; *Hum* **elles se haïssent cordialement** they cordially detest each other; **je me hais de lui avoir menti** I hate myself for lying to him

*****haire** [ɛr] NF *(chemise)* hairshirt

*****haïssable** [aisabl] ADJ hateful, detestable

*****Haïti** [aiti] NF Haiti

*****haïtien, -ienne** [aisjɛ̃, -jɛn] ADJ Haitian
N H. Haitian

*****halage** [alaʒ] NM towing; **chemin de h.** towpath; **corde de h.** towing line

halal [alal] ADJ INV *(viande)* halal, slaughtered according to Muslim law

*****hâle** [αl] NM (sun)tan

*****hâlé** [αle] ADJ (sun)tanned

haleine [alεn] NF breath; **avoir l'h. fraîche** to have fresh breath; **avoir mauvaise h., avoir l'h. forte** to have bad breath; **à son h., j'ai compris qu'il avait bu** I could tell from his breath that he'd been drinking; **retenir son h.** to hold one's breath; **(tout) d'une h.** all in one breath, in the same breath; **reprendre h.** to get or catch one's breath, to get one's breath back; **sans avoir le temps de reprendre h.** without having time to get one's breath back; **perdre h.** to get out of breath, to lose one's breath; **courir à perdre h.** to run until one is out of breath; **discuter à perdre h.** to argue nonstop or *Fam* hammer and tongs; **hors d'h.** out of breath, breathless; **travail de longue h.** long and exacting task; **tenir qn en h.** to keep sb in suspense

*****haler** [ale] VT **1** *(navire)* to warp **2** *(péniche etc)* to tow **3 h. une embarcation au sec** to haul up a boat (onto the beach) **4** *Naut (cordage etc)* to pull, to haul in, to heave
VI *Naut* **h. sur une manœuvre** to haul or pull on a rope, to heave at a rope

*****hâler** [αle] VT *(du soleil etc)* to tan, to brown; **pour h. votre teint pâle** to tan your pale skin

*****haletant** [al(ə)tα̃] ADJ *(coureur)* panting, gasping, breathless, out of breath; *(malade)* panting, gasping; **respiration haletante** panting, gasping; **voix haletante** breathless or gasping voice

*****halètement** [alεtmα̃] NM *(d'un coureur)* panting, gasping (for breath), puffing (and blowing); *(d'un malade)* panting, gasping; *(d'une locomotive)* puffing

*****haleter** [al(ə)te] VI (**je halète; je halèterai**) *(d'un coureur)* to pant, to gasp (for breath), to puff (and blow); *(d'un malade)* to pant, to gasp; *Fig Litt (d'une locomotive)* to puff; *Fig* **le cinéaste fait h. son public** the film-maker keeps his audience on the edge of their seats

*****haleur, -euse** [alœr, -øz] N *(de bateaux)* hauler, tower

*****half-track** [aftrak] NM *Mil* half-track

*****hall** [ol] NM entrance hall; *(d'un hôtel)* foyer, lobby; *(d'un aéroport)* lounge; **h. d'accueil** reception, lobby; **h. d'aéroport** airport lounge; **h. d'entrée** entrance hall; **h. d'entrée d'hôtel** hotel lobby; **h. d'exposition** exhibition hall; **h. de réception** foyer, lobby; **h. de gare** station concourse; **c'est un vrai h. de gare ici!** it's like Piccadilly Circus here!; **h. des départs** departure lounge

*****hallage** [alaʒ] NM *Com* market trader's dues

hallali [alali] NM mort; **sonner l'h.** to blow the mort

*****halle** [al] NF **1** (covered) market; *(grande salle)* hall; **h. aux poissons** fish market; **h. au blé** corn exchange; **les Halles (centrales)** the Halles *(the central market in Paris)* **2** *Suisse (bâtiment)* hall; **h. d'exposition** exhibition centre; **h. des fêtes** community centre; **h. de gymnastique** sports centre, sports hall; **h. polyvalente** community centre

*****hallebarde** [albard] NF *Arch* halberd, halbert; *Fam* **il pleut ou tombe des hallebardes** it's raining cats and dogs

*****hallebardier** [albardje] NM *Arch* halberdier

*****hallier** [alje] NM **1** thicket, copse **2 halliers** brushwood

Halloween [alɔwin] NF Halloween

hallu [aly] NF *Fam (abrév* **hallucination***)* hallucination; **je dois avoir des hallus!** I must be seeing things!

hallucinant [alysinα̃] ADJ *(drogue etc)* hallucinatory; *(pensée)* haunting; *(ressemblance etc)* striking; **paysage h. de beauté** strikingly beautiful scenery; *Fig Fam* **c'est h.!** it's incredible!, I don't believe it!

hallucination [alysinasjɔ̃] NF hallucination, delusion; **avoir des hallucinations** *(d'un malade, d'un ivrogne)* to have hallucinations; *Fig (se tromper)* to imagine or see things; **une h. collective** a collective or mass hallucination

hallucinatoire [alysinatwar] ADJ hallucinatory

halluciné, -ée [alysine] ADJ hallucinating; *Fig Fam* mad
N person who suffers from hallucinations; *Fig Fam* madman, *f* madwoman; **il me regardait de son air d'h.** he looked at me like a madman or with that wild staring look in the eyes

halluciner [alysine] VT *Rare* to make hallucinate, to cause to hallucinate
VI *(avoir des hallucinations)* to hallucinate; *Fig Fam* **j'hallucine!** I don't believe it!

hallucinogène [alysinɔʒεn] *Pharm* NM hallucinogen
ADJ hallucinogenic

*****halo** [alo] NM **1** *Météo etc* halo; *Fig* **un h. de gloire** a cloud of glory; **s'entourer d'un h. de mystère** to shroud oneself in mystery **2** *Opt* blurring **3** *Phot* fogging, *Spéc* halation

halogène [alɔʒεn] ADJ halogenous
NM halogen; **lampe à h.** halogen lamp; **h. à quartz** quartz-halogen

*****halte** [alt] NF **1** *(arrêt)* stop, halt; **faire h.** to (make a) halt, to stop; **h.(-là)!** stop!, halt!; *Fig* **h.-là, je ne suis pas d'accord!** hold on or not so fast, I don't agree!; **h. à l'armement!** stop the arms build-up!; **dire h. à l'inflation** to put a stop or an end to inflation **2** *(lieu)* stopping place, resting place; *Rail* halt; **h. routière** (roadside) rest area

*****halte-garderie,** *pl* **haltes-garderies** [alt(ə)gardəri] NF crèche

haltère [altεr] NM dumb-bell; **des haltères de 3 kilos** 3-kilo dumb-bells; **faire des haltères** to do weightlifting or weight training

haltérophile [alterɔfil] N weightlifter

haltérophilie [alterɔfili] NF weightlifting; **elle fait de l'h.** she does weightlifting or weight training

*****halva** [alva] NM halva

*****hamac** [amak] NM **1** hammock; **accrocher/décrocher un h.** to sling/unsling a hammock **2** *(fiche)* suspension file

hamadryade [amadrijad] NF *Myth* hamadryad, dryad, wood nymph

hamamélis [amamelis] NM *Bot* witch hazel, *Spéc* hamamelis

*****Hambourg** [ɑ̃bur] N Hamburg

*****hambourgeois, -oise** [ɑ̃burʒwa, -waz] ADJ of Hamburg
N **H.** Hamburger

*****hamburger** [ɑ̃burgœr] NM *Culin* hamburger

*****hameau, -eaux** [amo] NM hamlet

hameçon [amsɔ̃] NM (fish-)hook; **h. sans œillet** blind hook; *Fig* **mordre à l'h.** to swallow or rise to the bait

hameçonner [amsɔne] VT **1** *(poisson)* to hook **2** *(ligne de pêche)* to put hooks on

*****hammam** [amam] NM Turkish baths

*****hammerless** [amεrlεs] NM hammerless sporting gun

*****hampe¹** [ɑ̃p] NF **1** *(d'un drapeau etc)* staff, pole; *(d'une lance etc)* stave, shaft; *(d'un harpon)* shank; *Typ (de lettre)* stem; *(qui dépasse vers le haut)* ascender; **la h. du p** the stem of the p; *Typ* **h. montante** ascender **2** *Bot* flower spike

*****hampe²** [ɑ̃p] NF *Culin (de bœuf)* = cut taken between the flank and the sirloin; *(de la venaison)* breast

*****hamster** [amstεr] NM *Zool* hamster; **h. doré** golden hamster

*****han** [ɑ̃] INT oof!; **pousser un h. à chaque coup** to (give a) grunt at every stroke

*****hanap** [anap] NM *Arch* goblet, tankard

*****hanche** [ɑ̃ʃ] NF **1** *Anat* hip; **déformation congénitale de la h.** congenital hip deformity; **les poings sur les hanches** (with his/her/*etc*) hands on (his/her/*etc*) hips, (with) arms akimbo; **il refusait d'avancer, les mains sur les hanches** hands on hips, he refused to go any further; **rouler les hanches** to swing one's hips; **être large des hanches** *Fam* to be broad in the beam; **tour de hanches** hip measurement; **perdre quelques centimètres de tour de hanches** to lose a few centimetres from one's hips **2** *(d'un cheval)* haunch; **hanches** hindquarters **3** *Naut (d'un navire)* quarter; **par la h.** on the quarter

*****hand** [ɑ̃d] NM *Fam* handball

*****hand-ball** [ɑ̃dbal] NM *Sport* handball; **jouer au h.** to play handball; **ballon de h.** handball

*****handballeur, -euse** [ɑ̃dbalœr, -øz] N *Sport* handball player

*****handicap** [ɑ̃dikap] NM *aussi Fig* handicap; *Fig* **la Pologne part avec un h.** Poland is handicapped from the outset; **elle partait dans la vie avec un sérieux h.** she started out in life with a serious handicap or seriously disadvantaged

handicapant [ɑ̃dikapɑ̃] ADJ *(maladie)* disabling; *Fam* **ça peut être très h.** that can be a great handicap; *Fam* **ne pas avoir de voiture à la campagne est h.** being without a car in the countryside is a handicap

handicapé, -ée [ɑ̃dikape] ADJ handicapped; *(physiquement)* handicapped, disabled; **h. mental** mentally handicapped; **h. physique** physically handicapped, (physically) disabled
N handicapped person; *(physique)* handicapped or disabled person; **h. moteur** person with motor impairment; **les handicapés mentaux** the mentally handicapped; **les handicapés (physiques)** the disabled, the physically handicapped

*****handicaper** [ɑ̃dikape] VT to handicap

*****handicapeur** [ɑ̃dikapœr] NM *Courses de chevaux* handicapper

handisport [ɑ̃dispɔr] ADJ *Sport* tennis/équipement h. tennis/sports equipment for the disabled or handicapped; **jeux handisports** games for the handicapped or disabled

*****hangar** [ɑ̃gar] NM **1** shed, shelter; *(grand)* warehouse; *(pour les trains, bus etc)* depot; **h. à bateaux** boathouse **2** *Aviat* hangar

*****hanneton** [an(ə)tɔ̃] NM cockchafer, maybug, *Am* June beetle or bug; *Fam* **une dispute/un examen pas piqué(e) des hannetons** a stinker of an argument/exam; *Fam* **une réponse pas piquée des hannetons** an astounding answer; *Fam* **je vous ai amené un petit vin pas piqué des hannetons** I've brought you an unbelievable little wine

Hanoi [anɔj] N Hanoi

*****Hanovre** [anɔvr] N Hanover

*****hanovrien, -enne** [anɔvrijε̃, -εn] *aussi Hist* ADJ Hanoverian
N **H.** Hanoverian

*****hanse** [ɑ̃s] NF *aussi Hist* Hanse, Hansa; **la H.** the Hanseatic league

*hanséatique [ãseatik] ADJ *Hist* Hanseatic

*hanté [ãte] ADJ haunted; **maison hantée** haunted house; **être h. par un souvenir/ une impression** to be haunted by a memory/a feeling

*hanter [ãte] VT *(d'un fantôme) (maison etc)* to haunt; **cette idée le hante** he is obsessed *or* haunted by the idea; **ce souvenir me hante** the memory haunts me; *Fig* **il passait ses nuits à h. les bistrots** he spent every night in the pub

*hantise [ãtiz] NF haunting memory *or* thought; **j'ai la h. de ce genre de réunion** I dread this kind of meeting

*happe [ap] NF **1** *Menuis* cramp *or* clamp iron **2** *(anneau)* staple; **anneau à h.** ring and staple

*happement [apmã] NM snapping (up), snatching, seizing

*happening [apniŋ] NM happening

*happer [ape] VT *(des oiseaux etc) (insectes etc)* to snap up, to catch; **la voiture a été happée par un train** the car was hit by a train; **la machine a happé sa main** his hand got caught in the machine; *Fig* **happer qn** to buttonhole sb

happy end, happy ending [apiɛnd(iŋ)] NM happy ending; **j'aime les happy ends** I love happy endings

haptonomie [aptɔnɔmi] NF *Obst* = technique of communication with foetus through sensory stimulation

*haquenée [akne] NF *Arch* palfrey

hara-kiri, *pl* **hara-kiris** [arakiri] NM hara-kiri; **(se) faire h.** to commit hara-kiri

*harangue [arãg] NF harangue; *Fam* **nous avons eu droit à une de ses harangues** we were treated to one of his/her harangues *or* lectures

*haranguer [arãge] VT to harangue, to lecture

*haras [ara] NM stud farm

*harassant [arasã] ADJ exhausting

*harassé [arase] ADJ worn out, exhausted; **h. de travail** overwhelmed with work

*harassement [arasmã] NM fatigue, exhaustion

*harasser [arase] VT to tire out, to exhaust

> Il faut noter que le verbe anglais **to harass** est un faux ami. Il signifie **harceler**.

*harcelant [arsəlã] ADJ harassing, pestering

*harcèlement [arsɛlmã] NM harassment, harassing; **le h. sexuel** sexual harassment

*harceler [arsəle] VT (**je harcèle; je harcèle-rai**) *(personne)* to harass; *Mil* to harry, to harass; *(animal)* to bait; **h. qn de ses questions** to badger *or* pester *or* plague sb with one's questions; **h. qn pour obtenir qch** to pester sb for sth; **elle est harcelée de soucis** she's plagued by worries; **les remords/regrets le harcèlent** he's tormented *or* plagued by remorse/regrets

*harceleur, -euse [arsələr, -øz] N tormentor, pesterer; **h. téléphonique** phone pest

*hard [ard] *Fam* ADJ **la scène était un peu h.** the scene was a little risqué; **porno h.** hard *or* hard-core porn
▪ NM *Mus* hard rock; *Ordinat* hardware; *(porno)* hard-core porn

*harde¹ [ard] NF *(de cerfs)* herd, bevy

*harde² NF *(pour la meute)* leash

*hardes [ard] NFPL rags

*hardeur [ardœr] NM *Fam* hard-porn actor

*hardi [ardi] ADJ *(audacieux)* bold, daring; *(téméraire)* rash; *(osé)* impudent, brazen; **écriture hardie** bold hand(writing); **faire un**

---

commentaire h. to make a bold comment; **jugement h.** rash judgement; **mensonge h.** barefaced lie; **un décolleté h.** a daring neckline; **une interprétation hardie** a bold interpretation
  INT *Arch* go on!, go to it!; **h. les gars!** come on lads!

*hardiesse [ardjɛs] NF *(audace)* boldness, daring; *(effronterie)* impudence, effrontery; *(originalité)* boldness; **avoir la h. de faire qch** to be so bold as to do sth; **il a eu la h. de m'écrire** he had the audacity to write to me; **remarque la h. du style de ce peintre** note the boldness of this painter's style; **hardies-ses liberties** liberties; **se permettre des hardiesses envers qn** to take liberties with sb

*hardiment [ardimã] ADV *(avec audace)* boldly, audaciously, daringly; *(avec effron-terie)* impudently; *(à la légère)* rashly; **vous avez agi bien h.** you acted very rashly

*hard-top, *pl* **hard-tops** [ardtɔp] NM *Aut* hard top

*hardware [ardwɛr] NM *Ordinat* hardware

*harem [arɛm] NM harem

*hareng [arã] NM herring; **h.** (**salé et**) **fumé** kipper; **h. saur** red *or* smoked herring; **h. bouffi** bloater; *Fam* **être sec comme un h.** to be as skinny *or* thin as a rake; *Fam* **on était serrés comme des harengs dans le bus** we were packed together like sardines in the bus VOIR GRAMMAIRE A12

*harengère [arãʒɛr] NF fishwife

*harenguier [arãgje] NM herring boat

*harfang [arfã] NM *Can* snowy owl

*hargne [arɲ] NF bad temper, surly disposi-tion; **parler/répondre/s'exprimer avec h.** to speak/answer/express oneself bad-temper-edly *or* aggressively; **... dit-il avec h. ...** he snapped; **propos pleins de h.** aggressive remarks

*hargneusement [arɲøzmã] ADV bad-temperedly, aggressively

*hargneux, -euse [arɲø, -øz] ADJ *(per-sonne)* bad-tempered, cantankerous, ag-gressive; *(femme)* nagging; *(chien)* snarling, vicious, fierce; **ton h.** aggressive tone

*haricot [ariko] NM **1** bean; **haricots en grains** dried beans; *Fam* **des haricots!** not a sausage *or* bean!; *Fam* **c'est la fin des hari-cots** we've had it now; *très Fam* **courir sur le h. à qn** to tee sb off, *Br* to get on sb's wick *or* up sb's nose; *Fam* **travailler pour des hari-cots** to work for peanuts **2** *Culin* **h. de mou-ton** = Irish stew **3** *(bol)* kidney dish
▸▸ **h. beurre** butter bean; **h. blanc** haricot bean; **h. d'Espagne** scarlet runner; **h. mange-tout** mange-tout; **h. à rames** runner bean; **h. rouge** (red) kidney bean; **h. vert** French *or Am* string bean

*haridelle [aridɛl] NF old horse, nag

*harissa [arisa] NF *Culin* harissa

*harki [arki] NM *Mil* harki *(Algerian soldier who fought on French side during the War of Independence; also his descendants)*

*harle [arl] NM *Orn* merganser

harmonica [armɔnika] NM *Mus* harmonica, mouth organ; **jouer de l'h.** to play the mouth organ *or* harmonica

harmonie [armɔni] NF **1** *Mus* harmony; **table d'h.** *(d'un piano)* sounding board **2** *(accord)* harmony; **être en h. avec qch** to be in keep-ing *or* in harmony with sth, to fit in with sth; **vivre en h.** to live in harmony *or* harmo-niously; **l'h. qui règne dans cette famille** the harmony which reigns within this family **3** *(de l'orchestre)* wind section **4** *(fanfare)* brass band

harmonieusement [armɔnjøzmã] ADV harmoniously; **des couleurs qui s'unissent h.** colours which go well together

---

harmonieux, -euse [armɔnjø, -øz] ADJ *(son)* harmonious, melodious, tuneful; *(ar-rangement etc)* harmonious; **couleurs har-monieuses** harmonious colours

harmonique [armɔnik] ADJ, NM *Mus* harmonic

harmoniquement [armɔnikmã] ADV harmonically

harmonisation [armɔnizasjɔ̃] NF harmon-ization, harmonizing; **h. fiscale** tax harmon-ization; *Ling* **h. vocalique** vowel harmony

harmoniser [armɔnize] VT **1** *Mus (mélodie etc)* to harmonize **2** *(mettre en accord)* to har-monize; *(couleurs)* to match
  VPR **s'harmoniser** to be in keeping *or* in har-mony, to harmonize, to agree (**avec** with); **ces couleurs s'harmonisent très bien** these colours go very well together; **s'h. avec qch** *(de couleurs)* to match *or* go well with sth

harmoniseur [armɔnizœr] NM *Radio etc* harmonizer

harmonium [armɔnjɔm] NM harmonium

*harnaché [arnaʃe] ADJ *(d'un cheval)* har-nessed; *Fam* **il part à la pêche tout h.** he goes off fishing all kitted out; *Fam* **curieuse-ment h.** wearing the strangest gear *or* get-up

*harnachement [arnaʃmã] NM **1** *(action)* harnessing **2** *(harnais)* harness; *(selles etc)* saddlery; *Fam (vêtements)* (absurd) rig-out, get-up; **sortir dans un curieux h.** to go out wearing the strangest gear *or* get-up

*harnacher [arnaʃe] VT *(cheval etc)* to har-ness; *Fam* **h. qn** to dress sb up, to rig sb out; **il fallait voir comment elle était harnachée** you should have seen the ridiculous outfit she was wearing
  VPR **se harnacher** to rig oneself out; **il faut toujours se h. pour aller en montagne** you must always get properly kitted out for the mountains

*harnais [arnɛ] NM **1** *(sellerie)* harness; *Fig* **reprendre le h.** to get back into harness, to go back to work again; **blanchir sous le h.** to spend one's life in the same occupation, to grow grey in service; *Aut* **h. de sécurité** safe-ty harness **2** *Arch (armure)* armour **3** *Tech* **h. d'engrenage** train of gear wheels, gearing

*harnois [arnwa] NM *Arch* = harnais 2

*haro [aro] NM **(clameur de) h.** outcry, hue and cry; **crier h.** to raise a hue and cry (**sur** about); **crier h. sur le baudet** to scream for blood

harpagon [arpagɔ̃] NM miser, skinflint, scrooge; **c'est un h.** he's a real miser

*harpe [arp] NF *Mus* harp; **jouer** *ou* **pincer de la h.** to play the harp; **h. éolienne** Aeolian harp

*harpie [arpi] NF **1** *Myth* harpy; *Fig* harpy, shrew; **j'ai vu la concierge, cette h.** I've seen the caretaker, the old battleaxe **2** *Orn* harpy eagle

*harpiste [arpist] N *Mus* harpist

*harpon [arpɔ̃] NM *Pêche* harpoon; **pêche** *ou* **chasse (sous-marine) au h.** (underwater) spear fishing

*harponnage [arpɔnaʒ], **harponnement** [arpɔnmã] NM harpooning

*harponner [arpɔne] VT **1** *Pêche* to harpoon **2** *très Fam (de la police) (personne)* to nab, to collar; *(coincer) (personne)* to stop, to cor-ner, to grab; **se faire h. par qn** to get corne-red *or* nabbed by sb

*harponneur [arpɔnœr] NM *Pêche* harpooner

*hasard [azar] NM **1** chance, luck; **coup de h.** stroke of luck, fluke; **c'est vraiment un coup de h., je ne m'y attendais pas du tout** it's a real stroke of luck, I wasn't expecting it at all; **par un coup de h.** by mere chance, by coincidence; **un heureux h. a fait qu'il a**

été muté dans la même région que moi by a stroke of luck he was transferred to the same area as me; **par un heureux h.** by a happy coincidence; **ne rien laisser au h.** to leave nothing to chance; **le h. a voulu** *ou* **a fait que je ...** as luck would have it I ...; **le h. fit que** + *ind,* **le h. voulut que** + *sub* (as) luck would have it; **le h. fait bien les choses!** what a stroke of luck!; **au h.** at random, *Péj* haphazardly; **j'en ai pris un au h.** I took one at random; **marcher au h.** to walk aimlessly; **au h. de ses voyages** in the course of his travels, as he travelled from one place to another; **au h. de mes lectures** in the course of my reading; **par h.** by accident, by chance; **par pur h.** quite by chance, entirely by accident; **par le plus grand des hasards** by the merest chance; **si par h. vous le voyez** if you (should) happen to see him; **sauriez-vous son adresse par h.?** do you happen to know his address?, do you know his address by any chance?; **et comme par h., il est tombé malade** and as if by chance, he fell ill; **à tout h.** on the off-chance, just in case; **je te le dis à tout h.** I'm telling you just in case; **à tout h., je vais lui demander** I'll ask him just in case *or* on the off-chance

2 *(danger)* risk, danger, hazard; **les hasards de la guerre** the hazards of war

> Il faut noter que le nom anglais **hazard** signifie uniquement **danger**.

***hasardé** [azarde] ADJ *(entreprise etc)* hazardous, risky, foolhardy; *(paroles etc)* rash

***hasarder** [azarde] VT *(sa vie etc)* to risk, to venture, to hazard; **h. une opinion** to hazard *or* venture an opinion; **h. 500 euros** to gamble 500 euros

VPR **se hasarder** to take risks; **se h. à faire qch** to venture to do sth, to risk doing sth; **se h. dans la jungle** to venture (out) into the jungle

***hasardeux, -euse** [azardø, -øz] ADJ hazardous, perilous, risky; **entreprise hasardeuse** risky business; **paroles hasardeuses** rash words

***hasch** [aʃ] NM *Fam (drogue)* hash, pot

***haschisch** [aʃiʃ] NM hashish; **fumer du h.** to smoke hashish

***hase** [az] NF *Zool (d'un lièvre, d'un lapin de garenne)* doe

***hassidisme** [asidism] NM *Rel* Chassidism, Hassidism

hast [ast] NM *Arch* shaft; **arme d'h.** shafted weapon

***hâte** [ɑt] NF haste, hurry; **avoir h. de faire qch** to be in a hurry to do sth; *(avoir envie)* to be eager *or* to long to do sth, to look forward to doing sth; **j'ai h. de trouver un nouvel appartement** I can't wait to find a new flat; **j'ai h. de te revoir** I'm looking forward to seeing you again; **mettre trop de h. à faire qch** to be in too great a hurry *or* too much of a hurry to do sth; **il n'a qu'une h.: que tout soit fini** all he wants is to get it over with; **à la h.** in a hurry, in haste, hastily, hurriedly; **travail fait à la h.** slapdash work; **déjeuner à la h.** to hurry over one's lunch, *Fam* to bolt one's lunch; **en h.** hastily, in haste, hurriedly; **ils sont venus en h.** they came hurriedly *or* without delay; **en toute h.** posthaste, as quickly as possible; **sans h.** without haste, in a leisurely way

***hâter** [ɑte] VT *(événement)* to hasten, to hurry along; *(fruit etc)* to force; **h. les choses** to hurry things up *or* along; **h. le pas** to quicken one's pace *or* step; **h. le mouvement** to hurry things up *or* along

VPR **se hâter** to hurry, to hasten; **se h. de faire qch** to hurry to do sth, to lose *or* waste no time in doing sth; **je vais me h. de prendre rendez-vous** I'm going to waste no time in

making an appointment; **hâtez-vous lentement** more haste, less speed

***hâtif, -ive** [atif, -iv] ADJ **1** *(printemps, fruit etc)* early **2** *(mesure, décision etc)* hasty, hurried, ill-considered, premature

***hâtivement** [ativmɑ̃] ADV hastily, in a hurry, hurriedly; **se diriger h. vers ...** to hurry towards ...

***hauban** [obɑ̃] NM **1** *Naut* shroud **2** *(corde, câble)* guy, stay

***haubaner** [obane] VT *Naut* to guy, to stay, to brace

***haubert** [obɛr] NM *Arch* coat of mail

***hausse** [os] NF **1** *(de prix, de la température)* rise, increase; **h. de prix** price rise *or* increase *or* hike; **la h. des matières premières** the rise *or* increase in the price of raw materials; **baromètre en h.** rising barometer; *Com, Fin* **marché à la h.** rising *or* bull market; **h. de 4%** 4% rise; *Bourse* **h. des cours** stock market rise; **nous avons dû réviser nos prix à la h.** we've had to revise our prices upwards; **les cours sont orientés à la h.** there is an upward trend in share prices; **pousser les actions à la h.** to bull the market; **l'immobilier est en h.** house prices are going up; **le blé a subi une h. considérable** wheat has gone up considerably (in price); **h. à la pompe** rise in the price of petrol; *Bourse* **jouer à la h.** to speculate on a rising market, to bull the market; *Bourse* **spéculateur à la h.** bull **2** *Tech* prop, block, stand **3** *Mil (de fusil)* (back)sight, sighting gear

***haussement** [osmɑ̃] NM **h. d'épaules** shrug (of the shoulders); **il accueillit la nouvelle par un h. d'épaules/avec un h. de sourcils** he welcomed the news with a shrug (of his shoulders)/with raised eyebrow(s)

***hausser** [ose] VT *(lever)* to raise, to lift; *(élever)* to raise, to make higher, to heighten; *(augmenter) (prix)* to put up, to increase, to raise; **h. la voix** to raise one's voice; **h. les épaules** to shrug (one's shoulders); **h. les sourcils** to raise one's eyebrows

VI *Naut (d'un terrain, d'un phare)* to rise (over the horizon)

VPR **se hausser** to raise oneself (up); **se h. sur la pointe des pieds** to stand on tiptoe *or* one's toes; **se h. jusqu'à qn** to raise oneself to sb's level; **je me suis haussé jusqu'à la fenêtre** I hauled myself up to the window; **se h. jusqu'au poste de PDG** to climb to the position of Chairman, to rise to be Chairman

***haussier, -ière** [osje, -jɛr] *Bourse* ADJ bullish

N bull

***haussmannien, -ienne** [osmanjɛ̃, -jɛn] ADJ Haussmannian

---

*HAUT, HAUTE [o, ot]

ADJ high **1, 3, 4, 6** ▪ tall **1** ▪ upper **2** ▪ top **2** ▪ loud **4**		
ADV high **1** ▪ aloud **1** ▪ above **1, 2** ▪ back **2**		
NM height **1** ▪ top **2**		
NF upper crust		

ADJ **1** high; *(herbe)* tall, long; *(édifice etc)* tall, high, lofty; **femme de haute taille** tall woman; **mur h. de six mètres** wall six metres high; **h. comme trois pommes** knee high to a grasshopper; **pièce haute de plafond** room with a high ceiling; **les pièces sont hautes de plafond** the rooms have high ceilings; **des talons hauts** high heels; **un front h.** a high forehead; **marcher la tête haute** *or* **le front h.** to hold one's head up; *Fig* to walk with one's head held high *or* one's head up; **h. sur pattes** long-legged; **la lune/Vénus était haute dans le ciel** the moon/Venus was high up in the sky; **les hautes latitudes** the high latitudes; **en haute montagne** high

in the mountains; **les hauts plateaux** the high plateaus *or* plateaux; **hautes terres** highlands, uplands; **les Hautes Terres (de l'Écosse)** the Highlands (of Scotland); **haute mer** open sea, high sea; **hautes eaux** high water; **à marée haute** at high tide, at high water; **la marée était haute** the tide was in *or* high; **je ne la tiens pas en haute estime** I don't hold her in very high regard *or* esteem; **avoir une haute idée de soi-même** to have a high opinion of oneself; *Fig* **avoir/garder la main haute sur ses affaires** to be in/to retain control of one's affairs

2 *(supérieur)* upper, higher; **les hautes branches** the upper branches, the top branches; **l'étage le plus h.** the top floor; **la haute branche** the topmost *or* uppermost branch; **ville haute** upper part of the town; **les hautes classes** *(de la société)* the upper classes; **les hautes mathématiques** higher mathematics; **le H.-Rhin** *(département)* the Haut-Rhin; **le h. Rhin** *(fleuve)* the upper Rhine; *Naut* **les hautes voiles** the upper sails **3** *(éminent)* exalted, important, great; **de la plus haute importance** of the greatest *or* utmost importance; **de h. rang** of high rank, high-ranking; **les plus hautes instances policières** the highest-ranking *or* most senior police authorities; **h. comique** high comedy **4** *(note de musique)* high; **voix haute** loud voice; *(aiguë)* high (-pitched) voice; **lire à haute voix** to read aloud; **elle parlait à haute voix** she spoke aloud *or* out loud; **pousser les hauts cris** to shout out loud; **elle n'a jamais une parole plus haute que l'autre** she never raises her voice; **avoir le verbe h.** to be high and mighty **5** *(ancien)* **la haute antiquité** remote *or* earliest antiquity; **le h. Moyen Âge** the Early Middle Ages **6** *(extrême)* **mécanisme de haute précision** precision device; **h. en couleurs** *(personnage, récit)* colourful; **haute pression** high pressure; **mécanisme de** *ou* **à haute sécurité** high security device; *Radio* **haute fréquence** high frequency; **à haute valeur ajoutée** high value added

ADV **1** high (up), above, up; **h. les mains!** hands up!; **h. les cœurs** cheer up!; **parler h.** to speak loudly; **parlez plus h.!** speak up!; **parle moins h.!** keep your voice down!; **une voix h. perchée** a high-pitched voice; **parler** *ou* **penser tout h.** to talk *or* think aloud *or* out loud; **dire tout h. ce que tout le monde pense tout bas** to say out loud what everyone else is thinking; **parler h. et clair** to speak one's mind; **je l'ai déjà dit h. et clair** I've already said it quite openly; **femme h. placée** woman in a high position; **des gens h. placés** highly placed people, people in high office; **viser h.** to aim *or* set one's sights high; **il la place très h. dans son estime** he has a very high opinion of her, he holds her in very high regard *or* esteem; *Naut* **l'ancre est h.** the anchor is up; **gagner h. la main** to win hands down; **ils ont remporté la course h. la main** they won the race hands down

2 *(en arrière)* back; **remonter plus h. (dans le temps)** to go further back; **comme il est dit plus h.** as indicated above *or* earlier; **ainsi que nous l'avons déjà vu plus h.** as we have already seen (above)

NM **1** height; **le mur a six mètres de h.** the wall is six metres high; *Fig* **regarder qn du h. de sa grandeur** to look down one's nose at sb; **tomber de (son) h.** to fall flat on the ground, to fall headlong; *(être surpris ou déçu)* to fall flat on one's back, to be floored *or* flabbergasted

2 *(partie supérieure)* top, upper part; *Mktg (du marché)* high end, top end; **h.!** *(sur caisse)* this side up!; **la poste se trouve dans le h. du village** the Post Office is at the top end of the village; **le h. de la robe est en den-**

---

telle the top of the dress is made of lace; **du h. de l'escalier** from the top of the stairs; **elle est tombée du h. de l'escalier** she fell all the way down the stairs; **les hauts et les bas** *(de la vie etc)* the ups and downs; **avoir** *ou* **connaître des hauts et des bas** to have one's ups and downs; **h. de l'eau** high water; **les hauts (d'un navire)** the topsides (of a ship); **l'étage du h.** the top floor; **le monsieur du h.** the gentleman upstairs; **arriver en h. de la côte** to reach the top of the hill; **une fois en h. de la côte, je me suis rendu compte que ...** once I was at the top of the hill, I realized ...; **dévaler du h. de la côte** to hurtle down the hillside; **vers le h.** upwards; **lever les bras vers le h.** to raise *or* lift one's arms; **pousser vers le h.** to push upwards; **gloire à Dieu au plus h. des cieux** Glory to God in the Highest; **de** *ou* **du h. en bas** downwards, from top to bottom; **regarder qn de h. en bas** to look sb up and down; **regarder qn de h.** to look down on sb; **traiter qn de h.** to patronize sb; **prendre les choses de h.** to be very aloof *or* detached; **il a pris sa remarque de h.** he took his remark very scornfully *or* disdainfully; **en h.** above, at the top; *Naut* aloft; *(étage supérieur)* upstairs; **lancer qch en h.** to throw sth (up)/in(to) the air; **en h. du placard** at the top of the cupboard; **tout en h.** at the very top, right at the top; *Naut* **le h. tout le monde!** all hands on deck!; **en h. de l'échelle** at the top of the ladder; **d'en h.** from above, from on high; *(vu de l'étage inférieur)* from upstairs; **les gens/l'appartement d'en h.** the people (from) upstairs/the flat upstairs; *Fig* **la décision vient d'en h.** the decision comes from the top

NF *Fam* **haute** upper crust; **un gars de la haute** a toff; **elle ne fréquente que la haute** *ou* **les gens de la haute** she only associates with the upper crust

▸▸ **le h. allemand** High German; *Compta* **h. de bilan** *(fonds propres)* shareholders' funds; *Géog* **h. le Canada** Upper Canada; *Typ* **h. de casse** upper case, *Fam* caps; **en h. de casse** upper case, in upper case; **haute Cour de justice** high court of justice; **haute couture** haute couture; **défilé de haute couture** designer fashion show; **haute cuisine** haute cuisine; **je vous préviens, ce n'est pas de la haute cuisine** I warn you, it's nothing fancy; *TV* **haute définition** high definition; *Ordinat* **haute densité** high density; *Com* **haute direction** senior management; **h. fait** act of bravery; *Mil* deed of valour; *Iron* infamous deed; **haute finance** high finance; **h. fonctionnaire** high-ranking official; **h. de gamme** top of the range; **h. lieu touristique** a tourist Mecca; **en h. lieu** in high places; **je dois en parler en h. lieu** I must go to the top about it; **la haute magistrature** the superior judiciary; **le h. du panier** the top of the heap, the pick of the bunch; **ils ne fréquentent que le h. du panier** they mix only with the cream of society; **haute performance** high-performance; **haute résolution** high resolution; **haute saison** high season; **haute société** high society; **les gens de la haute société** members of *or* people in high society; **haute technologie** high technology, high tech, hitech; **haute trahison** high treason

****hautain** [otɛ̃] **ADJ** haughty, lofty

****hautainement** [otɛnmɑ̃] **ADV** haughtily, loftily

****hautbois** [obwa] **NM** *Mus* oboe

****hautboïste** [oboist] **N** *Mus* oboe player, oboist

****haut-commissaire,** *pl* hauts-commissaires **NM** high commissioner

****haut-commissariat,** *pl* hauts-commissariats **NM** high commission

****haut-de-chausse(s),** *pl* hauts-de-chausse(s) [od(ə)ʃos] **NM** *Arch* breeches

****haut-de-forme,** *pl* hauts-de-forme [od(ə)fɔrm] **NM** top hat

****haute-contre,** *pl* hautes-contres [otkɔ̃tr] *Mus* **NF** *(voix)* counter-tenor **ADJ, NM** counter-tenor

****haute-fidélité** [otfidelite] **ADJ** hi-fi, high fidelity; **chaîne h.** hi-fi

****hautement** [otmɑ̃] **ADV** *(à un haut degré)* highly; *Vieilli (ouvertement)* openly

****hauteur** [otœr] **NF** height, elevation; *(d'une étoile, d'un triangle etc)* altitude; *Mus (d'une note de musique)* pitch; *(des idées etc)* loftiness; **l'immeuble a une h. de 400 mètres** the building is 400 metres high; **sa h. est telle qu'on s'en sert comme d'un point de repère dans la ville** it is so high that it serves as a landmark in the town; **prendre de la h.** *(d'un avion etc)* to climb, to gain height; **pour résoudre ce problème, il convient de prendre de la h.** in order to solve this problem, we must rise above it; **le peu de h. du plafond** the lowness of the ceiling; **le pont manque de h. pour laisser passer les camions** there isn't enough clearance for lorries under the bridge; **tomber de (toute) sa h.** to fall flat on one's face *or* headlong; **à la h. de qch** abreast of *or* level with sth; **l'eau nous arrivait à la h. des épaules** the water came up to our shoulders; **arriver à la h. de qn/qch** to draw level with sb/sth; **être** *ou* **se montrer à la h. d'une tâche** to be *or* to prove equal to *or* up to a task, *Fam* to be up to a job; **être à la h. de la situation** to be equal to *or* up to the situation; *Fam* **être à la h.** to be up to it; *Fig Litt* **la h. de vues d'un fonctionnaire** the loftiness *or* lofty attitude of a civil servant; **avoir une grande h. de vues** to be lofty-minded; *Naut* **à la h. du cap Horn** off *or* abreast of Cape Horn; **à la h. de Grenoble, il faudra commencer à penser à mettre les chaînes** when you get to Grenoble, you will have to start thinking about putting the snow chains on; **il y a un embouteillage à la h. du Mans** there is a traffic jam near Le Mans; **ils habitent à la h. de l'église** they live up by the church; *Sport* **saut en h.** high jump; **faire du saut en h.** to do the high jump; **à h. de** *(s'engager)* up to; *Bourse* **M. Martin, actionnaire de Perrier® à h. de 5%** Mr Martin, a shareholder in Perrier® with *or* holding 5% of the shares; **il participe à h. de 30%** he is contributing up to 30%

▸▸ **à h. d'appui** at elbow height; *Couture* **h. du dos** = length of back; **h. libre** *(d'un pont etc)* headroom; *Ordinat* **h. de ligne** line height; *Typ* **h. de page** page depth; **h. de passage** *(d'un pont etc)* headroom; *Aut* **h. au plafond** headroom; **h. sous plafond** ceiling height; **quelle est la h. sous plafond?** what is the height of *or* how high is the ceiling?

Haute-Volta [hotvɔlta] **NF** Upper Volta

****haut-fond,** *pl* hauts-fonds **NM** *(dans la mer, dans une rivière)* shoal, shallow; **contourner le h.** to negotiate the shallow waters

****haut(-)fourneau,** *pl* hauts(-)fourneaux [ofurno] **NM** *Métal* blast furnace

****haut-le-cœur** [ol(ə)kœr] **NM INV** *(de l'estomac)* heave; **avoir un/des h.** to retch, to heave; **j'ai eu un h. de dégoût** my stomach heaved in disgust; **cette vision me donna un h.** the sight of it made me feel sick

****haut-le-corps** [ol(ə)kɔr] **NM INV** (sudden) start, jump; **faire un h.** *(d'un cheval)* to start; **avoir un h.** *(d'une personne)* to give a start, to jump

****haut-mal NM INV** *Méd Arch* falling sickness

****haut-parleur,** *pl* haut-parleurs **NM** loudspeaker, Tannoy®; *Radio, TV etc* (loud)-speaker; **h. d'aigus** tweeter; **h. de graves** woofer; **h. d'interphone** intercom loudspeaker; **h. d'ordres** intercom loudspeaker

****haut-relief,** *pl* hauts-reliefs **NM** *Beaux-Arts* high relief, alto-rilievo

****hauturier, -ière** [otyrje, -jer] **ADJ** *Naut* of the high seas; **navigation hauturière** ocean navigation; **pilote h.** deep-sea pilot; **pêche hauturière** deep-sea fishing

****havage** [avaʒ] **NM** *Min* cutting

****havanais, -aise** [avanɛ, -ɛz] **ADJ** of/from Havana
N H. *(natif)* native of Havana; *(habitant)* inhabitant of Havana

****Havane** [avan] **NF La H.** Havana
NM h. Havana (cigar)
ADJ INV cuir h. (light) brown *or* tan leather

****hâve** [ɑv] **ADJ** *(visage)* haggard, emaciated, gaunt; *(joues)* sunken; *(peau)* pale, pallid

****haveuse** [avøz] **NF** *Min (machine)* coalcutter

****havrais, -aise** [avrɛ, -ɛz] **ADJ** of/from Le Havre
N H. *(natif)* native of Le Havre; *(habitant)* inhabitant of Le Havre

****Havre (le)** [ləavr] **NM** Le Havre

****havre** [avr] **NM** *Litt* haven, harbour, *Am* harbor; *Vieilli (port)* port; **un h. de paix** a haven of peace

****havresac** [avrəsak] **NM** haversack; *Mil* knapsack, pack

Hawaï [awai] **N** Hawaii; **les îles H.** Hawaii, the Hawaiian Islands

hawaïen, -ïenne [awajɛ̃, -jɛn] **ADJ** Hawaiian; **guitare hawaïenne** Hawaiian guitar
N H. Hawaiian

****Haye (La)** [laɛ] **NF** The Hague

****hayon** [ajɔ̃] **NM** *(d'une voiture)* hatchback, tailgate; *(d'un camion)* tailgate; *(d'une charrette)* tailboard

HCR [aʃseɛr] **NM** *(abrév* **Haut-Commissariat des Nations unies pour les réfugiés)** UNHCR

HD *Ordinat (abrév* **haute densité)** HD

HDL-cholestérol [aʃdeɛlkɔlesterɔl] **NM** *Méd* HDL cholesterol, high-density lipoproteins

****hé** [e] **INT 1** *(pour interpeller)* hey (there)! **2** *(pour renforcer)* **hé! hé!** well, well!; **hé oui!** yes indeed!

****heaume** [om] **NM** helm(et)

****heavy metal** [ɛvimetal] **NM** *Mus* heavy metal; **écouter du h.** to listen to heavy metal

hebdo [ɛbdo] **NM** *Fam (abrév* **hebdomadaire)** weekly; **h. télé** TV magazine

hebdomadaire [ɛbdɔmadɛr] **ADJ, NM** weekly

hebdomadairement [ɛbdɔmadɛrmɑ̃] **ADV** weekly, once a week

hébergement [ebɛrʒ(ə)mɑ̃] **NM** *(logement)* accommodation, *Am* accommodations; *(fait d'héberger)* putting up, taking in; *Ordinat (d'un site Internet)* hosting; **h. de courte durée** short-stay accommodation; **h. de transit** transit accommodation; **h. de vacances** holiday accommodation; **h. en pension complète** board and lodging

héberger [ebɛrʒe] **VT** (j'hébergeai(s); n. hébergeons) *(hôte payant)* to accommodate, to put up; *(ami)* to put up; *(sans-abri, réfugié)* to take in; *(fugitif)* to harbour, *Am* to harbor; *Ordinat (site Internet)* to host

hébergeur [ebɛrʒœr] **NM** *Ordinat (de site Internet)* host

hébété [ebete] **ADJ** *(expression etc)* dazed, bewildered; **h. de douleur** numb with grief; **h. par l'alcool** in a drunken stupor

hébétement [ebɛtmɑ̃] **NM** stupefaction, bewilderment

hébéter [ebete] **VT** (j'hébète; j'hébéterai)

(sens etc) to dull, to stupefy; *(personne)* to daze

hébétude [ebetyd] NF stupor

hébraïque [ebraik] ADJ Hebraic, Hebrew

hébraïsant, -ante [ebraizɑ̃, -ɑ̃t] N *(érudit, étudiant)* Hebraist

hébraïser [ebraize] VT to hebraize

hébraïsme [ebraism] NM Hebraism

hébraïste [ebraist] N Hebraist, Hebrew scholar

hébreu, -eux [ebrø] ADJ (**hébraïque** *is used for the feminine*) Hebrew
NM**1** *Ling* Hebrew; *Fam* **c'est de l'h. pour moi** it's double Dutch *or* all Greek to me **2** *(personne)* H. Hebrew; **les Hébreux** the Hebrews

Hébrides [ebrid] NFPL **les H.** the Hebrides

HEC [aʃəe] NF *(abrév* **Hautes Études Commerciales)** *(à Paris, à Montréal)* = prestigious business school; **faire H.** to study at the HEC; **les anciens élèves de H.** the former students of the HEC

hécatombe [ekatɔ̃b] NF slaughter, massacre, *Lit* hecatomb; *Fig Fam* **ça a été une h. cette année au bac!** the bac results were disastrous this year!

hectare [ɛktar] NF hectare (= 2.47 acres)

hectique [ɛktik] ADJ *Méd (fièvre)* hectic

hecto [ɛkto] NM *(hectogramme)* hectogram(me); *(hectolitre)* hectolitre, *Am* hectoliter

hectogramme [ɛktogram] NM hectogram(me)

hectolitre [ɛktolitr] NM hectolitre, *Am* hectoliter

hectomètre [ɛktɔmɛtr] NM hectometre, *Am* hectometer

hectométrique [ɛktɔmetrik] ADJ hectometric

hectopascal, -als [ɛktɔpaskal] NM *Météo* millibar

hectowatt [ɛktɔwat] NM *Élec* hectowatt

hédonisme [edɔnism] NM hedonism

hédoniste [edɔnist] N hedonist
ADJ hedonist(ic)

hégélianisme [egeljanism] NM *Phil* Hegelianism

hégélien, -ienne [egeljɛ̃, -jɛn] ADJ, N *Phil* Hegelian

hégémonie [eʒemɔni] NF hegemony; **l'h. des USA sur le monde** the USA's position of hegemony in the world

hégire [eʒir] NF *Rel* Hegira

*****hein** [ɛ̃] INT *Fam* eh?, what?; **h., que dis-tu?** what did you say?; **il fait beau aujourd'hui, h.?** fine *or* nice day, isn't it?; **et qu'est-ce que tu lui diras, h.?** so, what are you going to tell him/her now, eh?; **qu'est-ce que tu veux, h., que j'arrête de travailler?** you want me to stop working, is that it?; **ne refais jamais ça, h.!** don't ever do that again, OK?; **h. qu'il fait bien la cuisine!** he does cook well, doesn't he?

hélas [elɑs] INT alas!; **mais h., c'était trop tard** but sadly *or Fml* alas it was too late; **h., trois fois h.!** alas and alack!

Hélène [elɛn] N **H. de Troie** Helen of Troy

*****héler** [ele] VT (**je hèle; je hélerai**) *(personne, taxi, navire)* to hail

hélianthe [eljɑ̃t] NM *Bot* helianthus

hélianthine [heljɑ̃tin] NF *Chimie* helianthin(e), methyl orange

héliaque [eljak] ADJ *Astron* heliac(al)

hélice [elis] NF**1** *Math, Archit* helix; **escalier en h.** spiral staircase; *Biol* **double h.** double helix **2** *Aviat* propeller; *Naut* propeller, screw; *(d'un appareil ménager)* screw

hélico [eliko] NM *Fam (abrév* **hélicoptère)** 'copter, chopper

hélicoïdal, -ale, -aux, -ales [elikɔidal, -o] ADJ helicoid(al), helical; **mèche hélicoïdale** twist drill

hélicoïde [elikɔid] ADJ, NM *Math* helicoid

hélicon [elikɔ̃] NM *Mus* helicon

hélicoptère [elikɔptɛr] NM *Aviat* helicopter; *Mil* **h. de combat** helicopter gunship

héligare [eligar] NF heliport

héliocentrique [eljɔsɑ̃trik] ADJ *Astron* heliocentric

héliographe [eljɔgraf] NM heliograph

héliographie [eljɔgrafi] NF heliography

héliograveur [eljɔgravœr] NM photogravure worker

héliogravure [eljɔgravyr] NF photogravure

héliomarin [eljɔmarɛ̃] ADJ *Méd* **cure héliomarine** = course of treatment based on sun and sea air; **centre h.** = seaside convalescent home where heliotherapy is used

héliothérapie [eljɔterapi] NF *Méd* heliotherapy; **h. artificielle** sunray treatment

héliotrope [eljɔtrɔp] NM *Bot* heliotrope

héliport [elipɔr] NM heliport

héliportage [elipɔrtaʒ] NM transport by helicopter

héliporté [elipɔrte] ADJ**1** *(transporté par hélicoptère)* transported by helicopter; **troupes héliportées** airborne troops **2** *(effectué par hélicoptère)* **mission héliportée** helicopter mission

hélisurface [elisyrfas] NF *Naut, Pétr* helideck; *(sur un immeuble)* helipad

hélitreuiller [elitrøje] VT to winch into a helicopter

hélium [eljɔm] NM *Chimie* helium

hélix [eliks] NM *Anat, Zool* helix

hellébore [elebɔr] NM *Bot* hellebore

hellène [elɛn] ADJ Greek; *Hist* Hellenic
N **H.** Hellene

hellénique [elenik] ADJ Greek; *Hist* Hellenic; **la politique h. à l'égard de l'Union européenne** Greek policy in relation to the EU

hellénisant, -ante [elenizɑ̃, -ɑ̃t] ADJ Hellenistic
N Hellenist

hellénisation [elenizasjɔ̃] NF Hellenization

helléniser [elenize] VT to Hellenize

hellénisme [elenism] NM Hellenism

helléniste [elenist] N Hellenist

hellénistique [elenistik] ADJ *Hist* Hellenic

*****hello** [ɛllo] INT *Fam* hello

*****Helsinki** [ɛlsinki] N Helsinki

helvète [ɛlvɛt] ADJ *(suisse)* Helvetian
N **H.** Helvetian

Helvétie [ɛlvesi] NF *Hist* Helvetia

helvétique [ɛlvetik] ADJ Helvetic, Swiss; **le gouvernement h.** the Swiss government; **la Confédération h.** the Swiss Federal Republic

helvétisme [ɛlvetism] NM *Ling* Swiss French expression

*****hem** [ɛm] INT *(pour attirer l'attention, se racler la gorge)* ahem!; *(question)* eh?, what?; *(exprimant le doute, la gêne etc)* h'm; **enfin, h., je ne peux pas te le dire comme ça ...** well, h'm, you see, I can't really tell you just like that ...

hématie [emasi] NF *Physiol* red blood corpuscle

hématologie [ematɔlɔʒi] NF *Méd* haematology, *Am* hematology

hématologique [ematɔlɔʒik] ADJ *Méd* haematological, *Am* hematological

hématologiste [ematɔlɔʒist], **hématologue** [ematɔlɔg] N *Méd* haematologist, *Am* hematologist

hématome [ematom] NM *Méd* haematoma,

Am hematoma; **se faire un h.** to bruise oneself; **contre les hématomes** for bruises

héméralopie [emeralɔpi] NF night blindness, *Spéc* nyctalopia

hémicycle [emisikl] NM *Archit* hemicycle; **en h.** *(voûte etc)* semicircular; *Pol* **les députés présents dans l'h.** *(à l'Assemblée nationale)* the MPs present in the chamber

hémiplégie [emipleʒi] NF *Méd* hemiplegia

hémiplégique [emipleʒik] ADJ, N *Méd* hemiplegic

hémiptère [emiptɛr] ADJ hemipterous, hemipteran
NM hemipteran

hémisphère [emisfɛr] NM hemisphere; *Anat* **h. cérébral** cerebral hemisphere; *Géog* **l'h. nord/sud** the northern/southern hemisphere

hémisphérique [emisferik] ADJ hemispheric(al)

hémistiche [emistiʃ] NM hemistich

hémoculture [emɔkyltyr] NF haemoculture, *Am* hemoculture, blood culture

hémodialyse [emɔdjaliz] NF *Méd* haemodialysis, *Am* hemodialysis

hémoglobine [emɔglɔbin] NF haemoglobin, *Am* hemoglobin; **des flots d'h.** *(dans un film etc)* blood and gore

hémophile [emɔfil] *Méd* ADJ haemophilic, *Am* hemophilic
NM haemophiliac, *Am* hemophiliac

hémophilie [emɔfili] NF *Méd* haemophilia, *Am* hemophilia; **atteint d'h.** suffering from haemophilia, haemophiliac, *Am* hemophiliac

hémoptysie [emɔptizi] NF *Méd (des voies respiratoires)* haemoptysis, *Am* hemoptysis, spitting of blood

hémorragie [emɔraʒi] NF *Méd* haemorrhage, *Am* hemorrhage, bleeding; **h. interne** internal bleeding; *Fig* **il faut arrêter cette h. humaine** we must stop this squandering of human life; **h. des capitaux** drain of capital; **l'h. des réserves d'or** the heavy drain on the gold reserve; **l'h. des cerveaux** the brain drain

hémorragique [emɔraʒik] ADJ *Méd* haemorrhagic, *Am* hemorrhagic

hémorroïdaire [emɔrɔidɛr] ADJ, N *Méd* **(personne) h.** person suffering from haemorrhoids *or Am* hemorrhoids

hémorroïdal, -ale, -aux, -ales [emɔrɔidal, -o] ADJ *Méd* haemorrhoidal, *Am* hemorrhoidal

hémorroïdes [emɔrɔid] NFPL *Méd* piles, haemorrhoids, *Am* hemorrhoids; **traitement anti-h.** treatment for haemorrhoids *or* piles; **avoir des h.** to have haemorrhoids *or* piles

hémostatique [emɔstatik] *Méd* ADJ haemostatic, *Am* hemostatic
NM haemostat(ic), *Am* hemostat(ic)

hendécagone [ɛ̃dekagɔn] NM hendecagon

hendécasyllabe [ɛ̃dekasilab] ADJ hendecasyllabic
NM hendecasyllable

*****henné** [ene] NM *Bot* henna; **se faire un h.** to henna one's hair, to give one's hair a henna rinse; **les cheveux teints au h.** hennaed hair; **feuilles de h.** henna leaves; **h. naturel** natural henna

hennin [enɛ̃] NM *Hist* hennin

*****hennir** [enir] VI to whinny, to neigh; *(d'une personne)* to bray

*****hennissement** [enismɑ̃] NM *(action)* whinnying, neighing; *(d'une personne)* braying; *(cri)* whinny, neigh; *(d'une personne)* bray

*****henry, *pl* henrys** [ɑ̃ri] NM *Élec* henry

*****hep** [ɛp] INT hey (there)!

héparine [eparin] NF *Pharm* heparin

hépatique [epatik] ADJ hepatic
N person suffering from a liver complaint
NF *Bot* hepatic, liverwort

hépatisme [epatism] NM *Méd* liver ailments

hépatite [epatit] NF *Méd* hepatitis; **h. A/B/C** hepatitis A/B/C

hépatologie [epatɔlɔʒi] NF *Méd* hepatology

heptacorde [ɛptakɔrd] *Mus* ADJ seven-stringed
NM heptachord (instrument/scale)

heptaèdre [ɛptaɛdr] NM heptahedron

heptagonal, -ale, -aux, -ales [ɛptagɔnal, -o] ADJ heptagonal

heptagone [ɛptagɔn] NM heptagon

heptamètre [ɛptamɛtr] NM heptameter

heptasyllabe [ɛptasilab] ADJ heptasyllabic
NM heptasyllable

Heptateuque [ɛptatøk] NM *Bible* l'H. the Heptateuch

heptathlon [ɛptatlɔ̃] NM heptathlon

héraldique [eraldik] ADJ heraldic
NF heraldry

héraldiste [eraldist] N heraldry expert

***héraut** [ero] NM 1 *Hist* h. (d'armes) herald 2 *Litt (du printemps etc)* herald, harbinger

herbacé [ɛrbase] ADJ *Bot* herbaceous

herbage [ɛrbaʒ] NM *(prairie)* pasture; *(herbe)* grass, pasture; **mener les vaches dans les herbages** to put the cows out to grass or to pasture or to graze

herbager¹ [ɛrbaʒe] VT *(j'herbageai(s); n. herbageons)* *Agr* h. les bœufs to put cattle out to grass or to pasture or to graze

herbager², -ère [-ɛr] N *Agr* grazier

herbe [ɛrb] NF 1 *(de gazon etc)* grass; **brin d'h.** blade of grass; **touffe d'h.** tuft of grass; **faire de l'h.** *(pour les lapins etc)* to cut grass; **couper l'h.** to cut the grass; *Fig* **couper l'h. sous le pied à qn** to cut the ground from under sb's feet; **déjeuner sur l'h.** to picnic, to have a picnic (lunch); *Golf* **être dans l'h. longue** to be in the rough
2 *(plante)* herb; *Fam (drogue)* grass; *Culin* **fines herbes** mixed herbs; **omelette aux fines herbes** omelette with herbs; **herbes marines** seaweed; **herbes médicinales** medicinal herbs; **mauvaise h.** weed; *Fig* **le garçon a grandi comme une mauvaise h.** the boy has shot up or really sprouted
3 **en h.** *(blé etc)* green, unripe; *Fig (poète, pianiste etc)* budding; *Fig* **manger son blé en h.** to eat one's seed corn
▸▸ **h. au cœur** lungwort; **h. aux chats** catmint, *Am* catnip; **h. aux écus** moneywort; **h. à éternuer** sneezewort; **h. aux poumons** lungwort; *Can* **h. à la puce** poison ivy; **h. aux puces** fleawort; **h. sacrée** wild vervain; **h. à tous les maux** wild vervain

> Il faut noter que le nom anglais **herb** s'applique uniquement à des herbes aromatiques ou à des plantes médicinales.

herbeux, -euse [ɛrbø, -øz] ADJ grassy

herbicide [ɛrbisid] ADJ weed-killing, herbicidal; **produit h.** weedkiller, herbicide
NM weedkiller

herbier [ɛrbje] NM *(collection)* herbarium; **faire un h.** to build up a collection of dried plants

herbivore [ɛrbivɔr] *Zool* ADJ herbivorous
NM herbivore

herborisation [ɛrbɔrizasjɔ̃] NF botanizing, gathering of plants

herboriser [ɛrbɔrize] VI to botanize, to gather plants; **les enfants herborisent** the children are gathering plants

herboriste [ɛrbɔrist] N herbalist

herboristerie [ɛrbɔristəri] NF *(boutique)* herbalist's (shop); *(commerce)* herb trade

herbu [ɛrby] ADJ grassy

***hercher** [ɛrʃe] VI *Min (charbon, minerai)* to haul

Herculanum [ɛrkylanɔm] N Herculaneum

Hercule [ɛrkyl] NM Hercules; **travail d'H.** Herculean task; **il est bâti en h.** he's built like a tank; **c'est un h.** he's a real Hercules; **h. de foire** (professional) strong man

herculéen, -enne [ɛrkyleɛ̃, -ɛn] ADJ Herculean

hercynien, -ienne [ɛrsinjɛ̃, -jɛn] ADJ *Géol* Hercynian

***hère** [ɛr] NM **pauvre h.** poor creature or devil or *Br* blighter

héréditaire [erediter] ADJ *(titre etc)* hereditary; *(maladie)* hereditary, that runs in the family; **haine h.** inherited hatred; **c'est h.!** it runs in the family!, it's in the blood!

héréditairement [ereditermã] ADV hereditarily

hérédité [eredite] NF 1 *Biol* heredity; **avoir une h. chargée** ou **une lourde h.** to come from a family with a history of mental/physical illness; **h. de la couronne** royal succession by birth 2 *Jur (droit)* right of inheritance

hérésiarque [erezjark] NM heresiarch

hérésie [erezi] NF heresy; **considéré comme une h.** considered sacrilegious; *Fig* **c'est une h.!** that's sacrilege!; **boire ce vin avec ce repas, c'est une h.** it's absolute sacrilege to drink a wine like this with this meal

hérétique [eretik] ADJ heretical
N heretic

***hérissé** [erise] ADJ 1 *(garni)* bristling (**de** with); **planche hérissée de pointes** plank covered in or bristling with spikes; **mur h. de tessons de bouteilles** wall with broken glass all along the top 2 *(cheveux)* (standing) on end, spiky; *(moustache)* bristly; *(tige, fruit)* prickly; **les cheveux hérissés sur la tête** hair standing on end

***hérissement** [erismã] NM bristling

***hérisser** [erise] VT 1 *(d'un animal)* to bristle (up); **h. ses plumes** *(d'un oiseau)* to ruffle up its feathers 2 *(poil, cheveux)* to make stand on end; **les rochers hérissent la côte** the coastline is bristling with rock; **parcours hérissé d'obstacles** course scattered with obstacles; *Fig* **l'épreuve était hérissée de pièges** the test was full of pitfalls, the test had one pitfall after another; *Fig* **h. qn** to get sb's back up; **ta remarque l'a profondément hérissé** your comment really got his back up
VPR **se hérisser** to bristle (up); *(des poils, des cheveux)* to stand on end; *Fig (d'une personne)* to get one's back up, to bristle; **mes cheveux se sont hérissés d'horreur** my hair stood on end with horror

***hérisson** [erisɔ̃] NM 1 hedgehog; *Fig* bristly person; **h. de mer** sea urchin; *(poisson)* porcupine fish 2 *(pour bouteilles)* bottlebrush; *(de cheminée)* (sweep's) flue brush 3 *Agr* toothed cylinder or roller

héritage [eritaʒ] NM inheritance, heritage; *Fig (spirituel, intellectuel)* inheritance; **part d'h.** portion; **faire** ou **recueillir un h.** to receive a legacy; *(argent)* to come into money; **il l'a eu par h.** he inherited it, it was handed down to him; *Fig* **h. de honte** legacy of shame

hériter [erite] VI **h. d'une fortune** to inherit or succeed to or come into a fortune; **j'ai hérité de ce service de table** I inherited this table linen, this table linen was handed down to me; **elle a hérité de l'intelligence de son père** she inherited her intelligence from her father; **h. de qn** to receive an inheritance from sb; *Hum* **tu t'achètes encore une moto, tu as hérité ou quoi?** you're buying another motorbike, have you won the lottery? or have you come into a fortune?; **et c'est moi qui ai hérité de tous ses problèmes d'argent** and I'm the one who's been landed with all his money problems
VT **h. une fortune de son grand-père** to inherit a fortune from one's grandfather; *Fig* **h. une tradition** to inherit a tradition

héritier, -ière [eritje, -jɛr] N heir, f heiress; **lui donnera-t-elle un h.?** will she give him an heir?; **h. de qch/qn** heir to sth/sb; **les héritiers d'une longue tradition** the heirs to a long tradition; **h. présomptif** *Jur* next of kin; *(du trône)* heir apparent; **h. légitime** ou **naturel** rightful heir, *Spéc* heir-at-law

hermaphrodisme [ɛrmafrɔdism] NM *Biol* hermaphroditism

Hermaphrodite [ɛrmafrɔdit] N *Myth* Hermaphroditus

hermaphrodite [ɛrmafrɔdit] NM *Biol* hermaphrodite
ADJ hermaphrodite, hermaphroditic

herméneutique [ɛrmenøtik] ADJ hermeneutic
NF hermeneutics

Hermès [ɛrmɛs] N *Myth* Hermes

hermès [ɛrmɛs] NM **(buste en) h.** bust where the shoulders, chest and arms have been cut away at an angle

hermétique [ɛrmetik] ADJ 1 *(récipient)* hermetically sealed; *(joint)* (à l'air) airtight; *(à l'eau)* watertight 2 *Fig (abscons)* abstruse; *(visage)* impenetrable; **être h. à qch** to be impervious to sth; **je suis absolument h. à ce genre d'humour** that kind of humour goes straight over the top of my head

hermétiquement [ɛrmetikmã] ADV hermetically

hermétisme [ɛrmetism] NM *Littér* hermetism; *(d'un texte etc)* abstruseness, obscurity

hermine [ɛrmin] NF *Zool* stoat, ermine; *Com (fourrure)* ermine; **manteau d'h.** ermine coat

herminette [ɛrminɛt] NF adze

***herniaire** [ɛrnjɛr] ADJ *(tumeur etc)* hernial; **bandage h.** truss

***hernie** [ɛrni] NF *Méd* hernia, rupture; *Aut (dans un pneu)* bulge, swelling; **h. étranglée** strangulated hernia; **h. discale** slipped disc

***hernié** [ɛrnje] ADJ *Méd (intestin etc)* herniated

héro [ero] NF *Fam (abrév* **héroïne**) smack, scag, skag

Hérode [erɔd] N Herod

Hérodote [erɔdɔt] N Herodotus

héroï-comique, *pl* **héroï-comiques** [erɔi-kɔmik] ADJ mock-heroic

héroïne¹ [erɔin] NF *(de roman)* heroine

héroïne² NF *Chimie* heroin; **prendre de l'h.** to take heroin

héroïnomane [erɔinɔman] N heroin addict

héroïnomanie [erɔinɔmani] NF heroin addiction

héroïque [erɔik] ADJ heroic; **les temps héroïques de l'aviation** the pioneering days of aviation

héroïquement [erɔikmã] ADV heroically

héroïsme [erɔism] NM heroism; **faire preuve d'h.** to be heroic, to show heroism

***héron** [erɔ̃] NM heron; **h. cendré** (grey or *Am* gray or common) heron

***héros** [ero] NM hero; **un h. de la guerre/de la Révolution française** a war hero/a hero of the French Revolution; **le h. de la fête** the guest of honour; **le h. national** the national hero; **le h. du jour** the hero of the day or hour; **mourir en h.** to die like a hero, to die a hero's death VOIR GRAMMAIRE A12

herpès [ɛrpɛs] NM *Méd* herpes; *(buccal)* cold sore

herpétique [ɛrpetik] ADJ *Méd* herpetic

herpétologie [ɛrpetɔlɔʒi] NF herpetology

***hersage** [ɛrsaʒ] NM *Agr* harrowing

***herscher** [ɛrʃe] VI = hercher

***herse** [ɛrs] NF **1** *Agr* harrow **2** *Hist (de forteresse)* portcullis **3** *Théâtre* batten

***herser** [ɛrse] VT *Agr* to harrow

***herseur** [ɛrsœr] NM *Agr* harrower

***herseuse** [ɛrsøz] NF *Agr* harrow

hertz [ɛrts] NM *Élec* hertz

hertzien, -ienne [ɛrtsjɛ̃, -jɛn] ADJ *Élec, Radio* hertzian; *TV* terrestrial; *Radio* **réseau h.** radio relay system; *TV, Radio* **par voie hertzienne** terrestrially broadcast

hésitant, -ante [ezitɑ̃, -ɑ̃t] ADJ hesitant, wavering, undecided; *(voix, pas etc)* faltering

N **il faut convaincre les hésitants** we must convince the waverers

hésitation [ezitasjɔ̃] NF hesitation, hesitancy, wavering; **parler avec h.** to speak hesitatingly; **après bien des hésitations** after much hesitation; **sans h.** unhesitatingly, without hesitation; **sans h., je choisirai celui-ci** I have no hesitation in choosing this one

hésiter [ezite] VI **1** *(être dans l'incertitude)* to hesitate, to waver; **h. sur qch/entre deux choses** to hesitate over sth/between two things; **h. sur ce que l'on fera** to hesitate as to what one will do; **j'hésite sur la démarche à suivre** I'm hesitating as to *or* dithering over what to do; **je ne sais pas, j'hésite** I don't know, I can't make up my mind *or* I'm undecided; **elle hésitait à t'en parler** she didn't like *or* she wasn't sure whether to talk to you about it; **il n'hésita pas une seconde à se jeter à l'eau** without a moment's hesitation, he jumped into the water; *Fig* without a moment's hesitation he took the plunge; **il n'y a pas à h.** there's no room *or* time for hesitation; **il n'y a pas à h., c'est le premier qu'il faut choisir** there are no two ways about it, you have to choose the first one **2** *(en parlant)* to hesitate, to falter; **elle hésite trop dans ses réponses** she is too hesitant in her answers; **h. devant l'obstacle** *(d'un cheval)* to refuse a fence

Hespérides [ɛsperid] NFPL *Myth* **les H.** the Hesperides; **le Jardin des H.** the garden of the Hesperides

hétaïre [etair] NF *Antiq* hetaera

hétéro [etero] *Fam* ADJ, N straight, hetero

hétéroclite [eterɔklit] ADJ *(collection)* heterogeneous, ill-assorted; *(bizarre)* unusual, strange, odd, eccentric; **mélange h.** odd assortment

hétérodoxe [eterɔdɔks] ADJ heterodox

hétérodoxie [eterɔdɔksi] NF heterodoxy

hétérodyne [eterɔdin] *Radio* ADJ heterodyne
NF heterodyne receiver

hétérogène [eterɔʒɛn] ADJ *(différent)* heterogeneous; *(collection etc)* incongruous; *(assemblée)* mixed

hétérogénéité [eterɔʒeneite] NF heterogeneousness, heterogeneity

hétéroplastie [eterɔplasti] NF *Chir* heteroplasty

hétérosexualité [eterɔsɛksɥalite] NF heterosexuality

hétérosexuel, -elle [eterɔsɛksɥɛl] ADJ, N heterosexual

***hêtraie** [ɛtrɛ] NF beech grove *or* plantation

***hêtre** [ɛtr] NM *(bois, arbre)* beech; **h. rouge** *ou* **pourpre** copper beech

***heu** [ø] INT *(en hésitant)* er…

heur [œr] NM *Iron, Litt* **je n'ai pas l'h. de la connaître** I have not the pleasure of her acquaintance; **je n'ai pas eu l'h. de lui plaire** I did not have the good fortune to win his/her favour *or Am* favor

HEURE [œr]

| hour **1, 2** ▪ o'clock **2** ▪ time **4, 5** |

NF **1** *(soixante minutes)* hour; *Scol* **h. de cours** period; **elle a dix heures de cours par semaine** she has ten periods *or* ten hours of lessons a week; **une h. de cours, ça peut être trop long pour les enfants** one-hour lessons can be too long for children; **j'ai attendu une bonne h.** I waited a full *or* good *or* solid hour; **on met une bonne h./deux bonnes heures pour y aller** it takes a good hour/a good two hours to get there; **cent kilomètres à l'h.** a hundred kilometres an hour; **faire du cent kilomètres h.** to do 100 kilometres an hour; **être payé à l'h.** to be paid by the hour; **travailler à l'h.** to work by the hour; **toucher 30 euros l'h.** *ou* **de l'h.** to get 30 euros an hour; **semaine de 40 heures** 40-hour week **2** *(de la journée)* **à toute h. du jour** at all hours of the day; **à toute h.** at any time, at all hours of the day, round the clock; **ouvert à toute h.** open 24 hours (a day); **repas chauds à toute h.** hot meals 24 hours a day; **un médecin de garde peut être appelé à toute h. du jour ou de la nuit** a doctor is on call round the clock *or* at all times; **disponible/à votre service à toute h. du jour ou de la nuit** available/at your service round the clock; **tout à l'h.** *(dans le passé)* just now, a few minutes ago; *(dans le futur)* soon, presently, in a few minutes; **on repartira tout à l'h.** we'll be leaving again in a few minutes; **je l'ai vu tout à l'h.** I saw him just a few minutes ago; **à tout à l'h.!** *(dans un futur proche)* so long!, see you soon *or* later!; **de bonne h.** early, in good time; *(dans l'histoire)* at an early period; **il est de trop bonne h. pour rentrer** it's too early to go home; **d'h. en h.** hour by hour, hourly; **la situation s'aggrave d'h. en h.** the situation is getting worse by the hour *or Fml* deteriorating hourly; *Fig* **la situation peut s'inverser à toute h.** the situation can *or* could change at any time; *Journ* **nouvelles de dernière h.** latest news, stop-press (news); **quelle h. est-il?** what time is it?, what's the time?; **quelle h. avez-vous?** what time do you make it?; **est-ce que vous avez l'h. exacte** *ou* **juste?** do you have the right time?; **demande-lui l'h.** ask him/her the time *or* what time it is; **il est deux heures** it's two o'clock; **cinq heures moins dix** ten (minutes) to *or Am* of five; **dix-huit heures** eighteen hundred (hours); **vingt heures quarante** eight forty pm; **le train de neuf heures** the nine o'clock train; **où serai-je demain à cette h.-ci?** where will I be this time tomorrow?; **que fais-tu debout à cette h.-ci?** what are you doing up at this time?; **à cette h.-ci je devrais déjà être parti** I should have left by now; **à une h. avancée (de la journée)** late in the day; **à une h. avancée (de la nuit)** late on (in the night); *Fam* **se coucher à pas d'h.** to go to bed at all hours; **jusqu'à pas d'h.** until all hours; **à cinq heures juste(s)** *ou* **sonnant(es)** *ou* **tapant(es)** at five (o'clock) on the dot, at five o'clock sharp, (right *or* exactly) on the stroke of five; **mettre sa montre à l'h.** to set one's watch; **ma montre n'est pas à l'h.** my watch is wrong; **les trains partent à l'h.** the trains leave on the hour; *(sans retard)* the trains leave on time; *Rel* **livre d'heures** Book of Hours SEE GRAMMAR A80–1; B60 **3** *Fig* **le parti communiste est à l'h. de la Russie** the Communist party is under Russian influence; **vivre à l'h. espagnole** to adopt a Spanish lifestyle, to go Spanish; **les**

Britanniques vont devoir se mettre à l'h. européenne** the British are going to have to come into line with the rest of Europe; **mettre l'administration à l'h. de l'informatique** to bring (the) administration into the computer age **4** *(moment précis)* **l'h. du dîner/déjeuner** dinner/lunch time; **c'est l'h. du goûter/de la toilette** it's time for a snack/time to get washed and ready; **c'est l'h. des mamans** *(à la maternelle)* it's home time; **l'h. d'aller se coucher** bedtime; **son h. est venue** his time has come; **il va arriver, c'est son h.** he'll be here soon, it's his usual time; **à l'h. dite** at the appointed *or* agreed time; **être à l'h.** to be punctual *or* on time; **arriver à l'h. exacte** to arrive dead on time; **arriver/avoir fini avant l'h.** to arrive/have finished ahead of time; **il est** *ou* **c'est l'h.** it's time; **c'est l'h. de partir** it's time to go; *Journ* **h. d'imprimer** press time; **h. d'arrivée** arrival time; **h. d'arrivée prévue** estimated time of arrival, ETA; **h. de départ** *(d'un hôtel)* check-out time, departure time; **h. de départ prévue** estimated time of departure, ETD; **h. du vol** flight time; **cette mode a eu son h.** this fashion has had its day; **j'attends mon h.** I'm biding my time; **un partisan de la première h.** a supporter from the word 'go'; **un partisan de la dernière h.** a late convert to the cause, *Fam* a Johnny-come-lately **5** *(moment présent)* **pour l'h.** for the present, for the time being; **l'h. est grave** these are difficult times; **la question de l'h.** the question of the moment, the current question; **à l'h. qu'il est** by this time, by now; *(maintenant)* nowadays, now; **nous n'en savons pas plus à l'h. qu'il est** that's all we know for the time being, we don't know anything more at the moment; **faire qch sur l'h.** to do sth at once *or* right away **6** *Fig* **à ses heures, il était charmant** he could be charming when he liked *or* when he felt like it *or* when he was in the mood **7** **à la bonne h.!** well done!, good (for you)! ▸▸ **heures d'affluence** rush hour, peak period; **h. astronomique** sidereal time; *Can* **h. avancée** *Br* British Summer Time, *Am* daylight(-saving) time; **heures de bureau** office hours; *Bourse* **heures de cotation** trading time; **heures creuses** off-peak hours, slack period; *TV* **heures d'écoute** viewing hours; *Journ* **h. de l'édition** edition time; **h. d'été** *Br* British Summer Time, *Am* daylight(-saving) time; *TV etc* **h. de grande écoute** prime time, peak viewing time; **il a eu son h. de gloire** he has had his hour *or* his moment of glory; **l'h. de Greenwich** Greenwich mean time; **h. légale** official *or* standard time; **h. limite** deadline; **h. limite d'enregistrement** check-in time; **h. machine** machine-hour; **heures d'ouverture** opening hours; **heures de pointe** rush hour, peak period; **heures supplémentaires** overtime; **faire des heures supplémentaires** to do *or* to work overtime; **les heures supplémentaires ne sont pas payées** overtime is unpaid

heure-homme, *pl* **heures-homme** NF man-hour

heureusement [œrøzmɑ̃] ADV **1** *(par bonheur)* luckily, fortunately, *Fml* happily; **h. que j'étais là** it's a good thing I was there, fortunately I was there **2** *(avec succès)* successfully; **commencer h.** to begin auspiciously, to get off to a good start; **h. exprimé** well expressed; **vivre h.** to live happily; **il a décrit très h. leur vie ensemble** he gave a good description of their life together

heureux, -euse [œrø, -øz] ADJ **1** happy; **qu'est-ce que tu as, tu n'es pas h.?** what's wrong, are you unhappy?; **être h. en ménage** to be happily married; **ils vécurent h. et eurent beaucoup d'enfants** ≃ they lived happily ever after; **h. comme un poisson dans l'eau** as happy as a sandboy; **vivre h.** to live happily; **je suis très h. de ce cadeau** I'm very happy or pleased with this gift; **je suis très h. de vous faire savoir que ...** I'm very happy or pleased to inform you that ...; **nous sommes très h. de vous annoncer le mariage de ...** we are very happy or pleased to announce the marriage of ...; **nous serions h. que vous acceptiez** we would be glad if you accepted; **je serais très heureuse si ...** I would be very happy or pleased if ...; **époque heureuse** happy times; **heureuse année!** Happy New Year!; **heureuse jeunesse!** the joys of youth!

2 (favorable) successful; (formulation etc) apt, Litt happy, felicitous; **avoir une heureuse façon de s'exprimer** to express oneself well; **la formulation n'est pas toujours très heureuse dans ce texte** this text is not always very well worded; **h. mariage** joyful wedding (ceremony); **mariage h.** happy marriage; **un h. mariage de couleurs** a successful blend of colours; **l'issue heureuse des négociations** the successful outcome of the negotiations; **une solution heureuse** a happy solution; **un choix h.** a good choice; Fig **début h.** auspicious beginning; **le résultat n'est pas très h.** it wasn't very successful, it didn't work out

3 (favorisé) fortunate, favoured, Am favored; **h. au jeu/en amour** lucky at cards/in love; **il peut s'estimer h.** he can think or consider himself lucky; **estime-toi h. d'avoir été sélectionné** think or consider yourself lucky to have been chosen; Bible **h. sont les pauvres en esprit** blessed are the poor in spirit

4 (chanceux) lucky, fortunate; **c'est fort h. pour vous** that's very lucky for you; **c'est h. que vous soyez libre** it's a good thing or a good job that you're free; Fam **encore h. qu'il ait gardé le ticket de caisse!** it's just as well that he held on to the receipt!; Fam **elle m'avait prévenu, encore h.!** it's a good thing she warned me!; **par un h. hasard** by a happy coincidence

N **vous avez fait un h.** you have made one man very happy; **si tu le lui donnes, tu vas faire un h.** if you give it to him, you will make him a happy man

▸▸ **h. événement** happy event

heuristique [œristik] ADJ heuristic NF heuristics

*heurt [œr] NM (des intérêts, des couleurs etc) clash; (des véhicules) collision; **leur collaboration ne va pas sans heurts** their collaboration has its ups and downs or its rough patches; **tout s'est fait sans h.** everything went smoothly or without a hitch

*heurté [œrte] ADJ (style) abrupt, halting; (ton) abrupt; Beaux-Arts (couleurs) contrasting; **exécution ou jeu heurté(e) au piano** jerky style of playing the piano

*heurter [œrte] VT **1** (personne, chose) to knock (against), to run into, to bump into; (personne) to collide with; Naut (rocher) to hit, to strike; **h. qch de la tête** to knock or bump one's head against sth

2 (sentiments etc) to shock, to offend; **ces théories vont h. de front un bon nombre d'idées reçues** these theories will clash head-on with a good number of received ideas; **h. toutes les idées reçues** to go against or run counter to convention

VI **h. à la porte** to knock at or on the door; **sa tête a heurté contre le pare-brise** he hit his head against the windscreen, his head struck the windscreen

VPR **se heurter 1** (se cogner) to collide (with each other); **se h. à ou contre qn/qch** to run (slap) into or collide with or bang into or bump into sb/sth; **les deux voitures se sont**

heurtées à 120 km/h the two cars crashed into each other at 120 kph; **je me suis heurtée contre un mur** I crashed into a wall; **se h. la tête à ou contre qch** to knock or bump one's head against sth; Fig **se h. à l'indifférence générale** to come up against general apathy or indifference; **se h. à une difficulté** to come up against a difficulty; **se h. aux idées reçues** to come into conflict with or to clash with received opinion

2 (de couleur, intérêt etc) to clash; **des couleurs/goûts qui se heurtent** clashing colours/tastes, colours/tastes which clash; Fig **au cours de la réunion, ils se sont heurtés violemment** during the meeting they clashed violently; **il est très fréquent qu'ils se heurtent** they're always clashing (with each other) or crossing swords

*heurtoir [œrtwar] NM (de porte) (door) knocker; (amortisseur) catch, stop; Rail buffer

hévéa [evea] NM Bot hevea

hexacorde [ɛgzakɔrd] NM Mus hexachord

hexadécimal, -ale, -aux, -ales [ɛgzadesimal, -o] ADJ Ordinat hex, hexadecimal

hexaèdre [ɛgzaɛdr] ADJ hexahedral NM hexahedron

hexagonal, -ale, -aux, -ales [ɛgzagɔnal, -o] ADJ hexagonal; Fig French

hexagone [ɛgzagɔn] NM hexagon; **l'H.** France

hexamètre [ɛgzamɛtr] ADJ hexametric(al) NM hexameter

HF Radio etc (abrév haute fréquence) HF

hi INT (en riant) ha ha; (en pleurant) boo-hoo

hiatal, -ale, -aux, -ales [jatal, -o] ADJ Méd hiatal; **hernie hiatale** hiatus hernia

*hiatus [jatys] NM (dans une narration etc) gap, break, hiatus; Ling, Anat hiatus; Fig **le h. entre la production et les besoins** the gap or discrepancy between production and needs

hibernal, -ale, -aux, -ales [ibɛrnal, -o] ADJ (germination, sommeil etc) winter, Spéc hibernal

hibernant [ibɛrnɑ̃] ADJ (animal) hibernating

hibernation [ibɛrnasjɔ̃] NF hibernation; Fig **la gauche sort de son h.** the left is coming in from the cold; **mettre un dossier en h.** to shelve a document; **h. artificielle** suspended animation, Spéc cryogenic suspension

hiberner [ibɛrne] VI to hibernate

hibiscus [ibiskys] NM Bot hibiscus

*hibou, -oux [ibu] NM owl; **jeune h.** owlet; **des yeux de h.** eyes like saucers; Péj **quel vieux h.!** he is a real recluse!

*hic [ik] NM Fam **voilà le h.!** that's the snag or the trouble!; **le h., c'est que ...** the trouble or snag is that ...

*hickory [ikɔri] NM Bot hickory

hidalgo [idalgo] NM Fam Latin hunk

*hideur [idœr] NF (qualité) hideousness

*hideusement [idøzmɑ̃] ADV hideously

*hideux, -euse [idø, -øz] ADJ hideous; **h. à voir** hideous-looking; **un crime h.** a hideous or heinous crime

hiémal, -ale, -aux, -ales [jemal] ADJ Litt winter

hier [jɛr] ADV yesterday; **h. matin, h. dans la matinée** yesterday morning; **h. (au) soir** yesterday evening, last night; **on s'en souvient comme si c'était h.** I/we/etc can remember it as if it were (only) yesterday; **le journal d'h.** yesterday's paper; Fig **cela ne date pas d'h.** that's nothing new; Fam **je ne suis pas né d'h.** I wasn't born yesterday

NM **tu avais tout h. ou toute la journée d'h. pour te décider** you had all (day) yesterday to make up your mind

*hiérarchie [jerarʃi] NF hierarchy; **h. des valeurs sociales** scale of social values; **être en haut/bas de la h.** to be at the top/bottom of the hierarchy

*hiérarchique [jerarʃik] ADJ hierarchical; **c'est mon supérieur h.** he's my immediate superior; **par (la) voie h.** through (the) official channels

*hiérarchiquement [jerarʃikmɑ̃] ADV hierarchically; **il lui est h. supérieur** he is superior (in rank) to him

*hiérarchisation [jerarʃizasjɔ̃] NF **h. des fonctions** grading of jobs; **h. des tâches** prioritization of tasks

*hiérarchisé [jerarʃize] ADJ (système) hierarchical

*hiérarchiser [jerarʃize] VT **1** (organiser) to form into a hierarchy; (régler) (état etc) to structure or to classify according to a hierarchical system; **pour fonctionner, il est nécessaire qu'une société soit hiérarchisée** a society must have a hierarchy in order to function; **h. les emplois** to grade jobs **2** (tâches) to prioritize

*hiératique [jeratik] ADJ **1** (sacré) hieratic **2** (geste) solemn; **port de tête h.** regal carriage

*hiéroglyphe [jerɔglif] NM hieroglyph(ic)

*hiéroglyphique [jerɔglifik] ADJ hieroglyphic(al)

*hi-fi [ifi] ADJ INV, NF INV hi-fi; **chaîne h.** hi-fi; **magasin de h.** hi-fi shop

*hi-han, pl **hi-hans** [iɑ̃] INT, NM (dâne) hee-haw

hi hi [ii, hihi] INT (rire nerveux) hee-hee!; (pleurs) boo-hoo!

hilarant [ilarɑ̃] ADJ hilarious; Chimie **gaz h.** laughing gas

hilare [ilar] ADJ (visage) beaming, grinning; **il était h.** he was beaming or grinning all over his face

hilarité [ilarite] NF hilarity, mirth; **provoquer l'h. générale** to cause general hilarity

*hile [il] NM Anat, Bot hilum

Himalaya [imalaja] N **l'H.** the Himalayas

himalayen, -enne [imalajɛ̃, -jɛn] ADJ Himalayan; **la chaîne himalayenne** the Himalayan (mountain) range; Fig **les sommets himalayens de la bêtise** the (absolute) height of stupidity

*hindi [indi] ADJ NM Ling Hindi

hindou, -oue [ɛ̃du] ADJ Hindu N **H.** Hindu

hindouisme [ɛ̃duism] NM Hinduism

hindouiste [ɛ̃duist] ADJ, N Hindu

Hindoustan [ɛ̃dustɑ̃] N Géog Hindustan

hindoustani [ɛ̃dustani] NM Ling Hindustani

hinterland [interlɑ̃d] NM hinterland

*hippie [ipi] ADJ, N hippie

hippique [ipik] ADJ relating to horses, equine; **concours h.** horse show

hippisme [ipism] NM horseriding; (courses) horseracing

hippocampe [ipɔkɑ̃p] NM Myth hippocampus; (poisson) sea horse

Hippocrate [ipɔkrat] N Antiq Hippocrates; **le serment d'H.** the Hippocratic oath

hippocratique [ipɔkratik] ADJ Hippocratic

hippodrome [ipɔdrom] NM racecourse; Antiq hippodrome, circus

hippomobile [ipɔmobil] ADJ horse-drawn

hippophagique [ipɔfaʒik] ADJ **boucherie h.** horsemeat butcher

hippopotame [ipɔpɔtam] NM hippopotamus, Fam hippo; **il avait une carrure d'h.** he was built like an ox VOIR GRAMMAIRE A14

hippopotamesque [ipɔpɔtamɛsk] ADJ

Fam Hum hippopotamus-like, of a hippopotamus; **une lourdeur/grâce h.** the weight/grace of a hippo

hippotechnie [ipɔtɛkni] **NF** (technique of) horse breeding and training

*hippy [ipi] **ADJ, N** hippie

hirondelle [irɔ̃dɛl] **NF 1** (*oiseau*) swallow; *Prov* **une h. ne fait pas le printemps** one swallow doesn't make a summer; *Culin* **nid d'h.** bird's nest **2** *Fam Vieilli* (*agent de police*) cycle cop
▸▸ **h. de cheminée** swallow tern; **h. de fenêtre** house martin; **h. de mer** tern; **h. de rivage** sand martin

*hirsute [irsyt] **ADJ** (*personne*) hairy, *Spéc* hirsute; (*barbe, ours*) shaggy

hispanique [ispanik] **ADJ** Hispanic, Spanish

hispanisant, -ante [ispanizɑ̃, -ɑ̃t] **N** student of/expert on Spanish

hispaniser [ispanize] **VT** to Hispanicize

hispanisme [ispanism] **NM** *Ling* Hispanicism

hispano-américain, -aine, *pl* **hispano-américain(e)s** [ispanɔamerikɛ̃, -ɛn] **ADJ** Hispano-American, Spanish-American
N H. Hispano-American, *Fam* Hispanic

hispano-arabe, *pl* **hispano-arabes** [ispanɔarab], **hispano-moresque** *pl* **hispano-moresques** [ispanɔmɔrɛsk] **ADJ** Hispano-Moorish, Hispano-Moresque

hispanophone [ispanɔfɔn] **ADJ** Spanish-speaking
N Spanish speaker

hispide [ispid] **ADJ** *Bot* hairy, *Spéc* hispid

*hisser [ise] **VT** to hoist (up), to pull up; *Naut* (*embarcation*) to hoist in; **hissez!** hoist away!; *Naut* up sails!; **oh! hisse!** (yo-)heave-ho!; **h. une échelle par-dessus un mur** to haul a ladder over a wall; **h. qn vers soi** to lift sb up (towards one); **h. qn sur ses épaules** to hoist *or* lift sb onto one's shoulders
VPR se hisser se h. jusqu'à la fenêtre to pull *or* hoist oneself up to the window; **se h. sur la pointe des pieds** to stand on tiptoe; *Fig* **se h. jusqu'au pouvoir/gouvernement** to rise to a position of power/a position in government

histogramme [istɔgram] **NM** bar chart, histogram

HISTOIRE [istwar]

history **1** ▪ history book **2** ▪ story **3**
▪ fib **3** ▪ trouble **3** ▪ fuss **3**

NF 1 history; **l'h. seule jugera** history *or* posterity alone will be the judge; **h. du moyen âge/naturelle** medi(a)eval/natural history; **étudiant en h. de l'art** history of art student *or* art history student; **l'h. des sciences** the history of science; **la petite h.** sidelights on history, footnotes of history; **sachez, pour la petite h., qu'elle fut la maîtresse du roi** let me tell you, by the way *or* for the record, that she was the king's mistress; **l'h. de (la) France** the history of France, French history; *Fig* **tout cela, c'est de l'h. ancienne** that's all ancient history *or* dead and buried; **livre d'h.** history book
2 (*livre*) history book; **une h. d'Allemagne** a history of Germany
3 (*récit*) story, tale; *TV, Cin* story, narrative; *Fam* (*mensonge*) fib, story; **histoires pour enfants** children's stories; **auteur d'histoires pour enfants** children's author, author of children's stories; **j'ai l'impression que tu es en train de me raconter une h.** I have a feeling that you're pulling my leg *or* telling me a tall story; **je t'assure, je ne te raconte pas d'histoires!** I assure you, I'm not making it up!; **h. de marin** sailor's yarn; **livre d'histoires** story book; **c'est toujours la même h.** it's (always) the same old story; **c'est une autre**

h. it's quite a different matter *or* story; **tout ça, ce sont des histoires** that's all nonsense *or* rubbish; **tu crois encore ses histoires?** do you still believe his/her nonsense?; **le plus beau de l'h., c'est que ...** the best part of the story is that ...; **se fourrer dans une sale/drôle (d')h.** to get mixed up in a nasty/funny business; **il m'est arrivé une drôle d'h./une sale h.** a funny thing/a nasty thing happened to me; **figure-toi qu'il m'est arrivé une h. incroyable!** believe it or not, something incredible has happened to me!; *Fam* **il est sorti, h. de prendre un peu l'air** he went out just to get a breath of fresh air; **h. de rire un peu** just for a laugh, just for fun; **ce que j'en dis, c'est h. de parler** you can take *or* leave what I've said; **elle l'a dit, h. de dire quelque chose** she said it just for the sake of saying something; **c'est toute une h.** (*à raconter*) it's a long story; (*pour faire qch*) it's no end of a job, it's quite a business; **en voilà une h. pour pas grand-chose** what a fuss about nothing; *Fam* **en voilà une h.!** what a fuss!, what a song and dance!; (*c'est incroyable*) that's quite a story; **quelle h.!** that's quite a story!; *Fam* **faire des histoires** *ou* **un tas d'histoires** to make a fuss *or* a to-do; **tu fais bien des histoires!** you're making *or* kicking up such a fuss!; **s'attirer des histoires** to get oneself into trouble; **faire des histoires à qn** to make trouble for sb; **il faut éviter d'avoir des histoires** you/we/*etc* must keep out of trouble; *Fam* **pas d'histoires!** no fuss!; **au lit, et pas d'histoires** off to bed now, and I don't want any fuss
▸▸ **h. de fous** shaggy dog story; **c'est une h. de fous!** it's crazy!; **l'H. sainte** Biblical history

Attention: ne pas confondre **history** et **story** lorsque l'on traduit **histoire**. Le terme **history** désigne la discipline, alors que **story** signifie **récit**.

histologie [istɔlɔʒi] **NF** histology

histologique [istɔlɔʒik] **ADJ** histological

historicité [istɔrisite] **NF** historicity

historié [istɔrje] **ADJ** that tells a story; (*initiales, bible*) illuminated

historien, -ienne [istɔrjɛ̃, -jɛn] **N** historian; **h. d'art** art historian

historiette [istɔrjɛt] **NF** anecdote, short story; **c'est une jolie petite h.** it's a nice little story

historiographe [istɔrjɔgraf] **N** historiographer

historiographie [istɔrjɔgrafi] **NF** historiography

historique [istɔrik] **ADJ** (*qui concerne l'histoire*) historical; (*important, décisif*) historic; *Gram* **présent h.** historic present; **être classé monument h.** (*d'un monument*) to be listed *or* classified as an ancient monument *or* as a place of historic interest; **liste des monuments historiques français** list of ancient French monuments; **c'est un événement h. dans la famille** it's a historic event *or* a red-letter day for the family
NM historical record *or* account; *Ordinat* (*de document*) log; **faire l'h. des événements** to give a chronological account of events; **faire l'h. d'une association/d'un gouvernement/d'un mot** to trace the history of an association/a government/a word; **h. d'entretien** (*d'une voiture etc*) service history

Attention: ne pas confondre **historic** et **historical** lorsque l'on traduit **historique**. **Historic** signifie **important d'un point de vue historique**, alors que **historical** signifie **qui se rapporte à l'histoire**.

historiquement [istɔrikmɑ̃] **ADV** historically

histrion [istrijɔ̃] **NM** *Théâtre Arch* play actor; *Litt Péj* second-rate actor

hi-tech [aitɛk] **ADJ INV** hi-tech

hitlérien, -ienne [itlɛrjɛ̃, -jɛn] **ADJ** Hitlerite; **le gouvernement h.** the Hitler government
N Hitlerite

hitlérisme [itlɛrism] **NM** Hitlerism

*hit-parade [itparad] **NM** charts; **chanteur n° 1 au h.** chart-topping singer; **chanson n° 1 au h.** chart-topper, number 1 in the charts; **être au h. de l'actualité** to be a big news item, to be headline news

*hittite [itit] *Antiq* **ADJ** Hittite
N Hittite

HIV [aʃive] **NM** (*abrév* **human immunodeficiency virus**) HIV

hiver [ivɛr] **NM** winter; **l'h. sera doux/rude** it will be a mild/severe winter; **en h.** in winter; **temps d'h.** wintry weather; **depuis une semaine, il fait un temps d'h.** it's been like winter this last week; **vêtements/sports d'h.** winter clothes/sports; **jardin d'h.** winter garden; *Fam* **le bonhomme H.** Jack Frost **VOIR GRAMMAIRE A7**
▸▸ *Fig* **h. nucléaire** nuclear winter

hivernage [ivɛrnaʒ] **NM 1** (*du bétail, de navires, d'une expédition polaire etc*) wintering **2** (*endroit*) winter quarters; *Naut* winter harbour **3** (*fourrage*) winter fodder

hivernal, -ale, -aux, -ales [ivɛrnal, -o] **ADJ** (*froid etc*) winter; (*temps*) wintry; **station hivernale** winter sports resort, ski resort

hivernant, -ante [ivɛrnɑ̃, -ɑ̃t] **N** (*dans un lieu de vacances etc*) winter visitor *or* tourist

hiverner [ivɛrne] **VI** to winter; (*d'un navire*) to lie up (for the winter)
VT (*bétail*) to winter

HLM [aʃɛlɛm] **NF** *ou* **NM** (*abrév* **habitation à loyer modéré**) *Br* ≃ council flat/house, *Am* ≃ public housing unit; **vivre dans une** *ou* *Fam* **un H.** to live in a council flat/house

*ho [o] **INT** (*appel*) hey!; (*surprise*) oh!

*hobby [ɔbi] **NM** hobby

*hobereau, -eaux [ɔbro] **NM 1** *souvent Péj* (*gentilhomme*) (country) squire **2** *Orn* hobby

*hochement [ɔʃmɑ̃] **NM h. de tête** (*négatif*) shake of the head; (*affirmatif*) nod (of the head)

*hochepot [ɔʃpo] **NM** *Culin* meat and vegetable stew

hochequeue [ɔʃkø] **NM** *Zool* wagtail

*hocher [ɔʃe] **VT h. la tête** (*de dédain*) to toss one's head; (*pour dire non*) to shake one's head; (*pour dire oui*) to nod (one's head); (*d'un cheval*) to toss its head

*hochet [ɔʃɛ] **NM** (*d'enfant*) (child's) rattle; *Fig* bauble, toy

*hockey [ɔkɛ] **NM** *Sport* (*jeu*) (field) hockey; *Can* (*sur glace*) ice hockey; *Can* (*crosse*) (ice) hockey stick; **h. sur gazon** (field) hockey; **h. sur glace** ice hockey, *Am* hockey; **partie de h.** hockey game *or* match; **jouer au h.** to play hockey

*hockeyeur, -euse [ɔkɛjœr, -øz] **N** hockey player

hoirie [wari] **NF** *Jur* avance *ou* avancement d'h. advancement

*holà [ɔla] **INT** (*pour appeler*) stop!, hold on!; **h., on se calme, hein!** hey, quieten down, OK?; **h., je ne suis pas tout à fait d'accord avec vous, moi!** now hold on, I don't quite agree with you there!
NM mettre le h. à qch to put a stop to sth

*holding [ɔldiŋ] **NM** *ou* **NF** *Fin* holding company

*hold-up [ɔldœp] **NM INV** *Fam* hold-up, *surtout Am* stick-up; **faire un h.** to carry out a hold-up

*hollandais, -aise [ɔlɑ̃dɛ, -ɛz] ADJ Dutch
 NM Ling Dutch
 N H. Dutchman, f Dutchwoman; **les H.** the Dutch

*Hollande [ɔlɑ̃d] NF Holland

*hollande [ɔlɑ̃d] NM (fromage) Dutch cheese
 NF Tex holland

*hollywoodien, -ienne [ɔliwudjɛ̃, -jɛn] ADJ (acteur) Hollywood; (maison, cadre) Hollywood-style

holmium [ɔlmjɔm] NM Chimie holmium

holocauste [ɔlɔkost] NM 1 (sacrifice) sacrifice; (avec immolation) burnt offering; **l'H.** (des Juifs) the Holocaust 2 (victime) sacrifice

hologramme [ɔlɔgram] NM hologram

holographe [ɔlɔgraf] ADJ = olographe

holographie [ɔlɔgrafi] NF holography

holothurie [ɔlɔtyri] NF Zool sea cucumber, Spéc holothurian

*homard [ɔmar] NM lobster; **manger du h.** to eat lobster; **pinces de h.** lobster claws; **bisque de h.** lobster soup or bisque; Fam **rouge comme un h.** (de honte, de gêne) as red as a beetroot; (après un coup de soleil) as red as a lobster

*hombre [ɔ̃br] NM Cartes Arch (game of) ombre

*home [om] NM home; **h. d'enfants** residential leisure centre for children, summer camp; Belg **h. d'étudiants** student hall of residence or Am dormitory, student hostel; Belg, Suisse **h. pour personnes âgées** old people's home, retirement home

*home cinéma [omsinema] NM home cinema

homélie [ɔmeli] NF homily

homéopathe [omeopat] Méd ADJ homeopathic
 N homeopath

homéopathie [omeopati] NF homeopathy; **se soigner à l'h.** to take homeopathic medicine, to have homeopathic treatment

homéopathique [omeopatik] ADJ homeopathic

Homère [ɔmɛr] N Homer

homérique [ɔmerik] ADJ Homeric

homicide [ɔmisid] ADJ Arch, Litt homicidal; (arme) murderous
 N Litt (personne) homicide, murderer, f murderess
 NM Jur (crime) homicide; **commettre un h.** to commit homicide
 ▸▸**h. involontaire** ou **par imprudence** manslaughter (through negligence); **h. sans préméditation** culpable homicide; **h. volontaire** wilful homicide, murder

hominidés [ɔminide] NMPL hominids

hominoïdes [ɔminɔid] NMPL hominoids

hommage [ɔmaʒ] NM 1 homage; **rendre h. à qn** to pay homage or (a) tribute to sb; **nous rendons h. à votre courage** we are paying tribute to your courage 2 hommages respects, compliments; **présenter ses hommages à une dame** to pay one's respects to a lady; **transmettez-lui mes hommages** give him my regards or respects 3 (de respect, d'estime) tribute, token; **faire h. de qch à qn** to offer sth to sb as a token of (one's) esteem; **h. de l'éditeur** complimentary copy, presentation copy; **h. de l'auteur** with the author's compliments

hommasse [ɔmas] ADJ Péj (femme) masculine, mannish; **elle a des manières hommasses** she acts like a man

HOMME [ɔm]

man	mankind
1–3	3

NM 1 man, pl men; **l'h. et la femme** man and woman; **jeune h.** young man; **je ne suis plus un jeune h.** I'm not as young as I was; **merci jeune h.** thank you, young man; **h. âgé** old man, elderly man; Com **rayon hommes** men's department, menswear; **parler à qn d'h. à h.** to talk to sb man to man, to have a man-to-man talk with sb; **un bel h.** a handsome man; **soyez un h.!** be a man!; Fam **mon h.** my man/husband VOIR GRAMMAIRE A13
 2 (individu) (pl hommes ou gens) man, pl men; **j'ai trouvé ton h., je pense qu'il fera tout à fait l'affaire** I've found just the man for you, I think he'll do nicely; **trouver son h.** to meet one's match; **il n'est pas h. à laisser passer cela** he's not one to or the kind of man to let that happen; Mil **les officiers et les hommes** the officers and (the) men; **les hommes du président/du directeur** the President's/director's men; **les hommes (d'équipage)** the crew, the ship's company; **un h. de goût** a man of taste; **h. politique** politician; **un h. de droite/de gauche** a right-/left-winger; **c'est l'h. fort du parti** he's the strongman of the party; **l'abominable h. des neiges** the abominable snowman
 3 (genre humain) man, mankind; **tous les hommes** all men, all mankind; **de mémoire d'h.** within living memory; **les droits de l'h.** human rights; **comme un seul h.** as one man, in unison; Prov **l'h. propose, Dieu dispose** man proposes, God disposes
 ▸▸**h. d'affaires** businessman; Naut **h. de barre** helmsman; **h. de confiance** right-hand man; **h. d'église** man of the church; **h. d'entretien** maintenance man; **h. d'État** statesman; **h. à femmes** ladies' man; **h.-grenouille**, pl **hommes-grenouilles** frogman; **h. de journée** (day) labourer; **h. de lettres** man of letters; **h. de loi** man of law, lawyer; **h. de main** henchman; **h. de métier** professional; **h. du monde** gentleman; **h.-orchestre**, pl **hommes-orchestres** one-man band; **h. de paille** figurehead; **h. de parole** man of his word; **h. de peine** (day) labourer; Litt **h. de peu** worthless individual; Naut **h. de quart** watch; **l'h. de la rue** the man in the street; **h.-sandwich**, pl **hommes-sandwich(e)s** sandwich man; **h. à tout faire** odd-job man, handyman; **h. de troupe** ordinary soldier, private

---

Il faut noter que le terme anglais **man of the world** ne signifie pas **homme du monde** mais **homme d'expérience**.

---

homo [ɔmo] ADJ, N Fam gay

homocentrique [ɔmɔsɑ̃trik] ADJ Math homocentric

homogène [ɔmɔʒɛn] ADJ homogeneous

homogénéisation [ɔmɔʒeneizasjɔ̃] NF homogenization

homogénéiser [ɔmɔʒeneize] VT to homogenize; **lait homogénéisé** homogenized milk

homogénéité [ɔmɔʒeneite] NF homogeneousness, homogeneity

homographe [ɔmɔgraf] NM homograph
 ADJ homographic

homologation [ɔmɔlɔgasjɔ̃] NF Jur (d'un accord etc) confirmation; (d'un testament) probate; Sport (d'un record etc) ratification

homologie [ɔmɔlɔʒi] NF homology

homologue [ɔmɔlɔg] ADJ Biol etc homologous
 NM Biol etc homologue
 N counterpart, opposite number

homologuer [ɔmɔlɔge] VT Jur (accord etc) to confirm, to endorse; Jur (testament) to prove; (décision) to ratify; (comptes) to approve; Sport (record) to ratify; Admin **prix homologués** authorized charges; Sport **record homologué** official record

homoncule [ɔmɔ̃kyl] NM = homuncule

homonyme [ɔmɔnim] ADJ Ling homonymous
 NM (mot) homonym; (personne) namesake

homonymie [ɔmɔnimi] NF Ling homonymy

homoparental [ɔmɔparɑ̃tal] ADJ relating to gay parenting, Spéc homoparental

homoparentalité [ɔmɔparɑ̃talite] NF gay parenting

homophobe [ɔmɔfɔb] ADJ homophobic
 N homophobe

homophobie [ɔmɔfɔbi] NF homophobia

homophone [ɔmɔfɔn] ADJ Ling, Mus homophonic, homophonous
 NM Ling homophone

homophonie [ɔmɔfɔni] NF homophony

homosexualité [ɔmɔsɛksyalite] NF homosexuality

homosexuel, -elle [ɔmɔsɛksɥɛl] ADJ, N homosexual

homuncule [ɔmɔ̃kyl] NM Arch homunculus; Fig Péj manikin, dwarf

*Honduras [ɔ̃dyras] NM le H. Honduras

*hondurien, -ienne [ɔ̃dyrjɛ̃, -jɛn] ADJ Honduran
 N H. Honduran

*Hongkong, Hong-Kong [ɔ̃gkɔ̃g] N Hong Kong

*hongre [ɔ̃gr] ADJ (cheval) gelded, castrated
 NM gelding

*hongrer [ɔ̃gre] VT Vét to geld, to castrate

*Hongrie [ɔ̃gri] NF Hungary

*hongrois, -oise [ɔ̃grwa, -waz] ADJ Hungarian
 NM Ling Hungarian
 N H. Hungarian

honnête [ɔnɛt] ADJ 1 (intègre) (personne etc) honest, honourable, Am honorable; **ce n'est pas très h. de sa part** that isn't very honest of him; **homme h., h. homme** honest man, man of honour or Am honor; **h. homme** (au XVIIIᵉ siècle etc) man of culture, gentleman; **peu h.** dishonourable; **moyens honnêtes** fair or honest means; **être h. avec soi-même** to be honest with oneself
 2 (décent) (comportement etc) decent, seemly, becoming; **attitude peu h.** unseemly or unbecoming attitude; **je suis une femme h., moi, monsieur!** I'm not that sort of woman!
 3 (acceptable) (prix etc) reasonable, moderate, fair; **une note plus qu'h.** a more than reasonable mark; **un repas h. sans plus** a reasonable or an OK meal, but nothing more or nothing to write home about
 4 Arch courteous, polite, well-bred

honnêtement [ɔnɛtmɑ̃] ADV 1 (avec intégrité) honestly, honourably, Am honorably; **h., je pense que tu fais une erreur** honestly or to be honest, I think you're making a mistake; **conseiller qn h.** to give someone honest advice; **se comporter h. en affaires** to be an honest businessman/businesswoman
 2 (raisonnablement) reasonably, fairly
 3 Arch (avec courtoisie) courteously, politely

honnêteté [ɔnɛtte] NF 1 (intégrité) honesty, integrity 2 (décence) decency, propriety, decorum 3 (dans les rapports) fairness, fair dealing 4 Arch (courtoisie) courtesy, politeness

honneur [ɔnœr] NM 1 honour, Am honor; **homme d'h.** man of honour, honourable or Am honorable man; **mettre un point d'h. à faire qch, se faire un point d'h. de faire qch** to make it a point of honour to do sth; **déclarer/jurer sur l'h. que ...** to state/swear on one's honour that ...; **forfaire** ou **manquer à l'h.** to act dishonourably; **il faut sauver l'h.** honour must be saved; **l'h. est sauf** our/

his/*etc* honour is safe; **non, je ne l'ai pas vu, parole d'h.** no, I haven't seen him, I give you my word (of honour) *or* cross my heart; **se faire un h. de qch/de faire qch** to be proud of sth/to do sth; **en tout bien tout h.** *(proposition, affaire)* (fair and) aboveboard; **nous nous sommes vus en tout bien tout h.** it was all aboveboard, there was nothing underhand about it; **affaire d'h.** matter of honour; *(duel)* duel; **garçon d'h.** best man; **demoiselle d'h.** bridesmaid

2 *(hommage)* **réception en l'h. de qn** reception in honour *or Am* honor of sb *or* in sb's honour; **assis à la place d'h.** in the seat of honour; **cour d'h.** main courtyard; *Univ* main quadrangle; **escalier d'h.** main staircase, main stairs; *Mil etc* **garde d'h.** guard of honour, *Am* honor guard; **hôte d'h.** guest of honour; **président d'h.** honorary president; **faire h. à qn** to do honour to sb, to honour sb; **vous me faites un grand h.** you are doing me a great honour; **me ferez-vous l'h. de m'accompagner?** will you do me the honour of accompanying me?; **à qui ai-je l'h. (de parler)?** to whom have I the honour *or* the pleasure of speaking?; **j'ai l'h. de vous faire savoir que …** I beg to inform you that …; **j'ai l'h. de vous demander la main de votre fille** I have the honour of asking for the hand of your daughter; *Fam* **en quel h. vous voit-on ici?** to what do I/we *etc* owe the honour (of your visit)?; *Fam* **et en quel h. me demandes-tu ma voiture?** just who do you think you are, asking me for my car?; *Fam* **et en quel h. devrais-je t'aider?** give me one good reason why I should help you!; **à vous l'h.** after you; **jouer pour l'h.** to play for love; **être à l'h.** to have the place of honour; **le cricket est à l'h. en Angleterre** cricket holds a place of honour *or* holds pride of place in England; **les lignes floues sont en h. cette année en France** loose-fitting clothes are all the fashion in France this year

3 *Golf* **avoir l'h.** to have the honour *or Am* honor

4 *(gloire)* credit; **c'est à elle que revient tout l'h. de l'affaire** she must take all the credit for the matter; **être l'h. de son pays** to be an honour *or Am* honor *or* a credit to one's country; **son attitude lui fait h.** his attitude is a credit to him *or* does him credit; **on doit dire à leur h. que …** it must be said to their credit that …; **il en est sorti à son h.** he came out of it with flying colours; **son refus est tout à son h.** it speaks well for him *or* it is greatly to his credit that he did not accept; **avec h.** creditably

5 honneurs *(marques d'estime)* honours, *Am* honors; **rendre les derniers honneurs** *ou* **les honneurs suprêmes à qn** to pay a last tribute *or* one's last respects to sb; **rendre de grands honneurs aux vainqueurs** to hail the returning victors; *Mil* **rendre les honneurs à qn** to present arms to sb, to give *or* pay (military) honours to sb; **avec tous les honneurs de la guerre** with all the honours of war; **rechercher les honneurs** to be looking for honours; **avoir les honneurs de la première page** to appear on the front page; **faire (à qn) les honneurs de la maison** to (do the honours and) show sb round the house; **rendre les honneurs funèbres à qn** to bury sb with due ceremony; **honneurs militaires** military honours

6 faire h. à sa signature to honour *or Am* honor one's signature; **faire h. à ses engagements** to honour one's commitments; *Com* **faire h. à une traite** to honour *or* meet a bill; *Fam* **faire h. au dîner** to do justice to the dinner

7 *Cartes* **les honneurs** honours, *Am* honors; **quatre d'honneurs** four by honours; **honneurs partagés** honours even

****honnir** [ɔniʀ] VT to disgrace, to dishonour, *Am* to dishonor; **honni soit qui mal y pense** honi soit qui mal y pense, evil be to him who evil thinks; **honni de tous** spurned by all

honorabilité [ɔnɔʀabilite] NF honourableness, *Am* honorableness, worthiness; *(d'une famille, une profession etc)* respectability; **porter atteinte à l'h. de qn/qch** to bring dishonour on sb/sth; **l'h. de ses intentions ne fait aucun doute** his/her intentions are completely honourable; **c'est quelqu'un d'une très grande h.** he/she is a person of great integrity

honorable [ɔnɔʀabl] ADJ **1** *(sentiments, personne)* honourable, *Am* honorable; *(famille, profession etc)* honourable, respectable; **mes intentions sont honorables** my intentions are honourable; **vieillesse h.** respected old age; *Euph* **un h. correspondant** a secret agent, a special operative **2** *(performance)* creditable; **doctorat avec mention h.** = doctorate awarded with distinction; **des résultats plus qu'honorables** more than satisfactory results

honorablement [ɔnɔʀabləmã] ADV **1** honourably, *Am* honorably, with honour, *Am* with honor; **famille h. connue** family of good reputation; **gagner h. sa vie** to earn an honest living; **vivre h.** to lead a respectable life **2** *(correctement)* **s'acquitter h. de qch** to acquit oneself creditably in sth; **il s'en est h. tiré** he did quite creditably

honoraire [ɔnɔʀɛʀ] ADJ *(fonction, membre etc)* honorary; **professeur h.** emeritus professor

NMPL **honoraires** fee(s); *(d'une profession libérale)* fee, *Spéc* honorarium; *(d'un avocat)* retainer; **honoraires d'agréé en douane** customs broker's fees; **honoraires fixes** fixed fees

honorariat [ɔnɔʀaʀja] NM honorary membership

honoré, -ée [ɔnɔʀe] ADJ honoured, *Am* honored; **mon h. confrère** my respected colleague

NF **votre honorée du …** *(dans une lettre)* yours of the …

honorer [ɔnɔʀe] VT **1** to honour, *Am* to honor; *(qualités de qn etc)* to respect

2 *(gratifier)* *(personne)* to do honour *or Am* honor to; **h. qn de sa confiance** to honour sb with one's confidence; *aussi Iron* **h. une cérémonie de sa présence** to honour *or* grace a ceremony with one's presence

3 *Com (facture)* to honour, *Am* to honor, to meet; *Com, Jur* **refuser d'h. (un contrat)** to repudiate (a contract); **h. ses engagements** to honour one's commitments

4 *(valoir de l'estime à)* *(personne, chose)* to be an honour *or Am* honor to, to do credit to, to be a credit to; **c'est un sentiment qui vous honore** the sentiment does you credit

5 *(sexuellement)* *(d'un animal)* to mate with; *Hum (d'un homme)* to make love to

VPR **s'honorer s'h. de qch/d'avoir fait qch** to be proud of sth/of having done sth; **notre ville s'honore de ses peintres** our town is proud of its painters *or* takes pride in its painters

honorifique [ɔnɔʀifik] ADJ *(titre, rang etc)* honorary; **président à titre h.** honorary president

honoris causa [ɔnɔʀiskoza] ADJ INV honoris causa; **docteur h.** doctor honoris causa, honorary doctor

****honte** [ɔt] NF **1** shame; **avoir perdu toute h.** *ou* **tout sentiment de h., avoir toute h. bue** to have lost all sense of shame, to have no (sense of) shame, to be lacking in any sense of shame; **faire qch toute h. bue** to do sth quite shamelessly; **h. à vous!** shame on you!; **à ma grande h.** to my shame; **sans h.**

(comme adjectif) shameless; *(comme adverbe)* shamelessly; **avoir h.** to be ashamed (of oneself); **avoir h. de faire qch, avoir** *ou* **éprouver de la h. à faire qch** to be *or* feel ashamed to do sth *or* of doing something; **il ne faut pas avoir h. de le dire** you shouldn't be ashamed to say it; **avoir h. pour qn** to be ashamed of sb; **faire h. à qn** to make sb ashamed, to put sb to shame; **elle me faisait h., posant sans cesse ses questions ridicules** she made me so ashamed, continually asking her ridiculous questions; **couvrir qn de h., jeter la h. sur qn** to bring shame *or* disgrace (up)on sb; **fausse** *ou* **mauvaise h.** self-consciousness, bashfulness; **se cacher la visage de h.** to hide one's face in shame; **rougir de h.** to blush with shame

2 *(cause)* (cause of) shame, disgrace, dishonour, *Am* dishonor; **faire** *ou* **être la h. de qn** to be a disgrace to sb; **quelle h.!,** what a disgrace!; **c'est une h.** it's a disgrace; *Fam* **eh, t'as vu ses chaussures? la h.!** *ou* **oh là là, la h.!** have you seen his shoes? they're an absolute disgrace!

****honteusement** [ɔtøzmã] ADV shamefully, disgracefully; **il a fui h.** he fled in shame; **il a h. fui** to his shame, he fled

****honteux, -euse** [ɔtø, øz] ADJ **1** ashamed; **être h. de qch/d'avoir fait qch** to be ashamed of sth/having done sth **2** *(après une erreur)* shamefaced, sheepish **3** *Péj (conduite etc)* shameful, disgraceful, ignominious; *Vieilli* **maladie honteuse** venereal disease; **c'est h.!** it's a disgrace!, it's shameful!; **si c'est pas h. de voir des choses pareilles!** isn't it terrible!

****hooligan** [uligan] NM hooligan

****hooliganisme** [uliganism] NM hooliganism

****hop** [ɔp] INT **allez h.!** *(saute!)* jump!; *(pars!)* off you go!; **allez h., tout le monde dehors!** come on, everybody out!; **h.-là!** oops(-a-daisy)!

hôpital, -aux [ɔpital, -o] NM hospital; **il est très bien soigné à l'h.** he is being very well cared for in hospital; **être emmené à l'h.** to be taken to hospital *or Am* the hospital; **chambre d'h.** hospital room; *Naut* **navire-h.** hospital ship

▸▸**h. des armées** military hospital; **h. de campagne** field hospital; **h. militaire** military hospital; **h. psychiatrique** psychiatric hospital

****hoquet** [ɔkɛ] NM **1** *Physiol* hiccup, hiccough; **avoir le h.** to have (the) hiccups; **que faire contre le h.?** how can you get rid of hiccups? **2** *(de surprise, de terreur etc)* gasp; **avoir un h. de surprise** to catch one's breath, to gasp in surprise; **le moteur eut un dernier h. et rendit l'âme** the engine gave a final splutter and died

****hoqueter** [ɔk(ə)te] VI *(***je hoquette,** n. **hoquetons; je hoquetterai)** to hiccup, to hiccough; **le moteur hoqueta puis se décida à partir** the engine spluttered into life

horaire [ɔʀɛʀ] ADJ **1** *(qui correspond à une heure)* hourly; **salaire h.** hourly rate *or* wage; *Ind* **débit h.** hourly output, output per hour **2 fuseau h.** time zone

NM timetable, schedule; *(à l'école, pour les moyens de transport)* timetable, *Am* schedule; *(d'un magasin)* opening hours; **avoir un h. chargé** to have a busy schedule *or* full timetable; **être en retard sur l'h.** to be behind schedule; **horaires de bureau/de travail** office/working hours; **h. flexible** flexible hours, flexitime; **h. variable** flexible hours, flexitime; **h. fixe/flottant** fixed/variable working hours; **h. mobile** *ou* **à la carte** flexitime, flexible working hours; **horaires d'été** summer timetable; **horaires de départ** departure schedule; *(de bateau)* sailing schedule

*horde [ɔrd] NF horde

*horion [ɔrjõ] NM blow

horizon [ɔrizõ] NM **1** horizon; *(des toits d'une ville etc)* skyline; **la ligne d'h.** the horizon; **à l'h.** on the horizon, on the skyline; **personne à l'h.?** on peut y aller nobody around *or* nobody in sight? let's go; **le soleil descend sur l'h.** the sun goes down beneath the horizon **2** *Fig* horizon; **se profiler à l'h.** to loom up on the horizon; **l'h. se vide de toute espérance** the future is bleak; **à l'h. 2010** in the year 2010; **ouvrir des horizons nouveaux** to open up new horizons *or* vistas; **tour d'h.** overview, survey; **faire un tour d'h. de la situation du nucléaire en France** to give a general overview of nuclear power in France; **h. intellectuel** intellectual horizons *or* boundaries
▸▸ *Aviat* **h. artificiel** artificial horizon

horizontal, -ale, -aux, -ales [ɔrizõtal, -o] ADJ **1** *(dans l'espace)* horizontal; **c'est la position horizontale qui me convient le mieux** I'm most comfortable lying down; **quelle est la définition du trois h.?** *(dans les mots croisés)* what's three across? **2** *Écon (concentration, intégration)* horizontal
NF **horizontale 1** horizontal; **le livre est posé à l'horizontale** the book is lying flat **2** *(droite)* horizontal line

horizontalement [ɔrizõtalmã] ADV horizontally; *(dans les mots croisés)* across

horizontalité [ɔrizõtalite] NF horizontality

horloge [ɔrlɔʒ] NF clock; **il est deux heures à l'h.** it's two by the clock; **j'ai attendu une bonne heure d'h.** I waited a full *or* solid hour by the clock; **réglé comme une h.** as regular as clockwork
▸▸ **h. atomique** atomic clock; **h. biologique** biological clock; **h. contrôleuse** time clock; **h. horodatrice** time clock; **h. normande** grandfather clock; **l'h. parlante** the speaking clock; **h. de parquet** grandfather clock; **h. physiologique** biological clock; **h. pointeuse** time clock; **h. à quartz** quartz clock; *Ordinat* **h. du système** system clock; *Ordinat* **h. en temps réel** real-time clock

horloger, -ère [ɔrlɔʒe, -ɛr] ADJ **l'industrie horlogère** the clock and watchmaking industry
N clock and watchmaker; *Fig* **le grand h.** the Creator

horloger-bijoutier, *pl* **horlogers-bijoutiers** NM jeweller *or* Am jeweler and watchmaker

horlogerie [ɔrlɔʒri] NF *(fabrication)* clock and watchmaking; *(magasin)* clockmaker's *or* watchmaker's (shop); **l'h. (ouvrages)** clocks and watches; **mouvement d'h.** clockwork

*hormis [ɔrmi] *Litt* PRÉP *(no liaison,* **h. elle** [ɔrmiɛl]) except, but, save; **personne h. vous** no one but you, no one besides yourself
CONJ **h. que** except *or* save that; *Can (à moins que)* unless

hormonal, -ale, -aux, -ales [ɔrmɔnal, -o] ADJ *Méd* hormonal; **insuffisance hormonale** hormone deficiency; **traitement/dosage h.** hormone treatment/test

hormone [ɔrmɔn] NF hormone; **veaux aux hormones** hormone-fed calves

hormonothérapie [ɔrmɔnoterapi] NF *Méd* hormone therapy

*hornblende [ɔrnblɛ̃d] NF *Minér* hornblende

horodatage [ɔrodataʒ] NM time and date stamping

horodaté [ɔrodate] ADJ pay and display; **stationnement h.** pay and display parking; **ticket h.** pay and display sticker

horodateur [ɔrodatœr] NM time and date stamp; *(dans la rue)* pay and display machine

horoscope [ɔrɔskɔp] NM horoscope; **faire l'h. de qn** to cast sb's horoscope; **consulter son h.** to read *or* consult one's horoscope

horreur [ɔrœr] NF **1** *(effroi)* horror; **à ma grande h.** to my unspeakable horror; **frappé** *ou* **glacé** *ou* **saisi d'h.** horror-stricken, horror-struck; **paralysé d'h.** paralysed *or* helpless with horror; **une indicible h. me gagnait** I was overcome by an indescribable sense of horror; *Fam* **c'est l'h.** it's the pits, it sucks, *Am* it bites
2 *(répugnance)* horror, repugnance, disgust, abhorrence; **faire h. à qn** to horrify sb, to fill sb with horror; **tous ces gens me font une sainte h.** all these people make me sick, I can't stand all these people; **avoir qn/qch en h., avoir h. de qn/qch** to have a horror of sb/sth, to hate *or* detest *or* loathe sb/sth; **j'ai h. que l'on me dérange pendant le repas** I hate being disturbed during meals; **considérer qch dans toute son h.** to see sth in all its horror *or* in its full horror
3 *(chose horrible)* horrible thing; **sa voiture/montre est une h.** his car/watch is hideous *or* dreadful; **tu la trouves belle?, c'est une h.!** you think she's beautiful? she's hideous!; **quelle h.!** that's horrible!, how horrible!
4 les horreurs de la guerre the horrors of war; **commettre des horreurs** to commit atrocities; **dire des horreurs de qn** to say horrid *or* horrible *or* dreadful things about sb

horrible [ɔribl] ADJ *(effrayant)* horrible, dreadful, horrid, ghastly; *(répugnant)* gruesome; **spectacle h.** ghastly *or* hideous *or* gruesome sight; **une soif h.** a terrible thirst; **il est h. sans sa moustache** he looks awful *or* horrible without his moustache; **elle a été h. avec lui** she was horrible to him

horriblement [ɔribləmã] ADV awfully, dreadfully, horribly; **h. mal habillé** appallingly dressed; **il nous a h. déçus** he let us down very badly; **il a été h. déçu** he was dreadfully disappointed

horrifiant [ɔrifjã] ADJ horrifying, shocking, appalling

horrifier [ɔrifje] VT to horrify; **être horrifié de qch** to be horrified at sth

horrifique [ɔrifik] ADJ *Fam Hum* horrific

horripilant [ɔripilã] ADJ exasperating, maddening

horripilation [ɔripilasjõ] NF exasperation

horripiler [ɔripile] VT to exasperate; **qu'est-ce qu'il m'horripile avec ses histoires!** he really gets on my nerves with his stories

*HORS [ɔr] PRÉP *(liaison with* **r, h. elle** [ɔrɛl]) **1 h. de** out of; **h. d'usage** out of action *or* service *or* use; **h. de l'eau** out of the water; **tomber h. du lit** to fall out of bed; **h. de la ville** out of town, outside the town; **dîner h. de chez soi** to dine out; **h. d'ici!** get out (of here)!; **h. d'haleine** out of breath; **h. de combat** *(arme, navire, homme)* out of action; *Fig* **ça l'a mis h. de combat** that put him out of the contest *or* game *or* running; **être h. d'affaire** to be out of the woods; *(d'un malade)* to be out of danger, to be out of the woods; **te voilà h. d'affaire!** that's you over the worst; **h. de portée** out of *or* beyond reach; **à garder h. de portée des enfants** keep out of the reach of children; **h. d'atteinte** out of *or* beyond reach; **h. de danger** out of danger, out of harm's way; **h. de question** out of the question; **h. de là** apart from that, otherwise; **être h. de soi** *(de colère etc)* to be beside oneself; **ça l'a mise h. d'elle-même** that infuriated her; **c'est h. de prix** the price is prohibitive, it's too expensive; **des produits h. de prix** prohibitively expensive goods; *Archit* **h. d'œuvre** out of alignment, projecting
2 *Ftbl* **h. jeu** *(joueur)* offside; **le joueur était**

h. jeu the player was offside *or* in an offside position; **skier h. piste** to ski off piste; **longueur h. tout** overall length; **h. taxe** net of tax; *(exempt de taxe)* tax free; **boutique h. taxe** duty-free shop; **mettre qn/qch h. la loi** to outlaw sb/sth
3 *Litt (sauf)* except, save, but; **tous h. un seul** all but one; **h. des gens avec qui je travaille** except (for) *or* apart from the people I work with
▸▸ *TV, Radio* **h. antenne** off-air; *Compta* **h. bilan** off-balance sheet; **h. Bourse** after hours; **h. budget** not included in the budget; *TV, Cin* **h. caméra** off-camera; **h. champ** out of vision, out of shot; **h. comptabilité** off-balance sheet; **h. concours: être (mis) h. concours** to be disqualified; *Fig* **il est h. concours** he's in a class of his own; *Fin* **h. cote** unlisted; **h. d'état** out of order; *Journ* **h. enregistrement** off the record; *Radio* **h. fréquence** out-of-band; *TV, Cin* **h. plan** off-shot; *TV, Radio* **h. programmme** unscripted; **h. saison** off-season; *Journ* **h. série** special edition; **numéro h. série** special issue; *Fig* **un talent h. série** an exceptional talent, a talent (that is) out of the ordinary; **h. studio** remote; *(répétition)* pre-studio rehearsal; **une dissertation h. (du) sujet, un h. sujet** an essay that doesn't deal with the subject; *Ordinat* **h. sujet** *(dans un groupe de discussion)* off-topic; **h. synchronisation** out of sync; **h. TVA** net of VAT

*hors-bord NM INV motor boat *or* speedboat *(with outboard motor)*; **moteur h.** outboard motor

*hors-concours NM INV = person *or* exhibit ineligible for competition (because of superiority)

*hors-cote *Bourse* ADJ INV unlisted
NM INV *(marché)* unlisted securities market

*hors-d'œuvre [ɔrdœvr] NM INV **1** *Culin* hors d'oeuvre, starter **2** *Fig* starter, taster **3** *Archit* annexe, outwork

*horse power [ɔrspawœr] NM INV horsepower

*hors-jeu NM INV *Sport* offside

*hors-la-loi NM INV outlaw

*hors-média ADJ below-the-line

*hors-micro ADJ *Radio* off-mike

*hors-piste NM INV *Ski* off piste; **faire du h.** to ski off piste

*hors-route ADJ INV off-highway

*hors-série *Journ* ADJ special
NM special edition

*hors-texte NM INV *(inset)* plate, tip-in

hortensia [ɔrtãsja] NM *Bot* hydrangea

horticole [ɔrtikɔl] ADJ horticultural; **exposition h.** flower show

horticulteur [ɔrtikyltœr] NM horticulturist

horticulture [ɔrtikyltyr] NF horticulture

*hosanna [ozana] INT hosanna!
NM hosanna

hospice [ɔspis] NM **1** *(maison) (de Saint-Bernard etc)* hospice **2** *(foyer)* (old people's/children's) home; **mourir à l'h.** to die in the poorhouse **3** *(hôpital)* hospice

hospitalier, -ière [ɔspitalje, -jɛr] ADJ **1** *(accueillant)* hospitable; *Litt (rive, ombre)* welcoming **2** *(frais, service, personnel)* hospital; **personnel h.** hospital staff **3** *Rel* **religieux h.** hospitaller; **sœur hospitalière** Sister of Charity
N *Rel* Hospitaller

hospitalisation [ɔspitalizasjõ] NF *(admission, séjour)* hospitalization; **h. à domicile** home care

hospitalisé, -ée [ɔspitalize] N *(à l'hôpital)* (in-)patient

hospitaliser [ɔspitalize] VT to hospitalize;

faire h. qn to hospitalize sb, to send sb to hospital; **il est resté hospitalisé de longs mois** he was in hospital for several months

hospitalité [ɔspitalite] NF hospitality; **offrir l'h. à qn** to offer sb hospitality; **donner l'h. à qn pour la nuit** to put sb up for the night; **avoir le sens de l'h.** to be hospitable

hospitalo-universitaire, pl **hospitalo-universitaires** [ɔspitaloyniversiter] ADJ **centre h.** university or teaching hospital

hostellerie [ɔstɛlri] NF (fashionable) country inn

hostie [ɔsti] NF Rel host

hostile [ɔstil] ADJ hostile; (action) unfriendly; **être h. à qn/qch** to be hostile or opposed to sb/sth; **tenir des propos hostiles à qn** to make hostile or unfriendly remarks to sb

hostilement [ɔstilmɑ̃] ADV hostilely, in a hostile manner

hostilité [ɔstilite] NF **1** hostility (**contre, envers** to(wards)); **acte d'h.** act of war **2** **hostilités** hostilities

hosto [ɔsto] NM Fam hospital; **aller à l'h.** to go to hospital or Am to the hospital

*****hot-dog,** pl **hot-dogs** [ɔtdɔg] NM hot dog

hôte [ot] NM host; Vieilli (dans une taverne etc) landlord; **dîner à la table d'h.** to have the set menu or the table d'hôte
▪ N **1** (invité) guest, visitor; **h. de marque** VIP guest; **h. payant** paying guest **2** Biol (d'un parasite) host **3** Litt (habitant) dweller; **les hôtes des bois** the woodland creatures, the creatures of the woods; **les souris et les araignées sont les hôtes de mon grenier** my attic is inhabited by mice and spiders

hôtel [otɛl] NM **1** hotel; **h. de luxe/miteux** luxury/seedy hotel; **h. deux/trois étoiles** two/three star hotel; **une chambre d'h.** a hotel room; **descendre à l'h.** to stay at or put up at a hotel; **j'habitais un petit h. de banlieue** I was staying in a little hotel on the outskirts of town; **h. meublé** residential hotel (providing lodging but not board); **on n'est pas à l'h. ici!** this isn't a hotel, you know!; **rat d'h.** hotel thief **2** **h. (particulier)** mansion, town house **3** Admin public building
▶▶**h. d'aéroport** airport hotel; **h. balnéaire** seaside hotel; **h. classe touriste** tourist class hotel; **h.-club** leisure hotel; **h. de congrès** hotel with conference facilities; **h. familial** family-run hotel; **h. de gare** railway hotel; **h. homologué** hotel classified by the 'préfecture de région'; **h. des impôts** tax office; **h. médicalisé** spa hotel; **l'H. de la Monnaie** ≃ the Royal Mint; **h. non homologué** simple, basic hotel classified by the 'préfectures'; **h. de passe** (hotel used as a) brothel; **h. quatre étoiles luxe** five-star hotel, luxury hotel; **h. de tourisme** hotel classified by the ministry of Tourism; **h. de vacances** holiday hotel; **h. des ventes** auction rooms or salerooms; **h. de ville** town hall, Am city hall

hôtel-Dieu, pl **hôtels-Dieu** NM hospital

hôtelier, -ière [otəlje, -jɛr] N hotel keeper, hotelier
▪ ADJ **l'industrie hôtelière** the hotel industry or trade

hôtellerie [otɛlri] NF **1** (hôtel) inn **2** (secteur) **l'h.** the hotel trade or industry or business, the hospitality business; **crise de l'h.** crisis in the hotel trade; **h. de plein air** camping and caravanning **3** (dans un couvent) guest quarters

hôtel-restaurant, pl **hôtels-restaurants** NM hotel-restaurant

hôtesse [otɛs] NF **1** hostess; Vieilli (dans une taverne etc) landlady **2** Aviat hostess, stewardess
▶▶**h. d'accueil** (dans une entreprise, une foire etc) receptionist; (à une exposition) hostess; **h. d'accueil téléphonique** switch-

board operator; **h. de l'air** air hostess, cabin or flight attendant

hot line [ɔtlajn] NF hot line

hot rod, pl **hot rods** [ɔtrɔd] NM Aut hot rod

*****hotte** [ɔt] NF **1** (sur le dos) basket; (de maçon) (bricklayer's) hod; **la h. du père Noël** Father Christmas's or Santa's sack; Fam **en avoir plein la h.** to be bushed or Br knackered or Am beat **2** (dans un laboratoire, au-dessus d'une cuisinière, dans une forge) hood; **h. aspirante** extractor hood

*****hottentot, -ote** [ɔtɑ̃to, -ɔt] ADJ Hottentot
▪ N **H.** Hottentot

*****hou** [u] INT boo!; **h.! la vilaine!** tut-tut, you naughty girl!

*****houblon** [ublɔ̃] NM hop

*****houblonnier, -ière** [ublɔnje, -jɛr] ADJ **région houblonnière** hop(-growing) district
▪ NM hop grower
▪ NF **houblonnière** hop field

*****houe** [u] NF hoe

*****houille** [uj] NF coal; **mine de h.** coalmine, colliery; **h. blanche** hydroelectric power; **h. bleue** wave power

*****houiller, -ère** [uje, -ɛr] ADJ carboniferous, coal-bearing; **dépôt** ou **bassin h.** coal bed or basin; **production houillère** coal output
▪ NF **houillère** coalmine, colliery

*****houle** [ul] NF (de la mer) swell, surge; **grosse h.** heavy swell

*****houlette** [ulɛt] NF **1** (de berger) (shepherd's) crook; (crosse) (bishop's) crosier; Fig **sous la h. de notre guide** under the leadership of our guide **2** (petite bêche) trowel, spud

*****houleux, -euse** [ulø, -øz] ADJ (mer) swelling, surging; Fig (assemblée) surging, tumultuous; **réunion houleuse** stormy meeting

houmous [umus] NM houmous, hummus

*****houp** [up] INT = hop

*****houppe** [up] NF (de poils etc) tuft; (de plumes) crest, tuft; **h. à poudrer** powder puff

*****houppelande** [uplɑ̃d] NF cloak

*****houppette** [upɛt] NF (de plumes etc) small tuft; (à poudre) powder puff

*****hourdage** [urdaʒ] NM Constr roughcasting

*****hourder** [urde] VT Constr to roughcast

*****houri** [uri] NF Rel houri

*****hourra** [ura] INT hurrah!; **hip, hip, hip, h.!** hip, hip, hooray!
▪ NM hurrah; **pousser trois hourras** to give three cheers

*****hourvari** [urvari] NM Litt uproar, tumult

*****house** [auz] NF Mus **la h. (music)** house music

*****houspiller** [uspije] VT **h. qn** (le réprimander) to reprimand sb, Fam to tell sb off

*****housse** [us] NF **1** (de meubles) cover; (contre la poussière) dust sheet; (dans une voiture) seat cover; **h. à vêtements** suit carrier; **h. de couette** duvet cover **2** (pour cheval) trappings

*****houx** [u] NM holly

*****hovercraft** [ɔvɛrkraft] NM hovercraft

HP [aʃpe] NM Fam (abrév **hôpital psychiatrique**) psychiatric hospital

HS [aʃɛs] ADJ Fam (abrév **hors service**) **1** (objet) bust, Br knackered **2** (personne) bushed, Br knackered

HT 1 (abrév **haute tension**) ht **2** (abrév **hors taxe**) before tax, exclusive of tax; **le montant HT de la facture** the net amount of the invoice, the invoice net of tax

HTML [aʃteɛmɛl] NM (abrév **HyperText Markup Language**) HTML

H. TVA (abrév **hors TVA**) net of VAT

*****huard, huart** [ɥar] NM **1** osprey, Am fish hawk **2** Can black-throated diver

*****hub** [œb] NM Ordinat hub

*****hublot** [yblo] NM porthole; (dans un avion, une machine à laver) window; Aut scuttle; Fig Fam **des hublots** (lunettes) thick or Fam milk-bottle glasses; **h. de contrôle** sight glass

*****huche** [yʃ] NF (pétrin) kneading trough; (coffre) bin; **h. à pain** bread bin

*****hue** [y, hy] INT (à un cheval) gee up!; **tirer à h. et à dia** to pull in opposite or different directions; **l'un tire à h. et l'autre à dia** they're pulling in opposite or different directions

*****huée** [ɥe] NF (usu pl) **huées** booing, jeering; **quitter la scène sous les huées** to be booed off the stage

*****huer** [ɥe] VT (acteur etc) to boo; (orateur etc) to barrack
▪ VI (d'un hibou) to hoot

*****huerta** [wɛrta] NF = irrigated plain in Spain

*****huguenot, -ote** [yg(ə)no, -ɔt] Hist ADJ Huguenot
▪ N **H.** Huguenot

huilage [ɥilaʒ] NM oiling, lubrication

huile [ɥil] NF oil; **frit à l'h.** fried in oil; **tache d'h.** oil stain; Fig **faire tache d'h.** to spread; **évidemment, ça a fait tache d'h. et tout le monde l'a su** obviously it spread like wildfire and everyone knew about it; Fig **jeter** ou **verser de l'h. sur le feu** to add fuel to the fire; Fig **mettre de l'h. dans les rouages** to oil the wheels; **une mer d'h.** a glassy sea; Arg **les huiles** the big shots, the top brass; Beaux-Arts **peinture à l'h.** oil painting; **faire de la peinture à l'h.** to paint in oils; **des tubes de peinture à l'h.** tubes of oil paint; **portrait à l'h.** portrait in oils; **une de ses huiles** one of his oil paintings
▶▶**h. de bras** elbow grease; Can **h. de chauffage** heating oil; Aut **h. de damper** damper oil, hydraulic fluid; **h. détergente** detergent oil; **h. essentielle** essential oil; **h. de foie de morue** cod liver oil; **h. de graissage** lubricating or lubrication oil; **h. de lin** linseed oil; **h. lourde** heavy-duty oil; **h. de lubrification** lubricating or lubrication oil; **h. de machine** machine oil; **h. minérale** mineral oil; **h. moteur** engine oil; **h. multigrade** multi-grade or cross-grade oil; **h. d'olive** olive oil; **h. de paraffine** paraffin oil; **h. réfrigérante** refrigerant oil; **h. de ricin** castor oil; **h. solaire** suntan oil; **h. synthétique** synthetic oil; **h. de table** salad oil; **h. de tournesol** sunflower (seed) oil; **h. végétale** vegetable oil

huiler [ɥile] VT to oil, to lubricate; Fam **un spectacle très bien huilé** a very well put-together show

huilerie [ɥilri] NF Ind oil works; Com oil trade; **il s'est enrichi dans l'h.** he made his money in the oil business

huileux, -euse [ɥilø, -øz] ADJ oily, greasy

huilier [ɥilje] NM **1** (de table) oil and vinegar cruet **2** Ind oil manufacturer

huis [ɥi] NM Arch door; **entretien à h. clos** conversation behind closed doors; Jur **entendre une cause à h. clos** to hear a case in camera; **ordonner le h. clos** to order a case to be heard in camera

huisserie [ɥisri] NF Constr (d'une porte, d'une fenêtre) frame

huissier [ɥisje] NM **1** Jur process server, ≃ sheriff's officer, bailiff; **h. audiencier** court usher **2** (portier) usher

*****huit** [ɥit] ADJ INV **1** (as cardinal adj before a noun or adj beginning with a consonant sound [ɥi]) eight; **h. (petits) garçons** [ɥi(pti)garsɔ̃] eight (little) boys; **h. hommes** [ɥitɔm] eight men; **j'en ai h.** [ɥit] I have eight (of them); **h. jours** a week; **aujourd'hui/demain en h.** a week today/tomorrow, Fml today/tomorrow week; **donner ses h. jours à qn** to give sb a week's notice; Ordinat **à h. élé-**

ments binaires eight-bit **2** *(dans des séries)* eighth; **page/numéro h.** page/number eight; **Henri H.** Henry the Eighth
  NM INV eight; **le h. mai** [ɥime] (on) the eighth of May, (on) May the eighth, *Am* (on) May eight; *Cartes* **le h. de carreau** the eight of diamonds; **j'habite au h.** I live at number eight; *(figure de patinage)* figure of eight; **la route fait un h. dans les collines** the road snakes round the hills; **l'ivrogne avançait en faisant des h.** the drunk was reeling *or* staggering along; **le grand h.** rollercoaster

*****huitain** [ɥitɛ̃] **NM** *Littér* octet

*****huitaine** [ɥiten] **NF 1** (about) eight **2** *(une semaine)* week; **il faut compter une bonne h. (de jours) pour que le paquet arrive** you must allow a good week for the parcel to get there; **dans une h. de jours** in a week or so; **affaire remise à h.** case adjourned for a week

*****huitante** [ɥitɑ̃t] **ADJ NUM INV** *Suisse* eighty

*****huitantième** [ɥitɑ̃tjɛm] **ADJ NUM, N** *Suisse* eightieth

*****huitième** [ɥitjɛm] **ADJ, N** eighth
  NM *(fraction)* eighth; *Sport* **être en h. de finale** to be through to the last sixteen
  NF *Scol Anciennement* **(classe de) h.** ≃ third form of junior school, *Am* ≃ eighth grade

*****huitièmement** [ɥitjɛmmɑ̃] **ADV** eighthly, in eighth place

huître [ɥitr] **NF 1** oyster; **h. perlière** pearl oyster **2** *Fam (idiot)* fool, mug

*****huit-reflets** [ɥir(ə)flɛ] **NM INV** top hat

huîtrier, -ère [ɥitrije, -ɛr] **ADJ industrie huîtrière** oyster farming
  NM *Orn* oyster catcher
  NF huîtrière oyster bed

*****hulotte** [ylɔt] **NF** tawny owl

*****hululement** [ylylmɑ̃] **NM** hoot; **le h. d'un hibou** the hoot *or* hooting of an owl; **des hululements** hooting

*****hululer** [ylyle] **VI** *(du hibou)* to hoot

*****hum** [œm] **INT** hem!, h'm!

humain [ymɛ̃] **ADJ 1** human; **il est h. après tout** he's only human; **c'est h.** it's only human; **le genre h.** mankind; **tu ne vas pas t'en prendre au genre h.** you can't put the blame on the whole human race; **les êtres humains** human beings, humans; **c'est un être h.,** après tout he's a human being, after all; **des pertes humaines énormes** a huge loss of life; **à l'échelle humaine** on a human scale; **sciences humaines** social sciences; *Mus* **voix humaine** *(d'un orgue)* vox humana; **ressources humaines** human resources; **l'erreur est humaine** to err is human **2** *(compréhensif)* humane; **elle a toujours été très humaine avec moi** she has always treated me very considerately
  NM human (being)

  Attention: ne pas confondre **human** et **humane** lorsque l'on traduit **humain**. **Human** signifie qui se rapporte à l'être humain alors que **humane** signifie **bienveillant**.

humainement [ymɛnmɑ̃] **ADV 1** *(relatif à l'homme)* humanly; **si c'est h. possible** if humanly possible **2** *(avec bonté)* humanely

humanisation [ymanizasjɔ̃] **NF** humanization, humanizing

humaniser [ymanize] **VT 1** to humanize, to make human **2** *(rendre plus charitable)* **h. qn** to make sb more human *or* humane
  VPR s'humaniser 1 to become more human **2** *(devenir plus charitable)* to become more human *or* humane

humanisme [ymanism] **NM** *Litt, Phil* humanism

humaniste [ymanist] **N** humanist
  ADJ humanist(ic)

humanitaire [ymanitɛr] **ADJ** humanitarian; **organisation/aide h.** humanitarian organization/aid
  N *(personne)* humanitarian (aid) worker

humanitarisme [ymanitarism] **NM** humanitarianism

humanité [ymanite] **NF 1** *(genre humain)* humanity, mankind; **tu rendrais service à l'h.** you'd be doing mankind *or* humanity a favour **2** *Rel (du Christ)* human nature **3** *(bonté)* humanity, humaneness; **traiter qn avec h.** to treat sb humanely **4 humanités** humanities, classics; **faire ses humanités** to study the classics

humanoïde [ymanoid] **NM** humanoid

humble [œ̃bl] **ADJ** humble, lowly; **à mon h. avis** in my humble opinion

humblement [œ̃bləmɑ̃] **ADV** humbly

humectage [ymɛktaʒ] **NM** dampening, moistening

humecter [ymɛkte] **VT** to dampen, to moisten
  VPR s'humecter s'h. les lèvres to moisten one's lips; *Fam* **s'h. le gosier** to wet one's whistle

*****humer** [yme] **VT 1** *(aspirer)* to inhale; *(sentir)* to sniff; **h. l'air frais** to inhale *or* breathe in the fresh air; **h. le parfum d'une fleur** to smell a flower **2** *(liquide)* to suck in *or* up

huméral, -ale, -aux, -ales [ymeral, -o] **ADJ** *Anat* humeral

humérus [ymerys] **NM** *Anat* humerus

humeur [ymœr] **NF 1** *(disposition)* mood, spirits, humour, *Am* humor; **être de bonne h.** to be in a good mood *or* in good spirits; **un livre/film plein de bonne h.** a good-humoured book/film; **être de mauvaise h.** to be in a bad mood; **une personne de mauvaise h.** an ill-humoured person; **passer sa mauvaise h. sur qn/qch** to take one's bad mood out on sb/sth; **de méchante h.** in a (bad) temper; **être d'une h. massacrante** *ou Fam* **de chien** to be in a foul *or* filthy mood *or* temper; **être d'une h. noire** *(déprimé)* to be depressed; *(mécontent)* to be in a (bad) temper; **il est rentré d'h. noire** he came home in a bad temper; **être** *ou* **se sentir d'h. à refuser** to be in the mood to refuse
  2 *(caractère)* temper, temperament; **avoir l'h. vive** to be quick-tempered; **il y a incompatibilité d'h. entre nous** we are temperamentally unsuited; **homme d'h. égale** even-tempered man
  3 *Litt (mauvaise humeur)* ill humour *or Am* humor, bad mood; **mouvement d'h.** outburst of temper; **geste d'h.** ill-tempered gesture; **montrer de l'h.** to show (ill) temper; **avec h.** testily, irritably; **je redoute ses sautes d'h.** I dread his changes of mood; **épancher son h. sur qn** to vent one's spleen on sb
  4 *Méd Arch* humour, *Am* humor
  ▸▸ *Anat* **h. aqueuse** aqueous humour; **h. vitrée** vitreous humour

  Do not confuse with **humour**.

humide [ymid] **ADJ** *(maison, linge)* damp; *(climat)* damp, humid; **il fait h.** it *or* the weather is damp *or* humid; **couloir sombre et h.** dark, dank passage; **temps h. et chaud** muggy *or* close weather; **temps h. et froid** raw weather; **les yeux humides (de larmes)** eyes moist with tears; **elle me lançait des regards humides** she looked at me with moist eyes

humidificateur [ymidifikatœr] **NM** *(à usage domestique)* humidifier; *(pour les cigares)* humidor

humidification [ymidifikasjɔ̃] **NF** *(fait de rendre humide)* dampening, moistening; *(contre le dessèchement)* humidification; **pour l'h. des cigares** to prevent cigars drying out

humidifier [ymidifje] **VT** to dampen, moisten; *(contre le dessèchement)* to humidify

humidité [ymidite] **NF** *(d'une maison, du linge)* dampness; *(du climat)* humidity, dampness; **il faut beaucoup d'h. à cette plante** this plant needs a lot of moisture; **h. absolue/relative** absolute/relative humidity; **craint l'h.** *(sur un paquet)* keep dry, store in a dry place; **taches d'h.** damp patches, mildew; **teneur en h.** moisture content; **il y a de l'h. dans l'air** it's going to *or* it feels like rain; *(au bord de la mer)* there is moisture *or* dampness in the air

humiliant [ymiljɑ̃] **ADJ** humiliating, mortifying; **il lui fit des reproches humiliants** he upbraided him/her in a humiliating fashion

humiliation [ymiljasjɔ̃] **NF** humiliation, mortification; **elle en fut malade d'h.** she was totally mortified

humilier [ymilje] **VT** *(abaisser)* to humiliate; *Vieilli, Rel (rendre humble)* to humble
  VPR s'humilier *(s'abaisser)* to humiliate oneself; *(devenir humble)* to humble oneself; **je ne veux pas m'h. devant eux** I'm not going to go grovelling to them; **s'h. jusqu'à faire qch** to stoop to doing sth

humilité [ymilite] **NF** humility, humbleness; **ton d'h.** humble tone, tone of humility; **ce fut une grande leçon d'h.** it was a lesson in humility

humoral, -ale, -aux, -ales [ymɔral, -o] **ADJ** *Méd* humoral

humoriste [ymɔrist] **ADJ** *(écrivain etc)* humorous
  N humorist

humoristique [ymɔristik] **ADJ** *(orateur, écrivain etc)* humorous; **dessin h.** cartoon

humour [ymur] **NM** humour, *Am* humor; **faire preuve d'h.** to keep smiling, to keep one's sense of humour, *Fam* to grin and bear it; **avoir (le sens) de l'h.** to have a (good) sense of humour; **h. noir** sick humour, black humour; **h. anglais** English humour

  Do not confuse with **humeur**.

humus [ymys] **NM** humus

*****Hun** [œ̃] **NM** *Hist* Hun

*****hune** [yn] **NF** *Naut* top; **h. de vigie** crow's nest

*****hunier** [ynje] **NM** *Naut* topsail

*****huppe** [yp] **NF 1** *Orn* hoopoe **2** *(d'un oiseau)* tuft, crest

*****huppé** [ype] **ADJ 1** *(oiseau)* tufted, crested **2** *Fam* high-class, *Br Fam* posh; **les classes huppées** the upper classes, *Br Fam* the toffs; **des gens huppés** the upper crust, *Br Fam* toffs, posh folk; **ce quartier est des plus huppés** this is a very high-class *or Br Fam* posh area

*****hure** [yr] **NF 1** *(de sanglier etc)* head **2** *Culin* brawn, *Am* headcheese

*****hurlement** [yrləmɑ̃] **NM** *(d'un loup, d'un chien)* howl; *(d'une personne)* yell, scream; *(du vent)* howling; *(d'une sirène d'alarme)* shriek, wail; **hurlements** *(d'un loup etc)* howling; *(d'une personne)* yelling, screaming; **pousser un h.** to give a howl; **pousser des hurlements** to howl

*****hurler** [yrle] **VI** *(d'un loup, d'un chien)* to howl; *(du vent, de la tempête)* to howl, to roar; *(d'une alarme)* to howl, to wail; *(d'une personne)* to howl, to roar, to yell; **elle faisait h. sa radio dans la cuisine** she had her radio blaring in the kitchen; **h. de douleur** to howl *or* scream (out) with pain; **c'était à h. de rire** it was screamingly funny, it was a scream; **à la lune** to bay at the moon; **h. avec les loups** to follow the crowd; **couleurs qui hurlent** colours that clash (with one another)
  VT *(chanson, discours etc)* to roar out, to

The symbol * indicates that the initial **h** is aspirate and that hence there is no liaison, eg **les haricots** [leariko] and not [lezariko], or contraction in spelling, eg **la haine** and not **l'haine**.

bawl out; **elle me hurlait une recette par téléphone** she bawled a recipe down the telephone at me

***hurleur, -euse** [yrlœr, -øz] ADJ howling, yelling
N howler, yeller
NM *(singe)* howler (monkey)

hurluberlu [yrlyberly] NM eccentric (person); **cet h. de Michel** that oddball Michel; **quel h., celui-là!** he's really odd *or* strange

***huron, -onne** [yrɔ̃, ɔn] ADJ Huron; **le lac H.** Lake Huron
N H. Huron

husky [œski] NM husky

***hussard** [ysar] NM *Mil* hussar

***hussarde** [ysard] NF **à la h.** roughly, in a cavalier fashion, cavalierly; **partir à la h.** to leave unceremoniously

***hussite** [ysit] NM *Hist, Rel* Hussite

***hutte** [yt] NF hut

hyacinthe [jasɛ̃t] NF **1** *Arch (fleur)* hyacinth **2** *(pierre)* hyacinth, jacinth

hyalin [jalɛ̃] ADJ transparent, glassy; *Minér* **quartz h.** rock crystal

hybridation [ibridasjɔ̃] NF *Bot* hybridization; *Biol* cross-breeding

hybride [ibrid] ADJ hybrid; *(style de musique)* crossover
NM hybrid

hybrider [ibride] VT *Bot* to hybridize; *Biol* to cross(-breed)

hybridité [ibridite] NF hybridity, hybridism

hydracide [idrasid] NM *Chimie* hydracid

hydrante [idrɑ̃t] NF *Suisse* fire hydrant, *Am* fireplug

hydratant [idratɑ̃] ADJ *(crème)* moisturizing
NM moisturizer

hydratation [idratasjɔ̃] NF **1** *Chimie* hydration **2** *(de la peau)* moisturizing

hydrate [idrat] NM *Chimie* hydrate; **h. de potasse** caustic potash; **h. de carbone** carbohydrate

hydrater [idrate] VT **1** *Chimie* to hydrate **2** *(peau)* to moisturize
VPR **s'hydrater** to hydrate, to become hydrated *or* moisturized

hydraulicien [idrolisjɛ̃] NM hydraulic engineer

hydraulique [idrolik] ADJ hydraulic; **roue h.** waterwheel
NF **1** *(science)* hydraulics **2** *(technique)* hydraulic engineering

hydravion [idravjɔ̃] NM seaplane

hydre [idr] NF **1** *Zool* hydra; *Fig* **l'h. du chômage** the hydra of unemployment **2** *Myth* **H.** Hydra

hydrique [idrik] ADJ hydrous

hydrocarbure [idrokarbyr] NM *Chimie* hydrocarbon

hydrocéphale [idrosefal] *Méd* ADJ hydrocephalic, hydrocephalous
N hydrocephalic *or* hydrocephalous patient

hydrocortisone [idrokortizɔn] NF hydrocortisone

hydrocracking, hydrocraquage [idrokrakiŋ, -kaʒ] NM *Pétr* hydrocracking

hydrocution [idrokysjɔ̃] NF immersion syncope

hydrodynamique [idrodinamik] ADJ hydrodynamic
NF hydrodynamics

hydro-électricité [idroelɛktrisite] NF hydroelectricity

hydro-électrique, *pl* **hydro-électriques** [idroelɛktrik] ADJ hydroelectric

hydrofoil [idrofɔil] NM hydrofoil

hydrofuge [idrofyʒ] ADJ *(vêtement, tissu)* waterproof

hydrofuger [idrofyʒe] VT *(j'hydrofugeai(s); n. hydrofugeons) (vêtement, tissu)* to waterproof

hydrogénation [idroʒenasjɔ̃] NF hydrogenation

hydrogène [idroʒɛn] NM *Chimie* hydrogen; **h. lourd** heavy hydrogen

hydrogéné [idroʒene] ADJ hydrogenated

hydrogéner [idroʒene] VT to hydrogenate

hydroglisseur [idroglisœr] NM jetfoil

hydrographe [idrograf] ADJ, NM **(ingénieur) h.** hydrographer

hydrographie [idrografi] NF hydrography

hydrographique [idrografik] ADJ hydrographic(al)

hydrologie [idroloʒi] NF hydrology

hydrologique [idroloʒik] ADJ hydrological

hydrologiste [idroloʒist], **hydrologue** [idrolog] N hydrologist

hydrolyse [idroliz] NF *Chimie* hydrolysis

hydrolyser [idrolize] VT *Chimie* to hydrolize, to hydrolyse

hydromel [idromɛl] NM mead

hydromètre [idromɛtr] NM hydrometer; *(d'océan)* depth gauge
NF *Entom* water spider

hydrométrie [idrometri] NF *Phys* hydrometry

hydrométrique [idrometrik] ADJ hydrometric

hydrominéralisme [idromineralism] NM water cures

hydrophile [idrofil] ADJ *(coton etc)* absorbent

hydrophobe [idrofɔb] ADJ hydrophobic
N *Méd* hydrophobic patient

hydrophobie [idrofɔbi] NF *Méd* hydrophobia

hydropique [idropik] *Méd* ADJ dropsical
N dropsical patient

hydropisie [idropizi] NF *Méd* dropsy

hydroponique [idroponik] ADJ hydroponic

hydroptère [idroptɛr] NM hydrofoil

hydroquinone [idrokinɔn] NF *Chimie, Phot* hydroquinone

hydrosol [idrosɔl] NM *Chimie* hydrosol

hydrosoluble [idrosɔlybl] ADJ water-soluble

hydrospeed [idrospid] NM *Sport* = type of water sport consisting of shooting the rapids on a board

hydrosphère [idrosfɛr] NF hydrosphere

hydrostatique [idrostatik] ADJ hydrostatic
NF hydrostatics

hydrothérapie [idroterapi] NF *Méd (traitement)* hydrotherapy, water cure; *(science)* hydrotherapeutics

hydrothérapique [idroterapik] ADJ hydrotherapeutic

hydrothermal, -ale, -aux, -ales [idrotɛrmal, -o] ADJ hydrothermal

hydrothermalisme [idrotɛrmalism] NM *Méd* water therapy

hydroxyde [idroksid] NM *Chimie* hydroxide

hydrure [idryr] NM *Chimie* hydride

hyène [jɛn] NF *(when aspirated* **la hyène,** *when silent* **l'hyène)** hyena

hygiaphone [iʒjafɔn] NM *(au guichet)* grill; **parlez dans l'h.** speak through the grill

hygiène [iʒjɛn] NF hygiene; **h. publique/mentale** public/mental health; **produits d'h. courante** cleaning *or* cleansing products; **prendre des mesures d'h.** to take steps to deal with a hygiene problem; **mauvaise h.**

alimentaire bad eating habits, poor diet; **vous devriez surveiller votre h. alimentaire** you should watch your diet *or* what you eat

hygiénique [iʒjenik] ADJ **1** *(sanitaire)* hygienic, sanitary; **peu h.** unhygienic; **papier h.** toilet paper; **serviette h.** sanitary towel *or Am* napkin **2** *(bon pour la santé)* healthy; **une promenade h.** a healthy walk, a constitutional

hygiéniquement [iʒjenikmɑ̃] ADV **1** hygienically **2** *(bon pour la santé)* healthily

hygrométrie [igrometri] NF *Phys* hygrometry

hygroscope [igroskɔp] NM *Phys* hygroscope

hygroscopique [igroskɔpik] ADJ *Phys* hygroscopic

hymen [imɛn] NM **1** *Litt* marriage **2** *Anat* hymen

hyménée [imene] NM *Litt* marriage

hyménoptère [imenɔptɛr] *Entom* ADJ hymenopterous
NMPL **hyménoptères** Hymenoptera

hymne [imn] NM *(de louanges)* song (of praise); **un h. à la beauté** a hymn to beauty; **l'h. à la joie** the Ode to Joy; **h. national** national anthem
NM OU NF *Rel* hymn

hyoïde [jɔid] ADJ, NM *Anat* **(os) h.** hyoid (bone)

hyper [ipɛr] NM *Fam (abrév* **hypermarché)** hypermarket, superstore

hyper- [ipɛr] PRÉF **1** *(terme scientifique)* hyper- **2** *(en intensif)* **techniques h.-spécialisées** highly specialized techniques; *Fam* mega-; **h.-cool** hyper- *or* mega-cool; **h.-chiant** mega-boring

hyperacidité [iperasidite] NF *Méd* hyperacidity

hyperactif, -ive [iperaktif, -iv] ADJ hyperactive

hyperactivité [iperaktivite] NF hyperactivity

hyperbare [iperbar] ADJ *Tech* hyperbaric; **caisson h.** decompression chamber

hyperbole [iperbɔl] NF **1** *Littér* hyperbole **2** *Math* hyperbola

hyperbolique [iperbɔlik] ADJ *Littér, Math* hyperbolic(al)

hyperboliquement [iperbɔlikmɑ̃] ADV *Littér* hyperbolically

hyperboloïde [iperbɔlɔid] *Math* ADJ hyperboloidal
NM hyperboloid

hyperboréen, -enne [iperbɔreɛ̃, -ɛn] ADJ *Litt* hyperborean

hypercalorique [iperkalɔrik] ADJ hypercalorific

hypercritique [iperkritik] ADJ hypercritical, overcritical

hyperémotivité [iperemɔtivite] NF *Méd* hyperemotionalism, hyperemotivity

hyperfréquence [iperfrekɑ̃s] NF *Radio* ultra high frequency

hyperglycémie [iperglisemi] NF *Méd* hyperglyc(a)emia

hyperinflation [iperɛ̃flasjɔ̃] NF *Écon* hyperinflation

hyperlien [iperljɛ̃] NM *Ordinat* hyperlink

hypermarché [ipermarʃe] NM hypermarket, superstore

hypermédia NM *Ordinat* hypermedia

hypermétrope [ipermetrɔp] ADJ *Méd* hypermetropic

hypermétropie [ipermetrɔpi] NF *Méd* hypermetropia

hypernerveux, -euse [ipernɛrvø, -øz] ADJ highly strung
N highly strung person

hyperonyme [iperɔnim] **NM** hyperonym, superordinate

hyperpack [iperpak] **NM** multipack

hyperréalisme [iperrealism] **NM** *Beaux-Arts* hyperrealism

hyperréaliste [iperrealist] **ADJ** *Beaux-Arts* hyperrealistic

hypersensibilité [ipersãsibilite] **NF** hypersensitivity

hypersensible [ipersãsibl] **ADJ** hypersensitive

hypertendu, -ue [ipertãdy] *Méd* **ADJ** hypertensive, suffering from high blood pressure
N hypertensive patient, person suffering from high blood pressure

hypertensif, -ive [ipertãsif, -iv] **ADJ, N** *Méd* hypertensive

hypertension [ipertãsjɔ̃] **NF** *Méd* hypertension, high blood pressure

hypertexte [ipertɛkst] **NM** *Ordinat* hypertext

hyperthyroïdie [ipertirɔidi] **NF** *Méd* hyperthyroidism

hypertoile [ipertwal] **NF** *Ordinat* WorldWide Web

hypertrophie [ipertrɔfi] **NF** *Méd* hypertrophy; **h. des amygdales** enlarged tonsils; *Fig* **l'h. urbaine** urban sprawl; **elle souffre d'h. du moi** she's got a swollen ego

hypertrophié [ipertrɔfje] **ADJ** enlarged, *Spéc* hypertrophied

hypertrophier [ipertrɔfje] *Méd* **VT** to hypertrophy; **amygdales hypertrophiées** enlarged tonsils
VPR s'hypertrophier to hypertrophy, to become too large; *Fig (de sentiments)* to become strong, to grow

hypertrophique [ipertrɔfik] **ADJ** *Méd* hypertrophic

hyperventilation [ipervãtilasjɔ̃] **NF** *Méd* hyperventilation

hypervitaminose [ipervitaminoz] **NF** *Méd* hypervitaminosis

hypnose [ipnoz] **NF** hypnosis, (hypnotic) trance; **être en état d'h.** to be under hypnosis, to be in a hypnotic trance

hypnotique [ipnɔtik] **ADJ, N** hypnotic

hypnotiser [ipnɔtize] **VT** to hypnotize

hypnotiseur [ipnɔtizœr] **NM** hypnotist

hypnotisme [ipnɔtism] **NM** hypnotism

hypoallergénique [ipoalɛrʒenik] **ADJ** hypoallergenic

hypocalcémie [ipɔkalsemi] **NF** *Méd* hypocalcaemia

hypocalorique [ipɔkalɔrik] **ADJ** **régime h.** low-calorie diet

hypocentre [ipɔsãtr] **NM** *Géol* focus, hypocentre

hypocondre [ipɔkɔ̃dr] **NM** *Anat* hypochondrium
N hypochondriac

hypocondriaque [ipɔkɔ̃drijak] **ADJ, N** hypochondriac

hypocondrie [ipɔkɔ̃dri] **NF** hypochondria; **être atteint d'h.** to have hypochondria, to be (a) hypochondriac

hypocras [ipɔkras] **NM** *Arch* hippocras

hypocrisie [ipɔkrizi] **NF** hypocrisy

hypocrite [ipɔkrit] **ADJ** hypocritical
N hypocrite; **faire l'h.** to be a hypocrite

hypocritement [ipɔkritmã] **ADV** hypocritically

hypodermique [ipɔdermik] **ADJ** hypodermic

hypogastrique [ipɔgastrik] **ADJ** *Anat* hypogastric; *Méd* **ceinture h.** abdominal belt

hypogée [ipɔʒe] **NM** *Archéol* underground (burial) vault, *Spéc* hypogeum

hypoglycémiant [ipoglisemjã] **ADJ** *Pharm* hypoglycemic

hypoglycémie [ipɔglisemi] **NF** *Méd* hypoglycemia; **être en h.** to be hypoglycemic, to have low blood sugar

hypoïde [ipɔid] **ADJ** *(engrenage)* hypoid

hypokhâgne [ipɔkaɲ] **NF** = first-year arts class preparing for the entrance examination for the École normale supérieure

hypolipidémiant [ipolipidemjã] *Pharm* **ADJ** lipid-lowering
NM lipid-lowering drug

hyponyme [ipɔnim] **NM** hyponym

hypophosphite [ipɔfɔsfit] **NM** *Chimie* hypophosphite

hypophyse [ipɔfiz] **NF** *Anat* pituitary gland, *Spéc* hypophysis

hypostase [ipɔstaz] **NF** hypostasis

hypostatique [ipɔstatik] **ADJ** *Phil, Rel* hypostatic

hypostyle [ipɔstil] **ADJ** *Archit* hypostyle, pillared

hypotendu, -ue [ipɔtãdy] *Méd* **ADJ** hypotensive, suffering from low blood pressure
N hypotensive patient, person suffering from low blood pressure

hypotenseur [ipɔtãsœr] **NM** *Méd* hypotensive

hypotension [ipɔtãsjɔ̃] **NF** *Méd* low blood pressure, *Spéc* hypotension

hypoténuse [ipɔtenyz] **NF** hypotenuse

hypothalamus [ipɔtalamys] **NM** hypothalamus

hypothécable [ipɔtekabl] **ADJ** mortgageable

hypothécaire [ipɔtekɛr] **ADJ** **prêt h.** mortgage (loan); **contrat h.** mortgage deed;

créancier h. mortgagee; **débiteur h.** mortgager

hypothécairement [ipɔtekɛrmã] **ADV** *Jur* by *or* on mortgage

hypothèque [ipɔtek] **NF** mortgage; **franc** *ou* **libre d'hypothèques** unmortgaged; **prendre une h.** to take out a mortgage; **prêt sur h.** mortgage (loan); **emprunter sur h.** to borrow on mortgage; **h. de premier rang** first legal mortgage; **h. générale** blanket mortgage; **purger une h.** to pay off *or* clear *or* redeem a mortgage; **propriété grevée d'hypothèques** encumbered estate; *Fig* **ces difficultés font peser une lourde h. sur son avenir** these difficulties are posing a great threat to his/her future

hypothéquer [ipɔteke] **VT** (**j'hypothèque; j'hypothéquerai**) **1** *(propriété etc)* to mortgage; *Fig* **h. son avenir** to sign away one's future **2 h. une dette** to secure a debt by mortgage

hypothermie [ipɔtermi] **NF** *Méd* hypothermia

hypothèse [ipɔtez] **NF** hypothesis; **émettre une h.** to venture a hypothesis; **nous pouvons faire l'h. que ...** we can assume or make the assumption that ...; **en être réduit aux hypothèses** to be reduced to making hypotheses *or* to hypothesizing; **selon cette h.** on this assumption; *Écon* **h. du cycle de vie** life-cycle hypothesis VOIR GRAMMAIRE A14

hypothétique [ipɔtetik] **ADJ** hypothetical

hypothétiquement [ipɔtetikmã] **ADV** hypothetically

hypothyroïdie [ipɔtirɔidi] **NF** *Méd* thyroid deficiency, *Spéc* hypothyroidism

hypotrophie [ipɔtrɔfi] **NF** underdevelopment, hypotrophy

hypovitaminose [ipovitaminoz] **NF** *Méd* vitamin deficiency, *Spéc* hypovitaminosis

hypsomètre [ipsɔmetr] **NM** hypsometer

hypsométrie [ipsɔmetri] **NF** hypsometry

hypsométrique [ipsɔmetrik] **ADJ** hypsometric(al); **courbe h.** contour line; **carte h.** contour map

hysope [izɔp] **NF** *Bot* hyssop

hystérectomie [isterɛktɔmi] **NF** *Chir* hysterectomy

hystérésis [isterezis] **NF** *Phys* hysteresis

hystérie [isteri] **NF** *Méd* hysteria; **je ne veux pas de crise d'h.** I don't want any hysterics; *Fam* **c'est de l'h.** it's sheer hysterics
▸▸ **h. collective** mass hysteria

hystérique [isterik] *Méd* **ADJ** hysterical
N hysterical person, hysteric

hystérotomie [isterɔtɔmi] **NF** *Chir* hysterotomy; **h. abdominale** caesarean *or Am* cesarean section

---

The symbol * indicates that the initial **h** is aspirate and that hence there is no liaison, eg **les haricots** [leariko] and not [lezariko], or contraction in spelling, eg **la haine** and not **l'haine**.

I, i NM (lettre) I, i

IA [ia] NF Ordinat (abrév **intelligence artificielle**) AI

iambe [jãb] NM Littér **1** (pied) iamb, iambus **2** (vers) iambic **3 iambes** (poème satirique) iambics

iambique [jãbik] ADJ (vers, strophe) iambic

IAO [iao] NF Ordinat **1** (abrév **instruction assistée par ordinateur**) CAI **2** (abrév **ingénierie assistée par ordinateur**) CAE

IATA [jata] NF (abrév **Association internationale des transporteurs aériens**) IATA

ibère [iber] ADJ Iberian
N I. Iberian

ibérique [iberik] ADJ Iberian; **la péninsule i.** the Iberian peninsula

ibid [ibid], **ibidem** [ibidɛm] ADV ibid, ibidem

ibis [ibis] NM (oiseau) ibis

Icare [ikar] N Icarus

iceberg [ajsberg, isberg] NM iceberg; **la partie visible de l'i.** the part of the iceberg above water; Fig the tip of the iceberg; **la partie cachée de l'i.** the part of the iceberg under water; Fig **quand tu réaliseras ce qu'est la partie cachée de l'i.** when you realize the true scale of the task/problem

icelui [isəlɥi], **icelle** [isɛl], **iceux** [isø], **icelles** [isɛl] PRON, ADJ DÉM Arch, Jur, Hum voir **celui, celle, ceux, celles**

ichtyocolle [iktjɔkɔl] NF fish glue, isinglass

ichtyologie [iktjɔlɔʒi] NF ichthyology

ichtyologique [iktjɔlɔʒik] ADJ ichthyologic(al)

ichtyologiste [iktjɔlɔʒist] N ichthyologist

ichtyophage [iktjɔfaʒ] ADJ fish-eating, ichthyophagous
N ichthyophagist

ICI [isi] ADV **1** (dans l'espace) here; **i. et là** here and there; **i. même** on this very spot, in this very place; **les gens d'i.** the people (who live) here, the locals; **je ne suis pas d'i.** I'm not from (round) here; **d'i., on a un très beau point de vue** there is a very good view from here; **M. Leblanc, i.** this is Mr Leblanc, who is here; Fam **je vois ça d'i.!** I can just see it!, I can see it coming!; Fam **tu vois d'i. les problèmes!** you can see the problems there are going to be!; **il y a vingt kilomètres d'i. à Paris** it's twenty kilometres from here to Paris; **c'est à dix minutes d'i.** it's ten minutes away or from here; **c'est loin d'i.** it's a long way away (from here); **viens par i.** come (over) here; (en entrant) come in here; (en sortant) come out here; **regarde par i.** look (over) here; **c'est par i. que ça se passe** it's happening (over) here; (dans cette pièce etc) it's happening in here; (dans le jardin etc) it's happening out here; **il habite par i. ou près d'i.** he lives near here or around here; **passez par i.** (come) this way, please; **par i. la sortie** this way out, the exit is this way; **par i. la monnaie** let's have your money; **c'est i.** this is the place; **c'est i. que ça s'est passé/que je veux habiter** this is where it happened/where I want to live; **le car vient jusqu'i.** the bus comes as far as here or as far as this; Fig **je reprends i. ses propres paroles** and here I'm using his/her own words; Tél **i. Thomas** (it's) Thomas speaking, Thomas here; Radio **i. France Inter** this is France Inter; **i. le Palais de l'Élysée, à vous les studios** (Jean Lô au micro) this is Jean Lô at the Élysée Palace handing you back to the studio
2 (dans le temps) **jusqu'i.** until now, up to now; **d'i. lundi/la semaine prochaine/demain** by Monday/next week/tomorrow; **d'i. lundi, il peut se passer tellement de choses!** so many things can happen between now and Monday or before Monday!; **d'i. là** by that time, by then; **mais d'i. là, on a le temps** but we've got time until then; **d'i. peu** before long; **d'i. à ce que vous ayez fini, je serai parti** by the time you've finished, I'll have gone; **d'i. à ce qu'il la quitte, il n'y a pas loin** ou **il n'y a qu'un pas** it won't be long before he leaves her; **d'i. à ce qu'on y arrive, on a quelques efforts à faire** we've quite a bit to do before we get there; **ce voyage est tentant, mais d'i. à ce que j'aie la somme nécessaire!** this trip is tempting, but it's going to take me forever to get the money together

ici-bas ADV here below, on earth

ici-dans ADV Can here; **qu'est-ce qu'il fait froid i.** it's terribly cold in here!

icône [ikon] NF Rel icon, ikon; Ordinat icon; Ordinat **i. contrastée** highlighted icon; Ordinat **i. de la corbeille** wastebasket icon, Am trash icon

iconoclasme [ikɔnɔklasm] NM iconoclasm

iconoclaste [ikɔnɔklast] ADJ iconoclastic
N iconoclast

iconographe [ikɔnɔgraf] N **1** iconographer **2** (dans l'édition) art or picture editor

iconographie [ikɔnɔgrafi] NF **1** iconography **2** (dans l'édition) illustrations, art work

iconographique [ikɔnɔgrafik] ADJ iconographic(al)

iconoscope [ikɔnɔskɔp] NM TV iconoscope

ictère [iktɛr] NM Méd icterus, jaundice; **i. du nouveau-né** neonatal jaundice

ictérique [ikterik] Méd ADJ **1** (personne, yeux etc) jaundiced **2** (troubles) icteric(al)
N jaundice sufferer

IDE [ideə] NMPL (abrév **investissements directs étrangers**) DFI

idéal, -ale, -aux, -ales [ideal, -o] ADJ ideal; Litt **devenir i.** to become a shadow of its former self
NM 1 ideal; **avoir un i.** to have an ideal; **l'i. de la beauté chez les Grecs** the Greek ideal of beauty **2 l'i.** the ideal thing; **c'est l'i. pour se remettre en forme** it's the ideal thing for getting back into shape; **l'i., c'est de pouvoir s'exprimer** the ideal thing is to be able to express oneself; **l'i. serait que tu y ailles tout seul** ideally, you should go alone

idéalement [idealmã] ADV ideally; **elle est i. belle** she is beauty itself

idéalisation [idealizasjõ] NF idealization, idealizing

idéaliser [idealize] VT to idealize

idéalisme [idealism] NM idealism

idéaliste [idealist] ADJ idealistic
N idealist

IDÉE [ide]

| idea 1–4, 6 ▪ notion 2 ▪ view 3 |
| ▪ opinion 3 ▪ mind 4, 5 |

NF **1** idea; **je n'ai pas eu l'i. de lui téléphoner** the idea of phoning him didn't occur to me; **as-tu une i. de ce qu'on pourrait faire ce soir?** (do you have) any idea what we could do this evening?; **je n'arrive pas à avoir d'idées pour ma dissertation** I can't get any ideas for my essay; **i. de génie, i. lumineuse** brilliant idea, Br brainwave, Am brainstorm; **bonne i.!** good idea!; **c'etait une bonne i. de l'emmener au restaurant** it was a good idea to take him out to eat; **j'ai une i. de pièce de théâtre** I've got an idea for a play; **avoir la bonne i. de faire qch** to have the bright idea of doing sth; **j'ai du mal à accepter l'i. que tu vas partir** I'm finding it hard to accept the idea that or to come to terms with the fact that you're leaving; **qu'est-ce qui vous a donné l'i. de venir?** what gave you the idea or made you think of coming?; **l'i. ne lui viendrait pas à l'esprit qu'elle a peut-être ses problèmes?** doesn't it occur to you that she has problems too?; **à l'i. de …/que …** at the idea of …/that …; **je me sens très triste à l'i. de te voir partir** I feel very sad at the idea of seeing you go; **se faire à l'i. de …/que …** to get used to the idea of …/that …; **je n'arrive pas à me faire à cette i.** I can't get used to the idea; **l'i. de Pierre était de …** Pierre's idea was to …; **avoir une i. derrière la tête** to be up to something; **donner des idées à qn** to put ideas into sb's head, to give sb ideas; **ce livre me donne des idées de voyage** the book is giving me some ideas for holidays; **c'était juste une i. en l'air** it was just an idea; **avoir sa petite i. sur qch** to have one's own little ideas about sth; **il ne manque pas d'idées!** he's got some good ideas; **il a des idées** he's quite imaginative, he comes up with good ideas; **il y a de l'i.** it's got something; **il y a de l'i. mais le plan de devoir laisse à désirer** the idea is good but your presentation leaves something to be desired; **quelle (drôle d')i.!, en voilà une i.!** what an idea!, what a thought!, the very idea!; **où a-t-elle pu prendre** ou Fam **pêcher cette i.?**

where did she get that idea from?; **se faire des idées** to imagine things

2 *(notion)* idea, notion; **l'i. qu'il a du travail** his idea *or* notion of work; **il a une i. un peu étrange de l'amour** he has rather a strange idea of love; **juste pour vous donner une i. de la situation** just to give you an idea of the situation; **vous avez trois jours pour vous faire une i. de la situation** you've got three days to get a handle on the situation; **je me faisais une autre i. du métier de journaliste** I imagined journalism to be different; **as-tu (une) i. *ou* la moindre i. du prix que ça coûte?** have you any idea how much it costs?; **je n'en ai pas la moindre i.** I haven't the least *or* faintest idea, *Fam* I haven't a clue; **aucune i.!** no idea!; **j'ai (comme une) i. qu'il va venir ce soir** I've an idea he'll come tonight; *Fam* **on n'a pas i. de faire des choses pareilles!** whoever heard of doing things like that!; *Fam* **on n'a pas i.!** whoever heard of that!; **tu n'as pas i. du monde qu'il peut y avoir!** you've no idea how crowded it can be!; *Fam* **elle est belle, t'as pas i.!** you wouldn't believe how beautiful she is!

3 *(opinion)* view, opinion; **avoir une haute i. de qn/qch** to have a high opinion of sb/sth; **se faire une i. de qch** to get an *or* some idea of sth; **je préfère me faire une i. (par) moi-même** I prefer to make up my own mind; **avoir des idées arrêtées sur qch** to have set ideas *or* very decided views on sth; **il a les idées très à gauche** he has very left-wing ideas *or* views *or* opinions; **on a tous une i. différente sur la question** we all have a different opinion *or* view on the matter; **avoir les idées larges/étroites** to be broad-/narrow-minded; **combattre pour ses idées** to fight for one's ideas

4 *(esprit)* **ça ne m'est jamais venu à l'i.** it's never occurred to me, it's never entered my head *or* mind; **elle n'est pas bien ici? ça ne m'était même pas venu à l'i.** she's not happy here? the possibility never even crossed my mind; **il ne me viendrait pas à l'i. de lui reprocher** it wouldn't occur to me to blame him for it; **il me vient à l'i. que ...** it occurs to me that ...; **j'ai dans l'i. que ...** I have an idea that ...; **elle a dans l'i. d'ouvrir un magasin** she's thinking of opening a shop; **je ne peux pas lui ôter cela de l'i.** I can't get it out of his mind *or* head; **on ne m'ôtera pas de l'i. que c'est elle qui a volé le sac** you won't get me to believe that it wasn't her who stole the bag; **se mettre dans l'i. que ...** to get it into one's head that ...; **il s'est mis dans l'i. de repeindre la cuisine en bleu** he got it into his head to repaint the kitchen blue; **cela m'était sorti de l'i.** it had gone right out *or* clean out of my mind *or* head; **il me revient à l'i. que ...** now I remember that ...

5 *(goût, avis)* **agir à son i.** to act as one likes; **fais à ton i.** do as you like; **elle n'en fait qu'à son i.** she does just as she likes; **elle n'agit qu'à son i.** she acts just as she likes; **à ton i., je me coupe les cheveux?** you think I should cut my hair?; **changer d'i.** to change one's mind

6 *(suggestion)* **i.-...** ...idea; **des idées-vacances/-cadeaux** holiday/gift ideas; **ce livret contient des idées-repas** this booklet offers ideas for meals; **une i.-rangement astucieuse** a clever storage idea

▸▸**i. fixe** obsession, idée fixe; **i. force** main idea; **i. reçue** generally accepted idea; **idées noires** gloomy *or* black thoughts

idem [idɛm] ADV idem, ditto; *Fam* **je suis venu en voiture et lui i.** I came by car and so did he *or* and he did too; *Fam* **je veux une glace à la fraise – i. pour moi** I'd like a strawberry ice cream – me too *or* the same for me

identifiable [idãtifjabl] ADJ identifiable

identificateur [idãtifikatœr] NM *Ordinat* identifier; *Mktg* **i. de marque** brand identifier

identification [idãtifikasjõ] NF identification (**avec, à** with); *Méd* **i. des types (de bactéries/de virus)** typing (of bacteria/viruses); *Ordinat* **i. de l'utilisateur** user identification; *Mktg* **i. de marque** brand recognition; *Tél* **i. d'appel** caller ID

identifier [idãtifje] VT *(confondre)* to identify (**avec, à** with); *(reconnaître)* to identify; **i. des empreintes digitales** to identify fingerprints

VPR s'identifier to identify (oneself), to become identified (**avec, à** with)

identique [idãtik] ADJ identical; **je l'ai trouvé i. à lui-même** I found him the same as ever

ADV à l'i. identically; **j'en ai fait un à l'i.** I made an identical one; **à l'i. de** according to; **je fais refaire mon salon à l'i. du précédent** I'm having my lounge redecorated in exactly the same way as the last one

identiquement [idãtikmã] ADV identically; **les candidats ont répondu i.** the candidates gave identical answers

identitaire [idãtitɛr] ADJ **obsession i.** obsession with issues of identity; **les revendications identitaires des minorités ethniques** ethnic minorities' demands for recognition; **l'afflux d'immigrants a donné lieu à un phénomène de repli i.** the large influx of immigrants has given rise to a racist backlash

identité [idãtite] NF identity; **bracelet d'i.** identity bracelet; *Admin* **carte d'i.** identity card; **papiers *ou* pièces d'i.** identity papers; **avez-vous une pièce d'i.?** do you have some identification *or* Fam ID?; **l'I. judiciaire** ≃ Criminal Records Office; *Mktg* **i. graphique** logo; **i. visuelle** visual identity

idéogramme [ideogram] NM *Ling* ideogram, ideograph

idéographie [ideografi] NF *Ling* ideography

idéographique [ideografik] ADJ *Ling* ideographic(al)

idéologie [ideoloʒi] NF ideology

idéologique [ideoloʒik] ADJ ideological

idéologue [ideolog] N ideologist, ideologue

idiolecte [idjolɛkt] NM *Ling* idiolect

idiomatique [idjomatik] ADJ *Ling* idiomatic; **expression i.** idiom; **utiliser des tournures idiomatiques** to speak/write idiomatically SEE GRAMMAR A3; B2

idiome [idjom] NM *Ling* idiom

idiosyncrasie [idjosɛ̃krazi] NF idiosyncrasy

idiot, -ote [idjo, -ot] ADJ idiotic, stupid; *(accident)* stupid, silly; *Méd Vieilli* idiotic, imbecilic; **ce système n'est pas i. du tout** this system is pretty clever *or* smart; **si tu es assez i. pour le croire** if you're stupid enough to believe it; **tu as été i. de refuser son offre** you were stupid to refuse his offer; **ce serait i. de ne pas le faire** it would be stupid *or* idiotic not to; *Hum* **dis-moi son nom/comment faire, je ne veux pas mourir i.** tell me his name/how to do it or I'll die of suspense

N idiot, fool; *Méd Vieilli* idiot, imbecile; *Fam* **l'i. du village** the village idiot; **faire l'i.** *(faire des bêtises)* to act *or* play the fool; *(feindre de ne pas comprendre)* to act stupid; **elle me prend pour un i.** she takes me for an idiot *or* a fool; **c'est loin d'être un i.** he's far from stupid

idiotement [idjotmã] ADV idiotically, stupidly

idiotie [idjosi] NF **1** *(bêtise)* stupidity, idiocy; *(chose, parole idiote)* idiotic *or* stupid thing; **c'est idiot d'avoir fait ça** it's stupid *or* idiotic to have done that; **ne dites pas d'idioties!** don't talk rubbish *or* nonsense!; **faire une i.** to do something stupid *or* idiotic; **ne va pas voir cette i.!** don't go and see that rubbish! **2**

Méd Vieilli idiocy, imbecility, mental deficiency

idiotisme [idjotism] NM *Ling* idiom, idiomatic expression

idoine [idwan] ADJ *Jur, Arch, Hum* appropriate; *Jur* **apte et i. à tester** fit and competent to make a will

idolâtre [idolɑtr] ADJ idolatrous

N idolater, **f** idolatress

idolâtrer [idolɑtre] VT *(personne)* to idolize; *(chose)* to be passionately fond of

idolâtrie [idolɑtri] NF idolatry

idolâtrique [idolɑtrik] ADJ idolatrous

idole [idol] NF idol; **il en a fait son i.** he idolized him; **c'est l'i. des jeunes** he's/she's a teenage idol

IDS [idees] NF *Mil (abrév* **initiative de défense stratégique)** SDI

idylle [idil] NF *(aventure)* romance; *Littér* idyll

Il faut noter que le terme anglais **idyll** ne s'applique jamais à une liaison entre deux personnes.

idyllique [idilik] ADJ idyllic

IEP [iəpə] NM *(abrév* **Institut d'études politiques)** = higher education establishment of political science

if [if] NM **1** *(arbre)* yew (tree) **2** *(pour bouteilles)* draining rack

IFOP [ifop] NM *(abrév* **Institut français d'opinion publique)** = French market research institute

IGF [iʒeɛf] NM INV *Anciennement (abrév* **impôt sur les grandes fortunes)** wealth tax

igloo, iglou [iglu] NM igloo

IGN [iʒeɛn] NM *(abrév* **Institut géographique national)** *Br* ≃ Ordnance Survey, *Am* ≃ United States Geological Survey

IGN
Created in 1940, this state agency is responsible for the official map of France and for keeping a geographical database. It is organized into regional offices and sponsors a school which trains 200 students a year.

igname [iɲam] NF yam

ignare [iɲar] ADJ ignorant

N ignoramus

ignifugation [iɲifygasjõ] NF fireproofing

ignifuge [iɲifyʒ] ADJ non-(in)flammable, fireproof; *(qui retarde l'embrasement)* fire-resistant, flame-retardant

NM fireproof material

ignifugé [iɲifyʒe] ADJ *(matériau)* fireproofed

ignifugeant [iɲifyʒã] ADJ = **ignifuge** ADJ

ignifuger [iɲifyʒe] VT (**j'ignifugeai(s); n. ignifugeons)** to fireproof

ignoble [iɲobl] ADJ **1** *(personne)* ignoble, base; *(conduite, attitude etc)* vile, disgraceful, unspeakable; **tu as vraiment été i. avec elle** you were really vile to her **2** *(habitation, quartier etc)* wretched, filthy

ignoblement [iɲobləmã] ADV *(se conduire)* ignobly, basely, disgracefully; **une maison i. sale** a disgracefully dirty house

ignominie [iɲomini] NF **1** *(caractère)* ignominy, shame, disgrace; **se couvrir d'i.** to cover oneself in ignominy *or* shame, to bring ignominy *or* shame *or* disgrace upon oneself **2** *(action)* shameful *or* disgraceful action; **c'est une i.!** it's a disgrace!, it's shameful!; **s'abaisser aux pires ignominies** to stoop to the lowest kinds of behaviour

ignominieusement [iɲominjøzmã] ADV ignominiously

ignominieux, -ieuse [iɲɔminjø, -jøz] ADJ *(conduite)* ignominious, shameful, disgraceful; *(vie, mort, destin)* ignominious; *(accusation)* shameful, disgraceful

ignorance [iɲɔrɑ̃s] NF **1** ignorance; **par i.** through *or* out of ignorance; **être/tenir qn dans l'i.** to be/keep sb in the dark; **être/tenir qn dans l'i. de qch** to be/keep sb in the dark about *or* in ignorance of sth; *Fam* **il est d'une i. crasse** he is incredibly ignorant **2** ignorances gaps in one's knowledge

ignorant, -ante [iɲɔrɑ̃, -ɑ̃t] ADJ **1** *(inculte)* ignorant; **être i. en latin** not to know (any) Latin **2** *(non informé)* **i. de qch** ignorant *or* unaware of sth
▪ N ignoramus; **faire l'i.** to pretend one doesn't know; **ne fais pas l'i., je suis sûr que c'est toi** don't pretend you don't know what I'm talking about *or* don't know anything about it, I'm sure it was you

Il faut noter qu'en anglais l'adjectif **ignorant** signifie également **mal élevé**.

ignoré [iɲɔre] ADJ unknown; *(négligé)* ignored; **vivre i.** to live in obscurity; **i. de** *ou* **par ses contemporains** unknown to his contemporaries; *(négligé)* ignored by his contemporaries

ignorer [iɲɔre] VT **1** *(ne pas savoir)* not to know *(that)*, to be ignorant *or* unaware of; **il ignore tout de …** he knows nothing whatever about …; **nul n'est censé i. la loi** ignorance of the law is no excuse; **je n'ignore pas les difficultés** I am not unaware *or* I'm well aware of the difficulties; **je n'ignore rien de ses activités** I'm perfectly well aware of what he's up to; **elle ignorait vous avoir blessé** she wasn't aware that she had hurt you; **elle ignore qui je suis** she doesn't know who I am; **i. que** + *sub* or + *ind* not to know that, to be unaware that; **il ignore que vous avez déjà travaillé** he doesn't know *or* he's unaware that you've already got work experience; **il ignorait que vous le connaissiez** he didn't know *or* wasn't aware *(that)* you knew him; *Litt* **il ignorait que nous fussions déjà arrivés** he was not aware that we had already arrived; **personne n'ignore que …** everybody knows that …; **j'ignorais si vous viendriez** I didn't know whether you would come; **j'ignore comment il est venu/où il habite** I don't know how he came/where he lives; **un fusil qu'il ignorait être chargé** a gun which he didn't know was loaded
2 *(mépriser)* *(personne, conseil, panneau, interdiction etc)* to ignore
▪ VPR **s'ignorer 1** *(se mépriser l'un l'autre)* to ignore each other **2** *(se méconnaître)* **c'est un artiste/un homosexuel qui s'ignore** he is unaware of his artistic talents/his homosexuality

Il faut noter que le verbe anglais **to ignore** ne signifie jamais **ne pas savoir**.

IGP [iʒepe] NF *Com (abrév* **indication géographique protégée)** = designation of a product which guarantees its authentic origin and gives the name protected status

IGPN [iʒepeɛn] NF *(abrév* **Inspection générale de la police nationale)** = police disciplinary body; *Br* ≃ Police Committee

IGS [iʒeɛs] NF *(abrév* **Inspection générale des services)** = police disciplinary body for Paris, *Br* ≃ Metropolitan Police Commission

iguane [igwan] NM iguana

il, *pl* **ils** [il] PRON PERS SEE GRAMMAR A27–8; B18; B66 **1** *(personne)* he; *(bébé, animal)* he; *(chose)* it; *(bateau, pays)* it, she; **ils** they; **sont-ils arrivés?** have they arrived?; **ton père a-t-il ouvert la bouteille?** has your father opened the bottle?

2 *(interrogatif, emphatique)* **viendra-t-il?** will he come?; **ton père est-il toujours à l'hôpital?** is your father still in hospital?; **le lave-vaisselle est-il toujours en panne?** is the dishwasher still broken?; **qu'il est joli, ce foulard!** what a pretty scarf (that is)!; **ton cousin, il n'est pas prêt de me revoir** your cousin's not likely to see me again in a hurry
3 *(impersonnel)* it; **il est/il doit être six heures** it is/it must be six o'clock; **il est facile de s'en assurer** it's easy to make sure; **il est vrai que j'étais là** it's true that I was there; **il était une fois une fée** once upon a time there was a fairy; **il pleut/neige** it's raining/snowing; **il faut partir** it's time to go, we must go; **il y a quelqu'un à la porte** there's someone at the door SEE GRAMMAR A28; B29–30

île [il] NF island; **habiter dans une i.** to live on an island; **î. coralienne** coral island; **î. déserte** desert island; **les îles Anglo-Normandes** the Channel Islands
▸▸ *Culin* **î. flottante** floating island

Île-de-France NF l'î. = administrative region including Paris

iléon [ileɔ̃] NM *Anat* ileum

Iliade [iljad] NF l'I. the Iliad

iliaque [iljak] ADJ *Anat* iliac; **os i.** ilium

illégal, -ale, -aux, -ales [ilegal, -o] ADJ illegal, unlawful

illégalement [ilegalmɑ̃] ADV illegally, unlawfully

illégalité [ilegalite] NF *(d'une action)* illegality, unlawfulness; **commettre une i.** to break the law; **vivre dans l'i.** to live outside the law; **être** *ou* **entrer dans l'i.** to break *or* flout the law; **ils ont fait tout cela dans la plus parfaite i.** they did all that in complete defiance of the law

illégitime [ileʒitim] ADJ *(enfant)* illegitimate; *(mariage)* unlawful; *(demande)* unwarranted; *(soupçons)* unfounded, groundless; **il était vraiment i. de ne pas lui faire confiance** it was completely unwarranted not to trust him

illégitimement [ileʒitim(ə)mɑ̃] ADV *(hériter, bénéficier de qch)* illegitimately, unlawfully; *(se marier)* unlawfully; **faire un enfant i.** to have an illegitimate child

illégitimité [ileʒitimite] NF *(d'un enfant)* illegitimacy; *(d'un mariage)* unlawfulness; *(d'une demande)* unwarranted nature

illettré, -ée [iletre] ADJ illiterate
▪ N illiterate (person); **les illettrés** illiterate people

illettrisme [iletrism] NM illiteracy

illicite [ilisit] ADJ illicit, unlawful; *Sport* **coup i.** foul

illicitement [ilisitmɑ̃] ADV illicitly, unlawfully

illico [iliko] ADV *Fam* **i. (presto)** right away, pronto

illimité [ilimite] ADJ *(pouvoirs)* unlimited, limitless; *(moyens, fortune, crédit)* unlimited; *(empire)* limitless, boundless; *(confiance, mépris)* boundless, limitless, unbounded; **congé i.** indefinite leave

illisibilité [ilizibilite] NF illegibility

illisible [ilizibl] ADJ **1** *(qu'on ne peut pas déchiffrer)* illegible, unreadable; *Ordinat (fichier, disquette)* unreadable **2** *(qu'on ne peut pas comprendre)* unreadable

illisiblement [iliziblǝmɑ̃] ADV illegibly

illogique [ilɔʒik] ADJ illogical

illogiquement [ilɔʒikmɑ̃] ADV illogically

illogisme [ilɔʒism] NM illogicality; **procéder de cette manière est un i.** to proceed like that is illogical

illumination [ilyminasjɔ̃] NF **1** *(action d'illuminer)* lighting up, illumination; **i. (par**

projecteurs) floodlighting **2** *(lumière)* **illuminations** lights, illuminations **3** *(inspiration)* (flash of) inspiration; **j'ai eu une i.** I've had an inspiration *or* a brilliant idea

illuminé, -ée [ilymine] ADJ *(éclairé)* lit up, illuminated; *(par projecteur)* floodlit
▪ N visionary, *Péj* fanatic, *Fam* loony

illuminer [ilymine] VT **1** *(éclairer)* to light up, to illuminate; *(par projecteur)* to floodlight; *Fig (visage, yeux)* to light up; **un superbe sourire illumina son visage** a radiant smile lit up his face; **une étrange lueur illuminait ses yeux** a strange glow lit up his eyes; **cette nouvelle a illuminé la journée** this news brightened up the day **2** *Rel, Phil* to enlighten
▪ VPR **s'illuminer** to light up (**de** with)

illusion [ilyzjɔ̃] NF illusion; **se nourrir d'illusions, se bercer d'illusions, se faire des illusions** to delude oneself; **je ne me fais aucune i. sur ses intentions** I have no illusions about his/her intentions; **elle l'a entretenu dans cette i.** she encouraged him in this illusion; **ces paroles lui ont enlevé** *ou* **ôté toutes ses illusions** these words completely disillusioned him/her; **perdre ses illusions** to become disillusioned; **faire perdre ses illusions à qn** to disillusion sb; **donner des illusions à qn** to raise sb's hopes *or* expectations; **faire i.** to take people in, to delude people; **cela n'a pas fait i.** no-one was taken in; **cet éclairage donne une i. de lumière naturelle** the lighting gives an *or* the impression of natural light; **ces espoirs n'étaient qu'i.** these hopes were illusory
▸▸ *Phys* **i. d'optique** optical illusion

illusionner [ilyzjɔne] VT to delude
▪ VPR **s'illusionner** to delude oneself, to deceive oneself (**sur** about)

illusionnisme [ilyzjɔnism] NM conjuring

illusionniste [ilyzjɔnist] N illusionist, conjurer

illusoire [ilyzwar] ADJ illusory, illusive

illusoirement [ilyzwarmɑ̃] ADV illusorily

illustrateur, -trice [ilystratœr, -tris] N illustrator; *Journ* picture editor; *TV, Cin* **i. sonore** sound effects supervisor

illustration [ilystrasjɔ̃] NF **1** *(action)* illustration; *(dans l'édition)* picture editing **2** *(dessin)* illustration; **illustrations** *(dans l'édition)* artwork; **i. en couleur** colour illustration; **l'i. du livre** the illustrations *or* the artwork in the book; **texte et illustrations de …** text and illustrations by …

illustre [ilystr] ADJ illustrious; *Hum* **un i. inconnu** somebody no-one has ever heard of

illustré [ilystre] ADJ illustrated; **abondamment i.** copiously illustrated
▪ NM illustrated magazine; *(pour enfants)* comic

illustrer [ilystre] VT **1** *(livre etc)* to illustrate; **illustré de nombreux exemples** illustrated with numerous examples **2** *Arch, Litt (rendre illustre)* to make illustrious
▪ VPR **s'illustrer** to distinguish oneself (**par** by)

ILM [iɛlɛm] NM *(abrév* **immeuble à loyer moyen)** = apartment building with low-rent accommodation (more expensive than an HLM)

îlot [ilo] NM *(petite île)* islet, small island; *(groupe d'immeubles)* block of buildings; *Com* gondola; *Fig* **î. de verdure** island of greenery; *Fig* **î. de résistance** pocket of resistance
▸▸ **î. directionnel** *(sur une route)* traffic divider; *Com* **î. de vente** (display) stand, island

îlotage [ilotaʒ] NM community policing

ilote [ilɔt] N *Hist* Helot; *Fig Litt* slave

îlotier [ilɔtje] NM community policeman

ILV [iɛlve] NF (abrév **information sur le lieu de vente**) point-of-sale information

image [imaʒ] NF **1** (dans l'eau, dans un miroir etc) reflection, image; Cin (de la pellicule) frame; Cin, TV (sur l'écran) picture; Opt **i. réelle/virtuelle** real/virtual image; Cin, TV **25 images par seconde** 25 frames per second; **nous avons le son mais pas l'i.** ou **pas les images** we've got the sound but no picture; **nous n'avons plus d'i.** the picture's gone; **à l'i.** on-camera; **être à l'i.** to be on camera; **images en direct** live pictures; **i. à l'écran** screen image; **soigner son i.** to cultivate one's image; **i. par i.** single frame **2** Fig image; **l'i. de son père** the image of his father; **Dieu créa l'homme à son i.** God created man in his own image; **ils sont l'i. du bonheur/de la réussite** they are the picture of happiness/success; **donner une bonne/mauvaise i. de qch** to present a good/bad image of sth **3** (dessin) picture; **livre d'images** picture book; **récit en images** pictorial record; **images pieuses** holy pictures; Scol **voici une i.** (récompense) ≃ here's a gold star; Mktg **images à compléter** picture completion **4** (représentation) image, picture; **i. visuelle forte** strong visual image or picture or impression; **garder l'i. d'une personne en mémoire** to keep an image of sb in one's memory; **la première i. qui vient à l'esprit** the first image that comes to mind; **i. fidèle** truthful account; Compta true and fair view **5** Littér image; **images** imagery ▸▸ TV, Cin **i. animée** moving picture; TV, Cin **i. d'archives** library picture; TV, Cin **images d'archives** library footage, found footage; TV, Cin **i. arrêtée** hold frame; Ordinat **i. bitmap** bitmap image; TV, Cin **i. chassée** push-over wipe; Ordinat **i. cliquable** image map; Ordinat **i. digitalisée** digitized image; TV, Cin **i. divisée en quatre** quad split; Mktg **i. de l'entreprise** corporate image; TV **i. fantôme** ghosting; TV, Cin **i. fixe** still frame, stop frame, photostill; **i. institutionnelle** corporate image; Ordinat **i. intégrée** inline image; **i. de marque** (d'un produit) brand image; (d'un homme politique, d'une société etc) (public) image; Ordinat **i. mémoire** dump; **prendre une i. mémoire** to take a hard copy, to dump; **i. en négatif** negative image; Mktg **i. du produit** product image; **i. publique** public image; Phot **i. de solarisation** solarized image; Ordinat **images de synthèse** computer-generated images, CGI; Ordinat **i. tramée** raster image; Ordinat **i. vectorielle** outline image

imagé [imaʒe] ADJ (style, langage) vivid, full of imagery; (expression) vivid

imager [imaʒe] VT (j'imageai(s); n. imageons) Litt (style, discours) to colour, Am to color

imagerie [imaʒri] NF **1** Littér imagery **2** Com colour or Am color print trade; (usine) colour or Am color print works **3** Méd **i. cérébrale** brain imaging or scanning; **i. par résonance magnétique** magnetic resonance imaging

imageur [imaʒœr] NM Ordinat imager; **i. documentaire** document imager

imagier [imaʒje] NM **1** (peintre) painter; (sculpteur) sculptor, carver **2** (dessinateur) drawer of pictures **3** (imprimeur) colour or Am color print maker; Com colour or Am color print seller **4** (livre d'images) picture book

imaginable [imaʒinabl] ADJ imaginable, conceivable; **cela n'était pas i. il y a quelques années** it was unimaginable or inconceivable a few years ago; **toutes les solutions possibles et imaginables** every conceivable solution, every solution imaginable

imaginaire [imaʒinɛr] ADJ (personnage, pays, animal etc) imaginary; Hum **malade i.** hypochondriac
NM imagination; **toute cette histoire relève de l'i.** the whole story is a product of the imagination, the story is entirely imaginary

imaginatif, -ive [imaʒinatif, -iv] ADJ imaginative

imagination [imaʒinasjɔ̃] NF imagination; **faire preuve d'i.** to show some imagination; **avoir de l'i.** to have imagination, to be imaginative; **avoir une i. débordante** to have a very active imagination; **tu manques d'i.!** you have no imagination!; **tu as vraiment trop d'i.!** you imagine things!; **ces histoires sortent de son i.** these stories are a product or Péj figment of his imagination; **voir qch en i.** to see sth in one's mind's eye or in one's imagination; **vivre qch en i.** to experience sth in one's imagination

imaginer [imaʒine] VT **1** (inventer) (méthode, système, stratagème) to devise, to think up; (machine, dispositif) to devise; **bien imaginé** well thought out; **les enfants imaginaient qu'ils étaient sur la lune** the children were pretending they were on the moon
2 (concevoir) to imagine; **imaginez un peu mon étonnement** just imagine my surprise; **tu l'imagines avec des enfants!** just think of or imagine or picture him/her with children!; **j'imagine qu'il viendra vers 9 heures** I imagine he'll come about 9 o'clock; **je n'imaginais pas que cela soit faisable** I didn't think it could be done; **tout ce qu'on peut i. de plus beau** the finest thing imaginable; **que vas-tu i. là?** how can you think such a thing?; **vous plaisantez, j'imagine** you must be joking!
VPR **s'imaginer 1** (croire à tort) **elle s'imagine que tout le monde l'admire** she imagines or thinks (that) everyone admires her; **elle s'est imaginé qu'il allait tout lui dire** she imagined or got it into her head that he would tell her everything; **il s'imagine tout savoir** he imagines he knows everything
2 (se figurer) to imagine; **tu t'imagines la tête qu'il va faire** you can imagine how he'll take it; **comme on peut se l'i.** as you can (well) imagine; **je me l'imaginais bien plus grand** I imagined him much taller; **il est bien plus grand que je ne me l'imaginais** he's much taller than I imagined
3 (se voir) to picture or see oneself; **je m'imagine sur la scène/à quarante ans** I can (just) picture or see myself on the stage/at forty

imago [imago] NM Entom imago
NF Psy imago

imam [imam], **iman** [imã] NM imam

imbattable [ɛ̃batabl] ADJ (champion) invincible, unbeatable; (record) unbeatable, unbreakable; (prix) unbeatable

imbécile [ɛ̃besil] ADJ idiotic, stupid; Méd Vieilli imbecilic, idiotic
N idiot, fool, imbecile; Méd Vieilli imbecile, idiot; **le premier i. venu vous dira cela** any fool will tell you that; **c'est un i. heureux** he's a bit simple-minded; **faire l'i.** (faire des bêtises) to play or act the fool; (feindre de ne pas comprendre) to act stupid

imbécilement [ɛ̃besilmã] ADV idiotically, stupidly

imbécillité [ɛ̃besilite] NF **1** (stupidité) idiocy, stupidity; Méd Vieilli imbecility, idiocy **2** (parole, chose stupide) idiotic or stupid thing; **dire des imbécillités** to talk nonsense or rubbish

imberbe [ɛ̃bɛrb] ADJ beardless

imbibé [ɛ̃bibe] ADJ Fam smashed

imbiber [ɛ̃bibe] VT **i. qch (de qch)** to soak sth

(in or with sth); **imbibé d'eau** saturated (with water); (terrain) waterlogged; **chiffon imbibé d'huile** oil-soaked rag
VPR **s'imbiber 1** to become soaked (**de** with) **2** Fam **s'i. d'alcool** to hit the bottle; **s'i. d'alcool pour oublier ses problèmes** to drown one's sorrows (in drink)

imbit(t)able [ɛ̃bitabl] ADJ très Fam unfathomable, incomprehensible

imbrication [ɛ̃brikasjɔ̃] NF (de tuiles, d'écailles etc) overlap(ping); Ordinat embedding; (de commandes) nesting; **se dépêtrer d'une i. de problèmes** to extricate oneself from a mesh or web of problems; **je ne m'y retrouve pas dans cette i. de personnages** I can't get my bearings in this complex web of characters

imbriqué [ɛ̃brike] ADJ Ordinat embedded; (commande) nested

imbriquer [ɛ̃brike] VT to overlap; Ordinat to embed; (commandes) to nest
VPR **s'imbriquer** (de tuiles, d'écailles etc) to overlap; (de questions, problèmes, situations) to be interwoven; **tous ces problèmes s'imbriquent les uns dans les autres** all these problems are interwoven

imbroglio [ɛ̃brɔljo] NM imbroglio

imbu [ɛ̃by] ADJ **i. de sa personne** ou **de soi-même** full of one's own importance or of oneself

imbuvable [ɛ̃byvabl] ADJ undrinkable; Fig (personne) insufferable, unbearable; **je le trouve i., ce mec** I can't stand (the sight of) that guy, I can't stomach or Br stick that guy

IME [iɛmə] NM (abrév **Institut monétaire européen**) EMI

imitable [imitabl] ADJ imitable; **sa voix est facilement i.** his/her voice is easy to imitate or easily imitated

imitateur, -trice [imitatœr, -tris] N imitator; Théâtre impersonator
ADJ imitative

imitatif, -ive [imitatif, -iv] ADJ imitative

imitation [imitasjɔ̃] NF **1** (fait de copier) (de produit, style etc) imitation, imitating, copying; **à l'i. de qn/qch** in imitation of sb/sth **2** (de personne) imitation, mimicking, mimicry; Théâtre impersonation; (de cri d'animal, de chant d'oiseau) imitation; **elle fait d'excellentes imitations** she does excellent imitations, she is an excellent mimic **3** (de signature, de papier officiel etc) forgery, forging; (d'argent) counterfeiting **4** (copie) imitation, copy; **bijoux en i. argent** imitation silver jewellery; **manteau (en) i. loutre** imitation sealskin coat; Péj **une pâle i.** a pale imitation

imiter [imite] VT (personne) to imitate, to mimic, Fam to take off; Théâtre to impersonate; (faire comme) to imitate, to copy; (cri d'animal, chant d'oiseau) to imitate; (style) to imitate, to copy; (signature) to forge; (argent) to counterfeit; **il leva son verre et tout le monde l'imita** he raised his glass and everyone followed suit or did the same; **matière qui imite le cuir/le bois** material that simulates leather/wood; **je voudrais une table qui imite celle des bistrots parisiens** I'd like a table that looks like the ones in Parisian cafés

immaculé [imakyle] ADJ (draps, linge, blanc) spotless, immaculate; (réputation) spotless; Rel **l'Immaculée Conception** the Immaculate Conception

immanence [imanãs] NF immanence

immanent [imanã] ADJ immanent; **justice immanente** divine retribution

immangeable [ɛ̃mãʒabl] ADJ inedible, uneatable

immanquable [ɛ̃mãkabl] ADJ (événement,

conséquence etc) inevitable; *Vieilli (moyen, astuce etc)* infallible

immanquablement [ɛ̃mɑ̃kabləmɑ̃] **ADV** inevitably, without fail

immatérialité [imaterjalite] **NF** *Phil* immateriality

immatériel, -ielle [imaterjɛl] **ADJ** *Phil* immaterial; *Fin (actif)* intangible; *Litt (pâleur, minceur etc)* ethereal

immatriculation [imatrikylasjɔ̃] **NF** *(d'acte, de voiture etc)* registration, registering; *(d'étudiant)* registration, enrolment; *(à la Sécurité Sociale)* registration (à with); **numéro d'i.** registration number

> ### Immatriculation
> The last two numbers on French number plates refer to the "département" where the vehicle was registered. Vehicles from the Val-de-Marne, for example, bear the number 94.

immatriculer [imatrikyle] **VT** *(document, voiture etc)* to register; *(étudiant)* to register, to enrol; *(à la Sécurité Sociale)* to register (à with); **voiture immatriculée T 342 SPF/dans le Var** car with the registration number T 342 SPF/with a Var number plate *or Am* license plate; **Com i. des marchandises** to register goods

immature [imatyr] **ADJ** immature

immaturité [imatyrite] **NF** immaturity

immédiat [imedja] **ADJ 1** *(cause, successeur etc)* immediate, direct; *(sentiment)* direct; *Chimie* **analyse immédiate** proximate analysis **2** *(proximité)* close; **être en contact i. avec le feu/le patron** to be in direct contact with the fire/the boss **3** *(dans le temps) (changement)* immediate, instant; *(résultat)* immediate; **la mort a été immédiate** death was instantaneous; **(mécanisme) à action immédiate** quick-acting (mechanism)
NM dans l'i. for the moment, for the time being

immédiatement [imedjatmɑ̃] **ADV** immediately

immédiateté [imedjat(ə)te] **NF** *Phil* immediacy

immémorial, -ale, -aux, -ales [imemɔrjal, -o] **ADJ** *Litt* age-old; **de temps i.** from *or* since time immemorial; **en des temps immémoriaux** in ancient times

immense [imɑ̃s] **ADJ** *(maison, forêt, foule etc)* immense, vast, huge; *(tâche, sacrifice)* huge, immense; *(joie, soulagement)* tremendous, great; *(succès)* huge, great; **c'est un i. acteur/écrivain** he's a tremendous *or* great actor/writer

immensément [imɑ̃semɑ̃] **ADV i. grand/riche/généreux** immensely big/rich/generous; **ce cadeau me fait i. plaisir** this gift gives me tremendous *or* great pleasure, this gift pleases me greatly; **j'ai eu i. peur** I was terribly afraid

immensité [imɑ̃site] **NF** *(de parc, maison etc)* vastness, hugeness, immenseness; *(de tâche)* immensity, hugeness; **les yeux perdus dans l'i.** gazing into the far distance *or* into space

immergé [imɛrʒe] **ADJ** submerged; **plante immergée** aquatic plant; **bateau i. par 200 mètres de fond** boat lying 200 metres under(water)

immerger [imɛrʒe] **(j'immergeai(s); n. immergeons)** **VT** to immerse, to submerge (**dans** in); *(câble)* to lay underwater; *(déchets)* to get rid of *or* dispose of *or* dump at sea; *(mort)* to bury at sea
VPR s'immerger *(d'un sous-marin)* to submerge, to dive

immérité [imerite] **ADJ** unmerited, undeserved

immersion [imɛrsjɔ̃] **NF** immersion; *(de câble)* laying underwater; *(de déchets)* disposal *or* dumping at sea; *(d'un sous-marin)* submersion, submergence; *(de mort)* burial at sea

immettable [ɛ̃mɛtabl] **ADJ** unwearable

immeuble [imœbl] **NM 1** *(bâtiment)* building; *(d'appartements)* block of flats, *Am* apartment block; **i. de bureaux** office block; **i. de 10 étages** 10-storey building; **i. de rapport, i. locatif** rental property **2** *Jur* real estate
ADJ *Jur* real, fixed; **biens immeubles** real estate

immigrant, -ante [imigrɑ̃, -ɑ̃t] **ADJ, N** immigrant; **Can i. reçu** landed immigrant

immigration [imigrasjɔ̃] **NF** immigration; **agent du service de l'i.** immigration officer

immigré, -ée [imigre] **ADJ, N** immigrant

immigrer [imigre] **VI** to immigrate; **i. en Europe/aux États-Unis** to immigrate to Europe/the United States

imminence [iminɑ̃s] **NF** imminence

imminent [iminɑ̃] **ADJ** imminent, impending; **être i.** to be imminent

immiscer (s') [simise] **VPR** (**je m'immisçai(s); n. n. immisçons**) to interfere, to meddle (**dans** in); **il faut toujours qu'elle s'immisce dans les conversations** she always has to interrupt

immixtion [imikstjɔ̃] **NF** interference, meddling (**dans** in)

immobile [imɔbil] **ADJ 1** *(personne, mer etc)* motionless, still; *(pièce de machine)* fixed, immobile; *(visage)* immobile, set; **rester complètement i.** to remain totally still **2** *Fig (institution, dogme etc)* unchanging, changeless

immobilier, -ière [imɔbilje, -jɛr] *Jur, Com* **ADJ** property, real-estate; **biens immobiliers** real estate, *esp Am* realty; **vente immobilière** sale of property; **société immobilière** property company; **agence immobilière** estate agency, *Am* real estate office; **agent i.** estate agent, *Am* real estate agent, realtor
NM real estate, property, *Am* realty; **i. de loisir** holiday property; **l'i. locatif** *Br* the property *or Am* the real-estate rental business

immobilisation [imɔbilizasjɔ̃] **NF 1** *(fait de ne plus bouger)* immobilization; **l'i. du malade est essentielle** it is essential to immobilize the patient; **attendre l'i. complète du train** wait until the train comes to a complete stop *or* standstill **2** *Jur* conversion into real estate **3** *Fin (de capital)* locking up, tying up, immobilization **4** *Compta* asset; **immobilisations fixed** *or* capital assets; **i. de capitaux** tied-up capital, capital assets; **immobilisations corporelles** tangible fixed assets; **immobilisations financières** long-term investments; **immobilisations incorporelles** intangible fixed assets; **immobilisations non financières** physical fixed assets

immobiliser [imɔbilize] **VT 1** *(rendre immobile) (blessé)* to immobilize; *(train)* to bring to a standstill; **i. un véhicule** *(avec sabot)* to clamp a vehicle **2** *Jur* to convert into real estate **3** *Fin (capital)* to lock up, to tie up, to immobilize; *Fin* **i. des actifs** to freeze assets
VPR s'immobiliser *(d'un véhicule)* to come to a stop *or* a standstill; *(d'un corps en mouvement)* to come to rest

immobilisme [imɔbilism] **NM** opposition to progress, ultra-conservatism

immobiliste [imɔbilist] **ADJ** opposed to progress, ultra-conservative
N ultra-conservative

immobilité [imɔbilite] **NF** *(d'un animal, de*

l'eau, des feuilles, des arbres etc) stillness, motionlessness; *(d'un visage)* immobility; **être condamné à l'i. pour une semaine** *(d'un malade)* to be kept immobile for a week

immodération [imɔderasjɔ̃] **NF** immoderation, immoderateness

immodéré [imɔdere] **ADJ** immoderate, excessive, inordinate

immodérément [imɔderemɑ̃] **ADV** immoderately, excessively, inordinately

immodeste [imɔdɛst] **ADJ** *Vieilli* immodest

immodestement [imɔdɛstəmɑ̃] **ADV** *Vieilli* immodestly

immodestie [imɔdɛsti] **NF** *Vieilli* immodesty

immolateur [imɔlatœr] **NM** *Arch, Litt* immolator, sacrificer

immolation [imɔlasjɔ̃] **NF** *Litt* immolation, sacrifice

immoler [imɔle] *Litt* **VT** to immolate, to sacrifice
VPR s'immoler to immolate *or* sacrifice oneself; **s'i. par le feu** to die by setting fire to oneself

immonde [imɔ̃d] **ADJ 1** *(sale) (quartier, maison etc)* foul, filthy, vile **2** *(ignoble) (acte, comportement etc)* foul, vile **3** *(laid) (personne, objet)* vile **4** *Rel* unclean

immondices [imɔ̃dis] **NFPL** refuse, rubbish

immoral, -ale, -aux, -ales [imɔral, -o] **ADJ** immoral

immoralement [imɔralmɑ̃] **ADV** immorally

immoralisme [imɔralism] **NM** *Phil* immoralism

immoraliste [imɔralist] **ADJ, N** *Phil* immoralist

immoralité [imɔralite] **NF** immorality

immortaliser [imɔrtalize] **VT** to immortalize
VPR s'immortaliser to gain immortality, to win everlasting fame (**par** through, with)

immortalité [imɔrtalite] **NF** immortality; **entrer dans l'i.** to gain immortality, to win everlasting fame

immortel, -elle [imɔrtɛl] **ADJ** *(dieu, être)* immortal; *(réputation, amour etc)* everlasting, undying
N *(membre de l'Académie française)* = member of the Académie Française
NF immortelle *(plante)* everlasting (flower), immortelle

immotivé [imɔtive] **ADJ** *(action, renvoi)* unmotivated; *(peur)* groundless, baseless

immuabilité [imɥabilite] **NF** immutability

immuable [imɥabl] **ADJ** *(vérité)* unchanging, immutable; *(passion)* undying; *(opinion)* fixed, set; *(sourire)* fixed, perpetual

immuablement [imɥabləmɑ̃] **ADV** immutably, unalterably, perpetually

immun [imœ̃] **ADJ** immune

immunisant [imynizɑ̃] **ADJ** immunizing

immunisation [imynizasjɔ̃] **NF** *Méd* immunization

immuniser [imynize] **VT** *Méd* to immunize; **être immunisé contre qch** *Méd* to be immunized against sth; *Fig* to be immune to *or* from sth; *Fig* **je suis immunisé** I'm immune

immunitaire [imyniter] **ADJ** *Méd* **système i.** immune system; **réactions immunitaires** immune reactions *or* responses; **défenses immunitaires** immune defences

immunité [imynite] **NF** immunity; **i. diplomatique** diplomatic immunity; **i. fiscale** immunity from taxation; **i. naturelle/acquise** natural/acquired immunity; **i. parlementaire** parliamentary privilege *or* immunity

immunodéficience [imynɔdefisjɑ̃s] **NF** *Méd* immunodeficiency

immunodéficitaire [imynɔdefisitɛr] ADJ *Méd* immunodeficient

immunodépresseur [imynɔdepresœr] ADJ, NM *Méd* immunosuppressive

immunodépressif, -ive [imynɔdepresif, -iv] ADJ *Méd* immunosuppressive

immunodéprimé, -ée [imynɔdeprime] *Méd* ADJ with a weakened immune system N person with a weakened immune system

immunogène [imynɔʒɛn] ADJ *Méd* immunogenic

immunoglobuline [imynɔɡlɔbylin] NF *Méd* immunoglobulin

immunologie [imynɔlɔʒi] NF immunology

immunologique [imynɔlɔʒik] ADJ immunological

immunologiste [imynɔlɔʒist] N immunologist

immunosuppresseur [imynɔsypresœr] NM *Méd* immunosuppressive, immunosuppressant

immunothérapie [imynɔterapi] NF *Méd* immunotherapy

immutabilité [imytabilite] NF immutability

impact [ɛ̃pakt] NM impact; *Fig* avoir un i. sur qch to have an impact on sth, to impact on sth; **point d'i.** point of impact; **étude d'i.** impact study; **i. sur les ventes** sales impact, impact on sales

impair [ɛ̃pɛr] ADJ *(nombre, fonction etc)* odd, uneven; *(jour)* odd; *(côté de la rue)* odd-numbered; *(vers)* with an uneven number of syllables; *(organe)* unpaired
NM 1 *(aux jeux)* odd numbers 2 *(gaffe)* blunder; **faire** *ou* **commettre un i.** to make a blunder, *Fam* to put one's foot in it

impala [ɛ̃pala] NM impala

impalpable [ɛ̃palpabl] ADJ impalpable, intangible

impaludation [ɛ̃palydasjɔ̃] NF infection with the malaria virus

impaludé [ɛ̃palyde] ADJ *(personne)* suffering from malaria; *(région)* infected with malaria

imparable [ɛ̃parabl] ADJ *(tir, coup, botte etc)* unstoppable; *Fig (argument, logique)* irrefutable, unanswerable

impardonnable [ɛ̃pardɔnabl] ADJ unforgivable, unpardonable; **il serait i. de ne pas les aider** it would be unforgivable not to help them; **c'est vraiment i. d'avoir oublié l'anniversaire de ta femme** it's really unforgivable of you to have forgotten your wife's birthday; **j'ai encore pris votre parapluie, je suis i.** I've taken your umbrella again, I'm hopeless

imparfait [ɛ̃parfɛ] ADJ 1 *Litt (qui n'est pas achevé)* unfinished, uncompleted; **avoir une connaissance imparfaite de qch** to have an imperfect knowledge of sth 2 *(qui a des défauts)* imperfect, defective
NM *Gram* imperfect (tense); **à l'i.** in the imperfect (tense) SEE GRAMMAR B30

imparfaitement [ɛ̃parfɛtmɑ̃] ADV imperfectly

impartial, -iale, -iaux, -iales [ɛ̃parsjal, -jo] ADJ impartial, unbias(s)ed

impartialement [ɛ̃parsjalmɑ̃] ADV impartially, without bias

impartialité [ɛ̃parsjalite] NF impartiality, lack of bias

impartir [ɛ̃partir] VT *Jur, Litt (droit, faveur)* to grant (à to); *(tâche)* to assign (à to); *(don)* to bestow (à on); **délai imparti** time limit, time allowed; **le temps qui vous est imparti** the time allotted to you

impartition [ɛ̃partisjɔ̃] NF *Écon* subcontracting

impasse [ɛ̃pas] NF 1 *(cul-de-sac)* dead end, cul-de-sac; *(sur panneau)* no through road

2 *Fig* impasse, deadlock; **être** *ou* **se trouver dans une i.** to be at a dead end; **il faut sortir de l'i.** the deadlock has to be broken; **les négociations sont dans l'i.** the talks have reached an impasse *or* a deadlock *or* are deadlocked; **aboutir à une i.** to reach an impasse 3 *Fin Vieilli* i. budgétaire budget deficit 4 *Cartes* faire une i. to finesse; **faire l'i. au roi** to finesse against the king; *Scol* **faire une i. sur un sujet** to give a subject a miss when revising for an exam; **j'ai fait l'i. sur le Japon en géographie** I gave Japan a miss in my geography revision

impassibilité [ɛ̃pasibilite] NF impassiveness, impassivity

impassible [ɛ̃pasibl] ADJ impassive

impassiblement [ɛ̃pasibləmɑ̃] ADV impassively

impatiemment [ɛ̃pasjamɑ̃] ADV impatiently

impatience [ɛ̃pasjɑ̃s] NF 1 impatience; **avec i.** impatiently; **montrer des signes d'i.** to show signs of impatience; **elle brûle d'i. de te le dire** she's dying to tell you; **être dans l'i. de faire qch** to be really impatient to do sth 2 *Litt* impatiences fits of impatience

impatient, -ente [ɛ̃pasjɑ̃, -ɑ̃t] ADJ impatient; **d'un air i.** impatiently; **être i. de faire qch** to be impatient *or* eager to do sth; **être i. avec qn** to be impatient with sb
NF impatiente *(plante)* busy lizzie, *Spéc* impatiens

impatienter [ɛ̃pasjɑ̃te] VT *(personne)* to annoy, to irritate; **tes questions m'impatientent** I'm getting impatient with your questions, you're annoying *or* irritating me with your questions
VPR **s'impatienter** to get impatient, to lose patience (**de qch** at sth; **contre** *ou* **avec qn** with sb)

impavide [ɛ̃pavid] ADJ *Fml* composed, unruffled, impassive

impayable [ɛ̃pɛjabl] ADJ *Fam (blague, histoire etc)* priceless; **elle est i.!** she's priceless!, she's a scream!

impayé [ɛ̃peje] ADJ *(dette, facture)* unpaid; *(paiement)* outstanding
NM outstanding payment; **j'ai un tas d'impayés** I've got a stack of unpaid bills

impeachment [impitʃmɛnt] NM *Pol* impeachment

impec [ɛ̃pɛk] ADJ, ADV *Fam* = impeccable

impeccable [ɛ̃pekabl] ADJ *(propre) (costume, personne, chambre, voiture)* impeccable; *(parfait) (traduction, voiture, repassage)* impeccable, perfect; **un travail i.** an impeccable *or* a perfect piece of work; **d'une propreté i.** impeccably clean
ADV *Fam* **i.!** great!

impeccablement [ɛ̃pekabləmɑ̃] ADV impeccably

impécunieux, -euse [ɛ̃pekynjø, -øz] ADJ *Litt* impecunious

impédance [ɛ̃pedɑ̃s] NF *Élec* impedance

impedimenta [ɛ̃pedimɛ̃ta] NMPL impedimenta

impénétrabilité [ɛ̃penetrabilite] NF 1 *(densité) (d'une forêt)* impenetrability; *(à l'eau)* imperviousness 2 *(mystère)* inscrutability

impénétrable [ɛ̃penetrabl] ADJ 1 *(forêt, citadelle, murs etc)* impenetrable; **i. à l'eau** impervious to water 2 *(visage, caractère)* inscrutable; *(mystère, secret, énigme)* unfathomable, impenetrable; *(texte)* impenetrable; **prendre un air i.** to adopt an inscrutable air; **les voies du Seigneur sont impénétrables** God works in mysterious ways

impénitence [ɛ̃penitɑ̃s] NF *Rel* impenitence

impénitent [ɛ̃penitɑ̃] ADJ *Rel* impenitent,

unrepentant; *Fig* **un fumeur/buveur i.** an unrepentant *or* a confirmed smoker/drinker

impensable [ɛ̃pɑ̃sabl] ADJ unthinkable, inconceivable; **il est i. de faire/que ...** it's unthinkable *or* inconceivable to do/that ...

impense [ɛ̃pɑ̃s] NF *Fin* property improvement expense

imper [ɛ̃pɛr] NM *Fam* raincoat, *Br* mac

impératif, -ive [ɛ̃peratif, -iv] ADJ *(ton, geste etc)* imperious, imperative, peremptory; *(nécessité, besoin)* imperative; *Jur (loi, disposition)* mandatory; **il est i. de connaître l'anglais pour ce poste** knowledge of English is essential for this post
NM 1 *(exigence)* requirement; **savoir nager est un i.** it is essential to be able to swim; **les impératifs de la mode** the dictates *or* demands of fashion; *Hum* **ce sont les impératifs du direct** that's what you have to contend with when you're broadcasting live 2 *Gram* imperative (mood); **à l'i.** in the imperative (mood) SEE GRAMMAR A40; B34-5

impérativement [ɛ̃perativmɑ̃] ADV imperatively; **il faut i. que je la voie** it is imperative that I see her

impératrice [ɛ̃peratris] NF empress

imperceptibilité [ɛ̃pɛrsɛptibilite] NF imperceptibility

imperceptible [ɛ̃pɛrsɛptibl] ADJ imperceptible; **i. par l'oreille humaine** imperceptible to the human ear; **elle eut un sourire i.** she gave a barely perceptible smile

imperceptiblement [ɛ̃pɛrsɛptibləmɑ̃] ADV imperceptibly; **sourire i.** to give a barely perceptible smile

imperdable [ɛ̃pɛrdabl] ADJ **le match/le procès est i.** the match/the case can't be lost; **le match est i. pour la France** France can't lose the match
NF *Suisse (épingle de nourrice)* safety pin

imperfectible [ɛ̃pɛrfɛktibl] ADJ that cannot be perfected, imperfectible

imperfectif, -ive [ɛ̃pɛrfɛktif, -iv] ADJ *Gram* imperfective

imperfection [ɛ̃pɛrfɛksjɔ̃] NF *(état imparfait)* imperfection; *(défaut) (de texte)* imperfection, flaw; *(de peau)* imperfection, blemish; *(de prototype)* imperfection, defect, fault; *(d'une personne)* shortcoming, failing, fault

impérial, -ale, -aux, -ales [ɛ̃perjal, -o] ADJ 1 *(relatif à l'empire)* imperial; **prendre un air i.** to adopt an imperial *or* a magisterial air 2 *(de qualité supérieure)* imperial
NF **impériale** 1 *(de bus, wagon etc)* top (deck), upper deck; **autobus à i.** double-decker (bus) 2 *(barbe)* imperial

impérialement [ɛ̃perjalmɑ̃] ADV imperially

impérialisme [ɛ̃perjalism] NM imperialism

impérialiste [ɛ̃perjalist] ADJ imperialist(ic)
N imperialist

impérieusement [ɛ̃perjøzmɑ̃] ADV 1 *(avec autorité)* imperiously 2 *(de façon pressante)* urgently; **il a i. besoin de manger** he is urgently in need of *or* urgently needs something to eat

impérieux, -euse [ɛ̃perjø, -øz] ADJ 1 *(autoritaire)* imperious, domineering 2 *(impératif) (nécessité, désir etc)* urgent, pressing; **j'ai un besoin i. de voir le patron** I need to see the boss urgently

impérissable [ɛ̃perisabl] ADJ *(œuvre)* imperishable; *(gloire)* everlasting, eternal; *(vérité, valeur)* eternal, imperishable; *(souvenir)* unforgettable, enduring, indelible; **cette aventure lui a laissé un souvenir i.** this adventure made an unforgettable impression on him *or* stayed in his mind forever; **ce film/mec ne me laissera pas un**

souvenir i. that film's/guy's pretty forgettable

imperméabilisant [ɛ̃pɛrmeabilizɑ̃] **ADJ** waterproofing
NM waterproofing agent

imperméabilisation [ɛ̃pɛrmeabilizasjɔ̃] **NF** waterproofing

imperméabiliser [ɛ̃pɛrmeabilize] **VT** to waterproof

imperméabilité [ɛ̃pɛrmeabilite] **NF** impermeability; *Fig* imperviousness (**à** to)

imperméable [ɛ̃pɛrmeabl] **ADJ** impermeable; *Fig* impervious (**à** to); **i. (à l'eau)** waterproof; **i. à la poussière** dustproof; *Fig* **être i. à la critique** to be impervious to criticism
NM raincoat, *Br* mackintosh

impersonnalité [ɛ̃pɛrsɔnalite] **NF** impersonality

impersonnel, -elle [ɛ̃pɛrsɔnɛl] **ADJ** impersonal **SEE GRAMMAR A28; B29–30**

impersonnellement [ɛ̃pɛrsɔnɛlmɑ̃] **ADV** impersonally

impertinemment [ɛ̃pɛrtinamɑ̃] **ADV** impertinently

impertinence [ɛ̃pɛrtinɑ̃s] **NF** impertinence; **dire des impertinences à qn** to speak impertinently to sb; **répondre avec i.** to answer impertinently

impertinent, -ente [ɛ̃pɛrtinɑ̃, -ɑ̃t] **ADJ** impertinent
N impertinent person; **un petit i.** an impertinent little boy

imperturbabilité [ɛ̃pɛrtyrbabilite] **NF** imperturbability

imperturbable [ɛ̃pɛrtyrbabl] **ADJ** (*personne*) imperturbable; (*optimisme*) unshakeable; **il restait i.** he remained impassive *or* unruffled

imperturbablement [ɛ̃pɛrtyrbabləmɑ̃] **ADV** imperturbably

impétigo [ɛ̃petigo] **NM** *Méd* impetigo

impétueusement [ɛ̃petɥøzmɑ̃] **ADV** *Litt* impetuously

impétueux, -euse [ɛ̃petɥø, -øz] **ADJ 1** (*fougueux*) (*personne*) impetuous, hotheaded, impulsive; (*tempérament*) fiery; (*amour*) impetuous **2** *Litt* (*torrent, flot etc*) raging, wild

impétuosité [ɛ̃petɥozite] **NF 1** (*fougue*) impetuosity, impetuousness **2** *Litt* **l'i. du torrent/des flots** the raging *or* wild torrent/waves

impie [ɛ̃pi] **ADJ** impious, ungodly
N impious *or* ungodly person

impiété [ɛ̃pjete] **NF 1** (*caractère impie*) impiety, ungodliness **2** (*acte, parole impie*) impiety

impitoyable [ɛ̃pitwajabl] **ADJ** pitiless, merciless, ruthless (**envers, pour** towards)

impitoyablement [ɛ̃pitwajabləmɑ̃] **ADV** pitilessly, mercilessly, ruthlessly

implacable [ɛ̃plakabl] **ADJ** (*personne*) implacable, unrelenting; (*haine, vengeance, logique*) implacable; (*avancée*) relentless

implacablement [ɛ̃plakabləmɑ̃] **ADV** implacably; (*avancer*) relentlessly

implant [ɛ̃plɑ̃] **NM 1** *Méd* implant; **i. dentaire** dental implant; **implants capillaires** hair transplant; **il s'est fait faire des implants** he had a hair transplant **2** (*bureau de voyages*) in-house travel agency, *Am* in-plant agency

implantation [ɛ̃plɑ̃tasjɔ̃] **NF** (*d'un système, d'une mode, d'une coutume*) introduction; (*d'une industrie, d'une filiale, d'un parti politique etc*) setting up, establishment; *Méd* implantation; (*des cheveux, des dents*) line; **i. commerciale** business operation

implanter [ɛ̃plɑ̃te] **VT** (*système, mode, coutume*) to introduce; (*idée*) to implant; (*industrie, filiale, parti politique etc*) to set up, to

establish; *Méd* to implant; **cette entreprise japonaise a plusieurs usines implantées en Europe** this Japanese company has a number of factories located in Europe; **cette habitude est bien implantée chez eux** this habit is well established with them; **solidement implanté** (*croyance*) firmly established
VPR s'implanter (*d'un usage, d'un sport, d'un parti etc*) to become established; (*d'une société, d'une industrie*) to set up, to become established (**dans** in); **s'i. à l'étranger** to set up overseas; **s'i. sur un marché** to establish oneself in a market

implémentation [ɛ̃plemɑ̃tasjɔ̃] **NF** *Ordinat* implementation

implémenter [ɛ̃plemɑ̃te] **VT** *Ordinat* to implement

implication [ɛ̃plikasjɔ̃] **NF 1** (*engagement*) involvement; *Jur* implication (**dans** in) **2** **implications** (*conséquences*) implications

implicite [ɛ̃plisit] **ADJ** implicit, implied

implicitement [ɛ̃plisitmɑ̃] **ADV** implicitly

impliquer [ɛ̃plike] **VT 1** (*compromettre*) to implicate (**dans** in); **véhicule impliqué (dans un accident)** vehicle involved (in an accident) **2** (*entraîner*) to involve, to entail, to mean; **la carrière de chanteur implique de nombreux déplacements** a singing career involves *or* entails *or* means a lot of travelling; **s'occuper d'enfants implique d'être très disponible** looking after children means having a lot of free time; **i. que … + ind** to imply that …; **je n'implique pas que vous devez vous sentir responsable** I'm not implying that you should feel responsible **3** (*engager*) to involve (**dans** in)
VPR s'impliquer to become *or* get involved (**dans** in); **il s'est beaucoup impliqué** he became *or* got heavily *or* deeply involved

implorant [ɛ̃plɔrɑ̃] **ADJ** imploring; **d'un ton i.** imploringly

imploration [ɛ̃plɔrasjɔ̃] **NF** entreaty, plea; **i. de Dieu** entreaty *or* plea to God

implorer [ɛ̃plɔre] **VT** (*personne, Dieu, le Ciel*) to implore, to beseech, to entreat; **i. le pardon de qn** to beg sb's forgiveness; **i. qn du regard** to give sb an imploring look; **i. qn de faire qch** to implore *or* beseech *or* entreat sb to do sth

imploser [ɛ̃plɔze] **VI** to implode

implosion [ɛ̃plozjɔ̃] **NF** implosion

impoli [ɛ̃pɔli] **ADJ** impolite, rude, *Fml* discourteous

impoliment [ɛ̃pɔlimɑ̃] **ADV** impolitely, rudely, *Fml* discourteously

impolitesse [ɛ̃pɔlitɛs] **NF 1** (*caractère impoli*) rudeness, impoliteness, *Fml* discourtesy; **avec i.** rudely, impolitely, *Fml* discourteously **2** (*acte*) impolite act, act of rudeness; (*remarque*) rude *or* impolite remark; **dire des impolitesses** to be impolite *or* rude, to say impolite things; **dire une i. à qn** to make an impolite *or* rude remark to sb, to say something impolite *or* rude to sb; **c'est une i. de quitter la table avant la fin du repas** it is impolite *or* rude to leave the table before the end of the meal

impolitique [ɛ̃pɔlitik] **ADJ** impolitic, ill-advised

impondérabilité [ɛ̃pɔ̃derabilite] **NF** imponderability

impondérable [ɛ̃pɔ̃derabl] **ADJ** imponderable
NMPL les impondérables the imponderables

impopulaire [ɛ̃pɔpylɛr] **ADJ** unpopular

impopularité [ɛ̃pɔpylarite] **NF** unpopularity

import [ɛ̃pɔr] **NM 1** (*action d'importer*) import; *Ordinat* **i. de données** data import **2**

Belg (*montant*) amount; **une facture d'un i. de 3 000 euros** a bill for 3,000 euros

importable¹ [ɛ̃pɔrtabl] **ADJ** (*marchandises*) importable

importable² **ADJ** (*vêtement*) unwearable

importance [ɛ̃pɔrtɑ̃s] **NF 1** importance; **avoir de l'i.** to be important, to matter; **cela / elle a beaucoup d'i. pour moi** it's/she's very important to me, it/she matters a lot to me; **sans i.** unimportant; **c'est sans i.** it's not important, it doesn't matter; **cela n'a pas d'i.** it's not important, it doesn't matter, it's of no importance *or Fml* of no consequence; **cela n'a aucune i.** it doesn't matter one bit *or* in the slightest, it's not at all important; **c'est d'une i. capitale** it's extremely important; **événement de la première** *ou* **de la plus haute i.** event of outstanding importance, all-important event; **attacher de l'i. à qch** to attach importance to sth; **tu attaches** *ou* **tu donnes trop d'i. à cela** you attach too much importance to it; **et alors? quelle i.?** so what?; **affaire d'i.** important matter; **l'affaire est d'i.** the matter is of some importance; **de peu d'i.** of little importance, of no great significance; **se donner de l'i.** to give oneself airs **2** (*d'une ville, d'un campus etc*) size; (*de dommages, d'une catastrophe etc*) extent; (*d'une somme, d'un projet*) size, magnitude; (*d'une blessure*) seriousness; **on ne connaît pas encore l'i. de ses blessures** the extent of his injuries is not yet known; **prendre de l'i.** (*d'une société etc*) to expand; **le mouvement prend de l'i.** the movement is gaining ground

important, -ante [ɛ̃pɔrtɑ̃, -ɑ̃t] **ADJ 1** (*qui compte*) important, significant; **ce n'est pas i.** it's not important, it doesn't matter; **cette maison est très importante pour moi** this house is very important to me; **il est très i. que vous le sachiez** it is very important that you (should) know; **ce qui est vraiment i., c'est que …** what is really important *or* what really matters is that …; **peu i.** unimportant, immaterial; **rien d'i.** nothing important, nothing of any importance *or* significance; **personnage i.** important *or* influential person; **c'est quelqu'un d'i.** he is (somebody) important; **se donner des airs importants** to give oneself airs **2** (*considérable*) (*ville, société, projet etc*) large, major; (*somme d'argent, dégâts etc*) considerable, significant; **la recette a atteint un chiffre i.** the takings reached a high *or* a considerable figure; **un retard i.** a considerable delay
N *Péj* **faire l'i.** to act important *or* big, to put on airs
NM l'i. the important thing, the main point; **l'i., c'est que tu sois satisfait** the important *or* main thing is for you to be satisfied; **ce n'est pas là le plus i.** that's not the most important thing, that's not what matters most

Il faut noter que l'adjectif anglais **important** ne signifie jamais **considérable** et ne se rapporte donc jamais à des proportions ou à une quantité.

importateur, -trice [ɛ̃pɔrtatœr, -tris] **N** importer; **c'est l'i. exclusif de cette marque pour la France** they are the sole French importers of this brand
ADJ (*firme, pays etc*) importing; **les pays importateurs de pétrole** oil-importing countries, oil importers

importation [ɛ̃pɔrtasjɔ̃] **NF 1** (*de marchandises, de coutume*) import, importation, importing; **articles** *ou* **produits d'i.** imports; **licence d'i.** import licence; **i. en franchise** duty-free import **2** (*produit*) import; **i. grise** grey import; **importations invisibles** invisible imports; **importations parallèles** parallel imports

importer[1] [ɛ̃pɔʀte] **vt 1** *(marchandises, coutume)* to import **2** *Ordinat* to import; **i. qch depuis qch** to import sth from sth

importer[2] *(used only in the third person, participles and inf)* **vi 1** *(compter)* to matter, to be of importance; **les choses qui importent** (the) things that matter *or* that are important; **est-ce que cela importe vraiment?** does it really matter?, is it really of any importance?; **ton opinion m'importe beaucoup** your opinion is very important *or* matters a lot to me; **les vacances lui importent peu** holidays don't matter much to him; **ce qui importe, c'est que tu viennes** the important thing is for you to come; **que m'importe la vie!** what is life to me!; **les diplômes importent de moins en moins** degrees are becoming less and less important, degrees matter less and less **2 il importe que …** + *sub* it is important that …; **il importe qu'elle soit consciente de ses responsabilités** it is important that she should be *or Am* she be aware of her responsibilities; **je vais être en retard – peu importe** I'm going to be late – no matter *or* it doesn't matter; **tu veux aller au cinéma ou au restaurant? – peu importe** do you want to go to the cinema or to the restaurant? – I don't mind; **peu importe que le voile soit blanc ou écru** it doesn't matter much whether the veil is white or beige; **peu m'importe** I don't mind, it's all the same to me; **peu m'importe qu'il vienne ou pas** it doesn't matter to me whether he comes or not; **peu m'importe le temps que ça prendra** I don't mind *or* care how long it takes; **peu importe le prix** the price isn't important *or* doesn't matter; **qu'importe?** what does it *or* that matter?; **qu'importe qu'il vienne ou non?** what does it matter whether he comes or not?; **que m'importe?** what do I care? **3 faire qch n'importe où/quand** to do sth no matter where/when, to do sth anywhere/ (at) any time; **tu l'as fait n'importe comment** you did it any old how; *Fam* **n'importe comment, c'est trop tard** anyway, it's too late; **tu peux venir n'importe quand** you can come at any time, you can come when you like, it doesn't matter when you come; **mets-le n'importe où** put it anywhere *or* wherever you like; **tu arrives n'importe quand et tu t'attends à ce que je sois là** you arrive at all hours *or* no matter when and expect to find me here; **n'importe** never mind; **le vert ou le bleu? – n'importe** the green or the blue? – either *or* it doesn't matter; **n'importe quel gamin aurait pu faire ce travail** any child could have done the work; **n'importe quelle autre personne** anybody else; **venez n'importe quel jour** come any day; **donnez-moi n'importe lequel** give me any of them, give me whichever you like; **n'importe qui** anybody, no matter who; **n'importe qui d'autre aurait compris** anybody else would have understood; **n'importe qui réagirait de la même manière** anyone would have the same reaction; **coucher avec n'importe qui** to sleep around; **je ne suis pas n'importe qui, je suis ta femme** I'm not just anybody, I'm your wife; *Fam* **ce n'est pas n'importe qui** he isn't just anybody; **n'importe quoi** anything (at all); **elle ferait n'importe quoi pour avoir le poste** she would do anything *or* no matter what to get the job; *Péj* **il dit n'importe quoi!** he's talking nonsense!; *Fam* **n'importe quoi!** nonsense!, rubbish!

import-export **NM** *Com* import-export (business); **il fait de l'i.** he works in the import-export business

importun, -une [ɛ̃pɔʀtœ̃, -yn] *Fml* **ADJ** *(personne)* troublesome, tiresome, *Fml* importunate; *(visiteur)* unwelcome; *(arrivée,*

remarque) ill-timed; *(question)* tiresome; **je crains de vous être i.** I'm afraid I'm disturbing you

N *(personne)* nuisance; **les importuns de son espèce** tiresome people like him

importunément [ɛ̃pɔʀtynemɑ̃] **ADV** *Fml* importunately

importuner [ɛ̃pɔʀtyne] **vt** *(ennuyer)* to bother, to pester, to badger; *(déranger)* to disturb, to trouble, to inconvenience; **ses questions m'importunent au plus haut point** I find his questions extremely annoying; **j'espère que je ne vous importune pas** I hope I'm not disturbing you; **la fumée/la musique m'importune** the smoke/the music bothers me

importunité [ɛ̃pɔʀtynite] **NF** *Fml* importunity

imposable [ɛ̃pozabl] **ADJ** *(personne, revenu)* taxable; *(propriété)* rateable, assessable

imposant [ɛ̃pozɑ̃] **ADJ** *(figure, cérémonie)* imposing; *(personne)* commanding, stately, dignified; **d'une stature imposante** of imposing stature; **une imposante majorité** an impressive majority

imposé [ɛ̃poze] **ADJ 1** *Sport* **figures imposées** compulsory figures; *Com* **prix i.** fixed price **2** *Admin (personne)* taxed

imposer [ɛ̃poze] **vt 1** *(une punition, un travail etc)* to impose; *(tâche)* to set; **i. des conditions** to impose *or* dictate conditions; **le règlement nous impose le secret absolu** the rules compel us to absolute secrecy; **i. une règle** to lay down a rule; **i. (le) silence à qn** to impose silence on sb; **elle veut toujours i. ses caprices à tout le monde** she always wants to force her whims on everyone; **i. sa présence à qn** to impose *or* force one's presence on sb; **i. sa manière de voir les choses à qn** to force one's opinions on sb; **cela nous a été imposé par les circonstances** it was forced on us by circumstances; **il a imposé son chouchou dans le service** he foisted his favourite on the department; **i. sa loi** to lay down the law; **i. le respect** to command *or* compel respect; **i. un blocage des prix** to impose a price freeze **2** *Admin (soumettre à l'impôt) (personne, objet)* to tax; **i. des droits sur qch** to impose *or* put a tax on sth, to tax sth; **être lourdement imposé** to be heavily taxed; **i. un immeuble** to levy a rate on *or* to assess a building **3** *Typ (feuille)* to impose **4** *Rel (mains)* to lay on **vi en i.** to command *or* inspire respect, to be awe-inspiring; **en i. à qn** to impress sb **VPR s'imposer 1** *(faire reconnaître sa valeur)* to assert oneself; **elle s'est imposée par sa compétence** she made a name for herself through sheer ability; **le coureur kenyan s'est imposé sans difficulté dans le 110 m haies** the Kenyan runner easily dominated the 110m hurdles; **la joueuse espagnole s'est imposée face à la Japonaise en 2 sets** the Spanish player powered her way past the Japanese player in straight sets; **il s'est imposé comme le meilleur boxeur de sa génération** he has stood out *or* made a name for himself as the best boxer of his generation; **le libéralisme économique s'impose comme la seule doctrine viable** free enterprise stands out as the only viable doctrine **2** *(déranger)* **je ne voulais pas m'i.** I didn't want to impose; **s'i. à qn** to foist *or* thrust *or* force oneself on sb; *(importuner)* to impose on sb **3** *(être nécessaire)* to be essential; **la discrétion s'impose** discretion is imperative *or* essential; **prendre les mesures qui s'imposent** to take the necessary steps; **s'i. à l'attention** to command attention; **la conviction s'impo-**

sa à mon esprit que … the conviction forced itself upon me that …; **une visite au Louvre s'impose** you/we/*etc* must visit the Louvre, *Fam* a visit to the Louvre is a must; *Hum* **cette gifle ne s'imposait peut-être pas** that slap was perhaps not called for; **cette solution/ décoration s'est imposée d'elle-même** it seemed the obvious solution/style of decoration, the solution/decor suggested itself **4** *(se contraindre)* **s'i. un labeur** to set oneself a task; **s'i. un sacrifice** to force oneself to make a sacrifice; **s'i. de faire qch** to make it a rule to do sth; **s'i. un régime sévère** to follow a strict diet; **elle s'impose plusieurs heures de sport par jour/de travailler huit heures par jour** she makes it a rule to do several hours sport a day/to work eight hours a day

imposition [ɛ̃pozisjɔ̃] **NF 1** *Fin* taxation; **avis d'i.** notice of assessment; **avis de non-i.** notice of exemption; **tranche d'i.** tax bracket; **double i.** double taxation; **i. à la source** taxation at source; **i. en cascade** cascade taxation; **i. des entreprises** business taxation; **i. forfaitaire** basic-rate taxation **2** *Typ* imposing, imposition; **i. en demi-feuille** work and turn **3** *Rel* **i. des mains** laying on of hands

impossibilité [ɛ̃pɔsibilite] **NF** impossibility; **être** *ou* **se trouver dans l'i. de faire qch** to find it impossible to do sth; **je suis dans l'i. de quitter mon lit** I can't get out of bed; **vu l'i. dans laquelle je me trouve de vous téléphoner** since I am unable to contact you by telephone; **en cas d'i.** if that is not possible

impossible [ɛ̃pɔsibl] **ADJ 1** *(irréalisable)* impossible; **i. à déchiffrer** impossible to decipher; **c'est i. à faire** it can't be done, it's impossible; **il est i. qu'il revienne avant lundi** he can't possibly be back before Monday; **il est i. de croire ce qu'il dit** you can't believe what he says; **c'est matériellement i.** it's (physically) impossible; **la résolution du problème est i.** it is impossible to solve the problem, the problem cannot be solved; **cela m'est i.** it's not possible for me, I can't (possibly); **il m'est i. de le faire** I can't (possibly) do it, it's impossible for me to do it; **il n'est pas i. que je vous rende visite** you might well get a visit from me, a visit from me is not out of the question; **est-ce que tu vas venir? – ce n'est pas i.** are you going to come? – it's not impossible; **i. n'est pas français** there's no such word as can't **2** *(insupportable) (situation)* intolerable, impossible; **il a fallu nous lever à une heure i.** we had to get up at an unearthly *or* a ridiculous hour; **avoir des horaires impossibles** to work ridiculous hours; **vous lui rendez la vie i.** you're making life impossible for him, you're making his life a misery; **tu es i.!** you're impossible! **3** *(farfelu)*, *Fam (chapeau etc)* extravagant, absurd, ridiculous; **encore une de tes histoires impossibles!** another one of your incredible *or* ridiculous stories!

NM 1 l'i. the impossible; **tenter l'i.** to attempt the impossible; **il a fait l'i. pour nous secourir** he did his utmost *or* did everything possible to help us; *Prov* **à l'i. nul n'est tenu** you can't do the impossible **2 si par i. il est encore vivant** if, by some remote chance *or* some miracle, he is still alive

imposte [ɛ̃pɔst] **NF** *Archit* **1** impost; *(d'arcade)* springer **2** *(fenêtre)* fanlight, *Am* transom (window)

imposteur [ɛ̃pɔstœʀ] **NM** impostor

imposture [ɛ̃pɔstyʀ] **NF** imposture; **c'est une i.!** he's/she's an impostor!; **rendu célèbre par ses impostures** famed as an impostor

impôt [ɛ̃po] **NM** tax; *(taxes)* taxes, taxation; **je ne paie pas d'impôts** I don't pay any tax;

déductible des impôts tax deductible; **payer mille euros d'impôts** to pay a thousand euros in tax(es); **déclaration d'impôts** income tax form *or* statement *or* return; **faire sa déclaration d'impôts** to fill out one's income tax form, *Fam* to do one's taxes; **frapper qch d'un i.** to tax sth, to put a tax on sth; *Fam* **les impôts m'ont envoyé une lettre** the taxman *or Am* IRS has sent me a letter; *Fam* **il faut que j'aille aux impôts** I have to see the taxman *or Am* go to the IRS; **i. retenu à la source** tax deducted at source, ≃ pay as you earn, PAYE, *Am* ≃ pay as you go ► ► **i. sur les bénéfices** corporation tax; **i. de Bourse** transaction tax; **i. sur le capital** capital tax; **i. sur le chiffre d'affaires** turnover tax, sales tax; **i. à la consommation** output tax; **i. dégressif** sliding scale taxation, degressive taxation; **i. déguisé** hidden tax; **i. différé** differed taxation; **i. direct** direct tax; **i. sur les dividendes** dividend tax; **i. sur les donations et les successions** gift and inheritance tax; **i. extraordinaire** emergency tax; **i. foncier** land *or* property tax; **i. sur les gains exceptionnels** windfall tax; *Anciennement* **i. sur les grandes fortunes** wealth tax; **i. sur l'hôtellerie** hotel tax; **i. indirect** indirect tax; **impôts locaux** local taxes, *Br* ≃ council tax; **i. sur la masse salariale** payroll tax; **i. sur les plus-values** capital gains tax; **i. progressif** graduated income tax; **i. sur le revenu** income tax; **i. sur les sociétés** corporation tax; **i. de solidarité sur la fortune** wealth tax; **i. sur les traitements et salaires** tax on wages and salaries; **i. sur le transfert des capitaux** capital transfer tax

---

Impôts locaux

These are taxes levied to finance local, departmental or regional government. The best-known are the "taxe d'habitation" (paid by rent-paying tenants), the "taxe foncière" (paid by homeowners) and the "taxe professionnelle" (paid by the self-employed). The rate of each tax is decided at local level.

---

impotence [ɛ̃pɔtɑ̃s] NF disability; *(causée par la vieillesse)* infirmity

impotent, -ente [ɛ̃pɔtɑ̃, -ɑ̃t] ADJ crippled **N** disabled person, cripple

---

Il faut noter que l'adjectif anglais **impotent** est un faux ami. Il signifie **impuissant**.

---

impraticabilité [ɛ̃pratikabilite] NF impracticability

impraticable [ɛ̃pratikabl] ADJ **1** *(où l'on ne peut pas passer)* impassable; **chemin i. aux** *ou* **pour les automobiles** road unfit for motor vehicles **2** *Sport (terrain)* unplayable, unfit for play; **annulé pour cause de terrain i.** cancelled because of the state of the pitch **3** *(irréalisable)* impractical

imprécateur, -trice [ɛ̃prekatœr, -tris] N doomsayer

imprécation [ɛ̃prekasjɔ̃] NF *Litt* curse, oath, *Fml* imprecation

imprécatoire [ɛ̃prekatwar] ADJ *Litt* imprecatory

imprécis [ɛ̃presi] ADJ **1** *(vague) (témoignage, proposition, rapport, contours)* vague, imprecise, indefinite; *(souvenir)* vague **2** *(tir, balance)* inaccurate

imprécision [ɛ̃presizjɔ̃] NF **1** *(caractère vague)* imprecision; *(d'un témoignage, souvenir, rapport)* vagueness; *(de contours)* lack of definition **2** *(de tir, d'une balance)* inaccuracy

imprégnation [ɛ̃preɲasjɔ̃] NF impregnation, permeation; **i. alcoolique** blood alcohol content

imprégner [ɛ̃preɲe] *(j'imprègne; j'imprégnerai)* VT to impregnate, to permeate *(de* with); *Fig* **imprégné de préjugés** full of prejudice; **ses vêtements sont imprégnés de l'odeur de fumée** his clothes stink of smoke; **leur famille est imprégnée des idées du grand-père** the grandfather's ideas have been imprinted on the family ▶ VPR **s'imprégner** to become impregnated *or* permeated *(de* with); **s'i. d'eau** to be saturated *or* soaked with water; *Fig* **s'i. d'un auteur** to immerse oneself in an author

imprenable [ɛ̃prɑ̃abl] ADJ impregnable; **vue i.** unobstructed view *(* sur of)

impréparation [ɛ̃preparasjɔ̃] NF unpreparedness

impresario [ɛ̃presarjo] NM manager

imprescriptibilité [ɛ̃preskriptibilite] NF *Jur* imprescriptibility, indefeasibility

imprescriptible [ɛ̃preskriptibl] ADJ *Jur* imprescriptible, indefeasible

impression [ɛ̃presjɔ̃] NF **1** *(sensation)* impression; **il nous a donné l'i. que ...** he gave us the impression that ...; **elle nous donne** *ou* **nous fait l'i. de** *ou* **d'être quelqu'un d'intelligent** she gives us the impression that she is intelligent; **il me donne** *ou* **fait l'i. d'être heureux** he seems happy to me; **il donne toujours l'i. d'être ailleurs** he always gives the impression that he's miles away; **faire i.** to make an impression, to be impressive; **il ne fait pas assez i.** he doesn't make enough of an impression, he's not impressive enough; **faire forte i.** to have *or* make a strong impression; **faire bonne/mauvaise i. (sur qn)** to make a good/bad impression (on sb); **c'est quelqu'un de très sympathique mais qui fait mauvaise i.** he's extremely nice but he gives people the wrong impression; **pour faire bonne i. chez mes parents** to make a good impression on my parents, to impress my parents; **il ne m'a pas fait une grande i.** he did not make a great impression on me; **elle m'a fait une i. favorable** she made a favourable impression on me, she impressed me favourably; **ça fait une drôle d'i. de s'entendre parler** it's a funny feeling, hearing yourself speak; **j'ai l'i. de l'avoir déjà vue** *ou* **que je l'ai déjà vue** I've an idea *or* a feeling that I've seen her before; **j'ai l'i. qu'elle est assez timide** I have the impression that *or* my impression of her is that she's rather shy; **l'i. que j'ai d'elle n'est pas excellente** I do not have an excellent opinion of her; **quelles sont vos impressions?** what are your impressions? **2** *(action d'imprimer), Typ, Tex* printing; *(copie)* printout, computer printout; **livre à l'i.** book in (the) *or* at press; **envoyer un manuscrit à l'i.** to send a manuscript off to press *or* the printer; **faute d'i.** misprint; **troisième i. d'un livre** third impression *or* printing of a book; **i. en bichromie** two-colour *or Am* two-color printing; **i. en colonnes** column printing; **i. en couleurs** colour *or Am* color printing; *Phot* **double i.** double exposure; *Ordinat* **i. rapide** draft; *Typ* **i. continue** web-offset printing; **i. en arrière-plan** background (mode) printing, spooling; **i. en relief** relief printing; **i. sans presse** plateless printing; **i. tremblée** slurring; **i. verso** backing up; *Ordinat* **i. en continu** continuous printout; **i. en deux couleurs** two-colour printing; **i. laser** laser printing; *(copie)* laser printout; **i. proportionnelle** proportional printing; *Ordinat* **i. en quadrichomie** four-colour; **i. en qualité brouillon** draft quality printing; *(copie)* draft printout; **i. recto-verso** double-sided printing; *Ordinat* **i. écran** screen dump; **i. jet d'encre** ink-jet printing; *(copie)* ink-jet printout **3** *(image)* print; **i. en couleurs** colour print

4 *(première couche de peinture)* primer, undercoat **5** *(motif)* **tissu à impressions florales** material with a flower pattern *or* print **6** *Vieilli (sur cire, sol etc)* impression, imprint; **i. de pas** footprint

impressionnabilité [ɛ̃presjɔnabilite] NF **1** *(sensibilité)* impressionability **2** *Phot* sensitivity

impressionnable [ɛ̃presjɔnabl] ADJ **1** *(sensible)* easily upset **2** *Phot (plaque etc)* sensitive

---

Il faut noter que l'adjectif anglais **impressionable** est un faux ami. Il signifie **influençable**.

---

impressionnant [ɛ̃presjɔnɑ̃] ADJ impressive; **tout ce sang partout était très i.** the sight of all that blood was extremely disturbing

impressionner [ɛ̃presjɔne] VT **1** *(frapper, bouleverser)* to impress, to make an impression on; *(d'une mauvaise nouvelle, d'un accident)* to upset; **ils ont été très impressionnés par les trapézistes** they were very impressed by *or* with the trapeze artists; **il ne faut pas se laisser i.** don't let yourself be overawed; **vision** *ou* **vue qui impressionne** impressive sight; **j'ai été très impressionné** it/ he/etc made a strong impression on me **2** *Opt (rétine)* to act on; *Phot (papier sensibilisé etc)* to produce an image on; *(film)* to expose

impressionnisme [ɛ̃presjɔnism] NM *Beaux-Arts* impressionism

impressionniste [ɛ̃presjɔnist] *Beaux-Arts* ADJ impressionist(ic) **N** impressionist

imprévisibilité [ɛ̃previzibilite] NF unpredictability; **elle est d'une telle i. que ...** she is so unpredictable that ...

imprévisible [ɛ̃previzibl] ADJ *(temps, réaction, personne)* unpredictable; *(événement, circonstances)* unforeseeable; **ce qu'il aime surtout chez elle, c'est son caractère i.** what he especially likes about her is her unpredictability *or* is that she's unpredictable

imprévoyance [ɛ̃prevwajɑ̃s] NF lack of foresight, improvidence

imprévoyant [ɛ̃prevwajɑ̃] ADJ lacking in foresight, improvident

imprévu [ɛ̃prevy] ADJ unexpected, unforeseen; **leur arrivée était tout à fait imprévue** they arrived quite unexpectedly **NM 1** *(caractère) (d'événement)* unexpectedness; **elle aime l'i.** she likes the unexpected **2** *(incident)* unexpected *or* unforeseen event; **sauf i., à moins d'un i.** barring accidents, unless something unforeseen *or* unexpected happens; **en cas d'i.** in (case of) an emergency; **en cas d'i., on se retrouve à la répétition** if something crops up *or* failing that, we'll see each other at the rehearsal

imprimable [ɛ̃primabl] ADJ printable

imprimante [ɛ̃primɑ̃t] NF printer; **i. à aiguilles** dot matrix printer; **i. 24 aiguilles** 24-pin printer; **i. à bulles (d'encre)** bubble-jet printer; **i. à chaîne** chain printer; **i. couleur** *ou Am* color printer; **i. feuille à feuille** sheet-fed printer; **i. à grand chariot** wide carriage printer; **i. graphique** graphics printer; **i. à impact** impact printer; **i. à jet d'encre** ink-jet printer; **i. (à) laser** laser printer; **i. ligne, i. par lignes** line printer; **i. à marguerite** daisywheel (printer); **i. page par page** page printer; **i. par pages** page printer; **i. par points** *ou* **matricielle** dot matrix (printer); **i. parallèle** parallel printer; **i. à petit chariot** narrow carriage printer; **i. par points** dot matrix printer; **i. de qualité courrier** letter quality printer, LQ printer; **i. sans impact**

non-impact printer; **i. série** serial printer; **i. (à transfert) thermique** thermal (transfer) printer

imprimatur [ɛ̃primatyr] NM INV imprimatur

imprimé [ɛ̃prime] ADJ printed; **tissu i.** printed fabric, print; *Électron* **circuit i.** printed circuit

NM **1** *(formulaire)* form; **imprimés** *(journaux etc)* printed matter; **département/catalogue des imprimés** *(dans une bibliothèque)* department/catalogue of printed books; **i. fiscal** tax return; **i. sans adresse** mailshot; **i. publicitaire** advertising leaflet, publicity handout **2** *Ordinat* **i. ligne par ligne** line printout **3** *Tex* print; **un i. à fleurs/à motifs géométriques** a flower/geometric print

imprimer [ɛ̃prime] VT **1** *(marquer)* to (im)print, to impress, to stamp; *Tex (tissu)* to print; *Fig* **un moment imprimé dans mon cœur/ma mémoire** a moment imprinted *or* stamped *or* engraved on my heart/in my memory **2** *Typ (livre)* to print; *Ordinat* to print (off), to print (out); **i. en offset** to offset; **i. en retiration, i. au verso** to back up, to perfect; **i. en surcharge** to overprint; *Ordinat* **i. un écran** to do a print screen; **presse à i.** printing press **3** *(direction)* to communicate; **i. un mouvement à un corps** to impart *or* transmit motion to a body

imprimerie [ɛ̃primri] NF **1** *(technique)* (art of) printing **2** *(atelier, usine)* printing house, printing works, (printing) press; **l'Imprimerie nationale** *Br* ≃ HMSO (Her Majesty's Stationery Office), *Am* ≃ Government Printing Office; **i. intégrée** in-house printing office

imprimeur [ɛ̃primœr] NM printer; **i.-éditeur** printer and publisher

impro [ɛ̃pro] NF *Fam (abrév* **improvisation)** improvisation

improbabilité [ɛ̃prɔbabilite] NF improbability

improbable [ɛ̃prɔbabl] ADJ improbable, unlikely; **son retour est très i.** he/she is very unlikely to come back, it's very improbable that he/she will come back; **dans le cas, très i., où …** in the very unlikely event that …

improbité [ɛ̃prɔbite] NF *Litt* dishonesty, lack of integrity

improductif, -ive [ɛ̃prɔdyktif, -iv] ADJ unproductive; *(capital)* non-productive, idle

N administrative employee *(as opposed to one working on the production side)*; **les improductifs** *(d'une compagnie)* the administrative staff, management; *(d'une nation)* the unwaged

improductivité [ɛ̃prɔdyktivite] NF unproductiveness

impromptu [ɛ̃prɔ̃pty] ADJ *(départ, arrivée, visite, réflexion)* impromptu, unexpected; *(repas)* impromptu; *(discours)* impromptu, off the cuff, *Fml* extempore; **il a fait une arrivée impromptue** he turned up unexpectedly; **sa réflexion était si impromptue qu'elle a laissé tout le monde sans voix** the remark was so unexpected that it left everyone speechless; **je vais lui faire une visite impromptue un de ces jours** I'll drop in on him unannounced one of these days

ADV *(parler)* off the cuff, impromptu; *(répondre)* off the cuff; **elle est venue i. hier soir** she turned up unexpectedly last night

NM *Théâtre, Mus* impromptu

imprononçable [ɛ̃prɔnɔ̃sabl] ADJ unpronounceable

impropre [ɛ̃prɔpr] ADJ **1** *(terme)* inappropriate, incorrect **2 i. à qch** unfit *or* unsuitable for sth; **i. à la consommation** unfit for human consumption

improprement [ɛ̃prɔprǝmɑ̃] ADV improperly, incorrectly

impropriété [ɛ̃prɔprijete] NF **1** *(mot)* inap-

propriate *or* incorrect term **2** *(caractère)* inappropriateness, incorrectness

improuvable [ɛ̃pruvabl] ADJ unprovable

improvisateur, -trice [ɛ̃prɔvizatœr, -tris] N improviser; **avoir un talent d'i.** to have a talent for improvising

improvisation [ɛ̃prɔvizasjɔ̃] NF improvisation; *(remarque, trait d'esprit)* ad-lib; **en cuisine, elle adore l'i.** she loves to improvise in the kitchen; **i. sur un thème** improvisation on a theme; **faire une i.** to improvise; **être doué pour l'i.** to be good at improvising; *(d'un comique)* to be good at ad-libbing

improvisé [ɛ̃prɔvize] ADJ *(discours, remarque)* improvised, off-the-cuff; *(sketch, siège)* improvised; *Sport (équipe)* scratch; **nous avons fait un barbecue i.** we had an impromptu barbecue

improviser [ɛ̃prɔvize] VT to improvise; **i. un discours** to make an impromptu speech, to speak off the cuff, to ad-lib; **je dus m'i. infirmière pour la circonstance** I had to act as nurse

VI to improvise; *(de comique)* to ad-lib; **i. à l'orgue** to improvise on the organ

VPR **s'improviser l'organisation, ça ne s'improvise pas** organization isn't something you can improvise; **on ne s'improvise pas danseur étoile comme ça** you don't just become a principal dancer overnight

improviste (à l') [alɛ̃prɔvist] ADV unexpectedly, without any warning; **prendre qn à l'i.** to take *or* catch sb unawares *or* by surprise; **visite à l'i.** surprise visit

imprudemment [ɛ̃prydamɑ̃] ADV imprudently, rashly, unwisely; *(conduire)* recklessly

imprudence [ɛ̃prydɑ̃s] NF **1** *(caractère)* imprudence, foolhardiness, rashness, recklessness; *Jur* **homicide par i.** = manslaughter **2** *(action)* **commettre une i.** to act rashly *or* imprudently; **j'ai peur qu'il fasse une i.** I'm afraid he may do something rash; **(ne fais) pas d'imprudences** don't do anything rash

imprudent, -ente [ɛ̃prydɑ̃, -ɑ̃t] ADJ imprudent, foolhardy, rash, reckless; **il serait très i. de la laisser partir seule** it would be very unwise to let her go off on her own; **c'est un peu i. de ne pas mettre sa ceinture de sécurité** it's rather unwise not to wear a safety belt

N imprudent *or* rash *or* reckless person

impubère [ɛ̃pybɛr] ADJ impubescent

N *Jur* impubescent minor

impubliable [ɛ̃pyblijabl] ADJ unpublishable

impudemment [ɛ̃pydamɑ̃] ADV impudently; *(avec cynisme)* brazenly, shamelessly; **il ment i.** he's a brazen *or* shameless liar

impudence [ɛ̃pydɑ̃s] NF **1** *(caractère)* impudence; *(effronterie)* effrontery; *(cynisme)* shamelessness; **quelle i.!** what impudence!; **il est d'une telle i. que …** he is so impudent that …; **il n'aura pas l'i. de revenir** he won't have the impudence *or* be impudent enough to come back **2** *(action, parole)* impudent action/remark

impudent [ɛ̃pydɑ̃] ADJ impudent, *(cynique)* shameless, brazen

impudeur [ɛ̃pydœr] NF shamelessness, immodesty

impudicité [ɛ̃pydisite] NF shamelessness; *(obscénité)* lewdness

impudique [ɛ̃pydik] ADJ shameless, *(obscène)* lewd

impudiquement [ɛ̃pydikmɑ̃] ADV shamelessly; *(d'une manière obscène)* lewdly

impuissance [ɛ̃pɥisɑ̃s] NF **1** *(incapacité)* powerlessness, helplessness, impotence; **i.**

à faire qch powerlessness *or* inability to do sth; **il leva les bras au ciel en un geste d'i.** in a gesture of helplessness, he raised his arms to the heavens **2** *Méd* impotence

impuissant [ɛ̃pɥisɑ̃] ADJ **1** *(incapable)* powerless, helpless, impotent; **i. devant sa douleur** powerless *or* helpless in the face of his pain; **i. à faire qch** powerless *or* unable to do sth **2** *Méd* impotent

NM *Méd* impotent man

impulsif, -ive [ɛ̃pylsif, -iv] ADJ impulsive

N person who acts on impulse; **c'est une impulsive** she's impulsive

impulsion [ɛ̃pylsjɔ̃] NF **1** *(influence)* impulse; **faire qch sous l'i. de la colère/de l'enthousiasme** to do sth in a fit of anger/enthusiasm **2** *(élan)* impulse, impetus, boost; **donner de l'i. au commerce** to give a boost to trade; **les affaires ont reçu une nouvelle i.** business has received fresh impetus *or* shows renewed activity **3** *Tech* impulse; **force d'i.** impulsive force; *Élec* **i. de courant** current impulse; **radar à impulsions** pulse radar; **i. électrique** electrical impulse

impulsivité [ɛ̃pylsivite] NF impulsiveness

impunément [ɛ̃pynemɑ̃] ADV with impunity; **tu ne crois tout de même pas qu'on va te laisser faire tes bêtises i.** I hope you don't think you're going to get away with being so stupid

impuni [ɛ̃pyni] ADJ unpunished

impunité [ɛ̃pynite] NF impunity; **agir en toute i.** to act with impunity

impur [ɛ̃pyr] ADJ impure; *(personne)* (morally) impure; *Rel (viande)* unclean

impureté [ɛ̃pyrte] NF **1** *(état)* impurity; *(d'une personne)* (moral) impurity; *Rel* uncleanness **2 impuretés** *(saletés)* impurities

imputabilité [ɛ̃pytabilite] NF imputability

imputable [ɛ̃pytabl] ADJ **1** attributable, ascribable, imputable (**à** to); **erreur i. à la distraction** mistake attributable to *or* caused by absent-mindedness; **cet accident ne m'est pas i.** I cannot be held responsible for the accident **2** *Fin* chargeable; **frais imputables sur un compte** expenses chargeable to an account

imputation [ɛ̃pytasjɔ̃] NF **1** *(accusation)* charge, imputation **2** *Com (des dépenses etc)* charge, charging; *Fin* **i. à charge to**; **i. d'une somme au crédit/débit d'un compte** crediting/debiting an amount to an account; **i. des charges** cost allocation

imputer [ɛ̃pyte] VT **1** *(crime etc)* to ascribe, to attribute (**à** to); **ils ont imputé cette erreur à son ignorance** they attributed the mistake to *or* put the mistake down to his ignorance **2** *Com* **i. des frais sur un compte** to charge expenses to an account

imputrescibilité [ɛ̃pytresibilite] NF **l'i. du bois/du plastique fait que …** the fact that the wood/plastic does not rot means …

imputrescible [ɛ̃pytresibl] ADJ which is not subject to rot

in [in] ADJ INV *Fam* in; **l'endroit le plus in de Paris** the most in spot in Paris; **être in** to be in

INA [ina] NM *(abrév* **Institut national de l'audiovisuel)** = French national television archive

inabordable [inabɔrdabl] ADJ *(endroit)* unapproachable, inaccessible; *(prix)* unaffordable; *(fruits, légumes etc)* overpriced; *Vieilli (personne)* unapproachable

inabrogeable [inabrɔʒabl] ADJ *Jur* unrepealable

inaccentué [inaksɑ̃tɥe] ADJ *(voyelle)* unaccented; *(syllabe)* unstressed

inacceptable [inaksɛptabl] ADJ unacceptable; *(conduite, méthodes)* unacceptable, objectionable

inaccessibilité [inaksesibilite] NF inaccessibility

inaccessible [inaksesibl] ADJ 1 *(inabordable)* inaccessible; **ils vivent dans un coin i.** they live in an out-of-the-way place; **se fixer un objectif i.** to set oneself an unattainable goal; **i. au grand public** *(livre)* not accessible to the general public 2 *(personne)* unapproachable 3 **i. à la pitié** incapable of pity; **i. à la flatterie** impervious to flattery

inaccompli [inakɔ̃pli] ADJ *Litt (tâche)* unaccomplished; *(rêve, vœu)* unfulfilled

inaccoutumé [inakutyme] ADJ 1 *(inhabituel)* unusual 2 *Litt (pas habitué)* unaccustomed, unused (**à** to)

inachevé [inaʃ(ə)ve] ADJ unfinished, uncompleted

inachèvement [inaʃɛvmɑ̃] NM incompletion

inacquitté [inakite] ADJ *Fin (effet)* unreceipted

inactif, -ive [inaktif, -iv] ADJ *(personne)* inactive, idle; *(fonds)* unemployed, idle; *Écon* **la population inactive** the non-working population; *Com* **marché i.** sluggish *or* slack market
▸ N *Écon* **un i.** a person without paid employment; **les inactifs** the non-working population

inaction [inaksjɔ̃] NF inaction, idleness; **c'est l'i. qui est parfois responsable de la délinquance** *(due aux circonstances)* a lack of things to do can be a cause of delinquency; *(due à la paresse)* idleness can be a cause of delinquency; **je ne supporte pas l'i.** I can't bear being idle *or* having nothing to do

inactivité [inaktivite] NF inactivity; *Com (du marché)* sluggishness, slackness; **sa maladie l'a réduit à l'i. pendant plusieurs mois** his illness put him out of action for several months; **j'ai été forcée à l'i. à cause de mon accident** I've had to give up all forms of activity *or* give up doing anything active since I had my accident; **elle ne supporte pas l'i.** she can't bear being idle *or* having nothing to do; **période d'i.** period of inactivity; *Com* dead period; **en i.** *Admin* (temporarily) unemployed; *Mil* not on the active list

inadaptation [inadaptasjɔ̃] NF *(sociale)* maladjustment; *(physique, mentale)* handicap; **i. familiale/scolaire** inability to adjust to family life/school

inadapté, -ée [inadapte] ADJ *(personne)* (*socialement*) maladjusted; *(physiquement, mentalement)* handicapped; *(matériel)* unsuitable; **l'enfance inadaptée** children with special needs; **matériel i. à ses besoins** equipment unsuited to *or* unsuitable for one's needs
▸ N *(socialement)* maladjusted person; *(physiquement, mentalement)* handicapped person; **les inadaptés** the maladjusted/the handicapped

inadéquat [inadekwa] ADJ *(insuffisant)* inadequate; *(mal adapté)* unsuitable

inadéquation [inadekwasjɔ̃] NF *(inadaptation)* unsuitability; *(insuffisance)* inadequacy; **étant donné l'i. des moyens au problème** since the means are not suited *or* are unsuited to the problem

inadmissibilité [inadmisibilite] NF inadmissibility

inadmissible [inadmisibl] ADJ *(attitude, négligence, erreur)* unacceptable, inadmissible; *(demande, proposition)* unacceptable; **il est i. qu'on ne l'ait pas reçu à l'examen** it's unacceptable that they should have failed him

inadvertance [inadvɛrtɑ̃s] NF **par i.** inadvertently, by mistake

inaliénabilité [inaljenabilite] NF *Jur (d'un droit)* inalienability, indefeasibility

inaliénable [inaljenabl] ADJ *Jur (droit)* inalienable, indefeasible

inalliable [inaljabl] ADJ *Métal* that cannot be alloyed, non-alloyable

inaltérabilité [inalterabilite] NF *(d'un matériau, un revêtement)* resistance to deterioration, permanence

inaltérable [inalterabl] ADJ 1 *(métal, revêtement)* that does not deteriorate, permanent; *(couleur)* fast; **i. à l'air/l'eau** unaffected by air/water 2 *Fig (bonne humeur)* unfailing, unvarying; *(espoir)* steadfast, unwavering; *(calme)* unwavering; **sa croyance en sa propre réussite semblait i.** his belief in his own success never seemed to waver *or* seemed steadfast

inaltéré [inaltere] ADJ *(bois, pierre)* unweathered

inamical, -ale, -aux, -ales [inamikal, -o] ADJ unfriendly; **avoir un geste i. envers qn** to act in an unfriendly way towards sb

inamovibilité [inamɔvibilite] NF *Admin* security of tenure; *(d'un juge, magistrat)* irremovability

inamovible [inamɔvibl] ADJ *(four, autoradio)* built-in; *Admin (poste)* held for life; *(juge, magistrat)* holding appointment for life; *Fam* **il est vraiment i.** he's a permanent fixture

inanimé [inanime] ADJ 1 *(matière)* inanimate, lifeless 2 *(personne, corps) (mort)* lifeless; *(inconscient)* motionless; *Fig (marché boursier)* sluggish; **tomber i.** to faint, to fall down in a faint

inanité [inanite] NF *(futilité) (de conversation)* inanity; *(inutilité) (d'effort)* futility; **des conversations d'une i. terrifiante** incredibly inane conversations

inanition [inanisjɔ̃] NF starvation; **tomber d'i.** to faint from hunger; **mourir d'i.** to die of starvation, to starve to death

inapaisable [inapɛzabl] ADJ *(faim)* insatiable; *(soif)* unquenchable; *(chagrin)* unappeasable

inapaisé [inapeze] ADJ *(faim)* unsatiated; *(soif)* unquenched; *(chagrin)* unappeased

inaperçu [inapɛrsy] ADJ **passer i.** to escape notice, to pass unnoticed; *Euph* **cet événement ne passa pas i.** the event did not go unnoticed

inappétence [inapetɑ̃s] NF *Méd (manque d'appétit)* lack of appetite; *(manque de désir)* lack of desire

inapplicable [inaplikabl] ADJ unenforceable

inapplication [inaplikasjɔ̃] NF 1 *(défaut d'application)* **i. d'une loi** failure to put a law into effect 2 *(manque de soin) (d'une personne)* lack of application

inappliqué [inaplike] ADJ 1 *(non mis en service) (méthode, procédé, technique)* not applied; *(loi)* in abeyance 2 *(peu soigneux) (personne)* lacking in application

inappréciable [inapresjabl] ADJ 1 *(impossible à évaluer) (quantité etc)* inappreciable; *(différence etc)* imperceptible 2 *(inestimable) (qualité, avantage, don)* invaluable, priceless, inestimable

inapprécié [inapresje] ADJ unappreciated

inapprivoisable [inaprivwazabl] ADJ untamable

inapproprié [inaprɔprije] ADJ inappropriate; **i. à qch** inappropriate to *ou* unsuitable for sth

inapte [inapt] ADJ 1 *(non apte) (personne)* *(pour raisons médicales)* unfit (**au travail** to work); *(intellectuellement)* unsuited (à to); **i.**

à faire qch incapable of doing sth; **i. à travailler** unfit to work 2 *Mil* unfit *(for military service)*
▸ NMPL *surtout Mil* **les inaptes** the unfit

inaptitude [inaptityd] NF *(intellectuelle)* inaptitude; *(médicale, militaire)* unfitness (**au travail** at work); **son i. à travailler a été prouvée à maintes reprises** it has been proved many times over that he is unfit for *or* to work

inarticulé [inartikyle] ADJ *(difficilement audible) (son, cris)* inarticulate

inassimilable [inasimilabl] ADJ which cannot be assimilated, unassimilable

inassouvi [inasuvi] ADJ *(faim)* unsatiated; *(soif)* unquenched; *(désir)* ungratified, unfulfilled; **ma vengeance est restée inassouvie pendant longtemps** my desire for revenge remained unsatisfied for a long time

inassouvissable [inasuvisabl] ADJ *Litt* insatiable

inattaquable [inatakabl] ADJ *(position, forteresse, tour, argumentation, projet de loi)* unassailable; *(personne)* unassailable, *Fam* untouchable; *(testament)* incontestable; *(preuves)* unimpeachable; *Chimie* **i. par les acides** acid-proof, acid-resisting

inattendu [inatɑ̃dy] ADJ *(visite, réponse, lettre, nouvelle, comportement)* unexpected; *(événement)* unexpected, unforeseen; **ce qui était très i. de leur part** which was very unexpected of them, which I wasn't/we weren't/*etc* expecting at all

inattentif, -ive [inatɑ̃tif, -iv] ADJ inattentive; **il est i. à tout ce qu'on lui dit** he doesn't pay any attention *or* heed to what you say to him; **i. aux conseils** heedless of advice

inattention [inatɑ̃sjɔ̃] NF inattention, carelessness; **faute d'i.** slip, careless mistake; **l'accident est dû à un moment d'i. du conducteur** the accident was due to a lapse of concentration by the driver

inaudible [inodibl] ADJ inaudible

inaugural, -ale, -aux, -ales [inogyral, -o] ADJ *(discours, séance)* inaugural; **voyage i.** maiden voyage

inauguration [inogyrasjɔ̃] NF *(d'une usine, d'un bâtiment, d'une route)* (official) opening, inauguration; *(d'une statue, d'un monument)* unveiling; **discours d'i.** inaugural speech; **depuis l'i. du nouveau tronçon d'autoroute** since the new section of the motorway was opened

inaugurer [inogyre] VT *(édifice, hôpital, route)* to (officially) open, to inaugurate; *(statue, monument)* to unveil; *Fig (nouvelle politique)* to inaugurate; *(époque)* to usher in

inauthenticité [inotɑ̃tisite] NF unauthentic nature

inauthentique [inotɑ̃tik] ADJ *(document)* not authentic, not genuine, unauthentic; *(fait)* incorrect; *(ouvrage)* inaccurate

inavouable [inavwabl] ADJ shameful

inavoué [inavwe] ADJ unconfessed

INC [iɛnse] NM *(abrév* **Institut national de la consommation***)* national consumer institute

inca [ɛ̃ka] ADJ INV Inca
▸ N **I.** Inca

incalculable [ɛ̃kalkylabl] ADJ *(conséquences, risques)* incalculable; **un nombre i. de vieux journaux/de gens** countless old newspapers/people

incandescence [ɛ̃kɑ̃desɑ̃s] NF incandescence; *Élec* **lampe à i.** incandescent lamp

incandescent [ɛ̃kɑ̃desɑ̃] ADJ incandescent; *Fig (imagination)* ardent

incantation [ɛ̃kɑ̃tasjɔ̃] NF incantation

incantatoire [ɛ̃kɑ̃tatwar] ADJ incantatory

incapable [ɛ̃kapabl] **ADJ 1** *(personne)* incapable, incompetent; *Jur* (legally) incompetent **2 être i. de faire qch** to be incapable of doing sth; *(par impossibilité physique)* to be unable to do sth; **i. de mentir/d'en vouloir à qn** incapable of lying/being cross with sb; **elle est i. de se détendre** she is incapable of relaxing, she cannot relax; *Fam* **il est i. de se faire cuire un œuf** he can't boil *or* he's incapable of boiling an egg; **i. de lâcheté/d'honnêteté/de mensonge** incapable of cowardice/of honesty/of lying
N 1 *(personne incompétente)* incompetent **2** *Jur* person who is legally incompetent

incapacité [ɛ̃kapasite] **NF 1** *(incompétence)* *(d'une personne)* incompetence; **i. à faire qch** incapability of doing sth, incapacity to do sth, inability to do sth; **il est dans l'i. de vous répondre** he is incapable of giving *or* unable to give you an answer **2** *(invalidité)* **i. (de travail)** disability; *Admin* **i. permanente** permanent disablement **3** *Jur* (legal) incompetence

incarcération [ɛ̃karserasjɔ̃] **NF** imprisonment, *Fml* incarceration

incarcérer [ɛ̃karsere] **VT** **(j'incarcère; j'incarcérerai)** to imprison, *Fml* to incarcerate; **il a été incarcéré à la prison des Baumettes** he has been sent to Baumettes prison; **il est incarcéré à la prison des Baumettes** he is (being held) in Baumettes prison

incarnat [ɛ̃karna] **ADJ** pinkish red; *Bot* **trèfle i.** red clover
NM *(de l'aurore)* rosy tint; *(du teint)* rosiness

incarnation [ɛ̃karnasjɔ̃] **NF** *Rel, Myth (de personne)* incarnation; *Fig (du mal, de l'honnêteté)* incarnation, embodiment (**de** of)

incarné [ɛ̃karne] **ADJ 1** *Rel* incarnate; *Fig* **la vertu/méchanceté incarnée** virtue/nastiness incarnate *or* personified; **c'est le diable i.!** he's the devil incarnate! **2** *Méd (ongle)* ingrowing

incarner [ɛ̃karne] **VT 1** *Rel* to incarnate; *Fig* to embody, to personify **2** *Théâtre, Cin* **i. qn** *ou* **le rôle de qn** to play (the part of) sb; **il incarne magistralement Hamlet** he is an authoritative Hamlet, he gives an authoritative performance as Hamlet
VPR **s'incarner 1** *Rel* to become incarnate **2** *Méd (d'un ongle)* to become ingrown

incartade [ɛ̃kartad] **NF 1** *(léger écart de conduite)* indiscretion **2** *Équitation (de cheval)* sudden swerve

incassable [ɛ̃kasabl] **ADJ** unbreakable

incendiaire [ɛ̃sɑ̃djɛr] **ADJ** *(bombe)* incendiary; *Fig (discours)* inflammatory
N *(personne)* arsonist, fire raiser

incendie [ɛ̃sɑ̃di] **NM** (outbreak of) fire, *Fml* conflagration; **provoquer un i.** *(d'une personne)* to start a fire; *Jur* to commit arson; *(d'une explosion, un court-circuit etc)* to cause *or* start a fire; **i. de forêt** forest fire; **i. volontaire** *ou* **criminel** arson; **la police pense qu'il s'agit d'un i. volontaire** the police suspect arson; **70% des incendies de forêt sont en fait des incendies volontaires** 70% of forest fires are caused by arson; **le nombre d'incendies volontaires** the number of cases of arson; *Litt* **l'i. du soleil couchant** the blaze of the setting sun

incendié, -ée [ɛ̃sɑ̃dje] **ADJ** *(détruit par les flammes) (villa, ville)* destroyed by fire, burnt to the ground *or* down
N victim of a/the fire

incendier [ɛ̃sɑ̃dje] **VT 1** *(mettre le feu à)* to set on fire, to set fire to; *Litt (le ciel, les nuages)* to set ablaze *or* on fire; *Fig (imagination)* to fire; **toute la ville a été incendiée** *(détruite)* the entire city was burnt down *or* burnt to the ground; **la nouvelle risque d'i. les esprits** the news may well have an in

flammatory effect **2** *Fam (accabler de reproches)* **i. qn** to give sb hell; **se faire i.** to catch hell; **on m'a incendié de reproches** I was bitterly reproached

incertain [ɛ̃sɛrtɛ̃] **ADJ** *(fait, donnée)* uncertain, doubtful; *(résultat)* uncertain; *(temps)* unsettled; *(mémoire)* unreliable; *(personne)* indecisive; *(démarche, pas)* unsteady; **couleur incertaine** indeterminate colour; **d'un âge i.** of uncertain age; **à une date incertaine** *(passée)* at some uncertain date; *(future)* at a date still to be decided *or* specified; **i. de qch** *(d'une personne)* uncertain *or* unsure of *or* about sth; **l'époque où a été écrit ce texte reste incertaine** there is still some uncertainty as to when the text was written; **ma démarche était très incertaine** I was very unsteady (on my feet); **il avançait d'un pas i. en direction de sa mère** he walked unsteadily *or* tottered towards his mother
NM *Fin* variable exchange; **coter l'i.** to quote on the exchange rate

incertitude [ɛ̃sɛrtityd] **NF** *(d'une personne, de l'avenir etc)* uncertainty; *(de caractère)* indecisiveness; **être dans l'i.** to be uncertain *or* in a state of uncertainty *(quant à* about); **nager dans l'i.** to be completely uncertain; **depuis le début de cette affaire, on nage dans l'i.** there has been constant uncertainty since the whole thing started; **il reste encore bien des incertitudes dans cette affaire** there are still a great many uncertainties *or* unresolved questions in the matter; **i. du marché** market uncertainty; **son i. a charmé l'auditoire** his/her timidity charmed the public; **je comprends votre i.** I understand your uncertainty *or* indecision

incessamment [ɛ̃sesamɑ̃] **ADV** *(sans attendre)* immediately, without delay, at once; **elle arrivera i.** she'll be arriving (at) any moment now *or* very shortly *or Am* momentarily; *Hum* **i. sous peu** in the very near future, any moment now

> Il faut noter que l'adverbe anglais **incessantly** est un faux ami. Il signifie uniquement **sans cesse**.

incessant [ɛ̃sesɑ̃] **ADJ** incessant, constant

incessibilité [ɛ̃sesibilite] **NF** *Fin* non-transferability; *Jur* inalienability

incessible [ɛ̃sesibl] **ADJ** *Fin (pension, titre de propriété)* non-transferable, not negotiable; *Jur (droit)* inalienable

inceste [ɛ̃sɛst] **NM** incest

incestueux, -euse [ɛ̃sɛstɥø, -øz] **ADJ** *(personne, relation)* incestuous; **enfant i.** child of an incestuous relationship

inchangé [ɛ̃ʃɑ̃ʒe] **ADJ** *(prix, plan, emploi du temps, situation)* unchanged

inchangeable [ɛ̃ʃɑ̃ʒabl] **ADJ** unchangeable

inchantable [ɛ̃ʃɑ̃tabl] **ADJ** unsingable

inchauffable [ɛ̃ʃofabl] **ADJ** *(pièce, maison, voiture)* impossible to heat

inchavirable [ɛ̃ʃavirabl] **ADJ** *(bateau)* uncapsizable, self-righting

inchoatif, -ive [ɛ̃koatif, -iv] **ADJ, NM** *Ling* inceptive

incidemment [ɛ̃sidamɑ̃] **ADV** *(apprendre une nouvelle)* in passing, incidentally; *(demander qch)* in passing; **il a été i. question du problème des retards** the problem of lateness came up in passing *or* incidentally

> Il faut noter que l'adverbe anglais **incidentally** signifie le plus souvent **à propos** ou **soit dit en passant**.

incidence [ɛ̃sidɑ̃s] **NF 1** *(répercussion)* repercussion; *(impact)* effect, impact; **cette action qu'il pensait sans i.** this action which

he thought would have no repercussions; **quelle i. aura la démission du ministre sur la situation?** what effect *or* impact will the Minister's resignation have on the situation?, how will the Minister's resignation affect the situation?; **i. fiscale** tax implications **2** *Méd (d'une maladie)* incidence **3** *Tech* incidence; *Phys* **angle d'i.** angle of incidence

incident [ɛ̃sidɑ̃] **NM 1** *(événement sans conséquence)* hitch, difficulty; **se dérouler sans i.** to go off without a hitch *or* without incident *or* smoothly; **c'est juste un i.** it's nothing much, it's just a slight mishap **2** *(événement plus grave)* incident; **l'i. est clos** the incident is closed; **i. à la frontière** border incident **3** *Jur* point of law
ADJ 1 *(par hasard) (question, remarque)* incidental **2** *Phys (rayon)* incident
▸ ▸ **i. diplomatique** diplomatic incident; **i. de parcours** minor setback; **i. technique** technical hitch *or* problem

incinérateur [ɛ̃sineratœr] **NM** incinerator

incinération [ɛ̃sinerasjɔ̃] **NF** *(de déchets)* incineration; *(d'une personne)* cremation

incinérer [ɛ̃sinere] **VT** **(j'incinère; j'incinérerai)** *(objets, déchets)* to incinerate; *(personne)* to cremate

incirconcis [ɛ̃sirkɔ̃si] **ADJ** uncircumcised

incise [ɛ̃siz] **NF** *Gram* interpolated clause, incidental clause

inciser [ɛ̃size] **VT** *(gencive)* to incise, to make an incision in; *(abcès, furoncle)* to lance; *(arbre)* to tap *(for resin)*
VI to incise

incisif, -ive [ɛ̃sizif, -iv] **ADJ 1** *(remarque)* incisive, sharp, cutting; *(personne, style)* incisive **2 dent incisive** incisor tooth
NF incisive incisor

incision [ɛ̃sizjɔ̃] **NF 1** *(action) (de gencive)* incision; *(d'un furoncle, d'un abcès)* lancing; *(d'un arbre)* tapping *(for resin)* **2** *(coupure)* incision

incitation [ɛ̃sitasjɔ̃] **NF** *(à la violence, l'émeute)* incitement; *(encouragement)* stimulus, incentive; **i. fiscale** tax incentive; **i. à l'achat** incentive to buy; **i. à la débauche** corruption; **i. de mineurs à la débauche** corruption of minors; **i. à la vente** sales incentive

inciter [ɛ̃site] **VT** to encourage, *Péj* to incite (**qn à faire qch** sb to do sth); **i. au crime** to incite crime; **tu incites tes petits camarades à bavarder** you're encouraging your friends *or* egging your friends on to chatter; **il faut i. les jeunes à travailler** young people must be encouraged *or* given incentives to work; **cette réponse m'incite à la prudence** the answer makes me inclined to be cautious; **son attitude n'incite pas à l'aider** his attitude does not make you inclined to help him

incivil [ɛ̃sivil] **ADJ** *Litt* uncivil, rude

incivilisable [ɛ̃sivilizabl] **ADJ** which cannot be civilized

incivilité [ɛ̃sivilite] **NF** *Litt* **1** *(manque de politesse)* incivility, rudeness **2** *(remarque/action impolie)* rude remark/action

incivique [ɛ̃sivik] **ADJ** *Vieilli* with no sense of civic duty

inclassable [ɛ̃klasabl] **ADJ** unclassifiable; **un film i.** a film that cannot be classified *or* pigeonholed; **elle est vraiment i.** she's in a class all of her own

inclémence [ɛ̃klemɑ̃s] **NF** inclemency

inclément [ɛ̃klemɑ̃] **ADJ** inclement

inclinable [ɛ̃klinabl] **ADJ** *(siège)* reclining; *(table, plan)* tilting

inclinaison [ɛ̃klinɛzɔ̃] **NF** *(de colline)* incline, gradient, slope; *(de ligne)* inclination; *(de toit)* pitch, slant, cant; *(de tête, chapeau)* tilt; *(de bateau)* heel, list; *(de mât)* rake; *(d'ai *guille magnétique)* dip; *(de trajectoire)* angle; **comble à forte/faible i.** high-/low-pitched roof; **degré d'i. d'une courbe** steepness of a curve

▸▸ **i. magnétique** (magnetic) declination, magnetic variation

inclination [ɛ̃klinasjɔ̃] **NF 1** *Fig (tendance naturelle)* inclination, tendency; **suivre ses inclinations** to follow one's inclinations; **montrer de l'i. pour la musique/le français** to show an inclination for music/French; **avoir de l'i. pour qch** to have a liking for sth *or* an inclination for sth; **avoir de l'i. pour la musique** to have an inclination for music, to be musically inclined, *Fml* to have a musical bent; *Vieilli* **mariage d'i.** love match **2** *(du corps)* angle; *(de la tête)* angle, tilt; **on note une légère i. de la tête du personnage central du tableau** the head of the central figure in the painting is slightly tilted *or* is at a slight angle

incliné [ɛ̃kline] **ADJ** *(penché) (poteau, mât)* at an angle *or* slope, sloping; *(plan de travail)* tilted; **la tête inclinée** *(sur le côté)* with one's head (tilted) to one side; *(en avant)* with bowed head; **plan i.** inclined plane; **le poteau est légèrement i.** the stake is at a slight angle; **le mur était i.** the wall sloped

incliner [ɛ̃kline] **VT 1** *(pencher) (poteau, barre, tablette, dossier de siège)* to tilt; *Constr (toit)* to slant, to slope, to cant; *(planche)* to tip up, to tilt; **i. le buste en avant** to bend forward *or* from the waist; **i. la tête** *(en avant)* to bow one's head; *(en signe de salut)* to nod (one's head); *(sur le côté)* to tilt one's head to one side; **il inclina la tête dans ma direction** he nodded in my direction **2** *Fig* **i. qn à faire qch** to incline sb to do sth; **i. qn à la prudence** to incline sb to be cautious, *Fml* to predispose sb to caution; **la vue de tous ces malheureux l'inclinait à la pitié** the sight of all these wretched people inclined him/her towards pity; **j'incline à penser qu'elle a tort** I'm inclined to think she's wrong

VI 1 *(d'un mur etc)* to lean, to slope **2** *(être enclin à)* **i. à la pitié** to be inclined to feel pity; **i. à la modération** to be moderate

VPR s'incliner 1 *(d'un terrain)* to slant, to slope; *(d'un bateau)* to heel (over); *(d'un avion)* to bank **2** *(se pencher) (en avant)* to bend over *or* forward; *(sur le côté)* to bend to one side; *(pour saluer)* to bow *(devant before)*; *Fig* **s'i. devant qn/le génie de qn** to bow down before sb/sb's genius **3** *(se soumettre)* **s'i. devant les arguments de qn** to bow *or* yield to sb's arguments; **j'ai dû m'i.** I had to give in; **s'i. devant son adversaire** to yield to one's opponent, to admit defeat **4** *(être battu) (d'une équipe, d'un club)* to admit defeat, to lose; **s'i. face à** *ou* **devant qn** to be beaten by sb, to lose to sb; **l'équipe de France a dû s'i.** the French team had to admit defeat

inclinomètre [ɛ̃klinɔmɛtr] **NM** *Aviat* inclinometer

inclure [ɛ̃klyr] **VT** *(conj like* **conclure** *except pp* **inclus) 1** *(document, cassette, pièces de dossier)* to enclose **2** *Jur (clause, condition, disposition)* to insert, to include *(à in)*, to add *(à to)*; **l'accord inclut les conditions suivantes** the agreement includes the following conditions

inclus [ɛ̃kly] **ADJ 1** *(compris)* **jusqu'à la page 5 incluse** up to and including page 5; **je serai absente jusqu'à mardi i.** I will be away until Wednesday, *Am* I will be away through Tuesday; **du 7 au 18 i.** from the 7th to the 18th inclusive; **ils seront 35, professeurs i.** there will be 35 of them, including the teachers; **le service est-il i.?** is service included?; *Math*

A est i. dans B A is included in B **2 dent incluse** impacted tooth

inclusif, -ive [ɛ̃klyzif, -iv] **ADJ** *Ling* inclusive

inclusion [ɛ̃klyzjɔ̃] **NF 1** *(fait d'inclure qch)* inclusion, insertion; *(d'un document dans une lettre etc)* enclosure *(dans with)*; **on a décidé l'i. d'un nouveau paragraphe au traité** we decided to add a new clause to the treaty **2** *(objet décoratif)* = flower, shell etc set into plastic and used as paperweight, ornament, jewellery etc **3** *Math* inclusion **4** *(d'une dent)* impacting **5** *Ordinat (de fichier)* insertion

inclusivement [ɛ̃klyzivmɑ̃] **ADV** **du vendredi au mardi i.** from Friday to Tuesday inclusive, *Am* from Friday through Tuesday; **jusqu'au 14 mars i.** up to and including 14th March, *Am* through March 14th

incoercible [ɛ̃kɔɛrsibl] **ADJ** *Litt (toux)* uncontrollable; *(rire)* irrepressible

incognito [ɛ̃kɔɲito] **ADV** *(venir, voyager)* incognito

NM **garder l'i.** to remain incognito

incohérence [ɛ̃kɔerɑ̃s] **NF** *(d'une personne, dans un film, une histoire)* inconsistency; *(d'un discours)* disjointedness, incoherence; *(d'idées)* disjointedness; **le film est plein d'incohérences** the film is full of inconsistencies; **le discours était un tissu d'incohérences** the speech was totally incoherent; **d'une i. ahurissante** dreadfully inconsistent *or* incoherent

incohérent [ɛ̃kɔerɑ̃] **ADJ** *(personne, histoire, attitude)* inconsistent; *(idées, argumentation)* disjointed; *(discours)* incoherent, disjointed; **tenir des propos incohérents** to speak incoherently

incollable [ɛ̃kɔlabl] **ADJ 1** *(riz)* non-stick **2** *Fam* **elle est i. sur la question/en histoire** you can't catch her out on the subject/on history

incolore [ɛ̃kɔlɔr] **ADJ** colourless, *Am* colorless

incomber [ɛ̃kɔ̃be] **VI** *(used only in third person)* **les devoirs qui lui incombent** the duties which fall on him, *Fml* the duties incumbent on him; **la responsabilité incombe à l'auteur** the responsibility lies *or* rests with the author, it is the author's responsibility; **il m'incombe de pourvoir à leurs besoins** it is my duty *or Fml* it is incumbent on me to provide for their needs; **il incombe au gouvernement d'indemniser les sinistrés** the onus is on the government to compensate the victims

incombustibilité [ɛ̃kɔ̃bystibilite] **NF** incombustibility

incombustible [ɛ̃kɔ̃bystibl] **ADJ** incombustible, non-(in)flammable, fireproof

incommensurable [ɛ̃kɔmɑ̃syrabl] **ADJ 1** *(immense) (richesse)* immeasurable; *(rage)* tremendous; **il est d'une bêtise i.** his stupidity knows no bounds **2** *Math* incommensurate, incommensurable *(avec with)*; **racine i.** irrational root

incommensurablement [ɛ̃kɔmɑ̃syrabləmɑ̃] **ADV 1** *(immensément) (riche)* immeasurably; *(bête)* tremendously **2** *Math* incommensurably

incommodant [ɛ̃kɔmɔdɑ̃] **ADJ** *(odeur, promiscuité)* unpleasant, disagreeable; *(bruit)* annoying

incommode [ɛ̃kɔmɔd] **ADJ** *(horaire, arrangement)* inconvenient, awkward; *(situation)* awkward, uncomfortable; *(chaise)* uncomfortable; *(outil)* clumsy, awkward; *(appartement)* inconvenient; *Vieilli (personne)* unwelcome

incommodé [ɛ̃kɔmɔde] **ADJ** *(gêné)* **être i.** to feel unwell *or* off colour; **être i. par la chaleur** to feel *or* be bothered by the heat; **être i. par**

une odeur/un bruit to be bothered by a smell/noise

incommodément [ɛ̃kɔmɔdemɑ̃] **ADV** uncomfortably, awkwardly

incommoder [ɛ̃kɔmɔde] **VT** *(gêner)* to bother

incommodité [ɛ̃kɔmɔdite] **NF** *(d'une situation)* uncomfortableness, awkwardness; *(d'un arrangement, un horaire)* inconvenience, awkwardness; *(d'un appartement)* inconvenience; *(d'un outil)* awkwardness, clumsiness; **en raison de l'i. des horaires** because the timetables are so inconvenient *or* awkward

incommunicabilité [ɛ̃kɔmynikabilite] **NF** *Litt (d'un secret)* strict confidentiality; **l'i. des sentiments est souvent à l'origine de nombreuses incompréhensions** the fact that people don't talk about *or* aren't open about their feelings gives rise to numerous misunderstandings; **nous en étions arrivé à un point d'i. tel que …** we had stopped communicating to the point where …

incommunicable [ɛ̃kɔmynikabl] **ADJ** *(secret)* which cannot be revealed; *(sentiment)* indescribable; **ce que j'ai ressenti est i.** I cannot describe my feelings *or* how I felt

incommutable [ɛ̃kɔmytabl] **ADJ** *Jur (propriété)* non-transferable; *(droit)* indefeasible

incomparable [ɛ̃kɔ̃parabl] **ADJ** *(qualité, cuisinière)* incomparable, beyond compare; **vous sentez la différence? – c'est i.!** do you feel the difference? – there's just no comparison

incomparablement [ɛ̃kɔ̃parabləmɑ̃] **ADV** incomparably

incompatibilité [ɛ̃kɔ̃patibilite] **NF** incompatibility; **i. d'humeur** *ou* **de caractère** incompatibility of temperament; **il y a i. entre nous** we are incompatible

▸▸ *Pharm* **i. médicamenteuse** incompatibility of drugs; *Méd* **i. sanguine** incompatibility of blood groups

incompatible [ɛ̃kɔ̃patibl] **ADJ** incompatible *(avec with)*

incompétence [ɛ̃kɔ̃petɑ̃s] **NF 1** *(manque de compétence)* incompetence; **son i. en informatique/matière de voitures** his ignorance about *or* lack of knowledge of computers/ cars **2** *Jur (d'une personne, d'un tribunal)* incompetence, incompetency

incompétent [ɛ̃kɔ̃petɑ̃] **ADJ 1** incompetent; **je suis i. en cuisine** I'm an incompetent cook, I know nothing about cooking; **je suis i. en informatique/en matière de voitures/en matière de droit** I know nothing *or* I am completely ignorant about computers/ cars/the law **2** *Jur (non habilité) (tribunal)* not qualified, unqualified

incomplet, -ète [ɛ̃kɔ̃plɛ, -ɛt] **ADJ** incomplete

incomplètement [ɛ̃kɔ̃plɛtmɑ̃] **ADV** incompletely

incomplétude [ɛ̃kɔ̃pletyd] **NF** *Psy* sentiment d'i. (sense of) inadequacy *or* nonfulfilment

incompréhensibilité [ɛ̃kɔ̃preɑ̃sibilite] **NF** *Litt* incomprehensibility

incompréhensible [ɛ̃kɔ̃preɑ̃sibl] **ADJ** incomprehensible; **c'est i., je les avais posées là!** I don't understand it, I put them right there!

incompréhensif, -ive [ɛ̃kɔ̃preɑ̃sif, -iv] **ADJ** *(père, médecin, parents)* unsympathetic, lacking in understanding; *(esprit)* unsympathetic

incompréhension [ɛ̃kɔ̃preɑ̃sjɔ̃] **NF** lack of understanding *or* sympathy

incompressible [ɛ̃kɔ̃presibl] **ADJ** *Phys (matériau)* incompressible; *Jur (peine)* to be served in full; **dépenses incompressibles** expenditure which cannot be reduced *or* pared down; **il existe un chômage i.** there is a level below which unemployment cannot be reduced

incompris, -ise [ɛ̃kɔ̃pri, -iz] ADJ misunderstood

  N **je suis un i.** I am misunderstood, nobody understands me

inconcevable [ɛ̃kɔ̃s(ə)vabl] ADJ inconceivable, unthinkable, unimaginable; **il est i. que ...** it's inconceivable that ...; **c'est totalement i.** it's quite unthinkable

inconcevablement [ɛ̃kɔ̃s(ə)vabləmɑ̃] ADV inconceivably

inconciliable [ɛ̃kɔ̃siljabl] ADJ *(théorie)* irreconcilable (**avec** with); **le métier est i. avec une vie de famille** the profession is incompatible with family life

inconditionnalité [ɛ̃kɔ̃disjɔnalite] NF *(d'un partisan)* unwavering *or* unquestioning support

inconditionné [ɛ̃kɔ̃disjɔne] ADJ *Psy (réflexe, stimulus)* unconditioned

inconditionnel, -elle [ɛ̃kɔ̃disjɔnɛl] ADJ *(soutien, retrait etc)* unconditional; *(obéissance)* unquestioning, unconditional; *(partisan)* staunch, unwavering

  N fan(atic); enthusiast; **c'est un i. de la pêche** he's a fishing fanatic, he's fanatical about fishing; **je suis une inconditionnelle de Prévert** I am a great fan of Prévert, I am mad about Prévert; **je suis une inconditionnelle de l'Espagne/des îles grecques** I am mad about *or* I adore Spain/the Greek islands

inconditionnellement [ɛ̃kɔ̃disjɔnɛlmɑ̃] ADV *(soutenir qn)* unconditionally, without question; *(obéir)* unquestioningly, without question; **être i. favorable à qn/qch** to support sb/sth wholeheartedly

inconduite [ɛ̃kɔ̃dɥit] NF *Litt* loose living; *Jur* misconduct

inconfort [ɛ̃kɔ̃fɔr] NM *(manque de confort matériel)* discomfort; *(malaise moral)* uncomfortableness

inconfortable [ɛ̃kɔ̃fɔrtabl] ADJ *(siège, voiture), Fig (situation)* uncomfortable

inconfortablement [ɛ̃kɔ̃fɔrtabləmɑ̃] ADV uncomfortably

incongru [ɛ̃kɔ̃gry] ADJ *(remarque, réponse)* incongruous, inappropriate, out of place; *(question, comportement)* inappropriate, improper, unseemly; *(bruit)* rude, unseemly; **il allait travailler dans une tenue des plus incongrues** he wore a really extravagant outfit to work

incongruité [ɛ̃kɔ̃grɥite] NF **1** *(caractère déplacé) (d'une remarque, réponse)* incongruity, inappropriateness; *(d'un comportement, d'une question)* inappropriateness, unseemliness, impropriety; *(de vêtements)* extravagance **2** *(remarque déplacée)* inappropriate *or* improper remark; *(action qui choque)* inappropriate *or* improper action

incongrûment [ɛ̃kɔ̃grymɑ̃] ADV *Litt* respondre, parler) in an unseemly fashion

inconnaissable [ɛ̃kɔnɛsabl] ADJ, NM unknowable

inconnu, -ue [ɛ̃kɔny] ADJ *(auteur, civilisation, destination)* unknown (**de, à** to); **se retrouver dans un lieu i.** to find oneself in a strange place; **il m'était i.** I didn't know him, he was a stranger to me; **il était i. de tout le monde** nobody knew him, he was a stranger to everybody; **né de père i.** *(sur document administratif)* father unknown; **elle est née de père i.** she doesn't know who her father was; **visages inconnus** strange faces; **c'est un problème qui lui est totalement i.** the problem is totally foreign to him, it's a pro-

blem he knows absolutely nothing about; **i. à cette adresse** not known at this address; *Fam* **Durand? i. au bataillon!** Durand? never heard of him!

  N *(étranger)* stranger; **c'est un i. qui a remporté le prix Nobel** someone no-one has ever heard of has won the Nobel prize

  NM **l'i.** the unknown; **la peur de l'i.** the fear of the unknown; **faire un saut dans l'i.** to take a leap in the dark

  NF *Math* **inconnue** unknown (quantity); *Fig* **il y a beaucoup trop d'inconnues dans cette affaire** there are two many unknowns in the matter

inconsciemment [ɛ̃kɔ̃sjamɑ̃] ADV **1** *(dans l'inconscient)* subconsciously **2** *(sans réfléchir)* without thinking, thoughtlessly; **il a signé un peu i.** he signed without giving it too much thought

inconscience [ɛ̃kɔ̃sjɑ̃s] NF **1** *(physique)* unconsciousness; **sombrer** *ou* **tomber dans l'i.** to lapse into unconsciousness, to become unconscious **2** *(manque de jugement)* recklessness, irresponsibility; **faire preuve d'i.** to be reckless *or* irresponsible; **c'est de l'i. pure et simple!** it's sheer madness!, how irresponsible can you get!

inconscient, -ente [ɛ̃kɔ̃sjɑ̃, -ɑ̃t] ADJ **1** *(sans connaissance) (personne, blessé)* unconscious **2** *(irréfléchi) (personne)* irresponsible; *(geste)* rash, ill-considered; **c'est i. ce que tu as fait là** it was irresponsible of you **3** *(non conscient) (acte)* unconscious; **i. de ce qui se passe autour de lui** oblivious to *or* unaware of what is going on around him

  N irresponsible person; **tu n'es qu'une inconsciente!** you really are irresponsible!

  NM *Psy* **l'i.** the unconscious, the subconscious

  ▸▸ *Psy* **l'i. collectif** the collective unconscious

inconséquence [ɛ̃kɔ̃sekɑ̃s] NF *(caractère inconséquent)* thoughtlessness; *(action inconséquente)* rash *or* irresponsible act; **on me blâmait pour mes inconséquences** I was reproached for being rash *or* irresponsible

inconséquent [ɛ̃kɔ̃sekɑ̃] ADJ **1** *(illogique, versatile) (argument, personne)* inconsistent; **être i. dans ses propos** to contradict oneself, to speak illogically; **il dit des choses inconséquentes** he speaks incoherently **2** *(irréfléchi) (personne, démarche)* thoughtless, rash

inconsidéré [ɛ̃kɔ̃sidere] ADJ **1** *(acte, remarque)* thoughtless, rash, *Fml* ill-considered; *(dépenses)* rash, reckless; **faire des dépenses inconsidérées** to spend recklessly **2** *Vieilli (personne)* irresponsible

inconsidérément [ɛ̃kɔ̃sideremɑ̃] ADV *(agir, parler)* thoughtlessly, without thinking, rashly; *(dépenser)* recklessly

inconsistance [ɛ̃kɔ̃sistɑ̃s] NF **1** *(manque de consistance) (d'une pâte)* runniness; *(de la boue)* softness; *(du sol)* looseness **2** *(d'une personne, d'un acte)* inconsistency; *(d'une intrigue)* thinness, flimsiness; *(d'un film, d'un roman)* thinness; *(d'une accusation)* flimsiness, insubstantial nature; **le film/roman était d'une i. telle que ...** the film/novel was so lacking in substance that ...

inconsistant [ɛ̃kɔ̃sistɑ̃] ADJ **1** *(liquide)* *(pâte, crème)* thin, runny; *(boue)* soft; *(sol)* loose **2** *(intrigue)* thin, flimsy, insubstantial; *(film, roman)* insubstantial; *(accusation)* flimsy, without substance; *(personne)* vacuous

Il faut noter que l'adjectif anglais **inconsistent** est un faux ami. Il signifie **incohérent**.

inconsolable [ɛ̃kɔ̃sɔlabl] ADJ *(personne, chagrin, tristesse)* inconsolable

inconsolé [ɛ̃kɔ̃sɔle] ADJ unconsoled

inconsommable [ɛ̃kɔ̃sɔmabl] ADJ unfit for consumption

inconstance [ɛ̃kɔ̃stɑ̃s] NF **1** *(d'une personne) (de caractère)* changeableness; *(en amour)* fickleness, *Fml* inconstancy **2** *Litt (du temps, de la mode)* fickleness, changeableness

inconstant [ɛ̃kɔ̃stɑ̃] ADJ **1** *(personne) (caractère)* changeable; *(en amour)* fickle, *Fml* inconstant; **être i. en amour** to be fickle **2** *Litt (mode)* fickle, changeable

inconstatable [ɛ̃kɔ̃statabl] ADJ unascertainable, unverifiable

inconstitutionnalité [ɛ̃kɔ̃stitysjɔnalite] NF *Jur* unconstitutionality

inconstitutionnel, -elle [ɛ̃kɔ̃stitysjɔnɛl] ADJ *Jur* unconstitutional

inconstitutionnellement [ɛ̃kɔ̃stitysjɔnɛlmɑ̃] ADV *Jur* unconstitutionally

inconstructible [ɛ̃kɔ̃stryktibl] ADJ *(zone, terrain)* that cannot be developed

incontestabilité [ɛ̃kɔ̃tɛstabilite] NF *Jur* incontestability

incontestable [ɛ̃kɔ̃tɛstabl] ADJ *(fait, preuve, victoire)* undeniable, indisputable, *Fml* incontestable; *(vérité)* undeniable, indisputable; **il est i. que ...** it is undeniable that ..., it cannot be denied that ...

incontestablement [ɛ̃kɔ̃tɛstabləmɑ̃] ADV undeniably, indisputably, beyond all doubt, *Fml* incontestably

incontesté [ɛ̃kɔ̃tɛste] ADJ *(droit)* uncontested, undisputed; *(maître, victoire)* undisputed

incontinence [ɛ̃kɔ̃tinɑ̃s] NF **1** *Méd* incontinence; **i. nocturne** bedwetting **2** *Arch, Litt (luxure)* incontinence, lack of restraint; **souffrir d'i. verbale** to have verbal diarrhoea

incontinent[1] [ɛ̃kɔ̃tinɑ̃] ADJ **1** *Méd* incontinent **2** *Arch, Litt (pas chaste)* incontinent, unrestrained; **être i. dans ses propos** to talk far too much; **un orateur complètement i. dans ses propos** an orator who goes on and on *or* who doesn't know when to stop

incontinent[2] ADV *Arch, Litt* at once, forthwith

incontournable [ɛ̃kɔ̃turnabl] ADJ **c'est i.** you can't get away from it; **son argument était i.** there was no getting away from his argument; **Harrods est un magasin i.** Harrods should not be missed, Harrods is a must; **son dernier film est absolument i.** his latest film is an absolute must

incontrôlable [ɛ̃kɔ̃trolabl] ADJ **1** *(affirmation)* difficult to verify *or* to check, unverifiable **2** *(incendie, supporter)* uncontrollable; **très vite, l'incendie fut i.** the fire very quickly got out of control *or* out of hand; **des éléments incontrôlables** rowdy elements

incontrôlé [ɛ̃kɔ̃trole] ADJ **1** *(non vérifié)* unchecked, unverified **2** *(non surveillé)* uncontrolled

inconvenance [ɛ̃kɔ̃v(ə)nɑ̃s] NF *(caractère inconvenant)* impropriety; **comme si j'avais dit/commis une i.** as if I had said/done something improper *or* out of place *or* out of turn

inconvenant [ɛ̃kɔ̃v(ə)nɑ̃] ADJ *(propos, remarque, acte)* improper, out of place, out of turn; **il est vraiment i.** he doesn't know how to behave, he has no manners; **il serait totalement i. d'aller à un enterrement habillé de rouge** it would be totally inappropriate to go to a funeral dressed in red

inconvénient [ɛ̃kɔ̃venjɑ̃] NM drawback, disadvantage; **les inconvénients qu'il y a à vivre si loin de la ville** the disadvantages *or* drawbacks *or* inconvenience of living so far from town; **le seul i., c'est que ...** the only drawback is that …; **l'i., c'est que …** the problem is that …; **je n'y vois pas d'i.** I can't see any objection(s) (to it), I've got nothing against it; **si vous n'y voyez aucun i., je voudrais …** if you have no objection, I'd like to …; **si je t'emprunte ta voiture, est-ce que tu y vois un i.?** would you have any objections if I borrowed your car?; **il n'y a pas d'i. à cela** that doesn't pose any problem; **nous pouvons sans i. modifier notre itinéraire** we can easily change our route

inconvertible [ɛ̃kɔ̃vɛrtibl] ADJ *(monnaie)* inconvertible, non-convertible

incoordination [ɛ̃kɔɔrdinasjɔ̃] NF lack of coordination; *Méd* ataxia

incorporable [ɛ̃kɔrpɔrabl] ADJ *Rare (appelé)* eligible for military service

incorporation [ɛ̃kɔrpɔrasjɔ̃] NF **1** *(mélange)* incorporation, blending, mixing (**de qch dans qch** of sth into or with sth); **opérer l'i. d'une poudre à un mélange** to incorporate a powder into a mixture; *Fin* **i. des réserves au capital** capitalization of reserves **2** *Mil* conscription; **sursis d'i.** deferment of call-up

incorporéité [ɛ̃kɔrpɔreite] NF incorporeity, incorporality

incorporel, -elle [ɛ̃kɔrpɔrɛl] ADJ *(qui n'a pas de corps)* incorporeal; *Jur* **biens incorporels** intangible property

incorporer [ɛ̃kɔrpɔre] VT **1** *(amalgamer)* **i. qch à** ou **avec qch** to incorporate or blend or mix sth into or with sth **2** *(intégrer) (terrain)* to incorporate (**dans un domaine** in(to) an estate); *(paragraphe)* to incorporate (**à** in(to)), to insert (**à** in); **le flash est incorporé à l'appareil photo** the flash is built into the camera; **un magnétophone avec micro incorporé** a tape recorder with a built-in microphone **3** *Mil (troupes)* to draft
VPR s'incorporer **chercher à s'i. dans un groupe** to try to join a group

incorrect [ɛ̃kɔrɛkt] ADJ **1** *(impropre) (emploi d'un mot, réponse, traduction)* incorrect, wrong **2** *(défectueux) (montage)* defective, faulty; *(tracé)* incorrect, wrong **3** *(inconvenant)* contrary to etiquette; **tenue incorrecte** *(débraillée)* slovenly clothes; *(déplacée)* unsuitable clothes **4** *(personne)* impolite, ill-mannered, rude; *(attitude)* improper; **être i. en affaires** to be unscrupulous in business

incorrectement [ɛ̃kɔrɛktəmɑ̃] ADV **1** *(en faisant des erreurs) (employer, écrire, traduire)* incorrectly, wrongly **2** *(d'une façon défectueuse) (monté)* defectively; *(tracé)* incorrectly, wrongly **3** *(habillé) (de façon débraillée)* in a slovenly manner; *(de façon déplacée)* unsuitably **4** *(avec impolitesse) (agir, se comporter)* improperly; **se conduire i. avec qn, agir i. avec qn** to behave improperly towards sb

incorrection [ɛ̃kɔrɛksjɔ̃] NF **1** *(impolitesse)* rudeness, impoliteness, lack of (good) manners; **pour i. envers ses professeurs** for being rude to his teachers; **elle est d'une i. avec les gens!** she is incredibly rude to people! **2** *Gram* incorrect expression; **le mot était considéré comme une i.** the word used to be considered incorrect **3** *(action incorrecte)* impolite or rude action; *(propos incorrect)* impolite or rude remark; **à la suite d'une grave i. envers un professeur** after being extremely rude to a teacher

incorrigibilité [ɛ̃kɔriʒibilite] NF incorrigibility

incorrigible [ɛ̃kɔriʒibl] ADJ incorrigible; **d'une gourmandise i.** incorrigibly greedy

incorrigiblement [ɛ̃kɔriʒibləmɑ̃] ADV *Rare* incorrigibly; **elle est i. bavarde** she is an incorrigible chatterbox

incorruptibilité [ɛ̃kɔryptibilite] NF incorruptibility

incorruptible [ɛ̃kɔryptibl] ADJ incorruptible
N incorruptible person

incoté [ɛ̃kɔte] ADJ *Fin* unquoted

incoterms [ɛ̃kɔtɛrm] NMPL *Com* incoterms

incrédibilité [ɛ̃kredibilite] NF incredibility

incrédule [ɛ̃kredyl] ADJ *(sceptique)* incredulous; *Rel* unbelieving; **il hochait la tête d'un air i.** he shook his head in disbelief or incredulously; **je suis très i. quant à la véracité de ce qu'il raconte** I'm very sceptical or Am skeptical about what he says
N *(personne sceptique)*, *Rel* unbeliever

incrédulité [ɛ̃kredylite] NF incredulity; *Rel* unbelief; **avec i.** incredulously

incrémenter [ɛ̃kremɑ̃te] VT *Ordinat* to increment

increvable [ɛ̃krəvabl] ADJ **1** *(pneu)* puncture-proof **2** *Fam (personne)* full of energy or *Fam* beans, tireless; *(personne âgée, voiture, moteur)* indestructible; **les enfants sont increvables** children never seem to get tired

incriminé [ɛ̃krimine] ADJ *Jur (personne)* accused, charged

incriminer [ɛ̃krimine] VT *(personne) Jur* to accuse, to charge, to indict; *(tenir responsable)* to blame, to accuse; *(actions, paroles de qn)* to condemn

incrochetable [ɛ̃krɔʃtabl] ADJ *(serrure)* unpickable; *(coffre)* burglar-proof

incroyable [ɛ̃krwajabl] ADJ *(histoire, chance, paresse)* incredible, unbelievable, extraordinary; *(chapeau)* incredible, extraordinary; **une histoire tout à fait i.** an altogether incredible story; **il est d'une paresse i.** he's incredibly lazy; **j'ai eu une chance i.** I was incredibly lucky, I had incredible luck; **je trouve ça i. que …** I think it's incredible or extraordinary that …; **tu es vraiment i.!** you're the limit!, I don't believe you!; **c'est i. ça!** I don't believe it!
N *Hist* incroyable *(beau or belle of the French Directoire period)*

incroyablement [ɛ̃krwajabləmɑ̃] ADV *(beau, vulgaire)* incredibly, unbelievably, extraordinarily; *(vêtu, maquillé)* incredibly, extraordinarily; **il s'est i. bien comporté** he behaved incredibly well

incroyance [ɛ̃krwajɑ̃s] NF *Rel* unbelief

incroyant, -ante [ɛ̃krwajɑ̃, -ɑ̃t] ADJ unbelieving
N unbeliever, non-believer

incrustation [ɛ̃krystasjɔ̃] NF **1** *(action)* encrusting; *Menuis* inlaying **2** *(dépôt) (dans une chaudière, une bouilloire)* fur, scale **3** *(ornement)* encrustation, inlay, inlaid work; **i. de dentelle** lace inlay; **avec incrustations de nacre** inlaid with mother of pearl **4** *Couture* insertion **5** *TV* inlay, inset

incruste [ɛ̃kryst] NF *Fam* **si on l'invite, il va encore taper l'i.** if we invite him, we'll never get rid of him; **il a tapé l'i. à ma soirée** he gatecrashed my party

incruster [ɛ̃kryste] VT **1** *Menuis* to inlay (**de** with) **2** *(former un dépôt)* to encrust; *(d'une eau calcaire) (tuyaux, chaudière, bouilloire)* to scale, to fur (up) **3** *(pour orner)* to encrust **4** *TV* to inlay
VPR s'incruster **1** *(adhérer)* to become encrusted **2** *(d'une chaudière, une bouilloire)* to fur up **3** *Fam (s'imposer)* **quand on l'invite, il s'incruste** once you invite him you can't get rid of him; **je ne voudrais pas m'i.** I wouldn't want to overstay my welcome; **ils font une fête, on s'incruste?** they're having a party, let's gatecrash

incubateur, -trice [ɛ̃kybatœr, -tris] ADJ *(appareil etc)* incubating
NM **1** *(couveuse)* incubator **2** *Écon* incubator

incubation [ɛ̃kybasjɔ̃] NF **1** *(d'œufs)* incuba-

tion; *(de poules)* sitting **2** *Méd* incubation; **période d'i.** incubation period

incube [ɛ̃kyb] NM incubus

incuber [ɛ̃kybe] VT *(œufs)* to incubate, to hatch (out)

inculcation [ɛ̃kylkasjɔ̃] NF *Litt* inculcating, inculcation

inculpation [ɛ̃kylpasjɔ̃] NF indictment; **depuis son i.** since his indictment, since he was indicted or charged; **le juge lui a notifié son i.** the judge informed him that he was being charged; **sous l'i. d'assassinat** charged with murder; **i. de trois responsables du club de football pour détournement de fonds** *(titre de journal)* three football club managers charged with embezzlement

inculpé, -ée [ɛ̃kylpe] N *Jur* **l'i.** the accused, the defendant

inculper [ɛ̃kylpe] VT to indict, to charge (**de, pour** with); **les trois hommes inculpés pour trafic de drogue** the three men charged with drug trafficking

inculquer [ɛ̃kylke] VT to instil, *Am* to instill, *Fml* to inculcate (**à qn** in sb)

inculte [ɛ̃kylt] ADJ *(non cultivé) (jardin)* uncultivated, wild; *(terre)* waste; *(non soigné) (barbe)* unkempt; *(ignorant) (personne)* uneducated

incultivable [ɛ̃kyltivabl] ADJ *(terre)* untillable, irreclaimable

incultivé [ɛ̃kyltive] ADJ *(terre)* untilled, uncultivated

inculture [ɛ̃kyltyr] NF lack of culture

incunable [ɛ̃kynabl] NM *Hist, Typ* incunabulum, *pl* incunabula

incurable [ɛ̃kyrabl] ADJ incurable; **d'une paresse/bêtise i.** incurably lazy/stupid
N person with an incurable disease

incurablement [ɛ̃kyrabləmɑ̃] ADV *(atteint, paresseux, bête)* incurably

incurie [ɛ̃kyri] NF *Fml* negligence; **faire preuve d'i.** to be negligent, to be guilty of negligence

incursion [ɛ̃kyrsjɔ̃] NF **1** *(invasion)* raid, foray, incursion **2** *Fig (entrée soudaine)* intrusion, interruption; **faire une i. dans une pièce/une réunion** to burst into a room/a meeting

incurvation [ɛ̃kyrvasjɔ̃] NF bend, curve

incurvé [ɛ̃kyrve] ADJ bent, curved

incurver [ɛ̃kyrve] VT to bend, to curve
VPR s'incurver to bend, to curve

indatable [ɛ̃databl] ADJ that cannot be dated

Inde [ɛ̃d] NF India; *Vieilli* **les Indes** the Indies; *Hist* **les Indes occidentales** the West Indies; **les Indes orientales** the East Indies

inde [ɛ̃d] NM dark blue

indéboulonnable [ɛ̃debulɔnabl] ADJ *Fam* unbudgeable; **elle est i.** they just can't get rid of her or they're stuck with her

indébrouillable [ɛ̃debrujabl] ADJ *(situation)* inextricable, tangled; *(histoire)* tangled

indécemment [ɛ̃desamɑ̃] ADV indecently

indécence [ɛ̃desɑ̃s] NF indecency

indécent [ɛ̃desɑ̃] ADJ *(tenue, décolleté, jupe)* indecent; *(gaspillage)* sinful, immoral; *(luxe, étalage de richesses)* obscene

indéchiffrable [ɛ̃deʃifrabl] ADJ **1** *(qu'on ne peut pas lire) (inscription, message)* indecipherable; *(écriture)* illegible; *(partition)* impossible to sight-read **2** *(incompréhensible)* unintelligible, incomprehensible; *(personne)* impenetrable, inscrutable

indéchirable [ɛ̃deʃirabl] ADJ tearproof, impossible to tear

indécis, -ise [ɛ̃desi, -iz] ADJ **1** *(peu net) (question)* undecided, unsettled; *(victoire)* indecisive, doubtful; *(contour)* vague, blurred; *(flamme)* wavering **2** *(personne) (de caractère)* indecisive, *Fml* irresolute; *(ponctuellement)* undecided; **être i. quant à l'attitude à adopter/sur le choix des couleurs** to be undecided *or* in two minds about what attitude to adopt/about the choice of colour; **je suis encore indécise** I still haven't decided *or* made my mind up

N c'est un i. he can never make his mind up; *Pol* **les i.** the floating voters; *(dans un sondage)* the don't knows

indécision [ɛ̃desizjɔ̃] NF *(de caractère)* indecisiveness; *(ponctuelle)* indecision; **l'i. n'est pas possible dans un travail comme le vôtre** you cannot afford to be indecisive in a job like yours

indécollable [ɛ̃dekɔlabl] ADJ *(papier peint)* that cannot be removed *or* peeled off

indécomposable [ɛ̃dekɔ̃pozabl] ADJ *(élément etc)* irresolvable

indécrottable [ɛ̃dekrɔtabl] ADJ *Fam (personne, cancre, ignorance)* hopeless; **être d'une ignorance/une bêtise i.** to be hopelessly ignorant/stupid; **c'est un i. paresseux** he's hopelessly *or* incurably lazy; **elle est vraiment i.** she's a hopeless case, there's no hope for her

indéfectibilité [ɛ̃defɛktibilite] NF *Rel (de l'Église etc)* indefectibility

indéfectible [ɛ̃defɛktibl] ADJ **1** *Rel (l'Église etc)* indefectible **2** *Litt (amitié, attachement etc)* everlasting, indestructible; *(mémoire)* unfailing

indéfendable [ɛ̃defɑ̃dabl] ADJ indefensible

indéfini [ɛ̃defini] ADJ **1** *(illimité)* indefinite **2** *(non précis) (nombre)* indefinite; *(tristesse, malaise)* vague, undefined **3** *Gram (pronom, article)* indefinite SEE GRAMMAR A5–6; A34–8; B4–5; B15–16

indéfiniment [ɛ̃definimɑ̃] ADV *(ajourner une réunion, attendre)* indefinitely; **répéter qch i.** to say sth over and over again, to keep repeating sth

indéfinissable [ɛ̃definisabl] ADJ *(terme)* indefinable, undefinable; *(goût, sentiment, charme, personne)* indefinable, impossible to describe

indéformable [ɛ̃defɔrmabl] ADJ *(chapeau, tissu)* that keeps its shape; *(acier)* that does not buckle

indéfrisable [ɛ̃defrizabl] NF *Vieilli* permanent wave, perm

indélébile [ɛ̃delebil] ADJ *(encre)*, *Fig (souvenir)* indelible; *(tache)* permanent, indelible

indélicat [ɛ̃delika] ADJ **1** *(personne, réflexion, action, démarche)* tactless, insensitive; **il est i. au possible** he's an insensitive lout **2** *(malhonnête)* dishonest, unscrupulous

indélicatement [ɛ̃delikatmɑ̃] ADV **1** *(sans délicatesse)* tactlessly, insensitively, *Fml* indelicate **2** *(malhonnêtement)* unscrupulously

indélicatesse [ɛ̃delikatɛs] NF **1** *(manque de tact) (d'une action, une personne)* tactlessness, insensitivity, *Fml* indelicacy; *(acte indélicat)* tactless action **2** *(malhonnêteté)* unscrupulousness; *(acte malhonnête)* unscrupulous action; **commettre une i.** to behave dishonestly

indémaillable [ɛ̃demajabl] ADJ *(bas)* nonrun, run-proof, *Br* ladderproof

NM non-run *or* run-proof fabric

indemne [ɛ̃dɛmn] ADJ *(sauf)* uninjured, unhurt, unharmed, unscathed; **elle est sortie i. de l'accident** she escaped uninjured

indemnisable [ɛ̃dɛmnizabl] ADJ *(personne)* entitled to compensation; *(dommages, dégâts)* compensable

indemnisation [ɛ̃dɛmnizasjɔ̃] NF *(de victimes, sinistrés)* compensation, *Fml* indem-

nification; **avoir droit à une i.** to be entitled to compensation

indemniser [ɛ̃dɛmnize] VT *(victime, sinistré)* to compensate, *Fml* to indemnify; **i. qn d'une perte** to compensate sb for a loss; **i. qn en argent** to pay sb compensation in cash

indemnitaire [ɛ̃dɛmnitɛr] ADJ **prestation i.** compensation

indemnité [ɛ̃dɛmnite] NF **1** *(pour perte encourue)* compensation, indemnity; *(pour délai, non-livraison etc)* compensation to other party, penalty **2** *Admin* allowance, grant

▸ ▸ **i. de chômage** unemployment benefit; *Fin* **i. de clientèle** compensation for loss of custom; **i. compensatrice** compensation; **i. compensatrice de congés payés** pay in lieu of holidays; **i. complémentaire** additional allowance; **i. conventionnelle** contractual allowance; **i. de déménagement** relocation grant *or* allowance; **i. de départ** *ou* **de licenciement** severance pay, redundancy payment; **i. de déplacement** *ou* **de transport** travel *or* transport allowance; **i. de guerre** war indemnity; **i. journalière** daily allowance; **i. kilométrique** ≃ mileage allowance; **i. de logement** accommodation allowance; **i. de maladie** sickness benefit; **i. parlementaire** *Br* ≃ MP's salary; **i. de représentation** entertainment allowance; **i. de résidence** housing allowance; *Fin* **i. de retard** late payment penalty; *Fin* **i. de rupture** severance pay; *Fin* **i. de rupture abusive** compensation for breach of contract; **i. de séjour** living expenses; **i. de vie chère** cost of living allowance

indémodable [ɛ̃demɔdabl] ADJ **un tailleur i.** a classic suit, a suit that will never go out of fashion

indémontable [ɛ̃demɔ̃tabl] ADJ *(serrure, armoire)* which cannot be dismantled; **c'est i.** it doesn't dismantle

indémontrable [ɛ̃demɔ̃trabl] ADJ unprovable, undemonstrable

indéniable [ɛ̃denjabl] ADJ undeniable; **il est i. que ...** it cannot be denied that ..., there's no denying that ...

indéniablement [ɛ̃denjablamɑ̃] ADV undeniably

indénombrable [ɛ̃denɔ̃brabl] ADJ innumerable, uncountable

indentation [ɛ̃dɑ̃tasjɔ̃] NF *Litt* indentation; *Typ* **i. à droite/gauche** right/left indent

indenter [ɛ̃dɑ̃te] VT *Typ* to indent

indépassable [ɛ̃depasabl] ADJ *(limite)* which cannot be exceeded

indépendamment [ɛ̃depɑ̃damɑ̃] ADV independently *(de* of*)*; **i. de l'ancienneté** irrespective *or* regardless of seniority; **i. de ce que je t'ai dit hier** regardless of *or* despite what I said to you yesterday; **i. des avantages que cette méthode comporte** leaving aside the advantages of this method

indépendance [ɛ̃depɑ̃dɑ̃s] NF independence; **accéder à l'i.** to gain independence; **guerre d'i.** war of independence; **on note chez lui une grande i. d'esprit et de caractère** he is very independently minded, he thinks for himself

indépendant, -ante [ɛ̃depɑ̃dɑ̃, -ɑ̃t] ADJ **1** *(personne, pays, vie)* independent *(de* of*)*; *(travailleur)* self-employed; *(traducteur, photographe etc, profession)* freelance; *(appartement)* self-contained; **circonstances indépendantes de ma volonté** circumstances beyond my control; **député i.** independent (MP); *Aut* **roues (avant) indépendantes** independent (front-wheel) suspension **2** *Gram* **proposition indépendante** independent clause

N *(travailleur)* self-employed worker; *(tra-*

ducteur, photographe etc) freelancer; *Pol* independent

indépendantisme [ɛ̃depɑ̃dɑ̃tism] NM *Pol* independence movement; **l'i. fait entendre sa voix** the desire for independence is making itself felt

indépendantiste [ɛ̃depɑ̃dɑ̃tist] N *Pol (membre actif)* freedom fighter; *(supporter de l'indépendance)* supporter of independence

indépensé [ɛ̃depɑ̃se] ADJ *Fin* unspent

indéracinable [ɛ̃derasinabl] ADJ *(arbre)* impossible to uproot; *Fig (personne)* impossible to move; *(préjugés)* deep-rooted, deep-seated, *Fml* ineradicable

indéréglable [ɛ̃dereglabl] ADJ *(mécanisme)* foolproof

indescriptible [ɛ̃dɛskriptibl] ADJ indescribable

indésirable [ɛ̃dezirabl] ADJ, N undesirable; *Méd* **effets indésirables: assoupissements, nausées** may cause drowsiness or nausea

indestructibilité [ɛ̃dɛstryktibilite] NF indestructibility

indestructible [ɛ̃dɛstryktibl] ADJ indestructible

indétectable [ɛ̃detɛktabl] ADJ undetectable

indéterminable [ɛ̃detɛrminabl] ADJ indeterminable

indétermination [ɛ̃detɛrminasjɔ̃] NF **1** *(d'idées)* vagueness **2** *(d'une personne)* indecisiveness, *Fml* irresoluteness; **faire preuve d'i.** to be indecisive

indéterminé [ɛ̃detɛrmine] ADJ **1** *(vague)* *(date, heure)* unspecified; *(idées)* indefinite, vague, *Fml* indeterminate; **pour une raison indéterminée** for some unknown reason; **la réunion est reportée à une date qui reste encore indéterminée** the meeting has been postponed to a date which has still to be decided **2** *(personne)* undecided; **elle est encore indéterminée sur ce point** she still has not made her mind up on the issue

index [ɛ̃dɛks] NM VOIR GRAMMAIRE A14 **1** *Anat* forefinger, index finger **2** *(aiguille) (de balance)* pointer, needle **3** *(de livre)* index; *Cathol* **l'I.** the Index; *Fig* **mettre qn/qch à l'i.** to blacklist sb/sth **4** *Ordinat* index; **i. de totalisation** hashed index

indexage [ɛ̃dɛksaʒ] NM indexing

indexation [ɛ̃dɛksasjɔ̃] NF *Écon (des salaires etc)* indexation, index-linking; *Ordinat* indexing

indexé [ɛ̃dɛkse] ADJ *(salaire etc)* index-linked

indexer [ɛ̃dɛkse] VT **1** *Écon (prix, salaires)* to index-link, to peg, to index; **salaires indexés sur le coût de la vie** salaries indexed to the cost of living **2** *(ajouter un index à) (ouvrage, collection), Ordinat* to index

indic [ɛ̃dik] N *Arg* grass, informer

indicateur, -trice [ɛ̃dikatœr, -tris] ADJ **poteau i.** signpost; **panneau i. (de route)** road sign

NM **1** *Péj (informateur)* informer

2 *(livre)* **i. des rues de Paris** Paris (street) directory *or* street finder; **i. horaire** timetable; **i. des chemins de fer** (railway) timetable

3 *(instrument)* **i. de niveau (de carburant)** (fuel) gauge; **i. de pression** pressure gauge; **i. de vitesse** speed indicator, tachometer; *Aut* speedometer; *Aviat* airspeed indicator; *Aviat* **i. d'altitude** altimeter; *Radio* **i. de direction** direction finder; *Aut* **i. (de changement) de direction** (directional) indicator, direction indicator; *Aut* **i. d'usure** *(de pneu)* tread depth gauge, tread wear indicator; *Aut* **i. de pression d'huile** oil pressure gauge; *Aut* **i. de pression de pneu** tyre pressure gauge; *Aut* **i. de température** temperature indicator *or* gauge; *Aut* **i. lumineux de porte ouverte** door-open warning light; **i. à diodes électroluminescentes** LED indicator

4 *Chimie* indicator

5 *Écon, Fin* **indicateurs d'alerte** economic indicators, business indicators; **i. de développement humain** human development index; **i. économique** economic indicator; **i. de marché** market indicator; **i. statistique** statistical indicator; **i. de tendance** market indicator

indicatif, -ive [ɛ̃dikatif, -iv] ADJ **1** *(qui indique) (signe)* indicative (**de** of); **à titre i.** as an indication, *Fam* to give me/you/*etc* an idea; **ces prix/chiffres ne sont fournis qu'à titre i.** these prices/figures are supplied for information only **2** *Gram* **mode i.** indicative (mood)

NM **1** *Gram* indicative (mood); **à l'i.** in the indicative VOIR GRAMMAIRE A40 **2** *Tél* dialling code; *TV, Radio* theme tune; *Ordinat* prompt; *Ordinat* **i. (du) DOS** DOS prompt; *Tél* **i. d'appel** dialling code; *Radio* **i. (musical) (de programme)** signature tune, theme tune; *TV* **i. de générique** theme tune; *Radio* **i. de station** station ident(ification)

indication [ɛ̃dikasjɔ̃] NF **1** *(action)* indication, indicating, pointing out; **l'i. de la date de péremption est obligatoire** the use-by date must be shown *or* indicated; **i. d'origine** indication of origin

2 *(renseignement)* (piece of) information; **sauf i. contraire** unless otherwise specified; **sauf i. contraire de ta mère** unless your mother says otherwise *or Fam* different; **donne-lui quelques indications pour se servir de l'ordinateur** can you show him how to use the computer; **une de tes indications était fausse ce qui fait que je me suis perdue** I got lost because one of your directions was wrong; **à titre d'i.** as an indication, *Fam* to give me/you/*etc* an idea

3 *(signe)* sign, token

4 *Géog* **indications topographiques** survey marks *or* data

5 **indications** *(sur mode d'emploi)* instructions; *(sur notice pharmaceutique)* for *(tonsillitis etc)*; **indications du mode d'emploi** directions for use; **indications spéciales** special indications; **quelles sont les indications pour ce médicament?** what is this medicine for?

▸▸ *Théâtre* **indications scéniques** stage directions

indice [ɛ̃dis] NM **1** *(signe)* sign, indication; *(d'un crime)* clue; **les indices du crime** the clues to the crime; **c'est l'i. de la reprise** it's the sign of a recovery; **j'ai vu là un i. de ta fatigue** to me that was a sign *or* an indication you were tired **2** *(chiffre indicateur)*, *Math* index (number); *Typ* subscript; **b i. 3** b subscript *or* inferior 3; **3 en i.** subscript 3 VOIR GRAMMAIRE A14

▸▸ *Mktg* **i. ad hoc** specific indicator; *Bourse* **i. boursier** share index; *Fin* **i. CAC 40** ≃ FTSE; *Aut* **i. de cétane** cetane number; *Écon* **i. de confiance** consumer confidence index; *Écon* **i. corrigé des variations saisonnières** seasonally adjusted index; *Bourse* **i. des cours d'actions** share price index; *Écon* **i. du coût de la vie** cost of living index; *Écon* **i. de croissance** index of growth; **i. d'écoute** *Radio* ratings; *TV* ratings, viewing figures; *Radio, TV* **avoir un bon i. d'écoute** to stand high in the ratings, to attract a large listening/viewing audience; **avoir un mauvais i. d'écoute** to have a low (audience) rating, to get bad ratings; **l'i. d'écoute a baissé** the ratings have dropped; **i. hiérarchique** salary scale code; **i. inférieur** suffix; *Fin* **l'i. Nikkei** the Nikkei index; *Écon* **i. non-corrigé des variations saisonnières** non-seasonally adjusted index; *Chimie* **i. d'octane** octane rating *or* number;

Aut **i. d'octane méthode moteur** motor octane number, MON; *Écon* **i. pondéré** weighted index; **i. de popularité** (popularity) rating; **l'i. de popularité du Président est en baisse** the President has dropped in the popularity ratings; *Écon* **i. des prix** price index; *Écon* **i. des prix à la consommation** consumer price index; *Écon* **i. des prix de détail** retail price index; *Écon* **i. des prix de gros** wholesale price index; *Écon* **i. des prix et des salaires** wage and price index; **i. de profit** profit indicator; **i. de protection** *(d'une crème solaire)* SPF; *Écon* **i. de rémunération** salary grading; **i. spécifique** specific indicator; *Écon* **i. de traitement** salary grading; *Bourse* **i. des valeurs boursières** share index; *Aut* **i. de viscosité** viscosity index

indiciaire [ɛ̃disjɛr] ADJ *Écon* index-based; **impôt i.** wealth tax

indicible [ɛ̃disibl] ADJ *Litt (plaisir, joie, bonheur)* indescribable; *(chagrin, rage, peur)* indescribable, unspeakable; **d'une saleté i.** indescribably *or* unspeakably filthy

indiciblement [ɛ̃disiblǝmɑ̃] ADV *Litt (d'une façon inexprimable)* inexpressibly

indiciel, -ielle [ɛ̃disjɛl] ADJ *Écon* index

indien, -ienne [ɛ̃djɛ̃, -jɛn] ADJ **1** Indian; **l'océan i.** the Indian Ocean **2 en** *ou* **à la file indienne** in single *or* Indian file

N **I.** *(d'Inde, d'Amérique)* Indian

NF **indienne** *Tex* cotton print, *surtout Am* printed calico; **nage (à l')indienne** overarm stroke

indifféremment [ɛ̃diferamɑ̃] ADV *(sans faire de différence)* indiscriminately, equally; **vous pouvez prendre i. la route de gauche ou celle de droite** you can take either the left-hand or the right-hand road *or* it doesn't really matter which road you take (they're equally good); **il va i. dans l'un ou l'autre de ces restaurants** it doesn't matter to him which restaurant he goes to; **traduire i. en chinois et en russe** to translate into Chinese and Russian equally well; **elle mange de tout i.** she'll eat anything **2** *Vieilli (avec froideur)* indifferently

indifférence [ɛ̃diferɑ̃s] NF indifference; **répondre avec i.** to answer with indifference *or* indifferently; **i. à (l'égard de)** *ou* **pour** *ou* **face à** *(pour la politique)* indifference to, lack of interest in; *(devant la misère du monde)* indifference to, lack of concern about; **elle est d'une i. totale face à tout ce qui ne concerne pas son métier** she is totally indifferent to anything that is not work-related

indifférenciable [ɛ̃diferɑ̃sjabl] ADJ indistinguishable; **ces jumeaux sont absolument indifférenciables** it's impossible to tell the twins apart

indifférenciation [ɛ̃diferɑ̃sjasjɔ̃] NF lack of differentiation

indifférencié [ɛ̃diferɑ̃sje] ADJ undifferentiated

indifférent, -ente [ɛ̃diferɑ̃, ɑ̃t] ADJ **1** *(peu ou pas intéressé)* indifferent (**à** to); *(sans émotion)* indifferent, cold, emotionless; **être i. au sort de qn** to be indifferent to sb's fate; **il m'est i.** I'm indifferent to him; **il a été i. à tous mes arguments** he was unmoved by my arguments; **rester i. à tout** to take no interest in anything; **toutes ses avances l'ont laissée indifférente** she was indifferent to his advances, *Fam* his advances left her cold; **elle ne le laisse pas i.** he is not indifferent *or* unattracted to her; **cela ne peut vous laisser i.** it can't leave you indifferent *or* unmoved; **ta requête ne pourra pas le laisser i.** he can't fail to respond to your request

2 *(sans importance)* immaterial, unimportant; **recherchons baby-sitter, sexe i.** baby-sitter wanted, male or female; **cela m'est i.**

it's all the same to me, I don't care either way; **cela m'est complètement i.** I couldn't care less, it's all the same to me; **il m'est i. de faire cela ou autre chose** it doesn't matter to me *or* it's all the same to me whether I do that or something else; **parler de choses indifférentes** to chat (about nothing in particular)

N uncaring person; **c'est un i.** he doesn't care about people, he's very uncaring; **elle se plaint que son mari est un i.** she complains that her husband doesn't care about her *or* is indifferent to her; **jouer les indifférents** to pretend to be indifferent, to put on a show of indifference

indifférer [ɛ̃difere] VT *used with pronoun complement only* (**il indiffère; il indiffèrera**) **cela m'indiffère** I couldn't care less (about it); **mon sort l'indiffère complètement** he/she couldn't care less what happens to me

indigence [ɛ̃diʒɑ̃s] NF **1** *(dénuement)* destitution; **être/tomber dans l'i.** to be/become destitute; **vivre dans l'i.** to live in dire poverty **2** *Fml Fig (manque)* **faire preuve d'i. d'idées** to be totally devoid of ideas; **l'i. de ses idées** the poverty of his/her ideas; **l'i. d'esprit dont fait preuve la télévision** the dearth of intelligent programmes on television

indigène [ɛ̃diʒɛn] ADJ *Zool, Bot* indigenous (**à** to); *(population)* native, indigenous; *(coutume)* native

N native

indigent, -ente [ɛ̃diʒɑ̃, -ɑ̃t] ADJ **1** *(personne)* destitute, poverty-stricken, *Fml* indigent **2** *Fig (esprit)* impoverished, poor; **avoir une imagination indigente** to be totally lacking in imagination

N person who is destitute; **les indigents** the destitute

indigeste [ɛ̃diʒɛst] ADJ *(nourriture)*, *Fig (livre)* indigestible, difficult to digest

indigestion [ɛ̃diʒɛstjɔ̃] NF indigestion; **avoir une i.** to have (an attack of) indigestion; **j'ai mangé tellement de chocolat que je m'en suis donné une i., j'ai mangé du chocolat jusqu'à l'i.** I ate so much chocolate I gave myself indigestion; *Fig Fam* **j'en ai une i.** I'm fed up with it, I've had my fill of it

indignation [ɛ̃diɲasjɔ̃] NF indignation; **faire éclater** *ou* **crier son i.** to give one's indignation free rein; **éclater** *ou* **exploser d'i.** to explode in indignation; **avec i.** *(parler, protester etc)* indignantly, with indignation

indigne [ɛ̃diɲ] ADJ **1** *(qui n'est pas digne) (personne)* unworthy, undeserving; **ces bassesses sont indignes de vous** such behaviour is unworthy of you; **i. de notre confiance** unworthy of our confidence; **je suis i. de votre dévouement** I don't deserve such devotion; **cet auteur est i. de figurer aux programmes des écoles** this author is not fit to be included in the school syllabus; **il est i. de vivre** he doesn't deserve to live, he's not fit to live; **être i. d'un poste/d'une tâche** to be unworthy of a position/a task; **ce travail est i. de lui** this work is not good enough for him *or* is beneath him; **conduite i. d'une sœur/d'un père** unsisterly/unfatherly conduct

2 *(méprisable) (action, conduite)* shameful; **c'est une mère i.** she's not a fit mother

indigné [ɛ̃diɲe] ADJ indignant; **je suis absolument i. par votre manque de sérieux** I am quite indignant about *or* at your lack of professionalism; **d'un air/ton i.** indignantly

indignement [ɛ̃diɲmɑ̃] ADV shamefully

indigner [ɛ̃diɲe] VT **i. qn** to make sb indignant, to outrage sb

VPR **s'indigner** to become *or* get *or* be indignant; **je m'indigne de voir ce crime impuni** it makes me indignant to see this crime go unpunished; **s'i. de** ou **contre qch/qn** to be indignant at or about sth/with sb; **s'i. que** + sub ou **de ce que** + ind ou sub to be indignant that

indignité [ɛ̃diɲite] NF **1** (d'une personne) unworthiness; (d'une action) baseness, vileness **2** (action) shameful act
▸ ▸ Jur **i. nationale** loss of citizenship rights (imposed on those who collaborated with the Germans in World War II)

indigo [ɛ̃digo] NM, ADJ INV indigo(-blue)

indiqué [ɛ̃dike] ADJ (recommandé) advisable; **un sujet de plaisanterie tout i.** an obvious subject for jokes; **il est tout à fait i. pour ce poste** he's the very man or just the man for the job; **dans votre cas, un séjour à la montagne me paraît tout à fait i.** a stay in the mountains seems to me to be just the thing you need; **il n'est pas très i. de mélanger l'alcool et les médicaments** it's not very advisable to mix alcohol and medication

indiquer [ɛ̃dike] VT **1** (montrer) (de personne) to show, to point out, to indicate; **i. qch du doigt** to point to or at sth, to point sth out, to indicate sth; **i. le chemin à qn** to show sb the way, to direct sb; **tu peux m'i. le chemin** ou **la route pour aller au cinéma?** can you show me the way or direct me to the cinema?; **i. une rue à qn** to tell sb where a street is; **indique-lui où ça se trouve** show him/her where it is; **elle m'indiqua comment utiliser cet outil** she showed me how to use the tool
2 (marquer) to show, to indicate; **le compteur indique cent** the meter reads or shows one hundred; **point indiqué sur la carte** point shown or marked on the map; **la maison indiquée sur le bordereau ci-joint** the firm shown or given or mentioned on the enclosed slip; **le panneau vert indique la sortie** the green panel indicates the exit; **suivre les pointillés comme indiqué** follow the dotted line as shown or indicated; **la loi oblige à i. le prix des marchandises en vitrine** by law, you have to show the price of goods displayed in the window; **le prix n'est pas indiqué** there's no price on it
3 (recommander) **elle m'a indiqué un dentiste/garage qui est vraiment excellent** she told me about or recommended a really excellent dentist/garage; **s'il vous plaît, indiquez-moi un bon médecin** can you recommend a (good) doctor?
4 (dénoter) to point to, to indicate; **ce genre d'attitude indique un manque de professionnalisme total** this sort of attitude points to or indicates a total lack of professionalism; **tout dans la maison indique un goût raffiné** everything in the house indicates or shows good taste
5 (donner) (jour, date) to give, to indicate; (ligne d'action etc) to prescribe, to lay down; **à l'heure indiquée** at the appointed or agreed time; **veuillez i. vos nom et adresse** please give your name and address; **pourriez-vous m'i. le prix de ce vase?** could you tell me how much the vase is?; **i. un prix** to quote a price

indirect [ɛ̃dirɛkt] ADJ **1** (non direct) (itinéraire, critique) indirect; (chemin) roundabout; (attaque) indirect, covert; Jur (héritiers) collateral; **éclairage i.** indirect or concealed lighting; **elle l'a dit d'une façon indirecte** she said it in an indirect or a roundabout way; **je l'ai appris de manière indirecte** I learned of it indirectly; **contributions indirectes** indirect taxation **2** Gram (objet) indirect SEE GRAMMAR B18–19 ; **discours i.** indirect speech, reported speech; **au discours i.** in indirect or reported speech VOIR GRAMMAIRE A63 **3** Jur (preuves) circumstantial

indirectement [ɛ̃dirɛktəmã] ADV indirect-

ly; **dire les choses i.** to say things in an indirect or a roundabout way

indiscernable [ɛ̃disɛrnabl] ADJ indiscernible, imperceptible

indiscipline [ɛ̃disiplin] NF indiscipline, lack of discipline; **faire acte** ou **preuve d'i.** to show a lack of discipline

indiscipliné [ɛ̃disipline] ADJ (élève) undisciplined, unruly; (soldat) undisciplined; Fig **cheveux indisciplinés** unruly or unmanageable hair

indiscret, -ète [ɛ̃diskrɛ, -ɛt] ADJ (personne, remarque, question, bavardage) indiscreet; (inquisiteur) inquisitive; **serait-il i. de vous demander où vous allez?** would it be indiscreet to ask you where you're going?; **à l'abri des regards indiscrets** safe from prying eyes; **une question fort indiscrète** a very personal question; **je ne voudrais pas être i. mais …** I don't want to be indiscreet but …; **je me méfie des oreilles indiscrètes** I'm on my guard against eavesdroppers
N indiscreet person, Fam Péj nosy parker; **à l'abri des indiscrets** away from eavesdroppers or prying eyes

indiscrètement [ɛ̃diskrɛtmã] ADV indiscreetly

indiscrétion [ɛ̃diskresjɔ̃] NF **1** (manque de discrétion) indiscretion, indiscreetness; (curiosité excessive) inquisitiveness; **peut-on vous demander sans i. …?** would it be indiscreet or rude to ask …?; **elle a eu l'i. de venir elle-même vérifier** she was so indiscreet as to come and see for herself; **il a poussé l'i. jusqu'à demander des détails** he was so indiscreet as to ask for details **2** (action, remarque) indiscretion; **commettre une i.** to commit an indiscretion, to be indiscreet

indiscutable [ɛ̃diskytabl] ADJ indisputable, unquestionable; **il est i. que vous ayez raison** you're indisputably or unquestionably right; **il est i. qu'il faille améliorer la production** there's no question but that production needs to be improved

indiscutablement [ɛ̃diskytabləmã] ADV indisputably, unquestionably

indiscuté [ɛ̃diskyte] ADJ undisputed, unquestioned

indispensable [ɛ̃dispɑ̃sabl] ADJ indispensable (à qn to sb; à ou pour qch for sth; pour faire qch for doing sth), essential (à qch for sth, to sth); **une condition i.** an essential condition; **il est i. que j'aie/d'avoir votre autorisation écrite** it is essential that I have/to have your authorization in writing; **anglais i.** (dans une offre d'emploi) knowledge of English indispensable or essential; **votre aide m'est i.** your help is indispensable (to me); **tu crois donc i.?** so you think you're indispensable?; **personne n'est i.** no-one is indispensable; **il nous est i.** he is indispensable to us, we can't do without him
NM **l'i.** the essentials, what is/was strictly necessary; **ne prenez que l'i.** only take the essentials or what you really need or what is strictly necessary

indisponibilité [ɛ̃disponibilite] NF **1** (d'une personne) unavailability **2** Jur inalienability

indisponible [ɛ̃disponibl] ADJ **1** (personne, argent) unavailable, not available **2** Jur (biens) inalienable; (domaine) entailed

indisposé [ɛ̃dispoze] ADJ (fatigué) indisposed, unwell, Fam out of sorts; **se sentir vaguement i.** to feel unwell or Br off colour; Euph **elle est indisposée** she's indisposed, it's her time of the month

indisposer [ɛ̃dispoze] VT **1** (rendre légèrement malade) **i. qn** to make sb unwell; (de la nourriture) to upset sb, to disagree with sb; **cette odeur m'indispose** that smell makes

me (feel) sick **2** (contrarier) to antagonize, to annoy; **i. qn contre qn** to set sb against sb; **tout l'indispose** everything annoys him/her; **elle indispose tout le monde par son attitude** her attitude antagonizes everybody

indisposition [ɛ̃dispozisjɔ̃] NF indisposition, slight illness, upset; Euph **souffrir d'une i. passagère** to be temporarily indisposed

indissociable [ɛ̃disɔsjabl] ADJ indissociable

indissolubilité [ɛ̃disɔlybilite] NF (du mariage) indissolubility

indissoluble [ɛ̃disɔlybl] ADJ (lien, amitié) indissoluble

indissolublement [ɛ̃disɔlybləmã] ADV indissolubly

indistinct [ɛ̃distɛ̃(kt)] ADJ (voix, bruits) indistinct; (visuellement) (contour, lumière, forme) vague, indistinct

indistinctement [ɛ̃distɛ̃ktəmã] ADV **1** (indifféremment) without distinction **2** (voir) indistinctly, vaguely; (parler) indistinctly

individu [ɛ̃dividy] NM **1** Biol individual **2** (être humain) individual; **tout i. est unique** every individual is unique; Fam **soigner son i.** to look after number one **3** souvent Péj (homme) individual, fellow; **i. louche** shady customer, suspicious character; **quel drôle d'i.!** what an odd character!; **un triste i.** a sad character

individualisation [ɛ̃dividɥalizasjɔ̃] NF individualization; **i. de l'enseignement/des peines** adapting or tailoring of education/ sentences to individual needs

individualiser [ɛ̃dividɥalize] VT to individualize; **i. l'enseignement/les peines** to adapt or tailor education/sentences to individual needs; **i. les salaires** to award salaries on an individual basis
VPR **s'individualiser** (d'une personne) to develop a personality of one's own; Biol to take on individual characteristics

individualisme [ɛ̃dividɥalism] NM individualism

individualiste [ɛ̃dividɥalist] ADJ (attitude, comportement, morale) individualistic
N individualist

individualité [ɛ̃dividɥalite] NF individuality

individuel, -elle [ɛ̃dividɥɛl] ADJ (cas, qualité) individual; (liberté, responsabilité, opinion) personal; (maison) detached; (chambre) single; **faire qch à titre i.** to do sth as an individual; **fiche individuelle** personal record card; **secrétaire i.** personal or private secretary; Sport **épreuve individuelle** individual event

individuellement [ɛ̃dividɥɛlmã] ADV individually; Jur severally; **responsables individuellement** severally liable

indivis [ɛ̃divi] ADJ Jur (domaine, succession) undivided, joint; (propriétaires) joint; **par ou en i.** jointly

indivisaire [ɛ̃divizɛr] N Jur joint owner

indivisément [ɛ̃divizemã] ADV Jur jointly

indivisibilité [ɛ̃divizibilite] NF indivisibility

indivisible [ɛ̃divizibl] ADJ indivisible

indivisiblement [ɛ̃divizibləmã] ADV indivisibly

indivision [ɛ̃divizjɔ̃] NF Jur joint possession; **propriété en i.** jointly held property

Indochine [ɛ̃dɔʃin] NF Indochina

indochinois, -oise [ɛ̃dɔʃinwa, -waz] ADJ Indochinese
N I. Indochinese

indocile [ɛ̃dɔsil] ADJ intractable, disobedient; **une mèche i.** a cowlick

indocilité [ɛ̃dɔsilite] NF intractability, disobedience

indo-européen, -enne, pl **indo-euro-péens, -ennes** [ɛ̃dɔørɔpeɛ̃, -ɛn] **ADJ** (langue) Indo-European
N I. Indo-European
NM Ling Indo-European

indolemment [ɛ̃dɔlamɑ̃] **ADV** indolently

indolence [ɛ̃dɔlɑ̃s] **NF** indolence

indolent [ɛ̃dɔlɑ̃] **ADJ 1** (nonchalant) indolent; **démarche indolente** slow or lazy walk **2** Méd (tumeur) indolent, painless

indolore [ɛ̃dɔlɔr] **ADJ** painless

indomptable [ɛ̃dɔ̃tabl] **ADJ 1** (animal) untam(e)able; (nation) unconquerable **2** Fig (orgueil, caractère) indomitable; (passion) ungovernable, uncontrollable

indompté [ɛ̃dɔ̃te] **ADJ** (animal) untamed; (nation) unconquered; Fig (passion, orgueil) uncontrolled; (esprit) unbroken

Indonésie [ɛ̃dɔnezi] **NF** Indonesia

indonésien, -ienne [ɛ̃dɔnezjɛ̃, -jɛn] **ADJ** Indonesian
N I. Indonesian

indou, -oue [ɛ̃du] Rel **ADJ** Hindu
N I. Hindu

in-douze **ADJ INV, NM INV** Typ duodecimo, twelvemo

indu [ɛ̃dy] **ADJ** (hâte) undue; (remarque, protestation) unwarranted; **à une heure indue** at an ungodly hour; **il rentre à des heures indues** he comes home at all hours of the night

indubitable [ɛ̃dybitabl] **ADJ** (preuves, détails) indisputable, indubitable; **c'est lui le vainqueur, c'est i.** he's the winner, there's no doubt about it or it's beyond doubt; **il est i. que ...** there's no doubt that ...

indubitablement [ɛ̃dybitabləmɑ̃] **ADV** undoubtedly, indubitably, unquestionably

inductance [ɛ̃dyktɑ̃s] **NF** Élec inductance; Aut induction

inducteur, -trice [ɛ̃dyktœr, -tris] Élec **ADJ** (capacité, champ) inductive; (courant) inducing
NM inductor; (de dynamo) field magnet

inductif, -ive [ɛ̃dyktif, -iv] **ADJ** Élec inductive

induction [ɛ̃dyksjɔ̃] **NF 1** (en logique) induction; **raisonner par i.** to reason by induction **2** Élec **courant d'i.** induced current; **bobine d'i.** induction coil

induire [ɛ̃dɥir] **VT** (prp induisant; pp induit; pr ind j'induis, n. induisons, ils induisent; p hist j'induisis; fu j'induirai) **1** (entraîner) i. **qn à faire qch** to induce sb to do sth; **i. qn en erreur** to mislead sb, to lead sb astray; Litt **i. qn au mal** to lead sb astray **2** (conclure) to infer, to induce; **que pouvez-vous en i.?** what can you infer from that?

induit [ɛ̃dɥi] Élec **ADJ** (circuit) induced, secondary; **courant i.** induction current
NM (circuit) induced circuit; (de dynamo) armature, rotor; **charge d'i.** induced charge

indulgence [ɛ̃dylʒɑ̃s] **NF 1** (tolérance) indulgence, leniency; **avec i.** indulgently, leniently; **avoir** ou **montrer de l'i. pour** ou **envers qn, faire preuve d'i. envers qn** to be indulgent with sb, to make allowances for sb; **regard plein d'i.** indulgent look; **par avance, je demande votre i.** I request your indulgence in advance; **rires sans i.** merciless laughter; **il me fit d'elle une portrait sans i.** he described her to me warts and all **2** Rel indulgence

indulgent [ɛ̃dylʒɑ̃] **ADJ** (personne, attitude) indulgent, lenient; (regard) indulgent; **être i. avec** ou **envers qn** to be indulgent or lenient with sb; **être trop i. avec soi-même** to be easy on oneself

indûment [ɛ̃dymɑ̃] **ADV** (protester) unduly; (facturé) incorrectly; **s'ingérer i. dans les af-faires d'autrui** to interfere unduly or without justification in other people's affairs

industrialisation [ɛ̃dystrijalizasjɔ̃] **NF** industrialization; **économie en voie d'i.** industrializing economy

industrialisé [ɛ̃dystrijalize] **ADJ** industrialized

industrialiser [ɛ̃dystrijalize] **VT** to industrialize
VPR **s'industrialiser** to become industrialized

industrialisme [ɛ̃dystrijalism] **NM** Hist industrialism

industrie [ɛ̃dystri] **NF 1** Écon (secteur) industry, manufacturing; (entreprise) industry; **travailler dans l'i.** to work in industry or in manufacturing; **être à la tête d'une i.** to head an industry; **capitaine d'i.** captain of industry **2** Arch, Litt (activité) activity; (des abeilles) industry; (ingéniosité) ingenuity, cleverness
▸ ▸ **i. alimentaire** food industry; **l'i. automobile** the motor or automotive industry; **i. de base** basic industry; **l'i. du bâtiment** the building trade, the construction industry; **i. clé** key industry; **i. de consommation** consumer goods industry; **i. de fabrication** manufacturing industry; **i. de haute technologie** high-tech industry, sunrise industry; **i. hôtelière** ou **de l'hôtellerie** hotel industry; **i. de l'hôtellerie et de la restauration** hotel and catering industry; Ling **les industries de la langue** the language professions; **l'i. légère** light industry; **i. des loisirs** leisure industry; **l'i. lourde** heavy industry; **i. manufacturière** manufacturing industry; **i. nationalisée** nationalized or state-owned industry; **i. pétrolière** oil industry; **l'i. pharmaceutique** the pharmaceutical industry, pharmaceuticals; **i. de pointe** high-tech or state-of-the-art industry; **i. primaire** primary industry; **i. de la restauration** catering industry; **i. secondaire** secondary industry; **i. de service** service industry; **i. des services** service industry; **l'i. du spectacle** the entertainment industry, show business; **i. de transformation** processing industry; **i. de volume** volume industry

industriel, -elle [ɛ̃dystrijɛl] **ADJ** (produit, secteur, fabrication) industrial; **zone industrielle** (d'une ville) industrial estate or Am park; Fam **des magazines en quantité industrielle** vast quantities of magazines
NM manufacturer, industrialist

Il faut noter que l'adjectif anglais **industrial** ne signifie pas toujours **industriel**. Il s'emploie également à propos des relations entre employeurs et employés dans des expressions du type **industrial relations** ou **industrial unrest**.

industriellement [ɛ̃dystrijɛlmɑ̃] **ADV** industrially; **vins produits i.** mass-produced wines

industrieux, -euse [ɛ̃dystrijø, -øz] **ADJ** Litt (qui travaille beaucoup) industrious; (qui montre de l'habileté) skilful, Am skillful, ingenious

inébranlable [inebrɑ̃labl] **ADJ** (mur, pilier, rocher) immovable, solid, firm; Fig (personne, foi, amitié) unshakeable, steadfast; (confiance) unshakeable; (courage) unwavering; **il en a une conviction i.** he is firmly convinced of it, his conviction is unshakeable

inébranlablement [inebrɑ̃labləmɑ̃] **ADV** unshakeably

inéchangeable [ineʃɑ̃ʒabl] **ADJ** non-exchangeable; Fin (devise) non-convertible

inécoutable [inekutabl] **ADJ** unbearable, impossible to listen to

inécouté [inekute] **ADJ** unheeded

inédit [inedi] **ADJ 1** (non publié) (livre, disque, nouvelles) unpublished; **ce film est i. en France** this film has never been released in France **2** (original) (spectacle, projet) new, original; **elle a des idées inédites** she has some original ideas
NM 1 (texte) unpublished work; **un i. de Gide** an unpublished work by Gide **2** **l'i.** the new, the original

ineffable [inefabl] **ADJ** ineffable, unutterable

ineffablement [inefabləmɑ̃] **ADV** ineffably

ineffaçable [inefasabl] **ADJ** (marque, tache, mémoire) indelible, ineffaceable

ineffaçablement [inefasabləmɑ̃] **ADV** ineffaceably

inefficace [inefikas] **ADJ** (personne) ineffective, ineffectual; (dans son travail) inefficient; (remède, méthode, loi) ineffective, ineffectual

inefficacement [inefikasmɑ̃] **ADV** ineffectively; (travailler) inefficiently

inefficacité [inefikasite] **NF** (de personne) ineffectiveness, ineffectualness; (dans son travail) inefficiency; (d'un remède) ineffectiveness, ineffectualness, inefficacy

inégal, -ale, -aux, -ales [inegal, -o] **ADJ 1** (non égal) (parts, partage, segments, force, lutte) unequal; **force est de constater que les citoyens sont inégaux face à la loi** we have to recognize that not all citizens are equal in the eyes of the law **2** (irrégulier) (sol) uneven; (pouls) irregular; (vent) changeable; Fig (travail, écrivain, style) inconsistent, erratic; (qualité) inconsistent, varying; **être d'une humeur inégale** to be as changeable as the weather

inégalable [inegalabl] **ADJ** incomparable, matchless; (record) unbeatable

inégalé [inegale] **ADJ** unequalled, unmatched; **le record reste jusqu'à ce jour i.** the record remains unbeaten to this day

inégalement [inegalmɑ̃] **ADV 1** (injustement) unequally, unevenly; **i. partagé** unequally or unevenly shared **2** (irrégulièrement) unevenly; **carreaux i. disposés** unevenly arranged tiles; **son cœur battait i.** his heart was beating irregularly; **le film a été i. apprécié par les critiques** the film received mixed reviews from the critics

inégalitaire [inegaliter] **ADJ** non-egalitarian, elitist

inégalité [inegalite] **NF 1** (injustice) inequality (**entre** between); **inégalités sociales** social inequalities **2** (différence) disparity, difference (**de** between); **les inégalités de salaire sont énormes dans cette entreprise** the differences in salary are huge in this company **3** (du sol) unevenness; **les inégalités du chemin** the bumps in the road, the unevenness of the road; Fig **i. d'humeur** capriciousness **4** Math inequality

inélastique [inelastik] **ADJ** Phys inelastic

inélégamment [inelegamɑ̃] **ADV** Litt inelegantly

inélégance [inelegɑ̃s] **NF** Litt inelegance

inélégant [inelegɑ̃] **ADJ** Litt inelegant; **il eût été i. d'insister** it would have been inappropriate to insist; **une action inélégante** an improper or unfitting act

inéligibilité [ineliʒibilite] **NF** ineligibility

inéligible [inéliʒibl] **ADJ** ineligible

inéluctabilité [inelyktabilite] **NF** inescapability, Fml ineluctability

inéluctable [inelyktabl] **ADJ** inescapable, Fml ineluctable

inéluctablement [inelyktabləmɑ̃] **ADV** inescapably, Fml ineluctably

inemployable [inãplwajabl] **ADJ** unusable

inemployé [inãplwaje] **ADJ** unused; *(ressources)* untapped; *(forces)* unchannelled

inénarrable [inenarabl] **ADJ** comical, funny; **dommage que vous ne l'ayez pas vu, c'était i.!** it was a shame you didn't see it, it was priceless!

inentamé [inãtame] **ADJ** intact; *(pain, camembert, gâteau)* uncut; *(fortune)* intact, untouched

inéprouvé [inepruve] **ADJ 1** *(non mis à l'épreuve)* untried, untested **2** *(non ressenti)* not yet experienced *or* felt

inepte [inɛpt] **ADJ** *(remarque, réponse)* inept, foolish

ineptie [inɛpsi] **NF 1** *(caractère stupide)* ineptitude, ineptness **2** *(action, remarque)* **dire des inepties** to talk nonsense; **ce traité est une i.** this treaty is nonsense *or* an absurdity; **c'est une i. de dire que …** it's absurd to say that …

inépuisable [inepɥizabl] **ADJ** *(réserves, sujet, curiosité)* inexhaustible; **un stock i. d'histoires drôles** an inexhaustible supply of funny stories; **une imagination i.** a limitless imagination; **sur ce sujet-là, il est i.** you can never get him off the subject

inéquation [inekwasjɔ̃] **NF** *Math* inequation

inéquitable [inekitabl] **ADJ** inequitable, unfair

inerte [inɛrt] **ADJ** *(masse, corps, matière)* inert; *(nature)* sluggish; *(personne déprimée)* in a state of inertia; **elle gisait par terre, i.** she lay on the ground, motionless; **un visage i.** an expressionless face; **le visage i.** *(écouter etc)* impassively

inertie [inɛrsi] **NF 1** *Phys* inertia; **force d'i.** force of inertia; **moment d'i.** moment of inertia **2** *(manque de réaction)* passivity, inertia; *(de l'esprit, du corps)* sluggishness, inertness

inescomptable [inɛskɔ̃tabl] **ADJ** *Fin* undiscountable

inespéré [inɛspere] **ADJ** unexpected, unhoped-for

inesthétique [inɛstetik] **ADJ** unaesthetic

inestimable [inɛstimabl] **ADJ** *(dégâts, coût, richesse)* incalculable, inestimable; **bijoux d'une valeur i.** priceless jewels; **votre aide a été i.** your help was invaluable; **être en bonne santé est une chance i.** good health is something to be treasured

inévitable [inevitabl] **ADJ** *(accident, contretemps)* unavoidable; *(résultat, conséquences)* inevitable, inescapable, unavoidable; **c'est i.** it's inevitable; *Hum* **l'i.** Lulu **était là** Lulu was there as per usual; *Hum* **nous eûmes droit à l'i. gâteau aux cerises** we were treated to the inevitable *or* the usual cherry cake

inévitablement [inevitabləmã] **ADV** inevitably, unavoidably; **si on passe par là, il va i. nous voir** if we go that way he's bound to see us

inexact [inɛgzakt] **ADJ 1** *(incorrect) (réponse, données, description, version, détail)* inaccurate, incorrect, inexact; *(somme, calcul)* wrong, incorrect; **des renseignements inexacts** inaccurate *or* incorrect information; **mais c'est i.** but that's wrong *or* incorrect **2** *(manquant de ponctualité) (personne)* unpunctual

inexactement [inɛgzaktəmã] **ADV** inaccurately, incorrectly

inexactitude [inɛgzaktityd] **NF 1** *(caractère erroné, imprécision) (de renseignement, données)* inaccuracy, incorrectness; *(faute)* mistake, inaccuracy; **relever des inexactitudes dans une traduction** to find mistakes *or* inaccuracies in a translation **2** *(manque de ponctualité)* unpunctuality

inexaucé [inɛgzose] **ADJ** *(prière)* unanswered; *(désir)* unfulfilled

inexcusable [inɛkskyzabl] **ADJ** *(action, retard, négligence)* inexcusable, unforgivable; **vous êtes i.!** you're unforgivable!

inexécutable [inɛgzekytabl] **ADJ** *(projet)* impracticable, impractical, unworkable; *(ordre)* that cannot be carried out *or* executed

inexécuté [inɛgzekyte] **ADJ** *(promesse, contrat)* unfulfilled; *(ordres, travaux)* not (yet) carried out *or* executed; **l'ordre de tirer sur les civils resta i.** the order to shoot civilians was not carried out; **le projet resta i.** the project did not go ahead

inexécution [inɛgzekysjɔ̃] **NF** *(d'un contrat)* non-performance; *(d'une promesse)* non-fulfilment

inexercé [inɛgzɛrse] **ADJ 1** *(sans entraînement)* untrained **2** *(sans expérience) (œil, oreille)* untrained

inexhaustible [inɛgzostibl] **ADJ** *Litt* inexhaustible

inexigible [inɛgziʒibl] **ADJ** *Fin* not due

inexistant [inɛgzistã] **ADJ** non-existent; *Fam* **il est totalement i.** he's a complete non-entity; *Fam* **lors de la réunion, il a été i.** at the meeting he just merged into the wallpaper; *Fam* **Hewitt a été quasiment i. pendant le premier set** Hewitt seemed totally out of it in the first set

inexistence [inɛgzistãs] **NF** non-existence; *(absence d'importance)* worthlessness

inexorabilité [inɛgzɔrabilite] **NF** inexorability

inexorable [inɛgzɔrabl] **ADJ** *(volonté, rigueur, fatalité)* inexorable; *(juge)* unrelenting, inflexible, inexorable

inexorablement [inɛgzɔrabləmã] **ADV** inexorably

inexpérience [inɛkspɛrjãs] **NF** inexperience

inexpérimenté [inɛksperimãte] **ADJ 1** *(sans expérience) (personne, pilote)* inexperienced; *(main etc)* unpractised, unskilled **2** *(non testé) (procédé)* untried, untested

inexpert [inɛkspɛr] **ADJ** *Litt* inexpert, unpractised

inexpiable [inɛkspjabl] **ADJ** *(faute, péché, crime)* inexpiable, irremissible; *(qu'on ne peut apaiser)* merciless

inexpié [inɛkspje] **ADJ** unexpiated, unatoned

inexplicable [inɛksplikabl] **ADJ** *(comportement, accident, peur, joie)* inexplicable, unexplainable; **le sentiment que j'ai est i.** I can't explain the feeling I have

inexplicablement [inɛksplikabləmã] **ADV** inexplicably, unaccountably

inexpliqué [inɛksplike] **ADJ** unexplained

inexploitable [inɛksplwatabl] **ADJ** *(mine, terre)* unworkable, inexploitable

inexploité [inɛksplwate] **ADJ** *(mine)* unworked; *(terre)* undeveloped, unworked; **ressources inexploitées** untapped resources

inexplorable [inɛksplɔrabl] **ADJ** inexplorable

inexploré [inɛksplɔre] **ADJ** unexplored

inexplosible [inɛksplozibl] **ADJ** nonexplosive

inexpressif, -ive [inɛkspresif, -iv] **ADJ** inexpressive; *(visage, personne)* expressionless

inexprimable [inɛksprimabl] **ADJ** inexpressible

inexprimé [inɛksprime] **ADJ** unexpressed

inexpugnable [inɛkspygnabl] **ADJ** *(forteresse, position)* impregnable; *(force, âme)* invincible, unassailable

inextensible [inɛkstãsibl] **ADJ** *(tissu)* nonstretch; *(matière)* inextensible

in extenso [ɛkstɛso] **ADV** in full, in extenso

inextinguible [inɛkstɛ̃g(ɥ)ibl] **ADJ** *(feu, vengeance, haine)* inextinguishable, unquenchable; *(rire)* irrepressible, uncontrollable

in extremis [inɛkstremis] **ADV** at the (very) last minute; **baptiser/marier qn in extremis** to baptize/marry sb on his/her deathbed

inextricable [inɛkstrikabl] **ADJ** inextricable; **nous nous trouvâmes dans un i. labyrinthe** we found ourselves in an impassable maze

inextricablement [inɛkstrikabləmã] **ADV** inextricably

infaillibilité [ɛ̃fajibilite] **NF** infallibility

infaillible [ɛ̃fajibl] **ADJ** infallible

infailliblement [ɛ̃fajibləmã] **ADV** infallibly

infaisable [ɛ̃fəzabl] **ADJ** not feasible, impossible; **ces mots croisés sont vraiment infaisables** this crossword is just impossible *or* just can't be done

infalsifiable [ɛ̃falsifjabl] **ADJ** *(carte d'identité)* forgery-proof

infamant [ɛ̃famã] **ADJ 1** *(déclaration, accusation)* defamatory, slanderous **2** *Jur* **peine infamante** penalty involving loss of civil rights

infâme [ɛ̃fam] **ADJ** *(mensonge, trafic)* infamous; *(acte, crime, créature)* foul, vile, unspeakable; *(taudis)* vile, squalid; *(odeur, nourriture)* vile, foul, revolting

infamie [ɛ̃fami] **NF 1** *(caractère infâme)* infamy **2** *(action infâme)* foul *or* vile action; *(remarque infâme)* piece of slander; **dire des infamies de qn** to vilify *or* slander sb

infant, -ante [ɛ̃fã, -ãt] **N** *Hist* infante, *f* infanta

infanterie [ɛ̃fãtri] **NF** *Mil* infantry; **soldat d'i.** infantryman, foot soldier; **i. aéroportée** *ou* **de l'air** airborne infantry; **i. de marine** marine corps, marines

infanticide [ɛ̃fãtisid] **N** *(personne)* infanticide, child killer
  ADJ infanticidal
  NM *(crime)* infanticide, child murder

infantile [ɛ̃fãtil] **ADJ 1** *(maladie, affection)* infantile; **mortalité i.** infant mortality; **psychiatrie i.** child psychiatry **2** *Péj (attitude, réaction, personne)* infantile, childish

infantiliser [ɛ̃fãtilize] **VT** *Péj* **la télévision infantilise les gens** television reduces people to the level of two-year-olds

infantilisme [ɛ̃fãtilism] **NM 1** *Méd* infantilism, retarded development **2** *Péj* **c'est de l'i.** how infantile!, how childish!

infarctus [ɛ̃farktys] **NM** *Méd* infarct, infarction; **i. du myocarde** myocardial infarction, coronary thrombosis

infatigable [ɛ̃fatigabl] **ADJ** indefatigable, tireless, untiring

infatigablement [ɛ̃fatigabləmã] **ADV** tirelessly, untiringly, indefatigably

infatuation [ɛ̃fatɥasjɔ̃] **NF** *(suffisance)* self-conceit, self-importance

infatué [ɛ̃fatɥe] **ADJ 1** *(suffisant)* conceited; **i. (de soi-même)** conceited, full of oneself *or* of one's own importance **2** *Vieilli* infatuated

infatuer [ɛ̃fatɥe] **VT** *Vieilli* to infatuate
  VPR **s'infatuer 1** **s'i. (de soi-même)** to become conceited, to become full of oneself *or* full of one's own importance **2** *Vieilli* **s'i. de qn/qch** to become infatuated with sb/sth

infécond [ɛ̃fekɔ̃] **ADJ** *(femelle, femme, esprit)* infertile, sterile, barren; *(terre)* barren, infertile

infécondité [ɛ̃fekɔ̃dite] **NF** *(de femelle, femme, d'esprit)* infertility, sterility, barrenness; *(de terre)* barrenness, infertility; **pé-**

riode d'i. *(de femelle, femme)* period of infertility

infect [ɛ̃fɛkt] ADJ *(nourriture, repas)* vile, revolting; *(air)* foul; *(goût)* foul, revolting; **odeur infecte** foul *or* revolting smell, stench, stink; **taudis i.** filthy hovel; **temps i.** filthy *or* foul weather; **elle a été infecte avec sa sœur** she was vile *or* rotten to her sister; **c'est quelqu'un d'i.** he's/she's a vile person *or* really obnoxious

infectant [ɛ̃fɛktɑ̃] ADJ *Méd (virus)* infectious

infecter [ɛ̃fɛkte] VT **1** *Méd, Ordinat* to infect **2** *(atmosphère, air)* to poison, to contaminate, to pollute; *(eau, sol)* to contaminate, to taint, to pollute
▶ VPR **s'infecter** *(de blessure, plaie, pied etc)* to become infected, to turn *or* go septic

infectieux, -euse [ɛ̃fɛksjø, -øz] ADJ *Méd* infectious

infection [ɛ̃fɛksjɔ̃] NF **1** *Méd, Ordinat* infection; **i. virale** viral infection **2** *(puanteur)* stench, stink; **quelle i. dans cette pièce!** this room stinks!

inféodation [ɛ̃feɔdasjɔ̃] NF **1** *Pol* allegiance (**à** to) **2** *Hist (d'un vassal)* enfeoffment; *(d'une terre)* giving in fief

inféoder [ɛ̃feɔde] VT **1** *(soumettre)* to subjugate **2** *Hist (vassal)* to enfeoff; *(terre)* to give in fief
▶ VPR **s'inféoder** *Pol* **s'i. à un groupe/un parti** to give one's allegiance to a group/a party; **être inféodé à** to be subservient to

inférence [ɛ̃ferɑ̃s] NF inference

inférer [ɛ̃fere] VT (**j'infère; j'inférerai**) to infer, to gather (**de** from)

inférieur, -eure [ɛ̃ferjœr] ADJ **1** *(qui est en bas)* *(étagère, niveau)* bottom; *(étages)* lower; *(lèvre, paupière, mâchoire)* lower, bottom; **partie inférieure** lower part, bottom (part); **membres inférieurs** lower limbs; **allez voir à l'étage i.** go and look on the floor below *or* the next floor down; *Astron* **planète inférieure** inferior planet; *Géog* **le cours i. d'un fleuve** the lower course of a river; **i. au niveau de la mer** below sea level
2 *(dans une hiérarchie)* *(qualité, marchandises)* inferior, poor; *(intelligence)* inferior; *Bot, Zool (plante, animal)* lower; **d'un rang i.** of a lower rank, lower in rank; **être rétrogradé à l'échelon i.** to be demoted to the grade below; **elle ne lui est pas inférieure** she is his equal, she's not inferior to him; **elle n'est en rien inférieure à ses collègues** she is in no way inferior to her colleagues; **son dernier roman est i. aux précédents** his latest novel is inferior to *or* not as good as his previous ones; *Litt* **il est i. à sa tâche** he is not equal to the task, he is not up to the job
3 *(plus petit)* **6 est i. à 8** 6 is less than 8; **a est i. ou égal à 3** a is less than *or* equal to 3; **note inférieure à douze** mark below twelve; **vitesse i. à 500 km/h** speed below *or* under 500 km/h; **température i. à -30** temperature below -30; **i. en nombre** fewer in number; **i. à la normale** *(de la température)* below normal; **i. à la moyenne** below average; **ce mois-ci la production est inférieure à celle des mois précédents** this month production is lower than *or* less than *or* below that of previous months
▶ N inferior

inférieurement [ɛ̃ferjœrmɑ̃] ADV **1** *(en bas)* in a lower position **2** *(moins bien)* in an inferior manner (**à** to), less well (**à** than)

infériorité [ɛ̃ferjɔrite] NF inferiority; **i. numérique** *ou* **en nombre** numerical inferiority, inferiority in numbers; *Psy* **avoir un complexe d'i.** to have an inferiority complex; **i. de niveau** difference *or* drop in level; **se sentir/être en position d'i.** *(par rap-*

---

port à qn) to feel/be in a position of inferiority *or* in an inferior position (in relation to sb)

infernal, -ale, -aux, -ales [ɛ̃fɛrnal, -o] ADJ **1** *(de l'enfer)* infernal, of hell; *Fig* **cruauté/méchanceté infernale** diabolical cruelty/wickedness **2** *Fam (insupportable)* *(chaleur, bruit)* infernal; **nous dévalions la pente à une vitesse infernale** we hurtled down the slope at (a) breakneck speed; **la direction nous impose des cadences infernales** the management wants us to work at an impossible speed; **cet enfant est i.** this child's a little devil; **elle est infernale, à toujours se plaindre** she's really awful, she's always complaining; **c'est i.!** it's hellish!, it's sheer hell!

infertile [ɛ̃fɛrtil] ADJ *(terre, imagination, esprit)* infertile, barren

infertilité [ɛ̃fɛrtilite] NF infertility

infestation [ɛ̃fɛstasjɔ̃] NF *Méd* infestation

infester [ɛ̃fɛste] VT *(de la vermine etc)* to infest, to overrun; **infesté d'insectes/de pirates** infested *or* overrun with insects/pirates

infeutrable [ɛ̃føtrabl] ADJ which does not felt *or* mat

infibulation [ɛ̃fibylasjɔ̃] NF infibulation

infichu [ɛ̃fiʃy] ADJ *Fam (incapable)* incapable (**de** of)

infidèle [ɛ̃fidɛl] ADJ **1** *(déloyal)* *(ami)* unfaithful, disloyal (**à** to); *(mari, femme)* unfaithful (**à** to); *Litt* **être i. à sa promesse** to be false *or* untrue to one's promise, to break one's promise **2** *(inexact)* *(traduction, rapport etc)* inaccurate, incorrect; *(mémoire, témoignage)* unreliable, untrustworthy; **c'est une traduction i.** it is not an accurate *or* a faithful translation **3** *Rel* infidel
▶ N *Rel* infidel

infidèlement [ɛ̃fidɛlmɑ̃] ADV **1** *(déloyalement)* unfaithfully **2** *(inexactement)* inaccurately, incorrectly

infidélité [ɛ̃fidelite] NF **1** *(déloyauté)* *(d'ami)* unfaithfulness, disloyalty (**à** to); *(de mari, femme)* unfaithfulness, infidelity (**à** to); **faire des infidélités à sa femme** to be unfaithful to one's wife; *Hum* **faire une i. à son boucher/son coiffeur** to be unfaithful to one's butcher/hairdresser, to go to a different butcher/hairdresser (just for once) **2** *(manque d'exactitude)* *(dans une traduction, un compte-rendu, un rapport)* inaccuracy; **infidélités** inaccuracies

infiltration [ɛ̃filtrasjɔ̃] NF **1** *(d'un liquide)* *(dans qch)* infiltration (**dans** into), seepage; *(à travers qch)* seepage, percolation (**à travers** through); **il y a des infiltrations dans le plafond** there are some leaks in the ceiling **2** *Fig (de nouvelles idées, coutumes, espions etc)* infiltration **3** *Méd (injection)* injection; **faire des infiltrations à qn** to give sb injections

infiltrer [ɛ̃filtre] VT **1** *(noyauter)* *(parti, pays etc)* to infiltrate **2** *Méd* to inject (**dans** into)
▶ VPR **s'infiltrer** **1** *(d'un fluide)* **s'i. dans qch** to seep into sth, to infiltrate (into) sth; **s'i. à travers qch** to seep through sth, to percolate through sth **2** *Fig (d'une idée, d'une théorie etc)* to infiltrate; **s'i. dans** to infiltrate **3** **s'i. dans un groupuscule/une organisation** to infiltrate a group/an organization; *Mil* **s'i. dans un pays** to infiltrate a country

infime [ɛ̃fim] ADJ **1** *(quantité, nombre, proportion, pourcentage, différence)* tiny, minute, infinitesimal **2** *(rang etc)* lowly, mean

infini [ɛ̃fini] ADJ *(espace, univers)* infinite, boundless; *(soin, bonté, patience etc)* infinite; *(bonheur)* *(intense)* utter, intense; *(arguments etc)* innumerable; **prendre d'infinies précautions** to take innumerable *or* countless precautions; **être d'une** *ou*

---

avoir une patience infinie to be infinitely patient, to have infinite patience; **vous m'avez fait un plaisir i. en venant me voir** you have given me enormous pleasure in coming to see me; **auriez-vous l'infinie bonté de me donner l'heure, monsieur?** would you do me the great kindness of telling me the time, sir?; **il est resté au téléphone un temps i.** he stayed on the phone for an eternity; *Math* **ensemble i.** infinite set
▶ NM **l'i.** *Phil* the infinite; *Phys* infinity; *Phot* **mettre au point sur l'i.** to focus to infinity; **à l'i.** *(s'étendre, se refléter)* to infinity; *(discutailler)* ad infinitum

infiniment [ɛ̃finimɑ̃] ADV *(bon, généreux, patient)* infinitely; **i. plus intelligent** infinitely more intelligent; **i. petit** infinitesimally small; **l'i. petit** the infinitesimal; **l'i. grand** the infinitely great; **i. grand** enormously large; **se donner i. de peine** to give oneself an infinite *or* an enormous amount of trouble; **il parle à ses enfants avec i. de douceur** he is incredibly gentle when speaking to his children; **je regrette i.** I'm extremely sorry; **je vous suis i. reconnaissant de m'avoir aidé** I'm extremely *or* enormously grateful to you for helping me

infinité [ɛ̃finite] NF **1** *Math, Phys* infinity; **l'i. de l'espace** the infinity *or* boundlessness of space **2** *(grand nombre)* **une i. de personnes/raisons** an infinite number of people/reasons

infinitésimal, -ale, -aux, -ales [ɛ̃finitezimal, -o] ADJ infinitesimal

infinitif, -ive [ɛ̃finitif, -iv] SEE GRAMMAR A40-2; B35-7 *Gram* ADJ infinitive
▶ NM infinitive; **à l'i.** in the infinitive

infirmation [ɛ̃firmasjɔ̃] NF *Jur* invalidation, nullification, quashing

infirme [ɛ̃firm] ADJ disabled, crippled, *Arch, Litt* weak; **i. du bras gauche** crippled in the left arm; **il est resté i. à la suite de son accident** his accident left him disabled *or* crippled *or* a cripple
▶ N cripple, disabled person; **les infirmes** the disabled, the crippled

infirmer [ɛ̃firme] VT **1** *(montrer la faiblesse de)* *(théorie)* to pinpoint the weakness of; *(contredire)* *(témoignage)* to invalidate; *(information, nouvelle)* to refute **2** *Jur (jugement)* to invalidate, to nullify, to quash

infirmerie [ɛ̃firməri] NF *(de prison, caserne etc)* infirmary; *(à l'école, dans un bateau)* sick bay

infirmier [ɛ̃firmje] NM *(male)* nurse; **i. militaire** medical orderly

infirmière [ɛ̃firmjɛr] NF nurse; *Mil* medical orderly; **i. diplômée** ≃ state-registered nurse, *Am* registered nurse; **i. en chef** nursing officer, *Am* quality control officer; **i. visiteuse** district nurse, *Am* home health nurse

infirmité [ɛ̃firmite] NF *(invalidité)* (physical) disability, *Arch, Litt* weakness, frailty

inflammabilité [ɛ̃flamabilite] NF inflammability, flammability

inflammable [ɛ̃flamabl] ADJ inflammable, flammable

inflammation [ɛ̃flamasjɔ̃] NF *Méd* inflammation

inflammatoire [ɛ̃flamatwar] ADJ *Méd* inflammatory

inflation [ɛ̃flasjɔ̃] NF *Écon* inflation; **politique d'i.** inflationary policy; **i. fiduciaire** inflation of the currency; **i. monétaire** monetary inflation; **i. rampante/galopante** rampant/galloping inflation; **l'i. du nombre des ...** the marked increase in the number of ...; **i. des prix** price inflation; **i. des salaires** wage inflation; **i. par la demande** demand-pull inflation; **i. par les coûts** cost-push inflation

inflationniste [ɛ̃flɑsjɔnist] *Écon* **N** inflationist
ADJ inflationary

infléchi [ɛ̃fleʃi] **ADJ 1** *Gram (voyelle)* inflected **2** *Opt (rayon etc)* inflected, bent

infléchir [ɛ̃fleʃir] **VT 1** *Opt (rayon)* to bend, to inflect, to curve **2** *(politique)* to change the direction of; **i. le cours des événements** to change *or* alter the course of events **3** *Bourse (faire diminuer)* to cut, to reduce
VPR s'infléchir 1 *(dévier) (d'une route, d'une ligne etc)* to bend, to curve; *Opt (d'un rayon)* to be inflected *or* bent **2** *(d'un plancher, d'une poutre)* to sag, to bow **3** *(changer) (de politique)* to change direction, to shift **4** *Bourse (diminuer) (cours)* to fall

inflexibilité [ɛ̃flɛksibilite] **NF** inflexibility, rigidity

inflexible [ɛ̃flɛksibl] **ADJ** *(personne)* inflexible, rigid, unyielding; *(règle, loi)* inflexible, rigid, hard and fast; **une volonté i.** an iron *or* inflexible *or* unbending will; **demeurer i. dans une résolution** to remain firm in *or* stick to a resolution

inflexiblement [ɛ̃flɛksibləmɑ̃] **ADV** inflexibly, rigidly

inflexion [ɛ̃flɛksjɔ̃] **NF 1** *(mouvement)* **i. du corps** bend(ing) of the body; *(pour saluer)* bow; **i. de (la) tête** tilt(ing) of the head; *(pour saluer, acquiescer)* nod **2** *(de la voix)* inflection, modulation **3** *(de courbe, rayon)* inflection **4** *Ling* inflection **5** *Bourse (diminution)* reduction, fall

infliger [ɛ̃fliʒe] **(j'infligeai(s); n. infligeons) VT** *(correction, punition, musique pénible etc)* to inflict *(à* on); **i. une peine/une amende à qn** to impose a penalty/a fine on sb; **i. des épreuves à qn** to bring hardship on sb; **il nous a infligé sa présence** he inflicted himself *or* his presence on us
VPR s'infliger s'i. des privations ou **des épreuves** to bring hardship on oneself

inflorescence [ɛ̃flɔresɑ̃s] **NF** *Bot* inflorescence

influençable [ɛ̃flyɑ̃sabl] **ADJ** easily influenced

influence [ɛ̃flyɑ̃s] **NF** influence (**sur** on); **avoir une bonne/mauvaise i. sur qn** to have a good/bad influence on sb; **exercer une i. bénéfique/néfaste sur qch/qn** to have a beneficial/harmful influence *or* effect on sth/sb; **sous l'i. de l'alcool/la drogue** under the influence of drink/drugs; *Fam* **être sous i.** to be under the influence of drugs; **agir sous l'i. de la colère/la jalousie** to act in a fit of anger/jealousy; **sous ton i.** under your influence; **il a beaucoup d'i.** he has a lot of influence, he's very influential; **cet incident n'a eu aucune i. sur ma décision** this incident had no influence on *or* didn't influence my decision; **sphère d'i.** sphere of influence; **trafic d'i.** corrupt practice

influencer [ɛ̃flyɑ̃se] **VT** **(j'influençai(s); n. influençons)** to influence, to have an influence on; *(opinion publique)* to influence, to sway, to have an influence on; **ce peintre a été très influencé par le cubisme** this painter was greatly influenced by cubism; **il ne faut pas te laisser i. par ce type-là!** you mustn't let yourself be influenced by that fellow!; **il se laisse facilement i.** he's easily influenced

influent [ɛ̃flyɑ̃] **ADJ** influential

influer [ɛ̃flye] **VI** **i. sur qch/qn** to have influence on sth/sb, to influence sth/sb; **le temps influe sur son humeur** the weather affects *or* has an effect on his mood

influx [ɛ̃fly] **NM 1** *Physiol* **i. nerveux** nerve impulse **2** *(fluide)* influx

info [ɛ̃fo] **NF** *Journ, Radio, TV Fam (nouvelle)* news item; **les infos** the news

infogérance [ɛ̃foʒerɑ̃s] **NF** facilities management

infographe [ɛ̃fograf] **N** graphics artist, graphics designer

infographie [ɛ̃fɔgrafi] **NF** computer graphics

infographiste [ɛ̃fografist] **N** graphics artist, graphics designer

in-folio **ADJ INV, NM INV** folio

infomercial [ɛ̃fomɛrsjal] **NM** infomercial

infondé [ɛ̃fɔ̃de] **ADJ** unfounded, groundless

informateur, -trice [ɛ̃fɔrmatœr, -tris] **N** informant; *(de police)* informer; *(de journaliste)* inside source

informaticien, -ienne [ɛ̃fɔrmatisjɛ̃, -jɛn] **N** computer scientist
ADJ ingénieur i. computer engineer

informatif, -ive [ɛ̃fɔrmatif, -iv] **ADJ** informative

information [ɛ̃fɔrmasjɔ̃] **NF 1** *(renseignement)* (piece of) information; **informations** information; **pour votre i.** for your information; **nous vous adressons ce catalogue à titre d'i.** we are sending you this catalogue for your information; **à titre d'i.** for information; **une i. de première importance** a very important piece of information; **c'est la seule i. dont je dispose** it's the only information I have; **je vous envoie pour votre i. ...** I'm sending you for your information ...; **assurer l'i. du public en matière de santé** to ensure that the public is (kept) informed about matters of health; **le droit à l'i.** freedom of information; **centre d'i.** information centre; *Mktg* **i. sur le lieu de vente** point-of-sale information; *Mktg* **informations primaires** primary data
2 *Journ, Radio, TV (nouvelle)* news (item), item *or* piece of news; **une i. de dernière minute** some last minute news, a late (news) item; *Journ* **des informations de dernière minute** stop press (news); **des informations de dernière minute semblent indiquer que le cessez-le-feu est intervenu** latest reports seem to indicate that there has been a ceasefire; **cette i. n'a pas été confirmée** this news is unconfirmed; **des informations économiques** economic news, news about the economy; **l'i. financière de la journée** the day's financial news; **un journal d'i.** a serious *or* quality newspaper; *Radio, TV, Journ* **les informations** *(émission)* the news (bulletin); **c'est passé aux informations** it was on the news; **je l'ai entendu aux informations** I heard it on the news; **informations radiodiffusées** radio news; **informations télévisées** television news
3 *(médias)* **l'i.** the media; **mettre la main sur l'i.** to take control of the media; **qui fait l'i.?** who decides what goes in the news?
4 *Ordinat* data, information; **traitement de l'i.** data processing; **théorie de l'i.** information theory
5 *Jur (enquête)* **i. (judiciaire)** (judicial) inquiry; *(instruction préparatoire)* preliminary investigation; **ouvrir une i.** to begin legal proceedings

informatique [ɛ̃fɔrmatik] **NF** *(traitement de l'information)* data processing, DP; *(science)* computer science, computing, information science *or* technology, IT; **travailler dans l'i.** to work *or* be in computing; **i. d'entreprise** business data processing; **i. individuelle** personal computing; **société/magazine d'i.** computer company/magazine; **cours d'i.** computer *or* data-processing course; **i. à domicile** home computing
ADJ *(mobilier, réseau etc)* computer

informatiquement [ɛ̃fɔrmatikmɑ̃] **ADV** by *or* on computer; **toutes les données sont traitées i.** all the data is processed by *or* on computer

informatisation [ɛ̃fɔrmatizasjɔ̃] **NF** computerization

informatiser [ɛ̃fɔrmatize] **VT** to computerize; **service informatisé** computerized department

informe [ɛ̃fɔrm] **ADJ** *(masse, amas, objet)* shapeless, formless; *(chapeau, pull, chaussures)* shapeless; *(plan)* crude, rough; *(monstre, être)* misshapen, ill-formed

informé [ɛ̃fɔrme] **ADJ** informed; **dans les milieux informés** in informed circles
NM *Jur* inquiry; **ordonner un plus ample i.** to order a broadening of the inquiry; **jusqu'à plus ample i.** until we have further information *or* are better informed

informel, -elle [ɛ̃fɔrmɛl] **ADJ** informal

informer [ɛ̃fɔrme] **VT** **i. qn de qch** to inform sb of sth, to tell sb *or* let sb know about sth; **i. qn d'un fait** to inform sb of *or* acquaint sb with a fact, to tell sb a fact; **personne ne m'a informé du fait qu'il devait rester plusieurs jours!** no one informed me (of the fact) that *or* told me that *or* let me know that he was to stay several days!; **veuillez m'en i.** please let me know, please inform me, please tell me; **i. qn que ...** to inform *or* tell sb that ..., to let sb know that ...; **nous informons les voyageurs que ...** we would like to inform passengers that ...; **bien informé** well informed; **mal informé** ill-informed; **on vous a mal informé, vous avez été mal informé** you've been misinformed *or* wrongly informed
VI *Jur* **i. sur un crime** to investigate a crime, to inquire into a crime; **i. contre qn** to begin legal proceedings against sb
VPR s'informer *(se renseigner)* to inquire, to ask, to make inquiries (**de qch** about sth; **au sujet de qn** about sb); *(se tenir au courant)* to keep oneself informed; **s'i. de l'état de santé de qn** to inquire *or* ask after *or* about sb's health

informulé [ɛ̃fɔrmyle] **ADJ** unformulated

inforoute [ɛ̃forut] **NF** *Ordinat* information superhighway

infortune [ɛ̃fɔrtyn] **NF** *surtout Litt* misfortune; **compagnons d'i.** companions in adversity, fellow sufferers; **tomber dans l'i.** to meet with misfortune

infortuné, -ée [ɛ̃fɔrtyne] **ADJ** unfortunate, unlucky, wretched
N (poor *or* unfortunate) wretch; **les infortunés** the unfortunate, the wretched

infospectacle [ɛ̃fospɛktakl] **NF** infotainment

infoutu [ɛ̃futy] **ADJ** *très Fam* downright incapable (**de** of)

infraction [ɛ̃fraksjɔ̃] **NF** *(à un règlement, une règle)* infringement, contravention; *(à la loi)* infringement, breach; *(à une coutume)* violation (**à** of); *(délit)* offence; **i. au code de la route** traffic offence, *Am* traffic violation; **être en i.** to be committing an offence *or* *Am* offense, to be breaking the law; **i. politique** ≃ offence/offences against the state

infranchissable [ɛ̃frɑ̃ʃisabl] **ADJ** *(rivière, col, gouffre)* impassable; *(obstacle, difficulté)* insurmountable, insuperable

infrangible [ɛ̃frɑ̃ʒibl] **ADJ** *Litt* infrangible

infrarouge [ɛ̃fraruʒ] **ADJ, NM** *Phys* infrared

infrason [ɛ̃frasɔ̃] **NM** *Phys* infrasonic vibration

infra(-)sonore, *pl* **infra(-)sonores** [ɛ̃frasɔnɔr] **ADJ** infrasonic

infrastructure [ɛ̃frastryktyr] **NF 1** *Constr* substructure **2** *Écon, Tech (de chemins de fer, d'hôpitaux etc)* infrastructure; **i. routière/touristique** road/tourist infrastructure; **i. organisationnelle** organizational infrastructure

infréquentable [ɛ̃frekɑ̃tabl] ADJ **gens infréquentables** people one doesn't want to associate with

infroissable [ɛ̃frwasabl] ADJ *Tex* crease-resistant

infructueux, -euse [ɛ̃fryktɥø, -øz] ADJ **1** *(effort, tentative)* fruitless, unfruitful, unsuccessful; *(investissement)* unprofitable **2** *Vieilli (terre etc)* unfruitful, barren

infumable [ɛ̃fymabl] ADJ unsmokable

infus [ɛ̃fy] ADJ *(connaissance)* inborn, innate; **je n'ai pas la science infuse!** I can't be expected to know everything!

infuser [ɛ̃fyze] VT **1** *(faire pénétrer)* to instil, *Am* to instill, to infuse (**dans** into); **i. le doute dans l'esprit de qn** to instil *or* infuse doubt into sb's mind; *Fig* **i. un sang nouveau à un organisme** to inject new blood into an organization **2** *(herbes)* to infuse; **le thé est assez infusé** the tea has brewed for long enough ▸ VI **faire i. le thé** to brew *or* infuse the tea; **laisser i. le thé** to let the tea brew *or* infuse

infusible [ɛ̃fyzibl] ADJ infusible, non-fusible

infusion [ɛ̃fyzjɔ̃] NF **1** *(action) (d'herbes, de thé)* infusion; *(plantes etc)* steeping **2** *(boisson)* herb tea, infusion; **une i. de camomille** some camomile tea, an infusion of camomile

ingagnable [ɛ̃ɡaɲabl] ADJ impossible to win; **la partie est i. pour l'Angleterre** England can't win (the game)

ingambe [ɛ̃ɡɑ̃b] ADJ *Vieilli (physiquement)* nimble, sprightly; *(esprit)* alert

ingénier (s') [sɛ̃ʒenje] VPR **s'i. à faire qch** to strive *or* make great efforts to do sth; **il s'ingénie à me rendre la vie impossible/à me contredire** he goes out of his way to make my life impossible/to contradict me

ingénierie [ɛ̃ʒeniri] NF engineering; **i. assistée par ordinateur** computer-aided engineering; **i. inverse** reverse engineering; **i. financière** financial engineering

ingénieur [ɛ̃ʒenjœr] NM engineer; **femme i.** female *or* woman engineer; *Mil* **Corps des Ingénieurs géographes** ≃ Ordnance Survey ▸ ▸ **i. civil** civil engineer; **i. commercial** sales engineer; *Naut* **i. des constructions navales** naval constructor; **i. de diffusion** broadcasting engineer; **i. éclairagiste** lighting director; **i. électricien** electrical engineer; **i. électronicien** electronics engineer; **i. logiciels** software engineer; **i. magnétoscope** videotape engineer; **i. mécanicien** mechanical engineer; **i. de méthodes** methods engineer; **i. des mines** = engineer who has graduated from the École des Mines; **i. des ponts et chaussées** = (government) civil engineer; **i. du son** sound *or* recording engineer; *(chargé du mixage ou doublage)* dubbing mixer; **i. technico-commercial** sales engineer *or* technician; **i. des télécommunications** telecommunications engineer; **i. des travaux publics** civil engineer; **i. des ventes** sales engineer; **i. de la vision** vision control operator, vision mixer; **i. de vol** flight engineer

ingénieur-conseil, *pl* **ingénieurs-conseils** NM consulting engineer

ingénieusement [ɛ̃ʒenjøzmɑ̃] ADV ingeniously, cleverly

ingénieux, -euse [ɛ̃ʒenjø, -øz] ADJ ingenious, clever

ingéniosité [ɛ̃ʒenjozite] NF ingenuity, cleverness

ingénu, -ue [ɛ̃ʒeny] ADJ *(personne)* ingenuous, artless, simple; *(regard)* ingenuous ▸ N ingenuous *or* artless *or* simple person; **faire l'i.** to affect simplicity ▸ NF *Théâtre* **ingénue** ingénue

ingénuité [ɛ̃ʒenɥite] NF ingenuousness, artlessness, simplicity

ingénument [ɛ̃ʒenymɑ̃] ADV ingenuously, artlessly

ingérence [ɛ̃ʒerɑ̃s] NF interference, meddling (**dans** in)

ingérer [ɛ̃ʒere] **(j'ingère; j'ingérerai)** VT *Physiol (nourriture)* to ingest ▸ VPR **s'ingérer s'i. dans qch** to interfere *or* meddle in sth

ingestion [ɛ̃ʒɛstjɔ̃] NF *Physiol* ingestion

ingouvernable [ɛ̃ɡuvɛrnabl] ADJ *(nation etc)* ungovernable; *(bateau etc)* unmanageable

ingrat, -ate [ɛ̃ɡra, -at] ADJ *(personne)* ungrateful (**envers** to, towards); *(sol, terre)* unproductive, barren; *(matière)* intractable; *(tâche)* thankless; *(travail, sujet)* unrewarding; *(apparence, visage etc)* unattractive, unpleasant; **l'âge i.** the awkward age ▸ N ungrateful person

ingratement [ɛ̃ɡratmɑ̃] ADV *Litt* ungratefully

ingratitude [ɛ̃ɡratityd] NF ingratitude, ungratefulness

ingrédient [ɛ̃ɡredjɑ̃] NM ingredient

inguérissable [ɛ̃ɡerisabl] ADJ *Méd* incurable; *(chagrin)* inconsolable

ingurgitation [ɛ̃ɡyrʒitasjɔ̃] NF ingurgitation

ingurgiter [ɛ̃ɡyrʒite] VT *(manger)* to gulp down, to swallow (down); *(boire)* to gulp down, to knock back; **faire i. qch à qn** to force sb to swallow sth, to make sb swallow sth; *Fig Fam* to cram sth into sb's head; **le prof nous a fait i. toutes les déclinaisons en une semaine** the teacher crammed all the declensions into our heads in a week; **j'ai ingurgité tout le programme d'histoire la veille de l'examen** I crammed the whole history syllabus into my head the day before the exam

inhabile [inabil] ADJ *Litt (malhabile)* unskilled (**à** in), unskilful, *Am* unskillful; *Jur* **i. à tester** incompetent to make a will

inhabileté [inabilte] NF lack of skill (**à faire qch** in doing sth); **c'est quelqu'un d'une grande i. en matière de commerce** he is extremely unskilful *or Am* unskillful in commercial matters

inhabilité [inabilite] NF *Jur* incapacity, disability; **i. à succéder** incompetency to succeed

inhabitable [inabitabl] ADJ uninhabitable

> Il faut noter que l'adjectif anglais **inhabitable** est un faux ami. Il signifie **habitable**.

inhabité [inabite] ADJ *(maison)* unoccupied, uninhabited; *(région)* uninhabited; *Astron* **vol i.** unmanned flight

> Il faut noter que l'adjectif anglais **inhabited** est un faux ami. Il signifie **habité**.

inhabituel, -elle [inabitɥɛl] ADJ unusual; **c'est i. de ne pas les trouver à la maison le dimanche** it's unusual not to find them at home on a Sunday

inhalateur, -trice [inalatœr, -tris] ADJ *(appareil)* inhaling ▸ NM *Méd* inhaler

inhalation [inalasjɔ̃] NF *Physiol* inhalation; *Méd* **faire des inhalations** to inhale

inhaler [inale] VT to inhale

inharmonieux, -ieuse [inarmɔnjø, -jøz] ADJ *(son)* inharmonious, discordant

inhérence [inerɑ̃s] NF inherence, inherency

inhérent [inerɑ̃] ADJ inherent (**à** in)

inhibé, -ée [inibe] ADJ inhibited, repressed ▸ N inhibited *or* repressed person

inhiber [inibe] VT to inhibit

inhibiteur, -trice [inibitœr, -tris] ADJ *Biol, Physiol (réflexe, nerf etc)* inhibitory ▸ NM *Pharm* inhibitor; *Aut* **i. d'oxydation** oxidation inhibitor; *Aut* **i. de corrosion** corrosion inhibitor

inhibition [inibisjɔ̃] NF inhibition

inhospitalier, -ière [inɔspitalje, -jɛr] ADJ inhospitable

inhumain [inymɛ̃] ADJ inhuman

inhumainement [inymɛnmɑ̃] ADV *Litt* inhumanly

inhumanité [inymanite] NF *Litt* inhumanity

inhumation [inymasjɔ̃] NF burial, interment

inhumer [inyme] VT to bury, to inter

inimaginable [inimaʒinabl] ADJ unimaginable, inconceivable, unbelievable

inimitable [inimitabl] ADJ inimitable

inimité [inimite] ADJ matchless; **un artiste extraordinaire resté i. à ce jour** an extraordinary artist whose like has never been seen since

inimitié [inimitje] NF enmity, hostility, ill feeling

ininflammable [inɛ̃flamabl] ADJ non-(in)-flammable, fireproof

inintelligemment [inɛ̃teliʒamɑ̃] ADV unintelligently

inintelligence [inɛ̃teliʒɑ̃s] NF **1** *(manque d'intelligence)* lack of intelligence; **elle a eu l'i. d'accepter son invitation** she rather unwisely accepted his invitation **2** *(incompréhension)* **son i. du problème** his inability to understand *or* his lack of understanding of the problem

inintelligent [inɛ̃teliʒɑ̃] ADJ unintelligent

inintelligibilité [inɛ̃teliʒibilite] NF unintelligibility

inintelligible [inɛ̃teliʒibl] ADJ unintelligible

inintelligiblement [inɛ̃teliʒibləmɑ̃] ADV unintelligibly

inintéressant [inɛ̃teresɑ̃] ADJ uninteresting

ininterrompu [inɛ̃terɔ̃py] ADJ *(efforts)* continued, uninterrupted, unremitting; *(discussions)* uninterrupted; *(sommeil, pluie)* uninterrupted, unbroken; *(progrès)* steady, continued; *(suite)* uninterrupted; **le flot i. des voitures** the steady *or* unbroken stream of cars; **deux heures de musique ininterrompue** two hours of non-stop *or* uninterrupted *or* continuous music

inique [inik] ADJ iniquitous

iniquement [inikmɑ̃] ADV iniquitously

iniquité [inikite] NF iniquity

initial, -iale, -iaux, -iales [inisjal, -jo] ADJ *(lettre, coût etc)* initial; **vitesse initiale** *(d'un projectile)* muzzle velocity ▸ NF **initiale** initial (letter); **il a signé le document de ses initiales** he signed the document with his initials, he initialled the document

initialement [inisjalmɑ̃] ADV initially

initialisation [inisjalizasjɔ̃] NF *Ordinat* initialization; **i. du compteur** counter initialization, zeroing of the counter

initialiser [inisjalize] VT *Ordinat (disque)* to initialize; *(ordinateur)* to boot (up)

initiateur, -trice [inisjatœr, -tris] N *(d'un projet, d'une réforme etc)* initiator, originator; **elle fut son initiatrice** she initiated him into it ▸ ADJ initiatory

initiation [inisjasjɔ̃] NF initiation (**à** into); **une i. à la musique** an introduction to music; **rite d'i.** initiation rite

initiatique [inisjatik] ADJ initiatory

initiative [inisjativ] NF initiative; **sur l'i. de qn** on sb's initiative; **prendre l'i. d'une ré-**

forme to initiate a reform; **prendre l'i. de faire qch** to take the initiative in doing sth; **faire qch de sa propre i.** to do sth on one's own initiative; **faire preuve d'i.** to show initiative; **manquer d'i.** to lack initiative; **il n'a aucune i.** he's got no initiative; **syndicat d'i.** tourist information bureau; *Mil* **i. de défense stratégique** strategic defence initiative; **i. gouvernementale** = governmental prerogative to propose legislation; *(idée)* government initiative; *Pol* **i. de paix** peace initiative *or* overture; **i. parlementaire** = parliamentary prerogative to legislate; **i. populaire** citizen's initiative

initié, -ée [inisje] N *Rel, Fig* initiate; **les initiés** the initiated, the initiates; *Bourse* **délit d'i.** insider trading

initier [inisje] VT to initiate (**à** into); **i. qn au grec/aux échecs/à l'harmonica** to introduce sb to Greek/chess/the harmonica
▶ VPR **s'initier** **s'i. à** *(matière, discipline)* to start learning; *(sport)* to start to play

injectable [ɛ̃ʒɛktabl] ADJ injectable

injecté [ɛ̃ʒɛkte] ADJ *(visage)* congested; **yeux injectés de sang** bloodshot eyes

injecter [ɛ̃ʒɛkte] VT *(substance)* to inject (**dans** into); **i. des capitaux dans une entreprise** to inject capital into a business
▶ VPR **s'injecter** *(des yeux)* to become bloodshot

injecteur, -trice [ɛ̃ʒɛktœr, -tris] *Tech* ADJ *(tube)* injecting
▶ NM injector; *Aviat* nozzle; *Aut* **i. de carburant** fuel injector; **i. multi-trous** multi-hole injector, multi-hole nozzle

injection [ɛ̃ʒɛksjɔ̃] NF *(de pénicilline, de capital etc)* injection; *Aut, Tech* **moteur à i.** fuel injection engine; *Aut* **i. diesel** diesel injection; *Aut* **i. directe** direct injection; *Aut* **i. monopoint** single-point fuel injection; *Aut* **i. multipoint** multi-point injection, multi-port fuel injection

injoignable [ɛ̃ʒwaɲabl] ADJ *(personne)* unreachable; **elle est i. au téléphone** she can't be reached *or* is unreachable on the *or* by phone

injonction [ɛ̃ʒɔ̃ksjɔ̃] NF injunction; *Jur* injunction, order; **recevoir l'i. de faire qch** to get the order to do sth; **faire qch sur l'i. de qn** to do sth on sb's orders; *Bourse* **i. à la vente** sell order

injouable [ɛ̃ʒwabl] ADJ unplayable; **le premier acte est i.** the first act is impossible to stage; **la sonate est i.** the sonata is impossible to play; **la balle est i.** the ball is unplayable

injure [ɛ̃ʒyr] NF *(insulte)* insult; *Jur (délit)* = slander without object; **injures** abuse, insults; **en venir aux injures** to start insulting *or* abusing each other; **couvrir qn d'injures** to hurl insults *or* abuse at sb; **faire i. à qn** to insult sb; **elle m'a fait l'i. de ne pas venir à ma soirée** she insulted me by not coming to my party; *Litt* **l'i. des ans** the ravages of time

> Il faut noter que le nom anglais **injury** est un faux ami. Il signifie le plus souvent **blessure**.

injurier [ɛ̃ʒyrje] VT to abuse, to insult

> Il faut noter que le verbe anglais **to injure** est un faux ami. Il signifie le plus souvent **blesser**.

injurieux, -euse [ɛ̃ʒyrjø, -øz] ADJ insulting, abusive

injuste [ɛ̃ʒyst] ADJ unjust, unfair (**envers, avec** to, towards)

injustement [ɛ̃ʒystəmɑ̃] ADV unjustly, unfairly

injustice [ɛ̃ʒystis] NF **1** *(iniquité)* injustice,

unfairness (**envers** to, towards); **i. sociale** social injustice; **lutter contre l'i.** to fight (against) injustice **2** *(acte, parole)* injustice

injustifiable [ɛ̃ʒystifjabl] ADJ unjustifiable

injustifié [ɛ̃ʒystifje] ADJ unjustified, unwarranted

inlassable [ɛ̃lasabl] ADJ *(efforts, patience)* untiring, unflagging; *(personne)* tireless

inlassablement [ɛ̃lasabləmɑ̃] ADV untiringly, tirelessly; *(répéter)* ceaselessly

inné [ine] ADJ innate, inborn

innervation [inɛrvasjɔ̃] NF *Physiol* innervation

innerver [inɛrve] VT *Physiol* to innervate

innocemment [inɔsamɑ̃] ADV innocently; **j'ai posé la question i.** I asked the question in all innocence, I meant no harm by my question

innocence [inɔsɑ̃s] NF innocence; *(d'une plaisanterie)* harmlessness; **prouver l'i. de qn** to prove sb innocent, to prove sb's innocence; **il a posé la question/l'a invitée en toute i.** he asked the question/invited her in all innocence, he meant no harm by his question/by inviting her

innocent, -ente [inɔsɑ̃, -ɑ̃t] ADJ *(non coupable, pur, naïf)* innocent; *(plaisanterie, remarque)* harmless, innocent; **i. comme l'enfant qui vient de naître** as innocent as a newborn babe; **il est i. du crime dont on l'accuse** he is innocent of the crime of which he is accused
▶ N *(non coupable)* innocent person; *(idiot)* simpleton; **les (saints) Innocents** the Holy Innocents; **ne fais pas l'i.!** don't act so innocent *or* the innocent!; **l'i. du village** the village idiot; *Prov* **aux innocents les mains pleines** fortune favours fools

innocenter [inɔsɑ̃te] VT **1** **i. qn** *(d'une accusation/d'un crime)* to clear sb (of a charge/ of a crime); *(d'un juge, d'un jury)* to find sb not guilty *or* to clear sb (of a charge/of a crime) **2** *(justifier)* *(conduite)* to excuse, to justify

innocuité [inɔkɥite] NF harmlessness, innocuousness; **il est d'une i. totale** he's completely harmless

innombrable [inɔ̃brabl] ADJ innumerable, countless; *(foule)* huge, vast

innommable [inɔmabl] ADJ *Péj (comportement, conduite, actes)* unspeakable; *(nourriture, odeur)* vile, revolting; **des monstres innommables** loathsome monsters

innom(m)é [inɔme] ADJ unnamed, nameless

innovant [inɔvɑ̃] ADJ innovative

innovateur, -trice [inɔvatœr, -tris] ADJ innovative, innovatory
▶ N innovator; *Mktg* **i. continu** continuous innovator

innovation [inɔvasjɔ̃] NF innovation; *Mktg* **i. continue** continuous innovation; *Mktg* **i. de produit** product innovation

innover [inɔve] VI to introduce innovations, to break new ground, to innovate; **il a beaucoup innové en matière de musique contemporaine** he has broken a lot of new ground or has introduced many innovations or has been a great innovator in the field of contemporary music
▶ VT to introduce, to invent

inobservable [inɔpsɛrvabl] ADJ unobservable

inobservance [inɔpsɛrvɑ̃s] NF non-observance, inobservance

inobservation [inɔpsɛrvasjɔ̃] NF *Jur* non-observation (**de** of), non-compliance (**de** with)

inobservé [inɔpsɛrve] ADJ **1** *(non observé)*

unobserved; *(non remarqué)* unobserved, unnoticed **2** *(loi, règlement)* unobserved

inoccupé [inɔkype] ADJ **1** *(libre)* *(siège, poste)* unoccupied, vacant; *(maison)* unoccupied, empty, uninhabited **2** *(personne)* idle, unoccupied

inoculation [inɔkylasjɔ̃] NF *Méd* inoculation

inoculer [inɔkyle] VT **1** **i. un virus/un vaccin à qn** to inoculate sb with a virus/a vaccine; **i. une maladie à qn** to infect sb with a disease; *Fig* **elle nous a inoculé sa gaieté** she infected us with her cheerfulness **2** **i. qn (contre une maladie)** to inoculate sb (against a disease)

inodore [inɔdɔr] ADJ odourless, *Am* odorless; *Hum Péj* **incolore, i. et sans saveur** *(personne)* totally colourless *or Am* colorless, *Fam* wishy-washy

inoffensif, -ive [inɔfɑ̃sif, -iv] ADJ *(personne)* inoffensive, harmless; *(drogue, livre, jeu, action)* harmless, innocuous

inondable [inɔ̃dabl] ADJ *(terre)* liable to flooding

inondation [inɔ̃dasjɔ̃] NF flood, *Fml* inundation; *(action)* flooding, *Fml* inundation; *Fig (invasion)* deluge, flood

inondé, -ée [inɔ̃de] ADJ flooded; **populations inondées** flood victims; **visage i. de larmes** face streaming with tears; **i. de lumière** flooded *or* bathed with light; **i. d'invitations** inundated *or* swamped with invitations
▶ N flood victim

inonder [inɔ̃de] VT *(champs, route, maison, habitant)* to flood, *Fml* to inundate; *Fig (marché)* to flood, to inundate, to swamp (**de** with); **être inondé d'invitations/de prospectus** to be inundated with invitations/brochures; **i. un pays de voitures bon marché** to flood a country with cheap cars; **le soleil inonda la chambre de son insoutenable clarté** blinding sunlight flooded *or* poured into the room; **un bonheur ineffable m'inonda le cœur** an indescribable happiness flooded my heart
▶ VPR **s'inonder** **s'i. de parfum** to douse oneself in perfume

inopérable [inɔperabl] ADJ *Chir* inoperable

inopérant [inɔperɑ̃] ADJ ineffective, inoperative

inopiné [inɔpine] ADJ unexpected

inopinément [inɔpinemɑ̃] ADV unexpectedly

inopportun [inɔpɔrtœ̃] ADJ inopportune, untimely, ill-timed; **le moment est i.** it isn't the best *or* most opportune moment

inopportunément [inɔpɔrtynemɑ̃] ADV inopportunely

inopportunité [inɔpɔrtynite] NF *Litt* inopportuneness, untimeliness

inorganique [inɔrganik] ADJ *Chimie* inorganic

inorganisé [inɔrganize] ADJ *(personne, entreprise, service etc)* disorganized; *(maind'œuvre)* unorganized, non-union; *Biol, Chimie* inorganic; *(pas encore structuré)* unorganized

inoubliable [inublijabl] ADJ unforgettable

inouï [inwi] ADJ **1** *(nouveau)* unheard of, unprecedented **2** *(ahurissant)* incredible, extraordinary; **avec une violence inouïe** with incredible *or* extraordinary violence; **il lui est arrivé une histoire inouïe** something incredible *or* extraordinary happened to him; **c'est/vous êtes i.!** it's/you're incredible *or* unbelievable!

inox® [inɔks] ADJ INV **acier i.** stainless steel
▶ NM stainless steel; **évier en i.** stainless steel sink

inoxydable [inɔksidabl] ADJ **1** *(qui résiste à*

l'oxydation) rustproof, rust-resistant; **acier i.** stainless steel **2** *Fam (inaltérable)* enduring
NM stainless steel

INPI [ienpei] **NM** (*abrév* **Institut national de la propriété industrielle**) ≃ Patent Office

input [input] **NM** *Ordinat* input

inqualifiable [ɛ̃kalifjabl] **ADJ** *(comportement, propos)* unspeakable

in-quarto [inkwarto] **ADJ INV, NM INV** quarto

inquiet, -ète [ɛ̃kjɛ, -ɛt] **ADJ 1** *(anxieux) (personne, air, regard)* worried, anxious, uneasy; *(au sujet de* about); *(voix)* worried, anxious; *(attente)* anxious, uneasy; **elle est inquiète de ne pas avoir de nouvelles** she's worried *or* anxious at not having any news; **sommeil i.** uneasy *or* troubled *or* broken sleep **2** *Litt (agité)* restless
N worrier

inquiétant [ɛ̃kjetɑ̃] **ADJ 1** *(alarmant) (nouvelles, situation etc)* worrying, disturbing; *(état de santé)* worrying **2** *(qui effraie) (air, sourire)* frightening

inquiéter [ɛ̃kjete] **(j'inquiète; j'inquiéterai) VT** to worry, to trouble, to make anxious; *(ennemi, adversaire)* to harass, to worry; *(tranquillité de qn etc)* to disturb; **la santé de ma mère m'inquiète** I'm worried *or* anxious about my mother's health, my mother's health is worrying me *or* troubling me *or* making me anxious; **l'homme n'a pas été inquiété par la police** the man wasn't harassed *or* bothered *or* troubled by the police; **il n'a pas assez d'expérience pour vraiment i. le champion du monde** he doesn't have enough experience to give the world champion any real trouble, he doesn't have enough experience really to trouble *or* worry the world champion
VPR s'inquiéter 1 *(s'en faire)* to worry, to get worried; **il n'y a pas de quoi s'i.** there's nothing to get worried *or* to worry about; **je ne m'inquiète pas pour lui** I'm not worried *or* bothered about him; **il s'inquiète de ce qu'elle n'ait pas donné de nouvelles** he's worried that she hasn't been in touch
2 s'inquiéter de *(s'occuper de, faire attention à)* to bother about; **ne vous inquiétez pas de cela** don't worry *or* don't bother about that; **elle ne s'est jamais inquiétée de savoir si j'avais besoin de quelque chose** she never bothered *or* troubled *or* took the trouble to find out if I needed anything; **sans s'i. de rien** without a care in the world

inquiétude [ɛ̃kjetyd] **NF 1** *(souci)* anxiety, uneasiness; **dissiper les inquiétudes de qn** to set sb's mind at rest; **état d'i.** state of anxiety, anxious state of mind; **sujet d'i.** cause for concern *or* worry; **sois sans i., je m'en occupe** don't worry (about a thing), I'll take care of it; **éprouver quelques inquiétudes** to have a few worries, to feel a bit worried *or* anxious **2** *Arch, Litt (agitation)* agitation, restlessness

inquisiteur, -trice [ɛ̃kizitœr, -tris] **NM** inquisitor
ADJ *(regard)* inquisitive, prying

inquisition [ɛ̃kizisjɔ̃] **NF** inquisition; *Hist* **l'I.** the Inquisition

inquisitorial, -iale, -iaux, -iales [ɛ̃kizitɔrjal, -jo] **ADJ** inquisitorial

INRA [inra] **NM** (*abrév* **Institut national de la recherche agronomique**) = national institute for agronomic research

inracontable [ɛ̃rakɔ̃tabl] **ADJ** *(trop complexe)* not easily describable; *(trop scabreux ou insoutenable)* unrepeatable

inratable [ɛ̃ratabl] **ADJ** *(que l'on ne doit pas rater)* (spectacle) unmissable

insaisissable [ɛ̃sezisabl] **ADJ 1** *(que l'on ne peut attraper) (fugitif, voleur)* difficult to catch, elusive; *(son, différence, nuance)* im-

perceptible **2** *Jur (biens)* not distrainable, not attachable

insalissable [ɛ̃salisabl] **ADJ** dirt-proof

insalubre [ɛ̃salybr] **ADJ** *(climat)* insalubrious, unhealthy; *(occupation)* unhealthy; *(habitation, pays)* insalubrious

insalubrité [ɛ̃salybrite] **NF** *(de climat)* insalubrity, unhealthiness; *(d'habitation, de pays)* insalubrity

insanité [ɛ̃sanite] **NF** *(de raisonnement, propos)* insanity; **proférer des insanités** to talk insanely; **sa dissertation est un tissu d'insanités** his essay is a mishmash of complete nonsense

insatiabilité [ɛ̃sasjabilite] **NF** insatiability

insatiable [ɛ̃sasjabl] **ADJ** *(soif)* insatiable, unquenchable; *(appétit, curiosité)* insatiable; **d'une curiosité i.** insatiably curious

insatiablement [ɛ̃sasjabləmɑ̃] **ADV** insatiably

insatisfaction [ɛ̃satisfaksjɔ̃] **NF** dissatisfaction

insatisfaisant [ɛ̃satisfəzɑ̃] **ADJ** unsatisfactory

insatisfait, -aite [ɛ̃satisfɛ, -ɛt] **ADJ** *(personne)* dissatisfied; *(désir)* unsatisfied
N c'est un (éternel) i. he's never satisfied (with anything), he's always dissatisfied (with things)

inscriptible [ɛ̃skriptibl] **ADJ** *Ordinat* writable

inscription [ɛ̃skripsjɔ̃] **NF 1** *(action) (d'un nom, d'une date etc)* writing down, noting down; *(dans un journal, un registre)* entering, recording; *(immatriculation)* registration, enrolment, *Am* enrollment; *Univ* **les inscriptions auront lieu …**; registration *or* enrolment will take place …; *Fam* **faire son i. à l'université** to register *or* enrol *or Am* enroll at university; **depuis son i. au club** since he joined the club; **avez-vous fait votre i. sur les listes électorales?** have you registered to vote?, have you put your name down on the electoral roll?; **i. sur le registre du commerce** registration in the trade register; **droit/ feuille d'i.** registration fee/form; *(pour concours)* entry *or* entrance fee/form; *(pour club, association)* enrolment fee/form; **prendre une i.** *(s'incrire)* to enter one's name
2 *(sur une tombe, un mur etc)* inscription; *(dans un livre de comptes)* entry; *(sur un poteau indicateur)* directions; *Compta* **i. comptable** accounting entry
▸▸ *Bourse* **i. à la cote** quotation on the (official) list; *Jur* **i. de** *ou* **en faux** plea of forgery; *Jur* **i. hypothécaire** registry *or* registration of mortgages; *Fin* **inscriptions nominatives** registered shares

inscrire [ɛ̃skrir] *(prp inscrivant; pp inscrit; pr ind j'inscris, il inscrit, n. inscrivons; p hist j'inscrivis; fu j'inscrirai)* **VT 1** *(renseignements, date etc)* to write down, to note down; *(dans un journal, registre etc)* to enter, to record; **i. une adresse sur qch** to address sth; **i. une question à l'ordre du jour** to put *or* place a question on the agenda; **i. une dépense au budget** to include an item in the budget; **inscrivez la date en haut à droite** write the date in the top right-hand corner
2 i. un enfant à un club to enrol *or Am* enroll a child in a club; **i. un enfant à une école** to put a child *or* a child's name down for a school; **i. qn à une activité** to put sb's name down *or* enrol sb for an activity; **il m'a inscrit au marathon** he put me *or* my name down for the marathon, he entered me *or* put me in for the marathon
3 *(dans la pierre)* (épitaphe etc) to inscribe, to engrave; **il a inscrit ses initiales dans l'écorce de l'arbre** he inscribed *or* carved his initials in the bark of the tree; *Fig* **cette**

date restera inscrite dans ma mémoire à **tout jamais** that date will remain etched *or* inscribed on my memory for all time
4 *Géom (triangle, carré)* to inscribe (**dans** in)
5 *Suisse (envoyer en recommandé)* **i. qch** to send sth registered (post)
VPR s'inscrire *(à l'université, à une école)* to register, to enrol (**à** at); *(à la Sécurité sociale, au chômage)* to register (**à** with); *(sur les listes électorales)* to have one's name put on the electoral roll; *(à un tournoi, un concours)* to put oneself *or* one's name down, to enter (**à** for); *(cours, atelier)* to put oneself *or* one's name down, to enrol (**à** for); **s'i. dans un club/à un parti** to join a club/party, to enrol in a club/party; **s'i. en faux contre qch** to deny sth; *Jur* to contest the validity of sth; *Fin* **s'i. en baisse** to fall; *Fin* **s'i. en hausse** to rise; **cette décision s'inscrit dans le cadre de la politique gouvernementale** this decision is in keeping with the general pattern of government policy; **noter l'adresse qui va s'i. sur vos écrans** note down the address which is coming up on your screens

inscrit, -ite [ɛ̃skri, -it] **ADJ 1** *(électeur, candidat)* registered **2** *Géom* inscribed **3** *Bourse* **i. à la cote officielle** listed
N *(à l'université)* registered student; *(dans un club, parti)* registered member; *(à un concours)* registered entrant; *(électeur)* registered voter
NM *Naut* **i. maritime** = certified navigator

insécable [ɛ̃sekabl] **ADJ** indivisible; *Ordinat* hard

insecte [ɛ̃sɛkt] **NM** insect

insecticide [ɛ̃sɛktisid] **ADJ** insecticidal; **poudre i.** insect powder
NM insecticide

insectifuge [ɛ̃sɛktifyʒ] **NM** insect repellent

insectivore [ɛ̃sɛktivɔr] *Zool* **ADJ** insectivorous
NM insectivore; **insectivores** insectivores, *Spéc* Insectivora

insécurité [ɛ̃sekyrite] **NF 1** lack of safety **2** *Psy* insecurity

INSEE [inse] **NM** (*abrév* **Institut national de la statistique et des études économiques**) = national institute of statistics and information about the economy

inséminateur, -trice [ɛ̃seminatœr, -tris] **ADJ** inseminating
NM inseminator

insémination [ɛ̃seminasjɔ̃] **NF** insemination; **i. artificielle** artificial insemination

inséminer [ɛ̃semine] **VT** to inseminate

insensé, -ée [ɛ̃sɑ̃se] **ADJ** *(action, geste)* extravagant, wild; *(projet, idée)* crazy, harebrained; *(espoir)* wild; *(dépenses)* extravagant, wild; *Vieilli (fou)* mad, insane; **il m'a dit des paroles insensées** what he said to me was mad; **c'est i.!** it's crazy!; **c'est i. ce qu'il peut boire!** it's crazy the amount he can drink!
NM madman
NF insensée madwoman

insensibilisation [ɛ̃sɑ̃sibilizasjɔ̃] **NF** anaesthetization, *Am* anesthetization

insensibiliser [ɛ̃sɑ̃sibilize] **VT** to anaesthetize, *Am* to anesthetize

insensibilité [ɛ̃sɑ̃sibilite] **NF** insensitivity (**à** to)

insensible [ɛ̃sɑ̃sibl] **ADJ 1** *(à la douleur, au froid etc)* insensitive (**à** to); **i. à la critique** impervious to criticism; **il demeura i. à leurs larmes** he remained unmoved by their tears **2** *(différence, changement)* imperceptible, hardly perceptible

insensiblement [ɛ̃sɑ̃sibləmɑ̃] **ADV** imperceptibly

inséparable [ɛ̃separabl] ADJ inseparable
  NMPL **inséparables** *(oiseaux)* lovebirds; **ce sont deux inséparables** *(de personnes)* they are inseparable

inséparablement [ɛ̃separabləmɑ̃] ADV inseparably

insérable [ɛ̃serabl] ADJ insertable

insérer [ɛ̃sere] *(j'insère; j'insérerai)* VT to insert (**dans** in); *TV, Cin* to edit in, to intercut; **i. une annonce dans un journal** to insert *or* put an advertisement in a paper; **prière d'i.** *(formule)* for publication (in your columns); *(feuille)* publication details
  VPR **s'insérer 1** *(s'attacher)* to be attached (**sur** to) **2** *(s'intégrer)* *(réformes, politique etc)* to fit (**dans** into); *(immigrés)* to integrate (**dans** into); **ces mesures s'insèrent dans le cadre des nouvelles réformes** these measures fit into the general pattern of the new reforms

Inserm [inserm] NM *(abrév* **Institut national de la santé et de la recherche médicale)** = national institute for medical research

insert [ɛ̃sɛr(t)] NM *TV, Cin* cut-in, insert

insertion [ɛ̃sɛrsjɔ̃] NF insertion; *Typ* insert; **l'i. sociale des immigrés** the (social) integration of immigrants; **l'i. professionnelle des jeunes** the integration of young people into the job market; *Ordinat* **mode d'i.** insert mode; **i. de caractères** character insert; **i. de ligne** line insert; **i. publicitaire** advertisement; **l'i. d'une petite annonce dans un journal** inserting *or* putting an advertisement in a newspaper

insidieusement [ɛ̃sidjøzmɑ̃] ADV insidiously

insidieux, -euse [ɛ̃sidjø, -øz] ADJ insidious

insigne[1] [ɛ̃siɲ] ADJ **1** *(remarquable)* remarkable; **faveur i.** signal favour; **j'ai eu l'honneur i. d'être invité à sa table** I had the great honour of being invited to his table **2** *Péj (indiscrétion, erreur, maladresse)* glaring; *(menteur, escroc etc)* notorious

insigne[2] NM *(de club, parti, militaire)* badge; **insignes de la royauté** insignia of royalty

insignifiance [ɛ̃siɲifjɑ̃s] NF insignificance, unimportance

insignifiant [ɛ̃siɲifjɑ̃] ADJ insignificant, unimportant; *(perte, somme)* trivial, trifling

insincère [ɛ̃sɛ̃sɛr] ADJ *Litt* insincere

insinuant [ɛ̃sinɥɑ̃] ADJ ingratiating

insinuation [ɛ̃sinɥasjɔ̃] NF insinuation, innuendo; **par insinuations** by insinuation, by innuendo; **il procède toujours par i.** he always speaks in innuendos

insinuer [ɛ̃sinɥe] VT to insinuate, to suggest, to hint at; **que voulez-vous i.?** what are you insinuating *or* implying *or* hinting at?
  VPR **s'insinuer le lierre s'insinuait dans les moindres fissures** the ivy was creeping (its way) into the smallest of cracks; **le froid s'insinue dans la pièce par tous les interstices** the cold is creeping into the room through all the cracks; **s'i. dans les bonnes grâces de qn** to insinuate oneself *or* worm one's way into sb's good books; **il a réussi à s'i. jusque dans les plus hautes sphères du pouvoir** he managed to worm his way into the higher reaches of power; **le doute/l'idée qui s'insinue dans mon esprit** the doubt/the idea that is creeping into my mind; **s'i. entre les voitures** to thread one's way through the traffic

insipide [ɛ̃sipid] ADJ *(personne, conversation, histoire, film etc)* insipid, dull, uninteresting; *(nourriture, boisson)* insipid, tasteless; *(fin)* tame

insipidité [ɛ̃sipidite] NF insipidness, dullness; *(de nourriture, boisson)* insipidness, tastelessness

insistance [ɛ̃sistɑ̃s] NF insistence (**à faire qch** on doing sth); **avec i.** insistently

insistant [ɛ̃sistɑ̃] ADJ insistent

insister [ɛ̃siste] VI to insist; **i. sur un fait** to stress a fact; **nous insistons particulièrement sur la ponctualité** we lay particular stress *or* emphasis on punctuality; **elle a beaucoup insisté** she was very insistent; **i. pour faire qch** to insist on doing sth; **elle a insisté pour que nous restions la nuit** she insisted on our staying the night; **i. auprès de qn** to take up a matter strongly with sb; **n'insistez pas trop** don't push it; **j'insiste là-dessus** I insist on it; **n'insistez pas trop là-dessus** don't put too much emphasis on it, don't overstress it; **elle a essayé la planche à voile mais elle n'a pas insisté** she tried windsurfing but soon gave (it) up; **j'ai dit non! n'insistez pas!** *ou* **inutile d'i.!** I said no! don't go on (about it)!; **ça ne répond pas – insiste encore un peu** there's no answer – hang on a bit; **j'ai essayé de la convaincre puis je me suis aperçu que ça ne servait à rien d'i.** I tried to convince her, then I realized that it was useless to keep on trying; **insiste sinon la tache ne partira jamais** keep rubbing or the stain will never come out

in situ [sity] ADJ, ADV in situ

insociabilité [ɛ̃sɔsjabilite] NF unsociability

insociable [ɛ̃sɔsjabl] ADJ unsociable

insolation [ɛ̃sɔlasjɔ̃] NF **1** *(exposition au soleil)* exposure to the sun; *Méd* sunstroke; *(d'une région etc)* hours of sunshine; **attraper une i.** to get sunstroke; **tu risques l'i. si … ** you'll risk getting sunstroke if … **2** *Phot* exposure

insolemment [ɛ̃sɔlamɑ̃] ADV insolently, impertinently

insolence [ɛ̃sɔlɑ̃s] NF **1** *(impertinence)* insolence, impertinence, impudence; **répondre avec i.** to answer insolently *or* impertinently *or* impudently; **cet enfant est d'une i.!** that child is so insolent *or* impertinent *or* impudent! **2** *(remarque, action)* impertinence

insolent, -ente [ɛ̃sɔlɑ̃, -ɑ̃t] ADJ **1** *(impertinent)* insolent, impertinent, impudent (**envers, avec** to); **répondre sur un ton i.** to answer insolently *or* impertinently *or* impudently **2** *(dans la victoire)* haughty, arrogant **3** *(succès)* outrageous; *(luxe)* unashamed, blatant, indecent; **il a une chance insolente** he's got the luck of the devil
  N insolent person; **petit i./petite insolente!** you insolent little boy/girl!

insolite [ɛ̃sɔlit] ADJ unusual, strange
  NM **l'i.** the unusual

insolubilité [ɛ̃sɔlybilite] NF *(de substance)* insolubility; *(de problème)* insolvability

insoluble [ɛ̃sɔlybl] ADJ **1** *(substance)* insoluble **2** *(problème)* insoluble, insolvable

insolvabilité [ɛ̃sɔlvabilite] NF *Com* insolvency

insolvable [ɛ̃sɔlvabl] ADJ *Com* insolvent

insomniaque [ɛ̃sɔmnjak] ADJ, N insomniac

insomnie [ɛ̃sɔmni] NF insomnia, sleeplessness; **nuit d'i.** sleepless night; **souffrir d'i., avoir des insomnies** to have insomnia

insondable [ɛ̃sɔ̃dabl] ADJ **1** *(océan, gouffre)* unfathomable, fathomless **2** *(mystère)* unfathomable, impenetrable **3** *(stupidité, désespoir)* immense, unbelievable

insonore [ɛ̃sɔnɔr] ADJ *(studio, matériau)* soundproof

insonorisation [ɛ̃sɔnɔrizasjɔ̃] NF *(de studio, d'appartement)* soundproofing

insonoriser [ɛ̃sɔnɔrize] VT *(studio, appartement)* to soundproof

insouciance [ɛ̃susjɑ̃s] NF *(absence de soucis)* carefreeness; *(détachement)* unconcern, lack of concern, *Litt* insouciance; **vivre dans l'i.** to live a carefree life

insouciant [ɛ̃susjɑ̃] ADJ *(sans soucis)* carefree; *(détaché)* unconcerned; *(léger)* thoughtless, casual, happy-go-lucky; **i. de son avenir** unconcerned about his future; **i. du danger/des conséquences possibles** heedless of the danger/the possible consequences; **ils sont jeunes et insouciants** they are young and carefree

insoucieux, -euse [ɛ̃susjø, -øz] ADJ *Litt (attitude, air)* unconcerned, casual; *(humeur)* carefree; **il est i. de l'avenir/du qu'en-dira-t-on** he is unconcerned about *or* pays no heed to the future/what people say; **i. du danger, il … ** heedless of the danger, he …

insoumis, -ise [ɛ̃sumi, -iz] ADJ **1** *(gens, peuple, tribus)* unsubdued **2** *(personne)* insubordinate, rebellious, refractory **3** *Mil (soldat)* absentee
  N rebellious *or* insubordinate person
  NM *Mil* absentee

insoumission [ɛ̃sumisjɔ̃] NF **1** *(indiscipline)* insubordination, rebelliousness **2** *Mil* absence without leave

insoupçonnable [ɛ̃supsɔnabl] ADJ *(personne)* beyond *or* above suspicion; **il est d'une probité i.** his probity is unquestionable *or* beyond question

insoupçonné [ɛ̃supsɔne] ADJ unsuspected (**de** by)

insoutenable [ɛ̃sutnabl] ADJ **1** *(opinion, théorie)* untenable; *(affirmation)* unwarrantable; *(position)* indefensible, untenable **2** *(agonie, pression, tension, spectacle, odeur)* unbearable
  NM **l'i.** the unbearable; **à la limite de l'i.** verging on the unbearable

inspecter [ɛ̃spɛkte] VT *(troupes, école, établissement)* to inspect; *(champ de bataille)* to survey; *(travail, bagages)* to examine, to inspect; **i. des marchandises** to examine goods

inspecteur, -trice [ɛ̃spɛktœr, -tris] N inspector; *(des travaux)* overseer; *(des mines)* surveyor
  ▸▸ *Scol* **i. d'Académie** school inspector, *Br* ≃ HMI; **i. des contributions directes** inspector of taxes, tax inspector; **i. des contributions indirectes** customs and excise official; **i. des finances** ≃ senior Treasury official; **i. de police** police inspector; **i. (de l'enseignement) primaire** primary school inspector; **i. d'une société d'assurances** insurance inspector; **i. de la sûreté** detective inspector; **i. du travail** factory inspector; *Hum* **i. des travaux finis** idler, *Br* skiver *(who arrives after the work has been done)*; **i. des ventes** sales coordinator

inspection [ɛ̃spɛksjɔ̃] NF **1** *(examen)* inspection; *(de bagages)* examination, inspection; **faire l'i. de** to inspect; *Mil* **faire l'i. des armes** to inspect arms; *Mil* **passer l'i. d'une compagnie** to inspect a company; **passer à l'i.** to undergo an inspection; **une i. en règle** a thorough inspection **2** *(fonction)* inspectorship, inspectorate **3** *(service)* inspectorate
  ▸▸ *Scol* **i. académique** school inspectorate; **entrer à l'i. académique** to become a school inspector; *Admin* **i. générale des finances** = department responsible for auditing public bodies; **i. de la Sécurité sociale** Social Security Inspectorate; **i. du travail** factory inspectorate

inspectorat [ɛ̃spɛktɔra] NM *Admin* inspectorship, inspectorate

inspirateur, -trice [ɛ̃spiratœr, -tris] ADJ **1** *(pensée, idée)* inspiring **2** *Anat (muscle)* inspiratory
  N *(d'activité créatrice)* inspiration; *(d'une intrigue)* instigator; **c'était elle mon inspiratrice** she was my inspiration

inspiration [ɛ̃spiʀasjɔ̃] **NF 1** *(créatrice)* inspiration; **avoir de l'i.** to be inspired, to have inspiration; **un poème d'i. romantique** a poem in the romantic style; **elle est pour lui une source d'i.** *(d'une femme)* she's his muse; *(d'une ville etc)* it's a source of inspiration for him **2** *(influence)* instigation, prompting; **sous l'i. de qn** at sb's instigation *or* prompting **3** *Physiol* inspiration, breathing in **4** *(idée)* inspiration; **i. soudaine** sudden inspiration, *Fam Br* brainwave, *Am* brainstorm; **elle a eu la lumineuse i. de venir me chercher** she had the bright idea to come for me; **selon l'i. du moment** on the spur of the moment

inspiré, -ée [ɛ̃spiʀe] **ADJ 1** *(style, poète, artiste, air)* inspired; **une toile inspirée de Bosch** a painting inspired by Bosch **2 il serait bien/mal i. de changer de métier** he'd be well-advised *or* he'd do well/he'd be ill-advised to change profession; **tu as été bien/mal i. de l'inviter à ta soirée** it was a good/bad idea of yours to invite him to your party **N** mystic, visionary

inspirer [ɛ̃spiʀe] **VT 1** *(suggérer)* **i. confiance/le respect** to inspire confidence/respect; **i. confiance à qn** to inspire sb with confidence, to inspire confidence in sb; **i. le respect à qn** to command *or* win sb's respect; **i. de l'admiration à qn** to fill sb with admiration; **spectacle qui inspire l'horreur/le dégoût** horrific/disgusting spectacle; **cet enfant ne peut i. que de la tendresse** you can't help but feel affectionate towards the child; **l'état du malade nous inspire la plus grande inquiétude** the patient's condition is giving us great cause for concern; **votre discours m'a inspiré plusieurs réflexions** your speech has given me food for thought *or* has set me thinking; **inspiré par la jalousie** prompted by jealousy **2** *(artiste, poète etc)* to inspire; **cet événement m'a inspiré une chanson/un poème** this event inspired me to write a song/a poem; **la vie de sa grand-mère lui a inspiré ce roman** his/her grandmother's life was the inspiration for the novel; **l'histoire est largement inspirée de la vie du grand homme** the story is largely drawn from *or* based upon the great man's life; *Iron* **cette question ne m'inspire guère** the subject doesn't exactly inspire me **3** *Physiol (air)* to breathe in, *Spéc* to inspire **VI** *Physiol* to breathe in, *Spéc* to inspire **VPR s'inspirer s'i. de qn/qch** to take *or* draw one's inspiration from sb/sth, to be inspired by sb/sth

instabilité [ɛ̃stabilite] **NF** *(de caractère, situation, gouvernement etc)* instability; *(du temps)* changeability, unsettled nature; *Chimie* instability; *Naut (d'un bateau)* crank; **i. des cours** unsteadiness of prices; **i. mentale** mental instability

instable [ɛ̃stabl] **ADJ 1** *(branlant)* *(échafaudage, plateau etc)* unstable, unsteady, wobbly; *(marché boursier)* unsettled; **équilibre i.** unsteady balance **2** *(personne, nature)* unstable **3** *(temps)* unsettled, changeable; *Naut (bateau)* crank; *(situation politique)* unstable, uncertain; *(gouvernement)* unstable; **la paix est encore i.** the peace is still fragile *or* uncertain **4** *Chimie (solution, mélange)* unstable

installateur [ɛ̃stalatœʀ] **NM** fitter

installation [ɛ̃stalasjɔ̃] **NF 1** *(fait d'installer)* *(d'une machine, d'un ascenseur etc)* installation; *(d'une cuisinière, d'un réfrigérateur)* installation, putting in; *(d'une machine à laver, lave-vaisselle)* plumbing in, installation; *(de chauffage, d'un téléphone etc)* putting in, installation; *(d'électricité, de gaz, d'eau)* putting in, *Br* laying on; *(d'une usine, d'un atelier)* fitting up *or* out, equipping; *(d'un appartement, d'une cuisine)* fitting out; *(de rideaux, d'une tenture)* putting up, hanging; *(de fenêtres)* fitting, installation; *(d'un ecclésiastique, magistrat)* installation, induction **2** *(emménagement)* **fêter son i.** to celebrate moving in; **prévoir son i. dans une région** to plan to settle in an area; **comment s'est passée votre i. dans votre nouvelle maison?** how did the move into your new house go? **3** *Ordinat* **programme d'i.** installation program; **i. en réseau** network installation **4 installations** *(d'une maison)* fixtures and fittings; *(d'un atelier)* fittings, equipment; *Ind* plant; **installations portuaires** port installations; **installations sanitaires** sanitary installations *or* fittings; *(tuyauterie)* plumbing; **installations techniques** plant and machinery; **installations touristiques** tourist facilities, visitor facilities; **l'i. électrique n'est pas conforme** the wiring is not up to standard; **installations de lavage** washing bay; **installations au sol** *(dans un aérodrome)* ground installations

installé [ɛ̃stale] **ADJ** *Ordinat (RAM)* on board

INSTALLER [ɛ̃stale]

VT to install ▪ to settle ▪ to put in ▪ to fit out ▪ to fit ▪ to put ▪ to set up
VPR to set up ▪ to settle down ▪ to settle

VT *(sa famille, son fils etc)* to settle; *(machine, ascenseur etc)* to install, *Am* to instal; *(cuisinière, réfrigérateur)* to install, to put in; *(machine à laver, lave-vaisselle)* to plumb in, to install; *(chauffage, téléphone etc)* to put in, to install; *(électricité, gaz, eau)* to put in, *Br* to lay on; *(usine, atelier)* to fit up *or* out, to equip; *(appartement, cuisine)* to fit out; *(rideaux, tenture)* to put up, to hang; *(fenêtres)* to fit, to install; *(ecclésiastique, magistrat)* to install, to induct; **i. le câble** to install cable; **où va-t-on i. le buffet?** where are we going to put the sideboard?; **il a installé son ordinateur dans sa chambre à coucher** he set up *or* put his computer in his bedroom; **i. qn dans un fauteuil/son lit** to settle sb comfortably *or* make sb comfortable in an armchair/in his/her bed; **i. qn devant la télévision** to settle sb down *or* install sb in front of the television; **je les ai installés dans la chambre bleue** I've put them in the blue room; **les nouveaux bureaux sont très bien installés** the new offices are very well fitted out *or* equipped; **i. la cuisine/la salle de bain dans une pièce** to turn a room into a kitchen/bathroom; **il a installé son bureau au grenier** he set up his office in the attic, he turned the attic into his office; **ils ont installé le musée dans une ancienne gare** they set up the museum in a former station; **i. son cabinet** *(d'un médecin)* to set up (in) practice **VPR s'installer** *(de supermarché, cirque)* to set up; *(de personne)* *(devant la télé)* to settle down, to install oneself; *(dans la vie)* to settle (down); *(chez qn)* to make oneself at home; **confortablement installé dans un fauteuil** comfortably settled in an armchair; **s'i. au bar** to install oneself at the bar; **s'i. à la campagne/à Madagascar** to settle in the country/in Madagascar; **des bourgeois bien installés** comfortably off middle-class people; **s'i. comme médecin** to set (oneself) up as a doctor; **s'i. à son compte** to set up in business on one's own; **un climat d'insécurité s'est installé dans le pays** a climate of insecurity has taken hold of the country

instamment [ɛ̃stamɑ̃] **ADV** *(recommander)* earnestly; **je vous demande i. de revenir sur votre décision** I beg *or* urge you to reconsider your decision; **elle l'a prié i. de la suivre** she begged him to follow her

instance [ɛ̃stɑ̃s] **NF 1** *(insistance)* demander qch à qn avec i. to beg *or* plead with sb for sth; **c'est avec i. qu'ils m'ont demandé d'accepter** they begged *or* urged me to accept **2 instances** entreaties, pleas; **j'ai dû plier devant ses instances** I had to give in to his entreaties *or* pleas; **sur** *ou* **devant les instances de son frère** in the face of his brother's entreaties *or* pleas **3** *Jur* process, suit; **introduire une i. (en justice)** to institute an action; **tribunal d'i.** *Eng* ≃ magistrates' court, *Scot* ≃ sheriff court; **tribunal de grande i.** *Eng* ≃ county court, *Scot* ≃ sheriff court; **tribunal de première i.** court of first instance; **acquitté en seconde i.** acquitted on appeal **4** *(autorité)* authority; **les instances internationales** the international authorities; **l'i. compétente/supérieure** the relevant/higher authority; **i. de contrôle** regulatory body; **instances dirigeantes** governing body; **les instances économiques/communautaires** the economic/EU authorities; **les plus hautes instances du parti** the leading bodies of the party **5** *(cours)* **ils sont en i. de divorce** they are waiting for a divorce, their divorce proceedings are under way; **être en i. de départ** to be on the point of departure *or* about to leave; **courrier en i.** mail waiting *or* ready to go out; **tout est encore en i.** everything is still pending

---

Il faut noter que le nom anglais **instance** est un faux ami. Il signifie **exemple**.

---

instant¹ [ɛ̃stɑ̃] **ADJ** *Litt* **1** *(imminent)* *(péril)* pressing **2** *(pressant)* *(prière etc)* insistent

instant² **NM** moment, instant; **à chaque** *ou* **tout i.** continually, all the time; **par instants** now and then; **il a eu un i. d'inattention** he had a momentary lapse of concentration; **pendant un i.** for a moment; **pendant un i., j'ai cru que j'allais gagner** for a moment *or* for one instant I thought I was going to win; **j'ai cru l'espace d'un i. que …** I thought for a *or* one (split) second that …; **un i.!** one moment!; **nous n'avons pas un i. à perdre** we don't have a moment to lose; **profiter de chaque i.** to enjoy every moment; **nous avons vécu ensemble des instants de bonheur parfait** we've shared some blissfully happy moments; **elle va arriver d'un i. à l'autre** she'll be arriving any moment now *or* at any moment; **à l'i.** *(dans le passé)* (just) a moment ago; *(tout de suite)* immediately, instantly, at once; **il vient de partir à l'i.** he has just this minute gone, he went (just) a moment ago; **j'en reviens à l'i.** I've just come back from there; **on m'apprend à l'i. que …** I've just (this minute) found out that …; **il est entré dans le bureau à l'i. même où …** he went into the office at the very *or* exact moment that …; **pour l'i.** for the moment, for the time being; **dans un i.** in a moment; **en un i.** in no time (at all); **un soin de tous les instants** unremitting *or* ceaseless care; **dès l'i. où je l'ai vue** *(dès que)* from the moment I saw her; **dès l'i. que tu as réussi tous tes examens** *(du moment que)* since you've *or* seeing that you've passed all your exams

instantané [ɛ̃stɑ̃tane] **ADJ** *(mort)* instantaneous; *(riposte)* instantaneous, immediate; *(café, soupe, bouillie)* instant **NM** *Phot* snapshot, *Fam* snap

instantanément [ɛ̃stɑ̃tanemɑ̃] **ADV** instantaneously

instar [ɛ̃staʀ] **ADV** *Litt* **à l'i. de** following the example of; **à l'i. de son père il a choisi d'être facteur** following his father's example *or* following in his father's footsteps, he chose to be a postman

instaurateur, -trice [ɛ̃stɔʀatœʀ, -tʀis] **N** *Litt* establisher

instauration [ɛ̃stɔrasjɔ̃] NF establishment, institution

instaurer [ɛ̃stɔre] VT to establish; *(usage)* to institute; *(mode de scrutin, système)* to introduce; **i. des mesures** to bring in new measures
VPR **s'instaurer** to be established

instigateur, -trice [ɛ̃stigatœr, -tris] N instigator

instigation [ɛ̃stigasjɔ̃] NF instigation, incitement; **agir à l'i. de qn** to act at *or* on sb's instigation

instiguer [ɛ̃stige] VT *Belg* to incite; **ils ont été instigués à se mettre en grève** they were incited to strike

instillation [ɛ̃stilasjɔ̃] NF *Méd* instillation

instiller [ɛ̃stile] VT *Méd, Fig* to instil, *Am* to instill (**dans** into, in); **i. le doute dans l'esprit de qn** to instil doubt into *or* in sb's mind

instinct [ɛ̃stɛ̃] NM instinct; **se fier à/suivre son i.** to trust to/follow one's instinct(s); **i. maternel** maternal instinct; **i. de conservation** instinct of self-preservation; **faire qch d'i.** to do sth by instinct *or* instinctively; **avoir l'i. du commerce** to have an instinct *or* a feel for business; **être guidé par un heureux i.** to be well guided by one's instinct

instinctif, -ive [ɛ̃stɛ̃ktif, -iv] ADJ *(personne, réaction etc)* instinctive

instinctivement [ɛ̃stɛ̃ktivmɑ̃] ADV instinctively

instit [ɛ̃stit] N *Fam* (primary school) teacher

instituer [ɛ̃stitɥe] VT 1 *(établir)* (impôt, règlement, suffrage universel)* to introduce, *Fml* to institute; *(commission d'enquête)* to set up, *Fml* to institute 2 *(fonctionnaire, héritier)* to appoint
VPR **s'instituer** *(climat de confiance, relations commerciales)* to become established; **il s'est institué juge/arbitre dans cette affaire** he has appointed himself judge/referee in the matter

institut [ɛ̃stity] NM 1 *(établissement)* institute, institution; **i. de crédit** credit institution; **i. national de recherche** national research institute 2 **l'I. (de France)** the Institute *(composed of the five Académies)*
▸▸**i. de beauté** beauty salon *or* parlour; **I. d'Études politiques** = grande école for political sciences in Paris, commonly known as Sciences-Po; **i. médico-légal** forensic laboratory; **I. monétaire européen** European Monetary Institute; **I. national de la consommation** = French consumer research organization; **I. national de la propriété industrielle** ≃ Patent Office; **Institut national de la statistique et des études économiques** = French national institute of statistics and information about the economy; **I. Pasteur** Pasteur Institute; **I. de sondage** polling company; **I. universitaire de technologie** = vocational higher education college

instituteur, -trice [ɛ̃stitytœr, -tris] N *Scol* (primary school) teacher
NF *Arch* **institutrice** governess

institution [ɛ̃stitysjɔ̃] NF 1 *(établissement)* institution, institution; **i. de crédit** credit institution; **i. financière** financial institution; *Fam* **c'est devenu une véritable i.** it has become an institution 2 *Jur (d'héritier)* appointing 3 *Pol* **institutions** institutions 4 *(coutume)* institution; **le mariage est une i. menacée** the institution of marriage is under threat 5 *(d'enseignement)* establishment

institutionnalisation [ɛ̃stitysjɔnalizasjɔ̃] NF institutionalization

institutionnaliser [ɛ̃stitysjɔnalize] VT *(pratique, procédure)* to institutionalize

institutionnel, -elle [ɛ̃stitysjɔnɛl] ADJ institutional
NMPL **institutionnels** institutional investors

instructeur [ɛ̃stryktœr] NM instructor, teacher
ADJ *Jur* **juge i.** examining magistrate; *Mil* **sergent i.** drill sergeant

instructif, -ive [ɛ̃stryktif, -iv] ADJ instructive

instruction [ɛ̃stryksjɔ̃] NF 1 **instructions** instructions, directions; **il faut suivre les instructions à la lettre** you must follow the instructions to the letter; **conformément aux instructions** as directed; **conformément à vos instructions** in accordance with your instructions, as instructed; **instructions de facturation** invoicing instructions; **instructions pour l'expédition** shipping instructions
2 *Ordinat* instruction; **i.-machine** machine instruction; **i. d'entrée-sortie** input/output instruction; **i. de code machine** machine code instruction
3 *Scol* education, schooling; *Mil* training (of troops); *Scol* **i. primaire/secondaire** primary/secondary education; **i. professionnelle** vocational training; **avoir de l'i.** to be well educated; **sans i.** uneducated; **i. religieuse** religious instruction; **i. musicale/militaire** musical/military training; **i. civique** civics
4 *Jur (d'une affaire)* preliminary investigation; **juge d'i.** examining magistrate
5 *(circulaire)* (official) memo, circular

instruire [ɛ̃strɥir] *(prp* **instruisant**; *pp* **instruit**; *pr ind* **j'instruis, il instruit**, n. **instruisons**; *p hist* **j'instruisis)** VT 1 *(enseigner à)* to teach, to educate, to instruct; **lisez Jünger, ça vous instruira** read Jünger, that will educate you 2 *(informer)* **i. qn de qch** to inform sb of sth 3 *(troupes)* to train, to drill 4 *Jur (affaire)* to examine, to investigate
VI to teach; **i. par le jeu/l'exemple** to teach through play/by example
VPR **s'instruire** to educate oneself, to improve one's mind; **s'i. de** to find out *or* get information about; **il s'instruisit des événements survenus pendant son absence** he brought himself up to date on what had happened during his absence; *Fml* **je viens m'i. de la santé de Madame votre femme** I've come to inquire after your wife's health

instruit [ɛ̃strɥi] ADJ educated, learned, well-read

instrument [ɛ̃strymɑ̃] NM instrument; *Jur* (legal) instrument; *Mus* **i. (de musique)** (musical) instrument; **i. de mesure/de précision** measuring/precision instrument; **i. de travail** work instrument; **i. de navigation** navigation(al) instrument; *Aviat* **atterrissage aux instruments** instrument landing; *Aviat* **naviguer aux instruments** to fly on instruments; **i. de chirurgie** surgical instrument; **i. de commerce** instrument of commerce; **i. de couverture** hedging instrument; **i. de crédit** credit instrument; **i. financier** financial instrument; **i. financier à terme** financial future; **i. négociable** negotiable instrument; **i. de paiement** payment instrument; **i. de placement** investment instrument; *Fig* **servir d'i. à la vengeance de qn** to serve as the instrument of sb's revenge; **elle fut l'i. de sa vengeance** she was the instrument of his revenge; **il n'a été qu'un i.** he was merely a tool; **être l'i. de qn** to be sb's tool *or* instrument; **sa femme a été l'i. de sa réussite** his success was solely due to his wife; *Mus* **jouer d'un i.** to play an instrument; **i. à anche/clavier/vent/cordes** reed/keyboard/wind/string instrument

instrumentaire [ɛ̃strymɑ̃tɛr] ADJ *Jur* **témoin i.** witness to a deed

instrumental, -ale, -aux, -ales [ɛ̃strymɑ̃tal, -o] ADJ *(musique etc)* instrumental
NM *Ling* instrumental

instrumentation [ɛ̃strymɑ̃tasjɔ̃] NF *Mus* scoring, instrumentation, orchestration

instrumenter [ɛ̃strymɑ̃te] VI *Jur* to draw up a document; **i. contre qn** to order proceedings to be taken against sb
VT *Mus (opéra)* to score, to orchestrate

instrumentiste [ɛ̃strymɑ̃tist] N *Mus* instrumentalist

insu [ɛ̃sy] NM **à l'i. de** without the knowledge of; **à l'i. de ses parents** without his parents' knowledge, unbeknownst to his parents; **à mon i.** without my knowledge, unbeknownst to me

insubmersible [ɛ̃sybmɛrsibl] ADJ unsinkable

insubordination [ɛ̃sybɔrdinasjɔ̃] NF insubordination

insubordonné [ɛ̃sybɔrdɔne] ADJ insubordinate

insuccès [ɛ̃syksɛ] NM lack of success, failure

insuffisamment [ɛ̃syfizamɑ̃] ADV insufficiently, inadequately; **cette pièce est i. éclairée** there's not enough light in this room; **être i. affranchi** to have insufficient postage

insuffisance [ɛ̃syfizɑ̃s] NF 1 *(manque)* insufficiency, deficiency; *(de personnel, de réserves en devises)* shortage; *(de moyens)* inadequacy; **l'i. de nos ressources est telle que …** our resources are so inadequate that …; **i. de capitaux** insufficient capital; **i. d'espèces** cash shortage; **i. de provision** insufficient funds 2 *Méd (d'un organe)* failure; **i. respiratoire** respiratory insufficiency; **i. cardiaque** cardiac insufficiency, *Fam* heart failure; **i. rénale** kidney failure 3 *(incompétence)* incompetence, inefficiency; **son travail révèle de graves insuffisances** his/her work shows serious shortcomings

insuffisant [ɛ̃syfizɑ̃] ADJ 1 *(quantité)* insufficient; *(moyens, mesures)* inadequate, insufficient; **nous disposons de médicaments mais en quantité insuffisante** we have drugs at our disposal but not enough of them *or Fml* but in insufficient quantity; **nos soldats sont en nombre i.** we do not have enough *or* sufficient soldiers; **vos résultats en physique sont insuffisants!** your physics results are not good enough!; **notre chiffre d'affaires est i. pour que l'on puisse envisager de recruter davantage de personnel** our sales aren't good enough to allow us to take on more staff 2 *Fml (incapable)* incapable, incompetent

insufflateur [ɛ̃syflatœr] NM *Méd* insufflator

insufflation [ɛ̃syflasjɔ̃] NF *Méd* insufflation

insuffler [ɛ̃syfle] VT 1 to blow, to breathe; *Méd* to insufflate; *Méd* **i. de l'air dans les poumons d'un malade** to insufflate a patient; **i. du dégoût à qn** to fill sb with disgust; **ce succès a insufflé un nouvel élan à l'entreprise** this success gave the company a new lease of life *or* breathed new life into the company 2 *Méd (gorge etc)* to spray

insulaire [ɛ̃sylɛr] ADJ island, *Spéc* insular
N islander

Il faut noter que l'adjectif anglais **insular** signifie le plus souvent **borné, étriqué**.

insularité [ɛ̃sylarite] NF insularity; **l'i. du pays a grandement contribué à sa puissance maritime** the fact that the country is an island has a great deal to do with its status as a maritime power; **leur i. leur donne un complexe de supériorité** the fact that they are an island race gives them a superiority complex

insuline [ɛ̃sylin] NF *Méd* insulin

insulinodépendant [ɛ̃sylinodepɑ̃dɑ̃] ADJ *Méd* insulin-dependent

insulinothérapie [ɛ̃sylinɔterapi] NF *Méd* insulin therapy

insultant [ɛ̃syltɑ̃] ADJ insulting; **c'est i.!** it's insulting!, it's an insult!; **il s'est comporté de façon insultante à mon égard** he behaved insultingly to me

insulte [ɛ̃sylt] NF insult; **insultes** insults, abuse; **c'est la pire des insultes** that's the worst possible insult; **il lui a lancé les pires insultes** he called him/her every name under the sun; **faire i. à qn** to insult sb; **une i. à notre intelligence/au bon goût** an insult to our intelligence/to good taste

insulté, -ée [ɛ̃sylte] ADJ insulted
N injured party

insulter [ɛ̃sylte] VT to insult
VI **i. au malheur** to jeer at misfortune; **i. au bon goût** to insult good taste

insupportable [ɛ̃sypɔrtabl] ADJ *(douleur, chaleur, froid)* unbearable, unendurable; *(vacarme)* unbearable, intolerable; *(conduite)* intolerable; *(personne)* unbearable, insufferable; **la luminosité du soleil était i.** the sun was unbearably bright; **il fait une chaleur i.** it's unbearably hot; **cette pensée m'était i.** the thought was unbearable

insupportablement [ɛ̃sypɔrtabləmɑ̃] ADV unbearably

insurgé, -ée [ɛ̃syrʒe] ADJ, N rebel, *Fml* insurgent

insurger (s') [sɛ̃syrʒe] VPR (**je m'insurgeai(s); n. n. insurgeons**) to rise up (in rebellion), to revolt, to rebel; **il s'est insurgé contre ces mesures** he rebelled against these measures

insurmontable [ɛ̃syrmɔ̃tabl] ADJ *(difficulté, obstacle)* insurmountable, insuperable; *(aversion, dégoût)* unconquerable; **il m'inspire un dégoût i.** I cannot overcome or conquer the disgust I feel for him

insurmontablement [ɛ̃syrmɔ̃tabləmɑ̃] ADV insurmountably

insurpassable [ɛ̃syrpasabl] ADJ unsurpassable

insurrection [ɛ̃syrɛksjɔ̃] NF uprising, rebellion, insurrection; **en état d'i.** *(paysans, étudiants)* up in arms, in a state of rebellion; *(pays)* in a state of insurrection or rebellion

insurrectionnel, -elle [ɛ̃syrɛksjɔnɛl] ADJ *(troupes, mouvement, gouvernement)* rebel, *Fml* insurrectionary

intact [ɛ̃takt] ADJ intact

intaille [ɛ̃taj] NF *Spéc* intaglio

intangibilité [ɛ̃tɑ̃ʒibilite] NF intangibility

intangible [ɛ̃tɑ̃ʒibl] ADJ intangible; *(loi, institution)* sacred

intarissable [ɛ̃tarisabl] ADJ *(puits, imagination)* inexhaustible; *(bavardage)* endless; **le puits/la source est i.** the well/the spring never dries up; **quand il commence à parler de football, il est i.** once he starts to talk about football he never shuts up

intarissablement [ɛ̃tarisabləmɑ̃] ADV *(parler)* endlessly, inexhaustibly

intégrable [ɛ̃tegrabl] ADJ *Math* integrable; *Ordinat (lecteur etc)* integratable

intégral, -ale, -aux, -ales [ɛ̃tegral, -o] ADJ **1 paiement/remboursement i.** payment/refund in full, full payment/refund; **après le versement i. de la rançon** after the ransom has been paid in full; **nous demandons le maintien i. des prestations de la Sécurité sociale** we ask that social security benefits be maintained at their current levels; **texte i.** complete and unabridged; **édition intégrale** (complete and) unabridged edition; *Cin* **version intégrale** uncut or full-length version; **elle pratique le bronzage i.** she goes in for an all-over tan, she sunbathes in the nude; **nu i.** total nudity; **un spectacle de nu i.** a nude show; *Fam* **un fumiste i.** an out-and-out clown or joker; *Fam* **un crétin i.** a

complete (and utter) idiot, an unmitigated idiot; *Fam* **un menteur i.** an absolute or unmitigated liar; *Fam* **c'est un profiteur i.** he's just out for what he can get **2** *Math* **calcul i.** integral calculus
NF **intégrale 1** *Math* integral **2 l'intégrale des symphonies de Beethoven** the complete set of Beethoven symphonies; **l'intégrale des œuvres de Shakespeare** the complete works of Shakespeare

intégralement [ɛ̃tegralmɑ̃] ADV *(citer, rembourser)* fully, in full; **il a vidé i. son compte épargne pour s'acheter une moto** he took all the money out of his savings account to buy a motor bike; *Fam* **se moquer i. de qch** not to give a damn about sth; *Fin* **i. libéré** fully paid up

intégralité [ɛ̃tegralite] NF **l'i.** the whole; **l'i. de son salaire** the whole of his salary, his entire salary; **ils lui ont remboursé l'i. de ses dépenses** they refunded his expenses in full; **dans son i.** in its entirety, in full

intégrante [ɛ̃tegrɑ̃t] ADJ f **une partie i. de** an integral part of; **faire partie i. de** to be an integral part of, *Fam* to be part and parcel of

intégrateur [ɛ̃tegratœr] NM *Ordinat* integrator

intégration [ɛ̃tegrasjɔ̃] NF *(d'une population)* (social) integration; *Math* integration; **i. d'un candidat à Polytechnique** admission of a candidate to the École Polytechnique
▸▸ *Écon* **i. en amont** backward integration; *Écon* **i. en aval** forward integration; **i. économique** economic integration; **i. européenne** European integration; *Ordinat* **i. à grande échelle** large-scale integration; *Écon* **i. horizontale** horizontal integration; *Ordinat* **i. à moyenne échelle** medium-scale integration; *Ordinat* **i. à petite échelle** small-scale integration; *Ordinat* **i. à très grande échelle** very large-scale integration; *Écon* **i. verticale** vertical integration; *Écon* **i. verticale en amont** vertical backward integration; *Écon* **i. verticale en aval** vertical forward integration

intégré [ɛ̃tegre] ADJ *Ordinat* integrated; *Aut* built-in; *Ordinat* **commandes intégrées** embedded commands; *Can* **système i. de gestion** management information system
NM *Ordinat* integrated package

intègre [ɛ̃tegr] ADJ upright, honest; **une femme i.** a woman of integrity

intégrer [ɛ̃tegre] (**j'intègre; j'intégrerai**) VT **1** to integrate (**à, dans** into); **i. une somme dans une facture** to include a sum in an invoice **2** *(devenir membre de)* *(entreprise)* to join; *(école)* to enter; **il a intégré une grande école de commerce** he entered a prestigious business school **3** *Ordinat (commande)* to embed
VPR **s'intégrer** to become integrated (**à, dans** into, with)

intégrisme [ɛ̃tegrism] NM *Rel* fundamentalism

intégriste [ɛ̃tegrist] ADJ, N *Rel* fundamentalist

intégrité [ɛ̃tegrite] NF **1** *(totalité)* integrity, completeness, entirety; *Ordinat* **i. des données** data integrity **2** *(honnêteté)* integrity, uprightness, honesty

intellect [ɛ̃telɛkt] NM intellect

intellectualiser [ɛ̃telɛktɥalize] VT to intellectualize

intellectualisme [ɛ̃telɛktɥalism] NM intellectualism

intellectualiste [ɛ̃telɛktɥalist] ADJ, N intellectualist

intellectualité [ɛ̃telɛktɥalite] NF *Litt* intellectuality

intellectuel, -elle [ɛ̃telɛktɥɛl] ADJ intellectual, *Péj* highbrow; *(fatigue, effort)* mental;

(travail, travailleur) white-collar, non-manual
N intellectual, *Péj* highbrow

intellectuellement [ɛ̃telɛktɥɛlmɑ̃] ADV intellectually

intelligemment [ɛ̃teliʒamɑ̃] ADV intelligently

intelligence [ɛ̃teliʒɑ̃s] NF **1** *(compréhension)* understanding, comprehension; **avoir l'i. des affaires** to have a good head for business; **pour l'i. de ce qui va suivre** in order to understand what follows
2 *(intellect)* intelligence, intellect, mind; **aiguiser l'i. de qn** to sharpen sb's wits; **le développement de l'i.** intellectual development; **un homme d'une vive i.** an extremely intelligent man, *Fml* a man of lively intelligence; **d'une i. extraordinaire** extraordinarily intelligent; **elle a eu l'i. de se taire** she had the intelligence or *Fam* the wits or the brains to keep quiet
3 *(connivence)* **un regard/sourire d'i.** a knowing look/smile; **faire des signes d'i. à qn** to signal to sb; **être d'i. avec qn** to be in collusion with sb; **entretenir des intelligences avec qn** to keep up a secret correspondence with sb; **avoir des intelligences avec l'ennemi** to have (secret) dealings with the enemy
4 *(entente)* **vivre en bonne/mauvaise i. avec qn** to be on good/bad terms with sb
▸▸ **i. artificielle** artificial intelligence; **i. mercatique** marketing or market intelligence

intelligent [ɛ̃teliʒɑ̃] ADJ intelligent, bright, clever; *Ordinat* smart, intelligent; **une femme intelligente** an intelligent woman, a woman of intelligence; *Iron* **ah, franchement, c'est i.!** that's really clever!

intelligentsia [ɛ̃telidʒɛnsja] NF **l'i.** the intelligentsia

intelligibilité [ɛ̃teliʒibilite] NF intelligibility

intelligible [ɛ̃teliʒibl] ADJ *(compréhensible)* intelligible, understandable; *(clair)* clear, distinct; **à haute et i. voix** in a loud, clear voice

intelligiblement [ɛ̃teliʒibləmɑ̃] ADV intelligibly

intello [ɛ̃telo] *Fam souvent Péj* N intellectual, highbrow
ADJ highbrow

intempérance [ɛ̃tɑ̃perɑ̃s] NF intemperance

intempérant [ɛ̃tɑ̃perɑ̃] ADJ intemperate

intempérie [ɛ̃tɑ̃peri] NF **1 intempéries** bad weather; **exposé aux intempéries** exposed to the elements **2** *Arch (du temps)* inclemency

intempestif, -ive [ɛ̃tɑ̃pɛstif, -iv] ADJ untimely, ill-timed, inopportune; **pas de démarches intempestives!** don't let's rush into this, let's not be hasty

intemporalité [ɛ̃tɑ̃pɔralite] NF timelessness

intemporel, -elle [ɛ̃tɑ̃pɔrɛl] ADJ *(hors du temps)* timeless

intenable [ɛ̃t(ə)nabl] ADJ *(chaleur, situation)* intolerable, unbearable; *(position)* untenable; *Fam* **enfant i.** uncontrollable child

intendance [ɛ̃tɑ̃dɑ̃s] NF **1** *Scol* bursary; *(bureau)* bursar's office **2** *Mil* Commissariat **3** *Hist (d'une province)* administration **4** *Arch (d'un domaine)* stewardship

intendant, -ante [ɛ̃tɑ̃dɑ̃, -ɑ̃t] NM **1** *Scol* bursar **2** *Mil* senior Commissariat officer **3** *Hist (d'une province)* administrator **4** *Arch (d'un domaine)* steward
NF **intendante 1** *Scol* (woman) bursar **2** *Hist (d'une province)* wife of the administrator **3** *Rel* Mother Superior **4** *Arch* steward's wife

intense [ɛ̃tɑ̃s] ADJ *(plaisir, froid, chaleur, activité)* intense; *(douleur)* intense, severe; *(couleur)* intense, deep; *(circulation)* dense, heavy; *(tir)* heavy; **temps d'un froid i.** intensely cold weather; **des yeux d'un bleu i.** intensely blue eyes, deep blue eyes

intensément [ɛ̃tɑ̃semɑ̃] ADV *(vivre)* intensely; *(regarder qn)* intently, intensely

intensif, -ive [ɛ̃tɑ̃sif, -iv] ADJ *(entraînement, cours, soins, bombardement)* intensive; *Agriculture* **intensive** intensive farming *or* cultivation

intensification [ɛ̃tɑ̃sifikasjɔ̃] NF intensification; **l'i. des échanges commerciaux** the strengthening of trade links, the increase in trade

intensifier [ɛ̃tɑ̃sifje] VT *(bombardements)* to intensify, *Fam* to step up; *(échanges commerciaux)* to increase, *Fam* to step up
▸ VPR **s'intensifier** to intensify, to become more intense; *(de lueur)* to get brighter *or* stronger; *(de douleur)* to become more intense, to get worse

intensité [ɛ̃tɑ̃site] NF **1** *(d'un sentiment)* intensity; *(d'un regard)* intentness, intensity; *(de la lumière)* intensity, brightness; *(du vent)* force; *(d'une couleur)* intensity, depth; *(du froid)* severity, intensity; *Élec (du courant)* strength; *(d'un champ magnétique)* density; **i. acoustique** loudness; **i. lumineuse** light intensity; *Cin, TV* candlepower; **l'i. de la lumière était telle que …** the light was so intense *or* bright that …; **donner plus d'i. à un morceau de musique** to give more feeling to a piece of music; **il y a dans ce spectacle des moments d'une grande i.** there are some very intense moments in the show; *Radio, Tél, TV* **i. du signal** signal strength **2** *Ling* **accent d'i.** stress mark

intensivement [ɛ̃tɑ̃sivmɑ̃] ADV *(répéter, s'entraîner etc)* intensively

intenter [ɛ̃tɑ̃te] VT *Jur* **i. une action/un procès à** *ou* **contre qn** to bring an action against sb, to institute proceedings against sb

intention [ɛ̃tɑ̃sjɔ̃] NF **1** *(projet)* intention, purpose, design; *Jur* intent; *Jur* **avec i. délictueuse** with malicious intent; **sans mauvaise i.** with no ill intent; **dans l'i. de nuire** with intent to harm; **sans i. de nuire** with no intent to harm, without malice; *Mktg* **i. d'achat** intention to buy, purchase intention; *Pol* **intentions de vote** voting intentions; **ils enregistrent 28 pour cent des intentions de vote** 28 percent of those polled said that they would vote for them; **avoir l'i. de faire qch** to intend *or* mean to do sth; **il n'a pas l'i. de se laisser faire** he doesn't intend to be cheated; **je n'ai nullement l'i. d'accepter** I have no *or* not the slightest intention of accepting; **à cette i.** with that in mind, to that end; **dans l'i. de faire qch** with a view to *or* with the intention of doing sth; **il a de bonnes intentions** he means well, his intentions are good; **il est plein de bonnes intentions** he's full of good intentions; **c'est l'i. qui compte** it's the thought that counts; *Prov* **l'enfer est pavé de bonnes intentions** the road to hell is paved with good intentions
 2 **ils ont organisé un banquet à l'i. de leurs invités** they organized a banquet in honour of their guests; **une messe à l'i. des disparus** a mass for the dead; **voici une écharpe que j'ai achetée à votre i.** here's a scarf I bought especially for you; **c'était une remarque à mon i.** the remark was meant for me; **livres écrits à l'i. des enfants** books for children, books aimed at children; *Com* **à l'i. de …** for the attention of …

intentionné [ɛ̃tɑ̃sjone] ADJ **bien/mal i.** well-/ill-disposed (**envers** towards); **personne bien intentionnée** well-intentioned

or well-meaning person; **c'était une démarche bien intentionnée** it was well-intentioned

intentionnel, -elle [ɛ̃tɑ̃sjonɛl] ADJ intentional, deliberate; **mon geste n'était pas i.** I didn't do it deliberately *or* intentionally *or* on purpose; **de façon intentionnelle** deliberately, intentionally

intentionnellement [ɛ̃tɑ̃sjonɛlmɑ̃] ADV deliberately, intentionally; **c'est i. que je ne l'ai pas invitée** I deliberately didn't invite her, I didn't invite her on purpose

inter [ɛ̃tɛr] NM **1** *Ftbl* **i. droit/gauche** inside right/left **2** *Tél Vieilli* trunk (line)

interactif, -ive [ɛ̃tɛraktif, -iv] ADJ *Ordinat* interactive

interaction [ɛ̃tɛraksjɔ̃] NF interaction

interactivité [ɛ̃tɛraktivite] NF interactivity, interactiveness

interafricain, -aine [ɛ̃tɛrafrikɛ̃, -ɛn] ADJ Pan-African

interallié [ɛ̃tɛralje] ADJ allied

interaméricain, -aine [ɛ̃tɛramerikɛ̃, -ɛn] ADJ Pan-American, Inter-American

interarabe [ɛ̃tɛrarab] ADJ Pan-Arab, Pan-Arabic

interarmées [ɛ̃tɛrarme] ADJ INV *Mil* **état-major i.** joint staff

interarmes [ɛ̃tɛrarm] ADJ INV *Mil (opération, manœuvre)* combined

interastral, -ale, -aux, -ales [ɛ̃tɛrastral, -o] ADJ *Rare* interstellar

interbancaire [ɛ̃tɛrbɑ̃kɛr] ADJ interbank

interblocage [ɛ̃tɛrblɔkaʒ] NM *Ordinat* deadlock

intercalaire [ɛ̃tɛrkalɛr] ADJ **1** **feuille i.** interpolated sheet; **feuillet i.** insert **2** **carte i.** *(de fichier)* guide (card) **3** *(jour)* intercalary
 NM insert, interpolated sheet; *(dans classeur)* divider

intercalation [ɛ̃tɛrkalasjɔ̃] NF *(dans un texte)* insertion; *Élec (d'une résistance)* switching in

intercaler [ɛ̃tɛrkale] VT *(dans un texte, un film)* to insert, to include; *(dans un programme, entre deux événements)* to slot in; *Élec (résistance)* to cut in, to switch in; *(jour dans une année bissextile)* to intercalate; *Typ* to insert, to insert; **i. des citations dans un discours** to intersperse *or* sprinkle a speech with quotations; **i. un court métrage entre les deux grands films** to slot a short in between the two features; **i. un mot dans un texte** to insert a word in a text
 VPR **s'intercaler** to come in between

intercantonal, -ale, -aux, -ales [ɛ̃tɛrkɑ̃tɔnal, o] ADJ *Suisse (entre cantons)* inter-canton, between cantons; *(qui concerne plusieurs cantons)* cross-canton

intercéder [ɛ̃tɛrsede] VT *(conj like* **céder***)* to intercede (**auprès de** with)

intercepter [ɛ̃tɛrsɛpte] VT *(lettre, avion, ballon, personne etc)* to intercept; *(bruit, lumière)* to shut *or* cut out

intercepteur [ɛ̃tɛrsɛptœr] NM *Aviat* interceptor

interception [ɛ̃tɛrsɛpsjɔ̃] NF *(d'une lettre, d'un avion, d'un ballon)* interception; *(du bruit, de la lumière)* cutting *or* shutting out; **avion d'i.** interceptor (aircraft)

intercesseur [ɛ̃tɛrsɛsœr] NM *Litt* mediator; **il fut mon i. auprès du patron** he interceded with the boss on my behalf

intercession [ɛ̃tɛrsɛsjɔ̃] NF *Litt* intercession

> Do not confuse with **intersession**.

interchangeable [ɛ̃tɛrʃɑ̃ʒabl] ADJ interchangeable

interclasse [ɛ̃tɛrklas] NM *Scol* (short) break (between classes)

interclassement [ɛ̃tɛrklasmɑ̃] NM *Ordinat* **i. du courrier** mail merge

interclasseuse [ɛ̃tɛrklasøz] NF *(de documents)* collator

intercom [ɛ̃tɛrkɔm] NM *TV etc* **i. de production** production talkback system

intercommunalité [ɛ̃tɛrkɔmynalite] NF *Pol* cooperation between neighbouring communes

intercommunication [ɛ̃tɛrkɔmynikasjɔ̃] NF intercommunication

interconnexion [ɛ̃tɛrkɔnɛksjɔ̃] NF *Élec* interconnection

intercontinental, -ale, -aux, -ales [ɛ̃tɛrkɔ̃tinɑ̃tal, -o] ADJ intercontinental; **fusée intercontinentale** intercontinental ballistic missile

intercooler [ɛ̃tɛrkulœr] NM *Aut* intercooler

intercostal, -ale, -aux, -ales [ɛ̃tɛrkɔstal, -o] *Anat* ADJ *(muscle)* intercostal; **des douleurs intercostales** pains in the side
 NM intercostal muscle

intercours [ɛ̃tɛrkur] NM *Scol* (short) break (between classes)

interculturel, -elle [ɛ̃tɛrkyltyrɛl] ADJ cross-cultural

interdépartemental, -ale, -aux, -ales [ɛ̃tɛrdepartəmɑ̃tal, -o] ADJ interdepartmental

interdépendance [ɛ̃tɛrdepɑ̃dɑ̃s] NF interdependence

interdépendant [ɛ̃tɛrdepɑ̃dɑ̃] ADJ interdependent; *(problèmes)* linked, related

interdiction [ɛ̃tɛrdiksjɔ̃] NF **1** *(défense)* prohibition, banning, forbidding; **i. des essais atomiques** atomic test ban; **i. de fumer/stationner** no smoking/parking, smoking/parking prohibited; **i. de tourner à droite** no right turn; **i. d'un livre par la censure** banning of a book by the censor; **i. absolue de toucher aux objets exposés** please do not touch the exhibits; **i. absolue de toucher à mon ordinateur** don't touch my computer, *Fam* hands off my computer **2** *Jur* **i. d'un aliéné** certifying of an insane person **3** *Tech* inhibit
 ▸▸ **i. de commerce** trade ban; **i. d'exportation** export ban; **i. d'importation** import ban; **i. légale** suspension *or* (temporary) deprivation of civil rights; *Admin, Pol* **i. de séjour** ban(ning order), exclusion order; **i. de vol** aircraft grounding

interdigital, -ale, -aux, -ales [ɛ̃tɛrdiʒital, -o] ADJ *(espace, pli)* between the fingers, *Spéc* interdigital

interdire [ɛ̃tɛrdir] *(conj like* **dire***, except pr ind* v. **interdisez** *and imp* **interdisez***)* VT **1** *(défendre)* *(parti politique)* to ban; *(la vente d'un produit, un meeting etc)* to ban, to prohibit; **i. qch à qn** to forbid sb sth; **il est interdit de marcher sur l'herbe** keep off the grass; **nos parents nous interdisaient les sorties** our parents forbade us to go out; **le centre-ville est interdit aux camions** lorries are banned from *or* are not allowed in the centre of town, the centre of town is closed to lorries; **la passerelle est interdite aux voyageurs** passengers are not allowed on the bridge; **le médecin lui a interdit l'alcool** the doctor has forbidden him to drink; **ils ont décidé d'i. l'accès du club aux femmes/aux mineurs** they've decided to ban women/minors from the club; **son propre père lui a interdit sa porte** his own father has forbidden him the house; **il nous est interdit de révéler …** we are not allowed to reveal …; **i. à qn de faire qch** to prohibit sb from doing sth, to forbid sb to do sth; **je t'interdis de fumer/de toucher à mes affaires/de parler à des étrangers** I forbid you to smoke/to touch my things/to talk to strangers; **i. à un pilote de voler** to ground a pilot

2 *Jur* **faire i. qn** to have sb declared incapable of managing his own affairs

3 *(empêcher)* to prevent, to stop; **le temps nous interdit de sortir** the weather is preventing *or* stopping us from going out *or* is making it impossible for us to go out

VPR s'interdire s'i. l'alcool/le tabac to give up drinking/smoking; **il s'interdit d'y penser** he doesn't let himself think about it

interdisciplinaire [ɛ̃terdisipliner] ADJ interdisciplinary

interdit, -ite [ɛ̃terdi, -it] ADJ **1** *(non autorisé)* forbidden; **(il est) i. de fumer** no smoking; **entrée interdite (au public)** no admittance, no entry; **affichage i.** billposters will be prosecuted; **passage/stationnement i.** no thoroughfare/parking; **c'est un sujet i. ici** it's a forbidden *or* taboo subject here; *Cin* **i. aux moins de 18 ans** adults only, *Br* ≃ 18, *Am* ≃ NC-17; *Cin* **i. aux moins de 13 ans** *Br* ≃ PG, *Am* ≃ PG-13; **i. de séjour** *(dans un pays)* banned; **il est i. de séjour en France** he is banned from France, he is persona non grata in France; *Banque* **être i. de chéquier** to have had one's cheque book withdrawn; *Banque* **être i. bancaire** to have had all banking facilities withdrawn; *Ordinat* **i. d'écriture** *(disquette)* write-protected; **avion i. de vol** grounded aircraft **2** *(déconcerté)* disconcerted, nonplussed, taken aback

N *Jur* **(aliéné) i.** certified person; **i. de séjour** = ex-convict prohibited from entering a certain area

NM **1** *(dans la société)* taboo; *Rel* interdict; **elle fait fi de tous les interdits** she flouts all the conventions; **fumer en public constituait un i. pour les femmes** it used to be frowned on *or* to be taboo for women to smoke in public; *Rel* **des interdits alimentaires** food forbidden by dietary law; **frapper qn/qch d'i.** to impose a ban on sb/sth **2** *Banque* **i. bancaire** ban on writing cheques; **être frappé d'i. bancaire** to be banned from writing cheques

intéressant, -ante [ɛ̃teresɑ̃, -ɑ̃t] ADJ **1** *(attirant)* interesting; **peu i.** dull, uninteresting; **il n'y a pas grand-chose d'i. à la télévision** there's not much of interest on television, *Fam* there's not much on television; **chercher à se rendre i.** to try to make oneself interesting, to draw attention to oneself **2** *(avantageux)* worthwhile; *(prix)* attractive; *(placements)* profitable

N *Fam* **faire l'i.** to show off, to draw attention to oneself

> Il faut noter que l'adjectif anglais **interesting** ne signifie jamais **avantageux**.

intéressé, -ée [ɛ̃terese] ADJ **1** *(concerné)* **les parties intéressées** the interested parties, the persons concerned *or* involved **2** *(égoïste)* selfish, self-seeking; **amour i.** cupboard love; **son amour pour lui est i.** his/her love for him is self-interested; **une amitié intéressée** a self-interested friendship; **agir dans un but i.** to have an axe to grind; **encore un conseil i.!** another piece of biased advice!

N **les intéressés** the interested parties, the persons concerned *or* involved; **les premiers intéressés** those most directly affected; **c'est vous le premier i.** you're the one most affected *or* most closely concerned

intéressement [ɛ̃teresmɑ̃] NM *Com, Ind* **i. (aux résultats)** employee profit-sharing scheme

intéresser [ɛ̃terese] VT **1** *(captiver)* to interest, to be interesting to; **un sujet qui m'intéresse beaucoup** a subject which interests me greatly; **la politique/l'astronomie m'in-**

téresse beaucoup I am very interested *or* I take a great deal of interest in politics/astronomy; **ceci peut vous i.** this may interest you *or* be of interest to you; **savoir i. les enfants** to know how to get children's interest; **i. qn à qch** to interest sb in sth; **le sort des réfugiés n'intéresse personne** no-one is interested in the fate of the refugees; **on va au cinéma, est-ce que ça t'intéresse?** we're going to the cinema, are you interested?; *Iron* **continue ou cause toujours, tu m'intéresses** how interesting!

2 *(concerner)* to concern, to affect; **question qui intéresse le monde entier** question of worldwide interest *or* of concern to the entire world

3 *Ind, Com* **i. les employés (aux bénéfices)** to initiate a profit-sharing scheme; **être intéressé dans une affaire** to have a share in a business

VPR s'intéresser s'i. à qn/qch to take an interest in sb/sth, to be interested in sb/sth; **un jeune romancier qui mérite qu'on s'intéresse à lui** a young novelist who merits some attention; **il s'intéresse beaucoup à elle** he's very interested in her, he's showing a great deal of interest in her

INTÉRÊT [ɛ̃terɛ]

stake **1** · share **1** · interest **2, 3, 5** · advantage **2** · importance **4**

NM **1** *(dans une affaire etc)* share, stake; **avoir des intérêts dans une affaire** to have financial interests in a business; **il y a de gros intérêts en jeu** there's a lot at stake; **les intérêts économiques de notre pays dans cette région** our country's economic interests in that region

2 *(avantage)* interest; **j'ai i. à le faire, c'est dans mon i. de le faire** it's in my interest to do it; **tu aurais tout i. à le faire** you would be well advised to do it; **on a i. à réserver si on veut avoir des places** it is advisable to book if we want seats; *Fam* **tu n'as pas i. à recommencer!** you'd better not do it again!; **agir dans son i.** to act in one's own interest(s); **agir dans/contre l'i. de qn** to act in/against sb's interest(s); **ce n'est pas dans mon i. (de le faire)** it's not in my interest (to do it); **je n'ai aucun i. à le faire** it's not at all in my interest; **quel i. aurait-elle à te nuire?** why should she want to harm you?; **agir par i. personnel** to act out of self-interest; **son i. personnel** his/her own interests; **il a fait un mariage d'i.** he married for money; **il sait où se trouve son i.** he knows where his advantage lies *or Fam* which side his bread is buttered on; **l'i. des vacances en groupe, c'est de faire des rencontres** the advantage of *or Fam* the great thing about group holidays is that you meet people; *Rail* **ligne d'i. local** branch line, local line; **très** *Fam* **tu viens à la réunion du syndicat? – y'a i.!** are you coming to the union meeting? – you bet (I am)!

3 *(attention, curiosité)* interest; **d'i. historique/architectural** of historical/architectural interest; **ressentir de l'i. pour qn/qch** to feel interested in sb/sth; **prendre de l'i. à qch** to take an interest in sth; **montrer un i. pour qch** to show an interest in sth; **livre sans i.** *ou* **dépourvu d'i.** uninteresting book, book devoid of interest; **elle a perdu tout son i. pour son travail/cet ami** she has lost all interest in her work/friend

4 *(importance)* importance; **du plus haut i.** of the greatest importance; **quelques paroles sans i.** some unimportant words; **c'était sans i.** it wasn't important

5 *Fin* interest; **i. simple/composé** simple/compound interest; **placer son argent à 12% d'i.** to invest one's money at 12% interest; **prêt à i.** interest-bearing loan

▸ ▸ *Fin* **i. bancaire** bank interest; *Fin* **i. capi-**

talisé capitalised interest; *Fin* **intérêts compensatoires** damages; **i. du consommateur** consumer welfare; *Fin* **intérêt(s) couru(s)** accrued interest; *Fin* **intérêts débiteurs** debt interest; *Fin* **intérêts dus** interest due; *Fin* **intérêts à échoir** accruing interest; *Fin* **intérêts échus** accrued interest; *Fin* **intérêts exigibles** interest due and payable; *Fin* **i. fixe** fixed interest; *Fin* **i. légal** statutory (rate of) interest; *Fin* **intérêts moratoires** default interest, penalty interest; *Fin* **i. négatif** negative interest; **i. public** public interest; **c'est dans l'i. public** it's in the public interest; *Bourse* **i. de report** contango; *Fin* **i. de retard** interest on arrears; *Fin* **i. à taux flottant** floating-rate interest; *Fin* **i. variable** variable-rate interest

interfaçage [ɛ̃terfasaʒ] NM *Ordinat* interfacing

interface [ɛ̃terfas] NF **1** *Ordinat* interface; **i. commune de passerelle** common gateway interface, CGI; **i. de communication** communication interface; **i. d'imprimante** printer interface; **i. graphique** graphic interface; **i. numérique** digital interface; **i. parallèle** parallel interface; **i. pour petit système informatique** small computer system interface; **i. série** serial interface; **i. utilisateur** user interface; **i. utilisateur graphique** graphical user interface, GUI; **i. vidéo numérique** digital video interface **2** *(intermédiaire)* interface

interfacer [ɛ̃terfase] VT *Ordinat* to interface

interférence [ɛ̃terferɑ̃s] NF **1** *Phys, Radio* interference; *Radio, Tél* **à cause des interférences** because of the interference; **i. électrique** electrical interference **2** *(d'événements)* combination

interférent [ɛ̃terferɑ̃] ADJ *Phys (rayons etc)* interfering

interférer [ɛ̃terfere] VI (**il interfère; il interférait; il interférera**) **1** *Phys (des ondes lumineuses etc)* to interfere **2** *(d'un projet)* to interfere (**avec** with); *(de projets, politiques)* to interfere with each other

interféron [ɛ̃terferɔ̃] NM *Biol* interferon

interfolier [ɛ̃terfɔlje] VT *Tech* to interleave, to interpage

intergalactique [ɛ̃tergalaktik] ADJ intergalactic

intergouvernemental, -ale, -aux, -ales [ɛ̃terguvɛrnəmɑ̃tal, -o] ADJ intergovernmental

intergroupe [ɛ̃tergrup] NM *Pol* joint committee

intérieur [ɛ̃terjœr] ADJ **1** *(dans l'espace) (escalier)* interior, inner, inside; *(cour)* inner; *(poche)* inside; *(partie)* inside, internal; *(mer)* inland

2 *(national) (administration, politique, marché, dette, commerce)* domestic, internal, home; **vol i.** domestic flight; **(tarif d')affranchissement en régime i.** inland postage rate

3 *(vie, sentiments, force)* inner

NM **1** *(dedans) (d'une maison, d'une voiture)* inside, interior; *(d'un four, d'un récipient, d'une boîte etc)* inside; *Cin* interior (shot); **à l'i.** inside, on the inside; *(à la maison)* inside, indoors; **à l'i. de la gare/de la malle** inside the station/the trunk; **à l'i. du parti** within *or* inside the party; **à l'i. de lui-même il savait que …** deep down he knew that …; **la porte était verrouillée de l'i.** the door was bolted on *or* from the inside; **il veut transformer le parti de l'i.** he wants to change the party from the inside *or* from within; *Cin* **tourné en i.** shot indoors *or* inside; **l'i. du pays** the interior of the country; **dans l'i. du pays** inland; **avancer vers l'i. du pays** to advance inland; **Ministère de l'I.** Ministry of the

Interior, *Br* ≃ Home Office, *Am* ≃ Department of the Interior; **i. cuir** *(de voiture)* leather trim; **i. sport** *(de voiture)* sports trim **2** *(maison)* interior, home; **un i. douillet** a cosy interior *or* home; **vie d'i.** home life, domestic life; **femme d'i.** houseproud housewife; **elle est très femme d'i.** she's very houseproud; **vêtements d'i.** indoor clothes **3** *Ftbl* **i. gauche/droit** inside left/right

intérieurement [ɛ̃terjœrmɑ̃] ADV *(savoir)* inwardly, inside, within oneself; *(maudire qn)* inwardly; **rire i.** to laugh to oneself *or* inwardly

intérim [ɛ̃terim] NM interim; *(travail intérimaire)* temporary work, temping; **dans l'i.** in the interim, (in the) meantime; **par i.** *(président, ministre)* acting; *(gouvernement, cabinet)* caretaker; **gouverner par i.** to govern in the interim *or* for an interim period; **secrétaire par i.** acting *or* temporary secretary; **faire de l'i.** to do temporary work, to temp; **assurer l'i.** to deputize *or* stand in (**de qn** for sb); *Méd* to act as locum (for sb)

intérimaire [ɛ̃terimɛr] ADJ *(fonction, fonctionnaire etc)* temporary; *Pol* **cabinet i.** caretaker cabinet; **directeur i.** acting manager; **dividende/rapport i.** interim dividend/report

▶ N *(travailleur)* temporary worker; *(secrétaire)* temporary secretary, temp; *Méd* locum (tenens); **travailler comme i.** to temp, to work as a temp

intériorisation [ɛ̃terjɔrizasjɔ̃] NF internalization, interiorization

intérioriser [ɛ̃terjɔrize] VT to internalize, to interiorize

interjectif, -ive [ɛ̃terʒɛktif, -iv] ADJ interjectional

interjection [ɛ̃terʒɛksjɔ̃] NF **1** *Gram* interjection **2** *Jur (d'appel)* lodging

interjeter [ɛ̃terʒəte] VT *(conj like* **jeter***) Jur* **i. appel** to lodge an appeal, to give notice of appeal

interlettrage [ɛ̃terletraʒ] NM *Ordinat* inter-character spacing

interlignage [ɛ̃terliɲaʒ] NM *Typ* leading, interline spacing, line spacing; **i. simple** single spacing

interligne [ɛ̃terliɲ] NM *Typ* leading, interline spacing, line spacing; *Mus (sur une portée)* space; **dans les interlignes** between the lines; **tapé en simple/double i.** typed with single/double spacing, single-/double-spaced

▶ NF *Typ (lame)* lead; **i. réglable** adjustable line space

interligner [ɛ̃terliɲe] VT **1** *(insérer) (mot)* to write between the lines, *Spéc* to interline **2** *Typ (séparer)* to lead out

interlinéaire [ɛ̃terlineɛr] ADJ *(notes)* interlinear

interlocuteur, -trice [ɛ̃terlɔkytœr, -tris] N speaker, *Fml* interlocutor; **mon i.** the person I was/am speaking to, *Fml* my interlocutor; **i. privilégié** = person *or* country with whom one has a special relationship; **les États-Unis ont toujours été un i. privilégié pour la Grande-Bretagne** the United States has always had a special relationship with Great Britain; **un i. valable** *(de négociation)* an acceptable negotiating partner

interlocutoire [ɛ̃terlɔkytwar] *Jur* ADJ interlocutory

▶ NM interlocutory judgement

interlope [ɛ̃terlɔp] ADJ *(établissement)* suspect, dubious, shady; *Rare (commerce)* unauthorized, illegal; **c'était le lieu de rendez-vous de tout un monde i.** it was the meeting place of the underworld

interloqué [ɛ̃terlɔke] ADJ dumbfounded, flabbergasted, taken aback

interloquer [ɛ̃terlɔke] VT *(personne)* to take aback, to dumbfound

interlude [ɛ̃terlyd] NM *Mus, Théâtre, TV* interlude

intermède [ɛ̃termɛd] NM *Théâtre, Fig* interlude

intermédiaire [ɛ̃termedjɛr] ADJ *(état, temps etc)* intermediate, intermediary; **couleur i. entre le bleu et le vert** colour halfway between blue and green; **sentiment i. entre la tristesse et le désespoir** feeling halfway between sadness and despair; **trouver une solution i.** to find a solution somewhere in-between; **une peinture i.** a size in-between; *Tech* **arbre i.** countershaft

▶ N *(personne)* intermediary, go-between; *Com* middleman; **i. commercial** merchant middleman; **i. financier** financial intermediary; **i. négociateur** trading member; **i. remisier (en Bourse)** intermediate broker

▶ NM **par l'i. de qn/qch** through sb/sth; **par l'i. de la presse** through (the medium of) the press; **sans i.** directly; **sans l'i. de** without the intermediary of

intermédiation [ɛ̃termedjasjɔ̃] NF intermediary financing

intermezzo [ɛ̃termedzo] NM *Mus* intermezzo

interminable [ɛ̃terminabl] ADJ never-ending, endless, interminable

interminablement [ɛ̃terminabləmɑ̃] ADV endlessly, interminably

interministériel, -ielle [ɛ̃terministerjɛl] ADJ *(entre ministres)* interministerial; *(entre ministères)* interdepartmental, interministerial

intermission [ɛ̃termisjɔ̃] NF *Méd* intermission

intermittence [ɛ̃termitɑ̃s] NF **1** *(irrégularité)* intermittence, intermittency; *(de la production, du pouls etc)* irregularity; **par i.** sporadically, intermittently; **il a plu par i.** it rained on and off **2** *Méd (intermission)* intermission

intermittent, -ente [ɛ̃termitɑ̃, -ɑ̃t] ADJ intermittent, sporadic; *(pouls)* irregular; **travail i.** casual work; *Élec* **courant i.** make-and-break current

▶ N casual worker

intermoléculaire [ɛ̃termɔlekylɛr] ADJ intermolecular

internalisation [ɛ̃ternalizasjɔ̃] NF *Écon* internalization

internaliser [ɛ̃ternalize] VT *Écon* to internalize

internat [ɛ̃terna] NM **1** *Scol (système)* boarding; *(pensionnat)* boarding school **2** *Méd (concours)* entrance examination for a housemanship *or Am* an internship; *(formation)* clinicals, *Am* internship; **faire l'i.** to be a house doctor *or* a houseman *or Am* an intern

international, -ale, -aux, -ales [ɛ̃ternasjɔnal, -o] ADJ international

▶ N *Sport (joueur)* international; **il a été trois fois i. de rugby** he played rugby three times for his country *or* at international level, *Br* he was capped three times *or* he won three caps at rugby

▶ NM *Écon* **i.** world markets; **ces entreprises réalisent près de la moitié de leur chiffre d'affaires à l'i.** these companies make almost half their profits in international trade *or* on the international market

▶ NF **l'Internationale** *(groupement)* the International; *(chant)* the Internationale

internationalement [ɛ̃ternasjɔnalmɑ̃] ADV internationally

internationalisation [ɛ̃ternasjɔnalizasjɔ̃] NF internationalization

internationaliser [ɛ̃ternasjɔnalize] VT to internationalize

▶ VPR **s'internationaliser** to become international

internationalisme [ɛ̃ternasjɔnalism] NM internationalism

internationaliste [ɛ̃ternasjɔnalist] ADJ, N internationalist

internationalité [ɛ̃ternasjɔnalite] NF internationality

internaute [ɛ̃ternot] N Internet user, net surfer; **i. novice** newbie

interne [ɛ̃tern] ADJ *(structure, paroi, hémorragie)* internal; *(de l'entreprise)* in-house; *(côté)* inner; *Math (angle)* interior; **le gouvernement connaît des difficultés internes** the government is experiencing internal difficulties; *Anat* **face i. du bras** inside of the arm; *Scol* **élève i.** boarder

▶ N *Scol* boarder; *Méd* **i. (des hôpitaux)** *Br* house doctor, houseman, *Am* intern; **réaliser qch en i.** to do sth in-house

interné, -ée [ɛ̃terne] N *Pol* internee; *Méd* inmate

internégatif [ɛ̃ternegatif] NM *Cin, TV* dupe

internement [ɛ̃ternəmɑ̃] NM *(d'un étranger)* internment; *(d'un malade mental)* commitment

interner [ɛ̃terne] VT *(étranger)* to intern; *(malade mental)* to commit

Internet [ɛ̃ternɛt] NM Internet; **I. 2** Internet 2; **sur (l') I.** on the Internet; **naviguer sur (l') I.** to surf the Internet; **l'I. mobile** the mobile Internet

interocéanique [ɛ̃terɔseanik] ADJ interoceanic

interopérabilité [ɛ̃terɔperabilite] NF interoperability

interparlementaire [ɛ̃terparləmɑ̃tɛr] ADJ *Pol* interparliamentary; **commission i.** joint committee

interpellateur, -trice [ɛ̃terpelatœr, -tris] N heckler; *Pol* questioner

interpellation [ɛ̃terpelasjɔ̃] N *(appel)* calling out; *(par sentinelle)* challenge; *Pol (question)* question; **répondre à une i.** *(au Parlement)* to answer a question; **interpellation(s)** *(à une réunion, à un spectacle)* heckling; **la police a procédé à plusieurs interpellations** the police took several people in for questioning

interpeller [ɛ̃terpele] VT **1** *(appeler)* to call (out) to; *Pol (ministre)* to question, to put a question to; *(à une réunion politique, un spectacle)* to heckle; *(d'une sentinelle)* to challenge; **se faire i. par la police** to be questioned by the police; **i. le ministre pour qu'il s'explique sur sa politique** to call on *or* challenge the Minister to explain his policy **2** *Fam (toucher)* **ce film/roman m'interpelle vraiment** I can really relate to this film/novel, this film/novel really says something to me

▶ VPR **s'interpeller** to call (out) to each other; **les deux automobilistes s'interpellaient grossièrement** the two drivers were exchanging insults *or* shouting insults at each other

interpénétration [ɛ̃terpenetrasjɔ̃] NF *(de phénomènes, domaines, cultures)* interpenetration

interpénétrer (s') [sɛ̃terpenetre] VPR to interpenetrate

interphone [ɛ̃terfɔn] NM *(dans un bureau)* intercom; *(à l'entrée d'un immeuble)* entryphone; *TV, Radio* talkback; **à l'i.** on the intercom; *TV, Radio* **i. commuté** switched talkback; **i. de studio** studio talkback

interplanétaire [ɛ̃terplanetɛr] ADJ interplanetary; **voyage i.** space flight

interpolation [ɛ̃tɛrpɔlasjɔ̃] NF interpolation

interpoler [ɛ̃tɛrpɔle] VT to interpolate

interposé [ɛ̃tɛrpoze] ADJ agir par personnes interposées to act through intermediaries; il m'a contacté par personne interposée he contacted me through an intermediary

interposer [ɛ̃tɛrpoze] VT to interpose (entre between)
▶ VPR s'interposer (se mettre entre) to come between; (intervenir) to intervene

interposition [ɛ̃tɛrpozisjɔ̃] NF 1 (intervention) intervention; Mil force d'i. intervention force 2 (situation) interposition

interprétable [ɛ̃tɛrpretabl] ADJ interpretable; c'est i. de plusieurs façons it can be interpreted in several ways

interprétariat [ɛ̃tɛrpretarja] NM interpreting

interprétatif, -ive [ɛ̃tɛrpretatif, -iv] ADJ (note, déclaration) interpretative, explanatory

interprétation [ɛ̃tɛrpretasjɔ̃] NF (explication) (de texte, déclaration, discours, rêves) interpretation; (métier) interpreting; Mus interpretation, performance, rendition; Théâtre, Cin interpretation, performance; selon l'i. que l'on donne au texte according to the interpretation put on the text, according to how the text is interpreted; i. erronée misinterpretation; donner une i. erronée d'un passage to misinterpret a passage; i. d'un contrat interpretation of a contract; TV, Cin i. visuelle visual interpretation

interprète [ɛ̃tɛrprɛt] N 1 (acteur) performer, player; (chanteur) singer; (danseur) dancer; les interprètes (d'un film) the cast; l'i. de Cyrano n'était pas à la hauteur the actor playing Cyrano wasn't up to the part 2 (dans une autre langue) interpreter; i. de conférence conference interpreter; servir d'i. à qn to act as interpreter to sb, to interpret for sb; (porte-parole) to act as sb's spokesman/spokeswoman; se faire l'i. de qn to act as sb's spokesman/spokeswoman; il s'est fait l'i. des paysans auprès du gouvernement he spoke with the government on behalf of the peasants; je ne suis que son i. I'm just passing on what he said

interpréter [ɛ̃tɛrprete] VT (j'interprète; j'interpréterai) 1 Mus, Théâtre to perform, to interpret; un morceau de musique magistralement interprété a brilliantly performed or interpreted piece of music; i. les grands rôles/Cinna to perform the great roles/Cinna; il a interprété tous ses grands succès he performed all his great hits; elle va maintenant nous i. un concerto she will now perform or play a concerto for us 2 (texte, déclaration, discours, geste, rêves) to interpret; ils ont interprété mon silence/son sourire comme ... they interpreted my silence/his smile as ...; mal i. les paroles de qn to misinterpret sb's words; mal i. un signe to misread a sign

interpréteur [ɛ̃tɛrpretœr] NM Ordinat interpreter; i. de commande command interpreter

interprofessionnel, -elle [ɛ̃tɛrprɔfesjɔnɛl] ADJ interprofessional

interrègne [ɛ̃tɛrɛɲ] NM interregnum

interro [ɛ̃tɛro] NF Fam (abrév interrogation) test (at school)

interrogateur, -trice [ɛ̃tɛrɔgatœr, -tris] ADJ (air, regard) questioning, inquiring; d'un air i. inquiringly, questioningly
▶ N questioner, interrogator; Scol (oral) examiner

interrogatif, -ive [ɛ̃tɛrɔgatif, -iv] ADJ 1 (air, ton) inquiring, questioning 2 Gram (pronom, phrase etc) interrogative

▶ NM Gram interrogative (word/pronoun/adjective) SEE GRAMMAR A31–2; B16–18
▶ NF Gram **interrogative** interrogative (clause)

interrogation [ɛ̃tɛrɔgasjɔ̃] NF 1 (d'un prisonnier, d'un suspect etc) questioning, interrogation; les yeux emplis d'une secrète i. with secretly enquiring eyes 2 (question) question; i. directe/indirecte direct/indirect question; Scol i. orale/écrite oral/written test 3 Ordinat (d'une base de données) inquiry, enquiry, query; (activité) interrogation; i. à distance remote access

> Do not confuse with **interrogatoire**.

interrogativement [ɛ̃tɛrɔgativmɑ̃] ADV interrogatively, questioningly

interrogatoire [ɛ̃tɛrɔgatwar] NM Jur (de prisonniers, d'inculpé) questioning, interrogation; (au tribunal) cross-examination; pendant l'i. le témoin a dit ... under cross-examination, the witness stated ...; subir un i. en règle to undergo a thorough questioning or interrogation; faire subir un i. en règle à qn to question or interrogate sb thoroughly

> Do not confuse with the French word **interrogation**.

interrogeable [ɛ̃tɛrɔʒabl] ADJ Ordinat i. en langage naturel which can be interrogated using natural language; i. à distance with a remote interrogation facility; Tél répondeur i. à distance answering machine with remote-access facility

interroger [ɛ̃tɛrɔʒe] (j'interrogeai(s); n. interrogeons) VT 1 (de la police) to question, to interrogate; Jur (au tribunal) to cross-examine; (candidat, élève) to examine; Mktg to interview; (les faits, l'histoire etc) to consult; (sa conscience) to examine; il m'a longuement interrogé à ton sujet he asked me a lot of questions about you; la moitié des personnes interrogées a répondu oui half the people questioned answered yes; i. qn du regard to look at sb questioningly or inquiringly, to give sb a questioning or an inquiring look; il a interrogé les élèves oralement/par écrit he gave the pupils an oral/a written test 2 Ordinat (base de données) to query, to interrogate
▶ VPR s'interroger to ask oneself, to wonder (sur about)

interrompre [ɛ̃tɛrɔ̃pr] (conj like rompre) VT (couper la parole à) to interrupt, to cut in on; (au cours d'une réunion, au travail etc) to interrupt; (conversation, représentation, match etc) to interrupt; (trafic) to hold up, to stop; (négociations, tournée, traitement médical etc) to break off; (voyage) to break; (courant d'une rivière etc) to intercept, to interrupt; Élec (courant) to break, to switch off; je ne voulais pas vous i. dans votre travail I didn't want to interrupt you while you were working; prière de ne pas nous i. please don't interrupt (us); le match a été interrompu par la pluie rain stopped play; Radio, TV nous interrompons nos programmes pour un flash spécial d'information we interrupt our programmes for a special newsflash; toutes les nuits, mon sommeil est interrompu par les cris du bébé every night my sleep is broken by the baby's cries; l'entreprise a décidé d'i. la production de ce produit the company decided to discontinue production of the product
▶ VPR s'interrompre to break off, to stop

interrupteur, -trice [ɛ̃tɛryptœr, -tris] N interrupter
▶ NM Élec (commutateur) switch; i. marche-arrêt on-off switch; i. à bascule toggle switch; i. à gradation de lumière dimmer (switch); i.

d'escalier two-way switch; Ordinat i. DIP ou à plusieurs positions DIP switch; Aut i. d'allumage ignition cut-off switch, ignition switch; Aut i. de démarrage starter switch; Ordinat i. à effleurement touch-sensitive switch

interruption [ɛ̃tɛrypsjɔ̃] NF interruption; (de négociations) breaking off; Élec (de courant) disconnection, switching off, breaking; sans i. (travailler, parler, lire etc) without a break, nonstop, continuously; le magasin sera ouvert de 9h à 22h sans i. the shop will be open all day from 9 a.m. to 10 p.m.; des avions cargo assureront le ravitaillement, et ce, sans i. cargo planes will ensure the continuous provision of fresh supplies; Radio, TV nous nous excusons pour cette i. momentanée de l'image/du son we apologize for the momentary loss of picture/of sound; Ordinat fonction d'i. interrupt function
▶▶ Méd i. de grossesse termination (of pregnancy); Méd i. de grossesse spontanée spontaneous abortion, miscarriage; Méd i. volontaire de grossesse voluntary termination of pregnancy

intersaison [ɛ̃tɛrsɛzɔ̃] NF off season

interscolaire [ɛ̃tɛrskɔlɛr] ADJ inter-school

intersecté [ɛ̃tɛrsɛkte] ADJ 1 Archit intersecting, interlacing 2 Math (ligne etc) intersected

intersection [ɛ̃tɛrsɛksjɔ̃] NF intersection, junction; à l'i. des deux rues at the junction of the two streets, where the two streets meet; à l'i. de deux écoles de pensée where two schools of thought converge; point d'i. point of intersection

intersession [ɛ̃tɛrsesjɔ̃] NF Parl recess

> Do not confuse with **intercession**.

intersidéral, -ale, -aux, -ales [ɛ̃tɛrsideral, -o] ADJ intersidereal, interstellar; l'espace i. outer space

interstellaire [ɛ̃tɛrsteler] ADJ Astron interstellar; l'espace i. outer space

interstice [ɛ̃tɛrstis] NM chink, crack, Fml interstice

interstitiel, -ielle [ɛ̃tɛrstisjɛl] ADJ interstitial

intersyndical, -ale, -aux, -ales [ɛ̃tɛrsɛ̃dikal, -o] ADJ interunion
▶ NF intersyndicale interunion group; (réunion) interunion meeting

intertexte [ɛ̃tɛrtɛkst] NM Littér intertext

intertextualité [ɛ̃tɛrtɛkstɥalite] NF Littér intertextuality

intertitre [ɛ̃tɛrtitr] NM Journ subheading, crosshead; Cin insert title

intertropical, -ale, -aux, -ales [ɛ̃tɛrtrɔpikal, -o] ADJ intertropical

interurbain [ɛ̃tɛryrbɛ̃] ADJ interurban; Tél Vieilli lignes interurbaines long-distance or Br trunk lines; c'est pour une communication interurbaine? is it a long-distance or Br trunk call?
▶ NM Tél Vieilli long-distance or Br trunk service; il faut passer par l'i. you have to go through the long-distance operator

intervalle [ɛ̃tɛrval] NM 1 (dans le temps) interval; un i. d'une heure an hour's interval, an interval of an hour, a one-hour interval; visites à de longs intervalles visits at long intervals; à intervalles réguliers at regular intervals; à deux mois d'i. two months apart; par intervalles at intervals, now and then; dans l'i. in the meantime, meanwhile 2 (dans l'espace, entre des paragraphes etc) gap, space; Mus interval; à deux mètres d'i. two metres apart; laissez deux mètres d'i. entre chaque piquet leave a gap or space of two metres *or* a two-metre gap *or* space between each stake **3** *Math* interval; **i. ouvert/fermé** open/closed interval

intervenant, -ante [ɛ̃tɛʀvənɑ̃, -ɑ̃t] ADJ *Jur* intervening

▸N **1** *Jur* intervening party **2** *(dans une conférence, un débat)* participant, contributor **3** *Mktg* **i. sur le marché** market participant

intervenir [ɛ̃tɛʀvəniʀ] VI *(conj like* venir, *aux* être) **1** *(agir)* to intervene (**dans** in); *(dans une discussion, un débat)* to intervene (**dans** in), to cut in (**dans** on); **i. pour faire qch** to intervene *or* step in to do sth; **elle va i. en ta faveur** she will intervene *or* intercede on your behalf; **i. auprès de qn** to intercede with sb; **au besoin, je pourrais i.** I could intervene if necessary; **faire i. la force armée** to call out the military, to bring in the army **2** *(arriver) (de facteurs, d'éléments, de considérations)* to arise, to come up; **un accord est intervenu** an agreement has been reached; **les changements intervenus depuis 1998** the changes that have occurred since 1998 **3** *(jouer un rôle)* to play a part (**dans** in); **ces facteurs n'interviennent pas dans le processus de l'inflation** those factors have no effect *or* bearing on the rise in inflation **4** *Méd* to operate

intervention [ɛ̃tɛʀvɑ̃sjɔ̃] NF **1** *(dans une crise etc)* intervention; **i. divine** divine intervention; **i. en faveur de qn** intervention on behalf of sb; **i. auprès de qn** intervention with sb; **par son i.** through his intervention; **offre d'i.** offer of mediation; **il a fallu l'i. de la police pour séparer les deux hordes de supporters** the police had to intervene *or* step in to separate the two hordes of supporters; **i. de l'État** state intervention; **i. gouvernementale** government intervention; *Mil, Aviat* **i. aérienne** air strike **2** *(prise de parole)* intervention; **l'i. du premier ministre à l'Assemblée nationale** the Prime Minister's speech to the National Assembly **3** *Cin, TV* personal appearance, PA **4** *Méd* **i. (chirurgicale)** operation, surgery **5** *UE* **prix d'i.** intervention price

interventionnisme [ɛ̃tɛʀvɑ̃sjɔnism] NM *Pol* interventionism

interventionniste [ɛ̃tɛʀvɑ̃sjɔnist] ADJ, N *Pol* interventionist

interversion [ɛ̃tɛʀvɛʀsjɔ̃] NF *(de termes, dates etc)* inversion, transposition, reversal

intervertébral, -ale, -aux, -ales [ɛ̃tɛʀvɛʀtebʀal, -o] ADJ *Anat* intervertebral; **disque i.** (intervertebral) disc

intervertir [ɛ̃tɛʀvɛʀtiʀ] VT *(l'ordre de qch)* to invert, to reverse; *(objets, éléments)* to switch (round); **maintenant les rôles sont intervertis** now the roles are reversed

interview [ɛ̃tɛʀvju] NF interview; **i.-déclaration** interpretative interview; **i.-document** documentary interview; **i. exclusive** exclusive (interview); **i.-explanation** interpretative interview; **i. question-réponse** question-and-answer interview; **i. téléphonique** telephone interview; **i. télévisée** television interview; **i.-témoignage** informational interview

interviewé, -ée [ɛ̃tɛʀvjuve] N interviewee

interviewer [ɛ̃tɛʀvjuve] VT to interview

interviewe(u)r [ɛ̃tɛʀvjuvœʀ] NM interviewer

intervocalique [ɛ̃tɛʀvɔkalik] ADJ *Ling* intervocalic

intestat [ɛ̃tɛsta] ADJ INV *Jur* **mourir i.** to die intestate

intestin¹ [ɛ̃tɛstɛ̃] ADJ internal; *(guerre)* internecine; **luttes intestines** infighting

intestin² NM *Anat* intestine; **intestins** intestines, bowels; **gros i.** large intestine; **i. grêle** small intestine

intestinal, -ale, -aux, -ales [ɛ̃tɛstinal, -o] ADJ intestinal

intifada [intifada] NF intifada

intimation [ɛ̃timasjɔ̃] NF *Jur* notification; *(citation devant un tribunal)* summons; **i. de vider les lieux** notice to quit

intime [ɛ̃tim] ADJ *(relations, endroit, atmosphère etc)* intimate; *(pièce)* cosy; *(dîner, fête)* intimate, quiet; *(ami)* intimate, close; **être i. avec qn** to be close to sb; **hygiène** *ou* **toilette i.** personal hygiene; **avoir la conviction i. de qch** to be thoroughly convinced of sth; **elle a l'i. conviction** *ou* **la conviction i. que ...** she is thoroughly convinced that ...; **pensées intimes** intimate *or* inmost *or* innermost thoughts; **journal i.** (private *or* personal) diary; *Phys* **la structure i. de la matière** the intimate *or* innermost structure of matter

▸N close *or* intimate friend, intimate; **Solange, Sosso pour les intimes** Solange, Sosso to my/her friends

> Il faut noter qu'en anglais **to be intimate with someone** signifie le plus souvent avoir des rapports sexuels avec quelqu'un.

intimé, -ée [ɛ̃time] N *Jur* respondent, defendant

intimement [ɛ̃timmɑ̃] ADV intimately; **i. liés** *(amis)* very close; *(phénomènes)* closely *or* intimately linked; **je suis i. persuadé que ...** I'm thoroughly convinced that ...

intimer [ɛ̃time] VT **1 i. à qn l'ordre de faire qch** to order sb to do sth **2** *Jur* **i. qn** to summons sb to appear before the Court of Appeal

intimidable [ɛ̃timidabl] ADJ easily intimidated; **ce n'est pas quelqu'un de facilement i.** he's/she's not someone who can be easily intimidated

intimidant [ɛ̃timidɑ̃] ADJ intimidating

intimidateur, -trice [ɛ̃timidatœʀ, -tʀis] ADJ *(paroles, propos)* intimidating

intimidation [ɛ̃timidasjɔ̃] NF intimidation; **ils ont usé d'i. pour lui faire signer la déclaration** they intimidated him into signing *or* used intimidation to make him sign the declaration

intimider [ɛ̃timide] VT *(effrayer)* to intimidate; *surtout Jur* to exert undue influence on; **elle ne se laisse pas facilement i.** she is not easily intimidated; **nullement intimidé** nothing daunted

intimisme [ɛ̃timism] NM *Littér, Beaux-Arts Spéc* intimism

intimiste [ɛ̃timist] ADJ, N *Littér, Beaux-Arts Spéc* intimist; **c'est un cinéaste très i.** his films explore the world of people's feelings and relationships; **des peintres intimistes** painters whose paintings portray interior domestic scenes

intimité [ɛ̃timite] NF **1** *(vie privée)* privacy; *(entre amis)* intimacy, closeness; **dans l'i.** in private (life); **dans l'i. de notre foyer** in the privacy of our own home; **dans l'i. conjugale** in one's private married life; **il vit dans l'i. des grands de ce monde** he is on close *or* intimate terms with people in high places; **le mariage a été célébré dans la plus stricte i.** only close family attended the wedding **2** **dans l'i. de son être** in the depths of one's being; **dans l'i. de sa conscience** in one's innermost conscience, in the depths of one's conscience

intitulé [ɛ̃tityle] NM *(de document, livre etc)* title; *(de chapitre)* heading, title; *(d'un article)* catchline; **i. de compte** account particulars

intituler [ɛ̃tityle] VT *(livre, film, opéra)* to

call, to entitle; **livre intitulé ...** book entitled ..., book with the title of ...; **article intitulé ...** article headed ..., article with the heading ...; **pourquoi avez-vous intitulé votre livre 'Colère'?** why did you call your book 'Anger'?

▸VPR **s'intituler** *(de livre, morceau de musique etc)* to be entitled, to be called; *(de personne)* to call oneself; **ce livre s'intitule 'Reflets'** this book is entitled *or* called 'Reflections'

intolérable [ɛ̃tɔleʀabl] ADJ intolerable, insufferable

intolérablement [ɛ̃tɔleʀabləmɑ̃] ADV intolerably

intolérance [ɛ̃tɔleʀɑ̃s] NF intolerance; *Méd* **i. à une substance** intolerance to a substance

intolérant [ɛ̃tɔleʀɑ̃] ADJ intolerant

intonation [ɛ̃tɔnasjɔ̃] NF intonation; **une voix aux intonations très douces** a very soft voice

intouchable [ɛ̃tuʃabl] ADJ, N untouchable

intox [ɛ̃tɔks] NF *Pol Fam* brainwashing; *(par la presse)* managed news

intoxicant [ɛ̃tɔksikɑ̃] ADJ *Méd* poisonous, toxic

intoxication [ɛ̃tɔksikasjɔ̃] NF *Méd* poisoning; *Fig Fam* indoctrination, brainwashing; **i. alimentaire** food poisoning

intoxiqué, -ée [ɛ̃tɔksike] ADJ poisoned; *(à la suite d'une intoxication alimentaire)* suffering from food poisoning; **les personnes intoxiquées se fournissaient toutes chez le même boucher** the people who got food poisoning all bought their meat from the same butcher

▸N addict

> Il faut noter que l'adjectif anglais **intoxicated** est un faux ami. Il signifie le plus souvent **ivre**.

intoxiquer [ɛ̃tɔksike] VT *Méd* to poison; *Fam* **les médias intoxiquent le public** the media indoctrinate *or* brainwash people; **intoxiqué par la publicité** brainwashed by advertising

▸VPR **s'intoxiquer** to poison oneself; **il s'est intoxiqué avec des champignons** he got food poisoning from (eating) mushrooms

intracellulaire [ɛ̃tʀaselylɛʀ] ADJ *Biol* intracellular

intracommunautaire [ɛ̃tʀakɔmynotɛʀ] ADJ intra-Community

intradermique [ɛ̃tʀadɛʀmik] *Méd* ADJ intradermic, intradermal

▸NF intradermic *or* intradermal injection

intrados [ɛ̃tʀado] NM *Archit (d'une voûte)* intrados; *Aviat (d'une aile)* undersurface

intraduisible [ɛ̃tʀaduizibl] ADJ untranslatable

intraitable [ɛ̃tʀɛtabl] ADJ uncompromising, inflexible; **il est i. sur le chapitre de la propreté** he is a stickler for cleanliness, he is uncompromising *or* inflexible where cleanliness is concerned

intra-muros [ɛ̃tʀamyʀos] ADV *(habiter)* within the town/city, in the town/city itself; **Londres/Paris i.** inner London/Paris

intramusculaire [ɛ̃tʀamyskylɛʀ] *Méd* ADJ intramuscular

▸NF intramuscular injection

Intranet [ɛ̃tʀanɛt] NM *Ordinat* Intranet

intransférable [ɛ̃tʀɑ̃sfeʀabl] ADJ not transferable; *Jur (droit)* unassignable

intransigeance [ɛ̃tʀɑ̃ziʒɑ̃s] NF intransigence; **faire preuve d'i.** to be intransigent *or* uncompromising

intransigeant, -ante [ɛ̃tʀɑ̃ziʒɑ̃, -ɑ̃t] ADJ *(personne)* intransigent, uncompromising, inflexible; *(code moral, ligne de conduite)* uncompromising, strict; *(ton)* peremptory; **il est très i. avec les gens qui ne pensent pas exactement comme lui** he takes a hard line with those who don't exactly share his views **N** *Pol* hardliner, intransigent

intransitif, -ive [ɛ̃trɑ̃zitif, -iv] **ADJ, NM** *Gram* intransitive

intransitivement [ɛ̃trɑ̃zitivmɑ̃] **ADV** *Gram* intransitively

intransitivité [ɛ̃trɑ̃zitivite] **NF** *Gram* intransitivity

intransmissible [ɛ̃trɑ̃smisibl] **ADJ** intransmissible, untransferable

intransportable [ɛ̃trɑ̃spɔrtabl] **ADJ** *(objet)* untransportable; *(blessé)* unfit to travel

intrant [ɛ̃trɑ̃] **NM** *Écon* input

intra-utérin, *pl* **intra-utérins, -ines** [ɛ̃trayterɛ̃] **ADJ** *Anat* intra-uterine; **la vie i.** life in the womb

intraveineux, -euse [ɛ̃travɛnø, -øz] **ADJ** intravenous
NF intraveineuse intravenous injection

intrépide [ɛ̃trepid] **ADJ 1** *(courageux)* intrepid, fearless **2** *(que rien ne rebute)* **buveur i.** hardened drinker; **menteur i.** barefaced liar **N** fearless *or* intrepid person

intrépidement [ɛ̃trepidmɑ̃] **ADV** fearlessly, intrepidly

intrépidité [ɛ̃trepidite] **NF** fearlessness, intrepidity; **avec i.** fearlessly, intrepidly

intrigant, -ante [ɛ̃trigɑ̃, -ɑ̃t] **ADJ** scheming, plotting, conniving
N schemer, intriguer

intrigue [ɛ̃trig] **NF** *(machination)* intrigue; *(liaison amoureuse)* (love) affair, intrigue; *Théâtre, Cin, Littér* plot; **déjouer/ourdir une i.** to foil/hatch a plot

intriguer [ɛ̃trige] **VT** *(étonner)* to intrigue **VI** *(manœuvrer)* to scheme, to intrigue

intrinsèque [ɛ̃trɛ̃sɛk] **ADJ** intrinsic

intrinsèquement [ɛ̃trɛ̃sɛkmɑ̃] **ADV** intrinsically

intro [ɛ̃tro] **NF** *Fam* intro; *(musicale)* theme tune

introducteur, -trice [ɛ̃trɔdyktœr, -tris] **N** *(d'une mode, d'un courant)* initiator; **il fut l'i. du tabac en France** he introduced tobacco (in)to France; **il fut mon i. auprès de la comtesse** he introduced me to the countess **NM** *Ordinat* **i. feuille à feuille** sheet feeder; *Ordinat* **i. manuel** manual feed

introductif, -ive [ɛ̃trɔdyktif, -iv] **ADJ** *Jur* introductory

introduction [ɛ̃trɔdyksjɔ̃] **NF 1** *(d'un livre, d'une dissertation, d'un morceau de musique)* introduction; *TV etc* introduction, lead-in; **quelques mots/pages d'i.** a few introductory words/pages, a few words/pages of introduction **2** *(de nouvelles techniques, du suffrage universel etc)* introduction **3** *(présentation)* introduction; **ce roman constitue une bonne i. à la littérature russe** this novel is a good introduction to Russian literature; **après mon i. auprès de quelques personnages influents** after I was introduced to a few influential people; **lettre d'i.** letter of introduction (**de la part de** from; **auprès de** to) **4** *(insertion)* insertion, *Fml* introduction (**dans** into) **5** *Rugby* put-in
▸▸ **i. en Bourse** listing on the stock market; *Ordinat* **i. de données** data input

introduire [ɛ̃trɔdɥir] *(prp* introduisant; *pp* introduit; *pr ind* j'introduis, il introduit, n. introduisons; *p hist* j'introduisis; *fu* j'introduirai*)* **VT** *(coutume, réforme, mesures etc)* to introduce; *(clé dans une serrure, doigt dans un trou etc)* to insert, to put, *Fml* to introduce (**dans** into); *Ordinat (données)* to enter, to input; *(marchandises)* to bring in; *(mode)* to introduce, to initiate; *(étranger, visiteur)* to

show in, to usher in; **i. des marchandises en contrebande dans un pays** to smuggle goods into a country, to bring goods illegally into a country; **i. le tabac/la mode des cheveux longs en France** to introduce tobacco/the fashion for long hair (in)to France; **introduisez ce monsieur** show the gentleman in; **il fut introduit dans une salle d'attente** he was shown into a waiting room; **i. qn auprès de qn** to show sb in to see sb; *(présenter)* to introduce sb to sb; **il est bien introduit dans les milieux de la finance** he is well established *or* has a firm foothold in the financial world; **i. en Bourse** to list on the stock market, to introduce on the Stock Exchange; **i. sur le marché** to bring onto the market, to launch; **i. une action en justice** to start legal proceedings, to bring an action; **i. une instance** to start legal proceedings
VPR s'introduire s'i. dans une maison *(d'un intrus)* to get into *or* enter a house; **s'i. dans un tunnel/tuyau** to work *or* worm one's way into a tunnel/pipe; **s'i. dans un club très fermé** to get into a very exclusive club; **l'eau s'introduit partout** water is getting in everywhere; *Ordinat* **s'i. en fraude dans un réseau** to hack into a network

---

Il faut noter que le verbe anglais **to introduce oneself** est un faux ami. Il signifie **se présenter.**

---

intromission [ɛ̃trɔmisjɔ̃] **NF** intromission

intronisation [ɛ̃trɔnizasjɔ̃] **NF 1** *(d'un évêque, d'un roi)* enthronement, enthroning **2** *(d'un système, d'une politique nouvelle)* establishment

introniser [ɛ̃trɔnize] **VT** *(roi, évêque)* to enthrone

introspectif, -ive [ɛ̃trɔspɛktif, -iv] **ADJ** introspective

introspection [ɛ̃trɔspɛksjɔ̃] **NF** introspection

introuvable [ɛ̃truvabl] **ADJ** *(produit, denrées)* unobtainable; **mes clés sont introuvables** my keys are nowhere to be found, I can't find my keys anywhere; **l'assassin reste i.** the murderer is still at large *or* still hasn't been found

introversion [ɛ̃trɔvɛrsjɔ̃] **NF** *Psy* introversion

introverti, -ie [ɛ̃trɔvɛrti] *Psy* **ADJ** introverted
N introvert

intrus, -use [ɛ̃try, -yz] **N** *aussi Ordinat* intruder; *(dans une réception, une soirée)* gatecrasher; *Jur* trespasser

intrusion [ɛ̃tryzjɔ̃] **NF** intrusion; *(dans une affaire)* interference (**dans** in), intrusion (**dans** into); **il fit i. dans la salle en plein milieu de la réunion** he came into the room and interrupted the meeting; *Géol* **roches d'i.** intrusive rocks

intubation [ɛ̃tybasjɔ̃] **NF** *Méd* intubation

intuber [ɛ̃tybe] **VT & VI** *Méd* to intubate

intuitif, -ive [ɛ̃tɥitif, -iv] **ADJ** intuitive
N c'est un i. he's an intuitive sort *or* person

intuition [ɛ̃tɥisjɔ̃] **NF** intuition; **par i.** intuitively, by intuition; **avoir une i.** to have an intuition; **avoir l'i. que ...** to have a hunch *or* a feeling that ...

intuitivement [ɛ̃tɥitivmɑ̃] **ADV** intuitively

intuitivité [ɛ̃tɥitivite] **NF** *Ordinat (de logiciel, interface)* intuitiveness

intumescence [ɛ̃tymɛsɑ̃s] **NF** intumescence

intumescent [ɛ̃tymɛsɑ̃] **ADJ** intumescent

inuit [inɥit] **ADJ INV** Inuit
N I. Inuit

inusable [inyzabl] **ADJ** *(souliers, veste, tissu, ustensile, thème, explication)* hard-wearing;

ces chaussures sont pratiquement inusables these shoes will last for ever *or* never wear out

inusité [inyzite] **ADJ** *(mots)* uncommon, not in common use; *Rare (bruit, sensation, parfum etc)* unusual

in utero [inyterɔ] **ADJ, ADV** in utero

inutile [inytil] **ADJ** *(qui ne sert à rien)* useless; *(effort)* vain, pointless, useless; *(non nécessaire) (précautions, démarche)* pointless, unnecessary; *(bagages)* unnecessary; **je suis i. ici** I'm (of) no use here; **c'est i.!** it's pointless!; *(ce n'est pas la peine)* you needn't bother; **bouches inutiles** unproductive people; **i. de dire que ...** needless to say ...; **i. de vous dire que ...** I don't have to tell you that ...; **i. d'attendre/de retenir** it's pointless waiting/ booking, there's no point in waiting/booking; **i. d'insister, je ne viens pas, un point, c'est tout** don't go on about it, I'm not coming and that's that; **c'est complètement i. de lui demander, jamais il n'acceptera** it's totally pointless asking him *or* there's absolutely no point in asking him, he'll never accept; **il n'est pas i. de préciser que ...** it is useful to point out that ...; **quelques leçons particulières ne seraient pas inutiles** a few private lessons wouldn't go amiss *or* would be useful

inutilement [inytilmɑ̃] **ADV** needlessly, unnecessarily; **se déranger i.** to put oneself out needlessly *or* unnecessarily, to go to unnecessary trouble; **c'est i. que je lui ai parlé** it was pointless talking to him, talking to him served no purpose

inutilisable [inytilizabl] **ADJ** unusable, useless; **sans la prise adéquate, cet appareil est i.** without the right plug this machine is useless; **ces statistiques sont trop vieilles, elles sont inutilisables** these statistics are too old, they are unusable

inutilisé [inytilize] **ADJ** unused; *(ressources, talent)* untapped, unused

inutilité [inytilite] **NF** uselessness, pointlessness, needlessness

invaincu [ɛ̃vɛ̃ky] **ADJ** *(pays)* unconquered, undefeated; *(armée)* unvanquished, undefeated; *Sport* unbeaten, undefeated

invalidant [ɛ̃validɑ̃] **ADJ** incapacitating, disabling

invalidation [ɛ̃validasjɔ̃] **NF** *Jur (de document, d'élection)* invalidation; *(d'un membre élu)* unseating

invalide [ɛ̃valid] **ADJ 1** *(personne)* disabled; *Jur Vieilli (loi, mariage etc)* invalid **2** *Ordinat (mot de passe, nom du fichier)* invalid
N disabled person; **les grands invalides** the severely disabled
▸▸ **i. de guerre** disabled *or* invalid ex-serviceman/ex-servicewoman; **i. du travail =** person disabled in an industrial accident

invalider [ɛ̃valide] **VT** *Jur (testament, élection etc)* to invalidate; *(membre élu)* to unseat

invalidité [ɛ̃validite] **NF** *(de personne)* disability, invalidity; *(d'une procédure, d'un contrat etc)* invalidity; **pension d'i.** disability pension

invariabilité [ɛ̃varjabilite] **NF** invariability

invariable [ɛ̃varjabl] **ADJ** invariable, unvarying; *Gram* invariable; **être i. dans ses opinions** to be unwavering in one's opinions

invariablement [ɛ̃varjabləmɑ̃] **ADV** invariably

invariance [ɛ̃varjɑ̃s] **NF** invariance, invariancy

invasif, -ive [ɛ̃vazif, -iv] **ADJ** *Méd (traitement)* invasive

invasion [ɛ̃vazjɔ̃] **NF** invasion; **i. de sauterelles** invasion of locusts; *Fig* **l'i. des touristes** the tourist invasion

invective [ɛ̃vɛktiv] NF invective; **invectives** abuse; **se répandre en invectives contre** to let out or let loose a stream of abuse at

invectiver [ɛ̃vɛktive] VI i. **contre qn** to inveigh or rail against sb

VT (personne) to hurl abuse at; **il s'est fait i. par des manifestants** he had abuse hurled at him by the demonstrators

invendable [ɛ̃vɑ̃dabl] ADJ unsaleable, unsellable

invendu [ɛ̃vɑ̃dy] ADJ unsold

NM **invendus** unsold goods; (journaux) unsold copies; (livres) unsold copies; (revendus moins cher) remainders

inventaire [ɛ̃vɑ̃tɛr] NM **1** (liste) inventory; **faire** ou **dresser un i.** to draw up or make an inventory; **sous bénéfice d'i.** conditionally, with reservations; Jur **accepter une succession sous bénéfice d'i.** to accept an estate without liability to debts beyond the assets descended; **un i. à la Prévert** a mixed bag **2** Com stocklist, inventory; **(établissement** ou **levée d')i.** stocktaking; **faire** ou **dresser l'i.** to take stock, to stocktake; **fermé pour cause d'i.** closed for stocktaking; Compta **i. comptable** book inventory; **i. de stock** physical inventory; **i. des marchandises** inventory of goods; **i. effectif** physical inventory; **i. d'entrée/de sortie** ingoing/outgoing inventory; **i. de fin d'année** accounts for the end of the Br financial or Am fiscal year; **i. intermittent** periodical inventory; **i. périodique** periodic inventory; **i. permanent** perpetual inventory; **i. physique** physical inventory; **i. théorique** theoretical inventory **3** (de monuments anciens, peintures, richesses artistiques) survey **4** Fin (d'un portefeuille de titres) valuation

inventer [ɛ̃vɑ̃te] VT (machine etc) to invent, to devise; (imaginer) (concept, moyen) to think up, to dream up; (histoire, excuse) to make up, to think up; (expression) to coin; Fam **il n'a pas inventé la poudre** ou **l'eau chaude** ou **l'eau tiède** ou **le fil à couper le beurre** he'll never set the Thames on fire; **il ne sait plus quoi i. pour la distraire** he doesn't know what else he can think up or dream up to keep her amused; **non, il ne dit pas de mal de toi derrière ton dos, qu'est-ce que tu vas i.?** no, he doesn't criticize you behind your back, you're making it (all) up!; **mais qu'est-ce qu'il va i. là?** what's he on about?; **cette histoire a été inventée de toutes pièces** this story has been completely fabricated or is a complete fabrication; **i. de faire qch** to hit on the idea of doing sth; **je n'invente rien** (c'est vrai) I'm not making anything up

VPR **s'inventer ça ne s'invente pas** (ce don etc) you've either got it or you haven't; (des détails comme ça etc) you can't make something like that up; **il s'inventa un nouveau passé** he invented a new past for himself

inventeur, -trice [ɛ̃vɑ̃tœr, -tris] N **1** (d'une machine, d'un processus etc) inventor **2** Jur (d'un objet perdu) finder

inventif, -ive [ɛ̃vɑ̃tif, -iv] ADJ inventive

invention [ɛ̃vɑ̃sjɔ̃] NF **1** (action) invention, inventing; (faculté) inventiveness, invention; **nécessité est mère d'i.** necessity is the mother of invention; **c'est encore une plaisanterie de son i.!** it's another one of his jokes! **2** (découverte) invention; (mensonge) fabrication, invention; **brevet d'i.** patent (for an invention); **pure i. (que) tout cela!** that's sheer fabrication or invention!; Com **i. de produit** product invention; Mktg **i. rétrograde** backward invention **3** Jur **i. d'un trésor** finding of treasure trove

inventivité [ɛ̃vɑ̃tivite] NF inventiveness

inventorier [ɛ̃vɑ̃tɔrje] VT (marchandises) to make an inventory of, to inventory

invérifiable [ɛ̃verifjabl] ADJ unverifiable, uncheckable

inverse [ɛ̃vɛrs] ADJ inverse; **en sens i. (de qch)** in the opposite direction (to sth); **dans l'ordre i.** in (the) reverse order; **dans le sens i. des aiguilles d'une montre** Br anticlockwise, Am counterclockwise; Math **en raison i. de qch** in inverse proportion to sth; Math **fonction i.** inverse function

NM **1 l'i.** the opposite, the reverse; **faire l'i.** to do the opposite or the reverse (de of); **c'est parce qu'il était déprimé qu'il s'est mis à boire et non l'i.** he started drinking because he was depressed and not the other way round or and not vice versa; **dans mon cas, c'est l'i. qui se passe** it's the reverse or the opposite in my case; **c'est quelqu'un de très renfermé, à l'i., son frère est très exubérant** he's very withdrawn, whereas his brother is very exuberant; **à l'i. de** unlike; **à l'i. de ce que nous avions prévu** contrary to our predictions **2** Math **l'i. d'un nombre** the inverse or reciprocal of a number

inversé [ɛ̃vɛrse] ADJ Ordinat inverse; Typ, Phot reversed out; Tech **carburateur i.** down-draught carburettor; **vidéo inversée** reverse video

inversement [ɛ̃vɛrsəmɑ̃] ADV Math inversely; Fig conversely; **... ou i.** ... or the other way round, ... or vice versa

inverser [ɛ̃vɛrse] VT (ordre) to reverse, to invert; (deux mots d'une phrase) to invert, to change round; (tendance) to reverse; Élec (courant) to reverse; Typ, Phot to reverse out

inverseur [ɛ̃vɛrsœr] NM reverser, reversing device; Élec **i. du courant** current reverser, change-over switch

inversion [ɛ̃vɛrsjɔ̃] NF **1** Gram, Mus etc inversion SEE GRAMMAR A78–9; B62 **2** (du courant électrique) reversal, reversing; Phot reversal; **i. de marche** reverse gear; **i. de chiffres** inversion of figures; Ordinat **i. vidéo** reverse video **3** Psy inversion

invertébré [ɛ̃vɛrtebre] ADJ, NM invertebrate; **les invertébrés** the invertebrates, Spéc the Invertebrata

inverti, -ie [ɛ̃vɛrti] ADJ **sucre i.** inverted sugar

N homosexual, Fml invert

invertir [ɛ̃vɛrtir] VT (chiffres) to invert

investigateur, -trice [ɛ̃vɛstigatœr, -tris] ADJ investigative; (regard) searching, inquiring

N investigator

investigation [ɛ̃vɛstigasjɔ̃] NF investigation

investir [ɛ̃vɛstir] VT **1** (argent), Fig (temps, énergie) to invest (**dans** in) **2** (encercler) (ville, édifice) to besiege, to encircle; (occuper) (ville, pays, bâtiment, locaux) to occupy **3** **i. qn d'une fonction** to invest or vest sb with an office; **i. qn d'une mission** to entrust sb with a mission

VI Fin to invest (**dans** in); **i. à court terme** to make a short-term investment; **i. à long terme** to make a long-term investment

VPR **s'investir il ne s'investit pas assez dans son travail** he doesn't put enough effort into his work; **il s'investit beaucoup dans son club de théâtre** he puts a lot of time and effort into his drama club

investissement [ɛ̃vɛstismɑ̃] NM **1** Fin, Psy investment; (action) investing; **i. de l'étranger** inward investment; **i. à l'étranger** outward or overseas or foreign investment; **i. de capitaux** capital investment; **i. direct** direct investment; **i. à court terme** short-term investment; **investissements directs étrangers** direct foreign investments; **i. éthique**

ethical investment; **i. immobilier** investment in real estate, property investment; **i. institutionnel** institutional investment; **i. locatif** investment in rental property; **i. privé** private investment; **investissements productifs** interest-bearing investments; **i. à revenu variable** floating-rate investment **2** (encerclement) (d'une ville, d'un édifice) besieging, encircling; (occupation) occupation

investisseur [ɛ̃vɛstisœr] NM Fin investor; **i. institutionnel** institutional investor; **i. minoritaire** minority investor; **i. privé** private investor

investiture [ɛ̃vɛstityr] NF investiture; (d'un évêque) induction, investiture; Pol (d'un candidat) nomination

invétéré [ɛ̃vetere] ADJ **1** (haine, manie, orgueil etc) inveterate, deeply rooted **2** (ivrogne, criminel, menteur) inveterate, confirmed, habitual

invincibilité [ɛ̃vɛ̃sibilite] NF invincibility

invincible [ɛ̃vɛ̃sibl] ADJ (armée, adversaire etc) invincible; (courage) invincible, indomitable; (difficulté, obstacle) insuperable, insurmountable

invinciblement [ɛ̃vɛ̃sibləmɑ̃] ADV invincibly

inviolabilité [ɛ̃vjɔlabilite] NF inviolability; (d'un office) immunity, inviolability; **i. diplomatique** diplomatic immunity; **i. parlementaire** Br ≃ Parliamentary privilege, Am ≃ congressional immunity

inviolable [ɛ̃vjɔlabl] ADJ inviolable; (office) immune, inviolable

inviolé [ɛ̃vjɔle] ADJ Litt inviolate, inviolated; (sommet) unconquered; (forêt) virgin

invisibilité [ɛ̃vizibilite] NF invisibility

invisible [ɛ̃vizibl] ADJ invisible; Fig **il restait i.** he was nowhere to be seen; **un danger i.** a hidden danger

NMPL **invisibles** Écon **les invisibles** (échanges) invisibles, invisible trade; (exportations) invisibles, invisible exports; **la balance des invisibles** the balance of invisible trade

invisiblement [ɛ̃vizibləmɑ̃] ADV invisibly

invitant [ɛ̃vitɑ̃] ADJ attractive, inviting; **gouvernement i.** host country

invitation [ɛ̃vitasjɔ̃] NF invitation; **venir sur l'i. de qn** to come at sb's invitation; **venir sans i.** to come uninvited; **lettre d'i.** letter of invitation; **carton d'i.** invitation card; **envoyer une i. à qn** to send sb an invitation; **une i. à dîner** an invitation to dinner; **être une i. à la réflexion** to be thought-provoking; **ce roman est une i. au voyage** this novel takes you out of yourself

invite [ɛ̃vit] NF **1** Litt invitation; **répondre à l'i. de qn** to respond to sb's advances **2** Ordinat prompt; **i. du DOS** DOS prompt; **i. du système** system prompt

invité, -ée [ɛ̃vite] N guest; **i. d'honneur** guest of honour; **i. de marque** distinguished guest

inviter [ɛ̃vite] VT **1** (convier) to invite; **i. qn à dîner** to invite or ask sb to dinner; **elle m'a invité à aller avec elle au théâtre** she invited me (to go) to the theatre with her; **personne ne l'invite jamais à sortir** no one ever asks him/her out; **être déjà invité** to have a previous engagement

2 (inciter) **i. qn à faire qch** to ask sb to do sth; **j'invite tous les locataires à signer la pétition** I urge all tenants to sign the petition; **les passagers à destination de Rome sont invités à se présenter à la porte d'embarquement numéro deux** passengers for Rome are requested to proceed to gate number two; **i. qn à entrer** to ask sb (to come) in; **d'un geste de la tête, il m'invita à le suivre**

he motioned with his head that I should follow him; **i. à la réflexion** to be thought-provoking; **tout l'invitait à partir** everything indicated or suggested to him that he should leave

vɪ (payer) **ce soir, c'est moi qui invite!** it's my treat this evening!, I'm paying this evening! vPR **s'inviter** to invite oneself; **s'i. à dîner** to invite oneself to dinner

in vitro [vitro] ADV, ADJ in vitro; **fécondation i.** in vitro fertilization

invivable [ɛ̃vivabl] ADJ unbearable, intolerable; (existence) not worth living, unbearable; (Fam (personne) impossible to live with, unbearable

in vivo [vivo] ADJ, ADV in vivo

invocation [ɛ̃vɔkasjɔ̃] NF invocation

invocatoire [ɛ̃vɔkatwar] ADJ Litt invocatory

involontaire [ɛ̃vɔlɔ̃tɛr] ADJ **1** (machinal) (mouvement, geste etc) involuntary **2** (pas intentionnel) (erreur, réaction etc) unintentional; **le témoin i. d'une scène de ménage** the unwilling witness of a domestic dispute

involontairement [ɛ̃vɔlɔ̃tɛrma] ADV involuntarily; (vexer qn) unintentionally; **je lui ai i. donné des renseignements confidentiels sur le projet** I unwittingly gave him confidential information about the project

involution [ɛ̃vɔlysjɔ̃] NF involution

invoquer [ɛ̃vɔke] VT **1** (raison, prétexte) to put forward; (loi, texte) to refer to; **il a invoqué l'étourderie/la maladresse pour expliquer son erreur** he pleaded absent-mindedness/clumsiness to explain his mistake **2** (Dieu, divinité) to call upon, to invoke; (esprit) to invoke, to call forth; **i. l'aide de la justice** to appeal to the law; **i. l'aide de ses amis** to call upon the help of one's friends

invraisemblable [ɛ̃vrɛsãblabl] ADJ unlikely, improbable; (excuses, alibi) implausible; (aventure) incredible, unbelievable; **histoire i.** tall or unlikely story; **chapeau i.** incredible hat; **ces gens-là sont invraisemblables** those people are extraordinary or incredible

invraisemblablement [ɛ̃vrɛsãblabləma] ADV incredibly, improbably

invraisemblance [ɛ̃vrɛsãblãs] NF **1** (improbabilité) unlikelihood, unlikeliness, improbability; (d'un récit, d'alibi) implausibility **2** (dans une déclaration etc) implausibility

invulnérabilité [ɛ̃vylnerabilite] NF invulnerability

invulnérable [ɛ̃vylnerabl] ADJ invulnerable; **i. à la fatigue** immune to fatigue; **i. à l'injure** immune or impervious to insults

iode [jɔd] NM iodine; **teinture d'i.** tincture of iodine; **lampe à i.** halogen lamp

iodé [jɔde] ADJ (eau, air) iodized

ioder [jɔde] VT to iodize

iodique [jɔdik] ADJ Chimie iodic

iodler [jɔdle] VI to yodel

iodoforme [jɔdɔfɔrm] NM Chimie iodoform

iodure [jɔdyr] NM Chimie iodide

ion [jɔ̃] NM Phys ion

ionien, -ienne [jɔnjɛ̃, -jɛn] ADJ Ionian; (dialecte) Ionic
ɴ **I.** Ionian

ionique[1] [jɔnik] ADJ Archit (ordre) Ionic

ionique[2] ADJ Phys ionic; **accélération i.** ion acceleration

ionisant [jɔnizã] ADJ Phys ionizing

ionisation [jɔnizasjɔ̃] NF Phys ionization

ioniser [jɔnize] VT Phys to ionize

ionosphère [jɔnɔsfɛr] NF ionosphere

iota [jɔta] NM (lettre grecque) iota; Fam **on n'y a pas changé un i.** not an iota of it has been

changed; **j'ai accepté de faire des compromis mais lui n'a pas bougé d'un i.** I accepted the need for compromise but he didn't budge an inch

iourte [jurt] NF yourt, yurt

IPC [ipese] NM Écon (abrév **indice des prix à la consommation**) CPI

ipéca(cuana) [ipeka(kwana)] NM Pharm ipecac(uanha)

IPR [ipeɛr] NM (abrév **Inspecteur pédagogique régional**) = locally-based education inspector

ipso facto [ipsofakto] ADV ipso facto

Ipsos [ipsos] NM = French market research institute

Irak [irak] NM Iraq

irakien, -ienne [irakjɛ̃, -jɛn] ADJ Iraqi
ɴM Ling Iraqi
ɴ **I.** Iraqi

Iran [irã] NM Iran

iranien, -ienne [iranjɛ̃, -jɛn] ADJ Iranian
ɴM Ling Iranian
ɴ **I.** Iranian

Iraq [irak] NM Iraq

iraquien, -ienne [irakjɛ̃, -jɛn] ADJ, ɴ = **irakien**

irascibilité [irasibilite] NF irascibility, irritability, testiness

irascible [irasibl] ADJ irascible, irritable

ire [ir] NF Litt ire, wrath

iridescent [iridesã] ADJ Litt iridescent

iridié [iridje] ADJ iridic; **platine i.** iridioplatinum

iridium [iridjɔm] NM Chimie iridium

iris [iris] NM **1** Anat (de l'œil) iris **2** Bot (plante) iris, flag; **i. jaune** ou **des marais** yellow iris; **racine d'i.** orris root **3** Opt iris; Phot **(diaphragme) i.** iris (diaphragm)

irisation [irizasjɔ̃] NF iridescence, irisation

irisé [irize] ADJ iridescent

iriser [irize] VT to make iridescent
vPR **s'iriser** to become iridescent

irlandais, -aise [irlãdɛ, -ɛz] ADJ Irish
ɴM Ling Irish
ɴ **I.** Irishman, f Irishwoman; **les I.** the Irish; **un I. du Nord** a Northern Irishman, an Ulsterman; **les I. du Nord** the Northern Irish

Irlande [irlãd] NF Ireland; **I. du Nord** Northern Ireland, Ulster; **I. du Sud** Southern Ireland, Eire

IRM [iɛrɛm] NF Méd (abrév **imagerie par résonance magnétique**) MRI

ironie [irɔni] NF irony; **avec une pointe d'i.** with a touch or note of irony; **par une i. du sort** by an irony of fate; **avec i.** ironically, with irony

ironique [irɔnik] ADJ ironic(al)

ironiquement [irɔnikma] ADV ironically

ironiser [irɔnize] VI to be ironical (**sur** about)

ironiste [irɔnist] ɴ ironist

iroquois, -oise [irɔkwa, -waz] ADJ Iroquois, Iroquoian; **coiffure iroquoise** mohican (hairstyle)
ɴM Ling Iroquoian
ɴ **I.** Iroquois, Iroquoian
ɴF **iroquoise** mohican (hairstyle)

irrachetable [iraʃtabl] ADJ (obligation) irredeemable

irradiation [iradjasjɔ̃] NF Phys, Méd (ir)radiation; Phot halation

irradier [iradje] VI to (ir)radiate; (d'une douleur) to radiate, to spread
VT **1** to irradiate, to expose to radiation; **aliments irradiés** irradiated food **2** (illuminer) to illuminate; Fig (paix, joie etc) to radiate
vPR **s'irradier** to glow

irraisonné [irɛzɔne] ADJ (action) unreasonable; (peur) irrational

irrationalisme [irasjɔnalism] NM irrationalism

irrationalité [irasjɔnalite] NF irrationality

irrationnel, -elle [irasjɔnɛl] ADJ irrational
ɴM **l'i.** the irrational

irrationnellement [irasjɔnɛlma] ADV irrationally

irrattrapable [iratrapabl] ADJ (retard) that cannot be made up; (erreur) irredeemable; **une gaffe i.** a blunder you cannot do anything about

irréalisable [irealizabl] ADJ **1** (rêve) unrealizable, unachievable; (projet) impracticable, unfeasible **2** Fin (valeurs) unrealizable

irréalisé [irealize] ADJ unrealized

irréalisme [irealism] NM lack of realism; **faire preuve d'i.** to be unrealistic

irréaliste [irealist] ADJ (personne, proposition, projet) unrealistic

irréalité [irealite] NF unreality

irrecevabilité [irəsəvabilite] NF Jur inadmissibility

irrecevable [irəsəvabl] ADJ Jur (preuve, demande) inadmissible; (théorie) unacceptable

irréconciliable [irekɔ̃siljabl] ADJ irreconcilable; (haine) implacable

irrécouvrable [irekuvrabl] ADJ irrecoverable, unrecoverable

irrécupérable [irekyperabl] ADJ (argent) irrecoverable; (personne) irredeemable, incorrigible; **cette machine à laver est i.** this washing machine is beyond repair or unrepairable
ɴ **c'est un i.** he's beyond redemption, he's irredeemable; **les irrécupérables** those beyond redemption

irrécusable [irekyzabl] ADJ **1** (indéniable) (preuve, signe) indisputable, undeniable **2** Jur (témoignage, juge) unimpeachable

irréductibilité [iredyktibilite] NF (d'opposition) implacability; Math irreducibility

irréductible [iredyktibl] ADJ **1** (personne, optimisme) indomitable, invincible; (attachement à qn) unshakeable; (opposition) unyielding, relentless, implacable; **un ennemi i. du parti** an inveterate or implacable enemy of the party **2** Math, Méd (équation, fraction, dislocation) irreducible
ɴ **une poignée d'irréductibles** a handful of diehards

irréel, -elle [ireɛl] ADJ unreal
ɴM **l'i.** the unreal; Gram **l'i. du présent/passé** the hypothetical present/past

irréfléchi [irefleʃi] ADJ (personne) hasty, rash, unthinking; (action, réponse) thoughtless, unconsidered; **avoir un mouvement/geste i.** to make an instinctive movement/gesture

irréflexion [irefleksjɔ̃] NF thoughtlessness; **faire preuve d'i.** to be thoughtless

irréformable [irefɔrmabl] ADJ Jur (décision etc) irrevocable

irréfragable [irefragabl] ADJ indisputable, irrefragable

irréfutabilité [irefytabilite] NF irrefutability

irréfutable [irefytabl] ADJ indisputable, irrefutable; **il a prouvé de manière i. que ...** he proved irrefutably or indisputably that ...

irréfutablement [irefytabləma] ADV indisputably, irrefutably

irréfuté [irefyte] ADJ unrefuted

irrégularité [iregylarite] NF (du sol, d'un terrain) unevenness; (du pouls, de traits, d'horaires etc) irregularity; **les irrégularités d'une élection** the irregularities of an election; **i. comptable** accounting irregularity;

on a relevé quelques irrégularités dans les comptes a few irregularities have been found in the accounts

irrégulier, -ière [iʀegylje, -jɛʀ] **ADJ 1** *(verbe)* irregular; *(sol, terrain)* uneven; *(sommeil)* fitful, irregular; *(rythme, horaire)* irregular; *(pouls, respiration)* irregular, erratic; *(visage, traits)* irregular; *(résultats, athlète)* inconsistent, erratic; *(efforts)* uneven, inconsistent; *(marché boursier)* unsteady; **troupes irrégulières** irregular troops, irregulars **2** *(peu honnête) (procédure, situation)* irregular; **il a été i. dans cette affaire** he acted irregularly in this business; **il est en situation irrégulière, il risque l'expulsion si on le retrouve** he's in the country illegally, he risks being deported if he's discovered; **les voyageurs en situation irrégulière devront payer une amende** passengers without a valid ticket will have to pay a fine **NMPL** *Mil* **irréguliers** irregulars

irrégulièrement [iʀegyljɛʀmɑ̃] **ADV 1** *(respirer, disposer etc)* irregularly; **il n'assiste que très i. aux réunions** he attends the meetings only very irregularly *or* only on a very irregular basis **2** *(pas légalement)* irregularly

irréligieux, -ieuse [iʀeliʒjø, -jøz] **ADJ** irreligious

irréligion [iʀeliʒjɔ̃] **NF** irreligion

irremboursable [iʀɑ̃buʀsabl] **ADJ** *(obligation)* irredeemable

irrémédiable [iʀemedjabl] **ADJ** *(préjudice, perte, problème)* irreparable; *(désastre)* irremediable; *(maladie)* incurable **NM l'i.** the inevitable

irrémédiablement [iʀemedjabləmɑ̃] **ADV** irreparably; **être i. hors d'usage** to be beyond repair

irrémissible [iʀemisibl] **ADJ** *Littl* **1** *(crime)* unpardonable, irremissible **2** *(irrémédiable)* irreversible

irremplaçable [iʀɑ̃plasabl] **ADJ** irreplaceable

irréparable [iʀepaʀabl] **ADJ** *(tort, perte, erreur)* irreparable; *(affront)* unpardonable; *(souliers, voiture, télévision etc)* beyond repair, unrepairable **NM commettre l'i.** to go beyond the point of no return; **éviter l'i.** to stop before (one has reached) the point of no return

irréparablement [iʀepaʀabləmɑ̃] **ADV** irreparably

irrépréhensible [iʀepʀeɑ̃sibl] **ADJ** blameless

irrépressible [iʀepʀesibl] **ADJ** irrepressible

irréprochable [iʀepʀɔʃabl] **ADJ** *(personne, conduite)* irreproachable; *(tenue, travail)* impeccable; **une nappe d'une propreté i.** an impeccably clean tablecloth

irréprochablement [iʀepʀɔʃabləmɑ̃] **ADV** *Littl* irreproachably; *(vêtu)* impeccably

irrésistible [iʀezistibl] **ADJ** irresistible; *(envie, besoin etc)* irresistible, compelling; **elle était i. avec son petit chapeau** she was irresistible in that hat

irrésistiblement [iʀezistibləmɑ̃] **ADV** irresistibly

irrésolu [iʀezɔly] **ADJ 1** *(personne, nature)* irresolute, indecisive; *(pas)* faltering, unsteady, uncertain **2** *(problème)* unresolved, unsolved

irrésolution [iʀezɔlysjɔ̃] **NF** irresolution, irresoluteness, indecisiveness, indecision

irrespect [iʀɛspɛ] **NM** disrespect (**envers** to, towards)

irrespectueusement [iʀɛspɛktɥøzmɑ̃] **ADV** disrespectfully

irrespectueux, -euse [iʀɛspɛktɥø, -øz] **ADJ** disrespectful (**envers** to, towards)

irrespirable [iʀɛspiʀabl] **ADJ** unbreathable; **aère ta chambre, c'est i. ici!** air your room, it's stifling in here!; *Fig* **l'atmosphère du bureau est devenue i.** the atmosphere in the office has become unbearable

irresponsabilité [iʀɛspɔ̃sabilite] **NF 1** *(inconscience)* irresponsibility; **c'est de l'i.!** that's irresponsible! **2** *Jur (du chef de l'État)* non-accountability; **i. parlementaire** *Br* ≃ parliamentary privilege, *Am* ≃ congressional immunity

irresponsable [iʀɛspɔ̃sabl] **ADJ** irresponsible; **avoir une conduite i.** to behave irresponsibly **N** irresponsible person; **espèce d'i.!** you irresponsible idiot!

irrétrécissable [iʀetʀesisabl] **ADJ** unshrinkable, non-shrink

irrévérence [iʀeveʀɑ̃s] **NF 1** *(caractère)* irreverence, disrespect **2** *(acte, propos)* irreverence; **il lui a fait l'i. de ne point la raccompagner après le bal** he paid her the irreverence of not taking her home after the ball

irrévérencieusement [iʀeveʀɑ̃sjøzmɑ̃] **ADV** irreverently, disrespectfully

irrévérencieux, -euse [iʀeveʀɑ̃sjø, -øz] **ADJ** irreverent, disrespectful

irréversibilité [iʀeveʀsibilite] **NF** irreversibility

irréversible [iʀeveʀsibl] **ADJ** irreversible

irréversiblement [iʀeveʀsibləmɑ̃] **ADV** irreversibly

irrévocabilité [iʀevɔkabilite] **NF** irrevocability

irrévocable [iʀevɔkabl] **ADJ** irrevocable; *(accord)* binding; *Jur* **décret i.** decree absolute **NM l'i.** the irrevocable

irrévocablement [iʀevɔkabləmɑ̃] **ADV** irrevocably

irrigable [iʀigabl] **ADJ** irrigable

irrigateur [iʀigatœʀ] **NM 1** *(pour arrosage)* irrigator **2** *Méd (pour blessures)* irrigator

irrigation [iʀigasjɔ̃] **NF 1** *Agr* irrigation; **canal d'i.** irrigation canal **2** *Méd* irrigation, supply of blood

irriguer [iʀige] **VT 1** *Agr* to irrigate **2** *Méd (blessure)* to irrigate; **si le cerveau n'est pas irrigué pendant plus de trois minutes …** if there is no blood supply to the brain for more than three minutes …

irritabilité [iʀitabilite] **NF** irritability

irritable [iʀitabl] **ADJ** aussi *Méd* irritable

irritant [iʀitɑ̃] **ADJ 1** *(énervant)* irritating, annoying **2** *Méd* irritant (**pour** to) **NM** *Méd* irritant

irritation [iʀitasjɔ̃] **NF** irritation, annoyance; *Méd* irritation

irrité [iʀite] **ADJ 1** *(en colère)* irritated, annoyed (**contre** with) **2** *Méd (blessure)* inflamed; **avoir la gorge irritée** to have an inflamed throat

irriter [iʀite] **VT 1** *(agacer)* to irritate, to annoy **2** *(provoquer une inflammation de) (les yeux, la peau)* to irritate **3** *Littl (passions etc)* to excite; **i. la curiosité de qn** to excite sb's curiosity **VPR s'irriter 1 s'i. contre qn/de qch** to get irritated *or* annoyed with sb/at sth **2** *(s'enflammer)* to become irritated *or* inflamed

irruption [iʀypsjɔ̃] **NF** *(arrivée brusque) (de barbares etc)* invasion; **les forces de l'ordre ne purent empêcher l'i. de la foule sur le terrain/sur la place** the police couldn't stop the crowd from pouring on to the pitch/into the square; **il a fui juste avant l'i. de la police dans la boîte de nuit** he fled just before the police burst into the nightclub; **faire i. dans**

une salle to burst into a room; **elle a fait i. chez nous à deux heures du matin** she burst in on us at two o'clock in the morning; **l'eau a fait i. dans les champs** the water flooded the fields; **l'i. de nouveaux fondamentalismes religieux** the upsurge of new (religious) fundamentalist groups

Do not confuse with **éruption**.

IRSM [iɛʀɛsɛm] **NM** *(abrév* **impact sur la rentabilité de la stratégie marketing)** PIMS

ISA [iɛsa] **NM** *(abrév* **imprimé sans adresse)** mailshot

Isaac [izak] **N** Isaac

isabelle [izabɛl] **ADJ INV** biscuit- *or* cream-coloured; **cheval i.** light-bay horse, light bay **NM** light-bay horse, light bay

Isaïe [izai] **N** *Bible* Isaiah

isard [izaʀ] **NM** izard

ISBN [iɛsbeɛn] **NM** *(abrév* **International Standard Book Number)** ISBN

ISF [iɛsɛf] **NM** *(abrév* **impôt de solidarité sur la fortune)** wealth tax

Islam [islam] **NM** *Rel* Islam

islamique [islamik] **ADJ** Islamic

islamisation [islamizasjɔ̃] **NF** Islamization

islamiser [islamize] **VT** to Islamize

islamisme [islamism] **NM** Islamism

islamiste [islamist] **N** Islamic fundamentalist

islandais, -aise [islɑ̃dɛ, -ɛz] **ADJ** Icelandic **NM** *Ling* Icelandic **N I.** Icelander

Islande [islɑ̃d] **NF** Iceland

ISO [izo] **NM** *(abrév* **International Standards Organization)** ISO

isobare [izɔbaʀ] *Météo* **ADJ** isobaric **NF** isobar

isocèle [izɔsɛl] **ADJ** *Math (triangle)* isosceles

isochrone [izɔkʀɔn] **ADJ** *Spéc* isochronous, isochronal

isoclinal, -ale, -aux, -ales [izɔklinal, -o] **ADJ** *Géol* isoclinal

isocline [izɔklin] *Math, Phys* **ADJ** *(ligne)* isoclinal **NF** isocline, isoclinal line

isolable [izɔlabl] **ADJ** *Chimie* isolable

isolant [izɔlɑ̃] **ADJ 1** *Constr, Élec* insulating; **bouteille isolante** vacuum flask; **matériau i.** *(contre le froid)* insulation, insulating material; *(contre le bruit)* soundproofing (material); *Élec* insulating material; **ruban i.** insulating tape **2** *Ling (langues)* isolating **NM** *(contre le froid)* insulation, insulating material; *(contre le bruit)* soundproofing (material); *Élec* insulating material; *Aut* insulator

isolateur, -trice [izɔlatœʀ, -tʀis] *Élec* **ADJ** insulating **NM** insulator

isolation [izɔlasjɔ̃] **NF 1** *Élec* insulation **2** **i. acoustique** *ou* **phonique** soundproofing; **i. contre le froid** insulation; **i. thermique** thermal insulation **3** *Psy* isolation

Do not confuse with **isolement**.

isolationnisme [izɔlasjɔnism] **NM** *Pol* isolationism

isolationniste [izɔlasjɔnist] **ADJ, N** *Pol* isolationist

isolé, -ée [izɔle] **ADJ 1** *(personne)* isolated; *(endroit, maison)* isolated, lonely, remote; *(cas)* isolated; *Pol (pays)* isolated; **se sentir i.** to feel isolated; **il vit trop i.** he lives too much in isolation, he leads too isolated a life; **quelques arbres isolés au milieu du champ** a few isolated trees in the middle of the field; **l'attentat est l'œuvre de quelques activistes isolés** the attack is the work of a few isolated *or* lone activists **2** *Élec (câble)* insulated

▪ N *(dans un parti, un mouvement etc)* maverick

isolement [izɔlmɑ̃] NM **1** *(de personne, maison etc)* isolation; **vivre dans un i. complet** to live in complete isolation; *Pol* **l'i. diplomatique d'un pays** the diplomatic isolation of a country **2** *Élec* insulation

> Do not confuse with the French word **iso-lation**.

isolément [izɔlemɑ̃] ADV *(interroger des gens)* separately, individually; *(employer un mot)* in isolation; **le malfaiteur a agi i.** the criminal acted in isolation *or* on his own

isoler [izɔle] VT **1** *(malade, dissident etc)* to isolate (**de** from); *Méd, Phys (virus, gène, corps)* to isolate; **sa maladie/son handicap l'isole** her illness/his handicap cuts her off from other people **2** *Élec* to insulate **3** *(protéger du bruit)* to soundproof

▪ VPR **s'isoler 1** *(se séparer)* to isolate oneself; **avoir besoin de s'i. quelques instants** to need to be alone for a few moments **2** *(vivre seul)* to cut oneself off, to isolate oneself

isoloir [izɔlwar] NM polling booth

isomère [izɔmɛr] *Chimie* ADJ isomeric

▪ NM isomer

isométrique [izɔmetrik] ADJ *Math* isometric(al)

isomorphe [izɔmɔrf] ADJ *Math, Chimie* isomorphous, isomorphic

isomorphisme [izɔmɔrfism] NM *Math, Chimie* isomorphism

isorel® [izɔrɛl] NM *Constr* hardboard

isotherme [izɔtɛrm] *Météo* ADJ isothermal; **sac i.** cool bag

▪ NF isotherm

isotope [izɔtɔp] NM *Chimie* isotope

isotrope [izɔtrɔp] ADJ *Chimie, Phys* isotropic

Israël [israɛl] NM Israel

israélien, -ienne [israeljɛ̃, -jɛn] ADJ Israeli

▪ N **I.** Israeli

israélite [israelit] ADJ Jewish; *Bible* Israelite

▪ N **I.** Jew, f Jewess; *Bible* Israelite

ISSN [iesɛsɛn] NM *(abrév* **International standard serial number)** (numéro) I. ISSN

issu [isy] ADJ **il est i. d'une grande famille périgourdine/d'un milieu artistique** he was born into an important family from the Perigord/into an artistic milieu; **cousins issus de germains** second cousins; **enfant i. d'un se-**

cond mariage child from a second marriage; *Fig* **être i. de** to stem from, to derive from

issue [isy] NF **1** *(sortie)* exit, way out; *(de tunnel, de conduit etc)* outlet; **i. de secours** emergency exit; **voie sans i.** cul-de-sac, dead end; *(sur panneau)* no through road; *Fig* dead end; *Fig* **en faisant ça, tu t'engages sur une voie sans i.** doing that will get you absolutely nowhere; **ses études l'ont mené sur une voie sans i.** his studies led to a dead end; *Fig* **la seule i. possible** the only possible solution; **il n'y a pas d'autre i.** there is no other way out; **elle est dans une situation sans i.** there's no way out of her situation; *Fig* **se ménager une i.** to leave oneself a way out

2 *(fin) (de match, conférence de paix etc)* outcome; **l'affaire a eu une i. heureuse** the matter had a happy ending *or* conclusion *or* outcome, the matter ended happily; **à l'i. de la réunion** at the end *or* close *or* conclusion of the meeting

> Il faut noter que le nom anglais **issue** est un faux ami. Il signifie le plus souvent **problème, question.**

Istanbul [istãbul] N Istanbul

isthme [ism] NM *Géog, Anat* isthmus

isthmique [ismik] ADJ isthmian

italianisant, -ante [italjanizɑ̃, -ɑ̃t] N expert on Italy, Italianist; *Ling* Italian specialist, Italianist

italianiser [italjanize] VT to Italianize

italianisme [italjanism] NM *Ling* Italianism

Italie [itali] NF Italy

italien, -ienne [italjɛ̃, -jɛn] ADJ Italian

▪ NM *Ling* Italian

▪ N **I.** Italian

▪ NF *Ordinat* **imprimer à l'italienne** to print landscape

italique [italik] ADJ **1** *Typ (caractère)* italic **2** *Hist* Italic

▪ NM **1** *Typ* italics; **en italique(s)** in italics **2** *Ling* Italic

▪ N *Hist* **I.** Italic

item [item] ADV *Com* ditto, item

▪ NM *Ling, Psy* item

itératif, -ive [iteratif, -iv] ADJ **1** *Jur (interdiction etc)* reiterated, repeated **2** *Gram (verbe)* iterative **3** *Ordinat* iterative

itération [iterasjɔ̃] NF *Math, Ordinat, Psy* iteration

Ithaque [itak] NF Ithaca

itinéraire [itinerɛr] NM route, itinerary; **tracer un i.** to map out a route *or* an itinerary;

changer d'i. to change one's route *or* itinerary; **i. touristique** tourist route; **il a eu un i. sentimental mouvementé** his love life has had its ups and downs

▪▪ *Aut* **i. bis: prendre un i. bis** to take a less busy route

itinérance [itinerɑ̃s] NF *Tél* roaming

itinérant [itinerɑ̃] ADJ *(prédicateur)* itinerant; **ambassadeur i.** roving ambassador; **camp (de marche) i. de deux semaines** two-week camping hike

itinérer [itinere] VI *Tél* to roam

itou [itu] ADV *Fam Vieilli* likewise, also, too; **et moi i.!** (and) me too!

IUFM [iyɛfɛm] NM *(abrév* **Institut universitaire de formation des maîtres)** ≃ teacher training college

IUT [iyte] NM *(abrév* **Institut universitaire de technologie)** = vocational higher education college

IV ADJ *Méd (abrév* **intra-veineux)** IV

I.V.C. [ivese] NF *Can (abrév* **indemnité de la vie chère)** COLA

IVG [iveʒe] NF *Méd (abrév* **interruption volontaire de grossesse)** termination *(of pregnancy)*

ivoire [ivwar] NM **1** *(matière)* ivory; **crucifix d'i.** *ou* **en i.** ivory crucifix; **noir d'i.** ivory black; *Fig* **dents d'i.** teeth like ivory; *Géog* **la Côte d'I.** the Côte d'Ivoire; *Fig* **tour d'i.** ivory tower **2** *(statuette etc)* ivory

ivoirien, -ienne [ivwarjɛ̃, -jɛn] ADJ of/from the Ivory Coast

▪ N **I.** *(natif)* native of the Côte d'Ivoire; *(habitant)* inhabitant of the Côte d'Ivoire

ivoirier, -ière [ivwarje, -jɛr] N worker in ivory

ivraie [ivrɛ] NF *Bot* **i. vivace, fausse i.** rye grass; *Fig* **séparer l'i. d'avec le bon grain** to separate the wheat from the chaff

ivre [ivr] ADJ drunk; **i. mort** blind *or* dead drunk; **i. de joie** beside oneself with joy, wild with joy; **i. de colère** raging, wild with anger

ivresse [ivrɛs] NF drunkenness; *(extase)* exhilaration, intoxication; **se laisser griser par l'i. du succès** to become intoxicated by success, to let success go to one's head; **dans l'i. du moment** in the excitement of the moment; *Jur* **conduite en état d'i.** drink driving, *Am* driving while intoxicated

▪▪ *Méd* **i. des profondeurs** bends

ivressomètre [ivrɛsɔmetr] NM *Can* breathalyser, *Am* breathalyzer

ivrogne [ivrɔɲ] N drunkard

ivrognerie [ivrɔɲri] NF drunkenness

J, j [ʒi] NM (*lettre*) J, j; **le jour J** D-day

j' [ʒ] PRON PERS (*used before a verb beginning with a vowel or h mute; also before* **en, y**) = **je**

jabot [ʒabo] NM **1** (*d'un oiseau*) crop **2** (*de chemise, blouse*) frill, ruffle, jabot

jacasse [ʒakas] NF magpie

jacassement [ʒakasmɑ̃] NM (*d'une pie, d'une personne*) chatter(ing); **leurs jacassements incessants** their constant chatter(ing)

jacasser [ʒakase] VI (*d'une pie, d'une personne*) to chatter

jacasserie [ʒakas(ə)ri] NF chatter(ing); **leurs incessantes jacasseries** their incessant chatter(ing)

jachère [ʒaʃɛr] NF fallow (land); **champ en j.** fallow field; **laisser en j.** (*champ*) to leave fallow, to let lie fallow; *Fig* (*talent*) to leave undeveloped, to ignore; *Fig* **laisser qn en j.** to ignore sb's talents

jacinthe [ʒasɛ̃t] NF hyacinth; **j. sauvage** *ou* **des bois** bluebell, wild hyacinth

jack [(d)ʒak] NM *Élec, Tél etc* jack

jackpot [dʒakpɔt] NM **1** (*combinaison*) jackpot; *aussi Fig* **toucher le j.** to hit the jackpot **2** (*machine*) slot machine

Jacob [ʒakɔb] N Jacob

jacobin, -ine [ʒakɔbɛ̃, -in] NM **1** *Hist* J. Jacobin **2** *Rel* Dominican friar
ADJ Jacobin
NF *Rel* **jacobine** Dominican nun

jacobinisme [ʒakɔbinism] NM *Hist, Pol* Jacobinism

jacobite [ʒakɔbit] ADJ, NM *Hist* Jacobite

jacquard [ʒakar] NM (*métier à tisser*) Jacquard loom; (*tissu*) Jacquard (weave); (*pull*) Jacquard
ADJ **pull j.** Jacquard sweater

jacquerie [ʒakri] NF peasant revolt; *Hist* J. Jacquerie; *Fig* **la j. des agriculteurs français** the rising up of French farmers

Jacques [ʒak] NM **Maître J.** factotum; *Hist* **J. (Bonhomme)** the French peasant; *Fam* **faire le J.** to act *or* play the fool

jacquet [ʒakɛ] NM backgammon

Jacquot [ʒako] NM (*perroquet gris*) grey parrot

jactance [ʒaktɑ̃s] NF **1** *Litt* (*vanité*) boastfulness **2** *Fam* (*bavardage*) chatter

jacter [ʒakte] VI *Fam* to chatter, *Péj* to spout; **t'as trop jacté, maintenant, ils savent tout** you've been opening your mouth too much, now they know everything

jacuzzi® [ʒakyzi] NM jacuzzi

jade [ʒad] NM **1** *Minér* jade **2** (*statuette etc*) jade object

jadis [ʒadis] ADV *Litt* in times past, formerly; **les chevaliers de j.** the knights of old
ADJ **le temps j.** the olden days, days gone by; **contes du temps j.** tales of long ago *or* of days gone by

jaguar [ʒagwar] NM jaguar

jaillir [ʒajir] VI **1** (*de l'eau, du pétrole, du sang*) to gush (out), to spurt (out); (*de source*) to gush (out); (*d'étincelles*) to fly (out), to shoot out; (*de flammes*) to shoot out *or* up; (*de la lumière*) to flash

2 (*apparaître soudainement*) (*concrètement*) **des pierres jaillirent de tous côtés** stones flew from all sides; **une foule de gens jaillit soudain de la rue** a crowd of people suddenly shot out of the street; **des curieux jaillissaient de toutes les maisons** inquisitive people were shooting out of all the houses; **tout à coup, on vit j. des mitraillettes des buissons environnants** suddenly the surrounding bushes sprouted submachine guns

3 (*abstraitement*) (*rires, cris*) to burst out; **des idées très bizarres jaillissent parfois de son cerveau** some very strange ideas pop out of his head sometimes; **on ne peut pas dire que les bonnes réponses aient jailli** correct answers didn't exactly fly thick and fast; **la vérité jaillira d'elle-même** the truth will out

jaillissant [ʒajisɑ̃] ADJ (*liquide*) gushing, spurting; (*étincelles*) flying, shooting

jaillissement [ʒajismɑ̃] NM (*d'un liquide*) gush(ing) (out), spurt(ing) (out); **j. d'étincelles** sparking

jaïnisme [ʒainism] NM *Rel* Jainism

jais [ʒɛ] NM *Minér* jet; **yeux (noirs) de j.** jet-black eyes

Jakarta [dʒakarta] N Jakarta

jalon [ʒalɔ̃] NM (*piquet*) (surveyor's) staff *or Am* rod; *Fig* **poser** *ou* **planter des jalons** *ou* **les premiers jalons** to prepare the ground; **poser les jalons d'un accord** to pave the way for *or* to prepare the ground for an agreement

jalonnement [ʒalɔnmɑ̃] NM marking out, staking out

jalonner [ʒalɔne] VT (*délimiter*) (*ligne, parcelle, piste d'atterrissage etc*) to mark out, to stake out; **de petits panneaux jalonnent le parcours** small signs mark out the course; *Fig* **la route est jalonnée de jolies maisons** the road is lined with pretty houses; **événements qui jalonnent la vie de qn** events that stand out as landmarks *or* milestones in sb's life; **sa vie est jalonnée de rencontres déterminantes/drames** his life has been punctuated with decisive encounters/drama

jalousement [ʒaluzmɑ̃] ADV (*regarder, garder etc*) jealously

jalouser [ʒaluze] VT to be jealous of

jalousie [ʒaluzi] NF **1** (*sentiment*) jealousy, envy; (*en amour*) jealousy; **éprouver de la j. envers qn** to be *or* feel jealous of sb; **j'en crève** *ou* **j'en suis malade de j.** I'm green with envy; **ce sont de petites jalousies** they're just petty jealousies **2** (*store*) Venetian blind

jaloux, -ouse [ʒalu, -uz] ADJ (*envieux*) jealous, envious (**de** of); (*en amour*) jealous; **il est j. comme un tigre** he's wildly jealous; **j. de sa réputation** jealous of one's reputation; **il exerce une surveillance jalouse sur son trésor** he guards his treasure jealously
N **c'est un j.** he's a jealous man; **faire des j.** to make people jealous

jamaïcain, -aine, jamaïquain, -aine [ʒamaikɛ̃, -en] ADJ Jamaican
N **J.** Jamaican

Jamaïque [ʒamaik] NF Jamaica

JAMAIS [ʒame] ADV **1** (*positif*) ever; **plus que j.** more than ever; **plus cher que j.** dearer than ever; **pire que j.** worse than ever; **si j. il revenait** if he ever came back; **avez-vous j. entendu chose pareille?** did you ever hear such a thing?; **avez-vous j. été à Rome?** have you ever been to Rome?; **c'est le film le plus drôle que j'aie j. vu** it's the funniest film I've ever seen; **c'est la maison la plus chère qui ait j. été construite** it's the most expensive house ever (to have been) built; **il désespère de j. avoir raison** he despairs of ever being right; **c'est à se demander s'il a j. vu un peigne** he doesn't seem to know what a comb's for *or* what a comb is; **à (tout) j.** for good, for ever; **je te quitte à j.** I'm leaving you for good; **ils sont séparés à tout j.** they've parted for good; **ils sont unis à tout j.** they are united for ever(more) *or* for ever and ever; **elle a renoncé à écrire à j.** she's given up ever writing again; **j'ai renoncé à tout j. à connaître le fin mot de l'histoire** I've given up ever trying to get to the bottom of the matter

2 (*négatif*) never; **je ne l'ai j. vu** I've never seen him; **n'a-t-il j. appris à conduire?** has he never learnt to drive?; **je n'ai j. pu supporter ce genre d'individus** I've never been able to bear *or* I never could bear that sort of individual; **je suis heureuse comme j.** je ne l'avais été I'm happier than I ever have been; **je ne partirai j. sans ma femme** I'll never go without my wife; **il a passé toute sa vie sans j. boire un verre d'alcool** he's gone all his life without touching a drop of alcohol; **sans j. y avoir pensé** without ever having thought of it; **vous prenez un petit verre, commissaire? – j. pendant le service!** you'll have a quick one, superintendent? – not while I'm on duty!; **on ne sait j.** you never know; **j. homme ne fut plus admiré** never was a man more admired; **j. je n'aurais pensé ça de lui** I would never have thought of it; **j. le dimanche** never on a Sunday; **c'est maintenant ou j.,** **c'est le moment ou j.** it's now or never; **c'est le moment ou j. d'investir dans la pierre** now's the time (if ever there was one) to invest in bricks and mortar; **on ne le voit presque j.** we hardly ever see him; **on ne le verra plus j.** *ou* **plus** we shall never see him again; **tu vas refaire du bateau? – j. plus** *ou* **plus j.** are you going sailing again? – never; **elle n'a j. fait que se plaindre toute sa**

vie she's done nothing *or* never done anything but complain all her life; **cela ne fait j. qu'une semaine que nous attendons ce colis** we've been waiting for this parcel for no more than a week; **il n'a j. que dix minutes de retard** he's only ten minutes late (at the most); **ce n'est j. qu'une faute de frappe** it's only *or* just a typing error (after all); **tu vas accepter son offre? – j. de la vie!** are you going to accept his offer? – never (in a million years)! *or* not on your life! *or* certainly not!; **tu as bu! – j. de la vie!** you've been drinking! – I certainly have not!; **t'es amoureuse de lui, hein? – j. de la vie!** you're in love with him, aren't you? – certainly not!; **je n'ai j. fait ça de ma vie** I've never done that in my life; **j. de ma vie, je n'ai été aussi heureuse** I've never been so happy in (all) my life; **j. de sa vie, il n'avait vu un spectacle aussi bête** never in his life had he seen anything so stupid; *Prov* **mieux vaut tard que j.** better late than never; **il n'est j. trop tard** it's never too late; **il n'est j. trop tard pour bien faire** it's never too late to mend; **j., au grand j., je n'admettrai cela** I shall never, (repeat) never, admit it; **j. deux sans trois** it never rains but it pours; *Fam* **j. tu t'excuses/frappes avant d'entrer?** don't you ever say sorry/knock before coming in? SEE GRAMMAR A21; B62–3

jambage [ʒɑ̃baʒ] NM **1** *(de porte, fenêtre, cheminée etc)* jamb **2** *(de lettre)* downstroke; *Ordinat* descender

jambe [ʒɑ̃b] NF **1** *Anat, Zool* leg; **être jambes nues** to be bare-legged; **aux longues jambes** long-legged, with long legs; **être tout en jambes** to be all legs; **avoir de bonnes jambes** to have a good pair of legs, to be a good walker; **je n'ai plus mes jambes de vingt ans** I'm not as young as I was; **il tire** *ou* **traîne la j.** *(de fatigue)* he's dragging his feet *or* heels; *(en boitant)* he's dragging one foot behind him; **se mettre en jambes** to limber up, to warm up; **mise en jambes** warming-up exercises; **il s'est sauvé à toutes jambes** he ran off as fast as his legs could carry him, he ran off at full *or* top speed; **la peur/la faim lui donnait des jambes** fear/hunger gave him wings; *Fam* **prendre ses jambes à son cou** to take to one's heels, to show a clean pair of heels; **il est toujours dans mes jambes** he's always under my feet *or* in my way; **tirer dans les jambes de qn** to make things *or* life difficult for sb, to create problems for sb; *Fam* **travail fait par-dessous** *ou* **par-dessus la j.** sloppy *or* slipshod work; **traiter qn par-dessous** *ou* **par-dessus la j.** to treat sb in an offhand manner, to be offhand with sb; *Fam* **ça me/lui fait une belle j.!** a (fat) lot of good that will do me/him!; *Fig Fam* **j'en avais les jambes sciées** you could have knocked me over with a feather, I was absolutely flabbergasted; **avoir dix kilomètres dans les jambes** to have walked ten kilometres; *Fig Fam* **n'avoir plus de jambes** to be tired out *or* worn out *or* exhausted; **je ne tiens plus sur mes jambes** my legs are giving way, I can't keep on my feet; *Fam* **tenir la j. à qn** to bore sb with one's talk; *Fam* **lâche-moi la j.** get off my back, leave me alone; *Fam* **en avoir plein les jambes** to be on one's last legs, to be absolutely worn out *or* exhausted; **j'avais les jambes en coton** my legs were like jelly **2** *(de pantalon, compas)* leg

▸▸ *Naut* **j. de chien** sheepshank; **j. de force** *Constr* strut, prop, brace; *Aut* stay (rod), torque rod

jambier, -ière [ʒɑ̃bje, -jɛr] ADJ, NM *Anat* **(muscle)** leg muscle

NF **jambière** *(au cricket)* pad; *Ftbl* (shin) pad *or* guard; *(d'armure)* greave; **jambières** *(grandes chaussettes)* leggings; *(sans pied, en laine)* legwarmers

jambon [ʒɑ̃bɔ̃] NM **1** *Culin* ham **2** *Fam (cuisse)* thigh

▸▸ **j. de Bayonne** Bayonne ham; **j. blanc** boiled ham; **j. braisé** braised ham; **j. cru** raw ham; **j. fumé** smoked ham; **j. de montagne** raw ham; **j. à l'os** ham on the bone; **j. de Paris** boiled ham; **j. de Parme** Parma ham; **j. de pays** raw ham

jambonneau, -eaux [ʒɑ̃bɔno] NM **1** *(viande)* knuckle of ham **2** *Fam (cuisse)* thigh

jamboree [ʒɑ̃bɔre, ʒɑ̃bɔri] NM jamboree

janissaire [ʒanisɛr] NM *Hist, Mil* janissary, janizary

jansénisme [ʒɑ̃senism] NM *Hist, Rel* Jansenism

janséniste [ʒɑ̃senist] ADJ, N *Hist, Rel* Jansenist

jante [ʒɑ̃t] NF *(de vélo, de roue de voiture)* rim; *Aut* **j. (en) alliage** alloy wheel; *Aut* **j. en aluminium, j. alu** aluminium wheel; *Aut* **j. de roue** wheel rim; *Fig Fam* **rouler sur la j.** to be going round the bend, to be losing one's marbles

janvier [ʒɑ̃vje] NM January; **en j.** in January; **au mois de j.** in (the month of) January; **le sept j.** (on) the seventh of January, (on) January the seventh, *Am* (on) January seventh SEE GRAMMAR A81–2; B60–2

Japon [ʒapɔ̃] NM **1** Japan; **être au J.** to be in Japan; **aller au J.** to go to Japan **2** **j.** *(porcelaine)* Japanese porcelain **3** **j.** *(papier)* Japanese vellum

japonais, -aise [ʒapɔnɛ, -ɛz] ADJ Japanese NM *Ling* Japanese

N **J.** Japanese; **les J.** the Japanese

japonaiserie [ʒapɔnɛzri], **japonerie** [ʒapɔnri] NF piece of Japanese art; *(bibelot)* Japanese curio

japonisant, -ante [ʒapɔnizɑ̃, -ɑ̃t] N expert on Japan; *Ling* Japanese specialist

jappement [ʒapmɑ̃] NM yelp(ing), yap(p)ing); **jappements** yelping, yapping

japper [ʒape] VI to yelp, to yap

jaquette [ʒakɛt] NF **1** *(d'homme)* morning coat, cutaway; *(de femme)* jacket; *Can (chemise de nuit)* nightdress; *Suisse (en tricot)* cardigan **2** *(de livre)* (dust) jacket, (dust) cover; *(d'une fiche)* jacket **3** *(de dent)* crown, cap **4** *très Fam* **la j. (flottante)** *(les homosexuels)* poofs, *Am* fags; *très Fam* **être** *ou* **refiler de la j. (flottante)** to be a *Br* poof *or Am* fag

jardin [ʒardɛ̃] NM garden; *Fig* **c'est mon j. secret** I keep it very much to myself; *Fig* **ça, c'est une pierre dans mon j.** that's a dig at me, that's aimed *or* directed at me, that's meant for me

▸▸ **j. d'acclimatation** zoological garden(s); **j. d'agrément** pleasure garden; **j. à l'anglaise** landscape(d) garden; **j. botanique** botanical garden(s); *Scol* **j. d'enfants** kindergarten; **j. à la française** formal garden; **j. fruitier** orchard; **j. d'hiver** winter garden; **j. japonais** miniature Japanese garden; **jardins ouvriers** allotments; **j. potager** kitchen garden; **j. public** (public) park, public gardens; **j. de rapport** market garden; **jardins suspendus** hanging gardens; **j. zoologique** zoological garden(s)

jardinage [ʒardinaʒ] NM gardening

jardiner [ʒardine] VI to do some gardening, to do the garden, to garden; **j'aime j.** I like gardening; **je n'ai pas peur de me salir quand je jardine** I'm not afraid of getting dirty when I do the garden(ing)

jardinerie [ʒardinri] NF garden centre

jardinet [ʒardinɛ] NM small garden

jardinier, -ière [ʒardinje, -jɛr] ADJ **plantes jardinières** garden plants

N *(personne)* gardener; *(d'un parc etc)* groundskeeper

NF **jardinière 1** *(pour le balcon)* window box; *(à l'intérieur)* jardinière **2** *Culin* **jardinière (de légumes)** mixed vegetables, jardinière **3** *Scol* **jardinière d'enfants** kindergarten teacher

jargon [ʒargɔ̃] NM **1** *(argot)* jargon, lingo; **j. administratif** official jargon, officialese; **j. communautaire** Eurospeak; **j. journalistique** journalese, newspaper jargon; **j. du métier** professional jargon; **le j. du palais** legal jargon, legalese **2** *(baragouin)* gibberish

jargonner [ʒargɔne] VI **1** to talk jargon **2** *(baragouiner)* to talk gibberish

jargonneux, -euse [ʒargɔnø, -øz] ADJ jargony, jargon-laden

Jarnac [ʒarnak] *voir* **coup**

jarre [ʒar] NF (earthenware) jar

jarret [ʒarɛ] NM **1** *(de personne)* back of the knee, *Fam* ham; *(de cheval, zèbre etc)* hock; **avoir des jarrets d'acier** to have a good *or* sturdy pair of legs **2** *Culin (de veau)* knuckle; *(de bœuf)* shin

jarretelle [ʒartɛl] NF suspender, *Am* garter

jarretière [ʒartjɛr] NF **1** garter **2** *Naut* gasket

jars [ʒar] NM gander

jas [ʒa] NM *Naut (d'ancre)* stock; **sans j.** stockless

jasant [ʒazɑ̃] ADJ *Can Fam (bavard)* chatty; *(cancanier)* gossipy

jaser [ʒaze] VI **1** *Vieilli, Can (bavarder)* to chatter, to prattle **(de** about) **2** *(médire)* to gossip; **cela va faire j.** that'll set tongues wagging *or* people talking **3** *(moucharder)* to grass, to talk

jasette [ʒazɛt] NF *Can Fam* chat, conversation; **faire une petite j.** to have a chat *or* chinwag, *Am* to shoot the breeze

jaseur, -euse [ʒazœr, -øz] ADJ gossiping; **ce qu'il est j.** what a gossip he is N gossip NM *(oiseau)* waxwing

jasmin [ʒasmɛ̃] NM jasmine

jaspe [ʒasp] NM **1** *Minér* jasper; **j. noir** touchstone; **j. sanguin** bloodstone **2** *(statuette etc)* jasper object

jasper [ʒaspe] VT to marble, to mottle

jaspiner [ʒaspine] *Fam* VT **il jaspine bien l'anglais** he speaks English well VI to chatter, *Br* to natter; **qu'est-ce qu'il jaspine bien!** he's got the gift of the gab

jaspure [ʒaspyr] NF marbling, mottling

jass [jas] NM *Suisse* = popular Swiss card game

JAT [ʒiate] *Com (abrév* **juste à temps)** JIT

jatte [ʒat] NF **1** bowl **2** *Belg (récipient)* coffee cup; *(contenu)* cup of coffee

jattée [ʒate] NF bowlful

jauge [ʒoʒ] NF **1** *(de tonneau, réservoir etc)* gauge, capacity **2** *Naut (de navire)* tonnage **3** *Tech (instrument)* gauge; **j. d'essence** petrol gauge; **j. de niveau d'huile** oil-level indicator; *(manuelle)* dipstick; **j. de vapeur** steam gauge; **robinet de j.** gauge cock; **j. de carburant** fuel gauge; *Aut* **j. manuelle** dipstick; *Aut* **j. à flotteur** float indicator **4** *Com* **j. brute** gross registered tonnage; **j. nette** net registered tonnage

jaugeage [ʒoʒaʒ] NM *(de tonneau, réservoir etc)* gauging; *Naut* measurement *(of tonnage)*

jauger [ʒoʒe] VT (**je jaugeais; n. jaugeons) 1** *(mesurer) (tonneau, réservoir etc)* to gauge, to measure the capacity of; *(navire)* to measure the tonnage of **2** *Fig (personne, situation)* to size up **3** *(de un navire)* **j. 300 tonneaux** to be of 300 tons burden; **pétrolier qui jauge quarante mille tonneaux** forty-thousand-ton tanker; **j. deux mètres d'eau** to draw two metres of water

jaunâtre [ʒonɑtr], **jaunasse** [ʒonas] ADJ yellowish; *(teint)* sallow, yellowish

jaune [ʒon] ADJ **1** yellow; **avoir le teint j.** to have a sallow complexion; **avoir les dents jaunes** to have yellow teeth; **j. comme un coing** *ou* **comme un citron** as yellow as a lemon; **la race j.** the yellow-skinned race(s) **2** *Can (lâche)* yellow(-bellied)

ADV **rire j.** to force a laugh, to give a forced laugh; **elle a ri, mais j.** she laughed, but it was forced

NM **1** *(couleur)* yellow; **tirer sur le j.** to be yellowish; **porter du j.** to wear yellow **2** *(colorant)* **j. d'ocre** yellow ochre; **j. de chrome** chrome yellow **3** **j. d'œuf** (egg) yolk **4** *Ind Fam* scab, rat, *Br* blackleg, *Am* fink **5** *Can (lâche)* yellowbelly **6** *Fam (apéritif anisé)* pastis

N *Péj (terme injurieux)* **J.** *(Asiatique)* Asian; *(Chinois)* Chink; *(Japonais)* Jap, Nip

▸▸ **j. canari** canary yellow; **j. citron** lemon yellow; *Fam* **j. cocu** garish yellow; **j. moutarde** mustard yellow; **j. d'or** golden yellow; **j. paille** straw-coloured; *Fam* **j. pipi** piss yellow; **j. safran** saffron (yellow); **j. serin** canary yellow

jauni [ʒoni] ADJ *(par le temps, le soleil etc)* yellowed

jaunir [ʒonir] VT to turn yellow, to yellow
VI to turn *or* become yellow, to yellow ▪

jaunissant [ʒonisɑ̃] ADJ yellowing; **blés jaunissants** ripening corn

jaunisse [ʒonis] NF *Méd* jaundice; *FigFam* **en faire une j.** to get into a state about it, to get worked up about it; **il n'y a pas de quoi en faire une j.** there's nothing to get into a state about *or* to get worked up about

jaunissement [ʒonismɑ̃] NM yellowing; *(du blé)* ripening

Java [ʒava] NF Java
NM *Ordinat* Java

java [ʒava] NF **1** *(danse)* = type of popular waltz **2** *Fam (fête)* **faire la j.** to live it up, to have a wild time

javanais, -aise [ʒavanɛ, -ɛz] ADJ Javanese
NM *Ling* **1** Javan(ese) **2** *(argot)* = a form of slang consisting of introducing 'av' or 'va' into words; *Fam* **c'est du j.** *(baragouin)* it's gibberish *or Br* double Dutch
N **J.** Javanese; **les J.** the Javanese

Javel [oʒavɛl] NF *(eau de)* **J.** bleach

javeline [ʒavlin] NF javelin

javelle [ʒavɛl] NF *Agr (de blé etc)* swath

javellisation [ʒavelizasjɔ̃] NF chlorination

javelliser [ʒavelize] VT to chlorinate

javelot [ʒavlo] NM javelin; *Sport* **le (lancer du) j.** the javelin

jazz [dʒaz] NM jazz

jazzman [dʒazman] NM *Mus* jazzman, jazz musician

J.-C. *(abrév* **Jésus-Christ)** JC; **av. J.-C.** BC; **ap. J.-C.** AD

je, j' [ʒ(ə)] PRON PERS SEE GRAMMAR A27; B18 **1** *(non accentué)* I; **je vois** I see; **j'ai** I have, I've; **j'en ai** I have some; **que vois-je?** [vwaʒ] what do *or* can I see? **2** *Fam (remplace une autre personne)* **et je tourne sans mettre de clignotant** and he/she goes and turns without indicating; **et que je te marche sur les pieds et que je te dis pas pardon!** fancy treading on your toes and not saying sorry! **3** *Admin* **je, soussigné …** I, the undersigned …
NM **employer le je** *(dans un récit)* to use the first person

Jean [ʒɑ̃] N **(saint)** **J.-Baptiste** [batist] (St) John the Baptist; **la Saint-J.** Midsummer('s) Day; *Can* **la Saint-J.-Baptiste** *(public holiday in Quebec)* Saint-Jean-Baptiste Day

jean [dʒin] NM *(pantalon)* (pair of) jeans; *(tissu)* denim; **j. en velours** velvet trousers; *(cô-*

telé) cord(uroy) jeans, corduroys, cords; **veste en j.** denim jacket

jean-foutre [ʒɑ̃futr] NM INV *très Fam* good-for-nothing, ne'er-do-well

Jeanne [ʒan] N **J. d'Arc** Joan of Arc; **cheveux à la J. d'Arc** bobbed hair with a fringe *or Am* bangs

jeannette [ʒanɛt] NF **1** *(croix)* gold cross **2** *(de planche à repasser)* sleeveboard **3** *(plante)* **j. jaune** daffodil **4** *(scout)* Brownie **5** *Belg Fam (homosexuel)* queer, poof, *Am* fag

Jeannot [ʒano] NM *Fam* **J. lapin** bunny (rabbit)

jeep® [(d)ʒip] NF jeep

Jéhovah [ʒeɔva] N Jehovah

jéjunum [ʒeʒynɔm] NM *Anat* jejunum

je-m'en-fichisme [ʒmɑ̃fiʃism] NM *Fam* couldn't-care-less attitude; **faire preuve de j.** to show one couldn't care less

je-m'en-fichiste [ʒmɑ̃fiʃist] N *Fam* couldn't-care-less type

je-m'en-foutisme [ʒmɑ̃futism] NM *très Fam* couldn't-give-a-damn attitude; **ce n'est pas parce que tu ne savais pas le faire, c'est du j.** it's not because you didn't know how to do it, it's because you couldn't give a damn

je-m'en-foutiste [ʒmɑ̃futist] N *très Fam* couldn't-give-a-damn type

je-ne-sais-quoi [ʒənsɛkwa] NM INV **un j.** a certain *or* an indefinable something; **il y a un j. qui ne me plaît pas** there's something about it I don't like

jennérien, -ienne [ʒenerjɛ̃, -jɛn] ADJ *Méd* Jennerian

jenny [ʒeni] NF *Tex* spinning jenny

jérémiades [ʒeremjad] NFPL whining, complaining, moaning

Jérémie [ʒeremi] N *Bible* Jeremiah

jerez [xeres, kseres, gzeres] NM **(vin de) j.** sherry

Jéricho [ʒeriko] N Jericho

jerk [dʒɛrk] NM *(danse)* jerk

jéroboam [ʒerɔbɔam] NM jeroboam

jerrican(e), jerrycan [(d)ʒerikan] NM jerrycan

Jersey [ʒɛrzɛ] NF Jersey

jersey [ʒɛrzɛ] NM *(tissu)* jersey; **j. de laine** wool jersey; **j. de soie** silk jersey; *Tricot* **point (de) j.** stocking stitch

jersiais, -aise [ʒɛrzjɛ, -ɛz] ADJ of *or* from Jersey; **vache jersiaise** Jersey cow
N **J.** *(natif)* native of Jersey; *(habitant)* inhabitant of Jersey
NF **jersiaise** Jersey cow

Jérusalem [ʒeryzalɛm] N Jerusalem

jésuite [ʒezɥit] NM *Rel* Jesuit
ADJ **1** *Rel* Jesuit; **prêtre j.** Jesuit priest **2** *Péj* Jesuitical, jesuitical

jésuitique [ʒezɥitik] ADJ **1** *Rel* Jesuitic **2** *Péj* Jesuitical, jesuitical

jésuitisme [ʒezɥitism] NM **1** *Rel* Jesuitism **2** *Péj* Jesuitry, jesuitry

Jésus [ʒezy] N Jesus; **J.-Christ** [ʒezykri] Jesus Christ; **en l'an 44 avant/après J.-Christ** in the year 44 BC/AD

jésus [ʒezy] NM **1** *(statue)* statue of the baby Jesus *or* of the Christ Child **2** *Typ* = superroyal, king of royal paper; **grand j.** = imperial **3** *Culin* **j. (de Lyon)** = type of pork salami

jet¹ [ʒɛ] NM **1** *(action)* *(de pierre, balle, grenade etc)* throwing; *Arch, Litt (de filet, dé)* casting; *(résultat)* *(de pierre, balle, grenade etc)* throw; *Arch, Litt (de filet, dé)* cast; **à un j. de pierre de nous** a stone's throw away from us, within a stone's throw of us; **force de j.** impetus; **armes de j.** projectiles, missiles **2** *Métal* cast, casting; **couler qch d'un seul j.** to cast sth in one piece; *Fig* **faire qch d'un seul**

j. to do sth at *or* in one go; **premier j.** *Beaux-Arts* first *or* rough sketch; *Littér* first *or* rough draft **3** **j. (de marchandises)** à la mer jettisoning (of cargo), throwing overboard (of cargo) **4** *(de liquide)* jet; *(de sang)* spurt, gush; *(de lumière)* flash; *(de flammes)* jet, burst; *(de vapeur)* jet of steam; **j. d'incendie** jet of water from a fire hose; **j. d'eau** *(fontaine)* fountain; **il parle à j. continu** he talks non-stop *or* continuously; *Tech* **j. de sable** sand blast; **j. d'encre** ink jet **5** *Bot (d'arbre)* young shoot; **elle est tout d'un j.** she is tall and slender **6** *(de tuyau)* nozzle; *(de pompe, d'arrosoir etc)* spout; **j. de gaz** gas jet; **diriger le j. de la douche vers le mur** to turn the shower-head towards the wall

jet² [dʒɛt] NM *Aviat* jet

jetable [ʒətabl(ə)] ADJ disposable, throwaway

jeté [ʒ(ə)te] NM **1** *(en danse)* jeté **2** *Tricot* wool over *or* forward; **j. simple/double** make one/two **3** *Sport (en haltérophilie)* jerk **4** **j. de table** (table) runner; **j. de lit** bedspread
ADJ *Fam* crazy, nuts

jetée [ʒ(ə)te] NF jetty, pier

⸻

JETER [ʒ(ə)te] (**je jette, n. jetons; je jetterai**)

| VT to throw **1, 7, 8** ▪ to throw away **2** |
| ▪ to hurl **1, 4** ▪ to throw into **6** |
| VPR to throw oneself |

VT **1** *(lancer)* to throw; *(plus fort)* to fling, to hurl; *Arch, Litt (filets, dés)* to cast; *(faire tomber)* to throw down; **j. qch à qn** to throw sb sth, to throw sth to sb; **j. qn à la porte** *ou* **dehors** to throw sb out; **j. qch à la tête de qn** to throw sth at sb; *Fig* **elle nous jette ses diplômes à la tête** she harps on to us about her qualifications, she rams her qualifications down our throats; **j. qch à terre** *ou* **par terre** to throw sth to *or* on the ground; **j. qn à terre** to throw sb to the ground; **j. qn en prison/à la rue** to throw sb in jail/out (into the street); **j. qch à la mer** *ou* **par-dessus bord** to jettison sth, to throw sth overboard; **objets jetés à la mer** jetsam; **navires jetés à la côte par la tempête** ships driven ashore by the storm; **il rêve de j. bas le gouvernement** he dreams of bringing down *or* overthrowing the government; *Boxe, Fig* **j. l'éponge** to throw in the sponge *or* towel; *Fig Fam* **n'en jetez plus (la cour est pleine)!** enough, enough!, you're making me blush!

2 *(se défaire de)* to throw away, to throw out; **j. qch à la poubelle** to throw sth in the (dust)bin *or Am* garbage can, *Br* to bin sth; **j. qch au panier** to throw sth in the wastepaper basket, *Br* to bin sth; **j. qch au** *ou* **dans le feu** to throw sth on *or* in the fire; **à j.** to be thrown away *or* out; *Fig Fam* **ce devoir/livre est (bon) à j.** this homework/book is trash *or* rubbish; **elle est vraiment à j., cette fille** that girl's really the pits; *Fam* **il n'y a rien à j. dans ce livre** this book's as good as you'll get; **j. son argent par la fenêtre** to throw (one's) money away, to throw (one's) money down the drain; *très Fam* **se faire j.** to get chucked out (**de** of); **quand je l'ai invitée à danser, elle m'a jeté/je me suis fait j.** when I asked her to dance she gave me the brush-off/I was given the brush-off; **j. le bébé avec l'eau du bain** to throw the baby out with the bath water

3 *(émettre)* **j. un cri** to utter a cry; **j. un regard sur qn** to glance at sb, to throw *or* cast a glance at sb; **elle lui jetait des regards désespérés** she glanced at him despairingly *or* in despair, she threw *or* cast despairing glances at him; **j. un (coup d')œil** to have a (quick) glance (**sur** at)

4 *(dire)* **j. des reproches à la tête de qn** to hurl reproaches at sb; **j. des insultes à qn** to hurl abuse at sb; **elle m'a jeté à la figure que**

je n'étais qu'une pauvre idiote she told me straight to my face that I was just a stupid fool; **'bien vu', lui jeta-t-il en passant** 'well done', he called out to him as he went by **5** *(construire)* j. **un pont sur une rivière** to hastily construct a bridge over a river; **j. les fondements d'un édifice** to lay the foundations of a building

6 *(mettre)* j. **qn dans l'embarras** to throw sb into confusion; **j. qn dans le désespoir** to plunge sb into despair; **j. qn dans l'angoisse** to throw sb into a state of distress; **j. le discrédit sur qn/qch** to bring discredit on sb/sth, to bring sb/sth into disrepute; **sa remarque a jeté le doute/le trouble dans mon esprit** his remark cast *or* sowed doubt in my mind/troubled *or* disturbed me; **ça a jeté un froid** it cast a chill

7 *(mettre rapidement)* to throw; **j. quelques affaires dans un sac** to throw a few things in a bag; **j. un châle sur ses épaules** to throw a shawl over one's shoulders, to throw on a shawl; **j. une lettre à la boîte** to pop a letter in the postbox *or Am* mailbox; **j. quelques notes sur une feuille** to jot down a few notes on a sheet of paper

8 *(faire un mouvement du corps)* j. **la tête/ les épaules en arrière** to throw one's head/ shoulders back; **j. ses bras autour du cou de qn** to throw *or* fling one's arms around sb's neck

VPR se jeter to throw oneself; **cours d'eau qui se jette dans la Seine** stream that flows into the Seine; **se j. à l'eau** to throw oneself *or* plunge into the water; *Fig* to take the plunge; **se j. par la fenêtre** to throw oneself out of the window; **elle s'est jetée du troisième étage de la tour Eiffel** she threw herself from the third level of the Eiffel Tower; **il s'est jeté sous le métro/dans la Seine** he threw himself beneath an underground train/in the Seine; **se j. aux pieds de qn** to throw oneself at sb's feet; **se j. sur qn** to throw oneself upon *or* at sb; **elle s'est jetée sur moi** *ou* **dans mes bras pour m'embrasser** she rushed up to me and kissed me; *Fig* **se j. à la tête de qn** *(draguer outrageusement)* to throw oneself at sb; **il s'est jeté sur le buffet/ le champagne** he pounced on the buffet/the champagne; **se j. (à corps perdu) dans une entreprise** to throw oneself (body and soul *or* wholeheartedly) into an undertaking; *Fam* **s'en j. un** *(derrière la cravate)* to have a quick one *or* a quickie

VI *Fam* **ça jette!** it's really something!, it's brilliant!; **elle en jette, ta bagnole** your car's really something, that's some car you've got

jeteur, -euse [ʒ(ə)tœr, -øz] **N** j. **de sort** wizard; **jeteuse de sort** witch

jeton [ʒ(ə)tɔ̃] **NM 1** *Cartes etc* counter, chip; *(pour téléphone etc)* token; **j. de présence** *(objet)* tally, token *(issued as voucher for attendance at meeting)*; *Com (honoraires)* director's fees; **toucher ses jetons** to draw one's fees **2** *très Fam (coup de poing)* whack, thump; **il s'est pris un j. pendant la bagarre** he got a whack *or* a thump during the brawl; **dans l'accident, ma bagnole a pris quelques jetons** *(coups)* my car got a bit of a bashing *or* got a few dents in the accident **3** *très Fam (peur)* **avoir les jetons** to have the jitters, to be scared stiff; **j'ai les jetons que mon père apprenne que j'ai séché** I'm scared stiff my father'll find out I've skipped school; **ça/il m'a donné les jetons** it/he gave me the jitters, it/he put the wind up me

jet-set [dʒɛtsɛt], **jet-society** [dʒɛtsɔsajti] **NF** jet-set

jet-ski [dʒɛski] **NM** jet-skiing

jet-stream, *pl* **jet-streams** [dʒɛtstrim] **NM** *Météo* jet stream

---

JEU, *pl* **jeux** [ʒø]

play **1**	game **2, 5**	hand **3**
gambling **4**	acting **7**	set **8**

NM 1 *(amusement)* le j. play; **salle de jeux** playroom; *(dans hôtel etc)* games room; **j. de main** horseplay, rough and tumble; *Prov* **jeux de mains, jeux de vilains** all this fooling around is going to end in tears; *Fig* **c'est un j. d'enfant** it's child's play; **se faire (un) j. de (faire) qch** to make light work *or* easy work of (doing) sth; *Fig* **à quel j. joues-tu?** what's your game?, what are you playing at?; **faire qch par j.** to do sth for fun; **cessez ce j. cruel!** stop this cruel game!; **les jeux de l'amour** *ou* **amoureux** love-play

2 *(activité comportant un gagnant)* game; *Ordinat* **jeux électroniques** computer games; **les jeux du cirque** *(antiquité)* the games of the circus; **la règle du j.** the rules of the game; *Fam* **ce n'est pas du j.** that's not fair; **jouer le j.** to play the game; **on aurait beau j. de répondre** it would be quite easy to answer that; *Fig* **faire le j. de qn** to play into sb's hands; **entrer dans le j. de qn** to go along with sb; **le j. n'en vaut pas la chandelle** the game isn't worth the candle; **se prendre** *ou* **se laisser prendre au j.** to get caught up in it; **se piquer au j.** to get into it; **être pris à son propre j.** to be caught out at one's own game, *Fml* to be hoist with one's own petard; **jouer un j. dangereux** to play a dangerous game; **voir clair/lire dans le j. de qn** to see through sb's game; **jouer franc j.** *(avec qn)* to play fair (and square) (with sb); **se prêter au j.** to join in with *or* to go along with the game; **j. grand public** game(s) show

3 *(cartes que le joueur a en main)* hand; **avoir un beau j.** *ou* **du j.** to have a good hand, to have good cards; **cacher son j.** *Cartes* to hide one's hand *or* one's cards; *Fig* to keep one's cards close to one's chest; *Cartes, Fig* **montrer/laisser voir son j.** to show one's hand *or* one's cards; *Fig* **sortir le grand j.** to go all out, to pull out all the stops

4 *(activité soumise au hasard)* le j. *(au casino etc)* gambling, *Fml* gaming; **j. de bourse** stock market gamble; **maison de j.** gaming house; **perdre une fortune au j.** to gamble away a fortune, to lose a fortune gambling; **se ruiner au j.** to ruin oneself gambling; **dettes de j.** gambling debts; **table de j.** card table, gaming table; **jouer gros j.** to play for high stakes; **les jeux sont faits** *(à la roulette)* les jeux sont faits; *Fig* the die is cast; *(situation critique)* the chips are down; **faites vos jeux!** place your bets!; **mettre qch en j.** *(argent, voiture, carrière etc)* to stake sth; *Fig* **mettre tout en j.** to stake one's all, to risk everything; **être en j.** to be at stake; **les intérêts en j.** the interests at stake *or* at issue *or* involved; **les forces en j.** the forces at work, the forces involved

5 *Tennis (division d'une partie)* game; **j., set et match** game, set and match; **j.** Pierce game *(to)* Pierce; *Ftbl* **être hors j.** *(ballon)* to be out of play; *(joueur)* to be offside; **où en est le j.?** what's the score?; **terrain de jeux** playing field, sports ground; **en j.** in play; **mettre la balle en j.** to bring the ball into play; *(au hockey)* to bully off

6 *Fig (système)* **le j. de l'offre et de la demande** the system of supply and demand; **j. du marché** market forces; *Fig* **le j. des alliances** the interplay *or* interaction of alliances; **il a obtenu cette faveur par le j. des relations diplomatiques** he obtained this favour through the exercise of diplomatic relations; **le j. des événements** the turn of events; **entrer en j.** to come into play

7 *Théâtre, Mus (d'un acteur)* acting; *(d'un musicien)* playing; **il a un j. très subtil** *Mus* his playing is very subtle, he has a very subtle manner

of playing; *Théâtre* his acting is very subtle; *Théâtre* **jeux de scène** stage business; **le j. de main d'un pianiste** a pianist's technique

8 *(ensemble)* *(d'outils, de clés etc)* set; **j. d'échecs/de dominos** chess set/set of dominoes; **j. de boules/quilles** set of bowls/skittles *or* ninepins; **j. de cartes** pack *or* deck of cards; *Typ* **j. de caractères** character set; *Com* **j. complet de connaissements** full set of bills of lading; **j. de fiches** card index; **j. de lettres de change** set of bills of exchange

9 *Tech (fonctionnement d'un mécanisme)* **j. d'une serrure** action of a lock; **j. d'un piston** length of stroke of a piston

10 *Tech, Aut* play; *Tech* **j. (utile)** play; **il faut rattraper le j.** it needs to be tightened up; **il y a du j.** it's rather loose, there's a bit of play; **donner du j. à qch** to ease *or* loosen sth; **j. (nuisible)** play, looseness; **prendre du j.** to work free *or* loose; *Vieilli Fig* **donner du j. à des négociations** to allow (some) scope for negotiations

▸▸ jeux d'adresse games of skill; **j. d'arcade** arcade game; *Tennis* **j. blanc** love game; **j. de Bourse** gambling *or* speculating on the Stock Exchange; **j. d'eau** fountain; *Fin* **j. d'écritures** creative accounting; **jeux éducatifs** educational games; **j. électronique** computer game; *Aut* **j. d'embouts** socket set; *Aut* **j. d'engrenages** gearing; **j. d'esprit** witticism; *Sport* **j. de jambes** *(d'un boxeur, d'un joueur de tennis etc)* footwork; **j. de lumière** play of light; *Théâtre* **jeux de lumière** lighting effects; **j. de mots** play on words, pun; *Sport* **Jeux olympiques** Olympic Games, Olympics; **j. d'ombre et de lumière** interplay of light and shade; *Mus* **j. d'orgue** *(organ)* stop; *Sport* **Jeux paralympiques** special Olympics, Paralympics; **j. radiophonique** game show *(on radio)*; **j. de rôles** role-playing, role play; **jeux de société** *(charades, devinettes etc)* parlour games; *(petits chevaux, jeu de l'oie etc)* board games; *Aut* **j. de soupapes** valve clearance; **j. télévisé** *(television)* game show; *(avec questions)* *(television)* quiz *(show)*; **j. vidéo** video game

---

jeu-concours, *pl* **jeux-concours** [ʒøkɔ̃kur] **NM** *Radio, TV, Journ* competition; *(émission)* game show; *(avec questions)* quiz *(show)*

jeudi [ʒødi] **NM** Thursday; **j. saint** Maundy Thursday; *Fam* **la semaine des quatre jeudis** when pigs fly *(voir aussi* **samedi)** SEE GRAMMAR A81; B61

jeun (à) [aʒœ̃] **ADJ** *(pas ivre)* sober; **être à j.** *(sans avoir mangé ni bu)* to have eaten or drunk nothing; **boire à j.** to drink on an empty stomach

JEUNE [ʒœn] **ADJ 1** *(personne, âge)* young; *(apparence, allure etc)* youthful; *(coiffure, vêtement)* young, that makes one look young; **j. homme** young man, youth; **elle n'est plus très** *ou* **toute j.** she's not as young as she was; **j. fille** girl, young woman; **jeunes gens** young people; *(hommes)* young men, youths; **j. aveugle** blind boy, *f* girl; **un j. Français/Anglais** a French/an English boy; **une j. Indienne** an Indian girl; **j. détenu** juvenile offender; **j. délinquant** juvenile delinquent; **le plus j. de mes frères** my youngest brother, the youngest of my brothers; **je suis plus j. que lui de quatre ans** I'm four years younger than him *or* than he is; **dans son j. âge** in his younger days, when he was younger; **être j. d'allure** to be young-looking, to be youthful-looking, to have a youthful appearance; **j. d'esprit** young at heart, youthful in outlook; **il est trop j. dans la société pour qu'on lui confie de telles responsabilités** he hasn't been with the firm long enough to be given such responsibilities; **faire j.** *(de personne)* to look young; **faire** *ou* **paraître plus j. que son âge** to look younger than one's age *or* one's years *or* one is

2 *(en comparaison)* younger; **mon j. frère** my younger brother; **M. Martin J.** Mr Martin junior, young Mr Martin

3 *(vert) (vin, industrie)* young, new; *(fromage)* young

4 *Fam (juste)* **c'est un peu j.!** it's a bit on the short side!; **c'est un peu j. pour le vin, on est un peu j.** en vin the wine's a bit on the short side; **je trouve ses arguments un peu jeunes** I find his arguments a bit flimsy *or* thin

N 1 *(personne jeune)* **un j.** a youngster, a youth; **une j.** a girl; *Fam* **un petit j.** a young guy; **les jeunes** (the) young people; **les jeunes d'aujourd'hui** *ou* **de maintenant** the young people *or* the youth of today, young people today **2** *(d'un animal)* young animal; **jeunes** young

ADV ça fait j. it makes you/her/*etc* look young(er); **s'habiller j.** to wear young clothes, to dress in a youthful style; **se coiffer j.** to wear one's hair in youthful styles/in a youthful style

---

jeûne [ʒøn] **NM 1** *(période)* fast; **rompre le j.** to break one's fast; **j. de protestation** hunger strike **2** *(pratique)* fasting; **jour de j.** day of fasting, fast day

jeûner [ʒøne] **VI** to go without food, to fast; *Rel* to fast

jeunesse [ʒœnɛs] **NF 1** *(période)* youth; **dans ma j.** in my youth, in my younger days, when I was young; **ne pas être de (la) première j.** *(de personne)* not to be as young as one was, to be no longer in one's first flush of youth, to be getting on; *(d'objet)* to have seen better days; **erreurs/péchés de j.** errors of youth/ youthful indiscretions; *Prov* **il faut que j. se passe** youth will have its fling **2** *(fraîcheur)* youthfulness; **j. de peau** youthful appearance of the skin; **j. d'esprit** youthful outlook **3** *(du vin)* newness **4** *(les jeunes)* young people; **il aime se retrouver au milieu de la j.** he likes to be surrounded by young people; **la j. nous rejoindra plus tard** the young people will join us later; **la j. dorée** the bright young things, *Litt* gilded youth; **club pour la j.** youth club; **livres pour la j.** books for young people; **la j. du village** the young people *or* the youth of the village; *Fam* **salut la j.!** hi (there), guys!; *Fam* **roulez j.!** let's go!; *Prov* **si j. savait, si vieillesse pouvait** if youth but knew, if age but could **VOIR GRAMMAIRE A11 5** *Vieilli (jeune fille)* girl

jeunet, -ette [ʒœnɛ, -ɛt] **ADJ** *Fam* youngish; **elle est un peu jeunette pour faire ce travail** she's a bit on the young side to do this job

jeûneur, -euse [ʒønœr, -øz] **N** faster

jeunot, -otte [ʒœno, -ɔt] *Fam* **ADJ** youngish, on the young side **NM** *Péj* youngster; **un petit j.** a young little fellow

JF *abrév* **jeune fille/femme**

JH *abrév* **jeune homme**

jingle [dʒiŋgəl] **NM** *Radio* jingle

jiu-jitsu [ʒ(j)yʒitsy] **NM INV** *Sport* j(i)ujitsu

JJ [ʒiʒi] *Bourse (abrév* **au jour le jour)** overnight

Jne *(abrév* **jeune)** jr, jnr, jun

JO [ʒio] **NM** *abrév* **Journal officiel**
NMPL *abrév* **Jeux olympiques**

joaillerie [ʒɔajri] **NF 1** *(magasin)* jeweller's *or Am* jeweler's shop **2** *(marchandises)* jewellery, *Am* jewelry **3** *(commerce)* jewellery *or Am* jewelry trade

joaillier, -ière [ʒɔaje, -jɛr] **N** jeweller, *Am* jeweler

Job [ʒɔb] **N** *Bible* Job; **pauvre comme J.** poor as a church mouse

job [dʒɔb] **NM,** *Can* **NF** *Fam* job

---

jobard, -arde [ʒɔbar, -ard] *Fam* **ADJ** gullible, naive
N sucker, *Br* mug

jobarderie [ʒɔbard(ə)ri], **jobardise** [ʒɔbardiz] **NF** *Fam* gullibility; **c'est de la j.** it's a mug's game

jobine [ʒɔbin] **NF** *Can Fam* casual job; **faire des jobines** to do odd jobs *or* casual work

jobiste [ʒɔbist] **N** *Belg Fam* student with a casual job

JOC [ʒɔk] **NF** *(abrév* **Jeunesse ouvrière chrétienne)** = Christian youth organization

jockey [ʒɔkɛ] **NM** *Courses de chevaux* jockey; *Arch* outrider

Joconde [ʒɔkɔ̃d] **NF** **la J.** the Mona Lisa

jodler [ʒɔdle, jɔ-] **VI** to yodel

joggeur, -euse [(d)ʒɔgœr, -øz] **N** jogger

jogging [(d)ʒɔgiŋ] **NM 1** *(vêtement)* jogging suit, tracksuit **2** *(activité)* jogging; **faire du j.** to go jogging, to jog

Johannesburg [ʒɔanesbur] **N** Johannesburg

joie [ʒwa] **NF** joy, delight; **plein de j.** full of joy; **dans la j. et la bonne humeur** happily and cheerfully; **elle était folle de j.** she was wild with joy *or* delight; **être au comble de la j.** to be overjoyed; **mettre qn au comble de la j.** to make sb deliriously happy; **sauter de j.** to jump for joy; **ne plus se sentir de j.** to be beside oneself with joy; *Fam* **c'est pas la j.!** it's no fun; **à ma grande j.** to my great delight; **une j. profonde** great pleasure; **accepter avec j.** to accept with pleasure, to accept gladly; **ça me met en j.** I'm delighted by it; **aller au concert ce soir me met en j.** I'm delighted *or* thrilled about going to the concert this evening; **ma fille faisait ma j.** my daughter was my (pride and) joy; **le film a fait la j. de Simon** the film delighted Simon; **c'est une j. de le voir rétabli** it's a joy *or* a delight to see him on his feet again; **se faire une j. de faire qch** to delight *or* take a delight in doing sth; **quand vais-je avoir la j. de faire sa connaissance?** when will I have the pleasure of making his acquaintance?; **pour ma plus grande j.** much to my delight, to my great delight; **feu de j.** bonfire; **j. de vivre** joy of living, joie de vivre; **il se faisait une j. de vous voir** he was looking forward (so much) to seeing you; **il se fera une j. de vous guider** he'll be only too pleased to guide you; **elle vous a fait une fausse j.** she gave you false cause for celebration; *Iron* **les joies de la famille/la plomberie!** the joys of family life/plumbing!

joignable [ʒwaɲabl] **ADJ** contactable

joindre [ʒwɛ̃dr] *(prp* **joignant;** *pp* **joint;** *pr ind* **je joins, il joint, n. joignons, ils joignent;** *impf* **je joignais;** *p hist* **je joignis;** *fu* **je joindrai)** **VT 1** *(réunir)* to join; **j. les mains** to clasp one's hands, to put one's hands together; **j. deux tuyaux bout à bout/un tuyau au bout d'un autre** to join two pipes end to end/one pipe to the end of another; **j. nos efforts** to combine *or* unite our efforts; *Fam* **j. les deux bouts** to make ends meet **2** *(ajouter)* to add (à to); *(dans une lettre, un colis etc)* to enclose (à with); **le bon sens joint à l'intelligence** common sense combined with intelligence; **j. le geste à la parole** to suit the action to the word; **j. l'utile à l'agréable** to combine business with pleasure; **j. sa voix aux protestations** to add one's voice to *or* join in the protests; **l'échantillon joint à votre lettre** the sample enclosed with *or* attached to your letter; **j. une carte à un bouquet de fleurs** to attach a card to a bouquet of flowers; **veuillez j. CV et photo d'identité** please attach a copy of your CV *or Am* resumé and a photograph **3** *(contacter) (personne)* to contact, to get in contact *or* in touch with, to reach
VI *(de planches, tuiles etc)* to meet, to fit; **fe-**

---

nêtre qui joint mal window that doesn't shut properly
VPR se joindre se j. à to join; **se j. à la conversation** to join in the conversation; **voulez-vous vous j. à nous?** would you like to join us?; **Marie se joint à moi pour vous remercier** Marie joins me in thanking you; **je voudrais me j. à vous pour le cadeau de Marie** I'd like to contribute to Marie's present

joint [ʒwɛ̃] **PP** *de* **joindre**
ADJ joined; **sauter à pieds joints** to do a standing jump, to jump from a standing position; **les mains jointes** with clasped hands, with hands together; **efforts joints** combined *or* united efforts; **pièces jointes** *(dans une lettre)* enclosures
NM 1 *Menuis, Tech, Aut* joint, join; *(de réservoir)* seam; *(produit d'étanchéité)* sealant **2** *Fam* **chercher/trouver le j. pour faire qch** to look for/find a way of doing sth; **faire le j. (entre deux personnes)** to act as a go-between (between two people) **3** *Fam (drogue)* joint
► ► **j. en about** butt joint; **j. abouté** butt joint; **j. articulé** knuckle (joint); **j. biseauté** scarf joint; **j. à brides** flange joint; **j. brisé** universal *or* cardan joint, coupling; **j. de cardan** universal *or* cardan joint, coupling, constant-velocity joint; **j. carré** butt joint; **j. en charnière** knuckle (joint); *Aut* **j. de culasse** cylinder head gasket, head gasket; **j. d'étanchéité** gasket, seal; *Aut* **j. d'huile** oil seal; *Aut* **j. moteur** engine gasket; **j. plat** butt joint; **j. à rotule** ball(-and-socket) joint; **j. sphérique** ball(-and-socket) joint; *Aut* **j. de transmission** universal joint; **j. universel** universal *or* cardan joint, coupling

jointif, -ive [ʒwɛ̃tif, -iv] **ADJ** *Tech* joined, placed edge to edge, contiguous

jointure [ʒwɛ̃tyr] **NF** *Anat* joint; *Tech* joint, join; *(d'un cheval) (boulet)* fetlock (joint); *(paturon)* pastern; **les jointures des doigts** the knuckles

joint venture [dʒɔjntventʃœr] **NF** *Fin* joint venture

jojo [ʒoʒo] *Fam* **NM** **affreux j.** little horror *or* monster
ADJ INV **il n'était pas j.** he wasn't a pretty sight

jojoba [ʒoʒoba] **NM** *Bot* jojoba

joker [ʒɔker] **NM** *Cartes* joker; *Ordinat* wildcard; *Fig* **sortir son j.** to play one's trump card

joli [ʒɔli] **ADJ** *(enfant, fille)* pretty, attractive, good-looking; *(ville, tableau)* pretty, attractive; *(voix, chanson)* pretty, lovely; *(promenade, histoire, image)* lovely, nice; *(expression)* attractive; **le j. mois de mai** the merry month of May; **j. comme un cœur, j. à croquer** pretty as a picture; **il est j. garçon** he's good-looking, he's attractive; **faire le j. cœur** to flirt; **il a une jolie fortune** he's pretty well off; **c'est bien j. tout ça mais ...** that's all well and good *or* all very well but ...; **c'est bien j. de vouloir acheter un bateau, mais avec quels sous?** it's all well and good *or* all very well to want to buy a boat, but where's the money coming from?; *Fam Iron* **c'est pas j. j.** *(blâmable)* that's not very nice; *(laid)* it's not a pretty sight; **ah te voilà dans une jolie situation!** what a fine mess you've got yourself into!; *Fam* **une jolie pagaille/merde** a fine old shambles/mess
NM **le j. de l'affaire, c'est que ...** the best thing (about it) *or* the beauty of the thing is that ...; *Iron* **c'est du j.!** that's marvellous *or* wonderful!; **c'est du j., de mentir** that's nice, lying; **faire du j.** to make a mess of everything; **faire du j. avec qch** to make a mess of sth

> Il faut noter que l'adjectif anglais **jolly** est un faux ami. Il signifie **joyeux**.

joliesse [ʒɔljɛs] **NF** *Litt* prettiness

joliment [ʒɔlimɑ̃] **ADV 1** *(bien)* nicely; **c'est j. dit!** that's neatly *or* nicely put; **elle parle très j. de sa fille** she talks quite charmingly about her daughter **2** *Fam (extrêmement)* really; **vous avez j. raison** you're dead right; **on s'est j. amusé(s)** we had a great *or* marvellous time; **elle s'est j. fait engueuler** she got a right telling-off **3** *Fam Iron (très mal)* **te voilà j. arrangé!** you're in a right mess *or* state!; **on a été j. reçu** we got a less than warm welcome; **il a été j. arrangé par la critique** the critics didn't leave a hair on him

jonc [ʒɔ̃] **NM 1** *(plante)* rush; **(canne de) j. Malacca** cane **2** *(en vannerie)* rush; *(baguette)* malacca cane, rattan (walking stick) **3** *(bague)* ring; *(bracelet)* bangle
▸▸ *Aut* **j. d'enjoliveur** wheel trim; *Bot* **j. fleuri** flowering rush; *Bot* **j. d'Inde** rattan; *Bot* **j. des marais** bulrush

joncher [ʒɔ̃ʃe] **VT** to strew; **j. la terre de fleurs** to strew the ground with flowers; **les débris de la statue jonchaient le pavé** fragments of the statue lay strewn about the pavement; **plancher jonché de débris** floor strewn *or* littered with rubbish

jonchets [ʒɔ̃ʃɛ] **NMPL** jackstraws, spillikins, pick-up sticks

jonction [ʒɔ̃ksjɔ̃] **NF** junction; *(fait de joindre)* joining; **point de j.** meeting point, junction; **j. de deux routes** junction of two roads; *Tech* **tuyau de j.** joint pipe; *Mil* **opérer une j.** *(de troupes)* to join forces; *Jur* **j. d'instance** joinder; *Ordinat* **j. physique** physical interface

jongler [ʒɔ̃gle] **VI 1** to juggle (**avec** with); *Fig* **j. avec les concepts/les chiffres/les problèmes** to juggle with concepts/figures/problems **2** *Can (rêvasser)* to daydream

jonglerie [ʒɔ̃gləri] **NF** juggling

jongleur, -euse [ʒɔ̃glœr, -øz] **N 1** *(acrobate)* juggler **2** *Hist (ménestrel)* jongleur, (wandering) minstrel **3** *Can (rêveur)* daydreamer

jonque [ʒɔ̃k] **NF** *Naut* junk

jonquille [ʒɔ̃kij] **NF** daffodil, jonquil
   NM bright yellow, daffodil (yellow)
   ADJ INV bright yellow, daffodil (yellow)

Jordanie [ʒɔrdani] **NF** Jordan

jordanien, -ienne [ʒɔrdanjɛ̃, -jɛn] **ADJ** Jordanian
   N J. Jordanian

joseph [ʒozɛf] **ADJ papier j.** fine transparent filter paper

Josué [ʒozɥe] **N** *Bible* Joshua

jouable [ʒwabl] **ADJ** playable

joual [ʒwal] **NM** *Can Ling* joual (French Canadian dialect)

jouasse [ʒwas] **ADJ** *Fam* pleased, *Br* chuffed; **qu'est-ce que t'as, t'es pas j.?** got a problem?

joubarbe [ʒubarb] **NF** houseleek

joue [ʒu] **NF 1** *(de personne, cheval)* cheek; **elle sentit le rouge lui monter aux joues** she felt herself going red in the face; **fard à joues** blusher; **danser j. contre j.** to dance cheek to cheek; **tendre la j.** to offer *or* present one's cheek; *Fig* **tendre** *ou* **présenter l'autre j.** to turn the other cheek; *Culin* **j. de bœuf** ox cheek **2 mettre** *ou* **coucher qn en j.** to aim at sb, to take aim at sb; **mettre** *ou* **coucher un fusil en j.** to aim a gun, to take aim with a gun; **tenir qn en j.** to keep sb in one's sights; *Mil* **en j.!** take aim! **3** *(de fauteuil etc)* side; *(de palier, mortaise etc)* cheek; *(de roue etc)* flange; *(de poutre etc)* web **4** *Arch* **joues** *(d'un bateau)* bows

JOUER [ʒwe]

VI to play **1–3** ▪ to act **5** ▪ to gamble **6** ▪ to work **7**	
VT to play **2–5** ▪ to act **4** ▪ to stake **1** ▪ to trick **6**	
VPR to be played **1** ▪ to trifle with **4** ▪ to be on **6**	

VI 1 *(s'amuser)* to play; **va j. ailleurs** go and play somewhere else; **j. avec ses lunettes** to play *or* fiddle *or* toy with one's glasses; **j. sur les mots** to play with words; **j. avec une idée** to toy with an idea; *Fig* **j. avec les sentiments de qn** to play *or* toy *or* trifle with sb's feelings; **j. avec qn** *(s'en moquer)* to play games with sb; **il joue avec son avenir** he's gambling with *or* risking his future

2 *Sport etc* to play; **j. à qch** to play (at) sth; **j. au tennis/aux cartes** to play tennis/cards; **j. aux soldats/charades** to play (at) soldiers/charades; **j. au docteur** to play doctors and nurses; **j. aux gendarmes et aux voleurs** to play cops and robbers; **j. à la marchande** to play (at) shops; **j. à faire des pâtés** to make sandcastles *or* sandpies; **j. au détective** *(quand on n'en est pas un)* to play detective; *Sport* **j. en finale** to play in the final; **j. dans l'équipe de France** to play in *or* for the French team; **je ne joue plus!** I'm not playing any more!; **c'est à qui de j.?** whose turn *or* go is it?; *(aux échecs, dames etc)* whose move is it?; *Cartes, Fig* **à vous de j.** it's your turn; *Fig* **j. au plus malin/au plus fort avec qn** to try to outwit/outdo sb; *très Fam* **j. au con** to act like a prat

3 *Mus* to play; **j. du piano/de la harpe** to play the piano/the harp; **j. dans un groupe** *(d'un musicien)* to play in a group

4 *(manier avec habileté) (éventail)* to wave; *(couteau, pistolet, hache etc)* to wield *or* brandish

5 *Théâtre, Cin, TV (d'un acteur)* to act; *(d'une troupe)* to perform; **j. dans un film** to be in a film; **il joue très mal** he's a very bad actor, he acts very badly; *(dans un film)* he gives a bad performance; **je joue/cette troupe joue demain à Paris** I'm playing *or* performing *or* acting/this company is playing *or* performing in Paris tomorrow

6 *(parier)* to gamble; *Bourse* to speculate; **j. en Bourse** to speculate on the Stock Market; **j. aux courses** to bet on *or* back horses; **j. 200 euros sur un cheval** to bet *or* stake 200 euros on a horse; **j. à la hausse** to gamble on a rise in prices, to bull the market; **j. à la baisse** to gamble on a fall in prices, to bear the market

7 *(fonctionner)* to work, to function; **clef qui ne joue pas bien** key that is hard to turn; **faire j. un ressort** to work *or* trigger *or* release a spring; *Fig* **faire j. ses relations pour obtenir qch** to pull a few strings to get sth; **faire j. la corde sensible** to strike *or* touch a chord

8 *(intervenir)* **l'augmentation des salaires joue depuis le 1er janvier** the rise in salaries has been effective since 1 January; **cette considération ne joue pas** that consideration doesn't apply *or* is irrelevant; **votre situation a joué dans l'obtention de ce dédommagement** your situation has been a factor *or* has played a role in obtaining this compensation; **cela jouera en sa faveur/défaveur** that will work in his favour/against him; **cela a joué contre lui** that worked against him

9 *(du bois)* to warp; *(d'une pièce)* to fit loosely, to have too much play

10 *(locutions)* **j. des coudes** to elbow one's way through; *Fig* to use some manoeuvring; **une fille qui joue de l'œil** a girl who's making eyes at sb *or* who's giving sb the eye; **elle joue de son expérience/de sa maladie** she's playing on her experience/her illness; *Fam* **j. petits bras** to hold back

11 *Suisse (convenir)* to be alright; **cela ne joue pas** it's not right; **avec un peu de chance ça pourrait j.** with a bit of luck it could work out

VT 1 *(parier)* to stake; *(cheval)* to back, to bet on; **j. cinq euros** to stake five euros; **j. sa tête** to risk one's neck; **j. un cheval gagnant et placé** to back a horse each way

2 *Sport* **j. la finale** to play in the final; **j. la revanche** to play the return match

3 *(carte)* to play; *(pion)* to move, to play; *Cartes* **j. trèfle** to play clubs; *(au début)* to lead clubs; *Échecs* **j. une pièce** to move *or* play a piece

4 *Théâtre, Cin, TV (rôle)* to act, to play, to perform; **j. (du) Genet** *(d'une troupe)* to perform *or* put on a Genet play; *(d'un acteur)* to act in a Genet play; **j. Phèdre** *(d'une actrice)* to play Phaedra; *Fig* **j. un rôle dans l'affaire** to play a part in the affair; **j. la surprise** to feign surprise, to pretend to be surprised; **j. les héros/les séducteurs** to play the hero/the seducer; **arrête de j. les incompris** stop acting as though no one understands you; **qu'est-ce qu'on joue?** what's on?; **ils jouent un film d'horreur au cinéma du coin** there's a horror film on at the local cinema, the local cinema's showing a horror film; *Fam* **où t'as vu jouer ça?** are you mad?, have you got a screw loose?, are you off your rocker?

5 *Mus* **j. un air au piano/à la flûte** to play a tune on the piano/flute; **j. du Bach** to play (some) Bach

6 *(duper) (personne)* to trick, to fool, to make a fool of

7 *Bourse* **j. la livre à la hausse/à la baisse** to speculate on a rising/falling pound

VPR se jouer 1 c'est un jeu qui se joue à plusieurs it's a game you need several people to play; **le match se jouera la semaine prochaine** the match will be played next week; **des sommes énormes se jouent au casino tous les soirs** huge sums are gambled in the casino every night

2 *(se décider)* **son sort est en train de se j.** his fate is hanging in the balance

3 faire qch (comme) en se jouant to do sth easily *or* without any difficulty, to make child's play of sth

4 se j. de qn to trifle with sb; *(se moquer)* to mock sb, to make fun of sb; **se j. des lois/des difficultés** to make a mockery of the law/to make light of difficulties; **il se joue de tous les chasseurs de prime lancés à ses trousses** he makes a mockery of all the bounty hunters at his heels

5 *Litt (de la brise, de la lumière, d'un filet de lune)* to play; **une brise légère se jouait dans ses cheveux** a gentle breeze caressed her hair

6 *Théâtre* **qu'est-ce qui se joue actuellement?** what's on *or* playing at the moment?

7 *Fam* **se la j.** to show off, to pose

jouet [ʒwɛ] **NM 1** *(d'enfant)* toy; *(terme plus général)* plaything **2** *Fig* **son mari n'est qu'un j. pour elle** her husband is just her plaything; **être le j. d'une illusion/des événements** to be the victim of an illusion/of events

jouette [ʒwɛt] **ADJ** *Belg* **enfant j.** child who loves playing

joueur, -euse [ʒwœr, -øz] **N 1** *(d'un jeu)* player; **j. de tennis** tennis player; **j. de golf/cricket** golfer/cricketer; **j. de cartes** card player; **être bon j.** to be a good player; **être beau/mauvais j.** to be a good/bad loser **2** *Mus* player **3** *(au casino etc)* gambler; *Bourse* speculator
   ADJ *(enfant, chien)* playful

joufflu [ʒufly] **ADJ** *(bébé, angelot)* chubby-cheeked; *(visage)* chubby
   NM *Fam (postérieur)* butt, *Br* bum, *Am* fanny

joug [ʒu] **NM 1** *Agr* yoke; **mettre les bœufs sous le j.** to yoke the oxen; *Fig* **être sous le j. d'un tyran** to be under the yoke of a tyrant; **secouer le j.,** **s'affranchir du j.** to throw off the yoke **2** *(d'une balance)* beam

jouir [ʒwir] **VI 1** *(sexuellement)* to have an orgasm, *Fam* to come; *Fig* **ça le fait j. de nous voir peiner** he gets a kick out of seeing us struggle **2** *(profiter)* **j. de la vie** to enjoy life

3 *(être en possession)* **j. de toutes ses facultés** to be in full possession of one's faculties; **j. d'une bonne réputation** to have a good reputation; **j. d'une bonne santé** to enjoy good health **4** *Fam (souffrir)* to go through hell

jouissance [ʒwisɑ̃s] **NF 1** *(plaisir)* enjoyment, pleasure; *(sexuel)* orgasm, climax; **il tire une véritable j. du travail** he gets real enjoyment or pleasure from work **2** *Jur (possession)* possession, tenure; **avoir la j. de certains droits** to enjoy certain rights; **entrer en j. de ses biens** to enter into possession of one's property; **maison à vendre avec j. immédiate** house for sale with vacant possession; **avec j. de la cuisine** *(d'un logement)* with use of kitchen; *Fin* **j. d'intérêts** entitlement to interest; **j. locative** tenure; **j. en commun** *(d'un bien)* communal tenure; **la période de j. est de sept ans** the period of tenure is seven years

jouisseur, -euse [ʒwisœr, -øz] **N** sensualist, *Litt* sybarite

jouissif, -ive [ʒwisif, -iv] **ADJ** *Fam* **1** *(agréable)* really great; **tirer un plaisir j. de faire qch** to get a great kick out of doing sth **2** *(douloureux)* *Br* bloody or *Am* goddamn painful; **s'écraser le petit orteil, c'est j.!** stubbing your little toe is a real barrel of laughs!

joujou, -oux [ʒuʒu] **NM** *Fam* toy; *(terme plus général)* plaything; **faire j.** to play; **faire j. avec une poupée/des explosifs** to play with a doll/explosives

joule [ʒul] **NM** *Phys* joule

JOUR [ʒur]

> day **2, 3** ▪ daylight **1** ▪ light **6, 10**
> ▪ gap **7** ▪ nowadays *(de nos jours)* **4**
> ▪ to give birth to *(donner le jour à)* **5**

NM 1 *(clarté)* day, (day)light; **au petit j.** at daybreak, at break of day, at dawn; **avant le j.** before dawn, before daybreak, before break of day; **en plein j.** in broad daylight; **à la tombée du j.** at nightfall; **il fait j.** it's (getting) light; **l'été, il fait j. à 4h30** in the summer it gets light at 4.30; **il fait à peine j.** it's hardly light; **vous me cachez le j.** you're in my light; **mets-toi face au j.** face the light; **le j. se fit dans mon esprit** I began to understand or to see daylight; **la vérité se fait j. dans son esprit** the truth is dawning on him; **voyager le ou de j.** to travel by day or in the day(time); **travailler j. et nuit** to work day and night or night and day; *Min* **travail au j.** surface work; *Fig* **elle et son mari c'est le j. et la nuit** she and her husband are like chalk and cheese; **elle est belle comme le j.** she's a real beauty

2 *(journée)* day; **huit jours** a week; **quinze jours** two weeks, *Br* a fortnight; **à quelques jours de là** a few days after (that); **500 euros/trois pages par j.** 500 euros/three pages a day; **une à deux fois par j.** once or twice a day; **c'est à un j. de voyage** it's a day's journey (away); **quel j. sommes-nous?** *(de la semaine)* what day (of the week) is it (today)?; *Prov* **les jours se suivent et ne se ressemblent pas** who knows what tomorrow holds?; *Fam* **il y a les jours avec et les jours sans** there are good days and (there are) bad days, there are days when everything goes right and others when everything goes wrong; **je l'ai vu l'autre j.** I saw him the other day; **un j. ou l'autre** one day, some time (or other); **de j. en j.** day by day, from day to day; **nous l'attendons d'un j. à l'autre** we're expecting him any day (now); **un j. que je me promenais** one day when I was out walking; **un (beau) j.** *je vous le dirai* one day or some day I'll tell you; **un beau j., il décida de …** one day he decided to …; **du j. au lendemain** overnight, from one day to the next; **tous les jours** every day, each day; **mes vête-** ments de tous les jours my everyday clothes; **vivre au j. le j.** *(sans faire de prévisions sur l'avenir)* to live from day to day; *(financièrement)* to live from hand to mouth; *Bourse* **argent au j. le j.** overnight money; **leur beauté n'est que d'un j.** their beauty is ephemeral or short-lived; **à j.** up to date; **mettre à j.** to update, to bring up to date; **tenir à j.** to keep up to date; **un de ces jours** one of these days; **j. de présence/d'absence** day at/off work; *Fam* **à un de ces jours!** I'll be seeing you!, see you soon! SEE GRAMMAR A81–2; B60–2

3 *(date)* day; **quel j. (du mois) sommes-nous?** what's the date (today)?, what's today's date?; **un j. d'été** a summer('s) day; **j. de Noël** Christmas Day; **le j. de mes 20 ans** my 20th birthday; **fixer un j. pour qch/pour faire qch** to fix a day or date for sth/for doing sth; **il y a six ans j. pour j.** six years ago to the (very) day; **à ce j. nous n'avons toujours pas reçu votre lettre** to date we still have not received your letter; **le journal du j.** today's paper; **quelles sont les nouvelles du j.?** what is today's news?; **le grand j.** the big day; **plat du j.** *(au restaurant)* dish of the day, today's special; **jours de consultation: mardi et jeudi de 9h à 18h** consulting or surgery hours: Tuesday and Thursday, 9 a.m. to 6 p.m.; **ce n'est pas le j. du boucher, aujourd'hui** this isn't the day the butcher comes; **décidément ce n'est pas mon j.!** it really isn't my day today!; **vas-y, je suis dans un bon j.** go ahead, I'm in a good mood today; **je t'invite, c'est mon j. de bonté** my treat, I'm feeling generous today

4 *(époque)* **de nos jours** these days, nowadays; **l'homme du j.** the man of the moment; **les beaux jours** the fine days of summer; **ils ont connu des jours difficiles** they've been through or seen hard times; **vieux jours** old age; **je l'ai connue dans ses beaux jours** I knew her in her prime

5 *(vie)* **donner le j. à un enfant** to give birth to a child; **il vit le j. à Paris** he was born in Paris; **mettre fin à ses jours** to put an end to one's life

6 *(éclairage)* light; *Fig* **jeter le j. sur une affaire** to throw (some) light on a matter; **voir qch sous un j. nouveau/sous son vrai j.** to see sth in a new light/in its true light; **se montrer sous son vrai j.** to show one's true colours; **présenter une affaire sous un j. favorable** to present a matter in a favourable light

7 *(ouverture)* *(entre des planches, tuiles, rideaux etc)* gap, chink; *(d'un escalier)* well; **pratiquer un j. dans un mur** to cut an opening or a hole in a wall; *Fig* **percer qn/qch à j.** to see through sb/sth; *Fig* **mettre qch au j.** to bring sth to light; *Fig* **au grand j.** publicly

8 *Couture* **à jours** *(passementerie, tricot, chemisier)* openwork; **draps ornés de jours** sheets decorated with openwork

9 *Mil* **service de j.** day duty; **officier de j.** duty officer; **être de j.** to be on (day) duty; **travailler de j.** to work days; **hôpital de j.** day hospital, *Am* outpatient clinic; **infirmière de j.** day nurse

10 *Beaux-Arts (d'un tableau)* light

▸▸ **j. de bourse** trading day; **j. chômé** public holiday; **j. de congé** day off; **j. des élections** election or polling day; **j. férié** public holiday, *Br* bank holiday; **j. franc** clear day; *Com* **j. de grâce** day of grace; *Fin* **jours d'intérêt** interest days; *Fin* **j. de liquidation** settlement day; **j. ouvrable** or **ouvré** working day; **j. de paiement** payment day; **j. plein** clear day; **j. de repos** day off; **j. du scrutin** election or polling day; *Bourse* **j. du terme** term day; *Fin* **j. de valeur** value date

Jourdain [ʒurdɛ̃] **NM le J.** the Jordan

journal, -aux [ʒurnal, -o] **NM 1** *(publication)* (news)paper; *(spécialisé)* journal; **c'est dans** le j. it's in the paper; **j. du matin/du soir** morning/evening paper; **j. gratuit** free paper, free sheet, giveaway paper; **les journaux** *(la presse)* the newspapers, the press; **marchand de journaux** newsagent, *Am* news dealer; *(dans la rue)* (news)paper seller or vendor, newsvendor; **livreur de journaux** paperboy, *Am* newsboy; **dans du (papier) j.** (wrapped) in newspaper; *Radio Vieilli* **j. parlé** radio news; *TV* **j. (télévisé)** (television) news

2 *(bureau)* office; *(équipe)* newspaper (staff); **le j. va déménager** the (news)paper will be moving (office)

3 *Radio, TV (informations)* news; **ce j. est présenté par…** the news is presented or *Br* read by…

4 *(récit d'événements, d'expériences)* journal, record; *Fin* ledger; *Ordinat* log; *Vieilli (livre)* **j.** account book; **tenir un j.** to keep a journal

▸▸ *Compta* **j. des achats** purchase ledger; *Compta* **j. analytique** analysis ledger; **j. d'annonces** advertising newspaper; *Fin* **j. de banque** bank book; *Naut* **j. de bord** log (book); *Compta* **j. de caisse** cash book; **j. sur CD-Rom** CD-Rom newspaper; **j. à diffusion contrôlée** controlled circulation newspaper; **j. à diffusion nationale** national newspaper, national; *Compta* **j. des effets à payer** bills payable ledger; *Compta* **j. des effets à recevoir** bills receivable ledger; **j. électronique** electronic newspaper; **j. d'entreprise** staff magazine, company magazine; **j. factures-clients** sales invoice ledger; *Compta* **j. factures-fournisseurs** purchase invoice ledger; **j. grand format** broadsheet; **j. gratuit** free paper, giveaway paper; **j. d'information** newspaper; **j. interne d'entreprise** in-house or staff news-sheet or newsletter, company magazine; **j. intime** diary; *Can* **j. jaune** scandal sheet; **j. en ligne** online newspaper; *Ordinat* **j. logique** logical log; **j. de mode** fashion magazine; *Admin* **J. officiel** = French government publication giving information to the public about new laws, government business, new companies etc, *Br* ≃ Hansard, *Am* ≃ Federal Register; **j. d'opinion** = political weekly/monthly (with a particular stance); *Compta* **j. de paie** wages ledger; **j. de petites annonces** advertising magazine; **j. plein format** broadsheet newspaper; **j. professionnel** trade journal; *Compta* **j. des rendus** returns ledger or book; **j. à scandale** scandal sheet; **j. à sensation** scandal sheet; **j. sportif** sports paper; **j. télévisé** television news; **j. de trésorerie** cash book; *Compta* **j. des ventes** sales ledger; **j. vidéo** video diary

> **Journal officiel**
> This bulletin prints information about new laws and summaries of parliamentary debates, and informs the public of any important government business. When new companies are established, they are obliged by law to publish an announcement in the "Journal officiel".

journaleux [ʒurnalø] **NM** *Fam Péj* hack (journalist)

journalier, -ière [ʒurnalje, -jɛr] **ADJ** *(tâche, salaire, souci)* daily
NM day labourer, *Am* day laborer

journaliser [ʒurnalize] **VT** to enter, to write up in the books

journalisme [ʒurnalism] **NM** journalism; **faire du j.** to be a journalist; **j. d'enquête** ou **d'investigation** investigative journalism; **j. de radiodiffusion** broadcast journalism; **j. de télévision** television journalism, broadcast journalism; **j. engagé** campaigning journalism; **j. militant** politically-orientated journalism; **j. sportif** sports journalism; **j. électronique** electronic journalism, EJ; **j. électronique de télévision** electronic news gathering

journaliste [ʒurnalist] **N** journalist; **j. politique/sportif/économique** political/sports/economics correspondent *or* journalist; **elle est j. au Monde** she's a journalist for *or* with Le Monde; **les journalistes de la rédaction** the editorial staff; **j. économique** economics correspondent *or* journalist; **j. politique** political correspondent *or* journalist; **j. d'investigation** investigative journalist; **j. de télévision** television journalist; *(présentateur)* newscaster; **j. indépendant** freelance journalist; **j. parlementaire** parliamentary reporter; **j. permanent(e)** staff reporter

journalistique [ʒurnalistik] **ADJ** journalistic; **style j.** journalistic style, *Péj* journalese

journée [ʒurne] **NF 1** *(par opposition à nuit)* day(time); **pendant la j.** in the daytime, during the day; **dans la j.** in the course of the day, during the day; **toute la j.** all day (long), the whole day; **il ne fait rien de la j.** he does nothing all day (long); **elle soupire/bavarde à longueur de j.** she sighs/chats for days on end; **par une belle j. d'été** on a fine summer's day
2 *(ensemble des activités)* day; **quelle j., je suis épuisée!** what a day, I'm exhausted!; **j'ai eu une j. bien remplie/mouvementée** I've had a very full *or* busy/eventful day; **j. de travail** *(jour non chômé)* working day, workday; *(quantité de travail)* day's work; **journées de travail perdues** lost working days; **j. de huit heures** eight-hour day; **faire la j. continue** *(d'une personne)* to work through lunch(time); *(d'un magasin)* to remain open at lunchtime; **travailler à la j.** to work by the day; *Vieilli* **homme de j.** (day) labourer *or Am* laborer; *Vieilli* **femme de j.** cleaning lady, *Br* char(woman), *Br* daily (help); *Vieilli* **faire des journées** *(d'une femme de ménage)* to do cleaning work, to work as a cleaning lady SEE GRAMMAR B61
3 *(salaire)* day's pay *or* wages; **tu as gagné ta j.** you've earned your (day's) pay *or* wages; *Iron* **j'ai gagné ma j.!** it's not my day!
4 *Vieilli (distance)* day's journey; **Valence était à une j. de Lyon** Valence was a day's journey from Lyons
▸▸*Compta* **j. comptable** accounting day; *Aut* **j. jaune** = day with no serious motorway congestion; *Aut* **j. noire** = day with very severe motorway congestion; *Aut* **j. orange** = day with some motorway congestion; *Pol* **les journées (parlementaires) du parti** *Br* ≃ the Party Conference, *Am* ≃ the Party Convention; **j. portes ouvertes** open day, *Am* open house; *Aut* **j. rouge** = day with heavy motorway congestion

> Il faut noter que le nom anglais **journey** est un faux ami. Il signifie **voyage, trajet**.

journellement [ʒurnɛlmɑ̃] **ADV** daily, every day

joute [ʒut] **NF 1** *(combat médiéval)* joust, tilt **2** *(jeu actuel)* **j. nautique** *ou* **lyonnaise** water joust; *Fig* **j. oratoire** verbal sparring (match) **3** *Can Sport* game, match; *(duel)* joust, duel

jouter [ʒute] **VI 1** *(combattre)* *(à cheval)* to joust, to tilt; *(sur l'eau)* to joust **2** *(rivaliser)* to spar (**avec qn** with sb)

jouteur, -euse [ʒutœr, -øz] **N 1** *(dans une discussion, un débat)* adversary **2** *(à cheval)* jouster, tilter; *(sur l'eau)* jouster

jouvence [ʒuvɑ̃s] **NF** *Litt* **cela a été un bain** *ou* **une cure de j.** it has rejuvenated me, it has made me feel years younger

jouvenceau, -eaux [ʒuvɑ̃so] **NM** *Arch* stripling, youth, lad

jouvencelle [ʒuvɑ̃sɛl] **NF** *Arch* maiden, damsel

jouxter [ʒukste] **VT** *Litt* to adjoin, to be adjacent to

jovial, -iale, -iaux, -iales [ʒɔvjal, -o] **ADJ** jovial, jolly

jovialement [ʒɔvjalmɑ̃] **ADV** jovially

jovialité [ʒɔvjalite] **NF** joviality, jolliness

joyau, -aux [ʒwajo] **NM** jewel, gem; **les joyaux de la couronne** the crown jewels; *Fig* **j. de la civilisation italienne** jewel (in the crown) of Italian civilization; **le Tadj Mahall est un véritable j. de l'art indien** the Taj Mahal is a real jewel *or* gem of Indian art

joyeusement [ʒwajøzmɑ̃] **ADV** joyfully, *Litt* joyously

joyeux, -euse [ʒwajø, -øz] **ADJ** *(personne, équipe)* joyful, *Litt* joyous; *(cris, nouvelles, mine)* joyful, cheerful; **une bande de j. drilles** a group of cheerful fellows; **joyeuses Pâques!** Happy Easter!; **j. anniversaire, Louis!** Happy Birthday, Louis!; **j. Noël!** Happy *or* Merry Christmas!
NFPL *très Fam* **joyeuses** *(testicules)* balls, nuts, *Br* bollocks

JT [ʒite] **NM** *(abrév* **journal télévisé)** TV news

jubé [ʒybe] **NM** *Archit* rood loft *or* screen, jube

jubilaire [ʒybilɛr] **ADJ** **année j.** jubilee year

jubilation [ʒybilasjɔ̃] **NF** jubilation

jubilé [ʒybile] **NM** jubilee

jubiler [ʒybile] **VI** to be jubilant; *(méchamment)* to gloat; **il jubilait de me voir humilié** he gloated over my humiliation

jucher [ʒyʃe] **VT** to perch
VI *(d'oiseaux) (pour dormir)* to roost
VPR se jucher *(d'oiseaux, de personnes)* to perch

juchoir [ʒyʃwar] **NM** roost(ing place); *(perche)* perch

judaïcité [ʒydaisite] **NF** *Rel* Jewishness

judaïque [ʒydaik] **ADJ** *Rel (loi, héritage)* Judaic, Jewish

judaïser [ʒydaize] **VI** to Judaize

judaïsme [ʒydaism] **NM** Judaism

judas [ʒyda] **NM 1** *Bible* **J.** Judas; **baiser de J.** Judas kiss **2** *(traître)* Judas, traitor, betrayer **3** *(ouverture)* peephole, spyhole, judas (hole); **j. (optique)** *(avec lentille)* peephole

Judée [ʒyde] **NF** *Bible* Judaea; **arbre de J.** Judas tree

judéité [ʒydeite] **NF** Jewishness

judéo-allemand, *pl* **judéo-allemand(e)s** [ʒydeoalmɑ̃, -ād] **ADJ** Yiddish
NM *Ling* Yiddish

judéo-chrétien, -ienne [ʒydeokretjɛ̃, -jɛn] **N, ADJ** Jud(a)eo-Christian

judiciaire [ʒydisjɛr] **ADJ** *Jur (pouvoir, enquête, acte)* judicial; *(aide, autorité)* legal; *(vente)* court-ordered; **frais judiciaires** legal charges; **erreur j.** miscarriage of justice; **vente j.** sale by order of the court; **poursuites judiciaires** legal proceedings

judiciairement [ʒydisjɛrmɑ̃] **ADV** judicially

judiciarisation [ʒydisjarizasjɔ̃] **NF** judicialization

judicieusement [ʒydisjøzmɑ̃] **ADV** judiciously

judicieux, -euse [ʒydisjø, -øz] **ADJ** *(remarque, choix, personne, esprit)* sensible, *Fml* judicious; *(peu j.* injudicious; **il serait j. de téléphoner avant d'y aller** it would be sensible *or* wise to phone before going

judo [ʒydo] **NM** judo

judoka [ʒydɔka] **N** *Sport* judoka

juge [ʒyʒ] **NM 1** *Jur* judge; **Monsieur le J.** Your Honour, *Am* Your Honor, *Br* M'Lord, M'Lud; **les juges** the bench **2** *(arbitre)* judge **3** **je vous en fais j., je vous laisse j.** judge for yourself, I leave it to you to judge; **on ne peut pas à la fois être j. et partie** you can't be (the)

judge in your own case; **tu es seul j.** you alone can judge, only you can (be the) judge
▸▸**j. aux affaires matrimoniales** divorce court judge; **j. de l'application des peines** = judge responsible for supervising the way a sentence is carried out; **j. consulaire** commercial court judge; **j. des enfants** juvenile court judge; **j. d'instance** police court magistrate, ≃ Justice of the Peace; **j. d'instruction** examining magistrate *(in commercial cases)*; *Tennis* **j. de ligne** line judge; *Arch* **j. de paix** police court magistrate, ≃ Justice of the Peace, *Arch* conciliation magistrate *(in commercial cases)*; **j. rapporteur** inquiry judge; **j. des référés** = judge sitting in chambers to deal provisionally with matters of special urgency; **j. de touche** *Ftbl* linesman; *Rugby* touch judge

jugé [ʒyʒe] **NM tirer au j.** to fire blind; **calculer/estimer au j.** to calculate/estimate roughly

jugeable [ʒyʒabl] **ADJ** *Jur* subject to a legal decision

jugement [ʒyʒmɑ̃] **NM 1** *Jur (d'une affaire)* trial; **faire passer qn en j.** to bring sb to trial, to put sb on trial; **mettre en j.** to commit for trial, to arraign; **mise en j.** committal for trial, arraignment; **passer en j.** to be brought to trial, to stand trial, to go on trial; **j. par défaut** judg(e)ment by default
2 *Jur (décision)* decision, award; *(dans des affaires criminelles)* sentence; **prononcer un j.** to pass judg(e)ment; **rendre un j. arbitral** to make an award; **j. provisoire** decree nisi; **j. déclaratif de faillite** adjudication in bankruptcy
3 *(opinion)* judg(e)ment, opinion; **porter un j. sur qch** to pass judg(e)ment *or* give an opinion on sth; **j. de valeur** value judg(e)ment; **soumettre qch au j. de qn** to submit sth to sb for his/her judg(e)ment
4 *(discernement)* judg(e)ment; **faire preuve de j.** to show (sound) judg(e)ment *or* good sense; **manquer de j.** to lack (good) judg(e)ment; **erreur de j.** error of judg(e)ment
▸▸**J. dernier** Last Judg(e)ment; **le jour du J. dernier** Judg(e)ment Day, Doomsday; *Hist* **J. de dieu** *(ordalie)* ordeal

jugeote [ʒyʒɔt] **NF** *Fam* common sense, *Br* gumption, *Br* nous; **avoir de la j.** to have one's head screwed on (the right way), to know what's what; **il n'a pas deux sous de j.** he hasn't got a scrap of common sense, *Br* he's got no gumption at all

JUGER[1] [ʒyʒe] *(je jugeai(s); n. jugeons)* **VT 1** *Jur (affaire)* to try, to judge; *(prévenu)* to try; *(demande, litige)* to adjudicate, to arbitrate
2 *(donner son avis sur) (situation, candidat, qualités de qn, livre etc)* to judge; *(condamner) (personne)* to judge; **j. les gens sur la mine** to judge people by *or* from appearances
3 *(croire)* **j. que** to think *or* consider that, to be of the opinion that; **on le jugeait fou** people thought *or* considered him mad; **j. à propos/nécessaire/superflu de faire qch** to think *or* consider it advisable/necessary/superfluous to do sth; **j'ai jugé bon de vous prévenir** I thought *or* considered it right *or* a good idea to warn you
VI 1 to judge; **à toi de j.** it's up to you to judge; **tu ne peux pas j.** you're in no position to judge
2 j. de qch to judge sth; **j. de qn** to form an opinion of sb, to judge sb; **j. favorablement d'un candidat** to form a favourable opinion of a candidate, to judge a candidate favourably; **jugez de ma surprise** imagine my surprise; **à en j. par ...** to judge by ..., judging *or* going by ...; **autant que je puisse en j.** as far as I can judge, to the best of my judg(e)ment; **à vous d'en j.** it's up to you to judge
VPR se juger to be judged; **un homme se juge par ses actions** a man is judged by his actions

juger² NM = jugé

jugulaire [ʒygylɛr] ADJ *Anat (veine)* jugular NF 1 *Anat* jugular (vein) 2 *(de casque)* chin strap

juguler [ʒygyle] VT 1 *(révolte, rébellion)* to put down, to suppress, to stifle; *(inflation)* to curb, to damp down, to check; *(épidémie)* to arrest, to halt 2 *Arch* to strangle, to throttle

juif, juive [ʒɥif, ʒɥiv] ADJ Jewish N J. Jew; le J. errant the Wandering Jew NM *Anat Fam* le petit j. the funny *or Am* crazy bone

juillet [ʒɥijɛ] NM July; en j. in July; au mois de j. in (the month of) July; le sept j. (on) the seventh of July, (on) July the seventh, *Am* (on) July seventh; le 14 j. Bastille Day *(day of national celebration in France)* SEE GRAMMAR A81–2; B61–2

> **La fête du 14 juillet**
> The celebrations to mark the anniversary of the storming of the Bastille begin on 13 July with outdoor public dances ("les bals du 14 Juillet") and firework displays, and continue on the 14th with a military parade in the morning. Firework displays are also held on the evening of "Bastille Day".

juilletiste [ʒɥijetist] N July holiday-maker *or Am* vacationer

juin [ʒɥɛ̃] NM June; en j. in June; au mois de j. in (the month of) June; le sept j. (on) the seventh of June, (on) June the seventh, *Am* (on) June seventh SEE GRAMMAR A81–2; B61–2

juiverie [ʒɥivri] NF *Arch (juifs, quartier juif)* Jewry

jujube [ʒyʒyb] NM 1 *Bot, Pharm* jujube 2 *Can (friandise)* fruit-flavoured sweet

jujubier [ʒyʒybje] NM *Bot* jujube (tree)

juke-box, *pl* **juke-boxes** [(d)ʒykbɔks] NM jukebox

julep [ʒylɛp] NM *Pharm* julep

Jules [ʒyl] N Julius; J. César Julius Caesar

jules [ʒyl] NM 1 *très Fam (mari, petit ami)* man, guy 2 *très Fam (vase de nuit)* chamber pot, *Br* jerry

julien, -ienne¹ [ʒyljɛ̃, -jɛn] ADJ *Antiq* Julian; année julienne Julian year

julienne² NF 1 *(plante)* rocket 2 *Culin (soupe)* julienne; j. de légumes vegetables julienne, julienne of vegetables 3 *Zool (poisson)* ling

jumbo(-jet), *pl* **jumbo-jets** [(d)ʒœmbo(dʒɛt)] NM *Fam* jumbo (jet)

jumeau, -elle, *pl* **jumeaux, -elles** [ʒymo, -ɛl] ADJ 1 frères jumeaux twin brothers; sœurs jumelles twin sisters; lits jumeaux twin beds; maisons jumelles semi-detached houses 2 *(fruits)* double NM *Anat* gemellus muscle N *(frère)* twin (brother); *(sosie)* double, twin; jumelle twin (sister); vrais jumeaux identical twins; faux jumeaux fraternal twins

jumelage [ʒymlaʒ] NM 1 *(assemblage) (de poutres, roues)* coupling, pairing 2 *(de villes)* twinning; j. d'entreprises twinning of companies

jumelé [ʒymle] ADJ maison jumelée semi-detached house; villes jumelées twin(ned) towns; *Aut* pneus jumelés twin *or* dual tyres; Courses de chevaux pari j. dual forecast *(of first two horses in a race)*

jumeler [ʒymle] VT *(je jumelle, n. jumelons; je jumellerai) (villes)* to twin (avec with); *(mât, poutre)* to fish, to reinforce

jumelles [ʒymɛl] NFPL 1 *Opt* (paire de) j. (pair of) binoculars; j. de théâtre opera

glasses; j. de campagne field glasses VOIR GRAMMAIRE A10 2 *Aut (spring)* shackles

jument [ʒymɑ̃] NF mare; j. poulinière brood mare

jumping [(d)ʒœmpiŋ] NM *Équitation* show jumping

jungle [ʒœ̃gl] NF jungle; *Fig* c'est une vraie j. *(le monde du travail etc)* it's a jungle out there, it's a real rat race, it's dog eat dog; la j. de la haute finance the financial jungle; la loi de la j. the law of the jungle

junior [ʒynjɔr] ADJ INV junior; *Hum* M. Martin j. Mr Martin junior; *Com* style *ou* mode j. junior fashion N *Sport* junior

junk bond [dʒœnkbɔd] NM *Fin* junk bond

junkie [dʒœnki] N *Fam* junkie

Junon [ʒynɔ̃] N *Astron, Myth* Juno

junte [ʒœ̃t] NF *Mil* junta

jupe [ʒyp] NF 1 skirt; j. à fleurs/à carreaux floral/checked skirt; j. droite/plissée straight/pleated skirt; *Fam* pendu aux jupes de sa mère tied to his mother's apron strings; *Vieilli* retrousser ses jupes to hitch up one's skirts 2 *Tech* skirt; *Aut* j. de pare-chocs bumper skirt

jupe-culotte, *pl* **jupes-culottes** NF culotte(s), divided skirt

jupette [ʒypɛt] NF skirt; *Sport* j. de tennis tennis skirt

Jupiter [ʒypitɛr] N *Myth* Jupiter, Jove NF *Astron* Jupiter

jupon [ʒypɔ̃] NM 1 underskirt, slip, (waist) petticoat 2 *Vieilli, Péj* courir le j. to chase after women, to chase the girls; coureur de j. womanizer

Jura [ʒyra] NM *(massif)* le J. the Jura (Mountains)

jurassien, -ienne [ʒyrasjɛ̃, -jɛn] ADJ of/from the Jura N J. *(natif)* native of the Jura; *(habitant)* inhabitant of the Jura

jurassique [ʒyrasik] ADJ, NM *Géol* Jurassic

juratoire [ʒyratwar] ADJ *Jur* caution j. guarantee given on oath

juré, -ée [ʒyre] ADJ *(qui a prêté serment)* sworn; expert j. sworn expert; *Fig* ennemi j. sworn enemy N juror, juryman; jurée juror, jurywoman; les jurés the jury; mesdames, messieurs les jurés ladies and gentlemen of the jury; un des jurés one of the jury, a member of the jury

jurer [ʒyre] VT to swear; j. sa foi to pledge one's word; j. sur la Bible to swear on the Bible; j. fidélité à qn to swear *or* pledge loyalty to sb; faire j. le secret à qn to swear sb to secrecy; j. de faire qch to swear *or* vow to do sth; j. de se venger to swear *or* vow (to take) revenge; je vous jure que c'est vrai I swear (to you) that it's the truth; *Fam* je le jure sur la tête de ma mère/mon père cross my heart and hope to die; j. ses grands dieux to swear blind, to swear to God; j'en jurerais I would swear to it; c'est drôle, j'aurais juré que la voiture était bleue that's funny, I could have sworn that the car was blue; *Prov* il ne faut j. de rien you never can tell VI 1 *(blasphémer)* to swear, to curse; *Fam* j. comme un charretier to swear like a trooper 2 *(des couleurs, vêtements etc)* to clash (avec with) VPR se jurer 1 *(l'un l'autre)* se j. un éternel amour to swear eternal love; les époux se sont juré fidélité the married couple swore to be faithful to each other 2 *(soi-même)* se j. de faire qch to swear *or* vow to do sth; se j. que to swear *or* vow that

juridiction [ʒyridiksjɔ̃] NF *(compétence)* jurisdiction; *(tribunaux)* courts (of law); sous

la j. de ... within the jurisdiction of ...; j. nationale national jurisdiction; j. commerciale commercial jurisdiction

juridictionnel, -elle [ʒyridiksjɔnɛl] ADJ jurisdictional

juridique [ʒyridik] ADJ legal; conseiller j. legal adviser; il a une formation j. he has studied law; un vide j. a gap in the law

juridiquement [ʒyridikmɑ̃] ADV legally

jurisconsulte [ʒyriskɔ̃sylt] NM jurisconsult, legal expert

jurisprudence [ʒyrisprydɑ̃s] NF *(doctrine)* jurisprudence; *(décision)* precedent *(of a case)*; *(ensemble des décisions)* case law; faire j. to set a precedent

juriste [ʒyrist] N *(spécialiste du droit)* jurist, legal expert; *(étudiant)* law student; j. d'entreprise company lawyer

juron [ʒyrɔ̃] NM oath, curse; *(gros mot)* swearword; lâcher *ou* pousser un j. to curse, to swear

jury [ʒyri] NM 1 *Jur* jury; dresser la liste du j. to draw up the jury list; membre du j. member of the jury, juror VOIR GRAMMAIRE A11 2 *(d'une exposition, d'un jeu-concours, d'un prix)* (panel of) judges; j. (d'examen) examining board, board of examiners; j. de concours d'entrée board for the entrance examination; *Mktg* j. de consommateurs consumer jury

jus [ʒy] NM 1 *(de pamplemousse, de tomate etc)* juice; j. de fruit fruit juice; j. de fruit pressé freshly squeezed fruit juice; j. de poire/d'abricot pear/apricot juice; plein de j. juicy, full of juice; un j. d'orange, s'il vous plaît! an orange juice, please 2 *Culin (de viande)* juice(s); *(sauce)* gravy; j. de viande juice(s) from the meat, meat juices; mon rôti n'a pas fait beaucoup de j. my roast hasn't given off *or* produced much juice; cuire *ou* mijoter dans son j. *(de volaille, rôti)* to stew in its own juice; *Fig Fam* to stew in one's own juice 3 *Arg* il est tombé au j. he fell in(to) the water; au j.! into the water with him/her! 4 *Arg (café)* coffee 5 *Fam (courant électrique)* juice; j'ai pris du j.! I got an electric shock!; mets le j.! switch on! 6 *Fam (essence)* juice 7 *Fam* ça vaut le j. it's really something ►► *Fam* j. de chaussettes *(café)* dishwater

jusant [ʒyzɑ̃] NM ebb (tide)

jusqu'au-boutisme [ʒyskobutism] NM INV *Fam* hardline attitude; je n'aime pas son j. I don't like the way he always has to go the whole hog *or* his hardline attitude

jusqu'au-boutiste, *pl* **jusqu'au-boutistes** [ʒyskobutist] N *Fam* hardliner, extremist; *(fidèle à un parti, des principes)* diehard ADJ hardline

JUSQUE [ʒysk(ə)] PRÉP 1 *(espace, mesure)* up to, as far as; jusqu'ici up to here, as far as here; venez jusqu'ici come over here; j.-là up to *or* as far as there *or* that point; jusqu'où? how far?; depuis Londres jusqu'à Paris all the way from London to Paris; avoir de l'eau jusqu'à la taille to have water (coming) right up to one's waist, to be waist-deep in water; jusqu'au bout (de la rue) (right) to the end (of the street); *Fig* aller jusqu'au bout d'un raisonnement/d'une action to follow an argument/action through; *Fig* jusqu'à un certain point up to a certain point, to a certain extent; *Fig* jusqu'où ira-t-il? how far will he go?; aller jusqu'à faire qch to go so far as to do sth; il a poussé la curiosité/le culot jusqu'à me demander si ... he was so curious/cheeky as to ask me if ..., his curiosity/cheek was such that he asked me if ...; j. chez lui (up) to his door; rougir jusqu'aux oreilles to blush to the roots of one's hair, to go as red as a beetroot; la nouvelle est venue jusqu'à lui the news reached him; ce

scandale va remonter jusqu'au directeur this scandal will go as far up as the director, this scandal will go right to the top; **nous avions de la paille j. dans nos sous-vêtements** the straw even got inside our underwear; **compter jusqu'à dix** to count (up) to ten; **je veux bien mettre jusqu'à 200 euros** I'm prepared to put in up to 200 euros; **jusqu'à concurrence de 2000 euros** (up) to 2,000 euros; **jusqu'à 250 gr** not exceeding 250g, up to 250g
2 *(temps)* until, till; **attendez jusqu'après les vacances** wait until *or* till after the holidays; **jusqu'ici, jusqu'à maintenant, jusqu'à présent, j.-là** *(en référence au présent)* until now, up to now, to date, as yet, so far; **j.-là, jusqu'alors** *(en référence au passé)* until then, up to then; **jusqu'ici** *ou* **j.-là, tout va bien** so far so good; **jusqu'à hier/dix heures** until *or* up to yesterday/ten o'clock; **jusqu'à (l'âge de) 15 ans** up to the age of 15, up to 15 (years old); **jusqu'à aujourd'hui** until today; **jusqu'à fin mai** until the end of May; **jusqu'à nouvel ordre** until further notice; **jusqu'à plus ample informé** pending further information, until further information is available; **jusqu'à mon dernier jour** to my dying day; **jusqu'au jour** *ou* **moment où ...** until the time when ..., until ...; **si nous remontons jusqu'en** *ou* **jusqu'à 1800** if we go back as far as 1800, if we go right back to 1800
3 *(indique un point extrême)* **tous jusqu'au dernier** every last one (of them); **jusqu'à dix personnes l'ont vu** as many as ten people saw it; **tout en lui, jusqu'à son sourire, a changé** everything about him, right down to *or* even his smile, has changed; **il se montrait sévère jusqu'à la cruauté** he was severe to the point of cruelty; *Fam* **s'en mettre j.-là** to stuff oneself *or* one's face; *Fam* **en avoir j.-là** to have had it up to here (**de** with)
CONJ jusqu'à ce que ... + *sub*, *Vieilli* **jusqu'à tant que ...** + *sub* until ..., till ...; **jusqu'à ce que les portes soient fermées** until *or* till the doors are shut

jusques [ʒyskə] PRÉP *Arch, Litt* = **jusque**; **j. et y compris ...** [ʒyskəzeikɔ̃pri] up to and including ...

justaucorps [ʒystokɔr] NM **1** *(pour la gymnastique)* leotard **2** *(pourpoint)* jerkin

JUSTE [ʒyst]

| ADJ | fair **1** ▪ just **1** ▪ right **2, 3** ▪ accurate **2** ▪ tight **5** |
| ADV | accurately **1** ▪ exactly **2** ▪ right **2** ▪ just **2, 3** ▪ only **3** |

ADJ **1** *(équitable)* *(personne, décision, punition, revendication)* fair, just; **ce n'est pas j.** it's not fair, it's unfair; **il est en colère, et à j. titre!** he's angry, and quite rightly (so) *or* and with good reason!; **ce n'est que j. récompense** it's nothing more than he/she/*etc* deserves, he/she/*etc* thoroughly deserves it; **ce n'est que j. récompense s'il a eu le premier prix** it's only right that he got first prize, he thoroughly deserves his first prize; **j. indignation** righteous indignation; **j. colère** righteous *or* justifiable anger; **elle se mit dans une j. colère** she became justifiably angry; **être j. avec** *ou* **vis-à-vis de** *ou* **envers qn** to be fair to sb; **pour être j. envers elle** to be fair to her, to give her her due; *Vieilli* **j. ciel!** heavens above!
2 *(exact)* *(calcul, réponse, données)* right, accurate, correct; *(raisonnement)* sound; **quelle est l'heure j.?** what is the right *or* exact time?; **le mot j.** the exact *or* right word; **se faire une idée j. de la situation** to get a true *or* an accurate picture of the situation; **j. milieu** happy medium; **votre réponse n'est pas j.** your answer is not right *or* is wrong *or* is incorrect; **c'est j.** that's right; **c'est très j. ce**

que vous dites-là what you say is quite right; **balance j.** accurate scales; **ma balance/ma montre n'est pas très j.** my scales are not/ my watch is not very accurate *or* exact *or* precise; **ma montre est j.** my watch is right *or* accurate; **arriver à l'heure j.** to arrive right on time, *Fam* to arrive on the dot
3 *Mus (en accord) (note)* right; **quarte j.** perfect fourth
4 *(qui suffit à peine) (indemnité)* scanty; **c'est bien j.** *(plat, boisson etc)* there's barely *or* scarcely enough to go round; **un aussi petit gâteau pour six, tu ne trouves pas que c'est trop j.?** do you think such a little cake is anywhere near enough for six?; **une bouteille de champagne pour sept, c'est j.** one bottle of champagne for seven is cutting it a bit fine; **cent euros pour une semaine, c'est un peu j.!** a hundred euros for a week, it's not a lot!; *Com* **au plus j. prix** at a rock bottom price, at a keen price; **ses résultats sont trop justes pour qu'elle passe dans la classe supérieure** she is not quite good enough to move up a class
5 *(trop petit) (chaussures)* tight(-fitting); *(vêtement)* tight(-fitting), skimpy; **je te donne cette veste, moi elle m'est un peu j.** you can have this jacket, it's a bit tight on me
6 *Fam (gêné financièrement)* **on est un peu justes en ce moment** we're a bit pushed for money *or* strapped for cash at the moment
ADV **1** *(avec exactitude) (viser, parler)* accurately, **frapper j.** to land a perfect blow; *Fig* to strike *or* hit home; **je ne pouvais pas frapper plus j. en mentionnant ce sujet** I couldn't have struck *or* hit home harder when I mentioned this subject; **chanter j.** to sing in tune; **elle ne chante pas très j.** she can't sing in tune very well; **sonner j.** *(cloche, carillon)* to ring in tune; *Fig (discours, arguments)* to ring true; *Fig* **voir j.** to guess correctly *or* right; **raisonner j.** to argue soundly; **deviner** *ou Fam* **tomber j.** to guess right; **tout j.!** you said it!, that's right!
2 *(précisément)* exactly, precisely, just; **il est midi j.** it's exactly *or* precisely twelve o'clock; **arriver à dix heures j.** to arrive on the stroke of ten, to arrive at ten o'clock sharp *or Fam* on the dot; **c'est j. au coin/en face/à côté** it's just *or* right on the corner/opposite/next door; **j. au milieu** right in the middle; **ça fait dix euros (tout) j.** that's ten euros exactly; **c'est j. l'homme qu'il nous faut** he's just the man *or* he's the very man we want *or* need; **c'est j. ce qu'il me fallait** it's just what I wanted, it's the very thing, it's just the job; *Iron* **un coup de téléphone de ma mère, c'est j. ce qu'il me fallait!** a phone call from my mother, that's all I needed!
3 *(seulement, à peine)* just, only; **j'ai bu j. une gorgée pour goûter** I just *or* only drank a mouthful to get the taste; **mets-m'en j. un fond s'il te plaît** give me just *or* only give me a drop, please; **c'est tout j. s'il sait lire** he can only just *or* he can barely read; **il ne manque jamais son train, mais c'est tout j.** he never misses his train, but he cuts it fine *or* it's a close thing; **c'est tout j. si elle ne m'a pas raccroché au nez!** she very nearly hung up on me!; **avoir j. le temps (de faire qch)** to have just (enough) time (to do sth); **vous avez tout j. le temps** you haven't a moment to spare; **j. à temps** just in time, in the nick of time; *Ind* just in time; **je suis arrivée j. à temps pour le voir** I arrived just in time to see him; **arriver j. à l'heure** to arrive just in time *or* in the nick of time; **il échappa tout j. à la mort** he narrowly escaped death; **on a tout j. évité la catastrophe** we narrowly avoided a catastrophe; **ils ont tout j. fini de manger** they've very only just finished eating
4 *(trop peu)* **voir** *ou* **prévoir** *ou* **calculer trop j.** not to allow enough, to allow too little (**pour** for)

5 au j., tu fais quoi cet été? by the way, what are you doing this summer?; **je ne sais pas au j. si ...** I don't exactly know whether ...; **comme de j.** of course, as usual, naturally, as one would expect
N *Bible* **les justes** the just, the righteous

justement [ʒystəmɑ̃] ADV **1** *(avec justesse)* rightly; **comme tu le disais si j. hier** as you so rightly said yesterday; **je lui ai j. fait remarquer que ...** I rightly pointed out to him that ... **2** *(avec justice)* justly, rightly; **être j. récompensé** to be justly rewarded **3** *(précisément)* exactly, precisely; **je vais faire des courses – tiens, j., si tu pouvais m'acheter ...** I'm going shopping – oh, well, if you could buy me ...; **voici j. la lettre que j'attendais** this is exactly *or* precisely the letter *or* here is the very letter I was waiting for; **j'ai toujours voulu voir Venise – j., on y va** I've always wanted to visit Venice – well that's just *or* exactly *or* precisely where we're going; **tu ne vas pas partir sans lui dire au revoir? – si, j.!** you're not going without saying goodbye to him? – that's precisely *or* exactly what I'm doing! *or* indeed I am!; **c'est drôle, on parlait de lui et j. le voilà** that's funny, we were just talking about him and here he is; **j., à ce propos, je voulais te dire que ...** well, while we're on the subject, I wanted to tell you that ...; **ah, vous tombez bien, j. je voulais vous parler de ...** ah, you've come at the right moment, I was just wanting to talk to you about ...

justesse [ʒystes] NF **1** *(précision) (d'une balance, d'un instrument de mesure)* accuracy, precision, exactness; *(d'une opinion)* soundness; *(d'une expression)* aptness, appropriateness; *(d'une comparaison)* exactness; **raisonner avec j.** to argue soundly **2 de j.** (only) just; **j'ai eu mon train de j.** I (only) just got my train

justice [ʒystis] NF **1** *(équité)* justice; **c'est j., ce n'est que j.** it's only right *or* fair *or* just; *Hum* **il n'y a pas de j.!** there's no justice (in the world)!; **demander j./que j. soit faite** to demand justice/that justice be done; **faire régner la j.** to establish justice; **en toute** *ou* **bonne j.** in all fairness; **avec j.** *(agir)* justly, in a just manner; **faire** *ou* **rendre j. à qn** to do justice to sb, to give sb his/her due; **se faire j.** *(à soi-même)* to take the law into one's own hands; *(se suicider)* to take one's own life, to commit suicide; **faire j. de qch** to judge sth for what it is **2** *Jur* **la j.** the law; **la j. civile/militaire/administrative** civil/military/administrative law; **gens de j.** *(juges)* magistrates; *(avocats)* lawyers; **action en j.** action at law; **aller en j.** to go to law; **poursuivre qn en j.** to bring proceedings against sb, to take legal action against sb, to take sb to court; **traduire qn en j.** to bring sb before the courts

justiciable [ʒystisjabl] ADJ *Jur* **j. d'un tribunal** justiciable to *or* in a court, amenable to a court; *Méd* **cas j. d'un certain traitement** case in which a certain treatment is indicated
N person subject to be tried

justicier, -ière [ʒystisje, -jɛr] N **1** dispenser of justice, righter of wrongs **2** *Jur Vieilli* dispenser of justice, justiciary

justifiable [ʒystifjabl] ADJ justifiable; **peu j.** unjustifiable

justificateur, -trice [ʒystifikatœr, -tris] ADJ justifying, *Fml* justificatory
N *Typ* justifier

justificatif, -ive [ʒystifikatif, -iv] ADJ justificatory; **pièce justificative** *Com* voucher (copy); *Admin (document écrit)* written proof; *Jur* relevant document; **pièces justificatives** *(pour une inscription)* supporting documents
NM **1** *Admin* written proof; *Jur* relevant do-

cument **2** *(exemplaire d'un journal)* free copy *(of newspaper sent to those who have an
advertisement or a review etc in it)*; **j. de paiement** proof of payment

justification [ʒystifikasjɔ̃] **NF 1** *(explication)* justification; **demander/chercher des
justifications** to demand/seek justification;
avez-vous une j. de votre absence d'hier? is
there any justification for *or* can you justify
your absence yesterday?; **cela ne doit pas
être une j. de la violence** that cannot be a
justification for *or* of violence; **son livre est
une j. du régime** his book is a justification of
the regime; **il n'y a pas de j. possible à un
acte aussi barbare** there is no possible justification for such a barbaric act **2** *(preuve)
(de fait, d'identité)* proof; **j. de paiement**
proof of payment **3** *Typ, Ordinat (de lignes)*
justification; **j. à droite/gauche** right/left
justification; **j. de tirage** limitation notice; **j.
horizontale/verticale** horizontal/vertical
justification

justifié [ʒystifje] **ADJ 1** *(action, comportement, réponse, colère etc)* justified, justifiable; **peu j.** unjustified, unwarranted **2** *Jur*
préjudice j. proved damages **3** *Typ* justified;
j. à droite flush right, right justified; **j. à gauche** flush left, left justified

justifier [ʒystifje] *(impf, pr sub* n. justifiions,
v. justifiiez) **VT 1** *(faire apparaître comme légitime) (action, conduite, erreur, décision etc)*
to justify; *(dépenses) (de personne)* to justify;
(de voyage, activité professionnelle) to warrant, to justify; **les faits ont justifié nos
craintes** the facts have justified *or* borne
out *or* vindicated our fears; **son échec ne justifie pas cette crise de nerfs** his failure
doesn't justify *or* warrant such hysterics **2**
Typ, Ordinat (ligne de caractères) to justify;
j. à droite/gauche to right-/left-justify **3** *Jur*
j. de ses mouvements to account for one's
movements; **j. de son identité** to prove one's
identity

VPR se justifier 1 to justify oneself; **se j.**

d'une accusation to clear oneself *or* one's
name of an accusation; **inutile de te j.**
there's no point in trying to justify yourself
2 *Typ* to justify

jute [ʒyt] **NM** jute; **toile de j.** hessian

juter [ʒyte] **VI** to be juicy, to drip (with) juice

juteux, -euse [ʒytø, -øz] **ADJ** *(fruit)* juicy;
Fam **une affaire juteuse** a juicy *or* lucrative
piece of business
  NM *Mil Arg* warrant officer

juvénile [ʒyvenil] **ADJ** youthful; **délinquance
j.** juvenile delinquency

juvénilité [ʒyvenilite] **NF** *Litt* youthfulness

juxtalinéaire [ʒykstalineɛr] **ADJ** **traduction
j.** parallel translation

juxtaposer [ʒykstapoze] **VT** to juxtapose, to
place side by side

juxtaposition [ʒykstapozisjɔ̃] **NF** juxtaposition

K, k¹ [kɑ] NM (*lettre*) K, k; *Phys* **échelle K** (= *Kelvin*) Kelvin *or* absolute scale (*of temperatures*)

k² (*abrév* **kilo**) k

K7 [kaset] NF (*abrév* **cassette**) tape; **radio-K7** radiocassette

Kaboul [kabul] N Kabul

kabyle [kabil] ADJ Kabyle
   NM *Ling* Kabyle
   N **K.** Kabyle

Kabylie [kabili] NF **la (Grande/Petite) K.** (Great/Lesser) Kabylia

kafkaïen, -ïenne [kafkajɛ̃, -jɛn] ADJ Kafkaesque

kaiser [kajzɛr] NM kaiser

kakatoès [kakatɔɛs] NM = **cacatoès**

kaki¹ [kaki] ADJ INV, NM (*couleur*) khaki, *Am* olive-drab

kaki² NM (*arbre, fruit*) persimmon

kakou [kaku] NM *Fam* **faire le k.** to act smart

kalachnikov [kalaʃnikɔf] NM kalashnikov

Kalahari [kalaari] NM **le (désert du) K.** the Kalahari (Desert)

kaléidoscope [kaleidɔskɔp] NM *Opt, Fig* kaleidoscope

kaléidoscopique [kaleidɔskɔpik] ADJ *Opt, Fig* kaleidoscopic

kalmouk, -ouke [kalmuk] ADJ Kalmuck
   NM *Ling* Kalmuck
   N **K.** Kalmuck

kamikaze [kamikaz] NM kamikaze; *Fig* **être k.** to have a death wish
   ADJ INV kamikaze; **opération k.** kamikaze operation, suicide mission

Kampuchéa [kãmputʃea] NM *Anciennement* Kampuchea

kanak [kanak] ADJ, N = **canaque**

kangourou [kãguru] NM **1** *Zool* kangaroo; **k. de rochers** wallaby; *Géog* **île des Kangourous** Kangaroo Island **2 (sac) k.** baby carrier; **slip k.** Y-fronts® **3** *Com* **exportation k.** piggybacking

kantien, -ienne [kãtjɛ̃, -jɛn] ADJ *Phil* Kantian

kantisme [kãtism] NM *Phil* Kantianism

kaolin [kaɔlɛ̃] NM kaolin

kaolinisation [kaɔlinizasjɔ̃] NF *Géol* kaolinization

kapok [kapɔk] NM kapok

kapokier [kapɔkje] NM kapok tree

Kaposi [kapozi] N *Méd* **maladie** *ou* **sarcome de K.** Kaposi's sarcoma

kaput [kaput] ADJ INV *Fam* kaput; **la téloche est k.; impossible de regarder le match!** the TV's kaput, we can't watch the match!

karakul [karakyl] NM (*animal, laine*) caracul, karakul

karaoké [karaɔke] NM karaoke

karaté [karate] NM karate; **faire du k.** to do karate

karatéka [karateka] NM karate expert, karateka

karbau [karbo] NM water buffalo

kardex [kardɛks] NF (*d'un client dans un hôtel*) guest history card

karité [karite] NM (*arbre*) shea (tree); **beurre de k.** shea butter

karma [karma] NM *Rel* karma

Karpathes [karpat] NFPL = **Carpates**

karst [karst] NM *Géol* karst

karstique [karstik] ADJ *Géol* karstic

kart [kart] NM (go-)kart, (go-)cart

karting [kartiŋ] NM karting, go-kart racing; **faire du k.** to go karting

kasba(h) [kazba] NF = **casbah**

kascher [kaʃɛr] ADJ INV *Rel* kosher

Katmandou [katmãdu] N Katmandu

kava, kawa [kava] NF (*arbuste, boisson*) kava

kayak [kajak] NM **1** canoe, kayak; **faire du k.** to go canoeing, to canoe **2** (*embarcation des Esquimaux*) kayak

kayakiste [kajakist] N canoeist

kazakh, -e [kazak] ADJ Kazakh
   N **K.** Kazakh

Kazakhstan [kazakstã] NM Kazakhstan

Kb NM (*abrév* **kilobit**) Kb

keffieh [kefje] NM keffiyeh

kéfir [kefir] NM *Culin* kefir

keiretsu [kɛjretsu] NM *Écon* keiretsu

kelvin [kɛlvin] *Phys* ADJ INV **échelle K.** Kelvin *or* absolute scale (*of temperatures*)
   NM kelvin

kendo [kɛndo] NM kendo

Kenya [kenja] NM Kenya

kenyan, -ane [kenjã, -an] ADJ Kenyan
   N **K.** Kenyan

képhir [kefir] NM *Culin* kefir

képi [kepi] NM kepi

kérabau [kerabo] NM water buffalo

kératine [keratin] NF keratin, ceratin

kératite [keratit] NF *Méd* keratitis

kératoplastie [keratɔplasti] NF *Chir* keratoplasty, corneal grafting

kératose [keratoz] NF *Méd, Vét* keratosis

Kerguelen [kɛrgelɛn] NFPL **les (îles) K.** Kerguelen

kermesse [kɛrmɛs] NF **1** (*dans les Flandres*) kermis, village fair **2** (*fête de bienfaisance*) (charity) fête; **la k. de l'école** the school fête

kérosène [kerozɛn] NM *Aviat* kerosene; *Chimie* paraffin (oil), *Am* kerosene

ket [kɛt] NM *Belg Fam* (*enfant*) kid

ketch [kɛtʃ] NM *Naut* ketch

ketchup [kɛtʃœp] NM *Culin* (tomato) ketchup

keuf [kœf] NM *très Fam* cop; **les keufs** the fuzz, the cops

keum [kœm] NM *Fam* guy, *Br* bloke

kevlar® [kevlar] NM kevlar

keynésianisme [kenezjanism] NM *Écon* Keynesianism

keynésien, -ienne [kenezjɛ̃, -jɛn] ADJ, N *Écon* Keynesian

KF [kɑef] NM *Anciennement* (*abrév* **kilofrancs**) thousand francs; **poste de directeur à 500 KF** director's post, salary 500 K

kg (*abrév* **kilogramme(s)**) kg

KGB [kɑgebe] NM KGB

khâgne [kɑɲ] NF = **cagne**

khâgneux, -euse [kɑɲø, -øz] N *Fam* = **cagneux**

khalifat [kalifa] NM = **califat**

khalife [kalif] NM = **calife**

khamsin [kamsin] NM *Météo* khamsin

khan [kã] NM khan

Khartoum [kartum] N Khartoum

khédive [kediv] NM khedive

khmer, -ère [kmɛr] ADJ Khmer
   NM *Ling* Khmer
   N **K.** Khmer; *Pol* **les Khmers rouges** the Khmer Rouge

khôl [kol] NM kohl

kibboutz, *pl* **kibboutz** [kibuts], **kibboutzim** [kibutsim] NM kibbutz VOIR GRAMMAIRE A14

kick-down [kikdawn] NM *Aut* kick-down

kick(-starter), *pl* **kick(-starter)s** [kik(starter)] NM (*pour moto etc*) kick-starter; **démarrer une moto au k.** to kick-start a motorbike; **donner un coup de k.** to kick the starter

kidnapper [kidnape] VT to kidnap

kidnappeur, -euse [kidnapœr, -øz] N kidnapper

kidnapping [kidnapiŋ] NM kidnapping

Kiev [kjev] N Kiev

kievien, -ienne [kjevjɛ̃, -jɛn] ADJ Kievan; *Hist* **Russie kievienne** Kievan Russia, Kiev Rus
   N **K.** Kievan

kif¹ [kif] NM cannabis, hemp

kif², kif-kif ADJ INV *Fam* **c'est k., c'est k.-k. (bourricot)** it's all the same, it makes no difference *or Br* no odds

kiffer [kife] VT *Fam* **k. qch** to get a kick out of sth

kiki [kiki] NM *Fam* **1** (*cou*) neck, throat; **serrer le k. à qn** (*de personne*) to throttle sb, to wring sb's neck; **couper le k. à qn** (*lui couper le sifflet*) to shut sb up **2** *Région Fam* (*petit ruban*) bow **3** (*sexe des petits garçons*) willy **4** **c'est parti mon k.!** here we go!

kil [kil] NM *Fam* litre, *Am* liter; **un k. de rouge** a litre of red (wine)

Kilimandjaro [kilimãdʒaro] NM **le K.** (Mount) Kilimanjaro

kilo [kilo] NM kilo

kilobar [kilobar] NM kilobar

kilobaud [kilobo] NM *Ordinat* kilobaud

kilobit [kilobit] NM *Ordinat* kilobit

kilocalorie [kilokalɔri] NF kilocalorie

kilocycle [kilosikl] NM kilocycle

kilofranc [kilofrã] NM *Fin Anciennement* thousand francs

kilogramme [kilogram] NM kilogram(me)

kilohertz [kiloɛrts] NM kilohertz

kilojoule [kiloʒul] NM kilojoule

kilométrage [kilɔmetraʒ] NM **1** *(d'une route)* marking off with milestones **2** *(distance)* ≃ mileage; **location de voiture avec k. illimité** car rental with unlimited mileage; **k. maximal autorisé** maximum permitted mileage

kilomètre [kilɔmɛtr] NM kilometre, *Am* kilometer; **k. carré/cube** square/cubic kilometre; **100 kilomètres à l'heure, 100 kilomètres-heure** 100 kilometres per *or* an hour; *Fam* **bouffer** *ou* **avaler du k.** *ou* **les kilomètres** to eat up the miles; *Fam* **des kilomètres de pellicule** miles of film; **taper du texte** *ou* **faire de la saisie de texte au k.** to type text straight in *(and leave the formatting etc until later)*; *Cyclisme* **k. arrêté** standing-start kilometre

kilomètre-passager, *pl* **kilomètres-passagers** NM *Admin, Aviat* passenger-kilometre, *Am* passenger-kilometer

kilométrer [kilɔmetre] VT *(je kilomètre, n. kilométrons; je kilométrerai)* *(route)* to mark off with kilometre *or Am* kilometer stones

kilomètre-voyageur, *pl* **kilomètres-voyageurs** NM *Admin* passenger-kilometre, *Am* passenger-kilometer

kilométrique [kilɔmetrik] ADJ **borne k.** kilometre *or Am* kilometer stone, ≃ milestone; **distance k.** distance in kilometres *or Am* kilometers

kilo-octet, *pl* **kilo-octets** NM *Ordinat* kilobyte

kilotonne [kilotɔn] NF kiloton

kilovolt [kilovɔlt] NM *Vieilli* kilovolt

kilowatt [kilowat] NM *Vieilli* kilowatt

kilowattheure [kilowatœr] NM *Phys* kilowatt-hour

kilt [kilt] NM kilt; *(de femme)* pleated tartan skirt

kimono [kimɔno] NM kimono; **manche k.** kimono sleeve

kinase [kinaz] NF *Biol, Chimie* kinase

kiné [kine] N *Fam (abrév* **kinésithérapeute, kinésithérapie)** physio

kinéscopage [kineskɔpaʒ] NM kinescope transfer, kinescope recording

kinéscope [kineskɔp] NM kinescope

kinésithérapeute [kineziterapøt] N physiotherapist, *Am* physical therapist

kinésithérapie [kineziterapi] NF physiotherapy, *Am* physical therapy

kinesthésie [kinɛstezi] NF kinaesthesia, *Am* kinesthesia

king-charles [kinʃarl] NM INV King Charles spaniel

kinkajou [kɛ̃kaʒu] NM kinkajou, honey bear

Kinshasa [kinʃasa] N Kinshasa

kiosque [kjɔsk] NM **1** *(pavillon)* pavilion; *(où l'on vend qch)* kiosk; **k. de** *ou* **à musique** bandstand; **k. à journaux** newspaper kiosk, newsstand **2** *Naut (d'un sous-marin)* conning tower; **k. de la barre** *(d'un navire)* wheelhouse; **k. de veille/de navigation** pilot house/chart house *or* room **3** *Tél (de Minitel)* ≃ (telephone) viewdata service; **k. télématique®** Minitel information service

kip [kip] NM *Fin* kip

kippa [kipa] NF kippa

kipper [kipœr] NM kipper

kir [kir] NM kir *(white wine with blackcurrant liqueur)*; **k. royal** kir royal *(champagne with blackcurrant liqueur)*

kirghiz, -e [kirgiz] ADJ Kirg(h)iz
 NM *Ling* Khirg(h)iz
 N **K.** Khirg(h)iz

Kirghizistan [kirgizistã] NM, **Kirghizie** [kirgizi] NF Kirghizia

kirsch [kirʃ] NM kirsch

kit [kit] NM (home- *or* self-assembly) kit; **étagère vendue en k.** shelf unit sold in kit form, shelf unit sold for home- *or* self-assembly; **acheter une table en k.** to buy a table in kit form; *Pharm* **k. de dépistage** home testing kit; **k. développeur** *(pour imprimante)* developer kit; *Ordinat* **k. d'extension** *ou* **d'évolution** upgrade kit; **k. de téléchargeur** download kit

kitch [kitʃ] ADJ INV, NM INV kitsch

kitchenette [kitʃənɛt] NF kitchenette

kitsch [kitʃ] ADJ INV, NM INV kitsch

kiwi [kiwi] NM **1** *(oiseau)* kiwi **2** *(fruit)* kiwi fruit, Chinese gooseberry

klaxon® [klaksɔn] NM *Aut* horn; **donner un coup de k.** to sound one's horn, *Br* to hoot (one's horn); **k. italien** tune-playing horn

klaxonner [klaksɔne] VI *Aut* to sound one's horn, *Br* to hoot (one's horn)
 VT **k. qn** to sound one's horn at sb, *Br* to hoot (one's horn) at sb

klébard [klebar], **klebs** [klɛp(s)] NM *très Fam voir* **clébard**

kleenex® [klinɛks] NM INV Kleenex®, *(paper)* tissue, paper hanky

kleptomane [klɛptɔman] ADJ, N kleptomaniac

kleptomanie [klɛptɔmani] NF kleptomania

klondike [klɔndajk] NM *Can Fam* high-paying job, plum job

klystron [klistrɔ̃] NM *Électron* klystron

km *(abrév* **kilomètre(s))** km

km/h *(abrév* **kilomètres à l'heure, kilomètres-heure)** km/h, kph

knicker [nikœr] NM, **knickers** [nikœr] NMPL knickerbockers, *Am* knickers

knock-out [nɔkawt] *Boxe* ADJ INV **mettre qn k.** to knock sb out; **être k.** to be knocked out
 NM INV knockout

knout [knut] NM knout

Ko NM *(abrév* **kilo-octet)** K, KB

k-o [kao] NM *Boxe abrév* **knock-out**
 ADJ INV **1** *Boxe abrév* **knock-out 2** *Fam (fatigué)* shattered; **mettre qn k.** to shatter sb

koala [kɔala] NM koala (bear)

kobold [kɔbɔld] NM *Myth* kobold

Koch [kɔk] N *Méd* **bacille de K.** Koch's bacillus

kola [kɔla] NM *(fruit)* **(noix de) k.** cola *or* kola nut

kolatier [kɔlatje] NM cola (tree), kola (tree)

kolkhoze [kɔlkoz] NM kolkhoz, collective farm

kolkhozien, -ienne [kɔlkɔzjɛ̃, -jɛn] ADJ kolkhoz
 N kolkhoznik

Komintern [kɔmintɛrn] NM *Hist, Pol* Comintern

kommandantur [kɔmãdãtur] NF *Hist* German military command

komsomol [kɔmsɔmɔl] NM *Hist, Pol* Komsomol member

kopeck [kɔpɛk] NM kopeck; *Fam* **ça ne vaut pas un k.** it's not worth a bean

Koran [kɔrã] NM **le K.** the Koran

korrigan, -ane [kɔrigã, -an] N *(en Bretagne)* goblin

ko/s *Ordinat (abrév* **kilo-octets par seconde)** kbps

kosovar, -e [kɔsɔvar] ADJ Kosovan
 N **K.** Kosovan

Kosovo [kosovo] NM Kosovo

kot [kɔt] *Belg* NM **1** *(chambre d'étudiant)* bedroom; *(for student)* **2** *(abri)* shack, hut

kotch [kɔtʃ] NM *Belg (cagibi)* storeroom

koteur, -euse [kɔtœr, -øz] N *Belg Fam* = student in rented accommodation

kouglof [kuglɔf] NM *Culin* kugelhopf

koukri [kukri] NM kukri, Gurkha knife

koulak [kulak] NM kulak

Kouriles [kuril] NFPL **les (îles) K.** the Kuril(e) Islands

Koweït [kɔwɛ(j)t] NM *(État)* Kuwait
 N *(ville)* Kuwait

koweïtien, -ienne [kɔwɛ(j)tjɛ̃, jɛn] ADJ Kuwaiti
 N **K.** Kuwaiti

kraal [kral] NM kraal

krach [krak] NM **k. (boursier)** (Stock Market) crash; **le k. de Wall Street** the Wall Street Crash

kraft [kraft] NM **(papier) k.** brown (wrapping) paper, manil(l)a paper; **enveloppe en papier k.** manil(l)a envelope

kraken [krakɛn] NM kraken

Kremlin [krɛmlɛ̃] NM **le K.** the Kremlin

kremlinologie [krɛmlinɔlɔʒi] NF Kremlinology

kremlinologue [krɛmlinɔlɔg] N Kremlinologist, *Fam* Kremlin-watcher

kriek [krik] NF *Belg* = beer made from cherries, kriek

kriss [kris] NM kris, Malay dagger

kroumir [krumir] NM *(chausson)* pump

krypton [kriptɔ̃] NM *Chimie* krypton

ksar, *pl* **ksour** [ksar, ksur] NM fortress, fortified village *(in North Africa)*

kumquat [kɔmkwat, kum-] NM *(fruit)* kumquat, cumquat

kung-fu [kuŋfu] NM INV kung fu; **faire du k.** to do kung fu

kurde [kyrd] ADJ Kurdish
 NM *Ling* Kurdish
 N **K.** Kurd

Kurdistan [kyrdistã] NM Kurdistan

kvas [kvas] NM kvas(s)

kW *Élec (abrév* **kilowatt(s))** kW

kwas [kvas] NM kvas(s)

K-way® [kawɛ] NM cagoule, waterproof jacket, *Am* K-way; **pantalon de K.** waterproof leggings

kWh *Élec (abrév* **kilowatt(s)-heure)** kWh

kyat [kjat] NM kyat

kymographe [kimɔgraf] NM *Méd* kymograph

kymrique [kimrik] ADJ, NM Cymric, Kymric

kyrie [kirje] NM *Rel* Kyrie (eleison)

kyrielle [kirjɛl] NF *(de mots, raisons, mensonges)* string; *(de reproches)* string, stream; *(d'enfants)* swarm, crowd; **une k. de pièces/ de photos** a whole series of rooms/photos; **elle a une k. d'amis** she has masses *or* a mass of friends; **il m'a fait une k. de reproches** he reproached me again and again

kyste [kist] NM *Méd* cyst; **k. synovial** ganglion

kystique [kistik] ADJ *Méd* cystic

L, l [ɛl] NM **1** *(lettre)* L, l **2** *Ling* **l** mouillé liquid l, palatal(ized) **3** *Fin* L £

l 1 *(abrév* **litre)** l **2** *(abrév* **livre)** lb

l', la [la] *art déf, pron f voir* **le**¹, **le**²

la ² NM INV *Mus* **1** *(note)* A; **donner le la** to give the or an A; *Fig* to set the tone **2** *(tonalité) (au solfège)* la

LÀ [la] ADV **1** *(endroit où se trouve celui qui parle)* here; *(là-bas)* there; **là où vous êtes** where you are; **il est là** *(présent)* he's here; **viens là!** come here!; **quand il n'est pas là** when he isn't here/there, when he's away; **le patron n'est jamais là le jeudi** the boss isn't here/there on Thursdays; **est-ce que le patron est là?** is the boss in?; **de là au village il y a un kilomètre** it's one kilometre from there to the village; **à cinq pas de là se tenait l'agent de police** five paces away stood the policeman; **c'est là qu'il demeure** that's where he lives; *Fam* **ôtez-vous de là!** get out of there!; **si tu vas par là** *(dans cette direction)* if you're going that way; *Fig* **si tu vas par là, pourquoi ne pas rétablir le travail des enfants?** why not bring back child labour while you're at it?; **quelque part par là** somewhere around here/there; **là, en bas/en haut** down/up there

2 *(à ce point)* **les choses en sont là** that's how things stand at the moment; **restons-en là** let's leave it at that; **la question n'est pas là** that's not the point; **c'est bien là le problème** that's the problem; **c'est là où nous ne sommes plus d'accord/que nos opinions divergent** that's where we disagree/where we or our opinions differ; **c'est là qu'elle fut interrompue** that's when she was interrupted, it was at that moment that she was interrupted; *Fig* **je m'en suis mis jusque-là** *(j'ai beaucoup et bien mangé)* I'm full up to here; *Fam* **j'en ai jusque-là de vos histoires** I've had it up to here with your stories, I've had your stories up to here

3 *(ici, à ce moment)* **qu'est-ce que je vois là? mais ce sont mes gants!** if it isn't my gloves!; **mais qu'est-ce que je vois là? ma fille avec un garçon** what's this (I see)? my daughter with a boy?; *Mil* **halte! qui va là?** halt! who goes there?; **que dites-vous là?** what's that you're saying?; *(qu'est-ce que vous voulez dire?)* what are you saying?, what do you mean?; **là tu exagères** now you're exaggerating; **je ne vois là aucune raison de s'inquiéter** I don't see that there's anything to worry about; **il n'y a là rien d'étonnant** there's nothing surprising about that

4 *(ce moment)* then; **d'ici là** between now and then, in the meantime; **en l'an 2036, mais d'ici là ...** in the year 2036, but by then ...; **à quelques jours de là** some days after (that), a few days later

5 *(ceci, ça)* **de là à croire que tout est facile, il y a une marge!** but to conclude from that that everything's easy!; **mais de là à dire qu'ils sont tous antipathiques!** but to conclude from that that they're all unpleasant!; **mais de là à ce qu'il nous donne son accord ...** but as to giving us his agreement ...; **qu'entendez vous par là?** what do you mean by that?; **de là on peut conclure que ...** from this or hence, it may be concluded that ...; **de là sa réaction** hence his reaction

6 **ce ...-là** that ...; **ces ...-là** those ...; **ces gens-là sont ennuyeux** those people are boring; **il est taré ce mec-là!** the guy's crazy!; **il est bête à ce point-là?** is he (really) that stupid?; **je savais qu'il buvait beaucoup, mais pas à ce point-là!** I knew he drank a lot but not that much or not to that extent!; *voir* **ce**², **celui**, **celle**

7 *Iron* **il se pose (un peu) là, comme plombier!** he's an absolutely hopeless plumber! INT **1** *(doucement)* **hé là! doucement!** gently does it!; **là, là!** there now, there there

2 **oh là là!** oh dear!; **oh là là! ce qu'il fait chaud!** goodness, it's warm!

3 **alors là, ce n'est pas étonnant!** well, that's not surprising!

4 **oh là! il a failli tomber!** oh dear or goodness, he almost fell!; **oh là doucement! je n'ai pas dit ça!** now wait a minute or *Fam* hang about a bit, I didn't say that

là-bas ADV over there; *(dans cette région, ce pays)* there; **tiens! le voilà l.** there he is over there

label [label] NM **1** *Com* quality label; **l. NF** ou **norme française** *(délivré par l'AFNOR)* French industry standards label; **l. de garantie** guarantee label; **l. d'exportation** export label; **le produit porte un l. de qualité** the product carries a quality label; *Fig* **il fera probablement campagne sous le l. socialiste** he will probably campaign as a Socialist **2** *(maison de disques)* label; **l. indépendant** independent record label **3** *Ordinat* **l. de volume** volume label

labelisé [labelize] ADJ which carries a seal of approval

labeur [labœr] NM **1** *Litt* labour, *Am* labor, toil, hard work **2** *Typ* **imprimerie de l.** book printing works

labial, -iale, -iaux, -iales [labjal, -jo] ADJ **1** *Anat (muscle etc)* labial **2** *Ling* **consonne labiale** labial

NF *Ling* **labiale** labial

labialisation [labjalizasjɔ̃] NF *Ling* labialization

labialiser [labjalize] VT *Ling* to labialize

labié [labje] ADJ *Bot* lipped, *Spéc* labiate

labiodental, -ale, -aux, -ales [labjodɑ̃tal, -o] *Ling* ADJ labiodontal

NF **labiodentale** labiodental

labo [labo] NM *Fam* lab; **l. photo** darkroom; **l. de langues** language lab; **les élèves qui font du l.** the pupils doing lab work

laborantin, -ine [labɔrɑ̃tɛ̃, -in] N laboratory or *Fam* lab assistant

laboratoire [labɔratwar] NM laboratory; **l. de recherche/de langues** research/language laboratory; **l. d'analyses (médicales)** pathology laboratory; **l. d'idées** think tank; **l. spatial/orbital** spacelab/orbiting laboratory; **l. d'essai de produits** testing laboratory; **l. photographique** photo laboratory

laborieusement [labɔrjøzmɑ̃] ADV laboriously; **gagner l. sa vie** to work hard for a living

laborieux, -euse [labɔrjø, -øz] ADJ **1** *(difficile)* laborious; *Péj (style)* laboured, *Am* labored; *Péj* **ce roman a quelque chose de l.** the novel is rather laboured; *Fam* **il n'a pas encore fini? c'est l.!** hasn't he finished yet? it's taking a long time or he's making heavy weather of it!; **j'ai réussi à la convaincre, mais ça a été l.!** I managed to convince her but it was a laborious task or but it was heavy going! **2** *(travailleur)* hard-working; *Litt* **les masses laborieuses** the toiling masses

labour [labur] NM *Agr* **1** *(labourage)* ploughing, *Am* plowing, tilling; **l. à la bêche** digging; **cheval de l.** plough or *Am* plow horse **2** **labours** ploughed or *Am* plowed land; **le semeur dans les labours** the sower in his ploughed fields

labourable [laburabl] ADJ *Agr (terre)* ploughable, *Am* plowable

labourage [laburaʒ] NM *Agr* ploughing, *Am* plowing, tilling

labourer [labure] VT **1** *Agr (terre)* to plough, *Am* to plow, to till; *(de char, moto)* to churn up; **l. la terre à la bêche** to dig the soil **2** *Naut* **l. le fond** *(d'un bateau)* to graze the bottom; *(d'une ancre)* to drag **3** **visage labouré de rides** face furrowed with wrinkles; **les griffes du tigre lui ont labouré la poitrine** his chest was lacerated by the tiger's claws; **mon sac à dos me laboure le bas du dos** my rucksack is digging into my back; *Fam* **les flics lui ont labouré les côtes (de coups)** the cops gave him a going-over or roughed him up

laboureur [laburœr] NM *Agr* ploughman, *Am* plowman

Labrador [labradɔr] NM *Géog* Labrador

labrador [labradɔr] NM *(chien)* Labrador

labyrinthe [labirɛ̃t] NM **1** maze, labyrinth; *Fig* maze **2** *Anat (de l'oreille)* labyrinth

labyrinthique [labirɛ̃tik] ADJ labyrinthine

lac [lak] NM *Géog* lake; **l. de cirque** tarn; **les lacs d'Écosse** the Scottish lochs; **le l. Léman** ou **de Genève** Lake Geneva; **l. artificiel** artificial lake; *(pour fournir de l'eau)* reservoir; **l. de montagne** mountain lake; *Fig* **être dans le l.** to have fallen through

laçage [lasaʒ] NM *(de chaussures, bottes)* tying (up); *(de corset)* lacing (up)

lacer [lase] *(je laçai(s); n. laçons)* VT *(corset)* to lace up; **l. ses chaussures/ses bottes** to tie one's shoe/boot laces, to tie up or do up one's shoes/boots

VPR se lacer *(de chaussures, bottes)* to tie up, to do up; **ce corset se lace sur le côté** this corset laces (up) at the side

lacération [laserasjɔ̃] NF **1** *(action)* laceration; *(avec un couteau)* slashing **2** *(blessure)* laceration; *(faite avec un couteau, des ciseaux)* slash

lacérer [lasere] VT (**je lacère, n. lacérons; je lacérerai**) *Méd* to lacerate; **il a été lacéré de coups de couteau** he was slashed with a knife; **le chat a lacéré le fauteuil avec ses griffes** the cat has clawed the armchair to pieces; **la douleur lui lacère le dos** the pain is like a knife in his back, he has a lacerating pain in his back

lacet [lasɛ] NM **1** *(de chaussure)* (shoe)lace; *(de botte)* (boot)lace; *(de corset)* lace; **chaussures à lacets** lace-up shoes, lace-ups; **faire ses lacets** to tie one's laces **2** *(tournant)* (hairpin) bend, sharp bend; **sentier en lacets** winding *or* twisting *or* zigzag path; **la route monte en lacets** the road winds steeply up; **la route fait des lacets** the road zigzags, the road twists and turns **3** *Tech, Aviat* yaw(ing) **4** *(collet) (pour lapins, oiseaux etc)* noose, snare; **tendre un l.** to set a snare **5** *Couture* braid

lâchage [lɑʃaʒ] NM *(d'un parachutiste etc)* dropping; **un l. de vivres** a supply drop; *Fig* **ce n'est pas le l. de quelques-uns qui nous forcera à abandonner** we're not going to give up just because one or two people have backed out

lâche [lɑʃ] ADJ **1** *(non serré, large) (ressort, nœud etc)* loose, slack; *(vêtement)* loose-fitting; *(discipline)* lax; *(style)* woolly **2** *Péj (peureux)* cowardly **3** *Péj (vil) (acte, attitude, attaque)* cowardly **4** *Litt Péj (mou) (personnage)* weak, feeble
  N coward

lâchement [lɑʃmɑ̃] ADV **1** *(non serré)* loosely, slackly **2** *(sans courage)* like a coward; **un crime l. perpétré** a cowardly act

LÂCHER [lɑʃe] VT **1** *(donner du mou à) (corde)* to slacken, to loosen; *Aut* **l. la pédale du frein** to take one's foot off the brake **2** *(ne plus tenir) (corde etc)* to let go of; *(laisser tomber)* to drop; *Aviat (bombe)* to release, to drop; *(parachutiste)* to drop; **lâchez-moi!** let me go!, let go of me!; **l. sa proie** *(d'un animal)* to drop its prey; *Fam* **il ne m'a pas lâché d'une semelle** he stuck to me like a leech; *Fam* **l. des sous**, *très Fam* **les l.** to fork out; **il a du mal à les l., il ne les lâche pas facilement** he hates putting his hand in his pocket; **il les lâche avec un élastique** he's a real scrooge *or Am* tightwad **3** *Fam (abandonner) (associé, mari, famille, société)* to walk out on; *(amant)* to drop, to ditch; *(fiancé)* to jilt; *(ami)* to drop; *(emploi)* to chuck in; **la voiture nous a lâchés** the car died on us *or* packed in on us; **l. ses études** to drop out (of university) **4** *(distancer) (reporter, poursuivant etc)* to shake off; **il vient de l. le peloton** he has just left the rest of the field behind *or* gone way out in front **5** *Fam (cesser d'importuner)* to leave alone; **lâche-moi les baskets** *ou Vulg* **la grappe** give it a rest, get off my back **6** *(libérer)* to release; **le sergent nous lâchait toujours à la dernière minute** the sergeant never used to let us go until the last minute; **l. un chien** to unleash a dog, to let a dog loose; *(Chasse)* to slip a dog; **l. le chien contre qn** to set the dog on sb **7** *Ordinat (icône)* to drop **8** *(laisser échapper) (juron, cri de surprise), Vulg (pet, rot)* to let out; *(sottise, plaisanterie)* to come out with; *(phrase)* to say; *Arg* **l. le paquet** *ou* **le morceau** to spill the beans, to come clean

VI *(d'une corde, d'un câble)* to break; *(d'un mécanisme, d'une pièce)* to go; *(d'un moteur)* to die, to pack in; *Fam (d'un organe)* to give out, to pack in; **mes freins ont lâché** my brakes failed; *Fig* **ses nerfs ont lâché** he broke down, his nerves gave way

lâcher² NM *(de pigeons, ballons etc)* release; *Ordinat* **l. d'icônes** icon drop

lâcheté [lɑʃte] NF **1** *(couardise)* cowardice, cowardliness; **il se tait par l.** he is keeping quiet out of cowardice **2** *Litt (faiblesse, mollesse)* weakness **3** *(acte lâche)* act of cowardice

lâcheur, -euse [lɑʃœr, -øz] N *Fam (traître)* rat

lacis [lasi] NM *(de nerfs, fils etc)* network; **un fin l. de veines bleutées** a delicate web of blue veins; **l. de ruelles** maze of back streets; **un l. d'intrigues** a web of intrigue

laconique [lakɔnik] ADJ laconic; **répondre de façon l.** to answer laconically

laconiquement [lakɔnikmɑ̃] ADV laconically

laconisme [lakɔnism] NM *(d'une réponse)* laconicism; **elle ne supporte pas son l.** she cannot bear the fact that he is so taciturn

lacrymal, -ale, -aux, -ales [lakrimal, -o] ADJ *(conduit)* tear, *Spéc* lachrymal; **glande lacrymale** tear gland

lacrymogène [lakrimɔʒɛn] ADJ **gaz/grenade l.** tear-gas/tear-gas grenade

lacs [lɑ] NM **1** *(motif décoratif)* **l. d'amour** love knot **2** *Arch, Litt (piège)* noose, snare; *Fig Litt* **tomber dans le l.** to fall into the trap

lactaire [laktɛr] ADJ *Physiol* lacteal
  NM *Bot (champignon)* lactarius; **l. délicieux** saffron milk cap

lactation [laktasjɔ̃] NF *Physiol* lactation

lacté [lakte] ADJ *Physiol (sécrétion)* lacteal; *(produit)* which contains milk; *(régime)* milk; *Litt (chair)* milky

lactescent [laktesɑ̃] ADJ milky

lactifère [laktifɛr] ADJ *Anat* lactiferous; *(conduit)* lacteal

lactique [laktik] ADJ *Chimie (acide)* lactic

lactose [laktoz] NM *Chimie* lactose

lacunaire [lakynɛr] ADJ **1** *(documentation, informations)* incomplete **2** *Anat, Bot (incomplet)* lacunar(y), lacunal

lacune [lakyn] NF **1** *(manque) (dans un texte, un dictionnaire, ses connaissances, ses souvenirs)* gap, *Fml* lacuna; *(de mémoire)* blank; **cette liste comporte plusieurs lacunes** there are several gaps in the list, the list is incomplete; **cette loi n'est pas sans lacunes** there are loopholes in this law; **malgré ses lacunes en physique** despite his shortcomings in physics **2** *Biol, Anat* lacuna; *Bot* air cell

lacuneux, -euse [lakynø, -øz] ADJ **= lacunaire**

lacustre [lakystr] ADJ *(flore, faune, habitat)* lakeside, lakeshore, *Spéc* lacustrine; **habitation l.** lake dwelling, pile dwelling; **cité l.** lake village, collection of lake dwellings

lad [lad] NM stable lad, boy

là-dedans [lad(ə)dɑ̃] ADV inside; *(dans un lieu, objet indiqué)* in there; *(dans une boîte, un sac)* in it, in this; **il y a l. quelque chose que je ne comprends pas** there's something here I don't understand; **ça ne m'étonnerait pas qu'elle soit impliquée l.** it wouldn't surprise me if she was involved (in it); **il n'a rien à voir l.!** he's got nothing to do with it!; *Fam* **debout l.!** rise and shine!; *Fam* **il y en a l.!** he's/she's got a lot up top

là-dessous [latsu] ADV under that, under there, underneath; *Fig* **il y a quelque chose l.** there's something behind it; **il y a un secret l.** something is being kept secret

là-dessus [latsy] ADV on that, on it; **tout le monde est d'accord l.** everybody agrees about that; **l., il est sorti** *or Fml* thereupon, he went out; **nous reviendrons l.** we'll come back to that; **c'est l. qu'il faut se concentrer** that's what you/we/*etc* have to concentrate on

ladre [ladr] ADJ **1** *Vét (porc)* measly, measled **2** *Arch (lépreux)* leprous **3** *Arch, Litt (avare)* miserly
  N *Arch* **1** *(lépreux)* leper **2** *Litt (avare)* miser

ladrerie [ladrəri] NF **1** *Vét (des porcs)* measles **2** *Arch (léproserie)* leper house **3** *Arch, Litt (avarice)* miserliness

lagon [lagɔ̃] NM *Géog* lagoon

lagopède [lagɔpɛd] NM *Orn* lagopus; **l. des Alpes** ptarmigan; **l. d'Écosse** red grouse

lagune [lagyn] NF *Géog* lagoon

là-haut ADV up there; *(à un étage supérieur)* upstairs; *(dans cette région, ce pays)* there

lai¹ [lɛ] NM *Littér* lay

lai² ADJ *Rel* **frère/sœur lai(e)** lay brother/sister

laïc [laik] ADJ, NM **= laïque**

laîche [lɛʃ] NF *Bot* sedge

laïcisation [laisizasjɔ̃] NF secularization, laicization

laïciser [laisize] VT to secularize, to laicize

laïcisme [laisism] NM secularism, laicism

laïcité [laisite] NF *(des écoles)* secularity; *Pol* secularism

laid, laide [lɛ, lɛd] ADJ **1** *(personne, visage)* ugly; *(imperfection, tache, édifice)* ugly, unsightly; *Fam* **l. comme un pou** *ou* à faire peur as ugly as sin, *Fam* plug ugly **2** *(méprisable) (action etc)* despicable; **c'est l. de mentir (à un enfant)** it's very naughty to tell lies; **comme c'est l. de faire des grimaces!** it's not nice to make faces!
  N *(physiquement)* ugly person
  NM **le l.** ugly things; **le l. et le beau** the ugly and the beautiful; **c'est d'un l.!** it's so ugly!

laidement [lɛdmɑ̃] ADV **1** *(sans goût, mal)* in an ugly way **2** *(ignoblement)* meanly, dishonestly

laideron [lɛdrɔ̃] NM *Péj* ugly girl/woman; **un petit l.** an ugly duckling

laideur [lɛdœr] NF **1** *(physique) (d'une personne, d'un visage)* ugliness; *(d'une imperfection, d'une tache, d'un édifice)* ugliness, unsightliness; **d'une l. épouvantable** horrifically ugly **2** *(bassesse) (d'une conduite etc)* meanness, lowness, nastiness **3** **les laideurs de la vie** the ugly side of life

laie¹ [lɛ] NF *Zool* (wild) sow

laie² NF *(sentier)* forest track, ride

laie³ NF *Tech* bush hammer

lainage [lɛnaʒ] NM **1** *(étoffe)* woollen *or Am* woolen fabric **2** *(vêtement en laine)* woollen *or Am* woolen garment *or* article, *Fam* woolly, *Am* wooly; *Com* **lainages** woollen goods, woollens, *Am* woolens **3** *Tex* teaseling, napping **4** *(toison)* fleece

laine [lɛn] NF **1** wool; **jupe en** *ou* **de l.** woollen *or Am* woolen skirt; **tapis de haute l.** thick-pile wool carpet; **pure l.** pure wool; **ensemble pure l.** pure wool outfit; *Fig* **se laisser manger** *ou* **tondre la l. sur le dos** *(voler)* to (let oneself) be fleeced; *(exploiter)* to (let oneself) be taken advantage of **2** *(vêtement)* **mettre une petite l.** to put on something warm
  ▸▸ **l. de bois** wood fibre *or Am* fiber; **l. cardée** carding wool; **l. à matelas** stuffing; **l. peignée** worsted; **l. perlée** crochet wool; **l. à tricoter** knitting wool; **l. de verre** glass wool; **l. vierge** virgin wool

lainer [lene] VT *Tex (tissu)* to teasel, to nap
  NM *Tex (d'un tissu)* nap

lainerie [lɛnri] NF **1** *(fabrication)* manufacture of woollens *or Am* woolens **2** *(usine, atelier)* woollen *or Am* woolen mill **3** *(magasin de gros)* (wholesale) wool shop

laineur, -euse [lɛnœr, -øz] N *Tex* teaseler, napper

laineux, -euse [lɛnø, -øz] ADJ *(tissu etc)* fleecy; *(mouton, cheveux)* woolly, *Am* wooly

lainier, -ière [lɛnje, -jɛr] ADJ *(commerce, industrie)* wool
▪ N *Ind (ouvrier)* worker in a woollen *or Am* woolen mill, wool worker

laïque [laik] ADJ lay; *(vie, état)* secular; **école/enseignement l.** = (non-religious) state school/education
▪ N layman, *f* laywoman, lay person; **les laïques** the laity

lais [lɛ] NM *(laisse)* foreshore

laisse [lɛs] NF **1** leash, lead; *(à la chasse)* slip; **tenir un chien en l.** to keep a dog on a lead *or* on the leash; *Fam* **mener** *ou* **tenir qn en l.** to keep a tight rein on sb **2** *Géog* foreshore; **l. de haute/basse mer** high-water/low-water mark

laissé(e)-pour-compte, *pl* **laissé(e)s-pour-compte** [lesepurkɔ̃t] ADJ **1** *Com (article)* rejected, returned **2** *(non désiré, non voulu) (personne)* rejected, unwanted
▪ NM *Com* reject
▪ N *(personne)* unwanted person, castoff; **les laissés-pour-compte** the castoffs of society; **les ouvriers métallurgiques sont les laissés-pour-compte du redéploiement industriel** industrial redeployment is throwing steel workers on the scrap heap

LAISSER [lese] VT **1** *(permettre)* to let; **il le laissa partir** he let him go, he allowed him to go; **laissez-moi passer** let me past; **laisse-le passer devant** let him (go) in front; **laisse sortir les gens avant de monter** let the people out before you get in; **je les ai laissés dire** I let them speak; **l. dire** to let people talk; *Fam* **il ne m'a laissé en placer une** he wouldn't let me get a word in edgeways; **je vous laisse libre d'agir** you are free to do as you like; **le toit laissait passer la pluie** the roof let the rain in; **l. voir son mécontentement** to show one's displeasure *or* disapproval; **ne rien l. deviner** to give nothing away; **l. tomber qch/qn** to drop sth/sb; *Fam* **laissez-moi rire!** don't make me laugh!; **l. sécher la peinture** to let the paint dry, to allow the paint to dry; **laissez-les boire un verre de vin** let them have a glass of wine; **laisse faire** never mind, don't bother; **laissez-le faire!** leave it to him, let him get on with it; **laisse-moi faire, ça ira plus vite** just leave me to it *or* let me get on with it and it'll soon be done; *Fam* **l. courir** to leave (things) alone
SEE GRAMMAR A41; B35
2 *(quitter) (mari, femme)* to leave, *Fam* to walk out on; **vous n'allez pas me l. tout seul?** you're not going to leave me (all) on my own?; **bon, je vous laisse!** well, I'm going *or* I'm off; **merci, vous pouvez nous l.** thank you, that will be all; **il a laissé une veuve et trois enfants** he left a widow and three children; **nous l'avions laissé pour mort** we had left him for dead; **laissez-moi!** let me go!; *(ne me dérangez pas)* I don't want to be disturbed!; **laissez-moi tranquille!** leave me alone!; **elle a laissé son mari planté sur le trottoir** she left her husband standing on the pavement looking like a fool; **l. là qn** to leave sb in the lurch
3 *(ne pas prendre)* to leave; **l. qch de côté** to put sth aside *or* to one side; **laissez-lui du gâteau** leave *or* save some cake for him; **l. le meilleur pour la fin** to leave *or* save the best till last; *Fam* **c'est à prendre ou à l.** take it *or* leave it
4 *(traces, cicatrices etc)* to leave; **ne laisse**

pas traîner tes affaires partout dans la maison don't leave your things lying everywhere about the house; **l. la fenêtre ouverte** to leave *or* keep the window open; **laissons cela jusqu'à demain** let's leave that until tomorrow; **laissez, c'est moi qui paie** leave that, I'm paying; **laisse, je m'en occupe** don't bother about that, I'll look after it
5 *(donner)* **je vous laisse le soin de le faire** I'll leave it to you (to do it), I'll leave you to do it; **je vous laisse le soin de décider** I'll leave it (up) to you to decide; **cela nous laisse le temps de …** that leaves *or* gives us time to …; **il m'a laissé entendre que …** he gave me to understand that …; **je te laisse imaginer la suite** I'll leave the rest to your imagination; **elle ne m'a pas laissé le choix** she left *or* gave me no choice; **l. à qn un héritage** to leave sb a legacy; **laissez-moi vos clefs** leave me your keys, let me have your keys; **ils ont laissé les enfants à la grand-mère** they left the children with their grandmother; **partir sans l. d'adresse** to go away without leaving one's address; **je vous le laisse pour 100 euros** I'll let you have it *or* you can have it for 100 euros; **je laisse maintenant la parole à mon collègue** I now hand over to my colleague
6 *(perdre) (fortune, vie, membre)* to lose
7 *Littr* **il ne laissera pas d'y aller** he won't fail to go; **cela ne laisse pas de m'inquiéter** nevertheless, I cannot help worrying about it; **cela n'a pas laissé de le surprendre** it could not fail to surprise him
▪ VPR **se laisser elle se laisse vivre** she takes life as it comes; **se l. aller** to let oneself go; **ne vous laissez pas aller comme ça!** pull yourself together!; **se l. aller au découragement** to let oneself become discouraged; **se l. aller au pessimisme** to give way to pessimism; **je me suis laissé aller à reprendre trois fois du gâteau** I went so far as to have three pieces of cake; **se l. décourager** to let oneself be discouraged; **se l. emporter par la colère/l'enthousiasme** to get carried away by anger/enthusiasm; **elle se laissa embrasser** she allowed herself to be kissed, she let herself be kissed, she let him/her/etc kiss her; **je me suis laissé dire que …** I hear that …; *Fam* **ce vin se laisse boire** this wine is definitely quite drinkable; **ce livre n'est pas de la grande littérature mais il se laisse lire** it's not great literature but it's quite readable *or* pleasant enough
▪ VI **je vous laisse à penser quel fut son bonheur en apprenant …** you can imagine how happy he was when he learned …; **tout laisse à penser que l'affaire aura des suites** there is every indication that the affair will have repercussions; **cela laisse (beaucoup) à désirer** it leaves much to be desired

laisser-aller NM INV **1** *(désinvolture)* casualness **2** *Péj (relâchement) (de l'apparence, la tenue etc)* carelessness, slovenliness; *(du travail)* carelessness, sloppiness; **il règne trop de l. dans ce bureau** things are too slack in this office

laisser-faire NM INV *Pol* laisser-faire, laissez faire

laissez-passer [lesepase] NM INV pass, permit; *Naut* sea pass; *(de douane)* transire

lait [lɛ] NM **1** milk; **petit l.** whey; *Fig Fam* **boire du petit l.** to lap it up; **ce punch se boit comme du petit l.** this punch is very moreish; **vache à l.** dairy cow; *Fam* **je ne suis pas une vache à l.** I'm not made of money; **pot à l.** milk jug; **frère/sœur de l.** foster brother/sister; **cochon de l.** suckling *or* sucking pig **2** *(cosmétique)* **l. démaquillant** cleansing lotion, cleanser; **l. bronzant** suntan lotion; **l. hydratant** moisturizing lotion, moisturizer
▪ ▪ **l. caillé** curd, curdled milk; **l. de chaux** limewater, whitewash; **l. de coco** coconut

milk; **l. concentré** evaporated milk; **l. condensé** condensed milk; **l. cru** unpasteurized milk; **l. demi-écrémé** semi-skimmed milk; **l. écrémé** skimmed milk; **l. entier** whole milk; **l. de ferme** unpasteurized milk; **l. longue conservation** long-life milk; **l. maternel** mother's milk; **l. en poudre** powdered *or* dried milk; *Am (pour bébé)* formula; **l. de poule** egg flip, egg nog

laitage [lɛtaʒ] NM dairy product

laitance [lɛtɑ̃s], **laite** [lɛt] NF *(de poisson)* milt; *Culin* soft roe

laité [lete] ADJ *(poisson)* soft-roed

laiterie [lɛtri] NF **1** *(dans la ferme)* dairy **2** *(usine)* factory producing dairy products; *(industrie)* dairy industry **3** *Vieilli (crémerie)* dairy

laiteron [lɛtrɔ̃] NM *Bot* sow thistle, milkweed

laiteux, -euse [lɛtø, -øz] ADJ *(teint)* creamy; *(couleur)* milky; *(lumière)* milky(-white)

laitier,¹ -ière [lɛtje, -jɛr] ADJ *(industrie, produit, vache)* dairy
▪ NF **laitière** dairy cow; **ces vaches sont de bonnes laitières** these cows are good milkers
▪ N **1** *(livreur)* milkman, *f* milkwoman **2** *(crémier)* dairyman, *f* dairywoman

laitier² NM *Métal etc* dross, slag

laiton [lɛtɔ̃] NM brass; **(fil de) l.** brass wire

laitue [lɛty] NF *(légume)* lettuce; **l. romaine** cos (lettuce), *Am* romaine (lettuce)

laïus [lajys] NM **1** *Fam (discours)* speech; *(long et ennuyeux)* long-winded speech; **faire un l.** to make a speech; *(long et ennuyeux)* to hold forth, to make a long-winded speech *(sur* about) **2** *Péj (baratin)* **quel l.!, venons-en au fait!** what a lot of waffle! let's get to the point!

lama¹ [lama] NM *Rel* lama; **le Grand l., le dalaï-l.** the Dalai Lama

lama² NM *Zool, Tex* llama

lamantin [lamɑ̃tɛ̃] NM *Zool* manatee, sea cow

lamaserie [lamazri] NF *Rel* lamasery

lambada [lɑ̃bada] NF *Mus* lambada

lambda [lɑ̃bda] ADJ INV *Fam* average; **un garçon l.** an average boy; **le contribuable l.** the average *or* ordinary taxpayer

lambeau, -eaux [lɑ̃bo] NM *(de tissu, papier, viande etc)* scrap, bit, shred; *(de musique, conversation etc)* scrap, fragment; **vêtements en lambeaux** clothes in rags *or* in tatters; **mettre qch en lambeaux** to tear sth to shreds *or* to pieces; **réduire qch en lambeaux** to reduce sth to shreds; **tomber en lambeaux** to fall to pieces

lambin, -ine [lɑ̃bɛ̃, -in] *Fam* ADJ slow; **ce qu'il peut être l., celui-là!** what a dawdler *or* slowcoach *or Am* slowpoke that one is!
▪ N dawdler, slowcoach, *Am* slowpoke

lambiner [lɑ̃bine] VI *Fam* to dawdle

lambourde [lɑ̃burd] NF **1** *(d'arbre)* fruit shoot **2** *Constr (pour parquet)* bridging joist; *(de plancher)* wall plate, bearing joist

lambrequin [lɑ̃brəkɛ̃] NM **1** *Hér* mantling, lambrequin **2** *(de rideau)* valance, pelmet

lambris [lɑ̃bri] NM *Constr (en bois)* panelling, wainscot(t)ing; *(en marbre, stuc)* lining; **l. d'appui** dado

lambrissage [lɑ̃brisaʒ] NM *Constr (de bois)* panelling, wainscot(t)ing; *(de marbre, stuc)* lining

lambrissé [lɑ̃brise] ADJ *Constr (de bois)* panelled; *(de marbre, de stuc)* lined; **plafond l.** panelled ceiling

lambrisser [lɑ̃brise] VT *Constr* **1** *(revêtir de lambris) (de bois)* to panel, to wainscot; *(de* *marbre, stuc)* to line **2** *(avec du plâtre) (mur, plafond)* to plaster

lambswool [lãbswul] NM *Tex* lambswool; **un pull en l.** a lambswool sweater

lame [lam] NF **1** *(d'épée, de couteau etc)* blade; *(épée)* sword, blade; **l. de rasoir** razor blade; **l. ressort** spring blade; *Fig Litt* **c'est une fine l.** he's a fine swordsman; **visage en l. de couteau** hatchet face **2** *(bande plate) (de métal, verre etc)* strip; *(de ressort)* leaf; *(de microscope)* slide; *(de store)* slat; **l. de parquet** strip of parquet flooring **3** *Anat, Bot* lamina; *(de champignon)* gill **4** *(vague)* wave; **l. de fond** ground swell; **le creux de la l.** the trough of the wave

lamé [lame] ADJ lamé; **robe lamée d'or** gold lamé dress
▷ NM lamé; **une robe en l.** a lamé dress

lamellaire [lamelɛr] ADJ *Minér etc* lamellar, lamellate, foliated

lamelle [lamɛl] NF **1** *(de fer, plastique etc)* thin strip; *(de mica)* scale, flake; *Bot (de champignon)* lamella, gill; *Culin* **couper en (fines) lamelles** to cut into (wafer-)thin slices **2** *(de microscope)* cover glass

lamellé [lamɛle], **lamelleux, -euse** [lamɛlø, -øz] ADJ lamellate(d)

lamentable [lamãtabl] ADJ **1** *(déplorable) (histoire, fait divers etc)* appalling, dreadful, terrible, awful; **sort l.** terrible fate **2** *Péj (mauvais)* appalling, awful; *(personne)* hopeless, pathetic **3** *(triste) (voix, ton)* mournful, woeful

lamentablement [lamãtabləmã] ADV *(échouer)* miserably, lamentably

lamentation [lamãtasjɔ̃] NF **1** *(cri de douleur extrême)* lament, lamentation; **cri de l.** wail; **les lamentations d'une femme qui a perdu son enfant** the wailing of a woman who has lost her child **2** *Péj (plainte, jérémiades)* moaning, complaining; **elle ne cesse de se répandre en lamentations** she never stops complaining or moaning

lamenter (se) [səlamãte] VPR **se l. sur son sort** to bemoan or lament one's fate; **se l. de son ignorance** to deplore or regret one's ignorance; **se l. d'avoir laissé passer sa chance** to moan about missing one's chance; **cesse donc de te l.!** stop feeling sorry for yourself!

lamento [lamento] NM *Mus* lament

laminage [laminaʒ] NM **1** *Métal* lamination, rolling, flatt(en)ing; **l. à chaud/à froid** hot-/cold-rolling **2** *Fig (de parti politique)* near annihilation

laminaire [laminɛr] NF oarweed

laminer [lamine] VT **1** *Métal* to laminate, to roll **2** *Fig (écraser, diminuer)* to erode; *(personne)* to destroy, to annihilate; **ses revenus sont laminés par les impôts** his income is swallowed up or gobbled up by taxes; **la gauche a été laminée aux législatives** the left were nearly annihilated in the parliamentary elections

lamineur [laminœr] *Métal* ADJ **cylindre l.** roller
▷ NM rolling mill operator

laminoir [laminwar] NM *Métal* **1** rolling mill, flatting mill; **l. de finissage** finishing rolls; *Fig* **faire passer qn au l.** to put sb through the mill **2** *(pour le papier)* plate glazing calender

lampadaire [lãpadɛr] NM **1** *(lampe sur haut support)* standard lamp, *Am* floor lamp **2** *(réverbère)* lamp post

lampant [lãpã] ADJ **pétrole l.** paraffin (oil), *Am* kerosene

lamparo [lãparo] NM *Pêche* lamp *(used to attract fish)*; **aller à la pêche au l.** to go fishing by lamplight

lampe [lãp] NF **1** *(appareil d'éclairage)* lamp; *Élec* lamp, light; **à (la lumière de) la l.** by lamplight **2** *Électron* **l. (de radio)** (radio) valve or tube; **l. d'amplification** amplifying tube **3** *Arg* **s'en mettre plein la l.** to have a good blowout
▸ ▸ **l. à alcool** spirit lamp; **l. à arc** klieg light; **l. à bronzer** sun lamp; **l. de bureau** desk lamp or light; **l. de camping** camping gas lamp; **l. de chevet** bedside lamp; **l. à gaz** gas lamp; **l. halogène** halogen lamp; **l. à huile** oil lamp; **l. à incandescence** incandescent lamp; *Aut* filament lamp; *Aut* **l. de lecture** reading light, map light; **l. de mineur** miner's (safety) lamp; **l. murale** wall light or lamp; **l. au néon** neon light or lamp; **l. à pétrole** oil lamp, paraffin lamp, *Am* kerosene lamp; **l. de poche** torch, *Am* flashlight; **l. à souder** blowlamp, *Am* blowtorch; *Mil Arg* machine gun; **l. de sûreté** miner's (safety) lamp; **l. témoin** warning light or lamp; **l. tungstène halogène au quartz** tungsten-halogen lamp

lampée [lãpe] NF *Fam (d'eau, de vin etc)* gulp, swig; *(de soupe)* gulp; **finir son verre d'une seule l.** to down (the rest of) one's drink in one; **boire qch à grandes lampées** to gulp sth down

lamper [lãpe] VT *Fam (eau, vin etc)* to gulp down, to swig (down)

lampe-tempête, *pl* **lampes-tempêtes** NF hurricane lamp, storm lantern

lampion [lãpjɔ̃] NM *(lanterne)* paper lantern, Chinese lantern; *Fam* **crier sur l'air des lampions** *(slogan)* to chant

lampiste [lãpist] NM **1** *Tech* light maintenance man; *Rail* lampman **2** *Fig Fam (subalterne)* underling; *(dupe)* scapegoat, fall guy; **ce sont toujours les lampistes qui trinquent** it's always the little man that gets the blame; **s'en prendre au l.** to bully one's subordinate(s) **3** *Arch (fabricant)* lamp maker; *(vendeur)* lamp seller

lampisterie [lãpistəri] NF *Rail etc* lamp room

lamproie [lãprwa] NF *Zool* lamprey; *(de rivière)* river lamprey

lance [lãs] NF **1** *(pique)* spear; **percer un animal d'un coup de l.** to spear an animal **2** *Fig Litt* **rompre une l. ou des lances avec ou contre qn** to cross swords with sb; **rompre des lances pour qn** to take up the cudgels for sb **3** *(tuyau)* **l. d'arrosage** water hose; **l. d'incendie** fire hose

lance-bombes NM INV *Aviat* bomb launcher

lancée [lãse] NF **1** momentum, impetus; **continuer sur sa l.** to forge ahead, to press on; **je ne voulais pas t'interrompre sur ta l.** I didn't want to interrupt you (while you were) in full flow; **j'ai fait les exercices 5, 6, et 7 et sur ma l. j'ai fait le 8** I did exercises 5, 6 and 7 and while I was at it I did 8 as well **2** *Suisse (douleur)* shooting pain

lance-flammes NM INV *Mil* flamethrower

lance-fusées NM INV *Mil* rocket launcher

lance-grenades NM INV *Mil* grenade launcher

lancement [lãsmã] NM **1** *(projection)* throwing; *(de missile, fusée)* launch(ing); *(de bombe)* dropping, releasing; *(de grenade)* throwing, launching; **rampe de l.** launching ramp; **dégager l'aire de l.** to clear the launch(ing) area **2** *Sport* **l. du javelot/du disque/du marteau** throwing the javelin/the discus/the hammer; **l. du poids** putting the shot; **il a gagné au l. du poids/du javelot** he won (in) the shot, the javelin **3** *(de bateau)* launching **4** *(de moteur)* starting (up) **5** *(de projet, d'attaque)* launch(ing) **6** *Com (de compagnie, produit, modèle)* launch(-

ing); *(de compagnie)* floating; *Bourse (d'une souscription)* start; **l. de produit** product launch; *Mktg* **l. sur le marché** market entry; **l. parallèle/tardif** parallel/late entry; **campagne de l.** launch campaign **7** *Ordinat (d'impression)* start; *(de programme)* running **8** *Belg* stabbing pain

lance-missiles NM INV *Mil* missile launcher

lancéolé [lãseɔle] ADJ *Bot* lanceolate

lance-pierres NM INV catapult, *Am* slingshot; *Fig Fam* **manger avec un l.** to wolf one's food (down); *Fam* **être payé au l.** to be paid a pittance, to be paid next to nothing

lancequiner [lãskine] *Arg* V IMPERS *(pleuvoir)* **il lancequine** it's pissing down
▷ VI *(uriner)* to pee, to piss

LANCER¹ [lãse] (**je lançai(s); n. lançons**)

VT to throw **1, 2** ▪ to send out **3** ▪ to launch **4** ▪ to start **6**
VPR to throw oneself **1** ▪ to embark on *(se lancer dans)* **2** ▪ to make a name for oneself **3**

VT 1 *(projeter)* to throw, *Litt* to cast; *(violemment)* to fling, to hurl; *(flèche)* to shoot; *(fusée, torpille)* to launch; *(bombe)* to drop, to release; *(grenade)* to throw, to launch; **l. des pierres à qn** to throw stones at sb; **l. de la fumée** to send out smoke; **l. des étincelles** to shoot out sparks; **les joyaux lançaient mille feux** the jewels were sparkling brightly; **l. ses bras en avant** to throw one's arms out in front; *Pêche* **l. la ligne** to cast the line; **l. qch/qn en l'air** to throw or toss sth/sb into the air; *Constr* **l. un pont sur une rivière** to throw a bridge over a river; **une proposition que j'ai lancée à tout hasard** a suggestion that I threw out just on the off-chance; **l. une idée** to throw out an idea; **l. un coup d'œil à qn** to dart or shoot a glance at sb; **l. un regard plein de haine à qn** to shoot a look of hatred at sb; **l. un mandat d'arrêt contre qn** to issue a warrant for sb's arrest; **l. un ultimatum** to issue an ultimatum; **l. un juron** to let out a swearword; **l. un mot d'esprit/une remarque désagréable** to come out with a witty remark/an unpleasant remark; **l. une bordée d'injures** to let fly or let loose a torrent of abuse; **l. une plaisanterie** to crack or make a joke

2 *Sport (balle)* to throw; *(au base-ball)* to pitch; **l. le disque/le javelot/le marteau** to throw the discus/the javelin/the hammer; **l. le poids** to put the shot

3 *(envoyer) (signaux de détresse, SOS)* to send out; **l. un cheval** to start a horse off at full gallop; **l. un chien contre qn** to set a dog on sb; *Fig* **si vous le lancez sur ce sujet il ne s'arrêtera plus** if you start him (off) on this subject he'll never stop; **une fois lancé sur ce sujet il est intarissable** once he's (off) on this subject or once he's launched on this subject he can go on for ever

4 *(navire, projet, attaque, société, produit)* to launch; *Bourse (société)* to float; *(acteur, carrière etc)* to launch; *(mode)* to start, to launch; **l. une souscription** to start a fund; **l. qn (dans les affaires)** to give sb a start or set sb up (in business); **maintenant qu'il est lancé il pourra demander plus cher** now that he's made a name for himself he can ask for more money; *Fin* **l. des titres sur le marché** to issue shares; *Fin* **l. un emprunt** to issue a bond; **l. un appel d'offres** to invite tenders

5 *(faire démarrer) (moteur)* to start (up); **une fois lancés, les skieurs ...** once they got going, the skiers ...; **le train lancé à toute vapeur ne put freiner à temps** the train was rushing along at full speed and couldn't brake in time

6 *Ordinat (impression)* to start; *(programme)* to run, to start (up)

vi *Fam* **ma jambe/mon abcès m'a lancé toute la nuit** my leg/my abscess has been giving me shooting pains *or* has been giving me twinges all night; **ça me lance dans le bras** I've got shooting pains in my arm, I've got twinges in my arm

vpr se lancer 1 *(se jeter)* **le malheureux s'est lancé dans le vide** the poor wretch threw himself into the abyss; **se l. en avant** to rush *or* dash *or* shoot forward; **se l. à l'attaque** to throw oneself into the attack; **se l. à l'assaut d'une place forte** to launch an assault on a fortress; **se l. à la poursuite de qn** to dash off *or* rush off in pursuit of sb
2 *(s'engager)* **se l. dans** *(affaire, discussion)* to embark on, to get involved in; *(aventure)* to embark on; *(dépenses)* to get involved in; **se l. dans les affaires** to launch out into the world of business; **se l. sur le marché** to enter the market; **il s'est lancé dans des digressions interminables** he went off into endless digressions
3 *(se faire connaître)* **elle veut se l.** she wants to make a name for herself

lancer² **nm 1** *(pêche au)* **l.** rod-and-reel fishing **2** *Sport* throw; *(au base-ball)* pitch; **l. du javelot/du disque/du marteau** throwing the javelin/the discus/the hammer; **l. du poids** putting the shot; **l. franc** *(au basket)* free throw

lance-roquettes **nm inv** *Mil* rocket launcher

lance-satellites **nm inv** satellite launcher

lance-torpilles **nm inv** *Mil* **(tube) l.** torpedo tube

lancette [lɑ̃sɛt] **nf 1** *Chir* lancet **2** *Archit* **(arc à) l.** lancet (arch)

lanceur, -euse [lɑ̃sœr, -øz] **n** *(au cricket)* bowler; *(au base-ball)* pitcher; **l. de javelot/disque/marteau** javelin/discus/hammer thrower; **l. de poids** shot putter
nm *(de satellite, vaisseau spatial etc)* launcher; **l. d'engins** underwater missile launcher

lancier [lɑ̃sje] **nm 1** *Mil* lancer **2 (quadrille des) lanciers** lancers

lancinant [lɑ̃sinɑ̃] **adj 1** *(douleur)* shooting **2** *(obsédant)* *(souvenir)* haunting; *(regret)* nagging; *(air, musique)* insistent, haunting

lanciner [lɑ̃sine] **vi** *Litt (d'une douleur)* to shoot; *(d'un doigt etc)* to throb
vt *(d'une idée, des remords etc)* to haunt, to trouble, to plague

lançon [lɑ̃sɔ̃] **nm** *Zool* sand eel, launce

landais, -aise [lɑ̃dɛ, -ɛz] **adj** of/from the Landes (region); **le paysage l.** the landscape of the Landes (region); **race landaise** breed of cattle from the Landes (region)
n L. *(natif)* native of the Landes (region); *(habitant)* inhabitant of the Landes (region)

landau [lɑ̃do] **nm 1** *(voiture d'enfant)* pram, *Am* baby carriage **2** *(sorte de fiacre)* landau

lande [lɑ̃d] **nf 1** *(terre)* moor, heath **2 les Landes** the Landes (region) *(in south-west France)*

Landerneau [lɑ̃dɛrno] **nm** *Hum* community; **dans le L. universitaire** in the academic community, in academic circles; **ça va faire du bruit dans L.!** that'll set tongues wagging!

landier [lɑ̃dje] **nm** andiron, fire dog

land rover® [lɑ̃drɔvɛr] **nf** *Aut* Land Rover®

langage [lɑ̃gaʒ] **nm 1** *Ling* language; **l'étude du l.** the study of language; **l'apprentissage du l.** language learning *or* acquisition; *Méd* **troubles du l.** speech problems *or* difficulties
2 *(style, façon de s'exprimer)* language; **l. administratif/scientifique** official/scientific

language *or Péj* jargon; **l. enfantin** children's language; **l. populaire** popular speech; **tenir un l. grossier à qn** to speak rudely to sb; **il a un l. très grossier** his language is very coarse; **vous tenez là un drôle de l.** that's a strange way to talk; **changer de l.** to change one's tune; **en voilà un l.!** that's no way to talk!; **surveillez votre l.!** watch your language!
3 *(code)* **le l. des fleurs/de l'amour** the language of flowers/of love; **l. chiffré** cipher, code; **l. du corps** body language; **parler le l. de la raison** to be reasonable
4 *Ordinat* language; **l. assembleur** *ou* **d'assemblage** assembly language; **l. auteur** authoring language; **l. chiffré** cipher; **l. de commande** command language; **l. de description de page** page description language; **l. évolué** high-level language; **l. d'imprimante par pages** page printer language; **l. interactif** interactive language; **l. d'interrogation** query language; **l. machine** machine language; **l. naturel** natural language; **l. à objets** object-oriented language; **l. de procédures** procedural language; **l. de programmation** programming language; **l. source** source language; **l. utilisateur** user language

> Do not confuse with **langue**.

langagier, -ière [lɑ̃gaʒje, -jɛr] **adj** linguistic
n *Can* language professional

lange [lɑ̃ʒ] **nm 1** *(pour emmailloter)* (baby) blanket; *Arch* **langes** swaddling clothes **2** *(couche)* nappy, *Am* diaper **3** *Fig* **être encore dans les langes** to be still in its infancy

langer [lɑ̃ʒe] **vt** (**je langeai(s), n. langeons**) *(bébé)* *(mettre une couche à)* to put a nappy *or Am* diaper on; *Arch* *(emmailloter)* to wrap in swaddling clothes

langoureusement [lɑ̃gurøzmɑ̃] **adv** languorously

langoureux, -euse [lɑ̃gurø, -øz] **adj** languorous

langouste [lɑ̃gust] **nf** crayfish, spiny *or* rock lobster

langoustine [lɑ̃gustin] **nf** langoustine, Dublin Bay prawn

langue [lɑ̃g] **nf 1** *Anat* tongue; **se mordre/se brûler la l.** to bite/burn one's tongue; **coup de l.** lick; **la vache me donna un coup de l.** the cow gave me a lick *or* licked me; **tirer la l.** to stick out one's tongue (**à qn** at sb); *Fam* *(avoir soif)* to be very thirsty; *Fam* *(être dans le besoin)* to be strapped for cash; **après dix kilomètres de marche, je tirais drôlement la l.** after walking ten kilometres, my tongue was really hanging out; *Fam* **j'ai tiré la l.** *(peiné)* it was hard *or* tough going; **l. pâteuse** *ou* **chargée** coated *or* furred tongue; **ils me regardaient manger mon sandwich la l. pendante** they watched me eating my sandwich with their tongues hanging out; *Culin* **l. de bœuf** ox tongue
2 *(parole)* **délier la l. à qn** to loosen sb's tongue; **avoir la l. bien pendue** to have the gift of the gab; **ne pas avoir la l. dans sa poche** never to be at a loss for words; **elle a la l. trop longue** she can't keep her mouth shut, she talks too much; **il ne sait pas tenir sa l.** he can't keep a secret; **tiens ta l.** keep quiet about it; **je l'avais sur le bout de la l.** I had it on the tip of my tongue; **je donne ma l. au chat** *(par référence à une devinette etc)* I give up, I can't guess; **tu donnes ta l. au chat?** give up?; **tu ne dis plus rien? tu as avalé** *ou* **perdu ta l.?** you've gone all quiet, (has the) cat got your tongue?; **alors, tu as retrouvé ta l.?** well, have you found your tongue?; *Fam* **se mordre la l.** *(pour ne pas parler)* to bite one's tongue; *Fam* **s'en mordre la l.** to be

kicking oneself for having spoken; **tourner sept fois la l. dans sa bouche** to take one's time *or* think before one speaks
3 *Ling* language, *Litt* tongue; **langues étrangères** foreign languages; **elle parle deux langues couramment** she speaks two (foreign) languages fluently; **avoir le don des langues** to be a good linguist, to have a gift for languages; *Rel* to have the gift of tongues; **peuples/pays de l. anglaise** English-speaking people/countries; **l. diplomatique** language of diplomacy; **l. officielle** official language SEE GRAMMAR A8; B4
4 *(manière de s'exprimer)* language; **l. parlée/écrite** spoken/written language; **la l. bien reconnaissable de Proust** the easily recognizable language of Proust
5 *(jargon)* language; *Péj* jargon; **l. scientifique** scientific language *or Péj* jargon
6 *(personne)* **une mauvaise l.** a backbiter, a scandalmonger; **une l. de vipère** a spiteful gossip
7 *(chose allongée)* **l. de terre** strip *or* spit of land
▶▶ **l. d'arrivée** target language; **l. de bois** platitudes, clichés; **les politiciens qui parlent la l. de bois** politicians who mouth platitudes *or* clichés; **l. cible** target language; **l. de départ** source language; **l. maternelle** mother tongue; **l. morte** dead language; **l. verte** slang; **langues de feu** tongues of flame; **langues O** Oriental languages; *(institut)* = centre for Oriental studies in Paris, *Br* ≃ School of Oriental Studies; **langues vivantes** living languages; *(comme matière)* modern languages

> Do not confuse with the French word **langage**.

langue-de-bœuf, *pl* **langues-de-bœuf** **nf 1** *(champignon)* beefsteak fungus **2** *(outil)* (heart-shaped) trowel

langue-de-chat, *pl* **langues-de-chat** **nf** *Culin* (flat) finger biscuit, langue de chat

languedocien, -ienne [lɑ̃gdɔsjɛ̃, -jɛn] **adj** of/from the Languedoc; **la région languedocienne** the Languedoc region *(of southern France)*
n L. *(natif)* native of the Languedoc (region); *(habitant)* inhabitant of the Languedoc (region)

languette [lɑ̃gɛt] **nf 1** *(objet en forme de petite langue)* *(de bois, métal, terre etc)* tongue; *(de papier)* strip; *(de soulier)* tongue; *Menuis* **assemblage à rainure et l.** tongue-and-groove (joint) **2** *Élec* **contact à l.** snap contact **3** *Ordinat* slider

langueur [lɑ̃gœr] **nf 1** *(apathie)* listlessness; *Litt, Arch* **se mourir de l.** to pine away **2** *Litt (mélancolie douce, rêverie)* languor, languidness; **regard plein de l.** languishing look **3** *Litt, Arch* **(maladie de) l.** wasting disease

languide [lɑ̃gid] **adj** *Litt* languid

languir [lɑ̃gir] **vi 1** *(se mourir)* to languish, to pine, to waste away; *(d'une plante)* to wilt; **l. d'amour** to be lovesick; **la conversation languit** the conversation is flagging; **les affaires languissent** business is slack **2** *(désirer, attendre avec impatience)* **ne nous faites pas l.** don't keep us on tenterhooks *or* in suspense; *Litt* **je languis d'être avec vous** I am longing *or* pining *or* yearning to be with you; *Litt* **l. après qn/qch** to long *or* pine *or* yearn for sb/sth
vpr se languir to languish; *Litt* **se l. d'amour** to be lovesick; *Litt* **je me languis de toi** I am longing *or* pining for you

languissamment [lɑ̃gisamɑ̃] **adv** *Litt* languidly

languissant [lɑ̃gisɑ̃] **adj** *Litt* **1** *(sans énergie)* *(conversation, récit)* flagging, dragging;

(santé) failing; *(économie)* slack, inactive; *(foi)* declining, dwindling **2** *(amoureux)* *(yeux, regard)* languishing, lovesick

lanière [lanjɛr] **NF** strap; *(de fouet)* lash; **découper qch en lanières** to cut sth in(to) strips

lanifère [lanifɛr], **lanigère** [laniʒɛr] **ADJ** wool-bearing

lanoline [lanɔlin] **NF** lanolin(e)

lanterne [lɑ̃tɛrn] **NF 1** *(lampe)* lantern; *Fig* **elle veut nous faire prendre des vessies pour des lanternes** she's trying to pull the wool over our eyes; *Fam* **éclairer la l. de qn** to enlighten sb **2** *(de véhicule)* (side)light, *Am* parking light; **se mettre en lanternes** to put one's (side)lights *or Am* parking lights on **3** *Cin* projector **4** *Hist (pendant la Révolution)* **à la l.!** string them up! **5** *Archit* lantern
▸▸ **l. chinoise** Chinese lantern; **l. magique** magic lantern; **l. de projection** (slide) projector; **l. rouge** *(d'un convoi)* rear *or* tail light; *Arch (d'un bordel)* red light; **la l. rouge** *Sp, Fig* the back-marker, the tail-ender; *(dans un classement)* the one at the bottom; **l. sourde** dark lantern; **l. vénitienne** paper lantern, Chinese lantern

lanterneau, -eaux [lɑ̃tɛrno] **NM** *(au-dessus d'un escalier)* skylight

lanterner [lɑ̃tɛrne] **VI** *Fam (traînailler)* to dawdle; **faire l. qn** to keep sb hanging about *or* waiting

Laos [laɔs] **NM** Laos

laotien, -ienne [laɔsjɛ̃, -jɛn] **ADJ** Laotian **N L.** Laotian

La Palice [lapalis] **N** **vérité de L.** truism, statement of the obvious

lapalissade [lapalisad] **NF** truism, statement of the obvious

laparoscopie [laparɔskɔpi] **NF** *Méd* laparoscopy

lapement [lapmɑ̃] **NM** *(de lait etc)* lapping (up); *(bruit)* lapping

laper [lape] **VT** *(d'un chien, chat etc)* *(eau, lait etc)* to lap up **VI** to lap

lapereau, -eaux [lapro] **NM** young rabbit

lapidaire [lapidɛr] **ADJ** *(inscription)* lapidary; *(concis) (style, formule)* concise, succinct **NM** lapidary

lapidation [lapidasjɔ̃] **NF** stoning

lapider [lapide] **VT** *(jeter des pierres à)* to stone, to throw stones at; *(mettre à mort)* to stone to death; *Fig (critiquer)* to criticize severely

lapin [lapɛ̃] **NM** rabbit; *Culin* **un civet de l.** (a) rabbit stew, jugged rabbit; *Com* **peau de l.** rabbit(skin), cony (skin); **manteau en (peau de) l.** rabbitskin coat; *Fam* **poser un l. à qn** to stand sb up; *Fam* **un chaud l.** a randy devil; *Fam* **c'est un fameux l.** he's quite a guy; **se sauver** *ou* **courir** *ou Fam* **détaler comme un l.** to run like hell; **coup du l.** rabbit punch; *(dans un accident de la circulation)* whiplash injury; **mon petit l.** my pet, sweetheart
▸▸ **l. domestique** rabbit *(bred for food)*; **l. de garenne** wild rabbit

lapine [lapin] **NF** doe (rabbit)

lapiner [lapine] **VI** *(d'un lapin)* to litter

lapinière [lapinjɛr] **NF** rabbit hutch

lapis [lapis], **lapis-lazuli** [lapislazyli] **NM INV** *Minér* lapis lazuli **ADJ** **ciel l.** bright blue sky

lapon, -one [lapɔ̃, -ɔn] **ADJ** Lapp **NM** *Ling* Lapp, Lappish **N L.** Lapp, Laplander

Laponie [lapɔni] **NF** Lapland

laps [laps] **NM** **un l. de temps** a period of time; **un l. de temps de trois heures** a period of three hours

lapsus [lapsys] **NM** *(oral)* slip of the tongue;

(par écrit) slip of the pen; **l. de mémoire** lapse of memory; **faire un l.** to make a slip (of the tongue/pen); **un l. révélateur** a Freudian slip

laquage [lakaʒ] **NM** lacquering

laquais [lakɛ] **NM** footman, lackey; *Fig Péj* lackey, flunkey

laque [lak] **NF 1** *(naturelle)* lac; **l. en feuilles** shellac **2** *(vernis)* lacquer **3** *(pour les cheveux)* (hair) lacquer, hair spray **4** *(peinture)* gloss (paint)
NM 1 *(vernis)* lacquer; **de** *ou* **en l.** lacquered; **l. de Chine** japan **2** *(objet d'art)* **des laques** lacquerware; **un l.** a piece of lacquerware

laqué [lake] **ADJ 1** *(de laque naturelle)* lacquered **2** *(vaporisé de fixateur)* *(cheveux)* lacquered **3** *Culin* **canard l.** Peking duck

laquelle *voir* **lequel**

laquer [lake] **VT 1** *(de laque naturelle)* to lacquer **2** *(de vernis)* to lacquer; *(de peinture)* to paint with gloss; **meubles laqués blanc** furniture painted with *or* in white gloss

larbin [larbɛ̃] **NM** *Fam souvent Péj* flunky; **je ne suis pas ton l., débrouille-toi tout seul!** I'm not your servant, sort it out yourself!

larcin [larsɛ̃] **NM 1** *(vol)* (petty) theft **2** *Vieilli (objet volé)* loot; **ses larcins** his/her loot

lard [lar] **NM 1** *(morceau de viande)* bacon; *(gras du cochon)* fat; **l. maigre** streaky bacon; **l. gras** fatty bacon; **l. fumé** smoked bacon; **omelette au l.** bacon omelette **2** *Arg (graisse)* **(se) faire du l.** to (sit around and) get fat; **gros l.** big fat slob **3** *Fig* **se demander si c'est du l. ou du cochon** to wonder what to make of it; **c'est une vraie tête de l.** he is so pigheaded; *Fig Fam* **rentrer dans le l. à qn** to lay into sb, to let sb have it

Il faut noter que le nom anglais **lard** est un faux ami. Il signifie **saindoux**.

larder [larde] **VT** *(morceau de viande)* to lard; *Fam* **l. qn de coups de couteau** to hack at sb with a knife; *Fam* **l. un texte de citations** to lard *or* pepper a text with quotations; *Tech* **l. un morceau de bois** to stud a piece of wood with nails

lardoire [lardwar] **NF 1** *Culin* larding needle *or* pin **2** *Fam (épée)* sword

lardon [lardɔ̃] **NM 1** *Culin* lardon; **lardons** lardons, diced bacon fat **2** *Arg (enfant)* kid **3** *Vieilli (raillerie)* jibe, cutting remark

lare [lar] *Antiq* **ADJ** **les dieux lares** lares, the household gods
NM household god; **les lares** lares, the household gods

largable [largabl] **ADJ** *Aviat (container, équipement)* releasable

largage [largaʒ] **NM** *Aviat (de parachutistes, vivres etc)* dropping; *(de bombe)* releasing, dropping

large [larʒ] **ADJ 1** *(grand, étendu)* *(route, rivière, table, porte, chaussures etc)* wide; *(visage, nez, mains)* broad; **l. d'épaules** broad-shouldered; **elle a les hanches larges** she has broad hips, she is broad in the hips; **chapeau à larges bords** wide-brimmed *or* broad-brimmed hat; **route l. de dix mètres** road ten metres wide; **vêtements larges** loose-fitting clothes; **d'un geste l.** with a (broad) sweeping gesture; **terme employé dans son sens l.** term used in its wide *or* broad sense; **avoir l'esprit l.** to be broad-minded; *Beaux-Arts* **style l.** broad *or* bold *or* free style
2 *(important, considérable)* large; **de larges ressources** ample resources; **dans une l. mesure** to a large extent; **avoir une l. part de responsabilité dans qch** to bear a large part of the responsibility for sth; **ils font une part très l. à l'esprit d'initiative** they give a lot of

importance to the spirit of enterprise; **dans son spectacle il fait une l. part à l'improvisation** improvization plays a large part in his show, he devotes a lot of his show to improvization
3 *(généreux)* **mener une vie l.** to spend freely; **il n'a pas été très l.** he wasn't very generous
NM 1 *(espace)* room, space; **être au l.** to have plenty of room; *(financièrement)* to be well off
2 *Naut* open sea; **brise du l.** sea breeze; **prendre le l.** to take to the open sea; *Fam (s'enfuir)* to beat it, to clear off; **gagner le l.** to get to the open sea; **au l.!** keep away!; **au l. de Cherbourg** off Cherbourg; **trop au l.** too far from the shore
3 *(largeur)* width, breadth; **avoir** *ou* **faire dix mètres de l.** to be ten metres wide; **se promener de long en l.** to walk up and down *or* to and fro; **il parcourait la pièce en long et en l.** he was walking up and down the room; *Fam* **il examina la question en long et en l.** *ou* **en long, en l. et en travers** he examined the question from every angle, he looked into every aspect of the question
ADV **calculer l.** to allow a margin for error; **compter l.** to allow for more; **cette robe habille** *ou* **taille l.** this dress is loose-fitting; **ces chaussures chaussent l.** these shoes are wide-fitting; **voir l.** to think big; **il n'en mène pas l.** he has his heart in his boots

Il faut noter que l'adjectif anglais **large** signifie **grand, important**.

largement [larʒəmɑ̃] **ADV 1** *(dans l'espace)* widely, broadly; **la porte était l. ouverte** the door was wide open; **opinion l. répandue** widely held opinion; **l. critiqué** widely criticized; *Beaux-Arts* **peindre l.** to paint in a free *or* broad style
2 *(amplement)* amply; *(généreusement)* generously; **on l'a l. récompensé** he has been amply *or* handsomely rewarded; **si tu aimes les musées il y a l. de quoi faire à Paris** if you like museums there's more than enough to do in Paris; **dépasser l. qch** to exceed sth by a long way, to go way *or* far beyond sth; **le quota est l. dépassé** the quota has been greatly exceeded; **il a été l. devancé par ses adversaires** he was left far *or* a long way behind by his opponents; **il s'est l. inspiré de Rabelais pour écrire son roman** he drew a great deal of inspiration from Rabelais in writing his novel; **avoir l. de quoi vivre** to have ample means; **services l. rétribués** highly paid services; **avoir l. le temps** to have plenty of time; **c'est l. suffisant, ça suffit l.** it's more than enough *or* sufficient; **elle a l. quarante ans** she's at least *or* easily forty (if not more); **il en a eu l. assez** he's had more than enough; **je me suis l. servi** I've taken a generous helping

Il faut noter que l'adverbe anglais **largely** est un faux ami. Il signifie **en grande partie**.

largesse [larʒɛs] **NF 1** *(générosité)* generosity, largesse (**envers** towards); **avec l.** generously **2** **largesses** generous gifts; **faire des largesses** to make generous gifts

largeur [larʒœr] **NF 1** width, breadth; *(de voie ferrée)* gauge; *(de bateau)* breadth, beam; **avoir** *ou* **faire trois mètres de l.** to be three metres wide; **en l., dans la l.** widthwise, breadthwise; **distance en l.** distance across; **les policiers barraient la rue sur toute sa l.** the policemen blocked off the whole width of the street; *Radio* **l. de bande** bandwidth; *Ordinat* **l. de papier** paper width; *Aut etc* **l. aux coudes** elbow room; *Aut* **l. de faisceau** beamwidth **2** *Fig* **l. de vues** broadness of outlook; **l. d'esprit** broadmindedness, broadness of mind; *Fam* **dans les grandes largeurs** in a big way, well and truly

largo [largo] *Mus* **ADV** largo
NM largo

largue [larg] **ADJ** *(cordage)* loose, slack; *(vent)* free; **naviguer vent l.** to sail free
NM grand l. quartering (wind), (wind) on the quarter

largué [large] **ADJ** *Fam (qui ne comprend pas/plus)* lost; *(qui n'est plus à la page)* out of touch

larguer [large] **VT 1** *(cordage)* to let go *or* loose; **l. les amarres** to cast off *or* to slip the mooring ropes; *Fig* to slip one's moorings; **l. la grand-voile** to unfurl the mainsail **2** *Aviat (parachutiste, vivres etc)* to drop; *(bombe)* to release, to drop **3** *Fam (se débarrasser de) (personne)* to chuck, to ditch, to dump; **il a tout largué et est parti vivre aux Caraïbes** he packed *or* chucked everything in and went to live in the Caribbean
VI *Vulg (émettre des gaz intestinaux)* to fart

larme [larm] **NF 1** *(des yeux)* tear; **fondre en larmes** to burst into tears, to break down in tears; **verser des larmes de joie** to weep tears of joy; **pleurer à chaudes larmes** to weep bitterly; **avoir les larmes aux yeux** to have tears in one's eyes; **mettre les larmes aux yeux** to bring tears to one's eyes; **elle était en larmes** she was in tears; **avec des larmes dans la voix** in a tearful voice; **au bord des larmes** on the verge of tears, close to tears; *Fam* **avoir toujours la l. à l'œil** to cry easily, to be easily moved to tears; **un rien lui met la l. à l'œil** he cries over nothing; **il a ri (jusqu')aux larmes** he laughed till he cried *or* till the tears rolled down his face; **pleurer toutes les larmes de son corps** to cry one's eyes *or* heart out; **larmes de crocodile** crocodile tears **2** *Fam (petite quantité)* drop; **une l. de rhum** a drop of rum

larmichette [larmiʃɛt] **NF** *Fam* tiny drop

larmier [larmje] **NM 1** *Anat* inner corner of the eye, *Spéc* inner canthus **2** *(de cerf)* tear bag; *(de cheval)* temple **3** *Archit* drip-(stone)

larmoiement [larmwamã] **NM 1** *Méd (des yeux)* watering **2** *Péj (pleurnicheries)* snivelling

larmoyant [larmwajã] **ADJ 1** *Méd* yeux larmoyants watering eyes **2** *(pleurnicheur) (voix, ton)* tearful, snivelling **3** *Péj (histoire, film, sentimentalité etc)* maudlin, mawkish; *Hist, Littér (comédie, drame)* sentimental

larmoyer [larmwaje] **VI** (**je larmoie, n. larmoyons; je larmoierai**) **1** *(des yeux)* to water **2** *(pleurnicher)* to snivel

larron [larɔ̃] **NM** *Arch* thief; *Fam* **s'entendre comme larrons en foire** to be as thick as thieves; **l'occasion fait le l.** opportunity makes the thief; *Bible* **le bon l. et le mauvais l.** the thief that was saved and the thief that was damned

larsen [larsɛn] **NM** effet l. feedback

larvaire [larvɛr] **ADJ 1** *Zool* larval **2** *Fig (stade, état etc)* rudimentary, embryonic

larve [larv] **NF 1** larva VOIR GRAMMAIRE A14 ; *(d'insecte)* grub; *Fig* worm; *Péj* **vivre comme une l.** to live like the lowest of God's creatures **2** *Fam (personne apathique)* wimp **3** *Litt* spectre

larvé [larve] **ADJ 1** *Méd (fièvre etc)* larvate **2** *Fig (non déclaré) (guerre, conflit etc)* latent

laryngé [larɛ̃ʒe] **ADJ** *Anat* laryngeal

laryngectomie [larɛ̃ʒɛktɔmi] **NF** *Chir* laryngectomy

laryngien, -ienne [larɛ̃ʒjɛ̃, -jɛn] **ADJ** *Méd, Anat* laryngeal

laryngite [larɛ̃ʒit] **NF** *Méd* laryngitis

laryngologie [larɛ̃gɔlɔʒi] **NF** *Méd* laryngology

laryngologiste [larɛ̃gɔlɔʒist], **laryngologue** [larɛ̃gɔlɔg] **N** *Méd* laryngologist

laryngoscope [larɛ̃gɔskɔp] **NM** *Méd* laryngoscope

laryngotomie [larɛ̃gɔtɔmi] **NF** *Chir* laryngotomy

larynx [larɛks] **NM** *Anat* larynx

las¹ [lɑs] **INT** *Arch* alack!, alas!

las², **lasse** [lɑ, lɑs] **ADJ** tired, weary; **être l. de qch** to be tired *or* weary of sth; **de guerre lasse il consentit** tired of resisting, he agreed; **être l. de vivre** to be tired *or* weary of life *or* of living

lasagnes [lazaɲ] **NFPL** *Culin* lasagne

lascar [laskar] **NM** *Fam* smart *or* streetwise character; **c'est un sacré l.** he's really smart *or* streetwise; **un drôle de l.** a shady *or* dubious character; **à nous deux mon l.!** you rascal!

lascif, -ive [lasif, -iv] **ADJ 1** *(sensuel)* sensual, lascivious **2** *(lubrique) (comportement)* lascivious, lewd, lecherous

lascivement [lasivmã] **ADV** lasciviously, lustfully

lasciveté [lasivte], **lascivité** [lasivite] **NF** lasciviousness, lustfulness

laser [lazer] **NM** *Phys* laser; **disque l.** compact disc; **rayon l.** laser beam; **faire qch au l.** to do sth using a laser

lassant [lɑsɑ̃] **ADJ** wearisome, tedious

lasser [lɑse] **VT** to tire, to weary; **ses explications me lassent** I find his/her excuses so tiresome; **l. la patience de qn** to try *or* tax sb's patience
VPR se lasser to tire; **se l. de qn/de qch/de faire qch** to get tired of sb/of sth/of doing sth, to tire *or* weary of sb/of sth/of doing sth; *Litt* **faire qch sans se l.** to do sth without tiring

lassitude [lɑsityd] **NF** weariness, lassitude

lasso [laso] **NM** lasso; **prendre au l.** to lasso

lasure [lazyr] **NF** lasure

latence [latɑ̃s] **NF** latency; **une période** *ou* **un temps de l.** a period of latency, a latent period

latent [latɑ̃] **ADJ** *(maladie, chaleur etc)* latent; **état l.** latent state, latency

latéral, -ale, -aux, -ales [lateral, -o] **ADJ 1** *(de côté) (vent, choc)* lateral; **entrée/rue latérale** side entrance/street; *Théâtre* **projecteurs latéraux** side projectors **2** *Ling* **consonne latérale** lateral (consonant)
NF *Ling* **latérale** lateral

latéralement [lateralmã] **ADV** *(se déplacer)* sideways, laterally; *(être situé)* at *or* on the side, laterally; **le vent soufflait l.** the wind was blowing from the side

latéralisation [lateralizasjɔ̃] **NF** **l. à droite/à gauche** right-/left-handedness

latex [latɛks] **NM** *Bot, Ind* latex

latifundium, *pl* **latifundia** [latifɔ̃djɔm, latifɔ̃dja] **NM** *Agr* large farm

latin, -ine [latɛ̃, -in] **ADJ 1** *(qui parle une langue romane) (peuple)* Latin; **les langues latines** the Romance languages; **le caractère l.** the Latin temperament **2** *Naut* **voile latine** lateen sail **3** *Ling* Latin; **une tournure latine** a Latin expression; **une version latine** a translation from Latin
NM *Ling* Latin; **l. classique** classical Latin; **bas l.** low Latin; **l. de cuisine** dog Latin; *Fig* **j'y perds mon l.** I can't make head (n)or tail of it
N L. Latin

latinisation [latinizasjɔ̃] **NF** Latinization

latiniser [latinize] **VT** to Latinize

latinisme [latinism] **NM** Latinism

latiniste [latinist] **N** *(spécialiste)* Latinist, Latin scholar; *(étudiant)* Latin student, student of Latin

latinité [latinite] **NF** *(civilisation)* Latin civilization *or* world; *(caractère)* Latin character

latino [latino] **NM** *Fam* latino

latino-américain, -aine, *pl* **latino-américain(e)s** **ADJ** Latin-American
N L. Latin-American

latitude [latityd] **NF 1** *Géog* latitude; *(région)* latitude, region; **à 30° de l. nord** at latitude 30° north; **il faut vivre différemment sous ces latitudes** you have to adopt a different way of life in this part of the world *or* in these latitudes **2** *(liberté)* latitude, scope, freedom; **avoir/donner à qn toute l. pour agir** to have/give sb total freedom of action *or* full discretion to act; **vous avez toute l. de dire oui ou non** you are completely free *or* at liberty to say yes or no

latitudinaire [latitydinɛr] **ADJ, N** latitudinarian

lato sensu [latosɛ̃sy] **ADV** loosely *or* broadly speaking

latrines [latrin] **NFPL** latrines

lattage [lataʒ] **NM** *(du plafond, mur etc)* lathing

latte [lat] **NF 1** lath, batten, slat; **l. volige** slate lath, roof batten **2** *Fam (pied)* foot; *(chaussure)* shoe; **donner un coup de l. à qn** to kick sb, to give sb a kick; **prendre un coup de l.** to get kicked, to get a kick

latter [late] **VT 1** *(toit, plancher)* to lath; *(jointures, tuiles)* to batten **2** *Arg* **l. qn** to give sb a kicking

lattis [lati] **NM** lathing, lathwork

laudanum [lodanɔm] **NM** *Pharm* laudanum

laudateur, -trice [lodatœr, -tris] **N** *Litt* lauder, praiser

laudatif, -ive [lodatif, -iv] **ADJ** *(discours, article etc)* laudatory; **il a été très l.** he was full of praise

lauréat, -ate [lɔrea, -at] **ADJ** *(élève, candidat etc)* (prize)winning
N (prize)winner; **les lauréats du prix Nobel** the Nobel prizewinners

lauréole [lɔreɔl] **NF** daphne

laurier [lɔrje] **NM 1** *(plante)* laurel; **l. commun** bay laurel, sweet bay; *Culin* **feuille de l.** bay leaf; *Culin* **du l.** (some) bay leaves **2** *Fig (gloire)* **lauriers** laurels; **les lauriers du vainqueur** the victor's laurels; **couronne de lauriers** laurel wreath; **se reposer** *ou* **s'endormir sur ses lauriers** to rest on one's laurels; **il est revenu de ses campagnes militaires couvert de lauriers** he returned from his military campaigns covered with glory

laurier-rose, *pl* **lauriers-roses NM** *(plante)* common oleander, rose laurel

laurier-sauce, *pl* **lauriers-sauce NM** bay

LAV [lav] **NM** *Méd abrév* **lymphadenopathy associated virus**

lavable [lavabl] **ADJ** washable; **l. en machine** machine-washable; **l. à la main** washable by hand

lavabo [lavabo] **NM 1** *(appareil sanitaire)* washbasin **2** *(salle de bain)* bathroom, washroom **3** *Euph* **lavabos** *(toilettes)* toilets **4** *Rel* lavabo

lavage [lavaʒ] **NM** washing; *(avec une brosse)* scrubbing; **toutes mes affaires sont au l.** all my things are in the wash; **ma chemise a rétréci/déteint au l.** my shirt has shrunk/run in the wash; **il a fallu trois lavages pour venir à bout des taches** it took three washes to get rid of the stains
▸▸ **l. auto** carwash; **l. de cerveau** brainwashing; **faire subir un l. de cerveau à qn**

to brainwash sb; *Méd* **l. d'estomac** pumping out of the stomach; **faire un l. d'estomac à qn** to pump sb's stomach; *Fam* **l. de tête** dressing-down, telling-off

lavage-balayage, *pl* **lavages-balayages** NM *Aut* wash-wipe

lavallière [lavaljɛr] NF **(cravate) l.** necktie with a large bow, *Spéc* lavallière

lavande [lavɑ̃d] NF *Bot (fleur)* lavender; **(eau de) l.** lavender water; **bleu l.** lavender blue

lavandière [lavɑ̃djɛr] NF **1** *(blanchisseuse)* washerwoman, laundress **2** *(oiseau)* wagtail

lavaret [lavarɛ] NM *Région (poisson)* lavaret, pollan

lavasse [lavas] NF *Fam Péj (boisson)* dishwater; **son café, c'est de la l.** his coffee tastes like dishwater

lave [lav] NF *Géol* lava

lavé [lave] ADJ *(couleur)* pale, faint; *(délavé)* washed-out, faded; *Tech, Beaux-Arts* **dessin l.** wash drawing

lave-auto, *pl* **lave-autos** NM *Can* carwash

lave-dos [lavdo] NM INV back-scrubber

lave-essuie-phare, *pl* **lave-essuie-phares** NM *Aut* headlamp wash/wipe

lave-glace, *pl* **lave-glaces** NM *Aut* windscreen *or Am* windshield washer, screen wash

lave-linge NM INV washing machine

lave-mains NM INV (small) handbasin

lavement [lavmɑ̃] NM *Méd* enema; **l. baryté** barium enema

lave-phares NM INV *Aut* headlamp washer

laver [lave] VT **1** *(nettoyer avec un liquide)* to wash; **l. qch à l'eau froide** to wash sth in cold water; **l. à grande eau** *(plancher, bateau, voiture)* to swill down; *(cuisine, atelier)* to swill out, to sluice down; **l. à la brosse** to scrub; **l. qch à l'éponge** to sponge sth (down); **l. qch au jet** to hose sth (down); *(pièce, cuve etc)* to hose sth (out); **l. la vaisselle** to wash *or* do the dishes, *Br* to wash up, *Br* to do the washing-up; **l. une tache** to wash out a stain; **l. une plaie** to bathe *or* cleanse a wound; *Fig Fam* **l. la tête à qn** to tell sb off, to haul sb over the coals; *Fig* **il faut l. son linge sale en famille** one shouldn't wash one's dirty linen in public; *Fig* **l'affront a été lavé dans le sang** the insult was paid for *or* avenged in blood **2** *Fig Litt (disculper)* **l. qn d'une accusation/ de tout soupçon** to clear sb of an accusation/of all suspicion **3** *(mélanger d'eau) (peinture)* to dilute, to water down; **l. un dessin** to wash a drawing **4** *Tech* **l. un minerai** to wash an ore

VI **cette lessive lave très bien** this powder washes very well

VPR **se laver 1** *(se nettoyer)* to wash (oneself), to have a wash, *Am* to wash up; **se l. les dents** to clean *or* brush one's teeth; **se l. les cheveux** *ou* **la tête** to wash one's hair; **se l. les mains** to wash one's hands; *Fig* **je m'en lave les mains** I wash my hands of it **2** *(pouvoir être lavé)* **ce tissu ne se lave pas** this material won't wash *or* isn't washable; **comment ça se lave, la viscose?** how should viscose be washed?

laverie [lavri] NF **1** *Ind* washing plant, washery **2 l. automatique** launderette, *Am* laundromat

lave-tête [lavtɛt] NM INV shampoo basin

lavette [lavɛt] NF **1** *(de vaisselle)* dishcloth **2** *Suisse (gant de toilette)* face cloth *or* flannel, *Am* washcloth **3** *Fig Fam (homme)* spineless creature, drip, wet

laveur, -euse [lavœr, -øz] N *(personne)* washer; **laveuse (de linge)** washerwoman; **l. de vaisselle** dishwasher, *Br* washer-up; **l. de vitres** window cleaner

NM scrubber

lave-vaisselle NM INV dishwasher

lave-vitre, *pl* **lave-vitres** NM *Aut* windscreen washer, *Am* windshield washer

lavis [lavi] NM **1** *(procédé) (de dessin)* washing, tinting **2** *(dessin)* wash drawing

lavoir [lavwar] NM **1** *(établissement)* **l. (public)** (public) washhouse **2** *(bassin)* (cement) washtub **3** *Tech, Ind (machine)* washer; *(atelier)* washing plant **4** *Belg (blanchisserie)* **l. (automatique)** self-service laundry

lavomatic [lavomatik] NM launderette, *Am* laundromat

laxatif, -ive [laksatif, -iv] ADJ, NM *Méd* laxative

laxisme [laksism] NM **1** *Rel* latitudinarianism **2** *(manque de fermeté)* laxness, laxity

laxiste [laksist] ADJ **1** *(qui manque de fermeté)* lax **2** *Rel* latitudinarian

N **1** *(qui manque de fermeté)* lax person **2** *Rel* latitudinarian

layette [lɛjɛt] NF baby clothes, layette; *Com* babywear; **bleu/rose l.** baby blue/ pink

layon [lɛjɔ̃] NM forest track *or* trail; *(pour monter à cheval)* bridle path

lazaret [lazarɛ] NM lazaret(to)

lazariste [lazarist] NM Lazarist (priest)

lazulite [lazylit] NM *Minér* lazulite, blue spar

lazzi [lazi, ladzi] NMPL gibes

l/c NF *Fin (abrév* **lettre de crédit)** L/C

LCR [ɛlseɛr] NF *Fin (abrév* **lettre de change relevé)** bills of exchange statement

LDL-cholestérol [ɛldɛelkɔlesterɔl] NM *Méd (abrév* **low-density lipoprotein-cholestérol)** LDL-cholesterol

LE¹, LA¹, LES¹ [lə, la, le] ART DÉF SEE GRAMMAR A5–8; B3–4 (**le** *and* **la** *are elided to* **l'** *before a vowel or h mute;* **le** *and* **les** *contract with* **à, de** *into* **au, aux, du, des) 1** *(précisant le nom ou pronom)* the; **ouvrez la porte** open the door; **il est venu la semaine dernière** he came last week; **j'apprends le français** I'm learning French; **j'étudie l'économie/la physique** I'm studying economics/physics; **la ville a perdu le quart/le tiers de ses habitants** the city has lost a quarter/a third of its inhabitants; **l'un … l'autre** the one … the other; **mon livre et le tien** my book and yours; **j'ai l'impression qu'il ne dit pas tout** I have the impression *or a or* the feeling that there's something he's not saying; **j'ai la certitude qu'il ment** I'm certain *or* sure that he's lying; **il est arrivé le lundi 12** he arrived on Monday the 12th; **ça s'est passé la veille de Noël** it happened on Christmas Eve; **oh! le beau chat!** what a beautiful cat!; **debout, les enfants!** time to get up, children!; **voilà le livre que j'ai préféré** this is the book that I liked best; **ce n'est plus la Claire que je connaissais** she's no longer the Claire I used to know; **le Paris de l'après-guerre/que nous aimions** post-war Paris/the Paris we knew and loved; **l'Amérique de Mark Twain n'existe plus** Mark Twain's America no longer exists

2 *(noms de lieux)* **la France** France; **l'Afrique** Africa; **le Mont Blanc** Mont Blanc; **les Alpes** the Alps; **la Seine** the Seine; **le lac de Constance** Lake Constance; **les Maldives** the Maldives; **la Réunion** Réunion (Island); **l'île de Pâques** Easter Island; **la vallée du Rhône** the Rhône Valley; **dans le Berry** in the Berry (region)

3 *(noms de personnes)* **l'empereur Guillaume** the Emperor William; **le roi Édouard** King Edward; **le cardinal Richelieu** Cardinal Richelieu; **le roi de France** the king of France; *Fam* **la Marie** Marie; *Fam* **le Pierre** Pierre

4 *(avec certains noms italiens, certains noms d'actrices et de cantatrices)* **le Tasse** Tasso; **la Callas** Callas; **le Caravage** Caravaggio

5 *(devant un nom déposé)* **la Renault® de mon père** my father's Renault

6 *(noms de villes)* **Le Havre** Le Havre; **je reviens du Havre** I'm just back from Le Havre; **La Rochelle** La Rochelle; **Le Mans** Le Mans; **Le Caire** Cairo; **La Havane** Havana; **La Nouvelle-Orléans** New Orleans; **La Haye** The Hague

7 *(noms de famille)* **les tableaux de Le Brun** Le Brun's pictures; **les Curie** the Curies; **comment vont les Dupond?** how are the Duponds?

8 *(avec la plupart des jours de fête)* **la Toussaint** All Saints' Day; **quand tombe la Saint Simon?** what day does Saint Simon's day fall on?; *Fam* **à la Noël** at Christmas

9 *(parties du corps)* **j'ai mal à la gorge** I've got a sore throat; **elle a les yeux bleus** she has blue eyes; **elle a les cheveux longs/ blonds** she has long/blond hair; **elle a les hanches larges** she has wide hips; **hausser les épaules** to shrug one's shoulders; **elle ferma les yeux** she closed her eyes; **il s'est coincé le doigt dans la porte** he caught his finger in the door; **le bras me fait mal** my arm hurts

10 *Fam (environ)* **il a téléphoné vers les trois heures** he phoned (at) about *or* around three o'clock; **ça fera dans les 500 euros** it'll come to about *or* to something in the region of 500 euros

11 *(formant les superlatifs)* **les jours les plus longs** the longest days; **le meilleur vin de sa cave** the best wine in his cellar; **mon amie la plus intime** my closest friend; **c'est elle (qui est) la plus jolie** she's the prettiest; *(avec des adverbes)* **c'est elle qui travaille le mieux** she's the one who works (the) best; *(avec un superlatif absolu)* **c'est lorsqu'elle est seule qu'elle est le plus heureuse** she's happiest when she's by herself

12 *(généralisant le nom)* **je préfère le café au thé** I prefer coffee to tea; **aimer la musique/la littérature/le football** to like music/literature/football; **aller au théâtre/au cinéma** to go to the theatre/the cinema; **ils ne vont jamais au restaurant** they never go to a restaurant, they never eat out; **il méprise les pauvres** he scorns poor people *or* the poor; **l'homme est un animal social** man is a social animal; **le dauphin est un mammifère marin** the dolphin is a marine mammal; **il fume la pipe/la cigarette** he smokes a pipe/cigarettes; **je n'ai pas eu la patience d'attendre/le courage de refuser** I didn't have the patience to wait/the courage to refuse; **il a eu le culot de me réclamer de l'argent** he had the cheek to demand money from me; **j'ai le droit de vivre** I have a right to live; **donner l'exemple** to set an example; **la paresse est un des sept péchés capitaux** sloth is one of the seven deadly sins; **demander le divorce** to sue for (a) divorce; **la belle excuse!** a fine excuse!

13 *(distributif)* **trois fois l'an** three times a year; **cinq euros la livre** five euros a pound; **il vient le jeudi/(tous) les jeudis** he comes on Thursdays/every Thursday; **il a passé le samedi chez ses parents** he spent Saturday at his parents' house; **il a passé la nuit dehors** he spent the night outdoors; **il a bu toute la nuit** he drank all night; **je n'ai pas mangé de la journée** I haven't eaten all day

14 *(avec un adjectif)* **je vous donne les livres neufs et je reprends les vieux** I'll give you the new books and take back the old ones; **tu préfères la rouge ou la jaune?** do you prefer the red (one) or the yellow (one)?

15 à la française/l'italienne in the French/ Italian fashion *or* style *or* way; **champignons à la grecque** mushrooms à la grecque; **un**

travail fait à la va-vite *ou* à la hâte a piece of work done in a hurry; **encore une blague à la Marie** another one of Marie's little jokes **16** *(partitif)* **du, de la, des** *voir* **de**

le², **la²**, **les²** PRON PERS **1** *(remplaçant le nom) (pour un homme)* him; *(pour une femme)* her; *(pour un bébé, un animal)* it, him, her; *(pour une chose, une idée)* it; *(pour un navire)* it, her; *(au pluriel)* them; **je vous le/la présenterai** I'll introduce him/her to you; **je ne le lui ai pas donné** I didn't give it to him/her; **les voilà!** there they are!; **ne l'abîmez pas!** don't spoil it!; **ce pays, je le connais** I know this country **2** *(remplaçant l'adjectif ou le nom utilisé adjectivement)* **malheureux, je l'étais certainement** I certainly was unhappy; **son frère est médecin, il voudrait l'être aussi** his brother is a doctor, he would like to be one too; **j'étais fatigué mais maintenant je ne le suis plus** I was tired, but now I'm not **3** *(remplaçant une proposition)* **il me l'a dit** he told me so; **je le pense aussi** I think so too; **il est plus riche que vous (ne) le pensez** he's richer than you think (he is); **tiens-le-toi pour dit** I'm telling you once and for all; **tu le sais aussi bien que moi** you know (it) as well as I do

lé [le] NM *(de tissu)* width, breadth; *(de papier peint)* strip

leader [lidœr] NM **1** *Pol, Sp, Mktg* leader; **cette entreprise est le l. mondial de la micro-informatique** this company is the world leader in microcomputing; **l. sur le marché** market leader **2** *Journ* **(article) l.** editorial, *Br* leader, leading article

leasing [liziŋ] NM leasing; **acheter une auto en l.** to lease a car

léchage [leʃaʒ] NM licking; *Fam* **l. de bottes** bootlicking

lèche [lɛʃ] NF *très Fam* bootlicking; **faire de la l.** to be a bootlicker; **faire de la l. à qn** to suck up to sb, to lick sb's boots

lèche-bottes *Fam* ADJ INV **elle est l.** she's a bootlicker
▪ N INV bootlicker

lèche-cul NM INV *Vulg* arse-licker, *Am* asslicker, brown-nose

lèchefrite [lɛʃfrit] NF **1** *Culin* dripping pan **2** *Can (moule à gâteau)* cake tin; *(moule à pain)* loaf tin **3** *Can (marmite)* maple syrup boiler

lécher [leʃe] *(je lèche, n. léchons; je lécherai)* VT **1** *(glace, cuiller, plaies etc)* to lick; **l. le beurre d'une tartine** to lick the butter off a slice of bread; *Fig* **l. les vitrines** to go window-shopping; *Péj* **l. les bottes** *ou Vulg* **le cul à qn** to lick sb's boots, *Vulg* to lick *or* kiss sb's arse *or Am* ass **2** *(fignoler) (travail, style)* to polish; **trop léché** overpolished, overdone **3** *(effleurer) (des vagues)* to lap against; *(des flammes)* to lick; **les vagues léchaient le sable** the waves were lapping on the sand
▪ VPR **se lécher se l. les doigts** to lick one's fingers; *Fam* **il s'en léchait les doigts** *ou* **les babines** he licked his lips *or* his chops over it; *Fam* **quel beau gâteau, c'est à s'en l. les doigts** *ou* **les babines** what a lovely cake, it's really mouthwatering

lécheur, -euse [leʃœr, -øz] N *Fam Péj* bootlicker, toady

lèche-vitrines NM *Fam* window-shopping; **faire du l.** to go window-shopping

lécithine [lesitin] NF *Chimie* lecithin

leçon [ləsɔ̃] NF **1** *Scol (cours)* lesson, class; *(ce qu'on doit étudier)* lesson; **il ne connaît pas sa/ses leçon(s)** he hasn't learned his lesson(s); **réciter sa l.** to recite one's lesson; *Fig* to recite one's answers/etc parrot-fashion; *Fig* **ils avaient bien appris leur l.** they had learnt their lines well, they

had rehearsed what to say very well; **leçons de chant** singing lessons; **le bricolage en dix leçons** DIY in ten (easy) lessons **2** *(conseil)* **leçon(s)** advice; **faire la l. à qn** *(le guider)* to give sb instructions, to tell sb what to do; *(le réprimander)* to lecture sb, to give sb a lecture; **faire une l.** *ou* **des leçons de morale à qn** to lecture sb (on his/her morals); **je n'ai pas de l. à recevoir de toi** I don't need your advice *or* (any) advice from you; **je n'ai de l. à recevoir de personne** I don't need anybody's advice *or* (any) advice from anybody **3** *(enseignement)* lesson; **donner une l. à qn** to teach sb a lesson; **espérons qu'il en aura tiré une l.** let's hope he's learnt his lesson; **que cela vous serve de l.** let that be a lesson *or* a warning to you **4** *(de manuscrit)* reading **5** *Rel* lesson
▪▪ **l. de choses** general science *(in primary school)*; **leçons particulières** private lessons, private tuition

lecteur, -trice [lɛktœr, -tris] N **1** *(personne qui lit)* reader; **c'est un grand l. de romans** he reads a lot of novels, he's a great novel reader **2** *(dans l'édition)* proofreader **3** *Univ* foreign language assistant, lector
▪ NM **1** *TV etc (dispositif)* player, playback deck, reproducer; **l. de badges** badge reader; **l. de carte** *Aut* map light, spot lamp; *(de cartes de crédit)* credit card reader; **l. de carte à puce** smartcard reader; **l. de cartes magnétiques** magnetic card reader; **l. de cartes à mémoire** smartcard reader, card reader; **l. de cartouche** cartridge player; **l. de cassettes** cassette deck, cassette player; **l. de codes barres** bar code reader *or* scanner; **l. de disques compacts** compact disc player, CD player; **l. de DVD** DVD player; **l. optique** optical reader; *Cin etc* **l. de ruban perforé** punchtape reader; **l. de son** sound head, sound reader; **l. de télé-cinéma** film scanner; **l. de vidéodisque** video disc player **2** *Ordinat* reader; **l. (de disquettes)** (disk) drive, floppy (disk) drive; **l. de bandes** tape drive *or* reader; **l. de bande audionumérique** DAT drive; **l. de CD-Rom** *ou* **de disque optique** CD-Rom drive; **l. de CD-ROM double vitesse** double-speed CD-ROM drive; **l. de courrier** mail reader; **l. DAT** DAT drive; **l. par défaut** default drive; **l. de destination** destination drive; **l. de disque dur** hard disk drive; **l. de lignes/de pages** line/page scanner; **l. de MP3** MP3 player; **l. OCR** OCR reader; **l. Zip®** Zip drive

lecteur-encodeur, *pl* **lecteurs-encodeurs** NM *Ordinat* reader-encoder

lectorat [lɛktɔra] NM **1** *Univ* assistantship **2** *(lecteurs)* readership

lecture [lɛktyr] NF **1** *(action de lire)* reading; **enseigner la l. à qn** to teach sb to read; **livre de l.** reading book, reader; **livre d'une l. agréable** book that makes pleasant reading; **salle de l.** *(de bibliothèque)* reading room; **méthode de l. rapide** rapid-reading method; *Mus* **l. à vue** sight-reading; **s'informer par la l. des journaux** to keep oneself informed by reading the newspapers; **l. à haute voix** *ou* **à voix haute** reading aloud; **faire la l. à qn** to read aloud to sb; **à la l. de sa lettre, j'ai souri** on reading his letter, I smiled; *Fml* **donner l. d'un document** to read out a document (**à qn** to sb); *Pol* **projet repoussé en deuxième l.** bill rejected at the second reading; **l. des épreuves** proofreading **2** *(ce qu'on lit)* reading, reading material; **l. pour la jeunesse** reading *or* books for young people; **Balzac fait partie de mes lectures** Balzac is part of my reading; **il m'a apporté de la l.** he brought me something to read; **avoir de saines/mauvaises lectures** to read the right/wrong things, to read wholesome/unwholesome books

3 *(interprétation)* reading, interpretation; **une nouvelle l. de Balzac** a new reading *or* interpretation of Balzac; **l. marxiste/psychanalytique** Marxist/psychoanalytic(al) reading *or* interpretation; **tous les sociologues n'ont pas la même l. des faits** not all sociologists read *or* interpret the facts in the same way; **grille de l.** interpretative framework **4** *Ordinat* read(ing); **en l. seule** in read-only mode; **mettre un fichier en l. seule** to make a file read-only; **l. optique** optical reading; **l. au scanneur** scan; **l. destructive** destructive read; **l. non destructive** non-destructive read; **l. sur disque** reading to disk **5** *Cin* **l. du son** sound reproduction

> Il faut noter que le nom anglais **lecture** est un faux ami. Il signifie **conférence**.

lecture-écriture NF *Ordinat* read-write (mode); **être en l.** to be in read-write (mode)

ledit, ladite, *pl* **lesdits, lesdites** [lədi, ladit, ledi, ledit] ADJ *(contractions avec* **à** *et de: voir* **le¹***)* the aforesaid, the aforementioned, the said

légal, -ale, -aux, -ales [legal, -o] ADJ legal; *(action)* legal, lawful; **avoir recours aux moyens légaux** to take legal action, to institute legal proceedings; **suivre la procédure légale** to follow the legal procedure; **par les voies légales** legally, by legal means; *Fin* **taux l.** official rate of interest; **monnaie légale** legal tender

légalement [legalmɑ̃] ADV legally, lawfully

légalisation [legalizasjɔ̃] NF legalization; *(de signature)* authentication, certification

légaliser [legalize] VT *(rendre légal) (pratique, drogue etc)* to legalize; *(authentifier) (signature, procuration)* to authenticate, to certify; **l. des documents** to certify documents

légalisme [legalism] NM legalism

légaliste [legalist] ADJ, N legalist

légalité [legalite] NF **1** *(de mesure, décision, licenciement etc)* legality, lawfulness **2** *(situation légale)* **la l.** the law; **rester dans/respecter la l.** to keep within/respect the law; **cet acte l'a fait sortir de la l.** this act has brought *or* put him/her outside the law; **agir en toute l.** to act within the law; **il l'a ainsi dépouillé de ses biens en toute l.** he thus stripped him of his possessions quite legally

légat [lega] NM *Rel, Antiq* legate; **l. du Pape** papal legate

légataire [legatɛr] N *Jur* legatee, heir; **l. universel** sole legatee; **l. d'une succession** heir to an estate

légation [legasjɔ̃] NF legation

legato [legato] ADV *Mus* **jouer l.** to play legato

légendaire [leʒɑ̃dɛr] ADJ legendary

légende [leʒɑ̃d] NF **1** *(histoire, fable)* legend; *Fig (mensonge)* fairy tale *or* story; **entrer dans la l.** to become a legend; **entrer vivant dans la l.** to become a living legend *or* a legend in one's own lifetime; **la l. napoléonienne** the Napoleonic legend; **pays/personnage de l.** legendary country/character **2** *(sur une pièce, médaille)* inscription, legend; *(de dessin, photo)* caption; *(de diagramme, carte etc)* key, legend; **consulter la l.** to refer to the key

légender [leʒɑ̃de] VT *(photo, dessin etc)* to provide with a caption; *(plan, carte etc)* to provide with a key; **voir photo légendée** see photo with caption

LÉGER, -ÈRE [leʒe, -ɛr] ADJ **1** *(de peu de poids)* light; **l. comme une plume** as light as a feather; **armes légères** light weaponry; **un croiseur l.** a light cruiser; **industrie légère** light industry; **repas l.** light meal; **avoir le cœur l.** to be light-hearted; **partir le cœur l.** to leave with a light heart; **marcher d'un pas**

l. to walk with a light step *or* with a spring in one's step; *Fig* **je me sens plus l. depuis que je lui ai tout avoué** telling him everything has taken a (great) weight off my mind *or* shoulders

2 *(faible) (douleur, erreur, blessure)* slight; *(brise)* light, gentle; *(couche de peinture, vin, parfum)* light; *(tabac)* mild; *(thé, café)* weak; *(goût, odeur)* slight, light, faint; *(son, nuance)* faint; **avoir le sommeil l.** to be a light sleeper; **il y a eu quelques blessés légers** some people were slightly injured; *Jur* **peine légère** light sentence, mild punishment; **il y a un l. mieux** there is a slight improvement; **perte légère** slight *or* small *or* trivial loss; **une légère pointe d'ail/d'ironie** a slight *or* little touch of garlic/irony; **elle a eu un l. sourire** she gave a slight *or* little smile

3 *(insuffisant) (preuves, arguments)* thin, lightweight; **c'est un peu l.** it's a bit on the thin side; **c'est un peu l. comme résultat** there's not much to show for it; **la musique légère** light music, easy listening music; **c'est un film l.** it's a light film

4 *(désinvolte, frivole) (personne)* thoughtless; *(en amour)* fickle; **le responsable s'est montré un peu l.** the person in charge was quite offhand about it; **femme légère** *ou* **de mœurs légères** woman of easy virtue, loose woman; **avoir la cuisse légère** to sleep around; **propos légers** frivolous *or* idle talk

NF agir à la légère to act without due consideration *or* thoughtlessly; **parler à la légère** to speak unthinkingly *or* thoughtlessly; **ce nouveau parti est un danger pour la démocratie, je ne parle pas à la légère** this new party is a danger to democracy, and I'm not saying that lightly *or* I mean that very seriously; **prendre** *ou* **traiter qch à la légère** to make light of sth, not to take sth seriously, to treat sth lightly

ADV manger l. to eat lightly *or* light meals; **s'habiller l.** to wear light clothes; *Fam* **il faut y aller l. avec les tranquillisants** you have to go easy with tranquillizers

légèrement [leʒεrmã] **ADV 1** *(avec légèreté)* *(habillé, armé)* lightly; **manger l.** to eat lightly *or* light meals/a light meal **2** *(un peu) (ennuyeux, surpris, plus grand etc)* slightly, somewhat; *(blessé)* slightly; **ça sent l. le moisi** there's a slight smell of mildew; **pourrais-tu reculer l.?** could you go back slightly *or* a bit? **3** *(avec souplesse)* nimbly, gracefully; **elle se déplace l.** she moves gracefully **4** *(avec désinvolture)* **agir l.** to act without due consideration *or* thoughtlessly; **traiter qch l.** to make light of sth, not to take sth seriously, to treat sth lightly

légèreté [leʒεrte] **NF 1** *(poids faible)* lightness; *(d'un danseur, sportif, cheval)* agility; **l. de main** *(d'un pianiste, d'une infirmière)* lightness of touch **2** *(faiblesse) (de blessure)* slightness; *(de brise)* lightness, gentleness; *(du tabac)* mildness; *(de vin)* lightness; *(du thé, café)* weakness; *(de son, nuance)* faintness **3** *(désinvolture)* thoughtlessness; **agir avec l.** to act without due consideration *or* thoughtlessly; **parler avec l.** to speak unthinkingly *or* thoughtlessly **4** *(en amour)* fickleness; *(des mœurs)* looseness

leggings [legiŋz] **NFPL** leggings

légiférer [leʒifere] **VI** (**je légifère, n. légiférons; je légiférai**) to legislate (**sur** on)

légion [leʒjõ] **NF** legion; **la L. (étrangère)** the Foreign Legion; **la L. d'honneur** the Legion of Honour *or Am* Honor; *Fig* **l. de moucherons/touristes** host *or* swarm of gnats/tourists; **elle a une l. d'oncles et tantes** she has a huge number of uncles and aunts; **ils sont l.** they are legion

---

Légion d'honneur

Intended to reward not only acts of military bravery but also outstanding civilian achievements, the Legion of Honour is the highest distinction that can be conferred by the French state. It can be awarded regardless of the nationality of its recipients. It is divided into five ranks ("chevalier", "officier", "commandeur", "grand officier" and "grand-croix"). The order of the Legion of Honour is currently made up of one-third civilians and two-thirds soldiers.

---

légionnaire [leʒjɔnεr] **NM 1** *Hist* legionary **2** *(à la Légion étrangère)* legionnaire, Foreign Legionary **3** *(membre de la Légion d'honneur)* member of the Legion of Honour *or Am* Honor **4** *Méd* **maladie du l.** legionnaire's disease

législateur, -trice [leʒislatœr, -tris] *Jur* **N** *(personne qui fait les lois)* legislator, lawmaker
  NM *(corps législatif)* legislature
  ADJ legislative, lawmaking; **puissance législatrice** legislative power

législatif, -ive [leʒislatif, -iv] **ADJ** *Jur* legislative; *Hist* **l'Assemblée législative** the Legislative Assembly; **élections législatives** parliamentary elections; **le pouvoir l.** the legislature
  NM *Pol* **le l.** legislative power
  NF 1 *Hist* **la Législative** the Legislative Assembly **2** *Pol* **législatives** parliamentary elections

législation [leʒislasjõ] **NF** *Jur* legislation, law(s); **l. criminelle/fiscale/du travail** criminal/tax/employment legislation *or* law; **l. française/anglaise** French/English legislation *or* laws; **l. antitrust** antitrust *or Br* antimonopoly legislation *or* law; **l. commerciale** commercial legislation *or* law; **l. sur la consommation** consumer legislation; **l. douanière** customs legislation; **l. européenne** EU legislation; **l. financière** financial legislation; **l. sur la sécurité** safety legislation

législature [leʒislatyr] **NF** *Jur* **1** *(durée)* term of office *(of legislative body)* **2** *(corps)* legislature, legislative body

légiste [leʒist] **NM** *Jur* jurist
  ADJ **médecin l.** pathologist

légitimation [leʒitimasjõ] **NF 1** *(d'enfant)* legitimization **2** *(de délégué, titre etc)* official recognition **3** *Litt (de conduite)* justification

légitime [leʒitim] **ADJ 1** *(légal)* legitimate; *(action)* lawful; **propriétaire l.** legal owner; **union l.** marriage *(as opposed to living together)*; **héritier l.** rightful heir; **enfant l.** legitimate child; *Jur* **l. défense** self-defense, *Am* self-defence; **il était en état de l. défense** he was acting in self-defence **2** *(juste) (récompense, motif, désir etc)* legitimate, justified, justifiable; **il est tout à fait l. qu'il soit en colère, sa colère est tout à fait l.** he is quite justified in his anger, it's quite legitimate *or* justifiable for him to be angry, his anger is quite justified *or* legitimate
  NF *Arg* **ma l.** my old lady, *Br* the wife, the missus

légitimement [leʒitimmã] **ADV** legitimately; *(en colère)* justifiably; *(appartenir à qn)* rightfully; *Jur* lawfully

légitimer [leʒitime] **VT 1** *Jur (enfant, union etc)* to legitim(at)ize, to legitimate **2** *(action, demande etc)* to justify **3** *(titre, pouvoir)* to recognize

légitimiste [leʒitimist] **ADJ, N** *Hist* legitimist

légitimité [leʒitimite] **NF 1** *Jur (d'un enfant, d'une union etc)* legitimacy **2** *(bien-fondé) (de démarche, conduite etc)* legitimacy, justi-

fiability; **tes soupçons sont sans l.** your suspicions are unjustified *or* without foundation

legs [lε, lεg] **NM 1** *Jur* legacy, bequest; **l. universel** universal bequest; **l. particulier** specific bequest; **faire un l. particulier à son neveu** to make a specific bequest to one's nephew; **faire un l. à qn** to leave sb a legacy, to make a bequest to sb **2** *Fig Litt (héritage)* **le l. du passé** the legacy of the past

léguer [lege] **VT** (**je lègue, n. léguons; je léguerai**) **1** *Jur* to bequeath, to leave (**à qn** to sb) **2** *(transmettre) (tradition, qualité etc)* to hand down, to pass on (**à** to)

légume [legym] **NM 1** vegetable; **légumes verts** green vegetables, greens; **soupe de légumes** vegetable soup; **légumes secs** pulses **2** *Fig Fam (personne végétative)* vegetable; **il est devenu un vrai l. après son accident** he's become a complete vegetable since his accident
  NF *Fam* **grosse l.** bigwig, big shot

légumier, -ière [legymje, -jεr] **ADJ** **culture légumière** vegetable growing
  NM *(plat)* vegetable dish
  N *Belg (commerçant)* greengrocer

légumineux, -euse [legyminø, -øz] *Bot* **ADJ** leguminous
  NF **légumineuse** leguminous plant; **les légumineuses** Leguminosae

leitmotiv, *pl* **leitmotive** [lajtmɔtiv, lεmɔtiv] **NM** *Mus, Fig* leitmotif, leitmotiv, recurring theme

lem [lεm] **NM** *Astron* lunar exploration module, LEM, *Fam* moon buggy

Léman [lemã] **N** **le lac L.** Lake Geneva

lemme [lεm] **NM** *Math, Phil* lemma

lemming [lemiŋ] **NM** lemming

lémure [lemyr] **NM** *Antiq* lemur

lémurien [lemyrjε̃] **NM** *Zool* lemur

lendemain [lãdmε̃] **NM 1** *(jour suivant)* **le l.** the next day, the following day; **le l. de la bataille** the day after the battle; **le l. matin** the next morning, the morning after; **le l. après-midi, (dans) l'après-midi du l.** the next afternoon, the afternoon after; **il devint célèbre du jour au l.** he became famous overnight; *Fam* **un l. de cuite** *ou* **de fête** the morning after (the night before) **2** *(avenir)* **il faut penser au l.** one must think of the future *or* of tomorrow; **des lendemains prometteurs** a promising future; *Hum* **des lendemains qui chantent** a better *or* bright(er) future; **avoir d'heureux lendemains** to have happy consequences; **des succès/aventures (amoureuses) sans l.** short-lived successes/(love) affairs **3** *(période qui suit)* **au l. de la guerre/de ce scandale** soon after *or* in the days following the war/this scandal

lénifiant [lenifjã] **ADJ** *Méd, Fig* soothing

lénifier [lenifje] **VT** *(pr sub, impf n. lénifiions, v. lénifiiez)* **1** *Méd* to soothe, to alleviate **2** *Fig (apaiser)* to soothe, to calm

Lénine [lenin] **N** Lenin

léninisme [leninism] **NM** *Pol* Leninism

léniniste [leninist] **ADJ, N** *Pol* Leninist

lénitif, -ive [lenitif, -iv] **ADJ, NM** lenitive

lent [lã] **ADJ** *(mouvement, développement etc)* slow; *(poison)* slow(-acting); *(tortue etc)* slow-moving; **mort lente** slow *or* lingering death; **être l. à faire qch** to be slow to do sth; **vous êtes l. à faire la vaisselle** you're slow at *or* taking your time doing the dishes; **vous êtes l. à manger** you're a slow eater, you eat slowly; **vous êtes l. à comprendre** you're slow to understand *or Fam* slow on the uptake; **avoir l'esprit l.** to be slow-witted, to be slow in understanding, *Fam* to be slow on the uptake

lente [lãt] **NF** nit

lentement [lãtmã] ADV slowly; **ruisseau qui coule l.** slow-flowing stream; **l. mais sûrement** slowly but surely

lenteur [lãtœr] NF **1** (*développement lent*) slowness; **avec l.** slowly **2 lenteurs** (*actions lentes*) slowness; **les lenteurs de la justice** the slowness of the law

lentigo [lãtigo] NM *Méd* lentigo

lentille [lãtij] NF **1** *Culin, Bot* lentil **2** *Bot* **l. d'eau** duckweed; *Spéc* lemna **3** *Opt* lens; **lentilles de contact** *ou* **cornéennes** contact lenses; **lentilles souples/dures** soft/hard lenses

lento [lɛnto] ADV, NM *Mus* lento

léonin [leɔnɛ̃] ADJ leonine; **partage l.** lion's share

léopard [leɔpar] NM **1** leopard; **manteau de l.** leopard skin coat **2** *Hér* leopard

LEP [ɛløpe, lɛp] NM **1** *Anciennement* (*abrév* **Lycée d'enseignement professionnel**) ≃ technical college **2** (*abrév* **livret d'épargne populaire**) = special tax-exempt savings account

lepeniste [ləpenist] N *Pol* = supporter of Jean-Marie Le Pen

lépidoptère [lepidɔptɛr] ADJ lepidopterous ◊ NM (*insecte*) lepidopteran; **les lépidoptères** Lepidoptera

lèpre [lɛpr] NF **1** *Méd* leprosy **2** *Fig* (*pourriture, ce qui ronge*) **mur rongé par la l.** peeling *or* flaking *or* crumbling wall **3** *Litt* (*mal*) canker, scourge; **l'envie le ronge comme une l.** envy eats away at him like a cancer

lépreux, -euse [leprø, -øz] ADJ **1** *Méd* leprous **2** *Fig* (*mur*) peeling, flaking, crumbling; (*quartier*) dilapidated, rundown ◊ N leper; **traiter qn comme un l.** to treat sb like a leper

léproserie [leprozri] NF leper hospital

leptine [lɛptin] NF leptin

LEQUEL, LAQUELLE, LESQUELS, LESQUELLES
[ləkɛl, lakɛl, lekɛl] (*contracted with* **à** *and* **de** *to* **auquel, auxquel(le)s, duquel, desquel(le)s**) PRON REL (*personne*) who; (*après prép*) whom; (*chose*) which; **le père de cette jeune fille, l. est très riche** this girl's father, who is very rich; **le père de cette jeune fille, laquelle est très riche** the father of this girl, who is very rich; **ont comparu trois témoins, lesquels ont déclaré ...** three witnesses appeared, who stated ...; **la dame avec laquelle elle était sortie** the lady with whom she had gone out; **les deux officiers entre lesquels elle était assise** the two officers between whom she was sitting; **j'ai retrouvé mon parapluie, l. était sous mon lit** I've found my umbrella, which was under my bed; **l'adresse à laquelle il devait m'écrire** the address at which he was to write to me; **la farine avec laquelle j'ai fait ce gâteau** the flour (that) I used to make this cake *or* with which I made this cake; **l'actrice à laquelle je pense est plus jeune** the actress (that) I'm thinking of *or* of whom I'm thinking is younger; **la personne par laquelle il faut passer pour obtenir ce dossier** the person (that) you have to go through to get this file; **décision par laquelle ...** decision whereby ...; **n'importe l. fera l'affaire** any (one) of them will do; **il y avait beaucoup de gens, parmi lesquels mon cousin Paul** there were a lot of people, among whom was my cousin Paul; **la dame chez laquelle je l'ai rencontré** the lady at whose house I met him; **l'homme sans l'avis duquel on ne peut rien faire** the man without whose advice one can do nothing; **la maison sur la porte de laquelle vous trouverez une plaque** the house with a plaque on the door; **le roman d'après l. il a tiré son film** the book his film from *or* on which he based his film SEE GRAMMAR A32–3; B22 ◊ ADJ REL **voici cent euros, laquelle somme vous était due par mon père** here's a hundred euros, (which was) the sum my father owed you; **j'ai**

vu son adversaire, **l. adversaire est impressionnant** I've seen his opponent, (who is) an impressive one; **il écrira peut-être, auquel cas ...** perhaps he will write, in which case ... SEE GRAMMAR A31; B17 ◊ PRON INTERR which (one); **lesquel(le)s** which; **l. (de ces chapeaux) préférez-vous?** which (one) (of these hats) do you prefer?; **l. d'entre nous?** which (one) of us?; **de laquelle de ces deux régions êtes-vous originaire?** which (one) of these two regions do you come from?; **auquel de ces deux hommes faites-vous confiance?** which (one) of these two men do you trust?

lerch(e) [lɛrʃ] ADV *Arg* **pas l.** damn all, *Br* bugger all

lérot [lero] NM lerot, garden dormouse

les [le] *voir* **le¹, le²**

lesbianisme [lɛsbjanism] NM lesbianism

lesbien, -ienne [lɛsbjɛ̃, -jɛn] ADJ lesbian ◊ NF **lesbienne** lesbian

lèse-majesté [lɛzmaʒɛste] NF INV *Jur* high treason, lese-majesty

léser [leze] VT (**je lèse, n. lésons; je léserai**) **1** (*désavantager*) to wrong; (*intérêts de qn*) to harm, to damage; *Jur* **l. les droits de qn** to encroach *or* infringe upon sb's rights; **la partie lésée** the injured party **2** *Méd* (*organe*) to injure

lésine [lezin] NF *Litt, Vieilli* stinginess

lésiner [lezine] VI to skimp (**sur** on); **ils n'avaient pas lésiné sur le vin** they hadn't skimped on the wine; **ne pas l. sur les moyens** not to go in for penny-pinching; (*pour une fête, en vacances etc*) to really push the boat out

lésineur, -euse [lezinœr, -øz] N *Vieilli* niggard, miser

lésion [lezjɔ̃] NF *Méd, Jur* lesion

lessivable [lesivabl] ADJ (*papier peint, tissus etc*) washable

lessivage [lesivaʒ] NM (*de linge, mur etc*) washing; *Chimie* leaching; *Fig* **c'est le grand l. dans la compagnie** there's a big clear-out (of personnel) going on in the company

lessive [lesiv] NF **1** (*produit*) (*en poudre*) washing powder; (*liquide*) liquid detergent; *Chimie* lye **2** (*action de laver*) wash(ing); **faire la l.** to do the washing; **jour de l.** wash(-ing) day; **j'ai fait trois lessives ce matin** I've done three washes this morning; **une l. de blanc et une l. de couleurs** one wash of whites and one wash of coloureds **3** (*linge sale*) (dirty) washing **4** (*linge propre*) (clean) washing; **une l.** a batch of washing **5** *Fig* (*assainissement*) shake-out, clear-out (operation); **il faut faire une grande l. dans cette famille** this family really needs sorting out

lessivé [lesive] ADJ *Fam* (*fatigué*) washed out, worn out, done in

lessiver [lesive] VT **1** (*nettoyer*) (*sol, mur etc*) to wash **2** *Chimie* to leach **3** *Fig très Fam* (*battre*) to lick, to wipe the floor with; **se faire l.** (*au jeu*) to be cleaned out **4** *Fig Fam* (*fatiguer*) to wear out, to do in; **ce match m'a lessivé** this match has worn me out *or* done me in

lessiveuse [lesivøz] NF **1** *Anciennement* boiler, *Br* copper **2** *Belg* (*machine à laver*) washing machine

lessiviel [lesivjɛl] ADJ detergent; **produit l.** detergent (product)

lest [lɛst] NM (*de bateau, ballon*) ballast; *Naut* **naviguer sur son l.** to sail in ballast *or* without a cargo; **jeter** *ou* **lâcher du l.** to discharge ballast; *Fig* (*faire des concessions*) to make concessions

lestage [lɛstaʒ] NM (*de bateau, ballon*) ballasting

leste [lɛst] ADJ **1** (*agile*) (*personne, animal*) nimble, agile; (*mouvement*) brisk, nimble **2**

Fig (*grivois*) (*manières, gestes, mot*) crude; (*plaisanteries, roman etc*) risqué

lestement [lɛstəmã] ADV nimbly, smartly; (*avec une légèreté choquante*) offhandedly, casually

lester [lɛste] VT **1** (*bateau, ballon*) to ballast **2** *Fam* (*poche, portefeuille etc*) to stuff, to fill; **l. son estomac** to fill one's stomach ◊ VPR **se lester 1** (*plongeur etc*) to weigh oneself down **2** *Fam* **se l. (l'estomac)** to stuff oneself; **se l. les poches de petite monnaie/de bonbons** to stuff *or* fill one's pockets with small change/sweets

létal, -ale, -aux, -ales [letal, -o] ADJ lethal; *Biol* **gène l.** lethal gene; **dose létale** lethal dose

letchi [lɛtʃi] NM *Bot* lychee, litchi

léthargie [letarʒi] NF lethargy; *Méd* coma; *Méd* **tomber en l.** to sink into a coma; *Fig* **en l.** in a state of lethargy

léthargique [letarʒik] ADJ lethargic

lette [lɛt] NM *Ling* Lettish, Latvian

letton, -onne [lɛtɔ̃, -ɔn] ADJ Latvian; (*personne*) Lett, Latvian ◊ NM *Ling* Lettish, Latvian ◊ N **L.** Latvian, Lett

Lettonie [lɛtɔni] NF Latvia

lettrage [lɛtraʒ] NM *Typ* lettering

LETTRE [lɛtr] NF **1** (*de l'alphabet*) letter; **l. majuscule/minuscule** capital/small letter; **mot de sept lettres** seven-letter word, word of seven letters; **écrire qch en toutes lettres** to write sth out in full; **écrire une somme en (toutes) lettres** to write an amount in words; *Fig* **c'est écrit en toutes lettres** it's there in black and white; **je l'ai vu écrit en toutes lettres dans les journaux** I saw it in black and white in the newspapers; *Typ* **le corps de la l.** the body of the letter; *Fig Litt* **c'est gravé en lettres d'or** it will remain in my/our/*etc* memory for all time; **c'est gravé en lettres de feu** it's written in letters of fire; **écrit/gravé en lettres de sang** written in blood

2 (*missive*) letter; **petite l.** note, short letter; **mettre une l. à la poste** *ou* **à la boîte** to mail or *Br* to post a letter; *Vieilli* **c'est pour moi lettres closes** it's a mystery to me; *Fam* **c'est passé comme une l. à la poste** it went off without a hitch, it went off smoothly; **ce couscous est passé comme une l. à la poste** this couscous went down with no trouble; **la nouvelle est passée comme une l. à la poste** the news was received without any fuss

3 **selon la l. de la loi** according to the letter of the law; **au pied de la l.** literally; **traduire à la l.** to translate word for word; **il prend les choses à la l.** he takes everything literally; **j'ai suivi vos instructions à la l.** I've followed your instructions to the letter; **il fut surréaliste avant la l.** he was a surrealist before the word had been invented

4 lettres (*littérature*) literature, *Litt* letters; *Univ* arts subjects, humanities; *Litt* **les belles lettres** literature; **homme/femme de lettres** man/woman of letters; **avoir des lettres** to be well read; *Univ* **faculté de lettres** faculty of arts *or* humanities

▸ ▸ **l. d'accompagnement** covering letter; **l. d'affaires** business letter; **l. d'amour** love letter; **l. anonyme** anonymous letter; **l. par avion** airmail letter; **l. d'avis** advice note; *Hist* **l. de cachet** = order under the King's private seal; *Fin* **l. de change** bill of exchange, B/E; *Fin* **l. de change relevé** bills of exchange statement; **l. circulaire** form letter; **lettres classiques** ≃ classics; **l. commerciale** business letter; **l. de confirmation** letter of confirmation; *Pol* **lettres de créance** credentials; *Banque, Com* **l. de crédit** letter of credit; *Com* **émettre une l. de crédit** to open a letter of credit; *Com* **l. de crédit docu-**

mentaire documentary letter of credit; *Com* **l. de crédit irrévocable** irrevocable letter of credit; **l. de démission** letter of resignation; **l. d'embauche** written offer of employment; **l. d'excuse** letter of apology; **l. exprès** express letter; **l. de félicitations** letter of congratulations, congratulatory letter; *Fin* **l. de gage** debenture bond; *(pour hypothèque)* mortgage bond; *Fin* **l. de garantie** letter of guarantee; *Fin* **l. de garantie bancaire** bank guarantee; **l. de grâce** reprieve; **l. d'injures** abusive letter; *Jur* **l. d'intention** letter of intent; **l. de licenciement** letter of dismissal; **l. de menace** threatening letter; *Jur* **l. missive** letter missive; **lettres modernes** *(section scolaire ou universitaire)* French; *Belg* **l. de mort** death announcement; **ce règlement est resté l. morte** this regulation was not enforced *or* stayed a dead letter; **ce projet est resté l. morte** this project was never put into operation; **toutes ses bonnes résolutions sont restées l. morte** he never put any of his good resolutions into practice; **l. de motivation** covering *or Am* cover letter *(in support of one's job application);* **lettres de noblesse** letters patent of nobility; *Fig* **donner ses lettres de noblesse à qch** to establish *or* prove the worth of sth; *Fig* **conquérir** *ou* **gagner ses lettres de noblesse** to establish *or* prove its worth; *Journ* **l. ouverte** open letter *(*à* to);* *Hist* **lettres patentes** letters patent; **l. de poursuite** letter threatening legal action, chasing letter; **l. de rappel** reminder; **l. de réclamation** letter of complaint; **l. de recommandation** letter of recommendation, reference; **l. recommandée** registered letter; **l. recommandée avec accusé de réception** = registered letter with confirmation of receipt; **l. de relance** follow-up letter; **l. de relance des impayés** debt chasing letter; **lettres supérieures** = preparatory classes for the Normale Supérieure littéraire; **lettre-transfert,** *pl* **lettres-transferts** transfer *or Am* decal letter; *Com* **l. de transport aérien** air waybill; **l. type** *(pour mailing)* form letter; **l. de vente** sales letter; *Com* **l. de voiture** waybill, consignment note; *Com* **l. de voiture CIM** CIM waybill; *Com* **l. de voiture CMR** CMR waybill; *Com* **l. de voiture fluviale** inland waterway waybill

lettré, -ée [letre] ADJ **1** *(personne)* well-read, cultured **2** *Belg (sachant lire et écrire)* **il est l.** he can read and write
N **1** well-read person **2** *Belg (personne sachant lire et écrire)* = person who can read and write

lettrine [letrin] NF *Typ (au début des chapitres)* drop cap; *(dans un dictionnaire)* running head(line)

leu,[1] *pl* **lei** [lø, lɛ] NM *(monnaie)* leu, *pl* lei

leu[2] NM **à la queue l. l.** in single file, in Indian file

leucémie [løsemi] NF *Méd* leukaemia, *Am* leukemia

leucémique [løsemik] *Méd* ADJ leukaemic, *Am* leukemic
N leukaemia *or Am* leukemia sufferer

leucocytaire [løkositer] ADJ *Physiol* leucocytic

leucocyte [løkosit] NM *Physiol* leucocyte, leukocyte

leucocytose [løkositoz] NF *Méd* leucocytosis

leucome [løkom] NM *Méd* leucoma, albugo

leucorrhée [løkɔre] NF *Méd* leucorrh(o)ea

leucose [løkoz] NF *Méd* leukaemia, *Am* leukemia

leur[1] [lœr] ADJ POSS their; **l. oncle et l. tante** their uncle and (their) aunt; **l. père et l. mère,** *Litt* **leurs père et mère** their mother and father; **ils ont mis l. chapeau et leurs**

gants they put on their hat and (their) gloves; **elles ont pris l. sac** *(il n'y a qu'un sac)* they took their bag; *(chacune a son sac)* they took their bags; **elles ont pris leurs sacs** they took their bags; **un(e) de leurs ami(e)s** a friend of theirs, one of their friends; **un professeur de leurs amis** a teacher friend of theirs; *Fam* **ils auront l. chambre à eux** *(il n'y a qu'une chambre)* they'll have their own room; *(chacun aura sa chambre)* they'll have their own rooms; *Fam* **l. imbécile de frère** their idiot of a brother; *Fam* **leurs artistes de mari** their artist husbands; *Fam* **ils ont eu l. vendredi** they got Friday off SEE GRAMMAR A30; B21

PRON POSS **le l., la l., les leurs** theirs; **ils me prêtent le l.** I can borrow theirs; **tu n'as qu'à prendre le l.** just take theirs; **il ressemble au l.** it looks like theirs; **ils veulent bien te donner du l.** you can have some of theirs; **ils n'en ont pas besoin, ils ont le l.** they don't need it, they've got their own; **je n'en ai pas besoin, j'ai le l.** I don't need it, I've got theirs; **les deux leurs** their two, the two *or* both of theirs; *(en insistant)* their own two; **ils nous ont laissé deux des leurs** they gave us two of theirs; *(ils en ont sacrifié deux)* they gave us two of their own; *très Fam* **le l. bébé est plus intelligent** their baby is more intelligent; *Fam* **à la l.!** *(en buvant)* let's drink to them! SEE GRAMMAR A30; B21-2

NM **le l.** *(ce qui leur appartient)* theirs; **ils devraient y mettre du l.** they should really do their share
NMPL **les leurs** *(leur famille)* their family, *Fam* their folks; *(leurs partisans)* their followers; *(leurs coéquipiers)* their team-mates; **ils font leurs vos principes** they have adopted these principles of yours; **ils font leurs les félicitations que je vous adresse** they join me in congratulating you

leur[2] PRON *voir* **lui**[1]

leurre [lœr] NM **1** *(pour faucons)* lure; *(pour gibier)* decoy; *(pour poissons)* (artificial) bait, lure **2** *(illusion)* illusion, delusion **3** *Mil* chaff

leurrer [lœre] VT **1** *(en fauconnerie)* *(faucon)* to lure **2** *(tromper)* to deceive, to delude; **l. qn par des promesses** to deceive sb with promises; **il se laisse facilement l.** he is easily taken in
VPR **se leurrer** to delude oneself *(sur* about)

lev, *pl* **leva** [lɛv, leva] NM *(monnaie)* lev, *pl* leva

levage [ləvaʒ] NM **1** *Tech* lifting (up), hoisting, raising; **câble de l.** hoisting cable; **appareil de l.** lifting apparatus; **cric de l.** lifting jack **2** *Culin (de pâte etc)* rising

levain [ləvɛ̃] NM leaven; **pain au/sans l.** leavened/unleavened bread; *Fig Litt* **ils furent le l. de la révolte/du changement** they sowed the seeds of revolt/change

levant [ləvɑ̃] ADJ **soleil l.** rising sun; **il est parti au soleil l.** he left at sunrise *or Am* at sun-up
NM **1** *Litt* **le l.** the east, the orient; **du l. au couchant** from East to West **2** *Vieilli* **le L.** the Levant

levantin, -ine [ləvɑ̃tɛ̃, -in] *Vieilli* ADJ Levantine
N **L.** Levantine

levé [ləve] ADJ **1** *(en l'air) (main, poing)* raised; **voter à mains levées** to vote by a show of hands; **dessin à main levée** freehand drawing; **pierre levée** standing stone **2** *Culin* **pâte bien levée** well-risen dough **3** *(debout)* up, out of bed; *(du soleil etc)* up; **je suis l. de bonne heure tous les jours** I'm up early every day **4** *Belg Fam* **bien/mal l.** in a good/bad mood
NM **1** *(de terrain)* plan, survey; **l. aérophotogrammétrique** aerial survey; **faire le l. d'un terrain** to survey a piece of land **2** *Mus* up beat

levée [ləve] NF **1** *(action de faire cesser)* *(d'embargo, de peine, d'interdiction, de sanctions etc)* lifting; *(de séance)* adjournment; *(d'immunité parlementaire)* stripping; *Mil (de siège)* raising; *(de scellés)* removal, breaking; *Jur* **demander la l. de la séance** to ask for an adjournment **2** *(enrôlement) (de troupes)* levy(ing) **3** *(collecte) (de lettres)* collection; **heures de l.** collection times; **la l. est faite** the post has been collected *or* has gone; **il y a trois levées par jour** there are three collections a day; *Vieilli* **la l. d'un impôt** the levying of a tax; **l. des impôts** tax collection, collection of taxes; *Fin* **l. des titres** taking delivery of shares; *Fin* **l. des actions** taking up of stock **4** *Cartes* trick; **faire une l.** to take a trick
▸▸ **l. de boucliers** general outcry; **levées de compte** personal withdrawals; **l. du corps** = removal of the coffin; **pendant la l. du corps la veuve s'est évanouie** the widow fainted as the coffin was being removed *or* carried out; *Jur* **l. d'écrou** release from prison; *Jur* **l. de jugement** transcript of the verdict; **l. en masse** levy en masse; *Jur* **l. d'option** exercising of an option; **l. de terre** levee

lève-glace(s) [lɛvglas] NM INV *Aut* window winder

LEVER[1] [ləve] *(je lève, n. levons; je lèverai)*
VT **1** *(objet)* to lift, to raise; *(filet de pêche)* to raise; *(store)* to open; *(vitre)* to wind up; **l. son verre (à qn/qch)** to raise one's glass (to sb/sth); **je lève mon verre à votre réussite/aux futurs époux** here's to your success/the happy couple; **l. un étendard** to raise a standard; *Fig Litt* **l. l'étendard de la révolte** to raise the standard of revolt; *Naut* **l. l'ancre** to weigh *or* lift anchor; *Fig Fam* to take off, to hit the road
2 *(parties du corps)* to raise, to lift; **l. la tête** to look up, to raise one's head; *Fig Litt (se montrer digne)* to hold one's head high; **l. les yeux (sur qn)** to look up (at sb); **lève les yeux quand je te parle!** look at me when I'm talking to you!; **l. les yeux au ciel** to raise one's eyes to heaven *or* the heavens; **l. les sourcils** to raise one's eyebrows; **l. les bras au ciel** to throw up one's hands; *Fig Fam* **l. le coude** to (be able to) knock it back; **l. la main droite** to raise one's right hand; *Fig* **l. la main sur qn** to raise *or* lift one's hand to sb; **l. le doigt** *(à l'école)* to put one's hand up; **il n'a pas levé le petit doigt** he didn't lift a finger, he didn't do a thing; **lève les pieds quand tu marches** lift your feet up when you walk; *Fam* **on conseille aux automobilistes de l. le pied ce soir** motorists are advised to drive slowly this evening; *Fam* **lève le pied** *(ralentis)* slow down; **ça me lève le cœur** it makes my stomach turn; *très Fam* **lève ton cul!** move your arse!; *Fam* **l. la patte** *(d'un chien)* to cock *or* lift its leg
3 *(faire cesser) (embargo, peine, interdiction)* to lift; *(difficulté, doute, ambiguïté, inhibitions)* to remove; *(audience)* to adjourn; *Mil (siège)* to raise; **l. la séance** to close a/the meeting; *Jur* to adjourn; **l. le camp** to strike *or* break camp; *Fig Fam* to take off, to hit the road, to go; *Fig* **cet article lève le voile sur l'affaire des diamants** this article reveals the truth about the affair of the diamonds
4 *Jur (enlever)* **l. les scellés** to break the seals
5 *(débusquer) (perdrix)* to flush; *Arg (femme)* to pick up, *Br* to pull; *(de prostituée) (client)* to pick up; **l. un lièvre** to start a hare; *Fig* to open a can of worms
6 *(faire sortir du lit) (enfant, malade)* to get up
7 *(collecter) (lettres, courrier)* to collect; *Fin (actions, titres, options)* to take up; **l. des impôts** to collect *ou Vieilli* levy taxes
8 *(enrôler) (troupes, armée)* to raise, to levy
9 *Cartes* **l. les cartes** to pick up a trick

10 *(plan)* to make, to draw
11 *Culin* **l. les filets** to remove the fillets
VI 1 *Litt (du blé, du grain)* to shoot
2 *(de la pâte)* to rise
3 *Cartes* to pick up a trick
VPR se lever 1 *(se mettre debout)* to stand up, to get up, to rise; **levez-vous** stand up, get up; **se l. de sa chaise** to get up (from one's chair), to rise (from one's chair), to stand up; *Jur* **accusé, levez-vous** the accused will rise; **va aider grand-mère à se l.** go and help grandma (to get) up; **se l. de table** to leave the table; **le peuple se leva en masse** *ou* **en foule contre l'oppresseur** the nation rose up as one against the oppressor
2 *(quitter le lit)* to get up, to get out of bed; **je me lève de bonne heure** I'm an early riser, I get up early; *Fam* **se l. du pied gauche** to get out of bed on the wrong side
3 *(apparaître) (du soleil, d'un astre, de la lune)* to rise; *(de la brise, du vent)* to rise, to get up; **le jour se lève** day is breaking *or* dawning; *Fig Litt* **le désespoir/la tristesse se lève dans mon cœur** despair/sadness is welling up inside me
4 *(s'éclaircir) (du temps)* to clear up; *(de la brume)* to lift, to clear up
5 *(se mouvoir vers le haut) (des mains)* to go up; *Théâtre (du rideau)* to go up, to rise; *(vitre)* to wind up

lever² NM **1** *(du lit)* getting up, *Fml* rising; *Hist (du roi)* levee; **programme de la journée: l. 6h30, petit-déjeuner 7h30** today's schedule: get up 6.30, breakfast 7.30; **au l., il est bon de boire un jus d'orange** first thing in the morning, it's good to have a drink of orange juice **2** *(apparition)* **l. du soleil** sunrise; **l. du jour** daybreak **3** *(montée), Théâtre (du rideau)* rising, rise; **le l. du rideau est à 19h** the curtain rises at 7 pm; *Fig* **un l. de rideau** a curtain raiser **4** *(croquis)* = **levé** NM **1**

lève-tard [lɛvtar] NM INV *Fam* late riser

lève-tôt [lɛvto] NM INV *Fam* early riser

lève-vitre, *pl* **lève-vitres** [lɛvvitr] NM *Aut* window winder

levier [ləvje] NM **1** *(outil)* crowbar, lever; **soulever/ouvrir qch avec un l.** to prize *or* prise *or* lever sth up/open **2** *Phys* lever; **bras de l.** lever arm; **force de l.** leverage; **faire l.** to act as a lever; **ce poids fait l. et permet de bouger la caisse** this weight acts as a lever and allows the crate to be moved **3** *(commande)* lever, handle; *Tech* **l. d'arrêt** shut-off lever; **l. de frein** brake lever; **l. de commande** control lever; *Fig* **être aux leviers de commande** to be in control *or* in command; **l. de dégagement du chariot** *(de machine à écrire)* carriage release arm; **l. de dégagement du papier** *(de machine à écrire)* paper release arm; *Aut* **l. (de changement) de vitesse** gear lever, gear stick, *Am* gearshift; *Aut* **l. de direction** steering lever; *Aut* **l. de débrayage** clutch release lever; *Aut* **l. de vitesses au plancher** floor shift; *Aut* **l. de vitesses sur colonne de direction** column change; *Aut* **l. sélecteur** selector lever; **à fourche** forked lever **4** *Fig (motif d'action)* spur, lever **5** *Écon* **l. financier** financial leverage

lévitation [levitasjɔ̃] NF levitation; **être en l.** to be levitating

lévite [levit] NM *Rel* Levite

levraut [ləvro] NM leveret

lèvre [lɛvr] NF **1** *Anat* lip; **avoir les lèvres charnues** *ou* **pleines/minces** to have thick *or* full/thin lips; **la l. inférieure** the lower lip; **se mettre du rouge à lèvres** to put on lipstick; **il avait un cigare aux lèvres** he had a cigar in his mouth; **le sourire aux lèvres** with a smile on his lips; **j'ai son nom sur les lèvres** *ou* **le bord des lèvres** his name is on the tip of my tongue; **son nom est sur toutes les lèvres** his name is on everybody's lips; **manger du bout des lèvres** to nibble *or* pick at one's food; **il accepta, mais du bout des lèvres** he grudgingly accepted; **rire du bout des lèvres** to force a laugh; *Fig* **nous étions tous suspendus à ses lèvres** we were all hanging on his every word; **pincer les lèvres** *(pour ne pas rire, pour exprimer son dédain)* to purse one's lips **2** *Anat (de la vulve)* **lèvres** lips, labia; **les grandes/petites lèvres** the labia majora/minora **3** *(bord) (de plaie)* lip; *(de cratère)* rim **4** *Bot* lip, *Spéc* labium

levrette [ləvrɛt] NF **1** greyhound bitch; **l. (d'Italie)** (small) Italian greyhound **2** *très Fam* **en l.** doggy fashion

lévrier [levrije] NM greyhound; **l. irlandais** *ou* **d'Irlande** Irish wolfhound; **l. d'Italie** Italian greyhound; **l. afghan** Afghan hound; **l. à poil long** borzoi; **courses de lévriers** greyhound racing

levure [ləvyr] NF yeast; **l. de boulanger** fresh *or* baker's yeast; **l. de bière** brewer's yeast; **l. chimique** = baking powder; **l. en sachet** yeast in a packet *or* sachet

lexème [lɛksɛm] NM *Ling* lexeme

lexical, -ale, -aux, -ales [lɛksikal, -o] ADJ lexical

lexicalisation [lɛksikalizasjɔ̃] NF lexicalization

lexicalisé [lɛksikalize] ADJ lexicalized

lexicographe [lɛksikɔgraf] N lexicographer

lexicographie [lɛksikɔgrafi] NF lexicography

lexicographique [lɛksikɔgrafik] ADJ lexicographical

lexicologie [lɛksikɔlɔʒi] NF lexicology

lexicologique [lɛksikɔlɔʒik] ADJ lexicological

lexicologue [lɛksikɔlɔg] N lexicologist

lexie [lɛksi] NF lexical unit

lexique [lɛksik] NM **1** *(dictionnaire)* lexicon, small dictionary; *(glossaire)* glossary; **l. financier** financial glossary **2** *(à la fin d'un livre)* list of terms **3** *(mots d'un auteur)* vocabulary, *Spéc* lexis

lézard [lezar] NM **1** *(reptile)* lizard; **l. gris/des murailles** grey/wall lizard; **l. vert** green lizard; **faire le l.** to bask *or* lounge in the sun **2** *(cuir)* lizard skin **3** *Fam* **il y a un l.** there's a catch, there's something fishy about it; **il n'y a pas de l.** there's no catch, it's kosher

lézarde [lezard] NF crack

lézardé [lezarde] ADJ *(mur, plâtre)* cracked, full of cracks

lézarder [lezarde] VT *(plâtre, ciment)* to crack
VI *Fam* to bask *or* lounge in the sun
VPR se lézarder *(de mur)* to crack

LFAJ [ɛlɛfaʒi] NF *(abrév* **Ligue française des auberges de jeunesse)** = French youth hostel association

liais [ljɛ] NM *Minér* hard limestone

liaison [ljɛzɔ̃] NF **1** *(enchaînement logique)* connection; **il y a un manque de l. dans l'expression de vos idées** you express your ideas in a disjointed fashion; **des idées sans l.** unconnected ideas; **en l. avec ce qui a été dit** in connection with *or* leading on from what has been said **2** *Tél* communications link; **l. radio/téléphonique** radio/telephone link; **l. vidéo** video link; **l. par satellite** satellite link *or* link-up; **la l. est mauvaise** it's a bad connection; **la l. est coupée entre la plateforme et le continent** all shore contact with the rig has been lost; **établir une l. radio** to establish radio contact; *Ordinat* **l. alternat** half duplex; *Ordinat* **l. par modem** modem link; *Ordinat* **l. spécialisée** dedicated line

3 *(entre des personnes)* close contact *or* relationship; **assurer la l. entre deux personnes/services** to liaise between two people/departments; **les différents services sont en (étroite) l.** the various departments are in close contact *or* liaise closely (with each other); **les différents services sont en l. permanente** the various departments are constantly in touch with each other; **être en l. avec qn** to be in touch with sb; **rester en l.** to stay in touch; **se mettre en l. avec qn** to get in touch with sb; **travailler en l. (étroite) avec qn** to work (closely) with sb; *esp Mil* to liaise with sb; **l. (amoureuse)** (love) affair, *Fml* liaison; **agent de l.** go-between; *Mil* liaison officer

4 *(dans les transports)* **l. aérienne/maritime/ferroviaire/routière** air/sea/rail/road link; **toutes les liaisons Paris-Téhéran sont suspendues** all services between Paris and Tehran have been suspended; **une navette assure la l. entre l'aéroport et le centre-ville** there is a shuttle service between the airport and the town centre; **un avion hebdomadaire assure la l. entre Paris et Moscou** there is one flight a week between Paris and Moscow; **les liaisons sont bonnes entre ces deux villes, que ce soit par le train ou par la route** there are good rail and road services between the two towns **5** *Ling* liaison *(sounding of final consonant before initial vowel sound)*; **faire la l.** to make *or* sound the liaison; *Gram* **mot** *ou* **terme de l.** linkword **6** *Constr (de briques etc)* bonding; *(produit)* mortar, cement; **maçonnerie en l.** bonded masonry; *Tech* **l. élastique** rubber joint; *Aut* **l. transversale** cross-tie **7** *Mus (pour lier deux notes)* slur; *(pour lier une suite de notes)* tie, ligature **8** *Chimie* bond **9** *Culin (pour sauce)* thickening

liaisonner [ljɛzɔne] VT *Constr (briques)* to bond; *(en maçonnerie)* to grout, to point

liane [ljan] NF *Bot* creeper, *Spéc* liana

liant [ljɑ̃] ADJ sociable, friendly; **il est très l.** he's quick to make friends
NM 1 *Tech* binder, binding agent **2** *Litt (sociabilité)* **avoir du l.** to be sociable **3** *(souplesse)* flexibility/pliability

liard [ljar] NM *Arch* half farthing; **il n'a pas un l.** he hasn't (got) a farthing, he hasn't (got) a penny to his name

lias [ljas] NM *Géol* lias

liasse [ljas] NF *(de lettres)* bundle, packet; *(de billets)* wad; *(de papiers)* bundle; **l. carbonée** print-through paper

libage [libaʒ] NM *Constr* bastard ashlar

Liban [libɑ̃] NM **le L.** (the) Lebanon

libanais, -aise [libanɛ, -ɛz] ADJ Lebanese
N L. Lebanese; **les L.** the Lebanese

libanisation [libanizasjɔ̃] NF disintegration *(due to ethnic or religious strife)*

libation [libasjɔ̃] NF **1** *Antiq, Rel* libation **2** *Fig* **faire des libations** to partake of libations

libelle [libɛl] NM *Litt* lampoon, scurrilous satire

libellé [libele] NM *(de document)* wording, terms used; **le l. du chèque/de la pièce comptable est incorrect** the cheque *or Am* check voucher is not made out correctly

libeller [libele] VT *Admin (document, acte, contrat)* to word, to draw up; *Fin* to denominate; **l. un chèque** to make out *or* write out a cheque; **chèque libellé à l'ordre de Y. Mourier** cheque made out *or* payable to Y. Mourier; **télégramme libellé comme suit ...** telegram worded as follows *or* that reads as follows ...; **l. une facture** to make out an invoice; **libellé au porteur** *(chèque)* made out to bearer; **libellé en** *(chèque)* made out in;

(cours) quoted *or* given in; *Fin* **libellé en dollars** denominated in dollars

libellule [libɛlyl] **NF** *(insecte)* dragonfly

libérable [liberabl] *Mil* **ADJ** *(soldat)* dischargeable, who can be demobbed; **congé** *ou* **permission l.** demob leave
▸ **NM** = soldier about to finish his military service

libéral, -ale, -aux, -ales [liberal, -o] **ADJ 1** *(tolérant) (personne, éducation)* lenient, liberal; *(idées)* liberal **2** *(indépendant)* **il exerce une profession libérale** he's a professional man; **défendre la médecine libérale** to defend private medicine **3** *(généreux)* generous **4** *Pol* liberal; **le parti l.** the Liberal Party **5** *(économie, doctrine)* free-market
▸ **N 1** *Pol* liberal **2** *Écon* free-marketeer

libéralement [liberalmɑ̃] **ADV 1** *(généreusement)* liberally **2** *(avec tolérance)* leniently, liberally

libéralisation [liberalizasjɔ̃] **NF 1** *Écon (de l'économie, des échanges commerciaux)* liberalization; **la l. de la presse** the liberalization of the press, the easing of restrictions on the press; **l. du commerce** liberalization of trade; **l. du cours de l'euro** freeing of the euro **2** *Jur* liberalization

libéraliser [liberalize] **VT** *(économie)* to liberalize

libéralisme [liberalism] **NM** *Pol, Écon* liberalism

libéralité [liberalite] **NF 1** *(libéralisme)* liberality **2** *(générosité)* generosity **3** *(cadeau)* generous gift; *Litt* **faire des libéralités à qn** to give liberally *or* freely to sb; **vivre des libéralités de ses amis** to live off the generosity of one's friends

libérateur, -trice [liberatœr, -tris] **ADJ** *(soldats, force)* liberating; **guerre libératrice** war of liberation; **le pouvoir l. du rire** the liberating power of laughter
▸ **N** liberator

libération [liberasjɔ̃] **NF 1** *(mise en liberté)* liberation, freeing, release; *(de prisonnier)* discharge, release; *(de soldat)* discharge; **l. conditionnelle** release of prisoner on parole **2** *(d'un joug)* liberation; **le mouvement de l. de la femme** the women's liberation movement, *Fam* women's lib; *Hist* **la L.** the Liberation *(from the Germans in 1944-45)* **3** *(déréglementation) (des prix, des échanges commerciaux)* freeing; *(de dette)* payment in full, discharge; *Fin* **l. d'une action** paying up of a share; **l. des échanges commerciaux** deregulation of trade **4** *Phys (émission)* liberation, release; **l. de chaleur/d'hormones** the liberation *or* release of heat/hormones; *Astronaut* **vitesse de l.** escape *or* parabolic velocity

libératoire [liberatwar] **ADJ** *Jur* **paiement l.** payment in full discharge from debt

libéré [libere] **ADJ 1** *(physiquement)* liberated, free; **jeune homme l. des obligations militaires** young man who has carried out his national service duties **2** *(moralement)* liberated **3** *Fin (action)* (fully) paid-up; **l. d'impôt** tax paid
▸ **NM** released prisoner

libérer [libere] **(je libère, n. libérons; je libérerai) VT 1** *(rendre sa liberté à) (otage, prisonnier)* to free, to set free, to release; *(pays, peuple)* to liberate; *(soldat)* to discharge; **l. qn de ses chaînes** to free sb from his chains; **le prof a libéré les élèves plus tôt** the teacher let the children go *or* let the children out early; **l. qn de sa promesse** to release sb from his promise
2 *(soulager)* **l. sa conscience** to salve one's conscience; **cela me libérera d'un souci** *ou* **poids** that will take a load off my mind; **l. les jeunes des tabous sexuels** to free *or* liberate

young people from sexual taboos
3 *(rendre disponible) (appartement, chambre d'hôtel)* to vacate
4 *(débloquer), Fin (prix, échanges commerciaux)* to free; *(cran de sûreté, mécanisme)* to release; *(instincts, passions)* to unleash; **l. le passage** to clear the way
5 *(décharger) (d'une dette)* to free; *(d'un engagement)* to release; **l. entièrement une action** to make a share fully paid-up, to pay up a share in full; **l. un débiteur** to discharge a debtor, to release a debtor
6 *(émettre) (gaz, hormone, énergie, chaleur)* to release
▸ **VPR se libérer 1** *(de liens, chaînes, oppresseur, passion)* to free oneself **2** *(se rendre disponible) (d'une personne)* to get away; **je n'ai pas pu me l. plus tôt** I couldn't get away any earlier; **se l. pour deux jours** to (arrange to) take two days off; **il y a une place de parking qui vient juste de se l.** someone's just left a parking space; **il y a un poste qui vient de se l.** a job vacancy has just come up **3** *(se dégager)* **se l. (d'une dette)** to redeem *or* liquidate a debt; **se l. d'un engagement** to free oneself from a commitment

Liberia [liberja] **NM** Liberia

libérien, -ienne [liberjɛ̃, -jɛn] **ADJ** Liberian
▸ **N** **L.** Liberian

libéro [libero] **NM** *Ftbl* sweeper

libertaire [libertɛr] **ADJ, N** libertarian

liberté [libɛrte] **NF 1** *(de personne, d'animal)* liberty, freedom; **l'assassin est toujours en l.** the murderer is still at large; **animaux en l.** animals in the wild, animals running free; **vivre en l.** *(d'un animal)* to live in the wild; **rendre sa l. à qn** *(fiancé etc)* to let sb go; **rendre sa l. à un animal** to let an animal go, to set an animal free; **reprendre sa l.** *(de conjoint)* to regain one's freedom; **être mis en l.** to be set free, to be released, to be allowed to go free; *(d'un inculpé)* to be discharged; **(re)mettre qn en l.** to set sb free, to free *or* release sb; *Jur* **mise en l.** *(d'un prisonnier)* release; *Jur* **(mise en) l. provisoire** *ou* **sous caution** (released on) bail; **mettre qn en l. provisoire** to release sb on bail; *Jur* **l. conditionnelle** parole; **mettre qn en l. conditionnelle** to release sb on parole; *Jur* **l. surveillée** probation; **mettre qn en l. surveillée** to release sb on probation
2 *Pol (droit de l'individu)* freedom, liberty; **l. civile** civil liberty; **atteinte aux libertés individuelles** infringement of one's individual freedom; **l., égalité, fraternité** liberty, equality, fraternity
3 *(absence de contrainte)* freedom; **l. d'entreprise** free enterprise; **avoir toute** *ou* **pleine l. d'action** to have complete freedom of action, to have a free hand; **vous avez toute l. pour organiser la rencontre** you have a free hand *or* complete freedom to organize the meeting as you wish; **vous avez pleine (et entière) l. d'agir comme bon vous semble** you are quite free *or* you are completely at liberty to act as you see fit; **parler en toute l.** to speak freely *or* without restraint; **j'ai pris la l. de dire ...** I took the liberty of saying ...; **si je puis prendre une telle l.** if I may be so bold
4 *(temps libre)* **jour de l.** free day, day off; **un moment de l.** a spare *or* free moment; **avec tout ce travail je n'ai pas beaucoup de l.** with all this work I haven't (got) much spare *or* free time
5 *Fin, Écon (déréglementation) (des échanges)* deregulation; *Aviat* **libertés commerciales** commercial freedoms; **l. des prix** freedom from price controls; **instaurer la l. des prix** to end *or* to abolish price controls
6 *(familiarités)* **prendre** *ou* **se permettre des libertés avec qn/un texte** to take liberties

with sb/a text; **se permettre des libertés de langage** to be rather free in one's use of language
▸▸ **l. d'association** freedom of association; **libertés du citoyen** civil liberties; **libertés civiques** civil liberties; **l. de communication** freedom of communication; **l. de conscience** freedom of conscience; **l. du culte** freedom of worship; **l. d'enseignement** freedom of educational choice; **l. d'expression** freedom of expression *or* of speech; **l. d'information** freedom of information; **l. de mouvement** freedom of movement; **l. d'opinion** freedom of opinion; **l. de pensée** freedom of thought; **l. de la presse** freedom of the press; **libertés publiques** civil liberties; **l. de réunion** freedom of assembly; **l. syndicale** freedom of association

libertel [libɛrtɛl] **NF** *Ordinat* freenet

libertin, -ine [libɛrtɛ̃, -in] **ADJ 1** *(aux mœurs libres) (personne)* libertine, dissolute; *(livre, propos)* licentious **2** *Hist* free-thinking
▸ **N 1** *(de par ses mœurs)* libertine **2** *Hist* free-thinker

libertinage [libɛrtinaʒ] **NM 1** *(débauche)* licentiousness **2** *Hist* free-thinking

Liberty® [libɛrti] **NM** Liberty® fabric; **une housse de coussin en L.** a liberty cushion cover

libidineux, -euse [libidinø, -øz] **ADJ** libidinous, lustful; **des regards l.** lustful *or* lascivious glances

libido [libido] **NF** libido; **avoir une forte l.** to be highly sexed

libraire [librɛr] **N** *Com* bookseller

> Il faut noter que le nom anglais **librarian** est un faux ami. Il signifie **bibliothécaire**.

libraire-éditeur, *pl* **libraires-éditeurs NM** *Com* publisher and bookseller

librairie [librɛri] **NF 1** *(magasin)* bookshop, *Am* bookstore; **l. d'art** art bookshop; **l.-papeterie** bookshop and stationer's **2** *Com (activité)* bookselling; **ouvrages en l.** published books

> Il faut noter que le nom anglais **library** est un faux ami. Il signifie **bibliothèque**.

LIBRE [libr]

free **1, 2, 6, 11**	▪ vacant **2**	▪ spare **2**
▪ unrestrained **3**	▪ clear **5**	▪ open **5**
▪ independent **7**	▪ disengaged **8**	

ADJ 1 *(non soumis) (personne, pays)* free; **le monde l.** the free world; *Hist* **zone l.** unoccupied France; *Hist* **la France l.** Free France; **l'homme est l.** man is a free agent; **laisser qn l. d'agir** to leave sb a free hand, to leave sb free to act; **laisser qn l. de choisir** to leave sb free to choose; **il nous laisse libres de partir** he lets us go when we want; **vous êtes l. de le faire, à vous de le faire** you are quite free *or* at liberty to do it; **l. à vous d'essayer** you're free *or* welcome to try; **donner l. cours à son enthousiasme/sa curiosité/son imagination** to give one's enthusiasm/curiosity/imagination free rein; **être l. de tout souci** to be free from care, to be carefree; **l. de préjugés** free from prejudice; **l. d'impôt** tax-free
2 *(disponible) (personne)* free, not tied down; *(sentimentalement)* unattached; *(temps)* free, spare; *(appartement, maison, chambre)* available; *(toilettes) (sur la porte)* vacant; *(table, place de parking, fauteuil)* free, unoccupied; **vous êtes l.?** are you free?; **vous êtes l. ce soir?** are you free this evening?; **avoir du temps (de) l.** to have some free *or* spare time, to have some time free *or* to spare; **je suis l. de onze heu-**

res à midi I'm free between eleven and twelve; *Fam* le lundi est mon jour de l. Monday is my day off, I have Mondays free; **je n'ai pas eu une minute de l. aujourd'hui** I haven't had a spare minute today; **être l. comme l'air** to be as free as the air *or*a bird; **j'ai les mains libres** I'm not carrying anything; *Fig* I'm a free agent; *Fig* **laisser les mains libres à qn** to give sb a free rein *or*hand; **studio à louer, l. de suite** *(annonce)* one-room flat to rent, available immediately; **j'ai trouvé une place l. pour me garer** I found a place to park; *Tél* **la ligne n'est pas l.** the line is engaged *or esp Am* busy

3 *(non attaché) (mouvement etc)* unrestrained; **robe qui laisse la taille l.** dress which fits loosely round the waist; **elle a les cheveux libres** she wears her hair down *or* loose

4 être l. avec qn to be free with sb, to treat sb in a familiar way; **allures** *ou* **manières libres** free and easy manner

5 *(non bloqué) (route)* clear, open; **laisser le champ l.** to leave the field clear; **je vous laisse le champ l.** I'll leave you to it, you're free to do as you think best; *Fig* **la voie est l.** the coast is clear; *Rail* **voie l.** line clear

6 *(non imposé) (adaptation, traduction, vers)* free; *Scol* **sujet l., texte l.** free choice of subject

7 *(privé)* **enseignement l.** independent Catholic education system; **école l.** independent Catholic school; **radio l.** independent radio

8 *Tech* disengaged; **roue l.** *(de bicyclette, voiture)* freewheel; **descendre une côte en roue l.** to freewheel *or*coast down a hill; *Fig* **être en roue l.** to be coasting

9 *Com* **entrée l.** *(dans un magasin)* please come in and look around, no obligation to buy; *(entrée gratuite)* admission free

10 *Sport* free, freestyle; **les figures libres** freestyle skating; **escalade l.** free climbing

11 *(non réglementé) (prix)* free; **le l. jeu de la concurrence** the free play of competition; **défendre la l. entreprise** to defend free *or* private enterprise; **il pratique les honoraires libres** = he's in private practice; **bibliothèque en l. accès** public library; **l. circulation des personnes** freedom of movement; **l. circulation des marchandises** free movement of goods; **l. échange international** international free trade

▸▸ **l. arbitre** free will; *Écon* **l.-échange** free trade; *Écon* **l.-échangisme** free trade **l. parole** free speech; **l. pensée** free thinking, free thought; **l. penseur/penseuse** free thinker

libre-échangiste, *pl* **libre-échangistes** *Écon* **ADJ** *(politique, théorie)* free trade
N free trader

librement [librəmã] **ADV** freely

libre-service, *pl* **libres-services NM 1** *(principe)* self-service; **magasin/restaurant en l.** self-service shop *or Am* store/restaurant; **station-service en l.** self-service petrol *or Am* gas station **2** *(magasin, restaurant)* self-service

librettiste [librɛtist] **N** *Mus* librettist

libretto, *pl* **libretti, librettos** [libreto, libreti] **NM** *Mus* libretto

Libreville [librəvil] **N** Libreville

Libye [libi] **NF** Libya

libyen, -yenne [libjɛ̃, -jɛn] **ADJ** Libyan
N L. Libyan

lice [lis] **NF** *Hist (barrière, enclos)* lists; *Fig* **entrer en l.** to enter the lists *or*the fray; **les athlètes français entreront en l. à 10 heures pour les épreuves de saut en hauteur** the French high jumpers will enter the competition at 10 a.m.; **trois concurrents sont en l.** there are three competitors, three people are in contention

licence [lisãs] **NF 1** *(permis)* licence, *Am* license; **accorder une l. à qn** to license sb; **accorder une l. sur un nom** to license a name; **l. d'utilisation** user licence; **l. de brevet** patent licence; **l. de fabrication** manufacturing licence; **l. de vente** sales licence; **l. exclusive** exclusive licence; **fabriqué sous l.** made under licence; **l. d'importation/d'exportation** import/export licence; **l. individuelle d'utilisation** single user licence; **l. de logiciel** software licence **2** *Sport* permit, certificate *(giving right of entry into competition)* **3** *Univ* bachelor's degree; **l. ès** *ou* **de lettres/ès** *ou* **de sciences/en droit** bachelor's degree in arts/in science/in law, arts/science/law degree; **passer sa l.** to sit *or* take one's degree exams *or*one's finals; **faire une l.** to do a degree **4** *(liberté)* licence, *Am* license; **l. poétique** poetic licence; **l. syntaxique** syntactic licence; **donner** *ou* **laisser à qn la l. de faire qch** to give sb licence to do sth; **je vous laisse toute l. pour la décoration du stand** I leave the decoration of the stand entirely up to you, you can decorate the stand as you like; *Arch* **prendre des licences avec qn** to take liberties with sb **5** *Vieilli (dérèglement)* licentiousness

licencié, -ée [lisãsje] **ADJ 1** *Univ* **il est l.** he's a graduate; **professeur l.** graduate teacher **2** *(renvoyé)* (made) redundant; **un ouvrier l.** *(pour raisons économiques)* a redundant worker; *(pour faute professionnelle)* a dismissed worker
N 1 *Univ* **l. ès lettres/ès** *ou* **en sciences/en droit** bachelor of arts/of science/of law, arts/science/law graduate **2** *Sport* member

licenciement [lisãsimã] **NM** *(pour raisons économiques)* redundancy; *(pour faute professionnelle)* dismissal; *Mil (de troupes)* disbanding; **recevoir une lettre de l.** to receive a redundancy notice/notice of dismissal; **il y a eu beaucoup de licenciements** many (people) were made redundant, there were a lot of redundancies; **l. économique** redundancy; **l. collectif** mass redundancies; **l. abusif** unfair dismissal; **l. avec/sans préavis** dismissal with/without notice

licencier [lisãsje] **VT** *(pr sub, impf n. licenciions, v. licenciiez)* *(pour raisons économiques)* to make redundant; *(pour faute professionnelle)* to dismiss; *Mil (troupes)* to disband

licencieusement [lisãsjøzmã] **ADV** *Litt* licentiously

licencieux, -euse [lisãsjø, -øz] **ADJ** *Litt* licentious

lichen [likɛn] **NM** lichen

lichette [liʃɛt] **NF** *Fam (de pain, fromage etc)* tiny bit, smidgen; *(de vin)* drop, smidgen

licite [lisit] **ADJ** licit, lawful, permissible

licitement [lisitmã] **ADV** licitly, lawfully

licol [likɔl] **NM** halter

licorne [likɔrn] **NF 1** *Myth, Hér* unicorn **2** *Zool* **l. de mer** sea unicorn, narwhal

licou [liku] **NM** halter

LICRA [likra] **NF** *(abrév* **Ligue internationale contre le racisme et l'antisémitisme)** = anti-racist movement

licteur [liktœr] **NM** *Antiq* lictor

lido [lido] **NM** *Géog* sand bar

lie [li] **NF** *(dépôt)* dregs; **l. (de vin)** lees *or* sediment of wine; *Fig* **la l. de la société** the dregs of society
ADJ INV **l.(-)de(-)vin** purplish red, wine-coloured

lié [lje] **ADJ 1** *(attaché)* bound; **avoir les mains liées** to have one's hands tied; *Fig* **j'ai les mains liées** my hands are tied **2** *(en relation étroite)* **être (très) l. avec qn** to be (great) friends *or* intimately acquainted with sb; **nous sommes très liés** we are great friends,

we are very close; **avoir partie liée avec qn** to be in league with sb **3** *Mus* **notes liées** slurred notes; *(deux notes différentes)* tied notes

lied, *pl* **lieder** [lid, lidœr] **NM** *Mus* lied, song

liège [ljɛʒ] **NM** *(matière naturelle)* cork; **semelle de l.** cork sole; **cigarette à bout (de) l.** cork-tipped cigarette; **bouchon de l.** cork

liégeois, -oise [ljeʒwa, -waz] **ADJ 1** of/from Liège **2** *Culin* **café/chocolat l.** coffee/chocolate ice cream topped with crème Chantilly
N L. *(natif)* native of Liège; *(habitant)* inhabitant of Liège

lien [ljɛ̃] **NM 1** *(attache)* tie, *esp Litt* bond; **il s'est libéré de ses liens** he freed himself (from his bonds) **2** *Fig* **liens du sang** blood ties; **l. de parenté** *ou* **de famille** family relationship; **il y a un l. de parenté entre ces deux familles** the two families are related; **des liens de famille avec le PDG expliquent sa nomination à ce poste** the fact that he is related to the Chairman *or*is a relation of the Chairman accounts for his appointment; **les liens du mariage** the bonds of marriage *or* matrimony; **je vous déclare unis par les liens du mariage** = I now pronounce you man and wife; **l. d'amitié** bond of friendship; **l. social** civic bond **3** *Ordinat* link; **l. hypertexte** hypertext link **4** *(relation)* link, connection; **j'ai du mal à faire le l. avec ce qu'il a dit avant** I can't see the connection with what he said before; **il y a un l. entre ces événements** there's a connection *or* link between these events

lier [lje] *(pr sub, impf n. liions, v. liiez)* **VT 1** *(attacher)* to bind, to fasten, to tie, to tie up; *(d'un contrat)* to be binding on; **l. qch avec une corde** to bind sth *or* tie sth up with a rope; **l. les pieds et les mains à qn** to bind sb hand and foot; **l. un fagot** to tie up a bundle of sticks; **on l'a lié à un arbre** he's been tied (up) to a tree; **vous êtes lié par ce contrat** you are bound by this agreement, this agreement binds you *or* is binding on you; **l'intérêt nous lie** we have common interests; **cela les a intimement liés** that has formed a close bond between them; **un même amour de l'art les lie** they are united by a mutual love of art; **l. les paragraphes** to connect *or* link the paragraphs; **tout est lié** everything is connected; **ce jardin est lié au souvenir de sa grand-mère** the garden is linked to the memory of his grandmother; **l. deux mots** to link two words (in pronunciation), to sound the liaison; *Mus* **l. deux notes** to slur (two notes); *(deux notes différentes)* to tie two notes **2** *Culin (sauce)* to thicken **3** **l. amitié/conversation avec qn** to strike up a friendship/conversation with sb
VPR se lier 1 *(socialement)* **se l. avec qn** to form *or* strike up a friendship with sb; **il se lie facilement** he makes friends easily; **je me suis lié d'amitié avec son père** I have made friends with his father **2** *(se mélanger)* **le lait et le jaune d'œuf se lient facilement** milk and egg yolk blend easily

lierre [ljɛr] **NM** ivy; **l. terrestre** ground ivy

liesse [ljɛs] **NF** *Arch, Litt* jubilation, gaiety; *Litt* **en l.** jubilant, in celebratory mood

LIEU¹, *pl* **lieux** [ljø]

place **1** ▪ premises *(lieux)* **3** ▪ scene *(lieux)* **3** ▪ to take place *(avoir lieu)* **4** ▪ instead of *(au lieu de)* **7**

NM 1 *(endroit)* place; **mettre qch en l. sûr** to put sth in a safe place; *Litt* **en tous lieux** everywhere; *Litt* **en aucun l.** nowhere; **visiter les lieux saints** to visit the Holy Places; **elle y a ses lieux de promenade** she goes for walks there; **c'est un drôle de l. de promenade** it's a funny place for a walk; **les mendiants se**

mettent de préférence sur les lieux de passage beggars prefer busy areas *or* areas where there are lots of people going past; cette ville n'est qu'un l. de passage people merely pass through the town

2 *(dans l'espace ou le temps)* en premier l. in the first place, first of all, first(ly); c'est le saumon que je mettrais en premier l. I would put salmon first; peut-être devrais-tu lui poser la question en premier l. perhaps you should put the question to him first; en troisième l. third(ly); en dernier l. last of all, last(ly), finally; en temps et l. at the proper time and place; en son l. in due course

3 lieux *(local)* premises; *(d'un accident, d'un crime)* scene; avant de quitter ces lieux before leaving the premises; quitter *ou* vider les lieux to vacate the premises; la police est sur les lieux de l'accident the police are at the scene of the accident; quand je suis arrivé sur les lieux (du crime) when I arrived on the scene/at the scene of the crime; j'étais sur les lieux bien avant vous I was there well before you; rendez-vous immédiatement sur les lieux go there immediately; *Litté* il vous faut prendre congé du maître de ces lieux it's time to bid your host farewell; *Litté* ces lieux de tristesse this place of sorrow

4 avoir l. to take place; la réunion aura l. à ... the meeting will take place *or* be held at ...

5 *(raisons)* il y a (tout) l./j'ai tout l. de supposer que ... + *ind* there are/I have (good) grounds for supposing that ..., there is/I have (every) reason to suppose that ...; il y a l. d'attendre it would be advisable *or* as well to wait; je vous écrirai s'il y a l. I'll write to you if necessary; donner l. à *(une querelle, des problèmes)* to cause, to give rise to; son retour a donné l. à une réunion de famille his return was the occasion for a family gathering; donner l. à des désagréments to cause inconvenience; tout donne l. de croire que ... everything leads me/us/*etc or* there is every reason to believe that ...

6 *(fonction)* tenir l. de qch to take the place of sth; elle lui a tenu l. de mère she has been a mother to him

7 au l. de instead of, *Fml* in lieu of; au l. de te plaindre instead of complaining; au l. de cela, elle ... but instead she ...; *Litté* au l. que + *sub* instead of + *gerund*

▸▸ *Vieilli* lieux (d'aisances) lavatory; l. commun commonplace; l. de départ point of departure; l. de destination destination; l. d'émission place of issue; *Math* l. géométrique locus; l. de livraison point of delivery; l. de naissance place of birth; *Fin* l. de paiement place of payment; l. public public place; l. de rassemblement assembly point; l. de réception place of receipt; l. de rencontre meeting place; l. de rendez-vous meeting place; quel est le l. de rendez-vous? where are we/they/*etc* meeting?; *Cin* l. de tournage location; l. de travail place of work; sur le l. de travail in the workplace; l. de vacances holiday resort; l. de vente point of sale

lieu ², *pl* lieus **NM** *(poisson)* l. jaune pollack, pollock; l. noir coalfish

lieu(-)dit, *pl* lieux(-)dits **NM** (named) place, locality

lieue [ljø] **NF** *(mesure)* league; *Naut* l. marine league; j'étais à cent *ou* mille lieues de penser/croire que ... I would never (in a million years) have dreamt/believed that ...

lieur, -euse [ljœr, -øz] *Agr* **N** *Arch (de gerbes, de bottes etc)* binder

NF lieuse *(machine)* (mechanical) sheaf binder

lieutenant [ljøtnɑ̃] **NM 1** *Mil* lieutenant; *Aviat* flying officer, *Am* first lieutenant; *(dans la marine marchande)* mate; *Naut* premier l. second mate; *Naut* l. de vaisseau lieutenant **2** *(proche collaborateur)* right-hand man

lieutenant-colonel, *pl* **lieutenants-colonels NM** *Mil* lieutenant-colonel; *Aviat* wing commander

lièvre [ljɛvr] **NM** hare; *Fig* courir deux lièvres à la fois to try to do two things at once; *Culin* pâté de l. hare pâté

lift [lift] **NM** *Sport* topspin; faire un l. to give a ball topspin, to put topspin on a ball

lifter [lifte] **VT 1** *Sport* l. une balle to give a ball topspin, to put topspin on a ball **2** *(faire un lifting à)* to perform a face lift on; *Fig (rénover)* to give a face lift to, to face-lift

liftier [liftje] **NM** lift attendant, *Am* elevator operator

lifting [liftiŋ] **NM** *Chir, Fig* face lift; elle s'est fait faire un l. she's had a face lift

ligament [ligamɑ̃] **NM** *Anat* ligament

ligature [ligatyr] **NF 1** *(fait d'attacher)* tying, binding; la l. des greffes the binding of (the) grafts **2** *Élec (au moyen d'un fil, câble)* splice **3** *Chir, Typ* ligature; l. des trompes tying of tubes

ligaturer [ligatyre] **VT** *(attacher)* to bind; *Élec (câble, fil)* to splice; *Chir* to ligature, to tie; *Typ* to ligature

lige [liʒ] **ADJ** *Hist* liege

ligérien, -ienne [liʒerjɛ̃, -jɛn] **ADJ** from the Loire

light [lajt] **ADJ INV** *(plat, préparation)* light, low-fat; *(boisson)* light, slimline

lignage [liɲaʒ] **NM 1** *Arch* lineage, descent **2** *Typ* linage, lineage

LIGNE [liɲ]

> line **1–10, 13** ▪ outline **3** ▪ route **6**
> ▪ range **10**

NF 1 *(trait)* line; l. droite straight line; l. brisée broken line; tracer une l. à main levée to draw a line freehand; les lignes de la main the lines of the hand; votre l. de vie/de cœur est courte you have a short life-/heart-line; avancer en l. droite to advance in a straight line; *Mus* l. supplémentaire ledger line; *Naut* la l. (équatoriale) the line, the Equator; passer la l. (équatoriale) to cross the line; l. de coke line of coke; *TV* définition de 625 lignes definition of 625 lines

2 *(d'écriture)* line; le prof m'a donné cent lignes *(en punition)* the teacher gave me a hundred lines; elle m'a juste envoyé deux lignes she just dropped me a line; je vous envoie ces quelques lignes pour vous donner les dernières nouvelles this is just a note to give you the latest news; *Fig* lire entre les lignes to read between the lines; aller à la l. to begin a new line *or* a new paragraph; à la l. *(en dictant)* new paragraph, new line; passer *ou* sauter une l. to leave a line; être payé à la l. to be paid by the line; tirer à la l. to pad (out) an article *(because it is being paid by the line)*; *Fig* mettre sur la même l. to compare; sa rapidité et son intelligence sont à mettre sur la même l. he is as quick as he is intelligent, his speed is matched by his intelligence; *Fig* entrer en l. de compte to be taken into consideration; les sentiments ne doivent pas entrer en l. de compte dans ton jugement feelings should not influence *or* enter into your decision; cela n'entre pas en l. de compte that doesn't enter *or* come into it; faire entrer un facteur en l. de compte to take a factor into account; c'est un facteur à faire entrer en l. de compte it's something to be considered *or* taken into account *or* consideration

3 *(contour, silhouette)* (out)line; la l. du nez the line *or* contour of the nose; la pureté des lignes purity of line; la l. élégante d'une voiture the elegant lines of a car; garder/soigner sa l. to keep/watch one's waistline *or* one's figure; avoir la l. to have a good figure; perdre la l. to lose one's figure

4 *(rangée)* line; se mettre en l. to line up; plantés en l. planted in a line *or* row; *Mil, Fig* en première l. in the front line; *Fig* sur toute la l. all along the line

5 *(direction, règle)* line; redéfinir sa l. d'action to adopt a different line *or* course of action; la l. du parti communiste the communist party line; *Fig* grandes lignes d'une œuvre broad *or* general outline(s) of a work; *Journ* l. éditoriale editorial policy, editorial line; je vais vous expliquer le projet dans ses grandes lignes I'll explain the broad outline(s) of the project to you

6 *(transports)*, *Aviat (destination)* route; *Rail* line; *Rail* grandes lignes main lines; l. maritime/aérienne shipping line/airline; *Aviat* lignes intérieures domestic services; *(destinations)* domestic routes; *Aviat* nous espérons vous revoir sur nos lignes we hope we will soon have the pleasure of welcoming you on board again; l. d'autobus bus service; *(parcours)* bus route; il n'y a que deux lignes de bus qui fonctionnent la nuit there are only two late-night bus services; l. de banlieue commuter service; *Aviat* l. radiale minor domestic air route; *Aviat* l. transversale domestic or international air route not serving the capital

7 *Élec* (power) line; l. télégraphique telegraph line

8 *Tél* line; l. téléphonique telephone line; être en l. *(téléphonique)* to be on a call; la l. est occupée the line is engaged *or esp Am* busy; la l. a été coupée I've/we've/*etc* been cut off; il y a quelqu'un sur la l. there's someone on the line; vous êtes en l. you're connected, you're through; il est déjà en l. he's on another line; l. commutée dial-up line; l. directe accessible 24 heures sur 24 twenty-four-hour hotline; l. extérieure outside line; l. ouverte open line; l. principale switchboard line, main line; l. privée private line; l. spécifique dedicated line; l. téléphonique directe direct dial telephone

9 *(fil)* line; *Pêche* (fishing) line; planter des arbres à la l. to plant trees straight by using a line *or* a cord

10 *Com* line, range; l. de produits line of products, product line; Lancôme lance une nouvelle l. de cosmétiques Lancôme are launching a new line *or* range of cosmetics; l. pour hommes range for men

11 *(filiation)* descendre en l. directe *ou* en droite l. de ... to be directly descended from ..., to be descended in a direct line from ...

12 *Can (mesure)* line, = 2.3 mm

13 *Ordinat* line; en l. on line; sur l. on line; hors l. off line; changer de l. to do a line feed; l. de commande command line; *(type de commande)* line command; l. d'état status line; l. louée leased line; l. ouverte open line; l. RNIS ISDN line; l. spécialisée dedicated line; l. vide blank line

▸▸ l. d'arrivée finishing line; l. d'attaque line of attack; l. de bataille line of battle, fighting line; *Aut* l. blanche white line, *Am* yellow line; l. de changement de date *ou* de jour International Date Line; *Naut* l. de charge load line; l. de combat line of battle; l. continue *(aussi sur la route)* continuous line; *Fin* l. de cotation line of quotation; *Fin* l. de crédit line of credit, credit line; l. de découvert line of credit, credit line; *Fin* l. de démarcation boundary; *Mil* demarcation line; l. de départ starting line; l. directrice keynote, thrust; l. discontinue *(sur la route)* broken line; *Aut* l. d'échappement exhaust system; *Ordinat* **l.-écran**, *pl* **lignes-écran** screen line; *Naut* **l. de flottaison** waterline; **l. de fond** *Pêche* ledger line; *Tennis* base line; **lignes de force** *(grandes lignes)* dominating *or* guiding principles; *Phys* lines of force; *Mil* **l. de front** front line; **l. à haute tension** high-tension wire *or* line; **l. d'horizon** (line of the) horizon; *Aut* **l. jaune** white line; *Am* yellow line; *Hist* **L. Maginot** Maginot Line; **l. magnétique** magnetic *or* black strip; *Com* **l. maritime de conférence** conference line; **l. médiane** centre line; **l. de mire** line of sight; *Fam (d'un fusil à lunette)* sights; *Fig* **avoir qn dans sa l. de mire** to have sb in one's sights; **l. du partage des eaux** watershed; *Typ* **l. de pointillé** dotted line; *Mus* **l. de portée** stave line; **l. de sonde** plumb line; **l. de substitution** backup line; **l. de tir** line of fire; *Ftbl* **l. de touche** touch line; *Typ* **l. veuve** widow; *Mil* **l. de visée** line of sight

lignée [liɲe] NF (line of) descendants; *(origine)* line, lineage; **une nombreuse l.** a large number of descendants; **ce clan est très fier de sa nombreuse l. de combattants** the clan is very proud of its many warrior descendants; **de bonne l. allemande** of good German stock; *Fig* **un philosophe dans la l. de Russell** a philosopher in the tradition of Russell

ligneux, -euse [liɲø, -øz] ADJ ligneous, woody

lignite [liɲit] NM *Minér* lignite, brown coal

ligoter [ligɔte] VT to tie up; **être ligoté à qch** to be tied to sth

ligue [lig] NF league, confederacy; *Hist* **la (Sainte) L.** the (Holy Catholic) League; *Hist* **L. des droits de l'homme** = organization set up in 1898 to defend Dreyfus

liguer [lige] VT *(nations, clans etc)* to league together; **être ligué avec qn** to be in league with sb
    VPR **se liguer** to form a league (**avec** with, **contre** against); **ils se liguent contre moi** they're ganging up on me

ligueur, -euse [ligœr, -øz] N member of a league

lilas [lila] NM *Bot* lilac
    ADJ INV lilac

lilliputien, -ienne [lilipysjɛ̃, -jɛn] ADJ Lilliputian
    N **L.** Lilliputian

lillois, -oise [lilwa, -waz] ADJ of/from Lille
    N **L.** *(natif)* native of Lille; *(habitant)* inhabitant of Lille

Lima [lima] N Lima

limace [limas] NF **1** *(mollusque)* slug; *Fam* **c'est une vraie l.** he's such a slowcoach *or Am* slowpoke, *Am* he's as slow as molasses in winter **2** *Arg (chemise)* shirt

limaçon [limasɔ̃] NM **1** *Vieilli* snail **2** *Anat (de l'oreille)* cochlea

limage [limaʒ] NM filing (down)

limaille [limaj] NF filings; **l. de fer** iron filings

limande [limɑ̃d] NF *(poisson)* dab; **l.-sole** lemon sole; *Fam* **plate comme une l.** *(d'une femme)* as flat as a pancake

lime¹ [lim] NF **1** *(outil)* file; **l. sourde** deadsmooth file; **l. à ongles** nail file; **l. émeri** emery board; **aiguiser un outil à la l.** to file up a tool **2** *(mollusque)* lima

lime² NF *Bot* lime

limer [lime] VT **1** *(réduire)* to file (down); *(polir)* to file (up); **l. les barreaux** to file through the bars **2** *Vulg* to screw
    VI *Vulg* to screw, to have one's end away
    VPR **se limer se l. les ongles** to file one's nails

limier [limje] NM *(chien)* bloodhound; *Fig* sleuth; *Bourse* investigator

liminaire [liminɛr] ADJ *(note, remarque etc)* introductory

limitatif, -ive [limitatif, -iv] ADJ limiting, restrictive, restricting; **dispositions limitatives** restrictions; **une liste non limitative** an open-ended list; **la liste n'est pas limitative** the list is not exhaustive

limitation [limitasjɔ̃] NF limitation, restriction; **l. des armements** arms limitation; **l. des naissances** birth control, family planning; **l. des salaires** imposition of wage restraints; *(volontaire)* (voluntary) wage restraint; **l. de vitesse** speed limit; **ce test se fait sans l. de temps** there is no time limit for the test; **l. de poids** weight limit; **l. des prix** price restrictions *or* controls; **l. de responsabilité** limitation of responsibility

limite [limit] NF **1** *(de pays, champ etc)* boundary; **les limites d'un terrain de football** the boundary (lines) of a football pitch; **marquer les limites du terrain** to mark out the ground; **à la l. du jardin, il y a une forêt** just beyond the garden there is a forest
    2 *(de pouvoir, compréhension etc)* limit; **fixer** *ou* **imposer des limites à l'autorité de qn** to set limits *or* bounds on sb's authority; **son ambition/sa générosité/son amour pour elle ne connaît pas de limites** his ambition/his generosity/his love for her knows no bounds; **je connais mes limites** I know my limits; **il y a des limites!** there are limits!; **ma patience a des limites!** there are limits to my patience!, my patience is wearing thin!; **la bonté a des limites** there are limits to my/ her/*etc* kindness; **mettre une l./des limites à qch** to set a limit/limits to sth, to limit sth; **franchir** *ou* **dépasser les limites** to go too far, to be out of line; **l'Irak a franchi les limites de l'horreur** the horror of what is happening in Iraq is beyond belief; **vous avez vraiment dépassé les limites du supportable** what you did is quite intolerable; **c'est à la l. de la vulgarité/du supportable** it's bordering on vulgarity/the unacceptable; **je vous aiderai dans les limites du possible** I'll do everything possible *or* everything I possibly can to help you, I'll help you as far as is humanly possible; **dans les limites du raisonnable** within reasonable limits; **dans les limites du sujet** within the limits of the subject; **veuillez rester dans les limites du sujet** please keep to the subject; **dans la l. des places disponibles** subject to availability; **dans la l. des stocks disponibles** while stocks last; **dans une certaine l.** up to a point, to a certain extent; **je suis prêt à vous prêter de l'argent dans une certaine l.** I am ready to lend you money up to a point; **à la l., j'accepterais de le voir** if pushed *or* if I have to, I'll agree to see him; **ça va? – oui, à la l.** is that OK? – yes, just about; **se battre/résister/travailler jusqu'à la dernière l.** to fight/resist/work to the last; **il est à la l. de ses forces** he's completely exhausted, he's at the limit of his endurance; **sans limites** unbounded, limitless; *Boxe* **gagner avant la l.** to win inside the distance
    3 *Math* limit, limiting value
    ADJ **cas l.** borderline case; **vitesse l.** maximum speed; **charge l. d'un pont** maximum load of a bridge; **date l.** deadline; *(pour candidature etc)* deadline, closing date; *Fam* **50 euros, c'est le prix l. que j'accepterais de payer** 50 euros is my top price; *Fam* **je ne lui ai pas mis une claque, mais c'était l.** I didn't slap him but I came very close to it *or* but it was touch and go; *Fam* **elle est l., ta dissertation** your essay's a borderline case *or* only just this side of acceptable; *Fam* **je suis un peu l. financièrement** I'm a bit short (of cash), my bank account's not very healthy;

Fam **j'ai trouvé qu'il était l. avec elle** I thought he was a bit hard on her
    ▸ ▸ **l. d'âge** age limit; **l. de crédit** credit limit; *Tech* **l. d'élasticité** elastic limit; *Tech* **l. élastique** yield point; **l. d'endettement** borrowing limit; **l. de poids** weight limit; *Bourse* **l. de position** position limit; **l. de rupture** breaking *or* yield point

limité [limite] ADJ **1** limited; **vitesse limitée à 60 km/heure** speed restricted to 60km/hour; **en temps l.** in a limited amount of time; **n'avoir qu'une confiance limitée dans une machine/l'honnêteté de qn** to have a limited amount of confidence in a machine/a person's honesty; **avec lui, la conversation est limitée** conversation is limited with him, you can't have much of a conversation with him; *Fam* **il est un peu l. ce mec** the guy's a bit thick **2** *Can* Limited, Ltd; **Desrochers et Cie limitée** Desrochers and Co. Ltd.

limiter [limite] VT **1** *(délimiter) (pays, territoire etc)* to bound, to mark the bounds of **2** *(restreindre)* to limit, to restrict; *(pouvoir, droits etc de qn)* to set bounds *or* limits to; *Fam* **l. les dégâts** to limit the damage; **je ne connaissais pas vraiment le sujet de l'examen, mais j'ai limité les dégâts** I didn't really know anything about the exam subject but I managed to make something of it; **l. la production** to limit production
    VPR **se limiter il faut apprendre à se l.** you have to learn to limit yourself *or* to keep within limits; **quand il commence à boire, il est incapable de se l.** once he starts drinking he doesn't know when to stop; **se l. à …** to limit *or* restrict *or* confine oneself to …; **elle se limita à dire que …** she confined herself to saying that …; **son œuvre se limite à quelques essais** his works amount to no more than a few essays; **l'intérêt touristique de la ville se limite à un château en ruines** the only tourist attraction in the town is a ruined castle, all the town has to offer in the way of tourist attractions is a ruined castle

limiteur [limitœr] NM *Aut* limiter; **l. de freinage** *(correcteur)* pressure limiter; **l. de régime** over-run valve, rev limiter

limitrophe [limitrɔf] ADJ adjacent (**de** to), bordering (**de** on); **les pays limitrophes** the neighbouring *or Am* neighboring countries; **être l. d'un autre pays** to border on another country

limogeage [limɔʒaʒ] NM *(d'officier)* superseding; *(de fonctionnaire)* dismissal

limoger [limɔʒe] VT *(officier)* to supersede; *(fonctionnaire)* to dismiss

limon¹ [limɔ̃] NM **1** *(alluvion)* silt, *Spéc* alluvium; **le l. employé comme engrais** silt used as a fertilizer **2** *Géol* limon

limon² NM **1** *(brancard)* shaft **2** *Constr (d'escalier)* stringboard, stringer

limon³ NM *Bot, Arch* lemon

limonade [limɔnad] NF *(boisson gazeuse)* (fizzy) lemonade

limonadier, -ière [limɔnadje, -jɛr] N **1** *Ind* soft drinks manufacturer **2** *Arch (cafetier)* café owner

limoner [limɔne] VI *Can Fam* **1** *(se plaindre)* to moan, to whinge; *(pleurnicher)* to whinge **2** *(hésiter)* to dither

limoneux, -euse [limɔnø, -øz] ADJ *(eau etc)* muddy, silty; *Géol* alluvial

limousin, -ine¹ [limuzɛ̃, -in] ADJ of/from (the province of) Limousin
    N **L.** *(natif)* native of (the province of) Limousin; *(inhabitant)* inhabitant of (the province of) Limousin
    NM *Ling* Limousin dialect

limousine² NF *Aut* limousine

limpide [lɛ̃pid] ADJ *(quartz, eau etc)* limpid, clear; *(explication)* clear, lucid; *(style)* limpid, lucid; **un regard l.** a clear *or Litt* limpid expression

limpidité [lɛ̃pidite] NF *(de quartz, eau)* clarity, limpidity; *(d'explication)* clarity, lucidity; *(de style)* limpidity, lucidity; *(de regard)* limpidity

lin [lɛ̃] NM **1** *(plante)* flax; **graine de l.** linseed; **huile de l.** linseed oil **2** *Tex* **(tissu/toile de) l.** linen

linceul [lɛ̃sœl] NM winding sheet, shroud

linéaire [lineɛr] ADJ **1** *Math* linear **2** *dessin* **l.** geometrical drawing **3** *Fig Litt* **récit l.** linear narrative
NM *(dans un magasin)* shelf-space

linge [lɛ̃ʒ] NM **1** *(draps etc)* linen; **gros l.** household linen; **armoire à l.** linen cupboard **2** *(dessous)* **(petit) l.** underwear; *Fig Fam* **c'est du beau l.** they're society people **3** *(vêtements)* clothes **4** *(lessive)* washing; **corde à l.** clothesline; **corbeille à l.** laundry basket **5** *(morceau de tissu)* cloth **6** *Suisse (serviette de toilette)* towel
▸▸ **l. de corps** underwear; **l. de maison** household linen; **l. de table** table linen

lingère [lɛ̃ʒer] NF linen-keeper

lingerie [lɛ̃ʒri] NF **1** *(dessous féminins)* underwear, lingerie **2** *(pour rangement)* linen room; *(pour entretien)* laundry

lingette [lɛ̃ʒet] NF *(pour bébés)* baby wipe

lingot [lɛ̃go] NM **1** *(masse de métal)* ingot; **l. d'or** gold bar *or* ingot; *Fin* **or/argent en lingots** (gold/silver) bullion **2** *Typ* space, slug

lingual, -ale, -aux, -ales [lɛ̃gwal, -o] ADJ *Anat, Ling* lingual

linguiste [lɛ̃gyist] N linguist

linguistique [lɛ̃gyistik] ADJ linguistic; **un séjour l.** a stay in a foreign country *(for the purposes of learning the language)*; **une communauté l.** a speech community
NF linguistics

linguistiquement [lɛ̃gyistikmɑ̃] ADV linguistically

liniment [linimɑ̃] NM *Méd* liniment

lino [lino] NM *Fam (abrév* linoléum) lino

linoléum [linɔleɔm] NM linoleum

linon [linɔ̃] NM *Tex* lawn

linotte [linɔt] NF *(oiseau)* linnet; *Fam* **tête de l.** scatterbrain

linotype® [linotip] NF *Typ* Linotype®

linotypie [linotipi] NF *Typ* Linotype® setting

linotypiste [linotipist] N *Typ* linotypist

linteau, -eaux [lɛ̃to] NM *Constr* lintel

lion [ljɔ̃] NM **1** lion; **la part du l.** the lion's share; *Fam* **il a mangé** *ou Arg* **bouffé du l.** he's being all hyper; **tourner comme un l. en cage** to prowl around; **l. de mer** sea lion VOIR GRAMMAIRE A12 **2** *Arch, Litt* celebrity; *(littéraire)* lion **3** *Astron, Astrol* **le L.** Leo; **être (du signe du) L.** to be (a) Leo

lionceau, -eaux [ljɔ̃so] NM lion cub

lionne [ljɔn] NF lioness; *Vieilli Fig* **une l.** a handsome *or* elegant-looking woman

lipase [lipaz] NF *Biol, Chimie* lipase

lipide [lipid] NM *Biol, Chimie* lipid

liposome [lipozom] NM *Biol, Chimie* liposome

liposuccion [liposysjɔ̃] NF liposuction

lippe [lip] NF (thick) lower lip; **faire la l.** *(faire la moue)* to pout; *(bouder)* to sulk

lippu [lipy] ADJ *(personne)* thick-lipped; *(lèvre)* thick

liquéfaction [likefaksjɔ̃] NF liquefaction

liquéfiable [likefjabl] ADJ liquefiable

liquéfiant [likefjɑ̃] ADJ liquefactive, liquefying

liquéfier [likefje] *(pr sub, impf n.* liquéfiions, v. liquéfiiez) VT to liquefy

VPR **se liquéfier** to liquefy; *Fig* to be drained (of energy); *(avoir peur)* to turn to jelly

liquette [liket] NF *Fam* shirt

liqueur [likœr] NF **1** *(spiritueux)* liqueur; **verre à l.** liqueur glass; **l. de cassis** blackcurrant liqueur **2** *Can* **l. (douce)** soft drink **3** *Chimie* solution; **l. titrée** standard solution; *Méd* **l. de Dakin** Dakin's solution

> Il faut noter que le terme **liquor**, utilisé en anglais américain, est un faux ami. Il signifie **alcool**.

liquidateur, -trice [likidatœr, -tris] N **1** *Jur* liquidator; **l. judiciaire** official liquidator **2** *Bourse* **l. officiel** official assignee

liquidation [likidasjɔ̃] NF **1** *Jur* liquidation; **l. forcée/volontaire** compulsory/voluntary liquidation; **l. judiciaire** official receivership; **l. des biens** liquidation of assets; **entrer en l.** to go into liquidation; **mettre en l.** to put into liquidation, to liquidate **2** *(de comptes)* settlement, clearing; *Bourse* settlement; *Bourse (d'une position)* liquidation; *Bourse* **l. en espèces** cash settlement; **chambre de l.** (bankers') clearing house; *Compta* **l. de fin de mois/de quinzaine** end-of-month/fortnightly settlement **3** *Com (de stocks)* selling off; **l. totale** *(sur panneau)* closing down sale, everything must go **4** *Fam (fait de tuer)* liquidation, elimination

liquide [likid] ADJ liquid; **la soupe est trop l.** the soup is too watery *or* too thin; **argent l.** cash, ready money, hard cash; *Fin* **actif l.** liquid asset; *Fin* **peu l.** illiquid
NM **1** *(substance)* liquid, fluid; **il ne pourra prendre que des liquides pendant une semaine** he'll be on liquids for a week **2** *Fig (espèces)* (ready) cash; **je n'ai pas assez de l.** I haven't enough (ready) cash; **vous payez par chèque ou en l.?** are you paying by cheque or (in) cash?
NF *Ling* liquid
▸▸ *Méd* **l. céphalo-rachidien** cerebrospinal fluid; **l. correcteur** correction fluid; *Aut* **l. de direction assistée** power steering fluid; *Aut* **l. de frein** brake fluid; *Aut* **l. hydraulique de frein** hydraulic brake fluid; **l. de nettoyage** cleaning fluid; **l. de refroidissement** coolant, coolant fluid; *Méd* **l. synovial** synovial fluid; *Aut* **l. pour transmission automatique** automatic transmission fluid

liquider [likide] VT **1** *Jur (affaire)* to liquidate, to wind up **2** *(compte)* to settle, to clear; *Bourse (une position)* to liquidate, to close out; **l. une dette** to pay off a debt **3** *Fam (tuer)* to liquidate, to eliminate; **l. une tâche** to get through a task, to get a task finished **4** *(stock)* to sell off; **ils liquident chez Martin** they're selling off stock at Martin's

liquidité [likidite] NF liquidity; *Fin* **liquidités** liquid assets; **liquidités excédentaires** excess liquidities; **liquidités obligatoires** mandatory liquid assets

liquoreux, -euse [likɔrø, -øz] ADJ *(vin)* liqueur-like

lire¹ [lir] *(prp lisant; pp lu; pr ind je lis, il lit; impf je lisais; p hist je lus; fu je lirai)* VT **1** *(livre, auteur, disquette, données, musique etc)* to read; **elle sait l.** she can read; **l. tout haut** *ou* **à haute voix** to read aloud; **l. en diagonale** to scan, to cast a quick eye over, to skim through; **l. qch dans un livre** to read sth in a book; **l. qch à qn** to read sth (out) to sb; **avoir beaucoup lu** to be well read; **c'est un auteur qui est très lu** he's a widely read author; **lu et approuvé** read and approved; **dans l'attente de vous l.** *(dans une lettre)* hoping to hear from you soon; *Fig* **l. entre les lignes** to read between the lines; *Ordinat* **l. au scanneur** to scan; **l. les épreuves de tirage** to proof-read

2 *(interpréter)* to read; **on peut le l. de deux façons différentes** you can read it two different ways

3 *(déchiffrer)* **l. dans la pensée de qn** to read sb's thoughts; **l. dans le jeu de qn** to know sb's game, to know what sb is up to; **elle a voulu me l. les lignes de la main** she wanted to read my hand; **l. dans une boule de cristal** to read a crystal ball; **l. dans le marc de café** ≃ to read the tea leaves

4 *Fig (deviner) (sur un visage, dans un regard)* to read
VPR **se lire 1 ce livre se lit bien** *ou* **se laisse l.** it's a readable book, this book is very readable *or* a good read; **ce roman se lit en une soirée** this novel can be read in an evening; **ce genre de fautes se lit couramment** you read this sort of mistake a lot **2** *(se deviner)* **cela se lit sur votre visage/dans vos yeux** it shows in your face/in your eyes, it's written all over your face/you can read it in your eyes

lire² NF *(monnaie)* lira

lis [lis] NM lily; **l. blanc** white lily; **l. des vallées** lily of the valley; **l. d'eau** *ou* **d'étang** water lily; **teint de l.** lily-white complexion

Lisbonne [lizbɔn] N Lisbon

liséré [lizre], **liséré** [lizere] NM *Couture* border, edging

liseron [lizrɔ̃] NM bindweed, convolvulus

liseur, -euse [lizœr, -øz] N reader
NF **liseuse 1** *(couverture amovible)* book cover **2** *(vêtement de femme)* (lady's) bed jacket **3** *(en train, en avion)* reading light

lisibilité [lizibilite] NF **1** *(d'une écriture)* legibility **2** *(d'un texte, fichier informatique)* readability

lisible [lizibl] ADJ **1** *(qu'on peut déchiffrer)* legible, readable; **l. par ordinateur** machine-readable **2** *(qu'on peut comprendre)* readable

lisiblement [lizibləmɑ̃] ADV legibly

lisière [lizjer] NF **1** *(de champ, forêt)* edge, border **2** *(bande de tissu)* selvage, selvedge

lissage [lisaʒ] NM *(de pierre etc)* smoothing, polishing; *(de cuir)* sleeking; *(de papier etc)* glazing; *Ordinat* **l. de courbes/des caractères** curve/character smoothing

lisse¹ [lis] NF *Naut* **1** *(de coque)* ribband; **lisses de l'avant** harpings **2** *(du bastingage)* handrail

lisse² ADJ smooth; *(poli)* polished; *(pneu)* bald; **cheveux lisses** sleek hair

lisser [lise] VT *(cheveux)* to smooth down, to sleek down; *(pli)* to smooth out; *(pierre etc)* to smooth, to polish; *(cuir)* to sleek; *(papier etc)* to glaze
VPR **se lisser se l. les plumes** *(d'un oiseau)* to preen its feathers *or* itself

lisseur [lisœr] NM **l. de fontes** font smoother

listage [listaʒ] NM *Ordinat* listing, printout

liste [list] NF list; **dresser/faire une l.** to draw up/make (out) a list; **être en tête/en fin de l.** to be at the top/the bottom of the list; **l. officielle des taux** schedule of charges; *Tél* **être sur (la) l. rouge** to be ex-directory, *Am* to have an unlisted number, to be unlisted
▸▸ **l. des actionnaires** list of shareholders; **l. d'adresses** mailing list, address list; **l. des arrivées** arrivals list; **l. d'attente** waiting list, waitlist; **l. bloquée** set list of candidates *(which electors cannot modify)*; **l. civile** civil list; **l. de clients** customer *or* client list; *(d'hôtel)* guest list; *Com* **l. de colisage** packing list; **l. commune** joint list (of candidates); **l. des correspondants** list of correspondents; **l. des départs** departure list; **l. de diffusion** mailing list; **l. électorale** electoral roll; **l. d'émargement** payroll; **l. d'envoi** mailing list; *Ordinat* **l. de fichiers à imprimer** print list, print queue; **l. de mariage** wedd-

ing list; **l. de naissance** = list of presents requested by the parents of a newborn baby; **l. noire** blacklist; **mettre qn sur la l. noire** to blacklist sb; **l. d'opposition** list of opposition candidates; *Pol* **l. panachée** = ballot paper in which a voter votes for candidates from different lists rather than for a list as a whole; *TV, Cin* **l. des prises de vue** shot list; **l. de prix** price list; *Ordinat* **l. à puces** bulleted list; *Ordinat* **l. rapide** draft; **l. récapitulative** checklist; **l. des réservations** reservations list; **l. des signatures autorisées** authorized signatory list; *Ordinat* **l. de signets** bookmark list; **l. des tarifs** price list, tariff; *(de transport)* fare list

listel, -els, **listeau, -eaux** [listɛl, -o] NM **1** *Archit etc* listel, fillet **2** *(de pièce de monnaie)* rim

lister [liste] VT to list

listériose [listerjoz] NF *Méd* listeriosis

listing [listiŋ] NM *Ordinat* listing, printout

lit [li] NM **1** *(meuble)* bed; **l. moelleux/dur** soft/hard bed *or* mattress; **l. de fer** iron bedstead; **aller au l.** to go to bed; **se mettre au l.** to get into bed; **l. pour deux personnes, grand l.** double bed; **mettre un enfant au l.** to put a child to bed; **au l. les enfants!** time for bed, children!, bedtime, children!; **au saut du l.** just after one has got up; **être au l.** to be in bed; **prendre le l.** to take to one's bed; **garder le l.** to stay in bed; **tirer qn du l.** to get sb out of bed; **je ne te tire** *ou* **sors pas du l. au moins?** I hope I didn't get you out of bed; **faire le l.** to make the bed; *Fig* **faire le l. de** to pave the way for; **faire l. à part** to sleep in separate beds; **un hôtel de 200 lits** a 200-bed hotel, a hotel with 200 beds; **chambre à un l./à deux lits** single-/twin-bedded room; **mourir dans son l.** to die in (one's) bed; **bois de l.** bedstead

2 *Jur* **enfant du second l.** child by one's second marriage

3 *(couche)* *(d'argile, de pierre etc)* bed, layer; **l. de cendres** bed of ashes; *Culin* **placer les filets sur un l. d'épinards** place the fillets on a bed of spinach

4 *(de rivière etc)* bed; **la rivière est sortie de son l.** the river has burst its banks

5 *Naut (de marée etc)* set; **être dans le l. de marée** to be in the tideway; **dans le l. du vent** in the wind's eye

▸▸**l. à baldaquin** canopied four-poster (bed), tester bed; **l.-bateau,** *pl* **lits-bateaux** = bed with curved sides, higher at the ends; **l.-cage,** *pl* **lits-cages** cot, *Am* crib; **l. de camp** camp bed, *Am* cot; **l. en cathédrale** = bed placed upright with sleeper in it; **l. clos** box bed; **l. à colonnes** four-poster (bed); **l. conjugal** marital bed; *Littr* **l. de douleur** sick bed; **l. d'enfant** cot, *Am* crib; **l. escamotable** Murphy bed; **l. de long séjour** *(dans un hôtel)* long-stay bed; **l. majeur** *(d'un fleuve)* flood plain; *Tech* high water *or* bed; *Tech* **l. mineur** mean water *or* bed; *Vieilli* **l. de misère** childbed; **l. de mort: être sur son l. de mort** to be on one's death bed; **l.-nacelle,** *pl* **lits-nacelles** carry cot; **l. pliant** folding *or* foldaway bed; **l. en portefeuille** apple-pie bed; **l. de repos** couch; **l. une place** single bed; **lits gigognes** beds that fit into each other; **lits jumeaux** twin beds; **lits superposés** bunk beds, bunks

litanie [litani] NF **1** *Rel* litanies litany **2** *Péj (de griefs, plaintes)* litany; **c'est toujours la même l.** it's the same old story

litchi [litʃi] NM *(fruit)* lychee, litchi

liteau, -eaux [lito] NM **1** *Constr* batten, rail, ribband **2** *Tex (sur linge de table etc)* band, stripe

litée [lite] NF *(d'animaux)* litter

literie [litri] NF bedding

lithiase [litjaz] NF *Méd* lithiasis

lithine [litin] NF *Chimie* lithia

lithiné [litine] ADJ **eau lithinée** lithia water
NMPL **lithinés** lithium salts

lithium [litjɔm] NM *Chimie* lithium

litho [lito] NF *Fam (abrév* **lithographie***)* litho

lithographe [litograf] N lithographer

lithographie [litografi] NF **1** *(technique)* lithography; **l. offset** offset lithography **2** *(estampe)* lithograph

lithographier [litografje] VT *(pr sub, impf* n. **lithographiions, v. lithographiiez***)* to lithograph

lithographique [litografik] ADJ lithographic

lithosphère [litosfɛr] NF *Géol* lithosphere

litière [litjɛr] NF **1** *(d'écurie)* litter; **la l. du chat** the cat's litter **2** *Hist (palanquin)* litter; **être porté en l.** to be carried in a litter

litige [litiʒ] NM dispute; *(poursuite)* lawsuit; *(recours à la loi)* litigation; **objet** *ou* **point de l.** bone of contention; *Jur* subject of the action; **être en l.** to be in dispute, to be disputed; **l. commercial** commercial dispute

litigieux, -euse [litiʒjø, -øz] ADJ *(affaire, héritage, contrat)* disputed, in dispute; *(question, cas)* contentious

litote [litɔt] NF *Littér* litotes, understatement

litre [litr] NM **1** *(mesure)* litre, *Am* liter **2** *(récipient d'un litre)* litre *or Am* liter bottle

litron [litrɔ̃] NM *Fam* litre *or Am* liter of wine

littéraire [literɛr] ADJ *(critique, prix, langue etc)* literary; **la vie l.** the literary world, literary life; **avoir l'esprit l.** to have a literary turn of mind

N **1** *(personne douée pour la littérature)* literary person **2** *(étudiant)* student of literature **3** *(professeur)* teacher of literature

littérairement [literɛrmɑ̃] ADV in literary terms; *(intéressant)* from a literary point of view

littéral, -ale, -aux, -ales [literal, -o] ADJ **1** *(traduction, sens etc)* literal; *Math* **coefficient l.** literal coefficient **2** *(par écrit)*, *Jur* **preuve littérale** documentary evidence; **arabe l.** written Arabic

littéralement [literalmɑ̃] ADV literally

littéralité [literalite] NF *Litt* literality, literalness

littérateur [literatœr] NM literary man, man of letters, *Péj* literary hack

littérature [literatyr] NF literature; **se lancer dans la l.** to embark on a literary career; **faire carrière dans la l.** to make a career in writing; **l. commerciale** sales literature; *Fig Péj* **tout ça c'est de la l.** all that's of trifling importance; **on a publié une importante l. sur le sujet** a considerable amount of literature has been published on the subject

littoral, -ale, -aux, -ales [litɔral, -o] ADJ coastal, *Spéc* littoral
NM coast(line), *Spéc* littoral

Lituanie [litɥani] NF Lithuania

lituanien, -ienne [litɥanjɛ̃, -jɛn] ADJ Lithuanian
NM *Ling* Lithuanian
N **L.** Lithuanian

liturgie [lityrʒi] NF *Rel* liturgy

liturgique [lityrʒik] ADJ *Rel* liturgical

livarde [livard] NF *Naut* sprit; **voile à l.** spritsail

livarot [livaro] NM *Culin* Livarot (cheese)

livide [livid] ADJ **1** *(teint)* pallid **2** *Litt (bleuâtre)* livid

lividité [lividite] NF pallor, pallidness; *Méd* **l. cadavérique** livor mortis, post-mortem lividity

living(-room), *pl* **living(-room)s** [liviŋ(-rum)] NM living room

livrable [livrabl] ADJ **1** *Com* that can be delivered; **marchandises livrables à domicile** goods delivered to your home **2** *Bourse* deliverable

livraison [livrɛzɔ̃] NF **1** *(de marchandises etc)* delivery; **l. gratuite,** *Spéc* **l. franco** free delivery, delivered free; **l. franco par nos soins** carriage paid; **payable à la l.** payable on delivery; **l. contre remboursement, paiement à la l.** *Br* cash on delivery, *Am* collect on delivery; **faire une l.** to make a delivery; **faire la l. de qch** to deliver sth; **faire la l. de pain/journaux** to deliver the bread/the newspapers; **prendre l. de qch** to take delivery of sth; **défaut de l.** non-delivery; **voiture de l.** delivery van; *Fin* **l. des titres** delivery of securities; *Com* **l. immédiate** available for delivery, ready delivery; **l. le jour même** same-day delivery; *Com* **l. à terme** future delivery, forward delivery; *Com* **l. à domicile** door-to-door delivery, home delivery; *(de journaux)* direct door delivery; **'l. à domicile'** home deliveries; **la l. est arrivée** *(marchandise)* the delivery has arrived **2** *(d'ouvrage publié en fascicules)* part

livre¹ [livr] NF **1** *(poids)* half kilo, ≃ pound; *Can* pound VOIR GRAMMAIRE A13 **2** **l. (sterling)** pound (sterling) VOIR GRAMMAIRE A13 **3** *Hist (monnaie)* livre

livre² NM **1** *(objet)* book; **un l. sur les papillons** a book on *or* about butterflies; **connaître qch par les livres** to know sth from *or* through books; **elle a toujours le nez dans les livres** she's always got her nose in a book; **l. cartonné** *ou* **relié** hardback (book); **l. de classe** *ou* **scolaire** schoolbook; **l. de grammaire** grammar (book); **l. de lecture** reader, reading book; **l. de cuisine** cookery book, cookbook; **l. d'images/pour enfants** picture/children's book; **l. musical** musical book; **parler comme un l.** to talk like a book; **traduire un passage à l. ouvert** to translate a passage at sight; **il lit Cicéron à l. ouvert** he can read Cicero at sight

2 *(édition)* **l'industrie du l., le l.** the book trade; **les ouvriers du l.** printworkers

3 *Com (registre)* **grand l.** ledger; **tenir les livres** to keep the accounts *or* the books; **tenue des livres** book-keeping

4 *(de la Bible etc)* book; **le premier l. des 'Fables' de La Fontaine** the first book of La Fontaine's Fables

▸▸ *Compta* **l. d'achats** purchase ledger; **l. d'actionnaires** register of shareholders; **l. blanc** official report; **l. de bord** *Naut* log(-book); *Scol* (teacher's) record book; *(à la maison)* housekeeping book; **l. de caisse** cashbook; **l. de chevet** bedside book; **l. de commandes** order book; **l. de comptes** journal, ledger, account book; **l. de coupures de presse** cuttings book; *Compta* **l. des créanciers** accounts payable ledger; *Compta* **l. des débiteurs** accounts receivable ledger; *Compta* **l. de dépenses** cash book; **l. d'échéance** bill book; *Compta* **l. des effets à payer** bills payable ledger; *Compta* **l. des effets à recevoir** bills receivable ledger; **l. électronique** e-book; *Compta* **l. des entrées** purchase ledger; **l. électronique** e-book; **l. d'heures** book of hours; *Compta* **l. des inventaires** stock book; **l. journal** *Com* daybook, journal; *Compta* book of original entry; **l. de la Loi** book of the Law; **l. de messe** missal, prayer book; **l. numérique** e-book; **l. d'or** visitors' book; **l. de paie** payroll; *Compta* wages ledger; **l. de petite caisse** petty cash book; **l. de poche** paperback; **l. de prières** prayer book; **l. de prix** prize book; *Arch* **l. de raison** family record book; *Compta* **l. des réclamations** claims book; *Compta* **l. des rendus** returns ledger; **l. de réservation** reservations book, hotel register; *Compta* **l. des sorties** sales ledger; *Compta* **l. de trésorerie géné-**

rale general cash book; **l. des ventes** sales ledger

livre-cassette, *pl* **livres-cassettes** NM spoken word cassette; *(pour les aveugles)* talking book

livrée [livʀe] NF **1** *(habit de domestique)* livery; **valet en l.** servant in livery, liveried servant **2** *(pelage)* coat; *(plumage)* plumage

livre-jeu, *pl* **livres-jeux** NM activity book

livrer [livʀe] VT **1** *(marchandises etc)* to deliver; **nous avons bien été livrés** we have received the delivery; Com **l. à terme fixe** to deliver at a fixed term; **nous livrons à domicile** we deliver (anywhere) or to your door; **vous serez livrés dès demain** you'll receive delivery tomorrow; Com **livré franco domicile** delivered free at domicile

2 *(abandonner)* to abandon; *(remettre)* to deliver (à to); **l. un village au pillage/un pays à l'anarchie** to abandon a village to pillage/a country to anarchy; **l. qn à la justice** to deliver or hand over sb to justice or to the authorities; **il a finalement livré ses complices** he finally delivered up his accomplices; **l. une place forte à l'ennemi** to give up a fortress to the enemy; **l. qn à la mort** to send sb to his death; **l. qn/qch aux flammes** to commit sb/sth to the flames; *Litt* **un épouvantail livré aux vents** a scarecrow left to the mercy of the four winds; **bateau livré à la tempête** boat at the mercy of the storm; **livré à soi-même** left to oneself or to one's own devices

3 *(donner, dévoiler)* **l. un secret** to divulge a secret (à to); **je vous livre un secret … ** I'll let you in on a secret …; **l. ses secrets à qn** to confide one's secrets to sb; **l. un peu/beaucoup de soi-même** to reveal a little/a lot of oneself, to open up a bit/a lot; **elle livre peu d'elle-même au bureau** she doesn't reveal much of herself or doesn't open up much at the office

4 l. passage à qn to let sb pass; **l. bataille** *ou* **combat** to join battle (à with), to give battle (à to); *Fig* **l. bataille à la pauvreté/à la famine** to battle against poverty/famine

VPR **se livrer 1** *(se rendre)* to give oneself up (à to); **se l. à la justice** to surrender to the authorities, to give oneself up

2 *(se confier)* to open up; **se l. à qn** to confide in sb

3 *(s'abandonner à)* **se l. à un vice/à des pratiques ignobles** to indulge in a vice/disgraceful practices; **se l. à des spéculations/des plaisirs coupables** to indulge in or give oneself over to speculation/guilty pleasures; **se l. au désespoir** to give way to despair; **se l. à la violence** to behave violently, to turn violent; *Litt* **elle s'est livrée à son amant** she gave or offered herself (up) to her lover; *Arch, Litt* **se l. à la boisson** to take to drink

4 *(s'occuper à)* **se l. à des recherches** to be engaged in research; **se l. à ses occupations habituelles** to indulge in one's usual activities; **se l. à une enquête** to set up or hold an inquiry; **se l. à l'étude/à la lecture** to devote oneself to study/reading; **se l. à un sport** to practise a sport

livresque [livʀɛsk] ADJ **1** *(théorique)* acquired from books; **connaissances livresques** book learning **2** *Péj (esprit)* bookish

livret [livʀɛ] NM **1** *(petit livre)* booklet; **l. (de caisse) d'épargne** bankbook, passbook; **compte sur l.** savings account **2** *Mus (d'opéra)* libretto, book **3** *Suisse (table de multiplication)* multiplication table

▸▸ *Banque* **l. de compte** bankbook; *Banque* **l. de dépôts** deposit book, passbook; **l. d'épargne logement** *Br* ≃ building society passbook, *Am* ≃ savings and loan association passbook; *Admin* **l. de famille** = family record book for registration of births and

deaths; **l. militaire** service record; **l. scolaire** school report book

livreur, -euse [livʀœʀ, -øz] N delivery man, *f* woman

LJM [ɛlʒiɛm] NF Com *(abrév* **livraison le jour même)** same-day delivery

LOA [ɛloa] NF *(abrév* **location avec option d'achat)** lease purchase

lob [lɔb] NM *Tennis* lob; **faire un l.** to hit a lob, to lob

lobby, *pl* **lobbies** [lɔbi] NM *Pol* lobby

lobbying [lɔbiiŋ] NM *Pol* lobbying; **faire du l.** to lobby

lobbyiste [lɔbiist] N *Pol* lobbyist

lobe [lɔb] NM **1** *Anat, Bot* lobe; **l. de l'oreille** ear lobe **2** *Archit* foil **3** *Radio* lobe

lobé [lɔbe] ADJ **1** *Bot* lobed, lobate **2** *Archit* foiled

lobectomie [lɔbɛktɔmi] NF *Chir* lobectomy

lobélie [lɔbeli] NF *Bot* lobelia

lober [lɔbe] VI *Tennis, Ftbl* to lob

VT *Ftbl* **l. le gardien de but** to lob the goalkeeper

lobotomie [lɔbɔtɔmi] NF *Chir* lobotomy; **on lui a fait une l.** he's had a lobotomy, he's been lobotomized

lobulaire [lɔbylɛʀ] ADJ *Anat* lobular

lobule [lɔbyl] NM *Anat* lobule

local, -ale, -aux, -ales [lɔkal, -o] ADJ *(autorité, radio, administration etc)*, *Méd* local; **coutumes locales** local customs; **averses locales demain dans la matinée** scattered showers tomorrow morning; **le journal l.** the local paper; **anesthésie locale** local anaesthetic

NM **1** *(lieu, endroit) (de société, d'organisation)* premises; **l. d'habitation** dwelling; **l. professionnel** premises used for professional purposes; **locaux commerciaux** business premises; **ils cherchent un l. pour leur réunion** they need a place to hold their meeting **2** *(bureau, permanence)* office(s), premises; **rendez-vous au l. à dix heures pour préparer le matériel** meeting at the office at ten o'clock to prepare the equipment **3** *Can Tél* extension

NF *Journ* **locale** local column

> Il faut noter que le nom anglais **local** ne désigne jamais une pièce ou un bâtiment.

localement [lɔkalmɑ] ADV locally

localier [lɔkalje] NM *Journ* local reporter

localisable [lɔkalizabl] ADJ locatable; *(appel téléphonique)* traceable

localisation [lɔkalizasjɔ̃] NF **1** *(circonscription)* localization, confinement **2** *(repérage)* location, locating; *(d'un appel téléphonique)* tracing; **l. de logiciel** software localization

localisé [lɔkalize] ADJ localized

localiser [lɔkalize] VT **1** *(circonscrire) (épidémie, incendie etc)* to localize, to confine **2** *(repérer) (bruit, gène etc)* to locate; *(appel téléphonique)* to trace; **l. qch dans sa mémoire** to place sth; **ne quittez pas, je vais essayer de le l.** hold the line, I'll try to locate him or find out where he is

localité [lɔkalite] NF *(ville)* town; *(village)* village

locataire [lɔkatɛʀ] N *(de propriété louée, de locaux commerciaux)* tenant; *(chez le propriétaire)* lodger, *Am* roomer; *(avec bail)* lessee, leaseholder

locateur [lɔkatœʀ] NM *Jur* lessor

locatif¹, -ive [lɔkatif, -iv] ADJ concerning the renting of premises; **risques locatifs =** tenant's obligations and responsibilities *(as regards damage etc)*; **valeur locative** rental value; **réparations locatives** repairs incum-

bent upon the tenant; **le marché locatif** the property rental market

locatif², -ive Gram ADJ locative

NM locative (case)

location [lɔkasjɔ̃] NF **1** *(de voiture, d'équipement, de costume etc) (par le locataire)* renting, *Br* hiring; *(par le propriétaire)* renting (out), rental, *Br* hiring (out); **prendre qch en l.** to rent sth, *Br* to hire sth; **donner qch en l.** to rent sth (out), *Br* to hire sth (out); **l. de voitures (sans chauffeur)** (self-drive) car rental or *Br* hire; **voiture de l.** rented or hire car, *Am* rental car; **vélos en l.** bikes for hire or *Am* rent **2** *(de logement) (par le locataire)* renting; *(par le propriétaire)* renting (out), *Br* letting (out); **prix de l.** rent; **dans cette agence ils ne font pas la l.** they don't rent (out) or *Br* let (out) property in this agency, they don't deal with rented property in this agency **3** *(propriété à louer)* rented property; *(pour y vivre uniquement)* rented accommodation; **nous n'avons pas trouvé de l. pour cet été** we haven't found anywhere to rent this summer **4** *(de places)* booking, reservation; **(bureau de) l.** box office, booking office

▸▸ **l.-bail,** *pl* **locations-bails** leasing, lease purchase; **l. gérance** rented business; **l. avec option d'achat** lease purchase; **l.-vente,** *pl* **locations-ventes** hire purchase, *Am* installment plan; **acheter qch en l.-vente** to buy sth on hire purchase or *Am* on the installment plan

> Il faut noter que le nom anglais **location** est un faux ami. Il signifie **endroit, emplacement**.

loch [lɔk] NM *Naut* (ship's) log; **ligne de l.** log line; **livre de l.** log

loche [lɔʃ] NF **1** *(poisson)* loach **2** *(mollusque)* grey slug **3** *Vulg (sein)* tit, boob

lock-out [lɔkawt] NM INV *Ind* lockout

lock-outer [lɔkawte] VT *Ind* to lock out

locks [lɔks] NFPL *Fam* dreadlocks

lock-up [lɔkœp] NM INV *Aut* lock-up

loco [loko] NF *Fam (abrév* **locomotive)** loco

locomoteur, -trice [lɔkɔmɔtœʀ, -tʀis] ADJ *(organe, troubles etc)* locomotor

NF *Rail* **locomotrice** electric engine

locomotion [lɔkɔmɔsjɔ̃] NF locomotion; **moyens de l.** means of transport

locomotive [lɔkɔmɔtiv] NF **1** *Rail* locomotive, engine; **l. diesel (à transmission) électrique** diesel electric locomotive **2** *Fig (élément moteur)* motive force; *(leader)* pacemaker, pacesetter; *(en politique)* dynamic or forceful leader

locus [lɔkys] NM *Biol* locus

locuteur, -trice [lɔkytœʀ, -tʀis] N *Ling* speaker; **l. natif** native speaker

locution [lɔkysjɔ̃] NF *(expression)* expression, phrase, locution; **l. figée** set phrase or expression; **l. vicieuse** incorrect expression; *Gram* **l. adverbiale** adverbial phrase; **l. conjonctive** complex conjunction

loden [lɔdɛn] NM *Tex* loden; *(manteau)* loden coat

lœss [løs] NM *Géol* loess

lof [lɔf] NM *Naut* windward side; **venir** *ou* **aller au l.** to sail into the wind, to luff; **virer l. pour l.** to wear

lofer [lɔfe] VI *Naut* to luff

loft [lɔft] NM converted warehouse/garage/etc

logarithme [lɔgaʀitm] *Math* NM logarithm, log; **table de logarithmes** log(arithm) table

ADJ **fonction l.** logarithmic function

logarithmique [lɔgaʀitmik] ADJ *Math* logarithmic

loge [lɔʒ] NF **1** *(d'artiste)* dressing room **2** *(de spectateur)* box; **première l.** first-tier box; *Fig* **être aux premières loges** to have a ringside seat **3** *(maçonnique, de concierge)* lodge **4** *Beaux-Arts, Mus* individual exam room *(for the Prix de Rome)* **5** *Archit* loggia **6** *Bot* cell

logeable [lɔʒabl] ADJ *(habitable)* habitable, fit for occupation

logement [lɔʒmɑ̃] NM **1** *(habitation)* accommodation, *Am* accommodations; *(maison)* house; *(appartement)* flat, *Am* apartment; **chercher un l.** to look for somewhere to live, to look for accommodation; **l. garni** *ou* **meublé** furnished rooms *or* flat *or Am* apartment; **l. collectif** block of flats, *Am* apartment block; **l. à demeure** live-in accommodation **2** *(action)* *(de gens)* housing; *(de troupes)* quartering; *(dans maison privée)* billeting; *(de chevaux)* stabling; **crise du l.** housing shortage **3** *Mil (local)* quarters; *(dans maison privée)* billet **4** *(de pièce de machine)* seating; *(de manche)* housing

LOGER [lɔʒe] **(je logeai(s); n. logeons)** VI to live; *(de troupes)* to be quartered; *(dans maison privée)* to be billeted; **l. à l'hôtel** to stay *or* put up at *or* in a hotel; *Mil* **l. chez l'habitant** to be billeted in private houses; **je compte l. chez l'habitant pendant les vacances** I'm intending to stay in a private house when I go on holiday
▶ VT **1** *(héberger)* *(étudiants, touristes etc)* to accommodate; *(troupes)* to quarter; *(dans maison privée)* to billet; *(chevaux)* to stable; **l. un ami pour la nuit** to put a friend up for the night; **l'auberge de jeunesse peut l. jusqu'à 200 personnes** the youth hostel can accommodate up to 200 people; **crois-tu qu'on arrivera à l. tous les invités dans la salle à manger?** do you think we'll manage to accommodate all the guests in the dining room?; **être logé et nourri** to have board and lodging *or* bed and board; **être bien/mal logé** to be well-/poorly-housed; **il est mal logé dans cet appartement** he's not very comfortable in that apartment
2 *(placer)* to put; **l. une balle dans qch** to put *or* lodge a bullet in sth; **j'ai réussi à l. ton sac entre les deux valises** I managed to put your bag between the two cases; **il faudra bien l. toutes nos affaires dans ce placard** we'll have to put all our belongings in that cupboard
3 *Fam (repérer)* to track down
▶ VPR **se loger 1** *(pour s'installer)* to find accommodation, to find somewhere to live; *(pour la nuit)* to find accommodation, to find somewhere to stay; **nous avons trouvé à nous l.** we've found accommodation, we've found somewhere to live/stay
2 *(se placer)* **mon ballon est allé se l. entre l'antenne de télé et la cheminée** my ball got stuck *or* lodged itself between the television aerial and the chimney; **où a-t-il bien pu aller se l.?** where has it got to?; **la balle se logea dans le mur** the bullet embedded itself in the wall; **le malheureux s'est logé une balle dans la tête** the poor wretch put a bullet in *or* through his head; **la poignée repliée se loge dans un creux spécialement prévu à cet effet** the folded handle fits into a hollow specially designed for the purpose; **la jalousie s'est logée dans son cœur** jealousy filled his heart; **la souris s'est logée sous le lit** the mouse went and hid under the bed; **on a réussi à tous se l. dans son canapé** we all managed to fit *or* squeeze on to his sofa

logeur [lɔʒœr] NM landlord *(of furnished apartments)*

logeuse [lɔʒøz] NF landlady *(of furnished apartments)*

loggia [lɔdʒja] NF *Archit* loggia

logiciel [lɔʒisjɛl] NM *Ordinat* software; **un l.** a software package, a package; *(programme)* a piece of software, a computer program; **un l. très utile** a very useful software package; **l. d'application** application software; **l. auteur** authoring software; **l. bureautique** business software (package); **l. client** client software; **l. de communication** communications package, comms package, communications software; **l. de compression de données** data compression software; **l. de comptabilité** accounts package, accounts software; **l. de conception assistée par ordinateur** computer-aided design package; **l. contributif** shareware; **l. à contribution volontaire** shareware; **l. de conversion** conversion software; **l. de courrier électronique** e-mail software; **l. de cryptage** encryption software; **l. de décompression** decompression software, decompressor; **l. de dessin** art package, drawing program; **l. d'édition d'images** image editing program, image editor; **l. espion** spyware; **l. d'exploitation** operating system software; **l. de filtrage** filtering software; **l. grapheur** graphics package, graphics software; **l. graphique** illustration software; **l. de groupe** groupware; **l. intégré** integrated software; **l. de jeu** games software; **l. libre** freeware; **l. ludique** games software; **l. de mise en page** desktop publishing package; **l. monoposte** single-user software package; **l. multi-utilisateur** multi-user software; **l. de navigation** (Web) browser; **l. de PAO** DTP software; **l. de planification** scheduler; **l. de présentation** presentation software; **l. (du domaine) public** freeware; **l. de reconnaissance de caractères** OCR software, character recognition software; **l. de reconnaissance vocale** voice recognition software; **l. de récupération** recovery program; **l. de réseau** network software; **l. de SGBD** DBMS software; **l. système** system software; **l. système d'exploitation** operating system software; **l. de télémaintenance** remote access software; *(pour base de données)* server software; **logiciels de traitement de texte** word-processing software, word-processing software packages, WP packages; **l. utilisateur** user software; **l. utilitaire** utility program

logicien, -ienne [lɔʒisjɛ̃, -jɛn] N logician

logique [lɔʒik] ADJ **1** *(cohérent)* *(raisonnement, déduction, esprit etc)* logical; **voyons, soyons logiques** come on, let's be logical about this; **il est tout à fait l. que tu n'aies pas envie de le revoir** it's quite natural that you don't want to see him again; **c'est l.** it stands to reason, it's only natural; **je trouve ça l.** it sounds logical to me; **tu n'es pas l.!** you're being illogical!; **il faut être l. avec soi-même** you have to be logical; **le candidat doit avoir l'esprit l.** the candidate must have a logical mind **2** *(analytique)* logical, methodical; *Ordinat* **analyseur l.** logic analyser; *Gram* **analyse l.** *(de phrase)* analysis
▶ NF **1** *Phil, Math* logic; **faire de la l.** to do logic; **l. formelle/pure** formal/pure logic **2** *(cohérence, raisonnement)* logic; **la l. de la passion/de la folie** the logic of passion/madness; **la l. des enfants** children's logic, the way children's minds work; **nous sommes entrés dans une l. de guerre** war is inevitable, war is the next logical step; **en toute l., voilà ce qui devrait se passer** logically, that's what ought to happen; **c'est dans la l. des choses que les enfants ne vivent pas éternellement chez leurs parents** it's logical *or* natural that children shouldn't live with their parents for ever; **ça manque de l.** there's no logic in it, it's illogical; **là, vous manquez de l.** you're not being very logical

▶▶ *Ordinat* **l. câblée** wired logic; **l. floue** fuzzy logic

logiquement [lɔʒikmɑ̃] ADV *(rationnellement)* logically; *(normalement)* all going well, all things being equal; **l., il devrait déjà être là** he should already be here, there's no reason why he shouldn't already be here

logis [lɔʒi] NM *Vieilli, Litt (maison)* home, dwelling, abode; **trouver un l.** to find accommodation

logistique [lɔʒistik] ADJ logistic; **soutien l.** logistic(al) support
▶ NF *Mil etc* logistics; *Mktg* **l. commerciale** marketing mix

logo [logo] NM *(abrév* **logotype)** logo; *Radio etc* **l. audio/sonore** audio/sound logo; *Journ* **l. de page** page logo

logomachie [lɔgɔmaʃi] NF logomachy; *(assemblage de mots, vide de sens)* verbiage, verbosity; **une l.** a lot of verbiage

logopédiste [lɔgɔpedist] N *Belg, Suisse (orthophoniste)* speech therapist

logorrhée [lɔgɔre] NF *Psy* logorrhea; *Hum* verbal diarrhoea; *Hum* **j'ai tendance à la l.** I tend to witter on

LOI [lwa] NF **1** *Jur* **la l.** *(le droit)* the law; **tomber sous le coup de la l.** to come under the law; **avoir la l. pour soi** to have the law on one's side; **je suis désolé mais c'est la l.** I'm sorry but that's the law *or* the law's the law; **respecter la l.** to respect *or* obey the law; **nul n'est censé ignorer la l.** ignorance is no defence in (a court of) law; **homme de l.** lawyer, legal practitioner
2 *(prescription de l'État)* **une l.** a law, an act (of Parliament); **projet de l., proposition de l.** bill; **la l. anti-tabac n'est pas très respectée** not many people respect *or* abide by the anti-smoking laws; **l. fiscale** tax law, fiscal law; **l. bancaire** banking law
3 *(autorité individuelle)* law; **faire la ou sa l.** to lay down the law; **dicter sa l.** to lay down the law, to impose one's will; **faire la l. chez qn** to lay down the law *or* dictate to sb; **c'est lui qui fait la l.** he's the master *or Fam* the boss; **la l. du plus fort** might is right; **dans la cour de récréation c'est la l. du plus fort** it's the law of the jungle in the playground; *Litt* **ce qu'il dit fait l.** his word is law; **nécessité fait l.** needs must when the devil drives; *Litt* **se faire une l. de faire qch** to make a rule *or* a point of doing sth; *Litt* **subir la l. de qn** to be ruled by sb, to be under sb's thumb
4 *(règle qui s'impose)* law; **l. de la nature** law of nature; **l. de la jungle** law of the jungle; **les lois économiques** the laws of economics; **l. phonétique** law of phonetics; **l. de l'offre et de la demande** law of supply and demand; **lois tarifaires** tariff laws; **lois de l'esthétique** rules of aesthetics; **lois de la mode** dictates of fashion; **les lois de la politesse/de l'honneur** the rules of etiquette/the code of honour
5 *Phys, Math* law
6 *Rel* **la l. divine** divine law, the law of God; *Fig* **c'est la l. et les prophètes** its/his/etc word is law

▶▶ *Pol, Jur* **l. d'amnistie** amnesty law; **l. antitrust** antitrust *or Br* anti-monopoly law; **l. électorale** electoral law; **l. d'exception** emergency legislation; *Pol, Jur* **l. de finances** Finance Act; *Pol, Jur* **l. d'habilitation** enabling act; **L. Informatique et Libertés** ≃ Data Protection Act; **l. martiale** martial law; **l. naturelle** natural law; *Pol* **l. d'orientation** = act laying down the basic principles for government action in a given field; **l. sur les sociétés anonymes** public company law; **la l. du talion** an eye for an eye (and a tooth for a tooth)

loi-cadre, *pl* **lois-cadres** NF outline law

LOIN [lwɛ̃] **ADV 1** *(dans l'espace ou le temps)* far (de from); **c'est encore l. le théâtre/Annecy?** is it far to the theatre/Annecy?; **est-ce l. d'ici?** is it far from here?; **ce n'est pas l.** it's not far; **la poste est l.** the post office is a long way off, it's a long way to the post office; **plus l.** farther *or* further (on); **moins l.** less far, not so far; **il y a l. d'ici à Paris** it's a long way to Paris; **l. de moi la prétention de vous apprendre quelque chose** far be it from me to tell you what to do; *Fig aussi Iron* **l. de moi cette idée!** I wouldn't dream of it!, the thought never entered my head!; **l. de moi l'idée d'insinuer que …** far be it from me to insinuate that …, I wouldn't dream of insinuating that …; **le prisonnier s'est échappé mais il n'est pas allé très l.** the prisoner escaped but he didn't get very far; **la voiture est vieille, elle n'ira pas l.** the car is old and on its last legs; *Fig* **ce jeune homme ira l.** this young man will go far; *Fig* **tu n'iras pas l. avec des théories pareilles!** you won't get very far with theories like that!; *Fig* **on pourrait même aller plus l. et dire que …** you could even go further and say that …; *Fig* **ça va (très) l. ce que vous dites** that's taking things a bit far; *Fig* **vous allez trop l.** you're going too far; **ça peut aller très l.** you don't realize what you're getting into; **si je m'en mêle ça peut aller très l.** if I decide to do something about it they'd better watch out; **voir l.** to be far-sighted; *Fig* to be far-sighted *or* shrewd; **voir plus l.** *(dans un texte)* see below/see following pages; *Fig* to look further ahead, to look to the future; **l. derrière lui** far *or* way behind him; *Fig* **laisser ses souvenirs l. derrière soi** to leave one's memories far behind; **j'étais l. de la vérité, ça m'a coûté 2000 euros!** I was way out (in my calculations), it cost me 2,000 euros!; *Prov* **l. des yeux, l. du cœur** out of sight, out of mind; *Fig* **de là à l'accuser de mensonge il n'y a pas l.** that's not far from *or* it's close to calling him a liar; **il ne voit pas plus l. que le bout de son nez** he can't see any further than the end of his nose, he can't see beyond the end of his nose; *Prov* **il y a l. de la coupe aux lèvres** there's many a slip 'twixt the cup and the lip; **nous étions l. de penser/croire/d'imaginer que …** we never thought/believed/imagined for a moment that …; **je ne suis pas l. de penser que …** I've more or less come to the conclusion that …; **elle est l. d'être bête** she is far from stupid; **il est l. d'avoir compris** he still hasn't understood by a long chalk; **je suis encore l. d'avoir fini** I'm still far from finished; **ne pas être l. d'une découverte** to be on the brink of a discovery; **je ne suis pas fâché, l. de là!** I'm not angry, far from it *or* anything but!; **cette époque est bien l.** those days are long gone; **c'est l. tout ça** *(c'est du passé)* that all happened a long time ago; **ça remonte à l. maintenant** it happened a long time *or* years or ages ago; **leur brouille remonte à l.** their quarrel is of long standing, they quarrelled a long time ago; **comme c'est l., tout ça!** that all happened a long time ago!, that's ancient history!; **ce jour est encore l.** that day is still a long way off *or Fnl* is still distant; **c'est encore l. les vacances?** is it still a long time (to go) till the holidays?; **il ne devait pas être l. de midi** it must have been getting on for twelve (o'clock); **ils ont payé pas l. de cent millions pour leur maison** they paid close to a hundred million *or* not far off a hundred million for their house
2 *(dans locutions)* **je l'ai reconnu de l.** I recognized him from a distance *or* from a long way off; **admirer qn de l.** to admire sb at *or* from a distance *or* from afar; **ils sont parents, mais de l.** they are only distantly related; *Litt* **d'aussi l. ou du plus l. qu'il se souvienne** as far back *or* for as long as he can remember; *Fig* **de l.** *(de beaucoup)* by far; **il est de l. plus intelligent que moi** he is far more intelligent than I am; **c'est de l. son meilleur roman** it's by far his best novel; **l. de l'affoler** far from upsetting him; **de l. en l.** *(de temps en temps)* at long intervals, now and then
3 *Suisse (absent)* **il est l.** he's not here
NM au l. in the distance; **apercevoir qn au l.** to see sb a long way off *or* a long way away *or* in the distance

lointain [lwɛ̃tɛ̃] **ADJ** distant, far off, faraway; *(île)* remote; *(ressemblance)* vague; **mes souvenirs les plus lointains** my earliest recollections; **dans un avenir l.** in the distant future; **elle avait l'air l.** she looked as if she was miles away, she had a faraway look on her face; **elle écoutait la conversation, l'air l.** she was listening to the conversation with a faraway look on her face
NM distance; **dans le l.** in the distance; **regard plongé dans le l.** faraway look; *Beaux-Arts* **les lointains** the distances

loi-programme, *pl* **lois-programmes NF** *Fin, Pol* = law providing framework for long-term government programme

loir [lwar] **NM** *(mammifère)* dormouse; **dormir comme un l.** to sleep like a log

Loire [lwar] **NF la L.** the Loire; **le Val de L.** the Loire valley

loisible [lwazibl] **ADJ** *Litt* **il lui est l. de refuser** he is at liberty *or* entitled to refuse

loisir [lwazir] **NM 1** *(temps libre)* leisure; **dans mes heures de l., pendant mes loisirs** in my spare time; **activités de l.** leisure *or* spare-time activities; **avoir des loisirs** to have some spare time **2** *(activité)* **le l., les loisirs** leisure *or* spare-time activities; **un professionnel du l.** *ou* **des loisirs** = specialist travel agency; **le ski/la lecture est mon l. préféré** skiing/reading is my favourite pastime; **société de loisirs** leisure society; **les loisirs sportifs** sporting activities **3** *(possibilité, temps nécessaire)* opportunity; **je n'ai pas encore eu le l. de lui parler/de le lire** I haven't had a chance *or* (the) time to speak to him/ to read it; *Litt* **donner** *ou* **laisser à qn le l. de faire qch** to give sb the opportunity to do sth, to allow sb to do sth; **on ne m'a pas laissé le l. de me reposer** I wasn't given the opportunity *or* any time to rest; **on ne m'a pas laissé le l. de donner mon avis** I wasn't given a chance *or* an opportunity to express my opinion; *Litt* **examiner qch à l.** to examine sth at one's leisure

lolette [lɔlɛt] **NF** *Suisse (tétine)* dummy, *Am* pacifier

lolo [lolo] **NM** *Fam* **1** *Enf (lait)* milk **2** *(sein)* booby

lombaire [lɔ̃bɛr] *Anat* **ADJ** *(douleur, région, vertèbre)* lower back, *Spéc* lumbar; **ponction l.** lumbar puncture
NF lumbar

lombalgie [lɔ̃balʒi] **NF** *Méd* lower back pain

lombard, -arde [lɔ̃bar, -ard] **ADJ** Lombard, of/from Lombardy; *Hist* **la ligue lombarde** the Lombard League
NM *Ling* Lombard dialect
N L. Lombard

Lombardie [lɔ̃bardi] **NF** Lombardy

lombes [lɔ̃b] **NFPL** *Anat* loins

lombric [lɔ̃brik] **NM** earthworm

Lomé [lɔme] **N** Lomé

londonien, -ienne [lɔ̃dɔnjɛ̃, -jɛn] **ADJ** London
N L. Londoner

Londres [lɔ̃dr] **N** London

londrès [lɔ̃drɛs] **NM** Havana cigar

LONG, LONGUE [lɔ̃, lɔ̃g]

┌─────────────────────────┐
│ **ADJ** long **1, 2** ▪ slow **3** │
│ **NM** length **1** ▪ along *(le long de)* **2** │
└─────────────────────────┘

ADJ 1 *(dans l'espace)* long; **avoir un l. nez/de longues jambes** to have a long nose/long legs; **elle a les cheveux longs** she has long hair; **corde longue de 5 mètres** rope 5 metres long, 5-metre rope; **prendre le chemin le plus l.** to go the longest way (round); **un vieillard l. et maigre le regardait fixement** an old man, tall and slim, was staring at him; *Vieilli* **il est l. comme un jour sans pain** he's a real beanpole; **le voyage/discours est l. comme un jour sans pain** this journey/ speech seems to be lasting for ever *or* dragging on for ever; *Fig* **avoir le bras l.** to be able to pull strings, *Fam* to have pull; **phare longue portée** high-intensity light; **navigation au l. cours** deep-sea navigation
2 *(dans le temps)* long; **les jours sont de plus en plus longs** the days are getting longer (and longer); **dix jours, c'est l.** ten days is a long time; **pendant de longues années** for many years; **discours un peu l.** rather long *or* somewhat lengthy speech; **c'est une longue histoire** it's a long story; **je trouve le temps l.** time seems to drag; **je trouve les jours longs** I find the days long, time seems to drag; **l. soupir** long-drawn *or* lengthy sigh; **un ami de longue date** an old friend, a friend of long standing; **projet à longue échéance** long-term project; **à l. terme** long-term; **longue durée** *(chômage)* long-term; *(pile)* long-life; *(cassette)* extended play; *(disque)* long-playing; **à plus ou moins longue échéance, à plus ou moins l. terme** sooner or later
3 *(lent)* slow; **être l. à faire qch** to take a long time to do sth, to be slow to do sth; **qu'est-ce que tu es l.!** you're so slow!, you're taking forever!; **il est l. ce feu** these lights take forever to change; **être l. à réagir** to be slow to react; **j'ai été l. à comprendre** it took me a long time to understand; **je ne serai pas l.** I won't be long; **ce ne sera pas l.** it won't take long; **c'est un travail l. à faire** it's slow work, this work takes a long time; **il s'en sortira, mais ce sera l.** he'll recover but it'll take a long time *or* it will be a slow process
4 *Ling* **une voyelle longue** a long vowel; **'a' l. long 'a'**
5 *Culin (sauce)* thin
NM 1 *(dans l'espace)* length; **table qui a 2 mètres de l.** table 2 metres long *or* in length; **le l. de** along; **se faufiler/grimper le l. du mur** to creep along/to climb up the wall; **tout l. du rivage** all along the shore; **en l.** *(couper, fendre)* lengthwise; **de l. en large** up and down, to and fro; **il arpentait la pièce de l. en large** he paced up and down the room; *Fam* **expliquer qch en l. et en large** *ou* **en l. en large et en travers** to explain sth in great detail *or* at great length; **étendu de tout son l.** stretched out (at) full length; **tomber de tout son l.** to fall flat on one's face
2 *(dans le temps)* **tout le l. du jour/de la nuit** all day/night long, throughout the day/ night; **tout au** *ou* **du l. de l'entretien** throughout *or* all through the conversation
ADV 1 *(beaucoup)* **je crois qu'il est inutile que j'en dise plus l.** need I say more?; **regard qui en dit l.** meaningful *or* eloquent look, look that speaks volumes; **cette action en dit l. sur …** this action speaks volumes for …; **en savoir l./plus l./trop l.** to know a lot/ more/too much; **j'en sais l./je pourrais en dire l. sur cette affaire** I know/I could say quite a lot about this business
2 **s'habiller l.** to wear long clothes
NF longue 1 *Ling* long syllable
2 à la longue in time, in the end, eventually
3 *Mus* long note
4 *Cartes* **longue à pique/trèfles** long suit of spades/clubs

longanime [lɔ̃ganim] **ADJ** *Litt* forbearing

longanimité [lɔ̃ganimite] NF *Litt* forbearance

long-courrier, *pl* **long-courriers** ADJ *(navire)* ocean-going; *(avion)* long-haul, long-range
NM *Naut* ocean-going ship, ocean-goer, ocean liner; *Aviat* long-haul *or* long-range aircraft

longe¹ [lɔ̃ʒ] NF *(pour mener le cheval)* leading rein, halter; *(pour l'attacher)* tether; *(pour le dresser)* lunge, longe

longe² NF *Culin (de veau, porc)* loin

longer [lɔ̃ʒe] VT (je longeai(s); n. longeons) **1** *(suivre) (de personne, voiture) (route, rivière)* to follow, to go along; *(mur, côte)* to follow, to hug **2** *(s'étendre le long de) (de sentier, canal, voie ferrée)* to follow, to run alongside, to border; **la route longe un bois/la côte/la rivière** the road skirts a wood/follows *or* hugs the coastline/follows the river

longeron [lɔ̃ʒrɔ̃] NM **1** *Constr (de pont de chemin de fer)* stringer, longitudinal girder; *(maîtresse poutre)* beam, member **2** *Aut (de châssis)* side member, side sill **3** *Aviat (sur fuselage)* longeron; *(d'aile)* spar

longévité [lɔ̃ʒevite] NF *(durée de vie)* longevity; *(longue vie)* long life; *(de produit)* life; **table de l. d'une population** life-expectancy table of a population

longiligne [lɔ̃ʒiliɲ] ADJ willowy

longitude [lɔ̃ʒityd] NF *Géog* longitude; **par 10° de l. ouest** at 10° longitude west

longitudinal, -ale, -aux, -ales [lɔ̃ʒitydinal, -o] ADJ longitudinal, lengthwise

longitudinalement [lɔ̃ʒitydinalmɑ̃] ADV longitudinally, lengthwise, lengthways

long-métrage, *pl* **longs-métrages** NM *Cin* full-length movie *or Br* film, feature-length movie *or Br* film; **l. d'animation** feature-length cartoon

longrine [lɔ̃grin] NF **1** *Constr* longitudinal beam *or* girder *or* member **2** *Rail* longitudinal sleeper

LONGTEMPS [lɔ̃tɑ̃] ADV **1** *(pendant un long moment)* a long time; **attendre l.** to wait (for) a long time; **ça fait l. que tu attends?** have you been waiting long?; *Iron* **tu peux attendre l.** you'll have a long wait; **cela ne pouvait pas durer l.** it couldn't last (for) long; **est-ce que ça va durer l.?** will it take long?; **ça va durer encore l. ce vacarme?** is this racket going to go on for much longer?; **ça ne va plus durer l.** maintenant it won't be long now; **rester trop l.** to stay too long
2 *(long espace de temps)* **il y a l.** long ago, a long time ago; **il n'y a pas l.** not long ago; **il y a l. qu'il est mort** he has been dead (for) a long time *or Fam* for ages; **il y a l. que je ne l'ai vu** it's a long time *or Fam* ages since I saw him; **pendant l.** for a long time; **(pendant) l. j'ai cru qu'elle reviendrait** I believed for a long time that she would come back; **mettre l. à faire qch** to take a long time *or Fam* ages to do sth; **je n'en ai pas pour l.** I shan't be long, it won't take me long; **tu en as encore pour l.?** are you going to be much longer?; **il n'en a plus pour l.** he hasn't much longer (to live); **cela existe depuis l.** it has existed for a long time *or Fam* for ages; **l. avant/après** long before/after; **avant l.** before long; **cela ne se fera pas avant l.** it won't happen for a long time (to come); **je ne pensais pas vous revoir avant** *ou* **de l.** I didn't expect to see you again for a long time

longuement [lɔ̃gmɑ̃] ADV *(pendant longtemps) (attendre, réfléchir, s'attarder)* for a long time; *(parler)* for a long time, at great length; *(expliquer)* at great length, lengthily; **il la regarda l.** he gazed earnestly at her; **parler l. avec qn** to have a (good) long talk with sb; **il a l. insisté pour que je vienne** he kept

---

on insisting *or* was extremely insistent that I should come; **il faudrait analyser plus l. les personnages** the characters must be analysed in greater detail

longuet, -ette [lɔ̃gɛ, -ɛt] ADJ *Fam (livre, discours, spectacle, attente)* rather long, longish; **c'est un peu l.** it's a bit long
NM *Région* breadstick

longueur [lɔ̃gœr] NF **1** *(dimension)* length; **l. totale, l. hors tout** length over all, overall length; **mesures de l.** linear measures; **unité de l.** unit of length; **jardin de cent mètres de l.** *ou* **d'une l. de cent mètres** garden a hundred metres long; **couper/scier qch en l.** *ou* **dans le sens de la l.** to cut/saw sth lengthwise; *Sport* **mener/gagner d'une l.** to lead/win by a length; **le cheval A prend une l. d'avance sur le cheval B** horse A is now one length ahead of horse B; *Fig* **la ville de Grenoble avait une l. d'avance sur les autres pour la prévention du sida** Grenoble had a clear lead over other cities as regards preventive measures against Aids; *Fig* **cette entreprise a plusieurs longueurs d'avance** this company has a good lead *or* is way ahead; *Péj* **traîner en l.** *(de discours, repas etc)* to drag (on), to drag on for ever; **faire traîner qch en l.** to drag sth out; *Typ* **l. de ligne** line width; *Typ* **l. de page** page length **2** *(état de ce qui est long)* **son discours/le film était d'une l.!** his speech/the film was incredibly long *or* dragged on for ever; **d'une l. incroyable/excessive** incredibly/excessively long **3** *Péj* **à l. de journée/de semaine/d'année** all day/week/year long; **je n'entends que ça à l. de journées** that's all I hear day after day **4** *Péj (développement trop long)* **roman plein de longueurs** novel full of long drawn-out passages **5** *(en nageant)* length; **faire des longueurs** to do lengths
▸▸ *Radio, Fig* **l. d'ondes** wavelength; *Fig* **nous ne sommes pas sur la même l. d'ondes** we're not on the same wavelength

longue-vue, *pl* **longues-vues** [lɔ̃gvy] NF telescope, field glass

look [luk] NM *Fam* look; **soigner son l.** to cultivate one's image; **changer de l.** to change one's look *or* image; *très Fam* **il a un l. d'enfer** he looks out of this world

looké [luke] ADJ *Fam* **être l. punk/grunge** to have a punky/grungy look *or* image

looping [lupiŋ] NM *Aviat* loop; **faire un l./des loopings** to loop the loop

lope [lɔp], **lopette** [lɔpɛt] NF **1** *Vulg (homosexuel)* poof, *Am* fag **2** *Fam (lâche)* wimp, wuss

lopin [lɔpɛ̃] NM **l. de terre** piece *or* patch *or* plot of ground

loquace [lɔkas] ADJ talkative, *Fml* loquacious

loquacité [lɔkasite] NF talkativeness, *Fml* loquacity; **elle a retrouvé sa l. d'antan** she's her old talkative self again

loque [lɔk] NF **1** rag; **être en loques** to be in rags *or* in tatters; **ses vêtements tombent en loques** his clothes are falling to pieces **2** *Fig (personne)* **l. (humaine)** wreck; **l'alcool a fait de lui une l.** alcohol has turned him into a human wreck **3** *Belg (serpillière)* mop

loquet [lɔkɛ] NM *(de porte)* latch; *Arch* **fermer la porte au l., pousser le l.** to put the latch on the door, to latch the door

loqueteau, -eaux [lɔkto] NM *(pour volet)* small latch, catch

loqueteux, -euse [lɔktø, -øz] ADJ *(personne)* in rags, in tatters; *(vêtements)* ragged, tattered; **un vieillard l.** an old man (dressed) in rags, a ragged old man
N ragamuffin

lord [lɔr(d)] NM lord; **la Chambre des lords** the House of Lords

---

lord-maire, *pl* **lords-maires** NM *(de Londres etc)* Lord Mayor

lordose [lɔrdoz] NF *Méd* hollow-back, *Spéc* lordosis

lorgner [lɔrɲe] VT **1** *(regarder indiscrètement) (personne, décolleté)* to eye; **l. une femme** to eye up *or* ogle a woman; **l. qch/ qn du coin de l'œil** to keep eyeing sth/sb, to cast a sidelong glance at sth/sb **2** *(convoiter) (héritage, poste etc)* to have one's eye on

lorgnette [lɔrɲɛt] NF (pair of) opera glasses; *Fig* **regarder/voir qch par le petit bout de la l.** to take a narrow-minded *or* blinkered view of sth

lorgnon [lɔrɲɔ̃] NM *(avec une tige)* lorgnette; *(avec ressort)* pince-nez

loriot [lɔrjo] NM **l. (jaune)** (golden) oriole

lorrain, -aine [lɔrɛ̃, -ɛn] ADJ from/of Lorraine
NM *Ling* Lorraine dialect
N **L.** *(habitant)* inhabitant of Lorraine; *(natif)* native of Lorraine
NF **la Lorraine** Lorraine

lorry [lɔri] NM *Rail* (platelayer's) trolley, pushcar

lors [lɔr] ADV **1** *Litt* **depuis l.** from that time, ever since then; **dès l.** *(à partir de ce moment-là)* from that moment on; **dès l. que tu refuses, tu es mis à la porte** should you *or* if you should happen to refuse, you're dismissed; **l. même qu'il souffre, il ne le dit pas** even though he is in pain, he says nothing; **espérez l. même qu'il n'y a plus d'espoir** you must hope against hope **2 l. de** *(pendant)* during; **l. de mon séjour à Hawaï** during my stay in Hawaii, while I was in Hawaii; **l. mon accident** at the time of my accident

lorsque [lɔrsk(ə)] CONJ *(becomes* **lorsqu'** *before* **il(s), elle(s), on, en, un(e)**) when SEE GRAMMAR B31–2

losange [lɔzɑ̃ʒ] NM **1** *(forme)* diamond; *Géom* rhomb(us) **2** *Hér* lozenge

losangé [lɔzɑ̃ʒe] ADJ *(boucle d'oreille etc)* diamond-shaped; *(frise)* with a diamond pattern; *Hér* lozengy

loser [luzœr] NM *Fam* loser

lot [lo] NM **1** *(à une loterie)* prize; **gros l.** first prize, jackpot; *Fig Fam* **en l'épousant, tu as gagné le gros l.** you've hit the jackpot marrying him; **l. de consolation** consolation prize; *Fin* **emprunt à lots** lottery loan **2** *(articles vendus ensemble) (de marchandises etc)* batch; *(de serviettes, casseroles)* set; *(de chaussettes, collants, savonnettes etc)* pack; *(aux enchères)* lot; **vendus par lots** *(casseroles, serviettes)* sold in sets; *(chaussettes, collants)* sold in packs; *Fig* **dans le l. il y en aura au moins un de bon** *(choses, personnes)* at least one out of this lot *or* batch should be some good; *Fig* **se détacher** *ou* **être au-dessus du l.** to stand out from the crowd **3** *(dans un partage)* share; **diviser un terrain en lots** to divide a piece of land into plots, to parcel up a piece of land **4** *Litt (sort)* lot, fate; **la souffrance est son l.** suffering is his lot; **son l. est d'être toujours seul** he is destined to remain alone all his life; **chacun son l.** we all have our cross to bear **5** *Ordinat* **traitement par lots** batch processing **6** *Bourse (d'actions)* parcel

loterie [lɔtri] NF lottery; **l. nationale** national lottery; **gagner à la l.** to win the lottery; *Fig* **c'est une l.** it's a lottery, it's the luck of the draw

loti [lɔti] ADJ **être bien/mal l.** to be well/badly off

lotion [losjɔ̃] NF lotion; **l. tonique** toning lotion, toner; **l. capillaire** hair lotion; **l. après-rasage** after-shave (lotion)

lotionner [losjɔne] VT *(épiderme, cuir chevelu)* to apply lotion to

lotir [lɔtir] **VT 1** *(diviser en lots) (terrain)* to divide into plots; *(immeubles)* to divide into lots; **terrains à l.** development site, building land **2** *(donner)* **l. qn de qch** to allot sth to sb

lotissement [lɔtismɑ̃] **NM 1** *(résidence)* housing estate *or* development **2** *(mise en lots) (de terrain)* parcelling out; *(de marchandises etc)* dividing into lots

loto [lɔto] **NM 1** *(jeu de hasard)* lotto; **un (jeu de) l.** *(matériel)* a lotto set; *Fig* **il me regarda avec des yeux en boules de l.** he looked at me with eyes like saucers **2** *(jeu national)* national lottery; **il joue au l. tous les mercredis** he buys a lottery ticket *or* takes part in *or* enters the national lottery every Wednesday; **le l. sportif** ≃ the pools; **il a gagné au l.** he won the lottery

lotte [lɔt] **NF** *(poisson)* burbot; *(de mer)* monkfish, anglerfish

lotus [lɔtys] **NM 1** *(plante)* lotus; **l. sacré** Indian lotus **2** *(arbre)* lotus tree **3** *Myth* Lotus

louable[1] [lwabl] **ADJ** *(acte, courage)* laudable, praiseworthy, commendable; *(intentions, efforts)* laudable; **c'est tout à fait l. de ta part** it is highly laudable of you, it is highly commendable on your part

louable[2] **ADJ** *(appartement, magasin etc)* rentable; **appartement difficilement l.** apartment that is difficult to rent

louage [lwaʒ] **NM** *(cession)* letting; *(jouissance)* renting; **prendre qch à l.** to rent sth; **contrat de l.** rental agreement *or* contract; **l. de services** contract of employment; **voiture de l.** hired carriage

louange [lwɑ̃ʒ] **NF** *(éloge)* praise; **digne de louange(s)** *(personne)* praiseworthy; *(action)* praiseworthy, commendable; **chanter les louanges de qn** to sing sb's praises; **couvrir qn de louanges** to shower sb with praise, to heap praise on sb; **faire un discours à la l. de qn** to make a speech in praise of sb; **c'est tout à sa l.** *(à son honneur)* it's to his credit, it's very commendable of him

louanger [lwɑ̃ʒe] **VT** *Litt* to sing the praises of

louangeur, -euse [lwɑ̃ʒœr, -øz] **ADJ** *Litt* *(poème, paroles)* laudatory

loubard, -e [lubar, -ard] **N** *Fam* yob(bo), lout, *surtout Am* hoodlum

louche[1] [luʃ] **ADJ 1** *(conduite, caractère, personne)* shady, suspicious, shifty; *(situation)* dubious; *(quartier, bar)* sleazy; *(passé)* shady; **c'est l.** there's something suspicious *or* *Fam* fishy about it; **il n'y a rien de l. là-dedans** it's all fair and above board, *Fam* there's nothing fishy about it **2** *(lumière, éclairage)* murky

NM il y a du l. dans cette affaire this business is a bit shady *or* *Fam* fishy

louche[2] **NF 1** *(ustensile de cuisine)* (soup) ladle **2** *Fam* *(main)* mitt, paw; **serrer la l. à qn** to shake hands with sb

loucher [luʃe] **VI** to squint; *(être atteint de strabisme)* to be cross-eyed, to have a squint; **l. de l'œil gauche** to have a squint in the left eye; *Fam* **l. vers** *ou* **sur qch** to eye *or* ogle sth; *Fig Fam* **l. sur l'héritage** to have one's eye on the inheritance

loucherie [luʃri] **NF** squint(ing)

loucheur, -euse [luʃœr, -øz] **N** cross-eyed *or* squint-eyed person

louer[1] [lwe] **VT 1** *(donner en location) (chambre, maison etc)* to rent (out), *Br* to let (out); *(équipement, véhicule, costume etc)* to rent (out), *Br* to hire (out) (**à** to); **maison à l.** house *Br* to let *or* for rent; **l. une ferme à bail** to lease out a farm **2** *(prendre en location) (chambre, maison etc)* to rent (**à** from); *(voiture, équipement, costume etc)* to rent, *Br* to hire; *(place de théâtre etc)* to reserve, to book; **l. une maison pour l'été** to take *or* rent a house for the summer

VPR se louer 1 *(être à louer) (de maison, chambre etc)* to be for rent, *Br* to be to let; *(d'équipement)* to be for rent *or* *Br* for hire; **cet appartement se loue très cher** this flat is very expensive to rent **2** *Arch (d'ouvrier agricole)* to hire oneself out

louer[2] **VT** *(personne, courage de qn)* to praise; *(officiellement)* to commend; **il n'a pas cessé de l. tes qualités** he has had nothing but praise for your qualities; **l. qn de** *ou* **pour qch** to praise sb for sth; **louons le seigneur!** praise the Lord!; **Dieu soit loué!** thank God!; **loués soient les philanthropes qui …** praise be to the philanthropists who …

VPR se louer 1 *(se féliciter)* **se l. de qch** to be pleased *or* well satisfied with sth; **je me loue chaque jour de notre collaboration** not a day goes by without my realizing the value of our collaboration; **je n'ai qu'à me l. de lui/de ses services** I have nothing but praise for him/for his services; **je n'ai qu'à me l. de mon choix** I must congratulate myself on my choice; **se l. d'avoir fait qch** to congratulate oneself on having done sth; **2** *(être loué)* **les locaux situés au centre de la capitale se louent à prix d'or** city centre premises are very expensive to rent

loueur, -euse [lwœr, -øz] **N** *Jur* lessor; **l. de bateaux/chevaux/costumes** person who rents (out) *or* *Br* hires (out) boats/horses/costumes

loufdingue [lufdɛ̃g] **ADJ** *Fam* crazy

loufiat [lufja] **NM** *Arg Vieilli (dans un café)* waiter

loufoque [lufɔk] *Fam* **ADJ** crazy
N crackpot, nut

loufoquerie [lufɔkri] **NF** *Fam* **1** *(absurdité)* craziness **2** *(acte)* crazy act; **loufoqueries** crazy behaviour

lougre [lugr] **NM** *Naut* lugger

louis [lwi] **NM** *Hist* **l. (d'or)** louis (d'or)

Louisiane [lwizjan] **NF** Louisiana

loukoum [lukum] **NM** **(rahat-)l.** Turkish delight; **j'ai mangé quatre loukoums** I've eaten four pieces of Turkish delight

loulou, -oute [lulu, -ut] **N** *Fam* **1** *(chéri, chérie)* dear, darling **2** *Fam (voyou)* lout, yob(bo), *Am* hoodlum
NM *(chien)* spitz; **l. de Poméranie** Pomeranian (dog), *Fam* pom

loup [lu] **NM 1** wolf; **une meute de loups** a pack of wolves; **à pas de l.** stealthily; **marcher à pas de l.** to creep along, to steal along, to walk stealthily; *Fig* **avoir une faim de l.** to be absolutely starving, to be ravenous; *Fig* **il fait un froid de l.** it's freezing (cold), it's bitterly cold; *Fig* **faire entrer le l. dans la bergerie** to set the fox to mind the geese; *Fig Fam* **se jeter dans la gueule du l.** to throw oneself into the lion's mouth; *Fig* **il est connu comme le l. blanc** everybody knows him; *Prov* **quand on parle du l. on en voit la queue** talk of the devil; *Fig* **avoir vu le l.** to have lost one's virginity; *Fig* **l'homme est un l. pour l'homme** it's dog eat dog in this world; *Prov* **les loups ne se mangent pas entre eux** there is honour among thieves; *Fig* **jeune l.** young go-getter; *Pol* **Young Turk**; *Fig Fam* **mon petit l., mon gros l.** *(terme d'affection)* (my) darling, (my) pet VOIR GRAMMAIRE A12 **2** *(poisson)* sea perch, sea dace; **l. de mer** *(poisson)* sea perch, sea dace; *Fig Fam (marin)* old salt, seadog; *(tricot rayé)* striped tee-shirt **3** *Tech (dans le bois etc)* flaw; *Ind* defect **4** *(demi-masque)* eye mask, domino

loup-cervier, *pl* **loups-cerviers** [lusɛrvje] **NM** lynx

loupe [lup] **NF 1** *Opt* magnifying glass; **regar-der qch à la l.** to look at sth through *or* with a magnifying glass; *Fig* to put sth under a *or* the microscope; **étudions-en tous les aspects à la l.** let's look at it very closely from every angle **2** *Méd* wen **3** *(sur arbre)* burr, burl; **un meuble en l. de noyer** a piece of furniture made of burr walnut

louper [lupe] *Fam* **VI** **tu n'as pas voulu m'écouter et ça n'a pas loupé, tu t'es coupé** you wouldn't listen to me and sure enough you've cut yourself; **je lui ai dit qu'il attraperait froid et ça n'a pas loupé** I told him he would catch cold and sure enough he did; **si tu continues comme ça tu vas tout faire l.** if you carry on like that you'll mess everything up *or* make a mess of everything
VT 1 *(ne pas réussir) (travail, discours, tarte etc)* to botch, to bungle, to make a botch *or* a mess of; *(examen)* to fail, *Am* to flunk; *Théâtre* **l. son entrée** to fluff one's entrance; **loupé!** missed!; **la soirée est loupée** the party's a flop; **la fin du film est complètement loupée** the end of the film is completely botched *or* bungled **2** *(ne pas prendre) (son tour, occasion, train)* to miss; **il n'en loupe pas une!** it's one stupid thing after another!; *(en parlant)* he's always opening his big mouth!; **je ne vais pas le l.** I won't let him get away with it
VPR se louper il a déjà fait plusieurs tentatives de suicide et cette fois-ci, il ne s'est pas loupé he's made several suicide attempts in the past and this time he didn't bungle it; **tu as vu son maquillage? – elle ne s'est pas loupée!** have you seen her make-up? – she's put it on with a trowel

loup-garou, *pl* **loups-garous** [lugaru] **NM 1** *Myth* werewolf **2** *(pour les enfants)* = bogeyman; **si tu ne manges pas ta soupe, attention au l.!** if you don't eat your soup, the bogeyman will get you!

loupiot [lupjo] **NM** *Fam (enfant)* kid

loupiote [lupjɔt] **NF** *Fam (lampe)* small light *or* lamp

[lur, lurd] **ADJ 1** *(objet, chargement, nourriture, repas etc)* heavy; *(sommeil)* heavy, deep; **démarche lourde** heavy gait; **artillerie/industrie lourde** heavy artillery/industry; **sol l.** heavy soil; **le terrain est l. aujourd'hui** *Sport* the ground is heavy *or* soft today; *(courses de chevaux)* the going is heavy *or* soft today; **marcher/quitter la pièce d'un pas l.** to walk/leave the room with a heavy tread *or* step; **yeux lourds de fatigue** eyes heavy with tiredness; **avoir le sommeil l.** to be a heavy *or* deep sleeper; **j'ai la tête lourde** I've got a thick head, my head feels fuzzy; **avoir l'estomac l.** to feel bloated; **c'est l. à digérer** it's difficult to digest, it's heavy on the stomach; **avoir le cœur l.** to feel very sad, *Litt* to have a heavy heart; **avoir la main lourde** *(punir)* to mete out punishment with a heavy hand; *(verser en quantité généreuse)* to be overgenerous; **ce travail est trop l. pour elle** this work is too much for her **2** *(à l'aspect pesant) (personne)* heavily-built; *(forme, silhouette, tentures etc)* heavy; **un visage aux traits lourds** a face with heavy features

3 *(qui manque de subtilité) (personne, comique, scène)* unsubtle, heavy-handed; *(plaisanterie)* unsubtle, obvious, clumsy; *(mouvement, style)* heavy, ponderous; **un gros garçon pataud aux mouvements lourds** a big fat lumbering oaf; **avoir l'esprit l.** to be slow(-witted) *or* dull-witted

4 *(sérieux, grave) (erreur)* serious, grave; *(perte)* heavy, severe, serious; *(dépenses, charges)* heavy; *(tâche, responsabilité)* heavy, weighty; **une lourde hérédité** a history of mental/physical illness in the family

5 *(temps)* close, sultry, muggy; **un parfum l.** a heavy *or* strong fragrance; **il fait l.** it's

close *or* sultry *or* muggy
6 incident/refus l. de conséquences incident/refusal fraught with consequences; **silence/nuages lourd(s) de menaces** ominous silence/clouds; **un discours l. de sousentendus** a speech packed *or* loaded with innuendos

ADV **peser l.** to weigh a lot, to be heavy; *Fig* **peser l. (dans la balance)** to count for a lot; *Fig* **ça ne pèse pas l.** that doesn't count for much; **en avoir l. sur le cœur** to have a heavy heart, to feel very sad; *Fam* **il n'en reste pas l.** there isn't much left; *(dénombrable)* there aren't many left; **je n'en fais pas l.** I don't exactly overwork; **il n'en sait pas l. sur l'histoire de son pays** he doesn't know much about the history of his country; **il travaille beaucoup mais ne gagne pas l.** he works a lot but doesn't earn much; **ça ne fait pas l.** it's not much to show for it

NF *Arg* **lourde** door; **ferme la l.** put the wood in the hole

lourdaud, -aude [lurdo, -od] *Péj* **ADJ** *(maladroit)* awkward, clumsy; *(bête)* oafish
N oaf

lourdement [lurdəmã] **ADV** **1** *(avec un matériel pesant)* heavily; **l. chargé/équipé** heavily laden/equipped **2** *(pesamment)* *(se déplacer)* heavily; **elle avance l.** she lumbers forward; **il est tombé l.** he fell heavily **3** *(grandement)* heavily; **se tromper l.** to be greatly mistaken; **ces changements vont peser l. sur notre budget** these changes will weigh heavily on our budget; **elle insistait l.** she *would* keep on insisting; **il insiste toujours l. sur les défauts de ses collègues** he always lays great stress on his colleagues' failings **4** *Péj (sans finesse)* *(rire)* coarsely

lourder [lurde] **VT** *Fam* **l. qn** to give sb the boot *or* the elbow; **se faire l. par sa petite amie** to get the boot *or* the elbow from one's girlfriend, to be given the boot *or* the elbow by one's girlfriend

lourdeur [lurdœr] **NF** *(d'objet, de charge etc)* heaviness; *(de bâtiment, d'architecture)* heaviness, massiveness; *(de traits de visage)* heaviness; *(d'administration, de bureaucratie)* unwieldiness, cumbersomeness; *(de personne)* *(dans les mouvements, de style)* clumsiness, awkwardness; *(manque de vivacité d'esprit)* slow (-witted)ness, dull-wittedness; *(de responsabilité)* weight; *(du temps)* sultriness, closeness; **l. d'esprit** slow(-witted)ness, dull-wittedness; *Vieilli* **avoir des lourdeurs de tête** to have fits of drowsiness, to feel headachy; **j'ai des lourdeurs d'estomac** my stomach feels heavy

lourdingue [lurdɛ̃g] **ADJ** *Fam (style)* heavy; *(personne, plaisanterie)* unsubtle

loustic [lustik] **NM** **1** *Fam (farceur)* joker; **il fait le l.** he's playing the fool, he's fooling around **2** *c'est un drôle de l.* *(louche)* he's a strange guy, he's an oddball

loutre [lutr] **NF** otter; *(fourrure)* otter (skin); **manteau de l.** otter-skin coat; **l. marine** *ou* **de mer** sea otter

louve [luv] **NF** she-wolf

louvet, -ette [luvɛ, -ɛt] **ADJ** dun

louveteau, -eaux [luvto] **NM** **1** *Zool* wolf cub **2** *(jeune scout)* cub (scout)

louvoiement [luvwamã] **NM** *Naut* tacking; *Fig* hedging

louvoyer [luvwaje] **VI** (**je louvoie, n. louvoyons; je louvoierai**) *Naut* to tack, to beat about, to beat to windward; *Fig* to hedge, to beat about the bush

Louvre [luvr] **NM** **le (palais du) Louvre** the Louvre; **le Grand Louvre** the enlarged Musée du Louvre *(including all the new constructions and excavations)*; **l'école du Louvre** = art school in Paris

---

Louvre
This former royal palace became a museum in 1791–1793. It houses one of the richest art collections in the world. The museum was extended in 1989, with the construction of the glass "pyramide du Louvre" in the main courtyard, and again in 1993 when the Richelieu wing, formerly occupied by the ministry of finance, was inaugurated.

---

lover [love] **VT** *(corde)* to coil; **lové dans un canapé** curled up on a couch
VPR **se lover** *(de serpent, d'anguille etc)* to coil up; **se l. dans un canapé moelleux** to curl up on a soft couch

loxodromique [loksodromik] **ADJ** *Naut (courbe, navigation)* loxodromic; **navigation l.** plane sailing

loyal, -ale, -aux, -ales [lwajal, -o] **ADJ** **1** *(honnête)* *(personne)* honest, fair, upright; *(procédés)* honest; *(combat)* clean; **être l. en affaires** to be straightforward *or* honest in one's business dealings; **il a été l. avec moi** he was honest *or* straight with me; **jeu l.** fair play; **ce n'est pas un adversaire l.** he doesn't play fair **2** *(serviteur, ami)* loyal, faithful, trusty; **après 25 ans de bons et loyaux services** after 25 years of good and faithful service

NF *Fam* **se battre à la loyale** to fight cleanly

loyalement [lwajalmã] **ADV** **1** *(honnêtement)* *(agir)* honestly, fairly; *(se battre)* fairly **2** *(fidèlement)* *(servir)* loyally, faithfully

loyalisme [lwajalism] **NM** *Pol* loyalty

loyaliste [lwajalist] **ADJ, N** *Pol* loyalist

loyauté [lwajote] **NF** **1** *(honnêteté)* honesty, fairness, uprightness **2** *(fidélité)* loyalty, faithfulness (**envers** to)

loyer [lwaje] **NM** **1** rent; *Arch* **prendre une maison à l.** to rent a house; *Arch* **donner à l.** to rent (out), *Br* to let (out); *Can* **être à l.** to be a tenant, to be in rented accommodation; **vous êtes encore en retard pour payer votre l.** you're late with your rent again; **j'ai trois loyers de retard** I'm three months behind with my rent; **l. arriéré** rent arrears; **l. commercial** commercial rent; **l. nominal** nominal rent **2** *Fin* **l. de l'argent** cost of money

LP [ɛlpe] **NM** *(abrév* **lycée professionnel**) technical college

LSD [ɛlɛsde] **NM** *Chimie* LSD

LTA [ɛltea] **NF** *(abrév* **lettre de transport aérien**) AWB

lubie [lybi] **NF** whim, fad, craze; **il a des lubies, il lui prend des lubies** he has whims *or* fads *or* crazes; **il lui prit la l. de manger à 4 heures du matin** he took it into his head *or* got the crazy idea to have something to eat at 4 o'clock in the morning

lubricité [lybrisite] **NF** *(de personne, de regard)* lustfulness, lechery; *(de propos)* lewdness

lubrifiant [lybrifjã] **ADJ** lubricating
NM lubricant; **l. EP** EP lubricant; **l. extrême pression** extreme pressure lubricant

lubrification [lybrifikasjɔ̃] **NF** lubrication

lubrifier [lybrifje] **VT** *(pr sub, impf n.* **lubrifiions, v. lubrifiiez**) to lubricate

lubrique [lybrik] **ADJ** *(homme, regard)* lustful, lecherous; *(propos)* lewd

lubriquement [lybrik(ə)mã] **ADV** *(regarder)* lustfully, lecherously; *(parler)* lewdly

Luc [lyk] **N** *saint* **L.** Saint Luke

lucane [lykan] **NM** *Entom* stag beetle

lucaniste [lykanist], **lucanophile** [lykanofil] **N** kite enthusiast *or* fan

lucarne [lykarn] **NF** **1** *(fenêtre dans un toit)* dormer (window); *(tabatière)* skylight; **l.**

---

rampante dormer (window) **2** *Ftbl (de filet)* top corner

lucide [lysid] **ADJ** **1** *(perspicace)* *(esprit, raisonnement etc)* lucid, clear; *(personne)* lucid, clear-headed; **il jette sur la société contemporaine un regard très l.** he casts a very lucid *or* clear gaze on *or* eye on contemporary society; **elle ne se fait pas d'illusion sur ce qui l'attend, elle est l.** she has no illusions about what awaits her, she sees things clearly **2** *(conscient)* lucid

lucidement [lysidmã] **ADV** lucidly, clearly

lucidité [lysidite] **NF** **1** *(perspicacité)* *(d'analyse, d'exposé)* lucidity, clearness; *(de personne)* lucidity, clear-headedness **2** *(état conscient)* lucidity; **elle a encore toute sa l.** she still has all her wits about her *or* all her faculties; **elle a des moments de l., puis remet à délirer** she has lucid moments *or* moments of lucidity, then sinks back into delirium

Lucifer [lysifɛr] **N** Lucifer

luciférien, -ienne [lysiferjɛ̃, -jɛn] **ADJ** *(propre à Lucifer)* Luciferian
N *Hist* Satanist

luciole [lysjɔl] **NF** firefly, *Spéc* luciola

lucratif, -ive [lykratif, -iv] **ADJ** *(entreprise, opération)* lucrative, profitable; *(emploi)* well-paid, lucrative; **à but l.** profit-making; **sans but l.** non-profit-making, *Am* not-for-profit

lucrativement [lykrativmã] **ADV** lucratively

lucre [lykr] **NM** *Péj* lucre

ludiciel [lydisjɛl] **NM** *Ordinat* computer game

ludion [lydjɔ̃] **NM** *Phys* Cartesian diver; *Fig (jouet des circonstances)* plaything, toy

ludique [lydik] **ADJ** play; **activité l.** play activity; **il doit y avoir une dimension l. dans ...** there has to be an aspect of play in ...

ludo-éducatif, -ive *pl* **ludo-éducatifs, -ives** [lydoedykatif, -iv] **ADJ** edutainment

ludothèque [lydotɛk] **NF** toy and game library

luette [lɥɛt] **NF** **1** *Anat* uvula **2** *Can Fam* **se mouiller/se rincer la l.** *(prendre un verre)* to wet one's whistle, to have a drink; *(se soûler)* to get wasted *or Am* ratted

lueur [lɥœr] **NF** **1** *(lumière faible)* *(de lampe, feu, allumette, soleil etc)* glow, glimmer; *(de couteau, épée)* gleam; **à la l. d'une bougie** by candlelight; **à la l. des étoiles** by starlight; **à la l. des derniers événements** in the light of recent events; **les premières lueurs de l'aube** the first light of dawn **2** *(lumière soudaine)* **l. soudaine** flash; **l'allumette jeta une dernière l. avant de s'éteindre** the match flared one last time, then went out **3** *Fig (moment bref)* *(de lucidité, colère)* flash; *(d'intelligence)* spark, glimmer; *(d'espoir)* glimmer, gleam

luge [lyʒ] **NF** toboggan, sledge, *Am* sled; *Sport* luge; **faire de la l.** to go tobogganing *or* sledging *or Am* sledding; *Sport* to luge

lugeur, -euse [lyʒœr, -øz] **N** *Sport* luger

lugubre [lygybr] **ADJ** *(atmosphère, humeur, personne, récit)* lugubrious, gloomy, dismal; *(endroit)* gloomy, grim; *(son, cri)* doleful, mournful

lugubrement [lygybrəmã] **ADV** lugubriously, gloomily

LUI[1] [lɥi] **PRON PERS** *(pour un homme)* (to) him; *(pour une femme)* (to) her; *(pour un bébé, un animal)* (to) it, (to) him, (to) her; *(pour une chose, une idée)* (to) it; *(pour un pays, navire)* (to) it, (to) her; *(au pluriel)* (to) them; **je le l. donne** I give it (to) him/her, I give him/her it; **donnez-l.-en** give him/her some; **donnez-le-l.** give it (to) him/her, give him/her it; **cette maison leur appartient** this house belongs to them, this house is theirs; **je le leur ai reproché** I reproached them for it; **je l. trouve mauvaise mine** I think he/she looks ill; **je l. ai serré la main** I shook his/her hand; **je l. ai entendu dire …** I heard him/her say that …; **il l. vint une envie de tout l. dire** he/she felt a desire to tell him/her everything; **il leur jeta une pierre** he threw a stone at them; **montrez-le-leur** show it (to) them, show them it

LUI² [lɥi] PRON PERS

he/she/it *(subject)* **1** ▪ him/her/it *(object)* **2** ▪ himself/herself/itself *(reflexive)* **3**

1 *(sujet) (pour un homme)* he; *(pour un bébé, un animal)* it, he; *(pour une chose)* it; *(pour un pays, navire)* it, she; *(au pluriel)* they; **ce sont eux, Fam c'est eux** it's them; **c'est l.** it's him; *(en le désignant)* that's him; **c'est l. qui nous a présentés** he's the one who introduced us, he introduced us; **c'est l. le coupable** he's the culprit *or* guilty one, he's guilty; **elle est blonde, l. est brun** she's blonde, he's dark-haired; **eux deux/tous** the two of/all of them; **Jacques et l. l'ont fait** he and Jacques did it, *Fam* Jacques and him did it; **l., au moins, il a fait un effort** he, at least, made an effort; **elle veut vendre la maison, mais est-ce que l. est d'accord?** she wants to sell the house, but does he agree to it?; **si j'étais l., je me méfierais** if I were him I'd be careful; **l.? il ne ferait jamais ça!** him? he'd never do that!; **mon frère, l., n'est pas venu** as for my brother, he didn't come; **il doit suivre un régime: il est malheureux, l. qui est si gourmand!** he has to go on a diet, and loving his food as he does, he's not happy about it; **ils jouent tous les deux au tennis, elle très bien, l. plutôt mal** they both play tennis, she very well, he rather badly; **elle aime le cinéma, l. non** she likes the cinema, he doesn't **2** *(objet) (pour un homme)* him; *(pour un bébé, un animal)* it, him; *(pour une chose)* it; *(pour un pays, un navire)* it, her; *(au pluriel)* them; **j'accuse son frère et l.** I accuse him and his brother; **l., je le connais, je le connais, l.** I know him; **l., je le connais, les autres non** him I know *or* I know him but not the others; **des deux frères, c'est l. que je connais le mieux** of the two brothers I know him *or* it's him I know best; **elle est plus grande que l.** she's taller than him *or* than he is; **elle gagne plus que l.** she earns more than him *or* than he does; **j'ai plus bu que l.** I've drunk more than him *or* than he has; **j'apprécie Marie plus que l.** *(plus qu'il ne l'apprécie)* I like Marie more than he does *or* than him; *(je préfère Marie)* I like Marie more than him; **elle m'a présenté à l.** she introduced me to him; **elle pense encore à l.** she still thinks about him; **ce livre est à l./à eux** this book is his/theirs; **à l. tout seul, il n'y arrivera pas** on his own he won't manage it; **à l. seul, il possède la moitié de la ville** he owns half of the town himself; **voilà une photo de l.** here's a photo of him; **c'est pour l.** it's for him; **c'est par l. que je l'ai su** it's *or* it was through him that I found out; **j'ai confiance en l.** I trust him; **c'est à l. de décider** it's for him to decide; **c'est un ami à l.** it's *or* he's a friend of his; **l'enfant n'est pas de l.** the child is not his; **maintenant tout le monde va vouloir faire comme eux** now everyone will want to do as they do **3** *(réfléchi) (pour un homme)* him(self); *(pour un bébé, un animal)* it(self), him(self); *(pour une chose)* it(self); *(pour un pays, un navire)* it(self), her(self); *(au pluriel)* them(selves); **il les rassembla autour de l.** he gathered them round him; **il ne pense qu'à l.** he thinks only of himself

lui-même PRON PERS *(pour un homme)* himself; *(pour un bébé, un animal)* itself, himself; *(pour un objet)* itself; **c'est l. qui me l'a dit** he told me so himself; **chacun d'eux travaille pour l.** each of them works for himself; *voir* **même** ADJ 3

luire [lɥir] VI *(prp* **luisant**, *pp* **lui**, *invariable in feminine; pr ind* **il luit, ils luisent**; *p hist* **il luit, ils luirent**, *parfois* **il luisit**; *fu* **il luira**) *(de métal, surface propre)* to gleam, to shine; *(de surface de l'eau, trottoirs mouillés etc)* to glisten; *(d'étoile, de soleil)* to shine; *(de feu, bougie)* to glow; *(d'yeux)* to gleam; *(de cheveux)* to be shiny, to shine; **l. au soleil** to gleam *or* shine in the sun

luisant [lɥizɑ̃] ADJ *(étoile, métal etc)* shining, bright; *(surface, pelage, peau)* shiny, glossy; *(yeux)* gleaming; *(braise)* glowing; **front l. de sueur** forehead glistening with sweat; **manteau l. d'usure** coat shiny with wear
▪ NM *(d'étoffe, de vernis)* shine, sheen

lumbago [lœbago] NM *Méd* lumbago

lumen [lymɛn] NM lumen

lumière [lymjɛr] NF **1** *(clarté)* light; **l. du jour** daylight; **l. du soleil** sunlight; **l. des étoiles** starlight; **l. électrique** electric light; **il n'y a plus de l.** the light's gone out; **la fenêtre donne de la l.** the window lets in (the) light; **à la l. de la lune** by moonlight; **allume la l., on n'y voit rien** put the light on, we can't see anything in here; **il y a de la l. chez lui** there's a light on *or* there are lights on at his place; **as-tu pensé à éteindre toutes les lumières?** did you remember to switch off all the lights?; **les lumières de la ville** the lights of the city, the city lights; *Aut Fam* **allume tes lumières, il y a du brouillard** put your lights on, it's foggy; **l. d'ambiance** floodlight; *Cin, TV* **l. ambiante** ambient light; *Cin, TV* **l. de base** key light; *Cin, TV* **l. diffuse** scattered light; **l. stroboscopique** strobe light; **l. tamisée** soft light
2 *Fig (compréhension)* light; **à la l. de son exposé, tout paraît évident** in the light of his presentation, everything seems clear; **mettre qch en l.** to bring sth out; **jeter une l. nouvelle sur qch** to throw *or* shed new light on sth; **faire (toute) la l. sur qch** to get (right) to the bottom of sth
3 *(connaissances rationnelles)* **les lumières de la raison** the light of reason; **avoir des lumières sur qch** to have some knowledge about sth; **j'ai besoin de tes lumières** I need the benefit of your knowledge; **le siècle des lumières** the Age of Enlightenment
4 *(homme de savoir)* **une des lumières de la science moderne/de son époque** one of the leading lights of modern science/of his age; *Fam* **ce n'est pas une l.** he's not very bright
5 *Tech (ouverture) (d'admission etc)* port; *(de mire)* aperture; **l. d'admission/d'échappement** inlet/exhaust port
6 *Phys, Astron* **l. oxhydrique** limelight; *Phys* **l. blanche** white light; **l. noire** *ou* **de Wood** black light; *Astron* **l. cendrée** earthlight, earthshine

lumignon [lymiɲɔ̃] NM **1** *(lampe)* dim light *or* lamp **2** *(bout de mèche)* candle end

luminaire [lyminɛr] NM **1** *(lampe)* light **2** *(dans une église)* lights

luminance [lyminɑ̃s] NF brightness

luminescence [lyminɛsɑ̃s] NF luminescence

luminescent [lyminɛsɑ̃] ADJ luminescent

lumineusement [lyminøzmɑ̃] ADV luminously, brightly; *Fig (expliquer)* lucidly, clearly

lumineux, -euse [lyminø, -øz] ADJ **1** *(corps, cadran)* luminous; *(pièce)* bright, filled with light; *(ciel)* bright, luminous; *Ordinat (bloc*

etc) highlighted; **montre à cadran l.** watch with a luminous dial, luminous watch; **enseigne lumineuse** illuminated sign; **couleur très lumineuse** very bright *or* intense colour; *Phys* **onde lumineuse** light wave **2** *Fig (explication, propos)* lucid, clear; **regard l.** radiant look *or* expression; **c'est une idée lumineuse** it's a brilliant idea *or* a brainwave *or Am* a brainstorm; **il est d'une intelligence lumineuse** he is extremely bright

luminosité [lyminozite] NF **1** *(de ciel)* brightness, luminosity; *(de regard)* radiance; **la l. est insuffisante pour prendre une photo** there is insufficient light (available) for taking a photo **2** *Phot (de l'objectif)* speed **3** *Ordinat* brightness; *(mise en relief)* highlighting

lump [lœp] NM lumpfish; **œufs de l.** lumpfish roe

lunaire [lynɛr] ADJ *(de la lune)* lunar; *(pareil à la lune)* moonlike; **paysage l.** lunar landscape; *Fig* **un visage l.** a moon-face
▪ NF *(plante)* honesty, moonwort, *Spéc* lunaria

lunaison [lynɛzɔ̃] NF *Astron* lunation, lunar month

lunatique [lynatik] ADJ *(personne)* moody

Il faut noter que l'adjectif anglais **lunatic** est un faux ami. Il signifie **fou, dément**.

lunch, *pl* **lunches, lunchs** [lœntʃ] NM buffet lunch

lundi [lœdi] NM Monday; **le l. de Pâques/de la Pentecôte** Easter/Whit Monday *(voir aussi* **samedi**)

lune [lyn] NF **1** *Astron* moon; **la pleine l.** the full moon; **la nouvelle l.** the new moon; **les phases de la l.** the phases of the moon; **(au) clair de l.** (in the) moonlight; **nuit sans l.** moonless night; **la l. se lève** the moon is rising; **face de l., visage de pleine l.** moon-face, moonlike face; *Fig* **demander la l.** to ask for the moon; **je ne te demande pas la l.** I'm not asking for the moon; *Fig* **promettre la l.** to promise the moon; **je ne vous promets pas la l.** I can't promise you the moon; *Fig Fam* **être dans la l.** to be miles away, to be in the clouds; *Fig très Fam* **être con comme la l.** to be dead from the neck up, *Br* to be as thick as two short planks; *Fig Fam* **tomber de la l.** to look flabbergasted **2** *Arch, Litt (mois)* moon, month **3** *Fam (derrière)* bottom, backside **4** **vieilles lunes** old-fashioned *or* outmoded ideas **5** *Vieilli* **il est dans une bonne/mauvaise l.** *(humeur)* he is in one of his good/bad moods; **lunes** vagary, caprice, whim **6** **l. de mer, poisson l.** (ocean) sunfish **7** **pierre de l.** moonstone
▪▪▸ *Bot* **l. d'eau** white water-lily; **l. de miel** honeymoon; **l. rousse** April moon

luné [lyne] ADJ *Fam* **être bien/mal l.** to be in a good/bad mood

lunetier, -ière [lyntje, -jɛr] N *(fabricant)* spectacle manufacturer
▪ ADJ **industrie lunetière** spectacle industry

lunette [lynɛt] NF **1 (paire de) lunettes** (pair of) glasses *or* spectacles *or Fam* specs *or Am* eyeglasses; **porter des lunettes** to wear glasses *or* spectacles *or Fam* specs; *Fam* **c'est un type à lunettes, facile à reconnaître** he wears specs, he's easy to recognize; *Fam* **c'est le type à lunettes** he's the guy in specs; **lunettes de vue** corrective glasses; **lunettes d'écaille** horn-rimmed glasses VOIR GRAMMAIRE A10 **2** *Opt* **l. (d'approche)** telescope, field glass; *Mil* **l. de pointage** sighting telescope; **l. de fusil** gun sight(s); **fusil à l.** gun with sights; **l. astronomique** astronomical telescope **3** *Archit* lunette **4** *(de guillotine)* lunette **5** *(siège des W.-C.)* seat
▪▪▸ *Aut* **l. arrière** rear window; **lunettes noir-**

es dark glasses, *Fam* shades; **lunettes de plongée** swimming goggles; **lunettes de protection** goggles; **lunettes de soleil,** *Belg* **l. solaires** sunglasses, *Fam* shades

lunetterie [lynɛtri] NF spectacle trade

lunule [lynyl] NF **1** *Math* lune **2** *Anat (d'ongle)* half-moon, *Spéc* lunula

lupanar [lypanar] NM *Litt Vieilli* brothel

lupin [lypɛ̃] NM *(plante)* lupin

lupus [lypys] NM *Méd* lupus

lurette [lyrɛt] NF *Fam* **il y a belle l.** ages ago; **il y a belle l. que je ne t'ai pas vu** I haven't seen you for ages, it's been ages since I saw you

luron, -onne [lyrɔ̃, -ɔn] N *Fam* **c'est un gai ou un joyeux l.** he's quite *or* a bit of a lad, *Vieilli* he's a gay dog; **c'est une sacrée luronne** she's quite a girl

lusitanien, -ienne [lyzitanjɛ̃, -jɛn] *Antiq* ADJ Lusitanian
▶ N **L.** Lusitanian

lusophone [lyzɔfɔn] ADJ Portuguese-speaking
▶ N Portuguese speaker

lustrage [lystraʒ] NM *(de tissu, cuir)* glossing, glazing, lustring; *(de verre)* polishing; **l. des fourrures** lustring of furs

lustre¹ [lystr] NM **1** *(lampe)* chandelier **2** *(brillant)* lustre, *Am* luster, gloss **3** *Litt (éclat, prestige)* lustre, *Am* luster; **il faut redonner du l. à cette ancienne demeure** some of the lustre needs to be brought back to this stately old dwelling; **redonner du l. à un parti politique** to give a political party a facelift

lustre² NM *Litt (cinq ans)* lustrum; *Fig* **ça fait des lustres qu'on t'attend!** we've been waiting for ages for you!; *Fig* **depuis des lustres** for ages

lustré [lystre] ADJ *(poterie)* glazed; *(fourrure, tissu, barbe, robe d'un cheval, cheveux)* glossy; **étoffe lustrée par l'usure** cloth shiny with wear

lustrer [lystre] VT *(glace, meuble, voiture)* to polish (up); *(par l'usure)* to make shiny; *Tech (tissu, cuir)* to glaze, to gloss, to lustre
▶ VPR **se lustrer ce tissu se lustre facilement** this material gets shiny very quickly

lustrerie [lystrəri] NF *Ind, Com* lighting industry

lustrine [lystrin] NF cotton lustre

lut [lyt] NM *Cér, Ind* lute, luting

Lutèce [lytɛs] N *Antiq* Lutetia

lutéine [lytein] NF *Biol, Chimie* lutein

luter [lyte] VT *Cér, Ind* to lute, to seal with luting

luth [lyt] NM **1** *Mus* lute **2** *Zool* **l. ou tortue l.** leatherback (turtle)

luthéranisme [lyteranism] NM *Rel* Lutheranism

lutherie [lytri] NF *Mus* **1** *(fabrication)* stringed instrument making **2** *(instruments)* stringed instruments

luthérien, -ienne [lyterjɛ̃, -jɛn] ADJ, N *Rel* Lutheran

luthier [lytje] NM stringed instrument maker

luthiste [lytist] N *Mus* lutanist, lutenist, lute player

lutin [lytɛ̃] NM **1** *(créature de conte etc)* imp, elf, goblin; *(irlandais)* leprechaun **2** *(enfant)* imp
▶ ADJ mischievous, impish

lutiner [lytine] VT **1** *(femme)* to fondle, to tickle **2** *(à la manière d'un lutin)* to plague, to torment; *(avec espièglerie)* to tease

lutrin [lytrɛ̃] NM **1** *Rel* lectern **2** *(pour soute-*

nir un livre, des feuilles) reading *or* book stand **3** *(endroit où se tient le chœur)* choir stall **4** *Belg, Can, Suisse Mus* music stand

lutte [lyt] NF **1** *Sport* wrestling; **l. libre** all-in *or* freestyle wrestling; **l. gréco-romaine** Graeco-Roman wrestling; **faire de la l.** to wrestle
2 *(combat, action violente)* fight, struggle; *(morale, de guerre)* conflict; **entrer/être en l. contre qn** to enter into/to be in conflict with sb; **après plusieurs années de l.** after several years of struggle; **la l. doit continuer!** the fight *or* struggle must go on!; **il faut soutenir les travailleurs en l.** we must support the workers in their fight *or* struggle; **les partis en l. pour le pouvoir** the opposing parties fighting for power; **luttes intestines** infighting; **l. d'influence** struggle for influence; **luttes parlementaires** parliamentary clashes; **l. armée** armed struggle; **se livrer à une l. acharnée pour qch** to be engaged in a desperate struggle for sth; **gagner de haute l.** to win by sheer force; **l. à mort** life-and-death struggle, fight to the death
3 *(pour venir à bout d'un mal)* **l. contre l'alcoolisme/le cancer** fight against alcoholism/cancer; **l. pour la liberté** struggle for freedom; **l. antipollution** fight against pollution
4 *Biol, Fig* **l. pour la vie** struggle *or* fight for survival; *(d'un malade)* fight for life
5 *(antagonisme)* conflict; **la l. entre le devoir et la passion/le bien et le mal** the conflict between duty and passion/good and evil; **l. d'intérêts** conflict *or* clash of interests; **la l. des classes** the class struggle *or* conflict

lutter [lyte] VI **1** *Sport* to wrestle (**avec, contre** with) **2** *(se battre)* to struggle, to fight; **l. contre la maladie** to fight (against) *or* to combat disease; **l. contre le vent** to battle with *or* against the wind; **l. contre un incendie** to fight a fire; **l. pour l'indépendance** to fight for independence; **l. contre le sommeil** to fight off sleep; **l. contre la tentation** to fight (against) temptation; **l. contre l'alcoolisme** to fight (against) alcoholism **3** *(rivaliser)* **l. de vitesse avec qn** to race sb; **elles luttent d'adresse** they're using all their skills to outdo each other

lutteur, -euse [lytœr, -øz] N **1** *Sport* wrestler **2** *(pour une cause etc)* fighter; **un tempérament de l.** a fighting *or* fighter's temperament

lux [lyks] NM *Phys* lux

luxation [lyksasjɔ̃] NF *Méd (d'articulation)* dislocation, *Spéc* luxation; **l. congénitale** congenital dislocation

luxe [lyks] NM **1** *(abondance, richesse)* luxury; *(de maison, pièce, ameublement etc)* luxuriousness, sumptuousness; **vivre dans le l.** to live in luxury; **goûts de l.** luxurious *or* extravagant tastes; **un l. tapageur** a flashy display of wealth; **étaler son l.** to flaunt one's wealth
2 *(qualité)* luxury, luxuriousness; **articles de l.** luxury articles; **édition de l.** de luxe edition; **voiture de l.** de luxe car, luxury car; **boutique de l.** luxury goods shop; **taxe (sur les produits) de l.** tax on luxury goods
3 *(bien superflu, coûteux)* luxury; **mon seul l., c'est d'aller au cinéma** my only luxury *or* indulgence is going to the cinema; **elle ne peut pas s'offrir le l. de refuser cet emploi** she can't afford the luxury of turning this job down; **je me suis payé le l. de le lui dire** I gave myself the pleasure of telling him so; **se payer le l. d'un cigare** to indulge in (the luxury of) a cigar; **je vais faire nettoyer ce vieil**

imperméable, ce ne sera pas du l. I'm going to have this old raincoat cleaned, it really needs it; **j'ai acheté un nouveau tapis, ce n'était pas du l.** I bought a new carpet, it had to be done *or* it was an essential purchase
4 *(profusion)* abundance; **un l. de précautions** a wealth of precautions; **l. de détails** wealth *or* abundance of details

Luxembourg [lyksɑ̃bur] NM *(pays, ville)* Luxembourg

luxembourgeois, -oise [lyksɑ̃burʒwa, -waz] ADJ of/from Luxembourg
▶ N **L.** Luxembourger

luxer [lykse] VT *(articulation, coude etc)* to dislocate, *Spéc* to luxate
▶ VPR **se luxer se l. un membre** to dislocate a limb; **se l. l'épaule** to dislocate one's shoulder, to put one's shoulder out

luxueusement [lyksɥøzmɑ̃] ADV luxuriously, sumptuously

luxueux, -euse [lyksɥø, -øz] ADJ luxurious, sumptuous

luxure [lyksyr] NF *Litt* lust

> Il faut noter que le nom anglais **luxury** est un faux ami. Il signifie **luxe**.

luxuriance [lyksyrjɑ̃s] NF luxuriance

luxuriant [lyksyrjɑ̃] ADJ *(végétation, forêt etc)* luxuriant, lush; *(chevelure)* luxuriant; *(imagination)* fertile; *Archit, Littér* **un style l.** a luxuriant style

luxurieux, -euse [lyksyrjø, -øz] ADJ lascivious, lewd, lustful, sensual

luzerne [lyzɛrn] NF *(plante)* lucerne, alfalfa

lycaon [likaɔ̃] NM wild dog

lycée [lise] NM **1** *Scol Br* ≃ secondary school, *Am* ≃ high school *(for pupils aged 15 to 18)*; *Anciennement* **l. (d'enseignement) professionnel** technical school; **l. technique** technical high school; **l. technique hôtelier** hotel school; **il se souvient du l. comme de ses meilleures années** he looks back on his schooldays as the best years of his life **2** *Antiq* **le L.** the Lyceum

lycéen, -éenne [liseɛ̃, -eɛn] N *Br* ≃ secondary school pupil, *Am* ≃ high school pupil
▶ ADJ *Br* ≃ secondary school, *Am* ≃ high school

lycra® [likra] NM Lycra®; **pantalon en l.** Lycra® trousers

lymphatique [lɛ̃fatik] ADJ **1** *(glande etc)* lymphatic **2** *(personne)* lethargic, apathetic
▶ NM lymphatic (duct)

lymphe [lɛ̃f] NF lymph

lymphocyte [lɛ̃fɔsit] NM lymphocyte

lymphoïde [lɛ̃fɔid] ADJ *(cellules, tissu)* lymphoid

lymphome [lɛ̃fɔm] NM lymphoma

lynchage [lɛ̃ʃaʒ] NM lynching

lyncher [lɛ̃ʃe] VT to lynch

lynx [lɛ̃ks] NM lynx; *Fig* **avoir des yeux de l.** to have eyes like a hawk, to be hawk-eyed

Lyon [ljɔ̃] N Lyons

lyonnais, -aise [ljɔnɛ, -ɛz] ADJ of/from Lyons
▶ N **L.** *(natif)* native of Lyons; *(habitant)* inhabitant of Lyons
▶ NM **le L.** *(région)* Lyonnais

lyophilisation [ljɔfilizasjɔ̃] NF *Tech* freeze-drying

lyophiliser [ljɔfilize] VT *Tech (café, soupe etc)* to freeze-dry; **café lyophilisé** freeze-dried coffee

lyre [lir] NF *Mus* lyre; *Fam* **toute la l.** the whole lot (of them), the whole shoot; **(oiseau-)l.** lyre bird

lyrique [lirik] ADJ **1** *Littér (poème, poète etc)* lyric **2** *(mis en musique)* **art l.** opera; **artiste l.** opera singer; **drame l.** lyric drama, opera; **comédie l.** comic opera, operetta; **théâtre l.** opera house **3** *(poétique, passionné)* lyrical; **des envolées lyriques** flights of lyricism; **parler de qch/qn d'une façon l.** *(avec lyrisme)* to wax lyrical about sth/sb

NM lyric poet

lyrisme [lirism] NM **1** lyricism; **parler avec l. de qch** to wax lyrical about sth; **s'exprimer avec l.** to wax lyrical **2** *(exaltation)* excessive

M, m¹ [ɛm] NM *(lettre)* M, m

m² **1** *(abrév* **mètre)** m; **1 m 50** 1.5 m **2** *Gram* *(abrév* **masculin)** m

M. *(abrév* **Monsieur)** Mr

m' *voir* **me**

ma [ma] *voir* **mon**

maboul [mabul] *Fam* **ADJ** *(fou)* crazy, nuts
N nut

mac [mak] NM *Arg (maquereau)* pimp

Macabées [makabe] NMPL *Bible* = **Maccabées**

macabre [makabʀ] **ADJ** *(découverte, histoire)* macabre, gruesome, grisly; *(humour)* macabre; **danse m.** dance of death, danse macabre

macache [makaʃ] **ADV** *Fam* **m. (bono)** *(absolument pas)* no way!, nothing doing!, not likely!; *(absolument rien)* not a sausage, *surtout Am* zilch

macadam [makadam] NM **1** *(revêtement)* macadam; **m. goudronné** tarmac(adam) **2** *(route)* road

macadamisage [makadamizaʒ] NM, **macadamisation** [makadamizasjɔ̃] NF *(de route)* tarmacking

macadamiser [makadamize] VT *(route)* to tarmac

macaque [makak] NM *(singe)* macaque; **m. rhésus** rhesus monkey
N *Fam (personne)* ugly ape

macareux [makaʀø] NM puffin

macaron [makaʀɔ̃] NM **1** *Culin* macaroon **2** **macarons** *(coiffure)* coils *(over the ears)*; *Fam* earphones **3** *(badge)* badge; *(décoration)* rosette; *(autocollant)* sticker; *Journ* **m. de presse** press badge

macaroni [makaʀɔni] NM **1** *Culin* piece of macaroni; **des macaronis** macaroni VOIR GRAMMAIRE A14 **2** *Arg Péj (Italien)* wop, *Br* Eyetie, *Am* guinea

Maccabées [makabe] NMPL *Bible* Maccabees

macchabée [makabe] NM *très Fam (mort)* stiff, corpse

Macédoine [masedwan] NF **la M.** Macedonia

macédoine [masedwan] NF **1** *Culin* **m. de fruits** fruit salad; **m. de légumes** mixed vegetables, *Spéc* macedoine of vegetables **2** *Fam Vieilli (mélange)* medley, miscellany, *Péj* hotchpotch

macédonien, -ienne [masedɔnjɛ̃, -jɛn] **ADJ** Macedonian
N M. Macedonian

macération [maseʀasjɔ̃] NF **1** steeping, soaking **2** *Rel* mortification

macérer [maseʀe] *(* **je macère; je macérerai** *)* **VT 1** to steep, to soak; **laisser m. qch** to leave something to steep *or* soak **2** *Rel (chair)* to mortify

VI to steep, to soak; **la viande doit m. plusieurs jours** the meat should be left to steep *or* soak for several days; *Fig Fam* **laissons-le m. quelques jours** let's leave him stewing for a few days

Mach [mak] NM *Aviat* **(nombre de) M.** Mach (number)

mâche [maʃ] NF *Bot* corn salad, lamb's lettuce

mâchefer [maʃfɛʀ] NM *Tech* clinker, slag

mâchement [maʃmã] NM *Rare* chewing, *Fml* mastication

mâcher [maʃe] VT *(nourriture)* to chew, *Fml* to masticate; *(quelque chose qui croustille ou qui croque)* to munch; *(d'un animal) (fourrage)* to champ, to chomp; **m. le mors** *(d'un cheval)* to champ at the bit; **ne pas m. ses mots** not to mince (one's) words; **m. le travail ou la besogne à qn** to spoon-feed sb; **m. le bois** *(d'un outil émoussé etc)* to chew up the wood

machette [maʃɛt] NF machete

Machiavel [makjavɛl] **N** Machiavelli

machiavélique [makjavelik] **ADJ** *(ruse etc)* Machiavellian

machiavélisme [makjavelism] NM Machiavellianism

mâchicoulis [maʃikuli] NM *Archit* machicolation; **à m.** machicolated

machin [maʃɛ̃] NM *Fam* **1** *(objet)* thing(ummy), thingumajig, thingumabob, whatsit(sname), what-d'you-call-it; **qu'est-ce que c'est que ce m.-là?** what's that thing(ummy) *or* thingumajig *or* thingumabob? **2** *(personne)* **monsieur M.** Mr What's-his-name, what-d'you-call-him, Thingummy; **madame M.** Mrs What's-her-name, what-d'you-call-her, Thingummy; **j'ai vu m.-chouette aujourd'hui** I saw what's-his-name *or* what-d'you-call-him *or* thingummy today

machinal, -ale, -aux, -ales [maʃinal, -o] **ADJ** *(action, geste)* mechanical, unconscious; *(réaction)* automatic, instinctive; *(travail)* mechanical; **faire qch de façon machinale** to do sth mechanically *or* unconsciously

machinalement [maʃinalmã] **ADV** *(agir)* mechanically, unconsciously; *(réagir, répondre etc)* automatically

machination [maʃinasjɔ̃] NF plot, machination

machine [maʃin] NF **1** *(appareil)* machine; *Ind* **les machines** the machinery, the plant; **machines agricoles** agricultural machinery *or* machines; **écrire une lettre à la m.** to type a letter; **écrit à la m.** typed, typewritten; **travailler le métal à la m.** to machine metal; **fait à la m.** *(objets)* machine-made; *(opération)* done by machine; **laver qch en m.** to machine-wash sth, to wash sth in a machine; *Fig* **la m. administrative/judiciaire** the administrative/judicial machinery *or* machine;

Fig **la m. est usée/fatiguée** *(corps humain)* the old body has had it/is tired out; *Fig Péj* **il n'est qu'une m. à penser/à faire de l'argent** he's nothing but a thinking/money-making machine; *Théâtre* **pièce à machines** play with stage effects **2** *(locomotive)* locomotive, engine; *Fam (moto)* machine; **m. volante** flying machine **3** *Naut (moteur)* engine; **salle des machines** engine room; **stopper les machines** to stop the engines; **faire m. arrière** to reverse the engine; *Fig* to backtrack

▸▸ **m. à adresser** addressing machine; **m. à affranchir** franking machine; **m. agrafeuse** stapling machine, stapler; **m. à aléser** boring machine, fine borer; **m. à battre** threshing machine; **m. de bureau** office machine; **m. à café** coffee machine; **m. à calculer** calculator; *(plus grande)* adding machine, calculating machine; *Typ* **m. à composer** typesetting machine; **m. comptable** accounting machine; **m. à coudre** sewing machine; **m. à écrire** typewriter; **m. à écrire à mémoire** memory typewriter; *Aut* **m. d'équilibrage des roues** wheel-balancing machine; **m. à fraiser** milling machine; **m. de guerre** engine of war; **m. infernale** explosive device; **m. interprète de cartes perforées** punch card reader; **m. à laver** *Belg* **m. à lessiver** washing machine, washer; **m. à laver la vaisselle** dishwasher; **m. à plier les documents** paper folding machine; **m. poinçonneuse** *(de cartes perforées)* punch; **m. à polycopier** duplicating machine; **m. à rayons X** X-ray machine; *Tech* **m. de rectification** grinding machine; **m. à repasser** ironing machine; **m. à sous** slot machine, *Fam* one-armed bandit, *Br* fruit machine; **m. de traitement de l'information** data processor; **m. à** *ou* **de traitement de texte** word processor; **m. à tricoter** knitting machine; **m. trieuse** sorter; **m. à vapeur** steam engine

machine-outil, *pl* **machines-outils** NF machine tool

machiner [maʃine] VT *Vieilli* to plot, to scheme; *(complot)* to hatch; **affaire machinée d'avance** put-up job; **qu'est-ce qu'il machine?** what's he plotting?; **c'est lui qui a tout machiné pour les faire accuser** he's the one who fixed *or* engineered everything so that they'd be blamed

machinerie [maʃinʀi] NF **1** *(machines)* machinery; *Ind* machinery, plant **2** *(salle)*, *Ind* machine room; *Naut* engine room

machinisme [maʃinism] NM mechanization

machiniste [maʃinist] NM **1** *Théâtre* scene-shifter, stagehand; *Cin, TV* grip; **m. de plateau** grip; **m. caméra** dolly operator; **m. de travelling** tracker **2** *(chauffeur) (d'autobus, de tramway)* driver; **'faire signe au m.'** 'request stop'

machisme [ma(t)ʃism] NM *Péj (virilité)* machismo; *(phallocratie)* male chauvinism

machiste [ma(t)ʃist] ADJ, NM *Péj* = macho

machmètre [makmɛtr] NM *Aviat* Machmeter

macho [matʃo] *Péj* NM *(phallocrate)* male chauvinist (pig)
ADJ INV *(comportement, attitude)* male chauvinist, macho

mâchoire [maʃwar] NF 1 *Anat (d'une personne, d'un animal)* jaw; **rire à s'en décrocher la m.** to split one's sides (laughing); *Fam* **jouer** *ou* **travailler des mâchoires** *(manger avec appétit)* to get stuck in 2 **mâchoires** *(d'un étau, d'une tenaille, d'une pince)* jaws; *Tech* **m. d'une poulie** flange of a pulley; *Aut* **mâchoires de frein** brake shoes

mâchonnement [maʃɔnmɑ̃] NM chewing; *Méd* tooth-grinding, *Spéc* bruxism

mâchonner [maʃɔne] VT 1 *(nourriture, cigare)* to chew (on); *(d'un cheval)* to chew on, to munch; **m. son crayon** to chew (the end of) one's pencil 2 *(marmonner) (menace)* to mutter; *(prière)* to mumble, to mutter

mâchouiller [maʃuje] VT *Fam* to chew away at *or* on

mâchure [maʃyr] NF *Tex (dans velours, drap)* flaw

mâchurer[1] [maʃyre] VT *(noircir)* to soil, to dirty; *Typ (feuille)* to mackle, to blur

mâchurer[2] VT *Tech (partie métallique d'un étau)* to dent, to bruise

macis [masi] NM *Bot, Culin* mace

macle [makl] NF *Bot* water chestnut

maçon, -onne [masɔ̃, -ɔn] ADJ mason; **abeille maçonne** mason bee
NM 1 *(artisan)* bricklayer; *(avec des pierres)* (stone)mason 2 *(franc-maçon)* Mason, freemason

mâcon [mɑkɔ̃] NM **m., vin de Mâcon** Mâcon (wine)

maçonnage [masɔnaʒ] NM *(action)* bricklaying; *(avec des pierres)* laying of stones; *(ouvrage)* masonry

maçonner [masɔne] VT *(construire)* to build; *(recouvrir de pierres) (mur)* to face with stone; *(condamner) (porte, fenêtre)* to wall up; *(avec des briques)* to brick up

maçonnerie [masɔnri] NF 1 *(avec des briques)* brickwork, masonry; *(avec des pierres)* masonry, stonework; **grosse m.** work on the superstructure; **petite m.** interior building work; **entreprise de m.** building *or* construction firm 2 *(organisation secrète)* (free)masonry

maçonnique [masɔnik] ADJ masonic

macramé [makrame] NM macramé; **faire du m.** to do macramé; **un set de table en m.** a set of macramé table mats

macre [makr] NF *Bot* water chestnut

macreuse [makrøz] NF 1 *(oiseau)* scoter (duck) 2 *Culin* shoulder of beef

macrobiotique [makrobjɔtik] ADJ macrobiotic
NF macrobiotics

macrocéphale [makrosefal] ADJ macrocephalic

macroclimat [makroklima] NM macroclimate

macro-commande, *pl* **macro-commandes** [makrokɔmɑ̃d] NF *Ordinat* macro (command)

macrocosme [makrokɔsm] NM macrocosm

macroéconomie [makroekɔnɔmi] NF macroeconomics

macroéconomique [makroekɔnɔmik] ADJ macroeconomic

macroenvironnement [makroɑ̃virɔnmɑ̃] NM macroenvironment

macroinstruction [makroɛ̃stryksjɔ̃] NF *Ordinat* macroinstruction

macrolangage [makrolɑ̃gaʒ] NM *Ordinat* macrolanguage

macromarketing [makromarketiŋ] NM, **macromercatique** [makromɛrkatik] NF macromarketing

macromolécule [makromolekyl] NF *Chimie* macromolecule

macroordinateur [makroordinatœr] NM mainframe

macrophotographie [makrofɔtografi] NF *Phot* macrophotography

macropode [makropɔd] NM *(poisson)* paradise fish

macroscopique [makroskɔpik] ADJ macroscopic

macrostructure [makrostryktyr] NF macrostructure

macula [makyla] NF *Anat* macula

maculage [makylaʒ] NM *(action de salir)* soiling, staining; *Typ* off-setting, mackling; *(tache)* stain, spot

maculature [makylatyr] NF *Typ (pour l'emballage)* waste; *(feuille tachée)* smudged *or* mackled sheet; *(feuille intercalaire)* interleaf

macule [makyl] NF 1 *Typ (pour l'emballage)* waste sheet 2 *Arch, Litt (tache)* stain, spot 3 *Méd* macula 4 *Typ (salissure)* mackle, smudge; *(feuille tachée)* smudged *or* mackled sheet; *(feuille intercalaire)* interleaf

maculer [makyle] VT *Litt (de sang)* to stain, to spot; *(de boue)* to spatter, to spot (**de** with); *Typ* to mackle; **maculé de taches d'encre** smeared with ink stains

Madagascar [madagaskar] NM Madagascar; **aller à M.** to go to Madagascar

madame, *pl* **mesdames** [madam, medam] NF 1 *(titre)* Mrs; **M. Martin** Mrs Martin; **Mesdames Martin** the Mrs Martin; **M. Veuve Martin** Mrs Martin, widow of David/*etc* Martin; **m. la marquise/la comtesse de X** the Marchioness/the Countess of X; **je voudrais parler à m. la directrice** *(du magasin, d'un service)* I would like to speak to the manager; *(d'une école)* I would like to speak to the headmistress; *Fml* **comment va m. votre mère?** how is your mother?
2 *(utilisé seul)* **voici le chapeau de m.** here is your hat, madam; *(dit par vendeur)* the lady *or* this lady *or* *Fml* madam is complaining that …; *(dit par un domestique)* the mistress *or* *Fml* madam is complaining that …; **M. est sortie** Madam is not at home; **M. a sonné?** you rang, madam?; **M. est servie** dinner is served(, madam); **occupez-vous de M.** *(à un employé de magasin)* see to the *or* this lady
3 *(apostrophe)* madam, *surtout Am* ma'am; *(à une dame titrée)* your ladyship; *(dans la police, l'armée etc)* ma'am; **non/au revoir, m.** no/goodbye, *Fml* no/goodbye, madam; *(à une femme qui s'appelle Martin)* no/goodbye, Mrs Martin; **oui, m. la colonelle** yes, colonel; *(épouse du colonel Martin)* yes, Mrs Martin; **entrez, mesdames** come in, ladies; **m.?** *(dans un magasin)* can I help you?, *Fml* can I help you, madam?
4 *(dans une lettre) (always written in full)* **Madame** Dear Madam; **chère Madame** *(qui s'appelle Martin)* Dear Mrs Martin
5 *Fam (dame)* **jouer à la m.** to put on airs (and graces)

Madeleine [madlɛn] NF 1 *Bible* Magdalen(e); *Fam* **pleurer comme une M.** to cry one's eyes *or* heart out 2 *Culin* **m.** madeleine

mademoiselle, *pl* **mesdemoiselles** [madmwazɛl, medmwazɛl] NF 1 *(titre)* Miss; **M. Martin** Miss Martin; **Mesdemoiselles Martin et Durand** the Misses Martin and Durand, Miss Martin and Miss Durand; *Fml Vieilli* **comment va m. votre cousine?** how is your cousin? 2 *(utilisé seul)* **M. se plaint que …**

(dans un magasin) the *or* this young lady is complaining that … 3 *(apostrophe)* **merci m.** thank you, miss; *(à une femme qui s'appelle Martin)* thank you, Miss Martin; **m. est servie** dinner is served(, madam); *Fml (à Caroline)* dinner is served, Miss Caroline; **m., avez-vous choisi?** *(au restaurant)* are you ready to order(, miss)?; **mesdemoiselles, un peu de silence je vous prie!** *(dans une classe)* let's have some quiet, girls, please! 4 *(dans une lettre) (always written in full)* **Mademoiselle** Dear Madam; **chère Mademoiselle** *(qui s'appelle Martin)* Dear Miss Martin

Madère [madɛr] N *Géog* Madeira
NM **m., vin de M.** Madeira (wine)

madone [madɔn] NF madonna; *Fig* **un visage de m.** a madonna-like face

madras [madra(s)] NM *(tissu)* madras (cotton); *(foulard)* (cotton) headscarf

madré, -ée [madre] *Litt* ADJ sly, crafty, wily
N sly fox, crafty devil

madrépore [madrepɔr] NM *Zool* madrepore

Madrid [madrid] N Madrid

madrier [madrije] NM (piece of) timber; *(façonné)* thick board *or* plank; *(poutre)* beam

madrigal, -aux [madrigal, -o] NM *Mus* madrigal

madrilène [madrilɛn] ADJ of/from Madrid
N **M.** *(natif)* native of Madrid; *(habitant)* inhabitant of Madrid

maelstrom [malstrɔm] NM maelstrom

maestria [maɛstrija] NF mastery; **avec m.** in a masterly manner, brilliantly

maestro [maɛstro] NM *Mus* maestro

maf(f)ia [mafja] NF 1 **la M.** the Mafia 2 *(groupe aux intérêts communs)* gang; **le monde du spectacle est une vraie m.** show business is a real Mafia

maf(f)ieux, -ieuse [mafjø, -jøz] ADJ Mafia
N mafioso

maf(f)ioso, *pl* **maf(f)iosi** [mafjozo, -zi] NM mafioso

mafflu [mafly] ADJ *Arch, Litt (personne)* chubby-cheeked, chubby-faced; *(visage)* chubby

maganer [magane] VT *Can (chose)* to spoil, to waste; *(personne)* to manhandle

magasin [magazɛ̃] NM 1 *(boutique)* shop, *surtout Am* store; **grand m.** department store; **chaîne de magasins** chain of shops *or* stores; **employé(e) de m.** shop assistant, *Am* (sales)clerk; **courir** *ou* **faire les magasins** to go shopping 2 *(entrepôt)* store, warehouse, storeroom; *TV etc* **m. de décors** scene dock; **marchandises en m.** stock in hand; **nous n'avons pas cet article en m.** we don't have that item in stock 3 *(de fusil, de projecteur)* magazine; **m. à papier** *(d'une imprimante etc)* paper tray
▸▸**m. d'alimentation** grocery shop *or Am* store; **m. d'armes** armoury, *Am* armory; **m. de décors** scene dock; **m. détaxé** duty-free shop *or Am* store; **m. discompte** discount store; **m. électronique** on-line shop *or Am* store; **m. franchisé** franchise; *Can* **m. général** general store; **magasins généraux** (public) bonded warehouse(s); *Mktg* **m. laboratoire** = model test-shop used to monitor consumer behaviour; **m. à libre service** self-service store; **m. minimarge** discount store; **m. de proximité** convenience store; *Can* **m. à rayons** department store; **m. à succursales multiples** chain store; **m. d'usine** factory (retail) outlet, factory shop; **m. vidéo** video shop *or Am* store

magasinage [magazinaʒ] NM 1 *Com (de marchandises)* warehousing, storing 2 **(droits de) m.** warehouse dues, storage (charges) 3 *Can* **faire du m.** to go shopping

magasiner [magazine] vi *Can* to go shopping

magasinier [magazinje] NM warehouseman, storekeeper

magazine [magazin] NM 1 *(journal)* magazine; **elle est dans tous les magazines en ce moment** her photo is in all the magazines at the moment; **m. féminin** women's magazine; **m. hebdomadaire/mensuel** weekly/monthly (magazine); **m. d'actualités** current affairs magazine; **m. électronique** ezine, e-zine; **m. d'information** news magazine; **m. littéraire** literary magazine *or* review; **m. people** celebrity magazine; **m. à sensation** trashy magazine; **m. télé, m. télévision** magazine programme; **m. en couleur** colour magazine 2 *Radio, TV* magazine (programme); **m. d'actualités** news programme; **m. d'information** current affairs (magazine) programme; **m. culturel** arts programme

magdalénien, -ienne [magdalenjɛ̃, -jɛn] ADJ, NM *Hist* Magdalenian

mage [maʒ] NM 1 *Antiq* magus; *Bible* **les (trois) Rois Mages** the Three Wise Men, the (Three) Magi 2 *(voyant)* seer

magenta [maʒɛta] ADJ INV, NM magenta

Maghreb [magrɛb] NM **le M.** the Maghreb *(French-speaking North Africa)*

maghrébin, -ine [magrebɛ̃, -in] ADJ of/from the Maghreb
N **M.** person from the Maghreb

Maghrébin

This term usually refers to people from Algeria, Morocco and Tunisia, although it can also refer to Libyans and Mauritanians. It has a particular resonance in contemporary France, where immigrants from these countries constitute the largest ethnic minority.

magicien, -ienne [maʒisjɛ̃, -jɛn] N 1 *(qui pratique la magie)* magician, sorcerer, *f* sorceress 2 *(illusionniste), Fig* magician

magie [maʒi] NF magic; **c'est de la m.!** it's magic!; **comme par m.** as if by magic; *Fig* **la m. du verbe** the magic of language *or* words ▸▸**m. blanche** white magic; **m. noire** black magic

magique [maʒik] ADJ 1 *(pouvoirs)* magic, magical; *(mot, formule, baguette)* magic; **c'est m.!** it's magic! 2 *Fig (formidable) (spectacle, musique etc)* magical

magiquement [maʒikmɑ̃] ADV magically

magister [maʒistɛr] NM 1 *Arch (maître d'école)* (village) schoolmaster 2 *Péj (pédant)* pedant

magistère [maʒistɛr] NM 1 *Univ* post-graduate vocational qualification 2 *Fig (autorité)* authority 3 *(titre)* Grand Master; **M. de l'Ordre de Malte** Grand Master of the Order of Malta

magistral, -ale, -aux, -ales [maʒistral, -o] ADJ 1 *(admirable) (œuvre, interprétation, démonstration)* masterly, authoritative; *(réussite)* brilliant, resounding; *Fig (rossée, engueulade)* sound, proper, thorough; *(gifle)* resounding; *(erreur)* colossal, monumental; **il s'est fait rembarrer de façon magistrale** he was told in no uncertain terms where to go; **réussir un coup m.** to pull off a master stroke 2 *(docte) (ton)* magisterial, authoritative 3 *Univ* **cours m.** lecture; **enseignement m.** lecturing 4 *Pharm* **préparation magistrale** prescribed medication specially made up by the pharmacist for the particular patient

magistralement [maʒistralmɑ̃] ADV authoritatively

magistrat [maʒistra] NM 1 magistrate; **il est m.** he's a magistrate, he sits on the Bench; **m. du parquet** public prosecutor 2 **premier m. de France** supreme judicial officer of France

magistrature [maʒistratyr] NF 1 *(personnes)* magistrature; **la m. assise** = the judges, the Bench; **la m. debout** = the (body of) public prosecutors; **entrer dans la m.** *(devenir juge)* to be appointed a judge; *(devenir fonctionnaire public)* to be appointed a public prosecutor 2 *(période)* magistrature

magma [magma] NM *Chimie, Géol* magma; **un m. informe de boue et de pierres** a shapeless heap *or* pile of mud and stones; *Fig* **un m. d'idées confuses** a jumble of confused ideas

magnanerie [maɲanri] NF 1 *(élevage)* silkworm breeding, *Spéc* sericulture 2 *(bâtiment)* silkworm house

magnanier, -ière [maɲanje, -jɛr] N silkworm breeder, *Spéc* sericulturist

magnanime [maɲanim] ADJ magnanimous; **se montrer m.** to show magnanimity, to be magnanimous

magnanimement [maɲanimmɑ̃] ADV magnanimously

magnanimité [maɲanimite] NF magnanimity

magnat [magna] NM 1 *Com, Ind* magnate, tycoon; **m. des médias** media mogul; **magnats du pétrole** oil magnates *or* tycoons; **m. de la presse** press baron, press lord 2 *Hist (de Pologne, Hongrie)* magnate, grandee

magner (se) [s(ə)maɲe] VPR *Fam* to get a move on, to get one's skates on; *très Fam* **magne-toi le train!** get your backside *or Am* butt into gear!

magnésie [maɲezi] NF *Chimie, Pharm* magnesia, magnesium oxide; *Pharm* **sulfate de m.** Epsom salts

magnésite [maɲezit] NF *(carbonate de magnésium)* magnesite; *(silicate de magnésium)* meerschaum

magnésium [maɲezjɔm] NM *Chimie* magnesium; **éclair de m.** magnesium light *or* flash

magnétique [maɲetik] ADJ magnetic; **champ m.** magnetic field; **enregistrement sur bande m.** recording on magnetic tape, tape-recording; *Fig* **exercer un pouvoir m.** to exert a hypnotic *or* magnetic power (**sur** on, over)

magnétiquement [maɲetikmɑ̃] ADV magnetically

magnétisable [maɲetizabl] ADJ magnetizable; *(personne)* hypnotizable

magnétisation [maɲetizasjɔ̃] NF 1 *Phys* magnetization 2 *(d'une personne)* hypnotizing, mesmerizing

magnétiser [maɲetize] VT 1 *(fer etc)* to magnetize 2 *(personne)* to hypnotize, to mesmerize; *Fig* **auditoire magnétisé** hypnotized *or* spellbound audience; **orateur qui magnétise les foules** speaker who hypnotizes *or* mesmerizes the crowds, speaker who holds the crowds in his spell

magnétiseur [maɲetizœr] NM *(guérisseur)* healer; *(hypnotiseur)* hypnotist

magnétisme [maɲetism] NM 1 *Phys* magnetism; **le m. terrestre** the earth's magnetism; **m. rémanent** residual magnetism 2 *(hypnotisme)* hypnotism, mesmerism; *Fig* **m. personnel** personal magnetism; **une personne qui a beaucoup de m.** a person with a great deal of charisma *or* personality; **m. animal** animal magnetism

magnétite [maɲetit] NF *Minér* magnetite, lodestone

magnéto [maɲeto] NF *Élec* magneto
NM *Fam (magnétophone)* tape recorder

magnétocassette [maɲetokasɛt] NM cassette deck *or* recorder; *Ordinat* **m. numérique** digital cassette recorder

magnétomètre [maɲetomɛtr] NM *Tech* magnetometer

magnétophone [maɲetofɔn] NM tape recorder; **m. (enregistreur) à cassettes** cassette recorder; **m. à bande** audio tape recorder; **m. à bobines** reel-to-reel tape recorder

magnétoscope [maɲetoskɔp] NM video, video recorder, *Am* VCR; **enregistrer qch au m.** to video sth, to record sth on video; **m. d'enregistrement** recording deck; **m. de lecture** playback deck; **m. de standard professionel** video(tape) recorder, VTR; **m. à cassette** video cassette recorder, VCR; **m. à cassette vidéo numérique** digital video recorder

magnétoscoper [maɲetoskɔpe] VT to videotape, to video, to record on video

magnificat [magnifikat] NM INV *Rel* magnificat

magnificence [maɲifisɑ̃s] NF *(richesse, éclat)* magnificence, *Br* splendour, *Am* splendor; *Litt (générosité)* munificence, lavishness

magnifier [maɲifje] VT *(pr sub, impf n. magnifiions, v. magnifiiez)* 1 *(exalter)* to magnify, to glorify 2 *(idéaliser)* to idealize

magnifique [maɲifik] ADJ 1 *(château, palais, meubles etc)* magnificent, splendid; *(temps)* glorious, superb, splendid, magnificent; *(corps)* superb, magnificent; *(film, tableau, fruits, cadeau etc)* splendid, marvellous, wonderful; **on a une vue m. depuis le deuxième étage** there is a magnificent *or* superb view from the second floor; **(c'est) m.!** (it's) marvellous *or* great *or* fantastic!; **elle était m. dans sa robe de mariée** she looked magnificent *or* wonderful *or* superb in her wedding dress; **un bébé m.** a bonny (little) *or* lovely (little) baby; **il est m. dans le rôle** he is magnificent *or* superb *or* brilliant in the role 2 *Vieilli (généreux, prodigue) (personne)* liberal, munificent; **Laurent le M.** Lorenzo il Magnifico; **Gatsby le M.** the Great Gatsby

magnifiquement [maɲifikmɑ̃] ADV *(décoré, vêtu)* magnificently, splendidly; *(réussir)* brilliantly; **un morceau de musique m. exécuté** a brilliantly performed piece of music; **la soirée s'est m. passée** the party went splendidly *or* marvellously *or* wonderfully

magnitude [maɲityd] NF *Astron, Géol* magnitude; **un séisme de m. 5 sur l'échelle de Richter** an earthquake measuring 5 on the Richter scale

magnolia [maɲɔlja], **magnolier** [maɲɔlje] NM magnolia (tree)

magnum [magnɔm] NM magnum

magot¹ [mago] NM *Fam (d'argent)* hoard, pile; *(économies)* savings, nest egg; **il a dû amasser un joli m.** he must have built up a nice little nest egg *or* a nice little pile; **dis-nous où tu as mis le m.!** tell us where you've stashed the loot!

magot² NM 1 *(singe)* Barbary ape 2 *(figurine)* magot

magouillage [magujaʒ] NM, **magouille** [maguj] NF *Fam* scheming, shady dealing; **faire des magouillages** to scheme; **magouillages électoraux** pre-election scheming

magouiller [maguje] *Fam* VT to scheme; **il magouille un mauvais coup** he's cooking up a dirty trick
VI **il est toujours en train de m.** he's always wheeling and dealing, he's always scheming; **il magouille pour avoir des ordinateurs gratuits** he's trying to wangle some free computers, he's scheming to get some free computers; **il a dû m. pour avoir ce poste** he had to do some scheming to get the job

magouilleur, -euse [magujœr, -øz] N *Fam* schemer, wheeler-dealer

magret [magrɛ] NM *Culin (d'oie, de canard)* fillet, breast

magyar, -are [magjar] ADJ Magyar
N **M.** Magyar

maharaja [maaradʒa] NM maharaja(h)

maharani [maarani] NF maharanee

mahatma [maatma] NM mahatma

mah-jong [maʒɔ̃g] NM mah-jong(g)

Mahomet [maɔmɛ] N Mohammed, Mahomet

mahométan, -ane [maɔmetɑ̃, -an] ADJ, N *Vieilli* Mohammedan, Mahometan

mahométisme [maɔmetism] NM *Vieilli* Mohammedanism

mai [mɛ] NM May; **en m.** in May; **au mois de m.** in (the month of) May; **le sept m.** (on) the seventh of May, (on) May the seventh, *Am* (on) May seventh; **le premier m.** the first of May; *Admin* May Day SEE GRAMMAR A81; B60–1

> **Mai 68**
> The events of May 1968 came about when student protests, coupled with widespread industrial unrest, culminated in a general strike and rioting. De Gaulle's government survived the crisis, but the issues raised made the events a turning point in French social history.

MAIF [maif] NF *abrév* Mutuelle assurance des instituteurs de France

maigre [mɛgr] ADJ *(personne, animal, bras, cou)* thin, *Péj* skinny; *(viande)* lean; *(revenu, récolte, résultats)* meagre, *Am* meager, poor; *(végétation)* sparse, scanty; *(barbe)* straggly, sparse; *(conclusions, explication)* thin; *(succès)* very limited; **m. comme un clou** as thin as a rake; *Can Fam* **m. comme un chicot ou un manche à balai** as thin as a rake; **homme grand et m.** tall, thin man; **fromage m.** low-fat cheese; **m. filet d'eau** thin trickle of water; **m. repas** scanty *or* frugal meal; **jour m.** day of abstinence; *Typ* **caractères maigres** light-face type
N *(personne)* **un grand m.** a tall, thin man; **c'est une fausse m.** she's not as thin as she looks
NM **1** **maigres** *(de rivière)* shallows **2** *(viande)* **un morceau de m.** a piece of lean (meat)
ADV **manger ou faire m.** not to eat meat, to abstain from meat

maigréchine [mɛgreʃin] ADJ *Can Fam* scrawny, skinny

maigrelet, -ette [mɛgrəlɛ, -ɛt] *Péj* ADJ skinny
N skinny person

maigrement [mɛgrəmɑ̃] ADV meagrely, *Am* meagerly, poorly; **il est m. payé** he's poorly paid, he gets a meagre pay

maigreur [mɛgrœr] NF *(de personne)* thinness, *Péj* skinniness; *Fig (de végétation)* sparseness, scantiness; *(de récolte, salaire)* meagreness, *Am* meagerness, poorness; **d'une m. effrayante** frighteningly thin

maigrichon, -onne [mɛgriʃɔ̃, -ɔn], **maigriot, -otte** [mɛgrijo, -ɔt] ADJ, N *Fam* = **maigrelet**

maigrir [mɛgrir] VI to get thin(ner), to lose weight; **elle essaie de m.** she's trying to lose weight, she's slimming; **j'ai maigri de dix kilos** I've lost ten kilos; **régime pour m.** (weight-loss) diet
VT **1 m. qn** *(d'une maladie)* to make sb thin(ner); *(d'un vêtement)* to make sb look thin(ner) **2** *(pièce de bois)* to thin

mail [maj] NM **1** *Vieilli (allée)* mall, avenue, promenade **2** *Hist (jeu, lieu)* pall-mall **3** *Arch (marteau)* mallet

mailing [melin] NM mailshot; **faire un m.** to do a mailshot

maillage [majaʒ] NM *Pêche (dimension des mailles d'un filet)* meshing **2** *(structuration en réseau)* **le m. de la région est insuffisant pour ce qui est des transports en commun** the region's public transport network *or* infrastructure is underdeveloped

maille¹ [maj] NF **1** *(en tricot etc)* stitch; **m. (à l')endroit** plain (stitch); **m. (à l')envers** purl (stitch); **une m. à l'endroit, une m. à l'envers** knit one, purl one; **m. qui file** ladder, *Am* run **2** *(tissu tricoté)* knitwear; **une robe en m. de coton** a knitted cotton dress **3** *(d'une chaîne)* link; **j'aime la m. de son bracelet** I like the style of link in her bracelet; **cotte de mailles** coat of mail **4** *(de filet, de grillage etc)* mesh; **filet à larges mailles** wide-mesh net; **passer entre ou à travers les mailles du filet** to slip through the net

maille² NF avoir **m. à partir avec qn** to have a set-to with sb; **avoir m. à partir avec la justice** to have a brush with the law

maillechort [majʃɔr] NM nickel silver

mailler [maje] VT **1** *(fil)* to net, to mesh **2** *Naut* to shackle **3** *(organiser en réseau)* to network **4** *Suisse (tordre, fausser)* to warp
VI **1** *Pêche* to be netted **2** *Suisse (s'énerver, se mettre en colère)* to get worked up
VPR **se mailler** *Suisse (se tordre)* **se m. la cheville/le genou** to twist one's ankle/one's knee; *Fig* **se m. de rire** to kill oneself (laughing), to be in stitches

maillet [majɛ] NM **1** *(outil)* mallet **2** *Sport (au polo)* stick, mallet; *(au croquet)* mallet

mailloche [majɔʃ] NF **1** *(outil)* beetle, large mallet **2** *Mus* bass drumstick

maillon [majɔ̃] NM **1** *(de chaîne)* link; **m. tournant** swivel; *Fig* **n'être qu'un m. de la chaîne** to be just one link in the chain **2** *Naut* shackle

maillot [majo] NM **1** *(tee-shirt)* T-shirt, tee-shirt; *(pour la danse)* leotard; *Sport (de footballeur, d'équipe)* shirt, jersey; *(de coureur, rameur)* vest, singlet; **m. (de bain)** *(pour femme)* swimsuit, *Br* swimming *or* bathing costume; *(pour homme)* (swimming *or* bathing) trunks; **leur nouvelle collection de maillots** their new swimwear collection; **m. de corps** *(pour homme)* vest, *Am* undershirt; **m. une pièce/deux pièces** one-piece/two-piece swimsuit; **être m. jaune** to be the overall leader of the Tour de France; **m. de marin** striped teeshirt; *(pull)* striped sweater **2** *(pour bébé)* swaddling clothes

MAIN [mɛ̃] NF **1** hand; **faire qch de la m. droite/gauche** to do sth right-handed/left-handed *or* with one's right/left hand; **faire qch à la m.** to do sth by hand; *(fabriquer)* to make sth by hand; **fait à la m.** *(pull etc)* handmade; **travailler de ses mains** to work with one's hands; **écrire une lettre de sa propre m.** to write a letter in one's own hand; **notes écrites à la m.** handwritten notes; **d'une (seule) m.** with one hand; **je n'ai que deux mains** I only have one pair of hands; **prendre un plateau/son courage à deux mains** to take a tray/one's courage in both hands; *Fig* **signer qch des deux mains** to sign sth eagerly; *Fig* **souscrire à deux mains à qch** to subscribe unreservedly to sth; **je lui ai serré la m.** I shook hands with him, I shook his hand; **dire adieu de la m. à qn** to wave goodbye to sb; **donner la m. à qn** to hold sb's hand; **donne ta m. à Philippe** *(pour traverser la rue)* give Philippe your hand, take *or* hold Philippe's hand; **ils se tenaient (par) la m., ils se donnaient la m.** they were holding hands; *Fig* **se donner la m.** to give each other a helping hand; *Fig* **ces deux-là peuvent se donner la m.** they're two of a kind, those two are as bad as each other; **prendre qn par la m.** to take sb's hand, to take sb by the hand; *Fig* **tu n'as qu'à te prendre par la m.** just go

for it, just do it; **il n'a qu'à se prendre par la m. et le faire** he just has to do it; *Fig* **se prendre en m.** to take oneself in hand; **prendre qn en m.** to take sb in hand; **prendre une affaire/une situation en m.** to take a matter/a situation in hand; **il a sa voiture bien en m.** he's got the feel of his car; **j'ai la situation en m.** I've got the situation in hand *or* under control; **la m. dans la m.** hand in hand; **avoir/tenir qch dans la m.** to have/hold sth in one's hand; **avoir une canne/une craie à la m.** to have a stick/a piece of chalk in one's hand; **mourir les armes à la m.** to die on the battlefield; **ne rien savoir faire de ses mains** to be hopeless with one's hands; **je ne suis pas très adroite de mes mains** I'm not very good with my hands; **la bouteille m'a échappé des mains** the bottle slipped out of *or* from my hands; **de m. en m.** from hand to hand; **passer de m. en m.** *(d'un objet)* to pass *or* be passed from hand to hand *or* from person to person; *Fig (d'une maison, d'un livre etc)* to go *or* pass through several hands; **passer aux mains de ...** to pass *or* fall into the hands of ...; **haut les mains!, les mains en l'air!** hands up!; **faire qch d'une m. habile ou experte ou exercée** to do sth with a skilled *or* an expert hand, to do sth skilfully; **en venir aux mains** to come to blows; **se battre à main(s) nue(s)** to fight with bare hands *or* fists; **combat à mains nues** bare-fisted *or* bare-knuckle fight; **attaque/vol à m. armée** armed attack/robbery; **venir/repartir les mains vides** to come/return empty-handed; *Fig* **arriver les mains dans les poches** to arrive unprepared; **donner d'une m. et reprendre de l'autre** to give with one hand and take back with the other; **demander la m. d'une jeune fille à ses parents** to ask a girl's parents for her hand (in marriage); **accorder/refuser sa m. à qn** *(d'une femme)* to give/refuse sb one's hand in marriage; **tendre la m.** to hold *or* stretch out one's hand *(à qn to sb)*; *Fig (pour l'aider)* to hold *or* stretch out a hand (to sb); **tendre à qn une m. secourable** to hold *or* stretch out a helping hand to sb; *Fig* **on le soupçonna de vouloir tendre la m. aux protestants** he was suspected of making conciliatory moves towards the Protestants; *Fig* **passer la m. dans le dos à qn** to butter sb up; **porter la m. à son chapeau** *(pour saluer)* to touch one's hat, to tip one's hat; *Fig* **on ne le voit pas souvent mettre la m. à son portefeuille** you don't often see him putting his hand in his pocket; **porter ou lever la m. sur qn** to lift *or* raise one's hand to sb; *Fam* **tu veux ma m. sur la figure?** do you want my hand across your face?; **mettre la m. sur qn ou au collet de qn** *(de la police)* to catch sb, *Fam* to collar *or* nab sb; *(le trouver)* to find sb; **mettre la m. sur qch** *(trouver qch que l'on cherchait)* to lay one's hands on sth, to put one's hand on sth; *(trouver par hasard)* to come across sth, to find sth; **je n'en mettrais pas ma m. au feu ou à couper** I shouldn't like to swear to it; **j'en mettrais ma m. au feu ou à couper** I'd swear to it; **mettre la m. à la pâte ou à l'ouvrage** to lend a hand; **mettre la dernière m. à qch** to put the finishing touches to sth; *Arg* **mettre la m. au panier de qn** to grope sb's behind; **prendre qn la m. dans le sac** to catch sb red-handed; **ne pas y aller de m. morte** *(en frappant, insultant qn)* not to pull one's punches; *(exagérer)* to overdo it; **faire m. basse sur qch** to get one's hands on sth; **avoir qch sous la m. ou à portée de (la) m.** to have sth handy *or* within easy reach *or* close at hand; **le premier objet qui lui est tombé sous la m.** the first object that came to hand; **faire qch en sous-m.** to do sth in an underhand way; **ne pas laisser ce produit à portée de m. des enfants** keep out of the reach of children; *Fam* **donner un coup de m. à qn** to lend *or* give sb a hand; **prêter la m. à qn pour faire qch** to lend sb a hand to do sth; **prêter la m. à qch** to have a hand in sth; **se faire la m.** to get one's hand in; **pour garder la m.** in order to keep your hand in; **il avait gardé la m.** he hadn't lost the knack or his touch; **il a perdu la m.** he's lost the knack or his touch; *(d'un sportif, musicien)* he's out of practice; **avoir le coup de m. (pour faire qch)** to have the knack (of doing sth); **ce n'est pas à mettre entre toutes les mains** it mustn't fall into the wrong hands; **une m. de fer dans un gant de velours** an iron hand or fist in a velvet glove; **d'une m. de fer** with an iron hand; **il empoigna le kalachnikov à pleines mains** he grabbed the kalashnikov with both hands; **il puise à pleines mains dans la caisse** he's got his hand in the till; **il a puisé à pleines mains dans les caisses de l'État** he liberally helped himself from the state coffers; **donner de l'argent à pleine(s) main(s)** to dish out money by the handful; **prendre qch à pleines mains** to take handfuls of sth; **il prit le livre à pleines mains** he took the book in both hands; **payer de la m. à la m.** to pay cash in hand; **tomber entre les mains** ou **aux mains** ou **sous la m. de qn** to fall into sb's hands or clutches; **tomber aux mains de l'ennemi** to fall into enemy hands; **l'affaire est entre les mains du juge Martin** the case is in the hands of Mr Justice Martin; **mon avenir est entre vos mains** my future is in your hands; **la décision est entre vos mains** the decision is in your hands or is up to you or is yours; **être en** ou **entre (de) bonnes mains** to be in good hands; **remettre qch à qn en mains propres** to deliver sth to sb in person; **acheter qch en première/seconde m.** to buy sth first-hand/second-hand; **article de seconde m.** second-hand article; **renseignements de première m.** first-hand information; **avoir la m. verte** to have green fingers or Am a green thumb; **ça nous laisse les mains libres pour agir** that gives us a free hand; **garder les mains libres** to keep a free hand; **j'ai les mains liées** my hands are tied; **avoir la m. légère** to have a delicate touch; Litt *(être habile)* to be clever with one's hands; *(être délicat)* to act with restraint or discretion; *(ne pas faire sentir son autorité)* to rule with a light hand; *(ne pas assaisonner suffisamment)* to underseason; **tu as eu la m. légère avec la crème/le sucre** you haven't put enough cream/sugar in; **avoir la m. lourde** *(avec le poivre, le whisky etc)* to be overgenerous, to be a bit heavy-handed (**avec** with); *(punir)* to mete out punishment with a heavy hand; **ce commerçant a la m. un peu lourde** this shopkeeper always gives you a bit over the weight; **avoir la m. leste** *(baladeuse)* to have wandering hands; *(être prompt à gifler)* to be a bit too quick with one's hands; **avoir la m. heureuse** to be lucky; **j'ai eu la m. heureuse** I was or got lucky, I had a lucky break; **mains criminelles/sacrilèges** criminal/sacrilegious hands; **dessin à m. levée** freehand drawing; **voter à m. levée** to vote by a show of hands; **gagner haut la m.** to win easily or hands down; Vieilli **de longue m.** for a long time (past); Fig **se laver les mains de qch** to wash one's hands of sth; Fig **se frotter les mains** to be rubbing one's hands with glee; **grand comme la m.** tiny; **leur maison est grande comme la m.** their house isn't big enough to swing a cat in; Prov **aux innocents les mains pleines** fortune favours fools, beginners have all the luck; Mus **morceau à quatre mains** piece for four hands, duet; **m. de maître** master hand; **de m. de maître** by a master('s) hand; **un concerto exécuté de m. de maître** a masterfully performed concerto; **la cérémonie a été organisée de m. de maître** the ceremony was a masterpiece of organiza-

tion; **c'est fait de m. de maître** it's a masterpiece; **on reconnaît la m. du maître** this is obviously the work of a master; **reconnaître la m. d'un peintre** to recognize a painter's style; **à m. droite/gauche** on the right-hand/left-hand side **2** Cartes lead; **avoir/perdre la m.** to have/lose the lead; **passer la m.** Cartes to pass the lead; Fig to stand aside, to give someone else a chance; **passer la m. à son fils** to hand over the reins to one's son **3** Ordinat pointing hand **4** Couture **petite m.** junior assistant **5** Typ *(de papier)* quire **ADV** **tricoté/fait/cousu m.** hand-knitted/made/sewn

▸▸**m. d'accoucheur** claw-like hand; **m. courante** *(d'escalier)* handrail; Com daybook; Com **m. courante de caisse** counter cash book; Com **m. courante de dépenses** paid cash book; **m. courante de justice** *(dans un commissariat de police)* incident book; Com **m. courante de recettes** received cash book; **m. de Fatma** hand of Fatima; Tél **mains libres** *(appareil)* hands-free; **kit mains libres** hands-free kit

mainate [mɛnat] **NM** myna(h) (bird)

main-d'œuvre [mɛ̃dœvr] **NF** *(personnes, travail)* manpower, workforce; Écon labour, Am labor; **embaucher de la m.** to take on workers; **m. étrangère** foreign labour(ers); **frais de m.** labour costs; **m. contractuelle** contract labour; **m. qualifiée** skilled labour; **m. temporaire** temporary labour

main-forte [mɛ̃fɔrt] **NF INV prêter m. à qn** to come to sb's assistance or aid

mainlevée [mɛ̃lve] **NF** Jur *(d'un acte)* lifting; **m. de saisie** restoration of goods *(taken in distraint)*

mainmise [mɛ̃miz] **NF** seizure (**sur** of); Fig **la m. du gouvernement sur les médias** the government's appropriation or takeover of the media

maint [mɛ̃] **ADJ** Litt many a; **m. auteur** many an author; **maintes et maintes fois, à maintes reprises, en maintes (et maintes) occasions** time and (time) again

maintenance [mɛ̃tnɑ̃s] **NF 1** Ind *(entretien)* maintenance, service; **m. sur site** on-site maintenance **2** Mil keeping up to strength

maintenant [mɛ̃tnɑ̃] **ADV** now; **vous devriez être prêt m.** you ought to be ready by now; **à vous m.** now it's your turn; **dès m., à partir de m.** from now on(wards), in future, Fml henceforth; **m. que tu es grand** now (that) you're a big boy; **je vous donne ce conseil, m. vous en faites ce que vous voulez** that's my advice to you, (now) take it or leave it; **m. reste à savoir si les employés voudront reprendre le travail** the question now is whether the employees will be willing to go back to work; **les jeunes de m.** young people today or nowadays, the young people or the youth of today VOIR GRAMMAIRE A21

mainteneur [mɛ̃tnœr] **NM** Bourse **m. de marché** market maker

MAINTENIR [mɛ̃tnir] *(conj like* **tenir***)* **VT 1** *(soutenir, retenir, tenir fermement)* to keep or hold in position; **colonnes qui maintiennent la voûte** columns that hold up or support the vault; **m. la foule** to hold back the crowd; **m. son cheval** to keep one's horse under control **2** *(entretenir, garder)* *(tradition)* to maintain, to keep, to uphold; *(discipline)* to maintain, to keep; *(paix)* to keep, to maintain, to preserve; *(décision)* to abide by; **m. qn dans ses fonctions** to maintain or keep sb in office; **m. sa position** to maintain one's position; **je maintiens que c'est faux** I maintain that it's untrue; **les médecins font tout pour le m. en vie** the doctors are doing everything pos-

sible to keep him alive; **m. qch à température constante** to keep or maintain sth at a constant temperature; **nos programmes sont maintenus malgré la grève** the station is maintaining normal service despite the strike; **on accuse le gouvernement de m. cette entreprise en activité de façon artificielle** the government has been accused of using artificial means to keep the company operating

VPR se maintenir *(de prix, dollar, taux de change, cours de la Bourse)* to remain steady, to hold up or steady; **se m. dans les bonnes grâces de qn** to keep in favour with sb, to stay in sb's good books; Fam **comment ça va? – je me maintiens** how are you? – (I'm) bearing up; **cela ne peut pas se m. longtemps** it can't last long; **le temps se maintient** the weather is holding

maintien [mɛ̃tjɛ̃] **NM 1** *(fait de conserver dans le même état)* maintenance; *(de la loi, d'un principe)* upholding; *(de la discipline)* maintenance, keeping; **le m. du pouvoir d'achat des salariés doit être une priorité** maintaining wage-earners' purchasing power must be a priority; Mil **force de m. de la paix** peacekeeping force; **m. de l'ordre** policing, maintenance of law and order; Jur **m. dans les lieux** right(s) of occupancy, security of tenure; Ordinat **m. majuscule** caps lock **2** *(allure, posture)* bearing, deportment; **leçons de m.** lessons in deportment

maire [mɛr] **NM** mayor; *(en Écosse)* provost; **monsieur/madame le m.** the Mayor, His/Her Worship (the Mayor); *(en s'adressant à lui/elle)* Your Worship; Hum **passer devant (monsieur) le m.** to tie the knot, to get hitched

Maire
In France, the mayor has obligations not only to the community but also to national government. He or she is responsible for promulgating national law as well as supervising the local police and officiating at civic occasions. Mayors are elected by the "conseil municipal" (and thus indirectly by the town's residents).

mairesse [mɛrɛs] **NF** Vieilli *(femme du maire)* mayoress; Rare *(femme maire)* mayor

mairie [mɛri] **NF** *(lieu)* town hall, Am city hall; *(administration municipale)* town or city council, Am city hall; **la m. a organisé un voyage pour les personnes âgées de la ville** the council has organized a trip for the town's senior citizens; **c'est un employé de m.** he works for the council, he's a council worker

Mairie
Also called the "hôtel de ville", this is the centre of municipal government. The "mairie" serves as a vital information source for town residents. People go there to ask about taxes, to get married in a civil ceremony, to enrol in certain community-sponsored classes, etc.

mais [mɛ] **ADV** Litt **n'en pouvoir m.** to be unable to do anything about it

CONJ 1 *(marque l'opposition)* but; **famille riche m. honnête** rich but honest family; **il n'est pas très intelligent m. il est très travailleur** he's not very intelligent but he's a hard worker; **non seulement ..., m. aussi** ou **encore ...** not only ..., but also ... **2** *(emphatique)* **m. oui!** oh yes!, of course!; **m. non!** oh no!, not at all!, of course not!; **m. c'est vrai!** but it's true!, it really is true!; **m. enfin!**

well really!; **m. enfin je te l'avais bien dit!** I told you!; **elle ne fait rien de la journée, m. vraiment rien** she does nothing all day, absolutely nothing **3** *(transition)* **m. qu'avez-vous donc?** whatever's the matter?; **m. à quoi penses-tu?** whatever's got into you?; **m. tu l'as déjà vu?** what, you've already seen it?; **m. j'y pense, je ne l'ai pas encore appelé!** I've just thought, I haven't rung him yet!

NM il y a un m. there's one snag; **il n'y a pas de m. (qui tienne)** there are no buts about it

maïs [mais] NM *(plante)* maize, *Am* corn; *(légume)* (sweet) corn; **farine de m.** cornflour, *Am* cornstarch

maison [mɛzɔ̃] NF **1** *(habitation)* house; **m. individuelle** detached house; **m. bourgeoise** luxurious house; **il porte des pantoufles dans la m.** he wears slippers indoors *or* around the house

2 *(foyer)* home; **tenir la m. de qn** to keep house for sb; **à la m.** at home; **retournons à la m.** let's go home, let's go back to the house; **elle travaille à la m.** she works at *or* from home; **ça fait longtemps que tu n'es pas venu à la m.** it's a long time since you came to our house; **dépenses de (la) m.** household expenses; **ça ne va pas fort à la m. en ce moment** things aren't too good at home just now; **toute la m. dort** the whole house is asleep; **le fils de la m.** the son of the house; **ami de la m.** friend of the family; **chez eux, c'est la m. du Bon Dieu** they keep open house, their door is always open

3 *(entreprise)* firm, company; **cela fait vingt ans qu'elle est dans la m., elle a vingt ans de m.** she's been with the firm *or* company for twenty years; **la m. décline toute responsabilité en cas de perte ou de vol** we accept no responsibility for loss or theft; **la m. ne fait pas crédit** we do not give credit; **la M. du Stylo** the Pen Shop; **l'esprit de la m.** the company spirit

4 *(lignée)* **la m. de Bourbon** the House of Bourbon

5 *(domestiques)* household, staff; **la m. du Roi** the Royal Household; **gens de m.** servants, (domestic) staff

6 *Astrol* house

ADJ INV 1 home-made; **spécialité m.** speciality of the house **2** *Fam (énorme)* colossal; **on s'est pris une engueulade m.** we got an almighty telling-off **3** *Fam (très réussi)* fantastic

▶▶*Banque* **m. affiliée** affiliated company, *Am* affiliate; **m. d'acceptation** accepting house; **m. d'arrêt** ≃ remand centre; **m. de campagne** *(résidence secondaire)* house in the country, country house; *(de style campagnard)* country cottage; **m. centrale** prison; **m. close** brothel; **m. de commerce** business; **m. de convalescence** convalescent home; *Vieilli* **m. de correction** reformatory; **m. de courtage** brokerage house; **m. de couture** fashion house; **m. de la culture** = arts centre; **m. de détail** retail business; **M. de Dieu** house of God; **m. de disques** record company; **m. d'édition** publisher, publishing house; **m. d'éducation surveillée** approved school, *Am* reformatory; **m. d'enfants** children's holiday centre, *Am* camp; **m. familiale** holiday *or Am* vacation home *(for families on low incomes)*; *Fig Fam* **m. de fous** madhouse; **m. de gros** wholesale business; **m. des jeunes et de la culture** = youth club and arts centre; **m. de jeux** gambling club, gaming club; **m. de maître** large luxurious house; **m. mère** parent company; *Rel* mother house; **m. de passe** brothel; **m. de poupées** doll's house; **m. de la presse** newsagent's; **m. de prêt** loan office company; **m. de rapport** rental property; **m. de redressement** reformatory; **m. religieuse** convent; **m. de rendez-vous** love nest; **m. de repos** rest home; **m. de retraite** old people's home; **m. de santé** *(établissement hospitalier)* nursing home; *(psychiatrique)* mental home; **M. du Seigneur** house of God; **m. à succursales multiples** multiple outlet company; *Fin* **m. de titres** securities firm; **m. de tolérance** brothel; **m. de vente par correspondance** mail order firm *or* house

Maison-Blanche (la) [lamɛzɔ̃blɑ̃ʃ] NF the White House

maisonnée [mɛzɔne] NF household, family

maisonnette [mɛzɔnɛt] NF small house; *(à la campagne)* cottage

maistrance [mɛstrɑ̃s] NF *Naut* petty officers

maître, maîtresse¹ [mɛtr, mɛtrɛs] NM **1** *(personne qui contrôle)* master, *f* mistress; **je veux être m. chez moi** I insist on being master in my own house; **ce chien n'obéit qu'à son m.** the dog obeys nobody but its master; **agir/parler en m.** to act/speak authoritatively; **être m. de la situation** to be master of *or* in control of the situation; **un dictateur fou qui veut devenir le m. du monde** a mad dictator who wants to take over *or* rule the world; **trouver son m.** to meet one's match; **être/rester son propre m.** to be/remain one's own master; **être/rester m. de soi** to be/remain self-possessed, to be/remain in control of one's emotions; **il n'était plus m. de lui-même** he lost control (of himself); **être m. de son véhicule** to be in control of one's vehicle; **le conducteur n'était plus m. de son véhicule** the driver (had) lost control of the car; **se rendre m. de qch** to take possession of sth; **tableau de m.** masterpiece; **les grands maîtres de la peinture flamande/de la musique** the great masters of Flemish painting/the great composers; **coup de m.** masterstroke; **être passé m. dans l'art de (faire) qch** to be a past master at (doing) sth; *Naut* **second m.** petty officer; **premier m.** chief petty officer; **être le seul m. à bord** to be sole master on board; *Fig* to be free to choose, to be free to do whatever one wants; *Fig* **c'est toi le seul m. à bord** you're the boss, you're in charge

2 *Scol* (school)teacher

3 *Jur (forme d'adresse) (pour un avocat qui s'appelle Martin)* Mr/Mrs/Miss Martin, *Am* counselor; **M. Dupont s'occupera de l'affaire** Mr/Mrs/Miss Dupont will be dealing with the case

4 *(titre octroyé à un peintre etc)* Maestro

ADJ chief, principal, main; **m. mot** key word; **poutre maîtresse** *(en métal)* main girder; *(en bois)* main beam; **cheville maîtresse** kingpin; **idée maîtresse d'un ouvrage** governing *or* key idea of a work; **maîtresse femme** capable woman; **carte maîtresse** *Cartes, Ordinat* master card; *Fig (principal atout)* trump card

▶▶ **m. d'armes** fencing master; *Univ Anciennement* **m. assistant** = assistant lecturer; *Rel* **m.-autel**, *pl* **maîtres-autels** high altar; *Scol Anciennement* **m. auxiliaire** supply *or Am* substitute teacher; **m. de cérémonies** master of ceremonies; **m. chanteur** blackmailer; **m. de chapelle** choirmaster; **m. charpentier** master carpenter; **m.-chien**, *pl* **maîtres-chiens** dog-handler; *Univ* **m. de conférence** ≃ (senior) lecturer, *Am* assistant professor; **m.-coq**, *pl* **maîtres-coqs** executive chef; *Aut* **m.-cylindre**, *pl* **maîtres-cylindres** master cylinder; **m. de danse** dancing master; **m. d'école** primary school *or Am* elementary school teacher; **m. d'équipage** boatswain; **m. de forges** ironmaster; **m. d'hôtel** *(dans une maison)* butler; *(dans un restaurant)* head waiter, *Am* maître d' ['mɛtr(ə)di]; *Naut* chief steward; **m. d'internat** housemaster, *Am* house director; **m. maçon** master mason; **m. de maison** *(pour un invité)* host; **pourrais-je parler au m. de maison?** could I speak to the man *or* the master of the house?; **m. de manège** riding instructor *or* master; **m. nageur** swimming instructor; **m. d'œuvre** prime contractor, project manager, master of works; **m. d'ouvrage** *ou de* l'ouvrage contracting authority; *Ordinat* **m. des postes** postmaster; *Culin* **m. queux** chef

maîtresse² NF **1** *(personne qui contrôle)* voir **maître** NM **2** *(d'un homme)* mistress; **avoir une m.** to have a mistress; **être la m. de qn** to be sb's mistress

▶▶ **m. d'école** primary school *or Am* elementary school teacher; **m. de maison** *(pour un invité)* hostess; *(ménagère)* lady of the house; **pourrais-je parler à la m. de maison?** could I speak to the lady of the house?

maîtrisable [mɛtrizabl] ADJ controllable

maîtrise [mɛtriz] NF **1** *Univ* ≃ master's degree, MA; **une m. d'anglais** ≃ a master's degree in English, an MA in English **2** *(contrôle) (de ses passions, d'un art, un sujet etc)* mastery, command; **m. de soi** self-control; *Mil* **m. des mers** command *or* control of the seas **3** *Ind* supervisory staff **4** *(école)* choir school; *(chorale)* choir; *(poste)* post of choirmaster

maîtriser [mɛtrize] VT *(agresseur)* to overpower; *(élèves, animal)* to control; *(flammes, opposition)* to subdue; *(incendie, épidémie)* to control, to get under control; *(passion, impatience)* to control, to curb, to contain; *(ses nerfs)* to control; *(ses peurs)* to master, to overcome; *(langue, sujet etc)* to master; **il ne maîtrise pas la langue** he has no command of the language

VPR se maîtriser to control oneself; **ne pas savoir se m.** to have no self-control

Maïzena® [maizena] NF *Culin* cornflour, *Am* cornstarch

majesté [maʒɛste] NF **1** *(souverain)* majesty; **Sa M. le roi/la reine** His Majesty the King/Her Majesty the Queen; **Leurs Majestés** their Majesties; *Gram* **pluriel de m.** royal we **2** *(de port)* majesty, dignity, stateliness; *(de style, paysage)* majesty, grandeur

majestueusement [maʒɛstɥøzmɑ̃] ADV majestically

majestueux, -euse [maʒɛstɥø, -øz] ADJ *(port)* majestic, stately; *(silhouette)* majestic, imposing; **paysage m.** majestic *or* magnificent landscape

majeur, -eure [maʒœr] ADJ **1** *(plus grand) (préoccupation, intérêt, difficulté)* major; **la majeure partie de** the greater part of, the major part of; **en majeure partie** for the most part; **prémisse majeure** major premise; *Rel* **les ordres majeurs** the major orders; **raison majeure de qch** chief reason for sth; **il n'y a pas de raison majeure pour que vous veniez** there's no real reason for you to come; **être absent pour raison majeure** to be unavoidably absent; *Cartes* **couleur majeure** major suit **2** *Jur* **être m.** to be of age; **le jour où il a été m.** the day he came of age; *Fig* **il est m., il sait ce qu'il fait** he's old enough *or* grown up, he knows what he's doing; *Hum* **je suis m. et vacciné** I'm old enough to look after myself; *Fig* **un peuple m.** a mature *or* responsible nation; *Jur* **m. incapable** mentally incompetent person **3** *Mus (clé etc)* major; **en sol bémol m.** in G flat major

N *(personne)* person who has come of age *or* reached the age of majority

NM *(doigt)* middle finger

NF *Cartes* **majeure** major suit

majolique [maʒɔlik] NF *Cér* majolica

major [maʒɔr] NM **1** *Mil* regimental adjutant *(with administrative duties)*; **m. général** chief of staff *(of a commander-in-chief in the field)*; **m. du camp** camp commandant; **(médecin) m.** medical officer, MO **2** *Univ* **être m. de promotion** = to be top of one's year

NF les **(grandes) majors** *Cin* the Majors; *(dans l'industrie de la musique)* major music conglomerates

majoration [maʒɔrasjɔ̃] **NF 1** *(surestimation) (de biens)* overestimation, overvaluation **2** *(augmentation) (d'une facture)* surcharge, additional charge (**de** on); *(d'un prix)* increase (**de** in); *(pour plus de bénéfices)* mark-up; **m. pour retard de paiement** additional charge *or* surcharge for late payment

majordome [maʒɔrdɔm] **NM** butler, major-domo

majorer [maʒɔre] **VT 1** *(surestimer) (biens)* to overestimate, to overvalue **2** *(augmenter) (facture)* to put a surcharge *or* an additional charge on; *(prix)* to raise, to put up, to increase; *(pour faire plus de bénéfices)* to mark up; *(salaires)* to increase; **m. les prix de dix pour cent** to raise *or* put up *or* increase prices by ten per cent; **m. une facture de dix pour cent** to put a surcharge of ten per cent on an invoice, to increase an invoice by ten per cent

majorette [maʒɔrɛt] **NF** (drum) majorette

majoritaire [maʒɔritɛr] **ADJ** majority; *Pol* **vote/parti m.** majority vote/party; *Fin* **actionnaire m.** majority shareholder, *Am* majority stockholder; **être majoritaires** to be in the *or* a majority; **c'est un métier où les hommes ont toujours été largement majoritaires** it's a profession where men have always been in a large majority *or* where there has always been a large majority of men; **il a une participation m. dans la société** he has a majority interest *or* shareholding in the company

N *Pol* member of the majority (party); *Fin* majority shareholder *or Am* stockholder

majorité [maʒɔrite] **NF 1** *(supériorité en nombre)* majority; **la m. silencieuse** the silent majority; **la m. des personnes interrogées …** the majority of (the) people *or* most of the people questioned …; **être en m.**, **avoir la m.** to be in a *or* the majority; **les citoyens pensent en m. que …** the majority of citizens *or* most citizens think that …; **dans la m. des cas** in the majority of cases, in most cases; **nous sommes une m. à vouloir combattre ce fléau** the *or* a majority of us want to fight against this scourge VOIR GRAMMAIRE A11

2 *(dans des élections)* majority; **remporter la m. des suffrages** to win a *or* the majority of the votes, to win a majority; **élu avec dix voix de m.** elected by a majority of ten; **m. relative/absolue** relative/absolute majority; **m. qualifiée** qualified majority; **m. simple** simple majority; **décision prise à la m. (des voix)** decision taken by a majority, majority decision

3 *Parl (parti)* majority party; **m. gouvernementale** parliamentary majority; **être dans la m.** to be a member of the majority party; **m. parlementaire** legislative majority; **m. plurielle** plural majority

4 *Jur* majority, coming of age; **atteindre la m.** to come of age, to attain one's majority; **m. légale** (minimum) voting age; **m. pénale** = minimum age in law at which a person is deemed capable of distinguishing between right and wrong

Majorque [maʒɔrk] **NF** Majorca

majorquin, -ine [maʒɔrkɛ̃, -in] **ADJ** Majorcan

N M. Majorcan

majuscule [maʒyskyl] **ADJ** *(lettre)* capital, upper-case; **les lettres majuscules** upper-case letters

NF capital (letter); *Typ* upper-case letter; **en majuscules** in capitals; **majuscules** caps; **majuscules d'imprimerie** block letters, block capitals

majuscule-clic, *pl* **majuscules-clics NM** *Ordinat* shift-click

majuscule-glisser, *pl* **majuscules-glisser NM** *Ordinat* shift-drag

making-of [mekinɳɔv] **NM** *Cin* featurette

MAL¹, *pl* **maux** [mal, mo]

pain **1** • harm **2** • evil **3** • difficulty **4**	

NM 1 *(douleur, sensation désagréable)* pain, ache; *(maladie)* illness, sickness; **souffrir d'horribles maux de ventre** to suffer from *or* to have terrible stomach pains; *Fam* **prendre** *ou* **attraper (du) m.** to catch cold, to catch a chill; **avoir m. à l'estomac/à la tête/au dos** to have stomach ache *or* a sore stomach/a headache *or* a sore head/backache *or* a sore back; **avoir m. à la gorge/au bras** to have a sore throat/arm; **avoir m. aux dents** to have toothache; *Fam* **avoir m. aux cheveux** to have a hangover; **où avez-vous m.?** where does it hurt?, where is the pain?; **vous me faites (du) m.** you're hurting me; **mon genou me fait m.** my knee hurts; **se faire m.** to hurt oneself; **spectacle qui fait m. (au cœur** *ou* **au ventre)** painful sight; **ça fait m. au ventre de voir des choses pareilles!** it makes you sick *or* it's sickening to see things like that!; *Fig* **ça me ferait m. (au ventre)!** it would make me sick!; *très Fam* **ça me ferait m. aux seins!** it would really piss me off!; *Fam* **tu vas lui prêter ta robe? – ça me ferait m.!** are you going to lend her your dress? – no way!; **être un m. de qch** to be yearning *or* desperate for sth, to be badly in need of sth; **je ne me laisserai pas calomnier par des journalistes en m. de copie** I'm not going to be slandered by journalists with nothing better to write about *or* who are short of copy; **femme en m. d'enfants** woman desperate for children *or* to have children

2 *(préjudice, tort, souffrance)* harm, hurt; **faire du m.** to do harm; **faire du m. à qn** to harm sb, to do sb harm; **ne bougez pas et aucun m. ne vous sera fait** don't move and nobody will get hurt; **allez, un p'tit coup de gnôle, ça n'a jamais fait de m. à personne!** go on, a little tipple never did anyone any harm!; **mettre qch à m.** to damage sth; *Fig Vieilli* **il avait mis à m. toutes les servantes** he had ravished all the maidservants; **il fait plus de bruit que de m.** *(chien, personne)* his bark is worse than his bite; **s'en tirer sans aucun m.** to escape uninjured *or* unhurt *or* unscathed; **il ne ferait pas de m. à une mouche** he wouldn't hurt a fly; **je ne lui veux pas de m.** I mean him no harm; **cela fera plus de m. que de bien** it will do more harm than good; **le m. est fait** the harm *or* damage has been done; *Prov* **aux grands maux les grands remèdes** desperate situations call for desperate remedies; **souffrir de trois grands maux** to suffer from three great evils; **entre deux maux il faut choisir le moindre** you have to choose the lesser of two evils; **entre deux maux j'ai choisi le moindre** it was the lesser of two evils; **un m. nécessaire** a necessary evil; **il n'y a pas de m. à cela** there's no harm in that; **quel m. y a-t-il à cela?** what harm can that do?, what harm is there in it?; *Fam* **il n'y a pas de m. (à qn qui s'excuse)** there's no harm done; **m. lui en a pris** he has had cause to regret it *or* to rue it; **dire du m. de qn, parler en m. de qn** to speak ill of sb; **il a changé en m.** he has changed for the worse

3 *(contraire au bien)* wrong; *(vice)* evil; *(mauvaises actions)* wrongdoing; **le bien et le m.** right and wrong, good and evil; **faire la différence entre le bien et le m.** to know the difference between right and wrong; **rendre le m. pour le m.** to answer evil with evil, to render evil for evil; **il ne pense pas à m.** he doesn't mean any harm; **voir le m. partout** to see bad in everything; *Rel* **délivre-nous du m.** deliver us from evil; **les forces du m.** the forces of evil; **faire le m.** to do evil

4 *(difficulté)* non sans m. not without difficulty; **se donner du m. pour faire qch** to go to a lot of trouble to do sth, to take pains to do sth; **je me suis vraiment donné du m. pour que la soirée soit réussie** I really went to a lot of trouble *or* I took great pains to make the party a success; **je me suis donné beaucoup de m. pour faire cette traduction** I worked really hard on this translation; *Fam* **se donner un m. de chien** to go to a hell of a lot of trouble; **donner du m. à qn** to give sb (some) trouble; **avoir du m. à faire qch** to have difficulty *or* trouble (in) doing sth; **avoir le plus grand m. à faire qch** to have the utmost *or* a great deal of difficulty doing sth; **avoir de plus en plus de m. à faire qch** to find it harder and harder to do sth; **tu ne peux pas savoir le m. que j'ai eu pour trouver cet objet** you don't know the trouble I've had finding this thing; *Fam* **avoir un m. de chien à faire qch** to have a hell of a job to do sth; **prendre son m. en patience** to try to put up with it, to be patient; **on n'a rien sans m.** you don't get anything easily

▶ ▶ m. de l'air airsickness; **avoir le m. de l'air** to be airsick; **m. blanc** whitlow; **m. de cœur** sickness, nausea; **m. de dents** toothache; **m. de gorge** sore throat; **m. de mer** seasickness; **avoir le m. de mer** to be seasick; **m. des montagnes** altitude sickness; *Arch* **m. napolitain** pox; **m. du pays** homesickness; **avoir le m. du pays** to be homesick; **m. des rayons** radiation sickness; **m. de la route** carsickness; **avoir le m. de la route** to be carsick; *Litt* **m. du siècle** world-weariness; **la dépression est le nouveau m. du siècle** depression is the new scourge of the century; **m. de tête** headache; **m. des transports** travelsickness; **m. de vivre** weariness with life; **avoir le m. de vivre** to be tired of life

MAL²

badly **1** • poorly **1** • ill **2** • wrong **4** • bad **4**	

ADV 1 *(jouer, nager, traiter qn, se conduire etc)* badly; *(payer)* poorly, badly; **tout cela finira m.** it will all end in tears; **leur histoire a m. fini** their story had a sad *or* an unhappy ending; **je n'aime pas ce livre, il finit m.** I don't like this book, it's got a sad *or* an unhappy ending; **si tu crois qu'elle va accepter, c'est m. la connaître!** if you think she's going to say yes, you don't know her very well!; **tout va m. en ce moment** everything's going wrong at the moment; **je dors très m. en ce moment** I'm sleeping very badly *or* I'm not sleeping at all well just now; **qu'est-ce qu'on mange m. ici** the food's really bad here; **cette cafetière verse m.** this coffee pot doesn't pour properly; **m. à l'aise** ill at ease; **vous avez m. agi** you did wrong, you acted badly; **je ne pensais pas m. faire** I didn't think I was doing anything wrong; **il se tient m. à table** he has bad table manners; **redresse-toi, tu te tiens m.** straighten up, you're not standing/sitting properly; *Prov* **bien m. acquis ne profite jamais** nobody ever profits by ill-gotten gains; **cette robe lui va m.** that dress doesn't suit her; **ça lui va m. de traiter les autres de paresseux** he's got a nerve calling other people lazy; **travail m. fait** badly done work, shoddy work; **tant bien que m.** as best one can/could; *(réussir)* after a fashion; **on a tout rangé tant bien que m.** we tidied everything up as best we could; **aller de m. en pis** to go from bad to worse; **s'y prendre m.** to go about it the wrong way; **s'y prendre**

m. avec qn to handle sb the wrong way; **tu t'y es m. pris pour assembler la bibliothèque** you've gone the wrong way about assembling the bookcase; **m. choisir** to make the wrong choice, to choose wrongly; **tu as m. choisi ton jour pour te plaindre** you've chosen the wrong day to complain; **m. tourner** *(d'une situation)* to turn sour; *(d'une dispute)* to turn ugly; *(d'une personne)* to go to the dogs; **avoir l'esprit m. tourné** to have a dirty or one-track mind; **m. comprendre** to misunderstand; **m. interpréter qch** to misinterpret sth, to misconstrue sth; **on voit m. d'ici** you can't see (very) well or properly from here; **on voit m. comment …** it's difficult or not easy to see how …; **m. informé** ill-informed; **m. embouché** foul-mouthed; **m. famé** disreputable, of ill repute; **il a très m. pris la chose, il l'a très m. pris** *(cela l'a blessé, chagriné, irrité)* he took it very badly; **se mettre m. avec qn** *(se brouiller)* to fall out with sb; *Fam* **être m. avec qn** to be on bad terms with sb; **vous ne feriez peut-être pas m. de …** it wouldn't be a bad thing (if you were) to …, it might not be a bad idea to …

2 *(en mauvaise santé)* **se sentir m.** to feel ill; *(avoir la nausée)* to feel sick; *(sur le point de s'évanouir)* to feel faint; **se trouver m.** to faint; **aller ou se porter m.** to be in poor health, to be ill; **être au plus m.** to be critically ill or at death's door; **elle est ou elle va très m.** she's in a very bad way

3 *(une certaine quantité)* **pas m. (de qch)** quite a lot (of sth); **il (n')y en a pas m.** there is quite a lot of it/there are quite a lot of them; **cela m'a pris pas m. de temps** it took me quite a time, it took me a fair time

4 *(avec fonction adjectivale)* **vous savez ce qui est bien et ce qui est m.** you know what's right and what's wrong, you know the difference between right and wrong; **c'est très m. de faire ça** *(en parlant à un enfant)* it's very naughty to do that; **c'est pas m.** it's not bad, it's quite good; **ce n'était pas m. du tout** it wasn't at all bad; **elle n'est pas m.** she's quite good-looking; **qu'est-ce que tu penses de ce pull? – pas m.** what do you think of this pullover? – it's not bad or it's OK; *Fam* **il déconne pas m. en ce moment** he's really arsing about at the moment; **nous ne sommes pas m. ici** we're quite comfortable or not badly off here

---

malabar [malabar] NM *Fam* hulk

malachite [malakit] NF *Minér* malachite

malade [malad] ADJ **1** *(souffrant)* *(personne)* ill, *Am* sick, unwell, *Fam* poorly; *(organe)* diseased; *(dent)* bad; *(jambe)* bad, *Fam* gammy; *Fig (industrie)* ailing; **tomber m.** to fall or be taken ill; **m. de la fièvre typhoïde** ill with typhoid; **être m. d'inquiétude/de jalousie** to be sick with worry/jealousy; **il a été m. comme un chien** ou **une bête** he was as sick as a dog; *très Fam* **j'ai été m. à crever** I was horribly or dreadfully ill; **être m. du cœur, avoir le cœur m.** to have heart trouble, to have a bad heart; **être m. de l'estomac, avoir l'estomac m.** to have stomach trouble; **ça me rend m. de le voir gâcher sa vie** it makes me sick to see him waste his life; *Fam* **il en est m.** he feels sick or he's sick about it; **à l'idée de le voir demain, j'en suis m.** I feel or I'm sick at the thought of seeing him tomorrow; *Mil etc* **se faire porter m.** to report or go sick **2** *(fou)* mad, crazy; **esprit m.** sick or unhealthy mind; *Fam* **t'es pas un peu m.?** are you right in the head?, are you off your rocker?

N **1** *Méd* patient; **un grand m.** a seriously ill person; **un m. mental** a mentally ill or sick person; *(dans un hôpital)* a mental patient; **les malades** the sick; **m. imaginaire** hypochondriac; **faire le m.** to pretend to be ill, to malinger **2** *(mentalement)* **c'est un m.** he's mentally ill; *Fam* **c'est un m., ce mec!** that

guy isn't right in the head!; *Fam* **comme un m.** *(travailler, courir, pousser)* like mad or crazy; *(conduire)* like a lunatic or a madman; *Fam* **un m. de Schubert/de ski** a Schubert/skiing fanatic; *Fam* **c'est un m. des films de Fellini/de la bouffe indienne** he's mad about Fellini's films/Indian food

maladie [maladi] NF **1** illness, disease; **c'est une petite m.** it's just a minor illness; **m. bénigne** minor illness; **m. grave** serious illness; **m. émergente** new disease; **m. mortelle** fatal illness or disease; **m. contagieuse** contagious disease or illness; **m. mentale** mental illness; **attraper une m.** to catch a disease; **cet hiver, le petit nous a fait toutes les maladies** this winter, our little boy's had all the diseases under the sun; **maladies des plantes** plant diseases; **par suite de m.** through illness; **congé de m.** sick leave; *Fig Fam* **il en fait une m.** he's making a song and dance about it; *Fam* **c'est quoi, cette m. de toujours tout critiquer?** what's with this mania for or obsession with criticizing everything?; *Fam* **c'est une m. chez toi, le piment/le foot** chilli's/football's an obsession with you VOIR GRAMMAIRE A10 **2** *Vét (des chiens)* (canine) distemper

▸▸ **m. d'Alzheimer** Alzheimer's (disease); **m. de Basedow** Graves' or Basedow's disease; **m. bleue** blue disease; **m. de Carré** (canine) distemper; **m. du charbon** anthrax; **m. des chiens** (canine) distemper; **m. de cœur** heart complaint or disease; **m. de Crohn** Crohn's disease; **m. cutanée** skin disease; **m. de foie** liver complaint or disease; **m. de Hodgkin** Hodgkin's disease; *Vieilli* **m. honteuse** venereal disease; **m. infantile** childhood illness; **m. du légionnaire** legionnaire's disease; **m. orpheline** orphan disease or illness; **m. de Parkinson** Parkinson's (disease); **m. de peau** skin disease; **m. professionnelle** occupational illness; **m. sexuellement transmissible** sexually transmitted disease; **m. du sommeil** sleeping sickness; *Vét* **m. de la vache folle** mad cow disease; **m. vénérienne** venereal disease

maladif, -ive [maladif, -iv] ADJ *(enfant)* sickly; *(curiosité, pensées)* morbid, unhealthy; **elle était d'une pâleur maladive** she was unhealthily pale; **sa maniaquerie est presque maladive** his fussiness is almost pathological; **être d'une jalousie maladive** to be pathologically jealous; **la propreté, chez lui, c'est m.** cleanliness is an obsession with him

maladivement [maladivmã] ADV *(jaloux)* pathologically; *(inquiet, ordonné)* obsessively

maladresse [maladrɛs] NF *(inhabileté)* clumsiness, awkwardness; *(manque de tact)* tactlessness; *(bévue, impair)* blunder; **quelle m. de lui avoir dit que tu n'aimais pas sa robe** how tactless of you to tell her that you didn't like her dress; **il y a quelques maladresses de style** there are a few awkward or clumsy turns of phrase

maladroit, -oite [maladrwa, -wat] ADJ *(inhabile)* clumsy, awkward; *(qui manque de tact)* tactless

N *(personne inhabile)* awkward or clumsy person; *(personne sans tact)* tactless person

maladroitement [maladrwatmã] ADV *(de façon gauche)* clumsily; *(sans tact)* tactlessly

mal-aimé, -ée N unpopular person; **il a toujours été le m. de la famille** he's always been the black sheep or misfit of the family

malais, -aise [malɛ, -ɛz] ADJ Malaysian, Malay(an)

NM *Ling* Malay

N **M.** Malaysian, Malay(an)

malaise [malɛz] NM **1** *(moral)* uneasiness, discomfort; *(social, politique)* unrest; **sa re-**

marque a provoqué un certain m. his remark aroused a certain uneasiness; **sentiment de m.** uneasy feeling, feeling of unease; *Fam* **il y a comme un m.** there's a bit of a snag or a hitch **2** *(physique)* feeling of sickness or ill-health; *(étourdissement)* dizzy spell; **avoir un m.** to feel faint

malaisé [malɛze] ADJ difficult; **certains auteurs sont d'une traduction malaisée** certain authors are difficult to translate

malaisément [malɛzemã] ADV with difficulty

Malaisie [malɛzi] NF Malaysia

malandrin [malãdrɛ̃] NM *Vieilli, Litt* brigand, robber

malappris, -ise [malapri, -iz] *Vieilli* ADJ uncouth, ill-bred, loutish

N uncouth or ill-bred person, lout

malard [malar] NM drake

malaria [malarja] NF malaria

malavenant, -ante [malavənã] *Can* ADJ *(désagréable)* unpleasant; *(hargneux)* grumpy; *(peu serviable)* disobliging

N *(personne désagréable)* unpleasant person; *(personne hargneuse)* grump, grumpy person; *(personne peu serviable)* disobliging person

malavisé [malavize] ADJ *Vieilli, Litt (action)* ill-advised, unwise; *(personne)* unwise, injudicious; **être m. de faire qch** to be ill-advised or unwise to do sth

Malawi [malawi] Malawi

malaxage [malaksaʒ] NM *(de pâte, d'argile)* kneading; *(de beurre)* creaming; *(de ciment)* mixing

malaxer [malakse] VT *(pâte, argile)* to knead; *(beurre)* to cream; *(ciment)* to mix

malaxeur [malaksœr] NM mixer, mixing machine; *(pour beurre)* butter creamer; *(pour ciment)* cement mixer

mal-baisée [malbɛze] NF *Vulg* **c'est une m.** she needs a good fuck

malbouffe [malbuf] NF *Fam* junk

malchance [malʃãs] NF **1** *(guigne)* bad luck, ill luck; **par m.** as ill luck would have it; **vous jouez de m.** you're not having much luck **2** *(mésaventure)* mishap, misfortune

malchanceux, -euse [malʃãsø, -øz] ADJ unlucky

N unlucky person

malcommode [malkɔmɔd] ADJ *(appareil)* impractical; *(vêtement)* unsuitable

Maldives [maldiv] NFPL **les (îles) M.** the Maldives

maldonne [maldɔn] NF *Cartes* misdeal; **faire (une) m.** to misdeal; *Fig Fam* **il y a m.** something's gone wrong somewhere

mâle [mɑl] ADJ **1** *Biol* male; *(oiseau)* cock; *(lapin, lièvre, antilope)* buck; *(renard, loup)* dog; *(éléphant)* bull; **un ours m.** a he-bear; **héritier m.** male heir **2** *(courage, assurance)* manly; *(style)* virile **3** *Élec* male; **prise m.** plug; *Tech* **pièce m.** male component

NM male; **un beau m.** *(animal)* a beautiful male specimen; *Hum (homme)* a real hunk

Il faut noter qu'en anglais le terme **male** signifie également **masculin**.

malédiction [malediksjɔ̃] NF *Litt (imprécation)* curse, *Fml* malediction; **une m. pèse sur elle** she is under a curse, a curse is hanging over her

INT *Vieilli* **m.! nous sommes enfermés** cursed! or curse it! we're locked in

maléfice [malefis] NM evil spell

maléfique [malefik] ADJ *Litt* maleficent; *(étoile)* unlucky; *(influence, pouvoirs)* evil

malencontreusement [malãkɔ̃trøzmã] ADV unfortunately

malencontreux, -euse [malɑ̃kɔ̃trø, -øz] ADJ (événement, remarque) unfortunate, untoward; **par un hasard m.** by a stroke of bad luck

malengueulé, -ée [malɑ̃gøle] Can ADJ Fam vulgar, uncouth
   N Fam vulgar or uncouth person

mal(-)en(-)point [malɑ̃pwɛ̃] ADJ INV in a bad way; **être très/un peu m.** to be in a very bad/a bit of a bad way

malentendant, -ante [malɑ̃tɑ̃dɑ̃, -ɑ̃t] N person who is hard of hearing, hearing-impaired person; **les malentendants** the hard of hearing, the hearing-impaired
   ADJ enfant m. child who is hard of hearing, hearing-impaired child

malentendu [malɑ̃tɑ̃dy] NM misunderstanding, Fml misapprehension

mal-en-train [malɑ̃trɛ̃] ADJ Can unwell, Br poorly; **avoir l'air m.** to look peaky or out-of-sorts

mal-être NM INV malaise

malfaçon [malfasɔ̃] NF (défaut) defect

malfaisance [malfəzɑ̃s] NF Litt maleficence, evil-mindedness

malfaisant [malfəzɑ̃] ADJ (personne) evil-minded, harmful; (influence) evil, harmful; (propos) harmful

malfaiteur, -trice [malfɛtœr, -tris] N criminal, lawbreaker, Litt wrongdoer, Fml, Vieilli malefactor; **un dangereux m.** a dangerous criminal; **association de malfaiteurs** criminal conspiracy

malfamé [malfame] ADJ disreputable

malformation [malfɔrmasjɔ̃] NF malformation

malfrat [malfra] NM Fam crook

malgache [malgaʃ] ADJ Madagascan, Malagasy
   NM Ling Malagasy
   N M. Madagascan, Malagasy

malgracieux, -ieuse [malgrasjø, -jøz] ADJ 1 Vieilli (qui manque de politesse) ungracious, churlish, rude 2 Litt (qui manque d'élégance) inelegant, ungainly, clumsy

malgré [malgre] PRÉP in spite of, despite, Fml notwithstanding; **m. tout** in spite of or despite everything; (pourtant) all the same, nevertheless; **m. sa fortune** for all his wealth; **je l'ai fait m. moi** I did it in spite of myself or against my better judgment
   CONJ (seulement dans **m. que j'en aie/que tu en aies/etc) m. que vous en ayez** whether you like it or not

malhabile [malabil] ADJ clumsy, awkward; **mains malhabiles** unskilled hands

malhabilement [malabilmɑ̃] ADV clumsily, awkwardly

MALHEUR [malœr]

| misfortune 1, 2 ▪ accident 1 |
| ▪ adversity 2 ▪ bad luck 3 |

NM 1 (drame, catastrophe) misfortune; (accident) (serious) accident; **la disparition de sa femme a été son plus grand m.** the death of his wife was the greatest misfortune ever to afflict him; **depuis quelques années, je n'ai que des malheurs** for some years now I've had nothing but misfortune; **ils ont eu des malheurs** they have been through difficult times; **il n'arrête pas de me raconter ses petits malheurs** he's forever telling me (about) all his petty cares and woes; Prov **un m. n'arrive ou ne vient jamais seul** misfortunes never come singly, it never rains but it pours; **un m. est si vite arrivé** accidents happen so easily; **l'argent qu'il met de côté en cas de m.** the money he puts aside just in case something should happen; **quel m.!** what a

tragedy!; **le m., c'est que ...** the unfortunate thing is that ...; Prov **à quelque chose m. est bon** it's an ill wind that blows nobody any good; Fam **je crois qu'on va déménager à Londres – parle pas de m.!** I think we're moving to London – God forbid!; **faire un m.** (tuer qn) to commit murder; Fam **s'il entre ici, je fais un m.!** if he comes in here, I'll say something I'll regret!; Fam **sa nouvelle pièce a fait un m.** his latest play was a big hit; Fam **les pantalons pattes d'éléphant font un m. en France** bell-bottomed trousers are all the rage in France

2 (chagrin, infortune) adversity, misfortune; **ils sont dans le m.** they are going through hard times; **il est resté très digne dans le m.** he remained very dignified in (his) adversity; **c'est dans le m. qu'on reconnaît ses amis** it's when things are going badly that you find out who your friends are; Prov **à friend in need is a friend indeed; enfant qui fait le m. de ses parents** child who brings sorrow to his parents; Prov **le m. des uns fait le bonheur des autres** one man's joy is another man's sorrow

3 (malchance) bad luck, ill luck; **par m.** unfortunately; **quel m. que je ne l'aie pas su** what a pity I didn't know (about it); **je le connais pour mon m.** unfortunately for me or unluckily for me, I know him; **porter m. à qn** to bring sb bad luck; **ceux qui ont le m. de le connaître** those who are unfortunate or unlucky enough to know him; **j'ai eu le m. de lui dire que je n'étais pas d'accord avec lui** I made the (big) mistake of telling him that I didn't agree with him; **jouer de m.** to be unlucky or out of luck; Fam **ces lettres de m.!** these blasted letters!; **m. à eux!** woe betide them!
   INT hell!

malheureusement [malœrøzmɑ̃] ADV unfortunately

malheureux, -euse [malœrø, -øz] ADJ 1 (triste) (personne, enfance) unhappy, miserable; (expression, air, regard) unhappy, sad, miserable; (affaire) unfortunate, unhappy; **m. comme les pierres** wretched, utterly miserable 2 (malchanceux) (personne) unlucky; (candidat) unsuccessful, unlucky; (tentative) unsuccessful; **avoir la main malheureuse** to be unlucky; **m. au jeu** unlucky at gambling; Prov **heureux au jeu, m. en amour** lucky at cards, unlucky in love; **amour m.** unrequited love; **amours malheureuses** unhappy love affairs 3 (regrettable) (geste, mot) unfortunate; **c'est bien m. pour vous!** it's hard for you!; **il est bien m. que ...** + subj it's very unfortunate or a great pity that ...; Fam **si ça n'est ou très Fam si c'est pas m. tout de même de voir ces enfants obligés de travailler!** it's such a terrible pity or shame to see these children having to work!; Fam **le voilà enfin, ce n'est pas m.!** here he comes at last, and a good job too! 4 Fam (négligeable) miserable, wretched, paltry; **tout ça pour une malheureuse faute!** all that because of a stupid little mistake!
   N **les m.** the poor, the needy; **une famille de m.** a poor family; **le m.!/la malheureuse!** poor man/woman!, poor wretch!; **m.! qu'avez-vous fait?** you wretch! what have you done?

malhonnête [malɔnɛt] ADJ 1 (employé, commerçant etc) dishonest, Fam crooked; **des procédés malhonnêtes** underhand or dishonest methods 2 Vieilli (impoli) (personne) rude, impolite 3 Vieilli (indécent) (geste) indecent; (suggestion) improper

malhonnêtement [malɔnɛtmɑ̃] ADV dishonestly

malhonnêteté [malɔnɛtte] NF 1 dishonesty; **la m. de ses procédés** the underhanded-

ness or the dishonesty of his methods 2 Vieilli (manque de politesse) rudeness, impoliteness; (remarque impolie) rude remark

Mali [mali] NM Mali

malice [malis] NF 1 (ruse, espièglerie) mischief, mischievousness, roguishness; **plein de m.** full of mischief, mischievous; **la m. de ses réflexions** the mischievousness of his remarks 2 Vieilli (méchanceté) malice, spitefulness; **ne pas entendre m. à qch** (ne voir rien de mal à qch) to see no harm in sth; (ne pas avoir l'intention de faire du mal) to mean no harm by sth; **il ne faut pas y entendre m.** he/she/etc didn't mean any harm; **être sans m.** to be harmless 3 sac/boîte à malices bag/box of tricks

---
Il faut noter que le terme anglais **malice** est un faux ami. Il signifie **méchanceté** ou **préméditation**, selon le contexte.
---

malicieusement [malisjøzmɑ̃] ADV mischievously

malicieux, -ieuse [malisjø, -jøz] ADJ 1 (espiègle) (personne, sourire, remarque) mischievous, roguish, impish; (solution) clever, smart 2 Vieilli (méchant) malicious

---
Il faut noter que l'adjectif anglais **malicious** est un faux ami. Il signifie **méchant**.
---

malien, -ienne [maljɛ̃, -jɛn] ADJ Malian
   N M. Malian

malignement [maliɲmɑ̃] ADV maliciously

malignité [maliɲite] NF 1 malice, spite(fulness) 2 Méd (d'une maladie, d'une tumeur) malignancy

malin, -igne [malɛ̃, -iɲ] ADJ 1 (espiègle, futé) shrewd, cunning, crafty; **regard m.** knowing look; **il est plus m. que ça** he knows better; **est m. comme un singe** he's a crafty devil; (d'un enfant) he's a little monkey; **elle n'est pas bien maligne** ou Fam maline she's not very clever or not all that bright; **ce n'est pas la peine de jouer au plus m.** there's no point in trying to outwit or outsmart each other; **bien m. qui le trouvera!** it will take a smart one to find that!; **tu te crois m.?** do you think you're clever?; **ce n'était pas très m. (de ta part)** that wasn't very bright, was it?; Iron **c'est m.! tu as tout gâché!** that was clever! now you've spoiled everything!; Fam **c'est pas bien m.!** that's dead easy!, that's simple! 2 (plaisir, joie) malicious; Arch (influence) malignant, evil; **l'esprit m.** the Evil One, the Devil; **éprouver un m. plaisir à faire souffrir qn** to take a sadistic or malicious pleasure in making sb suffer 3 Méd (cancer) malignant
   N **c'est un m.** he has his wits about him, Fam he knows what's what; **un petit m.** a crafty one, Péj a smart Aleck; **c'est une petite maligne** ou Fam maline she's a sly one, she's a little imp; **faire le m.** to show off, to try to be smart; Iron **gros m.!** smarty-pants!, smart Aleck!, Br clever Dick!; Prov **à m., m. et demi** there's always somebody cleverer than you
   NM **le M.** the Evil One, the Devil

malingre [malɛ̃gr] ADJ (personne, corps) puny

malintentionné [malɛ̃tɑ̃sjɔne] ADJ (personne) ill-intentioned

mal-jugé, pl mal-jugés [malʒyʒe] NM Jur miscarriage of justice

malle [mal] NF 1 (valise) trunk, Vieilli box; **faire sa m. ou ses malles** to pack (one's trunk); Fam **se faire la m.** to clear off, Br to scarper, Br to do a runner 2 Aut boot, Am trunk; **m. arrière** luggage compartment, load area 3 Hist (voiture de la poste) mail coach; **la m. des Indes** the Indian mail 4 Can mettre une lettre à la m. to mail or Br post a letter

malléabilité [maleabilite] NF malleability

malléable [maleabl] ADJ malleable

malle-poste, pl **malles-poste** NF Hist (voiture de la poste) mail coach

mallette [malɛt] NF 1 overnight bag; (valise) small (suit)case; (porte-documents) attaché case, briefcase; **une m. en osier** a wicker (picnic) basket **2** Belg (musette d'ouvrier) (canvas) haversack; (sacoche) bag; (cartable d'écolier) satchel

mal-logé, -ée, pl **mal-logés, -ées** [maloʒe] N **les mal-logés** = person living in inadequate housing conditions

malmener [malmǝne] VT (conj like **mener**) (brutaliser) (personne) to manhandle, to treat roughly; Fig (en paroles) to run down; (objet) to handle or treat roughly; **il malmène sa voiture** he's really rough with his car; **il a été malmené par la critique** he was slated by the critics; **notre équipe a été malmenée durant tout le match** our team was given a rough time or ride all through the match; **m. la grammaire** to misuse grammar, to make grammatical mistakes

malnutrition [malnytrisjɔ̃] NF malnutrition

malodorant [malɔdɔrã] ADJ foul-smelling, smelly, Fml malodorous

malotru, -ue [malɔtry] N lout, Br yob

malouin, -ine [malwɛ̃, -in] ADJ of/from Saint-Malo

N **M.** (natif) native of Saint-Malo; (habitant) inhabitant of Saint-Malo

Malouines [malwin] NFPL **les (îles) M.** the Falkland Islands, the Falklands; **la guerre des M.** the Falklands War or conflict; **un habitant des îles M.** a Falkland Islander

malpoli, -ie [malpɔli] Fam ADJ rude, impolite N rude or impolite person; **petit m.** rude or impolite (little) boy

malpropre [malprɔpr] ADJ **1** (sale) (mains) dirty, grubby; (apparence) slovenly, untidy; (travail) slovenly, slipshod **2** (inconvenant) (histoire, attitude etc) smutty **3** (malhonnête) (individu, conduite etc) despicable

N **se faire traiter comme un m.** to be treated like dirt; **se faire renvoyer comme un m.** to be sent packing

malproprement [malprɔprǝmã] ADV (manger) messily; (se conduire) despicably

malpropreté [malprɔprǝte] NF dirtiness; Fig (d'histoire) smuttiness

malsain [malsɛ̃] ADJ (maladif) (personne) unhealthy(-looking); (dangereux pour la santé) (nourriture) unhealthy, unwholesome; (climat, maison) unhealthy; (pernicieux) (littérature, atmosphère etc) unhealthy, unwholesome; (personne) unwholesome; (curiosité, attitude) unhealthy; **c'est très m. de vivre près des marécages** it's very unhealthy to live close to marshland; Fig **ça devient m. par ici** things are or it's looking a bit dodgy round here

malséant [malseã] ADJ Litt unseemly, unbecoming; **il serait tout à fait m. que tu m'accompagnes** it would be quite unseemly or unbecoming for you to accompany me

malsonnant [malsɔnã] ADJ offensive; (malséant) unseemly

malt [malt] NM malt

maltage [maltaʒ] NM (procédé) malting

maltais, -aise [maltɛ, -ɛz] ADJ Maltese NM Ling Maltese N **M.** Maltese

Malte [malt] NF Malta; **croix de M.** Maltese cross

malter [malte] VT (houblon) to malt

malterie [maltəri] NF (usine) malt house, malting

malthusianisme [maltyzjanism] NM Malthusianism

malthusien, -ienne [maltyzjɛ̃, -jɛn] ADJ, N Malthusian

maltose [maltoz] NM Chimie, Ind maltose

maltraitance [maltrɛtãs] NF ill-treatment, abuse

maltraiter [maltrete] VT **1** (brutaliser) to maltreat, to mistreat, to handle or treat roughly; **enfants maltraités** abused or maltreated children **2** (en paroles) to run down; **il a été maltraité par la critique** he was slated by the critics **3** (grammaire, langue) to misuse

malus [malys] NM (assurance) loss of no-claims bonus

malveillance [malvɛjãs] NF (hostilité, animosité) spite, malice, malevolence; **avec m.** spitefully, maliciously, malevolently; **un incident dû à la m.** malicious incident

malveillant [malvɛjã] ADJ spiteful, malicious, malevolent

malvenu [malvǝny] ADJ **1** (déplacé) out of place, inappropriate; **elle serait malvenue de se plaindre** she's scarcely in a position to complain; **il serait tout à fait m. de le critiquer** it would be quite inappropriate to criticize him **2** (mal développé) (plante) malformed

malversation [malvɛrsasjɔ̃] NF malversation(s) misappropriation of funds, embezzlement

malvoisie [malvwazi] NM **m., vin de M.** malmsey (wine)

maman [mamã] NF mum(my), Am mom; **les mamans regardent** the mothers or mums or moms are watching

mambo [mãmbo] NM mambo

mamelle [mamɛl] NF **1** (de vache) udder; (de chienne, truie etc) teat, dug; Prov **labourage et pâturage sont les deux mamelles de la France** ploughing and grazing are the lifeblood of France **2** Anat, Vieilli (sein) breast; **enfant à la m.** child at the breast

mamelon [mamlɔ̃] NM **1** Anat (de femme) nipple **2** Géog hillock, knoll

mamelonné [mamlɔne] ADJ (paysage) hillocky

mamel(o)uk [mamluk] NM Hist Mameluke

m'amie, mamie[1] [mami] NF Fam Arch (mon amie) my dear

mamie[2] NF Fam **1** (grand-mère) gran(ny) **2** (vieille dame) old lady

mamillaire [mamilɛr] ADJ Anat mamillary

mammaire [mamɛr] ADJ mammary

mammalogie [mamalɔʒi] NF mammalogy

mammectomie [mamɛktɔmi] NF Méd mastectomy

mammifère [mamifɛr] ADJ mammalian NM mammal

mammographie [mamɔɡrafi] NF Méd mammography

mammouth [mamut] NM mammoth

mamours [mamur] NMPL Fam **faire des m. à qn** to caress or fondle sb

mam'selle, mam'zelle [mamzɛl] NF Fam miss

MAN [ɛmaɛn] N Can Pol (abrév **Membre de l'Assemblée Nationale**) MNA

manade [manad] NF (dans le dialecte provençal) (taureaux) herd of bulls; (chevaux) herd of horses

management [manadʒmɛnt] NM management

manager[1], **manageur** [manadʒɛr] NM Ind, Sp etc manager; Cin, Théâtre agent

manager[2] [mana(d)ʒe] VT to manage

managérial [manaʒerjal] ADJ managerial

manant [manã] NM **1** Hist (villageois) villager; (paysan) peasant **2** Litt (mufle) churl, boor

manceau, -elle [mãso, -ɛl] ADJ of/from Le Mans

N **M.** (natif) native of Le Mans; (habitant) inhabitant of Le Mans

manche[1] [mãʃ] NF **1** (de vêtement) sleeve; **manches longues/courtes** long/short sleeves; **robe sans manches** sleeveless dress; **être en manches de chemise** to be in one's shirtsleeves; **relever ou retrousser ses manches** to roll up one's sleeves; Fig to roll up one's sleeves, to get down to work; Fig **avoir qn dans sa m.** to have sb in one's pocket; Fam **ça, c'est une autre paire de manches** that's quite another matter, that's a different kettle of fish; Fam **faire la m.** to busk **2** Aviat (de ballon) neck **3** (en athlétisme) heat; Boxe round; Tennis set; Cartes hand, game

▸ ► **m. à air** Aviat windsock; Naut windsail; Tech **m. d'arrosage** hose(pipe); **manches ballon** puff sleeves; Tech **m. à eau** hose(pipe); **manches gigot** leg-of-mutton sleeves; **m. à incendie** fire hose; **manches kimono** kimono sleeves; **manches raglan** raglan sleeves; **manches trois-quarts** three-quarter sleeves; Aviat **m. à vent** wind sock

manche[2] NM **1** (de marteau, casserole etc) handle; (de poignard) handle, haft; (de club de golf) shaft; (de fouet) stock; (de violon, guitare etc) neck; **couteau à m. d'ivoire** ivory-handled knife, knife with an ivory handle; Fam **être du côté du m.** to be well in with those who count; **branler dans le m.** to have a loose handle; Fig to be shaky **2** Ordinat joystick, control column or stick; Aviat joystick **3** Culin (de gigot) knuckle; **m. à gigot** leg-of-mutton holder (for carving) **4** Fam (personne maladroite) clumsy idiot; **s'y prendre comme un m.** to make a right mess of things; **avec les femmes, il s'y prend comme un m.** he's absolutely useless with women; **il conduit/danse comme un m.** he's a lousy or hopeless driver/dancer

▸ ► **m. de ou à balai** broomstick; **m. à balai** Ordinat joystick, control column or stick; Aviat joystick

Manche (la) [lamãʃ] NF **1** the (English) Channel **2** (en Espagne) La Mancha

manchette [mãʃɛt] NF **1** (extrémité de la manche) cuff **2** (pour protéger les vêtements) oversleeve, cuff protector **3** Sport (au catch) forearm smash; (au volley-ball) dig **4** Journ (de journal) (front-page) headline; **la nouvelle a fait la m. de tous les journaux** the news made the headlines or the story was headline news in all the papers **5** (dans l'édition) (note) side note

manchon [mãʃɔ̃] NM (vêtement) muff; Tech (pour axe, arbre etc) sleeve; (de palier) bush(ing); (pour pivot etc) socket; **m. d'accouplement** coupling sleeve; Aut etc **m. d'embrayage** clutch; **m. à incandescence** incandescent (gas) mantle

manchot, -ote [mãʃo, -ɔt] ADJ (privé d'un bras) one-armed; (privé d'une main) one-handed; (privé des deux bras) armless, with no arms; (privé des deux mains) with no hands; Fam **il n'est pas manchot** (adroit) he's clever with his hands; (il peut le faire lui-même) he's got hands, hasn't he?

N (privé d'un bras) one-armed person; (privé d'une main) one-handed person; (privé des deux bras) armless person, person with no arms; (privé des deux mains) person with no hands

NM Zool penguin

mandala [mãdala] NM mandala

mandale [mãdal] NF très Fam clout, slap (in the face)

mandant [mãdã] NM **1** Jur (dans une transaction) principal **2** Pol **le député et ses mandants** the member and his/her constituents

mandarin [mɑ̃darɛ̃] NM **1** *Hist* mandarin; *Fig Péj (fonctionnaire, intellectuel)* mandarin **2** *Ling* Mandarin (Chinese) **3** *(oiseau)* **(canard) m.** mandarin duck

mandarinal, -aux [mɑ̃darinal, -o] ADJ mandarin

mandarinat [mɑ̃darina] NM *Hist* mandarinate; *Fig Péj* **le m.** the intellectual establishment

mandarine [mɑ̃darin] NF **1** mandarin (orange) **2** *TV, Cin (éclairage)* redhead ▪ ADJ INV tangerine(-coloured)

mandarinier [mɑ̃darinje] NM *Bot* mandarin (orange) tree

mandat [mɑ̃da] NM **1** *(autorité) Hist* mandate; **territoires sous m.** mandated territories; **m. de député** member's (electoral) mandate; **m. de maire** mayoralty; **m. présidentiel** president's *or* presidential term of office **2** *Jur (procuration)* power of attorney, proxy **3** *Jur (ordre)* warrant **4** *Fin (mode de paiement)* order (to pay), money order; *(mandat-poste)* postal order, *surtout Am* money order
▶▶ **m. d'action** receiving order (in bankruptcy); **m. d'amener** ≃ summons; **m. d'arrêt** arrest warrant; **m.-carte,** *pl* **mandats-cartes** postal order, *surtout Am* money order *(in postcard form)*; **m. de comparution** summons (to appear), subpoena; **m. de dépôt** committal order; **placer qn sous m. de dépôt** to commit sb; **m. d'expulsion** eviction order; **m. international** international money order; **m.-lettre,** *pl* **mandats-lettres,** *surtout Am* money order *(in letter card form)*; **m. de paiement** order to pay; **m. de perquisition** search warrant; **m. postal** postal order, *surtout Am* money order; **m.-poste,** *pl* **mandats-poste** postal order, *surtout Am* money order; **m. télégraphique** telegraphic money order; **m. de virement** transfer order

mandataire [mɑ̃datɛr] N *(représentant) (d'électeurs etc)* representative; *(à une réunion)* proxy; *Com* agent; **m. général** general agent

mandatement [mɑ̃datmɑ̃] NM mandating

mandater [mɑ̃date] VT **1** *(charger d'une mission) (représentant etc)* to commission; *(membre parlementaire)* to give a mandate to **2 m. des frais** *(payer par mandat)* to pay expenses by money order

mandchou, -oue [mɑ̃dʃu] ADJ Manchurian
▪ NM *Ling* Manchu
▪ N **M.** Manchurian

Mandchourie [mɑ̃dʃuri] NF Manchuria

mandement [mɑ̃dmɑ̃] NM **1** *Arch (ordre)* mandate, order **2** *Rel* pastoral (letter)

mander [mɑ̃de] VT *Arch* **1** *(personne)* to summon **2 m. une nouvelle à qn** to convey *or* send news to sb *(by letter)*

mandibule [mɑ̃dibyl] NF *Anat, Zool* mandible; *Fam* **jouer des mandibules** to feed one's face

mandoline [mɑ̃dɔlin] NF *Mus* mandolin(e)

mandragore [mɑ̃dragɔr] NF mandrake

mandrill [mɑ̃dril] NM mandrill

mandrin [mɑ̃drɛ̃] NM *Tech (de tour)* chuck; *(de vilebrequin)* pad; *(pour faire un trou)* punch; *(pour élargir un trou)* drift

manécanterie [manekɑ̃tri] NF choir school

manège [manɛʒ] NM **1** *Équitation (exercices)* exercises; *(dressage) (de cheval)* training, breaking in; **(salle de) m.** riding school; **m. découvert** open-air riding school **2 m. (de chevaux de bois)** merry-go-round, roundabout, *surtout Am* carrousel; **aller aux manèges** *(fête foraine)* to go to the fair **3** *(manigances)* ploy, trick; **j'observais leur m.** I was watching their little game

mânes [mɑn] NMPL *Antiq, Rel* manes, shades, spirits *(of the dead)*; **les m. de mes ancêtres** the spirits of my ancestors

maneton [mantɔ̃] NM *Aut* crankpin

manette [manɛt] NF (hand) lever; *Aut* stalk; *(ouverture capot)* lever; *Aviat* **m. des gaz** throttle lever; **m. de jeux** joystick; *Fam* **à fond les manettes** at full speed, *Br* like the clappers, *Am* like sixty

manga [mɑ̃ga] NM manga

manganate [mɑ̃ganat] NM *Chimie* manganate

manganèse [mɑ̃ganɛz] NM *Chimie* manganese

manganite [mɑ̃ganit] NM *Chimie* manganite

mangeable [mɑ̃ʒabl] ADJ **1** *(comestible)* edible, eatable **2** *(médiocre)* (just about) eatable

mangeaille [mɑ̃ʒaj] NF **1** *Arch (pour animaux domestiques)* feed **2** *Fam (nourriture)* grub, *Br* nosh

mange-disque, *pl* **mange-disques** [mɑ̃ʒdisk] NM slot-feed record player

mangeoire [mɑ̃ʒwar] NF *Agr (feeding)* trough; *(pour chevaux, bétail)* manger; *(de canari)* feeding dish

manger¹ [mɑ̃ʒe] (**je mangeai(s), n. mangeons**) VT to eat; **qu'est-ce qu'on mange?** what are we having to eat?, what's for lunch/dinner/*etc?*; **il a tout mangé** he's eaten everything (up); **il mange de tout** he'll eat anything; **je ne mange pas de viande** I don't eat meat; **mange ta soupe** eat (up) *or* drink (up) your soup; **j'ai faim, je mangerais bien un morceau** I'm hungry, I could do with a bite to eat; *Fig* **il est conscient d'avoir mangé son pain blanc le premier** he knows that he had it easy for a while; **je me rends compte que je mange mon pain blanc le premier** *ou* **avant mon pain noir** I realize that I had it easy to start with; **ça ne mange pas de pain** it doesn't cost anything; *Fam* **je ne mange pas de ce pain-là** I don't go in for that sort of thing; *Fam* **m. du curé** to be violently anticlerical; *Fam* **elle ne vous mangera pas** she won't eat you; **la rouille mange l'acier** rust eats into steel; *Fam* **chaudière qui mange beaucoup de charbon** boiler that is very heavy on coal *or* that eats up coal; **mangé aux** *ou* **par les mites** moth-eaten; **ses yeux lui mangent le visage** his eyes seem to fill his face; **ses cheveux lui mangent le visage** her face is almost hidden by her hair; **m. ses mots** to mumble; *Arg* **m. le morceau** to spill the beans, to talk; *Fam* **m. son argent** to squander one's money, to run through one's money; *Fam* **il a mangé du lion aujourd'hui** he's full of beans today; *Fam* **m. de la vache enragée** to have a hard time of it; *Fam* **m. la laine sur le dos de qn** to sponge shamelessly off sb; *Fam* **tu vas bientôt me m. la soupe sur la tête** you'll soon be taller than me; **m. qn/qch des yeux** to look at sb/sth longingly; **m. qn de baisers** to smother sb with kisses; *Fam* **m. les pissenlits par la racine** to be pushing up the daisies; *Belg* **m. sa parole** to break one's promise, to fail to keep one's word
▪ VI to eat; **je les ai invités à m.** I've invited them for something to eat *or* for a meal; **m. dans une assiette** to eat off *or* from a plate; **c'est tellement propre chez elle qu'on mangerait par terre** her house is so clean you could eat off the floor; **bon à m.** good to eat; **m. sur le pouce** to have a (quick) snack, to have a bite to eat; **maman, je vais être obligé de m. sur le pouce** I'm going to have to eat and run, Mum; **m. au restaurant** to eat out, to go out for a meal; **m. dehors** *(dans le jardin)* to eat outside; *(ailleurs que chez soi)* to eat out, to go out for a meal; **donner à m. à**

qn to feed sb, to give sb something to eat; **donner à m. à un animal/bébé** to feed an animal/a baby; **m. comme quatre** *ou* **comme un ogre** to eat like a horse; **m. comme un oiseau** *ou* **un moineau** to eat like a sparrow; **m. du bout des dents** to pick at one's food; **m. à sa faim** to eat one's fill; **m. léger** to eat a light meal; **nous avons bien mangé** we had a very good meal; **d'habitude on mange très bien en France** you usually eat very well in France
▪ VPR **se manger 1** to be eaten; **le fromage se mange avec du pain** cheese is eaten with bread **2** *Fam* **se m. qch** *(percuter)* to go head-first into sth

manger² NM food; **chez eux, vous aurez le boire et le m.** you'll get something to eat and drink *or* you'll get food and drink at their place; **je ne pourrai pas rentrer avant m.** I won't be able to get back before lunch/dinner/*etc*; **à prendre après m.** to be taken after meals

mange-tout [mɑ̃ʒtu] ADJ INV, NM INV **(pois) m.** mangetout, sugar pea; **(haricot) m.** runner bean, *Am* string bean

mangeur, -euse [mɑ̃ʒœr, -øz] N eater; **gros** *ou* **grand m.** big eater; **c'est un gros m. de pommes de terre** he eats a lot of potatoes, he's a big potato eater; **mangeurs d'hommes** cannibals, man-eating savages; **tigre m. d'hommes** man-eating tiger

manglier [mɑ̃glije] NM *Bot* mangrove (tree)

mangoustan [mɑ̃gustɑ̃] NM *(arbre, fruit)* mangosteen

mangouste [mɑ̃gust] NF **1** *Zool* mongoose **2** *(fruit)* mangosteen

mangue [mɑ̃g] NF mango

manguier [mɑ̃gje] NM mango (tree)

maniabilité [manjabilite] NF *(d'outil)* handiness; *(d'avion)* manoeuvrability, *Am* maneuverability; *(de véhicule)* handling ability; *(d'un logiciel)* user-friendliness

maniable [manjabl] ADJ *(valise etc)* manageable; *(outil)* handy; *(véhicule)* easy to handle *or* control *or* drive; *(avion)* easy to control, easy to manoeuvre *or Am* maneuver

maniaco-dépressif, -ive [manjakodepresif, -iv] ADJ, N manic-depressive

maniaque [manjak] ADJ fussy, finicky, pernickety
▪ N **1** *(pointilleux)* fusspot, *Am* fussbudget; *(capricieux)* crank; **c'est une m. de l'hygiène/de l'ordre** she's fanatical about *or* obsessed with hygiene/tidiness **2** *(fou)* maniac, raving lunatic, *m* madman, *f* madwoman; **m. sexuel** sex maniac

> Il faut noter que le terme anglais **maniac** ne signifie jamais **pointilleux**.

maniaquerie [manjakri] NF fussiness, finickiness

manichéen, -enne [manikeɛ̃, -ɛn] ADJ Manichean

manichéisme [manikeism] NM Manicheism

manicle [manikl(ə)] NF = **manique**

manie [mani] NF **1** *Psy* mania, obsession; **m. de la persécution** persecution mania *or* complex **2** *(passion)* mania, craze; *(habitude, petite obsession)* odd habit; **avoir la m. de la propreté** to have a mania for cleanliness, to be fanatical about *or* obsessed with cleanliness; **elle a la m. de tout ranger** she has a compulsive habit of tidying everything up; **il a ses petites manies** he has his little ways *or* his little fads; **c'est ta nouvelle m., de fumer la pipe?** is that your latest fad *or* craze, smoking a pipe?; **c'est une m. chez lui de dire du mal des autres** it's become a habit with him to run other people down;

mais quelle **m. de claquer les portes!** why do people always have to slam doors? **3** *Méd Arch* mental derangement

maniement [manimɑ̃] **NM** *(d'outils, d'affaires, de langue etc)* handling; *Mil* **m. d'armes** drill

manier [manje] *(impf, pr sub* n. **maniions,** v. **maniiez)* **VT 1** *(outil, corde, armes etc)* to handle **2** *(diriger, contrôler) (hommes, cheval etc)* to handle, to manage; *(avion)* to control, to manoeuvre, *Am* to maneuver; **m. les avirons** to ply *or* pull the oars; **savoir m. la parole** to know how to handle words, to be good with words **3** *Arch (tissu)* to feel
VPR se manier *Fam* = **se magner;** *voir* **magner (se)**

manière [manjer] **NF 1** *(façon)* way, manner; **d'une m. assez particulière** in a rather unusual way *or* manner; **sa m. de s'habiller, la m. dont elle s'habille** the way she dresses, her way of dressing; **la m. qu'elle a de regarder les gens par en dessous** the furtive way she has of looking at people; **c'est sa m. d'être** that's the way he/she is; **laissez-moi faire à ma m.** let me do it my (own) way; **m. de voir** *ou* **de penser** way of looking at things; **s'y prendre de la bonne m.** to set about it the right way; **je comprends qu'il t'ait critiqué, mais il y a la m.** I can understand him criticizing you, but there are ways of doing these things; **employer la m. forte** to use strong-arm tactics, to use force; **de cette m.** (in) this way, (in) that way; **d'une m. ou d'une autre** one way or another; **de m. à ce que** so that, in such a way that; **de telle m. que** in such a way that; **d'une m. générale** generally speaking; **en aucune m.** under no circumstances, not under any circumstances; **de toute m.** in any case; **d'une certaine m.** in a manner of speaking, in a sense; **de la même m.** in the same way **2** *(conduite)* **manières** manners; **avoir de bonnes** *ou* **de belles manières** to have good manners, to be well-mannered; **avoir de mauvaises manières** to have bad manners, to be ill-mannered; **en voilà des manières!** what a way *or* that's no way to behave!; *Fig* **apprendre les bonnes manières à qn** to teach sb some manners; **faire des manières** *(être poseur)* to put on airs and graces; *(se faire prier)* to stand on ceremony, to make a fuss; **elle est sans manières** she is unaffected, she doesn't give herself airs and graces; **elle a accepté notre invitation sans (faire de) manières** she accepted our invitation just like that *or* without any fuss; **venez dîner ce soir, mais vous savez, ce sera sans manières** come and have dinner tonight, but you know, it'll only be a simple meal **3** *Beaux-Arts, Littér etc* **tableau à la m. de Degas** painting after (the manner of) Degas; **un Truffaut première m.** an early Truffaut

maniéré [manjere] **ADJ 1** *(poseur) (personne, politesse etc)* affected **2** *Beaux-Arts, Littér (style)* mannered

maniérisme [manjerism] **NM 1** affectation **2** *Beaux-Arts, Littér* mannerism

manieur, -ieuse [manjœr, -jøz] **N** *(d'hommes, d'affaires etc)* manager; **m. d'argent** financier

manif [manif] **NF** *Fam* demo

manifestant, -ante [manifɛstɑ̃, -ɑ̃t] **N** demonstrator

manifestation [manifɛstasjɔ̃] **NF 1** *(de sentiment, tendance, opinion etc)* expression; **avec de grandes manifestations de joie** with a great show of joy, with great expressions of joy **2** *(politique)* demonstration **3** *Rel* revelation **4** *(événement)* event; **m. sportive/culturelle** sporting/cultural event

manifeste [manifest] **ADJ** obvious, manifest; **il est m. que ses études ne l'intéressent pas** it's obvious that he isn't interested in his studies; **il est d'une incompétence m.** he is obviously *or* manifestly incompetent

manifeste [manifest] **NM 1** *Pol* manifesto **2** *Naut, Aviat* manifest; **m. de douane** customs manifest; **m. d'entrée/de sortie** inward/outward manifest

manifestement [manifɛstəmɑ̃] **ADV** obviously, manifestly

manifester [manifɛste] **VT** *(ses intentions, ses sentiments, son étonnement etc)* to show, to reveal; *(de l'intérêt)* to show, to manifest; *(son courage)* to show, to display; **m. sa volonté** to make one's wishes clear; **il m'a manifesté sa sympathie** he expressed his sympathy to me
VI *Pol* to demonstrate
VPR se manifester 1 *(de personne)* to turn up, to show up, to appear; **ça fait très longtemps qu'il ne s'est pas manifesté** he hasn't been in touch for ages, I/we/*etc* haven't heard from him for ages; **je n'ai pas osé me m.** I didn't dare (to) show myself **2** *(de sentiment, maladie etc)* to show *or* manifest itself (**par** in)

manigance [manigɑ̃s] **NF** scheme, plot; **manigances** scheming, schemes

manigancer [manigɑ̃se] **VT** (**je manigançai(s),** n. **manigançons)** to scheme, to plot; **qu'est-ce qu'ils manigancent?** what's their (little) game?, what are they up to?; **je ne sais pas ce que je vais pouvoir m. pour ne pas le rencontrer** I don't know what I'll be able to come up with to avoid meeting him

maniganceux, -euse [manigɑ̃sœr, -øz] **ADJ** *Can Fam* scheming
N schemer

Manille [manij] **N** Manila

manille [manij] **NM** *(cigare)* Manila (cigar)

manille [manij] **NF** *Cartes* = type of game in which the ten is the highest card

manille [manij] **NF** shackle

manillon [manijɔ̃] **NM** *Cartes* ace *(in the game of manille)*

manioc [manjɔk] **NM** manioc, cassava

manip [manip] **NF** *Fam abrév* manipulation

manipulateur, -trice [manipylatœr, -tris] **N 1** *(de machine)* operator; *(d'argent, de biens etc)* handler; **m. radio(graphe)/de laboratoire** X-ray/lab(oratory) technician *or* assistant **2** *Péj (de personne)* manipulator **3** *(prestidigitateur)* conjuror
NM 1 *(en robotique)* manipulator **2** *Tél* (sending) key

manipulation [manipylasjɔ̃] **NF 1** *(de produits chimiques)* handling; **m. génétique** genetic engineering; **les manipulations génétiques inquiètent l'opinion** the public is concerned about genetic engineering; **produit créé grâce à des manipulations génétiques** genetically engineered product **2** *Méd* manipulation; **m. vertébrale** manipulation of the spine; **un ostéopathe m'a fait des manipulations** an osteopath manipulated my spine **3** *Scol* **manipulations** *(surtout en science)* experiments, practical work **4** *(en prestidigitation)* sleight of hand **5** *Péj* manipulation; *Pol* **manipulations électorales** vote-rigging **6** *Ordinat* **m. de colonnes** column handling; **m. de données** data manipulation; **m. de documents** document handling; **m. d'images** image manipulation

manipuler [manipyle] **VT 1** *(outil compliqué)* to manipulate; *(appareil, produits chimiques, marchandise)* to handle; *Tél* to operate; **m. un colis avec précaution** to handle a parcel with care **2** *Péj (personne, électeurs)* to manipulate; *(statistiques)* to massage

manique [manik] **NF** *(pour la cuisine)* oven glove; *Tech* protective glove

manitou [manitu] **NM 1** *(d'Indiens d'Améri-*

que) manitou **2** *Fig Fam* **(grand) m.** big shot, big noise; *(patron)* big boss

manivelle [manivɛl] **NF 1** *Tech* crank; *(pour un vélo)* pedal crank; *(pour un moteur)* crank (handle); *Aut* starting handle; *(de lève-glace)* window winder; **retour de m.** backfire; *Fig* **il y eut un retour de m.** it backfired **2** *Cin (sur les anciennes caméras)* winding handle; *Fig* **dès le premier tour de m.** as soon as shooting started

manne [man] **NF** *Bible* manna; *Fig (don inespéré)* godsend, manna from heaven

manne [man] **NF** *(panier)* basket, hamper

mannequin [mankɛ̃] **NM 1** *Beaux-Arts* manikin, lay figure; *Couture* dress stand; *(qui a la forme du corps)* (dressmaker's) dummy **2** *(personne)* model, *Vieilli* mannequin; **elle est m. chez Chanel** she works for Chanel as a model, she models for Chanel

mannequin [mankɛ̃] **NM** *(panier)* small (wicker) basket

mannequinat [mankina] **NM** modelling

manocontact [manokɔ̃takt] **NM** *Aut etc* pressure switch

manœuvrabilité [manœvrabilite] **NF** manoeuvrability, *Am* maneuverability

manœuvrable [manœvrabl] **ADJ** manoeuvrable, *Am* maneuverable; **cette voiture est peu m.** the car is not at all easy to manoeuvre *or* handle

manœuvre [manœvr] **NF 1** *(conduite, direction) (de machine, grue etc)* operation; *(de véhicule)* manoeuvring, *Am* maneuvring; **m. de stationnement** parking manoeuvre; **est-ce que tu connais les manœuvres pour allumer la chaudière?** do you know how to go about lighting the boiler?; *Aut* **faire une m.** to (do a) manoeuvre *or Am* maneuver; **faire une fausse m.** *Fig* to do something wrong; *Aut* to manoeuvre badly; *Fig* **il n'a pas fait une seule fausse m.** he didn't put a foot wrong; *Fig* **vous avez toute liberté de m.** you have a completely free hand, you have complete freedom of action **2** *Naut (action)* manoeuvre, *Am* maneuver; **m. d'accostage** docking manoeuvre *or Am* maneuver; **3** *Mil* drill, exercise; *(dans une bataille)* manoeuvre, *Am* maneuver; **en manœuvres** on manoeuvres *or* exercises; **grandes manœuvres** army manoeuvres *or* exercises; **m. d'encerclement** encircling movement **4** *Rail (de trains)* shunting, marshalling; **voie de m.** shunting *or Am* switching track **5** *Fig* manoeuvre, *Am* maneuver; **m. électorale** vote-catching manoeuvre; **manœuvres** scheming, manoeuvring; *Jur* **manœuvres frauduleuses** embezzling **6** *Naut (cordage)* rope; **manœuvres dormantes** standing rigging; **manœuvres courantes** running rigging

manœuvre [manœvr] **NM** unskilled worker; **travail de m.** unskilled work

manœuvrer [manœvre] **VT** *(faire fonctionner) (machine, grue etc)* to operate; *(conduire, diriger) (véhicule)* to manoeuvre, *Am* to maneuver, to handle; *Rail (wagons à plate-forme)* to shunt, to marshal
VI to manoeuvre, *Am* to maneuver; *Fig* to manoeuvre, to scheme; **il se laisse m. par sa femme** he lets himself be manipulated *or* manoeuvred by his wife

manœuvrier, -ière [manœvrije, -jɛr] **N 1** *(soldat, marin etc)* tactician **2** *Fig Vieilli* manoeuvrer, *Am* maneuverer

manoir [manwar] **NM** *(petit château)* manor; *(grande maison)* manor (house), country house

manomètre [manɔmɛtr] **NM** pressure gauge; *(en forme d'U)* manometer; *Aut* **m. de compression** cylinder compression gauge; *Aut* **m. de pression d'huile** oil pressure gauge

manométrique [manɔmetrik] ADJ *Phys* manometric(al); **hauteur m.** head of water

manouche [manuʃ] N *Péj* gipsy, gypsy

manquant, -ante [mãkã, -ãt] ADJ *(personne) (dans une classe, une réunion)* absent, missing; *(objet)* missing; **une pièce manquante d'un puzzle** a piece missing from *or* a missing piece of a jigsaw
   N *(personne)* absentee; **les manquants** the absentees, those absent, those missing
   NM *Com* shortage; **m. en caisse** cash shortage; **m. en stock** stock shortage; **éviter des manquants dans la marchandise** to prevent short delivery

manque [mãk] NM 1 *(carence) (de nourriture, d'argent, de main-d'œuvre, d'informations etc)* lack, shortage; *(de vitamines, calcium etc)* lack, deficiency; *(par rapport à un total désiré)* shortfall; *(de courage, goût, sommeil, d'humour, d'enthousiasme etc)* lack; **par m. de** through lack of; **m. de chance** *ou Fam* **de pot** *ou Fam* **de bol!** bad luck!; *Fam* **m. de bol j'ai du travail** it's just (my) tough *or* rotten luck that I've got work to do; *Méd* **(crise de) m.** withdrawal symptoms; **il est en m.** *(de drogue)* he's got withdrawal symptoms; *très Fam* **elle est en m. ou quoi, celle-là!** *(sexuellement)* is she not getting enough, or what?
   2 *(vide)* emptiness; **je ressens un grand m. depuis sa mort** I feel a great emptiness since his death; **elle souffre d'un m. affectif** she suffers from a lack of affection
   3 *Fam* **à la m.** lousy, pathetic; **espèce d'électricien à la m.!** call yourself an electrician!; **quelle voiture à la m.!** what a pile of scrap *or* junk this car is!; **toi et tes idées à la m.!** you and your useless ideas!
   4 *(lacunes)* **avoir conscience de ses manques** to be aware of one's shortcomings *or* failings
   5 *(au casino)* manque
   ▸▸ *Compta* **m. de caisse** cash unders; **m. de fonds** lack of funds; *Com, Fin* **m. à gagner** loss of earnings *or* profit *or* revenue

   Do not confuse with **manquement**.

manqué [mãke] ADJ *(occasion)* missed, lost; *(rendez-vous)* missed; *(tentative, expérience)* unsuccessful, abortive; *(photo)* unsuccessful; **coup m.** *(tir etc)* miss; **vie manquée** wasted life; **c'est un médecin m.** he ought to have been a doctor
   NM *Culin* = biscuit with almond-flavoured or fruit-flavoured icing; **moule à m.** (round) cake tin

manquement [mãkmã] NM **m. à une règle** breach *or* violation of a rule; **m. à la discipline** breach of discipline; **m. au devoir** breach *or* dereliction of duty

   Do not confuse with **manque**.

┌─────────────────────────────────────┐
│ **MANQUER** [mãke]   │
│   │
│ VI to be lacking **3** ▪ to be missing **4** │
│ ▪ to be missed **5** ▪ to be short of │
│ *(manquer de)* **1**   │
│ V IMPERS to be missing   │
│ VT to miss   │
│ VPR to miss each other **1**   │
└─────────────────────────────────────┘

VI **1 m. de** *(argent, main-d'œuvre)* to be short of, to lack; *(courage, bon sens, charme etc)* to lack, to be lacking in; **nous manquons de sucre/vin** we're short of sugar/wine; *(nous n'en avons plus)* we're out of sugar/wine; **m. de temps** to be short of time; **nous manquons de l'essentiel** we lack *or* we're short of the basics; **ne m. de rien** to have all that one needs; **elle m'a manqué de respect** she showed a lack of respect towards me; **la chambre manque de lumière** the room doesn't get

enough light, the room is lacking in *or* lacks light; **on manque d'air ici** there isn't enough air *or* there's no air in here; **ils ont fini par m. d'air et mourir** they finally ran out of air and died; **tu ne manques pas d'audace** *ou* **de culot** *ou Fam* **d'air!** you're not lacking in nerve!; **elle ne manque pas d'admirateurs** she's not short of *or* not lacking in admirers
   2 *(faillir)* **il a manqué (de) tomber** he nearly *or* almost fell
   3 *(faire défaut)* to be lacking, to be in short supply; **commencer à m.** *(de vivres, d'eau etc)* to begin to run short *or* run out; **quand l'eau vint à m.** when the water ran short; **le bouton qui manque à ma veste** the button that's missing from my jacket, the missing button on my jacket; **une pièce manque au puzzle** there's a piece missing from the jigsaw puzzle, a piece of the jigsaw puzzle is missing; **les mots me manquent pour exprimer …** I'm at a loss for words to express …; **la voix me manqua** words failed me; **le pied lui manqua** he lost his footing; **le temps nous manque pour finir ce projet** we don't have enough time *or* the time to complete this project; **la place me manque** I don't have enough room; **ce n'est pas l'envie qui m'en manque** it's not that I don't want to, I would if I could; *Litt* **le cœur lui manqua** his heart failed him; **les occasions ne manquent pas, ce ne sont pas les occasions qui manquent** there's no lack of opportunity (**de faire** *or* **de**)
   4 *(dans une classe, une réunion)* to be absent, to be missing; *(avoir disparu)* to be missing; **m. à l'appel** to be absent from roll call; *Scol* **elle a beaucoup manqué le mois dernier** she was off (school) a lot *or* missed a lot of classes last month
   5 *(être regretté)* **tu me manques** I miss you; **est-ce que je t'ai manqué?** did you miss me?; **sa mère/sa maison lui manque** he's missing his mother/his house; **c'est au parti qu'il manque le plus** it's the party that's missing him most
   6 *(faillir à qch)* **m. à** *(son devoir, son honneur)* to fail in; *(sa parole, ses promesses)* to break; *Hum* **je manque à tous mes devoirs** I'm neglecting my duties; **m. à la consigne** to disregard orders; **m. à une règle** to break *or* violate a rule; **m. à la livraison** to miss a delivery; **m. à ses engagements financiers** to fail to meet one's financial liabilities
   7 *(échouer)* to fail
   8 *(à la forme négative)* **personne ne peut m. d'avoir observé …** no one can fail to have noticed …; **il n'a pas manqué d'être étonné** he couldn't help but be surprised; **cela ne pouvait m. d'arriver** it was bound to happen, it had to happen; **j'étais sûr qu'il allait casser l'assiette et, bien sûr, ça n'a pas manqué** I was sure he'd break the plate and, sure enough, he did; **ne manquez pas de nous écrire** don't forget to *or* be sure to write to us; **elle ne manquera pas de t'en faire la remarque** she'll be quite sure *or* she's bound to point it out to you; **remerciez bien votre mère! – je n'y manquerai pas** be sure to thank your mother! – I won't forget *or* I'll do that
   V IMPERS **il ne manque pas de candidats** there's no lack *or* no shortage of candidates; **il manque quelques pages** there are a few pages missing; **il me manque dix euros** I'm ten euros short, I need another ten euros; **il lui manque un bras** he has only one arm, he has lost an arm; **il ne lui manque que la parole** *(d'un animal)* the only thing it can't do is speak; *Fam* **il lui manque une case** he's got a screw loose; **il s'en manque de beaucoup** far from it; **il ne manquait plus que cela!** that's all I/he/etc needed!; *Fam* **il ne manquerait plus que ça!** that would be all I'd/he'd/etc need!; **il ne manquerait plus que ça,**

qu'il vienne avec sa nouvelle maîtresse! it would be the last straw if he came with his new mistress! SEE GRAMMAR B29
   VT *(rater) (cible, train etc)* to miss; *(occasion)* to miss, to lose; **j'ai manqué le train de trois minutes** I missed the train by three minutes; **M. Martin? vous l'avez manqué de peu** Mr Martin? you('ve) just missed him; **un film superbe, à ne m. sous aucun prétexte** a superb film, not to be missed under any circumstances; *Fig Hum* **je crois que j'ai manqué une étape** *ou* **un épisode** I think I've missed something; **il ne faut surtout pas m. ça** you really mustn't miss it; *Fam* **tu as manqué le coche** you've missed your chance *or* opportunity; *Br Fam* **you've missed the bus**; *Fam* **tu as encore manqué une occasion de te taire** *ou très Fam* **de fermer ta gueule** why didn't you just keep your big mouth shut for once?; **m. son coup** to miss; *Fig* to miss one's chance; **elle a manqué son coup, elle n'a pas réussi à le convaincre** she failed (in her attempt) to convince him; *Fam* **il n'en manque pas une** he's always putting his foot in it; **m. sa vocation** to miss one's vocation
   VPR **se manquer 1** to miss each other *(by not being in the same place at the same time)*
   2 *(rater son suicide)* to fail in one's suicide attempt

mansarde [mãsard] NF *(chambre)* attic; *Archit* **(toit** *ou* **comble en) m.** mansard roof

mansardé [mãsarde] ADJ **chambre mansardée** attic (room)

mansuétude [mãsɥetyd] NF *Litt* leniency

mante [mãt] NF mantis; **m. religieuse** praying mantis; *Fig (femme)* man-eater

manteau, -eaux [mãto] NM **1** *(vêtement)* coat; **m. de pluie** raincoat; **m. de fourrure** fur coat; *Fig* **m. neigeux** mantle *or* blanket of snow; **sous le m. de la nuit** under (the) cover of darkness; **faire qch sous le m.** to do sth secretly *or Fml* clandestinely **2** *Zool (de mollusque)* mantle
   ▸▸ *Théâtre* **m. d'Arlequin** proscenium arch; **m. de cheminée** mantel(piece)

mantelé [mãtle] ADJ *Zool (corbeau)* hooded

mantelet [mãtlɛ] NM **1** *Rel* mantelletta **2** *(de femme)* cape

mantille [mãtij] NF mantilla

manucure [manykyr] N *(personne)* manicurist
   NF *(technique)* manicure; **se faire faire une m.** to have a manicure

manucuré [manykyre] ADJ manicured

manuel¹, -elle [manɥɛl] ADJ *(travail, activité etc)* manual; **je ne suis pas manuel pour deux sous** I'm no good at all with my hands; **un cours de travaux manuels** a handicrafts class; **commande manuelle** manual controls; **corrections manuelles** corrections by hand, manual corrections
   N **1** *(adroit de ses mains)* **c'est un manuel** he is good with his hands **2** *(qui exerce une profession manuelle)* manual worker

manuel² NM *(livre)* manual, handbook; **un m. scolaire/d'histoire** a school/history textbook; **m. de l'utilisateur, m. d'utilisation** user *or* instruction manual; **m. d'entretien** service manual, maintenance manual, workshop manual; **m. d'installation** installation manual; **m. de référence** reference manual; *(dans l'édition)* **m. de style** style book

manuellement [manɥɛlmã] ADV manually; **m., je ne vaux rien** I'm useless with my hands

manufacture [manyfaktyr] NF **1** *Vieilli (usine)* factory; **la M. de porcelaine de Sèvres** the Sèvres porcelain factory **2** *Arch (fabrication)* manufacture

manufacturer [manyfaktyre] VT to manufacture; **produits manufacturés** manufactured goods, manufactures

manufacturier, -ière [manyfaktyrje, -jɛr] **ADJ** manufacturing
  N *Vieilli* manufacturer

manu militari [manymilitari] **ADV** by force

manuscrit [manyskri] **ADJ** *(page, texte)* manuscript
  NM *(texte à publier)* manuscript; **sous forme de m.** in manuscript (form); **m. dactylographié** manuscript, typescript; **un m. du XIIIᵉ siècle** a 13th-century manuscript; **les manuscrits de la mer Morte** the Dead Sea Scrolls

manutention [manytãsjɔ̃] **NF 1** *(action)* handling (of goods); **il fait de la m.** he's a goods handler **2** *(lieu)* storehouse, store(s)

manutentionnaire [manytãsjɔnɛr] **N** goods handler; *(dans un entrepôt)* storekeeper, storeman

manutentionner [manytãsjɔne] **VT** *(marchandises)* to handle

maoïsme [maɔism] **NM** *Pol* Maoism

maoïste [maɔist] **ADJ, N** *Pol* Maoist

maori, -ie [maɔri] **ADJ** Maori
  NM *Ling* Maori
  N M. Maori

maous, -ousse [maus] **ADJ** *Fam* ginormous, enormous

mappemonde [mapmɔ̃d] **NF** *(carte)* map of the world in two hemispheres; *(globe)* globe

maquer [make] *très Fam* **VT je pense pas qu'elle soit maquée** I don't think she's got a man; **on va essayer de le m.** we're going to try and fix him up (with a woman); **elle est maquée avec lui** she's shacked up with him; **on a réussi à les m. ensemble** we managed to fix them up with each other
  VPR se maquer se m. avec qn to be shacked up with sb; **depuis qu'elle s'est maquée …** since she got herself a man …

maquereau¹, -eaux [makro] **NM** *(poisson)* mackerel **VOIR GRAMMAIRE A12**

maquereau², -eaux NM *Arg (souteneur)* pimp

maquerelle [makrɛl] **NF** *Arg* **(mère) m.** madam

maquette [makɛt] **NF 1** *Beaux-Arts* model **2** *Théâtre (de mise en scène)* model **3** *(de livre)* dummy; *(de pages)* paste-up, layout **4** *Ind* scale model **5** *Cin* miniature **6** *(jouet)* model; **il fait des maquettes** he makes models; **m. d'avion/de bateau** model plane/boat

maquettiste [makɛtist] **N 1** model maker **2** *Typ* layout artist, layout compositor

maquignon [makiɲɔ̃] **NM 1** *(marchand de chevaux)* horse trader *or* dealer **2** *Fig (entremetteur malhonnête)* dishonest *or* crooked dealer

maquignonnage [makiɲɔnaʒ] **NM 1** *(vente de chevaux)* horse trading, horse dealing **2** *(trafic)* sharp practice

maquignonner [makiɲɔne] **VT** *Péj* **1** *(cheval)* to trade dishonestly **2** *Fig (affaire)* to conduct dishonestly; **affaire maquignonnée** put-up job

maquillage [makijaʒ] **NM 1** *(action) (de visage)* making up; **elle met beaucoup de soin dans son m.** she takes a lot of care with her make-up **2** *(produits)* make-up; **m. correcteur** corrective make-up **3** *(modification frauduleuse) (de voiture volée)* disguising; *(de documents)* forging; *(de photos)* faking; *(de comptes)* falsification, doctoring, *Br Fam* fiddling

maquiller [makije] **VT 1** *(personne, visage)* to make up **2** *(déguiser, falsifier) (voiture volée)* to disguise; *(documents)* to forge; *(photos)* to fake; *(comptes)* to falsify, to doctor, *Br Fam* to fiddle

VPR se maquiller to put (one's) make-up on, to make up; **elle se maquille trop** she uses too much make-up, she puts too much make-up on

maquilleur, -euse [makijœr, -øz] **N** *Théâtre, Cin* make-up artist; *Cin, TV* **elle est maquilleuse de studio** she works at a studio as a make-up artist

maquis [maki] **NM 1** *Géog* maquis; *Fig* **le m. de la procédure** the jungle of legal procedure **2** *Hist* maquis, underground movement *(in WWII)*; **les m. d'Afghanistan** the Afghan freedom fighters; **prendre le m.** to go underground; *(fuir à la campagne)* to take to the hills

maquisard [makizar] **NM** *Hist* member of the maquis, Resistance fighter *(in WWII)*

marabout [marabu] **NM 1** *Rel (ermite, tombeau)* marabout **2** *(sorcier)* witchdoctor **3** *(oiseau, plume)* marabou **4** *Can (personne acariâtre)* bad-tempered person
  ADJ *Can* bad-tempered, grumpy

marabouter [marabute] **VT** to put a spell on

maracas [marakas] **NFPL** maracas

maraîchage [mareʃaʒ] **NM** market gardening, *Am* truck farming

maraîcher, -ère [mareʃe, -ɛr] **ADJ** **culture maraîchère** market gardening, *Am* truck farming; **produits maraîchers** market garden produce, *Am* truck
  N market gardener, *Am* truck farmer

marais [marɛ] **NM 1** marsh; *(dans un pays chaud)* swamp; *(dans l'est de l'Angleterre)* fen; *(terres marécageuses)* marshland; **m. salant** salt marsh; **m. tourbeux** peat bog **2** *(terrain consacré à la culture maraîchère)* market garden, *Am* truck farm **3** *Fig* **le m. d'une vie sans surprises** a humdrum, uneventful existence **4** *Météo* **m. barométrique** shallow depression

marasme [marasm] **NM 1** *Méd* emaciation, *Spéc* marasmus; *Fig* **il était en plein m.** he was totally drained *(of energy, inspiration)* **2** *Écon* stagnation, slump; **dans le m. économique actuel** in the present economic slump

marasque [marask] **NF** marasca cherry

marasquin [maraskɛ̃] **NM** maraschino; **cerise au m.** maraschino cherry

marathon [maratɔ̃] **NM** *Sp, Fig* marathon; *Fig* **m. de danse** dance marathon; **c'est toujours la m. entre la famille, les amis, les expos** it's always an endless round of family, friends, exhibitions; *Pol* **m. diplomatique** diplomatic marathon; **m. électoral** electoral marathon

marathonien, -ienne [maratɔnjɛ̃, -jɛn] **N** marathon runner

marâtre [maratr] **NF** *(belle-mère)* stepmother; *(mère dénaturée)* cruel mother

maraud, -aude [maro, -od] **N** *Arch* villain, rascal, rogue

maraudage [marodaʒ] **NM =** **maraude 1**

maraude [marod] **NF 1** *(vol)* pilfering, petty thieving *(from orchards etc)* **2** **taxi en m.** cruising taxi

marauder [marode] **VI 1** *(voler)* to thieve, to pilfer *(from orchards etc)* **2** *(de taxi)* to cruise (for fares)

maraudeur, -euse [marodœr, -øz] **N** pilferer, petty thief
  ADJ 1 taxi m. cruising taxi **2 loup m.** prowling wolf

marbre [marbr] **NM 1** *(roche)* marble; **un escalier/une statue en m.** a marble staircase/statue; *Fig* **ce n'est pas écrit dans le m.** it's not written in (tablets of) stone, it's not carved in stone; **elle est restée de m.** she remained impassive; **avoir un cœur de m.** to have a heart of stone **2** *(statue)* marble (statue); *(de*

cheminée, commode etc) marble top **3** *(en reliure)* marbling **4** *Tech* surface plate, face plate **5** *Typ (de presse)* (forme) bed; **livre sur le m.** book in type *or* at press; **mettre un journal sur le m.** to put a paper to bed **6** *Journ (texte en attente de mise en page)* reserve feature; *Fam* **avoir du m.** to have copy over; **ne vous inquiétez pas pour l'édition de demain, j'ai du m.** don't worry about tomorrow's edition, I've got some items left over (from today); **rester sur le m.** to be excess copy

marbré [marbre] **ADJ** *(surface, couverture de livre)* marbled, mottled; *(peau)* mottled, blotchy; *(pierre)* veined, mottled; **il avait la peau toute marbrée de coups** his skin was all marked with bruises; **gâteau m.** marble cake

marbrer [marbre] **VT** *(surface)* to marble, to mottle; *(peau)* to mottle; **le froid lui avait marbré la peau** his skin was mottled *or* blotchy from the cold

marbrerie [marbrəri] **NF 1** *(art)* marble working *or* cutting; **m. funéraire** monumental sculpture *or* masonry **2** *(lieu)* marble mason's yard

marbrier, -ière [marbrije, -jɛr] **ADJ** *(industrie etc)* marble
  NM monumental sculptor *or* mason
  NF marbrière marble quarry

marbrure [marbryr] **NF 1** *(jaspure)* marbling, veining **2** *(de peau)* mottling; *(d'ecchymose)* mark, blotch

marc¹ [mar] **NM 1** *(mesure)* mark; **un m. d'or/ d'argent** a gold/silver mark (coin) **2** *Jur Vieilli* **au m. le franc** pro rata

marc² **NM 1** *(de raisins, d'olives etc)* marc **2** **(eau de vie de) m.** marc (brandy) **3** **m. de café** coffee grounds; **lire dans le m. de café** ≃ to read the tea leaves

marcassin [markasɛ̃] **NM** young wild boar

marcassite [markasit] **NF** *Minér* marcasite

marcel [marsɛl] **NM** *Hum (maillot de corps sans manches)* vest

marchand, -ande [marʃã, -ãd] **N** *(dans un magasin)* shopkeeper, *Am* storekeeper; *(de vin)* merchant; **m. de chevaux/tableaux/ meubles** horse/picture/furniture dealer
  ADJ 1 *Com* commercial, market; **denrées marchandes** saleable *or* marketable goods; **prix m.** trade price; **un tableau sans aucune valeur marchande** a painting of no saleable *or* marketable value **2 galerie marchande** shopping centre, *Am (shopping)* mall **3 marine marchande** merchant navy *or* marine
  ►► **m. ambulant** hawker; *Péj* **m. de canons** arms dealer; **m. de couleurs** ironmonger, *Am* hardware dealer; **m. au détail** retailer; **m. en gros** wholesaler; **m. de journaux** *(en boutique)* newsagent; *(en kiosque)* newstand man, newsvendor; **m. de légumes** greengrocer; **m. des quatre saisons** street merchant *(selling fruit and vegetables)*, *Br* barrow boy, *Vieilli* costermonger; **m. de sable: le m. de sable est passé** the sandman's on his way; *Péj* **m. de sommeil** slum landlord; *Fig Péj* **m. de soupe** *(restaurateur)* second-rate restaurant owner; *(directeur d'institution)* = money-grubbing headmaster of a private school; **m. de tabac** tobacconist; **m. de tapis** carpet dealer; *Fig Péj* haggler; **des discussions de marchands de tapis** haggling; **m. de vin** wine merchant, vintner; *Culin* in a red wine sauce

marchandage [marʃãdaʒ] **NM 1** bargaining, haggling; *Fig Péj* horse-trading **2** *Jur* subcontracting

marchander [marʃãde] **VT 1 m. qch avec qn** to haggle *or* bargain with sb over sth **2** *Jur* to subcontract
  VI to haggle, to bargain

marchandeur, -euse [marʃɑ̃dœr, -øz] **N 1** haggler **2** *Jur* subcontractor

marchandisage [marʃɑ̃dizaʒ] **NM** merchandising; **m. du distributeur** distributor merchandising; **m. du producteur** manufacturer merchandising

marchandisation [marʃɑ̃dizasjɔ̃] **NF** merchandization

marchandise [marʃɑ̃diz] **NF** (denrée) commodity, piece of merchandise; **marchandises** goods, merchandise, *Vieilli* wares; **la m. est bien arrivée** the goods have arrived safely; **vanter** *ou* **étaler** *ou* **faire valoir sa m.** to show one's wares to good *or* best advantage; *Fig* to make the most of oneself; *Fig* **je remballe ma m.** forget I said it; **tromper qn sur la m.** *(fournir un article de qualité inférieure)* to sell sb a dud; *(fournir un article différent)* to sell sb the wrong thing; *Fig* **j'ai été trompée sur la m.** he/they/*etc* didn't live up to my expectations; **train de marchandises** goods train, freight train; **gare de marchandises** goods station

▸▸ **marchandises acquittées** duty-paid goods; **marchandises avariées** spoiled *or* damaged goods; **marchandises au détail** retail goods; **marchandises franches de douane** duty-free goods; **m. hors taxes** duty-free goods; **m. libérée** duty-paid goods; **m. libre à la sortie** goods free of exit duty; **marchandises périssables** perishable goods, perishables; **m. prohibée** prohibited goods; **marchandises en souffrance** unclaimed goods; **marchandises en transit** goods in transit; **marchandises en vrac** bulk goods

marchandiser [marʃɑ̃dize] **VT** to merchandize

marchandiseur [marʃɑ̃dizœr] **NM** merchandiser; **m. de grande distribution** mass merchandiser

marchant [marʃɑ̃] **ADJ aile marchante** *Mil* outer flank *(of wheeling movement)*; *Fig (de groupement politique)* leading wing

marche¹ [marʃ] **NF** *Géog* march(es), border country

MARCHE²

> step **1** ▪ walking **2** ▪ march **3**
> ▪ running **4, 5** ▪ course **6**

NF 1 step; *(d'escalier)* step, stair; *Tech (pédale) (de métier à tisser etc)* treadle; *(d'orgue etc)* pedal; **la m. du bas** the bottom step *or* stair; **volée de marches** *(à l'extérieur)* flight of steps; *(à l'intérieur)* flight of stairs; **attention à la m.!** mind the step!; **rater une m.** to miss a step

2 *(action de marcher)* walking; *(promenade)* walk; **aimer la m.** to be fond of walking; **nous avons fait une longue m. dans la campagne** we went for a long walk in the country; **ralentir sa m.** to slacken one's pace; **continuer sa m.** to walk on; **se mettre en m.** to set off *or* out, to start off *or* out; **deux heures de m.** two hours' walk(ing); **une m. lente/rapide** a slow/rapid pace; **elle a réglé sa m. sur celle de la vieille dame** she adjusted her pace to the old lady's; **chaussures de m.** walking shoes; *Can* **prendre une m.** to go for a walk

3 *(défilé, manifestation)* march; **une m. silencieuse pour protester contre la mort d'un de leurs camarades** a silent protest march following the death of one of their comrades; **ouvrir la m.** to lead the way; **fermer la m.** to bring up the rear; **colonne en m.** column on the march; **ordre(s) de m.** marching orders; *Hist* **la Longue M.** the Long March; **en avant, m.!** forward, march!; *Mus* **m. nuptiale/funèbre/militaire** wedding/funeral/military march

4 *(mouvement) (de trains, d'autobus etc)*

running; *(de bateaux)* sailing, running; *Aut* **m. avant** forward gear; **m. arrière** *(pour un véhicule)* reversing, reverse, reverse gear; *Cin* reverse motion; *Fig* backtracking; **faire m. arrière** *(de voiture)* to reverse; *Fig* to backtrack; **entrer dans le garage en m. arrière** to back *or* reverse into the garage; **en m.** moving, in motion; **navire en m.** ship under way; **se mettre en m.** *(de véhicule)* to move off; **assis dans le sens de la m.** *(dans un train)* sitting facing the engine; *(dans un bus)* sitting facing forward; **assis dans le sens contraire de la m.** *(dans un train)* sitting with one's back to the engine; *(dans un bus)* sitting facing backwards

5 *(fonctionnement) (de machine)* running, working; **être en m.** *(de machine)* to be running; *(de fourneau)* to be in blast; **(re)mettre une machine en m.** to (re)start a machine; **en état de m.** in working order; **se mettre en m.** *(de machine)* to start; **il est responsable de la bonne m. de l'entreprise** he is responsible for the smooth running of the firm

6 *(des événements, de l'histoire etc)* course; **la m. du temps** the march of time; **m. à suivre** procedure

marché [marʃe] **NM 1** *(accord)* deal, bargain; *(plus officiel)* contract; **faire** *ou* **conclure un m.** to strike a deal *or* bargain; **m. conclu!** it's a deal!, *Fam* done!; **mettre à qn le m. en main** to invite sb to take it or leave it; **par-dessus le m.** into the bargain, on top of (all) that; **acheter/vendre qch (à) bon m.** to buy/sell sth cheaply *or* cheap; **(à) meilleur m.** more cheaply, cheaper; **articles bon m.** cheap *or* inexpensive articles

2 *(lieu public de vente)* market; **jour de m.** market day; **m. aux fleurs/à la volaille** flower/poultry market; **m. couvert** covered market; **aller au m.** to go to (the) market; **faire son m.** to go shopping *or* to do one's shopping (at the market)

3 *Com* market; **lancer un produit sur le m.** to launch a product; **produit qui n'a pas de m.** product for which there is no market; **conquérir un m.** to break into a market; **le m. mondial des bijoux** the world market in precious stones; *Bourse* **le m. de Londres** the London (Stock) Market; **économie de m.** market economy; **étude de m.** market research

▸▸ **m. d'acheteurs** buyers' market; *Bourse* **m. actions** securities market; *Bourse* **m. des actions** share market; **m. amont** market from which a company buys; **m. aval** sales market; **m. à la baisse** sellers' market; *Bourse* **m. baissier** bear market; **m. boursier** stock market; *Fin* **m. cambiste** foreign exchange market; *Fin* **marchés de capitaux** capital markets; **m. captif** captive market; *Bourse* **m. des changes** currency (exchange) market, foreign exchange market; **m.-cible** target market; **M. commun** Common Market; **m. compensatoire** compensation deal; *Fin* **m. au comptant** spot market; **m. des consommateurs** *ou* **de consommation** consumer market; *Bourse* **m. de cotation** securities market; *Bourse* **m. en coulisse** outside market; **m. effectif** available market; **m. des entreprises** business market; **m. environnant** substitution market; **m. d'équipement** capital goods market; **m. de l'eurodevise** *ou* **des eurodevises** euromarket; **m. à l'export** *ou* **à l'exportation** export market; **m. extérieur** foreign market, overseas market; **m. ferme** steady *or* strong *or* firm market; **m. financier** money *or* financial market; **m. de la grande consommation** mass market; **m. grand public** consumer market; **m. de gré à gré entre banques** interbank wholesale market; **m. à la hausse** buyers' market; *Bourse*

m. haussier bull market; *Bourse* **m. hors cote** unlisted securities market, USM, over-the-counter market, OTC market; **m. hypothécaire** mortgage market; **m. industriel** industrial market, business market; **m. interbancaire** interbank market; **m. intérieur** home market, domestic market, national market; **m. libre** free market; **m. monétaire** money market; **m. monopolistique** monopoly market; **m. national** national market, home market; *Bourse* **m. du neuf** primary market; **m. noir** black market; *Bourse* **m. des nouvelles émissions** new issue market; *Bourse* **m. obligataire** bond market; **m. officiel** official market; *Bourse* **m. orienté à la hausse** bull market; **marchés d'outre-mer** overseas markets; **m. ouvert** open market; **m. parallèle** parallel market, black market; *Fin* **m. à primes** options market; **m. principal** core market; **m. aux puces** flea market; **m. de référence** core market; **m. régional** regional market, area market; **m. à règlement mensuel** monthly settlement market; **m. secondaire** secondary market; **m. témoin** control market, test market; **m. à terme** futures market; **m.-test** test market; *Bourse* **m. des titres** securities market; **m. du travail** labour market; **M. unique (européen)** Single (European) Market; **m. utile** adressable market; *Bourse* **m. des valeurs mobilières** share market; **m. visé** target market

marchéage [marʃeaʒ] **NM** *Mktg* marketing mix spectrum; **m. de distribution** retailing mix

marchéisation [marʃeizasjɔ̃] **NF** marketization

marchepied [marʃəpje] **NM** *(d'autel)* steps; *(de train)* step; *Vieilli (de voiture)* running board; *(escabeau)* (pair of) steps; *(avec plusieurs marches)* stepladder; *Fig* **servir de m. à qn** to serve as a stepping-stone for sb

MARCHER [marʃe] **VI 1** *(se déplacer à pied)* to walk; **l'enfant ne marche pas encore** the child isn't walking yet; **il boite en marchant** he walks with a limp; **façon de m.** way of walking, gait; **m. à quatre pattes/sur les mains** to walk on all fours/on one's hands; **m. sur les pieds de qn** to tread on sb's toes; *Fig* **ne te laisse pas m. sur les pieds** don't let them walk all over you, don't let yourself be taken advantage of; **défense de m. sur les pelouses** keep off the grass; *Fig* **m. droit** to keep on the straight and narrow; *Fig* **m. sur les traces** *ou* **les pas de qn** to follow in sb's footsteps; **m. sur des œufs** *(avoir une démarche ralentie)* to walk gingerly; *(devoir être prudent)* to tread carefully *or* gently; **l'État marche à la ruine** the State is heading for ruin; **un peuple qui marche vers la liberté** a people marching *or* on the march towards liberty *or* freedom; *Mil* **m. contre l'ennemi** to advance on *or* move against the enemy; *Fam* **c'est marche ou crève!** it's do or die!, it's sink or swim!; *Fig Fam* **faire m. qn** to pull sb's leg, to have *or* *Am* put sb on, *Br* to wind sb up; *Fam* **et il a marché** and he fell for it, and he swallowed it

2 *(fonctionner) (de machine)* to work, to run, to go; *(de plans etc)* to work; **ma montre ne marche plus** my watch isn't working *or* going; **faire m. une machine** to work *or* operate a machine; **comment ça marche?** how does it work?; *Fig* **les affaires marchent (bien)** business is going *or* doing well, business is brisk; **les affaires ne marchent plus** business is at a standstill *or* is (very) slack; **cela fait m. le commerce** it's good for business; **ça marche pour ce soir? – ça marche!** is it OK for this evening *or* are we on for this evening? – definitely *or* sure!; *Fam* **m. (dans la combine)** to get involved; **tu es sûr qu'il va m. dans la combine?** are you sure he'll come in on it?; *Fam* **on vole une voiture ce soir? –**

OK, je marche! how about stealing a car tonight? – OK, count me in!; *Fam* **je ne marche pas** I'm having nothing to do with it, count me out; **on partage les bénéfices 50/50, ça marche?** we'll share the profits 50/50, (is that) agreed *or* OK?; **ça marche comme sur des roulettes** it's going like clockwork *or* like a dream *or* really smoothly; **ça ne marche pas si mal** we're not doing too badly; **la répétition a bien/mal marché** the rehearsal went well/badly

marchette [marʃɛt] NF *Can (chariot d'enfant)* baby-walker; *(déambulateur)* walking frame, zimmer frame

marcheur, -euse [marʃœr, -øz] N walker ADJ **1** *Zool* **oiseaux marcheurs** flightless birds **2 navire bon m.** fast ship

marcottage [markɔtaʒ] NM *Bot* formation of runners; *(artificiel)* layering

marcotte [markɔt] NF *Bot* layer

marcotter [markɔte] VT *Bot* to layer

mardi [mardi] NM Tuesday; **M. gras** Shrove Tuesday, *Br* Pancake Day; *Iron* **ce n'est pas m. gras aujourd'hui** are you going to a fancy-dress ball? (*voir aussi* **samedi**) SEE GRAMMAR A81–2; B61–2

Mardi gras
This is a very popular festival, falling on the eve of Ash Wednesday, at the end of the carnival. On this day, crêpes are prepared and eaten, and children dress up at school.

mare [mar] NF pool; *(dans un parc, une ferme)* pond; **m. aux canards** duck pond; **m. de sang** pool of blood

marécage [marekaʒ] NM marsh, bog; *(dans un pays chaud)* swamp; *(dans l'est de l'Angleterre)* fen; *(terres marécageuses)* marshland

marécageux, -euse [marekaʒø, -øz] ADJ **1** *(de la nature des marécages)* marshy, boggy; *(dans un pays chaud)* swampy **2** *(qui vit dans les marécages)* marsh; **une plante marécageuse** a marsh plant

maréchal, -aux [mareʃal, -o] NM **1 m. (de France)** *Mil* ≃ field marshal; *Hist (de maison royale etc)* ≃ marshal **2** *Mil* **m. des logis** sergeant; **m. des logis-chef** sergeant-major

maréchalat [mareʃala] NM *Mil* ≃ rank of field marshal

maréchale [mareʃal] NF *Mil* ≃ field marshal's wife

maréchalerie [mareʃalri] NF *(métier)* horse-shoeing, *Br* farriery; *(atelier)* smithy, forge

maréchal-ferrant [mareʃalfɛrɑ̃] *pl* **maréchaux-ferrants** [mareʃoferɑ̃] NM blacksmith, *Br* farrier

maréchaussée [mareʃose] NF *Hist* mounted constabulary; *Fam Hum* **la m.** the boys in blue, the constabulary, the police

marée [mare] NF **1** *(mouvement de la mer)* tide; **à m. haute/basse** at high/low tide; **m. montante/descendante** flood/ebb tide; **grande m.** spring tide; **horaire des marées** tide tables; **fleuve à m.** tidal river; *Fig* **m. humaine** surging mass of people, human tidal wave; **m. noire** oil slick; *Can Fig* **manquer la m.** to be left on the shelf, to stay unmarried **2** *Pêche* fresh (sea) fish; **arriver comme m. en carême** to come as surely as night follows day

marelle [marɛl] NF *(jeu)* hopscotch; *(figure)* (set of) hopscotch squares

marémoteur, -trice [maremɔtœr, -tris] ADJ *(énergie)* tidal; **usine marémotrice** tidal power station

marengo [marɛ̃go] NF *Culin* **poulet/veau (à la) m.** chicken/veal marengo
NM *(tissu)* ≃ black cloth with white speckles

marennes [marɛn] NF Marennes oyster

mareyage [marɛjaʒ] NM fish trade

mareyeur, -euse [marɛjœr, -øz] N fish wholesaler

margaille [margaj] *Belg Fam* NF **1** *(rixe)* fight **2** *(tapage)* row

margarine [margarin] NF margarine

marge [marʒ] NF **1** *(de livre, de page manuscrite)* margin; **écrire qch dans la m.** to write sth in the margin; **laissez une m. de trois centimètres** leave a margin of three centimetres; **note en m.** marginal note, note in the margin; **m. de droite/gauche** right-/left-hand margin, right/left margin; **m. du haut** *ou* **supérieure** top margin; **m. inférieure** *ou* **du bas** bottom margin; **m. de reliure** inside margin
2 *Fig* **accorder** *ou* **donner de la m. à qn** to allow sb some latitude *or* leeway *or* scope; *(temps)* to allow sb extra time; **avoir de la m.** to have plenty of scope; *(temps)* to have time in hand *or* to spare; **m. de négociation/manœuvre** room for negotiation/manoeuvre
3 en m. de on the fringe(s) of; **il y a une grande exposition de photos en m. du festival** there's a big exhibition of photographs as a fringe event; **en m. de cet enseignement, les élèves sont censés avoir des activités culturelles nombreuses** in addition, the pupils are supposed to have many extracurricular cultural activities; **rester en m. de l'histoire** to remain a footnote in history; **vivre en m. (de la société)** to live on the fringe(s) of society
4 *Com* margin; **avoir une faible/forte m.** to have a low/high (profit) margin; **nous faisons 30% de m. sur ce produit** we make a 30% margin on this product; *Bourse* **appel de m.** margin call
▸▸ **m. avant impôt** pretax margin; **m. bénéficiaire** profit margin; *Compta* **m. brute d'autofinancement** cashflow, funds generated by operations; **m. commerciale (brute)** gross profit margin; **m. commerciale moyenne** average gross profit margin; *Compta* **m. sur coûts variables** contribution; **m. de crédit** credit margin; **m. du détaillant** retailer margin; **m. du distributeur** distributor's margin; **m. d'erreur** margin of error; **m. du grossiste** wholesaler margin; **m. de l'importateur** importer margin; **m. initiale** initial margin; **m. nette** net margin; **m. nette d'exploitation** operating margin; **m. de profit** profit margin; **m. sectorielle** segment margin; **m. de sécurité** safety margin; **m. supplémentaire** additional margin; *Ind* **m. de tolérance** tolerance (margin)

margelle [marʒɛl] NF *(de puits)* coping, curb

marger [marʒe] VT *Typ* to feed in, to lay on; *Ordinat* **m. une page** to set the page margins
VI to set the margin(s); **m. à droite/à gauche** to set the right/left margin

margeur [marʒœr] NM *(de machine à écrire)* margin stop; *Typ* (paper) feed

marginal, -ale, -aux, -ales [marʒinal, -o] ADJ **1** *Écon (coût, revenu)* marginal **2** *Fig (secondaire)* marginal; **occupations marginales** side lines; **ce problème n'a qu'une importance marginale** this problem is of only marginal importance **3** *Géog (récif)* fringing
N dropout; **les marginaux** the fringe(s) of society

marginalisation [marʒinalizasjɔ̃] NF marginalization

marginaliser [marʒinalize] VT to marginalize; **un groupe social marginalisé** a marginalized social group, a group on the fringe(s) of society
VPR **se marginaliser** to become marginalized

marginalité [marʒinalite] NF nonconfor-

mism; **vivre dans la m.** to live on the fringe(s) of society

marginer [marʒine] VT to make margin notes in

margoulette [margulɛt] NF *Fam* **se casser la m.** to fall flat on one's face, to come a cropper

margoulin [margulɛ̃] NM rogue; *(homme d'affaires)* swindler

marguerite [margərit] NF **1** *Bot* **(petite) m.** daisy; **grande m.** marguerite; **effeuiller la m.** to play 'she/he loves me, she/he loves me not' **2** *(pour machine à écrire)* daisy wheel

marguillier [margije] NM *Vieilli* churchwarden

mari [mari] NM husband; *Fam* **son petit m.** her hubby

mariable [marjabl] ADJ marriageable

mariage [marjaʒ] NM **1** *(cérémonie)* wedding; **anniversaire de m.** wedding anniversary; **ils ont fêté leurs vingt-cinq ans de m.** they celebrated their 25th wedding anniversary *or* their silver wedding; **liste de m.** wedding list
2 *(union)* marriage; *(état)* marriage, matrimony; **elle a fait un mauvais m.** she made a bad marriage; **le m. ne lui a pas réussi** marriage *or* married life didn't suit him/her; **leur première année de m.** their first year of married life *or* marriage; **né hors m.** born out of wedlock; **demande en m.** proposal (of marriage); **acte de m.** marriage certificate
3 *Fig (d'esprit et de beauté etc)* combination, marriage; *(de couleurs)* blend(ing); **cette fille, c'est le m. de l'intelligence et de la beauté** this girl is a combination of *or* combines intelligence and beauty; *Fam* **c'est le m. de la carpe et du lapin** they make strange bedfellows
4 *Cartes* king and queen *(of a suit)*
▸▸ **m. d'amour** love match; **faire un m. d'amour** to marry for love; **m. d'argent: faire un m. d'argent** to marry for money; **m. en blanc** white wedding; **m. blanc** unconsummated marriage; **faire un m. blanc** to enter into a marriage of convenience *(primarily in order to acquire nationality)*; **m. civil** civil wedding, *Br* registry office wedding; **m. de convenance** marriage of convenience; **m. mixte** mixed marriage; **m. de raison** marriage of convenience; **m. religieux** church wedding

Attention: ne pas confondre **marriage** et **wedding** lorsque l'on traduit **mariage**. **Wedding** se rapporte uniquement à la cérémonie, alors que **marriage** se rapporte à l'institution.

Mariage
In France, a civil ceremony (which takes place at the "mairie") is required of all couples wishing to marry, though some choose to have a church wedding as well. The traditional wedding involves a long and sumptuous meal at which the wedding cake, a "pièce montée" is served.

Marianne [marjan] N *Fig* = the (French) Republic

Marie [mari] N *Rel* Mary

marié, -ée [marje] ADJ married; **non m.** unmarried, single
N *(homme)* (bride)groom; *(femme)* bride; **féliciter les mariés** to congratulate the bride and groom *or* the married couple; **jeune m./mariée** *(le jour du mariage)* (bride)groom/bride; *(dans les premiers temps)* newly married man/woman; **jeunes mariés** newly married couple, newlyweds; **robe de**

mariée wedding dress; *Prov* **se plaindre que la mariée est trop belle** not to know how lucky one is

Marie-Chantal [mariʃɑ̃tal] NF INV *Fam Br* ≃ Sloane (Ranger), *Am* ≃ preppy

marie-couche-toi-là [marikuʃtwala] NF INV *Péj* harlot, strumpet

marie-jeanne [mariʒan] NF *Fam (cannabis)* Mary Jane, pot

marier [marje] (*pr sub, impf n.* mariions, *v.* mariiez) VT **1** (*de prêtre etc*) (*homme et femme*) to marry; (*de père*) (*fille*) to marry (off); **je suis marié depuis trois ans** I've been married for three years; *Fig Fam* **nous ne sommes pas mariés!** we're not married to each other!, we're not Siamese twins! **2** (*deux qualités*) to combine; (*deux sociétés*) to merge; (*couleurs, senteurs*) to blend, to harmonize; (*vêtements, styles de meubles*) to harmonize; **il marie l'égoïsme à la plus parfaite indifférence** he is a combination of selfishness and total indifference
▶ VPR **se marier 1** (*de personnes*) to get married, to marry; **se m. avec qn** to marry sb **2** (*de couleurs, senteurs*) to blend, to harmonize (**avec** with); (*de vêtements, styles de meubles*) to go together, to harmonize; **le jaune se marie très bien avec le noir** yellow goes very well with black

marie-salope, *pl* **maries-salopes** [marisalɔp] NF **1** *Vulg* slut, *Br* slag **2** *Naut* (*mud*) dredger

marieur, -ieuse [marjœr, -jøz] N *Fam* matchmaker

marigot [marigo] NM (*dans les régions tropicales*) backwater (*of river*)

marihuana, marijuana [marirwana] NF marijuana

marin [marɛ̃] ADJ **1** (*en relation avec la mer*) (*air, brise*) sea; (*plante, animal*) marine; **algues marines** seaweed, *Spéc* marine algae; **sel m.** sea salt; **monstres marins** sea monsters **2** (*destiné à la navigation*) **carte marine** sea chart; **mille m.** nautical mile; **avoir le pied m.** to be a good sailor
▸ NM sailor, seaman, *Litt* seafarer, mariner; (*dans la flotte*) (*able*) seaman; **simple m.** ordinary seaman, rating; **costume m.** sailor suit ▶ ▶ **m. d'eau douce** landlubber; **m. pêcheur** (*deep-sea*) fisherman

marina [marina] NF marina

marinade [marinad] NF *Culin* **1** (*saumure*) pickle; (*avant de faire cuire*) marinade; **m. de poissons/de gibier** marinaded fish/game **2** *Can* **marinades** pickles

marine [marin] NF **1** (*flotte*) navy; **la m. marchande** the merchant navy; **la m. de guerre** the navy; **officier de m.** naval officer **2** (*navigation*) seamanship; **terme de m.** nautical term **3** *Beaux-Arts* seascape
▸ ADJ (**bleu**) **m.** navy (blue); **un chapeau bleu m.** a navy(-blue) hat; **une jupe m.** a navy(-blue) skirt
▸ NM *Mil Br* ≃ (Royal) Marine, *Am* ≃ (US) Marine

mariné [marine] ADJ *Culin* (*pour conserver*) pickled; (*avant cuisson*) marinaded

mariner [marine] *Culin* VT (*pour conserver*) to pickle; (*avant cuisson*) to marinade, to marinate
▸ VI to marinade, to marinate; **un poisson qui doit m. toute une nuit** a fish that should be left to marinade overnight; *Fig Fam* **il m'a fait m. pendant deux heures dans son bureau** he kept me hanging around in his office for two hours; **ça fait déjà six mois que je marine en attendant une lettre de lui** I've been hanging on for six months now waiting for a letter from him

maringouin [marɛ̃gwɛ̃] NM (*sous les tropiques, au Canada*) mosquito

marinier [marinje] ADJ **officier m.** petty officer
▸ NM bargee, *Am* bargeman

marinière [marinjer] NF **1** (*vêtement*) blouse **2** *Culin* **moules (à la) m.** moules (à la) marinière (*mussels cooked in white wine*)

mariol(le) [marjɔl] NM *Fam* sly or clever devil; **faire le m.** to try to be clever

marionnette [marjɔnɛt] NF **m. (à fil)** puppet, marionette; **m. à gaine** glove puppet; *Fig* **je ne suis pas une m.** I'm not a puppet; **spectacle/théâtre de marionnettes** puppet show/theatre; **faire les marionnettes** = to move one's hands and sing in order to amuse a young child

marionnettiste [marjɔnetist] N puppeteer

marital, -ale, -aux, -ales [marital, -o] ADJ (*union*) marital

maritalement [maritalmɑ̃] ADV **ils vivent m.** they're living as husband and wife, they're cohabiting; **vivre m. avec qn** to cohabit with sb

maritime [maritim] ADJ (*navigation, plante etc*) maritime; **ville m.** seaside town; **commerce m.** seaborne trade; **assurance m.** marine or shipping insurance; **courtier m.** shipbroker; **agent m.** shipping agent; **arsenal m.** naval dockyard; *Rail* **gare m.** harbour station; *Can Géog* **les Provinces Maritimes** the Maritime Provinces

maritorne [maritɔrn] NF *Vieilli* slattern, slut, sloven

marivaudage [marivodaʒ] NM *Litt* (*badinage*) light-hearted banter

marivauder [marivode] VI *Litt* to engage in light-hearted banter

marjolaine [marʒɔlɛn] NF *Bot* marjoram

mark [mark] NM *Anciennement* (German) mark

marketing [marketiŋ] NM marketing; **m. direct** direct marketing; **faire du m.** (*étudier*) to do marketing; (*avoir pour profession*) to be in marketing; **elle est chef du m.** she's (the) head of marketing; **m. 'à la carte'** customized or tailored marketing; **m. après-vente** after-sales marketing; **m. ciblé** target marketing; **m. électronique** e-marketing; **m. mix** marketing mix; **m. vert** green marketing

marlot [marlo] NM *Can Fam* (*bon à rien*) good-for-nothing

marlou [marlu] NM *Arg* pimp

marmaille [marmɑj] NF *Fam* (*noisy*) kids, brats; **rue pleine de m.** street swarming with (noisy) kids or brats; *Péj* **elle est venue avec toute sa m.** she brought the whole brood with her

marmelade [marməlad] NF **m. (d'oranges)** (orange) marmalade; *Fig Fam* **mettre qch en m.** to reduce sth to a pulp; **en m.** reduced to a pulp

marmite [marmit] NF **1** (*récipient*) (cooking) pot, pan; (*contenu*) potful, panful; **m. autoclave** pressure cooker; *Fig* **faire bouillir la m.** to bring home the bacon **2** *Mil Fam Vieilli* heavy shell **3** *Géol* **m. de géants** pothole

marmiton [marmitɔ̃] NM kitchen boy

marmonnement [marmɔnmɑ̃] NM mumbling, muttering

marmonner [marmɔne] VT & VI to mumble, to mutter; **qu'est-ce que tu marmonnes encore?** what's that you're muttering or mumbling (now)?

marmoréen, -enne [marmɔreɛ̃, -ɛn] ADJ *Litt* marmoreal, marmorean; **blancheur marmoréenne** marble whiteness

marmot [marmo] NM *Fam* (*enfant*) kid, *Péj* brat

marmotte [marmɔt] NF marmot; *Fig* sleepyhead; *Fig* **dormir comme une m.** to sleep like a log or a baby

marmottement [marmɔtmɑ̃] NM mumbling, muttering

marmotter [marmɔte] VT & VI **m. (entre ses dents)** to mumble, to mutter

marnage¹ [marnaʒ] NM *Agr* (*de sol*) marling

marnage² NM *Naut* tidal range

marne [marn] NF *Géol* marl

marner [marne] VT *Agr* (*sol*) to marl
▸ VI **1** *Arg Vieilli* (*travailler dur*) to slave, to slog **2** (*de la mer*) to rise

Maroc [marɔk] NM Morocco

marocain, -aine [marɔkɛ̃, -ɛn] ADJ Moroccan
▸ N **M.** Moroccan

maronite [marɔnit] ADJ, N Maronite

maronner [marɔne] VI *Fam* to grouse, to grumble

maroquin [marɔkɛ̃] NM **1** (*cuir*) morocco (leather) **2** *Fig* (*minister's*) portfolio

maroquinerie [marɔkinri] NF **1** *Ind* (*fabrication du maroquin*) morocco-leather tanning; (*du cuir*) leather working **2** (*atelier*) morocco-leather tannery **3** *Com* (*articles*) (fancy) leather goods; (*magasin*) (fancy) leather goods shop

maroquinier [marɔkinje] NM **1** (*tanneur*) morocco-leather tanner; (*personne qui fabrique des objets en cuir*) leather worker **2** (*commerçant*) dealer in (fancy) leather goods; **chez le m.** at the leather goods shop

marotte [marɔt] NF **1** (*manie, folie*) fad, craze; (*passe-temps*) hobby **2** (*de modiste, coiffeur*) dummy head

marouflage [maruflaʒ] NM *Beaux-Arts* remounting

maroufler [marufle] VT *Beaux-Arts* to remount

marquage [markaʒ] NM *aussi Sp* marking; *Com* branding; **m. de marchandises** marking of goods; *Aut* **m. au sol** road markings; **m. en zigzag** zigzag marking

marquant [markɑ̃] ADJ (*incident, personne, journée*) remarkable, outstanding; **un épisode m. de son adolescence** a significant episode in his adolescence; *Cartes* **carte marquante** card that counts

marque [mark] NF **1** (*signe, trace*) mark; *Ling* mark, sign; **la m. du pluriel** the mark or sign of the plural; **faire une m. dans la marge** to put a mark in the margin; **faire une m. au couteau sur qch** to make a mark with a knife or a knife mark on sth, to mark sth with a knife; **le cintre a fait une m. sur ce vêtement** the coat hanger has left a mark on this garment; **les roues avaient laissé des marques sur le sable** the wheels had left marks in the sand; **on voit encore la m. du coup qu'elle a reçu** you can still see where she was hit; *Com* **marques d'expédition** shipping marks; *Fig* **marques d'amitié** tokens of friendship
2 *Com* brand; (*de voiture*) make; (*sur l'article*) trademark; **j'ai eu des voitures de trois marques différentes** I've had three different makes of car; **les grandes marques d'électroménager** the main brands of electrical appliance(s); *Fig* **personnage de m.** person of distinction, distinguished or prominent person; **produits de m.** branded goods; **produits de m. courante** well-known branded goods; **vin de m.** wine from a well-known vineyard, choice or vintage wine; **produits sans m.** unbranded goods; **m. dominante** dominant brand; **m. milieu de gamme** middle-of-the-range brand; **m. numéro un** number-one brand; **m. ombrelle** umbrella brand; **m. économique** (*bon marché*) budget or economy brand
3 *Com* (*cachet*) stamp; **un produit qui porte la m. de la douane** goods that have been stamped at customs

4 *Sport* **à vos marques! prêts! partez!** on your marks! get set! go!; *Fig* **chercher ses marques** to try to find one's bearings **5** *(aux jeux)* score; **tenir la m.** to keep (the) score; **où en est la m.?** what's the score? **6** *Ordinat* marker, flag, tag; **m. d'insertion** insertion marker **7** *Naut* **la m. de l'amiral** the admiral's flag ▸▸**m. commerciale** *ou* **de commerce** brand, brand name, trademark; **m. déposée** registered trademark; **m. de détaillant** retailer brand; **m. de distributeur** distributor brand, retailer brand, private brand, private-label brand, own brand; **m. d'enseigne** retailer brand, shop's own brand; **m. de fabricant** manufacturer brand; **m. de fabrique** brand; *(de voiture)* make; *(sur l'article)* trademark; *Fig (caractéristique)* trademark; *Fig* **m. du génie: porter la m. du génie** to bear the stamp *or* the hallmark of genius; **m. de magasin** shop's own brand, store brand; **m. d'orfèvre** hallmark; **m. d'origine** origin of goods label; **m. pilote** brand leader; **m. de revendeur** dealer brand

marqué [marke] ADJ **1** *(qui porte une marque, un signe)* marked, bearing a mark; **être m.** *(de personne)* to have a lined *or* furrowed face; **visage m. par la petite vérole/l'âge** pockmarked face/face lined with age; *Fam* **qu'est-ce est m.** *ou* **qu'est-ce qu'il y a de m. sur l'enveloppe?** what does it say on the envelope?, what's written on the envelope?; *Fig* **j'ai été très m. par ce film** the film made a strong impression on me; **il est m. à vie par cette expérience** he has been marked for life by the experience; **elle guérira, mais restera marquée toute sa vie** she'll get better, but she'll carry *or* bear the marks of it *or* the scars for the rest of her life **2** *(prononcé) (différence, penchant etc)* marked, decided, distinct; *(traits)* pronounced; **robe à la taille marquée** dress with a fitted waist

marque-page, *pl* **marque-pages** NM bookmark

marquer [marke] VT **1** *(faire une marque, un signe sur)* to mark; *(écrire)* to write; *(enregistrer en écrivant)* to make a note of, to note down; **m. les prix** to mark prices; **m. du bétail (au fer)** to brand cattle; **tous les prisonniers ont été marqués au fer** all the prisoners were branded; *Fig* **c'est un événement/jour à m. d'une pierre blanche** it was a remarkable event/red-letter day; **marquez votre nom en haut à gauche** write your name in the top left-hand corner; **il est** *ou* **c'est marqué qu'il faut une pièce d'identité** it says that some form of identification is required **2** *(délimiter)* to mark; **cette clôture marque l'extrémité de la propriété** this fence marks the boundary of the property; **m. sa place** *(dans un train etc)* to reserve *or* *Fam* bag one's seat; *Fig* **cet événement a marqué la fin de son adolescence** this event marked the end of his/her adolescence **3** *Sport* **m. un adversaire** *(le surveiller)* to mark an opponent; **m. un but** to score a goal; **m. les points** to keep (the) score; **m. trente points** to score thirty (points); **ne m. aucun point** to fail to score (a single point); *Fig* **m. un point** *(dans une discussion)* to make a good point; **tu as raison, tu marques un point** you're right, one up to you; **tu as marqué plusieurs points** you scored several points **4** *(indiquer)* to indicate, to show; **la pendule marque dix heures** the clock says ten o'clock; **le thermomètre marque 25°** the thermometer shows *or* registers 25°; **elle n'a pas marqué beaucoup d'intérêt pour l'exposition** she didn't show much interest in the exhibition; *Mus* **m. la mesure** to beat time; **m. le pas** to mark time; **manteau qui**

marque bien la taille coat that shows off the figure; *Fig* **m. le coup** to mark the occasion **5** *(laisser une forte impression sur)* to mark; **la guerre l'a beaucoup marqué** the war certainly left its mark on him *or* left a deep impression on him; **le film ne m'a pas marqué** I wasn't very struck by the film **6** *Ordinat* to mark, to flag, to tag

VI **1** *(écrire)* **crayon qui ne marque pas** pencil that won't write **2** *(laisser une impression) (d'un événement)* to stand out; *(d'une personne)* to leave *or* make one's mark **3** **le verre a marqué sur la table** the glass left a mark on the table, the glass marked the table

marqueté [markǝte] ADJ *(bois)* inlaid; *(fourrure)* speckled

marqueterie [markɛtri] NF inlaid work, marquetry; **guéridon en m.** inlaid pedestal table; **bois de m.** marquetry wood

marqueteur [markǝtœr] NM worker in marquetry, inlayer

marqueur, -euse [markœr, -øz] N **1** *(de documents)* stamper; *(de bétail)* brander **2** *(aux jeux)* scorekeeper, scorer; *Ftbl etc* **m. (de but)** (goal) scorer; *Billard* **m. automatique** scoreboard

NM **1** (felt-tip) marker; **m. surligneur** highlighter **2** *Ordinat* marker, flag; **m. de fin de texte** end of text marker **3** *(biologique)* marker

marquis [marki] NM marquis, marquess

marquisat [markiza] NM marquisate

marquise [markiz] NF **1** *(noble)* marchioness **2** *(véranda) (de toile, tissu)* awning, canopy; *(de verre)* glass awning *or* canopy; *(de gare)* glass roof **3** *(canapé)* sofa, settee *(for two people)*, *Am* love seat **4** *(bague)* marquise (ring) **5** *Culin* **m. au chocolat** = chocolate marquise

Marquises [markiz] NFPL **les (îles) M.** the Marquesas Islands

marraine [marɛn] NF **1** *(d'enfant)* godmother; *(de bateau)* christener **2** *Hist* **m. de guerre** = female correspondent of soldier at the front

Marrakech [marakeʃ] N Marrakesh

marrant, -ante [marɑ̃, -ɑ̃t] *Fam* ADJ **1** *(drôle)* funny; **je ne vois pas ce qu'il y a de m. là-dedans** I can't see anything funny in it, I can't see what's so funny about it; **tu n'es vraiment pas m., tu ne veux jamais sortir** you're not much fun, you never want to go out **2** *(bizarre)* funny, odd, strange; **vous êtes m., vous, alors!** you're the limit!

N **c'est un m.**, **celui-là** that guy's a scream, that guy's hilarious; **le nouveau directeur, c'est vraiment pas un m.** the new manager doesn't fool around; **il a épousé une petite marrante** the woman he married is a real scream

marre [mar] ADV *Fam* **en avoir m. de qn/qch** to be fed up with *or* sick of sb/sth, to have had enough of sb/sth; **j'en ai m.!** I'm fed up!, I'm sick of it!, I've had enough (of it)!; **j'en ai m. de venir à pied tous les jours** I'm fed up with *or* I'm sick of walking here every day; **j'en ai m. que ce soit toujours moi qui fasse les courses** I'm fed up with always having to do the shopping; **il y en a m.** that's enough *(de* of); **il y en a m. de te voir ne rien faire** I'm sick (and tired) of seeing you laze around; **et c'est m.** and that's that

marrer (se) [sǝmare] VPR *Fam* to have a good laugh; **elle ne doit pas se m. tous les jours avec ce type-là** she can't have much fun with that guy; **quand elle me dit qu'elle va chercher du boulot, je me marre** when she tells me she's going to look for a job, I have to laugh; **faire m. qn** to make sb laugh; *Iron* **qu'est-ce qu'on se marre!** this is great fun, I don't think!; **tu me fais m. avec tes his-**

toires de télépathie! you make me laugh with all your stuff about telepathy!

marri [mari] ADJ *Arch* grieved, sad

marron [marɔ̃] ADJ INV NM **1** *Bot, Culin* chestnut; **m. d'Inde** horse chestnut; **crème de m.** chestnut purée; **marrons glacés** candied *or* sugared chestnuts, marrons glacés; **marrons chauds** roast chestnuts; *Fig* **tirer les marrons du feu pour qn** to pull sb's chestnuts out of the fire **2** *Fam (coup)* thump, wallop; **il s'est pris de ces marrons!** he got a real thumping *or* walloping!; **il s'est pris de ces marrons pendant son enfance** he took some real thumpings *or* wallopings as a kid **3** *(couleur)* brown

> Il faut noter que le mot anglais **maroon** est un faux ami. Lorsqu'il désigne une couleur, il signifie **bordeaux**.

marron², -onne [marɔ̃, -ɔn] ADJ **1** *Hist* esclave m. runaway slave **2** *(médecin, homme de loi)* quack **3** *Fam (dupé)* **être m.** to have been taken in *or* for a ride, *Am* to have been rooked; **faire qn m.** to take sb in *or* for a ride, *Am* to rook sb; **zut, voilà le contrôleur, on est marrons!** oh, no, we've had it now, here comes the ticket collector!

marronnier [marɔnje] NM chestnut tree; **m. d'Inde** horse chestnut tree

Mars [mars] N *Myth* Mars

NF *Astron* Mars

mars [mars] NM March; **en m.** in March; **au mois de m.** in (the month of) March; **le sept m.** (on) the seventh of March, (on) March the seventh, *Am* (on) March seventh; **blé de m.**, **les m.** spring wheat; **arriver comme m. en carême** to come as surely as night follows day SEE GRAMMAR A81–2; B60–2

marseillais, -aise [marsɛjɛ, -ɛz] ADJ (of/from) Marseilles

N **m.** *(natif)* native of Marseilles; *(habitant)* inhabitant of Marseilles

NF **la Marseillaise** the Marseillaise

Marseille [marsɛj] N Marseilles

marsouin [marswɛ̃] NM **1** *(mammifère)* porpoise **2** *Mil Fam Arch* marine **3** *Can Fam (malin)* rascal

marsupial, -iale, -iaux, -iales [marsypjal, -jo] ADJ, NM marsupial

marteau, -eaux [marto] NM *(outil)*, *Sport* hammer; *(de commissaire-priseur)* hammer, gavel; *(de porte)* (door) knocker; *(d'horloge)* striker; **coup de m.** hammer stroke *or* blow; *Fig* **être entre le m. et l'enclume** to be stuck in the middle; *Sport* **lanceur de m.** hammer thrower; **être premier au lancer de m.** to come first in the hammer; **requin m.** hammerhead (shark)

ADJ *Fam* nuts, crazy; **elles sont complètement marteaux** they're completely nuts *or* crazy

▸▸**m. à panne fendue** claw hammer; **m.-perforateur,** *pl* **marteaux-perforateurs** hammer drill; *Métal* **m.-pilon,** *pl* **marteaux-pilons** power hammer; **m.-piolet,** *pl* **marteaux-piolets** *(en alpinisme)* piton hammer; **m.-piqueur,** *pl* **marteaux-piqueurs** pneumatic drill; **m. pneumatique** pneumatic drill

martel [martɛl] NM **se mettre m. en tête** to be anxious, to worry

martelage [martǝlaʒ] NM hammering

martelé [martǝle] ADJ hammered; **argent m.** beaten silver; **paroles martelées** hammered-out words

martèlement [martɛlmɑ̃] NM hammering

marteler [martǝle] VT (**je martèle; je martèlerai**) to hammer; *Métal* **m. à froid** to cold-hammer; *Fig* **m. ses mots** to hammer out one's words; *Fig* **m. un air** to hammer out *or* pound out a tune; **la douleur martelait ma**

tempe the pain was hammering away at my temple

martial, -iale, -iaux, -iales [marsjal, -jo] **ADJ** *(musique)* martial; **arts martiaux** martial arts; *Mil* **loi martiale** martial law; *Mil* **code m.** articles of war; *Mil* **cour martiale** court martial; **passer devant la cour martiale pour haute trahison** to be court-martialled for high treason

martialement [marsjalmɑ̃] **ADV** martially

martien, -ienne [marsjɛ̃, -jɛn] **ADJ, N** Martian; **les martiens ont débarqué** the Martians have landed

martinet [martinɛ] **NM 1** *Métal* tilt hammer, drop stamp **2** *(fouet)* strap; **tu vas avoir six coups de m.** you'll get six of the strap *or* of the best **3** *(oiseau)* swift

martingale [martɛ̃gal] **NF 1** *(pour un cheval)* martingale; *(sur un vêtement)* half belt **2** *(au jeu) (façon de jouer)* doubling-up, martingale; *(combinaison)* (winning) formula

martiniquais, -e [martinikɛ, -ɛz] **ADJ** Martinican
  N M. Martinican

Martinique [martinik] **NF** la **M.** Martinique

martin-pêcheur, *pl* **martins-pêcheurs** [martɛ̃pɛʃœr] **NM** *(oiseau)* kingfisher

martre [martr] **NF** marten; **m. zibeline** sable; **m. du Canada** mink

martyr, -yre [martir] **N** martyr; **m. d'une cause** martyr to a cause; **se donner des airs de m., jouer les martyrs** to act the martyr, to put on a martyred expression *or* look; **ne prends pas cet air de m.** don't act the martyr **ADJ un enfant m.** an abused child; **un peuple m.** a martyred people

martyre [martir] **NM** martyrdom; **souffrir le m.** to suffer martyrdom; *Fig* to suffer agonies; **sa vie de couple a été un vrai m.** his married life was pure agony *or* a real martyrdom; **mettre qn au m.** to torture sb

martyriser [martirize] **VT** *Rel* to martyr; *Fig (faire souffrir)* to torture; **il a été martyrisé par ses parents** he was abused by his parents; **il martyrise sa petite sœur** he bullies his little sister

marxisme [marksism] **NM** Marxism

marxisme-léninisme [marksism(ə)leninism] **NM** Marxism-Leninism

marxiste [marksist] **ADJ, N** Marxist

marxiste-léniniste, *pl* **marxistes-léninistes** [marksist(ə)leninist] **ADJ, N** Marxist-Leninist

mas [mɑ(s)] **NM** *(en Provence) (ferme)* farm; *(maison)* farmhouse

mascara [maskara] **NM** mascara; **se mettre du m.** to put on mascara

mascarade [maskarad] **NF** masquerade; *Fig* sham, masquerade; **cette élection n'est qu'une m.** the election is nothing but a sham

mascaret [maskarɛ] **NM** *(dans un estuaire)* bore, tidal wave

mascaron [maskarɔ̃] **NM** *Archit (sur une clef de voûte etc)* grotesque mask

mascotte [maskɔt] **NF** mascot

masculin, -e [maskylɛ̃] **ADJ 1** *(sexe, voix, mode, métier etc)* male; *(qui a les caractères de l'homme) (orgueil, vanité etc)* masculine; *(femme)* masculine, mannish; **mes collègues masculins** my male colleagues **2** *Gram* masculine; **nom m.** masculine noun **3** *(en poésie)* **rime masculine** masculine rhyme
  NM *Gram* masculine (gender); **ce mot est du m.** this word is masculine; **au m.** in the masculine SEE GRAMMAR B5–7

masculinisation [maskylinizasjɔ̃] **NF** *Méd* masculinization; **la m. d'une profession** the increase in the number of men in a profession

masculiniser [maskylinize] **VT m. qn** *(de vêtement, coupe etc)* to make sb look masculine; *(de médicaments)* to produce male characteristics in sb, to masculinize sb; **m. une profession** to increase the number of men in a profession

masculinité [maskylinite] **NF** masculinity

maskinongé [maskinɔ̃ʒe] **NM** *Can (poisson)* muskellunge, *Fam* muskie

maso [mazo] **N, ADJ INV** *Fam (masochiste)* masochist; **tu es complètement m. d'avoir accepté!** you must be a masochist *or* a glutton for punishment if you agreed!

masochisme [mazɔʃism] **NM** masochism

masochiste [mazɔʃist] **ADJ** masochistic
  N masochist

masquage [maskaʒ] **NM** *Ordinat, Phot* masking

masque [mask] **NM 1** mask; **un m. de carnaval** a carnival mask; *Fig* **sa gentillesse n'est qu'un m.** his kindness is only a façade *or* front; **ôter** *ou* **arracher le m. à qn** to unmask sb; **lever le m.** to throw off one's mask; **m. (de beauté)** *(pour la peau)* face pack **2** *Ordinat, Phot* mask; **m. d'entrée, m. de saisie** input mask; **m. d'écran** screen mask **3** *Mil (dispositif de camouflage) (d'arme)* shield, hood
  ▸▸ *Méd* **m. de chirurgien** operating *or* surgeon's mask; **m. à gaz** gas mask; **m. de grossesse** brown patches on the skin, *Spéc* chloasma; **m. mortuaire** death mask; *Méd* **m. à oxygène** oxygen mask; **m. de plongée** diving mask; **m. de soudeur** welding mask

masqué [maske] **ADJ** *(personne)* masked; *(porte)* concealed, hidden; **bal m.** masked ball; *Mil* **tir m.** hidden *or* concealed fire

masquer [maske] **VT** *(mettre un masque à) (personne)* to put a mask on, to mask; *(cacher à la vue) (paysage etc)* to mask, to hide, to conceal; *(sentiments, amour)* to hide, to conceal; *(déguiser) (goût, odeur, peine)* to disguise, to mask; *(lumière)* to shade; *Naut (navire)* to darken; *Mil* **m. une batterie** to conceal *or* hide a battery; *Naut* **naviguer à feux masqués** to sail without lights; **on ne peut m. la vérité plus longtemps** the truth cannot be (kept) hidden any longer; **m. ses véritables intentions** to conceal *or* disguise one's true intentions
  VPR se masquer to put a mask on

massacrante [masakrɑ̃t] **ADJ** être d'une humeur m. to be in a filthy *or* vile temper

massacre [masakr] **NM 1** *(tuerie)* massacre, slaughter; *(d'animaux)* slaughter; *Hist* **le m. de la Saint-Barthélemy** the St Bartholomew's Day Massacre; **envoyer des soldats au m.** to send soldiers to the slaughter *or* to be slaughtered; *Fig* **le match a été un vrai m.** the match was a real massacre; **jeu de m.** ≃ Aunt Sally; *Fig* demolition job **2** *Fam (travail mal fait)* mess; **ils ont voulu faire un gâteau, mais c'est un véritable m.!** they wanted to make a cake but they've made a right mess of it *or* it's a right mess!; **jouer Shakespeare comme cela, c'est un m.!** it's absolutely massacring *or* murdering Shakespeare to perform him like that! **3** *Fam (grand succès)* **faire un m.** *(pièce, spectacle)* to be a smash hit, to be a roaring success; *(artiste, chanteur)* to be a roaring success; *(homme d'affaires)* to make a killing **4** *(tête de daim, de cerf)* stag's head *(displayed as a hunting trophy)*

massacrer [masakre] **VT 1** *(tuer, exterminer)* to massacre, to slaughter; *(animaux)* to slaughter; *Fig* **notre équipe s'est fait m.** our team was massacred; **le film a été massacré par la critique** the film was torn to pieces *or* savaged by the critics; **lors du débat, il s'est vraiment fait m. par son interlocuteur** he was really savaged by his opponent in the

debate **2** *Fam (travail)* to bungle, to botch, to make a mess *or* hash of; *(musique, texte)* to murder, to massacre; *(vêtements)* to ruin

massacreur, -euse [masakrœr, -øz] **N 1** *(tueur)* slaughterer, butcher **2** *Fam (gâcheur)* bungler, botcher

massage [masaʒ] **NM** massage; **se faire faire un m.** to have a massage
  ▸▸ *Méd* **m. cardiaque** cardiac *or* heart massage; **m. thaïlandais** Thai massage: **faire des massages thaïlandais** to work in a massage parlour

masse [mas] **NF 1** *Phys, Tech* mass; **le kilogramme est l'unité de m.** the kilogram is the unit of mass
  2 *(grande quantité)* mass; *(de gens)* mass, crowd; **m. d'eau** body of water; *(en mouvement)* mass of water; *Météo* **m. d'air** mass of air, air mass; **tomber comme une m.** to fall in a heap; **taillé dans la m.** carved from the block; *Fam* **un grand type taillé dans la m.** a big, heavily built sort of chap; **en m.** *(en grand nombre)* in large numbers, en masse; **'arrivée en m. des estivants sur les plages'** 'holidaymakers invade the beaches *or* take to the beaches in droves'; **les villageois se préparent à une arrivée en m. des touristes** villagers are bracing themselves for a tourist invasion; **la m. des connaissances** the total sum of knowledge; **la grande m. des employés** the vast majority of employees, virtually all employees; **les masses** the masses; culture de **m.** mass *or* popular culture; *Fam* **il y avait des masses de livres** there were masses (and masses) of books; *Fam* **il y a une m. de gens qui votent pour lui** masses of people *or* a whole mass of people are voting for him; *Fam* **il n'y avait pas des masses de gens** there weren't exactly masses of people there; *Fam* **il n'y en a pas des masses** *(objets)* there aren't masses of them; *(sucre, farine etc)* there isn't masses (of it); *Fam* **t'as faim? – pas des masses** are you hungry? – not really
  3 *Fin* fund, stock; **il faut établir la m. d'équipement dans le budget de cette année** we have to establish the total amount of (money allowed for) capital goods in this year's budget
  4 *Élec* earth, *Am* ground; **mettre le courant à la m.** to earth *or Am* ground the current; *Fig Fam* **être à la m.** to be mad, to be off one's head
  ▸▸ *Fin* **m. active** assets; *Phys, Nucl* **m. critique** critical mass; **masses laborieuses** (working) masses, *Litt* toiling masses; *Fin* **m. monétaire** money supply, (total amount of) money in circulation; *Fin* **m. passive** liabilities; **m. salariale** wage bill, staff costs; **faire partie de la m. salariale** to be on the payroll; *Phys* **m. spécifique** *ou* **volumique** density

masse [mas] **NF 1** *(marteau)* sledgehammer; **m. en bois** beetle; *Fig Fam* **coup de m.** *(dû à une émotion)* crushing blow; *(dû à un prix exorbitant)* (very) nasty shock *(when one sees the bill)*; **il a reçu le coup de m.** *(quand il a appris qu'il était renvoyé)* it came as a crushing blow; **ça a été le coup de m.** *(quand il nous a annoncé le total)* it came as a (very) nasty shock **2** *(d'huissier)* (ceremonial) mace; **m. (d'armes)** *(arme ancienne)* mace

masselotte [maslɔt] **NF** *Tech* bob weight; *(de régulateur)* flyweight

massepain [maspɛ̃] **NM** marzipan

masser [mase] **VT** *(réunir) (personnes)* to gather together, to assemble; *(soldats)* to mass; *Beaux-Arts (figures etc)* to group; **elle massait ses cheveux dans sa nuque** she gathered her hair (together) at the back of her neck
  VPR se masser to gather, to form a crowd; la

foule s'est massée devant le tribunal the crowd gathered in front of the courtroom

masser² VT *(frotter)* to massage; **il m'a massé le dos** he massaged my back; **elle a massé le patient** she gave the patient a massage, she massaged the patient; **se faire m.** to have a massage, to be massaged

massette [mɑsɛt] NF **1** *(outil)* two-handed hammer **2** *Bot* bulrush, reed mace, cat's tail

masseur, -euse [mɑsœr, -øz] N *(personne)* masseur, *f* masseuse
NM *(appareil)* (vibro)massager

masseur-kinésithérapeute, *pl* **masseurs-kinésithérapeutes** N physiotherapist

massicot¹ [masiko] NM *Chimie* massicot

massicot² NM *Tech* guillotine, trimmer

massicoter [masikɔte] VT *Tech* to guillotine

massif, -ive [masif, -iv] ADJ **1** *(gros, épais)* massive, bulky; *(homme)* heavily built; **des traits massifs** heavy features **2** *(plein) (argent, acajou etc)* solid; **bijoux en or m.** solid gold jewellery **3** *Fig (en masse, en grande quantité) (dose, bombardements)* massive; **départs massifs** mass exodus; **un 'oui' franc et m.** a clear and overwhelming 'yes'
NM **1** *(d'arbustes, d'arbres)* clump; **m. de fleurs** bed of flowers, flowerbed **2** *Géog* massif; **le M. central** the Massif Central *(mountain range in central France)*

massique [masik] ADJ *Phys* mass; **puissance m.** power-to-weight ratio

massivement [masivmɑ̃] ADV *(répondre, voter etc)* en masse, in large numbers

mass media [masmedja] NMPL mass media

massue [masy] NF club, bludgeon; **coup de m.** blow with a club; *Fig* **ça a été le coup de m.** *(prix excessif)* it was a rip-off; *(choc émotionnel)* it was a bolt from the blue, it was a staggering blow; **quand on a reçu la facture, ça a été le coup de m.** when we got the invoice, we had a (very) nasty shock; **argument m.** sledgehammer argument

mastard [mastar] NM *Fam* hefty man

mastectomie [mastɛktɔmi] NF mastectomy

master [mastɛr] NM *TV etc* master; **m. monté** edited master

mastère [mastɛr] NM *Univ (d'ingénieur)* DEng; *(de commerce)* MBA

mastic [mastik] NM **1** *(résine)* mastic (resin); *(pour fenêtres etc)* putty; *(pour bois etc)* filler, mastic; **m. de colmatage** filler paste **2** *Typ* transposition; **faire un m.** to (accidentally) transpose characters
ADJ INV putty-coloured *or Am* -colored

masticage [mastikaʒ] NM *(de fenêtre)* puttying; *(de bois)* filling

masticateur, -trice [mastikatœr, -tris] ADJ masticatory

mastication [mastikasjɔ̃] NF chewing, *Fml* mastication

masticatoire [mastikatwar] ADJ, NM masticatory

mastiquer¹ [mastike] VT *(mâcher)* to chew, *Fml* to masticate

mastiquer² VT *(fissures etc)* to fill (in); *(fenêtre, vitre)* to putty
VI **couteau à m.** putty knife

mastite [mastit] NF *Méd* mastitis

mastoc [mastɔk] ADJ INV **1** *Fam (personne)* hulking, lumpish; *(construction)* cumbersome **2** *Belg (fou) (personne)* daft, dippy

mastodonte [mastɔdɔ̃t] NM **1** *Zool* mastodon **2** *Fam (véhicule)* juggernaut; *(personne)* colossus

mastoïde [mastɔid] NF *Anat* mastoid

mastoïdien, -ienne [mastɔidjɛ̃, -jɛn] ADJ *Anat* mastoid

mastose [mastoz] NF *Méd* mastosis

mastroquet [mastrɔkɛ] NM *Vieilli* **1** *(cafetier)* bar owner, *Br* publican **2** *(bistro)* bar, *Br* pub

masturbation [mastyrbasjɔ̃] NF masturbation; **c'est de la m. intellectuelle** it's intellectual self-indulgence *or* masturbation

masturbatoire [mastyrbatwar] ADJ masturbatory

masturber [mastyrbe] VT to masturbate
VPR **se masturber** to masturbate

m'as-tu-vu, -vue [matyvy] ADJ INV *Fam* show-off; **qu'est-ce qu'elle est m'as-tu-vue** what a show-off she is; **ce genre de voiture, ça fait très m.** it's a really flashy type of car

masure [mazyr] NF tumbledown cottage, *Péj* hovel

mat¹ [mat] ADJ *(métal)* mat(t), unpolished, dull; *(couleur)* mat(t), flat; **teint m.** mat(t) complexion; **son m.** dull sound, thud

mat² *Échecs* ADJ INV checkmated; **le roi est m.** the king is checkmated *or* in checkmate
NM INV (check)mate; **faire m. en trois coups** to mate in three

mat' [mat] NM *Fam (abrév* **matin)** **deux/trois heures du m.** two/three a.m. *or* in the morning

mât [mɑ] NM **1** *Naut* mast; **grand m.** mainmast; **m. d'artimon** mizzenmast; **m. de misaine** foremast; **m. de hune** topmast; **m. de charge** cargo boom, derrick; **navire à trois mâts** three-masted ship, three-master **2** *(poteau)* pole; **m. de tente** tent pole; **m. de cocagne** greasy pole; *Rail* **m. de sémaphore** signal post, signal mast

matador [matadɔr] NM matador

mataf [mataf] NM *Arg (matelot)* tar, sailor

matamore [matamɔr] NM braggart, boaster; **faire le m.** to boast, to brag

match, *pl* **matchs, matches** [matʃ] NM *Sport* match; **disputer un m.** to play a match; **on fait un m.?** shall we have *or* play a match?; **m. de barrage** relegation match; **m. de boxe** boxing match; *Ftbl* **m. de championnat (professionnel)** league match; **m. aller** first leg; **m. retour** return match, second leg; **m. amical** friendly (match); **m. nul** draw; **faire m. nul** to draw, to tie; **ils ont fait m. nul** they drew, the match ended in a draw

maté [mate] NM maté

matelas [matla] NM **1** mattress; **m. à ressorts** spring mattress; **m. pneumatique** inflatable mattress, air bed, *Br* Lilo®; **toile à m.** ticking; *Constr* **m. d'air** air space **2** *Fam (fortune)* pile (of money); **un m. de billets de banque** a wad of banknotes

matelassé [matlase] ADJ *Tex* quilted; **blouson m.** quilted *or* padded jacket; **enveloppe matelassée** padded envelope, Jiffy bag®
NM quilted material; **du m. de soie** quilted silk

matelasser [matlase] VT *(meuble)* to upholster; *(tissu)* to quilt; *(recouvrir de tissu matelassé)* to cover with quilted material

matelassure [matlasyr] NF *(de matelas, selle etc)* padding, stuffing

matelot [matlo] NM *Naut* **1** *(personne)* sailor; **m. (breveté) de première classe** leading seaman; **m. de deuxième classe** able seaman; **servir comme simple m.** to sail before the mast **2** *(bateau)* consort (ship); **m. d'avant/d'arrière** next ship ahead/astern

matelotage [matlɔtaʒ] NM **1** *(connaissances)* seamanship **2** *(paye)* sailor's pay

matelote [matlɔt] NF *Culin* matelote, fish stew; **m. de morue** cod stew; **sauce m.** red wine and onion sauce

mater¹ [mate] VT **1** *Échecs* to (check)mate **2** *Fig (dresser, dompter) (personne, chien)* to bring to heel, to subdue, to tame

mater² VT **1** *(métaux, verre etc)* to mat(t), to dull **2** *(joints de chaudière etc)* to caulk, to hammer

mater³ *Fam* VT to ogle, to eye up; **mate un peu la gonzesse!** just take a look at *or* get an eyeful of that chick!; **se faire m.** to be ogled, to be eyed up
VI to eye up *or* ogle (the) women; **qu'est-ce que ça mate, ici!** all these men eyeing us up!

mâter [mɑte] VT *(navire)* to mast

matérialisation [materjalizasjɔ̃] NF *(d'espoir, de projet)* materialization, realization; **la m. de Dieu sur terre** the materialization of God on earth

matérialisé [materjalize] ADJ *Admin* **voie matérialisée** = section of road delimited by a white line

matérialiser [materjalize] VT *(idée, espoir, projet), Fin* to realize
VPR **se matérialiser** to materialize

matérialisme [materjalism] NM materialism

matérialiste [materjalist] ADJ materialistic
N materialist

matérialité [materjalite] NF **1** *(caractère de ce qui est réel, matériel)* materiality **2** *(matérialisme)* materialism

matériau [materjo] NM *Constr* material; **m. composite** composite

---
Do not confuse with **matériel.**
---

matériaux [materjo] NMPL **1** *Constr* material(s); **m. de construction** building *or* construction material(s) **2** *Fig* material; **il n'a pas tellement de m. pour rédiger sa thèse** he doesn't have much material for his thesis

matériel, -ielle [materjɛl] ADJ *(confort, besoins, aide etc)* material; *(financier)* financial; **tu n'en as pas la preuve matérielle** you don't have material *or* solid *or* firm proof of it; **l'organisation matérielle de la fête a posé de gros problèmes** the practical organization of the party posed great problems; **je n'ai pas le temps m. de le faire** I simply don't have time to do it; **être dans l'impossibilité matérielle de bouger** to find it physically impossible to move
NM **1** equipment; *(d'usine)* plant; *Mil* equipment, *Spéc* matériel; *Mil* **service du m.** ordnance; **m. de camping/de laboratoire** camping/laboratory equipment; **m. d'exploitation** working plant; **m. de guerre** weaponry; **m. d'emballage** packaging; **m. de bureau** office equipment; **m. hi-fi** hi-fi equipment; **m. industriel** plant; *Rail* **m. roulant** rolling stock **2** *Ordinat* hardware; **m. de composition** film setting hardware; **m. informatique** computer hardware

---
Do not confuse with **matériau.**
---

matériellement [materjɛlmɑ̃] ADV materially; *(financièrement)* financially; **avoir de quoi vivre m.** to have enough for one's material needs; **chose m. impossible** physical impossibility; **je ne peux m. pas accepter un travail à temps complet** it is physically impossible for me to take on a full-time job; **je n'ai m. pas le temps de venir te voir** I simply don't have time to come and see you

maternage [maternaʒ] NM mothering

maternel, -elle [maternɛl] ADJ maternal; *(soins, gestes)* motherly; **lait m.** mother's milk; **allaitement m.** breastfeeding; **l'instinct m.** the maternal instinct; **elle est très maternelle avec ses collègues** she acts in a very maternal *or* motherly way towards her colleagues; **un cousin du côté m.** a cousin on one's mother's side; **grand-père m.** maternal grandfather; **langue maternelle** mother tongue, native tongue; **centre de protection maternelle et infantile** mother-

and-baby clinic; **école maternelle** nursery (school)

NF maternelle 1 *(école)* nursery (school) **2** *Fam (mère)* old lady, *Br* old dear *(mother)*

Maternelle

Nursery education for children from two to six years old is provided by the state and is available to all families in France. Although it is not compulsory, a vast majority of children attend nursery schools and are thus well-prepared for entry into primary school.

---

maternellement [matɛrnɛlmɑ̃] **ADV** maternally, in a motherly way

materner [matɛrne] **VT** to mother

maternisé [matɛrnize] **ADJ lait m.** milk suitable for infants

maternité [matɛrnite] **NF 1** *(fait d'être mère)* motherhood; **un corps déformé par des maternités successives** a body misshapen by one pregnancy after another; **en congé de m.** on maternity leave **2** *(hôpital)* maternity hospital **3** *Beaux-Arts* Madonna and Child

mateur, -euse [matœr, -øz] **N** *très Fam* ogler

mathématicien, -ienne [matematisjɛ̃, -jen] **N** mathematician

mathématique [matematik] **ADJ** mathematical; *Fig (esprit)* (very) logical; *(rigueur)* mathematical; **c'est m.!** it's perfectly obvious!

NFPL mathématiques mathematics; **mathématiques pures/appliquées** pure/applied mathematics **VOIR GRAMMAIRE A10**

mathématiquement [matematikmɑ̃] **ADV** mathematically; **m., je ne pourrai pas être à l'heure** it's physically impossible for me to be on time

matheux, -euse [matø, -øz] **N** *Fam* mathematician; *(élève, étudiant)* maths *or Am* math student

math(s) [mat] **NFPL** *Fam* maths, *Am* math; *Univ* **m. sup/spé** = first/second-year maths class *(for candidates for the grandes écoles)*

Mathusalem [matyzalɛm] **NM 1** Methuselah; *Fam* **ça date de M.** *(objet)* it's as old as the hills; *(nouvelle)* it's ancient history **2** **m.** *(bouteille)* Methuselah

matière [matjɛr] **NF 1** *(substance)* material; **en quelle m. est ton pantalon?** what material are your trousers made of?; **matière(s) plastique(s)** plastic(s); **sachet en m. plastique** plastic bag; **matières consommables** consumables

2 *Phys, Phil* matter; **m. inanimée** inanimate matter; **m. solide inflammable** flammable solid; **la désintégration de la m.** the disintegration of matter; *Biol* **m. vivante** living matter

3 *Fig (sujet, contenu) (de discours)* subject (matter); *(pour discussion)* subject, topic, theme; *(pour en faire un film, un livre, une étude etc)* material; *Scol* subject; **table des matières** (table of) contents; **faire une entrée en m.** to give an introduction; **il n'y a pas m. à rire** it's no laughing matter; **cela donne m. à réflexion** it's food for thought; **il y a m. à procès/dispute** there are grounds for going to court/for contesting it; **il n'y avait pas m. à discuter** there was nothing to be said about it; **en m. de** as regards; **être bon juge en m. de musique** to be a good judge of music; **être bon juge en la m.** to be a good judge of the subject

▸▸ *Méd* **m. fécale** faecal *or Am* fecal matter; **matières grasses** fat; **fromage à 20% de matières grasses** cheese with a 20% fat content; **m. grise** grey matter; *Fin* **m. imposable** taxable income; *Ind* **matière(s) première(s)** raw material(s)

Matif [matif] **NM** *(abrév* **marché à terme des instruments financiers)** *(French)* international financial futures market

Matignon [matiɲɔ̃] **N** = French Prime Minister's offices; **M. a décidé que …** the Prime Minister's office has decided that …

Matignon

The name of the Prime Minister's offices is often used to refer to the Prime Minister and his or her administrative staff, for example "L'Élysée et Matignon ont fini par se mettre d'accord".

---

matin [matɛ̃] **NM** morning; **du m. au soir** from morning till night; **quatre heures du m.** four o'clock in the morning, 4 a.m.; **le jeudi deux au m.** on the morning of Thursday the second; **c'est le m. que je travaille le mieux** I work best in the morning; **elle travaille seulement le m.** she only works mornings, she only works in the morning; **demain m.** tomorrow morning; **tous les lundis m.** every Monday morning; **de grand** *ou* **bon m., le m. de bonne heure** early in the morning, in the early morning; **être du m.** to be an early bird *or* an early riser; **rentrer au petit m.** to come home in the small *or* early hours; **un de ces (quatre) matins, un beau m.** one of these (fine) days **SEE GRAMMAR A80~1; B60**

ADV early in the morning; **se lever très m.** to get up very early

mâtin, -ine [matɛ̃, -in] **NM** *(chien)* mastiff, watchdog

N *Arch Fam (coquin)* sly dog, *f* minx

INT *Arch* by Jove!

matinal, -ale, -aux, -ales [matinal, -o] **ADJ 1** *(brise)* morning; **à cette heure matinale** at this early hour; **promenade matinale** morning walk **2** **être m.** to be an early riser; **comme tu es m. aujourd'hui!** you're an early bird!

N early riser

mâtiné [matine] **ADJ** crossbred; *(chien)* mongrel, crossbred; **un teckel m. de caniche** a cross between a dachshund and a poodle; *Fig* **il parle un français m. d'anglais** his French is full of anglicisms; **un humour m. d'une touche de mépris** humour tinged with scorn

matinée [matine] **NF 1** *(matin)* morning; **dans la m.** in (the course of) the morning; **en fin de m.** towards the end of the morning; **j'ai passé toute ma m. à l'attendre/au lit** I spent the whole morning waiting for him/in bed; **je ne l'ai pas vu de toute la m.** I haven't seen him all morning; **une m. de lecture** a morning (spent) reading; *Fam* **faire la grasse m.** to have a lie -in **SEE GRAMMAR B61 2** *Théâtre* matinee, afternoon performance; *Cin* matinee, afternoon showing *or* screening; **on joue ce film en m.** there's an afternoon performance *or* a matinee performance of this film

matines [matin] **NFPL** *Rel* matins

matir [matir] **VT** = **mater²**

matité [matite] **NF** *(de son)* dullness

matois, -oise [matwa, -waz] *Litt* **ADJ** sly, cunning, crafty

N crafty person; **fin m.** sly devil

maton, -onne [matɔ̃, -ɔn] **N** *Arg (de prison)* screw

matos [matos] **NM** *Fam* equipment

matou [matu] **NM** tom (cat)

matraquage [matrakaʒ] **NM** bludgeoning, *Br* coshing, *Am* blackjacking; *Fig* **m. idéologique** ideological brainwashing; **m. publicitaire** hype; **c'est vraiment du m. qu'ils font pour la sortie de ce film** they're really hyping *or* plugging the release of this film; **avec**

---

les élections, ça va être le m. à la télé! with the elections, it'll be total overkill on TV!

matraque [matrak] **NF** bludgeon, *Br* cosh, *Am* blackjack; *(d'agent de police)* surtout *Br* truncheon, *Am* billy (club); *Fig Fam* **c'est le coup de m.** it's a rip-off

matraquer [matrake] **VT** *(frapper)* to bludgeon, *Br* to cosh; *Fam (auditeur, consommateur)* to bombard; *(disque, chanson)* to plug; *Fig Fam* **m. le client** to rip off *or* fleece the customer; *Fig* **la radio matraque ses annonces/cette chanson toute la journée** the radio churns out its announcements/that song all day long

matriarcal, -ale, -aux, -ales [matrijarkal, -o] **ADJ** matriarchal

matriarcat [matrijarka] **NM** matriarchy

matricaire [matrikɛr] **NF** *Bot* pineapple weed

matrice [matris] **NF 1** *Math* matrix; *Tech* matrix, die; *Typ* matrix, type mould; *(de disque)* matrix **VOIR GRAMMAIRE A14 2** *Ordinat* array; **m. active/passive** active/passive matrix; **m. d'aiguilles** dot matrix; **m. de vérité** truth table **3** *Admin (du rôle des contributions)* original **4** *Anat* uterus, womb

matricide [matrisid] **ADJ** matricidal

N matricide

NM *(crime)* matricide

matriciel, -ielle [matrisjɛl] **ADJ** *Math* matrix; *Ordinat* **imprimante matricielle** dot matrix printer

NF *Ordinat* **matricielle** dot matrix

matricule [matrikyl] **ADJ** *Mil, Admin* **numéro m.** number

NM *Mil, Admin* number; *Fam* **ça va chauffer pour ton m.** you'll be in hot water

NF 1 *(liste) (de prison, d'hôpital)* roll, register, list; *Mil* (regimental) roll; *(immatriculation)* registration **2** *(extrait)* registration certificate

matrimonial, -iale, -iaux, -iales [matrimɔnjal, -jo] **ADJ** matrimonial; **agence matrimoniale** dating agency; **régime m.** marriage settlement; **juge des affaires matrimoniales** divorce court judge

matrone [matrɔn] **NF** *Antiq* matron; *Péj (femme imposante)* stout *or* portly woman; **vieille m.** fat old woman

maturation [matyrasjɔ̃] **NF** maturation; *(de fruit, céréale, fromage)* ripening; *(de tabac)* maturing; *Physiol* **m. sexuelle** sexual maturation

mature [matyr] **ADJ** mature

mâture [mɑtyr] **NF** *Naut* masts (and spars); **dans la m.** aloft

maturité [matyrite] **NF 1** *(de personne, d'animal)* maturity; *(de fruit, fromage)* ripeness; **arriver** *ou* **venir à m.** to come to maturity, to mature; **cette jeune femme ne manque pas de m.** that young woman is very mature; **elle manque totalement de m.** she's totally immature; **sa m. d'esprit est remarquable** he/she has a remarkably mature mind **2** *Suisse (baccalauréat)* **m. fédérale** school-leaving diploma *(from a gymnase, granting admission to university)*

matutinal, -ale, -aux, -ales [matytinal, -o] **ADJ** *Litt* morning

maudire [modir] **VT** *(prp* **maudissant**; *pp* **maudit**; *pr ind* **je maudis, n. maudissons, v. maudissez, ils maudissent**; *pr sub* **je maudisse**; *p hist* **je maudis**; *fu* **je maudirai**) to curse; *Litt* **maudit sois-tu!** a curse on you!

maudit, -ite [modi, -it] **ADJ 1** *(crime, science)* accursed **2** *(avant nom) (voiture, ville etc)* damn(ed), blasted, cursed; **quel m. temps!** what filthy weather!

N le M. the Devil; **les maudits** the damned, the accursed

maugréer [mogree] **VI** to grumble, to grouse (**contre** about, at)

maure [mɔr] **ADJ** Moorish
N M. Moor

mauresque [mɔrɛsk] **ADJ** *(architecture, motif etc)* Moorish
NF 1 M. Moorish woman **2** *(boisson)* = pastis with barley water and water

Maurice [mɔris] **N l'île M.** Mauritius

mauricien, -ienne [mɔrisjɛ̃, -jɛn] **ADJ** Mauritian
N M. Mauritian

Mauritanie [mɔritani] **NF** Mauritania

mauritanien, -ienne [mɔritanjɛ̃, -jɛn] **ADJ** Mauritanian
N M. Mauritanian

mausolée [mozɔle] **NM** mausoleum

maussade [mosad] **ADJ 1** *(de mauvaise humeur)* sullen, morose; *(triste)* glum; **ça l'a rendu m.** *(amer)* that disgruntled him **2** *(temps)* dull, gloomy; **paysage m.** gloomy countryside

maussaderie [mosadri] **NF** *Litt* sullenness, moroseness

MAUVAIS, -AISE [mɔvɛ, ɛz] **ADJ 1** *(repas, haleine, rêve, avis, organisation, qualité etc)* bad; **m. pour la santé/la digestion** bad for one's health/the digestion; **de plus en plus m.** worse and worse; **le plus m.** the worst; **m. temps** bad weather; **mauvaise mer** rough sea; **être en mauvaise posture** to be in a difficult situation; **cela a fait m. effet** it looked bad, it made a bad impression; **elle a reçu une mauvaise nouvelle** she has had some bad news; **ce n'est pas m.** *(c'est bon)* it's not bad; **je l'ai trouvé mauvaise** I didn't appreciate it; **il risque de la trouver mauvaise quand il apprendra** he's not going to be very happy when he finds out; **l'avoir m.** to be very put out, *Br Fam* to be miffed; **elle a mauvaise mine** she doesn't look well; **avoir une mauvaise santé** to be in bad *or* poor health; **mauvaise vue** bad *or* poor eyesight; **il a fait une mauvaise bronchite** he's had a bad attack of bronchitis; **faire de mauvaises affaires** to be involved in some bad business deals; **la récolte sera mauvaise** it will be a bad *or* poor harvest; **les freins sont m.** the brakes are defective; **c'est un m. banquier** he's a poor *or* bad banker; **m. en anglais** bad *or* poor at English; **une mauvaise excuse** a poor excuse

2 *(inapproprié)* wrong; **c'est la mauvaise clef** it's the wrong key; **arriver au m. moment** to come at a bad *or* an inconvenient time *or* at a bad *or* an awkward moment; *Tél* **m. numéro** wrong number

3 *(méchant)* *(personne)* bad, nasty; *(augure)* bad, ill; **être m. avec qn** to be nasty to sb; **qu'est-ce qu'elle est mauvaise aujourd'hui!** she's in a nasty mood today!; **mauvaise action** wrong(doing); **avoir l'air m.** *(de personne)* to look nasty; *(de chien)* to look fierce *or* vicious; **c'est un m. sujet** *ou* **un m. garçon** he's a bad lot; **né sous une mauvaise étoile** born under an unlucky star; **elle n'a pas un m. fond** deep down she's not bad, she's not bad at heart; **elle a vraiment un m. fond!** she's a really nasty character!

ADV sentir m. to smell (bad), to stink; **il fait m.** the weather's bad

N villain; *Fam* baddie; **dans le film, il joue le rôle du m.** he plays the baddie in the film

▸▸ **mauvaise langue** (spiteful) gossip; **c'est vraiment une mauvaise langue** he's got a really spiteful *or* nasty tongue; **ce que tu peux être mauvaise langue, alors!** you can be a real gossip!; **m. œil** evil eye; **elle est persuadée d'avoir le m. œil** she's convinced that somebody has put the evil eye on her; **m. plaisant** practical joker

mauve [mov] **NM** *(couleur)* mauve
NF *Bot* mallow
ADJ mauve

mauviette [movjɛt] **NF** *Fam (physiquement)* wimp, *Br* weed; *(moralement)* wimp, drip; **quelle m. tu fais!** you're such a wimp!

MAV [ɛmave] **NM** *(abrév* **marketing après-vente***)* after-sales marketing

max [maks] **NM INV** *(abrév* **maximum***)* **1** *(dans annonce)* max **2** *Fam* **un m.** loads, lots; **ça lui plaît un m.** he/she likes it loads *or* lots; **un m. de fric** loads of money; **on s'est éclaté un m. à la soirée de Caroline** we had a really fantastic time at Caroline's party

maxi [maksi] *Fam* **ADJ INV** maxi; **une m.(-)bouteille** a giant-size *or* jumbo-size bottle
ADV on sera 20 m. there'll be 20 of us max *or* tops; **ça prendra deux heures m.** it'll take two hours max *or* tops
NM *Vieilli (manteau)* maxi (coat); **la mode du m.** the maxi fashion
NF *Vieilli (jupe)* maxi (skirt)

maxillaire [maksilɛr] *Anat* **ADJ** maxillary; **os m.** jawbone, *Spéc* maxilla
NM jawbone, *Spéc* maxilla

maximal, -ale, -aux, -ales [maksimal, -o] **ADJ** *(effet, excitation, peine etc)* maximum; *(température)* maximum, top; **vitesse maximale autorisée: 60 km/h** speed limit: 60 kmph

maxime [maksim] **NF** maxim

maximisation [maksimizasjɔ̃] **NF m. du profit** profit optimization

maximiser [maksimize] **VT** to maximize

maximum [maksimɔm], *pl* **maximums** *ou* **maxima** [maksima] **NM** maximum; **faire le m. (pour faire qch)** to do one's utmost *or* one's best (to do sth); **m. de rendement** maximum output; **porter la production au m.** to increase production to a maximum, to maximize production; **je vais essayer de t'aider au m.** I'll try my very hardest *or* my very best to help you; **thermomètre à maxima** maximum thermometer; **on sera 20 au m.** there will be 20 of us at (the) most; **nous avons de la place pour 20 personnes au m.** we have room for a maximum of 20 (people) *or* for 20 (people) at (the) most; *Fam* **un m.** *(beaucoup)* loads, lots; *Fam* **ça lui plaît un m.** he likes it loads *or* lots
ADJ SOUVENT INV maximum; **rendement m.** maximum *or* peak output

maya [maja] **ADJ** Maya, Mayan
NM *Ling* Mayan
N M. Maya, Mayan

Mayence [majɑ̃s] **N** Mainz

mayonnaise [majɔnɛz] **NF** *Culin* mayonnaise; *Fig Fam* **faire monter la m.** to stir things up; *Fig Fam* **la m. n'a pas pris** it didn't work; **la m. a pris** it worked

mazagran [mazagrɑ̃] **NM** *(en verre, faïence)* goblet

mazette [mazɛt] **INT** *Hum* my word!, *Br* goodness gracious!

mazout [mazut] **NM** (fuel) oil; **chauffage central au m.** oil-fired central heating; **poêle à m.** oil stove

mazouté [mazute] **ADJ** *(plage)* oil-polluted, polluted with oil; *(oiseau)* oil-covered, covered in oil, oiled

mazurka [mazyrka] **NF** mazurka

mb **NM** *Météo abrév* **millibar**

MBA [ɛmbea] **NF** *Compta (abrév* **marge brute d'autofinancement***)* cashflow, funds generated by operations

Mbps *Ordinat (abrév* **mégabits par seconde***)* mbps

MDD [ɛmdede] **NF** *Com (abrév* **marque de distributeur***)* distributor's brand name, own brand

me *(before a vowel sound* **m'***)* [mə] **PRON PERS** SEE GRAMMAR A27; B18–19 **1** *(objet direct)* me; **il m'aime** he loves me; **me voici** here I am **2** *(objet indirect)* (to) me; **il m'a écrit** he wrote to me; **il me l'a dit** he told me (so); **donnez-m'en** give me some; *Fam* **tu veux bien m'éteindre la lumière?** would you switch off the light (for me)? **3** *(verbe pronominal)* myself; **je m'amusais** I was enjoying myself; **je ne m'en souviens plus** I don't remember any more; **je me suis dit que …** I said to myself that … SEE GRAMMAR A29; B28–9

mea-culpa [meakylpa] **NM INV faire** *ou* **dire son m.** to own up *or* to confess (to one's mistake)

méandre [meɑ̃dr] **NM** *(de rivière)* meander, loop; *(de route)* bend; *Fig* **se perdre dans les méandres d'un raisonnement** to get lost in the intricacies of an argument

mec [mɛk] **NM** *Fam* guy, *Br* bloke; **t'en fais pas, m.!** don't worry about it, mate *or* pal *or surtout Am* man!; **son nouveau m.** her new guy *or* man; **eh les mecs! venez voir!** hey guys! come and have a look!

mécanicien, -ienne [mekanisjɛ̃, -jɛn] **N 1** *Aut* (garage *or* motor) mechanic; *Naut* engineer; *Aviat* **m. de bord** *ou* **navigant** flight engineer; **c'est une bonne mécanicienne** she's a good mechanic; **ouvrier m.** mechanic; **ingénieur m.** mechanical engineer **2** *Rail* engine driver, *Am* engineer
NF *Couture* **mécanicienne** machinist

mécanicien-dentiste, *pl* **mécaniciens-dentistes NM** *Vieilli* dental technician

mécanique [mekanik] **ADJ** *Tech etc (fonctionnement, système)* mechanical; *(dentelle, tuiles etc)* machine-made; **jouet m.** clockwork toy; **métier à tisser m.** power loom; **atelier(s) de constructions mécaniques** engineering works; **nous avons eu des ennuis mécaniques en route** we had mechanical problems on the way; **moyens mécaniques de contraception** barrier methods of contraception; *Fig* **un geste m.** a mechanical *or* an automatic movement; **c'est devenu m. pour lui** it's become automatic for him; **c'est un travail très m.** it's very mechanical work
NF 1 *(science du mouvement)* mechanics; **m. des fluides** fluid mechanics; **m. quantique** quantum mechanics **2** *(des moteurs, machines)* mechanical engineering; *Aut* **il adore la m.** he likes fiddling about with cars/motorbikes; *Fam* **rouler les mécaniques** to walk with a swagger **3** *(mécanisme)* mechanism, piece of machinery; *(d'une imprimante laser)* engine; **c'est une belle m., cette moto** that motorbike's a lovely piece of machinery

> Il faut noter que le nom anglais **mechanic** est un faux ami. Il signifie **mécanicien**.

mécaniquement [mekanikmɑ̃] **ADV** mechanically

mécanisation [mekanizasjɔ̃] **NF** mechanization

mécaniser [mekanize] **VT** to mechanize

mécanisme [mekanism] **NM 1** mechanism; *(de montre)* works; **le m. du corps humain** the workings of the human body; **m. de défense** defence mechanism; *UE* **m. des taux de change** Exchange Rate Mechanism; **m. de l'offre et de la demande** supply and demand mechanism; **m. budgétaire** budgetary mechanism; **m. des prix** price mechanism; *Aut* **m. d'avance automatique** automatic advance mechanism; *Aut* **m. d'avance centrifuge** centrifugal advance mechanism; *Aut* **m. de basculement** tipping gear; *Aut* **m. de direction** steering gear **2** *(de la pensée, parole)* mechanics

mécano [mekano] NM *Fam* mechanic, grease monkey

mécanographe [mekanɔgraf] N punch card operator

mécanographie [mekanɔgrafi] NF *(procédé)* (mechanical) data processing; *(service)* data processing department

mécanographique [mekanɔgrafik] ADJ **service m.** data processing department; **fiche m.** punch(ed) card

Meccano® [mekano] NM Meccano®

mécénat [mesena] NM sponsorship; *(des arts)* sponsorship, patronage; **m. d'entreprise** corporate *or* business sponsorship

mécène [mesɛn] NM sponsor; *(des arts)* sponsor, patron

méchamment [meʃamɑ̃] ADV **1** *(de façon méchante)* spitefully, nastily, maliciously **2** *Fam (vrai, bon etc)* damn(ed); *(trompé, déçu)* horribly, terribly; **il avait m. bu** he'd drunk a hell of a lot; **ça a m. cartonné hier au bar** there was one hell of a punch-up in the bar yesterday; **ce qu'il m'a dit m'a m. refroidi** what he said really put me off *or Br* didn't half put me off

méchanceté [meʃɑ̃ste] NF **1** *(de personne, remarque etc)* spitefulness, nastiness, maliciousness; *(d'enfant)* naughtiness; **faire qch par m.** to do sth out of spite *or* malice; **il l'a dit sans m.** he didn't mean to be unkind; **je dis ça sans m. aucune** I say that without any malice **2** *(action, parole)* spiteful *or* nasty action/remark; **quelle m.!** what a spiteful *or* nasty thing to do/say!

méchant, -ante [meʃɑ̃, -ɑ̃t] ADJ **1** *(personne, remarque etc)* spiteful, nasty, malicious; *(enfant)* naughty; *(animal)* vicious, bad-tempered; **attention chien m.** *(sur panneau)* beware of the dog; **il n'est pas si m. que ça!** he's not as bad as all that!; *Fam* **pas m.** harmless **2** *(désagréable) (affaire)* unpleasant, disagreeable; *(blessure, grippe)* nasty, bad; **être de méchante humeur** to be in a foul mood **3** *Fam (sacré)* terrific, incredible; **avoir une méchante dégaine** to look incredible; **j'avais une méchante envie de dormir/lui casser la figure** I had an incredible urge to sleep/to smash his face in **4** *(médiocre)* miserable, wretched, poor, sorry; **un m. billet de cinq euros** a paltry five-euro note; **une méchante excuse** a lame excuse **5** *Can Fam (mauvais)* bad, foul; **la soupe n'est pas méchante** the soup isn't at all bad, the soup is pretty good; **il fait m.** the weather is bad **6** *Can Fam (incorrect)* wrong; **le m. numéro** the wrong number
▪ N **petit m.!/petite méchante!** you naughty little boy/girl!; *Fam* **les bons et les méchants** the goodies and the baddies

mèche[1] [mɛʃ] NF **1** *(de bougie, lampe)* wick; *(pour mettre le feu à des explosifs)* match; *(de mine)* fuse; *Fam* **vendre la m.** to give the game away, to spill the beans; **éventer** *ou* **découvrir la m.** to uncover the plot **2** *(de cheveux)* lock; *(de laine)* wisp, tuft; **elle se fait faire des mèches tous les mois** she has streaks *or* highlights put in her hair every month; **m. postiche** hairpiece **3** *Chir* dressing **4** *(de câble etc)* core, heart; *Élec* **charbon à m.** cored carbon **5** *Menuis* auger, gimlet; **m. anglaise** *ou* **à trois pointes** centre bit; **m. hélicoïdale** twist bit, twist drill

mèche[2] NF INV *Fam* **1 être de m.** to be in cahoots (**avec qn** with sb) **2 il n'y a pas m.** nothing doing

méchoui [meʃwi] NM *Culin* spit-roasted lamb

mécompte [mekɔ̃t] NM **1** *Litt (désillusion)* disappointment; **il a eu un grave m.** he has had a serious disappointment, he has been badly let down **2** *Vieilli (erreur)* miscalculation, error

méconium [mekɔnjɔm] NM *Physiol* meconium

méconnaissable [mekɔnɛsabl] ADJ unrecognizable

méconnaissance [mekɔnɛsɑ̃s] NF **1** *Litt (du talent de qn)* lack of recognition; *(de faits, situation)* ignorance, lack of knowledge; **elle a toujours fait preuve d'une m. totale de la politique** she has never had any grasp *or* understanding of politics whatsoever **2** *(refus de reconnaître comme valable) (d'un droit, d'une loi)* disregard

méconnaître [mekɔnɛtr] VT *(conj like* **connaître***)* **1** *(talent de qn, écrivain etc)* to fail to appreciate, to fail to recognize; *(les faits)* to fail to take account of; *(l'importance d'une découverte)* to underrate, to misjudge **2** *(devoir)* to disregard

méconnu [mekɔny] ADJ *(talent, écrivain etc)* unrecognized, unappreciated

mécontent, -ente [mekɔ̃tɑ̃, -ɑ̃t] ADJ *(insatisfait)* displeased, dissatisfied, discontented (**de** with); *(fâché)* annoyed; **je ne suis pas m. de mon sort** I am not discontented with my lot; **être m. que ... + *sub*** to be annoyed that ...
▪ N grumbler, moaner; *Pol* **les mécontents** the discontented

mécontentement [mekɔ̃tɑ̃tmɑ̃] NM *(insatisfaction)* discontent, dissatisfaction; *(contrariété)* annoyance; **c'est un sujet de m.** it's a source of discontent *or* dissatisfaction; **marquer** *ou* **exprimer son m.** to show *or* express one's annoyance *or* displeasure

mécontenter [mekɔ̃tɑ̃te] VT to displease

Mecque (La) [lamɛk] NF Mecca; **pendant le festival, Juan-les-Pins est La M. des amateurs de jazz** during the festival, Juan-les-Pins becomes a Mecca for jazz fans

mécréant, -ante [mekreɑ̃, -ɑ̃t] *Vieilli* ADJ infidel, unbelieving
▪ N unbeliever, heathen

Il faut noter que le nom anglais **miscreant** est un faux ami. Il signifie **scélérat**.

mecton [mɛktɔ̃] NM *Fam* guy, *Br* bloke

MÉDAF [medaf] NM *Fin (abrév* **modèle d'évaluation des actifs***)* CAPM

médaille [medaj] NF **1** *(récompense)* medal; *Sport* **la m. d'or/d'argent/de bronze** the gold/silver/bronze (medal); **détenir la m. du 60 mètres** to hold the medal for the 60 metres; **être m. d'or** *(de sportif)* to be a gold medallist, to be a gold medal winner; **m. du travail** medal for long service, long-service medal; *Fig* **le revers de la m.** the other side of the coin; *Fig* **je ne lui donnerais pas la m. du courage!** he wouldn't win any medals for bravery! **2** *(en hommage à qn)* medal; **m. pieuse** holy medal **3** *(insigne)* (official) badge; *(plaque d'identité) (de chat, chien)* identity disc *or* tag

médaillé, -ée [medaje] ADJ holding a medal; *(soldat)* decorated
▪ N *Mil* medal-holder; *Sport* medallist; **le m. du 400 mètres nage libre** the 400 metres freestyle medallist; **un m. du travail** a holder of a long-service medal

médaillier [medaje] NM medal collection *(in cabinet)*

médaillon [medajɔ̃] NM **1** *(médaille)* medallion **2** *Culin* medallion **3** *(bijou)* medallion; *(avec photo)* locket **4** *TV, Cin, Journ* inset

médecin [medsɛ̃] NM doctor, *Fml* physician; **aller chez le m.** to go to the doctor('s); **femme m.** woman doctor
▪ ▪ **m. de bord** ship's doctor; **m. de campagne** country doctor; **m.-conseil,** *pl* **médecins-conseils** medical consultant *or* adviser; **m. consultant** consultant; **m. de famille** fa-

mily doctor; **m. généraliste** general practitioner, GP, *Am* family practitioner; **m. légiste** forensic pathologist, *Am* medical examiner; **m. militaire** army medical officer, MO; **Médecins sans frontières** = charitable organization providing medical aid, especially to Third World countries; **m. traitant** consulting physician; **qui est votre m. traitant?** who is your (regular) doctor?; **m. du travail** = doctor who carries out the annual examination, required by law, of a company's employees

médecine [medsin] NF **1** *(science)* medicine; *Fam* **elle fait m.** she's doing medicine; **docteur en m.** doctor of medicine, MD; **étudiant en m.** medical student, *Fam* medic; **école de m.** medical school **2** *(profession du médecin)* medicine; **exercer la m.** to practise medicine
▪ ▪ **m. douce** alternative medicine; **m. générale** general medicine; **m. légale** forensic medicine, *Fam* forensics; **service de m. légale** forensic department, *Fam* forensics; **m. naturelle** natural medicine; **m. parallèle** alternative medicine; **m. préventive** preventive medicine; **m. sportive** sports medicine; **m. du travail** industrial medicine

Il faut noter que le nom anglais **medicine** signifie également **médicament, remède**.

Medef [medef] NM *(abrév* **Mouvement des entreprises de France***)* French employers' association, *Br* ≃ CBI

média [medja] NM medium, *pl* media; **le pouvoir des médias** the power of the media; **faire campagne dans tous les médias** to carry out a media-wide advertising campaign; **la télévision est un m. privilégié** television is the most efficient medium; **m. grand public** mass media; **m. planneur** media planner; **médias de télécommunication** telecommunications media; **médias numériques interactifs** interactive digital media; **médias électroniques** electronic media VOIR GRAMMAIRE A11

médial, -iale, -iaux, -iales [medjal, -jo] ADJ *Ling (lettre)* medial
▪ NF **médiale** *(en statistique)* median

médian, -iane [medjɑ̃, -jan] ADJ *(nerf, ligne etc)* median
▪ NF **médiane 1** *Ling* mid vowel **2** *(en statistique)* median

médiateur, -trice [medjatœr, -tris] ADJ mediating, mediatory
▪ N *(personne)* Ind mediator; *Admin* ≃ ombudsman; **agir en tant que m., servir de m.** to act as (a) mediator; **m. d'entreprises** arbitrator; **le M. européen** the European Ombudsman; **le M. de la République** *Br* ≃ the Parliamentary Commissioner, the Ombudsman

médiathèque [medjatɛk] NF media library

médiation [medjasjɔ̃] NF mediation

médiatique [medjatik] ADJ *(couverture, personnalité etc)* media; **d'un intérêt m.** newsworthy; **événement m.** media event; **c'est quelqu'un de très m.** he/she is well suited to *or* comes over well in the media

médiatisation [medjatizasjɔ̃] NF **la m. d'un événement** the media coverage *or* attention given to an event; **la m. à outrance des faits et gestes des hommes politiques** the excessive media coverage given to politicians' behaviour, the media hype surrounding politicians' behaviour

médiatiser [medjatize] VT *(événement)* to give media coverage to; **m. la guerre** to turn the war into a media event

médiator [medjatɔr] NM *Mus* plectrum

médiatrice [medjatris] NF *Géom* median

médical, -ale, -aux, -ales [medikal, -o] ADJ medical; **examen m. (complet)** medical examination, check-up; **certificat m.** medical certificate

médicalement [medikalmã] ADV medically

médicalisation [medikalizasjɔ̃] NF *(de population)* provision of medical care (**de** for); **la m. de la grossesse** the treatment of pregnancy as a medical matter, the medicalization of pregnancy; **m. à outrance** pill-pushing

médicalisé [medikalize] ADJ **logement m.** nursing home

médicaliser [medikalize] VT *(personne)* to give medical care to; *(population)* to provide with medical care, to make medical care available to; *(la ménopause, la grossesse)* to treat as a medical matter, to medicalize

médicament [medikamɑ̃] NM medicine, drug, medication; **tu as pris tes médicaments?** have you taken your medicine?; **est-ce que vous prenez des médicaments?** are you on any kind of medication?; **m. de confort** palliative

médicamenteux, -euse [medikamɑ̃tø, -øz] ADJ medicinal

médication [medikasjɔ̃] NF medication, medical treatment

médicinal, -ale, -aux, -ales [medisinal, -o] ADJ medicinal

medicine-ball, *pl* **medicine-balls** [medisinbol] NM medicine ball

médico-légal, -ale, -aux, -ales [medikolegal, -o] ADJ forensic

médico-pédagogique, *pl* **médico-pédagogiques** [medikopedagɔʒik] ADJ **institut m.** special school *(for children with special learning needs)*

médico-social, -iale, -iaux, -iales [medikosɔsjal, -jo] ADJ **centre m.** health centre

médiéval, -ale, -aux, -ales [medjeval, -o] ADJ medieval

médiéviste [medjevist] N medievalist

médina [medina] NF medina

médiocre [medjɔkr] ADJ mediocre; *Scol (appréciation)* poor
N *(personne)* nonentity
NM *(médiocrité)* mediocrity

médiocrement [medjɔkrəmɑ̃] ADV indifferently, poorly; **m. riche** not very rich; **elle chante très m.** she's a very mediocre singer; **il a m. réussi ses examens** he scraped through his exams

médiocrité [medjɔkrite] NF mediocrity

médire [medir] VI *(conj like* dire, *except pr ind and imp* médisez*)* **m. de qn** to speak ill of sb, to run sb down; **il médit facilement** he is always ready to run people down; **je ne voudrais pas m. mais …** I don't like to gossip, but …

médisance [medizɑ̃s] NF **1** *(action)* scandal-mongering, slander **2** *(propos)* (bit of) scandal *or* gossip; **médisances** scandal, gossip

médisant, -ante [medizɑ̃, -ɑ̃t] ADJ *(paroles)* slanderous; *(personne)* scandalmongering; **qu'est-ce que tu peux être m.!** what a scandalmonger you are!; **je ne voudrais être m. mais …** I don't like to gossip, but …
N scandalmonger, slanderer

méditatif, -ive [meditatif, -iv] ADJ meditative, thoughtful

méditation [meditasjɔ̃] NF meditation; **plongé dans la m.** lost in thought; **entrer en m.** to start to meditate; **faire de la m.** to meditate; **m. transcendantale** transcendental meditation

méditer [medite] VI to meditate (**sur** on); **m. de faire qch** to be contemplating doing sth; **m. de prendre sa revanche** to plot one's revenge
VT to contemplate; **m. un projet** to reflect on

or mull over a plan; **m. une vengeance** to contemplate vengeance

Méditerranée [mediterane] NF **la (mer) M.** the Mediterranean (Sea), *Fam* the Med; **en M.** in the Mediterranean

méditerranéen, -enne [mediteraneɛ̃, -ɛn] ADJ Mediterranean
N M. **1** *(natif)* native of a Mediterranean country; *(habitant)* inhabitant of a Mediterranean country **2** *(en France)* Southerner

médium [medjɔm] NM **1** *Mus (de voix)* middle register **2** *(en parapsychologie)* medium VOIR GRAMMAIRE A13

médius [medjys] NM *Anat* middle finger

médoc [medɔk] NM Médoc (wine)

médullaire [medylɛr] ADJ *Anat, Bot* medullary

méduse [medyz] NF **1** *Zool* jellyfish, *Spéc* medusa **2** *Myth* M. Medusa

méduser [medyze] VT to transfix, to dumbfound

meeting [mitiŋ] NM *Pol, Sp etc* meeting; **m. aérien** air show; **m. d'athlétisme** athletics meeting *or* meet

méfait [mefɛ] NM misdeed; *Jur* misdemeanour, *Am* misdemeanor; *(d'un orage)* damage; **les méfaits de l'alcoolisme** the ill effects *or* the damage done by alcoholism; **les méfaits de la surinformation** the evils of over-information; **se déclarer l'auteur du m.** to own up (to the deed)

méfiance [mefjɑ̃s] NF *(manque de confiance)* distrust; *(suspicion)* mistrust, suspicion; **m.!** be on your guard!; **avoir de la m. envers qn** to distrust sb; *(avoir de la suspicion)* to mistrust sb; **avec m.** distrustfully; *(avec suspicion)* mistrustfully, suspiciously; *Prov* **m. est mère de sûreté** better safe than sorry

méfiant, -ante [mefjɑ̃, -ɑ̃t] ADJ distrustful; *(suspicieux)* mistrustful, suspicious (**à l'égard de, envers** of)

méfier (se) [səmefje] VPR *(impf, pr sub n. n.* méfiions, v. v. méfiiez*)* to be on one's guard, to take care; **se m. de qn** to distrust sb; *(avoir de la suspicion)* to mistrust sb; **méfiez-vous des pickpockets** beware of pickpockets; **se m. de qch** to be wary of sth, to be on one's guard against sth; **il faut se m. des apparences** you shouldn't trust appearances

méforme [mefɔrm] NF *Sport* poor form, lack of form; **être en m.** to be off form

méga¹ [mega] NM *Ordinat* megabyte, meg

méga² ADJ INV *Fam* mega

mégabase [megabaz] NF mega-database

mégabit [megabit] NM *Ordinat* megabit; **mégabits par seconds** megabits per second

mégacycle [megasikl] NM *Élec* megacycle

mégaflop [megaflɔp] NM *Ordinat* megaflop

mégahertz [megaɛrts] NM *Élec* megahertz

mégajoule [megaʒul] NM megajoule

mégalithe [megalit] NM megalith

mégalithique [megalitik] ADJ megalithic

mégalomane [megalɔman], *Fam* **mégalo** [megalo] ADJ, N megalomaniac

mégalomanie [megalɔmani] NF megalomania

mégalopole [megalɔpɔl] NF megalopolis

mégamarketing, [megamarkətiŋ] NM, **mégamercatique** [megamɛrkatik] NF mega-marketing

méga-octet, *pl* **méga-octets** NM *Ordinat* megabyte

mégaphone [megafɔn] NM megaphone; *(électrique)* loud-hailer, *Am* bullhorn

mégapixel [megapiksɛl] NM *Ordinat* megapixel

mégarde (par) [parmegard] ADV inadvertently, accidentally

mégatonne [megatɔn] NF megaton

mégawatt [megawat] NM *Phys* megawatt

mégère [meʒɛr] NF shrew, termagant

mégot [mego] NM *Fam (de cigarette)* (cigarette) butt, *Br* fag end; *(de cigare)* stump, butt

mégotage [megotaʒ] NM *Fam* skimping

mégoter [megote] VI *Fam* to skimp (**sur, pour** on);**arrête de m., achète du vrai Champagne!** don't be stingy, buy real champagne!; **il a pas mégoté sur le piment** he didn't skimp on the chilli

méhari [meari], *pl* **méhara** [meara] *ou* **méharis** NM racing camel, mehari

méhariste [mearist] NM camel driver, meharist; *Mil Arch* member of the camel corps *(in the Sahara)*

meilleur, -eure [mɛjœr] ADJ **1** *(comp de* bon*)* better; **elle est meilleure que lui** she is better than him *or* than he is; **il est m. en anglais qu'en allemand** he is better at English than German; **il est m. danseur que coureur** he is a better dancer than he is a runner, he is better at dancing than running; **les fraises, c'est m. avec de la crème** strawberries are better with cream; **rendre qch m.** to make sth better, to improve sth; **devenir m.** to get better, to improve; **je ne connais rien de m.** I don't know anything better; **les choses prennent une meilleure tournure** things are taking a turn for the better; **m. marché** cheaper; *Suisse* **avoir m. temps de faire qch** to be better off doing sth; **tu as m. temps de te taire** you'd be better off keeping quiet
2 *(superl de* bon*)* **le m./la meilleure** *(de plusieurs)* the best; *(de deux)* the better; **m. ami** best friend; **nous sommes les meilleurs amis du monde** we're the best of friends; **meilleurs vœux** *(dans une lettre)* with all good wishes, (with) best wishes
N **que le m. gagne** may the best man win; **j'en passe et des meilleures** and that's the least of it, and that's not the half of it, and I could go on; *Fam* **tu connais la meilleure? elle va se marier!** you know the best bit? she's going to get married!; *Fam* **c'est la meilleure (de l'année)!** that's the best (one) I've heard in a long time!
NM **le m.** the best; **garder le m. pour la fin** to keep the best till last; **pour le m. et pour le pire** for better or (for) worse; **donner le m. de soi-même** to give of one's best; **le m. de son temps/de la journée** the best part of one's time/of the day; **il a passé le m. de sa vie à l'aider** he spent the best years of his life helping him/her; *Sport* **prendre le m. sur son adversaire** to get the better of one's opponent
ADV **il fait m.** it's warmer

méiose [mejoz] NF *Biol* meiosis

méiotique [mejɔtik] ADJ *Biol* meiotic

méjuger [meʒyʒe] *(conj like* juger*)* VI **m. de qn/qch** to underestimate sb/sth
VT to underestimate
VPR **se méjuger** to underestimate oneself

mél, mel [mel] NM *(adresse électronique)* e-mail address; *(courrier électronique)* e-mail

melæna, méléna [melena] NM *Méd* melaena

mélamine [melamin] NF *Chimie* melamine

mélaminé [melamine] ADJ *Chimie* melamine-covered

mélancolie [melɑ̃kɔli] NF melancholy, gloom; *Méd* melancholia; **elle a un accès de m.** she's (feeling) a bit down *or* a bit gloomy; **ne pas engendrer la m.** to be great fun

mélancolique [melɑ̃kɔlik] ADJ melancholy, gloomy; *Méd* melancholic

Mélanésie [melanezi] NF Melanesia

mélanésien, -ienne [melanezjɛ̃, -jɛn] ADJ Melanesian NM Ling Melanesian N M. Melanesian

mélange [melɑ̃ʒ] NM 1 (action) mixing; (de thés, vins, tabacs) blending; (d'espèces) crossing 2 (résultat) mixture; (de thés, vins, tabacs) blend; (de ciment, de plâtre) mix; **m. pharmaceutique** pharmaceutical mixture; **m. explosif** ou **détonant** explosive mixture; **m. air/carburant** fuel/air mixture; Aut **m. carburé** explosive mixture; Aut **m. gazeux** gas mixture; **pas de whisky après le vin, je ne fais pas de mélanges** no whisky after my wine, I don't mix my drinks; **un curieux m. de timidité et d'orgueil** a strange mixture or blend of shyness and arrogance; Fig **sans m.** unadulterated, unalloyed 3 (ouvrage) **mélanges** miscellany

mélangé [melɑ̃ʒe] ADJ (coton, laine) mixed; **en coton m.** in a cotton mixture

mélanger [melɑ̃ʒe] (je mélangeai(s), n. mélangeons) VT (ingrédients etc) to mix; (thés, vins, tabacs) to blend; (confondre) (idées, documents etc) to mix up; **m. le citron à la crème** to mix the lemon (in) with the cream; Cartes **m. les cartes** to shuffle the cards VPR se **mélanger 1** to mix; **l'eau et l'huile ne se mélangent pas bien** water and oil don't mix well 2 Fam se **m. les pédales** ou **les pinceaux (dans qch)** to get (oneself) into a muddle (with sth), to get (sth) muddled up 3 très Fam (avoir des rapports sexuels) to exchange bodily fluids

mélangeur [melɑ̃ʒœr] NM mixer; (robinet) **m.** mixer tap, Am mixing faucet; Électron **m.** (de son) mixer, production switcher; TV etc **m. (de production)** production mixer or switcher; TV etc **m. de son** dubbing or sound mixer; TV etc **m. numérique 16 entrées** 16-source digital mixer; TV, Cin **m. vidéo** vision mixer

mélanine [melanin] NF melanin

mélanome [melanom] NM Méd melanoma

mêlant [mɛlɑ̃] ADJ Can **c'est pas m.** there's no doubt about it

mélasse [melas] NF (black) treacle, Am molasses; **m. raffinée** golden syrup; Fam **être dans la m.** to be in a mess or in the soup; Fam **quelle m.!** what a mess!

Melba [mɛlba] ADJ INV Culin Melba; **pêche/ poire M.** peach/pear Melba

mêlé [mele] ADJ 1 (mélangé) (sentiments, compagnie) mixed; (sons) mingled; **du rouge m. d'un peu de bleu** red mixed with a bit of blue; **fierté mêlée d'une certaine crainte** pride mixed or mingled with fear 2 (emmêlé) (affaires) involved, tangled; **dans cette histoire, la politique et le crime sont très mêlés** politics and crime are closely linked in this business; **tout est m. dans son suicide: la drogue, sa célébrité déclinante …** everything played a part in his suicide: drugs, his declining fame …

mêlée [mele] NF 1 (conflit) fray, mêlée; Fam (bagarre) scuffle, tussle, free-for-all; Fig **au-dessus de la m.** above the fray; **entrer dans la m.** to enter the fray 2 Rugby scrum(mage); **m. ouverte** ruck

mêler [mele] VT 1 (ingrédients, substances etc) to mix; (sons différents, plusieurs cultures etc) to combine; **m. qch à ou avec qch** to mix/ combine sth with sth; **m. son vin d'eau** to put water in one's wine; **m. deux races de chien** to cross two breeds of dog 2 **m. qn à qch** to involve sb in sth; **il a mêlé à plusieurs scandales financiers** he's involved in or mixed up in several financial scandals; **m. qn à la conversation** to bring sb into the conversation; **il est mêlé à tout** he's got a finger in

every pie 3 (mettre en désordre) (papiers) to mix up, to muddle (up); (idées etc) to confuse, to mix up; Cartes **m. les cartes** to shuffle the cards VPR se **mêler** (de sons, parfums) to blend; (de substances) to mix, to blend; **se m. à la foule** to mingle with or blend into the crowd; **se m. à la conversation** to join in the conversation; **quand l'amour propre se mêle à la colère** when self-esteem is mingled or combined with anger; **mêlez-vous de ce qui vous regarde** mind your own business; Fam **mais de quoi je me mêle?** what's it got to do with you?, what business is it of yours?; **ce n'est pas à moi de m'en m.** it's not for me to interfere; **se m. de politique** to dabble in politics

mélèze [melɛz] NM larch (tree)

méli-mélo, pl mélis-mélos [melimelo] NM Fam (d'objets) jumble; (de faits) jumble, hotchpotch, Am hodgepodge; (de gens) mix, mixture; **quel m.!** what a mess!

mélioratif, -ive [meljɔratif, -iv] ADJ meliorative

mélisse [melis] NF Bot (lemon) balm

mélo [melo] Fam NM melodrama; **nous sommes en plein m.!** this is melodramatic stuff! ADJ (qui tient du mélodrame) melodramatic; (qui donne dans la sensiblerie) sentimental, mawkish

mélodie [melɔdi] NF 1 Mus melody, tune 2 (de vers, d'une langue etc) melodiousness

mélodieusement [melɔdjøzmɑ̃] ADV melodiously, tunefully

mélodieux, -ieuse [melɔdjø, -jøz] ADJ melodious, tuneful

mélodique [melɔdik] ADJ Mus melodic

mélodiste [melɔdist] N melody writer

mélodramatique [melɔdramatik] ADJ melodramatic

mélodrame [melɔdram] NM melodrama

mélomane [melɔman] ADJ music-loving N music lover

melon [mǝlɔ̃] NM 1 (fruit) melon; **m. cantaloup** cantaloup(e) (melon), Am rock melon; **m. d'hiver** ou **de garde** honeydew melon; **m. d'eau** watermelon 2 (chapeau) **m.** bowler (hat), Am derby 3 Arg (terme raciste) Arab, Br ≃ wog

melonnière [mǝlɔnjɛr] NF melon bed

mélopée [melɔpe] NF Mus 1 (chant récitatif) chant, recitative 2 (chant monotone) threnody

MEM [mɛm] NF Ordinat (abrév **mémoire morte**) ROM

membrane [mɑ̃bran] NF 1 Anat, Biol membrane 2 Tech (dans un microphone etc) diaphragm

membraneux, -euse [mɑ̃branø, -øz] ADJ Anat, Méd membranous

membre [mɑ̃br] NM 1 Anat limb, Fml member; **m. supérieur/inférieur** upper/lower limb 2 (d'une association, d'une classe etc) member; **membres** membership, members; **les membres de l'ONU/du Parlement européen** the members of the UN/of the European Parliament; **être/devenir m. de …** to be/become a member of …; **m. du comité** committee member; **m. du conseil d'administration** member of the board, board member; **m. fondateur** founding or founder member; **m. honoraire** honorary member; **m. du parti** party member; **m. perpétuel** life member; **les États membres** the member states; Can **Membre de l'Assemblée nationale** Member of the National Assembly; **carte de m.** membership card, member's card 3 (part constituante), Ling, Archit member; Math **premier/second m. d'une équation** left-hand/right-hand side of an equation 4 (de bateau) rib, timber

▸▸Bourse **m. de compensation** clearing member; Méd **m. fantôme** phantom limb; **m. viril** (male) member, penis

membré [mɑ̃bre] ADJ limbed; **bien/mal m.** strong-/weak-limbed; Fam Hum **bien m.** (homme) well-hung

membrure [mɑ̃bryr] NF 1 (d'édifice etc) frame(work); (de bateau) ribs, timbers 2 Litt (de personne) limbs; **homme à forte m.** strong-limbed or powerfully built man

MÊME [mɛm]

ADJ same 1 • very 2 • self (-même) 3	
ADV even 1 • too (de même) 2 • to be able to (être à même de) 3	
PRON INDÉF same	

ADJ 1 (avant le nom) (semblable, identique) same; **j'ai la m. voiture qu'elle** I have the same car as her or as she does; **une seule et m. chose** one and the same thing; **ils sont du m. âge** they're the same age; **ce m. jour** that same day; **tous rassemblés en un m. lieu** all gathered in the same place; **en m. temps** at the same time SEE GRAMMAR B15 2 (après le nom) very; **aujourd'hui m.** this very day; **il habite ici m.** he lives in this very place/house; **c'est cela m.** that's right; **donner les chiffres mêmes** to give the actual figures; **c'est le titre m. que vous avez à traduire** it's the title itself or the actual title that you have to translate; **elle est la bonté/la beauté m.** she's kindness/beauty itself or personified SEE GRAMMAR B10 3 …-m. self; **moi-m.** myself; **toi-m.** yourself; **lui-m.** himself/itself; **elle-m.** herself/itself; **soi-m.** oneself; **nous-mêmes** ourselves; **vous-mêmes** yourselves; **eux-mêmes/elles-mêmes** themselves; **moi-m., quand j'y pense, j'en ai des frissons** I get shivers myself when I think about it; **par toi-m.** by yourself; **j'ai dû y aller car elle-m. ne peut plus se déplacer** I had to go because she can't get about herself any more; **il l'a fait lui-m.** he did it himself; **faire qch de soi-m.** to do sth of one's own accord; **c'est lui-m. qui me l'a dit, il me l'a dit lui-m.** he told me himself; **je l'ai trouvée pareille à elle-m.** I found she hadn't changed, I found her the same as ever; **rester/être égal à soi-m.** to remain/be true to form; **égale à elle-m., elle est restée très calme** typically or true to form, she remained calm; Enf **menteur! – toi-m.!** liar! – liar yourself!; **la chose n'est pas mauvaise en elle-m.** the thing is not bad in itself or per se; **un autre lui-m.** a second self; **je pensais en moi-m. que …** I was thinking to myself that …

ADV 1 even; **je le pense et m. j'en suis sûr** I think so, in fact I am sure of it; **je n'ai pas m. ou je n'ai m. pas le prix de mon voyage** I haven't even enough to pay my fare; **m. lui l'affirme** even he says so; **m. si je le savais** even if I knew; Fam **il va venir, m. qu'il me l'a promis!** he'll come, what's more he promised me he would! 2 **je vous souhaite le bonsoir – moi de m.** I wish you goodnight – likewise; **la France a privatisé ses banques et la Grande-Bretagne de m.** France has privatized its banks and so has Great Britain or and Great Britain has too; **la France a privatisé ses banques et ses compagnies d'assurance de m.** France has privatized its banks and its insurance companies too; **faire de m.** to do likewise, to do the same; **il en est de m. des autres** it's the same for the others, the same is true or holds good for the others; **il a refusé de travailler pour eux, de m. qu'il avait refusé de le faire pour moi** he refused to work for them, just as or just like he had refused to for me; **je déteste la Bretagne de m. que la Normandie** I hate Britanny just as much as

Normandy; **tout de m., quand m.** all the same, even so; **je trouve que tu aurais quand m. pu t'excuser** all the same or even so, I think you could have apologized; **mais tout de m.!, enfin quand m.!** well really!

3 boire à **m.** la bouteille to drink (straight) from or out of the bottle; **couché à m. le sable** lying on the bare sand; **banc taillé à m. la pierre** bench cut out of the rock; **à m. la peau** next to the skin; **être à m. de faire qch** to be able or in a position to do sth; **il n'est pas à m. de faire le voyage** he's not up to making the journey; **cela me met à m. de le faire** that enables me or puts me in a position to do it

PRON INDÉF **on prend les mêmes et on recommence** it's the mixture as before; **tu n'es plus le m.!** you're not the same!; **cela revient au m.** it comes (down) or amounts to the same thing; Fam **c'est du pareil au m.** it's all the same, it comes to the same thing, it makes no difference

mémé [meme] NF Fam (grand-mère) grandma, gran(ny); (vieille dame) old dear; Fam Péj **ça fait m. cette robe!** that dress makes you look ancient!

mémento [memɛ̃to] NM **1** (de service) memo(randum), note **2** (pour se souvenir) memo, reminder **3** (livre) handbook; Scol **m. de chimie** chemistry revision notes

mémérage [memɛraʒ] NM Can Fam gossip

mémère [memɛr] Fam NF **1** (grand-mère) grandma, gran(ny), nan **2** Péj **une grosse m.** a fat middle-aged woman; **tu fais m. avec cette robe** that dress makes you look fat and middle-aged; **qu'est-ce qu'elle fait m., cette fille!** she looks so dowdy, that girl!; **le petit chien-chien à sa m.** mummy's little doggie-woggie

ADJ frumpy, frumpish

mémérer [memere] VI Can Fam to gossip

mémo [memo] NM memo

mémoire¹ [memwar] NF **1** (faculté) memory; **je n'ai pas la m. des noms/dates** I've no memory for names/dates; **tu perds la m.?** are you losing your memory?; **il n'a pas de m.** he's got a bad memory; **avoir la m. courte** to have a short memory; **je n'ai plus son nom en m.** his/her name has slipped my memory, his/her name escapes me; **son nom est resté dans toutes les mémoires** his/her name is remembered by everyone; **c'est gravé dans ma m.** it's engraved in my memory; **rappeler qch à la m. de qn** to remind sb of sth; **je vais lui rafraîchir la m.** I'll refresh his memory; **réciter qch de m.** to recite sth from memory; **si j'ai bonne m.** if I remember rightly, if my memory serves me right; **avoir une m. d'éléphant** to have a long memory or a memory like an elephant; **m. collective** collective memory

2 (souvenir) memory; **de m. d'homme** within living memory; **de m. de pêcheur, je n'avais jamais vu de si gros poisson** in all my years as an angler, I've never seen such a big fish; **à la m. de qn** (de monument etc) in memory of sb, to the memory of sb; **faire qch à la m. de qn** to do sth in memory of sb; **je signale, pour m., que …** I might mention, for the record, that …; **je vous signale pour m. que …** I would remind you that …; **de sinistre m.** of evil memory

3 Ordinat memory; **m. de 40 méga-octets** 40-megabyte memory; **mettre un dossier en m.** to write a file to memory; **carte d'extension de m.** memory expansion card; **m. bloc-notes** scratchpad memory; **m. à bulles** bubble memory; **m. cache** cache memory; **m. centrale** main memory; **m. conventionnelle** conventional memory; **m. disponible** available memory, RAM disk; **m. à disque** disk memory, RAM disk; **m. écran** screen memory; **m. étendue** extended memory; **m. expansée**

expanded memory; **m. haute** high memory; **avoir chargé en m. haute** to have memory loaded high; **m. d'images** picture memory; **m. intermédiaire** buffer memory; **m. de masse** mass storage; **m. morte** read-only memory, ROM; **m. morte masquée** masked ROM; **m. non effaçable** non-erasable memory; **m. paginée** expanded memory; **m. principale** main memory; **m. standard** standard memory; **m. tampon** buffer store, buffer (memory); **m. tampon de données** data buffer; **m. tampon d'imprimante** ou pour imprimante printer buffer; **m. tampon de sortie** output buffer; **m. tampon de texte** text buffer; **m. vidéo** video memory; **m. vive** random access memory, RAM; **m. vive dynamique** DRAM, dynamic random access memory; **m. vive statique** SRAM, static RAM, static random access memory

mémoire² NM **1** (rapport) report; Jur (de procès) (written) statement; Univ thesis, dissertation; **m. de maîtrise** ≃ master's thesis or dissertation **2** (d'entrepreneur) account; (de coûts) bill **3** Littér **mémoires** memoirs; **écrire ses mémoires** to write one's memoirs **4** **mémoires** (de société savante etc) transactions

mémorable [memɔrabl] ADJ memorable

mémorandum [memɔrɑ̃dɔm] NM **1** (note) memorandum, note, memo; Naut **m. de combat** battle orders VOIR GRAMMAIRE A13 **2** (carnet) notebook

mémorial, -iaux [memɔrjal, -jo] NM **1** (monument) memorial **2** (mémoires) memoir **3** Com daybook

mémorisation [memɔrizasjɔ̃] NF memorization, memorizing; Ordinat writing to memory; Mktg **m. de la marque** brand awareness; **m. un jour après** day after recall

mémoriser [memɔrize] VT to memorize, to commit to memory; Ordinat to write to memory

menaçant [mənasɑ̃] ADJ threatening, menacing; **il fait un temps m.** the weather's looking ominous, it's threatening to rain

menace [mənas] NF threat; Jur **menaces** intimidation; **obtenir qch par la m.** to obtain sth by threats or intimidation; **faire qch sous la m.** to do sth under duress; **mettre ses menaces à exécution** to carry out one's threats; **m. de tempête/d'épidémie** threat of a storm/an epidemic; **m. de guerre** threat of war; **recevoir des menaces de mort** to receive death threats; **silence lourd de menaces** ominous silence

menacé [mənase] ADJ threatened; **vos jours sont menacés** your life is in danger or threatened

menacer [mənase] (je **menaçai(s), n. menaçons**) VT to threaten, Fml to menace; **m. qn du doigt/poing** to shake one's finger/fist at sb; **m. qn d'un procès** to threaten sb with legal proceedings; **cette longue séparation menace leur mariage** this long separation is threatening their marriage or is putting their marriage at risk; **m. de faire qch** to threaten to do sth; **le procès menace d'être long** the trial threatens to be lengthy

VI (de tempête, d'orage, de révolution) to be brewing; **la pluie menace** it's threatening to rain, it looks like rain; **l'incendie menace** there's a danger of fire

ménage [menaʒ] NM **1** (nettoyage) **faire le m.** to do the housework, Am to clean house; **le grand m.** the spring-cleaning; Fig **faire le (grand) m.** (dans un parti, une entreprise) to have a shake-up; **faire des ménages** to go out cleaning; **tenir le m. de qn** to keep house for sb; **femme de m.** cleaner, Br cleaning lady, Am cleaning woman **2** (meubles) **monter son m.** to furnish one's house; **m. de poupée** set of doll's furniture **3** (couple)

(married) couple; (famille) household, family; Écon household; **jeune m.** young (married) couple; **se mettre en m.** to live together; **se mettre en m. avec qn** to live with sb, to move in with sb; **heureux en m.** happily married; **faire bon/mauvais m. (ensemble)** to get on well/badly (together); **m. à trois** ménage à trois; Écon **la consommation des ménages** household consumption **4** Vieilli **de m.** (pain etc) home-made

ménagement [menaʒmɑ̃] NM care, caution, circumspection; (tact) consideration; **avec ménagement(s)** carefully, cautiously; (avec tact) considerately, tactfully; **parler/annoncer une nouvelle sans m.** to speak/break a piece of news bluntly; **traiter qn sans m.** to treat sb unceremoniously or without consideration

ménager¹, -ère [menaʒe, -ɛr] ADJ **1** (équipement) household; **appareils ménagers** household appliances; **travaux ménagers** housework; **arts ménagers** domestic science; **eaux ménagères** waste water; **salon des arts ménagers** ≃ Ideal Home Exhibition **2** Can (économe) thrifty, careful (with money)

NF **ménagère 1** (femme) housewife; **elle est bonne ménagère** she's a good housekeeper; Écon **le panier de la ménagère** the shopping basket **2** (service de couverts) canteen of cutlery

ménager² (je **ménageai(s), n. ménageons**) VT **1** (utiliser avec parcimonie) to use sparingly, to be sparing with; **essayez de m. vos jambes pendant quelques jours** try not to use your legs too much for a few days; **sans m. ses paroles** without mincing one's words; **ne pas m. sa peine** to put in a lot of effort **2** (traiter avec soin) **m. sa santé** to take care of one's health; **m. qn** to treat sb tactfully or with consideration; **ne le ménagez pas** don't spare him; **ses parents le ménagent trop** his parents are too soft with him; **elle cherche toujours à m. les uns et les autres** she always tries to do right by everybody; Fig **m. la chèvre et le chou** to keep everyone happy, Prov to run with the hare and hunt with the hounds **3** (arranger) (entrevue, réunion etc) to arrange, to organize; (réconciliation) to bring about; **m. une surprise à qn** to prepare a surprise for sb; **m. une ouverture pour les fils** to make an opening for the wires; **m. une sortie** to provide an exit

VPR **se ménager 1** (prendre soin de soi) to take care of oneself, to look after oneself, Péj to coddle oneself **2** (disposer) **se m. une sortie** to provide oneself with a way out; **se m. une petite place dans le train** to make some space for oneself to sit down in the train

ménagerie [menaʒri] NF menagerie

mendélien, -ienne [mɛ̃deljɛ̃, -jɛn] ADJ Biol Mendelian

mendélisme [mɛ̃delism] NM Biol Mendelism

mendiant, -ante [mɑ̃djɑ̃, -ɑ̃t] ADJ (moine, ordre) mendicant

N beggar; Culin **les (quatre) mendiants** = almonds, raisins, hazelnuts and figs (served as dessert)

mendicité [mɑ̃disite] NF begging; **réduit à la m.** reduced to begging or beggary

mendier [mɑ̃dje] (impf, pr sub n. mendiions, v. mendiiez) VI to beg

VT (du pain, des bonbons, des caresses) to beg for; Fig Péj (votes) to canvass; **m. des compliments** to fish for compliments

mendigot, -ote [mɑ̃digo, -ɔt] N Arg beggar

meneau, -eaux [məno] NM Archit **m. vertical** mullion; **m. horizontal** transom

menées [məne] NFPL scheming, machinations; **déjouer les m. de qn** to thwart or outwit sb

MENER [məne] (**je mène; je mènerai**) **VT 1** *(accompagner)* to take; **m. qn à sa chambre** to take *or* show sb to his room; **m. qn à sa dernière demeure** to accompany sb to his final resting place; **m. une ligne entre deux points** to draw a line between two points **2** *(être devant)* to lead, to be at the head of; **m. le deuil** to be chief mourner; *Sport* **m. la France mène la Belgique (par) 2 à 1** France is leading Belgium (by) 2 to 1; **m. la danse** *ou* **le bal** to lead the dance; *Fig* to call the tune **3** *Fig (conduire)* to lead; **cette petite somme ne te mènera pas bien loin** that won't get you very far; **cela nous mène à croire que …** this leads us to believe that …; **cette affaire peut le m. loin** this business could get him into deep water **4** *(diriger) (entreprise)* to run, to manage; *(personnel)* to manage, to control; **m. les débats** to lead *or* chair the discussions; **mari mené par sa femme** henpecked husband; **m. son personnel au doigt et à l'œil** *ou* **à la baguette** to have one's staff under one's thumb; **m. qn par le bout du nez** to lead sb by the nose; **elle se laisse m. par le bout du nez par son fiancé** her fiancé has got her under his thumb; **chez eux, c'est elle qui mène la barque** she wears the trousers in their house **5** *(bateau)* to steer; *Fig* **m. qn en bateau** to take sb for a ride; **m. de front plusieurs affaires** to have several irons in the fire; **comment peux-tu m. de front tes études et ton engagement politique?** how do you manage to fit in both your studies and your political commitments?; *Tech* **roue menée** driven wheel **6** *(affaire, enquête, campagne)* to conduct; **m. à bonne fin** *ou* **à bien** to bring to a successful conclusion; *(plan)* to carry through, to carry out; **m. un combat de tous les instants contre qch** to wage a constant fight against sth; **m. une vie triste** to lead a sad life; **m. la vie dure à qn** to give sb a hard time; **m. grand train** to live in grand style

VI chemin qui mène à la ville road that leads to the town; **cela ne mène à rien** this is getting us nowhere; *Fig* **elle n'en menait pas large** her heart was in her mouth

ménestrel [menɛstrɛl] **NM** minstrel

ménétrier [menetrije] **NM** (strolling) fiddler

meneur, -euse [mənœr, -øz] **N** *(de parti politique etc)* leader; *(de révolte, chahuteurs)* ringleader

NF meneuse de revue principal chorus girl; *Can Sport* **meneuse de claques** cheerleader, pompom girl

▸ ▸ **m. de bœufs** cattle drover; **m. d'hommes** leader of men; **le grand m. d'hommes que fut de Gaulle** De Gaulle, that great leader of men; **m. de jeu** *(de spectacle)* master of ceremonies, *Fam* emcee; *Br* compère; *TV, Radio (de jeu)* question master, quizmaster; *Ftbl* play maker

menhir [menir] **NM** menhir

méninge [menɛ̃ʒ] **NF** *Anat* meninx; *Fam* **se creuser les méninges** to rack one's brains; **il ne se fatigue pas les méninges** he doesn't exactly overtax his brain

méningé [menɛ̃ʒe] **ADJ** *Anat* meningeal

méningite [menɛ̃ʒit] **NF** *Méd* meningitis; *Fig* **il ne risque pas d'attraper une m.!** there's no risk of him overtaxing his brain!

ménisque [menisk] **NM** *Anat, Phys* meniscus

ménopause [menɔpoz] **NF** *Physiol* menopause; **faire sa m.** to go through the menopause

ménopausée [menɔpoze] **ADJ F** post-menopausal; **des femmes ménopausées** women who have gone through the menopause

ménorragie [menɔraʒi] **NF** *Méd* menorrhagia

menotte [mənɔt] **NF 1** *Enf* little hand **2 menottes** handcuffs; *Arch* manacles; **mettre** *ou* **passer les menottes à qn** to handcuff sb, to put handcuffs on sb

mensonge [mãsɔ̃ʒ] **NM 1** *(propos)* lie; **faire** *ou* **dire un m.** to tell a lie; **petit m., pieux m.** white lie; **gros m.** downright lie, *Fam* whopper, *Br Fam* porky; *Hum* **c'est vrai, ce m.?** do you expect me to believe that?, pull the other one *or* leg! **2** *(acte)* lying; **vivre dans le m.** to live a lie; **détester le m.** to hate lying *or* lies

mensonger, -ère [mãsɔ̃ʒe, -ɛr] **ADJ** *(histoire)* untrue; *(regard)* deceitful, false; *(promesse)* false, empty; *(publicité)* false

menstruation [mãstryasjɔ̃] **NF** *Physiol* menstruation

menstruel, -elle [mãstryɛl] **ADJ** *Physiol* menstrual

menstrues [mãstry] **NFPL** *Physiol* menses

mensualisation [mãsɥalizasjɔ̃] **NF** *(du personnel, des salaires, des impôts)* monthly payment; **remboursement par mensualisations** repayment in monthly instalments

mensualiser [mãsɥalize] **VT** to pay monthly *or* on a monthly basis, to make payable by the month; **je me suis fait m. pour tout** I pay everything monthly *or* on a monthly basis; **il est payé au trimestre mais il a demandé à être mensualisé** he is paid quarterly but has asked to be paid monthly

mensualité [mãsɥalite] **NF** monthly payment; **payer par mensualités** to pay monthly *or* by monthly instalments; **m. de remboursement** monthly repayment

mensuel, -elle [mãsɥɛl] **ADJ** monthly **NM** *(publication)* monthly (magazine) **N** employee paid monthly

mensuellement [mãsɥɛlmã] **ADV** monthly, every month

mensuration [mãsyrasjɔ̃] **NF** *(action)* measurement, measuring; **prendre les mensurations de qn** to take sb's measurements; **mensurations** *(de femme)* vital statistics; *Jur* **mensurations judiciaires** height and weight (as shown on criminal record)

mental, -ale, -aux, -ales [mãtal, -o] **ADJ** *(activité)* mental; **calcul m.** *(matière)* mental arithmetic; *(opération)* mental calculation; **maladie mentale** mental illness; **aliénation mentale** insanity

NM mental attitude; **un m. d'acier** a positive mental attitude

mentalement [mãtalmã] **ADV** mentally; *(calculer)* in one's head, mentally; *(prier)* silently; **j'ai préparé m. ce que j'allais lui répondre** I prepared in my head the answer I was going to give him/her; **se dire m. que** to tell oneself that

mentalité [mãtalite] **NF** mentality; **elle a une m. de petite bourgeoise** she has a lower middle-class mentality; **avoir une sale m.** to have a nasty mind; **il vole chez ses copains – jolie m.!** he steals from his friends – very nice!; **les mentalités ont évolué** (people's) attitudes have changed

menteur, -euse [mãtœr, -øz] **ADJ** *(personne)* untruthful, lying; *(discours, compliments)* deceitful

N liar

menthe [mãt] **NF** *(plante)* mint; **m. verte** spearmint, garden mint; **m. anglaise** *ou* **poivrée** peppermint; **pastilles de m.** (pepper)mints; **boire une m. à l'eau** to drink a glass of peppermint cordial; **sirop à la m.** peppermint cordial; **thé à la m.** mint tea; **gigot à la m.** leg of lamb with mint

menthol [mãtɔl] **NM** menthol; **bonbons/ci-** garettes au m. menthol(ated) sweets/cigarettes

mentholé [mãtɔle] **ADJ** menthol(ated)

mention [mãsjɔ̃] **NF** mention; **faire m. de qn/qch** to mention *or* refer to sb/sth; **m. écrite** written indication; **mentions obligatoires** *(sur étiquette)* essential information; *Scol* **reçu avec m.** ≃ passed with distinction; **décrocher la m. bien** ≃ to get a distinction

mentionner [mãsjɔne] **VT** to mention; **mentionné ci-dessus** above-mentioned, aforesaid; *TV, Cin* **m. au générique** to acknowledge in the credits, to give a credit to

mentir [mãtir] (*prp* **mentant;** *pp* **menti;** *pr ind* **je mens, il ment, n. mentons, ils mentent;** *p hist* **je mentis;** *fu* **je mentirai**) **VI** to lie (**à qn** to sb); **sans m.!** honestly!; **tu mens comme tu respires** you're a compulsive liar; **m. à sa réputation** not to live up to one's reputation; **elle ment à son mari** she is deceiving her husband

VPR se mentir to fool oneself

menton [mãtɔ̃] **NM** chin; **m. en galoche** jutting chin; **m. fuyant** receding chin; **double m.** double chin

mentonnier, -ière [mãtɔnje, -jɛr] **ADJ** of the chin

NF mentonnière *Mil* chin strap; *(de casque)* chinpiece; *Mus* chin rest

mentor [mãtɔr] **NM** *Litt* mentor

menu¹ [məny] **ADJ 1** *(petit)* small; *(gravier)* fine; *(silhouette)* slender, slim, slight; *(fragment)* tiny; **m. plomb** small shot, bird shot; **menue monnaie** small change; *Compta* **menus frais** petty expenses, incidental expenses **2** *(incident)* trifling, petty; **menues réparations** minor repairs; **menus détails** minute details; **menus frais, menues dépenses** minor expenses; **menus propos** small talk

ADV *(piler)* small, fine; **hacher m.** to chop fine *or* small; *(très fin)* to mince; **écrire m.** to write small

N raconter qch par le m. to relate sth in detail

menu² **NM 1** *(repas)* meal; **composer son m.** to plan one's meal; **m. équilibré** balanced meal **2** *(liste) (au restaurant)* menu; **prendre le m. (à 50 euros)** to have the (50-euro) set meal; **m. touristique/gastronomique** economy/gourmet menu; **m. déjeuner** lunch menu; **m. enfant** children's menu; **m. table d'hôte** table d'hôte menu; **m. à prix fixe** set menu, fixed-price menu **3** *Ordinat* menu; **contrôlé par menu(s)** menu-driven; **m. primaire/secondaire/principal** primary/secondary/main menu; **m. d'impression** print menu; **m. déroulant** pull-down menu; **m. d'aide** help menu; **m. de césure** hyphenation menu; **m. édition** edit menu; **m. fichier** file menu; **m. flottant** tear-off menu; **m. hiérarchique** hierarchical menu; **m. local** pop-up menu, pop-up; **m. principal** main menu; **menus en cascade** pull-down menus, cascading menus

menuet [mənɥe] **NM** minuet

menuiserie [mənɥizri] **NF 1** *(travail)* joinery, woodwork **2** *(atelier)* (joiner's) workshop **3** *(résultat)* joinery, woodwork

menuisier [mənɥizje] **NM** joiner

méphistophélique [mefistofelik] **ADJ** Mephistophelean

méphitique [mefitik] **ADJ** foul, noxious

méplat [mepla] **NM** flat surface; *(de rocher)* ledge

méprendre (se) [səmeprãdr] **VPR** *(conj* **prendre** *)* to be mistaken (**sur, quant à** about); **il imitait le maître à s'y m.** he could give a lifelike imitation of the master

mépris [mepri] **NM** contempt, scorn, disdain; **m. des richesses** contempt for wealth; **avoir le m. de l'argent/des conventions** to scorn or despise money/convention; **avoir du m. pour qn** to despise sb; **je n'éprouve que du m. à son égard** I have nothing but contempt for him/her; **au m. de qch** regardless of sth; **m.** scornfully, contemptuously; **sourire de m.** contemptuous or scornful smile

méprisable [meprizabl] ADJ contemptible, despicable

méprisant [meprizɑ̃] ADJ contemptuous, scornful

méprise [mepriz] NF mistake; **il y a m. sur le destinataire** it has been delivered to the wrong person; **par m.** by mistake

mépriser [meprize] VT (personne, argent) to despise, to scorn; (conseil, offre, danger) to scorn

mer [mɛr] NF **1** (étendue d'eau) sea; **en haute ou pleine m.** (out) at sea; **m. fermée ou intérieure** inland sea, landlocked sea; **la m. Rouge/Noire** the Red/Black Sea; **la m. Baltique** the Baltic (Sea); **la m. du Nord** the North Sea; **m. d'huile** sea as calm as a millpond; **au bord de la m.** at or by the seaside, by the sea; **aller à la m.** to go to the seaside; **une maison à la m.** a house by the sea(side); **grosse m.** heavy sea; **par grosse m.** when the sea is heavy; **il y a de la m.** the sea is running high, there's a heavy sea; **essuyer un coup de m.** to be struck by a heavy sea; **un homme à la m.!** man overboard!; **servir sur m.** to serve afloat or at sea; **voyager par m.** to travel by sea; **prendre la m.** to set sail, to put (out) to sea; **ce capitaine/navire n'a pas pris la m. depuis vingt ans** this captain/boat hasn't been to sea for twenty years; **mettre une embarcation à la m.** to get out a boat; (d'un navire) to lower a boat; **tenir la m.** (rester au large) to remain at sea; (la contrôler) to hold the seas, to rule the waves; **navire qui tient bien la m.** ship that behaves well in a heavy sea; **droit de la m.** maritime law; Fam **ce n'est pas la m. à boire** it's no big deal; Fig **m. de sable** vast expanse of sand **2** (marée) tide; **m. haute, pleine m.** high tide; **basse m.** low tide

mer-air ADJ INV Mil **missile m.** sea-to-air missile

mercanti [mɛrkɑ̃ti] NM (marchand) bazaar-keeper, Péj profiteer, shark

mercantile [mɛrkɑ̃til] ADJ **1** Péj **esprit m.** money-grabbing mentality **2** Arch (opération etc) mercantile, commercial

mercantilisme [mɛrkɑ̃tilism] NM **1** Péj money-grabbing, profiteering **2** Écon, Hist mercantilism

mercaphonie [mɛrkafɔni] NF Mktg telemarketing, telephone marketing

mercaticien, -ienne [mɛrkatisjɛ̃, -jɛn] N Mktg marketeer, marketer, marketing expert

mercatique [mɛrkatik] NF marketing; **m. après-vente** after-sales marketing; **m. ciblée** niche or target marketing; **m. commerciale** trade marketing; **m. de contact** direct marketing; **m. défensive** defensive marketing; **m. écologique** green marketing; **m. expansionniste** rollout marketing; **m. de grande consommation** mass marketing; **m. indifférenciée** undifferentiated marketing; **m. non lucrative** not-for-profit marketing; (résultats insatisfaisants) unprofitable marketing; **m. de relance** remarketing; **m. relationnelle** relationship or direct marketing; **m. de stimulation** stimulation or incentive marketing; **m. stratégique** strategic marketing; **m. sur mesure** customized marketing; **m. test dirigé** controlled test marketing; **m. téléphonique** telephone marketing; **m. de la valeur** value marketing

mercenaire [mɛrsənɛr] ADJ, N mercenary

mercerie [mɛrsəri] NF **1** (marchandise) haberdashery, Am notions **2** (magasin) haberdasher's (shop), Am notions store

merceriser [mɛrsərize] VT Tex to mercerize; **coton mercerisé** mercerized cotton

merchandising [mɛrʃɑ̃dajziŋ] NM Écon merchandising

merci [mɛrsi] INT thank you, thanks; (refus) no thank you, no thanks; **dire m.** to say thank you or thanks; **il ne m'a pas dit m.** he didn't say thank you to me; **m. bien, m. beaucoup** thank you very much, thanks a lot; **m. de ou pour votre offre** thank you for your offer; Fam **m. qui? m. mon chien!** don't bother to say thank you!; **grand m.!** no thank you!; Iron **m'excuser? m. bien, après ce qu'il m'a fait!** apologize? no way or no thanks, not after what he did to me!; Iron **m. du compliment!** thanks for the compliment!; **mille mercis de ou pour votre invitation** thank you so much or many thanks for your invitation

NM thank you; **il a pris le livre sans un m.** he took the book without a word of thanks or without saying thank you or without so much as a thanks

NF mercy; **être à la m. de qn/qch** to be at the mercy of sb/sth; **tenir qn à sa m.** to have sb at one's mercy; **crier m.** to cry for mercy; **sans m.** (adjectif) merciless, pitiless, ruthless; (adverbe) mercilessly, pitilessly, ruthlessly

mercier, -ière [mɛrsje, -jɛr] N haberdasher, Am notions dealer

Mercosur [mɛrkosyr] NM Écon Mercosur

mercredi [mɛrkrədi] NM Wednesday; **le m. des Cendres** Ash Wednesday (voir aussi **samedi**) SEE GRAMMAR A81–2; B61
INT Euph sugar!

mercure [mɛrkyr] NM **1** Chimie mercury **2** Myth **M.** Mercury
NF Astron **M.** Mercury

mercuriale[1] [mɛrkyrjal] NF Bot mercury

mercuriale[2] NF Litt (réprimande) reprimand, rebuke

mercuriale[3] NF Com commodity price list

mercuriel, -ielle [mɛrkyrjɛl] ADJ Pharm mercurial

Mercurochrome® [mɛrkyrokrom] NM mercurochrome®

merde [mɛrd] très Fam NF (excrément) shit, crap; (étron) turd; **j'ai marché dans une m. de chien** I've trodden in a dog turd or in some dog shit; **il y a une m. d'oiseau sur le pare-brise** there's some bird shit on the windscreen; **il ne se prend pas pour de la m.** he thinks he's God's gift to the world, Br Vulg he thinks the sun shines out of his arse; **c'est de la m.** (ce qu'il vient de dire) that's a load of shit or crap; (ce tissu, ce film etc) it's crap; **c'est une vraie m.** it's a right load of crap; **une m. à 5 euros** some cheap rubbish costing 5 euros; **de m.** (voiture, idée etc) shitty, crappy; **c'est la m.** things are shitty, Am this sucks; **c'est la m. dans le pays en ce moment** the country's a Br bloody or Am goddamn mess or shambles at the moment; **foutre la m.** to create havoc; **être dans la m.** to be in the shit, to be up shit creek; **il a de la m. dans les yeux** he never sees a thing, he can't see what's going on right in front of him; **il m'est arrivé une m.** something shit's happened; **traîner qn dans la m.** to drag sb's name through the mud
INT shit!; **m. alors, je ne m'attendais pas à ça** oh shit, I didn't expect that; **et m., j'en ai marre!** to hell with it or Br sod it, I've had enough!; **et m. au boulot, je vais au ciné** to hell with work or Br sod work, I'm off to the cinema; **t'es d'accord, oui ou m.?** are we agreed or not, for Christ's sake?; **dire m. à**

qn to tell sb to piss off or Br bugger off; **je te dis m.!** (bonne chance!) ≃ break a leg!; **avoir un œil qui dit m. à l'autre** to have a squint

merder [mɛrde] VI très Fam **ma bagnole merde depuis huit jours** my car's been playing up for the past week; **j'ai envie de partir en vacances, mais j'ai l'impression que ça va m.** I want to go on holiday, but I've a feeling it'll come to nothing; **j'ai complètement merdé dans les explications que je t'ai données** I made a real hash or mess of the instructions I gave you; **ils ne savent pas trop ce qui a merdé entre eux** they don't really know what screwed things up between them

merdeux, -euse [mɛrdø, -øz] Vulg ADJ (linge etc) shitty; Arch **c'est un bâton m.** he's a shit; **elle se sent merdeuse** she feels shitty
N **1** (personne) jerk; **un petit m.** a jerk or prat **2** (enfant) brat

merdier [mɛrdje] NM Vulg (désordre) mess; **je ne sais pas par quel bout ranger, tellement c'est le m.** it's such a mess or pigsty I don't know where to start tidying up; **c'est le m. dans ma vie** my life's (in) a real mess; **je suis dans un sacré m.** I'm really in the shit

merdique [mɛrdik] ADJ Vulg shitty, crappy

merdouiller [mɛrduje], **merdoyer** [mɛrdwaje] VI (je merdoie, n. merdoyons; je merdoierai) Vulg to make a cockup or balls-up or Am ball-up, Br to cock up

mère [mɛr] NF **1** (parent) mother; Zool dam; **elle est m. de famille** she is a wife and mother; **elle est m. de trois enfants** she is the mother of three children, she is a mother of three; **elle a été une vraie m. pour son frère** she's been like a mother to her brother; **sœur par la m.** half-sister on the mother's side; Fam **la m. Martin** old Mrs Martin; Fam **et dites donc, la petite m.!** well, missus!
2 (source, origine) **l'oisiveté est (la) m. de tous les vices** the devil finds work for idle hands (to do)
3 Beaux-Arts, Cér (pour moules en plâtre etc) mould, Am mold, matrix
4 **langue m.** mother tongue; Biol **cellule m.** mother cell; Com **maison m.** parent company; **la reine m.** the Queen Mother
▸▸ Rel **m. abbesse** abbess; **m. biologique** natural or biological mother; **m. célibataire** single or Vieilli unmarried mother; **m. d'emprunt** surrogate mother; **m. génétique** natural or biological mother; **m. nourricière** foster mother; **m. patrie** mother country, motherland; **m. porteuse** surrogate mother; **m. poule** mother hen; **m. de substitution** surrogate mother; Rel **M. supérieure** Mother Superior (of convent); **m. de vinaigre** mother of vinegar

merguez [mɛrgɛz] NF merguez (spicy North African sausage)

méridien, -ienne [meridjɛ̃, -jɛn] ADJ (ligne etc) meridian, meridional; **chaleur méridienne** midday heat; **ombre méridienne** shadow at noon
NM meridian; **sous le m. de vingt degrés à l'ouest de Greenwich** twenty degrees west of Greenwich
NF **méridienne 1** Astron meridian line; (altitude) meridian altitude **2** Arch (sieste) midday siesta or nap **3** (canapé) day bed

méridional, -ale, -aux, -ales [meridjɔnal, -o] ADJ (du Sud) southern; (du Sud de la France) Southern French
N (du Sud) southerner; (du Sud de la France) Southern Frenchman, f Frenchwoman; **méridionaux** (du Sud de la France) Southern French people

meringue [mərɛ̃g] NF Culin meringue

meringuer [mərɛ̃ge] VT Culin to cover with meringue; **tarte à la rhubarbe meringuée** rhubarb meringue pie

mérinos [merinos] NM *(mouton, laine, tissu)* merino; *Arg* **laisse pisser le m.!** don't let it get to you!

merise [məriz] NF *(fruit)* wild cherry

merisier [mərizje] NM *(arbre)* wild cherry (tree); *(bois)* cherry (wood)

méritant [meritã] ADJ deserving; **peu m.** undeserving

mérite [merit] NM *(qualité estimable)* merit; *(honneur)* credit; *(valeur)* worth; **ses remarques avaient le m. d'être franches** his/her remarks had the merit of being frank; **tu n'as même pas le m. de l'avoir fait tout seul** you can't even take credit for doing it yourself; **je n'ai aucun m.** I deserve no credit, I can't take any credit (for it); **s'attribuer le m. de qch** to take the credit for sth; **tout le m. lui revient** the credit is all his, all the credit is due to him/her; **son m. est grand d'avoir tout accepté, il a le grand m. d'avoir tout accepté** it is greatly to his credit that he accepted everything; **au seul m.** on merit alone; **augmentation au m.** merit increase; **par ordre de m.** in order of merit; **selon ses mérites** according to one's merits; **homme de m.** man of merit *or* talent *or* ability

mériter [merite] VT **1** to deserve, to merit; **il mérite des baffes** he deserves to be slapped; **il n'a que ce qu'il mérite** he's got what he deserves, it serves him right; **livre qui mérite d'être lu** book worth reading; **cela mérite réflexion** it's worth thinking about; **tu mérites qu'on te fasse la même chose** you deserve to have the same thing happen to you; **tu mériterais que je te laisse là tout seul** it would serve you right if I left you there on your own **2 voilà ce qui lui a mérité cette renommée** this is what earned him this fame; **bien m. de la patrie** to deserve well of one's country

méritocratie [meritokrasi] NF meritocracy

méritoire [meritwar] ADJ commendable, praiseworthy, meritorious

merlan [merlã] NM **1** *(poisson)* whiting; *Fam* **faire des yeux de m. frit à qn, regarder qn avec des yeux de m. frit** *(parce qu'on n'a pas compris)* to gape at sb; *(parce qu'on est amoureux de lui)* to make sheep's eyes at sb **2** *Arg (coiffeur) (pour hommes)* barber, hairdresser; *(pour femmes)* hairdresser

merle [merl] NM *(oiseau)* blackbird; *Fig* **vilain m.,** *Iron* **beau m.** nasty customer, *Br* nasty piece of work; **m. blanc** rare bird; **chercher le m. blanc** to ask for the moon

merlin[1] [merlɛ̃] NM *Naut* marline

merlin[2] NM *(hache)* axe, *Am* ax; *(pour abattre les arbres)* felling axe; *(pour abattre le bétail)* poleaxe

merlu [merly] NM hake

merluche [merly ʃ] NF **1** *(poisson)* hake VOIR GRAMMAIRE A12 **2** *Culin* dried (unsalted) cod, stockfish

mer-mer ADJ INV *Mil* **missile m.** sea-to-sea missile

mérou [meru] NM *(poisson)* grouper

mérovingien, -ienne [merovɛ̃ʒjɛ̃, -jɛn] *Hist* ADJ Merovingian
N **M.** Merovingian

mer-sol ADJ INV *Mil* **missile m.** sea-to-ground missile

merveille [mɛrvɛj] NF **1** marvel, wonder; **les merveilles de la technologie** the marvels *or* wonders of technology; **les sept merveilles du monde** the seven wonders of the world; **ma nouvelle machine à laver est une m.** my new washing machine is a marvel; **faire m.** to work *or* do wonders *(sur* with, for); **faire des merveilles** to work *or* do *or* perform wonders; **c'est m. que vous soyez à l'heure** it's a wonder that you're on time; **à m.** per-

fectly, wonderfully (well); **se porter à m.** to be in excellent health *or* in the best of health; **ce chèque tombe à m.** this cheque has arrived at exactly the right moment **2** *Culin* = sweet fritter

merveilleusement [mɛrvɛjøzmã] ADV marvellously, wonderfully; **il fait m. beau** it's marvellous *or* wonderful weather, the weather's marvellous *or* wonderful; **aller m. bien** to be wonderfully well, to be in excellent health; **elle a m. réussi son examen** she passed her exam with excellent results

merveilleux, -euse [mɛrvɛjø, -øz] ADJ marvellous, wonderful; **il a fait un temps m.** it was marvellous *or* wonderful weather, the weather was marvellous *or* wonderful; **c'est m. ce qu'il a changé** it's marvellous how he's changed
NM **le m.** the supernatural
NF *Hist* **merveilleuse** merveilleuse, fine lady

mes [me] *voir* **mon**

mésadapté, -ée [mezadapte] *Can* ADJ maladjusted
N misfit, maladjusted person; **m. social** social misfit

mésalliance [mezaljãs] NF unsuitable marriage; **faire une m.** to marry beneath oneself

mésallier (se) [səmezalje] VT *(conj like* **allier)** to marry beneath oneself

mésange [mezãʒ] NF tit; **m. bleue** bluetit; **m. charbonnière** great tit; **m. noire** coaltit

mésaventure [mezavãtyr] NF misadventure, mishap, misfortune

mescal [meskal] NM mescal

mescaline [meskalin] NF mescalin(e)

mésentente [mezãtãt] NF disagreement; **climat de m.** coolness

mésestimation [mezɛstimasjɔ̃] NF *Litt* underestimation, underrating, undervaluing

mésestime [mezɛstim] NF *Litt* low esteem; **tenir qn en m.** to hold sb in low esteem

mésestimer [mezɛstime] VT to underestimate

mésintelligence [mezɛ̃teliʒãs] NF *Litt* disagreement; **être en m. avec qn** to be at loggerheads with sb

mesmérisme [mesmerism] NM mesmerism

Mésopotamie (la) [lamezɔpɔtami] NF Mesopotamia

mésopotamien, -ienne [mezɔpɔtamjɛ̃, -jɛn] ADJ Mesopotamian
N **M.** Mesopotamian

mésothérapie [mezoterapi] NF *Méd* mesotherapy *(method of treatment involving intradermal injections with mini-needles)*

mésozoïque [mezɔzɔik] ADJ, NM *Géol* Mesozoic

mesquin [meskɛ̃] ADJ *(méchant)* mean, petty; *(avare)* mean, stingy, niggardly; *(excuse)* paltry, petty; **un coup m.** a mean *or* shabby trick; **il a vraiment un esprit m.** he's really small-minded *or* mean *or* petty

mesquinement [meskinmã] ADV meanly

mesquinerie [meskinri] NF *(de caractère, procédé)* meanness, pettiness; *(avarice)* meanness, stinginess, niggardliness; **je ne te savais pas capable de telles mesquineries** I would never have thought you capable of such meanness *or* pettiness, I didn't think you could be so mean *or* petty

mess [mes] NM *Mil* mess; **m. des officiers** officers' mess

message [mesaʒ] NM message; **prendre un m.** to take a message; **veuillez laisser un m. après le signal sonore** please leave a message after the tone; **chanson/pièce à m.** song/play with a message; **m. codé** coded message; **m. électronique** e-mail; **envoyer**

un m. électronique à qn to e-mail sb; **m. enregistré** recorded message; **m. subliminal** subliminal message; **m. télex** telex (message); **m. téléphonique** telephone message; **m. de détresse** distress message; **m. publicitaire** advertisement, advertising message; *Ordinat* **messages publicitaires** *(envoyés par e-mail)* junk mail, spam; *Ordinat* **m. d'accueil** welcome message; *Ordinat* **m. d'aide** help message; *Ordinat* **m. d'alerte** warning message, alert box; *Ordinat* **m. d'attente (du système)** (system) prompt; *Ordinat* **m. d'erreur** error message; *Ordinat* **m. d'invite** *(du système)* prompt; *Ordinat* **m. guide-opérateur** prompt

messager, -ère [mesaʒe, -ɛr] N messenger; **m. de malheur** bearer of bad news; *Litt* **m. du printemps** harbinger of spring
NM *(de colis, cargaison)* carrier

messagerie [mesaʒri] NF service de messageries parcel delivery service; *Ordinat* **m. de dialogue en direct** chat; **m. électronique** electronic mail service, e-mail; **m. instantanée** instant messaging; **m. de presse** newspaper distributing service; **m. rose** = interactive Minitel services enabling individuals seeking companionship to make contact; **m. vocale** voice mail; **messageries maritimes** shipping line; **messageries aériennes** air freight company; **bureau de(s) messageries** *Naut* shipping office; *Rail* parcel(s) office; *Hist* stagecoach office

messe [mes] NF *Rel* mass; **aller à la m.** to go to mass; **célébrer** *ou* **dire la m.** to celebrate *or* say mass; **faire dire une m. pour qn** to have a mass said for sb; *Mus* **m. en si mineur** mass in B minor; *Fig* **la m. est dite** the die is cast; *Can Fig* **il y a du monde à la m.!** the place is jam-packed!
▸ ▸ **m. basse** low mass; *Fig Fam* **pas de messes basses!** stop whispering!; **m. de minuit** midnight mass; **m. des morts** requiem mass; **m. noire** black mass

messeigneurs [mesɛɲœr] NMPL *voir* **monseigneur**

messeoir [meswar] VI *(prp* **messeyant;** *no pp; pr ind* **il messied, ils messeyent;** *pr sub* **il messeye;** *impf* **il messeyait;** *no p hist; fu* **il messiéra)** *Arch, Litt* to be unbecoming *or* unseemly; **il lui messied de ...** it ill becomes him to ...

messianique [mesjanik] ADJ Messianic

messianisme [mesjanism] NM Messianism

messidor [mesidor] NM *Hist* = tenth month of the French Republican calendar *(19-20 June – 19-20 July)*

Messie [mesi] NM Messiah; **on l'a attendu comme le M.** we were waiting eagerly for him

messin, -ine [mesɛ̃, -in] ADJ of/from Metz
N **M.** *(natif)* native of Metz; *(habitant)* inhabitant of Metz

messire [mesir] NM *Arch* Sir, Master

mestrance [mestrãs] NF *Naut* petty officers

mesurable [məzyrabl] ADJ measurable, *Spéc* mensurable

mesurage [məzyraʒ] NM measuring, measurement

mesure [məzyr] NF **1** *(dimension)* measurement; *(action)* measuring, measuring; **appareil de m.** measuring apparatus; **prendre les mesures de qn** to take sb's measurements, to measure sb; **prendre les mesures de qch** to measure sth; *Fig* **prendre la m. de qn** to size sb up, to get the measure of sb; **sur m.** made to measure, tailor-made; **complet (fait) sur mesure(s)** made-to-measure *or Am* custom-made suit; **faire faire un complet sur m.** to have a suit made to measure or tailor-made; *Fig* **être en m. de faire qch** to be in a position to do sth; **le producteur lui a trouvé un rôle sur m.** the producer found him a role that was tailor-made for him; *Fig* **donner toute sa m.** to show what one is capable of; *Fig* **être à la m. de qn/qch** to measure up to sb/sth; *Sp, Fig* **trouver un adversaire à sa m.** to meet one's match **SEE GRAMMAR B59**

2 dans une certaine m. to some or a certain extent or degree; **dans une large m.** to a large extent or degree, in large measure; **dans la m. où** insofar as; **je vous aiderai dans la m. de mes forces** ou **du possible** I'll help you to the best of my ability or as much as I can or as best I can; **ces dépenses ne sont pas dans la m. de mes moyens** this expenditure is beyond my means

3 (au fur et) à m. as one goes along; **je vérifie les chiffres (au fur et) à m.** I check the figures as I go along; **à m. que** as; **à m. que je reculais, il s'avançait** as I retreated, he advanced

4 (*action*) measure, step, action; **m. de sécurité** safety measure or precaution; **par m. de sécurité/d'hygiène** for reasons of safety/hygiene, as a safety/hygiene measure; **par m. d'économie** as a cost-saving measure, for reasons of economy; **prendre des mesures** to take measures or steps or action; **prendre des mesures pour faire qch/pour que ...** to take measures or steps to do sth/so that ...; **prendre des mesures contre qch** to take action against sth; **prendre ses mesures** to make arrangements; **j'ai pris mes mesures pour que les enfants soient gardés** I've made arrangements for the children to be looked after; **mesures d'austérité** austerity measures; **m. conservatoire** protective measure; **m. fiscale** fiscal measure; **m. incitative** incentive (measure); **mesures protectionnistes** protectionist measures; **mesures protectrices** protective measures; **mesures provisoires** temporary measures; **m. de rétorsion** retaliatory measure, reprisal; **m. d'urgence** emergency measure

5 (*quantité, unité*) measure; **verser une m. de vin à qn** to pour sb out a measure of wine; **faites-moi bonne m.** give me good measure; *Fig* **il n'y a pas commune m. entre ces deux vins** there is no comparison between the two wines; **sans commune m.** unrivalled; **m. de longueur** measure of length; **m. de surface** ou **de superficie** square measure; **m. de volume** cubic measure; **poids et mesures** weights and measures

6 pièces qui ne sont pas de m. pieces that are not the right size or that are not to size; **rester dans la juste m.** to keep within bounds; **elle n'a pas le sens de la m.** she has no sense of moderation; **(dé)passer la m.** to overstep the mark, to go too far; **ne garder aucune m., oublier toute m.** to fling aside all restraint, to lose all sense of moderation or proportion; **ambition sans m.** unbounded or limitless ambition

7 *Escrime* measure, reach, distance

8 *Mus* (*temps*) time; (*division*) bar; **m. à quatre temps** four-four time, common time; **battre la m.** to beat time; **barre de m.** bar line; **en m.** in (strict) time; **aller en m.** to keep time; **deux mesures plus loin** two bars further on

9 *Littér* (*de vers*) metre, *Am* meter

mesuré [məzyre] **ADJ** (*pas*) measured; (*langage, personne*) moderate, restrained

mesurément [məzyremã] **ADV** in moderation

mesurer [məzyre] **VT 1** (*dimensions, taille*) to measure; (*farine, sucre etc*) to measure out; (*bois, terre*) to measure (up); (*tissu*) to measure off; (*carburant*) to meter; *Fig* (*personne, chose*) to size up; **m. deux mètres** (*de personne*) to be two metres tall; **la colonne me-**

sure **dix mètres** the column measures ten metres or is ten metres high; **on mesure le travail au résultat** the work is measured by results; **m. la nourriture à qn** to ration sb's food; **le temps vous sera mesuré pour cette épreuve** you will have a limited amount of time for this test; **m. sa dépense sur ses profits** to cut one's coat according to one's cloth; **m. la distance à la vue** to judge or estimate or gauge the distance with one's eyes **2** (*ménager, régler*) **m. le châtiment à l'offense** to make the punishment fit the crime; **m. ses paroles** ou **son vocabulaire** to moderate one's language; **il ne mesure pas la portée de ses paroles** he says things without thinking

VPR se mesurer se m. avec ou **à qn** to measure one's strength against sb, to measure or pit oneself against sb; **vous n'êtes pas de force** ou **de taille à vous m. avec lui** you're no match for him; **les adversaires se mesurèrent des yeux** the opponents sized each other up

mesurette [məzyret] **NF 1** (*pour doser*) measuring spoon **2** (*décision sans grande portée*) petty reform

mesureur [məzyrœr] **NM** (*personne, appareil*) measurer; **m. de pression** pressure gauge

mésuser [mezyze] **VI m. de son bien** to misuse one's wealth; **m. de son pouvoir** to abuse one's power

métabolique [metabolik] **ADJ** metabolic

métabolisme [metabɔlism] **NM** metabolism

métacarpe [metakarp] **NM** *Anat* metacarpus

métacarpien, -ienne [metakarpjɛ̃, -jɛn] **ADJ, NM** *Anat* metacarpal

métairie [meteri] **NF** small farm (*worked by share-cropper*)

métal, -aux [metal, -o] **NM 1** metal; **métaux précieux** precious metals; **m. blanc** white metal; **m. antifriction** Babbit metal, bearing metal **2** *Fin* **m. en barres** bullion

métalangage [metalãgaʒ] **NM** metalanguage

métalangue [metalãg] **NF** metalanguage

métallifère [metalifɛr] **ADJ** metal-bearing, metalliferous

métallique [metalik] **ADJ** metallic; **câble m.** wire rope; **plume m.** metal nib; **rendre un son m.** to clang, to clank; *Fin* **réserve m.** bullion reserve

métallisation [metalizasjɔ̃] **NF** metallization

métallisé [metalize] **ADJ** *surtout Aut* (*peinture*) metallic; **voiture bleu m.** metallic blue car

métalliser [metalize] **VT** to metallize

métallo [metalo] **NM** *Fam* metalworker

métallurgie [metalyrʒi] **NF** metallurgy; **crise dans la m.** crisis in the metallurgical industry

métallurgique [metalyrʒik] **ADJ** metallurgical

métallurgiste [metalyrʒist] **NM 1** (*scientifique*) metallurgist **2** (*ouvrier*) metalworker

métamorphique [metamɔrfik] **ADJ** *Géol* metamorphic

métamorphiser [metamɔrfize] **VT** *Géol* to metamorphose

métamorphisme [metamɔrfism] **NM** *Géol* metamorphism

métamorphose [metamɔrfoz] **NF** transformation, metamorphosis; *Fig* transformation; *Fig* **quelle m.!** what a transformation!

métamorphoser [metamɔrfoze] **VT** to transform, to metamorphose; *Fig* to transform

VPR se métamorphoser to change completely, to be transformed

métaphore [metafɔr] **NF** metaphor; **parler par métaphores** to speak in metaphors; **elle parle beaucoup par métaphores** she is very metaphorical in her speech, she uses a lot of metaphor(s) when she speaks

métaphorique [metafɔrik] **ADJ** (*expression, style*) metaphorical, figurative; **cela n'a qu'une valeur m.** it's purely metaphorical or figurative

métaphoriquement [metafɔrikmã] **ADV** metaphorically, figuratively

métaphysicien, -ienne [metafizisjɛ̃, -jɛn] **N** metaphysician, metaphysicist

métaphysique [metafizik] **ADJ** metaphysical
NF metaphysics

métaphysiquement [metafizikmã] **ADV** metaphysically

métapsychique [metapsiʃik] **ADJ** (*phénomène*) psychic
NF parapsychology

métastase [metastaz] **NF** *Méd* metastasis, secondary cancer; **former des métastases** to metastasize

métatarse [metatars] **NM** *Anat* metatarsus

métatarsien, -ienne [metatarsjɛ̃, -jɛn] **ADJ, NM** *Anat* metatarsal

métathèse [metatez] **NF** *Ling* metathesis

métayage [metejaʒ] **NM** *Agr* sharecropping

métayer, -ère [meteje, -ɛr] **N** *Agr* sharecropper

métazoaire [metazɔɛr] **NM** *Biol* metazoan; **métazoaires** Metazoa

métempsycose [metãpsikoz] **NF** transmigration of the soul, *Spéc* metempsychosis

météo [meteo] *Fam* **NF 1** weather forecast or report; **la m. est mauvaise pour toute la semaine** the weather forecast is bad for the whole week; **je n'ai pas eu le temps d'écouter/de regarder la m.** I didn't have time to listen to/to look at the weather (forecast) **2** (*bureau*) weather office, *Br* ≃ Met Office, *Am* ≃ Weather Bureau
NM Monsieur M. the weather man
ADJ weather, meteorological; **bulletin m.** weather report or forecast; **station m.** meteorological or weather station; **frégate** ou **navire m.** weather ship

météore [meteɔr] **NM** meteor

météorique [meteɔrik] **ADJ** meteoric

météorite [meteɔrit] **NM OU F** meteorite

météorologie [meteɔrɔlɔʒi] **NF** meteorology; **le bureau central de m.** = the meteorological or weather office

météorologique [meteɔrɔlɔʒik] **ADJ** = météo **ADJ**

météorologiste [meteɔrɔlɔʒist], **météorologue** [meteɔrɔlɔg] **N** meteorologist

métèque [metɛk] **NM** *très Fam* (*terme injurieux*) = racist term used to refer to any dark-skinned foreigner living in France, especially one from the Mediterranean

méthadone [metadon] **NF** methadone

méthane [metan] **NM** *Chimie* methane

méthanier [metanje] **NM** *Naut* methane tanker

méthanol [metanɔl] **NM** methanol

méthode [metɔd] **NF 1** (*démarche*) method, way; **m. pour faire qch** method or way of doing sth; **une bonne m. pour apprendre les langues** a good method for or way of learning languages; **c'est quoi ta m. pour rester aussi mince?** how do you manage to stay so slim?; **elle a sa m.** she has her own method or way of doing things; **je vais changer de m.** I'm going to change my methods; **tu as suivi quelle m.?** which method did you use?; **c'est**

la seule m. à suivre it's the only way to do it; **il n'y a pas 36 méthodes** it's the only way; *Fam* **je n'ai pas la m. avec lui** I don't know how to handle him; **tu as vraiment la m. avec les enfants!** you really have a way with *or* know how to handle children!; *Fam* **trouver la m. pour faire qch** to find out how to do sth, to find a way of doing sth; **m. de lecture** reading method; **m. de financement** funding method; **m. de gestion** management technique; **m. de travail** work method; *UE* **m. communautaire** Community method; *Compta* **m. par** *ou* **à échelles** daily balance interest calculation; **m. des coûts variables** direct costing; **m. des coûts marginaux** cost pricing; **m. du coût de revient complet** full costing, full cost accounting (method); **m. de vente** sales *or* selling technique

2 *(ordre)* method; **il a beaucoup de m.** he's very methodical *or* systematic; **avec m.** methodically, systematically; **sans m.** unmethodically, without method, unsystematically

3 *(livre)* primer, grammar; **m. de piano** piano tutor

méthodique [metɔdik] ADJ methodic(al), systematic

méthodiquement [metɔdikmɑ̃] ADV methodically, systematically

méthodisme [metɔdism] NM *Rel* Methodism

méthodiste [metɔdist] ADJ, N *Rel* Methodist

méthodologie [metɔdɔlɔʒi] NF methodology

méthodologique [metɔdɔlɔʒik] ADJ methodological

méthyle [metil] NM *Chimie* methyl

méthylène [metilɛn] NM *Chimie* methylene

méthylique [metilik] ADJ *Chimie* methyl(ic)

méticuleusement [metikyløzmɑ̃] ADV meticulously

méticuleux, -euse [metikylø, -øz] ADJ meticulous; **par trop m.** over-meticulous; **elle est d'une propreté méticuleuse** she keeps everything immaculate *or* everything spotless(ly clean)

méticulosité [metikylozite] NF *Litt* meticulousness; **d'une m. exaspérante** exasperatingly meticulous

métier [metje] NM **1** *(travail)* trade, profession, occupation; **les métiers artistiques** the artistic professions; **j'ai fait tous les métiers** I've done a bit of everything; **quel est votre m.?** what do you do (for a living)?, what's your job?; **exercer** *ou* **faire un m.** to carry on a trade *or* a profession; **j'exerce le m. de journaliste** I'm a journalist (by profession); **quel m. veux-tu faire plus tard?** what do you want to be when you grow up?; **il n'est pas** *ou* **il n'y a pas de sot m.** a job's a job; **m. de banquier** banking profession, banking; **les métiers de bouche** the food and catering trade; *Euph* **le plus vieux m. du monde** the oldest profession in the world; **il est charpentier de son m.** he's a carpenter by trade; **elle a un bon m.** she has a good job; **il sent qu'il est temps de changer de m.** he feels it's time he changed his job; **ils sont du m.** they're in the business *or* trade; *Fig* **ce n'est pas mon m.** it's not my job; **il connaît son m.** he knows what he's doing; **ce n'est pas toi qui vas m'apprendre mon m.** don't teach me my business, I know what I'm doing; **ils font leur m.** they're only doing their job; **parler m.** to talk shop; *Fam* **quel m.!** what a life!; **quel m. de fou!** you don't have to be crazy to do this job, but it helps!; **chacun son m. (et les vaches seront bien gardées)** you do your job and I'll do mine; **terme de m.** technical term SEE GRAMMAR B5

2 *(savoir-faire, expérience)* experience; **il a**

du m. he has experience, he is experienced; **elle a plusieurs années de m.** she has several years' experience; **homme de m.** professional; **gens de m.** experts, professionals; **ficelles** *ou* **trucs du m.** tricks of the trade; *Fig* **c'est le m. qui rentre** put it down to experience, that's how you learn

3 *Tex* **m. à tisser** loom; **m. mécanique** power loom; **m. à filer** spinning frame; **m. à tapisserie** tapestry frame; **m. à broder** embroidery frame, tambour frame; *Fig* **avoir un ouvrage sur le m.** to have a piece of work in hand

métis, -isse [metis] ADJ **1** *(personne)* half-caste; *(animal)* crossbreed; *(chien)* mongrel; **plante métisse** hybrid plant **2** *Tex* **tissu m.** linen-cotton mixture

▸ N *(personne)* halfcaste, *Péj* halfbreed; *(animal)* crossbreed; *(chien)* mongrel

▸ NM *Tex* linen-cotton mixture

métissage [metisaʒ] NM crossbreeding

métisser [metise] VT to cross(breed); **une population très métissée** a highly intermixed population

métonymie [metɔnimi] NF *Ling* metonymy

métrage [metraʒ] NM **1** *(action)* measuring, measurement; *Constr* quantity surveying **2** *(longueur)* (metric) length; **grand/petit m.** *(tissu)* cut lengthways/crossways; **des métrages de lin** lengths of linen; **vous le voulez en quel m.?** what width would you like? **3** *Cin* footage; **long m.** feature film; **moyen m.** medium length film; **court m.** short

mètre [mɛtr] NM **1** metre, *Am* meter; **m. carré/cube** square/cubic metre; *Sport* **elle se prépare à courir un 200 mètres (haies)** she's training for the 200 metres (hurdles); **l'épreuve du 400 mètres** the 400 metres (race) **2** *(pour mesurer)* tape measure; *(en bois)* rule; **m. pliant** folding rule; **m. à ruban** tape measure **3** *Littér* metre, *Am* meter

métré [metre] NM *Constr (de terrain à construire etc)* measurement(s); *(devis)* bill of quantities

métrer [metre] VT (**je mètre; je métrerai**) **1** to measure (by the metre *or Am* meter) **2** *Constr* to survey (for quantities)

métreur, -euse [metrœr, -øz] N **m.** *(vérificateur)* quantity surveyor

métrique [metrik] ADJ **1** metric; **adopter le système m.** to adopt the metric system, *Fam* to go metric **2** *Littér* metric(al)

▸ NF *Littér* prosody, metrics

métro [metro] NM underground, *Am* subway; **le m. de Paris/de Montréal** the Paris/Montreal metro; **le m. de Londres** the London underground (system), *Am* the tube; **aller quelque part en m.** to go somewhere by metro/underground/tube/subway; **il y a un m. direct de la gare jusque chez moi** you can get a metro/tube/subway directly from the station to my place; **au m. Charonne** at Charonne metro (station); *Fam* **avoir un m. de retard** to be behind the times; *Fam* **m., boulot, dodo** the daily grind, the daily routine; **depuis que j'habite à Paris, ma vie c'est vraiment m., boulot, dodo** life has become very humdrum *or* routine since I moved to Paris

métrologie [metrɔlɔʒi] NF metrology

métrologique [metrɔlɔʒik] ADJ metrological

métrologiste [metrɔlɔʒist] N metrologist

métronome [metrɔnɔm] NM *Mus* metronome

métropole [metrɔpɔl] NF **1** *(grande ville)* metropolis; **faire de Marseille une m. d'équilibre** to turn Marseilles into a second capital **2** *(État)* mother country; **les Français de la M.** the French of Metropolitan France **3** *Rel* metropolis; *(d'archevêque)* see

métropolitain, -aine [metrɔpɔlitɛ̃, -ɛn] ADJ **1** *Admin* metropolitan; **armée métropoli-**

taine home army **2** *Rel* metropolitan; *(église etc)* archiepiscopal

▸ NM **1** *Admin* underground (railway), *Am* subway **2** *Rel* archbishop; *(de l'Église orthodoxe)* metropolitan

mets [mɛ] NM food

mettable [metabl] ADJ **1** *(vêtements etc)* wearable; **pas m.** not fit to wear; **elle dit n'avoir plus rien de m.** she says she has nothing to wear **2** *Vulg (personne)* fuckable, *Br* shaggable

metteur, -euse [metœr, -øz] N *Typ* compositor, comp; **m. en scène** *Cin* director; *Théâtre, Radio* director, *Br* producer; *Radio* **m. en ondes** programme director; *Typ* **m. en pages** layout artist; **m. en œuvre** *(de bijoux etc)* mounter

METTRE [mɛtr] *(prp* **mettant;** *pp* **mis;** *pr ind* **je mets, il met, n. mettons, ils mettent;** *p hist* **je mis;** *fu* **je mettrai)**

VT to put **1, 8** ▪ to put on **2, 5, 6** ▪ to take **3** ▪ to spend **4** ▪ to wear **5** ▪ to turn on **6** ▪ to lay **7** ▪ to put up **7** ▪ to suppose **9** ▪ to write **10**
VPR to go **1** ▪ to start + ing *(se mettre à faire)* **3** ▪ to put on **4**

VT **1** *(placer)* to put; **ne mets pas les coudes sur la table!** don't put your elbows on the table!; **m. qn au lit/dans le train** to put sb to bed/on the train; **il a mis le pied sur une peau de banane** he stepped on a banana skin; **il mit la main sur mon épaule** he put *or* laid his hand on my shoulder; **m. genou à terre** to go down on one knee; **mettez tout cela par terre** put all that on the floor; **m. qch debout** to stand sth upright; **mets les livres debout** stand the books on end; **m. qch à plat** to put *or* lay sth down flat; **m. un manche à un balai** to put a handle on *or* fit a handle to a broom; **m. une annonce dans les journaux** to put an advertisement in the (news)papers; **il a mis de la boue sur le tapis** he's got mud on the carpet; **m. une lettre à la poste** to post a letter; **m. de l'argent sur un compte** to put money into an account; **qu'est-ce qui vous a mis cela dans la tête?** what put that into your head?; **il met ses parents avant tout le reste** he puts his parents first; *Sport* **m. le ballon au fond des filets** to put the ball in the back of the net; **nous avons mis 3 km entre nous et nos poursuivants** we put 3 km between us and our pursuers

2 *(appliquer)* *(fond de teint, maquillage, parfum, pansement, couche de peinture etc)* to put on

3 *(consacrer)* **m. du temps à faire qch** to take time to do sth; **j'ai mis deux ans à faire cela** I took *or* it took me two years to do that; *Fam* **tu y as mis le temps, pour comprendre** it took you a while to catch on; **combien de temps met-on pour aller de Paris à Marseille en voiture?** how long does it take to get from Paris to Marseilles by car?; **le train met deux heures pour le trajet** the trip takes two hours by train, it takes the train two hours to do the trip; **m. toute son énergie/tout son enthousiasme à faire qch** to put all one's energy/enthusiasm into doing sth; **j'y mettrai tous mes soins** I'll give it my full attention

4 *(dépenser une somme d'argent)* to spend; *(investir)* to sink; **m. 500 euros dans qch** to spend 500 euros on sth; **il faudra m. dans les 2000 euros** you'll have to spend about 2,000 euros; **m. 20 000 euros dans une affaire** to sink 20,000 euros into a business venture; **je serais prêt à m. tout ce que j'ai dans cette entreprise** I'd be willing to put everything I have into this venture; *Fam* **y m. le prix** to pay for it; **mais il faudra que vous y mettiez le prix** but it'll cost you; **m. un enjeu** to lay a stake; **m. de l'argent sur**

un cheval to put money on a horse, to back a horse **5** *(revêtir)* *(vêtements, lunettes, chaussures etc)* to put on; **qu'est-ce que je vais m.?** what shall I wear?; **mettez votre robe bleue** put your blue dress on; **elle ne met que des mini-jupes** all she wears is mini-skirts; **je n'ai plus rien à m.** I've nothing to wear; **je ne mets plus cette robe** I don't wear this dress any more, I've stopped wearing this dress; **j'ai du mal à m. mes souliers** I find it difficult to get my shoes on; **n'oubliez pas de m. un collier anti-puce à votre chien** don't forget to put a flea collar on your dog

6 *(faire fonctionner)* *(gaz, chauffage, lumière, radio, télévision etc)* to put on, to turn on, to switch on; **m. en marche** *(machine à laver, télévision etc)* to turn on; *(moteur)* to turn on, to start (up); **m. une machine en route** to turn a machine on, to set a machine going; *Aut* **m. le contact** to start the engine *or* car; **m. un peu le chauffage** to put *or* turn the heating on low; **m. la radio plus fort** to turn up the radio; **m. de la musique** to put on some music, to put some music on; **mets le film de la deux** put on the film that's on Channel 2; **m. sa montre à l'heure** to set one's watch to the correct time; **m. le réveil à cinq heures** to set the alarm for five o'clock

7 *(installer)* *(moquette, parquet, gazon)* to lay; *(papier peint, étagères)* to put up; **elle a décidé de (faire) m. le chauffage central/l'électricité** she decided to have central heating/electricity put in; **m. la table** *ou* **le couvert** to lay *or* set the table; **m. des rideaux aux fenêtres** to put curtains at the windows, to put up curtains

8 *(placer dans une situation, un état)* *(en prison, en pension, à l'asile etc)* to put; **m. qn au désespoir** to cause sb to despair; **m. qn au régime/sous antibiotiques** to put sb on a diet/on antibiotics; **m. qn à la torture** to subject sb to torture; **m. qn à la porte** *(le renvoyer)* to dismiss *or Fam* sack sb; **m. ses enfants à l'école publique** to send one's children to a state school; **m. le feu à qch** to set fire to sth, to set sth on fire; **m. du linge à sécher**, **m. à sécher du linge** to hang some washing up *or* out (to dry); **m. du linge à tremper** to put some washing in to soak; **m. de l'eau à chauffer** to put some water on to heat (up); **ça le met dans tous ses états** that gets him into a state; **m. qn dans l'embarras** to embarrass sb; **m. qn dans l'angoisse** to cause sb great anxiety; **m. qn dans l'obligation de faire qch** to force *or* compel sb to do sth; **m. qn en colère** to make sb angry; **la réunion l'a mise d'une humeur exécrable** the meeting put her in a very bad mood *or* made her very bad-tempered; **m. qch en œuvre** to implement sth; **m. une pièce en scène** to direct a play; **m. des vers en musique** to set verse to music; **il a fallu m. le texte en espagnol** the text had to be put into Spanish; **m. le nom au pluriel** to put the noun into the plural; **m. de la gaieté dans une pièce** to brighten up a room; **ça mettra de la couleur dans la pièce** it will give the room a bit of colour

9 *(admettre)* **ça va prendre, mettons, trois mois** it'll take, say, three months; **mettons que vous avez** *ou* **ayez raison** suppose *or* let's say you're right; **mettons que ça fasse cent euros** (let's) call it *or* say a hundred euros; **mettons qu'il en soit ainsi** let's assume that that's the case; **mettez que je n'ai rien dit** pretend I didn't say anything

10 *(écrire)* to write; **que faut-il m. dans les cases de droite?** what do you have to put *or* write in the right-hand boxes?; **mettez votre signature au bas de la page** put your signature at the bottom of the page; **qu'est-ce qu'elle met, dans sa lettre?** what does she say in her letter?; **tu veux lui m. un petit**

mot? *(sur la carte, lettre)* do you want to write him/her a little note?; **tu n'as qu'à m. que je le remercie** *(dans une lettre)* tell him thanks; **m. un texte au propre** to make a fair copy of a text; **m. qch par écrit** to put sth in writing; **tu as oublié de m. une virgule** you forgot to put a comma; **je t'ai mis sur la liste des invités** I've put you on the guest list

11 *(flanquer)* **j'ai bien envie de lui m. une gifle** I feel like slapping him *or* giving him a slap; **m. son poing dans la figure à qn** to punch sb's face, to give sb a punch in the face; **m. douze balles dans la peau à qn** to put twelve bullets in sb; *Fam* **on va leur m. la pâtée** *(les battre, les frapper)* we're going to hammer them *or* beat the living daylights out of them; **qu'est-ce qu'il leur a mis!** he gave them a real roasting!

12 *Arg* **il va falloir m. les bouts** *ou* **les voiles!**, **il va falloir les m.!** we'd better make a move!

13 *Naut* **m. une voile au vent** to hoist *or* set a sail

14 *Vulg (posséder sexuellement)* to fuck, to screw, *Br* to shag; **va te faire m.!** up yours!, fuck off!; **se faire m.** to get fucked *or* laid

VPR se mettre 1 *(se placer)* to go, to get; **se m. derrière un arbre** to go *or* get behind a tree; **se m. au lit** to get into bed; **se m. à table** to sit down at the table; **se m. au soleil/à l'ombre** to sit in the sunshine/shade; **se m. à l'abri** to take shelter; **mettez-vous auprès du feu** sit (down) by the fire; **mettez-vous autour de grand-mère pour la photo** gather round grandmother for the photo; **se m. contre un mur** to stand *or* lean against a wall; **se m. debout** to stand up; **mets-toi là et ne bouge plus** stand/sit there and don't move; **où dois-je me m.?** where do you want me to stand/sit?; *Fig* **je ne savais plus où me m.** I didn't know where to put myself; **se m. sur le dos/le ventre** to lie on one's back/stomach; **les tasses se mettent dans le placard de droite** the cups go in the right-hand cupboard; **cette pièce se met facilement/se met dans cette case** this piece goes *or* fits in easily/goes *or* fits in this box

2 se m. dans *(situation, état)* to get into; **se m. en rage** to get into a rage; **je me suis mis de la peinture dans les cheveux/de la confiture sur les doigts** I've got paint in my hair/jam on my fingers; **se m. dans tous ses états** to get into a state; **se m. au service de qn** to enter sb's service; **se m. en avant** to push oneself forward; **se m. une idée dans la** *ou* **en tête** to get an idea into one's head; **elle s'est mis dans la tête l'idée que …** she's got it into her head that …; **on a fini par se m. d'accord** we finally reached agreement; **se m. au vert** to go to the country, to get some fresh air; **se m. nu** to undress, to strip off

3 *(commencer)* **se m. à (faire) qch** to begin *or* start *or* set about (doing) sth; **se m. à rire/chanter/pleurer** to begin *or* start to laugh/sing/cry, to start laughing/singing/crying; **il s'est mis à boire après le dessert** he started drinking after dessert; **c'est quand sa femme est morte qu'il s'est mis à boire** he started drinking *or* took to drink after his wife died; **il s'est mis à pleuvoir** it began *or* started to rain, the rain came on; **se m. au travail** to set to work; **il est temps de s'y m.** we'd better get down to it *or* get on with it; **se m. au régime** to put oneself on a diet, to go on a diet; **se m. à l'allemand** to start (learning) German; **se m. à la politique** to go in for *or* take up politics; **se m. en route** to start off, to set off; **se m. au pas** *(dans un défilé)* to fall into step; *Fam* **elle est insupportable once she gets started *or* going; *Fam* **si tu t'y mets aussi** if you join in, if you start on me/her/etc too

4 *(revêtir)* *(vêtement)* to wear; *(vernis à ongles, fard à paupières)* to put on; **se m. un pull chaud** to put on a warm pullover; **je n'ai rien à me m.** I haven't got anything to wear, I haven't a thing to wear; **elle ne se met jamais en pantalon/en rouge** she never wears trousers/red; **pourquoi ne te mets-tu pas en jupe ce soir?** why don't you put on *or* wear a skirt this evening?

5 le temps se met au beau the weather's turning out fine; **le temps se met à la pluie** it's turning to rain; *Vulg* **son contrat, il peut se le m. quelque part!** he can shove his contract up his *Br* arse *or Am* ass!

6 *(se grouper)* **on a dû se m. à trois pour bouger l'armoire** it took three of us to move the wardrobe; **ils se sont mis à trois pour écrire ce livre** the three of them wrote the book together; **on a préféré se m. à cinq pour faire l'exposé** we thought it preferable if five of us gave the presentation; **se m. avec qn** *(faire équipe)* to team up with sb; *Fam (vivre)* to move in *or* live with *or Am Fam* to shack up with sb

7 *Fam* **qu'est-ce qu'ils se sont mis!** *(ils se sont battus)* they went at it hammer and tongs!, they really laid into each other!

8 *Fam* **s'en m. jusque là** *(manger en grande quantité)* to stuff oneself *or* one's face; **qu'est-ce qu'on s'est mis!** we really stuffed ourselves *or* our faces!

VI *Naut* **m. à la voile** to set sail

---

meublant [mœblɑ̃] **ADJ** *Jur* **meubles meublants** movables

meuble [mœbl] **ADJ** movable; *Jur* **biens meubles** movables, personal estate, chattels; *Agr* **terre m.** light soil

NM 1 piece of furniture; **meubles** furniture; **être dans ses meubles** to have a place of one's own; *Fam* **faire partie des meubles** to be part of the furniture; **je manque de meubles de rangement** I don't have much storage space; **m. d'angle** corner unit; **meubles de bureau** office furniture; **m. hi-fi** hi-fi unit **2** *Jur* movable, chattel; **meubles corporels** tangible assets *or* movables; **meubles à demeure** fixtures; **meubles incorporels** intangible assets *or* movables

> Do not confuse with **mobilier**.

meublé [mœble] **ADJ** *(chambre etc)* furnished; **non m.** unfurnished

NM furnished room; *(appartement)* furnished flat *or Am* apartment; **habiter en m.** to live in lodgings; *(dans un appartement)* to live in a furnished flat

meubler [mœble] **VT** *(pièce)* to furnish; *(ferme)* to stock (**de** with); **ils sont entièrement meublés en Empire/en chêne** all their furniture is Empire style/oak; **m. la conversation** to make conversation

VPR se meubler to furnish one's home; **je me meuble chez IKEA** I buy *or* get my furniture at IKEA

meuf [mœf] **NF** *très Fam* female, *Br* bird, *Am* chick; *(épouse)* old woman, better half, *Am* old lady

meuglement [møɡləmɑ̃] **NM** *(de vache)* lowing, mooing; *(de sirène)* moaning, wailing

meugler [møɡle] **VI** *(de vache)* to low, to moo; *(de sirène)* to moan, to wail

meulage [mølaʒ] **NM** grinding (down)

meule [møl] **NF 1** *(de foin, de paille)* stack, rick; *(fumier)* mushroom compost; **mettre le foin en m.** to stack *or* rick the hay; **m. de foin** haystack, hayrick **2** *(de moulin)* millstone; **m. à aiguiser** grindstone; **m. à polir** buff(ing) wheel **3 m. de fromage** (whole) cheese **4** *Fam* **les meules** *(les fesses)* *(d'une femme)* arse, *Am* ass; *(d'un homme)* buns;

elle a de belles meules she's got a great arse *or Am* ass **5** *Fam (Mobylette®)* moped

meuler [møle] **VT** *(burin etc)* to grind; *(lentille etc)* to grind (down)

meulette [mølɛt] **NF** small haystack

meulière [møljɛr] **ADJ F pierre m.** millstone (grit)
NF 1 *(carrière)* millstone quarry **2** *(pierre)* millstone (grit)

meunerie [mønri] **NF 1** *(activité)* (flour) milling **2** *Ind* milling trade

meunier, -ière [mønje, -jɛr] **NM** miller
ADJ 1 *(industrie, méthode etc)* (flour-)milling **2** *Culin* **truite/sole meunière** trout/sole meunière *(coated with flour and fried in butter)*
NF meunière 1 miller's wife **2** *(oiseau)* long-tailed tit

meuron [mørɔ̃] **NM** *Suisse Bot (mûre)* mulberry

meurtre [mœrtr] **NM** murder; **au m.!** murder!

meurtri [mœrtri] **ADJ** *(bras, fruit etc)* bruised; **visage m.** bruised *or* battered face; *(par la fatigue)* ravaged face; **être tout m.** to be black and blue all over; **elle est sortie très meurtrie de cette expérience** she was bruised by the experience, it was a very bruising experience for her; **je suis m. dans mon cœur** *ou* **âme** I am heartbroken

meurtrier, -ière [mœrtrije, -jɛr] **ADJ 1** *(guerre, attentat, colère)* murderous; *(arme)* deadly, lethal; *(épidémie)* lethal; **ce croisement est m.** this junction is a death trap; **l'imprudence rend la route meurtrière** reckless driving turns roads into death traps; **le lundi de Pâques est souvent m.** there are often a lot of deaths on the road on Easter Monday **2** *Arch (personne)* murderous, guilty of murder
N murderer, murderess
NF *Archit, Mil* **meurtrière** loophole

meurtrir [mœrtrir] **VT** *(son bras, fruit etc)* to bruise; **m. qn de coups** to beat sb black and blue; **tu as meurtri mon cœur** you broke my heart

meurtrissure [mœrtrisyr] **NF** bruise

Meuse [møz] **NF la M.** the Meuse, the Maas

meute [møt] **NF** *(de chiens courants)* pack; *Fig* mob, pack, crowd; **chiens de m.** hounds; **lancer la m.** to loose the pack *or* hounds

MEV [mɛv] **NF** *Ordinat (abrév* **mémoire vive)** RAM

mévente [mevɑ̃t] **NF 1** *(des affaires)* slump, stagnation **2** *Vieilli (de biens)* sale at a loss

mexicain, -aine [mɛksikɛ̃, -ɛn] **ADJ** Mexican
N M. Mexican

Mexico [mɛksiko] **N** Mexico City

Mexique (le) [ləmɛksik] **NM** Mexico

mézigue [mezig] **PRON PERS** *Arg (moi)* yours truly; **c'est pour m.** it's for yours truly; **les plaintes, c'est pour m.** yours truly has to cope with the complaints; **et m.?** what about me?

mezzanine [mɛdzanin] **NF 1** *(étage)* mezzanine (floor) **2** *(fenêtre)* mezzanine window **3** *Théâtre* dress circle, *Am* mezzanine

mezzo-soprano, *pl* **mezzo-sopranos** [mɛdzosoprano] *ou* **-soprani** [-soprani] *Mus* **NM** mezzo(-soprano) (voice)
NF *(femme)* mezzo(-soprano)

mezzo-tinto [mɛdzotinto] **NM INV** mezzotint

MF [ɛmɛf] **NF** *Radio (abrév* **modulation de fréquence)** FM

mg *(abrév* **milligramme)** mg

MGP [ɛmʒepe] **NM** *(abrév* **marché grand public)** consumer market

Mgr *Rel (abrév* **Monseigneur)** Mgr

---

mi¹ [mi] **ADV la mi-avril/-mai** mid-April/-May; **à mi-hauteur** halfway up *or* down; **elle avait de l'eau jusqu'à mi-jambe/mi-cuisse** the water was halfway up her legs/thighs; **il la regardait, mi-amusé, mi-intrigué** he was looking at her half-amused, half-puzzled *or* with a mixture of amusement and puzzlement; **mi-figue, mi-raisin** half one thing and half another; **un petit sourire mi-figue, mi-raisin** a half-hearted *or* wry *or* forced smile; **ton mi-figue, mi-raisin** tone (of voice) half in jest and half in earnest; **acier mi-doux** semi-mild steel; **tissu mi-laine mi-soie** wool-silk mixture

mi² **NM INV** *Mus* **1** *(note)* E; *(de solfège)* mi; **morceau en mi** piece in E **2** *(d'un violon)* first string, E string

miam-miam [mjammjam] **INT** yum, yum

miaou [mjau] **NM** miaow, mew; **faire m.** to miaow, to mew

miasmatique [mjasmatik] **ADJ** *Litt* miasmic

miasme [mjasm] **NM** miasma

miaulement [mjolmɑ̃] **NM** mewing, miaowing; *(plus aigu)* caterwauling

miauler [mjole] **VI** to mew, to miaow; *(de façon plus aiguë)* to caterwaul

miauleur, -euse [mjolœr, -øz] **ADJ** mewing, miaowing

mi-bas **NM INV** knee-high; *(tricoté)* knee(-length) sock, *Com* half-hose

mica [mika] **NM** *Minér* mica

mi-carême, *pl* **mi-carêmes NF** mid-Lent

micaschiste [mikaʃist] **NM** *Minér* mica-schist

miche [miʃ] **NF 1** *(pain)* round loaf, *Br* cob (loaf) **2** *Fam* **miches** *(fesses)* bum, *Am* butt; **vire tes miches** move yourself, move your backside; **gare à tes miches** look out, mind yourself

Michel-Ange [mikɛlɑ̃ʒ] **N** Michelangelo

micheline [miʃlin] **NF** *Rail* railcar *(invented and equipped by the Michelin Tyre Company)*

mi-chemin (à) **ADV** halfway, midway; **on est à m.** we're halfway there

micheton [miʃtɔ̃] **NM** *Fam* trick, *Am* john; **elle s'est fait cinq michetons dans la soirée** she turned five tricks that evening

michetonner [miʃtone] **VI** *Fam* **1** *(avoir recours à une prostituée)* to go to a hooker **2** *(se prostituer)* to turn tricks

Michigan [miʃigan] **NM le M.** Michigan; **le lac M.** Lake Michigan

mi-clos, *pl* **mi-clos(es) ADJ** *(yeux, lèvres etc)* half-closed, half-shut

micmac [mikmak] **NM 1** *Fam* scheme; *(résultat)* put-up job; *(désordre)* muddle; **j'en ai assez de tes micmacs** I've had enough of your schemes *or* scheming **2** *Can Fam (désordre)* mess; **as-tu nettoyé le m. dans ta chambre?** have you cleaned up the mess in your room?

mi-corps (à) **ADV** portrait à **m.** half-length portrait; **avoir de l'eau jusqu'à m.** to be in water up to one's waist

mi-côte (à) **ADV** halfway up the hill

mi-course (à) **ADV** at the halfway mark

micro [mikro] **NM** *Fam* **1** *(microphone)* mike; *(tenu à la main)* baton *or* stick mike; **parler dans le m.** to speak into the mike; **m. caché** concealed microphone **2** *Ordinat* micro(-computer)
▸▸**NF** *Ordinat* microcomputing
▸▸**m. canon** rifle *or* gun mike; **m. sur casque** headphone talkback; **m. à condensateur** condenser mike; **m.-cravate,** *pl* **micros-cravates** tie mike; **m. directionnel** directional mike; **m. électrodynamique** dynamic mike; **m. sur perche** boom mike; **m. portatif** hand microphone; **m. suspendu** hanging *or* slung mike; **m. de table** desk mike

---

microampère [mikroɑ̃pɛr] **NM** *Phys* microampere

microanalyse [mikroanaliz] **NF** *Chimie* microanalysis

microbalance [mikrobalɑ̃s] **NF** *Phys* microbalance

microbe [mikrob] **NM** microbe; *(bactérie)* germ, *Fam* bug; **je ne veux pas que tu me donnes tes microbes** I don't want your germs; *Fig* **écrase-toi, m.!** push off, you little squirt!

microbicide [mikrobisid] **ADJ** germ-killing, *Spéc* microbicidal
NM germ-killer, *Spéc* microbicide

microbien, -ienne [mikrobjɛ̃, -jɛn] **ADJ** *(maladie, culture etc)* microbial, microbic

microbiologie [mikrobjolɔʒi] **NF** microbiology

microbiologique [mikrobjolɔʒik] **ADJ** microbiological

microbiologiste [mikrobjolɔʒist] **N** microbiologist

microcéphale [mikrosefal] **ADJ** microcephalous, microcephalic
N microcephalic

microchirurgie [mikroʃiryrʒi] **NF** *Méd* microsurgery

microcircuit [mikrosirkɥi] **NM** *Ordinat* microcircuit; **microcircuits** microcircuitry

microclimat [mikroklima] **NM** microclimate

microcosme [mikrokɔsm] **NM** microcosm

microcosmique [mikrokɔsmik] **ADJ** microcosmic

microcoupure [mikrokupyr] **NF** *Électron* power blip

microdisquette [mikrodiskɛt] **NF** *Ordinat* microfloppy

microéconomie [mikroekɔnɔmi] **NF** microeconomics

microéconomique [mikroekɔnɔmik] **ADJ** microeconomic

microédition [mikroedisjɔ̃] **NF** *Ordinat* desktop publishing, DTP

microélectronique [mikroelɛktrɔnik] **NF** microelectronics

micro-environnement, *pl* **micro-environnements NM** micro-environment

micro(-)espace, *pl* **micro(-)espaces NM** *Ordinat* micro-space

microfiche [mikrofiʃ] **NF** microfiche

microfilm [mikrofilm] **NM** microfilm

microfilmer [mikrofilme] **VT** to microfilm

microfinance [mikrofinɑ̃s] **NF** microfinance

micrographie [mikrografi] **NF** micrography

micrographique [mikrografik] **ADJ** micrographic

micro-informatique NF *Ordinat* microcomputing

micro-interrupteur, *pl* **micro-interrupteurs NM** *Ordinat* microswitch

micromarché [mikromarʃe] **NM** micromarket

micromarketing [mikromarketiŋ] **NM** micromarketing

micromercatique [mikromɛrkatik] **NF** micromarketing

micromètre [mikromɛtr] **NM** micrometer

micrométrique [mikrometrik] **ADJ** micrometric(al); **vis m.** micrometer screw

micron [mikrɔ̃] **NM** micron

Micronésie [mikronezi] **NF** Micronesia

micronisation [mikronizasjɔ̃] **NF** *Ordinat* downsizing

microniser [mikronize] **VT** *Ordinat* to downsize

micro-onde, *pl* **micro-ondes** [mikrɔɔ̃d] **NF** microwave; **four à micro-ondes** microwave oven

micro-ondes **NM INV** microwave (oven); **faire cuire qch au m.** to cook sth in the microwave, to microwave sth

micro-ordinateur, *pl* **micro-ordinateurs** **NM** *Ordinat* micro(computer)

micro-organisme, *pl* **micro-organismes** **NM** micro-organism

micropaiement [mikropɛmɑ̃] **NM** *Ordinat* micropayment

microphone [mikrɔfɔn] **NM** microphone; *(de téléphone)* mouthpiece; **m. à condensateur** condenser microphone; **m. sur girafe** sound-boom microphone; **m. sur pied** stand microphone

microphotographie [mikrɔfɔtɔgrafi] **NF 1** *(activité)* microphotography, photomicrography **2** *(résultat)* microphotograph, photomicrograph

microphotographique [mikrɔfɔtɔgrafik] **ADJ** microphotographic, photomicrographic

microphysique [mikrɔfizik] **NF** microphysics

micropilule [mikropilyl] **NF** *Pharm* minipill

microplaquette [mikrɔplakɛt] **NF** *Électron* chip

microprocesseur [mikrɔprɔsɛsœr] **NM** *Ordinat* microprocessor; **m. en tranches** bit slice microprocessor

microprogramme [mikrɔprɔgram] **NM** *Ordinat* microprogram

microscope [mikrɔskɔp] **NM** microscope; **regarder au m.** to look through a microscope; **regarder qch au m.** to look at sth through *or* under a microscope; **visible au m.** visible under the microscope; **m. électronique** electron microscope; **m. électronique à balayage** electron scanning microscope; **m. optique** light microscope

microscopie [mikrɔskɔpi] **NF** microscopy

microscopique [mikrɔskɔpik] **ADJ** microscopic

microseconde [mikrɔsəgɔ̃d] **NF** microsecond

microserveur [mikrɔsɛrvœr] **NM** *Ordinat* bulletin board service

microsillon [mikrɔsijɔ̃] **NM 1** *(sillon)* microgroove **2** *(disque)* **m.** long-playing record, LP

microsociété [mikrɔsɔsjete] **NF** miniature society, society in miniature

microsociologie [mikrɔsɔsjɔlɔʒi] **NF** = sociology of small groups

microtome [mikrɔtɔm] **NM** microtome

micro-trottoir, *pl* **micros-trottoirs** **NM** street interview, *Br Fam* vox pop

miction [miksjɔ̃] **NF** urination, *Spéc* micturition

MidCAC [midkak] **NM** *Bourse* **le M.**, **l'indice M.** = Paris stock exchange index comprised of 100 medium-range shares, ≃ MidCap

midi [midi] **NM 1** *(heure)* midday, (twelve) noon, twelve o'clock; **il est m.** it's twelve o'clock; **avant/après m.** before/after twelve (o'clock); **m. et demi** half-past twelve; **entre m. et deux** at lunch time; *Fig* **chercher m. à quatorze heures** to look for difficulties where there are none, to complicate matters **2** *(moment du déjeuner)* lunch time; **tu fais quoi, ce m.?** what are you doing at lunch time *or* for lunch?; **à m.** at lunch time; **à m., j'ai mangé des frites** I had chips at lunch time *or* for lunch; **repas de m.** midday meal **3** *(milieu du jour)* **en plein m.** at the height of noon **4** *(sud)* south; **chambre au m.** room facing south; **le M. (de la France)** the South of France

ADJ INV *(de taille moyenne)* **chaîne m.** midi system

midinette [midinɛt] **NF 1** silly young girl; **des lectures de m.** slushy novels **2** *Vieilli (ouvrière)* shop girl; *(couturière)* young dressmaker

mi-distance (à) **ADV** halfway, midway; **nous sommes à m. de notre but** we are halfway to our goal

midship, *pl* **midships** [midʃip] **NM** midshipman

mie[1] [mi] **NF** crumb *(of loaf, as opposed to crust)*; **pain de m.** sandwich loaf

mie[2] **NF** *Arch, Litt* truelove, ladylove; **ma m.** my beloved

miel [mjɛl] **NM** honey; **une tartine de m.** a slice of bread and honey; **m. rosat** rose honey; *Fig* **faire son m. de qch** to make capital out of sth; *Fig* **elle était (tout sucre et) tout m.** she was all sweetness and light **INT** *Fam* **et m.!** oh, sugar!

miellé [mjele] **ADJ** *Litt (parfum)* honeyed; *(boisson)* tasting of honey

mielleusement [mjɛløzmɑ̃] **ADV** *Péj (dire)* in honeyed tones; **sourire m.** to give a sweet, sugary smile

mielleux, -euse [mjɛlø, -øz] **ADJ 1** *(boisson, bonbon etc)* tasting of honey **2** *Péj (discours, sourire etc)* sugary; *(personne)* sugary, smooth

mien, mienne [mjɛ̃, mjɛn] **PRON POSS le m.**, **la mienne**, **les miens**, **les miennes** mine; **je te prête le m.** you can borrow mine; **tu n'as qu'à prendre la mienne** just take mine; **il ressemble au m.** it looks like mine; **je veux bien te donner du m.** please have some of mine; **tu n'en as pas besoin, tu as le m.** you don't need it, you've got mine; **les deux miens** my two, both of mine; *(en insistant)* **my own two; je lui ai laissé deux des miens** I gave him two of mine; *très Fam* **le m. de bébé est plus intelligent** my baby is more intelligent; *Fam* **à la mienne!** *(en buvant)* here's to me! **SEE GRAMMAR A30; B21–2**

NM le m. *(ce qui m'appartient)* mine; **je devrais y mettre du m.** I should really do my share

NMPL les miens *(ma famille)* my family, *Am* my folks; *(mes partisans)* my followers; *(mes coéquipiers)* my team-mates

ADJ POSS *Litt* mine; **un m. cousin** a cousin of mine; **je fais miens tes principes** I've adopted your principles as my own; **je fais miennes les félicitations qu'il vous adresse** I join (with) him in congratulating you

miette [mjɛt] **NF** *(de pain)* crumb; *(morceau)* morsel, scrap; **miettes de crabe/thon** flaked crab/tuna; **elle m'a laissé quelques miettes de son gâteau** she left me a few crumbs of her cake; **ils n'en ont pas laissé une m.** they didn't leave a crumb, they scoffed the lot; **mettre** *ou* **réduire qch en miettes** *(objet)* to smash sth to pieces *or* bits *or* smithereens; **je n'en prendrai qu'une m.** I'll just have a morsel *or* a very little *or* *Fam* a smidgeon; *Fig* **elle n'a pas perdu une m. de la conversation** not one scrap of the conversation escaped her *or* passed her by

MIEUX [mjø]

ADV	better **1** ▪ best **2**
ADJ	better ▪ best
NM	best

ADV 1 *(comp)* better; **elle danse m. que moi** she dances better than I do; **j'avais espéré m.** I had hoped for better *or* more; **je ne peux pas m. dire** *ou* **dire m.** that's all I can say, what more can I say?; **il ne parle pas m. l'italien que l'espagnol** his Italian isn't any *or* is no better than his Spanish, he speaks Italian no better than he does Spanish; **on va vivre**

ensemble, m. on va se marier! we're going to live together, better still, we're getting married!; **je ne demande pas m.!** I'd be delighted!, there's nothing I'd like better!; **je ne demande pas m. que (de) te rendre service** I'd be delighted to help, there's nothing I'd like better than to help; **il vaut m. les surveiller** you should watch them more closely; **vous feriez m. de m'écouter** you'd do better to *or* you'd be well advised to listen to me, you'd better listen to me; *Prov* **m. vaut tard que jamais** better late than never; *Prov* **m. vaut prévenir que guérir** prevention is better than cure; **elle va m. que jamais** she has never been better; **il va m.** he's (feeling) better; **il ne va pas m.** he is no better, he isn't any better; **ça va m.** things are improving, *Fam* **ça va m.?** feeling better?; *Fam* **j'ai l'impression que, Bernard, ça va m. aujourd'hui** I'm under the impression that Bernard is feeling better today; **comment ça va, la santé/l'école/avec ton mari? – ça va m.** how are you/things at school/things with your husband? – better; **ça ira m. demain** it'll *or* things'll be better tomorrow; *Hum* **je vois que ça ne va pas m.!** you've not improved one bit!, there hasn't been any change for the better!; *Scol* **'peut m. faire'** 'can do better'; **moins je travaille, m. je me porte** the less I work, the better I feel; **plus je le vois, m. je l'apprécie** the more I see of him, the more I appreciate him *or* the better I like him; **de m. en m.** better and better; **au bureau, ça va de m. en m.** it's getting better and better at the office, things are improving all the time at the office; **m. encore … better still …; m. encore, je dirais que c'est un artiste** I'd go even further and describe him as an artist; **on dirait m. 'pallier les inconvénients'** 'pallier les inconvénients' is more correct; **qui dit m.?** *(pour faire monter les enchères)* any advance?; **elle va on ne peut m.** she's in the best of health; **ce travail est on ne peut m. fait** no one could have done better, he has/you have/*etc* done a perfect job; **elle coud on ne peut m.** no one sews better than she does; **faire qch à qui m. m.** to vie with one another in doing sth; **ils criaient à qui m. m.** it was a case of who could shout the loudest **VOIR GRAMMAIRE A41**

2 le m., la m., les m. (the) best; **la femme la m. habillée de Paris** the best-dressed woman in Paris; **c'est à Paris que les femmes sont le m. habillées** you find the best-dressed women in Paris; **c'est à ce bureau que je travaille le m.** I work best at this desk; **le plus tôt sera le m.** the sooner the better; **il s'en est acquitté le m. du monde** nobody could have done it better; **un service des m. organisés** an extremely well-organized department; **fais du m. que tu peux** do the best you can

ADJ vous serez m. dans ce fauteuil you'll be more comfortable *or* better in this armchair; **il est m.** he's (feeling) better; **vous ne trouverez pas m. comme hôtel** you won't find a better hotel; **tu ne trouveras rien de m.** you won't find anything better; *Fam* **c'est ce qu'il y a de m., c'est ce qu'on fait de m.** it's the best there is; **ce qu'il y a de m. sur le marché** the best (there is) on the market; **c'est ce qu'il y a de m. si … it's ideal if …; c'est ce qu'il y a de m. (à faire) dans votre cas** that's the best thing (to do) in your case; **ce que vous avez de m. à faire, c'est de …** the best thing you can do is to …; **si tu n'as rien de m. à faire** if you've nothing better to do; **tu ne crois pas que tu as m. à faire que …?** don't you think there are better things to do than …?; *Iron* **elle n'a rien trouvé de m. que d'aller le répéter à sa mère** what did she do but go and tell her mother; **c'est m. comme ça** its better like that; *Fam* **c'était la m. des trois sœurs** she was the best of the three sisters; *(la plus jo-*

lie) she was the best-looking of the three sisters

NM le m. est l'ennemi du bien leave well (enough) alone, *Fam* if it ain't broke, don't fix it; **faute de m.** for want *or* lack of anything better; **il y a un m.** *ou* **du m.** there's been a change for the better, there's been an improvement; **faire** *ou* **agir pour le m.** to act for the best; **mais on fera pour le m.** but we'll do our best, but we'll do the best we can; **le m. serait de ...** the best thing would be to ..., it would be best to ...; **le m. serait qu'il se désiste de lui-même** it would be best if he withdrew of his own accord; **(en mettant les choses) au m., je ferai ce travail en deux mois** I can do the job in two months at best; **(en mettant les choses) au m., je ne pourrai pas être là avant six heures** I can't be there before six o'clock at the earliest; **au m., il la vendra 100 euros** he'll get 100 euros at most for it; **agir au m. des intérêts de qn** to act in sb's best interests; **être au m. avec qn** to be on the best of terms with sb; **faire de son m.** to do one's best, to do the best one can

mieux-disant, *pl* **mieux-disants** [mjødizɑ̃] **NM** elite

mieux-être NM improved condition; **les progrès techniques doivent servir au m. des hommes** technical progress must improve the human condition

mieux-vivre NM better *or* higher standard of living; **la lutte pour le m.** the struggle for a better *or* higher standard of living

mièvre [mjɛvr] **ADJ** *Péj (fille)* insipid; *(ton)* simpering; **des trucs mièvres à la télé** stupid things on TV

mièvrerie [mjɛvrəri] **NF** *Péj* insipidness; **d'une m. exaspérante** exasperatingly insipid; **ces mièvreries qu'on nous sert à la télé** these stupid programmes *or* the pap they show on TV

mi-fin, *pl* **mi-fins ADJ** *Com* medium

mignard [miɲar] **ADJ 1** = **mignon 2** *Péj* affected

mignardise [miɲardiz] **NF 1** *(caractère mignon)* charm, *Péj* affectedness **2** *(œillet)* **m.** garden pink

mignon, -onne [miɲɔ̃, -ɔn] **ADJ** delightful, charming; *(enfant)* darling, *surtout Am* cute; **un mec super m.** a great-looking guy; **est-elle mignonne!** isn't she a darling!; **c'est m. comme tout chez eux** they have a delightful *or* charming home; **sois m., va me chercher mes cigarettes** be a dear *or* an angel and get my cigarettes

N 1 *(terme d'affection)* pet, darling, dear **2** *Arch (favori)* minion

mignonnet, -ette[1] [miɲɔnɛ, -ɛt] **ADJ** pretty-pretty

mignonnette[2] **NF 1** *(plante) (saxifrage ombreuse)* London pride; *(chicorée sauvage)* wild chicory; *(œillet mignardise)* garden pink **2** *Tex* mignonette lace **3** *(poivre)* coarse-ground pepper **4** *(gravier)* gravel **5** *(flacon)* miniature

migraine [migrɛn] **NF** migraine; *Fam (mal de tête)* headache; **elle a des migraines** she has migraines; **elle a la m.** she has a headache; **m. ophtalmique** headache caused by eyestrain

migraineux, -euse [migrɛnø, -øz] **N** migraine sufferer

migrant, -ante [migrɑ̃, -ɑ̃t] **ADJ** migrant

N migrant; **m. économique** economic refugee

migrateur, -trice [migratœr, -tris] **ADJ** *(animaux)* migrating, migratory; *(personnes)* migrant

migration [migrasjɔ̃] **NF** *Orn* migration; *Fig* exodus; **au moment des vacances, les migra-**

---

tions sont impressionnantes the number of people on the move at holiday time is staggering

migratoire [migratwar] **ADJ** migratory

migrer [migre] **VI** to migrate (**vers** to); *Ordinat* **faire m.** to transmit

mi-jambe(s) (à) **ADV** halfway up the leg(s)

mijaurée [miʒɔre] **NF** *Péj* conceited *or* affected woman; **ne fais pas la** *ou* **ta m.!** don't give yourself such airs!

mijoter [miʒɔte] **VT** *Culin* to simmer, to let simmer; *Fig (projet, vengeance)* to mull over; **elle mijote avec amour de bons petits plats à son mari** she lovingly prepares wonderful meals for her husband; **m. un complot** to hatch a plot; **qu'est-ce que vous mijotez encore?** now what are you scheming *or* up to?

VI to simmer; *Fig* **je vois bien que ça mijote dans sa tête** I know he's up to something

VPR se mijoter *Fig* **il se mijote quelque chose** there's something in the wind, something's brewing

mikado [mikado] **NM** mikado

mil[1] [mil] **ADJ** thousand *(used only in writing out dates AD)*; **l'an m. neuf cent quatre-vingt-un** (the year) nineteen hundred and eighty-one

mil[2] [mij, mil] **NM** *(céréale)* millet

milady, *pl* **miladys** [miledi] **NF** *(titre)* my Lady; *(noble)* titled (English) lady

milan [milɑ̃] **NM** *(oiseau)* kite

milanais, -aise [milanɛ, -ɛz] **ADJ** Milanese

N M. Milanese; **les M.** the Milanese

mildiou [mildju] **NM** mildew; *(de la vigne)* brown rot; **atteint de m.** mildewed

mildiousé [mildjuze] **ADJ** *(vigne etc)* mildewed

mile [majl] **NM** *(mesure)* mile (= *1.609 m)*

miliaire [miljɛr] *Méd* **ADJ** *(glande, fièvre etc)* miliary

NF prickly heat, *Spéc* miliaria

milice [milis] **NF 1** militia **2** *Belg (service militaire)* military service; **la m.** the army

milicien, -ienne [milisjɛ̃, -jɛn] **N** member of a/the militia, *m* militiaman

milieu, -ieux [miljø] **NM 1** *(centre)* middle; **couper/plier qch en son m.** to cut sth through/to fold sth in the middle; **il est entré en plein m. d'une discussion** he came in right in the middle of a discussion; **au m. de** in the middle of, *Litt* amid(st), in the midst of; **au beau m. de la rue/la cour** right in the middle of the street/the yard; **au m. du courant** in midstream; **au m. de l'été** in the middle *or* at the height of summer; **au m. de l'hiver** in the middle *or* depth(s) of winter; **au m. de la nuit** in the middle of the night, *Litt* at dead of night; **vers le m. du mois** about the middle of the month; **la table du m.** the middle table

2 *(environnement) (physique)* environment, surroundings, milieu; *(social)* (social) sphere, circle; *Phys* medium; **le m. familial** the home environment, family surroundings; **dans les milieux financiers** in financial circles; **les animaux dans leur m.** animals in their environment *or* natural surroundings; **je n'appartiens pas à leur m., je ne suis pas de leur m.** I don't belong to *or* I'm not part of their set *or* circle, I don't move in their circles; **dans les milieux bien informés** in well-informed circles *or* quarters; **elle ne tient pas à changer de m.** she's not keen on a change of surroundings; **c'est parce qu'elle n'est pas dans son m.** it's because she's not in her usual surroundings

3 le m., les gens du m. the underworld; **c'est un type du m.** he's a member of the underworld

4 *(moyenne)* middle course; **il n'y a pas de**

---

m. there's no middle course; **le juste m.** the happy medium, the golden mean; **tenir le m. entre ... et ...** to steer a middle course between ... and ...

militaire [militɛr] **ADJ** *(discipline, service, hôpital, opération etc)* military; **véhicule m.** military *or* army vehicle; **à huit heures, heure m.** at eight o'clock sharp; **la marine m.** the Navy; **port m.** naval port

NM serviceman, soldier; **les militaires** the military, the armed forces, the services; **m. de carrière** career *or* professional soldier

militairement [militɛrmɑ̃] **ADV** militarily; **saluer m.** to give a military salute; **occuper une ville m.** to occupy a town by force of arms

militance [militɑ̃s] **NF** militancy

militant, -ante [militɑ̃, -ɑ̃t] **ADJ** militant

N militant; *(d'un parti)* member; **m. de base** grassroots member; **m. syndical** trade union militant *or* activist

militantisme [militɑ̃tism] **NM** militancy

militarisation [militarizasjɔ̃] **NF** militarization

militariser [militarize] **VT** to militarize

militarisme [militarism] **NM** militarism

militariste [militarist] **ADJ, N** militarist

militer [milite] **VI** to militate (**pour, en faveur de** in favour of; **contre** against); **m. au PS** to be a member of the Socialist Party

milk-shake, *pl* **milk-shakes** [milkʃɛk] **NM** milk shake; **m. à la vanille** vanilla milk shake

millage [milaʒ] **NM** *Can* mileage

mille[1] [mil] **ADJ INV 1** thousand; **m. hommes** a thousand men, one thousand men; **deux m.** two thousand; **trois cent m. hommes** three hundred thousand men; **m. un** a thousand and one, one thousand and one; **Les M. et une Nuits** the Arabian Nights, the Thousand and One Nights; **l'an m.** the year one thousand; **l'an m. neuf cent avant J.C.** (the year) nineteen hundred BC **2** *Fig (beaucoup de) (exemples, raisons)* countless, numerous, many; **je vous l'ai dit m. fois** I've told you a thousand times, I've told you time and time again; **vous avez m. fois raison** you are so right; **m. baisers** much love; **m. mercis** many thanks, thank you so much; **m. pardons** *ou* **regrets** I am so sorry; **c'est m. fois trop grand** it's miles *or* way too big; **casser qch en m. morceaux** to smash sth to smithereens; **souffrir** *ou* **endurer m. morts** *(physiquement)* to suffer agonies, to go through hell; *(moralement)* to go through hell, to die a thousand deaths; **j'étais à m. lieues de me douter que ...** I never for a moment suspected that ...; **je te le donne en m.** you'll never guess in a million years **SEE GRAMMAR A12–13; B58–9**

NM INV 1 *(chiffre)* thousand; **m. plus m.** a thousand plus a thousand, one thousand plus one thousand; **par m. de briques vendu(es)** per thousand bricks sold, for every thousand bricks sold; **un habitant sur m.** one inhabitant in a thousand; **les chances de guérison sont de dix pour m.** there's a one in a hundred chance of a cure; **un taux de natalité de 5 pour m.** a birth rate of 0.5 per cent; **ils sont morts par centaines de m.** they died in (their) hundreds of thousands **2** *Fig* **mettre** *ou* **donner dans le m.** to hit the bull's-eye; *Fam* **il gagne des m. et des cents** he makes a mint

mille[2] **NM** *(mesure)* mile (= *1.609 m)*; **m. (marin** *ou* **nautique)** nautical mile

mille-feuille, *pl* **mille-feuilles** [milfœj] **NF** *Bot* milfoil, yarrow

NM *Culin* millefeuille, *Am* napoleon

millénaire [mil(l)enɛr] **ADJ** *(arbre, monument)* a thousand years old; **cette superstition est plusieurs fois m.** the superstition has existed for several thousands of years

NM thousand years, millennium; *(anniversaire)* millennium, millenary; **dater du premier m. av. J.-C.** to date from the first millennium BC; **cette tradition est vieille d'au moins un m.** the tradition has existed for at least a thousand years VOIR GRAMMAIRE A13

millénarisme [milenarism] **NM** millenarianism

millénariste [milenarist] **ADJ, N** millenarian, millenary

millénium [milenjɔm] **NM** millennium VOIR GRAMMAIRE A13

mille-pattes [milpat] **NM INV** centipede, millipede

mille-pertuis, millepertuis [milpertɥi] **NM INV** *Bot* St John's wort

mille-raies [milrɛ] **NM INV** needlecord **ADJ INV** velours m. needlecord

millésime [milezim] **NM** *(de voiture)* year of manufacture; *(de vin)* year, vintage; *(sur pièce, timbre)* date; **il ne boit que de grands millésimes** he only drinks vintage wine

millésimé [milezime] **ADJ** *(vin)* vintage; *(pièce)* dated

millet [mijɛ] **NM** *Bot* millet; **(grains de) m.** birdseed, canary seed

milliampère [miljɑ̃pɛr] **NM** milliamp(ere)

milliard [miljar] **NM** billion, *Br Vieilli* thousand million, milliard VOIR GRAMMAIRE A76

milliardaire [miljardɛr] **ADJ, N** billionaire

milliardième [miljardjɛm] **ADJ, N** billionth, *Br Vieilli* thousand millionth

millibar [milibar] **NM** *Météo* millibar

millième [miljɛm] **ADJ, N** thousandth

millier [milje] **NM** thousand; **un m. de personnes** a thousand people; **des milliers de personnes** thousands of people; **les gens sont venus par milliers** people came in their thousands; **ils en vendent par milliers** they sell them by the thousand

milligramme [miligram] **NM** milligram(me)

millilitre [mililitr] **NM** millilitre, *Am* milliliter

millimètre [milimɛtr] **NM** millimetre, *Am* millimeter

millimétré [milimetre], **millimétrique** [milimetrik] **ADJ** échelle millimétrique millimetre *or Am* millimeter scale; **papier m.** graph paper

million [miljɔ̃] **NM** million; **quatre millions d'hommes** four million men; **riche à millions** worth millions; **il n'y en a pas des millions à s'appeler comme ça** there can't be too many people with a name like that VOIR GRAMMAIRE A12–13

millionième [miljɔnjɛm] **ADJ, N** millionth

millionnaire [miljɔnɛr] **ADJ, N** millionaire

milliseconde [milis(ə)gɔ̃d] **NF** millisecond

millivolt [milivɔlt] **NM** millivolt

milliwatt [miliwat] **NM** milliwatt

milord [milɔr] **NM 1** *(titre)* my Lord; *(noble)* (English) nobleman; *Fig* immensely wealthy man **2** *Arch (voiture)* victoria

mi-lourd, *pl* **mi-lourds ADJ, NM** *Boxe* **(poids) m.** light heavyweight (boxer)

mime [mim] **NM** mime, (art of) miming; **faire du m.** to mime, to do mime; **spectacle de m.** mime show
N *(personne)* mime; *(imitateur)* mimic

mimer [mime] **VT 1** to mime; **m. une scène** to mime a scene, to act a scene in dumb show **2** *(imiter)* to mimic

mimétique [mimetik] **ADJ** *Zool* mimetic; **le pouvoir m. de sa voix** his ability to imitate other people's voices

mimétisme [mimetism] **NM** *Zool* mimicry, *Spéc* mimesis; **par m., elle a fini par faire aussi de la peinture** taking the attitude that

'if you can't beat 'em, join 'em', she ended up doing painting too; **ils le font tous par m.** they can't help copying each other, they can't help mimicking each other

mimi [mimi] **NM** *Enf* **1** *(chat)* pussy (cat), kitty; **mon petit m.** my darling, my pet **2** *(baiser)* kiss; **fais m. à ta sœur** give your sister a kiss; **faire un gros m. à qn** to give sb a big kiss; **elle adore faire des mimis à son petit frère** she loves cuddling her little brother
ADJ INV *Fam (mignon)* lovely, cute

mimique [mimik] **ADJ langage m.** sign language
NF *(expression)* expression; *(grimace)* grimace; *(de sourd-muet)* sign language; **il s'exprime beaucoup par m.** he uses his face to convey his feelings

mimodrame [mimɔdram] **NM** *Théâtre* mime

mimolette [mimɔlɛt] **NF** *Culin* = type of firm cheese

mimosa [mimoza] **NM** mimosa

mi-moyen, *pl* **mi-moyens ADJ, NM** *Boxe* **(poids) m.** welterweight (boxer)

min *(abrév* **minimum)** min

minable [minabl] *Péj* **ADJ** *(appartement, apparence)* shabby, seedy; *(personne)* pathetic; **salaire m.** mere pittance (of a wage), miserable *or* pathetic wage; **c'est m., ce que tu lui as fait** that was a rotten trick you played on him
N failure, loser; **quelle bande de minables** what a pathetic *or* useless bunch

minaret [minarɛ] **NM** minaret

minauder [minode] **VI** to simper

minauderie [minodri] **NF** simpering; **minauderies** simpering (manner)

minaudier, -ière [minodje, -jɛr] **ADJ** *(personne)* simpering, affected

mince [mɛ̃s] **ADJ 1** *(fin)* *(planche, étoffe, tranche, mur etc)* thin; *(personne)* slim, slender **2** *(insuffisant)* *(prétexte)* slim, thin; *(preuves)* slim, thin, scant; *(profit)* small, slight; *(chance)* slight; **mes connaissances dans ce domaine sont trop minces** I know too little about this field, my knowledge in this field is too scanty; **d'un intérêt un peu m.** of little interest; **m. revenu** slender *or* small *or* scanty income; **tes arguments sont un peu minces** your arguments are a bit poor *or* feeble; *Fam* **ce n'est pas une m. affaire** it's not an easy job, it's not easy
INT *Fam* **m. (alors)!** *(surprise)* well, I'm blowed!; *(déception)* blast (it)!
ADV thinly

minceur [mɛ̃sœr] **NF 1** *(de couche, de peau)* thinness; *(de personne)* slimness, slenderness; **elle est d'une m. extraordinaire** she is extraordinarily slim **2** *(insuffisance)* scantiness; **étant donné la m. de mes revenus** since my income is so small

mincir [mɛ̃sir] **VI** to get thinner *or* slimmer, to lose weight

mine¹ [min] **NF 1** *(gisement)* mine; **travailler à la m.** to work in the mine, to be a miner; **exploitation des mines** mining; **m. de charbon** coalmine, colliery, pit; **m. d'or** goldmine; *Fig* **ce travail est loin d'être une m. d'or** you won't get rich doing this job; **m. à ciel ouvert** opencast mine; *Fig* **une m. de renseignements** a mine of information
2 *Admin* **les Mines** = government department responsible for supervising all construction projects involving tunnelling; **École des Mines,** *Fam* **les Mines** = grande école of engineering studies; **ingénieur des Mines** = engineer (who has graduated from the École des Mines); **service des Mines** = government department which verifies the roadworthiness of cars which have been involved in accidents
3 m. (de crayon) (pencil) lead; **crayon à m.**

grasse/dure soft/hard pencil; **m. de plomb** graphite, blacklead
4 *Mil, Constr etc* mine; **poser** *ou* **mouiller une m.** to lay a mine; **faire jouer une m.** to fire a blast *or* a mine; **coup de m.** blast; **attention aux coups de m.!** *(sur panneau)* danger, blasting; **m. flottante** floating mine; **mouilleur de mines** minelayer; **champ de mines** minefield; **m. terrestre** landmine

mine² **NF** *(de personne)* appearance, look; **mines** *(de bébé)* gestures, expressions; **avoir bonne/mauvaise m.** to look well/ill; *Iron* **nous avons bonne m. maintenant!** we do look good *or* silly!; **plat qui a bonne m.** dish that looks good *or* appetizing; **sa bonne m. fait plaisir à voir** it's a pleasure to see him looking so well; **avoir une m. resplendissante** to look in the best of health; **vous avez meilleure m.** you're looking better; **il en a une (sale) m.!** he does look ill!; **avoir une m. de papier mâché** *ou* **de déterré** to look like death warmed up; **m. boudeuse** sulky expression; **elle a toujours une m. réjouie** she always looks happy; **prendre une m. contrite** to look offended; **ne fais pas cette m.** don't look like that; **faire** *ou* **avoir triste m.** to look down in the dumps; **faire bonne m.** to put a good face on it *or* on things; **faire bonne m. à** *ou* **devant qn** to be pleasant to sb, to greet sb pleasantly *or* with a smile; **faire grise m.** to look miserable *or* po-faced; **faire grise m. à qn** to give sb a cool reception; **juger les gens sur la m.** to judge people by *or* on appearances; **sous sa m. d'homme rangé** behind that sober exterior of his; **il ne faut pas vous fier à sa m. de petite fille sage** don't trust that butter-wouldn't-melt-in-my-mouth expression of hers; *Fig* **ça/il ne paie pas de m.** it/he isn't much to look at; **faire m. d'être fâché** to pretend to be *or* look as though one is angry; **il a fait m. de me suivre** he made as if to follow me; *Fam* **m. de rien,** essaie de vérifier try to check on it without letting on (what you're up to); *Fam* **m. de rien, l'affaire progresse** the work is progressing, though you wouldn't think so to look at it; *Péj* **faire des mines** to simper; **elles font des mines devant le miroir** they're making faces in the mirror

miner [mine] **VT 1** *(saper)* *(forteresse etc)* to mine; **la mer mine les falaises** the sea is undermining the cliffs *or* is eating the cliffs away **2** *Fig* **la fièvre l'a miné** fever has undermined *or* sapped his strength; **ses soucis la minent** her worries are wearing her down; **miné par l'envie** eaten up *or* consumed with envy **3** *(poser des mines dans)* to mine

minerai [minrɛ] **NM** ore; **m. de fer** iron ore

minéral, -ale, -aux, -ales [mineral, -o] **ADJ** mineral
NM mineral

minéralier [mineralje] **NM** ore tanker

minéralisation [mineralizasjɔ̃] **NF** mineralization

minéraliser [mineralize] **VT** to mineralize

minéralogie [mineralɔʒi] **NF** mineralogy

minéralogique [mineralɔʒik] **ADJ 1** *Géol* mineralogical **2** *Aut, Admin* **numéro m.** registration number, *Am* license *or* Can licence number; **plaque m.** numberplate, *Am* license *or* Can licence plate

minéralogiste [mineralɔʒist] **N** mineralogist

Minerve [minɛrv] **N** *Myth* Minerva

minerve [minɛrv] **NF** *Méd* (surgical) collar

minestrone [minɛstrɔn] **NM** *Culin* minestrone

minet, -ette [minɛ, -ɛt] **N** *Fam* **1** *(chat)* pussy (cat), kitty; **mon m./ma minette** *(terme d'affection)* my darling, my pet **2** *Péj (jeune)* *(garçon)* trendy young guy, pretty boy; *(fille)* trendy chick, babe

mineur¹ [minœr] NM **1** *(ouvrier)* (coal) miner, collier; **m. de fond** underground worker **2** *Mil* sapper

mineur², **-eure** ADJ **1** *(inférieur)* minor, lesser; **Asie Mineure** Asia Minor **2** *Jur* under age **3** *Mus (note, gamme etc)* minor; **en ut m.** in C minor **4** *(de moindre importance)* minor; **ce sont des soucis mineurs** these are minor worries
▸ N *Jur* minor; **ce film est interdit aux mineurs** this film is restricted to over-18s; **cet établissement est interdit aux mineurs** these premises are banned to persons under 18
▸ NM *Mus* minor key

mini [mini] *Fam* ADJ INV mini; **la mode m. est de retour** the mini is back (in fashion)
▸ NF mini(skirt)
▸ ADV **s'habiller m.** to wear miniskirts

miniature [minjatyr] NF miniature; **peintre de miniatures** miniature painter, miniaturist; **en m.** in miniature, on a small scale; **c'est tout sa mère en m.** she's a miniature version of her mother
▸ ADJ INV miniature

miniaturisation [minjatyrizasjɔ̃] NF miniaturization; **la m. de l'informatique** computer (circuitry) miniaturization

miniaturiser [minjatyrize] VT to miniaturize; **un téléviseur miniaturisé** a mini *or* miniature television
▸ VPR **se miniaturiser** to become miniaturized; **la hi-fi se miniaturise** sound systems are getting much smaller

miniaturiste [minjatyrist] N miniaturist, miniature painter

minibar [minibar] NM **1** *(dans le train)* trolley; **un service de m. est assuré dans ce train** there is a trolley service on this train **2** *(à l'hôtel)* minibar; **avez-vous consommé au m.?** did you have anything from the minibar?

minibus [minibys] NM minibus

minicassette [minikasɛt] NF mini-cassette
▸ NM portable tape recorder

minichaîne [miniʃɛn] NF mini system

minidisc® [minidisk] NM MiniDisc®

mini-disquette, *pl* **mini-disquettes** NF minidisk, mini-floppy

minier, -ière [minje, -jɛr] ADJ *(industrie, région etc)* mining
▸ NF **minière** surface *or* opencast mine

minigolf [minigɔlf] NM crazy golf

minijupe [miniʒyp] NF miniskirt

minima [minima] *voir* **minimum**

minimal, -ale, -aux, -ales [minimal, -o] ADJ *(température, durée)* minimum; *(art)* minimal; *Ling* **paire minimale** minimal pair

minimalisme [minimalism] NM *Beaux-Arts* minimalism

minimaliste [minimalist] ADJ, N *Beaux-Arts* minimalist

minime [minim] ADJ *(dégâts, implication)* minimal; *(rôle)* minor; *(perte)* trivial; *(valeur)* trifling
▸ N *Sport* junior *(to 15 years old)*
▸ NM *Rel, Hist* Minim friar

mini-message, *pl* **mini-messages** NM *Tél* text message; **envoyer un m. à qn** to text sb, to send sb a text message

minimisation [minimizasjɔ̃] NF minimization; **ce n'est pas la m. de nos problèmes qui va les résoudre** we won't solve our problems by minimizing them *or Fam* by playing them down

minimiser [minimize] VT to minimize, to reduce to the minimum; *Fig (rôle, situation, problème)* to play down, to downplay

minimum [minimɔm], *pl* **minima** [minima] *ou* **minimums** NM minimum; **avec un m. d'ef-**
forts with a minimum of effort; **un m. de temps** a minimum amount of time; **en un m. de temps** in as short a time as possible; **nous exigeons un m. de garanties** we demand the minimum guarantees; **trois mois, c'est un m. pour s'habituer au climat** three months is the minimum it takes *or* it takes at least three months to get used to the climate; **c'est vraiment le m. que tu puisses faire pour elle** it's the least you can do for her; **il ne fait même plus le m. pour donner le change à sa femme** he's stopped making even the slightest attempt to keep his wife in the dark; **m. vital** minimum living wage; **m. vieillesse** basic old-age pension; **les minima sociaux** = basic income support; **réduire les frais au m.** to reduce expenses to a minimum; *Fam* **je n'y resterai que le m. de temps** I'll make it as brief as I can; **dépenser le m.** to spend as little as possible; *Fam* **bouger le** *ou* **au m.** to move as little as possible; **au m. 200 euros/cinq ans d'expérience** at least 200 euros/five years' experience, a minimum of 200 euros/five years' experience; **m. imposable** tax threshold
▸ ADJ minimum; **les largeurs minimums** *ou* **minima** the minimum widths; **vitesse m.** minimum speed; **prix m.** *(à une vente aux enchères)* reserve price; *Élec* **charge m.** *(de génératrice)* base load

mini-ordinateur, *pl* **mini-ordinateurs** NM minicomputer, mini

minipilule [minipilyl] NF minipill

mini-séjour, *pl* **mini-séjours** NM minibreak, short break

mini-série, *pl* **mini-séries** NF *TV* miniseries

mini-slip, *pl* **mini-slips** NM tanga

ministère [ministɛr] NM **1** *(département)* government department; **m. des Affaires étrangères** *Br* ≃ Foreign (and Commonwealth) Office, *Am* ≃ State Department, *Can* ≃ External Affairs Department; **m. de l'Agriculture** Ministry *or* Department of Agriculture; **m. du Commerce** Ministry of Trade, *Br* ≃ Department of Trade and Industry; **m. du Commerce extérieur** Foreign Trade Department; **m. de la Communication** Ministry for Communications; **m. de la Culture** Ministry of Culture, Ministry for the Arts; **m. de la Défense (nationale)** *Br* ≃ Ministry of Defence, *Am* ≃ Department of Defense; **m. de l'Économie et des Finances** Treasury; **m. de l'Éducation nationale** ≃ Department of Education; **m. de l'Environnement** ≃ Department of the Environment; **m. des Finances** Ministry of Finance, *Br* Exchequer; **m. de l'Intérieur** *Br* ≃ Home Office, *Am* ≃ Department of the Interior; **m. de la Justice** Department of Justice; **m. de la Santé et de la Sécurité sociale** *Br* ≃ Department of Social Security, *Am* ≃ Department of Health and Human Services; **m. du Tourisme** Ministry of Tourism; **m. du Travail** *Br* ≃ Department of Education and Employment, *Am* ≃ Department of Labor; **m. des Travaux publics** *Can* ≃ Department of Public Works, *Br Hist* ≃ Ministry of Public Works **2** *(gouvernement)* government; **entrer dans un m.** to take office; **former un m.** to form a government; **sous le m. Raffarin** under Raffarin's government
3 *Jur* **le m. public** *Br* ≃ the (Department of the) Director of Public Prosecutions, *Am* ≃ the District Attorney's Office **4** *Rel* **le (saint) m.** the ministry **5** *Arch, Litt (aide)* agency; **user du m. de qn** to make use of sb's services; *Jur* **l'accusé a droit au m. d'un avocat** the accused has the right to counsel *or Am* a lawyer

ministériel, -ielle [ministerjɛl] ADJ *(arrêté, décret, entourage)* ministerial; *(crise, rema-*
niement) cabinet; *Vieilli* **journal m.** newspaper supporting the government, government organ; *Jur* **officier m.** *(avoué, huissier, notaire)* officer of the court

ministrable [ministrabl] *Pol* ADJ likely to become a minister
▸ N likely candidate for minister, ministerial hopeful

ministre [ministr] NM **1** *(de gouvernement)* minister; **Premier m.** Prime Minister; *Can (d'une province)* Premier; **m. des Affaires étrangères** *Br* ≃ Foreign Secretary, *Am* ≃ Secretary of State, *Can* ≃ Secretary of State for External Affairs; **m. de l'Agriculture** Agriculture Minister, Minister for Agriculture; **m. du Commerce** *Br* ≃ Secretary of State for Trade and Industry, *Am* ≃ Secretary of Commerce; **m. de la Communication** Minister for Communications; **m. de la Culture** Minister for Culture, Arts Minister; **m. de la Défense (nationale)** ≃ Secretary of State for Defence, Minister of Defence; **m. de l'Éducation nationale** ≃ Secretary of State for Education; **m. de l'Environnement** ≃ Secretary of State for the Environment; **m. des Finances** *Br* ≃ Chancellor of the Exchequer, *Am* ≃ Secretary of the Treasury, *Can* ≃ Minister of Finance; **m. de l'Intérieur** *Br* ≃ Home Secretary, *Am* ≃ Secretary of the Interior; **m. de la Justice** *Br* ≃ Lord Chancellor, *Am* ≃ Attorney General, *Can* ≃ Minister of Justice and Attorney General; **m. de la Santé et de la Sécurité sociale** *Br* ≃ Secretary of State for Social Security, *Am* ≃ Secretary for Health and Human Services; **m. du Tourisme** Minister for Tourism; **m. des Transports** *Br* ≃ Secretary of State for Transport, *Am* ≃ Transportation Secretary; **m. du Travail** *Br* ≃ Secretary of State for Education and Employment, *Am* ≃ Labor Secretary; **m. des Travaux publics** *Br Hist, Can* ≃ Minister of Public Works; **m. sans portefeuille** minister without portfolio; **papier m.** ≃ official foolscap
2 *Rel* (Protestant) minister, clergyman **3** *Arch, Litt (de Dieu, d'un prince etc)* servant, agent

Minitel® [minitɛl] NM = viewdata service, *Am* ≃ Minitel®; **sur M.** on viewdata, *Am* on Minitel®; **m. rose** = erotic viewdata service

> **Minitel®**
> The domestic viewdata service run by France Télécom has become a familiar part of French life. The basic monitor and keyboard are provided free of charge, and the subscriber is charged for the services used on his or her ordinary telephone bill. The subscriber dials a four-figure number (typically 3615); a code word then gives access to the particular service required. Some Minitel® services are purely informative (the weather, road conditions, news etc); others are interactive (enabling users to carry out bank transactions, book tickets for travel, register for and obtain the results of nationwide examinations, for example). The Minitel® also serves as an electronic telephone directory. Nowadays the services offered by Minitel® are increasingly available on the Internet.

minitéliste [minitelist] N Minitel® user

mini-tour, *pl* **mini-tours** NF *Ordinat* mini tower

minium [minjɔm] NM *Chimie* red lead, minium; *(antirouille)* red lead paint

minivague [minivag] NF body wave

minois [minwa] NM *(d'enfant, de jeune*

femme) (pretty) face; **une jeune fille au frais m.** a fresh-faced young girl

minoration [minɔrasjɔ̃] **NF** *(de tarifs, temps de travail)* reduction, decrease

minorer [minɔre] **VT** *(minimiser) (incident)* to downplay; *(faire baisser) (chiffre, somme, prix, impôt etc)* to lower, to reduce

minoritaire [minɔritɛr] **ADJ** *(parti, participation)* minority; **ils sont minoritaires à l'Assemblée** they are in the minority in the Assembly; **très minoritaires** very much in the minority
N member of a minority

minorité [minɔrite] **NF** minority; *Jur* minority, infancy, nonage; **le service ne fonctionne qu'avec une m. de gens** the department is run by a skeleton staff; **être en m.** to be in the *or* in a minority; **mettre en m.** to defeat; **la gauche a été mise en m. lors des dernières élections** the left became the minority party at the last elections; **m. ethnique** ethnic minority; **m. de blocage** blocking minority vote; **m. agissante** active minority VOIR GRAMMAIRE A11

Minorque [minɔrk] **NF** Minorca

minorquin, -ine [minɔrkɛ̃, -in] **ADJ** Minorcan
N M. Minorcan

minoterie [minɔtri] **NF** *(moulin)* (large) flour mill; *(activité)* flour-milling

minotier [minɔtje] **NM** (flour) miller

minou [minu] **NM 1** *Fam (chat)* pussy (cat), kitty; **mon m.** my darling, my pet **2** *très Fam (sexe de la femme)* pussy, beaver, snatch

minuit [minɥi] **NM** midnight, twelve (o'clock) (at night); **m. et demi** half-past twelve (at night)

minus [minys] **NM** *Fam* **1** *(nabot)* midget, shortie, runt **2** *(incapable)* no-hoper, nobody **3 m. habens** half-wit, moron

minuscule [minyskyl] **ADJ 1** *(très petit)* tiny, minute, minuscule **2** *Typ* lower-case; **lettre m.** small letter; *Typ* lower-case letter
NF small letter; *Typ* lower-case letter; **en minuscules** (in) lower case

minutage [minyta3] **NM** timing; **faire un m. exact de qch** to time something to the minute

minute [minyt] **NF 1** *(d'heure, de degré)* minute; **à deux minutes près, vous le ratiez** a couple of minutes later and you would have missed him; **toutes les vingt minutes** every twenty minutes; **de dernière m.** last-minute; **faire qch à la m.** to do sth at a minute's *or* a moment's notice; *Fam* **on n'est pas à la m.** we've got plenty of time, there's no rush; **il sera là d'une m. à l'autre** he'll be here any minute now; *Fam* **m. (papillon)!** just a minute!, hold on! SEE GRAMMAR A80; B60 **2** *(court moment)* minute; **ne pas avoir une m. à perdre/de répit** not to have a moment *or* minute to lose/a moment's *or* minute's rest; **ne pas avoir une m. à soi** not to have a minute *or* a moment to oneself; **une m. de silence** a moment's silence; **la m. de vérité** the moment of truth; **nettoyage-m.** dry-cleaning while you wait; **talons/clés m.** heel/key bar; **réparations (à la) m.** repairs while you wait; **repas-m.** convenience meal; **steak m.** minute steak **3** *(de contrat etc)* minute, draft; *(d'acte, de jugement)* record; **faire la m. d'un acte** to draft an act; **faire la m. d'une réunion** to draw up the minutes of *or* to minute a meeting

minuter [minyte] **VT 1** *(dans le temps)* to time; **sa journée est soigneusement minutée** every minute of his day is carefully planned *or* accounted for **2** *(accord etc)* to minute, to draw up, to draft; *(acte, jugement)* to record, to enter

minuterie [minytri] **NF 1** *(appareil) (de lumière)* timer, (automatic) time switch **2** *(méca-*

nisme) (d'une horlogerie) motionwork, train of wheels; **as-tu mis en route la m. du four?** did you set the oven timer?

minuteur [minytœr] **NM** timer

minutie [minysi] **NF 1** *(caractère)* meticulousness, attention to detail; **avec m.** meticulously; **d'une m. remarquable** remarkably meticulous **2** *Vieilli (détail)* minute detail; **minuties** trifles, petty details, *Fml* minutiae

minutieusement [minysjøzmɑ̃] **ADV** meticulously, with attention to detail; **très m.** very meticulously, with great attention to detail; **examiner qch m.** to examine sth minutely, to scrutinize sth

minutieux, -ieuse [minysjø, -jøz] **ADJ** *(personne)* meticulous; *(inspection, examen)* close, thorough, minute, detailed; *(dessin, sculpture)* detailed; **la broderie est un travail très m.** embroidery demands close work *or* attention to detail

miocène [mjɔsɛn] **ADJ, NM** *Géol* Miocene

mioche [mjɔʃ] **N** *Fam* kid(die), tot, *Péj* brat

mi-pente (à) **ADV** halfway up/down the hill

MIPS [mips] **NM** *Ordinat (abrév* **million d'instructions par seconde)** MIPS

mirabelle [mirabɛl] **NF** mirabelle plum

mirabellier [mirabelje] **NM** mirabelle plum tree

miracle [mirakl] **NM 1** miracle; **ne t'attends pas à un m.** don't expect any miracles; **faire un m.** to perform *or* work a miracle; *Fig* **faire des miracles** to work miracles *or* wonders; **croire aux miracles** to believe in miracles; **cela tient du m.** it's miraculous; **m. d'architecture** marvel *or* miracle of architecture; **m. économique** economic miracle; **le m. industriel français** the French industrial miracle; **par m.** miraculously, by a miracle; **échapper par m.** to have a miraculous escape; **c'est (un) m. que …** it's a miracle *or* a wonder that …; **crier (au) m.** to go into raptures **2** *Hist, Littér* miracle (play)
ADJ INV *Fam* **produit m.** miracle *or* wonder product; **une crème m. contre la cellulite** a cream that works miracles *or* wonders on cellulite; **je ne crois pas aux solutions m.** I don't believe in miracle cures; **elle a toujours des solutions m.** she can always come up with a solution

miraculé, -ée [mirakyle] **ADJ** *(personne)* miraculously cured/saved, cured/saved by a miracle
N je suis un m. I'm lucky to be alive; **l'explosion n'a laissé que quelques miraculés** only a few people escaped death in the explosion; **les miraculés de Lourdes** the miracle cures of Lourdes

miraculeusement [mirakyløzmɑ̃] **ADV** by a miracle, miraculously; **m. vite** miraculously quickly

miraculeux, -euse [mirakylø, -øz] **ADJ** miraculous, wonderful; **remède m.** miracle cure; **cette crème est miraculeuse contre les rides** this cream works miracles *or* wonders on wrinkles

mirador [miradɔr] **NM 1** *Archit* mirador, belvedere **2** *Mil (dans un arbre etc)* observation post; *(de camp de prisonniers)* watchtower

mirage [mira3] **NM** mirage

miraud [miro] **ADJ** *Fam* = **miro**

mire [mir] **NF 1** *(de fusil)* foresight **2** *(signal)* sighting mark; *TV* test pattern, *Br* test card; **m. de réglage** test pattern, *Br* test card **3** *(piquet)* (surveyor's) ranging pole

mirer [mire] **VT 1** *Vieilli (viser)* to aim at, to take aim at **2** *Littér (refléter)* to reflect, to mirror **3** *(œufs)* to candle
VPR se mirer *(dans un miroir, l'eau etc)* to

look *or* gaze at oneself; *Litt* **les arbres se mirent dans l'eau** the trees are reflected in the water

mirettes [mirɛt] **NFPL** *Fam (yeux)* peepers, *Am* baby blues; **on s'en est pris plein les m.** we feasted our eyes on it

mirifique [mirifik] **ADJ** *Fam* wonderful, fabulous

mirliflor(e) [mirliflɔr] **NM** *Hum, Fig Vieilli* dandy, fop

mirliton [mirlitɔ̃] **NM** *(sifflet)* kazoo, mirliton; **des vers de m.** doggerel, bad verse

mirmidon [mirmidɔ̃] **NM** *Vieilli* whippersnapper, pipsqueak, little runt

miro [miro] **ADJ** *Fam* short-sighted; **il est complètement m.** he's as blind as a bat

mirobolant [mirɔbɔlɑ̃] **ADJ** *Fam* fabulous, wonderful, marvellous; **son travail n'est vraiment pas m.** his work is not exactly brilliant

miroir [mirwar] **NM** mirror, *Fml* (looking) glass; **m. (pliant) à trois faces** triple mirror; **m. grossissant** magnifying mirror; **m. déformant** distorting mirror; *Fig* **le m. d'une société** the mirror of a society; **ce journal est-il réellement le m. de ce que pensent les gens?** does this newspaper really mirror *or* reflect what people think?
▸ ▸ **m. aux alouettes** = lure for attracting birds; *Fig* snare, delusion; **m. de courtoisie** vanity mirror

miroitant [mirwatɑ̃] **ADJ** *(argent)* glistening, gleaming, flashing; *(lac, soie)* shimmering; *(bijou)* sparkling

miroité [mirwate] **ADJ** *(cheval)* dappled bay

miroitement [mirwatmɑ̃] **NM** *(d'argent)* glistening, gleam(ing), flash(ing); *(de lac, de soie)* shimmer(ing); *(de bijou)* sparkle, sparkling

miroiter [mirwate] **VI** *(d'argent)* to glisten, to gleam, to flash; *(de lac, de soie)* to shimmer; *(de bijou)* to sparkle; *Fig* **faire m. l'avenir à qn** to lure sb with bright prospects, to hold out *or* dangle the prospect of a bright future in front of sb; **ils m'ont fait m. une promotion/un voyage** they dangled the prospect of promotion/a trip in front of me

miroton [mirɔtɔ̃], *Fam* **mironton** [mirɔ̃tɔ̃] **NM** *Culin (bœuf)* **m.** = beef boiled in sauce with onions

mis [mi] **ADJ** *Vieilli* **être bien/mal m.** to be well/badly attired

misaine [mizɛn] **NF** *Naut* **(voile de) m.** (square) foresail; **mât de m.** foremast

misanthrope [mizɑ̃trɔp] **NM** misanthropist, misanthrope
ADJ misanthropic

misanthropie [mizɑ̃trɔpi] **NF** misanthropy

misanthropique [mizɑ̃trɔpik] **ADJ** *Litt* misanthropic

miscible [misibl] **ADJ** miscible

mise [miz] **NF 1** *(placement)* placing, putting in place; **m. à l'eau** *(d'un bateau)* launch, launching; **m. en bouteilles** bottling; **m. en boîtes** canning; **m. à terre** *(de marchandises)* landing; **m. en pratique** carrying out, putting into practice; **m. en musique d'un poème** setting a poem to music; **m. en eau** *(d'un barrage)* filling (of a reservoir); **m. au net** *(d'un document etc)* finalizing; **m. à exécution** *(d'une mesure)* implementation; **toute une série de mesures avec m. à exécution immédiate** a whole series of measures to be implemented immediately; **on craint la m. à exécution des menaces** there is concern that the threats will be carried out; **m. en italiques** italicization; **m. en valeur** *(d'un terrain, d'arguments)* development; **pour assurer la m. en valeur de sa collection** to show his collection off to better advan-

tage *or* better effect; **m. en vigueur** implementation; **m. en application** *(d'un règlement, d'une décision)* implementation, application; **la m. en application du règlement avait connu quelques difficultés** there had been some difficulties in implementing *or* applying the regulation; **m. en place** setting up, putting into place; **nous avons dû retarder la m. en place du nouveau système** we have had to postpone setting up the new system; **la m. en place du nouveau réseau demandera plusieurs mois** it will take several months to set up the new system *or* to get the new system up and running; **m. en vente** putting up for sale, putting on the market; **elle attend la m. en vente de sa maison pour commencer à en chercher une autre** she's waiting for her house to go on the market before she starts looking for another; **j'ai confié la m. en vente de la maison à un notaire** I put the sale of the house in the hands of a notary; **m. en exploitation** *(d'une machine)* commissioning; **m. en veille** putting on standby; *Tél* **m. en attente d'appels** call holding; *Ordinat* **m. en attente des fichiers à imprimer** printer spooling; *Ordinat* **m. en ligne** putting on-line; *Ordinat* **m. en mémoire** saving; **la m. en mémoire n'a pas été faite** it hasn't been saved; *Ordinat* **m. en relief** highlighting; *Ordinat* **m. en réseau** networking; **m. sur pied** setting up
2 *(habillement)* dress, clothing, *Fml* attire; **elle est simple dans sa m.** she dresses simply; **on voit à sa m. qu'elle n'est pas très riche** you can see from the way she dresses *or* the clothes she wears that she's not very rich
3 *Cartes* stake; *(à une vente aux enchères)* bid; **m. à prix** reserve price, upset price; *Fig* **son arrivée m'a sauvé la m.** his arrival got me out of a tight spot
4 être de m. to be obligatory; **le tutoiement n'est pas de m.** it's not the done thing to say 'tu'; **si tu y vas, sache que la cravate est de m.** if you go, you'll have to wear a tie, mind
▸▸ **m. en accusation** committal (for trial); *Fig* **on a assisté à une véritable m. en accusation du président du club** accusations were hurled at the club chairman; **m. bas** *(d'animal)* dropping *(of young)*; **assister à la m. en bière** to be present when the body is placed in the coffin; **m. en cause** *(de l'honnêteté etc de qn)* questioning; *(dans une affaire)* involvement; **m. en circulation** *(de billets)* issue; **m. en demeure** summons; *Journ* injunction; *(de paiement)* formal demand; **m. en dépôt** warehousing; **m. en disponibilité** leave of absence; *Can Ind* layoff; **demander sa** *ou* **une m. en disponibilité** to ask for leave of absence; **m. sur écoutes (téléphoniques)** bugging; **c'est pourquoi ils ont décidé de la m. sur écoutes** that's why they decided to bug his/her/etc phone; *Jur* **m. en examen** indictment; **m. à feu** *(de fusée etc)* firing; *Com* **m. de fonds** investment; *Typ, Ordinat* **m. en forme** formatting; **m. en gage** pawning, pledging; **m. en garde** warning, caution; **m. hors** *(action)* disbursement; *(somme)* sum advanced; **m. hors tension** power-down; **m. en jeu** *(au début)* *Ftbl, Rugby* kick off; *Hockey* bully-off; *(à la touche)* *Ftbl* throw-in; *Rugby* line-out; **m. à jour** *(réactualisation) (action)* updating, update, bringing up to date; *(résultat)* update, updated version; *(d'un secret etc)* bringing to light; *Ordinat* updating; **m. en liberté** release; *Jur* **m. en liberté provisoire** release on bail; **m. en marche** *(de moteur etc)* starting, start up; **m. à mort** killing; *Ordinat* **m. à niveau** upgrade; *Scol* **faire une m. à niveau en maths** = to catch up in maths *(after switching to another specialization)*; **m. en œuvre** *(d'un projet)* implementation; *Radio* **m. en ondes** production; *Astronaut* **m. en orbite** putting into

orbit; **depuis sa m. en orbite** since it was put into orbit; **la m. en orbite est prévue pour 15 h** the satellite is scheduled to be sent into orbit at 3 pm; *Typ* **m. en pages** page make-up *or* design *or* layout; **m. en pension** borrowing against securities, pledging; **m. à pied** *(disciplinaire) (permanent)* dismissal; *(temporaire)* suspension; *Can (chômage)* layoff; **donner trois jours de m. à pied à qn** to give sb three days' suspension, to suspend sb for three days; **m. en plis** set; **faire une m. en plis à qn** to set sb's hair, to give sb a set; **shampooing et m. en plis** shampoo and set; **m. au point** *(d'un objectif)* focusing; *(d'une technique)* perfecting; *(d'un moteur)* tuning; *(d'un mécanisme)* adjustment; *(d'un document, d'un rapport)* finalization, finalizing; *Journ* correction; **je voudrais faire une m. au point** I'd like to clarify something; *Ordinat* **m. en relation** *(avec un service)* logon; *Typ* **m. en retrait** indent; **m. à la** *ou* **en traite** pensioning (off), retirement on a pension; **il y aura 50 mises en retraite** 50 people will be retired; **m. en route** start-up; **m. à sac** *(par des soldats)* sacking; *(par des voleurs)* ransacking; **après la m. à sac de la maison** after the house was ransacked; **se livrer à une m. à sac** *(de voyous)* to go on a looting spree; **m. en scène** *(d'une pièce)* staging, production; *(d'un film)* direction; **c'est elle qui fera la m. en scène** she'll be responsible for staging the play; *Fig* **toute cette histoire n'était en fait qu'une vaste m. en scène** the entire story was just one big set-up; **m. en service** *(d'une machine)* commissioning; **mais sa m. en service ne se fera qu'en septembre** but it won't come into service until September; *Ordinat, Élec* **m. sous tension** *(d'un ordinateur, d'une turbine)* power-up; **m. en train** *(d'un projet etc)* start-up; **quelques minutes d'exercice pour assurer sa m. en train** a few minutes' exercise to get oneself started *or* going in the morning

miser [mize] **VT** to stake (**sur** on)
VI m. sur un cheval to back a horse, to (put a) bet on a horse; *Fig* **m. sur les deux tableaux** to try to have it both ways; *Fam* **m. sur qn** to count *or* bank on sb; *Bourse* **m. sur une hausse/une baisse** to speculate on a rising/falling market

misérabilisme [mizerabilism] **NM** sordid realism

misérabiliste [mizerabilist] **ADJ** sordidly realistic

misérable [mizerabl] **ADJ 1** *(indigent)* poor, wretched, impoverished, miserable; *(condition, existence)* wretched; **quartier m.** poor *or* poverty-stricken district **2** *(insignifiant)* wretched, miserable, worthless; **un m. salaire** a miserable wage, a mere pittance (of a wage); **pour la m. somme de 20 euros** for a paltry 20 euros **3** *Vieilli (action etc)* despicable, mean
N *Arch (malheureux)* poor wretch; *Vieilli (fripouille)* scoundrel, wretch, villain; **comment as-tu pu faire une chose pareille, m.?** how could you have done such a thing, you scoundrel *or* wretch?

Il faut noter que l'adjectif anglais **miserable** est un faux ami. Il signifie le plus souvent **malheureux**, **triste**.

misérablement [mizerabləmã] **ADV** miserably

misère [mizer] **NF 1** *(indigence)* extreme poverty, destitution; **être dans la m.** to be poverty-stricken *or* destitute; **ils sont dans une m. noire** they have nothing, they are quite destitute; **vivre dans la m.** to live in poverty; **tomber dans la m.** to become destitute; **réduire qn à la m.** to reduce sb to penury; **crier** *ou* **pleurer m.** to plead poverty;

salaire de m. starvation wage **2** *(ennui)* trouble, misfortune; **les misères de l'âge** the afflictions of old age; **faire des misères** *ou* *Can* **de la misère à qn** to tease sb unmercifully **3** *Vieilli (malheur)* misery; **reprendre son collier de m.** to get back to the treadmill; **c'est vraiment une m. de la voir si malheureuse!** it is dreadful to see her so unhappy!; **lit de m.** sick bed **4** *(vétille)* **une m.** a trifle; **cent euros? une m.!** a hundred euros? a mere nothing!; **je l'ai eu pour une m.** I got it for a song **5** *Cartes* misère **6** *Bot* tradescantia
INT m.! damn!, blast!

Il faut noter que le nom anglais **misery** est un faux ami. Il signifie **malheur** ou **tristesse**.

miserere, **miséréré** [mizerere] **NM INV** *Rel, Mus* miserere

miséreux, **-euse** [mizerø, -øz] **ADJ** poverty-stricken, destitute
N poverty-stricken *or* destitute person

miséricorde [mizerikɔrd] **NF** mercy
INT *Vieilli* mercy on us!

miséricordieux, **-ieuse** [mizerikɔrdjø, -jøz] **ADJ** merciful (**envers** to)

misogyne [mizɔʒin] **ADJ** misogynous
N misogynist, woman-hater

misogynie [mizɔʒini] **NF** misogyny; **d'une m. invraisemblable** incredibly misogynous

miss, *pl* **miss(es)** [mis] **NF 1** *(reine de beauté)* beauty queen; **M. Monde/France** Miss World/France **2** *Fam* **voilà, m.** there you are(, miss); **et comment va m. Martin?** how is Miss Martin?; *(en s'adressant directement à la personne)* and how are we today, Miss Martin? **3** *Arch (gouvernante)* (English) governess

missel [misel] **NM** *Rel* missal

missile [misil] **NM** *Mil* missile; **m. à tête chercheuse à infrarouge** heat-seeking missile; **m. ballistique de moyenne portée** *ou* **de portée intermédiaire** intermediate-range ballistic missile; **m. de courte/longue portée** short-/long-range missile; **m. de croisière** cruise missile; **m. stratégique** strategic missile; **m. tactique** tactical missile; **m. anti-sous-marins** anti-submarine missile

mission [misjɔ̃] **NF 1** *(tâche)*, *Pol, Mil etc* mission; *(d'employé)* job, task, assignment; **j'ai (pour) m. de faire qch** my job *or* task is to do sth; **ministre en m. spéciale à Paris** minister on a special mission to Paris; **chargé de m.** representative; **envoyer qn en m. aux États-Unis** to send sb to the United States; **partir en m.** *(d'un cadre)* to go away on business; *(d'un diplomate)* to go off on a mission; *Mil* **en m. de reconnaissance** on a reconnaissance mission, on reconnaissance; **m. accomplie** mission accomplished; **m. vous avait été confiée de faire …** you were given the job of doing …, *Fml* you were assigned the task of doing …; **il s'était donné pour m. de sauver les enfants** he had taken it upon himself to save the children; *Hum* **viens ici, j'ai une m. à te confier** *(à un enfant)* come here, there's something I'd like you to do for me
2 *(groupe)* delegation; *Pol* delegation, mission; **m. scientifique** scientific expedition; **partir en m. au pôle Nord** to go on an expedition to the North Pole
3 *Rel (vocation, organisation)* mission; *(bâtiment)* mission (station)
4 *(rôle)* *(de l'art etc)* task, rôle, function; **la m. civilisatrice de l'école** the civilizing mission of schools
▸▸ **m. de bons offices** goodwill mission; **m. commerciale** business assignment; *(gouvernementale)* trade mission; **m. diplomatique** diplomatic mission

missionnaire [misjɔnɛr] ADJ, N missionary

Mississippi [misisipi] NM le M. *(le fleuve)* the Mississippi (River); *(l'État)* Mississippi

missive [misiv] NF *Litt, Hum* missive, letter

mistigri [mistigri] NM *Fam (chat)* puss

mistoufle [mistufl] NF *Fam Vieilli* 1 être dans la m. to be broke *or* hard up *or* skint 2 faire des mistoufles à qn to annoy *or* tease *or* plague sb

mistral [mistral] NM *Météo* mistral

mitaine [mitɛn] NF *Can (moufle)* mitten; *(qui laisse les doigts nus)* fingerless glove

mitan [mitã] NM *Fam Vieilli* le m. the underworld, gangland

mitard [mitar] NM *Fam* disciplinary cell; se retrouver au m. to end up in solitary

mite [mit] NF 1 mite; m. du fromage cheese mite 2 *(petit papillon)* moth; mangé des *ou* aux mites, troué aux mites moth-eaten

mité [mite] ADJ moth-eaten

mi-temps NF INV *Ftbl etc* half-time; première/seconde m. first/second half; la police craint la troisième m. the police fear after-match trouble *or* violence

NM part-time job; l'emploi à m. part-time work *or* employment; travailler *ou* être à m. to work part-time, to have a part-time job; *Scol* m. pédagogique part-time teaching position; l'avantage d'un m. the advantage of a part-time job *or* of working part-time

miter (se) [səmite] VPR to become moth-eaten

miteux, -euse [mitø, -øz] ADJ *(vêtements, quartier, boîte)* seedy, shabby, tatty; *(personne)* seedy-looking, shabby, down-at-heel
N *Fam* shabby *or* down-at-heel *or* seedy-looking person; tes amis, c'est une bande de m.! your friends are a seedy lot!

Mithridate [mitridat] N Mithridates

mithridatiser [mitridatize] VT m. qn to make sb immune (to poison)

mitigation [mitigasjɔ̃] NF *Jur* mitigation

mitigé [mitiʒe] ADJ *(enthousiasme)* moderate, *Fml* mitigated; *(sentiments, impressions)* mixed; le public était assez m. the public was quite mixed in its reaction; morale mitigée lax morals; *Jur* peine mitigée reduced sentence

mitiger [mitiʒe] VT *(je mitigeai(s), n. mitigeons)* *Vieilli (mal)* to mitigate; *(peine)* to reduce, to mitigate; *(règlement, loi)* to relax

mitigeur [mitiʒœr] NM mixer tap

mitochondrie [mitokɔ̃dri] NF mitochondrion

mitonner [mitɔne] VT 1 *Culin* to prepare, to cook; *(cuire à feu doux)* to simmer; sa femme lui mitonne de bons petits plats his wife cooks nice little meals for him 2 *Fig (projet etc)* to concoct, to cook up 3 *Litt (enfant)* to coddle, to pamper, to cosset
VI *Culin* to simmer

mitose [mitoz] NF *Biol* mitosis

mitoyen, -enne [mitwajɛ̃, -ɛn] ADJ intermediate; mur m. party wall; cloison mitoyenne dividing wall *(between two rooms)*; maisons mitoyennes semi-detached houses; *(plus de deux)* terraced houses

mitoyenneté [mitwajɛnte] NF *Jur (de mur, de haie)* joint ownership

mitraillade [mitrajad] NF *(volley of)* shots, machine-gun fire; une m. a burst of machine-gun fire

mitraillage [mitrajaʒ] NM machine-gunning

mitraille [mitraj] NF 1 *Mil (projectiles)* case shot, canister shot, grapeshot; *(décharge)* hail of bullets 2 *Fam (monnaie)* small change

mitrailler [mitraje] VT to machine-gun; *Phot Fam* to click away at, to snap away at,

to take snaps of; les vedettes ont été abondamment mitraillées lots of photographs were taken of the film stars; *Fig* m. qn de questions to fire questions at sb, to bombard sb with questions

mitraillette [mitrajɛt] NF submachine gun, *Fam* tommy gun

mitrailleur [mitrajœr] NM machine-gunner; *Mil, Aviat* m. arrière rear gunner
ADJ fusil m. Bren gun

mitrailleuse [mitrajøz] NF machine gun

mitral, -ale, -aux, -ales [mitral, -o] ADJ *Anat* mitral

mitre [mitr] NF 1 *(d'évêque)* mitre, *Am* miter 2 *Tech (de cheminée)* cowl

mitré [mitre] ADJ *(abbé)* mitred, *Am* mitered

mitron [mitrɔ̃] NM baker's boy

mi-voix (à) ADV in an undertone, under one's breath

mix [miks] NM *Mktg (marchéage)* mix; m. de produits product mix

mixage [miksaʒ] NM *Cin, Radio (procédé)* mixing; *(résultat)* (sound) mix; m. magnétique final master soundtrack

mixer [mikse] VT 1 *Cin, Radio* to mix 2 *Culin* to blend, to liquidize

mixe(u)r [miksœr] NM mixer; *(pour rendre liquide)* liquidizer

mixité [miksite] NF *Scol* co-education

mixte [mikst] ADJ 1 *(des deux sexes)* mixed; école m. mixed *or* co-educational school; *Tennis* double m. mixed doubles 2 *(combiné)* train m. composite train *(goods and passengers)*; commission m. joint commission; billet m. combined rail and road ticket; mariage m. mixed marriage; cuisinière m. gas and electric cooker

mixtion [mikstjɔ̃] NF *Pharm (action) (de drogues etc)* compounding; *(médicament)* mixture

mixture [mikstyr] NF 1 *Pharm* mixture 2 *Culin, Fig* concoction

MJC [ɛmʒize] NF *(abrév* maison des jeunes et de la culture) = youth club and arts centre

ml *(abrév* millilitre(s)) ml

MLF [ɛmɛlɛf] NM *abrév* Mouvement de libération des femmes

Mlle *(abrév* mademoiselle) Miss

Mlles *(abrév* mesdemoiselles) Misses

MM *(abrév* Messieurs) Messrs

mm *(abrév* millimètre(s)) mm

Mme *(abrév* Madame) Mrs

Mmes *abrév* Mesdames

MMS [ɛmɛmɛs] NM *Tél (abrév* multimedia messaging service) MMS

mnémonique [mnemɔnik] ADJ, NF mnemonic

mnémotechnie [mnemɔtɛkni] NF mnemonics

mnémotechnique [mnemɔtɛknik] ADJ mnemonic; un moyen m. a mnemonic
NF mnemonics

Mo [ɛmo] NM *Ordinat (abrév* méga-octet) Mb

mob [mɔb] NF *Fam* = Mobylette®

mobile [mɔbil] ADJ 1 *(qui peut être bougé) (cloison)* mobile, movable; *(feuillets)* loose; album à feuilles mobiles loose-leaf album 2 *(expression, regard)* shifting, changing; *(visage)* lively, expressive; *(organe, cartilage)* mobile, having freedom of movement; *(cible)* moving; *(personne âgée)* mobile; *(employé, main d'œuvre)* willing to move *or* relocate; *(population)* mobile, shifting; dans les pays pauvres les populations ont tendance à être plus mobiles people in poor countries tend to move around more; le boxeur est très m. the boxer is very nimble, the boxer is very quick on his feet; *Tech* organes mobi-

les sliding *or* working *or* moving parts 3 *Mil* gendarmerie m. ≃ flying squad; gendarme *ou* garde m. ≃ member of the flying squad; *Hist* garde nationale m. *(de 1848, de 1868-71)* militia; *Hist* la garde républicaine m. = the (State) security police 4 *Vieilli (humeur)* changeable

NM 1 *(motif) (du crime)* motive *(*de for); *Mktg* m. d'achat buying inducement, purchasing motivator 2 *(téléphone portable)* mobile (phone) 3 *Phys etc* moving body, body in motion 4 *(en décoration)*, *Beaux-Arts* mobile; *Mktg* m. publicitaire advertising mobile

mobile home, *pl* mobile homes [mɔbilom] NM mobile home

mobilier, -ière [mɔbilje, -jɛr] ADJ *Jur* movable, personal; biens mobiliers personal property, chattels; *Fin* valeurs mobilières stocks and shares, transferable securities
NM *(ameublement)* furniture; m. de bureau office furniture; m. de présentation display stands
▸ ▸ m. national government property; m. urbain street furniture

> Do not confuse with **meuble**.

mobilisable [mɔbilizabl] ADJ 1 *Mil (troupes)* which can be mobilized; les jeunes de moins de 18 ans ne sont pas mobilisables young people under 18 are not eligible for call-up 2 *(créance)* discountable

mobilisateur, -trice [mɔbilizatœr, -tris] ADJ motivating; slogan m. rallying cry; un appel m. a call to rally the troops

mobilisation [mɔbilizasjɔ̃] NF *(de troupes)* mobilization; *Fin (de capital)* raising; m. de fonds raising of funds; *Mil* ordre de m. générale general mobilization order; les syndicats comptent beaucoup sur la m. des enseignants contre ce projet de réforme the unions are relying heavily on the teachers rallying to fight this proposed reform; nous avons besoin d'une m. des électeurs/ consommateurs pour dire non à … we need voters/consumers to mobilize *or* rally and say no to …; on sent un manque de m. total chez les étudiants en faveur de/contre ces nouvelles mesures students seem to be totally unwilling to rally in order to support/ fight these new measures

mobilisé, -ée [mɔbilize] ADJ *(troupes)* mobilized; *(réservistes)* called up
N serviceman, f servicewoman; un m. de la guerre de 14 a soldier in the First World War; les mobilisés de la dernière guerre those who served in the last war

mobiliser [mɔbilize] VT *(troupes)* to mobilize; *(réserviste)* to call up; *(syndicat, électorat)* to rally; *(ressources)* to mobilize; *(créances)* to discount; *(capital, argent)* to raise; m. toute son énergie to summon up all one's energy; *(de son travail, ses enfants)* to use up all one's energy; il faut m. les énergies we'll have to mobilize people
VPR se mobiliser to mobilize; se m. contre/ en faveur de qch to rally against/in support of sth

mobilité [mɔbilite] NF *(de la population etc)* mobility; *(dans le travail)* willingness to move *or* relocate; *(des organes)* freedom of movement; *Fig (de caractère, d'humeur)* changeability; la m. de son visage est remarquable he has a remarkably lively face; personnes à m. réduite people of reduced mobility; la m. de la mâchoire inférieure est affectée the movement of the lower jaw is affected; *Écon* m. sociale upward mobility

Mobylette® [mɔbilɛt] NF moped; faire de la M. to ride a moped; elle y va en *ou* à M. she goes there on her moped

mocassin [mɔkasɛ̃] NM moccasin

moche [mɔʃ] ADJ *Fam* **1** *(individu, chose)* hideous, ugly; **qu'est-ce qu'elle est m. aujourd'hui!** she looks a real sight today!; **c'est m. ces rideaux bleus avec ce canapé rose!** those blue curtains look really hideous with that pink sofa!; **je ne trouve pas qu'il soit m.** I don't think he's bad-looking **2** *(appréciation morale)* rotten, nasty; **c'est m. ce qu'ils t'ont fait** it's rotten what they did to you; **c'est trop m. de mourir à vingt ans** it's terrible to die at twenty

mocheté [mɔʃte] NF *Fam (laideur)* ugliness; **c'est d'une m.!** what an eyesore!, it's absolutely hideous!; **la mode de cet été est d'une m.!** this summer's fashions are hideous!; **quelle m., cette fille!** that girl's such a dog!

modal, -ale, -aux, -ales [mɔdal, -o] ADJ, NM *Ling* modal SEE GRAMMAR A57–61; B39–40

modalité [mɔdalite] NF **1** method, mode; *(d'application d'une loi)* mode; *Jur* **modalités** *(restrictive)* clauses; **modalités de paiement** *(liquide, chèque etc)* methods of payment; *(conditions)* terms or conditions of payment; **modalités d'examen** examination procedure; *Fin* **modalités d'une émission** terms and conditions of an issue; **modalités de financement** financing terms or conditions **2** *Phil, Mus, Gram* modality

mode[1] [mɔd] NF **1** fashion; **la m. est aux couleurs pastel** pastels are in (fashion); **la m. des pantalons pattes d'éléphant est revenue** flares are back (in fashion); **la m. du long est passée** long skirts are out (of fashion); **lancer la m. de qch** to set the fashion for sth, to make sth fashionable; **être à la m.** to be in fashion or in vogue, to be all the rage; **ta sœur est très à la m.** your sister's very fashionable or *Fam* trendy; **robe à la m.** fashionable or stylish dress; **revenir à la m.** to come back (into fashion); **passer de m.** to go out of fashion; **tu ne trouves pas que c'est un peu passé de m.?** don't you think it's a bit old-fashioned?; **à l'ancienne m.** in the old style; **journal de m.** fashion magazine; **un professionnel de la m.** a fashion professional; **à la m. de …** after the style or manner of …; **neveu/nièce à la m. de Bretagne** first cousin once removed **2** *Arch* **modes** *(vêtements)* fashions; **gravures de modes** fashion plates; **magasin de modes** milliner's shop

ADJ INV **le coloris m.** fashionable shades or colours, the shades or colours in fashion; **elle est toujours habillée très m.** she's always dressed very fashionably; **c'est très m.** it's very fashionable, it's very much in fashion

mode[2] NM **1** *(d'éducation etc)* method, mode; **m. d'emploi** instructions; **m. de vie** lifestyle, way of life; **m. de cuisson** cooking instructions; **m. opératoire** modus operandi; **m. de gestion** management method or style; **m. d'expression** means of expression; **m. d'expédition** method of delivery; **m. de classement** filing system; **m. de codification** coding method; **m. de paiement** *ou* **de règlement** method of payment; *Pol* **m. de scrutin** voting system; **m. de transport** method of transport; *Aut* **m. de conduite hiver** winter driving mode; *Aut* **m. de sélecteur de vitesses** gear selector; *Aut* **m. dégradé** limp-home mode **2** *Gram* mood; *Mus, Ordinat* mode SEE GRAMMAR A40; B32–5

▸▸ *Ordinat* **m. ajout** append mode; **m. amélioré** enhanced mode; **m. brouillon** draft mode; **m. caractère** character mode; **m. continu** continuous mode; *(de transmission)* burst mode; **m. conversationnel** *(d'un modem)* conversation mode; **m. dialogue** *(d'un modem)* dialog(ue) mode; **m. différé** non real-time mode, off-line mode; **m. direct** real-time mode; *Typ* **m. 'à la française'** portrait mode; **m. insertion** insert mode; *Typ* **m.**

'à l'italienne' landscape mode; **m. lecture seule** read-only mode; **m. linéaire** straight-line method; **m. machine à écrire** typewriter mode; **m. multitâche** multitask(ing) mode; **m. paysage** landscape mode; **m. point** bit-map; **m. portrait** portrait mode; **m. de prévisualisation** preview mode; **m. survol** browse mode; **m. sélectif** veto mode; **m. texte** text mode

modelage [mɔdlaʒ] NM *(action)* *(de l'argile etc)* modelling; *(résultat)* model

modèle [mɔdɛl] NM **1** *(exemple)* model; **m. d'écriture** handwriting copy; **m. de lettre** standard letter; **machines toutes bâties sur le même m.** machines all built to one pattern or on or along the same lines; **faites un résumé de ce texte en vous aidant du m.** summarize this text along the same lines; **prendre qn pour m.** to take sb as one's (role) model, to model oneself on; **Anne n'est pas un m. (à suivre)** don't follow Anne's example or lead; **le m. américain/japonais** the American/Japanese model; **m. de générosité/fidélité** model of generosity/fidelity; **m. de vertu** paragon or model of virtue

2 *Com (version)* model; **m. sport/deux portes** sports/two-door model; **m. dernier cri** car of the latest design; **ils ont présenté leur nouveau m. au salon de l'auto** they unveiled their new model at the car show; **ce m. existe aussi en rouge** this model also comes in or is also available in red

3 *Couture (de robe)* style; *(de tricot)* pattern; *Beaux-Arts (artist's)* model; **vous n'auriez pas un plus grand m.?** do you have it in a larger size?; **dessiné d'après m.** drawn from life; **servir de m. à un artiste** to sit or model for an artist

4 *Écon, Math, Ling etc (représentation schématique)* model; **m. de décision** decision model; **m. de décision en arborescence** decision-tree model; **m. du chemin critique** critical path model; **m. décisionnel** *ou* **déterministe** decision model; **m. mathématique** mathematical model

ADJ **époux m.** model or exemplary husband; **l'employé m.** the model employee; **adopter une conduite m.** to behave in an exemplary manner; **appartement/maison m.** show flat/house

▸▸ *Com, Ind* **m. déposé** registered pattern or model; **m.-phare** flagship; **m. réduit** scale model; **m. réduit de yacht/d'avion** model yacht/airplane; **amateurs de modèles réduits** model enthusiasts

modelé [mɔdle] NM **1** *Beaux-Arts* relief; *(de sculpture)* contours **2** *Géog* relief

modeler [mɔdle] (**je modèle; je modèlerai**) **VT** *(argile, cire)* to model, to mould, *Am* to mold; *Fig (caractère)* to shape, to mould; *(destinée)* to shape; **il avait un corps d'athlète, modelé par l'exercice physique** he had the body of an athlete, shaped by physical exercise; **un lobe d'oreille délicatement modelé** a delicately shaped earlobe; **l'eau/l'érosion a modelé le relief de la côte** water/erosion has shaped the coastline; **m. sa personnalité sur celle de qn** to model oneself on sb

VPR se modeler sur qn to take sb as one's model, to model oneself on sb

modeleur, -euse [mɔdlœr, -øz] N *Beaux-Arts* modeller; *Tech, Ind* pattern maker

modélisation [mɔdelizasjɔ̃] NF modelling

modélisme [mɔdelism] NM model-making; **un passionné de m.** a keen model-maker

modéliste [mɔdelist] N **1** *(de maquette)* model-maker **2** *(de vêtements)* dress designer

modem [mɔdɛm] NM *Ordinat* modem; **carte m.** modem card; **m. externe** external modem; **m. fax** fax modem; **m. interne** internal modem; **m. longue distance** long-haul

modem; **m. nul** null modem; **m. RNIS** ISDN modem; **envoyer qch à qn par m.** to modem sth to sb, to send sth to sb by modem

modem-câble, *pl* **modems-câbles** NM cable modem

modem-télécopieur, *pl* **modems-télécopieurs** NM fax-modem

modérateur, -trice [mɔderatœr, -tris] ADJ moderating, restraining

N moderating influence

NM **1** *(de moteur etc)* regulator, governor; *Nucl* moderator **2** *(dans un forum Internet)* regulator

modération [mɔderasjɔ̃] NF **1** *(retenue)* moderation, restraint; **sa réponse était pleine de m.** his answer was very restrained; **tu devrais faire preuve d'un peu plus de m. dans tes propos** you should curb your tongue a bit more; **avec m.** in or with moderation **2** *(réduction) (de prix)* restriction; *(fiscale)* reduction; **promettre une m. des impôts** to promise lower taxes

modéré, -ée [mɔdere] ADJ *(personne, propos)* moderate, restrained; *(ton, attitude)* restrained; *(température)* moderate; *(prix etc)* reasonable, moderate; *(acclamations)* subdued

N *Pol* moderate

modérément [mɔderemɑ̃] ADV moderately, in moderation; **j'aime m. le whisky** I'm moderately fond of whisky; **il fume, mais m.** he smokes, but in moderation; *Iron* **j'ai m. apprécié sa conduite** I was less than overwhelmed by his behaviour; **j'ai m. apprécié qu'il dise que je ronflais!** I didn't exactly appreciate his saying I snored!; **j'apprécie m. qu'on mette le nez dans mes affaires** I'm not very keen on people sticking their noses into my business

modérer [mɔdere] (**je modère; je modérerai**) **VT 1** *(passions, désirs, envies)* to moderate, to restrain, to curb; *(vitesse)* to reduce, to slacken; *Ind* **m. les cadences** to reduce or lower production rates; **m. ses ambitions** to lower one's sights, to be less ambitious; **je te prie de m. ton langage!** please mind your tongue! **2** *(réduire) (prix)* to restrict

VPR se modérer *(s'apaiser)* to control oneself, to calm down; *(faire preuve de sobriété)* to restrain oneself

moderne [mɔdɛrn] ADJ *(concept, monde, médecine, musique, danse)* modern; *(équipement, méthode, technologie, idée, pensée)* modern, up-to-date; **studio équipé de tout le confort m.** studio flat with all modern conveniences; **découverte m.** recent discovery; **la femme m. travaille** the modern woman goes out to work; *Hist* **la période m.** the modern period, recent history; **grec m.** modern Greek; **étudier les lettres modernes** *(en France)* to study French language and literature

NM **le m.** *(style)* (the) modern style; **nous avons tout meublé en m.** all our furniture is modern; **mélanger le m. et l'ancien** to mix old and new

N *(personne)* modern

modernisation [mɔdɛrnizasjɔ̃] NF modernization; **les efforts de m. de l'enseignement** the attempts to modernize education

moderniser [mɔdɛrnize] VT to modernize, to bring up to date

modernisme [mɔdɛrnism] NM modernism

moderniste [mɔdɛrnist] ADJ, N modernist

modernité [mɔdɛrnite] NF modernity; **on est tout d'abord frappé par sa m.** the first thing that strikes you is how modern it is; **il a toujours été un défenseur de la m.** he has always defended what is modern

modern style [mɔdɛrnstil] NM art nouveau

ADJ INVart nouveau; **balcon m.** art nouveau balcony

modeste [mɔdɛst] ADJ **1** *(sans orgueil) (personne)* modest, unassuming, self-effacing **2** *(sans faste) (revenu, hôtel, appartement, repas)* modest; *(milieu)* modest, humble; *(personne)* humble, simple; **avoir un train de vie m.** to have a modest lifestyle *or* way of life; **être d'une origine m.** to be of humble origin; **une pièce aux dimensions modestes** a small room, a room of modest dimensions **3** *Litt Vieilli (pudique)* modest ▸ Nne faites pas le/la m. don't be (so) modest; **elle joue les modestes** she's acting modest

modestement [mɔdɛstəmã] ADV *(sourire, parler)* modestly; **être m. logé** to live in modest surroundings

modestie [mɔdɛsti] NF **1** *(de personne, revenu)* modesty; **fausse m.** false modesty **2** *Litt Vieilli (pudeur)* modesty

modicité [mɔdisite] NF *(de moyens, revenus)* slenderness; *(de prix)* moderateness, lowness, reasonableness; **la m. de ses revenus l'empêchait de partir en vacances** his income was too small *or* low to allow him to go on holiday; **malgré la m. du loyer** despite the low rent

modifiable [mɔdifjabl] ADJ modifiable; **jouet m.** Transformer®; **après cela, le texte ne sera plus m.** after that, the text cannot be amended

modificateur, -trice [mɔdifikatœr, -tris] ADJ modifying ▸ NM modifier

modificatif, -ive [mɔdifikatif, -iv] ADJ modifying

modification [mɔdifikasjɔ̃] NF *(à un discours, un texte, une déclaration)* alteration, change, amendment, modification; *(à une loi, une convention, un contrat)* amendment; *(à un plan, un programme, une carte)* alteration, change; *(physique)* change; **apporter** *ou* **faire une m. à qch** to make an alteration to *or* modify sth

modifier [mɔdifje] *(pr sub, impf n.* **modifiions, v. modifiiez)** VT **1** *(texte, discours, déclaration)* to alter, to change, to amend, to modify; *(projet de loi, convention)* to amend; *(plan, programme, façon de faire)* to alter, to change; **ne modifiez rien** don't change anything, don't make any changes *or* alterations; **j'ai modifié la disposition des meubles** I've moved *or* changed the furniture around; *Naut* **la route** to alter course **2** *Gram (verbe)* to qualify, to modify ▸ VPR **se modifier** to alter, to be modified *or* altered

modique [mɔdik] ADJ *(coût, prix etc)* moderate, modest, reasonable; *(revenu)* modest, slender; **pour la m. somme de 50 euros** for the modest sum of 50 euros, for a mere 50 euros; *Iron* **sa voiture a coûté la m. somme de 50 000 euros** his car cost a cool 50,000 euros

modiquement [mɔdikmã] ADV **m. payé** poorly paid

modiste [mɔdist] NF milliner

modulable [mɔdylabl] ADJ *(horaires, tarif)* flexible; *(salle)* multi-purpose; *(espace intérieur)* adjustable

modulaire [mɔdylɛr] ADJ modular

modulateur, -trice [mɔdylatœr, -tris] *Radio etc* ADJ *(valve etc)* modulating ▸ NM modulator; **m. de fréquence** converter

modulation [mɔdylasjɔ̃] NF **1** *Mus* modulation, transition; *Fig* **une m. des paiements serait souhaitable pour les nouveaux adhérents** it would be desirable to adjust the rate of payment for new members **2** *(de la voix)* modulation, inflexion **3** *Radio etc* modulation, mod; **m. d'amplitude** ampli-

tude modulation; **m. de fréquence** frequency modulation **4** *Ling* modulation

module [mɔdyl] NM *(élément constitutif d'un tout)* unit; *Archit, Astronaut, Ordinat* module; *Math, Tech, Phys* modulus; *Univ* **m. (d'enseignement)** module; *Astronaut* **m. lunaire/de commande** lunar/command module; *Ordinat* **m. d'aide** help module; *Ordinat* **m. d'extension** plug-in

moduler [mɔdyle] VT*(des sons),* Phys *(amplitude etc)* to modulate; *(sa voix)* to inflect, to modulate; *Fig* **m. des paiements** to adjust the rate of payment; **m. la thérapeutique en fonction des résultats obtenus** to adjust the treatment in the light of results ▸ VI *Mus* to modulate

modus vivendi [mɔdysvivɛ̃di] NM INV modus vivendi

moé [mwe] PRON *Can Fam* me

moelle [mwal] NF **1** *(d'os)* marrow, *Spéc* medulla; **m. épinière** spinal cord; **m. osseuse** bone marrow; **greffe de m. osseuse** bone marrow transplant; **os à m.** marrowbone; *Fig* **anglais jusqu'à la m.** English to the core; *Fig* **glacé jusqu'à la m.** frozen to the bone *or* to the marrow; *Fig* **corrompu** *ou* **pourri jusqu'à la m.** rotten to the core **2** *Bot* pith

moelleusement [mwaløzmã] ADV snugly; **s'enfoncer m. dans un coussin de plumes** to snuggle down into a feather cushion; **être m. installé dans son lit** to be snuggled up in bed, to be snugly tucked up in bed; **être m. installé dans un fauteuil/sous une couette** to be snuggled up in an armchair/under an eiderdown

moelleux, -euse [mwalø, -øz] ADJ *(tapis, étoffe, pull)* (velvety) soft; *(coussin, lit)* soft; *(couverture, couette)* soft, downy; *(caramel, substance)* smooth; *(gâteau)* moist; *(vin, voix)* mellow, smooth ▸ NM *(d'un tapis, d'une étoffe, d'un pull)* (velvety) softness, velvetiness; *(d'un lit, de coussins)* softness; *(d'une couverture)* softness, downiness; *(d'une voix, d'un vin)* mellowness, smoothness; **un vin qui a du m.** a mellow *or* smooth wine

moellon [mwalɔ̃] NM quarry stone; **m. brut** rubble(stone); **m. d'appareil** ashlar

mœurs [mœr(s)] NFPL **1** *(coutumes) (de gens)* manners, customs; *(de pays, d'époque etc)* customs, *Fml* mores; *(d'animaux)* habits; **vivre avec les m. de son temps** to be in tune with the times; **il a de drôles de m.!** he's got some funny habits *or* ways!; **entrer** *ou* **passer dans les m.** to become part of everyday life **2** *(conduite en matière sexuelle) Jur* **certificat de bonne vie et m.** certificate of good character; **la brigade des m.,** *Fam* **les M.** ≃ the vice squad; **attentat aux m.** sexual offence; **affaire de m.** sex case; **il a des m. spéciales** *ou* **particulières** he's the other way inclined; **femme de m. légères** *ou* **faciles** woman of easy virtue **3** *(sens moral)* morals; **gens sans m.** unprincipled people; *Arch* **bonnes m.** morality; **c'est contraire aux bonnes m.** it is immoral *or* indecent; *Arch* **avoir des m.** to be of good moral character

mofette [mɔfɛt] NF *(mammifère)* skunk

moffler [mɔfle] VT *Belg Fam* **j'ai été mofflé** I failed my exam

mogette [mɔʒɛt] NF *Région* bean

mohair [mɔɛr] NM *Tex* mohair; **laine m.** mohair wool; **un pull en m.** a mohair sweater

Mohican [mɔikã] NM Mohican

moi [mwa] PRON PERS VOIR GRAMMAIRE A27; B20–1 **1** *(sujet)* I; **c'est moi** it's me, *Fml* it is I; **il est plus âgé que moi** he is older than me *or* than I am; **elle est invitée et m. aussi** she's invited and so am I; **qui vient avec nous? – m.** who's coming with us? – I am *or* me; **m. m'sieur, m. m'sieur, je connais la réponse!** me sir,

me sir, I know the answer; **m., je veux bien (le faire)** I don't mind (doing it); **m. qui vous parle** I'm telling you; **m., quand je serai grand** when I grow up; *très Fam* **m., les femmes, c'est fini** I've had it with women

2 *(objet)* me; **il nous accuse mon frère et m.** he's accusing my brother and me; **et m.? vous m'oubliez?** what about me? have you forgotten me?; **vous me soupçonnez, m.!** you suspect me!; **avec m.** with me; **venez à m.** come to me; **à m.!** help!; **à m., au secours!** help! help!; **ce livre est à m.** this book is mine *or* belongs to me; **un ami à m.** a friend of mine; **ces vers ne sont pas de m.** these verses are not mine; **de vous à m.** between you and me, between ourselves, *Fam* between you, me and the gatepost; **c'est pour m.** *(quand on apporte l'addition)* I'll get this *or* it **3** *(après impératif)* **laissez-moi tranquille** leave me alone; **donnez-le-moi** give it to me; **dis-moi, où est-ce que tu as mis le dossier bleu?** (by the way *or* by the by *or* Am say,) where have you put the blue file?; **dites-moi, Jérôme, si nous allions à la mer cet été?** how about going to the seaside this year, Jérôme?, *Am* say, Jérôme, how about going to the seaside this year? ▸ NM ego, self; **culte du m.** egoism; **la psychanalyse nous aide à découvrir notre vrai m.** psychoanalysis helps us discover our true selves VOIR GRAMMAIRE A12

moignon [mwaɲɔ̃] NM *(de membre amputé etc)* stump

moi-même PRON PERS myself; *voir* même

moindre [mwɛ̃dr] ADJ **1** *(comp)* less(er); *(prix)* lower; *(quantité)* smaller; *(vitesse)* slower, lower; **question de m. importance** question of less(er) importance *or of* minor importance; **deux sur dix c'est un m. mal** two out of ten is not as bad as it might have been; **ce qui est un m. mal** so things aren't as bad as they might have been; **s'il arrive à s'en sortir avec seulement une jambe cassée, ce sera un m. mal** if he comes out of it with just a broken leg he'll be lucky VOIR GRAMMAIRE A26

2 *(superl)* **le/la m.** the least; **pas la m. chance** not the slightest *or* remotest *or* faintest chance; **c'est la m. des choses** *ou* **politesses** it's the least I/he/*etc* can do; **au m. reproche, il se met à pleurer** he bursts into tears at the slightest reproach; **au m. sourire il s'imagine qu'on s'intéresse à lui** the least little smile and he thinks you're interested in him; **il n'y a pas le m. espoir de les retrouver vivants** there isn't the slightest hope of finding them alive; **je ne lui ai pas fait le m. reproche** I didn't reproach him in the slightest *or* in the least **3** *Suisse Fam (malade)* ill; **se sentir m.** to feel ill *or* sick ▸ N **de deux maux il faut choisir le m.** you have to choose the lesser of two evils; **un expert, et non des moindres** no mean expert

moindrement [mwɛ̃drəmã] ADV *Litt, Can (souvent avec nég)* **sans être le m. intéressé/gêné** without being in the least bit interested/embarrassed; **je vous dérange? – pas le m.** am I disturbing you? – not at all *or* not in the slightest *or* not in the least

moine [mwan] NM **1** *Rel* monk, friar; *Prov* **l'habit ne fait pas le m.** clothes do not make the man; *Fig* **être gras comme un m.** to be fat, *esp Am* to be a real butterball; **mener une vie de m.** to live like a monk **2** *Arch (bassinoire)* bed warmer

moineau, -eaux [mwano] NM *(oiseau)* sparrow; *Fam* **c'est un vilain m.** he's a bad lot *or* a nasty piece of work; *Com* **têtes de m.** nuts *(of coal)*

moinillon [mwaniɲɔ̃] NM *Fam* young monk

MOINS [mwɛ̃]

ADV less **1** ▪ fewer **1** ▪ unless (à moins que) **2** ▪ the least **3** ▪ at least (du moins, au moins) **4**
PRÉP minus ▪ to

ADV 1 (comparatif) less; **je gagne m. que vous** I earn less than you (do); **elle gagne peu et lui m. encore** she doesn't earn much and he earns even less or Fml still less; **elle est m. intelligente que sa sœur** she's not as intelligent as her sister, she's less intelligent than her sister; **il est m. pingre qu'économe** he's not so much stingy as thrifty; **beaucoup m. long** much shorter; **m. d'argent** less money, not so much money, not as much money; **m. d'hommes/d'occasions** fewer or not so many men/opportunities; **j'ai eu m. de remords** I felt less remorse; **un peu m. de fierté** a little less pride; **plus on le punit, m. il travaille** the more he's punished, the less he works; **plus il vieillit, m. il a de cheveux** the older he gets, the less hair he has; Fam **m. je le vois, mieux je me porte** the less I see of him the better; **il travaille de m. en m.** he's working less and less; **m. de dix euros** less than or under ten euros; **celui-ci coûte dix euros de m. que l'autre** this is ten euros less than the other one; **il y a eu 20% de visiteurs de m.** ou en m. there have been 20% fewer visitors; **je ne peux pas vous le laisser à m.** I can't let you have it for less; **il a m. de trente ans** he's less than or under thirty; **les m. de trente ans** the under-thirties; **les jeunes et les m. jeunes** the young and the not so young; **vous compterez cela en m.** you can deduct that, you can take that off the total; **il est revenu avec un œil/un bras/une jambe en m.** he came back minus an eye/an arm/a leg; **nous étions à m. d'un kilomètre de l'église** we were less than a kilometre from the church, we were within one kilometre of the church; **en m. de dix minutes** in less than ten minutes; **en m. de temps qu'il ne faut pour le dire**, Fam **en m. de deux** in no time (at all); Fam **c'était m. une** it was a close shave, it was a close or near thing; **il est on ne peut m. soigneux/honnête** he's extremely untidy/dishonest, Fml he is untidy/dishonest in the extreme; **je n'en suis pas m. décidée à le faire** I'm still going to do it nonetheless; **il est gentil mais il n'en est pas m. vrai que …** he's very nice but it's true nonetheless that …; **pas m. de 200 personnes** no fewer than 200 people, Fam no less than 200 people; **pas m. de 2 000 euros/trois jours** no less than 2,000 euros/three days; **rien m. que** nothing less than; **ce n'est rien m. qu'un héros** he's nothing less than a hero; **ce n'est rien (de) m. qu'un miracle** it's nothing short of a miracle; **elle mérite des éloges non m. que son frère** she deserves no less praise than her brother, she deserves praise quite as much as her brother **VOIR GRAMMAIRE A26**

2 à m. d'avis contraire unless I/you/etc hear to the contrary; **à m. d'un imprévu/un miracle/une catastrophe** barring something unforeseen/a miracle/a catastrophe, unless something unforeseen happens/a miracle happens/there's a catastrophe; **à m. de partir tout de suite** unless I/you/etc leave at once; **à m. que … + sub** unless …; **à m. que vous (ne) l'ordonniez** unless you order it

3 (superlatif) **le m.** the least; **les élèves les m. appliqués** the least industrious pupils; **le m. de gens possible** the smallest possible number of people, as few people as possible; **pas le m. du monde** not in the least or slightest, by no means; Prov **qui peut le plus peut le m.** you've/he's/etc done much more complicated things in your/his/etc time

4 du m. at least, that is to say, at all events;

c'est (tout) du m. ce qu'il dit that's what he says, at least; **au m.** at least; **gagner 20 000 euros par an au m.** to earn 20,000 euros a year at (the very) least; Fam **tu as fait ton travail, au m.?** you've done your work, I hope?; **c'est pour le m. surprenant** it's surprising, to say the least

PRÉP minus, less; **une heure m. cinq** five (minutes) to or Am of one; **six m. quatre égale deux** six minus four equals two; **il fait m. dix (degrés)** it's minus ten (degrees)
NM Math minus (sign)
N Fam un/une m. que rien a rat

> Attention: ne pas confondre **fewer** et **less** lorsque l'on traduit **moins**. Fewer s'utilise uniquement avec des termes dénombrables; **less** s'utilise avec des termes indénombrables ou dénombrables (bien que ce dernier emploi soit contesté).

moins-disant, pl **moins-disants** [mwɛ̃dizɑ̃] NM lowest bidder

moins-perçu, pl **moins-perçus** NM Fin outstanding amount, amount due or owing

moins-value, pl **moins-values** [mwɛ̃valy] NF Fin depreciation, drop in value; (après une vente) capital loss

moirage [mwaraʒ] NM (de soie etc) (action de moirer) watering

moire [mwar] NF **1** Tex moire, moiré; **m. de soie** watered silk **2** (reflet) shimmer

moiré [mware] ADJ **1** Tex (soie etc) watered, moiré **2** (aux reflets changeants) shimmering
NM = **moirure**

moirer [mware] VT **1** Tex (soie etc) to water **2** Litt to make shimmer

moirure [mwaryr] NF **1** Tex watered effect, moiré **2** Litt shimmer, shimmering

mois [mwa] NM **1** month; **au m. d'août** in (the month of) August; **louer qch au m.** to hire sth by the month; **pendant deux m.** for two months; **cent euros par m.** a hundred euros a month; **un m. de vacances/salaire** a month's holiday/wages; **le treizième m.** = one month's salary paid as a bonus; Bourse **m. d'échéance** trading month **VOIR GRAMMAIRE A81; B60–1 2** (de paie) month's wages or salary; **je n'ai pas encore touché mon m.** I still haven't received this month's wages or salary; **je dois deux m. à l'épicier** I haven't paid the grocer for two months

Moïse [mɔiz] N Bible Moses

moïse [mɔiz] NM (berceau) Moses basket

moisi [mwazi] ADJ (pain, gâteau, fromage) mouldy, Am moldy; (mur, tissu etc) mildewed, mildewy; (goût) musty; (odeur) musty, fusty
NM (sur pain, confiture, fromage) mould, Am mold; (sur mur, tissu) mildew; **odeur de m.** musty or fusty smell; **avoir un goût de m.** to taste mouldy or musty; **sentir le m.** to smell musty or fusty

moisir [mwazir] VI (de pain) to go mouldy or Am moldy; (de raisins) to go mouldy, to mildew; (de linge) to mildew; Fig **j'avais l'impression de m. dans cette ville** I felt I was mouldering away in that town; **il m'a laissé m. deux heures** he left me cooling my heels for two hours; Fig Fam **on ne va pas m. ici** (partons) let's not hang about here
VT (pain) to make mouldy or Am moldy; (raisins, linge) to mildew

moisissure [mwazisyr] NF **1** (partie moisie) mould, Am mold; **moisissures** mouldy bits, mould **2** (processus) (formation of) mould or Am mold; **une forte odeur de m.** a strong musty smell

moisson [mwasɔ̃] NF **1** (action) (de céréales) harvest(ing); (époque) harvest time; **faire la m.** ou **les moissons** to harvest; Fig **une m. de**

documents a pile or sheaf of documents; **une m. d'idées** a wealth of ideas **2** (récolte) crop, harvest; **rentrer la m.** to bring in the crops or the harvest

moissonnage [mwasɔnaʒ] NM harvesting, reaping

moissonner [mwasɔne] VT **1** (céréales) to reap, to harvest; (champ) to reap; (récoltes) to harvest, to gather (in); **lundi prochain, on commence à m.** we'll start harvesting next Monday; Litt Fig **m. des informations** to gather a wealth of information; **m. des lauriers** to reap or win laurels **2** Litt **la guerre moissonne les vies humaines** war cuts short many lives

moissonneur, -euse [mwasɔnœr, -øz] N harvester, reaper
NF **moissonneuse** (machine) reaper, reaping machine

moissonneuse-batteuse, pl **moissonneuses-batteuses** NF combine (harvester)

moissonneuse-lieuse, pl **moissonneuses-lieuses** NF reaper-binder

moite [mwat] ADJ (mains, front) sweaty, clammy; (atmosphère, air) muggy; (chaleur) moist; **j'avais les mains moites de sueur** my hands were sweaty, my hands were damp with sweat

moiteur [mwatœr] NF (de mains, du front) sweatiness, clamminess; (de terre) wetness; (d'atmosphère, d'air) mugginess

moitié [mwatje] NF **1** half; **quelle est la m. de dix?** what is half of ten?; **la m. de la production** half (of) the production; **qui veut la m. d'une banane?** who wants half (of) a banana?; **la bouteille était à m. pleine/vide** the bottle was half full/empty; **deux moitiés** two halves; **partagé en deux moitiés** divided into two halves, halved; **vendre qch à m. prix** to sell sth (at) half price; **réduit de m.** reduced by half; Fam **m.-m.** fifty-fifty; **faire m.-m.** to go halves or fifty-fifty; **ça devrait faire à peu près m.-m.** that should be us just about even; **se mettre** ou **être de m. avec qn** to go halves with sb, to go fifty-fifty with sb; **il est pour m. responsable** he is equally or just as much to blame, half the responsibility is his; **à m. half;** à **m. mort/cuit/nu/endormi** half-dead/-cooked/-naked/-asleep; **faire les choses à m.** to do things by halves; **elle ne fait pas les choses à m.** she doesn't do things by halves **VOIR GRAMMAIRE A5; A12 2** Hum Fam (époux, épouse) **ma (chère) m.** my better half

ADV half; **m. riant, m. pleurant** half laughing, half crying; **m. anglaise, m. écossaise** half English, half Scottish; **m. plus** half as much again; **il y a m. de plus de monde que l'année dernière** there are half as many people again as there were last year; **m. moins gros/cher** fifty per cent smaller/cheaper; **c'est m. moins gros que l'autre** it's half the size of the other one; **ça m'a coûté m. moins cher** it cost me half the price; **m. moins de monde** fifty per cent fewer people; **il y a m. moins de monde qu'à la première représentation** there are half the people there were at the first performance

moitir [mwatir] VT Vieilli Tech (papier etc) to moisten

moka [mɔka] NM (café) mocha (coffee); (gâteau) mocha or coffee cake; **glace au m.** coffee ice cream
N Géog **M.** Mocha, Mokha

mol voir **mou**[1]

molaire[1] [mɔler] NF molar

molaire[2] ADJ Phys molar

molasse [mɔlas] NF Géol molasse

moldave [mɔldav] ADJ Moldavian
N **M.** Moldavian

Moldavie [mɔldavi] NF Moldavia

mole [mɔl] NF *Phys* mole

môle [mol] NM *(brise-lames)* breakwater, mole; *(quai)* pier

moléculaire [mɔlekylɛr] ADJ molecular

molécule [mɔlekyl] NF molecule

molécule-gramme, *pl* **molécules-grammes** NF *Phys* gram(me) molecule

molène [mɔlɛn] NF *Bot* mullein

moleskine [mɔleskin] NF imitation leather; *(coton)* moleskin

molester [mɔleste] VT m. qn to rough sb up; **se faire m. par la police** to be roughed up by the police

> Il faut noter que le verbe anglais **to molest** est un faux ami. Il signifie le plus souvent **faire subir des sévices sexuels**.

moletage [mɔltaʒ] NM milling, knurling

moleter [mɔlte] VT (je molette; je moletterai) to mill, to knurl

molette [mɔlɛt] NF **1** *(d'éperon)* rowel; *(de briquet)* wheel; *(de jumelles)* focus wheel; **m. de réglage** control knob **2** *(pour le verre etc)* cutting wheel **3** *Ordinat* **m. de défilement** scroll wheel

Molières [mɔljɛr] NMPL les M. *(cérémonie)* = French theatre awards ceremony

moliéresque [mɔljeresk] ADJ *(situation, verve)* reminiscent of Molière

mollah [mɔla] NM *Rel* mullah

mollard [mɔlar] NM *Vulg* gob of spit

mollarder [mɔlarde] VI *Vulg* to spit, *Br* to gob

mollasse [mɔlas] ADJ flabby; *Fig Fam (personne) (physiquement)* lethargic; *(moralement)* spineless
▪ N *Fam* **un/une m.** a lazy lump (of a man/woman)

mollasson, -onne [mɔlasɔ̃, -ɔn] *Fam* ADJ *(personne) (physiquement)* lethargic; *(moralement)* spineless
▪ N **un m./une mollassonne** a lazy lump (of a man/woman)

molle *voir* mou¹

mollement [mɔlmɑ̃] ADV **1** *(avec abandon)* languidly; *(avec lenteur)* gently; **les barques se balançaient m. sur l'eau** the small boats were bobbing gently on the water; **m. étendu sur sa couche** stretched out languidly on his couch **2** *(sans énergie) (répondre, se déplacer)* feebly, weakly; *(serrer la main)* limply; *(protester, réagir)* feebly

mollesse [mɔles] NF **1** *(manque d'énergie)* lethargy; *(de tissus, muscles)* flabbiness; *(de style)* flabbiness, limpness; *(de gouvernement)* laxity, laxness; *Beaux-Arts* **la m. du trait** the lack of vigour in the brushstrokes **2** *(de coussin, matelas, chaise etc)* softness

mollet¹ [mɔlɛ] ADJ M *(œuf)* soft-boiled; **pain m.** (soft) bread roll

mollet² NM *Anat* calf; **des mollets de coq** spindly legs VOIR GRAMMAIRE A12

molletière [mɔltjɛr] ADJ F **bandes molletières** puttees
▪ NF puttee

molleton [mɔltɔ̃] NM *(en coton)* flannelette; *(en laine)* flannel; *(de table)* table felt

molletonné [mɔltɔne] ADJ *(gants, veste)* fleece-lined

molletonner [mɔltɔne] VT to line with fleece

mollir [mɔlir] VI *(du vent)* to die down, to abate; *(de courage, d'enthousiasme)* to flag, to slacken; **je sentis mes jambes m.** I felt my legs give way (beneath me); **le sol mollissait sous mes pieds** the ground was giving way beneath my feet
▪ VT *Naut (cordage)* to slacken, to ease, to slack off; *(barre)* to ease

mollo [mɔlo] ADV *Fam* **y aller m.** to take it easy

mollusque [mɔlysk] NM **1** *Zool* mollusc, *Am* mollusk **2** *Fam (personne)* lazy lump

molosse [mɔlɔs] NM watchdog, guard dog

molybdène [mɔlibdɛn] NM *Minér* molybdenum

môme [mom] N *Fam (enfant)* kid
▪ NF *Arg (femme, fille)* chick; *(petite amie)* girl ADJ *Fam* **quand j'étais (tout) m.** when I was (just) a kid

moment [mɔmɑ̃] NM **1** *(espace de temps)* moment; **le m. venu** *(passé)* when the time came; *(futur)* when the time comes; **à ce m.-là** then; *Fig (dans ces conditions)* if that's the case, in that case; **s'il ne peut pas te ramener, à ce m.-là tu m'appelles et je passerai** if he can't bring you back, then ring me and I'll come and get you; **à un m. donné** at one point; **c'est le bon m. pour ...** now is the (right) time to ...; **c'est le m. ou jamais** it's now or never; **c'est le m. ou jamais de lui dire ce que tu penses** now's the time (if ever there was one) to tell him what you think; **un m.!** one moment!, just a moment!; **je suis à vous dans un m.** I'll be with you in a moment; **en ce m.** at the moment, just now, at present; **à quel m. de l'année/la semaine?** at what time of the year/the week?; **à quel m. de l'histoire/sa vie?** at what stage of *or* point in the story/his life?; **il ne me faut rien pour le m.** I don't need anything at the moment *or* for the moment *or* for the time being; **sur le m.** at the time; **dans ces moments, on ne réfléchit pas** at times like that, you don't think; **passer un bon m.** to have a good time; **attendre le m. opportun** to wait for an opportune moment *or* the right moment; **arriver au bon m.** to arrive at just the right time; **ce n'est qu'un mauvais m. à passer** it'll soon be over with; **j'ai eu un m. de honte** for a moment I felt ashamed; **elle n'a pas eu un m. de repos aujourd'hui** she hasn't had a moment's rest today; **elle n'a pas un m. à elle** she hasn't a moment *or* minute to herself; **elle en a pour un m. avec ce travail** the work'll keep her busy for a (good) while; **par moments** at times, now and again; **d'un m. à l'autre** (at) any moment *or* time *or* minute; **à tout m., à tous moments** *(sans cesse)* constantly; *(n'importe quand)* at any moment; **il vaut mieux lui demander dans un de ses bons moments** it's better to ask him when he's in one of his good moods; **dans un m. de bonté** in a moment of kindness; **au m. de partir** just as I/he/etc was leaving *or* about to leave; **il attend toujours le dernier m. pour nous dire ce qu'il a décidé** he always waits till the last moment *or* minute to tell us what he's decided; **les derniers moments de sa vie** the last moments of his life; **au m. de sa naissance/de l'accident/des élections** at the time of his birth/of the accident/of the elections; **jusqu'au m. où ...** until ...
2 du m. que ... seeing that ..., since ...
3 *(temps présent)* **le m.** the moment; **c'est le disque/la star du m.** it's the record/she's the star of the moment
4 *Phys (de force, d'inertie etc)* moment

momentané [mɔmɑ̃tane] ADJ *(effort, coup de cafard)* brief; *(absence, interruption)* brief, temporary; *(panne)* temporary; **je suis bloqué chez moi mais c'est m.** I'm stuck at home, but it won't be for long; **je prends ce bureau mais ce n'est que m.** I'm taking this office, but it's only a temporary measure

momentanément [mɔmɑ̃tanemɑ̃] ADV *(perdre connaissance, s'assoupir)* momentarily, for a moment, briefly; *(être absent, arrêter de fumer)* temporarily; *TV* **nos programmes sont m. interrompus** there is a temporary break in transmission

momerie [mɔmri] NF *Litt Vieilli* mummery; *(pratique insincère)* insincerity

mômerie [momri] NF *(enfantillage)* childishness, childish behaviour; **cesse tes mômeries** stop being so childish

momie [mɔmi] NF mummy

momification [mɔmifikasjɔ̃] NF mummification

momifier [mɔmifje] *(impf, pr sub* **n. momifiions, v. momifiiez)** VT to mummify
▪ VPR **se momifier** to become mummified; *Fig* to become fossilized

mon, ma, mes [mɔ̃, ma, me] ADJ POSS SEE GRAMMAR A30; B21 (**mon** *is used instead of* **ma** *before f words beginning with vowel or mute* **h**) **1** my; **m. ami/amie** my friend; **m. meilleur ami/ma meilleure amie** my best friend; **m. oncle et ma tante** my uncle and (my) aunt; **m. père et ma mère**, *Litt* **mes père et mère** my mother and father; **j'ai mis m. chapeau et mes gants** I put on my hat and (my) gloves; **un(e) de mes ami(e)s** one of my friends, a friend of mine; **un professeur de mes amis** a teacher friend of mine; *Fam* **j'aurai ma chambre à moi** I'll have my own room; *Fam* **m. imbécile de frère** my idiot of a brother; *Fam* **m. artiste de mari** my husband, the artist; *Fam* **alors, tu veux le rencontrer, m. artiste?** do you want to meet this artist of mine, then?; *Fam* **et voilà m.** Simon qui se met à rouspéter then old Simon starts grumbling; *Fam* **j'ai eu m. vendredi** I got Friday off
2 *(pour s'adresser à qn)* non, **m. général/capitaine** no, General/Captain; *Rel* **oui, ma sœur/ma mère/m. père** yes, Sister/Mother/Father; *Fml* **m. oncle, je vous écris pour demander ...** I'm writing to you, uncle, to ask you ...; **viens, m. enfant** come here, child

monacal, -ale, -aux, -ales [mɔnakal, -o] ADJ *(vie, calme)* monastic

monachisme [mɔnaʃism] NM monasticism

Monaco [mɔnako] N **(la principauté de) M.** (the principality of) Monaco

monade [mɔnad] NF *Phil* monad

monarchie [mɔnarʃi] NF monarchy; **m. constitutionnelle/absolue** constitutional/absolute monarchy; **m. parlementaire** parliamentary monarchy

monarchique [mɔnarʃik] ADJ monarchic(al)

monarchisme [mɔnarʃism] NM monarchism

monarchiste [mɔnarʃist] ADJ, N monarchist

monarque [mɔnark] NM monarch

monastère [mɔnastɛr] NM *(de moines)* monastery; *(de religieuses)* convent

monastique [mɔnastik] ADJ monastic

monaural, -ale, -aux, -ales [mɔnɔral, -o] ADJ monaural

monceau, -eaux [mɔ̃so] NM heap, pile

mondain, -aine [mɔ̃dɛ̃, -ɛn] ADJ **1** *(lieu)* fashionable; **réunion/soirée mondaine** society gathering/evening; *Journ* **carnet m., rubrique** *ou* **chronique mondaine** society news, gossip column; **écrivain/chroniqueur m.** society writer/columnist; **la brigade mondaine** ≃ the vice squad **2** *Péj (qui aime les mondanités)* **il est très m.** he likes moving in fashionable circles, he's a great socialite **3** *Rel (plaisirs etc)* worldly, earthly
▪ N socialite
▪ NF *Fam* **la Mondaine** ≃ the vice squad

> Il faut noter que l'adjectif anglais **mundane** est un faux ami. Il signifie **terre-à-terre**.

mondanité [mɔ̃danite] NF **1** society life; **je ne supporte pas sa m.** I can't bear his love of society **2 mondanités** social gatherings; *(politesses, conversations superficielles)* social niceties; *Journ* society news, gossip column **3** *Rel* worldliness

monde [mɔ̃d] NM **1** *(univers, humanité)* world; **le m. entier** the whole world; **dans le m. entier** *(connu, en vente)* worldwide, all over the world, the world over; **(que) le m. est petit!** it's a small world!; **faire le tour du m.** to go round the world; **faire le tour du m. à la voile** to sail round the world; **les quatre coins du m.** the four corners of the world *or* globe; **il est allé/a travaillé aux quatre coins du m.** he's been/worked all over the world; **parcourir** *ou* **courir le m.** to travel the world; **mettre qn au m.** to bring sb into the world, to give birth to sb; **être seul au m.** to be alone in the world; **il est encore de ce m.** he is still with us, he is still alive; **je ne te ferais souffrir pour rien au m.** I wouldn't hurt you for (anything in) the world; *Fam* **c'est un m.!**, **c'est quand même un m.!** that's a bit much!; *Fam* **c'est tout de même** *ou* **quand même un m. de ne pas pouvoir faire ce qu'on veut chez soi!** it's a bit much if you can't do what you want in your own home!; *Fam* **elle se fait toujours un m. de tout** she always gets worked up about everything; *Fam* **il n'y a pas de quoi s'en faire un m.** it's not worth getting worked up about, it's no big deal; **personne au m. ne me fera changer d'avis** no one in the world will make me change my mind; **un des seuls êtres en ce m. qui ...** one of the few people in the world who ...; **les meilleurs amis du m.** the best friends in the world; **vieux comme le m.** (as) old as the hills; **depuis que le m. est m.** since time began, since the beginning of time; **elle a volé à la face du m.** she stole things right under everybody's nose; *Fig* **c'est le m. à l'envers** the world's gone mad, the whole world's topsy-turvy; **le bout du m.** the ends of the earth; **ils habitent au bout du m.** they live at the back of beyond; *Fig Fam* **ce n'est pas le bout du m.!** *(c'est faisable)* it's not the end of the world!, it's no big deal!; *Fig Fam* **c'est le bout du m. s'il me faut deux jours pour terminer ce travail** I'll finish the job in two days at the outside *or* at the very most; **il faut de tout pour faire un m.** it takes all sorts (to make a world); **ainsi va le m.** it's the way of the world; **refaire le m.** to put the world to rights; *Iron* **tout est pour le mieux dans le meilleur des mondes** everything is for the best in the best of all possible worlds; **l'autre m.** the next world; **il vit dans un autre m.** he lives in another world; **elle est dans son m.** she's in her own little world; **en ce bas m.** here on earth

2 *(milieu)* world; **le m. de la haute finance** the world of high finance; **je ne suis pas de leur m.** I'm not in their set *or* crowd; **le (beau) m.** (fashionable) society, *Fam* the glitterati; **le grand m.** high society; **aller (beaucoup) dans le m.** to go out a great deal, to move in fashionable circles; **homme du m.** society man; *Iron* **embarquez-moi tout ce joli m. dans le panier à salade** throw this bunch *or* crew into the back of the van

3 *(gens)* people; **tout le m.** everybody, everyone; **il y a du m.** *(le lieu n'est pas désert)* there are some people; *(il y a foule)* there are a lot of people; *très Fam* **il y a du m. au balcon** she's well-endowed; **il y a trop de m.** it's too crowded, there are too many people; **peu de m.**, **pas grand m.** not many people, not a large crowd; **avoir du m. à dîner** to have people to dinner; **tu te moques du m.? je te demande d'arriver à 9 h et ...** what do you take me for? I asked you to be here by 9 o'clock and ...; *Fam* **les politiciens se fichent vraiment du m.** politicians really must think we're stupid; *très Fam* **je n'aime pas qu'on se foute du m.! quand on me dit une chose un jour ...** I don't like being taken for a bloody idiot! if I'm told one thing one day ...; **il connaît son m.** he knows the people he has to deal with; **comment va tout**

votre m.? how is your *or* the family?
4 *Arch (domestiques)* servants, men, hands
5 *(vie séculière)* **se retirer du m.** to withdraw from the world

mondial, -iale, -iaux, -iales [mɔ̃djal, -jo] ADJ *(crise, conflit, problème, ampleur)* worldwide, global; **à l'échelle mondiale** on a world(wide) scale, on a global scale; **la première/seconde guerre mondiale** the First/Second World War, World War One/Two
NM *Ftbl* **le M.** the World Cup

mondialement [mɔ̃djalmɑ̃] ADV throughout the world, universally; **m. reconnu pour son génie** known throughout the world *or* universally for his genius; **m. célèbre** world-famous, celebrated throughout the world

mondialisation [mɔ̃djalizasjɔ̃] NF globalization; **la m. libérale** liberal globalization

mondialiser [mɔ̃djalize] VT to globalize
VPR **se mondialiser** to become globalized; **la crise s'est rapidement mondialisée** the crisis has rapidly taken on an international dimension

mondovision [mɔ̃dovizjɔ̃] NF *TV* world television

monégasque [mɔnegask] ADJ Monacan, Monegasque
N **M.** Monacan, Monegasque

monème [mɔnɛm] NM *Ling* moneme

MONEP [mɔnɛp] NM *(abrév* **marché des options négociables de Paris)** MONEP

monétaire [mɔnetɛr] ADJ *(unité, système, questions)* monetary; **quelle est l'unité m. du Pérou?** what is the currency of Peru?; **marché m.** money market; **masse m.** money supply; *UE* **le serpent m.** the (currency) snake

monétarisme [mɔnetarism] NM *Écon* monetarism

monétariste [mɔnetarist] ADJ, N *Écon* monetarist

Monétique® [mɔnetik] NF *Fin* electronic money, e-money; *Banque* electronic banking

monétisation [mɔnetizasjɔ̃] NF *Écon* monetization

monétiser [mɔnetize] VT *Écon* to monetize

mongol, -ole [mɔ̃gɔl] ADJ **1** *(de Mongolie)* Mongol, Mongolian **2** *Fam Péj* moronic
NM *Ling* Mongolian
N **1** *Géog* **M.** Mongol, Mongolian **2** *Fam Péj* moron

Mongolie [mɔ̃gɔli] NF Mongolia

mongolien, -ienne [mɔ̃gɔljɛ̃, -jɛn] *Méd* ADJ **bébé m.** Down's syndrome baby, *Vieilli* mongol baby
N *(bébé)* Down's syndrome baby, *Vieilli* mongol (baby); *(personne)* person with Down's syndrome, *Vieilli* mongol

mongolique [mɔ̃gɔlik] ADJ Mongol(ian)

mongolisme [mɔ̃gɔlism] NM *Méd* Down's syndrome, *Vieilli* mongolism

mongoloïde [mɔ̃gɔlɔid] *Méd* ADJ *(traits)* mongoloid; *(individu)* affected by Down's syndrome
N *Vieilli* mongoloid

moniteur, -trice [mɔnitœr, -tris] N **1** *Sport* instructor, *f* instructress, coach; **m. d'auto-école/de ski** driving/ski instructor **2** *(dans une colonie de vacances)* assistant, *Am* (camp) counselor
NM *Tech, Méd, TV* monitor; *Ordinat (écran)* display unit; *Méd* **m. cardiaque** cardiac *or* heart monitor; *Ordinat* **m. SVGA** SVGA monitor; *Ordinat* **m. basse radiation** low-radiation monitor; **m. couleur** colour monitor; *Ordinat* **m. pleine page** A4 monitor; **m. à cristaux liquides** liquid crystal monitor; *Ordinat* **m. à tube cathodique** cathode ray tube monitor; **m. à écran plat** flat screen monitor

monitorage [mɔnitɔraʒ] NM monitoring; **écran de m.** monitor

monitorat [mɔnitɔra] NM *(fonction)* instructorship; *(période de formation)* instructor training; **m. sportif** sports instruction

monitoring [mɔnitɔriŋ] NM monitoring

monnaie [mɔnɛ] NF **1** *Fin (argent)* money; *(d'un pays)* currency; **pièce de m.** coin; **m. électronique** electronic money, e-money; **m. légale** legal tender; **m. scripturale** bank money, deposit money; **fausse m.** counterfeit money; **frapper la m., battre m.** to coin *or* mint money; **(l'hôtel de) la M.** = the French Mint, *Br* ≃ the Royal Mint; **m. de papier** paper money; **m. de compte (convertible)** (convertible) money of account; *UE* **m. commune** common currency; **m. faible** soft currency; **m. fiduciaire** fiduciary money *or* issue, paper money, *Am* fiat money; **m. forte** hard currency; **m. de réserve** reserve currency; **m. unique** single currency; *Fam* **m. de singe** worthless currency; *Fam* **c'est de la m. de singe!** it's worthless!; *Fam* **payer qn en m. de singe** to fob sb off, to let sb whistle for his/her money; **c'est m. courante dans ce milieu** it's common in these circles **2** *(pièces etc)* change; **petite m.** small change; **vous auriez de la m. pour le parc-mètre?** do you have some change for the parking meter?; **vous auriez la m. de cent euros?** could you give me change for a hundred-euro note, could you change a hundred-euro note for me?; **faire de la m.** to get some change; **pourriez-vous me faire de la m.?** could you give me some change?; **faire la m. de 50 euros** to get change for a 50-euro note; *(du commerçant)* to give change for a 50-euro note; *Fig* **rendre à qn la m. de sa pièce** to pay sb back in his/her own coin *or* in kind

> Il faut noter que le nom anglais **money** est un faux ami. Il signifie **argent**.

monnaie-du-pape, *pl* **monnaies-du-pape** NF *Bot* honesty

monnayable [mɔnɛjabl] ADJ convertible into money; *Fig* **cette formation/son expérience est m.** this training/his experience is worth money; **ce diplôme n'est pas m.** this diploma is of no value financially

monnayage [mɔnɛjaʒ] NM minting, coining

monnayer [mɔnɛje] (**je monnaye, je monnaie; je monnayerai, je monnaierai**) VT **1** *(argent)* to coin, to mint **2** *Fig (son influence, son talent etc)* to capitalize on, to cash in on; **il refusa de m. son silence** he refused to put a price on his silence
VPR **se monnayer ça se monnaye** there's money to be made out of it, there's money in it; **je veux bien faire ce que vous me demandez mais ça se monnaye** I'm happy to do what you ask, but it'll cost you; **ici tout se monnaye** money can buy (you) anything here, everything here has its price

monnayeur [mɔnɛjœr] NM coiner, minter; **faux m.** counterfeiter

mono¹ [mɔno] ADJ INV *Fam (disque)* mono; **en m.** in mono

mono² N *Fam* = moniteur

monoacide [mɔnoasid] ADJ *Chimie* monoacid(ic)

monobloc [mɔnoblɔk] ADJ INV *(cylindres, châssis)* made in one piece, cast solid

monocaméra [mɔnokamera] NF single camera

monocaméral, -ale, -aux, -ales [mɔnokameral, -o] ADJ *Pol* unicameral

monocamérisme [mɔnokamerism], **monocaméralisme** [mɔnokameralism] NM *Pol* unicameralism

monochrome [mɔnɔkrom] ADJ monochrome; *Ordinat* **écran m.** monochrome screen
　NM *Beaux-Arts* monochrome

monochromie [mɔnɔkromi] NF monochromaticity

monocle [mɔnɔkl] NM monocle

monocoque [mɔnɔkɔk] ADJ **avion m.** monocoque; **carrosserie m.** *(de voiture)* monocoque body; **bateau m.** monohull
　NM *(bateau)* monohull

monocorde [mɔnɔkɔrd] ADJ **1** *Mus (instrument)* single-stringed **2** *(son, ton, voix)* monotonous
　NM monochord

monocorps [mɔnɔkɔr] ADJ *Aut* monobox

monocotylédone [mɔnɔkɔtiledɔn] NF *Bot* monocotyledon

monoculaire [mɔnɔkylɛr] ADJ *(jumelles, vision, microscope)* monocular; **cécité m.** blindness in one eye

monoculture [mɔnɔkyltyr] NF *Agr* monoculture

monocycle [mɔnɔsikl] NM unicycle, monocycle

monocylindre [mɔnɔsilɛ̃dr] NM *Aut* single-cylinder engine

monocylindrique [mɔnɔsilɛ̃drik] ADJ *Aut (moteur)* single-cylinder

monoéthylèneglycol [mɔnɔetilɛnglikɔl] NM monoethylene glycol

monogame [mɔnɔgam] ADJ monogamous

monogamie [mɔnɔgami] NF monogamy

monogamique [mɔnɔgamik] ADJ monogamous

monogramme [mɔnɔgram] NM monogram

monographie [mɔnɔgrafi] NF monograph

monoï [mɔnɔj] NM scented coconut oil

mono-insaturé, *pl* **mono-insaturés** [mɔnoɛ̃satyre] ADJ *(lipide)* mono-unsaturated

monokini [mɔnɔkini] NM monokini; **faire du m.** to wear a monokini, to go topless

monolingue [mɔnɔlɛ̃g] ADJ monolingual

monolinguisme [mɔnɔlɛ̃gɥism] NM monolingualism

monolithe [mɔnɔlit] ADJ monolithic
　NM monolith

monolithique [mɔnɔlitik] ADJ monolithic; *Fig (organisation, parti)* monolithic; *(caractère, personne)* uncompromising

monologue [mɔnɔlɔg] NM monologue; *Théâtre (de Hamlet etc)* soliloquy, monologue; **m. intérieur** interior monologue

monologuer [mɔnɔlɔge] VI *(parler seul)* to talk to oneself; *Théâtre* to soliloquize, to talk to oneself

monomaniaque [mɔnɔmanjak] ADJ monomaniacal
　N monomaniac

monomanie [mɔnɔmani] NF monomania

monôme [mɔnom] NM *Math* monomial, single term

monométallisme [mɔnɔmetalism] NM *Fin* monometallism

monomoteur [mɔnɔmɔtœr] ADJ M single-engined
　NM single-engined aircraft

mononucléose [mɔnɔnykleoz] NF *Méd* mononucleosis; **m. infectieuse** glandular fever, *Spéc* infectious mononucleosis

monoparental, -ale, -aux, -ales [mɔnɔparātal, -o] ADJ *(famille)* single-parent, one-parent

monoparentalité [mɔnɔparātalite] NF single parenthood

monophasé [mɔnɔfaze] *Élec* ADJ *(courant)* single-phase
　NM single-phase current

monophonique [mɔnɔfɔnik] ADJ monaural

monoplace [mɔnɔplas] ADJ *(avion, voiture)* single-seater
　NM OU F *Aut* single-seater (car)
　NM *Aviat* single-seater (plane)

monoplan [mɔnɔplā] NM *Aviat* monoplane

monopole [mɔnɔpɔl] NM monopoly; **m. d'État** State monopoly; *Écon* **m. d'achat** buyer's monopoly; **m. bilatéral** bilateral monopoly; **m. d'émission** issuing monopoly; **m. d'exploitation** operating monopoly; **m. de fabrication** manufacturing monopoly; **m. naturel** natural monopoly; **m. de vente** sales monopoly; **avoir le m. de qch** *Écon* to have the monopoly of sth, to have a monopoly on sth; *Fig* to have a monopoly on sth; **exercer un m. sur un secteur** to monopolize a sector

monopoleur [mɔnɔpɔlœr] NM monopolist

monopolisateur, -trice [mɔnɔpɔlizatœr, -tris] N monopolizer, monopolist
　ADJ monopolizing

monopolisation [mɔnɔpɔlizasjɔ̃] NF monopolization

monopoliser [mɔnɔpɔlize] VT to monopolize; **m. la parole** not to let anyone else speak

monoposte [mɔnɔpɔst] NM *Ordinat* stand-alone

monorail [mɔnɔraj] ADJ INV monorail
　NM monorail

monoski [mɔnɔski] NM *Sport* monoski; **faire du m.** to monoski

monospace [mɔnɔspas] NM *Aut* people carrier

monosyllabe [mɔnɔsilab] ADJ monosyllabic
　NM monosyllable

monosyllabique [mɔnɔsilabik] ADJ monosyllabic

mono-tâche ADJ INV *Ordinat* single-tasking

monothéisme [mɔnɔteism] NM monotheism

monothéiste [mɔnɔteist] ADJ monotheistic
　N monotheist

monotone [mɔnɔtɔn] ADJ monotonous; *(existence)* monotonous, humdrum

monotonie [mɔnɔtɔni] NF monotony; **rompre la m.** to break the monotony

Monotype® [mɔnɔtip] NF *Typ* Monotype® (machine)

monovalent [mɔnɔvalā] ADJ *Chimie* monovalent, univalent

monoxyde [mɔnɔksid] NM **m. de carbone** carbon monoxide

monseigneur [mɔ̃sɛɲœr] NM **1** *pl* **nosseigneurs** *ou* **messeigneurs** *(référence à un prince)* His Royal Highness; *(à un cardinal)* His Eminence; *(à un duc, archevêque)* His Grace; *(à un évêque)* His Lordship; **m. l'évêque de …** the Lord Bishop of … **2** *pl* **messeigneurs** *(en s'adressant au prince)* Your Royal Highness; *(au cardinal)* Your Eminence; *(au duc, à l'archevêque)* Your Grace; *(à l'évêque)* My Lord (Bishop), Your Lordship

monsieur [məsjø], *pl* **messieurs** [mesjø] NM **1** M. Robert Marceau Mr Robert Marceau; **Messieurs Marceau et Cie** Messrs Marceau and Co; **m. le duc/le comte de Montignac** the Duke/the Earl of Montignac; **m. le duc/le comte est servi** dinner is served, your Grace/my Lord
　2 *Vieilli (à un petit garçon)* **M. Robert** Master Robert

3 *Fml (utilisé seul)* **voici le chapeau de m.** *(en s'adressant à lui)* here's your hat, sir; *(sans s'adresser à lui)* here's the gentleman's hat; *(à quelqu'un qui s'appelle Martin etc)* here's Mr Martin's/*etc* hat; **m. n'est pas là** Mr Martin/*etc* is out; **m. a sonné?** you rang, sir?
　4 *(à un homme)* sir; *(à un duc)* sir, Your Grace; *(à un comte)* sir, Your Lordship; **au revoir, m.** goodbye, *Fml* goodbye sir; **bonsoir, messieurs** goodnight, gentlemen; **que prendront ces messieurs?** what will you have, gentlemen?; **Mesdames, Messieurs** ladies and gentlemen; **bonjour, Messieurs-Dames!** good morning/afternoon!
　5 *(dans une lettre)* **M.** *(à un étranger)* (Dear) Sir; **M. et cher Confrère, M. et cher Collègue** *(qui s'appelle Martin etc)* Dear Mr Martin/*etc*; **Cher M.** *(à une connaissance qui s'appelle Martin etc)* Dear Mr Martin/*etc*
　6 *(sur enveloppe)* **M. T. Marceau** Mr T. Marceau, *Fml* T. Marceau Esq
　7 *(homme)* (gentle)man; *Enf* **dis bonjour au m.** say hello (to the gentleman); **il y a un m. qui veut vous parler** there is a (gentle)man here who wants to speak to you; **c'est un vilain m.** he's a nasty piece of work
　▸▸ **m. je-sais-tout** Mr Know(-it)-all; **il va encore nous jouer son m. je-sais-tout** here he goes again, the know(-it)-all; *TV etc* **M. Météo** the weatherman; **m. tout-le-monde** the man in the street, *Am* Joe Public, Joe Blow

monstre [mɔ̃str] NM *Myth, Fig* monster; **les monstres marins** the monsters of the deep; *Fig* **m. d'ingratitude/d'égoïsme** ungrateful/selfish monster *or* brute, *Fml* monster of ingratitude/selfishness; *Fig Fam* **petit m.!** you little monster *or* horror!
　ADJ *Fam* huge, colossal, mammoth; *(succès)* enormous, huge, wild; **un travail m.** a mammoth task; **j'ai eu une chance m.** I was incredibly lucky; **elle avait une trouille m.** she was scared stiff *or* to death
　▸▸ **m. sacré** *(du cinéma, de la danse etc)* giant, idol

monstrueusement [mɔ̃stryøzmā] ADV *(laid, gros)* monstrously, hideously; *(égoïste)* horrendously, outrageously

monstrueux, -euse [mɔ̃stryø, -øz] ADJ **1** *(malformé)* monstrous, deformed **2** *(énorme)* *(erreur, gaffe)* huge, colossal; *(prix)* extortionate, exorbitant **3** *(scandaleux)* monstrous; **elle est d'un égoïsme m.** she is a selfish monster

monstruosité [mɔ̃stryozite] NF **1** *(difformité)* monstrosity **2** *(de crime, criminel etc)* monstrousness, monstrosity

mont [mɔ̃] NM **1** mountain; **le m. Sinaï/Everest** Mount Sinai/Everest; **le m. des Oliviers** the Mount of Olives; **le m. Blanc** Mont Blanc; *Fig* **par monts et par vaux** up hill and down dale; *Fig* **être toujours par monts et par vaux** to be always on the move; *Fig* **promettre monts et merveilles à qn** to promise sb the earth *or* the moon **2** *Anat* **m. de Vénus** mons veneris

montage [mɔ̃taʒ] NM **1** *(pose)* *(de bijou)* setting, mounting; *(de pneu)* fitting (on); *(d'appareil, de meuble etc)* assembling, assembly; *(d'atelier etc)* fitting out; *(de porte)* hanging; *Ind* **chaîne de m.** assembly line; **atelier de m.** assembly shop; *Tech* **m. serré** push fit; *Tech* **m. à la presse** press fit **2** *Cin, Radio, TV* editing; *Phot, Cin, TV (image truquée)* montage; *Typ* make-up; **couper qch au m.** to edit sth out; **m. original** edited master; **m. vidéo** video(tape) editing, tape editing; *Cin, TV, Radio* **m. sonore** sound editing; *(avec truquage)* sound montage; *Cin* **salle de m.** cutting room; *Cin* **film de m.** film montage **3** *Écon* **le m. financier d'un projet** the financial arrangements for a project; **le m. financier a été difficile** it wasn't easy getting the money together; **le m. financier du projet**

sera le suivant money for the project will be provided as follows **4** *Élec* connecting (up), wiring (up) **5** *(de matériaux de construction etc)* taking up, carrying up

montagnard, -arde [mɔ̃taɲar, -ard] ADJ mountain, highland

N **1** *(habitant)* mountain dweller, highlander **2** *Hist* member of the Mountain

montagne [mɔ̃taɲ] NF **1** mountain; *(région)* mountains, mountain region; **la haute m.** the high mountains; **la moyenne m.** the uplands; **passer ses vacances à la m.** to spend one's holiday in the mountains; **aimer les paysages de montagnes** to like mountain scenery; *Fig* **une m. de choux/repassage** a huge pile of cabbages/ironing; *Fig* **se faire une m. de qch** to make a great song and dance *or* a great to-do about sth; **tu t'en fais une m.!** you're making a mountain out of a molehill!; *Fig* **c'est la m. qui accouche d'une souris** what a lot of fuss for nothing, *Litt* the mountain laboured and brought forth a mouse

2 *Sport* **faire de la m.** *(alpinisme)* to go mountain climbing; *(randonnée)* to go hill walking; **sports de m.** mountain sports

3 *Hist* **la M.** the Mountain

▸▸ *UE* **m. de beurre** butter mountain; **montagnes russes** *(à la foire)* big dipper, roller coaster; *Fig* **faire des montagnes russes** *(d'une route)* to switchback; **m. à vaches** hills

montagneux, -euse [mɔ̃taɲø, -øz] ADJ mountainous

montant [mɔ̃tɑ̃] ADJ rising; **chemin m.** uphill road; **marée montante** rising tide, flood tide; **col m.** high *or* stand-up collar; *Rail* **train/quai m.** up train/platform; *Mil* **garde montante** new guard, relieving guard

NM **1** *(somme)* amount, sum; **cinq versements d'un m. de 500 euros** five payments of 500 euros (each); **j'ignore le m. de mes dettes** I don't know what my debts amount to; **m. brut/total** gross/total (amount); **m. du retour net** net return; **m. exonéré de TVA** VAT exempt amount; **m. forfaitaire** lump sum; **m. maximum/minimum** maximum/minimum (amount); **m. net** net (total); **m. prévisionnel des ventes** forecast sales level; *UE, Écon* **montants compensatoires (monétaires)** subsidies, *Spéc* compensatory amounts; **m. à reporter** amount brought forward

2 *(partie verticale)* *(d'échelle)* upright; *(de lit)* post; *(de fenêtre)* jamb; *(de portail)* post; *(de bride)* cheek strap; *Sport* **les montants** *(de but)* the goalposts; *Aut* **m. de pare-brise** screen pillar, windscreen pillar, A-pillar; *Aut* **m. de porte** door pillar, B-pillar

mont-de-piété, *pl* **monts-de-piété** NM *Arch* pawnshop; **mettre qch au m.** to pawn sth

monte [mɔ̃t] NF **1** *Courses de chevaux (action)* mounting; **jockey qui a eu trois montes dans la journée** jockey who has ridden three times *or* who has had three mounts *or* rides in the day **2** *(façon de monter à cheval)* horsemanship; **m. à l'obstacle** jumping **3** *(accouplement)* covering; *(époque de l'accouplement)* breeding *or* mating season

monté [mɔ̃te] ADJ **1** *(à cheval)* *(police, troupes)* mounted **2** *(bijou)* set, mounted; **m. sur or** gold-mounted; **médaille montée en pendentif** medal mounted as a pendant; **photographies non montées** unmounted photographs **3** *(approvisionné)* **cave/boutique bien montée** well-stocked cellar/shop; **être bien monté en vaisselle** to be well supplied with crockery **4** *Fam* **il était m.** *ou* **il avait la tête montée contre elle** he had it in for her; **il est drôlement m., ce matin, le patron!** the boss is really worked up *or* wound

up this morning! **5** *Vulg* **bien m.** *(homme)* well-hung

monte-charge, *pl* **monte-charges** NM hoist, *Br* goods lift, *Br* service lift, *Am* goods elevator

montée [mɔ̃te] NF **1** *(mouvement)* rise, rising; *(ascension)* ascent; *Fig (du nationalisme, fascisme etc)* rise, growth, increase; **pendant la m. du col** as he was/we were/*etc* going uphill; *Tech etc* **tuyau de m.** uptake pipe, riser; **m. des eaux** *(dans un réservoir)* inflow; **la m. des prix** the rise in prices, rising prices; *Physiol* **m. de lait** onset of lactation **2** *Aut, Aviat* **essai de m.** climbing test; **vitesse en m.** *Aviat* climbing speed; *Aut, Rail* speed on a gradient **3** *(côte)* *(sur une route)* slope, hill; **en haut de la m.** at the top of the slope *or* hill; **il y a une méchante m. avant d'arriver chez lui** there's a stiff climb before you reach his house

monte-en-l'air NM INV *Fam Vieilli* cat burglar

monte-plats NM INV *(au restaurant)* dumbwaiter

MONTER [mɔ̃te]

VI to go up **1, 4, 5** ▪ to climb on/in **1, 2, 4** ▪ to get on/in **2** ▪ to rise **3–5**	
VT to go up **1** ▪ to bring up **2** ▪ to set **3** ▪ to fit **3** ▪ to set up **3** ▪ to edit **3** ▪ to ride **5**	
VPR to come to *(se monter à)* **1** ▪ to equip oneself **2** ▪ to be ridden **4**	

VI *(aux souvent être, parfois avoir)* **1** *(se déplacer vers le haut)* to go up, to climb (up); *(vu d'en haut)* to come up; *(en haut de l'escalier)* to go up(stairs); *(vu d'en haut)* to come up(stairs); *(d'un oiseau)* to soar, to fly up; *(d'un avion)* to climb, to fly up; **m. à** *ou* **sur un arbre/une échelle** to climb (up) (into) a tree/(on to) a ladder; **m. en haut d'une colline** to climb *or* go up (right) to the top of a hill; **m. en courant/en rampant** to run/crawl up; **m. se coucher** to go (up) to bed; **faire m. qn** to show sb up; **montez chez moi** come up to my place; **après ses études, il est monté à Paris** after college, he moved up to Paris; **elle monte souvent à Paris pour voir sa sœur** she often goes up to Paris to see her sister; *Aut* **m. en régime** to rev; *Mil* **m. en ligne** to go to the front (line); **m. à l'assaut** to go into the attack; *Tennis* **m. au filet** to come up/go up to the net; *Naut* **faire m. tous les hommes** to order all hands on deck

2 *(pour s'installer etc)* to climb *or* get on/in; *(dans le train, l'autobus etc)* to get on; **où êtes-vous monté?** where did you get on?; **m. sur une chaise** to stand *or* get on a chair; **m. en chaire** to ascend the pulpit; **m. à cheval** to get on a horse, to mount (a horse); *(faire de l'équitation)* to ride, to go riding; **montez-vous (à cheval)?** do you ride?; *Fam* **m. sur ses grands chevaux** to get on one's high horse; **m. à** *ou* **en bicyclette** to ride a bicycle; **m. en voiture** to get into a car; *Naut, Aviat* **m. à bord** to go on board, to board; **faire m. qn (en voiture) avec soi** to give sb a lift; *Théâtre* **m. sur les planches** to go on the stage

3 *(d'un ballon, du soleil etc)* to rise; *(d'un prix, du baromètre etc)* to rise, to go up; *(de la marée)* to rise, to come in; **les frais montent** the costs are mounting (up); **la somme monte à cent euros** the total amounts to *or* comes to a hundred euros; **m. en flèche** *(de prix)* to soar; **faire m. les prix** to put up *or* increase *or* raise prices; **empêcher les prix de m.** to keep prices down, to stop prices rising; **le sang lui monta à la tête** the blood rushed to his head; **faire m. les larmes aux yeux de qn** to bring tears to sb's eyes

4 *(d'une route etc)* to climb, to go up, to rise;

la rue va en montant the street climbs

5 m. dans l'estime de qn to go up *or* rise in sb's estimation; **faire m. qn dans l'estime de qn** to raise sb in sb's estimation

VT *(aux avoir)* **1** *(colline, escalier etc)* to go/come up, to climb (up); **m. la rue en courant** to run up the street

2 *(porter)* to bring up; *(vu d'en bas)* to take up; **m. du vin de la cave** to fetch *or* bring wine up from the cellar; **m. le courrier** to bring the post; **m. le son** to turn up the volume; *Fig* **m. (la tête à) qn contre qn** to set sb against sb

3 *(bijou)* to set, to mount; *(photo, hameçon etc)* to mount; *(pneu)* to fit (on); *(appareil, machine)* to set up, to erect; *(porte)* to hang; *(atelier)* to fit out, to equip; *Théâtre (scène)* to set; *(pièce)* to put on, to stage, to produce; *Cin (film)* to edit; *Couture (vêtement)* to make up; *(en imprimerie)* to paste up; **m. une entreprise** to set up a business; **m. un magasin** to set up *or* open a shop; **elle commence à m. son trousseau** she's beginning to put her trousseau together; **m. un complot/un coup** to hatch a plot/plan a job; *Fam* **m. le coup à qn** to take sb in, to take sb for a ride; *Fam* **m. qch en épingle** to blow sth up out of all proportion; *Tricot* **m. les mailles** to cast on (the stitches)

4 *Mil etc* **m. la garde** to mount *or* keep guard **5** *(cheval)* to ride **6** *Élec* to connect up, to wire (up)

VPR **se monter 1** *(d'un prix etc)* **se m. à** to come to, to add up to, to amount to; **à combien se monte tout cela?** how much does all this come to *or* add up to *or* amount to?

2 *(s'équiper)* to equip oneself, to fit oneself out (**en** with); **se m. en vaisselle** to supply oneself with crockery; **se m. en affaires** to set up (in business) on one's own

3 *Fam (s'énerver)* to get worked up *or* wound up; **elle s'est montée contre lui** she's got it in for him

4 *(d'un cheval)* to be ridden; **Flicka se monte facilement** Flicka is easy to ride

monteur, -euse [mɔ̃tœr, -øz] N *(de bijoux)* setter; *(d'images)* mounter; *Cin* editor; *Tech* fitter; *Aut* engine fitter; *TV, Cin* **m. vidéo** videotape editor, VT editor

Montevideo [mɔ̃tevideo] N Montevideo

montgolfière [mɔ̃gɔlfjer] NF hot-air balloon

monticule [mɔ̃tikyl] NM *(petite colline)* hillock, mound; *(plus petit)* hummock; *Can Baseball* mound

montoir [mɔ̃twar] NM *(de cheval)* mounting block; **côté (du) m.** nearside; **côté hors (du) m.** offside

montrable [mɔ̃trabl] ADJ presentable, fit to be seen

montre [mɔ̃tr] NF **1** *(instrument)* watch; **m. (de poignet)** (wrist)watch; **m. de plongée** diver's watch; **m. à quartz** quartz watch; **à ma m., il est midi** by my watch, it's twelve o'clock; **cela lui a pris dix minutes m. en main** it took him exactly ten minutes; **course contre la m.** race against the clock; *Fig* **on est dans une course contre la m.** we're racing against time *or* the clock; *Fig* **jouer la m.** to play for time **2** *(preuve)* show, display; **faire m. de patience/d'un grand courage** to show *or* display patience/great courage; *Litt* **faire qch pour la m.** to do sth merely for show **3** *(vitrine)* shop window, display window; *(dans meuble)* showcase; **mettre qch en m.** to put sth in the window *or* on show *or* on display

Montréal [mɔ̃real] N Montreal

montréalais, -aise [mɔ̃realɛ, -ɛz] ADJ (of/from) Montreal

N **M.** Montrealer

montre-bracelet, *pl* **montres-bracelets** NF wristwatch

montrer [mɔ̃tre] VT *(révéler)* to show; *(désigner)* to show, to point out; *(faire preuve de)* to show, to display; **elle nous a montré où nous allions dormir** she showed us *or* pointed out to us where we were to sleep; **il a montré un grand courage** he showed *or* displayed great courage; **il faudrait que tu montres ta fille/cette vilaine blessure à un médecin** you should let a doctor have a look at *or* see your daughter/that nasty wound; **une robe décolletée qui montre les épaules** a low-cut dress which leaves the shoulders bare *or* which exposes the shoulders; **elle a montré une jolie paire de jambes en s'asseyant** she showed a pretty pair of legs as she sat down; **elle adore m. ses charmes** she loves showing off *or* displaying her charms; **il n'y montre jamais le nez** he never shows his face there; **m. qn/qch du doigt** to point sb/sth out, to point to *or* at sb/sth; *Fig* to point the finger at sb/sth; **m. le chemin à qn** to show sb the way; **m. la ville à qn** to show sb round the town; **il a réussi à ne pas m. qu'il était au courant** he managed not to show that he knew about it; **cela te montre qu'il faut être prudent** that (just) shows that you have to be careful; **montre-lui la manière de le faire** *ou* **comment le faire** show him how to do it *or* how it's done; **peux-tu me m. comment ça marche?** can you show me how it works?; **m. le poing à qn** to shake one's fist at sb; **m. les dents** to show *or* bare one's teeth; **m. la porte à qn** to show sb the door

VPR **se montrer 1** *(se présenter)* to show oneself, to appear; **il n'ose plus se m.** he doesn't dare show himself *or* his face **2** *(se révéler)* **il s'est montré très gentil/courageux** he was very kind/courageous, he showed great kindness/courage; **il s'est montré incapable de faire face à la situation** he proved (to be) *or* he was incapable of facing up to the situation

montreur, -euse [mɔ̃trœr, -øz] N *(dans une foire etc) (de bêtes sauvages)* exhibitor; **m. d'ours** bear leader; **m. de marionnettes** puppeteer

montueux, -euse [mɔ̃tɥø, -øz] ADJ hilly

monture [mɔ̃tyr] NF **1** *(de bijou)* setting; *(de scie, parapluie, lunettes etc)* frame; *(de fusil, revolver)* stock; *(d'épée)* guard; **lunettes sans m.** rimless spectacles **2** *(cheval etc)* mount

monument [mɔnymɑ̃] NM **1** *(statue etc)* monument, memorial; **élever un m. à la mémoire de qn** to erect a monument in memory of *or* to the memory of sb; **m. funéraire** monument *(over a tomb)*; **m. aux morts** war memorial **2** *(édifice public)* monument; **m. historique** historic monument *or* building; **être classé m. historique** to be a listed building **3** *Fam* **cette armoire est un m.** this cupboard's enormous; **être un m. d'absurdité** to be monumentally absurd **4** *Fig (livre, film)* masterpiece

monumental, -ale, -aux, -ales [mɔnymɑ̃tal, -o] ADJ monumental; **une erreur monumentale** a monumental blunder; **elle est d'une bêtise monumentale** she's monumentally stupid

mooniste [munist] N *(membre de la secte Moon)* moonie

mope [mɔp] NF *Can (balai)* mop

moque [mɔk] NF **1** *Naut* cringle **2** *Suisse Fam (morve)* snot

moquer [mɔke] VT *Arch* to mock

VPR **se moquer 1** *(railler)* **se m. de qn/qch** to make fun of *or* laugh at *or* poke fun at *or* mock sb/sth; **vous vous moquez?** what are you laughing at?, what's so funny? **2** *(ne pas faire cas)* **se m. de qch** not to care *or* not to

give a damn about sth; **je me moque de ce que les gens pensent** I don't care *or* I don't give a damn what people think; **je m'en moque** I don't care, I don't give a damn; **elle s'en moque éperdument** she doesn't give a damn, she just couldn't care less; **il se moque du tiers comme du quart** he doesn't care *or* give a damn about anybody or anything; *Fam* **je m'en moque comme de l'an quarante** *ou* **comme de ma première chemise** I don't give a damn, I don't care two hoots *or* a tinker's cuss **3** *(tromper)* **vous vous moquez** *ou* **c'est se m. du monde!** you've got a nerve!

moquerie [mɔkri] NF mockery, jeering, ridicule; **leurs moqueries continuelles** their constant mockery *or* jeering *or* ridicule

moquette [mɔket] NF **1** fitted carpet, wall-to-wall carpet; **faire poser une** *ou* **de la m.** to have a (fitted *or* wall-to-wall) carpet laid **2** *Tex* moquette

moquetter [mɔkete] VT to carpet

moqueur, -euse [mɔkœr, -øz] ADJ **1** *(remarque, rires etc)* mocking, jeering, derisive **2** *(personne)* given to mockery
N *(personne)* mocker, scoffer
NM *(oiseau)* mockingbird

moqueusement [mɔkøzmɑ̃] ADV mockingly

moraillon [mɔrajɔ̃] NM *(de serrure)* hasp

moraine [mɔren] NF *Géol* moraine

moral, -ale, -aux, -ales [mɔral, -o] ADJ **1** *(conduite, sens, certitude, courage, victoire)* moral; **cette histoire n'est pas morale** this is not a very edifying story; **facultés morales** ability to distinguish between right and wrong; **je me fais une obligation morale de le faire** I'm under a moral obligation *or* I'm morally obliged to do it **2** *Jur* **personne morale** legal entity, corporation
NM morale; **c'est bon pour le m.** it's good for morale; **le m. est bas** morale is low; **son m. est bas** his spirits are low, he's in low spirits; **je n'ai pas le m. en ce moment** I'm feeling down just now; **avoir le m. au beau fixe** to be in fine spirits; **elle a un m. d'acier** nothing gets her down; *Fam* **avoir le m. à zéro** to feel down in the dumps; **remonter le m. de** *ou* **à qn** to raise sb's spirits, to cheer sb up; **il se marie avec elle? il a le m.!** he's marrying her? he's got guts *or* he's a brave chap!

morale [mɔral] NF **1** *(bien)* morals, morality; **contraire/conforme à la m.** immoral/moral **2** *(règles)* morality, ethics; **tu ne vas quand même pas me faire une leçon de m.?** you're not going to start lecturing me, are you now?; **faire la m. à qn** to lecture sb; **adopter une m. d'ascète** to adopt an ascetic philosophy *or* way of life **3** *(d'une histoire)* moral

moralement [mɔralmɑ̃] ADV morally; **m., tu ne peux pas lui faire ça** morally (speaking), you can't do that to him

moralisant [mɔralizɑ̃] ADJ moralizing

moralisateur, -trice [mɔralizatœr, -tris] ADJ **1** *(personne)* moralizing **2** *(principes)* elevating, edifying
N moralizer

moralisation [mɔralizasjɔ̃] NF moralization

moraliser [mɔralize] VI to moralize
VT **1** *(politique, le marché financier etc)* to clean up **2** *(personne)* to lecture

moraliste [mɔralist] ADJ moralistic
N moralist

moralité [mɔralite] NF **1** *(mérite)* morality, (good) moral conduct; **certificat de m.** character reference **2** *(attitude)* morals, morality; **elle est d'une m. douteuse** her morals are dubious, she has dubious morals, she is of dubious morality; **quelqu'un d'une haute m./d'une m. au-dessus de tout soupçon** someone with high/impeccable moral

standards **3** *(d'une histoire)* moral; **m.: rien ne sert de courir, il faut partir à point** the moral of the story is that it's better to start on time than to try to catch up later; **il n'a pris aucune précaution, m.: il est mort** he didn't take any precautions and as a result he's dead **4** *Hist, Littér* morality (play)

morasse [mɔras] NF *Typ (de journal)* brush proof

moratoire [mɔratwar] *Jur* ADJ *(accord etc)* moratory; *(paiement)* delayed by agreement; **intérêts moratoires** interest on overdue payments
NM moratorium

moratorium [mɔratɔrjɔm] NM *Jur* moratorium

morbide [mɔrbid] ADJ morbid

morbidement [mɔrbidmɑ̃] ADV morbidly

morbidité [mɔrbidite] NF morbidness, morbidity

morbier [mɔrbje] NM **1** *(fromage)* Morbier (cheese) **2** *Suisse (horloge)* grandfather clock

morbleu [mɔrblø] INT *Arch* 'sdeath!, zounds!

morce [mɔrs] NF *Suisse (bouchée)* mouthful; **manger une m.** to have a bite to eat

morceau, -eaux [mɔrso] NM **1** *(de nourriture)* piece, bit; **m. de choix** choice morsel; **bas morceaux** *(de viande)* cheap(er) cuts; **aimer les bons morceaux** to like good things (to eat); *Fam* **manger** *ou* **prendre un m.** to have a bite to eat *or* a snack; *Fig Fam* **emporter le m.** to win (the day) *(in deal, court case etc)*; *Fig Fam* **lâcher** *ou* **cracher le m.** to spill the beans **2** *(de savon, tissu, laine, ficelle etc)* piece, bit; *(de papier)* piece, bit, scrap; *(de sucre)* lump; *(de terre)* piece, patch; *Mus* piece; **en morceaux** in pieces; **sucre en morceaux** lump sugar, cube sugar; **mettre qch en morceaux** to pull *or* tear sth to pieces *or* to bits; **il va me mettre en morceaux** he'll tear me limb from limb; **tomber en morceaux** to fall to pieces *or* bits; *Mus* **m. pour trombone** piece for trombone; *Littér* **morceaux choisis** selected passages *or* extracts; **m. d'anthologie** anthology piece; **m. de bravoure** purple passage, purple patch; *Fam* **cette fille, c'est un beau m.** she's a bit of all right, that girl

morceler [mɔrsəle] VT (**je morcelle; je morcellerai**) to divide (up); **m. une propriété** to break up *or* parcel out *or* divide (up) an estate

morcellement [mɔrselmɑ̃] NM division

mordacité [mɔrdasite] NF *Litt (de critique)* mordancy

mordant [mɔrdɑ̃] ADJ *(esprit, ironie, discours)* biting, caustic, scathing, *Fml* mordant; *(remarque, ton)* cutting, caustic, scathing; *(personne)* scathing; **froid m.** biting cold
NM *(d'esprit, d'ironie)* bite, *Litt* mordancy; *(d'analyse)* scathing nature; *(de troupes, d'équipe etc)* keenness; *(d'outil)* bite; *(pour teinture)* mordant; **le m. de son ton** his cutting *or* caustic *or* scathing tone

mordée [mɔrde] NF *Can (bouchée)* bite; **prendre une m. dans qch** to take a bite out of sth, to bite sth

mordicus [mɔrdikys] ADV *Fam* stubbornly, doggedly; **elle l'affirme m.** she's quite stubborn *or* dogged about it

mordieu [mɔrdjø] INT *Arch* 'sdeath!, zounds!

mordillage [mɔrdijaʒ] NM, **mordillement** [mɔrdijmɑ̃] NM nibbling

mordiller [mɔrdije] VT to nibble

mordoré [mɔrdɔre] ADJ, NM *(couleur)* bronze

mordorer [mɔrdɔre] VT *Litt* to bronze

mordorure [mɔrdɔryr] NF *(couleur)* bronze

mordre [mɔrdr] VT **1** (*d'une personne, d'un chien etc*) to bite; **m. une pomme** to bite into an apple; **m. qn au bras** to bite sb's arm, to bite sb on the arm; **elle s'est fait m. par un rat** she was bitten by a rat; **approche, je ne vais pas te m.** come here, I won't bite you; **le froid lui mordait les doigts** the cold was nipping *or* biting his fingers; *Fig Fam* **m. la poussière** to bite the dust **2** (*accrocher*) to bite into; **acide qui mord les métaux** acid that eats into metals **3** *Beaux-Arts* **m. une planche** to etch a plate

VI **1** (*d'une personne, d'un chien etc*) to bite; **m. dans une pomme** to bite into *or* take a bite out of an apple; *Fig* **m. sur qch** to encroach (up)on sth; **la route mord sur mon terrain** the road encroaches on my land; *Tennis* **m. sur la ligne** to have one's foot (just) over the line; *Pêche, Fig* **m. à l'appât** *ou* **à l'hameçon** to rise to *or* swallow the bait; **le public a bien mordu** the public responded well; *Fam* **il mord au latin** he's taking to Latin; *Pêche* **ça mord** I've got a bite; **ça mord?** are they biting? **2** (*accrocher*) to bite; **lime/vis qui mord** file/screw that bites *or* has a good bite; **l'ancre ne mord pas** the anchor won't hold *or* grip

VPR **se mordre** to bite oneself; **se m. la langue** to bite one's tongue; **se m. la langue d'avoir parlé** to regret bitterly having spoken; **se m. les lèvres pour ne pas rire/pour ne pas hurler** to bite one's lip so as not to laugh/scream; *Fig* **il s'en mord les doigts** he's kicking himself; **si vous outrepassez mes ordres, vous vous en mordrez les doigts** if you exceed my orders, you'll be sorry *or* you'll regret it

mordu, -ue [mɔrdy] ADJ bitten; *Fig Fam* madly in love; *Fig Fam* **elle est m. de ski/tricot** she's been bitten by the skiing/knitting bug, she's mad on skiing/knitting
◾ N *Fam* enthusiast; **m. du bridge/du cinéma** bridge/film fanatic *or* enthusiast

more [mɔr] ADJ, N = **maure**

morelle [mɔrɛl] NF *Bot* nightshade

moresque [mɔrɛsk] ADJ, NF = **mauresque**

morfal, -ale, -als, -ales [mɔrfal] N *Fam* greedy-guts, *Br Fam* gannet; **il a un appétit de m.** he eats like a horse

morfler [mɔrfle] *Fam* VT **1** (*recevoir*) to get; **il a morflé une claque dans la tronche** he got a slap in the face **2** (*se voir infliger une peine de*) to get, to cop
◾ VI **1** (*être abîmé*) to get smashed up; (*être blessé*) to get injured **2** (*être sévèrement puni*) to catch it, *Br* to cop it

morfondre (se) [səmɔrfɔ̃dr] VPR **1** (*s'ennuyer*) to be bored to death; (*être triste*) to mope; **la fillette était là à se m. en attendant son père, qui avait déjà deux heures de retard** the little girl was waiting dejectedly for her father, who was already two hours late **2** *Can* (*s'épuiser*) to wear oneself out

morfondu [mɔrfɔ̃dy] ADJ gloomy, dejected

morganatique [mɔrganatik] ADJ morganatic

morgue¹ [mɔrg] NF (*insolence*) pride, haughtiness, arrogance; **regard plein de m.** haughty *or* arrogant look

morgue² NF (*dans un hôpital*) mortuary, morgue

moribond, -onde [mɔribɔ̃, -ɔ̃d] ADJ dying, *Fml* moribund
◾ N dying man, *f* woman; **les moribonds** the dying

moricaud, -aude [mɔriko, -od] *Fam Péj* ADJ dark-skinned, dusky, swarthy
◾ N dark-skinned person; (*terme raciste*) darky, darkie

morigéner [mɔriʒene] VT (**je morigène; je morigénerai**) to lecture, to take to task, to give a good talking-to

morille [mɔrij] NF *Culin* morel

morillon [mɔrijɔ̃] NM **1** (*oiseau*) tufted duck **2** (*pierre précieuse*) rough emerald

mormon, -one [mɔrmɔ̃, -ɔn] ADJ, N Mormon

mormonisme [mɔrmɔnism] NM Mormonism

morne [mɔrn] ADJ (*personne, regard*) gloomy, glum; (*silence*) gloomy; (*temps, vacances*) dismal, dreary, dull; **parler d'un ton m.** to speak drearily *or* in a dreary voice

mornifle [mɔrnifl] NF *Fam* clout, slap

morose [mɔroz] ADJ (*personne, humeur*) morose, sullen, glum; (*temps, année*) miserable

morosité [mɔrozite] NF (*de personne*) moroseness, sullenness; (*de climat*) miserableness; (*du paysage*) gloominess

Morphée [mɔrfe] N Morpheus; **dans les bras de M.** in the arms of Morpheus

morphème [mɔrfɛm] NM *Ling* morpheme

morphine [mɔrfin] NF morphine, morphia

morphing [mɔrfiŋ] NM *Cin* morphing

morphinisme [mɔrfinism] NM *Méd* morphinism

morphinomane [mɔrfinɔman] ADJ addicted to morphine
◾ N morphine addict

morphinomanie [mɔrfinɔmani] NF addiction to morphine

morphologie [mɔrfɔlɔʒi] NF morphology

morphologique [mɔrfɔlɔʒik] ADJ morphological

morphologiquement [mɔrfɔlɔʒikmɑ̃] ADV morphologically

morphopsychologie [mɔrfɔpsikɔlɔʒi] NF = study of the relationship between people's morphology and their psychological make-up

morpion [mɔrpjɔ̃] NM **1** *Arg* (*pou du pubis*) crab **2** *Arg* (*gamin*) kid **3** (*jeu*) noughts and crosses, *Am* tick-tack-toe

mors [mɔr] NM **1** (*d'un étau*) jaw **2** (*de livre*) joint **3** (*de harnais*) bit; **prendre le m. aux dents** (*d'un cheval*) to take the bit in its teeth; *Fig* (*d'une personne*) to take the bit between one's teeth

morse¹ [mɔrs] NM *Zool* walrus

morse² NM (*code*) Morse (code)

morsure [mɔrsyr] NF **1** bite; **une m. de chien** a dog bite **2** (*d'acide*) biting

mort¹, morte [mɔr, mɔrt] ADJ **1** (*personne, peau, feuille, langue etc*) dead; **m. et enterré** dead and buried, dead and gone; **je le veux m. ou vif** I want him dead or alive; **plus m. que vif** (*à demi mort*) more dead than alive; (*très effrayé*) half-dead with fright; **il est m.** he's dead; **il est m. hier** he died yesterday; **si tu fais un geste, tu es un homme m.** one move and you're a dead man; **il est m. pour la France** he died for France; *Prov* **morte la bête, m. le venin** dead men tell no tales; **m. de peur/d'inquiétude/de froid** frightened/worried/frozen to death; *Fam* **je n'en peux plus, je suis m. (de fatigue)** I can't go on, I'm dead tired; *Fam* **être m. de rire** to be killing oneself (laughing); **elle avait le regard m.** her eyes were lifeless; **la mer Morte** the Dead Sea; **au mois d'août, la ville semble morte** in August the town seems dead
◾ **2** *temps m. Sport* (*dans un match*) injury time, stoppage time; (*dans le travail, la conversation*) lull; **poids m.** *Tech* dead weight; *Constr* dead load; **point m.** (*de la course d'un piston*) dead centre; (*d'un levier etc*) neutral position; *Aut* neutral; *Aut* **mettre le levier au point m.** to put the (gear) lever into neutral; *Fig* **arriver à un point m.** to come to a standstill; **angle m.** (*dans une voiture etc*)

blind spot; **eau morte** stagnant water; *Beaux-Arts* **nature morte** still life; **balle morte** spent bullet
◾ **3** *Fam* (*hors d'usage*) (*piles, appareil etc*) finished; **ma voiture est morte** my car's had it
◾ N dead person, dead man, *f* woman; **les morts** the dead; **le nombre des morts sur la route** the number of deaths on the roads; **cet accident a fait trois morts** the accident claimed three lives, three people died *or* were killed in the accident; **la drogue fait de nombreux morts chaque année** drugs claim many lives each year, many people die from drugs each year; *Rel* **jour** *ou* **fête des Morts** All Souls' Day; **l'office des morts** the burial service; **faire le m.** to pretend to be dead, to play dead; **je lui ai écrit il y a trois semaines, mais depuis, il fait le m.** I wrote to him three weeks ago, but since then he's been as silent as the grave *or* I haven't heard a thing; *Aut* **la place du m.** the passenger *or Am Fam* the death seat; *Fig* **c'est un m. vivant** he's half dead, he's more dead than alive; *Fig* **les morts vivants** the walking dead, the zombies
◾ NM *Cartes* dummy; **faire le m.** to be dummy

mort² NF death; **m. accidentelle/violente/clinique** accidental/violent/clinical death; **trouver la m. dans un accident** to die in an accident; **se donner la m.** to take one's (own) life; *Fam* **vous allez attraper la m.!** you'll catch your death (of cold)!; *Fam* **c'est pas la m.!** it won't kill you/him/*etc*!; **mourir de sa belle m.** *ou* **de m. naturelle** to die a natural death, to die of natural causes; **mourir de m. violente** to die a violent death; **être à la m.** *ou* **à l'article de la m.** to be at death's door; **à la m. de son père** on his father's death; **pâle comme la m.** as pale as death, deathly pale; **il n'y a pas eu m. d'homme** there was no loss of life; **mettre qn à m.** to put sb to death; **condamner qn à m.** to condemn *or* sentence sb to death; **sentence** *ou* **arrêt de m.** death sentence, sentence of death; **à m. les traîtres!** death to the traitors!; *Arg* **m. aux vaches!** down with the cops!; **blessé à m.** fatally *or Litt* mortally wounded; **lutte à m.** fight to the death *or* the end; *Fam* **freiner à m.** to jam on the brakes; **haïr qn à m.** to hate sb's guts, to loathe and detest sb; *Arg* **s'emmerder à m.** to be bored to death *or* out of one's mind, to be bored rigid; **nous sommes fâchés à m.** we are at daggers drawn; **en vouloir à qn à m.** to have a huge grudge against sb; **je lui en veux à m. d'avoir dit ça** I'll never forgive him for saying that; **ennemis à m.** deadly enemies; **silence de m.** deadly *or* deathlike silence *or* hush; **il avait la m. dans l'âme** he was sick at heart, he had a heavy heart; **partir la m. dans l'âme** to leave with a heavy heart; **souffrir m. et passion** to suffer agonies; **je m'en souviendrai jusqu'à la m.** I'll remember it until my dying day; **à la vie, à la m.** for ever, for life; **jamais je ne t'abandonnerai, à la vie, à la m.** I'll never leave you, we're in this together; **le monopole est la m. de l'industrie** monopoly means the end *or* is the ruin of industry; **ce fut un arrêt de m. pour notre entreprise** it spelt the end *or* was the death knell for our company
◾ ▸▸ *Bot* **m. aux loups** wolfsbane; *Bot* **m. aux poules** henbane; *Méd, Sp* **m. subite** sudden death; *Méd* **m. subite du nourrisson** cot death, *Spéc* sudden infant death syndrome

mortadelle [mɔrtadɛl] NF mortadella

mortaise [mɔrtez] NF *Menuis* mortise; **assemblage à tenon et à m.** mortise (and tenon) joint

mortaiser [mɔrteze] VT *Menuis* to mortise

mortalité [mɔrtalite] NF **1** mortality, death

rate; **taux de m.** mortality *or* death rate; **m. infantile** child *or* infant mortality **2** *Arch (condition mortelle)* mortal nature

mort-aux-rats [mɔrora] **NF INV** rat poison

mort-bois, *pl* **morts-bois NM** underwood, brushwood

morte-eau, *pl* **mortes-eaux NF** neap tide

mortel, -elle [mɔrtɛl] **ADJ 1** *(sujet à la mort)* mortal **2** *(qui tue) (blessure, maladie, accident)* fatal; *(coup)* fatal, lethal; *Fml* mortal; *(dose)* lethal; *(champignon)* poisonous, deadly; **poison m.** deadly poison; **rayon m.** death ray; **il a fait une chute mortelle de 100 mètres** he fell 100 metres to his death; *Fam* **il fait un froid m. dans cette chambre!** it's freezing in this bedroom!, you could freeze to death in this bedroom! **3** *(haine, péché)* deadly; *(silence)* deathly; **ennemi m.** deadly enemy, mortal enemy; **d'une pâleur mortelle** deathly pale **4** *Fam (ennuyeux)* deadly dull, dead boring; **je l'ai attendu deux mortelles heures** I waited two solid *or* whole hours for him; **le sport, je trouve ça m.** I find sport deadly dull; **d'un ennui m.** deadly dull, dead boring **5** *Fam (excellent)* wicked, awesome

▪ **N** mortal

mortellement [mɔrtɛlmã] **ADV** *(blessé)* fatally; *Fml* mortally; **m. pâle** deathly pale; **m. offensé** mortally offended; *Fam* **s'ennuyer m.** to be bored to death, to be bored rigid; **m. ennuyeux** deadly dull, dead boring; *Rel* **pécher m.** to commit a mortal sin

morte-saison, *pl* **mortes-saisons NF** *Com* slack period, off season

mortier [mɔrtje] **NM 1** *Culin* mortar; **pilon et m.** mortar and pestle **2** *Mil* mortar; **obus/tirs de m.** mortar shell/fire; **attaque au m.** mortar attack **3** *Constr* mortar; **m. liquide** *ou* **clair** grout(ing); **planche à m.** mortarboard

mortifiant [mɔrtifjɑ̃] **ADJ** mortifying, humiliating

mortification [mɔrtifikasjɔ̃] **NF 1** *(de la chair, des passions etc)* mortification **2** *(humiliation)* mortification, humiliation; **il a subi une terrible m.** he felt mortified *or* humiliated; **infliger une m. à qn** to mortify *or* humiliate sb **3** *Culin (de gibier)* hanging **4** *Méd Vieilli (de membre)* gangrene, mortification

mortifié [mɔrtifje] **ADJ 1** mortified, humiliated **2** *Méd Vieilli* gangrenous

mortifier [mɔrtifje] *(pr sub, impf n.* **mortifiions, v. mortifiiez)** **VT 1** *(chair, passions)* to mortify **2** *(humilier)* to mortify, to humiliate; **elle en a été mortifiée** she was mortified **3** *Culin (gibier etc)* to hang **4** *Méd Vieilli (membre)* to make gangrenous

▪ **VPR se mortifier** to mortify oneself

mortinatalité [mɔrtinatalite] **NF (taux de) m.** stillbirth rate, number of stillbirths

mort-né, -née, *pl* **mort-né(e)s ADJ** *(enfant, animal)* stillborn; *Fig* **projet m.** plan destined to fail

▪ **N** stillborn child

mortuaire [mɔrtɥɛr] **ADJ** **drap m.** pall; **masque m.** death mask; **registre m.** register of deaths; **la maison m.** the house of the deceased; **chambre m.** death chamber; **dépôt m.** mortuary; **cérémonie m.** funeral; **couronne m.** funeral wreath

morue [mɔry] **NF 1** *(poisson)* cod; **huile de foie de m.** cod-liver oil VOIR GRAMMAIRE A12 **2** *Vulg (prostituée)* tart

morutier, -ière [mɔrytje, -jɛr] **ADJ** *(industrie)* cod-fishing

▪ **NM 1** *(bateau)* cod-fishing boat **2** *(pêcheur)* cod-fisher(man)

morve [mɔrv] **NF 1** *(de nez)* (nasal) mucus, *Fam* snot; **ce gamin a toujours la m. qui lui**

coule du nez that kid has always got a snotty nose **2** *Vét* glanders

morveux, -euse [mɔrvø, -øz] **ADJ 1** *(enfant etc)* runny-nosed; *Fam* snotty-nosed; *(nez)* runny, *Fam* snotty; *Prov* **qui se sent m. se mouche** if the cap fits, wear it **2** *Vét* glandered

▪ **N** *Fam (gamin)* kid, *Péj* brat; *(plus âgé)* snot, (little) jerk, snotty-nosed kid

MOS [mɔs] **NM** *(abrév* **métal-oxyde-semiconducteur)** *Ordinat* **M. complémentaire** complementary MOS

mosaïque¹ [mɔzaik] **ADJ** *Bible (loi)* Mosaic

mosaïque² **NF 1** *Beaux-Arts, Fig* mosaic; **dallage en m.** mosaic flooring; *Fig* **une m. de couleurs** a kaleidoscope of colours **2** *TV (procédé)* pixellation

mosaïste [mɔzaist] **N** *Beaux-Arts* worker in mosaic

Moscou [mɔsku] **N** Moscow

moscovite [mɔskɔvit] **ADJ** Muscovite

▪ **N M.** Muscovite

mosquée [mɔske] **NF** mosque

mot [mo] **NM** word; **les mots me manquent pour t'exprimer ma gratitude** I cannot find the words to express my gratitude; **les mots me manquent!** words fail me!; **manger** *ou* **avaler ses mots** to mumble; **répéter qch m. pour m.** to repeat sth word for word *or* verbatim; **traduire m. à m., faire du m. à m.** to translate word for word *or* literally; **prendre qn au m.** to take sb at his/her word; **groupe de mots** word group; **sans dire** without (saying) a word; **il n'a pas dit un m. de toute la soirée** he didn't say a (single) word the entire evening; **qui ne dit m. consent** silence is tantamount to consent; **ne pas souffler m. de qch** not to breathe a word about sth; **dire un m.** *ou* **deux mots à qn** to have a word with sb; **il n'a pas dit un seul m. en ta faveur** he didn't put in a single good word for you; **avoir des mots avec qn** to have words with sb; **lâche? en effet, je crois que c'est le m.** a coward? yes, I think that's just the word for him; **avoir le dernier m.** to have the last word; **je ne sais pas un (traître) m. de russe** I don't know a word of Russian; **sur ces mots, il se leva** and with these words *or* so saying, he got up; **en un m./quelques mots** in a word/a few words; **en un m. comme en cent** in a nutshell; **il faut compter au bas m. trois heures/500 euros** you'll have to allow at least three hours/500 euros; **gros m.** swearword; **ne dis pas de gros mots!** don't swear!; **des mots doux, des mots d'amour** loving words, *Fam* sweet nothings; **il ne dit jamais un m. plus haut que l'autre** he never raises his voice, he never utters a cross word; **voilà le fin m. de l'affaire!** so that's what's at the bottom of it!; **on ne saura jamais le fin m. de l'affaire** we'll never get to the bottom of it, we'll never know the truth of the matter; **dire qch à mots couverts** to hint at sth, to say sth in a roundabout manner; **faire comprendre qch à qn à mots couverts** to give sb to understand sth in a roundabout manner; **se donner le m.** to pass *or* give the word; **ils ont dû se donner le m.** they must have agreed on it, they must have passed the word around; **envoyer** *ou* **écrire un (petit) m. à qn** to drop sb a line, to write sb a note; **il m'a laissé un m. sur mon bureau** he left a note on my desk; **un m. d'excuse pour l'institutrice** a note for the teacher; **je lui en toucherai un m.** I'll have a word with him about it, I'll mention it to him; **avoir son m. à dire** to have one's say; **tu n'as qu'un m. à dire** just say the word, you just have to say the word; **je ne pouvais pas placer un m.** I couldn't get a word in edgeways; **il a toujours le m. pour rire** he's always ready with a joke; **m. historique** historic remark, mem-

orable saying; **bon m.** witty remark, witticism; *Ordinat* **m. de 6 bits** 6-bit byte; *Ordinat* **m. binaire** binary word

▪ ▪ *aussi Ordinat* **mot-clé,** *pl* **mots-clés** keyword; **mots croisés** crossword puzzle, crossword; **faire des mots croisés** to do crosswords *or* crossword puzzles; **m. d'ordre** *Mil* password; *(de politique)* keynote; *(de parti politique, d'organisation)* watchword, slogan; **m. de passe** password; *Mil* **m. de ralliement** password

motard [mɔtar] **NM** *Fam* **1** biker **2** *(de police)* motorcycle policeman

motel [mɔtɛl] **NM** motel

motet [mɔtɛ] **NM** *Mus* motet

moteur, -trice [mɔtœr, -tris] **ADJ 1** *Tech* **arbre m.** drive shaft, main shaft; *Tech* **unité motrice** power pack *or* unit; **force motrice** driving force; **roue motrice** driving wheel; **voiture à roues avant motrices** car with front-wheel drive; **temps m.** power stroke **2** *Anat (nerve)* motor; **troubles moteurs** motor deficiencies; **un handicapé m.** a person with motor deficiencies

▪ **NM 1** motor, engine; *Cin* **m.!** camera!; **à m.** motor(-driven), power(-driven); **bateau à m.** motorboat; **caméra à m.** motor-driven camera; **commandé par m.** motor(-driven), power(-driven); **à moteurs multiples,** *ou* **à plusieurs moteurs** *(aircraft etc)* multi-engine(d) **2** *Fig* **c'est lui le m. de l'entreprise** he's the driving force behind the undertaking; *Fig* **le m. principal de la pensée hégélienne** the mainspring of Hegelian thought; **sans autre m. que l'amour de la gloire** for no other reason than love of glory

▪ **NF** *Rail* **motrice** motor coach, *surtout Am* motor car

▪ ▪ **m. ACT** ohc engine; **m. à allumage par bougie** spark-ignition engine; **m. à allumage par compression** compression-ignition engine; **m. alternatif à combustion interne** internal combustion (reciprocating) engine; **m. d'avion** aero-engine; **m. carré** square engine; **m. à combustion interne** internal combustion engine; **m. à cylindres à plat** boxer engine; **m. à deux temps** two-stroke engine; **m. diesel** diesel engine; **m. électrique** electric motor; **m. à explosion** internal combustion engine; **m. à gaz** gas engine; **m. hydrogène** hydrogen engine; **m. d'impression** *(d'une imprimante laser)* printer engine; **m. à injection** fuel-injected engine; **m. 'lean burn'** lean-burn engine; **m. en ligne** in-line engine; **m. multicylindre** multi-cylinder engine; **m. multisoupape** multi-valve engine; **m. pas à pas** stepper motor; **m. à pistons** piston engine; **m. à plat** flat engine; **m. polycarburant** multi-fuel engine; **m. polycylindre** multi-cylinder engine; **m. à quatre temps** four-stroke engine; **m. à réaction** jet engine; *Ordinat* **m. de recherche** search engine; **m. à refroidissement par air** air-cooled engine; **m. rénové** reconditioned engine, recon; **m. seize soupapes** sixteen-valve engine; **m. turbocompressé** turbocharged engine; **m. turbodiesel** turbo-diesel engine; **m. en V** vee engine; **m. V6** V6 (engine); **m. à vapeur** steam engine

motif [mɔtif] **NM 1** motive, reason; **un m. valable** a valid reason; **m. de licenciement** grounds for dismissal; **m. de mécontentement** cause *or* grounds for discontent; **m. de réclamation** reason for claim; **avoir un m. pour faire qch** to have a motive *or* a reason for doing sth; **c'est un faux m.** that's not the real reason; **pour quel m. a-t-il été puni?** what was the reason for punishing him?, why was he punished?; *Fam Vieilli* **courtiser qn pour le bon m.** to court sb with honourable intentions; **quel est le m. de ce coup de téléphone?** what is the reason for *or* behind this telephone call?; **quel m. avez-vous de vous plaindre?** what cause or grounds have you for complaint?; **soupçons sans m.** groundless or unfounded suspicions; **il s'est fâché sans m.** he got angry for no reason at all or without any reason; **insulter qn sans m.** to insult sb for no reason at all or Fml gratuitously; **il semble que l'individu ait agi sans m.** it seems that he acted without any motive; **le crime avait-il un m.?** did the crime have a motive?, was there a motive to the crime?; Jur **motifs d'un jugement** grounds upon which a judgment has been delivered **2** Beaux-Arts motif; Couture (pour la broderie) design, pattern, motif; Mus theme, motif, motto; **m. à fleurs** flower(ed) pattern; **papier peint à m. à fleurs** flowered wallpaper; **une veste avec des motifs noirs et blancs** a jacket with a black and white design

motion [mosjɔ̃] NF motion; **proposer une m.** to propose a motion, to move a proposal; **la m. a été adoptée** the motion was carried; **présenter une m.** to table a motion; **m. de censure** motion of censure

motivant [mɔtivɑ̃] ADJ (travail) motivating; (salaire, rémunération) worthwhile

motivation [mɔtivasjɔ̃] NF Psy motivation; **quelles sont vos motivations?** what motivates you?; **joindre une lettre de m. à votre CV** send a covering letter with your CV telling us why you're interested in the job or what prompted you to apply; **m. d'achat** buying motivation

motivé [mɔtive] ADJ **1** (personne) motivated; **élève très m.** very keen or motivated pupil **2** (action) justified; **refus m.** justifiable refusal; **non m.** unjustified, unwarranted; Jur **sentence arbitrale motivée** = award stating the reasons on which it is based; Jur **avis m.** counsel's opinion

motiver [mɔtive] VT **1** (causer, stimuler) (action, personne) to motivate; **l'ambition les motive** they are motivated by ambition; **des crimes motivés par l'argent** crimes motivated by money or with money as the motive **2** (justifier) to justify, to warrant; (refus etc) to state the reason for; **la situation motive nos craintes** the situation gives us (just) cause for concern

moto [moto] NF Fam motorbike; **aller au travail à ou en m.** to go to work on a motorbike, to ride a motorbike to work; **faire de la m.** to ride a motorbike; **m. tout terrain** motocross bike

motocross [motokrɔs] NM Sport motocross

motoculteur [motokyltœr] NM Agr motor cultivator

motoculture [motokyltyr] NF mechanized farming

motocycle [motosikl] NM Admin motorcycle

motocyclette [motosiklɛt] NF motorcycle, Fam motorbike

motocycliste [motosiklist] N motorcyclist, Fam biker; Mil dispatch rider

motomarine [motomarin] NF Can jet ski

motonautique [motonotik] ADJ **sport m.** motorboating

motonautisme [motonotism] NM motorboating

motoneige [motonɛʒ] NF snowmobile, surtout Can skidoo

motopompe [motopɔ̃p] NF motor(-driven) pump

motorisation [mɔtorizasjɔ̃] NF mechanization

motorisé [mɔtorize] ADJ mechanized; Mil **troupes motorisées** mechanized troops; Fam **vous êtes m.?** have you got a car or

transport or Am Fam wheels?, are you mobile?

motoriser [mɔtorize] VT to mechanize

motoriste [mɔtorist] NM engine manufacturer

mot-outil, pl **mots-outils** NM Ling form word, link word

motrice [mɔtris] ADJ, NF voir **moteur**

motricité [mɔtrisite] NF Physiol motor function

motte [mɔt] NF **1** (de terre) clod, clump; (sur les racines d'un arbre) root ball; **m. de gazon** sod, turf; **m. de tourbe** (turf of) peat; **m. de beurre** pat or block of butter; **du beurre à la m.** butter in blocks **2** Archéol motte

motteux [mɔtø] NM (oiseau) wheatear, stonechat

motus [mɔtys] INT **m. (et bouche cousue)!** mum's the word!

mou[1], **molle** [mu, mɔl] ADJ (the masc form **mol** is used before vowel or h mute) (beurre, matelas, substance) soft; (personne) spineless; (gouvernement, chef) spineless, lax, soft; (geste) lifeless, limp; (corde) slack; (pédale) slack, spongy; (chair, main, ventre) flabby, soft; (poignée de main) limp, flabby, feeble; (muscle) soft, Fml flaccid; (style) feeble, flabby; **ce que tu peux être m.!** God you're feeble or useless!; **j'ai les jambes molles** my legs are like cotton wool; **m. au toucher** soft to the touch; **un mol (et doux) oreiller** a (soft and) downy pillow; **des collines molles, des collines au relief m.** rolling hills; Fam **il est m. comme une chiffe** ou **comme une chique** he's an absolute wimp; Fam **je ne me sens pas bien, je suis** ou **je me sens tout m.** I'm not well, I feel like a wet rag; **il m'a fait de molles excuses** he gave me some lame or feeble excuses

N Fam wimp

NM (de corde, fil) slack; **donne-moi un peu de m.** give me some slack; **donner du m. à un cordage** to slacken a rope; **prendre du m.** (d'une corde) to slacken

ADV **1** **elle joue trop m.** she doesn't put enough verve into her playing **2** très Fam **vas-y m.!** go easy!, take it easy!; **vas-y m. avec le whisky** go easy on the whisky

mou[2] NM (abats) lights, lungs; Fig Fam **il est en train de te bourrer le m.** he's spinning you a yarn or handing you a line; Fig Fam **je vais lui rentrer dans le m.** I'll punch him one

mouais [mwɛ] ADV Fam well, yeah; **alors, t'as aimé le film? – m., j'ai vu pire** did you like the movie, then? – well, yeah, I've seen worse

mouchage [muʃaʒ] NM **1** (de nez) wiping, blowing **2** (de chandelles) snuffing (out)

mouchard, -arde [muʃar, -ard] N Fam (informateur) grass, informer, stool pigeon; Scol sneak

NM **1** Tech (tachymètre) spy in the cab **2** (contrôleur) watchman's clock **3** Aviat observation plane **4** (dans une porte) peephole **5** Ordinat **m. électronique** cookie

moucharder [muʃarde] VT Fam (personne) to grass or squeal on, to grass up; Scol to sneak on; **tu n'as pas intérêt à m.** you'd better not grass or squeal

mouche [muʃ] NF **1** (insecte) fly; **on aurait entendu une m. voler** you could have heard a pin drop; **gober les mouches, regarder les mouches voler** to gaze or stare into space; Fam **prendre** ou Suisse **piquer la m.** to fly off the handle; Fam **quelle m. vous pique?** what's up with you?, what's bitten you?, who rattled your cage?; **elle ne ferait pas de mal à une m.** she wouldn't hurt a fly; **tomber comme des mouches** to be dropping like flies; **c'est une fine m.** he's a sharp customer, he's a fly one; **j'ai des mouches devant les**

yeux I've got spots before my eyes; **Pêche m. mouillée** wet fly; **Pêche m. à saumon** salmon fly; **pêche à la m. sèche** dry-fly fishing; Boxe **poids m.** flyweight **2** (de cible) bull's-eye; **faire m.** to hit the bull's-eye, to score a bull; Fig **il a fait m. avec cette proposition** he hit the jackpot or he scored with that suggestion **3 bateau m.** river bus, bateau mouche **4** Hist (faux grain de beauté) patch; (sur menton) tuft of hair **5** Escrime button **6** Arch (tache) spot, speck; (sur vêtement etc) stain

▸ ▸ **m. bleue** bluebottle, blowfly; **m. domestique** housefly; Can **m. à feu** firefly; très Fam **m. à merde** (bleue) bluebottle; (verte) greenbottle; **m. à miel** honey bee; **m. tsé-tsé** tsetse fly; **m. de la viande** blowfly, bluebottle

moucher [muʃe] VT **1** (nez) to wipe, to blow; **m. un enfant** to wipe a child's nose; **je mouche du sang** there's blood on my handkerchief when I blow my nose **2** (chandelle) to snuff (out); Fam **m. qn** to put sb in his/her place

VPR **se moucher** to blow one's nose; Fam **il ne se mouche pas du coude** ou **du pied** he thinks a lot or he's got a high opinion of himself

moucheron [muʃrɔ̃] NM gnat, midge

moucheronner [muʃrɔne] VI (de poisson) to be rising, to be on the rise

moucheté [muʃte] ADJ **1** (poisson, œuf) speckled; (robe de cheval) dappled; **mer mouchetée d'écume** foam-flecked sea; **nez m. de taches de rousseur** freckled nose; **une écharpe blanche mouchetée de noir** a white scarf flecked or specked with black, a white scarf with black flecks **2** Escrime (fleuret) buttoned

moucheter [muʃte] VT (je mouchette; je mouchetterai) **1** (étoffe, papier) to speckle, to fleck **2** Escrime to button, to put a button on

mouchette [muʃɛt] NF **1 mouchettes** (pour chandelles) (pair of) snuffers **2** Archit (de larmier) outer fillet

moucheture [muʃtyr] NF speck, speckle; **une écharpe blanche avec des mouchetures noires** a white scarf with black flecks, a white scarf specked or flecked with black

mouchoir [muʃwar] NM handkerchief; (autour du cou) kerchief; **m. en papier** paper handkerchief, tissue; **m. en tissu** handkerchief; Fig **je vais faire un nœud à mon m.** I'll tie a knot in my handkerchief; **jardin grand comme un m. (de poche)** pocket handkerchief (of a) garden; **arriver dans un m. de poche** to come in neck and neck

mouchure [muʃyr] NF (du nez) mucus

moudjahidin [mudʒaidin] NMPL mujaheddin, mujahedeen

moudre [mudr] VT (prp moulant; pp moulu; pr ind je mouds, il moud, n. moulons, ils moulent; pr sub je moule; p hist je moulus; fu je moudrai) **1** (grain) to grind, to mill; (café, poivre) to grind; Fig **m. qn de coups** to beat sb to a pulp **2** Vieilli (air) (sur orgue de Barbarie) to grind out

moue [mu] NF pout; **faire la m.** to pout, to look sulky; **faire une m.** to purse one's lips; **m. boudeuse** sulk; **il eut une m. désapprobatrice** he looked disapproving; Fig **le public fit la m. et la pièce fit un four** the public stayed away in droves and the play flopped; **les critiques firent la m.** the critics turned up their noses

mouette [mwɛt] NF (sea)gull

mouf(f)ette [mufɛt] NF skunk

moufle [mufl] NF (gant) mitten, mitt
N Tech **1** tackle block, pulley block **2** (palan) (block and) tackle

mouflet, -ette [muflɛ, -ɛt] N Fam (enfant) kid, Péj brat

mouflon [muflɔ̃] NM mouf(f)lon, wild sheep

moufter [mufte] VI Fam **ne pas m.** to keep shtum, to keep one's mouth shut

mouillage [mujaʒ] NM **1** (de tissu, linge) moistening, damping; (du vin) (fraudulent) watering down **2** Naut (de bateau) anchoring; (de mine) laying; (de bouée) putting down **3** Naut (emplacement) anchorage, moorage; **être au m.** to be riding at anchor; **prendre son m.** to anchor

mouillé [muje] ADJ **1** wet; **tout m.** soaked; **m. jusqu'aux os** wet through, soaked to the skin; **elle avait les yeux mouillés de larmes** her eyes were wet with tears **2** Ling (consonne) palatalized

mouillement [mujmɑ̃] NM Ling palatalization

mouiller [muje] VT **1** (rendre humide) to wet; (linge à repasser) to moisten, to damp(en); Culin (ragoût) to add liquid to; (vin, boisson alcoolisée, lait) to dilute, to water down; **il a mouillé le bas de son pantalon en traversant la rivière à gué** he got the bottom of his trousers wet wading across the river; **l'averse a mouillé le linge** the clothes got wet in the rain; **on s'est fait m. par l'averse** we got soaked in the downpour; Fig **m. sa chemise** to put one's back into it, to work up a sweat, to get stuck in; **ce n'est pas avec le travail qu'il fournit qu'il risque de m. sa chemise** ou **son maillot** he's not likely to break into a sweat with the amount of work that he does **2** Naut (ancre) to cast, to drop **3** Naut (mine) to lay; (bouée) to put down **4** Fam (compromettre) to involve, to drag in **5** Ling (consonne) to palatalize **6** Can Fam (fêter) **il va falloir m. ça!** we'll have to have a drink to celebrate!, this calls for a celebration!
VI **1** Naut to anchor; (de navire) to lie at anchor; **mouillez!** let go (the anchor)! **2** Fam (avoir peur) to wet oneself **3** très Fam (être excitée sexuellement) to be wet **4** Can Fam (pleuvoir) to rain; **m. à siau** ou **à verse** ou **à boire debout** to rain buckets
VPR **se mouiller 1** to get wet; (des yeux) to fill with tears; **se m. les pieds** to get one's feet wet **2** Fam (dans un crime, une affaire louche) to get involved; **il ne veut pas se m.** (prendre parti) he doesn't want to stick his neck out

mouillette [mujɛt] NF (de pain) finger, surtout Br soldier

mouilleur [mujœr] NM **1** Naut **m. de mines** minelayer **2** (pour timbres) damper

mouillure [mujyr] NF **1** (marque) damp mark, stain **2** Ling (de consonne) palatalization

mouise [mwiz] NF Arg (misère) poverty; (ennuis) hassle; **être dans la m.** to be hard up or in dire straits; **tirer qn de la m.** to get sb out of a hole

moujik [muʒik] NM moujik

moujingue [muʒɛ̃g] N Arg (enfant) kid, Péj brat

moukère [mukɛr] NF (femme maghrébine) Maghrebi woman; Arg (femme) female; (prostituée) pro

moulage[1] [mulaʒ] NM (du grain) grinding, milling

moulage[2] NM **1** (fait de mouler) casting, moulding, Am molding; (de fer) founding; **m. à cire perdue** lost wax process **2 m. au** ou **en plâtre** plaster cast

moule[1] [mul] NM **1** mould, Am mold; Tech mould, Spéc matrix; **m. à gelée** jelly mould; **m. à gâteaux** cake tin; **m. à beurre** butter mould or print **2** Fig **on n'en fait plus des comme lui, on a cassé le m.** they broke the mould when they made him; **elle a rejeté le m. de son éducation** she has broken out of the mould of her upbringing; **ils ont été coulés dans le même m.** they're cast in the same mould, they're out of the same mould;

l'école est un m. qui étouffe la créativité de l'enfant school stifles children's creativity by forcing them into a mould; **une fille faite au m.** a girl with a great figure

moule[2] NF **1** Zool, Culin mussel **2** Arg (personne molle) wimp, drip; (idiot) fool, idiot **3** Vulg (sexe de femme) pussy, cunt

moulé [mule] ADJ cast, moulded, Am molded; **statue de plâtre m.** plaster cast; **pain m.** tin loaf; **écriture moulée** copperplate handwriting; **lettres moulées** printing; **je me trouve trop moulée dans cette robe** this dress clings too much

mouler [mule] VT to mould, Am to mold; Métal to cast; **robe qui moule la taille** tightly fitting or figure-hugging dress; Fig **m. sa conduite sur qn** to model one's behaviour on sb
VPR **se mouler** Fig (prendre pour modèle) to model oneself (**sur** on)

moules-frites [mulfrit] NM INV Belg **1** Culin mussels and chips or Am French fries **2** (restaurant) = restaurant specializing in mussels and chips or Am French fries

mouleur [mulœr] NM caster, moulder, Am molder

moulière [muljɛr] NF mussel bed

moulin [mulɛ̃] NM **1** mill; **roue de m.** millwheel; **on y entre comme dans un m.** people or all and sundry can just walk in; **ce n'est pas un m. ici!** you can't just walk in or breeze in as if you own the place! **2** Fam (de voiture) engine
▸▸ **m. à café** coffee grinder; (manuel) coffee mill; **m. à eau** watermill; **m. à légumes** food mill; **m. à minerai** ore crusher; Fig **m. à paroles** chatterbox, gasbag; **m. à poivre** pepper mill; Rel **m. à prières** prayer wheel; **m. à vent** windmill; Fig **se battre contre les moulins à vent** to tilt at windmills

mouliner [muline] VT **1** Culin to pass through a food mill **2** Pêche (ligne) to reel in

moulinet [mulinɛ] NM **1** Tech winch; Pêche reel **2 faire des moulinets (avec sa canne)** to twirl one's (walking) stick; **faire des moulinets (avec les bras)** to wave one's arms around

Moulinette® [mulinɛt] NF food mill; **passer la viande à la M.** to put the meat through the food mill; Fig **il m'a passé à la M.** he put me through it or through the mill; Fig **passer qch à la M.** to tear sth to shreds

moult [mult] ADV Hum, Vieilli a multitude of; **avec m. remerciements** with many thanks

moulu [muly] ADJ (café, poivre) ground; Fig (personne) shattered, worn-out, dead-beat; **m. (de coups)** black and blue

moulure [mulyr] NF Archit, Menuis (ornamental) moulding or Am molding

moulurer [mulyre] VT Constr to cut a moulding or Am molding on; **profils moulurés** mouldings

moumoute [mumut] NF **1** (veste) fleece (jacket) **2** Fam (perruque) wig, rug, Br syrup

mourant, -ante [murɑ̃, -ɑ̃t] ADJ dying; (voix) faint
N dying man, f woman; **les mourants** the dying

mourir [murir] (prp **mourant;** pp **mort;** pr ind **je meurs, il meurt, n. mourons, ils meurent;** pr sub **je meure, n. mourions;** p hist **il mourut;** fu **je mourrai** [murre]; aux **être**) VI **1** (de personne, d'animal, de plante) to die; **il est mort hier** he died yesterday; **il est mort assassiné** he was murdered; **il est mort de vieillesse** he died of old age; **m. de faim** to die of starvation, to starve to death; (avoir très faim) to be starving; **m. de soif/de chaleur/d'épuisement** to die of thirst/heat/exhaustion; **m. de froid** to freeze to death; **m.**

accidentellement to die in an accident; **elle l'aimait à en m.** she was desperately in love with him; **m. avant l'âge** to die before one's time; **m. à la tâche** to die in harness, Fam to die with one's boots on; **au moment de m.** in the hour of death; **au moment de m., il a fait venir toute sa famille** just before he died, he sent for his entire family; **faire m. qn** to put sb to death; **faire m. qn à petit feu** to kill sb by inches; Fam **il me fera m.** he'll be the death of me; **vous me faites m. d'impatience** the suspense is killing me; **je mourais de peur** I was dying of fright, I was frightened to death; **m. d'inquiétude** to be worried to death; **elle me fera m. d'inquiétude** she'll worry me to death, she'll be the death of me; **m. de chagrin** to be weighed down with grief, to be grief-stricken; (littéralement) to die of grief; **m. d'ennui** to die of boredom; **ennuyer qn à m.** to bore sb to death; **être à m. d'ennui** (de film, roman, conversation) to be deadly boring; **m. d'envie de faire qch** to be dying to do sth; **j'ai cru m. de rire** I thought I would die laughing, I nearly died laughing; **être à m. de rire** (de film, roman, personne) to be uproariously funny; très Fam **plus bête/avare que lui, tu meurs** there's nobody on God's earth who's as stupid/mean as he is; Fig **tu ne vas pas en m., tout de même!** it won't kill you, you know!
2 (d'un feu, d'une coutume, d'une industrie, d'une civilisation) to die out; (d'une région) to die; **la plainte s'enfla, envahit l'espace, puis finit par m.** the wailing grew, filled the whole space, then finally died away or faded away; **les vagues qui viennent m. sur la plage** the waves which break and spend themselves on the beach
V IMPERS **il meurt des milliers d'enfants chaque jour** thousands of children die every day
VPR **se mourir** Litt to be dying; (d'une habitude) to die out; (d'un feu) to die down; **je sens que je me meurs** I feel that I am dying; **la lampe se mourait** the lamp was fading or giving out

mouroir [murwar] NM Fam Péj old people's home; **ces foyers de personnes âgées sont des mouroirs** these homes are just places where old people are left to die

mouron [murɔ̃] NM Fam **se faire du m.** to worry; **je commence à me faire du m.** I'm beginning to worry or get worried

mousquet [muskɛ] NM musket

mousquetaire [muskətɛr] NM musketeer; **gants (à la) m.** gauntlets

mousqueterie [muskətri] NF musketry; **feu de m.** musket fire

mousqueton [muskətɔ̃] NM **1** Mil (fusil court) carbine **2** (d'escalade etc) (anneau) karabiner; (système d'accrochage) snaphook

moussage [musaʒ] NM foaming

moussaillon [musajɔ̃] NM Fam ship's boy

moussaka [musaka] NF Culin moussaka

moussant [musɑ̃] ADJ (gel) foaming; **être très m.** to produce a lot of lather; **il est peu m.** it doesn't produce or give much of a lather

mousse[1] [mus] NF **1** Bot moss; **couvert de m.** covered with moss, moss-grown, mossy; Prov **pierre qui roule n'amasse pas m.** a rolling stone gathers no moss; Tricot **point m.** moss stitch **2** (de mer, dans cours d'eau pollué, de cappuccino) froth, foam; (sur verre de bière) head; (de savon) lather; Culin mousse; **les assiettes sont encore pleines de m.** the plates are still covered in suds; **les vêtements sont encore pleins de m.** the clothes are still full of soap; Fam **une m.** (bière) a beer; Fam **se faire de la m.** to fret, to worry; Culin **m. au chocolat/de saumon** chocolate/salmon mousse; **m. à raser** shaving foam **3 (caoutchouc) M.**® foam rubber; **matelas en M.** foam rubber mattress

mousse [2] **NM 1** *(dans la marine)* ship's boy **2** *Can Fam (terme d'affection)* darling, sweetheart

mousse [3] **ADJ** *Tech (lame, pointe etc)* blunt

mousseline [muslin] **NF 1** *Tex* muslin; **m. de soie** chiffon **2** *Culin* **pommes (de terre) m.** puréed potatoes

mousser [muse] **VI** *(de bière)* to froth, to foam; *(d'eau savonneuse, de savon, de lessive)* to lather; *(de vin, d'eau gazeuse)* to sparkle, to fizz; **ce savon/cette lessive ne mousse pas beaucoup** this soap/washing powder doesn't lather very well *or* doesn't give much of a lather; **ce champagne mousse beaucoup** there are a lot of bubbles in this champagne, this champagne is very fizzy; *Arg* **faire m. qn** *(mettre en colère)* to make sb lose his/her temper *or* flare up; *(faire valoir)* to boast about sb, to sing sb's praises; **se faire m.** to show off

mousseron [musrɔ̃] **NM** edible mushroom, *surtout* St George's agaric

mousseux, -euse [musø, -øz] **ADJ 1** *(écumeux) (eau)* frothy, foaming; *(chocolat, cappuccino, crème)* frothy; *(bière)* frothy, with a lot of head **2** *(vin, cidre)* sparkling
NM sparkling wine

moussoir [muswar] **NM** whisk

mousson [musɔ̃] **NF** monsoon

moussu [musy] **ADJ** mossy, mossgrown

moustache [mustaʃ] **NF 1 m., moustaches** moustache; **m. à la gauloise** walrus moustache; **m. en brosse** toothbrush moustache; **porter la m., avoir une m.** to have a moustache **2** *(de chat, rongeur)* whiskers

moustachu [mustaʃy] **ADJ** *(homme)* with a moustache; **être m.** to have a moustache
NM man with a moustache

moustiquaire [mustiker] **NF** mosquito net; *Can (à la fenêtre)* screen

moustique [mustik] **NM 1** *(insecte)* mosquito VOIR GRAMMAIRE A12 **2** *Fam (personne maigrichonne)* weed; *(enfant)* kid, nipper

moût [mu] **NM** *(de raisins)* must; *(de bière)* wort

moutard [mutar] **NM** *Arg (enfant)* kid, nipper

moutarde [mutard] **NF** mustard; **m. forte** *ou* **de Dijon** strong *or* Dijon mustard; **graine de m.** mustard seed; *Fig* **la m. lui est montée au nez** he lost his temper *or* flared up; **je sens la m. qui me monte au nez** I'm beginning to lose my temper
ADJ INV gaz m. mustard gas; **(jaune) m.** mustard (yellow)

moutardier [mutardje] **NM 1** *(fabricant)* mustard maker; *(vendeur)* mustard seller; *Fam* **il se croit le premier m. du pape** he thinks he's the cat's pyjamas *or* the bee's knees **2** *(pot)* mustard pot

moutier [mutje] **NM** *Arch* monastery

mouton, -onne [mutɔ̃, -ɔn] **NM 1** *Zool* sheep; *Culin* mutton; **(peau de) m.** sheepskin; *Culin* **ragoût de m.** mutton stew; **éleveur de moutons** *(pour la viande)* sheep farmer; *(pour la laine)* woolgrower; **doux comme un m.** as meek as a lamb; **être frisé comme un m.** to have curly hair; *Fig* **revenons à nos moutons** let's get back to the subject; **ils ont tous suivi comme des moutons** they all followed like sheep; **compter les moutons** *(pour s'endormir)* to count sheep; *Fig* **c'est un m. à cinq pattes** he's a rare breed; **vous recherchez le m. à cinq pattes** you're looking for something that doesn't exist, you want the impossible VOIR GRAMMAIRE A12 **2** *Fam (dans les prisons)* grass **3 moutons** *(sur les vagues)* white horses; *(dans le ciel)* fluffy *or* fleecy white clouds; **la mer fait des moutons**

there are white horses on the sea **4 moutons** *(sous les meubles)* fluff, *Am* dust bunnies **5** *Constr* drop hammer
ADJ *Fig* sheeplike

moutonnant [mutɔnɑ̃] **ADJ** *(mer)* covered with white horses

moutonné [mutɔne] **ADJ** *(ciel)* dotted with fleecy clouds; **tête moutonnée** curly head of hair

moutonnement [mutɔnmɑ̃] **NM** *(de la mer)* breaking into white horses, frothing; **m. du ciel** dotting of fleecy clouds in the sky

moutonner [mutɔne] **VI** *(de la mer)* to break into white horses, to froth; *(du ciel)* to become dotted with fleecy clouds

moutonneux, -euse [mutɔnø, -øz] **ADJ 1** *(mer)* foam-flecked, covered with white horses **2** *(ciel)* dotted with fleecy clouds

moutonnier, -ière [mutɔnje, -jɛr] **ADJ** *(élevage)* sheep; *Fig (foule)* sheeplike; *(personne)* easily led

mouture [mutyr] **NF 1** *(de blé)* grinding, milling; *(de café)* grinding; **avec ce moulin à café, la m. est excellente** this mill grinds the coffee really well; **si la m. était plus fine** if it were ground more finely; **vous voulez quelle m.?** how would you like it ground?; *Fig Vieilli* **tirer deux moutures d'un sac** to profit twice over from sth **2** *(d'un ouvrage, d'un livre)* version, *Péj* rehash; **c'est la deuxième m. du texte** this is the second version of *or* draft of *or Fam* go at the text

mouv' [muv] **NM** *Fam (abrév* **mouvement)** **c'est dans le m.** it's dead hip, it's totally cool

mouvance [muvɑ̃s] **NF 1** *(de pays)* sphere of influence; **elle a été dans la m. surréaliste pendant un temps** she moved in surrealist circles for a time; **il se situe davantage dans la m. du Parti socialiste** he is closer to *or* tends more towards the Socialist Party **2** *Litt (instabilité)* flux, constant change; **tout est en m.** everything is in a state of flux

mouvant [muvɑ̃] **ADJ** *(terrain)* unstable; *(cible)* moving; *(feuillage, herbe)* swaying; **les blés mouvants sous le ciel d'orage** the swaying corn under the stormy sky; *Fig* **être sur un terrain m.** to be on shifting *or* unsteady ground

mouvement [muvmɑ̃] **NM 1** *(déplacement)* movement, motion; *(geste)* gesture; **m. vers l'arrière** backward movement *or* motion; **il tomba du cheval et resta sans m.** he fell from his horse and lay motionless on the ground; **il y eut un m. de panique dans la foule** the crowd panicked; **il y eut un m. de foule** a ripple ran through the crowd; **il y eut un m. de foule et je perdis mon frère de vue** I lost sight of my brother in the crush; **un m. de panique à la Bourse** panic *or* a panicky reaction on the Stock Exchange; **faire un m.** to move; **faire un faux m.** *(qui provoque une douleur)* to move the wrong way; **j'ai fait un faux m. et j'ai renversé le verre de vin** I clumsily knocked the glass of wine over; **surveiller les mouvements de qn** to monitor sb's movements; **il aime le m.** *(voyager)* he likes to move around, he can't stay in one place; **être toujours en m.** *(d'une personne)* to be always on the move; **répondre d'un m. de tête** *(pour dire non)* to answer with a shake of the head, to shake one's head; *(pour dire oui)* to answer with a nod, to nod; **elle me fit signe d'entrer d'un m. de tête** she signalled to me to come in; **avoir un m. de dégoût** to recoil in disgust; **il a eu un m. de recul** he recoiled, he started backwards; **mettre un mécanisme en m.** to set a machine in motion, to start a machine; **se mettre en m.** to start off, to move off; **c'est une ville toujours en m.** it's a bustling *or* very lively city; **quelques mouvements de gymnastique** a few exercises; **des mouvements**

pour soulager son mal de dos exercises to relieve one's backache; **on ne pouvait pas faire un m.** you couldn't move; **un film d'action où il y a beaucoup de m.** an action film with lots going on; **pièces en m.** *(de machine)* moving parts; **contrôler le m. des marchandises/des capitaux** to monitor the flow *or* movement of goods/capital; *Aut* **m. de caisse** body roll; *Mil* **m. de troupes** troop movement; **guerre de m.** mobile warfare; **amorcer un m. de repli** to start falling back; *Fam* **il faut accélérer le m.** we'll have to get a move on; **m. perpétuel** perpetual motion

2 *(changement)* **m. de terrain** undulation; **un m. de personnel** staff changes; **suivre le m.** to go with the flow; **le m. des idées** the evolution of ideas; **le m. des naissances** the trend in the birth rate; *Fam* **être dans le m.** to be with it, to be abreast of the times *or* up to date; *Bourse* **connaître un m. à la hausse/à la baisse** to move up/down; **m. ascensionnel** upward movement; **m. de baisse** downward movement; **m. boursier** Stock Market movement; **mouvements de compte** account transactions; **m. des capitaux** movement of capital; **m. des cours/des prix** price fluctuation; **m. des devises** currency fluctuation; **m. des valeurs** share movements; **mouvements monétaires** monetary fluctuations

3 *(élan)* **mon premier m. fut de …** my first impulse was to …; **m. d'humeur** outburst (of temper); **dans un m. de colère** in a fit of anger; **de son propre m.** of one's own accord; **avoir un bon m.** to act on a kindly impulse; **allez! un bon m.!** be a good sort!

4 *Pol etc* movement; **le m. syndical/ouvrier** the union/labour movement; **M. de libération de la femme** Women's Liberation Movement, *Fam* Women's Lib; **m. pacifiste** peace movement; **m. de contestation** protest movement; **m. de défense des consommateurs** consumer movement; **les cheminots vont reconduire leur m. de grève** the railwaymen want to extend their strike action; **lancer un m. de grève/révolte** to instigate a strike/revolt; **m. indépendantiste** independence *or* separatist movement; **m. insurrectionnel** uprising; **m. ouvrier** labour movement; **m. séparatiste** separatist *or* independence movement; **mouvements sociaux** workers' protest movements; **m. syndical** trade-union *or Am* labor-union movement

5 *(aspect)* *(de draperies, cou, reins)* line(s); *(de terrain)* contours

6 *(dans un port, un aéroport, une gare)* traffic; **un quartier où il y a toujours beaucoup de m.** a very busy area, an area with a lot of traffic; *Rail* **mouvements des trains** train arrivals and departures; *Rail* **chef de m.** traffic manager; **mouvements des navires** shipping intelligence

7 *Mus* movement; **symphonie à trois mouvements** symphony in three movements; **presser/ralentir le m.** to quicken/slow the tempo

8 *(d'horloge)* works, movement; **m. d'horlogerie** clockwork

mouvementé [muvmɑ̃te] **ADJ 1** *(discussion, débat)* animated, lively; *(journée, voyage, traversée, vie)* eventful; **une partie mouvementée** an exciting game **2 terrain m.** undulating ground

mouvoir [muvwar] *(prp* **mouvant**, *pp* **mû**, *f* **mue**; *pr ind* **je meus, il meut, n. mouvons, ils meuvent**; *pr sub* **je meuve, n. mouvions, ils meuvent**; *p hist* **je mus** *(rare)*, *fu* **je mouvrai***)* **VT 1** *(machine)* to drive, *Fml* to actuate; *(bateau)* to propel; **mû par la vapeur** steam-driven; **mû par un ressort** spring-loaded; *Fig* **mû par la colère** moved *or* prompted by anger; **mû par l'intérêt** prompted by interest **2** *(objet)* to move
VPR se mouvoir to move

moyen¹, -enne [mwajɛ̃, -ɛn] ADJ **1** (*du milieu*) middle; **les classes moyennes** the middle class(es); *Scol* **cours m.** intermediate class; **cours m. première/deuxième année** *Br* ≃ primary IV/V, *Am* ≃ fourth/fifth grade; *Géog* **le cours m. d'un fleuve** the middle reaches of a river; **moyenne saison** (*en tourisme*) shoulder period **2** (*coût, prix, durée, consommateur, élève, altitude etc*) average; (*pression, vitesse, température, temps de réaction*) average, *surtout Spéc* mean; (*qualité*) average, medium; **la durée moyenne de travail du Français** the average hours of work in France; **le Français m.** the average Frenchman, the man in the street; **à m. terme** in the medium term; **choisir un m. terme** to choose a middle course; **entre la passivité et la guerre, il doit y avoir un m. terme** there must be a middle ground between passiveness and war; **de taille** *ou* **grandeur moyenne** medium-sized; **femme de taille moyenne** woman of average height; *Péj* **travail/vin d'une qualité très moyenne** very average work/wine, work/wine of a very indifferent quality; **il est trop m. en physique** his physics marks aren't good enough

MOYEN² NM **VOIR GRAMMAIRE A13** **1** means; *Prov* **la fin justifie les moyens** the end justifies the means; *Prov* **qui veut la fin veut les moyens** you can't make an omelette without breaking eggs; **par tous les moyens** any way I/you/*etc* can/could, *Péj* by fair means or foul; **j'emploierai tous les moyens** I'll use whatever means I have to, I'll do whatever I have to; **employer les grands moyens** to take extreme measures; **au m.** *ou* **par (le) m. de qch** by means of *or* with the help of sth; **il a calé la table au m. d'un ticket de métro** he used a metro ticket as a wedge for the table, he wedged the table with a metro ticket; **y a-t-il m. de le faire?** is there any way it can be done?, is it possible (to do it)?; **y a-t-il m. d'éviter le centre-ville?** is there any way of avoiding the centre of town?; **y aurait-il m. de s'arrêter cinq minutes?** would it be possible to *or* could we stop for five minutes?; **y aurait-il m. d'avoir un vol moins cher/d'avoir un peu de pain avec mon fromage?** is there any chance of a cheaper flight/a bit of bread with my cheese?; **il y a m. de la contacter par l'intermédiaire de ses parents** she can be contacted through her parents; **il n'y a pas m.** it can't be done, it's impossible; **j'ai essayé d'ouvrir le pot, il n'y a pas m.** I've tried to open the jar but it's impossible, *Fam* I've tried but no way can I get the jar open; **il n'y a pas m. de lui faire comprendre** there's no way of making him understand, it's impossible to *or Fam* no way can you make him understand; **j'ai essayé de le convaincre mais il n'y a pas eu m.** I tried to convince him but it was impossible *or* but I couldn't budge him; *Fam* **j'ai essayé de lui faire entendre raison/de le faire changer d'avis: pas m.!** I tried to make him see reason/change his mind, but no way!; *Fam* **j'ai essayé de le joindre au téléphone tout l'après-midi: pas m.!** I tried all afternoon to get him on the phone but it was impossible *or* but nothing doing; *Fam* **y a m.!** can do!; **trouver un m. de faire qch** to find a way *or* means of doing sth; **trouver le m. de faire qch** to discover *or* find out how to do sth; **il a encore trouvé le m. de se faire dispenser** he's managed to get out of it again; *Iron* **elle a trouvé le m. de se mettre mal avec tous ses collègues** she's managed to get *or* she's succeeded in getting on bad terms with all her colleagues; **inventer un m. de s'échapper** to come up with a way of escaping; **faire qch par ses propres moyens** to do sth on one's own *or* unaided; **elle est venue par ses propres moyens** she came under her own steam; **m. de transport** means of transport; **disposes-tu d'un m. de transport?** do you have transport?; **moyens de production** means of production; **moyens de communication** means of communication; **avec les moyens du bord** with the means at one's disposal; **nous avons fait avec les moyens du bord** we made do with what we had; **si tu veux réussir, il faut t'en donner les moyens** if you want to succeed, you have to equip yourself to do so; **dans la mesure de mes moyens** to the best *or* to the utmost of my ability, as best I can; **enfant qui a des moyens** bright *or* talented child; **il a peu de moyens** he's not very bright; **perdre tous ses moyens** to lose one's head, to go to pieces; **faire perdre tous ses moyens à qn** to make sb lose his/her head **2** *Fin* **moyens** means; **moyens de paiement** means of payment; **moyens financiers** financial means; **moyens liquides** liquid resources; **vivre au-dessus de ses moyens** to live beyond one's means; **il a largement les moyens de faire construire** he can well afford to build; **je n'en ai pas les moyens** I can't afford it; **ils ont les moyens** (*ils ont de l'argent*) they're well off; (*ils peuvent se le permettre*) they can afford it; **dans la mesure de mes moyens** as best I can, as far as my finances permit

Moyen Âge [mwajɛnaʒ] NM **le M.** the Middle Ages; **le haut M.** the early Middle Ages; **coutumes du M.** medieval customs

moyenâgeux, -euse [mwajɛnaʒø, -øz] ADJ medieval; *Fig Péj* medieval, old-fashioned, outdated

moyen-courrier, *pl* **moyens-courriers** ADJ, NM (*avion*) **m.** medium-range *or* medium-haul aircraft

moyen-métrage, *pl* **moyens-métrages** NM *Cin* medium-length film

moyennant [mwajɛnɑ̃] PRÉP (in return) for; **louer qch m. cent euros par jour** to hire sth for *or* at (a charge of) a hundred euros a day; **m. paiement** in exchange for payment, subject to payment; **faire qch m. finance** to do sth in return for payment *or* for a consideration; **je veux bien nettoyer ton jardin, mais m. finance** I'm willing to tidy up your garden, but I'll want to be paid for it; **m. dix euros** for ten euros, on payment of ten euros; **m. quoi** in return for which, *Fml* in consideration of which; **je l'ai aidé à faire son devoir d'anglais, m. quoi il … ** I helped him with his English homework, and in return he …

moyenne [mwajɛn] NF average; *Math* mean; *Scol* pass mark; **j'ai 8/20 de m. en mathématiques** I averaged 40% in maths; *Scol* **améliorer sa m. de français** to improve one's average (mark) in French; **en m.** on (an) average; **m. (horaire)** (hourly) average; *Aut* average (speed); **faire du 100 de m.** to do an average of *or* to average 100 kilometres per hour; **supérieure/inférieure à la m.** above/below average, higher/lower than average; **enfant d'une intelligence au-dessus/au-dessous de la m.** child of above/below average intelligence; **m. de temps entre deux pannes** mean time between failures, MTBF; *Compta* **m. mobile** moving average; **m. pondérée** weighted average

moyennement [mwajɛnmɑ̃] ADV moderately, fairly; **travailler m.** to work fairly well

Moyen-Orient [mwajɛnɔrjɑ̃] NM **le M.** the Middle East

moyen-oriental, -ale, -aux, -ales [mwajɛnɔrjɑ̃tal, -o] ADJ Middle Eastern

moyette [mwajɛt] NF *Agr* (*de blé*) shock

moyeu, -eux [mwajø] NM (*de roue de voiture*) hub; (*de roue de charrette*) nave; (*d'hélice*) boss

mozambicain, -aine [mɔzɑ̃bikɛ̃, -ɛn] ADJ Mozambican
▸ N **M.** Mozambican

Mozambique [mɔzɑ̃bik] NM Mozambique

mozzarella [mɔdzarɛla], **mozzarelle** [mɔdzarɛl] NF mozzarella

MRAP [mrap] NM (*abrév* **Mouvement contre le racisme, l'antisémitisme et pour la paix**) = French antiracist pacifist movement

MS-DOS [ɛmɛsdɔs] NM *Ordinat* (*abrév* **Microsoft Disk Operating System**) MS-DOS

MST¹ [ɛmɛste] NF *Méd* (*abrév* **maladie sexuellement transmissible**) STD

MST² NF (*abrév* **Maîtrise de Sciences et Techniques**) **M. hôtellerie-restauration** = higher vocational qualification in hotel management and catering

mû *voir* **mouvoir**

muance [mɥɑ̃s] NF *Arch* (*à la puberté*) breaking of the voice

mucilage [mysilaʒ] NM mucilage, gum

mucilagineux, -euse [mysilaʒinø, -øz] ADJ mucilaginous, viscous

mucosité [mykozite] NF mucus, mucosity

mucoviscidose [mykovisidoz] NF *Méd* cystic fibrosis

mucus [mykys] NM mucus

mue [my] NF **1** (*d'oiseaux, de mammifères, de crustacés*) moult(ing), *Am* molt(ing); (*de cerf*) shedding *or* casting of the antlers; (*de reptiles*) sloughing; (*époque*) moulting season; (*dépouille*) (*d'oiseau*) discarded feathers; (*de crustacé*) discarded shell; (*de cerf*) discarded antlers; (*de serpents*) slough; **serin en m.** moulting canary **2** *Physiol* (*à la puberté*) breaking of the voice **3** (*cage*) (*pour faucons*) mew; (*pour volaille*) coop

muer [mɥe] VT *Littr* **m. sa tête** (*de cerf*) to shed *or* cast its antlers
▸ VI **1** (*d'oiseau, de mammifère, de crustacé*) to moult, *Am* to molt; (*de cerf*) to shed *or* cast its antlers; (*de reptile*) to slough, to cast its skin **2** (*de voix*) (*à la puberté*) to break; **il commence à m.** his voice is breaking
▸ VPR **se muer se m. en** to change (in)to

muesli [mɥɛsli, mysli] NM muesli

muet, -ette [mɥɛ, -ɛt] ADJ (*personne*) (*privé de l'usage de la parole*) dumb; (*silencieux*) silent, dumb, mute; (*film, cinéma, complicité*) silent; *Ling* silent; (*rôle, acteur*) non-speaking, walk-on; (*carte géographique*) blank; (*clavier de machine à écrire*) blank, unmarked; **m. de naissance** born dumb, dumb from birth; *Fig* **la stupeur m'a rendu m.** I was struck dumb with astonishment; **j'écoutais, m. d'étonnement** I listened, speechless with astonishment *or* in mute astonishment; **m. de colère** speechless with anger; **rester m.** to remain silent; **m. comme une tombe** (as) silent as the grave; **il est resté m. comme une carpe** (*il n'a pas répondu à la question*) he didn't say a word, he clammed up; **tu es resté m. comme une carpe toute la soirée** you didn't open your mouth *or* say a word all evening; **les grandes douleurs sont muettes** great sorrow is often silent; **le cinéma m.** silent cinema *or* films
▸ N mute
▸ NM *Cin* **le m.** silent films

muezzin [mɥɛdzin] NM muezzin

mufle [myfl] NM **1** (*du bœuf, bison etc*) (hairless part of) muzzle, muffle; (*de lion, taureau etc*) nose, *Fam* snout **2** *Fam* (*malotru*) boor, lout

muflée [myfle] NF *Fam* **prendre une m.** to get wrecked *or* wasted *or Br* legless; **il tenait une sacrée m.** he was totally wrecked *or* wasted *or Br* legless

muflerie [myfləri] NF Fam **1** (caractère) boorishness **2** (action) boorish behaviour; lassée de ses **mufleries** tired of his boorish behaviour or boorishness **3** (parole) boorish remark

muflier [myflije] NM Bot antirrhinum, snapdragon

mufti [myfti] NM Rel mufti

muge [myʒ] NM (poisson) mullet

mugir [myʒir] VI **1** (de vache) to low, to moo; (de taureau) to bellow **2** (du vent) to moan, to howl; (d'un torrent) to roar; (d'une sirène) to wail

mugissement [myʒismɑ̃] NM **1** (de vache) lowing, mooing; (de taureau) bellowing **2** (du vent) moaning, howling; (d'un torrent) roaring; (d'une sirène) wailing

muguet [mygɛ] NM **1** (plante) lily of the valley **2** Méd thrush

> **Muguet**
> On May Day in France, bunches of lily of the valley are sold in the streets and given as presents. The flowers are supposed to bring good luck.

mulâtre [mylɑtr] ADJ mulatto, half-caste N (f **mulâtre, mulâtresse** [mylɑtrɛs])mulatto

mule[1] [myl] NF **1** Zool mule **2** Fam (passeur de drogue) mule

mule[2] NF (pantoufle) mule; **la m. du Pape** the Pope's slipper; **baiser la m. du Pape** to kiss the Pope's toe

mulet[1] [mylɛ] NM Zool mule

mulet[2] NM (poisson) grey mullet

muletier, -ière [myltje, -jɛr] ADJ (chemin, sentier) mule; **équipage m.** mule train NM mule driver, muleteer

mulot [mylo] NM field mouse

multibancarisation [myltibɑ̃karizasjɔ̃] NF growth in the number of banks

multicantonal, -ale, -aux, -ales [myltikɑ̃tɔnal, -o] ADJ Suisse involving many cantons

multicarte [myltikart] ADJ, N (représentant) **m.** rep for several companies

multicellulaire [myltiselylɛr] ADJ multicellular

multicolonnage [myltikɔlɔnaʒ] NM Ordinat multicolumn working

multicolore [myltikɔlɔr] ADJ multicoloured, Am multicolored

multicoque [myltikɔk] NM Naut multihull

multicritère [myltikritɛr] NM Ordinat multicriterion

multiculturalisme [myltikyltyralism] NM multiculturalism

multiculturel, -elle [myltikyltyrɛl] ADJ multicultural

multidevise [myltidəviz] ADJ multicurrency

multidimensionnel, -elle [myltidimɑ̃-sjɔnɛl] ADJ multidimensional; Fig (expérience, compétence etc) multifaceted

multidisciplinaire [myltidisiplinɛr] ADJ multidisciplinary

multidistribution [myltidistribysjɔ̃] NF multidistribution

multi-écran, pl **multi-écrans** [myltiekrɑ̃] NM TV multiscreen, split screen

multiemploi [myltiɑ̃plwa] NM = holding several jobs at the same time

multiflore [myltiflɔr] ADJ Bot multiflora

multifonctions [myltifɔ̃ksjɔ̃] ADJ multifunctional; Ordinat **clavier m.** multi-functional keyboard

multiforme [myltifɔrm] ADJ multiform; Fig (pays, problème etc) multifaceted

multigrade [myltigrad] ADJ (huile) multigrade

multi-image, pl **multi-images** [myltiimaʒ] ADJ TV etc multi-image

multilatéral, -ale, -aux, -ales [myltilatéral, -o] ADJ (accord) multilateral

multimarque [myltimark] NF Mktg multibrand

multimédia [myltimedja] ADJ, NM multimedia

multimilliardaire [myltimiljardɛr], **multimillionnaire** [myltimiljɔnɛr] ADJ, N multimillionaire

multimode [myltimɔd] ADJ Ordinat multimode

multinational, -ale, -aux, -ales [myltinasjɔnal, -o] ADJ multinational NF **multinationale** multinational (company)

multinorme [myltinɔrm] ADJ TV multistandard

multipare [myltipar] ADJ multiparous NF multipara

multipartisme [myltipartism] NM Pol multiparty system

multipartite [myltipartit] ADJ Pol multiparty, multipartite

multipassage [myltipasaʒ] ADJ Ordinat multistrike

multipiste [myltipist] ADJ multitrack

multiplace [myltiplas] ADJ, NM (avion) **m.** passenger aircraft

multiplateforme [myltiplatfɔrm] ADJ Ordinat cross-platform

multiple [myltipl] ADJ **1** (raisons, résidences, talents, dangers) many, numerous; Psy (personnalité) multiple; **les causes sont multiples** the reasons are many or Fml manifold; **à usages multiples** multipurpose; **maison à succursales multiples** multiple store, chain store; Scol **question à choix multiples** multiple-choice question; **nous avons essayé de vous joindre à de multiples reprises** we tried repeatedly to contact you; Ordinat **à accès m.** multi-access **2** (complexe) (monde, âme etc) complex, multifaceted NM Math multiple; **le plus petit commun m.** the lowest common multiple

multiplex [myltiplɛks] ADJ INV, NM Radio, TV multiplex

multiplexage [myltiplɛksaʒ] NM multiplexing

multiplexe [myltiplɛks] NM multiplex (cinema)

multiplexé [myltiplɛkse] ADJ multiplex

multiplexer [myltiplɛkse] VT to multiplex

multiplexeur [myltiplɛksœr] NM multiplexer, multiplexor

multipliable [myltiplijabl] ADJ multipliable; **tout nombre est m.** any number can be multiplied

multiplicande [myltiplikɑ̃d] NM Math multiplicand

multiplicateur, -trice [myltiplikatœr, -tris] ADJ multiplying; **engrenage m.** step-up gear NM Math, Élec multiplier

multiplicatif, -ive [myltiplikatif, -iv] ADJ multiplicative, multiplying

multiplication [myltiplikasjɔ̃] NF **1** Math multiplication; **la m. des vols de voitures/des clubs sportifs** the increase in car theft/in the number of sports clubs; Bible **la m. des pains** the miracle of the loaves and fishes **2** Tech gear (ratio); **grande/petite m.** high/low gear; **m. du levier** leverage

multiplicité [myltiplisite] NF multiplicity

multiplier [myltiplije] (pr sub, impf n. **multipliions,** v. **multipliiez**) VT **1** Math to multiply

(par by) **2** (répéter) **m. les mises en garde** to issue repeated warnings; **m. les erreurs** to make mistake after mistake; **le chef de l'État a multiplié les appels au calme** the head of state has called repeatedly for calm; **ses erreurs/efforts multiplié(e)s** his repeated mistakes/efforts **3** Tech **m. la vitesse de révolution** to gear up VPR se **multiplier 1** to increase; **les crimes se multiplient** crime is on the increase; **les lapins se multiplient rapidement** rabbits multiply rapidly **2** Fig (être partout à la fois) to be in half a dozen places at once; **se m. pour aider qn** to bend over backwards to help sb

multipolaire [myltipɔlɛr] ADJ **1** Élec, Biol multipolar **2** Pol multipolar

multipostage [myltipɔstaʒ] NM volume mailing

multiposte [myltipɔst] ADJ Ordinat multistation

multiprocesseur [myltiprɔsesœr] NM Ordinat multiprocessor

multiprogrammation [myltiprɔgramasjɔ̃] NF Ordinat multiprogramming

multipropriété [myltiprɔprijete] NF timeshare, multi-ownership; **acheter un appartement/une maison en m.** to buy a timeshare (flat/house)

multiracial, -iale, -iaux, -iales [myltirasjal, -jo] ADJ multiracial

multirécidiviste [myltiresidivist] N persistent offender, repeat offender

multirisque [myltirisk] ADJ **assurance m.** comprehensive insurance

multisalles [myltisal] ADJ INV **complexe m.** multiplex (cinema) NM INV multiplex (cinema)

multisectoriel, -ielle [myltisektɔrjɛl] ADJ multisector

multisoupape [myltisupap] NM Aut multivalve (engine)

multistandard [myltistɑ̃dar] ADJ INV TV multistandard

multitâche [myltitaʃ] ADJ Ordinat multitasking

multithérapie [myltiterapi] NF Méd combination therapy

multitraitement [myltitrɛtmɑ̃] NM Ordinat multiprocessing

multitude [myltityd] NF **1** multitude (de of); **une m. de gens** hosts or crowds or swarms of people; **il y avait sur la cheminée une m. de bibelots** the mantelpiece was crowded with ornaments **2** Litt Péj **la m.** the masses

multi-utilisateur, pl **multi-utilisateurs** [myltiytilizatœr] ADJ Ordinat multi-user

multivision [myltivizjɔ̃] NF TV multivision

munichois, -oise [mynikwa, -waz] ADJ of/from Munich N **1 M.** (natif) native of Munich; (habitant) inhabitant of Munich **2** Hist, Pol (partisan des accords de Munich) Munich supporter **3** (capitulard) defeatist

municipal, -ale, -aux, -ales [mynisipal, -o] ADJ (élection, employé) municipal, local-government; (bibliothèque, stade, patinoire, piscine) municipal, local; **conseil m.** town council, local council; **arrêté m.** bylaw; Hist **la garde municipale** the military police (of Paris) NFPL **les municipales** municipal or local (-government) elections

> **Municipales**
> These are the elections where residents choose the town council. Electors vote for a list of council members whose leader or "tête de liste" will become the mayor, a ceremonial and political post.

municipalisation [mynisipalizasjɔ̃] NF municipalization; **la m. des sols a été votée** there has been a vote in favour of placing land under municipal control

municipaliser [mynisipalize] VT to municipalize

municipalité [mynisipalite] NF **1** (ville) municipality, town **2** (région) local administrative area **3** (maire et conseillers municipaux) (local) council, corporation

munificence [mynifisɑ̃s] NF Litt munificence

munificent [mynifisɑ̃] ADJ Litt munificent

munir [mynir] VT (personne) to supply, to provide, Fml to furnish (**de** with); (voiture, chambre) to fit, to equip (**de** with); **muni des sacrements de l'Église** fortified with the rites of the Church
▪ VPR **se munir se m. de** (vêtements chauds, cartes routières, provisions) to equip or provide oneself with; (crème solaire, parapluie) to take; **il faut se m. d'un passeport** you need (to take) a passport

munition [mynisjɔ̃] NF **1 munitions (de guerre)** ammunition, munitions; **des armes et des munitions** arms and ammunition **2** Arch (d'armée) munitioning, provisioning; **munitions de bouche** provisions

munster [mœstɛr] NM Munster (cheese)

muon [myɔ̃] NM Phys muon

muphti [myfti] NM Rel mufti

muqueux, -euse [mykø, -øz] ADJ (membrane) mucous
▪ NF **muqueuse** mucous membrane

mur [myr] NM Constr, Fig (d'eau, de policiers) wall; **m. de clôture** surrounding wall; **m. d'appui** low wall; **m. de soutènement** retaining wall; **m. de refend** partition (wall); **m. mitoyen** party wall; **m. porteur** load-bearing wall; **m. d'escalade, m. de varappe** climbing wall; **gros murs** main walls; Fam **les cambrioleurs n'ont laissé que les (quatre) murs** the burglars took everything but the kitchen sink, the burglars stripped the place bare; **rester entre quatre murs** (en prison) to be inside; **j'en ai marre de rester entre quatre murs toute la journée** I'm tired of being cooped up all day; Fig **mettre qn au pied du m.** to put sb on the spot, to drive sb into a corner, to have sb with his back to the wall; **être au pied du m.** to have one's back to the wall; **l'ennemi est dans nos murs** the enemy is within the gates; Fig **il est à présent dans nos murs** (en visite dans notre ville) he is in town at the moment; (dans nos locaux) he is on the premises at the moment; Fig **c'est à se taper la tête contre les murs** it's enough to drive or send you up the wall; Fig **se heurter à un m.** to come up against a brick wall; **se heurter à un m. d'incompréhension** to come up against a wall or a barrier of incomprehension; Fig **j'ai l'impression de parler à un m.** it's like talking to a brick wall; Fig **les murs ont des oreilles** walls have ears; **faire le m.** to sneak out
▸▸ Hist **le m. de Berlin** the Berlin Wall; Ordinat **m. coupe-feu** firewall; **le m. des Lamentations** the Wailing Wall; **m. du son** sound barrier; **franchir le m. du son** to break the sound barrier

mûr [myr] ADJ **1** (fruit) ripe; (vin) mellow; (personne, esprit) mature; **trop m.** (fruit) overripe; **il est très m. pour son âge** he is very mature for his age; **l'abcès est m.** the abscess has come to a head; **l'âge m.** maturity; **homme d'âge m.** man of mature years; **après mûre réflexion** after careful or Fml mature consideration; **m. pour qch** ripe or ready for sth; Litt **les temps sont mûrs** the time has come, the time is ripe **2** Arg (saoul) plastered, canned

murage [myraʒ] NM (de porte, fenêtre) walling up, blocking up

muraille [myrɑj] NF **1** (mur) (high) wall; **la Grande M. de Chine** the Great Wall of China; **les murailles de la ville** the town walls **2** (de bateau) side

mural, -ale, -aux, -ales [myral, -o] ADJ wall; **peinture murale** mural; **pendule murale** wall clock; **carte murale** wall map; Archit **console murale** wall bracket

mûre [myr] NF **1 m. (sauvage** ou **de ronce)** blackberry **2** (fruit du mûrier) mulberry

mûrement [myrmɑ̃] ADV **après avoir m. réfléchi** after careful or Fml mature consideration; **un plan m. réfléchi** a carefully thought-out plan; **tout cela a été m. préparé** it was all very carefully planned

murène [myrɛn] NF (poisson) moray (eel)

murer [myre] VT **1** (entourer de murs) (ville, cité) to wall in **2** (bloquer) (porte, fenêtre) to wall up, to block up; (personne) to wall up
▪ VPR **se murer** to shut oneself away; **elle se mure dans le silence/la solitude** she has retreated or withdrawn into silence/solitude; **muré chez soi** shut away at home

muret [myrɛ] NM, **murette** [myrɛt] NF low wall; (de pierres posées les unes sur les autres) dry-stone wall

murge [myrʒ] NF Fam **prendre une m.** (s'enivrer) to get wasted or Br legless

mûrier [myrje] NM Bot mulberry (tree or bush); **m. (sauvage)** blackberry bush, bramble

mûrir [myrir] VT (fruit) to ripen; Fig (projet, pensées) to nurture; **les épreuves l'ont beaucoup mûri** his hardships have made him much more mature; **laisser m. un abcès** to let an abscess come to a head
▪ VI (de fruit) to ripen; (d'abcès) to come to a head; (de projet, processus) to evolve, to develop; (de sentiment) to ripen; **cet enfant a beaucoup mûri** this child has become much more mature or has greatly matured

mûrissant, -ante [myrisɑ̃] ADJ (fruit) ripening; (personne) of mature years

mûrissement [myrismɑ̃] NM (de fruits) ripening; Fig (de projet) development

murmure [myrmyr] NM (à voix basse) murmur, murmuring; (de ruisseau) babbling; **murmures** murmuring, murmurs; (plaintes) murmuring, muttering, grumbling; **un m. d'approbation** a murmur of approval; **ce fut accepté sans un m. (de réprobation)** this was accepted without a murmur

murmurer [myrmyre] VT to murmur; **on murmure qu'il va démissionner** rumour has it or there are rumours that he's going to resign
▪ VI (à voix basse) to murmur; (se plaindre) to grumble, to complain; (cancaner) to say things, to talk; (de ruisseau) to babble; **m. entre ses dents** to mutter

mûron [myrɔ̃] NM Bot wild raspberry

musaraigne [myzarɛɲ] NF Zool shrew

musard, -arde [myzar, -ard] Fam Vieilli ADJ dawdling
▪ N dawdler

musarder [myzarde] VI to dawdle, to amble; (fainéanter) to dither

musc [mysk] NM musk

muscade [myskad] NF **1** Bot **(noix) m.** nutmeg; **fleur de m.** mace **2** (d'escamoteur) vanishing ball; **passez m.!** hey presto!

muscadier [myskadje] NM Bot nutmeg (tree)

muscadin [myskadɛ̃] NM Arch dandy, fop

muscardin [myskardɛ̃] NM Zool dormouse

muscat [myska] ADJ muscat; **raisin m.** muscat grape, muscatel grape; **vin m.** muscatel (wine)

NM (raisin) muscat or muscatel grape; (vin) muscatel (wine)

muscle [myskl] NM muscle; **avoir des muscles** to be muscular, to be brawny; **il est tout en muscles** he's all muscle; **m. antagoniste** antagonistic muscle; **m. biceps** biceps

musclé [myskle] ADJ (personne, bras, jambes) muscular, brawny; **il est bien m.** he is very muscular, he has well-developed muscles; Fig **cet écrivain écrit dans un style m.** this author has a sinewy or robust style; **un café m.** a good strong coffee; **une campagne électorale musclée** a punchy electoral campaign; **un discours m.** a punchy or forceful speech; **l'intervention musclée de la police** the strong-arm tactics of the police; **un régime m.** a strong-arm regime; **politique musclée** hardline or tough policy

muscler [myskle] VT to develop the muscles of; **il faut te m. les jambes** you must develop your leg muscles; Fig **tout faire pour m. l'industrie française** to do everything to give French industry some muscle or to beef up French industry
▪ VI Fam **le sport, ça muscle** sport builds up your muscles
▪ VPR **se muscler** to develop one's muscles

muscu [mysky] NF Fam = **musculation**

musculaire [myskylɛr] ADJ (système, tissu, force) muscular; **fibre m.** muscle fibre

musculation [myskylasjɔ̃] NF body-building; **faire de la m.** to do body-building

musculature [myskylatyr] NF musculature; **il a une belle m.** he has a fine set of muscles

musculeux, -euse [myskylø, -øz] ADJ aussi Anat muscular

muse [myz] NF muse; Myth **les Muses** the Muses; **invoquer sa m.** to invoke or call on one's muse; **taquiner la M.** to write the odd bit of verse

museau, -eaux [myzo] NM **1** (d'animal) muzzle, snout; Culin **m. vinaigrette** = brawn in vinaigrette **2** Fam (visage) face; **vilain m.** ugly mug

musée [myze] NM museum; **m. (de peinture ou d'art)** art gallery; **m. des arts et traditions populaires** folk museum; **m. des transports** transport museum; **Venise, ville-m.** the historical city of Venice; Fam **chez eux, c'est le m. des horreurs!** their place is full of things I wouldn't give house room to!; **tu as vu le m. des horreurs!** (ce groupe) what an ugly looking crew!

muséifier [myzeifje] VT Péj (quartier, ville) to museumify

museler [myzle] VT (je muselle; je musellerai) (animal) to muzzle; Fig (personne, la presse, l'opposition) to muzzle, to gag

muselière [myzəljɛr] NF muzzle; **mettre une m. à** (un chien), Fig (la presse) to muzzle

musellement [myzɛlmɑ̃] NM (d'animal) muzzling; (de personne, la presse) muzzling, gagging

muséographie [myzeɔgrafi] NF museography

muser [myze] VI **1** Arch, Litt to idle (about); (flâner) to dawdle, to amble **2** Belg (fredonner) to hum

muserolle [myzrɔl] NF Équitation noseband

musette [myzɛt] NF **1** Mus (instrument) musette (type of bagpipe); **orchestre m.** accordion band; **bal m.** dance to an accordion band; (lieu) dance hall with an accordion band **2** (de cheval) m. (mangeoire) nosebag **3** (sac) bag; Mil haversack; Arch (d'écolier) satchel
▪ NM Mus Fam **le m.** accordion music

muséum [myzeɔm] NM natural history museum

musical, -ale, -aux, -ales [myzikal, -o] **ADJ** *(son, soirée)* musical; **l'art m.** music; **avoir l'oreille musicale** to have an ear *or* a good ear for music

musicalement [myzikalmã] **ADV** musically

musicalité [myzikalite] **NF** musicality, musical quality

music-hall, *pl* **music-halls** [myzikol] **NM** *(spectacle)* variety, *Br* music hall, *Am* vaudeville; *(salle)* variety theatre, *Br* music hall, *Am* vaudeville theater; **faire du m.** to do variety *or Br* music hall *or Am* vaudeville; **numéros de m.** variety turns

musicien, -ienne [myzisjɛ̃, -jɛn] **ADJ** musical
N musician

musicographe [myzikɔgraf] **N** musicographer

musicologie [myzikɔlɔʒi] **NF** musicology

musicologue [myzikɔlɔg] **N** musicologist

musicos [myzikos] **NM** *Fam* muso

musicothérapie [myzikoterapi] **NF** music therapy

musique [myzik] **NF** music; **mettre des paroles en m.** to set words to music; **instrument de m.** musical instrument; **boîte à m.** music(al) box; **chef de m.** bandmaster; **m. classique** classical music; **m. légère** light music; **m. folklorique** folk music; **m. pop** pop music; **m. religieuse** church music; **m. de chambre** chamber music; **m. d'ambiance** *ou* **de fond** background music; **m. de supermarché** Muzak®, piped music; **m. militaire** *(formation)* military band; *(composition)* military music; **faire de la m.** to make music, to play; **lire la m.** to read music; *Fig Fam* **je connais la m.** I've heard it all before, it's the same old story; **il veut acheter la m. du film** he wants to buy the soundtrack of the film; *Fam* **en avant la m.!** let's get started!; **Can faire face à la m.** to face the music; *TV* **m. d'archives** library music; *TV etc* **m. de générique** title music, theme tune; *TV etc* **m. (de générique) de fin** playout music; *TV etc* **m. d'ouverture** introductory music

musiquette [myzikɛt] **NF** *Péj* piped music, Muzak®

musoir [myzwar] **NM** pierhead, jetty head

musqué [myske] **ADJ 1** *(odeur, parfum)* musky **2 bœuf m.** musk ox; **rat m.** muskrat, musquash; **canard m.** muscovy duck, musk duck **3** *Arch (poète, style etc)* affected

must [mœst] **NM** *Fam* must

mustang [mystãg] **NM** mustang

musulman, -ane [myzylmã, -an] **ADJ, N** Muslim, Moslem

mutabilité [mytabilite] **NF** mutability

mutable [mytabl] **ADJ** mutable

mutant, -ante [mytã, -ãt] **ADJ, N** mutant

mutation [mytasjɔ̃] **NF 1** *(de personnel)* transfer; **il a demandé/obtenu sa m. pour raison de santé** he asked for/obtained a transfer for health reasons **2** *(changement)* change, alteration; *Biol* mutation; *Ling (de voyelle)* gradation; *(de consonne)* shift; *Jur* change of ownership; *(de propriété)* transfer; **l'Europe de l'Est est en pleine m. politique** Eastern Europe is undergoing profound political change; **le secteur sidérurgique a subi de profondes mutations** the steel industry has undergone extensive change(s)

muter [myte] **VT** *(personnel)* to transfer
VI *Biol* to mutate

mutilateur, -trice [mytilatœr, -tris] **N** mutilator
ADJ *Fig (expérience)* crippling

mutilation [mytilasjɔ̃] **NF** *(de personne)* mutilation, maiming; *(de statue, d'objet d'art)* mutilation, defacement; *(de texte)* mutilation; **m. volontaire** self-mutilation

mutilé, -ée [mytile] **ADJ** *(personne)* mutilated, maimed; **il est m. du bras** he's lost an arm; **m. au visage** disfigured
N disabled person; **mutilés de guerre** disabled ex-servicemen

mutiler [mytile] **VT** *(personne)* to mutilate, to maim; *(statue, objet d'art)* to mutilate, to deface; *(arbre, texte)* to mutilate; *(paysage)* to disfigure; **il a eu les deux jambes mutilées à la guerre** he lost both legs in the war; **il a eu la main mutilée dans un accident du travail** his hand was badly injured in an industrial accident
VPR se mutiler to mutilate oneself

mutin [mytɛ̃] **ADJ 1** *(malicieux)* mischievous, impish, playful **2** *Arch (désobéissant)* disobedient, unruly, unbiddable
NM *(rebelle)* mutineer

mutiné [mytine] **ADJ** rebellious; *(troupes)* mutinous
NM mutineer

mutiner (se) [səmytine] **VPR** to rebel (**contre** against); *Naut, Mil* to mutiny

mutinerie [mytinri] **NF** rebellion; *Naut, Mil* mutiny

mutique [mytik] **ADJ** *Méd (personne)* suffering from mutism

mutisme [mytism] **NM 1** silence; **les responsables observent un m. absolu** the officials are maintaining (a) total silence; **s'enfermer dans le m.** to maintain a stubborn silence **2** *Méd* mutism

mutité [mytite] **NF** *Méd* mutism

mutualisme [mytɥalism] **NM 1** *Biol* symbiosis, mutualism **2** *Écon* mutual insurance

mutualiste [mytɥalist] **ADJ 1** *Biol* symbiotic, mutualistic **2** *Écon* **pharmacie m. =** chemist associated with a private insurance company, which may offer reduced rates on certain items to members of the company
N *Écon* member of a mutual insurance company

mutualité [mytɥalite] **NF** *Écon* mutual insurance; **société de m.** mutual insurance company, *Br* friendly society

mutuel, -elle [mytɥɛl] **ADJ** *(amour etc)* mutual; **société d'assurance mutuelle** mutual insurance company, *Br* friendly society
NF mutuelle *(société)* mutual insurance company, *Br* friendly society; *(assurance)* private insurance; **prendre une mutuelle** to take out private insurance

---

Mutuelle

A "mutuelle" is a non-profit-making health insurance company which provides insurance complementary to that of the "Sécurité sociale". Often these companies are set up for a particular profession: there is a "mutuelle" for students, one for teachers etc.

---

mutuellement [mytɥɛlmã] **ADV** each other, one another; **ils se sont aidés/critiqués m.** they helped/criticized each other *or* one another

Myanmar [mjanmar] **NM** Myanmar

Mycènes [misɛn] **N** *Hist* Mycenae

mycénien, -ienne [misenjɛ̃, -jɛn] **ADJ** *Hist* Mycenaean

mycologie [mikɔlɔʒi] **NF** *Bot* mycology

mycose [mikoz] **NF** *Méd* fungal infection, *Spéc* mycosis; *(sur les pieds)* athlete's foot

myéline [mjelin] **NF** *Anat* myelin

myélite [mjelit] **NF** *Méd* myelitis

myélome [mjelom] **NM** *Méd* myeloma

mygale [migal] **NF** trapdoor spider

myocarde [mjɔkard] **NM** *Anat* myocardium

myocardite [mjɔkardit] **NF** *Méd* myocarditis

myologie [mjɔlɔʒi] **NF** *Anat* myology

myome [mjom] **NM** *Méd* myoma

myopathe [mjɔpat] **N** *Méd* person with muscular dystrophy

myopathie [mjɔpati] **NF** *Méd* muscular dystrophy

myope [mjɔp] **ADJ** shortsighted, *Spéc* myopic; *Fig* **m. comme une taupe** as blind as a bat
N shortsighted person, *Spéc* myope

myopie [mjɔpi] **NF** *Méd* shortsightedness, *Spéc* myopia; *Mktg* **m. mercatique** marketing myopia

myosotis [mjɔzɔtis] **NM** *(fleur)* forget-me-not, *Spéc* myosotis

myriade [mirjad] **NF** myriad; **des myriades d'étoiles** myriads of stars, a myriad stars

myrmidon [mirmidɔ̃] **NM** *Fam* pipsqueak

myrrhe [mir] **NF** myrrh

myrte [mirt] **NM** *(plante)* myrtle; **m. des marais** bog myrtle

myrtille [mirtij] **NF** *(baie)* bilberry, whortleberry

Mystère® [mistɛr] **NM** *Culin* = ice-cream dessert coated with hazelnuts and with a meringue centre

mystère [mistɛr] **NM 1** mystery; **rester un m.** to remain a mystery; **on n'a jamais pénétré ce m.** no one has ever got to the bottom of this mystery; **si tu veux réussir, il faut travailler, il n'y a pas de m.!** if you want to succeed, you have to work, there's no mystery about it *or* it's as simple as that!; **ce garçon est un m. pour moi** that boy's a mystery to me; *Fam* **m. et boule de gomme** *(je n'en ai aucune idée)* I've no idea, search me; *Fig* **ne fais pas tant de mystères!** don't be so mysterious!; **je n'en fais pas m.** I make no secret of it **2** *Hist, Littér* mystery (play); **m. de la Passion** Passion play **3** *Antiq, Myth* mystery

mystérieusement [misterjøzmã] **ADV** mysteriously

mystérieux, -ieuse [misterjø, -jøz] **ADJ** mysterious; *(secret)* secret; **un rendez-vous m.** a secret rendezvous
NM 1 jouer le(s) m. to behave very mysteriously **2 le m.** the mysterious

mysticisme [mistisism] **NM** mysticism

mystifiable [mistifjabl] **ADJ** gullible

mystifiant [mistifjã] **ADJ** deceiving

mystificateur, -trice [mistifikatœr, -tris] **ADJ** *(coup de téléphone, lettre, annonce)* hoax; **avoir un côté m.** to have a mischievous streak
N hoaxer

mystification [mistifikasjɔ̃] **NF** *Péj (tromperie)* deception; *(farce)* hoax; **m. collective** mass deception

mystifier [mistifje] **VT** *(pr sub, impf n.* **mystifiions, v. mystifiiez)** **m. qn** *(faire marcher)* to pull sb's leg; *(leurrer)* to fool sb, to take sb in; **se laisser m. par qch** to (let oneself) be taken in *or* fooled by sth

---

Il faut noter que le verbe anglais **to mystify** est un faux ami. Il signifie **déconcerter, laisser perplexe.**

---

mystique [mistik] **ADJ** mystical
N *(personne)* mystic
NF mystique

mystiquement [mistikmã] **ADV** mystically

mythe [mit] **NM** myth

mythique [mitik] **ADJ** mythical

mytho [mito] N *Fam* (*abrév* **mythomane**) compulsive liar

mythologie [mitɔlɔʒi] NF mythology

mythologique [mitɔlɔʒik] ADJ mythological

mythologiquement [mitɔlɔʒikmɑ̃] ADV mythologically

mythologue [mitɔlɔg] N mythologist

mythomane [mitɔman] ADJ **être m.** to be a compulsive *or* pathological liar ▪ N compulsive *or* pathological liar; *Psy* mythomaniac

mythomanie [mitɔmani] NF *Psy* mythomania

mytiliculteur, -trice [mitilikyltœr, -tris] N mussel farmer

mytiliculture [mitilikyltyr] NF mussel farming

myxœdème [miksedɛm] NM *Méd* myxoedema, *Am* myxedema

myxomatose [miksɔmatoz] NF myxomatosis

N¹, n [ɛn] **NM** *(lettre)* N, n

N² *(abrév* **Nord)** N

na [na] **INT** *Fam* **(et) na!** so there!

nabab [nabab] **NM** nabob

nabot, -ote [nabo, -ɔt] *Péj* **N** dwarf, midget **ADJ** *(personne)* dwarfish, tiny

Nabuchodonosor [nabykɔdɔnɔzɔr] **NM 1** *Bible, Hist* Nebuchadnezzar **2** *(bouteille de champagne)* n. Nebuchadnezzar

nacelle [nasɛl] **NF 1** *(de montgolfière)* basket; *(de dirigeable)* gondola, car; *(d'avion)* nacelle; *(de laveur de carreau)* cradle, aerial work platform **2** *(de landau, poussette) (détachable)* carrycot; *(fixe)* carriage **3** *Vieilli (bateau)* skiff, wherry

nacre [nakr] **NF** mother-of-pearl; **un collier de** *ou* **en n.** a mother-of-pearl necklace

nacré [nakre] **ADJ** pearlescent

nacrer [nakre] **VT 1 n. qch** to give sth a pearly finish **2** *Litt* to cast a pearly glimmer onto

nadir [nadir] **NM** *Astron* nadir

nævus [nevys] **NM** *Méd* naevus, *Am* nevus

nage [naʒ] **NF 1** swimming; *(style)* stroke; **atteindre le rivage à la n.** to swim to the shore; **traverser une rivière à la n.** to swim across a river; **je pratique trois nages** I can do three strokes; **épreuve du 100 m quatre nages** 4 x 100 m relay; **n. libre** freestyle; **n. sur le dos** backstroke; **n. (à l')indienne** overarm stroke **2 être (tout) en n.** to be bathed in perspiration **3** *(aviron)* rowing, sculling; **banc de n.** thwart; **chef de n.** stroke **4** *Culin* **à la n.** poached in white wine

nageoire [naʒwar] **NF 1** *(de poisson)* fin; *(de dauphin, cétacé etc)* flipper; **n. caudale** caudal fin, tail fluke; **n. dorsale** dorsal fin; **n. anale** anal fin; **n. pelvienne** pelvic fin; **n. pectorale** pectoral fin **2** *(d'hydravion)* fin

nager [naʒe] *(je nageais, nous nageons)* **VI 1** to swim; *(de bois, bouchon etc)* to float; **on va n.?** shall we go for a swim?; **tu sais n.?** can you swim?; *Fig* **savoir n.** to know one's way around, to know how to take care of oneself; **n. vers la côte** to swim for the shore; **n. sous l'eau/sur le dos** to swim underwater/on one's back; **n. comme un poisson** to swim like a fish; **n. comme un fer à repasser** to swim like a brick; **n. entre deux eaux** to be floating beneath the surface; *Fig* not to commit oneself; **légumes qui nagent dans le beurre** vegetables swimming in butter; *Fig* **n. dans son sang** to be bathed in blood; **n. dans l'abondance** to be rolling in money; **on ne peut pas dire que la région nage dans l'abondance** the region is not exactly well-off or blessed with prosperity; **n. dans le bonheur** to be blissfully happy; *Fam* **tu nages dans ce costume** the suit drowns you; **tu nages vraiment trop dans ce short** the shorts really are far too big for you; **depuis qu'il a perdu 20 kg il nage dans tous ses vêtements** his clothes just hang on him since he lost 20 kilos; *Fig*

Fam **je nage** I'm all at sea; **je nage complètement!** I'm totally at sea *or* lost!

2 *Fig Litt (de vapeurs, nuages, effluves)* to drift

3 *Naut* to row; **nagez partout!** pull away!; **n. en arrière** *ou Spéc* **à culer** to back water; **n. plat** to feather; **n. à** *ou* **en couple** to (double) scull; **n. en pointe** to row

VT 1 *(la brasse, le crawl etc)* to do, to swim **2** *(disputer)* **n. le 100 mètres/le quatre fois 100 mètres** to swim (in) the 100 metres/the 4 x 100 metres relay

nageur, -euse [naʒœr, -øz] **N 1** swimmer; **être bon/mauvais n.** to be a good/bad swimmer, to swim well/badly; *Mil* **n. de combat** frogman **2** *Naut (rameur)* oarsman, *f* oarswoman, rower; **n. de l'arrière** stroke; **n. de l'avant** bow (oar)

NM *(maillot de bain une pièce)* one-piece swimsuit *or* swimming costume

ADJ *(animal)* swimming

naguère [nagɛr] **ADV** *Litt* not long ago, a short time ago, lately; *(autrefois)* formerly

naïade [najad] **NF** naiad, water nymph

naïf, -ïve [naif, -iv] **ADJ** *(innocent)* naive, ingenuous, innocent; **elle était assez naïve pour croire ses mensonges** she was naive enough to believe his lies; *Beaux-Arts* **un peintre n.** a naive painter

N 1 vous me prenez pour un n.! what sort of a fool do you take me for?; **jouer les naïfs/les naïves** to act *or* play the innocent **2** *Beaux-Arts* naive (painter)

nain, naine [nɛ̃, nɛn] **VOIR GRAMMAIRE A12 N 1** dwarf, midget **2** *Arg (enfant)* kid, brat

NF naine *(étoile)* dwarf

ADJ *(personne, étoile)* dwarf; **haricots nains** dwarf beans; **poule naine** bantam; **caniche n.** toy poodle; **rosier n.** miniature rosebush

▶▶ **n. de jardin** garden gnome; *Cartes* **n. jaune** Pope Joan

Nairobi [nerobi] **N** Nairobi

naissain [nɛsɛ̃] **NM** *(d'huître, de moule)* spawn, spat

naissance [nɛsɑ̃s] **NF 1** *aussi Fig* birth; **date de n.** date of birth; **lieu de n.** birthplace; **acte de n.** birth certificate *(original)*; **extrait de n.** birth certificate *(copy of original)*; **contrôle** *ou* **limitation** *ou* **régulation des naissances** birth control; **donner n. à un enfant** to give birth to a child; **à sa n., il avait les cheveux blonds** his hair was blond when he was born; **sourd/aveugle de n.** deaf/blind from birth, born deaf/blind; **paresseux de n.** bone idle; **qu'est-ce que tu es paresseuse! – oui, je sais, chez moi, c'est de n.** you're so lazy! – I know, I was born that way *or* I've been like that since the day I was born; **français de n.** French by birth; **de haute/d'obscure n.** of high *or* noble/humble birth; *Fig Litt* **la n. du printemps** the birth of spring; *Litt* **la n. du jour** dawn, daybreak, the break of day; **donner n. à une rumeur/de nouvelles habi-**

tudes de vie to give rise to a rumour/new lifestyles **2** *(de langue, d'ongle etc)* root; *(de rivière)* source; *Archit (de pilier, d'arche)* spring; **n. du cou** base of the neck; **cicatrice à la n. des cheveux** scar just where the hair begins *or* at the hairline; **à la n. des seins** at the top of one's cleavage; **prendre n.** to originate, to start; *(d'une rivière)* to rise

naissant [nɛsɑ̃] **ADJ 1** *(jour)* dawning; *(beauté)* nascent; **à l'aube naissante** at break of day; **une barbe naissante** the beginnings of a beard; **ses seins naissants** her budding breasts; **les rondeurs naissantes de sa gorge** the blossoming curves of her breasts **2** *Chimie* **à l'état n.** nascent

naître [nɛtr] **VI** *(prp naissant; pp né; pr ind je nais, il naît, nous naissons, ils naissent; pr sub je naisse; p hist je naquis; fu je naîtrai; aux être)* **1** to be born; **il naquit** *ou* **est né en 1880** he was born in 1880; **enfant/poussin qui vient de n.** newly born child/newly hatched chick; **je l'ai vu n.** I have known him from birth *or* since he was a baby; **né de parents anglais** born of English parents, of English parentage; **né de parents inconnus** of unknown parentage; **enfant à n.** unborn child; **il naît plus de filles que de garçons** more girls are being born than boys, there's a higher level of female births than male births; **Casanova était né pour l'amour** Casanova was destined to be a great lover; **il est né pour être musicien/réussir/diriger** he was born *or* destined to be a musician/to succeed/to be a manager; **elle est née pour emmerder le monde** it seems to be her mission in life to get up people's noses; *Litt* **n. à l'amour** to know love for the first time, to awaken to love; **il est né poète/bricoleur** he is a born poet/handyman; **je ne suis pas né d'hier** *ou* **de la dernière pluie** I wasn't born yesterday; **il n'est pas encore né, celui qui me fera manger des escargots!** the man who can make me eat snails hasn't been born yet! **2** *(d'espoirs)* to spring up, to (a)rise, to be born; *(de peur)* to (a)rise; *(de projet, d'idée)* to originate (**de** in), to arise (**de** out of); **faire n.** *(espoir, doute)* to give rise to, to raise; *(soupçon)* to give rise to, to arouse, to cause; *(sourire)* to provoke, to raise; **cette peur du noir est née du fait qu'enfant, il avait été laissé seul** his fear of the dark originates *or* arises from his being left alone as a child; **l'espoir de paix est né de la rencontre des deux présidents** the meeting between the two presidents has given rise to hopes of peace **3** *(de plantes)* to begin to grow *or* come up, to appear; *(du jour)* to dawn

naïvement [naivmɑ̃] **ADV** naively

naïveté [naivte] **NF 1** *(innocence)* naivety; **elle a eu la n. de croire à ses promesses** she was naive enough to believe his promises **2** *(remarque)* naive remark

Namibie [namibi] NF Namibia

namibien, -ienne [namibjɛ̃, -jɛn] ADJ Namibian

N **N.** Namibian

nana [nana] NF Fam **1** (jeune fille) girl, bird, Am chick; **une n. qu'elle a rencontrée cet été** a girl she met last summer; **c'est là qu'on trouve les plus belles nanas** that's where the best-looking birds or chicks are; **c'est plein de nanas, mais il n'y a pas un seul mec** it's full of women/girls but there isn't a single man **2** (petite amie) girlfriend

nanar [nanar] NM Fam **1** (marchandise sans valeur) junk, trash, garbage **2** (mauvais film) lousy film, Am turkey

nandou [nãdu] NM Zool rhea

nanisme [nanism] NM Méd dwarfism

Nankin [nãkɛ̃] N Nanking

nankin [nãkɛ̃] ADJ INV, NM Tex nankeen

nanomètre [nanɔmɛtr] NM nanometre, Br nanometer

nanoseconde [nanos(ə)gɔ̃d] NF nanosecond

nansouk [nãzuk] NM Tex nainsook

nanti, -ie [nãti] ADJ (personne, pays) well-off, rich

N rich person; **les nantis** the well-off, the rich

nantir [nãtir] VT **1** n. qn de qch to provide sb with sth; **être bien nanti** to be well-off or well provided for **2** Jur (créancier) to give security to; **n. des valeurs** to deposit shares as security; **n. un prêt** to secure a loan

VPR **se nantir** Litt **se n. d'un parapluie** to provide oneself or arm oneself with an umbrella

nantissement [nãtismã] NM security; (pour prêt) collateral, security; **déposer des titres en n.** to lodge stock as security; Banque **n. flottant** ou **général** floating charge; Bourse **n. d'actions** lien on shares

napalm [napalm] NM napalm; **bombe au n.** napalm bomb

naphtaline [naftalin] NF naphthalene; Can Fig **sortir qch de la n.** to take sth out of mothballs; **boules de n.** mothballs

naphte [naft] NM naphtha, mineral oil; **n. de goudron** coal-tar naphtha

Napoléon [napɔleɔ̃] NM **1** Napoleon **2** Anciennement **n.** (pièce) twenty-franc piece (bearing the effigy of Napoleon)

napoléonien, -ienne [napɔleɔnjɛ̃, -jɛn] ADJ (guerre, empire) Napoleonic

napolitain, -aine [napɔlitɛ̃, -ɛn] ADJ Neapolitan

NM (dialecte) Neapolitan

N **N.** Neapolitan

nappage [napaʒ] NM Culin coating, covering

nappe [nap] NF **1** (de table) tablecloth; **mettre/ôter la n.** to lay/remove the cloth; **n. à thé** tea cloth; Rel **n. d'autel** altar cloth **2** Fig (vaste étendue) (de glace) sheet; **n. de feu** sea of flames

▸▸**n. d'armature** belt; **n. de brouillard** fog patch; **n. carcasse** casing ply; **n. croisée** cross-ply; Géog **n. d'eau** water table; **n. éruptive** lava flow; **n. de pétrole** oil slick; **n. pétrolifère** oil layer; Géog **n. phréatique** water table

napper [nape] VT **1** Culin to coat, to cover (**de** with); **glace à la vanille, nappée de chocolat** vanilla ice cream topped with chocolate or with chocolate topping **2** Vieilli (recouvrir) (table) to cover with a cloth

napperon [naprɔ̃] NM mat

Narcisse [narsis] N Myth Narcissus

narcisse [narsis] NM **1** (plante) narcissus; **n. des poètes** pheasant's eye; **n. sauvage** ou **des prés** daffodil **2** Psy narcissist

narcissique [narsisik] ADJ Psy narcissistic

narcissisme [narsisism] NM Psy narcissism

narcodollars [narkodɔlar] NMPL drug money

narcolepsie [narkolɛpsi] NF Méd narcolepsy

narcose [narkoz] NF Méd narcosis

narcotique [narkɔtik] Méd ADJ narcotic

NM narcotic, drug; **faire prendre un n. à qn** to give sb a narcotic, to drug sb

narcotrafic [narkotrafik] NM drug trafficking

narcotrafiquant, -ante [narkotrafikã, -ãt] N drug trafficker

nard [nar] NM Bot, Pharm spikenard, nard

narguer [narge] VT to taunt, to scoff at; (la mort, le danger) to flout

narguilé, narghilé, narghileh [nargile] NM hookah, narghile

narine [narin] NF nostril

narquois [narkwa] ADJ (ton, sourire) taunting, mocking

narquoisement [narkwazmã] ADV tauntingly, mockingly

narrateur, -trice [naratœr, -tris] N (de roman, de film) narrator; (conteur) storyteller

narratif, -ive [naratif, -iv] ADJ (style, contenu) narrative

narration [narasjɔ̃] NF **1** narration; Gram **présent de n.** historic present **2** (d'événement) narrative, account; Scol Vieilli narrative composition

narrer [nare] VT Litt to narrate, to relate

narval, -als [narval] NM narwhal, unicorn whale

nasal, -ale, -aux, -ales [nazal, -o] ADJ (os, son, cloison) nasal

NF Ling **nasale** nasal

nasaliser [nazalize] VT (son) to nasalize

Nasdaq® [nasdak] NM Écon Nasdaq®

nase [naz] Fam ADJ **1** (fatigué) (personne) shattered, whacked, dead beat; (voiture etc) clapped out **2** (idiot) thick; **il est tout n., ce mec** the guy's a complete idiot **3** (nul) bloody useless or hopeless

N **c'est un n., ce mec** this guy's rubbish, this guy's bloody useless

naseau, -eaux [nazo] NM (de cheval, bœuf) nostril; Fam **les naseaux** (nez) the hooter, the conk

nasillard [nazijar] ADJ nasal; (vieux disque etc) tinny; **ton n.** (nasal) twang; **parler d'une voix nasillarde** to talk through one's nose

nasillement [nazijmã] NM (son nasillard) (nasal) twang

nasiller [nazije] VI to speak through one's nose or with a twang; (de radio, vieux disque) to make a tinny sound; (du canard) to quack

nasique [nazik] NM (singe) proboscis monkey

nasse [nas] NF lobster pot; (pour oiseaux) hoop net; (pour rats) trap; Fig Vieilli **tomber dans la n.** to fall into the trap

natal, -ale, -als, -ales [natal] ADJ (village) native; **ville natale** birthplace; Fam home town; **mon pays n.** my native land; **mon Écosse/ma France natale** my native Scotland/France; **ma maison natale** the house where I was born

Do not confuse with **natif.**

nataliste [natalist] ADJ **politique n.** policy to increase the birth rate, pro-birth policy

natalité [natalite] NF (taux de) **n.** birth rate; **forte n.** high birth rate; **courbe de n.** birth rate

natation [natasjɔ̃] NF swimming; **club de n.**

swimming club; **faire de la n.** to swim; **n. synchronisée** synchronized swimming

natatoire [natatwar] ADJ Zool (organe, membrane) natatory, natatorial; **vessie n.** (de poisson) swim bladder, air bladder

Natel [natɛl] NM Suisse (abrév **Nationales Autotelefon**) mobile (phone), Am cellphone

natif, -ive [natif, -iv] ADJ **1** native; **je suis n. de Londres** I'm a native Londoner, I'm a Londoner (by birth) **2** Minér (or etc) native, virgin **3** Litt (inné) natural, inborn; **bon sens n.** mother or native wit

N native

Do not confuse with **natal.**

nation [nasjɔ̃] NF nation; **n. commerçante** mercantile nation; **Nations unies** United Nations

national, -ale, -aux, -ales [nasjɔnal, -o] ADJ (équipe, gloire) national; **l'hymne n.** the national anthem; **à l'échelle nationale et internationale** nationally and internationally

NMPL **nationaux** nationals

NF Aut **nationale** main road, Br ≃ A road, Am ≃ highway

nationalement [nasjɔnalmã] ADV nationally

nationalisation [nasjɔnalizasjɔ̃] NF nationalization

nationaliser [nasjɔnalize] VT (industrie) to nationalize; **nationalisé** nationalized

nationalisme [nasjɔnalism] NM Pol nationalism

nationaliste [nasjɔnalist] N Pol nationalist

ADJ nationalist, Péj nationalistic; **la Chine n.** Nationalist China

nationalité [nasjɔnalite] NF nationality; Naut **acte de n.** (ship's) certificate of registry; **les personnes de n. française** people of French nationality, French nationals; **il est de quelle n.?** what nationality is he?; **n. à la naissance** nationality at birth; **code de la n.** = rules and regulations defining entitlement to French nationality **VOIR GRAMMAIRE A19; B11–12**

national-populisme NM Pol national populism

national-socialisme NM Hist, Pol National Socialism

national-socialiste Hist, Pol ADJ National Socialist

N National Socialist

nativité [nativite] NF Rel nativity; Beaux-Arts nativity (scene)

natron [natrɔ̃] NM, **natrum** [natrɔm] NM Minér natron

natte [nat] NF **1** (de cheveux, fil d'or etc) plait, surtout Am braid; **porter des nattes** to wear one's hair in plaits or pigtails, to have plaits or pigtails; **porter** ou **avoir une n.** to have a pigtail **2** (de jonc, paille) mat

natter [nate] VT **1** (cheveux, paille etc) to plait, to braid **2** (mur etc) to cover with mats

naturalisation [natyralizasjɔ̃] NF **1** Admin naturalization **2** (de plante, d'animal) naturalization; (de mot) adoption, naturalization **3** (de spécimen botanique etc) preservation, mounting; **n. d'animaux** taxidermy

naturalisé, -ée [natyralize] ADJ naturalized

N naturalized subject or citizen

naturaliser [natyralize] VT **1** Admin to naturalize; **se faire n. français** to take French citizenship **2** (plante, animal) to naturalize, to acclimatize; (mot) to adopt, to naturalize **3** (préserver) (spécimen botanique etc) to preserve, to mount; (empailler) (animal) to stuff

naturalisme [natyralism] NM naturalism

naturaliste [natyralist] N **1** (savant) naturalist **2** (artisan) taxidermist

ADJ naturalistic

nature [natyʁ] NF **1** *(univers)* nature; **les lois de la n.** the laws of nature; **une merveille de la n.** a wonder of nature; **une force de la n.** a force of nature; **laisser faire la n.** to let nature take its course; **tous les goûts sont dans la n.** everyone to his own taste; **vice contre n.** unnatural vice; **c'est contre n. qu'une femme ait des enfants après la ménopause** it's unnatural *or* it's against nature for a woman to have children after the menopause; **la n. fait bien les choses** *ou* **est bien faite** Mother Nature does wonderful things, isn't nature wonderful?; *Fam* **la pauvre fille n'est pas gâtée par la n.** nature hasn't been kind to the poor girl; **à l'état de n.** in the natural state

2 *(milieu végétal et animal)* nature; **une n. luxuriante s'offrit à nos yeux** a luxuriant landscape opened up before us; **les amoureux de la n.** nature lovers; **protection de la n.** protection of the environment; **maison en pleine n.** house deep in the country; **se promener dans la n.** to go for a walk in the country; *Fig* **se perdre** *ou* **disparaître dans la n.** to vanish into thin air; *Aut Fam* **partir dans la n.** to run into a ditch/a field; *Beaux-Arts* **n. morte** still life

3 *(caractère)* nature; **n. du climat/du sol** nature of the climate/the soil; **ce n'est pas dans ma n.** it's not in my nature; **c'est dans la n. des choses** it's in the nature of things; **une découverte de n. à révolutionner la science** a discovery likely to revolutionize science; **ce genre de détail n'est pas de n. à les inquiéter** that kind of detail is unlikely to bother them; **faits de n. à nous étonner** facts of an astonishing nature, astonishing facts; **un programme de cette n.** a programme of this kind *or* nature; **être d'une n. douce** to have a gentle nature; **être timide de** *ou* **par n., être d'une n. timide** to be naturally shy, to be shy by nature; **c'est une bonne n.** he's/she's a kind soul *or* a kindly (sort of) man/woman; **c'est une n. violente** he's/she's a violent sort; **c'est une n.** he's/she's a real character; *Fam* **c'est une petite n.** *(n'a pas une santé solide)* he's/she's got a weak constitution

4 *(réalité)* **plus grand que n.** larger than life; **peindre d'après n.** to paint from nature *or* from life; **payer en n.** *(avec des marchandises)* to pay in kind

ADJ INV **1** *Culin (yaourt, omelette)* plain; **riz n.** (plain) boiled rice; **thé n.** tea without milk **2** *(conforme à la réalité)* **grandeur n.** full-scale, life-size(d) **3** *Fam (personne)* natural, unaffected

naturel, -elle [natyʁɛl] ADJ **1** *(inhérent à la nature) (phénomène, loi, frontière, gaz)* natural; *(besoin, fonction)* bodily; **mort naturelle** death from natural causes; **il est mort de mort naturelle** he died from natural causes; **les défenses naturelles de l'organisme** the body's natural defences **2** *(inné) (don, tendance)* natural, innate; **il a des dispositions naturelles pour la peinture** painting comes naturally to him; **il a une grâce naturelle** he is naturally graceful **3** *(non artificiel) (procréation, couleur de cheveux, jus de fruit etc)* natural; **soie naturelle** pure *or* real silk **4** *(normal)* natural; **son inquiétude est tout à fait naturelle** it's only natural that he should be worried; **c'est n. de le faire** it's only natural *or* reasonable to do so; **mais c'est tout n.** don't mention it, you're welcome **5** *(non affecté) (personne, air, style)* natural, unaffected; *(réponse)* simple, straightforward; **vin n.** unfortified wine **6** *Mus* **note naturelle** natural

NM **1** *(tempérament)* nature, character, disposition; **d'un bon n.** kind, of a kind disposition; **elle est d'un n. généreux/peureux/jaloux** she has a generous/timid/jealous

nature, she is generous/timid/jealous by nature; *Prov* **chassez le n., il revient au galop** what's bred in the bone (will come out in the flesh) **2** *(simplicité, spontanéité)* naturalness; **elle joue la comédie avec beaucoup de n.** she's a natural (as a) comic actor; **parler avec n.** to speak naturally **3** *Culin* **thon au n.** tuna (packed) in brine; **poires au n.** pears in natural fruit juice

naturellement [natyʁɛlmɑ̃] ADV naturally; **n. timide** naturally shy, shy by nature; **se conduire n.** to behave naturally *or* without affectation; **vous vous en êtes fâché? – n.!** you resented it? – naturally! *or* of course (I did)!

naturisme [natyʁism] NM naturism; **adepte du n.** naturist, nudist

naturiste [natyʁist] N naturist, nudist
ADJ naturist; **centre n.** nudist colony *or* camp

naufrage [nofʁaʒ] NM (ship)wreck; *Fig (d'entreprise)* failure; **lors du n. du Titanic** when the Titanic sank; **faire n.** *(de bateau)* to be wrecked; *(de marin)* to be shipwrecked; *Fig (d'entreprise, de mariage)* to collapse; **périr dans un n.** to be lost at sea; *Fig* **le pays va vers le n.** the country is heading for disaster; *Fig* **le n. de ses ambitions** the collapse of his ambitions

naufragé, -ée [nofʁaʒe] ADJ *(bateau)* wrecked; *(marin)* shipwrecked, castaway
N castaway, shipwrecked man/woman

naufrageur, -euse [nofʁaʒœʁ, -øz] N *(de bateaux)* wrecker; **bateau n.** wrecker

naupathie [nopati] NF *Méd* seasickness

nauséabond [nozeabɔ̃] ADJ *(odeur)* nauseating, foul; *(personne, pièce)* foul-smelling; *Fig (thèses etc)* sickening, nauseating

nausée [noze] NF **1** *(envie de vomir)* nausea; *(chez la femme enceinte)* morning sickness; **avoir la n.** *ou* **des nausées** to feel sick *or* nauseous; **avoir des nausées** *(d'une femme enceinte)* to have morning sickness; **donner des nausées à qn** to make sb feel sick **2** *Fig* disgust; **l'hypocrisie me donne la n.** hypocrisy makes me sick *or* nauseates me

nauséeux, -euse [nozeø, -øz] ADJ **1** *(odeur)* nauseating; **se sentir n.** to feel sick *or* nauseous **2** *Fig (hypocrisie etc)* nauseating, sickening

nautile [notil] NM *Zool* nautilus

nautique [notik] ADJ *(terme, instrument etc)* nautical; **sports nautiques** water sports; **carte n.** (sea) chart; **salon n.** boat show

nautisme [notism] NM *Sport* water sports

naval, -ale, -als, -ales [naval] ADJ *(architecture, base, combat)* naval; **termes navals** nautical *or* sailing terms; **construction navale** shipbuilding; **chantier n.** shipyard; **les forces navales** the navy; **l'École navale** the Naval College
NF *Fam* **faire Navale** to attend Naval College

navarin [navaʁɛ̃] NM *Culin* lamb stew *or* casserole

navel [navɛl] NF navel orange

navet [navɛ] NM **1** turnip **2** *Fam (film, pièce de théâtre)* **c'est un n.** it's a load of rubbish *or* nonsense

navette¹ [navɛt] NF **1** *Tex* shuttle **2** *Aviat etc* shuttle (service); **navettes fréquentes entre la gare et la ville** frequent (shuttle) service between station and town; **faire la n. entre deux endroits/services** *(de véhicule, personne, dossier etc)* to shuttle back and forth between two places/two departments; **je fais la n. entre Glasgow et Édimbourg tous les jours** I commute between Glasgow and Edinburgh; **n. de transfert** transfer bus; **n. gratuite** courtesy bus; **n. parlementaire** =

successive readings of bills by the Assemblée nationale and the Sénat **3** *(fusée)* shuttle **4** *Rel* incense box
▸▸ **n. spatiale** space shuttle

navette² NF *Bot* rape; **(huile de) n.** rape (seed) oil, colza oil

navetteur, -euse [navɛtœʁ, -øz] N *Belg* commuter

navigabilité [navigabilite] NF **1** *(de rivière etc)* navigability **2** *(de bateau)* seaworthiness; *(d'avion)* airworthiness; **en (bon) état de n.** *(bateau)* seaworthy; *(avion)* airworthy

navigable [navigabl] ADJ **1** *(rivière, voie)* navigable **2** *(bateau)* seaworthy; *(avion)* airworthy

navigant [navigɑ̃] ADJ **personnel n.** navigation crew, flight crew
NMPL **les navigants** the navigation crew, the flight crew

navigateur, -trice [navigatœʁ, -tʁis] N **1** *(de bateau, d'avion etc)* navigator **2** *(voyageur sur mer)* navigator, seafarer; **n. solitaire** lone *or* single-handed yachtsman *or* sailor
NM *Ordinat* (Web) browser
ADJ **peuple n.** seafaring people

navigation [navigasjɔ̃] NF **1** *Naut, Aviat* navigation; **école de n.** *(de la marine marchande)* nautical school; **compagnie de n.** shipping company; **compagnie de n. aérienne** airline; **permis de n.** ship's passport, sea letter; **après un mois de n.** after a month at sea **2** *Ordinat* **n. sur (l')Internet** browsing the Web, Internet surfing; **n. rapide/sécurisée** rapid/secure browsing
▸▸ **n. côtière** coastal navigation; **n. à l'estime** dead reckoning; **n. extérieure** deep-sea navigation; **n. fluviale** inland navigation; **n. hauturière** deep-sea *or* ocean navigation; *Aviat* **n. aux instruments** instrument flying; **n. intérieure** inland navigation; **n. au long cours** deep-sea *or* ocean navigation; **n. maritime** deep-sea *or* maritime navigation; **n. de plaisance** sailing, yachting, pleasure cruising; *Astronaut* **n. spatiale** space navigation, astronautics; **n. à voile** sailing; *Aviat* **n. à vue** visual flying

naviguer [navige] VI **1** *(de bateau, marin)* to sail (**vers** to); **navire qui navigue bien** ship that handles well at sea *or* that behaves well; **n. au compas** to sail *or* navigate by the compass; *Fig Fam* **savoir n.** to know the ropes **2** *(se déplacer) (de personne, dossier)* to move around; **le dossier a navigué entre les différents responsables du projet** the file moved around from *or* was passed from project manager to project manager **3** *Ordinat* **n. sur (l')Internet** to surf the Net, to browse the Web
VT *(bateau, avion)* to navigate

navire [naviʁ] NM ship, vessel; **les navires du port** the ships *or* shipping in the harbour
▸▸ **n. amiral** flagship; **n.-citerne** tanker; **n. de combat** battleship; **n. de commerce** merchant ship, merchantman; **n. de conférence** conference ship; **n.-école** training ship; **n. frigorifique** refrigerated vessel; **n. de guerre** warship; **n.-hôpital** hospital ship; **n.-jumeau** twin ship; **n. au long cours** ocean-going ship; **n. marchand** merchant ship, merchantman; **n. mixte** mixed passenger and cargo ship; **n. porte-conteneurs** container ship; **n.-usine** factory ship; **n. à voiles** sailing ship

navrant [navʁɑ̃] ADJ *(nouvelle, attitude etc)* distressing, upsetting; **un film n. de bêtise** an incredibly stupid film; **un contretemps n.** an unfortunate *or* regrettable mishap

navré [navʁe] ADJ *(personne, expression, ton)* distressed; **être n.** *(désolé)* to be very *or* terribly sorry; **je suis n. (de l'apprendre)** I'm terribly *or* very sorry (to hear that); **n. de vous avoir fait attendre** sorry to have kept you waiting

navrer [navʀe] **VT** to distress, to upset

nazaréen, -enne [nazaʀeɛ̃, -ɛn] **ADJ, N** *Bible* Nazarene

naze [naz] **ADJ, N** *Fam* = **nase**

nazi, -ie [nazi] **ADJ, N** *Hist, Pol* Nazi

nazillon, -onne [nazijɔ̃, -ɔn] **N** *Fam* little Nazi

nazisme [nazism] **NM** *Hist, Pol* Nazism

NB [ɛnbe] (*abrév* **nota bene**) NB

NbP *Typ* (*abrév* **note de bas de page**) footnote

NC [ɛnse] **NM** (*abrév* **network computer**) NC

NCM **NFPL** [ɛnseem] (*abrév* **négociations commerciales multilatérales**) multilateral trade negotiations

NDLR (*abrév* **note de la rédaction**) Ed

NdT (*abrév* **note du traducteur**) translator's note

NE, N' [n(ə)] **ADV** SEE GRAMMAR B62–3 **1** (*forming neg verb with* **pas**) **je ne la connais pas** I don't know her; (*emphatique*) I do not know her; **il ne m'avait pas vu** he hadn't seen me (NOTE *for the use of* **ne** *in conjunction with* **aucun, aucunement, goutte, guère, jamais, mot, personne, plus, point, que, rien** *see these words*) **2** (*used alone, chiefly in literary style, with* **cesser, oser, pouvoir, savoir, importer** *and often as an archaism with other verbs*) **il ne cesse de parler** he is forever *or* always talking, he doesn't stop *or* never stops talking; **je n'ose lui parler** I dare not speak to him; **je ne puis vous le promettre** I cannot promise you that; **je ne sais que faire** I do not know what to do; **je ne saurais vous le dire** I cannot tell you **3** (*in the following constructions*) **qui ne connaît cette œuvre célèbre?** who does not know this famous work?; **que ne ferait-elle pour vous?** what would she not do for you?; **je n'ai d'autre désir que celui de vous plaire** I have no other desire than to please you; **si je ne me trompe** *ou* **m'abuse** if I am not mistaken, unless I am mistaken; **voilà six mois que je ne l'ai vue** it is now six months since I (last) saw her, I haven't seen her for six months; **il n'y a personne à qui il ne se soit adressé** there is no one whom he didn't speak to; **il n'eut garde d'y aller** he took good care not to go; **qu'à cela ne tienne!** never mind (about) that!, that's no problem!; **je n'ai que faire de votre aide** I have no need of your help **4** (*used optionally in literary style with a vague negative connotation*) **je crains qu'elle (ne) prenne froid** I am afraid she may catch cold; **évitez** *ou* **prenez garde qu'on (ne) vous voie** take care not to be seen; **peu s'en fallut qu'elle (ne) tombât** she very nearly fell; **je ne nie pas que cela (ne) soit vrai** I don't deny that it's true; **il est plus vigoureux qu'il n'y paraît** he is stronger than he looks; **elle agit autrement qu'elle ne parle** her actions belie *or* don't match her words

né [ne] **ADJ** born; *Litt* **c'est un conteur/conducteur né** he's a born story-teller/driver; **enfant né d'un premier mariage** child from a first marriage; **né d'une famille bourgeoise** born into a middle-class family; *Fig* **un film né de la rencontre d'un réalisateur et d'une actrice** a film born of *or* that grew out of a meeting between a director and an actress; **Mme Martin, née Dupond** Mrs Martin, née Dupond; *Arch* **être bien né** to be well born *or* of noble birth

néanmoins [neɑ̃mwɛ̃] **ADV** nevertheless, nonetheless, yet; **il est sérieux mais n. décontracté** he's serious but nevertheless *or* but nonetheless *or* yet relaxed

néant [neɑ̃] **NM 1** (*ce qui n'existe pas*) nothingness, void; **sortir du n.** to rise from nothing; **réduire qch à n.** to reduce sth to nothing, to destroy sth; **tous ses espoirs furent réduits à n.** all his hopes were dashed **2** (*sur formulaire, feuille de déclaration d'impôts etc*) none, nil; **signes particuliers: n.** distinguishing marks: none

nébuleux, -euse [nebylø, -øz] **ADJ** (*ciel, vue*) cloudy, hazy, misty; (*idées, raisonnement, explications*) vague, hazy, nebulous; (*écrivain, théorie, propos*) obscure

NF *Astron* **nébuleuse** nebula; *Fig* **toute une nébuleuse de sociétés-écrans** a whole cluster of umbrella companies

nébuliseur [nebylizœr] **NM** nebulizer

nébulosité [nebylozite] **NF 1** *Météo* (*nuage très fin*) wispy cloud; (*ciel couvert*) cloud cover; **forte n.** heavy cloud cover **2** (*d'une idée etc*) vagueness, haziness

nécessaire [nesesɛʀ] **ADJ 1** necessary; **cela ne sera pas n.** that won't be necessary; **n. à** *ou* **pour qn/qch** necessary *or* required for sb/sth; **n. pour faire qch** necessary to do sth; **avoir l'argent/le temps/la patience n.** to have the necessary money/time/patience; **il est n. de bien lire les instructions** the instructions need to be read properly, it is necessary to read the instructions properly; **il n'est pas n. d'être impoli** there is no need to be rude; **il n'est pas n. de passer par le standard** there is no need *or* it is not necessary to go through the switchboard; **ils n'ont pas jugé n. de venir s'excuser** they didn't think *or* consider it necessary to come and apologize; **il est n. que vous teniez compte de cela/procédiez de cette manière** you need to *or* you must take notice of this/proceed like this; **peu n.** unnecessary, needless **2** *Phil* necessary

NM le strict n. the bare necessities *or* essentials; **il ne fait que le strict n.** he does no more than that which is strictly necessary; **manquer du n.** to lack the necessities *or* basics of life; **faire le n.** to do what is necessary, *Fam* to do the necessary; **je vais faire le n.** I'll see to it; **pour les billets ne t'inquiète pas, je ferai le n.** don't worry about the tickets, I'll see to them; **merci de faire le n. pour qu'il soit accueilli à l'aéroport** thank you for arranging for him to be met at the airport

▸▸ **n. à chaussures** shoe-cleaning kit; **n. de couture** sewing kit; **n. à ongles** manicure set; **n. de toilette** (set of) toiletries; **n. de voyage** overnight bag

nécessairement [nesesɛʀmɑ̃] **ADV** necessarily; **ce n'est pas n. une mauvaise idée** it's not necessarily a bad idea; **mais c'est complètement idiot! – pas n.** but it's completely stupid! – not necessarily

nécessité [nesesite] **NF 1** (*caractère nécessaire*), *Phil* necessity; **être dans la n. de faire qch** to have no choice but to do sth; **c'est une n.** it's essential; **quelle n. y avait-il de faire cela?** what need was there to do that?; **faire qch par n.** to do sth out of necessity, to be compelled to do sth; **faire de n. vertu** to make a virtue (out) of necessity; *Vieilli de* **(toute) n.** necessarily, of necessity; **il est de toute n. de faire quelque chose** it is essential that we do something, we simply must do something; **objets** *ou* **articles de première n.** essential items, essentials; **denrées de première n.** essential commodities; **être dans la n.** (*être pauvre*) to be in need **2** (*chose nécessaire*) necessity; **les nécessités de la vie** the necessities of life; **à cause des nécessités du service** due to operational requirements

nécessiter [nesesite] **VT** to require, to need, to necessitate; **une telle question nécessite qu'on prenne le temps de réfléchir** such a

question requires *or* needs time to be considered

nécessiteux, -euse [nesesitø, -øz] **ADJ** needy, in need

NMPL les n. the needy, the poor, the destitute

nec plus ultra [nɛkplyzyltʀa] **NM INV le n.** the best there is; **le n. des voitures** the best car there is; **le n. du confort/luxe** the last word in comfort/luxury

nécrologe [nekʀɔlɔʒ] **NM** necrology, death roll

nécrologie [nekʀɔlɔʒi] **NF** (*notice*) obituary (notice); *Journ* (*rubrique*) obituary column

nécrologique [nekʀɔlɔʒik] **ADJ avis/rubrique n.** obituary notice/column

nécromancie [nekʀɔmɑ̃si] **NF** necromancy

nécromancien, -ienne [nekʀɔmɑ̃sjɛ̃, -jɛn] **N** necromancer

nécrophage [nekʀɔfaʒ] **ADJ** necrophagous

nécrophile [nekʀɔfil] **ADJ** necrophiliac

nécrophilie [nekʀɔfili] **NF** necrophilia

nécrophore [nekʀɔfɔʀ] **NM** carrion beetle

nécropole [nekʀɔpɔl] **NF** necropolis

nécrose [nekʀoz] **NF** *Biol* necrosis

nécroser [nekʀoze] *Biol* **VT** (*tissu*) to necrose
VPR se nécroser to necrose

nectaire [nɛktɛʀ] **NM** *Bot* nectary

nectar [nɛktaʀ] **NM** (*jus de fruit, Litt boisson exquise*), *Myth, Bot* nectar; **n. de poire/d'abricot** pear/apricot nectar

nectarine [nɛktaʀin] **NF** (*fruit*) nectarine

néerlandais, -aise [neɛʀlɑ̃dɛ, -ɛz] **ADJ** Dutch, (of the) Netherlands; **le gouvernement n.** the Dutch government, the government of the Netherlands

NM *Ling* (*aux Pays-Bas*) Dutch; (*en Belgique*) Flemish

N N. Dutchman, *f* Dutchwoman; **les N.** the Dutch

nef [nɛf] **NF 1** (*d'église*) **n. (centrale)** nave; **n. latérale** aisle **2** *Litt* (*navire*) ship

néfaste [nefast] **ADJ** (*effet, conséquence, influence*) harmful; **jour n.** ill-fated *or* evil day

nèfle [nɛfl] **NF** (*fruit*) medlar; *Fig Fam* **des nèfles!** no fear!, nothing doing!; **n. du Japon** loquat

néflier [neflije] **NM** medlar (tree); **n. du Japon** loquat (tree)

négateur, -trice [negatœʀ, -tʀis] *Litt* **ADJ une doctrine négatrice** a negative doctrine
N denier

négatif, -ive [negatif, -iv] **ADJ** negative; *Phot* **épreuve négative** negative
NM *Phot* negative
NF *Gram* **négative** negative; **je réponds par la négative** my answer is in the negative
ADV *Fam* **n.!** negative!

négation [negasjɔ̃] **NF 1** (*fait de nier*) negation, denial **2** *Gram* negative SEE GRAMMAR A47–8; B62–3

négationnisme [negasjɔnism] **NM** revisionism (*denying that the Holocaust ever happened*)

négationniste [negasjɔnist] **ADJ** revisionist (*denying that the Holocaust ever happened*)
N revisionist (*who denies that the Holocaust ever happened*)

négativement [negativmɑ̃] **ADV** (*réagir*) negatively; (*répondre*) in the negative

négativisme [negativism] **NM** negativism

négligé [negliʒe] **ADJ 1** (*peu soigné*) (*tenue, apparence, personne*) slovenly, untidy, scruffy; (*travail, devoir, style*) slovenly, careless **2** (*auquel on ne porte pas assez d'attention*) (*enfant, femme etc*) neglected
NM 1 (*caractère*) slovenliness, untidiness **2** (*vêtement*) negligee, negligée

négligeable [negliʒabl] **ADJ** (*détail, risque,*

quantité) negligible, insignificant; **un avantage non n.** a not inconsiderable advantage; **une quantité non n. de** a significant quantity of; **il me traite comme (une) quantité n.** he treats me as if I'm not there *or* as if I don't exist

négligemment [negliʒamā] ADV **1** *(habillé)* carelessly, untidily, scruffily **2** *(répondre, lire)* casually, nonchalantly; *(pour feindre l'inattention)* casually; **elle était n. installée dans le canapé** she was draped over the sofa

négligence [negliʒās] NF **1** *(manque de soin)* negligence, carelessness; *(de quelqu'un, d'un devoir)* neglect; **avec n.** *(travailler)* carelessly; **par (pure) n.** through (sheer) carelessness *or* negligence **2** *(insouciance)* casualness, nonchalance; **il me répondit avec n. qu'il viendrait peut-être** he casually *or* nonchalantly replied that he would perhaps come **3** *(acte négligent)* act of carelessness, careless act; *(oubli)* oversight; **l'accident est dû à une n.** the accident was due to carelessness; **je reconnais que c'est une n. de notre part** I admit that it is an oversight on our part; **n. de style** stylistic error, error of style; *Jur* **n. coupable** *ou* **criminelle** criminal negligence

négligent [negliʒā] ADJ *(parent, touriste, campeur)* negligent, careless; *(remarque, attitude, coup d'œil)* casual

négliger [negliʒe] (**je négligeai(s); nous négligeons**) VT **1** *(délaisser)* *(sa santé, son devoir, ses enfants)* to neglect, to be neglectful of; *(son apparence, sa tenue)* not to care about **2** *(omettre, oublier)* *(avis, conseil)* to disregard; *(occasion)* to miss; *(élément, détail)* to overlook, to disregard; **il ne faut jamais rien n.** you must never leave anything to chance; **n. de faire qch** to neglect *or* fail to do sth
▪ **VPR se négliger** to neglect one's appearance, to let oneself go

négoce [negɔs] NM trade; *Arch* **faire du n.** to be in trade; **le n. international** international trade *or* trading; *Bourse* **n. de titres** share dealing

négociabilité [negɔsjabilite] NF *Fin* negotiability

négociable [negɔsjabl] ADJ *(salaire, prix, conditions d'emploi)* negotiable; *Fin (bon, traite)* negotiable, transferable, trad(e)able; **n. en banque** bankable; **n. en Bourse** negotiable on the Stock Exchange

négociant, -ante [negɔsjā, -āt] N **1** *(de commerce)* merchant, dealer; **n. en gros** wholesaler; **n. en vins** wine merchant; **n. exportateur** export merchant **2** *Bourse* trader; **n. courtier** broker-dealer

négociateur, -trice [negɔsjatœr, -tris] N *(de traité, marché etc)* negotiator

négociation [negɔsjasjɔ̃] NF **1** *(de traité, paix)* negotiation (**sur** on); **entamer des négociations** to enter into negotiations; *UE* **négociations d'adhésion** accession negotiations; **négociations collectives** joint negotiations; *(au sein d'une entreprise)* collective bargaining; **négociations commerciales multilatérales** multilateral trade negotiations; **négociations pour la paix** peace negotiations; **négociations précontractuelles** precontractual negotiations; **en n.** *(conditions etc)* under negotiation; **nous sommes en n. avec la direction** we are negotiating *or* we are in negotiation with management **2** *Com* negotiation, transaction; **n. d'un effet** negotiation of a bill of exchange; **négociations au comptant** spot trading; **négociations à prime** options trading; **négociations à terme** futures trading

négocier [negɔsje] *(impf, pr sub nous négociions)* VI **1** *(traiter, discuter)* to nego-

tiate (**avec** with) **2** *Arch (faire du commerce)* to trade
▪ VT **1** *(prêt, traite, salaire, paix)* to negotiate; *Bourse* to trade; **modalités du contrat: à n.** terms negotiable **2** *Aut* **n. un virage** to negotiate a bend

nègre [nɛgr] NM **1** *Péj (Noir)* Negro; **la traite des nègres** the slave trade; *Fam* **travailler comme un n.** to work like a slave [VOIR GRAMMAIRE A12] **2** *Fig (écrivain)* ghost (writer); **être le n. de qn** to ghost for sb
▪ ADJ **1** *(art)* Negro **2** *Péj (race)* Negro **3** *inv (couleur)* nigger(-brown)
▪▸ **n. blanc** White Negro; **propos n. blanc** double talk; *Culin* **n. en chemise** = chocolate dessert with whipped cream

négresse [negrɛs] NF *Péj* Negress

négrier [negrije] NM **1** *(trafiquant d'esclaves)* slave trader; *(employeur, surveillant)* slave driver **2** *(bateau)* slave ship, slaver
▪ ADJ **vaisseau n.** slave ship, slaver

négrillon, -onne [negrijɔ̃, -ɔn] N *Péj* piccaninny

négritude [negrityd] NF negritude

négro [negro] NM *très Fam (terme raciste)* Negro, nigger

négroïde [negrɔid] ADJ *(traits, type)* Negroid

neige [nɛʒ] NF **1** snow; **tempête de n.** blizzard, snowstorm; *Can* **banc de n.** snow bank; **être bloqué par la n.** to be snowed up *or* snowbound; **aller à la n.** to go on a skiing holiday; **sports de n.** winter sports; **fondre comme n. au soleil** to melt away (like snow in the sun); **blanc comme (la) n.** white as snow, snow-white; *Fig* **être blanc comme n.** to be as pure as the driven snow; *Culin* **blancs d'œufs battus en n.** stiffly beaten egg whites **2** *Arg (cocaïne)* snow
▪▸ **n. artificielle** artificial snow; **n. carbonique** dry ice, (carbon dioxide) snow; **neiges éternelles** perpetual snow; **n. fondue** *(qui tombe)* sleet; *(par terre)* slush; **n. fraîche** freshly fallen snow; **n. poudreuse** powdery snow; *Ski* **n. pourrie** hazardous *or* crumbly snow; *Ski* **n. tôlée** crusted snow

neiger [neʒe] V IMPERS *(il neigeait)* to snow

neigeux, -euse [neʒø, -øz] ADJ **1** *(pic, temps)* snowy; *(toit, pente etc)* snow-covered **2** *Fig (barbe)* snow-white, snowy

nem [nɛm] NM *Culin* spring roll

nématode [nematɔd] NM *Zool* nematode (threadworm)

néné [nene] NM *Fam* tit, boob

nénette [nenɛt] NF *Fam* **1** *(jeune fille)* bird, *Am* chick **2** *(petite amie)* girl **3** *(tête)* **se casser la n. (à faire qch)** to go to a lot of bother (to do sth); **tu ne t'es pas trop cassé la n. pour faire ta rédaction** you didn't exactly strain yourself *or* exert yourself over your essay; **te casse pas la n.** don't worry about it, don't let it bother you

nénuphar [nenyfar] NM waterlily; **n. des étangs, n. jaune** yellow pond lily

néo- [neo] PRÉF neo-

néo-calédonien, -ienne, *pl* **néo-calédoniens, -iennes** ADJ New Caledonian
▪ N **N.-C.** New Caledonian

néocapitalisme [neokapitalism] NM neocapitalism

néocapitaliste [neokapitalist] ADJ, N neocapitalist

néoclassicisme [neoklasisism] NM neoclassicism

néoclassique [neoklasik] ADJ *(style, architecture)* neoclassical

néocolonial, -iale, -iaux, -iales [neokɔlɔnjal, -jo] ADJ neocolonial

néocolonialisme [neokɔlɔnjalism] NM neocolonialism

néofascisme [neofasism, -ʃism] NM neofascism

néofasciste [neofaʃist] ADJ, N neofascist

néogothique [neogɔtik] ADJ, NM *Archit* neogothic

néo-hébridais, -aise, *pl* **néo-hébridais, -aises** [neoebride, -ez] ADJ of the New Hebrides
▪ N **N.-H.** *(natif)* native of the New Hebrides; *(habitant)* inhabitant of the New Hebrides

néo-impressionnisme NM *Beaux-Arts* neo-impressionism

néolibéralisme [neoliberalism] NM neoliberalism

néolithique [neolitik] ADJ, NM Neolithic

néologisme [neolɔʒism] NM neologism

néon [neɔ̃] NM *Chimie* neon; **tube au n.** neon tube

néonatal, -ale, -als, -ales [neonatal] ADJ *Méd* neonatal

néonazi, -ie [neonazi] ADJ, N neo-Nazi

néonazisme [neonazism] NM neo-Nazism

néophyte [neofit] N **1** *Rel (converti)* neophyte **2** *Fig (novice)* novice, tyro; **je suis totalement n.** I'm a complete novice

Néoprène® [neopren] NM *Tech* neoprene

néoréalisme [neorealism] NM *Cin* neorealism

néoréaliste [neorealist] ADJ *Cin (film, cinéaste)* neorealist

néorural, -ale, -aux, -ales [neoryral] N neo-rural

néo-zélandais, -aise, *pl* **néo-zélandais, -aises** [neozelāde, -ez] ADJ New Zealand
▪ N **N.-Z.** New Zealander

Népal [nepal] NM Nepal

népalais, -aise [nepale, -ez] ADJ Nepalese, Nepali
▪ NM *Ling* Nepali
▪ N **N.** Nepalese, Nepali

népérien, -ienne [neperjē, -jɛn] ADJ *(logarithmes)* Napierian

néphrétique [nefretik] ADJ **colique n.** renal colic
▪ N sufferer from nephritis

néphrite [nefrit] NF **1** *Méd* nephritis; **n. chronique** Bright's disease **2** *Minér* nephrite, jade

néphrologie [nefrolɔʒi] NF *Méd* nephrology

néphron [nefrɔ̃] NM *Méd* nephron

népotisme [nepotism] NM nepotism

Neptune [nɛptyn] NM *Myth* Neptune *m*
▪ NF *Astron* Neptune *f*

néréide [nereid] NF nereid, sea nymph

nerf [nɛr] NM **1** *(optique, spinal)* nerve; **viande pleine de nerfs** meat full of gristle, gristly meat; *Fam* **il a les nerfs en pelote** *ou* **à vif** *ou* **en boule** his nerves are *or* he is on edge; *Fam* **porter** *ou* **taper** *ou* *Can* **tomber sur les nerfs à qn** to get on sb's nerves; **avoir les nerfs à fleur de peau** to be all on edge; **je suis à bout de nerfs** I'm at the end of my tether; *Fam* **c'est un paquet** *ou* **une boule de nerfs** he is a bundle *or* bag of nerves; **être** *ou* **vivre sur les nerfs** to live on one's nerves; **passer ses nerfs sur qn/qch** to take it out on sb/sth; **guerre des nerfs** war of nerves; *Fam* **avoir les nerfs** to be really fed up; **avoir les nerfs solides** to have strong *or* steady nerves, to have nerves of steel; **être malade des nerfs** to suffer from nerves, to have bad nerves; *Fam* **foutre les nerfs à qn** to hack sb off, to get sb's back up
2 *Vieilli (tendon)* sinew, tendon, ligament; **un grand athlète tout en n.** a tall sinewy athlete
3 *(force)* **un peu de n.!, du n.!** put some energy into it!; **avoir du n.** *(d'un moteur, d'une voiture)* to be responsive *or* lively; *(d'une personne)* to have some go about

one; **l'argent est le n. de la guerre** money is the sinews of war

4 *(de reliure)* band, cord

▸▸ **n. de bœuf** cosh, *Am* blackjack; *Anat* **n. crânien** cranial nerve; *Anat* **n. sciatique** sciatic nerve

nerprun [nɛrprœ̃] NM *Bot* buckthorn

nervation [nɛrvasjɔ̃] NF *Bot, Zool* nervation, venation

nervé [nɛrve] ADJ *Bot* nervate, veined

nerveusement [nɛrvøzmɑ̃] ADV **1** nervously **2** *(avec énergie)* energetically

nerveux, -euse [nɛrvø, -øz] ADJ **1** *(relatif aux nerfs) (système, maladie)* nervous; **centre n.** nerve centre; **dépression nerveuse** nervous breakdown; **influx n.** nerve impulse **2** *(émotif) (personne, tempérament)* nervous, excitable, highly-strung, *Br Fam* nervy; *(en un moment précis, avant un examen etc)* nervous, tense; *(rire, toux)* nervous; **être d'une nature nerveuse** to be of a nervous disposition; **rendre qn n.** to make sb nervous; **le café me rend n.** coffee makes me hyper **3** *(aux tendons apparents) (corps, mains)* sinewy; *(viande)* stringy **4** *(dynamique) (personne)* dynamic, energetic; *(style)* vigorous, terse; *Aut (conduite)* dynamic; **votre conduite est trop nerveuse** your driving is jerky; **moteur n.** responsive *or* lively engine

N nervous person

nervi [nɛrvi] NM henchman, thug

nervosité [nɛrvozite] NF nervousness; *(irritabilité)* irritability; **donner des signes de n.** to show signs of agitation

nervure [nɛrvyr] NF *(de feuille, d'aile d'insecte)* nervure, vein, rib; *Tech* flange, rib; *(de radiateur etc)* gill; *Aviat (d'aile)* rib; *(au dos d'un livre)* rib, raised band; *Archit* **voûte à nervures** ribbed vault; **plafond à nervures** filleted ceiling; *Couture* **nervures** pin tucks

nervuré [nɛrvyre] ADJ *(feuille, aile)* veined; *(vêtement)* ribbed

n'est-ce pas [nɛspa] ADV **tu viendras, n.?** you'll come, won't you?; **tu l'as déjà vue, n.?** you've already seen her, haven't you?; **n. qu'elle est mignonne?** isn't she cute, isn't she?; **le problème, n., c'est qu'elle est un peu prude** the problem, you see, is that she's something of a prude VOIR GRAMMAIRE A47

Net [nɛt] NM **le N.** the Net, the Internet

NET, NETTE [nɛt] ADJ **1** *(propre) (assiette, pièce, miroir, mains)* clean; *Fig (conscience)* clear; **j'ai la conscience nette** I have a clear conscience, my conscience is clear; *Fig* **j'ai les mains nettes** my hands are clean; **faire place nette** to clear everything out; *Cartes etc* **faire tapis n.** to sweep the board

2 *(clair, précis) (vue, idée, style)* clear; *(contour)* sharp; *(réponse)* plain, straight; **je n'ai pas les idées très nettes aujourd'hui** I'm not quite with it today; **écriture nette** neat handwriting; **il fait plus froid ici, c'est très n.** it's noticeably *or* definitely colder here; *Phot, TV, Opt* **image nette** sharp image; **cassure nette** clean break; **division nette** clear-cut division; **elle a gardé des souvenirs très nets de sa petite enfance** she remembers her childhood quite clearly *or* vividly

3 *(différence, amélioration, refroidissement etc)* clear, marked, distinct

4 *Fam* **il n'est pas n.** *(un peu dérangé)* he's not all there; *(louche)* he's a bit shady

5 *(poids, prix, salaire)* net; *(profit)* net, clear; **n. d'impôt** net of tax; **le montant n.** the net amount, the net

ADV **1** *(de manière précise, brutale) (parler)* plainly, frankly; **refuser (tout) n.** to refuse point-blank *or* flatly; **je lui ai dit tout n. ma façon de penser** I told him plainly *or* frankly what I thought; **s'arrêter n.** to stop dead; **se**

casser n. to break clean through; **coupé n.** cut clean through; **tué n.** killed outright; **mets ton exercice au n.** copy the exercise out neatly

2 *Com* **cent euros n.** a hundred euros net; **gagner mille euros n.** to earn a thousand euros net, to net a thousand euros

▸▸ *Compta* **n.** commercial net profit; **n. financier** net interest income; *(à payer)* net interest charges; **n. à payer** net payable

netéconomie [nɛtekɔnɔmi] NF *Écon, Ordinat* Internet economy

netiquette [nɛtikɛt] NF *Ordinat (sur l'Internet)* netiquette

netsurfer [nɛtsœrfœr] NM *Ordinat* net surfer

nettement [nɛtmɑ̃] ADV **1** *(distinctement) (voir, se dessiner)* clearly, distinctly; **profil n. découpé** clear-cut profile **2** *(incontestablement)* distinctly, markedly; **ce livre est n. pacifiste** this book is distinctly *or* markedly pacifist **3** *(beaucoup)* much, distinctly; **ça va n. mieux comme ça** it's a lot *or* much better like this; **elle est n. moins bonne que lui** she's not nearly as good as him; **il est arrivé n. en retard** he was more than a little late, he arrived quite late

netteté [nɛte] NF **1** *(propreté)* cleanliness, cleanness **2** *(précision) (de rupture)* cleanness; **s'exprimer avec n.** to express oneself clearly **3** *(clarté) (de pensée, style)* clearness, clarity; *(de vision, d'objet)* distinctness; *(d'image)* sharpness; *(de mémoire)* vividness; *(de refus)* flatness; **l'image manque de n.** the picture isn't very sharp; *Phot* **régler la n.** to focus

nettoiement [nɛtwamɑ̃] NM *(de rues)* cleaning; *(du sol)* cleaning, clearing; *(de forêt)* clearing; **service du n.** refuse collection service

nettoyage [nɛtwajaʒ] NM **1** cleaning; **faire le n.** to do the cleaning; **grand n. de printemps** spring-cleaning; **produit de n.** cleaning product; **entreprise de n.** cleaning firm **2** *(par la police)* cleaning *or* clearing out; **les policiers ont opéré un véritable n. du quartier** the police officers really cleaned out *or* cleared out the district; *Mil* **opérations de n.** mopping-up operations

▸▸ *Pol* **n. ethnique** ethnic cleansing; **n. à sec** dry-cleaning; **n. par le vide** vacuum cleaning; *Fig* **faire le n. par le vide** to throw everything out

nettoyant [nɛtwajɑ̃] ADJ cleaning
NM cleaning product

nettoyer [nɛtwaje] (**je nettoie; je nettoierai**) VT **1** *(pièce, vêtements, casserole, blessure)* to clean; *(bouteille)* to wash out; *Naut (pont)* to swab; **n. à sec** to dry-clean **2** *Fig Fam (de cambrioleur) (maison)* to strip, to clean out; **se faire n. au jeu** to be *or* get cleaned out gambling; **la police est en train de n. le quartier** the police are cleaning out *or* clearing out the district; *Mil* **n. les poches de résistance** to mop up **3** *Fam (tuer)* to wipe out; **se faire n.** to be *or* get wiped out
VPR **se nettoyer un tic les mains** to clean one's ears/hands; **le four se nettoie automatiquement** the oven cleans itself automatically *or* is self-cleaning

nettoyeur, -euse [nɛtwajœr, -øz] N *(personne)* cleaner
NF **nettoyeuse** *(machine)* cleaning machine, cleaner

neuf¹ [nœf, *before* ans *and* heures nœv] ADJ **1** nine; **à n. heures** at nine o'clock; **n. fois sur dix** nine times out of ten **2** *(dans une séries)* ninth; **page/numéro n.** page/number nine; **Louis N.** Louis the Ninth
NM INV nine; **le n. mai** (on) the ninth of May, (on) May the ninth, *Am* (on) May ninth; *Cartes* **le n. de carreau** the nine of diamonds;

j'habite au n. I live at number nine; *Math* **faire la preuve par n.** to cast out the nines

neuf², neuve [nœf, nœv] ADJ **à l'état n.** in new condition, as new; *(timbre postal, livre)* in mint condition, unused; **'état n.'** *(dans petite annonce)* 'as new'; **tout n.** brand new; **comme n.** as good as new; **aborder/considérer/regarder qch d'un œil n.** to approach/consider/look at sth with a fresh eye; **la curiosité (toute) neuve d'un enfant** a child's newly awakened curiosity; **être n. dans un métier** to be new to a job; **quoi de n.?** what's new?; **il n'y a rien de n.** there's nothing new

NM **vendre du n. et de l'occasion** to sell new and second-hand goods; **habillé de n.** wearing new clothes; **meublé de n.** newly furnished; **acheter du n.** *(dans l'immobilier)* to buy new; **refaire/repeindre une maison à n.** to redo/repaint a house completely; **remettre qch à n.** to make sth as good as new; *(machine)* to recondition sth, to renovate sth; **tu as du n. pour ton visa?** any developments on the visa front?, have you heard anything about your visa?

neurasthénie [nørasteni] NF *Méd* neurasthenia; *Vieilli* **faire de la n.** *(dépression)* to be depressed

neurasthénique [nørastenik] ADJ *Vieilli* depressed; *Méd* neurasthenic
N *Vieilli* depressive, depressed person; *Méd* neurasthenic

neurobiologie [nørobjɔlɔʒi] NF neurobiology

neuroblaste [nøroblast] NM *Biol* neuroblast

neurochirurgie [nøroʃiryrʒi] NF *Chir* neurosurgery

neurochirurgien, -ienne [nøroʃiryrʒjɛ̃, -jɛn] N *Chir* neurosurgeon

neuroleptique [nørolɛptik] *Méd* ADJ *(médicament)* neuroleptic
NM neuroleptic, *Fam* tranquillizer; **être sous neuroleptiques** to be on tranquillizers

neurologie [nørolɔʒi] NF *Méd* neurology

neurologiste [nørolɔʒist] N, **neurologue** [nørolɔg] N *Méd* neurologist, nerve specialist

neuromusculaire [nøromyskyler] ADJ neuromuscular

neuronal, -ale, -aux, -ales [nøronal, -o] ADJ neuronal; **réseau n.** neural net

neurone [nøron, -ron] NM *Biol, Ordinat* neuron, neurone

neuronique [nøronik] ADJ neuronic

neuropathologie [nøropatolɔʒi] NF neuropathology

neuropsychiatrie [nøropsikjatri] NF neuropsychiatry

neuropsychologie [nøropsikolɔʒi] NF neuropsychology

neurovégétatif, -ive [nørovɛʒetatif, -iv] ADJ *Anat (système)* neurovegetative

neutralisation [nøtralizasjɔ̃] NF *(de pays, d'acide etc)* neutralization, neutralizing; *Mil* **tir de n.** neutralizing fire

neutraliser [nøtralize] VT *(pays, acide)* to neutralize; *(efforts, concurrence, agents ennemis etc)* to thwart; *(agresseur)* to overpower; *(circulation)* to stop
VPR **se neutraliser** *(s'annuler réciproquement)* to cancel each other out

neutralisme [nøtralism] NM *Pol* neutralism

neutraliste [nøtralist] ADJ, N *Pol* neutralist

neutralité [nøtralite] NF *Pol, Chimie, Élec etc* neutrality; **garder la n.** to remain neutral; **sortir de sa n.** to take sides; *Pol* **to abandon one's neutrality** *or* one's neutral position; **violer la n. d'un État** to violate a state's neutrality

neutre [nøtr] ADJ **1** *(ni masculin, ni féminin)*

neuter; *Gram* **pronom n.** neuter pronoun; **abeille n.** neuter *or* worker bee **2** *(qui n'a pas pris position) (nation, navire, position, article de presse)* neutral; *Mil* **la zone n.** no-man's land; **rester n.** to remain neutral, not to take sides **3** *(sans caractéristique distinctive) (ton de voix, couleur)* neutral **4** *Chimie, Élec (sel, fil)* neutral

NM 1 *Gram* neuter; **au n.** in the neuter **2** *Can Aut* neutral; **se mettre sur le n.** to go into neutral

neutrino [nøtrino] **NM** *Phys* neutrino

neutron [nøtrɔ̃] **NM** *Phys* neutron; **bombe à neutrons** neutron bomb

neuvaine [nøvɛn] **NF** *Rel* novena

neuvième [nœvjɛm] **ADJ** ninth; **le n. art** *(la bande dessinée)* cartoons

N *(personne, chose)* ninth; **la n. de Beethoven** Beethoven's Ninth

NM *(fraction)* ninth

NF *Mus* ninth; *Scol Anciennement (école primaire)* Br ≃ third year of primary school, Am ≃ third grade

neuvièmement [nœvjɛmmɑ̃] **ADV** ninthly

névé [neve] **NM** *Géol* névé, firn

neveu, -eux [nœvø] **NM** nephew; *Fam* **un peu mon n.!** [nvø] you bet!

névralgie [nevralʒi] **NF** neuralgia; **avoir des névralgies** to suffer from neuralgia

névralgique [nevralʒik] **ADJ** neuralgic; *Fig* **point n.** *(d'une situation)* sensitive area

névrite [nevrit] **NF** *Méd* neuritis

névritique [nevritik] **ADJ** neuritic

névropathe [nevrɔpat] **N** *Vieilli* neuropath

névrose [nevroz] **NF** *Méd* neurosis; **n. post-traumatique** post-traumatic stress disorder

névrosé, -ée [nevroze] **ADJ, N** neurotic

névrotique [nevrɔtik] **ADJ** *Psy (désordre etc)* neurotic

new-look [njuluk] **NM INV, ADJ INV** New Look

newsgroup [njuzgrup] **NM** *Ordinat* newsgroup

new-yorkais, -aise [njujɔrkɛ, -ɛz] **ADJ** *(of/from)* New York; **un bar/théâtre n.** a bar/theatre in New York

N N.-Y. New Yorker

nez [ne] **NM 1** nose; **parler/respirer du n.** to speak/breathe through one's nose; **j'ai le n. bouché** my nose is stuffed up *or* blocked; **se casser le n.** to break one's nose; *Fig (trouver porte close)* to find nobody at home; *(échouer)* to come a cropper; **le bout du n.** the tip of the nose; *Fig* **elle ne voit pas plus loin que le bout de son n.** she can't see beyond the *or* further than the end of her nose; **montrer (le bout de) son n.** to show oneself *or* one's face, to put in an appearance; **mener qn par le bout du n.** to have sb wrapped round one's little finger; **se laisser mener par le bout du n.** to let oneself be manipulated; **avoir le n. en l'air** to look up in the air; *Fig (rêvasser)* to have one's head in the clouds; **partir/se promener le n. au vent** to stroll *or* dawdle off/along; **où est mon dictionnaire? – il est sous ton n. ou tu as le n. dessus** where's my dictionary? – it's (right) under your nose; **avoir le n. dans son journal/ses bouquins** to have one's nose in one's newspaper/one's books; **sans lever le n.** *(lire, travailler)* without a break; **ça se voit comme le n. au milieu de la figure** it's as plain as the nose on your face; **se trouver n. à n. avec qn** to find oneself face to face with sb; **fourrer ou mettre son n. dans les affaires d'autrui** to poke one's nose *or* pry into other people's affairs; **je n'aime pas qu'on mette le n. dans mes affaires** I don't like people poking their noses *or* prying into my affairs; **baisser le n.** to hang one's head, to look sheepish; **cela lui pend au n.** he's got

it coming (to him); *Arg* **je l'ai dans le n.** I can't stand him, *Br* he gets up my nose; **avoir un verre ou un coup dans le n.** to be a bit merry *or* tipsy; **ça m'est passé sous le n.** it slipped through my fingers; **regarder qn sous le n.** to stare sb in the face; **dire qch au n. de qn** to say sth to sb's face; **rire au n. de qn** to laugh in sb's face; **raccrocher au n. de qn** to hang up on sb, to put the phone down on sb; **s'évader au n. et à la barbe des gendarmes** to escape right under the police's noses; **dérober qch au n. et à la barbe de qn** to steal sth from right under sb's nose; *Fam* **se manger ou se bouffer le n.** to be at each other's throats; **fermer ou claquer la porte au n. de qn** to shut the door in sb's face; **je n'ai pas mis le n. dehors de la journée** I didn't set foot outside the door all day; **il fait un temps à ne pas mettre le n. dehors** it's not the kind of weather to be out in; **ton n. remue ou s'allonge!** *(tu mens)* your nose is getting longer!; **sentir l'ail à plein n.** to smell strongly of garlic; **sentir le renfermé à plein n.** to smell very musty; *Fig* **ça sent le discours préparé à plein n.** you can tell it's a well-rehearsed speech; *Fig* **ça sent l'entourloupe à plein n.** there's some dirty business going on **2** *(odorat)* sense of smell; *(de chiens)* scent; **avoir le n. fin** *(avoir un bon odorat)* to have a good nose *or* a keen sense of smell; *Fig* **avoir le n. fin ou creux, avoir du n.** *(avoir de l'intuition)* to be shrewd

3 *(de bateau)* nose, bow, head; *(d'avion)* nose; *(de marche)* nosing; *(de moteur)* nosepiece; *Com* **n. de caisse** checkout display; **piquer du n.** *(d'un avion)* to nosedive; *(s'endormir)* to nod off, to doze off

▸▸ **n. en pied de marmite** bulbous nose; **n. en trompette, n. retroussé** turned-up *or* snub nose

NF [ɛnɛf] **NF** *(abrév* **norme française)** = label indicating compliance with official French standards, *Br* ≃ BS, *Am* ≃ US standard

NfD *Typ (abrév* **note de fin de document)** endnote

NGP **NF** [ɛnʒepe] *Com (abrév* **nomenclature générale des produits)** customs nomenclature

ni [ni] **CONJ** (**ne** *is either expressed or implied)* nor; **ni moi** nor me (either), *Fml* nor I, *Fam* me neither; **sans argent ni bagages** without money or luggage, with neither money nor luggage; **il ne mange ni ne boit** he neither eats nor drinks; **il est parti sans manger ni boire** he left without (either) eating or drinking; **ni … ni** neither … nor; **ni Pierre ni Henri ne sont ou n'est là** neither Pierre nor Henri is there; **je n'ai ni femme ni enfant ni amis** I have neither wife nor children nor friends; **ni l'un ni l'autre ne se souvient** neither (of them) remembers; **lequel a été pris sur les deux? – ni l'un ni l'autre** which of the two was taken? – neither of them *or* neither one nor the other; **ni plus ni moins** neither more nor less **SEE GRAMMAR B62–3**

niacoué, -ée [njakwe] **N** *très Fam (terme raciste)* slant-eye, *Am* gook

niais, -aise [njɛ, -ɛz] **ADJ** *(personne, réponse, air)* simple, foolish, silly; *(sourire)* inane, silly

N fool, simpleton; **espèce de n.!** you silly fool!

niaisage [njɛzaʒ] **NM** *Can* idleness

niaisement [njɛzmɑ̃] **ADV** foolishly; **rire n.** to give a silly laugh, to laugh inanely

niaiser [njɛze] *Can* **VT n. qn** *(faire tourner en bourrique)* to drive sb crazy; *(se moquer de)* to laugh at sb; *(raconter des histoires à)* to pull sb's leg

VI *(ne rien faire)* to hang around doing nothing

niaiserie [njɛzri] **NF 1** *(caractère stupide)* sil-

liness, foolishness **2** *(une bêtise, une ânerie)* silly thing; **dire des niaiseries** to talk nonsense

niaiseux, -euse [njɛzø, -øz] *Can Fam* **ADJ** idiotic, stupid

N idiot

nibard [nibar] **NM** *Fam (sein)* tit, knocker, jug

Nicaragua [nikaragwa] **NM** Nicaragua

nicaraguayen, -enne [nikaragwajɛ̃, -ɛn] **ADJ** Nicaraguan

N N. Nicaraguan

Nicée [nise] **NF** *Antiq* Nicaea; **le symbole de N.** the Nicene Creed

niche¹ [niʃ] **NF 1** *(renfoncement)* niche, recess, alcove **2** *(de chien)* kennel **3** *Mktg* niche (market)

niche² **NF** *Fam Vieilli (farce)* trick, prank

nichée [niʃe] **NF** *(d'oisillons)* nest(ful), brood; *(de souris, de chiots)* litter; *Hum (d'enfants)* brood

nicher [niʃe] **VI** *(d'oiseaux)* to nest, to build a nest (**dans** in); *Fam (de personnes)* to hang out; **maison nichée dans la montagne** cottage nestling in *or* hidden away in the mountains; **niché dans un fauteuil** curled up in an armchair

VPR se nicher 1 *(d'oiseaux)* to nest, to build a nest **2** *(se cacher)* **où est-il allé se n.?** where's he hiding (himself)?, where's he got to?; **où ce chat a-t-il bien pu se n.?** where's the cat got to?

VT *(blottir)* **n. sa tête au creux de l'épaule de qn** to nuzzle *or* nestle one's head against sb's shoulder

nichet [niʃɛ] **NM** *(œuf factice)* nest egg

nichoir [niʃwar] **NM** nesting box

nichon [niʃɔ̃] **NM** *Fam (sein)* boob, tit

nickel [nikɛl] **NM** *Métal* nickel

ADJ INV *Fam (propre)* clean as a whistle

ADV *Fam* **faire qch n. ou n. chrome** to do something really well

nickelage [niklaʒ] **NM** nickel plating

nickelé [nikle] **ADJ** nickel-plated, nickelled; *Vieilli* **avoir les pieds nickelés** to sit tight, to refuse to budge

nickeler [nikle] **VT** (**je nickelle, nous nickelons; je nickellerai**) to nickel

nickélifère [nikelifɛr] **ADJ** nickel-bearing

niçois, -oise [niswa, -waz] **ADJ** of/from Nice

N N. *(natif)* native of Nice; *(habitant)* inhabitant of Nice

nicotine [nikɔtin] **NF** *Chimie* nicotine

nictation [niktasjɔ̃] **NF, nictitation** [niktitasjɔ̃] **NF** nictation, nictitation

nictitant [niktitɑ̃] **ADJ** *Zool (membrane)* nictitating

nid [ni] **NM 1** *(d'oiseaux, de souris, de fourmis etc)* nest; *aussi Fig* **n. d'aigle** eyrie; *Fig* **n. de brigands/d'espions** den of ruffians/of spies; *Mil* **n. de mitrailleuses** nest of machine guns; *Prov* **petit à petit l'oiseau fait son n.** slow and steady wins the race **2** *(logis confortable)* nest; **un petit n. douillet** a cosy little nest; **n. d'amour(eux)** love nest

▸▸ **Couture nid(s) d'abeilles** smocking, honeycomb stitch; **un torchon nid(s) d'abeilles** a honeycomb cloth; **n. d'ange** *(pour les bébés)* (baby's) sleeping bag, *Am* bunting (bag); **n. à poussière** dust trap

nid-de-pie, *pl* **nids-de-pie NM** *Naut* crow's nest; *Mil (retranchement)* lodg(e)ment

nid-de-poule, *pl* **nids-de-poule NM** pothole

nièce [njɛs] **NF** niece

nielle¹ [njɛl] **NF 1** *(maladie du blé)* smut, blight **2** *(fleur)* **n. des blés** corncockle

nielle² **NM** *Beaux-Arts* niello

niellé [njele] **ADJ** **blé n.** blighted wheat

nieller [njele] VT *Beaux-Arts* to inlay with niello

niellure [njelyr] NF *Beaux-Arts* niello work

nier [nje] (*impf, pr sub* **nous niions**) VT (*un fait, l'existence de qch*) to deny; **je nie l'avoir vue** I deny having seen her; **je nie qu'il m'ait vu** I deny that he saw me; **n. l'évidence** to deny the obvious *or* what's obvious; **je ne nie pas que j'ai parfois tort** I don't deny that I'm sometimes wrong; **on ne peut pas n. que ...** there's no denying *or* one can't deny *or* it's undeniable that ...
 VI **l'accusé nie** the accused denies the charge

niet [njet] INT *Fam* no way!, not a chance!

nigaud, -aude [nigo, -od] N ninny, fool; **gros n.!** you great *or* big ninny!
 ADJ (*sourire, réponse*) silly

nigelle [niʒɛl] NF (*fleur*) nigella, love-in-a-mist

Niger [niʒɛr] NM Niger

Nigeria [niʒerja] NM Nigeria

nigérian, -ane [niʒerjã, -an] ADJ Nigerian
 N **N.** Nigerian

nigérien, -ienne [niʒerjɛ̃, -jɛn] ADJ of/from Niger, Nigerien
 N **N.** Nigerien

nihilisme [niilism] NM *Phil* nihilism

nihiliste [niilist] *Phil* ADJ nihilist(ic)
 N nihilist

Nil [nil] NM **le N.** the Nile; **vert N.** (*couleur*) eau-de-nil

nilgaut [nilgo] NM (*mammifère*) nilgai

nilotique [nilɔtik] ADJ of the Nile, Nilotic

nimbe [nɛ̃b] NM halo, nimbus

nimbé [nɛ̃be] ADJ haloed

nimbus [nɛ̃bys] NM *Météo* nimbus

ninas [ninas] NM INV small cigar

nipper [nipe] *Fam* VT (*habiller*) to deck out; **bien nippé** well turned out
 VPR **se nipper** (*s'habiller*) to dress; **je me nippe chez Tati** I get my clothes at Tati's

nippes [nip] NFPL *Fam* (*vêtements*) gear, togs; **à part les n., rien ne l'intéresse** he isn't interested in anything apart from clothes

nippon, -one [nipɔ̃, -ɔn] ADJ Japanese
 N **N.** Japanese; **les Nippons** the Japanese

nique [nik] NF *Fam* **faire la n. à qn** to cock a snook at sb

niquer [nike] VT **1** *Vulg* (*posséder sexuellement*) to screw, to shag **2** *très Fam* (*duper*) to shaft, to screw; **c'est un faux, tu t'es fait n.!** it's a fake, you've been shafted *or* screwed! **3** *Fam* (*endommager*) to knacker, to bugger

niquet [nikɛ] NM *Belg Fam* snooze, nap

nirvana [nirvana] NM Nirvana

nissart [nisar] NM = dialect of occitan spoken in the Nice region of France

nitrate [nitrat] NM *Chimie* nitrate

nitre [nitr] NM *Chimie* nitre, saltpetre, *Am* niter, saltpeter

nitré [nitre] ADJ *Chimie* nitrated; **composé n.** nitro compound

nitrer [nitre] VT *Tech* to nitrate

nitreux, -euse [nitrø, -øz] ADJ *Chimie* nitrous

nitrifier [nitrifje] VT *Chimie* to nitrify

nitrique [nitrik] ADJ *Chimie* (*acide*) nitric

nitrobenzène [nitrobɛzɛn] NM *Chimie* nitrobenzene

nitroglycérine [nitrogliserin] NF *Chimie* nitroglycerine

nitrure [nityr] NM *Chimie* nitride; **n. de fer** iron nitride

nitrurer [nityre] VT *Métal* to nitride

niveau, -eaux [nivo] NM **1** (*hauteur*) level; **n. d'eau/d'huile** water/oil level; **n. de l'eau/**

de la mer water/sea level; **au n. de la mer** at sea level; **n. des basses/hautes eaux** low-water/high-water mark; **elle a une cicatrice au n. de la cuisse** she has a scar on her leg at about thigh-level; **l'eau nous arrivait au n. de la taille** the water came up to our waists; **les deux encadrements ne sont pas au même n.** the two frames are not level (with each other) *or* are not on the same level; **la Saône n'avait jamais atteint un n. aussi haut** the Saône had never reached such a high level *or* had never been so high; **quand tu arrives au n. de la place des Jacobins, prends à gauche** when you get to the Place des Jacobins, turn left; **au n. régional/local** at regional/local level; **au n. matériel/du travail** on the financial/work front, financewise/workwise, where finance/work is concerned; **au n. sentimental** as far as one's love life is concerned; *aussi Fig* **se mettre au n. de qn** to come down to sb's level; **être de n.** to be level; **mettre qch de n.** to make sth level
 2 (*étage*) level; **jardin à trois niveaux** garden on three levels; **immeuble à dix niveaux** ten-storey building; **le supermarché se trouve au troisième n.** the supermarket is on the third level; **n. arrivée** (*d'un aéroport*) arrivals level; **n. départ** (*d'un aéroport*) departures level
 3 (*degré*) level; *Scol* standard; **n. de pollution** pollution level; **n. sonore** noise level; *Radio* **n. de transmission** transmission level; **n. scolaire** academic standard; **tous les élèves ne sont pas du** *ou* **n'ont pas le même n.** not all the pupils are of *or* have reached the same (academic) standard, not all the pupils are of the same level of ability; **quel est son n. en anglais?** what is his standard in English?; **il a un très bon n. en physique** his physics is of a very high standard; **avoir le n. (requis), être au n.** to be up to standard, *Fam* to be up to scratch; **votre fils n'a pas le n. pour passer le concours** your son is not of a high enough standard to take the examination; **évaluer le n. des candidats** to evaluate the candidates' level of ability; **test de n.** assessment; **être au n. de qn/qch, être de n. avec qn/qch** to be on a level *or* on a par with sb/sth; **nous recherchons un candidat n. baccalauréat/maîtrise** we are looking for a candidate of baccalauréat/master's degree standard; **ils sont d'un n. social différent** they come from different social backgrounds; **au plus bas n. de l'échelle** at the very bottom of the ladder; **au plus haut n. de la hiérarchie** at the highest level of the hierarchy, at the very top; **les salaires augmentent régulièrement à tous les niveaux** there are regular salary increases for all grades *or* at all levels; **la production n'avait jamais atteint un n. aussi haut** production had never reached such a high level *or* had never been so high; **n. d'occupation** (*d'un hôtel*) occupancy level; **n. des prix** price levels; **n. des salaires** salary levels; **n. des stocks** inventory *or* stock level; **n. record** record level
 ▸▸ *Ordinat* **n. d'accès** (*dans un réseau*) access level; **n. à bulle d'air** spirit level; *Bourse* **n. de cours des actions** stock price level; *Bourse* **n. de dépôt requis** margin requirement; *Ordinat* **n. de gris** greyscale; *Ling* **n. de langue** register, language level; *Tech* **n. à lunette** surveyor's level; *Tech* **n. de maçon** vertical *or* plumb level; *Tech* **n. à plomb** vertical *or* plumb level; **n. tarifaire** fare level; *Écon* **n. de vie** standard of living

nivelage [niv(ə)laʒ] NM *Constr* levelling

niveler [nivle] VT (**je nivelle; je nivellerai**) **1** (*aplanir*) (*sol, terrain*) to level, to make level **2** (*les fortunes*) to level, to even out *or* up; **n. les prix** to level prices; **n. par le bas** to level down

niveleur, -euse [nivlœr, -øz] N leveller
 NM *Hist* Leveller
 NF *Constr* **niveleuse** grader

nivellement [nivɛlmã] NM (*de terrain, des classes sociales*) levelling; **n. par le bas** levelling down; **repère de n.** (*dans l'arpentage*) bench mark

nivéole [niveɔl] NF (*plante*) snowflake

nivôse [nivoz] NM *Hist* = fourth month of the Republican calendar (*December-January*)

NNTP [ɛnɛntepe] NM *Ordinat* (*abrév* **Network News Transfer Protocol**) NNTP

nobélisable [nobelizabl] ADJ (*chercheur, écrivain*) potential Nobel prizewinning
 N potential Nobel prizewinner

nobiliaire [nobiljɛr] ADJ **titre n.** title; **particule n.** nobiliary particle
 NM peerage (list)

noble [nobl] ADJ **1** (*famille, origine*) noble **2** (*imposant*) (*air, allure*) noble, stately **3** (*hautement apprécié*) (*cause, motif, entreprise*) noble; **il n'est animé que par de nobles sentiments** he is acting out of noble sentiments; **le n. art** (*boxe*) the noble art **4** (*précieux*) noble; **la soie est une matière n.** silk is a noble fabric
 N noble, nobleman, *f* noblewoman; **les nobles** the nobility, the nobles

noblement [nobləmã] ADV nobly

noblesse [noblɛs] NF **1** (*par la descendance*) nobility; **famille de n. récente** recently ennobled family; **la haute et la petite n.** the nobility and the gentry; **se marier dans la n.** to marry into nobility, to marry a title; **n. oblige** noblesse oblige **2** (*de style, de conduite*) nobility, nobleness; **agir avec beaucoup de n.** to act very nobly
 ▸▸ *Hist* **n. d'épée** old nobility; *Hist* **n. de robe** noblesse de robe

nobliau, -iaux [noblijo] NM *Péj* lesser noble(man)

noce [nos] NF **1** (*cérémonie du mariage*) wedding; (*fête*) wedding festivities; (*ensemble des assistants*) wedding party; **repas de n.** wedding breakfast; **noces d'argent/de vermeil/d'or/de diamant** silver/ruby/golden/diamond wedding; **il l'avait épousée en secondes noces** she was his second wife **2** *Fam* **faire la n.** to go on a binge, to live it up; **être à la n.** to have the time of one's life, to have a whale of a time; **je n'étais pas à la n.** it was no picnic

noceur, -euse [nosœr, -øz] N *Fam* fast liver, *Br* raver

nocif, -ive [nosif, -iv] ADJ (*produit, émanation*) harmful, noxious

nocivité [nosivite] NF harmfulness, noxiousness

noctambule [noktãbyl] N (*qui aime sortir la nuit*) night owl, night bird

noctuelle [noktɥɛl] NF *Entom* noctua, owlet moth

nocturne [noktyrn] ADJ (*animal*) nocturnal; (*attaque, visite*) night; *Bot* night-flowering; **évasion n.** escape by night
 NM **1** (*rapace*) nocturnal bird (of prey) **2** *Rel* nocturn **3** *Beaux-Arts, Mus* nocturne
 NF (*d'un magasin etc*) late-night opening; *Sport* **match (disputé) en n.** evening game

nodal, -ale, -aux, -ales [nodal, -o] ADJ (*point, ligne*) nodal
 NM *TV* master control room

nodosité [nodozite] NF *Bot, Méd* (*nodule*) node, nodule; (*état*) nodosity

nodule [nodyl] NM *Géol, Méd etc* nodule

Noé [noe] N *Bible* Noah

Noël [noɛl] NM **1** (*fête*) Christmas; **à N., *Région* à la N.** at Christmas (time); **le jour de N.** Christmas Day; **la nuit** *ou* **la veillée de N.**

Christmas Eve; **bûche de N.** yule log; **vacances de N.** Christmas holidays, *Am* Christmas vacation; **arbre** *ou* **sapin de N.** Christmas tree; **joyeux N.!** Happy *or* Merry Christmas! **2** *(chanson)* (Christmas) carol **3** *(cadeau)* **offrir qch à qn pour son (petit) n.** to give sb sth for Christmas *or* as a Christmas present

nœud [nø] **NM 1** *(entrecroisement)* knot; *Naut* hitch, bend; **corde à nœuds** knotted rope; **faire** *ou* **serrer un n.** to make *or* tie a knot; *Fig* **faire un n. à son mouchoir** to tie a knot in one's handkerchief; *Fig* **avoir un n. dans l'estomac** to have a knot in one's stomach; *Fig* **avoir un n. dans la gorge** to have a lump in one's throat; *Fig* **le n. du problème** the crux of the problem *or* matter; *Fig* **quel sac de nœuds!** what a muddle! **2** *(ornement)* bow; **faire un n.** to tie a bow; **mettre un n. dans ses cheveux** to put a bow in one's hair; **n. de diamants** diamond cluster **3** *(de serpent)* coil **4** *(d'orbite, de courbe, d'oscillation),* *Ordinat* node **5** *(sur un arbre, une planche)* knot, knur(l) **6** *(carrefour de grandes lignes)* **n. autoroutier/ferroviaire** major road/rail junction *or* intersection **7** *Naut (vitesse)* knot; **filer** *ou* **faire vingt nœuds** to do *or* make twenty knots **8** *Littér, Théâtre* knot, crux **9** *Vulg (pénis)* prick, dick, cock; **à la mords-moi le n.** lousy, crappy, *Br* poxy
▸▸ **n. coulant** *(pour serrer)* slipknot; *(pour étrangler)* noose; **n. de cravate** tie knot; **faire son n. de cravate** to knot one's tie; **n. gordien** Gordian knot; **trancher le n. gordien** to cut the Gordian knot; *Tech* **n. de grappin** fisherman's bend; *Anat* **n. lymphatique** lymph node; **n. papillon,** *Fam* **n. pap** bow tie; **n. plat** reef knot; *Tech* **n. de vache** carrick bend; **n. de vipères** nest of vipers

noir, noire [nwar] **ADJ 1** *(couleur)* black; **n. comme de l'encre** as black as ink, inky black; *Litt* **n. comme (de) l'ébène** as black as ebony, ebony black; *Litt* **n. comme (du) jais** jet black; *Litt* **n. comme de la poix** pitch-black; **n. d'ivoire** ivory black; **la place était noire de monde** the square was thick *or* swarming with people
2 *(très sombre) (cheveux, yeux, ciel, lunettes)* dark; **il est rentré n. de ses vacances** he was incredibly brown when he came back from his holidays
3 *(relatif à la race) (peau, race, origine, quartier, chanteuse)* black
4 *(plongé dans l'obscurité) (nuit, cellule)* dark; **il fait n.** it's dark; **il faisait nuit noire** *ou* **n. comme dans un four** it was pitch-dark *or* pitch-black
5 *(pessimiste) (pensées, vision)* black, gloomy; **avoir des idées noires** to be down in the dumps; **il m'a fait un tableau très n. de la situation** he painted a very black *or* gloomy picture of the situation; **le lundi/jeudi n.** Black Monday/Thursday; **rien n'est tout blanc ou tout n.** nothing is completely black and white
6 *(sale) (visage, mains, ongles, linge)* black, filthy, dirty; **tu es tout n.** you're all black *or* filthy *or* dirty; **être n. de crasse** to be black with grime; **être n. comme du charbon** to be as black as soot
7 *(inspiré par la colère) (regard)* black; *Litt (crime)* heinous, foul; *(ingratitude)* utter; *(calomnie)* wicked; **regarder qn d'un œil n.** to give sb a black look; *Litt* **de noirs desseins** evil designs; **être d'une humeur noire** to be in a black *or* foul mood
8 *(illicite)* **le marché n.** the black market
9 *(intense)* **colère noire** towering rage; **se mettre dans une colère noire** to fly into a towering rage; **misère noire** dire *or* abject poverty, utter destitution; **être dans une misère noire** to be utterly destitute
10 *Arg (ivre)* blind drunk

11 *Cin, Littér* **film n.** film noir, gangster thriller; **roman n.** gangster novel
▸ **N.** Black (man), *f* Black (woman); **il est N.** he's (a) Black; *Hist* **traite des Noirs** slave trade
▸ **NM 1** *(couleur)* black; **j'aime le n.** I like black; **le n. et blanc** *Cin* black and white; *Phot* black-and-white photography; *TV* black-and-white television; **en n. et blanc** *(film, photographie)* black-and-white; **être vêtu de n., être en n.** to be dressed (all) in black; *Fam* **se mettre du n. aux yeux** to put eyeliner on; **d'un n. d'ébène** as black as ebony, ebony black; **c'était écrit n. sur blanc** it was there in black and white
2 *(obscurité)* dark, darkness; **avoir peur du n. ou dans le n.** to be afraid of the dark
3 *(trace de salissure)* **tu as du n. sur le visage** you've got a black mark on your face; **j'ai mis plein de n. sur mon pantalon** I've got black marks all over my trousers
4 *(pessimisme)* **voir tout en n.** to look on the black side of everything; **broyer du n.** to be down in the dumps
5 *(travail illicite)* **le travail au n.** moonlighting, work on the side; **travailler au n.** to moonlight; **il a été engagé au n.** he was employed illegally; **il est chauffeur de taxi au n.** he moonlights *or* works on the side as a taxi driver; **faire des petits boulots au n.** to do some little jobs on the side
6 *(d'une cible)* bull's-eye
7 *(café)* **un (petit) n.** a (small) black coffee
▸ **NF** *Mus* **noire** crotchet, *Am* quarter note
▸▸ **Typ n. au blanc** reverse printing, white-on-black; **n. de Chine** Indian ink, *Am* India ink; **n. de fumée** lampblack; *Typ* **n. au gris** black-on-tone

noirâtre [nwaratr] **ADJ** blackish

noiraud, -aude [nwaro, -od] **ADJ** dark, swarthy
▸ **N** dark *or* swarthy person, *Péj* darky, darkie

noirceur [nwarsœr] **NF 1** *(d'encre etc)* blackness; *Litt (d'un crime)* heinousness, foulness **2** *Can (obscurité)* dark, darkness; **dans la n.** in the dark *or* darkness; **avoir peur dans la n.** to be afraid of the dark

noircir [nwarsir] **VI** to turn *or* go black, to darken
▸ **VT** *(mur, pierres etc)* to blacken, to make black; *Fig* **n. du papier, n. des pages et des pages** to write page after page; **il a noirci trois feuilles sans s'interrompre** he covered three sheets of paper without stopping; **tout ce qu'il est capable de faire, c'est n. du papier** the only thing he's good at is putting ink on paper; **n. qn** *ou* **la réputation de qn** to blacken sb's reputation; **n. le tableau** *ou* **la situation** to paint things blacker than they are
▸ **VPR** **se noircir** *(de métal, pierre, mur etc)* to turn *or* go black, to darken; *(du ciel)* to darken, to become overcast; *Fig Fam (se soûler)* to get blind drunk *(à la vodka/etc* on vodka/*etc);* **se n. le visage** to black one's face; *Théâtre* to black up

noircissement [nwarsismɑ̃] **NM** blackening

noircissure [nwarsisyr] **NF** black mark

noise [nwaz] **NF** *Litt* **chercher n.** *ou* **des noises à qn** to try to pick a quarrel with sb

noisetier [nwaztje] **NM** hazel (tree *or* bush); *(bois)* hazel (wood)

noisette [nwazet] **NF 1** *Bot, Culin* hazel(nut) **2** *(petite quantité) (de beurre)* knob; *(de mousse coiffante)* small ball **3** *Culin* **n. d'agneau** noisette of lamb **4** *(café)* espresso coffee with milk
▸ **ADJ INV** **yeux n.** hazel eyes

noix [nwa] **NF 1** *(fruit)* walnut **2** *Fam* **quelle n.!** *(imbécile)* what a twerp!; **comment vas-tu, vieille n.?** how are you, old thing?; *Fig Fam* **à la n. (de coco)** rubbishy, lousy; **excu-** ses à la n. paltry *or* trivial excuses **3** *Culin* **n. de bœuf, n. de côtelette, n. de gigot** pope's eye; **rôti dans la n. de veau** cushion *or* topside of veal **4** *(petite quantité)* **n. de beurre** knob of butter
▸▸ **n. d'acajou** cashew nut; **n. du Brésil** Brazil nut; **n. de cajou** cashew nut; **n. de coco** coconut; **n. de pécan** pecan; **n. vomique** nux vomica

nolisation [nɔlizasjɔ̃] **NF** chartering

nolisement [nɔliz(ə)mɑ̃] **NM** chartering

noliser [nɔlize] **VT** to charter

nom [nɔ̃] **NM 1** *(de personne)* name; **quel est votre n.?** what's your name?; **n. ..., prénom ...** *(sur formulaire)* surname ..., first name ...; **n. et prénoms** full name; **vos n., prénoms et adresse** your full name and address; **quelqu'un dont je tairai le n.** someone who shall remain nameless; **je porte le n. de ma grand-mère** I'm called after my grandmother; **tu porteras le n. de ton mari ou pas?** will you take your husband's name or not?; **je la connais de n. seulement** I only know her by name; **je n'arrive pas à mettre un n. sur sa tête/sur sa voix** I can't put a name to him; **voyager sous un faux n.** to travel under a false name *or* an alias; **on le connaissait sous le n. de Leduc** he went by *or* was known by the name of Leduc; **se faire un n.** to make a name for oneself; **un grand n. de la musique** one of the great names of music; **les grands noms de la littérature russe** the great names of Russian literature; **il n'est médecin que de n.** he's a doctor in name only; **faire une proposition au n. de qn** to make a proposal for sb *or* on behalf of sb; **parler en son n.** to speak for oneself; **je parlerai en votre n.** I'll speak for you *or* in your name; **un homme du n. de Pierre** a man by the name of *or* named Pierre; **Louis, treizième du n.** Louis, thirteenth king of that name; **traiter qn de tous les noms** to call sb names; **je lui ai donné tous les noms d'oiseaux** I called him every name under the sun; *Fam* **avoir un n. à coucher dehors** to have a totally unpronounceable name SEE GRAMMAR B8
2 *(de plantes, d'animaux, d'objets etc)* name; **c'est quoi le n. de ta rue?** what's the name of your street?; **appeler les choses par leur n.** to call a spade a spade; **impolitesse sans n.** unspeakable rudeness; *Fam* **n. de n.!, n. d'une pipe!, n. d'un chien!, n. de Dieu!** hell!; **au n. de la loi** in the name of the law; **faire qch au n. de l'amitié/la justice** to do sth in the name of friendship/justice
3 *Gram* noun SEE GRAMMAR A9–17; B5–8
▸▸ **n. de baptême** first name, Christian name, *Am* given name; *Ordinat* **n. de champ** field name; **n. commercial** company *or* trade name; *Gram* **n. commun** common noun; *Gram* **n. composé** compound (noun); *Com* **n. déposé** (registered) trademark; *Ordinat* **n. de domaine** domain name; *Bourse* **n. de domaine** nominee name; **n. de famille** surname; *Mktg* **n. de famille global** blanket family name; *Ordinat* **n. de fichier** file name; *Mktg* **n. générique** generic name; **n. de guerre** assumed name, pseudonym; *(d'un écrivain, d'un journaliste)* pseudonym, pen name; *(d'un acteur)* stage name; **n. de jeune fille** maiden name; **n. de marque** brand name; **n. à particule** = name with a nobiliary particle; **n. de plume** nom de plume, pen name, pseudonym; *Gram* **n. propre** proper noun; SEE GRAMMAR B8 *Fam* **n. à rallonges** long aristocratic surname, double-barrelled name; **n. de scène** stage name; *Théâtre* **n. de théâtre** stage name; *Fam* **n. à tiroirs** long aristocratic surname, double-barrelled name

nomade [nɔmad] **ADJ** *(vie, tribu)* nomadic, wandering

N (du désert) nomad; Jur (gitan) traveller; Ordinat, Tél road warrior

nomadisme [nɔmadism] **NM** nomadism

nombre [nɔ̃br] **NM 1** number; **(bon) n. de gens, un certain n. de gens, un assez grand n. de gens** a number of people, a good many people; **le plus grand n. est de cet avis** the majority are of this opinion; **un grand/petit n. d'entre nous** many/a few of us; **ils finirent par succomber sous le n. des assaillants** they were finally overcome by the sheer number of their attackers; Ordinat, Typ **n. de caractères** character count; Journ **n. de lecteurs** readership; Ordinat, Typ **n. de mots** word count; Typ **n. de pages** extent; Litt **surpasser en n.** to outnumber; **supérieur en n.** superior in number(s); **nous sommes en n. suffisant** there are enough of us; (dans une réunion) we have a quorum; **sans n.** (foule) huge, vast; **venez pour faire n.** come and make up the numbers; **venir/se précipiter en n.** to come/rush in large or great numbers; **les voitures/manifestants convergeaient en (très) grand n. vers le centre de la ville** the cars/demonstrators were converging in huge numbers on the town centre; Litt **en n. écrasant** by an overwhelming majority; **ils sont au n. de huit** there are eight of them; **être au n. ou du n. des élus** to be one of or be among the elect; Fml **mettre ou compter qn au n. de ses intimes** to number sb among one's friends; **sur le n.** among or out of (all) those; Bible **Le Livre des Nombres** (the Book of) Numbers SEE GRAMMAR A76-7; B58-60 **2** Gram number; **s'accorder en genre et en n.** to agree in gender and number
  ▸▸**n. atomique** atomic number; Phys **n. d'Avogadro** Avogadro number; Math **n. complexe** complex number; Math **n. décimal** decimal (number); Math **n. entier** whole number, integer; **n. d'or** golden section; Math **n. premier** prime number

nombreux, -euse [nɔ̃brø, -øz] **ADJ** (membres, objets) numerous, many; (famille, armée, groupe) large; **auditoire peu n.** small audience; **pendant de nombreuses générations** for many generations; **nous sommes peu n.** there are not many of us, there are very few of us; **n. sont ceux qui ...** there are/were many who ...; **venir (très) n.** to come in (very) large numbers; **venez n.!** all (are) welcome!, everyone (is) welcome!

nombril [nɔ̃bri(l)] **NM 1** Anat navel; Fam Hum **être décolletée jusqu'au n.** to be showing a lot of cleavage; **il avait une chemise ouverte jusqu'au n.** his shirt was open to the waist; Fam **il se prend pour le n. du monde ou de la terre** he thinks the whole world revolves around him; Fig **se regarder le n.** to contemplate one's navel; **Can ne pas avoir le n. sec** to be (still) wet behind the ears, to be green **2** Bot hilum

nombrilisme [nɔ̃brilism] **NM** self-absorption, self-centredness; **faire du n.** to contemplate one's navel

nombriliste [nɔ̃brilist] **ADJ** self-absorbed, self-centred

nomenclature [nɔmɑ̃klatyr] **NF** (ensemble de termes techniques) nomenclature; (liste des objets d'une collection etc) list, catalogue; (d'un dictionnaire) word list; (d'une voiture etc) parts list; **n. douanière ou générale des produits** customs nomenclature

nominal, -ale, -aux, -ales [nɔminal, -o] **ADJ 1** (prix, puissance en chevaux, autorité) nominal; Fin nominal, par; Fin **valeur nominale** face value; Élec **courant n.** (d'une machine) rated current **2** (relatif au nom de famille) appel n. roll call; **liste nominale** list of names, name list; **vérification ou contrôle nominal(e)** name check **3** Gram (emploi, fonction) nominal

NM Fin (d'une action) nominal value; (d'une obligation) par value

nominalement [nɔminalmɑ̃] **ADV 1** (appeler qn) by name; **rester n. propriétaire d'un immeuble** to remain the owner of an apartment block in name only **2** Gram (comme un nom) nominally, as a noun

nominalisme [nɔminalism] **NM** Phil nominalism

nominatif, -ive [nɔminatif, -iv] **ADJ 1** (qui comporte un nom) (carte d'adhérent, billet) nontransferable; **état n.** list of names, name list; **votre carte bancaire est nominative** (inscription sur carte) this banker's card may be used only by the authorized signatory or by the person whose name it bears; **les places de concert ne sont pas nominatives** the seats for the concert are transferable **2** Fin **titres nominatifs** registered securities

NM 1 Gram nominative (case); **au n.** in the nominative (case)
  2 Fin **dividende au n.** dividend on registered securities

nomination [nɔminasjɔ̃] **NF 1** (à un poste) appointment (à to); **attendre sa n.** to expect to be appointed; **n. à un grade supérieur** promotion **2** (pour une récompense) nomination; **ce film a trois nominations pour les Césars** this film has received three César nominations **3** Phil naming

nominativement [nɔminativmɑ̃] **ADV** by name

nominé [nɔmine] **ADJ** (film, acteur) nominated (à une récompense for an award)

nominer [nɔmine] **VT** to nominate

nommage [nɔmaʒ] **NM** Ordinat (de site Internet) designation

nommé, -ée [nɔme] **ADJ** (personne, objet) named
  N le n. Antoine the man named or called Antoine; **la nommée Chantal** the woman named or called Chantal; **un n. Bertrand a appelé** someone named or called Bertrand rang

nommément [nɔmemɑ̃] **ADV 1** accuser/dénoncer/désigner qn n. to accuse/denounce/refer to sb by name **2** (spécialement) especially, in particular

nommer [nɔme] **VT 1** (appeler) to name, to give a name to; **on le nomma Paul** they named or called him Paul; **on nomme aumôniers les prêtres attachés à un régiment** priests attached to a regiment are called chaplains **2** (désigner) (personne) to name, to mention by name; **un homme que je ne nommerai pas** a man who shall remain nameless or whom I won't (mention by) name; Hum **M. Dutronc, pour ne pas le n.** without mentioning any names or naming no names, Mr Dutronc; Vieilli **à jour nommé** on the appointed day; **elle est arrivée à point nommé** she arrived just at the right moment or just when she was needed **3** (à un poste) to appoint (à to); Mil (un officier) to commission; **n. qn directeur** to appoint sb manager; **n. des experts** to appoint experts; **elle a été nommée responsable des ventes** she was appointed sales director; **être nommé au grade supérieur** to be promoted; **être nommé à Lille** to be posted to Lille
  VPR se nommer 1 (avoir pour nom) to be called or named; **comment vous nommez-vous?** what is your name? **2** (s'identifier) to give one's name

non [nɔ̃] SEE GRAMMAR B62-3 **ADV 1** (en réponse) no; **répondre par oui ou n.** to answer yes or no; **n., n. et n.!** no, no, no!; **c'est dégoûtant, n.?** it's disgusting, isn't it?; **il est pas mal, n.(, tu ne trouves pas)?** he's not bad-looking, is he?; **il a commencé comme éboueur – n.!** (c'est pas possible!) he started as a dustman – no! or really?; **alors, ton augmentation? – c'est n.** what about your pay rise? – I didn't get it; **mais n.!, dame n.!, mon Dieu n.!,** Hum **que n.!** certainly not!, definitely not!; **n. mais! je ne te permets pas** no, really! I can't allow that; **tu es content? – ma foi n.!** ou **certes n.!** are you happy? – certainly not! or far from it!; Litt **n. pas!** not so!, not at all!; **n., je vous en prie** please don't; **je pense que n.** I don't think so, I think not; **je dis que n.** I say no; **faire signe que n.** (de la tête) to shake one's head; (avec le doigt) to indicate no; **il voulait traverser la rue, mais sa mère lui fit signe que n.** he was about to cross the road, but his mother signalled to him not to; **tu viens, oui ou n.?** are you coming, yes or no?; **qu'elle vienne ou n.** whether she comes or not SEE GRAMMAR B64 **2** (pas) not; **n. loin de la ville** not far from the town; **n. sans raison** not without reason; **n. seulement ..., mais encore** ou **aussi ...** not only ..., but also ...; **moi n. plus** me neither; **le problème est cette fois n. plus d'ordre économique mais social** the problem is now not economic but social; **ton frère est studieux, toi n.** your brother is studious, but you're not or unlike you; **il faut que ce soit toi qui lui parles et n. l'inverse** it's you who have to talk to him and not the other way round; **n. content de conduire sans permis, l'individu était ivre** not content with driving without a licence, the man was also drunk; **n. coupable** not guilty; **n. solvable** insolvent; **n. (pas) que je le craigne** not that I fear him; **n. que je ne vous plaigne** not that I don't pity you VOIR GRAMMAIRE A23-4
  NM INV no; **répondre par un n.** to answer with a no or in the negative; **les n. l'emportent** the noes have it; **se fâcher/pleurer pour un oui, pour un n.** to flare up/cry at the least (little) thing

non-acceptation [nɔnakseptasjɔ̃] **NF** Banque (d'une lettre de change) non-acceptance

non-accomplissement [nɔnakɔ̃plismɑ̃] **NM** (d'un contrat) non-fulfilment

non-activité [nɔnaktivite] **NF** Admin **mettre en n.** (employé) to suspend; Mil (officier) to put on half pay; **mise en n.** (d'un employé) suspension; Mil (d'un officier) putting on half pay

nonagénaire [nɔnaʒenɛr] **ADJ, N** nonagenarian, ninety-year-old

non-agression [nɔnagresjɔ̃] **NF** non-aggression; **pacte de n.** non-aggression pact

non-alcoolisé [nɔnalkɔlize] **ADJ** non-alcoholic

non-aligné, pl **non-alignés** [nɔnaliɲe] Pol **ADJ** (pays) nonaligned
  NMPL **les non-alignés** the nonaligned countries

non-alignement [nɔnaliɲ(ə)mɑ̃] **NM** Pol nonalignment

nonantaine [nɔnɑ̃tɛn] **NF** Belg, Suisse **1** (quantité) **une n.** around or about ninety, ninety or so; **une n. de voitures** around or about ninety cars **2** (âge) **avoir la n.** to be around or about ninety

nonante [nɔnɑ̃t] **ADJ, NM INV** Belg, Suisse ninety

nonantième [nɔnɑ̃tjɛm] **ADJ, N** Belg, Suisse ninetieth

non-assistance [nɔnasistɑ̃s] **NF** Jur **n. à personne en danger** failure to render assistance to a person in danger

non-autorisé [nɔnɔtɔrize, nɔ-] **ADJ** Ordinat (nom de fichier etc) illegal

non-banque **ADJ** non-bank

non-belligérance **NF** nonbelligerence

non-belligérant, -ante **ADJ, N** non-belligerent

nonce [nɔ̃s] **NM** n. du Pape Papal Nuncio

non-cessible **ADJ** *(billet etc)* not transferable

nonchalamment [nɔ̃ʃalamɑ̃] **ADV** nonchalantly; **marcher n.** to saunter along

nonchalance [nɔ̃ʃalɑ̃s] **NF** nonchalance

nonchalant [nɔ̃ʃalɑ̃] **ADJ** nonchalant

nonciature [nɔ̃sjatyr] **NF** **1** *(charge d'un nonce)* nunciature **2** *(résidence)* nuncio's residence

non-combattant, *pl* **non-combattants** **ADJ, NM** non-combatant

non-comparution **NF** non-appearance

non-conciliation **NF** failure to settle out of court

non-confirmé **ADJ** unconfirmed

non-conformisme **NM** *Rel, Fig* nonconformism

non-conformiste, *pl* **non-conformistes** **ADJ, N** *Rel, Fig* nonconformist

non-conformité **NF** n. d'un produit nonconformity of a product

non-connecté **ADJ** *Ordinat* off-line

non-consigné **ADJ** non-returnable

non-coté [nɔ̃kɔte] **ADJ** *Bourse* unquoted

non-cumul **NM** n. des peines concurrence of sentences; *Pol* les règles de n. des mandats = the laws prohibiting politicians from holding more than one post at a time

non-dit, *pl* **non-dits** **NM** le n. what is unspoken *or* unvoiced; **non-dits** unspoken *or* unvoiced comments; **un film riche en non-dits** a film full of meaningful silences

non-droit **NM** zone de n. area in which law and order have/had broken down; **état de n.** situation in which law and order have/had broken down

none [nɔn] **NF** *Antiq (heure)* ninth hour; **nones** *(jour)* nones

non-encaissé [nɔnɑ̃kese] **ADJ** *(chèque)* uncashed

non-engagé, *pl* **non-engagés** [nɔnɑ̃gaʒe] *Pol* **ADJ** neutral
NM neutral country

non-engagement [nɔnɑ̃gaʒmɑ̃] **NM** *Pol* neutrality

non-être [nɔnɛtr] **NM** *Phil* nonbeing, nonexistence

non-événement [nɔnevenmɑ̃] **NM** non-event

non-exécution [nɔnegzekysjɔ̃] **NF** *(d'un accord)* non-fulfilment; *(d'un contrat)* non-performance

non-existence [nɔnegzistɑ̃s] **NF** non-existence

non-ferreux, -euse **ADJ** *Métal* nonferrous

non-figuratif, -ive *Beaux-Arts* **ADJ** non-figurative
N nonfigurative artist

non-formaté **ADJ** *Ordinat* unformatted

non-fumeur, -euse **ADJ** nonsmoking; **fumeur ou n.?** smoking or nonsmoking?
N nonsmoker

non-gage **NM** *Aut* certificat de n. certificate of ownership

non-ingérence [nɔnɛ̃ʒerɑ̃s] **NF** noninterference

non-initialisé [nɔninisjalize, nɔ̃-] **ADJ** *Ordinat* uninitialized

non-initié, -ée [nɔninisje] **ADJ** uninitiated
N uninitiated person; **les non-initiés** the uninitiated

non-inscrit, -ite [nɔnɛ̃skri] **N** *Pol* independent

non-intervention [nɔnɛ̃tervɑ̃sjɔ̃] **NF** nonintervention

non-interventionniste, *pl* **non-inver-**

ventionnistes [nɔnɛ̃tervɑ̃sjɔnist] **ADJ, N** non-interventionist

non-jouissance **NF** *Jur (d'un bien)* nonenjoyment

non-justifié **ADJ** *Typ* ragged, unjustified; **n. à droite** ragged right; **n. à gauche** ragged left

non-lieu, *pl* **non-lieux** **NM** *Jur* **bénéficier d'un n.** to be discharged through lack of evidence; **ordonnance ou arrêt de n.** nonsuit

non-livraison **NF** *Com* non-delivery

non-modifiable **ADJ** *(billet etc)* not alterable

nonne [nɔn] **NF** *Rel* nun

non-négociable **ADJ** non-negotiable

nonnette [nɔnɛt] **NF** **1** *Rel Fam* young nun **2** *Culin* small iced gingerbread cake **3** *(oiseau)* tit

non-nuisible **ADJ** n. à l'environnement environmentally friendly, environment-friendly

nono, -ote [nɔno, -ɔt] **N** *Can Fam* idiot

nonobstant [nɔnɔpstɑ̃] **PRÉP, ADV** *Vieilli* notwithstanding; **ce n.** this notwithstanding

non-paiement **NM** nonpayment

nonpareil, -eille [nɔ̃parɛj] **ADJ** *Vieilli* peerless

non-partant, *pl* **non-partants** **NM** *(cheval)* nonstarter

non-polluant **ADJ** environmentally friendly

non-prolifération **NF** nonproliferation

non-recevoir **NM** opposer une fin de n. à une réclamation to refuse; *Jur* to put in a plea in bar of a claim

non-récupérable **ADJ** *Ordinat* non-recoverable

non-relationnel, -elle **ADJ** *Ordinat* non-relational

non-remboursable **ADJ** non-refundable

non-représentation **NF** *Jur* n. d'enfant refusal to comply with the access *or* visiting rights of a child

non-résident, -ente **N** nonresident

non-respect **NM** failure to respect; **le n. de la loi** failure to respect the law

non-retour **NM** point de n. point of no return

non-salarié, -ée **ADJ** unsalaried
N self-employed person; **les non-salariés** the self-employed

non-sens **NM INV** **1** *Scol (dans une traduction)* meaningless word *or* phrase **2** **c'est un n.** it's (a) nonsense

non-spécialiste, *pl* **non-spécialistes** **N** nonspecialist

non-stop [nɔnstɔp] **ADJ INV, ADV** *Fam* nonstop

non-structuré **ADJ** *Ordinat* unstructured

non-suspendu **ADJ** *Aut (freins)* outboard

non-syndiqué, -ée **ADJ** *(employé)* non-union, *Am* non-unionized
N non-union *or Am* non-unionized worker

non-taxable **ADJ** non-dutiable

non-tissé [nɔ̃tise] **NM** *Tex* nonwoven material

non-trié [nɔ̃trije] **ADJ** *Ordinat* unsorted

non-usage [nɔnyzaʒ] **NM** non-use

non-valeur, *pl* **non-valeurs** **NF** *Jur (état)* unproductiveness; *(bien)* unproductive asset; *Fin* bad debt; *(créance)* worthless amount; **terres en n.** unproductive land

non-vérifié [nɔ̃verifje] **ADJ** *Compta* unaudited

non-viable **ADJ** *Méd* nonviable

non-violence **NF** nonviolence

non-violent, -ente **N** supporter of non-violence
ADJ nonviolent

non-voyant, -ante **N** unsighted person; **les non-voyants** the unsighted

nopal, -als [nɔpal] **NM** *Bot* nopal

noquette [nɔket] **NF** *Belg (petite quantité)* **une n. de beurre** a knob of butter

noradrénaline [nɔradrenalin] **NF** *Biol, Chimie* noradrenalin(e)

nord [nɔr] **NM** *(no pl)* **1** *(point cardinal)* north; **au n., dans le n.** in the north; **où est le n. ?** which way is north?; **la partie la plus au n. de l'île** the northernmost part of the island; **le vent vient du n.** it's a north *or* northerly wind, the wind is coming from the north; **un vent du n.** a northerly wind; **le vent du n.** the north wind; **aller au ou vers le n.** to go north *or* northwards; **les trains qui vont vers le n.** trains going north, north-bound trains; **rouler vers le n.** to drive north *or* northwards; **aller droit vers le n.** to head due north; **la cuisine est plein n.** *ou* exposée au n. the kitchen faces due north; **n. géographique** true *or* geographic north; **n. magnétique** magnetic north; *Fig Fam* **perdre le n.** to go bonkers, to lose it **2** *(partie d'un pays, d'un continent)* north, northern area *or* regions *(partie d'une ville)* north; **la mer du N.** the North Sea; **le Grand N.** the Far North; **le n. de l'Italie** northern Italy, the north of Italy; **dans le n. de l'Espagne** in northern Spain, in the north of Spain; **elle habite dans le n.** she lives in the north; **il habite dans le n. de Paris** he lives in the north of Paris; **elle est du n.** she's from the north; **les gens du n.** people who live in the north
ADJ INV *(côté, face)* north; *(banlieue, partie, région)* northern; **le pôle N.** the North Pole; **la façade n. d'un immeuble** the north-facing wall of a building; **la chambre est côté n.** the bedroom faces north; **dans la partie n. de la France** in the north of France, in northern France; **suivre la direction n.** to head *or* to go northwards

nord-africain, -aine, *pl* **nord-africains, -aines** **ADJ** North African
N N.-A. North African

nord-américain, -aine, *pl* **nord-américains, -aines** **ADJ** North American
N N.-A. North American

nord-coréen, -enne, *pl* **nord-coréens, -ennes** **ADJ** North Korean
N N.-C. North Korean

nord-est [nɔrest] **NM INV** *(point cardinal)* north-east
ADJ INV north-east

nordicité [nɔrdisite] **NF** *Can* northerliness

nordique [nɔrdik] **ADJ** Nordic; *Hist* Norse; **langues nordiques** Nordic *or* Scandinavian languages
NM *Ling* Norse
N N. Scandinavian

nordir [nɔrdir] **VI** *Naut (du vent)* to veer north(ward)

nordiste [nɔrdist] **ADJ** **1** *Am Hist* Northern **2** *Sport (club)* northern
NM *Am Hist* Northerner

nord-nord-est **NM INV** north-north-east
ADJ INV north-north-east

nord-nord-ouest **NM INV** north-north-west
ADJ INV north-north-west

nord-ouest **NM INV** **1** *(point cardinal)* north-west **2** *(vent)* north-west wind, north-wester, nor'wester
ADJ INV north-west

nord-vietnamien, -ienne, *pl* **nord-vietnamiens, -iennes** **ADJ** North Vietnamese
N N.-V. North Vietnamese

NOREX [nɔrɛks] *Com* = source of information on standards and rules governing goods for export

noria [nɔrja] NF **1** *(machine)* noria **2** *(de véhicules qui vont et viennent)* endless stream

normal, -ale, -aux, -ales [nɔrmal, -o] ADJ **1** *(dans la norme) (état, cours)* normal; **elle n'est pas dans son état n.** she's not her normal *or* usual self; **en temps n.** in *or* under normal circumstances **2** *(naturel)* normal; **c'est tout à fait n. que la jeunesse se rebelle** it's only normal *or* natural for young people to rebel; **c'est bien n.** it's quite normal *or* natural; **tu trouves ça n. toi?** do you think that's all right *or* OK?; **ce n'est pas n.** it's not right (**que** that) **3** *(moyen) (poids, taille)* standard; **cet enfant n'a pas encore atteint la taille normale pour son age** this child is still below the average height for his age; **vitesse normale** normal *or* Spéc rated speed **4** *(intellectuellement) (personne)* normal **5** *Typ* roman
NF **normale 1 la normale** normal, the norm; **la température est revenue à la normale** the temperature is back to normal; **intelligence/température au-dessus/au-dessous de la normale** above-/below-average intelligence/temperature; **température au-dessous des normales saisonnières** temperature below the seasonal norm *or* average **2** *Univ Fam* **Normale Sup** = École normale supérieure

normalement [nɔrmalmã] ADV **1** *(de façon normale)* normally; **depuis un certain temps, il ne se comporte plus n.** for some time, he's not been behaving normally **2** *(habituellement)* usually, normally; **n. il passe nous voir le dimanche** he usually *or* normally calls to see us on Sundays **3** *(si tout va bien)* **n., nous devrions arriver pour le déjeuner** all being well *or* if all goes well, we should arrive in time for lunch; **n. elle devrait déjà être arrivée** she should be here by now

> Il faut noter que l'adverbe anglais **normally** ne s'emploie jamais dans le sens "si tout va bien".

normalien, -ienne [nɔrmaljɛ̃, -jɛn] N *Scol* student/former student of a teacher training college; *Univ* student/former student of the École normale supérieure

normalisation [nɔrmalizasjɔ̃] NF **1** *Pol* normalization **2** *Ind* standardization

normalisé [nɔrmalize] ADJ *(produit)* standard

normaliser [nɔrmalize] VT *(relations)* to normalize; *(équipement)* to standardize

normalité [nɔrmalite] NF normality

normand, -ande [nɔrmã, -ãd] ADJ **1** *(de Normandie)* Norman, (of) Normandy; **armoire normande** large rustic wardrobe **2** *Hist* Norman; **la conquête normande** the Norman Conquest
N **N.**Norman; **c'est un fin N.** he's shrewd; **réponse de N.** non-committal *or* equivocal *or* evasive answer **2** *Hist* **les Normands** the Normans

Normandie [nɔrmãdi] NF Normandy

norme [nɔrm] NF **1** *(règle)* norm, standard; **échapper à la n.** to be an exception; **être d'une intelligence qui échappe à la n.** to be exceptionally intelligent **2** *Ind, Com* standard; **normes européennes** European standards; **n. française** French standard, *Br* ≃ British standard, *Am* ≃ US standard; **jouet conforme aux normes de sécurité** toy which conforms to safety standards; **n. de production** production norm; **n. de productivité** productivity norm; **n. de travail** work standard; **n. technique** technical standard; **n. d'application** relevant standard; **normes**

d'application obligatoires compulsory standards; **normes d'application volontaires** voluntary standards; **normes publicitaires** advertising standards **3** *Math* norm

normographe [nɔrmɔgraf] NM stencil

norois, noroît [nɔrwa] NM *(vent)* northwest wind, northwester, nor'wester

Norvège [nɔrvɛʒ] NF Norway

norvégien, -ienne [nɔrveʒjɛ̃, -jɛn] ADJ Norwegian
NM *Ling* Norwegian
N **N.** Norwegian
NF **norvégienne** round-stemmed boat

nos *voir* **notre**

nosocomial, -ale, -aux, -ales [nozokɔmjal, -o] ADJ *Méd (maladie, infection)* nosocomial

nostalgie [nɔstalʒi] NF nostalgia; *(mal du pays)* homesickness; **j'ai la n. de ces temps-là** I look back on that time with nostalgia, I feel nostalgia for that time; **avoir la n. de son foyer** to long *or* yearn for home, to be homesick; **avoir la n. du pays** to be homesick; **penser à qch avec n.** to think of sth nostalgically *or* with nostalgia

nostalgique [nɔstalʒik] ADJ *(humeur, souvenirs, sentiments, personne)* nostalgic
N nostalgic person; **les nostalgiques des années 80** people who pine for the 1980s, people who are nostalgic for the 1980s

nostalgiquement [nɔstalʒikmã] ADV nostalgically

nota [nɔta] NM INV *(en bas de texte)* footnote; *(en marge)* marginal note; **nota bene** [nɔtabene] nota bene, NB

notabilité [nɔtabilite] NF *(personne, caractère)* notability

notable [nɔtabl] ADJ **1** *(remarquable)* notable, worthy of note; **sans variation n.** without appreciable change **2** *(personne)* notable, distinguished
NM notable (person), distinguished person, person of note *or* distinction; **les notables de la ville** the leading citizens, *Hum* the local worthies

notablement [nɔtabləmã] ADV notably, appreciably

notaire [nɔtɛr] NM *Jur* notary (public); **par-devant n.** before a notary

notamment [nɔtamã] ADV notably

notarié [nɔtarje] ADJ *Jur* certified by a notary; **acte n.** notarized deed

notation [nɔtasjɔ̃] NF **1** *Scol (d'un travail, d'un élève)* marking **2** *(par des symboles)* notation; *Ordinat* **n. hexadécimale** hex *or* hexadecimal code **3** *Fin* rating; *Bourse* **n. AAA** triple-A rating

note [nɔt] NF **1** *(mots, phrases)* note; **prendre des notes** to take (down) notes; **jeter quelques notes sur le papier** to jot down a few notes; **prendre n. de qch, prendre qch en n.** to note sth, to make a note of sth; **prendre bonne n. de qch** to take due note of sth; *Typ* **n. de bas de page** footnote; **n. de couverture** cover note; **n. marginale** note in the margin; **n. de renvoi** cross reference; *Journ* **n. de la rédaction** editor's note; **notes prises en sténo(graphie)** shorthand notes **2** *Scol, Univ (appréciation)* mark, *Am* grade; **bonne/mauvaise n.** good/bad mark; **notes trimestrielles** (end-of-term) report; **carnet** *ou* **relevé de notes** school report **3** *Mus* note; **fausse n.** wrong note; *Fig* false note; **donner la n.** *(aux chanteurs etc)* to sound the keynote; *Fig* **forcer la n.** to exaggerate; *(faire du zèle)* to overdo it; **sa robe n'était pas/ses blagues n'étaient pas dans la n.** her dress/his jokes struck the wrong note; **une n. d'originalité/de gaieté** a touch *or* note of originality/gaiety **4** *(facture), Com* bill; *(dans un hôtel etc)*

bill, *Am* check; **n. de téléphone** phone bill; *Fin* **n. de commission** commission note, fee note; **n. de crédit** credit note; **n. de débit** debit note; **n. de rappel** reminder
▸ ▸ **n. diplomatique** diplomatic note; *Ordinat, Typ* **n. de fin de document** end note; **n. de frais** expense account; *(présentée après coup)* expenses; **mettre qch sur sa n. de frais** to put sth on one's expense account; *Admin* **n. de service** memorandum, memo

noté [nɔte] ADJ **1** **être bien/mal n.** *(d'élève, d'employé)* to have a good/bad record; *(de devoir)* to have received a good/poor mark **2** *Bourse* **n. triple A** triple-A rated

notebook [nɔtbuk] NM *Ordinat* notebook

noter [nɔte] VT **1** *(mettre par écrit)* to note *or* put *or* jot down, to make a note of; **vas-y, je note** go ahead, I've got something to write with; **n. un passage** to mark a passage; **n. une commande** to log *or* note an order; **n. que** to note down *or* make a note that **2** *(remarquer)* to note, to take notice of; **à n.: les bus ne circulent pas le dimanche** note: there are no buses on Sundays; **notez bien cela** take good note of this, note this well; **il est à n. que ...** it is to be noted that ...; **c'est bon à n.** it's worthy noting *or* making a note of; **notez bien ce que je vous dis** mark my words; **note bien que cela n'a pas d'importance/je pourrais faire autrement** but it really doesn't matter/I could always do something else; **très bien, chef, c'est noté** *ou* **je note** OK boss, I've got it **3** *Scol, Univ (travail)* to mark, *Am* to grade

notice [nɔtis] NF **1** *(notes sommaires)* note; **n. bibliographique** bibliographical note **2** *(préface de livre)* note **3** *(mode d'emploi)* instructions, directions; *(livret)* instruction book(let), handbook, manual; **n. explicative** directions for use, explanatory leaflet; **n. du constructeur** manufacturer's instructions; **n. technique** technical specification

> Il faut noter que le nom anglais **notice** est un faux ami. Il signifie le plus souvent **avertissement**, **écriteau** ou **attention**, selon le contexte.

notification [nɔtifikasjɔ̃] NF *Jur* notification, notice; **recevoir n. de qch** to receive notification *or* be notified of sth

notifier [nɔtifje] VT *(impf, pr sub* **n. notifiions, v. notifiiez)** *(faire savoir)* **n. qch à qn** to notify sb of sth; *Jur* **n. son consentement** to signify one's consent (**à qn** to sb); **on lui notifia qu'il aurait à déménager dans les vingt-quatre heures** he received notice to quit within twenty-four hours

notion [nosjɔ̃] NF **1** *(concept)* notion, concept; **l'amitié est une n. abstraite** friendship is an abstract notion *or* concept; **perdre la n. du temps/de la réalité** to lose track of time/all sense of reality **2** *(connaissance succincte)* **des notions de** a smattering of, the basics of; **avoir des notions de chimie/russe** to have a smattering *or* know the basics of chemistry/Russian

notoire [nɔtwar] ADJ *(connu de tous)* well-known, *Péj* notorious; **son avarice est n.** his miserliness is notorious *or* legendary

> Il faut noter que l'adjectif anglais **notorious** signifie "tristement célèbre".

notoirement [nɔtwarmã] ADV manifestly, *Péj* notoriously; **fait n. faux** manifestly false fact; **un malfrat n. connu** a notorious gangster

notoriété [nɔtɔrjete] NF **1** *(d'un fait, d'une personne)* reputation; **avoir de la n.** to be well known, to have a (good) reputation; **cela lui a valu une certaine n.** that brought *or* earned him a certain reputation; **il est de**

n. publique que … it is public or common knowledge that …; *Mktg* n. de la marque brand awareness **2** *Jur* acte de n. attested affidavit

> Il faut noter que le nom anglais **notoriety** signifie uniquement "mauvaise réputation".

notre, nos [nɔtr, no] ADJ POSS our; *(de roi, de reine)* Our; **n. oncle et n. tante** our uncle and (our) aunt; **n. père et n. mère**, *Litt* nos père et mère our father and mother; **ils ont mis n. chapeau et nos gants** they put on our hats and (our) gloves; **nous avons pris n. sac** *(il n'y a qu'un sac)* we took our bag; *(chacun a son sac)* we took our bags; **nous avons pris nos sacs** we took our bags; *Fam* **nous aurons n. chambre à nous** *(il y a une chambre)* we will have our own room; *Fam* **à nous de frère** our idiot of a brother; *Fam* **nos artistes de maris** our artist-husbands; **nous retrouvons n. héros dix ans plus tard …** we meet our hero again ten years later …; *Fam* **nous avons n. vendredi** we've got Friday off SEE GRAMMAR A30; B21–2

nôtre [notr] PRON POSS **le n., la n., les nôtres** ours; **il ressemble au n.** it looks like ours; **nous voulons bien te donner du n.** you can have some of ours; **il n'en avons pas besoin, nous avons le n.** we don't need it, we've got our own; **tu n'en as pas besoin, tu as le n.** you don't need it, you've got ours; **les deux nôtres** our two, the two of ours; *(en insistant)* our own two; **nous devrions y mettre du n.** we should do our share; *Fam* **le n. de bébé est plus intelligent!** our baby is more intelligent!; *Fam* **à la n.!** *(en buvant)* here's to us! SEE GRAMMAR A30; B21

NMPL **les nôtres** *(notre famille)* our family, *Am* our folks; *(nos partisans)* our followers; *(nos coéquipiers)* our team-mates; **est-il des nôtres?** *(de notre côté)* is he one of us?; **vous serez des nôtres, n'est-ce pas?** *(pour dîner)* you will join us, won't you?

ADJ POSS *Litt* **un n. cousin** a cousin of ours; **nous ferons nôtres ses principes** we shall adopt these principles of his; **nous faisons nôtres les félicitations qu'ils vous adressent** we join them in congratulating you

Notre-Dame [nɔtrədam] NF *Rel* Our Lady; **la fête de N.** the feast of the Assumption

nouba [nuba] NF **1** *Fam* party; **faire la n.** to party **2** *(musique)* (Algerian) military band

noue¹ [nu] NF *(terre grasse)* marshy meadow, water meadow

noue² NF *Constr* **1** *(arête)* valley **2** *(tuile)* gutter tile; *(bande de plomb)* flashing

nouer [nwe] VT *(ficelle, corde, ruban)* to tie, to knot; **n. qch serré** to knot sth tightly, to make a tight knot in sth; **n. ses cheveux** to tie up one's hair; **n. sa cravate** to knot one's tie; **n. ses lacets** to tie (up) one's laces; **n. son tablier** to tie one's apron; **elle noua ses bras autour du cou de son ami** she wrapped her arms around her friend's neck; **avoir la gorge nouée** to have a lump in one's throat; **avoir l'estomac noué** to have a knot in one's stomach; **n. conversation avec qn** to enter into conversation with sb; **n. des relations avec qn** to establish relations with sb; **n. l'intrigue d'un roman** to bring the action of a novel to a head *or* climax

VI *(de fleur)* to set

VPR **se nouer 1 se n. les cheveux** to tie up one's hair **2** *(se faire)* **des amitiés qui se nouent** friendships which are formed *or* which form **3** *Littér, Théâtre, Cin* to take shape; **l'intrigue se noue dès le premier acte** the plot takes shape right from Act One

noueux, -euse [nwø, -øz] ADJ *(ficelle, bois)* knotty; *(tronc d'arbre, mains, doigts)* gnarled

nougat [nuga] NM **1** *(confiserie)* nougat **2** *Fam* **nougats** *(pieds)* feet

nougatine [nugatin] NF nougatine

nouille [nuj] NF **1** *Culin* noodle **2** *Fam (personne molle)* drip; *(bébête)* dimwit, noodle

nouméne [numɛn] NM *Phil* noumenon

nounou [nunu] NF *Fam* nanny

nounours [nunurs] NM *Enf* teddy (bear)

nourri [nuri] ADJ **1** *(alimenté)* fed; **bien n.** well fed; **mal n.** undernourished, underfed; **être logé (et) nourri (blanchi)** to get (one's) bed and board; **avoir 500 euros par mois logé et nourri** to get 500 euros a month with board and lodging **2** *(riche)* *(style)* rich; *(ligne en dessin)* broad, firm; *(ton, son)* full; *(applaudissements)* sustained, prolonged; **discussion nourrie** heated debate, lively discussion; *Mil* **feu n.** heavy *or* sustained fire

nourrice [nuris] NF **1** *(assistante maternelle)* child-minder; **n. agréée** registered childminder **2** *(personne qui allaite)* (wet) nurse; **mettre un enfant en n.** to put a child out to nurse **3** *Tech* auxiliary tank, service tank; *Aut (de carburant)* spare can

nourricier, -ière [nurisje, -jɛr] ADJ *Bot (sève, suc)* nutritive; *Anat (artère, canal)* nutrient; *Litt (terre)* nourishing

N **père n.** foster father; **mère nourricière** foster mother

nourrir [nurir] VT **1** *(donner à manger à) (personnes, animaux)* to feed (**de, avec** with, on); **nourri au biberon/sein** bottle-/breast-fed; **n. sa famille** to provide for *or* feed one's family; **j'ai cinq personnes à n.** I've five mouths to feed; **travail qui nourrit son homme** job that provides a living; **le lait nourrit** milk is nourishing; *Fig* **lectures qui nourrissent l'esprit** reading that improves the mind; *Mus* **n. le son** to give fullness *or* body to the tone **2** *(de crème, lotion) (peau, visage, cuir)* to nourish; *(feu)* to feed **3** *Litt (entretenir) (haine)* to foster; *(idées de vengeance, illusion etc)* to harbour, *Am* to harbor; *(espoir)* to cherish, to harbour, to entertain; *(projet)* to nurse; **je nourris l'espoir de le revoir** I cherish the hope of seeing him again

VPR **se nourrir** *(manger)* to eat; **il refuse de se n.** he won't eat; **chasser pour se n.** to hunt for one's food; **il gagne juste de quoi se n.** he earns just enough to live on; **se n. de lait/ fruits** to live on milk/fruit

nourrissant [nurisɑ̃] ADJ *(repas, aliments)* nourishing, nutritious; *(crème pour le visage, le cuir)* nourishing

nourrisseur [nurisœr] NM **1** *(de bétail, de boucherie)* stockbreeder; *(de vaches laitières)* dairyman **2** *Tech (pour l'alimentation des animaux)* feed roll

nourrisson [nurisɔ̃] NM young baby, infant

nourriture [nurityr] NF *(aliments)* food; **retrouver une n. saine et équilibrée** to get back to a healthy and balanced diet; **priver qn de n.** to starve sb, to deprive sb of food; **il refuse toute n. depuis trois jours** he has been refusing food *or* refusing to eat for three days; **n. de l'esprit** food for the mind; **les nourritures terrestres** the fruits of the earth

nous [nu] PRON PERS SEE GRAMMAR A27; B18–19 **1** *(sujet)* we; *Fam* **n. sommes allés au restaurant avec mon mari** *(lui et moi)* me and my husband went to the restaurant **2** *(objet direct)* us; *(objet indirect)* to us; **il ne n. connaît pas** he does not know us; **lisez-le-n.** read it to us; **elle n. en a parlé** she spoke to us about it **3** *(réfléchi)* **n. n. réchauffons** we are warming ourselves; **n. n. sommes versé du vin** we poured ourselves some wine; **n. n. battions avec l'ennemi** we were fighting the enemy SEE GRAMMAR A29–30; B28–9 **4** *(réciproque)* **n. n.**

connaissons we know each other **5** **n. deux/ tous** *(sujet)* both/all of us, we two/all; *(objet)* both/all of us, us two/all; **c'est n. qui sommes fautifs** we are to blame, it is us *or* surtout *Fml* we who are to blame; **n. autres Anglais** we English; **un ami à n.** a friend of ours; **ce livre est à n.** that book is ours *or* belongs to us; **bon, à n. maintenant** so, we can have a talk now; **à n. deux** *(sur ton menaçant)* let's have a little talk; *(avant de se battre)* let's fight it out; **c'est à n. de jouer** it's our turn; **il était avec n.** he was with us; **entre n. (soit dit)** (this is) between ourselves **6** (**nous de majesté ou de modestie, employé pour je**) we; **n. sommes désolés de l'apprendre** we are grieved to hear it

nous-même PRON PERS *(après nous de majesté, de modestie)* ourself; *voir* **même**

nous-mêmes PRON PERS ourselves; **nous l'avons fait n.** we did it ourselves; *voir* **même**

nouveau, -el, -elle, -eaux [nuvo, -ɛl] ADJ (**nouvel** *is used before m sing nouns beginning with a vowel or h mute*) **1** *(récent)* new; **nouvelles voitures** new cars; **livres nouveaux** new books; **il est n., ce manteau?** is this coat new?; **techniques nouvelles** new *or* up-to-date techniques; **je suis n. dans ce métier** I'm new to this business; *Fam* **tu sais ce que c'est, tout n. tout beau, ça lui passera** you know what it's like, it's all new and exciting at first, but she'll get over it; **il n'y a rien de n.** there's nothing new, there are no new developments; **il y a quelqu'un de n. au bureau** there's someone new in the office; **c'est n. ça!** that's new!; **il n'y a rien de n. sous le soleil** there's nothing new under the sun; **nouvel utilisateur** first-time user

2 *(qui succède à un autre)* *(télévision, directeur, épisode, gouvernement, adresse, collection)* new; **les nouveaux pères** modern(-day) fathers; **nouvelle technologie** new technology; *Fin* **nouvelle émission** *(d'actions)* new issue; **nouveaux emprunts** new borrowings; *Cin etc* **nouvelle version** remake; **faire une nouvelle version de** to do a remake of, to reversion; **jusqu'à nouvel ordre** until further notice; **que font-ils au sujet des enfants? – jusqu'à nouvel ordre, rien** what are they doing about the children? – they haven't decided yet; **la nouvelle Marilyn Monroe** the new Marilyn Monroe; **la nouvelle mode** the latest fashion; **la nouvelle génération** the new *or* rising generation; **j'ai besoin d'une nouvelle voiture** I need a new car; **il met tous les jours une nouvelle chemise** he wears a clean *or* different shirt every day; **n. et amélioré** *(sur emballage)* new improved

3 *(autre)* new; **sous un jour n.** in a new light; **un n. chapitre** a new *or* fresh chapter; **une nouvelle raison/hausse des prix** a further *or* an additional *or* another reason/price rise; **se faire de nouveaux amis** *(supplémentaires)* to make new friends; **elle a eu un nouvel enfant** she has had another child; **faire de nouveaux efforts** to make new *or* fresh efforts; *Jur* **n. procès** retrial

4 *(nouvellement produit)* *(carotte, pomme de terre)* new; **du vin n.** new *or* young wine; **le beaujolais n.** the new Beaujolais *or* Beaujolais nouveau; **herbe nouvelle** young grass

5 *(avec une fonction adverbiale)* **le nouvel arrivé** the newcomer; **les nouveaux arrivés** the newcomers; **les nouveaux élus** those newly elected; **les nouveaux convertis** the new converts, the newly converted; **n. pays industrialisé** newly industrialized country

6 à n., de n. *(once or over)* again; **recommencer à n.** to start afresh; **elle est de n. malade** she is ill again; **la terre a à n.** *ou* **de n. tremblé en Californie** there has been another earthquake in California

NM **il y a du n.** there's been a new development; **j'ai du n. au sujet de … ** I've got news about …; **tu as du n. pour ton billet d'avion?** have you heard anything more about your plane ticket?

N *(personne)* new person; *Scol* new pupil
▸▸ **Nouvel An** New Year; **passer le Nouvel An chez des amis** to spend New Year's Eve at friends'; **nouvelle cuisine** nouvelle cuisine; *Pol* **la nouvelle droite** the New Right; **nouvelle économie** new economy; *Anciennement* **n. franc** new franc; *Pol* **la nouvelle gauche** the New Left; **les nouveaux médias** the new media; **Nouveau Monde** New World; **nouveaux pauvres** new poor; *Beaux-Arts* **n. réalisme** New Realism; **n. réaliste** New Realist; *Péj* **n. riche** nouveau riche; **n. roman** nouveau roman, new novel; **Nouveau Testament** New Testament; *Cin* **la nouvelle vague** the New Wave, the Nouvelle Vague

Nouveau-Brunswick [nuvobrœzvik] **NM** New Brunswick

Nouveau-Mexique [nuvomɛksik] **NM** New Mexico

nouveau-né, -née, *pl* **nouveau-nés, -nées** **ADJ** newborn
N newborn child

nouveauté [nuvote] **NF 1** *(caractère nouveau)* newness, novelty; **recherche constante de la n.** constant search for something new *or* for novelty **2** *(produit récent) (livre)* new publication; *(invention)* new invention; **le cinéma n'est plus une n.** the cinema is no longer a novelty *or* anything new; **vous trouverez ce disque/livre au rayon des nouveautés** you'll find that record in the new releases rack/that book on the new titles shelf; *Fam* **tu sais qu'il trompe sa femme? – c'est pas une n.!** do you know he's cheating on his wife? – that's nothing new! **3 les nouveautés de printemps** *(vêtements)* the new spring fashions; *Vieilli* **magasin de nouveautés** draper's shop, *Am* dry goods store

nouvelle [nuvɛl] **NF 1** *(annonce d'un événement)* (piece of) news; **bonne/mauvaise n.** good/bad news; **j'ai une bonne n.!** (I've) good news!; **une n. plutôt décevante** a rather disappointing piece of news; **première n.!** that's news to me!, that's the first I've heard of it!; **la n. de sa mort** the news of his death; **la n. a été confirmée par le gouvernement** the news *or* report was confirmed by the government; **vous connaissez la n.?** have you heard the news *or* the latest? VOIR GRAMMAIRE A10
2 *(informations)* **nouvelles (de qn/qch)** news (of *or* about sb/sth); **demander** *ou* **(aller) prendre des nouvelles de (la santé de) qn** to inquire *or* ask about sb('s health); **j'ai eu des nouvelles de Pierre** *(par lui-même)* I've had news from *or* I've heard from Pierre; *(par qn d'autre)* I've had news about *or* of Pierre; **envoyez-moi de vos nouvelles** let me know how you're doing; **on n'eut plus jamais de leurs nouvelles** they were never heard of again; **je suis sans nouvelles de lui** *(directement)* I've had no news from him, I've not heard from him; *(indirectement)* I've had no news of *or* about him; **aux dernières nouvelles, il était à Lima** he was last heard of in Lima; **les nouvelles vont vite!** news travels fast!; **goûtez cela, vous m'en direz des nouvelles** taste this, I'm sure you'll like it; **vous aurez de mes nouvelles!** you'll be hearing from me!; **pas de nouvelles, bonnes nouvelles** no news is good news
3 *Journ* news item; **les nouvelles** the news; **les dernières nouvelles** the latest news; **à quelle heure sont les nouvelles?** when's the news on?
4 *Littér* short story

Il faut noter que le nom anglais **novel** est un faux ami. Il signifie **roman**.

Nouvelle-Angleterre **NF** New England

Nouvelle-Calédonie [nuvɛlkaledɔni] **NF** New Caledonia

Nouvelle-Écosse **NF** Nova Scotia

Nouvelle-Galles du Sud **NF** New South Wales

Nouvelle-Guinée **NF** New Guinea

nouvellement [nuvɛlmā] **ADV** newly, recently

Nouvelle-Orléans [nuvɛlɔrleā] **NF** **La N.** New Orleans

Nouvelles-Hébrides [nuvɛlzebrid] **NFPL** New Hebrides

Nouvelle-Zélande [nuvɛlzelād] **NF** New Zealand

nouvelliste [nuvelist] **N** short story writer

nova, *pl* **novæ** [nɔva, -e] **NF** *Astron* nova

novateur, -trice [nɔvatœr, -tris] **ADJ** innovative
N innovator

novélisation [nɔvelizasjɔ̃] **NF** novelization

novembre [nɔvābr] **NM** November; **en n.** in November; **au mois de n.** in (the month of) November; **le premier n.** (on) the first of November, (on) November the first SEE GRAMMAR A81–2; B60–2

novice [nɔvis] **N** *(personne sans expérience)* novice, beginner; *(au couvent)* novice
NM *(jeune marin)* junior seaman
ADJ **être n. à** *ou* **dans qch** to be new to *or* inexperienced in sth

noviciat [nɔvisja] **NM** *Rel* noviciate, novitiate

noyade [nwajad] **NF 1** drowning; **sauver qn de la n.** to save sb from drowning; **mort par n.** death by drowning **2** *Hist* execution by drowning

noyau, -aux [nwajo] **NM 1** *(de fruit)* stone, *Am* pit; **fruit à n.** stone fruit; **enlever** *ou* **retirer le n. d'un fruit** to stone *or Am* pit a fruit; **n. de cerise** cherry stone *or Am* pit **2** *(centre) (d'atome, de cellule, de comète)* nucleus; *(de la terre)* core; **n. de bombe nucléaire** nuclear bomb core VOIR GRAMMAIRE A14 **3** *(petit groupe)* **un n. de joueurs** a small group of players; **un n. d'opposants/d'irréductibles** a small group of opponents/hardliners; **un n. d'amis** a small circle of friends; **le n. dur** the hard core; *Bourse* = group of stable shareholders chosen for a company by the government on its flotation; **noyaux de résistance** pockets of resistance **4** *Archit (d'escalier)* newel; **escalier à n. plein** winding staircase **5** *Él (d'armature), Métal (de moule)* core; *Ordinat* node; *Géol* **n. volcanique** volcanic bomb

noyautage [nwajotaʒ] **NM** *Pol* infiltration

noyauter [nwajote] **VT** *Pol (syndicat, parti, organisation)* to infiltrate

noyé, -ée [nwaje] **ADJ** *(par noyade)* **mourir n.** to die by drowning; *Fig* **être n.** to be out of one's depth
N drowned person; **secours aux noyés** first aid for the drowning; **on a repêché un n. dans la rivière** a drowned man was fished out of the river

noyer¹ [nwaje] **NM** *(arbre)* walnut (tree); *(bois)* walnut; **n. (blanc) d'Amérique** hickory

noyer² (**je noie, nous noyons; je noierai**) **VT** **1** *(personne, animal)* to drown; *(la terre etc)* to swamp, to inundate, to deluge; *(soute)* to flood; **les polders ont été noyés sous des mètres cubes d'eau** the polders were submerged under several cubic metres of water; **n. une rébellion dans le sang** to quash a rebellion with bloodshed; *Fig* **n. son chagrin (dans l'alcool)** to drown one's sorrows (in drink); **noyé dans la foule** lost in the crowd; **n. le poisson** *(à la ligne)* to play the fish; *Fig* to confuse the issue deliberately, to muddy the waters
2 *Aut* **n. le moteur** to flood the engine
3 *(mouiller abondamment)* **les larmes noyaient son visage/ses joues** his face was/his cheeks were drenched with tears, tears poured down his face/cheeks; **yeux noyés de larmes** eyes brimming with tears; **elle avait les yeux noyés de larmes** her eyes were brimming with tears; **n. la sauce** to make the sauce too thin; **n. le vin** to drown the wine
4 *(recouvrir entièrement) (de brouillard, brume)* to shroud, to envelop; **le village était noyé dans la brume** *ou* **noyé de brume** the village was shrouded *or* enveloped in mist; **la chambre était noyée dans la pénombre/de lumière** the room was shrouded in darkness/bathed in light; **les points essentiels sont noyés dans le détail** the essential points are buried *or* lost in too many details
5 *(contours, couleurs)* to blend, to blur
6 *Constr* to sink in cement; *(vis)* to countersink; *(clou)* to drive in flush
VPR **se noyer** *(mourir par noyade) (accidentellement)* to be drowned, to drown; *(volontairement)* to drown oneself; *Fig* **se n. dans les détails/des explications** to get bogged down in details/in explanations; **elle se noierait dans un verre d'eau** she makes a mountain out of a molehill

NPI [ɛnpei] **NM** *(abrév* **nouveau pays industrialisé)** NIC

NTI [ɛntei] **NFPL** *(abrév* **nouvelles technologies de l'information)** NIT

nu [ny] **ADJ 1** *(dévêtu) (personne)* naked; *(épaules, bras, jambe)* bare; *Beaux-Arts* nude; **mettez-vous torse nu** strip to the waist; **il était torse nu** *ou* **nu jusqu'à la ceinture** he was stripped to the waist; **être tout nu** to be stark naked; **se baigner tout nu** to bathe in the nude, *Fam* to go skinny-dipping; **avoir les seins nus** to be topless, to have bare breasts; **nu comme la main** *ou* **comme un ver** stark naked, *Fam* in the buff; **danseuse nue** striptease artist; (**NOTE nu** *before the noun that it qualifies is invariable and is joined to the noun by a hyphen*) **aller tête nue** *ou* **nu-tête** to go bareheaded *or* without anything on one's head; **aller pieds nus** *ou* **nu-pieds** to go barefoot; **se battre à main(s) nue(s)** to fight with bare fists; **la boxe à main(s) nue(s)** bare-knuckle boxing **2** *Fig (style)* plain, unadorned; *(épée)* unsheathed, naked; **la vérité (toute) nue** the plain *or* naked truth; *Élec* **fil nu** bare wire **3** *(dégarni) (paysage, arbre, pièce, mur)* bare
NM *Beaux-Arts (personne, œuvre)* nude; **le nu** *(genre)* the nude; **mettre à nu** to lay bare, to expose, to uncover; *(fil électrique)* to strip; **il a mis son cœur à nu** he laid bare his heart; *Équitation Vieilli* **monter un cheval à nu** to ride (a horse) bareback

nuage [nɥaʒ] **NM** cloud; **nuages pommelés** fleecy *or* fluffy clouds; **nuages en flocons** fluffy clouds; **ciel couvert** *ou* **chargé de nuages** overcast *or* cloudy sky; **n. de poussière/fumée/sauterelles** cloud of dust/smoke/locusts; **n. radioactif** cloud of radioactive dust; **sans nuages** *(ciel)* cloudless; *Fig (vie, avenir)* unclouded; *Fig* **bonheur sans nuages** perfect bliss; *Fig* **un n. de tristesse assombrissait son front** his face was clouded with sadness; *Fig* **être dans les nuages** to have one's head in the clouds, to be daydreaming; **n. de lait** drop *or* dash of milk

nuageux, -euse [nɥaʒø, -øz] **ADJ** *(temps)* cloudy; *(ciel)* overcast, cloudy; **masse nuageuse** cloud mass

nuance [nɥās] **NF 1** *(de couleur)* shade, hue; **toutes les nuances de bleu** all shades of blue **2** *(légère trace)* **une n. d'amertume/de mépris/de regrets** a touch *or* hint *or* suggestion of bitterness/contempt/regret **3** (subtilité) nuance; (légère différence) slight or subtle difference; **les nuances de la langue** the nuances of the language; **récit tout en nuances** story full of nuances; **je ne saisis pas la n.** I don't quite see the difference; **il y a une n.!** there's a slight difference!; **j'ai dit peut-être, pas oui, n.!** I said perhaps, not yes, there's a slight difference!; *Fig* **il est sans nuances** he sees everything in black and white **4** *Mus* nuance; **il joue sans nuances** he plays without any light and shade

nuancé [nɥɑ̃se] **ADJ** (couleur, ton) subtle; *Fig* (discours, propos, attitude) full of nuances; **ses réponses sont toujours très nuancées** he always qualifies his answers a lot

nuancer [nɥɑ̃se] **VT** (**je nuançai(s); nous nuançons**) **1** (en dessin, peinture) (couleurs) to shade; (mélanger) to blend (**de** with); **n. une couleur avec une autre** to shade one colour into another **2** (modérer) (pensée, jugement, propos) to qualify **3** *Mus* **n. son jeu** to introduce light and shade into one's playing

nuancier [nɥɑ̃sje] **NM** (de couleurs), *Com* sample card or chart; *Phot* colour chart; *Typ* swatch; *Aut* graduated tint shadeband

nubile [nybil] **ADJ** nubile, marriageable; **âge n.** (en sociologie) age of nubility

nubilité [nybilite] **NF** nubility

nucléaire [nykleɛr] **ADJ 1** *Phys, Mil* (énergie, fission, armes) nuclear; **particule n.** elementary particle **2** *Biol* (membrane) nuclear **3** (en sociologie) **la famille n.** the nuclear family
NM le n. nuclear power

nucléarisation [nyklearizasjɔ̃] **NF** *Ind* = introduction of nuclear power to replace conventional energy sources; *Mil* nuclearization

nucléariser [nyklearize] **VT** to supply with nuclear power; *Mil* to supply with nuclear weapons, to nuclearize
VPR se nucléariser 1 (choisir l'énergie nucléaire) to go nuclear **2** *Mil* (se doter d'armes nucléaires) to go nuclear, to nuclearize

nucléé [nyklee] **ADJ** *Biol* (cellule) nucleate

nucléique [nykleik] **ADJ** (acide) nucleic

nucléole [nykleɔl] **NM** *Biol* nucleolus

nucléon [nykleɔ̃] **NM** *Phys* nucleon

nucléonique [nykleɔnik] *Phys* **ADJ** nucleonic
NF nucleonics

nucléus [nykleys] **NM** *Biol* nucleus

nudisme [nydism] **NM** nudism; **faire du n.** to be a nudist, to practise nudism

nudiste [nydist] **N** nudist; **camp de nudistes** nudist camp

nudité [nydite] **NF 1** (de personne) nudity, nakedness; (de rocher, de mur) bareness; *Fig* **l'horreur étalée dans toute sa n.** the horror displayed in all its starkness **2** *Beaux-Arts* nude (figure)

nue [ny] **NF** *Arch, Litt* high cloud(s); **nues skies**; **l'oiseau fendait les nues** the bird was cleaving its way through the skies; *Fig* **porter qn/qch aux nues** to laud or praise sb/sth to the skies; *Litt* **se perdre dans les nues** to have one's head (completely) in the clouds, to be lost in the clouds or in daydreams; *Fig* **tomber des nues** to be flabbergasted, to be thunderstruck

nuée [nɥe] **NF** *Litt* cloud, storm cloud; (d'insectes, de criquets) cloud, swarm; *Fig* **une n. de journalistes/touristes** a horde or swarm of journalists/tourists; **n. ardente** nuée ardente (cloud of ash, gas etc)

nue-propriété, *pl* **nues-propriétés NF** reversionary ownership

nuire [nɥir] (*ppr* **nuisant;** *pp* **nui;** *pr ind* **je nuis, nous nuisons;** *pr sub* **je nuise;** *p hist* **je nuisis;** *fu* **je nuirai**) **VI** (desservir) **n. à qn/à**

qch (de personne) to harm sb/sth; (de chose) to harm or be harmful to sb/sth; **cela ne nuira en rien** it won't do any harm; **cela nuira à sa réputation** it will damage or harm his reputation, it will be harmful to his reputation; **n. aux intérêts de qn** to prejudice or harm or damage sb's interests; **le tabac nuit gravement à la santé** smoking seriously damages your health; **dans l'intention de n.** maliciously; *Prov* **abondance de biens ne nuit pas** you can't have too much of a good thing; *Prov* **trop parler nuit** too much talking is harmful
VPR se nuire to do oneself (a great deal of) harm

nuisance [nɥizɑ̃s] **NF** nuisance; **nuisances acoustiques** noise pollution; **nuisances chimiques** chemical pollution

nuisette [nɥizɛt] **NF** baby doll (nightie)

nuisibilité [nɥizibilite] **NF** harmfulness

nuisible [nɥizibl] **ADJ** harmful (**à** to); **plantes nuisibles** noxious plants; **animaux nuisibles** vermin, pests
NM pest; **les nuisibles** vermin, pests

nuit [nɥi] **NF 1** night; **la n. dernière** last night; **cette n.** tonight; (passée) last night; **cela s'est passé dans la n. de samedi à dimanche** it happened during Saturday night or the night of Saturday to Sunday; **la n. où il est mort** the night (when) he died; **bonne n.!** good night!; **as-tu passé une bonne n.?** did you have a good night?; **veiller jusqu'à une heure avancée de la n.** to sit up far into the night; **passer la n. à faire qch** to stay up or spend all night doing sth; **on a passé la n. à faire la fête** we made a night of it; **passer la n. chez des amis** to stay overnight or the night with friends; **passer la n. à l'hôtel** to spend or stay the night at a hotel; **une chambre à 100 euros la n.** a room at 100 euros a or per night; **le train/bateau/voyage de n.** the night train/boat or ferry/journey; **vêtements de n.** nightwear; **médecin de n.** night doctor; *Beaux-Arts* **effet de n.** night effect; **être de n.** to be on night shift or night duty or *Fam* nights; **voyager de n.** ou **la n.** to travel by night or at night; **conduire de n.** to drive at night or in the dark; **n. et jour** [nɥitezur] night and day; **il ne passera pas la n.** he won't last the night; **je n'ai pas dormi de la n.** I didn't sleep a wink all night; **le bébé fait ses nuits** the baby sleeps through the night; **il commence à faire n.** night is falling, it is growing or getting dark; **il fait déjà n.** it is dark already; **à la n. tombante** at nightfall, at dusk; **une fois la n. tombée, à (la) n. tombée** after dark; **la n. porte conseil** it would be best to sleep on it; *Prov* **la n., tous les chats sont gris** all cats are grey in the dark
2 *Fig* darkness; *Litt* **la n. de l'ignorance** the darkness of ignorance; **perdu dans la n. des temps** lost in the mists of time; **c'est le jour et la n.** they're (like) chalk and cheese
▸▸ *Cin* **n. américaine** day for night; **tourné en n. américaine** shot in day for night; **n. blanche** sleepless night; **passer une n. blanche** (par insomnie) to spend a sleepless night; (volontairement) to stay up all night; **n. bleue** night of bomb attacks; **n. d'hôtel** (dans l'hôtellerie) bed-night; **payer une n. d'hôtel** to pay for a night at a hotel; *Hist* **la N. des longs couteaux** the Night of the Long Knives; **n. de noces** wedding night; **la n. de la Saint-Jean** Midsummer Night

nuitamment [nɥitamɑ̃] **ADV** *Litt* by night

nuitée [nɥite] **NF** (dans l'hôtellerie) overnight stay, bed-night; **deux nuitées pour quatre personnes** two nights for four people; **la n. va de midi à midi le lendemain** a night runs from noon to noon the next day

nul, nulle [nyl] **ADJ 1** (inexistant) (différence, risques, écart, récolte) nil; (élection) null and void, invalid; **rendre n.** to nullify, to annul;

Sport **score n. zéro (à) zéro** (en fin de match) match drawn nil-nil; (à la mi-temps) score nil-nil; **le score est n.** (en fin de match) the game is drawn, the result is a draw; (à la mi-temps) neither team has scored yet, the game so far is drawn; **match n.** draw, drawn match; **faire match n.** to draw, to tie; **bulletin (de vote) n.** spoilt (ballot) paper; **le solde est n.** the balance is nil; *Phys* **tension nulle** zero tension; *Jur* **n. et non avenu** invalid, null and void **2** *Fam* (qui ne vaut rien) (réponse, personne) useless, hopeless; (film, livre, chanson, blague) rubbish, très *Fam* crap; (argument) useless; *Vulg* **c'est n. à chier!** it's a load of crap! **3** *Fam* (incompétent) (élève, employé) hopeless, useless; **être n. en qch** to be hopeless or useless at sth
ADJ INDÉF (avec ne exprimé ou compris) no; *Litt* **n. espoir** no hope; **il n'a nulle raison de se plaindre** he has no reason to complain; **sans nulle vanité** without boasting; **n. doute qu'il y serait parvenu** there's no doubt that he would have managed it; *Litt* **à nul(le) autre pareil(le)** unparalleled; **n. autre que moi ne le sait** I alone know of it [SEE GRAMMAR B63]
PRON INDÉF no one, nobody; *Prov* **n. n'est prophète en son pays** no man is a prophet in his own country; **à l'impossible n. n'est tenu** you can't be expected to do the impossible
N *Fam* useless idiot, prat

nullard, -arde [nylar, -ard] très *Fam* **ADJ** (personne) useless, hopeless
N dimwit, *Br* plonker

nullement [nylmɑ̃] **ADV** (avec ne exprimé ou compris) not at all, by no means; **cela vous dérange-t-il? – n.!** does that bother you? – not at all! or by no means!; **nous ne sommes n. surpris** we are not in the least or at all surprised; **je n'ai n. l'intention d'y aller** I haven't the slightest or least intention of going; **il n'est n. sot** he is no fool

nulle part ADV nowhere; **je ne les vois n.** I can't see them anywhere; **je n'ai vu ça n. (ailleurs)** I've not seen that anywhere (else), I've seen that nowhere (else)

nullification [nylifikasjɔ̃] **NF** nullification

nullissime [nylisim] **ADJ** *Fam* totally useless, pathetic

nullité [nyl(l)ite] **NF 1** *Jur* (de contrat, de mariage etc) nullity, invalidity; **frapper une clause de n.** to render a clause void; **lors d'un mariage, la bigamie est une cause de n.** bigamy is grounds for the annulment of a marriage **2** (stupidité) (de personne) uselessness, hopelessness; (de remarque, plaisanterie) crassness; **elle est d'une n.!** she's totally useless!; **cette blague est d'une n. totale** that joke is completely pathetic **3** *Fam* (personne incompétente) dead loss

nûment [nymɑ̃] **ADV** *Litt* frankly, without embellishment

numéraire [nymerɛr] **ADJ** (monnaie) legal; **valeur n.** cash value
NM specie, (current) coin; **payer en n.** to pay in cash or *Spéc* in specie

numéral, -ale, -aux, -ales [nymeral, -o] **ADJ, NM** numeral

numérateur [nymeratœr] **NM** *Math* numerator

numération [nymerasjɔ̃] **NF** *Math* numeration, notation; *Méd* **n. globulaire** blood count; **n. et formule sanguine** full blood count

numérique [nymerik] **ADJ 1** (valeur, supériorité etc) numerical **2** *Ordinat* (ordinateur, donnée) digital; **balance à affichage n.** digital scales; **enregistrement/disque n.** digital recording/record
NM digital (broadcasting); **n. hertzien** ou **terrestre** digital terrestrial (broadcasting)

numériquement [nymerikmɑ̃] ADV **1** numerically **2** *Ordinat* digitally

numérisation [nymerizasjɔ̃] NF *Ordinat* digitization; **n. en lots** batch capture

numériser [nymerize] VT *Ordinat* to digitize

numériseur [nymerizœr] NM *Ordinat* digitizer; **n. d'image** image digitizer

numéro [nymero] NM **1** *(chiffre)* number; **tirer le bon n.** to draw the lucky *or* winning number; *Fig* to strike (it) lucky; **le n. gagnant** the winning number; **n. de page** page number; *Typ* folio; **le n. un/deux du parti** the number one/two in the party; **j'habite au n. 10** I live at number 10; **l'ennemi public n.** un public enemy number one; **la chambre n. 20** room (number) 20; **n. de téléphone** telephone number; **est-ce que tu as son n.?** have you got his number?

2 *(de périodique)* issue (**sur** on, about); *(d'émission)* edition; **le n. du jour/de la semaine/du mois, le dernier n.** the current issue; **ancien n., n. déjà paru** back issue *or* number; **deux numéros en un** double issue; **n. spécial** special issue; **n. zéro** zero edition; **vente au n.** single copies sold; **acheter un magazine au n.** to buy a magazine as it appears; **il faudra chercher dans de vieux numéros** we'll have to look through some back issues; **la suite au prochain n.** *(dans un magazine)* (to be) continued in the next issue, to be continued; *Fig Fam* watch this space

3 *(d'artiste)* spot; **n. de cirque** circus act; *Fam* **il aime faire son petit n.** he likes doing his little act

4 *(personne)* **quel n.!** what a character!

▶▶ **n. d'appel** telephone number; **n. d'appel gratuit** Freefone® number, *Am* toll-free number; *Tél* **n. azur** = type of Freefone® number in which costs are shared between caller and company; **n. de chambre** room number; *Aut* **n. de châssis** chassis *or* commission number; **n. de commande** order number; *Journ* **n. de commission paritaire** publication registration number; **n. de compte** account number; **n. d'enregistre-ment** booking number; **n. d'identification** identification number; **n. d'identité bancaire** bank sort code; **n. d'immatriculation** registration number; *Ordinat* **n. Internet** Internet number; *Ordinat* **n. IP** IP number; *Ordinat* **n. de licence** registration number; **n. d'ordre** running *or* serial *or* order number; *Belg, Suisse* **n. postal** postcode, *Am* zip code; *Tél* **n. de poste** extension number; **n. de référence** reference number; **n. de sécurité sociale** social security number; **n. de série** serial number; **n. de sociétaire** *(d'une assurance)* insurance *or* policy number; *Tél* **n. surtaxé** premium rate number; **n. de téléphone** telephone number; **VOIR GRAMMAIRE** **A77** *Tél* **n. d'urgence** hot-line; *Tél* **n. vert** *Br* ≃ Freefone® number, 0800 number, *Can* ≃ Zenith number, *Am* ≃ 0800 number, toll-free number; **n. de vol** flight number

numérologie [nymerɔlɔʒi] NF numerology

numérotage [nymerɔtaʒ] NM numbering; **n. de pages** page numbering, pagination

numérotation [nymerɔtasjɔ̃] NF numbering; *(téléphone)* dialling, *Am* dialing; *Tél* **n. abrégée** short code dialling; *Ordinat* **n. alphanumérique** alphanumeric numbering; *Ordinat* **n. décimale** decimal numbering

numéroter [nymerɔte] VT *(maisons, pages de livre etc)* to number; **les places ne sont pas numérotées** the seats are not numbered; *Mil* **numérotez-vous (à partir de la droite)!** (from the right) number! VI *Tél* to dial

numéroteur [nymerɔtœr] NM numbering device

numismate [nymismat] N numismatist

numismatique [nymismatik] ADJ numismatic NF numismatics, numismatology

nummulaire [nymylɛr] NF *Bot* moneywort, creeping Jenny

nunuche [nynyʃ] ADJ *Fam* silly

nu-pieds NM INV sandal ADV barefoot

nu-propriétaire, nue-propriétaire, *pl* **nu(e)s-propriétaires** N reversionary owner

nuptial, -iale, -iaux, -iales [nypsjal, -jo] ADJ wedding; **anneau n.** wedding ring; **marche nuptiale** wedding march; **chambre nuptiale** bridal suite; **cortège n.** bridal procession; **robe nuptiale** wedding dress, bridal gown; **messe nuptiale** nuptial mass

nuptialité [nypsjalite] NF marriage rate

nuque [nyk] NF nape *or* back of the neck; **elle veut une coupe de cheveux qui dégage bien la n.** she wants her hair cut short at the back; **saisir qn par la n.** to catch hold of sb by the scruff of the neck

nurse [nœrs] NF *Vieilli* nanny, (children's) nurse

nursery, *pl* **nurseries** [nœrsəri] NF *(d'hôpital)* nursery

nutation [nytasjɔ̃] NF nutation

nu-tête ADV bare-headed

nutritif, -ive [nytritif, -iv] ADJ nutritive; *(aliment)* nutritious, nourishing; **valeur nutritive** food *or* nutritional value

nutrition [nytrisjɔ̃] NF nutrition; **une mauvaise n.** a bad *or* an unbalanced diet

nutritionniste [nytrisjɔnist] N nutritionist

nyctalope [niktalɔp] ADJ day-blind, *Spéc* hemeralopic

Nylon® [nilɔ̃] NM nylon; **des bas (de) N.** nylon stockings, nylons

nymphe [nɛ̃f] NF **1** *Myth* nymph **2** *Entom* nymph, pupa, chrysalis

nymphéa [nɛ̃fea] NM *Bot* nymphea, white waterlily

nymphette [nɛ̃fɛt] NF nymphet

nympho [nɛ̃fo] NF *Fam* (abrév **nymphomane**) nympho

nymphomane [nɛ̃fɔman] ADJ, NF nymphomaniac

nymphomanie [nɛ̃fɔmani] NF nymphomania

O¹, o [o] **NM** *(lettre)* O, o

O² *(abrév* **Ouest)** W

ô [o] **INT** *Litt* O!

OAA [oaa] **NF** *(abrév* **Organisation de l'alimentation et l'agriculture)** FAO

OACI [oasei] **NF** *(abrév* **Organisation de l'aviation civile internationale)** ICAO

OAS [oaɛs] **NF** *Hist abrév* **Organisation de l'armée secrète**

oasien, -ienne [ɔazjɛ̃, -jɛn] **ADJ** oasis
N oasis dweller

oasis [ɔazis] **NF** *(parfois m)* oasis; *Fig* **une o. de calme/bonheur** a haven of peace/happiness VOIR GRAMMAIRE A14

OAT [oate] **NF** *(abrév* **obligation assimilable du Trésor)** = French government bond

obédience [ɔbedjɑ̃s] **NF 1** *(appartenance)* **musulman/catholique de stricte o.** strict or devout Muslim/Catholic; **pays d'o. communiste** countries under Communist rule; **des communistes d'o. trotskiste** Communists of the Trotskyist tendency **2** *Rel* obedience

> Il faut noter que le nom anglais **obedience** signifie le plus souvent **obéissance**.

obéir [ɔbeir] **VI** to obey; **o. à qn** to obey sb; **o. à qn au doigt et à l'œil** to be at sb's beck and call; **mes enfants m'obéissent peu** my children aren't very obedient; **il est obéi de ses enfants** he is obeyed by his children; **un prof pas du tout obéi de ses élèves** a teacher with no control over his pupils; **se faire o.** to command obedience; **o. à un règlement/une loi** to obey a rule/a law, to abide by a rule/a law; **o. à un ordre** to obey an order, to comply with an order; **o. à la force/une contrainte** to yield to force/a constraint; **o. à son instinct** to follow or obey one's instinct; **o. à une impulsion** to act on or follow an impulse; **o. à une envie très forte** to give in to a very strong desire; **o. à sa conscience** to follow the dictates of or to obey one's conscience; **o. à la mode** to follow (the dictates of) fashion; *Naut* **o. à la barre** to answer the helm; *Aviat* **o. aux commandes** to respond to the controls

obéissance [ɔbeisɑ̃s] **NF** obedience (**à** to); **refus d'o.** insubordination; **devoir o. à qn** to owe sb obedience or allegiance; **jurer o. au roi** to swear allegiance to the king

obéissant [ɔbeisɑ̃] **ADJ** obedient

obélisque [ɔbelisk] **NM** *Archit* obelisk

obérer [ɔbere] **VT** (**j'obère; j'obérerai**) *Fml (personne, secteur etc)* to burden with debt; **très** ou **fort obéré** heavily burdened with debt, deeply in debt, debt-ridden

obèse [ɔbɛz] **ADJ** obese
N obese person

obésité [ɔbezite] **NF** obesity

obier [ɔbje] **NM** guelder rose, snowball tree

objecter [ɔbʒɛkte] **VT** *(rétorquer)* to raise as an objection; **je n'ai rien à o. à la proposition** I have no objection to the proposal, I have nothing (to say) against the proposal; **qu'avait-il à o.?** what was his objection?, what did he have against it?; **o. des arguments à une théorie** to put forward arguments against a theory; **o. qch à qn** to put sth forward as an argument to sb; **que puis-je lui o.?** how can I answer him?, what can I say in response?; **tout ce qu'il m'a objecté, j'y avais déjà réfléchi** I'd already given some thought to what arguments he might use; **o. que ...** to object that ...; **on vous objectera que ...** they will object that ...; **on lui objecta sa jeunesse** they took exception to his youth, his youth counted or was held against him

objecteur [ɔbʒɛktœr] **NM o. de conscience** conscientious objector

objectif, -ive [ɔbʒɛktif, -iv] **ADJ** *(impartial)* objective; **observateur o.** neutral or objective observer
NM 1 *(but)* object(ive), aim; *Mil* objective; *(cible)* target; **atteindre son o.** to attain one's object(ive); **o. de chiffre d'affaires** sales target; **o. de vente** sales target or objective; **o. à terme** short-term objective **2** *Phot, Cin, TV* lens; *Phys (d'un microscope)* object glass, objective; **régler l'o.** to adjust the focus; **braquer son o. sur qch** to train one's camera on sth; **fixer l'o.** to look into the camera; **devant l'o.** in front of the camera; **o. fish-eye** fish-eye lens; **o. grand angle** wide-angle lens; **o. normal** normal-angle lens; **o. ultra grand angle** fish-eye lens; **o. zoom** zoom lens; *TV, Cin* **o. à courte focale** short-focus lens; *TV, Cin* **o. à distance focale variable** zoom lens; *TV, Cin* **o. à focale fixe** prime lens

objection [ɔbʒɛksjɔ̃] **NF** objection; **faire** ou **formuler** ou **soulever une o.** to make or raise an objection, to object (**à qch** to sth); **on me fit l'o. que ...** they objected or argued that ...; **voyez-vous une o. à son départ/à ce que je lui en parle?** do you have any objection to his leaving/to my talking to him about it?; *Jur* **o. (votre honneur)!** objection or I object, m'lud or Am your honor!
▸▸**o. de conscience** conscientious objection

objectivement [ɔbʒɛktivmɑ̃] **ADV** objectively

objectiver [ɔbʒɛktive] **VT** to objectivize

objectivisme [ɔbʒɛktivism] **NM** objectivism

objectivité [ɔbʒɛktivite] **NF** objectivity, objectiveness

objet [ɔbʒɛ] **NM 1** *(chose)* object, thing; **o. de luxe** luxury article or item; **o. de première nécessité** essential or basic item; **objets trouvés** lost-property office, *Am* lost and found
2 *Gram* object; **o. direct/indirect** direct/indirect object SEE GRAMMAR A78–9; B52–3
3 *Phil* object; **femme-o.** woman as an object

4 *(sujet) (d'une dispute, d'un colloque)* subject; *(d'une conversation)* topic, subject; **l'o. du litige** the matter at issue; **o. d'un contrat** subject matter of a contract; **quel est l'o. de l'anthropologie?** what does anthropology cover?; **les enfants sont l'o. de nombreux soins** children receive a lot of care; **votre requête sera l'o. de toute notre attention** your request will receive our full attention; **cela fera l'o. de ma conférence/d'une recherche approfondie** this will be the subject of my lecture/of a thorough investigation; **o. de pitié/haine** object of pity/hatred

5 *(but) (d'une action)* object, aim, purpose; **l'o. de ma visite** the purpose of my visit; **remplir son o.** to achieve or fulfil its object or aim or purpose; **cet appareil/cette nouvelle mesure remplit tout à fait son o.** the device/the new measure does exactly what it's supposed to; **sans o.** *(remarque, réclamation, préoccupation)* unjustified

6 *Ordinat* object
▸▸**o. d'art** objet d'art; **objets de valeur** valuable items, valuables; **aucun o. de valeur n'a disparu** nothing valuable was taken; **ne laissez pas d'o. de valeur dans votre voiture** don't leave valuables in your car; *Astron* **o. volant non identifié** unidentified flying object

objurgation [ɔbʒyrgasjɔ̃] **NF** objurgation

oblat, -ate [ɔbla, -at] **N** *Rel* oblate

oblation [ɔblasjɔ̃] **NF** *Rel* oblation, offering

obligataire [ɔbligatɛr] *Fin* **N** bondholder, debenture holder
NM *(obligation)* debenture bond
ADJ **emprunt/marché o.** debenture or bond loan/market

obligation [ɔbligasjɔ̃] **NF 1** *(contrainte, devoir)* obligation; **tu viens si tu veux, mais ce n'est pas une o.** you can come if you want, but you're not obliged to or you don't have to; **avoir l'o. de faire qch** to be under an obligation to do sth, to be obliged to do sth; **être dans l'o. de faire qch** to be obliged to do sth; **je me sens dans l'o. de vous avertir** I feel obliged to warn you; **je me vois dans l'o. de me taire** I find myself obliged to keep silent; **sans o. d'achat** no purchase necessary; **sans o. de votre part** without any obligation (on your part); **tu manques à toutes tes obligations** you're not facing up to any of your responsibilities; *Fin* **honorer ses obligations** to honour or meet one's obligations; **remplir ses obligations** to meet one's obligations; **avoir/se sentir des obligations envers qn** to be/feel under an obligation to sb; **avoir des obligations (familiales)** to have (family) obligations; **obligations militaires** liability to military service; **ayant rempli ses obligations militaires** having completed one's military service; **o. contractuelle** contractual obligation SEE GRAMMAR A60–1; B39

2 *Jur (acte)* recognizance, bond; **o. alimen-**

taire maintenance order; **contracter une o. irrévocable** to enter into a binding agreement

3 *Fin* bond, debenture; **obligations** bonds, loan stock *or* notes; **o. assimilable du Trésor** = French government bond; **o. cautionnée** secured bond; **o. convertible** *ou* **échangeable** convertible bond; **o. garantie** guaranteed bond; **o. hypothécaire** mortgage bond; **o. indexée** index-linked bond; **o. à intérêt variable** floating rate bond; **o. nominative** registered bond; **o. au porteur** bearer bond; **o. à revenu fixe** fixed rate bond; **o. à revenu variable** floating rate bond; **o. à taux progressif** step-up bond; **o. à taux variable** variable-income bond, floating-rate bond; **o. transférable, o. transmissible** transferable bond

obligatoire [ɔbligatwar] ADJ obligatory, compulsory, mandatory; **école laïque, gratuite et o.** free, compulsory and non-religious education; **l'uniforme est o.** uniform is compulsory *or* obligatory *or* must be worn; *Fam* **c'était o.** *(c'était forcé)* it had to happen, it was bound to happen, it was inevitable

obligatoirement [ɔbligatwarmɑ̃] ADV **vous devez o. montrer votre passeport** you are required to show your passport; *Fam* **elle lui demandera o. des comptes sur ce qui s'est passé** she's bound to ask him for an explanation of what happened; **est-ce qu'il faut porter une robe habillée? – pas o.** do you have to wear an evening dress? – not necessarily

obligé, -ée [ɔbliʒe] ADJ **1** *(contraint)* obliged, compelled (**de faire qch** to do sth); **tu y es allé? – (bien) o.!** did you go? – I had to! **2** *(indispensable)* necessary; **c'est un passage o.** it's something that has to be done **3** *Fam (inévitable)* inevitable; **c'est o.** it's inevitable; **c'est o. qu'il rate son examen** he's bound to fail his exam **4** *Fml (reconnaissant)* obliged, grateful (**de** for); **je vous serais très o. de …** *(dans une lettre)* I would be most obliged *or* grateful (to you) if you would … **5** *Mus* **récitatif o.** recitative ob(b)ligato

N person under an obligation; *Jur* obligee; *Vieilli* **je suis votre o.** I am in your debt

obligeamment [ɔbliʒamɑ̃] ADV obligingly; **il m'a o. aidé à porter ma valise** he obligingly helped me to carry my suitcase

obligeance [ɔbliʒɑ̃s] NF obligingness; **ayez** *ou* **veuillez avoir l'o. de fermer la porte** would you oblige me by closing the door, would you be so kind as to close the door

obligeant [ɔbliʒɑ̃] ADJ obliging, helpful, kind

obliger [ɔbliʒe] (**j'obligeai(s); n. obligeons**) VT **1** *(contraindre)* **o. qn à faire qch** *(d'une personne)* to compel *or* force sb to do sth, to make sb do sth; *(d'une situation etc)* to force *or* oblige sb to do sth; **ce travail m'oblige à me lever à cinq heures tous les matins** this job means I have to get up at five o'clock every morning; **ne m'oblige pas à me mettre en colère** don't make me lose my temper; **personne ne t'oblige à aller travailler à l'étranger** nobody's forcing you to go and work abroad; **son état de santé l'oblige à de longs moments de repos** the state of his health means he has to rest for long periods; **le temps nous oblige à rester enfermés** the weather is keeping us indoors; **ma signature m'y oblige** my signature binds me *or* holds me to it; **la loi m'y oblige** I'm required to by law, the law requires me to; **votre devoir/honneur vous y oblige** you are duty-/honour-bound to do it; **être obligé de faire qch** to be obliged *or* compelled to do sth, to have to do sth; **ne te sens pas obligé de le faire** don't feel obliged *or* compelled to do

it, don't feel you have to do it; **ne te crois pas obligé de tout manger** don't feel you have to eat everything; **rien ne t'y oblige** you don't have to, nobody's forcing you **2** *Fml (rendre service à)* **o. qn** to oblige sb; **vous m'obligeriez en fermant la porte** I'd be obliged if you would close the door, you would oblige me by closing the door

VPR **s'obliger s'o. à faire qch** *(ne pas manquer de)* to make a point of doing sth; *(se forcer à)* to force oneself to do sth

oblique [ɔblik] ADJ *(ligne)* oblique; *(rayon)* slanting, oblique; *(regard)* sideways *or* sidelong glance; **manœuvre o.** *(malhonnête)* underhand move; *Gram* **cas o.** oblique case

NM *Anat* oblique muscle

NF oblique (line); *Typ* slash; **en o.** diagonally; **stationner en o.** to angle-park

obliquement [ɔblikmɑ̃] ADV obliquely, slantwise; **regarder qn o.** to look sideways *or* sidelong at sb

obliquer [ɔblike] VI **obliquez à gauche/à droite!** bear left/right!

obliquité [ɔblikɥite] NF obliqueness

oblitérateur, -trice [ɔbliteratœr, -tris] ADJ *Tech* cancelling

NM *(pour timbres)* franker

oblitération [ɔbliterasjɔ̃] NF **1** *Méd* obstruction **2** *(de timbres)* cancellation, cancelling; **(cachet d')o.** postmark

oblitérer [ɔblitere] (**j'oblitère, n. oblitérons**) **j'oblitérerai**) VT **1** *(timbre)* to cancel, to frank; **timbre oblitéré** used stamp; **la lettre n'a pas été oblitérée** the letter hasn't been postmarked **2** *Méd (obstruer)* to obstruct **3** *Litt Fig (souvenirs, le passé etc)* to obliterate

VPR **s'oblitérer** *Litt* **peu à peu le passé s'oblitérait dans sa mémoire** little by little, every trace of the past disappeared from his memory

oblong, -ongue [ɔblɔ̃, -ɔ̃g] ADJ **1** oblong; **un coquillage de forme oblongue** an oblong shell **2** *Typ* **format o.** oblong format

obnubiler [ɔbnybile] VT *(obséder)* to obsess; **elle est obnubilée par l'idée que …** she is obsessed by the idea that …

obole [ɔbɔl] NF **1** *(argent)* small offering; *(dans la Bible)* widow's mite; **apporter** *ou* **verser son o. (à qch)** to make a contribution (to sth); *esp Litt* **il ne m'a pas fait l'o. d'un sourire** he didn't deign to smile at me **2** *Hist (monnaie grecque)* obol(us); *(monnaie française)* obole

OBSA [ɔbsa] NF *Fin (abrév* **obligation avec bon de souscription d'actions)** bond with share warrant attached

obscène [ɔpsɛn] ADJ *(langage, livre)* obscene; *(geste)* obscene, lewd

obscénité [ɔpsenite] NF *(d'un langage, d'un livre)* obscenity, smuttiness; *(d'un geste)* obscenity, lewdness; **dire des obscénités** to make obscene remarks

obscur [ɔpskyr] ADJ **1** *(sombre)* *(nuit, chambre)* dark **2** *(inexplicable, confus)* obscure **3** *(vague)* *(pressentiment)* vague, dim; *(impression)* vague **4** *(inconnu)* *(écrivain, peintre etc)* obscure; *(humble)* *(naissance)* lowly, humble

obscurantisme [ɔpskyrɑ̃tism] NM obscurantism

obscurantiste [ɔpskyrɑ̃tist] ADJ, N obscurantist

obscurcir [ɔpskyrsir] VT **1** *(assombrir)* *(lumière)* to obscure; *(chambre, ciel)* to darken; **yeux obscurcis par les larmes** eyes misty *or* dim with tears **2** *(rendre confus)* **il avait le jugement/les idées obscurci(es) par l'alcool/la douleur** his judgment/thinking was clouded by alcohol/pain

VPR **s'obscurcir** *(d'une pièce, du paysage)* to darken, to grow dark; *(du ciel)* to darken, to grow dark, to cloud over; *(de l'esprit, de la*

vue) to grow dim; **son regard s'obscurcit** his face clouded over *or* darkened

obscurcissement [ɔpskyrsismɑ̃] NM *(du sens)* obscuring; *(d'une chambre, du ciel)* darkening; *(de l'esprit, de la vue)* dimming

obscurément [ɔpskyremɑ̃] ADV obscurely, dimly; *(sentir)* vaguely; **j'ai o. l'impression que …** I've a vague impression that …; **mourir o.** to die in obscurity

obscurité [ɔpskyrite] NF **1** *(noirceur)* darkness; **dans l'o.** in the dark; **j'ai peur dans l'o.** I'm scared in the dark; **elle doit rester dans l'o.** she has to stay in darkness *or* in a darkened room; **soudain, l'o. se fit** everything suddenly went dark **2** *(caractère complexe, confusion)* obscurity; **la solution de cette énigme restera à jamais dans l'o.** the answer to this enigma will for ever remain shrouded in obscurity **3** *(anonymat)* obscurity; **vivre dans l'o.** to live in obscurity; **sortir de l'o.** to emerge from obscurity, to become known

obsédant [ɔpsedɑ̃] ADJ *(souvenir, musique)* haunting; *(pensée)* obsessive

obsédé, -ée [ɔpsede] N fanatic; **un o. du cinéma/du rangement** a film/tidiness fanatic *or* freak; **un o. (sexuel)** a sex maniac

obséder [ɔpsede] VT (**j'obsède; j'obséderai**) *(d'une pensée, d'un souvenir)* to obsess; **son souvenir m'obsède** I'm obsessed by his memory; **être obsédé par qch** to be obsessed by *or* with sth; **elle est obsédée par ses enfants** she is obsessed with her children; **c'est un problème, mais ne te laisse pas o.** it's a problem, but don't become obsessed by it *or* don't let it become an obsession

obsèques [ɔpsɛk] NFPL funeral; **avoir droit à des o. nationales** to be given a state funeral; **les o. se feront dans la plus stricte intimité** the funeral will be strictly private

obséquieusement [ɔpsekjøzmɑ̃] ADV obsequiously

obséquieux, -ieuse [ɔpsekjø, -jøz] ADJ obsequious

obséquiosité [ɔpsekjozite] NF obsequiousness

observable [ɔpsɛrvabl] ADJ observable; **un fait o. uniquement dans certaines couches de la population** a phenomenon that can be observed only in certain segments of the population

observance [ɔpsɛrvɑ̃s] NF *(d'un règlement)* observance; **communiste de stricte o.** hardline communist; **un bénédictin d'ancienne o.** a Benedictine of the old school

observateur, -trice [ɔpsɛrvatœr, -tris] N **1** *(d'événements, d'un phénomène, des mouvements de l'ennemi etc)* observer; *Mil (qui règle les tirs)* spotter; **o. des Nations unies** United Nations observer **2** *(des règlements, des lois)* observer, keeper

ADJ observant

observation [ɔpsɛrvasjɔ̃] NF **1** *(surveillance)* observation; **être en o.** to be under observation; **mettre/(main)tenir qn en o.** to put/keep sb under observation; **malade en o.** patient under observation; **poste d'o.** observation *or* lookout post; **avion d'o.** spotter plane; **observations par satellite** satellite observations; **il a l'esprit d'o.** he is very observant **2** *(remarque)* observation, remark, comment; *(critique)* remark; **faire des observations** to make observations *or* remarks *or* comments; *(critiques)* to make *or* pass remarks; **je peux faire une petite o.?** can I make one tiny remark?; **si je puis me permettre une o.** if I may make an observation *or* say something; **il faisait toujours des observations à ses élèves** he was always finding fault with his pupils; **à la moindre o. de ma part, elle se met en colère** the slightest remark from me and she gets angry, she gets angry if I make the slightest remark **3** *(respect) (des lois)* observance, keeping **4** *(étude) (des étoiles, des insectes, des oiseaux etc)* observation

observatoire [ɔpsɛrvatwar] NM *Astron* observatory; *Mil* observation post

observer [ɔpsɛrve] VT **1** *(surveiller, regarder) (personne, chose)* to watch, to observe; **on nous observe** we are being watched; **se sentir observé** to feel one is being watched; **elle adore o. les gens dans le métro** she loves watching people *or* she loves to peoplewatch in the metro **2** *(remarquer)* to notice; **nous observons un retour à …** we are seeing *or* witnessing a return to …; **faire o. qch à qn** to draw sb's attention to sth, to point sth out to sb; **faire o. à qn que …** to point out to sb that …; **je vous ferai o. que …** I must point out to you that … **3** *(suivre, respecter) (règlements, lois etc)* to observe, to keep (to), to comply with; *(promesse)* to keep; **o. le silence** to keep silent; **o. une minute de silence** to observe a minute's silence; **o. la loi** to observe the law; **faire o. la loi** to enforce (obedience to) the law; **o. un contrat** to comply with a contract **4** *(étudier) (les étoiles, les insectes, les peuplades etc)* to observe; *(un angle)* to take, to read; **il passait des heures à o. les oiseaux** he spent hours bird-watching; *Naut* **o. le soleil** to take the sun, to take a sight at the sun
VPR **s'observer 1** *(d'un phénomène, d'une attitude)* to be seen; **ce phénomène ne s'observe que dans ce pays tropicaux** this phenomenon can be seen only in tropical countries **2** *(de deux personnes)* to watch *or* observe each other **3** *(d'une personne)* to keep a check on oneself

obsession [ɔpsɛsjɔ̃] NF obsession; **mais c'est une o. ou de l'o.!** you're/he's/*etc* obsessed (with the idea)!; **il ne faudrait pas en faire une o.,** il ne faudrait pas que cela devienne de l'o.** it shouldn't become an obsession; **avoir l'o. de qch** to be obsessed with sth

obsessionnel, -elle [ɔpsɛsjɔnɛl] *Psy* ADJ obsessional; **névrose obsessionnelle** obsessional neurosis
N **c'est un o.** he's obsessive, he has *or* is an obsessive personality

obsidienne [ɔpsidjɛn] NF *Minér* obsidian

obsolescence [ɔpsɔlɛsɑ̃s] NF obsolescence; **o. calculée** *ou* **planifiée** built-in *or* planned obsolescence

obsolescent [ɔpsɔlɛsɑ̃] ADJ obsolescent

obsolète [ɔpsɔlɛt] ADJ obsolete; **un mot devenu o.** a word that has become obsolete, an obsolete word

obstacle [ɔpstakl] NM obstacle; *Courses de chevaux* fence, jump; *Sport* hurdle; *Fig* obstacle, hindrance, impediment; **il continua sa route/il a atteint son but sans rencontrer d'o.** he continued on his way/he achieved his aim without meeting any obstacles; **se heurter à un o.** to come up against an obstacle; **venir à bout d'un o.** to overcome an obstacle; **faire o. à qch** to be an obstacle to sth, to stand in the way of sth; **plus rien ne faisait o. à mon départ** *ou* **à ce que je parte** there was no longer any reason for me not to go; **je n'y vois pas d'o.** I don't see any difficulty *or* problem (about it); **course d'obstacles** *Courses de chevaux* steeplechase; *Sport* hurdle race

obstétrical, -ale, -aux, -ales [ɔpstetrikal, -o] ADJ obstetric

obstétricien, -ienne [ɔpstetrisjɛ̃, -jɛn] N obstetrician

obstétrique [ɔpstetrik] NF obstetrics

obstination [ɔpstinasjɔ̃] NF obstinacy, stubbornness, *Fam Péj* pigheadedness

obstiné [ɔpstine] ADJ *(personne, caractère)* obstinate, stubborn, *Fam Péj* pigheaded; *(résistance)* stubborn, dogged; *(travail)* determined, dogged

obstinément [ɔpstinemɑ̃] ADV obstinately, stubbornly; *(travailler, avancer)* determinedly, doggedly; *(répondre)* stubbornly

obstiner (s') [ɔpstine] VPR to persist; **obstine-toi!** be persistent!, don't give up!; **s'o. à faire qch** *(continuer)* to persist in doing sth; *(vouloir)* to be set *or Fml* bent on doing sth; **elle s'obstine sur cette question** she won't let go, she won't give up, *Fam* she's like a dog with a bone; **s'o. dans son silence** to remain stubbornly *or* obstinately silent; **s'o. dans ses idées/convictions** to cling stubbornly *or* doggedly to one's ideas/convictions

obstruction [ɔpstryksjɔ̃] NF *(d'une rue, d'un passage)* blocking, obstruction; *(d'un égout)* blocking; *Méd* **o. intestinale** obstruction of the bowels; **faire de l'o.** *Pol* to be obstructive, to use obstructive tactics; *Sport* to obstruct

obstructionnisme [ɔpstryksjɔnism] NM *Pol* obstructionism

obstructionniste [ɔpstryksjɔnist] ADJ, N *Pol* obstructionist

obstruer [ɔpstrye] VT *(rue, passage)* to block, to obstruct; *(tuyau)* to block; **il a des artères obstruées** he has blocked arteries; **le tuyau est obstrué par des cheveux** the pipe is clogged up with hair

obtempérer [ɔptɑ̃pere] VI (**j'obtempère,** n. **obtempérons;** j'**obtempérerai**) **o. à** *(ordre, assignation)* to obey, to comply with; *Jur* **refus d'o.** obstruction

obtenir [ɔptənir] *(conj like* **tenir***)* VT *(biens, permission, réponse etc)* to obtain, to get; *(promesse)* to obtain, to secure, to get; *(le consentement de qn)* to obtain, to gain, to get; *(résultat)* to obtain, to achieve, to get; **o. la libération des otages** to obtain the release of the hostages; **si on mélange ces deux substances, qu'obtient-on?** what do you get if you mix these two substances?; **si on ajoute les deux, on obtient 500** if you add the two together, you get 500; **j'ai travaillé sur ce dossier pendant trois mois et qu'ai-je obtenu? – rien!** I've worked on this case for three months and what have I got to show for it *or* what have I achieved? – nothing!; **o. qch de qn** to obtain *or* get sth from sb; **n'espère plus rien o. de moi** don't expect (to get) anything else from me; **c'est lui qui m'a fait o. ces renseignements** he's the one who got (hold of) *or* obtained the information for me; **j'ai obtenu de le voir** I obtained *or* got permission to see him; **j'ai obtenu d'elle qu'elle vérifie tout** I got her to agree to check everything; **j'ai obtenu qu'elle revienne** I arranged for her to come back
VPR **s'obtenir où cela s'obtient-il?** where can you get it?

obtention [ɔptɑ̃sjɔ̃] NF obtaining; **depuis l'o. de son diplôme** since obtaining his diploma, since he got his diploma; **ajoutez du blanc jusqu'à o. de la couleur désirée** add white until the desired colour is obtained; **pour l'o. de qch** (in order) to obtain sth; **o. d'un prêt** obtaining of a loan

obturateur, -trice [ɔptyratœr, -tris] ADJ closing; *Anat (membrane, muscle)* obturator
NM **1** *Anat, Chir (d'une ouverture)* obturator **2** *(clapet)* shutter, stop valve; *Aut* throttle; *Phot* shutter; **armer/déclencher l'o.** to set/to release the shutter; *Phot* **o. de plaque** focal-plane shutter; *Phot* **o. au diaphragme** diaphragm shutter; *Aut* **o. de bloc** core plug; *Aut* **o. papillon** throttle valve

obturation [ɔptyrasjɔ̃] NF *(d'un tuyau, d'une ouverture)* sealing; *(d'une dent)* filling

obturer [ɔptyre] VT *(tuyau, ouverture)* to seal; *(dent)* to fill

obtus [ɔpty] ADJ **1** *(angle)* obtuse **2** *(personne)* obtuse, dim-witted

obus [ɔby, oby] NM *Mil* shell; **o. à balles** *ou* à **mitraille** shrapnel (shell); **o. de mortier** mortar shell; **o. traçant** tracer shell

obusier [ɔbyzje] NM *Mil* howitzer

obvier [ɔbvje] VI *(impf, pr sub* n. **obviions,** v. **obviiez)** *Litt* **o. à qch** to obviate sth; **o. à un accident** to take precautions *or* to guard against an accident

OC [ose] NFPL *Radio (abrév* **ondes courtes)** SW

oc [ɔk] ADV *Hist, Ling* **langue d'oc** langue d'oc *(language of southern France)*

ocarina [ɔkarina] NM *Mus* ocarina

occase [ɔkaz] NF *Fam* **1** *(affaire)* bargain **2** *(article de seconde main)* second-hand item; **elle est neuve, ta voiture? – non, c'est une o.** is your car new? – no, it's second-hand; **je cherche une o. pas trop chère** I'm looking for a second-hand one, not too expensive; **acheter qch d'o.** to buy sth second-hand

occasion [ɔkazjɔ̃] NF **1** *(circonstance favorable)* opportunity, chance; *(moment)* occasion; **saisir l'o.** to take *or* seize the opportunity; *Fam* **sauter sur l'o.** to jump at the chance *or* the opportunity; *Fam* **c'est l'o. ou jamais** it's now or never; *Fam* **c'est l'o. ou jamais de le faire** now's the time to do it; *Fam* **c'était l'o. ou jamais de changer de boulot!** if ever there was a time to change jobs, it was then!; **avoir l'o. de faire qch** to have the opportunity *or* chance of doing *or* to do sth; **tout le monde n'a pas l'o. de faire ça** not everybody gets the chance *or* opportunity to do that; **je n'ai jamais eu l'o. de le regretter** I've never had cause *or* reason to regret it, I've never had any cause for regret; **donner à qn l'o. de faire qch** to give sb the *or* an opportunity *or* a *or* the chance to do sth; **si l'o. se présente** if you get the chance, if the opportunity arises, *Fml* should the opportunity arise; **laisser passer l'o.** to let the opportunity slip (by); **profiter de l'o. pour faire qch** to take the opportunity to do sth; *Iron* **tu as encore perdu l'o. de te taire** why can't you keep your mouth shut?; *Iron* **il ne perd jamais une o. d'être désagréable/de se faire remarquer** he never misses an opportunity to be unpleasant/to get himself noticed; **attendre l'o.** to bide one's time; **à l'o.** when the opportunity presents itself; **voir qn à l'o.** to see sb occasionally *or* from time to time; **venez boire un coup à l'o.** come for a drink when you get a *or* the chance; **elle sait être très virulente à l'o.** she can be very harsh on occasions; **il faudra que je m'en assure, à l'o.** I'll have to check it myself, when I get the chance; **à la première o.** at the first *or* earliest opportunity; **je m'en débarrasserai à la premiere o.** I'll get rid of it the first chance I get; **à** *ou* **en plusieurs occasions** on several occasions; **s'habiller pour l'o.** to dress for the occasion; **on a bu du champagne pour l'o.** we drank champagne to celebrate, we drank champagne to mark the occasion; **à l'o. de son mariage** on the occasion of his marriage; **je l'ai rencontré à l'o. d'un concert** I met him at a concert; **je m'en suis rendu compte à l'o. d'une visite de routine** I realized it during a routine visit; **à l'o. de sa venue** upon his arrival; **en pareille o.** in circumstances like these, in similar circumstances; **à cette o.** on that occasion; **dans/pour les grandes occasions** on/for great occasions; *Prov* **l'o. fait le larron** opportunity makes the thief; **être l'o. de qch** to be the occasion of sth; **ce sera l'o. de faire la fête** that will be a good excuse for a party; *Fin* **o. de profit** profit opportunity
2 *(affaire)* bargain; **le marché de l'o.** the

second-hand market; **faire le neuf et l'o.** to sell new and second-hand goods; **marchandises/voitures/livres/meubles d'o.** second-hand goods/cars/books/furniture; **elle est neuve, ta voiture? – non, c'est une o.** is your car new? – no, it's secondhand; **je l'ai acheté d'o.** I bought it secondhand; **ça, c'est une o.!** it's a bargain!

occasionnel, -elle [ɔkazjɔnɛl] ADJ occasional; *(rencontre)* chance; *(aide)* casual; **je vais parfois au restaurant mais cela reste très o.** I sometimes go to the restaurant but only very occasionally; **cause occasionnelle d'une révolte** event that triggered or *Fml* occasioned a revolt

occasionnellement [ɔkazjɔnɛlmã] ADV occasionally

occasionner [ɔkazjɔne] VT to cause, to give rise to, *Fml* to occasion; **un bébé occasionne de nombreux frais** having a baby is a costly business

occident [ɔksidã] NM west, *Fml* occident; *Pol* **l'O.** the West

occidental, -ale, -aux, -ales [ɔksidãtal, -o] ADJ west, western; **côte occidentale** west coast; **l'Europe occidentale** Western Europe; **les Indes occidentales** the West Indies N Westerner, *Fml* Occidental

occidentalisation [ɔksidãtalizasjɔ̃] NF westernization

occidentaliser [ɔksidãtalize] VT to westernize
VPR **s'occidentaliser** to become westernized

occipital, -ale, -aux, -ales [ɔksipital, -o] *Anat* ADJ occipital
NM occipital (bone)

occiput [ɔksipyt] NM *Anat* occiput

occire [ɔksir] VT (*used only in inf & pp* occis) *Arch, Hum* to slay; **se faire o.** to be slain

occitan [ɔksitã] ADJ of the langue d'oc
NM *(langue)* langue d'oc *(dialect spoken in parts of southern France)*

occlusif, -ive [ɔklysif, -iv] *Ling* ADJ occlusive
NF **occlusive** occlusive consonant, stop

occlusion [ɔklyzjɔ̃] NF occlusion; *Méd* **o. intestinale** intestinal obstruction, *Spéc* ileus

occultation [ɔkyltasjɔ̃] NF *Astron* occultation; *Fig* concealment

occulte [ɔkylt] ADJ *(surnatural)* occult; *(secret)* *(comptabilité)* secret; *(cause)* hidden; *(rôle)* clandestine, covert; **les sciences occultes** the occult, the occult sciences

occulter [ɔkylte] VT *Astron* to occult; *(signal lumineux)* to block out, *Spéc* to occult; *Fig (informations, intentions etc)* to conceal

occultisme [ɔkyltism] NM occultism

occupant, -ante [ɔkypã, -ãt] ADJ *(locataire, armée)* occupying
N *(d'une maison)* occupier, occupant; *(d'un poste)* occupant; *Jur* **premier o.** occupant; *Mil* **l'o.** the occupying forces

occupation [ɔkypasjɔ̃] NF 1 *(fait d'être ou de rester quelque part)* occupancy, occupation; *(fait de posséder ou d'entrer en possession) (d'une maison)* possession; *Mil (d'un territoire conquis)* occupation; **armée d'o.** army of occupation; *Hist* **l'O.** the Occupation; **grève avec o. des lieux** sit-down strike, sit-in; **manifestation estudiantine avec o. des locaux** student sit-in; **o. des chambres/des lits** *(dans un hôtel)* room/bed occupancy; **o. double** double occupancy; **o. maximale** capacity occupancy 2 *(besogne, ouvrage)* occupation; **avoir de l'o.** to be busy, to have things to do; **être sans o., ne pas avoir d'o.** to have nothing to do; **j'ai bien assez d'occupations comme cela!** I've got enough to do or enough on my plate already!; **vaquer à ses**

occupations to go about one's business; *Admin* **o. principale** main occupation

occupé [ɔkype] ADJ 1 *(personne) (travaillant)* busy; *(avec un autre client)* busy, engaged; **o. aux préparatifs du départ** busy with the preparations for departure, busy getting ready to leave; **o. à relire le texte** busy rereading the text; **c'est un homme fort o.** he's a very busy man; **elle a des journées/semaines très occupées en ce moment** her days/weeks are very full at present 2 *(place)* taken; *Tél (ligne)* engaged, *Am* busy; *(sur la porte des toilettes)* engaged; *Ordinat (imprimante)* busy; **en territoire o.** in occupied territory

occuper [ɔkype] VT 1 *(maison)* to occupy; *(place)* to take up, to occupy; **ce lit occupe beaucoup trop de place** this bed takes up or occupies far too much room; **les livres d'art occupent trois étagères de la bibliothèque** the art books take up or occupy or fill three shelves of the bookcase; **le magasin n'occupe que le rez-de-chaussée** the shop takes up or occupies only the ground floor
2 *Mil etc (par la force) (ville, bâtiment)* to occupy; **les ouvriers ont décidé d'o. l'usine** the workers have decided to occupy the factory; **o. le terrain** *Mil* to hold the field; *Com* to make one's presence felt in the market
3 *(remplir) (temps)* to fill, to occupy; **faire qch pour o. le temps** to do sth to fill or occupy the time; **o. ses loisirs** to fill or occupy one's free time; **les enfants occupent la majeure partie de mon temps** the children take up the greater part of my time; **o. sa journée à faire qch** to spend one's day doing sth
4 *(poste etc)* to have, to hold
5 **o. qn** *(employer)* to employ sb; *(donner une activité à)* to keep sb busy or occupied, to give sb something to do, to occupy sb; **la lecture de ce livre m'a occupé toute la soirée** reading this book took up my entire evening or kept me busy all evening; **ces problèmes m'ont occupé pendant un certain temps** these problems have kept me busy or kept me occupied or given me something to think about for some time; **fais un peu de ménage, ça occupe!** ou **ça t'occupera!** do a bit of housework, that'll pass or fill the time!
VPR **s'occuper 1** to keep oneself busy or occupied; **s'o. à faire qch** to be busy doing sth, to be occupied in doing sth; **s'o. en lisant** to spend one's time reading; **on a toujours de quoi s'o.** there's always something to keep you busy or occupied, there's always something that needs doing; **je trouverai bien de quoi m'o. en attendant** I'll find something to keep me busy or to occupy myself with while I wait
2 **s'o. de** *(être intéressé par) (photographie, littérature etc)* to be interested in; *(se charger de) (quelque chose)* to deal with, to take care of, to attend to; *(personnes, enfants)* to take care of, to look after; **s'o. de qch** to see about doing sth; **cette maison son s'occupe surtout d'argenterie** this firm specializes in silverware; **nous allons maintenant nous o. du bilan** we will now turn (our attention) to the balance sheet; **ce n'est pas la peine de vous o. de cela pour l'instant** it's not worth worrying or bothering about that at the moment; **il s'occupe de trop de choses** he takes on too much, he has too many irons in the fire; **je m'en occuperai** I'll see to it, I'll deal with it, I'll take care of it; *Fam* **occupe-toi de ce qui te regarde** ou **de tes affaires** ou **de tes oignons!** mind your own business!; **de quoi tu t'occupes?** what business is it of yours?, what's it got to do with you?; *Fam* **t'occupe (pas)!** keep your nose out!, mind your own business!; *Iron* **je vais m'o. de lui** I'll take care of him; *Com* **est-ce qu'on s'occupe de**

vous? are you being attended to or being served?

occurrence [ɔkyrãs] NF 1 *(circonstance)* **en l'o.** in this case, as it happens/happened; **et en l'o., il s'agissait d'une ville romaine** and as it happened or as it turned out, it was a Roman town; **mais en l'o., tu as tort** but in this case or but this time or but as it happens, you're wrong 2 *Ling (apparition)* occurrence

OCDE [osede] NF *(abrév* Organisation de coopération et de développement économique*)* OECD

océan [ɔseã] NM ocean; **l'o. Atlantique** the Atlantic (Ocean); **l'o. Indien** the Indian Ocean; **l'o. Pacifique** the Pacific (Ocean); **l'o. Antarctique** ou **Austral** the Antarctic Ocean; **l'o. Arctique** the Arctic Ocean; **d'un o. à l'autre** from coast to coast; *Fig* **un o. de fleurs/couleurs** a sea of flowers/colour

océane [ɔsean] ADJ F 1 *Culin (salade, sauce)* seafood 2 *Litt (de l'Océan)* **une brise o.** a sea breeze
NF **l'O.** *(autoroute)* = the Paris-Nantes motorway

Océanie [ɔseani] NF Oceania

océanien, -ienne [ɔseanjɛ̃, -jɛn] ADJ Oceanian
N **O.** Oceanian; *(de Polynésie, Mélanésie)* South Sea Islander

océanique [ɔseanik] ADJ *(courant, climat)* ocean, oceanic

océanographe [ɔseanɔgraf] N oceanographer

océanographie [ɔseanɔgrafi] NF oceanography

océanographique [ɔseanɔgrafik] ADJ oceanographic(al)

océanologie [ɔseanɔlɔʒi] NF oceanology

ocelle [ɔsɛl] NM *Zool (d'un insecte)* simple eye, *Spéc* ocellus; *(d'une plume, de l'aile d'un insecte)* eye, *Spéc* ocellus

ocelot [ɔslo] NM ocelot

ocre [ɔkr] NF, ADJ INV ochre, *Am* ocher

ocré [ɔkre] ADJ ochre(-coloured), *Am* ocher(-colored)

ocreux, -euse [ɔkrø, -øz] ADJ ochreous

octaèdre [ɔktaɛdr] ADJ octahedral
NM octahedron

octaédrique [ɔktaedrik] ADJ octahedral

octal, -ale, -aux, -ales [ɔktal, -o] ADJ *Ordinat* octal

octane [ɔktan] NM *Chimie* octane; **essence à haut indice d'o.** high-octane petrol or *Am* gasoline

octante [ɔktãt] ADJ INV *Région* eighty

octave [ɔktav] NF octave; **jouer à l'o.** *(plus haut)* to play an octave higher; *(plus bas)* to play an octave lower

octet [ɔktɛ] NM *Ordinat* (eight-bit) byte; **milliard d'octets** gigabyte; **o. de contrôle** check byte

octobre [ɔktɔbr] NM October; **en o.** in October; **au mois d'o.** in (the month of) October; **le premier o.** (on) October the first, (on) the first of October, *Am* (on) October first SEE GRAMMAR A81–2; B60–2

octogénaire [ɔktɔʒenɛr] ADJ, N octogenarian

octogonal, -ale, -aux, -ales [ɔktɔgɔnal, -o] ADJ octagonal

octogone [ɔktɔgon] NM octagon

octopode [ɔktɔpɔd] ADJ, NM octopod

octosyllabe [ɔktɔsilab] ADJ octosyllabic
NM octosyllable

octosyllabique [ɔktɔsilabik] ADJ octosyllabic

octroi [ɔktrwa] NM 1 *(concession) (d'une faveur)* concession, granting; *Com* **o. de licence** licensing 2 *Hist (impôt)* town dues, city toll; *(bureau)* tollhouse

octroyer [ɔktrwaje] (**j'octroie, n. octroyons; j'octroierai**) VT **o. qch à qn** to grant or concede sth to sb; **o. du temps à qn** to allow sb time; **o. une permission à qn** to give or grant sb leave; **o. sa grâce à un condamné a mort** to reprieve a condemned man; **o. des faveurs à qn** to bestow favours on sb; **o. un prêt** to grant a loan
VPR **s'octroyer il s'est octroyé un jour de vacances supplémentaire** he gave himself or awarded himself an extra day's holiday

octuor [ɔktɥɔr] NM Mus octet

octuple [ɔktypl] ADJ octuple; (montant) eightfold
NM octuple

oculaire [ɔkylɛr] ADJ 1 (visuel) **témoin o.** eyewitness 2 (de l'œil) **hygiène o.** eye care, care of the eyes; **globe o.** eyeball
NM Opt eyepiece, Am ocular; Phot viewfinder; **o. de visée** (d'une caméra) eyepiece

oculiste [ɔkylist] N eye specialist, ophthalmologist

odalisque [ɔdalisk] NF odalisque, odalisk

ode [ɔd] NF ode

odeur [ɔdœr] NF (généralement désagréable) smell, odour; (agréable) scent, smell; **il a une drôle d'o., ce poisson** this fish has a funny smell or smells funny; **o. de brûlé** smell of burning; **je sentais une o. de brûlé** I could smell something burning; **sans o.** odourless, Am odorless; **bonne o.** lovely or pleasant smell; **mauvaise o.** bad or unpleasant smell, Fam stink; Fig **mourir en o. de sainteté** to die in the odour of sanctity; Fig **être en o. de sainteté auprès de qn** to be in sb's good books; **ne pas être en o. de sainteté auprès de qn** to be in sb's bad books; **je ne suis pas en o. de sainteté** I'm not popular, Fam I'm in the doghouse, Fam I'm not flavour of the month; Prov **l'argent n'a pas d'o.** money has no smell

odieusement [ɔdjøzmɑ̃] ADV odiously, hatefully

odieux, -ieuse [ɔdjø, -jøz] ADJ (personne) odious, hateful; (crime, vice) odious, abominable

odomètre [ɔdɔmɛtr] NM (pour véhicule) odometer; (pour piéton) pedometer

odontologie [ɔdɔ̃tɔlɔʒi] NF Méd odontology

odorant [ɔdɔrɑ̃] ADJ (agréable) sweet-smelling, fragrant; (désagréable) strong-smelling, Fam smelly

odorat [ɔdɔra] NM (sense of) smell; **avoir l'o. développé** to have a keen sense of smell

odoriférant [ɔdɔriferɑ̃] ADJ sweet-smelling, Litt odoriferous

odyssée [ɔdise] NF 1 Littér **l'O.** the Odyssey 2 Fig odyssey; **ce voyage a été une véritable o.** it was a truly epic journey

OEA [oɛa] NF (abrév **Organisation des États américains**) OAS

œcuménique [ekymenik, ø-] ADJ Rel ecumenical

œcuménisme [ekymenism, ø-] NM Rel ecumenicalism

œcuméniste [ekymenist, ø-] N, ADJ Rel ecumenist

œdème [edɛm, ø-] NM Méd oedema, Am edema; **avoir un o. aux poumons** to have pulmonary oedema

Œdipe [edip, ø-] N Littér Oedipus; Psy **complexe d'O.** Oedipus complex

œil, pl **yeux** [œj, jø] NM 1 Anat eye; **avoir de grands/petits yeux** to have large/small eyes; **avoir les yeux bleus** to have blue eyes; **avoir les yeux globuleux/enfoncés** to have protruding/deep-set eyes; **j'ai le soleil dans les yeux** ou **dans l'o.** the sun's in my eyes, I've got the sun in my eyes; **se maquiller** ou **se**

faire les yeux to do one's eyes, to put on one's eye make-up; **visible à l'o. nu** visible to the naked eye; **voir qch de ses (propres) yeux** to see sth with one's own eyes; **je l'ai de mes yeux vu** I saw it with my (very) own eyes; Fam **avoir un o. qui dit zut** ou **merde à l'autre, avoir un o. qui joue au billard et l'autre qui compte les points, avoir les yeux qui se croisent les bras** to be cross-eyed, to have a squint; **avoir un o. de verre** to have a glass eye; Fam **avoir une coquetterie dans l'o.** to have a cast in one's eye; **avoir les yeux injectés de sang** to have bloodshot eyes; **fermer/ouvrir les yeux** to close/open one's eyes; **je n'ai pas fermé l'o. de la nuit** I didn't sleep a wink all night; **ne dormir que d'un o.** to sleep with one eye open; **j'étais tellement inquiète que je n'ai pu dormir que d'un o.** I was so worried I couldn't sleep properly; Fig **je pourrais le faire les yeux fermés** I could do it with my eyes shut or closed; **chez eux, j'achète les yeux fermés** I buy things from them with complete confidence; **ouvrir un o.** to half-open one's eyes; **ouvrir de grands yeux** to look surprised; **faire les gros yeux (à qn)** to glare (at sb); **lever les yeux au ciel** to raise one's eyes heavenward or to heaven; **baisser les yeux** to lower one's eyes or gaze, to look down; Fam **avoir de petits yeux** to look tired; **j'ai les yeux qui se ferment (tout seuls), je ne peux plus garder les yeux ouverts** I can't keep my eyes open; **avoir un o. au beurre noir** ou **un o. poché** to have a black eye; **regarder qn dans les yeux** to look sb in the eye; **parler à qn entre quat'z'yeux** [katzjø] in private; (avec franchise) man to man/woman to woman, frankly; **les yeux dans les yeux** face to face, facing each other; (amoureusement) gazing into each other's eyes; **n'avoir d'yeux que pour une personne** to have eyes for only one person; Prov **o. pour o., dent pour dent** an eye for an eye, a tooth for a tooth; **épouser une femme pour ses beaux yeux** to marry a woman for her (good) looks; **je ne travaille pas pour les beaux yeux de mon patron!** I don't do this job for the love of it!; **je ne le fais pas pour ses beaux yeux** I'm not doing it just to please him; Fam **avoir des yeux de merlan frit** to look like a lovesick calf; **coûter les yeux de la tête** to cost a fortune or an arm and a leg; **tu as les yeux plus gros** ou **grands que le ventre** your eyes are bigger than your belly; **n'avoir plus que les** ou **ses yeux pour pleurer** to have nothing left apart from the clothes on one's back; **ça saute aux yeux** it's glaringly obvious; **ça crève les yeux qu'il est amoureux d'elle** it's glaringly obvious that he's in love with her; Fam **je m'en bats l'o.** I don't give a damn, I couldn't care less; Fam **mon o.!** my eye!; **tourner de l'o.** to keel over, to faint; Fam **à l'o.** free, gratis, for nothing; **le mauvais o.** the evil eye; **porter un o. critique sur qch** to be critical about sth; **nous voyons ça du même o.** we see eye to eye (with each other) about it; **nous ne voyons pas du tout les choses de cet o.-là** we see things in that light at all; **voir** ou **regarder qn/qch d'un bon o.** to look favourably or approvingly on sb/sth; **voir** ou **regarder qn/qch d'un mauvais o.** to look unfavourably or disapprovingly on sb/sth, to frown on sb/sth; **je n'en croyais pas mes yeux** I couldn't or didn't believe my eyes; **faire les yeux doux à qn** to make eyes at sb; Fam **faire de l'o. à qn** to give sb the eye; Fam **taper dans l'o. à qn** to take sb's fancy

2 (vue) (eye)sight, eyes; **avoir de bons/mauvais yeux** to have good/bad (eye)sight; **je n'ai plus mes yeux de 20 ans** I can't see as well as I used to; **s'user** ou **s'abîmer les yeux** to ruin one's eyes or eyesight; **fatiguer les yeux** to strain one's eyes; **cette lumière me fatigue les yeux** I'm straining my eyes in this

light; **dès que j'eus jeté les yeux sur lui** as soon as I had set eyes on him; **chercher qn des yeux** to look around for sb; **suivre qn des yeux** to follow sb with one's eyes; **couver** ou **manger** ou **dévorer qn des yeux** to look lovingly or fondly at sb; **regarder qn avec les yeux de l'amour** to look at sb through the eyes of love; Fam **se rincer l'o.** to get an eyeful; **elle n'a pas froid aux yeux** she's not afraid of anything; **aux yeux de la loi** in the eyes of the law; **aux yeux de Dieu** in the eyes or sight of God; **à mes yeux** in my opinion; **l'accident s'est déroulé sous mes yeux** the accident happened right before my eyes; **sous l'o. jaloux/inquisiteur/bienveillant de qn** under the jealous/inquisitive/kindly eye of sb; **avoir qch sous les yeux** to have sth right in front of one or one's eyes; **je n'ai pas encore eu leur projet sous les yeux** I haven't had sight of or I haven't seen their plan yet

3 (attention) **avoir** ou **garder l'o. ouvert** ou **les yeux ouverts** to keep one's eyes open; **avoir l'o. sur qch** to keep an eye on sth; **avoir l'o. sur qn, avoir l'o. à qn** to keep an eye on sb; **avoir l'o. à tout** to keep an eye on everything; Fam **ouvrir l'o. (et le bon)** to keep one's eyes open or peeled or skinned; **ne pas avoir les yeux en face des trous** to be half-asleep; Fam **elle n'a pas les yeux dans sa poche** she keeps her eyes open, she's very observant; **fermer les yeux sur qch** (par indulgence) to turn a blind eye to sth; (par refus de la réalité) to close one's eyes to sth; **ouvrir les yeux à qn sur qch** to open sb's eyes to sth; **coup d'o.** glance; **au** ou **du premier coup d'o., d'un seul coup d'o.** at a glance; **jeter un coup d'o. sur qch** to have a quick look at sth, to have a glance at sth; **il y a un joli coup d'o. d'ici** there's a lovely view from here; **avoir le coup d'o.** to have a good eye (for things); **ça vaut** ou **ça mérite le coup d'o.** it's worth a look
4 (d'une aiguille etc) eye; (d'une charnière) (screw-)hole; (sur une corde) eye (splice); (dans du pain, du gruyère) hole; (dans la soupe) globule or speck of fat; **piton à o.** eye bolt
5 Typ (pl **œils**) typeface
6 Élec, TV **o. électrique** electric eye; Radio **o. magique, o. cathodique** magic eye
7 Météo (d'un cyclone) eye

œil-de-bœuf, pl **œils-de-bœuf** NM bull's-eye (window)

œil-de-chat, pl **œils-de-chat** NM Minér cat's-eye

œil-de-perdrix, pl **œils-de-perdrix** NM (au pied) (soft) corn

œillade [œjad] NF glance; **lancer** ou **jeter une o. à qn** to give sb the eye; **lancer des œillades à qn** to make eyes at sb, to give sb the eye

œillère [œjɛr] NF 1 (pour un cheval) blinker, Am blinder; Fig **avoir des œillères** (être borné) to be narrow-minded; (ignorer la réalité) to wear blinkers 2 Méd eyebath, Am eyecup

œillet [œjɛ] NM 1 (fleur) carnation; **o. des fleuristes** carnation, clove pink; **o. de poète** sweet william; **o. des prés** ragged robin; **o. d'Inde** French marigold 2 (trou) (d'une botte, d'une voile etc) eyelet 3 (en papeterie) (gummed) reinforcement

œilleton [œjtɔ̃] NM 1 Opt (d'un viseur) eyepiece 2 (d'une plante) eye (bud)

œillette [œjɛt] NF oil poppy, opium poppy; **huile d'o.** poppy seed oil

œnologie [enɔlɔʒi, ø-] NF wine-making, Spéc oenology, Am enology; **cours d'o.** wine appreciation course

œnologique [enɔlɔʒik, ø-] ADJ wine, Spéc oenological, Am enological; **croisière o.** wine-tasting cruise

œnologue [enɔlɔg, ø-] N wine expert, *Spéc* oenologist, *Am* enologist

œsophage [ezɔfaʒ, ø-] NM *Anat* oesophagus, *Am* esophagus

œstre [ɛstr] NM *(mouche)* gadfly, warble fly

œstrogène [ɛstrɔʒɛn, ø-] ADJ, NM *Physiol* oestrogen, *Am* estrogen

œstrus [ɛstrys] NM *Physiol* oestrus, *Am* estrus

œuf, *pl* **œufs** [œf, ø] NM **1** egg; **blanc/jaune d'o.** egg white/yolk; **o. du jour** freshly laid egg; **o. frais** fresh egg; **œufs battus** *ou* **montés en neige** beaten egg whites; **en forme d'o.** egg-shaped; *Fig* **mettre tous ses œufs dans le même panier** to put all one's eggs in one basket; *Fig Fam* **marcher sur des œufs** to tread warily; **il tondrait un o.** he's a skinflint; *Prov* **qui vole un o. vole un bœuf** he that will steal a penny will steal a pound; **tuer la poule aux œufs d'or** to kill the goose that lays the golden egg(s); *Fam* **quel o.!** what an idiot *or* fool!; *Fam* **une tête d'o.** an egghead; *Fam* **va te faire cuire un o.!** take a running jump!, go jump in the lake!; **c'est comme l'o. de Christophe Colomb, il fallait y penser** it's easy when you know how **2** *Biol* egg; *(d'écrevisse, de homard)* berry; *(d'insecte)* egg; **œufs** *(de grenouille)* spawn; *(de poisson)* spawn, hard roe; *Fam* **étouffer ou tuer qch dans l'o.** to nip sth in the bud **3** *Ski (télécabine)* cable car

▸ ▸ **œufs brouillés** scrambled eggs; **o. en chocolat** chocolate egg; **o. à la coque** boiled egg; **o. dur**, *Belg* **o. cuit dur** hard-boiled egg; **œufs au lait** egg custard; **œufs à la liqueur** small liqueur-filled Easter eggs; **œufs de lump** lumpfish roe; **œufs mimosa** eggs mimosa *(egg whites filled with mayonnaise and crushed egg yolk)*; **o. (au) miroir** fried egg; **o. mollet** soft-boiled egg; **œufs à la neige** floating islands; **o. de Pâques** Easter egg; **o. au plat** *ou* **sur le plat** fried egg; *Péj Fig Fam* **elle n'a que des œufs sur le plat** she's as flat as a pancake; **o. poché** poached egg; **o. en poudre** dried *or* dehydrated *or* powdered egg; *Couture* **o. à repriser** darning egg

œufrier [œfrije] NM egg holder *or* stand *(for boiling eggs)*

œuvre [œvr] NF **1** *(travail)* work; **faire o. utile** to do useful work; **leur rencontre était son o.** *(grâce à lui)* it was thanks to him that they met; *(à cause de lui)* it was because of him that they met; **être à l'o.** to be at work; **mettre qn à l'o.** to set sb to work; **se mettre à l'o.** to get down to *or* set to work; **quand le médecin arriva, la mort avait déjà fait son o.** by the time the doctor arrived, the patient had already died; **la maladie/cette idée néfaste a déjà fait son o.** the disease/this dangerous idea has already done its work; **mettre en o.** to use, to make use of; *(traité, loi, système)* to implement; **mettre tout en o.** to do everything possible; **les bonnes œuvres** charitable work; **quête au profit d'une o.** collection in aid of a charity **2** *(création)* work; **œuvres d'un peintre** works of a painter; **œuvres complètes/choisies** complete/selected works

NM *Constr* **gros o. (d'un bâtiment)** fabric (of a building); **à pied d'o.** on site; *Fig* ready to start work

NM *ou* F *Beaux-Arts, Littér (ensemble de créations)* works; **l'o. entière** *ou* **entier de Beethoven** the complete works of Beethoven

▸ ▸ **o. d'art** work of art; **o. de bienfaisance** charity, charitable institution; **o. cinématographique** cinematic work; **o. de charité** charity, charitable institution; *Naut* **œuvres mortes** dead works, upper works, topsides; *Naut* **œuvres vives** quick works, vitals

œuvrer [œvre] VI *Littér* to work

---

off [ɔf] ADJ INV **1** *Cin (hors champ)* off-screen; **voix o.** voice off **2** *(festival)* fringe

NM fringe festival

offensant [ɔfɑ̃sɑ̃] ADJ offensive, insulting

offense [ɔfɑ̃s] NF **1** *(affront)* insult; **faire (une) o. à qn** to offend sb; **o. envers un chef d'État** insult to a head of state; **soit dit sans o.** with all due respect; *Fam* **il n'y a pas d'o.** no offence taken **2** *Rel* transgression, trespass; **pardonne-nous nos offenses** forgive us our trespasses

offensé, -ée [ɔfɑ̃se] ADJ offended, insulted

N offended *or* injured party

offenser [ɔfɑ̃se] VT **1 o. qn** to offend sb, to give offence *or Am* offense to sb; **sans (vouloir) vous o., monsieur le ministre** with all due respect, Minister; **sans vouloir t'o., Jean-Pierre, j'ai bien l'impression que … ** no offence (intended), Jean-Pierre *or* I don't wish to offend, Jean-Pierre, but I get the feeling that … **2** *Litt (bon goût, délicatesse etc)* to offend against; **o. les regards** to be an eyesore, *Litt* to offend the eye

VPR **s'offenser** to be offended (**de** by), to take offence *or Am* offense (**de** at)

offenseur [ɔfɑ̃sœr] NM offending person *or* party

offensif, -ive [ɔfɑ̃sif, -iv] ADJ *(guerre, arme)* offensive

NF **offensive** offensive; **passer à l'o.** to go on the *or* over to the offensive; *Fig* **l'o. de l'hiver est particulièrement précoce cette année** winter has come particularly early this year; **o. du froid** sudden cold spell, cold snap; **o. diplomatique** diplomatic offensive; **o. de paix** peace offensive

offertoire [ɔfɛrtwar] NM *Rel, Mus* offertory

office [ɔfis] NM **1** *(charge)* office; **le secrétaire n'a pas rempli son o.** the secretary didn't carry out his duties; **la pénicilline a rempli son o.** the penicillin did its job; **faire o. de secrétaire/témoin** to act as secretary/witness; **une robe blanche toute simple a fait o. de robe de mariée** a simple white dress served as a wedding gown; **d'o.** automatically, as a matter of course; **un nommé ou commis d'o.** appointed by the court; **être mis à la retraite d'o.** to be automatically retired **2** *(assistance)* **accepter les bons offices de qn** to accept sb's good offices; **proposer ses bons offices** to offer to act as mediator; *Fam* **monsieur bons offices** mediator **3** *Rel* service, office; **l'o. des morts** the burial service, the Office for the Dead; **livre d'o.** prayer book; **aller à l'o.** to go to church

NM *ou* F *Vieilli (pièce)* back kitchen, scullery

▸ ▸ **O. du commerce extérieur** foreign trade office; **O. national de la navigation** French national shipping and inland waterways office; *Suisse* **o. de poste** post office; **o. de publicité** advertising agency; **o. du tourisme(-syndicat d'initiative)** tourist information centre *or Am* center

officialisation [ɔfisjalizasjɔ̃] NF officialization, officializing

officialiser [ɔfisjalize] VT to officialize

officiant [ɔfisjɑ̃] *Rel* ADJ *(prêtre)* officiating

NM officiant

officiel, -ielle [ɔfisjɛl] ADJ *(déclaration, langage, visite, source)* official; **la version officielle est le suicide** the official version is suicide; **c'est o.** it's official; **à titre o.** officially, formally; **le Journal o.** = French government publication giving information to the public about new laws, *Br* ≃ Hansard, *Am* ≃ Federal Register

NM **1** official; **les officiels du Parti** the Party officials **2 l'O.** *Br* ≃ Hansard, *Am* ≃ Federal Register

officiellement [ɔfisjɛlmɑ̃] ADV officially; **o., il a donné sa démission** officially, he re-

signed; **il a donné sa démission o.** he formally resigned

officier¹ [ɔfisje] NM **1** *(fonctionnaire)* official, officer **2** *Mil* officer; **o. de marine** naval officer

▸ ▸ **o. d'état civil** ≃ registrar (of births, marriages and deaths); **o. général** *Mil* general officer; *Naut* flag officer; **O. de la Légion d'honneur** Officer of the Legion of Honour *or Am* Honor; *Jur* **o. ministériel** *(notaire)* notary (public); *(huissier)* officer of the court; *Naut* **o. de pont** deck officer; **o. de port** harbour *or Am* harbor master; *Mil* **o. supérieur** field officer

officier² VI *(impf, pr sub* **n. officiions**, v. **officiiez)** to officiate; *Hum, Fig* to do the honours *or Am* honors

officieusement [ɔfisjøzmɑ̃] ADV unofficially

officieux, -ieuse [ɔfisjø, -jøz] ADJ unofficial; *Journ* **note d'origine officieuse** inspired piece; **à titre o.** unofficially

officinal, -ale, -aux, -ales [ɔfisinal, -o] ADJ *Pharm (plante)* medicinal; **préparation officinale** patent medicine

officine [ɔfisin] NF **1** *Pharm* dispensary, pharmacy **2** *Fig (d'une intrigue)* hotbed; *(d'espions)* nest

off-line [ɔflajn] ADJ *Ordinat* off-line

offrande [ɔfrɑ̃d] NF **1** offering, gift; **apporter son ou une o.** to make a donation (**à** to) **2** *Rel (don)* offering; *(cérémonie)* offertory; **o. votive** votive offering

offrant [ɔfrɑ̃] NM **le plus o.** the highest bidder; **vendre au plus o.** to sell to the highest bidder; **on me propose deux emplois et j'ai décidé de dire oui au plus o.** I've got two job offers and I've decided to accept the one offering the most money

offre [ɔfr] NF offer; *(dans un appel d'offres)* tender, bid; *(dans une vente aux enchères)* bid; **faire o. de qch** to offer sth; **recevoir/accepter une o.** to receive/accept an offer; **faire des offres de service à qn** to offer to help sb; *Com* to solicit orders from sb; *Écon* **l'o. et la demande** supply and demand

▸ ▸ *Mktg* **o.-ami** introduce-a-friend scheme; **o. de base** basic offer; **o. de bon de réduction** coupon offer; **o. commerciale** bid; **o. d'emploi** job offer, offer of employment; *Journ* **offres d'emploi** situations vacant; **o. d'essai** trial offer; **o. excédentaire** excess supply; **o. export** export bid; **o. globale** aggregate supply; **o. de lancement** introductory offer; **o. promotionnelle** promotional offer; *Fin* **o. publique** takeover bid; *Fin* **o. publique d'achat** takeover bid; **faire ou lancer une o. publique d'achat** to make a takeover bid (**sur** for); *Fin* **o. publique d'échange** takeover bid for shares; *Fin* **o. publique de vente** public offering, public share offer; **o. de remboursement** money-back offer; **o. de service** offer of services; **o. spéciale** special offer, bargain offer; **o. de vente** offer for sale

offreur, -euse [ɔfrœr, -øz] N *Écon* seller

OFFRIR [ɔfrir] *(prp* **offrant**; *pp* **offert** [ɔfɛr], *pr ind* **j'offre**, **n. offrons**; *p hist* **j'offris**; *fu* **j'offrirai)** VT **1** *(cadeau)* to give; *(sacrifice)* to offer up; **c'est pour o.** it's a gift *or* present; **c'est pour o.?** would you like it giftwrapped?; **o. à déjeuner à qn** to offer sb lunch; **essaie de te faire o. un repas au restaurant** try to get yourself invited out for a meal; **je t'offre un verre** I'll buy *or* stand you a drink **2** *(proposer)* to offer; **o. de faire qch** to offer to do sth; **o. mille euros (pour** *ou* **de qch)** to offer a thousand euros (for sth); *(aux enchères)* to bid a thousand euros (for sth); **combien t'en a-t-il offert?** how much did he offer you for it?; **o. des marchandises** to offer goods for sale; **o. un prix** to offer a price; **on lui a offert une place de mécanicien** he was offered a job as a mechanic; **o. la main de sa fille à qn** to offer one's daughter's hand in marriage to sb

3 *(présenter)* **o. une résistance acharnée** to put up stiff *or* fierce resistance; **la campagne offre des vues splendides** the countryside offers *or Fml* affords magnificent views; **l'histoire en offre plusieurs exemples** history gives *orFml* affords several examples of it **VPR s'offrir 1 s'o. comme guide** to offer to act as a guide, to offer oneself *or* one's services as a guide; **s'o. pour faire qch** to offer to do sth; **s'o. à faire qch** to offer *or* volunteer to do sth; **s'o. aux regards** *(d'un spectacle, d'une vue)* to meet *or* greet the eyes; *(d'une personne)* to expose oneself to the public gaze, *Péj* to flaunt oneself

2 s'o. un bon cigare/une semaine de vacances to treat oneself to a good cigar/a week's holiday; **tu ne peux vraiment pas t'o. une soirée au cinéma?** can you really not afford a night out at the cinema?; **je ne peux pas m'o. une secrétaire** I can't afford (the luxury of) a secretary

offset [ɔfsɛt] *Typ* **ADJ** offset
NM offset (process)
NF offset (printing) machine

off-shore [ɔfʃɔr] **ADJ 1** *Sport* **bateau o.** speedboat, powerboat; **course o.** speedboat *or* powerboat race; *Pétr* **plate-forme/forage o.** offshore oil rig/drilling **2** *Fin* **placement o.** offshore investment
NM *(bateau)* speedboat, powerboat; *(course)* speedboat *or* powerboat racing

offusquer [ɔfyske] **VT** *(personne)* to offend, to shock
VPR s'offusquer s'o. de qch to take offence *or Am* offense at sth; **il s'offusque d'un rien** he takes offence at the slightest thing

ogival, -ale, -aux, -ales [ɔʒival, -o] **ADJ** *Archit* ogival

ogive [ɔʒiv] **NF 1** *Archit* (diagonal) rib; **voûte d'ogives** ribbed vault **2** *Mil (d'un obus)* head; *(d'une roquette)* nose cone; **o. nucléaire** nuclear warhead

OGM [ɔʒeɛm] **NM** *(abrév* **organisme génétiquement modifié***)* GMO

ogre [ɔgr] **NM** ogre; **manger comme un o.** to eat like a horse

ogresse [ɔgrɛs] **NF** ogress

oh [o] **INT** oh!; **oh! hisse!** (yo-)heave-ho!

ohé [ɔe] **INT** hey!; **o. du bateau!** ahoy!

ohm [om] **NM** *Élec* ohm

ohmique [omik] **ADJ** *Élec* ohmic

ohmmètre [ommɛtr] **NM** *Élec* ohmmeter

oie [wa] **NF** goose; **o. sauvage** wild goose; *Culin* **confit d'o.** = goose preserved in goose fat; **graisse d'o.** goose fat; **conte de ma mère l'O.** Mother Goose story; **pas de l'o.** goose step; **jeu de l'o.** ≃ snakes and ladders
▸▸ *Fam* **o. blanche** naive young girl; **je ne suis pas une o. blanche** I'm no innocent

oignon [ɔɲɔ̃] **NM 1** *(légume)* onion; **petits oignons** *(pour les salades)* spring onions; *(pour les conserves)* pickling onions; **aux petits oignons** *Culin* with baby onions; *Fig Fam (parfait)* first-rate; *Fig Fam* **chez eux, je suis toujours soigné aux petits oignons** I always get the VIP treatment when I stay with them; **en rang d'oignons** in a row *or* line; **se mettre en rang d'oignons** to line up in a row *or* line, to line up; *Fam* **occupe-toi** *ou* **mêle-toi de tes oignons** mind your own business; *Fam* **ce ne sont pas tes oignons** it's none of your business **2** *Bot* bulb; **oignons de tulipe** tulip bulbs **3** *Méd* bunion **4** *(montre)* turnip (watch)

oïl [ɔjl] **ADV** *Hist, Ling* **langue d'o.** langue d'oïl *(language of northern France)*

oindre [wɛ̃dr] **VT** *(conj like* **craindre***)* **1** *Vieilli (enduire)* to (rub with) oil **2** *Rel (roi etc)* to anoint

oint, ointe [wɛ̃, wɛ̃t] **ADJ, N** anointed; **l'O. du Seigneur** the Lord's anointed

oiseau, -eaux [wazo] **NM** bird; *Prov* **petit à petit, l'o. fait son nid** slow and steady wins the race; **avoir un appétit d'o., manger comme un o.** to eat like a bird; **à vol d'o.** as the crow flies; *Fig Fam* **l'o. s'est envolé** the bird has flown; *Fig Fam* **c'est un drôle d'o.** he's an odd type *or* sort *or* customer, he's a funny old bird; **mon petit o.** my pet; **donner à qn des noms d'o.** to call sb bad names
▸▸ **oiseaux de basse-cour** poultry; *Fig* **o. de malheur, o. de mauvais augure** bird of ill omen; **o. de nuit** nocturnal bird; *Fig* night owl; **o. de passage** bird of passage; **o. de proie** bird of prey; **c'est l'o. rare** he's/she's a rare bird; **elle cherche l'o. rare** *(comme époux)* she's looking for the ideal man; *(comme employé)* she's looking for the ideal employee

oiseau-lyre, *pl* **oiseaux-lyres NM** lyrebird

oiseau-mouche, *pl* **oiseaux-mouches NM** hummingbird

oiseleur [wazlœr] **NM** bird catcher

oiselier [wazəlje] **NM** bird seller

oiselle [wazɛl] **NF** hen bird; *Fig Fam* naive young girl

oisellerie [wazɛlri] **NF** *(élevage)* bird breeding; *(vente)* bird selling

oiseux, -euse [wazø, -øz] **ADJ** *(conversation)* idle; *(débat)* pointless; **explication oiseuse** unsatisfactory explanation

oisif, -ive [wazif, -iv] **ADJ** idle, unoccupied; *(capital)* idle; **vie oisive** idle life, life of idleness
N person of leisure

oisillon [wazijɔ̃] **NM** fledgling

oisivement [wazivmɑ̃] **ADV** idly

oisiveté [wazivte] **NF** idleness; *Prov* **l'o. est (la) mère de tous les vices** the Devil finds work for idle hands to do

oison [wazɔ̃] **NM** gosling

OIT [oite] **NF** *(abrév* **Organisation internationale du travail***)* ILO

OK [ɔkɛ] *Fam* **ADV** OK, okay
ADJ OK, okay; **c'est OK en ce qui me concerne!** that's OK *or* fine by me!

okapi [ɔkapi] **NM** okapi

olé [ɔle] **INT** olé!

oléagineux, -euse [ɔleaʒinø, -øz] **ADJ** oleaginous, oil-yielding; **graines oléagineuses** oilseeds
NMPL oleaginous *or* oil-yielding plants

oléiculteur, -trice [ɔleikyltœr, -tris] **N** olive grower

oléiculture [ɔleikyltyr] **NF** olive growing

oléifère [ɔleifɛr] **ADJ** oil-producing

oléine [ɔlein] **NF** olein, triolein

oléique [ɔleik] **ADJ** *Chimie (acide)* oleic

oléoduc [ɔleɔdyk] **NM** pipeline

olé olé ADJ INV *Fam (propos, spectacle)* risqué; *(robe)* daring; *(gens, soirée)* wild; **elle est très o. depuis qu'elle a divorcé** she's been leading a pretty wild life since her divorce; **il y a quelques scènes o.** some of the scenes are a bit close to the bone *or* risqué *or Br* near the knuckle

oléopneumatique [ɔleɔpnømatik] **ADJ** air/hydraulic

olfactif, -ive [ɔlfaktif, -iv] **ADJ** *(nerfs, sens, bulbe)* olfactory

olibrius [ɔlibrijys] **NM** *Fam Péj* oddball

olifant [ɔlifɑ̃] **NM** (ivory) horn

oligarchie [ɔligarʃi] **NF** oligarchy

oligarchique [ɔligarʃik] **ADJ** oligarchic(al)

oligarque [ɔligark] **NM** oligarch

oligoélément [ɔligoelemɑ̃] **NM** *Biol* trace element

oligopole [ɔligɔpɔl] **NM** *Écon* oligopoly

oligopolistique [ɔligɔpɔlistik] **ADJ** *Écon* oligopolistic

oligopsone [ɔligɔpsɔn] **NM** *Écon* oligopsony

oliphant [ɔlifɑ̃] **NM** (ivory) horn

olivaie [ɔlivɛ] **NF** olive grove *or* plantation

olivâtre [ɔlivɑtr] **ADJ** olive-greenish; *(teint)* sallow

olive [ɔliv] **NF 1** olive; **huile d'o.** olive oil **2** *Élec* switch
ADJ INV olive (green)

oliveraie [ɔlivrɛ] **NF** olive grove *or* plantation

olivette [ɔlivɛt] **NF 1** *(raisin)* = variety of grape; *(tomate)* plum tomato **2** *(olivaie)* olive plantation *or* grove

olivier [ɔlivje] **NM 1** *(arbre)* olive (tree); *Bible* **le mont des Oliviers** the Mount of Olives; **se présenter un rameau d'o. à la main** to hold out the olive branch **2** *(bois)* olive (wood); **saladier en o.** olive-wood salad bowl

olographe [ɔlɔgraf] **ADJ** *Jur* **testament o.** holograph will

OLP [ɔɛlpe] **NF** *(abrév* **Organisation de libération de la Palestine***)* PLO

Olympe [ɔlɛ̃p] **NM** *Myth* **l'O.** (Mount) Olympus; **les dieux de l'O.** the gods of Olympus

olympiade [ɔlɛ̃pjad] **NF** Olympiad

olympien, -ienne [ɔlɛ̃pjɛ̃, -jɛn] **ADJ** Olympian; *Fig* **calme o.** Olympian calm
N O. Olympian

olympique [ɔlɛ̃pik] **ADJ** *(jeux, champion, flamme)* Olympic; **Comité international o.** International Olympic Committee; **stade/piscine o.** Olympic stadium/pool

ombelle [ɔ̃bɛl] **NF** *Bot* umbel; **en o.** umbellate

ombellifère [ɔ̃belifɛr] *Bot* **ADJ** umbelliferous
NFPL ombellifères Umbelliferae, umbellifers

ombilic [ɔ̃bilik] **NM** *Anat* navel, *Spéc* umbilicus

ombilical, -ale, -aux, -ales [ɔ̃bilikal, -o] **ADJ** umbilical; *Obst, Astronaut* **cordon o.** umbilical cord; *Fig* **couper le cordon o.** to cut the apron strings

omble [ɔ̃bl] **NM o.(-chevalier)** char

ombrage [ɔ̃braʒ] **NM 1** *(des arbres)* shade **2** *Ordinat* shading **3** *Fig* **prendre o. de qch** to take umbrage *or* offence *or Am* offense at sth; **porter** *ou* **faire o. à qn** to give offence to sb

ombragé [ɔ̃braʒe] **ADJ** shaded, shady

ombrager [ɔ̃braʒe] **VT** *(il ombrageait)* *(d'un arbre)* to shade

ombrageux, -euse [ɔ̃braʒø, -øz] **ADJ** *(personne)* touchy, easily offended, quick to take offence *or Am* offense; *(cheval)* skittish

ombre¹ [ɔ̃br] **NF 1** *(forme)* shadow; **projeter une o.** to cast a shadow; *Fig* **suivre qn comme son o.** to stick to sb like glue; *(espionner)* to shadow sb; **avoir peur de son o.** to be afraid of one's own shadow; **lâcher la proie pour l'o.** to catch at shadows
2 *(d'un arbre)* shade; **se reposer à l'o. d'un arbre** to rest in the shade of a tree; **quarante degrés à l'o.** forty degrees in the shade; **elle a grandi à l'o. de la tour Eiffel** she grew up in the shadow of *or* within a stone's throw of the Eiffel Tower; *Fig Fam* **mettre qn à l'o.** to put sb inside, *Br* to put sb behind bars; *Fig* **jeter une o. sur la fête** to cast a shadow *or* a gloom over the festivities; *Fig* **vivre dans l'o. de qn** to live in sb's shadow, to be (always) overshadowed by sb; **faire de l'o. à qn** to be

in sb's light; *Fig* to put sb in the shade; *Fam* **marche à l'o.!** *(conseil)* keep a low profile!; *(menace)* stay out of my sight!

3 *(obscurité)* darkness; *Fig (anonymat)* obscurity; **ils disparurent dans l'o. de la nuit** they were swallowed up by the darkness; **leurs agissements délictueux se faisaient dans l'o. de la nuit** their criminal schemes were carried out under cover of darkness; *Fig* **rester dans/sortir de l'o.** to remain in/emerge from obscurity; *Fig* **laisser qch dans l'o.** to leave sth dark; *Fig* **travailler dans l'o.** to work behind the scenes

4 *(être de l'au-delà)* ghost, *Litt* shade; **le royaume des ombres** the nether world; *Fig* **n'être plus que l'o. de soi-même** to be a mere shadow of one's former self

5 *(trace)* **vous n'avez pas l'o. d'une chance** you haven't the ghost of a chance; **il n'y a pas l'o. d'un doute** there isn't the *or* a shadow of a doubt; **elle n'a pas l'o. d'un scrupule!** she's totally unscrupulous *or* without scruples!; **une o. de méchanceté/jalousie** a hint of malice/jealousy

6 *Astron* umbra

7 *Beaux-Arts* **l'o. et la lumière** light and shade; *Fig* **il y a une o. au tableau** there's a fly in the ointment

▸▸ **ombres chinoises** shadow play; **théâtre d'ombres chinoises** shadow theatre; **o. à paupières** eye shadow

> Attention: ne pas confondre **shadow** et **shade** lorsque l'on traduit **ombre**. **Shadow** décrit une forme projetée par un objet se trouvant dans une source de lumière, alors que **shade** s'applique simplement à un lieu se trouvant à l'abri du soleil.

ombre² NF terre d'o. umber

ombre³ NM *(poisson)* o.(-chevalier) char; **o. de rivière** grayling

ombré [ɔ̃bre] NM *Ordinat* shading

ombrelle [ɔ̃brɛl] NF sunshade, parasol; *Zool (d'une méduse)* umbrella

> Il faut noter que le nom anglais **umbrella** est un faux ami. Il signifie **parapluie**.

ombrer [ɔ̃bre] VT *(serre, dessin)* to shade; **o. ses paupières de bleu** to put blue eye shadow on

ombreux, -euse [ɔ̃brø, -øz] ADJ *Litt (promenade, bosquet)* shady

Ombrie [ɔ̃bri] NF Umbria

ombudsman, *pl* **ombudsmans** [ɔ̃bydsman] NM ombudsman

OMC [oɛmse] NF *(abrév* **Organisation mondiale du commerce)** WTO

OMCI [oɛmsei] NF *(abrév* **Organisation de la navigation maritime consultative et intergouvernementale)** IMCO

oméga [omega] NM omega

omelette [ɔmlɛt] NF omelette, *Am* omelet; **o. au jambon** ham omelette; **o. norvégienne** baked Alaska; *Prov* **on ne fait pas d'o. sans casser des œufs** you can't make an omelette without breaking eggs

omettre [ɔmɛtr] VT *(conj like* **mettre)** *(mot, détail)* to omit, to miss out, to leave out; **o. de faire qch** to fail *or* omit *or* neglect to do sth

OMI [oɛmi] NF *(abrév* **Organisation maritime internationale)** IMO

omission [ɔmisjɔ̃] NF *(d'un mot, détail)* omission; *(oubli)* oversight; **péché/mensonge par o.** sin/lie of omission; *Typ* **signe d'o.** caret

omnibus [ɔmnibys] NM **1** *(train)* slow train, *Br* stopping train **2** *Arch (bus)* omnibus
▪ ADJ INV **train o.** slow train, *Br* stopping train; *Élec* **barre o.** busbar

omnidirectionnel, -elle [ɔmnidirɛksjɔnɛl] ADJ *(microphone, antenne, transmetteur)* omnidirectional

omnipotence [ɔmnipɔtɑ̃s] NF omnipotence

omnipotent [ɔmnipɔtɑ̃] ADJ omnipotent, all-powerful

omnipraticien, -ienne [ɔmnipratisjɛ̃, -jɛn] N *Méd* general practitioner, GP

omniprésence [ɔmniprezɑ̃s] NF omnipresence

omniprésent [ɔmniprezɑ̃] ADJ omnipresent

omniscience [ɔmnisjɑ̃s] NF omniscience

omniscient [ɔmnisjɑ̃] ADJ omniscient

omnisports [ɔmnispɔr] ADJ INV **stade/centre o.** sports stadium/centre

omnium [ɔmnjɔm] NM **1** *Écon* combine; *Bourse* **o. de valeurs** = type of investment trust **2** *Sport* open; *Courses de chevaux* open handicap **3** *Belg* comprehensive insurance

omnivore [ɔmnivɔr] ADJ omnivorous
▪ NM omnivore

omoplate [ɔmɔplat] NF shoulder blade, *Spéc* scapula

OMS [oɛms] NF *(abrév* **Organisation mondiale de la santé)** WHO

on [ɔ̃] PRON INDÉF *(sometimes becomes* **l'on**, *especially after vowel sound)* **1** *(indéterminé)* you, people, *Fml* one; *(quelqu'un)* someone, somebody; **on ne sait jamais** you never know, *Fml* one never knows, you *or Fml* one never can tell; **on n'en sait rien** nobody knows anything about it; **on n'aime pas être traité comme ça** people don't like to be treated like that; **on dit qu'elle est folle** it's said *or* they say *or* people say that she's mad, she's said to be mad; **on le dit dans les milieux autorisés** that's what is being said in official circles; **partout où l'on trouve de ces fossiles** wherever these fossils are found; **on ne connaît jamais son bonheur** you never know how lucky you are, *Fml* one never knows how lucky one is; **quand on demande à une femme de vous épouser** when a man asks a woman to marry him, when you ask a woman to marry you; **on était le sept mars** it was the seventh of March; **on frappe à la porte** someone's *or* somebody's (knocking) at the door, there's a knock at the door; **on sonne** there's the (door)bell, there's someone *or* somebody at the door; **on a enfoncé la porte** the door was burst open; **on m'a volé mon sac** my bag has been stolen, someone's stolen my bag; **on demande une bonne cuisinière** *(annonce)* wanted, good cook

2 *(précisé) (a following adj, noun or pp agrees in gender and number as the sense requires)* **on parlait très peu au déjeuner** we didn't talk much over lunch; **on ne s'était jamais séparés** we had never been separated; **on n'est pas toujours jeune et belle** women can't be young and beautiful forever; **où va-t-on?** where are we going?; **alors, on s'en va comme ça?** are you really leaving just like that?; **on est dix en tout** there are ten of us in all; *Fam* **nous, on est tous égaux** we're all equal here; *Fam* **on est allés au cinema avec les parents** we went to the pictures with our parents

onagre¹ [ɔnagr] NF *Bot* evening primrose

onagre² NM *Zool* onager, wild ass

onanisme [ɔnanism] NM onanism

once¹ [ɔ̃s] NF *(mesure)* ounce; **il n'a pas une o. de bon sens** he doesn't have an ounce of common sense

once² NF *Zool* ounce, snow leopard

oncle [ɔ̃kl] NM uncle; **o. à la mode de Bretagne** first cousin once removed; **o. d'Amérique** rich uncle; **o. à héritage** rich uncle *(from whom one expects to inherit)*; **O. Sam** Uncle Sam

oncogène [ɔ̃kɔʒɛn] ADJ *Méd* oncogenic

onction [ɔ̃ksjɔ̃] NF *Rel, Fig* unction; *Méd Vieilli* = massage or rubbing with oil

onctueusement [ɔ̃ktɥøzmɑ̃] ADV *Péj* unctuously

onctueux, -euse [ɔ̃ktɥø, -øz] ADJ *(yaourt, sauce)* smooth, creamy; *Péj (manières, paroles)* smooth, unctuous

onctuosité [ɔ̃ktɥozite] NF *(de yaourt, d'une sauce)* smoothness, creaminess

onde [ɔ̃d] NF **1** *Phys* wave; **o. calorifique/lumineuse/sonore** heat/light/sound wave; *Radio* **ondes** airwaves; **sur les ondes** on the air; **passer sur les ondes** *(d'une émission)* to be broadcast; *(d'une personne)* to be on air; **mettre en ondes** to produce; **petites ondes** short wave; **grandes ondes** long wave; **sur grandes ondes** on long wave; *Fig Fam* **nous ne sommes pas sur la même longueur d'o.** we're not on the same wavelength **2** *Métal* corrugation **3** *Litt (eau)* waters; **sur la terre et sur l'o.** on land and water
▸▸ **o. de choc** shock wave; **ondes courtes** short wave; **ondes hertziennes** airwaves, hertzian waves, radio waves; **ondes longues** long wave; **ondes moyennes** medium wave; **ondes radio** radio waves; **ondes très courtes** very high frequency; **ondes ultra-courtes** ultrashort waves

ondé [ɔ̃de] ADJ *Litt (cheveux)* wavy; *(soie)* watered

ondée [ɔ̃de] NF sudden downpour

ondemètre [ɔ̃dmɛtr] NM *Radio* wavemeter

ondin, -ine [ɔ̃dɛ̃, -in] N *Myth* water sprite

on-dit NM INV rumour, *Am* rumor, hearsay; **il ne faut pas croire à ces o.** you shouldn't believe these rumours; **ce ne sont que des o.** it's only hearsay

ondoiement [ɔ̃dwamɑ̃] NM **1** *(des roseaux, du maïs etc)* swaying, undulation **2** *Rel* summary baptism *(conducted in cases of emergency)*

ondoyant [ɔ̃dwajɑ̃] ADJ **1** *(sol)* undulating; *(cheveux)* wavy; *(foule, mouvement)* swaying; *(roseaux)* swaying, undulating **2** *Litt (personne, caractère)* changeable

ondoyer [ɔ̃dwaje] *(j'ondoie; j'ondoierai)* VI *(des blés)* to sway, to undulate; *(d'un drapeau)* to wave; *(de la surface de l'eau)* to undulate; *(de flammes)* to flicker
▪ VT *Rel* to baptize summarily *(in cases of emergency)*

ondulant [ɔ̃dylɑ̃] ADJ *(courbe, ligne)* undulating; *(plaine)* rolling, undulating; *(roseaux)* swaying, undulating; *(crinière)* flowing; **avoir une démarche ondulante** to swing one's hips

ondulation [ɔ̃dylasjɔ̃] NF *(de l'eau, du sol etc)* undulation; *(dans les cheveux)* wave; *TV* **o. de l'image** picture weave

ondulatoire [ɔ̃dylatwar] ADJ undulatory; *Phys* **mouvement o.** wave motion

ondulé [ɔ̃dyle] ADJ *(sol)* undulating; *(cheveux)* wavy; *(tôle, carton)* corrugated; **route ondulée** switchback road; **trait o.** wavy line

onduler [ɔ̃dyle] VI to undulate; *(de cheveux)* to be wavy
▪ VT *(cheveux)* to wave

onduleur [ɔ̃dylœr] NM *Ordinat* uninterruptible power supply, UPS

onduleux, -euse [ɔ̃dylø, -øz] ADJ = **ondulant**

onéreux, -euse [ɔnerø, -øz] ADJ *(dépense)* heavy; *(achat)* expensive, costly; **à titre o.** subject to payment

> Il faut noter que l'adjectif anglais **onerous** est un faux ami. Il signifie **lourd, pénible**.

ONF [oɛnɛf] NM (abrév **Office national des forêts**) Br ≃ Forestry Commission, Am ≃ National Forestry Service

ONG [oɛnʒe] NF (abrév **organisation non gouvernementale**) NGO

ongle [ɔgl] NM (finger)nail; (des orteils) (toe)nail; (d'un animal) claw; (d'un oiseau de proie) talon, claw; **coup d'o.** scratch; **se faire les ongles** to do one's nails; Fam **avoir les ongles en deuil** to have dirty nails; Méd **o. incarné** ingrowing nail; **se ronger les ongles** to bite one's nails; Fig **avoir les ongles crochus** to be mean or tight-fisted; **connaître ou savoir qch sur le bout des ongles** to know sth perfectly; **il est français jusqu'au bout des ongles** he's French to his fingertips, he's every inch a Frenchman

onglée [ɔgle] NF tingling, aching (of numbed fingertips); **j'ai l'o.** my fingers are numb with cold

onglet [ɔglɛ] NM **1** (d'un répertoire) tab; (d'un canif) thumbnail groove; **dictionnaire à onglets** thumb-indexed dictionary; **o. à fenêtre** (d'une fiche etc) window tab **2** Typ (béquet) tab; (d'un livre) guard **3** Menuis mitre, Am miter; **boîte à onglets** mitre box; **tailler à o.** to mitre **4** Culin flank of beef

onglier [ɔglije] NM manicure set

onguent [ɔgɑ̃] NM Litt ointment, unguent

ongulé [ɔgyle] ADJ, NM Zool ungulate

onirique [ɔnirik] ADJ Litt dreamlike

onirisme [ɔnirism] NM (state of) hallucination

onirologie [ɔnirɔlɔʒi] NF interpretation of dreams

ONN [oɛnɛn] NM (abrév **Office national de la navigation**) = French national shipping and inland waterways office

onomasiologie [ɔnɔmazjɔlɔʒi] NF Ling onomasiology

onomastique [ɔnɔmastik] Ling NF onomastics

ADJ onomastic

onomatopée [ɔnɔmatɔpe] NF onomatopoeia

onomatopéique [ɔnɔmatɔpeik] ADJ onomatopoeic

Ontario [ɔ̃tarjo] NM l'O. Ontario; **le lac O.** Lake Ontario

ontogenèse [ɔ̃tɔʒənɛz] NF ontogenesis, ontogeny

ontogénétique [ɔ̃tɔʒenetik] ADJ ontogenetic, ontogenic

ontogénie [ɔ̃tɔʒeni] NF = **ontogenèse**

ontologie [ɔ̃tɔlɔʒi] NF Phil ontology

ontologique [ɔ̃tɔlɔʒik] ADJ Phil ontological

ONU [ony, oɛny] NF (abrév **Organisation des Nations unies**) UN

ONUDI, Onudi [onydi] NF (abrév **Organisation des Nations unies pour le développement industriel**) UNIDO

onusien, -ienne [ɔnyzjɛ̃, -jɛn] ADJ (of the) UN; **la politique onusienne** UN policy
N UN official

onyx [ɔniks] NM Minér onyx

onze [ɔ̃z] (the **e** of **le** and **de** is not, as a rule, elided before **onze** and its derivatives) ADJ INV eleven; **o. cent trente** eleven hundred and thirty; **nous n'étions que o.** [kɔ̃z], **nous n'étions qu'o.** there were only eleven of us; **le o. avril** the eleventh of April, Am April eleventh; **Louis O.** Louis the Eleventh
NM INV Ftbl **le o. de France** the French team, the French eleven

onzième [ɔ̃zjɛm] ADJ eleventh; **le o. jour** the eleventh day
N (personne, chose) eleventh
NM (fraction) eleventh
NF Mus eleventh

onzièmement [ɔ̃zjɛmmɑ̃] ADV in the eleventh place

oolithe [ɔɔlit] NM Minér oolite

oolithique [ɔɔlitik] ADJ Minér oolitic

OPA [opea] NF (abrév **offre publique d'achat**) takeover bid; **lancer une O.** to make a takeover bid (**sur** for); **O. amicale/inamicale** friendly/hostile takeover bid; **être l'objet d'une O.** to be the subject of a takeover bid

opacification [ɔpasifikasjɔ̃] NF making opaque

opacifier [ɔpasifje] VT to make opaque

opacité [ɔpasite] NM (d'un corps, d'un liquide) opacity, opaqueness; (d'une forêt) darkness, denseness; (d'un texte) opaqueness, impenetrability; Typ opacity

opale [ɔpal] NF opal
ADJ **verre o.** opal glass; Élec **ampoule o.** pearl bulb

opalescence [ɔpalɛsɑ̃s] NF opalescence

opalescent [ɔpalɛsɑ̃] ADJ opalescent

opalin, -ine [ɔpalɛ̃, -in] ADJ (nuance, reflet) opaline
NF **opaline** opaline

opaque [ɔpak] ADJ opaque; (forêt) dark, dense; Fig (texte, explications) opaque, impenetrable; Typ (papier) opaque; **collant o.** opaque tights; **o. aux rayons X** impervious to X-rays; Ling **mot o.** opaque word

op art [ɔpart] NM op art

OPCVM [opeseveɛm] NM Bourse (abrév **organisme de placements collectifs en valeurs mobilières**) unit trust, Am mutual fund; **O. actions** equity-based unit trust

OPE [opeə] NF abrév **offre publique d'échange**

opéable [ɔpeabl] ADJ ripe for takeover

opeamania [opeamanja] NF Fin takeover fever

open [ɔpɛn] ADJ INV open; **une compétition o.** an open competition; **un billet o.** an open ticket
NM Sport open; **un o. de tennis** a tennis open

OPEP [ɔpɛp] NF (abrév **Organisation des pays exportateurs de pétrole**) OPEC

opéra [ɔpera] NM **1** (genre, œuvre) opera; **il aime beaucoup l'o.** he loves opera; **c'est une chanteuse d'o.** she's an opera singer; **grand o.** grand opera **2** (lieu) opera house; **je vais rarement à l'o.** I rarely go to the opera; **l'O. (de Paris)** the Paris Opera House; **les petits rats de l'O.** = the ballet pupils at the Paris Opera House
▸▸ **o. bouffe** comic opera, opera buffa

opérable [ɔperabl] ADJ Chir (tumeur) operable; (malade) who can be operated on, operable

opéra-comique, pl **opéras-comiques** NM opéra comique (opera with spoken dialogue)

opérande [ɔperɑ̃d] NM Ordinat operand

opérant [ɔperɑ̃] ADJ effective; **les mesures ont été opérantes** the measures (taken) were effective

opérateur, -trice [ɔperatœr, -tris] N (personne) (machine) operator; Typ machine setter; Journ copytaker; Fin trader; Tél telecommunications company; Cin cameraman, f camerawoman
NM **1** Math operator **2** (d'une machine) working piece
▸▸ TV, Cin **o. banc-titre** rostrum cameraman, f rostrum camerawoman; Ordinat **o. booléen** Boolean operator; Fin **o. boursier** stock-exchange dealer; Ordinat **o. de comparaison** comparator; Bourse **o. en couverture** hedger; Ordinat **o. logique** logical operator; TV, Cin **o. magnétoscope** video-

tape operator, VT operator; TV, Cin **o. de prise de vue** camera operator; **o. de radio** radio operator; Ordinat **o. relationnel** relational operator; Ordinat **o. de saisie** keyboard operator, keyboarder; TV, Cin **o. steadicam** steadicam operator; Ordinat **o. système** systems operator, SYSOP; Com **o. de transport multimodal** multi-modal operator; **o. vidéo** video operator, VT operator; TV, Cin **o. de la vision** video control operator

opération [ɔperasjɔ̃] NF **1** Chir **o. (chirurgicale)** operation; **subir une o.** to have or undergo an operation; **salle d'o.** operating theatre or Am room
2 Math, Mil, Ordinat operation; Com, Fin, Banque deal, transaction; **o. de change** exchange transaction; **o. financière** financial transaction; **o. imposable** taxable transaction; **opérations militaires** military operations; **o. de police** police operation; **o. publicitaire** advertising campaign; Fin **opérations fermes** firm transactions; Scol **j'ai des opérations à faire pour demain** I've got some sums to do for tomorrow
3 (démarche) operation, process; **par l'o. du Saint-Esprit** by the working of the Holy Ghost; Fig Fam by magic
▸▸ Bourse **o. blanche** break-even transaction; **opérations de Bourse** Stock Exchange dealings or business or transactions; Banque **opérations de caisse** counter transactions; Compta **o. en capital** capital transaction; Méd **o. à chaud** emergency operation (for appendicitis etc); Compta **o. de clearing** clearing transaction; Chir **o. à cœur ouvert** open-heart surgery; Com **opérations en commun** joint ventures; **la police a effectué une o. coup de poing contre les revendeurs de drogue du quartier** the police launched a crackdown on drug pushers in the area; '**o. coup de poing sur les chaînes hi-fi**' 'hi-fi prices slashed'; Compta **o. courante** normal business transaction; Compta **opérations courantes** ordinary activities; Bourse **opérations de couverture** hedging; **o. escargot** go-slow or Am slow-down by lorry/bus/car drivers; Bourse **o. de journée** day trade; Bourse **o. jumbo** jumbo trade; Ordinat **o. 'si-alors'** if-then operation; Bourse **opérations à terme** futures trading

opérationnel, -elle [ɔperasjɔnɛl] ADJ operational

opératoire [ɔperatwar] ADJ Chir (procédure) operating; **médecine o.** surgery; **choc o.** post-operative shock

opercule [ɔpɛrkyl] NM Tech cover, lid, cap; Biol (d'un poisson, d'un mollusque) operculum; Naut **o. de hublot** deadlight

operculé [ɔpɛrkyle] ADJ Biol operculate(d)

opéré, -ée [ɔpere] N patient (who has/had had an operation)

opérer [ɔpere] (j'opère; j'opérerai) VT **1** (accomplir, faire) (réforme) to carry out; (multiplication), Chimie (synthèse) to perform; **o. une retraite** to (effect a) retreat; **o. un sondage** Tech to sink a borehole; (d'opinion) to carry out or conduct an opinion poll; Banque **o. un virement** to make a transfer **2** Chir to operate on; **être opéré de l'appendicite** to be operated on for appendicitis, to have an operation for appendicitis; **o. qn des amygdales** to take sb's tonsils out; **se faire o.** to have or undergo an operation; **se faire o. des amygdales** to have one's tonsils taken out; **tu t'es déjà fait o.?** have you been operated on or had an operation before?
VI (d'un médicament) to take effect, to work; **laisser o. la nature** to let nature take its course; **laissons les choses o. par elles-mêmes** let's allow things to take their own course; **son éloquence/charme opéra sur la foule** his eloquence/charm had an effect on

or worked on the crowd; **la façon dont les cambrioleurs ont opéré** the way the burglars went to work; **je ne sais pas comment il opère en de telles circonstances** I don't know how he proceeds in such circumstances

VPR s'opérer *(d'un changement, d'une transformation)* to come about, to take place; **un changement complet s'est opéré dans sa vie** there's been a complete change in his life, his life has changed completely

opérette [ɔpɛʀɛt] **NF** operetta; **chanteuse d'o.** operetta singer; *Fig* **héros d'o.** cardboard *or* two-dimensional hero

ophidien, -ienne [ɔfidjɛ̃, -jɛn] **ADJ, NM** ophidian

ophite [ɔfit] **NM** *Minér* ophite, serpentine

ophrys [ɔfʀis] **NM** *Bot* ophrys; **o. abeille** bee orchid; **o. araignée** spider orchid

ophtalmie [ɔftalmi] **NF** *Méd* ophthalmia; **o. des neiges** snow blindness

ophtalmique [ɔftalmik] **ADJ** *Méd* ophthalmic

ophtalmo [ɔftalmo] **N** *Méd Fam* ophthalmologist

ophtalmologie [ɔftalmɔlɔʒi] **NF** *Méd* ophthalmology

ophtalmologiste [ɔftalmɔlɔʒist], **ophtalmologue** [ɔftalmɔlɔg] **N** *Méd* ophthalmologist

ophtalmoscope [ɔftalmɔskɔp] **NM** *Méd* ophthalmoscope

opiacé [ɔpjase] *Pharm* **ADJ** containing opium, opiate
NM opiate

opiner [ɔpine] **VI o. pour/contre qch** to come down in favour of/against sth; **o. du chef** *ou* **de la tête** *ou* **du bonnet** to nod (one's) assent, to nod in agreement

opiniâtre [ɔpinjɑtʀ] **ADJ** *(tenace) (personne)* obstinate, stubborn; *(toux)* stubborn, persistent; *(opposition)* stubborn, unyielding; *(résistance)* stubborn, dogged

opiniâtrement [ɔpinjɑtʀəmɑ̃] **ADV** obstinately, stubbornly; *(résister)* stubbornly, doggedly

opiniâtreté [ɔpinjɑtʀəte] **NF** *Vieilli (obstination)* obstinacy, stubbornness; *(persévérance)* perseverance, determination

opinion [ɔpinjɔ̃] **NF** opinion (**de** of; **sur** about, on); **opinions politiques/religieuses** political/religious opinions *or* views; **liberté d'o.** freedom of thought *or* opinion; **journal d'o.** = political weekly/monthly (with a particular stance); **créer un mouvement d'o.** to create a groundswell of opinion; **sondage d'o.** opinion poll; **se faire une o. sur qch** to make up one's mind about sth, to form an opinion about sth; **mon o. est faite** I've made up my mind; **émettre** *ou* **exprimer une o.** to express an opinion; **sans o.** *(dans un sondage)* don't know; **les opinions sont partagées** opinion is divided; **partager l'o. de qn** to agree with sb, to share sb's opinion; **partager les opinions de qn** to share sb's opinions *or* views, to think the same way as sb; **avoir le courage de ses opinions** to have the courage of one's convictions; **amener qn à son o.** to bring sb round to one's way of thinking; **avoir bonne/mauvaise o. de qn/ qch** to have a good/bad opinion of sb/sth; **donner bonne o. de soi** to make a good impression

▸▸**o. publique** public opinion

opiomane [ɔpjɔman] **N** opium addict

opium [ɔpjɔm] **NM** opium; *Fig* **la religion est l'o. du peuple** religion is the opium of the people; *Hist* **guerre de l'o.** opium war

opossum [ɔpɔsɔm] **NM** opossum

opportun [ɔpɔʀtœ̃] **ADJ** *(arrivée)* timely, opportune, well-timed; *(moment, jour)* right;

arriver au moment o. to come at the right time *or* an opportune moment

opportunément [ɔpɔʀtynemɑ̃] **ADV** at the right time, opportunely

opportunisme [ɔpɔʀtynism] **NM** opportunism

opportuniste [ɔpɔʀtynist] **ADJ** opportunist; *(maladie)* opportunistic
N opportunist

opportunité [ɔpɔʀtynite] **NF** *(d'une arrivée)* timeliness, *Fml* opportuneness; *(d'un projet, d'une décision)* advisability; **o. commerciale** market opportunity; **o. mercatique** marketing opportunity

opposable [ɔpozabl] **ADJ** opposable (**à** to); **rien n'est o. à ses arguments** there is no answer to his arguments, nothing can be said against his arguments

opposant, -ante [ɔpozɑ̃, -ɑ̃t] **ADJ** *(minorité)* opposing
N opponent (**à** of); *Pol* member of the Opposition

opposé [ɔpoze] **ADJ 1** *(armées, caractères etc)* opposing; *(côtés, rivage, direction)* opposite; *(intérêts, conseil)* conflicting; **angles opposés par le sommet** vertically opposite angles; **leurs opinions sont diamétralement opposées** their views are poles apart *or* diametrically opposed; **elle est plutôt artiste, lui est diamétralement o.** she is rather artistic, he is the exact opposite; **tons opposés** contrasting colours **2 être o. à une mesure** to oppose *or* be opposed to *or* be against a measure; **je suis o. à ce qu'une centrale soit construite dans cette région** I'm opposed to *or* I'm against a power station being built in this area
NM 1 *(contraire)* **l'o.** the opposite, the reverse; **à l'o.** *(dans l'espace)* opposite, on the other side; *Fig* on the other hand; **le deuxième film de ce réalisateur est vraiment l'o. du premier** the director's second film is the complete opposite of *or* is in complete contrast to his first; **mon avis est à l'o. du sien** my opinion is the opposite of his; **à l'o. de ce que nous attendions** contrary to expectation *or* to what we expected; **cela va à l'o. de ce que l'on m'avait promis/de notre politique** that goes against what I was promised/our policy **2 la gare est à l'o.** the station is in the opposite direction; **à l'o. de la gare** opposite the station

opposer [ɔpoze] **VT** *(deux adversaires)* to bring into conflict (with each other); **o. des arguments valables à une théorie** to put forward valid arguments against a theory; **je n'ai rien à o. à ce raisonnement** I cannot counter this argument; **que peut-il t'o.?** what objection can he have to that?, what can he say against that?; **o. une résistance vigoureuse** to put up *or* offer vigorous resistance, *Fam* to resist tooth and nail; **o. un farouche refus à qch** to be fiercely opposed to sth; **o. son veto** to exercise one's veto; **o. des idées/théories l'une à l'autre** to contrast ideas/theories; **o. Mozart à Debussy** to contrast Mozart with Debussy; **cette course oppose les meilleurs athlètes de toute l'Europe** this race brings together Europe's finest athletes; **ce match opposera le joueur français au joueur américain** this match will pit the French player against the American; **la finale opposera la France à l'Italie** France will meet Italy *or* come up against Italy in the final
VPR s'opposer s'o. à qch to oppose sth, to be opposed to sth, to be against sth; **nous nous opposons à ce que la centrale soit construite** we oppose the building of the power station, we are opposed to *or* are against the power station being built; **nous nous opposons à ce qu'il arrête ses études** we are

against *or* we are opposed to the idea of him giving up his studies; **il n'y a pas de loi qui s'y oppose** there is no law against it; **rien ne s'oppose à votre succès** nothing stands between you and success; **rien ne s'oppose à votre projet** nothing stands in the way of your plan; **rien ne s'oppose à ce que vous fassiez ce que vous souhaitez** there's nothing to stop you doing what you want to; **les meilleurs joueurs d'échecs s'opposent dans ce tournoi** this tournament pits the best chess players against one another, the best chess players come up against each other in this tournament

opposite [ɔpozit] **NM à l'o. de** opposite, facing; *Fig* opposed to

opposition [ɔpozisjɔ̃] **NF 1** *(résistance)* opposition; *Pol* **l'o.** the Opposition; **faire o. à un chèque** to stop a cheque, to stop payment of a cheque; **à chaque fois qu'on parle d'un nouveau projet, il fait de l'o.** every time there is talk of a new plan, he is opposed to it *or* against it **2** *Jur* caveat; **o. sur titre** attachment against securities; **jugement susceptible d'o.** judgment liable to stay of execution **3** *(contraste)* contrast; **c'est en o. totale avec les principes qu'il expose dans ses livres** it is in complete contrast to *or* is totally at odds with *or* totally contradicts the principles that he puts forward in his books; **tout cela est en o. totale avec ce que je pense** all that is the complete opposite of what I think; **par o. à qch** as opposed to sth; **couleurs en o.** contrasting colours **4** *Astron (des planètes)* opposition

oppositionnel, -elle [ɔpozisjɔnɛl] *Pol* **ADJ** oppositional, opposition
N oppositionist

oppressant [ɔpʀɛsɑ̃] **ADJ** *(chaleur, sentiment)* oppressive

oppresser [ɔpʀɛse] **VT 1** *(d'une situation, d'une atmosphère etc)* to oppress **2** *(de problèmes, de responsabilités)* to weigh down **3** *Litt* = **opprimer**

> Do not confuse with **opprimer**.

oppresseur [ɔpʀɛsœʀ] **NM** oppressor
ADJ M oppressive

oppressif, -ive [ɔpʀɛsif, -iv] **ADJ** *(gouvernement, autorité etc)* oppressive

oppression [ɔpʀɛsjɔ̃] **NF 1** *(d'un peuple)* oppression **2** *Méd* **o. de la poitrine** tightness of the chest, difficulty in breathing

opprimé [ɔpʀime] **ADJ** oppressed, downtrodden
NMPL les opprimés the oppressed

opprimer [ɔpʀime] **VT** *(peuple, nation)* to oppress; *(liberté)* to suppress

> Do not confuse with **oppresser**.

opprobre [ɔpʀɔbʀ] **NM** *Litt* opprobrium; **jeter l'o. sur qn** to cast opprobrium on sb; **accabler** *ou* **couvrir qn d'o.** to heap opprobrium on sb

optatif, -ive [ɔptatif, -iv] **ADJ, NM** *Ling* optative

opter [ɔpte] **VI o. entre deux choses** to choose between two things; **o. pour qch** to opt for sth

opticien, -ienne [ɔptisjɛ̃, -jɛn] **N** optician

optimal, -ale, -aux, -ales [ɔptimal, -o] **ADJ** optimum, optimal

optimalisation [ɔptimalizasjɔ̃] **NF** optimization; *Fin* **o. des profits** profit optimization

optimisation [ɔptimizasjɔ̃] **NF** *aussi Ordinat* optimization

optimiser [ɔptimize] **VT** *Ordinat, Mktg etc* to optimize

optimiseur [ɔptimizœʀ] **NM** *Ordinat* optimizer

optimisme [ɔptimism] NM optimism; **avec o.** optimistically

optimiste [ɔptimist] ADJ optimistic; **sois un peu o.** try to be optimistic, try to look on the bright side; **nous ne sommes pas très optimistes quant à la guérison de ce malade** we're not very optimistic about the patient's chances of recovery or that the patient will recover

N optimist

optimum [ɔptimɔm], *pl* **optimums**, *parfois* **optima** [ɔptima] ADJ *(conditions)* optimum; **la température o. ne dépasse pas 5 degrés** the optimum temperature does not exceed 5 degrees

NM optimum

option [ɔpsjɔ̃] NF option, choice (**de** of; **entre** between); **prendre une o. sur qch** to take (out) an option on sth; **le flash est en o.** the flash is optional or is an optional extra; *Bourse* **jour d'o.** option day; *Scol* **matières à o.** optional or elective subjects; **il avait le latin en o. au baccalauréat** he took Latin as an option or an optional subject or an elective subject for the baccalauréat

▸▸ *Bourse* **o. d'achat** call (option), option to buy; *Bourse* **o. sur actions** option on shares; *Bourse* **o. américaine** American-style option; *Fin* **o. de change** foreign currency option; **o. cotée** traded option; **o. d'échange** swap option; *Bourse* **o. européenne** European-style option; *Ordinat* **o. d'impression** print option; *Bourse* **o. sur indice** index option; *Ordinat* **o. de menu** menu option; *Bourse* **o. négociable** traded option; *Ordinat* **o. de sauvegarde** save option; *Bourse* **o. de vente** put (option), option to sell; *Pol* **o. zéro** zero option

optionnel, -elle [ɔpsjɔnɛl] ADJ optional

optique [ɔptik] ADJ *(nerf)* optic; *(angle)* visual; *(verre)* optical; **télégraphie o.** visual signalling

NF **1** *(science)* optics; **instruments d'o.** optical instruments; **o. électronique** electron optics; **transmettre par o.** to communicate by visual signals **2** *(perspective)* perspective; **nous ne travaillons pas dans la même o.** we're working towards different aims; **o. du théâtre** stage perspective; *Mktg* **o. mercatique** marketing orientation; *Mktg* **o. produit** product orientation; *Mktg* **o. vente** sales orientation, sales philosophy **3** *(d'un projecteur)* optical system

optométrie [ɔptɔmetri] NF optometry

optométriste [ɔptɔmetrist] N optometrist

opulence [ɔpylɑ̃s] NF opulence, affluence; *Fig (de la poitrine, des formes etc)* fullness, ampleness; **nager** ou **être dans l'o.** to be rolling in money; **vivre dans l'o.** to have an opulent lifestyle, to live in opulence

opulent [ɔpylɑ̃] ADJ *(mobilier, environs)* opulent; *(personne)* opulent, wealthy, affluent; *Fig (moisson, pâturage)* abundant; **une poitrine opulente** an ample or full bosom

opus [ɔpys] NM opus

opuscule [ɔpyskyl] NM opuscule

OPV [opeve] NF *Fin (abrév* **offre publique de vente)** public offer for sale

or [ɔr] NM **1** *(métal)* gold; **or pur/fin** pure/fine gold; **la ruée vers l'or** the gold rush; **chercheur d'or** gold-prospector; *Min, Fig* **mine d'or** gold mine; *Fig* **cette boutique est une véritable mine d'or pour les collectionneurs** this shop is a real gold mine or treasure trove for collectors; **or en barre** ou **en lingots** (gold) bullion; *Fig* **c'est de l'or en barre** it's as safe as the Bank of England or as houses; *Fin* **étalon or** gold standard; **poudre d'or** gold dust; **montre en or** ou **d'or** gold watch; **bracelet doré à l'or fin** a fine gold-

(-plated) bracelet; **en or massif** (in) solid gold; **or en feuille(s)** gold leaf or foil; **feuille d'or** gold leaf; **payer qch à prix d'or** to pay a fortune for sth; **revendre qch à prix d'or** to resell sth for a fortune; **affaire en or** *(achat)* excellent bargain; *(commerce, combine)* lucrative line of business; *Fam* **j'ai une femme en or** I've a wonderful wife; **il/ça vaut son pesant d'or** he's worth his/it's worth its weight in gold; **pour tout l'or du monde** for all the money in the world, for all the tea in China; **l'âge d'or** the golden age; **cœur d'or** heart of gold; **parler d'or** to speak words of wisdom; **livre d'or** (official) visitors' book; **rouler sur l'or, être (tout) cousu d'or** to be rolling in money, to have money coming out of one's ears; **il ne roule pas sur l'or** he isn't exactly rolling in it; *Prov* **tout ce qui brille n'est pas or** all that glitters or glistens is not gold; **le silence est d'or** silence is golden

2 *(couleur)* gold; *Hér* or; **vieil or** old gold; **murs/voiture vieil or** old gold walls/car; **chevelure d'or** golden hair

▸▸ **or blanc** ou **gris** white gold; **or noir** black gold, oil; **or rouge** red gold

or [ɔr] CONJ now; *(pour conclure)* well; **or, pour revenir à ce que nous disions** now, to come back to what we were saying; **or …, donc …** now …, therefore …; **avant de le lire, je pensais que le livre était bon – or, il ne l'était pas** before reading it, I thought the book was good – well, it wasn't; **il n'achète jamais de chocolats, or … et …** he never buys chocolates, but …

oracle [ɔrakl] NM oracle; **parler d'un ton d'o.** to speak with assurance

orage [ɔraʒ] NM (thunder)storm; **temps d'o.** thundery or stormy weather; **le temps est à l'o.** there's thunder in the air, there's a storm brewing; *Fig* **l'atmosphère est à l'o. au bureau** there's trouble or a storm brewing in the office; **il va faire de l'o., il y a de l'o. dans l'air** there's a storm brewing; *Fig* there's trouble or a storm brewing, there's trouble in the air; *Fig* **laisser passer l'o.** to let the storm blow over

▸▸ **o. magnétique** magnetic storm

orageusement [ɔraʒøzmɑ̃] ADV stormily

orageux, -euse [ɔraʒø, -øz] ADJ *(temps)* thundery, stormy; *(saison, mer)* stormy; *Fig (vie)* stormy, tempestuous; *(discussion)* stormy, heated

oraison [ɔrezɔ̃] NF prayer; **faire** ou **dire** ou **réciter une o.** to say a prayer; **o. funèbre** funeral oration

oral, -ale, -aux, -ales [ɔral, -o] ADJ *(tradition, enseignement, examen)* oral; *(déposition, communication)* oral, verbal; *Anat (cavité)* oral; **par voie orale** orally; *Psy* **stade o.** oral stage

NM oral examination; *surtout Univ* oral or viva voce examination; *Fam* oral, viva

oralement [ɔralmɑ̃] ADV orally

orange [ɔrɑ̃ʒ] NF *(fruit)* orange; **peau d'o.** orange peel; *Fig* orange-peel skin

NM *(couleur)* orange; *Aut* **passer à l'o.** to go through (the lights) on amber; **le feu était à l'o.** the lights were at amber

ADJ INV orange; *Aut* **feu o.** amber light; **carte o.** *(pour les transports parisiens)* = combined monthly pass for the underground, bus and suburban train

▸▸ **o. amère** bitter orange, Seville orange; **o. givrée** orange sorbet; **o. pressée** freshly-squeezed orange juice; **o. sanguine** blood orange

orangé [ɔrɑ̃ʒe] ADJ orange-coloured or Am -colored

NM orange colour or Am color

orangeade [ɔrɑ̃ʒad] NF orangeade

oranger [ɔrɑ̃ʒe] NM orange tree; **fleur d'o.**

orange blossom; **eau de fleur d'o.** orange-flower water

orangeraie [ɔrɑ̃ʒrɛ] NF orange grove

orangerie [ɔrɑ̃ʒri] NF orangery

orangiste [ɔrɑ̃ʒist] N **1** *(en Irlande du Nord)* Orangeman, f Orangewoman **2** *Hist* Orangist

ADJ Orange

orang-outan(g) [ɔrɑ̃utɑ̃], *pl* **orangs-outan(g)s** NM orang-outang, orang-utan

orateur, -trice [ɔratœr, -tris] N orator; *(dans un dîner)* speaker

oratoire [ɔratwar] ADJ oratorical; **l'art o.** (the art of) oratory, public speaking; **il a pris des précautions oratoires** he chose his words carefully; **joutes oratoires** verbal sparring matches

oratoire [ɔratwar] NM *Rel* **1** *(chapelle)* oratory, chapel for private prayer **2** **l'O.** the Oratory

oratorio [ɔratɔrjo] NM *Mus* oratorio

orbe [ɔrb] NM orb

orbe [ɔrb] ADJ **mur o.** blind wall

orbitaire [ɔrbitɛr] ADJ *Anat* orbital

orbital, -ale, -aux, -ales [ɔrbital, -o] ADJ *Astron* orbital

orbite [ɔrbit] NF **1** *(d'une planète, d'un vaisseau spatial, d'un électron)* orbit; **en** ou **sur o.** in orbit; **mettre** ou **placer un satellite en** ou **sur o.** to put a satellite into orbit **2** *(sphère d'influence)* orbit, (sphere of) influence **3** *Anat (de l'œil)* socket, orbit

orbiter [ɔrbite] VI to orbit

Orcades [ɔrkad] NFPL **les O.** the Orkneys, the Orkney Islands

orchestral, -ale, -aux, -ales [ɔrkestral, -o] ADJ orchestral

orchestration [ɔrkestrasjɔ̃] NF **1** *Mus* orchestration; **faire une nouvelle o. d'un morceau** to re-orchestrate a piece **2** *Fig (d'une campagne électorale ou commerciale)* orchestration, organization

orchestre [ɔrkestr] NM *Mus* orchestra; **diriger un o.** to conduct an orchestra; **chef d'o.** conductor; **o. de jazz** jazz band; **o. de chambre** chamber orchestra; *Théâtre* **(fauteuil d')o.** seat in the stalls or Am orchestra; **deux fauteuils d'o., deux orchestres** two stalls, two stall or Am orchestra seats `VOIR GRAMMAIRE A11`

orchestrer [ɔrkestre] VT *Mus* to orchestrate; *Fig (organiser) (campagne électorale ou commerciale etc)* to orchestrate, to organize

orchidée [ɔrkide] NF orchid

ordalie [ɔrdali] NF *Hist* ordeal; **o. par l'eau/le feu** ordeal by water/fire

ordinaire [ɔrdinɛr] ADJ *(habituel)* ordinary, usual, normal; **vêtements ordinaires** ordinary or everyday clothes; **vin o.** table or Am jug wine; **peu** ou **pas o.** unusual, uncommon, out of the ordinary; **gens ordinaires** ordinary people; **elle est vraiment o.** she's so ordinary; *Fam* **voilà une chose qui n'est pas o.!** that's not something you see every day!; *Math* **fractions ordinaires** vulgar fractions; *Fin* **actions ordinaires** ordinary shares, *Am* common stock; **votre fournisseur o.** your normal or regular or usual supplier; **votre médicin o.** your usual doctor; **médecin o. du roi** physician in ordinary to the king; **évêque o.** diocesan bishop; **de taille o.** ordinary-sized, normal-sized, *Am* regular-sized; *(personne)* of average height; **vin très o.** very ordinary wine; **une vie très o.** a very ordinary or run-of-the-mill life

NM **1** *(habitude)* **d'o., à l'o.** usually, as a rule; **plus en forme qu'à l'o.** fitter than usual; **comme à l'o.** as usual **2** *(moyenne)* **cela sort de l'o.** it's unusual, it's out of the ordinary; **beauté/intelligence qui sort de l'o.** exceptional beauty/intelligence **3** *(au restaurant)* standard fare; *Mil* (company) mess; **auberge où l'o. est excellent** inn where the food is excellent; *Mil* **fonds d'o.** mess fund **4** *Cathol* **l'o. de la messe** the ordinary of the Mass

ordinairement [ɔrdinɛrmɑ̃] ADV ordinarily, usually, as a rule

ordinal, -ale, -aux, -ales [ɔrdinal, -o] ADJ ordinal SEE GRAMMAR A76; B59

ordinateur [ɔrdinatœr] NM **1** *(machine)* computer; **o. autonome** stand alone (computer); **o. bloc-notes** notebook (computer); *Aut* **o. de bord** trip computer; **o. de bureau** business computer, desktop (computer); **o. central** mainframe (computer); **o. domestique** home computer; **o. à écran tactile** touch-screen computer; **o. familial** family computer; **o. final** front-end processor; **o. frontal** front end computer *or* processor, front end; **o. individuel** personal computer; **o. multimédia** multimedia computer; **o. numérique** digital computer; **o. de poche** palmtop (computer), pocket computer; **o. portable** *ou* **portatif** portable (computer), laptop (computer); **o. de réseau** network computer; **o. sans clavier** keyboardless computer; **o. serveur** host computer, server; **o. de table** desktop (PC) **2** *Rel* ordainer

ordination [ɔrdinasjɔ̃] NF *Rel* ordination

ordinogramme [ɔrdinɔgram] NM flow chart

ordonnance [ɔrdɔnɑ̃s] NF **1** *(disposition)* *(d'un bâtiment)* layout, (general) arrangement; *(d'un tableau)* organization **2** *(ordre)* order; *Jur* order, ruling; **o. d'amnistie** amnesty order; *Fin* **o. de paiement** order *or* warrant for payment, order to pay **3** *Méd* prescription; **délivré seulement sur o.** available only on prescription **4** *Mil* orderly; **bottes d'o.** standard issue boots; **revolver d'o.** service revolver; **officier d'o.** aide-de-camp; *Naut* flag lieutenant

ordonnancement [ɔrdɔnɑ̃smɑ̃] NM **1** *Fin* order to pay **2** *Ind* *(de production)* scheduling

ordonnancer [ɔrdɔnɑ̃se] VT *(j'ordonnançai(s); n. ordonnançons)* *Fin* to authorize; **o. un paiement** to order *or* authorize a payment

ordonnancier [ɔrdɔnɑ̃sje] NM *(du pharmacien)* prescription book; *(du médecin)* prescription pad

ordonnateur, -trice [ɔrdɔnatœr, -tris] N **1** organizer; *(d'un spectacle)* master of ceremonies; **o. des pompes funèbres** funeral director *(at the funeral itself)* **2** *Admin* person authorized to pass accounts; *Fin* payer; *Bourse* giver *or* placer of an/the order

ordonné, -ée [ɔrdɔne] ADJ **1** *(vie, rangement)* orderly, (well-) ordered; *Ordinat* **traitement non o.** random processing **2** *(personne)* tidy, orderly
NF *Math* **ordonnée** ordinate; **axe des ordonnées** Y-axis

ordonner [ɔrdɔne] VT **1** *(mettre de l'ordre dans)* to organize, to arrange; *Math* to arrange in order; **il faut davantage o. votre argumentation** you need to organize your arguments a bit more, you need to get more order into your arguments **2** *(commander)* to order; **o. à qn de faire qch** to order sb to do sth; **o. à qn de se taire** to tell sb to be quiet; **o. une grève** to call a strike; **o. une enquête** to order an enquiry; *Méd* **o. un remède à qn** to prescribe a remedy for sb **3** *Jur* *(statuer)* to ordain, to rule; *Rel* **o. qn prêtre** to ordain sb

ORDRE [ɔrdr] NM **1** *(organisation)* order; **o. alphabétique/chronologique** alphabetical/chronological order; **par o. alphabétique** in alphabetical order; **o. croissant/décroissant** ascending/descending order; **rangé par o.**

de grandeur arranged in order of size; **procéder par o.** to do things in order; *Théâtre* **distribution par o. d'entrée en scène** *ou* *Cin, TV* **par o. d'apparition à l'écran** cast in order of appearance; **numéro d'o.** serial number; **l'o. de classement des livres/dossiers est le suivant** books/files are arranged as follows; *Fig* **c'est dans l'o. des choses** it's in the nature of things; **avec o.** *(travailler)* methodically; **manque d'o.** untidiness; **manquer d'o.** to be untidy; **en bon o.** *(de façon réglée)* in an orderly manner; *(comme cela doit être)* in good order; **mettre bon o. à qch** to sort sth out; **homme d'o.** orderly man; *(qui est pour l'ordre public)* law-and-order man; **avoir de l'o.** *(ranger ses affaires)* to be tidy; *(être méthodique)* to be methodical; **(re)mettre de l'o. dans sa vie** to put *or* get one's life (back) in order; **(re)mettre de l'o. dans ses souvenirs** to get one's memories into some kind of order; **mettre de l'o. dans sa chambre, mettre sa chambre en o.** to tidy (up) one's room; **laisser une maison en o.** to leave a house tidy; **mettre de l'o. dans ses affaires, mettre ses affaires en o.** *(arranger, régler)* to put one's affairs in order, to settle one's affairs; *Fig* to set one's house in order; **tout est en o.** everything is in order; **en o. de marche** *(machine etc)* in working order **2** *(discipline)* order; **assurer l'o.** to preserve (law and) order; **maintenir l'o.** to maintain order; **rétablir l'o.** to restore order; **les forces de l'o.** the police, the forces of law and order *(especially at demonstration etc)*; **rappeler qn à l'o.** to call sb to order; **tout est rentré dans l'o.** everything has returned to normal; *(après une émeute etc)* order has been restored; **idées qui renversent l'o. établi** ideas that upset the established order (of things); **retour à l'o. moral** return to traditional moral values **3** *(catégorie)*, *Biol, Archit* order; **o. des carnivores** order of carnivores; **ordres grecs** classical orders; *Hist* **les trois ordres (de l'État)** the three orders *or* classes (of the State); **de premier o.** first-class, first-rate; **tireur de premier o.** crack shot; **un crétin de premier o.** a first-class cretin; **hôtel de troisième o.** third-rate hotel; **renseignements/ idées d'o. général** general information/ ideas; **d'o. privé** of a private nature; **dans un tout autre o. d'idées** in a quite different connection; **du même o.** of the same order; **de l'o. de dix tonnes** in the order *or* region of ten tonnes **4** *(communauté)* order; **o. religieux** religious *or* monastic order; *Rel* **les ordres** holy orders; **entrer dans les ordres** to take holy orders **5** *(acte d'autorité)* order; *Mil* order, command; **o. d'exécution** death warrant; *Ind etc* instruction to proceed; **donner l'o. à qn de faire qch** to order sb to do sth; **donner des ordres à qn** to give sb orders, to order sb about; **recevoir des ordres** to be given orders; **je n'ai d'ordres à recevoir de personne** I don't take orders from anyone; **je ne reçois** *ou* **prends mes ordres que de mes supérieurs** I only take orders from my superiors; **se mettre aux ordres de qn** to put oneself at sb's disposal; **être aux ordres de qn** to be at sb's disposal; **je ne suis pas à tes ordres!** I don't take orders from you!; **à vos ordres, mon général!** yes sir!; *Hum* **à vos ordres!** yes sir!; **c'est un o.!** that's an order!; **par o. ou sur l'o. de qn** on the order of sb; **jusqu'à nouvel o.** until further notice; *(pour le moment)* for the time being; **sauf o. contraire** unless otherwise stated; **mot d'o.** watchword **6** *Fin, Com* order; **à l'o. de ...** payable to (the order of) ...; **payez à l'o. de J. Martin** pay to the order of J. Martin; **faites votre chèque à l'o. de ...** make your cheque out to ..., make your cheque payable to ...; **c'est à quel o.?**

who should I make it out to?, who should I make it payable to?; **billet à o.** bill of exchange payable to order
▸▸ **o. d'achat** *Com* purchase order; *Bourse* buy order; *Mil* **o. d'appel (sous les drapeaux)** call-up papers, *Am* draft notice; **o. des avocats** Bar Association; *Mil* **o. de bataille** battle order *or* array; *Bourse* **o. de Bourse** Stock Exchange order; **o. de chevalerie** order of knighthood; *Jur* **o. de comparaître** summons; *Fin* **o. au comptant** cash order; *Bourse* **o. conditionnel** contingent order; *Bourse* **o. environ** discretionary order; *Fin* **o. ferme** firm order; **O. de la Jarretière** Order of the Garter; **o. du jour** *(du comité etc)* agenda; *Mil* general orders, order of the day; *Mil* **cité à l'o. du jour** mentioned in dispatches; *Fig* **le mariage de la princesse est à l'o. du jour** the princess's marriage is very much in the news; **o. de la Légion d'honneur** Order of the Legion of Honour; *Bourse* **o. lié** straddle; **l'o. des médecins** *Br* ≃ the British Medical Association, *Am* ≃ the American Medical Association; *Bourse* **o. au mieux** market order; *Bourse* **o. de négociation** trading order; *Fin* **o. de paiement** payment order; *Banque* **o. permanent** standing order; *Banque* **o. de prélèvement automatique** direct debit mandate; **o. public** law and order, public order; **atteinte à l'o. public** breach of the peace; **troubler l'o. public** to cause a breach of the peace; *Bourse* **o. à révocation** good-till-cancelled order; *Bourse* **o. stop à cours limité** stop-limit order; *Fin* **o. à terme** futures order; *Bourse* **o. 'tout ou rien'** all-or-none order; **o. de transfert permanent** banker's order, *Br* standing order; **o. de vente** order to sell; *Fin* **o. de virement** transfer order

ordré [ɔrdre] ADJ *Suisse (ordonné)* tidy, orderly, neat

ordure [ɔrdyr] NF **1** *(saleté)* dirt, filth, muck; **faire ses ordures sur le trottoir** *(d'un chien)* to make a mess on the pavement **2** *(objets)* **ordures** refuse, *Br* rubbish, *Am* garbage; **boîte à ordures** dustbin, *Am* garbage can *or* trash can; **jeter** *ou* **mettre qch aux ordures** to throw sth in the dustbin *or Am* garbage *or* trash can; **c'est bon à mettre aux ordures** it's fit for the dustbin *or Am* garbage can *or Am* the trash **3** *(dans un échange)* filth, dirt, smut; **dire/écrire des ordures** to talk/write filth *or* smut; *Litt* **se vautrer dans l'o.** to wallow in filth **4** *Fig Péj très Fam* **il exploite tout le monde, c'est vraiment une o.** he exploits everybody, he's a real shit *or* bastard
▸▸ **ordures ménagères** household refuse *or Br* rubbish *or Am* garbage

ordurier, -ière [ɔrdyrje, -jɛr] ADJ *(livre, chanson, langage)* filthy, dirty, smutty

orée [ɔre] NF **à l'o. de la forêt/du bois** on the edge of the forest/wood

oreillard [ɔrɛjar] NM **1** *Zool* long-eared bat **2** *(d'un fauteuil)* wing

oreille [ɔrɛj] NF **1** *(d'une personne, d'un animal)* ear; **il a les oreilles décollées** his ears stick out, he has protruding ears; *Fam* **avoir les oreilles en feuilles de chou** to have huge protruding ears; **avoir mal à l'o./aux oreilles** to have earache; **chien aux oreilles courtes/ longues** short-eared/long-eared dog; **mettre** *ou* **porter son chapeau sur l'o.** to wear one's hat over one ear; *Fig* **baisser l'o., avoir l'o. basse** to be crestfallen; **il partit l'o. basse** he went off with his tail between his legs; **coucher les oreilles** *(d'un cheval)* to set *or* lay its ears back; **tirer les oreilles à qn** to pull *or* tweak sb's ears; *Fig* to give sb a telling off; *Fig* **tu vas te faire tirer les oreilles** you'll get told off, you'll get a telling off; *Fam* **il s'est (bien) fait tirer l'o.** he took a lot of coaxing; *Fam* **il ne s'est pas fait tirer l'o.** he didn't have to be asked twice; *Fig* **montrer le bout de l'o.**

to show one's true colours; **rougir jusqu'aux oreilles** to go as red as a beetroot; **n'écouter que d'une o., écouter d'une o.** distraite to listen with half an ear; *Fam* **ça lui entre par une o. et ça sort par l'autre** it goes in one ear and out the other; **dire** *ou* **souffler qch à l'o. de qn** *ou* **dans le creux de l'o. de qn** to whisper sth in sb's ear; **dresser** *ou* **tendre l'o.** to prick up one's ears; **être tout oreilles** to be all ears; **prêter l'o.** to lend an ear; **je n'en crois pas mes oreilles** I can't believe my ears *or* what I'm hearing; **faire la sourde o. (à qch)** to turn a deaf ear (to sth); *Fig* **il doit avoir les oreilles qui sifflent** his ears must be burning; **ce n'est pas tombé dans l'o. d'un sourd** it did not fall on deaf ears; **il n'entend pas de cette o.-là** he is deaf in that ear; *Fig* **il ne l'entend pas de cette o.** he won't hear of it; *Fam* **(é)chauffer les oreilles à qn** to get on sb's nerves, to annoy sb; **casser les oreilles à qn** *(en faisant du bruit)* to deafen sb; *(en posant des questions ennuyeuses)* to drive sb crazy; **c'est le bouche à o. qui a fait le succès de ce film** it was word of mouth that made the film a hit; **quand ça m'est venu** *ou* **arrivé aux oreilles** when I got to hear of it; **mettre la puce à l'o. à qn** to set sb thinking, to make sb suspicious; **rebattre les oreilles à qn de qch** to go on and on to sb about sth; **être dur d'o.** to be hard of hearing; *Fig* **vous pouvez dormir sur vos deux oreilles** you can sleep easy in your bed; **avoir de l'o.** *(pour la musique)* to have a good ear, to have an ear for music; **avoir l'o. absolue** to have perfect pitch **2** *(d'un fauteuil)* wing; *(d'un plat, d'un vase)* handle; *(d'une casquette)* ear flap; **écrou à oreilles** wing *or* butterfly nut **3** *Journ* position to right/left of headline ▸▸**o.** *Anat* **o. externe** outer ear; **o. interne** inner ear; **o. moyenne** middle ear

oreiller [ɔrɛje] NM pillow; **taie d'o.** pillowcase, pillowslip; **sur l'o.** in bed; **confidences sur l'o.** pillow talk

oreillette [ɔrɛjɛt] NF **1** *Anat (du cœur)* auricle, atrium **2** *(écouteur)* earpiece **3** **fauteuil à oreillettes** wing chair; **casquette à oreillettes** cap with ear flaps

oreillons [ɔrɛjɔ̃] NMPL *Méd* mumps VOIR GRAMMAIRE A10

Orénoque (l') [ɔrenɔk] NM the Orinoco

ores [ɔr] ADV **d'o. et déjà** already

orfèvre [ɔrfɛvr] NM *(qui travaille l'or)* goldsmith; *(qui travaille l'argent)* silversmith; *Fig* **être o. en la matière** to be an expert in the matter

orfèvrerie [ɔrfɛvrəri] NF *(métier)* *(de l'or)* goldsmith's trade; *(de l'argent)* silversmith's trade; *(magasin)* *(d'objets d'or)* goldsmith's shop *or Am* store; *(d'objets d'argent)* silversmith's shop *or Am* store

orfraie [ɔrfrɛ] NF *Orn* sea eagle; *Fam* **pousser des cris d'o.** to shriek at the top of one's voice

organdi [ɔrgɑ̃di] NM *Tex* organdie

organe [ɔrgan] NM **1** *Physiol* organ; **les organes génitaux** the genital organs, the genitals, the genitalia **2** *(élément)* *(d'une machine)* part, component; **organes de transmission** transmission system; *Ordinat* **o. d'entrée** input unit; *Ordinat* **o. périphérique** peripheral device **3** *Fig (instrument)* organ; **o. de publicité** advertising agency; **o. de presse** *(publication)* organ of the press; **l'o. officiel du parti** the official organ of the party **4** *(voix)* voice; **o. mâle et sonore** manly voice; *Hum* **il a un bel o.** he has a fine voice

organigramme [ɔrganigram] NM organization chart; *Ordinat* (data) flow chart; **o. de production** production flow chart

organique [ɔrganik] ADJ *(maladie, chimie, loi)* organic

organiquement [ɔrganikmɑ̃] ADV organically

organisateur, -trice [ɔrganizatœr, -tris] ADJ organizing
N organizer; *(d'une rencontre sportive)* promoter, organizer; **o. de conférences** *ou* **de congrès** conference organizer; **o. de voyages** tour operator

organisation [ɔrganizasjɔ̃] NF **1** *(planification)* organization; **qualités d'o.** organizing *or* organizational ability; *Ordinat* **o. des données** data organization **2** *(groupement)* organization; **o. à but non lucratif** non profit-making organization, *Am* not-for-profit organization; **o. politique/syndicale** political/trade-union organization **3** *Biol (du corps humain)* structure
▸▸**O. de l'alimentation et l'agriculture** Food and Agriculture Organization; *Hist* **O. de l'armée secrète** Secret Army Organization *(right-wing group opposed to Algerian independence)*; **O. de l'aviation civile internationale** International Civil Aviation Authority; **O. de coopération et de développement économique** Organization for Economic Cooperation and Development; **o. humanitaire** aid agency; **O. internationale de normalisation** International Standards Organization; **O. internationale du travail** International Labour Organization; **O. de libération de la Palestine** Palestine Liberation Organization; **O. maritime internationale** International Maritime Organization; **O. mondiale de la santé** World Health Organization; **O. des Nations unies** United Nations Organization; **O. des Nations unies pour le développement industriel** United Nations Industrial Development Organization; **O. des Nations unies pour l'éducation, la science et la culture** United Nations Educational, Scientific and Cultural Organization; **O. de la navigation maritime consultative et intergouvernementale** Intergovernmental Maritime Consultative Organization; **o. non gouvernementale** non-governmental organization; **O. des pays exportateurs de pétrole** Organization of Petroleum Exporting Countries; **o. scientifique du travail** organization and methods, time and motion studies; **O. du traité de l'Atlantique Nord** North Atlantic Treaty Organization; **O. de l'unité africaine** Organization of African Unity

organisationnel, -elle [ɔrganizasjɔnɛl] ADJ organizational

organisé [ɔrganize] ADJ **1** *(planifié)* organized; **voyage o.** package tour; *Fam* **c'est du vol o.** it's a rip-off, *Br* it's daylight robbery; **il est bien o.** he is (well-)organized; **les manifestants n'étaient pas organisés** the demonstrators were not organized **2** *Biol (être)* organic

organiser [ɔrganize] VT *(réunion, affaires, fête, voyage etc)* to organize, to arrange; *(temps, emploi du temps)* to organize, to plan
VPR **s'organiser** to get organized

organiseur [ɔrganizœr] NM **o. personnel** *(logiciel)* personal organizer; **o. électronique** electronic organizer

organisme [ɔrganism] NM **1** *Biol* organism; *Anat* system; **le tabac est mauvais pour l'o.** tobacco is bad for the system; **o. génétiquement modifié** genetically modified organism **2** *(organisation)* organization, body; **o. d'aide** aid organization; **o. de contrôle** watchdog; **o. de crédit** credit institution; **o. de défense des consommateurs** consumer organization; **o. international** international organization; **o. de normalisation** standards committee; **o. professionnel** professional body; **o. de surveillance** watchdog

organiste [ɔrganist] N *Mus* organist

organoleptique [ɔrganɔlɛptik] ADJ organoleptic

orgasme [ɔrgasm] NM orgasm

orge [ɔrʒ] NF barley; **sucre d'o.** barley sugar
NM **o. mondé** hulled barley; **o. perlé** pearl barley

orgeat [ɔrʒa] NM **sirop d'o.** barley water

orgelet [ɔrʒəlɛ] NM *Méd* sty(e)

orgiaque [ɔrʒjak] ADJ orgiastic

orgie [ɔrʒi] NF *(sexuelle)* orgy; *(avec excès de boissons)* drunken feast; *Fig* **j'ai fait une o. de foie gras** I gorged myself on foie gras; **une o. de couleurs** a riot of colour; **une o. de lumières** a profusion of lights

orgue [ɔrg] NM *(pl souvent f)* **1** *Mus* organ; **un bel o., de belles orgues** a fine organ; **tenir l'o.** *ou* **les orgues** to be at *or* be playing the organ; **o. électrique/électronique** electric/electronic organ; **joueur d'o.** organ grinder; **point d'o.** pause; *Fig* **le point d'o. de la réunion** the climax *or* high point of the meeting **2** *Géol* **orgues de basalte** basalt columns
▸▸**o. de Barbarie** barrel organ

orgueil [ɔrgœj] NM pride; *Péj* pride, arrogance; **péché d'o.** sin of pride; **être gonflé** *ou* **bouffi d'o.** to be puffed up *or* swollen with pride; **tirer o. de qch** to take pride in sth; **être l'o. (et la joie) de qn** to be sb's pride and joy; **par o.** out of pride; **par o., il ne veut pas admettre son erreur** he is too proud to admit his error

orgueilleusement [ɔrgœjøzmɑ̃] ADV proudly; *Péj* proudly, arrogantly

orgueilleux, -euse [ɔrgœjø, -øz] ADJ proud; *Péj* proud, arrogant
N proud person; *Péj* arrogant person

oriel [ɔrjɛl] NM oriel (window), bay window

orient [ɔrjɑ̃] NM **1** *(est)* east, *Litt* orient; **l'O.** the East, the Orient; **en O.** in the East; **pays/peuples d'O.** Oriental nations/peoples; **tapis d'O.** oriental carpet; *Hist* **l'Empire d'O.** the Eastern (Roman) Empire **2** *(dans la franc-maçonnerie)* **Grand-O.** Grand Lodge

orientable [ɔrjɑ̃tabl] ADJ *(grue)* swivelling; *(lampe, antenne)* adjustable

oriental, -ale, -aux, -ales [ɔrjɑ̃tal, -o] ADJ *(région)* eastern; *(côte)* east; *(langue)* oriental; *Hist* **les Indes orientales** the East Indies
N **O.** Oriental

orientalisme [ɔrjɑ̃talism] NM Orientalism

orientaliste [ɔrjɑ̃talist] N Orientalist

orientateur, -trice [ɔrjɑ̃tatœr, -tris] N = **orienteur**

orientation [ɔrjɑ̃tasjɔ̃] NF **1** *(détermination de position)* orientation; **table d'o.** orientation *or* panoramic table; **avoir le sens de l'o.** to have a (good) sense of direction; **course d'o.** orienteering course **2** *Scol* **choisir une o.** to choose a course of study; **o. en fin de cinquième** = determination of future course of studies at the end of one's second year; **conseiller d'o.** course and careers adviser **3** *(d'une grue, d'une antenne)* positioning; **o. d'un canon** training of a gun; **à o. libre** free-moving, adjustable; *Aut* **o. de la roue** wheel alignment, tracking **4** *(d'une maison)* aspect, orientation; *(d'une politique)* thrust; **o. des voiles** set *or* trim of the sails; **o. de la Bourse** Stock Market trend; **o. du marché** market orientation; **o. stratégique de la société** corporate strategic orientation
▸▸**o. politique** *(d'un journal, d'une personne)* political leanings *or* tendencies; *(d'un parti)* political direction; **o. professionnelle** careers advice *or* guidance

orienté [ɔrjɑ̃te] ADJ **1** *(disposé)* **maison/pièce orientée au sud** house/room facing south, house/room with a southerly aspect; **le jardin est mal o.** the garden is badly positioned; *Bourse* **o. à la baisse** *(marché)* falling;

o. à la hausse *(marché)* rising **2** *(peu objectif)* bias(s)ed, slanted; **ouvrage o. politiquement** work with a political bias *or* slant **3** *Ordinat* **o. bloc** block-orientated; **o. ligne** line-orientated; **o. objet** object-orientated; **o. problème** problem-orientated; **o. procédure** procedure-orientated

orienter [ɔrjɑ̃te] **VT 1** *(bâtiment)* to orient(ate); *(canon, fusil)* to train **(vers** on); *(télescope)* to point, to direct; *(voile)* to trim **2** *(mener)* to direct, to guide; *Scol* **o. un élève vers la chimie** to steer a pupil towards chemistry, to advise a pupil to take up chemistry; *Scol* **on l'a mal/bien orienté** he was given the wrong/right academic advice; **o. la conversation vers d'autres sujets** to steer *or* turn the conversation to other topics; **j'ai essayé d'o. la conversation sur toi** I tried to bring *or* steer the conversation round to you **3** *(carte)* to orient(ate) **4** *Math* **o. une droite** to indicate the direction of a straight line

VPR s'orienter 1 *(déterminer sa position)* to get *or* find one's bearings, to orientate oneself; *(avec une boussole)* to take one's bearings **2** *(se destiner)* **elle veut s'o. vers le droit** she wants to go in for *or* specialize in law; **il a décidé de s'o. vers la carrière diplomatique** he has decided on a career in the diplomatic service; **cette politique s'oriente vers le communisme** this policy is tending *or* moving towards Communism; **s'o. vers la vente de produits écologiques** to specialize in the sale of environmentally friendly products; **s'o. en fonction des cours** to move in relation to prices

orienteur, -euse [ɔrjɑ̃tœr, -øz] **N** careers adviser
NM *(instrument)* orientator
ADJ *Mil* **officier o.** interviewing officer *(for candidates for military service)*

orifice [ɔrifis] **NM** opening, aperture; *(du corps)* orifice; *(d'un puits, d'une galerie)* mouth; *Tech* port; *Aut* **o. d'admission** inlet port; *Aut* **o. d'air** air port; *Aut* **o. d'alimentation** feed hole; *Aut* **o. d'arrivée d'essence** petrol port; *Aut* **o. d'écoulement d'huile** oil drain hole; *Aut* **o. de sortie** outlet port

oriflamme [ɔriflam] **NF 1** *Hist* oriflamme **2** *(bannière)* banner

origami [ɔrigami] **NM** origami

origan [ɔrigɑ̃] **NM** oregano

originaire [ɔriʒinɛr] **ADJ 1 o. de** *(personne)* originating from, coming from; **il est o. de Russie/du Havre** he is a native of *or* he comes from Russia/Le Havre; **le haggis est o. d'Écosse** haggis originates in *or* comes from Scotland **2** *(initial) (membre)* original, founding

originairement [ɔriʒinɛrmɑ̃] **ADV** originally

original, -ale, -aux, -ales [ɔriʒinal, -o] **ADJ 1** *(premier) (texte, manuscrit)* original; *(bande etc)* master; **édition originale** first edition; *Cin* **copie originale (du film)** master print **2** *(nouveau) (style, idée)* original **3** *(excentrique)* odd, eccentric
NM *(œuvre, document)* original; *(d'un fichier, d'une disquette)* master copy; **copier qch d'après l'o.** to copy sth from the original
N *(excentrique)* eccentric; **c'est un o.** he's (quite) a character, he's an eccentric

Do not confuse with **originel**.

originalité [ɔriʒinalite] **NF 1** *(nouveauté)* originality **2** *(excentricité)* eccentricity, oddness **3** *(trait original)* original feature; *(de personne)* eccentricity

origine [ɔriʒin] **NF 1** *(création, début)* origin; **l'o. de l'univers** the origin of the universe; **dès l'o.** from the very beginning, from the outset; **à l'o.** originally, in the beginning, at first; **à l'o. de** at the origin of; **des origines à nos jours** from the earliest times to the present day **2** *(ascendance)* origin; **être d'o. illustre/ouvrière** to be of noble/working-class descent; **être d'o. modeste** to be of humble origin *or* descent; **il est d'o. anglaise, il est anglais d'o.** he is English by birth; **il a des origines anglaises** he is of English extraction *or* has English origins; **d'o. française** *(produit, mot)* of French origin; **la colonie devait son o. aux baleiniers** the colony was founded by *or* owed its origins to whalers **3** *(source)* origin, source; *(d'un mot)* origin, derivation; *(d'une tradition)* origin; **l'o. de cette coutume est ...** the custom has its origins in ...; **tirer son o. de qch** to originate from sth, to have its origins in sth; **le mot tire son o. du latin** the word originates *or* derives from the Latin; **bureau d'o.** office of dispatch; **certificat d'o.** certificate of origin; **vins d'o.** vintage wines; **appellation d'o. contrôlée d'un vin** = official quality guarantee of a wine **4** *Math* **(point) o.** zero point

originel, -elle [ɔriʒinɛl] **ADJ** *(péché, forme)* original; *(cause, sens)* original, primary

Do not confuse with the French adjective **original**.

originellement [ɔriʒinɛlmɑ̃] **ADV** *(à l'origine)* originally; *(dès l'origine)* from the outset

orignal, -aux [ɔriɲal, -o] **NM** *Zool* moose

oripeaux [ɔripo] **NMPL** *(haillons)* rags, tatters; *(vêtements voyants)* loud *or* gaudy clothes

ORL [ɔɛrɛl] **N** *Méd (abrév* **oto-rhino-laryngologiste)** ENT specialist

orléaniste [ɔrleanist] **ADJ, N** *Hist* Orleanist

Orlon® [ɔrlɔ̃] **NM** Orlon®

ormaie [ɔrmɛ] **NF** elm grove

orme [ɔrm] **NM 1** *(arbre)* elm (tree); **o. blanc, o. de(s) montagne(s)** wych elm; **o. champêtre** *ou* **à petites feuilles** common elm, English elm; **maladie des ormes** Dutch elm disease **2** *(bois)* elm (wood)

ormeau, -eaux [ɔrmo] **NM** *(arbre)* (young) elm

orné [ɔrne] **ADJ** *(style)* ornate, florid; **lettre ornée** illuminated letter

ornement [ɔrnəmɑ̃] **NM** ornament; *(détail)* embellishment; *(parure)* adornment; **sans o.** plain, unadorned; **plantes d'o.** ornamental plants; *Rel* **ornements sacerdotaux** vestments; *Mus* **notes d'o.** grace notes, ornaments

ornemental, -ale, -aux, -ales [ɔrnəmɑ̃tal, -o] **ADJ** ornamental

ornementation [ɔrnəmɑ̃tasjɔ̃] **NF** ornamentation, decoration

ornementer [ɔrnəmɑ̃te] **VT** to ornament, to decorate

orner [ɔrne] **VT** to decorate **(de** with); **o. une robe de dentelles** to trim a dress with lace

ornière [ɔrnjɛr] **NF** rut; *Fig* **sortir de l'o.** to get out of trouble; *Fig* **tirer qn de l'o.** to get sb out of trouble

ornithologie [ɔrnitɔlɔʒi] **NF** ornithology

ornithologique [ɔrnitɔlɔʒik] **ADJ** ornithological

ornithologiste [ɔrnitɔlɔʒist], **ornithologue** [ɔrnitɔlɔg] **N** ornithologist

ornithorynque [ɔrnitɔrɛ̃k] **NM** *Zool* duck-billed platypus, *Spéc* ornithorhynchus

orogénèse [ɔrɔʒenɛz] **NF** *Géol* orogenesis

orogénie [ɔrɔʒeni] **NF** *Géol* orogeny

orogénique [ɔrɔʒenik] **ADJ** *Géol* orogenic

orographie [ɔrɔgrafi] **NF** orography

oronge [ɔrɔ̃ʒ] **NF** *Bot* royal agaric, Caesar's mushroom; **fausse o.** fly agaric

orpaillage [ɔrpajaʒ] **NM** gold washing *or* panning

Orphée [ɔrfe] **N** *Myth* Orpheus

orphelin, -ine [ɔrfəlɛ̃, -in] **N** orphan
ADJ orphan(ed); **o. de père** fatherless; **o. de mère** motherless
NF *Typ* **orpheline** orphan

orphelinat [ɔrfəlina] **NM** orphanage

orphéon [ɔrfeɔ̃] **NM 1** *(fanfare)* band **2** *Arch (chorale)* choral society

orphéoniste [ɔrfeɔnist] **N 1** *(d'une fanfare)* band member **2** *Arch (d'une chorale)* choral society member

orphie [ɔrfi] **NF** *Zool* garfish, garpike

orphisme [ɔrfism] **NM** orphisme

orpiment [ɔrpimɑ̃] **NM** *Tech* orpiment

orque [ɔrk] **NF** *Zool* killer whale, orc, grampus

Orsay [ɔrsɛ] **N** **le Quai d'O.** = the French Foreign Office

ORSEC [ɔrsɛk] *(abrév* **organisation des secours) le plan O.** = disaster contingency plan

Le plan ORSEC
This scheme is set in motion whenever there is a major disaster in France, such as flooding or forest fires. Under the provisions of the scheme, the "préfet", or chief of police, is empowered to mobilize both public and private resources to deal with a civil emergency.

orteil [ɔrtɛj] **NM** toe; **gros o.** big toe; **petit o.** little toe

ORTF [ɔɛrteɛf] **NM** *Anciennement (abrév* **Office de la radiodiffusion et télévision française)** = publicly owned broadcasting organization, divided into seven autonomous organizations in 1974

orthochromatique [ɔrtokrɔmatik] **ADJ** *Phot* orthochromatic

orthodontie [ɔrtodɔ̃ti] **NF** orthodontics

orthodontique [ɔrtodɔ̃tik] **ADJ** orthodontic

orthodontiste [ɔrtodɔ̃tist] **N** orthodontist

orthodoxe [ɔrtodɔks] **ADJ** *(église, doctrine, opinion)* orthodox; **peu o.** unorthodox, unconventional
N *Rel* person of orthodox beliefs; *(de l'Église orthodoxe)* member of the Orthodox Church; *Pol* follower of the (official) party line

orthodoxie [ɔrtodɔksi] **NF** orthodoxy

orthogénie [ɔrtoʒeni] **NF** *Méd* birth control, family planning

orthogonal, -ale, -aux, -ales [ɔrtogɔnal, -o] **ADJ** orthogonal

orthogonalement [ɔrtogɔnalmɑ̃] **ADV** orthogonally, at right angles

orthographe [ɔrtograf] **NF** spelling; **je ne connais pas l'o. de ce mot** I don't know how to spell this word *or* how this word is spelt; **mot qui a deux orthographes** word that has two spellings, word that can be spelt in two ways; **faute d'o.** spelling mistake; **réforme de l'o.** spelling reform; **o. d'usage/d'accord** literal/grammatical spelling; **être bon en o., avoir une bonne o.** to be good at spelling VOIR GRAMMAIRE A79-80

orthographier [ɔrtografje] **VT** *(impf, pr sub* **n. orthographiions, v. orthographiiez)** to spell; **mal o. un mot** to spell a word incorrectly, to misspell a word

orthographique [ɔrtografik] **ADJ** *Gram* orthographic(al); **réforme o.** spelling reform

orthopédie [ɔrtɔpedi] NF orthopaedics, Am orthopedics

orthopédique [ɔrtɔpedik] ADJ orthopaedic, *surtout Am* orthopedic; **chaussures orthopédiques** orthopaedic shoes; **semelles orthopédiques** built-up soles

orthopédiste [ɔrtɔpedist] N **1** *(médecin)* orthopaedist, *surtout Am* orthopedist; **chirurgien o.** orthopaedic *or surtout Am* orthopedic surgeon **2** *(fabricant)* maker of orthopaedic *or surtout Am* orthopedic apparatus

orthophonie [ɔrtɔfɔni] NF speech therapy

orthophoniste [ɔrtɔfɔnist] N speech therapist

orthoptie [ɔrtɔpsi] NF orthoptics

orthoptiste [ɔrtɔptist] N orthoptist

ortie [ɔrti] NF nettle; **o. brûlante** stinging nettle; **o. blanche** dead nettle

ortolan [ɔrtɔlã] NM *Orn* ortolan (bunting)

orvet [ɔrvɛ] NM *Zool* slow-worm, blindworm

oryx [ɔriks] NM oryx

OS [oɛs] NM *abrév* **ouvrier spécialisé**

os [ɔs, *pl* o] NM bone; **avoir de gros/petits os** to be big-boned/small-boned; **viande avec os** meat on the bone; **viande sans os** meat off the bone, boned meat; **cuiller en os** bone spoon; **n'avoir que la peau sur les os, n'être qu'un sac** *ou* **un paquet d'os** to be nothing but skin and bone, to be just a bag of bones; **elle est tellement maigre qu'on lui voit les os** she's a bag of bones; **voir qn en chair et en os** to see sb in the flesh; **mouillé** *ou* **trempé jusqu'aux os** soaked to the skin, wet through; **pourri jusqu'à l'os** thoroughly corrupt; **se rompre les os** to break one's neck; **il ne fera pas de vieux os** he's not long for this world, he won't make old bones; *Fig* **donner** *ou* **jeter un os à ronger à qn** to give sb something to keep him/her happy; *Fam* **tomber sur un os** to run up against *or* hit a snag; *Fam* **il y a un os** there's a snag *or* hitch; *très Fam* **je l'ai dans l'os** I've been shafted *or* screwed
► ► *Anat* **os malaire** cheek bone; **os à moelle** marrowbone; **os de seiche** cuttlebone

oscar [ɔskar] NM *Cin* Oscar; **elle a reçu l'o. du meilleur second rôle** she won the Oscar for best supporting actress

OSCE [oɛssəe] NF *(abrév* **Organisation pour la sécurité et la coopération en Europe)** OSCE

oscillant, -ante [ɔsilã, -ãt] ADJ *(pendule), Élec (décharge)* oscillating; *(tige)* rocking; *Radio* **circuit o.** oscillatory circuit; *Méd* **fièvre oscillante** irregular fever

oscillateur [ɔsilatœr] NM *Radio, Électron* oscillator

oscillation [ɔsilasjõ] NF **1** *(d'un pendule)* swing, oscillation; *Phys, Élec* oscillation; *Phys* **oscillations amorties/entretenues** damped/sustained oscillations **2** *(d'un bateau)* rocking **3** *Tech* vibration **4** *Fig (du marché, de l'opinion etc)* fluctuation; **oscillations saisonnières** seasonal fluctuations

oscillatoire [ɔsilatwar] ADJ *(mouvement, circuit)* oscillatory

osciller [ɔsile, -je] VI **1** *(d'un pendule)* to swing, to oscillate; *(de l'aiguille d'un compteur de vitesse)* to flicker; *(d'un bateau)* to rock; *Phys, Élec* to oscillate **2** *(hésiter)* **o. entre deux opinions/positions** to waver between two opinions/positions **3** *Fin (du marché)* to fluctuate

oscillogramme [ɔsilɔgram] NM oscillogram

oscillographe [ɔsilɔgraf] NM oscillograph; **o. cathodique** cathode ray tube

oscilloscope [ɔsilɔskɔp] NM oscilloscope

osé [oze] ADJ *(tentative, démarche, geste)* dar-

ing, bold, audacious; *(plaisanterie, scène d'un film)* daring, risqué; *(demande)* bold; **c'est vraiment o. de sa part** that's really daring *or* bold *or* audacious of him

oseille [ozɛj] NF **1** *Bot* sorrel **2** *Arg (argent)* dough, bread, *Br* lolly; **avoir de l'o.** to have bags *or* pots of money, to be loaded

oser [oze] VT **1** **o. faire qch** to dare (to) do sth; **elle n'ose (pas) le faire** she daren't do it, she doesn't dare (to) do it; **les mots qu'il n'a jamais osé dire** the words he never dared (to) say; **comment oses-tu répondre à ton père!** how dare you answer your father back!; **je voudrais qu'il vienne mais je n'ose l'espérer** I'd like him to come but I daren't hope *or* I don't dare hope that he will; **si j'ose dire** if I may (venture to) say so; *Litt* **o. qch** to dare sth; **il faut o.** nothing ventured, nothing gained; **comment osez-vous?** how dare you!; **approchez si vous osez!** come over here if you dare!; **il veut me parler? qu'il ose un peu!** he wants to talk to me? just let him dare!; **vous n'oseriez pas!** you wouldn't dare! SEE GRAMMAR A40-1; A61; B35 **2** *Suisse (avoir la permission de)* **est-ce que j'ose entrer?** may I come in?

oseraie [ozrɛ] NF osier bed

osier [ozje] NM **1** *Bot* osier; **brin d'o.** withy **2** *(en vannerie)* wicker; **panier d'o.** wicker basket

Oslo [ɔslo] N Oslo

osmonde [ɔsmõd] NF *Bot* **o. royale** royal fern

osmose [ɔsmoz] NF *aussi Fig* osmosis; *Fig (entre des personnes)* total empathy

ossature [ɔsatyr] NF **1** *Biol (d'un homme, d'un animal)* frame, skeleton; **d'une o. puissante** powerfully built, of powerful build **2** *Fig (structure) (d'un bâtiment)* frame(work); *(d'un pont)* main girders; *(d'un texte)* framework, structure

osselet [ɔslɛ] NM *(de mouton)* knucklebone; **jouer aux osselets** to play at knucklebones; *Anat* **les osselets de l'oreille** the ossicles of the ear, the otic bones

ossements [ɔsmã] NMPL bones

osseux, -euse [ɔsø, -øz] ADJ *(visage, main)* bony; *(tissu)* bone, *Spéc* osseous; **système o.** bone structure; **greffe osseuse** bone graft

ossification [ɔsifikasjõ] NF *Méd* ossification

ossifier [ɔsifje] VT to ossify
VPR **s'ossifier** to ossify, to become ossified

ossu [ɔsy] ADJ big-boned, raw-boned

ossuaire [ɔsɥɛr] NM ossuary, charnel house

OST [oɛste] NF *Com (abrév* **organisation scientifique du travail)** organization and methods, time and motion studies

ostensible [ɔstãsibl] ADJ open; *(mépris)* clear, patent

> Il faut noter que le terme anglais **ostensible** est un faux ami. Il signifie **prétendu, apparent**.

ostensiblement [ɔstãsibləmã] ADV openly

> Il faut noter que le terme anglais **ostensibly** est un faux ami. Il signifie **prétendument, en apparence**.

ostensoir [ɔstãswar] NM *Rel* monstrance

ostentation [ɔstãtasjõ] NF ostentation, show, display; *Litt* **faire o. de sa misère** to parade one's poverty; **agir par** *ou* **avec o.** to act ostentatiously; **sans o.** unostentatiously

ostentatoire [ɔstãtatwar] ADJ ostentatious

ostéologie [ɔsteɔlɔʒi] NF osteology

ostéomyélite [ɔsteɔmjelit] NF *Méd* osteomyelitis

ostéopathe [ɔsteɔpat] N *Méd* osteopath

ostéoporose [ɔsteɔpɔroz] NF *Méd* osteoporosis

ostracisme [ɔstrasism] NM **1** *(exclusion)* ostracism; **frapper qn d'o.** to ostracize sb **2** *(hostilité, attitude de rejet)* hostility

ostréicole [ɔstreikɔl] ADJ **l'industrie o.** oyster farming; **parc o.** oyster bed; **la région est l'un des plus grands parcs ostréicoles de la France** it is one of the largest oyster-producing regions in France

ostréiculteur, -trice [ɔstreikyltœr, -tris] N oyster farmer

ostréiculture [ɔstreikyltyr] NF oyster farming

ostrogot(h), ostrogot(h)e [ɔstrɔgo, -ɔt] N *Hist* **O.** Ostrogoth
NM *(homme malappris)* boor

OT NM *(abrév* **Office du Tourisme)** tourist office

otage [ɔtaʒ] NM hostage; **prendre qn en o.** to take sb hostage; **une prise d'o.** a hostage-taking

otalgie [ɔtalʒi] NF *Méd* earache, *Spéc* otalgia

OTAN [ɔtã] NF *(abrév* **Organisation du traité de l'Atlantique Nord)** NATO

otarie [ɔtari] NF sea lion, *Spéc* otary, eared seal

OTASE [ɔtaz] NF *(abrév* **Organisation du traité de l'Asie du Sud-Est)** SEATO

ôter [ote] VT to remove, to take away; *(vêtement)* to take off; *(tache)* to remove, to take out; *(assiettes)* to clear away; **ô. le couvert** to clear away, to clear the table; **ô. qch à qn** to take sth away from sb; **il faudrait leur ô. ces armes des mains** these weapons should be taken away from them; **ô. ses illusions à qn** to rid sb of his/her illusions; **ça lui a ôté ses illusions** that shattered his illusions; **cela lui a ôté l'appétit** it has taken away his appetite; **cela lui a ôté toute sa force** it has drained him of all his strength; **ô. à qn l'espoir/l'envie de faire qch** to deprive sb of all hope/all desire of doing sth; **tu ne m'ôteras pas de l'idée que ...** I'm quite convinced that ...; **cela n'ôte rien à sa valeur/à notre amitié** that in no way detracts from its value/from our friendship; **ô. qch à** *ou* **de qch** to remove sth from sth; **ôtez trois de cinq** take (away) *or* subtract three from five; **10 ôté de 30 égale 20** 30 minus 10 equals 20, 10 taken away from 30 leaves 20; **cela me l'a ôté tout à fait de l'esprit** that drove *or* put it right out of my head; **ô. le pain de la bouche à qn** to take the bread out of sb's mouth; **ô. la vie à qn** to take sb's life
VPR **s'ôter** *Fam* **ôtez-vous de là!** get out of the way!, move (yourself)!; **ôte-toi de mon chemin!** get out of my way!; **ôte-toi de là que je m'y mette!** get out and make room for me!; **il faut qu'il s'ôte cette idée de la tête** he has to get that idea out of his head; **elle ne peut pas s'ô. de l'idée que ...** she can't get it out of her head that ...

otique [ɔtik] ADJ *Anat* otic

otite [ɔtit] NF *Méd* otitis

OTM [oteɛm] NM *Com (abrév* **opérateur de transport multimodal)** multi-modal operator

otologie [ɔtɔlɔʒi] NF otology

oto-rhino, *pl* **oto-rhinos** [otorino] N *Méd Fam* ENT specialist

oto-rhino-laryngologie NF *Méd* ear, nose and throat medicine, *Spéc* otolaryngology, otorhinolaryngology

oto-rhino-laryngologiste, *pl* **oto-rhino-laryngologistes** N *Méd* ear, nose and throat specialist, *Spéc* otolaryngologist

otoscope [ɔtɔskɔp] NM *Méd* otoscope, ear speculum

OTSI [oteesi] NM (*abrév* **Office du tourisme-syndicat d'initiative**) tourist office

Ottawa [ɔtawa] N Ottawa

ottoman, -ane [ɔtɔmã, -an] ADJ *Hist* Ottoman
 N *Hist* **O.** Ottoman
 NM (*étoffe*) ottoman
 NF **ottomane** (*meuble*) ottoman

ou [u] CONJ or; **voulez-vous du bœuf ou du jambon?** would you like beef or ham?; **trois ou quatre fois par jour** three or four times a day; **l'un ou l'autre** one or the other; **entrez ou sortez** either come in or go out; **qu'il vienne ou non, nous irons** whether he comes or not, we'll go; **vous ou moi, nous lui en parlerons** (either) you or I will speak to him about it; **lui ou son frère va** *ou* **vont vous aider** he or his brother will help you; **l'un ou l'autre devait forcément être le chef** one or the other was bound to be leader; **j'appelle tout de suite ou j'attends demain?** shall I call straight away or wait till tomorrow?; **ou … ou (bien) …** either … or (else) …; **ou vous payez ou j'appelle la police** either you pay up or (else) I call the police; *Ordinat* **circuit OU** OR circuit

où [u] ADV **1** (*dans l'espace*) (*interr*) where; **où habite-t-il?** where does he live?; **où allez-vous?** where are you going?; **où en êtes-vous?** how far have you got (with it)?; **par où est-il passé?** which way did he go?; **jusqu'où les a-t-il suivis?** how far did he follow them?; **qui peut dire où nous vivrons dans dix ans** who can tell where we'll be living in ten years' time?
 2 (*dans l'espace*) (*rel*) where; **j'irai où vous voudrez** I'll go where(ever) you wish; **partout où il va** wherever he goes, everywhere he goes; **vous le trouverez là où vous l'avez laissé** you'll find it where you left it; **d'où on conclut qu'il est coupable** from which one concludes that he is guilty; **d'où sa tristesse** hence her sadness; **où que vous soyez** wherever you may be; **mettez-le n'importe où** put it down anywhere; **nous cherchons un studio où passer quelques jours** we're looking for a studio flat for a few days *or* where we can spend a few days; **dans l'état où elle est** in the state she's in; **au train où vont les choses** at this rate, at the rate things are going SEE GRAMMAR B23
 3 (*temps*) when; **à l'époque où il était jeune** in the days when he was young
 4 (= *dans lequel, auquel etc*) la maison où il habite the house he lives in, the house in which he lives

OUA [oya] NF (*abrév* **Organisation de l'unité africaine**) OAU

ouache [waʃ] NF *Can* bear's den

ouah [wa] INT woof!

ouaille [waj] NF *Bible, Litt* sheep; **le pasteur et ses ouailles** the minister and his flock

ouais [wɛ] INT *Fam* yeah!, yep!; (*sceptique*) oh yeah?

ouananiche [wananiʃ] NF *Can* freshwater salmon

ouaouaron [wawarɔ̃] NM *Can* bullfrog

ouate [wat] NF (*souvent* la ouate, *parfois* l'ouate) **1** (*pour rembourrage*) padding, wadding; **doublé d'o.** quilted **2** (*pour soins*) cotton wool, *Am* absorbent cotton; **o. hydrophile** absorbent cotton wool *or* cotton; *Fig* **avoir été élevé dans la o.** to have been brought up in cotton wool

ouaté [wate] ADJ (*vêtement*) quilted; *Fig* (*bruit de pas*) muffled, soft; (*contours*) vague, fuzzy

ouater [wate] VT to quilt

ouatine [watin] NF *Tex* quilting (material)

ouatiné [watine] ADJ (*tissu*) quilted

oubli [ubli] NM **1** (*acte d'oublier*) forgetting; (*défaillance de la mémoire*) forgetfulness; (*négligence*) (*du devoir*) neglect; **l'o. de soi** selflessness **2** (*général*) oblivion; **tomber dans l'o.** to sink *or* fall into oblivion, to be forgotten; **sortir de l'o.** to emerge from oblivion **3** (*trou de mémoire*) oversight; (*lacune*) omission; **réparer un o.** to rectify an oversight/omission; **je suis désolée de ne pas l'avoir fait, c'est un o.** I'm sorry I've not done it, it's an oversight on my part

oublier [ublije] (*impf, pr sub* n. **oubliions,** v. **oubliiez**) VT **1** (*ne pas se rappeler*) to forget; **j'ai oublié son nom** I've forgotten his name, his name has slipped my mind; **j'ai oublié son visage** I've forgotten what he looks like; **o. où/quand/qui …** to forget where/when/who …; **j'ai complètement oublié que nous avions rendez-vous aujourd'hui** I completely forgot that we'd agreed to meet today; **o. le passé** to forget the past; **oublions le passé** let's let bygones be bygones; **faire o. son passé** to live down one's past; **o. de faire qch** to forget to do sth; **on ne nous le laissera pas o.** we'll never hear the last of it *or* be allowed to forget it, we'll never live it down; **il mourut oublié de tous** he died forgotten by all, he died in obscurity; **n'oubliez pas à qui vous vous adressez** remember who you're talking to; *Hum* **il a oublié d'être bête** he's not lacking in brains, he's as clever as they come VOIR GRAMMAIRE A44
 2 (*ne pas prendre*) to forget, to leave (behind); (*omettre*) to leave out; (*rendez-vous*) to overlook; (*devoir*) to neglect; **j'ai oublié mes lunettes chez toi** I've left my glasses (behind) at your place; **o. l'heure** to forget the time, to lose track of the time
 VPR **s'oublier 1** (*se relâcher*) to forget oneself, to forget one's manners; **le chien s'est oublié sur le tapis** the dog's made a mess on the carpet
 2 (*s'exclure*) to forget oneself; *Fam* **il ne s'oublie pas** he always looks after himself, he always takes care of number one
 3 (*sortir de la mémoire*) **les langues étrangères s'oublient facilement quand on ne les pratique pas** foreign languages are easily forgotten when you don't use them; **des choses pareilles ne doivent jamais s'o.** things like that must never be forgotten; **c'est comme le vélo, ça ne s'oublie pas** it's like riding a bike, once you learn you never forget

oubliette [ublijɛt] NF dungeon, oubliette; *Fig Fam* **mettre qch aux oubliettes** to shelve sth indefinitely; **cet homme politique fut mis aux oubliettes pendant dix ans** this politician was condemned to ten years in the wilderness

oublieux, -ieuse [ublijø, -jøz] ADJ forgetful; **o. de** forgetful of; (*devoir*) neglectful of, forgetful of

oued [wɛd] NM *Géog* wadi

Ouessant [wɛsɑ̃] NM Ushant

ouest [wɛst] NM (*no pl*) **1** (*point cardinal*) west; **à l'o., dans l'o.** in the west; **où est l'o.?** which way is west?; **la partie la plus à l'o. de l'île** the westernmost part of the island; **le vent vient de l'o.** it's a west *or* westerly wind, the wind is coming from the west; **un vent d'o.** a westerly wind; **le vent d'o.** the west wind; **aller au** *ou* **vers l'o.** to go west *or* westwards; **les trains qui vont vers l'o.** trains going west, westbound trains; **rouler vers l'o.** to drive west *or* westwards; **aller droit vers l'o.** to head due west; **la cuisine est plein o.** *ou* **exposée à l'o.** the kitchen faces due west; **le soleil se couche à l'o.** the sun sets in the west **2** (*partie d'un pays, d'un continent*) west, western area *or* regions; (*partie d'une ville*) west; **l'o. de l'Italie** western Italy, the west of Italy; **dans l'o. de l'Espagne** in western Spain, in the west of Spain; **elle habite dans l'o.** she lives in the west; **il habite dans**

l'o. de Paris he lives in the west of Paris; **elle est de l'o.** she's from the west; **les gens de l'o.** people who live in the west
 ADJ INV (*côte, face*) west; (*banlieue, partie, région*) western; **la façade o. d'un immeuble** the west-facing wall of a building; **la chambre est côté o.** the bedroom faces west; **dans la partie o. de la France** in the west of France, in western France; **suivre la direction o.** to head *or* go westwards

ouest-allemand, -ande, *pl* **ouest-allemand(e)s** *Anciennement* ADJ West German
 N **O.** West German

ouf [uf] INT whew!, phew!; *Fam* **il n'a pas eu le temps de dire o.!** he didn't even have time to catch his breath!
 NM **pousser un o. de soulagement** to heave a sigh of relief

ouf² ADJ *Fam* crazy, *Br* mental, barking, *Am* nutso

Ouganda [ugãda] NM Uganda

ougandais, -aise [ugãdɛ, -ɛz] ADJ Ugandan
 N **O.** Ugandan

ougrien, -ienne [ugrijɛ̃, -jɛn] *Ling* ADJ Ugric
 NM Ugric

oui [wi] ADV yes; **vient-il? – o.** is he coming? – yes (he is); **je crois que o.** I think so; **faire signe que o., faire o. de la tête** to nod (one's head); **mais o., bien sûr que o.** (yes,) of course; **o., o., allez-y** yes, (yes,) get on with it; **êtes-vous content de partir? – o. et non** are you happy to be leaving? – yes and no; **eh o.! c'est encore moi!** yes! it's me again!; *Naut* **o., commandant!** aye, aye, sir!; **ah, o.?** really?, is that so?; *Fam* **tu viens, o.?** you're coming, aren't you?; *Fam* **tu viens, o. ou non** *ou très Fam* **o. ou merde?** are you coming or not?, are you coming or aren't you?, are you coming, yes or no? SEE GRAMMAR B64
 NM INV *Pol* **deux cents o. et trois cents non** two hundred ayes and three hundred noes; *Fam* **se quereller/pleurer pour un o. pour un non** to quarrel/cry over the slightest thing; **changer d'avis pour un o. pour un non** to change one's mind at the drop of a hat

ouï-dire [widir] NM INV hearsay; **ce sont des o.** it's hearsay; **je ne le sais que par o.** I know it only by *or* from hearsay

ouïe [wi] NF **1** (*sens*) (sense of) hearing; **avoir l'o.** fine to have keen *or* sharp ears, to have excellent hearing; **avoir l'o. défectueuse** to be hard of hearing; **à portée de l'o.** within earshot, within hearing distance; **être tout o.** to be all ears *or* all attention **2** *Mus* **ouïes** (*de violon*) sound holes **3** *Tech* (*d'un ventilateur*) ear **4** *Zool* **ouïes** gills

ouille [uj] INT ouch!, ow!

ouïr [wir] VT (*only used in inf, pp* **ouï,** *compound tenses, prp* **oyant** *and imp* **oyez;** *p hist* **j'ouïs** *and fu* **j'ouïrai** *sometimes used*) *Arch* to hear; **nous l'avons ouï dire à notre père** we have heard our father say so; **j'ai souvent ouï dire que …** I have often heard it said that …; *Jur* **o. les témoins** to hear the witnesses; *Arch* **oyez, oyez braves gens …** oyez, oyez *or* now hear this, good people …

ouistiti [wistiti] NM *Zool* marmoset; *Fig Fam* **un drôle de o.** an odd character

ouragan [uragã] NM hurricane; **entrer comme un o. dans une pièce** to burst into a room; **sa déclaration a déclenché un o. de protestations** his statement caused a storm of protest *or* an uproar

Oural (l') [lural] NM **1** (*fleuve*) the Ural **2** (*montagnes*) the Urals, the Ural Mountains

ourdir [urdir] VT **1** *Tex* (*lin, tissu*) to warp **2** (*paille*) to plait **3** *Fig* (*complot*) to hatch, to weave

ourdissage [urdisaʒ] NM *Tex* warping

ourdou [urdu] NM *Ling* Urdu

ourlé [urle] ADJ *Couture* hemmed; **des oreilles délicatement ourlées** delicately shaped ears

ourler [urle] VT **1** *Couture* to hem; **o. à jour** to hemstitch **2** *(border)* to edge (**de** with) **3** *Tech (feuilles de métal)* to lap-joint

ourlet [urlɛ] NM **1** *Couture* hem; **o. à jour** hemstitched hem; **faux o.** false hem; **point d'o.** hemstitch **2** *(repli, rebord) (d'un cratère)* edge; *(de l'oreille)* rim, *Spéc* helix **3** *Tech (de feuilles de métal)* lap joint, hem

ours, ourse [urs] N *Zool* bear, *f* she bear; **il vit comme un o.** he's a grumpy, unsociable sort; *Fig* **quel o.!** what a boor!; *Prov* **il ne faut pas vendre la peau de l'o. avant de l'avoir tué** don't count your chickens before they're hatched; *Arg* **avoir ses o.** *(d'une femme)* to have the curse, to have one's period
▪ NM *Journ* credit pages *(where contributors to a book or newspaper are acknowledged)*
▪ NF *Astron* **la Grande Ourse** *(constellation)* the Great Bear; *(sept étoiles)* the Plough, *Am* the Big Dipper; **la Petite Ourse** the Little Bear, *Am* the Little Dipper
▸ ▸ **o. blanc** polar bear; **o. brun** brown bear; **o. gris d'Amérique** grizzly bear; *Fam* **o. mal léché** uncouth individual; **o. marin** sea bear, fur seal; **o. en peluche** teddy bear; **o. polaire** polar bear

oursin [ursɛ̃] NM sea urchin; *Fam* **avoir des oursins dans le porte-monnaie** to be tight-fisted

ourson [ursɔ̃] NM bear cub

oust(e) [ust] INT *Fam* **allez o.!** *(avance!)* get a move on!; *(va-t'en!)* scram!, *Br* hop it!

out [awt] ADJ INV **1** *(personne)* out (of fashion); **ce chanteur est déjà o.** that singer is already out of fashion **2** *Tennis* out

outarde [utard] NF *Orn* **1** bustard **2** *(bernache du Canada)* Canada goose

outil [uti] NM **1** *(d'un ouvrier, artisan)* tool; *(d'un jardinier)* tool, implement; **o. coupant** *ou* **de coupe** *ou* **tranchant** cutting tool; *(pour bords ou bordures)* edging tool **2** *(moyen)* tool; **outils pédagogiques** teaching aids; *Bourse* **o. de spéculation** trading instrument; **o. de travail** tool, work instrument; **o. d'aide à la décision** decision-making tool; *Ordinat* **o. auteur** authoring tool; *Ordinat* **o. de création de pages Web** web authoring tool; **o. de gestion** management tool; *Ordinat* **o. de navigation sur le Web** web browser; **o. de production** production tool; **o. de recherche** research tool

outillage [utijaʒ] NM **1** *(ensemble d'outils)* (set of) tools **2** *(équipement) (d'une usine)* plant, equipment

outiller [utije] VT *(ouvrier)* to equip *or* supply with tools; *(usine)* to equip, to fit out, to tool up; **nous ne sommes pas outillés pour ce genre de réparation** we're not equipped *or* we don't have the tools for that sort of repair
▪ VPR **s'outiller** *(d'une usine)* to equip itself; *(d'un bricoleur)* to equip oneself with tools

outrage [utraʒ] NM *(injure) (au bon goût etc)* insult (**à** to); **c'est un o. aux convenances/à la morale** it offends against propriety/against morality; *Euph* **faire subir les derniers outrages à une femme** to violate a woman; *Litt* **l'o. des ans** *ou* **du temps** the ravages of time
▸ ▸ *Jur* **o. à agent** insulting behaviour; **o. aux bonnes mœurs** affront to public decency; **o. à magistrat** contempt of court; **o. à la pudeur** public indecency

outrageant [utraʒɑ̃] ADJ *(proposition, refus)* insulting; *(plaisanterie, propos)* offensive; *(accusation)* outrageous

outrager [utraʒe] VT (**j'outrageai(s)**) **1** *(insulter)* to insult; **o. un homme dans son honneur/sa dignité** to offend against a man's honour/dignity **2** *Vieilli (porter atteinte à) (la vérité)* to violate; *(la raison, le bon sens, le bon goût)* to offend against

outrageusement [utraʒøzmɑ̃] ADV **1** *(excessivement)* excessively, outrageously **2** *Vieilli* insultingly

outrageux, -euse [utraʒø, -øz] ADJ *Vieilli* insulting

outrance [utrɑ̃s] NF excess; *(d'une tenue, d'une attitude, de propos)* extravagance; **agressif/méfiant à o.** excessively aggressive/mistrustful; **combat à o.** fight to the death; **industrialisation à o.** all out industrialization; **travailler à o.** to work excessively *or* to excess

outrancier, -ière [utrɑ̃sje, -jɛr] ADJ *(personnalité, propos)* extreme

outre¹ [utr] NF wine skin; *(en peau de chèvre)* goatskin bottle

outre² PRÉP **1 o. mesure** *(travailler)* excessively; *(se soucier, s'exposer etc)* unduly, excessively; **se fatiguer o. mesure** to tire oneself out unduly, to overtire oneself; **je ne me sens pas fatigué o. mesure** I don't feel unduly *or* overly tired; **il n'est pas scrupuleux o. mesure** he's not excessively *or* overly scrupulous **2** *(en plus de)* besides, in addition to; **o. cette somme** besides *or* in addition to that sum; **o. cela** besides that, in addition to that
▪ ADV **passer o., aller o.** to go on *or* further; *Fig* **passer o.** to carry on regardless; **passer o. à une interdiction/la loi** to disregard *or* take no notice of *or* ignore a ban/the law; **en o.** besides, moreover; **j'ai, en o., deux neveux** I have two nephews besides
▪ CONJ **o. (le fait) qu'il est riche** apart from the fact that he's rich, apart from *or* besides *or* in addition to being rich; **o. qu'il est riche, il est extrêmement aimable** he's not only rich, he's also very nice

outré [utre] ADJ **1** *(indigné)* outraged, indignant; **je suis o. de voir que …** I'm outraged to see that … **2** *Litt (excessif) (éloge)* exaggerated, extravagant, overdone; **comédien dont le jeu est o.** actor who overacts, actor whose acting is overdone

outre-Atlantique ADV on the other side of the Atlantic, across the Atlantic

outrecuidance [utrəkɥidɑ̃s] NF **1** *(orgueil)* presumptuousness **2** *(insolence)* impertinence, effrontery; **il a eu l'o. de me dire que …** he had the impertinence *or* effrontery to tell me that …

outrecuidant [utrəkɥidɑ̃] ADJ **1** *(orgueilleux)* presumptuous **2** *(insolent)* impertinent

outre-Manche [utrəmɑ̃ʃ] ADV on the other side of the Channel, across the Channel

outremer [utrəmɛr] NM **1** *Minér* lapis lazuli **2 (bleu d')o.** ultramarine
▪ ADJ INV ultramarine

outre-mer [utrəmɛr] ADV overseas; **commerce d'o.** overseas trade; *Admin* **territoires d'o.** overseas territories

outrepasser [utrəpase] VT *(une limite, ses droits)* to exceed, to go beyond

outrer [utre] VT **1** *(exagérer)* to exaggerate; *(rôle)* to overdo **2** *(mettre en colère)* to outrage, to infuriate; **j'ai été outré par son attitude** I was outraged by *or* at his attitude

outre-Rhin [utrərɛ̃] ADV beyond *or* across the Rhine

outre-Sarine [utrəsarin] ADV *Suisse* in German-speaking Switzerland

outre-tombe (d') [dutrɔtɔb] ADV from beyond the grave; *Fig* **une voix d'o.** a sepulchral voice

outsider [awtsajdœr] NM *Courses de chevaux, Fig* outsider

ouvert [uvɛr] ADJ **1** *(porte, fenêtre, tiroir)* open; **entre, la porte est ouverte** *ou* **c'est o.** come in, the door's open; **porte grande ouverte** wide-open door; **plaie ouverte** open *or* gaping wound; **fracture ouverte** open fracture; **il a le crâne/le genou o.** he has a gaping wound in his skull/knee, his skull/knee has been split open; *Chir* **opérer qn à cœur o.** to perform open-heart surgery on sb; **accueillir qn à bras ouverts** to welcome sb with open arms; **il était dans son lit, les yeux ouverts** he was lying in bed with his eyes open; **tu ne peux pas les recevoir chemise ouverte** you can't greet them with your shirt open *or* undone; **manteau qui se porte le col o.** coat that is worn with the collar open *or* undone; **voyelle ouverte** open vowel; *Ftbl* **jeu o.** open play; **traduire à livre o.** to translate at sight *or* off the cuff; **elle lit le grec à livre o.** she can read Greek at sight; **ville ouverte** open *or* unfortified town; **o. de 10 heures à 5 heures** open (from) 10 to 5; *Fam* **l'épicier du coin reste o. jusqu'à minuit** the grocer on the corner stays open till midnight; **collection ouverte au public** collection open to the public; **o. à la navigation** open to navigation; *Banque* **compte o.** open account; **c'est la guerre ouverte contre les fumeurs** it's open war on smokers; **être o. guerre ouverte avec qn** to be openly at war with sb; **le gaz/robinet est o.** the gas/tap is on; **la séance est ouverte** I declare the meeting open; **la chasse/la campagne électorale est ouverte depuis ce matin** the hunting season/the election campaign began *or* started this morning; **les paris sont ouverts** *Courses de chevaux* bets are being taken; *Fig* it's anyone's guess **2** *Fig (franc, sans préjugé) (personne, caractère)* open, frank; **être o. à toute proposition** to be open to suggestions; **avoir l'esprit o.** to be open-minded; **parler à cœur o.** to speak openly *or* frankly **3** *Suisse (en pichet)* **du vin o.** wine in a carafe

ouvertement [uvɛrtəmɑ̃] ADV openly; *(parler)* openly, frankly

ouverture [uvɛrtyr] NF **1** *(d'une porte, d'un livre, d'une séance etc)* opening; *(de la saison de chasse, d'une campagne)* opening, start; **pour ne pas faire la queue, j'étais là avant même l'o.** to avoid queuing, I was there even before it *or* the doors opened; **elle travaille dans cette boutique depuis l'o.** she has worked in the shop since it opened; **j'ai fait l'o. de la galerie** I was at the opening of the gallery; *Bourse* **à l'o., le dollar était à 5,98 euros** at the start of trading, the dollar was at 5.98 euros, the dollar opened at 5.98 euros; **l'o. des portes du musée est prévue pour janvier** the museum is scheduled to open (its doors) in January; **l'o. des portes du lycée se fait tous les jours à huit heures** the school doors are opened every day at eight o'clock; **o. d'un compte** opening of an account; *Fin* **o. d'un crédit** granting of a loan; **o. des hostilités** outbreak of hostilities; *Ordinat* **o. de session** logon; *Aut* **o. sans clé** keyless entry; **conférence/discours d'o.** opening lecture/speech; *Bourse* **cours d'o.** opening price; **heures d'o.** opening hours; *Rugby* **il est demi d'o.** he plays stand-off *or* fly-half
2 ouvertures *(avances)* overtures; **faire des ouvertures à qn** to make overtures to sb; **des ouvertures de paix** peace overtures
3 *Mus* overture
4 *(accès) (dans un mur etc)* opening, aperture; *(d'une caverne)* mouth; *(d'une haie)* gap, break
5 *(écartement) (d'une voûte etc)* width, span; *(des branches d'un compas)* spread; *Élec* **o. d'induit** armature gap

6 *Phot* aperture, f-stop; **réduire l'o.** to stop down; **o. du diaphragme** aperture, f-stop **7** *Fig* **o. de cœur** openness, frankness; **o. d'esprit** open-mindedness; *Pol* **le Président pratique une politique d'o.** the President is following a policy of conciliation **8** *Cartes, Échecs* opening **9** *Mktg* window of opportunity; **l'o. de nouveaux marchés** the opening up of new markets

ouvrable [uvrabl] ADJ **jour o.** working day; **heures ouvrables** business hours, working hours

ouvrage [uvraʒ] NM **1** *(travail)* work; **se mettre à l'o.** to set to work, to get down to work; **avoir du cœur à l'o.** to put one's heart into one's work, to work with a will; **je n'ai pas le cœur à l'o. aujourd'hui** I'm not in the mood for work today, I don't feel like working today **2** *Constr* work; **entreprise spécialisée dans les ouvrages de maçonnerie** firm specializing in masonry work; **ouvrages d'art** civil engineering works **3** *(livre)* work, book; **o. en prose** prose work; **un o. de philosophie** a work of philosophy, a philosophy book; **un o. de géographie** a geography book; **o. de référence** reference work *or* book; **ouvrages de fonds** backlist titles **4** *(résultat)* piece of work, product; *(tricot, broderie)* work; *Vieilli* **o. de dames** needlework; **corbeille à o.** workbasket; **boîte à o.** workbox; **une rencontre qui est l'o. du hasard** a meeting which is due to chance, a chance meeting; **l'o. du temps** the work of time
NF *Fam* **c'est de la belle o.** that's a nice bit of work

ouvragé [uvraʒe] ADJ = **ouvré**

ouvrager [uvraʒe] VT *(j'ouvrageai(s))* *(métal, bijou)* to work; *(orner)* *(brocart)* to figure

ouvrant [uvrɑ̃] ADJ *Aut* **toit o.** sun roof, sliding roof
NM *Beaux-Arts (d'un triptyque)* panel

ouvré [uvre] ADJ **1** *Tech (fer)* wrought; **produits ouvrés et semi-ouvrés** finished and semi-finished products **2** *Litt (orné)* decorated; *(nappe)* embroidered

ouvre-boîte(s), *pl* **ouvre-boîtes** [uvrəbwat] NM can opener, *Br* tin opener; **o. électrique** electric can *or Br* tin opener

ouvre-bouteille(s), *pl* **ouvre-bouteilles** [uvrəbutɛj] NM bottle opener

ouvre-huître(s), *pl* **ouvre-huîtres** [uvrɥitr] NM oyster knife

ouvrer [uvre] VT **1** *Tech (bois, cuivre etc)* to work **2** *(orner)* *(nappe etc)* to work, to embroider

ouvreur, -euse [uvrœr, -øz] N *Cartes* opener
NF *Théâtre, Cin* usherette

ouvrez-moi [uvremwa] NM INV *Ordinat* read-me document

ouvrier, -ère [uvrije, -ɛr] ADJ **1** *(prolétaire)* *(quartier, tradition)* working-class; **la classe ouvrière** the working class(es); **agitation ouvrière** industrial unrest, labour unrest; **syndicat o.** trade union **2** *Zool* **abeille ouvrière** worker bee; **fourmi ouvrière** worker ant
N worker; *(prolétaire)* working man, f woman; *(de réparation, de travaux publics)* workman; *(d'une machine)* operative; **o. en bois** woodworker; **o. sur métaux** metalworker; **une famille d'ouvriers** a working-class family; *Litt Fig* **il est l'o. de sa fortune** he is a self-made man
NF *Zool* **ouvrière** worker
▸▸ **o. agricole** farm worker *or* hand, agricultural labourer; **o. non qualifié** unskilled manual worker; **o. qualifié** skilled worker; **o. spécialisé** semi-skilled worker

ouvriérisme [uvrijerism] NM *Pol (autogestion)* worker control; *(syndicalisme)* trade unionism

OUVRIR [uvrir] *(prp* **ouvrant**; *pp* **ouvert**; *pr ind* **j'ouvre**; *p hist* **j'ouvris)**

VT to open **1, 2, 4** ▪ to unfasten **1** ▪ to unlock **1** ▪ to turn on **1** ▪ to broaden **2** ▪ to cut through **3** ▪ to open up **4** ▪ to start **4**	
VI to open	
VPR to open **1** ▪ to open up **1** ▪ to cut open **2**	

VT **1** *(porte, fenêtre, boîte, bouteille etc)* to open; *(verrou)* to draw; *(loquet)* to unfasten; *(avec une clef)* to unlock; *(rideaux)* to open, to draw (back); **o. sa maison** *ou* **sa porte à qn** to throw open one's house to sb; *Fig* **o. la porte à qch** to open the door to sth; **il n'a pas ouvert la bouche,** *Fam* **il ne l'a pas ouverte** he didn't open his mouth; *Fam* **tu ferais mieux de ne pas l'o.!** you'd better keep your mouth *or* trap shut!; **o. le lit** to turn down the bed(clothes); **o. un robinet/le gaz** to turn on a tap/the gas; **o. l'électricité** to switch on (the electricity); *Fam* **o. le poste** to put on *or* switch on the radio; *Élec* **o. le circuit** to switch off *or* break the current
2 *Fig (découvrir)* **o. son cœur à qn** to open one's heart to sb, to unburden oneself to sb; **cette expérience lui a ouvert l'esprit** the experience broadened his mind; **cela ouvre l'appétit** it sharpens *or* whets the appetite
3 *(percer)* *(mur)* to cut through; *(mine)* to open up; *(canal)* to cut; *Méd (abcès)* to lance; **le chirurgien lui a ouvert l'estomac** the surgeon opened (up) his/her stomach
4 *(commencer, lancer)* *(une école, une boutique)* to open; *(un débat, une discussion)* to open, to start; **o. un compte chez qn** to open an account with sb; **o. un col en montagne** to open up a pass through *or* in the mountains; **cette discussion m'a ouvert de nouvelles perspectives** the discussion opened (up) new horizons for me; **ce sont des professions que nous voulons o. aux femmes** they are professions that we want to open up to women; **o. le bal** to open the ball; **o. boutique** to set up shop; **o. la marche** to lead the way; *Fin* **o. un crédit** to grant a loan; *Com* **o. un débouché à un produit** to open up a new outlet for a product; *Ordinat* **o. une session** to log in, to log on
VI to open; *(ouvrir la porte)* to open the door; **o. à qn** to open the door to sb, to let sb in; **les magasins n'ouvrent pas les jours de fête** the shops don't open *or* aren't open on public holidays; **la fenêtre n'ouvre plus** the window doesn't *or* won't open any more; **la porte n'ouvre que de l'intérieur** the door can only be opened from the inside, the door only opens from the inside; **la scène ouvre par un chœur** the scene opens with a chorus; **le salon/la fenêtre ouvrait sur le jardin** the drawing room/the window opened on(to) the garden; *TV, Cin* **o. en fondu** to fade in; *TV, Cin* **o. par un volet** to wipe on
VPR **s'ouvrir 1** *(devenir ouvert)* *(d'une porte, d'une fenêtre, des yeux etc)* to open; *(d'une fleur)* to open out, to open; **la porte s'ouvrit en coup de vent** the door flew open; **les fenêtres s'ouvrent sur le jardin** the windows open on(to) the garden; *Fig* **un gouffre s'ouvrait sous mes pieds** a chasm opened up *or* yawned under my feet; **les possibilités/nouvelles perspectives qui s'ouvrent aux jeunes diplômés** the possibilities/new horizons that are opening up for young graduates; **carrières qui s'ouvrent de plus en plus aux femmes** careers that are opening up more and more to women; **s'o. à de nouvelles technologies** to open (up) one's mind to new technologies; **tu ne peux pas ne pas**

t'o. à l'informatique you can't afford to close yourself off to computer technology, you have to be open to computer technology; **la séance s'ouvre par un discours** the meeting opens with a speech; **le bal s'ouvrit par une valse** the ball opened *or* began *or* started with a waltz
2 *(se couper)* **s'o. la main/le menton** to cut open one's hand/chin; **s'o. les veines** to slash one's wrists; **s'o. un chemin à travers la foule** to push one's way through the crowd
3 *(se confier)* **s'o. à qn** to unburden oneself to sb, to confide in sb; **s'o. à qn de qch** to open one's heart to sb about sth, to confide in sb about sth

ouvroir [uvrwar] NM workroom, sewing room

ouzbek [uzbɛk] ADJ Uzbek
N **O.** Uzbek

Ouzbékistan [uzbekistɑ̃] NM Uzbekistan

ovaire [ɔvɛr] NM *Anat, Bot* ovary; **kyste de l'o.** ovarian cyst

ovale [ɔval] ADJ oval; *Sport* **ballon o.** rugby ball; **le ballon o.** *(le rugby)* rugby; **les adeptes du ballon o.** rugby fans
NM oval; **en o.** oval

ovalisation [ɔvalizasjɔ̃] NF *Tech (des cylindres)* ovalization

ovalisé [ɔvalize] ADJ *Tech (cylindre)* ovalized

ovaliser [ɔvalize] VT *Tech* **l'usure ovalise les cylindres** cylinders become ovalized through wear

ovariectomie [ɔvarjɛktɔmi] NF *Méd* ovariectomy, oophorectomy

ovarien, -ienne [ɔvarjɛ̃, -jɛn] ADJ *Anat, Bot* ovarian

ovation [ɔvasjɔ̃] NF ovation; **faire une o. à qn** to give sb an ovation

ovationner [ɔvasjɔne] VT **o. qn** to give sb an ovation

ové [ɔve] ADJ *(fruit)* egg-shaped, ovate

overdose [ɔvœrdoz] NF *Méd, Fig* overdose; **mourir d'une o.** to die of *or* from an overdose; *Fig* **j'ai fait une o. de films japonais** I've overdosed on *or* I've had an overdose of Japanese films

overdrive [ɔvœrdrajv] NM *Aut* overdrive

ovidés [ɔvide] NMPL *Zool, Agr* Ovidae

oviducte [ɔvidykt] NM oviduct

ovin [ɔvɛ̃] *Agr* ADJ ovine
NMPL **ovins** sheep

ovipare [ɔvipar] *Zool* ADJ oviparous
NM oviparous animal

ovni [ɔvni] NM *(abrév* **objet volant non identifié)** UFO

ovocyte [ɔvɔsit] NM oocyte

ovoïde [ɔvɔid] ADJ ovoid, egg-shaped; *Élec* **maillon o.** egg insulator

ovovivipare [ɔvɔvivipar] *Zool* ADJ ovoviviparous
NM ovoviviparous animal

ovulaire [ɔvylɛr] ADJ ovular

ovulation [ɔvylasjɔ̃] NF ovulation

ovule [ɔvyl] NM **1** *Biol* ovum **2** *Pharm* **ovules gynécologiques** (vaginal) pessaries

ovuler [ɔvyle] VI to ovulate

oxalate [ɔksalat] NM *Chimie* oxalate

oxalide [ɔksalid] NF, **oxalis** [ɔksalis] NM *Bot* oxalis, wood sorrel

oxalique [ɔksalik] ADJ *Chimie* **acide o.** oxalic acid

oxford [ɔksfɔrd] *Tex* NM **une chemise en o.** an Oxford shirt
ADJ **de la flanelle o.** Oxford

oxhydrique [ɔksidrik] ADJ oxyhydrogen

oxyacétylénique [ɔksiasetilenik] ADJ *Tech (gaz, soudure)* oxyacetylene

oxycoupage [ɔksikupaʒ] NM *Métal* oxygen cutting

oxydable [ɔksidabl] ADJ **1** *Chimie* oxidizable **2** *(d'un métal)* liable to rust

oxydant [ɔksidɑ̃] ADJ oxidizing ▸ NM oxidizer, oxidizing agent

oxydation [ɔksidasjɔ̃] NF *Chimie* oxidization, oxidation

oxyde [ɔksid] NM *Chimie* oxide; **o. de carbone** carbon monoxide; **o. d'azote** nitrogen oxide; **o. nitrique** nitric oxide

oxyder [ɔkside] VT to oxidize ▸ VPR **s'oxyder** to oxidize

oxygénation [ɔksiʒenasjɔ̃] NF **1** *Chimie* oxygenation **2** *(application d'eau oxygénée)*

les méfaits de l'o. sur les cheveux the damaging effects of bleach on the hair

oxygéné [ɔksiʒene] ADJ *Chimie* oxygenated; **eau oxygénée** hydrogen peroxide; **cheveux oxygénés** peroxide blonde hair, bleached hair

oxygène [ɔksiʒɛn] NM **1** *Chimie* oxygen; *Méd* **tente à o.** oxygen tent **2** *Fam* **j'ai besoin d'o.** I need a change of air

oxygéner [ɔksiʒene] (il oxygène; il oxygénera) VT **1** *Chimie (liquide, tissu vivant)* to oxygenate, to oxygenize; *(élément, produit chimique)* to oxidize **2** *(cheveux)* to bleach, to peroxide ▸ VPR **s'oxygéner** *Fam (respirer)* to take or get a breath of fresh air; **partir à la campagne**

pour une quinzaine pour s'o. to go off to the countryside for two weeks to get some good clean air (in one's lungs)

oxymore [ɔksimɔr], **oxymoron** [ɔksimɔrɔ̃] NM *Ling* oxymoron

oxyton [ɔksitɔ̃] NM *Ling* oxytone

oxyure [ɔksjyr] NM *Méd* oxyuris

oyat [ɔja] NM *Bot* marram grass

Ozalid® [ɔzalid] NM *Typ* Ozalid®

ozone [ozon] NM *Chimie* ozone; **couche d'o.** ozone layer

ozonisation [ozɔnizasjɔ̃] NF *Chimie, Tech* ozonization

ozoniser [ozɔnize] VT to ozonize

P, p [pe] NM *(lettre)* P, p

PAC [pak] NF *(abrév* **Politique Agricole Commune)** CAP

PACA [paka] NF *(abrév* **Provence-Alpes-Côte d'Azur)** = region of southeastern France

pacage [pakaʒ] NM *Agr* **1** *(champ)* pasture(-land); **p. d'été** summer pasture **2** *(action de faire paître)* pasturing, grazing; *Jur* **droit(s) de p.** grazing rights

pacager [pakaʒe] (**je pacageai(s); n. pacageons**) VT *(troupeau)* to pasture, to graze
VI *(d'un troupeau)* to graze

pacane [pakan] NF pecan (nut); *Culin* **tarte aux pacanes** pecan pie

pacemaker [pɛsmɛkœr] NM *Sport, Méd* pacemaker

pacha [paʃa] NM pasha; *Fam* **mener une vie de p.** to live like a lord; **tu ne vas pas faire le p. tout le week-end!** don't expect to be waited on hand and foot all weekend!

pachyderme [paʃiderm] NM pachyderm; *Fig Fam (personne)* great *or* fat lump, tub of lard; **de p.** *(allure, démarche)* elephantine, lumbering; *(grâce)* elephantine

pacificateur, -trice [pasifikatœr, -tris] ADJ pacifying
N peacemaker

pacification [pasifikasjɔ̃] NF pacification

pacifier [pasifje] VT *(impf, pr sub* **n. pacifiions, v. pacifiiez**) to pacify

pacifique [pasifik] ADJ *(coexistence, manifestation etc)* peaceful; *(qui aime la paix)* peace-loving; **mesure à but p.** measure intended to bring about peace; **mener une existence p.** to lead a quiet *or* peaceful life; **l'océan P.** the Pacific (Ocean); *Jur* **possesseur p.** uncontested owner
N *Bible* **bienheureux les pacifiques** blessed are the peacemakers
NM **le P.** *(océan)* the Pacific

pacifiquement [pasifikmɑ̃] ADV peacefully; **le meeting s'est déroulé p.** the meeting went off peacefully *or* quietly

pacifisme [pasifism] NM *Pol* pacifism

pacifiste [pasifist] ADJ, N *Pol* pacifist

pack [pak] NM **1** *(des mers polaires)* pack ice, ice pack **2** *Rugby* pack **3** *(lot)* pack; **des cannettes de bière en p. de six** a six-pack (of beer); **lait vendu en p.** milk sold in multipacks

package [pakɛdʒ] NM *Com, Ordinat* package

packaging [pakɛdʒiŋ] NM packaging

pacotille [pakɔtij] NF *Péj (marchandises de)* **p.** shoddy goods; **c'est de la p.** it's junk; **de p.** shoddy, third-rate; **bijoux de p.** paste jewellery; **exotisme de p.** third-rate exoticism

Pacs [paks] NM *(abrév* **Pacte civil de solidarité)** civil solidarity pact *(law introduced in France in 1999 extending the legal rights of married couples to unmarried heterosexual couples and to homosexual couples, particu-*

larly with regard to inheritance and taxation)*; **faire** *ou* **conclure un P.** to enter into a Pacs agreement

pacser [pakse] *Fam* VI to sign a Pacs contract, to enter into a civil solidarity pact
VPR **se pacser** to sign a Pacs contract, to enter into a civil solidarity pact

pacson [paksɔ̃] NM *Fam (argent, paquet)* packet; **toucher le p.** to win a fortune

pacte [pakt] NM pact; **conclure** *ou* **faire** *ou* **sceller un p. avec / contre qn** to enter into a pact with/against sb; **signer un p. avec le diable** to sign a pact with the Devil
▸▸**p. pour l'emploi** = job creation scheme for young people; **p. de non-agression** non-aggression pact; **p. à quatre** four-power pact; *UE* **p. de stabilité** stability pact; *UE* **p. de stabilité et de croissance** stability and growth pact; **le P. de Varsovie** the Warsaw Pact

pactiser [paktize] VI **p. avec qn** to come to terms with sb; **p. avec le diable** to make a pact with the Devil; *Fig* **p. avec sa conscience** to come to terms with one's conscience

pactole [paktɔl] NM **1** *Litt (qui enrichit)* gold mine; **ce travail est un vrai p.** this type of work is a real gold mine **2** *Fam (argent mis en jeu)* kitty; **il rêvait de gagner le p.** *(au loto)* he dreamt of winning the lottery; **son job lui rapporte un sacré p.** his job brings in megabucks; **elle a touché un joli p. quand son grand-père est mort** she came in for a nice little sum when her grandfather died

paddle [padœl] NM *Sport* paddle tennis

paddock [padɔk] NM paddock; *Fam (lit)* bed; *Fam* **se mettre** *ou* **aller au p.** *(se coucher)* to hit the sack *or* hay

paddy [padi] NM INV paddy

Padoue [padu] N Padua

paella [paɛla, paɛja] NF *Culin* paella

PAF [paf] NM *(abrév* **paysage audiovisuel français)** **le P.** the broadcasting scene *or* set-up in France

paf [paf] INT slap!, bang!
ADJ INV *Fam* **être p.** *(saoul)* to be pissed; **il est complètement p.** he's as pissed as a newt

PAG [peaʒe] NF *Com (abrév* **procédure accélérée générale de dédouanement)** accelerated customs clearance procedure

pagaie [pagɛ] NF *(rame)* paddle

pagaïe, pagaille [pagaj] NF *Fam (d'objets)* disorder, clutter; **il y a une drôle de p. dans ce bureau** this office looks as if a bomb has hit it *or* is in a fine old mess; **c'est la p. dans les rues de Paris** the streets of Paris are completely snarled up; **quelle p.!** what a mess!, what a shambles!; *(à cause des embouteillages)* what a snarl-up!; **quelle p. dans cette pièce!** this room's (in) a real mess!; **en p.** *(maison, chambre)* in a mess; *(affaires, papiers)* all jumbled up, in a mess; **ses affaires étaient en p. avec les miennes/dans le sac**

his/her things were jumbled up with mine/in the bag; **j'ai mis mes papiers en p. dans mon cartable** I stuffed my papers into my briefcase any old how; **je les ai mis en p.** *(ces livres etc)* I've just bundled them up, they're not in any particular order; **évite de mettre tout en p.** don't get things all jumbled up *or* mixed up; **avec des cadeaux en p.** with presents galore, with masses *or* loads of presents; **il y en a en p.** there's masses *or* lots *or* loads of it; *(nombre)* there are masses *or* lots *or* loads of them; **semer la p.** to cause trouble *(* **parmi** among; **dans** in); **il adore semer la p.** he likes causing trouble, *Br Fam* he's a real stirrer

paganisme [paganism] NM paganism

pagayer [pageje] VI (**je pagaie, je pagaye**) to paddle

pagayeur, -euse [pagejœr, -øz] N paddler

page¹ [paʒ] NF *(de journal, de livre, de site Web)* page; **feuilleter les pages d'un magazine** to flick through a magazine; **un livre de 250 pages** a 250-page book; **être payé à la p.** to be paid by the page; **je gagne quatre euros de la p.** I earn four euros a page; **en première p. des journaux** on the front page of the newspapers; **faire la première p. des journaux** to hit the headlines; *Journ* **photo sur une double p.** two-page photo spread; *Journ* **article sur une double p.** two-page spread; **ouvrez vos livres à la p. 10** open your books at page 10 *or* and turn to page 10; **j'ai perdu la p.** I've lost my place; **je voudrais finir la p.** I'd like to finish the page I'm on; *Typ* **mettre en page(s)** to make up; *Typ* **mise en page(s)** pagination, page make-up; *Ordinat* **logiciel de mise en p.** desktop publishing package; *Typ* **belle p.** right-hand page, recto (page); *Typ* **fausse p.** dummy; **une des plus belles pages de Victor Hugo** one of Victor Hugo's finest passages; *Fig* **une des plus célèbres pages de l'histoire** one of the most famous pages *or* chapters in history; **une nouvelle p. de l'histoire de France était tournée** a new chapter had begun in the history of France; *Fam* **être à la p.** to be up to date; **je ne suis plus vraiment à la p. en matière de musique** I'm pretty out of touch with what's happening in music; **ne pas être à la p.** to be behind the times; **tu n'es plus du tout à la p.** you're totally behind the times *or* out of it; **il faut te mettre à la p.** you're going to have to get with it; **rester à la p.** to keep up to date
▸▸*Ordinat* **p. d'accueil** home page; *Journ* **p. d'actualités** news page; *Journ* **p. centrale** centre page; *Journ* **p. centrale dépliante** centre spread, centrefold; **p. de couverture** cover page; *Typ* **pages de départ** prelims; *Ordinat* **p.-écran** screen page; *Journ* **p. féminine** women's page; *Journ* **pages financières** financial *or Br* City pages; **p. de garde** *Typ* endpaper; *Ordinat* splash page; *(d'un fax)* cover(ing) sheet; **les pages jaunes (de l'an-**

nuaire) the yellow pages; *Journ* **p. de mode** fashion page; *Ordinat* **p. perso, p. personelle** personal home page; *Ordinat* **p. précédente** page up; **p. de publicité** *Journ* full-page advert; *Radio, TV* commercial break; *Ordinat* **p. suivante** page down; *Typ* **p. de titre** title page; **p. volante** slip page; *Ordinat* **p. Web** Web page

page² NM *Hist* page(boy)

page³ NM *Fam* = **pageot**

pageot [paʒo] NM *Fam* bed; **se mettre** *ou* **aller au p.** to hit the sack *or* hay

pageur [paʒœr] NM pager

pageux [paʒø] NM *Typ* compositor, comp

pagination [paʒinasjɔ̃] NF pagination, page numbering; **il y a une erreur de p.** the pages have been numbered wrongly

paginer [paʒine] VT to paginate, to number the pages of

pagne [paɲ] NM loincloth; *(en paille)* grass skirt

pagnoter (se) [sepaɲɔte] VPR *Fam (se coucher)* to hit the sack *or* hay

pagode [pagɔd] NF **1** *Archit* pagoda; **toit en p.** pagoda roof; **manches pagodes** pagoda sleeves **2** *(figurine à tête mobile)* mandarin

Pagsi [paksi] NM *(abrév* **Programme d'action gouvernemental pour la société de l'information)** = government scheme to promote the use of the Internet in education and in public services

paie [pɛ] NF pay; *(par semaine)* wages; **feuille** *ou* **bulletin de p.** pay (advice) slip; **jour de p.** pay day; **faire la p.** to pay (out) the wages; **toucher sa p.** to get paid, to get one's pay; *Fig Fam* **ça fait une p. que je ne l'ai pas vu** I haven't seen him for ages; **quand vous êtes-vous rencontrés? – ça fait une p.!** when did you meet? – donkey's years ago!

paiement [pemɑ̃] NM payment; **p. mensuel** monthly payment; **p. du solde** payment of the balance; **demander des délais de p.** to ask for time to pay; *aussi Fig* **c'est tout ce qu'il reçut en p. de son travail** that's all he got for his work; *Fig* **voilà donc le p. de mon aide!** so that's what I get (in return) for helping you!
▸▸ **p. par accomptes** payment by *or* in instalments *or Am* installments; **p. anticipatif** *ou* **anticipé** advance payment, payment in advance, prepayment; **p. par anticipation** payment in advance; **p. arriéré** payment in arrears; **p. d'avance** payment in advance, advance payment, prepayment; *TV* **p. à la carte** *(des programmes)* pay per view; *Banque* **p. par carte** card payment, payment by card; *Tél* **p. par carte prépayée** pay-as-you-go; **p. par chèque** payment by cheque; **p. à la commande** cash with order, CWO; **p. (au) comptant** cash payment, payment in cash; *TV* **p. à la consommation** pay per view; **p. contre documents** payment against documents; **p. différé** deferred payment; **p. échelonné** staged *or* staggered payment; **p. électronique** electronic payment, payment by electronic transfer; **p. en espèces** payment in cash, cash payment; **p. intégral** payment in full; **p. libératoire** payment in full discharge from debt; **p. à la livraison, p. contre livraison** *Br* cash on delivery, COD, *Am* collect on delivery; **p. en nature** payment in kind; **p. partiel** partial *or* part payment; **paiements périodiques** periodic payments; **p. préalable** prepayment; **p. progressif** graduated *or* increasing payments; **p. au prorata** payment pro rata; *TV* **p. à la séance** pay per view; *Ordinat* **p. sécurisé** secure (electronic) transaction; **p. en souffrance** overdue *or* outstanding payment; **p.**

à tempérament payment by *or* in instalments; **p. à termes** payment by *or* in instalments

païen, -ïenne [pajɛ̃, -jɛn] ADJ, N pagan, heathen; **jurer comme un p.** to swear like a trooper

paierie [pɛri] NF local government finance office

paillage [pɑjaʒ] NM *Agr* mulching

paillard, -arde [pajar, -ard] ADJ *(personne, chanson, plaisanterie)* bawdy, ribald; **regard p.** leer
N debauchee; *(homme)* debauchee, rake

paillardise [pajardiz] NF **1** *(d'une personne, chanson etc)* bawdiness, ribaldry **2** *Vieilli (histoire)* bawdy story

paillasse [pajas] NF **1** *(matelas)* straw mattress, paillasse, palliasse **2** *(de l'évier)* draining board; *(de laboratoire)* (laboratory) bench **3** *Fam* **crever** *ou* **trouer la p. à qn** to stab sb in the stomach (and kill him/her) **4** *Fam Vieilli (prostituée)* floozy, tart
NM clown, buffoon

paillasson [pajasɔ̃] NM *(tapis-brosse)* (door)mat; *Agr* straw matting; *Fig (personne)* doormat; *Fig* **mettre la clef sous le p.** to clear out, *Br Fam* to scarper

paille [pɑj] NF **1** straw; **p. de litière** loose straw; **menue p., p. d'avoine** chaff; **p. de riz** *ou* **d'Italie** rice straw; **chapeau de p.** straw hat; **chaise de p.** straw-bottomed chair; **vin de p.** straw wine *(wine made from grapes dried on straw mats before pressing)*; *Fig* **homme de p.** man of straw, *Am* straw man; **il leur fallait un homme de p.** they needed a front man *or* a figurehead; *Fig* **feu de p.** flash in the pan; **ce ne fut qu'un feu de p.** *(leur amour)* it was just a flash in the pan; *(ce scandale)* it was just a nine days' wonder; **cela leur passera comme un feu de p.** they'll soon get over it, it'll be a flash in the pan; **sur la p. humide des cachots** behind bars; *Fig* **sur la p.** destitute, *Fam* on one's uppers, down and out; **voilà ce qui t'a mis sur la p.** that's what put you on your uppers; **mourir sur la p.** to die destitute; **vieillir sur la p.** to be old and destitute; **c'est facile de voir la p. dans l'œil du voisin (et ne pas voir la poutre dans le sien)** it's easy to criticize, you/he/*etc* should take the mote out of your/his/*etc* own eye first; **c'est la p. et la poutre** you/he/*etc* should take the mote out of your/his/*etc* own eye first; **tirer à la courte p.** to draw lots; **on tira à la courte p. qui irait faire du café** we drew lots to see who would make the coffee; **on tira à la courte p. le nom du gagnant** the winner was chosen by lot, the name of the winner was drawn out of a hat; *Fam* **une p.!** *(peu de chose)* chickenfeed!, peanuts!

2 *(pour boire)* (drinking) straw; **boire qch avec une p.** to drink sth through *or* with a straw; **tirer sur une p.** to suck on a straw

3 **p. de fer** steel wool

4 *(défaut) (dans une pierre précieuse etc)* flaw

ADJ INV **1** straw-coloured *or Am* -colored; **jaune p.** pale yellow **2** *Culin* **pommes p.** thinly cut chips *or surtout Am* (French) fries

paillé¹ [pɑje] NM stable litter

paillé² ADJ **1** *(couleur)* straw-coloured *or Am* -colored **2** *(chaise)* straw-bottomed **3** *(métal, pierre précieuse etc)* flawed

pailler¹ [pɑje] NM *(hangar)* farmyard, straw yard; *(meule)* straw stack

pailler² VT **1** *(arbuste)* to protect *or* mulch with straw **2** *(chaise)* to put a straw bottom in

paillet [pɑje] NM *Naut* mat, fender; **p. d'abordage, p. makarov** collision mat

pailleté [pɑjte] ADJ spangled *(de* with), sequined

pailleter [pɑjte] VT *(* **je paillette; je paillette-rai**) to sequin, to spangle

paillette [pɑjɛt] NF **1** *(sur des vêtements)* sequin, spangle; **à paillettes** sequined **2** *(de maquillage)* **des paillettes** glitter **3** *(de mica etc)* flake; **p. d'or** grain of gold dust; **savon en paillettes** soap flakes **4** *(d'une pierre précieuse)* flaw

pailleux, -euse [pɑjø, -øz] ADJ **1** *Agr* **fumier p.** = manure which has not rotted down sufficiently **2** *Tech (acier)* flawed

paillis [pɑji] NM *Agr* mulch

paillote [pɑjɔt] NF straw hut

pain [pɛ̃] NM **1** *(aliment)* bread; *(unité)* loaf, *pl* loaves; **achète deux pains** buy two loaves; **quelle sorte de p. devrais-je acheter?** what kind of bread should I buy?; *Rel* **le p. et le vin** the bread and wine; *Rel* **le/notre p. quotidien** our daily bread; **mettre qn au p. (sec) et à l'eau/au p. sec** to put sb on bread and water/on dry bread; **bon comme du bon p.** *ou* **comme le p.** extremely kind-hearted; **long comme un jour sans p.** interminable; *Fig* **c'est p. bénit** it serves him/her/them right but it's a godsend for us; **acheter qch pour une bouchée de p.** to buy sth for a song *or* for next to nothing; **il ne vaut pas le p. qu'il mange** he isn't worth his salt; **avoir du p. sur la planche** to have a lot on one's plate, to have plenty of work to do; **gagner son p. (à la sueur de son front)** to earn one's living *or* make a living (by the sweat of one's brow); **ôter le p. de la bouche à qn** to take the bread out of sb's mouth; **je ne mange pas de ce p.-là** I'm not getting involved in that, I'm not having any of that; **ça ne mange pas de p.** it won't cost you/him/*etc* anything; **du p. et des jeux** bread and circuses; *Bot* **arbre à p.** breadfruit tree VOIR GRAMMAIRE A12

2 **petit p.** (bread) roll; *Fig* **ça part** *ou* **se vend comme des petits pains** it sells/it's selling like hot cakes; **ces foulards sont partis comme des petits pains** those scarves went *or* sold like hot cakes; *Culin* **p. de poisson** fish loaf

3 *(de savon)* bar, cake; *(de cire)* stick

4 *Fam (coup de poing)* punch; **flanque-lui un p.** sock him one, *Br* give him a bunch of fives; **il a pris un p. dans la gueule** he got socked in the kisser

▸▸ **p. azyme** unleavened bread; **p. bis** brown bread/loaf; *Fig* **p. blanc: il a mangé son p. blanc le premier** he was lucky to start with; **fais attention à ne pas manger ton p. blanc le premier** remember that tomorrow always comes, always keep something to fall back on; **p. brioché** = bread closely resembling brioche in texture; **p. de campagne** farmhouse loaf; **p. au chocolat** pain au chocolat *(chocolate-filled pastry)*; **p. complet** wholemeal bread/loaf; **p. d'épices** ≃ gingerbread; **p. de Gênes** Genoa cake; **p. grillé** toast; **p. au lait** sweet roll; **p. au levain** sourdough bread/loaf; **p. de ménage** homemade bread/loaf; **p. de mie** sandwich loaf; **p. noir** black bread; **p. parisien** short French stick; **p. paysan** farmhouse loaf; **p. perdu** *(cuit à la poêle)* French toast; *(cuit au four)* bread-and-butter pudding; **p. aux raisins** = circular pastry made from sweetened dough and raisins; **p. de seigle** rye bread/loaf; **p. au** *ou* **de son** bran bread/loaf; **p. de sucre** sugar loaf; *Géog* **(montagne en) p. de sucre** sugar loaf (mountain); **p. viennois** Viennese bread/loaf

pair [pɛr] ADJ *(nombre)* even; **jours pairs** even dates; *Ordinat* **parité paire** even parity; **organes pairs** paired organs
NM **1** *(égal)* equal, peer; **être jugé par ses pairs** to be judged by one's peers; *Litt* **être avec qn** *ou* **traiter qn de p. à compagnon** to treat sb as an equal; **hors (de) p.** *(habileté, talent, efficacité etc)* unequalled, unrivalled,

beyond compare; *(personne)* unequalled; **c'est un traducteur hors p.** as a translator, he's second to none *or* in a class by himself; **pour ce qui est de l'informatique, elle est hors p.** there is no one to equal *or* match her *or* she is unequalled when it comes to computers; **aller de p.** *(de deux choses)* to go together, to go hand in hand; **aller de p. avec qch** to go hand in hand with sth; **le chômage va de p. avec les crises économiques** unemployment and economic crises go hand in hand; **ça va de p.** the two go hand in hand **2** *(noble)* peer (of the realm); *Br* **Chambre des Pairs** House of Lords; *Br* **p. à vie** life peer **3** *Fin* par; *Com* **p. commercial** par; *Com* **p. du change** par of exchange; **au-dessous/au-dessus du p.** below/above par; **au p.** at par **4 travailler au p.** to work au pair, to do au pair work; **jeune fille au p.** au pair (girl); **elle est au p. dans une famille bordelaise/chez un médecin** she's working (as an) au pair for a family in Bordeaux/for a doctor; **elle envoie des jeunes filles au p. aux États-Unis** she sends girls to work au pair in the United States **5 jouer p./impair** to bet on the even/odd numbers

paire [pɛr] NF *(de chaussures, de lunettes, de ciseaux etc)* pair; *(de draps)* set; *(de gibier à plumes, de pistolets)* brace; **p. de bœufs** yoke of oxen; **une belle p. de seins** a great pair, *Arg* great boobs *or* tits; *Fam* **une belle p. de fesses** a nice arse *or Am* ass; **il a reçu une p. de claques** he got his face slapped; *Fig Fam* **ça, c'est une autre p. de manches** that's another matter, that's a different kettle of fish; **quant à lui faire comprendre cela, c'est une autre p. de manches** it's another matter *or* a different kettle of fish getting him to understand; *Fam* **ils font la p.** they're two of a kind; *Fam* **se faire la p.** to clear out, to beat it, *Br* to scarper; *Tech* **p. torsadée** twisted pair VOIR GRAMMAIRE A10

pairesse [pɛrɛs] NF *Br* peeress

pairie [pɛri] NF peerage; **p. à vie** life peerage

paisible [pezibl] ADJ peaceful; *(silence, sommeil)* peaceful, undisturbed; *(personne)* quiet; *(eau)* calm; *Jur* **p. possesseur d'un bien** uncontested owner of a piece of property; **dormir d'un sommeil p.** to sleep peacefully; **retrouver un sommeil p.** to sleep peacefully again

paisiblement [peziblǝmā] ADV peacefully

paître [pɛtr] *(prp paisant; pr ind je pais, il paît, ns paissons; pr sub je paisse; impf je paissais; fu je paîtrai; no p hist)* VT *(des animaux)* *(feuilles etc)* to feed on; *(herbe)* to crop; *Arch, Litt (bétail)* to feed, to graze VI *(des animaux)* to feed; *(manger de l'herbe)* to graze, to pasture; *(manger des feuilles)* to browse; *Fig Fam* **je l'ai envoyé p.** I sent him packing, I sent him off with a flea in his ear

paix [pɛ] NF **1** *(entre États)* peace; **en temps de p.** in peacetime, in times of peace; **demander la p.** to sue for peace; **troubler la p.** to break the peace; **faire la p.** to make peace (**avec** with); *Fig* **faire la p. avec qn** to make one's peace with sb, to make it up with sb; *Fig* **on fait la p.?** let's make up, let's be friends again; *Fig* **faire la p. avec son passé** to come to terms with one's past; **rester en p. avec un pays** to remain at peace with a country; **vivre en p. avec ses voisins** to live at peace with one's neighbours; *Fig* **je souhaite vivre en p. avec ma conscience/mon passé** I want to be able to live with my conscience/my past; *Jur* **juge de p.** magistrate, justice of the peace; **climat de p. sociale** *(absence de grève)* climate of industrial peace **2** *Rel (sérénité)* peace; **la p. du tombeau** the quiet of the grave; **p. à son âme** may his/her soul rest in peace; **qu'il repose en p.** may he rest in peace; **allez en p.** go in peace

3 *(tranquillité)* peace; **dormir en p.** to sleep peacefully; **avoir besoin de p. pour se concentrer** to need peace and quiet to concentrate; **troubler la p. de qn** to disturb sb; *(moralement)* to disturb sb's peace of mind; **troubler la p. de ce petit matin** to break the peace of the early morning; **il ne m'a pas laissé en p. tant que ...** he gave me no peace until ...; **laissez-moi en p.** leave me alone *or* in peace; **je suis pour la p. des ménages** I'm a great believer in marital harmony; *Fam* **avoir la p.** to get peace (and quiet); **impossible d'avoir la p. quand il est là** it's impossible to get any peace (and quiet) when he's around; **je peux avoir la p. cinq minutes?** can I have five minutes' peace (and quiet)?, can't I be left alone for five minutes?; *Fam* **je veux qu'on me fiche** *ou* **foute la p.** I want to be left alone; *Fam* **il faut lui ficher** *ou* **fiche** *ou* **foutre la p. avec tes questions** stop pestering him with your damn questions; *Fam* **fiche-moi** *ou* **fous-moi la p.!** leave me alone!, stop pestering me!, get off my back!; **fous-lui la p.!** bloody leave him alone!; *Fam* **la p.!** hush!, be quiet!

▸ ▸ **p. armée** armed peace; **p. séparée** separate peace; **p. universelle** universal peace

Pakistan [pakistā] NM Pakistan

pakistanais, -aise [pakistanɛ, -ɛz] ADJ Pakistani
  N **P.** Pakistani

PAL [pal] ADJ TV *(abrév* **Phase Alternation Line)** PAL

pal, -als [pal] NM **1** *(pieu)* pale, stake; *Arch* **le (supplice du) p.** impalement **2** *(plantoir)* planter, dibber

palabre [palabr] NM OU NF *(souvent pl)* palabres palaver, (endless) discussion; **après de long(ue)s palabres** after a long discussion; **s'éterniser en palabres** to drag on forever

palabrer [palabre] VI to palaver, to talk endlessly

palace [palas] NM luxury hotel; **tu verrais sa maison, c'est un vrai p.** you should see his house, it's palatial *or* luxurious

---

Il faut noter que le terme anglais **palace** est un faux ami. Il signifie **palais**.

Do not confuse with **palais**.

---

paladin [paladɛ̃] NM paladin; *(itinérant)* knight-errant

palais¹ [palɛ] NM **1** *(d'un roi etc)* palace **2** *Jur* **le p. de Justice, le p.** the law courts; **les gens du** *ou* **de p., le p.** the legal profession; **terme de p.** legal term; **le style du p.** legal language *or* jargon, the language of the courts

▸ ▸ **le P. Bourbon** = home of the French Parliament; **le P. Brongniart** = the Paris Stock Exchange; **p. des congrès** convention centre; **le p. de l'Élysée** the Élysée (Palace) *(official residence of the French President)*; **le p. Garnier** = the Paris Opera House; **le Grand P.** = science museum in Paris, originally built as part of the 1900 World Fair; **le P. du Luxembourg** = home of the French Senate in Paris; **le P. des Papes** = papal palace in Avignon, now the centre of a large arts festival; **le Petit P.** = art museum in Paris, originally built as part of the 1900 World Fair; **p. des sports** sports centre

---

Do not confuse with the French word **palace**.

---

palais² NM **1** *Anat* palate; **voûte du p., p. dur** hard palate; **voile du p., p. mou** soft palate; **p. fendu** cleft palate **2** *(goût)* (sense of) taste; **avoir le p. fin** to have a fine palate; **flatter le p.** to please the palate

palan [palā] NM *Tech* hoist, hoisting gear;

Naut pulley block, purchase tackle, whip; *Com* **sous p.** under ship's tackle

palanche [palāʃ] NF *(pour porter des seaux etc)* yoke

palanque [palāk] NF (timber) stockade

palanquée [palāke] NF *(multitude)* **une p. de...** a raft of...

palanquer [palāke] VT to stockade

palanquin [palākɛ̃] NM palanquin

palatal, -ale, -aux, -ales [palatal, -o] ADJ **1** *Ling (consonne)* palatal; *(voyelle)* front **2** *Anat (os etc)* palatal
  NF *Ling* **palatale** *(consonne)* palatal (consonant); *(voyelle)* front vowel

palatalisation [palatalizasjɔ̃] NF *Ling* palatalization

palataliser [palatalize] *Ling* VT to palatalize
  VPR **se palataliser** to be palatalized

palatin, -ine [palatɛ̃, -in] ADJ **1** *Hist* palatine; **comte p.** Count Palatine **2** *Géog* **le mont P.** the Palatine Hill
  N *Hist* palatine
  NF *Hist* **La Palatine** the Princess Palatine

Palatinat (le) [lǝpalatina] NM *Hist* the Palatinate

pale¹ [pal] NF **1** *(d'une rame, d'une hélice, d'un ventilateur etc)* blade; **hélice à trois/quatre pales** three-/four-bladed propeller **2** *(vanne)* sluice (gate)

pale² NF *Rel* chalice cover, pall(a)

pâle [pal] ADJ **1** *(livide, blafard)* pale; *Litt, Méd* pallid; **p. comme un linge** as white as a sheet; **p. comme la mort** deathly pale, ashen, as pale as death; **p. de colère** livid with rage; **p. de jalousie** green with envy; *Mil Fam* **se faire porter p.** to report sick; **les Visages pâles** the Palefaces **2** *(couleur, ciel)* pale; *(lumière)* pale, faint; *(sourire)* wan, faint; *(style)* colourless, *Am* colorless; **une p. imitation de Vermeer** a pale *or* poor imitation of Vermeer; **mes aventures semblent bien pâles auprès des vôtres** my adventures pale in comparison with yours; *Fam* **c'est un p. crétin** he's a complete idiot *or* fool

palefrenier [palfrǝnje] NM groom; *Arch (d'auberge)* ostler

palefroi [palfrwa] NM *Arch* palfrey

paléoanthropologie [paleoātrɔpɔlɔʒi] NF palaeoanthropology, *surtout Am* paleoanthropology

paléoanthropologue [paleoātrɔpɔlɔg] N palaeoanthropologist, *surtout Am* paleoanthropologist

paléographe [paleɔgraf] N palaeographer, *surtout Am* paleographer

paléographie [paleɔgrafi] NF palaeography, *surtout Am* paleography

paléographique [paleɔgrafik] ADJ palaeographic, *surtout Am* paleographic

paléolithique [paleɔlitik] ADJ Palaeolithic, *surtout Am* Paleolithic
  NM Palaeolithic age, *surtout Am* Paleolithic age

paléontologie [paleɔ̃tɔlɔʒi] NF palaeontology, *surtout Am* paleontology

paléontologique [paleɔ̃tɔlɔʒik] ADJ palaeontological, *surtout Am* paleontological

paléontologiste [paleɔ̃tɔlɔʒist], **paléontologue** [paleɔ̃tɔlɔg] N palaeontologist, *surtout Am* paleontologist

paléozoïque [paleɔzɔik] *Géol* ADJ Palaeozoic, *surtout Am* Paleozoic
  NM **le p.** the Palaeozoic *or surtout Am* Palezoic (era)

Palerme [palɛrm] N Palermo

paleron [palrɔ̃] NM *(de cheval, de bœuf etc)* shoulder blade, blade bone; *Culin* neck, *Am* chuck; *Culin* **p. de bœuf** chuck

Palestine [palɛstin] NF *Géog* Palestine

palestinien, -ienne [palɛstinjɛ̃, -jɛn] ADJ Palestinian
N **P.** Palestinian

palet [palɛ] NM **1** *(anneau)* quoit; **jouer au(x) palet(s)** to play quoits **2** *(pour hockey sur glace)* puck; *(pour curling)* stone

paletot [palto] NM *(short)* overcoat; *Fig Fam* **tomber sur le p. à qn** *(l'attaquer)* to jump sb; *(d'un voleur)* to mug sb; *(pour lui parler)* to buttonhole sb, to nab sb

palette [palɛt] NF **1** *(de peintre)* palette; *Fig (éventail) (d'activités, de produits etc)* range; *Fig* **la p. de Matisse** the range of colours used by Matisse, Matisse's palette; *Ordinat* **p. d'outils** tool palette; **p. graphique** graphics palette **2** *(pour la manutention)* pallet; **p. (en) bois** wooden pallet; *Com* **p.-avion** air freight pallet **3** *Culin (de mouton, de porc)* shoulder **4** *(d'une roue à aubes)* paddle **5** *Sport (raquette de bois)* (wooden) battledore **6** *(pour le linge)* (washerwoman's) beetle

palettisation [palɛtizasjɔ̃] NF *Tech* palletization

palettiser [palɛtize] ADJ *Tech* to palletize

palettiseur [palɛtizœr] NM *Com* palletizer

palétuvier [paletyvje] NM mangrove

pâleur [palœr] NF *(du teint)* paleness, pallor; *(de la lumière)* faintness; *(du style)* colourlessness, *Am* colorlessness; **d'une p. mortelle** deathly pale

pâlichon, -onne [paliʃɔ̃, -ɔn] ADJ *Fam* pale, green around the gills

palier [palje] NM **1** *Archit (d'escalier)* landing; **nous sommes voisins de p.** we live on the same floor; **tu connais tes voisins de p.?** do you know the people who live on the same floor as you?, do you know your next-door neighbours?; **p. intermédiaire** half-landing **2** *(étape)* stage; **par paliers** in stages **3** *Aut, Rail etc* level stretch; *Math etc (d'un graphique)* plateau; **atteindre un p.** *(devenir plat)* to reach a plateau; **le taux des naissances a atteint un p.** the birth rate has reached a plateau or has levelled off; **à partir d'un certain p., le taux change** the rate changes at a certain point; *Aut, Rail etc* **vitesse en p.** speed on the level or on the flat; *Aviat* **voler en p.** to fly level **4** *Tech* bearing; **p. d'arbre** shaft bearing; **p. d'appui** mounting; **p. de tête de bielle** big-end bearing

palière [paljɛr] ADJ **porte p.** landing door, door opening onto the landing; **marche p.** top step

palimpseste [palɛ̃psɛst] NM palimpsest

palindrome [palɛ̃drom] NM *Ling* palindrome

palinodie [palinɔdi] NF **1** *Littér* palinode **2** *Péj (revirement)* volte-face

pâlir [palir] VI *(d'une personne)* to turn or become or grow pale, to pale; *(d'une lumière, d'une étoile etc)* to fade, to grow dim; *(d'une couleur, d'un souvenir)* to fade; **ses joues ont pâli** his/her cheeks have lost their colour; **p. d'horreur/de peur** to turn pale or go white with horror/fright; **p. de rage/de colère** to become livid with rage/anger; **p. de jalousie** to turn green with envy; **faire p. qn de jalousie** to make sb green with envy; **à faire p.** *(cauchemar, histoire)* terrifying; *(revenus, succès, maison)* amazing, unbelievable; **ils ont une maison à faire p. (d'envie)** they have a house that would make you green with envy; *Fig* **p. sur un travail** to slave over a piece of work
VT *Littér* **p. qn** *(d'une couleur, un maquillage etc)* to make sb look pale

palis [pali] NM **1** *(clôture)* (picket) fence **2** *(espace clôturé)* enclosure **3** *(pieu)* picket

palissade [palisad] NF **1** *(clôture)* fence; *Mil* palisade **2** *(haie)* hedge

palissader [palisade] VT to fence in, to rail in, to enclose; *Mil* to palisade

palissandre [palisɑ̃dr] NM *(bois)* Brazilian rosewood

pâlissant [palisɑ̃] ADJ *(visage)* turning pale; *(lumière)* fading, waning; *(couleur)* fading

palladium [paladjɔm] NM *Chimie* palladium

palliatif, -ive [paljatif, -iv] ADJ palliative
NM *Méd* palliative; *Fig* stopgap measure, *Litt* palliative

pallier [palje] *(impf, pr sub* n. **palliions, v. palliiez)** VT *(atténuer) (douleur, maladie)* to alleviate, *Fml* to palliate; *(faute, erreur)* to lessen the impact of
VI **p. à** *(un manque de qch)* to compensate for, to make up for; *(conséquences, problèmes)* to lessen the impact of

palmarès [palmarɛs] NM *Scol etc* honours or *Am* honors list; *(à une distribution de prix)* (list of) prize winners; *Sport* (list of) winners; *Mus, Radio etc* **le p. (de la chanson)** the charts; **être** ou **figurer au p.** to be among the (prize) winners; *Mus* to be in the charts; **une chanteuse qui ne figure plus au p.** a singer who's dropped out of the charts; **être premier au p.** to be number one, to top the charts; **il est au p. des hommes les plus séduisants de France** he's been voted one of the most attractive men in France; **avoir un beau p.** *(d'un sportif)* to be having a good season or year; **il a** ou **compte 50 victoires à son p.** he has fifty wins to his credit, he has notched up fifty wins

palme [palm] NF **1** *(de palmier)* palm (branch); *Fig (symbole de la victoire)* palm; **le dimanche des Palmes** Palm Sunday; **p. du martyre** martyr's crown, crown of martyrdom; **avec p.** *(decoration)* ≃ with bar; **décerner la p. de qch** to award the prize for sth; **remporter la p.** to win, to be victorious, *Litt* to carry off the palm of victory; **la p. lui revient** he's the winner, the victory goes to him; *Fig* **pour ce qui est de la cuisine, c'est lui qui remporte la p.** when it comes to cooking, there's no one to beat him; *Hum* **on peut lui décerner la p. de la paresse** he takes the biscuit for sheer laziness **2** *Arch (arbre)* palm (tree); **huile/vin de p.** palm oil/wine **3** *(pour nager)* flipper
▸▸ **la P. d'or (du festival de Cannes)** the Palme d'or (of the Cannes Film Festival) *(top prize awarded to a film)*; *Admin* **les palmes (académiques)** = decoration awarded to teachers; **décerner les palmes académiques à qn** to decorate sb for services to teaching

palmé [palme] ADJ **1** *Bot (feuille)* palmate **2** *Orn* web-footed; **pied p.** webbed foot; *Fam* **les avoir palmées** to be bone idle or a complete layabout

palmer [palmɛr] NM *Tech* micrometer

palmeraie [palmərɛ] NF palm grove

palmier [palmje] NM **1** *(arbre)* palm (tree); **p. dattier** date palm; **cœur de p.** palm (tree) heart **2** *Culin* = small sweet heart-shaped pastry

palmipède [palmipɛd] *Orn* ADJ web-footed, *Spéc* palmiped(e)
NM web-footed bird, *Spéc* palmiped(e)

palmiste [palmist] NM *(plante)* cabbage palm or tree; **chou p.** palm tree heart

palombe [palɔ̃b] NF *Région* ringdove, wood pigeon

palonnier [palɔnje] NM *Aviat* rudder bar; *Aut* **p. de freinage** compensator

palot [palo] NM *très Fam* French kiss; **rouler un p. à qn** to French kiss sb, *Br* to snog sb

pâlot, -otte [palo, -ɔt] ADJ rather pale, peaky

palourde [palurd] NF *(mollusque)* clam

palpable [palpabl] ADJ **1** *(que l'on peut toucher)* palpable, tangible **2** *(réel, vérifiable) (erreur, mensonge)* palpable; *(vérité etc)* obvious, plain

palpation [palpasjɔ̃] NF *Méd* palpation

palper [palpe] VT **1** *(objet)* to feel (with one's hands); *Méd* to palpate **2** *Fam (somme)* to be paid, to get
VI *Fam* to get one's money, to get paid; **qu'est-ce qu'il a dû p.!** he must have made a mint!
NM *Méd* palpation

palpeur [palpœr] NM *(heat)* sensor; *Ordinat* sensor; *Aut* **p. de détonation** knock sensor

palpitant [palpitɑ̃] ADJ *(cœur, pouls)* fluttering; *(plus fort)* throbbing; *Méd* palpitating; *(personne) (d'émotion etc)* quivering; **p. (d'intérêt)** *(roman, film etc)* exciting, thrilling
NM *Arg (cœur)* ticker

palpitation [palpitasjɔ̃] NF *(du cœur, pouls)* fluttering; *(plus fort)* throbbing; *Méd* palpitation; *(d'une paupière)* fluttering; **avoir des palpitations** to have palpitations

palpiter [palpite] VI *(du cœur, pouls)* to flutter; *(plus fort)* to throb; *Méd* to palpitate; *(d'une paupière)* to flutter; *(d'une lumière etc)* to flicker; *(d'une personne) (de peur, rage)* to quiver (**de** with); **p. de froid** to tremble with cold

paltoquet [paltɔkɛ] NM *Fam Vieilli* jackanapes

paluche [palyʃ] NF *très Fam (main)* mitt, paw

paludéen, -enne [palydeɛ̃, -ɛn] ADJ *(plante, terrain etc)* marsh; *Méd* malarial

paludisme [palydism] NM malaria

palustre [palystr] ADJ *(plante etc)* marsh; *Méd* malarial

PAM [pam] NM *(abrév* **programme alimentaire mondial)** WFP

pâmer (se) [səpame] VPR *Vieilli (s'évanouir)* to swoon, to faint; *Fig Hum* to (practically) swoon; *Fig* **se p. devant qn** to practically swoon over sb; **se p. (d'aise)** to be blissfully happy; **se p. de rire** to be convulsed with laughter; **ça la faisait se p. de rire, cette histoire** the story sent her into hysterics; **se p. d'admiration** to be in raptures (**sur** over), to be overcome with admiration (**sur** for); **se p. d'amour** to be head over heels in love

pâmoison [pamwazɔ̃] NF *Vieilli* swoon; *Iron* **tomber en p.** to swoon; **tomber en p. devant qch** to go into raptures or to swoon over sth

pampa [pɑ̃pa] NF *(d'Amérique du Sud)* pampas

pamphlet [pɑ̃flɛ] NM lampoon, satirical tract

> Il faut noter que le terme anglais **pamphlet** est un faux ami. Il désigne le plus souvent une brochure.

pamphlétaire [pɑ̃fletɛr] ADJ *(ton, esprit)* pamphleteering
N lampoonist, pamphleteer

pamplemousse [pɑ̃pləmus] NM *(fruit)* grapefruit

pampre [pɑ̃pr] NM *Litt* vine branch *(with grapes)*

Pan [pɑ̃] N *Myth* Pan

pan¹ [pɑ̃] NM **1** *(de chemise, manteau)* tail; *(de jupe)* panel; **relever les pans de son manteau** to hitch up one's coat; **il l'a enveloppée des pans de son manteau** he wrapped his coat around her; **se promener en p. de chemise** to wander about in one's shirt-tails **2** *(morceau)* section, piece; *Fig (d'enfance, d'une époque)* section, portion; **p. de mur** section of wall; **p. de ciel** patch of sky **3** *(d'un* *polyèdre etc)* face, side; **tour à huit pans** eight-sided *or* octagonal tower; **p. coupé** cant; **en p. coupé** with the corner cut off

pan² INT **1** bang!, crash!, wham!; **et p.! je te tue!** bang! bang! you're dead!; **et p., le voilà qui entre!** and then, would you believe it, in he comes! **2** *Enf* **je vais te faire p. p. (cucul)!** I'll smack you!

panacée [panase] NF panacea

panachage [panaʃaʒ] NM **1** *(de couleurs etc)* mixing **2** *Pol* **p. électoral** splitting one's vote between candidates from different parties

panache [panaʃ] NM **1** *(aigrette)* plume, panache; *(de plumes etc)* plume, tuft; **p. de fumée** plume *or* wreath *or* trail of smoke **2** *(brio, éclat)* panache; **avec p.** with panache; **il avait le goût du p.** he did things in style *or* with panache

panaché [panaʃe] ADJ **1** *(oiseau, fleur)* multicoloured, *Am* multicolored; *(feuillage)* variegated; *(foule)* motley; **p. de blanc** streaked with white, with white streaks; *Culin* **salade panachée** mixed salad; **glace panachée** = selection of various flavours of ice cream; **demi p.** shandy **2** *Pol* **liste (électorale) panachée** = ballot paper in which votes are split among candidates from different parties
  NM shandy

panacher [panaʃe] VT **1** *(bigarrer) (couleurs)* to mix; **p. un bouquet** to put together a mixed bouquet **2** *Pol* **p. une liste électorale** to split one's votes *(among candidates from different parties)*

panade [panad] NF *Culin* = soup made from bread; *Fig Fam* **être dans la p.** to be in the soup *or* in a real fix; *(ne pas avoir d'argent temporairement)* to be short of cash; **ça m'a mise dans la p.** I was really up the creek; **quelle p.!** what a mess!

panafricain [panafrikɛ̃] ADJ *Pol* Pan-African

panafricanisme [panafrikanism] NM *Pol* Pan-Africanism

panais [panɛ] NM *(légume)* parsnip

Panama [panama] NM **1** *Géog* Panama; **le canal de P.** the Panama Canal **2** **p.** *(chapeau)* panama hat

Paname [panam] N *Géog Fam* = nickname given to Paris

panaméen, -enne [panameɛ̃, -ɛn] ADJ Panamanian
  N **P.** Panamanian

panaméricain [panamerikɛ̃] ADJ *Pol* Pan-American

panaméricanisme [panamerikanism] NM *Pol* Pan-Americanism

panarabe [panarab] ADJ *Pol* Pan-Arab

panarabisme [panarabism] NM *Pol* Pan-Arabism

panard [panar] ADJ *(cheval)* knock-kneed
  NM *très Fam (pied)* foot; **panards** feet, *Br* plates (of meat); *Fig* **quel p.!** great!, terrific!, fantastic!; **tu imagines, vivre au bord de la mer, quel p.!** just imagine how great *or* terrific *or* fantastic it would be to live at the seaside!; **ce n'est pas le p.** it's not exactly a load of laughs *or* a barrel of fun

panaris [panari] NM *Méd* whitlow

panavision [panavizjɔ̃] NF panavision

pan-bagnat, *pl* **pans-bagnats** [pɑ̃baɲa] NM = filled roll sliced and filled with salade niçoise

pancarte [pɑ̃kart] NF sign, notice; *(affiche)* placard

pancréas [pɑ̃kreas] NM *Anat* pancreas

pancréatique [pɑ̃kreatik] ADJ *Anat* pancreatic

panda [pɑ̃da] NM panda

pandémie [pɑ̃demi] NF *Méd* pandemic

pandémique [pɑ̃demik] ADJ *Méd* pandemic

pandémonium [pɑ̃demɔnjɔm] NM *(lieu de corruption)* den of vice *or* iniquity; *(lieu de désordre)* pandemonium

pandit [pɑ̃di] NM *(titre indien)* pandit, pundit

Pandore [pɑ̃dɔr] N *Myth* Pandora; **boîte de P.** Pandora's box

pané [pane] ADJ *Culin* coated with breadcrumbs, breaded

panégyrique [panegirik] NM eulogy, *Litt* panegyric; **faire le p. de qn** to extol sb's virtues *or* merits, to eulogize sb

panégyriste [panegirist] NM eulogist, *Litt* panegyrist

panel [panɛl] NM *(groupe)* panel; *(échantillon)* sample (group); *Mktg* **p. de consommateurs** consumer panel, shopping panel; *Mktg* **p. de distributeurs** distributor panel; *Mktg* **p. de détaillants** retail panel; *Mktg* **p. d'essayeurs de produits** product testing panel; **p. de téléspectateurs** television viewing panel

panéliste [panelist] N *Mktg* panellist, panel member

paner [pane] VT *Culin* to cover *or* coat with breadcrumbs, to bread

panetière [pantjɛr] NF bread bin

paneuropéanisme [panørɔpeanism] NM *Pol* Pan-Europeanism

paneuropéen, -enne [panørɔpeɛ̃, -ɛn] ADJ *Pol* Pan-European

pangermanisme [pɑ̃ʒɛrmanism] NM *Pol* Pan-Germanism

pangermaniste [pɑ̃ʒɛrmanist] ADJ, N *Pol* Pan-Germanist

panier [panje] NM **1** *(corbeille)* basket; *(de fruits etc)* basket(ful); **p. à anse(s)** basket; **un plein p. de fruits** a basketful of fruit; **mettre** *ou* **jeter qch au p.** to throw sth in the wastepaper basket; *Fig* to throw sth away *or* out, *Br Fam* to bin sth; **ton pantalon est bon à mettre au p.** your trousers aren't fit to be seen, your trousers should be thrown out; *Fig* **mettre tous ses œufs dans le même p.** to put all one's eggs in one basket; *Fig* **moi, les hommes, je les mets tous dans le même p.** men are all alike *or* the same, as far as I'm concerned; *Fig* **il ne faut pas tous les mettre dans le même p.** you can't lump them all together, they're not all tarred with the same brush; *Fig* **le dessus du p.** the elite; *Scol, Univ* the pick of the bunch, the cream of the crop; **il ne fréquente que le dessus du p.** he only mixes with the very best people; **faire partie du dessus du p.** to be out of the top drawer; *Scol, Univ* to be one of the best
  2 *Mktg (présentoir)* dump bin; **p. de présentation en vrac, p. présentoir** dump bin; **p. à la sortie** check-out display; **p. vrac** dump bin
  3 *Ordinat* shopping basket, *Am* shopping cart; **ajouter au p.** add to shopping basket *ou Am* shopping cart
  4 *(nasse)* lobster pot
  5 *Sport (au basketball)* basket; **réussir** *ou* **marquer un p.** to score (a basket)
  6 *(de tondeuse)* grass box
  7 *(pour diapositives)* slide magazine
  8 *(de crinoline)* hoop
  9 *Fam* **il a mis la main au p. de la serveuse** he groped the waitress's behind
  ▸▸ *Bourse* **p. d'actions** basket of shares; **p. à bouteilles** bottle carrier; *Fig* **p. de crabes: c'est un p. de crabes** they're constantly at each other's throats, they're always trying to stick knives in each other's backs; *Fin* **p. de devises** basket of currencies; **p. à légumes** *(pour cuisson vapeur)* steamer insert; *(de Cocotte-Minute®)* food basket; **p. à linge** linen basket; *Écon* **le p. de la ménagère** the shopping basket; **avec des conséquences sur le p. de la ménagère** with consequences

for the food bill; *Écon* **p. de monnaies** basket of currencies; **p. à ouvrage** sewing basket; *Fam* **p. percé** *(dépensier)* spendthrift; *Can (indiscret)* blabbermouth; **p. à provisions** shopping basket; **p. à salade** salad shaker; *Fam (convoi cellulaire)* police van *or Am* wagon, *Br Vieilli* Black Maria

panier-repas, *pl* **paniers-repas** NM *(panier)* lunch basket; *(repas)* packed lunch

panifiable [panifjabl] ADJ *(céréale)* suitable for making bread; **farine p.** bread flour

panifier [panifje] VT *(impf, pr sub n. panifiions, v. panifiiez)* **p. de la farine** to make bread

panique [panik] ADJ **peur p.** panic
  NF panic; **pris de p.** panic-stricken; **pris de p., ils s'enfuirent** they fled in (a) panic; **pris de p., je ne trouvais plus mes mots** I was panic-stricken and couldn't say a word; **être pris de p.** to panic; *Bourse* **stock market panic; ne pas céder à la p.** not to let oneself be panicked, not to give way to panic; **la police recommande à la population de ne pas céder à la p.** the police are urging people not to panic; *Fam* **pas de p., ce n'est pas la fin du monde!** don't panic, it's not the end of the world!; **c'était la p. totale** it was panic stations; **il y a eu un début de p.** people started to panic; **il y a eu un mouvement de p.** there was a stampede, there was panic; **la p. était générale** there was a general state of panic

paniqué [panike] ADJ *Fam* in a panic, panicky; **complètement p.** in a complete panic

paniquer [panike] *Fam* VT **p. qn** to get sb into a panic, to panic sb, to put the wind up sb
  VI to (get into a) panic, to get panicky

panislamique [panislamik] ADJ *Pol* Pan-Islamic

panislamisme [panislamism] NM *Pol* Pan-Islamism

panne¹ [pan] NF **1** *Tex* panne, plush **2** *(gras)* fat, lard; *Fig (d'une personne)* flab; *Fig* **tu prends/tu as de la p.** you're getting/you're flabby

panne² NF **1** *(arrêt de fonctionnement)* (mechanical) breakdown; *Aut* breakdown; *Élec* (power) failure, outage; *Ordinat* failure, crash; **p. de courant** *ou* **d'électricité** power failure *or* cut, blackout; *Radio, TV* **p. d'émission** technical fault *or* hitch; **p. de moteur** engine failure; **nous avons eu plusieurs pannes de moteur avec cette auto** the engine on the car has failed several times; **p. de secteur** power failure *or* outage, mains failure; *Ordinat* **p. du système** system crash; *Ordinat* **p. matérielle** hardware crash; **tomber en p.** *(d'une voiture, une machine)* to break down; *(d'un automobiliste)* to break down, to have a breakdown; **tomber en p. d'essence, tomber en p. sèche** to run out of petrol *or Am* gas; **en p.** *(ascenseur etc)* out of order; **je suis en p.** *(d'automobiliste)* I've broken down; *Fam* **rester en p. devant une difficulté** to be put off *or* floored by a difficulty; *Fam* **laisser qn en p.** to leave sb in the lurch, to let sb down; *Fam* **je suis en p. d'allumettes/de café/d'idées** I've run out of matches/coffee/ideas; **trouver la p.** to find the problem, to find the cause of the problem; **soudain, ce fut la p.** suddenly, we/they/it/etc broke down; *Fam Hum* **j'ai eu une p. d'oreiller** I overslept; *Fam* **il m'a fait le coup de la p.** he pretended we'd run out of petrol, he tried to pull the old 'we've run out of petrol' trick **2** *Naut* **en p.** hove to; **mettre un navire en p.** to bring a ship to

panne³ NF *Constr (d'un toit)* purlin

panne⁴ NF *Tech (d'un marteau)* peen, pane

panneau, -eaux [pano] NM **1** *(pour afficher)* board **2** *(élément plan) (de bois, contre-plaqué etc)* panel; **panneaux** panelling, panels; **porte à panneaux** panelled door; **p.**

vitré glass panel; **p. mobile/coulissant** movable/sliding panel **3** *(pour le gibier)* snare, net; *Fig* **tomber** *ou* **donner dans le p.** to fall into the trap **4** *Aut* signpost, direction sign **5** *Ordinat (d'écran d'ordinateur)* pane ▸▸ **p. d'affichage** notice *or Am* bulletin board; *Ordinat* bulletin board; *Naut* **p. de cale** hatch cover; *Aut* **p. de carrosserie** body panel; *Ordinat* **p. de configuration** control panel; *Mktg* **p. à crochets** *(présentoir)* pegboard; *Naut* **p. d'écoutille** hatch cover; **panneaux électoraux** noticeboards for election posters; *Aut* **p. indicateur** signpost; **p. publicitaire** hoarding, *Am* billboard; **p. de signalisation (routière)** roadsign; **p. solaire** solar panel

panneton [pantɔ̃] NM *(d'une clé)* web, bit

pano [pano] NM *(abrév* **panoramique)** *TV, Cin* **p. de poursuite** following pan; **p. filé** whip *or* zip pan

panonceau, -eaux [panɔ̃so] NM **1** *(de notaire etc)* plaque **2** *(pancarte)* sign **3** *Hist* escutcheon

panoplie [panɔpli] NF *(armure)* panoply; *(assortiment) (d'outils)* set; *Fig (de raisons)* array, multitude; *(d'arguments)* battery; *(de dettes)* multitude, *Fam* pile; **p. de soldat/d'infirmière** *(pour enfants)* soldier's/nurse's outfit *or* costume; **toute la p. du parfait bricoleur** a whole array of DIY equipment; *Iron* **j'ai eu droit à toute la p.** I got the works

panorama [panɔrama] NM panorama; *Fig* overview

panoramique [panɔramik] ADJ *(écran etc)* panoramic; *(restaurant)* with panoramic views; *Méd (radiographie)* all-over, total; **voiture avec carrosserie p.** car with panoramic *or* wrap-round windows; **vue p.** panoramic view; *Fig* overview; *Cin* **prise p.** panning shot NM *Cin, TV* pan (shot); **faire un p.** to pan; **p. horizontal** pan (shot); **faire un p. horizontal** to pan; **faire un p. vers le bas/le haut** to pan down/up; **p. vertical** tilt, tilted shot; **faire un p. vertical** to tilt

panoramiquer [panɔramike] VI *TV, Cin* to pan; **p. vers le bas/le haut** to pan down/up

panosse [panɔs] NF *Suisse (serpillière)* mop

panosser [panɔse] VT *Suisse (passer à la serpillière)* to mop

pansage [pɑ̃saʒ] NM *(d'un cheval etc)* grooming

panse [pɑ̃s] NF **1** *Fam (ventre)* belly, paunch, pot; **s'en mettre plein la p.** to gorge *or* stuff oneself; **manger à s'en faire crever la p.** to stuff oneself *or* one's face, to eat until one is fit to burst **2** *(d'un ruminant)* first stomach, paunch, rumen **3** *(d'une bouteille etc)* belly, bulge

pansement [pɑ̃smɑ̃] NM *Méd* **1** *(action) (d'une blessure)* dressing **2** *(élément protecteur)* dressing; *(enroulé autour d'une blessure)* bandage; **p. (adhésif)** (sticking) plaster; **faire un p.** to dress a wound, to apply a dressing; **refaire un p.** to change a dressing; **faire/refaire un p. à qn** to dress sb's wound(s)/change sb's dressing(s); **il est couvert de pansements** he's all bandaged up; **il faut mettre un p.** it needs a plaster ▸▸ **p. gastrique** *(liquide)* ≃ milk of magnesia; *(poudre)* stomach powder

panser [pɑ̃se] VT **1** *(blessure)* to dress, to put a dressing on; *(membre)* to bandage; *(avec un sparadrap)* to put a plaster on; **p. qn** to dress sb's wounds; *Fig* **p. ses blessures** to lick one's wounds; **six mois lui suffiront pour p. ses blessures** six months will be long enough for him to get over it **2** *(cheval)* to groom, to rub down

panslavisme [pɑ̃slavism] NM *Pol* Pan-Slavism

pansu [pɑ̃sy] ADJ *(personne)* potbellied, paunchy; *(bouteille)* potbellied

pantagruélique [pɑ̃tagryelik] ADJ *(repas, appétit)* enormous, gigantic

pantalon [pɑ̃talɔ̃] NM **1** (pair of) trousers *or Am* pants; **mettre un p.** to put on a pair of trousers; **mettre son p.** to put on one's trousers; **un p. neuf** a new pair of trousers, some new trousers; **p. cigarette** drainpipes; **p. fuseau** tapered trousers *or Am* pants, ski pants; **p. de golf** plus-fours; **p. à pattes d'éléphant** flared trousers *or Am* pants, flares; **p. à pinces** pleated trousers *or Am* pants; **p. de pyjama** pyjama trousers *or Am* pants; **p. de ski** ski pants; **p. de toile** canvas trousers *or Am* pants; **p. de velours côtelé** corduroy trousers *or Am* pants, cords; **elle porte un p.** *ou Vieilli* **des pantalons** she wears trousers; *Fig* **c'est elle qui porte le p.** she wears the trousers *or Am* pants VOIR GRAMMAIRE A10 **2** *Théâtre* P. Pantaloon

pantalon-jupe, *pl* **pantalons-jupes** NM palazzo pants

pantalonnade [pɑ̃talɔnad] NF **1** *Hist, Théâtre* burlesque farce **2** *(hypocrisie)* piece of hypocrisy

pantelant [pɑ̃tlɑ̃] ADJ **1** panting, gasping (**de** with); **tout p.** gasping for breath, out of breath; **la nouvelle m'a laissé p.** the news left *or* had me gasping **2** *(homme ou animal à l'agonie)* quivering, twitching; **chair pantelante** *(d'un animal à l'agonie)* twitching flesh

panteler [pɑ̃tle] VI *(je pantelle, n. pantelons; je pantellerai)* *Vieilli (respirer)* to pant; *Fig (d'émotion)* to gasp (**de** with); *(palpiter)* to quiver

panthéisme [pɑ̃teism] NM *Phil* pantheism

panthéiste [pɑ̃teist] *Phil* ADJ pantheistic(al) N pantheist

panthéon [pɑ̃teɔ̃] NM pantheon; **faire partie du p. des hommes célèbres** to have a place in the hall of fame; **le p. cinématographique** the film industry's hall of fame; **elle fait partie du p. cinématographique** she is one of the all-time movie greats; **mettre qn au p. des musiciens** to consider sb a great musician, to rank sb among the best musicians

panthère [pɑ̃tɛr] NF **1** *Zool* leopard; **p. des neiges** snow leopard; **p. noire** panther **2** *Pol* **les Panthères noires** the Black Panthers

pantin [pɑ̃tɛ̃] NM *(poupée)* jumping jack; *Péj (fantoche)* puppet, stooge; **elle a fait de son époux un p.** she has turned her husband into a puppet

pantographe [pɑ̃tɔgraf] NM *Rail* pantograph; *Aut* scissor jack

pantois [pɑ̃twa] ADJ astounded, *Fam* flabbergasted; **j'en suis tout p.** I'm astounded *or* speechless *or Fam* flabbergasted; **en rester p.** to be speechless *or Fam* flabbergasted

pantomime [pɑ̃tɔmim] NF **1** *Théâtre (art)* mime; *(spectacle)* mime show **2** *Péj (comédie)* scene; **que signifie cette p.?** what is all this nonsense?

> Il ne monte pas que le terme anglais **pantomime** est un faux ami. Il désigne un spectacle de Noël inspiré d'un conte de fées.

pantouflard, -arde [pɑ̃tuflar, -ard] ADJ, N *Fam* stay-at-home; **ils sont très pantouflards** they're real homebodies, they never go out; **ce qu'il est p.!** he's a real stay-at-home!

pantoufle [pɑ̃tufl] NF slipper; **il était en pantoufles** he was wearing slippers, he was in his slippers; **les pantoufles de vair** *ou* **de verre de Cendrillon** Cinderella's glass slippers; *Fig* **passer sa vie dans ses pantoufles** to live a quiet life; *Fig Fam* **raisonner comme une p.** to talk through one's hat

pantoufler [pɑ̃tufle] VI *Fam (d'un fonctionnaire)* to join the private sector

pantoute [pɑ̃tut] ADV *Can Fam (pas du tout)* absolutely not, no way; *(jamais de la vie)* never

panure [panyr] NF *Culin* breadcrumbs

Panurge [panyrʒ] N **agir comme les moutons de P.** to follow the herd

panurgisme [panyrʒism] NM herd mentality

PAO [peao] NF *Ordinat (abrév* **publication assistée par ordinateur)** DTP

paon [pɑ̃] NM **1** *(oiseau)* peacock; **pousser des cris de p.** to screech like a peacock; *Fig* **se parer des plumes du p.** to take all the credit; **être vaniteux comme un p.** to be as vain as a peacock; **faire le p.** to strut about **2** *(insecte)* peacock butterfly

paonne [pan] NF peahen

paonneau, -eaux [pano] NM peachick

PAP [pap] NM *(abrév* **prêt d'accession à la propriété)** = loan for first-time homebuyers

papa [papa] NM dad, *surtout Enf* daddy, *surtout Am* pop; **jouer au p. et à la maman** to play mummies and daddies; **c'est un fils à p.** he's a daddy's boy; *Fam* **faire qch à la p.** to do sth in a leisurely fashion; *Fam* **l'amour à la p.** boring sex; **nous allons faire ça à la p.** we'll take it easy, we won't rush things; **aller à la p.** *(en voiture)* to potter along; *Fam Péj* **de p.** old-fashioned, behind the times; *Fam* **le cinéma/l'armée de p.** the films/army of the past; **p. gâteau** indulgent father; **p. poule** doting father

papal, -ale, -aux, -ales [papal, -o] ADJ papal

paparazzi [paparadzi] NMPL paparazzi

paparazzo [paparadzo] NM paparazzo

papauté [papote] NF papacy

papaye [papaj] NF pawpaw, papaya

papayer [papaje] NM pawpaw *or* papaya (tree)

pape [pap] NM **1** *Rel* pope; *Fam* **heureux comme un p.** happy as a sandboy, happy as Larry; *Fam* **sérieux comme un p.** deadly serious, very solemn; **le P. Jean-Paul II** Pope John Paul II **2** *(d'une association, d'un mouvement etc)* leading light

papelard¹, -arde [paplar, -ard] *Péj* ADJ *(voix etc)* sanctimonious; **il a un air p.** he looks as if butter wouldn't melt in his mouth; **dit-il d'un air p.** he said sanctimoniously N sanctimonious *or* self-righteous person, hypocrite

papelard² NM *Fam (petit papier)* (piece of) paper; *(journal)* (news)paper; *Journ (article)* article, piece; **j'ai oublié mes papelards** I've forgotten my (identity) papers *or Fam* my ID

paperasse [papras] NF *Péj* papers, *Br Fam* bumf, bumph; *(fiches à remplir)* forms; **il y a plein de p. sur mon bureau** my desk is covered in paper; **c'est de la p.!** it's just a load of bumph!; **j'ai horreur de toutes ces paperasses** I hate all this red tape; **je passe mon temps à m'occuper de paperasses** I spend all my time doing paperwork

paperasserie [paprasri] NF *Péj* (accumulation of) papers, *Br Fam* bumf, bumph; *(à remplir)* forms; **la p. (administrative)** red tape; **il y a trop de p.** *(dans ce travail)* there's too much paperwork; *(pour obtenir un visa etc)* there's too much paperwork *or* red tape (involved)

paperassier, -ière [paprasje, -jɛr] *Péj* ADJ *(personne)* fond of paperwork; *(procédure)* cluttered up with red tape N **1** *(personne qui amasse les papiers)* hoarder of (old) papers, *Am Fam* pack rat **2** *(fonctionnaire)* bureaucrat

papet [papɛ] NM *Suisse Culin* = Swiss dish made with potatoes, leeks and sausages

papeterie [papɛtri] NF **1** *(fabrication)* paper manufacturing; *(usine)* paper mill; **la p.** *(industrie)* the paper industry **2** *(magasin)* stationer's (shop); *(articles)* stationery

papetier, -ière [pap(ə)tje, -jɛr] N **1** *Ind* paper manufacturer **2** *Com* stationer
   ADJ paper

papetier-libraire, *pl* **papetiers-libraires** NM *Com* bookseller and stationer

papi [papi] NM grandpa, granddad

papier [papje] NM **1** *(matière)* paper; **pâte à p.** pulp; **un p.** a sheet *or* piece of paper; **notez plutôt cela dans votre carnet que sur un p.** write it down in your notebook rather than on a scrap of paper; **son bureau est couvert de papiers** his desk is covered in paper(s); **classer ses papiers** to put one's papers in order; **jeter des idées sur le p.** to put some ideas down on paper; **ça n'est pas ce qui est dit sur le p.** that's not what it says here; *Fig* **sur le p.** on paper, in theory; **gratter du p.** *(comme métier)* to be a pen-pusher; *(en utiliser beaucoup)* to use a lot of paper; *Fig Fam* **être dans les petits papiers de qn** to be in sb's good books; *Fig Fam* **rayez cela de vos papiers** don't count on it, (you can) forget it **2 papiers** *(documents)* papers, documents; *Jur* **papiers d'une affaire** documents relating to a case; **les papiers de la vente/de la voiture** the sale/car documents; *Admin* **papiers (d'identité)** identity papers, *Fam* ID; **mes papiers sont en règle** my papers are in order; **vos papiers, s'il vous plaît!** can I see your identity papers, please?; *Aut* can I see your driving licence *or Am* driver's license, please?; **faux papiers** false ID **3** *Jur* **p. timbré** stamped paper *(for official and legal documents)* **4** *Fin* bill(s); **p. de commerce** commercial *or* trade paper; **p. long** *ou* **à long terme** long(-dated) bill **5** *Journ* article, piece; **faire un p. sur qch** to do a piece *or* an article on sth
   ▸▸ *Fam* **p. alu** (kitchen *or* aluminium) foil; **p. d'aluminium** aluminium foil, tinfoil; **p. d'argent** silver foil *or* paper; **p. avion** airmail paper; *Fin* **p. bancable** bankable paper; *Ordinat* **p. à bandes perforées** perforated paper; **p. bible** Bible paper; **p. de bonbon** sweet wrapper; **p. buvard** blotting paper; **p. cadeau** gift wrap, wrapping paper; **mettre un p. cadeau à qch** to giftwrap sth; **p. calque** tracing paper; **p. carbone** carbon paper; *Ordinat* **p. Caroll** perforated paper; **p. à cigarettes** cigarette paper; **fin comme du p. à cigarettes** like tissue paper; **un voile fin comme du p. à cigarettes** a gossamer-thin veil; *Fin* **p. commercial** commercial paper; *Fin* **p. commercial de premier ordre** prime bill; *Ordinat* **p. continu** continuous paper *or* stationery; *Ordinat* **p. continu plié en accordéon** fanfold paper; **p. couché** coated paper; *Beaux-Arts* art paper; *Vulg* **p. cul** bog paper; **p. à dessin** drawing paper; **p. d'emballage** wrapping *or* packing paper; **p. émeri** emery paper; **p. à en-tête** headed notepaper; **p. d'étain** tinfoil; **p. à étiquettes** sheets of labels; **p. à lettres** foreign bill; **p. filtre** filter paper; **p. glacé** glazed paper; **papiers gras** litter; **p. hygiénique** toilet paper, *Br Fam* loo paper; *Ordinat* **p. d'impression** printer paper; **p. journal** newsprint; *(vieux journaux)* newspaper; **p. kraft** manila paper; **p. à lettres** notepaper, writing paper; *Ordinat* **p. listing** listing paper; **p. mâché** papier mâché; **poupée en p. mâché** papier mâché doll; **avoir une mine de p. mâché** to look green about the gills; **p. machine** typing paper; **p. ministre** foolscap; *Fin* **p.-monnaie** paper money; *Ordinat* **p. multiple** multi-part stationery; **p. à musique** music

paper, manuscript paper; **être réglé comme du p. à musique** to be as regular as clockwork; **une vie réglée comme du p. à musique** a very orderly life; **un emploi du temps réglé comme du p. à musique** a very strict routine; **chez nous, le matin, c'est réglé comme du p. à musique** there's a strict routine in our house in the morning; *Fin* **p. négociable** negotiable paper; *Fin* **p. à ordre** instrument to order; **p. parcheminé** greaseproof paper; *aussi Ordinat* **p. peint** wallpaper; **p. pelure** onion skin; *Phot* **p. photo** photographic paper; *Fin* **p. au porteur** bearer paper; **p. réglé** ruled *or* lined paper; *Phot* **p. sensible** sensitized paper; **p. de soie** tissue paper; *Ordinat* **p. thermique** thermal paper; **p. toilette** toilet paper, *Br Fam* loo paper; *Fin* **papiers valeurs** securities; **p. vélin** vellum paper; **p. de verre** glasspaper, sandpaper; *Fin* **p. à vue** sight paper

papillaire [papilɛr] ADJ *Anat etc* papillary

papille [papij, -il] NF *Anat, Bot* papilla; **p. gustative** taste bud

papillon [papijɔ̃] NM **1** *(insecte)* butterfly; **p. de nuit** moth; *Fig* **être un p.** to be flighty; *Fam* **minute p.!** just a minute!, hold on a minute!; *Natation* **(brasse) p.** butterfly (stroke); **nager le p.** to do the butterfly **2** *(dans un livre)* inset; *(prospectus)* handbill; *(sur document)* flag; **p. publicitaire** advertising leaflet, flier **3** *Fam (contravention)* (parking) ticket **4** *Tech (de réglage)* butterfly valve, throttle; *(écrou)* thumb screw, butterfly *or* wing nut; *Aut* **p. des gaz** throttle

papillonnant [papijɔnɑ̃] ADJ fluttering, flitting; *Fig (personne)* flighty, fickle

papillonnement [papijɔnmɑ̃] NM fluttering; *(d'un lieu à un autre, d'une personne à une autre)* flitting; *Fig (d'une personne)* flightiness, fickleness

papillonner [papijɔne] VI *(des paupières)* to flutter; *(d'une personne à une autre)* to flit about; *(d'un sujet à un autre)* to pass rapidly; **les yeux des enfants papillonnaient devant le spectacle** the children blinked (in astonishment) at the sight

papillotage [papijɔtaʒ] NM **p. des yeux** blinking (of the eyes)

papillote [papijɔt] NF **1** *Culin (pour faire cuire les côtelettes etc)* buttered paper; *(en papier alu)* silver foil; **cailles en papillotes** quails in papillote **2** *(papier)* twist of paper; *(autour d'un jambon etc)* frill; *Fig* **tu peux en faire des papillotes** you can throw it away; *Fig* **ta dissertation, tu peux en faire des papillotes** your essay is rubbish, your essay isn't worth the paper it's written on **3** *Arch (pour les cheveux)* paper **4** *Région (bonbon)* = special kind of sweet with shiny wrapper, available at Christmas

papillotement [papijɔtmɑ̃] NM *(des yeux)* blinking; *(d'une lumière)* Cin, TV flicker

papilloter [papijɔte] VI **1** *(des yeux)* to blink; *(d'une lumière)* Cin, TV to flicker **2** *(scintiller)* to glitter; *(plus brillamment)* to dazzle
   VT *Arch* **p. ses cheveux** to put one's hair in curl papers

papisme [papism] NM (Roman) Catholicism, *Péj* popery, papistry

papiste [papist] N (Roman) Catholic, *Péj* papist

papoter [papɔte] VI *Fam* to chat, to have a natter; **nous avons passé la journée à p.** we spent the day nattering *or Am* shooting the breeze

papou, -oue [papu] ADJ Papuan
   NM *Ling* Papuan
   N **P.** Papuan

Papouasie-Nouvelle-Guinée [papwazi-nuvɛlgine] NF Papua New Guinea

papouille [papuj] NF *Fam* **faire des papouil-**

les à qn to cuddle *or* squeeze sb; **se faire des papouilles** to have a bit of a cuddle *or Br* a bit of slap and tickle; **il aime les papouilles** he likes a little cuddle

paprika [paprika] NM *Bot, Culin* paprika

papule [papyl] NF pimple; *Méd* papule; *(d'urticaire)* weal

papy [papi] NM granpa, granddad

papy-boom [papibum] NM *Hum (augmentation de la proportion du troisième âge dans la population)* grey *or Am* gray boom

papyrus [papirys] NM papyrus; *(feuille)* sheet of papyrus; **écrire sur des p.** to write on papyrus VOIR GRAMMAIRE A14

paqson [paksɔ̃] NM *Fam* = pacson

pâque [pɑk] NF *Rel* **P., la P. juive** Passover
   NFPL **pâques** Easter; **faire ses pâques** to take the sacrament at Easter
   NM *(contraction of* jour de Pâques, *used without article)* **Pâques** Easter; **le lundi de Pâques** Easter Monday; **œufs de Pâques** Easter eggs; *Fig Fam* **remettre qch à Pâques ou à la Trinité** to put sth off indefinitely; **il le fera, enfin, à Pâques ou à la Trinité** he'll never do it in a month of Sundays; **île de Pâques** Easter Island

> **Pâques**
>
> In France, Easter is traditionally symbolized not only by eggs but also by bells; according to legend, church bells fly to Rome at Easter. At this time of the year, people offer each other chocolate eggs, bells, fish or hens.

paquebot [pakbo] NM *Naut* (steam)ship; *(gros)* liner; **p. de ligne** liner; **p. de haute mer** ocean liner

paquégique [pakeʒik] NF *Mktg* packaging

pâquerette [pakrɛt] NF daisy; *Fam* **voler au ras des pâquerettes** *(conversation, plaisanterie)* to be a bit on the basic side

paquet [pakɛ] NM **1** *(de thé, pâtes)* packet; *(de café, sucre, riz)* bag, packet; *(de cigarettes)* packet, *Am* pack; *(postal)* parcel, package; *(ballot, liasse)* bundle; **expédier** *ou* **envoyer un p.** to send (off) a parcel; **faire un p.** to make up a parcel; **faire son p.** *ou* **ses paquets** to pack one's bags; **p. de billets** wad of notes; *Fam* **il a touché un joli p.** he's made a packet; **du riz/du café en p.** prepacked *or* packaged rice/coffee; **il fume un p. (de cigarettes) par jour** he smokes twenty *or* a packet *or Am* a pack a day; **il est tombé un p. de neige** it snowed heavily, there was a lot of snow; **des paquets d'eau tombaient** the rain was coming down in sheets; **c'est un p. d'os** he's/she's all skin and bone; **c'est un p. de nerfs** he's/she's a bag *or* bundle of nerves; *Fig Fam* **mettre le p.** to go all out, to pull out all the stops; *Fig Fam* **risquer le p.** to risk *or* chance everything one's got *or* the lot; *Fig Fam* **lâcher le p.** to spill the beans **2** *Ordinat* packet **3** *Rugby* **p. (d'avants)** pack
   ▸▸ *Fin* **p. d'actions** parcel *or* block of shares; *Com* **p. économique** economy pack; *Com* **p. familial** family-size packet; **p. fiscal** tax package; **p. de mer** *(vague)* big wave; **embarquer des paquets de mer** *(d'un bateau)* to take on a lot of water; *Com* **p. postal** parcel; *Com* **p. de présentation** display pack; *Fin* **p. de valeurs** parcel *or* block of shares

paquetage [paktaʒ] NM *Mil etc* (soldier's) pack; **faire son p.** to get one's kit ready

paquet-cadeau, *pl* **paquets-cadeaux** NM gift-wrapped parcel; **je vous fais un p.?** would you like it gift-wrapped?; **dans un joli p.** prettily gift-wrapped

paquet-poste, *pl* **paquets-poste** NM mailing box

PAR [par]

PRÉP by **4, 6** ▪ through **1** ▪ round here (*par ici*) **2** ▪ on **3** ▪ in **3** ▪ at **4** ▪ out of **5** ▪ with **6** ▪ according to **7** ▪ per **8**

PRÉP SEE GRAMMAR B56 **1** (*à travers*) (*porte, hall, trou de la serrure*) through; **il entra p. la fenêtre** he came in through or by the window; **regarder p. la fenêtre** (*de l'intérieur*) to look out (of) the window; (*de l'extérieur*) to look (in) through the window; **passer p. Calais** to travel or go through or via Calais or by way of Calais; **venez p. ici** come this way; **allez p. là** go that way; **p. ici la sortie** this is the way out, it's this way out; **p. où est-il passé?** which way did he go?; **p. où passe ce cordon électrique?** where does this wire go?; **p. où est-il entré?** how did he get in?; **il court p. les rues** he runs through the streets; **de p. le monde** all over the world

2 (*position*) **p. ici** round (about) here; **p. 10° de latitude nord** at a latitude of 10° North; **j'ai mal p. ici** it hurts round about here; **ça doit être p. là quelque part** it must be over there somewhere

3 (*pendant, durant*) **p. un jour d'hiver** on a winter's day; **p. cette chaleur/ces temps de pluie** in this heat/rainy weather; **p. le passé** in the past; **je l'ai averti p. trois fois** I warned him three times; *Litt* **p. trois fois, il fut blessé** he was wounded on three separate occasions

4 (*agent*) by; **tu as été appelé p. M. Alain** Mr Alain called you, you had a call from Mr Alain; **accablé p. l'inquiétude** overcome by or with anxiety; **soulagé p. cette nouvelle** relieved by or at the news; **faire qch p. soi-même** (*seul*) to do sth by oneself or on one's own; (*de sa propre volonté*) to do sth on one's own initiative; **examiner/juger/voir qch p. soi-même** to examine/judge/see sth for oneself; **elle est remarquable p. sa beauté** she is remarkable for her beauty; **elle est unique p. sa générosité/son intelligence** there is no one to equal her for generosity/intelligence; **j'ai appris p. les Martin que vous étiez malade** I heard through or from the Martins that you were ill; *Fam* **tu le sais p. qui, toi?** who did you get that from?, who told you that?; **faire faire qch p. qn** to have sth done by sb; **as-tu vu Don Juan p. Planchon?** have you seen Planchon's Don Juan?

5 (*motif*) (*habitude, négligence, curiosité, amitié etc*) out of; **j'ai fait cela p. amitié/respect pour vous** I did it out of friendship/respect for you; **p. pitié!** for pity's sake!; **p. hasard/erreur** by chance/mistake; **p. malheur** unfortunately, as bad luck would have it

6 (*au moyen de*) (*clou, chaîne etc*) with, by (means of); (*train, avion, voiture, bateau*) by; **il fut salué p. des acclamations** he was hailed with or by cheers; **remercié p. un bouquet** thanked with a bouquet; **conduire/prendre qn p. la main** to lead/take sb by the hand; **tenir qn p. la taille** to hold sb round the waist; **envoyer qch p. la poste** to send sth by post or through the post; **répondre p. oui ou p. non** to answer yes or no; **commencer** ou **débuter/finir** ou **achever** ou **terminer p. qch/faire qch** to begin/end with sth/by doing sth; **se terminer p. un divorce/une dispute** to end in divorce/an argument; **commençons p. le commencement** let's begin at the beginning; **il a essayé p. tous les moyens** he tried (by) every possible means, he tried everything; **il est monté p. l'escalier** he took the stairs up; **il a dû monter p. l'échelle** he must have climbed the ladder; **mon cousin p. alliance** my cousin by marriage; **société p. actions** joint-stock company; **obtenir qch p. la force** to obtain sth by

force; **p. la seule volonté** by sheer force of will; **appeler qn p. son nom** to call sb by his/her name; *Fig* **appeler les choses p. leur(s) nom(s)** to call a spade a spade; **p. route** by road

7 (*selon*) according to; **p. taille, p. ordre de grandeur** according to size; **p. ordre alphabétique/chronologique** in alphabetical/chronological order

8 (*distributif*) **entrer deux p. deux** to come in two by two, to come in in twos; **deux jours p. semaine** two days a week; **il gagne 200 euros p. semaine** he earns 200 euros a or per week; **10 000 euros p. an** 10,000 euros a year or per annum; **un siège p. personne** one seat per person; **un guide p. groupe de six** one guide per group of six or for each group of six; **actualité transmise heure p. heure** hourly news broadcasts

9 *Arch* (*au nom de*) **de p. le Roi** by order of the King, in the name of the King

ADV *Litt* **p. trop** far too, much too; **vous êtes p. trop aimable** you are much too kind

para [para] **NM** *Fam* (*abrév* **parachutiste**) para

parabole [parabɔl] **NF 1** (*allégorie*) parable; **parler par paraboles** to speak in parables **2** *Géom* parabola **3** *Tél, TV* (*antenne*) satellite dish, dish aerial, *Am* dish antenna

parabolique [parabɔlik] **ADJ** (*miroir*), *Géom* (*courbe*) parabolic; *Tél, TV* **antenne p.** satellite dish, dish aerial, *Am* dish antenna; **radiateur p.** electric fire (*with parabolic reflector*) **NM** electric fire (*with parabolic reflector*)

paracétamol [parasetamɔl] **NM** paracetamol; **prendre du p.** to take some paracetamol; **deux cachets de p.** two paracetamol

parachèvement [paraʃɛvmɑ̃] **NM** completion, finishing; (*perfectionnement*) perfecting, perfection

parachever [paraʃ(ə)ve] **VT** (*conj like* **achever**) to complete, to finish off; (*perfectionner*) to perfect

parachutage [paraʃytaʒ] **NM** parachuting, dropping (by parachute); *Pol Fam* (*d'un candidat*) parachuting in; *Fig Fam* **son p. dans le bureau** the way he was foisted on or parachuted into the office

parachute [paraʃyt] **NM** (*appareil de saut*) parachute, *Fam* chute; **p. dorsal/ventral** back(-pack)/lap-pack parachute; **saut en p.** parachute jump; **sauter en p.** to make a parachute jump; **faire du p.** to go parachuting; **p. ascensionnel** parascending

parachuter [paraʃyte] **VT** (*vivres*) to drop by parachute, to parachute in; (*soldats*) to parachute in; *Pol Fam* (*nommer*) to parachute in; *Fig Fam* **la façon dont il s'est fait p. dans le service** the way he was foisted on or parachuted into the department; *Fig Fam* **j'ai été parachuté à ce poste** I've been pitchforked into this job

parachutisme [paraʃytism] **NM** parachuting, parachute jumping

parachutiste [paraʃytist] **N** parachutist, parachute jumper **NM** *Mil* paratrooper; **parachutistes** (*corps d'armée*) paratroops **ADJ** parachute

parade [parad] **NF 1** (*défilé*) parade; **faire la p.** to parade; **comme à la p.** (*facilement*) like clockwork; **p. de cirque** circus parade **2** (*exhibition*) show, ostentation; **faire p. de** (*ses bijoux, ses connaissances*) to parade, to display, to show off; (*sa beauté*) to flaunt; **habits de p.** full-dress or ceremonial clothes; *Fig* **de p.** (*sourire, air etc*) insincere, forced **3** *Équitation* (*de cheval*) stopping, pulling up **4** *Zool* display; **p. nuptiale** (*des animaux*) courtship dance or ritual **5** *Escrime* parade, parry; *Boxe* parry **6** (*réplique*) riposte; **faire**

une p. to riposte, to parry; **je n'ai pas encore trouvé la p.** I haven't come up with a way of handling it/them yet

parader [parade] **VI** to show off; (*en se promenant*) to strut about; *Zool* to display

paradigmatique [paradigmatik] *Ling* **ADJ** paradigmatic **NF** study of paradigmatic relationships

paradigme [paradigm] **NM** *Ling* paradigm

paradis [paradi] **NM** paradise, heaven; *Fig* paradise; **un p. terrestre** heaven on earth, an earthly paradise; **les p. artificiels** drug-induced euphoria; **l'enfer et le p.** heaven and hell; **aller au** ou **en p.** to go to heaven or paradise; **il ne l'emportera pas au** ou **en p.** he won't get away with it, he'll be sorry; **un p. pour les enfants** a paradise for children; **c'est le p. des pêcheurs** it's a fisherman's paradise or idea of heaven; *Théâtre Fam* **le p.** the gods; **oiseau de p.** bird of paradise

▸▸ **p. fiscal** tax haven; **le P. terrestre** the Garden of Eden

paradisiaque [paradizjak] **ADJ** of paradise, *Fml* paradisiac(al), paradisaical; *Fig* (*vacances, lieu*) heavenly

paradisier [paradizje] **NM** (*oiseau*) bird of paradise

paradoxal, -ale, -aux, -ales [paradɔksal, -o] **ADJ** paradoxical; **c'est complètement p.** it's totally illogical

paradoxalement [paradɔksalmɑ̃] **ADV** paradoxically

paradoxe [paradɔks] **NM** paradox

parafe [paraf] **NM** = **paraphe**

parafer [parafe] **VT** = **parapher**

paraffinage [parafinaʒ] **NM** paraffining, waxing

paraffine [parafin] **NF** *Chimie* paraffin; *Com* paraffin (wax); *Méd* **huile de p.** liquid paraffin

paraffiner [parafine] **VT** to paraffin

parafiscal, -ale, -aux, -ales [parafiskal, -o] **ADJ** (*taxe*) exceptional, special

parafiscalité [parafiskalite] **NF** indirect taxation, special taxation

parage[1] [paraʒ] **NM** *Arch* **de haut p.** of high lineage, high-born

parage[2] **NM 1** *Naut* (*souvent pl*) **parages** waters, region(s); **les parages du cap Horn** the waters off Cape Horn; **se trouver dans les parages du cap Horn** to be off Cape Horn **2** (*toujours pl*) **dans les parages de ...** in the vicinity of ..., near ...; **que faites-vous dans ces parages?** what are you doing here or in this neck of the woods?; **est-ce qu'il est dans les parages?** is he around?; **il est dans les parages** he's around somewhere; **elle habite dans les parages** she lives round about here

paragraphe [paragraf] **NM 1** paragraph; *Journ* par; (*d'un texte de loi*) subsection **2** *Typ* section mark, paragraph

Paraguay [paragwɛ] **NM** Paraguay

paraguayen, -enne [paragwɛjɛ̃, -ɛn] **ADJ** Paraguayan **N** P. Paraguayan

para-hôtellerie **NF** serviced accommodation industry

paraître[1] [parɛtr] **NM** **l'être et le p.** appearance and reality; **s'intéresser davantage au p.** to be more interested in appearances; **juger sur le p.** to judge by appearances

PARAÎTRE[2] (*prp* **paraissant**; *pp* **paru**; *pr ind* **je parais, il paraît, n. paraissons**; *impf* **je paraissais**; *p hist* **je parus**; *fu* **je paraîtrai**)

VI to appear **1–3** ▪ to come out **2** ▪ to look **3** ▪ to seem **3** **V IMPERS** to seem **1, 2** ▪ to appear **2**

VI 1 *(se montrer)* to appear; *(d'une étoile, de la lune etc)* to appear, to come out; *(d'un acteur)* to appear, to come on; **le jour commençait à p.** day was dawning; **il n'a pas** *ou* **n'est pas paru de la journée** he hasn't appeared all day; **lorsque l'enfant paraît** when the baby arrives; **laisser p. ses sentiments/sa déception** to show one's feelings/disappointment; to let one's feelings/disappointment show; **il ne pouvait pas s'empêcher de laisser p. un certain agacement** he couldn't help showing or betraying a degree of annoyance; **un faible sourire a paru sur ses lèvres** he/she smiled weakly; **p. en public** to appear in public; *Théâtre* **c'est alors qu'elle parut sur la scène** it was at that moment that she appeared on stage *or* she came on (stage); **elle aime un peu trop p.** she likes to show off; **elle ne pense qu'à p.** all she thinks about is impressing people

2 *(d'un livre etc)* to come out, to appear, to be published; *(d'un périodique)* to appear, to come out; **faire p. un livre** to publish a book, to bring out a book; **vient de p.** just out; *(livre)* just published; **le dernier San Antonio vient de p.** the latest San Antonio has just come out

3 *(sembler)* to seem, to look, to appear; **il paraissait furieux** he looked furious; *(à l'entendre)* he sounded furious; **cette décision me paraît bizarre** it seems a strange decision to me, it strikes me as a strange decision; **cela me paraît (être) une très bonne idée** it sounds to me like *or* strikes me as a very good idea; **ça ne te paraît pas une bonne idée?** don't you think that's a good idea?; **l'endroit lui parut familier** the place seemed familiar to him; **il ne paraît pas remarquer leur présence** he doesn't seem *or* appear to notice their presence; **il paraît (avoir) trente ans** he looks about thirty; *(d'une personne plus âgée)* he looks no more than thirty; **elle a quarante ans, mais elle ne les paraît pas** she's forty, but she doesn't look it; **p. son âge** to look one's age; **il veut p. ce qu'il n'est pas** he wants to pass for *or* he wants to appear to be something that he isn't; **pourquoi ce besoin de p.?** why this need to appear to be what you're/he's/*etc* not?

V IMPERS SEE GRAMMAR B29 **1** *(sembler)* **je suis très mal – il n'y paraît pas** I'm very ill – you don't look it *or* it doesn't look as if you are; **demain, il n'y paraîtra plus** there'll be no trace of it tomorrow; **sans qu'il n'y paraisse** without it *or Fml* its being apparent; **il faut l'aider sans qu'il n'y paraisse** we must help him/her without making it obvious *or* without making it look as if we are doing; **il me paraît que ...** it seems to me *or* it strikes me that ...; **il me paraît utile de ...** I think it would be useful to ...

2 il paraît que *(on dit que)* it seems *or* appears that; **il paraît qu'elle s'en va, elle s'en va, paraît-il** it seems *or* appears *or* would appear that she's leaving, she's leaving apparently; **il paraît que ça fait maigrir** apparently it helps you lose weight; **à ce qu'il paraît** apparently, it would seem so; **à ce qu'il paraît, c'est plus rapide par la route que par avion** apparently *or* seemingly *or* it would appear that it's quicker by road than by air; **il paraît (que oui)** so it appears *or* would appear, it appears *or* seems so, apparently; **il paraît que non** it appears *or* would appear not, it seems not, apparently not

paralangage [paralãgaʒ] **NM** paralanguage
paralinguistique [paralɛ̃gɥistik] **ADJ** paralinguistic
NF paralinguistics

paralittéraire [paraliterɛr] **ADJ** œuvre p. work of popular literature; **écriture p.** popular writing

paralittérature [paraliteratyr] **NF** popular literature

parallaxe [paralaks] **NF** *Astron etc* parallax; *Opt etc* **erreur de p.** parallax error

parallèle [paralɛl] **ADJ** *Géom* parallel (**à** to, **with**); *Fig (expériences, destinées, carrières etc)* very similar; *Ordinat* **imprimante/interface p.** parallel printer/interface; *Gym* **barres parallèles** parallel bars; **faire des barres parallèles** to do exercises on the parallel bars; **rue qui est p. à la rivière** street that is *or* runs parallel to *or* with the river; **droites parallèles à l'infini** parallel straight lines extending into infinity; **mener une action p.** to take parallel *or* similar action; **mener une vie p.** to lead a secret life; **circuits parallèles de vente** parallel sales networks; **police p.** illegally constituted police force; *Écon* **marché p.** unofficial *or* illegal market
NF parallel (line)
NM *Géog (d'une latitude)* parallel; *(comparaison)* comparison, parallel; **en p.** *(employé adjectivement)* parallel; *(employé adverbialement)* in parallel; **mettre qch en p. avec qch** to compare sth with sth; **mettre deux événements/réactions en p.** to compare two events/reactions, to set two events/reactions side by side; **établir un p. entre ... et ...** to establish *or* draw a parallel between ... and ...

parallèlement [paralɛlmã] **ADV** parallel (**à** to, **with**); *(en même temps)* at the same time, *Fml* concurrently; *(de la même façon)* in the same way; **p. à la route** parallel to the road, alongside the road

parallélépipède [paralelepipɛd] **NM** *Géom* parallelepiped

parallélisme [paralelism] **NM** parallelism; *Aut* **p. (des roues)** (wheel) alignment; *Aut* **il y a un défaut de p.** there's something wrong with the alignment, the wheels aren't properly aligned

parallélogramme [paralelɔgram] **NM** *Géom* parallelogram

paralympique [paralɛ̃pik] **ADJ** *voir* **jeu**

paralysant [paralizã] **ADJ** *Méd, Fig (peur)* paralysing; *(timidité)* crippling, paralysing

paralysé, -ée [paralize] **ADJ** *Méd* paralysed; *Fig (pays)* crippled; *Fig* **p. de peur** paralysed with fear; *Fig* **je suis resté p.** I was paralysed *or* petrified; **nous sommes paralysés par l'absence de fonds suffisants** we are hamstrung by a lack of funds
N person who is paralysed; **les paralysés** the paralysed

paralyser [paralize] **VT** *(rendre infirme)* to paralyse; *Fig (empêcher d'agir, de fonctionner)* to paralyse, to incapacitate; *Fig (économie, pays)* to cripple; *Fig (circulation)* to bring to a standstill; **paralysé des deux jambes** paralysed in both legs; **le froid paralyse ses mains** his/her hands are numb with the cold; **ce genre de situation me paralyse** I'm petrified in that kind of situation; **paralysé par la peur** paralysed *or* helpless with fear

paralysie [paralizi] **NF** *Méd (d'une partie du corps)* paralysis; *Fig* state of paralysis; **p. agitante** Parkinson's disease; **p. générale (progressive)** creeping paralysis; **p. cérébrale** cerebral palsy; **p. faciale** facial palsy

paralytique [paralitik] **ADJ** paralytic
N person who is paralysed, paralytic

paramédical, -ale, -aux, -ales [paramedikal, -o] **ADJ** paramedical; **personnel p.** paramedics
NM **emplois du p.** jobs in paramedics, paramedic jobs

paramétrable [parametrabl] **ADJ** *Ordinat* configurable; **p. par l'utilisateur** user-definable

paramétrage [parametraʒ] **NM** *Ordinat* configuration

paramètre [parametr] **NM** *Math, Fig* parameter; *Ordinat* parameter, setting; *(du DOS)* switch

paramétrer [parametre] **VT** *Ordinat* to configure

paramilitaire [paramiliter] **ADJ** paramilitary
N paramilitary

parangon [parãgɔ̃] **NM** *Litt* paragon; **p. de vertu** paragon of virtue

parano [parano] *Fam* **ADJ** paranoid
NF *(paranoïa)* paranoia; **elle fait de la p.!** she's being paranoid!; **tu es en pleine p.!** you're being completely paranoid!; **arrête ta p.!** stop being paranoid!
N *(personne)* **c'est un/une p.!** he's/she's paranoid!

paranoïa [paranɔja] **NF** *Psy* paranoia; *Fig* **tu es en pleine p.** you're being completely paranoid

paranoïaque [paranɔjak] **ADJ, N** *Psy* paranoiac

paranoïde [paranɔid] **ADJ** paranoid

paranormal, -ale, -aux, -ales [paranormal, -o] **ADJ** paranormal

parapente [parapãt] **NM** *(activité)* paragliding; *(parachute)* paraglider; **faire du p.** to go paragliding

parapet [parapɛ] **NM** parapet

parapharmacie [parafarmasi] **NF 1** *(produits)* = personal hygiene products and cosmetics **2** *(rayon, boutique)* = chemist's selling personal hygiene products and cosmetics, *Am* ≃ drugstore

paraphe [paraf] **NM 1** *(ajouté à la signature)* flourish **2** *(de son nom)* initials

parapher [parafe] **VT** to initial; *(signer)* to sign

parapheur [parafœr] **NM** signature book

paraphrase [parafraz] **NF** paraphrase; **faire de la p.** to paraphrase

paraphraser [parafraze] **VT** to paraphrase

paraplégie [parapleʒi] **NF** *Méd* paraplegia

paraplégique [parapleʒik] **ADJ, N** *Méd* paraplegic

parapluie [paraplɥi] **NM** umbrella, *Br Fam* brolly; **p. de golf** golf umbrella; *Fig* **p. nucléaire** *ou* **atomique** nuclear umbrella

parapsychologie [parapsikɔlɔʒi] **NF** parapsychology

parapublic, -ique [parapyblik] **ADJ** *(entreprise)* part government-owned

parasciences [parasjãs] **NFPL** sciences of the paranormal

parascolaire [paraskɔlɛr] **ADJ** extra-curricular

parasismique [parasismik] **ADJ** anti-earthquake

parasitaire [paraziter] **ADJ** parasitic(al)

parasite [parazit] **NM** *Biol* parasite; *Fig* parasite, *Fam* sponger, freeloader; **un p. social** a social parasite; *Radio, TV* **parasites** interference, static, *Br* atmospherics
ADJ *Biol (insecte, plante etc)* parasitic; *Fig (mot)* unnecessary, superfluous; *Radio, TV* **bruits parasites** interference

parasiter [parazite] **VT** *Biol* to parasitize; *Radio, TV* to cause interference in; *Fig Fam* **p. la société** to be a parasite on society

parasitique [parazitik] **ADJ** parasitic(al)

parasitisme [parazitism] **NM** parasitism

parasitologie [parazitɔlɔʒi] **NF** *Méd* parasitology

parasitologique [parazitɔlɔʒik] **ADJ** *Méd* parasitological

parasitose [parazitoz] **NF** *Méd* disease caused by a parasite

parasol [parasɔl] NM parasol, sunshade; *(sur la plage)* beach umbrella; **pin p.** parasol *or* umbrella pine

parasympathique [parasɛ̃patik] ADJ *Anat* parasympathetic

parataxe [parataks] NF parataxis

paratonnerre [paratɔnɛr] NM lightning conductor

paratyphoïde [paratifɔid] ADJ, NF *Méd* **(fiè-vre) p.** paratyphoid fever

paravalanche [paravalɑ̃ʃ] ADJ **mur** *ou* **in-stallation p.** avalanche barrier *or* wall
NM avalanche barrier *or* wall

paravent [paravɑ̃] NM screen; *Fig* **ce n'est qu'un p.** it's just a smoke screen *or* a front; **cette société leur sert de p. pour d'autres ac-tivités** the company is a screen *or* front for their other activities

parbleu [parblø] INT *Vieilli* good Lord!

parc [park] NM **1** *(jardin)* park; *(d'un château etc)* grounds, park **2** *(pour enfant)* playpen **3** *(ensemble) (de bus, de voitures etc)* fleet; *Rail* rolling stock; **p. automobile** number of cars on the roads; **le p. automobile français** the number of cars in France; **le p. des télévi-seurs couleurs** the total number of colour te-levisions owned by the population; *Ordinat* **p. de micros** computer park; *Ordinat* **p. in-formatique** computer park; **p. immobilier** housing stock; **le p. nucléaire de la France** France's nuclear power stations
▸▸**p. aquatique** water park; **p. d'attractions** theme park; **p. à bestiaux** cattle pen; *Aut* **p. d'exposition** forecourt; **p. des expositions** exhibition centre; **p. industriel** industrial park, *Br* industrial estate; **p. de loisirs** leisure park; **p. à moules** mussel bed; **p. à moutons** sheep pen, sheepfold; **p. national** national park; **p. na-turel** nature reserve; **p. régional** regional park; **p. résidentiel de loisirs** chalet park, holiday camp; **p. de stationnement** car park, *Am* parking lot; **p. de stationnement à plusieurs niveaux** multi-storey car park, *Am* multi-story parking garage; **p. technolo-gique** technology park; **p. à thème** theme park; **p. zoologique** zoo, *Fml* zoological gardens

parcage [parkaʒ] NM **1** *(du bétail, de mou-tons)* penning, enclosing **2** *Tél* hold; **mettre en p.** *(correspondant)* to put on hold; *Ordinat (disque dur)* to park

parcellaire [parsɛlɛr] ADJ *(terrain)* divided into small portions *or* into parcels; **travail p.** work divided into sections

parcelle [parsɛl] NF (small) fragment, mor-sel; *(de terrain)* piece, parcel; *Fig* **pas la moindre p. de jugement/d'intelligence/de vérité** not an ounce of common sense/intel-ligence/truth; **il n'a pas la moindre p. de gé-nérosité** he doesn't have a generous bone in his body; **il ne cédera pas la moindre p. de son indépendance/sa liberté** he will not give up the least little bit of his independence/freedom

parcellisation [parsɛlizasjɔ̃] NF *(du terrain)* parcelling up; **p. du travail** breaking work down into sections

parcelliser [parsɛlize] VT *(terrain)* to divide into small portions, to parcel up; *(travail)* to break down into sections

parce que [pars(ə)kə] CONJ because; **p. c'est vrai** because it's true; **ce n'est pas p. tu n'ai-mes pas la cervelle que …** just because you don't like brains doesn't mean that …; **parce qu'on lui dit de le faire, il le fait** he does it (just) because he's told to do it; **pourquoi ne viens-tu pas? – p.** why aren't you coming? – (just) because (I'm not); **mais pourquoi pleures-tu comme ça? – p.** why are you cry-ing? – just because; **ce chandelier vous in-**

téresse? p. je pourrais … are you interested in the chandelier? because if you are *or* if so, I could …; **je le ferai, mais p. c'est vous!** I'll do it, but only because it's you!

parchemin [parʃəmɛ̃] NM parchment; *(de livre)* vellum; **papier p.** parchment paper; **un p.** a parchment; *Univ* a diploma; **des par-chemins** *(titres de noblesse)* titles of nobility

parcheminé [parʃəmine] ADJ parchment-like; *Fig (visage)* wizened, wrinkled

parcheminer [parʃəmine] VT *(papier)* to give a parchment finish to
VPR **se parcheminer** *(de la peau)* to shrivel up, to become shrivelled

parcimonie [parsimɔni] NF thrift; **avec p.** sparingly; **elle distribue les conseils avec p.** she is sparing with her advice

parcimonieusement [parsimɔnjøzmɑ̃] ADV sparingly; **distribuer les compliments p.** to be sparing with one's compliments

parcimonieux, -ieuse [parsimɔnjø, -jøz] ADJ *(personne, action)* thrifty; **une distribu-tion parcimonieuse du pain** a sparing distri-bution of bread

par-ci, par-là ADV *(dans l'espace)* here and there; *(dans le temps)* now and then, from time to time; **une virgule par-ci, un point d'exclamation par-là** a comma here, an ex-clamation mark there

parcmètre [parkmɛtr], **parcomètre** [parkɔ-mɛtr] NM (parking) meter; **ma voiture est au p.** I'm on a meter

parcourir [parkurir] VT *(conj like* **courir***)* **1** *(région, quartier)* to roam, to travel through; *(les rues)* to roam, to wander (through); **p. les mers** to sail the seas; **p. le pays de long en large** to travel the length and breadth of the country; **p. un endroit à la recherche de qn** to scour a place for sb; **p. une distance de plusieurs kilomètres** to cover a distance of several kilometres; **il reste deux kilomè-tres/un long chemin à p.** there are two kilo-metres/there is a long way to go; **le pays est parcouru de canaux** the country has a net-work of canals; **mesurer le chemin parcouru** to measure the distance covered; *Fig* to measure one's progress; *Fig* **un frisson me parcourut** a shiver went through me; *Fig* **un frisson me parcourut l'échine** *ou* **le dos** a shi-ver ran down my spine; *Fig* **un murmure a parcouru la foule** a murmur ran through the crowd
2 *(regarder) (texte, document)* to look at briefly, to read *or* run through *or* over; *(let-tre, journal)* to skim, to glance at; *(livre)* to skim (through), to glance through; *Ordinat* to scroll through; **p. qch des yeux** *ou* **du re-gard** to glance at *or* over sth, to run one's eyes over sth; **p. ses notes avant une réu-nion** to go over *or* look over one's notes be-fore a meeting

parcours [parkur] NM *(d'un défilé, de bus etc)* route; *(d'un fleuve)* course; *Sport (de voi-tures, motos etc)* circuit; *(de chevaux), Golf* course; *(distance)* distance covered; *(voyage en avion)* leg; *(itinéraire)* route; *Aviat* **p. à vide** deadhead flight, empty leg; **les che-vaux font un p. de 20 kilomètres** the horses run over a distance of 20 kilometres; *Golf* **un p. dix-huit trous** an eighteen-hole course; **le car fait le p. entre la ville et la côte** the bus runs between the town and the coast; **elle fait plusieurs fois le p. dans la journée** she does the journey several times a day; **je fais le p. à pied dans les deux sens** I walk both ways; **payer le p.** *(dans un taxi)* to pay the fare; **le prix du p.** the fare; **je ne connais pas le prix du p. pour aller à l'aéroport** I don't know the fare to the airport *or* how much it costs to get to the airport; *Courses de che-vaux* **reconnaître le p.** to walk the course; **faire un p. sans faute** *(d'un cheval)* to have

a clear round; *Fig (dans une carrière)* to have a copybook career; *Mil, Fig* **p. du combat-tant** obstacle course; **faire le p. du combat-tant** to do an obstacle course

par-delà PRÉP, ADV beyond

par-derrière ADV *(attaquer qn)* from be-hind; *(se boutonner)* at the back; **entrer p.** to come in the back way, to come in the back door; **des coups p.** underhand tricks; **elle a toujours fait des coups p.** she's always been underhand; **dire des choses p.** to say things behind people's backs; **mais p. je suis sûr qu'il dit autre chose** but I'm sure he says something quite different behind my back
PRÉP behind

par-dessous PRÉP under, beneath, under-neath
ADV underneath; **je suis passé p.** I crept un-derneath; **prendre qch p.** to get hold of sth underneath

pardessus [pardəsy] NM overcoat

par-dessus PRÉP over (the top of); **sauter p. la table** to leap over the table; **jeter qch p. bord** to throw sth overboard; *Fig* **p. le marché** into the bargain; **p. tout** above all; *(le com-ble)* to crown it all, on top of it all; *Fig Fam* **j'en ai p. la tête** I've had just about enough; **re-garder p. l'épaule de qn** to look over sb's shoulder
ADV over

par-devant PRÉP in front of; **passer p. la maison** to pass the house; *Jur* **acte signé p. (le) notaire** deed signed in the presence of a lawyer
ADV in front

par-devers [pardəvɛr] PRÉP **1 p. soi** in one's possession **2 p. le juge** before the judge

pardi [pardi] INT *Fam* of course!, naturally!

pardieu [pardjø] INT *Arch* zounds!

pardon [pardɔ̃] NM **1** *(grâce)* forgiveness; **ac-corder son p. à qn** to forgive *or* pardon sb; **demander p. à qn** to apologize to sb, to say sorry to sb; **demander p. à Dieu pour ses pé-chés** to ask God's forgiveness for one's sins; **mille pardons** a thousand apologies; **arrête de toujours (me) demander p.** stop apolo-gizing; **c'est à lui de te demander p.** it's up to him to apologize, he should apologize to you; **(je vous demande) p.** (I'm) sorry, I beg your pardon; *(pour passer, avertir, attirer l'attention de qn)* excuse me; **j'ai fait une grosse bêtise, je vous demande p.** I'm sorry *or* I do apologize, I've done something very stupid; **je vous demande p., quel est votre nom?** I'm sorry, what is your name?; **p., ce n'est pas ce que j'ai dit!** *(pour contredire)* ex-cuse me *or* pardon me, but that's not what I said!; **p. (qu'as-tu dit)?** what did you say?, excuse me?, (I beg your) pardon?; *Fam* **on dit qu'il n'est pas très malin, mais son fils, p.!** he's not very bright, it seems, but his son is even worse!; *Fam* **la mère est jolie, mais la fille, p.!** the mother's pretty, but the daughter, wow! **2** *Rel (en Bretagne)* religious festival; *Rel juive* **le Grand P., le jour du P.** the Day of Atonement, Yom Kippur

pardonnable [pardɔnabl] ADJ *(faute, erreur)* forgivable, excusable, pardonable; **il s'est trompé mais c'est p.** he made a mistake, but he can be forgiven *or* excused *or* it's ex-cusable; **tu es p. d'avoir oublié** you can be forgiven for forgetting; **vous n'êtes pas p.!** it's unforgivable *or* inexcusable of you!

pardonner [pardɔne] VT *(erreur, faute)* to forgive, to excuse, to pardon; *(personne)* to forgive; **est-ce que tu me pardonnes?** do you forgive me?, am I forgiven?; **p. qch à qn** to forgive sb sth; **elle m'a pardonné d'avoir oublié** she forgave me for forgetting; **par-donnez-moi si je vous contredis** I'm sorry to contradict you, excuse *or* forgive *or* pardon me for contradicting you; **pour me/te/**etc **faire p.** to make it up; **pour se faire p. son retard** as a way of saying sorry for being late; **tu es tout pardonné** you are forgiven

VI to forgive; **elle pardonne vite** she is quick to forgive; **maladie/faute qui ne pardonne pas** fatal illness/mistake; **ça ne pardonne pas** you don't get a second chance

VPR se pardonner je ne me le pardonnerai jamais I'll never forgive myself (for it); **c'est une erreur qui ne se pardonne pas** it's an unforgivable mistake; **ils se sont pardonné leurs paroles de colère** they forgave each other for being angry

paré [pare] **ADJ 1** *(prêt)* ready (à for); **être p. contre** *(le froid, les attaques etc)* to be prepared for; **vous voilà p.!** you're all set!; *Naut* **p. à virer!** ready about! **2** *(orné)* decorated, ornamented (**de** with); *(personne)* *(vêtu)* dressed (up) (**de** in); *(couvert de bijoux)* wearing jewels, covered in jewels **3** *Culin* *(viande)* dressed

pare-avalanches [paravalɑ̃ʃ] **NM INV** avalanche barrier *or* wall

pare-balles [parbal] **ADJ INV** bullet-proof; **gilet p.** bullet-proof vest

pare-boue [parbu] **NM INV** mudflap

pare-brise [parbriz] **NM INV** *Aut etc* windscreen, *Am* windshield; **p. feuilleté** laminated windscreen

pare-chocs [parʃɔk] **NM INV** *Aut* bumper; **on roulait p. contre p.** it *or* the traffic was bumper to bumper; **p. bouclier** bumper; **p. circonférenciel** *ou* **enveloppant** wrap-around bumper; **p. à absorption d'énergie** energy-absorbing bumper

pare-éclats [parekla] **NM INV** *Mil* splinter-proof shield *(on trench parapet etc)*

pare-étincelles [paretɛ̃sɛl] **NM INV** fire-guard

pare-feu [parfø] **NM INV 1** *(dans la forêt)* fire-break **2** *(de cheminée)* fireguard; **porte p.** fire door; *Aut* **p. de moteur** engine bulkhead, *Am* firewall **3** *Ordinat* firewall

pare-flammes [parflam] **NM INV** *Aut* flame arrester

parégorique [paregɔrik] **ADJ** *Pharm* pare-goric

pareil, -eille [parɛj] **ADJ 1** *(semblable)* alike, similar; **elles sont presque pareilles** they are almost the same; **ce n'est pas p.** it's not the same (thing); **une erreur et un oubli, ce n'est pas p.** a mistake and an oversight are not the same (thing); **ce n'est pas p. que l'année dernière** it's not the same as last year; **en voici un tout p.** here's one exactly the same *or* exactly like it; **il est vraiment p.** it's very similar; **l'an dernier à pareille époque** this time last year; *Litt* **à nul autre p.** without equal, unparalleled; **p. que** *ou* **à** the same as, just like; **et lui, qu'est-ce qu'on lui donne? – p., une orange** and what will we give him? – the same (thing), an orange; **ses deux chaussettes ne sont pas pareilles** his socks don't match; **ces bougeoirs ne sont pas pareils** these candlesticks aren't alike *or* the same; **il n'y en a pas deux (de) pareils** no two are alike; **les gens sont partout pareils** people are the same the world over; *Fam* **si ça ne te plaît pas, c'est p.** too bad if you don't like it; **toujours p. à lui-même** the same as always; **c'est toujours p. avec lui** it's always the same with him

2 *(tel)* such, like this/that; **en p. cas** in a case like this, in such cases; **dans de pareils moments, dans des moments pareils** at times like this; **dans** *ou* **en pareille situation** in a similar situation; **par un temps p.** in weather like this; **comment a-t-elle pu faire une chose pareille!** how could she do such a thing!; **je n'ai jamais vu (une) chose pareille**

I've never seen anything like it; **mais je n'ai jamais dit une chose pareille!** but I never said any such thing!; **tu ne vas pas croire une chose pareille!** you're not going to believe something like that!; **qu'a-t-il donc fait pour avoir une chance pareille?** how did he manage to get so lucky?; **j'ignorais que tu y portais un p. intérêt** I didn't realize you were so interested; **a-t-on idée de rentrer à des heures pareilles!** what kind of time is this to come home at?

N *(pair)* **il n'a pas son p. au monde** there's no one like him, he's second to none; **un cuisinier qui n'a pas son p. au monde** a chef in a class of his own; **cet endroit n'a pas son p. au monde** there's nowhere else like this; **comme sage-femme, elle n'a pas sa pareille** there's no one to equal *or* match her as a midwife; **elle n'a pas son p. pour faire le cassoulet** nobody can make cassoulet like her *or* the way she can; **sans p.** *(occasion, méchanceté)* unparalleled; *(richesse, beauté)* unparalleled, unrivalled, unequalled; *(gentillesse, imagination)* unparalleled, unequalled; **une soirée sans pareille** a wonderful evening; **c'est une cuisinière sans p.** she's a superb cook, no one can match her when it comes to cooking; **mes pareils** my equals; **lui et ses pareils** him and people like him

NF rendre la pareille à qn *(se venger)* to get one's own back on sb; *(faire preuve de reconnaissance)* to repay sb, to pay sb back; **elle ne manquera pas de lui rendre la pareille** she'll get her own back on (him/her); **si on me frappe, je rends la pareille** if anyone hits me, I hit back

NM *Fam* **c'est du p. au même** it's six of one and half a dozen of the other, it comes (down) to the same thing

ADV *Fam* **faire p.** to do the same thing; **je ne fais pas p.** that's not how I do it; **ils s'habillent/écrivent p.** they dress/write the same (way); **ils mangent/lisent p.** they eat/read the same kind of things; **elles se coiffent p.** they have the same hairdo, they do their hair the same way; **elle se coiffe p. depuis 10 ans** she's had the same hairdo for the past 10 years

pareillement [parɛjmɑ̃] **ADV 1** *(de la même manière)* in a similar manner, in the same way; **p. habillé** dressed the same **2** *(aussi)* also, likewise; **p!** *(en réponse à des vœux)* the same to you!; **et moi p.!** same here!; **ravi de vous rencontrer – et moi p.!** pleased to meet you – likewise!

parement [parmɑ̃] **NM 1** *(décoration)* ornament, decoration; *Couture (de manche, col)* facing; *Rel* **p. d'autel** (altar) frontal **2** *Constr* *(d'un mur)* facing; *(de la pierre)* (dressed) face

parent, -ente [parɑ̃, -ɑ̃t] **NM 1** *(always pl)* **parents** *(père et mère)* parents, mother and father; **les parents sortent ce soir** my parents *or surtout Am* my folks *or Fam* (my) mum and dad are going out this evening; **tu as prévenu les parents?** have you told mum and dad?; **la relation parents-enfant** the parent-child relationship **2** *Litt (always pl)* **parents** *(ancêtres)* forefathers, forebears **3** *Biol* parent

N *(personne appartenant à la proche famille)* relative, relation; **c'est mon seul p.** he's my only living relative; *Jur* **le p. survivant** the last surviving relative; **proche p.** close relative; **p. éloigné** distant relative; **être (proches) parents** to be (closely) related; **être p. avec qn, être un p. de qn** to be related to sb; **nous sommes parents par alliance/par mon père** we are related by marriage/on my father's side; *Fig* **p. pauvre** poor relation; *Fig* **traiter qn en p. pauvre** to treat sb like a poor relation

ADJ related; *(semblable)* similar; **sciences parentes** related sciences; **leurs œuvres révèlent des intelligences/sensibilités parentes** their work shows a similar intelligence/sensitivity

▸▸ **parents adoptifs** adoptive parents; **parents biologiques** biological parents; **parents d'élèves: association de parents d'élèves** parent teacher association, PTA

parental, -ale, -aux, -ales [parɑ̃tal, -o] **ADJ** *(autorité etc)* parental

parenté [parɑ̃te] **NF 1** *aussi Fig (rapport)* relationship; *Spéc (en sociologie)* kinship; **il n'y a entre eux aucune p.** they are not related in any way; **quel est le lien de p. entre eux?** what relation are they to each other?, how are they related?; **as-tu un lien de p. avec …?** are you related to *or* any relation of …?; **liens de p.** family connections **2** *(famille)* family, relations

parenthèse [parɑ̃tɛz] **NF** parenthesis, *Br* bracket; *Fig (dans un discours)* digression; **entre parenthèses** in parentheses, *Br* in brackets; *Fig* incidentally, by the way; **mettre qch entre parenthèses** to put sth in parentheses, *Br* to put sth in brackets; *Typ* **p. fermante/ouvrante** closing/opening bracket; *Fig* **cette époque a été une p. dans sa vie** that period was an interlude in his life; *Fig* **c'est une p. dans ma routine quotidienne** it's a break from my daily routine; **ouvrir/fermer une p.** to open/to close the brackets; *Fig* **je voudrais ouvrir une p.** *(pour aborder cette question)* I would like to digress for a moment; **je voudrais vous dire, dans une p.** *ou* **par p., que …** I would like to say by way of digression that …; **il est temps de fermer la p. et de revenir à notre sujet** enough of this digression, let's get back to our subject **VOIR GRAMMAIRE A14**

paréo [pareo] **NM** pareo; **jupe-p.** sarong (skirt)

parer[1] [pare] **VT 1** *(éviter)* *(attaque, coup)* to fend off, to ward off; *Escrime, Boxe, Fig (question)* to parry; *(en esquivant) (coup)* to dodge; *Naut (abordage)* to avoid, to fend off; *Fig* **ils savaient qu'une OPA se préparait et ils ont réussi à p. le coup** they knew a takeover was in the offing and managed to ward it off; *Naut* **p. un cap** to clear *or* double a headland **2** *(protéger)* to protect (**contre** against); **je suis paré contre le froid/l'hiver** I'm ready for *or* to face the cold/the winter

VI p. à *(accident)* to prevent, to guard against; *(difficulté, problème)* to avoid; *(défaite, désastre)* to ward off, to stave off; **pour p. à toute difficulté/à tout retard** in order to guard against any difficulties/delay; **p. à toute éventualité** to be prepared for anything; **on ne peut pas p. à tout** you can't guard against everything; **p. au plus pressé** to attend to the most urgent things first; **nous devons p. au plus pressé** first things first

parer[2] **VT 1** *(arranger)* *(viande, cuir)* to dress; *Naut (câble, ancre etc)* to clear **2** *(vêtir)* *(personne)* to deck out, to adorn (**de** with); *(décorer)* to decorate with taste; **p. la mariée** to dress the bride; *Fig* **p. qn de toutes les vertus/qualités** to endow sb with every virtue/quality

VPR se parer 1 to dress oneself up; **se p. de bijoux** to deck oneself out in jewels, to adorn oneself with jewels; **elle ne sort pas sans s'être parée de bijoux** she never goes out without her jewellery on; **se p. d'un faux titre** to assume a false title; **je me suis paré contre le froid** I've made sure that I'm not going to feel the cold **2** *Can (se préparer)* to get ready

pare-soleil [parsɔlɛj] **NM INV** *Aut* sun visor; *Phot* lens hood

paresse [parɛs] **NF 1** *(indolence)* laziness,

idleness; **par pure p.** out of sheer laziness; **d'une p. incroyable/incurable** incredibly/incurably lazy **2** *(lenteur)* **p. d'esprit** *ou* **intellectuelle** sluggishness of mind; *Méd* **p. intestinale** sluggishness of the bowels

paresser [parese] *vi* to laze (about *or* around)

paresseusement [paresøzmɑ̃] *ADV* lazily; **le fleuve coule p.** the river moves slowly *or* sluggishly

paresseux, -euse [paresø, -øz] *ADJ* **1** *(nonchalant)* lazy, *Fml* indolent; **p. comme une couleuvre** *ou* **un loir** bone idle; **il est p. le matin** he moves at a snail's pace in the morning **2** *(lent)* *(intestins)* sluggish; *(geste)* lazy; *(fleuve)* sluggish, slow-moving; **c'est un esprit p.** he won't use the brains God gave him, he's mentally lazy
▶ *N* lazy person, *Fam* lazybones
▶ *NM Zool* sloth

parfaire [parfɛr] *VT* *(conj like* **faire***; used chiefly in inf and pp) (travail etc)* to finish off, to complete; *(technique, compétences etc)* to perfect

parfait [parfɛ] *ADJ* **1** *(irréprochable)* perfect; *(performance)* faultless, perfect; *(diamant)* flawless; *(réputation)* unsullied; **en ordre p.** in perfect order; **le tout était rangé dans un ordre p.** there was not a thing out of place; **il est p. en toute occasion** he always knows what to do; **personne n'est p.** nobody's perfect; **il est loin d'être p.** he's far from perfect, he's no saint; **vous avez été p.** you were wonderful *or* splendid *or* marvellous; *Iron* you were just great; **(c'est** *ou* **voilà qui est) p.!** (that's) splendid! *or* fine! *or* wonderful!, *Fam Iron* great!; *Iron* (that's just) great!; **p., passons à autre chose** fine *or* good, let's go on to something else **2** *(complet)* *(bonheur)* perfect, complete; *(réussite)* complete; *(ressemblance)* exact; **un p. orateur** an accomplished speaker; **un p. meneur d'hommes** a wonderful leader; *Fam* **un p. imbécile** a perfect *or* complete idiot, an utter fool; **en p. accord** in full *or* perfect agreement; **je suis en p. accord avec ce qu'il a dit** I quite *or* totally agree with what he said; **nous travaillons en p. accord** *ou* **en parfaite harmonie l'un avec l'autre** we work in perfect harmony with each other; **être dans l'ignorance la plus parfaite de qch** to be completely ignorant of sth; *Mus* **accord p.** perfect chord
▶ *NM* **1** *Gram* perfect (tense) SEE GRAMMAR A50; B30 **2** *Culin* parfait; **p. au café** coffee parfait

parfaitement [parfɛtmɑ̃] *ADV* **1** *(admirablement)* perfectly, to perfection; **cela m'ira p.** that will suit me perfectly *or* just fine; **elle s'occupe p. de ses enfants** she looks after her children wonderfully well; **un vin qui accompagne p. le poisson** a wine that is the perfect accompaniment for fish; **elle parle p. (l')anglais** she speaks English perfectly, she speaks perfect English **2** *(totalement)* completely, thoroughly; *(compréhensible, clair, heureux)* perfectly; **elle est p. qualifiée pour faire le travail** she's perfectly *or* ideally qualified for the job; **il connaît p. son domaine** he knows his field thoroughly; **je comprends p.** I quite *or* perfectly understand; **il est p. idiot** he's a perfect idiot; **il a p. le droit de le dire** he has a perfect right *or* he is perfectly entitled to say so; **ceci m'est p. égal** it's really all the same to me; **j'ai p. conscience de ...** I'm fully aware of ...; **il a p. raison** he's perfectly right **3** *(tout à fait)* certainly, exactly; **vous dites que vous l'avez vu? – oui, p.** you say you saw it? – indeed I did *or* yes, I most definitely did; **oui, p., j'y étais** yes indeed, I was there

parfois [parfwa] *ADV* sometimes, at times; *(moins souvent)* occasionally, (every) now

and then; **p. elle lit, p. elle tricote** sometimes she reads, other times she knits

parfum [parfœ̃] *NM* **1** *(senteur, odeur) (de fleurs)* perfume, fragrance, scent; *(d'un vin)* bouquet, aroma; *Fig* **un p. de scandale** a whiff of scandal **2** *(à base d'essences)* perfume, *Br* scent **3** *Culin (de glace, yaourt)* flavour, *Am* flavor **4** *Fig Fam* **être au p.** to be in the know; **il n'était pas au p.** he didn't know anything (about it); **mettre qn au p.** to fill sb in, to put sb in the picture

parfumé [parfyme] *ADJ (fleur)* scented, fragrant, sweet-smelling; *(savon)* perfumed, scented; *(vin, air)* fragrant; *(au goût)* sweet-tasting; **des fruits très parfumés** fruit that is full of flavour *or Am* flavor; **glace parfumée au café** coffee-flavoured *or Am* -flavored ice cream; **l'air p. du soir** the balmy evening air; **elle est trop parfumée** she's wearing too much perfume

parfumer [parfyme] *VT* **1** *(embaumer)* to scent, to perfume; **les fleurs parfument la pièce** the flowers scent the room; **un potpourri pour p. votre maison** potpourri to scent *or* fragrance your house; **le gâteau parfume la cuisine** the kitchen smells of cake **2** *Culin* to flavour, *Am* to flavor (**à** with) **3** *(mettre du parfum sur) (mouchoir)* to scent; *(armoire à linge)* to perfume; *(eau de bain)* to scent, to fragrance; **je vous parfume?** *(à une cliente)* would you like to try some (perfume)?
▶ *VPR* **se parfumer** to wear *or* use perfume; *(mettre du parfum)* to put perfume on

parfumerie [parfymri] *NF (magasin)* perfume shop, perfumery; *(rayon)* perfume counter; *(produits)* perfumes, perfumery; *(industrie)* perfume industry

parfumeur, -euse [parfymœr, -øz] *N* perfumer

pari [pari] *NM* **1** *(convention)* bet, *Fml* wager; **faire un p.** to make *or* lay a bet; **faire un p. avec qn** to make a bet with sb; **je suis prêt à faire le p. que ...** I'm willing to bet that ...; **tenir un p.** to take a bet; *Fig* **les paris sont ouverts** it's anyone's guess **2** *(jeu)* betting; **p. mutuel** *Br* ≃ totalizator system, *Fam* tote, *Am* ≃ pari-mutuel

paria [parja] *NM (en Inde)* pariah; *Fig* pariah, (social) outcast

parier [parje] *(impf, pr sub* n. **pariions***, v.* **pariiez)** *VT* to bet, *Fml* to wager; **je parie une bouteille de vin qu'il ne viendra pas** I bet a bottle of wine he won't come; **je parie qu'il viendra** I bet he'll come, it's my bet he'll come; **tu veux p. qu'il te le reprochera?** what's the betting he'll blame you?; **il y a gros** *ou* **fort à p. que ...** it's virtually certain that ..., the odds are that ..., it's odds on that ...; **je te parie tout ce que tu veux ...** I bet you anything (you like) ...; **je l'aurais parié** I might have known (it) *or* guessed; *Fam* **tu en as assez, je parie?** I bet you've had enough
▶ *vi* to bet; **p. avec qn/sur qch** to bet with sb/ on sth; **p. sur un cheval** to bet on *or* back a horse; **on a parié gros** the betting ran high; **je te dis qu'il viendra – on parie?** he'll come, I tell you – (do you) want to bet?

pariétal, -ale, -aux, -ales [parjetal, -o] *ADJ* **1** *Anat (os)* parietal **2** *Beaux-Arts* **art p.** cave painting
▶ *NM Anat* parietal bone

parieur, -ieuse [parjœr, -jøz] *N* better, *Fam* punter; *Sport, surtout Courses de chevaux* backer; **c'est un p.** he'll bet on anything

parigot, -ote [parigo, -ɔt] *Fam Péj ADJ* Parisian
▶ *N* **P.** Parisian

Paris [pari] *N* Paris

parisianisme [parizjanism] *NM Ling* = expression particular to Paris

parisien, -ienne [parizjɛ̃, -jɛn] *ADJ* Parisian; *Péj* **esprit p.** superior Parisian outlook; **le Bassin p.** the Paris Basin; **la banlieue parisienne** the Paris suburbs
▶ *N* **P.** Parisian

paritaire [pariter] *ADJ Ind* with parity of representation; **commission p.** = board on which management and unions are equally represented

parité [parite] *NF* **1** *(égalité)* parity; *(de rang, de valeur)* equality; *Fin* **p. des monnaies** monetary parity; *Fin* **p. euro-dollar** euro-dollar parity; *Bourse* **à p.** at the money; *Bourse* **au voisinage de la p.** close to par; **p. du pouvoir d'achat** purchasing power parity; **parités du change** exchange rate parity; **p. fixe** fixed parity **2** *Math, Ordinat* parity; **p. paire/impaire** even/odd parity; **pas de p.** no parity

parjure [parʒyr] *NM* perjury; **commettre un p.** to commit perjury, to perjure oneself
▶ *N (personne)* perjurer
▶ *ADJ (personne)* who does not keep his/her word

parjurer (se) [səparʒyre] *VPR* to perjure oneself, to be guilty of *or* to commit perjury

parka [parka] *NM OU NF* parka

parking [parkiŋ] *NM (stationnement)* parking; *(emplacement)* car park, *Am* parking lot; **place de p.** parking place *or* spot, place to park; **il y a encore des places de p. derrière le restaurant** there's more parking space behind the restaurant; **mettre sa voiture au p.** to put one's car in the car park
▶▶ **p. courte durée** short-stay car park; **p. gratuit** free car park; **p. longue durée** long-stay car park; **p. payant** paying car park; **p. privé** private car park; **'p. privé'** 'private parking'

parkinsonien, -ienne [parkinsɔnjɛ̃, -jɛn] *Méd ADJ* Parkinson's
▶ *N* person with Parkinson's (disease), Parkinson's sufferer

parlant [parlɑ̃] *ADJ* **1** *(doué de parole)* speaking; *(portrait)* lifelike; *(geste)* eloquent, meaningful; *(description)* vivid; **cinéma p.** talking pictures, *Fam* talkies; **film p.** talking picture, *Fam* talkie; *Tél* **l'horloge parlante** the speaking clock; **être p.** *(d'une réaction, de preuve)* to speak for itself **2** *Fam (bavard)* talkative

parlé [parle] *ADJ* **l'anglais/le français p.** colloquial English/French; **ça se dit dans la langue parlée** it's a colloquial term, it's used colloquially; *TV, Radio* **journal p.** news (broadcast *or* programme); **présenter le journal p.** to present the news
▶ *NM (dans un opéra)* spoken part

parlement [parləmɑ̃] *NM* **1** **le P.** Parliament; **au P.** in Parliament VOIR GRAMMAIRE A11 **2** *Hist, Jur* high judicial court *(in Paris and provinces)*
▶▶ **p. bicaméral** bicameral *or* two-chamber parliament; **le P. européen** the European Parliament; **membre du P. européen** member of the European Parliament, MEP, Euro-MP

parlementaire [parləmɑ̃ter] *ADJ Pol (gouvernement, immunité, débat etc)* parliamentary
▶ *N* **1** *Pol* member of Parliament, *Am* Congressman, *f* Congresswoman; **p. européen** member of the European Parliament, Euro-MP, MEP **2** *Mil* negotiator, mediator

parlementarisme [parləmɑ̃tarism] *NM Pol* parliamentary government

parlementer [parləmɑ̃te] *vi (négocier)* to negotiate (**avec** with), *Vieilli* to parley, to hold a parley (**avec** with); **nous avons dû p. avant de pouvoir quitter le poste de police** we had to talk our way out of the police station

PARLER[1] [parle] **VI 1** to speak, to talk; *(avouer)* to talk; **je ne peux pas le faire p.** I can't get him to talk, I can't get a word out of him; **parlons peu mais parlons bien** let's be brief and to the point; **elle a perdu sa voix à force de p.** she lost her voice from talking so much; **s'enrouer à force de p.** to talk oneself hoarse; **son fils ne parle pas encore** her son isn't talking yet; **est-ce que ton perroquet parle?** can your parrot talk?; **le président va p.** the president is about to speak; **laissez-le p.** *(ne l'interrompez pas)* let him speak *or* have his say *or* say what he has to say; *(ne faites pas attention à ce qu'il dit)* let him talk; **elle aime s'écouter p.** she likes the sound of her own voice; **il parle bien/avec style** *(d'un orateur)* he's a good/stylish speaker; **p. haut/bas** to talk *or* speak loudly/quietly; **parlez plus haut ou plus fort!** speak up!; **il faut p. moins haut** don't speak so loud; **parle plus bas** lower your voice; **p. par signes** to sign, to use sign language; **p. avec les mains** to gesticulate, to talk with one's hands; **p. par gestes** *(des muets)* to use sign language; *(pour éviter de parler)* to gesture (**à qn** to sb); **p. entre ses dents** to mumble; **p. du nez** to talk through one's nose; **parlez-vous sérieusement?** are you serious?, do you really mean it?; **p. pour ne rien dire** to talk for the sake of talking; *Br Fam* to rabbit on; **p. en l'air** to make empty promises; **p. à tort et à travers** to talk drivel; **parlons franc** let's be frank, let's talk frankly; **généralement parlant** generally speaking; **on parlait très peu au petit déjeuner** there was very little talking over breakfast; **ils parlent très peu entre eux** they don't talk much to each other, they don't do much talking; **elle parle peu, ta sœur** your sister isn't very talkative, your sister doesn't have much to say for herself; **(c'est une) façon de p.** so to speak; **enfin, c'est une façon de p.** well, that's one way of putting it; **elle connaît six langues étrangères, enfin c'est une façon de p.** she can speak six languages more or less; *Fam* **tu peux (bien) p.!** you can talk!, you're a fine one to talk!; *Fam* **ses ambitions? parlons-en!** his ambitions? who are you kidding? or you've got to be joking!; *Fam* **tu parles!** you're telling me!, you bet!; *(pas question)* you must be joking!, no way!; *Fam Iron* **des progrès? tu parles!** progress? you must be joking!; *Fam Iron* **tu parles comme c'était intéressant!** talk about interesting!; *Fam* **tu parles d'une occasion/d'un idiot!** talk about an opportunity/an idiot!; *Fam* **parle pour toi!** speak for yourself!; *Fam* **tu parles d'un athlète!** some athlete!; *Fam* **que tu m'aides, tu parles!** you? help me? you must be joking!; *Fam* **tu parles si je te la prêterai!** no way will I lend it to you!, you must be joking if you think I'll lend it to you!; *Fam* **tu parles si c'est utile!** a fat lot of use that is!; *Fam* **voilà qui est parlé!** now you're talking!; **il trouvera à qui p.** he'll get more than he bargained for; **mais je parle, je parle, qu'en pense notre cher ami?** but I'm talking too much *or* I really mustn't go on so much, what do you think about it?; **je parle en toute connaissance de cause** I know what I'm talking about

2 p. à qn to talk *or* speak to sb; **je ne lui parle plus** *(je me suis disputé avec lui)* I'm not talking to him, I'm not on speaking terms with him; **je ne lui parle plus depuis cette date** I haven't said a word to him since; **je l'avais déjà rencontré, mais je ne lui avais jamais parlé** I'd met him but I'd never spoken to him; *Fam* **moi qui vous parle, je peux vous aider** I'm the one who can help you; **moi qui vous parle, j'ai fait trois guerres** listen, I've been in three wars; **c'est (comme) p. à un mur** it's like talking to a brick wall; *Fig* **cette peinture parle à l'imagination** this painting fires the imagination; *Fig Fam* **cette peinture ne me parle pas beaucoup/du tout** this painting doesn't do much/does absolutely nothing for me; **il est temps que nous parlions de ta conduite** it's time we had a talk about your behaviour; **je sais de quoi je parle** I know what I'm talking about; **nous avons dû p. de cette question une douzaine de fois!** we must have gone over this point a dozen times!; **son dernier film/livre parle de la guerre** his latest film/book is about the war; **ce tableau parle de …** the subject of the painting is …; **ça parle de quoi?** what's it about?; **on ne parle que de cela** everyone's talking about it, that's all people are talking about; **les journaux ne parlent que de ça** the newspapers are full of it; **faire p. de soi** to become famous; **il a beaucoup fait p. de lui dans les années 50** he was very much to the fore in the 50s; **tu lui en as parlé?** have you talked *or* spoken to him about it?, have you mentioned it to him?; **ne lui en parle surtout pas!** don't mention it to him!, don't say a word about it to him!; **nous en parlerons après déjeuner** we'll talk about it *or* discuss it after lunch; **toute la ville en parle** the whole town is talking about it, it's the talk of the town; *Fig* **ici, tout me parle de toi** everything here reminds me of you; **il n'en parle jamais** he never talks about *or* refers to *or* mentions it; **n'en parlez à personne** don't tell anyone about it, don't mention it to anyone; *Fam* **ne m'en parlez pas!** you're telling me!; **les voisins? ne m'en parlez pas!** the neighbours? don't mention them *or* their name to me!; **n'en parlons plus** let's drop the subject, let's say no more about it; **vacances, n'en parlons plus** let's drop the subject of holidays, let's say no more about holidays; **cela ne vaut pas la peine d'en p.** it isn't worth talking about, it's nothing to speak of; **on parle d'organiser une fête** there's some talk about *or* they're talking about (organizing) a party; **elle parle de déménager** she's talking about moving; **sans p. de …** to say nothing of …, not to mention …; **pour ne p. que des …** to mention only the …; **les résultats/faits parlent d'eux-mêmes** the results/facts speak for themselves; **mal p. de qn** to criticize sb, to run sb down; **p. pour/contre qn** to speak for/against sb; **j'entends beaucoup p. de lui** I hear a lot about him; **mon père ne veut pas en entendre p.** my father won't hear of it; **on m'a beaucoup parlé de vous** I've heard a lot about you; **elle ne veut pas entendre p. d'informatique** she doesn't want to hear a word about computers; **il veut p. de moi à son patron** he's going to mention *or* recommend me to his boss; **je n'en ai jamais entendu p.** I've never heard of it/him/her/etc

VT p. (le) français to speak French; **p. le langage des sourds-muets** to know (how to use) sign language *or* how to sign; **elle parlait français** she was speaking French *or* talking (in) French; **ici on parle français** *(dans un magasin)* French spoken; **p. chiffons/cuisine/vacances** to talk about *or* discuss clothes/cooking/holidays; **p. affaires/boutique/politique** to talk business/shop/politics

VPR se parler 1 *(d'une langue)* to be spoken; **l'anglais se parle partout** English is spoken everywhere

2 se p. à soi-même to talk to oneself; **ils ne se parlent plus** *(ils se sont disputés)* they're not speaking *or* talking to each other, they're not on speaking terms; **nous ne nous parlons plus** *(de conjoints)* we've stopped communicating, we don't talk any more; **ils ne s'étaient jamais parlé** they had never spoken (to each other)

---

parler[2] **NM** speech; *(régional)* dialect; **il a un p. rude** he's got a coarse way of speaking

parler-vrai, *pl* **parlers-vrai NM** straight talking

parleur, -euse [parlœr, -øz] **N** *Péj* **beau p.** smooth talker; **c'est un beau p.** he's all talk, *Fam* he's got the gift of the gab; *(il est enjôleur)* he's a smooth talker, *Fam* he's got the gift of the gab

parloir [parlwar] **NM 1** visiting room; *Rel* parlour, *Am* parlor **2** *Belg (salon)* parlour

parlot(t)e [parlɔt] **NF** *Fam* gossip, *Br* natter; **faire la p.** to gossip, to chat; **faire la p. avec qn** to have a chat *or Br* natter with sb; **j'en ai assez de ces parlottes** I've had enough of this chitchat *or* gossiping *or* chattering

Parme [parm] **N** Parma; **jambon de P.** Parma ham

parmentier [parmɑ̃tje] **NM** *Culin* **(au bœuf)** ≃ cottage pie; *(avec de la viande blanche)* = dish similar to cottage pie, made with white meat; *(au mouton)* ≃ shepherd's pie

parmesan [parməzɑ̃] **NM** *Culin* Parmesan (cheese)

parmi [parmi] **PRÉP** among; **p. la foule** among *or* in the crowd; **nous souhaitons vous voir bientôt p. nous** we hope that you'll soon be with us; **c'est une solution p. d'autres** that's one solution; **il figure p. les meilleurs** he's one of the best, he's among the best SEE GRAMMAR A68; B56

ADV *Suisse (mutuellement, les uns les autres)* **on s'invite p.** we invite each other *or* one another

Parnasse (le) [ləparnas] **NM 1** *Antiq* Parnassus **2** *Hist, Littér* the Parnassian School (of poetry)

parnassien, -ienne [parnasjɛ̃, -jɛn] **ADJ, NM** *Hist, Littér* Parnassian

parodie [parɔdi] **NF** *(pastiche)* parody; *(simulacre)* parody, mockery; **c'est une p. de procès** this trial is a mockery *or Fam* a joke

parodier [parɔdje] **VT** *(impf, pr sub* **n. parodiions, v. parodiiez)** *(personne, pièce de théâtre)* to parody

parodique [parɔdik] **ADJ** *Littér* parodic(al)

parodiste [parɔdist] **N** *Littér* parodist

paroi [parwa] **NF 1** *(cloison)* (entre des pièces) partition (wall) **2** *(mur)* (d'une tente etc), *Biol* (d'une cellule) wall; *(d'une maison)* (inner) wall; *(d'une falaise)* face; **p. artérielle** artery wall **3** *(face intérieure)* (d'un tunnel) lining; *(de l'estomac)* lining, wall; *(d'un vase etc)* inner side *or* surface; *Aut* **p. des cylindres** cylinder wall

paroisse [parwas] **NF 1** *(territoire)* parish; **il n'est pas de la p.** he's not from here **2** *(habitants)* parishioners

paroissial, -iale, -iaux, -iales [parwasjal, -jo] **ADJ** parish; **église paroissiale** parish church; **salle paroissiale** church hall

paroissien, -ienne [parwasjɛ̃, -jɛn] **N** parishioner; *Fam Vieilli* **un drôle de p.** a queer bird

NM *(livre)* prayer book

parole [parɔl] **NF 1** *(mot)* word; **paroles** *(d'une chanson)* lyrics, words; **elle n'a pas dit une p. de la journée** she hasn't said a word *or* spoken all day; **c'est la seule p. qu'il a prononcée** that's all he said; **ce sont ses propres paroles** those are his very words; **assez de paroles! des actes!** that's enough talk(ing)! let's see some action!; **être courageux en paroles** to be all talk, to talk big; **histoire sans paroles** cartoon without a caption; *TV, Cin* short silent film; **la p. de Dieu** the word of God; **p. blessante** hurtful remark; *Iron* **belles paroles** fine words; **ce sont encore de belles paroles, mais …** that's all very well and good, but …; **sur ces belles paroles …** on this note …; **voilà une bonne p.!** well said!, *Am Fam* right on!

2 *Fig (engagement)* promise, word; **tenir (sa) p.** to keep one's promise *or* word; **nous vous obligerons à tenir p.** we'll keep you to that *or* to your word; **manquer à sa p.** to break one's promise *or* word; **il est (homme) de p., il a sa p., il n'a qu'une p.** he's a man of his word; **donner sa p. d'honneur à qn que ...** to give sb one's word that ..., to promise sb that ...; **(ma) p. d'honneur!** (on) my word of honour!; **non, je ne l'ai pas vu, p. d'honneur** no, I haven't seen him, I give you my word (of honour); **je vous en donne ma p.** I give you my word, (you can) take my word for it; **je vous crois sur p.** I'll take your word for it; **il a promis de m'aider et je l'ai cru sur p.** he promised to help me and I took him at his word; **c'est votre p. contre la sienne** it's your word against his; **prisonnier sur p.** prisoner on parole

3 la p. *(faculté de parler)* speech; *(manière, diction)* delivery; **avoir le don de la p.** to be a good speaker; **perdre la p.** to lose the power of speech; **usage de la p.** power of speech; **si les animaux avaient l'usage de la p.** if animals could speak *or* talk *or* had the power of speech; **retrouver l'usage de la p.** to be able to speak again; *Hum* **tu as perdu l'usage de la p.?** cat got your tongue?; **il ne lui manque que la p.** *(d'un chien)* the only thing he can't do is talk; **retrouver l'usage de la p.** to be able to speak again; **adresser la p. à qn** to speak to sb, to address sb; **elle ne m'a pas adressé la p. de toute la soirée** she didn't say a word to me *or* speak to me the entire evening; **couper la p. à qn** to interrupt sb, to cut sb short; **prendre la p.** to speak; **je vous rends la p.** *(dans un débat)* the floor is yours again; *Radio, TV* back *or* over to you; *Radio, TV* **nous passons maintenant la p. à ...** we now hand over *or* go over to ...; **taisez-vous, vous n'avez pas la p.** be quiet, it's not your turn to speak; *(dans un débat)* be quiet, you don't have the floor; **la p. est à M. Renault** Mr Renault will now speak, Mr Renault has the floor

4 *Cartes* **p.!** pass!; *(au bridge)* no bid!

parolier, -ière [parɔlje, -jɛr] *N (de chanson)* lyricist; *(d'opéra)* librettist

paronyme [parɔnim] NM paronym

paronymie [parɔnimi] NF paronymy

paroxysme [parɔksism] NM *(de colère, violence, plaisir)* height, peak; *Méd (d'une maladie)* crisis (point); **être au p. de la joie** to be ecstatically happy; **être au p. de la douleur** to be in agony; **il était au p. de la colère** he was blazingly angry *or Fml* in a paroxysm of rage; **être au p. de la solitude** to be agonizingly lonely; **être au p. de l'angoisse** to be in anguish; **l'incendie était à son p.** the fire was at its height; **cela va pousser la crise à son p.** that's going to take the crisis to breaking point; **atteindre son p.** to reach a climax, to peak *or* climax; **la crise/la douleur a atteint son p.** the crisis/the pain is at its height *or* its worst

parpaing [parpɛ̃] NM *Constr* breeze block

Parque [park] NF *Myth* **les Parques** the Fates

parquer [parke] VT *(voiture)*, *Ordinat (disque)* to park; *(bétail, moutons)* to pen; *(prisonniers)* to confine, to pack in; **on nous a parqués comme des moutons dans la salle d'attente** we were herded into the waiting room; **des étudiants parqués dans des salles de cours trop petites** students packed into lecture theatres that are too small

parquet [parkɛ] NM **1** *Jur* public prosecutor's office; **(membres du) p.** public prosecutor and his deputies; **déposer une plainte au p.** to lodge a complaint in court **2** *Bourse* **le P.** the (trading) floor, *Am* the pit **3** *Constr* (wooden *or* parquet) floor *or* flooring; **lame de p.** floorboard

parquetage [parkətaʒ] NM **1** *(installation)* laying of wooden *or* parquet floors **2** *(sol)* wooden *or* parquet flooring *or* floor

parqueter [parkəte] VT (**je parquette, n. parquetons; je parquetterai**) **p. une pièce** to lay a wooden *or* parquet floor in a room, to parquet a room

parqueterie [parkɛtri, -kətri] NF *(installation)* laying of (wooden *or* parquet) floors; *(fabrication)* making of (wooden *or* parquet) floors

parqueteur [parkətœr] NM *(fabricant)* parquet maker; *(installateur)* parquet layer

parrain [parɛ̃] NM *Rel, Fig Péj* godfather; *(d'un enfant du tiers-monde, d'un sportif, d'une manifestation sportive)* sponsor; *(d'un nouveau membre d'un club)* sponsor, proposer; *(d'une fondation)* patron; *Mktg* promoter, sponsor; *Rel* **être p.** to be *or* stand godfather (**de** to); **être le p. d'un navire** to name a ship

parrainage [parɛnaʒ] NM *(d'un enfant du tiers-monde)* sponsorship, sponsoring; *(d'un nouveau membre)* sponsorship, sponsoring, proposing; *(d'un navire)* naming; *(d'une fondation)* patronage; *Mktg* sponsoring; **p.-partenariat** partnership sponsoring; **p.-télévision** television sponsorship *or* sponsoring

parrainer [parene] VT *Rel (enfant)* to act as godfather/godmother to; *(enfant du tiers-monde)* to sponsor; *(nouveau membre)* to sponsor, to propose; *(navire)* to name; *(fondation)* to act as patron of; *Mktg* to sponsor

parraineur [parɛnœr] NM sponsor

parricide [parisid] N parricide
 NM *(crime)* parricide; **commettre un p.** to commit parricide
 ADJ parricidal

parsemé [parsəme] ADJ **ciel p. d'étoiles** sky studded *or* spangled with stars; **champ p. de pâquerettes** field dotted with daisies; **texte p. de coquilles** text littered with misprints; **un visage p. de taches de rousseur** a freckled face; **ses affaires sont parsemées sur le sol de sa chambre** his things are scattered *or* strewn all over the floor of his room

parsemer [parsəme] VT *(conj like* **semer**) *(de papiers)* to strew (**de** with); *(de sucre)* to sprinkle (**de** with); *(de graines)* to scatter (**de** with); **des feuilles parsemaient le chemin** the path was scattered *or* strewn with leaves, leaves were scattered *or* strewn all over the path

parsi, -ie [parsi] ADJ, N *Rel* Parsee

PART [par]

> share **1, 2** ■ nowhere *(nulle part)* **3**
> ■ from *(de la part de)* **4** ■ apart *(à part)* **5**

NF**1** *(portion)* share, part, portion; **diviser un gâteau en parts égales** to divide a cake into equal portions; **combien de parts de gâteau faut-il faire?** how many pieces should I cut (the cake into)?; **une p. de gâteau** a piece of cake; *Fig* **avoir/vouloir sa p. du gâteau** to have/want one's share of the cake *or* slice of the cake; **sa p. des bénéfices** his/her share of the profits; **elle a eu sa p. de malheurs** she's had her share of misfortune; **professeur à p. entière** fully qualified teacher, *Fam* fully fledged *or Am* full-fledged teacher; **ils viennent pour une bonne p. des environs de Lille** a good many of them come from *or* they come very largely from the Lille area; **une grande/petite p. d'entre elles** a large/small proportion *or* number of them; **pour ma p.** for my part, as for me, as far as I am concerned, speaking for myself; *Fig* **prendre qch en bonne/mauvaise p.** to take sth in good/bad part, to take sth the right/wrong way, to take sth well/badly; *Fig* **ne le prends pas en mauvaise p. mais ...** don't take this

the wrong way but ...; *Fig* **comment veux-tu que je ne le prenne pas en mauvaise p.?** how else should I react?

2 *(participation)* share, part; **avoir p. à qch** to have a hand *or* a share in sth; **avoir p. aux bénéfices** to have a share of the profits; **prendre p. à** to take part in; *(conversation, débat, jeu)* to take part in, to join in; *(honneurs)* to share (in); *(la joie, la douleur, la déception de qn)* to share; **je n'y ai pris aucune p.** I had nothing to do with it, I had no part in it; **faire p. de qch à qn** to inform sb of sth, to tell sb about sth; **qui t'a fait p. de cette information?** who gave you this information?; **je tenais à vous faire p. de notre joie** I wanted to let you know how happy we are; **lettre de faire-p.** *(de mariage, de décès)* announcement; **faire la p. de qch** to take sth into account *or* into consideration, to make allowance(s) for sth; **faire la p. des choses** to make allowances

3 nulle p. nowhere; **je ne les ai vus nulle p.** I couldn't see them anywhere; **nulle p. ailleurs** nowhere else; **elle ne veut partir nulle p. ailleurs** she doesn't want to go anywhere else; **autre p.** somewhere else, *Fml* elsewhere; **quelque p.** somewhere; **de p. et d'autre** here and there; **faire des concessions de p. et d'autre** to make concessions on both sides; **de toute(s) part(s)** on all sides; **de p. en p.** through and through, right through; **d'une p. ... d'autre p. ...** on the one hand ... on the other hand ... SEE GRAMMAR B63

4 de la p. de from; **je viens de la p. de Madame Dubol** *(c'est elle qui m'envoie)* I've come on behalf of Madame Dubol; *(c'est elle qui m'a parlé de vous)* Madame Dubol gave me your name; **une indiscrétion de la p. de ...** an indiscretion on the part of ...; *Tél* **c'est de la p. de qui?** who's speaking *or* calling?; **dites-lui de ma p. que ...** tell him from me that ...; **ce serait bien aimable de votre p.** it would be very kind of you; **cela m'étonne de sa p.** that surprises me, coming from him; **je n'aurais jamais cru ça de sa p.** I would never have believed it of him/her

5 à p. apart, separately; **prendre qn à p.** to take sb aside; **il m'en a parlé à p.** he spoke to me about it in private; **mettre de l'argent à p.** to put money by *or* aside; **plaisanterie à p.** joking apart; **c'est une femme à p.** she's an exceptional woman, she's one of a kind; **un cas à p.** a special case, a case apart; **et à p. lui?** who besides him?, who apart from him?; **tu aimes le foot, et à p. ça?** what else do you like apart from *or* besides football?; **je me disais à p. moi que ...** I was saying to myself that ...; **à p. quelques exceptions/quelques pages** with a few exceptions/the exception of a few pages; **à p. quelques fautes d'inattention** apart from *or* except for a few careless mistakes; **à p. cela, tout va bien** apart from that, everything is fine; *Fam* **à p. que ...** apart from the fact that ...

▸▸ *TV* **p. d'audience** audience share; **p. du feu: faire la p. du feu** to cut down's losses; *Fin* **p. de fondateur** founder's share(s); **la p. du lion** the lion's share; *Com* **p. de marché** market share, share of the market; **p. patronale** employer's contribution; **p. salariale** employee's contribution; *Fin* **p. sociale** share of capital, capital share

partage [partaʒ] NM **1** *(action)* *(d'une fortune, d'un domaine, d'une propriété etc)* division, sharing out; *Pol, Jur (d'un pays, de biens)* partition; **faire le p. de qch** to divide sth up, to share sth out; **sans p.** *(amour, engagement etc)* total; **il y a p. d'opinions** opinions are divided; *Géog* **ligne de p. des eaux** watershed, *Am* divide **2** *(lot)* share, portion; **donner qch en p.** to give sth away *(as part of one's fortune)*; **recevoir qch en p.** to receive sth *(as part of one's inheritance)*;

il leur donna cet argent en p. he gave them the money (as their share of his fortune); **ce que les hommes reçurent en p. de la nature** nature's gifts to mankind; **la pauvre n'a pas reçu la beauté en p.** the poor girl isn't one of nature's beauties; **la souffrance est le p. du genre humain** suffering is the lot of mankind; **cela fait partie du p. de chacun** it's something we all have to put up with

▸▸ *Ordinat* **p. des données** data sharing; *Ordinat* **p. de fichiers** file sharing; *Ordinat* **p. d'imprimantes** printer sharing; **p. du pouvoir** power sharing; **p. de temps** time sharing; **p. du (temps de) travail** job-sharing; **p. des voix** distribution of votes; **regardons le p. des voix** let's look at how people voted; **en cas de p. des voix** in the event of a tied vote

partagé [partaʒe] ADJ **1** *(incertain)* **elle est partagée** *(elle a du mal à décider, à choisir)* she's torn; **je suis très p. sur ce point** I have very mixed feelings on the subject; **je suis partagée entre la tristesse et la joie** I don't know whether to feel sad or happy; **être p. entre son devoir et ses sentiments** to be torn between one's duty and one's feelings; **les avis sont partagés** opinions are divided **2** *(entre plusieurs personnes)* *(convictions, sentiments, impressions)* shared; **amour p.** mutual love; *Ordinat* **travail en temps p.** timesharing

partageable [partaʒabl] ADJ divisible, which can be divided

partager [partaʒe] (**je partageai(s); n. partageons**) VT **1** *(terrain, groupes etc)* to divide (up); *(biens etc)* to divide (up), to apportion; *(butin etc)* to divide (up), to share (out); **p. son temps entre deux occupations** to divide *or* split one's time between two occupations; **p. qch en deux** to divide sth in two, to halve sth; **le fleuve partage le pays en deux** the river divides *or* splits the country in two; **ce débat partage l'opinion** people are divided *or* split over the issue **2** *(avoir ou mettre en commun)* to share; **nous partageons la même chambre** we share a room; **je partage un appartement avec mon amie** I share a flat *or* I flat-share with a friend; **je ne partage vraiment rien avec ces gens-là** I really have nothing in common with those people; **p. l'avis de qn** to share sb's opinion; **p. la joie/la douleur de qn** to share (in) sb's joy/sorrow; **p. le repas de qn** to share sb's meal, to share a meal with sb; **je lui ai proposé de p. mon croissant** I offered him/her a share of my croissant

VI to share; **elle n'aime pas p.** she doesn't like sharing

VPR **se partager 1** *(être partagé)* to divide, to be divided; **le gâteau peut se p. en quatre morceaux** the cake can be cut into four portions **2** *(se communiquer)* **ces expériences ne se partagent pas si facilement** it's not very easy to share such experiences; **ça ne se partage pas** it's not something you can share **3** *(faire un partage entre soi)* to share; **ils se sont partagé les bénéfices** they shared *or* divided the profits between them **4** *(partager son temps)* to divide one's time; **elle se partage entre ses enfants et son travail** she divides her time between her children and her work

partageur, -euse [partaʒœr, -øz] ADJ willing to share; **il n'est pas p.** he doesn't like sharing, he's not very good at sharing; **on ne lui a jamais appris à être p.** he's never been taught to share

partagiciel [partaʒisjɛl] NM *Ordinat* shareware

partance [partɑ̃s] NF **en p.** *(train)* about to leave; *(avion)* about to take off; *(navire)* about to sail; **en p. pour Bordeaux** bound for Bordeaux; **train en p. pour Londres** train for London, London train

partant[1] [partɑ̃] ADV *Litt* consequently, therefore

partant[2]**, -ante** [-ɑ̃t] ADJ departing; *Fam* **je suis p.** you can count me in, I'm game; *Fam* **êtes-vous toujours p?** are you still game?, can I/we/*etc* still count you in?; *Fam* **elle est toujours partante pour aller au restaurant** she's always game for a meal out

N *Sport* starter; *(en athlétisme)*, *Courses de chevaux* runner, starter

partenaire [partənɛr] N partner; *(dans une affaire)* (business) partner; *(dans un film)* co-star; **partenaires commerciaux** trading partners; **les partenaires sociaux** employers and trade unions *or Am* labor unions, workers and management; **je suis son p. au tennis** I partner him at tennis, I'm his tennis partner

partenariat [partənarja] NM partnership; **p. public-privé** public-private partnership, private finance initiative; *Mktg* **p. télévision** television tie-in

parterre [partɛr] NM **1** *Fam* *(sol)* floor **2** *(de fleurs)* (flower)bed; *(plate-bande)* border **3** *Théâtre* *(places, le public)* pit

Parthe [part] NM **la flèche du P.** the Parthian shot

parthénogénèse [partenɔʒenɛz] NF *Biol* parthenogenesis

parthénogénétique [partenɔʒenetik] ADJ *Biol* parthenogenetic

Parthénon [partenɔ̃] NM *Antiq* **le P.** the Parthenon

PARTI[1] [parti]

> party **1, 2** ▪ side **1** ▪ to side with someone *(prendre parti pour quelqu'un)* **1** ▪ to resign oneself *(en prendre son parti)* **4** ▪ to take advantage of *(tirer parti de)* **5** ▪ bias *(parti pris)* **7**

NM **1** *(camp)* party, side; **prendre le p. de qn, se mettre** *ou* **se ranger du p. de qn** to take sb's side *or* part, to take sides with sb, to side with sb; **prendre p. pour qn** to side with sb, to take sb's side; **prendre p. contre qn** to side *or* take sides against sb; **je ne prends p. pour ou contre personne** I'm not taking sides; **j'hésite à prendre p.** I'm reluctant to come down on one side or the other; **il faut que tu prennes p. pour ou contre l'un ou l'autre** you're going to have to make your mind up one way or the other; **il ne faut pas que tu prennes p. contre l'un ou l'autre** you mustn't take sides

2 *Pol* party; **prendre sa carte du** *ou* **au p.** to join the party, to become a card-carrying member; **les partis de droite** the parties of the right, the right-wing parties; **les partis de gauche** the parties of the left, the left-wing parties; **le P. (communiste)** the Communist Party; **le P. communiste français** the French Communist Party; **le P. conservateur** *(en Grande-Bretagne)* the Conservative Party, the Tory Party; *(au Canada)* the Progressive Conservative Party; **le P. démocrate** the Democratic Party; **p. majoritaire** majority party; **p. minoritaire** minority party; **p. politique** political party; **le P. républicain** the Republican Party; **le P. socialiste** = left-of-centre French political party; **le P. travailliste** *(en Grande-Bretagne)* the Labour Party; **un p. unique** a single party

3 *(personne bonne à marier)* **un bon** *ou* **beau p.** a good match *or Fam* catch

4 *(choix, décision)* **prendre un p.** to decide, to make up one's mind, to come to a decision; **prendre le p. de faire qch** to decide *or* resolve to do sth; **il ne savait quel p. prendre** he didn't know what course to take; **en prendre son p.** to resign oneself, to make the best of it *or Fam* the best of a bad job

5 *(profit)* **tirer p. de qch** to take advantage of sth, to make (good) use of sth, to turn sth to (good) account; **il n'a jamais cherché à tirer p. de cet avantage** he's never tried to take advantage of it; **tirer le meilleur p. possible de ...** to make the best possible use of ...

6 **faire un mauvais p. à qn** to treat sb badly; **la presse lui fit un mauvais p.** he got rough treatment from the press

7 **p. pris** *(pour ou contre un concurrent etc)* bias; *(préjugé)* prejudice; **avoir un p. pris contre qn/qch** to be prejudiced about sb/sth, to have a prejudice towards sb/sth; **avoir un p. pris pour qn** to be bia(s)sed in sb's favour; **faire preuve de p. pris** to show bias; **sans p. pris** unbias(s)ed; **sans p. pris, elle est vraiment mauvaise dans son domaine, non?** speaking impartially, she's really bad in her field, isn't she?

parti[2] ADJ *Fam* *(ivre)* wasted, plastered; *(sous l'effet de la drogue)* high, spaced out; **il est complètement p.** *(ivre)* he's plastered; *(sous l'effet de la drogue)* he's totally spaced out

partial, -iale, -iaux, -iales [parsjal, -jo] ADJ *(personne)* bias(s)ed, partial; *(opinion, article)* bias(s)ed, one-sided

> Do not confuse with **partiel**.

partialement [parsjalmɑ̃] ADV in a bias(-s)ed way, with bias

partialité [parsjalite] NF bias **(envers** in favour of; **contre** against), partiality **(envers** for, to); **il juge toujours avec p.** he's always bia(s)sed in his judgments; **s'exprimer avec p.** to be bia(s)sed

participant, -ante [partisipɑ̃, -ɑ̃t] ADJ participating; **les personnes participantes** the participants, the people taking part

N *(à une réunion, une action)* participant (**à** in); *(à un concours)* participant, contestant; *(d'un club)* member; *Sport etc* competitor; **les participants à la manifestation** those taking part in the demonstration; **le nombre croissant des participants aux manifestations sportives** the increase in the number of people taking part in sporting activities

participation [partisipasjɔ̃] NF **1** *(collaboration)* participation (**à** in); *(aux élections)* turnout; *(à un cadeau)* contribution; **cela s'est fait sans ma p.** I didn't take any part in it, I had no part *or* hand in it; **cela s'est fait avec ma p.** I was involved in it; *Cin, TV* **avec la p. de Jean Martin (dans le rôle de ...)** with *or* featuring Jean Martin (as ...); **nous avons pu réaliser ce film grâce à la p. des Transports Dubout** our thanks to the Dubout Transport Company for helping us make this film; **sans la p. de M. Martin, rien de tout cela n'aurait vu le jour** none of this would have been possible without the help of Mr Martin; **représentation avec la p. de plusieurs vedettes** show with appearances by several stars; *Scol* **mauvaise p. d'un élève en classe** poor level of participation by a pupil; *Scol* **doit faire des efforts de p.** must try to take part more; **p. aux frais** (financial) contribution; **la p. aux frais est de 200 euros par personne** each person will contribute 200 euros; **taux de p.** level of participation; *(à un marathon, un jeu télévisé)* entries; **taux de p. électorale** voter turnout **2** *Com* share, interest (**à** in); *Fin* share, interest, holding (**à** in)

▸▸ **p. active** active participation; **p. aux bénéfices** profit sharing; **p. croisée** cross-holding; **p. majoritaire** major shareholding, majority holding; **p. minoritaire** minority interest; **p. ouvrière** worker participation; **p. des salariés aux bénéfices** profit-sharing scheme

participe [partisip] NM *Gram* participle **A44-6; B37-9**

participer [partisipe] **vi 1 p. à** *(réunion, jeu etc)* to take part in; *(discussion etc)* to take part in, to participate in; *(concours)* to take part in, to enter; *(marathon)* to take part in, to enter, to run in; *(complot etc)* to be involved in, to be (a) party to; *(d'un acteur) (spectacle)* to appear in; **p. à la joie/au chagrin de qn** to share (in) sb's joy/sadness; **elle participe activement au projet** she is taking an active part in the project **2 p. à** *(financièrement)* to contribute (money) to **3 p. à** *(partager) (bénéfices etc)* to share in, to have a share in; *Fin* **p. à une entreprise** to have an interest in a business **4** *Fml* **p. de qch** to partake of sth, to have some of the characteristics of sth; **sa théorie participe plus de la philosophie que des sciences exactes** his theory bears more of a resemblance to philosophy than to the exact sciences

participial, -iale, -iaux, -iales [partisipjal, -jo] *Gram* **ADJ** *(proposition etc)* participial **NF participiale** participial clause

particularisation [partikylarizasjɔ̃] **NF** particularization

particulariser [partikylarize] **vt** *(définir par ses particularités)* to particularize
VPR se particulariser to stand out; **il se particularise par ses cheveux roux** his red hair makes him stand out, he stands out by virtue of his red hair; **il s'habille toujours en noir pour se p.** he always wears black to make himself different *or* to make himself stand out

particularisme [partikylarism] **NM** *Pol, Rel etc* particularism

particularité [partikylarite] **NF 1** *(spécificité) (de quelque chose)* particularity, special nature **2** *(trait caractéristique)* characteristic, (distinctive) feature; *(qui sort de l'ordinaire)* peculiarity; **la p. de cette imprimante, c'est que …** what distinguishes this printer (from all the rest) *or* what is special about this printer is that … **3** *Litt (détail)* detail, particular

particule [partikyl] **NF 1** *(de poussière, sable etc)*, *Nucl* particle; **panneau de particules** particle board; *Nucl* **p. élémentaire** elementary particle; *Nucl* **p. alpha/bêta** alpha/beta particle; *Nucl* **physique des particules** particle physics **2** *Gram* particle; **avoir un nom à p.** ≃ to have a double-barrelled name

particulier, -ière [partikylje, -jɛr] **ADJ 1** *(spécial)* particular, special; *(propre)* characteristic (à of), peculiar (à to); **signes particuliers** *(sur passeport)* distinguishing features; **il a un humour qui lui est p.** he has his own special brand of humour; **sa démarche bien particulière** his own particular way of walking; **la saveur très particulière du citron vert** the very distinctive taste of the lime; **les besoins particuliers à l'enfant** the special *or* specific *or* particular needs of children; **revenir sur un point p.** to come back to a specific *or* particular point
2 *(remarquable)* unusual, exceptional; *(soin, attention, patience, intérêt)* particular; *Péj (style, gens, mœurs etc)* peculiar; **le médecin s'est occupé de lui avec une patience toute particulière** the doctor was particularly patient with him; **cas p.** special case; *Hum* **elle, c'est un cas p.** she's a real oddball
3 *(privé) (maison, voiture etc)* private; *(compte)* personal; *(salle de bain)* en-suite; **secrétaire p./particulière** private secretary; **cours particuliers, leçons particulières** private lessons *or* tuition; **j'ai des raisons particulières pour le désirer** I have my own (private *or* particular) reasons *or* I have reasons of my own for wishing it; **à titre p.** in a private capacity; **il a pris la voiture de l'entreprise pour s'en servir à titre p.** he took the company car for his own personal use

4 en p. *(spécialement)* in particular, particularly; **ses frères et en p. son frère cadet** his brothers, particularly his younger brother, his brothers and his younger brother in particular; **ce livre en p.** this book in particular
5 en p. *(en privé)* privately, in private; **recevoir qn en p.** to see sb privately *or* in private; **demander à être reçu en p.** to ask for a private meeting; **prendre qn en p.** to take sb aside; **je ne pourrai pas m'occuper de vous en p.** I won't be able to deal with you in person
N *(private)* individual; *Fam Péj Vieilli* individual; **simple p.** ordinary person, private citizen; *Vieilli* **que nous veut cette particulière?** what does she *or* that woman want?; **vente de p. à p.** private sale
NM le p. ne l'intéresse pas he's not interested in details; **aller du p. au général** to go from the specific to the general

> Attention: ne pas confondre **particular** et **peculiar** lorsque l'on traduit **particulier**. **Particular** signifie **spécifique**, alors que **peculiar** signifie **bizarre**.

particulièrement [partikyljɛrmɑ̃] **ADV 1** *(surtout)* particularly, (e)specially; **il aime tous les arts et p. la peinture** he is fond of all the arts, especially painting *or* and painting in particular **2** *(spécialement) (intelligent, beau, bête etc)* particularly, outstandingly, exceptionally; **j'attire tout p. votre attention sur cette question** I would particularly like to draw your attention to this question; **cela ne me fait pas p. plaisir** I'm not particularly happy about it; **je sais que cela lui fera p. plaisir** I know it will give him particular pleasure; **pas p.** not particularly **3** *(d'une façon intime)* intimately; **je ne la connais pas p.** I don't know her very *or* particularly well

PARTIE [parti]

> part **1, 6** ▪ partly *(en partie)* **2** ▪ to be part of *(faire partie de)* **3** ▪ field **5** ▪ party **7, 10, 11** ▪ game **8** ▪ to tell somebody off *(prendre quelqu'un à partie)* **12**

NF 1 *(morceau) (d'un tout)* part; **certaines parties ne sont pas mauvaises** it's not bad in parts, parts *or* bits of it aren't bad; **une p. de la maison est à louer** part of the house is to let; **une bonne p. du papier est abîmée** a good *or* great deal of the paper is damaged; **une bonne p. du personnel est en grève** a good portion of the staff *or* a good many of the employees are on strike; **une bonne p. des pistes de ski** a good many of the ski runs; **la plus grande p. du chemin** the best part of the way; **la plus grande p. de mon temps/du travail** the greatest part *or* most of *or* the majority of my time/the work; **il dépense la plus grande p. de son argent** he spends most of *or* the best part of his money; **les parties communes** *(d'une maison)* the communal areas; **les parties du corps** the parts of the body **SEE GRAMMAR B21**; **les parties génitales**, *Fam Vieilli* **les parties honteuses**, *Fam* **les parties** the genitals, *Fam* the private parts, *Fam* the privates; **une dissertation en trois parties** a dissertation in three parts *or* sections; *Hum* **je ne vais pas te faire une démonstration en trois parties** I won't go into the sordid details; **parties par million** parts per million
2 en p. partly, in part; **en p. responsable** partly responsible, responsible in part; **refait en p.** *(appartement)* partly redecorated; **nous avons été en p. remboursés** we got a part refund, we were partially refunded; **j'étais en p. surprise/déçue** I was slightly surprised/disappointed; **en grande** *ou* **majeure p.** largely, to a great extent, for the

most part; **ce sont en grande p. des adolescents** most of them are teenagers, they are teenagers for the most part
3 faire p. de qch to be *or* form part of sth; **cela fait p. de mes intentions** that's one of the things I intend to do; **cela ne fait pas p. de mes responsabilités** that isn't part of *or* one of my responsibilities; **cela ne fait pas p. des choses qui nous occupent aujourd'hui** that's not one of the things that concern us today; **je ne fais plus p. de ce cercle** I don't belong to this club any longer; **elle ne fait plus p. de nos amis** she is no longer a friend of ours; **faire p. de la famille** to be part of *or* one of the family; **tu fais un peu p. de la famille, maintenant** you're like one of the family now; **je n'ai pas l'impression de faire p. de cette famille** I don't feel like (I'm) part *or* a member of this family; *Fam* **faire p. des meubles** to be part of the furniture
4 *Fin* **p. double** double entry; **comptabilité en p. simple/double** single-/double-entry book-keeping
5 *(domaine)* field, subject; *(d'une entreprise, d'une profession)* line, particular branch; **ce n'est pas (de) ma p., je ne suis pas de la p.** that's not (in) my line, that's not up my street
6 *Mus (d'une voix, d'un instrument)* part; **parties d'orchestre** orchestral parts
7 *(fête, réunion)* party; *Fig* **voulez-vous être de la p.?** will you join us?; *Fig* **s'il voulait être de la p., nous pourrions bénéficier de ses conseils** if he was willing to come in with us we could benefit from his advice; **je n'étais pas de la p.** I wasn't invited; **elle ne pouvait pas être de la p. car …** she couldn't be here *or* join us because …
8 *(jeu) (de cartes, d'échecs, de tennis)* game; *(de golf)* game, round; **faire une p. de cartes/d'échecs** to have *or* play a game of cards/chess; **p. nulle** draw; **gagner la p.** to win the game; **après 30 minutes de jeu, elle avait la p. gagnée** the match was hers *or* she had the match won after 30 minutes; *Fig* **ce n'est que p. remise** we'll do it soon, *Am* let's take a rain check
9 *(combat)* struggle; *(pour un point d'honneur)* duel; **p. inégale** uneven struggle
10 *Jur (d'un litige, dans un contrat etc)* party; **la p. adverse** the other side; **entendre les avocats des deux parties** to hear counsel on both sides; *Fig* **être juge et p.** to be judge and jury; **p. prenante** party concerned; *(dans un projet)* participant
11 *(adversaire)* opponent; **les parties belligérantes** the belligerent parties, the belligerents; **avoir affaire à forte p.** to have a tough opponent on one's hands
12 prendre qn à p. to tell sb off; **il nous a pris à p. en nous reprochant de faire trop de bruit** he told us off for making too much noise
13 *avoir* **p. liée avec qn** to have joined forces with sb
▸▸ **parties annexes** *(dans l'édition)* end matter; **p. de campagne** picnic; *Fam* **p. carrée** foursome *(in bed)*; **p. de chasse** shooting party; *Jur* **p. civile** plaintiff claiming damages *(in criminal case)*; **se constituer** *ou* **se porter p. civile** to take civil action, to sue; *Gram* **parties du discours** parts of speech; *Fam* **p. fine** orgy; *Fam* **p. de jambes en l'air** roll in the hay; **ils commencent à m'énerver avec leurs parties de jambes en l'air en pleine nuit** they're beginning to get on my nerves doing it in the middle of the night; **p. de plaisir: ce n'est pas une p. de plaisir!** it's no picnic!, it's not my idea of fun!

partiel, -ielle [parsjɛl] **ADJ** partial; **paiement p.** part payment; *Pol* **élection partielle** by-election; *Univ* **épreuve partielle** class exam
NM *Univ* class exam
NF *Pol* **partielle** by-election

Do not confuse with the French word **partial**.

partiellement [parsjɛlmɑ̃] ADV *(cuit)* part, partly, partially; *(fini, guéri, satisfait etc)* partly, partially, in part

PARTIR [partir]

▪ to leave **1** ▪ to go away **1, 2** ▪ to go **1, 2** ▪ to depart **1** ▪ to set out **1** ▪ to start **1** ▪ to disappear **2** ▪ to come out **2** ▪ to come off **2** ▪ from *(à partir de)* **4**

VI *(prp* partant; *pp* parti; *pr ind* je pars, il part, n. partons, ils partent; *pr sub* je parte; *impf* je partais; *p hist* je partis; *fu* je partirai; *aux* être) **1** *(s'en aller)* to leave, *Fml* to depart; *(commencer un voyage)* to start, to set out, to set off; *(sans destination particulière)* to go off, to go away; *(à pied)* to walk off *or* away; *(d'un bateau)* to leave, to sail; *(d'un avion)* to leave, to take off; *Aut (d'un moteur)* to start; *(d'un fusil, d'un pétard)* to go off; *Euph (mourir)* to pass away; **nous partons demain** we're leaving tomorrow; **il est temps que je parte** it's time I went *or* I left *or* I was off; **partez!** get out!; *Sport* go!; **je pars de la maison à huit heures** I leave home at eight o'clock; **l'avion va p. dans une heure** the plane leaves *or* takes off in an hour; **toutes les heures un bus part pour le centre-ville** a bus leaves for the town centre every hour; **le train/bus est parti à temps** the train/bus left *or* pulled out on time; **la voiture est partie** the car drove away *or* off; **p. pour Paris/le Canada/la France/la campagne, p. à Paris/au Canada/en France/à la campagne** to leave *or Fam* take off for Paris/Canada/France/the country; **p. en vacances** to go (away *or* off) on holiday; **p. en promenade** *ou Fam* **en balade** to go for a stroll; **p. en excursion** to go off on a trip; **p. faire ses courses** to go and do one's shopping, to go out (to do one's) shopping; **p. chez qn** to go to sb's house *or Fam* place; **p. au front** to go off to war *or* to fight; *Fig* **p. de ce monde** *ou* **pour un monde meilleur** to depart this life, to die; **p. du bon/mauvais pied** to get off to a good/bad start; **p. à toute vitesse** *ou* **comme une flèche** *ou* **en courant** to shoot *or* speed off; **s'il m'en reparle, je pars à toute vitesse** *ou* **en courant** if he mentions it again, I'll be off like a shot *or* he won't see me for dust; **p. à la renverse** to fall over backwards; **la gifle est partie toute seule** I just slapped him/her automatically; **la réponse est partie trop vite** I/you/*etc* didn't take the time to think, I/you/*etc* should have thought first; **il est parti avec la femme de son meilleur ami** he's gone off with his best friend's wife; **p. gagnant** to think like a winner, to think positive; **p. perdant** to think like a loser; **si tu pars perdant, tu n'as aucune chance de réussir** if you think you won't win then you won't, if you think you'll be beaten you will be; **cette affaire est bien/mal partie** the business has got off to a good/bad start; **elle est mal partie si elle veut faire la paix avec moi** if she wants to make her peace with me she's not going the right way about it; **je voulais lui faire une surprise, mais c'est mal parti** I wanted to give him a surprise but it might not work now; *Fam* **c'est parti, mon kiki!** here we go!; *Vieilli* **p. d'un éclat de rire, p. à rire** to burst out laughing; **il est parti d'une longue tirade contre les …** he burst into *or* came out with a long tirade about the …; **p. de zéro** *(dans sa carrière)* to start from nothing; **je suis parti de zéro et j'ai lu tous les grands écrivains de la littérature anglaise** I started from scratch and read all the English classics; **on est bien partis pour se faire mouiller** we're in for a soaking; **on est partis pour se faire attraper** we're going

to get caught, we'll end up getting caught; **il est parti pour être malheureux** he'll end up being unhappy; **nous sommes partis pour une période de prospérité** we're in for a period of prosperity; **quand elle part sur ce sujet, on ne l'arrête pas** once she's off on *or* started on the subject, there's no stopping her; **faire p.** *(fusil)* to fire; *(feux d'artifice)* to let off; *(mine)* to set *or* touch off; *(moteur)* to start; *(courrier)* to send off; **p. c'est mourir un peu** you always leave a bit of yourself *or* your heart behind

2 *(disparaître) (de la douleur, d'un bleu)* to go (away), to disappear; *(d'une tache)* to come out *or* off; *(de la peinture, du vernis etc)* to peel, to come off; **la tache ne part pas** the stain won't come off *or* out; **ça part difficilement sur la soie** it's not easy to get it off silk *or* out of silk; **p. au lavage** to wash out; **faire p. une tache** to get a stain out, to remove a stain

3 *(émaner, sortir)* to spring, to emanate, to proceed (**de** from); **mot qui part du cœur** word (which comes) from the heart; **en partant du principe qu'il a raison** assuming that he's right; **si l'on part de l'idée que …** if we start from the assumption that …; **j'étais parti sur l'idée que …** I had assumed that …; **le chemin part du village** the path starts at the village; **ça partait pourtant d'un bon sentiment** it was for the best of motives; **ça partait des meilleures intentions** he/she/*etc* meant well, it was well meant; **et partant de la …** on that assumption …

4 à p. d'aujourd'hui from today (onwards); **à p. du 15** from the 15th (onwards), on and after the 15th; **à p. de maintenant** from now on, starting now; **à p. de cette date, les billets ne seront plus valables** tickets will not be valid from that date; **à p. de cette rencontre/discussion, ma vie a changé** my life changed after that meeting/discussion; **à p. de la route, tu peux courir** you can start running when you get to the road; **à p. de la haie, le champ est à lui** his part of the field starts at the hedge; **robes à p. de 50 euros** dresses from 50 euros (upwards); **c'est fait à p. de céréales** it's made from cereals

partisan, -ane [partizɑ̃, -an] N *(d'un homme politique)* supporter, follower; *(d'une politique, d'une cause etc)* supporter, advocate

NM *Mil* partisan; **guerre de partisans** guer(r)illa warfare

ADJ *(esprit)* partisan; **querelles partisanes** sectarian quarrels; **être p. de (faire) qch** to be in favour *or Am* favor of (doing) sth; **je suis p. de cette réforme** I'm in favour of *or Fam* all for the reform

partitif, -ive [partitif, -iv] ADJ, NM *Gram* partitive SEE GRAMMAR B5

partition [partisjɔ̃] NF **1** *Pol* partition, division **2** *Mus* score; **p. d'orchestre** full score; **elle joue sans p.** she plays without music

Il faut noter que le terme anglais **partition** signifie également **cloison**.

partitionner [partisjɔne] VT *Ordinat (disque dur)* to partition

partouse [partuz] NF *très Fam* orgy

partouser [partuze] VI *très Fam* to take part in an orgy

partout [partu] ADV **1** everywhere; **chercher qch p.** to look everywhere for sth, to hunt high and low for sth; **p. où** wherever; **p. où je suis allé** wherever I went, everywhere *or* every place I went; **p. ailleurs** everywhere else; **un peu p.** all over (the place); **souffrir de p.** to feel pain all over; **j'ai mal p.** I ache all over; **je ne peux pas être p. à la fois** I can't be everywhere *or* in two places at once VOIR GRAMMAIRE A21 **2** *Sport* all; **trois buts p.** three

(goals) all; *Tennis* **15/30 p.** 15/30 all; *Tennis* **40 p.** deuce

partouze [partuz] NF *très Fam* = partouse

partouzer [partuze] VI *très Fam* = partouser

parturiente [partyrjɑ̃t] NF *Méd* woman in childbirth *or Spéc* parturition

parturition [partyrisjɔ̃] NF *Méd* childbirth, *Spéc* parturition

parure [paryr] NF **1** *(décoration)* ornament; *(vêtements et bijoux)* costume, finery; *Fig* **une peau éclatante sera votre seule p.** a superb complexion will be your sole adornment **2** *(ensemble) (de bijoux, de diamants, de lingerie etc)* set; **p. de table/lit** set of table linen/bed linen

parution [parysjɔ̃] NF *(d'un livre, d'un article)* appearance, publication; *(d'une revue)* issue; **date de p.** *(d'un livre, article)* date of publication, publication date; *(d'une revue)* date of issue; **p. variable** occasional publication

parvenir [parvənir] VI *(conj like* venir; *aux* être) **1** *(arriver)* to arrive; **p. à un endroit** to arrive at *or* reach *or* come to a place; **quand le sang parvient au visage** when the blood reaches the face; **la lettre leur est parvenue** they received the letter, the letter reached them; **votre demande doit nous p. avant le 4** your application must be in *or* reach us by the 4th; **faire p. qch à qn** to send *or* forward sth to sb; **écrits anciens qui sont parvenus jusqu'à nous** ancient writings which have come down to us **2** *(atteindre)* **p. à** *(un grand âge etc)* to attain, to reach; *(la gloire, la célébrité)* to achieve; **p. à faire qch** to manage to do sth, to succeed in doing sth; **je croyais p. à le convaincre** I thought I could convince him; **p. à ses fins** to achieve one's ends **3** *(s'élever socialement)* to succeed *or* get on (in life)

parvenu, -ue [parvəny] N *Péj* upstart, *Fml* parvenu, f parvenue

parvis [parvi] NM *Archit (devant une église)* square, *Spéc* parvis

PAS¹ [pɑ] NM **1** *(enjambée)* step, pace; *(plus long)* stride; *(allure)* pace; *(de danse)*, *Mil* step; **à chaque p.** at every step; **p. à p.** step by step; *(progresser)* step by step, little by little; **allonger le p.** to lengthen one's stride; **à p. de loup** stealthily; **j'entrai à p. de loup dans la maison** I crept into the house; **aller à p. comptés** to walk with measured tread; **aller** *ou* **avancer** *ou* **marcher à grands p.** to stride along; *Fig* **avancer à grands p.** to make great strides (forward), to make great progress; **marcher à petits p.** *(d'un enfant etc)* to toddle (along); **aller** *ou* **marcher d'un p. lourd/léger/hésitant** to walk heavily/lightly/hesitantly; **faire un p.** to take a step *(vers* towards, in the direction of); *Fig* **elle a fait un p. vers la réussite/son but** she is one step closer to *or* nearer success/her goal; *Fig* **je ne peux pas faire un p. sans que …** I can't do a thing without …; *Fig* **faire le(s) premier(s) p.** to take the first step, to make the first move; **faire ses premiers p.** to take one's first steps; *Fig* **il n'y a que le premier p. qui coûte** the longest journey starts with a single step; **faire un p. en avant/en arrière** to step forward/back, to take a step forward/back; *Fig* **un p. en avant et deux p. en arrière** one step forward and two back; *Fig* **elle a fait un grand p. en avant** she has made great progress; **faire deux p. en avant** to take two steps *or* paces forward; **faire les cent p.** to pace up and down; *Fig* **c'est un grand p. de fait** it's a big step forward; *Fig* **il n'y a qu'un p.** it's a short step; *Fig* **et de là à conclure que Martin savait, il n'y a qu'un p.** and it doesn't take much (doing) to work out from that that Martin knew; **j'y vais de ce p.** I'll do it right now *or* right away; **il faut lui en parler, et j'y**

vais de ce p. somebody has to talk to him and I'm going to do it right now; **entendre des p.** *ou* **un bruit de p.** to hear footsteps; **je l'ai reconnu à son p.** I knew him by his step, I recognized his footstep; **ils habitent à deux p. d'ici** they live a few yards away *or* (within) a stone's throw from here; **c'est à deux p. d'ici** it's not very far away, it's a stone's throw away; **il était à deux p. de nous** he was a couple of paces *or* feet away from us; **à quelques p. de Piccadilly** just off Piccadilly; **aller d'un bon p.** to step out; **au p.** *(lentement)* at a walking pace; **avancer au p.** *(de la circulation)* to move at a crawl; **roulez au p.** *(sur panneau)* dead slow; **aller** *ou* **rouler au p.** *(en voiture)* to crawl along; **mettre son cheval au p.** to walk one's horse; *Fig* **mettre qn au p.** to bring sb into line; *Mil* **marcher au p.** to march in step *or* in time; **se mettre au p.** *Mil* to get in step; *Fig* to fall in line; **marquer le p.** to mark time; **allez! au p. de course!** go on! run!; *Mil* **changer le p.** to change step; **hâter** *ou* **presser le p.** to quicken one's pace; **ralentir le p.** to slow down; **avoir/prendre le p. sur qn/qch** to have/take precedence over sb/sth; **céder le p. à qn** to give way to sb; **je vais là où me conduisent mes p.** I just follow my nose, I just go where the fancy takes me **2** *(trace)* footprint; **marcher sur les p. de qn** to follow in sb's wake; *Fig* to follow in sb's footsteps; **arriver sur les p. de qn** to arrive just after sb, to arrive on sb's heels; **revenir** *ou* **retourner sur ses p.** to retrace one's steps **3** *Vieilli (d'un escalier)* step; **p. de la porte** doorstep; **il est sur le p. de la porte** he's standing on the doorstep **4** *(passage)* passage; *(de montagne)* (mountain) pass; *(détroit)* strait; *Fig* **tirer qn d'un mauvais p.** to get sb out of a hole *or* fix; *Fig* **sauter le p.** to take the plunge; *Litt (mourir)* to die **5** *Tech (d'une vis)* pitch, thread; *(d'une hélice)* pitch; *(entre les sièges d'un avion, d'un car etc)* distance, spacing; *Typ (des caractères)* pitch; **sièges au p. de 980 mm** seats 980 mm apart

▸▸ **p. de bourrée** *(en danse)* pas de bourrée; *Mil* **p. cadencé:** **marcher au p. cadencé** to march in quick time; **le p. de Calais** the Straits of Dover; **p. de deux** *(en danse)* pas de deux; *Typ* **p. d'écriture** pitch; **p. de gymnastique** jog trot; *Mil* **double time; p. de l'oie** goose step; *Mil* **p. ordinaire** normal pace; *Jur* **p. de porte** *(d'appartement)* key money; *Com* **p. de porte à vendre** business for sale; *Mil* **p. redoublé** double time; **p. de valse** waltz step

---

PAS² ADV SEE GRAMMAR A23–4; B62 **1** not; *(avant un nom)* no; **je ne sais p.** I don't know; **je ne l'ai p. encore vue** I haven't seen her yet; **je n'en dis p. plus** I won't say another word; **je n'en sais p. plus** that's all I know, I don't know any more; **elle ne te le dira p.** she won't tell you; **ça ne te suffit donc p.?** isn't that enough for you?; **prière de ne p. parler au conducteur** (please) do not speak to the driver; **prière de ne p. fumer** no smoking; **il est difficile de ne p. le lui dire** it's difficult not to tell him; **comment va-t-elle? – p. mieux** how is she? – no better; **p. du tout, absolument p.** not at all, absolutely not, *Fam* not a bit of it; **pourquoi p.?** why not?; **p. moi** not me; **qu'il vienne ou p., cela m'est égal** it's all the same to me whether he comes or not; **alors, c'est d'accord ou p.?** so, is that agreed or not?; **elle est libre, lui p.** *ou* **p. lui** she's free, he isn't; **il a de l'argent, elle p.** *ou* **p. elle** he has money, she hasn't; **elle le peut, moi p.** she can (do it), I can't; **il n'y a p. que ça** that's not all; **p. tant que ça** not that much, not as much as that; **jolie, mais p. tant que ça** pretty, but not that pretty; **est-ce que ça a coûté beaucoup? – p. tant que ça** did it cost a lot? – not all that much; **p. si fort, la radio!** turn that radio

down!; **p. si vite, quand tu manges/conduis/parles!** slow down when you eat/drive/talk!, don't eat/drive/talk so fast!; **p. si vite!** *(pas d'emballement)* steady on!, hold on!, not so fast!; **déçu, non p.** découragé disappointed but not discouraged; **ce n'est p. qu'il soit beau, mais il a énormément de charme** he's not exactly handsome *or* he's not what you would call handsome, but he's very charming; **ce n'est p. que j'y tienne particulièrement mais ...** it's not that I'm particularly keen on it but ...; **p. d'argent, p. de voiture** no money, no car; **allez, p. d'histoires!** come on, don't make a fuss!; **viendra?, viendra p.?/ passera?, passera p.?/***etc* will he come or won't he?, will he or won't he (come)?/will he make it or won't he?, will he or won't he (make it)?/*etc*; *Fam* **tu es heureuse, p. vrai?** you're happy, aren't you?; *Fam* **c'est magnifique, p. vrai?** it's wonderful, isn't it?; *Fam* **c'est p. vrai!** you're kidding!, no kidding!; *Fam* **c'est p. vrai, la presse a déjà les photos!** I don't believe it, the press has already got hold of the photos!; *Fam* **connais p.** I don't know him/her/*etc*; *Fam* **lui, la propreté, connaît p.!** he doesn't know what the word 'clean' means!; *Fam* **si c'est p. malheureux!** isn't that a shame!; **p. possible!** no! incredible!

2 *(qualifying an adj)* **des lilas p. fleuris** lilac not yet in bloom; **des fruits p. mûrs** unripe fruit; **p. décidé** undecided; **je déteste les gens p. sûrs d'eux** I hate people who are unsure of themselves

3 p. un mot ne fut dit not a word was spoken; **p. un n'a réagi** not a single person reacted; **fier comme p. un** prouder than anyone; **il fait les omelettes comme p. un** he makes omelettes better than anybody else *or Fam* like nobody else can; **il est menteur comme p. un** he's a terrible liar

---

pascal¹, -ale, -aux, -ales [paskal, -o] ADJ *Rel (agneau)* paschal; *(de la fête de Pâques chrétienne) (communion etc)* Easter

pascal² NM **1** *Phys* pascal **2** *Anciennement Fam (billet de 500 francs)* 500-franc note

pascalien, -ienne [paskaljɛ̃, -jɛn] ADJ *Phil* Pascal's; **la théorie pascalienne du pari** Pascal's wager

pasionaria [pasjɔnarja] NF *Pol* (political) militant

paso-doble [pasodɔbl] NM INV paso doble

passable [pasabl] ADJ fair, passable, acceptable; *Scol* **mention p.** ≃ (average to below average) pass; **c'est p.** it's not too bad

passablement [pasabləmɑ̃] ADV *(ivre, fatigué, déçu etc)* fairly; **dessiner p.** to draw tolerably well; **il a p. voyagé** he's done a bit of travelling, he's travelled a bit

passade [pasad] NF *(engouement)* passing fancy, whim; *(liaison courte)* passing fancy

passage [pasaʒ] NM **1** *(d'une route, d'une rivière)* crossing; *(d'un lieu)* passing, going past; *Naut* passage; **p. d'une région/d'une porte** passing through an area/a door; **p. de frontière** border crossing; *Élec* **p. du courant** flow of current; *Aut* **p. de l'huile** oil passage; *Aut* **p. de rapports** *ou* **de vitesses** gear shifting; **p. en douane** customs clearance; **p. à la télévision** *(de spot publicitaire, film)* screening; *(de personne)* screen appearance; **la rivière est de p. facile** the river is easy to cross; **elle guette le p. du facteur** she's watching for *or* she's on the lookout for the postman; **j'attends le p. de l'autobus** I'm waiting for the bus (to come); **chacun sourit sur son p.** everyone smiles as he goes by; **les hommes se retournaient sur son p.** she made heads turn; **les soldats ont tout détruit sur leur p.** the soldiers destroyed everything in their path *or* everything they came across; **après le p. des sauterelles, il**

ne restait plus rien dans les champs there was nothing left in the fields after the locusts had been there; **il y a toujours du p. ici** there are always a lot of people (coming and going) here; **livrer p.** to make way (à qn for sb); **lieu de p.** busy area; **de p.** *(client)* passing, *Am* transient; **oiseau de p.** bird of passage; **droit de p.** right of way; **être de p. dans une ville** to be passing through a town; **voyageur de p. à Paris** traveller passing through Paris; **la clientèle de p.,** *Fam* **le p.** passing *or* casual trade; *Mus* **note de p.** passing note; **j'ai pris un prospectus au p.** I picked up a brochure as I went past; *Fig* **au p., je te ferai remarquer ceci ...** and incidentally, let me draw your attention to this ...; *Naut* **payer son p.** to pay for one's passage; **p. du jour à la nuit** transition *or* change from day to night; **avec le p. du temps** with the passage of time, as the days passed/pass, as time went/goes on *or* by; *Scol* **le p. d'un élève en classe supérieure** the moving up of a child into a higher class; **examen de p.** end-of-year exam, *Am* final exam **2** *(chemin)* passage, way; *(ruelle)* alley(-way); *(magasins)* (shopping) arcade, *Am* mall; *Naut* channel; **se frayer un p.** to force *or* push one's way through; **barrer le p. à qn** to stand in *or* block sb's way, to block sb's passage; *Fig* to stand in sb's way **3** *(extrait)* *(d'un livre)* passage; *(d'un morceau de musique)* passage, piece **4** *Météo* **p. nuageux/pluvieux** cloudy/rainy spell **5** *(changement)* **p. à l'euro/à l'économie de marché** changeover *or* transition to the euro/to a market economy

▸▸ *Psy* **p. à l'acte** living out of a fantasy/of fantasies; *Aut* **p. d'air de roue** wheel vent; *Ordinat* **p. automatique à la ligne suivante** wordwrap; **p. clouté** pedestrian crossing, *Br* ≃ zebra crossing, *Am* ≃ crosswalk; *Aut* **p. d'huile** oil gallery, oilway; **p. interdit (au public)** no entry, no thoroughfare; *Rail* **p. à niveau** level crossing, *Am* grade crossing; **p. piéton** *ou* **pour piétons** pedestrian crossing, *Br* ≃ zebra crossing, *Am* ≃ crosswalk; *(sous-terrain)* pedestrian subway; *Aut* **p. protégé** priority over secondary roads; *Aut* **p. de roue** wheel arch; **p. souterrain** subway, underpass, *Am* underground passage; *Fam* **p. à tabac** beating up; **p. à vide:** **avoir un p. à vide** to go through a bad patch; *Sport* **il a eu un p. à vide dans la côte** *(d'un cycliste, d'un coureur)* he lost it on the hill

passager, -ère [pasaʒe, -ɛr] ADJ *(beauté, bonheur)* fleeting, short-lived, transitory; *(douleur, malaise)* momentary; **état p.** passing phase; **pluies passagères** occasional showers; **elle se crut amoureuse de lui, mais ce ne fut que p.** she thought she was in love with him, but it was a passing thing; **ils ont eu une petite brouille passagère** they fell out momentarily

N *(par bateau, par avion)* passenger; **p. clandestin** stowaway; *Aut* **p. arrière** back-seat passenger; **p. direct** through passenger; **p. en correspondance** transfer passenger; **p. en transit** transit passenger; **p. piéton** *ou* **à pied** foot passenger

passagèrement [pasaʒɛrmɑ̃] ADV temporarily, for a short while

passant, -ante [pasɑ̃, -ɑ̃t] ADJ *(rue)* busy

N passer-by

NM *(de ceinture, jean)* loop; **p. de courroie** strap loop

passation [pasasjɔ̃] NF *Jur (d'un accord)* signing; *Compta (d'écritures)* entering; *Pol* **des pouvoirs** transfer of power; *Fin* **p. d'un dividende** payment of a dividend; *Compta* **p. d'écriture** journal entry; *Fin* **p. de commande** placing of an order; **p. par pertes et profits** write-off

passavant [pasavã] **NM 1** *Naut* (fore-and-aft) gangway, catwalk **2** *Jur* transire; *Com* transire, transit bill

passe [pas] **NF 1** *Ftbl* pass; *Escrime* pass, thrust; *Escrime, Fig* **p. d'armes** passage of arms; *Ftbl* **p. en avant/en retrait** forward/back pass **2** *(manipulation)* **passes magnétiques** mesmeric *or* hypnotic passes **3** *Métal (sur un tour)* cut **4** *(d'une prostituée)* trick; **c'est combien la p.?** how much is it a time?; **j'ai fait dix passes** I've had ten clients *or Br* punters; **maison de p.** brothel; **hôtel de p.** = hotel used by prostitutes and their clients **5** *(à la roulette)* passe *(any number above 18)* **6** *Naut (chenal)* pass, channel; **p. étroite** narrows **7** *Fig* **être en p. de faire qch** to be on the way to doing sth; **être dans une mauvaise p.** to be in a fix *or* a tight corner; **tirer qn/se sortir d'une mauvaise p.** to get sb out of/get out of a tight corner; **elle est dans une bonne p.** everything's going right for her **8** *Typ* **(main de) p.** overs, overplus; **exemplaires de p.** surplus copies, over copies **9** *Fin* **p. de caisse** cashier error allowance

NM *Fam (clé)* skeleton *or* master *or* pass key

passé [pase] **ADJ 1** *(écoulé) (temps)* past; **la semaine/l'année passée** last week/year; **lundi p.** last Monday; **il est quatre heures passées** it's gone four, it's after four; **il a quarante ans passés** he's over forty; **à quinze ans passés, il ne savait toujours pas lire** he was over fifteen and he still couldn't read; **ça fait deux ans passés que je ne l'ai pas vu** it's over two years now since I saw him; **p. de mode** out of fashion **2** *(fini)* over; **l'orage/la crise est passé(e)** the storm/the crisis is over; **penser à son enfance/sa beauté passée** to think of one's vanished childhood/beauty **3** *(éteint, décoloré) (couleur, tissu etc)* faded; **mon salon est tout p.** my living room is looking old and drab

NM 1 *(temps révolu)* **le p.** the past; **dans le p.** in the past; **comme par le p.** as in the past; **tout ça, c'est du p.** that's all in the past; **avoir un p. chargé** *ou* **un lourd p.** to have a shady past; **oublier le p.** to forget the past; **oublions le p.** let's let bygones be bygones; **avoir honte/être fier de son p.** to be ashamed/proud of one's past **2** *Gram* past (tense); **les temps du p.** the past tenses; **p. simple** preterite, past historic; **p. composé** perfect (tense); **au p.** in the past (tense); **p. progressif** past continuous <small>SEE GRAMMAR A49–50; B30–1</small>

PRÉP after; **p. les arbres …** after *or* beyond the trees …; **p. cette date** after this date; **p. la première impression** once *or* after the first impression has worn off

passe-crassane [paskrasan] **NF INV** passe crassane *(type of pear)*

passe-droit, *pl* **passe-droits NM** (undeserved) privilege, favour, *Am* favor; **le fils du patron a eu un p., on a fait un p. au fils du patron** the boss's son got preferential treatment

passéisme [paseism] **NM** *Péj* attachment to the past, backward-looking attitude

passéiste [paseist] *Péj* **ADJ** backward-looking

N backward-looking person

passe-lacet, *pl* **passe-lacets NM** bodkin; *Fig Fam* **raide comme un p.** stony broke, *Am* stone broke

passement [pasmã] **NM** braid, braiding

passementer [pasmãte] **VT** to braid

passementerie [pasmãtri] **NF 1** *Com* haberdashery trade, *Am* notions trade **2** *(accessoire décoratif)* braid

passementier, -ière [pasmãtje, -jɛr] **ADJ** *(commerce, industrie)* haberdashery, *Am* notions

N haberdasher, *Am* dealer in notions

passe-montagne, *pl* **passe-montagnes NM** balaclava (helmet)

passe-partout NM INV 1 *(clef)* skeleton *or* master *or* pass key **2** *(scie)* cross-cut saw **3** *(cadre)* passe-partout **4** *Journ* filler

ADJ INV all-purpose; **réponse p.** stock *or* all-purpose reply *or* answer; **tenue p.** all-purpose outfit

passe-passe NM INV **tour de p.** (conjuring *or* magic) trick; *Fig (tromperie)* trick

passe-plat, *pl* **passe-plats NM** serving hatch

passepoil [paspwal] **NM** *(pour vêtements)* piping

passepoiler [paspwale] **VT** *(vêtement)* to pipe; **poche passepoilée** welted pocket

passeport [paspɔr] **NM** *Admin, Fig* passport; *Naut* passport, sea letter; **les enfants sont sur le p. de leur mère** the children are on their mother's passport

PASSER [pase]

VI to pass **1, 8, 9, 13** ▪ to go by **1, 9** ▪ to go through *(passer par)* **4, 7** ▪ to be on **5** ▪ to call on somebody *(passer chez quelqu'un)* **6** ▪ to disappear **8** ▪ to fade **8** ▪ to pass for *(passer pour)* **10** ▪ to be accepted **11** ▪ to filter **14**
VT to cross **1** ▪ to go over **1** ▪ to go through **1** ▪ to carry across **2** ▪ to pass **3, 4** ▪ to give **4** ▪ to put **5** ▪ to show **6** ▪ to excuse **8** ▪ to leave out **9** ▪ to enter into **10** ▪ to take **12** ▪ to sit **12**
VPR to happen **1** ▪ to take place **1** ▪ to go by **2** ▪ to pass **2** ▪ to go **2** ▪ to come to an end **2** ▪ to do without *(se passer de)* **3**

VI *(aux* **être)** **1** *(se déplacer, circuler)* to pass, to go/come past, *Fml* to proceed; **par où est-il passé?** which way did he go?; **je regardais p. la procession** I was watching the procession go by; **p. sur un pont** to cross (over) a bridge; **il est passé devant le magasin** he went/came by *or* passed (by) the shop; **p. par-dessus/par-dessous qch** to get over/under sth; **la voiture lui est passée** *ou* **lui a passé sur les jambes** the car ran over his legs; *Fig* **p. sur le corps de qn pour parvenir à qch** to trample all over sb to attain sth; **il faudrait me p. sur le corps pour que je dise oui** if you get me to say yes it'll be over my dead body; **la bouteille est passée** *ou* **a passé de main en main** the bottle was passed round; **faire p. les gâteaux/photos** to hand round *or* pass round the cakes/photos; **p. sur une difficulté** to pass over a difficulty; **passons!** let's leave it at that!; **en passant** in passing; **dire qch en passant** to mention sth in passing; **soit dit en passant** by the way, incidentally

2 *(aller d'un lieu à un autre, changer)* **p. à l'ennemi** to go over to the enemy; *(d'un espion)* to defect; **le chiffre d'affaires est passé de deux à trois millions** the turnover has gone up from two to three million; **p. à table** to come to *or* sit up at the table; **passons à table!** come to the table, everybody!; **passons à la salle à manger** let's go into the dining room; **il nous fit p. dans le bureau** he showed us into the office; *Scol* **p. dans la classe supérieure** to move up *or* be moved up (a class); *Sport* **p. en seconde division** *(être promu)* to go up to the second division; *(être relégué)* to go down to the second division; **passons à autre chose** let's move on to other matters; *(changeons de sujet)* let's change the subject; *Aut* **p. en seconde/troisième** to go *or* change into second/third (gear); **il est passé du rire aux larmes** his laughter turned to tears

3 *(se transmettre)* **p. à la postérité** to go

down to posterity; **l'héritage est passé à sa fille** the inheritance went to his daughter; **le mot est passé dans l'usage/dans le vocabulaire général** the word passed into common usage/into the general vocabulary; **c'est passé dans la tradition/les coutumes** it passed into tradition/custom; **c'est passé dans la langue** it's entered the language; **l'alcool passe très rapidement dans le sang** alcohol goes *or* gets into the bloodstream very quickly

4 *(traverser)* **la route passe par le village** the road runs *or* goes through the village; **passez par la fenêtre** go through the window; **on est passé par Bourges/la Belgique** we went through *or* via Bourges/Belgium; **mon dîner ne passe pas** my dinner won't go down; *Fig* **ce qu'il m'a dit, ça ne passe pas** what he told me sticks in my throat; **je ne peux pas p.** I can't get by *or* past; **empêcher qn de p.** to stop sb from getting by *or* past; **on ne passe pas** you're not allowed through; **laisser p.** *(lumière, air etc)* to let in; *(personne etc)* to let through; *Fig* **laisser p. une erreur** to overlook a mistake; **faire p. un tuyau à travers le mur** to run a pipe through the wall; **faire p. des gens d'un pays à un autre** to smuggle people out of one country and into another; *Fig* **il est passé par l'université** he did a university course; **il dit tout ce qui lui passe par la tête** he says anything *or* the first thing that comes into his head; **la première chose qui m'est passée** *ou* **m'a passé par la tête** the first thing that came into my head; **une idée m'est passée par la tête …** an idea has occurred to me …, I've had an idea …; *Can* **j'ai passé tout droit** I overslept

5 *Cin* to be on, to be showing; *Radio, TV* to be on; **p. à la radio** *(d'une émission, personne)* to be on the radio *or* the air; **p. à la télévision** *(de personne)* to be *or* appear on television; *(de film)* to be on television; **son documentaire n'est jamais passé** her documentary was never shown; **ça ne passe jamais à la radio/télévision** it's never on the radio/on television; **ce film est passé la semaine dernière** the film was on last week; **qu'est-ce qui passe ce soir?** what's on this evening?

6 *(aller)* **p. chez qn** to call on sb; **p. au pressing/à la boucherie** to call (in) at *or Fam* pop in at the dry cleaner's/butcher's; **je passerai chez vous ce soir** I'll come round *or* drop round this evening; **je passerai vous prendre vers 18 h** I'll pick you up *or* call for you *or* fetch you at about 6 o'clock; **en passant, je suis entré dire bonjour** I just looked in *or* dropped in on my way past; **il est passé prendre le courrier** he dropped by to pick up the mail; **je ne fais que p.** I'm not stopping; **est-ce que le facteur est passé?** has the postman been?, has the post come?

7 *(subir)* **elle est passée par des périodes vraiment difficiles** she has been *or* gone through some really difficult periods; **je suis passé par là** I've been through it, it's happened to me; *Fam* **quand il se met en colère, tout le monde y passe** when he gets angry, everybody bears the brunt of it; *Fam* **il a failli y p.** he nearly died; **toute sa fortune y est passée** he spent his entire fortune on it

8 *(disparaître, finir)* to disappear; **la douleur est passée** the pain has gone *or* passed *or* disappeared; **cela fera p. la douleur** that will get rid of the pain; **cela a fait p. mon mal de tête** it has cured my headache; **le vert est passé de mode** green is out of fashion; **le plus dur est passé** the worst is over; **ça lui passera (avec l'âge)** he'll grow out of it; **j'ai été un peu déprimé mais maintenant c'est passé** *ou* **ça m'a passé** I was a bit down but it's over now *or* I've got over it now *or* that's all in the past now; **couleurs qui passent** colours that fade; **le soleil a fait p. les couleurs**

the sun faded the colours; **il faut laisser p. l'orage** we must let the storm blow over; **la crise est passée** the crisis is over or past; **il fallait bien laisser p. cette période difficile** we just had to get through that difficult period; **laisser p. sa dernière chance** to miss one's last chance; **laisser p. une occasion** to miss or let slip an opportunity

9 (*s'écouler*) to go by, to pass; **des ou les années ont passé depuis …** years have passed or it's been years since …; **à mesure que les années passent** as the years go by; **comme le temps passe (vite)!** how time flies!; **faire le temps** to pass the time; **tout passe, tout lasse, tout casse** nothing lasts, everything comes to an end

10 (*être considéré*) **p. pour riche** to be considered rich, to pass for rich; **p. pour avoir fait qch** to be credited with having done sth; **ceci passe pour vrai** everyone believes this is true; **se faire p. pour …** to pass oneself off as …; **tu veux me faire p. pour un imbécile ou quoi?** do you want me to be taken for a fool or what?

11 (*être accepté*) to be accepted; **la loi est passée** the law has been passed or has gone through; **passe encore qu'il revienne demain, mais …, qu'il revienne demain, passe encore mais …** if he comes back tomorrow that's one thing or (that's all) well and good, but …; **cela peut p./ne passe pas** it will/won't do; *Fam* **cette excuse ne passera pas** that excuse won't wash; **alors, c'est passé, il a accepté?** well, did it work, did he accept?; *Fam* well, any joy, did he accept?

12 *Jur* **p. en jugement** to come up for judgment; **l'affaire passera demain/en janvier** the case will be heard tomorrow/in January

13 *Cartes* **passe!** pass!; (*au bridge*) no bid!

14 (*de café, liquide*) to filter

VT (*aux* **avoir**) **1** (*pont, rivière, frontière*) to cross, to go over; (*porte, barrière*) to go through, to pass through; (*douanes*) to go through, to clear; *Fig* (*limite*) to pass, to go beyond, to exceed; **vous avez passé la maison** you've gone past the house; *Fig* **il a passé la soixantaine** he's in his sixties; *Fig* **cela passe les limites** ou **les bornes** that's going too far; *Fig* **le vieux ne passera pas l'hiver** the old man won't last the winter (out); **p. son chemin** to carry on one's way

2 (*transporter*) to convey across, to carry across; **p. des marchandises en fraude** to smuggle goods

3 (*mettre en circulation*) to pass; **p. des faux billets** to pass forged banknotes

4 (*donner*) **p. qch à qn** to pass or give sth to sb; **voulez-vous me p. l'eau, s'il vous plaît?** would you pass me the water, please?; **est-ce que tu peux me p. ton stylo?** (*prêter*) could you lend me your pen?; **voulez-vous me p. le volant?** do you want me to drive?; **p. un message (à qn)** to pass on a message (to sb); **il m'a passé son rhume** he gave me his cold, I caught his cold; *Sport* **p. le ballon** to pass the ball; **p. la parole à qn** to hand over to sb; *Tél* **allô, je vous passe Paris/M. Robert** hello, I'm putting you through to Paris/Mr Robert; *Tél* **passez-moi M. Robert** put me through to or give me Mr Robert; *Tél* **passez-moi un coup de fil demain** call me tomorrow, give me a call or Br a ring tomorrow; **p. son tour** (*en jouant*) to miss one's go; (*exprès*) to pass

5 (*mettre, faire aller*) **p. l'éponge sur le tableau** to wipe the blackboard; *Fig* **passons l'éponge là-dessus** let's say no more about it; **p. l'aspirateur sur le tapis** to vacuum or Br hoover the carpet; **p. un coup de chiffon sur les meubles** to give the furniture a quick dust; **p. sa tête par la fenêtre** to put or stick one's head out of the window; **p. sa main dans qch** to put or slip one's hand in sth; **je lui ai passé mon bras autour de la taille** I

put or slipped my arm round his/her waist; **p. une chemise/une robe** to slip on a shirt/a dress; *Aut* **p. la seconde/la troisième** to go into or change into second/third (gear); *Naut* **p. une manœuvre** to reeve a rope; **p. sa colère sur qn** to vent one's anger on sb; **p. ses nerfs sur qn** to take it out on sb; **qu'est-ce que je vais lui p.!** I won't half tell him off!, he won't half catch it!; *Fam* **il s'est fait p. un savon** he got a telling-off; **je l'ai senti p.** I really caught it; **p. un couteau à la meule** to sharpen a knife; **p. un parquet à la cire** to polish a (parquet) floor; **p. des troupes en revue** to inspect or review troops

6 *Cin, TV* (*film*) to show, to screen; *Radio* (*émission*) to broadcast; **p. un disque** to put on or play a record; **p. une vidéo** to put on a video; **qu'est-ce qu'ils passent au cinéma cette semaine?** what's on or showing at the cinema this week?, what are they showing at the cinema this week?

7 (*temps, sa vie, vacances*) to spend; **p. l'après-midi à faire qch** to spend the afternoon doing sth; **la secrétaire qui passe son temps à ne rien faire** the secretary who sits there doing nothing; **on y passera le temps nécessaire** we'll spend as much time on it as necessary; **pour p. le temps** (in order) to while away or pass the time

8 (*pardonner*) to excuse; **on ne lui passe rien** he doesn't get away with anything; **elle lui passe tout** she lets him get away with everything; **passez-moi l'expression** (if you'll) pardon the expression

9 (*omettre*) to leave out, to omit; **p. qch sous silence** to make no mention of sth; (*fait gênant, secret inavouable*) to keep quiet about sth; **(et) j'en passe, et des meilleures** and that's not all, and that's not the half of it; **il est beau, intelligent, instruit, et j'en passe** he's handsome, intelligent, cultured, and that's not all

10 *Jur* (*accord, contrat*) to enter into, to sign; **p. un marché** to sign a deal; *Fin* **p. un montant** to post an amount; **p. une commande** to place an order (**de qch à qn** for sth with sb); **p. une loi** to pass a law

11 *Compta* **p. un article en compte** to post an entry; **p. par pertes et profits** to transfer to profit and loss

12 **p. un examen** to take or sit an exam; **p. le permis de conduire** to take one's driving test

13 (*liquide*) to strain; (*farine*) to sift; **p. le café** to filter the coffee

14 (*devenir*) **p. capitaine** to be promoted to captain; **elle est passée maître dans l'art du collage/l'art de mentir** ou **du mensonge** she's a past master at collage/lying

VPR se passer 1 (*se produire, arriver*) to happen, to take place; **cela s'est passé il y a dix ans** it happened ten years ago; **que se passe-t-il?, qu'est-ce qui se passe?** what's going on?, what's happening?; **tout s'est bien passé** everything went (off) smoothly; **comment ça c'est passé?** how did it go?; **mon histoire se passe en France** my story is set in France; *Fam* **ça ne se passera pas comme ça** I won't stand for it SEE GRAMMAR B29

2 (*cesser*) (*du temps*) to go by, to pass; **nos ennuis finiront par se p.** our troubles will come to an end eventually; **mon mal de tête se passe** my headache is going

3 **se p. de qn/qch** to do without sb/sth, to dispense with sb/sth; **je m'en passerai** I'll do or manage without it/them; **je m'en passerais** I can well do without it/them; **ces faits se passent de commentaires** these facts need no comment

4 **se p. la main dans les cheveux** to run one's fingers through one's hair; **se p. un mouchoir sur le visage** to wipe one's face with a handkerchief

5 **se p. une fantaisie** to indulge a whim

Il faut noter que l'expression **passer un examen** se traduit par **to sit an exam** ou **to take an exam**. To pass an exam signifie **réussir un examen**.

passereau, -eaux [pasro] NM *Orn* passerine; *Arch* (*moineau*) sparrow

passerelle [pasrɛl] NF **1** (*au-dessus d'une rue, d'un ruisseau*) footbridge **2** *Naut* boarding bridge; (*escalier*) boarding steps; (*de ferry*) linkspan, boarding ramp; **p. (de commandement)** bridge; **p. de navigation** navigation bridge **3** (*pont incliné*) **p. de débarquement** ou **d'embarquement** *Naut* gangway, gangplank; *Aviat* (*amovible*) steps; (*fixe*) passenger bridge **4** *Fig* (*intermédiaire*) link; **ce cours est une p. entre les deux niveaux** this course bridges the two levels **5** *Ordinat* **p. (de connexion)** gateway (**avec** to)

passe-temps NM INV pastime, hobby

passe-thé NM INV tea strainer

passeur, -euse [pasœr, -øz] N ferryman, f ferrywoman; **il est p.** (*de marchandises*) he's a smuggler; (*de gens*) he smuggles people across the border

passe-vite NM INV *Belg, Suisse* (*moulin à légumes*) vegetable mill

passible [pasibl] ADJ liable (**de** to, for); **p. d'une amende** liable to a fine; **p. de l'impôt** liable for tax; **p. de taxe** liable to tax

passif, -ive [pasif, -iv] ADJ passive; **rester p.** to remain passive; *Pol* **faire de la résistance passive** to offer passive resistance; *Gram* **forme passive** passive form; *Com* **dettes passives** liabilities; *Mil* **défense passive** civil defence

   NM **1** *Gram* passive; **au p.** in the passive SEE GRAMMAR A54-5; B39 **2** *Fin* liabilities; **l'actif et le p.** assets and liabilities; **p. reporté** deferred liabilities; **p. exigible** ou **circulant** current liabilities

passiflore [pasiflɔr] NF *Bot* passionflower

passing-shot, pl passing-shots [pasiŋʃɔt] NM *Sport* passing shot; **faire un p.** to play a passing shot

passion [pasjɔ̃] NF **1** passion; **avoir une p. pour la musique** to have a passion for music; **il a la p. des voitures** he has a passion for cars; **la moto est sa p., la moto est une p. chez lui** he's mad about motorbikes; **vivre une p.** to have a passionate love affair, to be passionately in love; **avec p.** passionately; **aimer qn à la** ou **avec p.** to love sb passionately; **parler avec/sans p.** to speak passionately/dispassionately; **lutter contre ses passions** to struggle against one's passions; **déchaîner les passions** to unleash passions or strong emotions **2** *Rel* **la P.** the Passion (of Christ); **la semaine de la P.** Passion Week; *Mus* **la P. selon saint Jean** the St John Passion

passionnant [pasjɔnɑ̃] ADJ (*histoire, livre, film*) gripping, fascinating; (*aventure*) thrilling, exciting; (*personne*) fascinating; **ce boulot n'est vraiment pas très p.** this job's really not very exciting

passionné, -ée [pasjɔne] ADJ passionate; **débat p.** heated or impassioned debate; **p. de** ou **pour qn/qch** passionately fond of sb/sth

   N enthusiast; **c'est une passionnée de moto(s)** she's mad about motorbikes, she's a motorbike fanatic

passionnel, -elle [pasjɔnɛl] ADJ passionate; **état p.** state of passion, passionate state; **crime p.** crime of passion

passionnément [pasjɔnemɑ̃] ADV passionately

passionner [pasjɔne] VT **1** (*inspirer un intérêt très vif à*) (*d'un livre, film etc*) to fascinate, to grip; **ce livre m'a passionné** I found this book fascinating or gripping, this book fascinated *or* gripped me; **le sport/travailler avec les enfants la passionne** sport/working with children is a passion with her; **son métier le passionne** he finds his job fascinating **2** *(animer) (débat)* to inflame

VPR se passionner se p. de *ou* **pour qch** to be passionately fond of sth, to have a passion for sth

passivement [pasivmɑ̃] **ADV** passively

passivité [pasivite] **NF** passivity, passiveness

passoire [paswar] **NF** *Culin* sieve; *(pour liquides)* strainer; **p. (à légumes)** colander; **sa mémoire est une (vraie) p., il a la tête comme une p.** he's got a memory *or* a head like a sieve; **cette frontière est une vraie p.** this border doesn't keep anyone in or out; *Fam* **ce gardien est une vraie p.!** this goalkeeper is really useless *or* lets everything in!; *Fam* **transformer qn en p.** to pump sb full of lead, to riddle sb with bullets

pastel [pastɛl] **NM 1** *Beaux-Arts* pastel; *(dessin)* pastel (drawing); **tableau au p.** picture in pastels **2** *Bot* woad
ADJ INV pastel; **bleu p.** pastel blue; **tons p.** pastel shades

pastelliste [pastelist] **N** *Beaux-Arts* pastellist

pastèque [pastɛk] **NF** watermelon; *Fam* **j'ai la tête comme une p.** my head's buzzing

pasteur [pastœr] **NM 1** *Litt (berger)* shepherd; **peuple p.** pastoral people; *Rel* **le bon P.** the Good Shepherd **2** *Rel* pastor, minister

pasteurisation [pastœrizasjɔ̃] **NF** pasteurization

pasteuriser [pastœrize] **VT** to pasteurize

pastiche [pastiʃ] **NM** parody

pasticher [pastiʃe] **VT** to parody

pasticheur, -euse [pastiʃœr, -øz] **N** writer of pastiches

pastille [pastij] **NF 1** *(bonbon, pilule) (molle)* pastille; *(dure)* lozenge; **p. contre la toux** cough drop *or Br* sweet; **p. de menthe** (pepper)mint; **p. pour purifier l'eau** water sterilizing tablet **2** *(motif)* circle **3** **p. verte** = green label on a low-emission vehicle indicating that it may be driven on days when restrictions are placed on traffic due to high levels of atmospheric pollution

pastis [pastis] **NM 1** *(boisson)* pastis **2** *Fig Fam* **être dans le p.** to be in a fix; **quel p.!** what a mess!

pastoral, -ale, -aux, -ales [pastɔral, -o] **ADJ** pastoral
NF pastorale *Littér* pastoral; *Mus* pastorale

pastorat [pastɔra] **NM** pastorate

pastoureau, -elle, -eaux, -elles [pasturo, -ɛl] **N** *Arch, Litt* shepherd lad, *f* shepherd lass
NF pastourelle *Mus* pastourelle; *(danse)* fourth figure of the quadrille

pat [pat] **NM INV** *Échecs* stalemate; **les Noirs sont p.** Black is stalemated

patachon [pataʃɔ̃] **NM** *Arg* **mener une vie de p.** to lead a wild life

Patagonie (la) [lapatagɔni] **NF** Patagonia

patapouf [patapuf] **INT** flop!
NM *Enf* **gros p.** fat lump

pataquès [patakɛs] **NM 1** *(faute de liaison)* incorrect liaison **2** *(faute de langage)* serious mistake *(in pronunciation etc)* **3** *Fam (gaffe)* boo-boo, *Br* boob

patata [patata] **INT** *voir* **patati**

patate [patat] **NF 1** *Fam (pomme de terre)* spud; *Can* **patates frites** French fries, *Br* chips; **la corvée de patates** peeling the spuds; *Mil* spud-bashing **2 p. (douce)** sweet potato **3** *Fam (imbécile)* clot, idiot **4** *Anciennement Fam (dix mille francs)* ten thousand francs **5** *Math* set diagram **6** *Fam* **en avoir**

gros sur la p. to be down in the mouth *or* down in the dumps **7** *Can Fam (cœur)* heart, *Br* ticker; **monter les escaliers, c'est dur pour la p.** going up the stairs is hard on the old ticker

patati [patati] **INT** *Fam* **et p. et patata** and so on and so forth

patatras [patatra] **INT** *Fam* crash!

pataud, -aude [pato, -od] **NM** *(chiot)* puppy with big paws
N *Vieilli* lump
ADJ *Fam (personne)* lumpish, clumsy; *(apparence, démarche)* clumsy, awkward

Pataugas® [patogas] **NM** = canvas walking shoe

pataugeoire [patoʒwar] **NF** paddling pool

patauger [patoʒe] **VI** (**je pataugeai(s); n. pataugeons**) **1** *(dans la boue)* to squelch; *(dans l'eau)* to paddle **2** *Fig Fam (s'empêtrer)* to flounder; **il patauge dans ses réponses** he's getting more and more bogged down trying to answer; **p. (dans la semoule)** to be totally lost **3** *Fam (ne pas progresser) (d'une enquête)* to get bogged down

patch [patʃ] **NM 1** *Pharm* (skin) patch **2** *Élec* jackfield

patchouli [patʃuli] **NM** patchouli

patchwork [patʃwœrk] **NM** patchwork

pâte [pat] **NF 1** *Culin (à tarte)* pastry; *(à pain)* dough; *(à gâteau)* mixture; **pâtes (alimentaires)** pasta; **pâtes fraîches** fresh pasta; *Fig* **c'est une bonne p.** he's a good sort; *Fig* **mettre la main à la p.** to lend a hand; *Fig* **être comme un coq en p.** to be in clover; *Fig* **une p. molle** a drip, a wimp **2** *(mélange, composition)* **fromage à p. dure/molle** hard/soft cheese **3** *Beaux-Arts* paint, colours, *Am* colors; *(plus épais)* paste **4** *Typ* (printer's) pie; **caractères tombés en p.** pied type
▸▸ **p. d'amandes** marzipan, almond paste; **p. brisée** short(crust) pastry; **p. à choux** choux pastry; **p. à crêpes** pancake batter; **p. dentifrice** toothpaste; **p. feuilletée** flaky pastry; **p. à frire** batter; **p. de fruits** fruit jelly; **p. à modeler** modelling *or Am* modeling clay; **p. à pain** bread dough; **p. à papier** pulp; **p. sablée** rich shortcrust pastry; **p. à tarte** pastry

pâté [pate] **NM 1** *Culin (terrine)* pâté; **p. de foie** liver pâté; **p. de campagne** pâté de campagne *(coarse pâté made with pork)*; **p. en croûte** pâté en croûte, *Br* raised (crust) pie; **p. impérial** spring roll **2 p. (de sable)** sandpie **3** *(tache d'encre)* blot; **faire un p. sur sa copie** to blot one's paper **4** *(bloc)* **p. de maisons** block of houses **5** *Belg (gâteau)* cake

pâtée [pate] **NF 1** *(pour volaille, cochon)* mash; *(pour chat/chien)* cat/dog food **2** *Fam (défaite)* **prendre la p.** to get a thrashing *or* a good hiding; **on leur a mis** *ou* **foutu la p.** they got a thrashing, they were thrashed

patelin [patlɛ̃] **ADJ** *Litt Péj (personne, manière, air)* unctuous
NM *Fam* village; **quel sale p.!** what a dump!, what a hole!

patelle [patɛl] **NF 1** *(mollusque)* limpet **2** *Archéol* patella

patène [patɛn] **NF** *Rel* paten

patenôtre [patnotr] **NF** *Fam* prayer, *Arch* paternoster; *Fig (paroles incompréhensibles)* gibberish

patent [patɑ̃] **ADJ 1** *(clair) (erreur, injustice)* obvious, patent; **il est p. que ...** it is patently obvious that ... **2 lettres patentes** letters patent

patentable [patɑ̃tabl] **ADJ** *Admin* subject to a licence, requiring a licence

patente [patɑ̃t] **NF 1** *Com (licence)* licence *(to exercise a trade or profession)*; *Anciennement (impôt)* tax *(paid by traders and profes-*

sional men); **payer p.** to be duly licensed **2** *Naut* **p. (de santé)** bill of health

patenté [patɑ̃te] **ADJ** *Com* licensed; *Fig Fam* **spécialiste/graphiste p.** recognized specialist/graphic designer; **imbécile/menteur/voleur p.** out-and-out fool/liar/thief

patenter [patɑ̃te] **VT** *Com* to license

pater [patɛr] **NM INV 1** *Rel* Paternoster **2** *Fam (père)* old man; **le p.** the old man, *Am* pop, *Br* Vieilli, Hum pater

patère [patɛr] **NF** (coat) peg

paternalisme [patɛrnalism] **NM** paternalism

paternaliste [patɛrnalist] **ADJ** paternalistic

paterne [patɛrn] **ADJ** *Litt* benevolent

paternel, -elle [patɛrnɛl] **ADJ** paternal; *(protecteur, bienveillant) (ton, conseil)* fatherly, kindly; *(attention)* fatherly; **du côté p.** on the father's side; **ma grand-mère paternelle** my grandmother on my father's side; **le domicile p.** (the family) home; **image paternelle** father figure; **l'amour p.** paternal *or* fatherly love
NM *Fam (père)* old man; **le p.** the old man, *Br* Vieilli, Hum pater, *Am* pop

paternellement [patɛrnɛlmɑ̃] **ADV** paternally, in a fatherly way

paternité [patɛrnite] **NF** paternity, fatherhood; *Jur* **p. légitime/naturelle** legitimate/natural paternity; *Jur* **recherche de p.** affiliation; **il vit mal sa p.** he's finding fatherhood difficult, he's finding it difficult being a father; *Fig* **revendiquer/désavouer la p. d'un livre** to claim/repudiate authorship of a book; **la p. d'une découverte/d'une invention** the paternity of a discovery/an invention

pâteux, -euse [patø, -øz] **ADJ 1** *(substance, crème)* pasty; *(pain)* doughy; **j'ai la langue pâteuse** my tongue is all furry; **j'ai la bouche pâteuse** my mouth is all dry *or Fam* is like the bottom of a parrot's cage **2** *(trop épais) (encre)* thick; *Péj* **style p.** woolly style

pathétique [patetik] **ADJ 1** *Litt (histoire, situation, ton)* pathetic, touching, moving **2** *Anat* **nerf p.** pathetic nerve
NM *Litt* pathos

Il faut noter que l'adjectif anglais **pathetic** est un faux ami. Il signifie souvent **lamentable**.

pathétiquement [patetikmɑ̃] **ADV** pathetically, movingly

pathétisme [patetism] **NM** *Litt* pathos

pathogène [patoʒɛn] **ADJ** *Méd* pathogenic

pathologie [patɔlɔʒi] **NF** *Méd* pathology

pathologique [patɔlɔʒik] **ADJ** *Méd* pathological; **c'est un cas p.** he/she's a pathological case; *Fam* **c'est p. chez lui** it's a neurosis with him, it's pathological

pathologiquement [patɔlɔʒikmɑ̃] **ADJ** *Méd* pathologically

pathologiste [patɔlɔʒist] **N** *Méd* pathologist

pathos [patos] **NM** *Litt* pathos

patibulaire [patibyler] **ADJ 1** *(sinistre)* **avoir une mine p.** to have a sinister look, to look sinister **2** *Vieilli* **fourches patibulaires** gibbet

patiemment [pasjamɑ̃] **ADV** patiently

patience[1] [pasjɑ̃s] **NF 1** patience; **avoir de la p., prendre p.** to be patient, to have patience; **avoir de la p. avec qn** to be patient with sb; **prendre son mal en p.** to suffer patiently; **faire preuve de p.** *ou* **montrer de la p. envers qn** to be patient with sb; **avoir une p. d'ange** to have the patience of a saint *or* of Job; **avec p.** patiently; **ma p. est à bout, je suis à bout de p.** my patience is exhausted *or* is at an end; **ma p. a des limites!** there are limits to my patience!; **s'armer de p.** to be as patient as one can; **(prenez) p.!** be patient!; **perdre p.** to lose patience; *Prov* **p. et longueur de temps (font plus que force ni que rage)** all things must take their time; **jeu de p.** (jigsaw) puzzle; *Fig* test of patience **2** *Cartes* patience, *Am* solitaire; **faire des patiences** to play patience *or Am* solitaire

patience² NF *Bot* patience (dock)

patient, -ente [pasjɑ̃, -ɑ̃t] ADJ patient; *(qui endure une épreuve)* long-suffering
▶ N *Méd* patient

patienter [pasjɑ̃te] VI to wait; **faire p. qn** to ask sb to wait; *Tél* to ask sb to hold; **pour vous faire p., je vais vous passer un film** I'll show you a film while you're waiting *or* to pass the time for you; **p. en lisant le journal** to read the newspaper to while away *or* pass the time

patin [patɛ̃] NM **1** *(de patineur)* skate; *(de traîneau)* runner; **patins à glace/à roulettes** ice/roller skates; **nous allons faire du p. à glace** we're going (ice)skating; **sais-tu faire du p. à glace/à roulettes?** can you (ice)skate/(roller)skate?; *Can Fam* **être vite sur ses patins** to be quick off the mark; *Can Fam* **accrocher ses patins** to hang up one's hat, to retire; *(d'un sportif)* to hang up one's boots, to retire **2** *(sur parquet)* cloth pad; *Arch (chaussure)* patten **3** *Tech* shoe; **p. (de frein)** (brake) shoe; *Aut* **p. amortisseur** damping slipper; *Fam* **donner** *ou* **filer un coup de p.** *(un coup de frein)* to slam on the brakes **4** *très Fam (baiser)* French kiss; **rouler un p. à qn** to French-kiss sb; **ils n'ont pas arrêté de se rouler des patins toute la soirée** they had their tongues down each other's throats the whole evening

patinage [patinaʒ] NM **1** *Sport* skating; **p. artistique** figure skating; **p. de vitesse** speed skating **2** *(d'une roue)* spinning; *Aut* **p. de l'embrayage** clutch slip; **p. des roues** wheel spin **3** *Tech* patination

patine [patin] NF patina; *Fig* **la p. du temps** the patina of age *or* time

patiner [patine] VI **1** *(faire du patinage)* to skate **2** *Aut* to skid; *(d'une roue)* to spin; *(d'une courroie, de l'embrayage)* to slip; *Fig (stagner)* to get nowhere; **ça patine!** it's slippery!; **faire p. l'embrayage** to slip the clutch ▶ VT *Tech* to give a patina to; **une table patinée par les ans** a table that has acquired a patina with age
▶ VPR **se patiner** to develop a patina

patinette [patinɛt] NF scooter

patineur, -euse [patinœr, -øz] N skater

patinoire [patinwar] NF skating *or* ice rink; **cette route est une vraie p.** this road is like a skating rink *or* an ice rink

patio [patjo] NM patio

pâtir [patir] VI to suffer (**de** because of); **c'est moi qui vais en p.** I'm the one that's going to suffer

pâtis [pɑti] NM *Agr* grazing ground, pasture

pâtisserie [pɑtisri] NF **1** *Culin (gâteau)* pastry, (small) cake; *(gâteaux)* pastries **2** *(confection de gâteaux)* pastry-making; **apprendre à faire de la p.** to learn pastry-making; **elle fait de la bonne p.** she makes good cakes **3** *(magasin)* cake shop; **p.-confiserie** confectioner's

pâtissier, -ière [pɑtisje, -jɛr] N *(de restaurant)* pastrycook; *(commerçant)* confectioner; **Papa est très bon p.** Dad makes very good cakes
▶ ADJ **crème pâtissière** confectioner's custard

patois [patwa] NM patois, (local) dialect
▶ ADJ patois

patoisant, -ante [patwazɑ̃, -ɑ̃t] ADJ *(personne)* patois- *or* dialect-speaking; **histoire patoisante** story in patois *or* dialect
▶ N patois *or* dialect speaker

patouiller [patuje] *Fam* VI to flounder
▶ VT to paw

patraque [patrak] ADJ *Fam (personne)* out of sorts, under the weather

pâtre [pɑtr] NM *Litt (pour bétail)* herdsman; *(pour moutons)* shepherd

patriarcal, -ale, -aux, -ales [patriarkal, -o] ADJ patriarchal

patriarcat [patriarka] NM **1** patriarchy **2** *Rel* patriarchate

patriarche [patriarʃ] NM patriarch

patricien, -ienne [patrisjɛ̃, -jɛn] ADJ, N patrician

patrie [patri] NF *(nation)* homeland; *(localité de naissance)* birthplace; **mère p.** mother country; **mourir pour la p.** to die for one's country; **une seconde p.** my/his/*etc* second home; *Fig* **la p. des arts/de la musique** the cradle of the arts/of music

patrimoine [patrimwan] NM heritage; *(d'un ancêtre)* patrimony, inheritance; *Fin* property, wealth, personal assets; *(actif net)* net worth; **faire partie du p.** to be part of our/one's/*etc* heritage; **p. familial** family wealth *or* heritage; *Fig* family heritage; *Banque* **p. social** social assets; **p. artistique** artistic heritage; **p. culturel** cultural heritage; *Biol* **p. génétique** gene pool; **p. héréditaire** genetic inheritance; **p. immobilier** property assets, *Am* real-estate assets

patrimonial, -iale, -iaux, -iales [patrimɔnjal, -jo] ADJ *Jur* patrimonial

patriotard [patrijɔtar] *Péj* ADJ jingoistic
▶ NM jingoist

patriote [patrijɔt] ADJ *(personne)* patriotic
▶ N patriot

patriotique [patrijɔtik] ADJ patriotic

patriotisme [patrijɔtism] NM patriotism

patron, -onne [patrɔ̃, -ɔn] N **1** *(d'une usine, d'une entreprise, d'un hôtel) (personne qui dirige)* boss; *(propriétaire)* owner; *Fam* **c'est moi le p.!** I'm the boss!, I'm in charge!; **eh la patronne, une bière!** a beer please, landlady!; **être son propre p.** to be one's own boss; **oui, p.** yes, boss, *Am* yes, chief; **il faut en parler au p.** you'll have to speak to the boss about it; **p. de presse** publisher *(newspaper owner)*; *Univ* **p. de thèse** thesis supervisor **2** *Fam (conjoint)* old man; *(conjointe)* old lady **3** *(protecteur) (d'une association, des arts, d'un artiste)* patron, *f* patroness; **le p. d'un club** the patron of a club **4** *Rel* patron saint; **le saint p.** the patron saint; **la patronne des musiciens** the patron saint of musicians **5** *Méd (dans un hôpital universitaire)* senior consultant; **les grands patrons** the leading specialists *or* consultants
▶ NM *Couture* pattern; **p. (ajuré)** stencil (plate)

Il faut noter que le terme anglais **patron** est un faux ami. Il signifie le plus souvent **client**.

patronage [patrɔnaʒ] NM **1** *(parrainage)* patronage; *Com* sponsoring; **placé sous le p. de ...** sponsored by ...; **sous le p. de** under the sponsorship of **2** *(organisation, siège)* youth club; *Fig Péj* **roman de p.** moralizing *or Fam* preachy novel

patronal, -ale, -aux, -ales [patrɔnal, -o] ADJ **1** *(de l'employeur)* employers', of employers; **syndicat p.** employers' association **2** *(relatif au saint patron)* patronal

patronat [patrɔna] NM employers; *(syndicat)* employers' organization, *Br* ≃ Confederation of British Industry, CBI; **le p. français** French employers

patronner [patrɔne] VT *(hôpital, charité etc)* to support; *(artiste, candidat)* to sponsor; **p. une candidature** to support a candidacy;

(avec aide financière) to sponsor a candidacy; **p. une entreprise** to back a business

patronnesse [patrɔnɛs] ADJ, NF *souvent Iron* **(dame) p.** patroness

patronyme [patrɔnim] NM patronymic

patronymique [patrɔnimik] ADJ patronymic

patrouille [patruj] NF *Mil etc* patrol; **aller en p.** to go on patrol; **être de p.** to be on patrol; *Aviat* **p. de chasse** fighter patrol

patrouiller [patruje] VI to patrol, to be on patrol

patrouilleur [patrujœr] NM **1** soldier/guard/*etc* on patrol; *Aviat* patrol plane; *Naut* patrol boat **2** *Suisse* **p. scolaire** school patroller

patte [pat] NF **1** *(de chien, chat etc)* paw; *(d'oiseau)* foot; *(d'insecte)* leg; *Fam (jambe)* pin, leg; *Fam (main)* hand, *Péj* paw; **se dresser sur ses pattes** to sit up and beg; **pattes de devant** forelegs; *(partie griffue)* forepaws; **pattes de derrière** hind legs; *(partie griffue)* back paws; **marcher/se mettre à quatre pattes** to walk/get down on all fours; *Fig* **retomber sur ses pattes** to land on one's feet; *Fig* **tirer dans les pattes de qn** to give sb a hard time; **court/haut sur pattes** short-/long-legged; **coup de p.** blow with the paw; *Fig* cutting remark, *Fam* dig; *Fam* **pattes (de lapin)** *(cheveux)* sideboards, sideburns; *Fam* **avoir le coup de p.** *(d'un peintre)* to have talent; *Fam* **tomber dans les pattes de qn** to fall into sb's clutches; *Fam* **bas les pattes!** hands off!; *Fig Fam* **graisser la p. à qn** to grease sb's palm **2** *(rabat) (d'une poche, d'une enveloppe)* flap; *(d'un portefeuille, d'une chaussure)* tongue **3** *(attache)* clamp, clip, fastening; *Naut (d'une ancre)* fluke, palm; *(d'un grappin)* claw **4** *Couture (sur un vêtement)* strap; **pattes d'épaule** shoulder straps **5** *Suisse (torchon)* cloth
▶ ▶ **p. blanche:** *Fig* **montrer p. blanche** to show one's credentials; **pattes d'éléphant: pantalon à pattes d'éléphant** bell-bottom(ed) *or* flared trousers; **p. folle: avoir une p. folle** to have a gammy *or Am* gimpy leg; **p. de lapin** rabbit foot; *Fam* **pattes de mouche(s)** cramped handwriting; **p. de velours: faire p. de velours** *(d'un chat)* to draw in its claws; *Fig* to be all sweetness and light

patte-d'oie, *pl* **pattes-d'oie** NF **1** *(carrefour)* crossroads **2** *(ride)* crow's-foot **3** *Bot* goosefoot

pattemouille [patmuj] NF damp cloth *(for ironing clothes)*

pâturage [pɑtyraʒ] NM **1** *(action)* grazing; *Jur (droit)* grazing rights **2** *(endroit)* pasture; **pâturages** pasture land

pâture [pɑtyr] NF **1** *(nourriture) (pour animaux)* food, feed, fodder; *Fig* **p. intellectuelle** food for the mind; *Fig* **donner qn/qch en p. au public** to serve sb/sth up for public consumption **2** *(pâturage)* pasture; *Jur* **vaine p.** (right of) common

pâturer [pɑtyre] VI *(du bétail)* to graze

paturon [patyrɔ̃] NM **1** *(du cheval)* pastern **2** *Fam (pied)* foot

paume [pom] NF **1** *Anat (de la main)* palm **2** *(jeu de)* **p.** real tennis; **jeu de p.** *(terrain)* real-tennis court

paumé, -ée [pome] *Fam* ADJ *(perdu)* lost; *(dans une explication)* all at sea, lost; *Fig* **il est complètement p.** he hasn't got a clue; **un bled complètement p.** a godforsaken hole
▶ N *(personne)* loser

paumelle [pomɛl] NF **1** *Naut* (sailmaker's) palm **2** *(des gonds d'une porte)* plate

paumer [pome] *Fam* VT to lose
▶ VPR **se paumer** to get lost

paupérisation [poperizasjɔ̃] NF impoverishment

paupériser [poperize] VT to impoverish

paupérisme [poperism] NM pauperism

paupière [popjɛr] NF *Anat* eyelid

paupiette [popjɛt] NF *Culin* (meat) olive; **paupiettes de veau** veal olives

pause [poz] NF **1** *(arrêt) (dans une activité)* break; *(en parlant)* pause; *(pour déjeuner)* meal break; **faire une p.** to have a break; *(en parlant)* to pause; **p. de midi** lunch break **2** *Mus* semibreve *or Am* whole-note rest
▸▸ **p.-café** coffee break; **p.-cigarette** cigarette break; **p.-repas** meal break

pause-carrière, *pl* **pauses-carrière** NF *Belg* sabbatical year *(on reduced pay)*

pauvre [povr] ADJ ⸢SEE GRAMMAR B10⸣ **1** *(qui manque de biens)* poor; **p. comme Job** poor as a church mouse; **minerai p. en métal** ore with a low metal content; **p. en vitamine C** with a low vitamin C content; *Aut* **mélange p.** weak mixture **2** *(malheureux)* poor, unfortunate; **le p. homme!** poor chap!; **p. de moi!** poor old me!; **p. Pierre** poor (old) Pierre; **p. vieux/vieille** poor old thing **3** *(misérable) (robe, meubles etc)* shabby; *(excuse)* paltry, poor, weak; *(sourire)* weak, thin; *(argument)* pathetic, weak, poor; *(orateur)* poor, bad; **c'est un p. type** he's pathetic, *Br très Fam* he's a poor sod; **p. idiot!** silly fool!; *très Fam* **p. con!** poor bastard!, *Br* sod! **4** *(stérile) (sol)* poor; **des terres pauvres** barren lands
N poor man, *f* woman; **les pauvres et les riches** the poor and the rich; *Fig* **p. d'esprit** half-wit; *Rel* **les pauvres d'esprit** the poor in spirit; **le p., il n'a pas de chance!** poor chap, he doesn't have much luck!; **la p., elle a encore loupé son examen** poor thing, she's failed her exam again; **mon p.!** you poor thing!

pauvrement [povrəmɑ̃] ADV poorly; **p. vêtu/meublé** poorly *or* shabbily dressed/furnished

pauvresse [povrɛs] NF poor girl/woman

pauvret, -ette [povrɛ, -ɛt] N *Fam* **le p./la pauvrette** the poor little thing

pauvreté [povrəte] NF poverty; *Fig (du langage)* poverty, poorness; *(d'un style)* poverty, baldness; *Rel* **vœu de p.** vow of poverty; **p. du sol** poorness of the soil

pavage [pavaʒ] NM **1** *(action)* paving; *(aux pavés ronds)* cobbling **2** *(revêtement)* paving; *(rond)* cobbles, cobblestones

pavane [pavan] NF *Mus* pavan(e)

pavaner (se) [səpavane] VPR to strut about

pavé [pave] N **1** *(morceau de grès)* paving stone; *(rond)* cobblestone; *Journ (encart)* block (of text); *Journ Fam (article)* prominent article; *Fam Péj (livre, thèse)* massive tome; *Fig* **un p. dans la mare** a bombshell; **jeter un p. dans la mare** to drop a bombshell; *Fig* **avoir un p. sur l'estomac** to have a weight on one's stomach; *Culin* **p. (de bœuf)** slab of beef; *Journ* **p. publicitaire** (large) display advertisement **2** *(revêtement)* pavement, paving; *(rond)* cobbles; *Fig* **le p. (rues)** the street, the streets; **brûler le p.** to tear along; *Fig* **tenir le haut du p.** to be at the top; *Fig* **céder le haut du p. à qn** to give pride of place to sb; **battre le p.** to loaf about the streets; **être sur le p.** to be on the street; **sous les pavés, la plage** = slogan dating from the 1968 student riots and referring both to the paving stones thrown at the police and to the ideal of a more fulfilling life beyond the confines of drab conformity **3** *Ordinat* keypad; **p. numérique** numeric keypad **4** *Typ* box **5** *Fam (dent)* tooth

pavement [pavmɑ̃] NM paving

paver [pave] VT to pave; *(avec des pavés ronds)* to cobble; **cour pavée** paved/cobbled

yard; *Fig* **l'enfer est pavé de bonnes intentions** the road to hell is paved with good intentions; *Can* **être pavé de monde** to be full of *or* packed with people

paveur [pavœr] NM paver

pavillon [pavijɔ̃] NM **1** *(petite maison)* (small) bungalow; **p. d'entrée** (gate) lodge; **p. de jardin** summerhouse, pavilion; **p. de chasse** hunting *or* shooting lodge **2** *(d'un hôpital)* pavilion, block, wing **3** *(partie évasée) (d'un Klaxon®, d'un haut-parleur, d'une sirène)* horn; *(d'un entonnoir)* mouth; *Mus (de cuivres)* bell; *Tél* **p. d'écouteur** earpiece; *Anat* **p. de l'oreille** auricle, pinna, external ear **4** *Naut (drapeau)* flag; **hisser *ou* arborer son p.** to hoist one's colours; **battre p. britannique** to fly the British flag; **baisser p.** to strike one's flag, to surrender; *Fig (céder)* to admit defeat, to give in **5** *Mil Arch* pavilion, tent **6** *Aut* roof, roof panel
▸▸ **p. de complaisance** flag of convenience; **p. de départ** Blue Peter; **p. de détresse** flag of distress; **p. noir** Jolly Roger; **p. de partance** Blue Peter; **p. de quarantaine** yellow flag

pavillonnaire [pavijɔnɛr] ADJ **banlieue p.** suburbia

pavois [pavwa] NM **1** *Naut (d'un navire)* bulwark **2** *Naut* **petit/grand p.** flags *(for dressing ship)*, dressing; **mettre *ou* hisser le grand p.** to dress over all **3** *Hist (grand bouclier)* (body) shield, pavis(e)

pavoiser [pavwaze] VT *(décorer) (rue, maison)* to deck with flags *or* bunting; *Naut (navire)* to dress
VI *(décorer)* to put out the flags; *Naut* to dress ship; *Fam (se réjouir)* to crow; *Fam* **il n'y a vraiment pas de quoi p.!** there's nothing to crow about!

pavot [pavo] NM *(fleur)* poppy; **p. somnifère** opium poppy; **tête de p.** poppyhead; **graine(s) de p.** poppy seed

payable [pɛjabl] ADJ payable; *Com* **p. à la livraison** payable on delivery; **p. à vue** payable at *or* on sight; **p. comptant** payable in cash; **p. à l'arrivée** payable on arrival; **p. à l'échéance** payable at maturity; **p. à la banque** payable at the bank; **p. à la commande** payable with order; **p. au porteur** payable to bearer

payant [pɛjɑ̃] ADJ *(qui paie) (hôte, élève)* paying; *(où il faut payer)* with charge for admission; **spectateur p.** ticket-holder who pays/paid (for admission); **spectacle p.** show with charge for admission; **l'entrée est payante** there is an admission charge *or* a charge for admission; *Fig* **affaire payante** *(bénéfique)* paying proposition; *Fig* **ça s'est avéré p.** it turned out to be worth it

paye [pɛj] NF = **paie**

payement [pɛjmɑ̃] NM = **paiement**

⸢PAYER⸣ [pɛje] *(je paye, je paie; je payerai, je paierai)* VT **1** *(somme)* to pay; **p. qn** to pay sb; **payez au porteur** pay to bearer; **tu l'as payé combien pour qu'il fasse tout cela?** how much did you pay him to do all that?; **je ne suis pas payé pour ça** that's not my job; **combien vous a-t-il fait p.?** how much did he charge you?; **elle ne nous/m'/etc a pas fait p. cher** she didn't charge a lot; **p. qn de ses services** to pay sb for his/her services; **trop payé** overpaid; **trop peu payé** underpaid; **bien/mal payé** well/badly paid; **ce travail est peu payé** this work isn't paid *or* doesn't pay very well; **se faire p.** to get *or* be paid; **il a accepté de nous aider mais il veut se faire p.** he has agreed to help us but he wants paying *or* he wants to be paid; **p. qn de paroles** *ou* **de mots** to put sb off with fine words; **il les méprise et il est payé de retour** he despises them and the feeling is mutual

2 *(acquitter, régler) (dette)* to pay, to settle, to discharge; **p. son loyer** to pay one's *or* the rent; **p. la note** to pay the bill; *Com* **p. un effet** to honour *or Am* honor a bill; **la prime de déplacement ne paie pas tous les frais de voyage** the relocation allowance doesn't cover all the travel costs; **congés payés** paid holidays; *Admin* **paid leave; tu as les congés payés?** do you get holiday pay?

3 *(acquérir contre de l'argent)* to pay for; **la viande a été payée** the meat's (been) paid for; **combien tu l'as payé?** how much did you pay for it?; **elle ne l'a pas payé très cher** she didn't pay a lot for it; **je ne vous fais pas p. le transport** I'm not charging you for transport; **je le lui ai payé cent euros** I paid him a hundred euros for it; **p. qch à qn** *(lui offrir)* to buy sth for sb; **ses parents lui paient tout ce qu'il veut** his parents pay for everything he wants, his parents buy him anything he wants; **elle va se le faire p. par son mari** she's going to get her husband to buy it for her; **p. le dîner à qn** to treat sb to dinner; **c'est moi qui paie la tournée** it's my round; **payé d'avance** prepaid; **port payé** post(age) paid; *Tél* **réponse payée** answer prepaid

4 *Fig (expier)* to pay for; **il a payé sa témérité de sa vie** he paid for his rashness with his life; **faire p. ses méfaits à qn** to bring sb to account; **vous me le paierez!** you'll pay for it!; *Fam* **je suis payé pour le savoir** I've learnt (it) the hard way; **il l'a payé cher** he paid dearly for it; **il paya cher son insolence** he paid dearly for his rudeness, his rudeness cost him

VI **1** *(verser de l'argent)* to pay; **vous payez comment?** how are you paying?, how would you like to pay?; **p. cash** *ou* **comptant** to pay cash; **p. en liquide/par carte (de crédit)** to pay (in) cash/by credit card; **p. par chèque** to pay by cheque *or Am* check; **p. à vue** to pay at sight; **p. de sa poche** to pay out of one's own pocket; **c'est toujours moi qui paie** I'm always the one who pays, it's always me who pays; **p. rubis sur l'ongle** to pay on the nail

2 **p. de ses dernières économies** to sacrifice the last of one's savings; *Fig* **p. de sa personne** to put oneself out; **il fallut p. d'audace** he had to be bold; **il ne paie pas de mine, mais il est doué** he doesn't look it, but he's very clever, he doesn't look very clever but he is

3 *(rapporter)* to pay; **le crime ne paie pas** crime doesn't pay; **la traduction en freelance, ça ne paie pas** freelance translation doesn't pay; **ça a payé** *(cette affaire)* it was worth it

VPR **se payer 1 voilà monsieur, payez-vous** here you are, take it out of that; *Fig* **se p. de mots** to talk a lot of fine words

2 *(s'offrir)* **je me suis payé une glace/une semaine de vacances** I treated myself to an ice cream/a week's holiday; **se p. le luxe de sortir deux fois par semaine** to treat oneself to two nights out a week; *Fig* **se p. le culot de partir sans régler ses dettes** to have the nerve to leave without paying one's debts; *Fig* **se p. la tête de qn** to make fun of sb; **je n'aime pas qu'on se paie ma tête** I don't like being made fun of; *Fam* **se p. un arbre/un mur** to crash into a tree/a wall; *Fam* **je me suis payé un bon rhume** I got a nasty cold; *Fam* **s'en p. (une tranche)** to have a good time; *Fam* **si il continue à m'énerver, celui-là, je vais me le p.!** if he carries on annoying me, I'm going to swing for him *or* thump him one!

payeur, -euse [pɛjœr, -øz] N payer; *Admin* pay clerk; *Mil* paymaster; **mauvais p.** bad payer

pays[1] [pei] NM **1** *(nation)* country; **un p. lointain** a faraway country *or* land; **l'Espagne, p.**

de la corrida Spain, land of the bullfight; **vi-siter des p. étrangers** to visit foreign countries *or* lands VOIR GRAMMAIRE A8; A28 **2** *(région)* region, district, locality; **voir du p.** to travel around; **p. du rêve** dreamland; **vous n'êtes donc pas du p.?** so you're not from these parts *or* from round here?; **être en p. de connaissance** to be among friends; *(sur un sujet)* to be on familiar *or* home ground; **vin de p.** *ou* **du p.** local wine; **miel/fruits du p.** locally produced honey/fruit; **c'est un gars/une coutume du p.** he's a local lad/it's a local custom; **revenir au p.** to go back home; **avoir le mal du p.** to be homesick; **p. de montagne(s)/lacs** mountain/lake country; **p. de chasse/pêche** hunting/fishing country **3** *Admin* = group of neighbouring communes which have joined together to promote distinctive aspects of the locality

▸▸ *UE* **p. candidat** applicant country; **p. de destination** country of destination; **p. développé** developed country; **p. émergent** newly industrialized country; **p. d'Europe centrale et orientale** Central and East European country; **p. d'Europe de l'Est** Eastern European country; **p. exportateur** exporting country; **p. hors communauté** non-EC country; **p. importateur** importing country; *UE* **p. in** = EU member state that has adopted the euro; **p. industrialisé** industrialized *or* developed country; **p. membre** member state; **p. d'origine** country of origin; *UE* **p. out** = EU member state that has not adopted the euro; *UE* **p. pré-in** = EU member state that has not adopted the euro; **p. de provenance** country of export; **p. riche** affluent country; **p. signataire** *(d'un accord)* signatory country; **p. sous-développé** developing country; *UE* **p. tiers** third *or* non-EU country; **p. du tiers-monde** Third World country; **p. en voie de développement** developing country; **p. en voie d'industrialisation** industrializing country

pays², **payse** [pei, peiz] N *Région* fellow-countryman, f fellow-countrywoman; **nous sommes p.** we're from the same area *or* place

paysage [peizaʒ] NM **1** landscape; *(vue)* scenery; *Fig (ensemble)* scene, set-up; **cette région offre de merveilleux paysages** this area has marvellous scenery; *Fam* **cela fait bien dans le p.** it looks good; **le p. urbain** the urban landscape; *Fig* **le p. audiovisuel français** the broadcasting scene *or* set-up in France; *Fig* **le p. politique** the political scene **2** *Beaux-Arts* landscape (painting) **3** *Ordinat* **mode** *ou* **format p.** landscape mode; **imprimer qch en p.** to print sth in landscape

paysager, -ère [peizaʒe, -ɛr] ADJ *(jardin, espace)* landscaped; **bureau p.** open-plan office

paysagiste [peizaʒist] N **1** *(peintre)* landscape painter **2** *(jardinier)* **p.** landscape gardener

paysan, -anne [peizã, -an] ADJ *(vie, famille)* peasant; *(façon de vivre, manières)* rustic, country

▪ N (small) farmer, *Péj* peasant, *Hum Péj* rustic; *Hist* peasant; *Agr* **p. (propriétaire)** farmer; *Hist* **les paysans** the peasants, the peasantry

paysannerie [peizanri] NF *Hist* peasantry

Pays-Bas (les) [lepeibɑ] NMPL the Netherlands

PC [pese] NM **1** *(abrév* **parti communiste)** CP **2 poste de commandement 3** *Ordinat* PC
▪ NF *Fin (abrév* **pièce de caisse)** cash voucher

PCC, Pcc [pesese] *abrév* **pour copie conforme**

PCF [peseɛf] NM *(abrév* **parti communiste français)** French Communist Party

PCG [peseʒe] NM *Compta (abrév* **plan comptable général)** chart of accounts

PCS [peseɛs] NFPL *(abrév* **professions et catégories sociales)** socio-economic categories

PCV [peseve] NM *Tél (abrév* **payable chez vous) (appel en) P.** reverse-charge call, *Am* collect call; **appeler en P., faire un appel en P.** to make a reverse-charge call, *Am* to call collect

pd *Com abrév* **port dû**

PDG [pedeʒe] NM INV *(abrév* **Président-directeur général)** chairman and managing director, CEO, chief executive officer, *Am* President

PDM [pedeɛm] NF *(abrév* **part de marché)** market share

PDV [pedeve] NM *(abrév* **point de vente)** POS

PEA [peøa] NM *Fin (abrév* **plan d'épargne en actions)** investment trust, *Br* ≃ PEP

péage [peaʒ] NM **1** *(droit)* toll; **pont à p.** toll bridge; *Hist* **barrière de p.** turnpike, tollgate **2** *(installation)* *Aut* tollbooth; *Hist* tollhouse **3** *TV* **chaîne (de télévision) à p.** pay channel; **p. à la consommation** pay per view, PPV

péagiste [peaʒist] N *Aut* tollbooth attendant

peau, peaux [po] NF **1** *(derme)* skin; **avoir la p. blanche/noire** to be white/black; **une belle p.** a beautiful skin *or* complexion; **avoir la p. grasse/sèche/mixte** to have greasy/dry/combination skin; **peaux mortes** dead skin; *Fig* **p. de pêche** (soft and) velvety skin; **avoir une p. de pêche** to have (soft and) velvety skin; *Fig* **avoir la p. dure** *(d'une personne)* to have a thick skin, to be thick-skinned; **ce genre de croyances stupides a la p. dure** this sort of stupid belief takes a long time to die out; *Fig* **attraper** *ou* **prendre qn par la p. du cou** *ou* **du dos** *ou* *Fam* **des fesses** *ou* *Vulg* **du cul** to grab *or* take sb by the scruff of the neck; *Fig* **faire p. neuve** *(d'une personne)* to turn over a new leaf; *(d'une entreprise, d'un parti etc)* to get a new image, to modernize itself; **elle n'a que la p. et les os** she's nothing but skin and bone; **je ne voudrais pas être dans sa p.** I wouldn't like to be in his shoes; **se mettre dans la p. de qn** to put oneself in sb's shoes; *Théâtre* **entrer dans la p. d'un personnage** to get right inside a character, to get under the skin of a character; *Fig* **j'ai ça dans la p.** it's in my blood; *Fig Fam* **avoir qn dans la p.** to be crazy about sb; *Fam* **se sentir bien/mal dans sa p.** to feel/not to feel good about oneself; *Fam* **craindre pour/tenir à sa p.** to fear for/value one's life; *Fam* **risquer sa p.** to risk one's neck *or* one's life; *Fam* **sauver sa p.** to save one's skin *or* bacon; *Fam* **se faire trouer** *ou* **crever la p.** to get bumped off, to get killed; *Fam* **recevoir** *ou* **prendre douze balles dans la p.** to be shot by a firing squad; *Fam* **faire la p. à qn** to kill sb; *Fam* **j'aurai sa p.!** I'll get *or* have him!; *Fam* **la p.!, p. de balle** *ou* *Vulg* **de zébi!** nothing doing!, no way!; *Fam* **ce qu'on nous a donné? p. de balle!** what did we get? *Br* bugger all! *or* **surtout** *Am* zilch!; *Arg Vieilli* **vieille p.** old hag **2** *(dépouille)* *(d'un animal)* skin, hide; *(d'un animal à fourrure)* pelt, fur; **p. de lapin** rabbit skin, cony(skin); **vêtu de peaux de bête** dressed in (animal) skins **3** *(cuir)* hide, leather; **p. de chamois** shammy (leather), chamois leather; **p. de chevreau** kid; **p. de daim** buckskin; **p. de mouton** sheepskin; **p. de requin** shagreen; **p. de serpent** snakeskin; **p. de veau** calfskin, box calf **4** *(de fruit)* skin, peel; **enlever la p. d'un fruit** to peel a fruit; *aussi Fig* **p. de banane** banana skin; **p. d'orange** orange peel; *Fig* orange-peel skin **5** *(pellicule)* *(du lait)* skin **6** *(autour des ongles)* hangnail

▸▸ *Fam* **p. d'âne** diploma; *Fig Fam* **p. de cha-**

grin diminishing asset; **diminuer comme une p. de chagrin** to dwindle away; *Arg* **p. de vache: c'est une p. de vache** *(cet homme)* he's a bastard; *(cette femme)* she's a cow *or* a bitch

peaucier [posje] ADJ, NM *Anat* (muscle) **p.** platysma

peaufiner [pofine] VT to clean with a shammy leather; *Fig Fam (fignoler) (texte)* to polish up, to add the final touches to

Peau-Rouge, *pl* **Peaux-Rouges** ADJ, N *Vieilli (amérindien)* Red Indian, redskin

peausserie [posri] NF **1** *(commerce)* skin trade **2** *(marchandise)* leatherwear

peaussier [posje] NM skinner, skin dresser

pébroc, pébroque [pebrɔk] NM *Fam* umbrella, *Br* brolly

pécari [pekari] NM peccary

peccadille [pekadij] NF peccadillo

pechblende [pɛʃblɛ̃d] NF *Minér* pitchblende

pêche¹ [pɛʃ] NF **1** *(fruit)* peach; **p.-abricot, p. jaune** yellow peach; **p. blanche** white peach; **p. Melba** peach Melba **2** *Fam (coup)* clout, blow; **se prendre une p.** to get a clout **3** *Fam* **se fendre la p.** *(rire)* to split one's sides (laughing); *(s'amuser)* to have a good laugh **4** *Fam (forme)* feeling of being on top of the world; **avoir la p.** to be feeling on top of the world, to be on top form; **ça va te donner la p.** it'll make you feel on top of the world
▪ ADJ INV peach(-coloured), *Am* peach(-colored)

pêche² NF **1** *(activité)* fishing; **aller à la p.** to go fishing; **p. à la truite** trout fishing; **p. aux crevettes** shrimping; **grande p.** deep-sea fishing; **canne à p.** fishing rod **2** *(produits pêchés)* catch; **faire une heureuse** *ou* **bonne p.** to get a good haul **3** *(endroit)* fishing ground(s); **p. gardée** restricted fishing area; **p. privée** private fishing ground

▸▸ **p. côtière** coastal *or* inshore fishing; **p. au large** deep-sea fishing; **p. à la ligne** angling; **la p. miraculeuse** *Bible* the miraculous draught of fishes; *(à la fête foraine)* ≃ the lucky dip; **p. à la mouche** fly fishing

péché [peʃe] NM sin, *Fml* transgression; **les sept péchés capitaux** the seven deadly sins; **vivre dans le p.** *Rel* to live in a state of sin, to lead a sinful life; *Hum (de concubins)* to live in sin; **à tout p. miséricorde** there is no sin that cannot be forgiven; *Fam* **ce n'est pas un p.!** it's not a crime!

▸▸ **p. de jeunesse** youthful indiscretion; **p. mignon: les éclairs au chocolat, c'est son p. mignon** chocolate éclairs are his weakness; **p. mortel** mortal sin; **le p. originel** original sin

pécher [peʃe] VI (je pèche, n. péchons; je pécherai) to sin, *Fml* to transgress; **p. par orgueil** to commit the sin of pride; **il pèche par excès de timidité/trop d'humilité** he is excessively shy/humble; **p. par manque de confiance** to lack sufficient confidence; **cette enquête pèche sur un point** the inquiry falls down on one point; **p. par excès/défaut** to exceed/fall short of what is required; **p. par omission** to sin by omission; **p. contre l'honnêteté** to act dishonestly; **p. contre le bon goût** to break the rules of good taste

pêcher¹ [peʃe] NM peach tree

pêcher² VT **1** *(truite etc)* to fish for; **p. le corail** to dive for coral; **p. la baleine** to hunt whales, to go whaling **2** *Fam (trouver)* **où avez-vous (été) péché cela?** where did you pick that up?, where did you get hold of that?; **je ne sais pas où elle a (été) péché que nous allions nous marier** I don't know where she got hold of the idea that we're getting married
▪ VI to fish, to go fishing; **p. à la ligne** to go

angling; **p. à la mouche** to go fly-fishing; **p. en mer** to go sea fishing; *Fig* **p. en eau trouble** to fish in troubled waters

pêcherie [peʃri] NF fishery, fishing ground

pêcheur, pécheresse [peʃœr, peʃrɛs] *Rel* N sinner, *Fml* transgressor
ADJ sinful

pêcheur, -euse [peʃœr, -øz] N fisherman, *f* fisherwoman; **p. à la ligne** angler; **p. de baleines** whaler; **p. de perles** pearl diver
ADJ **bateau p.** fishing boat

pêchu [peʃy] ADJ *Fam* on (top) form, full of go

pécloter [peklɔte] VI *Suisse Fam* **1** *(être en mauvaise santé)* to be in a bad way **2** *(mal fonctionner)* to play up

PECO [peko] *(abrév* **pays d'Europe centrale et orientale)** CEEC

pécore [pekɔr] *Fam* N *(paysan)* yokel, peasant, *Am* hick
NF *Fam* silly stuck-up girl/woman

pectine [pɛktin] NF pectin

pectique [pɛktik] ADJ *(acide)* pectic

pectoral, -ale, -aux, -ales [pɛktɔral, -o] ADJ *(muscle, nageoire etc)* pectoral; *Méd* **sirop p.** expectorant; *Méd* **pâte pectorale** cough lozenge
NM *Anat* pectoral muscle; **travailler ses pectoraux** to work on one's pecs

pécule [pekyl] NM **1** *(économies)* savings, nest egg **2** *Mil, Naut* gratuity *(on discharge)*

pécuniaire [pekynjɛr] ADJ *(avantage)* financial, *Fml* pecuniary; *(position)* financial

pécuniairement [pekynjɛrmɑ̃] ADV financially

PED [peəde] NM *(abrév* **pays en voie de développement)** DC

pédagogie [pedagɔʒi] NF pedagogy, pedagogics; **manquer de p.** to lack teaching skills

pédagogique [pedagɔʒik] ADJ *(voyage, sortie etc)* educational; *(méthode)* teaching, *Fml* pedagogical

pédagogiquement [pedagɔʒikmɑ̃] ADV pedagogically

pédagogue [pedagɔg] N educationalist, *Fml, Arch* pedagogue

pédale [pedal] NF **1** *(de vélo, de voiture, de piano etc)* pedal; *Tech (de tour)* pedal, treadle; **appuyer sur les pédales** *(à vélo)* to pedal hard; **p. d'embrayage** clutch pedal; **p. d'accélérateur** accelerator pedal; **p. de frein** brake pedal; *Fam* **perdre les pédales** to get all mixed up; *(s'affoler)* to lose one's head, to get in a tizzy; *Fam* **s'emmêler les pédales** to get all mixed up, to get hopelessly lost **2** *Mus* **(note de) p.** pedal (note); *Fig Fam* **mettre la p. douce** to go easy **3** *Fam Péj (homosexuel)* queer, poof(ter); **il est de la p.** he's queer

pédaler [pedale] VI **1** to pedal **2** *Fam* **p. dans la choucroute** *ou* **la semoule** to get nowhere

pédaleur, -euse [pedalœr, -øz] N pedaller

pédalier [pedalje] NM **1** *(de vélo)* crank gear **2** *(clavier d'orgue)* pedal board

Pédalo® [pedalo] NM pedal boat, pedalo

pédant, -ante [pedɑ̃, -ɑ̃t] N pedant
ADJ pedantic

pédanterie [pedɑ̃tri] NF pedantry

pédantesque [pedɑ̃tɛsk] ADJ pedantic

pédantisme [pedɑ̃tism] NM pedantry

pédé [pede] *Fam Péj* ADJ queer, *Br* bent; **p. comme un phoque** as bent as a nine-bob note *or* as a three-pound note, *Am* as queer as a three-dollar bill
NM *(homosexuel)* queer, poof(ter)

pédégé [pedeʒe] NM *Hum* MD, *Am* CEO

pédéraste [pederast] NM **1** pederast **2** *(homosexuel)* homosexual

pédérastie [pederasti] NF **1** pederasty **2** *(homosexualité)* homosexuality

pédestre [pedɛstr] ADJ *(voyage)* on foot; **chemin p.** footpath; **randonnée p.** hike

pédiatre [pedjatr] N *Méd* paediatrician, *Am* pediatrician

pédiatrie [pedjatri] NF *Méd* paediatrics, *Am* pediatrics

pedibus [pedibys] ADV *Fam Hum* **p. (cum jambis)** on foot, on Shanks's pony *or Am* mare

pédicelle [pedisɛl] NM *Biol, Bot* pedicel, pedicle

pédicule [pedikyl] NM *Biol, Anat* pedicle, peduncle

pédicure [pedikyr] N chiropodist

pédieux, -ieuse [pedjø, -jøz] ADJ *Anat* pedal

pedigree [pedigre] NM *(d'un animal)*, *Fig (d'une personne)* pedigree

pédomètre [pedɔmɛtr] NM pedometer

pédoncule [pedɔ̃kyl] NM *Biol* peduncle

pédophile [pedɔfil] ADJ paedophile, *Am* pedophile

pédophilie [pedɔfili] NF paedophilia, *Am* pedophilia

pedzouille [pɛdzuj] NM *Fam* peasant, country bumpkin, yokel, *Am* hick

PEE [peəə] NM *Fin (abrév* **plan d'épargne d'entreprise)** employee share *or Am* stock ownership plan

peeling [piliŋ] NM *(gommage)* facial scrub; *Méd* exfoliation treatment; **se faire un p.** to give oneself a facial scrub; *Méd* **se faire faire un p.** to have one's skin peeled

pègre [pɛgr] NF **la p.** the underworld

peignage [pɛɲaʒ] NM *Tex* carding, combing

peigne [pɛɲ] NM **1** *(démêloir, barrette)* comb; **p. fin** fine-tooth comb; *Fig* **passer qch au p. fin** to go through sth with a fine-tooth comb; **se donner un coup de p.** to run a comb through one's hair, to give one's hair a comb; **sale comme un p.** filthy **2** *Tex (pour la laine)* card, comb; *(pour le chanvre)* hackle; **p. de métier à tisser** reed **3** *(mollusque)* pecten, scallop
ADJ *Can Fam Péj (avare)* stingy

peigné [peɲe] ADJ **1** *(personne)* combed; **bien p.** *(personne)* well-groomed; *(cheveux)* tidy; **mal p.** *(personne)* unkempt; *(cheveux)* tousled **2** *Tex (fil)* worsted
NM worsted (yarn)

peigne-cul, *pl* **peigne-culs** NM *très Fam Péj* creep

peignée [peɲe] NF **1** *Tex (de laine, de lin, de chanvre)* cardful **2** *Fam (raclée)* thrashing, good hiding

peigner [peɲe] VT **1** *(coiffer) (cheveux)* to comb; **p. un enfant** to comb a child's hair; *Fig Fam* **p. la girafe** to waste one's time **2** *Tex (laine)* to card, to comb; *(chanvre)* to hackle
VPR **se peigner** to comb one's hair

peignoir [peɲwar] NM **1** *(vêtement d'intérieur)* housecoat; *(robe de chambre)* dressing gown; **p. (de bain)** bath robe **2** *(chez le coiffeur)* cape, overall

peinard [penar] ADJ *Fam (poste, situation)* cushy; **rester p.** to take it *or* things easy; **tiens-toi p.** keep quiet, keep your nose clean; **il est bien p.** he's having an easy time of it; **ils sont peinards dans leur nouvelle baraque** they're nice and comfortable in their new place; **il a trouvé un coin p. pour pioncer** he found a quiet corner to crash out
ADV *Fam (tranquillement)* in peace, peacefully; **inutile de se presser, on va y aller p.** there's no point in hurrying, we'll take our time

peindre [pɛ̃dr] *(prp* **peignant;** *pp* **peint;** *pr ind* **je peins, il peint,** *n.* **peignons;** *impf* **je peignais;** *p hist* **je peignis;** *fu* **je peindrai)** VT to paint; **p. qch en vert** to paint sth green; **p. au pinceau/au rouleau/à la brosse** to paint with a brush/a roller/a brush; **papier peint** wallpaper; *Fig* **elle peint la situation avec justesse** she portrays *or* depicts the situation accurately; *Fig* **p. tout en rose** to paint everything in rosy colours; *Suisse* **p. le diable sur la muraille** to be pessimistic
VI to paint
VPR **se peindre** *Fig* **l'innocence se peint sur son visage** innocence is written on his face

PEINE [pɛn]

| punishment **1** ▪ penalty **1** ▪ sorrow **2** ▪ trouble **3** ▪ difficulty **4** ▪ hardly *(à peine)* **5** |

NF **1** *(sanction)* punishment, penalty; **p. capitale** capital punishment; **la p. de mort** the death penalty; **condamné à la p. capitale** *ou* **de mort** sentenced to death; **p. de prison** prison sentence; **p. incompressible** sentence without remission; **p. de substitution** non-custodial sentence; **double p.** double punishment *(in the form of a prison sentence followed by expulsion from the country)*; **défense d'entrer sous p. d'amende** *ou* **de poursuites** trespassers will be prosecuted; **pour la** *ou* **ta p., tu vas descendre la poubelle** (just) for that, you can take the bin down

2 *(chagrin)* sorrow, sadness; *(tourment)* distress; **j'ai beaucoup de p.** I feel very upset, I'm very distressed; **faire de la p. à qn** to upset *or* distress sb, to cause sb distress; **je m'en suis séparé avec beaucoup de p.** I was very sorry to part with it; **cela fait p. à voir** it's painful *or* distressing to see; **elle fait p. à voir** she's a pitiful sight; **être dans la p.** to be in distress; **p. de cœur** heartache; **raconter ses peines de cœur à qn** to tell sb about one's troubled love life

3 *(effort)* trouble, pains; **se donner de la p. pour faire qch** to take the trouble *or* take pains to do sth; **se donner beaucoup de p. pour faire qch** to go to a lot of trouble *or* take great pains to do sth; **ils se sont donné beaucoup de p. pour leurs enfants** they went to a lot of trouble *or* they really put themselves out for their children; **ils se sont donné beaucoup de p. pour la décoration** they took a lot of trouble with *or* over the decoration; **en vous donnant un peu de p., vous y arriverez** with a little effort, you'll manage it; **donnez-vous** *ou* **prenez la p. d'entrer** please come in; **si au moins tu te donnais la p. de lui en parler** if you at least made the effort to talk to him about it; **ne vous donnez pas cette p.** don't bother; **se mettre en p. pour qn/qch** to put oneself out *or* put oneself to a lot of trouble for sb/sth; **c'est p. perdue** it's a waste of time; **elle n'est pas au bout de ses peines** her troubles aren't over yet; **en être pour sa p.** to have nothing to show for one's trouble; **il lui a donné 15 euros pour sa p.** he gave him 15 euros for his trouble; **cela vaut la p. d'essayer** it's worth trying; **cela vaut la p. que tu viennes** it's (well) worth your while coming; **ça ne vaut pas la p. qu'on y aille à trois** it's not worth all three of us going; **cela ne vaut pas la p.** it's not worth it, it's not worth the trouble; **non, ce n'est pas la p.** no, don't bother; **ce n'est pas la p. d'aller voir cette pièce/de lui en parler** it's not worth *or* it's a waste of time going to see that play/ talking to him about it; **ce n'est pas la p. de changer de robe** you needn't bother to change *or* it's not worth changing your dress; *Iron* **c'était bien la p. de venir!** we might just as well have stayed at home!; *Iron* **c'était bien la p. que je me dérange!** I'm glad I went to so much trouble!

4 *(difficulté)* difficulty; **j'ai eu toutes les peines du monde à le trouver** I had a real or terrible job finding it; **elle a de la p. à parler** *(après une opération)* she has difficulty speaking, she finds it difficult to speak; **elle a de la p. à en parler** it's difficult for her to talk about it, she finds it difficult to talk about; **j'ai (de la) p. à croire que ...** + *sub* I find it hard to believe that ...; **avoir p. à retenir ses larmes** to have difficulty holding back one's tears; **ne jamais être en p. de trouver une excuse** never to be at a loss for an excuse; **elle serait bien en p. de t'expliquer comment ça marche** she'd be hard put or hard pushed to explain or she'd have great difficulty explaining to you how it works; **elle n'est pas en p. pour trouver des amis avec qui sortir** she has no trouble or difficulty finding friends to go out with; **avec p.** with difficulty; **à grand-p.** with great difficulty; **faire qch sans p.** to do sth without difficulty or easily; **l'anglais sans p.** English made easy, English without tears; **cela n'a pas été sans p.** it was no easy matter; **sans p. aucune** without any difficulty or trouble

5 **à p.** hardly, barely, scarcely; **on tient à p. debout, tellement il y a de vent!** it's so windy, we can hardly or barely or scarcely stay on our feet!; **c'est à p. si je le connais** I hardly know him; **il est à p. 3 heures** it's barely 3 o'clock; **à p. étions-nous sortis qu'il se mit à pleuvoir** we had only just gone out when it began to rain, we were scarcely out of the door before it started to rain; **j'arrive à p.** I've only just arrived, I've arrived just this minute; **à p. arrivée, elle se mit à se plaindre** no sooner had she arrived than she began to complain; *Iron Fam* **à p.!** hardly!, not much! **SEE GRAMMAR B62**

peiner [pene] VT *(quelqu'un)* to upset, to sadden, to distress; **cette nouvelle m'a beaucoup peiné** I was very upset or saddened by the news; **d'un ton peiné** in a sad tone

VI to toil, to labour, *Am* to labor; *Aut (d'un moteur)* to labour; **il peinait sur son travail** he was toiling at or over his work; **p. à marcher** to have trouble or difficulty walking; **je peine à comprendre son point de vue** I find it hard to understand his point of view

peintre [pɛtr] NM **1** *(artiste)* p. painter, artist; **une femme p.** a woman artist **2** *(ouvrier, artisan)* **p. en bâtiment(s)** *(house)* painter; **p.(-)décorateur** painter and decorator; *TV etc* scenic artist **3** *Fig* portrayer; **cet auteur est un p. de la société parisienne** this author is a portrayer of or portrays Parisian society

peinture [pɛtyr] NF **1** *(art, action)* painting; **musée de p.** art or picture gallery; **faire de la p.** to paint **2** *(tableau)* painting, picture; *Fig* **p. des mœurs de l'époque** portrayal or description of the customs of the period; *Fig* **je ne peux pas le voir en p.** I can't stand the sight of him **3** *(matière)* paint; **attention p. fraîche!, attention à la p.!** wet paint; **p. à la colle** size; **p. en détrempe** distemper; **p. mate** matt emulsion (paint); **p. brillante** ou **laquée** gloss (paint); *Péj* **c'est un vrai pot de p.!** she wears make-up an inch thick! **4** *(surface peinte)* paintwork; **il faudra refaire les peintures** the paintwork will have to be done; **c'est moi qui ai fait la p. de la cuisine** I did the paintwork in the kitchen

▶▶ **p. en bâtiments** *(house)* painting; **p. à l'eau** watercolour or *Am* watercolor (painting); **p. figurative** figurative painting; **p. à l'huile** oil painting; **p. au pistolet** spray painting

peinturer [pɛtyre] VT *Can* to paint

peinturlurer [pɛtyrlyre] VT *Fam (toile, mur, morceau de papier etc)* to daub (with paint)

péjoratif, -ive [peʒɔratif, -iv] ADJ *(mot, sens)*

pejorative; *(remarque, ton)* disparaging
NM pejorative

péjoration [peʒɔrasjɔ̃] NF pejoration

péjorativement [peʒɔrativmɑ̃] ADV pejoratively

Pékin [pekɛ̃] N Peking, Beijing

pékin [pekɛ̃] NM **1** *Tex* Pekin (fabric) **2** *Mil Fam* civilian; **être en p.** to be in civvies **3** *Fam (individu)* guy, *Br* bloke

pékinois, -oise [pekinwa, -waz] ADJ of/from Peking or Beijing
NM **1** *(chien)* pekin(g)ese, *Fam* peke **2** *(dialecte)* Mandarin (Chinese), Pekinese
N **P.** Pekin(g)ese

PEL NM *(abrév* **plan épargne-logement)** *Br* ≃ building society account, *Am* ≃ savings and loan association account

pelade [pəlad] NF *Méd* alopecia

pelage [pəlaʒ] NM *(d'un animal)* coat, fur

pélagique [pelaʒik] ADJ pelagic, pelagian

pelant [pəlɑ̃] ADJ *Belg Fam (agaçant)* annoying; *(assommant)* boring; **c'est p.!** *(agaçant)* it's a real pain in the neck or a real nuisance!; *(assommant)* it's a real drag!

pélargonium [pelargɔnjɔm] NM pelargonium, *Fam* geranium

pelé, -ée [pəle] ADJ *(personne, fourrure)* bald; *Fig (paysage)* bare; *(tissu)* threadbare
N *Fam* baldie; **il n'y avait que trois pelés et un tondu** there was hardly anyone there

pêle-mêle [pɛlmɛl] ADV higgledy-piggledy; **tout est entassé p.** everything is piled up higgledy-piggledy or any old how; **mettre tout p.** to jumble everything up
NM INV jumble; *(cadre)* multiple (photo) frame

peler [pəle] VT *(légumes, fruit)* to peel, to skin
VI *(de la peau etc)* to peel; **j'ai le nez qui pèle** my nose is peeling; *Fig Fam* **je pèle (de froid)** I'm freezing (cold)
VPR **se peler** to peel; **la pêche se pèle facilement** peaches peel easily or are easy to peel; *Fig Fam* **on se pèle (de froid)** it's freezing (cold)

pèlerin, -ine[1] [pɛlrɛ̃, -in] N pilgrim
NM **1** *(requin)* **p.** basking shark **2** *(faucon)* **p.** peregrine falcon **3** *Fam (individu)* guy, *Br* bloke

pèlerinage [pɛlrinaʒ] NM *(action)* pilgrimage; *(lieu)* place of pilgrimage; **faire un p.** to go on a pilgrimage

pèlerine[2] [pɛlrin] NF cape; *(à capuche)* hooded cape

pélican [pelikɑ̃] NM pelican

pelisse [pəlis] NF pelisse

pellagre [pelagr] NF *Méd* pellagra

pelle [pɛl] NF *(d'enfant, de jardinier)* spade; *(pour charbon, cendres)* shovel; *(pour céréales, noix etc)* scoop; **ramasser qch à la p.** to shovel sth up; *Fig* **à la p.** by the bucketful; *Fig* **il y en a à la p., on les ramasse à la p.** there's masses or loads (of it); *(nombre)* there are masses or loads (of them); **remuer/ramasser l'argent à la p.** to be rolling in money/raking it in; **ça ne se trouve pas à la p.** **des mecs comme lui** guys like him are few and far between; *Fam* **ramasser** ou **se prendre une p.** to fall flat on one's face; *Fam* **rouler une p. à qn** to French-kiss sb; **ils étaient en train de se rouler une p.** they had their tongues down each other's throats
▶▶ **p. à charbon** coal shovel; *Constr etc* **p. mécanique** mechanical shovel; *(drague)* shovel dredger; **p. à ordures** dustpan; **p. à tarte** cake or tart slice

pelle-pioche, *pl* **pelles-pioches** NF combined pick and shovel

pelletée [pɛlte] NF shovelful, spadeful; *Fig Fam* **une p. d'injures** a stream of insults

pelleter [pɛlte] VT (**je pellette** [pɛlt], *n.* **pelletons; je pelletterai** [pɛltre]) to shovel (up); *Can* **p. des nuages** to dream up idle schemes

pelleterie [pɛltri] NF **1** *(fourrure)* pelt **2** *(confection)* fur making; *(commerce)* fur trade, furriery

pelleteuse [pɛltøz] NF *Constr* mechanical shovel

pelletier, -ière [pɛltje, -jer] N furrier

pellicule [pelikyl] NF **1** *(de glace, peinture)* thin layer; *(sur un liquide)* film **2** *(enveloppe du raisin)* grape skin **3** *Cin, TV, Phot* film; **p. en bobine** roll film; **p. inversible** reversal film **4** *(dans les cheveux)* **pellicules** dandruff; **avoir des pellicules** to have dandruff; **shampooing contre les pellicules** (anti-)dandruff shampoo

pelloche [pelɔʃ] NF *Fam* film (for camera)

pélo [pelo] NM *Fam (individu)* guy, *Br* bloke

Péloponnèse (le) [lapelɔpɔnɛz] NM the Peloponnese

pelotage [p(ə)lɔtaʒ] NM *Fam* petting

pelotari [p(ə)lɔtari] NM pelota player

pelote [p(ə)lɔt] NF **1** *(de laine, de ficelle)* ball; **p. (à épingles)** pincushion; *Fig Fam* **faire sa p.** to make one's pile; *(aux dépens d'autrui)* to feather one's nest; *Fig* **avoir les nerfs en p.** to be on edge, to be nervy; *Vieilli Fam* **envoyer qn aux pelotes** to send sb packing **2** *Can (boule)* **p. de neige** snowball **3** *Sport* **p. (basque)** pelota

peloter [p(ə)lɔte] *Fam* VT to feel up, to touch up; **elle s'est fait p. dans le métro** somebody groped her in the metro
VPR **se peloter** to pet

peloteur, -euse [p(ə)lɔtœr, -øz] N **1** *Fam* **c'est un sacré p.** he's got wandering hands, he can't keep his hands to himself **2** *Tex (ouvrier)* ball winder
NF *Tex* **peloteuse** *(machine)* balling machine

peloton [p(ə)lɔtɔ̃] NM **1** *(de laine, de ficelle etc)* (small) ball **2** *(de gens)* group; *(d'abeilles, de chenilles)* cluster; *Sport* **le p.** the pack, the bunch; **le p. de tête** *Sport* the leaders, the leading bunch, the front pack; *Fig* the front runners, the leaders **3** *Mil (de cavalerie)* troop; *(de tanks)* platoon
▶▶ **p. de discipline** punishment squad; **p. d'exécution** firing squad; **p. d'instruction** training unit; **p. de punition** punishment squad

pelotonner [p(ə)lɔtɔne] VT *(laine, ficelle etc)* to wind into a ball
VPR **se pelotonner** to curl up; *(pour avoir chaud)* to huddle up; **se p. dans un fauteuil** to curl up in an armchair; **se p. contre la cheminée** to huddle up to the fire; **se p. dans les bras de qn** to snuggle up in sb's arms

pelouse [p(ə)luz] NF lawn; *Courses de chevaux* **la p.** the public enclosure; **'p. interdite'** *(sur panneau)* 'keep off the grass'

peluche [p(ə)lyʃ] NF **1** *Tex* plush; **un jouet en p., une p.** a soft or cuddly toy **2** *(flocon, poil)* *(piece of)* fluff; **mon pull est plein de peluches** my sweater is all pilled

peluché [p(ə)lyʃe] ADJ *(tissu)* pilled

pelucher [p(ə)lyʃe] VI *(d'un tissu usé)* to pill

pelucheux, -euse [p(ə)lyʃø, -øz] ADJ fluffy

pelure [p(ə)lyr] NF **1** *(peau) (de fruit)* peel, skin; *(de légumes)* peelings; **p. d'oignon** *(vin)* dark rosé wine; **(papier) p.** onion skin **2** *Fam (vêtement)* coat

pelvien, -ienne [pɛlvjɛ̃, -jɛn] ADJ *Anat* pelvic

pelvis [pɛlvis] NM *Anat* pelvis

pénal, -ale, -aux, -ales [penal, -o] ADJ *(code)* penal; **clause pénale** penalty clause

pénalement [penalmɑ̃] ADV penally

pénalisation [penalizasjɔ̃] NF *Sport* penalization, penalizing; **point de p.** penalty point

pénaliser [penalize] VT *(punir, désavantager)* to penalize; **cette mesure pénalise les petits épargnants** this measure penalizes small savers

pénalité [penalite] NF *(Jur, Sp etc (sanction)* penalty; *Ftbl* **coup de pied de p.** penalty (kick); **donner le coup de pied de p.** to take the penalty (kick); *Fin* **p. de retard** late payment penalty; *(pour livraison tardive)* late delivery penalty; *Fin* **p. libératoire** full and final penalty payment

penalty, *pl* **penalties** [penalti] NM *Ftbl* penalty; **point de p.** penalty point; **tirer/marquer/ manquer un p.** to take/score/miss a penalty; **siffler un p.** to award *or* give a penalty

pénates [penat] NMPL *(dieux domestiques)* penates; *Fig* **regagner ses p.** to return home

penaud [pəno] ADJ sheepish; **d'un air p.** sheepishly

penchant [pɑ̃ʃɑ̃] NM **1** *(tendance)* propensity (**pour qch** for sth), tendency; *(préférence)* leaning (**vers** towards), penchant (**vers** for); **p. à faire qch** *(tendance)* tendency to do sth; *(préférence)* inclination to do sth, penchant for doing sth; **un p. pour la boisson** a fondness *or* partiality for drink; **avoir un p. pour qn** to be fond of sb **2** *Arch, Litt (pente)* slope; **p. de la colline** hillside

penché [pɑ̃ʃe] ADJ *(incliné)* leaning; *(écriture)* sloping, slanting; **la Tour penchée de Pise** the Leaning Tower of Pisa; *Fig* **prendre des airs penchés** to look pensive; **d'un air p.** pensively

pencher [pɑ̃ʃe] VT *(assiette, bouilloire, verre etc)* to tilt; **p. la tête en avant/en arrière** to bend *or* lean forward/backwards; **p. la tête à droite** to lean one's head to the right

VI *(s'écarter de la position verticale)* to lean (over); **le navire penche sur le côté** the ship is listing; **le tableau penche vers la droite** the picture is tilting to the right; *Fig* **faire p. la balance** to tip the scales; *Fig* **p. vers** *ou* **pour qch** to incline *or* lean towards sth; *Fig* **p. pour une solution** to prefer *or* favour *or Am* favor a solution; **il pencherait plutôt pour des vacances en Italie** he would prefer to take his holidays in Italy

VPR **se pencher** to lean over, to bend over; **p. en avant/en arrière/sur le côté** to bend *or* lean forward/backwards/to the side; **se p. (en** *ou* **au) dehors** to lean out; **se p. à** *ou* **par la fenêtre** to lean out (of) the window; *Fig* **se p. sur un problème/cas** to look into a problem/case

pendable [pɑ̃dabl] ADJ *(coup, histoire)* outrageous; *Arch (crime)* for which the penalty is/was hanging; *Vieilli Fam* **cas p.** reprehensible action; **jouer un tour p. à qn** to play a rotten trick on sb; **ce n'est pas un cas p.!** it's not a hanging matter!

pendaison [pɑ̃dɛzɔ̃] NF hanging; **p. de crémaillère** housewarming (party)

pendant¹ [pɑ̃dɑ̃] ADJ **1** *(qui pend)* hanging, *Fml* pendent; *(jambes)* dangling; **oreilles pendantes** floppy ears; **le chien le regardait, la langue pendante** the dog looked at him with its tongue hanging out **2** *(en attente)* pending

pendant² NM **1 p. (d'oreille)** drop earring; *Mil* **p. de ceinturon** sword-belt sling, frog **2** *(d'un tableau, d'un bibelot etc)* matching piece (**de** to); **ces deux tableaux (se) font p.** these two pictures make a pair

pendant³ PRÉP during; **p. l'été** during the summer, in summer; **p. toute ma jeunesse** all through my youth, during the whole of my youth; **restez là p. quelques minutes/un quart d'heure** stay there for a few minutes/a quarter of an hour; **il a été silencieux p. tout**

le trajet he was silent throughout the journey *or* for the whole journey; **route bordée d'arbres p. un kilomètre** road lined with trees for a kilometre; **j'irai faire les courses p. ce temps** I'll go shopping in the meantime; **et p. ce temps-là, tu ne penseras pas à tes problèmes** it will take your mind off your problems for a while; **avant la classe et p.** before and during the class, before the class and during it; **il te l'a dit après la réunion? – non, p.** did he tell you after the meeting? – no, during it SEE GRAMMAR A69; B56

CONJ **p. que** while, *Fml* whilst; **elle lisait p. que je repassais** she was reading while I was ironing, she read while I ironed; **p. que j'y pense** while I think of it; **p. que vous y êtes** while you're at *or* about it SEE GRAMMAR B31

pendard, -arde [pɑ̃dar, -ard] N *Fam Arch* rogue, scoundrel

pendeloque [pɑ̃dlɔk] NF *(de bijou)* pendant; *(de lustre)* pendant, crystal

pendentif [pɑ̃dɑ̃tif] NM **1** *(bijou)* pendant **2** *Archit* pendentive

penderie [pɑ̃dri] NF wardrobe, *Am* closet

pendiller [pɑ̃dije] VI to dangle

pendoir [pɑ̃dwar] NM *(meat)* hook

pendouiller [pɑ̃duje] VI *Fam* to dangle

pendre [pɑ̃dr] VT **1** *(accrocher)* to hang (up); **p. le linge (pour le faire sécher)** to hang the washing out (to dry); **p. la crémaillère** to have a housewarming (party) **2** *(mettre à mort)* to hang; **p. qn haut et court** to hang sb (by the neck); *Fig Fam* **qu'il aille se faire p. ailleurs** let him go hang *or* go to hell; *Fig* **je veux être pendu si …** I'll be hanged if …

VI to hang; *(des cheveux)* to hang down; *(de la langue d'un animal)* to hang out; **les voiles pendaient le long des mâts** the sails were flapping idly against the masts; **jupe qui pend par derrière** skirt that hangs down *or* dips at the back; *Fam* **ça lui pend au nez** he's got it coming to him

VPR **se pendre 1** *(se suicider)* to hang oneself **2** *(s'accrocher)* **se p. à qch** to hang from sth; **se p. au cou de qn** to hug sb

pendu, -ue [pɑ̃dy] ADJ hung up, hanging (up); *(personne)* hanged; **p. aux jupes de sa mère** clinging to his mother's skirts; *Fig* **avoir la langue bien pendue** to be a great talker, to be very talkative; **il est toujours p. au téléphone** he's never off the phone, he spends all his time on the phone; **elle est restée deux heures pendue au téléphone** she spent two hours on the phone

N hanged man, *f* woman; **le p.** *(jeu)* hangman

pendulaire [pɑ̃dylɛr] ADJ swinging, pendular; **train p.** tilting train

N *Suisse* commuter

pendule [pɑ̃dyl] NM pendulum

NF clock; **p. à coucou** cuckoo clock; *Fig* **remettre les pendules à l'heure** to get things straight; *Fam* **tu ne vas pas en faire** *ou Vulg* **chier une p.** you're not going to make a big fuss *or* a song and dance about it

pendulette [pɑ̃dylɛt] NF small clock; *(réveille-matin)* travelling clock, travel alarm

pêne [pɛn] NM bolt

pénéplaine [peneplɛn] NF *Géol* peneplain

pénétrabilité [penetrabilite] NF penetrability

pénétrable [penetrabl] ADJ **1** *(perméable)* penetrable (**à** by) **2** *(compréhensible)* understandable

pénétrant, -ante [penetrɑ̃, -ɑ̃t] ADJ penetrating; *(vent, froid)* piercing; *(pluie)* drenching; *(odeur)* penetrating, pervasive, obtrusive; *(regard)* penetrating, searching, keen; *(esprit)* penetrating, shrewd, acute

NF **pénétrante** = dual carriageway or motorway leading into the centre of a city

pénétration [penetrasjɔ̃] NF **1** *(d'un produit chimique, d'une balle etc)* penetration; *Fig* **la p. d'idées nouvelles** the penetration of new ideas **2** *(clairvoyance) (d'une personne)* penetration, insight, shrewdness; *(de l'esprit)* acuteness **3** *(sexuellement)* penetration **4** *Com (d'un produit)* (market) penetration; *(d'un marché)* penetration

pénétré [penetre] ADJ **p. d'humidité** *(mur etc)* riddled with damp; *Fig* **p. d'un sentiment/d'une idée** imbued with a feeling/an idea; *Péj* **il est p. de son importance** he's full of his own importance; **un candidat/orateur p. de son sujet** a candidate/speaker who is completely immersed in his subject; **d'un ton p.** in an earnest tone, earnestly; **d'un air p.** with an earnest air, earnestly

pénétrer [penetre] VI *(je* **pénètre,** *n.* **pénétrons; je** **pénétrerai)** VI to penetrate; **la baïonnette pénétra jusqu'au poumon** the bayonet penetrated to the lung; **un cambrioleur a pénétré dans la maison** a burglar got into the house; **ils pénétrèrent par la force** *(de policiers, soldats etc)* they broke in, they forced their way in; **l'armée a pénétré en territoire ennemi** the army penetrated enemy territory; **l'eau avait pénétré partout** the water had penetrated everywhere *or* got in everywhere; **le vent pénètre dans toute la maison** the wind gets into the whole house

VT to penetrate; **la balle pénétra l'os** the bullet penetrated *or* pierced the bone; **p. un secret** to penetrate *or* fathom a secret; **p. la pensée/les intentions de qn** to fathom sb's thoughts/intentions; *Com* **p. un marché** to penetrate a market; **le froid nous pénètre (jusqu'aux os)** the cold goes right through us, the cold chills us to the bone

VPR **se pénétrer se p. d'une idée** to let an idea sink in; **se p. de l'importance de qch** to be fully aware of the importance of sth

pénible [penibl] ADJ **1** *(qui demande de l'effort) (tâche)* laborious, arduous, hard; *(respiration, style)* laboured, *Am* labored, heavy; *(route)* rough; *(hiver, froid)* severe; **vie p.** hard *or* difficult life **2** *(dérangeant, insupportable) (spectacle, nouvelles etc)* painful, distressing; **l'idée m'est trop p.** the idea is too painful; **il m'est p. de devoir vous annoncer que …** it is my painful duty to inform you that …; **p. à voir** painful to see **3** *Fam (personne)* **ce qu'elle est p.!** she's such a pain!

péniblement [peniblamɑ̃] ADV with difficulty, laboriously; *(douloureusement)* painfully; **avancer** *ou* **marcher p.** to struggle along; **respirer p.** to breathe heavily

péniche [peniʃ] NF **1** *(de transport fluvial)* barge; *(pour embarquer des marchandises)* lighter; **il vit sur une p.** he lives on a houseboat *or* barge; *Mil* **p. de débarquement** landing craft **2** *Fam* **péniches** *(chaussures)* clodhoppers

péniche-hôtel, *pl* **péniches-hôtels** NF botel *(moored)*

pénicilline [penisilin] NF *Pharm* penicillin

péninsulaire [penɛ̃sylɛr] ADJ peninsular

péninsule [penɛ̃syl] NF peninsula; **la p. Ibérique** the Iberian Peninsula

pénis [penis] NM *Anat* penis

pénitence [penitɑ̃s] NF **1** *Rel (repentir)* penitence, repentance; *(peine)* penance; **pour votre p.** as a penance; **faire p.** to do penance (**de** for) **2** *(punition)* punishment; **mettre un enfant en p.** to punish a child; **il est en p.** he's in disgrace; **pour ta p.** as a punishment **3** *Vieilli (aux jeux)* forfeit

pénitencier [penitɑ̃sje] NM **1** *Rel* grand p. penitentier (priest) **2** *(maison d'arrêt)* prison, *Am* penitentiary

pénitent, -ente [penitɑ̃, -ɑ̃t] ADJ, N *Rel* penitent

pénitentiaire [penitãsjɛr] **ADJ système p.** prison system

pénitentiel, -ielle [penitãsjɛl] *Rel* **ADJ** penitential

NM penitential (book)

penne [pɛn] **NF** *(d'un oiseau)* quill, *Spéc* penna; *(d'une flèche)* flight

Pennsylvanie [pɛnsilvani] **NF** Pennsylvania

péno [peno] **NM** *Fam (penalty)* penalty, *Br* pen *(in football)*

pénombre [penɔ̃br] **NF** *(lumière faible)* half-light, semi-darkness, shadowy light; *Astron, Phys* penumbra; *Fig* **rester dans la p.** to remain in the background

pensable [pãsabl] **ADJ** thinkable; **ce n'est pas p.** it's unthinkable

pensant [pãsã] **ADJ** *(créature)* thinking; **mal p.** unorthodox

pense-bête, *pl* **pense-bêtes** [pãsbɛt] **NM** *Fam* memory jogger, reminder; *TV, Cin* goof sheet, idiot board

pensée[1] [pãse] **NF** *(fleur)* pansy

pensée[2] **NF** *(réflexion)* thought; *(esprit)* thought, mind; *(opinion)* thought, view; **absorbé** *ou* **perdu** *ou* **plongé dans ses pensées** lost in thought *or* in one's thoughts; **se représenter clairement qch par la p.** to have a clear conception *or* a clear idea of sth; **entrer dans la p. de qn** to understand sb's thinking; **deviner les pensées de qn** to read sb's mind, to guess what sb is thinking; **dire sa p.** to speak one's mind, to say what one thinks; **dire le fond de sa p.** to say what one really thinks; **saisir la p. de qn** to grasp sb's meaning; **il partage ma p.** he shares my opinion, he thinks the same way I do; **libre p.** free thought *or* thinking; **à la p. des vacances, ...** at the thought of the holidays, ...; **la seule p. de ce repas me met l'eau à la bouche** just thinking about *or* just the thought of this meal makes my mouth water; **la p. que tu seras là** the thought that you will be there; **la p. marxiste/bouddhiste** Marxist/Buddhist thought *or* thinking; **la p. unique** = new orthodoxy in politics driven by the principles of the free market; **en p., par la p.** in one's mind; **voyager par la p.** to be an armchair traveller; **je suis avec vous en p.** *ou* **par la p.** my thoughts are with you; **avoir une p. pour qn** to think of sb; **ayons une p. émue pour elle** let's spare a thought for her; **pensées affectueuses** *(dans une lettre)* fond(est) regards

penser[1] [pãse] **NM** *Arch, Litt* thought

PENSER[2]

[VI] to think **1–3** ▪ to think of/about *(penser à)* **1, 2** ▪ to remember to do something *(penser à faire quelque chose)* **2**
[VT] to think **1, 2** ▪ to believe **1** ▪ to expect **3** ▪ to be thinking of doing something *(penser faire quelque chose)* **3** ▪ to think out **4**

VI 1 *(songer, réfléchir)* to think; **p. à qn/qch** *(songer à)* to think of *or* about sb/sth; **il pense à elle tout le temps** he's always thinking about her; **il pense par lui-même** he thinks for himself; **à quoi pensez-vous?** what are you thinking of *or* about?, what's going through your mind?; *(où avez-vous la tête?)* what are you thinking of?, how could you *(think of such a thing)*?; **p. tout haut** to think aloud; **je l'ai fait sans y p.** I did it without thinking; **pensez-vous!** what an idea!; **est-ce qu'il a donné un bon pourboire? – pensez-vous!** did he give a good tip? – what do you think? *or* you're joking! *or* what, him!; **pensez donc!** just fancy!; **vous n'y pensez pas!** you're not serious!; **n'y pensons plus** let's forget (about) it; **ce n'est même pas la**

peine d'y p. it's not even worth thinking about; **ah, j'y pense!** by the way!; **rien que d'y p., ça me donne des frissons** just thinking about it *or* of it gives me the shivers, I shiver at the mere thought (of it); **elle l'a fait sans p. à mal** she didn't mean any harm by it; **je lui ai parlé de toi sans p. à mal** I didn't mean any harm by speaking to him about you

 2 *(se souvenir)* **p. à tout** to think of everything; **p. à faire qch** to remember to do sth; **c'est toujours moi qui dois p. à tout** I'm the one who always has to think of *or* remember everything; **tu penses à tout!** you think of everything!; **pourrais-tu me faire p. à vérifier que ...?** could you remind me to check that ...?; **il me fait p. à mon frère** he reminds me of my brother; **ça me fait p. à du Proust/ de la banane** it reminds me of Proust/banana

 3 *(estimer)* to think; **je pense comme vous** I think like you *or* as you do, I agree with you; **voilà ma façon** *ou* **manière de p.** that's my way of thinking, that's the way I see it; **je ne partage pas sa façon de p.** I don't share his way of thinking

 4 p. vacances to think (about) holidays; **il faut p. européen** we must think European

VT 1 *(estimer)* to think, to believe; *(imaginer)* to imagine, to picture; **est-ce que tu penses réellement ce que tu viens de dire?** do you really believe what you've just said?; **je le pensais bien** I thought as much, I thought so; **comment peux-tu p. une chose pareille?** how can you think such a thing?; **je pense que oui/non** I think/don't think so; **pensez si j'étais furieux** you can imagine how angry I was; **je ne savais plus que p.** I no longer knew what to think; **je le pense fou** I think he's mad

 2 p. qch de qn/qch to think sth of sb/sth; **qu'est-ce que tu penses de lui?** what do you think of him?; **je ne pense rien de ce genre de gens** I think nothing *or* I don't think anything of these sort of people; **qu'en penses-tu?** what do you think (of it)?; **j'en pense le plus grand bien** I have a very high opinion of him/her/it; **p. du mal de qn** to have a poor opinion of sb, not to think much of sb; **je lui ai dit carrément ce que j'en pensais** *ou* **ce que je pensais** I told him straight out what I thought; *(en se fâchant)* I gave him a piece of my mind

 3 p. faire qch *(espérer)* to expect *or* hope to do sth; *(avoir l'intention)* to be thinking of doing sth; **je pensais le voir demain** I was expecting to see him tomorrow; *Litt* **j'ai pensé mourir de rire** I thought I would die laughing

 4 *(concevoir)* **p. qch** to think sth out; **p. la ville en fonction des habitants** to think of the city in terms of its inhabitants; **les plans ont été mal pensés** the plans were badly thought out; **p. l'actualité en démocrate** to view current events from a democratic standpoint

 5 *Fam Euph* **il peut se le mettre où je pense** he knows where he can stick it; **elle lui a fichu un coup de pied où je pense** she gave him a kick up the you-know-where

penseur, -euse [pãsœr, -øz] **N** thinker; **libre p.** free thinker

pensif, -ive [pãsif, -iv] **ADJ** thoughtful, pensive

pension [pãsjɔ̃] **NF 1** *(allocation)* pension, allowance; *Fin* **mise en p.** borrowing against securities, pledging **2 être en p. chez qn** to board with sb; **prendre qn en p.** to take sb in as a lodger; **prendre p. chez qn** to take board and lodging with sb; *Hum* **tu es toujours fourré chez eux, tu prends p. ou quoi?** you're always round at their place, are you moving in with them or what?; **chambre et**

p. board and lodging **3** *(pensionnat)* boarding school; *(élèves)* boarders; **mettre un enfant en p.** to send a child to boarding school **4** *Belg (cessation d'activité)* retirement; **l'âge de la p.** retirement age; **prendre sa p.** to retire

▸▸ **p. alimentaire** maintenance, alimony; **verser/recevoir une p. alimentaire** to pay/ get alimony; **demander 1500 euros de p. alimentaire** to claim 1,500 euros' maintenance *or* alimony; **p. complète** full board, *Am* American plan; **sept jours en p. complète** seven days' full board *or Am* American plan; **p. de famille** boarding house; **p. d'invalidité** invalidity pension; **p. de retraite** (retirement *or* old age) pension; **p. de réversion** survivor's pension; **p. viagère** life annuity

pensionnaire [pãsjɔnɛr] **N 1** *(dans une pension de famille, à l'école)* boarder; *(à l'hôtel)* resident; *(dans une maison privée)* lodger, paying guest; *(dans une maison pour personnes âgées)* resident; *Fam (d'une prison)* inmate **2** *(personne qui reçoit une pension)* **p. de la Comédie-Française** member of the Comédie Française company; **p. de la villa Médicis** = scholarship student at the Villa Medicis

Il faut noter que le nom anglais **pensioner** est un faux ami. Il signifie le plus souvent **retraité**.

pensionnat [pãsjɔna] **NM** *Scol (établissement)* boarding school; *(élèves)* boarders

pensionné, -ée [pãsjɔne] **ADJ** *(soldat, employé)* pensioned

N pensioner

pensionner [pãsjɔne] **VT** to pension

VI *Can (être en pension)* to be a boarder

pensivement [pãsivmã] **ADV** pensively, thoughtfully

pensum [pɛ̃sɔm] **NM** *Scol Vieilli* imposition; *(lignes)* lines; *Fig* chore

pentagonal, -ale, -aux, -ales [pɛ̃tagɔnal, -o] **ADJ** *Math* pentagonal

pentagone [pɛ̃tagon] **NM 1** *Math* pentagon **2** *Am Mil* **le P.** the Pentagon

pentamètre [pɛ̃tametr] **ADJ, NM** *Littér* pentameter

Pentateuque (le) [ləpɛ̃tatøk] **NM** *Bible* the Pentateuch

pentathlon [pɛ̃tatlɔ̃] **NM** *Sport* pentathlon

pentatonique [pɛ̃tatɔnik] **ADJ** *Mus* pentatonic

pente [pãt] **NF 1** *(inclinaison)* slope; *Spéc (d'une colline)* gradient, *Am* grade; **p. ascendante/descendante** upward/downward slope *or Spéc* gradient; **à faible/forte p.** gently/steeply sloping; **p. à 10%** slope of 10%, 1-in-10 hill; **en p.** sloping; *(plage, côte)* shelving; **rue en p.** street on a slope; **p. d'une rivière** fall of a river; *Arg* **avoir la dalle en p.** to be a bit of a boozer; *Fig Fam* **être sur une mauvaise p.** to be going downhill, to be on a slippery slope, to be on a downward path; *Fig* **remonter la p.** to get back on one's feet **2** *(cambrure) (de la route)* camber; *(du toit)* pitch; *Math (d'une courbe)* slope; **angle de p.** *(sur un plan)* angle of slope **3** *Aviat (de la trajectoire de vol)* slope

Pentecôte [pãtkot] **NF** *Rel* Pentecost; *(jours fériés)* Whitsun(tide); **dimanche de la P.** Whit Sunday; **lundi de P.** Whit Monday

penthotal® [pɛ̃tɔtal] **NM** *Pharm* truth drug, *Spéc* penthotal

Pentium® [pɛ̃tjɔm] **NM** *Ordinat* Pentium®

pentu [pãty] **ADJ** sloping

penture [pãtyr] **NF** *Tech (de porte etc)* strap hinge; **p. et gond** hook and hinge; *Naut* **pentures du gouvernail** rudder braces

pénultième [penyltjɛm] **ADJ, NF** penultimate

pénurie [penyri] NF shortage, scarcity (**de** of); **p. de capitaux** shortage of capital; **p. de main-d'œuvre** labour *or Am* labor shortage; **organiser la p.** to maximize available resources in times of shortage

people [pipɔl] ADJ **la presse p.** celebrity magazines *or* press

PEP [pɛp] NM *Fin (abrév* **plan d'épargne populaire)** special savings scheme

pep [pɛp] NM *Fam* pep; **avoir du p.** to be full of pep

pépé [pepe] NM *Fam* grandad, grandpa; *(vieil homme)* grandad

pépée [pepe] NF *Fam (fille)* chick, *Br* bird, *Am* broad

pépère [peper] *Fam* NM **1** **c'est un gros p.** he's an old fatty; *(d'un enfant)* he's a chubby little fellow **2** *(grand-père)* grandad, grandpa ▪ ADJ **1** *(endroit)* quiet; *(repas)* quiet, relaxed; **un petit coin p.** a nice quiet little spot **2** **il est p.** *(dans une situation confortable)* he's got it easy; **un travail p.** a cushy little job *or* number ▪ ADV *Aut* **rouler p.** to potter along

pépettes, pépètes [pepɛt] NFPL *très Fam (argent)* dough, bread

pépie [pepi] NF *(d'oiseau)* pip; *Fam* **avoir la p.** *(avoir soif)* to be parched

pépiement [pepimã] NM cheep(ing), chirp(ing)

pépier [pepje] VI to cheep, to chirp

pépin¹ [pepɛ̃] NM **1** *(de pomme, de raisin etc)* pip; **sans pépins** seedless **2** *Fam (ennui)* hitch; **avoir un p.** to be in trouble *or* in difficulties; **elle a eu un gros p.** she had some trouble *or* problems

pépin² NM *Fam (parapluie)* umbrella, *Br* brolly

pépinière [pepinjɛr] NF **1** *(d'arbustes)* nursery **2** *Fig* training ground (**de** for); **p. de entreprises** business incubator

pépiniériste [pepinjerist] N nursery gardener

pépite [pepit] NF *(d'or)* nugget; **pépites de chocolat** chocolate chips

péplum [peplɔm] NM *Fam (film)* sword and sandals epic

PEPS [peøpɛɛs] *Com (abrév* **premier entré, premier sorti)** FIFO

pepsine [pepsin] NF *Biol, Chimie* pepsin

peptide [pɛptid] NM *Biol, Chimie* peptide

peptique [pɛptik] ADJ peptic

peptone [pɛptɔn] NF *Physiol, Chimie* peptone

péquenaud, -aude [pekno, -od], **péquenot, -notte** [pekno, -ɔt] N *Fam* peasant, country bumpkin, yokel, *Am* hick

péquiste [pekist] *Can Pol* ADJ (of the) Parti Québécois, PQ ▪ N *(membre)* member of the Parti Québécois *or* PQ; *(partisan)* supporter of the Parti Québécois *or* PQ

PER [peøɛr] NM *Fin (abrév* **plan d'épargne de retraite)** retirement savings scheme

perborate [pɛrbɔrat] NM *Chimie* perborate

perçage [pɛrsaʒ] NM *(de tissu, de la peau)* piercing; *(d'un grand trou)* boring; *(d'un plus petit trou)* drilling

percale [pɛrkal] NF *Tex* percale

percaline [pɛrkalin] NF *Tex* percaline

perçant [pɛrsã] ADJ *(regard, cri)* piercing; *(voix)* penetrating, *Péj* shrill; **vue perçante** sharp eyesight

perce [pɛrs] NF **1** *(machine)* borer; *(outil)* drill; *(poinçon)* punch **2** *(d'un instrument à vent)* hole **3 mettre en p.** to broach, to tap

percé [pɛrse] ADJ pierced; *(chaussures, poche)* with a hole/holes in; **p. de vers** *(fruit, bois)* worm-eaten; **oreilles percées** pierced

ears; **pantalon p. au genou** trousers with a hole in the knee, trousers out at the knee; **mes chaussures sont percées** I've got holes in my shoes

percée [pɛrse] NF **1** *(ouverture)* opening; *(dans un mur)* opening, breach, gap; *(dans une forêt)* clearing; **ouvrir** *ou* **faire une p. dans un bois** to cut a passage through a wood **2** *Mil, Sp, Fig* breakthrough; **faire une p.** to make a breakthrough, to break through; **p. technologique** technological breakthrough

percement [pɛrs(ə)mã] NM *(d'un trou, d'un passage)* boring; *(d'une avenue)* opening; *(d'un canal)* cutting; *(d'un tunnel)* driving

perce-muraille, *pl* **perce-murailles** [pɛrs(ə)myraj] NF *Bot* wall pellitory

perce-neige, *pl* **perce-neige** [pɛrs(ə)nɛʒ] NM OU NF INV *Bot* snowdrop

perce-oreille, *pl* **perce-oreilles** [pɛrsɔrɛj] NM earwig

perce-pierre, *pl* **perce-pierres** [pɛrs(ə)pjɛr] NF *Bot* samphire, sea fennel, saxifrage

percepteur, -trice [pɛrsɛptœr, -tris] ADJ *(organe)* of perception ▪ NM *Admin* tax collector, *Fam* tax man

perceptibilité [pɛrsɛptibilite] NF perceptibility

perceptible [pɛrsɛptibl] ADJ **1** *(que l'on peut percevoir)* perceptible (**à** to), discernible; **p. à l'oreille** audible **2** *Admin (impôt)* collectable

perceptiblement [pɛrsɛptibləmã] ADV perceptibly; *(à l'oreille)* audibly

perceptif, -ive [pɛrsɛptif, -iv] ADJ perceptive

perception [pɛrsɛpsjɔ̃] NF **1** *(par les sens)* perception **2** *Admin (d'impôts, de droits, de loyer)* collection; **(bureau de) p.** tax office; *Fin* **p. de dividende** receipt of a dividend; *Com* **p. douanière** collection of customs duties; *Fin* **p. à la source** tax deduction at source

perceptoscope [pɛrsɛptɔskɔp] NM *Mktg* perceptoscope

percer [pɛrse] (**je perçai(s); n. perçons**) VT **1** *(transpercer)* to pierce, to go through; *Fig* **ça me perce les oreilles** it's ear-splitting; *Litt* **p. la foule** to make *or* elbow one's way through a crowd; **p. un abcès** to lance an abscess; **le soleil perce les nuages** the sun is breaking through *or* piercing the clouds; **p. le cœur/bras à qn d'un coup de couteau** to stab sb through the heart/in the arm; *Fig* **p. un complot** to uncover a plot; **p. un mystère/une énigme** to solve a mystery/a riddle; **p. qch à jour** to see through sth; **ses yeux perçaient l'obscurité** his eyes penetrated the darkness **2** *(trouer)* to make a hole in, to pierce; *(trou)* to make, to pierce; *(avec une perceuse)* to drill, to bore; *(tunnel)* to drive; *(avenue)* to open; *(canal)* to cut; **p. un mur** to make *or* open a door in a wall; **se faire p. les oreilles** to have one's ears pierced ▪ VI **1** to come *or* break through; **le soleil commence à p.** the sun is breaking through *or* coming out; **ses dents percent** his teeth are coming through, he is cutting his teeth; **l'abcès a percé** the abscess has burst; *Fig* **rien n'a percé de leur entretien** nothing has emerged about *or* got out about their meeting; **auteur qui commence à p.** author who is beginning to make a name (for himself); **il laissa p. son impatience/sa jalousie** he let his impatience/jealousy show

perceur, -euse [pɛrsœr, -øz] N *(personne) (de feuille de métal etc)* driller, puncher ▪ NF **perceuse** *(machine)* boring *or* drilling machine; *(outil)* drill; **perceuse à percussion**

hammer drill; **perceuse électrique** electric drill ▪ NM **p. de coffres-forts** safe breaker

percevable [pɛrsəvabl] ADJ *Admin (impôt)* collectable

percevoir [pɛrsəvwar] VT *(prp* **percevant;** *pp* **perçu;** *pr ind* **je perçois, n. percevons, ils perçoivent;** *pr sub* **je perçoive, n. percevions, ils perçoivent;** *impf* **je percevais;** *p hist* **je perçus;** *fu* **je percevrai) 1** *(prendre conscience de) (par les sens, l'intellect)* to perceive, to discern; **p. un bruit** to hear *or* catch a sound; **je ne perçois pas la différence** I can't make out *or* sense the difference; **je n'ai pas perçu, dans sa voix, qu'elle était désespérée** I didn't sense, from her voice, that she was desperate; **être bien/mal perçu** to be well/badly thought of; *(d'une information)* to be well/badly received; *(d'un produit)* to be well/badly perceived; **risque perçu** perceived risk **2** *Admin (impôts, loyers)* to collect; *(intérêts)* to receive, to be paid; **p. l'allocation chômage** to receive unemployment benefit; **p. une commission** to receive a commission; **p. les impôts à la source** to collect tax at source

perchaude [pɛrʃod] NF *Can* yellow perch

perche¹ [pɛrʃ] NF *(pièce de bois)* pole; *Rail* coupling pole; *Cin, TV* boom; **p. à houblon** hop pole; *Sport* **saut à la p.** pole vault(ing); **conduire un bateau à la p.** to punt a boat; *Fig* **tendre la p. à qn** to give sb a helping hand; *(donner une indication)* to give sb a broad hint; *Fam* **une grande p.** *(personne)* a beanpole

perche² NF *(poisson)* perch

percheman, *pl* **perchemen** [pɛrʃman, -mɛn] NM ski-lift attendant; *Cin, TV* boom operator

percher [pɛrʃe] VI *(des oiseaux)* to perch; *(des poules)* to roost; *Fig Fam* **il perche au quatrième** he lives up on the fourth *or Am* fifth floor; *Fig Fam* **où perchez-vous?** where's your pad? ▪ VT *Fam* to perch, to stick; **p. un vase sur une armoire** to perch *or* stick a vase on top of a wardrobe ▪ VPR **se percher** **se p. sur une branche** *(d'un oiseau)* to perch on a branch; *Fam* **il s'est perché sur le mur pour mieux voir** he perched himself on the wall to see better

percheron [pɛrʃərɔ̃] NM *(cheval)* Percheron

perchette [pɛrʃɛt] NF *TV, Cin* fishing rod

percheur, -euse [pɛrʃœr, -øz] ADJ *(oiseau)* perching

perchiste [pɛrʃist] N *Sport* pole vaulter; *Cin, TV* boom operator

perchlorate [pɛrklɔrat] NM *Chimie* perchlorate

perchlorique [pɛrklɔrik] ADJ *Chimie* perchloric

perchman [pɛrʃman] NM = **percheman**

perchoir [pɛrʃwar] NM perch; *(pour la volaille)* roost; *Fig* perch; *Pol* = raised seat for the President of the French National Assembly; *Pol* **obtenir le p.** to become President of the (French) National Assembly

perclus [pɛrkly] ADJ paralysed, *Am* paralyzed; **p. de rhumatismes** crippled with rheumatism; *Fig* **p. de terreur/froid/timidité** paralysed with fright/cold/shyness

perçoir [pɛrswar] NM *(outil)* awl, gimlet, broach

percolateur [pɛrkɔlatœr] NM *(coffee)* percolator

perçu [pɛrsy] ADJ **1** *(valeur, importance)* perceived **2** *(somme, traitement, intérêt)* received

percussion [pɛrkysjɔ̃] NF *Tech* percussion; *Méd* sounding (by percussion), percussion; **fusil à p.** percussion gun; *Mus* **instruments à**

p. percussion instruments; *Mus* **aux percussions, Jack** on percussion, Jack

percussionniste [pɛrkysjɔnist] **N** *Mus* percussionist

percutané [pɛrkytane] **ADJ** *Méd* percutaneous

percutant [pɛrkytɑ̃] **ADJ 1** *(qui percute)* percussive; *Mil* **obus p.** percussion fuse shell **2** *Fig (discours, argument)* forceful, powerful; *(style)* incisive
NM *Mil* percussion fuse shell

percuter [pɛrkyte] **VT 1** *(heurter violemment) (voiture, avion etc)* to crash into; **p. l'amorce** *(sur une arme)* to strike the primer **2** *Méd* to sound by percussion, to percuss
VI 1 *(cogner)* **l'avion percuta contre le sol** the plane crashed to the ground; **la voiture est allée p. contre un arbre** the car crashed into a tree **2** *Fam (comprendre)* to catch on

percuteur [pɛrkytœr] **NM** *(d'une arme à feu, d'un fusible)* striker, hammer; *(d'un fusil)* needle; *(d'une mitrailleuse)* firing pin

percutiréaction [pɛrkytireaksjɔ̃] **NF** *Méd* percutaneous reaction

perdant, -ante [pɛrdɑ̃, -ɑ̃t] **ADJ** losing; **partir p.** to start out with low hopes
N loser; **être bon/mauvais p.** to be a good/bad loser

perdition [pɛrdisjɔ̃] **NF 1** *Rel* perdition; **lieu de p.** den of vice *or* iniquity **2** *Naut* **navire en p.** ship in distress; *Fig* **entreprise en p.** company in difficulties *or* in trouble

---

PERDRE [pɛrdr]

VT	to lose **1** ▪ to ruin **2**
VI	to lose **3** ▪ to lose out *(y perdre)* **4**
VPR	to disappear **1** ▪ to be lost **1** ▪ to go bad **3** ▪ to get lost **5**

VT 1 to lose; **j'ai perdu mes clés** I've lost my keys; **vous êtes en train de p. votre écharpe** you're losing your scarf; **il a perdu ses parents dans un accident** he lost his parents in an accident; **p. du terrain** to lose ground; **p. pied** *(d'un nageur)*, *Fig* to get out of one's depth; *(d'un grimpeur)* to lose one's footing; **p. la partie** to lose the game; **il perd son pantalon** his trousers are too big for him; **p. ses cheveux** to lose one's hair, to go bald; **le chien perd ses poils** the dog is losing *or* shedding his hair; **p. une dent/un bras** to lose a tooth/an arm; **p. du poids/quelques kilos** to lose weight/a few pounds; **p. de sa valeur** to lose value; **il n'a rien perdu de sa bonne humeur** he's as cheerful as ever; **p. la raison** *ou* **la tête** *ou Fam* **la boule** to go mad, *Fam* to go off one's head, to go round the bend; **faire p. la tête à qn** *(le rendre fou)* to drive sb mad *or Fam* round the bend; *(de passion)* to drive sb crazy; *Fam* **il ne perd pas le nord!** he's no fool!; *Fam* **il n'en perd pas une** he doesn't miss a trick; **p. son calme** to lose one's composure; **p. la face** to lose face; **p. le fil (de ses pensées)** to lose the thread; **courir à p. haleine** to run until one is out of breath; **p. courage/patience/espoir/confiance** to lose heart/patience/hope/confidence; **p. connaissance** to lose consciousness; **p. une habitude** to shake off *or* get rid of a habit; **j'aimerais bien que tu perdes l'habitude de m'appeler 'ma vieille'** I wish you'd get out of the habit of calling me 'old girl'; **faire p. une habitude à qn** to break sb of a habit; **tu ne perds rien pour attendre!** just you wait!; **n'avoir rien à p.** to have nothing to lose; **p. son chemin** to lose one's way; **p. son temps** to waste (one's) time; **p. du temps** to waste time; *(dans un programme de travail, un horaire)* to lose time; **faire qch sans p. de temps** to do sth without losing *or* wasting any time, to lose no time in doing sth; **il n'y a pas de temps à p.** there is no time to lose; **il n'y a pas un instant** *ou* **une minute** *ou* **une seconde à p.** there isn't a moment to lose; **elle ne perd pas un mot** *ou* **une miette** *ou* **une bouchée de la conversation** she isn't missing a (single) word of the conversation; **p. une occasion** to miss an opportunity; **p. qn/qch de vue** to lose sight of sb/sth; **vous n'y perdez rien** you're not missing anything **2** *(ruiner)* to ruin; **l'ambition l'a perdu** ambition was his undoing *or* his downfall; *Hum* **ce qui te perdra, toi, c'est la gourmandise** your greed will be your undoing; **des lectures qui perdent la jeunesse** the kind of reading that is ruining our youth
3 *Obst* **elle a perdu les eaux** her waters have broken
VI 1 **la marée perd** the tide is ebbing
2 *Naut* to fall *or* drop astern
3 *(ne pas remporter une partie, bataille etc)* to lose
4 **y p.** *(dans un échange)* to lose out; *(dans une vente)* to make a loss; **p. au change** to lose out on the deal
VPR se perdre 1 *(disparaître)* to disappear, to be lost; **le navire se perdit corps et biens** the ship was lost with all hands; **se p. dans la foule** to disappear into the crowd, to lose oneself in the crowd; **cela se perd facilement** it's easily lost, it's easy to lose; **cet usage se perd** this custom is dying out; *Fig* **se p. de vue** to lose touch *or* contact with each other
2 *(d'une puissance mécanique)* to be wasted
3 *(de la nourriture)* to go bad
4 **il y a des fessées qui se perdent** he/she needs a good spanking
5 *(s'égarer)* to lose one's way, to get lost; **il s'est perdu dans le bois** he got lost in the wood; **se p. en conjectures** to get lost in conjecture; **se p. dans des explications/dans les détails** to get bogged down in explanations/details; **se p. dans ses pensées** to be lost in thought; *Fam* **je m'y perds** I can't make head (n)or tail of it, I'm confused; **on s'y perd** it's confusing

perdreau, -eaux [pɛrdro] **NM 1** *(oiseau)* young partridge **2** *Fam (policier)* cop

perdrix [pɛrdri] **NF** partridge; **p. des neiges** ptarmigan **VOIR GRAMMAIRE A12**

perdu, -ue [pɛrdy] **ADJ 1** lost; *(égaré)* lost, missing; *(que l'on ne gagne pas)* lost; **dans ses pensées** lost in thought; **je suis p.** I'm lost; *Fig (je n'y comprends rien)* I'm lost, I'm confused; **les causes perdues d'avance** causes lost right from the start; **un match p.** a lost match, a defeat; **il habite un trou p.** he lives at the back of beyond *or* in the middle of nowhere; **à mes moments perdus, à mes heures perdues** in my spare time; *Com* **emballage p.** non-returnable *or* throw-away *or* disposable packaging; **ce n'est pas p. pour tout le monde** *(d'objet)* somebody's making good use of it **2** *(abîmé)* ruined; *(ruiné, fini) (personne)* ruined; **il est p.** *(de malade)* there's no hope for him; *Litt* **il est p. de réputation** his reputation is ruined; **âme perdue** lost soul **3** **à corps p.** without restraint, recklessly; **se jeter à corps p. dans une activité** to throw oneself into an activity; **se jeter à corps p. dans la mêlée** to hurl oneself into the fray
N crier comme un p./une perdue to shout like a madman/a madwoman

perdurer [pɛrdyre] **VI** *Litt* to continue

père [pɛr] **NM 1** *(géniteur)* father; **de p. en fils** from father to son, from generation to generation; *Prov* **tel p. tel fils** like father like son; **M. Martin p.** Mr Martin senior; **nos pères** our forefathers, our ancestors; *Fam* **un gros p.** a chubby fellow; *Fam* **c'est un p. tranquille** he's a quiet sort; *Fam* **(mon) petit p.** old chap, *Am* old buddy; **le p. Jean** old John; **il a été un vrai p. pour moi** he was like a father to me; *Fig* **le p. du cubisme** the father of cubism **2** *Rel* father; **le Saint-P.** the Holy Father; **le (Révérend) P. Martin** Father Martin; **mon p.** Father; **notre P. qui êtes aux cieux** our Father who art in heaven; **le P., le Fils et le Saint-Esprit** the Father, the Son and the Holy Ghost **3** *(dans un élevage)* sire
▸ ▸ **p. de famille** father, family man; **en bon p. de famille** wisely; **p. naturel** natural father; *Théâtre* **p. noble** heavy father; **le P. Noël** Father Christmas, Santa Claus; **croire au P. Noël** to believe in Father Christmas *or* Santa Claus; **p. spirituel** *Rel* father confessor; *Fig (d'un mouvement)* father; *Rel* **les Pères Blancs** the White Friars, the Carmelites

pérégrination [peregrinasjɔ̃] **NF** *Litt* peregrination

péremption [perɑ̃psjɔ̃] **NF 1** *Jur* lapsing; *(dans un procès)* time limitation **2** **date de p.** use-by date

péremptoire [perɑ̃ptwar] **ADJ 1** *(ton)* peremptory; **argument p.** unanswerable argument **2** *Jur* **délai p.** strict time limit

péremptoirement [perɑ̃ptwarmɑ̃] **ADV** peremptorily

pérenniser [perenize] **VT** to perpetuate

pérennité [perenite] **NF** *(d'une théorie, d'une tradition, d'une vérité)* timelessness; *(de fournisseur)* permanence

péréquation [perekwasjɔ̃] **NF** *Admin, Écon (d'impôts, de salaires)* equalization; *Rail (des charges de fret, de tarifs)* standardizing; *Can Admin* **fonds de p.** equalization fund

perestroïka [perɛstroika] **NF** *Pol* perestroika

perfectibilité [perfɛktibilite] **NF** *Litt* perfectibility

perfectible [perfɛktibl] **ADJ** perfectible

perfectif, -ive [perfɛktif, -iv] **ADJ, NM** *Gram* perfective

perfection [perfɛksjɔ̃] **NF 1** *(qualité)* perfection; **atteindre la p.** to achieve perfection; **à la p.** to perfection, perfectly **2** *Fam* **une p.** a gem

perfectionné [perfɛksjɔne] **ADJ** sophisticated

perfectionnement [perfɛksjɔnmɑ̃] **NM 1** *(action)* perfecting; *(amélioration)* improving; *(formation)* (further) training; **brevet de p.** patent relating to improvements; *Scol* **cours de p.** proficiency course; **faire un stage de p.** to do an advanced training course **2** *(résultat)* improvement

perfectionner [perfɛksjɔne] **VT** to perfect; *(améliorer)* to improve
VPR se perfectionner to improve; **se p. en allemand** to improve one's German

perfectionnisme [perfɛksjɔnism] **NM** perfectionism

perfectionniste [perfɛksjɔnist] **ADJ, N** perfectionist; **elle n'est pas assez p.** she is not enough of a perfectionist

perfecto [perfɛkto] **NM** short leather jacket

perfide [perfid] **ADJ** treacherous (**envers** to), *Litt* perfidious; **la p. Albion** perfidious Albion
N *Arch, Litt* traitor

perfidement [perfidmɑ̃] **ADV** treacherously, *Litt* perfidiously

perfidie [perfidi] **NF** *Litt* **1** *(déloyauté)* perfidiousness **2** *(action)* perfidy

perforage [perfɔraʒ] **NM** *(de cuir)* punching; *(de papier)* perforation; *(à travers du bois, un mur etc)* boring

perforant [perfɔrɑ̃] **ADJ** perforating; **obus p.** armour-piercing *or Am* armor-piercing shell

perforateur, -trice [perfɔratœr, -tris] **ADJ** perforating
N *(personne)* punch card operator
NF perforatrice 1 *Constr* rock drill **2** *(pour papier)* (hole) punch; *(pour cuir)* punch;

(pince) perforatrice ticket punch **3** *Ordinat* card punch, (key) punch; **perforatrice de bande** tape punch
NM *Chir* perforator

perforation [pɛrfɔrasjɔ̃] NF **1** *(action)* perforation, perforating; *Ordinat* punching **2** *(trou)* perforation; *Ordinat* punch (hole); *Méd* **p. intestinale** perforation of the intestine

perforer [pɛrfɔre] VT **1** *(trouer) (papier)* to perforate; *(bois, mur)* to bore (through), to drill; *(cuir)* to punch **2** *Ordinat (carte, bande)* to punch; **carte perforée** punch card; **bande perforée** punched tape

perforeuse [pɛrfɔrøz] NF perforator; *Ordinat* card punch

performance [pɛrfɔrmɑ̃s] NF *Sport* performance; *Fig (exploit)* feat, achievement; *Tech* **les performances d'une voiture/d'un ordinateur** a car's/computer's performance; **il faut améliorer les performances de notre entreprise** we must improve our company's performance; **moteur (à) haute p.** high-performance engine; **la p. éblouissante d'un acteur** the dazzling performance of an actor

performant [pɛrfɔrmɑ̃] ADJ *(machine)* high-performance; *(entreprise)* high-performance, efficient; *(investissement)* profitable, high-yield; **des résultats performants** outstanding *or* impressive results

perfuser [pɛrfyze] VT *Méd* to put on a drip; *(organe)* to attach a drip to

perfusion [pɛrfyzjɔ̃] NF *Méd* drip, *Spéc* perfusion; **être sous p.** to be on a drip

pergola [pɛrgɔla] NF pergola

péricarde [perikard] NM *Anat* pericardium

péricardite [perikardit] NF *Méd* pericarditis

péricliter [periklite] VI *(d'une affaire, d'une entreprise)* to be in jeopardy; **ses affaires périclitent** his business is about to collapse

péridot [perido] NM *(pierre)* peridot, chrysolite

péridural, -ale, -aux, -ales [peridyral, -o] *Méd* ADJ epidural; **anesthésie péridurale** epidural anaesthesia *or Am* anesthesia
NF **péridurale** epidural; **accoucher sous péridurale** to give birth under an epidural

périf [perif] NM *Fam (abrév* **boulevard périphérique)** **le p.** = the ring road around Paris

périgée [periʒe] NM *Astron* perigee

périglaciaire [periglasjer] ADJ *Géog* periglacial

périhélie [perieli] NM *Astron* perihelion

péri-informatique [periɛ̃fɔrmatik] NF *Tech* computer peripherals

péril [peril] NM peril, danger; *(particulier)* risk, hazard; **au p. de sa vie** at the risk of one's life; **en p.** in peril, in danger; **il y aurait p. à sortir en mer aujourd'hui** it would be unsafe to go out to sea today; **mettre qch en p.** to imperil *or* endanger *or* jeopardize sth; **les périls de cette affaire** the risks involved in this affair; **à ses risques et périls** at one's own risk; **il y a p. en la demeure** it's a matter of great urgency; **il n'y a pas p. en la demeure** there's no urgency about it; *Péj* **le p. jaune** the yellow peril

périlleusement [perijøzmɑ̃] ADV perilously

périlleux, -euse [perijø, -øz] ADJ perilous, dangerous, hazardous; **saut p.** somersault

périmé [perime] ADJ *(billet, passeport, coupon)* out of date, no longer valid; *(mandat)* lapsed; *(nourriture, marchandise)* past its sell-by date; **votre passeport est p.** your passport has expired *or* is out of date *or* is no longer valid; *Fig* **conceptions périmées** outdated *or* outmoded concepts

périmer [perime] VI **laisser p. un passeport** to let a passport expire; **laisser p. de la nourriture** to let food go off *or* bad
VPR **se périmer** *Jur* to lapse; *(d'un passeport, d'un billet)* to expire

périmètre [perimɛtr] NM *Géom* perimeter; **dans un p. de 50 km** within a 50-km radius; **p. de vision** zone of vision

périnatal, -ale, -als *ou* **-aux, -ales** [perinatal, -o] ADJ *Méd* perinatal

périnatologie [perinatɔlɔʒi] NF *Méd* perinatal medicine

périnée [perine] NM *Anat* perineum

période [perjɔd] NF **1** *(de temps)* period; **p. de changements sociaux** period of social change; **longue p. de beau temps** long spell of fine weather; **la p. bleue de Picasso** Picasso's Blue Period; **elle a eu sa p. jazz** she went through a jazz period; *Beaux-Arts* **la p. classique** the Classical Period *or* Age; **première p. de l'existence** early stages of life; *Mil* **p. (d'instruction)** training; **pendant la p. électorale** during the elections; **aller en France en pleine p. électorale** to go to France in the middle of elections; **pendant la p. de Noël** *ou* **des fêtes** during the Christmas period; **p. de fêtes** holiday period; **p. estivale** summer season; **p. de pointe** peak period **2** *(d'un phénomène récurrent, d'un cycle)* period; **nombre de périodes par seconde** *(d'une onde sonore etc)* frequency; *Math* **p. d'une fraction décimale** repetend of a (recurring) decimal; *Phys* **p. d'une onde** period of a wave **3** *Gram* period, complete sentence; *Mus* **p. (musicale)** phrase
▸▸ *Fin* **p. d'amortissement** depreciation period; *Rail* **p. blanche/bleue** = moderately busy/slackest period on the French rail system; *Fin* **p. comptable** financial *or Am* fiscal period; *UE* **p. de double circulation** *(de la monnaie nationale et de l'euro)* double circulation period; **p. d'essai** trial period; **p. d'essai gratuit** free trial period; *Biol* **p. d'incubation** incubation period; *Chimie* **p. de radioactivité** half-life; **p. de référence** reference period; **p. de réflexion** *(après signature d'un contrat)* cooling-off period; *Rail* **p. rouge** = busiest period on the French rail system; **p. de sûreté** minimum period of imprisonment

périodicité [perjɔdisite] NF periodicity; *(d'un périodique)* frequency of publication; *(d'une émission)* frequency of broadcast

périodique [perjɔdik] ADJ **1** periodic; **phases périodiques de récession et de progrès** periodic *or* cyclical phases of recession and economic progress; *Journ* **presse p.** periodical publications; *Math* **fraction p.** recurring decimal; *Math* **fonction p.** periodic function; *Méd* **fièvre p.** recurrent fever **2** *(hygiénique)* **tampons périodiques** tampons; **serviettes** *ou* **garnitures périodiques** sanitary towels *or Am* napkins
NM *Journ* periodical

périodiquement [perjɔdikmɑ̃] ADV periodically

périoste [perjɔst] NM *Anat* periosteum

péripatéticien, -ienne [peripatetisjɛ̃, -jɛn] ADJ *Phil* peripatetic
N *Phil* peripatetic
NF *Fam* **péripatéticienne** streetwalker, prostitute

péripétie [peripesi] NF *Litt* **1** *(dans un roman, dans la vie)* sudden change of fortune **2** **péripéties** adventures, incidents; *(de la vie)* ups and downs, vicissitudes

périph [perif] NM *Fam* = **périf**

périphérie [periferi] NF **1** periphery; *Géom* circumference **2** *(banlieue)* outskirts; **vivre à la p. de Paris** to live on the outskirts of Paris

périphérique [periferik] ADJ **1** *(situé autour)* peripheral; **boulevard p.** ring road, *Am* beltway; *Radio* **radio p.** = radio station broadcasting from outside national territory; *Anat* **système nerveux p.** peripheral nervous system **2** *Ordinat* peripheral
NM **1** *(ceinture routière)* ring road, *Am* beltway **2** *Ordinat* peripheral; **p. d'entrée** input device; **p. externe** external device; **p. d'impression** printer peripheral; **p. série** serial device; **p. de sortie** output device

périphrase [perifraz] NF circumlocution; *Gram* periphrasis, periphrase

périphrastique [perifrastik] ADJ circumlocutory; *Gram* periphrastic

périple [peripl] NM *(voyage)* (long) tour, journey; *(par mer)* (sea) voyage

périr [perir] VI *(aux* **avoir)** *(d'une personne)* to perish, to die; *(de la gloire, d'une réputation)* to be destroyed; *(d'un empire)* to fall; **p. dans un incendie/accident** to die *or* perish in a fire/an accident; **p. noyé** to drown, to be drowned; *Fig Litt* **p. d'ennui** to die of boredom; *Fig Litt* **s'ennuyer à p.** to be bored to death; **son nom ne périra pas** his name will live (on); **la démocratie ne peut p.** democracy cannot be destroyed

périscolaire [periskɔler] ADJ extra-curricular

périscope [periskɔp] NM periscope

périscopique [periskɔpik] ADJ periscopic

périssabilité [perisabilite] NF perishability

périssable [perisabl] ADJ perishable; **denrées périssables** perishable foodstuffs

périssoire [periswar] NF canoe

péristaltique [peristaltik] ADJ *Physiol (mouvement)* peristaltic

péristaltisme [peristaltism] NM *Physiol* peristalsis

péristyle [peristil] NM *Archit* peristyle

péritel® [peritɛl] ADJ INV **prise p.** SCART plug; *(qui reçoit)* SCART socket

péritéléphonie [peritelefɔni] NF *Tech* peripheral telephone equipment

péritoine [peritwan] NM *Anat* peritoneum

péritonite [peritɔnit] NF *Méd* peritonitis

périurbain [periyrbɛ̃] ADJ *(cité, lotissement)* suburban; *(parking, shopping)* out-of-town

perle [pɛrl] NF **1** *(naturelle)* pearl; *(de verre, de métal etc)* bead; *Fig (personne)* gem, treasure; **rang de perles** row *or* string of pearls; *Fig* **jeter des perles aux pourceaux** to cast pearls before swine; **c'est la p. des frères** he's the best brother in the world; **ma bonne est une p. (rare)** my maid is a (real) gem *or* treasure; *Fig Fam* **enfiler des perles** to waste one's time on trivia; **p. de rosée** dewdrop; **perles de sang** drops of blood; **perles de sueur** beads of sweat **2** *Scol* howler
▸▸ **p. de culture** cultured pearl; **p. fine** real pearl

perlé [pɛrle] ADJ **1** *(orné de perles)* set with pearls; *(de perles de verre)* beaded; **riz p.** husked *or* polished rice; **orge p.** pearl barley; **coton p.** pearl cotton; *Fig* **rire p.** rippling laughter **2** *(travail)* exquisitely done; *Mus* clear-cut

perler [pɛrle] VT *(travail)* to execute to perfection; *Mus* to play in clear-cut fashion
VI *(des larmes, de la sueur etc)* to form in beads; **la sueur perlait sur son front** sweat beaded his forehead, beads of sweat stood out on his forehead

perlier, -ière [pɛrlje, -jɛr] ADJ **huître perlière** pearl oyster; **industrie perlière** pearl industry

perlimpinpin [pɛrlɛ̃pɛ̃pɛ̃] NM **poudre de p.** magic *or* miracle powder

perlingual, -ale, -aux, -ales [pɛrlɛ̃gwal,

-o] ADJ *Méd* à prendre par voie perlinguale place under the tongue

perlouse, perlouze [pɛrluz] NF **1** *Arg* pearl **2** *Vulg (pet)* fart; **lâcher une p.** to fart

perm [pɛrm] NF *Fam* **1** *Mil* leave **2** *Scol* study room; **aller en p.** to go to the study room; **avoir deux heures de p.** to have two hours' private study

permanence [pɛrmanɑ̃s] NF **1** *(continuité)* permanence; **en p.** permanently, continuously **2** *(service d'accueil d'un organisme)* reception; **la p. est assurée le dimanche** there is someone on duty on Sundays; **être de p.** to be on duty; **p. électorale** committee rooms **3** *Scol* study room; **aller en p.** to go to the study room; **avoir deux heures de p.** to have two hours' private study

permanent, -ente [pɛrmanɑ̃, -ɑ̃t] ADJ *(ordre, commission)* standing; *(spectacle)* continuous; *(tribunal)* permanent; **en direct de notre envoyé p. à New York** live from our New York correspondent *or* from our permanent correspondent in New York; *Ordinat* **mémoire permanente** permanent memory; **cinéma p.** *(concept)* continuous showings; *(bâtiment)* cinema *or Am* movie theater with continous showings

NF **permanente** perm, permanent wave; **se faire faire une permanente** to have a perm, to have one's hair permed
N *Pol* official

permanenter [pɛrmanɑ̃te] VT to perm; **se faire p.** to have a perm, to have one's hair permed

permanganate [pɛrmɑ̃ganat] NM *Chimie* permanganate

perméabilité [pɛrmeabilite] NF permeability, perviousness; *Fig (à une influence)* susceptibility

perméable [pɛrmeabl] ADJ permeable, pervious **(à** to); *Fig* susceptible **(à** to)

PERMETTRE [pɛrmɛtr] *(conj like* **mettre***)* VT to allow, to permit; **p. qch à qn** to allow sb sth; **les médecins ne lui permettent pas l'alcool/ le sport** the doctors don't allow *or* permit him to drink/to do sport; **p. à qn de faire qch** to allow *or* permit sb to do sth, to let sb do sth; **mes moyens ne me le permettent pas** I can't afford it; **est-il permis d'entrer?** may I come in?; **s'il est permis de s'exprimer ainsi** if I/we may (be allowed to) say so; **il n'est pas permis de stationner là** you're not allowed *or* permitted to park there, parking there isn't allowed *or* permitted; **est-ce qu'il est permis de rapporter six bouteilles de vin?** am I allowed to bring back six bottles of wine?, are six bottles of wine allowable?; **cela ne devrait pas être permis** it shouldn't be allowed; *Hum* **être aussi beau/riche que ça, ça ne devrait pas être permis** nobody's got a right to be that good-looking/rich; **est-il permis de se montrer aussi insolent?** how can anyone be so insolent?; *Fam* **il est égoïste comme ce n'est pas permis!** he's incredibly selfish!; *Fam* **il boit comme c'est pas permis!** he drinks like there's no tomorrow!; **autant qu'il est permis d'en juger** as far as one can tell; **il se croit tout permis** he thinks he can do anything he likes *or* whatever he likes; **il n'est pas permis à tout le monde de …** not everyone can …; **permettez-moi de vous dire que vous avez tort** excuse me, but you're wrong; **permettez-moi de vous présenter ma sœur** allow me to introduce you to my sister, may I introduce you to my sister?; **permettez!** excuse me!, if you don't mind!; **vous permettez?** may I?, do you mind?; **si le temps le permet** weather permitting; **si mon emploi du temps le permet** if my schedule allows it
VPR **se permettre 1 se p. de faire qch** to take the liberty of doing sth; **je me permets d'attirer votre attention sur …** may I draw your

attention to …; **tu ne t'es pas servi un verre? – je ne me serais pas permis!** didn't you get yourself a drink? – I didn't like to!
2 se p. qch to allow oneself sth; **il se permet bien des choses** he takes a lot of liberties

permis [pɛrmi] ADJ allowed, permitted
NM *Admin* permit, licence, *Am* license; *Aut Fam* driving licence, *Can* driver's licence, *Am* driver's license; *(examen)* driving test
▸▸ **p. de chasse** hunting permit; *Aut* **p. de conduire** driving licence, *Can* driver's licence, *Am* driver's license; *(examen)* driving test; **p. de conduire international** international driving licence; **p. de construire** planning permission; **p. de débarquement** unloading note *or* permit; **p. de douane** customs permit; **p. d'embarquement** shipping note *or* permit; **p. d'exportation** export licence; **p. d'importation** import licence; **p. d'inhumer** burial certificate; **p. provisoire** = temporary licence issued after passing driving test; **p. de séjour** residence permit; **p. tous véhicules** full licence; **p. de travail** work permit

permissif, -ive [pɛrmisif, -iv] ADJ permissive

permission [pɛrmisjɔ̃] NF **1** *(autorisation)* permission; *Jur* leave; **demander/donner la p. à qn de faire qch** to ask/give sb permission to do sth; **il n'a pas même demandé la p.** he didn't even ask permission; **avec votre p.** with your permission, if I/we may SEE GRAMMAR A58–9; B40 **2** *Mil (congé)* leave (of absence); *(certificat)* pass; **en p.** on leave; **il s'est marié pendant sa p.** he got married during his leave *or* while (he was) on leave

permissionnaire [pɛrmisjɔnɛr] NM **1** *Mil* man on leave; *Naut* liberty man **2** *(détenteur d'un permis)* permit holder
ADJ **officier p.** officer on leave

permissivité [pɛrmisivite] NF permissiveness

permutabilité [pɛrmytabilite] NF permutability, interchangeability

permutable [pɛrmytabl] ADJ permutable, interchangeable

permutation [pɛrmytasjɔ̃] NF **1** *(échange)* exchange of posts; *Mil* transfer **2** *(de lettres, de chiffres)* transposition; *Math* permutation **3** *Ling* metathesis

permuter [pɛrmyte] VT **1** *(lettres, chiffres)* to transpose; *Math* to permute **2** *Vieilli (poste)* to exchange (**avec qn** with sb)
VI to exchange posts

pernicieusement [pɛrnisjøzmɑ̃] ADV perniciously

pernicieux, -ieuse [pɛrnisjø, -jøz] ADJ pernicious, harmful; *Méd* **anémie pernicieuse** pernicious anaemia *or Am* anemia

péroné [perɔne] NM *Anat* fibula

péronnelle [perɔnɛl] NF *Fam Péj* silly goose

péroraison [perɔrɛzɔ̃] NF peroration

pérorer [perɔre] VI *Péj* to hold forth, to speechify, to spout

Pérou [peru] NM Peru; *Fig Fam* **ce n'est pas le P., on peut se l'offrir** it doesn't cost a fortune, we can afford it

peroxyde [perɔksid] NM *Chimie* peroxide

peroxydé [perɔkside] ADJ peroxide; **une blonde peroxydée** a peroxide blonde

perpendiculaire [pɛrpɑ̃dikylɛr] ADJ perpendicular (**à, sur** to)
NF *Géom* perpendicular; **tirer une p.** to drop *or* draw a perpendicular (**à, sur** to)

perpendiculairement [pɛrpɑ̃dikylɛrmɑ̃] ADV perpendicularly; **p. à** perpendicular to

perpète [pɛrpɛt] ADV *Fam* **1** *(perpétuité)* **condamné à p.** sentenced to life; **il a pris p.** he got life; **je ne vais pas t'attendre jusqu'à p.!** I'm not going to wait for you for ever! **2**

(distance) **envoyer qn à p.** *(très loin)* to send sb miles away; **vivre à P.(-les-Oies)** to live at the back of beyond *or* in the sticks *or Am* in the boonies

perpétration [pɛrpetrasjɔ̃] NF *Jur* perpetration

perpétrer [pɛrpetre] VT (**je perpètre; je perpétrerai**) to perpetrate

perpette [pɛrpɛt] = **perpète**

perpétuation [pɛrpetɥasjɔ̃] NF perpetuation

perpétuel, -elle [pɛrpetɥɛl] ADJ perpetual; *(Dieu, amour)* everlasting; *(secrétaire, membre)* permanent; **rente perpétuelle** perpetuity; **mouvement p.** perpetual motion; **crainte perpétuelle** perpetual *or* constant fear; **de perpétuels reproches** perpetual *or* constant *or* endless reproaches

perpétuellement [pɛrpetɥɛlmɑ̃] ADV perpetually

perpétuer [pɛrpetɥe] VT *(nom, réputation)* to perpetuate; *(tradition)* to carry on, to perpetuate; **p. le souvenir de qn** to perpetuate sb's memory, to keep sb's memory alive
VPR **se perpétuer** to survive; *Fig (d'un problème)* to survive, to live on; **se p. dans son œuvre** to live on in one's work

perpétuité [pɛrpetɥite] NF perpetuity; **à p.** *(concession)* in perpetuity; *(emprisonnement)* for life; **être condamné (à la réclusion) à p.** to be sentenced to life (imprisonment)

perplexe [pɛrplɛks] ADJ perplexed, puzzled; **laisser qn p.** to perplex *or* puzzle sb

perplexité [pɛrplɛksite] NF perplexity; **être dans la plus grande p.** to be completely baffled *or* utterly perplexed; **plonger qn dans la plus grande p.** to completely baffle *or* utterly perplex sb; **avoir un air de p.** to look confused; **la p. se lisait sur son visage** you could see that he was confused

perquisition [pɛrkizisjɔ̃] NF *Jur* search; **mandat de p.** search warrant; **faire une p. chez qn** to search sb's premises; **procéder à une p.** to carry out a search

perquisitionner [pɛrkizisjɔne] VI *Jur* to make *or* conduct *or* carry out a search; **p. au domicile de qn** to search sb's house
VT to search

perré [pere] NM *Constr (d'une route, d'une digue)* stone pitching *or* facing

perron [perɔ̃] NM *Archit* (flight of) steps *(leading to building)*, *Spéc* perron

perroquet [perɔkɛ] NM **1** *Orn* parrot; **p. de mer** puffin; **répéter qch comme un p.** to repeat sth parrot-fashion **2** *(boisson)* pastis with mint **3** *Naut (voile)* topgallant **4** *(crochet)* hook

perruche [peryʃ] NF **1** *(oiseau)* budgerigar, *Fam* budgie; *Vieilli Fam (femelle du perroquet)* hen parrot; *Fam (femme bavarde)* chatterbox, chatterer **2** *Naut* mizzen topgallant sail

perruque [peryk] NF **1** *(postiche)* wig; *Hist* periwig, peruke **2** *Pêche* tangled line, *Fam* bird's nest

perruquier, -ière [perykje, -jɛr] N wig maker

pers [pɛr] ADJ *Litt* blue-green

persan, -ane [pɛrsɑ̃, -an] ADJ Persian; **chat p.** Persian cat; **tapis p.** Persian carpet *or (plus petit)* rug
NM *Ling* Farsi; *Hist* Persian

perse [pɛrs] NF **1** *Géog* **la P.** Persia; **tapis de P.** Persian carpet *or (plus petit)* rug **2** *Tex* chintz
ADJ of/from ancient Persia, (ancient) Persian
N **P.** Persian
NM *Hist, Ling* Persian

persécuté, -ée [pɛrsekyte] ADJ *(personne)* persecuted

N 1 *Psy* sufferer from persecution mania **2** *(victime)* victim of persecution

persécuter [pɛrsekyte] **VT** *(minorité, peuple)* to persecute; *(harceler)* to harass; *(élève, enfant)* to bully; **se sentir persécuté** to feel persecuted

persécuteur, -trice [pɛrsekytœr, -tris] **N** persecutor
▸ **ADJ** persecuting

persécution [pɛrsekysjɔ̃] **NF** persecution; *Psy* **manie** ou **délire de p.** persecution mania or complex; *Psy* **avoir la manie de la p.** to have a persecution complex

persévérance [pɛrseverɑ̃s] **NF** perseverance

persévérant [pɛrseverɑ̃] **ADJ** persevering

persévérer [pɛrsevere] **VI** (**je persévère, n. persévérons; je persévérerai**) to persevere (**dans** in); **p. dans une attitude de refus** to remain stubbornly opposed; **il persévère dans l'erreur** he refuses to admit that he is wrong; **il n'a guère persévéré** he didn't show much perseverance; *Litt* **p. à faire qch** to persevere in doing sth

persicaire [pɛrsikɛr] **NF** *Bot* persicaria, lady's thumb

persienne [pɛrsjɛn] **NF** (slatted) shutter

persiflage [pɛrsiflaʒ] **NM** mockery

persifler [pɛrsifle] **VT** to mock, to ridicule

persifleur, -euse [pɛrsiflœr, -øz] **N** mocker
▸ **ADJ** mocking, derisive

persil [pɛrsi] **NM** parsley

persillade [pɛrsijad] **NF** *Culin* persillade, = finely chopped garlic, parsley and lemon zest; *(plat)* beef seasoned with persillade

persillé [pɛrsije] **ADJ** *Culin* **1** **fromage à pâte persillée** veined cheese **2** *(viande)* marbled **3** *(assaisonné de persil)* sprinkled with chopped parsley

persique [pɛrsik] **ADJ** (ancient) Persian; **le golfe P.** the Persian Gulf

persistance [pɛrsistɑ̃s] **NF 1** *(constance)* persistence, persistency (**à faire qch** in doing sth); **avec p.** persistently; **p. dans le mensonge** persistent lying **2** *(continuité) (de la fièvre etc)* persistence, continuance; **p. rétinienne** persistence of vision

persistant [pɛrsistɑ̃] **ADJ** *(parfum, toux, fièvre etc)* persistent; *Bot (feuilles)* persistent, indeciduous

persister [pɛrsiste] **VI 1** *(persévérer)* to persist; **il faut p.** you must persevere, you must keep at it; **p. dans sa résolution** to persist in one's resolve; **p. dans sa décision/son choix** to stick to one's decision/choice; **p. à faire qch** to persist in doing sth; **p. à croire qch** to persist in thinking sth, to continue to believe sth; **je persiste et signe** I'm sticking to it **2** *(continuer) (de fièvre, mécontentement etc)* to persist, to continue; **(il) persiste un doute/une interrogation** there remains a doubt/question

perso [pɛrso] *Fam* **ADJ INV** personal; **pour un ailier, il est trop p.** for a winger, he hogs the ball too much *or* he is too much of a solo artist
▸ **ADV** *(dans les jeux de ballon)* **il joue trop p.** he hogs the ball too much

persona [pɛrsona] **ADJ INV** **p. grata/non grata** persona grata/non grata; **déclarer qn p. grata/non grata** to declare sb persona grata/non grata

personnage [pɛrsonaʒ] **NM 1** *(personne importante)* important person, *Fml* personage; **p. connu** ou **célèbre** celebrity; **p. officiel** VIP; **un grand p.** a great figure; **un grand p. de l'État** a State dignitary; **les grands personnages de l'histoire** the great names of history; **c'est devenu un p.** he's become an important person *or Fam* a big shot **2** *(individu)* indivi-

dual, character; **un curieux p.** an odd (sort of) character; **c'est un triste p.** he's a poor specimen; **cet homme-là, c'est un p.!** he's quite a character, that man! **3** *(image publique)* (public) image, persona; **il s'est construit un p.** he's created an image for himself **4** *Théâtre, Cin, TV, Littér* character; **p. principal** main *or* principal character; **jouer un p.** to play a part *or* role; *Fig* to play a part *or* role, to put on an act **5** *Beaux-Arts (de tableau)* figure

personnalisation [pɛrsonalizasjɔ̃] **NF** personalization; *Mktg* customization

personnalisé [pɛrsonalize] **ADJ** personalized; *(voiture, crédit)* customized; **nous vous promettons un accueil p.** we promise you a welcome with a personal touch

personnaliser [pɛrsonalize] **VT** to personalize; *(chambre, appartement, bureau etc)* to give a personal touch to; **p. une voiture** to customize a car; **p. sa retraite** to adapt one's pension to one's personal needs; **p. l'image de marque du personnel** to give the staff a corporate identity; **nous devons p. l'accueil** we must welcome our guests/clients/*etc* in a more personal manner

personnalité [pɛrsonalite] **NF 1** *(caractère)* personality; **trouble de la p.** personality disorder; **avoir de la p.** to be full of personality; **manquer de p.** to have no personality; **elle ne manque pas de p.** she's got plenty of personality, she doesn't lack personality; **c'est une forte p.** he/she has a strong personality; *Fam* **il a une sacrée p.** he's got one hell of a personality; **culte de la p.** personality cult **2** *(personnage important)* personality, VIP; **les personnalités politiques** the key political figures; **c'est une p.** he's/she's an important man/woman **3** *Jur* **p. juridique** legal personality *or* status

PERSONNE [pɛrsɔn]

| **NF** person **1, 4, 5** ▪ people **1** ▪ in |
| person *(en personne)* **3** |
| **PRON INDÉFINI** anybody **1** ▪ nobody **2** |

NF 1 *(individu)* person; **trois personnes** three people; **le respect de la p. (humaine)** respect for the individual's rights; **une tierce p.** a third party; **par p. interposée** through a third person *or* party; **toute p. intéressée doit** ou **toutes les personnes intéressées sont priées de me contacter au …** all interested parties *or* all those interested should contact me at …; **p. interrogée** respondent; **cela coûte 20 euros par p.** it costs 20 euros a head *or* per head *or* per person; **il y a deux oranges par p.** there are two oranges per person *or* each; **une p. âgée** an elderly person; **les personnes âgées** the elderly, elderly people, senior citizens; **p. handicapée** disabled person; **une grande p.** a grown-up; **une jeune p.** a young lady; **il y a erreur sur la p.** you've got the wrong person; **personnes à charge** dependants

2 *Jur* **p. morale** body corporate, corporate body, legal entity; **p. physique** natural person; **personnes physiques** ou **morales** individual and legal entities

3 *(soi-même)* **être satisfait/faire grand cas de sa (petite) p.** to be self-satisfied/full of (one's own) self-importance; **prendre soin de sa (petite) p.** to look after oneself; **il ne pense qu'à sa petite p.** he only thinks about number one, he's all self; **en p.** in person, personally; **le roi est venu en p.** the king came in person, the king himself came; **il est la bonté en p.** he is kindness itself, he is kindness personified; **elle est bien de sa p.** she's got a good figure; **il est bien/mal fait de sa p.** he's well/badly proportioned; **exposer sa p.** to expose oneself to danger, to risk one's life; **y aller** ou **donner**

de sa p. to give everything one has

4 *(personnalité)* person; **la gentillesse émane de toute sa p.** his/her whole person *or* being radiates kindness; **j'apprécie le cinéaste, mais je n'aime pas la p.** I like him as a film maker, but not as a person

5 *Gram* person; **écrire à la troisième p. du singulier** to write in the third person singular

PRON INDÉF SEE GRAMMAR B16 **1** *(quiconque)* anyone, anybody; **il le sait aussi bien** ou **mieux que p.** nobody knows it better than he does; **il est exclu que p. parle** nobody is allowed to speak; **elle danse comme p.** no one dances *or* can dance like her, she dances *or* can dance better than anyone; **sans nommer p.** without naming anybody, naming no names, without naming names

2 *(with* ne *expressed or understood)* no one, nobody; **p. n'est venu, il n'est venu p.** no one *or* nobody has come; **qui est là? – p.** who's there? – no one *or* nobody; **que p. ne sorte** no one *or* nobody is to leave; **il n'y a p. de blessé** no one *or* nobody has been injured, there are no casualties; **il n'y avait p. d'intéressé** no one *or* nobody was interested; **p. d'autre n'était à bord** there was no one else *or* nobody else on board; **je ne peux le dire à p. d'autre** I can't tell anyone *or* anybody else; **je ne dois rien à p.** I don't owe anyone anything; **dans cette maison p. ne se connaissait** in this house no one knew anyone else *or* nobody knew anybody else; **je n'y suis pour p.** I'm not at home to anybody *or* anyone, if anybody *or* anyone calls, I'm not at home; **je ne connais p. de plus hypocrite** I don't know anybody *or* anyone (who is) more hypocritical; **ne connaissez-vous p. qui puisse nous aider?** do you *or* don't you know anybody who could help us?; *Fam* **dès qu'il s'agit de travailler, il n'y a plus p.** as soon as there's work to be done, you can't see anyone for dust SEE GRAMMAR B62

personnel, -elle [pɛrsonɛl] **ADJ 1** *(lettre, entreprise, idées etc)* personal; *(titre de transport)* non-transferable; **objets personnels** personal belongings; **fortune personnelle** personal *or* private fortune; *Gram* **pronom p.** personal pronoun SEE GRAMMAR A27–9; B18–21 **2** *(égoïste)* selfish; *Sport* **joueur p.** selfish player; **il avait un intérêt p. à voir se détériorer les choses** he had a personal *or* vested interest in seeing things get worse; **elle a des intérêts personnels dans cette affaire** she has a vested interest in the matter
▸ **NM** *(d'une institution, d'une firme)* personnel, staff, employees; *(d'une école)* staff; *(d'une usine, dans l'industrie)* workforce, employees; *Mil* personnel, manpower; *Naut* complement; **faire partie de p. de …** to be on the staff of …; **p. réduit** reduced *or* skeleton staff; **manquer de p.** to be understaffed; **un membre du p.** a member of staff, *surtout Am* a staffer; **directeur du p.** personnel manager; **service du p.** personnel (department); **le p. politique/artistique** the political/artistic staff VOIR GRAMMAIRE A11
▸ ▸ **p. administratif** administrative staff; *Banque* **p. de back-office** back-office staff; **p. de bureau** office *or* clerical staff; *Aviat* **p. de cabine** flight personnel, cabin staff; **p. d'encadrement** management; *(animateurs)* activity organizers; *(moniteurs)* instructors; **p. extra** relief staff; *Aviat* **p. navigant** flight personnel *or* staff *or* crew; *TV etc* **p. de plateau** floor crew; **p. saisonnier** seasonal staff; *Aviat* **p. au sol** ground personnel *or* staff *or* crew; *Mktg* **p. de soutien commercial** sales support staff; **p. à temps partiel** part-time staff; **p. titulaire** permanent staff; **p. de vente** sales personnel

personnellement [pɛrsonɛlmɑ̃] **ADV** personally

personnification [pɛrsɔnifikasjɔ̃] NF personification, embodiment

personnifier [pɛrsɔnifje] VT (impf, pr sub n. **personnifiions**, v. **personnifiiez**) (objet, vertu, vice etc) to personify; **elle personnifie toute la bonté humaine** she is the embodiment or personification of all human kindness; **il est la bêtise personnifiée** he is stupidity personified, he is stupidity itself; **il personnifie son pays** he typifies his country

perspectif, -ive¹ [pɛrspɛktif, -iv] ADJ (plan) perspective

perspective² [pɛrspɛktiv] NF **1** (avenir, idée) prospect; **en p.** in prospect; **avoir qch en p.** to have sth in prospect or in view; **quels sont les projets en p.?** what projects are there lined up or in prospect?; **perspectives de reprise** outlook for recovery; **elle était très excitée à la p. de faire ce voyage** she was very excited at the prospect of going on the journey; **j'envisage avec plaisir la p. de le revoir** I am looking forward to seeing him again; **des perspectives d'avenir** future prospects **2** Beaux-Arts etc perspective; **p. à vol d'oiseau** bird's-eye view; **dessin en p.** drawing in perspective **3** (point de vue) viewpoint, point of view; **ce roman est analysé sous des perspectives différentes** this novel is analysed from several different viewpoints or points of view; **dans une p. marxiste** from a marxist viewpoint or point of view

perspicace [pɛrspikas] ADJ shrewd, perspicacious

perspicacité [pɛrspikasite] NF shrewdness, insight, perspicacity

persuader [pɛrsɥade] VT **1 p. qn** to persuade or convince sb; **p. qn de qch/de faire qch** to persuade or convince sb of sth/persuade sb to do sth; **j'ai fini par les p.** I convinced or persuaded them in the end, I talked them round in the end; **être persuadé de qch** to be convinced of sth; **être persuadé que ...** to be sure or convinced that ...; **j'en suis tout à fait persuadé** I'm quite convinced (of it); **je n'en suis pas persuadé** I'm not convinced (of it) **2** Vieilli **p. qch à qn** to persuade sb of sth, to make sb believe sth

▪ VPR **se persuader** (se convaincre) to persuade or convince oneself; **ils se sont persuadé(s) que ...** they have persuaded or convinced themselves that ...

persuasif, -ive [pɛrsɥazif, -iv] ADJ persuasive

persuasion [pɛrsɥazjɔ̃] NF **1** (fait ou action de persuader) persuasion; **à force de p.** through (the use of) persuasion; **agir par (la) p.** to use persuasion, to persuade; **avoir un grand pouvoir de p.** to have great powers of persuasion **2** (conviction, certitude) conviction, belief

perte [pɛrt] NF **1** (d'argent, d'un proche, d'un procès, de la vue, de la raison etc) loss; **des pertes importantes** considerable or significant losses; **de lourdes pertes en hommes et en matériel** heavy losses of men and equipment; Fig Fam **elle a été renvoyée avec p. et fracas** she was thrown out of her job; Fig Fam **il est sorti avec p. et fracas** he made a big scene when he left; **à p. de vue** as far as the eye can see; **ce n'est pas une grosse p.** it's no great loss; **p. de pouvoir d'achat** loss of purchasing power; **pertes et profits** profit and loss; **pertes et profits exceptionnels** extraordinary items; aussi Fig **passer qch par pertes et profits** to write sth off; **vendre qch à p.** to sell sth at a loss; **travailler** ou **fonctionner à p.** to operate at a loss

2 (gaspillage) waste; **une p. de temps** a waste of time; **en pure p.** to no purpose, fruitlessly; **expliquer qch à qn en pure p.** to

waste one's time or one's breath trying to explain sth to sb; **une dépense en pure p.** wasteful expenditure

3 (déperdition) loss; (de tuyau, récipient) leakage; **p. de chaleur** heat loss, loss of heat; Élec **p. de charge** drop in voltage; Élec **p. à la terre** earth or Am ground leakage; Aviat **avion en p. de vitesse** plane that is losing speed; Fig **le président/le cinéma semble en p. de vitesse** the President/the film industry seems to be running out of steam; **pertes de mémoire** memory losses; Méd **pertes de sang** bleeding

4 (destruction) ruin; **jurer la p. de qn** to swear to ruin sb; **il/l'entreprise court à sa p.** he/the company is heading for disaster ▸▸**p. de bénéfice** loss of profit; **p. brute** gross loss; **p. en capitaux** capital loss; Fin **p. de change** (foreign) exchange loss; **p. de connaissance** loss of consciousness; Ordinat **p. de données irréparable** irretrievable data loss; **p. envisagée** estimated loss; Fin **p. d'intérêts** loss of interest; Fin **p. latente** unrealized loss; Fin **p. nette** net loss; Fin **p. sèche** dead loss; Compta **p. supportée** loss attributable; Fin **p. totale** total loss; Compta **p. transférée** loss transferred; Méd **pertes blanches** vaginal discharge, Spéc leucorrhoea, surtout Am leukorrhea; **pertes humaines** loss of life

pertinemment [pɛrtinamɑ̃] ADV **1** Litt (s'exprimer) pertinently, to the point **2** **savoir qch p.** to know sth for a fact

pertinence [pɛrtinɑ̃s] NF pertinence, pertinency, relevance

pertinent [pɛrtinɑ̃] ADJ pertinent, relevant

pertuis [pɛrtɥi] NM **1** (canal) sluice **2** (d'un fleuve) narrows; (détroit) strait(s), (narrow) channel

perturbant [pɛrtyrbɑ̃] ADJ disturbing, upsetting

perturbateur, -trice [pɛrtyrbatœr, -tris] ADJ disruptive
▪ N troublemaker

perturbation [pɛrtyrbasjɔ̃] NF (de services publics) disruption; Astron perturbation; **p. (atmosphérique)** (atmospheric) disturbance; **perturbations du service aérien** disruption of air travel

perturber [pɛrtyrbe] VT (services publics, trains, métro) to disrupt; (personne) to perturb, to upset; Astron to perturb

péruvien, -ienne [peryvjɛ̃, -jɛn] ADJ Peruvian
▪ N **P.** Peruvian

pervenche [pɛrvɑ̃ʃ] NF **1** (plante) periwinkle; **(bleu) p.** periwinkle blue **2** Fam (contractuelle) (female) traffic warden, Am meter maid

pervers, -erse [pɛrvɛr, -ɛrs] ADJ (idée) perverse; (esprit, pratiques sexuelles) perverted; **goûts p.** unnatural or perverted tastes; **conseils p.** evil advice; **effet p.** perverse effect
▪ N twisted person; (vicieux) pervert

> Il faut noter que l'adjectif anglais **perverse** signifie également **contrariant**.

perversion [pɛrvɛrsjɔ̃] NF (des goûts, de la morale) perversion; (de l'esprit) warping; Fam **c'est de la p.!** that's twisted or perverted!; **p. sexuelle** sexual perversion

perversité [pɛrvɛrsite] NF perversity, depravity

perverti, -ie [pɛrvɛrti] ADJ (personne) perverted, depraved
▪ N pervert

pervertir [pɛrvɛrtir] VT (goût, sens) to pervert; (personne) to pervert, to deprave, to corrupt; (morale) to corrupt
▪ VPR **se pervertir** (d'un goût, d'un sens) to

come perverted; (d'une personne) to become perverted or depraved or corrupt(ed); (d'une morale) to become corrupt(ed)

pesage [pəzaʒ] NM **1** (pesée) weighing **2** Courses de chevaux weigh-in; (lieu) weighing room

pesamment [pəzamɑ̃] ADV heavily; **marcher p.** to walk with a heavy tread or heavily

pesant [pəzɑ̃] ADJ (valise, pas) heavy; (style, écrivain) heavy, ponderous; (esprit) slow, sluggish; (sommeil) deep; (ambiance) oppressive; **silence p.** heavy silence; **marcher à pas pesants** to walk with a heavy step or heavily; **le temps me semble p.** time hangs heavy on my hands
▪ NM **cela vaut son p. d'or** ou Fam **de moutarde** ou Fam **de cacahuètes** it's worth its weight in gold

pesanteur [pəzɑ̃tœr] NF **1** Phys gravity; **p. spécifique** specific gravity **2** (lourdeur) heaviness; (d'un mouvement, d'une démarche) inelegance, unwieldiness; (de l'esprit) slowness, sluggishness; **j'ai une p. d'estomac** there's something lying heavy on my stomach; Fig **pesanteurs intellectuelles** intellectual baggage or impedimenta; Fig **pesanteurs économiques** economic impedimenta

PESC [pɛɛsse] NF UE (abrév **politique étrangère et de sécurité commune**) CFSP

pèse-alcool [pɛzalkɔl] NM INV alcoholometer

pèse-bébé, pl **pèse-bébés** [pɛzbebe] NM baby scales

pesée [pəze] NF **1** weighing; Boxe, Courses de chevaux weigh-in; **faire la p. de qch** to weigh sth; **cette balance a une p. de 150 kilos** these scales can weigh up to 150 kilos **2** (pression) force, effort; **exercer une p. sur une porte** to try to force a door

pèse-lait [pɛzlɛ] NM INV lactometer

pèse-lettre, pl **pèse-lettre(s)** [pɛzlɛtr] NM letter scales

pèse-personne, pl **pèse-personnes** [pɛzpɛrsɔn] NM scales

peser [pəze] (je **pèse**, n. **pesons**; je **pèserai**) VT to weigh; **p. à vide** to tare; Fig **p. ses mots** ou **ses paroles** to weigh one's words, to think before one speaks; **et je pèse mes mots!** and I don't say it lightly!; **réponse bien pesée** considered or careful answer; Fig **tout bien pesé** all things considered; **p. tous les éléments** to weigh (up) all the facts; **p. une décision** to weigh up or ponder a decision; **p. le pour et le contre** to weigh (up) the pros and cons; Sport **se faire p.** to weigh in

▪ VI **1** (faire ou avoir comme poids) to weigh; (être lourd) to be heavy; (d'un argument) to carry weight; **ce paquet pèse deux kilos** this parcel weighs two kilos; **il ne pèse pas lourd** he doesn't weigh much, he's not very heavy; Fig he doesn't carry much weight or count for much; **mon avis ne pèse pas lourd** my opinion doesn't carry much weight or count for much; **cela me pèse de vous le demander** it isn't easy for me to ask you; **le temps lui pèse** time hangs heavy on his hands; **l'isolement/votre absence me pèse** this isolation/your absence gets me down or is a strain; **cette ambiance me pèse un peu** I'm finding this atmosphere a bit oppressive; **toutes ces discussions lui pèsent** all these discussions are a strain on him; **p. sur qch** to press on sth; **p. sur un levier** to press down or push down on a lever; Can **p. sur un bouton** to push a button; **aliment qui pèse sur l'estomac** food that lies heavy on the stomach; **p. sur le cœur à qn** to give sb a heavy heart; **un silence pesait sur l'assemblée** a heavy silence hung over the meeting; **une lourde responsabilité pèse sur lui** he is weighed

down by a heavy responsibility; **une menace qui pèse sur nous** a threat that is hanging over us; **ça lui pèse sur la conscience** it lies heavy on his conscience; **p. sur un choix** to weigh up *or* mull over a choice; **p. sur ou dans une décision** to carry weight in a decision; **p. sur un mot** to lay stress on a word, to stress a word
2 *(valoir) (d'une entreprise, d'une personne)* to be worth; **cette entreprise pèse 20 millions de dollars** this company is worth 20 million dollars
VPR se peser to weigh oneself

peseta [pezeta] **NF** *Anciennement* peseta

pèse-vin [pɛzvɛ̃] **NM INV** oenometer

peso [pɛzo] **NM** peso

peson [pəzɔ̃] **NM** balance

pessaire [pesɛr] **NM** *Méd* pessary

pesse [pɛs] **NF, pessereau** [pesro] **NM** *(plante)* horse tail, *Spéc* equisetum

pessimisme [pesimism] **NM** pessimism

pessimiste [pesimist] **ADJ** pessimistic
N pessimist

peste [pɛst] **NF 1** *Méd* plague, *Litt, Arch* pestilence; **être atteint de la p.** to have the plague, to be stricken with the plague; *Fam* **fuir qn/qch comme la p.** to avoid sb/sth like the plague; **je me méfie de lui/ça comme de la p.** I don't trust him/it one little bit, I wouldn't trust him/it as far as I could throw him/it; *Litt, Vieilli* **p.!** good gracious!, heavens!; *Litt, Arch* **soit du vieux fou!** a plague on the old fool!; *Vieilli* **que la p. t'étouffe!** a plague on you! **2** *Fig Péj (enfant)* pest, nuisance; **une petite p.** a little devil *or* pest
▸▸ **p. bovine** cattle plague; **la p. bubonique ou noire** the bubonic plague; *Hist* the Black Death; **p. porcine** swine fever

Il faut noter que le terme anglais **pest** est un faux ami. Il ne désigne jamais une maladie.

pester [peste] **VI p. contre qn/qch** to curse sb/sth, to rave at sb/sth; **il pestait** he was cursing

pesticide [pestisid] **ADJ** pesticidal
NM pesticide

pestiféré, -ée [pestifere] **ADJ** plague-stricken
N plague victim; **fuir qn comme un p.** to avoid sb like the plague

pestilence [pestilɑ̃s] **NF** stench, stink

pestilentiel, -ielle [pestilɑ̃sjɛl] **ADJ** stinking, fetid

pet [pɛ] **NM 1** *Fam (vent)* fart; **faire ou lâcher un p.** to fart; **ça ne vaut pas un p. (de lapin)** it isn't worth a monkey's fart *or* a damn; *Fig* **il a toujours un p. de travers** there's always something wrong with him *or* the matter with him **2** *Arg Vieilli (grabuge)* **il va y avoir du p.** there's going to be trouble **3** *Fam* **faire le p.** *(faire le guet)* to keep watch *or* a lookout **4** *Fam (choc)* [pɛt] **ta voiture a pris un p.** your car's had a bash; **j'ai fait un p. à la voiture** I've put a dent in the car; **plein de pets** all bashed up, full of dents

pétage [petaʒ] **NM** *Fam* **p. de plombs** *(fait de se mettre en colère)* going ballistic, hitting the roof *or* Am ceiling; *(fait de craquer nerveusement)* cracking up; **le patron nous a fait un p. de plombs maison quand il s'est aperçu de ce qui s'était passé** the boss went totally ballistic *or* totally hit the roof *or* Am ceiling when he saw what had happened; **il faut que je prenne des vacances parce que là je suis au bord du p. de plombs** I need to take a holiday because I'm on the verge of cracking up

pétainiste [petenist] *Hist* **ADJ** Pétainist
N follower of Pétain, Pétainist

pétale [petal] **NM** petal

pétanque [petɑ̃k] **NF** ≃ bowls *(played in the South of France)*

Pétanque
Originally invented in the South of France, where it has become a local institution, this bowling game is equally popular with tourists. The game, which requires two teams and is played up to a score of thirteen points, is played outdoors on a flat sandy or earth surface. Each team consists of two to three players, each of whom has three steel "boules". Each player tosses or rolls their "boule" so that it ends up as near as possible to the "cochonnet" (a small wooden ball thrown from a distance of 6 to 10 metres), at the same time trying to hit the other team's "boules" so as to scatter them. Players take turns, and whoever ends up closest to the "cochonnet" when all balls are played, wins.

pétant, -ante [petɑ̃, -ɑ̃t] **ADJ** *Fam* **à neuf heures pétantes** at nine o'clock sharp *or* on the dot, on the stroke of nine

Pétaouchnock [petauʃnɔk] **N** *Fam* = imaginary distant place; **ils l'ont envoyé à P.** they sent him to some place in the back of beyond

pétaradant [petaradɑ̃] **ADJ** *(moto, camion etc)* spluttering, sputtering

pétarade [petarad] **NF 1** *(d'un cheval)* (succession of) farts **2** *(de feux d'artifice, d'armes à feu)* crackling **3** *(de voiture, Mobylette® etc)* backfiring, backfire

pétarader [petarade] **VI 1** *(d'un cheval)* to let off a succession of farts **2** *(de feux d'artifice, d'armes à feu)* to crackle **3** *(de voiture, Mobylette® etc)* to backfire

pétard [petar] **NM 1** *(feu d'artifice)* (fire)cracker, *Br* banger; *Min* shot, blast; *Mil* explosive charge, *Arch* petard; *Rail* fog signal; **faire partir ou claquer un p.** to let off a (fire)cracker *or Br* banger; *Fig* **p. mouillé** damp squib **2** *Fam (grabuge)* **il va y avoir du p.** there's going to be a hell of a row; **faire du p.** to raise a stink; **être en p. (en colère)** to be raging (**contre** against), to be in a flaming temper; **se mettre en p.** to fly off the handle **3** *Fam (pistolet)* shooter, *Am* gat **4** *Fam (derrière)* bum, *Am* ass, fanny **5** *Fam (joint)* joint, *Br* spliff

pétasse [petas] **NF** *Vulg (terme injurieux)* bitch, slut; *(prostituée)* whore, hooker

pétaudière [petodjɛr] **NF** bedlam, bear garden; **la réunion a tourné en p.** the meeting turned into a bear garden

pet-de-nonne, *pl* **pets-de-nonne NM** *Culin* fritter

pété [pete] **ADJ** *Fam (ivre)* smashed, plastered

péter [pete] (**je pète, n. pétons; je péterai**) **VI 1** *Fam (d'une personne)* to fart; *Fig* **il l'a envoyé p.** he told him to piss off; *Fig* **p. dans la soie** to be stinking rich, to be loaded; *Fig* **il pète plus haut que son derrière ou son cul** he thinks he's really somebody *or* really it, he thinks he's God's gift to humanity **2** *Fam (exploser)* to blow up; **faire p. des pétards** to set off (fire)crackers; *Fig* **il faut que ça pète** let's have it all out in the open; **si les relations entre les deux pays continuent à se détériorer, ça va finir par p.** if relations between the two countries continue to deteriorate, all hell will break loose; **ça va p. entre eux** they're going to have one hell of a row **3** *(de bois qui brûle)* to crack, to crackle; *(d'un bouchon)* to pop **4** *Fam (casser)* to break; *(d'une ficelle, d'une branche, d'un câble)* to snap, to break; **ça va lui p. entre les mains** it'll break in his hands; **tous les boutons étaient prêts à p.** all the buttons were about to pop off **5** *Fam* **p. de joie/santé** to be jumping for joy/bouncing with health; **et je veux que ça pète!** chop, chop!, *Arg* and get your finger out!; **on a enfin l'impression que ça pète!** things seem to be moving at last!, we're seeing a bit of action at last!
VT *Fam* **1 p. le feu ou la forme** to be bursting with energy *or* vitality; **ça va p. des flammes** there's going to be a hell of a row **2** *(casser)* to bust; **je vais lui p. la gueule** I'll smash his face in **3 p. sa frime** to show off, to pose **4 la p.** *(avoir très faim)* to be starving *or* ravenous
VPR se péter *Fam* **1** *(d'une machine etc)* to break; **il s'est pété la gueule** *(il est tombé)* he came a cropper; *(il s'est saoulé)* he got smashed *or* plastered **2 se la p.** to show off, to pose; *Can* **se p. les bretelles** to brag, to be full of oneself

pète-sec [pɛtsɛk] *Fam* **NM INV** snappy person
ADJ INV curt

péteux, -euse [petø, -øz] *Fam Péj* **N 1** *(lâche)* yellowbelly, coward; **c'est un petit p.** he's yellow **2** *(prétentieux)* upstart
ADJ 1 *(lâche)* cowardly **2** *(prétentieux)* stuck-up, snooty

pétillant [petijɑ̃] **ADJ** *(feu)* crackling; *(vin)* sparkling; *(eau)* fizzy; *Fig (yeux)* sparkling; *Fig* **esprit p.** sparkling wit

pétillement [petijmɑ̃] **NM** *(du bois qui brûle)* crackling; *(du champagne)* sparkling, fizzing, bubbling; *(des yeux)* sparkling

pétiller [petije] **VI** *(de bois qui brûle)* to crackle; *(d'une boisson)* to sparkle, to fizz, to bubble; *Fig (des yeux)* to sparkle; *Fig* **p. d'esprit** to sparkle with wit; **elle pétillait de joie** she was bubbling over with joy; **un regard qui pétille de joie/d'intelligence** a look that sparkles with joy/with intelligence

pétiole [pesjɔl] **NM** *Bot* petiole

petiot, -ote [pətjo, -ɔt] *Fam* **ADJ** tiny, wee
N tiny child; **ma petiote** my little girl; **viens ici, p.** come here, little fellow

PETIT, -ITE [p(ə)ti, -it]

ADJ small **1, 5, 7** ▪ little **1–3, 6**
▪ insignificant **5** ▪ young **6** ▪ mean **8**
▪ petty **8**
N (little) boy/girl
NM young

ADJ 1 *(de taille réduite)* small, little; **un p. homme** a small *or* short *or* little man; **c'est un homme p.** he's small *or* short *or* little; **jouer avec des petits soldats/des petites voitures** to play with toy soldiers/toy cars; **une toute petite maison/boîte/entreprise** a tiny little house/box/firm; **petite distance** short distance; **un p. nombre de gens** a small number of people; **ces chaussures sont trop petites (pour moi)** these shoes are too small (for me); **faire de petits profits** to make a small profit; **rouler à petite vitesse** to drive slowly; **pendant un p. moment** for a little while; *Fam* **nous avons attendu un bon p. moment** we waited quite a time; *Fam* **j'y suis resté une petite demi-heure** I stayed there just under half an hour; *Fig* **se faire tout p.** to make oneself as inconspicuous as possible; **il s'est fait tout p. devant elle** he tried to do everything to please her; *Fig* **comme le monde est p.** it's a small world
VOIR GRAMMAIRE A17
2 *(méprisant)* **p. crétin/con!** little idiot/bastard!
3 *(affectueux)* little; **mais ma petite Louise ...** but my dear Louise ...; **Ma chère petite maman** *(dans une lettre)* Dear Mummy; **un**

p. coup de rouge a drop of red wine; **et si on se regardait une petite cassette vidéo?** how about watching a video?; **je prendrais bien une petite cigarette** I'd love a cigarette; **on s'en fume une petite?** shall we have a quick smoke or Br fag?

4 (de niveau inférieur) lesser, minor; Scol les **petites classes** the lower classes; **le p. personnel** the junior staff; **la petite industrie** light industry; **les petits propriétaires** the small landowners; Com **petite caisse** petty cash

5 (de moindre importance) (problème, erreur etc) small, minor, insignificant; (fait) insignificant, unimportant; Péj (plainte, affaire) petty; (événement) minor; **petites routes** minor roads; **entrer par la petite porte** to start off at the bottom; **ce n'est pas une petite affaire** it's no small matter; **p. accident** minor accident; **j'ai un p. rhume** I've a slight cold or a bit of a cold; **les petites gens** ordinary people

6 (jeune) little, young; **p. enfant** little or young child; **petite fille** little girl; **mon p. frère** my little brother; **tu es trop p. pour ça** you're too young for that; **quand tu étais p.** when you were little or small or young; **un p. Anglais** an English boy; **les petits Thomas** the Thomas children

7 (faible) **il a une petite santé** he's delicate; **une petite voix** a small voice

8 (borné) narrow-minded; (mesquin) petty; (remarque, acte) mean, petty; (dans ses compliments, ses défaites) ungenerous; **c'est vraiment p.** that's really mean or petty; **c'est un p. esprit** he's petty-minded

N (enfant) (little) boy, f (little) girl; **pauvre petit(e)** poor little thing; Scol **les petits** the juniors; **le p.** (dans une famille) the youngest (boy); Fam **bonjour, mon p.** (à une femme, un enfant) good morning, my dear

NM (d'un animal) young; **petits du chien** (dog's) puppies; **petits du chat** (cat's) kittens; **faire** ou **avoir des petits** to have young; (d'une chienne) to have pups, Spéc to pup, to whelp; (d'une lionne) to have cubs, Spéc to whelp; (d'une truie) to have piglets, Spéc to farrow; (d'une chatte) to have kittens, Spéc to kitten; (d'une louve) to have cubs, Spéc to cub; Fig Fam **faire des petits** (de l'argent) to increase, to multiply

ADV p. à p. little by little, bit by bit, gradually; **en p.** on a small scale, in miniature; **le même mais en plus p.** the same only smaller
▶ ▶ **p. ami** boyfriend; **petite amie** girlfriend; Journ **petite annonce** classified ad, small ad; Journ **petites annonces personnelles** personal column; **p. bois** kindling wood; Typ **petite capitale** small cap; Fam **le p. coin** the toilet, Br the loo, Am the john; **p. commerçant** shopkeeper; **p. commerce** (secteur) small retail trade; (endroit) small shop; Fam **p. copain** boyfriend; Fam **petite copine** girlfriend; Typ **petits corps** small type; **p. cousin/petite cousine** second cousin; **p. déjeuner** breakfast; **p. déjeuner américain** American breakfast; **p. déjeuner à l'anglaise** English breakfast; **p. déjeuner continental** continental breakfast; **p. doigt** little finger, Am, Scot pinkie; **le p. écran** television, the small screen; **la petite enfance** early childhood, infancy; **petits-fours** petits fours; **la petite mort** orgasm; **petites et moyennes entreprises** small (and medium-sized) businesses; **petites et moyennes industries** small (and medium-sized) industries; Fam **p. nom** first name; Fig **petites phrases** (des hommes politiques) soundbites; **il est connu pour ses petites phrases très médiatiques** he's the master of the soundbite; **petits pois** (garden) peas; Fin **p. porteur** small investor or shareholder; Culin **p. salé** = type of streaky bacon; **petits salariés** low wage-earners

petit-beurre, pl **petits-beurre** NM Culin butter biscuit or Am cookie

petit-bourgeois, petite-bourgeoise, pl **petit(e)s-bourgeois(es)** ADJ aussi Péj lower middle class, petit-bourgeois **N** member of the lower middle class; **les petits-bourgeois** the petty bourgeoisie

petit-déj' [p(ə)tideʒ] NM Fam breakfast

petite-fille, pl **petites-filles** [p(ə)titfij] NF granddaughter

petitement [pətitmɑ̃] ADV **1** (dans la pauvreté) poorly **2** (à l'étroit) **elle est logée p.** she lives in cramped accommodation **3** (bassement) meanly, pettily

petite-nièce, pl **petites-nièces** [p(ə)titnjɛs] NF great-niece

petitesse [p(ə)titɛs] NF **1** (d'un objet) smallness, small size; (d'une silhouette) slenderness **2** Péj (mesquinerie) meanness, pettiness; (d'un repas, d'une somme d'argent) paltriness; **p. d'esprit** narrow-mindedness; **p. de cœur** small-mindedness **3** Péj (action mesquine) shabby deed

petit-fils, pl **petits-fils** NM grandson

petit-gris, pl **petits-gris** NM **1** (écureuil) Siberian squirrel; (fourrure) squirrel (fur) **2** Culin = edible brown snail

pétition [petisjɔ̃] NF **1** petition; **adresser une p. à qn** to petition sb; **faire signer une p. à qn** to get sb to sign a petition **2 p. de principe** begging the question, Spéc petitio principii

pétitionnaire [petisjɔnɛr] N petitioner

pétitionner [petisjɔne] VI to petition

petit-lait, pl **petits-laits** NM whey; **cela se boit comme du p.** it goes down or slips down a treat; Fig **boire du p.** to lap it up

petit-maître, pl **petits-maîtres** NM Arch fop, dandy

petit-nègre NM Ling Fam **1** (mauvais français) bad French; **c'est du p.** it's gibberish **2** Vieilli (français parlé dans les colonies) pidgin French

petit-neveu, pl **petits-neveux** NM great-nephew

petits-enfants [p(ə)tizɑ̃fɑ̃] NMPL grandchildren

petit-suisse, pl **petits-suisses** NM Culin petit-suisse (small cream cheese dessert)

pétochard, -arde [petoʃar, -ard] N Fam yellowbelly, coward

pétoche [petoʃ] NF Fam jitters; **avoir la p.** to have the jitters, to be scared stiff; **ficher** ou **flanquer** ou très Fam **foutre la p. à qn** to give sb the jitters, to scare sb stiff

pétocher [petoʃe] VI Fam to be scared stiff or witless

pétoire [petwar] NF **1** (sarbacane) peashooter **2** (mauvais fusil) popgun **3** (moto) motorbike; (Mobylette®) moped

pétole [petol] NF Suisse (crotte de chèvre) goat shit

peton [pətɔ̃] NM Enf tootsy(-wootsy); **petons** tootsies, tootsy-wootsies

pétoncle [petɔ̃kl] NM scallop

pétouiller [petuje] VI Suisse Fam (traînasser) to loaf around

Pétrarque [petrark] N Petrarch

pétrel [petrɛl] NM petrel; **p. tempête** storm(y) petrel

pétri [petri] ADJ kneaded, moulded, Am molded (**de** out of); **un homme p. d'orgueil** a man puffed up with pride; **p. d'ignorance** steeped in ignorance; **p. de contradictions** riddled with contradictions

pétrifiant [petrifjɑ̃] ADJ (eau) petrifying, petrifactive; (nouvelle) stupefying

pétrification [petrifikasjɔ̃] NF petrification,

petrifaction; Fig **p. du cœur** hardening of the heart; **p. de l'esprit** sclerosis of the mind

pétrifier [petrifje] (impf, pr sub **n. pétrifiions, v. pétrifiiez**) VT **1** Minér to petrify; Fig **pétrifié de peur** petrified, paralysed or Am paralyzed with fear; **pétrifié de froid** frozen stiff **2** (couvrir de calcaire) to encrust with lime
  VPR se pétrifier Minér to petrify, to become petrified; Fig **son sourire se pétrifia** his smile froze; **son esprit se pétrifiait** he was developing sclerosis of the mind; **en entendant son nom, elle s'est pétrifiée** hearing his name, she froze

pétrin [petrɛ̃] NM kneading trough; **p. mécanique** kneading machine; Fam **mettre qn/se mettre dans le p.** to get sb/get into a mess or a fix; Fam **laisser qn dans le p.** to drop sb in it, to leave sb in a mess; Fam **être dans le p.** to be in a mess or a fix; **nous voilà dans un beau** ou **joli** ou **sale p.** that's a fine or right mess we're in

pétrir [petrir] VT (brasser) (pâte à pain) to knead; (façonner) (argile) to knead, to shape, to mould, Am to mold; Fig **p. l'esprit de qn** to mould or shape sb's mind; **il lui pétrissait le bras** he was kneading her arm; **il pétrissait son chapeau avec nervosité** he was nervously fiddling or toying with his hat; Méd **p. un muscle** to knead a muscle

pétrissage [petrisaʒ] NM kneading

pétrisseur, -euse [petrisœr, -øz] N (ouvrier) **p.** dough mixer
  NF **pétrisseuse** (machine) kneading machine

pétrochimie [petroʃimi] NF petrochemistry

pétrochimique [petroʃimik] ADJ petrochemical

pétrochimiste [petroʃimist] N petrochemist

pétrodollar [petrodɔlar] NM Fin petrodollar

pétrographie [petrografi] NF Géol petrography

pétrole [petrol] NM oil, petroleum; **p. brut** crude (oil); **p. lampant** paraffin (oil), Am kerosene; **gisement de p.** oil deposit, oilfield; **puits de p.** oil well; **lampe à p.** oil lamp; **bleu p.** inv petrol blue; **vert p.** inv deep turquoise

Il faut noter que le terme anglais britannique **petrol** est un faux ami. Il signifie **essence.**

pétrolette [petrolɛt] NF Fam moped

pétroleuse [petroløz] NF activist; Hist female incendiary (during the Paris Commune of 1871)

pétrolier, -ière [petrolje, -jɛr] ADJ **l'industrie pétrolière** the oil or petroleum industry; **société pétrolière** oil company; **pays p.** oil-producing country; **navire p.** (oil) tanker; **choc p.** oil crisis
  NM **1** (financier, industriel) oil magnate, oilman; (technicien) petroleum engineer **2** (navire) (oil) tanker

Do not confuse with **pétrolifère.**

pétrolifère [petrolifɛr] ADJ oil-bearing, Spéc petroliferous; **gisement p.** oilfield

Do not confuse with **pétrolier.**

pétromonarchie [petromonarʃi] NF oil kingdom

pétulance [petylɑ̃s] NF liveliness, exuberance

pétulant [petylɑ̃] ADJ lively, exuberant

Il faut noter que l'adjectif anglais **petulant** est un faux ami. Il signifie **irascible.**

pétunia [petynja] NM petunia

PEU [pø]

| ADV | little **1** ▪ few **2** ▪ not very **3** |
| NM | little **1** ▪ a little (un peu) **2, 3** ▪ a bit (un peu) **2, 3** |

ADV 1 ((en) petite quantité) little; **très/trop p.** very/too little; **de l'instruction, il en avait p. ou pas** he had little or no education, he had precious little education; **p. ou point** little or none; **manger p. (ou point)** to eat little (or nothing); **p. à p.** bit by bit, little by little, gradually; **c'est p. dire** that's an understatement; **c'est p. dire qu'il était content** it's an understatement to say that he was content; **ce n'est pas p. dire** that's saying a good deal or a lot; **il a p. fait pour nous** he has done (very) little for us; **quelque p.** somewhat, rather; **je suis quelque p. surpris** I am somewhat or rather surprised; **si tu m'aimais tant soit p.** if you loved me at all or even a little; **si tu es tant soit p. fatigué** if you're at all or the least bit tired; **p. s'en faut** ou **il s'en faut de p. pour que je me mette en colère** I'm on the verge of losing my temper, it won't take much to make me lose my temper; **p. s'en est fallu qu'il fasse tout rater, il s'en est fallu de p. qu'il fasse tout rater** he very nearly ruined everything; **pour p. qu'il soit de mauvaise humeur, on va passer une sacrée soirée** if he's in a bad mood at all, we're in for one hell of an evening; **il ne s'est pas découragé pour si p.** he didn't get discouraged by such a small thing; **p. de viande** not much meat, very little meat; **c'est p. de chose** it's nothing; **nous en savons p. de choses** we know little about it, we don't know much about it; **il suffirait de p. de choses pour que ça fonctionne** it wouldn't need much or it would take very little to get it to work; **nous sommes bien p. de choses** life is so fragile; **fort p.** (de sucre etc) very little, not much; Fam **très p. pour moi!** not for me!

2 (nombre) few; **p. en garderont un souvenir** few (people) will remember it; **p. de gens** ou **monde** few people; **très p. de gens** very few people, not very many people; **p. d'entre eux avaient voyagé** few of them had travelled; **en p. de mots** in a few words VOIR GRAMMAIRE A6

3 (pas, pas très) not very; **p. utile** not very useful; **p. intelligent** unintelligent, not very intelligent; **p. enviable** unenviable; **p. honnête** dishonest; **p. profond** shallow; **p. souvent** not very often, infrequently; **elle n'est pas p. séduisante** she's more than a little seductive

4 (de temps) **il reste p. de temps** there's not much time left; **très p. de temps** very little time, not very much time; **en très p. de temps** very quickly, in no time at all; **p. après** shortly after(wards), not long after(wards); **sous p., dans p., avant p., d'ici p.** soon, shortly, before long; **depuis p.** lately, recently; **j'ai manqué le train de p.** I (only) just missed the train; **il y a p.** not (very) long ago, recently; **j'ai p. de temps à vous accorder** I don't have much time

NM 1 (petite quantité) little; **le p. qu'il y a est à votre disposition** you are welcome to the little there is; **le p. que je sais de lui** the little I know about him; **le p. d'argent qu'il me reste** what little money I have left; **finis le plat, pour le p. qu'il reste** finish the dish, there's only a little bit left; **son p. d'instruction** what little education he has had

2 un p. a little, a bit; **un p. de** a little, a bit of; **il nous reste un p. de temps/sucre** we still have a little time/sugar left or a bit of time/sugar left; **elle a un p. moins/un p. plus de quarante ans** she's a little under/over forty; **j'en veux un p. plus/moins** I want a little or a bit more/less; **un tout petit p.** a tiny bit, a very little; **un tout petit p. de beurre** a tiny bit of butter, a very little butter; **encore un p.** a bit more, a little more; (encore quelques-uns) a few more; **encore un p. de lait** a bit or a little more milk; **j'ai besoin d'un petit p. de temps avant de donner une réponse** I need a little bit of time before giving an answer; **il sait un p. d'anglais** he knows a little English or a bit of English, he has a smattering of English; **vous êtes allé un p. loin!** you went a bit far!; **je suis un p. en retard** I'm a bit or a little late; **je suis un p. artiste** he's something of an artist; Fam **ça, c'est un p. fort!** that's a bit much!; **un p. plus et il tombait dans l'eau** he very nearly fell in the water; **pour un p. je l'aurais jeté dehors** I all but or I very nearly threw him out; **écoutez un p.** just listen; **viens un p. ici** come here a minute; **regarde un p. ce que tu as fait!** just look what you've done!; **il m'aime un p., beaucoup, passionnément, à la folie, pas du tout** (en effeuillant une marguerite) ≃ he loves me, loves me not; très Fam **t'as vu un p. comment il m'a parlé?** did you see the way he spoke to me?; Fam **je vous demande un p.!** I ask you!; Fam **tu ferais ça – un p.!** you'd do that? – you bet!; Fam **un p. mon neveu!** you bet!, sure! VOIR GRAMMAIRE A6

3 (de temps) **restez encore un p.** stay a bit longer, stay a little (while) longer; **j'aurais voulu prolonger encore un p. mon séjour** I would have liked to extend my stay a bit or a little

peuchère [pøʃɛr] INT Région heavens!, Br strewth!

peuh [pø] INT pooh!, bah!

peuplade [pœplad] NF (small) tribe

peuple [pœpl] NM VOIR GRAMMAIRE A11 **1** (nation) people, nation; **le p. français** the French people; **le p. élu** the chosen people **2** (ensemble des citoyens) people (considered as a political entity); **dans une démocratie, le p. gouverne** in a democracy, it is the people who govern; **le roi et son p.** the king and his people or subjects; **les gens du p.,** Vieilli **le bas** ou **petit p.** the lower classes; Fam **que demande le p.?** what more could you ask for? **3** Fam (foule) crowd (of people); Fam **quel p.!** what a crowd!, what a lot of people!; Fam **ça fait du p.** that's a lot of people; Fam **elle se fiche** ou **se fout** ou **se moque du p.** who does she think she is!

ADJ INV Fam Péj common, vulgar; **ça fait p.** that's common, that's vulgar

peuplé [pœple] ADJ inhabited; **p. de** inhabited by; **très/peu p.** densely/sparsely populated

peuplement [pœpləmɑ̃] NM (d'une région) populating; (d'un vivier, d'un parc à gibier etc) stocking; (d'une forêt) planting (with trees); **régions à faible p.** sparsely populated areas

peupler [pœple] VT **1** (pourvoir d'habitants) (pays) to populate, to people; (vivier, parc à gibier etc) to stock; (forêt) to plant (with trees) **2** (occuper) to inhabit; **rue peuplée de gens** street crowded with people, crowded street; Fig **ville peuplée de souvenirs** town full of memories

VPR se peupler (d'une région, ville) to become populated; **la rue s'est peuplée peu à peu** the street gradually filled (up) with people

peupleraie [pøpləre] NF poplar grove or plantation

peuplier [pøplije] NM poplar; **p. tremble** aspen

peur [pœr] NF fear; (subite) fright; **avoir p.** to be afraid or frightened; **avoir p. des chiens** to be afraid or frightened of dogs; Fig **n'ayons pas p. des mots** let's call a spade a spade, let's not mince our words; **ne pas avoir p. de mourir** not to be afraid or frightened of dying; **il ne faut pas avoir p. de le lui dire** you mustn't be afraid or frightened of telling him so; **j'avais p. de vous gêner** I was afraid I might be in your way; **elle n'a pas p. de déplaire** she doesn't care if she's not liked; **j'ai p. pour lui** I'm afraid or frightened for him; **n'ayez pas p.!** don't be afraid!; **n'aie pas p., tout va s'arranger** don't worry, everything will be all right; Fam **vous n'avez pas p.!** you've got a or some nerve!; **prendre p.** to take fright; **je n'avais qu'une p., qu'il dise oui** my only fear was that he might say yes; Fam **avoir une p. bleue** to be scared to death; **avoir une p. bleue des abeilles/de parler en public** to be scared to death of bees/of speaking in public; **avoir une p. panique des voyages en avion** to be terrified of flying; **avoir la p. au ventre** to be terrified or petrified; **en être quitte pour la p.** to get off with a fright; **il a eu plus de p. que de mal** he was more frightened than hurt; **il me fait p.** he frightens me; **tu m'as fait p.!** you frightened or startled me!, you gave me a fright!; **il m'a fait une de ces peurs!** he gave me such a fright!; **être laid à faire p.** to be as ugly as sin; **c'était d'un ennui à faire p.** it was dreadfully boring; **sans p.** (employé comme adj) fearless; (employé comme adv) fearlessly; **un chevalier sans p. et sans reproche** ≃ a very parfitt gentle knight; **j'en ai bien p.** I'm afraid so; **j'ai p. qu'il (ne) soit en retard** I'm worried in case he is or Fml should be late; **la p. des élèves (devant leur professeur)** the children's fear (of their teacher); Fam **la p. du gendarme** the fear of being caught; **c'est par p. des représailles que ...** it's for or through fear of reprisals that ...; **la p. de s'engager** the fear of committing oneself; **de p. de faire qch** for fear of doing sth; **de p. que ... (ne) + sub** in case ..., for fear that ...; **elle ne t'en a pas parlé de p. que tu ne t'offenses** she didn't tell you about it in case you took or for fear that you should take offence

peureusement [pœrøzmɑ̃] ADV fearfully

peureux, -euse [pœrø, -øz] ADJ (personne, regard) timid, fearful; Fml timorous

▶ **N** fearful or timid person; **quel p.!** what a coward!, Fam what a wimp!

peut-être [pøtɛtr] ADV perhaps, maybe, possibly; **p. que oui, p. que non** perhaps, perhaps not, maybe, maybe not; **elle est p. rentrée chez elle** perhaps or maybe she has gone home, she may have gone home; **je ne suis p. pas riche, mais j'ai mon honneur** I may not be rich or perhaps I'm not rich, but I have my honour; **p. bien qu'il viendra** he may (very) well come; Iron **tu le sais mieux que moi, p.?** you think you know better, do you?; **je ne sais pas faire la cuisine, p.?** you think I can't cook? SEE GRAMMAR B62

p. ex. (abrév par exemple) eg

pèze [pɛz] NM Arg (argent) dough, cash

pff [pf], **pfft** [pft], **pffut** [pfyt] INT pooh!

PgPr Ordinat (abrév page précédente) PgUp

PgSv Ordinat (abrév page suivante) PgDn

pH [peaʃ] NM Chimie pH

phacochère [fakɔʃɛr] NM warthog

phaéton [faetɔ̃] NM phaeton

phagocyte [fagɔsit] NM Biol phagocyte

phagocyter [fagɔsite] VT **1** Biol to phagocytose **2** Fig to swallow up, to engulf; **les zones industrielles phagocytent la banlieue** the suburbs are being swallowed up or engulfed by industrial estates

phagocytose [fagɔsitoz] NF Biol phagocytosis; Fig swallowing up

phalange [falɑ̃ʒ] NF **1** Antiq, Mil phalanx; Litt (armée) host, army; Hist, Pol **la P.** the Falange, the Falangist party **2** Anat phalanx

phalangette [falãʒɛt] NF *Anat (du doigt, de l'orteil)* top joint, *Spéc* ungual phalanx

phalangien, -ienne [falãʒjɛ̃, -jɛn] ADJ *Anat* phalangeal

phalangiste [falãʒist] N *Hist, Pol* Falangist

phalanstère [falãstɛr] NM *Hist, Écon* phalanstery; *Fig* **un p. de philosophes** a community of philosophers

phalène [falɛn] NF *(parfois nm en poésie)* geometrid (moth)

phallique [falik] ADJ phallic

phallo [falo] NM *Fam Péj (abrév* **phallocrate***)* male chauvinist (pig)

phallocrate [falɔkrat] NM *Péj* male chauvinist (pig)

phallocratie [falɔkrasi] NF male chauvinism

phalloïde [falɔid] ADJ *Biol* phalloid; **amanite p.** *(champignon vénéneux)* death cap, *Spéc* amanita phalloides

phallus [falys] NM phallus

phantasme [fɑ̃tasm] NM = **fantasme**

pharamineux, -euse [faraminø, -øz] ADJ *Fam* phenomenal, staggering

pharaon [faraɔ̃] NM **1** *Hist* Pharaoh **2** *Cartes* faro

pharaonique [faraɔnik], **pharaonien, -ienne** [faraɔnjɛ̃, -jɛn] ADJ **1** *Hist* Pharaonic **2** *Fig (gigantesque)* huge, enormous

phare [far] NM **1** *(tour lumineuse)* lighthouse; **p. à éclats** flashing light; **p. à feu fixe/à feu tournant** fixed/revolving light; **gardien de p.** lighthouse keeper **2** *Aviat* beacon; **p. d'atterrissage** landing light **3** *Aut* headlight, headlamp; **faire un appel de phares** to flash one's headlights; **mettre ses phares** to switch on one's headlights; **se mettre en phares** to dip *or Am* dim one's headlights; **rouler (en) pleins phares** to drive on full headlights *or Br* on full beam *or Am* on high beams; **p. anti-brouillard** foglight; **p. de recul** reversing *or Am* backup light

-phare [far] SUFF **personnalité-p.** leading light; **film-p.** seminal film

pharisaïque [farizaik] ADJ **1** *Péj (hypocrite)* hypocritical, *Litt* pharisaic(al) **2** *Hist, Rel* Pharisaic(al)

pharisien, -ienne [farizjɛ̃, -jɛn] N **1** *Péj (hypocrite)* hypocrite, *Vieilli, Litt* pharisee **2** *Hist, Rel* Pharisee

ADJ **1** *Péj (pointilleux)* self-righteous **2** *Hist, Rel* Pharisaic(al)

pharmaceutique [farmasøtik] ADJ pharmaceutical

pharmacie [farmasi] NF **1** *(science)* pharmacy, pharmaceutics **2** *(magasin)* pharmacy, chemist's (shop), *Am* drugstore; *(dispensaire)* dispensary; **la p. de l'hôpital** the hospital dispensary **3** *(médicaments)* pharmaceuticals; **(armoire à) p.** medicine chest *or* cabinet; **p. de premiers soins** first-aid kit; **p. de voyage** travelling *or Am* traveling first-aid kit

pharmacien, -ienne [farmasjɛ̃, -jɛn] N *(vendeur)* pharmacist, *Br* (dispensing) chemist, *Am* druggist; *(d'un laboratoire pharmaceutique, dans l'industrie)* pharmacist, *Br* chemist

pharmacodépendance [farmakodepãdãs] NF drug dependency

pharmacologie [farmakɔlɔʒi] NF pharmacology

pharmacologique [farmakɔlɔʒik] ADJ pharmacological

pharmacopée [farmakɔpe] NF pharmacopoeia

pharmacorésistance [farmakorezistãs] NF resistance to drugs

pharmacovigilance [farmakoviʒilãs] NF drug testing and control

pharyngé [farɛ̃ʒe], **pharyngien, -ienne** [farɛ̃ʒjɛ̃, -jɛn] ADJ *Méd, Anat* pharyng(e)al

pharyngite [farɛ̃ʒit] NF *Méd* pharyngitis

pharynx [farɛ̃ks] NM *Anat* pharynx

phascolome [faskɔlɔm] NM *Zool* wombat

phase [fɑz] NF *(période)* phase, stage; *Astron, Chimie, Phys* phase; **cancer en p. terminale** terminal cancer; **cancéreux en p. terminale** terminal cancer patient; *Ind* **p. de production** stage of production; **p. de croissance** growth phase; **être en p. de croissance** to be growing; *Phys* **en p.** in phase; *Fig* **être en p.** to be on the same wavelength; *Phys* **décalage de p.** difference of phase, phase displacement; *Élec* **(conducteur de) p.** phase conductor

phatique [fatik] ADJ *Ling* **fonction p.** phatic function

Phébus [febys] N *Myth* Phoebus

Phèdre [fɛdr] N *Myth* Phaedra

Phénicie [fenisi] NF Phoenicia

phénicien, -ienne [fenisjɛ̃, -jɛn] *Hist* ADJ Phoenician
NM *Ling* Phoenician
N P. Phoenician

phénix [feniks] NM *Myth* phoenix; *Fig Litt (personne unique en son genre)* paragon

phénol [fenɔl] NM *Chimie* phenol; *Com* carbolic acid

phénoménal, -ale, -aux, -ales [fenɔmenal, -o] ADJ *Phil, Fam (incroyable)* phenomenal

phénoménalement [fenɔmenalmã] ADV phenomenally

phénomène [fenɔmɛn] NM *(expérience, fait, personne)* phenomenon, *pl* phenomena; *(dans les foires)* freak; **quel p.!** *(excentrique)* what a character!; **c'est un drôle de p.!** he's quite a character!

phénoménologie [fenɔmenɔlɔʒi] NF *Phil* phenomenology

Philadelphie [filadɛlfi] N Philadelphia

philanthrope [filãtrɔp] N philanthropist

philanthropie [filãtrɔpi] NF philanthropy

philanthropique [filãtrɔpik] ADJ philanthropic

philatélie [filateli] NF philately, stamp collecting

philatélique [filatelik] ADJ philatelic

philatéliste [filatelist] N philatelist, stamp collector

philharmonie [filarmɔni] NF philharmonic society

philharmonique [filarmɔnik] ADJ *(société, orchestre etc)* philharmonic

philhellène [filelɛn] NM philhellene
ADJ philhellenic

philhellénisme [filelenism] NM philhellenism

philippin, -ine [filipɛ̃, -in] ADJ Filipino, Philippine
N P. Filipino

Philippines (les) [lefilipin] NFPL the Philippines VOIR GRAMMAIRE AB

philistin [filistɛ̃] ADJ M, NM *Péj* philistine

philo [filo] NF *Scol Fam* philosophy

philodendron [filɔdɛ̃drɔ̃] NM philodendron

philologie [filɔlɔʒi] NF philology

philologique [filɔlɔʒik] ADJ philological

philologiquement [filɔlɔʒikmã] ADV philologically

philologue [filɔlɔg] N philologist

philosophale [filɔzɔfal] ADJ F **la pierre p.** the philosophers' stone

philosophe [filɔzɔf] N philosopher; **prendre les choses en p.** to take things philosophically

ADJ philosophical; **se montrer p. face à une déception** to react philosophically to a disappointment

philosopher [filɔzɔfe] VI to philosophize

philosophie [filɔzɔfi] NF *(science)* philosophy; **la p. de l'histoire/des sciences** the philosophy of history/science; **supporter une épreuve avec p.** to suffer a hardship philosophically; *Fam* **c'est ma p.** that's my philosophy, that's my outlook on life; *Scol Vieilli* **(classe de) p.** final-year arts and humanities class

philosophique [filɔzɔfik] ADJ philosophical

philosophiquement [filɔzɔfikmã] ADV philosophically

philtre [filtr] NM philtre, *Am* philter; **p. d'amour** love potion

phlébite [flebit] NF *Méd* phlebitis

phlébologie [flebɔlɔʒi] NF *Méd* phlebology

phlébologue [flebɔlɔg] N *Méd* vein specialist

phlébotomie [flebɔtɔmi] NF *Méd* phlebotomy

phlegmon [flɛgmɔ̃] NM *Méd* phlegmon

phlox [flɔks] NM phlox

pH-mètre [peaʃmɛtr] NM *Tech* pH-meter

phobie [fɔbi] NF *Psy, Méd* phobia, morbid fear; **avoir la p. de qch** to have a phobia about sth

phobique [fɔbik] ADJ, N *Psy, Méd* phobic

phocéen, -enne [fɔseɛ̃, -ɛn] ADJ Marseilles

phonation [fɔnasjɔ̃] NF *Physiol, Ling* phonation

phonatoire [fɔnatwar] ADJ phonatory

phone [fɔn] NM *Phys* phon

phonématique [fɔnematik] ADJ *Ling* phonemic

phonème [fɔnɛm] NM *Ling* phoneme

phonémique [fɔnemik] ADJ *Ling* phonemic

phonéticien, -ienne [fɔnetisjɛ̃, -jɛn] N phonetician

phonétique [fɔnetik] ADJ phonetic
NF phonetics

phonétiquement [fɔnetikmã] ADV phonetically

phoniatre [fɔnjatr] N *Méd* speech therapist

phoniatrie [fɔnjatri] NF *Méd* speech therapy

phonie [fɔni] NF *Radio, Électron* wireless telegraphy, radiotelegraphy

phoning [fɔniŋ] NM *Mktg* telesales

phonique [fɔnik] ADJ acoustic, *Vieilli* phonic; **isolation p.** soundproofing, sound insulation

phono [fono] NM *Fam Vieilli* = **phonographe**

phonographe [fɔnɔgraf] NM *(gramophone)* gramophone, *Am, Arch* phonograph

phonographique [fɔnɔgrafik] ADJ phonographic

phonologie [fɔnɔlɔʒi] NF *Ling* phonology

phonologique [fɔnɔlɔʒik] ADJ *Ling* phonological

phonologue [fɔnɔlɔg] N *Ling* phonologist

phonothèque [fɔnɔtɛk] NF sound archives, audio library

phoque [fɔk] NM **1** *(animal)* seal; **souffler comme un p.** to (puff and) wheeze *or* (puff and) blow like a grampus; *Vulg* **il est pédé comme un p.** he's a real queer *or Br* poofter **2** *(fourrure)* sealskin

phosgène [fɔsʒɛn] NM *Chimie* phosgene (gas)

phosphatage [fɔsfataʒ] NM *Agr* treating with phosphates

phosphate [fɔsfat] NM *Chimie* phosphate; **sans phosphates** phosphate-free

phosphaté [fɔsfate] ADJ *Chimie* phosphatic, phosphated; *(engrais etc)* phosphate-enriched

phosphater [fɔsfate] VT to treat with phosphates, to phosphate

phosphène [fɔsfɛn] NM *Physiol* phosphene

phosphore [fɔsfɔr] NM *Chimie* phosphorus

phosphoré [fɔsfɔre] ADJ *Chimie* phosphorated

phosphorer [fɔsfɔre] VI *Fam* to have one's thinking cap on; **alors, ça phosphore?** working hard, are we?

phosphorescence [fɔsfɔresɑ̃s] NF phosphorescence

phosphorescent [fɔsfɔresɑ̃] ADJ phosphorescent

phosphoreux, -euse [fɔsfɔrø, -øz] ADJ *Chimie* phosphorous

phosphorique [fɔsfɔrik] ADJ *Chimie* phosphoric

phosphure [fɔsfyr] NM *Chimie* phosphide

phot [fɔt] NM *Phys* phot

photo [foto] NF *(activité)* photography; *(cliché)* photo, shot; *(tirée d'un film, du tournage)* still, photostill; **faire de la p.** *(en professionnel)* to be a photographer; *(en amateur)* to be an amateur photographer; **prendre qn en p., prendre une photo de qn** to take sb's photo, to take a photo of sb; **prendre qch en p., prendre une p. de qch** to take a photo of sth; **se faire prendre en p. par qn** to have one's photo taken by sb; **il est bien en p.** he photographs well; *Fam* **tu veux ma p.?** who do you think you're staring at?, what are you staring at?; **appareil p.** camera; **p. d'identité** identity photo, passport-sized photograph; **p. souvenir** souvenir photo; **p. de mode** fashion photo

photobiologie [fotobjɔlɔʒi] NF photobiology

photochimie [fotoʃimi] NF photochemistry

photochimique [fotoʃimik] ADJ photochemical

photocomposer [fotokɔ̃poze] VTI to photocompose, to photoset, *Br* to filmset

photocomposeur [fotokɔ̃pozœr] NM = **photocompositeur**

photocomposeuse [fotokɔ̃pozøz] NF *(machine)* photocomposer, photosetter, *Br* filmsetter

photocompositeur, -trice [fotokɔ̃pozitœr, -tris] N photocomposer, photosetter, *Br* filmsetter

photocomposition [fotokɔ̃pozisjɔ̃] NF photocomposition, photosetting, *Br* filmsetting

photoconducteur, -trice [fotokɔ̃dyktœr, -tris] ADJ photoconductive

photoconductivité [fotokɔ̃dyktivite] NF photoconductivity

photocopie [fotokɔpi] NF photocopy

photocopier [fotokɔpje] VT *(conj like copier)* to photocopy

photocopieur [fotokɔpjœr] NM, **photocopieuse** [fotokɔpjøz] NF photocopier

photocopillage [fotokɔpijaʒ] NM = infringement of copyright through excessive use of photocopiers

photodiode [fotodjɔd] NF photodiode

photoélectricité [fotoelɛktrisite] NF photoelectricity

photoélectrique [fotoelɛktrik] ADJ *(cellule, effet)* photoelectric

photo-finish, *pl* **photos-finish** NM *Sport* photo finish; *(appareil)* photo-finish camera; **l'arrivée a dû être vérifiée au p.** it was a photo finish

photogénique [fotoʒenik] ADJ photogenic

photogramme [fotogram] NM *Cin* frame

photogrammétrie [fotogrametri] NF photogrammetry

photographe [fotograf] N *(professionnel de la photo)* photographer; **reporter p.** photojournalist; **p. de mode** fashion photographer; *Cin* **p. de plateau** still photographer, unit photographer; **p. de presse** press photographer; **p. indépendant(e)** freelance photographer

> Il faut noter que le terme anglais **photograph** est un faux ami. Il signifie **photographie, cliché**.

photographie [fotografi] NF **1** *(technique, hobby etc)* photography; **p. numérique** digital imaging; **p. journalistique** press photography; **p. par téléobjectif** long-lens photography; **faire de la p.** *(en professionnel)* to be a photographer; *(en amateur)* to be an amateur photographer **2** *(cliché)* photograph, photo, shot; **prendre qn en p., prendre une p. de qn** to take sb's photo, to take a photo of sb; **p. qch en p., prendre la p. de qch** to take a photo of sth; **p. aérienne** aerial photograph

photographier [fotografje] VT *(impf, pr sub n. photographiions, v. photographiiez)* to photograph, to take a photograph of; **se faire p.** to have one's photograph taken

photographique [fotografik] ADJ *(reproduction, description etc)* photographic; **appareil p.** camera

photographiquement [fotografikmɑ̃] ADV photographically

photograveur [fotogravœr] NM photoengraver

photogravure [fotogravyr] NF *(procédé, épreuve)* photogravure, photoengraving

photo-interprétation NF *Tech* photo-interpretation

photojournalisme [fotoʒurnalism] NM photojournalism

photojournaliste [fotoʒurnalist] N photojournalist

photolithographie [fotolitografi] NF photolithography

photolyse [fotoliz] NF *Chimie* photolysis

Photomaton® [fotomatɔ̃] NM *(automatic)* photo machine *or* booth

photomécanique [fotomekanik] ADJ *Tech (procédé)* photomechanical

photomètre [fotomɛtr] NM *Tech* photometer

photométrie [fotometri] NF *Phys* photometry

photométrique [fotometrik] ADJ *Phys* photometric

photomontage [fotomɔ̃taʒ] NM photomontage

photon [fotɔ̃] NM photon

photopériode [fotoperjɔd] NF *Bot* photoperiod

photopériodique [fotoperjɔdik] ADJ *Bot* photoperiodic

photopériodisme [fotoperjɔdism] NM *Bot* photoperiodism

photophobie [fotofɔbi] NF *Méd* photophobia

photophore [fotofɔr] NM **1** *(lampe)* reflective lamp *(esp of miner)* **2** *(pour bougie)* candle holder with glass shade

photopile [fotopil] NF *Tech* solar cell

photoreportage [fotorəpɔrtaʒ] NM **1** *(discipline)* photojournalism **2** *(reportage)* photo report

photo-robot, *pl* **photos-robots** NF Identikit® *or* Photofit® (picture)

photosensible [fotosɑ̃sibl] ADJ photosensitive

photosphère [fotosfɛr] NF *Astron* photosphere

photostat [fotosta] NM *Tech* photostat

photostoppeur, -euse [fotostɔpœr, -øz] N street photographer

photostyle [fotostil] NM *Ordinat* light pen

photosynthèse [fotosɛ̃tɛz] NF *Biol* photosynthesis

photothèque [fototɛk] NF photo *or* picture library; **p. électronique** electronic still store

photothérapie [fototerapi] NF *Méd* phototherapy

phototransistor [fototrɑ̃zistɔr] NM phototransistor

phototypie [fototipi] NF *Tech* phototype (process)

photovoltaïque [fotovɔltaik] ADJ photovoltaic; **cellule p.** photovoltaic cell; **effet p.** photovoltaic effect

phragmite [fragmit] NM **1** *Bot* reed **2** *Orn* sedge warbler

phrase [fraz] NF *Gram* sentence; *Mus* phrase; **p. toute faite** stock phrase; *Fig* **faire des phrases, faire de grandes phrases** to use high-flown language; **phrases à compléter** sentence completion; **sans phrases** straight out, without mincing one's words; *Gram* **membre de p.** phrase SEE GRAMMAR A78–9; B62–4

> Il faut noter que le nom anglais **phrase** est un faux ami. Il signifie **expression**.

phrasé [fraze] NM *Mus* phrasing

phraséologie [frazeɔlɔʒi] NF *(syntaxe)* phraseology; *Péj (verbiage)* flowery *or* high-flown language

phraser [fraze] VT *Mus* to phrase
VI to use high-flown language

phraseur, -euse [frazœr, -øz] N *Péj* phrasemonger

phrastique [fraztik] ADJ *Gram* sentence

phréatique [freatik] ADJ *Géol* **nappe p.** ground water

phrénologie [frenɔlɔʒi] NF phrenology

phrénologique [frenɔlɔʒik] ADJ phrenological

phrénologiste [frenɔlɔʒist] NM phrenologist

Phrygie [friʒi] NF *Antiq* Phrygia

phrygien, -ienne [friʒjɛ̃, -jɛn] ADJ *Antiq* Phrygian; *Hist* **bonnet p.** Phrygian cap *(in French Revolution)*
N *Antiq* **P.** Phrygian

phtisie [ftizi] NF *Méd Arch* consumption, *Spéc* phthisis; **p. galopante** galloping consumption

phylactère [filaktɛr] NM **1** *Rel juive* phylactery **2** *Beaux-Arts* scroll **3** *(de bande dessinée)* bubble, balloon

phylloxéra, phylloxera [filɔksera] NM *Entom* phylloxera

phylogénèse [filoʒenɛz] NF phylogenesis, phylogeny

physicien, -ienne [fizisjɛ̃, -jɛn] N physicist; **p. de l'atome** nuclear physicist

> Il faut noter que le terme anglais **physician** est un faux ami. Il signifie **médecin**.

physicochimie [fizikoʃimi] NF physical chemistry

physicochimique [fizikoʃimik] ADJ physicochemical

physicomathématique [fizikomatematik]

NF mathematical physics

ADJ relating to mathematical physics

physiocrate [fizjɔkrat] **NM** *Écon, Hist* physiocrat

physiocratie [fizjɔkrasi] **NF** *Écon, Hist* physiocracy

physiologie [fizjɔlɔʒi] **NF** physiology

physiologique [fizjɔlɔʒik] **ADJ** physiological

physiologiquement [fizjɔlɔʒikmɑ̃] **ADV** physiologically

physiologiste [fizjɔlɔʒist] **N** physiologist

physionomie [fizjɔnɔmi] **NF 1** *(traits du visage)* facial appearance, features, *Litt, Hum* physiognomy; **il a une p. joviale** he has a jolly face; **il ne faut pas juger les gens sur leur p.** you shouldn't judge by appearances **2** *(aspect)* face; **la p. de l'Europe va changer** the face of Europe will change

physionomiste [fizjɔnɔmist] **ADJ** **je ne suis pas p.** I've no memory for faces; **elle est très p.** she has a very good memory for faces
N c'est un p. he's got a good memory for faces

physiopathologie [fizjɔpatɔlɔʒi] **NF** *Méd* physiopathology

physiothérapie [fizjɔterapi] **NF** *Méd* natural medicine

physique [fizik] **ADJ** physical; **culture p.** physical training; *Scol* **éducation p.** physical education; **le monde p.** the physical *or* material world; *Fam* **je ne le supporte pas, c'est p.** I can't stand him, it's a physical thing
NF *(science)* physics; *Scol Vieilli (livre)* physics (text)book; **p. nucléaire** nuclear physics; *Géog* **p. du globe** geophysics VOIR GRAMMAIRE A10
NM *(d'une personne)* physique; *(apparence)* external appearance; **avoir un p. avantageux** to have a fine physique; **soigner son p.** to take care of *or* look after oneself; **il a le p. de l'emploi** he looks the part; **le p. et le moral** the mind and the body; **au p.** physically

physiquement [fizikmɑ̃] **ADV** physically

phytobiologie [fitobjɔlɔʒi] **NF** phytology

phytogéographie [fitoʒeografi] **NF** phytogeography

phytoplancton [fitoplɑ̃ktɔ̃] **NM** phytoplankton

phytosanitaire [fitosaniter] **ADJ** **produits phytosanitaires** plant-care products

phytothérapie [fitoterapi] **NF** herbal medicine

pi [pi] **NM** *(lettre)*, *Math* pi

piaf [pjaf] **NM** *Fam* sparrow

piaffement [pjafmɑ̃] **NM** *(d'un cheval)* pawing (the ground)

piaffer [pjafe] **VI** *(d'un cheval)* to paw the ground; *Fig (trépigner)* to stamp one's feet; **p. d'impatience** to fidget impatiently

piaillard, -arde [pjajar, -ard] **ADJ, N** *Fam* voir **piailleur**

piaillement [pjajmɑ̃] **NM** *Fam (d'un oiseau)* cheeping; *Fig (d'un enfant)* squealing, squalling

piailler [pjaje] **VI** *Fam (de petits oiseaux)* to cheep; *Fig (des enfants)* to squeal, to squall

piaillerie [pjajri] **NF** *Fam* = **piaillement**

piailleur, -euse [pjajœr, -øz] *Fam* **ADJ** *(oiseau)* cheeping; *(enfant)* squealing, squalling
N cheeping bird; *Fig Péj (enfant)* squealer, squaller

piane-piane [pjanpjan] **ADV** *Fam* **allez-y p.** gently does it, go easy

pianiste [pjanist] **N** pianist; **un p. (de) jazz** a jazz pianist

piano¹ [pjano] **NM** *(instrument)* piano; **jouer** *ou* **faire du p.** to play the piano
▸▸ *Fam* **p. à bretelles** squeezebox; **p. de concert** concert grand; **p. crapaud** boudoir grand; **p. demi-queue** baby grand; **p. droit** upright piano; **p. mécanique** player piano; **p. quart de queue** miniature grand; **p. à queue** grand piano

piano² **ADV** *Mus* piano; *Fig Fam* **allez-y p.** gently does it, go easy; **allez-y p. avec lui** go easy with *or* on him; **vas-y p. avec le café** go easy with *or* on the coffee

piano-bar, *pl* **pianos-bars NM** piano bar

pianoforte [pjanoforte] **NM** *Mus Arch* fortepiano

pianotage [pjanotaʒ] **NM** *Fam (sur le piano)* tinkling (away); *(des doigts)* drumming

pianoter [pjanote] **VI** *Fam* **1** *(mal jouer du piano)* to tinkle away (on the piano) **2** *(tapoter)* to drum one's fingers; **ses doigts pianotent sur la nappe** he's drumming his fingers *or* his fingers are drumming on the tablecloth

piastre [pjastr] **NF** piastre; *Can Arg (dollar)* buck

piaule [pjol] **NF** *Fam (logement)* pad

piaulement [pjolmɑ̃] **NM** *(des poussins)* cheeping; *Fig Fam (des enfants)* whimpering, whining

piauler [pjole] **VI** *(des poussins)* to cheep; *Fig Fam (des enfants)* to whimper, to whine

PIB [peibe] **NM** *Écon (abrév* **produit intérieur brut)** GDP

PIBOR [pibɔr] **NM** *Bourse (abrév* **Paris interbank offered rate)** PIBOR; **P. trois mois** three-month PIBOR

pic¹ [pik] **NM 1** *(pioche)* pick, pickaxe, *Am* pickax; **p. pneumatique** pneumatic drill; **p. de mineur** miner's pick; **p. à glace** ice pick **2** *(sommet)* (mountain) peak; *(d'une courbe)* peak; **à p.** *(chute, falaise)* sheer; *(tomber)* straight down; **sentier à p.** steep path; **promontoire à p.** sheer headland, bluff; **couler à p.** to sink like a stone; *Fig Fam* **tomber à p.** to come at just the right moment

pic² **NM** *(oiseau)* woodpecker

pica [pika] **NM** *Typ* pica

picador [pikadɔr] **NM** picador

picaillons [pikajɔ̃] **NMPL** *Arg (argent)* dough, bread

picard, -arde [pikar, -ard] **ADJ** *(of/from)* Picardy; *Culin* **ficelle picarde** = ham and cheese pancake
NM *Ling* Picardy dialect
N P. *(natif)* native of Picardy; *(habitant)* inhabitant of Picardy

Picardie [pikardi] **NF** Picardy

picaresque [pikaresk] **ADJ** *(roman)* picaresque

piccolo [pikɔlo] **NM** *Mus* piccolo

pichenette [piʃnɛt] **NF** flick (of the finger), flip; *(avec le pied)* flick

pichet [piʃɛ] **NM** (small) jug, *Am* pitcher

pickles [pikœlz] **NMPL** pickles

pickpocket [pikpɔkɛt] **NM** pickpocket

pick-up [pikœp] **NM INV 1** *(bras de lecture)* pick-up (arm); *Vieilli (électrophone)* record player **2** *(véhicule)* pick-up (truck)

picoler [pikɔle] **VI** *Fam* to booze, to knock it back; **qu'est-ce qu'il peut p.!** he's a real boozer!; **ici, ça picole dur** they're real boozers here!

picoleur, -euse [pikɔlœr, -øz] **N** *Fam* boozer

picolo [pikɔlo] **NM** *Mus* piccolo

picorer [pikɔre] **VI** *(d'un oiseau)* to pick *or* scratch about; *Fig (manger à peine)* to pick at one's food
VT *(d'un oiseau)* to peck (at); *(par manque*

d'appétit) (nourriture) to pick at; *(grignoter)* to nibble; **on a eu des olives à p.** we had olives to nibble, that's all

picoseconde [pikos(ə)gɔ̃d] **NF** picosecond

picot [piko] **NM 1** *(pointe)* splinter (of wood) **2** *Tech (de roue d'entraînement)* pin **3** *Couture* picot **4** *Pêche* fishing net *(for flatfish)*

picotement [pikɔtmɑ̃] **NM** *(dans la gorge, le nez)* tickle, tickling; *(dans les yeux)* stinging, smarting; *(sur la peau)* prickling; **j'ai des picotements dans les yeux** my eyes are stinging *or* smarting; **j'ai des picotements dans le nez** my nose is tickling, I've got a tickle in my nose

picoter [pikɔte] **VT 1** *(faire de petits trous dans)* to prick tiny holes in **2** *(d'un oiseau)* to peck (at) **3** *(irriter) (quelque chose)* to produce a tingling sensation in; *(gorge)* to tickle; *(peau)* to prickle; **la fumée me picotait les yeux** the smoke made my eyes sting *or* smart; **j'ai les yeux qui (me) picotent** my eyes are stinging *or* smarting; **j'ai la gorge qui (me) picote** I've a tickle in my throat, my throat is tickling; **j'ai la peau qui (me) picote** my skin is prickling

picotin [pikɔtɛ̃] **NM** *Agr (d'avoine) (mesure)* peck; *(ration)* feed, ration

picrate [pikrat] **NM 1** *Arg (vin)* cheap red wine, *Br* plonk **2** *Chimie* picrate

Pictes [pikt] **NMPL** *Hist* Picts

pictogramme [piktɔgram] **NM** pictogram, pictograph

pictographe [piktɔgraf] **NM** pictogram, pictograph

pictographie [piktɔgrafi] **NF** pictography

pictographique [piktɔgrafik] **ADJ** *Ling* pictographic

pictural, -ale, -aux, -ales [piktyral, -o] **ADJ** pictorial

pic-vert, *pl* **pics-verts** [pivɛr] **NM** green woodpecker

Pie [pi] **N** Pius

pie¹ [pi] **NF** magpie; *Fam (personne bavarde)* chatterbox; *Fam* **être bavard comme une p.** to be a real chatterbox; *Naut* **nid de p.** crow's nest
ADJ INV **cheval/jument p.** piebald (horse/mare), *Am* pinto (horse/mare); **vache p.** black and white cow; *Vieilli* **voiture p.** patrol car, *Br* Panda car

pie² **ADJ** **œuvre p.** good deed, act of charity

PIÈCE [pjɛs]

room **1** ▪ piece **2, 5, 9, 11, 12** ▪ coin **3** ▪ play **4** ▪ part **7** ▪ patch **8** ▪ bit **9** ▪ document **10**		

NF 1 *(salle, chambre)* room; **un appartement de trois pièces, un trois-pièces** a three-room(ed) flat *or Am* apartment; **un trois-pièces cuisine** a three-room(ed) flat with kitchen, *Am* a three and a half
2 *(élément)* piece; **p. de musée** museum piece; **p. de bétail/gibier** head of cattle/game; **p. de blé** wheatfield; **un service complet de trente-six pièces** a complete thirty-six-piece dinner service; **les pièces d'un uniforme** the items of a uniform; **costume deux-pièces/trois-pièces** two-piece/three-piece suit; **un (maillot de bain) une-p./deux-pièces** a one-piece/two-piece swimsuit; **ils coûtent dix euros (la) p.** they cost ten euros each *or* apiece; **ils se vendent à la p.** they are sold singly *or* separately; **travailler aux pièces** to do piece work; *Fam* **on n'est pas aux pièces** there's no hurry *or* rush
3 *Fin* coin; **p. de two euros** two-euro piece; **donner la p. à qn** to give sb a tip, to tip sb; **je ne vous demanderai qu'une petite p.** *(d'un mendiant)* have you got any loose change you don't need?

4 *Théâtre* play; **monter une p.** to put on *or* stage a play; **p. radiophonique** radio play, radio drama

5 *Mus, Littér* piece; **une p. de Couperin/en vers** a piece by Couperin/of verse

6 tout d'une p. all in one piece; *Fig* **être tout d'une p.** to be straightforward and uncompromising; **une histoire inventée de toutes pièces** a completely made-up story, a complete fabrication; **ce qu'il raconte est forgé de toutes pièces** he's making the whole thing up; **mensonge fait de toutes pièces** out-and-out lie

7 *(d'une machine, d'une horloge etc)* part, component; **pièces de rechange, pièces détachées** replacement parts, spare parts, spares; **p. de charpente** beam; *(sous le plancher)* joist; *Tech* **p. en croix** crosspiece; *Tech* **p. en mouvement** moving part; *Tech* **p. matricée** pressing

8 *(raccord)* patch; **mettre** *ou* **poser une p. à un vêtement** to put a patch on *or* to patch a garment

9 *(morceau, débris)* piece, bit, fragment; **être en pièces** to be in pieces; *(de vêtements)* to be in tatters; **mettre en pièces** *(vase)* to smash to bits *or* to pieces; *(livre)* to pull *or* tear to pieces; *(vêtement)* to tear to pieces; **tailler l'ennemi en pièces** to cut the enemy to pieces; *Fig* **se faire tailler en pièces** to be torn to pieces

10 *Jur, Admin etc (document)* document, paper; **p. justificative** *Admin* written proof; *Jur* relevant document; *Com* voucher (copy); *Compta* **p. de caisse** cash voucher; **p. à l'appui** supporting document; **juger sur pièces** to judge on the evidence; **p. jointe** *(à une lettre)* enclosure; **p. à joindre** *(à une lettre)* enclosure

11 *(quantité déterminée)* **p. de bœuf** cut *or* piece of beef; **p. d'étoffe** length *or* piece of material

12 *Échecs* piece; *(aux dames)* draught(s-man), *Am* checker

13 *Mil* **p. (d'artillerie)** gun, *Spéc* piece of ordnance; **p. de campagne** field gun; **chef de p.** number one, squad leader, *Am* chief of (piece) section

▸ ▸ *Jur* **p. à conviction** exhibit *(in criminal case)*; **p. détachée** component; *(de rechange)* spare part; **p. d'eau** ornamental lake; *(plus petite)* water feature, ornamental pond; **p. d'identité** identity paper(s), proof of identity; **p. de monnaie** coin; *Culin* **p. montée** ornamental cake; **p. rapportée** insert; *Couture* patch; *Fig (dans une famille)* in-law; **p. de résistance** *Culin* pièce de résistance, main dish; *Fig* pièce de résistance; **p. de théâtre** play; **p. de vin** barrel *or* cask of wine

---

Pièce

Flats in France are referred to in terms of the total number of rooms they have (excluding the kitchen and bathroom). "Un deux-pièces" is a flat with a living room and one bedroom; "un cinq-pièces" is a flat with five rooms.

---

piécette [pjesɛt] **NF** small coin

PIED [pje] **NM 1** *(d'une personne)* foot; **p. bot** / **plat** club/flat foot; **doigts de p.** toes; **sauter à pieds joints/sur un p.** to jump with (one's) feet together/hop (on one foot); **être/marcher pieds nus** to be/walk barefoot(ed), to be/walk in one's bare feet; **elle s'est mise pieds nus** she took off her shoes (and stockings); **il n'avait pas de chaussures aux pieds** he had no shoes on (his feet); **se jeter aux pieds de qn** to throw oneself at sb's feet; **avoir bon p. bon œil** to be hale and hearty; **se lever du p. gauche** to get out of bed on the

wrong side; **il ne peut pas mettre un p. devant l'autre** he can hardly put one foot in front of the other; **de la tête aux pieds, de p. en cap** [dəpjetᾶkap] from head to toe *or* foot, from top to toe; *Fig* **faire des pieds et des mains pour faire qch** to move heaven and earth to do sth; *Fam* **être bête comme ses pieds** to be unbelievably stupid, *Br* to be as thick as two short planks; *Fam* **faire du p. à qn** to play footsie with sb; *Fam* **ça lui fera les pieds!** that'll teach him a lesson!; *Fam* **c'est bien fait pour tes pieds!** it serves you right!; *Fam* **elle me casse les pieds** *(elle m'ennuie)* she bores the pants off me; *(elle m'agace)* she gets on my nerves *or* *Br* my wick; **ça fait deux mois qu'elle me casse les pieds pour que je t'en parle** she's been on at me for two months now to talk to you about it; **mettre p. à terre** [pjetatɛr] *(d'un cheval, d'un vélo)* to dismount; *(sans descendre de vélo)* to put one's foot down; *aussi Fig* **tomber sur ses pieds** to fall *or* land on one's feet; **je ne remettrai jamais les pieds chez lui** I'll never set foot in his house again; *Fam* **mettre les pieds dans le plat** to put one's foot in it; **attention où vous mettez les pieds!** mind where you're treading!, watch your step!; **avoir un p. dans la tombe** to have one foot in the grave; **marcher sur les pieds de qn** to tread on sb's toes; *Fig* **tu ne vas pas te laisser marcher sur les pieds par ton chef de service?** you're not going to let your head of department walk all over you *or* take advantage of you?; *Fam* **lever le p.** *(partir)* to run off, *Br* to scarper; *(en voiture)* to ease off; **faire qch au p. levé** to do sth at a moment's notice; **répondre au p. levé** to answer off the cuff; *Fig* **pieds et poings liés** bound hand and foot; **frapper du p.** to stamp (one's foot); **pousser qch du p.** to kick sth; **coup de p.** kick; **donner** *ou* **envoyer un coup de p. à qn** to kick sb, to give sb a kick; **il faut te donner un bon coup de p. (au derrière)** you need a good kick (up the backside); **recevoir un coup de p.** to be kicked, to get a kick; **chasser qn à coups de p.** to kick sb out; **enfoncer une porte à coups de p.** to kick a door in *or* down; **se prendre les pieds dans un tapis** to trip over a carpet; *Belg Fam* **jouer avec les pieds de qn** *(se moquer de)* to make fun of sb, *Br* to take the mick *or* the mickey out of sb; *(duper)* to take sb for a ride

2 à p. on foot; **aller à p.** to walk, to go on foot; **faire deux kilomètres à p.** to walk two kilometres; **vous en avez pour vingt minutes à p.** it will take you twenty minutes to walk (there) *or* twenty minutes on foot; **course à p.** (running) race; **mettre qn à p.** to suspend sb, *Can* to lay sb off

3 mettre une affaire sur p. to set up *or* start a business; **il est de nouveau sur p.** he's up and about again, he's getting about again; **portrait en p.** full-length portrait

4 *Fam* **jouer/chanter/conduire comme un p.** to be a lousy *or* terrible player/singer/driver; **je m'y suis pris comme un p. pour le réparer** I made a real mess of repairing it

5 *Fig* **elle a le p. marin** she's a good sailor, she never gets seasick; **avoir p.** to be within one's depth; *aussi Fig* **perdre p.** to get out of one's depth; **prendre p. (sur un marché/un territoire)** to get a foothold (in a market/a territory); **lâcher p.** to give in, to give way; **faire un p. de nez à qn** to cock a snook at sb; **faire un p. de nez au destin** to thumb one's nose at fate

6 *Fam* **prendre son p.** to get one's kicks; *(sexuellement)* to come; **c'est le p.!** it's fantastic!, it's great!; **ce n'est pas (vraiment) le p.** it's not much fun

7 *Fig (rang)* **être sur un p. d'égalité avec qn** to be on an equal footing with sb; **vivre sur un grand p.** to live on a grand scale

8 *(patte) (de cheval)* hoof; *(à la chasse)*

(trace) footprint; *(piste)* track(s); *Culin* **p. de veau/mouton/porc** knuckle of veal/leg of mutton/pig's trotter

9 *(partie inférieure) (d'un bas, d'un arbre, d'un escalier, d'un lit)* foot; *(d'une colonne, d'un mur)* foot, base; *(d'une montagne)* foot, bottom; *Math (d'une perpendiculaire)* foot; *Typ (d'une lettre)* foot; *Typ* **p. de page** footer; **à p. d'œuvre** *Constr etc* on site; *Fig* ready to get on with the job

10 *(support) (d'une chaise, d'une table etc)* leg; *(de télescope)* stand, rest; *(d'un verre)* stem; *Phot* foot; **p. (à trois branches)** tripod; **p. de lampe** *ou* **de lampadaire** lampstand; *TV, Cin* **p. de sol** *(d'une caméra)* high-hat

11 *(tige)* stalk; *(de vigne)* stock; **p. de céleri / d'asperges/de salade** head of celery/asparagus/lettuce

12 *Naut (du mât)* step, heel

13 *(mesure), Littér* foot; **p. carré/cube** square/cubic foot; **au petit p.** (in) miniature; **p. à p.** [pjeapjə] inch by inch; **six pieds sous terre** six foot under; **p. à coulisse** calliper VOIR GRAMMAIRE A13

Pied noir

This is the name given to the French settlers who settled in North Africa (most notably in Algeria) during the period of French colonial expansion. Most of them resettled in France (mainly on the south coast) after the colonies regained their independence. The largest wave of these settlers to arrive in France was in 1962, following the Algerian war.

---

pied-à-terre [pjetatɛr] **NM INV** pied-à-terre

pied-bot, pl pieds-bots NM *(personne)* club-footed person; *(infirmité)* club foot

pied-d'alouette, pl pieds-d'alouette NM *Bot* larkspur, delphinium

pied-de-biche, pl pieds-de-biche NM *(poignée de sonnette)* bell pull; *(outil)* nail claw, nail extractor; *(d'une machine à coudre)* presser foot; *(d'une chaise, d'une table etc)* cabriole leg

pied-de-coq, pl pieds-de-coq ADJ, NM *Tex* hound's-tooth

pied-de-poule, pl pieds-de-poule ADJ, NM *Tex* hound's-tooth

pied-de-roi, pl pieds-de-roi NM *Can* folding rule

pied-droit, pl pieds-droits NM *Constr* *(d'une voûte, d'un pont)* pier

piédestal, -aux [pjedɛstal, -o] **NM** pedestal

pied-noir, pl pieds-noirs *Fam* **N** Algerian-born Frenchman, *f* Frenchwoman
ADJ French Algerian, Algerian French

piédouche [pjeduʃ] **NM** small pedestal

piédroit [pjedrwa] **NM = pied-droit**

piège [pjɛʒ] **NM 1** *(pour les animaux)* trap, snare; **p. à souris** mousetrap; **p. à rats** rat trap; **dresser** *ou* **tendre un p.** to set a trap (**à** for); **prendre un animal au p.** to trap an animal, to catch an animal in a trap **2** *Fig (embuscade)* trap; **attirer l'ennemi dans un p.** to draw the enemy into a trap; **donner** *ou* **tomber dans un p.** to fall into a trap; **tendre un p. à qn** to set a trap for sb; **être pris à son propre p.** to be caught in one's own trap, *Prov* to be hoist by one's own petard; **dictée pleine de pièges** dictation full of pitfalls; *très Fam* **p. à cons** con, scam

piégeage [pjeʒaʒ] **NM** *(d'animaux)* trapping

piéger [pjeʒe] **VT** *(je piège, n. piégeons; je piégeai(s); je piégerai)* **1** *(attraper), Fig* to trap; **se faire p.** to be trapped; **se laisser p.** to fall into a trap, to get trapped **2** *(munir de pièges) (cour, forêt)* to set a trap/traps in **3** *(placer un explosif dans)* to booby-trap; **voi-**

ture piégée car bomb, booby-trapped car; **colis piégé** parcel bomb; **lettre piégée** letter bomb

piégeur [pjeʒœr] **NM** trapper

pie-grièche, pl **pies-grièches** [pigrijɛʃ] **NF** Orn shrike

pie-mère, pl **pies-mères NF** Anat pia mater

Piémont [pjemɔ̃] **NM** Piedmont

piémontais, -aise [pjemɔ̃tɛ, -ɛz] **ADJ** Piedmontese

   NM Ling Piedmont (dialect)

   N P. Piedmontese

piercé [pirse] **ADJ** Fam (partie du corps) pierced

piercing [pirsiŋ] **NM** piercing

piéride [pjerid] **NF** pierid; **p. du chou** cabbage white (butterfly)

pierraille [pjerɑj] **NF** loose stones

Pierre [pjɛr] **N** P. le Grand Peter the Great

pierre [pjɛr] **NF 1** (matière, caillou, bloc rocheux) stone; (rocher) rock, boulder; **pierres de gué** stepping stones; Prov **qui roule n'amasse pas mousse** a rolling stone gathers no moss; **attaquer qn à coups de pierres** to pelt sb with stones, to throw stones at sb; **on le fit partir à coups de pierres** they drove him away by throwing stones (at him); **jeter une p. à qn** to throw a stone at sb; Fig **jeter la p. à qn** to reproach sb; Fig **je ne serai pas le premier à lui jeter la p.** I will not be the one to throw the first stone; Fig **c'est une p. dans votre jardin** that's a dig at you; Fig **faire d'une p. deux coups** to kill two birds with one stone; Fig **être malheureux comme les pierres** to be bitterly unhappy; Fig **avoir un cœur de p.** to have a heart of stone; **mur de p.** stone wall; **mur en pierres sèches** drystone wall; **maison de** ou **en p.** stone(-built) house; **investir (son argent) dans la p.** to invest in bricks and mortar; **aimer les vieilles pierres** to like old buildings; **p. à p.** stone by stone; Fig (progressivement) bit by bit, little by little; **ils n'ont pas laissé p. sur p.** they didn't leave a stone standing; Fig **apporter sa p. à l'édifice** to make a contribution; **poser la première p.** to lay the foundation stone; Fig to lay the foundation (de for); Hist **âge de p.** Stone Age; **âge de la p. taillée/polie** Old/New Stone Age; **outils en p.** stone implements

   2 (en bijouterie) stone; **p. précieuse** precious stone, gem; **p. fine** ou **semi-précieuse** semi-precious stone

   3 (concrétion) piece of grit; **des fruits pleins de pierres** fruit full of grit

  ▸▸**p. d'achoppement** stumbling block; Tech **p. à aiguiser** whetstone, grindstone; Constr, Fig **p. angulaire** cornerstone; Constr **p. à bâtir** building stone; **p. à briquet** (lighter) flint; **p. à chaux** limestone; **p. à fusil** gun flint; **p. de lune** moonstone; **p. philosophale** philosopher's stone; **p. ponce** pumice (stone); **p. de taille** dressed stone; Minér, Fig **p. de touche** touchstone

pierreries [pjɛr(ə)ri] **NFPL** precious stones, jewels, gems

pierreux, -euse [pjɛrø, -øz] **ADJ 1** (couvert de pierres) (sol, route etc) stony; (lit de rivière) gravelly **2** (qui contient des concrétions) (poire) gritty **3** Méd (formation) calculous

pierrot [pjero] **NM 1** Théâtre **P.** Pierrot **2** Fam (oiseau) sparrow

pietà [pjeta] **NF INV** pietà

piétaille [pjetɑj] **NF** Mil Vieilli rank and file, infantrymen; Fig rank and file; (piétons) pedestrians

piété [pjete] **NF 1** (ferveur religieuse) piety; **articles de p.** devotional objects **2** (affection) **p. filiale** filial devotion

piétinement [pjetinmɑ̃] **NM** (bruit) stamp-

ing; (marche sur place) standing around; Fig (stagnation) lack of progress; **à cause du p. de l'enquête** because the enquiry is at a standstill or is marking time

piétiner [pjetine] **VT 1 p. qch** (en trépignant) to stamp on sth; (en marchant) to trample on sth; (écraser) to trample sth underfoot; **ils sont morts piétinés par la foule** they were trampled to death by the crowd **2** Fig (malmener) (les convictions de qn, les souhaits de qn, la mémoire de qn etc) to have no respect for, to trample underfoot

   VI (frapper des pieds) **p. d'impatience** to stamp (one's feet) impatiently or with impatience; **p. (sur place)** to stand around; Fig **l'instruction piétine** the investigation is marking time or is making no headway or is at a standstill; **je piétine depuis deux mois** I've been marking time for two months

piétisme [pjetism] **NM** Hist, Rel Pietism

piétiste [pjetist] **ADJ, N** Hist, Rel Pietist

piéton, -onne [pjetɔ̃, -ɔn] **N** pedestrian; **passage (pour) piétons** pedestrian crossing, Br ≃ zebra crossing, Am crosswalk

   ADJ rue piétonne pedestrianized street; **zone piétonne** pedestrian precinct

piétonnier, -ière [pjetɔnje, -jɛr] **ADJ** pedestrian; **rue piétonnière** pedestrianized street; **zone piétonnière** pedestrian precinct

piètre [pjɛtr] **ADJ** Litt (compagnon) wretched, poor; (excuse) lame, paltry; **faire p. figure** to cut a poor or sorry figure; **p. consolation** cold or small comfort

piètrement [pjɛtrəmɑ̃] **ADV** wretchedly, poorly

pieu[1], pieux [pjø] **NM 1** (piquet) stake, post; Constr pile; **enfoncer** ou **battre un p.** to drive (in) a pile; **p. creux** tubular pile; **p. de fondation** foundation pile **2** Fam (lit) bed; **se mettre au p., aller au p.** to hit the hay or the sack

pieusement [pjøzmɑ̃] **ADV** (dévotement) piously, devoutly; (avec grand respect) reverently

pieuter [pjøte] Fam **VI** (passer la nuit) to crash (out)

   VPR se pieuter to hit the hay or the sack

pieuvre [pjœvr] **NF** (animal) octopus; Fig Péj (personne) leech; Fig **la p. bureaucratique** the tentacles of bureaucracy; **la p.** (la Mafia) the Mob

pieux, -euse [pjø, -øz] **ADJ 1** (religieux) pious, devout; Fig **p. mensonge** white lie; **c'est un vœu p.** it's wishful thinking **2** Litt (dévoué) (silence) reverent; (fils) devoted

pif[1] [pif] **INT** bang!, smack!; **p., paf!** pow!; **p., paf, boum!** slap! bang! wallop!

pif[2] NM Fam **1** (nez) conk, Br hooter; **je l'ai dans le p.** I can't stand the sight of him, Br he gets right up my nose **2** Fig **faire qch au p.** to do sth by guesswork; **j'ai dit ça au p.** I was just guessing; **j'ai fait ça au p.** it was sheer guesswork, I made it up as I went along; **répondre à une question au p.** to guess at the answer to a question; **au p., je dirais qu'il y en a vingt** at a rough guess I'd say there are twenty; **au lieu d'y aller au p., tu ferais mieux de consulter un plan!** instead of just following your nose, you'd do better to consult a map!

pif(f)er [pife] **VT** Fam **je peux pas le p.** I can't stand (the sight of) him, I can't stomach him

pifomètre [pifɔmɛtr] **NM** Fam intuition; **en politique, il n'y a que le p. qui compte** in politics, having a nose for things or having intuition is all-important; **au p.** voir pif[2] 2

pige [piʒ] **NF 1** (mesure) measuring rod; Typ take (amount of copy to be set up in a given time); Journ freelance contribution; **être payé à la p.** to be paid by the line; **faire des piges,** Can **travailler à la p.** to work freelance **2** Fam (année) **il a 45 piges** he's 45; **à 60 piges**

at 60 **3** Fam **faire la p. à qn** to go one better than sb

pigeon [piʒɔ̃] **NM 1** (oiseau) pigeon; **p. mâle/femelle** cock/hen pigeon; **p. voyageur** carrier pigeon, homing pigeon; **p. colombin** ou **bleu** stock dove; **p. ramier** ring dove, wood pigeon; **p. paon** fantail (pigeon); **p. d'argile** clay pigeon; **tir aux pigeons d'argile** (sport) clay-pigeon shooting; (événement) clay-pigeon shoot; **p. vole** = children's game consisting of giving a yes or no answer to the question 'does X fly?' **2** Fam Péj (dupe) sucker, mug, Am fall guy **3** Constr builder's plaster; (morceau de pierre dans la chaux) hard lump

pigeonnant, -e [piʒɔnɑ̃] **ADJ** Fam **poitrine pigeonnante** high bust; **soutien-gorge p.** uplift bra

pigeonne [piʒɔn] **NF** hen pigeon

pigeonneau, -eaux [piʒɔno] **NM** young pigeon, Spéc squab

pigeonner [piʒɔne] **VT** Fam **p. qn** to take sb in; **je me suis laissé** ou **fait p.** I've been had, I've been taken for a ride or taken in

pigeonnier [piʒɔnje] **NM 1** dovecot(e) **2** Fig Fam (logement très petit) garret, attic

piger [piʒe] (je pigeai(s); n. pigeons) **VT** Fam (comprendre) to get; **tu piges la combine?** do you get what they're/we're/etc up to?; **je ne pige rien aux mathématiques** I haven't got a clue about mathematics; **je n'ai rien pigé à ce qu'il a raconté** I didn't get any of what he was on about, I didn't have a clue what he was on about

   VI tu piges? get it?; **il a pigé** he's got it, Br he's twigged, the penny's dropped; **il ne pige pas** (chaque fois) he doesn't get it; (cette fois-ci) he hasn't got it

pigiste [piʒist] **N 1** (journaliste) freelance journalist, freelancer; **travailler comme p.** to freelance, to work as a freelancer **2** Can (free-lance) freelancer

pigment [pigmɑ̃] **NM** pigment

pigmentaire [pigmɑ̃tɛr] **ADJ** pigmentary

pigmentation [pigmɑ̃tasjɔ̃] **NF** pigmentation

pigmenter [pigmɑ̃te] **VT** to pigment

pigne [piɲ] **NF** pine cone; (graine) pine nut or kernel

pignocher [piɲɔʃe] **VI** Vieilli to pick at one's food

pignon[1] [piɲɔ̃] **NM** Constr gable; **avoir p. sur rue** to have premises in a desirable location; Fig to be of some standing

pignon[2] NM Tech gear(wheel); (la plus petite de deux roues) pinion; **p. de chaîne** sprocket wheel, chain sprocket; **grand p.** (d'une bicyclette) front chain wheel; Tech **p. conique** bevel gear; **p. d'attaque** (de différentiel) driving pinion; **p. de distribution** timing gear; **p. fou** idler; **p. planétaire** planet gear, planet wheel; **p. satellite** (intermediate) planet gear, = gearing between sun gear and planet gear

pignon[3] NM Bot pine nut or kernel

pignoratif, -ive [piɲɔratif, -iv] **ADJ** Fin with a repurchase option

pignouf [piɲuf] **NM** Fam slob, Br yob(bo)

pilaf [pilaf] **NM** Culin pilaf, pilau; **riz p.** pilau rice

pilage [pilaʒ] **NM** pounding, crushing, grinding

pilaire [pilɛr] **ADJ** of the hair

pilastre [pilastr] **NM** Archit pilaster; (au bout d'une rampe) newel

Pilate [pilat] **N** Hist **Ponce P.** Pontius Pilate

pilchard [pilʃar] **NM** pilchard

pile[1] [pil] **NF 1** (tas) pile, stack; **mettre en p.** to stack (up), to pile (up) **2** (pilier) (d'un pont) pier **3** *Élec* battery, *Spéc* cell; **p. sèche** dry cell; **p. plate/ronde** square/round battery; **p. bouton** *(pour montre/appareil photo/calculatrice)* watch/camera/calculator battery; **la radio marche aussi avec des piles** the radio also works on *or* off batteries **4** *Nucl Vieilli* **p. atomique** atomic pile, nuclear reactor

pile² NF *Fam* **1** *(volée de coups)* belting, beating, thrashing; **flanquer** *ou* **donner une p. à qn** to give sb a thrashing *or* belting *or* beating **2** *(défaite)* hammering; **recevoir** *ou* **prendre une p.** to take *or* get a hammering, to get hammered; **flanquer une p. à une équipe** to hammer a team, to walk all over a team

pile³ NF *(d'une pièce)* reverse; **p. ou face?** heads or tails?; **jouer** *ou* **tirer à p. ou face** to toss for it; **on tira à p. ou face qui irait chercher de l'eau** we tossed (up) *or* tossed a coin to decide who was going to get some water

ADJ **côté p.** *(d'une pièce)* reverse side

ADV *Fam* **s'arrêter p.** to stop dead, to come to a dead stop; **vous tombez p.** you've come just at the right moment; **ça tombait p.** that's just what was wanted *or* just what the doctor ordered, that came just at the right time; **tu seras p. à l'heure** you'll be (there) right on time, you'll be (there) on the dot; **à six heures p.** at six on the dot, bang on six; **ma montre est p. à l'heure** my watch is dead on *or* bang on; **elle est arrivée p. le même jour que moi** she arrived on exactly the same day as I did; **nous étions p. dix à table** there were exactly ten of us at the table

pile-poil INT *Fam* wicked!, great!

piler [pile] VT **1** *(broyer)* to pound, to crush, to grind; *(amandes)* to grind **2** *Fam (battre)* to thrash, to hammer; **notre équipe s'est fait p.** our team got a good thrashing *or* hammering
VI *Fam* to slam on the brakes

pilet [pilɛ] NM **(canard) p.** pintail (duck)

pileux, -euse [pilø, -øz] ADJ *Anat* hair, *Spéc* pilose; **follicule p.** hair follicle; **système p.** hair

pilier [pilje] NM **1** *(colonne)* pillar, column; *(poteau, pieu)* post **2** *Rugby* prop (forward) **3** *Fig (soutien)* **ce point est le p. de notre théorie** that point is the mainstay of our theory, our theory rests on that point; **p. de l'Église/de la démocratie** *(personne, journal)* bastion *or* pillar of the Church/of democracy; *Fam Péj* **c'est un p. de bar** *ou* **de bistrot** he's always propping up the bar

pili-pili [pilipili] NM INV bird-pepper

pillage [pijaʒ] NM **1** *(ravage)* pillaging, looting, plundering; **mettre une ville au p.** to sack a town **2** *Fig (d'œuvre)* plagiarism

pillard, -arde [pijar, -ard] ADJ pillaging, looting
N pillager, plunderer; *(lors d'une émeute)* looter

piller [pije] VT **1** *(dévaster, ravager) (village)* to pillage, to plunder; *(magasin)* to loot; *(Rome etc)* to sack; *(maison, pièce)* to ransack **2** *Fig (livre, film)* to plagiarize; **p. un auteur** to plagiarize an author, to steal from an author; **p. les idées de qn** to steal sb's ideas

pilleur, -euse [pijœr, -øz] ADJ pillaging, plundering, looting
N pillager, plunderer; *(lors d'une émeute)* looter; **c'est un p. d'idées** he's always stealing ideas from people; *Naut* **p. d'épaves** plunderer of wrecks

pilon [pilɔ̃] NM **1** *Pharm etc* pestle; *Tech* (earth) rammer; **p. mécanique** power hammer; *Fig* **mettre un livre au p.** to pulp a book; **tous ces livres iront au p.** all these books will be pulped **2** *(cuisse de poulet)* drumstick **3** *(jambe de bois)* wooden leg

pilonnage [pilɔnaʒ] NM *(de produits phar-*

---

maceutiques etc) pounding; *(de terre, béton etc)* ramming; *Mil* bombardment, shelling

pilonner [pilɔne] VT **1** *(écraser) (produits pharmaceutiques etc)* to pound; *(papier)* to pulp; *(terre, béton etc)* to ram **2** *Mil* to bombard, to shell

pilori [pilɔri] NM pillory; *aussi Fig* **clouer** *ou* **mettre qn au p.** to pillory sb

pilosébacé [pilosebase] ADJ *Anat* pilosebaceous

pilosité [pilozite] NF *Anat* hairiness, *Spéc* pilosity; **p. normale/excessive** normal/excessive hair growth; **p. faciale** facial hair

pilot [pilo] NM **1** *Constr* pile; **p. de pont** bridge pile **2** *Tech (chiffons)* = cloth used in paper-making

pilotage [pilɔtaʒ] NM **1** *Naut* piloting; **(droits** *ou* **frais de) p.** pilotage (dues) **2** *Aviat* piloting, flying; **le p. d'un jumbo-jet ne s'apprend pas en un mois** you can't learn to fly a jumbo jet in the space of a month; **poste de p.** cockpit; *(dans un avion plus important)* flight deck; **p. automatique** automatic piloting; **école de p.** flying school **3** *Ordinat* control

pilote [pilɔt] NM **1** *Aviat, Naut* pilot; *(conducteur) (de voiture de course)* driver; *(de moto de course)* rider; *Aviat* **p. d'essai** test pilot; *Aviat* **p. de ligne** airline pilot; **p. breveté** *Aviat* licensed pilot; *Mil, Aviat* certified pilot; **p. automatique** automatic pilot, autopilot, *Br Fam* George; *Fig* **je vais lui servir de p.** I'll show him/her round, I'll act as his/her guide **2** *(poisson)* pilot fish **3** *Ordinat* driver; **p. d'affichage** display driver; **p. d'imprimante** printer driver; **p. de logiciel** software driver; **p. de périphérique** device driver; **p. de mise en attente des fichiers à imprimer** printer spooler **4** *TV* pilot

ADJ pilot; **étude p.** pilot study; **usine/installation p.** pilot factory/plant; **université p.** experimental university; **bateau(-)p.** pilot boat

piloter [pilɔte] VT **1** *(navire)* to pilot; *(avion)* to pilot, to fly; *(conduire) (voiture de course)* to drive; *(moto de course)* to ride; *Fig (projet)* to be in charge of; *Fig* **p. qn dans Londres** to guide *or* show sb round London **2** *Ordinat* to drive; **piloté par menu** menu-driven

pilotis [pilɔti] NM *Constr* piling, piles; **bâti sur p.** built on piles

pilou [pilu] NM *Tex* flannelette, cotton flannel

pils [pils] NF *Belg (bière blonde)* lager

pilulaire [pilylɛr] ADJ *Pharm* pilular

pilule [pilyl] NF *Pharm* pill, tablet; **la p. (contraceptive** *ou* **anticonceptionnelle)** the (contraceptive) pill; **prendre la p.** to be on the pill; **p. abortive** abortion pill; **p. du lendemain** morning-after pill; *Fig* **avaler la p.** to grin and bear it; *Fig* **vous aurez du mal à leur faire avaler la p.** you'll have a hard time getting them to accept that; *Fig* **la p. était amère** it was a bitter pill to swallow; *Fig* **dorer la p. (à qn)** to sugar the pill (for sb); *Fig* **très Fam on va prendre la p.** *ou* **une de ces pilules!** we'll get a hammering!, we'll get hammered!

pimbêche [pɛ̃bɛʃ] NF stuck-up girl/woman
ADJ stuck-up

piment [pimɑ̃] NM *Bot* pimento, capsicum; *Fig (piquant)* spice, piquancy; *Culin* **p. rouge** chilli; **p. doux** pepper, *Am* bell pepper, capsicum; **une histoire/vie qui ne manque pas de p.** a story/life that is anything but dull; **donner du p. à une histoire/une soirée** to add spice to a story/a party

pimenté [pimɑ̃te] ADJ *Culin* spicy, highly spiced, hot; *Fig (histoire)* spicy

pimenter [pimɑ̃te] VT *Culin* to spice up; *Fig (relever) (histoire)* to spice up, to add spice to

---

pimpant [pɛ̃pɑ̃] ADJ *(personne)* smart, spruce, trim

pimprenelle [pɛ̃prənɛl] NF *Bot* burnet

pin [pɛ̃] NM **1** *(arbre)* pine (tree); **p. maritime** maritime pine; **p. d'Écosse** *ou* **sylvestre** Scots pine; **p. pignon** *ou* **parasol** umbrella pine; **p. de montagne** silver pine, white pine; **p. de Virginie** scrub pine; **pomme de p.** pine cone; *(de sapin)* fir cone **2** *(bois)* pine(wood)

pinacle [pinakl] NM pinnacle; *Fig* **porter qn au p.** to praise sb to the skies; **être au p.** to be at the top

pinacothèque [pinakɔtɛk] NF picture gallery, art gallery

pinaillage [pinajaʒ] NM *Fam* quibbling, hair-splitting, nitpicking

pinailler [pinaje] VI *Fam* to quibble, to split hairs, to nitpick; **p. sur qch** to quibble over sth

pinailleur, -euse [pinajœr, -øz] *Fam* ADJ nitpicking
N quibbler, nitpicker

pinard [pinar] NM *Fam* vino, wine; *(de qualité inférieure)* cheap wine, *Br* plonk

pinasse [pinas] NF *Naut* pinnace, shallop

pinçage [pɛ̃saʒ] NM *(de bourgeons)* pinching off, nipping off

pince [pɛ̃s] NF **1** *(outil)* pliers; *(aux mâchoires recourbées)* pincers; *(de forgeron)* tongs; *Chir* forceps VOIR GRAMMAIRE A10 **2** *(patte) (de crabe etc)* pincer, claw **3** *Fam (main)* paw, mitt; **serrer la p. à qn** to shake hands with sb **4** *(d'un animal herbivore)* incisor **5** *(du sabot d'un cheval)* toe, point; *Fam* **aller à pinces (à pied)** to hoof it; *Fam* **il est parti à pinces** he left on foot **6** *Couture* dart

▸▸ **p. alligator** alligator clip; **p. à becs fins** needle-nosed pliers; **p. à becs pointus** pointed-nose pliers; **p. à circlip** circlip pliers; **pince(s) coupante(s)** cutting pliers, wire cutters; **pince(s) coupante(s) d'électricien** electrician's side cutters; **p. de cravate** tie clip; **p. crocodile** crocodile clip; **p. à épiler** tweezers; *Élec* **p. pour fil terminal** terminal clamp; *Chir* **p. hémostatique** artery clip; **p. à linge** clothes peg; **p. multiprise** combination pliers; **p. à ongles** nail clippers; *TV, Cin* **p. pour projecteur** gaffer grip; *Élec* **p. de raccordement** connecting clamp, connector; **p. à sucre** sugar tongs; **p. universelle** (universal) pliers, combination pliers; **p. à vélo** bicycle clip

pincé [pɛ̃se] ADJ *(air)* stiff, starchy; **sourire p.** tight-lipped smile; **répondre d'un ton p.** to answer stiffly *or* starchily; **nez p.** thin nose; **les lèvres pincées** with pursed lips *or* lips pursed, tight-lipped; **instrument à cordes pincées** plucked stringed instrument

pinceau, -eaux [pɛ̃so] NM **1** *(brosse)* (paint)brush; **p. en poils de martre** sable brush; **coup de p.** brush stroke; **on reconnaît facilement le coup de p. de l'artiste** the artist's brushwork is easily recognizable; **elle a un bon coup de p.** she paints well **2** *Fig (technique, manière)* brushwork **3** *Fam (pied)* foot; **s'emmêler les pinceaux** *(trébucher)* to trip up, to stumble; *(s'embrouiller)* to tie oneself in knots **4** *Opt* **p. de lumière** pencil of light

pincée [pɛ̃se] NF *(de sel, de tabac à priser etc)* pinch

pince-fesses NM INV *Fam Vieilli* knees-up, shindig, bash

pincement [pɛ̃smɑ̃] NM **1** *(fait de pincer)* pinching, nipping **2** *Fig (sensation vive, douloureuse) (de regret etc)* pang, twinge; **il a eu un p. au cœur** his heart missed a beat **3** *Mus (des cordes de guitare etc)* plucking **4** *(des bourgeons)* pinching off, nipping off

pince-monseigneur, *pl* **pinces-monsei-**

gneur NF jemmy, *Am* jimmy; **forcer une porte à la p.** to jemmy *or Am* jimmy a door

pince-nez NM INV pince-nez

pincer [pɛ̃se] (je pinçai(s); n. pinçons) VT **1** *(serrer)* to pinch, to nip; **son grand-père lui pinça la joue** his grandfather pinched his cheek; **p. les lèvres** to purse one's lips; **non mais pince-moi, je rêve!** pinch me, I'm dreaming!; *Fam* **ça pince dur ce matin!** it's pretty nippy this morning! **2** *(bourgeons)* to pinch off, to nip off; *(plante)* to top **3** *Mus (cordes de harpe etc)* to pluck **4** *Couture (vêtement)* to put darts in **5** *Fam (attraper) (personne)* to catch; **se faire p.** to be *or* get caught, to cop it; *Fam* **en p. pour qn** to be crazy about sb, to be gone on sb

VPR **se pincer se p. le doigt dans la porte** to catch one's finger in the door; **fais attention, tu vas te p.** watch out, you'll catch yourself; **se p. le nez** to hold one's nose

pince-sans-rire N INV person with a dry sense of humour

ADJ INV dry, deadpan; **répondre d'un air p.** to answer drily *or* deadpan

pincette [pɛ̃sɛt] NF **1** *(petite pince)* tweezers; **pincettes** (fire) tongs, pair of (fire) tongs; *Fig Fam* **il n'est pas à prendre avec des pincettes** *(il est sale)* he's absolutely filthy; *(il est de très mauvaise humeur)* he's like a bear with a sore head VOIR GRAMMAIRE A10 **2** *Suisse (pince à linge)* clothes peg

pinçon [pɛ̃sɔ̃] NM pinch mark

pindarique [pɛ̃darik] ADJ *Littér* Pindaric

pine [pin] NF *Vulg* dick, prick, cock

pinéal, -ale, -aux, -ales [pineal, -o] ADJ *Anat* pineal

Pineau [pino] NM Pineau *(apéritif made from unfermented grape juice and brandy)*

pinède [pinɛd], **pineraie** [pinrɛ] NF pine forest *or* wood

pinglot [pɛ̃glo] NM *Fam* foot, *Br* plate, *Am* dog

pingouin [pɛ̃gwɛ̃] NM penguin; *(de la famille des macareux)* auk; **p. royal** king penguin

ping-pong [piŋpɔ̃g] NM ping-pong, table tennis

pingre [pɛ̃gr] *Péj* ADJ stingy, niggardly, miserly
N miser, skinflint, *Am* tightwad

pingrerie [pɛ̃grəri] NF *Péj* stinginess, niggardliness, miserliness

pinot [pino] NM Pinot grape

pin's [pinz] NM INV lapel badge *or* pin

pinson [pɛ̃sɔ̃] NM chaffinch; **être gai comme un p.** to be as happy as a lark

pintade [pɛ̃tad] NF guinea fowl; **p. mâle** guinea cock; **p. femelle** guinea hen

pintadeau, -eaux [pɛ̃tado] NM young guinea fowl, guinea poult

pinte [pɛ̃t] NF **1** *Arch (mesure)* pint *(0.93 litres)*; *Br, Am* pint; *Can* quart **2** *Fam Vieilli* **se payer une p. de bon sang** to have a good time *or* a good laugh **3** *Suisse* café-bar **4** *Can* **se faire une p. de mauvais sang** to worry oneself sick

pinter [pɛ̃te] *très Fam* VI to booze
VPR **se pinter** to booze; *(s'enivrer)* to get sozzled *or* plastered; **il s'est pinté (la gueule)** he got plastered, *Am* he tied one on

pinteur, -euse [pɛ̃tœr, -øz] N *Belg, Suisse Fam (alcoolique)* boozer, alky

pin up [pinœp] NF INV *(photo)* pin-up; *(jolie fille)* sexy-looking girl

pinyin [pinjin] NM *Ling* Pinyin

pioche [pjɔʃ] NF **1** *(outil)* pick, pickaxe, *Am* pickax; *Agr* mattock; *Fig Fam* **tête de p.** pigheaded person **2** *(aux dominos)* stock, pile

piocher [pjɔʃe] VT **1** *(creuser)* to dig (with a pick) **2** *Scol Fam* **p. son allemand** to swot up *or* mug up one's German
VI **1** *(fouiller)* to dig, to delve (**dans** into) **2** *(aux dominos)* to draw from the stock

piocheur, -euse [pjɔʃœr, -øz] *Fam* ADJ hardworking
N *Scol Vieilli* slogger, *Péj* swot, *Am* grind

piolet [pjɔlɛ] NM **1** ice axe, *Am* ice ax **2** *Suisse (bâton de ski)* ski stick, ski pole

pion, -onne [pjɔ̃, -ɔn] N *Scol Fam* supervisor *(paid to supervise pupils outside class hours)*
NM **1** *Échecs* pawn; *(aux dames)* draught(s)man, *Am* checker; *(dans d'autres jeux)* piece; *Fig* **n'être qu'un p. (sur l'échiquier)** to be only a pawn in the game **2** *Tech* peg

> ### Pion
> In French lycées, the "pions" (officially called "surveillants") are responsible for supervising pupils outside class hours; they are often university students who do the job to make a little extra money.

pioncer [pjɔ̃se] VI (je pionçai(s); n. pionçons) *Fam* to sleep, *Br* to kip

pionnier, -ière [pjɔnje, -jɛr] N *aussi Fig* pioneer
ADJ pioneering; **son esprit p.** his pioneering spirit

pipe¹ [pip] NF **1** *(de fumeur)* pipe; **p. de bruyère/en terre** briar/clay pipe; **fumer la p.** to smoke a pipe; *Fig Fam* **casser sa p.** to kick the bucket; **nom d'une p.!** heavens above!; *Fam* **20 euros par tête de p.** 20 euros a head; *Fam* **se fendre la p.** *(rire)* to split one's sides (laughing); *(s'amuser)* to have a good laugh; *Vulg* **faire ou tailler une p. à qn** to give sb a blow job **2** *(contenu)* pipe(ful) **3** *Arg Vieilli (cigarette)* ciggy, *Br* fag **4** *Région (futaille)* (large) cask, barrel

pipe² [pajp] NM *(tuyau)* pipe(line) *(for liquid, gas)*

pipeau, -eaux [pipo] NM *Mus* (reed) pipe; **p. de chasse** bird call; **pipeaux** *(pour prendre les oiseaux)* limed twigs; *Fam* **c'est du p.** it's all claptrap

pipée [pipe] NF bird snaring, bird catching *(with bird calls and limed twigs)*

pipelet, -ette [piplɛ, -ɛt] *Fam* N *Vieilli* concierge, porter, *Am* janitor
NF **pipelette** *(personne bavarde)* gossip, chatterbox

pipe(-)line, *pl* **pipe(-)lines** [piplin, pajplajn] NM pipeline

piper [pipe] VT **1** *(attraper avec des appeaux) (oiseaux)* to lure by means of bird calls **2** *(truquer) (dés)* to load; *(cartes)* to mark; *Fig* **les dés sont pipés** the dice are loaded **3** *Fam* **ne pas p. (mot)** not to say a word, to keep silent, to keep mum

piperade [pip(ə)rad], **pipérade** [piperad] NF *Culin* piperade, = rich stew of tomatoes and sweet peppers, mixed with beaten eggs and slightly scrambled

pipette [pipɛt] NF pipette; *Suisse* **ça ne vaut pas p.** *(ça ne vaut rien)* it's not worth a bean *or Am* a red cent

pipi [pipi] NM *Fam* pee, *Enf* wee(-wee); **faire p.** to pee, *Enf* to wee(-wee), to have a wee(-wee); **aller faire p.** to go to the loo *or Am* john, to go for a pee; **faire p. au lit** to wet the bed; **le chien a fait p. sur le tapis** the dog's made a puddle on the carpet; *Fam Péj* **c'est du p. de chat** *(boisson)* it's dishwater; *(argument, discours etc)* it's tripe

pipi-room, *pl* **pipi-rooms** [pipirum] NM *Fam* loo, *Am* rest room; **où sont les pipi-rooms?** where's the loo?

pipistrelle [pipistrɛl] NF *Zool* pipistrelle

piquage [pika3] NM *Couture (machine)* stitching; *(d'une surface métallique)* pitting

piquant [pikɑ̃] ADJ **1** *(pointu) (objet)* pointed; *(plante)* prickly, thorny; *(ortie)* stinging; *(barbe)* bristly, prickly; *(sensation)* prickling **2** *(vent)* biting **3** *(goût)* spicy, hot, piquant; *(moutarde, radis)* hot **4** *Fig (caustique) (remarques etc)* cutting, caustic **5** *Fig (qui stimule la curiosité, l'intérêt) (beauté)* piquant, striking; **une petite brune piquante** a striking little brunette
NM **1** *(épine) (d'une plante)* prickle, thorn; *(d'un porc-épic)* quill, spine; *(d'un hérisson)* bristle; *(de fil de fer barbelé)* spike, barb **2** *Fam (agrément) (d'un style, d'une situation)* piquancy; *(d'une histoire)* spice; **cette fille a du p.** that girl is rather striking *or* is strikingly attractive; **le changement donne du p. à la vie** variety is the spice of life; **c'est ce qui fait tout le p. de la situation** it's what makes the situation so piquant

pique¹ [pik] NF *(arme)* pike; *(d'un picador)* lance
NM *Cartes (carte)* spade; *(couleur)* spades; **valet de p.** jack of spades; **jouer (un) p.** to play spades *or* a spade; **il me reste encore trois piques** I still have three spades left (in my hand)

pique² NF **1** *(méchanceté)* taunt, spiteful remark, *Fam* dig; **envoyer ou lancer des piques à qn** to get at sb, *Fam* to have a dig *or* a go at sb **2** *Vieilli (brouille)* tiff

piqué, -ée [pike] ADJ **1** *(dessus-de-lit, vêtement)* quilted; **p. à la machine** machine-stitched; *(matelassé)* machine-quilted **2** *(marqué par les vers) (bois, livre)* wormeaten; *(marqué par l'humidité) (miroir)* tarnished; *(page, gravure)* foxed; *(métal)* pitted; *Fig* **ciel p. d'étoiles** sky studded with stars; *Fam* **une histoire/recette qui n'est pas piquée des hannetons** *ou* **des vers** one heck of a story/recipe **3** *Fam (fou)* crazy, mad **4** *(acide) (vin)* sour, tart **5** *Mus (notes)* staccato
NM **1** *Aviat* **descente en p.** vertical dive, nose dive; **bombardement en p.** dive bombing **2** *Tex* piqué
N *Fam (fou, folle)* nutter, loony

pique-assiette, pl pique-assiettes N *Fam* scrounger, sponger, freeloader

pique-bœuf, pl pique-bœufs NM *Orn* oxpecker

pique-feu NM INV poker

pique-fleurs NM INV flower holder, frog

pique-nique, pl pique-niques NM picnic; **faire un p.** to have a picnic

pique-niquer VI to have a picnic, to picnic

pique-niqueur, -euse, pl pique-niqueurs, -euses [piknikœr, -øz] N picnicker

pique-notes NM INV spike

piquer [pike] VT **1** *(percer avec une pointe)* to prick; *(d'une guêpe, d'un moustique etc)* to sting; *(d'une puce)* to bite; *(aiguillonner) (cheval)* to spur on; *(bœuf)* to goad; *Fam* **quelle mouche vous a piqué?** what's eating *or* biting you?, what's got into you?, who rattled your cage?; **se faire p. par un insecte** to be bitten by an insect; **p. un cheval de l'éperon** to prick *or* spur a horse; **la fumée me pique les yeux** the smoke makes my eyes sting *or* smart; **ça me pique la gorge/le nez** it tickles my throat/nose
2 *Méd* **p. qn** to give sb an injection *or Br Fam* a jab; *Fam* **se faire p. contre qch** to be vaccinated against sth; *Fam* **p. un chien** to put a dog down, to put a dog to sleep; *Fam* **faire p. un chien** to have a dog put down *or* put to sleep
3 *(offenser, froisser)* to offend, to pique; **p. qn au vif** to cut sb to the quick

4 *(exciter)* **p. l'attention de qn** to arouse sb's attention; **p. la curiosité de qn** to arouse *or* excite sb's curiosity

5 *(trouer)* *(d'acide, de vers)* to eat into; *(tacheter)* to spot, to mark; **mains piquées de taches de rousseur** freckled *or* freckly hands

6 *(coudre)* to (back)stitch; *(dessus-de-lit etc)* to quilt; **p. (à la machine)** to machine (stitch); **p. du cuir** to stitch leather

7 *Culin* **p. de la viande** to lard meat; **rôti piqué d'ail** joint stuck with garlic

8 *Mus* **p. une note** to play a note staccato; *Naut* **p. l'heure** to strike the hour

9 *Fam (voler)* to pinch, to swipe (**qch à qn** sth from sb); **ils m'ont piqué ma voiture** they pinched *or* swiped my car; **je me suis fait p. mon stylo** my pen got pinched *or* swiped

10 *(enfoncer)* to stick (**dans** into)

11 *Fam* **p. un cent mètres** to sprint off; **p. une tête** to take a header, to dive; **p. un roupillon** to have forty winks *or* a nap *or* a snooze; **p. une crise** *ou* **une colère** to throw a fit; **p. une crise de nerfs** to have hysterics; **p. un soleil** *ou* **un fard** to go bright red, to blush

VI 1 *Aviat* **p. (du nez)** to nosedive; *Fig* **p. du nez** to nod off, to doze off; *(baisser les yeux)* to look down; *Naut* **p. de l'avant** to go down by the bows

2 *(picoter)* *(de plat)* to be hot *or* spicy; *(de vin)* to be sour *or* tart; **moutarde qui pique** hot mustard; *Fam* **eau qui pique** fizzy water; **vent qui pique** keen *or* biting wind; **ça pique** it stings; **tu piques!** *(à un homme mal rasé)* you're all bristly!

3 *(d'une abeille, d'un moustique, d'une plante)* to sting; *(d'une puce)* to bite

4 p. des deux to spur on one's horse; *(s'en aller à cheval)* to gallop off; *Fig* to rush *or* dash off

VPR se piquer 1 *(se blesser)* to prick oneself; **il s'est piqué le doigt en cousant un bouton** he pricked his finger sewing on a button

2 *(se faire une piqûre)* *(de malade, drogué)* to give oneself an injection, to inject oneself; **il se pique** he shoots up

3 *(se froisser)* to take offence *or Am* offense

4 se p. de faire qch to pride oneself on doing sth; **se p. de littérature** to pride oneself on one's knowledge of literature; **se p. au jeu** to get into it **5** *(se couvrir de taches) (de miroir)* to tarnish; *(de métaux)* to pit; *(du bois)* to become wormeaten, to get woodworm; *(des vêtements etc)* to become motheaten; *(de livres)* to become foxed; *(devenir acide) (du vin)* to turn acid, to (turn) sour

piquet¹ [pikɛ] **NM 1** *(pieu)* stake, post; *(plus petit)* peg; **mettre** *ou* **attacher les chevaux au p.** to tether the horses; **droit/raide comme un p.** as straight as a ramrod/stiff as a poker; **rester planté comme un p.** to stand there doing nothing, *Br Fam* to stand there like a lemon **2** *Scol* **mettre** *ou* **envoyer qn au p.** to send sb to stand in the corner; **être au p.** to stand in the corner

▸▸ *Ind* **p. de grève** strike picket, picket line; **p. d'incendie** fire picket; **p. de tente** tent peg

piquet² **NM** *Cartes* piquet; **faire un p.** to play a hand of piquet

piquetage [piktaʒ] **NM** *Tech* staking (out)

piqueter [pikte] **VT** (**je piquette, n. piquetons; je piquetterai**) **1** *(jalonner)* to stake out, to mark out **2** *(marquer)* to spot, to dot; **piqueté de noir** spotted *or* dotted with black

piquette [pikɛt] **NF 1** *Péj (vin)* cheap wine, *Br Fam* plonk **2** *Fam (défaite)* hammering, thrashing; **prendre une** *ou* **la p.** to get *or* take a hammering, to get a good thrashing

piqueur, -euse [pikœr, -øz] **NM 1** *(à la chasse)* whipper-in; *Équitation* groom **2** *Min* hewer, pickman **3** *Rail* platelayer, *Am* tracklayer

N *Ind* stitcher

ADJ *Zool* **insecte p.** stinging insect

piquouse [pikuz] **NF** *Fam* shot, *Br* jab; **se faire une p.** to have a jab

piqûre [pikyr] **NF 1** *(petite blessure) (de guêpe etc)* sting; *(de puce)* bite; **p. d'épingle** pinprick **2** *Méd* injection, *Fam* shot, *Br Fam* jab; **faire une p. à qn** to give sb an injection **3** *(trou)* (small) hole; *(dans le métal)* pit; **p. de vers** *(dans bois, livre)* wormhole; **p. d'aiguille** *(dans le cuir)* pinhole **4** *Couture (d'un tissu, du cuir)* (back)stitching; **(point de) p.** *(d'une machine à coudre)* lockstitch **5** *(tache) (de rouille, de poussière, de moisi)* spot, speck; **piqûres** *(dans le métal)* pitting

piranha [pirana] **NM** piranha

piratage [pirataʒ] **NM** piracy; **p. informatique** (computer) hacking, cracking

pirate [pirat] **NM 1** *(des mers)* pirate **2** *(voleur, filou)* crook

ADJ *Fig* pirate; *Radio* **station p.** pirate station; **enregistrement p.** pirate *or* bootleg recording

▸▸ **p. de l'air** hijacker, skyjacker; *Ordinat* **p. informatique** hacker, cracker; **p. de la route** robber *(who preys on motorists)*

pirater [pirate] **VT** *(enregistrement, cassette)* to pirate; *Ordinat* to hack; **p. un film** to make a pirate copy of a film

piraterie [piratri] **NF 1** *(sur les mers)* piracy; *(acte)* act of piracy; *Aviat* **p. aérienne** hijacking, skyjacking **2** *Fig (escroquerie)* swindling; *Ordinat* hacking; **p. audiovisuelle** unauthorized copying *or* reproduction, *Fam* bootlegging; **p. informatique** hacking; **p. commerciale** illegal copying of brand-name goods, counterfeiting

pire [pir] **ADJ 1** *(comp)* worse; **cela est bien p.** that's much worse; **c'est p. qu'avant** it's worse than before; **p. que jamais** worse than ever; **le remède p. que le mal** the cure is worse than the disease; *Prov* **il n'est p. eau que l'eau qui dort** still waters run deep; *Prov* **il n'est p. sourd que celui qui ne veut pas entendre** there is none so deaf as he who will not hear; **rien n'est p. que …** nothing is worse than …, there is nothing worse than …; **ce qui est p.** what is worse; **c'est de p. en p.** it's getting worse and worse **2** *(superl)* worst; **le p./la p./les pires** the worst; **un voyou de la p. espèce** a lout of the worst kind; **nos pires erreurs** our worst mistakes; **c'est mon p. ennemi** he's my worst enemy

NM le p. de l'histoire, c'est que … the worst thing about it is that …; **pour le meilleur et pour le p.** for better or for worse; **il est capable du meilleur comme du p.** he can be extremely good or extremely bad; **craindre le p.** to fear the worst; **s'attendre au p.** to expect the worst; **(en mettant les choses) au p.** if the worst comes to the worst, at worst

Pirée (le) [ləpire] **NM** Piraeus

piriforme [piriform] **ADJ** pear-shaped, *Spéc* pyriform

pirogue [pirɔg] **NF** pirogue, dugout (canoe)

piroguier [pirɔgje] **NM** boatman *(in a pirogue)*

pirouette [pirwɛt] **NF 1** *(de danseuse)*, *Équitation* pirouette; *Fig Fam* **répondre par une p.** *ou* **des pirouettes** to give a flippant answer **2** *Fig (revirement)* about-turn, volte-face

pirouetter [pirwete] **VI** to pirouette

pis¹ [pi] **NM** *(d'une vache etc)* udder

pis² **ADV** **aller de mal en p.** to go from bad to worse

ADJ *Litt* **1** *(comp)* worse; **cela serait encore p.** that would be worse still *or* even worse; **qui p. est** what is worse; **son état est p. que jamais** his condition is worse than ever **2** *(superl)* **ce qu'il y a de p.** what is worst

NM 1 *(comp)* worse; **il y a p.** there is/are

worse; **il a fait tout cela et p.** he did all that and (something even) worse; **dire p. que pendre de qn** to call sb every name under the sun, not to have a good word to say for sb; **on m'a dit p. que pendre de cet homme-là** I've been told the most dreadful things about that man **2** *(superl)* **le p.** the worst; **en mettant les choses au p.** if the worst comes to the worst, at worst; **au p. aller** at the very worst

pis-aller [pizale] **NM INV** *(solution temporaire)* stopgap (solution); **on va l'engager mais c'est un p.** we'll take him on but we're scraping the bottom (of the barrel), we'll take him on as the best of a bad lot; **j'ai pris ce travail, mais pour moi, c'est un p.** I took the job as the best thing available in the circumstances *or* although it's far from ideal

piscicole [pisikɔl] **ADJ** fish-breeding, *Fml* piscicultural

pisciculteur, -trice [pisikyltœr, -tris] **N** fish breeder, *Fml* pisciculturist

pisciculture [pisikyltyr] **NF** fish breeding, *Fml* pisciculture

pisciforme [pisiform] **ADJ** pisciform

piscine [pisin] **NF 1** *(bassin de natation)* (swimming) pool; **p. couverte/en plein air** indoor/open-air *or* outdoor pool; **p. d'eau de mer** sea-water pool; **p. d'eau douce** fresh-water pool; **p. intérieure** indoor pool; **p. publique** (public) swimming pool, *Br* swimming baths **2** *Arg* **la p.** = the French secret service

piscivore [pisivɔr] **ADJ** fish-eating, *Spéc* piscivorous

Pise [piz] **N** Pisa

pissaladière [pisaladjɛr] **NF** *Culin* = (open) onion, olive and anchovy tart, a speciality of Nice

pissat [pisa] **NM** *(de cheval, d'âne etc)* urine

pisse [pis] **NF** *Vulg* piss, pee; **c'est de la p. d'âne, ta bière!** your beer's like (gnat's) piss!

pisse-copie **N** *INV* *Fam* hack

pisse-froid **NM** *INV* *Fam (personne morose)* wet blanket

pissenlit [pisɑ̃li] **NM 1** dandelion; *Fam* **manger les pissenlits par la racine** to be pushing up the daisies, to be six feet under **2** *Can Fam (enfant souffrant d'énurésie)* bedwetter, child who wets his/her bed

pisser [pise] **VI 1** *très Fam* to (have a) piss, to (have a) pee; **il a pissé dans sa culotte** he's pissed in *or* peed in *or* wet his pants; **c'est comme si je pissais dans un violon** it's a complete waste of time, it's like pissing in the wind; **laisse p. (le mérinos)!** leave it!, forget it!, don't let it get to you!; **p. de rire** to piss oneself (laughing); **ça/il ne pisse pas loin** it's/he's not up to much; **ça l'a pris comme une envie de p.** he felt a sudden urge to do it, the urge suddenly took him to do it; **je pisse sur les intellectuels** I despise these fucking intellectuals; **ton patron, je lui pisse dessus!** I don't give a shit about your boss!; **je te pisse à la raie!** up yours! **2** *Fam (fuir)* *(d'un récipient)* to leak; *(d'un liquide)* to squirt out; **tonneau qui pisse** leaky barrel

VT *Fam* **son bras pissait le sang** there was blood gushing *or* pouring from his arm, his arm was pouring with blood; **elle pissait le sang** blood was pouring out of her; *Méd très Fam* **p. du sang** to pass blood; **le robinet pisse de l'eau continuellement** the tap is continually leaking

pissette [pisɛt] **NF 1** *Chimie* wash(ing) bottle **2** *Can Fam (pénis)* dick, prick

pisseur, -euse¹ [pisœr, -øz] *Vulg* **N 1 c'est un p.** he's always going for a piss *or* pee, he's got a weak bladder **2** *Journ Péj* **p. de copie** writer who churns/churned out rubbish

NF pisseuse *(petite fille)* little girl, *Péj* brat

pisseux, -euse² [pisø, -øz] ADJ Fam **1** (qui sent l'urine) smelling of piss; (taché par l'urine) stained with piss, piss-stained **2** Fig (couleur) washed out, wishy-washy, yellowy

pisse-vinaigre NM INV Fam (avare) skinflint, tightwad; (rabat-joie) killjoy

pissoir [piswar] NM, **pissotière** [pisɔtjɛr] NF Fam (public) urinal; (dans la rue) street urinal

pissou [pisu] NM Can Fam wimp, wuss

pistache [pistaʃ] NF pistachio (nut); Culin **glace à la p.** pistachio ice cream
ADJ INV pistachio (green)

pistachier [pistaʃje] NM pistachio (tree)

pistage [pistaʒ] NM (d'animal) tracking, trailing; (de personne) tailing

pistard, -arde [pistar, -ard] N Cyclisme track racer

piste [pist] NF **1** (trace) track, trail; **suivre la p.** to follow the track or the trail; **être sur la p. de qn/qch** to be on the track of sb/sth; **la police a plusieurs pistes** the police have several leads; **brouiller les pistes** to cover one's tracks; Fig to confuse the issue; **suivre une fausse p.** to be on the wrong track; **être sur la bonne p.** to be on the right track
2 Sport track; Courses de chevaux (race)track; (course automobile) (racing) track; Fig Fam Dial **aller en p.** to go clubbing; **p. cendrée** cinder track; **tour de p.** lap; Aut etc **p. de vitesse** racing track; **p. d'essai** test track; **p. de patinage** skating rink; **p. de ski** (ski) run, piste; **p. de luge** toboggan run; Ski **p. artificielle** artificial or dry ski slope; **p. de danse** dance floor; **p. (de cirque)** (circus) ring; **en p.!** into the ring!; Fig (au travail) get cracking!
3 Aviat runway; **p. d'envol** take-off runway; **p. d'atterrissage** landing runway; (dans la brousse etc) airstrip; **p. de fortune** airstrip, landing strip
4 (chemin) track, trail; **p. cyclable** cycle path; Tech **p. des billes** ball race; **p. en terre** dirt track
5 (de magnétophone), Ordinat (de disque), Cin track; **magnéto 4 pistes** 4-track tape recorder; Cin **p. sonore** soundtrack; **p. audio** sound track; Ordinat **p. d'amorçage** boot track; TV etc **p. de fond** backing track; **p. magnétique** magnetic track; Ordinat magnetic stripe; **p. optique** optical track; TV, Cin **p. pilote** control track; TV, Cin **p. son** sound track, audio track; **p. son non synchrone** wild track; TV, Cin **p. vidéo** video track; Ordinat **pistes par pouce** tracks per inch

pister [piste] VT (animal) to track, to trail; **p. qn** to tail or shadow or follow sb

pisteur [pistœr] NM ski-run attendant or supervisor

pistil [pistil] NM Bot pistil

pistoche [pistɔʃ] NF Fam (swimming) pool

pistole [pistɔl] NF pistole

pistolet [pistɔlɛ] NM **1** (arme à feu) pistol, gun; Tech **peinture au p.** spray painting, spraying **2** Culin (petit pain au lait) (milk) roll; Belg (petit pain) (bread) roll; **3** (de dessinateur) French curve **4** Fam (urinal) bottle **5** (type bizarre) **un drôle de p.** a queer or an odd sort or Fam fish **6** Can Fam **être en p.** (être en colère) to be hopping mad or fuming ▸▸ **p. à air comprimé** air pistol or gun; Hist **p. d'arçon** horse pistol; **p. à bouchon** popgun; **p. à eau** water pistol; Tech **p. à peinture** paint gun, spray gun; Sport **p. de starter** starting pistol; Mil etc **p. de tir** firing pistol; Tech **p. vaporisateur** paint gun, spray gun

pistolet-mitrailleur, pl **pistolets-mitrailleurs** NM submachine gun, tommy gun, sten gun

pistoleur [pistɔlœr] NM Tech spray(-gun) painter

piston [pistɔ̃] NM **1** Tech (de machine, de pompe, de cric etc) piston; **p. à air/eau** air/water piston; **tête de p.** piston head; **p. plongeur** (d'une pompe refoulante etc) plunger; (d'une presse hydraulique) ram; **p. de servo** booster piston **2** Fam (recommandation) string-pulling; **avoir du p.** to have friends in the right places; **il a eu la place par p.** someone pulled strings to get him the job; **faire jouer le p.** to pull strings **3** Mus valve; **(cornet à) p.** cornet

pistonné, -ée [pistɔne] N **c'est un p.** he got where he is thanks to a bit of string-pulling

pistonner [pistɔne] VT Fam **p. qn** to pull strings for sb; **il s'est fait p.** he got someone to pull strings for him

pistou [pistu] NM Culin pesto; **soupe de** ou **au p.** vegetable soup with pesto

pita [pita] NM pitta bread

pitance [pitɑ̃s] NF **1** Arch (dans un couvent) allowance (of food) **2** Péj Vieilli sustenance

> Il faut noter que le terme anglais **pittance** est un faux ami. Il désigne une somme dérisoire.

pit-bull, pl **pit-bulls** [pitbul] NM pit bull (terrier)

pitchoun, -oune [pitʃun] N Région (enfant) little one

pitchpin [pitʃpɛ̃] NM Bot pitch pine

piteusement [pitøzmɑ̃] ADV pitifully, miserably

piteux, -euse [pitø, -øz] ADJ **1** Vieilli (qui suscite la pitié) pitiful **2** (médiocre) **p. résultat** poor or miserable or pitiful result; **en p. état** in a sorry or pitiful state **3 faire une mine piteuse**, **faire piteuse mine** to look crestfallen; **il annonça d'un air p. que ...** he announced shamefaced that ...

pithécanthrope [pitekɑ̃trɔp] NM pithecanthropus

pithiviers [pitivje] NM Culin = cake made of puff pastry containing rum and almond-flavoured cream

pitié [pitje] NF **1** (compassion) pity, compassion; **avoir p. de qn** to pity sb; (s'apitoyer) to take or have pity on sb; (épargner) to have mercy on sb; **prendre p. de qn, prendre qn en p.** to take pity on sb; **être sans p.** to be pitiless or merciless or ruthless; **il les a jugés sans p.** he judged them pitilessly or mercilessly or ruthlessly; **par p.** out of pity; (en implorant) for pity's sake; **p.!** (grâce) (have) mercy!, have pity on me!; (arrête ça) for pity's sake!; **faire p.** to arouse pity; **il me faisait p.** I felt sorry for him; **cela faisait p. à voir** it was pitiful or Fml pitiable to see (it); Vieilli **c'est p. qu'il soit resté seul** it's pitiful or sad that he should have been left alone **2** (commisération mêlée de mépris) pity; **c'est (une) p. de voir des choses pareilles** it's pitiful to see such things

piton [pitɔ̃] NM **1** Tech eye (bolt); **p. (d'alpiniste)** piton, peg; **p. à vis** screw eye; **p. à boucle** ring bolt **2** (sommet de montagne) **p. (rocheux)** (rocky) peak **3** Can Fam (d'une sonnette) button; (d'un clavier) key

pitoune [pitun] NF Can **1** (bille de bois) pulpwood bolt **2** Fam (femme bien en chair) plump woman; **grosse p.** fat lump (of a woman) **3** Fam Péj (femme de mœurs légères) tramp, tart **4** Fam (terme d'affection) darling, sweetheart

pitoyable [pitwajabl] ADJ **1** (digne de pitié) (récit, condition etc) pitiful, Fml pitiable, piteous **2** Péj (lamentable) (excuse, plaisanterie etc) pathetic, pitiful

pitoyablement [pitwajabləmɑ̃] ADV pitifully; **échouer p.** to fail miserably

pitre [pitr] NM (clown) clown; **faire le p.** to clown (around), to play or act the fool

pitrerie [pitrəri] NF clowning around, tomfoolery

pittoresque [pitɔrɛsk] ADJ picturesque; (description, style) colourful, Am colorful, vivid
NM picturesqueness; (d'un style, d'une description) vividness

pituitaire [pitɥitɛr] ADJ Anat pituitary

pituite [pitɥit] NF Anat (vomissement) bile, Arch phlegm

pive [piv] NF Suisse (pomme de pin) pine cone

pivelé [pivle] ADJ Can (moucheté) spotted; (couvert de taches de rousseur) freckled

pivert [pivɛr] NM green woodpecker

pivoine [pivwan] NF Bot peony; Fig **rouge comme une p.** red as a beetroot

pivot [pivo] NM **1** (axe) pivot; (de fusil) swivel; (de levier) fulcrum; (en dentisterie) post; (de compas, de boussole) centre pin; **p. à rotule** ball pivot; **à p., monté sur p.** pivoted, swivelling; **canon à p.** swivel gun; Tech **p. de fusée** swivel pin, king pin **2** Fig (élément central) (d'un drame) mainspring, pivot **3** Bot tap root **4** (au basket) centre, Am center

pivotant [pivɔtɑ̃] ADJ **1** (qui tourne) pivoting, swivelling, revolving; **fauteuil p.** swivel chair; **base pivotante** swivel base **2** Bot **racine pivotante** tap root

pivoter [pivɔte] VI **1** (tourner) to pivot, to swivel, to turn (**sur** (up)on); Mil (des troupes) to wheel; **faire p. qch** to turn or swivel sth round; **p. sur ses talons** to swing round or pivot on one's heels **2** Bot (d'une plante) to form a tap root

pixel [piksɛl] NM Ordinat pixel

pixélisé [pikselize] ADJ Ordinat pixellated

pizza [pidza] NF pizza

pizzeria [pidzerja] NF pizzeria

pizzicato [pidzikato], pl **pizzicati** [pidzikati] NM Mus pizzicato

PJ¹ (abrév **pièce jointe**) encl

PJ² [peʒi] NF Fam (abrév **Police Judiciaire**) Br ≃ CID, Am ≃ FBI

placage [plakaʒ] NM **1** (fait de recouvrir) (de bois) veneering; (de métal) plating; **au chrome** chrome or chromium plating **2** (matériau) (bois) veneer; (métal) plating; **bois de p.** veneer **3** Rugby tackle

placard [plakar] NM **1** (armoire murale) cupboard; Fig Fam **mettre qn au p.** to sideline sb; Fam **mettre un projet au p.** to put a plan on ice or into cold storage, to shelve a project **2** (affiche) poster; Journ **p. publicitaire** ou **de publicité** display advertisement **3** Typ (format) broadsheet; **(épreuve en) p.** galley (proof) **4** Naut (sur une voile) patch **5** Tech (d'une porte) panel **6** Fam (prison) clink, Br nick; **faire 20 ans de p.** to do 20 years inside or in the clink

> Il faut noter que le terme anglais **placard** est un faux ami. Il signifie **pancarte**.

placarder [plakarde] VT **1** (affiche) to stick up, to put up; **p. un mur de posters** to stick or put posters (up) on a wall **2** Typ to set in galleys

placardisation [plakardizasjɔ̃] NF Fam (de personnes) sidelining

placardiser [plakardize] VT Fam (personnes) to sideline

PLACE [plas]

> place **1, 2, 5, 10** ▪ room **3** ▪ seat **4**
> ▪ job **6** ▪ square **7** ▪ market **8**

NF **1** (lieu, endroit) place; **changer sa chaise**

de p. to move *or* shift one's chair; **mettre qch en p.** to put sth in place; **tout est à sa p.** everything's in its place; **p. de parking** parking place *or* space; **je n'ai pas trouvé de p. en ville** I couldn't find any parking places *or* spaces in town; **remettez vos livres à leur p.** put your books away; **voulez-vous prendre ma p.?** would you like to take my place?; **il ne peut pas rester en p.** he can't keep still; **il ne tient pas en p. aujourd'hui** he is very fidgety today; **sur p.** on the spot; *Constr* on site; *Fam* **faire du sur p.** to mark time, to stand still; *(en voiture)* to crawl along; *Fam* **dans cette affaire, j'ai l'impression de faire du sur p.** I've a feeling I'm getting nowhere with this matter; **il lut la lettre sur p.** he read the letter there and then *or* on the spot; **personnel engagé sur p.** staff hired locally; **rester sur p.** to stay put; **la police sera sur p. dans quelques minutes** the police will be on the scene *or* spot in a few minutes; **on trouve tout sur p.** everything we need is here/will be there; **son nom a pris p. dans l'histoire** his name has found a place in history **2** *Fig (condition, situation)* place; **avoir sa p. au soleil** to have one's place in the sun; **il finira par trouver sa p. dans ce milieu** he'll eventually find his place *or* a niche among those people; **prendre sa p. dans la société** to take one's place in society; **je viens à la p. de mon père** I've come instead of my father, I've come in my father's place *or Fml* stead; **parler à la p. de qn** to speak for sb; **remettre qn à sa p.** to put sb in his/her place; **rester à sa p.** to know one's place; **à votre p., je ...** in your place *or* if I were you, I ...; **mets-toi à sa p.** put yourself in his position, look at things from his point of view **3** *(espace)* room, space; **prendre** *ou* **occuper beaucoup de p.** to take up a great deal of room *or* space; **nous n'avons pas de p. pour mettre un piano** we have no room *or* space for a piano; **gagner de la p.** to gain some (extra) room *or* space; **faire p. à qn/qch** to make way for sb/sth; *Vieilli* **(faites) p.!** stand aside!, make way!; **faites-lui un peu de p.** make room for him; *Fig* **céder la p. aux jeunes** to make way for the younger generation; *Aut* **p. aux pieds** footwell; *Aviat* **p. pour les jambes** legroom **4** *(siège)* seat; **céder sa p. à qn** to give up one's seat to sb, to give sb one's seat; **à vos places!** take your seats!; **restez à votre p.** stay in your seat, remain seated; **louer deux places au théâtre** to book two seats at the theatre; **prendre p.** *(s'asseoir)* to take a seat, to sit down; *(debout)* to take up one's place; **il n'y avait pas une p.** there wasn't a seat to be found *or* to be had; **voiture à deux/à quatre places** two-/four-seater (car); *Aut* **une deux places** a two-seater; **prix des places** *(transports publics)* fares; *(spectacles)* seat prices; **payer p. entière** *(transports publics)* to pay full fare; *(spectacles)* to pay full price; **p. assise** seat; **places debout 15** *(sur un écriteau)* standing room for 15 passengers; **p. côté couloir** aisle seat; **p. côté fenêtre** window seat; **p. fumeur** smoking seat; **p. non-fumeur** no-smoking seat; **p. du mort** (front) passenger seat **5** *(appartenance, rôle)* place; **la p. de l'homme dans le monde** man's place in the world; **sa famille tient une grande p. dans sa vie** his family has an important place in his life; **il aura toujours une p. dans mon cœur** he'll always have a place in my heart **6** *(emploi, poste)* job, post; **quitter/perdre sa p.** to leave/lose one's job; **le gouvernement en p.** the government in office *or* power; *Fig* **une personne en p.** a person in high office; *Fig* **les gens en p.** people in high places, people with influence **7** *(lieu public)* square; **la p. Rouge** Red

Square; **p. du marché** market place; *Suisse* **p. de jeu(x)** playground **8** *Com, Fin* market; **achats sur p.** local purchases; **prix sur p.** loco price; **être bien connu sur la p.** to be a well-known player in the market; **avoir du crédit sur la p.** to have credit (facilities) locally; **affaires sur la p. de Paris** business on the Paris market **9** *Mil* **p. (forte** *ou* **de guerre)** fortified place; *(ville)* fortress *or* fortified town; **p. d'armes** parade ground, drill ground **10** *(rang)* place, placing; **il a eu une bonne p. au concours** he was well placed in the competition; **une p. d'honneur** a place of honour **11** *Suisse* **p. de parc** parking space **12** *Belg (pièce d'habitation)* room ▸ ▸ **p. bancaire** banking centre; **p. boursière** stock market; **p. commerciale** trade centre; **p. financière** financial centre *or* marketplace; **p. marchande** market place; **p. monétaire** money market

placé [plase] *Courses de chevaux* **ADJ** placed; **arriver p.** to be placed **NM** placed horse

placebo [plasebo] **NM** placebo

placement [plasmɑ̃] **NM 1** *(fait de donner un emploi)* placement, placing; *(fait d'attribuer un siège)* seating; **bureau** *ou* **agence de placement(s)** employment bureau *or* agency, *Am* placement bureau **2** *Jur (d'un mineur dans une famille d'accueil ou dans un organisme)* placement **3** *Fin (d'argent)* investment, investing; *(argent)* investment; **faire des placements** to invest (money), to make investments; **faire un bon p.** to make a good investment; **p. avantageux** good investment; **p. en actions** equity investment; **p. éthique** ethical investment; *Fam* **p. de père de famille** blue chip (investment), gilt-edged investment; **p. à court terme** short-term investment; **p. obligataire** bond investment; **p. temporaire** temporary investment; **p. à revenus fixes** fixed income investment; **p. à revenus variables** variable income investment **4** *Mktg* **p. de produit** product placement

placenta [plasɛ̃ta] **NM** *Obst* placenta; *(expulsé après accouchement)* afterbirth, placenta

placentaire [plasɛ̃tɛr] **ADJ** *Obst* placental

PLACER [plase] (**je plaçai(s); n. plaçons**) **VT 1** *(mettre à sa place)* to place, to put; *(spectateurs, invités etc)* to seat; **p. qn** *(au spectacle)* to show sb to his/her seat; *Fig* **vous êtes mieux placés que moi pour en juger** you're better placed than I (am) to judge; *Fig* **vous êtes bien placés pour le savoir** you're in a position to know, you ought to know; **p. une sentinelle** to post a soldier on sentry duty; **maison bien placée** well-situated house; **p. l'honnêteté au plus haut rang** to put *or* set *or* place a high value on honesty; **je place le courage au-dessus de toutes les valeurs** I put *or* set *or* place courage above all other values; **confiance mal placée** misplaced confidence; *TV etc* **p. les bandes-son** to lay tracks **2** *(procurer un emploi à)* to find a job for; **p. qn comme apprenti chez qn** to apprentice sb to sb **3** *(vendre) (marchandises)* to sell; *Fin* **valeurs difficiles à p.** bills difficult to negotiate **4** *(situer)* to set; **c'est ici que l'auteur a placé son roman** this is where the author set his/her novel **5** *(dire)* to get in; **il voulait à tout prix p. son histoire** he was determined to get his anecdote in *(in the conversation etc)*; *Fam* **avec elle, on ne peut pas en p. une!** you can't get a word in edgeways *or Am* edgewise with

her!; **je n'ai pas pu p. un mot** I couldn't get a word in edgeways *or Am* edgewise **6** *Fin (argent)* to invest; **p. à court terme** to invest short-term; **p. à intérêts** to invest at interest

VPR se placer 1 *(prendre sa place)* to take one's seat *or* one's place *(at table etc)*; *Mil, Sp etc* to take up one's position; **dites-moi où me p.** tell me where to sit/stand; **il faut se p. dans son optique** you have to look at things from his point of view; **se p. sous la protection de qn** to place oneself under sb's protection; **marchandises qui se placent facilement** goods that sell readily **2** *(trouver un emploi)* to get *or* find a job; **se p. comme vendeuse** to get a job as a sales assistant *or Am* clerk

placet [plasε] **NM 1** *Arch* petition, address **2** *Jur* (plaintiff's) claim

placette [plasεt] **NF** (small) square

placeur, -euse [plasœr, -øz] **N 1** *(personne qui tient un bureau de placement)* employment agent *or* consultant **2** *(dans des réunions publiques)* steward; *Cin, Théâtre* usher, *f* usherette

placide [plasid] **ADJ** placid, calm

placidement [plasidmɑ̃] **ADV** placidly, calmly

placidité [plasidite] **NF** placidity, calmness

placier, -ière [plasje, -jɛr] **N** *Com* **1** *(représentant)* travelling salesman, *f* saleswoman, traveller **2** *(forain)* = person who allocates stall space in a market

Placoplâtre® [plakoplatr] **NM** plasterboard

placoter [plakɔte] **VI** *Can Fam* to chat

plafond [plafɔ̃] **NM 1** *Archit* ceiling; **p. à caissons** coffered ceiling; **chambre haute/basse de p.** high-/low-ceilinged room; *Fig Fam* **avoir une araignée au p.** to have bats in the belfry; *Fig Fam* **être bas de p.** to be a bit slow on the uptake **2** *(toit) (de voiture, de caverne)* roof **3** *(maximum)* ceiling; **prix p.** maximum price, ceiling (price); **fixer un p. à un budget** to fix *or* put a ceiling on a budget; **p. des charges budgétaires** spending limit, budgetary limit; *Fin* **p. du crédit** credit ceiling; *Banque* **p. d'autorisation** *ou* **de retrait** withdrawal limit; *Banque* **p. de découvert** overdraft limit **4** *Aviat (d'avion)* ceiling, maximum flying height; *Aut* top *or* maximum speed; *Météo* **p. (nuageux)** (cloud) ceiling

plafonnage [plafɔnaʒ] **NM** *Constr* ceiling work

plafonnement [plafɔnmɑ̃] **NM** **p. des salaires/cotisations** *(fait de limiter)* fixing *or* putting a ceiling on wages/contributions; *(fait d'atteindre un plafond)* peaking *or* levelling *or Am* leveling off of wages/contributions

plafonner [plafɔne] **VT 1** *(pièce)* to put a ceiling in **2** *(salaire etc)* to put a ceiling on; *Fin* **être plafonné** to have a ceiling of
VI 1 *Aviat* to fly at the ceiling; *Aut* to go at maximum *or* top speed **2** *Fig* to peak, to level out, to level off; **la production plafonne** output has reached its ceiling; **cette année, l'inflation a plafonné à 3%** inflation this year peaked at 3%

plafonneur [plafɔnœr] **NM** *Tech* plasterer of ceilings

plafonnier [plafɔnje] **NM** ceiling light; *Aut* courtesy *or* interior light

plage [plaʒ] **NF 1** *(grève)* beach; **p. de sable/de galets** sandy/pebble beach; **sac/robe de p.** beach bag/robe **2** *(lieu touristique)* seaside resort **3** *Naut (d'un cuirassé)* freeboard deck; **p. arrière** *Naut* quarterdeck; *Aut* window deck, (rear) parcel shelf **4** *(surface)* area; *Opt* **p. lumineuse** light area, high light **5** *(laps de temps)* time, period; *TV, Radio (d'émissions)* (time) segment; **p. horaire** time slot; **p. horaire très écoutée/regardée** peak listening/viewing time or period; Can **p. fixe** (dans un horaire variable) core time **6** Fig (éventail) range; Radio **p. de réception** tuning range; Com **p. de prix** price range; Aut **p. de régime** engine speed range, rev range **7** (d'un disque) track

plagiaire [plaʒjɛr] N plagiarist, plagiarizer

plagiat [plaʒja] NM plagiarism

plagier [plaʒje] VT (impf, pr sub n. **plagiions, v. plagiiez**) to plagiarize

plagiste [plaʒist] N beach attendant

plaid [plɛd] NM travelling rug

plaidable [plɛdabl] ADJ Jur pleadable

plaidant [plɛdɑ̃] ADJ Jur **avocat p.** ≃ lawyer, Br barrister; **les parties plaidantes** the litigants

plaider [plede] VT to plead; **p. la cause de qn** Jur to plead sb's case, to defend sb; Fig to speak in favour of or defend sb, to plead sb's cause; **p. sa propre cause** Jur to conduct one's own defence; Fig to speak in one's own defence; **son défenseur va p. la folie** his counsel will plead insanity or will put forward a plea of insanity; **p. le faux pour savoir le vrai** to lie in order to get at the truth; **p. coupable/non coupable** to plead guilty/not guilty
▸ VI (d'un avocat) to plead (**pour** for; **contre** against); (d'un plaignant) to go to court, to litigate; **p. contre qn** to take sb to court, to take proceedings against sb; Fig **p. pour** ou **en faveur de qn/qch** to speak for sb/sth, to defend sb/sth
▸ VPR **se plaider la cause s'est plaidée hier** the case was heard yesterday

plaideur, -euse [plɛdœr, -øz] N Jur litigant

plaidoirie [plɛdwari] NF Jur speech for the defence or Am defense

plaidoyer [plɛdwaje] NM Jur speech for the defence or Am defense; Fig (défense passionnée) plea

plaie [plɛ] NF **1** (blessure), Fig wound; (coupure) cut; Fig **rouvrir d'anciennes plaies** to reopen old wounds; **retourner** ou **remuer le couteau** ou **le fer dans la p.** to twist or turn the knife in the wound; **mettre le doigt sur la p.** to put one's finger on the source of the trouble **2** (fléau) affliction, scourge; (personne, chose) pest, nuisance; **quelle p.!** what a pest or nuisance!; Bible **les dix plaies d'Égypte** the ten plagues of Egypt; Prov **p. d'argent n'est pas mortelle** money isn't everything

plaignant, -ante [plɛɲɑ̃, -ɑ̃t] Jur ADJ **partie plaignante** plaintiff, complainant
▸ N plaintiff, complainant

plain [plɛ̃] ADJ Vieilli (terrain, surface) flat, level, even
▸ NM **le p.** high tide

plain-chant, pl **plains-chants** NM Mus plainsong, plainchant

plaindre [plɛ̃dr] (prp **plaignant**; pp **plaint**; pr ind **je plains, il plaint, n. plaignons, ils plaignent**; pr sub **je plaigne**; impf **je plaignais**; p hist **je plaignis**; fu **je plaindrai**) VT **1** (témoigner de la compassion à) to pity, to feel sorry for; **je vous plains de voyager dans ces conditions** I pity you or I feel sorry for you having to travel in those conditions; **il est fort à p.** he is greatly to be pitied; **elle n'est pas à p.** she hasn't anything to worry about, she's got it made; **il est plus à p. qu'à blâmer** he is more to be pitied than blamed **2** Région, Arch (donner parcimonieusement) to (be)grudge; **on n'a pas plaint l'argent** there was no stinting of money, no expense was spared; **il ne plaint pas sa peine** he spares himself no trouble
▸ VPR **se plaindre** to complain (à to); (se lamenter) to moan, to groan; **se p. de qn/qch**

to complain about sb/sth; **se p. de maux d'estomac** to complain of stomach pains; **il n'y a pas de quoi vous p., vous n'avez pas à vous p.** you've nothing to complain about, you shouldn't grumble; **se p. (de ce) que ... + sub** to complain (about the fact) that ...

plaine [plɛn] NF **1** Géog plain **2** Hist **la P.** the Plain (moderate deputies during the French Revolution) **3** Belg **p. de jeux** playground; **p. de(s) manœuvres** exercise ground; **p. de(s) sports** sports field or ground

plain-pied ADV **de p.** on the same level, on a level; (au même étage) on one floor; **salon de p. avec le jardin** sitting room on a level with or on the same level as the garden; **deux surfaces de p.** two surfaces flush with each other; Fig **nous sommes de p.** we are on an equal footing (with each other)

plainte [plɛ̃t] NF **1** (cri, gémissement) moan, groan **2** (revendication, protestation) complaint; **un sujet de p.** the subject of a complaint **3** Jur complaint; **porter p.** ou **déposer une p. contre qn** to lodge a complaint against sb (**auprès de** with); **p. en diffamation** action for libel; **p. contre X** complaint against a person or persons unknown

plaintif, -ive [plɛ̃tif, -iv] ADJ (ton) plaintive

plaintivement [plɛ̃tivmɑ̃] ADV plaintively

plaire [plɛr] (prp **plaisant**; pp **plu**; pr ind **je plais, il plaît, n. plaisons, ils plaisent**; pr sub **je plaise**; impf **je plaisais**; p hist **je plus**; fu **je plairai**) VI **1 cet homme me plaît** I like this man; **ce livre/film m'a plu** I liked or enjoyed this book/film; **elle te plaît, ta nouvelle voiture?** do you like your new car?; **la nouvelle robe lui plaît beaucoup** she's very pleased with or she really likes the new dress; **cette offre devrait lui p.** the offer should appeal to him; **il ne plaît pas aux femmes** women don't like him; (physiquement) women don't find him attractive; **cela ne me plaît pas du tout** I don't like that at all; **c'est ce qui plaît en ce moment** it's what people seem to like just now; **il plaît** people like him, he's popular; **ça plaît beaucoup** it's very popular; **tu devrais faire une tarte aux pommes, ça plaît toujours** you ought to make an apple tart, that's always popular or welcome or that always goes down well; **je le ferai, si cela me plaît** I'll do it if I want to or if I feel like it; Fam **si ça ne te plaît pas, c'est pareil!** if you don't like it, tough!; **que cela te plaise ou non** whether you like it or not; Fam Iron **tu commences à me p.!** you're beginning to annoy or irritate me!
  2 (se rendre agréable) **p. à qn** to please sb; **chercher à p. à qn** to try to please sb; **elle veut p.** (elle veut qu'on l'aime) she wants to be liked
  V IMPERS **s'il vous plaît** please, Vieilli if you please; Fam (pour insister) if you please; **s'il te plaît** please; **et pas n'importe qui, s'il vous plaît** and not just anybody, if you please or if you don't mind; **elle passe ses vacances à Saint-Tropez, s'il vous plaît** she goes to St-Tropez for her holidays, if you please or don't you know; **vous plairait-il de nous accompagner?** would you like to come with us?; Vieilli, Région **plaît-il?** I beg your pardon?, what did you say?; **comme il vous plaira** (just) as you like or please; **plaise à Dieu qu'il vienne!** please God let him come!, Fml God grant that he may come!; **à Dieu ne plaise (que ...)** God forbid (that ...); **plût au ciel que ...!** would to heaven that ...!
  VPR **se plaire 1** (s'aimer soi-même) to admire oneself, Fam to fancy oneself; **elle se plaît dans cette robe** she likes wearing that dress, she likes herself in that dress **2** (de deux personnes) to be attracted to each other, Fam to fancy each other **3** (se trouver bien) **je me plais beaucoup à Paris** I'm very happy in Paris; **se p. à faire qch** to enjoy or like doing sth;

il ne se plaît pas ici he doesn't like it here, he's unhappy here; **la vigne se plaît sur les coteaux** the vine does well or thrives on hillsides

plaisamment [plɛzamɑ̃] ADV **1** (agréablement) pleasantly **2** (drôlement) funnily, amusingly **3** Litt (d'une façon ridicule) ridiculously

plaisance [plɛzɑ̃s] NF **1 bateau de p.** pleasure boat; **port de p.** marina; **navigation de p., la p.** boating **2** Arch (plaisir) pleasure

plaisancier, -ière [plɛzɑ̃sje, -jɛr] N (amateur) yachtsman, f yachtswoman

plaisant [plɛzɑ̃] ADJ **1** (agréable) pleasant, agreeable; **p. à l'œil** pleasing to or Fam easy on the eye, pleasing to look at **2** (drôle) funny, amusing; (d'un humour sec ou ironique) droll **3** (always before the noun) Vieilli (ridicule) (personne, réponse) ridiculous, absurd, ludicrous
▸ NM **1 le (plus) p. de l'affaire, c'est que ...** the funniest thing about it is that ... **2** Arch (farceur) wag, joker; **faire le p.** to play or act the comedian; **mauvais p.** malicious joker

plaisanter [plɛzɑ̃te] VI **1** (s'amuser, rire) to joke, Fml to jest; **elle aime bien p.** she enjoys a joke; **il faut bien p., n'est-ce pas?** we all have to have a joke from time to time, don't we?; **dire qch en plaisantant** to say sth as a joke or in jest; **il n'est pas d'humeur à p.** he's not in a joking mood **2** (dire par jeu) to joke; **vous plaisantez!** you're joking!, you're kidding!, you don't mean it!; **je ne plaisante pas** I'm serious, I'm not joking; **c'est un homme avec qui on ne plaisante pas** he is not a man to be trifled with; **on ne plaisante pas avec la justice** the law is not to be trifled with; **on ne plaisante pas avec la santé** health is a serious matter; **il ne plaisante pas là-dessus** ou **sur ces choses-là** he doesn't joke about things like that; **dans leur famille, on ne plaisante pas avec la religion** you don't joke about religion in their family, religion isn't a joking matter in their family
▸ VT to tease (**sur qch** about sth), to poke fun at, to make fun of

plaisanterie [plɛzɑ̃tri] NF (blague) joke, Fml jest; (activité) joking, Fml jesting; **une fine p.** a subtle joke; **une mauvaise p.** (blague) a bad joke; (farce) a nasty trick; **faire des plaisanteries** to tell or crack jokes; **les plaisanteries les plus courtes sont les meilleures** brevity is the soul of wit; **tourner qch en p.** to laugh sth off, to make a joke out of sth; **entendre la p.** to know how to take a joke; **par p.** for fun, for a joke; Fig **c'est une p.!** it's a joke!, it's ridiculous or laughable!; **ce sera une p. pour toi** it'll be child's play for you; **pousser trop loin la p.** to take the joke too far, to go too far

plaisantin [plɛzɑ̃tɛ̃] NM joker; Fig Péj **c'est un (petit) p.** (on ne peut pas lui faire confiance) he's (a bit of) a joker

plaisir [plɛzir] NM **1** (sensation plaisante) pleasure, delight; **j'apprends avec p. que vous êtes de mon avis** I'm pleased or delighted or glad to hear you agree with me; **c'est avec p. que j'ai appris la nouvelle** I was pleased or delighted or glad to hear the news; **faire p. à qn** to please sb; **ça me ferait vraiment p. que tu acceptes ce travail** I would be really pleased or delighted if you accepted the job; **fais-moi p., viens danser** do me a favour, come and dance; **cela m'a fait p. de le revoir** I was pleased or delighted to see him again, it gave me great pleasure to see him again; **si cela peut te faire p., s'il n'y a que ça pour te faire p.** if it will make you happy; **je viens avec toi, mais c'est bien pour te faire p.** I'll come with you just to keep you happy!; **cela me fait grand p. de vous voir** I'm delighted to see you; **cela fait p. à voir** it's a pleasure to see; Iron **ça fait**

(toujours) p.! charming!; **faire à qn le p. de venir** to do sb the pleasure of coming; **voulez-vous me faire le p. de vous taire!** will you please be quiet!; **ils vous prient de leur faire le p. de dîner avec eux** they request the pleasure of your company at dinner; **j'ai le p. de vous apprendre que ...** I have pleasure in informing or I am pleased to inform you that ..., I'm pleased to be able to tell you that ...; **tout le p. est pour moi** the pleasure is all mine; **gâcher le p. de qn** to spoil sb's pleasure; **car tel est le bon p. du roi** because that is what His Majesty wishes; **le p. d'offrir/de recevoir** the pleasure of giving/receiving; **au p. de vous revoir** goodbye, I hope we'll meet again; **Fam au p.!** goodbye!, see you (again)!; **pour le plus grand p. de l'assistance/de ses collègues** to the great delight of the audience/of one's colleagues; **prendre (grand) p. à qch** to (really) enjoy sth; **prendre p.** ou **avoir du p. à faire qch** to enjoy doing sth; **prendre un malin p. à faire qch** to take a malicious pleasure in doing sth; **il va se faire un p. de te téléphoner demain** he'll be only too pleased to phone you tomorrow; **rougir/frissonner/gémir de p.** to flush/quiver/moan with pleasure; **avec p.!** with pleasure!

2 (agrément) pleasure, fun; **c'est par p. que vous faites cela?** are you doing that because you like it or for the fun of it?; **parler pour le p. de parler** to talk for talking's sake or for the sake of it; **elle le dit pour le p. de te faire souffrir** she said it because she wants to make you suffer; **elle travaille pour le p.** she works because she enjoys or likes it; **se tourmenter à p.** to worry for the sake of worrying or for the sake of it; **faire durer le p.** to make the pleasure last; Iron to prolong the agony; Iron **je vous souhaite bien du p.!** the best of luck (to you)!

3 (distraction) pleasure, enjoyment, amusement; **son plus grand p. est de faire des photos** what he likes doing most or best is taking photos; **les plaisirs de la table** fine food; **chaque âge a ses plaisirs** every age has its pleasures; **on prend son p. comme on peut** you take your pleasure where you find it; **s'accorder** ou **s'offrir un petit p.** to indulge oneself; **faire qch pour le p.** ou **pour son p.** to do sth for pleasure or for fun; **le planeur est un p. coûteux** gliding's an expensive pastime or hobby; Iron **ce n'est pas une partie de p.** it's no picnic

4 Litt (sensuel) **le p., les plaisirs** dissipation; **lieu de p.** place of amusement; (où l'on s'amuse la nuit) night haunt **5 le p. (sexuel)** (sexual) pleasure; **il y prit du p.** he got a (sexual) thrill out of it; **p. solitaire** self-abuse

PLAN¹ [plɑ̃] ADJ (terrain, surface) flat, level, even; Géom (surface etc) plane
NM **1** Math etc plane
2 Cin, TV shot; Beaux-Arts **premier p.** foreground; **second p.** middle ground; **au second p.** in the middle distance; Fig **ce problème occupe le premier p.** this question is very much to the fore or is very much in the foreground; Fig **reléguer qn au second p.** to push sb into the background; Fig **un artiste de premier p.** an artist of the first rank, a first-rate artist; Cin, TV **hors p.** off-shot; **sur le même p.** on the same level; **sur le p. politique/économique, au p. politique/économique** on the political/economic level; Phot, Cin **faire un gros p.** to take or shoot a close-up
3 Aviat **p. de sustentation** aerofoil, Am airfoil; **p. fixe horizontal** tail plane; **p. supérieur** (d'un biplan) upper wing or plane
▸▸ TV, Cin **p. accéléré** time-lapse shot; TV, Cin **p. américain** American shot, two-shot; TV, Cin **p. d'archives** stock shot; TV, Cin **p. de buste** bust shot; TV, Cin **p. ceinture** waist shot; TV, Cin **p. en contre-plongée** periscope shot; **p. de cuisson** hob; TV, Cin **p. de détail** detail or insert shot; **p. d'eau** stretch of water; (d'une rivière) reach; TV, Cin **p. éloigné** long shot; TV, Cin **p. d'ensemble** wide shot; TV, Cin **p. fixe** static shot; Opt **p. focal** focal plane; TV, Cin **p. général** full-length shot, long shot; **p. incliné** inclined plane; Tech **ball ramp**; TV, Cin **p. en intérieur** interior (shot); TV, Cin **p. de longue durée** continuous film sequence; TV, Cin **p. moyen** medium shot; TV, Cin **p. en plongée** high-angle shot, overhead shot; TV, Cin **p. rapproché** medium close-up, close-up, close shot; TV, Cin **p. de réaction** reaction shot; TV, Cin **p. refilmé** retake; TV, Cin **p. séquence** sequence shot; TV, Cin **p. serré** close-up, tight shot; TV, Cin **p. à la taille** waist shot; **p. de travail** (d'une cuisine) work(ing) surface, worktop; TV, Cin **p. travelling** travelling shot; TV, Cin **p. très éloigné** extra or extreme long shot; TV, Cin **p. très rapproché** extreme close-up; TV, Cin **p. très serré** big close-up; TV, Cin **p. de visage** face shot

PLAN² NM **1** (relevé) plan; Constr, Tech blueprint; (de ville) plan, map; **tracer un p.** to draw a plan; **relever le p. d'une région** to map out or survey an area; **p. de classement** filing method; **p. d'étage** floor plan; **p. géométral** ground plan; Typ **p. de maquette** layout card; **p. de mise en page** page plan
2 (projet) plan, scheme, project; **faire** ou **arrêter le p. de qch** to plan sth; **quels sont vos plans pour les années à venir?** what are your plans for the future?; Fig **tirer** ou **faire des plans sur la comète** to build castles in Spain or in the air; Fam **t'as un p. pour ce soir?** got any plans for tonight?; Fam **il a de bons plans pour bouffer à l'œil** he's got good ideas when it comes to finding cheap places to eat; **sans p. arrêté** without any set plan; **p. de carrière** career plan; **p. d'études** study plan or programme; **p. économique** economic plan, plan for the economy; **p. d'un roman/d'un devoir** plan for a novel/an essay
3 Fam **laisser qn en p.** to leave sb in the lurch; (sans moyen de transport) to leave sb stranded; **laisser son travail en p.** to leave one's work unfinished; **il a tout laissé en p. et il est rentré** he dropped everything and went home
▸▸ Mktg **p. d'activité** business plan; Compta **p. d'amortissement** depreciation schedule; Ordinat **p. calcul** = plan to establish a computer industry in France; Compta **p. comptable** chart of accounts; Compta **p. comptable général** chart of accounts; Compta **p. de comptes** chart of accounts; TV, Cin **p. des décors** floor plan; Fin **p. d'épargne** savings scheme or plan; Fin **p. d'épargne en actions** personal equity plan, PEP; Fin **p. d'épargne entreprise** employee share or Am stock ownership plan; Fin **p. d'épargne retraite** retirement savings plan or scheme; **p. d'évacuation** escape route; Compta **p. de financement** funding plan, financial plan; Mktg **p. de marchéage** marketing mix; Mktg **p. (des) médias** media planning; Mktg **p. mercatique (stratégique)** (strategic) marketing plan; Ordinat **p. de navigation** site map; **p. d'occupation des sols** land-use plan; TV, Cin **p. de positionnement sur le plateau** staging plan; Cin, TV **p. de production** production schedule; **p. quinquennal** five-year plan; **p. de redressement** recovery plan; Constr **p. de référence** datum plane or level; **p. social** (du gouvernement) social plan; Com = corporate restructuring plan, usually involving job losses; Mktg **p. stratégique d'entreprise** strategic business plan; Mktg **p. des supports** media planning; **p. de travail créatif** (publicité) creative brief; Aviat **p. de vol** flight plan

planage [planaʒ] NM Tech (de bois) planing; (de métal) planishing

planant [planɑ̃] ADJ Fam (drogue) relaxing; (musique) mellow

planche [plɑ̃ʃ] NF **1** (pièce de bois) plank; (plus large) board; (étagère) shelf; Fam (ski) plank; Fig **c'est ma p. de salut** it's my sheet anchor; (dernier espoir) it's my last hope; Natation **faire la p.** to float on one's back; Fig Fam **c'est une p. à pain, elle est plate comme une p. à pain** she's as flat as a pancake; Fig **avoir du pain sur la p.** to have a lot on one's plate **2** Naut **p. (de débarquement)** gangplank; **passer à la p.** to walk the plank; **jour de p.** lay day **3** Théâtre **les planches** the stage, the boards; **monter sur les planches** to go on the stage, to tread the boards; **être sur les planches** to be on the stage; Fig **l'amour des planches** love of the stage **4** (d'imprimerie, de gravure etc) plate, block; **planches en couleurs** colour plates **5** (de jardin potager) bed **6** Sport (de surf) surfboard; (à voile) sailboard **7 les planches** (sur une plage) the boardwalk
▸▸ **p. à billets** printing press (for printing banknotes); Fig **faire fonctionner la p. à billets** to print money; Aut **p. de bord** dashboard, fascia panel; **p. à découper** chopping board; **p. à dessin** drawing board; **p. à fromage** cheeseboard; **p. à hacher** chopping board; **p. à laver** washboard; Can **p. des neiges** (objet) snowboard; (sport) snowboarding; **p. à pain** breadboard; **p. à pâtisserie** pastry board; **p. à repasser** ironing board or Am table; **p. à roulettes** skateboard; **faire de la p. à roulettes** to go skateboarding, to skateboard; **p. de surf** surfboard; **p. à voile** sailboard; **faire de la p. à voile** to go windsurfing, to windsurf

planchéiage [plɑ̃ʃejaʒ] NM (de cloison, de plancher) boarding, planking; (d'une pièce) flooring

planchéier [plɑ̃ʃeje] VT (impf, pr sub n. planchéiions, v. planchéiiez) (cloison) to board, to plank; (plancher) to board over, to plank over; (pièce) to floor

plancher¹ [plɑ̃ʃe] NM **1** (sol) floor; Fam **le p. des vaches** dry land, terra firma; Fam **débarrassez-moi le p.!** get out!, clear out!, beat it!; Fam **avoir un feu de p.** = to be wearing trousers that are too short **2** Fig (minimum) minimum, lower limit; **le p. des versements** the minimum deposit; **prix p.** bottom price **3** Tech (de pont) planking; (de la salle des machines) floorplates; (de tranchée) flooring; Aut floor, floorpan; Aut **p. de chargement** load floor; Aut, Fig **mettre le pied au p.** to put one's foot down **4** Tech (de serrure) bottom **5** Anat (d'une cavité) floor; **p. pelvien** pelvic floor

plancher² VI Scol Fam to be tested, to have a test; **les ministres planchent sur ce problème** the ministers are working on the problem

planchette [plɑ̃ʃet] NF (petite planche) (small) board; (étagère) (small) shelf; Spéc (de topographe) plane table; Phot **p. d'objectif** lens panel

planchiste [plɑ̃ʃist] N Sport windsurfer

plançon [plɑ̃sɔ̃] NM (jeune arbre) sapling; (plante) set, slip

plan-concave, pl **plan-concaves** ADJ Opt (lentilles) plano-concave

plan-convexe, pl **plan-convexes** ADJ Opt (lentilles) plano-convex

plancton [plɑ̃ktɔ̃] NM plankton

plané [plane] ADJ Aviat **vol p.** gliding; **descendre en vol p.** to glide down; Fam **faire un vol p.** (tomber) to go flying

planéité [planeite] NF flatness, evenness

planer¹ [plane] VT Tech (bois) to plane; (métal) to planish

planer² vi **1** *(d'un oiseau)* to glide, to soar; *(voltiger)* to hover; *(d'un ballon)* to float; *(d'un planeur)* to glide; *(de la brume, fumée)* to hover, to hang; *Fig* **p. sur qn/qch** to hang *or* hover over sb/sth; **la menace plane** there's a sense of threat in the air **2** *Litt* **son regard planait au-delà des montagnes** he gazed out beyond the mountains; **son esprit planait au-dessus de la ville** his mind soared above the city **3** *Fig Fam (se sentir particulièrement bien)* to be on cloud nine, to be *or* feel on top of the world; *(perdre le sens des réalités)* to have one's head in the clouds; *(après s'être drogué)* to be high; *(penser à autre chose)* to be miles away, to have one's head in the clouds

planétaire [planeter] ADJ **1** *Astron (système)* planetary **2** *Tech* **engrenage p.** planetary gear **3** *Phys (électrons)* orbital, orbiting **4** *(expansion, action)* on a worldwide *or* global scale
◼ NM *Aut* sun gear

planétairement [planetermã] ADV **voir les choses p.** to look at things on a worldwide *or* global basis

planétarisation [planetarizasjõ] NF globalization; **la p. économique** the growth of a world economy

planétarium [planetarjom] NM *Astron* planetarium

planète [planɛt] NF *Astron* planet; **planètes inférieures/supérieures** inferior/superior planets; **sur toute la p.** over the whole planet, all over the planet

planétisation [planetizasjõ] NF = **planétarisation**

planétoïde [planetoid] NM *Astron* planetoid

planétologie [planetolozi] NF planetology

planeur¹ [plancer] NM *Aviat* glider; **faire du p.** to go gliding

planeur², -euse [plancer, -øz] *Tech* N *(ouvrier)* planisher
◼ NF **planeuse** *(machine)* planing machine; *(pour métal)* planishing machine

planifiable [planifjabl] ADJ *Écon* that can be planned

planificateur, -trice [planifikatœr, -tris] *Écon* ADJ *(autorité, mesures)* planning
◼ N planner

planification [planifikasjõ] NF *Écon* planning; **p. budgétaire** budget planning; **p. à court terme** short-term planning; **p. économique** economic planning; *Mktg* **p. de l'entreprise** corporate planning; **p. à long terme** long-term planning; **p. des naissances** population control; **p. nationale** state planning; **p. stratégique** strategic planning

planifier [planifje] VT *(impf, pr subj n. planifiions, v. planifiiez)* *Écon* to plan

planigramme [planigram] NM *Mktg* flowchart

planisme [planism] NM *Écon* planning

planisphère [planisfer] NM planisphere

planning [planiŋ] NM **1** plan, schedule; *(programme d'activités, de travail)* schedule; **p. Whitney** *(dans un hôtel)* Whitney rack; **p. d'occupation journalière** *(dans un hôtel)* daily occupancy chart; **p. de fabrication** manufacturing plan *or* schedule; *Compta* **p. des charges** expenditure plan; **p. à gouttières** slot-in planner; **nous avons un p. très chargé cette semaine** we have a very busy schedule this week **2 p. familial** family planning; *(lieu)* family planning clinic

plan-plan [plãplã] ADJ INV *Fam* routine, humdrum

planque [plãk] NF *Fam* **1** *(cachette)* *(pour une personne)* hideout, hideaway, hiding place; *(pour quelque chose)* hiding place; **la police est en p. devant la maison** the police

are staking out the house **2** *(travail facile)* cushy job *or* number; **vraiment, ce boulot, c'est la p.!** this job is really cushy!

planqué, -ée [plãke] N *Fam Péj* person with a cushy job; *Mil* dodger, shirker; **quelle planquée!** what a cushy job she's got!

planquer [plãke] *Fam* VT to hide (away), to stash (away); *(personne)* to hide
◼ VI *(de la police)* **p. devant la maison** to stake out the house
◼ VPR **se planquer** to hide; *(se mettre à l'abri)* to take cover

plant [plã] NM **1** *(pépinière)* *(d'arbres, d'arbustes)* nursery **2** *(carré)* patch, bed; **p. de choux** cabbage patch **3** *(bouture)* *(d'un arbre)* sapling; *(d'une plante)* set, slip; **jeunes plants** seedlings

plantage [plãtaʒ] NM *Fam (échec)* flop; *Ordinat* crash

plantain [plãtɛ̃] NM *Bot* plantain

plantaire [plãter] ADJ *Anat* plantar; **voûte p.** plantar arch

plantard [plãtar] NM = **plançon**

plantation [plãtasjõ] NF **1** *(fait de planter)* *(d'arbres, de graines)* planting **2** *(exploitation)* *(de sucre, thé)* plantation; **p. d'oranges** orange grove

plante¹ [plãt] NF *Anat* **p. du pied** sole (of the foot); **la p. des pieds** the soles (of the feet)

plante² NF *Bot* plant; **le Jardin des Plantes** = botanical gardens and zoo in Paris; *Fig Fam* **cette fille, quelle belle p.!** she's a stunner, that girl!
▸▸**p. d'appartement** pot *or* house plant; **p. à fleurs** flowering plant; **p. grasse** succulent (plant); **p. marine** seaweed; **p. potagère** *(herbe)* herb; *(légume)* vegetable; **p. de serre** hothouse plant; **plantes vertes** house plants, foliage

planté [plãte] ADJ **1 enfant bien p.** sturdy *or* healthy child; **bien p. sur ses jambes** sturdily built; **avoir les dents bien/mal plantées** to have straight/crooked teeth **2** *(debout)* standing; **il était p. au milieu de la pièce** he had planted himself *or* he was standing right in the middle of the room; *Fam* **ne la laissez pas plantée là** don't leave her standing there; **tu ne vas pas rester p. devant nous à ne rien faire** you're not just going to stand there doing nothing **3** *Ordinat Fam* **être p.** *(réseau, ordinateur)* to be down

planter [plãte] VT **1** *(graines, fleurs, arbres)* to plant; *(bouture)* to plant, to set out; **colline plantée d'arbres** hill planted with trees **2** *(clou)* to knock in, to hammer in; **p. un pieu dans le sol** to drive a stake into the ground; **p. un drapeau** to put up *or* hoist *or* raise a flag; **p. une échelle contre le mur** to stand a ladder (up) against the wall; **p. sa tente** to put up *or* pitch one's tent; *Fig* **p. les personnages** to build up the characters, to give substance to the characters; *Fam* **p. son chapeau sur la tête** to stick *or* put one's hat on one's head; **p. un baiser sur la joue de qn** to plant a kiss on sb's cheek; *Fig* **p. son regard sur qn** to fix one's gaze on sb; *Fam* **p. là qn** to dump sb; **il veut tout p. là** he wants to drop everything *or* give it all up; *Can Fig* **p. des clous** to doze off (in one's chair)
◼ VI *Ordinat Fam (ordinateur)* to crash
◼ VPR **se planter 1** *(se tenir immobile)* to plant oneself, to stand; **se p. devant qn** to plant oneself *or* stand in front of sb **2** *Fam (se tromper)* to get it wrong; **se p. dans ses calculs** to get one's calculations wrong **3** *Fam (en voiture)* to crash, to have an accident **4** *Fam (tomber)* to fall

planteur [plãtœr] NM **1** *(exploitant dans un pays tropical)* planter **2** *(cocktail)* planter's punch

planteuse [plãtøz] NF *Agr, Tech* potato planting machine

plantigrade [plãtigrad] ADJ, NM *Zool* plantigrade

plantoir [plãtwar] NM dibble, dibber

planton [plãtõ] NM *Mil* orderly; **être de p.** to be on orderly duty; *Fam* **faire le p.** to kick one's heels, to hang around

plantureusement [plãtyrøzmã] ADV copiously

plantureux, -euse [plãtyrø, -øz] ADJ **1** *(copieux)* *(repas)* copious, lavish; *(femme)* buxom; **poitrine plantureuse** ample bosom **2** *(fécond)* *(région)* fertile

plaquage [plakaʒ] NM = **placage 3**

plaque [plak] NF **1** *(feuille rigide)* *(de métal)* plate, sheet; *(de marbre)* slab; *(de chocolat)* block; *(de glace)* patch, sheet; *(de neige)* layer; *Phot* **appareil à plaques** plate camera **2** *Radio* plate, anode; **tension de p.** plate voltage, anode voltage **3** *(portant une inscription)* plaque; *(insigne)* *(d'un bureau)* badge; *(d'un ordre)* star; **p. de porte** door plate; *(avec nom)* nameplate; **p. de rue** street nameplate, street sign **4** *Méd (sur la peau)* patch, *Spéc* plaque; **p. (dentaire)** (dental) plaque; **plaques muqueuses** mucous plaque; **sclérose en plaques** multiple sclerosis **5** *Fig Fam* **être à côté de la p.** to be off-target, to be wide of the mark **6** *Suisse (à gâteau)* cake tin
▸▸*Élec* **p. d'accumulateur** accumulator plate; **p. d'auto-école** ≃ L-plate; **p. de blindage** armour *or Am* armor plate; **p. chauffante** hotplate; **p. de cheminée** fireback; **p. commémorative** commemorative plaque; *Com* **p. CSC** CSC plate; **p. d'égout** manhole cover; *Tech* **p. de fond** base plate; **p. de four** baking sheet *or* tray, *Am* cookie sheet; **p. funéraire** church brass; *Suisse* **p. à gâteau** cake tin; **p. à grille** grid plate; **p. d'identification** *(d'une machine)* model identification plate; *(avec nom)* nameplate; *(avec numéro)* numberplate; **p. d'identité** *(de soldat)* identity disc, *Am Fam* dog tag; *Aut* **p. d'immatriculation** *ou* **minéralogique** numberplate, *Am* license plate; **p. mortuaire** church brass; *Typ* **p. offset** offset plate; *Aut* **p. oscillante** *(de pompe d'injection rotative)* cam plate; **p. photographique** photographic plate; **p. de propreté** *(sur une porte)* fingerplate; **p. stéréoscopique** stereo slide; *Typ* **p. de tirage** printing plate; *Rail* **p. tournante** turntable; *Fig* **c'est la p. tournante du projet** the plan hinges on it; **cet aéroport est une p. tournante pour les industries régionales** this airport is the hub of industrial activity in the region; **cette ville deviendra la p. tournante de l'Europe** this city will become the hub of Europe

plaqué [plake] NM **1 p. or** gold plate; **montre en p. or** gold-plated watch; **c'est du p.** it's plated **2** *(bois)* veneered wood
◼ ADJ **p. or/argent** gold-/silver-plated

plaquemine [plakmin] NF *Bot* persimmon

plaqueminier [plakminje] NM *Bot* persimmon (tree)

plaquer [plake] VT **1** *(appliquer une plaque sur)* *(bois)* to veneer; *(métal)* to plate; *(appliquer) (plâtre)* to lay on **2** *(mettre à plat)* *(cheveux)* to plaster down; **le vent lui plaquait son manteau sur les jambes** the wind blew *or* flattened his coat against his/her legs; **p. qn contre un mur** to pin sb to a wall; **il avait les épaules plaquées au mur** he had his shoulders pinned *or* pressed to the wall **3** *Rugby (adversaire)* to tackle, to bring down **4** *Mus* **p. un accord** to strike (and hold) a chord **5** *Fam (abandonner)* *(amant, petit ami)* to ditch, to chuck; **j'ai envie de tout p.** I feel like chucking it all in **6** *Belg (coller)* to stick
◼ VPR **se plaquer se p. au sol/contre un mur** to

lie flat on the ground/flatten oneself against a wall

plaquette [plakɛt] NF **1** *(petite plaque) (de métal)* (small) plate; *(portant un nom, une inscription etc)* (small) plaque; *(bloc) (de métal)* block; *Ordinat* circuit board; **p. de circuits imprimés** printed circuit board, PCB; *Aut* **p. de frein** brake pad **2** *(petit livre)* booklet; **p. publicitaire** advertising brochure **3 plaquettes (sanguines)** (blood) platelets

plaqueur [plakœr] NM **1** *(sur métaux)* plater **2** *(sur bois)* veneerer

plasma [plasma] NM **1** *Biol* plasma; **p. sanguin** blood plasma **2** *Phys* **p. gazeux** gas plasma

plastic [plastik] NM plastic explosive

plasticage [plastikaʒ] NM bomb attack (**de** on)

plasticien, -ienne [plastisjɛ̃, -jɛn] N **1** *Tech* plastics technician **2** *Méd* plastic surgeon

plasticité [plastisite] NF plasticity

plastie [plasti] NF *Méd* plastic surgery

plastifiant [plastifjɑ̃] NM plasticizer

plastifier [plastifje] VT *(impf, pr sub* **n. plastifiions, v. plastifiiez)** **1** *(recouvrir de plastique)* to laminate; **jaquette plastifiée** laminated jacket **2** *Tech* to plasticize

plastiquage [plastikaʒ] NM = **plasticage**

plastique [plastik] ADJ **1** *(malléable)* plastic, malleable **2 arts plastiques** plastic arts; **chirurgie p.** plastic surgery; **statue aux formes plastiques** finely formed statue; **beauté p.** fine forms
▪ NF **1** *Beaux-Arts* plastic art, art of modelling **2** *(harmonie des formes) (d'une actrice, d'un danseur)* figure, physique
▪ NM plastic

plastiquement [plastikmɑ̃] ADV from the viewpoint of form; **cet athlète est p. très beau** this athlete has a very fine physique

plastiquer [plastike] VT to bomb *(using plastic explosive)*

plastiqueur, -euse [plastikœr, -øz] N bomber *(using plastic explosive)*

plastoc [plastɔk] NM *Fam* plastic

plastron [plastrɔ̃] NM **1** *(pièce d'armure)* breastplate, plastron; *(d'escrimeur)* plastron **2** *(de vêtement)* front; *(de chemise) (fixe)* shirt front; *(amovible)* dick(e)y, false shirt front

plastronner [plastrɔne] VT *(personne)* to put a plastron on
▪ VI to throw out one's chest; *Fig* to strut around, to swagger around

PLAT [pla] ADJ **1** *(qui a peu de relief)* flat, level; **pays p.** flat country; **chaussure plate** low-heeled *or* flat shoe; **avoir la poitrine plate/les pieds plats** to be flat-chested/-footed; *Fam* **elle est plate comme une limande** she's as flat as a pancake; **cheveux plats** flat hair; **mer plate** smooth *or* still sea; *Naut* **calme p.** dead calm; **c'est le calme p.** there's a dead calm; *Fig* things are dead quiet; **eau plate** still water; **vis à tête plate** flat-head(ed) screw; **assiette plate** dinner plate; *Ordinat* **écran p.** flat screen
2 *Fig (ennuyeux) (style, livre, film, intrigue)* flat, dull; *Fml* insipid; **vin p.** wine that lacks body
3 à p. *(pneu, batterie)* flat; **mettre qch à p.** to lay sth (down) flat; *Fig* **mettre un problème à p.** to look at a problem from all sides; **couché à p. sur le sol** lying flat on the ground; **dormir à p.** to sleep without a pillow; *Fig* **tomber à p.** *(d'une proposition, d'un projet etc)* to fall flat; **se mettre à p. ventre** to lie flat on one's stomach; *Péj Fig* **se mettre à p. ventre (devant qn)** to crawl *or* grovel *or* kowtow (to sb); *Fam* **être à p.** *(épuisé)* to be exhausted *or* all in; *(en mauvaise santé)* to be run down; *Aut* to

have a flat; **cette maladie l'a mis à p.** the illness has taken it out of him
▪ NM **1** *(partie plate) (de la main)* flat; *(d'un aviron)* blade; *(d'un marteau)* face
2 *Sport* **course de p.** flat race; *Natation* **faire un p.** to do a bellyflop
3 *Fam* **faire du p. à qn** *(chercher à séduire)* to make advances to sb; *(flatter)* to crawl to sb, *Br* to suck up to sb; *Fam* **il en fait un p.** *(il fait très chaud)* it's a scorcher, *Br* it's roasting
4 *Culin (contenant)* dish; **p. (de service)** serving dish; **p. à barbe** shaving dish; **p. de quête** *(dans une église)* collection plate; *Fig* **mettre les petits plats dans les grands** to put on a marvellous spread; *Fig* **mettre les pieds dans le p.** to put one's foot in it; *Fam* **en faire tout un p.** to make a great fuss about it
5 *Culin (mets)* dish; *(partie du menu)* course; **p. cuisiné** ready-cooked dish; *(à emporter)* takeaway dish; **p. du jour** today's special, dish of the day; **p. principal** main course; **p. de résistance** main course; *Fig* pièce de résistance

platane [platan] NM plane tree; *Fam* **rentrer dans un p.** to crash into a tree

plat-bord, *pl* **plats-bords** NM *Naut* gunwale, gunnel; **hauteur au-dessus du p.** height above the hull

plate [plat] NF *Naut* punt, flat-bottomed boat

plateau, -eaux [plato] NM **1** *(plat)* tray; **p. d'argent** silver tray *or* salver; **p. à fromages** *(objet)* cheeseboard; **p. de fromages** *(choix de fromages)* cheeseboard; **p. de fruits de mer** seafood platter; **p. petit déjeuner** breakfast tray; **p. de courtoisie** hospitality tray; *Fig* **(servi) sur un p.** on a plate; *Fig* **ça ne va pas t'arriver servi sur un p.** you're not going to get it handed to you on a plate
2 *(d'une balance)* pan; *(d'une platine, d'un four micro-ondes)* turntable; *(de table)* top; **p. tournant** *(de tourne-disque)* turntable
3 *Géog* plateau; **haut p.** high plateau; **p. continental** continental shelf
4 *Méd* plateau
5 *Théâtre* stage; *Cin, TV* set; *Cin, TV* **sur le p.** on set; **p. de tournage** film set; **p. fermé** closed set; **p. sonorisé** sound stage; **p. tournant** revolving stage
6 *Rail* flat truck *or* wagon *or* *Am* car
7 *Tech* plate, disc, *Am* disk; **p. absorbeur de couple** torque plate; **p. de chargement** load bed, load platform; **p. d'embrayage** clutch plate; **p. de friction** friction plate; *Aut* **p. menant** driving plate; *Aut* **p. mené** driven plate; *Aut* **p. oscillant** wobble-plate, swashplate; *Cyclisme* **p. de pédalier** front chain wheel; **p. de pression** pressure plate; *Aut etc* **raccordement à plateaux** flange assembly

plateau-repas, *pl* **plateaux-repas** NM meal on a tray

plate-bande, *pl* **plates-bandes** NF flowerbed; *Fig Fam* **marcher sur les plates-bandes de qn** to trespass on sb's patch; **ne marchez pas sur mes plates-bandes** keep off my patch

plate-forme, *pl* **plates-formes** NF **1** *(partie ouverte) (d'un bus)* platform; *(d'une locomotive)* footplate; **toit en p.** flat roof; **p. de chargement** loading platform; *Aut* load deck; **p. de déchargement** unloading *or* offloading platform; *TV, Cin* **p. de prise de vue** camera platform **2** *Géog* **p. continentale** continental shelf **3** *Rail (wagon)* flat truck *or* wagon *or* *Am* car **4** *Mil* **p. de tir** gun platform; **p. tournante** turntable **5** *Pol* platform; **p. électorale** electoral platform **6** *Ordinat* platform **7** *Pétr* **p. pétrolière** *ou* **de forage** oil rig

plate-longe, *pl* **plates-longes** NF *(longe)* leading rein

platement [platmɑ̃] ADV *(s'exprimer, écrire)* in a dull *or* flat way, dully, flatly; **s'excuser p.** to apologize humbly

platinage [platinaʒ] NM platinum plating

platine¹ [platin] NF *Tech (d'une serrure)* plate; *(d'une presse à imprimer, d'une machine à écrire)* platen; *(d'un microscope)* stage; *(tourne-disque)* (record) deck, *(record)* turntable; **p. cassettes** cassette *or* tape deck; **p. laser** CD player

platine² [platin] NM platinum
▪ ADJ INV platinum; **cheveux (blonds) p.** platinum blond hair

platiné [platine] ADJ **1** *(recouvert de platine)* platinum-plated; *Aut* **vis platinées** points **2 cheveux platinés** platinum blond hair; **une blonde platinée** a platinum blonde

platiner [platine] VT to plate with platinum

platitude [platityd] NF **1** *(de personnalité, style, discussion)* dullness; **ce film est d'une p.!** this film is so dull! **2** *(propos)* platitude, trite remark; **débiter des platitudes** to talk in platitudes, *Fml* to platitudinize; *Arch* **faire des platitudes à qn** to grovel to sb

Platon [platɔ̃] N Plato

platonicien, -ienne [platɔnisjɛ̃, -jɛn] ADJ *(école, philosophe)* Platonic
▪ N Platonist

platonique [platɔnik] ADJ **1** *(amour)* platonic **2** *(vain)* futile, vain

platoniquement [platɔnikmɑ̃] ADV *(aimer)* platonically

platonisme [platɔnism] NM Platonism

plâtrage [platraʒ] NM *Constr (action)* plastering; *(ouvrage)* plasterwork

plâtras [platra] NM *(débris)* (plaster) rubble; *(morceau)* lump of plaster

plâtre [platr] NM **1** *Constr* plaster; **les plâtres** the plasterwork; *Fig Fam* **essuyer les plâtres** *(d'une maison)* to be the first occupant; *(subir des conséquences fâcheuses)* to put up with the teething problems; *Fig Fam* **ce camembert, c'est du p.** this Camembert is like chalk **2** *Beaux-Arts* plaster; *(ouvrage)* plaster cast; **p. de moulage** plaster of Paris **3** *Méd* plaster; *(moule)* plaster cast; **poser un p.** to put a plaster cast on; **avoir la jambe dans le p.** to have one's leg in plaster

plâtrée [platre] NF *Fam* huge helping; **une p. de nouilles** a huge helping of noodles

plâtrer [platre] VT **1** *(enduire de plâtre) (mur, plafond)* to plaster; *(trou, fissure)* to plaster over *or* up **2** *Méd* to put in plaster **3** *Agr (sol)* to dress with sulphate

plâtrerie [platrəri] NF *(usine)* plasterworks; **travaux de p.** plasterwork, plastering

plâtreux, -euse [platrø, -øz] ADJ *(mur)* covered with plaster; *Fig (camembert)* chalky; **teint p.** pasty *or* chalky complexion

plâtrier [platrije] NM plasterer

plâtrière [platrijer] NF *(carrière)* gypsum quarry; *(four)* plaster kiln, gypsum kiln

plausibilité [plozibilite] NF plausibility

plausible [plozibl] ADJ plausible

plausiblement [plozibləmɑ̃] ADV plausibly

Plaute [plot] N Plautus

play-back [plɛbak] NM INV miming; **chanter en p.** to mime; **c'est du p.** he's/she's/*etc* miming

play-boy, *pl* **play-boys** [plɛbɔj] NM playboy

plèbe [plɛb] NF **1** *Antiq* **la p.** the plebs **2** *Litt Péj* **la p.** the hoi polloi, the plebs, the common people

plébéien, -ienne [plebejɛ̃, -jɛn] ADJ, N plebeian

plébiscite [plebisit] NM plebiscite

plébisciter [plebisite] VT **1** *(élire par plébiscite)* **p. qn/qch** to vote for sb/sth by plebiscite **2** *(élire à une très forte majorité)* **p. qn** to elect sb by a large majority **3** *Fig* to heartily approve of, to endorse

plectre [plɛktr] NM plectrum

pléiade [plejad] NF **1** *Astron* **les Pléiades** the Pleiades **2** *Littér* **la P.** the Pleiad; *Fig* **une p. de gens célèbres** a galaxy of famous people

---

PLEIN [plɛ̃]

> ADJ full **1–5** ▪ complete **2** ▪ right in the middle of *(en plein)* **5** ▪ pregnant *(pleine)* **6** ▪ drunk **7**
> ADV lots of *(plein de)*
> NM full tank (of petrol) **1** ▪ right in the middle of *(en plein dans)* **3**

ADJ **1** *(rempli)* full (**de** of); **une bouteille pleine** a full bottle; **une pleine bouteille** a whole bottle, a bottleful; **p. comme un œuf** chock-full, chock-a-block; **salle pleine à craquer** room full to bursting; **avoir le ventre p.** to be full (up), to have eaten one's fill; **ne parle pas la bouche pleine** don't speak with your mouth full; **suffit, j'ai la tête pleine!** that's enough, I've had it up to here!; **être p. de courage** to have a lot of courage; **être p. d'espoir** to be full of hope, to be hopeful; **une entreprise pleine de dangers/risques** an enterprise fraught with danger/risk; **il a les doigts pleins d'encre** his fingers are covered with ink; **être p. de certitudes** to be sure of things

2 *(complet)* *(accord, adhésion)* full, complete; **pleine lune** full moon; **p. sud** due south; **la chambre est (en) p. ouest** the room faces due west; **pleine mer** *(marée haute)* high tide; **en pleine mer** out at sea, on the open sea; **gagner la pleine mer** to reach the open sea; **p. tarif** full price; *(de transports)* full fare; *(dans un hôtel)* rack rate; **trois jours pleins** three full days; **reliure pleine peau** full leather binding; **p. format** *(de journal)* text-size format, broadsheet format; **p. pouvoir** full power; *Jur* power of attorney; **avoir les pleins pouvoirs** to have full powers; **de son p. gré** of one's own free will, of one's own accord

3 *(solide, qui occupe toute la masse)* *(pneu, essieu etc)* solid; *(ligne)* continuous, unbroken; *(visage)* full; **joues pleines** full *or* plump cheeks

4 *(intense)* **respirer à pleins poumons** to breathe deeply; **crier à pleine gorge** to shout at the top of one's voice; **rire à pleine gorge** to roar with laughter; **ça sent le brûlé à p. nez** there's a strong smell of burning; **apporter des fleurs à pleines brassées** to bring armfuls of flowers; **être en pleine forme** to be on top form; **être en pleine possession de ses moyens** to be in full possession of one's faculties; **à p. temps** full-time; **travailler à p. temps** to work full-time; **un p. temps** a full-time job

5 *(au milieu de)* **en p. (milieu du) cours** (right) in the middle of the lesson; **en pleine réunion/messe** (right) in the middle of the meeting/of Mass; **s'arrêter en p. milieu de la place** to stop right in the middle of the square; **en pleine figure**, *très Fam* **en pleine gueule** right *or* bang in the face; **il a reçu la balle en p. cœur/en pleine poitrine** he got the bullet right *or* bang in the heart/in the chest; **en p. hiver** in the depths *or* the middle of winter; **en p. air** in the open (air); **restaurant/piscine en p. air** open-air restaurant/swimming pool; **en p. soleil** in the full heat of the sun; **marché en p. vent** open-air market; **planté en pleine terre** planted in open ground; **en p. jour** in broad daylight; **en pleine nuit** in the middle of the night, at dead of night; **en pleine lumière** in the full light; **en pleine saison** at the height of the season; **prix de la pleine saison** high-season prices; **en p. tribunal** in open court; **être en p. travail** to be hard at work; **être en pleine croissance** to be growing fast; **à pleines**

voiles with all sails set, under full sail

6 *(animal)* pregnant; **jument pleine** mare in foal; **brebis pleine** ewe with lamb; **chèvre pleine** goat in kid

7 *Fam* **être p. (comme une barrique)** *(ivre)* to be (dead) drunk, to be plastered, to have had a skinful

ADV **il avait des larmes p. les yeux** his eyes were full of tears; **il a des billes/livres p. ses poches** his pockets are full of marbles/stuffed with books; **avoir de l'argent p. les poches** to have plenty of money; **elle avait de la colle p. les mains** her hands were covered with *or* in glue; **elle a des vêtements p. ses armoires** her cupboards are full of *or* stuffed with clothes; **elle en a p. la bouche** she's full of him/it/*etc*, she never shuts up about him/it/*etc*; *Fam* **en avoir p. le dos** *ou très Fam* **le cul** to be sick of it, to be fed up with it, *Fam* to have a bellyful; *Fam* **en avoir p. les jambes** *ou* **les bottes** to be on one's last legs; *Fam* **en mettre p. la vue à qn** to dazzle sb, to impress sb; *Fam* **s'en mettre p. la lampe** to have a good blowout; **à p.** *(travailler, fonctionner etc)* at full capacity; **l'avion part à p.** the plane is leaving with a full passenger load; **l'argument/la remarque a porté à p.** the argument/remark has had the desired effect; **elle est mignonne tout p.** she's awfully sweet; *Fam* **p. de gens/magasins/journaux** lots *or* loads of people/shops/newspapers; *Naut* **porter p.** to keep her full

NM **1** *(de carburant)* full tank; **faire le p. d'un réservoir** to fill up a tank; *Aut* **faire le p. (d'essence)** to fill up (with petrol *or Am* gas); **(faites) le p., s'il vous plaît** fill her up, please; *Fig* **faire le p. d'air pur/de soleil** to get a good dose of fresh air/sunshine; **on fait le p. une fois par semaine chez Casino** *(de courses)* we do a big shop *or* stock-up once a week at Casino; **avoir son p.** *(d'un bateau)* to be fully laden

2 *(phase maximale)* **le p. (de la mer)** high tide; **battre son p.** *(de la marée)* to be at the full; *Fig* **la saison bat son p., c'est le p. de la saison** the season is at its height *or* is in full swing; **la fête battait son p.** the party was in full swing

3 **en p. dans le centre** full *or* right in the middle, *Fam* slap bang in the middle; **en p. dans le mille** right in the bull's-eye; *Fig* spot on, **tomber p.** bang on

4 *(trait épais)* downstroke; *Typ* thick stroke

pleinement [plɛnmɑ̃] ADV fully; **je veux en profiter p.** I want to make the most of it *or* to take full advantage of it

plein-emploi [plɛnɑ̃plwa] NM INV full employment

pléistocène [pleistɔsɛn] ADJ, NM *Géol* Pleistocene

plénier, -ière [plenje, -jɛr] ADJ plenary

plénipotentiaire [plenipɔtɑ̃sjɛr] ADJ, NM plenipotentiary

plénitude [plenityd] NF *(d'une émotion, d'une expérience etc)* fullness, plenitude; *(d'une victoire etc)* completeness; *(d'un son)* fullness, richness

plénum [plenɔm] NM plenum

pléonasme [pleɔnasm] NM pleonasm

pléonastique [pleɔnastik] ADJ pleonastic

plésiosaure [plezjɔzɔr] NM plesiosaurus

pléthore [pletɔr] NF plethora (**de** of)

pléthorique [pletɔrik] ADJ **1** *Méd Vieilli* full-blooded, plethoric **2** *(très abondant)* superabundant; *(trop)* excessive

pleur [plœr] NM *Littt* tear; **verser des pleurs** to shed tears; **fondre en pleurs** to dissolve into tears; **cessez vos pleurs** dry your tears; **être (tout) en pleurs** to be (bathed) in tears; *Bible* **il va y avoir des pleurs et des grince-**

ments de dents there will be wailing and gnashing of teeth

pleurage [plœraʒ] NM *Tech* wow; **niveau de p.** wow level

pleural, -ale, -aux, -ales [plœral, -o] ADJ *Anat* pleural

pleurant, -ante [plœrɑ̃, -ɑ̃t] ADJ *Litt* weeping, crying
N *Beaux-Arts* weeper, mourner *(on a tomb)*

pleurard, -arde [plœrar, -ard] *Péj Vieilli* ADJ *(enfant)* whimpering, fractious; *(voix)* whining, whimpering, tearful
N whiner, *Fam* crybaby

pleurer [plœre] VT **1** **p. qn** to mourn (for) sb; **p. la mort de qn** to mourn sb's death; **p. sa jeunesse, p. ses vingt ans** to weep for *or* over one's lost youth; **mourir sans être pleuré** to die unmourned

2 *(laisser couler)* to cry, to shed, to weep; **p. toutes les larmes de son corps** to cry one's eyes out; **p. des larmes de sang** to weep bitterly, to shed bitter tears; **p. des larmes de bonheur** to cry *or* weep for joy; **p. misère** to bemoan one's lot

3 *Fig Fam Vieilli (ménager) (argent)* to stint; **elle ne pleure pas ses efforts** *ou* **sa peine/ses conseils** she spares no effort/is generous with her advice

VI **1** *(verser des larmes)* to cry, to weep (**sur** over; **pour** for); **et puis j'ai vu que je m'étais trompé et j'en aurais pleuré** when I saw I had made a mistake, I could have cried *or* wept; **elle pleure de ne pas avoir eu son examen** she's crying because she hasn't passed her exam; **p. sur soi-même** *ou* **sur son sort** to bewail *or* bemoan one's fate; **p. de joie** to cry *or* weep for joy; **p. à chaudes larmes** *ou Fam* **comme une madeleine** *ou Fam* **comme un veau** to sob *or* cry one's heart out; **s'endormir en pleurant** to cry oneself to sleep; **il était sentimental, c'était à en p.** he was ridiculously sentimental; **c'est à (faire) p.** it's enough to make you weep *or* cry; **bête/méchant à faire p.** terribly stupid/nasty

2 **j'ai les yeux qui pleurent** my eyes are watering *or* running

3 *Fig Péj (supplier)* to beg; **aller p. auprès de qn** to go begging to sb; **Fam et qu'il ne vienne pas me p. dans les bras!** and he needn't come begging to me!; **p. après une faveur** to beg for a favour

pleurésie [plœrezi] NF *Méd* pleurisy

pleurétique [plœretik] ADJ, N *Méd* pleuritic

pleureur, -euse [plœrœr, -øz] N *Péj Vieilli* whimperer
NF **pleureuse** *(dans un cortège funèbre)* (hired) mourner, *Arch* mute
ADJ *Péj* whimpering; **saule p.** weeping willow

pleurite [plœrit] NF *Méd* dry pleurisy

pleurnichard, -arde [plœrniʃar, -ard] N, ADJ = **pleurnicheur**

pleurnichement [plœrniʃmɑ̃] NM = **pleurnicherie**

pleurnicher [plœrniʃe] VI *Fam* to whine, to snivel, *Br (surtout d'un jeune enfant)* to grizzle

pleurnicherie [plœrniʃri] NF *Fam* whining, snivelling, *Br (surtout d'un jeune enfant)* grizzling

pleurnicheur, -euse [plœrniʃœr, -øz] *Fam* N whiner, sniveller; *(qui pleure facilement)* crybaby
ADJ whining, snivelling

pleurote [plœrɔt] NM oyster mushroom

pleutre [pløtr] *Littt Péj* ADJ craven, cowardly
NM craven, coward

pleuvasser [pløvase], **pleuviner** [pløvine] V IMPERS to drizzle

pleuvoir [pløvwar] *(prp* **pleuvant**; *pp* **plu;** *pr* *ind* **il pleut, ils pleuvent;** *impf* **il pleuvait;** *p hist* **il plut;** *fu* **il pleuvra** V IMPERS to rain; **il pleut** it's raining; **il pleut à verse** *ou* **à seaux** it's pouring (down) (with rain); **les jours où il pleut** on wet *or* rainy days; *Fam* **il pleut des cordes** *ou* **des hallebardes, il pleut comme vache qui pisse** it's raining cats and dogs, it's coming down in buckets, *Br* it's tipping it down; *Can* **il pleut à boire debout** it's pouring; **des cadeaux comme s'il en pleuvait** presents galore; **dépenser de l'argent comme s'il en pleuvait** to spend money as if there's no tomorrow *or* as if it's going out of fashion ▪ VI **faire p. des coups sur qn** to rain blows (down) on sb, to shower sb with blows; **les invitations pleuvent sur lui** invitations are pouring in to him, he's being inundated with invitations; **ce ne sont pas exactement les compliments qui pleuvent** I'm not exactly being showered with compliments

pleuvoter [pløvɔte] V IMPERS = **pleuvasser**

plèvre [plɛvr] NF *Anat* pleura, pleural membrane

Plexiglas® [plɛksiglas] NM Perspex®, *Am* Plexiglas®

plexus [plɛksys] NM *Anat* plexus; **p. solaire** solar plexus

pli [pli] NM **1** *(rabat)* *(de rideaux, tissu)* fold; *Couture* pleat; **(faux) p.** crease; *Couture* **p. creux** *ou* **rentré** *ou* **inverti, double p.** box pleat, inverted pleat; **p. couché** knife pleat; **petit p.** tuck; **jupe à plis** pleated skirt; **faire** *ou* **marquer le p. d'un pantalon** to put a crease in a pair of trousers; **faire des plis à une robe** to put pleats in a dress, to pleat a dress; *(la froisser)* to crease a dress
2 mise en plis set; **faire une mise en plis à qn** to set sb's hair
3 *Aut (d'un pneu)* ply; **p. diagonal** diagonal ply; **p. radial** radial ply
4 *Fig* **ça ne fait pas un p.** (there's) no doubt about it; **j'étais sûr qu'il allait se tromper, et ça n'a pas fait un p.!** I was sure he'd make a mistake, and I was right!; *Fig* **prendre le p. (de faire qch)** to get into the habit (of doing sth); **il a pris le p.** he got used to it, he got into the habit; **le p. était pris** I/he/*etc* had got used to it; *Fig* **prendre un mauvais p.** to get into a bad habit
5 *(du bras, de la jambe)* bend; *(de peau)* fold; *(petit)* wrinkle; **p. du jarret** hollow of the knee; **les plis du front** the lines on the forehead; **elle a de gros plis sur le ventre** she has big folds of skin on her stomach; **il a de petits plis autour des yeux** he has wrinkles round his eyes
6 *(enveloppe)* envelope; *(lettre)* letter; **sous p. séparé** under separate cover; **sous p. discret** under plain cover, *aussi Hum* in a plain brown wrapper; **nous vous envoyons sous ce p. ...** we are sending you herewith ..., please find enclosed ...; **p. cacheté** sealed envelope; *Naut* sealed orders; **envoyer qch sous p. cacheté** to send sth in a sealed envelope; **p. chargé** registered and insured letter; **p. recommandé** registered letter; **par p. recommandé** by registered mail
7 *Cartes* trick; **faire un p.** to take a trick
8 *Géol* **p. de terrain** fold

pliable [plijabl] ADJ *(chaise, lit)* foldable; **canot p.** folding boat

pliage [plijaʒ] NM *(d'un tissu)* folding; *(origami)* paper folding; *(objet)* folded-paper model

pliant [plijɑ̃] ADJ *(chaise, table)* folding, collapsible; **pied p.** folding tripod
▪ NM folding *or* collapsible stool

plie [pli] NF plaice

plié [plije] NM *(en danse)* plié

plier [plije] *(impf, pr sub* **n. pliions, v. pliiez)*
▪ VT **1** *(mettre en double)* *(draps, vêtements)* to fold; *(page)* to turn down; *(voile)* to furl; *(ra-*

battre) *(parapluie)* to fold up *or* away; *Fig* **p. bagage** to pack one's bags **2** *(courber)* *(branche, genou etc)* to bend; **plié en deux** *(personne)* bent double, doubled up; *Fig Fam* **être plié (de rire)** to be doubled up *or* bent double with laughter; **p. qn à la discipline/une règle/une contrainte** to impose discipline/a rule/a constraint on sb; **p. qn à une habitude** to get sb into a habit **3** *Fam (détruire)* to smash up, to wreck
▪ VI **1** *(se courber)* to bend (over); **p. sous le poids de qch** *(d'une poutre, de branches etc)* to bend *or* give *or* sag under the weight of sth **2** *(se soumettre)* to submit, to yield; *(des troupes dans une bataille)* to give way; **elle ne pliera pas devant lui** she will not submit to him *or* give in to him
▪ VPR **se plier** *(d'un parapluie, d'une chaise)* to fold (up); **se p. aux circonstances** to yield *or* bow *or* submit to circumstances; **se p. à la discipline** to submit to discipline; **se p. aux lois** to obey the law; **se p. aux caprices/volontés de qn** to give in to sb's whims/wishes

plieur, -ieuse [plijœr, -jøz] *Tech* N *(personne)* folder
▪ NF **plieuse** folding machine

Pline [plin] N **P. l'Ancien/le Jeune** Pliny the Elder/the Younger

plinthe [plɛ̃t] NF **1** *(lame de bois)* skirting (board), *Am* baseboard **2** *Archit (de colonne)* plinth

pliocène [plijɔsɛn] ADJ, NM *Géol* Pliocene

plioir [plijwar] NM *(coupe-papier)* paper knife

plissage [plisaʒ] NM *(d'un tissu)* pleating

plissé [plise] ADJ **1** *Couture* pleated **2 front p.** wrinkled brow; **visage tout p.** creased *or* wrinkled face
▪ NM *Couture* pleats; **p. soleil** sunray *or* *Am* sunburst pleats

plissement [plismɑ̃] NM **1** *(fait de plier)* *(d'un tissu)* pleating; *(de papier)* folding; *(de métal, de carton)* corrugation **2** *(froissement)* *(de papier, de tissu)* creasing, crumpling, crinkling **3** *(froncement)* *(des yeux)* screwing up **4** *Géol* fold; **le p. hercynien** the Armorican *or* Hercynian fold

plisser [plise] VT **1** *(plier)* *(vêtement)* to pleat; *(papier)* to fold; *(métal, carton)* to corrugate **2** *(froisser)* *(papier, tissu)* to crease, to crumple, to crinkle **3** *(froncer)* *(front)* to wrinkle; *(lèvres)* to pucker; **p. les yeux** to screw up one's eyes
▪ VI *(d'un vêtement)* to crease
▪ VPR **se plisser** *(d'une étoffe)* to crease; *(d'une bouche)* to pucker; **la soie se plisse facilement** silk creases easily; **ses yeux se plissent quand elle sourit** her eyes go all crinkly when she smiles; **son front se plissa** he frowned

plisseur, -euse [plisœr, -øz] *Tex* N *(personne)* pleater
▪ NF **plisseuse** pleating machine

plissure [plisyr] NF pleats

pliure [plijyr] NF *(action)* *(du papier)* folding; *(résultat)* *(d'un tissu)* fold; *(du genou)* bend

ploc [plɔk] INT plop!

ploiement [plwamɑ̃] NM bending

plomb [plɔ̃] NM **1** *(métal)* lead; **p.-étain** lead-tin; **p. laminé** *ou* **en feuilles** sheet lead; **tuyau de p.** lead pipe; **blanc de p.** white lead; *Fig* **sommeil de p.** deep *or* heavy sleep; **dormir d'un sommeil de p.** to sleep like a log; **ciel de p.** leaden sky; **teint de p.** livid complexion; **soleil de p.** blazing (hot) sun; *Fig* **n'avoir pas de p. dans la tête** to be scatterbrained; **espérons que cela lui mettra un peu de p. dans la tête** *ou* **dans la cervelle** let's hope that will knock some sense into him; **années de p.** dark years; **les années de p. de l'Occupation** the dark years of the Occu-

pation **2** *(poids)* lead (weight); *Pêche* sinker; *Naut* **jeter** *ou* **lancer le p. (de sonde)** to heave the lead; **fil à p.** plumb line; **à p.** upright, vertical **3** *Archit* **plombs** *(de fenêtre)* leadwork, leads; **mise en p.** leading **4** *Typ* type, metal; *(de chasse)* shot; **petit** *ou* **menu p.** small shot; **gros p.** buckshot; *Fig* **avoir du p. dans l'aile** to be in a bad way **5** *(sceau)* lead seal *(on meter etc)*; *Élec* **p. (fusible)** fuse; **faire sauter les plombs** to blow the fuses; *très Fam* **j'ai pété les plombs** I blew my top

plombage [plɔ̃baʒ] NM **1** *(fait de garnir avec du plomb)* covering with lead; *Cér* lead glazing **2** *(fait de mettre des plombs)* weighting with lead **3** *(d'une dent)* filling

plombagine [plɔ̃baʒin] NF *Minér* black lead, graphite

plombe [plɔ̃b] NF *Arg* hour; **quatre plombes, ce n'est pas une heure à rentrer** four o'clock is no time to come home; **on ne va pas l'attendre pendant des plombes** we're not going to wait for him for ever

plombé [plɔ̃be] ADJ *(fenêtre)* leaded; *(toit)* lead(-covered); *Fig (teint)* livid; *(ciel)* leaden

plomber [plɔ̃be] VT **1** *(couvrir de plomb)* to cover with lead; *Cér* to glaze **2** *(mettre des plombs à)* to weight with lead **3** *Fig (rendre livide)* *(teint, ciel)* to turn livid **4** *(dent)* to fill, to stop; **le dentiste m'a plombé une dent** the dentist gave me a filling **5** *(handicapper, compromettre)* to jeopardize, to undermine **6** *Constr (mur)* to plumb **7** *très Fam (transmettre une maladie vénérienne à)* **plomber qn** to give sb a dose
▪ VPR **se plomber** *(du teint)* to become livid; *(du ciel)* to become leaden

plomberie [plɔ̃bri] NF *(installations, métier)* plumbing; *(atelier)* plumber's shop

plombier [plɔ̃bje] NM *(technicien)* plumber; *Fig Fam Péj (policier spécialiste de l'écoute clandestine)* snooper, eavesdropper; *(au téléphone)* phone-tapper

plombières [plɔ̃bjer] NF *Culin* tutti-frutti (ice cream)

plonge [plɔ̃ʒ] NF *Fam (dans un restaurant)* dishwashing, *Br* washing up; **faire la p.** *(dans un restaurant)* to be a dishwasher; *(at home)* to wash the dishes, *Br* to do the washing up

plongeant [plɔ̃ʒɑ̃] ADJ *(tir, décolleté)* plunging; **vue plongeante** bird's-eye view *(sur* onto), view from above

plongée [plɔ̃ʒe] NF **1** *(de nageur)* diving; **faire de la p.** to dive; **partir en p.** to go diving; **p. sous-marine** skin *or* scuba diving **2** *(de sous-marin)* dive, diving, submersion; **effectuer sa p.** to dive, to submerge; **p. raide** crash-dive **3** *Cin, TV* elevated shot; *(verticale)* bird's-eye view **4** *Aut* **p. (au freinage)** dive

plongeoir [plɔ̃ʒwar] NM diving board

plongeon [plɔ̃ʒɔ̃] NM **1** *(fait de plonger)* dive; **p. de haut vol** high dive; **faire un p.** *(d'un nageur, gardien de but)* to dive; *Fig Fam* **faire le p.** *(dans les affaires)* to suffer heavy losses, *Am* to take a bath **2** *(oiseau)* diver, *Am* loon

plonger [plɔ̃ʒe] *(je plongeai(s); n. plongeons)* VI **1** *(s'immerger)* *(d'un nageur, sousmarin, avion etc)* to dive (**dans** into) **2** *Fig (descendre)* to plunge; **les murs plongent dans le fossé** the walls plunge into *or* run steeply down into the moat; **son regard plongea sur nous** he gazed down at us; **d'ici, on plonge sur la cathédrale** from here, you look down on the cathedral *or* you have a view down onto the cathedral; **p. dans le sommeil** to fall into a deep sleep; **p. dans la décadence** to sink rapidly into decline; **p. dans le travail pour oublier** to throw oneself into work *or* immerse oneself in work to take one's mind off things **3** *Fam (être envoyé en prison)* to be put inside *or* away, *Br* to be sent down

vt to plunge, to thrust (**dans** in(to)); **p. la main dans sa poche/un couteau dans le cœur de qn** to plunge *or* thrust one's hand into one's pocket/a knife into sb's heart; **il plongea son regard sur nous** he stared at us **vpr se plonger** to immerse oneself (**dans** in); *Fig* **être plongé dans ses pensées** to be immersed *or* lost *or* deep in thought; **être plongé dans le silence** to be plunged in silence; **être plongé dans le noir/l'angoisse** to be plunged in darkness/overcome by anguish; **se p. dans son travail/l'étude** to throw oneself into *or* to immerse *or* bury oneself in one's work/one's studies; **se p. dans Proust** to become absorbed *or* engrossed in Proust; **se p. dans le vice** to plunge into the world of vice

plongeur, -euse [plɔ̃ʒœr, -øz] **N 1** *(personne qui plonge dans l'eau)* diver; **cloche à plongeurs** diving bell; **p. sous-marin** skin *or* scuba diver **2** *Fam (dans un restaurant)* dishwasher, *Br* washer-up
NM 1 *Orn* diver, diving bird **2** *Tech (d'une pompe)* plunger

plot [plo] **NM** *Élec* contact (stud)

plouc [pluk] *Péj* **ADJ** *Fam* naff; **ça fait p.!** that's really naff!
NM yokel, (country) bumpkin

plouf [pluf] **INT** plop!; *(objet plus lourd)* splash!

ploutocrate [plutɔkrat] **N** plutocrat

ploutocratie [plutɔkrasi] **NF** plutocracy

ploutocratique [plutɔkratik] **ADJ** plutocratic

ployable [plwajabl] **ADJ** pliable, flexible

ployer [plwaje] (**je ploie, n. ployons; je ploierai**) **VI** *(courber)* to bend; *(d'un plancher, d'une poutre)* to sag; *(se casser, s'effondrer)* to give (way); *(sous un joug, un fardeau)* to bend, to bow; *(de troupes)* to give way, to submit, to yield
VT *(branche, genou)* to bend

pluches [plyʃ] **NFPL** *Mil Fam* **(corvée de) p.** potato-peeling, *Br* spud-bashing; **je suis de p.** I'm on potato-peeling *or Br* spud-bashing (duty)

pluie [plɥi] **NF 1** rain; **pluies acides** acid rain; **p. battante** driving *or* pelting *or* lashing rain; **p. diluvienne** pouring rain; **p. torrentielle** torrential rain; **p. fine** drizzle; **p. d'orage** cloudburst; **goutte de p.** raindrop; **il n'y a pas eu une goutte de p. dans la région depuis deux mois** the region hasn't had a drop of rain for two months; **eau de p.** rainwater; **le temps est à la p.** it looks like rain; **temps de p.** rainy *or* wet weather; **jour sans p.** dry day; **sous la p.** in the rain; **sous une p. diluvienne** in the pouring rain; **la saison des pluies** the rainy season; **ajoutez la farine en la versant en p.** sprinkle in the flour; *Fig* **parler de la p. et du beau temps** to talk about nothing in particular, to talk of this and that, *Am* to shoot the breeze; *Fig Fam* **il n'est pas tombé de la dernière p.** he wasn't born yesterday; *Prov* **après la p., le beau temps** it's a long road that has no turning; *Fam* **faire la p. et le beau temps** to rule the roost, to be the boss **2** *Fig (de coups, balles, pierres)* hail, shower; *(de reproches, compliments)* stream; **p. d'or** shower of gold

plumage [plymaʒ] **NM** *(ensemble des plumes)* plumage, feathers; *(fait de plumer)* plucking

plumard [plymar] **NM** *Fam* bed; **aller au p.** to hit the sack *or* the hay, to crash (out)

plume¹ [plym] **NF 1** *(d'oiseau)* feather; **oiseau sans plumes** unfledged bird; **gibier à plumes** game birds; *Fig Fam* **il y a laissé des plumes** he didn't come out of it unscathed, he didn't get off lightly; *Fig Fam* **on lui a volé dans les plumes** they laid into him; **léger comme une p.** (as) light as a feather; *Prov* **la belle p. fait le bel oiseau** fine feathers make fine birds; **lit de plume(s)** feather bed; **couette en plumes d'oie** goose-feather duvet; *Fig Hum* **perdre ses plumes** to go thin on top, to go bald; **poids p.** *Boxe* featherweight; *Fig* lightweight; **un poids p. en politique** a political lightweight **2** *(de stylo)* (pen) nib; **p. (d'oie)** quill (pen); **p. à dessin** drawing pen; **les idées se pressent sous sa p.** he can't write his ideas down quickly enough, his ideas are coming thick and fast; **écrire des mots/ses idées au courant** *ou* **au fil de la p.** to write down words/one's ideas as they come into one's head; **dessin à la p.** pen (and ink) drawing; **trait de p.** stroke of the pen; **prendre la p.** to put pen to paper; **j'ai pris ma plus belle p. pour écrire cette lettre** I made this the most beautiful letter I could; **vivre de sa p.** to make one's living by writing, to live by one's pen; **avoir la p. facile** to have a gift for writing **3** *Méd* **p. à vaccin** vaccine point

plume² **NM** *Fam* = **plumard**

plumeau, -eaux [plymo] **NM** feather duster

plumer [plyme] **VT** *(volaille)* to pluck; *Fam (personne)* to fleece
VPR se plumer *Fam* to hit the sack *or Am* the hay, to crash (out)

plumet [plymɛ] **NM** plume

plumetis [plymti] **NM** *Couture* **1** broderie au p. raised *or* satin stitch **2** *(étoffe)* Swiss muslin

plumeux, -euse [plymø, -øz] **ADJ** feathery

plumier [plymje] **NM** *(ouvert)* pen tray; *(à couvercle)* pencil box, pencil case

plumitif [plymitif] **NM** *Péj (employé de bureau)* penpusher; *(mauvais écrivain)* scribbler

plum-pudding, *pl* **plum-puddings** [plumpudiŋ] **NM** Christmas pudding, *Vieilli* plum pudding

plupart (la) [laplypar] **NF** most, the majority, *Fml* the greater part; **la p. des gens** most people, the majority of people; **la p. de mes clients** most of my customers, the majority of my customers; **la p. d'entre eux** most of them, the majority of them; **la p. du temps** most of the time; *(en général)* in most cases, generally; **il passe la p. du temps à lire** he spends most of his time reading; **dans la p. des cas** in most cases, in the majority of cases; **pour la p.** for the most part, mostly

plural, -ale, -aux, -ales [plyral, -o] **ADJ** **vote p.** plural voting

pluralisme [plyralism] **NM** *Pol, Phil* pluralism

pluraliste [plyralist] **ADJ** pluralist; **élections pluralistes** multi-party elections
N pluralist

pluralité [plyralite] **NF** *(multiplicité)* plurality, multiplicity; *Rel* **p. des bénéfices** pluralism; *Arch* **élu à la p. des voix** elected by a majority

pluriannuel, -elle [plyrianɥel] **ADJ** **récolte pluriannuelle** crop harvested every few years; **contrat p.** contract valid for a number of years

pluridisciplinaire [plyridisiplinɛr] **ADJ** *(approche, études)* multidisciplinary
NM le technicien doit être un p. the technician must possess a range of skills; **des pluridisciplinaires** people with a range of skills

pluridisciplinarité [plyridisiplinarite] **NF** multidisciplinary approach; **favoriser la p. dans les études universitaires** to encourage students to take up a range of subjects; **nous visons à une certaine p. dans nos services** we're aiming to widen the range of tasks undertaken in our departments

pluriel, -ielle [plyrjɛl] **ADJ** plural SEE GRAMMAR A9–15; B8; B10
NM plural; **au p.** in the plural

pluriethnique [plyrietnik] **ADJ** multiethnic

plurilingue [plyrilɛ̃g] **ADJ** multilingual

plurilinguisme [plyrilɛ̃gɥism] **NM** multilingualism

plurinational, -ale, -aux, -ales [plyrinasjɔnal, -o] **ADJ** multinational

plurinominal [plyrinɔminal] **ADJ** *Pol* **scrutin p.** = voting for more than one candidate

pluripartisme [plyripartism] **NM** *Pol* multiparty system

PLUS [ply] *(often* [plys] *at the end of a word group;* [plyz] *before a vowel* **plus on est de fous, plus on rit** [plyzɔ̃nɛdfuplyzɔ̃ri])

> ▪ more **1, 6** ▪ most **2** ▪ not any more **3**
> ▪ either *(non plus)* **4** ▪ plus **5** ▪ in addition *(en plus)* **7** ▪ more or less *(plus ou moins)* **8**

ADV 1 *(davantage)* more; **p. de** *(davantage)* more; *(au-delà de)* more than; **soyez p. réaliste!** be more realistic!; **p. courageux** braver, more courageous; **p. clair/fort** clearer/stronger; **ils sont (beaucoup) p. nombreux** there are (far) more of them; **c'est sa mère, en p. jeune** she's a younger version of her mother, she looks just like her mother, only younger; **le même, en p. petit** the same, only smaller; **il est p. grand que moi** he's taller than I am *or* than me; **je ne suis pas p. grand que lui** I'm no taller than he is *or* than him; **elle écoute p. attentivement** she listens more attentively; **une fenêtre p. haute que large** a window higher than it is wide; **elle est p. jolie que belle** she is pretty rather than beautiful; **deux fois p. grand/rapide (que)** twice as big/fast (as); **c'est mille fois p. adapté pour ce que tu fais** it's a thousand times more suitable for what you're doing; *Fam* **c'est p. que bien** it's more than just good; **des résultats p. que satisfaisants** more than satisfactory results; **je gagne p. que vous** I earn more than you (do); **p. qu'à moitié** *(souvent* [plyskamwatje]*) (fait etc)* more than half; **en vouloir toujours p.** to be always wanting more; **il a p. de patience/temps que moi** he has more patience/time than I have *or* than me; **p. d'une fois** more than once; **p. de dix hommes** more than ten men; **il a p. de vingt ans** he's over twenty; **pendant p. d'une heure/d'un kilomètre** for over *or* for more than an hour/a kilometre; **p. loin** further *or* farther (on); **p. tôt** earlier; **je n'étais pas p. tôt arrivé que le téléphone sonnait** no sooner had I arrived than the telephone rang; **p. ... (et) p. ...** the more ..., the more ...; **p. on est de fous, p. on rit** the more the merrier; **p. je lis, moins je retiens** the more I read, the less I remember; **et qui p. est** [plyzɛ] and what is more, and moreover; **j'en ai trois fois p. qu'il ne m'en faut** I've (got) three times as much/as many as I need; **il y en a tant et p.** there's an awful lot (of it); *(nombre)* there are an awful lot (of them); **c'est d'autant p. facile/compliqué que ...** it's all the easier/the more complicated since ..., it's particularly easy/complicated since ...; **c'est d'autant p. vrai qu'il l'a dit lui-même** it must be true, he said so himself SEE GRAMMAR A24–6; B11; B13–14

2 (le) p. (the) most; **la p. longue rue** *ou* **la rue la p. longue de la ville** the longest street in the town; **la p. belle femme que j'aie jamais vue** the most beautiful woman I've ever seen; **c'est la femme la p. capable de le faire** she's the woman most capable of doing it;

c'est vous qui avez fait le p. de fautes you've made (the) most mistakes; **le p. vite possible** as quickly as possible; **c'est à trente ans qu'elle a été la p. belle** she was at her most beautiful at thirty; **ce que je désire le p.** what I most desire, what I desire (the) most; **le p. drôle, ce qu'il y a de p. drôle** the funniest thing; **crier le p. fort** to shout (the) loudest; **faites le p. que vous pourrez** do the most you can *or* as much as you can; **(tout) au p.** at the (very) most, at the (very) outside; **c'est tout au p. s'il est midi** it's twelve o'clock at the latest; **c'est tout ce qu'il y a de p. simple** nothing could be simpler; **c'était des p. réussis** *(extrêmement)* it was most successful; **un gâteau des p. délicieux** a most delicious cake SEE GRAMMAR A24–6; B11; B13–14

3 *(négation)* **ne ... p.** not any more, not any longer, no more, no longer; **je ne les vois p.** I don't see them any more *or* any longer, I no longer see them; **je ne le ferai p.** I won't do it again *or* any more; **tu n'iras p.** you won't go again *or* any more; **je ne la verrai p.** *(jamais)* I'll never see her again; *Litt* **il n'est p.** *(mort)* he is no more; **je ne veux p. de cela** I don't want any more of that; **je n'ai** *ou Fam* **j'ai p. d'argent** I haven't any money left *or* any more money, I've (got) no more money; **nous n'avons p. d'espoir de la retrouver** we no longer have any hope *or* we have no hope any more of finding her; **il n'y a p. aucun espoir** I've/they've/*etc* given up hope; **sans p. attendre** without further ado; **(il n'y a) p. de doute** there is no longer any doubt about it; **il n'y a p. de jeunesse!** young people aren't what they used to be!, honestly, young people nowadays!; **p. de potage, merci** no more soup, thank you; **il (n')y en a p.** there is/are no more (left), there is/are none left; **il (n')y a p. rien** there's nothing left; **p. que dix minutes!** only ten minutes left!; **on procède non p. par ordre alphabétique, mais par thème** we shall no longer proceed in alphabetical order, but according to theme; **pas p. que no more than; pas p. qu'on ne doit voler, on ne doit mentir** it is no more acceptable to lie than it is to steal SEE GRAMMAR B62

4 **non p.** either *(in negative sentences)*; **je n'en ai pas non p.** I haven't got any either; **(ni) moi non p.** neither do I/did I/*etc*, I don't/didn't/*etc* either, *Fam* me neither; **jamais non p. je n'avais songé à ... nor** had I ever thought of ...; **vous n'en avez guère non p.** you haven't got much/many either

5 [plys] *surtout Math* plus; **sept p. neuf** seven plus nine; **il fait p. 20 (degrés)** it's plus 20 (degrees); **500 euros d'amende, p. les frais** 500 euros fine and *or* plus costs; *Golf* **p. quatre** [plyskatr] plus four

6 **de p.** more; **une journée de p.** one day more, one more day; **il a trois ans de p. que moi** he's three years older than I am *or* than me; **rien de p., merci** nothing else, thank you; **de p. en p.** more and more; **de p. en p. froid** colder and colder

7 **en p.** in addition, into the bargain; *(en sus)* extra; **la même maison, avec un balcon en p.** the same house, but with a balcony; *(avec un autre balcon)* the same house, but with an extra *or* additional balcony; **le vin est en p.** wine is extra; **il y en a trois en p. de lui** there are three more besides him; **en p. de ce qu'il me doit** over and above *or* in addition to *or* besides what he owes me; **sans p.** but no more than that; **elle a été aimable, sans p.** she was pleasant, but no more than that

8 **p. ou moins** [plyzumwɛ̃] more or less; **elle joue p. ou moins bien** she plays fairly well, she's not a bad player; **c'est un mensonge, ni p. ni moins** it's nothing more nor less than a lie, it's purely and simply a lie

NM [plys] **1** *Prov* **qui peut le p. peut le moins** you have/he has/*etc* done more difficult things than that before

2 *Math (signe)* plus (sign)

3 *Golf* **le p.** the odd

4 *Fig (atout)* plus; **c'est un p. pour vous** that's a plus for you

plusieurs [plyzjœr] **ADJ, PRON** several; **p. personnes l'ont remarqué** several people *or* a number of people have noticed it; **de p. manières** in more ways than one, in several ways; **j'en ai p.** I have several; **on s'y est mis à p.** several of us *or* a number of us got together (to do it) SEE GRAMMAR B15–16

plus-que-parfait, *pl* **plus-que-parfaits** [plyskəparfɛ] **NM** *Gram* pluperfect, past perfect SEE GRAMMAR A50; B30

plus-value, *pl* **plus-values** [plyvaly] **NF** *Écon, Fin (de biens, de terrains etc)* capital gain, appreciation, increase in value; *(excédent) (d'impôts)* surplus, excess yield; **les recettes présentent une p. de ...** the receipts show an increase of ...; **impôt sur les plus-values** capital gains tax; **p. sur titres** paper profit

Pluton [plytɔ̃] **N** *(dieu)* Pluto
NF *(planète)* Pluto

plutonium [plytɔnjɔm] **NM** *Chimie* plutonium

plutôt [plyto] **ADV 1** *(de préférence)* rather; **p. que de faire les choses en cachette** rather than do things in secret; **p. la mort que l'esclavage** death before slavery, rather *or* sooner death than slavery; **p. souffrir que mentir** it is better to suffer than to lie; **il récite p. qu'il ne chante** he recites rather than sings; **p. que de partir** rather than leave, instead of leaving; **demande p. à ta mère** ask your mother instead; **ne te plains pas, travaille p.!** don't complain, just work!; **il faudrait p. en rire** it's best to laugh

2 *(pour préciser)* rather; **il faisait p. froid (que chaud)** the weather was cold if anything, it was cold rather than anything (else); **elle n'est pas bête, p. étourdie** she's absent-minded rather than stupid, she's not so much stupid as absent-minded, she's not stupid, just absent-minded; **ses parents, ou p. son père** his parents, or rather *or* or more precisely his father; **il n'est pas satisfait, mais p., soulagé** he's relieved rather than satisfied

3 *(assez)* fairly, quite, rather, *Fam* pretty, *surtout Fml* somewhat; **son discours était p. long** his speech was fairly *or* quite *or* rather long *or* was on the long side; *Fam* **il est p. bien, ce type!** he's not bad-looking at all, that guy!; **c'est p. une bonne idée, tu ne trouves pas?** it's rather a good idea, isn't it?; **je suis en retard? – oui, p.!** am I late? – you can say that again! *or Br* not half! VOIR GRAMMAIRE A5

4 *Litt (à peine)* hardly, scarcely; **il ne nous avait pas p. annoncé la venue de son frère ...** hardly *or* scarcely had he announced the arrival of his brother before ..., no sooner had he announced his brother's arrival than ... VOIR GRAMMAIRE A78

pluvial, -iale, -iaux, -iales [plyvjal, -jo] **ADJ** *Géog* pluvial; **eau pluviale** rainwater

pluvier [plyvje] **NM** *Orn* plover

pluvieux, -ieuse [plyvjø, -jøz] **ADJ** wet, rainy

pluviner [plyvine] **VI** = pleuvasser

pluviomètre [plyvjɔmɛtr] **NM** *Météo* rain gauge, *Spéc* pluviometer

pluviôse [plyvjoz] **NM** *Hist* = fifth month of the French Republican calendar *(January-February)*

pluviosité [plyvjozite] **NF** *Météo* rainfall

PLV [peɛlve] **NF** *(abrév* **publicité sur le lieu de vente)** point-of-sale promotion

PMA [peɛma] **NF** *(abrév* **procréation médicalement assistée)** artificial *or* assisted reproduction
NMPL *(abrév* **pays les moins avancés)** LDCs

PME [peɛmə] **NF(PL)** *(abrév* **petite(s) et moyenne(s) entreprise(s))** small business(es), small and medium-sized business(es); **une P.** a small business

PMI [peɛmi] **NF** *(abrév* **petite et moyenne industrie)** small (and medium-sized) industries

PMU [peɛmy] **NM** *(abrév* **Pari mutuel urbain)** = state-run betting system, *Br* ≃ tote

PNB [peɛnbe] **NM** *Écon (abrév* **Produit national brut)** GNP

pneu [pnø] **NM 1** *Aut* tyre, *Am* tire; **avoir des pneus lisses** to have worn tyres; **avoir un p. à plat/crevé** to have a flat/a puncture **2** *(lettre exprès)* express letter *(sent through a pneumatic despatch system)*
▸▸ **p. à architecture radiale** radial-ply tyre; **p. à ceinture** braced *or* belted tyre; **p. à clous, p. clouté** studded tyre; **pneus jumelés** twin tyres; **p. neige** snow tyre; **p. pluie** wet-weather tyre; **p. sans chambre** tubeless tyre; **p. à structure diagonale** cross-ply tyre; **p. à structure radiale** radial tyre; **p. taille basse** low-profile tyre; **p. temps sec** dry-weather tyre; **p. tout-temps** all-weather tyre; **p. tout-terrain** all-terrain tyre; **p. à usage mixte** town-and-country tyre

pneumatique [pnømatik] **ADJ** pneumatic; *(canoë)* inflatable; **canot p.** rubber dinghy; **matelas/pistolet p.** air mattress/gun
NM = pneu

pneumocoque [pnømokɔk] **NM** *Biol* pneumococcus

pneumologie [pnømɔlɔʒi] **NF** *Méd* pneumology

pneumologue [pnømɔlɔg] **N** *Méd* lung specialist

pneumonie [pnømɔni] **NF** *Méd* pneumonia; **p. atypique** atypical pneumonia; *(SRAS)* SARS

pneumothorax [pnømotɔraks] **NM** *Méd* pneumothorax

PNUD [pnyd] **NM** *(abrév* **programme des Nations unies pour le développement)** UNDP

Pô (le) [lapo] **NM** *Géog* the (River) Po

PO 1 *Com (abrév* **par ordre)** by order **2** *Radio (abrév* **petites ondes)** MW

pochade [pɔʃad] **NF** quick sketch

pochard, -arde [pɔʃar, -ard] **N** *Fam* drunk(ard)

poche [pɔʃ] **NF 1** *(partie de vêtement)* pocket; **p. intérieure** inside pocket; **p. plaquée** patch pocket; **p. de poitrine** breast pocket; **p. revolver** hip pocket; *Fam* **faire les poches à qn** to go through *or* rifle sb's pockets; **argent de p.** pocket money; **calculatrice de p.** pocket calculator; **carnet de p.** pocketbook; **livre de p.** paperback; **j'en suis de ma p.** I'm out of pocket (by it); **payer de sa p.** to pay out of one's own pocket; *Fig* **connaître qn/ qch comme sa p.** to know sb/sth inside out *or* like the back of one's hand; *Fig Fam* **se remplir les poches, s'en mettre plein les poches** to make a packet; **j'ai cent euros en p.** I've got a hundred euros on me; **mettre qch dans sa p.** to put sth in one's pocket, to pocket sth; *Fam* **mettez ça dans votre p. (et votre mouchoir dessus)** put that in your pipe and smoke it; *Fig* **les mains dans les poches** without a care in the world; **il n'a pas sa langue dans sa p.** he's got plenty to say for himself; **ne pas avoir les yeux dans sa p.** to keep one's eyes open; **elle l'a mis dans sa p.** she's got him eating out of her hand; *Fam* **c'est dans la p.** it's in the bag

2 *(sac)* bag; **p. à cartes** map case *or* holder; **p. à tabac** tobacco pouch; *Fig* **acheter chat**

en p. to buy a pig in a poke **3** *(amas de substance)* pocket; **p. de pétrole** pocket of oil; **p. d'air** *Aviat* air pocket; *(dans une pipe)* airlock **4** *(déformation)* bag; **pantalon qui fait des poches aux genoux** trousers that are baggy *or* that bag at the knees; **poches sous les yeux** bags under the eyes **5** *Biol, Méd, Anat* sac; *(d'un kangourou etc)* pouch **6** *(filet de chasse)* purse *or* bag net; **p. de chalut** purse seine **7** *Fig (secteur)* pocket; **p. de résistance/pauvreté** pocket of resistance/deprivation **8** *Suisse (louche)* ladle

NM *Fam (livre)* paperback; **paru en (collection de) p.** published in paperback

▸▸ *Tech* **p. à couler** *ou* **de coulée** casting ladle; *Culin* **p. à douille** piping bag; *Méd* **p. des eaux** amniotic sac

poché [pɔʃe] ADJ **1** *Culin* **œuf p.** poached egg **2** *Fam* **œil p.** black eye

pocher [pɔʃe] VT **1** *Culin (œuf, poisson)* to poach **2** *Beaux-Arts* to dash off **3** *Fam* **p. l'œil à qn** to give sb a black eye; **la ferme, ou je te poche un œil!** shut up, or I'll give you one!

VI *(de vêtements)* to go *or* get baggy, to bag; **mon pantalon poche aux genoux** my trousers are going *or* getting baggy at the knees

pochetron [pɔʃtrɔ̃] NM *Fam* alky, boozer

pochette [pɔʃɛt] NF **1** *(enveloppe)* pouch; *(pour papiers)* envelope; *(pour stylos, articles de toilette)* case; *(d'un disque)* sleeve; *(pour protéger un document)* document cover; **p. d'expédition de disquette** disk mailer; **p. matelassée** Jiffy bag®, padded envelope; **p. d'allumettes** book of matches; **p.-surprise** lucky bag; *Fam* **il a eu son permis dans une p.-surprise** he's a lousy driver **2** *(petit mouchoir)* (breast) pocket handkerchief

pochoir [pɔʃwar] NM stencil; **passer qch au p.** to stencil sth; **motifs au p.** stencils, stencil(led) patterns; **brosse à p.** stencil(ling) brush

pochon [pɔʃɔ̃] NM *Région* **1** *(sac)* bag **2** *(grande louche)* ladle

pochothèque [pɔʃɔtɛk] NF paperback shop; *(rayon)* paperback section

podagre [pɔdagr] *Vieilli* NF *(goutte)* gout N gout sufferer

ADJ suffering from gout

podiatre [pɔdjatr] N *Can Méd* chiropodist, *Am* podiatrist

podium [pɔdjɔm] NM podium; **monter sur le p.** to mount the *or* take to the podium

podologie [pɔdɔlɔʒi] NF *Méd* chiropody, *Am* podiatry

podologue [pɔdɔlɔg] N *Méd* chiropodist, *Am* podiatrist

podomètre [pɔdɔmɛtr] NM pedometer

poêle[1] [pwal] NF frying pan, *Am* skillet; **passer qch à la p.** to fry sth

poêle[2] NM *(appareil de chauffage)* stove; **p. à feu continu** slow-burning stove; **p. à bois/à mazout** wood(-burning)/oil stove

poêle[3] NM *Hist (dans un mariage catholique)* canopy **2** *(drap)* pall; **tenir les cordons du p.** to be a pallbearer

poêlée [pwale] NF panful

poêler [pwale] VT to fry

poêlon [pwalɔ̃] NM casserole (dish)

poème [pɔɛm] NM poem; **p. symphonique/ en prose** symphonic/prose poem; *Fam* **c'est tout un p.** *(personne)* he's quite a character; *(situation)* it's quite a business *or* a palaver *or Br* a carry-on

poésie [pɔezi] NF **1** *(art)* poetry; **écrire** *ou* **faire de la p.** to write poetry; *Fig* **la p. du**

style/film the poetry of the style/film; **tu manques de p.** you don't have any soul; **une région pleine de p.** a region full of (poetic) charm; **la p. des grandes villes américaines** the romance of the great American cities **2** *(poème)* poem, piece of poetry

poète [pɔɛt] NM *aussi Fig* poet; **elle est devenue le grand p. de son temps** she became the greatest poet of her age

poétesse [pɔetɛs] NF woman poet, poetess

poétique [pɔetik] ADJ *(inspiration, licence etc)* poetic; **l'art p.** the art of poetry NF poetics

poétiquement [pɔetikmɑ̃] ADV poetically

poétiser [pɔetize] VT to poeticize

pogne [pɔɲ] NF *Arg (main)* paw, mitt

pognon [pɔɲɔ̃] NM *Fam (argent)* dough, bread, *Br* dosh

pogrom(e) [pogrom] NM *Hist* pogrom

POIDS [pwa] NM **1** weight; *(lourdeur)* weight, heaviness; **de tout son p.** with all one's weight, with the whole of one's weight; **surveiller son p.** to watch one's weight; **perdre du p.** to lose weight; **vendre au p.** to sell by weight; **être plié sous le p. d'un sac** to be weighed down by a sack; **ajouter qch pour faire le p.** to put sth in to make up the weight; **ne pas faire le p.** to fail to come up to weight *or* to make the (minimum) weight; *Fig Fam* **il ne fait pas le p.** he's not up to the job *or* up to scratch *or* up to it; **faire le p. face à la concurrence** to measure up to the competition; **le parti ne fait pas le p. devant le problème** the party does not measure up to the problem **2** *(charge) (dans une horloge, sur une balance)* weight; *Sport* shot; **un p. de 20 kilos** a 20-kilo weight; *Admin* **p. et mesures** weights and measures; **étalonnage des p.** standardization of weights; *Sport* **lancer le p.** to put the shot **3** *Fig (charge pénible, écrasante)* burden; *Litt* **le p. des ans** the weight of the years; **le p. des impôts** the burden of taxation; **p. de la fiscalité** tax burden; **le p. de ses soucis** the burden of his worries **4** *Fig (importance)* weight; **donner du p. à qch** to give weight to sth; **cette région finira par avoir autant de p. que Paris** this region will eventually carry as much weight as Paris; **son opinion a un certain p.** his opinion carries a certain weight

▸▸ **p. atomique** atomic weight; **p. brut** gross weight; **p. en charge** laden weight; *Boxe* **p. coq** bantamweight; **p. embarqué** shipped weight; *Boxe* **p. léger** lightweight; **p. lourd** *Aut* heavy goods vehicle, HGV, heavy lorry *or Am* truck; *Boxe* heavyweight; *Fig* **un p. lourd de la politique** a political heavyweight; *Boxe* **p. mi-moyen** welterweight; *Mktg* **p. mort** cash trap, dog, dodo; *Fig* **c'est un p. mort** he's a dead weight; *Boxe* **p. mouche** flyweight; *Boxe* **p. moyen** middleweight; **p. net** net weight; *Aut* **p. en ordre de marche** kerb weight; **p. plume** *Boxe* featherweight; *Fig* lightweight; **p. remorqué** tow weight; *Com* **p. rendu** delivered weight; **p. spécifique** *Phys* specific weight; *Chimie* specific gravity; *Com* **p. de taxation** chargeable weight; **p. total autorisé** maximum permissible weight; **p. utile** live weight; *Aviat* payload; **p. à vide** *Aut* unloaded weight, kerb weight; *Com* tare; *Boxe* **p. welter** welterweight

poignant [pwaɲɑ̃] ADJ *(moment, pensée)* poignant; *(expérience, spectacle, lecture etc)* harrowing

poignard [pwaɲar] NM dagger; **coup de p.** stab; **donner un coup de p. à qn** to stab sb; *Fig* **recevoir un coup de p. dans le dos** to get stabbed in the back

poignarder [pwaɲarde] VT to stab, *Fam* to knife; **se faire p.** to get stabbed *or Fam* knifed

poigne [pwaɲ] NF grip, grasp; *Fig* **homme à p.** *ou* **qui a de la p.** strong *or* forceful man; **un chef d'État à p.** a strong head of state, a head of state with a firm grip

poignée [pwaɲe] NF **1** *(quantité contenue dans une main) (de farine, de bonbons etc)* handful; *(de billets de banque)* fistful; **à** *ou* **par poignées** by the handful, in handfuls **2** *(petit nombre)* handful; **p. d'hommes** handful of men **3** *(de porte, sac)* handle; *(de pistolet)* grip; *(d'épée)* hilt; *Aut* **p. de maintien** passenger assist handle, grab handle; *Aut* **p. de portière** door handle **4** **p. de main** handshake; **donner une p. de main à qn** to shake hands with sb, to shake sb's hand **5** *Fam* **poignées d'amour** love handles

poignet [pwaɲe] NM **1** *Anat* wrist; *Fig* **faire qch à la force du p.** to do sth by sheer strength *or* brute force; *(à force de travail)* to do sth by sheer hard work **2** *(d'un vêtement)* cuff; *(bracelet, brassard)* wristband

poil [pwal] NM **1** *(d'un animal)* hair; *(pelage)* coat; **poils de chat** cat hairs; **p. de chameau** camelhair; **à p. long/ras** long-/short-haired; **cheval d'un beau p.** sleek horse; **chien au p. rude/à p. dur** wire-haired/rough-coated dog; *Fig* **caresser qn dans le sens du p.** to rub sb up the right way; *Fig Fam* **tomber sur le p. à qn** to lay into *or* go for sb; *Arch* **monter un cheval à p.** to ride a horse bareback; **les poils d'une brosse** the bristles of a brush **2** *Tex (d'un tissu)* nap; *(du velours)* pile **3** *(d'une personne)* hair; **poils du visage** facial hair; **poils follets** down; *Fam* **à p.** stark naked, *Br* starkers; *Fam* **se mettre à p.** to strip off; *Fam* **avoir un p. dans la main** to be bone idle *or* workshy; *Fam* **ne pas avoir un p. sur le caillou** to be as bald as a coot; *Fam* **avoir du p. aux pattes** to have hairy legs; *Fig* **reprendre du p. de la bête** to regain (one's) strength, to pick up, *Fam* to perk up; *Fig Fam* **de tous poils** of all sorts *or* kinds; *Fam* **être de bon/mauvais p.** to be in a good/bad mood; *Fam* **au quart de p.** perfectly; **démarrer au quart de p.** to start right away *or* first time; *Fam* **à un p. près** very nearly; **à un p. près, il ratait son examen** he very nearly failed his exam; **nous avons payé la même chose à un p. près** we paid more or less the same, we paid the same, or as near as makes no difference; *Fam* **un p. plus haut/moins vite** a fraction *or* a touch higher/slower; *Fam* **au (petit) p.** great, fantastic; **il est arrivé au p.** he turned up at just the right moment **4** *(d'une plante)* hair **5** **p. à gratter** itching powder

poilant [pwalɑ̃] ADJ *Fam* hilarious, screamingly funny

poiler (se) [səpwale] VPR *Fam* to kill oneself *or* die laughing

poilu [pwaly] ADJ *(qui a des poils)* hairy; **p. comme un singe** hairy as an ape NM *Fam* poilu *(French soldier 1914-1918)*

poinçon [pwɛ̃sɔ̃] NM **1** *(pointeau) (de graveur)* style, burin; *(de cordonnier)* awl, bradawl; *Couture* bodkin; **p. à glace** ice pick **2** *(matrice)* die, stamp; **p. à chiffrer** number punch **3** *(marque)* stamp; **p. de contrôle** hallmark *(stamp)*

poinçonnage [pwɛ̃sɔnaʒ], **poinçonnement** [pwɛ̃sɔnmɑ̃] NM *(de métal, cuir)* punching; *(contrôle par perforation)* punching, clipping; *(estampillage)* stamping; *(d'or, d'argent)* hallmarking

poinçonner [pwɛ̃sɔne] VT *(métal, cuir)* to punch; *(contrôler)* to punch, to clip; *(estampiller)* to stamp; *(or, argent)* to hallmark

poinçonneur, -euse [pwɛ̃sɔnœr, -øz] NM

(personne) Ind puncher; *(à la gare)* ticket puncher

NF **poinçonneuse** punching machine

poindre [pwɛ̃dr] VI *(prp* **poignant;** *pp* **point;** *pr ind* **il point, ils poignent;** *imp* **il poignait;** *p hist* **il poignit;** *fu* **il poindra;** *used esp in third person and in inf) (du jour)* to dawn, to break; *(des plantes, des étoiles)* to appear, to come out; **le jour point à l'horizon** day is breaking; **p. à l'horizon** *(apparaître)* to come into view

poing [pwɛ̃] NM fist; **se battre poings nus** to fight with one's bare fists; **sabre/revolver au p.** sword/revolver in hand; **serrer les poings** to clench one's fists; **menacer qn du p., montrer le p. à qn** to shake one's fist at sb; **les poings sur les hanches** hands on hips, arms akimbo; **dormir à poings fermés** to sleep soundly *or* like a log; **coup de p.** punch; **coup de p. (américain)** knuckleduster; **donner un coup de p. à qn** to punch sb; **recevoir un coup de p.** to be punched; *Fam* **envoyer son p. dans la figure de qn,** *très Fam* **mettre son p. sur** *ou* **dans la gueule de qn** to give sb a punch in the face, to bash *or* smash sb's face in; **taper du p. sur la table** to bang one's fist (down) on the table, to pound the table; *Fig* to put one's foot down; **lever le p.** to give a raised-fist salute; **ils défilaient le p. levé** they marched past with their fists raised *or* with raised fists; *Suisse* **faire le p. dans sa poche** to swallow one's anger

POINT¹ [pwɛ̃]

point **1–3, 11, 13, 14** ▪ spot **1, 10** ▪ place **1** ▪ stitch **4, 6** ▪ dot **9, 10** ▪ full stop **9** ▪ period **9** ▪ stage **11** ▪ extent **11**

NM **1** *(dans l'espace)* point, spot, place; *aussi Fig* **p. de départ** starting point, point of departure; **p. de vue** *(panorama)* view; *Fig (opinion)* point of view, viewpoint, standpoint; **au** *ou* **du p. de vue international/économique** from an international/economic point of view *or* viewpoint; *Fam* **du** *ou* **au p. de vue caractère/rapidité** as far as character/speed is concerned, character-/speed-wise; **en tous points** in every way, in all respects; *Tech, Fig* **p. critique** critical point; *Aviat* **essai au p. fixe** ground run

2 *(dans le temps)* point; **le p. du jour** daybreak, dawn; **être sur le p. de faire qch** to be about to do sth, to be on the point *or* verge of doing sth; **sur le p. de mourir** at *or* on the point of death; **arriver à p. nommé** *ou* **juste à p.** to arrive just at the right moment; **tout vient à p. à qui sait attendre** everything comes to him who waits

3 *(question)* point; **p. de droit** point of law; **le p. capital** the main point; **traiter un problème en trois points** to deal with a problem in three stages; **mettre son** *ou* **un p. d'honneur à ne pas céder** to make it a point of honour not to yield; **n'ayez aucune crainte sur ce p.** don't worry on that score *or* on that count; **je suis d'accord avec vous sur ce p.** I agree with you on that point; **exécuter un ordre p. par p.** to carry out an order exactly *or* to the letter

4 *Couture* stitch; **faire un p. à un vêtement** to put a few stitches in a garment; **p. arrière** backstitch; **p. de Bruxelles** Brussels lace; **p. de chaînette** chainstitch; **p. de chausson** herringbone stitch; **p. de croix** cross-stitch; **p. devant** *ou* **glissé** *ou* **coulé** running stitch; **p. de feston** buttonhole stitch; **p. de languette** blanket stitch; **p. noué** knot stitch; **p. perdu** blind *or* slip stitch; **coudre qch à points perdus** to blindstitch *or* slipstitch sth; **p. roulé** whipping

5 *Tricot* stitch; **p. de riz** moss stitch; **p. mousse** garter stitch

6 p. de côté *(douleur)* stitch (in one's side);

avoir un p. au dos to have a stabbing pain in one's back

7 *Naut, Aviat* **p. estimé** dead reckoning (position); **faire le p.** to take bearings, to find one's position

8 *Opt* **au p.** in focus; **mettre au p.** *(lentilles, objectif, caméra etc)* to focus; *(moteur)* to tune; *(mécanisme)* to adjust; *(technique)* to perfect; *(projet, stratégie)* to finalize; **mise au p.** *(de lentilles, d'objectif etc)* focusing; *(d'un moteur)* tuning; *(d'un mécanisme)* adjusting; *(d'une technique)* perfecting; *(d'un projet, d'une stratégie)* finalization, finalizing; **leur organisation n'est pas vraiment au p.** their organization is really not up to scratch; **faire le p.** to take stock; **faire le p. sur l'affaire Martin** to take stock of the Martin affair; *Vieilli* **recherche et mise au p.** research and development

9 *(marque)*, *Typ* dot; *(sur les dés)* pip; *(dans une adresse électronique)* dot; **p. (final)** full stop, *Am* period; **mettre les points sur les i** to dot one's i's; *Fig* to make one's meaning perfectly plain; **deux points** colon; **(trois) points de suspension** suspension points *(en parlant ou en dictant)* dot, dot, dot; *Fam* **tu restes ici, un p., c'est tout!** *ou* **p. final!** *ou* **p. à la ligne!** *ou* **p. barre!** you're staying here and that's final *or* that's that!, *Am* you're staying here, period!; *Tél* **points et traits** *(de l'alphabet Morse)* dots and dashes; *Typ* **caractères de huit points** eight-point type; *Typ* **points par pouce** dots per inch; *Ordinat* **gdupont arrobas transex, p., co, p., uk** *(adresse électronique)* gdupont at transex, dot, co, dot, uk

10 *(marque visible)* speck, spot, dot; **le navire n'est qu'un p. à l'horizon** the ship is a mere speck on the horizon

11 *(phase, degré)* point, stage; *(étendue)* degree, extent; *Culin* **(cuit) à p.** done to a turn; *(steak)* medium-rare; **jusqu'à un certain p.** to a certain extent, up to a (certain) point; **au p. où en sont les choses** as matters stand, as things are; **au p. où j'en suis** the way things are at the moment (for me); **à ce p. que …, à tel p. que …, au p. que …** to such a point *or* an extent that …, so much so that …; **ils étaient déçus au p. qu'ils ont préféré rentrer directement** they were so disappointed that they preferred to return right away; **vous n'êtes pas malade à ce p.-là** you're not as ill as all that; **au dernier p.** to *or* in the last degree

12 mal en p. in a bad way

13 *(de jeux)* point; *Scol* mark; **marquer les points** to keep (the) score; **elle a marqué 10 points** she scored 10 points; *Fig* **là, tu marques un p.!** that's one up to you!; *Boxe* **gagner aux points** to win on points; **rendre des points à qn** to give sb points; *Fig* to be more than a match for sb; *Scol* **bon p.** good mark

14 *(unité)* point; **l'indice des prix gagne/perd deux points** the retail price index has gone up/down (by) two points

15 *Ordinat* **en mode p.** bitmap, bitmapped ▸▸ *Aut* **p. allumage** firing point; *Aut* **p. d'ancrage** anchor(age) point; **p. d'appui** *Mil etc* base of operations; *Méd* pressure point; *Tech (de levier)* fulcrum; *Fig (d'un argument, d'une théorie)* basis; *Naut* **p. d'attache** mooring (post); *Géog* **points cardinaux** cardinal points, points of the compass; *Ordinat* **p. de césure** breakpoint, hyphenation point; **p. chaud** *(pendant une guerre)* hot spot, trouble spot; *Fig* **les points chauds de l'actualité** the most topical issues of the day; *Typ* **points de conduite** dotted leader; **p. de congélation** freezing point; *TV, Cin* **p. diffus** soft focus; *Mktg* **p. de distribution** distribution outlet; **p. d'eau** *(dans le désert)* waterhole; *(dans un camping)* water supply point; **p. d'ébullition à sec** dry boiling point;

p. d'éclair flash point; *TV etc* **p. d'entrée** *(d'une bande)* inpoint; **p. d'exclamation** exclamation mark *or Am* point; **p. faible** weak point; *TV, Cin* **p. focal** focus; **p. fort** strong point; **p. de fusion** melting point; **p. de graissage** lubricating point; *Aut* **p. d'inflammation** point of ignition; **p. d'interrogation** *Typ, Fig* question mark; *Mktg (produit)* question mark; *Fig* **ce qu'il lui a dit? on ne sait pas, c'est le p. d'interrogation** what did he say to him? we don't know, that's the question we're all asking; **p. d'intersection** (point of) intersection; *Aut* **p. de levage** *(au cric)* jacking *or* jack point; *Math* **points limites** limit points; **p. de mire** target; *Fig* **p. de mire de tous les yeux** *(critiqué)* target for criticism; *(admiré)* focus of attention, *Fml* cynosure; *TV, Cin* **p. de montage** edit point; **p. mort** *Aut* neutral; *Fin* breakeven (point); *Fig* **être au p. mort** to be at a standstill; *Fig* **p. noir** *(comédon)* blackhead; *Fig* problem; *(à l'avenir)* cloud on the horizon; *Aut* accident blackspot; *(embouteillage)* blackspot; *Mus* **p. d'orgue** pause, fermata; *Fig* climax, highpoint; *Aut* **p. de prise** *(d'embrayage)* take-up point; **p. prix** price point; **p. de référence** benchmark; **p. retrait** cashpoint; *Com* **p. de saturation** saturation point; *Tech* **p. de soudure** weld spot; **p. de tabulation** *Ordinat* tab marker; *Typ* tab set; *Aut* **p. talon** accelerator heel point; *Com* **p. de vente** point of sale; *(magasin)* sales outlet; **disponible dans votre p. de vente habituel** available at your local stockist; *Com* **p. de vente au détail** retail outlet; *Com* **p. de vente électronique** electronic point of sale, EPOS

point² ADV *Vieilli, Litt, Dial* = **pas²;** **peu ou p.** little or not at all; **le connaissez-vous? – p.** do you know him? – not at all; **depuis plusieurs semaines, p. de nouvelles** there's been no news (at all) for several weeks SEE GRAMMAR 862

pointage [pwɛ̃taʒ] NM **1** *(contrôle) (de noms sur une liste)* checking, ticking off; *(de votes)* counting; *Naut (d'une carte marine)* pricking; *(d'une position sur une carte)* plotting; *(à l'usine)* timekeeping; *(à l'arrivée)* clocking in; *(au départ)* clocking out; **p. des salariés** signing-in of employees **2** *Mus (d'une note)* dotting **3** *(d'un télescope)* pointing, levelling, training; *(de fusil)* aiming, training

pointe [pwɛ̃t] NF **1** *(extrémité) (d'aiguille, de couteau etc)* point; *(de flèche)* tip, head; *(de balle)* nose; *(de chaussure)* toe; *(d'une flèche d'église)* top; *(de sein)* nipple; *Rail* **p. d'une aiguille** point of a switchblade; **p. de l'épée** at the point of a sword; *Fig Vieilli* **j'ai obtenu mon contrat à la p. de l'épée** I had to fight hard to get my contract; **en p.** pointed; **partir en p., former une p.** to taper to a point; **tailler en p.** to cut (in)to a point; *(crayon)* to sharpen; *Fam* **je vais te tailler les oreilles en p.!** I'll box your ears!; **p. de lance** spearhead; **marcher/se tenir sur la p. des pieds** to walk/stand on tiptoe; **entrer sur la p. des pieds** to tiptoe in; **faire des pointes** *(en danse)* to go up on points

2 *(moment d'intensité)*, *Math, Élec, Méd (d'une courbe, d'une charge, de la fièvre)* peak; *Sport* **p. de vitesse** burst of speed, spurt; **faire une p. de vitesse** to put on a burst of speed *or* a spurt; **avec des pointes de vitesse de 160 km/h** with a top speed of 160 km/h; **dans les pointes de vitesse, on peut faire du 200 km/h** at top speed you can do 200 km/h; **vitesse de p.** top *or* highest speed; **heure de p.** rush hour; **période de p.** peak period; *Litt* **p. du jour** daybreak, dawn

3 *Mil (d'une sentinelle avancée)* point; **nous avons poussé une p. jusqu'à** *ou* **sur Paris** we pressed on *or* pushed on to Paris; *Naut* **tir en p.** firing ahead; **être à la p. du progrès/de la**

recherche to be in *or* at the forefront of progress/of research, to be at the cutting *or* leading edge of progress/of research; **à la p. de l'actualité** in the headlines, very much in the news; *Fig* **les secteurs de p.** the high-tech industries, the most advanced sectors of industry; **industrie de p.** high-tech *or* state-of-the-art industry; **technologie de p.** state-of-the-art technology, leading-edge technology; **c'est de la technologie de p.** it's very state-of-the-art

4 *(petite quantité, trace)* hint, touch, tinge; **parler avec une p. d'accent** to speak with a hint of an accent; **p. d'ironie** touch *or* hint *or* tinge of irony; **p. d'ail** touch of garlic; **p. de vanille** dash of vanilla

5 *(raillerie)* barb, pointed remark; **lancer des pointes à qn** to make digs at sb

6 *Géog* **p. (de terre)** headland, foreland

7 *(outil)* *(de maçon)* point; *Menuis* **p. carrée** bradawl; **p. à tracer** scribe

8 *(clou)* nail; *(pour tapis)* tack; *Sport (sur une chaussure)* spike; **chaussures à pointes** spiked shoes, spikes; **casque à p.** spiked helmet

9 *(lange)* nappy, *Am* diaper; *(écharpe, foulard)* (triangular) scarf

▸ ▸ **p. d'asperge** asparagus tip; **p. Bic®** ballpoint (pen), *Br* Biro®; *Méd* **pointes de feu** ignipuncture; *Beaux-Arts* **p. sèche** (dry) point; *(procédé)* dry-point (engraving); *Élec* **p. de tension** surge, spike

pointeau, -eaux [pwɛto] NM **1** *Tech* centre *or Am* center punch; *(de carburateur)* needle **2** *Vieilli (personne)* timekeeper **3** *(sur un autocuiseur)* pressure valve

pointer¹ [pwɛte] VT **1** *(vérifier) (noms sur une liste)* to check, to tick off; *(votes)* to count; *Naut (carte marine)* to prick; *(position sur une carte)* to plot

2 *(dresser)* **p. les oreilles** to prick up its ears; **le chien arriva en pointant le bout de son museau** the dog arrived with its muzzle in the air; *Fig* **il pointa son nez à la porte** his face appeared around the door, he peeped around the door; **s'il pointe son nez ici, je lui donne une gifle!** if he shows his face here, I'll give him one!; **il n'a pas pointé le bout de son nez depuis longtemps** he hasn't looked in *or* been round for a long time

3 *(diriger) (télescope)* to point (**sur** at), to train (**sur** on); *(fusil)* to aim, to level (**sur** at), to train (**sur** on); *(spot, projecteur)* to train (**sur** on); *Ordinat (curseur)* to position (**sur** on); *Ordinat* **pointé** *(mot, page)* where the cursor is/was; **j'ai pointé le doigt vers lui** I pointed (my finger) at him

4 *(signaler, révéler)* to point to

5 *Mus (note)* to dot; **note pointée** dotted note

6 *Vieilli (piquer) (avec une épée)* to stab; *(avec une aiguille)* to prick

VI **1** *(d'employé) (en arrivant)* to sign in; *(en partant)* to sign out; **p. (à l'arrivée/à la sortie)** *(à l'usine)* to clock in/out; **p. à l'ANPE** *au chômage* to register unemployed

2 *(apparaître)* to appear; *(d'une plante)* to come up; *(d'un oiseau)* to soar; *(d'un cheval)* to rear up; *(du jour)* to dawn; **ses seins pointaient sous son corsage** her firm breasts were clearly outlined beneath her bodice; **ses os pointaient** his bones were sticking out; **le clocher de l'église pointait vers un ciel d'azur** the church steeple soared into *or* rose towards a bright blue sky

3 *(au jeu de boules)* = to get one's ball nearest to the jack

VPR **se pointer** *Fam* to turn up, to show up

pointer² [pwɛtœr] NM *(chien)* pointer

pointeur, -euse [pwɛtœr, -øz] N *(contrôleur)* *Ind* timekeeper; *Sport* scorer, marker

NF **pointeuse** *(horloge)* (time)clock

NM *Ordinat* pointer; **p.-balle** beachball

pointer; **p.-croix** crosshair pointer; **p.-montre** watch pointer; **p. de pile** stack pointer; **p. en I** I-beam

pointillage [pwɛtijaʒ] NM *Beaux-Arts* dotting; *(plus serré)* stippling

pointillé [pwɛtije] ADJ *(ligne)* dotted; *(gravure)* stippled; *Tex (tissu)* pinhead

NM **1** *(trait)* dotted line; *(sur une feuille détachable)* perforations; **détacher suivant les pointillés** tear along the dotted line/the perforations **2** *(technique de dessin)* stippling; **dessin en p.** stippled design; **ligne en p.** dotted line; *Fig* **on pouvait lire en p. des allusions à son passé glorieux** reading between the lines, we saw certain allusions to his glorious past

pointiller [pwɛtije] VT **1** *(percer de petits trous)* to dot **2** *Beaux-Arts* to stipple

VI *Péj Arch* to cavil (over trifles), to split hairs

pointilleux, -euse [pwɛtijø, -øz] ADJ particular, fussy, finicky, *Fam* pernickety (**sur** about)

pointillisme [pwɛtijism] NM *Beaux-Arts* pointillism

pointilliste [pwɛtijist] ADJ, N *Beaux-Arts* pointillist

pointu [pwɛty] ADJ **1** *(en forme de pointe)* pointed; *(aigu) (couteau)* sharp, pointed; *(voix)* shrill **2** *Fig (susceptible) (ton de la voix, humeur)* touchy; **prendre un air p.** to bridle **3** *Fig (spécialisé)* specialized, specialist

ADV *Région Fam* **parler p.** to speak with a Parisian accent

pointure [pwɛtyr] NF *(de chaussures, de gants, de coiffure)* size; **quelle est votre p. (de gants/de chaussures)?, quelle p. faites-vous?** what size (gloves/shoes) do you take?, what's your (glove/shoe) size?; *Fig Fam* **une (grosse) p. du cinéma français/de la physique nucléaire** a big name in French cinema/in nuclear physics

point-virgule, *pl* **points-virgules** NM semicolon

poire [pwar] NF **1** *(fruit)* pear; **entre la p. et le fromage** at the end of the meal; *Fig* **garder une p. pour la soif** to put something by for a rainy day; *Fig* **couper la p. en deux** to compromise; *(faire la moyenne entre deux quantités)* to split the difference; **en forme de p.** pear-shaped **2** *(objet en forme de poire)* *(d'un appareil photo)* (pear-shaped) bulb; *(d'un interrupteur électrique)* (pear-shaped) switch; **p. à lavement** enema bag **3** *Fam (tête)* mug, face; **il a une bonne p.** he's got a nice enough face, he looks nice enough; **en pleine p.** right in the face **4** *Fam (idiot)* sucker, *Br* mug; **je ne suis pas une p.!** I'm no sucker *or Br* mug!; **je suis vraiment trop bonne p.,** je lui pardonne toujours tout I'm a real sucker *or Br* mug, I let him get away with everything; **et moi, bonne p., j'ai accepté** and like the sucker *or Br* mug that I am, I accepted

poiré [pware] NM perry

poireau, -eaux [pwaro] NM *(légume)* leek; *Fam* **faire le p.** to be kept hanging around *or* waiting, to kick *or* cool one's heels

poireauter [pwarote] VI *Fam* to be kept hanging around *or* waiting, to kick *or* cool one's heels; **faire p. qn** to keep sb hanging around *or* waiting, to leave sb to kick *or* cool his/her heels

poirée [pware] NF *Bot* white beet

poirier [pwarje] NM **1** *(arbre)* pear tree; *Gym* **faire le p.** to do a headstand, to stand on one's head **2** *(bois)* pear-tree wood

pois [pwa] NM **1** *(plante)* pea; *Culin* **petits p.** (garden) peas; **purée de p.** thick pea soup; *Fam (brouillard)* peasouper **2** *(rond)* spot, (polka) dot; **cravate bleue à p. blancs** blue tie with white spots, blue polka-dot tie; **tis-**

su/**robe à p.** spotted *or* polka-dot material/dress

▸ ▸ **p. carré** marrowfat pea; **p. cassés** split peas; **p. chiche** chickpea; **p. de senteur** sweet pea

poiscaille [pwaskɑj] NM *Fam* fish

poison [pwazɔ̃] NM **1** *(substance fatale)* poison **2** *Fig Fam* **quel p.!** what a drag *or* bind!, how boring!

N *Fam (personne, chien etc)* pest, horror

poissard, -arde [pwasar, -ard] ADJ vulgar, coarse

NF *Vieilli Péj* **poissarde** fishwife

poisse [pwas] NF *Fam* bad luck; **c'est la p.!** just my/our luck!; **porter la p. (à qn)** to bring (sb) bad luck

poisser [pwase] VT **1** *(engluer)* to pitch; **fil poissé** waxed thread **2** *(salir avec une matière gluante)* to make sticky **3** *Fam Vieilli (personne)* to nab, to collar

VI *(d'une substance)* to be sticky

poisseux, -euse [pwasø, -øz] ADJ sticky

poisson [pwasɔ̃] NM **1** fish; **p. d'eau douce/de mer** freshwater/saltwater fish; **prendre un/du p.** to catch a/some fish; **je n'aime pas le p.** I don't like fish; **manger du p.** to eat fish; **p. d'avril!** April fool!; **c'est un p. d'avril** it's an April fool's trick; **être (heureux) comme un p. dans l'eau** to be really in one's element; *Fam* **engueuler qn comme du p. pourri** to give sb a real mouthful; *Fam* **se faire engueuler comme du p. pourri** to get a real mouthful; *Prov* **petit p. deviendra grand** great oaks from little acorns grow VOIR GRAMMAIRE A12 **2** *Astron, Astrol* **les Poissons** Pisces; **être (du signe des) Poissons** to be (a) Pisces

▸ ▸ *Entom* **p. d'argent** silverfish; **p.-chat** catfish; **p. lune** sunfish; **p. pilote** pilot fish; **p. plat** flatfish; **p. rouge** goldfish; **p. volant** flying fish

---

Poisson d'avril

In France and in French-speaking countries, on the first of April, children cut fish shapes out of paper and stick them on their unsuspecting classmates' backs, and people play practical jokes on one another before crying out "Poisson d'avril!" ("April fool!"). This custom is referred to in Quebec as "courir le poisson d'avril".

---

poissonnerie [pwasɔnri] NF *(magasin)* fish shop, *Br* fishmonger's; *(marché)* fish market

poissonneux, -euse [pwasɔnø, -øz] ADJ full of fish

poissonnier, -ière [pwasɔnje, -jɛr] N *Com* fishmonger, *Am* fish merchant

NM *(bateau)* = small boat used to buy fish direct from fishing boats

NF **poissonnière** *(ustensile)* fish kettle

poitevin [pwatvɛ̃] ADJ *(de Poitiers)* of/from Poitiers; *(du Poitou)* of/from Poitou

N *(de Poitiers)* = inhabitant of or person from Poitiers; *(du Poitou)* = inhabitant of or person from Poitou

poitrail [pwatraj] NM **1** *(partie du corps de certains animaux)* breast; *Fig Fam (poitrine)* chest; **un homme au p. découvert** a man with a bare chest **2** *(partie de harnais)* breast strap, breastplate

poitrinaire [pwatrinɛr] ADJ, N *Vieilli* consumptive

poitrine [pwatrin] NF **1** *(poumons)* chest; **chanter à pleine p.** to sing at the top of one's voice; **être fragile de la p.** to have a weak chest; *Arch* **s'en aller de la p.** to be dying of consumption; *Mus* **voix de p.** chest voice **2** *(thorax)* chest, *Litt* breast; *(de femme)* bosom, bust, chest; **serrer qn contre** *ou* **sur sa p.** to hold *or* press *or* clasp sb to one's breast; **tour de p.** *(d'un homme, d'un enfant)* chest (measurement); *(d'une femme)* bust (measurement); **avoir une belle/forte p.** to have a shapely bosom/be well-endowed; **ne pas avoir de p.** to be flat-chested, to have no bust; **ne pas avoir beaucoup de p.** to be small-chested, to have a small bust; **elle n'a pas encore de p.** her bust hasn't started to develop yet **3** *Culin (de veau)* breast; *(de bœuf)* brisket; *(de porc)* belly

poivrade [pwavrad] NF *Culin (sauce)* = sauce made by reducing a heavily peppered mixture of wine and vinegar; **manger des artichauts à la p.** to eat artichokes (raw) with salt and pepper

poivre [pwavr] NM pepper; **p. blanc/noir** *ou* **gris** white/black pepper; **p. vert/rouge** green/red pepper; **p. de Cayenne** cayenne (pepper); *Culin* **steak au p.** pepper steak; **grain de p.** peppercorn; **des cheveux p. et sel** pepper-and-salt hair; **une femme p. et sel** a woman with pepper-and-salt hair

poivré [pwavre] ADJ **1** *(nourriture)* peppery; *(odeur)* pungent, spicy **2** *Fig (grivois) (histoire)* spicy, juicy **3** *Fam (ivre)* wasted, *Br* sloshed

poivrer [pwavre] VT to put pepper on/in, to season with pepper
▪ VPR **se poivrer** *Fam (boire)* to get plastered *or* smashed

poivrier [pwavrije] NM **1** *Bot* pepper plant **2** *(petit pot)* pepper pot; *(moulin)* pepper mill

poivrière [pwavrijer] NF **1** *(plantation)* pepper plantation **2** *(boîte)* pepper pot **3** *Archit* pepperpot (turret)

poivron [pwavrɔ̃] NM *Bot* (sweet) pepper, capsicum, *Am* bell pepper; **p. vert/rouge/jaune** green/red/yellow pepper

poivrot, -ote [pwavro, -ɔt] N *Fam* drunk, alky

poix [pwa] NF pitch; **p. sèche** resin; **p. liquide** tar; **noir comme (de la) p.** pitch black; **collant comme de la p.** sticky as glue

poker [pɔkɛr] NM *Cartes* poker; **faire un p.** to have a game of poker; **p. d'as** *(cartes)* four aces; *(dés)* poker dice; *Fig* **une partie de p.** a poker game, a game of bluff (and counter-bluff); *Fig* **c'est un coup de p.** it's a game of bluff

Polac, Polack [pɔlak] N *Fam Péj (Polonais)* Polack

polaire [pɔlɛr] ADJ polar; **l'étoile P.** the Pole Star; **froid p.** intense *or* Arctic cold; **expédition p.** polar expedition, expedition to the (North/South) Pole; **laine p.** fleece, fleecy material; **fourrure p.** fleecy jacket
▪ NF *Math* polar; *Astron* **la P.** the Pole Star

polar [pɔlar] NM *Fam (livre, film)* whodunnit

polard, -arde [pɔlar, -ard] *Arg* N swot
▪ ADJ **être p.** to be a swot

polarimètre [pɔlarimɛtr] NM *Phys* polarimeter

polarisable [pɔlarizabl] ADJ polarizable

polarisant [pɔlarizɑ̃] ADJ polarizing

polarisation [pɔlarizasjɔ̃] NF **1** *Phys (de la lumière, d'électrodes)* polarization, polarizing; *Électron* **p. de grille** grid bias; **résistance de p. de grille** bias resistor **2** *Fig (focalisation) (d'attention, d'énergies etc)* focusing

polariscope [pɔlariskɔp] NM *Opt* polariscope

polariser [pɔlarize] VT *Phys, Électron* to polarize; *Fig (attention)* to attract; **ce phénomène polarise l'attention de tous** this phenomenon is the focus of everybody's attention; **cette décision a polarisé le mécontentement des masses salariales** this decision has become the focus of the workers' discontent; **p. qn** *ou* **p. l'attention de qn sur qch** to focus sb's attention on sth
▪ VPR **se polariser** *Fam (de l'attention)* to focus;

se p. sur qch *(d'une personne)* to focus one's attention on sth

polariseur [pɔlarizœr] NM *Opt* polarizer

polarité [pɔlarite] NF polarity

Polaroïd® [pɔlarɔid] NM *Phot (appareil)* Polaroid® (camera)

polatouche [pɔlatuʃ] NM *Zool* flying squirrel

polder [pɔldɛr] NM *Géog* polder

pôle [pol] NM **1** *Géog* pole; **p. Nord/Sud** North/South Pole; *Phys* **pôles semblables** like poles; **pôles contraires** opposite poles; **pôles magnétiques** magnetic poles **2** *Fig* **p. d'intérêt** focus of interest; **p. d'attraction** centre of attention; **un p. d'attraction économique/touristique** a centre of economic/ tourist development; *Écon, Pol* **les pôles de croissance** the main centres of economic growth; **p. de reconversion** development *or* reconversion zone

polémique [pɔlemik] ADJ polemical
▪ NF argument, controversy, *Fml* polemic; **faire de la p.** to provoke arguments, to be controversial; **chercher la p.** to look for an argument; **une vive p. s'ensuivit** a heated argument ensued

polémiquer [pɔlemike] VI to argue

polémiste [pɔlemist] N polemicist

polémologie [pɔlemɔlɔʒi] NF study of war

polenta [pɔlɛnta] NF *Culin* polenta

pole position [pɔlpozisjɔ̃] NF *(dans une course automobile)* **être en p.** to be in pole position

poli¹ [pɔli] ADJ **1** *(lisse) (métal)* polished, burnished, buffed; *(pierre)* polished **2** *(élégant) (style)* polished, elegant
▪ NM shine, polish, gloss

poli² ADJ *(courtois) (personne, réponse, manières)* polite, civil; **être très p. avec qn** to be very polite *or* very courteous to sb; **il est trop p. pour être honnête** he's so polite that I'm suspicious of him; **peu p.** impolite, rude, discourteous

police¹ [pɔlis] NF **1** *(maintien de l'ordre)* maintenance of law and order; *(par la police)* policing; **exercer** *ou* **faire la p.** to maintain law and order, to keep order; *(au bureau, dans une classe etc)* to keep order; *Aut Vieilli* **numéro de p.** registration *or Am* license number; **intervention des forces de p.** police intervention, intervention by the police; *Jur* **tribunal de (simple) p.** magistrate's court; *Mil* **salle de p.** guardroom
2 *(institution)* **la p.** the police (force); **appeler la p.** to call the police; **appeler p. secours** ≃ to dial *Br* 999 *or Am* 911 (for the police); **être de** *ou* **dans la p.** to be in *or* to be a member of the police (force); *Fig Hum* **tu n'es pas de la p. à ce que je sache!** what is this, the Spanish Inquisition?, what is this, Twenty Questions?; **p.!, les mains en l'air!** police!, hands up!; **remettre qn entre les mains de la p.** to give sb up to the police; **la p. est à vos trousses** the police are after you *or* are (hot) on your heels; **la guerre des polices** = rivalry between different police departments; **toutes les polices de France sont à ses trousses** the entire French police force are hot on his heels; **p. de la circulation** traffic police; **p. administrative** = administrative branch of the police; **p. judiciaire** *Br* ≃ Criminal Investigation Department, *Am* ≃ Federal Bureau of Investigation; **p. municipale** local police; **la p. nationale** = national police force; **p. mondaine** *ou* **des mœurs** ≃ vice squad; **p. de l'air et des frontières** airport and border police; **p. de l'immigration** immigration police; **p. secrète** secret police; *Fam* **la p. des polices** *Br* ≃ Complaints Investigation Bureau, *Am* ≃ Internal Investigation Board; **p. montée** mounted police; **p.**

parallèle secret police; **agent de p.** police officer; *(de circulation)* traffic policeman; **inspecteur de p.** (police) inspector; **commissaire de p.** *Br* ≃ (police) superintendent, *Am* ≃ (police) captain; **préfet de p.** ≃ chief commissioner of police VOIR GRAMMAIRE A11

> ### Police nationale
> The "Police nationale" operates under the authority of the Ministry of the Interior, unlike the "Gendarmerie", which is an army corps.

police² NF **1** *Jur* (insurance) policy; **prendre une p.** to take out a policy; **p. d'assurance (sur la) vie/(contre l')incendie** life insurance/fire insurance policy; **p. d'assurance maritime** marine insurance policy; *Com* **p. de chargement** bill of lading; **p. individuelle crédit acheteur** individual buyer credit policy; **p. individuelle crédit fournisseur** individual supplier credit policy; *Com* **p. ouverte** open policy; **p. tous risques** comprehensive policy, all-risks policy; **p. universelle** worldwide policy; **p. au voyage** travel insurance policy **2** *Typ, Ordinat* **p. (de caractères)** font; **p. bâton** sans serif font; **p. bitmap** *ou* **pixélisée** bitmap font; **p. par défaut** default font; **p. proportionnelle** proportional font; **p. de taille variable** scalable font; **p. vectorielle** outline font

policé [pɔlise] ADJ civilized

policeman [pɔlisman] NM (British) policeman

policer [pɔlise] VT *(je poliçai(s); n. poliçons)* **1** *Arch (gouverner)* **p. un pays** to bring a country under orderly government **2** *Arch, Litt (civiliser)* to civilize

polichinelle [pɔliʃinɛl] NM **1** *(marionnette)* Punch; **théâtre de p.** ≃ Punch and Judy show; **secret de p.** open secret; *Fig Fam* **avoir un p. dans le tiroir** *(être enceinte)* to have a bun in the oven, to be in the pudding club **2** *Fig Péj* buffoon; **faire le p.** to act *or* play the fool

policier, -ière [pɔlisje, -jɛr] ADJ *(enquête, État, chien etc)* police; *(roman, film)* detective
▪ NM **1** *(officier de police)* policeman, police officer; **femme p.** woman police officer VOIR GRAMMAIRE A11 **2** *(roman)* detective novel; *(film)* detective film

policlinique [pɔliklinik] NF outpatients' clinic *or* department

poliment [pɔlimɑ̃] ADV politely

polio [pɔljo] *Méd* NF *(maladie)* polio
▪ N polio victim

poliomyélite [pɔljɔmjelit] NF *Méd* poliomyelitis

poliomyélitique [pɔljɔmjelitik] *Méd* ADJ *(vaccin)* polio; *(personne)* suffering from polio
▪ N polio victim

polir [pɔlir] VT **1** *(poncer) (métal)* to polish, to burnish, to buff; *(pierre)* to polish; **poli par l'usage** shiny with use; **poli par l'érosion/le temps** made smooth by erosion/the passage of time **2** *(perfectionner) (style, discours etc)* to polish (up); *(manières)* to refine
▪ VPR **se polir se p. les ongles** to polish *or* buff one's nails

Polisario [pɔlisarjo] N *Pol* **le Front P.** the Polisario

polissage [pɔlisaʒ] NM *(de métal)* polishing, burnishing, buffing; *(des ongles)* polishing, buffing

polisseur, -euse [pɔlisœr, -øz] N polisher
▪ NF **polisseuse** *(machine)* polishing machine, polisher

polissoir [pɔliswar] NM *Tech* buffing wheel; *(de graveur)* grinding disc; *(pour les ongles)* nail buffer

polissoire [pɔliswar] NF **1** *(brosse) (pour chaussures)* (polishing) brush **2** *Ind (atelier)* polishing shop

polisson, -onne [pɔlisɔ̃, -ɔn] N **1** *(enfant espiègle)* rascal, scamp **2** *Vieilli Fam (gamin des rues)* street urchin
▪ ADJ **1** *(méchant) (enfant)* naughty, mischievous **2** *(coquin, grivois)* smutty; **regard p.** leer

polissonner [pɔlisɔne] VI *Vieilli (d'un enfant)* to be mischievous *or* naughty

polissonnerie [pɔlisɔnri] NF **1** *(espièglerie)* mischievous trick **2** *Vieilli (parole)* smutty remark; *(plaisanterie)* smutty joke

politesse [pɔlites] NF politeness, courtesy; **il est toujours d'une grande p. avec les gens** he is always very polite *or* courteous to people; **dire/faire qch par p.** to say/do sth out of politeness *or* to be polite; **brûler la p. à qn** to leave sb abruptly, to leave without saying goodbye to sb; **faire des politesses à qn** to be polite to sb; **faire échange de politesses** to exchange compliments; **ce serait la moindre des politesses de le prévenir** it's only polite to warn him; **il m'a rendu la p.** he returned the favour *or Am* favor; *(invitation)* he returned my invitation; *(mauvais tour)* he paid me back

politicaillerie [pɔlitikajri] NF *Fam Péj* political scheming

politicard, -arde [pɔlitikar, -ard] *Fam Péj* N political schemer
▪ ADJ scheming

politicien, -ienne [pɔlitisjɛ̃, -jɛn] N politician, *Am Fam* politico
▪ ADJ *Péj* politicking; **politique politicienne** politicking; **faire de la politique politicienne** to politick

politique [pɔlitik] ADJ **1** *(de la société, du gouvernement)* political; **homme/femme p.** politician; **ambitionner une carrière p.** to have political ambitions; **le corps p.** the body politic; **détenu p.** political prisoner; **économie p.** economics, political economy **2** *Arch, Litt (réponse, choix, conduite)* politic
▪ NF **1** *(de gouvernement, d'entreprise)* policy; **p. intérieure/extérieure** domestic/foreign policy; **suivre** *ou* **adopter une nouvelle p.** to follow *or* adopt a new policy; **la p. de l'autruche** burying one's head in the sand; **pratiquer la p. de l'autruche** to bury one's head in the sand; **pratiquer la p. de la chaise vide** to make a political point by not attending meetings; **p. de la main tendue** policy of the outstretched hand; **pratiquer la p. de la main tendue** to make friendly overtures, to be conciliatory; **la p. du pire** = deliberately worsening the situation to further one's ends; *Écon* **p. de la porte ouverte** open-door policy; **p. de droite/gauche** right-wing/left-wing policy; *UE* **la p. agricole commune** the Common Agricultural Policy; **p. d'apaisement** policy of appeasement; **p. d'austérité** austerity policy; **p. budgétaire** budgetary *or* fiscal policy; **p. commerciale** trade policy; *UE* **p. communautaire** EU policy; *UE* **p. commune de la pêche** Common Fisheries Policy; *Mktg* **p. de communication** promotional policy; **p. conjoncturelle** economic policy *(responding to changes in the business cycle)*; *Pol* **p. conventionnelle** = policy relating to union-management agreements; *Fin* **p. de crédit** credit policy; **p. économique** economic policy; *Journ* **p. éditoriale, p. de la rédaction** *(principe)* editorial policy; **p. étrangère** foreign policy; *UE* **p. étrangère et de sécurité commune** Common Foreign and Security Policy; **p. fiscale** fiscal policy; **p. industrielle** industrial policy; **p. de libre-échange** free-trade policy; **p. monétaire** monetary policy; **p. d'ouverture** consensus politics; **p. de plein emploi** policy of full em-

ployment; **p. politicienne** party politics; *Mktg* **p. de vente** sales policy; **p. des prix** pricing policy; **p. de relance** reflationary policy; **p. de rigueur** policy of austerity; **p. des salaires** wages policy; **p. sécuritaire** repressive law-and-order policy
▪ **2** *(affaires publiques)* politics; **parler/discuter de p.** to talk/discuss politics; **se lancer dans la p.** to go into politics; **faire de la p.** to be in politics; **tu sais, moi, je ne fais pas de p.** I'm not politically inclined; *Fig* **p.-fiction** political fiction; **scénario de p.-fiction** scenario belonging to the realms of political fiction; **un roman de p.-fiction** a political novel VOIR GRAMMAIRE A10

polity NM **1** *(personne)* politician **2** *Fig (domaine)* politics; **le p. français** French politics

> **Attention:** ne pas confondre **politics** et **policy** lorsque l'on traduit **politique**. **Politics** est un terme indénombrable qui désigne la politique en tant que discipline, alors que le terme **policy** est un terme dénombrable qui désigne un ensemble de mesures.

politiquement [pɔlitikmɑ̃] ADV *Pol* politically; *Fig Litt* politically, diplomatically; **p. correct** politically correct

politiquer [pɔlitike] VI *Arch Fam* to talk politics

politisation [pɔlitizasjɔ̃] NF politicization

politiser [pɔlitize] VT *(chose)* to politicize, to bring politics into; *(personne)* to politicize; **plus/moins/très politisé** more/less/very politically inclined *or* political

politologie [pɔlitɔlɔʒi] NF political science

politologue [pɔlitɔlɔg] N political scientist

polka [pɔlka] NF polka

pollen [pɔlɛn] NM pollen

pollinisation [pɔlinizasjɔ̃] NF pollination

polliniser [pɔlinize] VT to pollinate

polluant [pɔlɥɑ̃] ADJ polluting; **produit p.** pollutant
▪ NM pollutant

pollué [pɔlɥe] ADJ polluted; **région fortement polluée** highly polluted region, region with a high level of pollution

polluer [pɔlɥe] VT to pollute

pollueur, -euse [pɔlɥœr, -øz] N polluter; **le principe du p.-payeur** 'the polluter pays' principle
▪ ADJ polluting

pollution [pɔlysjɔ̃] NF **1** *(dégradation de l'environnement)* pollution; **p. atmosphérique** atmospheric *or* air pollution; **p. automobile** traffic pollution **2** *Méd* **pollutions nocturnes** wet dreams, *Spéc* nocturnal emissions

polo [pɔlo] NM **1** *Sport* polo **2** *(chemise)* polo shirt

polochon [pɔlɔʃɔ̃] NM *Fam* bolster; **bataille de polochons** pillow fight; **se battre à coups de polochons** to have a pillow fight

Pologne [pɔlɔɲ] NF Poland

polonais, -aise [pɔlɔnɛ, -ɛz] VOIR GRAMMAIRE A19 ADJ Polish
▪ NM *Ling* Polish
▪ N **P.** Pole; *Fam* **soûl comme un P.** as drunk as a lord
▪ NF *Mus* **polonaise** polonaise

polonium [pɔlɔnjɔm] NM *Chimie* polonium

poltron, -onne [pɔltrɔ̃, -ɔn] ADJ cowardly
▪ N coward

poltronnerie [pɔltrɔnri] NF cowardice

polyacide [pɔliasid] ADJ, NM *Chimie* polyacid

polyamide [pɔliamid] NM *Chimie* polyamide

polyandre [pɔljɑ̃dr] ADJ polyandrous

polyandrie [pɔljɑ̃dri] NF polyandry

polyarthrite [pɔliartrit] NF *Méd* polyarthritis

polycentrisme [pɔlisɑ̃trism] NM *Pol* polycentrism

polychrome [pɔlikrom] ADJ polychrome, polychromatic

polychromie [pɔlikromi] NF polychromy

polyclinique [pɔliklinik] NF *Méd* polyclinic

polycopie [pɔlikɔpi] NF *(procédé)* duplicating, duplication; *(document)* duplicate

polycopié [pɔlikɔpje] ADJ duplicated
▪ NM duplicate; *Scol, Univ* (duplicated) course material; *(plus petit)* handout

polycopier [pɔlikɔpje] VT to duplicate

polyculture [pɔlikyltyr] NF *Agr* mixed farming

polydactyle [pɔlidaktil] ADJ polydactyl

polyèdre [pɔliɛdr] *Géom* ADJ polyhedral
▪ NM polyhedron

polyédrique [pɔliedrik] ADJ *Géom* polyhedral

polyester [pɔliɛstɛr] NM *Chimie* polyester

polyéthylène [pɔlietilɛn] NM polythene, *surtout Am* polyethylene

polygame [pɔligam] ADJ polygamous
▪ N polygamist

polygamie [pɔligami] NF polygamy

polyglotte [pɔliglɔt] ADJ, N polyglot

polygonal, -ale, -aux, -ales [pɔligɔnal, -o] ADJ polygonal

polygone [pɔligon] NM **1** *Géom* polygon **2** *Mil* shooting range

polygraphe [pɔligraf] N versatile writer

polyinsaturé [pɔliɛ̃satyre] ADJ *(lipide)* polyunsaturated

polymère [pɔlimɛr] *Chimie* ADJ polymeric
▪ NM polymer

polymérisation [pɔlimerizasjɔ̃] NF *Chimie* polymerization

polymorphe [pɔlimɔrf] ADJ polymorphous, polymorphic

polymorphie [pɔlimɔrfi] NF, **polymorphisme** [pɔlimɔrfism] NM polymorphism

Polynésie [pɔlinezi] NF Polynesia

polynésien, -ienne [pɔlinezjɛ̃, -jɛn] ADJ Polynesian
▪ N **P.** Polynesian

polynôme [pɔlinom] NM *Math* polynomial

polynucléaire [pɔlinykleɛr] ADJ *Biol* polynuclear

polype [pɔlip] NM *Méd, Zool* polyp

polypétale [pɔlipetal] ADJ *Bot* polypetalous

polypeux, -euse [pɔlipø, -øz] ADJ *Méd* polypous

polyphasé [pɔlifaze] ADJ *Élec (système)* polyphase, multiphase

polyphonie [pɔlifɔni] NF *Mus* polyphony

polypropylène [pɔliprɔpilɛn] NM polypropylene

polysémie [pɔlisemi] NF *Ling* polysemy

polysémique [pɔlisemik] ADJ *Ling* polysemous

polysoc [pɔlisɔk] NM *Agr* multiple plough *or Am* plow

polystyle [pɔlistil] ADJ *Archit (salle, temple)* polystyle

polystyrène [pɔlistirɛn] NM *Chimie* polystyrene; **boîte en p.** polystyrene box

polysyllabe [pɔlisilab] ADJ *(mot)* polysyllabic
▪ NM polysyllable

polysyllabique [pɔlisilabik] ADJ polysyllabic

polytechnicien, -ienne [pɔliteknisjɛ̃, -jɛn] N student at the École polytechnique; *(diplômé)* graduate of the École polytechnique

polytechnique [politɛknik] ADJ **École p.** = grande école specializing in technology
NF **P.** = grande école specializing in technology

Il faut noter que le nom anglais **polytechnic** est un faux ami. Il désigne un établissement d'enseignement supérieur comparable à un IUT.

École polytechnique
Founded in 1794, this prestigious engineering college has close connections with the Ministry of Defence. Formerly situated in the heart of the 5th arrondissement, the college moved to Palaiseau, near Paris, in the 1970s. It is popularly known as "l'X". Students are effectively enlisted in the army and must repay their education through government service.

polythéisme [politeism] NM polytheism
polythéiste [politeist] N polytheist
ADJ polytheistic
polythène [politɛn] NM *Chimie* polythene
polytransfusé, -ée [politrɑ̃sfyze] *Méd* ADJ who has/had received multiple blood transfusions
N person who has/had received multiple blood transfusions
polytraumatisé [politromatize] ADJ *Méd* suffering from multiple injuries
polyuréthane [poliyretan] NM *Chimie* polyurethane
polyvalence [polivalɑ̃s] NF *Chimie* polyvalency, multivalency; *Fig (d'une personne)* versatility
polyvalent [polivalɑ̃] ADJ **1** *Chimie* polyvalent, multivalent **2** *Fig (salle)* multipurpose; *(outil)* versatile, multipurpose; *(personne)* versatile; *Admin* **inspecteur p.** tax inspector
NM *Admin* tax inspector
polyvinyle [polivinil] NM *Chimie* polyvinyl; **chlorure de p.** polyvinyl chloride
polyvinylique [polivinilik] ADJ *Chimie* polyvinyl
pomélo [pomelo] NM pomelo
Poméranie [pomerani] NF *Géog* Pomerania; **loulou de P.** Pomeranian, *Fam* Pom
pommade [pomad] NF *Méd* ointment; *Arch (pour les cheveux)* pomade; **p. pour les lèvres** lip salve; *Fig Fam* **passer de la p. à qn** to butter sb up
pommader [pomade] VT *Arch (cheveux)* to pomade
pomme [pom] NF **1** *(fruit)* apple; **p. à cuire** cooking apple, *Br* cooker; **p. à couteau** eating apple; **p. à cidre** cider apple; **compote de pommes** stewed apples, *Am* applesauce; *Fig Fam* **c'est toujours pour ma p.** it's always yours truly that gets it; *Fam* **je ne veux pas voir sa p. ici** I don't want to see him/her here; *Fam* **ramener sa p.** to turn up, to roll up; *Fam* **haut comme trois pommes** knee-high to a grasshopper; *Fam* **tomber dans les pommes** to pass out, to faint; *Fam* **aux pommes** super, great; *Myth* **les pommes d'or du jardin des Hespérides** the golden apples of Hesperides **2** *(cœur)* *(de salade, de chou)* heart **3** *(partie arrondie)* *(de bois de lit, de canne etc)* knob; *(d'arrosoir)* rose; *Naut (de mât)* truck; **canne à p. d'or** gold-headed stick; **p. de douche** shower head **4** *Fam (personne naïve)* sucker, *Br* mug, *Am* patsy **5** *Suisse (eau de vie de pomme)* apple brandy ▶▶*Anat* **p. d'Adam** Adam's apple; **pommes allumettes** matchstick chips *or Am* potatoes; **p.**

d'amour *(tomate)* love apple; **p. d'api** = type of small red and white apple; **p. cannelle** custard apple; **p. de chêne** oak apple; **pommes chips** (potato) crisps *or Am* chips; **pommes dauphine** dauphine potatoes; *Fig* **p. de discorde** bone of contention; **pommes duchesse** duchesse potatoes; **p. épineuse** thorn apple; **pommes frites** (French) fries, *Br* chips; **pommes noisette** = small potato croquettes; **p. de pin** pine cone; *(de sapin)* fir cone; **p. reinette** pippin; **p. sauvage** crab apple; **p. de terre** potato; **pommes de terre à l'eau** boiled potatoes; **p. de terre au four** *ou* **en robe de chambre** *ou* **en robe des champs** baked potato, jacket potato; **pommes de terre frites** (French) fries, *Br* chips; **pommes vapeur** steamed potatoes
pommé [pome] ADJ **1** *(laitue, chou)* hearty, firm (and round) **2** *Fam Vieilli (idiot, gaffe)* complete, downright
pommeau, -eaux [pomo] NM *(d'un sabre, d'une selle)* pommel; *(d'une canne à pêche)* butt; *(d'une canne, d'un levier de vitesse)* knob; **p. de douche** shower head
pommelé [pomle] ADJ dappled, mottled; **gris p.** *(cheval)* dapple-grey; **ciel p.** mackerel sky
pommeler (se) [səpomle] VPR (**il se pommelle; il se pommellera**) **1** *(du ciel)* to become covered *or* dappled with small fleecy clouds **2** *(d'un chou, d'une laitue)* to form a head *or* heart
pommelle [pomɛl] NF grating *(over drainpipe etc)*
pommer [pome] VI *(d'un chou, d'une laitue)* to form a head *or* heart
pommeraie [pomrɛ] NF apple orchard
pommette [pomɛt] NF *Anat* cheekbone; **avoir les pommettes saillantes** to have high cheekbones
pommier [pomje] NM apple tree; **p. sauvage** crab (apple) tree
pompage [pɔ̃paʒ] NM pumping; *Aut (de moteur)* hunting; *TV, Radio (d'une bande)* flutter; **station de p.** pumping station
pompe[1] [pɔ̃p] NF *(cérémonie)* pomp, ceremony; **en grande p.** with great (pomp and) ceremony; **las de la cour et de ses pompes** tired of all the pomp and ceremony
pompe[2] NF **1** *(machine)* pump; **puiser l'eau à la p.** to pump out the water; **prendre de l'eau à la p.** to get water from the pump; *Fam* **avoir le** *ou* **un coup de p.** to feel done in *or* shattered all of a sudden; **une barre de chocolat pour le coup de p. de onze heures** a chocolate bar for when you need an energy boost; *Fam* **à toutes pompes** like lightning, at top speed; *Sport Fam* **faire des pompes** to do push-ups *or Br* press-ups **2** *Mus* **p. d'accord** *(d'un instrument à vent)* (tuning) slide **3** **serrure à p.** high security lock **4** *Fam* **pompes** *(chaussures)* shoes; **ça, c'est de la p.!** those are some shoes!; *Fig* **être bien/mal dans ses pompes** to have got it together/be mixed up; *Fig* **il est à côté de ses pompes** he's not with it, he's not himself **5** *Mil Arg* **(soldat de) deuxième p.** squaddie, *Am* grunt ▶▶**p. à air** air pump, pneumatic pump; **p. d'alimentation** *ou* **alimentaire** feed pump; **p. aspirante** suction pump, lift pump; **p. aspirante et foulante** lift-and-force pump; **p. de bicyclette** bicycle pump; **p. à bière** beer pump; **p. à carburant** fuel pump; **p. à chaleur** heat pump; *Aut* **p. distributrice** distributor pump; *Aut* **p. à eau** water pump; **p. à essence** *(de moteur)* fuel pump; *(distributeur)* petrol *or Am* gas pump; *(station-service)* petrol *or Am* gas station; **p. foulante** force pump; **pompes funèbres** undertaker's, funeral di-

rector's, *Am* mortician's; **ordonnateur** *ou* **entrepreneur de pompes funèbres** undertaker, funeral director, *Am* mortician; *Aut* **p. de graissage** grease gun; *Tech* **p. à graisse** grease gun; *Aut* **p. à huile** oil pump; **p. à incendie** water pump *(on a fire engine)*; *Aut* **p. d'injection** injection pump, injector pump; **p. pneumatique** air *or* pneumatic pump; **p. refoulante** force pump; *Aut* **p. de refoulement** *ou* **de relevage** lift pump; *Aut* **p. de reprise** accelerator *or* acceleration pump; *Fam* **p. à vélo** bicycle pump; **p. à vide** vacuum pump; *Aut* exhauster
pompé [pɔ̃pe] ADJ *Fam (épuisé)* bushed, *Br* knackered
Pompée [pɔ̃pe] N Pompey
Pompéi [pɔ̃pei] N Pompeii
pompéien, -ienne [pɔ̃pejɛ̃, -jɛn] ADJ Pompeiian
N **P.** Pompeiian
pomper [pɔ̃pe] VT **1** *(puiser)* *(eau, air)* to pump; *(faire monter)* to pump up; *(évacuer)* to pump out; **p. de l'eau du puits** to pump (up) water from the well; **p. de l'air dans un pneu** to pump air into a tyre; **des parasites qui pompent le sang** parasites that suck blood; *Fig Fam* **p. qn** *(épuiser)* to do sb in, to wear sb out; *Fam* **être pompé** to be done in *or* shattered; *Fam* **tu me pompes l'air** you're getting on my nerves **2** *Fam (boisson)* to knock back **3** *Scol Fam* to copy (**sur qn** from sb)
VI **1** *(faire marcher une pompe)* to pump **2** *Scol Fam* to copy (**sur qn** from sb)
pompette [pɔ̃pɛt] ADJ *Fam* tipsy, *Br* merry
pompeusement [pɔ̃pøzmɑ̃] ADV *Péj* pompously
pompeux, -euse [pɔ̃pø, -øz] ADJ *Péj* pompous
pompier [pɔ̃pje] NM **1** fireman, fire fighter; **p. de service** fire officer; **appeler les pompiers** to call the fire brigade *or Am* the fire fighters; *Fam* **fumer comme un p.** to smoke like a chimney **2** *Vulg (fellation)* blow job; **faire un p. à qn** to give sb a blow job
pompier, -ière [pɔ̃pje, -jɛr] *Beaux-Arts Péj* ADJ *(art, style, tableau)* pompous
NM artist with a pompous style
pompiste [pɔ̃pist] N *Aut* (petrol *or Am* gas) pump attendant, forecourt attendant
pom-pom girl, *pl* **pom-pom girls** [pɔmpɔmgœrl] NF cheerleader
pompon [pɔ̃pɔ̃] NM pompom, bobble; **bonnet à p.** bobble hat; *Fam* **ça, c'est le p.!** that's the limit!, that's the last straw!; *Iron* **avoir le p.** to be the limit, to take the biscuit *or Am* cake; *Fam Vieilli* **avoir son p.** to be tipsy
pomponner (se) [səpɔ̃pɔne] VPR *Fam* to doll oneself up
ponçage [pɔ̃saʒ] NM **1** *(action de poncer)* *(à la pierre ponce)* pumicing; *(au papier de verre)* sandpapering; *(de peinture)* rubbing down, sanding down; *(avec une ponceuse)* sanding **2** *Beaux-Arts* pouncing
ponce [pɔ̃s] NF **(pierre) p.** pumice (stone)
Ponce Pilate [pɔ̃spilat] N *Bible* Pontius Pilate
poncer [pɔ̃se] VT (**je ponçai(s); n. ponçons**) **1** *(passer à la pierre ponce)* to pumice; *(au papier de verre)* to sandpaper; *(peinture)* to rub down, to sand down; *(avec une ponceuse)* to sand **2** *Beaux-Arts* to pounce
ponceur [pɔ̃sœr] NM polisher
ponceuse [pɔ̃søz] NF sander, sanding machine
poncho [pɔ̃tʃo] NM poncho
poncif [pɔ̃sif] NM **1** *Beaux-Arts* pouncing pattern **2** *(banalité, évidence)* cliché, commonplace

ponction [pɔ̃ksjɔ̃] NF *Méd* puncture; *(de poumon)* tapping; **p. lombaire** lumbar puncture; *Fig* **faire une p./des ponctions dans ses économies** to draw on one's savings; *Admin* **p. fiscale** taxation; **c'est une p. importante sur mes revenus** it makes a big hole or dent in my income

ponctionner [pɔ̃ksjɔne] VT *Méd* to puncture; *(poumon, malade)* to tap; *Fig Fam (argent)* to draw on; **on nous ponctionne un tiers de notre salaire en impôts** a third of our salary goes in tax

ponctualité [pɔ̃ktɥalite] NF punctuality

ponctuation [pɔ̃ktɥasjɔ̃] NF punctuation

ponctuel, -elle [pɔ̃ktɥɛl] ADJ **1** *(à l'heure)* punctual **2** *Phys* **source ponctuelle de chaleur** pinpoint flame; **source lumineuse ponctuelle** point source; **projecteur p.** spotlight **3** *Fig (qui ne concerne qu'un point) (opération, aide)* ad hoc; **intervention ponctuelle du gouvernement** exceptional action by the government; **nous n'avons fait que des changements ponctuels** we have made only selective changes; **débrayage p.** one-off stoppage; **les terroristes ne se livraient qu'à des actions ponctuelles** the terrorists made only sporadic attacks

ponctuellement [pɔ̃ktɥɛlmɑ̃] ADV *(de façon limitée)* on an ad hoc basis

ponctuer [pɔ̃ktɥe] VT *(phrase)* to punctuate; **elle ponctua ses explications de silences** her explanation was punctuated with silences

pondaison [pɔ̃dɛzɔ̃] NF egg-laying time

pondérable [pɔ̃derabl] ADJ *Tech* weighable

pondéral, -ale, -aux, -ales [pɔ̃deral, -o] ADJ weight; **surcharge pondérale** excess weight

pondérateur, -trice [pɔ̃deratœr, -tris] ADJ stabilizing, balancing

pondération [pɔ̃derasjɔ̃] NF **1** *(d'une personne)* level-headedness; *(symétrie, équilibre)* balance; **parler/agir avec p.** to speak/act level-headedly **2** *Écon (d'un indice)* weighting; *Math* **coefficient de p.** weighting

pondéré [pɔ̃dere] ADJ **1** *(équilibré, calme) (esprit)* well-balanced; *(personne)* level-headed **2** *Écon* **indice p.** weighted index; **moyenne pondérée** weighted average

pondérer [pɔ̃dere] VT *(je pondère; je pondérerai)* **1** *(équilibrer)* to balance **2** *Écon (indice, moyenne)* to weight

pondéreux, -euse [pɔ̃derø, -øz] *Tech* ADJ *(marchandises etc)* heavy
NMPL **les p.** heavy goods

pondeur, -euse [pɔ̃dœr, -øz] ADJ (egg-)laying; **poule pondeuse** laying hen
NF **pondeuse** *(poule)* (good) layer; *Fig Péj* **quelle pondeuse!** *(femme)* she's like a battery hen!
NM *Péj* **p. de prose** prolific scribbler; **p. de tableaux** prolific dauber; **c'est un p. d'articles/de romans** he just churns out articles/novels

pondoir [pɔ̃dwar] NM nest box

pondre [pɔ̃dr] VT **1** *(œuf)* to lay; **œuf frais pondu** new-laid or newly laid or freshly laid egg **2** *Fam (mettre au monde) (enfant)* to produce **3** *Fig Fam (texte, solution)* to come up with; *(articles, romans)* to churn out; **elle a pondu une de ces traductions!** she came up with a great translation!; **p. une lettre tous les jours** to churn out a letter every day

poney [pɔnɛ] NM pony

pongiste [pɔ̃ʒist] N *Sport* table tennis player

Pont (le) [pɔ̃] NM *Antiq* **1** the (Kingdom of) Pontus **2** **le P.-Euxin** the Euxine Sea, the Black Sea

pont [pɔ̃] NM **1** *Constr* bridge; *Admin* **les Ponts et Chaussées** Department of Civil En-

gineering; **École des Ponts et Chaussées** = specialist institute of Civil Engineering; *Mil* **tête de p.** bridgehead; **vivre sous les ponts** to be a tramp; *Fig* **il est passé de l'eau sous les ponts** a lot of water has passed or flowed under the bridge; *Fig* **faire le p.** = to take the intervening day or days off; *Fig* **le p. de la Pentecôte** the (long) Whitsun Bank Holiday weekend
2 *Naut* deck; **faux p.** orlop deck; **navire à un p.** single-decker (ship), single-deck ship; **navire à deux/trois ponts** two-/three-decker; **homme** ou **matelot de p.** deck hand; *(dans la marine)* upper-deck rating; **sur le p.** on deck; **tout le monde sur le p.!** all hands on deck!; *(dans la marine)* clear lower deck!; *Com* **sur p.** free on board, fob
3 *Tech* live axle; *Aut* drive axle
4 *Fig* link; **assurer un p. entre Paris et la province** to provide a link between Paris and the provinces; **couper les ponts** to break off all relations or sever all links or sever all ties (**avec qn** with sb)
▸▸ **p. aérien** airlift; **p. aux ânes** *Géom* pons asinorum; *Fig* (piece of) common knowledge; **p. arrière** *Aut* rear or back axle; *Naut* afterdeck; **p. autoroutier** motorway bridge, overpass; **p. avant** foredeck; **p. basculant** ou **à bascule** drawbridge, bascule bridge; **p. de bateaux** floating or pontoon bridge; **p. cantilever** cantilever bridge; *Ind* **p. à chariot culbuteur** tipping stage; **p. à consoles** cantilever bridge; *Ind* **p. de décharge** tipping stage; **p. élévateur** *(dans un garage)* (repair) ramp; **p. des embarcations** boat deck; **p. des emménagements** saloon deck; **p. en encorbellement** cantilever bridge; **p. d'envol** *(d'un porte-avions)* flight deck; **p. des gaillards** upper deck; **p. de graissage** *(dans un garage)* ramp; **p. inférieur** lower deck; **p. de manœuvre** hurricane deck; **p. d'or** golden hello; **faire un p. d'or à qn** to offer a golden hello to sb; **p. pour piétons** footbridge; **p. pivotant** swing bridge; **p. des premières** saloon deck; **p. principal** main deck; **p. promenade** promenade deck; *(sur un paquebot)* sun deck, hurricane deck; *Ind* **p. roulant** travelling crane; *(support)* gantry; *Ordinat* **p. routeur** routing node; **p. supérieur** upper deck; **p. suspendu** suspension bridge; **p. tournant** swing bridge; **p. tubulaire** box (girder) bridge; **p. volant** flying bridge; *Élec* **p. de Wheatstone** Wheatstone bridge

pontage [pɔ̃taʒ] NM **1** *Constr* bridge building; *(travaux)* bridging **2** *Naut* decking **3** *Méd* bypass (operation); **p. coronarien** heart bypass (operation); **on lui a fait un p.** he's had a bypass, he's had bypass surgery

pont-bascule, *pl* **ponts-bascules** NM drawbridge, bascule bridge; *(pour peser les poids lourds)* weighbridge

ponte¹ [pɔ̃t] NF *(action)* (egg) laying; *(œufs)* eggs (laid); **p. ovulaire** ovulation

ponte² NM **1** *(aux jeux de hasard)* punter **2** *Fam (personnage important)* big shot; **un grand p. de la médecine** a big shot in medicine

ponté [pɔ̃te] ADJ decked; **non p.** open

pontée [pɔ̃te] NF *Naut* deck load, deck cargo

ponter¹ [pɔ̃te] VT *Naut (navire)* to lay the deck(s) of, to deck

ponter² VI *(aux jeux de hasard)* to punt

pontier [pɔ̃tje] NM *Tech* swing-bridge keeper

pontife [pɔ̃tif] NM *Rel* pontiff; *Fig Fam* big shot, bigwig; **le souverain p.** the Supreme Pontiff; *Fig Fam* **les pontifes de l'hôpital** the bigwigs or top brass at the hospital

pontifiant [pɔ̃tifjɑ̃] ADJ *Fam Péj* pontificating

pontifical, -ale, -aux, -ales [pɔ̃tifikal, -o]
ADJ pontifical, papal
NM pontifical

pontificat [pɔ̃tifika] NM pontificate; **sous le p. de Jean-Paul II** during the pontificate of John Paul II

pontifier [pɔ̃tifje] VI *(impf, pr sub n.* **pontifiions, v. pontifiiez***)* to pontificate

pont-l'évêque [pɔ̃levɛk] NM INV Pont-l'Évêque (cheese)

pont-levis, *pl* **ponts-levis** [pɔ̃l(ə)vi] NM drawbridge; **p. à fléau** ou **à balancier** lever drawbridge

Pont-Neuf [pɔ̃nœf] NM *Fig* **être solide comme le P.** to have the constitution of an ox, to be as fit as a fiddle

ponton [pɔ̃tɔ̃] NM **1** *(construction flottante)* pontoon; **p. d'incendie** fire float; **p. d'atterrissage** (floating) landing stage **2** *Naut Vieilli (prison flottante)* hulk, prison ship

pontonnier [pɔ̃tɔnje] NM **1** *Mil* pontoneer, pontonier **2** *(gardien)* swing-bridge keeper

pool [pul] NM **1** *Écon* pool; **p. d'assurances** insurance pool; **p. bancaire** banking pool **2** *(équipe)* **p. de dactylos** typing pool; **p. de secrétaires** secretarial pool

pop [pɔp] ADJ INV, NF *(musique)* **p.** pop (music); **chanteur p.** pop singer

pop art [pɔpart] NM *Beaux-Arts* pop art

pop-corn [pɔpkɔrn] NM INV popcorn; **on a mangé du p./des p.** we ate (some) popcorn

pope [pɔp] NM *Rel* pope (of the Orthodox Church)

popeline [pɔplin] NF *Tex* poplin

popote [pɔpɔt] NF **1** *Fam (cuisine)* cooking; **faire la p.** to do the cooking **2** *Mil* canteen; *(mess)* officers' mess
ADJ INV *Fam souvent Péj (personne)* stay-at-home

popotin [pɔpɔtɛ̃] NM *Fam* bum, *Am* butt; **se manier le p.** to get a move on

populace [pɔpylas] NF *Péj* rabble, riff-raff, mob

populacier, -ière [pɔpylasje, -jɛr] ADJ *Péj* vulgar, common

populage [pɔpylaʒ] NM *Bot* marsh marigold

populaire [pɔpylɛr] ADJ **1** *(du peuple)* popular; **démocratie p.** popular or people's democracy; **manifestation p.** mass demonstration **2** *(pour le peuple)* **chanson p.** popular song; **expression p.** vernacular expression; **un roman p.** a low-brow novel; **bal p.** (local) dance *(open to the public)*; **la soupe p.** the soup kitchen **3** *(ouvrier)* working-class; **les classes populaires** the working classes; **quartier p.** working-class district **4** *(qui plaît)* popular; **se rendre p.** to make oneself popular

populairement [pɔpylɛrmɑ̃] ADV *(s'exprimer, parler)* in the vernacular

populariser [pɔpylarize] VT to popularize

popularité [pɔpylarite] NF popularity; **cote de p.** popularity rating

population [pɔpylasjɔ̃] NF population
▸▸ **p. active** working population, labour force; *Mktg* **p. cible** target population; **p. inactive** non-working population; **p.-mère** basic population; **p. prévue** projected population

populationnisme [pɔpylasjɔnism] NM = policy of population growth

populationniste [pɔpylasjɔnist] ADJ **politique p.** policy of population growth; **gouvernement p.** government in favour of population growth

populeux, -euse [pɔpylø, -øz] ADJ populous, densely populated

populisme [pɔpylism] NM *Littér* populism

populiste [pɔpylist] ADJ, N *Littér* populist

populo [pɔpylo] NM *Fam* **1** le p. ordinary people, *Péj* the riffraff, the rabble **2** *(foule)* crowd (of people)

poquet [pɔkɛ] NM *Agr* seed hole

porc [pɔr] NM **1** *(animal)* pig, *Am* hog; *Fam (homme grossier)* pig, slob; **gardeur de porcs** pig keeper, pigman, *Arch* swineherd; **p. sauvage** wild boar; **(peau de) p.** pigskin; **sale comme un p.** filthy (dirty); **manger comme un p.** to eat like a pig **2** *Culin* pork; **côtelette de p.** pork chop

porcelaine [pɔrsəlɛn] NF **1** *Cér (matière)* porcelain, china; *(objet)* piece of porcelain or china; **p. de Chine** china; **p. de Saxe** Dresden china; **p. tendre (anglaise)** bone china **2** *(mollusque)* cowrie

porcelainier, -ière [pɔrsəlenje, -jer] ADJ industrie porcelainière porcelain or china industry
N porcelain or china manufacturer

porcelet [pɔrsəlɛ] NM piglet, young pig

porc-épic [pɔrkepik], *pl* **porcs-épics** [pɔrkepik] NM porcupine; *Fam (personne)* prickly person; **c'est un vrai p.** *(il pique)* his face is all bristly

porche [pɔrʃ] NM porch

porcher, -ère [pɔrʃe, -er] N pig keeper, *Arch* swineherd

porcherie [pɔrʃəri] NF piggery; *(enclos)* pigsty, *Am* pigpen; *Fig Péj* **quelle p.!** what a pigsty or pigpen!

porcin [pɔrsɛ̃] ADJ pig, *Fml* porcine; **élevage p.** pig breeding; **peste porcine** swine fever, *Am* hog cholera; *Fig Péj* **un visage p.** a piggy face; **yeux porcins** piggy eyes
NMPL **porcins** pigs, swine, *Am* hogs

pore [pɔr] NM *(de peau, de plante, de pierre)* pore; **avoir les pores dilatés** to have open pores; *Fig* **il sue la couardise par tous les pores** he exudes cowardice from every pore

poreux, -euse [pɔrø, -øz] ADJ porous

porno [pɔrno] *Fam* ADJ *(abrév* **pornographique)** *(film, magazine, scène)* porn, porno; **des photos pornos** dirty pictures
NM *(abrév* **pornographie)** **1** le p. *(genre)* porn; *(industrie)* the porn industry **2** *(film)* blue movie, *Br* porno film

pornographe [pɔrnɔgraf] N pornographer

pornographie [pɔrnɔgrafi] NF pornography

pornographique [pɔrnɔgrafik] ADJ pornographic

porosité [pɔrozite] NF porosity, porousness

porphyre [pɔrfir] NM *Minér* porphyry

porreau [pɔro] NM *Suisse (poireau)* leek

porridge [pɔridʒ] NM *Culin* porridge

port¹ [pɔr] NM **1** *(abri)* harbour, *Am* harbor; *(plus important)* port; **capitaine de p.** harbour master; **droits de p.** harbour dues, port charges; **entrer dans le p.** to enter harbour; **entrer au p.** to come into port; **quitter le p.** to leave port, to clear the harbour; *Fig* **arriver à bon p.** to arrive safe and sound; **Dunkerque est le premier p. de France** Dunkirk is the largest port in France; *Naut* **les ports de la métropole** the home ports
2 *Ordinat* port; *(pour Internet)* socket; **p. de communication** comms port, communications port; **p. d'entrée/sortie** input/output port; **p. d'E/S** I/O port; **p. d'extension** expansion port; **p. d'imprimante** printer port; **p. (de connexion pour) jeux** games port; **p. modem** modem port; **p. parallèle** parallel port; **p. SCSI** SCSI port; **p. série** serial port; **p. série universel** USB, universal serial bus; **p. souris** mouse port; **p. USB** USB port
▸▸ **p. d'armement** port of registry, *Am* port of documentation; **p. d'arrivée** port of arrival, port of entry; **p. artificiel** artificial port; **p. d'attache** home port, port of commission-

ing; *Com* port of registry; *Fig* home base; **p. de commerce** commercial port; **p. pour conteneurs** container port; *Com* **p. de départ** port of departure; *Com* **p. d'embarquement** port of loading, port of embarkation; **p. d'entrée** port of entry; **p. d'escale** port of call; **p. pour ferry** ferry port; **p. fluvial** river port; **p. franc** free port; **p. de guerre** naval port, naval base; **p. lacustre** lakeside port; **p. maritime** *ou* **de mer** seaport; *Com* **p. militaire** naval port, naval base; **p. naturel** natural harbour; **p. de pêche** fishing port; **p. de plaisance** marina; **p. de transit** port of transit

port² NM **1** *(fait de porter)* carrying; **permis de p. d'armes** permit for carrying firearms; *Mil* **se mettre au p. d'armes** to shoulder arms **2** *(fait de revêtir)* *(de vêtement, lunettes, barbe)* wearing; **le p. du casque est obligatoire** *(sur panneau)* safety helmets must be worn; *(en moto)* crash helmets must be worn **3** *(transport payant)* *(de marchandises)* carriage; *(de paquet, de lettre, de télégramme)* delivery; **ports de lettres, frais de p.** postage, postal charges; **en p. dû** carriage forward, freight collect; **p. avancé** carriage forward, freight collect, freight forward; **p. compris** postage included; **p. débours** carriage forward paid against invoice; **p. en lourd** deadweight, dwt; **p. et emballage** postage and packing, p&p; **p. forfait** = carriage forward paid in a lump sum in advance; **p. franc, p. payé, franc(o) de p.** *(de revue, de journal)* postage paid; *(de marchandise)* carriage paid or free, freight collect; **p. payé, assurance comprise** carriage insurance paid **4** *(allure)* *(d'une personne)* bearing, carriage; **un p. de reine** a regal or queenly bearing; **un gracieux p. de tête** a graceful manner of holding one's head **5** *Bot (d'une plante)* habit **6** *Naut (d'un navire)* burden, tonnage

port³ NM *(dans les Pyrénées)* pass

portabilité [pɔrtabilite] NF *Ordinat* portability

portable [pɔrtabl] ADJ **1** *(facilement transportable)* *(machine à écrire, ordinateur etc)* portable; *(ordinateur)* laptop; *Ordinat (programme)* portable; **téléphone p.** mobile (phone), *Am* cellphone **2** *(mettable)* *(vêtement)* wearable, presentable **3** *Jur* payable at the address of the payee
NM *Ordinat* laptop; *Tél* mobile (phone), *Am* cellphone

portage [pɔrtaʒ] NM **1** *(transport)* *(de marchandises)* porterage, conveyance, transport; *(de bateau)* portage; **frais de p.** porterage **2** *(partie d'un fleuve)* portage **3** *Banque* piggybacking

portager [pɔrtaʒe] VI *Can* to portage

portail [pɔrtaj] NM *aussi Ordinat* portal

portance [pɔrtɑ̃s] NF *Aviat* lift (per unit area)

portant [pɔrtɑ̃] ADJ **1** *(qui soutient)* **mur p.** load-bearing wall; **à bout p.** at point-blank range, point-blank; *Aviat* **surface portante** aerofoil, *Am* airfoil; *Naut* **vent p.** fair wind **2** **être bien p.** to be in good health, to be well; **être mal p.** to be in poor health, to be unwell; **enfants bien/mal portants** healthy/unhealthy children
NM **1** *Tech* upright; *(support)* stay, strut **2** *Vieilli (anse)* handle **3** *(chenille)* *(d'une roue)* tread **4** *(présentoir)* *(dans un magasin de vêtements)* rack

portatif, -ive [pɔrtatif, -iv] ADJ *(machine à écrire, radio)* portable; *(ordinateur)* laptop; **armes portatives** small arms
NM *Ordinat* laptop

Port-au-Prince [pɔropRɛ̃s] N Port-au-Prince

porte [pɔrt] NF **1** *(de maison, de placard etc)* door; **à ma p.** on my doorstep; **aller ouvrir la p.** to answer the door; **le musée ouvrira ses portes (au public) en juin** the museum will open its doors to the public in June; **le théâtre fermera ses portes à la fin du mois** the theatre will close at the end of the month; *Fam* **ce n'est pas la p. à côté** it's hardly just around the corner; **il y a deux kilomètres/on met deux heures de p. à p.** it's two kilometres/it takes two hours door to door; *Fam* **je lui ai parlé entre deux portes** I spoke to him for a brief moment or briefly, I had a quick word with him; *Fam* **on s'est vus entre deux portes** we saw each other briefly; **trouver p. close** to find nobody in; **j'ai voulu aller au musée mais j'ai trouvé p. close** I wanted to go to the museum but it was closed; **être à la p.** to be locked out; **mettre qn à la p.** to throw or kick sb out; *(d'un emploi)* to fire or *Br* sack sb; *Fam* **tais-toi ou tu vas prendre la p.** be quiet or you're out; **qu'il prenne la p. s'il n'est pas content** let him leave or he doesn't have to stay if he's not happy; **elle m'a fermé/claqué la p. au nez** she closed/slammed the door in my face; **refuser** *ou* **fermer** *ou* **défendre sa p. à qn** not to allow sb in, to refuse sb admission; *Fig* **vous avez frappé** *ou* **sonné à la bonne/mauvaise p.** you've come to the right/wrong person; *Fam* **entrer dans une profession par la petite p.** to start at the bottom; *Fig* **c'est la p. ouverte à toutes les atrocités** it leaves the door wide open to all sorts of atrocities; *Fig* **journée portes ouvertes** open day or house; *Prov* **il faut qu'une p. soit ouverte ou fermée** it has to be either one way or the other; **chassez-le par la p., il reviendra par la fenêtre** get rid of him one way and he'll come back another
2 *(voie d'entrée)* *(d'un parc)* gate(way); *(d'un immeuble)* doorway, entrance; *(dans un aéroport)* gate; **portes d'une ville** gates of a town; **l'entreprise est installée aux portes de Paris** the company is situated on the outskirts of Paris; **l'ennemi est à nos portes** the enemy is at our gates; **la guerre est à nos portes** the war is on our doorstep; *(temporel)* war is around the corner; **la campagne est à vos portes** the countryside is on your doorstep; **aux portes du désert** at the gateway to the desert; **être aux portes de la mort** to be at death's door; **les portes de l'enfer** the gates of hell; *Hist* **la (Sublime-)P., la P. ottomane** the (Sublime) Porte
3 *(portière)* *(de voiture, de train)* door; **attendre l'ouverture complète des portes** wait until the doors are fully open; **(voiture) deux/quatre/cinq portes** two-/four-/five-door car
4 *Ski* gate
5 *(fente)* *(d'une agrafe)* eye
6 *(usu pl)* portes *(dans la roche)* gorge; *(passage étroit)* defile, pass
7 *Ordinat* gate; **p. logique** logic gate
▸▸ **p. d'aérage** air gate, trap door; **p. battante** swing door; **p. cochère** carriage entrance; **portes communicantes** inter-connecting doors; **p. coulissante** sliding door; **p. de débarquement** (disembarkation) gate; **p. de derrière** back door; **p. à deux battants** double door; *Tech* **p. d'écluse** (lock) gate; **p. d'embarquement** (boarding) gate; **p. d'entrée**, *Belg* **p. de rue** front door; **p. roulante** sliding door; **p. de secours** emergency exit; **p. de service** *(de maison, d'appartement)* *(de derrière)* back door; *(sur le côté)* side door, *Vieilli* tradesman's entrance; **p. de sortie** way out, exit; *Fig* way out, means of escape; **p. tournante, p. à tambour** revolving door; *Tech* **p. de visite** inspection door; *(d'égout)* manhole cover; **p. vitrée** glass door

porté [pɔrte] ADJ **être p. à l'indulgence/la compréhension** to be inclined to be indulgent/understanding; **être p. à la discussion** to be inclined *or* prone to argue; **être p. à la colère** to be quick-tempered; **p. à faire qch** inclined to do sth, given to doing sth; **être p. à oublier** to be apt *or* inclined to forget; **p. sur qch** fond of sth; *Fam* **être p. sur la chose** to be sex-mad, to have a one-track mind

porte(-)à(-)faux [pɔrtafo] NM INV overhang; *Constr* cantilever; **en p.** overhanging; *Fig* **être en p.** to be awkwardly placed; **il est en p. avec la ligne officielle du parti** he's at odds with *or* out of step with the official party line

porte-affiche(s), *pl* **porte-affiches** NM notice *or Am* bulletin board

porte-aiguille, *pl* **porte-aiguille(s)** NM *Chir* needle holder

porte-aiguilles NM INV *Couture* needle case

porte-amarre, *pl* **porte-amarre(s)** NM *Naut* line-throwing apparatus; **flèche p.** line-throwing rocket

porte-à-porte NM INV door-to-door selling; **faire du p.** *(pour vendre)* to sell from door to door, to do door-to-door selling; *(faire des enquêtes etc)* to go from door to door

porte-avions NM INV *Naut* aircraft carrier

porte-bagages NM INV luggage rack; *(de bicyclette)* carrier; *(de voiture)* roof rack

porte-baïonnette, *pl* **porte-baïonnette(s)** NM bayonet frog

porte-balai, *pl* **porte-balai(s)** NM *Élec* brush holder

porte-bébé, *pl* **porte-bébés** NM baby carrier

porte-billets NM INV notecase, *Am* billfold

porte-bombes NM INV *Mil, Aviat* bomb rack

porte-bonheur NM INV (lucky) charm; *(animal, enfant)* mascot; **couleur/petit cochon p.** lucky colour/pig

porte-bouteilles NM INV *(pour stocker le vin)* wine rack, bottle rack; *(pour porter)* bottle carrier

porte-brosses [pɔrt(ə)brɔs] NM INV **p. (à dents)** toothbrush holder

porte-cartes NM INV **1** *(pour cartes de crédit, de visite)* card holder *or* wallet **2** *(pour cartes géographiques)* map case *or* holder

porte-chapeaux NM INV hat stand

porte-chars [pɔrtəʃar] NM INV *Mil* tank transporter

porte-chéquier, *pl* **porte-chéquiers** NM cheque *or Am* check book holder

porte-cigares NM INV cigar case

porte-cigarettes NM INV cigarette case

porte-clefs, porte-clés [pɔrtəkle] NM INV key ring

porte-conteneurs NM INV *Tech* container ship

porte-copie, *pl* **porte-copie(s)** NM *Typ* copy holder

porte-couteau, *pl* **porte-couteau(x)** NM knife rest

porte-croix [pɔrtəkrwa] NM INV *Rel* cross bearer

porte-documents NM INV briefcase

porte-drapeau, *pl* **porte-drapeau(x)** NM *Mil, Fig* standard bearer

portée [pɔrte] NF **1** *(petits)* litter, brood; *(d'une truie)* farrow

2 *(amplitude)* *(des bras)* reach; *(de la flèche d'une grue)* radius; *(d'un fusil, d'un émetteur)* range; *(d'un traité)* scope; *(de voix)* range, compass; **(à) courte p., (à) petite p.** (at) short range; **(à) grande p., (à) longue p.** (at)

long range; **canon à longue p.** long-range gun; **à p. (de tir)** within range; **à p. de fusil** within rifle range, within gunshot; **à p. de canon** within gun range; **à p. de (la) voix** within earshot; **à p. de (la) vue** (with)in sight; **des chaussures à la p. de toutes les bourses** shoes to suit every pocket *or* budget; **ce sport est maintenant à la p. de toutes les bourses** this sport is now within everyone's means, everyone can now afford this sport; **des chaussures à ce prix ne sont pas à la p. de tout le monde** not everyone can afford shoes at that price; **c'est à ma p.** *(cet objet)* it's within my reach; *(ce livre)* I can understand it; *(ce travail)* I can do it; **hors de ma p.** *(dans l'espace)* beyond my reach; *Fig (de compréhension)* beyond my understanding, *Fam* beyond me; **hors de p.** out of reach, beyond reach; **à mettre hors de (la) p. des enfants** keep out of the reach of children; **à p. de (la) main** within reach, to hand; **j'ai toujours un tube d'aspirine à p. de la main** I always have some aspirin handy; **livre à la p. de tout le monde** *(facile à lire)* book that anyone can understand; **cette musique/ce roman n'est pas à la p. de tout le monde** this music/novel is not accessible to everyone

3 *Mus* stave, staff

4 *Radio, TV* reach

5 *Fig (force) (d'une déclaration, des mots)* (full) significance *or Fml* import; **conséquences d'une p. incalculable** far-reaching consequences; **un changement/une décision d'une très grande p.** a very significant *or* a far-reaching change/decision

6 *Constr (charge)* bearing; *(distance)* span; *Naut* **p. en lourd** *ou* **en poids** deadweight (capacity)

7 *Tech* bearing surface; *(point d'appui) (d'un arbre)* boss; **portées** *(d'un arbre)* (main) journals

porte-étendard NM INV *Hist (dans la cavalerie)* standard bearer

portefaix [pɔrtəfɛ] NM *Hist* (street) porter

porte-fenêtre, *pl* **portes-fenêtres** NF French window *or Am* door

portefeuille [pɔrtəfœj] NM **1** *(pour l'argent)* wallet, *Am* billfold; *Fig* **avoir un p. bien garni** to be well-off, to be rich; *lit* **en p.** apple-pie bed; **jupe p.** wrapover *or* wraparound skirt **2** *(cartable)* portfolio; *Com* **p. d'assurances** *(d'un assureur)* portfolio; **p. d'actions** share portfolio; *Fin* **effets en p.** bills in hand, holdings; **p. (titres)** investments, securities; **p. de titres** securities portfolio; *Mktg* **p. d'activité** business portfolio, portfolio mix; **p. d'investissements** investment portfolio **3** *Pol (fonction de ministre)* portfolio; **ministre sans p.** minister without portfolio **4** *Aut (de semi-remorque)* jackknifing

porte-greffe(s) [pɔrtəgrɛf] NM INV *Bot* stock

porte-hélicoptères [pɔrtelikɔptɛr] NM INV *Naut* helicopter carrier

porte-jarretelles NM INV suspender *or Am* garter belt

porte-journaux NM INV newspaper rack

porte-jupe, *pl* **porte-jupe(s)** [pɔrtəʒyp] NM skirt hanger

porte-malheur NM INV bringer of bad luck, jinx; **les plumes de paon sont considérées comme un p.** peacock feathers are thought to bring bad luck

portemanteau, -eaux [pɔrtmɑ̃to] NM **1** *(accroché au mur)* coat rack; *(sur pied)* coat stand **2** *Arch (malle)* portmanteau

portement [pɔrtəmɑ̃] NM **p. de croix** (Christ's) bearing of the Cross

porte-menu NM INV menu holder

portemine [pɔrt(ə)min] NM propelling pencil

porte-monnaie NM INV purse; **p. électronique** electronic purse *or* wallet

porte-musique NM INV music case

porte-objet, *pl* **porte-objet(s)** NM *(de microscope)* (object) slide; *(platine)* stage

porte-outil, *pl* **porte-outil(s)** NM *(d'un machine-outil)* tool holder; *(d'une perceuse)* chuck; *(d'un tour)* slide rest

porte-papier NM INV **p. (hygiénique)** toilet paper holder; *(pour rouleau)* toilet roll holder

porte-parapluies NM INV umbrella stand

porte-parole NM INV spokesperson, spokesman, *f* spokeswoman; *(organe d'un parti politique)* organ; **se faire le p. de qn** to speak on sb's behalf

porte-pipes [pɔrtəpip] NM INV pipe rack

porte-plat, *pl* **porte-plat(s)** [pɔrtəpla] NM (dish) stand

porte-plume [pɔrtəplym] NM INV penholder

PORTER [pɔrte]

VT to carry **1** ▪ to produce **2** ▪ to wear **3** ▪ to take **4** ▪ to bring **4, 9** ▪ to direct **5** ▪ to enter **6** ▪ to bear **7** ▪ to incite **8** ▪ to have **10**	
VI to rest **1** ▪ to hit **2** ▪ to have effect **2**	
VPR to go **1** ▪ to turn to **3** ▪ to be well *(bien se porter)* **4** ▪ to be worn **6**	

VT 1 *(soutenir) (valise, enfant etc)* to carry; *(poids, charge)* to bear, to carry; **p. qn en triomphe** to carry sb in triumph *or* shoulder high (in triumph); **p. la tête haute** to hold *or* carry one's head high; **ces abus portent en eux leur propre châtiment** these abuses carry their own punishment; **une réforme qui porte en elle tous les abus** a reform that carries *or* has within it the seed of all sorts of abuse; **elle porte bien son âge** she's wearing well; **elle porte/ne porte pas son âge** she looks/doesn't look her age; **elle a 30 ans? elle ne les porte pas du tout** she's 30? she doesn't look it at all; **mes jambes ne me portent plus** my legs won't carry me any further; **je ne le porte pas dans mon cœur** he's not exactly my favourite *or Am* favorite person; *Mil* **portez armes!** shoulder arms!; *Naut* **p. tout dessus** *(d'un voilier)* to have all sails set

2 *(produire)* to produce; **p. des fruits** to bear fruit; **terres qui portent du blé** wheat-producing land; **p. intérêt** to yield interest; **argent qui porte intérêt** money that brings in *or* bears interest; **cela vous portera bonheur/malheur** that will bring you luck/bad luck; *Prov* **la nuit porte conseil** sleep on it

3 *(avoir avec ou sur soi) (vêtement, chapeau)* to wear; **p. des lunettes/une bague/du noir** to wear glasses/a ring/black; **p. une moustache/la barbe** to have or wear a moustache/a beard; **p. les cheveux courts/longs** to wear one's hair short/long, to have short/long hair; **il portait une cicatrice à la joue droite** he had a scar on his right cheek; *Fig* **p. la soutane** to be a priest; *Fig Fam* **faire p. le chapeau à qn** to make sb take the rap *or Br* carry the can, *Am* to leave sb holding the bag; *Fig Fam* **c'est elle qui porte la culotte** she wears the trousers in their house; **il porte le nom de son oncle** he's called after his uncle; **ce produit porte le nom de son inventeur** this product is named after its inventor, this product bears the name of its inventor; **p. le même prénom que qn** to have the same name as sb; **qu'est-ce qu'elle porte comme prénom?** what's her first name?; **elle porte bien/mal son nom/prénom** her name suits/doesn't suit her; **le chameau porte deux bosses** the camel has two humps

4 *(transporter) (là-bas)* to take; *(ici)* to bring; **p. qch dans la maison/dehors** to take/bring sth into the house/outside; **p. une chaise d'une pièce à une autre** to take *or* carry a chair from one room to another; **p. une lettre à la poste** *ou Fam* **boîte** to post *or Am* mail a letter; **je suis allée lui p. un message** I took him a message; **je suis allé lui p. la nouvelle** I went to give *or* to tell him the news; **p. à domicile** to deliver to domicile; **p. le lait à domicile** to deliver milk to the door; **il porta le verre à ses lèvres** he raised *or* lifted the glass to his lips; **p. qn en terre** to carry sb to his/her grave

5 *(diriger)* **p. un coup à qn, p. la main sur qn** to strike *or* hit sb; **s'il porte la main une seule fois sur toi, dis-le-moi** if he ever lays a hand on you *or* strikes you, tell me; **p. la main à sa nuque** to touch the back of one's neck; **il porta la main à sa casquette** he touched his cap; **p. la main à son front** to hold one's hand to one's forehead; **p. ses regards sur qn** to direct one's gaze towards sb, to look at sb; **p. son attention sur qch** to turn one's attention to sth, to give sth one's attention; *Fig* **p. qch devant un tribunal/les tribunaux** to take sth to court; **p. plainte** to make a complaint; *Fig* **p. un toast à qn** to drink *or* offer a toast to sb, to toast sb; **p. témoignage** to testify, to give evidence, to bear witness; **p. qch à la connaissance de qn** to bring sth to sb's attention, to make sth known to sb, to let sb know about sth

6 *(inscrire) (noms, chiffres)* to enter, to write; **p. une position sur une carte** to mark a position on a map; **p. une somme au crédit/au débit de qn** to credit/debit sb with a sum; **p. une somme au crédit/débit d'un compte** to credit/debit a sum to an account; **se faire p. malade** *ou Fam* **pâle** to report sick; *Mil etc* **p. qn manquant à l'appel** to report sb absent from roll call; **p. qn absent** to report sb absent; **p. qn déserteur** to declare sb a deserter; **être porté disparu** to be reported missing; *Naut* **p. un homme au rôle de l'équipage** to enter a seaman on the ship's books

7 *(être revêtu ou marqué de)* to bear; **la lettre porte la date du 2 juin** the letter is dated 2 June; **p. une signature** to bear a signature; **p. le titre de …** *(d'un livre)* to be entitled *or* called …

8 *(inciter à)* **p. qn à qch** to incite sb to sth; **p. qn à faire qch** to induce *or* prompt sb to do sth; **tout me porte à croire que …** everything leads *or* inclines me to believe that …

9 *(monter, transformer)* to bring; **p. la température à 100°** to raise the temperature to 100°; **p. qn au pouvoir** to bring sb to power; **p. une pièce classique à l'écran** to bring *or* transfer a classical drama to the screen; **p. la production au maximum** to raise *or* increase production to a maximum; **portez le liquide à ébullition** bring the liquid to the boil; **ça porte à dix le nombre des victimes** that brings the number of victims to ten; **cela portera à cent euros le prix du billet** that will bring the price of the ticket up to a hundred euros

10 *(avoir) (intérêt)* to have *(à* in); *(affection, amour)* to have, to feel *(à* for, towards)

11 *(donner)* **p. secours à un bateau en détresse/à qn** to come to the aid of a boat in distress/of sb; **p. assistance à qn** to come to sb's assistance, to offer assistance to sb

12 *(mentionner)* **le rapport ne porte aucune mention de tout cela** the report makes no mention of any of that; **la loi porte que cet usage est interdit** this practice is expressly forbidden by law; *Mil etc* **la décision porte que …** it is stated in orders that …

VI 1 *(appuyer)* to rest, to bear; **tout le poids porte sur cette poutre** all the weight rests *or* bears on this beam; **croyez-vous que la glace porte?** do you think the ice will hold?;

la discussion porte toujours sur le même sujet the discussion always deals with *or* turns on the same subject; **les questions ont porté sur un chapitre que je n'avais pas revu** the questions dealt with *or* were about a chapter that I hadn't revised; **faire p. son attention sur qch** to turn one's attention to sth, to focus one's attention on sth; **faire p. sa thèse sur qch** to choose sth as the subject for one's thesis

2 *(atteindre)* **sa tête a porté sur le rebord du trottoir/contre le volant** his/her head hit *or* struck the kerb/the wheel; **aucun des coups n'a porté** none of the blows struck home *or* hit their target; **ses attaques/critiques n'ont pas porté** his attacks/criticisms had no effect; **chaque mot a porté** every word hit home; **coup qui porte/qui a porté** telling blow; **sa voix porte bien** his voice carries well; **courant qui porte au sud** current that sets to the south; *Fam* **ce bruit me porte sur les nerfs** that noise gets on my nerves

3 *Naut (d'une voile)* to fill, to draw

4 *Naut* **laisser p.** to bear away; **laisser p. sur un navire** to bear down upon *or* run down a ship

5 *(être en gestation)* **les juments portent onze mois** the gestation period of a mare is eleven months

VPR se porter 1 *(aller)* to go, *Fml* to proceed; **se p. au secours de qn** to go to sb's assistance; **se p. au-devant de tout besoin** to anticipate every need; **la foule s'est portée vers la gare** the crowd made for *or* went towards the station

2 *(se livrer à)* **se p. à des voies de fait/à des extrémités** to commit assault/to go to extremes

3 *(se diriger)* **son regard se portait vers son frère** his gaze fell on his brother; *Mil* **se p. en avant** to advance; **la conversation s'est portée sur l'Extrême-Orient** the conversation turned to the Far East; **la conversation se porte toujours sur les mêmes sujets** the conversation always turns on *or* revolves around *or* is always about the same subjects

4 **se p. bien** to be well, to be in good health; **se p. à merveille** to be in the best of health; **comment vous portez-vous?** how are you?; **je ne m'en porte pas plus mal** I'm none the worse for it; **moins je le vois, mieux je me porte** the less I see him, the better I feel

5 *(se présenter comme)* **se p. acquéreur de qch** to offer to buy sth; **se p. candidat** to put oneself forward *or* up as a candidate, *Br* to stand as a candidate; **se p. caution** to stand surety; **se p. garant envers qn** to stand guarantor for, to stand surety for

6 *(devoir être porté)* to be worn; *(être à la mode)* to be fashionable; **le nœud papillon se porte de plus en plus** more and more people are wearing bow ties, bow ties are becoming more and more fashionable; **le bleu se porte beaucoup cette année** blue is being worn a lot *or* is very fashionable this year

porte-raclette, *pl* **porte-raclettes NM** *Aut* wiper arm

porte-revues NM INV magazine rack

porterie [pɔrtəri] **NF** *(d'un couvent etc)* gatehouse

porte-satellites NM INV *Aut* planet carrier

porte-savon, *pl* **porte-savon(s) NM** soapdish

porte-serviettes NM INV towel rail

porte-skis [pɔrt(ə)ski] **NM INV** *Aut* ski carrier, ski rack

porte-toasts [pɔrtətost] **NM INV** toast rack

porteur, -euse [pɔrtœr, -øz] **N 1** *(d'un message)* bearer; **p. de nouvelles** bearer *or* bringer of news; **j'arrivais p. d'heureuses nouvelles** I arrived bringing *or* bearing good

news; **par p.** by messenger **2** *(de gare, d'aéroport etc)* porter; **chaise à porteurs** sedan chair **3** *Méd* carrier; **p. de germes** (germ) carrier; **p. sain** unaffected carrier **4** *(détenteur)* holder; *Fin (d'un chèque)* bearer, payee, endorsee; **p. d'actions** shareholder; **les petits/gros porteurs** small/big shareholders; **p. de papiers volés/de faux papiers** person carrying stolen/false identity papers; **il était p. de faux papiers** he was carrying false papers; **p. d'une procuration** holder of a power of attorney, holder of a proxy; **p. de titres** holder of stock, stockholder; **p. d'une traite** bearer of a bill, holder of a bill; **payable au p.** payable to bearer; **effets au p.** bearer stock(s)

ADJ 1 *Tech* **essieu p.** bearing axle, carrying axle; **câble p.** suspension cable; *Élec* **fréquence porteuse** carrier frequency; **onde porteuse** carrier wave **2** *Méd* **les individus porteurs du virus** individuals who carry the virus, (individuals who are) carriers of the virus **3** *Fig (industrie, marché, créneau)* buoyant, flourishing

NF porteuse 1 *Tél* carrier **2** *Can (marraine)* godmother

> Do not confuse with **portier**, which means **doorman**.

porte-vélo, *pl* **porte-vélos NM** *Aut* bike carrier

porte-vent [pɔrtəvã] **NM INV** *Tech* air duct

porte-voix [pɔrtəvwa] **NM INV** megaphone; *(électrique)* loudhailer, *Am* bullhorn; **mettre ses mains en p.** to cup one's hands round one's mouth

portfolio [pɔrtfoljo] **NM** portfolio

portier, -ière [pɔrtje, -jɛr] **NM 1** *(gardien)* porter, doorman, doorkeeper; *(dans un hôtel)* commissionaire; **p. de nuit** night porter **2** *Litt (d'un domaine, monastère etc)* gatekeeper

N *Rel* **(frère) p.** porter; **(sœur) portière** portress

> Do not confuse with **porteur.**

portière [pɔrtjɛr] **NF 1** *(d'une voiture, d'un wagon)* door **2** *(rideau)* door curtain, portière

portillon [pɔrtijɔ̃] **NM** wicket (gate); *Rail (dans un passage à niveau)* side gate; *(dans une gare)* gate, barrier; *Fam* **cela se bouscule au p.** *(il y a une foule)* people are turning up in droves; *(il s'exprime difficilement)* he can't get his words out; *Fam* **ça ne se bouscule pas au p.** people are staying away in droves

portion [pɔrsjɔ̃] **NF** *(d'argent)* portion, share; *(de gâteau, fromage etc)* portion; *(de viande)* portion, helping; *(d'un groupe, d'une population etc)* portion, section; *(d'un livre)* section, part

portique [pɔrtik] **NM 1** *Archit* portico **2** *Gym (pour accrocher des agrès)* (cross)beam **3** *Rail* **p. à signaux** signal gantry **4** *Tech* **grue à p.** travelling gantry crane

portland [pɔrtlãd] **NM** *Tech* Portland cement

Porto [pɔrto] **N** *Géog* Oporto

porto [pɔrto] **NM** *(vin)* port

portoricain, -aine [pɔrtorikɛ̃, -ɛn] **ADJ** Puerto Rican

N P. Puerto Rican

Porto Rico [pɔrtoriko] **NM** *Géog* Puerto Rico

portos [pɔrtos] **N INV** *Fam Péj* Dago *(from Portugal)*

portrait [pɔrtrɛ] **NM 1** *(représentation)* portrait; *(photo)* portrait(-sized photo); **p. en pied/buste** full-/half-length portrait; **faire le p. de qn** to do *or* paint a portrait of sb; *(au crayon)* to do *or* draw a portrait of sb;

Fig **c'est le p. vivant de son père, c'est tout le p. de son père** he's the spitting image of his father; *Fam* **se faire tirer le p.** to have one's photo taken; **p. littéraire** character sketch **2** *(description)* description, portrayal; **faire le p. de qn/qch** to paint a picture of sb/sth, to describe or portray sb/sth; **il nous a fait un p. flatteur de la situation/de sa future femme** he painted a flattering picture of the situation/his future wife **3** *Fam (visage)* face, mug; **il s'est fait abîmer** *ou* **arranger le p.** someone's made a real mess of or *Fam* someone's rearranged his face **4** *Beaux-Arts* **le p.** *(genre)* portrait painting, portraiture; *Ordinat* **mode p.** portrait mode; **imprimer qch en p.** to print sth in portrait

portraitiste [pɔrtretist] N portrait painter, portraitist

portrait-robot, *pl* **portraits-robots** NM Photofit® (picture), Identikit® picture; *Fig* **faire le p. du candidat idéal** to draw up a profile of the ideal candidate

portraiturer [pɔrtretyre] VT *Rare* to portray

portuaire [pɔrtɥɛr] ADJ port, harbour, *Am* harbor; **installations portuaires** port facilities or installations

portugais, -aise [pɔrtygɛ, -ɛz] ADJ Portuguese

 NM *Ling* Portuguese

 N **P.** Portuguese

 NF **portugaise 1** *(huître)* Portuguese oyster **2** *Fam (oreille)* ear; **tu as les portugaises ensablées ou quoi?** are you deaf or what?

Portugal [pɔrtygal] NM *Géog* Portugal

pose [poz] NF **1** *(de rideaux)* putting up, hanging; *(d'un tableau)* hanging; *(de briques, de moquette etc)* laying; *(de pierres précieuses)* setting; *(de bombe)* planting; *(de verre de montre etc)* fitting; *(d'appareils)* installation; **p. de câbles** cable laying; *Typ* **p. de marges** margin setting; **p. de tabulations** tabbing, setting of tabs **2** *(attitude)* pose, posture; *Beaux-Arts, Phot etc* **garder la p.** to hold the pose; **prendre une p.** to assume or strike a pose **3** *Péj (airs)* posing, posturing, affectation; **sans p.** *(adverbe)* unaffectedly; *(adjectif)* unaffected **4** *Golf (d'une balle)* lie **5** *Phot (cliché, durée)* exposure; **temps de p.** exposure time; **p. instantanée** instantaneous exposure; **pellicule de 24 poses** 24-exposure film

posé [poze] ADJ **1** *(réfléchi, calme) (personne)* self-possessed, composed, calm; *Mus* **voix bien posée** even or steady voice **2** *(en train de couver) (oiseau)* sitting

posément [pozemã] ADV calmly, with composure; *(avancer, bouger)* steadily, deliberately

posemètre [pozmɛtr] NM *Phot* light meter

POSER	[poze]		
VI	to rest **1** ▪ to lie **1** ▪ to pose **2, 3** ▪ to show off **3**		
VT	to put **1** ▪ to place **1** ▪ to put down **1** ▪ to ask **2** ▪ to lay down **2, 6** ▪ to write down **3** ▪ to lay **4** ▪ to put up **4** ▪ to put forward **6**		
VPR	to land **1** ▪ to arise **2** ▪ to claim to be *(se poser en)* **3**		

VI **1** *(d'une poutre)* to rest, to lie (**sur** on)

2 *(comme modèle)* to pose; *(pour qu'on fasse son portrait)* to sit, to pose; **p. pour la postérité** to have one's portrait painted for posterity; **p. nu** to pose (in the) nude

3 *Péj (prendre des airs)* to show off, to pose; **p. pour la galerie** to play to the gallery; *Fam* **je ne pose pas à l'ange** I don't pretend to be an angel; **il pose au grand connaisseur** he plays or acts the great connoisseur

VT **1** *(mettre)* to put, to place; **pose-le sur la table** put it (down) on the table; **p. les armes** to lay down one's arms; **p. un avion** to land an aircraft; **p. sa candidature** *(aux élections)* to put oneself forward (as a candidate), *Br* to stand (as a candidate); *(à un poste)* to apply; **à peine avais-je posé la tête sur l'oreiller que …** no sooner had my head hit or touched the pillow than …; **l'examen est terminé, posez les stylos** the exam is over, put your pens down

2 *(formuler)* **p. une question** to ask a question; **p. une question à qn** to ask sb a question, to put a question to sb; *Pol* **p. la question de confiance** to table a motion of confidence; **p. un problème** to pose a problem (**à qn** for sb); **bien/mal p. le problème** *(dans une dissertation)* to identify the problem well/poorly; **p. une règle de conduite** to lay down a rule of conduct

3 *Math (écrire) (opération, équation)* to write down; **p. un chiffre** to put down or set down a number; **je pose deux et je retiens un** put down two (and) carry one

4 *(rideau, papier peint)* to put up, to hang; *(tableau)* to hang; *(briques, moquette, pierre de fondation, rails etc)* to lay; *(pierres précieuses, rivets)* to set; *(bombe)* to plant; *(chaudière)* to install; *(verre de montre etc)* to fit; **p. une vitre** to put in a pane of glass; **faire p. le téléphone** to have a telephone put in or installed; *Typ* **p. des tabulations dans** to tab; *Fig* **p. les jalons** to prepare the ground (**de** for); **p. la première pierre de qch** to lay the foundation stone for sth; *Fig* to lay the foundation(s) for sth

5 p. qn to establish sb's reputation; **une telle expérience, ça vous pose un homme** an experience like that sets you up for life

6 *(supposer, établir) (hypothèse)* to put forward; **p. des principes** to lay down principles; **posons le cas que cela soit** supposing or assuming or let's suppose or let's assume that that is the case; **cela posé** assuming this to be true

7 *Mus* **bien p. la voix** to pitch (one's voice) correctly

8 p. son regard sur qn/qch to look at sb/sth; **il posa sur elle son regard de myope** he peered at her shortsightedly

9 *Can (photographier)* to photograph, to take a photograph or picture of; **il s'est fait p. avec sa copine** he had his picture taken with his girlfriend

VPR **se poser 1** *(d'un oiseau)* to land, to settle, to alight (**sur** on); *(d'un avion)* to land

2 *(apparaître) (d'une question, d'un problème)* to arise, to come up, to crop up; **un nouveau problème se pose** we are faced with a new problem, a new problem has arisen; **la question se posera toujours** it's a perennial question; **la question qui se pose est la suivante** the question we are faced with is the following

3 *(se prétendre)* **se p. en réformateur/redresseur de torts** to set oneself up as or to claim to be a reformer/a righter of wrongs

4 *(devoir être posé)* **cette potiche se pose par terre/dans un coin** this vase should be (placed) or this vase goes on the ground/in a corner; **ça se pose comme du papier peint** you put it up or it goes on like wallpaper

5 se p. des questions to ask oneself questions; **je finis par me p. des questions** I'm beginning to have my doubts; **il se pose la question de savoir si …** he is wondering whether …

6 *Fam* **il se pose un peu là, comme bricoleur/cuisinier!** some handyman/cook(, I don't think)!; **comme enquiquineur, il se pose là!** he's a real pain in the neck!

poseur, -euse [pozœr, -øz] N **1** *Tech (de câble etc)* layer; **p. d'affiches** billsticker, billposter; *Rail* **p. de rails** platelayer, *Am* tracklayer; *Naut* **p. de mines** minelayer; **p. de bombes** bomb planter; **la police recherche activement les poseurs de bombes** the police have launched a manhunt for the people who planted the bombs **2** *Péj (pédant)* show-off, poser, poseur; **il est p.** he's always putting on airs, he's affected

posidonie [pozidɔni] NF posidonia

positif, -ive [pozitif, -iv] ADJ **1** *(sûr, certain) (résultat, fait)* positive, actual, real; *Méd (réaction, test)* positive **2** *Math, Élec etc (nombre, pôle etc)* positive; *Phot* **épreuve positive** positive **3** *(pratique) (personne, esprit)* practical, pragmatic **4** *(enthousiaste) (remarque, attitude, personne)* positive **5** *Jur* **droit p.** statute law

 NM *Phot* positive; **p. (en) couleur** colour positive; **p. transparent** transparency

POSITION [pozisjɔ̃] NF **1** *(emplacement) (de navire, d'avion etc)* position; *Golf (de la balle)* lie; **le coureur français est en première/deuxième p.** the French runner is in the lead or in first place or position/in second place or position; **prendre la première p.** to take the lead, to go into first place or position; **il est arrivé en troisième p.** he came third; *Aut* **feux de p.** sidelights; **p. d'atterrissage** *(d'un avion)* landing attitude; *Aut* **p. nuit antiéblouissement** *(de rétro intérieur)* anti-glare position; **p. clé** key position; **p. défensive** *ou* **de défense** defensive position; *Mil, Fig* **p. de repli** fall-back position

 2 *(attitude corporelle)* position, posture, attitude; *(debout)* stance; *(des pieds)* position; **s'endormir dans une mauvaise p.** to fall asleep in an uncomfortable or awkward position; **être/se mettre en p.** to be in/get into position; **la p. du missionnaire** the missionary position; **première/troisième p.** *(en danse)* first/third position; **en p. debout/assise** in a standing/sitting position; **trois cents passagers en p. debout** three hundred standing passengers

 3 *(opinion, avis)* position; **quelle est votre p. sur la guerre?** what is your position on the war?, what position do you take on the war?; **expliquer sa p.** to explain one's position; **elle est restée sur ses positions** she refused to back down, she stood her ground, she stood firm; **prendre p.** to take a stand; **prise de p.** stand; **la prise de p. de notre pays** our country's stand, the stand taken by our country; **une prise de p. devient nécessaire** it's becoming necessary to take a stand; **p. politique** political stance; **p. sociale** *(d'un journal)* social stance

 4 *(dans la société)* position; **p. sociale** social standing or position or status

 5 *(situation)* position, situation; **voici ma p.** this is how things stand with me, this is my position or situation; **être en p. de faire qch** to be in a position to do sth; *Fam* **être dans une p. intéressante** to be pregnant, *Vieilli* to be in an interesting situation; **p. gênante** embarrassing position or situation; **p. concurrentielle** competitive position; **p. sur le marché** market position

 6 *Fin* balance; **demander sa p.** to ask for one's balance; **p. d'un compte** balance of an account; *Fin* **p. de compte** balance; **p. créditrice** credit balance; **p. débitrice** debit balance; **p. financière** financial position

 7 *Bourse* **p. acheteur** long position; **p. (courte) couverte** covered (short) position; **p. élémentaire** simple position; **p. longue** long position; **p. non couverte** uncovered position; **p. vendeur** short position

positionnement [pozisjɔnmã] NM **1** *Tech* positioning **2** *Fin (d'un compte)* calculation of the balance **3** *Com* positioning; *Mktg* **p. concurrentiel** competitive positioning; **p. de la marque** brand positioning; **p. de prix** price positioning; **p. du produit** product po-

sitioning; **p. stratégique** strategic positioning

positionner [pozisjɔne] VT **1** *Tech, Ordinat*
(curseur, graphique etc) to position **2** *Fin*
(compte) to calculate the balance of **3** *Mktg*
(produit) to position
VPR se positionner se p. à la hausse sur le
marché to move upmarket; **se p. par rapport**
à la concurrence to position oneself in relation to the competition

positivement [pozitivmã] ADV positively;
je ne le sais pas p. I don't know for certain, I
can't be positive about it; *Élec* **chargé p.** positively charged

positiver [pozitive] VI *Fam* to be positive, to
look on the bright side; **arrête donc de te**
morfondre comme ça, essaye de p.! stop
moping around like that, try to look on the
bright side!

positivisme [pozitivism] NM *Phil* positivism

positiviste [pozitivist] ADJ, N *Phil* positivist

positivité [pozitivite] NF *Élec, Phil, Méd*
positivity

positon [pozitɔ̃] NM, **positron** [pozitrɔ̃] NM
Nucl positron

posologie [pozɔlɔʒi] NF *Méd (de produit*
pharmaceutique) dosage; *(science)* posology

possédant, -ante [posedɑ̃, -ɑ̃t] ADJ, N **les**
possédants, les classes possédantes the
propertied *or* moneyed classes, the wealthy

possédé, -ée [posede] ADJ *(par la passion,*
la jalousie etc) gripped, dominated (**par** by);
p. du diable *ou* **du démon** possessed by the
devil
N person possessed; *Fig* maniac, madman,
f madwoman; **hurler comme un p.** to wail
like a banshee, *Fml* to scream like one
possessed

posséder [posede] (je **possède**; je **posséde-**
rai) VT **1** *(avoir)* to possess, to own, to have;
p. un titre to have a title; **p. un million** to be a
millionaire; **je ne possède pas un centime** I
don't have a penny (to my name); **p. un**
grand talent/sens de l'humour to possess
or have a great talent/sense of humour; *Fig*
p. le cœur d'une femme to have won a woman's heart **2** *(connaître) (sujet)* to have a
thorough knowledge of, to be master of;
(langue, technique) to have mastered, to
have a good mastery of; **tu ne possèdes pas**
la vérité, tu sais you don't know everything,
you know; **p. son métier** to know one's job
inside out; **elle possède maintenant tous**
les automatismes now it comes automatically to her **3** *(dominer) (d'un démon, du dia-*
ble etc) to possess; **ils étaient tous possédés**
de la même illusion they all laboured under
the same delusion **4** *Fam (tromper) (per-*
sonne) to take in, to fool; **je me suis fait p.**
I've been taken in *or* had **5 p. une femme** to
possess a woman
VPR se posséder to control oneself; **elle ne**
se possédait plus de joie/rage she was beside herself with joy/rage; **elle ne se pos-**
sède plus! she's out of her mind!

possesseur [posesœr] NM owner; *(de titre)*
holder, possessor; **il se croit le p. de la vérité**
he thinks he knows everything; **p. de va-**
leurs share owner

possessif, -ive [posesif, -iv] ADJ **1** *Gram*
possessive **2** *Psy (mère, mari)* possessive
NM *Gram* possessive SEE GRAMMAR A30; B21–2

possession [posesjɔ̃] NF **1** *(fait de détenir,*
d'avoir) ownership; *(de titre)* holding, possession; **être en p. de qch** to be in possession of sth, to possess sth; *Jur, Fml* to be
possessed of sth; **Com nous sommes en p.**
de votre lettre du 4 mars we are in receipt
of *or* have received your letter of 4 March;
avoir qch en sa p. to have sth in one's possession; **entrer en p. d'un héritage** to enter

into possession of an inheritance; **entrée en**
p. d'un patrimoine accession to an estate;
prendre p. de qch to take possession of sth;
rentrer en p. de qch to gain possession of
sth; **comment ce manuscrit est-il tombé en**
votre p.? how did this manuscript come into
your possession?; **p. vaut titre** possession is
nine points *or* nine-tenths of the law; **p. de**
fait de facto possession
2 *(bien) (surtout bien immobilier, domaine)*
possession; **avoir quelques possessions** to
have a few possessions; *Fin* **possessions**
d'une société assets of a company
3 *Psy, Rel* possession *(by evil spirit)*
4 *(maîtrise)* self-control, self-possession;
reprendre p. de soi-même to regain *or* recover one's self-control *or* composure; **être en**
pleine p. de ses facultés, être en p. de toutes
ses facultés to be in (full) possession of
one's faculties; **elle était en pleine p. de ses**
moyens she was at the peak of her powers *or*
her abilities

possessivité [posesivite] NF possessiveness

possessoire [poseswar] *Jur* ADJ **intenter une**
action p. to undertake an action for possession (of land)
NM right of possession

possibilité [posibilite] NF **1** *(éventualité)*
possibility; *(d'un projet, d'une opération)* feasibility; **voir la p. de faire qch** to see the possibility of doing sth; **nous ne voyons aucune**
p. de changement we can't see any possibility of change; **il faut prendre en compte la**
p. du rejet (de greffe) we have to allow for
the possibility of rejection *or* for the possibility that the transplant will be rejected SEE
GRAMMAR A58–60; B40
2 *(cas)* possibility; **c'est une p. que je n'avais**
pas envisagée it's a possibility that I hadn't
envisaged
3 *(moyen, occasion)* opportunity, chance;
c'est la première fois qu'elle a la p. de le faire
this is the first opportunity *or* chance she's
had to do it *or* of doing it; **on ne m'en a jamais**
donné la p. I was never given the opportunity *or* chance; **si j'ai la p. de lui écrire** if it's
possible for me *or* if I can manage to write
to him; **p. d'emprunter** borrowing power;
Ordinat **possibilités d'extension** upgradeability
4 **possibilités** *(d'une personne)* capabilities;
(financières) means; **connaître ses possibili-**
tés to be aware of one's (own) capabilities;
chacun doit payer selon ses possibilités
from each according to his means; **la région**
dispose de nombreuses possibilités de va-
cances the region offers many holiday possibilities; **le nombre de touristes dépasse**
largement les possibilités de l'hôtel the
number of tourists easily exceeds the capacity of the hotel; **quelles sont vos possibili-**
tés d'embauche? what are your plans for
taking people on?; **quelles sont vos possibi-**
lités de logement? how many people can
you put up?

POSSIBLE [posibl] ADJ **1** *(faisable)* possible;
(projet, opération) feasible; **c'est (bien) p.** it's
(quite) possible, (very) possibly; **est-ce p.?,**
ce n'est pas p.!, Fam pas p.! it's not possible!,
impossible!, I don't believe it!; *Fam* **c'est pas**
Dieu p. it's unbelievable; **si (c'est) p.** if (it's)
possible; **est-il p. de faire des fautes pareil-**
les? how can people make such mistakes?;
il leur est p. de vous héberger it's possible
for them to put you up; **est-ce qu'il te serait**
p. de travailler demain? would it be possible
for you to work tomorrow?, could you possibly work tomorrow?; **il ne m'est pas p. de le**
faire it's impossible *or* not possible for me to
do it, I can't possibly do it; **il ne m'est guère**
p. de le faire it's a bit difficult for me to do it;
cela lui est tout à fait p. it's no trouble at all

for him; **il est p. qu'il soit mort** it's possible
that he's dead, he may *or* might be dead; **il**
n'est pas p. que j'y aille *(je ne peux pas)* it's
impossible *or* not possible for me to go; *(il*
n'est pas question) there's no possibility of
my going; **il est bien p. que …** it's quite possible that …; **aussitôt que p., dès que p.** as
soon as possible; *Fml* **le plus tôt qu'il vous**
sera p. at your earliest convenience; **est-ce**
que tu viens? – p. are you coming? – possibly; **il faut absolument qu'il nous conduise à**
l'aéroport, ce n'est pas p. autrement he'll
<u>have</u> to drive us to the airport, otherwise
we'll never make it
2 *(existant, maximum, minimum)* **le moins**
souvent p. as infrequently as possible; **le**
moins de détails possible(s) as few details as
possible; **elle nous en parle le moins p.** she
talks to us about it as little as possible; **tous**
les détails possibles every possible detail;
toutes les informations possibles all available information; **la boîte la plus grande p.**
the largest box possible, the largest possible box; **elle a eu tous les ennuis possibles**
et imaginables she's had every problem you
can think of; **dans la plus large mesure p.** as
far as possible
3 *(éventuel)* possible; **danger p.** possible *or*
potential danger; **il est p. qu'il y pense à la**
dernière minute he may well think of it at
the last minute; *Fam* **c'est dans les choses**
possibles it's a possibility
4 *Fam (supportable)* **cette fille/situation**
n'est pas p.! that girl/this situation is impossible!; **ça n'est plus p.** I can't take (it) any
more, I've had enough
NM **1** *(ce qui est possible)* what is possible;
dans la mesure du p. as far as possible; **faire**
tout son p. pour … to do all *or* everything
one (possibly) can (do) to …, to do one's
utmost *or* best to …, to try one's hardest to
…; **il s'est montré aimable au p.** he couldn't
have been nicer, he was extremely pleasant
2 *(chose réalisable)* possibility; **envisa-**
geons tous les possibles let's consider all the
possibilities

post-achat [postaʃa] ADJ *Mktg* post-
purchase

post-acheminement, *pl* **post-achemine-**
ments [postaʃ(e)minmã] NM transfer from
main airport

postal, -ale, -aux, -ales [postal, -o] ADJ
(tarif) mail, *Br* postal; *(train, camion, wagon)*
mail; **code p.** postcode, postal code, *Am* zip
code; **sac p.** mailbag, *Br* postbag; **carte pos-**
tale postcard; **colis p.** parcel sent by post; **les**
services postaux the postal *or Am* mail services; **les services postaux sont assez fia-**
bles dans ce pays the postal service is quite
reliable in this country

postcombustion [postkɔ̃bystjɔ̃] NF *Tech*
(d'une fusée, d'un turboréacteur) afterburn-
ing, reheat; **dispositif de p.** afterburner

postcommunion [postkɔmynjɔ̃] NF *Rel*
postcommunion

postcommunisme [postkɔmynism] NM
postcommunism

postcure [postkyr] NF *Méd* aftercare; **elle est**
en p. she's in aftercare

postdater [postdate] VT to postdate

poste[1] [post] NF **1** *(service)* mail, *Br* post; **la P.**
the mail *or Br* postal service, *Br* ≃ the Post
Office, *Am* ≃ the US Postal Service; **envoyer**
une lettre par la p. to send a letter by mail *or*
Br post; **mettre une lettre à la p.** to mail *or Br*
post a letter; **(bureau de) p.** post office; **p.**
principale, grande p. main post office; **aller**
à la p. to go to the post office; **receveur/rece-**
veuse des postes postmaster/postmistress;
grève des postes mail *or Br* postal strike **2**
Arch (relais de chevaux) post, relay; **chevaux**
de p. posthorses; **maître de p.** postmaster;

aller en p. to travel post; **courir la p.** to go posthaste

▸▸ **p. aérienne** airmail; **p. restante** poste restante, *Am* general delivery

poste ² NM **1** *(fonction)* job, position, post; **il y a des postes vacants** there are (job) vacancies; **présenter sa candidature à un p. de technicien** to apply for a job as a technician; **un p. clé** a key position; **occuper un p. de confiance** to hold a position of trust; *Ind* **p. de jour/nuit** day/night shift; **p. à pourvoir** vacancy

2 *Radio, TV* **p. (de) radio** radio set; **p. de télévision** television set; **p. récepteur** receiver, receiving set; *Fam* **ouvrir/fermer le p.** to switch the radio/television on/off; *Radio* **p. émetteur** *(endroit)* broadcasting station; *(équipement)* transmitter

3 *Tél* extension; **je voudrais le p. 35, s'il vous plaît** I'd like extension 35, please; **le p. est occupé** the extension *or* line is *Br* engaged *or Am* busy; **je vous passe le p.** I'm putting you through

4 *(bureau)* post; *(de police)* station; **passer la nuit au p.** to spend the night at the station; **p. de la Croix-Rouge** Red Cross station

5 *(salle)* quarters; **p. d'équipage** crew's quarters; *(dans la marine marchande)* forecastle; *Naut* **p. des maîtres** warrant officers' wardroom; **p. des aspirants** gunroom

6 *Compta* entry, item; **p. créditeur/débiteur** credit/debit item; **p. de bilan** balance sheet item; **p. extraordinaire** extraordinary item

7 *Mil (d'un soldat)* post, station; *Mil* **p. avancé** advanced *or* outlying post; *Mil, Naut* **chef de p.** guard commander; **à vos postes!** to your posts!, stand by!; **postes de combat** action stations; **être à son p.** to be at one's post; *Fig* **être solide** *ou* **fidèle au p.** to be still going strong

8 *Naut (emplacement)* berth; **p. de mouillage** anchoring berth; **p. d'amarrage** mooring berth, mooring(s); **mettre les ancres à p.** to stow the anchors

9 *Ordinat* **p. autonome** stand-alone; **p. terminal** terminal; **p. de travail** workstation

▸▸ *Rail* **p. d'aiguillage** signal box; **p. de commandement** headquarters, command post; *Naut* control room; **p. de contrôle** checkpoint; *Mil* **p. d'écoute** listening station; **p. d'essence** petrol *or Am* gas station, filling station; *Mil* **p. de garde** guardroom; **p. d'incendie** fire point; *Mil* **p. d'observation** observation post; **p. de péage** toll booth; *Aviat* **p. de pilotage** cockpit; *(dans un avion plus important)* flight deck; **p. de police** (police) station; *Mil* guardroom; **p. de secours** first-aid post

posté, -ée [pɔste] ADJ **travail p.** shift work; **ouvrier p.** shift worker

N shift worker

poster ¹ [pɔste] VT *(sentinelle)* to post; *(hommes, troupes)* to station

VPR **se poster** to take up a position, to station oneself

poster ² VT *(courrier)* to mail, *Br* to post

poster ³ [pɔstɛr] NM poster

postérieur [pɔsterjœr] ADJ **1** *(dans le temps)* later, subsequent; **p. à son décès** after his death; **la rechute est très postérieure à son opération** the relapse came a long time after his operation; **avoir lieu à une date postérieure** to be held at a later date; **être remis à une date postérieure** to be postponed to a later date; **à une date postérieure à notre coup de téléphone** at a date some time after our phone call **2** *(dans l'espace) (pattes)* back, hind, rear; *Anat* posterior; **partie postérieure** back part

NM *Fam (derrière)* behind, backside, *Hum* posterior

postérieurement [pɔsterjœrmɑ̃] ADV later, subsequently, at a later date; **p. à** after

postériorité [pɔsterjɔrite] NF posteriority

postérité [pɔsterite] NF posterity; *(famille, descendance)* posterity, descendants; **mourir sans (laisser de) p.** to die without issue; **nous travaillons pour la p.** we are working for posterity; *Fig* **la p. du nouveau-roman** the legacy of the nouveau roman; **entrer dans la p., passer à la p.** *(d'une personne)* to go down in history; *(d'une œuvre, d'un mot etc)* to be handed down to posterity

postface [pɔstfas] NF postscript

postglaciaire [pɔstglasjɛr] ADJ *Géol* postglacial

posthume [pɔstym] ADJ posthumous

postiche [pɔstiʃ] ADJ *(cheveux, cils etc)* false NM hairpiece

postier, -ière [pɔstje, -jɛr] N postal worker, post office employee

postillon [pɔstijɔ̃] NM **1** *Hist (cocher)* postilion **2** *(salive)* postillons shower(s) of spit; **envoyer des postillons** to splutter, to sputter

postillonner [pɔstijɔne] VI *(en parlant)* to splutter, to sputter

postindustriel, -ielle [pɔstɛ̃dystrijɛl] ADJ postindustrial

postmoderne [pɔstmɔdɛrn] ADJ postmodern

postmodernisme [pɔstmɔdɛrnism] NM postmodernism

postnatal, -ale, -als, -ales [pɔstnatal] ADJ postnatal

postopératoire [pɔstɔperatwar] ADJ *Méd* postoperative

postpartum [pɔstpartɔm] NM INV *Méd* postpartum period

postposer [pɔstpoze] VT **1** *Gram* **p. un adjectif/un verbe** to place *or* put an adjective/a verb after; **adjectif postposé** adjective placed after the noun, postpositive adjective **2** *Belg (remettre à plus tard)* to postpone

postposition [pɔstpozisjɔ̃] NF *Gram* postposition

post-production [pɔstprɔdyksjɔ̃] NF *TV etc* postproduction

postscolaire [pɔstskɔlɛr] ADJ *(cours)* continuation; **enseignement p.** further *or* continuing education

post-scriptum [pɔstskriptɔm] NM INV postscript, PS

postsonorisation [pɔstsɔnɔrizasjɔ̃] NF *Cin* post-synchronization, dubbing

postsonoriser [pɔstsɔnɔrize] VT *Cin* to post-synchronize, to dub

post-synchro [pɔstsɛ̃kro] NF *Cin* post-synching

postsynchronisation [pɔstsɛ̃krɔnizasjɔ̃] NF *Cin* post-synchronization, ADR

postsynchroniser [pɔstsɛ̃krɔnize] VT *Cin* to post-synchronize, to dub

postulant, -ante [pɔstylɑ̃, -ɑ̃t] N **1** *(à un emploi)* applicant, candidate **2** *Rel* postulant

postulat [pɔstyla] NM *Phil* postulate, assumption

postuler [pɔstyle] VT **1** *(demander) (poste, emploi)* to apply for **2** *Phil* to postulate

VI **1** *Jur* **p. pour un client** *(d'un avocat)* to act on behalf of *or* represent a client **2** **p. à** *ou* **pour un emploi** to apply for a job

posture [pɔstyr] NF **1** *(attitude du corps)* posture, position, attitude **2** **être en p. de faire qch** to be in a position to do sth; **être en bonne/mauvaise p. (pour faire qch)** to be in a good/bad position *or* well/badly placed (to do sth); **être en fâcheuse p.** to be in an awkward situation

pot [po] NM **1** *(récipient)* pot; **p. de terre**

earthenware pot; **p. à tabac** tobacco jar; *Fig Fam (personne petite et grosse)* tubby person; **p. à eau** water jug; **p. de fleurs** *(récipient)* flowerpot, plant pot; *(plante)* pot of flowers; **p. à lait, p. au lait** milk jug; *(en métal)* milk can; **p. de confiture** jam jar; *Fam* **le p.** *(pour enfant)* the potty; **aller sur le p.** to use the potty; **mettre en p.** *(plante)* to pot; **p. de colle** pot of glue; *Fig Fam* **quel p. de colle!** he sticks to you like glue!, you can't shake him off *or* get rid of him!; **quel p. de colle tu fais aujourd'hui!** stop annoying *or* bugging me!; **il est gentil mais c'est un p. de colle** he's nice but he tends to cling; *Fig Fam* **payer les pots cassés** to take the rap, *Br* to carry the can; *Fig* **découvrir le p. aux roses** [potoroz] to find out what's been going on; *Fam* **c'est le p. de terre contre le p. de fer** he doesn't stand a chance, he's more than met his match

2 *(contenu)* pot; **finir un p. de confiture** to finish a jar *or* pot of jam; **un p. d'eau** a jug of water; **petit p.** *(pour bébé)* (jar of) baby food; **p. d'accueil** welcoming drink; *Fam* **allons prendre un p.** let's go for a drink *or Br* jar; *Fam* **faire un p. (d'adieu/d'anniversaire)** to have a (farewell/birthday) drink

3 *Culin (marmite)* (cooking) pot; **manger à la fortune du p.** to take pot luck; **en trois coups de cuiller à p.** in less than no time, in no time (at all), in two shakes (of a lamb's tail); *Fig* **tourner autour du p.** to beat about the bush; **sourd comme un p.** as deaf as a post

4 *Fam (chance)* **avoir du p.** to be lucky; **avoir un coup de p.** to have a stroke of luck; **manque de p., pas de p.** just his/your/*etc* luck; **elle n'a vraiment pas de p.!** she has no luck at all!

5 *Fam* **plein p.** *(à toute vitesse)* like the clappers, *Am* like sixty; **ils croyaient qu'ils auraient droit à une réduction mais finalement ils ont payé plein p.** they thought they would be entitled to a discount but they ended up paying the full whack; **elle met toujours la musique à pleins pots** she always puts music on at full blast

▸▸ **p. à absorption** absorption silencer; **p. à catalyseur** catalytic converter; **p. catalytique** catalytic converter; **p. de chambre** chamber pot; **p. d'échappement** silencer, *Am* muffler; *(ensemble du système)* exhaust (system); *(tuyau)* exhaust (pipe), *Am* tail pipe; *Naut* **p. au noir** doldrums; *Aut* **p. de résonance** resonance chamber

potable [pɔtabl] ADJ **1** *(que l'on peut boire)* drinkable, fit to drink; **eau p.** drinking water **2** *Fam (correct)* passable, reasonable; *(tenue)* acceptable, decent

potache [pɔtaʃ] NM *Scol Fam* schoolboy *(attending a collège or lycée)*

potage [pɔtaʒ] NM **1** *(soupe)* soup; **p. aux légumes** vegetable soup; *Fam* **être dans le p.** *(être évanoui)* to be out cold; *(être dans une situation pénible)* to be in the soup **2** *Arch, Litt* **pour tout p.** all told, (all) in all

potager, -ère [pɔtaʒe, -ɛr] ADJ **herbes potagères** herbs for cooking, pot herbs; **plante potagère** vegetable; **jardin p.** vegetable *or* kitchen garden

NM vegetable *or* kitchen garden

potasse [pɔtas] NF *Chimie* potash; **chlorate de p.** potassium chlorate

potasser [pɔtase] *Fam* VT to bone up on, *Br* to swot up

VI to bone up, *Br* to swot

potassique [pɔtasik] ADJ *Chimie* potassium; *(sel)* potassic

potassium [pɔtasjɔm] NM *Chimie* potassium

pot-au-feu [pɔtofø] NM INV *Culin* = boiled beef with vegetables

ADJ INV *Fam Vieilli (personne)* stay-at-home

pot-de-vin, *pl* **pots-de-vin** NM bribe, *Fam* backhander; **donner un p. à qn** to bribe sb, *Fam* to give sb a backhander

pote [pɔt] NM *Fam* pal, chum

poteau, -eaux [pɔto] NM **1** post; *Min* pit prop; *Sport (de but)* (goal)post; **p. indicateur** signpost; **p. télégraphique** telegraph pole; **p. électrique** electricity pylon; *Sport* **p. de départ** starting post; *Sport* **p. d'arrivée** finishing post, winning post; **rester au p.** to be left at the post; **être coiffé sur le p.** to be pipped at the post, *Am* to be beaten by a nose; *Fam* **avoir des jambes comme des poteaux** to have legs like tree-trunks **2 p. (d'exécution)** execution post *or* stake *(for sb about to be shot)*; **mettre qn au p.** to put sb up against a wall and shoot him/her; **le général au p.!** down with the general! **3** *Fam (ami)* pal, chum

potée [pɔte] NF *Culin* stew *(especially cabbage and carrots with pork)*

potelé [pɔtle] ADJ chubby, plump

potence [pɔtɑ̃s] NF **1** *(gibet)* gallows, gibbet; **échapper à la p.** to cheat the gallows; **gibier de p.** gallows bird VOIR GRAMMAIRE A13 **2** *(charpente)* bracket, arm, support; *(de grue)* jib; *(d'un guidon de bicyclette)* stem; *(d'une perfusion)* stand; **en p.** bracket-shaped, L-shaped **3** *Naut, Mil* davit

potentat [pɔtɑ̃ta] NM potentate

potentialisation [pɔtɑ̃sjalizasjɔ̃] NF *Pharm* potentiation

potentialiser [pɔtɑ̃sjalize] VT **1** *Pharm* to potentiate **2** *Fig* to maximize
  VPR **se potentialiser** to maximize one's potential

potentialité [pɔtɑ̃sjalite] NF potentiality; **une p. inutilisée** unused potential

potentiel, -ielle [pɔtɑ̃sjɛl] ADJ potential; *Gram* **préfixe/sens p.** potential prefix/ meaning; *Tech* **énergie potentielle** potential energy
  NM **1** potential; **avoir un bon/fort p.** to have good/strong potential; **p. de croissance** growth potential; **p. de guerre** war establishment; **p. industriel** industrial potential; **p. de vente** sales potential; **p. du marché** market potential **2** *Élec* potential; *Radio* **p. de grille** grid potential **3** *Gram* potential (mood)

potentiellement [pɔtɑ̃sjɛlmɑ̃] ADV potentially

potentille [pɔtɑ̃tij] NF *Bot* **p. (rampante)** cinquefoil

potentiomètre [pɔtɑ̃sjɔmɛtr] NM *Électron* potentiometer; *Cin (de son)* fader; **p. de micro** microphone fader; **p. vidéo** video fader

poterie [pɔtri] NF **1** *(usine)* pottery (works); *(atelier)* potter's workshop *or* studio; *(art, techniques)* pottery; **cours de p.** pottery class; **faire de la p.** to do *or* make pottery **2** *(objet)* piece of pottery; *(objets)* pottery; **elle achète souvent de la p./des poteries** she often buys pottery; **p. (de terre)** earthenware; **p. de grès** stoneware **3** *Tech* **p. d'étain** pewter(ware)

poterne [pɔtɛrn] NF postern (gate)

potiche [pɔtiʃ] NF **1** *(vase)* (large) vase *(especially of Chinese or Japanese porcelain)* **2** *Fig* figurehead

potier, -ière [pɔtje, -jɛr] N potter

potin [pɔtɛ̃] NM *Fam* **1** **potins** gossip, tittle-tattle; **s'intéresser aux petits potins** to take an interest in idle gossip **2** *(bruit)* row, din, rumpus; **faire du p.** to kick up a row *or* rumpus, to make a din

potiner [pɔtine] VI to gossip

potion [posjɔ̃] NF *Méd* potion; **p. magique** magic potion

potiron [pɔtirɔ̃] NM pumpkin

pot-pourri, *pl* **pots-pourris** NM *Mus* potpourri, medley; *(fleurs séchées)* potpourri

potron-minet [pɔtrɔ̃minɛ] NM INV *Arch Fam* **dès p.** at daybreak, at the crack of dawn

pou, *pl* **poux** [pu] NM louse, *pl* lice; **p. du pubis** pubic louse, *Fam* crab (louse); *Fam* **laid comme un p.** as ugly as sin; **fier** *ou* **orgueilleux comme un p.** as proud as a peacock; **sale comme un p.** filthy dirty; **elle est vexée comme un p.** she's really really upset, *Br* she's really got the hump; *Fam* **chercher des poux dans la tête à qn** to pick a quarrel with sb (about nothing)

pouah [pwa] INT ugh!

poubelle [pubɛl] NF **1** *(pour les ordures)* (dust)bin, *Am* garbage *or* trash can; *Ordinat* wastebasket, *Am* trash; **p. à pédale** pedal bin; **jeter** *ou* **mettre qch à la p.** to throw *or* put sth in the (dust)bin, to throw sth away; *Fig Fam* to think sth is a load of rubbish; **c'est bon à jeter** *ou* **mettre à la p.** it should be thrown out, it's fit for the dustbin; *Fig* it's a load of rubbish; **qu'est-ce que j'en fais?** – **p.!** what do I do with this? – just bin it!; **descendre la p.** to take the rubbish *or Am* garbage down; **faire les poubelles** to scrounge in dustbins **2** *Fam (voiture)* heap, banger, rustbucket

pouce [pus] NM **1** *(doigt)* thumb; **sucer son p.** to suck one's thumb; *Fam* **donner un coup de p. à qn/qch** to help sb/sth along (a bit); **elle/le projet n'a besoin que d'un coup de p.** she/ the project just needs to be helped along a bit; *Fam* **manger sur le p.** to have a (quick) snack; **se tourner les pouces** to twiddle one's thumbs; **dire p.** to give up; *Scol* **p.!** truce!, *Br* pax!; *Suisse Fam* **tenir les pouces à qn** to keep one's fingers crossed for sb; *Can* **faire du p.** to thumb a lift *or Am* ride; *Can* **avoir les mains pleines de pouces** to be all thumbs, to be clumsy with one's hands **2** *(gros orteil)* big toe **3** *(mesure)* inch; **disquette de 3,5/5,25 pouces** 3.5-/5.25-inch disk; *aussi Fig* **ne pas bouger d'un p.** not to move an inch; *aussi Fig* **ne pas céder un p. de terrain** not to yield *or* budge an inch

poucer [puse] VI *Can Fam (faire de l'auto-stop)* to thumb a lift *or Am* ride

Poucet [pusɛ] NM **le Petit P.** Tom Thumb

poucettes [pusɛt] NFPL *Arch* = metal rings attached to the thumbs of prisoners

poucier [pusje] NM *(doigtier)* thumbstall

pouding [pudiŋ] NM = **pudding²**

poudingue [pudɛ̃g] NM *Géol* pudding stone

poudrage [pudraʒ] NM *Tech* powdering

poudre [pudr] NF **1** *(substance)* powder; **réduire qch en p.** to reduce sth to powder, to pulverize sth, to powder sth; **café en p.** instant coffee; **chocolat en p.** chocolate powder; **lait en p.** powdered milk; **sucre en p.** caster sugar; **lessive en p., p. à laver**, *Belg* **p. à lessiver** washing powder; **savon en p.** soap powder; **p. compacte/libre** *(maquillage)* pressed/loose powder; *Fam* **prendre la p. d'escampette** to make off, *Br* to do a bunk **2** *(explosif)* (explosive) powder; **p. à canon** gunpowder; *Fig* **être vif comme la p.** to flare up easily; *Fig* **mettre le feu aux poudres** to spark off a crisis; **la nouvelle s'est répandue comme une traînée de p.** the news spread like wildfire; **faire parler la p.** to let one's guns do the talking; *Fig* **ça sent la p.** there's trouble brewing **3** *Arch (poussière)* dust; *Fig* **jeter de la p. aux yeux de qn** to dazzle *or* impress sb **4** *Arg (héroïne)* smack; *(cocaïne)* coke, charlie
  ▸▸ **p. dentifrice** tooth powder; **p. d'encre** toner; **p. à éternuer** sneezing powder; *Suisse* **p. à lever** *(levure)* baking powder; **p. d'or** gold dust; **p. de perlimpinpin** magic *or* mira-

cle powder; **p. à récurer** scouring powder; **p. de riz** face powder

poudrer [pudre] VT to powder; **p. ses cheveux** to powder one's hair, to put powder on one's hair; **une femme poudrée** a woman with a powdered face
  V IMPERS *Can* **il poudre** it's snowing slightly
  VPR **se poudrer** to powder one's face *or* nose; **se p. le visage** to powder one's face

poudrerie [pudrəri] NF **1** *(fabrique de poudre)* (gun)powder factory **2** *Can (neige)* drifting snow

poudreux, -euse [pudrø, -øz] ADJ **1** *(qui a la consistance de la poudre)* powdery; **neige poudreuse** powder snow **2** *Vieilli (couvert de poussière)* dusty
  NF **poudreuse 1** *(neige)* powder snow **2** *(sucrier)* sugar sprinkler *or* caster

poudrier [pudrije] NM powder box; *(porté dans un sac à main etc)* (powder) compact

poudrière [pudrijɛr] NF *(entrepôt)* powder magazine; *Fig (région)* powder keg

poudrin [pudrɛ̃] NM spindrift

poudroiement [pudrwamɑ̃] NM dust haze

poudroyer [pudrwaje] VI *Litt* **(il poudroie; il poudroiera)** *(du soleil)* to pick out the dust in the air; **la route poudroie** the dust whirls up from the road

pouf [puf] INT bump!, thud!
  NM **1** *(meuble)* pouf(fe) **2** *Belg* **à p. (à crédit)** on tick; **taper à p. (au hasard)** to make a wild guess

pouffer [pufe] VI **p. (de rire)** to burst out laughing

pouffiasse [pufjas] NF *Vulg Vieilli (prostituée)* whore, tart; *Péj Vulg* **une grosse p.** a (great) fat cow, *Br* a fat slag; **quelle p.!** what a slag!

pouillerie [pujri] NF squalor; *(lieu)* filthy place, lousy hole

pouilleux, -euse [pujø, -øz] ADJ **1** *(couvert de vermine)* lousy, flea-ridden, verminous **2** *(misérable)* wretched, miserable; *(quartier, maison)* squalid, shabby **3** *Géog* **la Champagne pouilleuse** = the barren part of the Champagne region
  N **1** *(personne couverte de vermine)* louse-ridden *or* flea-ridden person **2** *(clochard)* tramp, *Am* bum

pouillot [pujo] NM *Orn* warbler

poujadisme [puʒadism] NM *Hist, Pol* Poujadism *(lower-middle-class, populist movement in the 1950s and 60s)*; *Fig Péj* narrow-minded *or* shopkeeper mentality

poujadiste [puʒadist] N *Hist, Pol* Poujadist; *Fig Péj* narrow-minded person

poulaille [pulaj] NF *Fam* **la p.** the cops, the pigs, *Br* the fuzz

poulailler [pulaje] NM **1** *(basse-cour)* hen house, hen roost **2** *Théâtre Fam* **le p.** the gods; **places de p.** seats in the gods

poulain [pulɛ̃] NM **1** *(cheval)* foal **2** *Fig* protégé **3** *Tech* **p. (de chargement)** *(pour décharger les tonneaux etc)* skid

poulaine [pulɛn] NF **1** *Naut* (ship's) head; **les poulaines** the latrines *(for crew)* **2** **soulier à la p.** long pointed shoe

poulamon [pulamɔ̃] NM *Can* tomcod

poularde [pulard] NF *Culin* fattened pullet

poulbot [pulbo] NM street urchin (of Montmartre)

poule¹ [pul] NF **1** *Zool* hen; *Culin (boiling)* fowl; **p. pondeuse** laying hen; **p. au pot** boiled chicken; *Fig* **ma (petite) p.!** my dear!, my pet!; *Fig* **la p. aux œufs d'or** the goose that lays the golden eggs; *Fig* **mère p.** mother hen; *Fig Péj* **p. mouillée** *(personne)* softie, wimp; *surtout Br Pol* wet; **se coucher comme** *ou* **avec les poules** to go to bed early; **lait de**

p. (non-alcoholic) egg flip *or* egg nog; *Fig* **quand les poules auront des dents** when pigs can fly; **p. d'eau** moorhen; **p. faisane** hen pheasant; **petite p. de bruyère** grey hen; **nid de p.** *(sur la route)* pothole **2** *Arg Péj (femme légère)* floozy, tart; *(maîtresse)* mistress; **p. de luxe** high-class call girl

> Do not confuse with **poulet**.

poule² NF **1** *(enjeu)* pool, kitty **2** *Escrime* pool, tournament; *Rugby* group **3** *Courses de chevaux* **p. d'essai** = early-season race for three-year-olds

poulet [pulɛ] NM **1** *Zool, Culin* chicken; *Culin* **p. fermier** *ou* **de grain** free-range chicken; **p. élevé en batterie** battery(-farmed) chicken; *Culin* **aile de p.** chicken wing; **cuisse de p.** chicken leg; **p. rôti** roast chicken; *très Fam* **et mon cul, c'est du p.?** oh come on, don't give me that crap! **2 mon (petit) p.** my darling, my pet, *Hum* my little chickadee **3** *Fam (policier)* cop **4** *Arch Fam (billet doux)* billet-doux

> Do not confuse with **poule**.

poulette [pulɛt] NF **1** *Vieilli (jeune poule)* pullet, young hen; *Culin* **sauce (à la) p.** = rich white sauce *(with onions, mushrooms, white wine etc)* **2** *Fam Vieilli (fille)* girl, *Am* dame **3** *Fam* **ma p.** my darling, my pet

pouliche [puliʃ] NF filly

poulie [puli] NF pulley; **p. simple/double** single/double block; **p. fixe** fixed pulley, standing block; **p. d'entraînement** drive pulley; **p. folle** loose pulley, idler

pouliner [puline] VI *(d'une jument)* to foal

poulinière [pulinjɛr] ADJ, NF **(jument) p.** brood mare

pouliot¹ [puljo] NM *Bot* pennyroyal

pouliot² NM *(sur charrette)* windlass

poulot, -otte [pulo, -ɔt] N *Enf* sweetheart, sweetie

poulpe [pulp] NM octopus

pouls [pu] NM pulse; **tâter le p. de qn** to feel sb's pulse; **prendre le p. à qn** to take sb's pulse; *Fig* **tâter** *ou* **prendre le p. de l'économie** to take the pulse of the economy; *Fig* **tâter** *ou* **prendre le p. de l'opinion** to sound out public opinion

poumon [pumɔ̃] NM *Anat* lung; **p. d'acier** iron lung; **respirer à pleins poumons** to breathe deeply, to take deep breaths/a deep breath; **crier à pleins poumons** to shout at the top of one's voice; **avoir de bons poumons** *ou* **des poumons** *(d'un chanteur etc)* to have good lungs; *Fam* **cracher ses poumons** to cough one's guts up *or* out; *Fig* **cette région était jadis le p. économique du pays** in days gone by this region was the economic lung of the country

poupard [pupar] NM **1** *Vieilli (gros bébé)* chubby baby **2** *Arch (poupée)* baby doll

ADJ *Vieilli* chubby(-cheeked); **visage p.** baby face

poupe [pup] NF *Naut* stern, poop; **avoir le vent en p.** to have the wind aft; *Fig* to have the wind in one's sails

poupée [pupe] NF **1** *(jouet)* doll, *Enf* dolly; **p. mannequin** doll for dressing up; **poupées gigognes** *ou* **russes** Russian dolls; **p. gonflable** inflatable doll; **maison de p.** doll's house; *Fig* doll's house, shoebox; **jouer à la p.** to play with dolls **2** *Fam (jolie fille)* doll **3** *(pansement au doigt)* finger bandage; *(le doigt lui-même)* bandaged finger; **faire une p. à qn** to bandage sb's finger **4** *Naut* **p. de cabestan** capstan head

poupin [pupɛ̃] ADJ *(personne)* chubby(-cheeked); *(air)* baby-like; **visage p.** baby face

poupon [pupɔ̃] NM **1** *(enfant)* (tiny) baby **2** *(poupée)* doll; **il a un visage de p.** he's baby-faced

pouponner [pupɔne] VI to play the doting mother/father

pouponnière [pupɔnjɛr] NF nursery *(for children up to three years old)*

poupoune [pupun] NF *Can Fam* sweetie, honey

POUR [pur]

> **PRÉP** for **1-8, 18** ▪ on behalf of **1** ▪ as **2** ▪ in favour of **7** ▪ in my/his opinion *(pour moi/lui)* **8** ▪ to **3, 9, 10, 12** ▪ in order to **10** ▪ if *(pour peu que)* **17**
> **NM INV** the pros and cons *(le pour et le contre)*

PRÉP 1 *(à la place de)* for; **dis-le-lui/allez-y p. moi** tell him/go for me; **agir p. qn** to act for sb *or* on sb's behalf; **p. le Président, son secrétaire …** on behalf of the President, his secretary …; *Fin* **p. acquit** received with thanks

2 *(comme)* for; **il la veut p. femme** he wants her for *or* as his wife; **tenir qn p. fou** to regard sb as mad, to consider sb mad; **prendre qn p. un autre** to take sb for somebody else; **laisser qn p. mort** to leave sb for dead; **une attitude p. le moins étrange** a somewhat strange attitude, a strange attitude to say the least; *Fam* **c'est p. de bon** *ou* **p. de vrai** I mean it, I'm serious; *Fam* **ça compte p. du beurre, on rejoue** that doesn't count, let's play again; **avec p. tout bagage …** with only … as luggage, taking only …

3 *(direction)* for; **je pars p. la France** I'm off to France, I'm leaving for France; **le train/ l'avion p. Paris** the Paris train/plane, the train/plane to *or* for Paris

4 *(temps)* for; **je vais en Suisse p. quinze jours** I'm going to Switzerland for two weeks; **p. dans trois jours** in three days, in three days' time; **p. toujours** for ever, for good; **p. le moment** for the moment; **il sera ici p. quatre heures** he'll be here for four hours; *(à quatre heures)* he'll be here by four o'clock; **j'en ai p. une heure** it'll take me an hour, I'll be an hour SEE GRAMMAR A70; B56–7

5 *(contre)* for; **il a acheté son vélo p. 50 euros** he bought his bike for 50 euros; **il me l'a vendu p. trois fois rien** he sold it to me for next to nothing; **trente p. cent** thirty per cent; **10 p. 1000** one percent; **mot p. mot** word for word; **jour p. jour** to the (very) day; **donnez-moi p. 50 euros d'essence** give me 50 euros' worth of petrol; **j'en ai p. mon argent** I've got my money's worth; **être p. beaucoup/peu dans qch** to play a large part/not to play much of a part in sth, to have a great deal to do/not to have much to do with sth; **je n'y suis p. rien!** it's got nothing to do with me!, I've got nothing to do with it!

6 *(cause, but)* for; **vêtements p. hommes** men's clothes, clothes for men; **livres p. enfants** children's books, books for children; **j'épargne p. quand je serai vieux** I'm saving for my old age *or* for when I'm old; **je le mets de côté p. ce soir** I'm putting it aside for tonight; **je suis ici p. affaires** I'm here on business; **voyager p. le plaisir** to travel for pleasure; **je viens p. la machine à laver** I've come about the washing machine; **je vous téléphone p. l'annonce parue dans le journal** I'm calling about the advertisement in the newspaper; **pommade p. les démangeaisons** ointment to relieve itching; **shampooing p. cheveux secs** shampoo for dry hair; *Ordinat* **moniteur p. graphismes** graphics monitor; **c'est p. cela qu'il est venu** that's why he came, that's the reason he came; **p. l'amour de Dieu** for God's sake, for heaven's sake; **faites-le p. moi** do it for me *or*

my sake; **nous devons y réfléchir p. les générations futures** we should think about it for the sake of future generations; **j'avais peur p. lui** I was afraid for him, I feared for him; **elle s'inquiète p. toi** she's worried about you; **il est bon p. les animaux** he's kind to animals; **l'art p. l'art** art for art's sake; **p. la forme** for form's sake; **beaucoup de bruit p. rien** a lot of fuss about *or* over nothing, *Litt* much ado about nothing; **tant pis p. moi** it's just hard luck on me; **tant mieux p. elle** good for her; **p. quoi faire?** what for?; *Fam* **c'est fait p.** that's what it's there for; *Fam* **c'est p. quoi?** what's that for?

7 *(en faveur de)* for, in favour *or Am* favor of; **parler p. qn** to speak in favour of sb; **je suis p. la libération de la femme** I'm (all) for *or* in favour of women's liberation; **moi, je suis p.** I'm (all) for it, I'm in favour of it

8 *(quant à, en ce qui concerne)* for; **p. mon compte (personnel)** for my part, as far as I'm concerned; **il est grand p. son âge** he's tall for his age; **p. ce qui est de …** as regards …, with regard to …; **p. (ce qui est de) moi** as for me, for my part, as far as I'm concerned; **p. moi, c'est absurde** in my opinion it's ridiculous, I think it's ridiculous; **ce ne sera une surprise p. personne** it will come as no surprise to anybody; **il n'en est pas plus intelligent p. cela** he's none the cleverer for all that; **et p. cela …** and so …; **en tout et p. tout** all in all, altogether, in total; *Fam* **p. de la chance, c'est de la chance** you're in luck and no mistake; **p. une surprise, c'est une surprise!** that's a surprise and no mistake!; **p. une déception/un anniversaire, ce fut une déception/un anniversaire!** it was some disappointment/birthday!, *Fam* it was one hell of a disappointment/birthday!

9 p. + *inf* (in order) to; **il faut manger p. vivre** one must eat (in order) to live; **p. ainsi dire** so to speak; **p. bien faire** to do things properly; **c'était p. rire** it was just for fun *or* for a laugh; **il s'en va p. ne jamais revenir** he's going away for good, he's leaving never to return; **nous nous sommes dépêchés p. ne pas être en retard** we hurried so as not to be late

10 p. que + *sub* so that, in order that; **je te dis cela p. que vous soyez sur vos gardes** I'm telling you this in order to put you on your guard *or* so that you'll be on your guard; **il est trop tard p. qu'elle sorte** it is too late for her to go out; **mettez-le là, p. qu'on ne l'oublie pas** put it there so that it won't be forgotten

11 *(ayant pour résultat)* **p. notre grand malheur, il nous a quittés bien tôt** most unfortunately for us, he died very young; **cela n'est pas p. me surprendre** that doesn't come as a surprise to me; **cette amitié n'était pas p. lui plaire** the friendship was not to his liking; **de telles remarques ne sont pas p. me déplaire** such remarks are not unwelcome

12 assez intelligent p. comprendre intelligent enough to understand; **être trop faible p. marcher** to be too weak to walk; **trop beau p. être vrai** too good to be true

13 *Litt (étant donné que)* **il est bien ignorant p. avoir étudié si longtemps** he's very ignorant considering how long he's studied

14 *Litt (concession)* (a)lthough; **p. être petit, il n'en est pas moins brave** though small, he is none the less brave

15 *Fam* **être p. partir** to be about to start out *or* set off, to be on the point of starting out *or* setting off

16 mourir p. mourir if I/we/*etc* must die; **ennuis p. ennuis, je préfère les miens** as troubles go, I prefer my own

17 p. peu que vous hésitiez, vous êtes fichu if you hesitate at all, you've had it; **p. peu qu'il se trompe, il est mis à la porte** if he makes any sort of mistake, he's out

18 (*à cause de*) for; **on l'apprécie p. sa gentillesse** he is liked for *or* on account of his kindness; **fermeture p. raisons familiales** closed for family reasons; **congé p. maladie** sick leave; **p. un rien** over nothing; **p. un peu, c'était trop tard** it was very nearly too late; **merci p. tout** thank you for everything; **être puni p. avoir désobéi** to be punished for having disobeyed *or* for disobeying *or* for disobedience; **je le sais p. l'avoir vu** I know from having seen it *or* from seeing it; **il est mort p. avoir trop travaillé** he died from overwork(ing) *or* from working too hard

NM INV **peser le p. et le contre** to weigh (up) the pros and cons; **entendre le p. et le contre** to hear both sides; **il y a du p. et du contre** there are pros and cons

pourboire [purbwar] NM tip, *Fml* gratuity; **donner un p. au porteur** to tip the porter, to give the porter a tip; **laisser 5 euros/10% de p.** to leave a 5-euro/10% tip; **être payé au p.** to depend on tips for one's pay

pourceau, -eaux [purso] NM pig, swine, *Am* hog

pourcentage [pursɑ̃taʒ] NM percentage; (*d'intérêts*) rate; (*pour représentant*) percentage, commission; **au p.** on a percentage basis, on a commission basis; **un p. fixe** a fixed percentage; **p. de grisé** shading percentage

pourchasser [purʃase] VT to pursue; (*criminel*) to pursue, to hunt (down); (*de créanciers, journalistes*) to harry; **pourchassé de rue en rue** hounded from street to street

> Il faut noter que le verbe anglais **to purchase** est un faux ami. Il signifie **acheter**.

pourfendeur, -euse [purfɑ̃dœr, -øz] N *Litt, Iron* **p. d'injustices** fighter against injustice

pourfendre [purfɑ̃dr] VT *Litt, Iron* (*injustices, crime etc*) to combat, to fight against

pourlécher (se) [səpurleʃe] (**je me pourlèche; je me pourlécherai**) VPR **se p. (les babines; je me pourléche les babines** that smells good, my mouth is watering already

pourliche [purliʃ] NM *Fam* tip (*in bar, restaurant*)

pourparlers [purparle] NMPL talks, discussions, negotiations; **entrer en p.** to enter into *or* begin talks *or* discussions *or* negotiations (**avec** with); **nous sommes en p. avec le Japon** we're having talks *or* discussions with Japan, we're in negotiation with Japan; **p. de paix** peace talks

pourpier [purpje] NM *Bot* purslane

pourpoint [purpwɛ̃] NM *Hist* pourpoint, doublet

pourpre [purpr] NF **1** (*teinte naturelle*) purple (dye) **2** *Fig* (*symbole de haute dignité*) purple; **né dans la p.** born in *or* to the purple NM **1** crimson, rich red; **le p. (de la honte) lui monta au visage** he/she turned crimson (with shame); *Physiol* **p. rétinien** visual purple **2** (*animal*) murex ADJ crimson; (*personne*) crimson, purple (**de rage** with rage)

pourpré [purpre] ADJ *Litt* crimson

pourquoi [purkwa] ADV, CONJ why; **p. cela?** why?; **p. êtes-vous venu?** why have you come?, what have you come for?; **dis-moi p.** tell me why; **mais p. donc?** but what on earth for?; **je voulais savoir p. (il était parti)** I wanted to know why (he had left); **voilà p.** that's (the reason) why; **c'est p. ...** and that's why ..., and so ...; **p. pas?, p. non?** why (ever) not?; **il a trouvé du travail, p. pas toi?** he's found a job, why haven't you?; **et p. ne pas aller voir un film?** why don't we go to see a film? VOIR GRAMMAIRE A41

NM INV (*raison*) reason (**de** for); **je ne sais**

pas le p. I don't know the reason why; **le p. et le comment** the whys and wherefores; **les p. des enfants** the questions that children ask

pourri [puri] ADJ **1** (*fruit*) rotten, bad; (*bois*) rotten; (*dent*) rotten, decayed; (*chair*) putrid; (*œufs*) bad; *Fam* (*corrompu*) (*chef, gouvernement etc*) corrupt; *Fam* **il est p. de vices** he's rotten to the core; *Fam* **ils sont pourris de fric** they're stinking rich, they're rolling in money; *Fam* **il est p. de talent** he's amazingly talented, he's bursting with talent **2** *Fam* (*insupportable*) (*ville, boulot, été, temps etc*) rotten; **cet enfant est p. gâté** that kid is spoiled rotten

NM **1** (*décomposition*) (*d'un fruit*) rotten *or* bad part; **sentir le p.** to smell rotten **2** *très Fam* (*terme injurieux*) bastard; **bande de pourris!** you bastards! **3** *Belg* (*paresseux*) lazy so-and-so

pourriel [purjɛl] NM *Ordinat* spam e-mail

pourrir [purir] VI to rot; (*d'un corps*) to putrefy, to decompose; (*de fruits, de la nourriture, d'œufs*) to go rotten, to go bad; **faire p.** to rot; *Fig* **p. en prison** to rot in prison; *Fig* **laisser p. les choses/la situation** to allow things/the situation to deteriorate; **laisser p. une grève** to allow a strike to drag on

VT **1** (*gâter*) (*fruits, bois*) to rot **2** *Fam* (*corrompre*) to spoil; **elle pourrit ses enfants en leur donnant tant d'argent** she's spoiling her children by giving them so much money; **elle me pourrit la vie** she's ruining my life **3** *Fam* (*dire du mal de*) to bad-mouth, *Br* to slag off

pourrissement [purismɑ̃] NM (*d'une situation*) deterioration

pourrissoir [puriswar] NM *Litt* muck heap

pourriture [purityr] NF **1** (*décomposition*) rotting, rot, decay; **p. sèche (du bois)** dry rot **2** (*état de décomposition*) rottenness; *Fig Fam* corruption **3** *très Fam* (*terme injurieux*) bastard

pour-soi NM INV *Phil* pour-soi

poursuite [pursɥit] NF **1** (*chasse*) pursuit; (*d'un criminel*) hunt (**de** for), pursuit, hunting, tracking (**de** of); **se mettre** *ou* **se lancer à la p. de qn** to set off in pursuit of sb, to chase after sb; **être à la p. de qch** (*bonheur, paix etc*) to be in pursuit *or* search of sth; (*travail, livre etc*) to be looking for sth; *Fig* **la p. du bonheur/de la sagesse** the pursuit of happiness/wisdom; *Cyclisme* (**course**) **p.** pursuit; *Cin* **scènes de p.** chase scenes **2** (*continuation*) continuation; **p. d'un travail** carrying on (with) a piece of work; **nous avons décidé de la p. de la grève** we've decided to continue the strike **3** *Électron* (*d'un avion, d'un missile etc*) tracking; **radar de p.** tracking radar **4** *Jur* **poursuites (judiciaires)** (legal) proceedings; (*en droit pénal*) prosecution; **engager** *ou* **entamer** *ou* **intenter des poursuites (judiciaires) contre qn** to start *or* institute (legal) proceedings against sb, to take legal action against sb; (*en droit pénal*) to prosecute sb; **s'exposer à des poursuites** to lay oneself open to prosecution **5** *Théâtre* (*projecteur*) follow spot

poursuiteur, -euse [pursɥitœr, -øz] N *Cyclisme* pursuit cyclist

poursuivant, -ante [pursɥivɑ̃, -ɑ̃t] ADJ *Jur* (*partie*) prosecuting

N **1** *Jur* plaintiff **2** (*personne qui poursuit*) pursuer

poursuivre [pursɥivr] (*conj like* **suivre**) VT **1** (*pourchasser*) (*personne, animal*) to pursue, to go after, to chase, to hunt (down); (*d'un songe, d'une idée, d'une crainte*) to haunt; **poursuivi par la malchance** dogged by bad luck **2** (*chercher à atteindre*) (*idéal, rêve, but*) to pursue, to chase (after) **3** (*harceler*) to pester, to plague (**de** with); (*débiteur*) to

hound, to harry; *Mil* (*ennemi*) to harry; **p. une femme de ses assiduités** to force one's attentions on a woman; **p. qn de sa colère** to vent *or* unleash one's anger on sb **4** *Jur* (**en justice**) to sue, to bring proceedings against, to take legal action against; (*en droit pénal*) to prosecute **5** (*continuer*) to pursue, to continue, to go on with, to proceed with; **p. un travail** to carry on (with) a piece of work

VI to go on, to continue; **poursuivez** (*votre histoire etc*) go on, continue; **bien, je poursuis ...** well, to continue ...

VPR **se poursuivre** (*de préparatifs, négociations etc*) to continue, to go on

pourtant [purtɑ̃] ADV yet, all the same; **un homme malade, et p. plein d'optimisme** a man who, though ill, is full of optimism; **il t'aime bien et p. s'il savait ...** he likes you and yet if he knew ...; **vous n'allez p. pas nous quitter?** you're surely not going to leave us?, you're not going to leave us though, are you?; **je ne peux p. pas l'empêcher de venir** all the same *or* even so, I can't stop him from coming; **je fume encore, p. j'aimerais bien m'arrêter** I still smoke, but I'd really like to stop; **tout avait p. bien commencé** and yet it all started so well; **ça n'est p. pas compliqué!** it's hardly complicated!; **on t'avait p. bien dit de ne pas y aller!** we did tell you not to go!; **les instructions étaient p. claires** the instructions were quite clear; **je sais que j'ai bien fait, et p. ...!** I know I did the right thing, and yet *or* but still ...!

pourtour [purtur] NM circumference, perimeter; **les pays du p. méditerranéen** the countries around the Mediterranean; **avec des rosiers sur le p.** with rose bushes around the edges

pourvoi [purvwa] NM *Jur* appeal; **p. en grâce** appeal for clemency; **p. en cassation** appeal to the Supreme Court

pourvoir [purvwar] (*prp* **pourvoyant**; *pp* **pourvu**; *pr ind* **je pourvois, n. pourvoyons**; *pr sub* **je pourvoie**; *impf* **je pourvoyais**; *p hist* **je pourvus**; *fu* **je pourvoirai**) VI **p. aux besoins de qn** to provide for *or* cater for *or* supply sb's needs; (*de façon plus immédiate*) to attend to *or* see to sb's needs; **p. à un emploi** to fill a job; **il y a un poste à p. à la comptabilité** there is a vacancy in Accounts; **on n'y a pas pourvu** no provision has been made for it

VT **p. qn de** to supply *or* provide *or* *Fml* furnish sb with; (*outils*) to equip sb with; **p. qn d'une charge** to appoint sb to an office; **être pourvu de tout l'équipement nécessaire** to be supplied *or* provided with all the necessary equipment; **nous étions bien pourvus pour la montagne** we were well equipped for the mountains; **p. une maison du chauffage central** to fit out *or* equip a house with central heating; **il est pourvu d'un grand talent** he is endowed with great talent; **la nature l'a pourvu d'une intelligence hors du commun** nature has endowed him with exceptional intelligence

VPR **se pourvoir 1** (*se munir*) to provide oneself (**de** with) **2** *Jur* to appeal, to lodge an appeal; **se p. en grâce** to appeal for clemency; **se p. en cassation** to take one's case to the Supreme Court of Appeal

pourvoyeur, -euse [purvwajœr, -øz] N supplier, provider, *Fml* purveyor; *Constr* contractor; **p. de drogue** drug dealer

pourvu que [purvykə] CONJ (+ *sub*) **1** (*exprimant une condition*) provided (that), so *or* as long as; **tu peux y aller p. tu sois rentré pour le dîner** you can go provided (that) *or* so long as *or* as long as you're back for dinner **2** (*exprimant un souhait*) **pourvu qu'il ne fasse pas de gaffes!** I just hope/let's just hope he won't make any blunders!; **p. ça dure!** let's just hope it lasts!

poussage [pusaʒ] NM *Tech* pushing

poussa(h) [pusa] NM *(jouet)* tumbler; *Fig (gros homme)* potbellied man

pousse [pus] NF **1** *(croissance) (des feuilles, des cheveux, des plumes)* growth; *(des dents)* cutting **2** *Bot (bourgeon)* (young) shoot, sprout; **p. de bambou** bamboo shoot; **cette plante a des pousses** this plant is putting out shoots **3** *Com* **jeune p. (d'entreprise)** start-up

poussé [puse] ADJ *(ornementation etc)* elaborate; *(étude)* thorough, searching, extensive; *(connaissances)* extensive; *(interrogatoire)* intensive; **il aboutit à un scepticisme assez p.** he carries scepticism to some lengths *or* rather far; **un pessimisme assez p.** a fairly deep pessimism; **faire des études très poussées** to pursue one's studies to a very advanced level; **des recherches très poussées** very advanced research; **des critiques très poussées** thoroughgoing criticism; *Aut* **moteur p.** hotted-up *or* souped-up engine

pousse-au-crime *Fam* ADJ INV that invites crime
NM INV **1 c'est du p.** it's an invitation to crime **2** *(eau-de-vie)* firewater, rotgut

pousse-café NM INV (glass of) liqueur *(after coffee)*

poussée [puse] NF **1** *(pression)*, *Phys* thrust; *(de liquide)* buoyancy; *(de la mer)* heave; **p. du vent** wind pressure; *Phys* **centre de p.** aerodynamic centre, centre of pressure; *(de liquide)* centre of buoyancy; *Phys* **axe de p.** aerodynamic axis; *Phys* **force de p.** upward thrust; **la p. de la foule** the pushing and shoving of the crowd **2** *(geste, fait de pousser qn)* push, shove; **écarter qch d'une p.** to push *or* shove sth aside **3** *(fait de croître)* growth; *Méd (accès) (de boutons, d'herpès)* eruption, outbreak; **p. de croissance** spurt of growth; **faire une p. de croissance** to shoot up; **p. de fièvre** sudden rise *of* or in temperature **4** *Fig (augmentation soudaine) (des prix, de l'inflation etc)* upsurge (**de** in)

pousse-pousse NM INV **1** rickshaw; **en p.** by rickshaw **2** *Suisse (poussette)* pushchair, *Am* stroller

POUSSER [puse]

| VT to push **1, 2** ▪ to shove **1** ▪ to urge on **2** ▪ to pursue **3** ▪ to grow **4** |
| VI to push **1** ▪ to push on **2** ▪ to grow **3** |
| VPR to move over **2** |

VT **1** *(soumettre à une force)* to push; *(rudement)* to shove; *(bétail)* to drive; *(bicyclette)* to push, to wheel; *(charrette, brouette)* to push (along); *(du vent) (embarcation)* to blow, to drive; **p. qn du coude/du genou** to nudge sb (with one's elbow/knee); **p. la porte/les volets** *(ouvrir)* to push the door/the shutters open; *(fermer)* to push the door/the shutters to; **on a poussé tous les meubles et on a dansé** we pushed all the furniture out of the way *or* aside and danced; **pousse un peu la chaise, je ne vois plus rien** push the chair out of the way *or* move the chair a bit, I can't see anything; **il poussa le moteur encore un peu plus** he pushed the engine a little harder, he squeezed a bit more out of the engine; **p. un pion** *(aux échecs)* to move a pawn; *Fig* **p. l'aiguille** to sew; *Fig Fam* **p. le bouchon trop loin** to go too far; *Fig Fam* **faut pas p. Mémé** *ou* **Mémère dans les orties!** don't push your luck!; *Fig Fam* **à la va comme je te pousse** slipshod; **fait à la va comme je te pousse** done in a slipshod way; *Fam* **pousse tes fesses** *ou* **très**

Fam **ton cul!** shift yourself!, shove over!
2 *(inciter) (quelqu'un)* to push, to urge on; *(cheval)* to urge on; **des élèves qu'il faut p.** pupils who need pushing *or* to be pushed; **il n'a pas fallu le p. beaucoup pour qu'il accepte** he didn't need much pushing *or* convincing to accept; **nous avons dû le p. à la roue pour qu'il …** we had to push him a bit to get him to …; **p. qn à faire qch** *(de la faim, la jalousie etc)* to drive sb to do sth, to lead sb to do sth; *(d'une personne) (contre son gré)* to push sb into doing sth; *(encourager)* to urge *or* encourage sb to do sth, to egg sb on to do sth; **p. qn à la dépense** to encourage sb to spend money; **les publicités sont faites pour p. à la consommation** advertisements are designed to encourage *or* stimulate consumption; **poussé par la pitié/la curiosité** prompted by pity/curiosity; *très Fam* **p. qn au cul** to give sb a kick up the back side **3** *(continuer) (études)* to pursue, to continue; **p. trop loin une plaisanterie** to take *or* carry a joke too far; **si l'on pousse encore plus loin cette explication/hypothèse** if we take this explanation/hypothesis further still; **p. qch jusqu'au bout** *ou* **jusqu'à l'extrême** to push *or* take sth to the limit; **il a même poussé la générosité jusqu'à …** he was so generous that he even …; **p. les enchères** to push up the bidding; **p. le chauffage/le son** to turn up the heating/volume; **p. le feu** to poke the fire; *Tech* **p. les feux** to raise steam, to stoke up **4** *(produire) (feuilles, racines)* to put out, to grow; *(d'un enfant) (dents)* to cut **5** *(exprimer)* **p. un cri** to shout, to give a shout; **p. des cris** to shout; **p. un cri de joie/de douleur** to shout with joy/pain, to give *or* *Fml* utter a shout of joy/pain; **p. un soupir** to sigh, to give *or* heave a sigh; **p. un gémissement** to groan, to moan, to give a groan *or* moan; **p. des acclamations** to cheer; **p. un juron** to swear; *Fam* **p. la chansonnette** *ou* **la romance, en p. une** to sing a song; *Fam* **il nous en a poussé une** he gave us a song; *très Fam* **p. une gueulante** to raise the roof, to kick up one hell of a stink

VI **1** *(faire un effort pour expulser qch)* to push; **ne poussez pas!** don't push!, don't shove!; *Fig* **p. à la roue** to do some pushing; *Fig Fam* **faut pas p.!** don't push your luck!; *Fam* **partir sans prévenir, vraiment, tu pousses!** going without saying anything, really, it's a bit much *or* you're taking things a bit too far!
2 *(continuer, avancer)* to push on; *Mil* to push forward; **p. jusqu'au bois** to push on as far as the wood
3 *(croître) (d'une plante, des cheveux, des ongles, d'une ville)* to grow; *(d'un bourgeon)* to sprout; *(des dents)* to come through; **laisser p. sa barbe** to grow a beard; **ses dents commencent à p.** his teeth are beginning to come through, he's beginning to cut his teeth; **p. comme du chiendent** to grow like a weed; **des villes qui ont poussé comme des champignons** towns that sprang up like mushrooms, towns that mushroomed; **tous ces enfants poussent** *(grandissent)* these children are all shooting up; **qu'est-ce qu'elle a poussé!** hasn't she grown!
4 *(inciter)* **p. à** to press *or* push for; **p. au changement** to press *or* push for change; **p. à la manifestation/la grève** to press *or* push for a demonstration/a strike; *Écon* **p. à la hausse/la baisse** to have an inflationary/a deflationary effect; **poussé par les profits** profit-driven

VPR **se pousser 1** *(se mettre en vue)* to push oneself forward; *(dans la société etc)* to make one's way
2 *(se presser) (pour faire de la place)* to move *or* shift over *or* up
3 *Can Fam (s'enfuir)* to take off, *Br* to scarper

poussette [puset] NF *(voiture d'enfants)* pushchair, *Am* stroller; *(Caddie®)* shopping trolley *or Am* cart

pousseur [pusœr] NM **1** *(bateau)* tug **2** *Astronaut* booster rocket

poussier [pusje] NM coal dust, *Spéc* screenings; *(charbon)* slack

poussière [pusjɛr] NF dust; **une p.** a speck of dust; **p. d'or** gold dust; **enlever la p. des meubles** to dust the furniture; *Fam* **faire la p.** *ou* **les poussières** to do the dusting, to dust; **couvert de p.** dusty, covered in dust; **s'en aller** *ou* **tomber en p.** to crumble (away) to dust; **réduire qch en p.** to reduce sth to dust; *Fig* to demolish sth; **mordre la p.** to bite the dust; **je lui ferai mordre la p.** I'll wipe the floor with him; *Fam* **dix euros/jours et des poussières** ten and a bit euros/days, ten euros/days and a bit; **poussières radioactives** radioactive dust

poussiéreux, -euse [pusjerø, -øz] ADJ dusty; *Fig (terne)* dull, humdrum; *(dépassé)* outmoded

poussif, -ive [pusif, -iv] ADJ *(personne)* wheezy, short-winded; *(cheval)* broken-winded; *(moteur)* wheezy

poussin [pusɛ̃] NM *Zool* chick; *Culin* spring chicken; *Fam* **mon p.** pet

poussivement [pusivmɑ̃] ADV wheezily

poussoir [puswar] NM *(d'une sonnerie électrique)* (push) button; *Tech (d'une valve)* push rod; *Aut* tappet, cam follower; *Ordinat (de souris)* button; **p. à ressort** trigger

poutou [putu] NM *Fam (baiser)* kiss

poutrage [putraʒ] NM, **poutraison** [putrɛzɔ̃] NF *Constr* framework of beams

poutre [putr] NF **1** *(en bois)* beam; **grosse p.** ba(u)lk; **p. de faîte** ridge piece, roof tree; **p. de plancher** ceiling joist; **poutres apparentes** exposed beams **2** *(en métal)* girder; **p. à âme pleine** plate girder; **p. à caisson** box girder; **p. maîtresse** main girder *or* beam

poutrelle [putrɛl] NF *Constr* girder

poutser [putse] VT *Suisse Fam* to clean

POUVOIR¹ [puvwar] NM **1** *(possibilité)* power, ability; **il n'est pas en mon p. de …** it is not within *or* it is beyond my power to …; **je ferai tout ce qui est en mon p.** I'll do everything (that's) in my power; **avoir le p. de faire qch** to have the power to do sth; **il a des pouvoirs surnaturels** he has supernatural powers
2 *Chimie, Phys etc (propriété)* **p. calorifique** calorific value; **p. rayonnant** radiating capacity; *Aut* **p. antidétonant** anti-knock rating; **p. absorbant** absorbency
3 *(puissance)* power; **p. politique** political power; **p. absolu** absolute power; **avoir un p. absolu sur qn** to have complete power over sb; **avoir un certain p. sur qn** to have a (certain) power over sb; **tenir qn en son p.** to have sb in one's power; **le p. des sens/des images/des mots** the power of the senses/of images/of words; **abuser de son p.** *ou* **de ses pouvoirs** to abuse one's power; **vouloir prendre le p.** to aim for power; **prendre le p.** to assume power; **arriver au p.** to come to power; **le parti au p.** the party in power; **quand les Libéraux sont au p.** when the Liberals are in (power); *Fig* **dans les milieux proches du p.** in the corridors of power; *Fig* **une affaire qui concerne le p.** a government matter; **huit ans de p.** eight years in power; **avoir un p. de décision** to have decision-making power *or* ability; **en vertu des pouvoirs qui me sont conférés …** by virtue of the powers invested in me …
4 *Jur (procuration)* power of attorney; **avoir/recevoir plein(s) pouvoir(s) pour agir** to have full powers/to be (fully) empowered *or* authorized to act; **se présenter sans pou-**

voirs réguliers to come without full credentials; **bon pour p.** good for proxy ▸▸*Écon* **p. d'achat** purchasing power, buying power; **p. exécutif** executive power; **p. judiciaire** judicial power; *(les juges)* judiciary; **p. législatif** legislative power; **les pouvoirs publics** the authorities, the public authorities

---

POUVOIR² *(prp* **pouvant;** *pp* **pu;** *pr ind* **je peux, je puis** *(always* **puis-je** [pɥiʒ]*),* **tu peux, il peut, n. pouvons, ils peuvent;** *pr sub* **je puisse, n. puissions;** *impf* **je pouvais;** *p hist* **je pus;** *fu* **je pourrai** [pure]*)*

> **VT** to be able to **1** ▪ to be allowed to **2**
> ▪ can **1–3** ▪ may **2–4** ▪ might **3**
> **V IMPERS** can, may, might

VT SEE GRAMMAR A58–60; B39–40 **1** *(être capable)* to be able; **faire tout ce qu'on peut** to do one's best, to do the best *or* all *or* everything one can; **si je peux** if I can, if I'm able to; **je ne peux pas** I can't, I'm unable to; **je ne peux (pas) le faire** I can't *or* cannot do it, I'm unable *or* not able to do it; **cela ne peut (pas) se faire** it can't *or* cannot be done; **comment a-t-il pu dire cela?** how could he say that?; **comment a-t-il pu?** how could he?; **il aurait pu le faire s'il avait voulu** he could have done it if he had wanted to; **si vous aviez pu le voir** if you could have seen him, if you'd been able to see him; **il ne pouvait pas l'accompagner** he couldn't go with him, he wasn't able *or* he was unable to go with him; **j'ai fait toutes les démarches que j'ai pu** I took every step that I possibly could; **j'ai pu le revoir** I managed *or* got *or* was able to see him again; **je n'y peux rien** I can't help it; **on n'y peut rien** it can't be helped, there's nothing that can be done about it; **il a été on ne peut plus grossier** he couldn't have been ruder, he was extremely rude; **des gens on ne peut plus aimables** extremely kind people; **il travaille on ne peut mieux** he's as good a worker as it's possible to be; **il n'en peut plus (de fatigue)** he's quite exhausted *or* worn out *or* tired out; **je n'en peux plus (de ses scènes/des voisins)** I've had enough *or* I can't take any more (of his scenes/the neighbours); **il n'en peut plus** *(d'impatience)* he can't take any more; **elle peut beaucoup** she's very capable; **sauve qui peut** every man for himself; **on ne peut pas ne pas l'admirer** you can't not admire him, you can't help but admire him, you have to admire him; **je viendrai aussitôt que je pourrai** I'll come as soon as I can *or* I'm able; **qu'est-ce qu'il peut bien me vouloir?** what(ever) can he want?; **où pouvait-il bien être à cette heure?** where(ver) could he be at this time?; **la loi ne peut rien contre lui** the law can't touch him; **nous ne pouvons rien pour vous** we can't do anything for you

2 *(avoir le droit, la permission (de))* to be allowed to; **vous pouvez partir** you can *or Fml* may go; **elle ne peut pas sortir seule** she can't go out alone, she isn't allowed out alone; **puis-je entrer?** can *or Fml* may I come in?; **quand pourrai-je emménager?** when can I move in?, when will I be able to move in?

3 *(être possible)* **la porte a pu se fermer toute seule** the door may have *or* could have closed on its own; **on peut se tromper, n'est-ce pas?** after all, we may *or* could be wrong; **nous pourrions le trouver si nous nous dépêchions** we might *or* could find him if we hurry; **elle pourrait le rencontrer, si elle le voulait** she could meet him if she wanted to; **elle peut bien s'excuser, je ne lui pardonnerai pas** she can apologize all she likes, but I shan't forgive her; **tout de même, vous auriez (bien) pu faire moins de bruit** all the

same, you could have *or* might have made less noise; **tu peux (bien) me raconter tout ce que tu veux …** you can say what you like …; **il pouvait être trois ou quatre heures du matin** it might have been three or four in the morning; *Fam* **qu'est-ce que ça peut (bien) te faire?** what's that got to do with you?

4 *Litt* **puisse-t-il défendre nos lois!** may he defend our laws!

V IMPERS cela se peut (bien) it may be *or* it could well be (the case), it's quite possible, maybe, possibly; **cela ne se peut pas** that's impossible, that's not possible; **ça se pourrait (bien)** that's quite possible; **advienne que pourra** come what may; **autant que faire se peut** as much as can/could be done; **il peut se faire** *ou* **il peut arriver que … +** *sub* it may be *or* may happen that …; **il se peut qu'il vienne** he may *or* might come; **il se peut qu'il ne soit pas coupable** he may not *or* might not be guilty

---

pp [pepe] **1** *abrév* **port payé 2** *(abrév* **par procuration)** *(à la fin d'une lettre)* pp

PPCM [pepeseɛm] NM *Math (abrév* **plus petit commun multiple)** LCM

ppm [pepeɛm] **1** *(abrév* **parties par million)** ppm **2** *(abrév* **pages par minute)** ppm

ppp [pepepe] NMPL *Ordinat (abrév* **pixels par pouce)** ppi

PQ [peky] NM **1** *Can Pol (abrév* **Parti Québécois)** PQ **2** *très Fam (papier hygiénique)* toilet paper, *Br* loo paper, *Br* bog roll

PR¹ [peɛʀ] *abrév* **poste restante**

PR² NM *abrév* **Parti Républicain**

pragmatique [pʀagmatik] ADJ pragmatic

pragmatisme [pʀagmatism] NM pragmatism

pragmatiste [pʀagmatist] ADJ, N pragmatist

Prague [pʀag] N Prague

praire [pʀɛʀ] NF clam

prairial [pʀɛʀjal] NM *Hist* = ninth month of the French Republican Calendar (May-June)

prairie [pʀeʀi] NF *(pré, champ)* meadow; *(large étendue)* grassland, *Am* prairie; **p. artificielle** cultivated grassland; *Géog* **la P.** the Prairies

pralin [pʀalɛ̃] NM *Culin* praline

praline [pʀalin] NF **1** *Culin* praline; *Péj Fam* **cucul la p.** silly, idiotic **2** *Fam (balle d'arme à feu)* bullet, slug

praliné [pʀaline] ADJ *Culin (chocolat)* praline-filled; *(crème, glace)* praline-flavoured; **amandes pralinées** = almonds coated in caramelized sugar

praticable [pʀatikabl] ADJ *(possible, réalisable),* Théâtre *(porte, fenêtre)* practicable; *(projet, idée)* feasible, practicable; *(route etc)* passable, negotiable
▪ NM *Théâtre (décor)* practicable scenery; *Cin,* TV dolly

praticien, -ienne [pʀatisjɛ̃, -jɛn] N **1** *Jur (legal)* practitioner; *Méd (medical)* practitioner **2** *(technicien)* practitioner **3** *Beaux-Arts (ouvrier)* sculptor's assistant

praticité [pʀatisite] NF *(caractère pratique)* practicality

pratiquant, -ante [pʀatikɑ̃, -ɑ̃t] *Rel* ADJ practising; **catholique p.** practising Catholic; **il est très p.** he's very religious, he's a strong believer; *(d'un chrétien)* he's a regular churchgoer, he goes to church regularly
▪ N religious person; *(chrétien)* (regular) churchgoer

pratique [pʀatik] ADJ *(méthode, personne etc)* practical; *(gadget, outil etc)* practical, handy; *(date, heure, jour)* convenient; **avoir l'esprit p.** to have a practical turn of mind, to be practically minded; **sens p.** practical

common sense; **c'est très p. d'avoir l'école si près de la maison** it's very practical *or* handy to have the school so close to the house; **cette crème n'est pas p. à appliquer** this cream isn't easy to apply
▪ NF **1** *(application)* practice; **mettre qch en p.** to put sth into practice; **c'est une p. courante** it's common practice, it's quite usual; **la théorie et la p.** theory and practice; **en p.** in practice

2 *(expérience)* (practical) experience; *Litt (de la vertu)* practice; **p. du théâtre** theatrical experience; **la p. du football m'a valu une jambe cassée** I got a broken leg *or* I broke my leg (through) playing football; **la p. d'un sport est encouragée** sporting activity *or* practising a sport is encouraged; **perdre la p. de qch** to lose the knack of sth; *(d'un sport, d'une activité)* to get out of practice at sth; **avoir une grande** *ou* **longue p. de qch** to have a lot of (practical) experience of sth

3 *Jur (de la loi)* practice; **terme de p.** legal term

4 *(action)* practice; **pratiques clandestines** underhand practices; **pratiques religieuses** religious practices; *Com* **pratiques restrictives** restrictive practices; **la p. de ce genre de vente est illégale en France** this kind of sales practice is illegal in France; *Jur* **libre p.** *(de sa religion etc)* free exercise; *Naut* **avoir libre p.** to be out of quarantine

5 *(d'avocat, de médecin)* practice; *(de fournisseur)* custom, business; *Vieilli (clientèle) (d'un avocat)* clients; *(d'un médecin)* patients; *(d'un fournisseur)* customers

6 *Arch* **il avait vécu dans la p. des hauts fonctionnaires** he had associated with high-ranking civil servants

pratiquement [pʀatikmɑ̃] ADV *(dans l'expérience)* in practice; *(en fait)* in actual fact; *(presque)* practically, virtually; **il ne vient p. jamais plus** he practically never comes any more

pratiquer [pʀatike] VT **1** *(exercer) (activité, sorcellerie, vertu, charité, religion etc)* to practise; *(méthode)* to employ, to use; *(langue)* to use; **il pratique le football** he plays football; **elle pratique la natation** she's a (keen) swimmer, she swims; **elle ne pratique aucun sport** she doesn't do *or* take part in *or* practise any sport; **il a appris le piano mais ne pratique plus beaucoup** he learnt the piano but doesn't play it much any more; *Com* **les cours pratiqués** the ruling prices; **les prix pratiqués ici** the prices being asked here **2** *Méd* **p. une intervention** to carry out an operation, to operate; **p. une petite incision** to make a small incision **3** *(ménager)* to make; **p. une ouverture dans un mur** to make an opening in a wall; **p. un sentier** to make a path, to open up a path **4** *(livre, auteur)* to study **5** *Arch (fréquenter)* to frequent, to associate with
▪ VI **1** *(travailler) (d'un médecin, avocat, conseiller)* to practise; **il ne pratique plus** he's no longer in practice, he no longer practises **2** *Rel* to observe the practices of one's religion; **ils sont catholiques mais ils ne pratiquent pas** they're Catholics but not practising Catholics
▪ VPR **se pratiquer** to be practised; **le commerce de l'ivoire se pratique encore** ivory trading still goes on *or* is still practised; **les mariages arrangés ne se pratiquent plus** arranged marriages no longer take place; **voilà comment ça se pratique** that's how it's done

praxis [pʀaksis] NF praxis

pré [pʀe] NM meadow; *Arch* **aller sur le p.** to fight a duel

pré-acheminement, *pl* **pré-acheminements** [pʀeaʃ(ə)minmɑ̃] NM transfer to main airport

préadhésion [preadezjɔ̃] NF *UE* pre-accession

préadolescence [preadɔlesɑ̃s] NF preadolescence

préadolescent, -ente [preadɔlesɑ̃, -ɑ̃t] N preadolescent, preteen

préalable [prealabl] ADJ previous, prior (**à** to); *(accord)* prior; **formalités préalables au débat** formalities that precede the debate; **mais il y a quelques formalités préalables** but there are a few formalities to be gone through first
▸ NM **1** *(condition)* prerequisite, precondition; **préalables d'un accord** pre-contract conditions; **au p.** first, beforehand **2** *Arch (préparation)* preliminary

préalablement [prealabləmɑ̃] ADV first, beforehand; **p. à ...** prior to ...

pré-allumage [prealymaʒ] NM *Aut* pre-ignition

Préalpes (les) [leprealp] NFPL the foothills of the Alps

préalpin [prealpɛ̃] ADJ of the foothills of the Alps

préambule [preɑ̃byl] NM *(d'un discours)* preamble (**de** to); *(d'une action)* prelude (**de** to); **il a abordé le sujet sans p.** he (dispensed with preliminaries and) came straight to the point; **sans p., elle lui a demandé son âge** she asked him straight off how old he was

préamplificateur [preɑ̃plifikatœr] NM *Électron* preamplifier

PréAO [preao] NF *Ordinat (abrév présentation assistée par ordinateur)* computer-assisted presentation

préapprentissage [preaprɑ̃tisaʒ] NM pre-apprenticeship training

préau, -aux [preo] NM **1** *(cour intérieure)* (court)yard **2** *(partie couverte)* covered part (of the playground)

préavis [preavi] NM (previous *or* advance) notice; **exiger un p. de trois mois** to require three months' notice; **sans p.** without notice *or* warning; **p. de licenciement** notice (of dismissal); **p. de paiement** payment advice; **p. de grève** strike notice; **déposer un p. de grève** to give notice of strike action

prébende [prebɑ̃d] NF *Rel* prebend; *Fig (profit)* sizeable income

prébendé [prebɑ̃de] ADJ *Rel* prebendal

prébendier [prebɑ̃dje] NM *Rel* prebendary

précaire [prekɛr] ADJ *(position, état de santé)* precarious; *(santé)* delicate; *(abri)* precarious, rickety; *(emploi)* insecure; **être dans un équilibre un peu p.** to be rather precariously balanced

précairement [prekɛrmɑ̃] ADV precariously

précambrien, -ienne [prekɑ̃brijɛ̃, -jɛn] ADJ *Géol* Precambrian, Pre-Cambrian

précarisation [prekarizasjɔ̃] NF jeopardizing; **p. de l'emploi** casualization of labour

précariser [prekarize] VT to jeopardize

précarité [prekarite] NF precariousness; **p. de l'emploi** lack of job security

précaution [prekosjɔ̃] NF **1** *(mesure)* precaution; **prendre des** *ou* **ses précautions** to take precautions (**pour** for); *Euph* **prendre ses précautions** to go *(to the toilet)*; **mesures de p.** precautionary measures; **par (mesure de) p.** as a precaution; **précautions oratoires** carefully chosen remarks; *Prov* **deux précautions valent mieux qu'une** you can never be too sure, better safe than sorry **2** *(soin)* caution, wariness, care; **avec p.** cautiously, warily, carefully; **pour plus de p.** to be extra safe, to be on the safe side, to err on the side of caution

précautionner [prekosjɔne] VT *Arch* to warn, to caution (**contre** against)
▸ VPR **se précautionner** to take precautions; **se p. contre qch** to take precautions *or* guard against sth

précautionneusement [prekosjɔnøzmɑ̃] ADV carefully

précautionneux, -euse [prekosjɔnø, -øz] ADJ careful

précédemment [presedamɑ̃] ADV previously, before

précédent [presedɑ̃] ADJ previous; **le jour/mois p.** the day/month before, the previous day/month
▸ NM precedent; **créer un p.** to create *or* set a precedent; **sans p.** unprecedented, without precedent

précéder [presede] *(conj like* **céder)** VT to precede; **la musique précède les troupes** the band marches in front of *or* precedes the troops; **il me précédait pour me guider** he went in front of *or* preceded me in order to guide me; **l'antichambre qui précède le salon** the antechamber leading to the drawing room; **je l'ai précédé de 10 minutes** I got there ten minutes before he did *or* before him *or* ahead of him; **nous serons précédés de quelques jours par nos enfants** our children will get there a few days before we do *or* before us *or* ahead of us; **le scandale a précédé la révélation de l'affaire** the scandal occurred before the affair came to light; **sa réputation le précédait** his reputation went before *or* preceded him; **p. qn (en dignité)** to have precedence over sb; **faire p. un concert d'un discours** to preface a concert with a speech
▸ VI **la page qui précède** the preceding *or* previous page, the page before; **dans les jours qui précèdent** in the days before, in the preceding days; **ce qui précède** the foregoing

précepte [presɛpt] NM precept

précepteur, -trice [preseptœr, -tris] N (private) tutor

préceptorat [preseptɔra] NM tutorship

précession [presesjɔ̃] NF precession

préchambre [preʃɑ̃br] NF *Tech (d'un moteur diesel)* precombustion chamber

précharge [preʃarʒ] NF *Aut* pre-load

préchargé [preʃarʒe] ADJ *(logiciel)* pre-loaded

préchauffage [preʃofaʒ] NM pre-heating; *(d'un appareil)* warm-up; **p. moteur diesel** pre-heating

préchauffer [preʃofe] VT to pre-heat

prêche [prɛʃ] NM sermon

prêcher [preʃe] VT *(enseigner)* to preach (**à** to); **p. qn** to preach to sb; **p. l'économie** to preach economy; *Iron* **p. la bonne parole** to spread the good word; **p. un converti** to preach to the converted *or Am* to the choir
▸ VI *(prononcer un sermon)* to preach; *Fig (moraliser)* to preach, to preachify, to sermonize; *Rel, Fig* **p. dans le désert** to be a voice crying in the wilderness; **p. d'exemple** *ou* **par l'exemple** to practise what one preaches; *Fig* **p. pour sa paroisse** to look after one's own interests

prêcheur, -euse [preʃœr, -øz] ADJ **1** *(moine)* preaching **2** *(moralisateur) (personne)* sermonizing
▸ N *Fig Péj* sermonizer, preacher

prêchi-prêcha [preʃipreʃa] NM INV *Fam Péj* preaching, preachifying, sermonizing

précieusement [presjøzmɑ̃] ADV **1** *(avec soin)* very carefully; **garder** *ou* **conserver qch p.** to treasure sth **2** *(avec préciosité)* preciously, affectedly

précieux, -ieuse [presjø, -jøz] ADJ **1** *(d'une grande valeur)* precious; **pierre précieuse** precious stone **2** *(conseil, temps etc)* valuable (**à** to) **3** *Litt (style)* precious, affected, mannered
▸ NF *Hist, Littér* **précieuse** = pedantic, over-refined woman

préciosité [presjozite] NF *Litt* affectation, affectedness, preciosity

précipice [presipis] NM chasm, abyss; *(bord d'une falaise, d'un ravin etc)* precipice; *Fig* abyss; **au bord d'un p.** on the edge of a precipice; *Fig* **être au bord du p.** to be on the brink, to be on the edge of a precipice

précipitamment [presipitamɑ̃] ADV hurriedly, hastily, *Fml* precipitately; **entrer/sortir p.** to rush *or* hurry *or* dash in/out; **agir trop p.** to be too hasty *or Fml* precipitate, to be overhasty, to act too hastily *or Fml* precipitately

précipitation [presipitasjɔ̃] NF **1** *(grande hâte)* haste, great hurry, *Fml* precipitation; **avec p.** hurriedly, hastily, *Fml* precipitately; **entrer/sortir avec p.** to hurry *or* rush *or* dash in/out **2** *Chimie, Phys* precipitation **3** *Météo* **précipitations** precipitation

précipité [presipite] ADJ *(action, décision)* hasty, hurried, *Fml* precipitate; *(départ)* hasty, hurried, abrupt; *(pouls)* racing; **s'avancer à pas précipités** to rush forward; **un bruit de pas précipités** (the sound of) hurried *or* quick footsteps
▸ NM *Chimie* precipitate

précipiter [presipite] VT **1** *(entraîner)* to throw down, to hurl down; *Fig* to plunge; **p. qn contre un mur/dans le vide** to hurl sb against a wall/over the edge; *Fig* **p. qn dans le désespoir/le malheur** to plunge sb into despair/misfortune; **p. un peuple dans la guerre** to plunge a nation into war **2** *(dépêcher, hâter) (un achat, une embauche, un mariage etc)* to speed up; *(événements)* to precipitate; *(la mort de qn, la perte de qn)* to hasten; **il ne faut rien p.** we mustn't rush things, we mustn't be overhasty **3** *Chimie (substance)* to precipitate
▸ VI *Chimie (d'une substance)* to precipitate, to form a precipitate
▸ VPR **se précipiter 1** *(se hâter)* to rush, to hurry **2** *(s'accélérer)* **les événements se sont précipités** things started happening quickly **3** *(se jeter)* to rush (**sur** at; **vers** towards); **se p. à la fenêtre** to rush to the window; **se p. aux pieds de qn** to throw oneself at sb's feet; **dès qu'il rentre à la maison, il se précipite devant la télévision** as soon as he gets home, he throws himself down in front of the television; **le fleuve se précipite dans la mer** the river rushes into the sea **4** *Chimie* to precipitate

précis [presi] ADJ *(description, vocabulaire, plan, but etc)* precise, exact; **à cet instant p.** at this precise *or* exact moment; **exiger d'une façon précise que ...** to call unambiguously for ...; **à deux heures précises** at two o'clock precisely *or* exactly *or* sharp; **je suis parti sans raison précise** I left for no definite reason *or* for no particular reason; **en termes p.** in precise terms, precisely; **il est très p. dans son travail** he's very meticulous *or* precise *or* exact in his work; **des gestes p.** precise movements; **pensez-vous à quelque chose de p.?** do you have something specific in mind?; **pour être plus p.** to be more precise
▸ NM précis, summary, abstract; *(livre)* handbook; **p. d'histoire de France** short history of France

précisément [presizemɑ̃] ADV **1** *(exactement)* precisely, exactly; **ou plus p. ...** or more precisely ..., or to be more precise ...; **ce n'est pas p. une réussite** it's not exactly a success, it's not (exactly) what you'd call a success; **a-t-il dit cela? – oui, p.** did he say that? – yes, those were his very words **2**

(justement) **c'est p. l'homme que je cherche** he's just the man I'm looking for; **c'est p. ce que je lui disais** that's just *or* exactly what I said to him/her; **p. il m'en fallait un aujourd'hui** as it happens *or* as a matter of fact, I needed one today

préciser [presize] VT **1** *(déterminer) (prix, date, informations)* to specify; **il faut p. vos affirmations/arguments** you must be (more) explicit *or* specific in your statements/arguments **2** *(rendre plus net)* to clarify; **je tiens à p. que …** I wish to make it clear that …; **p. la date de la réunion** to give the exact *or* precise date of the meeting; **la circulaire ne précise pas où aura lieu la réunion** the circular doesn't specify where the meeting will take place; **il n'a pas été précisé qu'il fallait être en tenue de soirée** it wasn't specifically stated that evening dress was to be worn, evening dress wasn't specified
VI to be (more) precise *or* explicit
VPR **se préciser** to become clear(er); *(des idées, d'un contrat)* to take shape; **les vacances se précisent** the holiday plans are taking shape

précision [presizjɔ̃] NF **1** *(exactitude) (d'information, d'une description, d'un travail)* accuracy; *(de mouvements)* preciseness, precision; **avec p.** accurately, precisely; **p. de tir** accuracy of fire; *Typ* **p. de frappe** keying accuracy; **instruments de p.** precision instruments **2** **une p.** a (precise) detail, a (point of) clarification; **donner** *ou* **apporter des précisions sur qch** to give precise details about sth; **demander des précisions sur qch** to ask for more *or* further information *or* details about sth; **merci de ces précisions** thank you for this information

précité [presite] ADJ aforesaid, aforementioned; *(plus haut sur une page, dans un document)* above(-mentioned)

préclassique [preklasik] ADJ *Hist* preclassical

précoce [prekɔs] ADJ *(enfant)* precocious; *(fruit, gel)* early; *(sénilité, calvitie)* premature; **l'été est p. cette année** summer is early this year; **enfant p. pour son âge** child who is advanced *or* precocious for his age; **sexuellement p.** sexually precocious

précocement [prekɔsmɑ̃] ADV *Litt* precociously

précocité [prekɔsite] NF precociousness, precocity; *(de fruits, d'une saison etc)* earliness; **p. sexuelle** sexual precociousness

précolombien, -ienne [prekɔlɔ̃bjɛ̃, -jɛn] ADJ *Hist* pre-Columbian

précombustion [prekɔ̃bystjɔ̃] NF *Tech* precombustion

précommercialisation [prekɔmɛrsjalizasjɔ̃] NF *Mktg* pre-marketing

précomptabilisation [prekɔ̃tabilizasjɔ̃] NF preparation of accounting entries

précompte [prekɔ̃t] NM *(d'un compte, d'un salaire)* (advance) deduction

précompter [prekɔ̃te] VT to deduct, to withhold *(sur* from)

préconception [prekɔ̃sɛpsjɔ̃] NF preconception; *(contre quelqu'un, quelque chose)* prejudice

préconçu [prekɔ̃sy] ADJ preconceived; *Péj* **idée préconçue** preconceived idea

préconditionné [prekɔ̃disjɔne] ADJ prepacked, pre-packaged

préconditionner [prekɔ̃disjɔne] VT to prepack, to pre-package

préconfiguré [prekɔ̃figyre] ADJ *Ordinat* preconfigured

préconisation [prekɔnizasjɔ̃] NF recommendation

préconiser [prekɔnize] VT to recommend, to advocate; *(remède)* to recommend

précontraint [prekɔ̃trɛ̃] ADJ, NM *Tech* **(béton) p.** prestressed concrete

précouche [prekuʃ] NF precoating

précuit [prekɥi] ADJ pre-cooked, ready-cooked

précurseur [prekyrsœr] NM precursor, forerunner
ADJ precursory; **signe p.** forewarning, portent

prédateur, -trice [predatœr, -tris] ADJ predatory
NM predator

prédécesseur [predesesœr] NM predecessor

prédécoupé [predekupe] ADJ pre-cut, ready-cut

prédéfinition NF *Ordinat* **p. des secteurs** hard sectoring

prédélinquant, -ante [predelɛ̃kɑ̃, -ɑ̃t] N potential delinquent

prédestination [predɛstinasjɔ̃] NF predestination

prédestiné [predɛstine] ADJ predestined, fated *(à faire qch* to do sth); **p. à qch** predestined for sth

prédestiner [predɛstine] VT to predestine *(à faire qch* to do sth; **à qch** sth)

prédétermination [predetɛrminasjɔ̃] NF predetermination

prédéterminer [predetɛrmine] VT to predetermine

prédicant [predikɑ̃] NM *Rel* preacher

prédicat [predika] NM *Gram* predicate

prédicateur, -trice [predikatœr, -tris] N preacher

prédicatif, -ive [predikatif, -iv] ADJ *Gram* predicative

prédication [predikasjɔ̃] NF **1** *Rel* preaching; *(sermon)* sermon **2** *Gram* predication

prédiction [prediksjɔ̃] NF **1** *(action de prédire)* prediction, predicting, foretelling **2** *(ce qui est prédit)* prediction, forecast

prédigéré [prediʒere] ADJ predigested

prédilection [predilɛksjɔ̃] NF predilection, partiality, fondness; **auteur/restaurant de p.** favourite *or Am* favorite author/restaurant; **avoir une p. pour qch** to be partial to sth, to have a predilection *or* fondness for sth

prédire [predir] VT *(conj like* **dire** *except pr ind & imp* **(v.) prédisez)** to predict, to prophesy, to foretell; **p. qch à qn** to predict sth for sb; **p. que** to predict that

prédisposer [predispoze] VT to predispose *(à qch* to sth; **à faire qch** to do sth)

prédisposition [predispozisjɔ̃] NF predisposition *(à* to)

prédominance [predɔminɑ̃s] NF predominance

prédominant [predɔminɑ̃] ADJ predominant

prédominer [predɔmine] VI to predominate; *(d'une préoccupation)* to be uppermost; **ce qui prédomine chez lui, c'est la générosité** generosity is his chief quality

préélectoral, -ale, -aux, -ales [preelɛktɔral, -o] ADJ *Pol* pre-electoral, pre-election

préemballé [preɑ̃bale] ADJ pre-packed

préemballer [preɑ̃bale] VT to pre-pack, to pre-package

pré-embarquement [preɑ̃barkəmɑ̃] NM *(à un aéroport)* pre-boarding

pré-embarquer [preɑ̃barke] VI *(à un aéroport)* to pre-board

prééminence [preeminɑ̃s] NF pre-eminence

prééminent [preeminɑ̃] ADJ pre-eminent

préempter [preɑ̃pte] VT *Jur* to pre-empt

préemption [preɑ̃psjɔ̃] NF *Jur* pre-emption

préencollé [preɑ̃kɔle] ADJ *(papier peint)* pre-pasted, ready-pasted

préenregistré [preɑ̃r(ə)ʒistre] ADJ *TV, Radio* pre-recorded

préenregistrement [preɑ̃rəʒistrəmɑ̃] NM *(à un aéroport)* pre-registration; *TV, Radio* pre-recording

préétablir [preetablir] VT to pre-establish

préexistant [preɛgzistɑ̃] ADJ pre-existing, pre-existent

préexistence [preɛgzistɑ̃s] NF pre-existence

préexister [preɛgziste] VI to pre-exist; **p. à qch** to exist *or* be in existence before sth

préfabrication [prefabrikasjɔ̃] NF prefabrication

préfabriqué [prefabrike] ADJ prefabricated; *Fig Péj* **sourire p.** artificial smile; **candidat p.** packaged candidate
NM *(maison)* prefabricated house, *Fam* prefab

préface [prefas] NF **1** *(avant-propos)* preface, foreword *(à, de* to) **2** *Rel* preface

préfacer [prefase] VT to write a preface to *or* for, to preface

préfacier [prefasje] NM preface writer

préfacturation [prefaktyrasjɔ̃] NF *Compta* prebilling

préfectoral, -ale, -aux, -ales [prefɛktɔral, -o] ADJ *Admin* prefectorial

préfecture [prefɛktyr] NF *Admin* prefecture; **la P. de police** police headquarters; **p. maritime** = area under command of a port admiral; *(bureau)* naval superintendent's office, port admiral's office

> **Préfecture**
> This refers to the main administrative office of each "département". The word has also come to refer to the town where the office is located. One goes to the "préfecture" to obtain a driving licence or a "carte de séjour", for example.

préférable [preferabl] ADJ preferable *(à* to); **il serait p. de le revoir** *ou* **qu'on le revoie** it would be preferable *or* better to see him again

préférablement [preferabləmɑ̃] ADV preferably

préféré, -ée [prefere] ADJ, N favourite, *Am* favorite

préférence [preferɑ̃s] NF preference; **de p.** preferably; **de p. à …** in preference to …; **donner** *ou* **accorder la p. à qn** to give sb preference *(sur* over); **il n'a pas de p.** he has no (particular) preference; **par ordre de p.** in order of preference; *Jur* **droits de p.** priority rights; *Fin* **actions de p.** preference shares, *Am* preferred stock; **la p. nationale** policy of discrimination in favour of a country's own nationals *(as opposed to immigrants)*; *Ordinat* **préférences** preferences

préférentiel, -ielle [preferɑ̃sjɛl] ADJ preferential; *Jur* **vote p.** preferential voting (system); **tarif p.** preferential rate

préférer [prefere] VT *(* **je préfère; je préférerai** *)* to prefer *(à* to); **je préférerais du thé** I'd prefer tea, I'd rather have tea; **je préférerais que vous veniez** I'd prefer it if you came, I'd rather you came; **p. faire qch** to prefer to do sth; **il préféra mourir plutôt que de se rendre** he preferred to die rather than surrender, he died rather than surrender; **je préfère ne pas y aller** I'd rather not go, I'd prefer not to go

préfet [prefɛ] NM *Admin* prefect; **p. de police** = chief commissioner of police; *Naut* **p. maritime** port admiral, commander-in-chief of the port

préfète [prefɛt] NF *Admin* prefect; *(épouse)* prefect's wife

préfiguration [prefigyrasjɔ̃] NF prefiguration, foreshadowing

préfigurer [prefigyre] VT to prefigure, to foreshadow

préfinancement [prefinɑ̃smɑ̃] NM *Fin* advance funding, pre-financing

préfixal, -ale, -aux, -ales [prefiksal, -o] ADJ *Gram* prefixal

préfixation [prefiksasjɔ̃] NF *Gram* prefixation

préfixe [prefiks] NM *Ling, Tél* prefix

préfixer [prefikse] VT to prefix

préformaté [prefɔrmate] ADJ *Ordinat* preformatted

préformater [prefɔrmate] VT *Ordinat* to preformat

pré-gardiennat [pregardjena] NM *Belg* *(jardin d'enfants)* nursery school, *Am* kindergarten

préglaciaire [preglasjɛr] ADJ *Géol* pre-glacial

préhellénique [preelenik] ADJ pre-Hellenic

préhenseur [preɑ̃sœr] ADJ M prehensile

préhensile [preɑ̃sil] ADJ prehensile

préhension [preɑ̃sjɔ̃] NF gripping, *Spéc* prehension

préhistoire [preistwar] NF prehistory

préhistorique [preistɔrik] ADJ prehistoric

préimpression [preɛ̃presjɔ̃] NF *Typ* pre-press

préimprimé [preɛ̃prime] NM preprinted form

préimprimée [preɛ̃prime] NF preprinted form

préimputation [preɛ̃pytasjɔ̃] NF *Compta* pre-input preparation

préindustriel, -ielle [preɛ̃dystrijɛl] ADJ pre-industrial

préinscription [preɛ̃skripsjɔ̃] NF pre-check-in

préinstallé [preɛ̃stale] ADJ *Ordinat* preinstalled

préinstaller [preɛ̃stale] VT *Ordinat* to preinstall

préjudice [preʒydis] NM *(à une cause, à la situation de qn etc)* prejudice, detriment; *(à une personne)* harm, wrong, injury; *(aux perspectives de qn)* damage; *Jur* tort; **subir un p. (matériel)** to sustain damage; **subir un p. (moral)** to be wronged; **porter p. à qn** to do sb harm; *(d'une action, d'une déclaration)* to be prejudicial to sb's interests; **p. financier** financial harm; **au p. de qn** to the prejudice *or* detriment of sb; **au p. de la justice** at the expense of justice; **sans p. de …** without prejudice to …

> Il faut noter que le terme anglais **prejudice** est un faux ami. Il signifie le plus souvent **préjugé**.

préjudiciable [preʒydisjabl] ADJ prejudicial, detrimental, harmful (**à** to)

préjudiciel, -ielle [preʒydisjɛl] ADJ *Jur* *(question)* interlocutory; *(action)* prejudicial

préjudicier [preʒydisje] VI *(pr sub, impf n. préjudiciions) Arch, Litt* to be detrimental *or* prejudicial (**à** to)

préjugé [preʒyʒe] NM *(opinion toute faite)* prejudice, bias; **p. de classe** class prejudice; **préjugés raciaux** racial prejudice; **avoir un p. pour** *ou* **envers/contre qn/qch** to be prejudiced *or* bias(s)ed in favour *or Am* favor

of/against sb/sth; **elle avait un p. favorable à son égard** he had created a favourable *or Am* favorable impression upon her; **bénéficier d'un p. favorable** *(dans une course)* to look a likely winner; *(avoir bonne réputation)* to be well thought of

préjuger [preʒyʒe] VI *(conj like juger)* **p. de qch** to prejudge sth; **autant qu'on peut en p.** as far as one can judge beforehand *or* in advance; **il ne faut jamais p. de l'avenir** you can't tell what the future has in store

prélart [prelar] NM tarpaulin

prélasser (se) [səprelase] VPR to lounge, to loll; *(au soleil)* to bask

prélat [prela] NM prelate

prélature [prelatyr] NF prelacy

prélavage [prelavaʒ] NM prewash

prèle, prêle [prɛl] NF *Bot* horsetail

prélèvement [prelɛvmɑ̃] NM **1** *Fin (action)* deduction, withholding (**sur** from); **p. sur le capital** *ou* **sur la fortune** capital levy; **faire un p. sur un compte** to debit an account; **p. fiscal** tax deduction; **p. de l'impôt à la source** taxation at source; **p. salarial** deduction from wages; **prélèvements sociaux** social security contributions **2** *Ind (action)* sampling; *(échantillon)* sample; **nous procéderons ensuite à un p. d'échantillons** next we shall proceed to take some samples **3** *Méd (action)* sampling; *(échantillon)* sample; *(d'un organe)* removal; *(de sécrétion)* swab; **faire un p. à qn** to take a sample from sb; **faire un p. de sang** *ou* **sanguin à qn** to take a blood sample from sb
▸▸ *Banque* **p. automatique** direct debit; **prélèvements obligatoires** = tax and social security contributions

prélever [prelve] VT *(conj like lever)* **1** *(somme d'argent)* to deduct, to withhold (**sur** from); *(impôt)* to levy; **p. des taxes** to withhold taxes, to deduct taxes; **p. une commission de deux pour cent** to deduct *or* charge a commission of two per cent; **p. qch à la source** to deduct sth at source **2** *(organe)* to remove; **p. un échantillon** to take a sample; **p. du sang** to take a blood sample; **p. un morceau de tissu organique** to take a sample of organic tissue

préliminaire [preliminɛr] ADJ preliminary
NMPL **préliminaires** preliminaries; *(discussions)* preliminary talks; *Typ* prelims

prélude [prelyd] NM *Mus, Fig* prelude (**de, à** to)

préluder [prelyde] VI *Mus* to warm up; *(jouer un prélude)* to play a prelude; *Fig* **p. à qch** to serve as *or* be a prelude to sth

prémaquette [premakɛt] NF rough layout

prématuré, -ée [prematyre] ADJ premature; *(mort)* premature, untimely; **il est p. de l'annoncer** it's too early to announce it, an announcement would be premature; **être p. de six semaines** *(de bébé)* to be six weeks premature *or* early
N premature baby

prématurément [prematyremɑ̃] ADV prematurely

prématurité [prematyrite] NF prematureness, prematurity

prémédication [premedikasjɔ̃] NF *Méd* premedication, *Fam* premed

prémédiquer [premedike] VT *Méd* to premedicate

préméditation [premeditasjɔ̃] NF premeditation; *Jur* **avec p.** *(agir, tuer)* with premeditation, with malice aforethought; **meurtre avec p.** premeditated murder; **meurtre sans p.** unpremeditated murder, murder without premeditation

préméditer [premedite] VT to premeditate; **elle n'avait pas prémédité de lui demander**

de rester she hadn't planned *or* intended to ask him to stay

prémenstruel, -elle [premɑ̃stryɛl] ADJ premenstrual; **syndrome p.** premenstrual tension *or* syndrome, PMT

prémices [premis] NFPL **1** *Hist (fruits)* first fruits **2** *Litt (début)* early beginnings

> Il faut noter que le nom anglais **premises** est un faux ami. Il signifie **locaux**. Do not confuse with **prémisse**.

PREMIER, -IÈRE [prəmje, -jɛr] ADJ **1** *(initial)* first; **le p. jour du mois** the first day of the month; **les trois premières années** the first three years; **les premières heures du matin** the early hours (of the morning), the (wee) small hours; **enseignement du p. degré** primary education; **professeurs du p. degré** primary(-school) teachers; **les premiers temps, elle n'osait pas parler** at first she didn't dare speak; **en p. (lieu)** in the first place, first, firstly; **la première fois** the first time; **il y a toujours une première fois** there's always a first time, there's a first time for everything; **dès le p. jour** from the first day, from the beginning *or* the outset; **du p. coup** at the first attempt; **les premiers arrivés** the first to arrive; **le p. venu vous dira cela** anybody *or* anyone will tell you that; **je ne vais pas coucher avec le p. venu** I'm not going to sleep with the first man that comes along; **ce n'est pas le p. venu** he isn't just anybody *or* anyone; **il n'a pas le p. sou** *Br* he hasn't (got) two halfpennies to rub together, *Am* he hasn't a cent; *Typ* **première épreuve** first proof; **première diffusion** *(d'un film)* first run; *Journ* **première page** front page SEE GRAMMAR B59

2 *(original)* primary, original; **sens p. d'un mot** primary *or* original meaning of a word; **cause première** prime *or* primary cause; **vérité première** basic truth; *Ind* **matières premières** raw materials

3 *(dans un ordre)* first; **habiter au p. étage** to live on the first *or Am* second floor; **p. plan** foreground; *Fig* forefront; **une personnalité de tout p. plan** a leading personality; **première marche** bottom stair; *Théâtre* **premières loges** first-tier boxes; *Fig* **être aux premières loges** to have a ringside seat; **s'asseoir au p. rang** to sit in the front row; **ce pays est au p. rang mondial pour l'exportation du nickel** this country is one of the world leaders in the export of nickel; **au tout p. rang** in the forefront; **prendre la première place** to take the lead

4 *(placé au sommet de la hiérarchie)* **le p. chirurgien de Paris** the leading *or* top surgeon in Paris; **la première dame de France** the First Lady of France; **capitaine en p.** senior captain; *Culin* **du p. choix** prime cuts (of meat); **un morceau du p. choix** a prime cut (of meat); **de première importance** of the highest importance, of prime importance; **de première nécessité** essential; **je suis concerné au p. chef** it affects me first and foremost; **je suis le p. intéressé/concerné** I'm the one with most at stake/the one most affected; **billet de première classe** first-class ticket; **voyager en première classe** to travel first-class; *Théâtre* **p. rôle** leading part, lead

5 *(en logique) (terme)* given; **nombre p.** prime number

N **1** *(dans un classement)* first; **il/elle est le p./la première de sa classe** he's/she's (the) top of his/her class; **arriver le p./la première** *ou* **en p.** to arrive first; **elle était la première à arriver** she was the first to arrive; **nous sommes arrivés les premiers** we were the first to arrive, we arrived first; **arriver bon p.** to come in an easy first; **être le p. à faire qch** to be (the) first to do sth; **au p. de ces messieurs** next, please

2 *Théâtre* jeune p./première (young) romantic lead; *Fig* il a des airs de jeune p. he looks like a matinée idol *or* film star

NF première 1 *Couture* head seamstress

2 *Théâtre* first *or* opening night, première; *Cin* première; *Fig* c'est une première! it's a first!; *Journ* première de couverture *ou* *Arg* de couve front cover

3 *(ascension)* first ascent

4 *Aviat, Rail etc* first class; billet de première first-class ticket; voyager en première to travel first-class

5 *Scol Br* ≃ lower sixth (form), *Am* ≃ eleventh grade

6 *(vitesse)* first (gear), bottom (gear); passer en première to go into first (gear)

7 *(de chaussure)* inner sole, insole

8 *Fin* première de change first of exchange

9 *Fam* de première first-rate, first-class

NM 1 *(date)* le p. janvier the first of January, January (the) first; le p. de l'an New Year's Day

2 *(premier étage)* first floor, *Am* second floor; les gens du p. the people on the first *or* *Am* second floor

▸▸p. commis principal clerk, head clerk; *Sport* p. de cordée leader; p. cycle *Scol* = first three years of secondary school; *Univ* = first two years of undergraduate course; première danseuse leading dancer; *Cin* première exclusivité first showing; *Naut* p. maître chief petty officer; P. ministre Prime Minister; *Can (d'une province)* Premier; *TV, Cin* p. montage rough cut; p. numéro first issue; *Cin, TV* p. rôle leading part; p. tirage first run; *(presse)* early edition; p. violon first violin; *(qui dirige)* leader, *Am* concertmaster

premièrement [prəmjɛrmɑ̃] ADV first, firstly, in the first place

premier-né, première-née, *pl* **premiers-nés, premières-nées** [prəmjene, prəmjɛrne] ADJ, N firstborn

prémilitaire [premiliter] ADJ premilitary

prémisse [premis] NF *Phil* premise, premiss

> Do not confuse with **prémices**.

prémix [premiks] NM alcopop

prémolaire [premɔlɛr] NF *Anat* premolar

prémonition [premɔnisjɔ̃] NF premonition

prémonitoire [premɔnitwar] ADJ premonitory

prémunir [premynir] VT *Vieilli* p. qn contre qch *(protéger)* to protect sb against sth; *(mettre en garde)* to put sb on his/her guard against sth

VPR se prémunir se p. contre qch *(être vigilant)* to be on one's guard against sth; se p. contre le rhume to take precautions against (catching) a cold

prenable [prənabl] ADJ *(ville, fort)* pregnable

prenant [prənɑ̃] ADJ **1** *Fin* partie prenante payee; *(d'argent, de biens)* recipient **2** *Zool (queue)* prehensile **3** *(voix)* captivating; *(livre, film, travail)* fascinating, absorbing

prénatal, -ale, -als, -ales [prenatal] ADJ antenatal, prenatal

PRENDRE [prɑ̃dr] *(prp* prenant; *pp* pris; *pr ind* je prends, il prend, n. prenons, ils prennent; *pr sub* je prenne, n. prenions; *impf* je prenais, n. prenions; *p hist* je pris, n. prîmes; *fu* je prendrai)

> **VT** to take **1, 3–6, 12, 18, 22, 23** ▪ to take away **4** ▪ to charge **5** ▪ to catch **8, 20** ▪ to collect **10** ▪ to get **11, 20** ▪ to take on **15, 21** ▪ to have **18**
> **VI** to set **1** ▪ to take **2, 3** ▪ to catch **3** ▪ to work **4** ▪ to go **6**
> **VPR** to get caught **1** ▪ to attack *(s'en prendre à)* **6** ▪ to go about it *(s'y prendre)* **7**

VT 1 *(saisir)* to take; p. qch dans un tiroir to take *or* get sth from *or* out of a drawer; p. qch sur la table to take sth from *or* off the table; p. brusquement qch to snatch sth (up), to seize sth; je suis allé p. mon parapluie I went to get my umbrella; il l'a prise par le bras/la main he took her (by the) arm/hand; p. qn par la taille to put one's arm round sb's waist; p. qn par les cheveux to take *or* grab sb by the hair; je l'ai prise dans mes bras I took her in my arms; p. les armes to take up arms; il faut savoir le p. you have to know how to handle him; où avez-vous pris cela? where did you get that (from)?; *(cette idée)* where did you get that idea (from)?; *Tech* p. en étau to clamp

2 p. qch sur soi to take responsibility for sth; p. sur soi de faire qch to take it upon oneself to do sth

3 *(accepter, recevoir)* to take; *(pensionnaire)* to take (in); vous avez mal pris mes paroles you took me *or* what I said the wrong way; il a très mal pris la chose he took it very badly; p. une commande to take an order; p. qch à bail to take out a lease on sth, to lease sth

4 *(enlever)* to take (away); p. qch à qn to take sth (away) from sb; *(voler)* to steal sth from sb, to rob sb of sth; *(priver)* to deprive sb of sth; cela me prend tout mon temps it takes (up) all my time; ça m'a pris deux heures it took me two hours; mon temps est entièrement pris I haven't a free minute, my time is completely taken up; toute sa semaine est déjà prise his whole week is already taken up; c'est toujours ça de pris that's something at least; j'ai dû p. sur mes économies I had to draw on my savings

5 *(en argent)* prenez ce que je vous offre take what I'm offering you; dites-moi ce que vous prenez pour cela how much do you charge for that?; il prend combien? how much does he charge?; *Fam* il prend cher he charges a lot, he's expensive

6 *(s'approprier)* to take; c'est à p. ou à laisser take it or leave it; il y a à p. et à laisser there are good things and bad things; il y a à p. et à laisser dans ce qu'elle dit some of what she says is right and some of it isn't

7 *(considérer)* à tout p. on the whole, all in all

8 *(s'emparer de)* *(fugitif, voleur)* to catch, to capture; *(ville, région)* to take, to capture, to seize; *(marchandises illégales)* to seize; *(poisson, lièvre etc)* to catch; p. une ville d'assaut to take a town by storm, to storm a town; *Prov* tel est pris qui croyait p. it's a case of the biter bit; se faire p. to be *or* get caught; se laisser p. to let oneself be *or* get caught; *Fig* to let oneself be taken in; il s'y est laissé p. he fell into the trap; p. qn à voler to catch sb stealing; être pris à faire qch to be caught doing sth; p. qn sur le fait to catch sb in the act *or* red-handed; que je vous y prenne! just *or* don't let me catch you (at it) again!; on ne m'y prendra plus I won't be caught (out) *or* taken in again; être pris par le brouillard/la tourmente to be caught in the fog/the gale; il s'est pris le pied dans une racine he caught his foot on a root

9 pris de panique panic-stricken; pris d'un sentiment d'angoisse overcome by a feeling of anxiety; être pris d'une faiblesse to feel suddenly faint; elle a été prise d'un fou rire she got (a fit of) the giggles; l'envie lui a pris *ou* il lui a pris l'envie de partir he got a sudden urge to leave, he was seized with a desire to leave; si jamais l'envie vous en prenait if ever you should feel so inclined; *Fam* ça te prend souvent? do you get like that often?; qu'est-ce qui lui prend? what's come over him?, what's up with him?; bien lui en a pris it was lucky for him that he did; *Fig très Fam* ça/il me prend la tête it/he really gets on my nerves

10 *(emmener)* to call for, to collect, to fetch; prends ton frère avec toi take your brother with you; le taxi s'est arrêté pour p. un client the taxi stopped to pick up a fare; passe me p. vers six heures call for *or* come for *or* fetch me at about six o'clock; p. des marchandises *(d'un bateau)* to take in cargo; le bateau prend l'eau the boat is leaking, the boat is letting in water; les murs prennent l'humidité the walls are getting damp

11 *(acheter)* to get, to buy; *(réserver)* to book, to reserve; p. une chambre *(dans un hôtel)* to take a room; *(réserver)* to book a room; j'ai pris un petit studio I took a little studio flat; p. une police d'assurance to take out an insurance policy

12 p. sa retraite to retire; il n'a pas pris de vacances l'année dernière he didn't take *or* have any holidays last year; tu devrais p. quelques jours (de vacances) you ought to take a few days off; p. du repos to take *or* have a rest

13 *(s'informer de)* p. des renseignements to make enquiries; tous renseignements pris ... after (making) thorough enquiries ...

14 *(noter)* p. des notes to take (down) notes; p. le pouls/la température de qn to take sb's pulse/temperature

15 *(embaucher)* *(personnel)* to take on, *Fml* to engage

16 p. qn/qch comme exemple to take sb/sth as an example; p. qn comme modèle to model oneself on sb

17 p. qn/qch pour ... to take sb/sth for ...; on le prenait pour un colonel we/they/*etc* took him for a colonel, we/they/*etc* took him to be a colonel

18 *(nourriture, boisson)* to have; *(médicament)* to take; *(bain)* to have, to take; qu'est-ce que vous pren(dr)ez? what will you have (to drink)?; il prend du sucre dans son thé he takes sugar in his tea; il prend toujours un petit verre avant d'aller se coucher he always has a small glass of something before going to bed

19 *Fam (recevoir)* qu'est-ce que tu vas p.! you're for it!, you'll catch it!; elle a pris une sacrée raclée she got a real good hiding *or* thrashing

20 *(attraper)* *(maladie)* to get; *(accent, habitudes)* to acquire; p. froid to catch cold

21 *(se mettre à avoir)* *(apparence)* to take on, to assume; *(attitude)* to strike, to assume; elle prit un ton sévère her voice took on a severe tone; p. du poids to put on *or* gain weight; p. de l'âge to be getting old *or* on; p. un coup de vieux to age

22 *Méd* p. du sang to take a blood sample

23 *(utiliser)* *(train, bus etc)* to take; j'ai pris l'avion I flew, I took the plane; prenez une chaise take *or* have a seat, sit down; p. la route de *ou* pour Paris to take the road to Paris; il est temps de p. la route it's time to set off *or* *Fam* to hit the road; *Aut* p. un virage to take a bend; *Naut* p. le large to take to the open sea; p. le trot *(d'un cheval)* to break into a trot; *TV, Radio* p. l'antenne to go on the air

VI 1 *(du mortier, de la gelée, du ciment, d'un flan etc)* to set

2 *(d'une plante)* to take (root)

3 *(du feu)* to take, to catch; *(d'une allumette)* to strike, to light; le feu a pris à sa robe her dress caught fire; le feu a pris vite et s'est propagé the fire took hold quickly and spread

4 *(réussir, marcher)* le vaccin a pris the vaccine has taken (effect); cette mode ne prendra pas this fashion won't catch on; *Fam* ce truc-là prend toujours this trick always works *or* is always successful; *Fam* ça ne prend pas avec moi! you can't fool me!, it won't wash with me!

5 p. sur soi to restrain *or* contain oneself

6 *(aller)* **p. à gauche** to bear (to the) left, to go left; **p. par la vieille ville** to go via the old town; **p. à travers champs** to strike across the fields

VPR se prendre 1 *(s'accrocher)* **son manteau s'est pris dans la porte/à un clou** her coat (got) caught in the door/on a nail; **ils se sont pris par la taille/le cou** they put their arms around each other('s waists/necks); **se p. par la main** to hold hands, to take each other by the hand

2 *(se saisir)* to be held; *(être attrapé)* to be caught; **le verre se prend par son pied** the glass is held *or* you hold the glass by the stem; **un médicament qui se prend le soir** a medicine which is (to be) taken in the evening

3 *(se considérer)* **se p. au sérieux** to take oneself seriously; **il se prend pour un héros** he thinks he's a hero

4 **se p. d'amitié pour qn** to take a liking to sb; *(devenir ami)* to form a friendship with sb; **se p. de dégoût pour qch** to take a (strong) dislike to sth

5 *Litt (commencer)* **se p. à faire qch** to begin *or* start to do sth, to begin *or* start doing sth

6 **s'en p. à qn** *(physiquement, verbalement)* to attack sb; *(moralement)* to blame sb, to put *or* lay the blame on sb; *(passer sa colère sur)* to take it out on sb; **ne t'en prends qu'à toi-même** you've only (got) yourself to blame

7 **il sait comment s'y p.** he knows how to go *or* set about it; **je sais comment m'y p. avec lui** I know how to deal with him *or* handle him; **vous vous y prenez mal** you're going about it (in) the wrong way; **il s'y prend bien** he sets *or* goes about it (in) the right way; **elle s'y prend bien pour le faire** she's going *or* setting about it (in) the right way; **s'y p. à deux fois** to make two attempts, to have two goes

8 *très Fam* **se p. la tête** to make life difficult for oneself

preneur, -euse [prənœr, -øz] **N 1** *Com, Fin* buyer, purchaser; *(d'un chèque)* payee; **je suis p.** I'll take it; **trouver p.** to find a buyer; *Fin* **p. de lettre de change** payee of a bill of exchange **2** *Jur (locataire)* lessee, leaseholder **3** **p. de son** sound engineer, sound technician **4** **p. d'otages** hostage taker

prénom [prenɔ̃] **NM** first *or Am* given name; *(dans les pays chrétiens)* Christian name

prénommé, -ée [prenɔme] **ADJ** called, named; *Jur* said, above-named, aforesaid; **le p.** Victor the man called *or* named Victor ▸ **N** *Jur* **le p./la prénommée** the above-named, the aforesaid

prénommer [prenɔme] **VT** to call, to name; **on la prénomma Irma** she was called *or* named Irma

VPR se prénommer il se prénomme Adam his first *or Am* given name is Adam, he is called Adam

prénuptial, -iale, -iaux, -iales [prenypsjal, -jo] **ADJ** premarital; **examen p.** premarital medical check

préoccupant [preɔkypɑ̃] **ADJ** worrying

préoccupation [preɔkypasjɔ̃] **NF 1** *(priorité)* concern, preoccupation; **ma seule p. a été d'assurer ...** my sole concern has been to ensure ...; **j'ai d'autres préoccupations** I have other things to worry about **2** *(tourment)* worry

préoccupé [preɔkype] **ADJ** preoccupied; *(inquiet)* worried; **tu as l'air p.** you look worried; **d'un ton p.** *(pensant à autre chose)* absentmindedly; *(inquiet)* in a worried tone; **d'un air p.** with a worried look (on his/her face)

préoccuper [preɔkype] **VT** *(tracasser)* to worry; *(obséder)* to preoccupy; **être préoc-** cupé par qch to be concerned *or* preoccupied with sth; **sa santé me préoccupe** I'm worried *or* anxious *or* concerned about his health; **elle a quelque chose qui la préoccupe** she's got something on her mind, something's worrying her; **le foot est tout ce qui le préoccupe** football is all he thinks about

VPR se préoccuper se p. de qn/qch to concern oneself with sb/sth; **il ne s'est pas beaucoup préoccupé de savoir si j'allais bien** he didn't bother himself much to find out if I was all right

préopératoire [preɔperatwar] **ADJ** *Méd* pre-operative

prépa [prepa] **NF** *Scol Fam* preparatory class *(for the entrance exam to the grandes écoles)*; **faire une p., être en p.** to be studying for the entrance exam to the grandes écoles

prépaiement [prepɛmɑ̃] **NM** prepayment

préparamétré [preparametre] **ADJ** *Ordinat (logiciel)* preconfigured

préparateur, -trice [preparatœr, -tris] **N** *(assistant)* assistant *(in laboratory)*; *Ind* demonstrator; **p. en pharmacie** pharmacist's *or Br* (dispensing) chemist's assistant

préparatifs [preparatif] **NMPL** preparations (**de** for); **faire ses p. de départ** to prepare to *or* get ready to leave, to make one's preparations for departure; **j'étais en plein p. de départ quand ...** I was in the middle of preparing *or* getting ready to leave when ...

préparation [preparasjɔ̃] **NF 1** *(fait de préparer, de se préparer)* preparation (**à** for); *(des repas)* preparation, *esp Am Fam* fixing; **faire un discours sans p.** to make an ad-lib *or* impromptu speech; **annoncer une nouvelle sans p.** to blurt out a piece of news; **tu ne peux pas le lui dire sans p.** you can't tell him without any preparation, you can't blurt it out; **faire une p. militaire** to do a training course in preparation for military service; **p. au mariage** preparation for marriage **2** *Scol (à un examen)* preparation (**de** for); *(composition, exercice préparé)* preparation; **faire une p. aux grandes écoles** to prepare for the entrance exam to the grandes écoles **3** *Pharm* preparation; *Culin* **p. pour gâteau/ sauce** cake/sauce mix **4** *(organisation)* preparation, planning

préparatoire [preparatwar] **ADJ** preparatory, preliminary; *Scol* **cours p.** *Br* ≃ first year infants' class, *Am* ≃ nursery school; **classes préparatoires** preparatory classes *(for the entrance exam to the grandes écoles)*; **école p.** = school that prepares students for higher education

préparer [prepare] **VT 1** *(organiser, apprêter)* to prepare, to get ready; *(réunions)* to make preparations *or* arrangements for, to arrange; *(lit)* to make (up); *(repas)* to prepare, *surtout Am Fam* to fix; *(poisson, poulet)* to prepare, to dress; *Pharm (ordonnance)* to make up; **elle prépare le déjeuner** she's getting lunch ready, she's preparing lunch; **plats (tout) préparés** ready-cooked meals

2 **p. qn à qch** to prepare sb for sth; *(entraîner)* to train *or* coach sb for sth; **p. qn à une nouvelle** to prepare sb for a piece of news; **rien ne m'y avait préparé** nothing had prepared me for this

3 *Univ (examen)* to prepare for, to study for

4 *(prévoir, ébaucher)* to plan, to prepare; **p. un coup** to be hatching something, to be cooking something up; **p. ses vacances** to plan *or* arrange one's holidays; **p. un discours** to prepare a speech; **p. son avenir** to prepare for one's future; **cette découverte a été préparée par toute une tradition scientifique** a whole scientific tradition prepared the ground *or* paved the way for this dis- covery; **je suis sûr qu'il nous prépare quelque chose** I'm sure he's up to something **VPR se préparer 1** *(être imminent)* to be in the offing; **un orage se prépare** a storm is brewing; **il se prépare quelque chose** there's something in the air; *(mauvais coup)* there's something fishy going on

2 *(s'apprêter)* **se p. à qch/à faire qch** to prepare (oneself) *or* to get ready for sth/to do sth; **se p. à ou pour un voyage** to get ready for a journey, to make preparations for a journey; **se p. au combat** to prepare for action *or* combat; **il est dans la salle de bain, il se prépare** he's in the bathroom getting ready

3 *(se faire)* **se p. un café** to make oneself a coffee; **tu te prépares bien des ennuis/des désillusions** you're in for trouble/a surprise

prépasserelle [prepasrɛl] **NF** pre-boarding bridge

prépayé [prepeje] **ADJ** prepaid

préplanification [preplanifikasjɔ̃] **NF** pre-planning

prépondérance [prepɔ̃derɑ̃s] **NF** predominance (**sur** over)

prépondérant [prepɔ̃derɑ̃] **ADJ** predominant; **sa voix sera prépondérante** he will have the casting vote

préposé, -ée [prepoze] **N** *(employé, agent)* employee; *Admin* official; *(dans un vestiaire)* attendant; **p. (des postes)** postman, *f* postwoman, *Am* mailman, *f* mailwoman; **à la caisse** cashier; **p. des douanes** customs officer; *Jur* **commettant et p.** principal and agent; **p. aux réservations** reservations clerk

préposer [prepoze] **VT** **p. qn à une fonction** to appoint sb to an office; **il a été préposé au poste de chargé des relations publiques** he was put in charge of public relations, he was appointed public relations officer

prépositif, -ive [prepozitif, -iv] **ADJ** *Gram (locution)* prepositional

préposition [prepozisjɔ̃] **NF** *Gram* preposition **SEE GRAMMAR A66–73; B54–7**

prépositionnel, -elle [prepozisjɔnɛl] **ADJ** *Gram* prepositional

préproduction [preprodyksjɔ̃] **NF** preproduction

préprogrammé [preprograme] **ADJ** *Ordinat* preprogrammed

prépubère [prepybɛr] **ADJ** prepubescent

prépublication [prepyblikasjɔ̃] **NF** prepublication

prépuce [prepys] **NM** *Anat* foreskin, *Spéc* prepuce

préraphaélisme [prerafaelism] **NM** *Beaux-Arts* Pre-Raphaelitism

préraphaélite [prerafaelit] **ADJ, N** *Beaux-Arts* Pre-Raphaelite

prérentrée [prerɑ̃tre] **NF** *Scol* = day before school begins, used by teachers for preparation

prérequis [prerəki] **NM** prerequisite

préretraite [prer(ə)trɛt] **NF** early retirement; *(pension)* early retirement pension; **partir en p.** to take early retirement; **être en p.** to have taken early retirement; **être mis en p.** to be given early retirement, to be pensioned off, *Fam* to be put out to grass

préretraité, -ée [prer(ə)trɛte] **N** = person who has taken early retirement; *(mis en préretraite)* = person who has been given early retirement

prérogative [prerɔgativ] **NF** prerogative

préromantique [preromɑ̃tik] **ADJ** *Hist, Littér* pre-Romantic

préromantisme [preromɑ̃tism] **NM** *Hist, Littér* pre-Romanticism

PRÈS [prɛ]

> **ADV** near **1** ▪ close **1** ▪ nearly *(à peu près)* **2** ▪ closely *(de près)* **4**
> **PRÉP** near (to) **1** ▪ close to **1**

ADV 1 *(dans l'espace)* near, close; *(dans le temps)* close; **il habite tout p.** he lives very near here *or* very close by; **c'est tout p.** it's very near *or* close; **vous êtes trop p.** you're too close *or* near; **plus p.** nearer, closer; **moins p.** farther away; **à un détail p.** except for *or* apart from one detail; **à cela p. que ...** except that ...; **à quelques exceptions p.** with a few exceptions; **à cinq centimètres p.** to within five centimetres; **il devinerait votre poids à un milligramme p.** he would guess your weight to the nearest milligram; **nous n'en sommes pas à un ou deux jours/dix euros p.** a day or two/ten euros more or less doesn't matter; **je l'ai raté à deux minutes p.** I missed him by two minutes; **à peu de choses p.,** *Fam* **à quelque chose p.** more or less **2 à peu p.** *(pas tout à fait)* nearly, almost; *(approximativement)* about, approximately; **le travail est à peu p. achevé** the work is nearly *or* almost *or* just about *or* more or less finished; **il était à peu p. certain que ...** it was fairly certain that ... **3** *Naut* **courir au plus p.** to sail on a wind *or* close to the wind *or* on a bowline **4 de p.** closely; *(voir quelqu'un)* close to, close up; **tirer de p.** to fire at close range; **examiner qch de p.** to examine sth closely; **suivre qn de p.** *(ne pas être loin derrière)* to follow sb closely, to follow close behind sb, to follow hard *or* close on sb's heels; *(d'un médecin, professeur etc)* to follow sb's progress closely; **de p., elles sont très différentes** (seen) close to *or* up, they are very different

PRÉP 1 p. de *(dans l'espace)* near (to), close to; *(dans le temps)* close to; **p. de là** nearby, close by; **p. de chez eux** near (to) *or* close to where they live; **tout p. de moi** very close *or* near to me; *Naut* **courir p. du vent** to sail close to the wind; **il est p. de midi** it's close on *or* nearly *or* almost twelve (o'clock); **il y a p. de dix ans** close on *or* nearly *or* almost ten years ago; **il a fallu p. de deux heures pour ...** we needed close on *or* nearly *or* almost two hours to ...; **être p. de faire qch** to be about to do sth, to be on the point *or* verge of doing sth; **elle était p. d'éclater en sanglots** she was about to burst into tears, she was close to tears *or* on the brink *or* the verge of tears; *Iron* **nous ne sommes pas p. de le revoir** we won't see him again in a hurry; **est-il p. d'avoir fini?** is he anywhere near finished?; *Fam* **être p. de ses sous** to be tight-fisted, to be mean **2** *Admin* **ambassadeur p. le gouvernement français** ambassador to France

présage [preza3] **NM** omen, sign, *Litt* presage, portent; *(de malheur)* foreboding; **mauvais p.** bad *or* ill omen

présager [preza3e] **VT** (**je présageai(s); n. présageons**) **1** *(annoncer)* to be an omen of, *Litt* to presage, to portend; *(malheur)* to (fore)bode; **cela ne présage rien de bon** it bodes no good, nothing good will come of it **2** *(prédire) (d'une personne)* to predict; **ces gros nuages noirs laissent p. un orage** those big black clouds are a sure sign of a storm

présalaire [presalɛr] **NM** (student) grant

pré-salé, *pl* **prés-salés NM** *(mouton)* salt-meadow sheep; *(viande)* salt-meadow lamb

presbyte [prɛzbit] **ADJ** long-sighted, *Spéc* presbyopic

presbytère [prɛzbitɛr] **NM** presbytery

presbytérianisme [prɛzbiterjanism] **NM** Presbyterianism

presbytérien, -ienne [prɛzbiterjɛ̃, -jɛn] **ADJ, N** Presbyterian

presbytie [prɛsbisi] **NF** long-sightedness, *Spéc* presbyopia

prescience [presjɑ̃s] **NF** *(de l'avenir)* foreknowledge, *Fml* prescience

prescient [presjɑ̃] **ADJ** prescient

préscolaire [preskɔlɛr] **ADJ** preschool

préscolarisation [preskɔlarizasjɔ̃] **NF** pre-school education

prescripteur, -trice [preskriptœr, -tris] **N** *(médecin)* prescriber; **le p. d'une ordonnance** the writer of a prescription
NM *Mktg* influencer

prescription [preskripsjɔ̃] **NF 1** *Jur* prescription; **invoquer la p.** to raise a defence under the statute of limitations; **après 50 ans, il y a p.** the statute of limitations runs out after 50 years; *Fin* **p. acquisitive** acquisition of a right due to the passage of time; *Fin* **p. extinctive** lapse of a right due to the passage of time **2** *Méd* prescription, direction(s) (for treatment) **3** *(instruction)* rule, regulation

prescrire [preskrir] (*conj like* **écrire**) **VT 1** *(ordonner) (conditions)* to stipulate, to lay down, to specify; *(remède)* to prescribe; **à la date prescrite** on the date laid down, on the prescribed date **2** *Jur* to prescribe, to bar by the statute of limitations **3** *(réclamer)* to demand, to require; **ce que l'honneur prescrit** the demands *or* dictates of honour
VPR se prescrire *Jur* **ces dettes se prescrivent par cinq ans** these debts are barred at the end of five years; *Méd* **ce médicament se prescrit en cas de ...** this medicine is prescribed for ...

préséance [preseɑ̃s] **NF** precedence, priority (**sur** over); **avoir la p. sur qn** to have precedence over sb

présélecteur [preselɛktœr] **NM** *Tech* preselector

présélection [preselɛksjɔ̃] **NF 1** *(premier choix)* preselection, preselecting; *(pour un emploi)* shortlisting **2** *Aut* **boîte de vitesses à p.** preselector gearbox

présélectionner [preselɛksjɔne] **VT** *Tech* to preselect; *(candidats)* to shortlist

présence [prezɑ̃s] **NF 1** *(fait d'être dans un lieu)* presence; *(aux cours etc)* attendance; **je désire sa p.** I want him to be here; **il ignore votre p.** he doesn't know you're here; **faire acte de p., faire de la p.** to put in an appearance; **feuille de p.** attendance sheet; *Ind* time card; **p. policière** police presence **2** *(personnalité)* presence; **avoir de la p.** to have great presence; **elle n'a aucune p. sur scène** she has no stage presence **3 en p.** face to face, facing one another; **mettre les deux parties en p.** to bring the two parties face to face *or* together; **en p. de toute la famille** in front of *or* in the presence of the whole family; **je ne parlerai qu'en p. de mon avocat** I'll only speak with my lawyer present; **en p. de la mort** in the presence of death; **en p. de ces faits/cette situation** faced with these facts/this situation, in view of these facts/this situation; **en p. du virus ...** when the virus is present ...; **mis en p. du réactif ...** when placed in the vicinity of the reagent ...; **cela s'est fait en ma p.** it was done in my presence; **cela s'est dit en ma p.** it was said in my presence *or* hearing **4** *(existence)* presence; **la p. de sang dans les urines** the presence of blood in the urine; **expliquez-moi la p. de cette arme ici** explain to me how this weapon comes to be here; **j'ai senti une p. à côté de moi** I felt a presence beside me

▸▸ **p. d'esprit** presence of mind; **je n'ai pas eu la p. d'esprit de le lui dire** I didn't have the

presence of mind to tell him; *Rel* **p. réelle** real presence

PRÉSENT, -ENTE [prezã, -ãt] **ADJ 1** *(qui est dans le lieu dont on parle)* present; **les personnes présentes** those present; **être p. à un spectacle/un mariage** to be present at a performance/a wedding; **Jacques Martin, ici p., vous le dira** Jacques Martin, who is here with us, will tell you; *Scol* **Tardi? – p!** Tardi? – here! *or* present!; *Hum* **dès qu'il s'agit de manger, tu peux être sûr qu'il répond p.** as soon as there's food on the go, you can be sure he'll be there; **cela m'est toujours p. à l'esprit** it's always in my mind; *(d'un conseil, d'un danger etc)* I always keep it in mind; **p. par la pensée** here/there in spirit
2 *(actuel) (situation, moment)* present; **vivre dans l'instant p.** to live for the moment; **la présente convention** this convention; *Jur* **par la présente lettre** hereby, by these presents
3 *Gram* present; **le temps p.** the present (tense)
N *(témoin)* person present; **le nom des présents à la réunion** the names of those present at the meeting
NM 1 *Gram* present (tense); **le p. du subjonctif/de l'indicatif** the present subjunctive/indicative; **mettre le texte au p.** to put the text into the present (tense) **SEE GRAMMAR A49; B30**
2 *(partie du temps)* present; **vivre dans le p.** to live for the moment *or* in the present
3 *Litt (cadeau)* present, gift; **faire p. de qch à qn** to make a present of sth to sb
NF *Jur, Admin* **par la présente** *ou* **les présentes** *(par cette lettre, ce texte)* hereby, by these presents
ADV à p. at present, (just) now; **jusqu'à p.** up to now, up to the present (time), until now; *(de qch qui ne s'est pas encore produit)* as yet; **dès à p.** from now on, *Fml* henceforth; **à p. que ...** now that ...

présentable [prezãtabl] **ADJ** presentable

présentateur, -trice [prezãtatœr, -tris] **N** *Radio, TV* presenter; *(d'un spectacle télévisé)* master of ceremonies, MC; **p. télé** TV presenter; **p. de journal télévisé** newscaster, newsreader; *TV, Radio* **p. principal** anchor

présentation [prezãtasjɔ̃] **NF 1** *(de faits, d'un travail, d'un titre de transport etc)* presentation; **10% de réduction sur p. de la carte** 10% discount on presentation of this card; *Banque* **p. à l'encaissement d'un chèque** paying in, *Br* encashment; *Admin Fml* presentation for collection; *Com* **payable à p.** payable on demand *or* on presentation *or* at sight; **p. au paiement** presentation for payment; *Fin* **p. à l'acceptation** presentation for acceptance
2 *(apparence) (d'une personne)* appearance; *(d'un document etc)* presentation; **soigner la** *ou* **sa p.** to take care over one's appearance *or* over how one looks; **recherche hôtesses, excellente p.** hostesses required, must have smart, attractive appearance; **livre de bonne p.** well-produced book; **la p. des objets dans une vitrine** the presentation *or* display of items in a shop window; **p. assistée par ordinateur** computer-aided presentation
3 *Obst* presentation; **p. par les pieds** breech presentation
4 *(dans un groupe etc)* introduction (**à qn** to sb); *(à la cour)* presentation; **lettre de p.** letter of introduction; **je vous laisse faire les présentations** I'll leave you to make the introductions
5 *Rel* **la P. de la Vierge** (the Feast of) the Presentation (of the Blessed Virgin Mary)
6 *(à un public) (d'un film)* showing, presentation; *Mil* **p. du drapeau** trooping the colour; *Com* **p. de collections, p. de mode**

fashion show; **la p. du nouveau modèle diesel** the unveiling or presentation of the new diesel model

7 Tél **p. du numéro de l'appelant** caller display

présentement [prezɑ̃tmɑ̃] ADV at present, Am presently

> Il faut noter que le terme anglais britannique **presently** est un faux ami. Il signifie **bientôt** ou **peu de temps après**, selon le contexte.

PRÉSENTER [prezɑ̃te]

> **VT** to show **1** ▪ to present **1, 3–5** ▪ to offer **2, 3**
> **VPR** to arise **1** ▪ to apply **2** ▪ to come **3** ▪ to introduce oneself **4** ▪ to present **5**

VT 1 (montrer) (passeport, billet etc) to show, to produce, to present; (spectacle, film, émission) to present; (bulletin d'informations) to present, to read; (jeu télévisé) to host; **p. son passeport au douanier** to show one's passport to the customs officer; **p. une pièce d'identité** (au commissariat etc) to show or produce or present proof of identity; **p. des factures** to present invoices; **p. à l'encaissement** to present for collection; **p. sa main à qn** to hold out one's hand to sb; **il m'a présenté son dos** he turned his back on or to me; **je lui ai présenté le meilleur fauteuil/des cacahuètes** I offered him the best chair/some peanuts; Mil **p. les armes** to present arms; **présentez armes!** present arms!

2 (dire, exprimer) **je vous présente mes excuses** I do apologize; **p. ses condoléances** to offer one's condolences; **p. ses hommages à qn** to pay one's respects to sb; **p. ses arguments/raisons** to present or set out one's arguments/reasons; **p. ses craintes** to express one's fears

3 (soumettre) (facture, addition) to present, to submit; **p. sa candidature à un poste** to apply for a job; Scol **p. le français (à un examen)** to take or offer French (as one of one's exam subjects)

4 (faire connaître) (motion) to table; (spectacle) to present, to compere, Am Fam to emcee; **il m'a présenté tous les faits** he set out or put or laid all the facts before me; **p. des conclusions** to submit conclusions; **p. un projet de loi** to bring in or introduce a bill; **son travail est bien présenté** his work is well presented or set out; **vitrine joliment présentée** attractively dressed window; **les chocolats sont présentés dans une très belle boîte** the chocolates are presented or packaged in a very attractive box

5 (comporter) **son projet présente des inconvénients** there are drawbacks to his plan, his plan has got drawbacks; **ceci ne présente aucun intérêt** it's totally pointless; **le produit présente de nombreux défauts** there are a lot of problems with this product; Méd **p. un symptôme** to present a symptom

6 p. qn à qn to introduce sb to sb; (à la cour) to present sb to sb; **nous n'avons pas été présentés** we haven't been introduced; **je voudrais vous p. ma cousine** I'd like you to meet my cousin, Fml allow me to introduce my cousin (to you); **p. qn comme candidat** to put sb forward as a candidate; **il a été présenté pour ce poste** he has been put forward or proposed for this post; **p. les meilleurs élèves pour le concours d'entrée** to enter the best pupils or put the best pupils forward for the entrance examination

VI Fam **il présente bien** he has a good appearance

VPR se présenter 1 (se produire) to arise; **si l'occasion se présente** if the opportunity

presents itself or arises (**de faire qch** to do sth); **si le cas se présente** if the case arises; **un beau spectacle s'est présenté à mes yeux** a beautiful sight met my eyes; **attendre que quelque chose se présente** to wait for something to turn up; **la chose se présente bien** things look promising; **l'affaire se présente sous un jour nouveau** the matter appears in a new light

2 (se porter candidat) to apply; **est-ce que beaucoup de gens se sont présentés?** did many people apply?, were there many applications?; **se p. à un examen** to take or Br sit an examination; **se p. aux élections** to be a candidate or Br stand (as a candidate) at the elections; **se p. comme candidat** to come forward as a candidate

3 (se rendre) (au commissariat), Mil to report; **se p. chez qn** to call on sb; **elle s'est présentée ivre chez son nouvel employeur** she arrived drunk at her new employer's; **prière de vous p. chez Monsieur Troc** please go to see Mr Troc, Fml please report to Mr Troc; **si vous êtes intéressé, présentez-vous à nos bureaux** if you're interested, come along to our office

4 (se faire connaître) **se p.** to introduce oneself (**à** to); **permettez-moi de me p.** may I introduce myself?

5 Méd, Obst to present; **l'enfant se présente mal** the child is presenting badly; **le bébé s'est présenté par la tête/les pieds** the baby was in a normal/breech position

présentoir [prezɑ̃twar] NM Com display unit, display shelf; **p. de caisse** check-out display; **p. au sol** floor display, floor stand

présérie [preseri] NF Tech test series, pilot series

préservateur, -trice [prezɛrvatœr, -tris] ADJ Arch preservative; (mesures) preventive ▪ NM (dans la nourriture) preservative

préservatif, -ive [prezɛrvatif, -iv] ADJ Vieilli (épaisseur, vêtement) protective; **des mesures préservatrices contre l'épidémie** steps to ward off the epidemic ▪ NM (condom) condom, sheath; **p. féminin** female condom, Femidom®; (diaphragme) diaphragm, cap

> Il faut noter que le terme anglais **preservative** est un faux ami. Il signifie **agent de conservation**.

préservation [prezɛrvasjɔ̃] NF (de l'environnement, des traditions etc) preservation, protection; (d'une personne, des récoltes) protection

préserver [prezɛrve] VT to preserve; (protéger) to protect (**de** from); **le ciel m'en préserve!** heaven forbid!; **à p. de l'humidité** to be kept dry ▪ VPR **se préserver** to protect oneself (**de** from); **se p. de l'ennui/de la solitude** to guard against boredom/loneliness

présidence [prezidɑ̃s] NF 1 Pol presidency; **sous sa p.** under or during his presidency; **un candidat à la p.** a presidential candidate, a candidate for the presidency; **p. d'une société** chairmanship of a company, Am presidency of a company; UE **p. tournante** rotating presidency **2** (de club etc) chairmanship; **prendre la p.** (à une réunion) to take the chair **3** (habitation) presidential residence

président, -ente [prezidɑ̃, -ɑ̃t] N 1 Pol president; **le P.** the President; **la Présidente** the President; Vieilli (femme du Président) the President's wife, Am the First Lady **2** (d'assemblée, d'un club etc) chairperson, chairman, f chairwoman; **être élu p.** to be voted into the chair, to be elected chairperson; **Monsieur le p./Madame la présidente**, per-

mettez-moi de ... Mr Chairman/Madam Chairwoman, allow me to ... **3** (magistrat) presiding judge

▸▸ **p. de l'Assemblée Nationale** President of the National Assembly; **p. de la Commission européenne** President of the European Commission; Hist, Pol **p. du Conseil** Prime Minister; Com **P. du conseil d'administration** Chairman of the Board; Ind, Com **p.-directeur général** chairman and managing director, chief executive officer, CEO; **p. du jury** Jur foreman of the jury; (dans un concours) chairman of the adjudicating committee; **p. du Parlement européen** President of the European Parliament; **p. du Sénat** President of the Senate; **p. à vie** life president

présidentiable [prezidɑ̃sjabl] N presidential hopeful

présidentialisme [prezidɑ̃sjalism] NM presidential (government) system

présidentiel, -ielle [prezidɑ̃sjɛl] ADJ presidential; **l'élection présidentielle** the presidential election, the election for president; **régime p.** presidency, presidential system of government ▪ NFPL **présidentielles** presidential elections

> ### Présidentielles
> In France, since 1873, the president has been traditionally elected for a renewable seven-year term ("le septennat"). However, as a result of a referendum held in September 2000 the French parliament ruled that the seven-year term of office was to be replaced in 2002 by a five-year term ("le quinquennat"). Candidates are usually nominated by the main political parties, but anyone who collects the requisite number of sponsors can run. If no candidate wins an outright majority in the first round of voting, a runoff between the two frontrunners is held two weeks later.

présider [prezide] VT 1 (diriger) (conseil) to preside over; (réunion) to chair **2** (être à la place d'honneur de) (banquet) to be the guest of honour or Am honor at ▪ VI 1 (diriger) to preside, to be in the chair; **p. à une réunion** to preside at or over a meeting **2** (veiller) **p. à** to preside over; **aux destinées de ...** to preside over the destinies of ...; **les codes qui président à ces cérémonies** the codes that govern these ceremonies

présomptif, -ive [prezɔ̃ptif, -iv] ADJ héritier **p.** heir presumptive; (fils aîné) heir apparent

présomption [prezɔ̃psjɔ̃] NF 1 (supposition), Jur presumption; **de fortes présomptions pèsent sur lui** he is under great suspicion; **ce ne sont que des présomptions de votre part** these are just presumptions or assumptions of yours; Jur **p. de responsabilité** presumption of liability **2** (suffisance) presumption, presumptuousness

présomptueusement [prezɔ̃ptɥøzmɑ̃] ADV presumptuously

présomptueux, -euse [prezɔ̃ptɥø, -øz] ADJ presumptuous ▪ N **un jeune p.** a presumptuous young man

présono [presono] NF TV, Radio playback

présonorisation [presonorizasjɔ̃] NF TV etc playback

presque [prɛsk(ə)] ADV 1 (à peu près) almost, nearly; **c'est p. impossible** it's almost or next to or all but or well-nigh impossible; **c'est p. sûr** it's almost or nearly or well-nigh certain; **ça n'est pas sûr mais p.** it's not certain, but just about or but as good as; **je les ai p. tous** I have nearly or almost all of them; **c'est p. de la folie/la répression** it's little short of madness/repression; **il est sourd ou p.** he's deaf or as good as or just about; **j'ai vu tout le monde ou p.** I saw everybody or almost or nearly or just about everybody

2 (+ nég) scarcely, hardly; **p. jamais** scarcely or hardly ever, almost never; **p. rien** scarcely or hardly anything, next to nothing; **je ne dors p. pas** I hardly or scarcely get any sleep; **je ne dors p. plus** I hardly or scarcely get any sleep any more; **p. personne** hardly or scarcely anyone; **je ne connais p. personne** I hardly or scarcely know anyone; **rien ou p.** nothing, or hardly or scarcely anything, nothing, or as good as (nothing)

3 (devant un nom) **la p. totalité de son œuvre** nearly or almost all (of) his/her works, the near totality of his/her works; Litt **la p. obscurité** the near darkness; **c'est une p. certitude** it's virtually certain, it's well-nigh certain

presqu'île [prɛskil] NF peninsula

pressage [prɛsaʒ] NM (des raisins, du linge, de disques etc) pressing

pressant [prɛsɑ̃] ADJ (besoin) pressing, urgent; (créancier, demande) insistent; **cas p.** urgent case; **il se faisait p.** he was very insistent; Euph Fam **avoir un besoin p.** to need to go (to the toilet)

press-book, pl **press-books** [prɛsbuk] NM press book; (d'un mannequin, d'un artiste etc) portfolio

presse [prɛs] NF **1** (ensemble des imprimés, des textes) press; **la grande p.** large-circulation newspapers and magazines; **la liberté de la p.** the freedom of the press, press freedom; **délits de p.** infringements of press laws; **je l'ai lu dans la p.** I read it in the papers; **c'est dans toute la p.** it's in all the papers; **photographe de p.** press photographer; **attaché de p.** press attaché; **service de p.** publicity (department); **agence de p.** news or press agency; **conférence de p.** press conference; **avoir bonne/mauvaise p.** to have a good/bad press; Fig to be well/badly thought of (**auprès de** by); **la p. affaires** business press; **la p. de charme** soft porn magazines; **la p. clandestine** underground press; **la p. du cœur** romance magazines; **la p. de distribution professionnelle** trade press; **la p. économique** the financial press; **la p. écrite** print media, press; **la p. féminine** women's magazines; **la p. généraliste** general(-interest) press; **la p. grand public** general press; **la p. d'information** newspapers and magazines; **la p. d'information professionnelle** trade press; **la p. magazine** news magazines; **la p. de midinette** romance press; **la p. musicale** music press; **la p. d'opinion** quality press; **la p. parlée/télévisée** radio/television news; **p. people** celebrity magazines; **la p. périodique** periodical press; **la p. professionnelle** trade press; **la p. de qualité** quality press; **la p. régionale** ou **de province** the regional press; **la p. à scandale, p. à sensation** popular press, gutter press, ≃ tabloids; **la p. du soir** the evening newspapers; **la p. spécialisée** specialist press; **la p. sportive** sports press

2 Tech press; **p. mécanique** power press; **p. à copier** letter press, copying press; **travailler du métal à la p.** to stamp metal; **p. étoupe** gland; **p. à pantalon** trouser-press; **p. monétaire** minting press

3 Typ (printing) press; **p. à imprimer** ou **d'imprimerie** printing press; **p. à bras** hand press; **p. à rogner** guillotine; **p. rotative** rotary press; **livre sous p.** book that has gone to press; **être mis sous p.** to go to press; **prêt à mettre sous p.** (livre) ready for press; (journal) ready to put to bed; **le livre sera**

mis sous p. fin septembre the book will go to press at the end of September; **à l'heure où nous mettons sous p.** at the time of going to press

4 Arch, Litt (foule) press, throng, crowd; **fendre la p.** to force one's way through the crowd

5 Naut Arch press (gang)

6 Can (urgence) **il n'y a pas de p.** there's no hurry or rush; **dans les moments de p.** at busy periods

pressé [prɛse] ADJ **1** (comprimé) pressed; **citron p.** freshly squeezed lemon juice; **p. à froid** cold-pressed **2** (serré) **il était p. contre le mur** he was pressed or squashed up against the wall; **pressés les uns contre les autres** pressed or crowded or packed or squashed together; (objets) pressed or packed or squashed together **3** (qui a hâte) in a hurry or rush; **je suis très p.** I'm in rather a hurry, I'm very pressed for time; **p. de faire qch** in a hurry to do sth; **être p. par le temps** to be pushed for time; **aller** ou **marcher d'un pas p.** to walk hurriedly; **avoir un air p.** to look as though one is in a hurry; **on n'est pas p.** there's no rush, we're not in a hurry **4** (urgent) urgent; **ce n'est pas p.** it's not urgent, there's no hurry or rush; **si vous n'avez rien de plus p. à faire** if you've got nothing more urgent to do

▶ NM **aller** ou **parer au plus p.** to deal with the most urgent thing(s) first

presse-agrumes [prɛsagrym] NM INV juice extractor, juicer

presse-ail [prɛsaj] NM INV garlic press

presse-bouton [prɛsbutɔ̃] ADJ INV push-button

presse-citron [prɛsitrɔ̃] NM INV lemon squeezer

pressentiment [prɛsɑ̃timɑ̃] NM presentiment; (d'un malheur) foreboding; **j'ai comme un p. que …** I have a (funny) feeling that …; **avoir le p. que quelque chose va se passer** to have the or a feeling that something is going to happen

pressentir [prɛsɑ̃tir] VT (conj like **sentir**) **1** (prévoir) to have a presentiment or premonition of, to sense; (malheur) to have a foreboding of; **p. que quelque chose va se passer** to have a (funny) feeling that something is going to happen; **faire** ou **laisser p. qch** to foreshadow or portend sth; (malheur) to forebode sth; **son attitude me fait p. que …** I get the feeling or I can sense from his attitude that …; **rien ne laissait p. une rage pareille** nothing could have prepared me/us/etc for such a rage **2 p. qn** (sur ou pour qch) to sound sb out or approach sb (about sth); **le candidat pressenti** the likely candidate (for the job)

presse-papiers [prɛspapje] NM INV paperweight; Ordinat clipboard

presse-purée [prɛspyre] NM INV potato masher

presser [prɛse] VT **1** (citron, éponge etc) to squeeze; (raisin, pommes), Tech (disque) to press; **p. à froid** to cold-press; **p. qn contre son cœur** to clasp sb in one's arms, to hug sb; **p. le bras à qn** to squeeze sb's arm; **il m'entraînait en me pressant le bras** he dragged me off clutching me by the arm; Fam **ici on vous presse comme un citron** they get as much out of you as they can here

2 (appuyer sur) (commutateur, bouton) to press, to push; Ordinat to hit

3 (harceler) to press; **pressé par ses créanciers** pressed by his creditors; **p. l'ennemi** to press the enemy; **p. qn de questions** to ply or bombard sb with questions; **p. qn de faire qch** to press or urge sb to do sth

4 (dépêcher) (quelqu'un) to hurry (up); (travail, mouvement) to speed up, to accelerate;

p. le pas ou **l'allure** to speed up, to quicken one's pace; **p. le départ de qn** to speed up or hasten sb's departure; **qu'est-ce qui vous presse?** why are you in such a hurry?, what's the hurry or rush?; **rien ne nous presse** we're not in any hurry or rush; **allons, pressons!** come on, let's get a move on!

▶ VI **le temps presse** there isn't much time (left), time is short or is pressing; **le temps ne presse pas** there's plenty of time (left), there's no need to hurry; **l'affaire presse** the matter is urgent; **il n'y a rien qui presse, rien ne presse,** Fam **ça ne presse pas** there's no hurry or rush

▶ VPR **se presser 1** (s'entasser) to press, to crowd; (contre des grilles) to squash up, to crush; **on s'y presse toujours à six heures** there's always a crowd there at six o'clock

2 (se serrer) **elle s'est pressée contre lui** she pressed (herself) against him; (de façon affectueuse) she snuggled (up) against him, she snuggled up to him; **les badauds se pressaient autour de la victime** the onlookers crowded or clustered around the victim; **on se pressa pour entrer** there was a crush to get in; **les mots se pressaient dans sa bouche** he had so much to say he could not express himself clearly

3 (se dépêcher) to hurry (up); **pressez-vous!** hurry (up)!; **presse-toi de répondre à l'annonce** hurry up and reply to the advertisement; **faire qch sans se p.** to take one's time over doing sth; **répondre sans se p.** to answer deliberately or leisurely, to give an unhurried answer; **il faut se p. d'oublier** we must forget as quickly as we can

4 Fam **se p. le citron** to rack one's brains

presse-raquette [prɛsrakɛt] NM INV racket press

pressing [prɛsiŋ] NM **1** (repassage à la vapeur) (steam) pressing **2** (magasin) dry cleaner's **3** Fig Fam pressure; **faire le p.** to put on pressure

pression [prɛsjɔ̃] NF **1** Fig (action insistante) pressure; **faire p. sur qn,** Fam **mettre la p. sur qn** to put pressure on sb, to pressure or pressurize sb; **ils vont faire p. sur lui pour qu'il signe** they're going to put pressure on him to sign, they're going to pressure or pressurize him into signing; **être soumis/céder à des pressions** to be subjected to/to give in to pressure; **faire monter la p.** to pile on or increase the pressure; **être sous p.** to be under pressure; **sous la p. des événements, il dut démissionner** the pressure of events was such that he had to resign; **je travaille mieux sous p.** I work better under pressure; **groupe de p.** pressure group; **p. sociale/démographique** social/demographic pressure; **p. fiscale** tax burden

2 (action de presser) **exercer une p. sur qch, faire p. sur qch** to exert pressure on sth; **faire monter** ou **augmenter la p.** to increase the pressure; **en exerçant une simple p. du doigt** by simply pressing with one's finger; **un bouton (à) p., une p.** a press stud, Am a snap fastener, Fam a popper

3 Tech pressure; **vis de p.** binding screw; **p. d'huile** oil pressure; Aut **p. de gonflage** tyre pressure; Aut **p. des pneumatiques** tyre pressure; Aut **p. du carburant** fuel pressure; Aut **jauge de p.** pressure gauge; Tech **machine à haute/basse p.** high-/low-pressure engine; **mettre sous p.** to pressurize; **mettre la chaudière sous p.** to get up steam; **cabine sous p.** pressurized cabin

4 Phys pressure; **p. atmosphérique/artérielle** atmospheric/blood pressure; Météo **zone de hautes/basses pressions** area of high/low pressure

5 bière (à la) p. draught or Am draft beer; **une p., s'il vous plaît** ≃ half a pint of lager or Am a beer, please

pressographe [prɛsɔɡraf] NM credit card machine, imprinter machine

pressoir [prɛswar] NM 1 *(presse) (pour faire du vin)* wine press; *(pour faire du cidre)* cider press; *(pour huile)* oil press 2 *(lieu)* press house, press room

pressurage [prɛsyraʒ] NM pressing

pressurer [prɛsyre] VT *(fruits)* to press; *Fig (exploiter)* to squeeze

pressurisation [prɛsyrizasjɔ̃] NF pressurization

pressuriser [prɛsyrize] VT to pressurize

prestance [prɛstɑ̃s] NF presence; **avoir de la p.** to have (great) presence; **il faut une certaine p. pour porter ces vêtements** you need a certain style to wear these clothes; **un homme de belle p.** a fine-looking man

prestataire [prɛstatɛr] NM 1 *Admin* person receiving benefits *or* allowances; **p. de service** service provider, service supplier 2 *TV* facilities man

prestation [prɛstasjɔ̃] NF 1 *(allocation)* benefit; *Admin* allowance; **prestations** services; **prestations familiales** family benefits; **prestations sociales** social security benefits; **p. compensatoire** *(en cas de divorce)* compensation; **prestations maladie** sickness benefit; **p. en nature** payment *or* allowances in kind; **recevoir des prestations** to receive benefits 2 *Com* service; **p. de service** provision of a service; **p. de capitaux** provision of capital 3 *(résultat, performance)* performance; **la p. d'un homme politique à la télévision** the performance of a politician on television 4 *Jur* **p. de serment** oath taking; *Hist* **p. de foi** oath of fealty

preste [prɛst] ADJ nimble; **avoir la main p.** to have nimble fingers

prestement [prɛstəmɑ̃] ADV promptly

prestidigitateur, -trice [prɛstidiʒitatœr, -tris] N conjurer, magician

prestidigitation [prɛstidiʒitasjɔ̃] NF conjuring, magic; **tour de p.** conjuring trick, magic trick; *Fig* **c'est de la p.!** it's magic!

prestige [prɛstiʒ] NM 1 *(d'une personne, d'une société importante etc)* prestige; *(séduction, attrait)* (d'une star de cinéma, d'une façon de vivre etc)* glamour, *Am* glamor; **sans p.** undistinguished; **publicité/magazine de p.** prestige advertising/magazine; **le p. de l'uniforme** the glamour of the uniform 2 *Arch (chose étonnante)* marvel

prestigieux, -ieuse [prɛstiʒjø, -jøz] ADJ 1 *(qui a du renom) (artiste, nom etc)* prestigious, famous, great; **produits p.** prestige products 2 *Litt (étonnant)* marvellous, wonderful, amazing

presto [prɛsto] ADV 1 *Mus* presto 2 *Fam* double-quick, at the double

présumable [prezymabl] ADJ presumable

présumer [prezyme] VT *(supposer)* to presume, to assume; **tu viens aussi, je présume?, je présume que tu viens aussi?** you're coming too, I presume *or* assume?, I presume *or* assume that you're coming too?; **p. qn innocent** to presume sb (to be) innocent; **le coupable présumé, le présumé coupable** the alleged culprit; **le voleur présumé** the alleged thief; **il est l'auteur présumé de cette œuvre** he is presumed to be the author *or* he is the presumed author of this work; **on présume qu'il est mort** he is assumed *or* presumed (to be) dead ▸ VI **trop p. de soi** to presume too much, to be overconfident; **trop p. de ses forces** to overestimate *or* overrate one's strength

présupposé [presypoze] ADJ presupposed ▸ NM presupposition

présupposer [presypoze] VT to presuppose

présupposition [presypozisjɔ̃] NF presupposition

présure [prezyr] NF rennet

prêt¹ [prɛ] ADJ ready; **p. à l'emploi** ready for use; **p. à servir** ready to serve; **se tenir p.** to hold oneself in readiness, to be ready; **être p. à tout** to be ready for anything; *(pour parvenir à son but)* to be prepared to do anything; **je le sens p. à tout** I think he will stop at nothing; **être p. à faire qch** to be ready to do sth, to be all set to do sth; **p. à partir** ready to leave *or* go, *Fam* ready for the off; **toujours p. à rendre service** always willing *or* ready to help

prêt² [prɛ] NM 1 *(action)* lending; *(somme)* loan; **p. de 1000 euros** loan of 1,000 euros; **faire/consentir/obtenir un p.** to make/grant/get *or* obtain a loan; **demander un p.** to ask for *or* apply for a loan; **p. à court/moyen/long terme** short-/medium-/long-term loan; **le service du p.** *(d'une bibliothèque)* the lending department 2 *Mil* pay 3 *(avance sur salaire)* advance

▸ ▸ *Banque* **p. pour l'accession à la propriété** home loan; **p. bancaire** bank loan; **p. bonifié** loan at reduced rate of interest, soft loan; **p. à la consommation** consumer loan; **p. à découvert** overdraft loan; **p. d'épargne-logement** home loan; **p. à fonds perdus** loan without security, unsecured loan; **p. sur gage(s)** pawnbroking; **p. garanti** guaranteed loan; **p. d'honneur** loan on trust; **p. hypothécaire** mortgage loan; **p. immobilier** *Br* property *or Am* real-estate loan; **p. à intérêts** loan at interest; **p. participatif** equity loan; **p. en participation** syndicated loan; **prêts aux particuliers** personal loans; **p. personnalisé** *ou* **personnel** personal loan; **p.-relais** bridging loan, *Am* bridge loan; **p. sans intérêt** interest-free loan; **p. en souffrance** non-performing loan; **p. sur titres** loan against securities; **p. à vue** loan at call, loan repayable on demand

prêt-à-diffuser, *pl* **prêts-à-diffuser** [prɛtadifyze] NM master tape

prêt-à-porter, *pl* **prêts-à-porter** [prɛtapɔrte] NM 1 ready-to-wear clothes; **en p.** off the peg *or Am* rack; **acheter du p.** to buy ready-to-wear *or Br* off-the-peg *or Am* off-the-rack clothes 2 *(secteur)* ready-to-wear (clothing business)

prêté [prɛte] ADJ borrowed ▸ NM **c'est un p. pour un rendu** it's tit for tat

prétendant, -ante [pretɑ̃dɑ̃, -ɑ̃t] N applicant, candidate (**à** for); *(à un bien, à un titre)* claimant (**à** to); *(au trône)* pretender ▸ NM suitor, admirer; *Mktg* challenger

prétendre [pretɑ̃dr] VT 1 *(déclarer)* to maintain, to assert, to claim; **je prétends que ce n'est pas vrai** I maintain that it is not true; **on prétend que ...** people say that ..., it is said that ...; **à ce qu'il prétend** according to him; **elle prétend pouvoir guérir le cancer** she claims to be able to cure cancer; **il ne prétend pas être artiste** he doesn't pretend to be artistic, he lays no claim to being an artist; **je ne prétends pas lui faire comprendre** I don't pretend to be able to make him understand; **on le prétend fou** they say he's mad 2 *(vouloir)* to mean; **je prétends être obéi** I mean to be obeyed 3 *Vieilli (exiger)* to require, to want; **que prétendez-vous de moi?** what do you require *or* want of me? 4 *Belg (avoir l'intention de)* **il ne prétend pas le faire** he doesn't intend to do it ▸ VI **p. à qch** to lay claim to sth; **p. aux honneurs** to aspire to honours; *Litt* **p. à la main de qn** to aspire to marry sb ▸ VPR **se prétendre** to claim to be; **elle se prétend trompée sur la qualité du produit** she claims to have been misled about the quality of the product

Il faut noter que le verbe anglais **to pretend** *est un faux ami. Il signifie* **faire semblant.**

prétendu, -ue [pretɑ̃dy] ADJ *(coupable, voleur etc)* alleged; *(héros, cantatrice etc)* would-be; **un p. baron** a self-styled baron; **prétendus progrès** so-called progress ▸ N *Arch, Région* **mon p.** my fiancé; **ma prétendue** my fiancée

prétendument [pretɑ̃dymɑ̃] ADV supposedly; **cet individu p. architecte nous avait construit une horreur** this so-called architect built us a monstrosity

prête-nom, *pl* **prête-noms** [prɛtnɔ̃] NM *Fig* figurehead; *Fin (société)* nominee company

prétenseur [pretɑ̃sœr] NM *Aut* **p. de ceinture** seatbelt pre-tensioner

prétentaine [pretɑ̃tɛn] NF *Vieilli* **courir la p.** to chase (after) women

prétentieusement [pretɑ̃sjøzmɑ̃] ADV pretentiously

prétentieux, -ieuse [pretɑ̃sjø, -jøz] ADJ *(écrivain, personne, style)* pretentious; *(tenue, apparence)* showy ▸ N pretentious person; **un jeune p.** a conceited young idiot; **regarde-la, quelle prétentieuse!** look at her, she's so full of herself *or* she really fancies herself!

prétention [pretɑ̃sjɔ̃] NF 1 *(revendication, ambition)* pretension, claim (**à** to); **je n'ai pas la p. d'avoir réponse à tout** I don't claim to know the answer to everything; **renoncer à ses prétentions** to renounce one's claims 2 *(fait d'être prétentieux)* pretentiousness, pretension; **homme sans prétention(s)** unassuming *or* unpretentious man; **repas sans p.** simple meal; **un style plein de p.** a very pretentious style 3 *(salaire demandé)* **envoyer curriculum vitae et prétentions** send curriculum vitae and state salary required; **quelles sont ses prétentions?** what sort of salary does he want?

PRÊTER [prɛte] VT 1 *(fournir temporairement)* to lend, *surtout Am* to loan; **p. qch à qn** to lend sth to sb, to lend sb sth; **p. sur gage(s)** to lend against security; **p. de l'argent à 6%** to lend money at 6%; *Prov* **on ne prête qu'aux riches** only lend to those who can repay; *Fig* people are judged according to their reputation; **p. sur titres** to lend against securities; **p. à intérêt** to lend at interest

2 *(donner)* to lend, to give; **p. son appui** *ou* **son concours à qn** to give *or* lend sb one's support; **p. assistance** *ou* **secours à qn** to lend *or* give assistance to sb; **p. main forte à qn** to lend *or* give sb a hand; **p. l'oreille** to listen, to lend an ear; **p. attention à qch** to pay attention to sth; **p. serment** to take an oath; **p. le flanc à la critique** to lay oneself open *or* expose oneself to criticism; **p. son nom à qch** to lend one's name to sth, to allow one's name to be used for sth; *Vieilli* **si Dieu me prête vie** God willing

3 *(attribuer) (propos, intentions etc)* to attribute, to ascribe (**à** to); **on me prête des discours que je n'ai jamais tenus** I am credited with speeches which I never made

▸ VI **1 p. à confusion/la critique** to give rise to confusion/to criticism; **privilège qui prête aux abus** privilege that lends itself to *or* that is open to *or* that invites abuse; **cela prête à rire** that's laughable

2 *(des gants, d'un tissu etc)* to give, to stretch ▸ VPR **se prêter 1** *(consentir)* to lend oneself, to be a party (**à** to); **se p. à un accommodement** to fall in with *or* consent to an arrangement **2** *(permettre)* to lend itself (**à** to); **roman qui se prête à des interprétations différentes** novel which lends itself to different interpretations; **domaine d'étude qui se prête à des développements variés** area of study that can be developed in different ways; **j'aurais voulu lui parler de ses enfants, mais la situation ne s'y prêtait pas** I'd have liked to talk to him about his children, but it was neither the time nor the place; **attends que la situation s'y prête** wait until the situation is right; **j'aimerais faire une grande fête mais mon appartement ne s'y prête guère** I'd like to have a big party but my flat is hardly the right place

prétérit [preterit] **NM** *Gram* preterite (tense); **au p.** in the preterite VOIR GRAMMAIRE A39

prétériter [preterite] **VT** *Suisse (faire du tort à) (personne)* to wrong

pré-test, *pl* **pré-tests** [pretest] **NM p. publicitaire** pre-testing advertisement; **pré-tests publicitaires** copy testing; **pré-tests** pre-testing

pré-tester [preteste] **VT** to pre-test

préteur [pretœr] **NM** *Antiq* praetor

prêteur, -euse [pretœr, -øz] **N** lender; **p. sur gages** pawnbroker
ADJ ready *or* willing to lend things; **je ne suis pas p.** I don't like lending things

prétexte [pretɛkst] **NM** pretext, excuse; **ce n'est qu'un p.** it's just a pretext *or* an excuse; **bon/mauvais p.** good/poor excuse; **se chercher des prétextes** to look for excuses; **sous p. de faire qch** on *or* under the pretext of doing sth; **sous p. d'amitié** on *or* under the pretext of friendship; **sous p. que ...** on *or* under the pretext that ...; **sous aucun p.** on no account, under no circumstances; **prendre p. de qch pour faire qch** to use sth as a pretext *or* an excuse for doing sth; **prendre** *ou* **saisir le premier p. pour ...** to take advantage of the first pretext one can to ...; **donner p. à** to provide an excuse for
NF *Antiq* toga praetexta
ADJ *Antiq* **toge p.** toga praetexta

prétexter [pretɛkste] **VT** to use *or* give as a pretext *or* an excuse; **il a prétexté qu'il était malade** he gave the excuse that he was ill; **p. la fatigue** to plead fatigue, to give fatigue as a pretext *or* an excuse

prétoire [pretwar] **NM 1** *Jur* court **2** *Antiq* praetorium

Pretoria [pretɔrja] **N** Pretoria

prétorien, -ienne [pretɔrjɛ̃, -jɛn] **ADJ** *Antiq* praetorian
NM *Antiq* praetorian; *Fig (de dictature)* praetorian guard, military bodyguard

prêtre [pretr] **NM** priest; **grand p.** high priest; **se faire (ordonner) p.** to be ordained (a priest), to become a priest

prêtre-ouvrier, *pl* **prêtres-ouvriers NM** worker priest

prêtresse [pretrɛs] **NF** priestess

prêtrise [pretriz] **NF** priesthood; **recevoir la p.** to take (holy) orders

preuve [prœv] **NF 1** *(d'innocence, d'amitié, de courage etc)* proof, evidence; **une p. de mauvaise organisation** evidence *or* proof of poor organization; **ce n'est pas une p.** that proves nothing *or* doesn't prove anything; **il nous faut des preuves** we need proof *or* evidence; **faire la p. de qch** to prove sth; **avoir la p. que/de ...** to have proof that/of ...; **faire p. d'intelligence/de générosité/***etc* to show intelligence/generosity/*etc*; **faire ses preuves** *(d'un élève, employé etc)* to prove oneself, to show what one can do; **cette méthode a fait ses preuves** this method has proved itself *or* has stood the test of time; **jusqu'à p. du contraire** until there's proof to the contrary; **comme p.** by way of proof, as proof; *Fam* **le directeur est un incapable, à p. le déficit de la maison** the manager is incompetent, witness the firm's deficit; *Fam* **on ne peut pas compter sur lui, la p. il est encore absent** you can't count on him, as you can see he's absent again; **à p. que ...** which (just) goes to show that ...; **j'en veux pour p. ...** the proof of it is ...; **être la p. vivante que ...** to be living proof that ...; **p. d'achat** proof of pur-

chase **2** *Math* **faire la p. d'une opération** to prove *or* test the validity of a mathematical operation; **faire la p. par neuf** to cast out nines **3** *Jur* evidence; **p. directe** direct evidence; **p. indirecte** circumstantial evidence; **preuves testimoniales** (witnesses') evidence; **le soin** *ou* **l'obligation de faire la p.** the onus *or* burden of proof

preux [prø] *Arch, Litt* **ADJ M** gallant, valiant
NM gallant *or* valiant knight

prévalence [prevalɑ̃s] **NF** *Méd* prevalence

prévaloir [prevalwar] *(conj like* **valoir** *except pr sub* **je prévale**) **VI** to prevail (**sur** over; **contre** against); **ce principe prévaut sur tous les autres** this principle takes precedence over all others; **faire p. ses droits** to assert one's rights; **faire p. son opinion** to win acceptance for one's opinion
VPR se prévaloir 1 se p. de *(profiter de)* to take advantage of **2 se p. de qch** *(s'enorgueillir)* to pride oneself on sth

prévaricateur, -trice [prevarikatœr, -tris] *Jur* **ADJ** *(fonctionnaire, magistrat)* dishonest
N dishonest official; *(dans une gestion)* betrayer of trust

prévarication [prevarikasjɔ̃] **NF** *Jur* breach of trust; *(dans une organisation)* maladministration

prévariquer [prevarike] **VI** *Jur* to be guilty of a breach of trust

prévenance [prevnɑ̃s] **NF** kindness, consideration; *(d'un geste, d'une bonne idée)* thoughtfulness; **une p.** a thoughtful *or* kind act *or* deed; **entourer qn de prévenances** to show sb great kindness *or* consideration; **avoir des prévenances pour qn** to show sb kindness *or* consideration

prévenant [prevnɑ̃] **ADJ** *(personne)* kind (**envers, avec** to), considerate (**envers, avec** towards); *(geste)* thoughtful (**envers, avec** towards); *(manière, apparence)* pleasing, prepossessing

prévenir [prevnir] **VT** *(conj like* **venir** *but with aux* **avoir**) **1** *(informer)* to inform, to tell, to let know (**de qch** about sth, of sth); *(avertir)* to warn; *(à l'avance)* to forewarn; **les personnes à p. en cas d'accident** those to be informed *or* notified in case of an accident; **je vais le p. que vous êtes ici** I'll tell him *or* let him know that you're here; **on m'avait prévenu que la police était à mes trousses** I had been warned that the police were after me; **vous auriez dû m'en** *ou* **me p.** you should have told me (about it) beforehand; **je l'ai prévenue, si ça ne s'améliore pas, c'est la porte!** I've warned her, if there's no improvement she'll be out of a job!; **tu es prévenu!** you've been warned!; **partir sans p.** to leave without telling anyone *or* without warning
2 *(empêcher) (maladie)* to prevent, to ward off, to avert; *(danger, accident)* to avert; *Prov* **mieux vaut p. que guérir** prevention is better than cure
3 *(devancer) (les désirs de quelqu'un)* to anticipate; *(question, objection)* to forestall
4 *Litt (agir, influencer)* **p. qn en faveur de qn** to predispose sb *or* bias sb in favour of sb; **p. qn contre qn** to prejudice sb against sb, to bias sb *or* make sb bias(s)ed against sb; **son visage prévient en sa faveur** he has a prepossessing face

préventif, -ive [prevɑ̃tif, -iv] **ADJ** preventive; **à titre p.** as a preventive (measure); **médecine préventive** preventive medicine; *Cartes* **ouverture préventive** pre-emptive bid; *Jur* **détention préventive** detention awaiting trial; **être en détention préventive** to be in custody

prévention [prevɑ̃sjɔ̃] **NF 1** *(d'une maladie etc)* prevention; **p. routière** road safety; **p. des accidents du travail** prevention of industrial accidents **2** *Jur* **mettre qn en p.** to

commit sb for trial; **mise en p.** committal for trial **3** *Litt (opinion, avis)* predisposition, bias (**en faveur de** in favour of), prejudice, bias (**contre** against); **observateur sans p.** unprejudiced *or* unbias(s)ed observer

préventivement [prevɑ̃tivmɑ̃] **ADV 1** as a preventive (measure) **2** *Jur* **arrêter qn p.** to arrest sb on suspicion; **détenu p.** committed for trial

préventorium [prevɑ̃tɔrjɔm] **NM** tuberculosis sanatorium

prévenu, -ue [prevny] **ADJ 1** *(qui a une opinion)* prejudiced, bias(s)ed **2** *Jur* **p. de vol** charged with theft
N *Jur* **le p./la prévenue** the accused

prévisibilité [previzibilite] **NF** foreseeability

prévisible [previzibl] **ADJ** foreseeable; **c'était difficilement p.** it was hard to foresee

prévision [previzjɔ̃] **NF** forecast; *(activité)* forecasting; *(description d'un événement futur)* forecast, prediction; **en p. de qch** in expectation *or* anticipation of sth; **dépasser les prévisions** to exceed all expectations; **au-delà de toute p.** beyond all expectation; **selon nos prévisions** according to our forecast; **prévisions météorologiques** *ou* **du temps** weather forecast; *Mktg* **prévisions aléatoires** probability forecasting; *Mktg* **p. de la base** grass-roots forecast; *Mktg* **p. depuis la base** bottom-up forecast; *Fin* **p. boursière** stock-exchange forecast; **prévisions budgétaires** budget estimates *or* forecasts; **prévisions de l'entreprise** company forecasting; *Mktg* **p. événementielle** hazard forecast; *(activité)* hazard forecasting; **prévisions hiérarchisées** top-down forecasting; **p. du marché** market forecast; *(activité)* market forecasting; **p. des ventes** sales forecast; *(activité)* sales forecasting; **p. des ventes et profits** sales and profit forecast; *(activité)* sales and profit forecasting

prévisionnel, -elle [previzjɔnɛl] **ADJ** forecast; *(budget, coûts)* estimated, provisional; *(analyse, étude)* preliminary; **la gestion prévisionnelle des entreprises** management by objectives; **étude prévisionnelle des ventes** sales forecast *or* projection

prévisionner [previzjɔne] **VT** *TV, Cin* to preview

prévisionniste [previzjɔnist] **N** *Écon* forecaster

prévisualisation [previzɥalizasjɔ̃] **NF** *Ordinat* print preview

prévoir [prevwar] **VT** *(conj like* **voir** *except in fu and cond* **je prévoirai, je prévoirais**) **1** *(penser, imaginer)* *(futur, désastre)* to foresee; *(météo, prix etc)* to forecast; *(réaction)* to anticipate; *(difficultés, retards)* to foresee, to anticipate; **il est difficile de p. ce qui va arriver** it's difficult to foresee *or* forecast what will happen; **nous n'avions pas prévu toutes ces dépenses** we didn't foresee *or* allow for *or* plan on all this expense; **tout laisse p. que ...** everything indicates that ...; **rien ne laisse p. un changement de temps** there appears to be no prospect of a change in the weather; **rien ne laissait p. qu'ils prendraient la fuite** there was nothing to indicate *or* suggest that they would run away; **comment aurais-je pu p. que ça n'allait pas me plaire?** how could I have foreseen *or* known in advance *or* anticipated that I wouldn't like it?; **cela n'était pas prévu au programme** that wasn't on the agenda; **ces incidents n'étaient pas prévus au programme** these incidents were totally unplanned; **heureusement qu'on avait prévu le coup!** luckily, we had anticipated this!
2 *(organiser) (quelque chose)* to provide for; **p. des mesures** to take measures; **p. des changements** to make changes; **dépenses prévues au budget** expenses provided for

or included in the budget; **la loi n'a pas prévu un cas semblable** the law makes no provision for a case of this kind; **les seuls cas prévus par la loi** the only cases covered by *or* provided for by the law; **le personnel prévu dans le contrat** the personnel provided for *or* laid down *or* stipulated in the contract; **l'argent que nous avions prévu pour le voyage n'a pas suffi** the money we allowed for *or* budgeted for *or* set aside for the trip wasn't enough; **la réunion est prévue pour demain** the meeting is arranged *or* scheduled for tomorrow; **on ne peut pas tout p.** you can't think of everything; **elle prévoit de demander une augmentation** she's planning to ask for *or* planning on asking for a rise; **comme prévu** as (was) planned, as expected; **cela s'est passé comme prévu** it went according to plan; **plus tôt/tard que prévu** sooner/later than expected; **vitesse prévue** *(d'un bateau)* designed speed; **charge prévue** *(d'un poids lourd etc)* specified load

3 *(préparer) (repas, pique-nique)* to provide, to arrange; **il faudra p. des vêtements de pluie** we'll have to take waterproof clothes; **on a prévu une tente en cas de pluie** we've brought a tent in case it rains

prévôt [prevo] NM **1** *Escrime* **p. de salle** *ou* **d'armes** assistant fencing master **2** *Mil* assistant provost marshal; **grand p.** provost marshal **3** *Hist, Jur* provost

prévoyance [prevwajɑ̃s] NF *(précaution)* precaution; *(dans le futur)* foresight, forethought; *Fin* contingency, provision for the future; **elle a manqué de p. en achetant cette voiture** it was rather short-sighted *or* unwise of her to buy the car; **il ne manque pas de p.** he thinks well ahead, he doesn't lack foresight; **faire preuve de p.** to show foresight, to be far-sighted, to look ahead; **fonds** *ou* **caisse de p.** contingency fund, reserve fund; **société de p.** provident society; **p. sociale** social security provisions

prévoyant [prevwajɑ̃] ADJ far-sighted, *Fml* provident; **un homme p. aurait ...** a man with foresight would have ...; **en bon père p., il avait prévu de ...** as a prudent father should, he had made arrangements to ...

priapisme [prijapism] NM priapism

prie-Dieu [pridjø] NM INV prie-dieu, prayer stool

prier [prije] *(impf, pr sub* **n. priions, v. priiez)** VT **1** *Rel (Dieu etc)* to pray to; **je prie Dieu qu'il en soit ainsi** I pray (to) God that it may be so **2** *(supplier)* to beg, *Fml, Litt* to beseech, to entreat; **se faire p.** to need a lot of persuasion *or* persuading *or* coaxing; **après s'être fait un peu p.** after a bit of persuasion *or* persuading *or* coaxing; **il ne s'est pas fait p. pour venir** he didn't need *or* take much persuading to come, he didn't need to be asked twice to come; **sans se faire p.** readily, willingly; **il est parti sans se faire p.** it didn't need any coaxing *or* persuasion to get him to go **3** *Fml (demander)* to ask, to request; **p. qn de faire qch** to ask sb to do sth; **je te prie de ne pas t'occuper de ça!** I'd be obliged if you minded your own business!, kindly *or* please mind your own business!; **taisez-vous, je vous prie!** please be quiet!; **puis-je vous p. de fermer la porte?** would you be so kind as to *or* be kind enough to close the door?; **dites-moi, je vous prie** would you mind telling me; **je te prie de croire qu'elle a été très surprise** she was very surprised, believe me *or* let me tell you; **je vous en prie!** *(faites-le)* please do!, of course!; *(ne le faites pas)* please don't!; *(il n'y a pas de quoi)* it's/it was a pleasure!, you're welcome!, not at all!; *Fml* **je vous prie de bien vouloir recevoir l'assurance de mes sentiments les meilleurs** *(dans une lettre)* yours sincerely *or*

truly; **Monsieur et Madame Hugo prient Monsieur et Madame Adam de leur faire l'honneur d'assister à ...** Mr and Mrs Hugo request the pleasure of Mr and Mrs Adam's company at ...; *Arch, Litt* **p. qn à dîner** to invite sb to dine

VI to pray (**pour qn/qch** for sb/sth); **nous avons prié pour qu'il revienne vivant** we prayed that he might return alive, we prayed for his safe return

prière [prijɛr] NF **1** *(formule)* prayer; **faire** *ou* **dire ses prières** to say one's prayers; *Hum* **tu peux faire ta p.** *ou* **tes prières** you can say your prayers **2** *(acte de prier)* **faire** *ou* **dire la p.** to offer prayer; **c'est l'heure de la p.** it's time for prayers; **être en prières** to be praying *or* at prayer; **aller à la p.** to go to prayers **3** *(demande)* request, *Fml, Litt* entreaty; **à la p. de qn** at sb's request; **céder aux prières de qn** to give in to sb, *Fml* to give way to sb's entreaties; **p. de ne pas fumer** no smoking please, thank you for not smoking, you are requested not to smoke; **p. de fermer la porte** please close the door

prieur, -eure [prijœr] N prior, *f* prioress

prieuré [prijœre] NM *Rel* priory

prima donna [primadɔna], *pl* **prime donne** [primedɔne] NF prima donna

primage [primaʒ] NM *Tech* priming

primaire [primɛr] ADJ **1** *(école, couleur etc)*, *Géol (ère)* primary; *Élec, Tech* **circuit p.** primary; *Écon* **secteur p.** primary sector **2** *Péj (simpliste) (personne)* narrow (in outlook), unsophisticated; *(réaction, attitude)* narrow-minded; *(racisme)* narrow-minded

NM 1 *Scol* primary education; **être en p.** to be at primary school; **les classes du p.** primary school classes **2** *Géol* primary era **3** *Élec* primary (winding) **4** *Écon* primary sector **5** *Péj (personne)* person of narrow outlook

NF *Am Pol* primary (election); **les primaires** the primaries

primat [prima] NM **1** *Rel* primate **2** *Phil* primacy

primate [primat] NM *Zool* primate

primauté [primote] NF **1** *Rel etc* primacy **2** *(supériorité)* supremacy; **avoir la p.** to have priority, to come first; **donner à qch la p. sur qch** to give sth priority over sth

prime¹ [prim] ADJ *Arch, Litt* first; **de p. abord** at first sight; **de p. abord, il a l'air très sympathique** he seems very nice; **dès sa p. jeunesse** since his/her early youth; **elle n'est plus dans sa p. jeunesse!** she's no spring chicken!

NF 1 *Rel* prime; **chanter p.** to sing the prime **2** *Math* **B p.** B prime

prime² NF **1** *Fin (d'assurance)* premium; *Bourse* **marché à p.** option market; *Fig* **faire p.** to come first, to take precedence over everything else; **faire p. sur qch** to come before sth, to take precedence over sth **2** *Com, Admin etc (allocation)* grant; *(sur salaire)* bonus **3** *Com (cadeau)* free gift; **et vous aurez droit à une cafetière en p.** and you will get a free coffee maker *or* a coffee maker as a free gift; *Fig* **en p.** into the bargain

▸▸ **p. acheteur** buyer's option; **p. d'ancienneté** long service award; **p. annuelle** annual premium; **p. d'assurance** insurance premium; *Mktg* **p. auto-payante** self-liquidator; **p. du change** agio; **p. à la construction** construction grant *(for people building their own homes)*; **p. contenant** *(pour bouteille etc)* container premium; **p. de conversion** conversion premium; **p. de déménagement** relocation allowance; *Mil* **p. de démobilisation** demobilization gratuity; **p. de départ** severance pay, golden handshake; **p. d'éloignement** isolated post allowance; *Bourse* **p.**

d'émission bond discount; **p. pour l'emploi** = tax credit awarded to low wage-earners, as an incentive to continue working and not claim benefit instead; **p. à l'exportation** export subsidy; **p. familiale** family allowance; **p. de fusion** merger premium; **p. d'intéressement** reversionary bonus; **p. à l'investissement** investment subsidy; **p. de licenciement** severance allowance; **p. de remboursement** premium on redemption, redemption fee; **p. de rendement** *Ind* productivity bonus, performance bonus; *(suite à une mission réussie)* success fee; **p. de renouvellement** renewal premium; **p. de risque** danger money; **p. de transport** transport allowance; **p. de vie chère** cost of living allowance

primer¹ [prime] VT *(avoir la priorité sur)* to take precedence over; **considération qui prime toutes les autres** consideration of the first importance, consideration that outweighs all others

VI *Fig* to come first, to take precedence; **le travail prime avant tout** work takes precedence over *or* comes before everything else; **il faut savoir ce qui prime pour toi** you have to know what comes first with you *or* matters most to you, you have to know what your priorities are; **le courage prime sur toutes les autres qualités** courage is the most important quality; **ce qui prime chez lui, c'est l'honnêteté** honesty is his outstanding quality *or* trait

primer² VT *(donner un prix honorifique à)* to award a prize to; **primé** *(taureau)* prize; *(roman, film)* prizewinning, award-winning; **vous avez été primé deux fois à Cannes** you have twice won an award *or* you have won two awards at Cannes

primerose [primroz] NF *(fleur)* hollyhock

primesautier, -ière [primsotje, -jɛr] ADJ *(personne, réaction, réponse)* spontaneous; *(esprit)* ready, quick; **au risque de paraître un peu trop p.** at the risk of appearing a little impulsive; **répondre de façon primesautière** to answer spontaneously

prime time [prajmtajm] NM *TV, Radio* prime time

primeur [primœr] NF **1** primeurs (early) fruit and vegetables; **marchand de primeurs** greengrocer *(selling early produce)* **2** *Journ* scoop; **avoir la p. d'une nouvelle** to be the first to hear a piece of news; *Journ, TV* **avoir la p. du reportage/de l'information** to be first with *or* to scoop the report/news; *Journ, TV* **c'est un mariage dont le chanteur nous a réservé la p.** the singer gave us a scoop on his forthcoming marriage; **je vous en réserverai la p.** you'll be the first to know; **nous réservons à nos lecteurs la p. de l'interview** this interview is exclusive to our readers

primevère [primvɛr] NF *(fleur)* primula; **p. à grandes fleurs** primrose; **p. commune** cowslip; **p. des jardins** polyanthus

primipare [primipar] ADJ primiparous
NF primipara

primitif, -ive [primitif, -iv] ADJ **1** *(qui est le plus près de l'origine) (instinct, l'homme)* primitive; *Opt* **couleurs primitives** primary colours; *Géol* **terrains primitifs** primitive strata, primitive terrain; *Gram* **temps primitifs** primary tenses **2** *(premier) (forme, couleur)* original; **la forme primitive d'une société** the earliest form of a society; **économie primitive** primitive economic system **3** *Péj (rudimentaire) (société, coutumes etc)* primitive; *(outil, méthodes)* primitive, crude

NM 1 *Beaux-Arts* primitive, early master **2** *(membre d'une tribu)* primitive tribesman

primitivement [primitivmɑ̃] ADV originally

primitivisme [primitivism] NM primitivism

primo [primo] ADV *Fam* first(ly), in the first place

primogéniture [primoʒenityr] NF *Jur* primogeniture

primo-infection, *pl* **primo-infections** NF *Méd* primary infection

primordial, -iale, -iaux, -iales [primɔrdjal, -jo] ADJ **1** *(premier)* primordial; *(instinct, besoin)* primal; **c'est un besoin p. que de communiquer** we have a primal need to communicate, communication is one of our most basic needs **2** *(capital) (question, rôle, point, caractéristique)* of the utmost importance, essential; *(souci, nécessité, importance)* prime; **d'une nécessité/importance primordiale** of prime necessity/importance; **il est p. que tu sois là** you must be there, your presence is essential; **il est p. de s'inscrire à temps** it is of prime or the utmost importance to register in time; **l'eau est un élément p. de la vie** water is essential to life

prince [prɛ̃s] NM prince; **p. héritier** *ou* **royal** *ou* **impérial** crown prince; **le fait du p.** high-handed government action; **c'est le fait du p., que pouvons-nous y faire?** that's what the government's decided or how the government wants it, so what can we do?; *Fig* **comme un p.** *(traité, élevé)* like a prince, like royalty; **il est habillé comme un p.** he's dressed like a prince; *Fig* **être bon p., se montrer bon p.** to be very decent; **il s'est montré bon p. en t'accordant un délai supplémentaire** it was very decent or good of him to give you more time; **allez, montre-toi bon p.** be a good sort; **je vais me montrer bon p. et ...** I'm going to be very generous or kind and ...
▸▸**le p. charmant** Prince Charming; **p. consort** prince consort; **le p. des ténèbres** the Prince of Darkness

prince de Galles [gal] ADJ, NM INV *Tex* Prince of Wales check

princeps [prɛ̃sɛps] ADJ INV **édition p.** first edition

princesse [prɛ̃sɛs] NF princess; **p. royale** princess royal

princier, -ière [prɛ̃sje, -jɛr] ADJ princely

princièrement [prɛ̃sjɛrmɑ̃] ADV *(dîner)* like a prince, in princely fashion; *(accueilli)* like royalty; **nous avons été reçu p.** we were treated like royalty or given the red carpet treatment

principal, -ale, -aux, -ales [prɛ̃sipal, -o] ADJ *(personne)* main, principal, chief, leading; *(question, bâtiment, but)* main, principal; *(agent), Gram (proposition)* main; *(actionnaire)* main, major; **associé p.** senior partner; **principale compétence** core competence; **les principaux intéressés** those most concerned
NM **1 le p.** the main thing, the most important thing **2** *Fin* principal, capital sum; *(de l'impôt)* = original amount of tax payable (before surcharges); **p. et intérêts** principal and interest **3** *Mus* principal
N principal, chief; *Scol (d'un collège etc)* principal, *Br* head (teacher), headmaster, *f* headmistress

principalement [prɛ̃sipalmɑ̃] ADV mainly, principally

principauté [prɛ̃sipote] NF principality

principe [prɛ̃sip] NM **1** *(fondement, loi)* principle; **les principes de la géométrie** the principles of geometry; **un accord de p.** an agreement in principle; **poser qch en p.** to lay sth down as a principle; **le p. de nos actions** the principle governing our actions, the mainspring of our actions; **partir du p. que ...** to assume that ..., to take it as given that ...; **p. de précaution** precautionary

principle; **p. de solidarité** solidarity principle; *Pol* **p. de subsidiarité** subsidiarity principle; *Compta* **p. de la partie double** double-entry method; *Bourse* **p. mark to market** mark-to-market principle
2 *Chimie (d'une substance)* element, constituent; **p. actif** active principle *or* constituent
3 principes *(rudiments)* rudiments; **avoir des principes de philosophie** to have a rudimentary knowledge of philosophy
4 *(règle de conduite)* principle; **déclaration de principes** statement or declaration of principle; **ne serait-ce que pour le p.** if only for the principle of the thing; **c'est une question de p.** it's a matter of principle; **par p.** on principle, as a matter of principle; **en p.** in principle, theoretically, in theory; **avoir pour p. de ...** to make it a matter of principle to ...
5 principes (moraux) *(moral)* principles; **avoir des principes** to have (high) principles; **manquer à ses principes** to fail to live up to one's principles; **sans principes** unprincipled

printanier, -ière [prɛ̃tanje, -jɛr] ADJ *(fleurs etc)* spring; *(température, couleur etc)* spring-like; **comme tu es printanière dans cette robe!** how (fresh and) spring-like you look in that dress!

printemps [prɛ̃tɑ̃] NM spring; **au p.** in (the) spring(time); *Can Fam* **avoir la fièvre du p.** to have spring fever; *Fig* **le p. de la vie** the springtime of one's life; **fêter ses 26 p.** to celebrate one's 26th birthday; *Litt* **ses 26 p.** her 26 summers; *Fig* **elle n'a que 26 p.** she's only 26; *Fig* **le p. de la démocratie** the flowering of democracy VOIR GRAMMAIRE A7

prion [prijɔ̃] NM prion

prioritaire [priɔritɛr] N *(automobiliste)* person with priority
ADJ (that has) priority; **être p.** to have priority; **droits prioritaires** priority rights; *Fin* **actions prioritaires** preference shares, *Am* preferred stock; **le véhicule venant de la droite est p.** the vehicle coming from the right has (the) right of way or has priority; **le véhicule p.** the vehicle with the right of way or with priority; **votre demande sera p. sur toutes les autres** your application will have priority over the others; **route p.** main road, road which has priority

priorité [priɔrite] NF **1** priority; **donner la p. à qn/qch** to give sb/sth priority; **une question qui vient en p.** a question which has priority; **régler une question en p.** to settle a question as a (matter of) priority; **leur dossier sera traité en p.** their file will get priority treatment; **la p. des priorités** top priority; **ce dossier a la p. absolue** this file is top priority; **avoir la p. sur** to have or take priority or precedence over; **réclamer la p.** to claim the right to speak first; **droits de p.** priority rights; *Fin* **actions de p.** preference shares, *Am* preferred stock; **carte de p.** = pass entitling its holder to move to the head of a queue **2** *Aut* **p. (de passage)** right of way, priority; **avoir la p.** to have priority or right of way; **accorder** *ou* **laisser la p. à une voiture** to give way or *Am* to yield to a car; **refuser la p.** to refuse to give way; **p. à droite** *(sur panneau)* ≃ give way to vehicles coming from the right; **route à p.** major road

pris [pri] ADJ **1** *(siège)* occupied, taken; **tout est p.** everything is taken; **avoir les mains prises** to have one's hands full; **tu ne vois donc pas que j'ai les mains prises!** can't you see my hands are full? **2** *(personne)* busy; **je suis très p. ce matin** I'm very busy this morning, I've got a lot on this morning; **je suis déjà p. ce jour-là** I've already got something on that day, that day's booked already; **désolé, toute ma journée est prise** sorry, I'm tied up

all day; **désolé, je suis p.** sorry, I'm tied up **3 p. de peur** seized with fear; **p. de panique** panic-stricken, in a panic; **p. de remords** smitten with remorse; **p. de rage** in a rage; **p. de colère, il a déchiré la lettre** he angrily tore up the letter; **p. de boisson** *(ivre)* the worse for drink or *Fam* wear; *Fml, Jur* under the influence (of alcohol) **4** *(flan, gelée etc)* set; *(rivière etc)* frozen (over); **avoir le nez p.** to have a blocked nose; **avoir la gorge prise** to have a sore throat **5 bien p.** *(taille)* trim **6** *(attrapé)* caught, captured

prise [priz] NF **1** *(fait de prendre) (d'une ville, de prisonniers etc)* taking, capture, seizure; *(de minerai etc)* sample; **la p. de la Bastille** the fall or storming of the Bastille; **de nombreuses prises de guerre** numerous war trophies; *Échecs* **la p. de la dame par le fou** the capture of the queen by the bishop; *Méd* **faire une p. de sang** to take a blood sample; *Tech* **faire une p. à une rivière/sur un câble** to tap a river/a cable; **la p. du médicament doit se faire à heures régulières** the medication must be taken regularly; **la p. de cette substance peut provoquer des hallucinations** (taking) this substance may cause hallucinations; **p. de conscience** awareness, realization; **sa première p. de conscience de la situation réelle** the first time he realized or grasped the truth of the situation; **la p. en considération de facteurs importants** the taking into consideration or account of important factors; **la p. de voile se fit à 39 ans** she took the veil at the age of 39; *Fam* **quelle p. de tête!** what a pain (in the neck)!
2 *(quantité) (de poissons)* catch; *(de médicament)* dose; *(de tabac à priser)* pinch
3 *Élec* socket, *Am* outlet; *(mâle)* plug; **p. pour rasoir électrique** shaver socket
4 *Phot, Cin, TV (cliché)* shot; *(de filmage continu)* take; *TV, Cin* **p. non-utilisée** outtake; *Cin* **entre les prises** between takes
5 *Tech* engagement, mesh(ing); **en p.** in gear, engaged; **mettre en p.** to engage, to put into gear; *Tech* **p. constante** constant mesh; **p. câblée** cable connection; **p. directe** direct drive; *Aut* **en p. (directe)** in top (gear); *Fig* **en p. (directe) sur** *ou* **avec qch** in touch or in contact with sth; **hors de p.** out of gear
6 *(solidification)* **faire p.** *(du ciment)* to set; **ciment à p. rapide** fast-setting cement
7 *(pour se retenir)* grasp, grip; *(en escalade)* hold; *(pour le pied)* foothold; **trouver (une) p. à** *ou* **sur qch** to get a grip or a hold on or of sth; *Tech, Fml* to gain a purchase on sth; **il faut trouver de bonnes prises** you have to get a good grip; **je n'avais pas de p. (pour me hisser)** I didn't have a good enough grip (to pull myself up); *Fig* **avoir p. sur qn** to have a hold on or over sb; **la morale n'a aucune p. sur ce garçon** preaching has no effect or makes no impression on that boy; **ce film n'a eu aucune p. sur moi** the film didn't grip me; **lâcher p.** to lose one's grip; *Fig* to give up, to throw in the towel; **donner p. aux reproches/critiques** to lay oneself open to reproach/criticism
8 *(de judo, de lutte)* hold; **faire une p. de judo à qn** to use a judo throw on sb; *Fig* **être aux prises avec qch** to grapple with sth; **elle est aux prises avec son chef de service** she is at odds with her boss; **leurs intérêts se sont trouvés aux prises** their interests have clashed
▸▸**p. d'air** air intake; *Tech* **p. d'alimentation** input socket; *Fin* **p. de bénéfices** profit-taking; **p. en charge** *(par taxi) (d'un passager)* picking up; *Admin (par Sécurité sociale)* (guaranteed) reimbursement; **p. de contact** contact; *Com* **p. de contrôle** takeover; *Ordinat* **p. de contrôle à distance** remote control; **p. de corps** *Jur* arrest; *Fin* charge; **p. de cou-**

rant *(mâle)* plug; *(femelle)* socket, plug *or* power point, outlet; **p. de décision** decision-making; *Com* **p. à domicile** receipt at domicile; **p. d'eau** *Tech* intake of water; *(dispositif)* cock, tap, valve; *(à incendie)* (fire) hydrant; *(point d'alimentation) (d'un canal, à partir d'une rivière etc)* offtake; *Jur, Pol* **p. illégale d'intérêt** = misuse of public office; *TV, Cin* **p. des marques** blocking; *Élec* **p. multiple** adapter; **p. de notes** note-taking; **p. d'otages** hostage-taking; **p. de participation** *(dans une entreprise)* acquisition of an interest in a company; *Ordinat* **p. péri-informatique** connector; **p. Péritel®** scart connector; **p. de position** stance, position; *Bourse* position taking; **une p. de position est nécessaire** we must take a stand; **p. de possession: la p. de possession de qch** taking possession of sth; **p. de pouvoir** *(légale)* (political) takeover; *(illégale)* seizure of power; *TV, Cin* **p. de repères** camera blocking; *TV, Cin* **p. de son** sound recording; **effectuer une p. de son** to shoot sound; *Élec* **p. de terre** earth *or Am* ground (connection); *Élec* **avoir une p. de terre** to be earthed *or Am* grounded; **p. de terre** to be earthed *or Am* grounded; **p. de vue** *Phot* photography; *TV, Cin (technique)* shooting; *(cliché)* (camera) shot; **p. de vue de couverture** cover shot; *TV* **p. de vue(s) en direct** live broadcast

prisée [prize] NF *Jur (de biens)* valuation

priser¹ [prize] VT **p. du tabac** to take snuff; **p. de la cocaïne** to sniff cocaine
   VI to take snuff; **tabac à p.** snuff

priser² VT **1** *Litt (estimer)* to prize, to value **2** *Arch (biens)* to appraise, to value

priseur, -euse [prizœr, -øz] N snuff-taker

prismatique [prismatik] ADJ prismatic

prisme [prism] NM prism; *Fig* **elle voit la situation à travers un p.** she has a distorted view of the situation; **jumelles à p.** prismatic binoculars; *TV, Cin* **p. diviseur (de faisceau)** (prism) beam splitter

prison [prizɔ̃] NF **1** *(lieu de détention)* prison, jail; **être/aller en p.** to be in/to go to prison *or* jail; **mettre qn en p.** to put sb in prison *or* jail, *Fml* to imprison sb; **sortir de p.** to come *or* get out (of prison *or* jail), to be released (from prison *or* jail); **s'échapper de p.** to escape from *or* break out of prison *or* jail; *Fig* **cette école est une vraie p.** this school is like a prison; *Péj Fam* **aimable comme une porte de p.** extremely unpleasant; **gardien de p.** prison officer, prison warder ▣VOIR GRAMMAIRE A6-7 **2** *(peine)* imprisonment; **il risque la p.** he risks going to prison *or* jail; **faire de la p.** to be in prison *or* jail, to serve a prison *or* jail sentence; **cinq ans de p.** five years' imprisonment; **elle a fait deux ans de p.** she spent two years in prison *or* inside; *Fam* **il a été condamné à cinq ans de p. ferme/avec sursis** he was given a five-year prison *or* jail sentence/a five-year suspended prison sentence; **p. à vie** *ou* **à perpétuité** life imprisonment; **on l'a condamné à la p. à vie** *ou* **à perpétuité** he was sentenced to life imprisonment, he received a life sentence, he was sent to prison for life

prisonnier, -ière [prizɔnje, -jer] N prisoner; **faire qn p.** to take sb prisoner; **se constituer p.** to give oneself up; **camp de prisonniers** prison camp; **p. condamné à perpétuité** prisoner serving a life sentence, *Fam* lifer
   ADJ imprisoned, in prison; *(pris, attrapé)* captive; **ils sont encore prisonniers sous les décombres** they are still trapped in the rubble; *Fig* **être p. de ses principes** to be a slave to one's principles; **être p. de ses habitudes** to be a creature of habit; **je suis p. du confort** I can't do without my creature comforts; **on est toujours p. de son milieu** you can never break free of your environment

▶▶*Jur* **p. de droit commun** prisoner; **p. de guerre** prisoner of war, POW; *Pol* **p. d'opinion** prisoner of conscience; **p. politique** political prisoner

Prisunic® [prizynik] NM = low-priced department store; *Péj* **il m'a donné un truc de P.** he gave me a real cheapo present; **le genre Marilyn des P.** the dyed blonde dollybird type

privatif, -ive [privatif, -iv] ADJ **1** *Gram* privative **2** *(particulier)* private
   NM *Gram* privative prefix

privation [privasjɔ̃] NF **1** *(perte, manque)* deprivation; **p. d'un droit/de la liberté** loss of a right/of freedom **2 privations** hardship, privation; **une vie de privations** a life of hardship; **s'imposer des privations** to deprive oneself, to go without

privatique [privatik] NF home video equipment

privatisable [privatizabl] ADJ which can be privatized, privatizable

privatisation [privatizasjɔ̃] NF privatization

privatiser [privatize] VT to privatize

privautés [privote] NFPL *(undue)* familiarity; **prendre** *ou* **se permettre des p. avec qn** to be over-familiar with sb

privé [prive] ADJ **1** *(individuel) (vie, entreprise, chemin, propriété etc)* private; **se réunir en séance privée** to sit in private *or* closed session; **visite privée** *(d'un président etc)* private *or* unofficial visit; **nous avons eu droit à une visite privée du château** we were given a private tour of the castle; *Hist* **le Conseil p.** the Privy Council; *Fig* **c'est un peu son domaine p.** it's his own private domain **2** *(libre) (école, patient etc)* private
   NM **1** *(vie)* private life; **en p.** *(parler à qn, voir qn)* in private; **connaître qn dans le p.** to know sb in private life; **dans le p., cet acteur est très modeste** off stage he's a very modest man **2** *Ind, Scol, Méd* **le p.** *(secteur libre)* the private sector; **dans le p., les médecins sont plus attentifs** private doctors are more attentive; *Scol* **elle a mis ses filles dans le p.** she sent her daughters to a private school **3** *Fam (détective privé)* private eye, *Am* dick, shamus

priver [prive] VT **p. qn de qch** to deprive sb of sth; **on l'a privé de sortie, il a été privé de sortie** *(à cause de ce qu'il a fait)* he wasn't allowed to go out, *Am Fam* he was grounded; **tu seras privé de dessert** you'll go without pudding, there'll be no pudding for you; **j'ai été privé de sommeil** I didn't get any sleep; **je suis privée de télévision depuis un mois** I've been without television for a month; **je ne vous en prive pas?** can you spare it?, I'm not depriving you, am I?; **ça te prive beaucoup si je te l'emprunte pour la nuit?** would it be too much to ask to borrow it overnight?; **ça ne le prive pas du tout de ne plus fumer** he doesn't find it a hardship not to smoke any more; **ce genre de situation me prive de tous mes moyens** I completely lose my head *or* I go completely to pieces in that kind of situation

   VPR **se priver** to do *or* go without; **se p. de** *(nourriture etc)* to do *or* go without; *(plaisir etc)* to deprive oneself of, to deny oneself; **toi, tu n'aimes pas te p.!** you certainly don't like to go *or* do without, do you?; **il ne se prive pas de le lui dire** he never misses a chance *or* an opportunity to tell him/her so; **je ne me suis pas privé de lui dire ce que je pensais** I didn't hesitate to tell him/her what I thought; **tu peux te reposer cinq minutes, elle ne s'en est pas privée!** you can have a rest for five minutes, she did!

privilège [privilɛʒ] NM **1** *(avantage, droit)* privilege; **jouir du p.** *ou* **avoir le p. de faire qch** to have the privilege of doing sth, to be

privileged to do sth; **cette méthode a le p. d'être très rapide** this method has the advantage of being very fast; **le p. de l'âge/de la beauté/de la naissance** the privileges of age/beauty/birth; **c'est le p. de l'âge que de pouvoir dire ce qu'on pense** speaking your mind is one of the privileges of age; **la raison fait partie des privilèges de l'homme** the ability to reason is one of the advantages enjoyed by man; **c'est un triste p.** it's a dubious privilege; *Iron* **il a le p. de me déplaire** I have a particular dislike for him; *Iron* **elle a le p. de nous agacer** we find her particularly annoying; *Hist* **abolition des privilèges** abolition of privilege **2** *(exclusivité)* licence, grant; *(d'une banque)* charter **3** *Jur* preferential claim

privilégié, -ée [privileʒje] ADJ *(favorisé)* *(classe)* privileged; *(situation)* privileged, favourable; **entretenir des relations privilégiées avec un pays** to have a special relationship with a country; **elle est privilégiée par son expérience** she is at *or* has an advantage on account of her experience; **jouir d'un climat p.** to be privileged *or* blessed in its climate; **le moyen d'expression p. de cet artiste** the artist's favourite *or* preferred means of expression, the means of expression favoured by the artist; **banque privilégiée** chartered bank; **créancier p.** preferential *or* preferred creditor; **action privilégiée** preference share
   N privileged person; **quelques privilégiés l'ont vu** a privileged few have seen it; **nous faisons partie des privilégiés** we are among the privileged; **c'est un p.** *(d'un milieu favorisé)* he comes from a privileged background; **tu es un p.** *(tu as de la chance)* you're one of the privileged

privilégier [privileʒje] VT *(pr sub, impf n. privilégiions, v. privilégiiez) (personne, groupe)* to privilege; *(facteur, aspect)* to prioritize; **c'est l'objectif à p.** it's the objective to be prioritized

prix [pri] NM **1** *(valeur)* value, worth; *(coût)* cost; *Fig* **à tout p.** at all costs, whatever the cost, at any price; **faire qch à p. d'argent** to do sth for money; **se vendre à p. d'or** *(de biens)* to fetch huge prices; **acheter qch à p. d'or** to pay a huge amount *or Fam* a fortune for sth; **à aucun p.** not on any terms, not at any price; **elle n'ira à aucun p.** she won't go on any terms *or* at any price, nothing will make her go; **à n'importe quel p.** no matter what it costs; **à tout p.** at all costs; **elle veut changer de travail à tout p.** she wants to change jobs no matter what it costs *or* takes; *Fig* **au p. de** at the cost of; **attacher beaucoup de p.** *ou* **un grand p. à qch** to set great store by sth, to set a lot of value on sth; **il attache beaucoup de p.** *ou* **un grand p. à l'apparence de sa voiture** he sets great store by his car's appearance, he prizes his car's appearance **2** *(en argent)* price; **acheter qch à juste p.** to buy sth at a fair price, to pay a fair price for sth; **je l'ai acheté à bas p.** I didn't pay very much for it, I paid a low price for it; *Fam* **faire un p. à qn** to give sb a good deal; **vous nous faites un p. si on en prend deux?** will you give us a good price if we take two?; **je vous ferai un p. (d'ami)** I'll let you have it cheap; **une voiture dans mes p.** a car I can afford *or* within my means *or* within my price range; **ce n'est pas du tout dans mes p.** I can't afford it, it's way beyond my means *or* well outside my price range; **c'est plus dans mes p.** that's more in my price range *or* my line; *Bourse* **actions cotées au p. de ...** shares quoted at the rate of ...; **articles de p.** expensive goods; **coûter un p. fou** to cost the earth *or Fam* an arm and a leg; **hors de p.** prohibitively expensive; **ne pas avoir de p.** to be priceless; **la santé/le bonheur, ça n'a pas de p.**

you can't put a price on health/happiness; **mettre à p. la tête de qn** to put a price on sb's head; **mise à p. d'une propriété** upset price of an estate; **mise à p.** *(aux enchères) (d'un article)* reserve price; **c'est mon dernier p.** that's my final offer; **votre p. sera le mien** name your price; *Fam* **au p. où sont les choses, au p. où est le beurre** given the price of things, seeing what things cost; *Écon* **hausse/baisse des p.** rise/fall in prices; **vous pouvez en trouver si vous y mettez le p.** you can get it if you're willing to pay for it; **mais elle a dû y mettre le p.** but it cost her SEE GRAMMAR B59

3 *(tarif)* charge; *(d'un voyage)* fare; **quel est le p. du billet?** how much do the tickets cost?; *(transports)* what's the fare?, how much is it?

4 *(récompense)* prize; *(d'une bonne action)* reward; *Fam* **au p. où sont les choses,** the prize, to carry off the prize; **distribution des p.** prizegiving, *Br Scol* speech day; **le jour de la distribution des p.** prizegiving day; *Scol* **livre de p.** prize book; **p. de consolation** consolation prize; *Scol* **p. d'excellence** prize for excellence; **le p. Nobel** the Nobel Prize *(de for)*; **le p. Nobel de la Paix** the Nobel Peace Prize; **un/le p. Nobel** *(personne)* a/ the Nobel prizewinner *or Am* laureate

5 *(œuvre, ouvrage primé)* prizewinning work; **j'ai lu le dernier p. Médicis** I've read the latest Prix Médicis *or* the latest Médicis prizewinner

6 *Sport* race; **Grand p. (automobile)** Grand Prix

▸▸ *Mktg* **p. d'acceptabilité** psychological price; **p. d'achat** purchase price; *Bourse* **p. acheteur** bid price; **p. affiché** posted price; **p. avantageux** bargain price; **p. catalogue** list price; **p. de la chambre** room rate; **p. au comptant** cash price; **p. conseillé** suggested retail price, recommended retail price; **p. contractuel** contract *or* contractual price; **p. courant** current price, market price; **p. coûtant** cost price; **à** *ou* **au p. coûtant, au p. de revient** at cost price; **acheter/vendre qch au p. coûtant** to buy/sell sth at cost; **p. départ usine** price ex-works; **p. de détail** retail price; **p. discompte** discount price; **p. élastique** elastic price; *Bourse* **p. d'émission** issue price; **p. de l'essence à la pompe** price of petrol at the pump; *Bourse* **p. d'exercice** *(d'option d'achat)* exercise price, strike price; **p. facturé** invoice *or* invoiced price; **p. fixe** fixed rate; **(repas à) p. fixe** set (price) meal; **p. forfaitaire** all-inclusive price; **p. fort** full price; **au p. fort, ça coûte ... the** full price is ...; **p. de gros** wholesale price; **p. hors taxe** price net of tax, price before tax; **p. imposé** fixed price; **p. indicatif** approximate price; **p. initial** prime cost; *Mktg* **p. magique** odd-numbers price; **p. adapté au marché** market-based price; **p. du marché** market price; **p. sur le marché** market price; *Bourse* **p. de négociation** trade price; **p. net** net rate; **p. d'offre** supply price; **p. optimum** optimal price; **p. plafond** ceiling price; **p. plancher** price floor; *Mktg* **p. de prestige** premium price; **p. promotionnels** promotional pricing; *Mktg* **p. psychologique** psychological price; **p. public** posted price; **p. réduit** discount price; **p. de référence** reference price; **p. seuil** floor price; **p. taxe comprise** price inclusive of tax; **p. de transport** freight price; **p. unique** one price, single price; **p. unitaire** unit price; **p. unitaire produit** unit price; **p. d'usine** factory price; *Bourse* **p. vendeur** offer price; **p. de vente** selling price

> Attention: ne pas confondre **price** et **prize** lorsque l'on traduit le terme **prix**. **Price** désigne une somme à payer, alors que **prize** désigne toujours une récompense.

pro [pro] **N** *Sport etc Fam* pro; **elle l'a fait en p.** she did it like a pro; **du travail de p.** professional work, the work of a pro; **ils ont fait du travail de p., tous les deux** they both worked like pros

proactif, -ive [proaktif, -iv] **ADJ** proactive

probabilité [probabilite] **NF** probability, likelihood; **selon toute p.** in all probability *or* likelihood, most probably; *Math* **calcul des probabilités** theory of probability; **il y a une forte p.** there's a strong probability; **il y a une faible p.** there's little probability *or* likelihood SEE GRAMMAR A59-61; B39-40

probable [probabl] **ADJ** probable, likely; **il est p. qu'elle viendra** she'll probably come; **il est fort p. que ...** it's very probable that ...; **peu p.** improbable, unlikely; **il est peu p. qu'elle vienne** she's not likely *or* she's unlikely to come, it's unlikely that she'll come; **c'est très p.** (it's) very likely; **c'est plus que p.** it's more than likely; *Fam* **tu pourras rester avec nous? – c'est p.** will you be able to stay with us? – probably (I will); *Fam* **p. qu'elle ne se souvient plus de ce que je lui ai dit** she probably doesn't remember what I told her

probablement [probabləmã] **ADV** probably

probant [probã] **ADJ** *(témoignage, argument etc)* convincing, conclusive; *(raison)* convincing; **peu p.** unconvincing; *Jur* **pièce probante** incriminating piece of evidence

probation [probasjõ] **NF** *Jur, Rel* probation

probatoire [probatwar] **ADJ** **stage p.** trial *or* probationary period; *Scol* **examen p.** grading examination; *Jur* **délai p.** probation

probe [prob] **ADJ** *Litt* honest, upright

probité [probite] **NF** probity, integrity

problématique [problematik] **ADJ** problematic(al)
  NF set of problems; *Phil* problematics

problématiquement [problematikmã] **ADV** problematically

problème [problem] **NM** problem; **un p. d'algèbre/de géométrie/de physique** an algebra/a geometry/a physics problem; **elle a soulevé le p. de la cantine** she brought up *or* raised the problem of the canteen; **poser un p.** to pose a problem; **si cela devait vous poser un p.** if that poses *or* creates a problem for you, if that's a problem for you; **cet emploi du temps pose p.** this schedule is (posing *or* creating) a problem; **ce n'est pas un p.** it's not a problem, that's no problem; **c'est tout un p.!** it's such a problem!; *Fam* **tu pourras passer me prendre? – oui, sans p.** could you come and pick me up? – sure, no problem; **tu n'auras aucun p. à la convaincre** you won't have any problem convincing her; *Fam* **(il n'y a) pas de p.! *(bien sûr!)*** no problem!; **avoir des problèmes** to have problems; *Psy* **un adolescent qui a des problèmes** a problem teenager; *Scol* **faire des problèmes** to do sums; *Fam* **il va nous faire des problèmes** he's going to cause *or* give us problems; **peau/cheveux à problèmes** problem skin/hair; *Fam* **encore un type à problèmes** another guy with problems; **avoir des problèmes familiaux/d'argent** to have family/money problems

procédé [prosede] **NM 1** *(façon de faire)* method; **des procédés peu recommandables** dubious methods; **échange de bons procédés** *(de formules de politesse)* exchange of courtesies *or* civilities; **c'est un échange de bons procédés** *(de petits services)* one good turn deserves another; **leur mésentente se traduit par des échanges constants de mauvais procédés** they don't get on and constantly play dirty tricks on each other; **cet échange de mauvais procédés finit par ...** the dirty tricks they played on each other ended up ... **2** *(technique)* process; *(de tra-*

vail) method; **p. de fonctionnement** operating procedure; **p. de fabrication** manufacturing process; *Péj* **ça sent le p.** it seems rather artificial **3** *(de queue de billard)* tip **4** *Litt (comportement)* conduct

procéder [prosede] **VI** *(conj like* **céder)** **1** *(venir de)* **p. de** to arise out of, to originate in; **sa maladie procède de l'humidité ambiante** his illness is caused by *or* is attributable to the dampness **2** *(agir)* to proceed, to act; **p. par ordre** to do things in order; **p. par tâtonnement** to feel *or* fumble one's way; **p. avec méthode** to proceed methodically **3 p. à** *(des recherches, une arrestation, une vérification etc)* to carry out; *(des élections)* to hold

procédure [prosedyr] **NF 1** *(méthode)* procedure; **il faut suivre la p.** you/we/*etc* have to follow procedure; *Ordinat* **p. de chargement** loading procedure; *Tél* **p. de connexion** dialup procedure **2** *Jur* procedure; *(démarche)* proceedings; **engager une p.** to take *or* institute proceedings; **engager une p. de divorce** to begin *or* institute divorce proceedings; **terme de p.** legal term; **vice** *ou* **incident de p.** procedural irregularity, legal technicality; **p. de codécision** codecision procedure; **p. douanière** customs procedure; *Fin* **p. de faillite** bankruptcy proceedings; **p. législative** legislative procedure; **p. parlementaire** parliamentary procedure; **p. d'urgence** emergency *or* special powers **3** *Ordinat* procedure

procédurier, -ière [prosedyrje, -jer] **ADJ** quibbling, *Fam* nit-picking; *(avocat)* pettifogging
  N quibbler, *Fam* nit-picker; *(avocat)* pettifogger

procès [prosE] **NM 1** *Jur (legal)* proceedings, action (at law); **p. civil** lawsuit; **p. criminel** *(criminal)* trial; **engager un p.** to take legal action; **faire** *ou* **intenter un p. à** *(un particulier)* to sue, to bring an action against, to institute proceedings against; *(un délinquant)* to prosecute; **engager** *ou* **entreprendre un p.** to institute proceedings **(contre qn** against sb); **être en p. avec qn** to be involved in legal proceedings with sb; **intenter un p. en divorce à qn** to institute divorce proceedings against sb; **le dossier du p.** the brief; **gagner/perdre son p.** to win/lose one's case; *Fam* **avoir un p. sur le dos** to be faced with a lawsuit *or* a court case; *Fig* **tu me/lui/** *etc* **fais un p. d'intention** you're jumping to conclusions; *Fig* **faire le p. de qn/qch** to attack sb/sth; *Fig* **sans autre forme de p.** without (any) further ceremony, without further ado; **renvoyé sans autre forme de p.** unceremoniously dismissed; *Fig* **c'est un p. contre la société** the whole of society is on trial; *Journ* **p. médiatique** trial by media **2** *Anat Vieilli* process

> Il faut noter que le nom anglais **process** est un faux ami. Il signifie le plus souvent **processus, procédé.**

processeur [prosesœr] **NM** *Ordinat* processor; **p. SQL** SQL engine; **p. audio** audio processor; **p. central** central processing unit, CPU; **p. de données** data processor; **p. frontal/graphique/maître/matriciel** front-end/display/master/array processor; **p. en tranches** bit-slice processor

processif, -ive [prosesif, -iv] **ADJ** *(mesures etc)* progressive

procession [prosesjõ] **NF** *aussi Fig* procession; **aller en p.** to walk in procession

processionnaire [prosesjoner] **ADJ** processionary

processionnel, -elle [prosesjonel] **ADJ** processional

processionnellement [prosesjonelmã] **ADV** *Litt* in procession

processus [prɔsesys] **NM 1** *(évolution)* process; **un p. de changement** a process of change; *UE* **p. de convergence** convergence process; **p. de paix** peace process; *Méd* **p. pathologique** pathology **2** *(méthode)* process, method; **l'introduction de nouveaux p.** the introduction of new methods; **p. industriel** industrial process **3** *Anat* process

procès-verbal, *pl* **procès-verbaux NM 1** *Jur* policeman's report *(about an offence)*; **avoir un p.** to get a (parking) ticket; **dresser le p. d'une contravention à qn, dresser (un) p. à** *ou* **contre qn** to report *or Fam* book sb **2** *(rapport)* (official) report; *(d'une réunion)* proceedings, minutes; *(d'un témoignage etc)* record; **approbation du p.** approval of the minutes; **registre des procès-verbaux** minute book

prochain, -aine [prɔʃɛ̃, -ɛn] **ADJ 1** *(qui suit)* next; **dimanche p.** next Sunday; **la semaine prochaine** next week; **le p. numéro** *(d'un magazine)* the next issue; **la prochaine fois** the next time; **ce sera pour une prochaine fois** another time perhaps, *Am* let's take a rain check; **à la prochaine fois!** be seeing you!, *Fam* see you (soon)! VOIR GRAMMAIRE A7 **2** *surtout Litt (imminent)* imminent; **son p. départ, son départ p.** his/her approaching *or* impending *or* imminent departure; **sa fin prochaine** his/her imminent death; **dans un avenir p.** in the near *or* not too distant future; **un jour p.** one day soon **N** neighbour, *Am* neighbor; *(tout être humain)* fellow human being; **aimer son p.** to love one's neighbour **NF prochaine** *Fam* **1 à la prochaine!** see you (soon)! **2 je descends à la prochaine** I'm getting off at the next stop

prochainement [prɔʃɛnmɑ̃] **ADV** shortly, soon; **p. sur vos écrans** coming soon to a cinema near you

PROCHE [prɔʃ] **ADV de p. en p.** little by little, step by step, by degrees **ADJ** near, close (**de** to), neighbouring, *Am* neighboring; **la ville la plus p.** the nearest *or* closest town; **tout p.** close at hand, nearby, close by; **le chalet est tout p.** the chalet is not very far away; **dans un avenir tout p.** in the very near future; **sa fin est p.** he/she is close *or* near to death, the end is not very far away; **la fin est p.** the end is nigh; **l'heure est p.** the hour is near *or* at hand; **cela me paraît pourtant si p.!** *(dans le passé)* it seems like only yesterday!; **p. de la ruine/la catastrophe** on the verge of *or* close to ruin/catastrophe; **p. de mourir** near death, close to death; **l'italien est p. du français** Italian is close to French; **des langues très proches** languages that are very close to each other; **je me sens p. de lui** I feel close to him; **nous sommes devenus très proches** we became very close; **ses proches parents** his/her near *or* close relations; *Jur, Fml* his next of kin; **nom et adresse des proches parents** name and address of next of kin; **ils sont proches parents** they are closely related; **les gens les plus proches de nous** the people closest to us, our nearest and dearest; **la guerre est p.** war is close; **les gens proches du pouvoir** those close to the seat of power; **une préoccupation p. de la névrose** a worry bordering on neurosis; **une description p. de la réalité** a realistic *or* true-to-life description **N réunir ses proches** to gather one's nearest and dearest (around one); **seuls ses proches étaient au courant** only his nearest and dearest *or* those closest to him knew

Proche-Orient (le) [ləprɔʃɔrjɑ̃] **NM** the Middle East, *Vieilli* the Near East

proclamateur, -trice [prɔklamatœr, -tris] **N** *Litt* proclaimer

proclamation [prɔklamasjɔ̃] **NF** proclamation

proclamer [prɔklame] **VT** to proclaim; **p. le résultat du scrutin** to declare the results of the election; **on proclama que ...** it was given out that ...; **tu ne vas pas aller p. ça partout, j'espère** you're not going to announce it to all and sundry *or* shout it from the rooftops, I trust; **elle est allée p. partout que ...** she went around telling everybody that ...; **p. son innocence** to proclaim *or* protest one's innocence; **p. qn roi** to proclaim sb king

proclitique [prɔklitik] **ADJ, NM** *Ling* proclitic

proconsul [prɔkɔ̃syl] **NM** *Hist* proconsul

proconsulaire [prɔkɔ̃sylɛr] **ADJ** *Hist* proconsular

proconsulat [prɔkɔ̃syla] **NM** *Hist* proconsulate

procréateur, -trice [prɔkreatœr, -tris] *Hum, Vieilli* **ADJ** procreative **N** procreator

procréation [prɔkreasjɔ̃] **NF** procreation; *Arch (des enfants)* begetting; **p. médicalement assistée** assisted conception

procréatique [prɔkreatik] **NF** artificial birth technology

procréer [prɔkree] **VT** *Litt* to procreate, *Arch* to beget

procurateur [prɔkyratœr] **NM** *Hist* procurator

procuration [prɔkyrasjɔ̃] **NF** *Com, Fin, Jur* proxy, power of attorney; **par p.** by proxy, *Spéc* per pro(curationem); **voter par p.** to vote by proxy; **vote par p.** proxy vote; **donner (la) p. à qn** to confer powers of attorney on sb, to give sb power of attorney; **elle lui a envoyé une p.** she sent him a power of attorney; *Fig* **elle avait le sentiment de vivre par p.** she felt she was living by proxy

procuratrice [prɔkyratris] **NF** *Jur* procurator, proxy

procurer [prɔkyre] **VT p. qch à qn** to get *or* obtain *or Fml* procure sth for sb; **p. un emploi à qn** to get sb a job; **p. un renseignement à qn** to get hold of information for sb; **le plaisir que cela nous procure** the pleasure that gives us, the pleasure we derive *or* get from that; **son travail lui procure d'importants revenus** his job provides him with *or* brings in a substantial income **VPR se procurer** to get (hold of), to obtain, *Fml* to procure; **se p. de l'argent** to get hold of *or* raise *or* find money; **où peut-on se p. ce livre?** where can you get hold of this book?

procureur [prɔkyrœr] **NM** *Jur* procurator, proxy; **p. de la République** *Eng* ≃ public prosecutor, *Scot* ≃ procurator fiscal, *Am* ≃ district attorney *(in lower courts)*; **p. général** *(in higher courts) Eng* ≃ public prosecutor, *Scot* ≃ procurator fiscal, *Am* ≃ district attorney *(in lower courts)*

prodigalité [prɔdigalite] **NF** *(défaut)* extravagance, prodigality; **une p. de** *(détails, anecdotes)* a wealth *or* an abundance of; *(objets)* an abundance of; **une p. de richesses** a king's ransom; **donner avec p.** to be extremely generous; **donner son temps avec p.** to be extremely generous with one's time; *Fig* **prodigalités** *(dépenses)* lavish *or* reckless expenditure

prodige [prɔdiʒ] **NM** wonder, marvel; *(personne)* prodigy; **faire des prodiges** to work *or* do wonders, to work miracles; **un p. d'ingéniosité** a marvel of ingenuity; **un p. de courage/patience** wonderful bravery/patience; **déployer des prodiges de courage/patience** to demonstrate wonderful bravery/patience; **tenir du p.** to be extraordinary, to be something of a miracle; *(être impossible)* to be impossible *or* a physical impossibility; **c'est un p.** *(personne)* he's a prodigy; *(fait)* it's amazing *or* incredible **ADJ enfant p.** child prodigy

prodigieusement [prɔdiʒjøzmɑ̃] **ADV** prodigiously

prodigieux, -ieuse [prɔdiʒjø, -jøz] **ADJ** *(quantité, force)* prodigious, extraordinary; *Fam (incroyable)* phenomenal, stupendous; *Iron* **sa bêtise est prodigieuse** his/her stupidity knows no bounds, he/she is phenomenally stupid; **d'un courage p.** extraordinarily brave

prodigue [prɔdig] **ADJ 1** *(généreux)* lavish, unsparing (**de** in, with); **il est p. pour ses enfants** he's very generous towards his children; **être p. d'excuses** to apologize profusely, to be profuse in one's apologies; **être p. de compliments** to be lavish in one's praise; **être p. de son argent** to spend lavishly, to be free with one's money; **il est très p. de conseils** he's very generous with his advice; *Iron* he's very free with his advice **2** *Péj (dépensier)* wasteful, spendthrift, *Fml* prodigal; *Bible* **l'enfant p.** the prodigal son **N** spendthrift, squanderer

prodiguer [prɔdige] **VT 1** *(donner abondamment) (aide)* to be unstinting in, to give unstintingly; *(compliments)* to be lavish *or* unstinting in; *(énergie)* to lavish; **p. sa patience** to show unstinting patience; **p. qch à qn** to lavish sth on sb; **p. ses conseils** to be generous with one's advice; *Iron* to be free with one's advice; **il lui prodiguait ses conseils** he was generous *or Iron* free with his advice; **p. son argent à ses enfants** to spend *or* lavish all one's money on one's children; **p. ses talents à qn** to treat sb to a display of one's talents **2** *Péj (gaspiller)* to waste, to squander

prodrome [prɔdrom] **NM 1** *(d'une maladie)* warning symptom **2** *(d'un traité)* preamble

producteur, -trice [prɔdyktœr, -tris] **ADJ** productive (**de** of); **pays p. de blé/pétrole** wheat-growing/oil-producing country; *Cin* **société productrice** production company **N** *(entreprise etc), Radio, TV, Cin* producer; **p. associé** associate producer, production associate; **p. délégué** executive producer

productible [prɔdyktibl] **ADJ** producible

productif, -ive [prɔdyktif, -iv] **ADJ** productive; *Fin* **p. d'intérêts** interest-bearing

production [prɔdyksjɔ̃] **NF 1** *Ind, Cin* production; *(d'électricité)* production, generation; **la p. textile/automobile** textile/car production; **augmenter la p.** to increase production *or* output; **les conditions de p. des œuvres artistiques** the conditions in which works of art are produced; **moyens de p.** means of production; **coût de p.** cost of production, production cost; *Cin* **directeur de p.** production manager; **assistant de p.** production assistant; *TV, Cin* **p. back-to-back** back-to-back production; **p. à la chaîne** mass production; **p. cinématographique** film production; *TV, Radio* **p. directe** live production; **p. de l'exercice** *(poste de bilan)* production for the period; *Fin* **p. immobilisée** fixed assets produced for use by the company; *Com* **p. JAT** JIT production; *Com* **p. juste à temps** just-in-time production; **p. en masse** mass production; **p. en série** mass production; **p. en studio** studio production; *TV, Cin* **p. à la suite** back-to-back production; *TV* **p. vidéo légère** electronic field production, EFP

2 *(produit)* product; *Cin* production; *Cin* **p. journalière** rushes, dailies; **productions** *Agr* produce; *(de la mine etc)* yield; *(d'une usine)* output; **p. stockée** *(poste de bilan)* stored production, production left in stock; *Compta* **p. vendue** sales; **p. littéraire** literary output; *Cin* **une p. franco-russe** a Franco-Russian (co-)production

3 *Jur* **p. des pièces** exhibition of documents

productique [prɔdyktik] NF production engineering

productivisme [prɔdyktivism] NM *Péj* obsession with productivity

productiviste [prɔdyktivist] ADJ *Péj* that emphasizes productivity to an obsessive degree

productivité [prɔdyktivite] NF productivity, productiveness; *(d'une usine)* productive capacity; **accroissement de la p.** increase in productivity

produire [prɔdɥir] *(prp* **produisant;** *pp* **produit;** *pr ind* **je produis,** n. **produisons;** *impf* **je produisais;** *p hist* **je produisis;** *fu* **je produirai)** VT **1** *Ind, Agr, Cin, TV, Radio* to produce; *(chaleur, électricité)* to generate, to produce; *Litt (descendance etc)* to bring forth, to bear; **argent qui produit de l'intérêt** money that yields *or* bears interest; **p. cent voitures par jour** to produce *or* turn out *or* have an output of a hundred cars a day; **p. une créance** to result in an account receivable; *TV, Cin* **produit par** produced by

2 *(résultat)* to produce, to bring about, to generate; *(effet)* to produce, to bring about; *(sensation)* to create, to generate; *(odeur)* to produce, to generate; *(irritation)* to cause; **p. une impression favorable sur qn** to produce *or* make a favourable impression on sb; **sa déclaration a produit un certain effet** his/her statement created *or* caused something of a stir; **il a produit son effet en annonçant cela** his announcement had the effect he wanted *or* was hoping for

3 *(créer)* to produce, to turn out; **elle vient de p. son premier roman** she's just produced *or* written *or* turned out her first novel; **les œuvres que ces années de guerre ont produites** the works that were the outcome of the war years *or* that the war years generated

4 *Jur etc (témoignage etc)* to produce, to bring forward; **p. des témoins** to produce witnesses

VI **1** *Écon* to produce, to be productive

2 *Jur* **sommation de p.** order *or* requirement to present one's ID papers/driving licence/etc

VPR **se produire 1** *(d'un événement)* to happen, to take place, to occur; **il pourrait se p. des incidents** there might be trouble; **cela se produit souvent** that often happens, it's a frequent occurrence

2 *(d'un acteur etc)* to appear

produit [prɔdɥi] NM **1** *(marchandise)* product; *Agr* **produits** produce; **produits agricoles** agricultural produce, farm products; **le p. de la terre** the produce of the land; **vivre du p. de la terre** to live off the land; **les services et les produits** goods and services

2 *(profit)* yield; **p. d'une vente** proceeds of a sale; *Com* **le p. de la journée** the day's takings *or* receipts; **le p. de dix années de travail** the product *or* result of ten years' work

3 *Math (d'une multiplication)* product

4 *(création)* product; **c'est le p. de son imagination** it's the *or* a product of his imagination; **toute cette histoire était le plus pur p. de son imagination** the entire story was a figment of his/her imagination

▸▸ **produits d'achat courant** convenience goods; *Mktg* **p. d'achat impulsif** *ou* **non prémédité** impulse item; *Mktg* **produits d'achat réfléchi** shopping goods; **p. alimentaire** food product; *Compta* **produits annexes** incidental income; **p. augmenté** augmented product; *Mktg* **p. d'avenir** rising star, potential market leader; *Banque* **p. bancaire** banking product; **p. de beauté** beauty product; *Compta* **p. brut** gross proceeds, gross income; **p. chimique** chemical; *Mktg* **p. ciblé** niche product; **p. de consommation courante** consumer product; *Compta* **p. cons-**

taté **d'avance** prepaid income; *Compta* **produits courants** current income; *Compta* **produits en cours** work in progress; *Mktg* **produits de dépannage** emergency goods; **produits dérivés** by-products, derivatives; *Mktg* **p. dodo** dodo; *Mktg* **p. drapeau** own-brand product; **p. écologique** green product; **produits d'entretien** *(household)* cleaning products; **p. d'étanchéité** sealing compound; *Compta* **produits exceptionnels** extraordinary income; *Compta* **produits d'exploitation** income from operations; **p. final** end product; *Fin* **p. financier** financial product; *Compta* **produits financiers** interest dividends and other financial income; **p. fini** finished product; *Mktg* **p. générique** generic, generic product; *Compta* **produits de gestion courante** income from operations; **p. de grande consommation** mass-market product; **produits de grande sommation** consumer goods; **p. hôtelier** hotel product; *Mktg* **p. d'imitation** imitative product; *Écon* **p. intérieur brut** gross domestic product; **produits intermédiaires** semi-finished products; **p. de luxe** luxury product; **p. manufacturé** manufactured product; **p. de marque** branded *or* brand-name product; **produits de marque** designer goods; *Mktg* **p. à marque de distributeur** own-brand product; **produits ménagers** *(household)* cleaning products; *Écon* **p. national brut** gross national product; *Compta* **p. net** net proceeds, net income; *Compta* **p. net partiel** accrued income; **p. novateur** innovative product; **produits de première nécessité** emergency convenience goods, staple convenience goods; **produits périssables** non-durable goods; **produits 'prêts-à-consommer'** convenience goods; *Compta* **produits à recevoir** accrued income, accruals; *Mktg* **p. sans marque** unbranded product, no-name product; *Mktg* **p. sans nom** no-name product; **produits de second choix** seconds, rejects; **produits semi-finis** semi-finished goods; **produits spécialisés** speciality goods; *Mktg* **p. substituable** substitutable product; **p. de substitution** substitute product; *Chimie* **p. de synthèse** product of synthesis, synthesized product; *Mktg* **p. tactique** me-too product; *Mktg* **p. vert** green product

proéminence [prɔeminɑ̃s] NF *(état)* prominence; *(ce qui fait saillie)* protuberance

proéminent [prɔeminɑ̃] ADJ prominent; *(pierre)* projecting; *(nez)* prominent, protuberant; *(grosseur)* protuberant

prof [prɔf] N *Fam* (school)teacher; *(maître de conférences)* prof; *(maître assistant)* lecturer

profanateur, -trice [prɔfanatœr, -tris] *Litt* ADJ profanatory

N profaner

profanation [prɔfanasjɔ̃] NF *(d'une tombe)* desecration, violation, *Fml* profanation

profane [prɔfan] ADJ profane; *(musique etc)* secular; *(cimetière)* unhallowed; *Fig* **elle est p. (en la matière)** she doesn't know much about it

N *Fig* layman; **aux yeux du p.** to the layman *or* the uninitiated, to the untrained eye; **je n'ai jamais fait de ski, je suis un p.** I've never skied, I'm a complete beginner

profaner [prɔfane] VT *(église)* to desecrate, *Fml* to profane; *(tombe)* to desecrate, to violate, *Fml* to profane; *(innocence)* to defile

profeciat [prɔfesjat] INT *Belg* congratulations!; **souhaiter à qn** to congratulate sb

proférer [prɔfere] VT *(je profère; je proférerai)* to utter; **sans p. une (seule) parole** without (so much as) a word

profès, -esse [prɔfɛ, -ɛs] *Rel* ADJ professed

N professed monk, *f* professed nun

professer [prɔfese] VT **1** *(religion, opinion)* to profess; *(point de vue)* to hold **2** *(enseigner)* to teach; **il professe la physique au lycée** he teaches physics at the lycée

VI *(être titulaire d'une chaire)* to be a professor; *(comme maître assistant)* to be a lecturer; *(dans une école)* to be a teacher; **il professe à la Sorbonne** he's a professor/lecturer at the Sorbonne, he teaches at the Sorbonne

professeur [prɔfesœr] NM (school)teacher, *Br Vieilli* master, *f* mistress; *(à l'université)* professor; *(maître assistant)* lecturer; **p. des écoles** primary schoolteacher; **elle est p. de piano** she's a piano teacher, she teaches (the) piano; **p. de terminale** *Br* ≃ sixth-form teacher, *Am* ≃ twelfth-grade teacher; **c'est un bon/mauvais p.** he's a good/bad teacher; **p. de chant** singing teacher; **p. principal** class *or* form teacher, *Am* homeroom teacher; *Br (dans une école privée)* form master, *f* form mistress

profession [prɔfesjɔ̃] NF **1** *(métier)* profession, occupation; *(pour artisans)* trade; **médecin de (sa) p.** doctor by profession; **menuisier de p.** carpenter by trade; *Fig Fam* **rouspéteur de p.** professional grumbler, full-time grumbler; **sans p.** unemployed; **je suis sans p.** I don't work, I don't have a job **SEE GRAMMAR B5 2 faire p. de qch** to profess sth

▸▸ **p. de foi** profession of faith; **p. libérale** (liberal) profession; **avoir une p. libérale** to be a professional person; **j'ai décidé d'avoir une p. libérale** I decided to take up a profession

professionnalisation [prɔfesjɔnalizasjɔ̃] NF professionalization; *(d'un sportif)* turning professional

professionnaliser (se) [səprɔfesjɔnalize] VPR *(d'un sportif)* to turn professional; *(d'un sport)* to become professional *or* a professional sport

professionnalisme [prɔfesjɔnalism] NM professionalism

professionnel, -elle [prɔfesjɔnɛl] ADJ **1** *(personne, attitude)* professional; *(enseignement)* vocational; **avoir des difficultés professionnelles** to have professional problems *or* problems at work; **maladies professionnelles** occupational diseases; **syndicat p.** trade association; **faire preuve de conscience professionnelle** to be conscientious (in one's work); **cela n'est pas très p.** it's not very professional **2** *(footballeur)* professional

N **1** *Sport* professional; **passer p.** to turn professional **2** *Ind etc* skilled worker; **le travail d'un p.** a professional job

professionnellement [prɔfesjɔnɛlmɑ̃] ADV professionally

professoral, -ale, -aux, -ales [prɔfesɔral, -o] ADJ *aussi Fig* professorial

professorat [prɔfesɔra] NM teaching profession *(esp in higher education)*; **choisir le p.** to choose teaching as a *or* one's profession

profil [prɔfil] NM **1** *(d'une personne)* profile; **dessiner qn de p.** to draw sb in profile; **se placer** *ou* **se mettre de p.** to turn one's face *(so it is in profile)*; **vue de p.** side view; *Fig* **adopter un p. bas** to adopt a low profile; **garder le p. bas** to keep a low profile, to keep one's head down; **le p. de l'employé idéal** the profile of the ideal employee; **p. de poste** job description; **elle a tout à fait le p. de l'emploi** she fits the job description exactly, she's exactly the type of person that's needed (for the job); **elle a le p. de celle que nous recherchons** she's exactly what we're looking for **2** *(d'un objet)* profile, contour, outline; *(dessin)* section; **p. en travers** cross section; **p. de l'hori-**

zon skyline; *Géol* le p. d'une rivière the profile of a river

▶▶ *Mktg* **p. des consommateurs** consumer profile; **p. grec** Greek profile; *Mktg* **p. du marché** market profile; **p. médical** medical history; *Banque* **p. patrimonial** personnel assets profile; **p. psychologique** psychological profile

profilage [prɔfilaʒ] NM **1** *Beaux-Arts* profiling; *Tech (de la carrosserie d'une voiture etc)* shaping, streamlining **2** *(en psychologie)* profiling

profilé [prɔfile] *Tech* ADJ *(métal etc)* shaped; *(voiture etc)* streamlined; **fers profilés** sectional irons, iron sections

NM section; **profilés en acier** steel sections, sectional steel; *Aut* **p. creux** box frame section; *Aut* **p. creux de châssis** channel frame section; *Aut* **p. en T** T section

profiler [prɔfile] VT *Tech* **1** *(représenter de profil)* to draw in section **2** *(morceau de métal)* to shape; *(voiture etc)* to streamline

VPR **se profiler** to stand out in profile, to be outlined, to be silhouetted (**à, sur, contre** against); **des nuages se profilent à l'horizon** clouds are looming on the horizon; *Fig* **les difficultés qui se profilent pour les années à venir** the difficulties building up for the future; *Fig* **tout se profile plutôt bien** everything is shaping up pretty well, things look pretty good

profileur [prɔfilœr] NM *(psychologue)* profiler

profit [prɔfi] NM **1** *(avantage)* profit, benefit; **faire (son) p. de qch** to profit by *or* from sth; **mettre qch à p.** to put sth to good use, *Fml* to turn sth to (good) account; **tirer p. de qch** to take advantage of sth, to derive benefit from sth; **tirer p. d'une situation** to take advantage of *or* make the most of a situation; **elle a su tirer p. de son stage** she made the most of her training period; **tirer le p. maximum de qch** to derive maximum benefit from sth; *Fam* **sa vieille auto m'aura fait du p.** his old car has served me well, I've got a lot of use out of his old car; **j'en ai eu peu de p.** I gained little advantage from it; **il doit y trouver son p.** he must be getting something out of it; **elle ne cherche que son p.** she's only interested in personal gain; **au p. de qn** on behalf of sb, for the benefit of sb; **au p. des pauvres** in aid of the poor; **concert donné au p. des orphelins** benefit concert for orphans; **elle l'a laissé tomber au p. de son frère** she dropped him for his brother; **les socialistes perdront au p. des communistes** votes will swing from the Socialists to the Communists, the Communists will pick up votes from the Socialists **2** *Écon* **un p.** a profit; **profits et pertes** profit and loss; **vendre à p.** to sell at a profit; **p. fait sur une vente** profit on a sale; **p. de 12%** 12% profit; **p. espéré** anticipated profit; **p. réel** real profit; **il n'y a pas de petits profits** every little helps

profitabilité [prɔfitabilite] NF profitability

profitable [prɔfitabl] ADJ profitable; *(situation)* advantageous; *(expérience, exercice)* beneficial

profitablement [prɔfitabləmā] ADV profitably

profiter [prɔfite] VI **1 p. de qch** to take advantage of sth, to (derive) benefit from sth, *Fml* to turn sth to (good) account; **il est de bonne humeur aujourd'hui, il faut en p.** he's in a good mood today, we'd better make the most of it; **p. de l'occasion** to make the most of *or* seize the opportunity; **je profite d'un moment de calme pour vous dire que …** I'm using these few moments of peace and quiet to tell you that …; **p. de la vie** to make the most of life, to enjoy life (to the full); **p. de sa jeunesse** to make the most of one's

youth; **elle n'a pas pu p. de ce moment de vacances** she was not able to benefit from the break; **nous sommes un peu en avance, j'en profite pour …** let me take advantage of the few moments we have in hand to …; **il a profité de ce que tout le monde dormait encore pour s'esquiver** he took advantage of the fact that everyone was still asleep to slip away; **il a profité de mon offre** he took me up on my offer; **elle a profité de ses petits-enfants pendant les vacances** she made the most of her grandchildren during the holidays

2 *Écon* **p. sur une vente** to make a profit on a sale

3 p. à qn to be to sb's advantage, to be of benefit to sb, to benefit sb; **ses idées révolutionnaires ne lui ont pas profité** his revolutionary ideas didn't do him any good (in the end); *Prov* **bien mal acquis ne profite jamais** ill-gotten goods never prosper; *Fam* **ces chaussures m'ont bien profité** these shoes have lasted me a long time, I've got a lot of use out of these shoes

4 *Fam (un enfant, d'une plante etc)* to thrive

profiterole [prɔfitrɔl] NF *Culin* profiterole

profiteur, -euse [prɔfitœr, -øz] N *Péj* profiteer; **les profiteurs de guerre** war profiteers

profond [prɔfɔ̃] ADJ **1** *(lac, bassin, trou, voix)* deep; **puits p. de six mètres** well six metres deep; **ces étagères ne sont pas profondes** these shelves are not very deep; **un décolleté p.** a plunging neckline; **une forêt profonde** a dense *or* thick forest; **révérence profonde, p. salut** low *or* deep bow; **peu p.** shallow

2 *(haine)* profound, deep-seated, deep-rooted; *(préjugé)* deep-seated, deep-rooted; *(cause)* underlying, deep-rooted; **des marques profondes, ineffaçables** deep, indelible scars; **cette expérience a laissé en elle des marques profondes** the experience marked her for life

3 *Fig (sagesse, érudition etc)* profound; *(connaissance, discussion)* thorough, in-depth; *(sommeil)* deep, sound; *(paroles)* profound, meaningful; *(personne)* profound, deep; **un bleu p.** a deep blue; **un silence p.** a profound *or* heavy silence; **un p. soupir** a deep *or* heavy sigh; **p. dégoût** profound *or* deep disgust; **un homme p.** a man who thinks deeply, a deep thinker; **elle leur reproche de ne pas être assez profonds** she reproaches them for their shallowness *or* with being shallow; **un esprit p.** a mind of great depth; **plongés dans de profondes discussions** deep in discussion; **ses intentions profondes étaient honorables** deep down his intentions were honourable; **je ne connais pas ses intentions profondes** I don't know what his/her intentions are deep down

ADV *(plonger, creuser etc)* deep; **ça descend p. sous la cave** it goes a long way down under the cellar

NM **au plus p. de mon cœur** in my heart of hearts, deep down; **au plus p. de la nuit** at dead of night, in the middle of the night

profondément [prɔfɔ̃demā] ADV *(choqué, vexé, déçu, touché)* deeply, profoundly; *(aimer qn)* deeply; **dormir p.** to sleep soundly; **p. endormi** sound *or* fast asleep; **s'incliner p.** to make a deep *or* low bow; **j'en suis p. convaincu** I am quite convinced of it; **se comprendre p.** to have a profound *or* deep understanding of each other; **je ne te demande pas d'aimer p. ma famille mais … I** don't expect you to like my family, but …

profondeur [prɔfɔ̃dœr] NF **1** *(de l'eau, d'un trou dans le sol etc)* depth; *(d'une voix)* deepness; **avoir dix mètres de p.** to be ten metres deep, to be ten metres in depth; **creuser en p.** to dig deep, to go down a long way; **les plongeurs ont effectué des répara-**

tions en p. the divers carried out repairs far beneath the surface; *Fig* **travailler en p.** to be working in depth; **travail en p.** in-depth work; **des changements en p.** in-depth *or* profound changes; **rien n'a changé en p.** deep down nothing has changed, the changes have all been superficial; **peu de p.** shallowness; **de peu de p.** *(trou), Fig (échanges)* shallow **2** *(de sentiment)* depth; *(d'esprit, d'un poème, d'une œuvre d'art)* profoundness, profundity; **un film sans p.** a film with no depth, a shallow *or* superficial film **3 profondeurs** *(de l'esprit)* depths, recesses; **la psychologie des profondeurs** psychoanalysis

▶▶ *Mktg* **p. de l'assortiment de produits** product-mix depth; *Phot* **p. de champ** depth of field; *Phot* **p. de foyer** depth of focus; *Mktg* **p. de gamme** depth of product mix; *Mktg* **p. de produit** product depth

pro forma [prɔfɔrma] ADJ INV **facture p.** pro forma invoice

profus [prɔfy] ADJ *Litt* profuse

profusément [prɔfyzemā] ADV *Litt* profusely

profusion [prɔfyzjɔ̃] NF profusion, abundance; **une p. de** a profusion *or* an abundance of; **avec une p. d'exemples** with abundant examples; **à p.** in profusion; **des bouteilles à p.** an abundance of bottles, bottles galore; **donner de l'argent à p.** to give a great deal of money

progéniture [prɔʒenityr] NF progeny, offspring; *Fam Hum* **il nous a présenté sa p.** he introduced his offspring to us

progestatif, -ive [prɔʒestatif, -iv] *Biol, Chimie* ADJ **corps p.** corpus luteum

NM progestin, progestogen

progestérone [prɔʒesterɔn] NF *Biol, Chimie* progesterone

progiciel [prɔʒisjel] NM *Ordinat* software package; **p. de communication** comms package; **p. intégré** integrated package

prognathe [prɔgnat] ADJ *(visage)* undershot, underhung, *Spéc* prognathous

programmable [prɔgramabl] ADJ *Électron* programmable

programmateur, -trice [prɔgramatœr, -tris] N *Radio, TV* programme planner, scheduler, programmer

NM *Tech* automatic control (device); *Ordinat* scheduler, programmer

programmation [prɔgramasjɔ̃] NF **1** *TV etc* programme planning, scheduling, programming; **un changement de p.** a change to the advertised *or* scheduled programme **2** *Ordinat* programming; **langage de p.** programming language; **p. orientée objet, p. par objets** object-oriented programming

programme [prɔgram] NM **1** *TV, Radio etc* programme, *Am* program; *(brochure)* *TV* TV guide, listings magazine; *Cin* programme, *Am* program; **hors p.** unscheduled; **un changement des programmes** a change to the advertised *or* scheduled programme; *Fig Fam* **changement de p., on ne part plus** there's been a change of plan, we're not going away after all; **quel est ton p. pour les vacances?** what have you got planned *or* arranged for the holidays?; **on n'a pas de p., on verra au jour le jour** we haven't any definite plans *or* anything definite planned, we'll play it by ear; **qu'est-ce que nous avons comme p. aujourd'hui?** what's on the agenda for today?; **nous n'avons rien au p. aujourd'hui** we haven't anything planned for today, *Fam* we haven't anything on today; **avoir un p. chargé** to have a busy schedule, *Fam* to have a lot on; **p. d'actualités** current affairs programme; **p. à la demande** programme-on-demand; **p. familial** family programme; **p.**

minimum skeleton programme; *TV, Radio* **p. phare** top-rating programme, banker; **p. radiodiffusé** radio programme; **p. radiophonique** radio programme; *TV, Radio* **p. de stock** programme with re-run potential; **p. télé**TV programme

2 *Scol* **p. (d'études)** curriculum; *(d'un cours)* syllabus; **être** *ou* **figurer au p.** to be on the syllabus; **ne pas sortir du p.** not to depart from the syllabus; **les auteurs au** *ou* **du p.** the set books; **des auteurs hors p.** books that are not on the syllabus; **une question hors p.** a question not covered by the syllabus VOIR GRAMMAIRE A13

3 *(d'un parti politique, d'une entreprise commerciale)* programme, *Am* program, platform; **p. de réformes sociales** programme of social reform; **p. électoral** (election) platform; *Fig* **c'est tout un p.** it's quite a job *or* a business *or* an undertaking; **P. alimentaire mondial** World Food Programme; *Mktg* **p. d'amélioration de la qualité** quality improvement programme, QIP; **p. de fidélisation** frequent user programme; **p. de formation** training programme; *Mktg* **p. marketing** marketing programme; *Mktg* **p. marketing de fidélisation** frequency marketing programme, FMP; *Mktg* **p. de stimulation** incentive scheme; *Mktg* **p. de vente pyramidale** pyramid selling scheme; **p. de voyage de stimulation** incentive travel programme

4 *Ordinat* program; **p. d'amorçage** boot program; **p. antivirus** antivirus program; **p. d'arrière-plan** background program; **p. assembleur** assembler program; **p. d'autotest** self-test program; **p. de césure** hyphenation program; **p. de commande** driver; **p. de commande d'impression** printer driver; **p. de commande de la souris** mouse driver; **p. de configuration** configuration program; **p. de conversion** conversion program; **p. de courrier électronique** e-mail program; **p. en cours d'exécution** active program; **p. de création de pages Web** web authoring program; **p. de dessin** drawing program, paint program; **p. détecteur de virus** virus detection program; **p. de diagnostic** malfunction routine; **p. éditeur de liens** link program, linker; **p. d'évaluation (de performance)** benchmark program; **p. de formatage** formatter; **p. de gestion** driver; **p. d'initialisation** initialization program; **p. d'installation** setup program, installer; **p. maître** master program; **p. objet** object program; **p. pilote** driver; **p. prioritaire** foreground program; **p. de publipostage** mailmerge program; **p. en recouvrement** overlay program; **p. résident** resident program; **p. de routage** router; **p. sentinelle** watchdog program; **p. source** source program; **p. système** system program; **p. de test** test program; **p. traducteur** interpreter; **p. de traitement par lots** batch program; **p. utilitaire** utility program; **p. virus** virus program

programmer [prɔgrame] **VT 1** *Ordinat* to program; **p. en assembleur** to program in assembly language **2** *TV, Radio (émission)* to schedule **3** *(organiser, mettre au point) (vacances, changements)* to plan, to schedule **VI 1** *TV, Radio* to schedule, to draw up a schedule **2** *Ordinat* to program

programmeur, -euse [prɔgramœr, -øz] **N** *Ordinat* programmer; **analyste-p.** systems analyst

progrès [prɔgrɛ] **NM 1** *(avance)* progress; *(d'une armée)* progress, advance; *(d'une épidémie)* progress, spread; *(d'un incendie, d'une inondation)* spread **2** *(d'un élève, d'un malade)* progress, improvement; *(d'une enquête)* progress; **faire des p.** *(d'un élève, d'un malade)* to make progress, to improve; *(dans une enquête)* to make progress *or* headway; *Scol* **il n'a pas**

fait beaucoup de p. he hasn't made much progress *or* hasn't improved much; **le malade fait des p. satisfaisants** the patient is making satisfactory progress *or* is progressing satisfactorily; **on guette les moindres p. du malade** the patient is being watched for the slightest signs of progress *or* improvement; **suivre les p. d'un malade/d'un élève** to follow *or* monitor a patient's/pupil's progress; **la science a fait de grands p.** science has made great progress *or* great strides (forward); **suivre les p. d'une science** to keep abreast of a science; **suivre les p. d'une affaire** *Jur* to monitor *or* keep track of a case; *Com* to monitor *or* keep track of a transaction; **être en p.** to be making progress; **il y a un net p. par rapport à l'an dernier** it's a distinct improvement over last year; **un p. sensible vers la démocratie** a significant step *or* advance towards democracy; *Fam* **il y a du p.** there's been an improvement

3 le p. progress; **croire au p.** to believe in progress; **c'est ça, le p.!** that's progress for you!; *Pol* **un parti de p.** a party of progress, a progressive party; **le parti du p.** the party of progress

progresser [prɔgrese] **VI 1** *(avancer) (d'une armée)* to advance, to progress; *(d'un marcheur)* to make progress; **p. lentement/rapidement** to make slow/rapid progress **2** *(évoluer) (d'une épidémie, d'un incendie)* to spread, to gain ground; **son cancer progresse** his cancer is spreading **3** *(faire des progrès) (d'un élève, d'un malade)* to make progress, to make headway, to improve; *(d'un projet)* to progress, to make progress; *(d'une enquête, d'un policier)* to make progress *or* headway; **p. lentement/rapidement** *(dans une étude/des recherches)* to make slow/rapid progress; **p. lentement/rapidement dans la lecture d'un livre** to make slow/rapid progress with a book, to get through a book slowly/quickly

progressif, -ive [prɔgresif, -iv] **ADJ** progressive; *(amélioration, expansion)* gradual; *(taux)* graduated, increasing; *Ling* **la forme progressive en anglais** the progressive *or* continuous form in English; **impôt p.** progressive *or* graduated tax VOIR GRAMMAIRE A49–52

progression [prɔgresjɔ̃] **NF 1** *(avance) (d'une armée)* advance, progress; **la p. des marcheurs** the walkers' progress **2** *(évolution) (d'un incendie, d'une maladie, d'un cancer, d'une épidémie, du sida)* spread; *(de la délinquance, du chômage)* rise; *(d'un secteur économique)* expansion; *Bourse (des actions)* rise, improvement; *(dans une carrière)* progress, advancement; *(dans la société)* advancement; *(amélioration)* upturn; **être en p.** *(d'un secteur économique)* to be growing *or* expanding; *(d'une maladie)* to be spreading; *(du chômage, de la criminalité)* to be increasing *or* rising, to be on the increase *or* rise

▸▸ *Math* **p. arithmétique** arithmetical progression; *Mus* **p. harmonique** harmonic progression

progressiste [prɔgresist] **ADJ, N** *Pol* progressive

progressivement [prɔgresivmɑ̃] **ADV** progressively

progressivité [prɔgresivite] **NF** progressiveness; *(d'impôt)* graduation

prohiber [prɔibe] **VT** to prohibit, to forbid; **l'alcool est prohibé là-bas** alcohol is prohibited *or* forbidden there; **marchandises prohibées** illegal goods; **le port d'armes est prohibé** it is illegal to carry weapons, people are forbidden to carry weapons

prohibitif, -ive [prɔibitif, -iv] **ADJ 1** *(prix)* prohibitive **2** *(loi etc)* prohibitory

prohibition [prɔibisjɔ̃] **NF** prohibition; **la p.**

du port d'armes the ban on carrying weapons; *Hist* **pendant la p.** during Prohibition; **p. d'importation** import ban

prohibitionnisme [prɔibisjɔnism] **NM** *Écon etc* prohibitionism

prohibitionniste [prɔibisjɔnist] **ADJ, N** *Écon etc* prohibitionist

proie [prwa] **NF** prey; *(à la chasse)* quarry; **oiseau de p.** bird of prey; **faire sa p. de qch** *(d'un animal)* to prey on sth; *Fig* **une p. facile/des proies faciles** easy prey *or* meat; **être la p. de qn** to be the prey *or* victim of sb; **une partie de la population est la p. de cette maladie** part of the population has fallen victim *or* prey to the disease; **les enfants sont la p. de la publicité** children are the victims of advertising; **la maison fut vite la p. des flammes** the house was soon devoured *or* consumed by the flames; **être en p. aux remords/au doute** to be racked *or* tormented by remorse/doubt, *Litt* to be prey to remorse/doubt; **une personne en p. à des obsessions/des hallucinations** a person prey to obsessions/hallucinations; **tomber en p. à la tentation** to fall prey to temptation

projecteur [prɔʒektœr] **NM 1** *Cin, Phot* projector; **p. de diapositives** slide projector; *TV, Cin* **p. de décors** scenic projector; **p. de films** film projector; **p. de télévision** telejector; **p. à arc** brute, arc light; **p. à faisceau concentré** spotlight **2** *(lampe)* searchlight; *(sur un bâtiment, sur un monument)* floodlight; *Théâtre* spotlight; *Aut* headlamp, headlight; **illuminé par des projecteurs** floodlit; *Fig* **sous les projecteurs de l'actualité** in the limelight *or* news; *Aut* **p. antibrouillard** fog lamp; **p. halogène** halogen headlight; **p. polyéllipsoïde** poly-ellipsoid headlight; **p. de poursuite** follow spot

projectif, -ive [prɔʒektif, -iv] **ADJ** *Géom, Psy* projective

projectile [prɔʒektil] **NM** projectile; *(autoguidé)* missile

projection [prɔʒeksjɔ̃] **NF 1** *(fait de projeter)* projection; *(d'un liquide)* splashing; *(de boue)* splashing, splattering; *(de graisse)* spattering; **des projections de boue** splashes *or* splatters of mud; *Géol* **projections volcaniques** volcanic ash, *Spéc* (volcanic) ejecta; *Aut* **p. de gravillons** loose chippings **2** *Cin, Phot* projection; *Cin (d'un film)* screening, showing; **une p. de diapositives** a slide show; *Cin* **la p. durera 45 minutes** it will take 45 minutes to show the film, the screening will last 45 minutes; **nous avons vu le film en p. privée** we were given a private screening *or* showing (of the film); **appareil de p.** projector; **cabine de p.** projection booth; **p. par transparence** rear projection; **conférence avec projections** lecture (illustrated) with slides **3** *(de lumière)* beam **4** *Math, Archit etc* projection, plan; **p. horizontale** ground plan **5** *(image)* (outward) manifestation; *Psy* projection (**dans** onto); **cette expression est la p. de sa pensée** that expression reveals what he is thinking; *Psy* **faire une p. sur qn** to project oneself onto sb **6** *(prévision)* projection; **p. des ventes** sales projection

projectionniste [prɔʒeksjɔnist] **N** *Cin* projectionist

projet [prɔʒɛ] **NM 1** *(plan)* plan, project, scheme; *(travaux)*, *Scol, Univ* project; **quels sont vos projets pour cet été?** what are your plans for the summer?; **avoir d'autres projets** to have other plans; **faire des projets** to make plans; **faire des projets d'avenir** to plan *or* make plans for the future; **faire** *ou* **former le p. de faire qch** to plan to do sth; **nous avons fait le p. de partir en Norvège l'an prochain** we're planning on *or* thinking about going to Norway next year; **p. d'entre-**

prise business plan; **p. d'OPA sur ...** planned takeover of ...; **p. de budget** draft budget; *Jur* **p. de contrat** draft agreement; *Jur* **p. de convention** draft treaty; *Jur* **p. de loi** bill; **mettre un p. de loi au vote** to vote on a bill; **adopter/repousser un p. de loi** to pass/reject a bill; **à l'état de p.**, **en p.** at the planning stage; **ça n'est resté qu'à l'état de p.** it never got off the ground **2** *(d'un bâtiment)* plan; *(d'une machine)* blueprint

projeter [prɔʒte] *(conj like* **jeter***)* VT **1** *(lancer)* to project; *(graisse)* to spatter; *(liquide)* to splash; *(boue)* to splatter, to splash; *(d'un volcan) (cendres)* to eject, to spew out; **le train projette des gravillons en passant** the train throws up loose stones as it passes; **la poêle chaude projette de la graisse** grease is spattering from the hot frying pan; **être projeté au sol/contre la vitre** to be thrown *or* flung *or* hurled to the ground/against the windscreen **2** *(ombre)* to cast, to throw **3** *Cin (film)* to show, to screen **4** *(voyage, expédition etc)* to plan, to think about; **p. de faire qch** to plan to do sth, to plan on doing sth **5** *Psy* to project (**sur** onto) **6** *Math* to project
▸ **se projeter** VPR **une ombre s'est projetée sur le mur** a shadow fell *or* was cast on the wall; *Psy* **il se projette sur son fils** he's projecting himself onto his son

projeteur [prɔʒtœr] NM *Tech* planner; *(d'une machine etc)* designer

projo [prɔʒo] NM *Fam* projector

prolapsus [prɔlapsys] NM *Méd* prolapse

prolétaire [prɔleter] ADJ, N proletarian

prolétariat [prɔletarja] NM proletariat VOIR GRAMMAIRE A11

prolétarien, -ienne [prɔleterjɛ̃, -jɛn] ADJ proletarian

prolétarisation [prɔletarizasjɔ̃] NF proletarianization

prolétariser [prɔletarize] VT to proletarianize

prolifération [prɔliferasjɔ̃] NF proliferation; **p. des armes** arms proliferation

prolifère [prɔlifer] ADJ *Biol* proliferous

proliférer [prɔlifere] VI (**il prolifère; il proliférera**) to proliferate; **les affichages illégaux prolifèrent** flyposting is on the increase

prolifique [prɔlifik] ADJ prolific

prolixe [prɔliks] ADJ wordy, verbose, *Fml* prolix

prolixement [prɔliksəmɑ̃] ADV at great length

prolixité [prɔliksite] NF verbosity, *Fml* prolixity

prolo [prɔlo] *Péj Fam* ADJ *(accent, goûts)* plebby, working-class
N pleb, prole, oik

prologue [prɔlɔg] NM prologue (**de** to)

prolongation [prɔlɔ̃gasjɔ̃] NF *(de discussions)* prolongation, protraction; *(de congé, séjour)* extension, prolongation; *Ftbl* **jouer les prolongations** to play extra time *or Am* overtime

> Do not confuse with **prolongement**, which conveys the idea of physical extension.

prolonge [prɔlɔ̃ʒ] NF *Mil* ammunition wagon; **p. d'artillerie** gun carriage *(at military funeral)*

prolongé [prɔlɔ̃ʒe] ADJ *(absence, séjour)* prolonged, lengthy; **visite très prolongée** very lengthy visit; **soupir p.** long-drawn-out sigh; **applaudissements prolongés** prolonged *or* sustained applause; **éviter tout séjour p. au soleil** do not stay in the sun too long, avoid prolonged exposure to the sun; **rue Crinas prolongée** = continuation of rue Crinas

prolongement [prɔlɔ̃ʒmɑ̃] NM **1** *(d'une rue etc)* prolongation, continuation; *(d'un mur, d'une voie de chemin de fer)* extension; **je veux installer le Frigidaire® dans le p. de l'évier** I want the fridge in line with the sink; *Fig* **ce départ était dans le p. de sa toute première décision** the departure was in line with *or* consistent with his original decision **2 prolongements** *(d'une action etc)* ramifications (**de** of)

> Do not confuse with **prolongation**, which only has to do with duration.

prolonger [prɔlɔ̃ʒe] (**je prolongeai(s); n. prolongeons**) VT *(la vie)* to prolong; *(séjour, absence)* to prolong, to extend; *(débat, discours, repas)* to prolong, to draw *or* spin out; *(mur, route, voie ferrée etc)* to extend (**jusqu'à** to, as far as); *Rail* **un billet** to extend a ticket; **des écuries prolongent les murs de la maison** stables are built on to the house; *Math* **p. une droite** to continue *or* produce a line
▸ VPR **se prolonger** *(d'une absence, une réunion)* to be prolonged; *(d'une rue etc)* to continue, to extend; *(d'une guerre, d'un film etc)* to go *or* carry on, to continue; **leur visite s'est prolongée jusqu'à minuit** they stayed until midnight; **la soirée ne s'est pas prolongée très tard** the party didn't go on till very late *or* finished quite early; **mais il ne faudrait pas que cela se prolonge** but it mustn't be for too long

promenade [prɔmnad] NF **1** *(balade)* walk; *(courte)* stroll; *(en voiture)* drive, outing, trip; **faire une p. (à pied)** to go for a walk; **faire une p. en voiture** to go for a drive *or* a run; **faire une p. à bicyclette** to go for a bike ride; **faire une p. à cheval** to go (horse)riding, to go for a ride; **p. en bateau** *(en canot)* row; *(en voilier)* sail; **être en p.** *(à pied)* to be out walking, to be out for a walk; *(à bicyclette)* to be out on a bike ride; *(à cheval)* to be out riding, to be out for a ride; **ils ne sont pas chez eux, ils sont en p.** they've gone out; **faire faire une p. à qn** to take sb (out) for a walk; **l'heure de la p.** *(d'un détenu)* exercise time; *Mil* **p. militaire** route march; *Mus* **concert p.** promenade concert, *Br* prom **2** *(avenue)* *(au bord de la mer)* promenade

promener [prɔmne] (**je promène; je promènerai**) VT **1** *(faire aller, conduire)* **p. qn** *(à pied)* to take sb (out) for a walk; *(en voiture)* to take sb (out) for a drive; **p. le chien** to take the dog for a walk, to walk the dog, to take the dog out; **p. son cheval** to exercise one's horse; **p. des amis à travers Paris** to show *or* take friends round Paris; *Fam* **cela vous promènera un peu** it'll get you out (of the house) a bit; **p. sa tristesse** to parade one's sadness; **je promenais toujours les mêmes idées sombres** I couldn't shake off my dark thoughts, the same dark thoughts were always with me; *Fig* **il m'a promené de musée en musée** he dragged me from museum to museum; *Fig Fam* **j'ai vraiment l'impression qu'il me promène** I really get the impression that he's having me on *or* taking me for a ride; **j'en ai assez qu'on me promène** I've had enough of being taken for a ride **2** *(faire aller) (sa main)* to run (**sur** over); **p. ses yeux sur** *(liste, texte)* to run one's eye(s) over, to scan; *(salle, foule)* to scan
▸ VPR **se promener 1** *(se balader)* to walk; *Ordinat* to browse; **je vais me p.** I'm going (out) for a walk *or* stroll; **se p. en Auvergne** to tour Auvergne; *Ordinat* **se p. dans** *(texte)* to scroll through; *(base de données)* to browse through; (**se** omitted) **mener p. les enfants** to take the children (out) for a walk; *Fam* **envoyer p. qn** to send sb packing, to send sb off with a flea in his/her ear; **va te p.!** get out!, *Fam* get lost!, *Am* take a hike!

2 *(des yeux, des pensées etc)* to wander; *Fig Fam* **cette vieille chaise s'est promenée dans toute la maison** that old chair has found its way into *or* has been in every room in the house; *Fam* **pourquoi ce dossier se promène-t-il sur ton bureau?** why is this file lying about on your desk?; *Fam* **il laisse se p. ses affaires partout** he leaves his things lying about *or* around all over the place

3 *Fam (éprouver de la facilité)* **il se promène en anglais** he finds English a pushover

promeneur, -euse [prɔmnœr, -øz] N *(dans un parc etc)* stroller, walker; *(randonneur)* walker, rambler

promenoir [prɔmnwar] NM promenade, (covered) walk; *(dans une cour de justice etc)* lobby; *Théâtre Vieilli* promenade

promesse [prɔmɛs] NF **1** *(serment)* promise; *Mktg* claim; **faire une p.** to make a promise; **je vais te faire une p.** I'm going to make you a promise; **tu pourrais me faire une p.?** will you promise me something?; **elle m'a fait la p. de ne plus en parler** she has promised me not to speak of it again; **elle m'avait fait de grandes promesses** she promised me great things; **tenir sa p.** to keep one's promise; **tu as ma p.** you have my word *or* promise; **manquer à sa p.** to break one's promise; *Com* **p. écrite** written promise, written undertaking; **p. de Gascon** empty *or* hollow promise; *Fig* **la p. d'un avenir meilleur** the promise of a better future; *Fig* **ces réunions sont la p. d'une paix future** these meetings held out the hope of peace; *Fig* **plein de promesses** full of promise, that shows a great deal of promise, very promising; **un avenir plein de promesses** a very promising *or* bright future; *Pol* **p. électorale** electoral promise; *Mktg* **p. mensongère** false claim **2** *Com etc* undertaking to pay; **p. d'achat/de vente** agreement *or* undertaking to purchase/undertaking *or* promise to sell

Prométhée [prɔmete] N Prometheus

prométhéen, -enne [prɔmeteɛ̃, -ɛn] ADJ *Litt* Promethean

prometteur, -euse [prɔmɛtœr, -øz] ADJ *(artiste, premier roman etc)* promising, full of promise; *(sourire)* full of promise; **des débuts prometteurs** a promising start; **c'est très p.!** it's very promising!

promettre [prɔmɛtr] *(conj like* **mettre***)* VT **1** to promise; **p. qch à qn** to promise sb sth, to promise sth to sb; **je ne peux rien te p.** I can't promise (you), I can't make any promises, I can't guarantee it; **tu (me) le promets?** (do you) promise?; **je (te) le promets!** I promise (you)!; **je te promets de lui en parler** I promise you that I'll talk to him/her about it, I promise to talk to him/her about it; **il m'a promis qu'il le ferait** he promised (me) he'd do it; **on promet une forte récompense** a handsome reward is being offered; **le médecin promet un prompt rétablissement** the doctor predicts a speedy recovery; **je te rembourserai, c'est promis** I'll pay you back, I promise; *Fam* **tu le regretteras, je te le promets!** you'll regret it, mark my words *or* take my word for it!; *Fam* **je m'en souviendrai du 1er mai, je te le promets!** you can take it from me *or* you can take my word for it that I won't forget the first of May!; *Fam* **je vous promets qu'on s'est amusé** we had a really great time **2** *(faire espérer)* **il promet d'éclipser tous ses rivaux** he looks set *or* he promises to eclipse all his rivals; **la soirée promet d'être amusante** it promises to be an amusing evening; **ça nous promet de gros orages** it looks as if we're in for some violent storms; **ce vent nous promet une mer agitée** we're in for rough seas judging from this wind; **la hausse des taux d'intérêt ne promet rien de bon pour l'industrie** the rise in interest rates does not look good *or Fml* does not augur well for industry

VI *(d'un projet etc)* to look promising; **un enfant qui promet** a child with promise; *Fam* **ça promet!** *(avant, au début d'une affaire)* that looks promising!; *Iron* great!, terrific!; *Iron* **eh bien, ça promet pour la fin de la semaine!** well then, it looks as if we're in for a great weekend!; *Iron* **vraiment, ça promet pour le reste de la soirée!** well now, the rest of the evening promises to be rather interesting!

VPR se promettre 1 *(mutuellement)* to promise (to) each other; **ils se sont promis de ne plus se disputer** they promised (each other) not to or that they wouldn't quarrel any more **2 se p. qch** to promise oneself sth **3** *(décider)* **se p. de travailler** to make up one's mind *or* to resolve to work; **je me suis promis de ne pas pleurer devant lui** I made up my mind *or* I promised myself that I wouldn't cry in front of him

promis, -ise [prɔmi, -iz] **ADJ** promised; **la Terre promise** the Promised Land; **p. à** destined for; **il est p. à un grand avenir** he is destined for a great future, he has a great future ahead of him

N *Vieilli, Région* fiancé, *f* fiancée, betrothed

promiscuité [prɔmiskɥite] **NF** overcrowding; **vivre dans la p.** to live in crowded accommodation; **je ne supportais plus la p. de cet appartement** I couldn't take the overcrowding in the flat any more; **je déteste la p. des transports en commun** I hate the crowding *or* the crowds on public transport; **je ne supporte pas la p.** I can't bear having people around me, I need lots of space; **la p. des plages en été** the overcrowding of beaches in summer

---

Il faut noter que le terme anglais **promiscuity** est un faux ami. Il désigne uniquement **un changement fréquent de partenaires sexuels.**

---

promo [prɔmo] **NF** *Fam* promo; **en p.** on special offer

promontoire [prɔmɔ̃twar] **NM** promontory, headland; *(plus grand)* cape

promoteur, -trice [prɔmɔtœr, -tris] **N 1** *Com* promoter; **p. (immobilier)** property developer **2** *(créateur)* originator (**de** of)

promotion [prɔmosjɔ̃] **NF 1** *(avancement)* promotion; *Rel* preferment; **p. à l'ancienneté** promotion by seniority; **p. interne** internal promotion, promotion from within the company; **p. sociale** upward mobility, *Fml* social advancement

2 *Univ* (students of the same) year, *Am* class; **camarade de p.** fellow student; **le premier de sa p.** the first in his year

3 *Com* promotion; **articles en p.** items on promotion *or Am* on special; **notre p. de la semaine** this week's special offer *or Am* special; **faire une p. sur un produit** to promote a product; **faire la p. de** to sell, to promote; **faire de la p. immobilière** to go in for property development; **contrat de p. immobilière** property development contract; **p. (en quatrième de couverture)** (back-cover) blurb; *Mktg* **p. auprès des intermédiaires** trade promotion order; *Mktg* **p. collective** tie-in promotion; *Mktg* **p. d'entreprises** corporate identity; *Mktg* **p. par une personnalité** personality promotion; *Mktg* **p. sur le lieu de vente** point-of-sale promotion; *Mktg* **p. sur point d'achat** point-of-purchase promotion; **p. spéciale** special promotion; **p. des ventes** sales promotion

NFPL *Suisse* **promotions** *(remise de diplômes)* = school prizegiving ceremony marking the move up to the next class

promotionnel, -elle [prɔmosjɔnɛl] **ADJ**

Com (brochure) promotional; *(tarif)* special; **vente promotionnelle** special offer

promouvoir [prɔmuvwar] **VT** *(conj like* **mouvoir***)* **1** *(donner un avancement à)* to promote; **être promu** to be promoted, to get promotion; **elle a été promue chef du personnel** she's been promoted *or* moved up to personnel manager **2** *Fig (favoriser)* *(recherche, création d'entreprise, relations entre États)* to promote, to further **3** *Com* to promote; *(à prix réduit)* to put on special offer *or Am* on special

prompt [prɔ̃] **ADJ** *(réaction, condamnation)* prompt, quick, swift; *(vengeance)* swift, speedy; **avoir la main prompte** to be quick with one's hands *or* to raise one's hand; **avoir la repartie prompte** to be always ready with an answer, *Fml* to have a ready wit; **nous vous souhaitons un p. rétablissement** we wish you a speedy recovery, get well soon; **esprit p.** quick mind; *(sens de l'humour)* ready wit; **être d'humeur prompte** to be quick-tempered; **il est p. à la colère** *ou* **à se fâcher** he loses his temper *or* flares up easily, *Fml* he is quick to anger; **p. à agir** quick *or* prompt to act; **p. à décider** decisive; **p. à la riposte** quick with a riposte

promptement [prɔ̃tmã, prɔ̃ptəmã] **ADV** *Litt* promptly, quickly, swiftly

prompteur [prɔ̃ptœr] **NM** teleprompt(er), Autocue®; **p. déroulant** roller prompter

promptitude [prɔ̃tityd] **NF** *Litt (d'une réaction etc)* promptness, quickness, swiftness; **avec toute la p. possible** with all possible dispatch

promu, -ue [prɔmy] **ADJ** (who has been) promoted

N person who has been promoted; *Univ* **les nouveaux promus** = this year's graduates *(of a grande école)*

promulgation [prɔmylgasjɔ̃] **NF** *(d'une loi)* promulgation; *(d'un décret)* publication

promulguer [prɔmylge] **VT** *(loi)* to promulgate; *(décret)* to publish, to issue

prône [pron] **NM** *Rel* sermon, homily

prôner [prone] **VT** *(patience, indulgence, tolérance)* to strongly recommend, to advocate, to urge; *(méthode)* to strongly recommend, to advocate

pronom [prɔnɔ̃] **NM** *Gram* pronoun; **p. défini/indéfini/interrogatif** definite/indefinite/interrogative pronoun `SEE GRAMMAR A27–38; B14–23`

pronominal, -ale, -aux, -ales [prɔnɔminal, -o] **ADJ** *Gram* pronominal

pronominalement [prɔnɔminalmã] **ADV** pronominally

prononçable [prɔnɔ̃sabl] **ADJ** pronounceable

prononcé [prɔnɔ̃se] **ADJ** *(traits)* strong; *(forme)* strong, definite; *(tendance)* marked; *(accent)* broad, strong, pronounced; **courbe prononcée** sharp curve; **avoir un goût p. pour qch** to have a strong *or* distinct taste for sth; **peu p.** *(accent)* faint, slight; *(forme)* indefinite, vague; *(relief)* flattish; **avoir un goût peu p. pour qch** to have little taste for sth

NM *Jur* decision; **p. du jugement** verdict

prononcer [prɔnɔ̃se] (**je prononçai(s); n. prononçons**) **VT 1** *(dire) (mot)* to say, to utter; **il a prononcé quelques paroles sur …** he said a few words about …; **c'est à peine s'il prononça quelques paroles** he hardly said a word; **sans p. un mot** without (uttering) a word; **il a prononcé quelques mots entre ses dents** he muttered a few words; **il ne faut jamais p. son nom** you must never mention him *or* his name

2 *(déclarer) (discours)* to deliver, to make; *Jur (arrêt)* to deliver; **p. une sentence** to pass *or* pronounce sentence; **p. un divorce** to

pronounce *or* declare a couple divorced; *Rel* **p. ses vœux** to take one's vows

3 *(articuler) (mot)* to pronounce; **mal p. un mot** to mispronounce a word

VI 1 *(articuler)* to pronounce (one's words); **apprendre à p.** to learn to pronounce one's words properly, to learn proper pronunciation; **p. bien/mal** to have good/bad pronunciation

2 *Jur (s'exprimer)* to give one's verdict (**sur qch** on sth); **p. en faveur de qn** to decide *or* declare in favour of sb; **p. sur une question** to adjudge *or* adjudicate a question

VPR se prononcer 1 *(être articulé)* to be pronounced; **ça s'écrit comme ça se prononce** it is written as it is pronounced; **comment se prononce …?** how do you pronounce …?; **le s ne se prononce pas** the s isn't pronounced, the s is silent

2 *(apparaître) (de différences)* to become more pronounced; *(de rides)* to become more marked

3 *(s'exprimer)* to give an opinion; *(d'un juge)* to give a decision; **le médecin ne s'est pas encore prononcé** the doctor has not yet given his prognosis; **j'ai mis longtemps avant de me p.** it took me a long time to make up my mind; **50 pour cent ne se prononcent pas** *(dans un sondage)* 50 per cent are undecided; **se p. pour** *ou* **en faveur de qn/qch** to express one's support for sb/sth; **ils se sont prononcés pour** *ou* **en faveur de/contre la construction du barrage** they said they were in favour of/against the dam being built; **se p. contre qn/qch** to express one's opposition to sb/sth

prononciation [prɔnɔ̃sjasjɔ̃] **NF 1** *(articulation)* pronunciation; **défaut de p.** speech defect; **faute de p.** mispronunciation, mistake in pronunciation; **elle a une très bonne/mauvaise p.** her pronunciation is very good/bad **2** *(d'un discours)* delivery; *Jur (d'une condamnation)* passing; *(d'un divorce)* pronouncement; *(d'un arrêt)* delivering

pronostic [prɔnɔstik] **NM 1** *(prévision)* forecast, prediction, prognosis; **quel est votre p. pour le match/la course?** what's your forecast for the match/race?, who do you tip to win the match/race? **2** *Méd* prognosis

pronostiquer [prɔnɔstike] **VT 1** *(prévoir)* to forecast, to predict; **je lui pronostique la première place** I predict that he'll come in first, I tip him for first place; **on pronostique qu'elle prendra la première place** she's being tipped for first place **2** *Méd* **p. un prompt rétablissement** to predict a speedy recovery

pronostiqueur, -euse [prɔnɔstikœr, -øz] **N** forecaster, pundit; *Sport* tipster

pronunciamiento [prɔnunsjamjɛnto] **NM** *Pol* pronunciamiento

propagande [prɔpagãd] **NF** *Péj* propaganda; *Pol* **faire de la p. pour qn** to electioneer on behalf of sb; **c'est de la p.!** it's propaganda!; **p. électorale** electioneering

propagandiste [prɔpagãdist] **ADJ, N** propagandist

propagateur, -trice [prɔpagatœr, -tris] **N** *(de nouvelles)* spreader; *(d'idées)* disseminator

propagation [prɔpagasjɔ̃] **NF** *(d'une plante, d'une espèce)* propagation; *(d'une épidémie, d'une rumeur, d'une nouvelle)* spreading; *(d'idées, d'une doctrine)* spreading, dissemination, *Fml* propagation; *Phys* **la vitesse de p. d'une onde** the velocity of propagation of a wave

propager [prɔpaʒe] (**je propageai(s); n. propageons**) **VT** *(plante, espèce)* to propagate; *(épidémie)* to spread; *(rumeur, nouvelle)* to spread, *Litt* to spread abroad; *(idées, doctrine)* to spread, *Fml* to propagate; **p. une mode** to spread *or* popularize a fashion

VPR se propager 1 *(d'une épidémie etc)* to spread **2** *Phys (de la lumière, du son)* to be propagated **3** *Biol (d'une plante etc)* to propagate, to reproduce

propane [prɔpan] NM *Chimie* propane

propanier [prɔpanje] NM *Naut* propane tanker

propédeutique [prɔpedøtik] NF **1** *(enseignement préparatoire)* propaedeutics **2** *Univ Anciennement* = first year of university course

propène [prɔpɛn] NM *Tech* propene

propension [prɔpɑ̃sjɔ̃] NF propensity, tendency, inclination (à to)

propergol [prɔpɛrgɔl] NM *Tech* (rocket) propellant

prophète, prophétesse [prɔfɛt, prɔfetɛs] N prophet, *f* prophetess, *Litt* seer; **parler en p.** to prophesy; **p. de malheur** prophet of doom, Jeremiah; **nul n'est p. en son pays** no man is a prophet in his own country

prophétie [prɔfesi] NF prophecy

prophétique [prɔfetik] ADJ prophetic

prophétiquement [prɔfetikmɑ̃] ADV prophetically

prophétiser [prɔfetize] VT to prophesy, to foretell

prophylactique [prɔfilaktik] ADJ *Méd* prophylactic

prophylaxie [prɔfilaksi] NF *Méd* prophylaxis

propice [prɔpis] ADJ propitious (à to); *(signe, commencement)* auspicious; *(conditions)* favourable, *Am* favorable; **attendre le moment p. pour faire qch** to wait for the right moment to do sth; **cet endroit est p. au repos** it's a restful spot; **un climat p. à la guérison des malades** a good climate for people who are ill; **ce festival est p. aux rencontres** the festival is a good place to meet people; **si la fortune nous est p.** if Fortune smiles on us; **peu p.** unpropitious; *(signe, commencement)* inauspicious; **c'est arrivé à un moment peu p.** it did not come at a very good time

propitiation [prɔpisjasjɔ̃] NF *Rel* propitiation

propitiatoire [prɔpisjatwar] ADJ *Rel* propitiatory

proportion [prɔpɔrsjɔ̃] NF **1** proportion; *Math* ratio; **il a bien respecté les proportions** he got the proportions right; **la p. du tronc et des jambes** the size of the trunk (as) compared with the legs; **varier en p. directe/inverse** to vary in direct proportion *or* ratio/in indirect proportion *or* inverse ratio (**de** to); **p. d'alcool dans un vin** percentage of alcohol in a wine, alcohol content of a wine; **les bénéfices ont augmenté dans une p. de 30 pour cent** profits have risen by 30 per cent; **à p., en p.** proportionally, proportionately, in proportion; **à p. de, en p. de** in proportion to; **payé en p. du travail fourni/des heures passées** paid in proportion to *or* according to the amount of work done/the number of hours; **tout augmente, et les salaires à p.** everything is going up, and salaries are keeping pace; **hors de (toute) p. avec** out of (all) proportion to; *Fig* **cette dispute est sans p. avec son objet** the argument is out of all proportion to the issue; **des travaux hors de p.** work of huge proportions; **toute(s) proportion(s) gardée(s)** up to a point, in certain respects SEE GRAMMAR B59

2 proportions size, proportions; **salle de vastes proportions** hall of vast proportions *or* dimensions; **dans de plus vastes proportions** on a much larger scale; **si les commandes diminuent dans de sérieuses proportions** if orders should decrease to any great

extent; **cette histoire a pris de sérieuses proportions** this business has assumed serious proportions; **pourquoi les choses ont-elles pris de telles proportions?** why have things escalated to such an extent?

proportionnalité [prɔpɔrsjɔnalite] NF **1** *Math* proportionality **2** *(rapport)* balance, (good) proportions **3** *(répartition)* equal distribution **4** *Écon* **p. de l'impôt** fixed rate system of taxation

proportionné [prɔpɔrsjɔne] ADJ **1 bien/mal p.** *(corps etc)* well/badly proportioned **2** proportionate, proportional (à to); *(de la même échelle, du même degré)* commensurate (à with); **la cotisation est proportionnée à vos revenus** payment is in proportion *or* proportional *or* proportionate to your income; **salaire p. aux qualifications** salary commensurate with qualifications

proportionnel, -elle [prɔpɔrsjɔnɛl] ADJ proportional (à to); *Pol* **représentation proportionnelle** proportional representation; *Ordinat* **espacement p.** proportional spacing; **inversement p.** inversely proportional, in inverse ratio (à to); **impôt p. (au revenu)** fixed-rate *or* fixed-percentage income tax

NF **proportionnelle 1** *Math* proportional **2** *Pol* proportional representation; **élu à la proportionnelle** elected by proportional representation

proportionnellement [prɔpɔrsjɔnɛlmɑ̃] ADV proportionally, proportionately, in proportion (à to)

proportionner [prɔpɔrsjɔne] VT to adapt, to adjust, to proportion (à to); **p. les dépenses aux ressources** to adjust expenditure to suit resources, *Fam Prov* to cut one's coat according to one's cloth

propos [prɔpo] NM **1** *(sujet)* subject, matter; **à ce p.** talking of which, while we're on the subject, in connection with that; **à p., avez-vous lu ce livre?** by the way *or* by the by *or* incidentally, have you read this book?; **à tout p.** constantly, at every turn; **dire qch à p.** to say sth to the point, to say sth suitable *or* appropriate; **elle n'est pas du tout intervenue à p.** what she had to say was entirely irrelevant; **vous avez réagi tout à fait à p.** you reacted quite appropriately; **jeté à p., fait à p.** *(mot, remarque)* timely; **faire qch à p.** to do sth at the right moment; **arriver fort à p.** to arrive at just the right moment *or* in the nick of time; **juger à p. de faire qch** to consider it advisable to do sth, to see fit to do sth; **mal à p.** at the wrong time *or* moment, *Fml* inopportunely; **tu ne pouvais pas tomber plus mal à p.** you couldn't have come at a worse time *or Fml* a more inopportune moment; **hors de p.** *(remarque)* irrelevant; **il est intervenu tout à fait hors de p.** what he had to say was entirely irrelevant; **à p. de** about, in connection with, with regard to, on the subject of; **à p. de rien** *(se disputer, se chamailler, s'agiter)* about nothing, for nothing at all, for no reason whatever; **à p. de tout et de rien** about anything and everything; **à p. de quoi?, à quel p.?** what about?; **à quel p. t'a-t-elle dit cela?** what did she say that to you for?; **c'est à quel p.?** what's it about?; **elle veut te voir – à quel p.?** she wants to see you – what about *or* what for?

2 *(intention)* purpose, intention, resolution; **avoir la ferme p. de faire qch** to firmly intend to do sth, to have the firm intention of doing sth; **de p. délibéré** deliberately, on purpose; **tel n'est pas mon p.** that is not my intention; **ce n'est pas le p.** that's not the point

3 *(parole)* **des p.** talk, words; **p. méchants/désagréables** nasty/unpleasant remarks; **les p. qu'ils échangèrent sont restés confidentiels** their talk *or* conversation has remained confidential; **des p. de table**

table talk; **changer de p.** to change the subject

proposer [prɔpoze] VT *(projet, solution, idée, plan d'action etc)* to propose, to suggest; *(théorie)* to propose, to suggest, *Fml* to propound; *(définition, interprétation, lecture d'un texte)* to suggest, to offer, to propose; *(appartement, somme d'argent, travail)* to offer; *Parl (amendement, décret, loi)* to table, to propose, to move, to put forward; **mais que propose-t-il d'autre?** but what else does he have to suggest?; **c'est tout ce que tu proposes comme idée?** is that all you have to offer by way of an idea?; **écoutez, voilà ce que je vous propose** listen, this is what I suggest; **'allons boire une bière', proposa-t-elle** 'let's go for a beer', she suggested; **ils (vous) proposent deux semaines aux Seychelles pour une misère** they're offering two weeks in the Seychelles for next to nothing; **le cinéma le César vous propose cette semaine …** this week at le César: …; **aujourd'hui le restaurant vous propose comme plat du jour …** today's special is …; **p. ses services à qn** to offer *or* volunteer one's services to sb; **je vous en propose 6000 euros/un bon prix** I'll give you 6,000 euros/a good price for it; **il m'a proposé un bon prix pour la voiture** he offered me a good price for the car; **p. un candidat** to put forward *or* put up *or* propose a candidate; **être proposé pour un emploi** to be suggested *or* proposed *or* recommended for a job; **son nom a été proposé plusieurs fois** his name has been suggested *or* put forward several times; **puis-je vous p. mon parapluie?** would you like *or* can I offer you my umbrella?; **p. que l'on fasse qch** to suggest *or* propose that sth should be done; **je propose que l'on passe d'abord au marché** I suggest going *or* that we go to the market first; **je propose que nous commencions par le problème du Brésil** *(en ouverture de discours)* I propose to start with the problem of Brazil; **je lui ai proposé de venir avec moi** I suggested (to him) that he should come with me; **je vous propose d'attendre jusqu'à ce que …** I suggest waiting *or* that you should wait until …; **elle m'a proposé de m'aider** she offered to help me

VI to propose; **je le laisse p.** I leave him to make the suggestions; **l'homme propose et Dieu dispose** man proposes and God disposes

VPR se proposer 1 *(se présenter)* to come forward, to offer one's services; **se p. comme secrétaire** to offer to act as secretary, to offer one's services *or* oneself as secretary; **se p. pour faire qch** to offer *or* volunteer to do sth **2 il s'est proposé cet objectif** he set himself this objective; **se p. de faire qch** to propose to do sth

> Il faut noter que le verbe anglais **to propose to somebody** signifie **demander quelqu'un en mariage**.

proposition [prɔpozisjɔ̃] NF **1** *(suggestion)* proposal, suggestion, proposition; *(d'emploi)* offer; **faire une p.** to make a suggestion *or* proposal; *(dans une assemblée)* to put *or* propose a motion; **si vous voulez acheter l'appartement, faites-moi une p.** if you want to buy the flat, make me an offer; **il a fait une p. pour l'appartement à 60 000 euros** he made an offer of *or* he offered 60,000 euros for the flat; **si quelqu'un a une p. à faire** if anyone has any suggestions; **je vais vous faire une p.: vous vous occupez de …** I've got a proposition for you: you deal with …; **de nombreux réalisateurs lui ont fait des propositions (de film)** lots of directors have offered him films, he's had lots of offers from directors; **faire des propositions à une femme** to proposition a woman; **mettre**

une **p. aux voix** to put a motion to the vote; **sur la p. de** at the suggestion of; **dernière p.** final offer; **p. de loi** *Br* ≃ private member's bill, *Am* ≃ private bill; **propositions de paix** peace proposals; **p. d'assurance** insurance proposal; *Mktg* **p. d'idées** ideation; **p. de paiement** payment proposal; **p. de prix** price proposal; **p. ferme** firm offer; **p. unique** unique proposition; *Mktg* **p. unique de vente** unique selling proposition, USP **2** *Phil, Math etc* proposition **3** *Gram* clause; **p. principale/subordonnée/relative** main/subordinate/relative clause; **p. circonstancielle de temps/lieu/but** adverbial clause of time/place/purpose SEE GRAMMAR A4; B2

PROPRE [prɔpr]

ADJ proper **1** ▪ characteristic **2** ▪ own **3** ▪ appropriate **4** ▪ clean **5** ▪ neat **5** ▪ tidy **5**
NM characteristic **1**

ADJ SEE GRAMMAR B10 **1** *(exact)* proper; **signification p. d'un mot** proper meaning of a word; **le mot est ici employé au sens p.** the word is used literally here; **un débile, au sens p. du mot** a mental defective in the true sense of the word; **chercher le mot p.** to try to find the right *or* appropriate word **2** *(particulier)* characteristic *(à of)*, *Fml* peculiar *(à to)*; **c'est une technique qui lui est p.** it's a technique that is characteristic of him; **une façon de marcher à lui p.** his own particular *or* characteristic way of walking **3** *(personnel)* own; **mon p. argent** my own money; **ses idées lui sont propres** his ideas are his own; **c'est par ta p. faute que …** it's your own fault if …; **de son p. chef** on one's own, *Fam* off one's own bat; **voir/entendre qch de ses propres yeux/oreilles** to see/hear sth with one's own eyes/ears; **je le lui ai remis en main(s) propre(s)** I delivered it to him/her personally; **à remettre en main p.** to be delivered to the addressee in person; **dans votre p. intérêt** in your own interest; **ce sont là ses propres paroles** those are his very words **4** *(convenable)* appropriate, suitable, proper, fitting; **p. à qch** adapted *or* fitted *or* suited to sth; **un lieu p. aux rencontres** a good place for meeting people; **l'endroit le plus p. au camping** the best *or* most suitable place for camping; **des conditions peu propres à la discussion** conditions that are not very conducive to a discussion; **exercice p. à aiguiser l'intelligence** exercise calculated to sharpen the wits; **p. à rien** good for nothing **5** *(impeccable)* *(linge, maison, hôtel)*, *Scol (copie)* clean; *(bureau, apparence)* neat; *(soigné, bien présenté)* *(travail)* neat, tidy; *(non polluant)* *(moteur, voiture)* clean, non-polluting; **n'utilise pas la serviette de ton frère, ce n'est pas p.!** don't use your brother's towel, it's not hygienic!; **une énergie p.** a clean form of energy; **chambre p. et nette** clean and tidy room; **je n'ai plus rien de p.** I haven't (got) anything clean to wear; **habillé de p.** wearing clean clothes; **p. comme un sou neuf** as clean as a new pin, spick and span; *(personne)* spick and span; **être p. sur soi** to be clean, to have clean habits; *Fam* **nous voilà propres!** we're in a fine *or* nice mess!; **le chat est un animal très p.** the cat is a very clean animal; **mon bébé était p. à vingt mois** my baby was potty-trained at twenty months; **la pianiste a un jeu très p.** the pianist has a very clean style **6** *Fig (réputation)* spotless; *(conscience)* clear; *Fam* **elle n'est pas p.**, **son affaire** there's something shady *or Fam* not quite kosher about the business; **ça ne me paraît pas très p., tout ça** it all seems a bit shady *or* dodgy to me; **ce n'est pas très p., tout ça** *(du point de vue moral)* that's a bit tacky

NM **1** *(d'une nation, d'une personne etc)* property, attribute, characteristic; *(caractère, nature)* nature; **le p. de l'homme** man's distinguishing feature **2** *(sens propre)* **au p.** in the literal sense; **employer un mot au p.** to use a word in its literal sense *or* literally **3** **avoir qch en p.** to possess sth in one's own right; **la maison m'appartient en p.** the house is mine, the house belongs to me; **il a un exemplaire en p.** he has a copy of his own **4** *Scol* **mettre qch au p.** to make a neat copy of sth, to copy sth out neatly; **recopier qch au p.** to make a fair *or* clean copy of sth, to copy sth (neatly) **5** **c'est du p.!** *(saleté)* what a mess!; *(action immorale)* that's not right!, *Fam* that's a bit tacky! **6** **ça sent le p.** it smells clean; **ça sent le p. dans toute la maison** the whole house smells clean

---

Il faut noter que l'adjectif anglais **proper** est un faux ami. Il ne se rapporte jamais à la propreté.

---

propre-à-rien, *pl* **propres-à-rien** N good-for-nothing, *Vieilli* ne'er-do-well

proprement [prɔprəmɑ̃] ADV **1** *(d'une manière propre)* cleanly; **une maison p. tenue** a well-kept house; **p. vêtu** correctly *or* properly dressed; **manger p.** not to make a mess when eating; **mange tes brochettes p.!** don't make a mess with your kebabs!; **tu ne sais pas encore manger p.!** you still can't eat without making a mess! **2** *Fam (convenablement)* well; *(de façon efficace)* efficiently; *(odieux, ridicule)* thoroughly, altogether, absolutely; **assez p.** tolerably well; *Iron* **se faire renvoyer p.** to be sent packing, to be sent off with a flea in one's ear; **il l'a p. ridiculisée** he made an absolute fool of her; **ils se sont fait p. battre par les concurrents** they were thoroughly *or* well and truly beaten *or Fam* they were hammered by the other side; **c'est p. scandaleux!** it's an absolute disgrace! **3** *(avec honnêteté)* *(se conduire)* decently, honourably, fairly; **se tirer d'affaire p.** to get out of a difficult situation with one's honour intact **4** **à p. parler** strictly speaking; **pas à p. parler** not exactly; **p. dit** actual; **pierres précieuses p. dites** precious stones according to the strictest definition of the term **5** *(strictement)* strictly (speaking); **c'est un problème p. urbain** it's purely *or* strictly an inner-city problem

---

Il faut noter que l'adverbe anglais **properly** est un faux ami. Il signifie **correctement**.

---

propret, -ette [prɔprɛ, -ɛt] ADJ neat, tidy

propreté [prɔprəte] NF **1** *(hygiène, soin)* cleanliness; *(des vêtements, de la vaisselle)* cleanness; *(d'une pièce, d'un travail)* neatness, tidiness **2** *(de moteur etc)* cleanness

propriétaire [prɔprijetɛr] N **1** *(d'une voiture, d'une propriété etc)* owner; *(d'une entreprise, d'un hôtel)* proprietor, f proprietress, owner; **devenir** *ou* **se rendre p. de qch** to acquire sth; **p. (de maison)** householder; **qui est le p. de cette terre?** who owns this land?; **p. foncier** landowner; **être p.** to be a man/woman of property *or* a landowner; *(de maison)* to be a property owner, to have a house *or* home of one's own; **maintenant que vous êtes p.** now that you're a homeowner, now that you own your own home; **vous voulez faire le tour du p.?** would you like a guided tour? **2** *(qui loue)* landlord, f landlady

propriété [prɔprijete] NF **1** *(fait de posséder)*

ownership, proprietorship; *(chose possédée)* *(terres)* property, estate; **une p. de 20 hectares** a 20-hectare estate; **p. privée/publique** private/public property; **titres de p.** title deeds; **p. littéraire** literary property; *(droit)* copyright; **p. artistique** copyright; **p. collective** social ownership; **p. de l'État** government *or* state property; **p. industrielle** patent rights, industrial property; **p. intellectuelle** intellectual property; **p. foncière** landed property, landed estate; **p. foncière (perpétuelle et) libre** freehold; **p. immobilière** property; **propriétés immobilières** real estate, *surtout Am* realty; **p. de l'État** government property; *Fin* **p. allégée, p.-loisirs, p.-vacances** = timeshare taken on a lease basis converting to ownership after a certain period **2** *(d'un métal, d'une plante etc)* property, characteristic, peculiar quality **3** *(de mot etc)* correctness, appropriateness **4** *Ordinat* **propriétés** *(de fichier)* properties

---

Il faut noter que le terme anglais **property** est un faux ami. Il signifie **bienséance**.

---

proprio [prɔprijo] N *Fam* landlord, f landlady

propulser [prɔpylse] VT to propel
VPR **se propulser** *Fam* to shoot; **il s'est propulsé dans le bureau du patron** he shot off to the boss's office; **se p. au sommet de la gloire** to shoot to the heights of fame; **se p. en tête du peloton** to shoot to the front of the pack

propulseur [prɔpylsœr] ADJ propellent, propulsive, propelling; **gaz p.** propellant, propellent
NM **1** *Aviat etc* propeller; **p. à hélice** screw propeller **2** *(gaz)* propellant, propellent

propulsif, -ive [prɔpylsif, -iv] ADJ = **propulseur** ADJ

propulsion [prɔpylsjɔ̃] NF propulsion, propelling; **réacteur de p.** propulsion jet; **sous-marin à p. nucléaire** nuclear-powered submarine; **véhicule à p. électrique** electrically powered vehicle; *Aut* **p. arrière** rear-wheel drive

propylène [prɔpilɛn] NM *Chimie* propylene

prorata [prɔrata] NM INV proportional part, proportion; **paiement au p.** payment pro rata; **au p. de qch** in proportion to sth

prorogatif, -ive [prɔrɔgatif, -iv] ADJ proroguing

prorogation [prɔrɔgasjɔ̃] NF **1** *surtout Jur* extension; *(de séance)* adjournment **2** *(de parlement)* prorogation

proroger [prɔrɔʒe] VT (je prorogeai(s); n. prorogeons) **1** *(contrat, bail)* to extend; **p. une échéance** to extend payment terms **2** *(parlement)* to prorogue; *(séance)* to adjourn

prosaïque [prɔzaik] ADJ prosaic, commonplace, pedestrian

prosaïquement [prɔzaikmɑ̃] ADV prosaically

prosaïsme [prɔzaism] NM prosaic nature *or* quality, prosaicness

prosateur [prɔzatœr] NM prose writer

proscenium [prɔsenjɔm] NM **1** *Théâtre (avant-scène)* proscenium, apron **2** *Antiq* proscenium (arch)

proscription [prɔskripsjɔ̃] NF *(d'une personne)* outlawing, *Fml* proscription; *(d'un mot, d'un usage)* outlawing, banning

proscrire [prɔskrir] VT *(conj like* **écrire***)* *(personne)* to outlaw, *Fml* to proscribe; *(mot, usage)* to outlaw, to ban, *Fml* to proscribe; **p. qn de la société** to ostracize sb; **p. un mot de son vocabulaire** to banish a word from one's vocabulary

proscrit, -ite [prɔskri, -it] ADJ *(personne)* outlawed, *Fml* proscribed; *(mot, usage)*

outlawed, banned, *Fml* proscribed
N outlaw

prose [proz] NF prose; **en p.** *(écrire)* in prose; *(texte, poème)* prose; *Fam Hum* **j'ai lu sa p.** I've read his literary masterpiece

prosélyte [prozelit] N proselyte; *Fig* convert; *Fig* **faire des prosélytes** to make *or* gain converts

prosélytisme [prozelitism] NM proselytism, proselytizing; **faire du p.** to proselytize

prosodie [prozodi] NF prosody

prosodique [prozodik] ADJ prosodic

prospect [prospɛ] NM prospective customer, prospect; *Mktg* **prospects à forte potentialité** hot prospect pool

prospecter [prospɛkte] VT **1** *Min* to prospect **2** *Com (client)* to canvass; *(marché)* to explore; **p. la clientèle** to canvass for new business

prospecteur, -trice [prospɛktœr, -tris] N **1** *Min* prospector **2** *Com* canvasser

prospectif, -ive [prospɛktif, -iv] ADJ prospective; **analyse prospective** *(en affaires)* forecast

prospection [prospɛksjɔ̃] NF **1** *Min* prospecting **2** *Com* canvassing; *Mktg* prospecting; **faire de la p.** to explore the market; **p. téléphonique** telephone marketing; **p. sur le terrain** field research

prospectus [prospɛktys] NM **1** *Bourse* prospectus **2** *(de publicité)* leaflet; *(de plusieurs pages)* brochure; *(donnant renseignements de base)* factsheet

prospère [prospɛr] ADJ *(ville, région)* prosperous, thriving, flourishing; *(personne, année)* prosperous; *(santé)* glowing; **les années prospères de sa vie** the prosperous period in his life, his/her years of prosperity

prospérer [prospere] VI **(je prospère; je prospérerai)** *(d'une personne)* to prosper, to do well; *(d'une société, d'un pays)* to prosper, to thrive, to do well

prospérité [prosperite] NF prosperity, prosperousness; *Com* **vague de p.** boom; **en période de p.** in times of prosperity, in prosperous times; **cette industrie est en pleine p.** the industry is thriving

prostaglandine [prostaglãdin] NF *Méd* prostaglandin

prostate [prostat] NF *Anat* prostate (gland)

prostatique [prostatik] ADJ *Anat* prostatic
NM prostate sufferer

prosternation [prosternasjɔ̃] NF *Litt* prostration; *Fig Péj* kowtowing

prosterné [prosterne] ADJ prostrate

prosternement [prosternəmã] NM prostration; *(état)* prostrate attitude

prosterner (se) [səprosterne] VPR *(se courber)* to prostrate oneself (**devant** before); *Fig Péj (s'abaisser)* to grovel, to kowtow (**devant** to)

prostitué, -ée [prostitye] N *(homme)* male prostitute; *(femme)* prostitute

prostituer [prostitye] VT *(personne, talent etc)* to prostitute
VPR **se prostituer** to prostitute oneself

prostitution [prostitysjɔ̃] NF prostitution; *Fig* **c'est de la p.** *(ton attitude)* you're just prostituting yourself

prostration [prostrasjɔ̃] NF **1** prostration **2** *Méd* (nervous) exhaustion

prostré [prostre] ADJ prostrate

protagoniste [protagonist] N protagonist

protal [protal] NM *Fam* head, headmaster, *f* headmistress, *Am* principal

prote [prot] NM *Typ* foreman

protecteur, -trice [protɛktœr, -tris] N **1** *(personne)* protector; *Can Admin* **Bureau du**

p. du citoyen Office of the Ombudsman **2** *(des arts etc)* patron, *f* patroness
NM protector, shield; *(pour machine-outil etc)* guard
ADJ *(appareil, tarif, vêtements etc)* protective; *Péj (ton etc)* patronizing, condescending; **il est très p. avec ses enfants** he is very protective towards his children; **crème protectrice** barrier cream; **société protectrice des animaux** = society for the prevention of cruelty to animals; **des mesures économiques protectrices** measures designed to protect the economy

protection [protɛksjɔ̃] NF **1** protection (**contre** from, against); *(de l'environnement etc)* protection, conservation; **p. civile** civil defence; **p. du consommateur** consumer protection; **p. de l'enfance** child welfare; **ne t'inquiète pas, tu es sous ma p.** don't worry, I'll protect *or* shield you; **assurer la p. rapprochée de qn** to act as a bodyguard for sb; **p. sociale** social welfare (system); **seul le préservatif assure une bonne p.** only condoms provide real protection; **sous la p. de la police** under police protection; **de p.** *(écran, visière, vernis)* protective; **dispositif de p.** safety device, protective device; *Can Admin* **Commissaire à la p. de la vie privée** Privacy Commissioner; *Ordinat* **p. d'accès logique** logical access protection; *Ordinat* **p. de bloc** block protection; *Ordinat* **p. contre l'écriture** *ou* **en écriture** write-protection; *Ordinat* **p. contre la copie** copy protection; *Ordinat* **p. de fichiers** file protection; *Ordinat* **p. de l'information** data protection; *Ordinat* **p. mémoire** protected location; *Ordinat* **p. par mot de passe** password protection; *Aut* **p. de phare** lamp guard **2** *(patronage)* patronage; *(mécénat) (des arts etc)* patronage, sponsorship; **prendre qn sous sa p.** to take sb under one's wing; *Péj* **par p.** through patronage *or* influence

protectionnisme [protɛksjonism] NM *Écon* protectionism

protectionniste [protɛksjonist] ADJ, N protectionist

protectorat [protɛktora] NM protectorate

protégé, -ée [proteʒe] ADJ protected; **p. contre l'inflation** inflation-proof; *Ordinat* **p. contre la copie** copy-protected; *Ordinat* **p. en écriture** write-protected; *Ordinat* **p. par mot de passe** password-protected; *Aut* **'passage p.'** = priority (over vehicles entering from minor road ahead)
N *(jeune artiste, sportif etc)* protégé, *f* protégée

protège-cahier, *pl* **protège-cahiers** [proteʒkaje] NM exercise-book cover

protège-dents [proteʒdã] NM INV *Boxe* gum shield

protéger [proteʒe] **(je protège, n. protégeons; je protégeai(s); je protégerai)** VT **1** *(personne, peau, mains)*, *Écon (industrie etc)* to protect (**contre** from); *Bourse (position)* to hedge; **p. une maison du froid/de l'humidité** to protect a house against *or* from the cold/dampness; **les arbres protègent la maison du vent** the trees shelter the house from the wind; **c'est pour p. son frère qu'elle a dit cela** she said it in order to protect *or* shield her brother; **p. qn contre un danger** to shield sb from danger; **p. une invention par un brevet** to patent an invention; **les verres fumés protègent bien les yeux** tinted lenses offer good protection for the eyes; **cet écran total vous protégera parfaitement** this sun block will provide complete protection; **on la protège en haut-lieu** she has friends in high places; **p. les droits acquis** to protect *or* defend hard-won rights; **que Dieu vous protège!** God keep you!; *Ordinat* **p. contre l'écriture** *ou* **en**

écriture to write-protect; *Ordinat* **p. contre la copie** to copy-protect **2** *(arts etc)* to patronize, to be a patron of; *(artiste)* to be a patron of
VPR **se protéger** to protect oneself; **l'usage du préservatif est le seul moyen de se p.** a condom is the sole means of protection *or* the only way you can protect yourself; **ils doivent absolument prendre l'habitude de se p.** *(du sida etc)* they must get into the habit of taking precautions *or* into the habit of safe sex; **se p. de** *ou* **contre** *(intempéries, soleil)* to protect *or* shield oneself from; *(maladie, excès de confiance en soi)* to guard against

protège-slip, *pl* **protège-slips** [proteʒ(ə)slip] NM panty-liner

protège-tibia, *pl* **protège-tibias** [proteʒtibja] NM *Sport* shin guard

protège-tympan [proteʒtɛ̃pã] NM INV earplug

protéiforme [proteiform] ADJ protean

protéine [protein] NF protein; **surveiller les protéines dans son alimentation** to watch one's protein intake; **alimentation faible/riche en protéines** food that is low/high in protein, low-/high-protein food

protéique [proteik] ADJ *Chimie* proteinic, proteinous, proteinaceous

protestable [protɛstabl] ADJ *Jur* which may be protested; *Fin* protestable

protestant, -ante [protɛstã, -ãt] ADJ, N *Rel* Protestant

protestantisme [protɛstãtism] NM *Rel* Protestantism; *(ensemble des protestants)* Protestant churches, Protestant community

protestataire [protɛstatɛr] ADJ *(lettre etc)* of protest
N protester, protestor

protestation [protɛstasjɔ̃] NF **1** *(affirmation)* protestation, declaration, affirmation; **protestations** protestations; **faire une p.** *ou* **des protestations d'innocence/d'amour** to protest *or* declare one's innocence/love; **ses protestations d'amour** his protestations *or* declaration of love **2** *(reproche, déclaration opposée)* protest; **voulez-vous signer notre p.?** will you sign our protest?; **émettre des protestations** to protest; **élever des protestations énergiques** to protest strongly; **paroles/geste de p.** words/gesture of protest; **réunion/manifestation/vote de p.** protest meeting/demonstration/vote; **démissionner en signe de p.** to resign in protest

protester [protɛste] VI to protest; **p. contre** *(une injustice, une décision) (en manifestant)* to protest *or* make a protest about *or* against, *Am* to protest; **p. contre une décision** *(devant la justice)* to challenge a ruling; **elle a protesté auprès du directeur** she complained to the manager; **p. de** *(son innocence, sa bonne foi)* to protest
VT *(affirmer)* to protest

protêt [protɛ] NM *Com, Jur* protest; **dresser un p.** to make a protest

prothèse [protɛz] NF **1** *Chir* prosthetics, prosthesis **2** **(appareil de) p.** prosthesis; **p. auditive** hearing aid; **p. dentaire** *(complète)* false teeth, denture(s); *(partielle)* bridge, *Spéc* dental prosthesis

prothésiste [protezist] N prosthesis maker

prothétique [protetik] NF prosthetics

protide [protid] NM protein

protocolaire [protokolɛr] ADJ formal, pertaining to protocol *or* etiquette; **clauses protocolaires d'accord** formal provisions of agreement

protocole [protokol] NM **1** *(procédés diplomatiques)* protocol; *(usage)* etiquette, formalities, social conventions; **le chef du p.**

the chief of protocol; **p. d'accord** protocol of agreement; *(contrat)* outline agreement **2** *Typ* list of proofreading symbols **3** *Ordinat* protocol; *(de réseau)* frame format; *(de traitement etc)* procedure; **p. Internet** Internet protocol; **p. multivoie/univoie** multi-channel/single-channel protocol; **p. de téléchargement** download protocol; **p. de transfert anonyme** anonymous FTP; **p. de transfert de fichiers** file transfer protocol; **p. de transmission** transmission protocol

protoétoile [prɔtoetwal] NF *Astron* proto-star

protohistoire [prɔtoistwar] NF protohistory

proton [prɔtɔ̃] NM *Nucl* proton

protoplasma [prɔtɔplasma] NM, **protoplasme** [prɔtɔplasm] NM *Biol* protoplasm

prototype [prɔtɔtip] NM prototype

protoxyde [prɔtɔksid] NM *Chimie* protoxide; **p. d'azote** nitrous oxide

protozoaire [prɔtɔzɔɛr] NM *Zool* protozoan, protozoon; **les protozoaires** the Protozoa

protractile [prɔtraktil] ADJ protractile

protrusion [prɔtryzjɔ̃] NF protrusion

protubérance [prɔtyberɑ̃s] NF protuberance; *(sur bâton etc)* knob; *Anat (sur le crâne)* bump

protubérant [prɔtyberɑ̃] ADJ protuberant

protuteur, -trice [prɔtytœr, -tris] N *Jur (d'un mineur)* acting guardian

prou [pru] ADV **peu ou p.** more or less

proue [pru] NF *(de navire)* prow, stem, bow(s)

prouesse [prues] NF **1** *Litt (acte héroïque)* deed of valour *or Am* valor **2** *(en sport etc)* feat, achievement; *Iron* **quelle p.!** that's quite a feat *or* an achievement!; **faire des prouesses** to do the impossible, to work miracles; **j'ai dû faire des prouesses pour le convaincre** it took everything I had *or* I had to work very hard to convince him

proustien, -ienne [prustjɛ̃, -jɛn] ADJ Proustian

prout [prut] NM *Fam (pet)* fart; **faire un p.** to fart

prout-prout ADJ *Fam* snobby, up oneself; **qu'est-ce qu'elle peut être p., sa copine!** his girlfriend can be so up herself

prouvable [pruvabl] ADJ provable; **c'est facilement/difficilement p.** it's easy/difficult to prove

prouver [pruve] VT **1** *(établir comme vrai)* *(fait)* to prove; **la police n'a rien pu p.** the police couldn't prove anything; **p. le bien-fondé d'une réclamation** to substantiate a claim, to prove the merits of a claim; **cela reste à p.** it still has to be proved; **elle dit qu'elle est experte mais cela reste à p.** she says she's an expert but that remains to be seen; **son dévouement n'est plus à p.** he has proved his devotion; **p. qch par A plus B** to prove sth in a logical fashion; **p. qch à qn** to prove sth to sb, to give sb proof of sth; **il y était aussi – prouve-le-moi!** he was there too – prove it!; **peux-tu me p. le contraire?** can you convince me otherwise *or* any differently? **2** *(être la preuve de)* to prove, to show; **ce qui prouve qu'on aurait dû écouter ce que je disais** which only goes to show that you should have listened to me

VPR **se prouver 1** *(à soi-même)* to prove to oneself; **que cherche-t-il à se p.?** what's he trying to prove to himself? **2** *(mutuellement)* **nous nous sommes prouvé que les deux versions étaient correctes** we proved to each other that both versions were correct **3** *(pouvoir être prouvé)* **ça ne se prouve pas** *(c'est une intuition)* you can't prove it, it's not the sort of thing you can prove

provenance [prɔvnɑ̃s] NF source, origin; **de p. anglaise** of English origin, English in origin; **marchandise de p. italienne** Italian merchandise, merchandise from Italy; **pays de p.** country of origin; **train en p. de Bordeaux** train from Bordeaux

provençal, -ale, -aux, -ales [prɔvɑ̃sal, -o] ADJ Provençal, of Provence
NM *Ling* Provençal
N **P.** person from Provence

provende [prɔvɑ̃d] NF *(pour élevage)* fodder, provender

provenir [prɔvnir] VI *(conj like* venir*)* **p. de** to come from; *(tirer son origine de)* to originate in; **d'où provient cet argent?** where does this money come from?; **des produits provenant du Japon** products from Japan; **des vins provenant des meilleurs crûs** wines from the best vintages; **les difficultés qui proviennent de cette situation** the difficulties arising from *or* out of the situation; *Jur* **les enfants provenant ou provenus de ce mariage** the children issuing from this marriage, the children of this marriage

proverbe [prɔvɛrb] NM proverb; **passer en p.** to become a proverb

proverbial, -iale, -iaux, -iales [prɔvɛrbjal, -jo] ADJ proverbial; *(beauté, sagesse, bonté, intelligence etc)* legendary, proverbial

proverbialement [prɔvɛrbjalmɑ̃] ADV proverbially

providence [prɔvidɑ̃s] NF providence; **c'est un secret de la p.** it's in the hands of providence; **être la p. de qn** *(d'une personne)* to be sb's guardian angel; **cette auberge est la p. des marcheurs** the inn is a godsend for walkers; **ce centre de conseils fut notre p.** the advice centre was a godsend *or* was heaven-sent; **l'État P.** the Welfare State

providentiel, -ielle [prɔvidɑ̃sjɛl] ADJ *(aide, rencontre etc)* providential, heaven-sent; **par une circonstance providentielle** by an act of providence

providentiellement [prɔvidɑ̃sjɛlmɑ̃] ADV providentially

province [prɔvɛ̃s] NF **1 la p.** the provinces; *(la campagne)* the country; **sa p. (d'origine)** the part of the country where he was born, *Litt, Hum* his native heath; **ça n'arriverait jamais dans ma p.** that type of thing would never happen where I come from; **elle s'est perdue dans le métro, elle arrive de sa p.** she got lost in the metro, she's new in town; **en p.** in the provinces; **aller en p.** to go to the country; **de p.** provincial; **vie de p.** provincial life, life in the provinces; *Péj* **mentalité de p.** small-town *or* provincial mentality **2** *Admin* province; *Can Géog* **les Provinces Maritimes** the Maritime Provinces, *Fam* the Maritimes; **la Belle P.** *(le Québec)* the Beautiful Province
ADJ INV *Fam Péj (attitude, personne)* provincial, parochial; *(air)* provincial

provincial, -iale, -iaux, -iales [prɔvɛ̃sjal, -jo] ADJ provincial; *Péj (manières)* provincial, countrified; *(mentalité, attitude)* provincial, parochial; **la vie provinciale** provincial life, life in the provinces; **manières provinciales** small-town *or* provincial ways
N provincial; **une jeune provinciale** a small-town girl, a girl from the provinces

provincialisme [prɔvɛ̃sjalism] NM *Ling* provincialism

provirus [prɔvirys] NM *Méd* provirus

proviseur [prɔvizœr] NM *Scol (d'un lycée)* headmaster, *f* headmistress

provision [prɔvizjɔ̃] NF **1** *(de pain, bois, nourriture)* supply, stock, store; *(d'eau)* supply; **faire des provisions ou faire p. de qch** to stock up on sth, to lay in a supply *or* stock

of sth; **nos provisions d'eau/de bois** our water/wood supply; **faire ses provisions** to go shopping; **provisions de guerre** munitions; *Vieilli* **provisions de bouche** food; **placard à provisions** store cupboard; **sac à provisions** shopping bag **2** *Com* funds; **verser une p.** *ou* **des provisions** to pay a deposit; **faire p. pour une lettre de change** to provide for a bill; **insuffisance de p.** *(pour honorer un chèque etc)* insufficient funds; **chèque sans p.** bad *or Fam* dud *or* rubber cheque, cheque that bounces/bounced; **faire un chèque sans p.** to write out a bad *or Fam* dud *or* rubber cheque; **il m'a fait un chèque sans p.** his cheque bounced; **un demi-mois de loyer par p.** a deposit of two weeks' rent; *Compta* **p. pour dépréciation** provision for depreciation, allowance for depreciation; **p. pour risques et charges** contingency and loss provision; *Fin* **provisions réglementées** regulated provisions **3** *Jur* retainer

provisionnel, -elle [prɔvizjɔnɛl] ADJ *Jur* provisional, interim; **tiers p.** = thrice-yearly income tax payment based on estimated tax due for the previous year

provisionnement [prɔvizjɔnmɑ̃] NM *Banque* funding

provisoire [prɔvizwar] ADJ *(arrêt)* temporary, provisional; *(arrangement, solution etc)* temporary, provisional, interim; **elle gère le centre, mais c'est p.** she manages the centre but it's a temporary arrangement, she's managing the centre but it's only on a temporary basis; **nommé à titre p.** appointed provisionally; **dividende p.** interim dividend; **habitation p.** emergency *or* temporary accommodation; *Jur* **détention p.** (temporary) custody; *Jur* **être en liberté p.** to be (out) on bail, to have been released on bail; **mis en liberté p.** released on bail
NM **ça n'est que du p.** it's only temporary, it's only for the time being; **il s'est installé dans le p.** he's got used to living on a day-to-day basis; **je ne veux plus vivre dans le p.** I'm tired of living in uncertainty

provisoirement [prɔvizwarmɑ̃] ADV provisionally, temporarily

provitamine [prɔvitamin] NF *Biol, Chimie* provitamin

provoc [prɔvɔk] NF *Fam (abrév* provocation*)* provocation

provocant [prɔvɔkɑ̃] ADJ **1** *(agressif)* *(paroles, langage, attitude)* provocative **2** *(sourire, robe)* provocative; **d'une manière provocante** provocatively

provocateur, -trice [prɔvɔkatœr, -tris] ADJ *(sourire)* provocative; *(attitude)* provocative, challenging; **agent p.** agent provocateur
N troublemaker, agitator

provocation [prɔvɔkasjɔ̃] NF **1** *(défi)* provocation; **un ton/air de p.** a challenging tone/look, a tone/look of provocation; **elle le fait par p.** she does it to provoke, she's being provocative; **il te l'a dit par p.** he said it to provoke you; **c'est de la p.!** it's deliberate provocation!; **p. en duel** challenge to a duel **2** *Jur* instigation; **p. au crime** incitement to crime

provoquer [prɔvɔke] VT **1** *(défier, sexuellement)* to provoke; **p. qn en duel** to challenge sb to a duel; *Fam* **tu me provoques, toi!** you're starting to get up my nose! **2** *(inciter)* *(crime, violence)* to instigate; **p. les jeunes à la violence/au crime** to incite young people to violence/to crime **3** *(effet)* to have; *(stupeur, incendie, mort)* to cause; *(malaise, crise cardiaque)* to cause, *Fam* to bring on; *Méd (sommeil, des vomissements)* to induce; *(critique)* to provoke, to give rise to, to generate; *(réaction)* to provoke, to produce; *(jalousie, ressentiment)* to arouse; *(courant d'air)* to cause, to create; **un coma provoqué par la**

drogue a drug-induced coma; **il faut p. l'accouchement** we'll have to induce you/her or labour
VPR se provoquer to provoke each other

proxénète [prɔksenɛt] N pimp, Litt, Arch pander; Jur procurer, f procuress

proxénétisme [prɔksenetism] NM pimping; Jur procuring

proximité [prɔksimite] NF proximity, nearness, closeness; (d'un événement) imminence, proximity; **j'apprécie la p. de la ville** I appreciate the fact that the town is nearby or is within easy reach; **la p. du départ rend la famille nerveuse** the family are becoming apprehensive as the day of departure draws near; **p. de parenté** near relationship; **à p.** close by, near at hand; **à p. de qch** near sth, close to sth, in the vicinity of sth; **police de p.** community policing; **justice de p.** = legal system in which the judiciary have closer links with the community they serve; **commerce de p.** neighbourhood shop or store

proyer [prwaje] NM (oiseau) **(bruant) p.** bunting

prude [pryd] Péj ADJ prudish
NF prude; **ne fais pas la p.!** don't be so prudish!, don't be such a prude!

prudemment [prydamã] ADV prudently, carefully, cautiously

prudence [prydãs] NF prudence, carefulness, cautiousness, caution; (d'un conducteur) cautiousnessness; **avec p.** (agir) cautiously, prudently; (conduire) carefully; **on conseille la p.** caution is advised; **son excès de p. l'exaspérait** she was sick of his overcautiousness; **donner des conseils de p. à qn** to advise sb to be cautious; **par (mesure de) p.** as a precaution; **par p., je n'ai pas voulu lui en parler tout de suite** I thought it wiser not to speak of it to him right away; Prov **p. est mère de sûreté** discretion is the better part of valour; Litt **des prudences** precautionary measures

prudent [prydã] ADJ (personne) careful, cautious, prudent; (conducteur) careful, cautious; (décision etc) wise, sensible, prudent; (ligne de conduite) prudent, advisable; **on n'est jamais trop p.** you can't be too careful; **vous avez raison, c'est plus p.** you're right, it's wiser or more sensible; **j'ai jugé p. de le prévenir tout de suite** I thought it wise or sensible to let him know right away; **un homme très p. en affaires** a very cautious businessman; **il faut être p. de ne pas décider trop vite** we must be careful not to decide too quickly; **attention brouillard, soyez prudents** fog warning, drive cautiously

pruderie [prydri] NF Péj prudery, prudishness

prud'homme [prydɔm] NM Ind, Jur industrial arbitrator; **conseil des prud'hommes** ≃ industrial tribunal; **aller aux** ou **devant les prud'hommes** ≃ to go before an industrial tribunal

prudhommerie [prydɔmri] NF Péj pomposity, sententiousness

pruine [prɥin] NF (sur fruit) bloom

prune [pryn] NF **1** (fruit) plum; (liqueur) plum brandy; **p. de Damas** damson; Fig Fam **pour des prunes** to work for nothing; **travailler pour des prunes** to work for nothing or for peanuts; **si j'y suis allée, ce n'est pas pour des prunes!** I didn't go just for the fun or hell of it!; Fig Fam **tu crois qu'elle m'en donnerait? – des prunes!** do you think she'll let me have some? – no way! or no fear! or not bloody likely!; **et qu'est-ce que j'ai reçu en remerciements? des prunes!** and what did I get by way of thanks? not a bloody thing! **2** Fam (coup de poing) punch, thump, clout **3** Fam (contravention) fine
ADJ INV plum(-coloured or Am -colored)

> Il faut noter que le terme anglais **prune** est un faux ami. Il signifie **pruneau**.

pruneau, -eaux [pryno] NM **1** (fruit) prune **2** Suisse (prune) red plum **3** Arg (balle d'arme à feu) slug, bullet

prunelle [prynɛl] NF **1** (fruit) sloe; **(liqueur de) p.** sloe gin **2** Anat (des yeux) pupil; Fig **j'y tiens comme à la p. de mes yeux** it's the apple of my eye, it's my pride and joy; Fam **jouer de la p.** to flutter one's eyelashes

prunellier [prynelje] NM blackthorn, sloe (bush)

prunier [prynje] NM plum tree; Fam **secouer qn comme un p.** to give sb a good shaking, Fam to shake sb till his/her teeth rattle; Fig to give sb a good telling-off, to tear sb off a strip; Fam **arrête de me secouer comme un p.** stop shaking me like that

prunus [prynys] NM (arbre) prunus, Japanese flowering cherry

prurigineux, -euse [pryriʒinø, -øz] ADJ Méd which causes itching, Spéc pruritic

prurit [pryrit] NM Méd itching, Spéc pruritus

Prusse [prys] NF Hist Prussia; **bleu de P.** Prussian blue; Fig Fam **travailler pour le roi de P.** to work for nothing or for peanuts

Prusse-Orientale [prysɔrjɑ̃tal] NF Ancien-nement **la P.** East Prussia

prussiate [prysjat] NM Chimie cyanide

prussien, -ienne [prysjɛ̃, -jɛn] Hist ADJ Prussian
N **P.** Prussian

prytanée [pritane] NM military school (for sons of officers)

PS [pees] NM **1** abrév **Parti socialiste 2** (abrév **post-scriptum**) P.S.

psallette [psalɛt] NF choir school

psalmiste [psalmist] NM psalmist

psalmodie [psalmɔdi] NF **1** Rel psalmody **2** (déclamation, formule monotone) droning

psalmodier [psalmɔdje] (pr sub, impf n. **psalmodiions, v. psalmodiiez**) VT **1** Rel (office etc) to intone, to chant **2** (dire avec monotonie) to drone out, to recite monotonously
VI **1** Rel to intone, to chant **2** (parler avec monotonie) to drone (on or away)

psaltérion [psalterjɔ̃] NM Mus psaltery

psaume [psom] NM psalm

psautier [psotje] NM Mus psalter, psalm book

pseudo [psødo] NM Fam (abrév **pseudonyme**) alias

pseudo- [psødo] PRÉF pseudo-; **des p.-intellectuels** pseudo-intellectuals; **un p.-médecin** a quack, a bogus or fake doctor

pseudo-membrane, pl **pseudo-membranes** NF Méd pseudomembrane, false membrane

pseudonyme [psødɔnim] NM pseudonym; **prendre un p.** to adopt a pseudonym; **elle a pris un p.** (cette écrivain) she writes under a pseudonym

pseudo-rubis NM INV Minér rose quartz

pseudo-saphir, pl **pseudo-saphirs** NM Minér blue quartz

psi [psi] NM psi

psitt [psit] INT psst!

psittacose [psitakoz] NF Méd, Vét psittacosis

psoriasis [psɔrjazis] NM Méd psoriasis

pst [pst] INT psst!

psy [psi] Fam ADJ = **psychiatrique, psychologique, psychanalytique**
NF = **psychiatrie, psychologie, psychanalyse**
N (psychologue, psychanalyste) shrink

psychanalyse [psikanaliz] NF (domaine) psychoanalysis; (traitement) (psycho)analysis; **faire une p.** to be in or undergoing (psycho)analysis; **commencer une p.** to start analysis, to go into (psycho)analysis; **il a fait une p. pendant cinq ans** he was in (psycho)analysis for five years; **faire de la p.** to psychoanalyse people

psychanalyser [psikanalize] VT (personne, rêves etc) to (psycho)analyse; **se faire p.** to be (psycho)analysed

psychanalyste [psikanalist] N psychoanalyst

psychanalytique [psikanalitik] ADJ psychoanalytical; **école p.** school of psychoanalysis

psyché [psiʃe] NF **1** Myth **P.** Psyche **2** Phil psyche **3** (miroir) cheval glass

psychédélique [psikedelik] ADJ psychedelic; Fam **la mode p.** the fashion for psychedelia

psychiatre [psikjatr] N psychiatrist

psychiatrie [psikjatri] NF psychiatry

psychiatrique [psikjatrik] ADJ psychiatric

psychique [psiʃik] ADJ psychic

psychisme [psiʃism] NM psyche, inner mind

psycho [psiko] NF = **psychologie**

psychodrame [psikodram] NM role-playing, Spéc psychodrama

psychographie [psikografi] NF psychographics

psychographique [psikografik] ADJ psychographic

psycholinguistique [psikolɛ̃gɥistik] NF psycholinguistics

psychologie [psikɔlɔʒi] NF psychology; Univ **faire de** ou **étudier la p.,** Fam **faire p.** to do or study psychology; Univ **études de p.** psychology (studies); **étudiants en p.** psychology students; **faire preuve de p.** to be a good psychologist, to use psychology; **tu manques de p.** you're not much of a psychologist, you don't have much idea of how people's minds work; **il a réellement manqué de p.** he showed a great lack of insight; **la p. des descriptions chez Proust** the psychological insights offered by Proust's descriptions; **une p. très fragile** a very fragile personality; **il faut comprendre sa p.** you have to understand the way his/her mind works

psychologique [psikɔlɔʒik] ADJ (roman, film etc) psychological; **le moment p.** the psychological moment; **son état p.** his psychological state, his state of mind; **son état p. n'était pas bon du tout** he wasn't in a good state of mind or frame of mind at all; **c'est p.!** it's psychological!

psychologiquement [psikɔlɔʒikmã] ADV psychologically

psychologue [psikɔlɔg] N psychologist; Fig **c'est un fin p.** he's a good psychologist
ADJ **elle n'est pas très p.** she's not much of a psychologist, she doesn't understand how people's minds work

psychonévrose [psikonevroz] NF psychoneurosis

psychopathe [psikɔpat] N psychopath

psychopathie [psikɔpati] NF psychopathy

psychopathologie [psikopatɔlɔʒi] ADJ psychopathology

psychopédagogie [psikopedagɔʒi] NF application of experimental psychology to education

psychopharmacologie [psikofarmakɔlɔ-ʒi] NF psychopharmacology

psychophysiologie [psikofizjɔlɔʒi] NF psychophysiology

psychose [psikoz] NF **1** Psy psychosis; Mil **p.**

traumatique post-combat stress syndrome, shellshock; **p. maniaco-dépressive** manic depression; **souffrir de p. maniaco-dépressive** to be a manic-depressive **2** *(obsession)* *(d'une maladie, une crise, une guerre)* psychosis (**de** about), fear (**de** of)

psychosociologie [psikosɔsjɔlɔʒi] NF social psychology

psychosomatique [psikosɔmatik] ADJ *Méd* psychosomatic

psychotechnique [psikotɛknik] ADJ psychological testing, *Spéc* psychotechnical ▸ NF psychological testing, *Spéc* psychotechnology, psychotechnics

psychothérapeute [psikoterapøt] N psychotherapist

psychothérapie [psikoterapi] NF (psycho)-therapy; **p. analytique** analytical (psycho)-therapy; **p. familiale** family therapy; **faire une p. de groupe** to go to *or* do group therapy

psychothérapique [psikoterapik] ADJ psychotherapeutic; **intervention p.** psychotherapeutic treatment

psychotique [psikɔtik] ADJ, N psychotic

psychotonique [psikotɔnik] ADJ *Pharm* psychoactive, psychotropic

psychotrope [psikɔtrɔp] NM *Pharm* psychotropic drug ▸ ADJ *Anat* psychotropic

ptérodactyle [pterɔdaktil] NM pterodactyl

ptérosaurien [pterɔsɔrjɛ̃] NM pterosaur

Ptolémée [ptɔleme] N *Antiq* Ptolemy; *Astron* **système de P.** Ptolemaic system

ptomaïne [ptɔmain] NF *Biol, Chimie* ptomaine

PTT [petete] NFPL *Anciennement (abrév* **Postes, Télécommunications et Télédiffusion)** = former French post office and telecommunications network

PU [pey] NM *Com (abrév* **prix unitaire)** UP

puant [pɥɑ̃] ADJ **1** *(qui sent mauvais)* stinking, foul-smelling; *Chimie Fam* **gaz p.** hydrogen sulphide, *Fam* stink bomb gas; **boule puante** stink bomb **2** *Fig (odieux)* cocky

puanteur [pɥɑ̃tœr] NF stink, stench, *Br Fam* pong

pub¹ [pyb] NF *Fam* = **publicité 1, 2**

pub² [pœb] NM pub

pubère [pybɛr] ADJ pubescent

puberté [pybɛrte] NF puberty

pubescent [pybesɑ̃] ADJ *Bot* pubescent

pubien, -ienne [pybjɛ̃, -jɛn] ADJ *Anat* pubic

pubis [pybis] NM *Anat* pubis, pubes; *(os)* pubic bone

publiable [pybliabl] ADJ fit for publication, publishable

public, -ique [pyblik] ADJ public; *(assemblée)* public, open (to the public); **la séance est publique** the meeting is open to the public; **la chose publique** res publica; **service p.** public utility (service), *Am* utility; **travailler pour le bien p.** to work for the common good; **la voie publique** the public highway; **il est de notoriété publique que ...** it is public *or* common knowledge that ...; *Admin* **ministère p.** = public prosecutor
▸ NM *(d'un spectacle, d'une émission)* audience; **cette émission a été enregistrée en p.** this programme was recorded before a live audience; **un p. cultivé** a cultured *or* an educated audience; *(lecteurs)* cultured *or* discerning readers; **cette chanteuse a encore son p.** this singer still has a following; **le p.** the public; **'interdit au p.'** 'no admittance *or* admission to the public', 'keep out'; **le grand p.** the general public; **un film pour le grand p.** a family film, a film (suitable) for

everybody; **électronique grand p.** consumer electronics; **en p.** in public, publicly; **faire une déclaration en p.** to make a public statement; **p. cible** target audience; **p. en studio** studio audience VOIR GRAMMAIRE A11

publicain [pyblikɛ̃] NM *Antiq* tax gatherer; *Bible* publican

publication [pyblikasjɔ̃] NF **1** *(fait de rendre public)* publication, publishing; **p. en feuilleton** serialization; **p. de vente aux enchères** notice of sale by auction; **date de p.** publication date, date of publication; **p. assistée par ordinateur** desk-top publishing **2** *(magazine etc)* publication; **p. périodique** periodical; **p. trimestrielle** quarterly (publication); **p. spécialisée** specialist journal; **p. interne** in-house publication

publiciste [pyblisist] N *Com Fam* person who works in advertising, *(homme)* adman

publicitaire [pyblisitɛr] ADJ *(concerned with)* publicity; *Com* (concerned with) advertising; **campagne p.** publicity campaign; *Com* advertising campaign; **agence p.** advertising agency; **vente p.** promotional sale; *TV, Radio* **spot/message p.** commercial, ad(vert)
▸ N person who works in advertising; *Fam (homme)* adman

publicité [pyblisite] NF **1** *(notoriété)* publicity; *Com* advertising; **être dans la p.** to be in advertising; **faire de la p. pour un savon** *(d'un acteur)* to advertise a soap; *(d'une agence)* to do the advertising for a soap; **l'animateur a fait de la p. pour cet album** the disc jockey plugged the album; **ça lui fait de la p.** it's publicity for him; **la p. paie** it pays to advertise; **une agence de p.** an advertising agency
 2 *(affiche)*, *Journ* ad(vert); *TV, Radio* ad(-vert), commercial; **une pleine page de p. dans le journal** a full page ad(vert) *or* advertisement in the paper; **il y a trop de p. à la télévision** there are too many ads *or* there's too much advertising on television
 3 *(caractère public) (d'un débat)* public nature

▸▸**p. associé** cooperative advertising; **p. clandestine** underhand advertising; **p. commerciale** commercial advertising; **p. comparative** comparative advertising; *(activité)* comparative *or* comparison advertising; **p. par correspondance** direct mail advertising; **p. directe** direct advertising *or* mail, below-the-line advertising; **p. d'entreprise** corporate advertising; **p. par l'événement** event advertising; **p. extérieure** outdoor advertising; **p. hors-médias** below-the-line promotion; **p. d'intérêt général** government advertisement; *(activité)* government advertising; **p. sur le lieu de vente** point-of-sale promotion; **p. média** *(publicité directe)* above-the-line *or* media advertising; **p. mensongère** false *or* misleading advertising; **p. sur panneau** billboard advertisement; *(activité)* billboard advertising; **p. plein page** full page advertisement; **p. par publipostage** direct mail advertising; **p. pure** above-the-line advertising; **p. de rappel** follow-up advertisement; *(activité)* follow-up publicity; **p. rédactionnelle** advertorial; **p. télévisée** television advertisement *or* commercial, TV ad; *(activité)* television advertising

public-relations [pœblikrilɛʃɑnz] NF public relations, PR; **le service de p.** the public relations department, the PR department
▸ N public relations officer, PR man, *f* woman

publier [pyblije] VT *(pr sub, impf* n. **publiions, v. publiiez)* **1** *(rendre public) (chiffres du commerce etc)* to publish, to make public, to make known; *(décret etc)* to proclaim; *(règlement)* to issue; **les bans ont-ils été pu-**

bliés? have the banns been published?; **p. la nouvelle que ...** to release the news that ... **2** *(livre)* to publish, to bring out; **ce journal est publié sur seize pages** the paper runs to sixteen pages

publi-information, *pl* **publi-informations** [pybliɛ̃fɔrmasjɔ̃] NF advertorial

Publiphone® [pyblifɔn] NM card phone

publipostage [pyblipostaʒ] NM mailshot; **logiciel de p.** mail merge software; **faire un p.** to do a mailshot; **p. groupé** volume mailing

publi-promotion, *pl* **publi-promotions** [pyblipromosjɔ̃] NF promotional offer

publiquement [pyblikmɑ̃] ADV publicly, in public; *(ouvertement)* openly; **se faire ridiculer p.** to be publicly insulted, to be insulted in public

publireportage [pyblirəpɔrtaʒ] NM advertorial, advertising feature, promotional article

puce [pys] NF **1** *(insecte)* flea; **p. de mer** sand hopper *or* flea; **herbe aux puces** fleawort; **jeu de p.** tiddlywinks; **piqûre de p.** fleabite; **le marché aux puces, les puces** the flea market; **les puces de Paris** the Paris flea market; *Fig* **mettre la p. à l'oreille à qn** to make sb suspicious, to arouse sb's suspicions; *Fam* **secouer les puces à qn** to give sb a good telling off; *Fam* **elle est excitée comme une p.** she can't sit still, she's jumping up and down with excitement; **elle est rentrée de l'école excitée comme une p.** she came home jumping up and down with excitement; *Fam* **mais oui, ma p.** yes, (my) dear *or* (my) love *or* (my) pet **2** *Ordinat* (micro)chip; **p. à ADN** DNA chip; **p. antiviolence** V-chip; **p. logique** logic chip; **p. mémoire** memory chip; **p. de reconnaissance vocale** voice recognition chip
▸ ADJ INV puce(-coloured *or Am* -colored)

puceau, -eaux [pyso] NM, ADJ M *Fam* virgin

pucelage [pyslaʒ] NM *Hum* virginity; **perdre son p.** to lose one's virginity

pucelle [pysɛl] ADJ F virgin
▸ NF virgin, *Arch, Euph* maid(en); *Hist* **la P. d'Orléans** the Maid of Orleans

puceron [pysrɔ̃] NM greenfly, aphid

pucier [pysje] NM *Arg (lit)* bed

pudding [pudiŋ] NM *Culin* **1** steamed pudding; *(pour Noël)* (plum) pudding, Christmas pudding **2** *(gâteau)* = filling type of cake made from stale bread

puddlage [pydlaʒ] NM *Métal* puddling

puddler [pydle] VT *Métal* to puddle

pudeur [pydœr] NF *(réserve)* modesty; **sans p.** *(adjectivement)* unblushing, shameless; *(adverbialement)* unblushingly, shamelessly; **avec p.** modestly; **rougir de p.** to blush with shame; **par p., il n'a pas abordé le sujet** out of a sense of decency *or* propriety, he did not mention the subject; **avoir la p. de faire qch** to have the decency to do sth

pudibond [pydibɔ̃] ADJ easily shocked, prudish

> Do not confuse with **pudique**.

pudibonderie [pydibɔ̃dri] NF prudishness

pudicité [pydisite] NF *Litt* modesty

pudique [pydik] ADJ modest; **une allusion p.** a discreet reference

> Do not confuse with **pudibond**.

pudiquement [pydikmɑ̃] ADV modestly

puer [pɥe] VI to stink, to reek; **ça pue!** what a stink *or Br Fam* pong!
▸ VT **ça pue le poisson** it stinks *or* reeks of fish; **il pue des pieds** his feet stink

puériculteur, -trice [pцerikyltœr, -tris] **N** nursery nurse

puériculture [pцerikyltyr] **NF** child care, infant welfare

puéril [pцeril] **ADJ** childish, *Fml* puerile

puérilement [pцerilmã] **ADV** childishly

puérilité [pцerilite] **NF** childishness, *Fml* puerility

puerpéral, -ale, -aux, -ales [pцɛrperal, -o] **ADJ** *Obst* puerperal

puffin [pyfɛ̃] **NM** (*oiseau*) shearwater

pugilat [pyʒila] **NM 1** (*combat de boxeurs*) boxing, *Fml* pugilism **2** (*dispute, bataille*) fight, brawl, *Fam* set-to

pugiliste [pyʒilist] **NM** boxer, *Fml* pugilist

pugnace [pygnas] **ADJ** *Litt* pugnacious

pugnacité [pygnasite] **NF** *Litt* pugnacity, pugnaciousness

puîné, -ée [pцine] *Vieilli* **ADJ** (*de deux*) younger; (*de plusieurs*) youngest ▸ **N** (*frère*) younger/youngest brother; (*sœur*) younger/youngest sister

puis [pцi] **ADV** then; **tourner à droite p. à gauche** turn right (and) then left; **et p.** and then; (*d'ailleurs*) moreover, (and) then; **et p. qu'est-ce qui s'est passé?** then what happened?, what happened then *or* next?; **et p., c'est tout** and that's all there is to it; **et p. (quoi)?, et p. après?** then what?, what next?; *Fam* (*qu'est-ce que ça peut faire*) so what?

puisage [pцizaʒ] **NM** (*d'eau*) drawing (up)

puisard [pцizar] **NM** (*pour ordures*) cesspool, sink; *Min, Tech etc* sump, well

puisatier [pцizatje] **NM** (*ouvrier*) well maker, well sinker; *Min* shaft sinker

puisement [pцizmã] **NM** = **puisage**

puiser [pцize] **VT** (*eau*) to draw (**à, dans** from); *Fig* (*inspiration, idée*) to derive, to get, to take (**dans, chez** from); **p. aux sources** to draw on the original sources, to go to the source, *Litt, Hum* to go to the fountainhead ▸ **VI** **elle puise dans ses réserves** she's drawing on her reserves; **elle ne s'est pas gênée pour p. dans ma trousse de maquillage** she felt no embarrassment about using my make-up *or* dipping into my make-up bag; **p. dans son porte-monnaie** to dip *or* put one's hand in one's wallet

puisque [pцisk(ə)] **CONJ** since, as, seeing that; **je le ferai, puisqu'il le faut** I'll do it, since I must; **p. tu veux savoir, je vais te le dire** since *or* seeing that you want to know, I'll tell you; **p. c'est comme ça** if that's how you feel/he feels/*etc*, if that's how things are; **d'accord, p. c'est ce que tu veux!** all right, if that's what you want!; **je te dis que je l'ai vu!** but I'm telling you I did see it!; **tu es sûr que tu peux y aller? – mais p. je te le dis!** are you sure you can go? – I said so, didn't I?

puissamment [pцisamã] **ADV** powerfully; *Fam* **p. riche** exceedingly rich

puissance [pцisãs] **NF 1** power; (*du vent*) force, strength; (*d'une armée*) strength; **p. d'une machine** power of an engine; *Mil* **p. de ou du feu** fire power; **p. en chevaux** horsepower; **p. au frein** brake horsepower; *Aut* **p. de traction** pulling power; **p. effective** power output; **p. nominale** rated power; **p. utile** usable brake horsepower, usable bhp; *Admin* **p. fiscale d'une voiture** = engine rating of a car for road tax purposes; **p. administrative** taxable horsepower; *Radio* **p. d'antenne** aerial capacity; **poste émetteur de haute p.** high-power radio transmitter **2** *Math* power; **élever un nombre à la nième p.** to raise a number to the nth power; **dix (à la) p. quatre** ten to the fourth, ten to the power of four **3** (*autorité*) power; **avoir qn en sa p.** to have sb in one's power; **la volonté de p.** the desire for power; **être en p. de mari** to be under a husband's control *or* authority; **p. paternelle** paternal authority **4** *Pol* **les grandes puissances** the great powers; *Fig* **les puissances célestes** the powers above; **les puissances des ténèbres** the powers of darkness **5** **en p.** (*assassin, meurtrier*) potential

puissant [pцisã] **ADJ 1** (*qui a du pouvoir*) (*armée, moteur, voiture, pays etc*) powerful **2** (*qui a de la force physique, fort*) (*homme, vent, musculature*), *Fig* (*envie*) strong; (*voix*) powerful; (*remède*) powerful, strong, potent **3** *Fam* (*remarquable*) wicked, *Br* fab, *Am* awesome ▸ **NMPL** **les puissants** the powerful, the mighty (ones)

puits [pцi] **NM 1** (*pour l'eau*) well; **p. de sondage** borehole; **p. artésien** artesian well; **p. absorbant, p. perdu** cesspool; *Fig* **c'est un p. de science** he's a mine of information; (*d'un esprit plus profond*) he's a fount of knowledge **2** (*de mine*) shaft, pit; **p. d'aération** *ou* **d'aérage** air shaft, ventilation shaft; **p. d'extraction** winding shaft **3** *Mil* **p. de lancement** launching silo **4** *Culin* **p. d'amour** = small round of puff pastry filled with pastry cream

pull [pyl] **NM** *Fam* jumper, sweater, pullover

pullman [pulman] **NM** *Rail* Pullman (car)

pull-over, *pl* **pull-overs** [pylɔvœr] **NM** jumper, sweater, pullover

pullulation [pylylasjɔ̃] **NF**, **pullulement** [pylylmã] **NM 1** (*d'organismes etc*) rapid multiplication, *Fml* pullulation **2** (*d'enfants etc*) swarm

pulluler [pylyle] **VI 1** (*se reproduire*) to multiply rapidly, *Fml* to pullulate **2** (*être en profusion*) to abound, to be found in profusion; (*en mouvement*) to swarm; **la rue pullule de monde** the street is swarming with people; **les marchands de chaussures pullulent dans ce coin de la ville** there are lots of shoe shops in this part of town, this part of town is full of *or* swarming with shoe shops

pulmonaire [pylmɔnɛr] **ADJ** pulmonary; **congestion p.** pulmonary congestion ▸ **NF** lungwort

pulpe [pylp] **NF 1** (*de fruit*) pulp; **yaourt à la p. de fruits** yoghurt with pieces of fruit in it; **réduire qch en p.** to reduce sth to a pulp, to pulp sth **2** (*partie molle*) (*des doigts ou des orteils*) pad; (*des dents*) pulp

pulpeux, -euse [pylpø, -øz] **ADJ** (*lèvres*) fleshy; **une fille pulpeuse** a sexy female

pulsar [pylsar] **NM** *Astron* pulsar

pulsation [pylsasjɔ̃] **NF** (*fait de battre*) (*du cœur*) beating, throbbing; (*battement*) throb

pulsative [pylsativ] **ADJ F** *Méd* **douleur p.** throbbing pain, *Spéc* pulsatory pain

pulser [pylse] **VT** (*air*) (*dans une pièce, dans un moteur*) to force

pulsion [pylsjɔ̃] **NF** *Psy* impulse; **p. sexuelle** sex drive; **p. de mort** death wish

pulsionnel, -elle [pylsjɔnɛl] **ADJ** impulsive, impulse; **phénomène p.** impulsive action, instinctive action; **c'était plus p. que réfléchi** it was more of a reflex *or* an impulse than a conscious act

pulsoréacteur [pylsoreaktœr] **NM** *Aviat* pulse jet

pulvérisable [pylverizabl] **ADJ** (*poudre etc*) which can be crushed; (*liquide*) that can be sprayed

pulvérisateur [pylverizatœr] **NM 1** (*de matières solides*) pulverizer **2** (*de liquide*) spray; *Tech* vaporizer, atomizer

pulvérisation [pylverizasjɔ̃] **NF 1** (*de matières solides*) pulverizing, crushing **2** (*de liquides*) spraying; *Tech* vaporization; **p. métallisée** metal-spraying

pulvériser [pylverize] **VT 1** (*roche*) to crush, to pulverize; **p. une matière** to grind *or* reduce a substance to powder **2** (*liquide, parfum*) to spray; *Ind* to vaporize **3** *Fig Fam* (*record*) to smash, to shatter; **la voiture a été pulvérisée lors de l'accident** the car was completely smashed up *or* was smashed to pieces in the accident; **p. qn** to beat the hell out of sb, to pulverize sb

pulvériseur [pylverizœr] **NM** *Agr* disc *or Am* disk harrow

pulvérulence [pylverylãs] **NF** powderiness, dustiness

pulvérulent [pylverylã] **ADJ** powdery, dusty

puma [pyma] **NM** puma, cougar, mountain lion

punaise [pynɛz] **NF 1** (*insecte*) bug; **p. des lits** bed bug; *Fam* **p. de sacristie** fervent churchgoer; *Fam* **oh p.!** golly!, goodness!, gosh! **2** (*pour accrocher*) drawing pin, *Am* thumbtack

punaiser [pyneze] **VT** *Fam* to pin (up); **p. des affiches au mur** to pin posters to the wall

punch¹ [pɔ̃ʃ] **NM** *Culin* punch; **bol à p.** punchbowl

punch² [pœnʃ] **NM** *Boxe, Fig Fam* punch; *Fig* **elle ne manque pas de p.** (*elle a de l'énergie*) she's full of energy; **ça vous donnera du p. pour la suite!** it'll give you energy *or* set you up for what's to come!; **un slogan qui a du p.** a punchy *or* catchy slogan; **cette aide de l'État a donné du p. à notre organisation** the government's assistance was a shot in the arm for our organization

punching-ball, *pl* **punching-balls** [pœnʃiŋbol] **NM** *Boxe* punchball

punique [pynik] **ADJ** *Hist* (*guerres etc*) Punic

punir [pynir] **VT** (*personne, crime*) to punish; **p. qn de mort/prison** to punish sb with death/imprisonment; **p. qn d'un crime/pour un mensonge** to punish sb for a crime/for lying; **être puni de ses crimes** to be punished *or* pay the penalty for one's crimes; **ça te punira de ta curiosité!** that'll teach you to be nosy!; **me voilà puni de ma gourmandise!** it serves me right for being greedy!, that'll teach me to be greedy!; **être puni par où l'on a péché** to reap what one has sown

punissable [pynisabl] **ADJ** punishable

punitif, -ive [pynitif, -iv] **ADJ** (*expédition, mesure etc*) punitive

punition [pynisjɔ̃] **NF** punishment; **p. corporelle** corporal punishment; **donner une p. à un enfant** to punish a child; **en p. de qch** as (a) punishment for sth; **par** *ou* **pour p.** for punishment, by way of punishment, as a punishment

punk [pœnk] **ADJ INV** (*musique etc*) punk ▸ **N** punk

pupe [pyp] **NF 1** (*enveloppe*) pupa case **2** (*chrysalide*) pupa, chrysalis

pupillaire¹ [pypilɛr] **ADJ** *Jur* pertaining to a ward, *Spéc* pupil(l)ary

pupillaire² [pypilɛr] **ADJ** *Anat* (*membrane etc*) pupil(l)ary

pupillarité [pypilarite] **NF** *Jur* wardship, *Spéc* pupil(l)age

pupille¹ [pypil, -ij] **N** *Jur* ward; **pupilles de la Marine/de l'Air** = children whose fathers have died while serving in the Navy/Air Force; **p. de l'État** child in (state) care; **pupilles de la Nation** war orphans

pupille² **NF** *Anat* (*de l'œil*) pupil

pupillomètre [pypijɔmɛtr] **NM** pupillometer

pupitre [pypitr] NM **1** *(d'écolier etc)* desk; *(d'où s'adresse un orateur)* lectern; **p. à musique** music stand **2** *Mus (d'instruments)* group; **chef de p.** front desk player **3** *TV, Radio* console; **p. de mixage** mixing desk; **p. de mélange vidéo** switcher; **p. de régie** studio control console, studio desk, control board; **p. son** audio (control) console **4** *Ordinat* **p. (de commande)** console (desk); **p. de visualisation** visual display unit

pupitreur, -euse [pypitrœr, -øz] N *Ordinat* console operator

pur, pure [pyr] ADJ **1** *(pas mélangé)* (or, laine, jus de fruits, style etc) pure; *(air)* clean, pure; *(ciel)* clear; *(whisky, gin etc)* straight, neat; **un peu d'air p. nous fera du bien** a bit of fresh air will do us good; **elle boit son whisky p.** she drinks her whisky straight *or* neat; **de l'eau de Javel pure** undiluted bleach; **liquide p. de tout mélange** liquid free from all admixture; **biscuits p. beurre** all-butter biscuits; **elle parle un italien très p.** her Italian is very pure; **cheval p. sang** thoroughbred horse; **c'est un p. produit de mai 68/du catholicisme** he's a true child of May 68/of the Catholic church; **être un p. produit de la bourgeoisie** to be middle-class through and through, to be a hundred per cent middle-class; **un p. produit du féminisme** a one hundred per cent red-blooded feminist; **c'est un p. produit de Polytechnique** he's a typical Polytechnique graduate

2 *(total)* pure; **p. hasard** pure chance, mere chance; **c'est un p. hasard qu'il se soit trouvé là** it was pure *or* sheer chance that he was there; **par p. hasard, il y avait un médecin dans le car** by sheer chance there was a doctor on the bus; **la pure vérité** the simple *or* plain *or* honest *or* unvarnished truth; **la vérité pure et simple** the plain and simple truth; **c'est de la folie pure (et simple)** it's sheer madness, it's pure folly; **un socialiste/trotskiste p. et dur** a hard-line Socialist/Trotskyist; **un bouddhiste p. et dur** a strict Buddhist; **c'est un Breton p. et dur** he's extremely proud of being a Breton; **l'invitation est de pure forme** the invitation is purely for form's sake; **par pure malice** out of pure *or* sheer malice; **travailler en pure perte** to work for nothing *or* to no purpose; **elle l'a fait en pure perte** she did it all for nothing, it was a sheer waste of her time

3 *Fig (moralement)* pure; *(esthétiquement)* *(lignes)* pure, clean, clean-cut; *(visage)* clean-cut; **conscience pure** clear conscience; **p. d'esprit** pure-minded

4 *(théorique)* *(science, mathématiques etc)* pure

N *Pol etc* diehard

purée [pyre] NF *Culin* purée; **p. (de pommes de terre)** mashed *or* creamed potato(es), *Br Fam* mash; **p. de carottes** puréed carrots; **p. de pois** thick pea soup; *Fam (brouillard)* peasouper; *Fam* **être dans la p.** *(dans la gêne financière)* to be hard up, to be down on one's luck; *(dans une situation difficile)* to be up the creek

INT *Fam (colère etc)* hell!, blast (it)!; *(surprise)* wow!

purement [pyrmɑ̃] ADV purely

pureté [pyrte] NF purity; *(du ciel)* clearness; *(de lignes)* purity, cleanness

purgatif, -ive [pyrgatif, -iv] *Méd* ADJ purgative

NM purgative, purge

purgation [pyrgasjɔ̃] NF *Méd* purging

purgatoire [pyrgatwar] NM *Rel* purgatory

purge [pyrʒ] NF **1** *Méd* purge, purgative **2** *Pol* purge **3** *(d'un liquide)* draining; *Aut (des freins)* bleeding; **robinet de p.** drain *or* bleed cock; *Aut* **p. de carburant** fuel bleed; **vis de p.** bleed screw **4** *Jur (d'une hypothèque)* redemption, paying off

purgeoir [pyrʒwar] NM *(d'une réserve d'eau etc)* purifying tank, filtering tank

purger [pyrʒe] (je purgeai(s); n. purgeons) VT **1** *Méd* to purge; **p. les intestins** to clean out *or* cleanse *or* purge the system; *Fig* **p. un pays de voleurs** to rid *or* purge a country of bandits; **p. une société des fainéants** to get rid of the shirkers in a company **2** *Jur (hypothèque)* to redeem, to pay off; *(dettes)* to pay off, to clear; **p. sa peine** to serve one's sentence **3** *Tech (freins)* to bleed; *(radiateur)* to bleed, to drain

VPR **se purger 1** *Méd* to take a purgative *or* a laxative **2** *Fig* **se p. d'une accusation** to clear oneself of an accusation

purgeur [pyrʒœr] NM *Tech* drain cock, bleed cock; *Aut* bleeder valve

purifiant [pyrifjɑ̃] ADJ purifying, cleansing

purificateur, -trice [pyrifikatœr, -tris] ADJ purifying, cleansing

NM purifier, cleanser; **p. d'air** *ou* **d'atmosphère** air purifier

purification [pyrifikasjɔ̃] NF purification; *(de métaux)* refining; *(du sang)* cleansing; **p. ethnique** ethnic cleansing

purifier [pyrifje] (*pr sub, impf n.* purifiions, *v.* purifiiez) VT *aussi Fig* to purify, to cleanse; *(langue)* to purify; *(métal)* to refine; *(sang)* to cleanse; **lotion qui purifie la peau** skin cleanser

VPR **se purifier** to become pure, to be purified

purin [pyrɛ̃] NM *Agr* slurry, liquid manure

purisme [pyrism] NM *(du langage etc)* purism

puriste [pyrist] N purist

puritain, -aine [pyritɛ̃, -ɛn] N puritan; *Hist* Puritan

ADJ puritan(ical); *Hist* Puritan

puritanisme [pyritanism] NM puritanism

purotin [pyrɔtɛ̃] NM *Arg Vieilli* down-and-out

purpura [pyrpyra] NM *Méd* purpura

purpurin [pyrpyrɛ̃] ADJ *Litt* deep crimson

pur-sang NM INV thoroughbred (horse)

purulence [pyrylɑ̃s] NF *Méd* purulence

purulent [pyrylɑ̃] ADJ *Méd* suppurating, *Spéc* purulent; **foyer p.** abscess

pus [py] NM *Méd* pus, matter

push-pull [puʃpul] NM INV, ADJ INV *Élec* push-pull

pusillanime [pyzilanim] ADJ *Litt* pusillanimous, faint-hearted

pusillanimité [pyzilanimite] NF *Litt* pusillanimity, faint-heartedness

pustule [pystyl] NF blister, pustule; *(de crapauds)* wart

pustuleux, -euse [pystylø, -øz] ADJ pus-filled, pustulous

put [put] NM *Bourse* put (option)

putain [pytɛ̃] *Arg Vulg* NF **1** prostitute, whore, *Am* hooker; **faire la p.** *(se prostituer)* to prostitute oneself; *Fig (chercher à plaire)* to prostitute oneself; *(renoncer à ses principes)* to sell out **2** **cette p. de guerre/machine** this bloody *or Vulg* fucking war/machine

INT *(colère etc)* shit!; *(surprise)* Christ!

putassier, -ière [pytasje, -jɛr] ADJ *Vulg* **a** *(tenue, manières)* tarty **2** *(servile, obséquieux)* ingratiating

putatif, -ive [pytatif, -iv] ADJ putative, supposed, presumed

pute [pyt] NF *Arg Vulg* = **putain** NF **1**; **la p.!** *(elle m'a menti etc)* the bitch!; **fils de p.!** bastard!, son of a bitch!

putois [pytwa] NM *(animal)* polecat; *(fourrure)* polecat (fur); **p. (d'Amérique)** skunk; *Fam* **crier comme un p.** to scream blue murder

putréfaction [pytrefaksjɔ̃] NF putrefaction; **matière en p.** putrefying matter

putréfier [pytrefje] VT to putrefy, to rot

VPR **se putréfier** to putrefy, to become putrid

putrescence [pytresɑ̃s] NF putrescence

putrescent [pytresɑ̃] ADJ putrescent

putrescible [pytresibl] ADJ liable to putrefy

putride [pytrid] ADJ putrid

putridité [pytridite] NF *Litt* putridness

putsch [putʃ] NM *Pol* putsch

putschiste [putʃist] *Pol* ADJ putsch

NM person involved in a putsch, putschist

puzzle [pœzl] NM (jigsaw) puzzle; *Fig* puzzle; *Fig* **le p. commence à prendre forme dans son esprit** the pieces of the puzzle are beginning to fall into place

PV [peve] NM *Fam (abrév* procès-verbal*)* (parking) ticket; **j'ai eu un P. ce matin** I got a ticket this morning

PVC [pevese] NM *Tech (abrév* polyvinyl chloride*)* PVC; **siège en P.** PVC seat

PVD [pevede] NM *(abrév* pays en voie de développement*)* developing country

pygmée [pigme] N pygmy, pigmy

pyjama [piʒama] NM pyjamas, *Am* pajamas; **un p.** a pair of pyjamas; **elle était encore en p.** she was still in her pyjamas; **c'est un vrai p.** *(ce vêtement)* it's loose and comfortable; **j'y suis comme dans un p.** it's really comfortable VOIR GRAMMAIRE A10

pylône [pilon] NM **1** *Élec* pylon; *(pour fils télégraphiques)* lattice mast; **p. électrique** electricity pylon; **grue à p.** tower crane **2** *Archit (de temples égyptiens)* pylon

pylore [pilɔr] NM *Anat* pylorus

pyorrhée [pjɔre] NF *Méd* pyorrhoea, *Am* pyorrhea

pyramidal, -ale, -aux, -ales [piramidal, -o] ADJ pyramidal

pyramide [piramid] NF pyramid; **p. des âges** age pyramid; **p. des salaires** wage pyramid; **entasser des oranges en p.** to pile up oranges in a pyramid; **structure en p.** pyramid-like *or* pyramidal structure

pyrénéen, -enne [pireneɛ̃, -ɛn] ADJ Pyrenean

N **P.** Pyrenean

Pyrénées (les) [lepirene] NFPL the Pyrenees

pyrèthre [piretr] NM *(plante)* feverfew, pyrethrum; **poudre de p.** insect powder

Pyrex® [pireks] NM Pyrex®; **plat en P.** Pyrex® dish; **c'est du P., ton plat?** is your dish (made of) Pyrex®?

pyrexie [pireksi] NF *Méd* pyrexia, fever

pyrite [pirit] NF *Minér* pyrites

pyrograveur, -euse [pirogravœr, -øz] N *Beaux-Arts* pyrographer

pyrogravure [pirogravyr] NF *Beaux-Arts* poker work, pyrography; *(gravure)* pyrograph

pyrolyse [pirɔliz] NF pyrolysis; **four à p.** self-cleaning oven

pyromane [pirɔman] N *Psy* pyromaniac; *Jur (incendiaire)* arsonist

pyromanie [pirɔmani] NF *Psy* pyromania

pyromètre [pirɔmɛtr] NM *Phys, Tech* pyrometer

pyrosis [pirɔzis] NM *Méd* heartburn, *Spéc* pyrosis

pyrotechnie [pirɔtɛkni] NF pyrotechnics

pyrotechnique [piroteknik] ADJ pyro-technic(al)

Pythagore [pitagɔr] N Pythagoras; **théorème de P.** Pythagoras' theorem

pythagoricien, -ienne [pitagɔrisjɛ̃, -jɛn] *Phil* ADJ Pythagorean
N P. Pythagorean

pythagorisme [pitagɔrism] NM *Phil*

Pythagoreanism

Pythie [piti] NF **1** *Myth* P. de Delphes Pythia of Delphi **2** *Litt* prophetess, oracle

python [pitɔ̃] NM python

Q, q [ky] NM *(lettre)* Q, q

Qatar [katar] NM Qatar

QCM [kyseεm] NM INV *(abrév* **questionnaire à choix multiple)** multiple-choice question-naire

QG [kyʒe] NM INV *Mil Fam (abrév* **quartier gé-néral)** HQ

QI [kyi] NM INV *(abrév* **quotient intellectuel)** IQ

quad [kwad] NM **1** *(moto)* quad bike **2** *(patin à roulettes)* quad (roller) skate

quadra [kwadra] N *Fam* = **quadragénaire**

quadragénaire [kwadraʒenɛr] ADJ, N forty-year-old, quadragenarian; **elle est q.** she's in her forties

Quadragésime [kwadraʒezim] NF *Rel* **(le di-manche de) la Q.** Quadragesima (Sunday)

quadrangulaire [kwadrãgyler] ADJ qua-drangular, four-angled; *(bâtiment)* four-cornered, four-sided

quadrant [k(w)adrã] NM *Géom* quadrant

quadratique [kwadratik] ADJ **1** *Math* qua-dratic **2** *Minér* quadratic, tetragonal

quadrature [kwadratyr] NF **1** *Géom* quadra-ture, squaring; *Fig* **c'est la q. du cercle** it's like trying to square the circle **2** *Astron, Phys* quadrature; **marées de q.** neap tides, neaps

quadriceps [kwadrisɛps] NM *Anat* quadri-ceps

quadrichromie [kwadrikrɔmi, kadrikromi] NF four-colour processing *or* printing

quadriennal, -ale, -aux, -ales [kwadri-jenal, -o] ADJ *(plan, période)* quadrennial, four-year; **les Jeux olympiques sont qua-driennaux** the Olympic Games take place every four years

quadrifolié [kwadrifɔlje] ADJ *Bot* four-leaved, quadrifoliate

quadrijumeaux [kwadriʒymo] NMPL quad-ruplets

quadrilatère [k(w)adrilatɛr] NM *Géom, Mil etc* quadrilateral

quadrillage [kadrijaʒ] NM **1** *(action) (d'un papier, d'une carte)* ruling in squares, cross-ruling; **la police a établi un q. du quartier** the police have the district under tight sur-veillance **2** *(motif)* squares; *(sur une carte)* grid

quadrille [kadrij] NM quadrille; **q. des lan-ciers** lancers

quadrillé [kadrije] ADJ *(papier)* squared, cross-ruled; **carte quadrillée** grid map

quadriller [kadrije] VT **1** *(papier)* to rule in squares, to cross-rule; **le quartier est qua-drillé par un réseau de ruelles** the district is criss-crossed by a network of alleys **2** *(quar-tier)* to put under tight surveillance; **tout le quartier est quadrillé** the whole district is under tight surveillance

quadrimoteur [k(w)adrimɔtœr] ADJ, NM *(avion)* **q.** four-engined plane

quadriparti [kwadriparti], **quadripartite** [kwadripartit] ADJ *(corolle, traité)* quadripar-tite; *(conférence, commission) (de partis)* four-party; *(de pays)* four-power

quadriphonie [kwadrifoni] NF quadraphony

quadriplégie [kwadriplezi] NF *Méd* quadriplegia

quadriréacteur [k(w)adrireaktœr] NM *Aviat* four-engined jet

quadrisyllabe [kwadrisilab] NM quadri-syllable

quadrisyllabique [kwadrisilabik] ADJ quadrisyllabic

quadrumane [k(w)adryman] *Zool* ADJ *(ani-mal)* quadrumanous, four-handed
NM quadrumane

quadrupède [k(w)adrypɛd] *Zool* ADJ *(ani-mal)* quadruped, four-footed
NM quadruped

quadruple [k(w)adrypl] ADJ quadruple, fourfold
NM quadruple; **au q.** fourfold; **payer le q. du prix** to pay four times the price; **elle gagne le q. de ce que je gagne** she earns four times as much as I do

quadrupler [k(w)adryple] VTI to quadruple, to increase fourfold

quadruplés, -ées [k(w)adryple] NPL qua-druplets, *Fam* quads

quai [kɛ] NM **1** *Naut* quay; *(d'embarquement, de débarquement)* wharf; *(construit au-dessus de l'eau)* pier; **amener un navire à q.** to bring a ship alongside, to berth a ship; **se mettre à q.** to berth; **navire à q.** berthed ship; **q. des pétroliers** oil wharf; **droits de q.** wharfage; *Com* **livrable à q.** *(marchandises)* ex-quay, ex-wharf VOIR GRAMMAIRE A12 **2** *(le long d'une rivière, d'un fleuve)* embankment **3** *Rail* platform; **accès aux quais** ≃ to the trains; **le train est à q.** the train is in
▸▸ **q. d'arrivée** *Naut* arrival quay; *Rail* arri-val platform; **q. de chargement** loading quay; *Naut* **q. de déchargement** unloading quay; **q. de départ** *Naut* departure quay; *Rail* departure platform; **le Q. des Orfèvres** Police Headquarters *(in Paris)*; **le Q. d'Orsay** the French Foreign Office

quaker, -eresse [kwɛkœr, -(ə)rɛs, kwa-] N Quaker, f Quakeress

quakerisme [kwɛkœrism, kwak(ə)rism] NM Quakerism

qualifiable [kalifjabl] ADJ *(que l'on peut qualifier)* definable; **sa conduite n'est pas q.** his/her behaviour is indescribable

qualificatif, -ive [kalifikatif, -iv] *Gram* ADJ *(adjectif etc)* qualifying
NM qualifier, modifier; *Fig* **il n'y a pas de q. assez fort pour la décrire** there's no word strong enough to describe her

qualification [kalifikasjɔ̃] NF **1** *(formation)* qualification; **q. professionnelle** profes-sional qualification **2** *Sport* qualification; **ob-tenir sa q.** to qualify; **obtenir sa q. pour la** *ou* **en finale** to qualify for the final; **match de q.** qualifying match; **il court les épreuves de q.** he's running in the heats; **leur q. est assurée** they are sure to qualify **3** *(nom)* designation, name; **s'attribuer la q. de colonel** to call one-self colonel; **elle n'est pas médecin spécia-liste, mais elle en a pris la q.** she's not a specialist doctor, but she's given herself that title **4** *Gram (d'un nom etc)* qualifying; *Jur (d'un crime etc)* legal definition **5** *Bourse* qualification *(by acquisition of shares)*

qualifié, -ée [kalifje] ADJ **1** *(compétent)* qualified; **q. pour faire qch** qualified to do sth; **je suis certainement q. pour en parler** I am certainly qualified to speak about it; **ou-vrier q./non q.** skilled/unskilled worker **2** *Jur (délit, vol)* aggravated **3** *Sport* **cheval/ coureur q.** qualifier; **équipe qualifiée** quali-fying team
N *Sport* qualifier

qualifier [kalifje] *(impf, pr sub* n. **quali-fiions)* VT **1 q. qn pour qch/pour faire qch** to qualify sb for sth/to do sth **2** *(appeler)* to describe; **q. qn/qch de ...** to call sb/sth ..., to describe sb/sth as ...; **q. qn de charlatan** to call sb a quack, to describe sb as a quack; **acte qualifié de crime** action termed a crime; **conduite qu'on ne saurait q.** unspeak-able behaviour **3** *Gram* to qualify
VPR **se qualifier 1** *Sport* to qualify; **il s'est qualifié pour la finale** he qualified for *or* got through to the final **2 se q. de génie/d'ar-tiste/etc** to call oneself a genius/an artist/ *etc*

qualitatif, -ive [kalitatif, -iv] ADJ qualita-tive; *Chimie* **analyse qualitative** qualitative analysis

qualité [kalite] NF **1** *(de produit etc)* quality; **bonne/mauvaise q.** good *or* high/bad *or* poor quality; **produit de (bonne) q.** (good-) quality product; **produit de mauvaise q.** poor-quality product, product of poor qua-lity; **de première q.** top-quality; **blé/viande de première q.** prime wheat/meat; **vin de première q.** choice wine; **chocolat de q. su-périeure** extra fine chocolate; **minerai de q. inférieure** low-grade ore; *Ordinat* **q. brouil-lon, q. liste rapide, q. listing** draft quality; *Ordinat* **q. courrier** (near) letter quality; **ga-rantie de q.** guarantee of quality; **améliorer la q. de la vie** to improve the quality of life; **q. de l'environnement** quality of the environ-ment; *Ordinat* **q. d'impression** print quality **2** *(de personne)* quality; **homme qui a beau-coup de qualités** man with many good qua-lities *or* points; **qualités de gestionnaire** management *or* managerial qualities; **elle n'a pas que des qualités** she isn't all good; **cet ordinateur a beaucoup de qualités** this computer has many good points; **les quali-**

tés littéraires d'un texte the literary qualities of a text **3** *(propriété)* quality, property; **c'est une des qualités de cette plante** it's one of the properties of this plant; **qualités fébrifuges** antifebrile properties **4** *(occupation)* occupation; *(fonction)* capacity; **décliner ses titres et qualités** to state one's titles and qualifications; *Admin* **nom, prénom et q.** surname, forename and occupation; **il nous révéla sa q. de prêtre** he disclosed the fact that he was a priest; **agir en q. de tuteur** to act (in one's capacity) as guardian; **en (ma) q. de citoyen, je voudrais …** (in my capacity) as a citizen, I would like …; **ès qualités** in one's official capacity; **avoir q. pour agir** to have authority to act; **avoir les qualités requises pour un emploi** to have the necessary qualifications *or* to be qualified for a job **5** *Vieilli* **gens de q.** people of quality, gentlefolk

QUAND [kɑ̃]

CONJ when **1** ▪ even if *(quand bien même)* **2** ▪ anyway *(quand même)* **3** ▪ still *(quand même)* **3**
ADV when

CONJ 1 when; **je lui en parlerai q. je le verrai** I'll mention it to him when I see him; **q. je lui téléphone, elle est toujours pressée** when I ring her she's always in a hurry, whenever I ring her she's in a hurry; *Fam* **je me souviens de q. tu as commencé à travailler ici** I remember when you started working here; *Fam* **q. je pense que le voyage devait être annulé** when I think that they were going to cancel the trip; *Fam* **q. je vous le disais!** I told you so!, didn't I tell you so! SEE GRAMMAR B31–2 **2** *Litt* **q. (même), q. (bien même)** even if, even though; **q. (bien même) il me l'affirmerait, je n'en croirais rien** even if he assured me, I wouldn't believe it; **je n'en voudrais pas q. (bien) même on me le donnerait** I wouldn't have it (even) as a gift **3** *Fam* **je le ferai q. même** I'll do it anyway; **q. même, ça serait plus gentil d'aller la chercher à la gare** still *or* even so, it would be nicer to meet her at the station; **c'est q. même gentil de sa part** still *or* even so, it's nice of him; **tu aurais pu me dire q. même!** you might have told me!; **elle ne sait pas compter – q. même!** she can't count – come on! **ADV** when; **q. viendra-t-il?** when will he come?; **dites-moi q. il viendra** tell me when he will come; **n'importe q.** no matter when, at any time; **jusqu'à q. serez-vous à Paris?** how long will you be in Paris?; **depuis q. êtes-vous à Paris?** how long have you been in Paris?; **à q. le mariage?** when will the wedding be?, when is the wedding?; **de q. est ce journal?** what is the date of this paper?; **pour q. est la réunion?** when is the meeting?; *Fam* **c'est prévu pour q.?** when is this supposed to be happening?

quant à [kɑ̃ta] **PRÉP** as for; **q. moi** as for me, for my part, as far as I am concerned; **q. cela …** as for *or* to that …, as far as that is concerned …; **q. l'avenir …** as for *or* to the future …, as far as the future is concerned …; **s'inquiéter q. à l'avenir** to be worried about the future; **q. le demander, je n'y aurais pas songé** as for asking for it, I wouldn't have dreamt of it

quant-à-soi [kɑ̃taswa] **NM INV** reserve; **rester sur** *ou* **se tenir sur son q.** to keep oneself to oneself

quantième [kɑ̃tjɛm] **NM** *Litt* day of the month; **quel q. (du mois) sommes-nous?** what day of the month is it?, what is the date?

quantifiable [kwɑ̃tifjabl] **ADJ** quantifiable; **données non-quantifiables** unquantifiable data

quantification [kwɑ̃tifikasjɔ̃] **NF** *Phil* quantification; *Phys* quantization

quantifier [kɑ̃tifje] **VT** to quantify; *Phys* to quantize

quantique [kɑ̃tik] **ADJ** *Phys etc (théorie, mécanique, nombre etc)* quantum

quantitatif, -ive [kɑ̃titatif, -iv] **ADJ** *(analyse, changement etc)* quantitative

quantitativement [kɑ̃titativmɑ̃] **ADV** quantitatively

quantité [kɑ̃tite] **NF 1** *(somme, dose)* quantity, amount; **en grande/petite q.** in large/small quantities *or* amounts; **dans la q. prescrite** in the prescribed dose; **en q.** in quantity; **nous en avons en q.** we have plenty of them; **q.** *ou* **des quantités de gens/réponses** a lot of *or* a great number of *or* a great many people/replies; **il n'en reste pas des quantités** there are not a lot left; **q. négligeable** negligible quantity *or* amount; *Fam* **il faut la considérer comme q. négligeable** what she thinks is of no consequence, her opinion is neither here nor there SEE GRAMMAR B59–60 **2** *Phys etc* quantity; *Math* **q. variable** variable quantity; *Phys* **q. de mouvement** momentum, impulse

quantum, *pl* **quanta** [k(w)ɑ̃tɔm, -a] **NM 1** *Phys* quantum; **théorie des quanta** quantum theory **2** *(quantité)* amount; **fixer le q. des dommages-intérêts** to fix the amount of damages, to assess the damages

quarantaine [karɑ̃tɛn] **NF 1** *(environ quarante)* about forty, forty or so; **une q. de personnes/jours** about forty *or* forty or so people/days **2** *(âge)* about forty, forty or so; **approcher de la q.** to be getting on for forty, to be almost forty; **avoir la q.** to be in one's forties; **elle doit avoir une petite q. d'années** she must be just over forty; **les problèmes typiques de la q.** the typical problems of the fortysomething generation **3** *(isolement)* quarantine; **pavillon de q.** quarantine flag; **mettre un navire en q.** to quarantine a ship, to put a ship in quarantine; **mettre qn en q.** to quarantine sb, to put sb in quarantine; *Fig Fam* to send sb to Coventry; **être en q.** to be in quarantine **4** *Ordinat* **mettre un fichier en q.** to quarantine a file

quarante [karɑ̃t] **ADJ INV, NM INV** forty; **page q.** page forty; **habiter au (numéro) q.** to live at number forty; **la semaine de q. heures** the forty-hour week; *Fam* **je m'en fiche comme de l'an q.** I couldn't care less, I don't give a damn; *Tennis* **q. à** *ou* **partout** deuce; **les années q.** the forties; **les Q.** the Académie française

quarante-cinq **ADJ INV q. tours** *(disque)* single, 45

quarantenaire [karɑ̃tnɛr] **ADJ 1** *(régulations etc)* quarantine **2** *Jur* forty-year, lasting for forty years

quarantième [karɑ̃tjɛm] **ADJ, N** fortieth

quark [kwark] **NM** quark

quart¹ [kar] **ADJ le q.-monde** *(pays)* the Fourth World; *(pauvres des pays riches)* the underclass *(of a developed country)*

quart² **NM 1** *(fraction)* quarter; **donner un q. de tour à une vis** to give a screw a quarter turn; **partir au q. de tour** *(d'une voiture)* to start first time; *Fig (d'une personne)* to fly off the handle; **il est parti** *ou* **a démarré au q. de tour** *(d'un moteur)* it started first time *or* right away; *Fam (d'un débat etc)* it got off to a great start, it took off right away; *Fam* **il est parti au q. de tour** he hit the roof, he blew up; *Fam* **il part au q. de tour** *(il est coléreux)* he's got a short fuse; *Fam* **elle a compris au q. de tour** she understood straight off *or* right

away; *Com* **remise du q.** 25% discount, discount of 25%; **un q. de siècle** a quarter (of a) century, twenty-five years; **un q. d'heure** a quarter of an hour; **dans un petit q. d'heure** in ten minutes or so; *Fam* **passer un mauvais q. d'heure** to have a bad time of it; **je vais lui faire passer un mauvais q. d'heure** I'm going to give him a bad time; **un q. de beurre** a quarter (of a) kilo of butter; **trois quarts** three quarters; **la mode du trois quarts** the fashion for three-quarter-length skirts and coats; **manteau trois quarts** three-quarter-length coat; *Fam* **les trois quarts du temps** most of the time; *Fam* **être aux trois quarts ivre/mort** to be three parts drunk/all but *or* as good as dead; *Fam* **elle était décidée aux trois quarts** she had all but *or* as good as decided; **il est deux heures et q.** *ou* **deux heures un q.** it's (a) quarter past *or Am* after two; **six heures moins le q., cinq heures trois quarts** (a) quarter to *or Am* of six **2** *(bouteille, pichet)* quarter litre *or Am* liter; *Mil (gobelet)* quarter litre *or Am* liter mug **3** *Naut* **q. (de vent)** point of the compass; **nord-est q. est** north-east by east **4** *Naut (veille)* watch; **officier de q.** officer of the watch; **homme de q.** watch keeper; **être de q.** to be on watch; **faire le q.** to keep watch; *Fam (d'une prostituée)* to walk her beat **5** *Arg (poste de police)* cop shop, police station
▸▸ *Fam* **q. de brie** *(nez)* beak, *Br* conk, hooter; **q. de cercle** quadrant; *Sport* **q. de finale** quarter final; **l'équipe va jouer en q. de finale** the team will play in the quarter final; *Mus* **q. de soupir** semiquaver *or Am* sixteenth rest

quarte [kart] **NF 1** *Mus* fourth **2** *Escrime* quarte, quart, carte; **parer en q.** to parry in carte

quarté [karte] **NM** = system of betting on four horses in the same race

quarteron, -onne [kart(ə)rɔ̃, -ɔn] **N** *(métis)* quadroon
NM *(petit nombre)* bunch; **un q. de manifestants** a bunch of demonstrators

quartette [kwartɛt] **NM** jazz quartet

quartier [kartje] **NM 1** *(quart)* quarter, *Fml* fourth part; **bois de q.** quartered logs; **la lune est au premier q.** the moon is in the first quarter; *Culin* **q. d'agneau/de bœuf** quarter of lamb/of beef; **cinquième q.** offal; *Hér* **quartiers de l'écusson** quarters *or* quarterings of the shield; **avoir quatre quartiers de noblesse** to belong to the established nobility **2** *(morceau) (d'un gâteau)* portion; *(d'une orange)* segment; *(d'une pomme)* piece; *(d'une terre)* plot; **q. de lard** side of bacon; **q. de chevreuil** haunch of venison **3** *(d'une ville)* district, area, neighbourhood, *Am* neighborhood; *Admin* district; **les beaux quartiers** the fashionable districts *or* areas; **les quartiers nord de la ville** the north side of (the) town; **q. des spectacles** theatreland, the theatre district; **je ne suis pas du q.** I'm not from around here, I'm not local; **demandez aux gens du q.** ask the locals *or* the local people; **médecin/cinéma de q.** local doctor/cinema *or Am* movie theater; **tout le q. en parle** the whole neighbourhood is talking about it **4** *Mil* **quartier(s)** quarters; **rentrer au q.** *ou* **aux quartiers** to return to quarters; **avoir q. libre** to be off duty; *Fig* **vous avez q. libre jusqu'à dix-huit heures** you're free until six o'clock, take a break until six o'clock, your time's your own till six o'clock; **quartiers d'hiver** winter quarters; *Fig* **un endroit idéal pour prendre nos quartiers d'hiver** an ideal place to spend the winter **5** *Vieilli* **demander q.** to ask for quarter;

faire q. à qn to give sb quarter; **ne pas faire de q.** to give no quarter; **pas de q.!** no quarter!; **il ne fait de q. à personne** he spares nobody
▸▸ **q. général** headquarters VOIR GRAMMAIRE A13 ; **grand q. général** general headquarters; **q. de haute sécurité** *(dans une prison)* top- *or* maximum-security wing; **q. réservé** red-light district

quartier-maître, *pl* **quartiers-maîtres NM** *Naut* leading seaman

quartile [kwartil] **NM** quartile

quartz [kwarts] **NM** *Minér, Électron* quartz; **piloté par q.** crystal-controlled; **horloge/montre à q.** quartz clock/watch

quartzeux, -euse [kwartsø, -øz] **ADJ** *Minér* **sable q.** quartz sand

quartzite [kwartsit] **NM** *Minér* quartzite

quasar [kazar] **NM** *Astron* quasar

quasi¹ [kazi] **NM** *Culin (de veau, de bœuf)* chump end

quasi² **ADV** almost, virtually; **q. aveugle** almost *or* virtually blind; **j'en ai la q.-certitude** I am practically *or* virtually certain of it; **une q.-collision** a near miss; **la q.-totalité du budget** almost the whole *or* entire budget; **la q.-totalité des femmes** almost all (the) women; **une q.-dispute/un q.-divorce** a sort of argument/divorce; *Jur* **q.-contrat** implied contract; **q.-délit** technical offence

quasiment [kazimã] **ADV** almost, nearly, as good as; **q. guéri** almost *or* nearly *or* as good as cured; **je n'ai q. rien senti** I hardly *or* barely *or* scarcely felt a thing

Quasimodo [kazimɔdo] **NF** *Rel* Low Sunday; **le lundi de (la) Q.** Low Monday

quaternaire [kwatɛrnɛr] **ADJ** *Chimie etc* quaternary; *Géol* Quaternary
NM Quaternary

quatorze [katɔrz] **ADJ INV, NM INV** fourteen; **le q. juillet** the fourteenth of July, Bastille Day; **page q.** page fourteen; **Louis Q.** Louis the Fourteenth; **habiter au (numéro) q.** to live at number fourteen; **la guerre de q.** the First World War, World War I, the 1914-18 War

quatorzième [katɔrzjɛm] **ADJ, N** fourteenth
NM *(fraction)* fourteenth

quatorzièmement [katɔrzjɛmmã] **ADV** in the fourteenth place, fourteenthly

quatrain [katrɛ̃] **NM** *Littér* quatrain

quatre [katr] **ADJ INV 1** four; **à q. heures** at four o'clock; *Fam* **ton q. heures** your afternoon snack; **trèfle à q. feuilles** four-leaf(ed) clover; **q. barré** *(à l'aviron)* coxed four; **par q.** in fours; **se mettre par q.** to get into *or* form fours; **manger comme q.** to eat like a horse; **monter l'escalier q. à q.** to go upstairs four at a time, to rush upstairs; *Sport Fam* **il est arrivé q. ou cinquième** he came in fourth or fifth; *Fig* **se mettre** *ou* **se couper en q. pour faire qch** to do one's utmost to do sth; *Fig* **clair comme deux et deux font q.** as clear as daylight *or* crystal; *Fig* **je me tenais à q. pour ne pas rire** it was all I could do not to laugh; *Fig* **plié en q.** doubled up with laughter; *Fig* **pull/livre de q. sous** cheap *or* inexpensive sweater/book; *Fig* **il a fait les q. cents coups dans sa jeunesse** he sowed his wild oats when he was young; *Fig* **les q. coins du monde** the four corners of the world; **il n'y est pas allé par q. chemins** he came straight to the point *or* he didn't beat about the bush; **être tiré à q. épingles** to be dressed to the nines; *Fam* **un de ces q.** one of these days; **dire ses q. vérités à qn** to tell sb a few home truths; *Mus* **jouer à q. mains** to play a duet; **se mettre à q. pattes** to go down on all fours **2** *(dans des séries)* fourth; **page/numéro q.** page/number four; **Henri Q.** Henry the Fourth
NM INV four; **le q. août** (on) the fourth of Au-

gust, (on) August the fourth, *Am* (on) August fourth; *Cartes* **q. de carreau** four of diamonds; **j'habite au q.** I live at number four

Quatre-Cantons [katr(ə)kãtɔ̃] **NMPL le lac des Q.** Lake Lucerne

quatre-cent-vingt-et-un [katsãvɛ̃teœ̃] **NM INV** = dice game in which the aim is to throw 4-2-1

quatre-mâts [katrəmɑ] **NM INV** *Naut* four-masted ship, four master

quatre-quarts [kat(rə)kar] **NM INV** *Culin* ≃ pound cake

quatre-quatre [katkatr] **NM OU NF INV** *Aut* four-wheel drive

quatre-saisons [kat(rə)sɛzɔ̃] **NFPL marchand des q.** street merchant *(selling fresh fruit and vegetables)*, *Br Vieilli* costermonger
NF INV *(fraise)* perpetual-fruiting strawberry

Quatre-Temps [katrətã] **NMPL** *Rel* Ember days

quatre-vingt-dix [katrəvɛ̃dis] **ADJ INV, NM INV** ninety

quatre-vingt-dixième [katrəvɛ̃dizjɛm] **ADJ, N** ninetieth

quatre-vingtième [katrəvɛ̃tjɛm] **ADJ, N** eightieth

quatre-vingts [katrəvɛ̃] **ADJ, NM INV** *(omits the final s when followed by another number or when used as an ordinal)* eighty; **ils étaient q.** there were eighty of them; **page quatre-vingt** page eighty; **quatre-vingt-un** eighty-one; **quatre-vingt-onze** ninety-one; **ça fait q.** that comes to eighty; **habiter au (numéro) quatre-vingt** to live at number eighty; **les années q.** the eighties

quatrième [katrijɛm] **ADJ** fourth; **habiter au q. étage** to live on the fourth *or Am* the fifth floor; **le q. âge** *(personnes)* the over-75s; *(état)* life after the age of 75
NF 1 *Cartes* sequence of four; **q. de couverture** *(d'un livre)* outside back cover **2** *Scol* **(classe de) q.** *Br* ≃ third form, *Am* ≃ seventh or eighth grade
NM monter au q. to go up to the fourth *or Am* fifth floor

quatrièmement [katrijɛmmã] **ADV** fourthly, in the fourth place

quattrocento [kwatrɔtʃɛnto] **NM** *Beaux-Arts* quattrocento

quatuor [kwatɥɔr] **NM** *Mus* quartet, quartette; **q. à cordes** string quartet

quat'zyeux [katzjø] *Fam* **entre q.** in private

QUE [k(ə)] **PRON REL 1** *(souvent omis en anglais) (personne)* that, *Fml* whom; *(chose)* that, which; **l'homme q. vous voyez** the man (that) you see, *Fml* the man whom you see; **montrez-moi les livres q. vous avez achetés** show me the books (that *or* which) you have bought; **la tarte q. j'ai fait cuire** the tart (that) I baked; **c'est le meilleur q. nous ayons** it is the best (that) we have; **il n'est venu personne q. je connaisse** no one I know has come; **il faut attendre le temps qu'elle se prépare** you'll need to wait till she's ready SEE GRAMMAR A32–3; B22

2 *(attribut)* **il mourut en brave soldat qu'il était** he died like the gallant soldier he was; **idiot q. je suis** fool that I am; **menteur q. tu es!** you liar!; **couvert qu'il était de poussière** covered with dust as he was; **purs mensonges q. tout cela!** that's all a pack of lies!; **le garçon/livre q. voilà** that boy/book (there); **c'est une théorie intéressante q. la vôtre** yours is an interesting theory

3 *(de temps)* **depuis trois mois q. j'habite Paris** for the three months I have been living in Paris; **un jour q. j'étais de service** one day when I was on duty; **il y a trois jours q. je ne l'ai vue** it's been three days since I saw her; *Vieilli* **les jours qu'il fait chaud** on hot days;

Vieilli **du temps q. les automobiles n'existaient pas** (in the time) before cars existed; *Vieilli* **les trois ans q. j'ai habité à Paris** the three years (during which) I lived in Paris
PRON INTERR what; **q. voulez-vous?** what do you want?; **q. dit Jean?** what does Jean say?; **qu'y a-t-il à voir dans cette ville?** what is there to see in this town?; **q. faire?** what can I/we/one do?, what's to be done?; **q. dire?** what can/could I say?; **il ne savait q. penser** he didn't know what to think; **je n'ai q. faire de vos souhaits** you can keep your good wishes; **qu'en sait-elle?** what does she know (about it)?; **q. prendrez-vous, du lait ou de la crème?** what *or* which would you like, milk or cream?; **qu'est-il arrivé?, q. s'est-il passé?** what has happened?; *Litt* **qu'est-ce?** what is it?; *Litt* **q. ne le disiez-vous?** why didn't you say so? SEE GRAMMAR A31–2; B17

PRON EXCLAMATIF **qu'il est beau!** how handsome he is!; **q. c'est vrai!** how true!; **q. de déceptions!** what a lot of disappointments!

CONJ SEE GRAMMAR B58 **1** that *(souvent omis en anglais)*; **je vois qu'il se trompe** I see (that) he's mistaken; **je pense qu'il a raison** I think (that) he's right; **je ne doute pas qu'elle y consente** I have no doubt (that) she will consent; **je désire qu'il vienne** I want him to come; **j'ai peur qu'il ne vienne** I'm afraid he will come; **je pense q. non** I think not; **il faut qu'elle le fasse** she has to *or* must do it; **peut-être qu'il est venu ce matin** perhaps he came this morning, he may have come this morning; **c'est q. je ne savais pas q. ...** it's because I didn't know (that) ...; **l'ennui est q. je n'ai rien préparé pour lui** the trouble is (that) I haven't prepared anything for him

2 *(pour exprimer un souhait)* **qu'elle entre!** let her come in!; **q. Dieu lui pardonne!** (may) God forgive him!; **q. je vous y reprenne!** don't let me *or* just let me catch you at it again!

3 *(pour exprimer une hypothèse)* **q. la machine chauffe, et il y aura un accident** let the machine get hot and there will be an accident; **qu'il essaie encore une fois, et il ...!** just let him try again and he'll ...!

4 *(dans une alternative)* **qu'il pleuve ou qu'il fasse du vent** whether it rains or blows; **q. tu le veuilles ou non** whether you like it or not

5 *(reliant deux conditionnels)* **il l'affirmerait q. je ne le croirais pas** even if he said it was true, I would not believe it

6 *(équivalent de* où*)* *Litt* **il ne se passe jamais une année qu'il ne nous écrive** a year never goes by without his writing to us

7 *(équivalent de* afin que, alors que, avant que, depuis que, puisque, sans que, tant que, *etc)* approchez qu'on vous entende** come nearer so that we can hear you; *Litt* **ne partez pas q. je ne vous aie parlé** don't go before I have had a talk with you

8 *(pour ne pas répéter une autre conjonction)* **quand il entrera et qu'il vous trouvera ici** when he comes in and finds you here; **c'est pour quand tu iras mieux et q. tu voudras sortir** it's for when you're better and you want to go out; **quoiqu'il pleuve et qu'il fasse froid** although it is rainy and cold; **si on vient et qu'on veuille me consulter** if anyone comes and wants to consult me

9 *(dans les comparaisons)* **plus grand/moins rapide q. moi** taller/slower than me; **aussi grand q. moi** as tall as I (am) *or* me; **c'est moins bien q. l'année dernière** it's not as good as last year; **il y a plus de monde q. la semaine dernière** there are more people than last week; **tout autre q. moi** anyone but me; **un autre parapluie q. celui-là** another umbrella besides that one; **vous écrivez plus correctement q. vous (ne) parlez** you write more correctly than you speak; **il habite la même maison q. moi** he lives in the same house as I do *or* as me

10 ne ... q. only; **il n'est q. blessé** he is only wounded; **il n'a qu'une jambe** he has only one leg, he only has one leg; **il n'a fait qu'entrer et sortir** he just slipped in and out again; **je ne fais q. passer** I'm not stopping, I won't stay; **elle ne fait q. (de) sortir** she has only just gone out; **je n'en ai q. trop** I have all too many; **je ne le connais q. trop** I know him only or all too well; **il n'y a pas qu'elle qui le sache** she is not the only one who knows it; **l'homme ne vit pas q. de pain** man does not live by bread alone; **il ne me reste plus q. vingt euros** I have only twenty euros left; **je ne bois jamais q. de l'eau** I never drink anything but water, I only ever drink water SEE GRAMMAR A22; B62–3

11 Arch, Litt **q. si vous savez la vérité, il est de votre devoir de la révéler** if you know the truth, it is your duty to reveal it

12 Fam **ah! q. non!/q. si** ou **oui!** ah! surely not!/yes indeed!; **il va au cercle – qu'il dit!** he goes to the club – so he says!; **ton manteau est dans un état, q. c'est une horreur!** your coat is in a terrible state!

Québec [kebɛk] NM Géog Quebec

québécisme [kebesism] NM Ling = word or expression peculiar to Quebec French

québécitude [kebesityd] NF Quebec identity

québécois, -oise [kebekwa, -waz] ADJ (of or from) Quebec
  NM Ling Quebec French
  N **Q.** Quebec(k)er

QUEL, QUELLE [kɛl] ADJ INTERR (personne) which; (chose) which, what; **q. livre avez-vous pris?** which or what book did you take?; **q. homme?** which man?; **quelle réponse a-t-elle faite?** what was her reply?; **quelle heure est-il?** what time is it?, what's the time?; **dites-moi quelle heure il est** tell me the time, tell me what time it is; **q. genre d'homme est-ce?** what sort of a man is he?; **si tu savais à q. point il tient à cette montre** if you knew how fond he is of this watch; **de quels hommes parlez-vous?** which men are you talking about?; **à q. projet faites-vous référence?** which project are you referring to?; **quels sont ces messieurs?** who are these gentlemen?; **quels sont ces livres?** what are these books? SEE GRAMMAR A31–2; B16
  ADJ EXCLAMATIF **q. homme!** what a man!; **quelle surprise!** what a surprise!; **quelle bonté!** how kind!; **q. dommage que personne n'en ait rien su** what a shame no one knew anything about it; **quelle bêtise d'avoir oublié le tire-bouchon** how stupid to have forgotten the corkscrew SEE GRAMMAR A5; B17
  ADJ REL (personne) whoever; (chose) whatever; **q. que soit le résultat** whatever the result may be; **quelle que soit mon affection pour vous** however great my affection for you, much as I love you; **quels que soient ces hommes** whoever these men may be; **q. que soit l'endroit où ...** wherever ..., no matter where ...; **il l'a rendu tel q.** he gave it back the way (it was when) he got it; **mettez-moi à n'importe quelle table** put me at any table you like VOIR GRAMMAIRE A33
  PRON INTERR which (one); **de vous trois, q. est le plus rapide?** which (one) of you three is the fastest?

quelconque [kɛlkɔ̃k] ADJ **1** (n'importe lequel) any, some ... or other; **s'il y a un q. problème** if there is any problem (whatever); **si pour une raison q. tu ...** if for some reason or other or for any reason you ...; **je prends un prétexte q. pour sortir** I get on some pretext or other; **décrire un cercle passant par trois points quelconques** to describe a circle passing through any three points; **le projet peut échouer pour une raison q.** the plan

can fail for any (of a) number of reasons
  2 (insignifiant, médiocre) ordinary, mediocre; **parler de choses quelconques** to talk about one thing and another; **une femme très q.** a very nondescript or average sort of woman; (physiquement) a very plain-looking woman; **on ne peut pas lui donner un emploi q.** we can't give him an ordinary job or Fam any old job; **son travail est q.** his work isn't up to much; **un q. général Alain** some General Alain or other

QUELQUE [kɛlk(ə)] ADJ **1** some; **quelques** some, a few; **pendant q. temps** for some time; **si j'avais q. argent** if I had some money; **je ressentais q. inquiétude** I felt some or a slight uneasiness; **avec quelques amis** with some friends, with a few friends; **il y a quelques jours** a few days ago; **cent et quelques mètres** a hundred metres plus, a hundred metres and a bit; Fam **nous étions quarante et quelques** there were forty or so of us, there were rather more than forty of us SEE GRAMMAR A34–5; B15
  2 (correlative to qui, que + sub) **q. ambition qui l'agite** whatever ambition moves him; **quelques erreurs qu'elle ait commises** whatever mistakes she has made; **je vous interdis de sortir sous q. prétexte que ce soit** I forbid you to go out for any reason whatsoever; **tout traité de q. nature qu'il soit** every treaty, whatever its nature; **de q. côté que vous regardiez** whichever way you look
  3 (un) some; **avez-vous q. ami qui puisse vous aider?** have you some or a friend who can help you?
  ADV **1** (environ) some, about; **q. dix ans** some or about ten years; **les q. mille euros qu'il m'a prêtés** the thousand euros or so or thereabouts that he lent me
  2 (correlative to que + sub) **q. grandes que soient ses fautes** however great his faults (may be); **q. méchant qu'il fût** wicked as he was

quelque chose [kɛlkəʃoz] PRON INDÉF INV SEE GRAMMAR A34; B16 something; (dans les phrases interrogatives ou conditionnelles) (chose indéfinie) anything, something; (chose définie) something; **q. me dit qu'elle viendra** something tells me she will come; **avez-vous q. à dire?** do you have anything or something to say?; **est-ce que je peux te dire q.?** can I tell you something?; **si je te dis q., est-ce que tu promets de ne pas te mettre en colère?** if I tell you something, do you promise not to get angry?; **q. de nouveau/plus moderne** something new/more modern; **q. d'autre** something else; **tu veux q. à manger/boire?** would you like something to eat/drink?; **il y a q. entre eux** there's something between them; **il y est pour q.** he has something to do with it; **il se doute de q.** he suspects something; **cela m'a fait q.** it had an effect on me; **ça te ferait vraiment q. si je m'en allais?** would it really matter to you if I went away?; **c'est déjà q.** that's something (anyhow); Fam **il a q.** there's something the matter with him; Fam **ah mais c'est q., ça!** that's a bit much!; Fam **q. comme deux ans** something like two years; Fam **je lui ai offert un petit q.** (cadeau) I gave him a little something; Fam **il tenait q. comme cuite!** he was totally plastered!; Fam **il lui a passé un savon, q. de bien** he gave him an almighty telling-off

quelquefois [kɛlkəfwa] ADV sometimes, at times

quelque part [kɛlkəpar] ADV **1** somewhere; **on ira q. où tu n'es jamais allé** we'll go somewhere you've never been before; **cela doit bien venir de q.** it must come from somewhere; Euph **je lui ai donné un coup**

de pied q. I kicked him in an unmentionable part of his anatomy; **son contrat, il peut se le mettre q.** he can shove his contract you know where **2** Litt, Vieilli (correlative to que + sub) **q. qu'il fouillât** wherever he searched

quelqu'un, quelqu'une [kɛlkœ, kɛlkyn], pl **quelques-uns, -unes** [kɛlkəzœ, -yn] PRON INDÉF **quelques-uns, quelques-unes** some, a few; **quelques-uns des magasins** some or a few of the shops; **j'ai lu quelques-unes des lettres** I have read some or a few of the letters; **quelques-un(e)s d'entre nous** some or a few of us SEE GRAMMAR A34; B16
  NM someone, somebody; (dans les phrases interrogatives ou conditionnelles) anyone, anybody, someone, somebody; **q. me l'a dit** someone or somebody told me; **de la part de q. qui pense à vous** from someone or somebody who is thinking of you; **si q. vient** if anyone or anybody or someone or somebody comes; **q. de plus** someone or somebody extra; **q. de trop** one too many; **y a-t-il eu q. de blessé?** was anyone or anybody or someone or somebody hurt?; **il faudra q. d'assez fort** it will need someone or somebody fairly strong; **c'est q. de très généreux** he's a very generous person; **ce doit être q. d'important** he must be someone or somebody important, he must be an important person; Fam **ça intéresse q.?** anyone or anybody interested?; Fam **je veux vraiment devenir q.** I really want to <u>be</u> somebody; Fam **c'est q., tu sais!** (c'est un homme remarquable) he's quite something, you know!; Fam **on ne me parle pas comme ça! je suis q., moi, monsieur!** don't talk to me like that! I'm not just anybody, you know!

quémander [kemɑ̃de] VT **q. qch à qn** to beg for sth from sb
  VI to beg

quémandeur, -euse [kemɑ̃dœr, -øz] N Litt beggar

qu'en-dira-t-on [kɑ̃diratɔ̃] NM INV gossip, tittle-tattle; **se moquer du q.** not to care what people say; **par souci du q.** for fear of what people might say

quenelle [kənɛl] NF Culin quenelle

quenotte [kənɔt] NF Enf (dent) toothy-peg, tooth

quenouille [kənuj] NF **1** Tex distaff; Fig **tomber en q.** (d'une succession) to fall to the distaff side; (d'une entreprise, d'un projet etc) to fall to pieces **2** (d'un lit à baldaquin) bedpost

quéquette [kekɛt] NF Fam willy, Am peter

querelle [kərɛl] NF quarrel, dispute, Fam row; **chercher q. à qn** to try to pick a quarrel with sb; **avoir une q. avec qn** to have a quarrel or Fam a row with sb; **q. d'argent** quarrel over money; **querelles de famille** family squabbles
  ▸▸ **q. d'Allemand** quarrel over nothing; **q. d'amoureux** lovers' tiff; **q. de clocher** petty feud; **q. d'ivrognes** drunken brawl

quereller [kərele] VT Vieilli (quelqu'un) to scold
  VPR **se quereller** to quarrel (with each other); (d'amoureux) to have a tiff

querelleur, -euse [kərelœr, -øz] N quarreller
  ADJ quarrelsome

quérir [kerir] VT Vieilli, Litt (used only in the inf after **aller, venir, envoyer**) **aller q. qn/qch** to go and fetch sb/sth

qu'est-ce que [kɛskə] PRON INTERR what; **q. vous voulez?** what do you want?; **q. la grammaire?** what is grammar?; **q. c'est que ça?** what's that?; **q. c'est que ce petit garçon qui ne veut pas se coucher?** what's all this about some little boy not wanting to go to bed?; Fam **q. tu avais besoin d'aller lui dire ça?**

what did you have to go and tell him that for? SEE GRAMMAR A31–2; B17

PRON EXCLAMATIF qu'est-ce qu'il fait beau! what lovely weather!; **qu'est-ce qu'on a rigolé!** we had such a good laugh!

qu'est-ce qui [kɛski] **PRON INTERR** what; **q. est arrivé?** what (has) happened? SEE GRAMMAR A31–2; B17

questeur [kɛstœr] **NM 1** *Antiq* quaestor **2** *Pol* parliamentary administrator

QUESTION [kɛstjɔ̃] **NF 1** *(interrogation)* question; *(demande de précisions)*, query (**sur** about, on); *Ordinat* query; **faire** *ou* **poser** *ou* **adresser une q. à qn** to ask sb a question, to put a question to sb; **sa fidélité ne fait pas q.** there is no doubt *or* no question about his/her loyalty; **quelle q.!** what a question!, what a thing to ask!; **tu te poses trop de questions** you worry too much; **je commence à me poser des questions sur son honnêteté** I'm beginning to wonder about *or* have my doubts about his/her honesty; **être en q.** to be called into question; **mettre en q.** to question, to call into question; *(affirmation)* to challenge; **elle ne cesse de tout remettre en q.** she questions absolutely everything; **le voyage est remis en q.** there's a question mark hanging over the trip; **voici un point qui fait q.** this is a debatable *or* moot point; **il n'y a pas de q.** there is no question *or* doubt about it SEE GRAMMAR A46–7; B63–4

2 *(affaire)* question, matter, issue; **je voudrais vous consulter sur une q. d'affaires** I would like to consult you on a business matter; **questions d'actualité** current affairs; **ce n'est qu'une q. d'argent/de temps** it is simply a question *or* matter of money/of time; **c'est une q. de minutes/d'habitude** it's a matter of minutes/of habit; **de quoi est-il q.?** what is it all about?; **il est q. de l'affaire de détournement de fonds** it's about this matter of embezzlement; **il est q. de lui élever une statue** there is some talk of putting up a statue to him/her; **il n'en est pas q.** it's out of the question; **il n'est pas q. de leur en parler** talking to them about it is out of the question; **il n'est pas q. que tu y retournes** it is out of the question for you to go back; **il ne saurait être q. de les inviter** we couldn't think of *or* there can be no question of inviting them; **la personne/l'affaire en q.** the person/the business in question; **sortir de la q.** to wander from the point; **ce n'est pas là la q., là n'est pas la q., la q. n'est pas là** that is not the point; *Iron* **c'est bien la q.!** that's completely beside the point!; **qu'il n'en soit plus q.** let us say no more about it, let's drop the subject; *Fam* **q. argent, ce n'est pas rose** moneywise *or* as far as money goes, things are pretty grim; **q. vacances, ça pourrait être mieux** as far as holidays go, it could be better; *Fam* **pas q.** no way, no chance

3 *Jur* (point at) issue; **q. de fait/droit** issue of fact/law

4 *Hist* **appliquer la q. à qn, mettre qn à la q.** to put sb to the question, to torture sb

▸▸ *Mktg* **q. cafétéria** multiple choice question; **q. à choix multiple** multiple choice question; *Pol* **q. de confiance** vote of confidence; **q. de contrôle** check question; **q. fermée** closed question; **q. fermée à choix unique** dichotomous question; *Mktg* **q. filtre** check question; **q. majeure** leading question; **q. ouverte** open question; **q. piège** trick question; *Mktg* **q. ricochet** boomerang question; **q. subsidiaire** *(d'un jeu)* tie-break, tiebreaker

questionnaire [kɛstjɔnɛr] **NM** questionnaire; **q. à choix multiple** *(à l'école etc)* multiple choice question paper; *(sondage)* multiple choice questionnaire; **q. d'évalua-**

tion *(remis aux clients)* customer satisfaction questionnaire; **q. pilote** pilot questionnaire

questionnement [kɛstjɔn(ə)mɑ̃] **NM** questioning; *Ordinat* **q. logique** logical querying

questionner [kɛstjɔne] **VT** *(quelqu'un)* to question (**sur** about)
VPR se questionner to question each other

questionneur, -euse [kɛstjɔnœr, -øz] **ADJ** *(enfant, air)* inquisitive
N *Rare* questioner

questure [kɛstyr] **NF 1** *Antiq* quaestorship **2** *Pol* = treasury and administrative department of the French Parliament

quête [kɛt] **NF 1** *(recherche)* quest, search (**de** for); **se mettre en q. de qn/qch** to set out *or* go in search of sb/sth, to go looking for sb/sth; **gens en q. de plaisirs** people in search of pleasure, pleasure-seekers **2** *(pour trouver du gibier)* beating; *(de la meute)* tracking, scenting **3** *(collecte)* collection; **faire la q.** *(pour amasser des fonds)* to make a collection, *Fam* to pass the hat round; *Rel* to take the collection

quêter [kete] **VT 1** *(argent etc)* to collect **2** *(approbation, louanges)* to seek; *(compliments)* to fish for, to angle for; *(de la meute) (gibier)* to seek
VI 1 *(faire la quête)* to collect money, to make a collection **2** *(de la meute)* to quarter

quêteur, -euse [kɛtœr, -øz] **N** collector; *Rel* collection taker, person taking the collection

quêteux [kɛtø] **NM** *Can* beggar

quetsche [kwɛtʃ(ə)] **NF 1** *(prune)* dark-red plum **2** *(eau-de-vie)* = plum liqueur similar to kirsch

queue [kø] **NF 1** *(d'animal)* tail; **couper la q. à un cheval** to dock a horse *or* a horse's tail; **cheval à longue q.** long-tailed horse; **cheval à q. écourtée** bobtail (horse); **q. de renard** fox's brush; **elle a des queues de rat** her hair is like rats' tail; *Fam* **il est parti la q. entre les jambes** he went off with his tail between his legs; *Fam* **pas la q. d'un** *ou* **d'une** not a blessed one

2 *(d'une comète, d'un cerf-volant)* tail; *(d'un météore)* trail; *(d'une noire, d'une croche)* stem; *(d'une casserole)* handle; *(d'un fruit, d'une fleur)* stalk; *Typ (d'une lettre)* stem, descender; *Typ (d'une page)* tail, foot; **habit à q.** tail coat; **piano à q.** grand piano; *Typ* **lettre à q. inférieure** descending letter

3 *(d'une procession)* (tail) end, rear; **venir en q.** *(d'un cortège etc)* to bring up the rear; **être en q.** *(d'un cortège etc)* to be at the rear; *Courses de chevaux* **arriver en q.** to come in at the tail end; **être à la q. de la classe, être en q. de classe** to be at the bottom of the class; *Fig* **une histoire/un film sans q. ni tête** a story/a film one can't make head or tail of, an incomprehensible story/film; **voiture en q. de train** *ou* **du train** carriage *or Am* car in the rear of the train; **wagon de** *ou* **en q.** end carriage, *Am* end car; **attaquer une armée en q.** to attack an army in the rear

4 *(de gens)* queue, *Am* line; **ce sont les premiers de la q.** they are (the) first in the queue *or Am* line; **faire la q.** to queue (up), *Am* to stand in line; **se mettre dans** *ou* **prendre la q.** to get in *or* join the queue *or Am* line; **faire une heure de q.** to queue *or* to stand in a queue *or Am* to stand in line for an hour

5 *Billard* cue; **faire fausse q.** to miscue

6 *Vulg (pénis)* prick, cock, dick

▸▸ **q. de cheval** *(coiffure)* ponytail; **avoir une q. de cheval** to have a ponytail, to wear one's hair in a ponytail; **q. de poisson: le conducteur m'a fait une q. de poisson** the driver cut (in) in front of me; *Fam* **finir en q. de poisson** *(d'une pièce de théâtre, d'un projet etc)* to fizzle out; *Suisse Fam* **ne pas se prendre pour la q. de la poire** to think one is the bee's knees

queue-d'aronde, *pl* **queues-d'aronde** **NF** *Menuis* dovetail; **assemblage à q.** dovetail(ed) joint

queue-de-cochon, *pl* **queues-de-cochon** **NF** *(outil)* auger bit, gimlet

queue-de-morue, *pl* **queues-de-morue** **NF 1** *(basques)* tail; **(habit à) q.** tail coat, *Fam* tails **2** *(brosse)* flat (paint)brush

queue-de-pie, *pl* **queues-de-pie** **NF =** **queue-de-morue**

queue-de-rat, *pl* **queues-de-rat** **NF 1** *(lime)* rat tail, rat-tailed file **2** *(pour les trous)* reamer

queuter [køte] **VI** *Fam (échouer)* to fail; **q. à un examen** to flunk an exam

QUI [ki] **PRON REL** SEE GRAMMAR A32–3; B22 **1** *(personne)* who, that; *(animal, chose)* which, that; **homme/femme q. parle français** man/ woman who *or* that speaks French; **phrases q. ne sont pas françaises** sentences which *or* that are not French; **vous q. êtes libres** you who are free; **c'est la plus âgée q. a répondu** it was the eldest who *or* that answered; **il y a peu de gens q. savent cela,** *Litt* **il est peu de gens q. sachent cela** there are few people who *or* that know that; **il n'y a personne q. ne comprenne cela** there is no one who *or* that does not understand that; **dans ce match, q. était son premier, l'équipe a fait preuve de résistance** in this their first match, the team showed great staying power; **je le vois q. vient** I can see him coming; **la voici q. arrive** she's coming (now), here she is (now); **le voilà q. râle à présent** there he goes, moaning; **c'est une femme charmante, et q. a du talent** she is a charming woman, and talented

2 *(= celui qui)* **q. vivra verra** time will tell; **tout vient à point à q. sait attendre** all things come to him who waits; **sauve q. peut** every man for himself; **adressez-vous à q. vous voudrez** apply to anyone you like; *Fam* **comme q. dirait** so to speak, as it were

3 *(= ce qui)* **q. plus est** what is more; **q. pis est** what is worse; **voilà q. me plaît** that's what I like

4 ce q. *voir* **ce**

5 *(après prép) (peut être omis en anglais)* who, *Fml* whom; **voilà l'homme à q. je pensais** there is the man (who) I was thinking of *or Fml* the man of whom I was thinking; **il cherche quelqu'un avec q. jouer** he is looking for someone to play with

6 *(indéf)* some; **on se dispersa, q. d'un côté, q. d'un autre** we scattered, some going one way, some another

7 q. que ce soit *(sujet)* whoever; *(objet)* anyone; **je défie q. que ce soit de le prouver** I challenge anyone to prove it

PRON INTERR who; *(complément d'objet ou après prép)* who, *Fml* whom; **q. a dit cela?** who said that?; **savez-vous q. a dit cela?** do you know who said that?; **q. désirez-vous voir?** who *or Fml* whom do you wish to see?; **q. vient à la réunion?** who is coming to the meeting?; **devinez q. est arrivé le premier** guess who was here first; **à q. est ce canif?** whose knife is this?, whose is this knife?; **de q. parlez-vous?** who are you talking about?, *Fml* of whom are you speaking?; **de q. êtes-vous le fils?** whose son are you?; **je me demande de q. il tient son mauvais caractère** I wonder who *or* where he gets his bad temper from; **q. d'autre?** who else?; **de vous me suivra?** which of you will follow me?; *Fam* **q. ça?** who's that?; **c'est à q. entrera le premier** it's a question of who comes in first; **c'était à q. l'aiderait** they vied with *or* outdid each other in helping him; *Fam* **il est là – q. donc?** he's here – who? SEE GRAMMAR A31; B17

quia (à) [akɥija] **ADV** *Vieilli* **être à q.** to be at a loss for an answer; **réduire** *ou* **mettre qn à q.** to nonplus sb

quiche [kiʃ] NF *Culin* quiche; **q. lorraine** quiche lorraine

quiconque [kikɔ̃k] PRON INDÉF **1** (*relatif*) whoever, anyone who, anybody who; **q. désobéira sera puni** whoever disobeys *or* anyone who *or* anybody who disobeys will be punished **2** (*n'importe qui*) anyone, anybody; **q. de mes amis** any of my friends

quid [kwid] PRON *Hum* **q. de …?** what about …?

quidam [kidam] NM *Fam* fellow, individual

qui est-ce que [kiɛskə] PRON INTERR (*objet*) who, *Fml* whom; **q. vous désirez voir?** who *or Fml* whom do you wish to see?

qui est-ce qui [kiɛski] PRON INTERR (*sujet*) who

quiet, -ète [kjɛ, -ɛt] ADJ *Arch* calm

quiétisme [kjetism] NM *Hist, Rel* quietism

quiétiste [kjetist] ADJ, N *Hist, Rel* quietist

quiétude [kjetyd] NF peace(fulness); **en toute q.** quite calmly

quignon [kiɲɔ̃] NM (*de pain*) (*morceau*) chunk, hunk; (*bout*) end crust

quillard [kijar] NM *Anciennement Fam* = soldier about to be discharged or nearing the end of his national service

quille[1] [kij] NF **1** skittle, ninepin; **jouer aux quilles** to play skittles *or* ninepins; *Fig* **être reçu comme un chien dans un jeu de quilles** to be treated as an intruder; *Fig* **se tenir droit comme une q.** to hold oneself as straight as a ramrod **2** *très Fam* (*jambe*) pin, leg; **il ne tient pas sur ses quilles** he's shaky on his pins **3** *Anciennement Fam* (*fin du service militaire*) discharge, *Br* demob; **à nous la q.!** civvy street, here we come!; **la q., c'est dans cent cinquante jours** we'll be back in civvy street in a hundred and fifty days

quille[2] NF *Naut* keel; **fausse q.** false keel, outer keel; **q. de roulis, q. latérale** bilge keel; **poser la q. d'un navire** to lay down a ship; **la q. en l'air** bottom up

quilleur, -euse [kijœr, -øz] N *Can* skittle player

quillier [kije] NM set of skittles

quincaillerie [kɛ̃kajri] NF **1** (*ustensiles*) hardware, *Br* ironmongery; *Fig Fam* **elle a mis toute sa q.** she's wearing every bit of jewellery she's got **2** (*commerce*) hardware business; (*magasin*) hardware shop, *Br* ironmonger's **3** *Fam* (*armes*) weapons; **il ne sort jamais sans toute sa q.** he's always armed to the teeth when he goes out

quincaillier, -ière [kɛ̃kaje, -jɛr] N hardware dealer, *Br* ironmonger

quinconce [kɛ̃kɔ̃s] NM quincunx; **arbres disposés en q.** trees arranged in staggered rows; **rivetage en q.** staggered *or* zigzag riveting

quinine [kinin] NF quinine

quinqua [kɛ̃ka] (*abrév* **quinquagénaire**) ADJ INV fifty-something
N fifty-something

quinquagénaire [kɛ̃kaʒenɛr] ADJ, N fifty-year-old, quinquagenarian; **elle est q.** she is in her fifties

Quinquagésime [kɛ̃kaʒezim] NF *Rel* Quinquagesima (Sunday)

quinquennal, -ale, -aux, -ales [kɛ̃kenal, -o] ADJ quinquennial; (*plan*) five-year; **une exposition quinquennale** a five-yearly exhibition

quinquennat [kɛ̃kena] NM five-year term; **pendant son premier q.** during his first term of office

quinquet [kɛ̃kɛ] NM **1** *Fam Vieilli* **quinquets** eyes; **ouvrez/fermez les quinquets!** open/close your eyes! **2** (*lampe*) oil lamp

quinquina [kɛ̃kina] NM **1** *Pharm* cinchona **2** (**vin de**) **q.** (apéritif) tonic wine

quint [kɛ̃] ADJ *Arch* fifth

quintal, -aux [kɛ̃tal, -o] NM quintal

quinte [kɛ̃t] NF **1 q. de toux** coughing fit, fit of coughing **2** *Mus* fifth; **q. juste** perfect fifth **3** *Cartes* straight; **q. flush** straight flush **4** *Escrime* quinte **5** *Vieilli* (*accès de mauvaise humeur*) fit of bad temper

quintefeuille [kɛ̃tfœj] NF *Hér, Bot* cinquefoil NM *Archit* cinquefoil

quinter [kɛ̃te] VI *Suisse* (*se mettre en colère*) to flare up, to lose one's temper

quintessence [kɛ̃tesɑ̃s] NF quintessence

quintette [k(ɥ)ɛ̃tɛt] NM *Mus* quintet(te)

quinteux, -euse [kɛ̃tø, -øz] ADJ (*personne*) crotchety, testy; (*cheval*) restive; (*toux*) fitful

quintuple [kɛ̃typl] ADJ fivefold, quintuple NM quintuple; **au q.** fivefold; **trente est (le) q. de six** thirty is five times (as much as) six

quintupler [kɛ̃typle] VT & VI to increase fivefold, to quintuple

quintuplés, -ées [kɛ̃typle] NPL quintuplets, *Fam* quins, *Am* quints

quinzaine [kɛ̃zɛn] NF **1** (*environ quinze*) about fifteen, fifteen or so, some fifteen; **une q. d'euros/personnes** about fifteen *or* fifteen or so *or* some fifteen euros/people **2** (*deux semaines*) **une q. (de jours)** two weeks, *Br* a fortnight; **remettre une cause à q.** to adjourn a case for two weeks *or Br* a fortnight **3** (*salaire*) two weeks' *or Br* a fortnight's pay

quinze [kɛ̃z] ADJ INV **1** fifteen; **Louis Q.** Louis the Fifteenth; **numéro q.** number fifteen **2 q. jours** two weeks, *Br* a fortnight; **tous les q. jours** every other *or* second week, *Br* every fortnight, once a fortnight, fortnightly NM INV **1** fifteen; **le q. mai** (on) the fifteenth of May, (on) May the fifteenth, *Am* (on) May fifteenth; **habiter au q.** to live at number fifteen; *Tennis* **q. partout** fifteen all **2 demain en q.** two weeks *or Br* a fortnight (from) tomorrow, *Br* tomorrow fortnight **3** *Rugby* **le q. de France** the French fifteen **4** *UE* **les Q.** = the fifteen member states of the European Union from 1995 to 2004

quinzième [kɛ̃zjɛm] ADJ, N fifteenth NM (*fraction*) fifteenth

quinzièmement [kɛ̃zjɛmmɑ̃] ADV in the fifteenth place, fifteenthly

quiproquo [kiprɔko] NM (*en prenant une personne pour une autre*) case of mistaken identity, mix-up; (*en prenant une chose pour une autre*) mix-up; **il y a eu un q.** there's been a mix-up

quittance [kitɑ̃s] NF receipt; **q. de loyer** rent receipt; **q. pour solde** receipt in full; *Banque* **q. pour solde de compte** closing account balance; *Fin* **q. finale** final payment *or* discharge; **q. comptable** accountable receipt

quittancer [kitɑ̃se] VT (**je quittançai(s)**) (*facture, dette*) to receipt

quitte [kit] ADJ **1** (*libéré*) **je suis q. envers vous** I'm no longer in debt to you; **nous sommes quittes** we're quits *or* all square; **tenir qn q. de qch** to let sb off (with) sth; **je vous tiens q. du reste** I'll let you off (with) the rest, never mind the rest; **il en a été q. pour la peur** he got off *or* escaped with a fright; **ils en ont été quittes à bon compte** they got off lightly; **jouer (à) q. ou double** to play double *or* quits; *Jur* **être q. de dettes** to be out of debt, to be clear of debts **2 q. à même** if it means; **je le ferai, q. à être grondé/m'ennuyer** I'll do it even if it means being scolded/getting bored; **il abandonne ce travail, q. à le reprendre plus tard** he's giving up this work but may resume it later NM **un q. ou double** double or quits

quitter [kite] VT (*endroit, personne*) to leave;

(*métier*) to leave, to quit; (*fonction, chambre d'hôtel*) to vacate; **q. la grande route** to turn off *or* leave the main road; **la voiture a quitté la route** (*par accident*) the car went off *or* left the road; (*délibérément*) the car turned off (the road); **q. les rails** (*d'un train*) to jump *or* leave the rails, to derail; *Naut* **q. la jetée** *ou* **le quai** to cast off; **q. l'hôtel** to check out (of the hotel); *Ordinat* **q. le système** to quit (the system); **q. le théâtre** to give up the stage; **q. les affaires** to retire from business; **q. une mauvaise habitude** to give up a bad habit; **q. la vie** to depart this life; **un ami très cher vient de nous q.** we have just lost a very dear friend, a very dear friend has just passed away; **quel plaisir de tout q.!** how nice to get away from it all!; **sa main n'a pas quitté la mienne** his/her hand didn't leave mine; **il ne l'a pas quittée des yeux** he didn't take his eyes off her; **ne le quittez pas des yeux** keep your eye on him, don't let him out of your sight, don't take your eyes off him; **c'est une idée qui ne me quitte pas** I can't get the idea out of my head; **elle veut q. son mari** she wants to leave her husband; **elle ne quitte pas sa mère** (*elle n'est pas indépendante*) she won't leave her mother, she never leaves her mother's side; **je dois vous q., il est tard** I must leave you, it's late; **vous ne quittez pas votre veste?** won't you take off your jacket?; **tu vas adorer ce pull, tu ne le quitteras plus** you'll love this sweater, you won't want to take it off; *Tél* **ne quittez pas (l'écoute)!** hold on!, hold the line!; **q. la partie** to give up
VPR **se quitter** (*des amis etc*) to part, to say goodbye; (*d'un couple*) to part, to split up, to break up; **il est tard, nous devons nous q.** it's late, we have to say goodbye now; **ils se sont quittés bons amis** they parted good friends

quitus [k(ɥ)itys] NM *Jur* (*d'une dette, d'une responsabilité etc*) quietus, final discharge; **q. fiscal** tax clearance

qui-vive NM INV **être** *ou* **se tenir sur le q.** to be on the alert *or* the qui vive

QUOI [kwa] PRON REL **1** what; **ce sur q. l'on discute** what is being discussed; **ce à q. je m'oppose** what I object to; **c'est en q. vous vous trompez** that is where you are wrong; **après q.** after which; **c'est ce pour q. il s'est battu des années durant** this is what he's been fighting for for years; **travaille, sans q. tu ne mangeras pas** work, otherwise you won't eat; **il a de q. vivre** he has enough to live on; **il a bien autre chose à q. penser!** he has other things to think about! SEE GRAMMAR A32–3; B22–3

2 il y a de q. vous faire enrager it's enough to drive you mad; **il n'y a pas de q. être fier/se réjouir** there's nothing to be proud of/to get excited about; **je suis en colère – je vous comprends, il y a de q.** I'm angry – I understand, you've every right *or* reason to be; **il n'y a pas de q.** (*en réponse à des remerciements, des excuses*) don't mention it, not at all; *Fam* **il a de q.** he's well *or* comfortably off; **avez-vous de q. écrire/manger?** have you anything *or* something to write with/to eat?; **il faut trouver de q. allumer le feu** we must find something to light the fire with

3 (*dans une exclamation*) *Fam* **comme q. ça n'était pas la peine de s'énerver** so it wasn't worth getting worked up about!

4 (*correlative to* **qui, que** + *sub*) **q. qui survienne, restez calme** whatever happens, keep calm; **q. qu'il en soit** be that as it may, however that may be; **q. qu'on fasse, il n'est jamais content** no matter what you do *or* whatever you do, he's never satisfied; **q. que ce soit** anything (whatever); **puis-je vous être utile en q. que ce soit?** can I be of use to you in any way?; **avez-vous dit q. que ce soit?** did you say anything (at all)?; **q. que ce soit qui l'en empêche** whatever may be preventing him

PRON INTERR what; **q. d'autre?** what else?; **q. de nouveau** *ou* **neuf?** what's new?; **q. de plus simple?** what could be simpler *or* easier?; **je ne sais q. penser/lui dire** I don't know what to think/to say to him; **à q. pensez-vous?** what are you thinking of *or* about?; **de q. parlez-vous?** what are you talking about?; **en q. puis-je vous être utile?** how can I help you?; **à q. bon (faire qch)?** what's the use *or* good (of doing sth)?; **en q. est-ce?, c'est en q.?** what's it made of?; *Fam* **eh bien! q.?** well, what about *or* of it?; *Fam* **tu es sourd ou q.?** are you deaf or what?; *Fam* **q.? je n'entends rien!** what? I can't hear you!; *très Fam* **vous désirez q.?** what is it you want?; *très Fam* **de q.?** what!, what's that? SEE GRAMMAR A31–2; B17

INT (mais) q.! what!; **q. donc!** what's that?; **q., c'est vous!** what, is it you?; **mais alors q.?** don't tell me it's all off!; **enfin q.! il ne peut pas se désister comme ça!** wait a minute, he can't back out like that!; **on ne va pas y passer la nuit, q.!** we're not going to spend the night there!

quoique [kwak(ə)] **CONJ 1** *(+ sub)* (al)though; **quoiqu'il soit pauvre, il est généreux** (al)though he is poor, he is generous; **je suis heureux q. malade** I am happy (al)though I'm ill; **q. jeune, il avait une certaine expérience** (al)though young, he had some experience **2** *(+ ind) (à la réflexion)* **nous recevons souvent des coups, q., vous savez, nous en donnons aussi** we often receive blows, but then, of course, we hit back

quolibet [kɔlibɛ] **NM** gibe, jeer; **poursuivre qn de ses quolibets** to gibe *or* jeer at sb

quorum [k(w)ɔrɔm] **NM** quorum; **atteindre le q.** to have a quorum

quota [k(w)ɔta] **NM** quota; **q. d'exportation** export quota; **q. d'importation** import quota; **quotas volontaires à l'export** voluntary export restraint; *Can Fig* **avoir son q.** to be fed up

quote-part, *pl* **quotes-parts** [kɔtpar] **NF** share, quota, portion

quotidien, -ienne [kɔtidjɛ̃, -jɛn] **ADJ** *(travail, promenade, journal, émission)* daily; *(ennuis)* everyday; **la vie quotidienne** everyday life

NM 1 *(journal)* daily (paper); **un grand q.** a (major) national daily **2 au q.** on a day-to-day basis; **la science-fiction au q.** science fiction in the everyday world

quotidiennement [kɔtidjɛnmɑ̃] **ADV** daily, every day

quotidienneté [kɔtidjɛnte] **NF** everyday nature

quotient [kɔsjɑ̃] **NM** *Math etc* quotient
▸▸ **q. électoral** electoral quota; *Admin* **q. familial** family allowance; **q. intellectuel** intelligence quotient, IQ; **son q. intellectuel est de 120** he/she has an IQ of 120

quotité [kɔtite] **NF** quota, share, proportion; *Jur* **q. disponible** disposable portion of estate; **impôt de q.** proportional tax; **q. garantie** *(en assurance)* guaranteed cover limit

QWERTY [kwɛrti] **ADJ INV clavier Q.** QWERTY keyboard

R, r [ɛr] NM *(lettre)* R, r; **rouler les r** to roll one's r's; **ne mangez des fruits de mer que pendant les mois en r** only eat seafood when there's an r in the month

r. *(abrév* **route)** Rd

rab [rab] NM *Fam (nourriture)* extra (food); *(temps)* overtime; **un r. de poulet** a second helping *or* seconds of chicken; **un r. de cigarettes** extra cigarettes; **faire du r.** to put in a bit of overtime; **avoir un r. de cinq minutes** to have an extra five minutes, to have five more minutes; **un r. de sommeil, c'est toujours agréable** it's always nice to get some extra sleep; **il reste du poulet en r.** there's some chicken going spare *or* up for grabs; **j'en ai encore en r.** I still have some left over

rabâchage [rabaʃaʒ] NM (tedious) repetition

rabâcher [rabaʃe] VI to say the same thing over and over again
▸ VT *(conseils, recommandations)* to keep on repeating; *(leçon)* to repeat parrot-fashion; **ils rabâchent toujours la même chose** they're always (harping) on about the same old thing; **elle nous a rabâché qu'il fallait faire attention au verglas** she kept on at us about being careful of the ice; **c'est ce qu'elle a passé son temps à me r.** that was what she kept on at me about; **le prof rabâche le même cours depuis dix ans** the teacher's been regurgitating *or* churning out the same old course for ten years

rabâcheur, -euse [rabaʃœr, -øz] ADJ repetitive; **il est très r.** he's always repeating himself *or* harping on about the same thing; **elle devient un peu rabâcheuse** she's starting to repeat herself
▸ N repetitive person

rabais [rabɛ] NM discount, reduction; **r. en cas de paiement comptant** cash discount; **r. différé** deferred rebate; **faire un r. (sur qch)** to give a discount (on sth); **faire un r. de 50 euros/de 15%** to give a 50-euro/15% discount, to take 50 euros/15% off the price; **vendre qch au r.** to sell sth at a discount *or* at a reduced price; **il m'a fait un r. de 20 pour cent** he gave me 20 percent off *or* a 20 percent discount; *Fig* **au r.** *(travail)* poorly or badly paid; *(système éducatif)* second-rate; **formation au r.** second-rate training, training on the cheap

rabaissement [rabɛsmɑ̃] NM *Rare* **1** *(de store)* lowering **2** *(critique)* disparagement

rabaisser [rabese] VT **1** *(store)* to lower; *(prix)* to reduce, to lower **2** *(personne, talents etc)* to belittle, *Fam* to put down
▸ VPR **se rabaisser** to belittle oneself, *Fam* to put oneself down; **se r. devant qn** to put oneself down with sb

rabane [raban] NF *Tex* raffia (fabric); **rabanes** (raffia) mats

rabat [raba] NM **1** *(de sac à main, d'une enveloppe)* flap; *(d'un costume officiel)* bands **2** *(pour gibier)* beating

rabat-joie [rabaʒwa] NM INV killjoy, *Fam* spoilsport, *Fam* wet blanket
▸ ADJ INV **elle est r.** she's such a killjoy *or* spoilsport *or* wet blanket

rabattable [rabatabl] ADJ *(siège, dossier)* folding, fold-down; *Aut* **capote r.** folding roof, drophead

rabattage [rabataʒ] NM *(du bois)* beating; *(du gibier)* driving

rabatteur, -euse [rabatœr, -øz] N **1** *(à la chasse)* beater **2** *(de clients)* tout; *(de partisans)* canvasser

rabattre [rabatr] *(conj like* **battre)** VT **1** *(capote)* to fold down; *(couvercle, siège de toilettes)* to close, to shut, to put down; *(store)* to lower, to pull down, to shut; *(col)* to turn down; *(siège)* *(vers le haut)* to fold up, to put up; *(vers le bas)* to fold down, to put down; *(remettre en place)* to fold *or* put back; **r. une couture** to press down *or* flatten a seam; **r. le bord d'une tôle** to flange a plate; **le vent rabat la fumée** the wind is blowing *or* driving the smoke in this direction; **le vent rabattait la fumée vers nous** the wind was blowing *or* driving the smoke in our direction; *Sport* **r. la balle** to smash the ball; **r. la foule vers la place** to drive the crowd back towards the square
2 *(diminuer) (prix)* to reduce, to cut; *(arbre, branche)* to cut back; **r. 100 euros du prix** to take *or Fam* knock 100 euros off the price; **je n'en rabattrai pas un sou** I won't take a penny less for it; **r. l'orgueil de qn** to humble sb; *Fam* **r. le caquet à qn** to shut sb up, to put sb in his/her place; *Fam* **se faire r. le caquet** to get put in one's place; **r. de ses prétentions, en r.** to lower one's sights; *Tricot* **r. les mailles** to cast off
3 *(gibier)* to drive; *(fugitifs)* to herd
▸ VPR **se rabattre 1** *(de siège de voiture)* to fold down; **table qui se rabat** folding *or* drop-leaf table **2** *(armée)* **se rabattit sur la ville** the army fell back on the town; **la fumée s'est rabattue sur nous** the smoke was blown *or* driven in our direction **3** **se r. sur** *(se contenter de) (un sujet)* to fall back on; *(un film, une personne)* to fall back on, to make do with; **elle finira par se r. sur ce qu'on lui propose** she'll end up accepting *or* making do with what she's offered **4** *Aut* to pull back in; *(s'écarter)* to move over

> Do not confuse with **rebattre**.

rabattu [rabaty] ADJ **col r.** turn(ed)-down collar; **couture rabattue** run and fell seam

rabbin [rabɛ̃] NM rabbi; **grand r.** Chief Rabbi

rabbinique [rabinik] ADJ rabbinical

rabbinisme [rabinism] NM rabbinism

rabbiniste [rabinist] N rabbinist

rabdomancie [rabdɔmɑ̃si] NF dowsing, *Spéc* rhabdomancy

rabelaisien, -ienne [rablɛzjɛ̃, -jɛn] ADJ *Littér* Rabelaisian

rabibochage [rabibɔʃaʒ] NM *Fam* patching up, repairing, mending; *Fig (entre amis)* making up, reconciliation

rabibocher [rabibɔʃe] *Fam* VT *Fig* **j'ai réussi à les r.** I managed to patch things up between them
▸ VPR **se rabibocher** to patch things up, to make it up (**avec** with)

rabiot [rabjo] NM *Fam Vieilli* = **rab**

rabioter [rabjɔte] *Fam* VI to scrounge, to cadge; *(de commerçant)* to give short measure; **elle rabiote sur la nourriture** she skimps on the food
▸ VT *(nourriture)* to snaffle; *(de commerçant)* to skimp on; **r. quelques centimes** ≃ to skim off a few pennies *or Am* cents; **j'ai réussi à r. cinq minutes** I managed to snatch *or* steal an extra five minutes

rabique [rabik] ADJ *(virus)* rabies

rabistoquer [rabistɔke] VT *Belg Fam (réparer)* to patch up; *(remonter le moral à)* to buck up

râble[1] [rɑbl] NM *(de lièvre, lapin)* back; *Culin* **r. de lièvre** saddle of hare; *Fam* **il m'a sauté sur le r.** he jumped on me; *Fam* **je ne pouvais pas me douter de ce qui allait me tomber sur le r.** I didn't suspect what was waiting for me round the corner

râble[2] NM fire rake

râblé [rɑble] ADJ *(personne)* stocky, stockily built

rabot [rabo] NM *Menuis* plane; **r. à languette** grooving plane, tongue plane; **passer le r. sur qch, donner un coup de r. à qch** to plane sth

rabotage [rabɔtaʒ] NM *Menuis* planing

raboter [rabɔte] VT *Menuis (avec un rabot)* to plane; *(avec un autre outil)* to scrape, to rub; *Fig Vieilli* **r. son style** to polish one's style

raboteur [rabɔtœr] NM *Menuis (personne)* planer

raboteuse [rabɔtøz] NF *Menuis* planing machine, planer

raboteux, -euse [rabɔtø, -øz] ADJ *(surface)* rough, uneven; *(bois)* knotty; *(route)* bumpy, uneven; *Fig (style)* unpolished

rabougri [rabugri] ADJ *(plante, personne)* stunted

rabougrir [rabugrir] VT & VI *(plante, fruit etc)* to shrivel up; *(personne)* to become shrivelled
▸ VPR **se rabougrir** to shrivel up

rabouter [rabute] VT to join end to end

rabrouer [rabrue] VT to berate

racaille [rakɑj] NF *(voyous)* scum; *Fam Vieilli (populace)* riff-raff, rabble

raccommodable [rakɔmɔdabl] ADJ which can be mended

raccommodage [rakɔmɔdaʒ] NM **1** *(action)*

(de vêtements) mending; *(de bas, chaussettes)* darning; **faire du r.** to do some mending **2** *(résultat)* mend; *(de bas)* darn

raccommodement [rakɔmɔdmɑ̃] NM *Fam* reconciliation

raccommoder [rakɔmɔde] VT **1** *(vêtement)* to mend; *(bas, chaussette)* to darn **2** *Fam (personnes)* to patch things up between

▸ **se raccommoder** VPR *Fam* to make it up, to patch things up; **se r. avec qn** to make it up *or* to patch things up with sb

raccommodeur, -euse [rakɔmɔdœr, -øz] N mender

raccompagner [rakɔ̃paɲe] VT **r. qn** to accompany sb back; **je vais vous r.** *(à pied)* I'll take you back, I'll go back with you, I'll see you home; *(en voiture)* I'll drive *or* take you home; **je te raccompagne jusqu'à ta voiture** I'll see *or* walk you to your car; **r. qn à la porte** to see *or* show sb to the door

raccord [rakɔr] NM **1** *(de papier peint)* join; **papier peint sans raccords** (wall)paper with no pattern repeat; **faire des raccords de peinture** to touch up the paintwork; **faire un r. à une bande magnétique** to splice a tape; *Fam* **faire un r.** *(de maquillage)* to touch up one's make-up; **j'ai eu du mal avec les raccords** *(de papier peint)* I had trouble matching up the pattern **2** *Tech* union; *(pièce d'assemblage)* connection, coupling, joint; *Élec* **r. mâle et femelle** plug and socket connection; **bouchon de r.** adapter; **r. de lampe** lamp adapter *or* connector; **r. de graissage** grease nipple **3** *Cin (liaison de scènes)* continuity; *(plan)* link shot; **faux r.** jump cut

raccordement [rakɔrdəmɑ̃] NM **1** *(en ajustant)* adjusting **2** *(pour relier)* joining, linking (up), connecting; **pièces de r.** *(de canalisations etc)* making-up lengths; *Rail* **voie de r.** junction line, loop line; *(vers une usine etc)* service siding; *Élec* **boîte de r.** *(pour câbles etc)* junction box **3** *Ordinat* link

raccorder [rakɔrde] VT **1** *(relier)* to join (up), to connect; *(bâtiments, routes)* to link up; *Ordinat* to connect; **r. qn au réseau téléphonique** to connect sb to the telephone system; **nous ne sommes toujours pas raccordés au réseau électrique** we still don't have mains electricity; *Élec* **r. à la masse** *ou* **à la terre** to earth, *Am* to ground **2** *(pièces)* to connect **3** *(bande magnétique)* to splice

▸ **se raccorder** VPR *aussi Fig* to fit together, to link up; *Ordinat* **se r. à** to link up to

raccourci [rakursi] NM **1** *(route plus courte)* short cut; **prendre un r.** to take a short cut; *Ordinat* **r. clavier** keyboard shortcut **2** *(résumé)* abridg(e)ment, shortened version; **en r.** briefly, in brief; **par un r. saisissant** in a facile way; **c'est un r. saisissant que d'affirmer que …** it is facile to say that … **3** *Beaux-Arts* foreshortening; **bras en r.** foreshortened arm

raccourcir [rakursir] VT **1** *(discours, texte, chemin etc)* to shorten *(* **de** *by)*; *Couture (manches, jupe etc)* to shorten, to take up *(* **de** *by)*; **r. ses cheveux** to have a bit taken off one's hair; *Fig Fam* **tomber à bras raccourcis sur qn** to pitch into sb **2** *Beaux-Arts* to foreshorten **3** *Fam* **r. qn** *(guillotiner)* to chop sb's head off

▸ VI to grow shorter, to shorten; **les jours raccourcissent** the days are growing shorter *or* drawing in; **son tee-shirt a raccourci au lavage** his/her tee-shirt has shrunk in the wash; *Fam* **les jupes raccourcissent encore cet hiver** skirts are getting even shorter this winter

raccourcissement [rakursismɑ̃] NM **1** *(action de raccourcir)* shortening **2** *Beaux-Arts* foreshortening **3** *(des jours)* drawing in; *(de vêtement) (au lavage)* shrinking; **le r. des ju-**

pes shortening hemlines, the rise in hemlines

raccroc [rakro] NM fluke, lucky stroke; **par r.** by a fluke, by a stroke of luck

raccrocher [rakrɔʃe] VT **1 r. qch** to hang sth up again, to put sth back on the hook; **elle ne pouvait pas r. la scie sur son crochet** she couldn't get the saw back on its hook; *Tél* **r. l'appareil** *ou* **le téléphone** to hang up; **ce boxeur devrait r. les gants** it's time this boxer hung up his gloves **2** *Fam (récupérer) (commande, contrat, affaire)* to salvage **3** *(personne dans la rue)* to accost, to stop; *(d'une prostituée)* to accost, to solicit

▸ VI **1** *Tél* to hang up; *Fam* **il m'a raccroché au nez** he hung up on me, he put the phone down on me; **je n'ai pas envie de me faire r. au nez** I don't want to have the phone put down on me **2** *Sport Fam* to retire; *(d'un boxeur)* to hang up one's gloves, to retire

▸ **se raccrocher** VPR **1 se r. à qch** to catch hold of sth, to catch on to sth; **se r. à une espérance** to cling to a hope; *Fig Fam* **se r. aux branches** to clutch at straws **2** *(se rapporter)* to be linked, to be connected; **cette idée ne se raccroche pas du tout au sujet** that idea has nothing to do with *or* is totally unrelated to the subject

race [ras] NF **1** *(famille)* ancestry, descent; **de r. noble** of noble blood *or* descent *or* extraction; *Fig* **être de la r. des gagnants** to be a born winner; **être fin de r.** to be decadent; **elle a de la r.** she's very distinguished-looking **2** *(ethnie)* race; **la r. blanche/noire** whites/blacks; **la r. humaine** the human race; **sans distinction de r.** without discrimination on the grounds of race, regardless of race; *Fam (injurieux)* **quelle sale r.!** what filth!; **les banquiers, quelle sale r.!** those bankers are nothing but bastards! **3** *Zool* breed; **la r. chevaline** the horse species; **améliorer/croiser les races** to improve/to cross breeds; **chien/taureau de r.** pure-bred dog/bull, pedigree dog/bull; **cheval de r.** thoroughbred (horse); **avoir de la r.** to be pure-bred; *(de cheval)* to be a thoroughbred

racé [rase] ADJ *(animal)* pure-bred; *(cheval)* thoroughbred; *(personne)* patrician, tall and aristocratic-looking; *Fam* **profil r.** *(d'une voiture, d'un bateau)* clean *or* elegant lines

racème [rasɛm] NM *Bot* raceme

rachat [raʃa] NM **1** repurchase, buying back; **ils ont convenu du r. des captifs** they came to an agreement over the prisoners' ransom; *Jur* **pacte de r.** covenant of redemption; *Jur* **avec faculté de r.** with option of repurchase *or* redemption; *Bourse* **r. gagnant** repurchase at a profit **2** *(de police d'assurance)* surrender; *(de valeur, police etc)* redemption; **valeur de r.** surrender value; *Compta* **r. forfaitaire des créances** lump-sum purchase of accounts receivable **3** *(de société)* buy-out; *Fin* **r. d'entreprise avec un fort levier financier** leveraged buy-out; **r. d'une société par la direction** management buy-out **4** *Rel* **r. d'un péché** atonement for a sin

rachetable [raʃtabl] ADJ **1** *(stock)* redeemable **2** *(péché)* for which atonement can be made

racheter [raʃte] *(conj like* **acheter***)* VT **1** *(objet perdu, objet cassé)* to replace; **je pourrai le r., je pourrai en r. un** I can replace it, I can buy another; **r. qch à qn** to replace sth for sb *(au propriétaire)* to buy back, to repurchase *(* **à** *from); (une société)* to buy out; **r. les parts de qn** to buy sb out; **je te le rachèterai si tu ne l'aimes pas** I'll buy it from you *or* *Fam* I'll take it off your hands if you don't like it **3** *(acheter davantage de)* to buy some more; **je n'ai plus de café, je dois en r.** I've no coffee left, I'll have to buy some more; **je vais r. de la lessive** I'm going to buy some

more soap powder **4** *(en assurances) (police)* to surrender; *Jur (rente, dette, gage)* to redeem; *(otage, prisonnier)* to pay a ransom for, to ransom; *Compta* **r. une créance** to purchase an account receivable; **r. une obligation** to retire *or* redeem a bond **5** *Fig (faute)* to make up for, to compensate for; *Jésus-Christ est mort pour r. les hommes* Christ died to redeem mankind; **r. ses péchés** to atone for one's sins; **r. son honneur/son nom** to retrieve one's honour/reputation; **la profusion de détails ne rachète pas la faiblesse du plan** the wealth of detail does not make up for *or* atone for the lack of planning

▸ **se racheter** VPR to redeem oneself; **que puis-je faire pour me r.?** what can I do to make up for it?, how can I redeem myself?

racheteur [raʃtœr] NM purchaser

rachicentèse [raʃisɛ̃tɛz] NF *Méd* lumbar puncture

rachidien, -ienne [raʃidjɛ̃, -jɛn] ADJ *Anat (bulbe, canal)* rachidian

rachis [raʃis] NM *Anat, Bot* rachis, spinal column, spine; *Anat* **r. cervical** cervical vertebrae; *Anat* **r. coccygien** coccyx; *Anat* **r. dorsal** dorsal vertebrae; *Anat* **r. lombaire** lumbar vertebrae; *Anat* **r. sacré** sacrum; *Anat* **r. thoracique** thoracic vertebrae

rachitique [raʃitik] *Méd* rickety, *Spéc* rachitic; *Fam (très maigre)* scrawny

rachitisme [raʃitism] NM *Méd* rickets, *Spéc* rachitis; **faire du r.** to have rickets VOIR GRAMMAIRE A10

racho [raʃo] ADJ *Fam (abrév* **rachitique***) (personne)* weedy, scrawny; *(portion)* mean, stingy

racial, -iale, -iaux, -iales [rasjal, -jo] ADJ racial

racine [rasin] NF **1** *(de plante, de cheveu, d'ongle, de dent etc)* root; *Bot* **r. pivotante** tap root; **r. de gingembre** root ginger; **prendre r.** *(d'une plante)*, *Fig (d'une personne)* to take root; *Fig* **attaquer** *ou* **couper le mal à la r.** to strike at the root of the evil; *Fig Fam* **manger les pissenlits par la r.** to be pushing up (the) daisies; *Fam* **se faire faire les racines** *(chez le coiffeur)* to have one's roots done **2** *Math* **r. carrée/cubique** square/cube root **3** *Ling (d'un mot)* root **4** *Fig (origine)* root; **être à la recherche de ses racines** to be searching for one's roots **5** *Ordinat* root

raciner [rasine] VT *(couvertures de livre)* to marble

racisme [rasism] NM rac(ial)ism; *Fig Fam* **c'est du r. anti-vieux** that's ageism; **r. anti-jeunes** prejudice *or* bias against young people

raciste [rasist] ADJ, N rac(ial)ist

racket [rakɛt] NM *Fam* racket; **faire du r.** to run a racket

racketter [rakete] VT *Fam* **r. qn** to extort money from sb; **se faire r.** to pay protection money

racketteur, -euse [raketœr, -øz] N *Fam* racketeer

raclage [raklaʒ] NM scraping

raclée [rakle] NF *Fam* thrashing, hiding; **flanquer** *ou* **administrer une r. à qn** to give sb a thrashing *or* hiding; *Fig* **son parti/son équipe a pris une belle r.** his party/team got a good thrashing *or* hiding *or* licking

raclement [rakləmɑ̃] NM scraping (noise)

racler [rakle] VT *(frotter) (peau, semelle)* to scrape; *(pour faire partir) (peinture, vernis etc)* to scrape off; *(pour nettoyer)* to scrape (out); **ce vin racle la gorge** this wine's (a bit) rough on the throat; *Péj* **r. du** *ou* **le violon** to scrape *or* saw on the fiddle; *Fig Fam* **r. les (fonds de) tiroirs** to scrape (the bottom of) the barrel

VPR se racler se r. la gorge to clear one's throat

raclette [raklɛt] **NF 1** *(racloir)* scraper; *Aut (de balai)* wiper blade **2** *(de jardin)* hoe **3** *Culin* raclette, = Swiss speciality consisting of melted cheese prepared at the table using a special heater or grill, served with potatoes and cold meats

racloir [raklwar] **NM 1** scraper **2** *Phot etc* squeegee

raclure [raklyr] **NF** *très Fam (homme méprisable)* bastard, *Am* son-of-a-bitch; *(femme méprisable)* bitch

racolage [rakɔlaʒ] **NM** *(d'une prostituée)* soliciting, accosting; *(d'un publicitaire)* touting for business *or* custom; *Hist (pour l'armée, la marine)* press-ganging; **faire du r.** *(d'une prostituée)* to solicit; *(d'un publicitaire)* to tout for business *or* custom; *(pour un parti)* to tout for votes; **r. de partisans** enlisting of supporters

racoler [rakɔle] **VT** *(d'une prostituée)* to solicit, to accost; *(clients)* to tout for; *(électeurs, partisans)* to canvass; *Hist (hommes pour l'armée, la marine)* to press-gang; **r. des clients** to tout for custom *or* business
VI *(d'une prostituée)* to solicit; *(d'un publicitaire)* to tout for custom *or* business; *(pour un parti)* to canvass votes

racoleur, -euse [rakɔlœr, -øz] **ADJ** *(publicité, affiche)* eye-catching; *(titre, journal)* sensationalist; *(campagne électorale)* vote-catching
N *(politicien)* = canvasser who attempts to recruit party members using unscrupulous means; *(commerçant)* tout
NM *Hist, Mil* crimp
NF racoleuse street walker

racontable [rakɔ̃tabl] **ADJ** relatable, tellable; **cette plaisanterie n'est pas r. devant des enfants** it's not the kind of joke you can tell in front of children

racontar [rakɔ̃tar] **NM** story, piece of gossip; **ce ne sont que des racontars** it's just gossip *or* tittle-tattle

raconter [rakɔ̃te] **VT** to tell, *Fml* to relate, to narrate, to recount; **r. une histoire à qn** to tell sb a story; **j'ai l'impression qu'elle m'a raconté une histoire** *ou* **des histoires** I have a feeling she wasn't telling me the truth; **r. sa vie à qn** to tell sb the story of one's life *or* one's life story; **raconte-nous tes dernières vacances** tell us about your last holiday; **on m'a raconté beaucoup de choses sur toi** I've heard a lot about you; **il en a raconté de belles** he told some pretty incredible stories; **on en raconte de belles sur toi!** I've heard quite a few tales about you!; **qu'est-ce qu'il raconte (là)?** what is he talking about?; **alors qu'est-ce que tu racontes (de beau ou de neuf)?** so what's new?; **est-ce que tu as quelque chose de beau à nous r.?** *(pour nous distraire)* haven't you got anything interesting to tell us?; *(à qn qu'on revoit)* so what's new?; **on raconte que ...** apparently, ..., people are saying that ...; **à ce qu'on raconte** judging by *or* from what people say; *Fam* **je te raconte pas!** you can't imagine!; **on s'est pris une de ces cuites, je te raconte pas ...** you can't imagine how plastered we got
VI r. bien/mal to be a good/bad storyteller; **il faut toujours qu'elle nous raconte!** she always has to tell us all about it!; **je vais tenter de vous r. en quelques mots** I'll try to tell you in a few words; **allez, raconte!** come on, out with it!

VPR se raconter to talk about oneself; **je ne tiens pas à me r. devant tout le monde** I'm not keen on talking about myself in front of lots of people; **ce sont des choses qui ne se racontent pas** it's not the type of thing you

can talk about; *Fam* **se r. des histoires** to fool *or* delude oneself; **elle se raconte des histoires si elle s'imagine qu'elle va avoir une augmentation** she's living in cloud-cuckoo-land if she thinks that she's going to get a rise; *Fam* **se la r.** to show off

raconteur, -euse [rakɔ̃tœr, -øz] **N** storyteller; *(d'un film, d'une pièce de théâtre)* narrator

racornir [rakɔrnir] **VT r. qch** to shrivel sth (up), to dry sth out
VPR se racornir *(des ongles)* to grow horny; *(du papier)* to grow brittle; *(de plante, chair)* to shrivel up, to dry out

racornissement [rakɔrnismɑ̃] **NM** hardening, toughening (up)

racrapoter (se) [sərakrapɔte] **VPR** *Belg (confortablement)* to curl up; *(dans l'inconfort)* to huddle up; *Fig* to retreat into *or* turn in on oneself

radar [radar] **NM** radar; **r. à ondes entretenues** continuous-wave radar; **balayage r.** radar scan; **écho r.** radar echo; **r. d'autoguidage** homing radar; *Fig Fam* **ce matin je suis** *ou* **j'avance au r.** I'm like a zombie this morning, I'm on autopilot this morning

radariste [radarist] **N** radar operator

rade[1] [rad] **NF 1** *Naut* roadstead; **r. foraine** *ou* **ouverte** open roadstead; **r. fermée** sheltered roadstead; **navire en r.** ship in the roads; **mettre un navire en r.** to lay up a ship; **en r. de Toulon** off Toulon **2** *Fam* **laisser en r.** *(personne)* to leave in the lurch; *(projet)* to jettison; *Fam* **tomber en r.** to break down

rade[2] **NM** *Arg (comptoir)* bar, counter; *(bistro)* bar

radeau, -eaux [rado] **NM** raft; **r. de sauvetage** life raft

radial, -iale, -iaux, -iales [radjal, -jo] **ADJ 1** radial; **pneumatique à carcasse radiale** radial(-ply) tyre **2** *Anat (muscle, nerf)* radial
NF radiale 1 radial road, urban motorway **2** *Anat* radial

radian [radjɑ̃] **NM** *Math* radian

radiance [radjɑ̃s] **NF** *Litt* radiance

radiant [radjɑ̃] **ADJ** *(chaleur)*, *Vieilli (beauté)* radiant; **pouvoir r.** radiating capacity
NM *Astron* radiant (point)

radiateur [radjatœr] **NM** radiator; **r. à accumulation** storage heater; **r. à ailettes** fin radiator; **r. à bain d'huile** oil-filled radiator; **r. à eau chaude** hot-water radiator; **r. électrique** electric fire; **r. à** *ou* **en nid d'abeilles** honeycomb radiator, cellular film-type radiator; **r. soufflant** fan heater; **r. transversal** cross-flow radiator; **r. vertical** vertical-flow radiator

radiation[1] [radjasjɔ̃] **NF** *(d'une liste)* striking out, crossing out; *(de dette)* cancellation; *(d'un avocat)* disbarment; *(d'un médecin)* striking off; *(d'un sportif)* banning; **vous risquez la r.** you risk being disbarred/struck off/banned

radiation[2] **NF** *Phys* radiation; **r. cosmique** cosmic radiation; *Électron* **r. (de) haute fréquence** high-frequency radiation; *Nucl* **r. alpha/bêta** alpha/beta radiation, alpha-ray/beta-ray emission

radical, -ale, -aux, -ales [radikal, -o] **ADJ** radical; *Pol* left of centre; *Math* **signe r.** radical *or* root sign; **c'est r.** *(d'un médicament, d'une méthode)* it does the trick, it works like magic (**contre** on)
N radical; *Pol* person who is left of centre; **être r. de droite/de gauche** to be right/left of centre
NM *Ling* root, radical; *Math* radical *or* root sign; *Chimie* radical; **radicaux libres** free radicals

radicalement [radikalmɑ̃] **ADV** radically

radicalisation [radikalizasjɔ̃] **NF** *Pol* radicalization; **la r. du conflit** the heightening of the conflict

radicaliser [radikalize] *Pol* **VT** to make more radical, to radicalize
VPR se radicaliser to become more radical, to radicalize

radicalisme [radikalism] **NM** *Pol* radicalism

radical-socialisme **NM** *Pol* liberalism; *Hist, Pol* radical socialism

radical-socialiste, *pl* **radicaux-socialistes ADJ, N** *Pol* liberal; *Hist, Pol* radical socialist

radicelle [radisɛl] **NF** *Bot* rootlet, *Spéc* radicel

radicule [radikyl] **NF** *Bot* radicle

radier[1] [radje] **NM** *Constr* frame, floor, bed; *(de porte d'écluse)* sill; *(de bassin)* apron; **r. de fondation** foundation raft

radier[2] **VT** *(impf, pr sub* **n. radiions)** to strike *or* cross out; **r. qn/qch d'une liste** to strike *or* cross sb/sth off a list

radiesthésie [radjɛstezi] **NF** dowsing, divination

radiesthésiste [radjɛstezist] **N** dowser, diviner

radieux, -ieuse [radjø, -jøz] **ADJ** *(soleil)* radiant, dazzling; *(temps)* glorious; *(personne)* radiant; **elle avait un regard r., son regard était r.** she was radiant *or* glowing

radin, -ine [radɛ̃, -in] *Fam* **N** skinflint, tightwad
ADJ stingy

radiner [radine] *Fam* **VI** to turn up, to show up, to roll up
VPR se radiner to turn up, to show up, to roll up; **c'est à cette heure-ci que tu te radines?** what kind of time do you call this?; **alors tu te radines?** are you coming or not?

radio [radjo] **NF 1** *(poste)* radio (set); **à la r.** on the radio; **écouter la r.** to listen to the radio; **passer à la r.** *(personne)* to be on the radio; *(chanson)* to be played on the radio; *(concert)* to be broadcast (on the radio); **travailler à la r.** to work on the *or* for (the) radio; **faire de la r.** to be *or* work as a radio presenter **2** *(station)* radio station; **sur toutes les radios** on all stations **3** *(radiotéléphonie)* radiotelephony **4** *Méd* X-ray (photograph); **passer une r.** *ou* **à la r.** to be X-rayed
NM *Vieilli* **1** *(télégramme)* radio(gram) **2** *(opérateur)* radio operator
ADJ INV radio
▸▸ **r. commerciale** commercial radio; *(station)* commercial radio station; **r. communautaire** community radio; *(station)* community radio station; **r. K7** radio-cassette player; **r. libre** independent local radio (station); **r. locale** local radio; **r. périphérique** = any independent radio broadcasting organization based outside France; **r. pirate** pirate radio (station); **r. scolaire** schools radio

radioactif, -ive [radjoaktif, -iv] **ADJ** radioactive

radioactivité [radjoaktivite] **NF** radioactivity

radioalignement [radjoaliɲ(ə)mɑ̃] **NM** *Aviat, Naut* radio-beacon route; **voler par r.** to fly airways

radioamateur NM radio ham

radioastronomie [radjoastrɔnɔmi] **NF** radio astronomy

radiobalisage [radjobalizaʒ] **NM** radio-beacon navigation; *Aviat* airways navigation

radiobalise [radjobaliz] **NF** radio beacon, marker beacon

radiocassette [radjokasɛt] **NF** radio cassette (player)

radiocommunication [radjokɔmynikasjɔ̃] **NF** radiocommunication

radiocompas [radjokɔ̃pɑ] NM *Aviat* radio compass

radioconducteur [radjokɔ̃dyktœr] NM *Phys* radio conductor

radiodermite [radjodɛrmit] NF *Méd* radiodermatitis, X-ray dermatitis

radiodiagnostic [radjodjagnɔstik] NM *Méd* X-ray diagnosis

radiodiffuser [radjodifyze] VT *Radio* to broadcast; **un concert radiodiffusé** a broadcast concert

radiodiffusion [radjodifyzjɔ̃] NF *Radio* broadcasting

radioélectricien, -ienne [radjoelɛktrisjɛ̃, -jɛn] N radio (and television) technician

radiogénique [radjoʒenik] ADJ *Fam* **il a une voix r.** he has a good broadcasting voice; **elle est très r.** she has a good voice for radio

radiogoniomètre [radjogɔnjɔmɛtr] NM direction finder, *Spéc* radiogoniometer

radiogoniométrie [radjogɔnjɔmetri] NF direction finding, *Spéc* radiogoniometry

radiogramme [radjogram] NM *(message)* radio telegram, radiogram

radiographie [radjografi] NF *Méd* **1** *(technique)* radiography, X-ray photography **2** *(cliché)* X-ray (photograph), radiograph

radiographier [radjografje] VT *(impf, pr sub* **n. radiographiions)** *Méd* to X-ray

radiographique [radjografik] ADJ *Méd* X-ray, radiographic; **examen r.** X-ray (examination)

radioguidage [radjogidaʒ] NM *Aviat, Naut* radio control *or* direction *or* guidance; *(de missile etc)* homing; *Radio (pour automobilistes)* traffic news *or* information

radioguidé [radjogide] ADJ radio-controlled; *(missile)* guided

radio(-)journal, *pl* **radio(-)journaux** NM *Radio* radio news, news bulletin

radiologie [radjolɔʒi] NF *Méd* radiology

radiologique [radjolɔʒik] ADJ *Méd* radiological; **examen r.** X-ray (examination)

radiologue [radjolɔg], **radiologiste** [radjolɔʒist] N *Méd* radiologist

radiomètre [radjomɛtr] NM *Phys* radiometer

radionavigant [radjonavigɑ̃] NM *Naut, Aviat* radio officer

radionavigation [radjonavigasjɔ̃] NF navigation by radar

radiophare [radjofar] NM *Naut, Aviat* radio beacon

radiophonie [radjofɔni] NF radio(tele)phony, wireless telephony, broadcasting

radiophonique [radjofɔnik] ADJ radio

radiorepérage [radjorəperaʒ] NM radio-location

radioreportage [radjorəpɔrtaʒ] NM *Radio* radio reporting; **un r.** a report

radioreporter [radjorəpɔrter] NM *Radio* radio reporter

radioréveil [radjorevɛj] NM radio-alarm (clock)

radioscopie [radjoskɔpi] NF *Méd* radioscopy, X-ray (examination)

radioscopique [radjoskɔpik] ADJ *Méd* **examen r.** X-ray (examination)

radiosondage [radjosɔ̃daʒ] NM *Météo* radiosonde exploration

radiosonde [radjosɔ̃d] NF **1** *Météo* radiosonde **2** *Aviat* radio altimeter

radio-taxi, *pl* **radio-taxis** NM radio taxi

radiotechnique [radjotɛknik] NF radiotechnology

radiotélégramme [radjotelegram] NM radio telegram

radiotélégraphie [radjotelegrafi] NF radio telegraphy, wireless telegraphy

radiotélégraphier [radjotelegrafje] VT *(conj like* **télégraphier)** *(télégramme)* to radio

radiotéléphone [radjotelefɔn] NM radiotelephone

radiotéléphonie [radjotelefɔni] NF radiotelephony, radio communication

radiotélescope [radjoteleskɔp] NM radio telescope

radiotélévisé [radjotelevize] ADJ simulcast, broadcast simultaneously on radio and television

radiotélévision [radjotelevizjɔ̃] NF radio and television

radiothérapeute [radjoterapøt] N *Méd* radiotherapist

radiothérapie [radjoterapi] NF *Méd* radiotherapy, X-ray treatment

radis [radi] NM radish; **r. noir** black radish; *Fig Fam* **ne pas/plus avoir un r.** to be (stony) broke, not to have a bean; **sans un r.** broke, *Br* skint

radium [radjɔm] NM radium

radius [radjys] NM *Anat* radius

radon [radɔ̃] NM radon

radotage [radotaʒ] NM twaddle, drivel; *(d'une vieille personne etc)* rambling talk

radoter [radote] VI *(divaguer)* to ramble on; *(rabâcher)* to keep on repeating oneself; **il commence à r.** *(par sénilité)* he *or* his mind is starting to wander; *(il se répète)* he's starting to repeat himself all the time

VT *Fam* **tu radotes toujours les mêmes histoires!** you keep on coming out with the same old thing!; **mais qu'est-ce qu'il radote?** what's he (rabbiting) on about?

radoteur, -euse [radotœr, -øz] N dotard; **c'est un (vieux) r.** he's always rambling on

radoub [radu] NM *(d'un bateau)* refitting, graving; **navire au r.** ship under repair *or* in dry dock; **bassin de r.** graving dock, dry dock

radouber [radube] VT **1** *(bateau)* to repair the hull of **2** *(filet)* to mend, to repair; *Fam Vieilli (vêtement)* to patch up

radoucir [radusir] VT *(personne)* to calm down, to mollify; *(caractère)* to soften; **r. le temps/la température** *(de la pluie, du vent)* to bring milder weather/temperatures

VPR **se radoucir** *(d'une personne)* to calm down; *(d'une voix)* to soften; *(du temps)* to become milder

radoucissement [radusismɑ̃] NM **1** *(de la voix)* softening; *(d'une personne)* calming down **2** *Météo* milder spell; **on prévoit un net r. de la température** distinctly milder temperatures are forecast

rafale [rafal] NF **1** *(de vent)* squall, strong gust, blast; *(de pluie)* burst; **vent à rafales** blustering *or* gusty wind; **temps à rafales** blustery *or* squally weather; **le vent soufflait par** *ou* **en rafales** the wind was blowing in strong gusts; **la pluie tombait par rafales** the rain was falling in great bursts **2** *(de coups de feu)* burst

raffermir [rafɛrmir] VT **1** *(chair)* to firm up, to make firm(er); *(peau, tissus)* to tone up **2** *(autorité)* to reinforce, to strengthen; *(courage)* to strengthen; **l'équipe gouvernementale est sortie raffermie du conflit** the government team came out of the conflict stronger *or* strengthened

VPR **se raffermir** *(du sol, des muscles, de la peau etc)* to firm up, to get firmer; *(des prix)* to steady; *(du gouvernement) (devenir plus intransigeant)* to take a stronger *or* firmer *or* tougher line; *(devenir plus fort)* to become stronger; **ses jambes se raffermissent** his/her legs are growing stronger again; **son au-**

torité se raffermit he is recovering *or* regaining his authority; **il se raffermit dans ses intentions** he is more determined than he used to be

raffermissement [rafɛrmismɑ̃] NM **1** *(du sol)* firming (up), making firm(er); *(des tissus, de la peau)* toning **2** *(des prix)* steadying **3** *(de l'autorité, du pouvoir)* strengthening

raffinage [rafinaʒ] NM *(du pétrole, du sucre etc)* refining

raffiné [rafine] ADJ **1** *(pétrole, sucre etc)* refined **2** *(esprit)* subtle, refined; *(goût)* refined; *(manières, style)* refined, polished

raffinement [rafinmɑ̃] NM *(des manières, de langage, de luxe)* refinement; *(de la pensée, d'une politique)* subtlety, refinement; **le comble du r.** the height of refinement; **avec des raffinements de cruauté** with sophisticated cruelty

raffiner [rafine] VT *(sucre, huile etc)* to refine; *(ses manières)* to refine, to polish

VI to be overmeticulous *or* fussy (**sur** about); **r. sur la propreté** to carry cleanliness to extremes; **on ne va pas r. sur les détails!** we won't be too fussy about the details!; **vous raffinez!** you're getting too hung up on detail!

raffinerie [rafinri] NF refinery; **r. de pétrole** oil refinery

raffineur, -euse [rafinœr, -øz] N refiner

raffoler [rafole] VI *Fam* **r. de qn/qch** to adore sb/sth, to be mad about *or* dote on sb/sth

raffut [rafy] NM *Fam (bruit)* din, racket, row; **faire du r.** *(bruit)* to make a din *or* racket *or* row; *(scandale)* to set tongues wagging; *(pour protester)* to kick up a fuss

raffûter [rafyte] VT *(outil)* to (re)sharpen, to (re)set

rafiau, **rafiot** [rafjo] NM *Naut* skiff *(with lateen sail)*; **vieux r.** old tub

rafistolage [rafistɔlaʒ] NM *Fam* patching up; **ça n'ira pas loin, c'est du r.** it won't last long, it's just a makeshift *or* patched-up job; **ces changements ne sont que du r.** these changes will do nothing more than patch things up

rafistoler [rafistɔle] VT *Fam* to patch up

rafle [rafl] NF **1** *(par la police)* raid; **la police a fait une r. dans le club** the police raided the club; *Hist* **la r. du Vel'd'Hiv** = the rounding-up of Jews in the Velodrome d'Hiver in Paris on 16 July, 1942 **2** *Vieilli* thieving; *Fam (par des voleurs etc)* clean sweep; **r. d'étalage avec bris de devanture** smash-and-grab raid

rafler [rafle] VT *Fam (de cambrioleurs)* to swipe, to nick; **ils m'ont tout raflé** they've totally cleaned me out, they've swiped the lot; **les enfants ont tout raflé dans la cuisine** the children have made off with everything in the kitchen; **le film qui a raflé tous les oscars** the film which made a clean sweep of the Oscars, the film which walked off with all the Oscars

rafraîchir [rafrɛʃir] VT **1** *(rendre frais) (personne)* to cool (down); *(pièce)* to air; **pour r. l'atmosphère** to cool the air (down) **2** *(couleur, maquillage)* to freshen up; *(peintures)* to freshen up, to do up, to renovate; *Fig* **r. sa coupe à qn** to trim sb's hair, to give sb('s hair) a trim; *Fig Fam* **r. la mémoire à qn** to refresh sb's memory; *Fig Fam* **je vais te r. les idées** I'll refresh your memory for you

VI **1** *Météo* to get cooler *or* colder; **le temps rafraîchit** it's getting colder **2** *Culin* to chill; **mettre qch à rafraîchir** to chill sth; **mettre le vin à r. à la cave** to put the wine to cool in the cellar **3** *Ordinat* to refresh

VPR **se rafraîchir 1** *(du temps)* to grow *or* turn cooler **2** *(d'une personne) (se laver)* to freshen up; *Fam (en buvant)* to have a refreshing drink

rafraîchissant [rafrɛʃisɑ̃] ADJ *(brise, boisson)* refreshing, cooling; *Fig (simplicité, spontanéité)* refreshing; **d'une simplicité/ spontanéité rafraîchissante** refreshingly simple/spontaneous

rafraîchissement [rafrɛʃismɑ̃] NM **1** *(de la température, d'un liquide etc)* cooling; **on prévoit un r. des températures ce week-end** temperatures are expected to drop *or* things are expected to be a bit cooler this weekend **2** *(boisson)* cold drink; **rafraîchissements** refreshments **3** *Ordinat* refresh

rafting [raftiŋ] NM rafting

raga [raga] NM INV *Mus* raga

ragaillardir [ragajardir] VT **r. qn** *(physiquement)* to revive sb, to make sb feel better; *(encourager)* to cheer sb up
  VPR **se ragaillardir** to cheer up, *Fam* to buck up

rage [raʒ] NF **1** *Méd, Vét* rabies **2** *Fig* rage, fury, frenzy; *(passion)* passion (**de qch** for sth); **la tempête fait r.** the storm is raging; **l'incendie faisait r.** the fire was blazing *or* raging (furiously); **avoir la r. du jeu/d'écrire** to have a passion for gambling/writing; **avoir la r. au cœur** to be bitterly angry; **fou de r.** furious, hopping mad; **se mettre en r.** to get into a rage, to get furious (**contre qn** with sb; **contre qch** about sth); **ça me met en r.** it infuriates me, it makes me furious *or* my blood boil; **r. de dents** raging toothache; *Fam* **ce n'est pas de l'amour, c'est de la r.** that's not love, it's madness

rageant [raʒɑ̃] ADJ *Fam* infuriating

rager [raʒe] VI **(je rageai(s); n. rageons)** *Fam* to rage, to be in a rage, to fume; **ça me fait r. de voir ça!** it makes me hopping mad to see that!, seeing that makes my blood boil!

rageur, -euse [raʒœr, -øz] ADJ *(ton, voix)* furious, infuriated; **dit-elle d'un ton r.** she said furiously; **'va au diable!', dit-il, r.** 'go to hell!', he said furiously

rageusement [raʒøzmɑ̃] ADV furiously

raglan [raglɑ̃] NM raglan coat
  ADJ INV **manches r.** raglan sleeves

ragondin [ragɔ̃dɛ̃] NM *Zool* coypu; *(fourrure)* nutria

ragot[1] [rago] NM *(sanglier)* boar in its third year
  ADJ *Vieilli* dumpy, squat

ragot[2] NM *Fam (commérages)* piece of gossip *or* tittle-tattle; **faire des ragots** to gossip, to tittle-tattle

ragoût [ragu] NM *Culin* stew, ragout; **r. de mouton** mutton stew; **(faire) cuire qch en r.** to stew sth

ragoûtant [ragutɑ̃] ADJ *(with neg)* **peu ou pas r.** *(plat)* unappetizing, uninviting; *(personne)* disgusting; **des choses peu ragoûtantes** some rather unpleasant *or* nasty things

ragréer [ragree] VT **1** *(maçonnerie, boiserie)* to finish off; *(jointure etc)* to clean up, to trim up **2** *(façade d'un bâtiment)* to clean

ragtime [ragtajm] NM *(danse), Mus* ragtime

rahat-lokoum [raatlokum], **rahat-loukoum** [raatlukum] NM piece of Turkish delight; **des rahat-lo(u)koums** Turkish delight

rai [rɛ] NM *(de lumière)* ray; *(d'étoile)* point

raï [raj] NM INV *Mus* = North African popular music influenced by music from the West

raid [rɛd] NM **1** *Mil* raid; **r. aérien** air raid; **lancer un r.** to launch *or* mount a raid *(contre* on) **2** *Sport* endurance test; *(en automobile)* long-distance rally; *(en avion)* long-distance flight **3** *Fin* raid; **lancer/financer un r.** to mount/to finance a raid

raide [rɛd] ADJ **1** *(membre, articulation)* stiff; *(câble etc)* taut, tight; **corde r.** tightrope; *Fig* **être sur la corde r.** to be walking a tightrope; **cheveux raides** straight hair; **mettre un**

câble au r. to take up the slack in a cable; **assis r. sur sa chaise** sitting bolt upright on his chair; **r. comme un piquet** as stiff as a ramrod, ramrod straight; *Fig Fam* **r. (comme un passe-lacet)** *(sans le sou)* (stony) broke **2** *(manières, mouvement, démarche)* stiff; *(caractère)* inflexible, unbending, unyielding **3** *(escalier, pente)* steep; **ça descend en pente r.** it slopes steeply **4** *Fam* **ça, c'est un peu r.!** that's a bit thick *or* a bit much!; **il en a vu de raides** he's had a tough life; **elle m'en a dit de raides sur toi** she told me some pretty nasty things about you **5** *très Fam (drogué)* stoned, wasted; *(ivre)* plastered, *Br* legless
  ADV **1** *(monter)* steeply **2 tomber r.** to collapse; **tomber r. (par terre)** to fall to the ground; **r. mort** dead as a doornail; **tomber r. mort** to drop dead; **il y avait une odeur à tomber r. mort** it stank to high heaven, the smell was enough to kill you; *Fam Vieilli* **il faut travailler r.** we're going to have to work like galley slaves

raider [rɛdœr] NM *Fin* (corporate) raider

raideur [rɛdœr] NF **1** *(d'un membre, d'une articulation, d'un mouvement)* stiffness; *(d'une corde)* tautness; **donne plus de r. à ta démarche** be a little bit more dignified; **avoir une r. dans le cou** to have a stiff neck **2** *(de manières)* stiffness, starchiness; *(de caractère)* inflexibility, rigidity; **répondre avec une certaine r.** to answer rather stiffly **3** *(d'une pente)* steepness, abruptness

raidillon [rɛdijɔ̃] NM steep path; *(sur une route)* (short and steep) rise

raidir [rɛdir] VT *(corde, câble etc)* to tighten, to pull tight *or* taut; *(tissu)* to stiffen; **r. les bras/jambes** to brace one's arms/legs; **un cadavre raidi par la mort** a body in rigor mortis
  VPR **se raidir 1** *(des membres, des articulations)* to stiffen up, to grow stiff(er); *(de câble)* to grow taut, to tauten **2** *(d'une personne)* to tense up, to grow tense; *Fig* **se r. contre le malheur** to steel *or* brace oneself against misfortune

raidissement [rɛdismɑ̃] NM stiffening; *(de corde)* tautening; *Fig* **r. des rapports internationaux** increase of tension in international relations; **il y a un net r. de la position des ouvriers face à la direction** the workers are quite clearly standing their ground with the management

raidisseur [rɛdisœr] NM *Tech* stiffener; *(pour fils de fer)* wire stretcher

raie[1] [rɛ] NF **1** *(motif)* stripe **2** *Opt* **raies du spectre, raies spectrales** spectrum lines **3** *(dans les cheveux)* parting, *Am* part; **porter la r. à droite** to part one's hair on the right; **porter la r. sur le** *ou* **de côté/au milieu** to part one's hair at the side/in the centre, to have a side/centre parting; **je ne porte pas de r.** I don't have a parting; **où portez-vous la r.?** where do you part your hair?; **avoir une coiffure sans r.** to wear one's hair without a parting **4** *Agr* furrow

raie[2] NF *(poisson)* skate, ray; **r. bouclée** thornback; *Culin* **r. au beurre noir** skate in brown butter sauce

raifort [rɛfɔr] NM horseradish

rail [rɑj] NM **1** rail; **rails mobiles** movable rails, switch rails; **r. conducteur** *(d'une voie ferrée électrifiée)* conductor rail, live rail; **quitter les rails, sortir des rails** *(d'un train)* to be derailed; *Fig* to go off the rails; *Fig* to go off the rails; *Fig* **remettre l'économie sur les rails** to get the economy back on the rails *or* (back) on its feet again; *Fig* **il faut le remettre sur les rails** we'll have to put him back on the rails *or* straighten him out **2** *(chemins de fer)* railways, *Am* railroads; **travailleurs du r.** railwaymen, *Am* railroaders; **le r. est un moyen de locomotion très développé en**

France the railway is a much-used means of transport in France **3** *(glissière)* **r. (de sécurité)** crash barrier **4** *(itinéraire)* lane; **les bateaux se déplacent sur quatre rails au large d'Ouessant** boats sail along four sea lanes off Ushant; **le respect des rails aériens** respect of air (traffic) lanes *or* air corridors

railler [rɑje] *Litt* VT *(personne)* to mock, to make fun of; **elle le raille sur sa timidité** she mocks *or* makes fun of his shyness
  VI to jest; **il me répondit en raillant** he answered me in jest
  VPR **se railler se r. de qn/qch** to mock sb/sth, to make fun of sb/sth

raillerie [rɑjri] NF *(plaisanterie)* jest; **sans r.** jesting apart; **recueillir des railleries** to be scoffed *or* mocked at; **il décida d'ignorer leurs railleries** he decided to ignore their scoffing; *Litt* **il n'entend pas r. sur les choses religieuses** he will not have jokes made about religion

railleur, -euse [rɑjœr, -øz] ADJ *(ton, voix, commentaire etc)* mocking, derisive
  N scoffer

railleusement [rɑjøzmɑ̃] ADV mockingly, derisively

rainer [rene] VT to groove

rainette [rɛnɛt] NF **1** *(grenouille)* tree frog **2** *(pomme)* pippin; **r. grise** russet

rainure [rɛnyr] NF **1** groove; **r. de clavette** keyway, key slot; **à rainure(s)** grooved **2** *Astron* rille

rainurer [rɛnyre] VT to groove

raiponce [rɛpɔ̃s] NF *Bot* rampion

raisin [rɛzɛ̃] NM **1 du r.** (some) grapes; **manger du r.** to eat grapes; **(grain de) r.** grape; **grappe de r.** bunch of grapes; **raisin(s) de table** dessert grapes; **raisins secs** raisins; **raisins de Corinthe** currants; **raisins de Smyrne** sultanas **2** *Bot* **r. de renard** herb Paris; *Bot* **r. d'ours** bearberry **3** *(mollusque)* **r. de mer** sea grapes, cuttlefish eggs **4** **grand r.** *(papier)* ≃ royal

Il faut noter que le terme anglais **raisin** est un faux ami. Il signifie **raisin sec**.

raisiné [rezine] NM **1** fruit preserved in grape jelly **2** *Arg (sang)* blood

raisinet [rezinɛ] NM *Suisse (groseille)* redcurrant

raison [rɛzɔ̃] NF **1** *(motif)* reason, ground (**de** for); **mais ce n'est pas une r. pour venir me déranger** but that's no reason to disturb *or* for disturbing me; **pour des raisons de convenance personnelle** for personal reasons; **pour quelle r.?** for what reason?; **sans r.** without (any) reason, for no reason; **elle s'est inquiétée sans r.** she worried needlessly; **en r. de qch** because of *or* on account of sth; **en r. d'un deuil récent** owing to a recent bereavement; **je me rends à vos raisons** I concede defeat; **rendre r. de qch** to give a reason for sth, to give an explanation of sth, to account for sth; **à plus forte r. puisqu'il suit un traitement** particularly since he's being given treatment; **à plus forte r. si elle est invitée** particularly if she's invited too; **r. de plus** all the more reason (**pour venir** to come); **r. de plus pour qu'elle fasse un effort** all the more reason for her to make an effort; **la r. pour laquelle il est venu** the reason (why) he came

2 *(entendement)* reason; **il n'a pas toute sa r.** he is not quite sane, he's not quite in his right mind; **il n'a plus toute sa r.** he's losing his faculties; **recouvrer la r.** to regain one's sanity; **heureusement, il a recouvré la r. et le mariage n'a pas eu lieu** luckily he came to his senses and the wedding was called off; **ramener qn à la r.** to make sb see reason *or* sense; **revenir à la r.** to come to one's senses,

to see reason; **se rendre à la r.** to see sense, to come to one's senses; **rends-toi à la r.!** see sense!, be sensible!; **vous perdez la r.!** have you taken leave of your senses?; **entendre r.** to listen to reason; **l'âge de r.** the age of reason; **mariage de r.** marriage of convenience **3 avoir r.** to be right; **avoir r. de faire qch** to be right to do or in doing sth; **elle a bien r. de ne pas lui demander son avis** she's quite right not to ask his/her opinion; **donner r. à qn** to admit that sb is right; **les événements lui donnèrent r.** events proved him/her right; **se faire une r.** to accept the inevitable, to resign oneself; **le travail n'était pas bon, mais il a bien fallu se faire une r.** the work wasn't well done but we just had to accept it as it was; **avec r.** rightly; **elle s'est mise en colère avec r.** she was right to get angry, she got angry and rightly so; **boire plus que de r.** to drink too much or more than is reasonable; **il avait bu, et plus que de r.** he had drunk too much, he had been drinking more than was reasonable; **il est inquiet plus que de r.** he is unreasonably concerned, his concern is slightly irrational; **gourmand plus que de r.** more than reasonably greedy; **comme de r.** as a matter of course, as one might expect **4** *(satisfaction)* satisfaction, reparation; **demander r. d'un affront** to demand satisfaction for an insult; **avoir r. de qn/qch** to get the better of sb/sth; **elle ne partira pas tant qu'elle n'aura pas eu r. de cet appareil** she won't leave until she's sorted that machine out **5** *Math* ratio; **r. géométrique/arithmétique** geometrical/arithmetical ratio; **r. directe/inverse** direct/inverse ratio or proportion; **le poids est en r. directe du volume** the weight is directly proportional or in direct proportion to the volume; **travail payé à r. de cinquante euros l'heure** work paid at the rate of fifty euros an hour; **je suis payé à r. de cinquante euros de l'heure** I am paid fifty euros an hour; **à r. de deux par minute** at the rate of two per or a minute; **à r. de huit mots par ligne** on the basis of eight words to a line
▶▶ *Com* **r. commerciale** trade name; **la r. d'État** reasons of State, raison d'état; **le gouvernement a invoqué la r. d'État pour justifier cette mesure** the government said that it had done this for reasons of State; **r. d'être: r. d'être de qch** raison d'être of or object of or reason for sth; **c'est ma seule r. d'être** it's my whole life or raison d'être; **sa petite fille est sa r. d'être** his granddaughter is his entire reason for living or his only raison d'être, he lives for his granddaughter; **c'est la r. d'être de cet organisme** that's the whole point of or reason for the institution, that's what the institution is there for; **cela n'a plus aucune r. d'être** there's no longer any need for it; *Com* **r. sociale** (company) name

raisonnable [rɛzɔnabl] **ADJ 1** *(sensé)* reasonable; **tu n'es pas r.** you're not being reasonable; **soyez r.!** be sensible or reasonable!, listen to reason!; **tu n'es pas r. de tellement fumer** you're silly to smoke so much, you're not being sensible smoking so much; **à son âge il devrait être plus r.** he is old enough to know better; **ce n'est pas r. de sortir avant la fin** it's silly to leave before the end; **tu ne peux pas sortir et travailler, ce n'est pas r.!** you can't go out (all the time) and work, it's stupid! **2** *(doué de raison)* rational; **l'homme est un animal r.** man is a rational or reasoning animal **3** *(condition, frais etc)* reasonable; **prix r.** reasonable or moderate or fair price; **à un prix r.** reasonably priced, at a reasonable price

raisonnablement [rɛzɔnabləmã] **ADV 1** *(avec bon sens)* reasonably, rationally; **tout ce qu'on pouvait r. demander** all that one

could reasonably ask for **2** *(assez)* *(grand etc)* reasonably, fairly; *(manger etc)* moderately, in moderation; *Fam (travailler etc)* fairly well, reasonably well

raisonné [rɛzɔne] **ADJ** *(argumentation)* reasoned; *(grammaire)* rational, analytical; **voilà qui est bien r.!** well worked out!; *Com* **catalogue r.** descriptive catalogue

raisonnement [rɛzɔnmã] **NM** *(pensée etc)* reasoning; **homme de r. juste** man of sense; **je comprends ton r.** I understand your reasoning or (line of) argument; **on ne peut pas tenir un tel r. avec lui** you can't take that line with him; **pas de raisonnements!** don't argue!

raisonner [rɛzɔne] **VI 1** *(penser)* to reason (**sur** about); **r. par induction/déduction** to reason by induction or inductively/by deduction or deductively **2** *(discuter)* to argue (**sur** about); **on ne peut r. avec ce genre de personnes** you can't reason with people like that; **ne raisonnez pas tant!** don't be so argumentative!
VT *(personne)* to reason with; **je vais essayer de le r.** I'll try and reason with him or make him see sense; **il faut absolument la r.** she must be made to see sense
VPR se raisonner to see reason; **raisonne-toi donc!** try to be reasonable!, do see reason!; **la jalousie ne se raisonne pas** jealousy cannot be reasoned with or knows no reason

raisonneur, -euse [rɛzɔnœr, -øz] **ADJ 1** reasoning, rational **2** *(qui discutaille)* argumentative
N 1 reasoner **2** *(discutailleur)* arguer

raja(h) [raʒa] **NM** raja(h)

rajeunir [raʒœnir] **VT 1** *(personne)* to rejuvenate; **ce chapeau te/la rajeunit (de dix ans)** that hat makes you/her look (ten years) younger; **ça me rajeunit** it makes me feel younger or feel young again; **ça ne nous rajeunit pas!** it brings it home or makes you realize that we're not getting any younger!; **tu la rajeunis, elle a passé la trentaine** she's not as young as you think, she's over thirty; **vous me rajeunissez, j'ai cinq ans de plus!** I'm five years older than that!, add five years to that figure!; **elle me rajeunit de cinq ans** she's taking five years off my age **2** *(robe, veste etc)* to update; *(organisation, bureau)* to modernize; **r. une équipe** to bring new blood into a team; **une équipe rajeunie** a younger team; **le comité a besoin d'être rajeuni** the committee needs new blood
VI to get younger, to grow young again; **je ne rajeunis pas** I'm not getting any younger; **il a rajeuni de dix ans** he's ten years younger
VPR se rajeunir *(pour paraître plus jeune)* to make oneself look younger; *(se dire, prétendre plus jeune)* to make oneself out to be younger than one is; **elle se rajeunit de quelques années** she's taking a few years off her age

rajeunissant [raʒœnisã] **ADJ** *(traitement, crème)* rejuvenating

rajeunissement [raʒœnismã] **NM** rejuvenation

rajout [raʒu] **NM** addition; **on ne peut plus faire de r.** nothing else can be added, we can't add anything else

rajouter [raʒute] **VT** to add; **r. du sel** add (more) salt, put in more salt

rajustement [raʒystəmã] **NM** readjustment, adjustment

rajuster [raʒyste] **VT** *(vêtement, chapeau, cravate)* to adjust, to straighten; *(chignon)* to fix, to tidy; *(prix)* to adjust; **r. les salaires** to bring wages into line with the cost of living; **il faut r. les salaires des femmes** women's wages have to be brought into line with men's

VPR se rajuster to tidy or smarten or straighten oneself up

râle¹ [rɑl] **NM** *(oiseau)* **r. d'eau** water rail; **r. des genêts** corncrake

râle², râlement [rɑlmã] **NM** *(venant de la gorge)* rattle; **le r. (de la mort)** the death rattle; *Méd* **un r. au poumon** a rale or *Fam* rattle in the lung

ralenti [ralãti] **ADJ** slow(er); **au trot r.** at a slow trot
NM 1 *Cin* slow motion; *Cin* **scène au** ou **en r.** scene in slow motion; *Aut* **prendre un virage au r.** to take a corner slowly; **l'usine tourne au r.** the factory's not working at full capacity, the factory's just ticking over; **elle travaille au r.** she's slowed right down; **la ville tourne au r.** things are pretty quiet in the city; **le malade a l'impression de vivre au r.** the patient feels he's living in slow motion or hardly living at all **2** *(de moteur)* idling, slow running, idle; **r. accéléré** fast idle; **tourner au r.** to idle, to tick over

ralentir [ralãtir] **VT** *(circulation, progression)* to slow (down); *(production, progrès, économie)* to slow (down or up); **r. la marche** to slow down, to walk a bit more slowly; **r. le pas** to slow down; **r. l'allure** to slow down; **r. ses efforts** to ease up
VI to slow down; *(d'un train, véhicule, convoi etc)* to slow (down), to reduce speed; *(de la progression)* to slow (down); *(de la production, des progrès, de l'économie)* to slow (down or up); **le train ralentit quand il entre en gare** the train slows down or reduces its speed when it pulls into a station; **ralentis, il y a du verglas!** slow down, there's black ice on the road!
VPR se ralentir *(de mouvements, de la circulation etc)* to slow (down); *(de la production, des progrès, de l'économie)* to slow (down or up)

ralentissement [ralãtismã] **NM** *(de la circulation, d'un rythme, de l'économie etc)* slowdown, slowing down, slowing up; *(des exportations, de la production, des ventes)* slowdown (**de** in); **des ralentissements** *(de la circulation)* hold-ups, delays; **périodes de r. dans les affaires** slow or slack periods in business; **il comptait sur un r. de la progression de l'armée allemande** he was counting on the German army's advance slowing down

ralentisseur [ralãtisœr] **NM** *Aut* speed bump, ramp, *Br Fam* sleeping policeman; *Tech, Élec* retarder; *Nucl* moderator

râler [rɑle] **VI 1** *Fam (se plaindre)* to moan, to grouse, to grumble; **elle râle contre notre retard** she's moaning about us being late; **ça me fait r.!** it gets up my nose!; **ça me fait r. de perdre du temps comme ça!** wasting time like that really bugs me!; **laisse-le r.** let him moan; **mais qu'est-ce qu'elle a encore à r.?** what is she moaning about now? **2** *(de douleur)* to moan, to groan; *(d'un mourant)* to give a or the death rattle **3** *(d'un tigre)* to growl

râleur, -euse [rɑlœr, -øz] *Fam* **ADJ** grumbling, moaning, grousing; **elle est très râleuse** she's a real moaner or grumbler
N moaner, grumbler

ralliement [ralimã] **NM 1** *(des troupes)* rallying; **mot de r.** *Mil* password; *Fig* rallying cry; **point de r.** rallying point, meeting place; **ce bar est un bon point de r.** the bar is a good meeting place; **Paris est le point de r. de tous les comédiens français** Paris is a magnet for all French actors; **signe de r.** rallying sign; **en signe de r., ils portent tous le même tee-shirt** they all wear the same tee-shirt as a kind of badge or so they can recognize each other **2** *(d'un avion)* homing **3** *(d'adhérents)* winning over; **son r. à notre**

parti fut immédiat he/she immediately came over or was won over to our party

rallier [ralje] (*impf, pr sub n.* ralliions) VT 1 (*troupes, navires etc*) to rally; *Fig* r. l'opinion autour d'une idée commune to mobilize or rally public opinion around a common idea 2 *Mil etc* (*d'un soldat etc*) (*unité*) to rejoin; (*base*) to return to, to make one's way back to; *Naut* r. le bord to rejoin one's ship 3 r. qn (*à un parti, mouvement*) to win sb over; (*à une opinion*) to win sb over, to bring sb round; *Fig* les groupuscules ont rallié le groupe majoritaire the small groups have united with or joined the majority group; *Fig* r. tous les suffrages to win unanimous approval or support
▶ VPR se rallier 1 (*des troupes etc*) to rally; *Hum* ralliez-vous à mon panache blanc! follow me! 2 (*des opposants, dissidents*) to rally; se r. à (*une opinion, un point de vue*) to come round to; (*un parti*) to join; (*une cause*) to rally to

rallonge [ralɔ̃ʒ] NF 1 (*d'une table*) (extension) leaf; *Can* (*d'un bureau*) runoff; *Tech* extension bar or piece; table à rallonge(s) extending table 2 (*électrique*) extension cord or lead 3 *Fam* additional or extra time/payment/*etc*; r. budgétaire addition to the budget; obtenir une r. de 30 000 euros to get an extra 30,000 euros; une r. de trois jours an additional or an extra or another three days

rallongement [ralɔ̃ʒmɑ̃] NM lengthening, extension

rallonger [ralɔ̃ʒe] (je rallongeai(s); n. rallongeons) VT (*prolonger*) to make longer; (*vacances, journée de travail, route*) to extend (de by); (*vêtement*) to let down, to lengthen; r. qch de dix centimètres/de deux heures to make sth ten centimetres/two hours longer; *Fam* ça me rallongerait de 20 minutes it would add twenty minutes onto my journey; ils ont rallongé le câble d'un mètre they lengthened the cable by a metre, they made the cable a metre longer; tu devrais r. ce paragraphe you should make this paragraph longer; j'ai fait r. cette jupe de dix centimètres I had this skirt let down or taken down ten centimetres
▶ VI (*des jours*) to get longer, to draw out; (*des nuits*) to get longer, to draw in

rallumer [ralyme] VT (*appareil électrique*) to turn on or switch on again; (*avec une allumette*) to light again; *Fig* (*querelle, colère, espoir etc*) to rekindle, to revive; r. l'électricité ou la lumière ou les lumières to turn on or switch on the light(s) again
▶ VI rallume, s'il te plaît switch or turn the light/television/*etc* on again, please
▶ VPR se rallumer (*de la lumière, d'un appareil électrique*) to come back or go back on; (*d'un feu*) to flare up again; *Fig* (*d'une guerre, dispute*) to flare up again; (*de l'espoir etc*) to rekindle, to revive; il tira sur la pipe, qui se ralluma he puffed on the pipe, which got going again

rally [rali] NM *Bourse* rally

rallye [rali] NM 1 *Sport* (car) rally 2 = series of dances held for young, upper-class people, ≃ the débutantes' season

RAM [ram] NF *Ordinat* RAM; R. sur carte onboard RAM

Ramadan [ramadɑ̃] NM *Rel* Ramadan; respecter le R., faire le R. to observe Ramadan

ramage [ramaʒ] NM 1 *Vieilli* (*feuillage*) foliage; (*motif*) floral design 2 (*des oiseaux*) song, twittering, chirping

ramas [ramɑ] NM *Vieilli* = ramassis

ramassage [ramasaʒ] NM 1 (*des ordures, de vêtements, de vieux journaux*) collection; (*de fruits, noix etc*) gathering, picking; r. scolaire school bus service; car de r. scolaire school

bus; il n'existe pas de service de r. scolaire there isn't a school bus 2 *Bourse* (*d'actions*) buying up

ramassé [ramase] ADJ 1 (*trapu*) thickset, stocky 2 (*recroquevillé*) (*person, village etc*) huddled; village r. autour de son église village huddled or clustering round its church 3 (*machine, style*) compact

ramasse-miettes [ramasmjɛt] NM INV table tidy (*a small brush and pan for clearing the crumbs off the table*)

ramasse-monnaie [ramasmɔnɛ] NM INV change tray

ramasse-poussière [ramaspusjɛr] NM INV 1 *Belg* dustpan 2 dust-trap; ces bibelots sont de véritables r. these ornaments just gather or collect the dust

---

RAMASSER [ramase]

> VT to pick up 1, 2 ▪ to collect 1, 2 ▪ to gather 1, 2 ▪ to dig up 1 ▪ to get 3 ▪ to catch 3
> VPR to gather oneself 1 ▪ to crouch 1 ▪ to fail 2

VT 1 (*prendre par terre*) (*objet tombé*) to pick up; (*fruits, noix, coquillages*) to gather, to collect, to pick up; (*champignons*) to pick, to gather, to collect; (*pommes de terre*) to dig up, to lift; r. qch avec une pelle et une balayette to sweep sth up (with a brush and dustpan); r. qch avec un chiffon to wipe sth up; r. des feuilles avec un râteau to rake up leaves; r. ses jupes (*pour ne pas se salir*) to gather one's skirts up; *Cartes* r. la mise to win the kitty; r. qn to help sb up or to his/her feet, to pick sb up; *Fam* (*de la police*) to pick sb up; *Fig* r. qn dans le ruisseau to pick sb up out of the gutter; *Fig* être à r. à la petite cuillère to be worn to a frazzle, to be fit to drop; *Fam* se faire r. (*par la police*) to be run in or picked up
2 (*regrouper*) (*des assiettes, copies, feuilles etc*) to collect, to gather (up); (*de l'argent*) to collect; (*informations*) to gather, to collect; (*des enfants, ouvriers, courrier*) to pick up, to collect; (*actions*) to buy up; r. les cartes to pick up the cards; r. ses affaires to collect one's belongings; r. ses cheveux dans une natte/sur le dessus de la tête to put one's hair (up) in a pigtail/to pile one's hair on top of one's head; r. (toutes) ses forces to gather or muster all one's strength; les quelques informations/connaissances qu'il a pu r. the scraps of information/knowledge he was able to pick up; le tigre ramasse son corps avant de bondir the tiger crouches before springing; *Fam* il a dû r. pas mal d'argent avec cette affaire he must have made quite a pile or a fair old whack out of the business
3 *Fig Fam* (*recevoir*) (*engueulade, gifle, râclée, procès-verbal*) to get; (*rhume*) to catch; r. une bûche ou une pelle to fall flat on one's face, to come a cropper
▶ VPR se ramasser 1 (*pour faire un effort*) to gather oneself; (*d'un tigre*) (*avant de bondir*) to crouch
2 (*après une chute*) to pick oneself up; *Fig Fam* (*échouer, tomber*) to fail, to fall flat on one's face, to come a cropper

---

ramassette [ramasɛt] NF *Belg* dustpan

ramasseur, -euse [ramasœr, -øz] N (*de champignons etc*) picker, collector, gatherer; *Tennis* r./ramasseuse de balles ball boy/girl; r. de lait milk collector (*who collects milk from farms*)

ramassis [ramasi] NM *Péj* (*de choses*) heap, pile, jumble; (*de gens*) bunch; (*d'idées*) collection, hotchpotch

ramassoire [ramaswar] NF *Suisse* (*pelle à poussière*) dustpan

rambarde [rɑ̃bard] NF *Naut etc* (guard)rail

ramdam [ramdam] NM *Fam* row, racket; faire du ou un sacré r. to make a heck of a din or racket

rame¹ [ram] NF (*pour faire pousser des pois etc*) stick, cane; haricots à rames stick beans

rame² NF (*aviron*) oar; aller à la r. to row; nous avons rejoint le port à la r. we rowed into port; faire force de rames to row hard; *Fam* elle n'en fiche pas une r. she does damn all, she never does a stroke (of work)

rame³ NF 1 (*de papier*) ream 2 *Rail* train; *Naut* (*de péniches*) string, tow; *Rail* la r. directe pour Tours the through coach(es) for Tours; r. (de métro) (underground or Am subway) train

rameau, -eaux [ramo] NM 1 (*d'arbre*) (small) branch or bough; un r. d'olivier an olive branch; *Rel* le dimanche des Rameaux, les Rameaux Palm Sunday 2 (*de familles, de langues*) branch 3 *Anat* ramification

ramée [rame] NF 1 *Litt, Vieilli* (*d'un arbre*) green or leafy boughs 2 (*branches coupées*) cut branches 3 *Fam* il n'en fiche pas une r. he does damn all, he never does a stroke (of work)

ramener [ramne] (*conj like* mener) VT 1 (*reconduire*) (*personne*), *Fam* (*objet*) (*vers le point de référence choisi*) to bring back; (*en s'éloignant du point de référence choisi*) to take back; (*l'ordre, la paix*) to restore; ramenez-nous-le vite! bring him back quickly!; on peut maintenant r. les enfants à l'école we can take the children back to school now; il a fallu la r. d'urgence à l'hôpital we had to rush her back to hospital; c'est lui qui est chargé de r. le journal it's his job to fetch or get the newspaper; r. qn chez lui en voiture to drive sb home; je peux vous r.? can I give you a lift or Am ride back?; la faim/la fatigue/le froid le ramènera he'll come back when he's hungry/tired/cold; la curiosité le ramènera curiosity will bring him back; la faim/la fatigue/le froid le ramena he came back because he was hungry/tired/cold; r. qn à la vie to bring sb back to life, to resuscitate sb; r. qn à la raison to make sb see reason or sense; r. la conversation sur un sujet to lead or bring the conversation back to a subject; *Fam* r. le compteur à zéro to reset the counter to zero, to zero the counter; ça me ramène des années en arrière! that really takes me back!; ça me ramène au temps de mon enfance/au temps où ... that takes me back to my childhood/to when ...; *Fam* r. sa fraise ou *très Fam* sa gueule, la r. (*s'immiscer*) to stick or shove one's oar in; ramène ta fraise, ramène-la (*viens ici*) get yourself over here a minute
2 (*réduire*) (*nombre de chômeurs, prix, inflation etc*) to reduce (à to); r. l'inflation à un taux inférieur to bring down inflation
3 (*remettre*) (*couverture*) to pull up (sur over); (*baisser*) (*chapeau, jupe*) to pull down (sur over); r. ses cheveux sur le côté to sweep one's hair to the side; *Fig* elle ramène tout à elle/à ses propres problèmes she always drags the conversation round to herself/her own problems
▶ VPR se ramener 1 voici à quoi se ramène son raisonnement this is what his/her argument boils down to 2 *Fam* (*arriver*) to roll up; c'est à cette heure-ci que tu te ramènes? what kind of time do you call this!

ramequin [ramkɛ̃] NM *Culin* ramekin

ramer¹ [rame] VT (*pois etc*) to stake

ramer² VI 1 (*pagayer*) to row, *Litt* to pull (at the oar/oars); r. en couple to scull; r. à rebours to back water 2 *Fig Fam* to sweat blood; qu'est-ce qu'on a ramé! we sweated blood!, we worked like dogs or like galley slaves!; **j'ai ramé pendant des années avant de trouver ce travail** I had a hard time of it for years before I found this job; **j'ai ramé pendant des années pour restaurer cette maison** it took years of hard graft to restore this house

rameur, -euse [ramœr, -øz] N *(à l'aviron)* rower, oarsman; *f* oarswoman; **r. de couple** sculler

rameux, -euse [ramø, -øz] ADJ branching, *Spéc* ramose

rami [rami] NM *Cartes* rummy

ramie [rami] NF *Bot* ramie

ramier [ramje] ADJ INV, NM **(pigeon) r.** ring dove, wood pigeon

ramification [ramifikasjɔ̃] NF *Bot* ramification, branching (out); *Fig (d'une secte, famille, science etc)* branch; *Fig* **ramifications** *(d'une affaire, d'un scandale)* ramifications

ramifier (se) [səramifje] VPR to branch out (en into); *Fig* **cette organisation se ramifie dans plusieurs pays** this organization has branches in several countries

ramille [ramij] NF twig

ramolli, -ie [ramɔli] ADJ *(beurre)* soft; *Fam (personne) (physiquement)* limp, washed out; *(mentalement)* soft in the head; **je suis ou je me sens tout r.** I feel like a wet rag *or* as if I've had all of the stuffing knocked out of me
▸ N *Fam* wimp; **c'est un r. du cerveau** he's going soft in the head

ramollir [ramɔlir] VT *(cire, beurre)* to soften; *Fig (volonté)* to sap; **ces vacances m'ont ramolli** this holiday has left me without any energy
▸ VPR **se ramollir** *(du beurre, goudron)* to go soft, to soften; *Fig (physiquement)* to go downhill; *(moralement)* to have no energy, *Fam* to have no get up and go; *Fam* **son cerveau se ramollit** he's going soft in the head

ramollissement [ramɔlismɑ̃] NM softening

ramollo [ramɔlo] *Fam* ADJ *(inv in f) (physiquement)* limp, washed out; **je me sens tout r.** I feel like a wet rag *or* as if I've had all of the stuffing knocked out of me; **son grand-père est un peu r.** his grandfather's a bit soft in the head
▸ N **c'est un r.** he's a wimp

ramon [ramɔ̃] NM *Belg (balai)* broom

ramonage [ramɔnaʒ] NM (chimney) sweeping *or* cleaning; *(en alpinisme)* climbing a chimney, chimneying

ramoner [ramɔne] VT *(cheminée)* to sweep, to clean
▸ VI to sweep *or* clean the chimney; *(en alpinisme)* to (climb a) chimney

ramoneur [ramɔnœr] NM (chimney) sweep

rampage [rɑ̃paʒ] NM *Aut (d'une boîte automatique)* creep

rampant, -e [rɑ̃pɑ̃] ADJ **1** *(plante)* creeping; *(animal)* crawling; *Aviat* **personnel r.** ground staff **2** *Péj (personne, caractère)* crawling, grovelling **3** *(inflation)* rampant; *Hér* **lion r.** lion rampant

rampe [rɑ̃p] NF **1** *(d'escalier)* ban(n)isters, handrail; **faire des glissades sur la r.** to slide down the banisters; *Fam* **tenir bon la r.** to be still going strong; *Arg* **lâcher la r.** to kick the bucket, to snuff it **2** *(pente)* slope, incline, rise; *(d'une route)* gradient; *Aut* **vitesse en r.** speed when (hill) climbing *or* going uphill; *Aut* **ralentir dans la r.** to slow down on the incline **3** *(passerelle etc)* ramp, gangway **4** *(de projecteurs etc)* bank **5** *Théâtre* footlights; *Fig* **être sous les feux de la r.** to be in the limelight; **pièce/acteur qui ne passe pas la r.** play that/actor who doesn't come across
▸▸ **r. d'accès** access ramp; **r. de graissage** lubricating rack, oil distributor; **r. de lance-**

ment *(de projectile)* launching ramp; *Aviat* **r. (lumineuse) d'atterrissage** illuminated landing strip; **r. mobile** portable ramp, movable gangway

rampement [rɑ̃pmɑ̃] NM creeping, crawling

ramper [rɑ̃pe] VI *(d'un animal, d'une personne)* to crawl; *(d'une plante)* to creep; **entrer/sortir en rampant** to crawl in/out; *Péj* **r. devant les chefs** to crawl *or* grovel to the bosses; **je n'aime pas les gens qui rampent!** I don't like crawlers!

rampon [rɑ̃pɔ̃] NM *Suisse (mâche)* lamb's lettuce

ramponneau, -eaux [rɑ̃pɔno] NM *Fam* clout, thump

ramure [ramyr] NF **1** *(d'arbre)* branches, boughs **2** *(d'un cerf)* antlers

rancard [rɑ̃kar] NM **1** *Fam (rendez-vous) (avec son petit ami)* date; *(chez le médecin, le dentiste etc)* appointment; **j'ai r. avec lui à deux heures** *(ami)* I'm meeting him at two o'clock; *(petit ami)* I've got a date with him at two o'clock; *(médecin)* I've got an appointment with him at *or* for two o'clock; **on s'est filé un r. pour la semaine prochaine** we arranged to meet next week, we made a date for next week **2** *Arg (renseignement)* tip

rancarder [rɑ̃karde] VT *Arg* **r. qn sur qch** to put sb on to sth; **on a dû les r.** they must have been tipped off

rancart [rɑ̃kar] NM *Fam* **mettre au r.** *(objet)* to discard; *(projet)* to shelve; *(personne)* to put on the sidelines, to sideline; **on a finalement décidé la mise au r. du projet** we finally decided to shelve the project

rance [rɑ̃s] ADJ rancid, rank
▸ NM **sentir le r.** *(du beurre)* to smell rancid; *(d'un placard)* to smell fusty; **un goût de r.** a rancid taste; **avoir un goût de r.** to taste rancid

ranch [rɑ̃tʃ] NM ranch; **exploiter un r.** to ranch

rancidité [rɑ̃sidite] NF rancidness

rancir [rɑ̃sir] VI to become *or* grow rancid

rancœur [rɑ̃kœr] NF resentment, bitterness, rancour; **j'ai de la r. contre lui** I feel resentment towards him, I resent him; **plein de r.** *(personne, ton)* resentful, bitter

rançon [rɑ̃sɔ̃] NF ransom; *Litt* **mettre qn à r.** to hold sb to ransom; *Fig* **la r. du progrès/de la gloire** the price of progress/fame; **c'est la r. du progrès!** that's the price you pay for progress!

rançonner [rɑ̃sɔne] VT **r. qn** to hold sb to ransom; *Fig Fam* to fleece sb; **r. un voyageur** to hold up (and rob) a traveller

rancune [rɑ̃kyn] NF spite; **garder r. à qn, avoir de la r. contre qn** to have a grudge against sb, to bear sb a grudge; **plein de r.** spiteful; **par r.** out of spite; **sans r.!** no hard feelings!; **il y a de vieilles rancunes entre eux** there is bad blood between them

rancunier, -ière [rɑ̃kynje, -jɛr] ADJ vindictive, spiteful
▸ N vindictive *or* spiteful person

randomisation [rɑ̃dɔmizasjɔ̃] NF randomization

randomiser [rɑ̃dɔmize] VT to randomize

randonnée [rɑ̃dɔne] NF ramble, hike; *(sport)* rambling, trekking; *(en voiture)* outing, trip; *(à vélo)* run, ride; *(en montagne)* hill-walking, climbing; *(à ski de fond)* cross-country skiing; *(avec peau de phoque)* ski-mountaineering; **r. à pied** *ou* **pédestre** hike; **r. équestre** pony trek; **chemin de grande r.** long-distance footpath; **faire de la r.** *(à pied)* to go hiking; *(en petite montagne)* to go hill-walking; *(en moyenne montagne)* to go climbing; *(en haute montagne)* to go moun-

taineering; **r. en VTT** mountain biking; **une r. en montagne** a hill-walk, a climb; **r. sac au dos** backpacking (tour); **r. à dos de poney** pony-trekking

randonneur, -euse [rɑ̃dɔnœr, -øz] N *(à pied)* rambler, hiker, walker; *(en petite montagne)* hill-walker; *(en moyenne montagne)* climber; *(en haute montagne)* mountaineer; *(à ski)* cross-country skier; *(avec peau de phoque)* ski-mountaineer

rang [rɑ̃] NM **1** *(d'arbres, de sièges etc)* row, line; *(d'oignons, de tricot)* row; *(d'avirons)* bank; *Mil* rank; **fauteuil au premier r.** front-row seat; *Scol* **être (assis) au premier/dernier r.** to sit in the front/back row, to sit at the front/back of the class; *Fig* **je le sais, j'étais au premier r. (pour le voir)** I should know, I have first-hand experience; **se mettre en r./rangs** to line up; *Hum* **se mettre en r. d'oignons** to stand (close together) in a line; **(un collier avec) trois rangs de perles** a triple strand of beads; **machine à quatre rangs de touches** four-bank typewriter; **sur deux rangs** in two ranks, two deep; **par rangs de trois** three abreast, three in a row; *Mil* **homme du r.** private; *Mil* **formez les rangs!** fall in!; *Mil, Fig* **serrer les rangs** to close ranks; *Mil* **en rangs serrés** in close order; *Fig* **nous sommes arrivés en rangs serrés dans le bureau du directeur** we trooped into the manager's office; *Fig* **s'il le faut, nous irons en rangs serrés lui en parler** we'll talk to him about it all together *or* as a group *or* en masse if necessary; *Mil, Fig* **rompre les rangs** to break ranks; *Mil* **sortir des rangs** to fall out (of line), to break rank; **officier sorti du r.** officer promoted from the ranks; *Fig* **un ancien ouvrier sorti du r.** a former worker who came up *or* rose through the ranks **2** *(classement)* rank, place; *(social)* station; *Mil, Fin (d'une créance)* rank; **r. élevé** high rank; **dame de haut r.** lady of rank; **un militaire de haut r.** a high-ranking *or* senior officer; **r. social** social status; **il faut tenir notre r.** we have to keep up our position (in life); **avoir r. de colonel** to hold the rank of colonel; **de premier/second r.** first-/second-class, first-/second-rate; **il est au r. des meilleurs** he ranks amongst the best; **il est au premier r. de sa profession** he is at the top of (the tree in) his profession; **par r. de** *(taille, ancienneté, âge)* by, according to; **occuper un r. supérieur à qn** to rank above *or* outrank sb; **prendre** *ou* **avoir r. avant/après qn** to come before/after sb (in rank); **il a pris r. parmi les grands poètes** he has taken his place *or* is counted among the great poets; **prendre r. dans un parti** to join a party; **sortir d'une École avec un bon r.** = to graduate near the top of one's class; **venir au** *ou* **en troisième r.** to rank third; **arriver au premier r.** to be in the forefront; **le chômage arrive au premier r. des préoccupations des Français** unemployment is one of the main concerns of the French; *Fig* **se mettre sur les rangs** to enter the lists, to join the fray, to put one's name forward; **il y avait déjà quelqu'un sur les rangs** there was already someone in the field; *Fig* **grossir les rangs des révoltés/des chômeurs** to swell the ranks of the rebels/the unemployed **3** *Can* concession road; *(quartier)* concession, rural district

rangé, -e [rɑ̃ʒe] ADJ **1** *(en ordre)* tidy, orderly; *(vie)* well-ordered, orderly; *(personne)* steady; **une jeune fille rangée** a well-behaved girl; **c'était un homme très r.** he was a very quiet kind of man; **une maison très bien rangée** a very tidy *or* well-kept house; **ce n'est pas bien r. chez elle** her place isn't very tidy; **ma petite vie bien rangée** my quiet *or* unexciting little life; *Fig Fam* **être r. des voitures** to be a reformed character, to have settled *or*

steadied down 2 bataille rangée pitched battle

rangée [rɑ̃ʒe] NF *(de personnes, boutons, sièges, d'arbres)* row, line; *(de gradins)* tier; **r. de cylindres** cylinder bank

rangement [rɑ̃ʒmɑ̃] NM **1** *(action)* tidying, putting in order; *Ordinat* storage; **avoir la manie du r.** to have a mania for tidiness, to be fanatically tidy; **volume de r.** storage space; **faire du r. (dans son bureau)** to do some tidying up (in one's office); **faire du r. dans ses affaires** to tidy up one's things **2** *(placard)* **(meuble de) r.** storage unit; **cette cuisine manque de rangements** this kitchen lacks storage space; **r. de cuisine** kitchen cabinet **3** *(disposition)* arrangement

ranger [rɑ̃ʒe] (je rangeai(s); n. rangeons) VT **1** *(pièce, maison)* to tidy (up), to put away; **tout est si bien rangé dans cette maison** this house is so beautifully tidy

2 *(affaires, vêtements)* to put or tidy away; *(par ordre alphabétique, de taille etc)* to arrange; *Com (marchandises)* to stow; *(voiture)* to park; **où as-tu rangé les fourchettes/ton livre?** where have you put the forks/your book?; **tu devrais r. tes classeurs (à leur place)** you should put your files away or put your files back where they belong; **tout est si bien rangé** everything is arranged so neatly or tidily; *Ordinat* **r. en mémoire** to store

3 r. qn parmi les grands écrivains to rank or count sb amongst the great writers; **on le range parmi les meilleurs médecins/psychanalystes** he is said to be one of the best doctors/psychoanalysts

4 *Mil (troupes)* to draw up, to marshal

VPR **se ranger 1** *(s'écarter)* **se r. (de côté)** *(d'un piéton)* to get out of the way, to stand aside; *(d'une voiture)* to pull over; **on se rangea pour nous laisser passer** they stood aside for us, they made way for us; **la voiture s'est rangée contre le mur** the car pulled in alongside the wall; *Naut* **se r. à quai** to berth **2** *Fig* **se r. du côté de qn** to side with sb, to take sb's side; **se r. à l'opinion de qn** to come round to sb's point of view

3 *Fam (s'assagir)* to settle down; **se r. des voitures** to settle down; *(criminel)* to go straight

rani [rani] NF ranee

ranimation [ranimasjɔ̃] NF resuscitation, reanimation

ranimer [ranime] VT *(personne qui s'évanouit)* to bring round; *Méd (après un arrêt cardiaque)* to resuscitate; *Fig (ville, industrie)* to revive, to put new life into; *(couleurs)* to brighten, to revive; *(feu)* to rekindle; *(colère, désir)* to reawaken, to rekindle; *(espoir)* to revive, to reawaken, to rekindle; *(souvenir, enthousiasme, débat)* to rekindle, to revive; *(conversation)* to liven up; **r. le courage de qn** to put new heart into sb; **un simple mouvement du bras suffit à r. la douleur** just moving the arm is enough to make the pain flare up

VPR **se ranimer** *(d'un feu)* to flicker into life; *(d'une conversation)* to pick up again, to come to life again; **son visage se ranima** his/her face lit up

rap [rap] NM *Mus* rap

rapace [rapas] ADJ predatory; *Fig (personne)* grasping, *Fml* rapacious; **oiseau r.** bird of prey

NM bird of prey

rapacité [rapasite] NF rapacity; *Fig* rapaciousness, rapacity; **avec r.** greedily, *Fml* rapaciously

râpage [rɑpaʒ] NM *(du métal, du bois)* rasping

rapatrié, -ée [rapatrie] N person who has been repatriated, repatriate; **les rapatriés**

d'Algérie the people repatriated from Algeria

rapatriement [rapatrimɑ̃] NM repatriation; **r. sanitaire** repatriation for health reasons

rapatrier [rapatrije] VT *(personne)*, *Fig (capitaux)* to repatriate; **se faire r.** to get or be repatriated

râpe [rɑp] NF **1** *(de cuisine)* grater; **r. à muscade/à fromage** nutmeg/cheese grater **2** *Tech* rasp **3** *Suisse Fam (avare)* miser

râpé [rɑpe] ADJ **1** *(fromage, carotte etc)* grated **2** *(usé) (vêtement)* worn out, threadbare **3** *Fam (raté)* **c'est r. pour ce week-end** this weekend's had it; **pour le pique-nique, c'est r.** the picnic's out, the picnic's had it

NM **1** *(vin)* rape wine **2** *(fromage)* grated cheese

râper [rɑpe] VT *(carotte, noix de muscade etc)* to grate; *(bois, métal)* to rasp; **ce vin râpe la gorge** this wine is rough or harsh on the throat

rapetassage [raptasaʒ] NM *Fam* patching up

rapetasser [raptase] VT *Fam (vêtement)* to patch up

rapetissement [raptismɑ̃] NM *(d'un objet) (dû à la distance)* reduction (in size); *(d'un vieillard)* shrinking

rapetisser [raptise] VT *(chose)* to make smaller, to reduce in size; *(vêtement)* to shrink; *Fig (succès)* to belittle; **la distance rapetisse les objets** distance makes things look smaller; **r. les mérites de qn** to belittle sb

VI *(d'un vêtement, d'une personne)* to shrink; **au pied de cet immeuble, on a l'impression de r.** you feel very small in front of this building, you feel dwarfed by this building; **j'aurais voulu r. pour qu'il ne me voie pas** I wanted to make myself invisible so that he didn't see me

VPR **se rapetisser** to make oneself shorter; **elle portait des talons plats pour essayer de se r.** she wore flat shoes in an attempt to make herself look shorter

râpeux, -euse [rɑpø, -øz] ADJ *(langue)* raspy; *(vin)* harsh; *(voix)* grating, rasping

raphia [rafja] NM *(fibre)* raffia; *(arbre)* raffia (palm)

rapiat, -ate [rapja, -at] *Fam* ADJ *(avare)* stingy, miserly, tight-fisted

N miser, skinflint, *Am* tightwad

rapide [rapid] ADJ **1** *(coureur, itinéraire, voiture etc)* fast; *(pouls, progrès, changement, récit etc)* rapid, fast; *(décision)* rapid, speedy; *(courant)* rapid, swift, fast; **être r. à la course** to be a fast or quick runner, to run fast; **il est r. dans son travail** he's a fast or quick worker; **il a l'esprit très r.** *(il comprend vite)* he's quick to grasp things, he has a quick mind; **la voiture la plus r. de sa catégorie** the fastest car in its category; **c'est plus r. si tu passes par là** it's faster or quicker if you go that way; **faire une lecture trop r. de qch** to read sth too quickly or fast; **une décision trop r.** a hasty decision; **r. comme une flèche, r. comme l'éclair** as swift as an arrow; *(réponse, coureur)* quick as lightning; **il est r. en affaires** he doesn't waste any time, he's a fast worker; **fusil à tir r.** quick-firing or rapid-fire rifle **2** *(abrupt) (pente)* steep

NM **1** *(de rivière)* rapid; **descendre les rapides** to shoot the rapids **2** *(train)* express (train)

N *(personne)* **c'est une r.** *(compréhension)* she's quick on the uptake; *(travail)* she's a fast worker

rapidement [rapidmɑ̃] ADV quickly, fast, rapidly; **le temps passe r.** time flies; **trop r.** too fast, too quick(ly); **je l'ai lu r.** I read through it quickly, I had a quick read through it; **parcourir r. le journal** to skim the newspaper

rapidité [rapidite] NF **1** *(d'actions)* speed, swiftness, rapidity; *(d'une décision)* speediness; *(d'une réponse)* swiftness; **célèbre pour sa r. à la course** famous for being a fast runner; **grâce à sa r. d'esprit** because of the speed with which he/she grasps things; **faire preuve d'une grande r.** *(dans son travail, dans un jeu)* to be very quick or fast; **le poison agit avec une r. fulgurante** the poison is incredibly fast-acting; *Ordinat* **r. d'impression** print speed; **r. de traitement** processing speed **2** *(d'une pente)* steepness

rapido [rapido], **rapidos** [rapidos] ADV *Fam* quickly; **boire un coup r.** to have a quick drink

rapiéçage [rapjesaʒ], **rapiècement** [rapjesmɑ̃] NM *(d'un vêtement)* patching (up), mending

rapiécer [rapjese] VT (je rapièce, n. rapiéçons; je rapiécerai) *(vêtement)* to patch, to put a patch on

rapière [rapjɛr] NF rapier

rapin [rapɛ̃] NM *Fam Péj (peintre)* dauber

rapine [rapin] NF *Litt* rapine, pillage; *(butin)* spoils; **habitudes de r.** predatory habits

raplapla [raplapla] ADJ INV *Fam (personne)* washed out; *(pneu, coussin)* flat as a pancake; **je me sens tout r. aujourd'hui** I don't have any go in me at all today

rappareiller [rapareje], **rapparier** [raparje] VT *(impf, pr sub n. rappariions)* *Rare* to match, to find a match for; *(chaussettes)* to pair

rappel [rapɛl] NM **1** *(d'un incident etc)* calling to mind, recalling; *(pour se souvenir)* reminder; **(lettre de) r.** (letter of) reminder; *Fin* **r. de compte** reminder of account outstanding; **r. de traitement/de solde/de salaire** back pay; *Radio, TV* **voici le r. des titres (de l'actualité)** here's a reminder of the headlines; **et les coussins sont assortis aux rideaux, quel joli r. de couleurs** the colour of the cushions is nicely picked up or repeated in the curtains

2 *(d'un général, ambassadeur, de réservistes)* recall; **lettres de r.** *(d'un ambassadeur)* letters of recall; *Mil* **battre le r.** to call or beat to arms; *Fig* to rally the troops, to send out a call to arms

3 *Com (d'une somme déjà avancée)* calling in; *(de marchandises défectueuses)* recall

4 *Méd* **(injection de) r.** booster (injection); **faire un r.** to have a booster

5 r. à l'ordre *(à un membre d'une assemblée)* call to order; *(à un employé)* warning; **un simple r. au bon sens suffira à le faire changer d'avis** an appeal to his common sense will make him change his mind

6 *Théâtre* curtain call; *(à un concert)* encore; **il y a eu plusieurs rappels** *Théâtre* he/she/etc took several curtain calls or was called back several times; *Mus* there were several encores

7 *Sport* abseil; **faire une descente** *ou* **descendre en r., faire du r.** to abseil down

8 *Ordinat (de texte)* restore; *Tech* **vis de r.** adjusting screw; **fil de r.** bracing or straining wire; **ressort de r.** return spring, drawback spring; **tige de r.** stay rod; *Aut* **r. latéral de clignotant** side repeat indicator

RAPPELER [rap(ə)le] *(conj like* **appeler***)*

VT	to call again **1** ▪ to ring again **1** ▪ to ring back **1** ▪ to recall **2, 3, 5** ▪ to remind sb of sth *(rappeler qch à qn)* **3**
VPR	to remember **1** ▪ to recollect **1**

VT **1** *(oralement) (personne)* to call back; *Tél (pour rendre un coup de téléphone)* to call or phone or Br ring back; *(quelqu'un que l'on a des difficultés à joindre)* to call or phone or Br ring again; *Tél* **je l'ai rappelé plusieurs fois** mais je n'ai jamais réussi à lui parler I called or phoned or Br rang (him) several times but I didn't get to speak to him; *Tél* je l'ai rappelé une cinquième fois I called or phoned or Br rang him for the fifth time; je (le) rappelle dans une minute I'll call (him) back/again in a minute

2 *(faire revenir)* to recall, to call or summon back; *(ambassadeur), Ordinat* to recall; *Mil* r. qn (sous les drapeaux) to call sb up; être rappelé trois fois *(d'un comédien)* to take three curtain calls; *(d'un musicien, chanteur)* to give three encores; r. son chien to call off one's dog; r. qn à l'ordre *(membre d'une association)* to call sb to order; *(élève)* to warn sb; tu vas te faire r. à l'ordre you're going to get a warning, you're going to be pulled up; r. qn à la vie *ou* à lui *(personne évanouie)* to bring sb round; *(blessé, noyé)* to resuscitate sb; *Fig* to bring sb back to life; r. qn à son *ou* au devoir to remind sb of their duty or where their duty lies; r. qn à la raison to make sb see reason or sense; être rappelé au chevet de qn to be called to sb's bedside; Dieu l'a rappelée à lui God called her to Him

3 *(pour se souvenir de) (quelque chose)* to recall; r. qch à qn to remind sb of sth; rappelez-moi votre nom what was your name again?; vous me rappelez mon oncle you remind me of my uncle; cela me rappelle mon enfance it brings back my childhood, it reminds me of my childhood; **ça me rappelle quelque chose** it reminds me of something, it rings a bell; **cela ne me rappelle rien** it doesn't ring a bell or any bells; **puis-je te r. que tu me dois 200 euros?** may I remind you that you owe me 200 euros?; **rappelez-moi à son bon souvenir** remember me (kindly) to him; **ce sont des choses qu'il vaut autant ne pas r.** these things are best forgotten; **il n'est pas nécessaire de r. que vous devez tous être ponctuels au cours** there's no need to remind you that you all have to be on time for class; *Com* **prière de r. ce numéro** in reply please quote this number

4 *Tech (pièce d'une machine etc)* to draw back; *Typ* r. le chariot to return the carriage; *(de quelques espaces)* to backspace

5 *(marchandises défectueuses)* to recall

VPR se rappeler **1** se r. qch, *Fam* se r. de qch to remember or recall or recollect sth, to call sth to mind; je ne me le rappelle plus, *Fam* je ne m'en rappelle plus I can't remember it; un rêve dont je ne me rappelle presque plus rien a dream I remember almost nothing about; se r. (d')avoir promis qch to remember promising sth; rappelez-vous que ce n'est qu'une enfant remember that or bear in mind that she's only a child

2 *Tél Fam* se rappelle la semaine prochaine *(au téléphone)* we'll talk again next week; on se rappelle, hein? talk to you on the phone

Attention: ne pas confondre les verbes **to remember** et **to remind** lorsque l'on traduit le verbe **rappeler**.
Se rappeler quelque chose se traduit **to remember something**, alors que **rappeler quelque chose à quelqu'un** se dit **to remind somebody of something**.

rappeur, -euse [rapœr, -øz] N *Mus* rapper

rappliquer [raplike] VI *très Fam* to turn or roll up, to show (up); r. à la maison to roll back home; je n'ai aucune envie de le voir r. ici I don't want him turning up here

RAPPORT [rapɔr]

relationship **1** ▪ relation **2**
▪ connection **2** ▪ ratio **3** ▪ report **4**
▪ return **5**

NM1 *(relation humaine)* mettre qn en r. avec qn to put sb in touch with sb; quelle est la nature de vos rapports avec elle? what is the nature of your relationship with her?, what exactly is your relationship with her?; nos rapports sont purement professionnels our relationship is purely professional; nous avons maintenu des rapports amicaux we've stayed on friendly terms; nous ne sommes plus en r. depuis des années we lost touch years ago, we haven't been in touch for years; rapports commerciaux business relations; avoir des rapports avec qn *(officiels)* to have dealings or relations with sb; *(sexuels)* to have sex with sb, *Fml* to have sexual intercourse with sb; les couples qui n'ont plus de rapports couples who no longer have sex or sexual relations; à quand remontent vos derniers rapports? when did you last have intercourse?; avoir de bons rapports avec qn to be on good terms with sb; les rapports qu'elle a avec son père sont très tendres/tendus she and her father have a very loving/tense relationship; les rapports qu'elle a avec son père sont très amicaux she and her father have a very friendly relationship or are on very friendly terms; ses difficultés relationnelles trouvent leur origine dans son r. à sa mère her difficulties in forming relationships stem from her own relationship with her mother; un r. de forces a battle of wills; entretenir des rapports d'affaires avec qn to have a business relationship with sb; cesser tout r. avec qn to break off all contact or relations with sb; *Pol* les rapports Est-Ouest East-West relations; entretenir des rapports de bon voisinage avec les pays européens to maintain good relations with European countries

2 *(lien)* relation, connection (avec with); sans r. avec le sujet without any bearing on or unconnected with or irrelevant to the subject; la question est sans r. avec ce que nous disions the question has no bearing on or is not relevant to what we were saying; ce n'est pas sans r. avec ce que je disais it is not unrelated to what I was saying; sa décision est sans r. avec ce qui se passe ici her decision has no bearing on or relevance to what's happening here; avoir r. à qch to be about sth, to have to do with sth, to relate to sth; mais ça n'a aucun r. avec ce que je disais! but that's got nothing to do with what I was saying!; question qui a un r. très étroit avec une autre question that is closely connected with another; un métier en r. avec ses goûts a trade that suits his/her tastes; un travail (plus) en r. avec vos capacités a job (more) in keeping with your abilities; il a un mode de vie parfaitement en r. avec ses revenus he has a lifestyle well within his means; une histoire en r. avec votre vie quotidienne a story about or that has to do with your daily life; parlez-lui de choses qui sont peut-être moins en r. avec votre passé talk to him about things that maybe have a bit less to do with your past; établir un r. entre deux choses to establish or make a connection between two things; elle n'a pas fait le r. she didn't make the connection; je ne vois pas le r. I can't see the connection or link; où est le r.? where's the link or connection?; par r. à qch *(en ce qui concerne)* with regard to sth; *(en comparaison)* compared or in comparison with sth; *Fin* par r. au dollar against the dollar; *Fam* je suis venu vous voir r. à mes allocs I've come to see you about my dole money; sous ce r. in this respect; analyser un texte sous le r. de la sémiologie to analyse a text from a semiotic angle; sous le r. de l'efficacité from the performance point of view; sous tous les rapports in all respects, in every respect; un homme bien sous tous rapports a fine

man in every respect or in every way; cherche jeune femme bien sous tous rapports pour garder deux enfants *(dans petite annonce)* wanted: respectable young woman to look after two children

3 *(proportion)* ratio, proportion; *Math* ratio; *(vitesse)* gear; en r. avec in proportion or proportional to; dans le r. de un à trois in a ratio of one to three; le r. maître-élèves est de 1 pour 20 the staff-student ratio is 1 to 20; le r. des forces entre le Nord et le Sud the balance of power between North and South; *Com* r. qualité-prix quality-price ratio; ce produit est d'un bon r. qualité-prix this product is good value for money; r. valeur-prix value-price ratio; *Aut* r. des engrenages gear ratio; changer de r. to change gear; r. avant forward gear ratio; r. course-alésage stroke-bore ratio; r. de boîte gearbox ratio; r. inférieur low (gear); r. intermédiaire intermediate gear

4 *(écrit etc)* report; *(des dépenses etc)* return; faire *ou* rédiger un r. sur qch to make a report on sth, to draw up a report on sth; r. d'activité progress report; *Com, Fin* r. annuel annual report; r. commercial market report; r. d'expertise valuation, expert's report; *Compta* r. d'exploitation operating statement; r. d'intelligence mercatique market intelligence report; r. d'étude de marché market study report; r. de gestion management report; *Com* r. de situation journalière daily trading report; *Com* r. de situation mensuelle monthly trading report; r. des affaires sociales social report; r. des commissaires aux comptes government auditors' report; r. financier financial report; r. récapitulatif summary report

5 *Fin* yield, return, profit; *Agr* yield; vivre du r. d'une terre to live off the money that a piece of land brings in; capital en r. interest-bearing or productive capital; arbre fruitier en plein r. fruit tree in full yield; *Agr* terre en plein r. extremely productive land; immeuble de r. rental property; d'un bon r. profitable, that brings in a good return, that pays well; d'un mauvais r. unprofitable, that brings in a poor return, that does not pay well; les rapports du tiercé winnings on the horse races

6 *Mil* daily assembly for issue of orders; salle des rapports orderly room

rapportage [rapɔrtaʒ] NM *Scol Fam* tale-telling, sneaking

rapporté [rapɔrte] ADJ *Couture* manche rapportée set-in sleeve; poches rapportées patch pockets

rapporter [rapɔrte] VT **1** *(pour rendre) (vers le locuteur)* to bring back, to return; *(en s'éloignant du locuteur)* to take back, to return; *(d'un chien) (gibier)* to retrieve; rapportez-moi un kilo de sucre bring me back a kilo of sugar; j'espère que tu nous rapportes de bonnes nouvelles! I hope you've brought us some good news!; je t'ai rapporté l'aspirateur I've brought back the or your vacuum cleaner; *(en le présentant)* here's the vacuum cleaner that I borrowed; veux-tu r. ce livre à la bibliothèque? will you take this book back to the library?, will you return this book to the library?; il n'en a rapporté que la déception all he got out of it was disappointment; allez! rapporte! *(à un chien)* fetch!; *Journ* r. une copie to file copy

2 *(relier à)* r. qch à une cause to attribute or ascribe sth to a cause; il faut r. l'événement à l'époque où il a eu lieu one must look at or consider the event in context; r. tout à soi to relate everything to oneself; *(parler de soi)* to drag the conversation round to oneself

3 *(faire le compte rendu de)* to report, to give an account of; tu me rapporteras sa réponse/ce qu'il dit de notre proposition let me know his answer/what he says about our proposal; **le journal rapporte l'anecdote suivante ...** the newspaper carries this story ...; **l'histoire rapporte que ...** history relates that ...; **on rapporte qu'il avait des pouvoirs surnaturels** he is said or reported to have had supernatural powers; **je vous rapporte ses paroles** I'm telling you what he said; **il rapporte tous les faits et gestes de ses collègues à son patron** he reports to his boss on everything that his colleagues do; **vous n'auriez pas dû le r.** you shouldn't have repeated it; **ce petit fayot est allé tout r. à l'instituteur** the little sneak has gone and told the teacher

4 Couture (poche, pièce) to sew on

5 Fin to bring in, to bear, to yield; Agr to yield; **r. de l'argent** to be profitable; **r. des bénéfices** to be profitable; **r. des intérêts** to yield interest; **placement qui rapporte dix pour cent** investment that brings in or yields ten per cent; **arbres qui rapportent beaucoup** trees that yield well; **cela ne rapporte rien** it doesn't pay; Fig **est-ce que tu crois que ça va te r. quelque chose?** do you think you're going to get anything out of it?, do you think it will do you any good?

6 Jur etc (décret) to rescind, to revoke; (ordre) to withdraw, to cancel; **r. un ordre de grève** to call off a strike, Fml to rescind a strike order

7 Géom (angle) to plot, to set off, to lay off; **r. des mesures à une autre échelle** to plot measurements on a different scale

8 Compta (écriture) to post

VPR se rapporter 1 (avoir rapport avec) **se r. à qch** to refer to sth, to relate to sth; **les documents qui se rapportent à l'affaire** the relevant documents, the documents relating to or connected with the case; **la réponse ne se rapporte pas à la question posée** the answer has nothing to do with or is irrelevant to the question asked; **les souvenirs qui se rapportent à cette expérience** the memories connected with the experience

2 s'en r. à qn/au témoignage de qn to rely on or to put one's faith in sb/sb's evidence; **je m'en rapporte à vous pour ce qui est des invitations** I can rely on you to arrange the invitations; **je m'en rapporte à votre jugement** I have every faith in your judgement

3 Tech (d'une pièce) to fit (**avec** with)

VI 1 (être rentable) to pay; **c'est un métier qui rapporte** it's a profitable career; **une affaire qui rapporte** a profitable business, a business that pays; **ça ne rapporte pas** it doesn't pay, there's no money in it; **vous croyez que ça rapporte?** do you think there's any money in it?; **ça peut r. gros** it can be very profitable

2 (en secret) to tell tales, to sneak; **r. sur le compte de qn** to tell on sb; **je n'aime pas les enfants qui rapportent** I don't like telltales

3 Litt (ressembler à) to be on a level or a par with

rapporteur, -euse [rapɔrtœr, -øz] **ADJ** telltale, sneaky

N telltale, sneak

NM 1 Admin, Pol reporter, recorder; **r. officiel** official recorder; **r. de la commission** = committee member who acts as spokesman **2** Mil judge advocate (at court martial) **3** Math protractor; **r. à limbe complet** circular protractor

rapprendre [raprɑ̃dr] **VT** (conj like **prendre**) **1** (apprendre) to learn (over) again; **elle a dû r. à marcher après son accident** she had to learn to walk (all over) again after her accident; **r. le bonheur** to learn how to be happy again **2** (enseigner) to teach again; **il faut leur r. sans cesse le code de la route** you

have to keep teaching them the Highway Code

rapproché [raprɔʃe] **ADJ** (dans l'espace, dans le temps) near; (yeux) close-set; **maisons très rapprochées** houses very close together, houses very close or near to one another; **des examens très rapprochés** ou **qui ont lieu à des dates très rapprochées** exams coming very close together or very close to each other; **j'ai trois réunions très rapprochées dans la journée** I've got three meetings one right after the other; **faits rapprochés dans le temps** events occurring close together (in time); Phot, Cin **plan r. sur un visage** close-up of a face; (sur script) close-up on a face

rapprochement [raprɔʃmɑ̃] **NM 1** (de faits, d'idées) comparison, setting side by side, putting together; **il n'a pas fait le r.** he didn't make the connection; **je ne peux m'empêcher de faire un r. entre ces deux faits** I can't help making a connection between or linking the two facts **2** (de deux objets) bringing or placing together; Fig (de deux personnes) reconciliation, bringing together; Pol rapprochement; Typ **r. de caractères** kerning; **un r. israélo-palestinien** an Israeli-Palestinian rapprochement; **le r. qui s'est opéré entre elles** their reconciliation; Compta **r. bancaire** bank reconciliation

rapprocher [raprɔʃe] **VT 1** (mettre plus près) (objet) to move or bring nearer or closer; (deux objets) to move nearer or closer together; **rapproche ta chaise de la table** move your chair closer to the table; **r. une chaise du feu** to draw a chair up to the fire; **le vent rapproche les nuages de la côte** the wind is blowing the clouds inshore; **et si on rapprochait les deux cousins à table?** how about sitting the two cousins closer to each other at the table?; **r. les lèvres d'une plaie** to draw together or join the lips of a wound; **une lunette rapproche les objets** a field glass makes objects look nearer; **il va falloir r. les rendez-vous** we'll have to meet more often; (en affaires) we'll have to have more frequent meetings; **chaque jour les rapproche de la fin** each day brings them nearer the end; **je te déposerai sur la place, ça te rapprochera (de chez toi)** I'll drop you off in the square, that'll get you a bit nearer home **2** (réconcilier) (deux personnes) to bring together; **un intérêt commun les rapproche** they are united or brought together or drawn together by a common interest; **cette épreuve nous a rapprochés** the ordeal drew or brought us closer together; **elle essaie de r. le père et le fils** she is trying to reconcile father and son

3 (lier) (des faits, des idées) to put together or side by side, to compare

VPR se rapprocher 1 se r. de (sa destination, un lieu) to get closer to, to approach; (la télévision, la table) to move closer to; **rapproche-toi de lui, il n'entend pas** move closer (to him), he can't hear; Fig **se r. de son idéal** to come close to one's ideal; **son costume se rapprochait d'un uniforme** his clothes looked almost like or came near to being a uniform; **se r. de la vérité** to get close to the truth; **ça n'est pas tout à fait ça, mais ça s'en rapproche** that's not quite it but it's close; **à mesure que nous nous rapprochons du premier anniversaire de sa mort ...** as we near or approach the first anniversary of his/her death ...; **plus on se rapprochait de la fin du trimestre, plus les enfants devenaient espiègles** the closer or nearer we got to the end of the term, the more mischievous the children became

2 Fig **se r. de qn** to become closer to sb; (après une brouille) to become reconciled with sb, to make it up with sb; **la France et**

l'Espagne s'étaient rapprochées a rapprochement had taken place between France and Spain

rapsodie [rapsɔdi] **NF** rhapsody

rapt [rapt] **NM** abduction, kidnapping

râpure [rɑpyr] **NF** Tech raspings, gratings, filings

raqué [rake] **ADJ** Can Fam (en panne, en ruine) broken-down, wrecked; Fig (épuisé) knackered, Am bushed

raquer [rake] **VT** Fam to fork out, to cough up, to stump up

raquette [rakɛt] **NF 1** (de tennis, badminton, squash) racket, racquet; (de ping-pong) bat; Aut Fam **coups de r.** jolts; Fig **une des meilleures raquettes du monde** one of the best (tennis/squash/table tennis/etc) players in the world **2** (pour marcher dans la neige) snowshoe; **ils sont montés en raquettes** they snowshoed up **3** Bot Fam prickly pear

rare [rar] **ADJ 1** (peu courant) (livre, plante, insecte etc) rare; **lors d'une de ses rares visites** on one of his/her rare or few visits; **elle ne nous fait plus que de rares visites** she rarely or seldom visits us now; **je n'ai que de rares visites** I seldom or rarely get visitors; **je suis un des rares à aimer la pluie** I'm one of the few people who like rain; **vous devenez r. comme les beaux jours** you're quite a stranger, we seldom see you (these days); **se faire r.** to be becoming rare; **il se faisait r. dans le quartier** he was rarely seen around the area; **la main-d'œuvre/l'argent était r.** there was a shortage of labour/money; **les denrées de base se font rares** basic food items are becoming scarce; **c'est (bien) r. qu'il pleuve ici** it (very) rarely rains here; **cela n'avait rien de r. à cette époque** it was quite common at that time; **il n'est pas r. qu'elle rentre au petit matin** it's not uncommon for her to go home in the small hours; Litt **rares sont ceux que la famine épargne** rare are they who are spared by the famine **2** (exceptionnel) (mérite, beauté, intelligence, talent etc) rare, uncommon, exceptional

3 (clairsemé) (végétation etc) thin, sparse, scanty; (jour, lumière) dim, poor; (oxygène) rare; **avoir le cheveu r.** to have thinning hair

raréfaction [rarefaksjɔ̃] **NF 1** Phys (de gaz, d'air) rarefaction **2** (d'un produit, de l'argent) growing scarcity

raréfier [rarefje] **VT 1** Phys to rarefy **2** Rare (rendre rare) to deplete, to make scarce

VPR se raréfier 1 Phys to become rarefied, to rarefy **2** (animal, plante) to become scarce

rarement [rarmɑ̃] **ADV** rarely, seldom

rareté [rarte] **NF 1** Phys (de gaz etc) rarity **2** (d'objets) scarceness, scarcity, Fml dearth; (de visites) infrequency; (d'un phénomène) novelty, singularity, unusualness; (d'un mot, d'une maladie etc) rare occurrence, rareness **3** (objet rare) **cabinet plein de raretés** cabinet full of rare objects or of rarities or curiosities

RAS [ɛraɛs] Fam (abrév **rien à signaler**) (à l'écrit) everything OK; **quoi de neuf? – R.!** what's new? – nothing much!

ras [rɑ] **ADJ 1** (cheveux, tête) close-cropped; (menton) close-shaven; (barbe) short; (tapis) short-pile; **chien à poil r.** short-haired dog; **pull r. du cou** crew-neck (sweater), round-neck sweater

2 mesure rase full (level) measure; **deux cuillerées rases de sucre** two level spoonfuls of sugar; **verser du vin à qn à r. bord** to fill sb's wineglass to the brim; **à r. de** (on a) level or flush with; **vaisseau chargé au r. de l'eau** vessel laden to the water line; **voler au r. du sol/de l'eau** to fly close to the ground/water, to skim (along) the ground/

water; *Fam* **voler** *ou* **rester au r. des pâquerettes** (*d'un livre, d'un film, d'une conversation*) to be very lowbrow; **son humour vole
ou reste au r. des pâquerettes** his/her sense
of humour is pretty basic *or* lowbrow; *Fam*
**elle portait une minijupe qui lui arrivait au
r. des fesses** she was wearing a mini-skirt
which was more like a belt; **en rase campagne** in the open country

3 *Fam* **en avoir r. le bol** *ou* **la casquette** *ou*
Vulg **le cul** to have had it up to here, to be
fed up (*to the back teeth*); **j'en ai** *ou* **il y en a
r. le bol (de tes histoires)** I'm fed up *or* I've
had it up to here (with your nonsense), I'm
sick to the back teeth (of your nonsense);
**j'en ai r. le bol de ne pas pouvoir lui parler
directement** I'm fed up with not being able
to talk to him/her directly; **r. le bol!** enough
is enough!

ADV se faire couper les cheveux r. to have
one's hair cropped

rasade [razad] **NF** (*de vin*) glassful

rasage [razaʒ] **NM** shaving; *Tex* shearing; lotion **après-r.** aftershave lotion

rasant [razɑ̃] **ADJ 1 tir r.** grazing fire; **trajectoire rasante** flat trajectory; **vol r.** flight that
skims the ground; **lumière rasante** oblique
or (almost) horizontal light **2** *Fam* (*personne, discours, film etc*) boring

rascasse [raskas] **NF** scorpion fish

rasé [raze] **ADJ** shaven; **r. de près** close-
shaven; (**entièrement**) **r.** (*visage*) (clean-)
shaven; (*tête*) shaven; **des enfants rasés**
children with shaven heads

rase-mottes [razmɔt] **NM INV** *Aviat Fam*
faire du *ou* **voler en r.** to hedgehop, to skim
the ground; **le vol en r.** hedgehopping

raser [raze] **VT 1** (*tête*) to shave; (*moustache,
barbe, cheveux*) to shave off; **r. un homme** to
shave a man, to give a man a shave; **r. une
femme/un enfant/un prisonnier** to shave a
woman's/a child's/a prisoner's head; **se faire
r.** to be given a shave **2** (*bâtiment, ville*) to
raze to the ground **3** (*frôler*) (*surface de qch*)
to graze, to brush; (*sol, eau*) to skim (over);
Fig Fam **r. les murs** to hug the walls **4** *Fam*
(*ennuyer*) to bore

VPR se raser 1 to shave, to have a shave; **je
dois me r.** I need a shave; **se r. les jambes/
les aisselles** to shave one's legs/armpits **2**
Fam (*s'ennuyer*) to be bored; **qu'est-ce qu'on
se rase chez eux!** they're really boring

raseur, -euse [razœr, -øz] **N** *Fam* bore

rasibus [razibys] **ADV** *Fam* **couper les cheveux** *ou* **tondre le crâne r. à qn, tondre qn r.**
to scalp sb; **la balle est passée r.** the bullet
whizzed past very close; **le couteau lui est
passé à côté du doigt r.** the knife only just
missed his/her finger; **il est passé en terminale mais r.** he made it into the sixth form
but only by the skin of his teeth

rasif [razif] **NM** *Fam* razor; **ils se sont battus à
coups de r.** they were going at each other
with open razors

ras-le-bol [ralbɔl] **NM INV** *Fam* (*sentiment*)
discontent, dissatisfaction; **le r. généralisé
qui s'empare des professeurs** the widespread feeling among teachers that they've
had as much as they can take *or Fam* that
they've had it up to here; **le r. des jeunes** *ou*
de la jeunesse the feeling among young
people that they've had it up to here

rasoir [razwar] **NM 1** razor; **r. de sûreté** safety
razor; **r. électrique** electric razor *or* shaver;
pierre à r. hone; **cuir à r.** strop; **couper
comme un r.** to be as sharp as a razor; **le
feu du r.** razor burn **2** *Fam* (*personne*) bore
ADJ INV boring

rassasié [rasazje] **ADJ** (*repu*) satisfied; *Fig
Fam* full, sated (**de** with); **ah non, plus de
films d'horreur, je suis r.!** no more horror

films, I've had enough *or* my fill!; **les Français
sont rassasiés de discours électoraux** the
French have had their fill of political speeches

rassasiement [rasazimɑ̃] **NM** *Rare* (*de la
faim*) satisfaction; *Fig* satiety, surfeit

rassasier [rasazje] **VT** (*faim*), *Fig* (*curiosité,
soif d'apprendre, passion pour qch*) to satis-
fy; **r. qn** to satisfy sb's hunger; *Fig* **r. son regard à contempler qch** to feast one's eyes
on sth; **les fruits ne rassasient pas** fruit isn't
very filling *or* doesn't satisfy your hunger;
Fam **je suis rassasiée de toutes vos histoires**
I've had more than enough *or* than my fill of
your stories

VPR se rassasier to eat one's fill; **se r. d'un
mets** to eat one's fill of *or Péj* gorge oneself
on a dish; *Fig* **se r. de plaisirs** to take one's fill
of pleasure; **je ne me rassasie pas de cette
vue/sa présence** I never tire of this view/his
presence

rassemblement [rasɑ̃bləmɑ̃] **NM 1** (*de
documents, de troupes, d'outils*) assembling,
collecting, gathering; *Mil* fall in, parade; *Mil*
sonner le r. to sound the assembly; *Mil* **r.!** fall
in!, form up!; *Pol* **œuvrer au r. de la gauche**
to work towards the union of the left **2** (*foule*)
crowd, gathering; **provoquer un r.** to draw
or attract a crowd; **disperser les rassemblements** to disperse the crowd; **r. pour la paix**
peace rally

rassembler [rasɑ̃ble] **VT** (*personnes, choses,
etc*) to collect, to gather together, to get together, to assemble; (*troupes*) to assemble,
to muster; **r. ses affaires** to collect one's
things, to get one's things together; **r. les
gens qui partagent la même opinion** to
bring together the people who share the
same viewpoint; **ce qui nous rassemble ici
ce soir, c'est la passion du théâtre** it is a passion for the theatre which has brought us
here this evening; **nous sommes rassemblés
ici pour fêter ...** we are gathered here this
evening to celebrate ...; **c'est pourquoi nous
avons voulu vous r. aujourd'hui** that's why
we wanted to gather you all together here
today; **c'est le besoin qui les rassemble** they
are brought together by need; **r. toutes les
pièces d'un procès** to bring together all the
documents in a case; **r. ses idées** to collect
or gather together one's thoughts; **r. ses esprits** to collect oneself, to regain one's
composure; *Fig* **r. son courage/toutes ses
forces** to muster *or* summon up one's cour-
age/all one's strength; *Équitation* **r. un cheval** to gather a horse

VPR se rassembler (*s'assembler*) to assemble,
to get together, to gather; (*d'une foule*) to collect, to gather; *Mil* to fall in, to muster; **les ouvriers se rassemblent sous l'égide du
syndicat** the workers are gathering *or* band-
ing together under the aegis of the union;
**nous nous rassemblons tous les jeudis dans
ce bar** we meet *or* get together in this bar
every Thursday

rasseoir [raswar] (*conj like* asseoir) **VT r. qn**
(*qui était debout*) to sit sb down again; (*qui
était couché*) to sit sb up again; **faire r. qn** to
make sb sit down again; **r. une statue sur sa
base** to replace a statue on its base; *Fig* **r.
l'école dans la démocratie** to re-establish
the educational system as one of the fundamental institutions of democracy; **il faut r.
la psychanalyse dans la pratique hospitalière** psychoanalysis must be restored
to its former prominence in hospital medicine

VPR se rasseoir 1 (*de personne*) to sit down
again, to sit back down **2** (*de liquide*) to
settle; **laisser r. le vin** to let the wine settle

rasséréner [raserene] (**je rassérène, n. ras-
sérénons; je rassérénerai**) **VT r. qn** to put sb's
mind at rest; **je suis rasséréné** my mind's at
rest

VPR se rasséréner 1 (*du ciel*) to clear (up) **2**
(*d'une personne*) to calm down

rassir [rasir] **VI** to go *or* get stale; **j'ai laissé r.
mon pain** I've let my bread go stale
VPR se rassir to go *or* get stale

rassis [rasi] **ADJ 1** pain **r.** stale bread **2** *Fig*
(*personne, caractère, disposition*) calm,
sedate

rassortir [rasɔrtir] **VT** = réassortir

rassurant [rasyrɑ̃] **ADJ** (*personne*) reassuring; (*nouvelle, paroles*) reassuring, heartening; **peu r.** disquieting; **c'est une nouvelle
peu rassurante** that's not very reassuring
news

rassurer [rasyre] **VT** (*d'une personne*) to reassure; (*d'une nouvelle, paroles*) to reassure, to
cheer, to hearten; **je ne suis pas trop rassuré
de la savoir seule** I have my worries about
her being alone; **il n'a pas l'air très rassuré**
he's not looking too cheery; **cela me rassure
(de savoir que ...)** it reassures me (to know
that ...); **ce n'est pas ça qui va me r.** that's not
enough to reassure me, that doesn't do
anything to calm my misgivings; **je te rassure tout de suite, je n'irai pas poser la question!** I can assure you, I won't be the one
who asks the question!; **eh bien, me voilà
rassuré!** that's a relief!; **ah, tu me rassures!**
well, that's a relief!, you've taken a weight
off my mind!

VPR se rassurer to feel reassured; **rassurez-
vous là-dessus** set your mind at rest on that
point; **rassurez-vous** rest assured; **vous pouvez vous r., ça ne fait pas mal du tout** you
can relax, it doesn't hurt at all

rasta [rasta] **ADJ, N** Rasta(farian)

rastaquouère [rastakwɛr] **NM** *Fam* **un drôle
de r.** a queer bird

rat [ra] **NM 1** (*animal*) rat; *Fig* **c'est un r.
d'église** he's never out of church; *Fig* **les rats
quittent le navire** the rats are leaving the
sinking ship; *Fam* **être fait comme un r.** to
be caught like a rat in a trap; *Fam* **s'ennuyer
comme un r. mort** to be bored out of one's
mind *or* skull, to be bored to death; **petit r.
(de l'Opéra)** ballet pupil; *Fam* **mon petit r.**
darling; *Fam* **ah le r., il ne m'a pas téléphoné!**
the rat didn't call me; *Fam* **face de r.!** ratface!
2 (*avare*) miser, skinflint, *Am* tightwad; *Fam*
c'est un r. he's stingy *or* a miser **3** *Can* (*sournois*) sly customer

ADJ INV *Fam* **1** (*avare*) stingy, tight; **ce qu'il
est r.!** what a skinflint *or Am* tightwad! **2**
Can (*sournois*) wily, sly

▸ **r. d'Amérique** coypu; *Fig* **r. de bibliothèque** bookworm; **r. des champs** field
mouse; **r. d'eau** water vole; **r. d'Égypte** mongoose; **r. géant (des Indes)** bandicoot; *Fig* **r.
d'hôtel** hotel thief; **r. musqué** muskrat, musquash; **r. noir** black rat; **r. de Pharaon** mongoose; **r. surmulot** brown *or* Norway rat

rata [rata] **NM** *Mil Fam Vieilli* grub, *Péj* pigswill

ratafia [ratafja] **NM** (*boisson*) ratafia

ratage [rataʒ] **NM** *Fam* botching, bungling,
messing up

rataplan [rataplɑ̃] **NM** (*d'un tambour*) rat-a-
tat

ratatiné [ratatine] **ADJ 1** (*à cause de l'âge, du
dessèchement, du feu*) shrivelled; **petite
vieille ratatinée** little old wizened *or* shrunken woman **2** *Fam* (*accidenté*) smashed-up

ratatiner [ratatine] **VT 1** (*pomme, visage etc*)
to shrivel (up) **2** *Fam* (*écraser*) to scrunch up
3 *très Fam* **r. qn** (*tuer*) to bump sb off; (*battre*)
to beat sb up; **se faire r. par l'équipe adverse**
to get thrashed *or* hammered by the other
side

VPR se ratatiner (*de cuir, d'une plante, d'un
parchemin*) to shrivel up; **une vieille dame
qui se ratatine** a shrunken little old lady; **je
commence à me r.** I'm beginning to shrink;

Fam **tu vas te faire r.** *(dans un concours, match)* you're going to get slaughtered; *(à un examen)* you're going to fail abysmally

ratatouille [ratatuj] NF *Culin* ratatouille

rate¹ [rat] NF *Anat* spleen; *Fam* **se dilater la r.** to laugh one's head off, to split one's sides laughing; *Fam* **ne pas se fouler la r.** not to strain oneself

rate² NF *(animal)* female rat

raté, -ée [rate] N *(personne)* failure, loser; **comme écrivain, je suis un r.** I'm a failure or a washout as a writer

  NM *(d'un fusil, d'un moteur)* misfire; *Fig* hitch, minor problem; *TV, Radio etc* fluff; **le moteur avait des ratés** the engine was misfiring; **avoir un r. (d'allumage)** to backfire, to misfire

râteau, -eaux [rato] NM **1** *(de jardin)* rake; **r. mécanique** raker; **r. faneur** tedder; **donner un coup de r. à l'allée** to give the path a rake; **ramasser les feuilles mortes avec un r.** to rake up the dead leaves

  2 *Naut* **r. de pont** squeegee
  3 *(de croupier)* rake
  4 *(de métier à tisser)* comb
  5 *Fam (peigne)* comb
  6 *Fam* **se prendre un r.** *(être rejeté)* to get turned down, *Br* to get a knockback
  7 *Suisse Fam (avare)* stingy, tight-fisted

râteler [ratle] VT (je râtelle, n. râtelons; je râtellerai) *(foin etc)* to rake up

râtelier [ratəlje] NM **1** *(dans une étable)* rack; *Fig* **manger au r. de qn** to live off sb; **il mange à tous les râteliers** he serves more than one master, he has his foot in more than one camp; *Fig Fam* **quand il n'y a plus de foin dans le r.** when I'm/we're/etc broke, when there's nothing left in the kitty **2** *(support)* **r. d'armes/à outils/à pipes** weapon/tool/pipe rack **3** *Fam (dents)* (set of) choppers

rater [rate] VI *(d'un fusil)* to misfire, to fail to go off; *(d'un moteur)* to misfire; *Fig (d'une entreprise, d'une expérience)* to fail; **c'est raté, la plaie s'infecte** it hasn't worked, the wound is becoming infected; **si tu voulais lui parler, c'est raté, il vient de partir** if you wanted to talk to him, you're too late, he's just gone; *Fam* **j'étais sûr qu'elle allait être en retard et ça n'a pas raté** I was convinced she was going to be late and, sure enough or right enough, she was; *Fam* **tu as tout fait r.!** you've ruined everything!

  VT **1** *(échouer à)* *(examen, bac, permis de conduire)* to fail; **le dîner était super mais j'ai raté mon gâteau** the dinner was great but I made a mess of the cake or my cake was a flop; **r. sa vie** to make a mess of one's life; **r. son coup** *(aux fléchettes etc)* to miss (one's shot or the target); *Golf* to foozle one's shot; *Fig Fam* to make a mess of it; **j'ai raté mon coup, maintenant elle ne viendra pas** I blew it, she won't be coming now; **elle n'a pas raté son coup, tout le monde l'a entendue** she got what she wanted, everybody heard her; *Aviat* **atterrissage raté** bad landing

  2 *(manquer)* *(train, avion, personne)* to miss; **j'ai raté l'occasion** ou **ma chance** I missed my opportunity or chance; **tu n'as pas raté grand-chose** you didn't miss much; **tu as raté un film extraordinaire** you missed or missed out on a great film; *Fam* **je ne vais pas le r.** I'm really going to let him have it; *Fam* **le coiffeur ne t'a pas raté, dis donc!** the hairdresser really did a job on you!; *Fam* **elle n'en rate pas une!** she's always putting her foot in it!

  VPR **se rater 1** *(manquer son suicide)* to make a failed suicide attempt

  2 **on avait rendez-vous à l'Arc de triomphe mais on s'est ratés** we were supposed to meet at the Arc de Triomphe but we missed each other

ratiboiser [ratibwaze] VT *très Fam* **1 r. qn** *(au jeu, en Bourse, dans une entreprise)* to clean sb out; **je suis complètement ratiboisé** I'm flat broke or *Br* stony broke or skint; **j'ai été complètement ratiboisé dans cette affaire** that business cleaned me out totally; **se faire r. la colline** to get scalped **2** *Fam Vieilli* **r. qch à qn** to do or swindle sb out of sth

ratiche [ratiʃ] NF *Fam* tooth

raticide [ratisid] NM rat poison

ratier [ratje] ADJ, NM **(chien) r.** ratter

ratière [ratjɛr] NF rat trap

ratification [ratifikasjɔ̃] NF ratification; **accord sous réserve de r.** agreement subject to ratification or confirmation

ratifier [ratifje] VT *(traité, acte)* to ratify; *(décision)* to confirm

ratio [rasjo] NM ratio; **r. de capitalisation** p/e ratio, price/earnings ratio; **r. capital-travail** capital-labour ratio; **r. cours-bénéfices** price-earnings ratio; *Compta* **r. d'exploitation** performance ratio, operating ratio; **r. de gestion** financial ratio, financial management ratio; **r. de levier** leverage; **r. de liquidités** quick ratio, acid test ratio; **r. de situation** financial ratio; **r. de solvabilité** solvency ratio; **r. de trésorerie** cash ratio; **r. des ventes** sales ratio

ratiocination [rasjɔsinasjɔ̃] NF *Litt* mulling or brooding over

ratiociner [rasjɔsine] VI *Litt* to brood; **r. sur qch** to mull or brood over sth

ration [rasjɔ̃] NF *(d'eau, de sucre etc)* ration; *(pour bête)* feed; *Fig (de critiques, de difficultés, de malheurs)* share; **r. alimentaire** food ration, ration of food; **r. calorique** calorie intake; **r. de combat** iron rations; **rations de survie** survival rations; **rations imposées en temps de guerre** wartime rations

rationalisation [rasjɔnalizasjɔ̃] NF rationalization, rationalizing, streamlining

rationaliser [rasjɔnalize] VT to rationalize, to streamline

rationalisme [rasjɔnalism] NM rationalism

rationaliste [rasjɔnalist] ADJ, N rationalist

rationalité [rasjɔnalite] NF rationality

rationnel, -elle [rasjɔnɛl] ADJ rational

rationnellement [rasjɔnɛlmɑ̃] ADV rationally

rationnement [rasjɔnmɑ̃] NM rationing

rationner [rasjɔne] VT *(population, malade, approvisionnement)* to ration

  VPR **se rationner** to ration oneself

ratissage [ratisaʒ] NM **1** *(du jardin)* raking **2** *Fam (au casino) (des mises)* raking in **3** *Fam (d'un quartier, par la police etc)* combing, thorough search

ratisser [ratise] VT **1** *(allée, sol)* to rake (over); *(feuilles)* to rake (up) **2** *Fam* **r. les mises** *(au casino)* to rake in the stakes **3** *Fam (quartier)* to comb, to search, to make a thorough search of **4** *Fam (voler) (personne)* to clean out; **se faire r.** *(au jeu)* to be cleaned out

  VI **r. large** to cast one's net wide

raton [ratɔ̃] NM **1** *(animal)* young rat; **r. laveur** raccoon **2** *Fam (terme injurieux)* = racist insult directed at Arabs from North Africa, *Br* ≃ wog

ratonnade [ratɔnad] NF *(contre des Maghrébins)* attack on North African Arabs, *Br* ≃ Paki-bashing

ratoureux, -euse [raturø, -øz] *Can* ADJ wily, devious; **parfois le bonheur est un peu r.** sometimes happiness is not all it seems

  N shady customer

RATP [ɛratepe] NF *(abrév* **Régie autonome des transports parisiens)** = Parisian municipal transport system

rattachement [rataʃmɑ̃] NM *(d'un objet à un autre)* re-attachment; **le r. de l'Alsace à la France** the return of Alsace to France; **la société a décidé votre r. au bureau de Londres** the company has decided that you should report to the London office

rattacher [rataʃe] VT *(attacher de nouveau)* *(lacets)* to do up or fasten or tie (up) again; *(cheveux)* to put up again; *(chien, objet)* to tie up again *(à* to); **r. un sac sur un vélo** to tie or fasten a bag onto a bike again; **r. l'Alsace à la France** to (re)unite Alsace with France; **nous sommes rattachés à l'Hôpital Broussais** we're attached to the Broussais Hospital; **il est rattaché au service de M. Benoît** he reports to Monsieur Benoît's department; *Fig* **les liens qui vous rattachent à la famille** the ties that bind you to your family; *Fig* **c'était la seule chose qui nous rattachait l'un à l'autre** it was the only thing that bound us together; **c'est tout ce qui le rattache à la vie** it's the only thing keeping him alive; **r. une idée à une autre** to link (up) or connect one idea with another; **r. un mot à un autre par son étymologie** to establish the origin of a word through its etymology; *Mil* **unité rattachée** attached unit

  VPR **se rattacher se r. à qch** to be connected with sth; **voici le rapport et toutes les pièces qui s'y rattachent** here is the report and its related documents

rattachiste [rataʃist] N = Belgian who supports the integration of French-speaking parts of Belgium into France

rattrapage [ratrapaʒ] NM *Scol* **cours de r.** remedial course; **être admis au r., être admis à passer les épreuves de r.** = to be allowed to sit further oral examinations to gain a pass mark in the baccalauréat; **l'oral de r.** = further oral examination to gain a pass mark in the baccalauréat; **j'ai eu mon bac au r.** I passed my bac at the oral; **r. des salaires/des prix** the catching up of wages/prices

rattraper [ratrape] VT **1** *(reprendre)* *(prisonnier, chien)* to recapture, to catch; *Tricot* **r. une maille qui file** to pick up a dropped stitch; **se faire r. par la police** to get caught by the police

  2 *(attraper) (objet ou personne qui tombe)* to catch

  3 *(rejoindre) (personne, voiture)* to catch up (with); **je vous rattraperai à l'angle de la rue** I'll catch you up or catch up with you at the corner

  4 *(regagner) (argent)* to recover, to get back; **r. le temps perdu** to make up for lost time; **nous avons rattrapé notre retard** we made up the time; **j'ai du sommeil à r.** I have to catch up on some sleep; **ce que tu perds d'un côté, tu le rattrapes de l'autre** what you lose on the swings, you gain on the roundabouts

  5 *(rétablir) (faute d'orthographe, de calcul etc)* to correct; *(situation, Culin (mayonnaise)* to salvage; **j'aurais voulu r. l'énorme gaffe que je venais de faire** if only I could have taken back the huge gaffe I'd just made; **ça, tu ne pourras pas le r.** you'll never be able to make up for it; **dis-moi comment r. le mal que je t'ai fait** tell me how I can make up for the hurt I've caused you

  6 *Scol* **r. un élève** = to award a borderline candidate a pass in the baccalauréat

  VPR **se rattraper se r. à qch** to catch hold of sth; *Fig Fam* **se r. aux branches** to clutch at straws; **se r. de justesse** to just stop oneself falling; **se r. (avant de faire une erreur)** to stop oneself (before making a mistake); … **mais je me suis rattrapé de justesse** … but I caught or stopped myself just in time; **je me suis rattrapé en l'invitant** I made up for it or I made amends by inviting him/her; **pas de soleil depuis trois mois, je vais me r.!** no sun for three months, I'm going to make up for it now *or* I'm going to make up for lost time!; **elle s'est bien rattrapée depuis** she's really made up for it since; **elle ne peut pas parler pendant le travail, mais le soir, elle se rattrape avec son mari** she can't talk at work but she makes up for it in the evening with her husband; **se r. de ses pertes** to make good *or* recoup one's losses

VI *Fam* to catch up

rature [ʀatyʀ] **NF** crossing-out, deletion; **faire une r.** to cross out *or* delete a word; **sans ratures ni surcharges** without deletions or additions

raturer [ʀatyʀe] **VT** *(mot, phrase etc)* to cross *or* score out, to delete; **les devoirs raturés ne seront pas corrigés** homework with too many crossings-out in it will not be marked

raucité [ʀosite] **NF** *Litt (enrouement)* hoarseness; *(caractère voilé)* huskiness; *(de rire)* raucousness

raugmenter [ʀogmɑ̃te] **VI** *Fam (d'un prix)* to go up again

rauque [ʀok] **ADJ** *(voix)* *(enroué)* hoarse; *(voilé)* husky; *(rire, cri)* raucous

ravage [ʀavaʒ] **NM** *(often pl)* **ravages** havoc, devastation; *(d'une guerre, d'une maladie)* ravages; **les ravages du feu/de la tempête** the devastation *or* destruction caused by the fire/the storm; **faire des ravages** to wreak *or* cause havoc; *Fig* **cette mode fait des ravages parmi les jeunes** this fashion is all the rage among the young; *Fam* **elle va faire des ravages avec son bronzage parfait** with that perfect suntan of hers, she'll have them queuing up at her door

ravagé [ʀavaʒe] **ADJ 1** *(pays)* ravaged, devastated; *(visage)* ravaged, haggard; **visage r. par la petite vérole** face pitted with *or* ravaged by smallpox; **un visage r. par la colère** a face disfigured *or* contorted by anger **2** *Fam (fou)* bonkers, crazy; **il n'est pas un peu r., ton copain?** your mate's got a screw *or* slate loose; **c'est un r. du cerveau** he's off his rocker *or* trolley

ravager [ʀavaʒe] **VT** *(je ravageai(s); n. ravageons)* *(ville, région etc)* to ravage, to devastate, to lay waste; *(récoltes)* to ravage, to devastate, to play havoc with; *(visage)* to ravage

ravageur, -euse [ʀavaʒœʀ, -øz] **ADJ** ravaging; *(orage)* devastating; *(oiseaux)* destructive

N ravager, destroyer

ravalement [ʀavalmɑ̃] **NM 1** *Constr (de la maçonnerie)* repointing; *(en recrépissant)* roughcasting; *(enduit)* (coat of) roughcast **2** *(d'un arbre)* pruning, cutting back **3** *Vieilli (d'une personne)* disparagement **4** *Fig Fam* **r. de façade** facelift

ravaler [ʀavale] **VT 1** *(avaler de nouveau)* *(salive)* to swallow; *Fig (sanglot, larmes)* to swallow, to choke (back); *(colère, indignation, rancunes)* to swallow, to suppress, to stifle; *(réplique)* to bite back; **je lui ferai r. ses paroles** I'll make him eat his words **2** *(abaisser)* *(personne)* to degrade, to lower; *(dévaluer)* *(personne, talents, qualités etc)* to run down, to disparage; **l'assistante du directeur s'est sentie ravalée au rang de secrétaire** the manager's assistant felt she was being effectively demoted to secretary **3** *(arbre)* to prune, to cut back **4** *Constr (maçonnerie)* to repoint; *(mur)* to roughcast; *Fig Fam* **se faire r. la façade** to have a facelift

VPR se ravaler 1 to degrade *or* lower *or* debase oneself; **vous ne vous ravaleriez pas jusque-là** you wouldn't stoop to that, you wouldn't lower yourself to that extent; **ce ne serait pas se r. que d'accepter** you wouldn't be demeaning yourself if you agreed

2 *Fam* **se r. la façade** to touch up one's warpaint

ravaleur [ʀavalœʀ] **NM** roughcaster, plasterer

ravaudage [ʀavodaʒ] **NM 1** *(action)* *(de vêtements)* mending, repairing; *(de chaussettes)* darning, mending; *Fig* **ce n'est que du r. mais ça fait de l'effet** it's just a quick repair job but it looks good **2** *(résultat)* *(d'un vêtement)* mend, repair; *(de chaussettes)* darn, mend; **mon r. ne dura pas longtemps** my makeshift repair *or* my bit of make-do and mend didn't last long

ravauder [ʀavode] **VT 1** *(vêtements)* to mend, to repair; *(chaussettes)* to darn, to mend **2** *Can (errer)* to wander about; *(faire l'idiot)* to fool *or* clown around **3** *Can (faire du bruit)* to make a racket

ravaudeur, -euse [ʀavodœʀ, -øz] **N** *(de vêtements)* mender; *(de chaussettes)* darner

rave[1] [ʀav] **NF** *(colza)* rape; *(radis)* radish; *(navet)* turnip; **céleri r.** celeriac

rave[2] [ʀɛv] **NF** *Fam* rave

ravi [ʀavi] **ADJ** delighted (**de** with); **je suis r. de vous voir** I'm delighted to see you; **r. de vous rencontrer** pleased to meet you; **un air r.** delightedly; **eh bien, tu m'en vois r.!** I'm positively delighted!; *Iron* oh great!, terrific!; *Iron* **r. de le savoir** *ou* **de l'apprendre** thanks for telling me

ravier [ʀavje] **NM** hors d'œuvres dish

ravigotant [ʀavigɔtɑ̃] **ADJ** *Fam* invigorating; **un verre de calva, c'est r.** a glass of calvados will put new life into you/him/*etc or* blow your/his/*etc* cobwebs away

ravigote [ʀavigɔt] **NF** *Culin* = hard-boiled eggs served with ravigote sauce and herbs; **sauce r.** ravigote sauce *(highly seasoned oil and vinegar dressing)*

ravigoter [ʀavigɔte] **VT** *Fam* **r. qn** to put new life into sb; **se sentir tout ravigoté** to feel rejuvenated; **après ce bon chocolat chaud, je me sens tout ravigoté!** that nice hot chocolate has really perked me up!

ravin [ʀavɛ̃] **NM** ravine

ravine [ʀavin] **NF 1** *(petit ravin)* gully **2** *(rivière)* (mountain) torrent

ravinement [ʀavinmɑ̃] **NM** gullying, channelling *(by running water)*

raviner [ʀavine] **VT** *(d'orage, de torrent)* *(sol)* to gully, to channel; *(route)* to furrow, to cut up; *Fig (visage)* to crease

ravioli, *pl* **ravioli** *ou* **raviolis** [ʀavjɔli] **NM** *Culin* piece of ravioli; **des ravioli(s)** ravioli

ravir [ʀaviʀ] **VT 1** *(plaire)* to delight; **sa gentillesse me ravit** I am delighted by his/her kindness; **ce film m'a ravi** I thought the film was delightful; **à r.** *(jouer, chanter)* delightfully, charmingly, beautifully; **belle à r.** ravishing, ravishingly beautiful; **elle est douce à r.** she is extremely gentle; **cela te va à r.** it suits you beautifully, you look delightful in it

2 *Litt (femme)* to carry off, *Arch* to ravish; *(enfant)* **r. qch à qn** to rob sb of sth, to steal sth from sb; **la mort nous l'a ravi bien trop tôt** death took him from us *or* snatched him away from us far too soon; **ceux que la mort a ravis** those whom death has taken from our midst

raviser (se) [səʀavize] **VPR** to change one's mind

ravissant [ʀavisɑ̃] **ADJ** delightful, entrancing, ravishing

ravissement [ʀavismɑ̃] **NM 1** *(extase)* rapture, ecstasy, delight; **être dans le r. le plus total** to be in raptures *or* in ecstasies; **ce qui la plongeait dans le r. le plus total** which sent her into raptures; **avec r.** *(écouter, contempler qch)* with delight; **c'est ce que nous**

avons découvert avec r. that's what we found out to our delight **2** *Litt (d'une femme)* carrying off, *Arch* ravishment

ravisseur, -euse [ʀavisœʀ, -øz] **ADJ** predatory

N abductor, kidnapper, *Arch* ravisher

ravitaillement [ʀavitajmɑ̃] **NM 1** *Mil etc (action)* supplying (**en** with); **r. (en carburant)** refuelling; **r. en munitions** ammunition supply; **convoi de r.** supply column; **r. à la mer** replenishment *or* refuelling at sea; *Aviat* **r. en vol** in-flight refuelling; **le r. des grandes villes est un des problèmes de la guerre** maintaining supplies in large cities is one of the problems of war; *Fam* **aller au r.** to go shopping **2** *(denrées)* supplies; **distribution du r.** issue of supplies

ravitailler [ʀavitaje] **VT** *(armée, camp, refuge)* to supply; *(avion, navire)* to refuel; **r. un avion en vol** to refuel an aircraft in flight

VPR se ravitailler to take in (fresh) supplies; *Fam (faire des courses)* to stock up, to do a big shop; **se r. (en carburant)** to refuel

ravitailleur [ʀavitajœʀ] **NM** *Mil etc (camion)* supply truck; *(bateau)* supply ship; *(avion)* supply aircraft

ADJ **navire/avion r.** supply ship/aircraft

ravivage [ʀavivaʒ] **NM** *(de couleur)* brightening up; *(de surfaces métalliques)* cleaning

raviver [ʀavive] **VT** *(feu)*, *Fig (colère)* to rekindle; *(couleur)* to brighten up; *(douleur)* to revive; *(surfaces à souder)* to clean; *Fig (souvenir, querelle)* to rekindle, to revive; *Fig* **r. une plaie** to reopen an old wound

VPR se raviver *(d'une conversation)* to revive, to pick up; *(de la colère, de l'inquiétude)* to flare up again

ravoir [ʀavwaʀ] **VT** *(only in inf)* **1** *(récupérer)* **r. qch** to have *or* get sth back again **2** *Fam (nettoyer)* to clean (up); **je n'arrive pas à r. cette casserole** I can't get this pan clean, I can't get the marks off this pan

VPR se ravoir *Belg (reprendre haleine)* to get one's breath back; *(retrouver ses esprits)* to come to one's senses

rayage [ʀɛjaʒ] **NM** *(d'arme à feu)* rifling

rayé [ʀɛje] **ADJ 1** striped, stripy; **tablier r. rouge et bleu** red and blue striped *or* stripy apron; **un animal r. noir et blanc** an animal with black and white stripes **2** *(papier)* lined, ruled **3** *(fusil)* rifled, grooved **4** *(disque, verre, parquet, carrosserie de voiture)* scratched

rayer [ʀɛje] **VT** *(je raie, je raye, n. rayons; je raierai, je rayerai)* **1** *(verre, parquet, carrosserie de voiture, disque etc)* to scratch; *(surface)* to score

2 *(papier)* to rule, to line

3 *(tissu)* to stripe

4 *(fusil)* to rifle; *(cylindre)* to groove

5 *(mot etc)* to strike out, to cross out, to delete; **on vous a rayé** *ou* **on a rayé votre nom de la liste** you have *or* your name has been struck off *or* crossed off *or* deleted from the list; **rayez les mentions inutiles** delete as appropriate; **on peut r. les articles que l'on a déjà achetés** we can cross off the things we've already bought; *Fig* **tu ne peux pas r. cet événement de ta vie** you can't banish *or* blot out the event from your life; *Fig* **il voudrait me r. de sa vie** he'd like to forget he ever knew me; *Fig* **une ville qui fut rayée de la carte** a town that was wiped off the map; *Mil* **r. qn des contrôles** to strike sb off the strength

rayon[1] [ʀɛjɔ̃] **NM 1** *(faisceau)* *(de lumière)* ray, beam, shaft; *Fig (d'espoir)* ray; **un faible r. de lumière** a faint gleam of light; **r. de soleil** sunbeam; *Fig* **c'est un peu mon r. de soleil** he/she has brought a ray of sunshine into my life; *Opt* **r. visuel** line of sight; **rayons X** X-rays; **passer qn/qch aux rayons X** to X-ray

sb/sth; *Méd* **mal des rayons** radiation sickness; **r. électronique** *ou* **cathodique** electron beam; **r. laser** laser beam
  2 *(périmètre)* range; *(d'un cercle)* radius; *Aut* **r. de braquage** turning circle; **dans un r. de deux kilomètres** within a radius of two kilometres (**autour de** of); **r. d'action** *(d'un avion)* range (of action *or* operation); **avion à grand r. d'action** long-range aircraft; *Fig* **r. d'action d'une campagne publicitaire** scope *or* coverage *or* range of an advertising campaign; **cette société a étendu son r. d'action** the firm has extended the scope of its operations
  3 *(de roue)* spoke

rayon² NM **1** *(dans un magasin)* department; **r. hommes/femmes** menswear/ladies' wear (department); **r. jardinage** gardening department; **chef de r.** head of department, department manager; **magasin à rayons multiples** department store; **r. des soldes** bargain counter; *Fig Fam* **ça ne c'est pas mon r.** *(ça ne me concerne pas)* that's nothing to do with me, that's none of my business; *(ça n'est pas dans mes compétences)* that's not my department; *Fig Fam* **elle en connaît un r. (sur la question)** she's well clued up (on the subject), she knows all there is to know (about the subject)
  2 *(de placard etc)* shelf; **rayons** shelves, shelving
  3 r. de miel honeycomb

rayon³ NM *Agr* drill; **r. d'oignons** row of onions

rayonnage [rɛjɔnaʒ] NM shelving, shelves

rayonnant [rɛjɔnɑ̃] ADJ *(chaleur, soleil, lumière)* radiant; *Fig (visage)* radiant, beaming; **r. de joie** radiant (with joy); **r. de santé/bonheur** glowing with health/radiant with happiness

rayonne [rɛjɔn] NF *Tex* rayon

rayonnement [rɛjɔnmɑ̃] NM **1** *Phys* radiation **2** *(du soleil etc)* radiance; *Fig* influence; **un r. émanait de toute sa personne** his/her entire being was radiant with joy

rayonner¹ [rɛjɔne] VI **1** *Phys* to radiate **2** *(du soleil)*, *Fig (du visage)* to beam, to shine; **il rayonnait (de joie)** he was radiant *or* beaming (with joy); **r. de bonheur** to radiate happiness; **son visage rayonnait de plaisir** his/her face *or* he/she was glowing *or* aglow with pleasure **3** *(à partir d'un centre)* to radiate; *Fig* **r. dans le monde** *(d'une culture, d'une école de pensée, d'art etc)* to have worldwide influence; **une douleur qui rayonne** a spreading pain; **r. autour d'Avignon** to use Avignon as a base *(for excursions)*

rayonner² VT *(pièce etc)* to fit with shelves, to put shelves up in

rayure [rɛjyr] NF **1** *(bande)* stripe; **tissu à rayures** striped *or* stripy material; **à rayures rouges et jaunes** with red and yellow stripes; **les rayures noires et blanches du zèbre** the black and white stripes *or* markings of the zebra **2** *(éraflure)* scratch; *TV, Cin (sur l'écran)* line **3** *(d'un fusil)* groove

raz [ra] NM **r. (de courant)** strong current; *Spéc* race *(in estuary)*; **r. de marée** tidal wave; *Fig* **cette nouvelle a eu l'effet d'un r. de marée** the news caused great upheaval; *Pol Fig* **ce fut un r. de marée (électoral) pour les** *ou* **en faveur des socialistes** it was a landslide (victory) for the Socialists, it was a Socialist landslide

razzia [razja] NF *(attaque)* incursion, raid; *Hist* razzia; *Fam* **faire une r. sur les articles en solde** to make a clean sweep of *or* to snap up the bargains; **faire une r. dans le frigo** to raid the fridge

RD [ɛrde] NF *abrév* **route départementale**

RDA [ɛrdea] NF *Anciennement (abrév* **République démocratique allemande)** GDR

rdc *abrév* **rez-de-chaussée**

RDS [ɛrdɛɛs] NM *(abrév* **Remboursement de la dette sociale)** = contribution paid by every taxpayer towards the Social Security deficit

ré [re] NM INV *Mus* **1** *(note)* D **2** *(en solfège)* re

réa [rea] NF *Fam abrév* **réanimation**

réabonnement [reabɔnmɑ̃] NM subscription renewal

réabonner [reabɔne] VT **r. qn** to renew sb's subscription (**à** to)
  VPR **se réabonner** to renew one's subscription (**à** to)

réabsorber [reapsɔrbe] VT to reabsorb

réabsorption [reapsɔrpsjɔ̃] NF reabsorption

réac [reak] ADJ, N *Pol Fam Péj* reactionary

réaccoutumer [reakutyme] VT to reaccustom (**à** to)
  VPR **se réaccoutumer se r. à qch** to get used to sth again, to become reaccustomed to sth; **j'aurais du mal à me r.** I would find it hard to get used to things again

réachat [reaʃa] NM repurchase

réacheminement [reaʃ(ə)minmɑ̃] NM *(de marchandises)* rerouting; *Ordinat (de message)* redirecting

réacheminer [reaʃ(ə)mine] VT *(marchandises)* to reroute; *Ordinat (message etc)* to redirect

réacheter [reaʃte] VT to repurchase

réactance [reaktɑ̃s] NF *Élec* reactance

réacteur [reaktœr] NM **1** *(moteur)* jet engine **2** *Nucl* reactor, pile; **r. propulseur de navire** ship-propulsion reactor; **r. nucléaire** nuclear reactor; *Tech* **r. thermique** thermal reactor

réactif, -ive [reaktif, -iv] ADJ reactive; **non r.** non-reactive; *Chimie* **papier r.** reagent paper, test paper; *Élec* **courant r.** reactive current
  NM *Chimie* reagent; **r. à base de mercure** mercury reagent

réaction [reaksjɔ̃] NF **1** *Chimie, Phys* reaction; **r. en chaîne** chain reaction; **r. nucléaire** nuclear reaction
  2 *Élec* reaction, feedback
  3 *(de machines etc)* reaction; *(de fusil)* kick; **moteur à r.** jet engine; **propulsion par r.** jet propulsion; **avion à r.** jet(-propelled) aircraft, jet plane, jet; *Fam* **la voiture a de très bonnes réactions (sur la glace)** the car responds well *or* handles well (on ice); **r. du moteur** engine response
  4 *Physiol (d'un organe etc)* reaction, response; **r. cutanée** skin reaction, *Spéc* cutaneous reaction; **temps de r.** response time; **il y a toujours un temps de r. avant qu'elle ne réponde** she always takes a while to answer; **avoir des réactions lentes** to be slow to react; *Physiol* **r. auditive** response to auditory stimulus
  5 *(à une remarque, à un incident, au stress etc)* reaction; **elle eut une r. de peur/de colère** her reaction was one of fear/anger; **faire qch par r.** to do sth as a reaction; **elle s'y oppose, simplement par r.** she is opposed to it as a matter of principle; **en r. à sa famille** in reaction to his/her family; **la décision a été prise en r. à …** the decision was taken in response to …; **je suis resté sans r.** I didn't react; **qu'a-t-il répondu? – rien, il n'a eu aucune r.** what did he reply? – nothing, he didn't react at all; **provoquer des réactions** to cause a reaction
  6 *Pol* **la r.** reaction, reactionary attitudes; *(personnes)* reactionaries

réactionnaire [reaksjɔnɛr] ADJ, N *Pol* reactionary

réactiver [reaktive] VT *(catalyseur, sérum)* to reactivate; *Fig (vieilles colères, anciens sentiments)* to rekindle, to arouse again, to stir up; **r. le feu** to revive *or* poke the fire; **cela a réactivé la douleur** it caused the pain to flare up again

réactivité [reaktivite] NF reactivity

réactualisation [reaktɥalizasjɔ̃] NF updating

réactualiser [reaktɥalize] VT to bring up to date, to update

réadaptation [readaptasjɔ̃] NF **1** *(d'un invalide, d'un prisonnier)* rehabilitation **2** *(de projets etc)* readjustment

réadapter [readapte] VT **1** *(invalide, prisonnier)* to rehabilitate **2** *(projets)* to readjust
  VPR **se réadapter** to readjust, to become readjusted; **il n'a pas eu de mal à se r.** he didn't have any problem readjusting

réadmettre [readmɛtr] VT *(conj like* **mettre)** to readmit

réadmission [readmisjɔ̃] NF readmission

réaffectation [reafɛktasjɔ̃] NF *(d'un employé)* reassignment; *aussi Ordinat* reallocation; *Ordinat (d'une touche)* reassignment

réaffecter [reafɛkte] VT *(personnel)* to reassign; *(crédits), Ordinat* to reallocate; *Ordinat (touche)* to reassign; **r. qn à son premier emploi** to reinstate sb in his/her former job; **r. une subvention à sa destination première** to reallocate funds to their original use

réafficher [reafiʃe] VT *Ordinat* to redisplay

réaffirmer [reafirme] VT to reaffirm

réagir [reaʒir] VI to react (**sur** on; **contre** against; **à** to); **on verra comment il réagira** we'll see how he reacts; **ça ne l'a pas du tout fait r.** he/she didn't react at all, it didn't provoke any reaction; **allez, secoue-toi, il faut r.!** come on, wake up, <u>do</u> something!; **elle a très fortement réagi à son vaccin** she had a very strong reaction to the vaccination; **tu réagis trop violemment** you're overreacting; **r. contre qch** to take a stand against sth, to stand up to sth

réajuster [reaʒyste] VT = **rajuster**

réal, -aux [real, -o] NM *(monnaie)* real

réalésage [realezaʒ] NM *Aut* rebore

réaléser [realeze] VT *Aut* to rebore

réalignement [realiɲmɑ̃] NM *(des taux de change)* realignment; **r. monétaire** realignment of currencies

réaligner [realiɲe] VT to realign

réalisable [realizabl] ADJ *(projet, proposition)* feasible, practical, workable; *Fin (avoirs)* realizable; *Fig (rêve)* attainable

réalisateur, -trice [realizatœr, -tris] N *Cin* (film) director; *Radio, TV* producer; *(d'une pièce, d'un feuilleton)* director

réalisation [realizasjɔ̃] NF **1** *(d'un projet)* implementation, carrying out, realization; *(d'une œuvre d'art)*, *Culin (d'une pièce montée)* creation; *(d'un bâtiment)* construction; **la dernière r. de Picasso** Picasso's final *or* last creation; **les autres projets sont en cours de r.** the other projects are still in progress; **la rénovation du quartier est en cours de r.** the renovation of the area is an ongoing project
  2 *(d'un rêve)* attainment; **tu verras s'accomplir la r. de ton rêve/ton souhait** you'll see your dream/wish come true
  3 *Radio, TV* production; *(d'un film, d'une pièce télévisée ou radiodiffusée)* direction; **r.: Claudine Rébersat** directed by Claudine Rébersat
  4 *Fin* realization; **r. d'un bénéfice** making a profit

réaliser [realize] VT **1** *(ambition)* to achieve, to realize; *(projet)* to carry out, to implement, to put into effect; *(œuvre d'art)*,

Culin (pièce montée) to create
2 *(rêve)* to attain; **elle a mis 30 ans avant de r. son rêve** her dream took 30 years to come true
3 *Cin* to direct; *Radio, TV* to produce
4 *Fin* **r. un capital** to realize an asset, to convert an asset into cash; **r. un profit** to make a profit; **r. un chiffre d'affaires de 10 millions d'euros** to have a turnover of 10 million euros, to have a 10 million euro turnover
5 *Fam (erreur, situation)* to realize, to understand; **elle n'arrive pas à r. que cela est vrai** she can't take it in, it hasn't sunk in *or* registered yet; **j'ai mis un certain temps avant de le r.** it was some time before I realized
VPR se réaliser 1 *(d'une prédiction, d'un rêve)* to come true
2 *(d'une personne)* to fulfil oneself
VI *Fam* to realize, to twig; **laisse-lui le temps de r.** give him time for it to sink in *or* register

réalisme [realism] **NM** realism; **faire preuve de r.** to be realistic; **faire preuve de r. politique** to demonstrate political realism *or* pragmatism; **décrire qch avec r.** to describe sth realistically; **décrire qn avec r.** to give a realistic portrayal of sb, to give a true-to-life description of sb

réaliste [realist] **ADJ** *(attitude, personne, proposition, description)* realistic; *(portrait)* lifelike
N realist

réalité [realite] **NF** reality; **la r. de la situation fait que nous ne pouvons …** the situation being what it is, we can't …; **il faut prendre en compte la r. de la situation** you/we/*etc* have to face facts *or* to look at the situation realistically; **c'est une r.** it's a reality *or* fact; **elle n'a pas le sens des réalités** she has no sense of reality, she doesn't live in the real world; **en r.** in reality, really, actually; **en r., ce n'est pas du tout comme cela que ça s'est passé** that's not really what happened, actually that's not what happened at all; **lorsque la r. dépasse la fiction** when truth is stranger than fiction; *Ordinat* **r. virtuelle** virtual reality

reality show [realitiʃo] **NM** reality show

realpolitik [realpɔlitik] **NF** *Pol* realpolitik

réaménagement [reamenaʒmɑ̃] **NM 1** *(d'un bâtiment)* refitting; **r. urbain** urban redevelopment **2** *(d'un horaire, d'un projet)* reorganization; *(d'une politique)* reshaping **3** *Fin (d'une dette)* rescheduling

réaménager [reamenaʒe] **VT 1** *(bâtiment)* to refit **2** *(horaire, projet)* to reorganize; *(politique)* to reshape **3** *Fin (dette)* to reschedule

réamorcer [reamɔrse] *Ordinat* **VT** to reboot
VPR se réamorcer to reboot

réanimation [reanimasjɔ̃] **NF** *Méd* resuscitation; **service de r.** intensive care (unit); **mettre qn en r.** to put sb in intensive care

réanimer [reanime] **VT** *Méd (patient)* to resuscitate

réapparaître [reaparɛtr] **VI** *(conj like* **apparaître**; *aux often* **être**) to reappear; *(d'une douleur)* to come back, to recur, to return; *Mus (d'un thème)* to be repeated, to recur, to return

réapparition [reaparisjɔ̃] **NF** *(d'une personne)* reappearance; *(d'une douleur)* recurrence; *(du nationalisme, d'une tendance, du choléra etc)* resurgence; *Mus (d'un thème)* recurrence, return

réapprovisionnement [reaprɔvizjɔnmɑ̃] **NM** restocking; **assurer le r.** to restock

réapprovisionner [reaprɔvizjɔne] **VT** *(magasin)* to restock a shop (**en** with); **r. qn** to replenish sb's supplies (**en** of)
VPR se réapprovisionner *(d'un magasin)* to stock up again, to restock (**en** with); *(d'une*

personne) to replenish one's supplies (**en** of), to stock up (**en** on)

réargenter [rearʒɑ̃te] **VT** to resilver

réarmement [rearmamɑ̃] **NM 1** *Pol* rearmament, rearming; *Pol, Rel* **r. moral** moral rearmament **2** *Naut* refitting, recommissioning

réarmer [rearme] **VT 1** *Pol* to rearm **2** *(arme à feu)* to recock; *(appareil photo)* to reset **3** *Naut* to refit, to recommission
VI *Pol* to rearm
VPR se réarmer *Pol* to rearm

réassort [reasɔr] **NM** *(d'une boutique)* restocking

réassortiment [reasɔrtimɑ̃] **NM 1** *(de couleurs)* matching **2** *(d'une boutique)* restocking; *(stock)* new stock

réassortir [reasɔrtir] *(conj like* **assortir**) **VT 1** *(tissu, parure de lit etc)* to match **2** *(magasin)* to restock
VPR se réassortir to restock

réassurance [reasyrɑ̃s] **NF** reinsurance

réassurer [reasyre] **VT** to reinsure

réassureur [reasyrœr] **NM** reinsurer

rebaptiser [rəbatize] **VT** *(rue etc)* to rename

rébarbatif, -ive [rebarbatif, -iv] **ADJ** *(sujet, tâche)* daunting; *(visage, mine)* forbidding, unprepossessing; *(style)* off-putting; *(logiciel, écran)* not user-friendly

rebâtir [rəbatir] **VT** *(maison)* to rebuild

rebattre [rəbatr] **VT** *(conj like* **battre**) **1** to beat again **2** *Cartes* to reshuffle **3** *Fam* **r. les oreilles à qn de qch** to shove sth down sb's throat; **il me rebat les oreilles de ses vacances au Maroc** he keeps shoving his holiday in Morocco down my throat, he keeps bending my ear about his holiday in Morocco

> Do not confuse with **rabattre**.

rebattu [r(ə)baty] **ADJ** *(histoire, thème)* hackneyed, trite; *(conversation)* trite; **c'est un sujet r.** it's a trite subject, *Fam* it's (a subject that's) been done to death; **avoir les oreilles rebattues de qch** to have had sth shoved down one's throat, to have had one's ear bent about sth

rebelle [rəbɛl] **ADJ** *(personne, esprit etc)* rebellious; *(camp, armée, troupes)* rebel; *(fièvre)* stubborn, obstinate; **pour les mèches rebelles** for unruly *or* unmanageable hair; **r. à toute discipline** unamenable to discipline; **r. aux antibiotiques** resistant to antibiotics
N rebel; **le chef des rebelles** the rebel leader

rebeller (se) [sərəbɛle] **VPR** to rebel, to revolt (**contre** against); *Fig (protester)* to protest

rébellion [rebɛljɔ̃] **NF** rebellion, (up)rising, revolt; **armer une r.** to arm a rebellion; **mater une r.** to curb a rebellion; **en état de r.** *(pays, jeunes)* in a state of rebellion; *(armée)* insurgent; **acte de r.** act of rebellion, rebellious act

rebelote [rəbəlɔt] **NF 1** *(aux cartes)* rebelote *(said when playing the second card of a pair of king and queen of trumps while playing belote)* **2** *Fam* **r.!** here we go again!

rebeu [rəbø] **NM** *Fam* = person born and living in France of North African immigrant parents

rebibes [rəbib] **NFPL** *Suisse (de fromage)* = thin slices of cheese; *(de viande)* = small pieces of cured meat

rebiffer (se) [sər(ə)bife] **VPR** *Fam* to hit back (**contre** at)

rebiquer [r(ə)bike] **VI** *Fam (de cheveux, col de chemise etc)* to stick up

reblochon [rəblɔʃɔ̃] **NM** Reblochon *(type of cheese from Savoie)*

reboire [rəbwar] **VT** *(conj like* **boire**) to drink

again; **jamais je ne reboirai de ce vin** I'll never drink *or* touch that wine again

reboisement [rəbwazmɑ̃] **NM** reforestation, *Br* (re)afforestation

reboiser [rəbwaze] **VT** to reforest, *Br* to (re)afforest

rebond [rəbɔ̃] **NM 1** *(d'un ballon)* bounce; *(ricochet)* rebound; **faux r.** spin; **saisir la balle au r.** to catch the ball on the rebound; *Fig* to seize the opportunity; *Aut* **r. des roues** wheel hop **2** *Fin (d'actions, de marché, de monnaie)* recovery

rebondi [rəbɔ̃di] **ADJ** *(joues)* round, chubby; *(personne)* plump, chubby; **ventre r.** paunch; **aux formes rebondies** with generous curves

rebondir [rəbɔ̃dir] **VI 1** *(d'un ballon)* to bounce; *(ricocher)* to rebound; **r. contre** *ou* **sur qch** to bounce off sth **2** *Fig* to flare up again; **faire r. l'intrigue/la conversation** to get the plot/conversation moving again; **c'est ça qui a fait r. toute l'affaire** that was what started the whole business up again; *Can* **son chèque a rebondi** his cheque bounced **3** *(se remettre) (économie)* to recover, to pick up again; **le dollar a rebondi** the dollar has bounced back, the (value of the) dollar has shot back up again; **il n'a jamais vraiment rebondi après cet échec** he never really recovered from that setback

rebondissement [rəbɔ̃dismɑ̃] **NM 1** rebound, bounce; **les rebondissements de la balle sur le parquet** the bouncing of the ball on the floor **2** *Fig (dans une affaire etc)* development

rebord [rəbɔr] **NM 1** *(d'une table, d'un puits)* edge; *(d'une assiette)* rim, edge; **r. d'une fenêtre** window sill *or* ledge **2** *Tech (surélevé)* raised edge, flange

reborder [rəbɔrde] **VT 1** *(vêtement)* to put a new edging *or* border on **2 r. qn dans son lit** to tuck sb up (in bed) again

reboucher [rəbuʃe] **VT 1** *(fermer de nouveau) (bouteille)* to recork, to put the cork back in; *(tube de colle, de dentifrice)* to put the top back on **2** *(obturer de nouveau) (évier)* to block *or* stop up again; *(trou)* to fill in again
VPR se reboucher 1 *(d'un évier, des W.-C.)* to get blocked up again **2 la bouteille se rebouche mal** it's not easy to get the cork back in (the bottle); **la bouteille se rebouche hermétiquement** once the cork is back in, the bottle is hermetically sealed

rebours [rəbur] **NM prendre qn à r.** to rub sb up the wrong way; **compter à r.** to count backwards; **compte à r.** countdown; **prendre à r. une rue à sens unique** to go the wrong way along a one-way street; **prendre tout à r.** to take everything the wrong way; **faire/commencer qch à r.** to do/start sth back to front *or* the wrong way round; **tu as compris à r.** you've got hold of the wrong end of the stick

rebouter [rəbute] **VT** *Fam (membre fracturé)* to set; *(articulation démise)* to put back

rebouteur, -euse [rəbutœr, -øz] **N** *Fam* bonesetter

reboutonner [rəbutɔne] **VT** to rebutton, to button up again
VPR se reboutonner to do oneself up again, to do up one's buttons again

rebrancher [rəbrɑ̃ʃe] **VT** to reconnect

rebrousse-poil (à) [arəbruspwal] **ADV brosser un chapeau à r.** to brush a hat against the nap *or* the wrong way; **caresser un chat à r.** to stroke a cat the wrong way *or* against its fur; *Fig Fam* **prendre qn à r.** to rub sb up the wrong way

rebrousser [rəbruse] **VT r. chemin** to turn back, to go back the way one came, to retrace one's steps

rebuffade [rəbyfad] NF rebuff, snub; **essuyer une r.** to be snubbed *or* rebuffed, to meet with a rebuff

rébus [rebys] NM rebus; *Fig* enigma, puzzle

rebut [rəby] NM **(article de) r.** reject; **habits de r.** cast-off clothing, cast-offs; *Ind* **pièces de r.** rejects, throw-outs; **marchandises de r.** rejects; **mettre au r.** *(voiture, ordinateur etc)* to discard, to scrap; **bon à mettre au r.** fit for the scrapheap; **bureau des rebuts** *(à la poste)* dead-letter office; *Fig* **le r. de la société/du genre humain** the dregs of society/ of the human race

rebutant [rəbytɑ̃] ADJ **1** *(tâche)* disagreeable, *Fam* off-putting; **j'ai trouvé l'administration particulièrement rebutante dans ce pays** I found having to deal with the administration in that country particularly disheartening **2** *(manière, personne)* disagreeable, unprepossessing, *Fam* off-putting

rebuter [rəbyte] VT **1** *(déplaire fortement) (d'une situation, de conditions de travail)* to put off; **ce qui me rebutait dans ce travail, c'est que …** what I found disagreeable about the job was that …; **son mauvais caractère l'a rebutée** she was disgusted by how nasty he was **2** *(dégoûter)* to disgust, to repulse
  VPR **se rebuter** to be put off; **c'est pour cela que je me suis rebuté** that's what put me off

recacheter [rəkaʃte] VT to reseal

recadrage [rəkadraʒ] NM *Phot* cropping; *Cin* framing

recadrer [rəkadre] VT *Phot* to crop; *Cin* to frame

recalage [rəkalaʒ] NM *Fam (à un examen)* failure

recalcification [rəkalsifikasjɔ̃] NF recalcification, recalcifying

recalcifier [rəkalsifje] VT to (re)calcify

récalcitrant, -ante [rekalsitrɑ̃, -ɑ̃t] ADJ *(personne, cheval)* recalcitrant, obstinate
  N recalcitrant

recalé, -ée [rəkale] N *Fam* failure; **il y a cinq recalés dans cette classe** five people in this class have failed

recaler [rəkale] VT *Fam (personne) (à un examen)* to fail; **être recalé, se faire r. (au baccalauréat/en maths)** to fail *or Fam* to flunk (the baccalauréat/(in) maths)

recapitalisation [rəkapitalizasjɔ̃] NF *Fin* recapitalization

recapitaliser [rəkapitalize] VT to recapitalize

récapitulatif, -ive [rekapitylatif, -iv] ADJ recapitulatory, recapitulative; *Ordinat* **carte récapitulative** summary card

récapitulation [rekapitylasjɔ̃] NF **1** recap, summing up, *Fml* recapitulation; **faire la r. des points importants** to recap *or* sum up the important points **2** *(résumé)* recap, summary, résumé

récapituler [rekapityle] VT to recap, to sum up, *Fml* to recapitulate
  VI to recap, to sum up; **alors, je récapitule** so, I'll recap

recapoter [rəkapɔte] VI *Aut* to put up the hood

recaser [rəkaze] *Fam* VT **1** *(dans une entreprise)* to find another job for **2** *(dans un logement)* to rehouse
  VPR **se recaser** *(retrouver du travail)* to find a new job; *(se remarier)* to get hitched again

recel [rəsɛl] NM *Jur (de biens volés)* receiving (and concealing), *Fam* fencing; *(d'un criminel)* harbouring, *Am* harboring

receler [rəs(ə)le] VT *(pr ind* **je recèle,** n. **recelons;** *fu* **je recèlerai) 1** *Jur (biens volés)* to receive; *Fam* to fence; *(criminel)* to harbour, *Am* to harbor **2 la terre recèle de grands tré-** sors great treasures lie hidden in the earth; *Littr* **un grand secret** to harbour *or* conceal a deep secret

recéler [rəsele] VT (**je recèle,** n. **recélons; je** **recélerai) = receler**

receleur, -euse [rəs(ə)lœr, -øz] N *Jur (de biens volés)* receiver, *Fam* fence

récemment [resamɑ̃] ADV recently, lately, *Fml* of late; **je le constatai encore r.** I noticed it again recently; **un livre r. publié** *ou* **publié r.** a recently published book; **encore r., elle me disait que …** she was saying to me only the other day that …

recensement [rəsɑ̃smɑ̃] NM *(de voitures, d'appartements libres etc)* count, inventory; *Admin (de la population)* census; *Pol (des votes)* counting; *Fin* stocktake; **r. du contingent** registration of those eligible for military service; **faire un r.** to make a count *or* an inventory; *(de la population)* to take a census; **agent chargé du r.** census official; **r. de la population** population census; **r. de la production** census of production; **r. des distributeurs** census of distribution; **r. des entreprises** company census

recenser [rəsɑ̃se] VT *(livres, disques etc)* to count, to make an inventory of; *Admin (ville, habitants etc)* to take a census of; *Pol (votes)* to count; *Mil* to register; **r. des marchandises** to inventory goods, to check off goods

recenseur, -euse [rəsɑ̃sœr, -øz] N *Admin* census taker; *Pol (des votes)* counter, teller

récent [resɑ̃] ADJ recent

recentrage [rəsɑ̃traʒ] NM **1** *Pol* move towards the centre *or Am* center; **le r. du Parti socialiste s'est opéré lentement mais sûrement** the Socialist party has moved slowly but surely towards the centre **2** *(d'activités)* **l'entreprise a décidé d'opérer un r. sur les activités multimédia** the company has decided to concentrate on the multimedia sector

recentrer [rəsɑ̃tre] VT *(parti politique)* to move towards the centre *or Am* center; *Sport (balle)* to centre again
  VPR **se recentrer** to refocus; **nous devons nous r. de façon à être plus compétitifs** we need to refocus our activities in order to be more competitive

recéper [rəsepe] VT **(je recèpe,** n. **recépons; je recéperai)** *(arbre, pied de vigne)* to cut back to the stump

récépissé [resepise] NM *(d'un dépôt, d'un envoi)* receipt; **r. aérien** airfreight consignment note; **r. de dépôt** deposit receipt; **r. de versement** receipt of payment; **r. des chemins de fer** rail consignment note

réceptacle [reseptakl] NM **1** receptacle; **la mer est le r. des déchets de la ville** the sea is the receptacle *or* dumping ground for the city's waste; *Fig* **cette région ne peut pas devenir le r. de tous les gangsters du pays** the region cannot become a meeting place for all the gangsters of the country **2** *Bot* receptacle **3** *Ordinat* **r. pour extension** extension slot

récepteur, -trice [reseptœr, -tris] ADJ *Radio (appareil, poste)* receiving
  NM **1** *Physiol (de stimuli)* receptor; **r. olfactif/ auditif/tactile** olfactory/auditory/tactile receptor **2** *(de radar), Tél, Radio, TV* receiver, communications receiver; *(de frein)* slave cylinder; **r. d'embrayage** clutch slave cylinder; **r. de poche** pager; *Tél* **décrocher le r.** to lift the receiver; *Tél* **r. Morse** Morse receiver; **r. de liaison terre/satellite** uplink receiver; *Ordinat* **r. de données** data receiver

réceptif, -ive [reseptif, -iv] ADJ receptive, responsive (**à** to)
  NM *Mktg* **r. précoce** early adopter

réception [resepsjɔ̃] NF **1** *(d'une lettre, d'une commande, de biens)* receipt; **prévoir quelqu'un pour la r. des marchandises** to ar- range for somebody to take delivery (of the goods); *Com* **à payer à la r.** cash on delivery, COD; *Com* **r. définitive** final hand-over, final acceptance; *Com, Ind* **r. des travaux** acceptance of work; **accuser r. de qch** to acknowledge receipt of sth
  2 *(accueil)* welcome; **faire une bonne r. à qn** to give sb a good reception *or* warm welcome, to receive *or* welcome sb warmly; **séance de r. de M. Yourcenar à l'Académie française** ceremony admitting M. Yourcenar to the Académie Française, *Fml* M. Yourcenar's induction into the Académie Française; **discours de r.** induction speech
  3 *(soirée)* reception, function; **salle de r.** reception room
  4 *(dans un hôtel)* reception (desk); **passer à la r.** to go to reception; **prière de laisser les clefs à la r.** please leave your keys at reception *or* the (front) desk
  5 *Tél, Radio, TV, Électron* reception; **appareil** *ou* **poste de r.** receiving set; **la r. est bonne/ mauvaise ici** the reception is good/bad here, you get good/bad reception here; **cet appareil n'a pas une bonne r.** the reception on this set isn't very good; **r. hertzienne** terrestrial signal reception
  6 *Sport (de gymnaste, sauteur)* landing; *Ftbl, Rugby (de ballon)* take; **il s'est blessé à la r.** *(d'un sauteur etc)* he hurt himself on landing; **mauvaise r. de Zidane** Zidane fumbles the pass; **et Zidane à la r.** to Zidane

réceptionnaire [resepsjɔner] N *(de marchandises)* consignee; *Com, Ind* receiving agent *or* clerk; *(dans un hôtel)* receptionist, *Am* desk clerk

réceptionner [resepsjɔne] VT **1** *Com, Ind (marchandises livrées)* to check and sign for, to take delivery of **2** *TV, Radio* to receive

réceptionniste [resepsjɔnist] N receptionist, *Am* desk *or* reception clerk; **r. de nuit** night porter

réceptivité [reseptivite] NF *(à des sensations, impressions)* receptiveness, responsiveness; *(à une infection)* susceptibility; **dans un état de r.** in a receptive *or* responsive mood

récessif, -ive [resesif, -iv] ADJ *Biol* recessive

récession [resesjɔ̃] NF *Écon* recession; **r. économique** economic recession

recette [rəsɛt] NF **1** *Fin* takings, receipts; *Sport* gate money; **dépenses et recettes** expenditure and receipts, outgoings and incomings; **les recettes de la boutique sont en hausse cette semaine** the shop's takings are *or Fam* take is up this week; **r. annuelle** annual income *or* receipts *or* revenue; **r. brute** gross income *or* receipts *or* earnings; **recettes en devises** foreign currency earnings; **r. des douanes** customs office; **recettes de l'État** public revenue, state revenue; **recettes fiscales** tax revenue; **r. journalière** daily takings; **r. nette** net income *or* receipts; **recettes publiques** government revenue; **faire r.** to be profitable *or* a success; *Théâtre, Cin* to be a (box-office) success, to be a hit at the box office; *Cin* **recettes en salles** box-office takings
  2 *(d'argent dû)* collection; *(bureau)* tax collector's office; **garçon de r.** bank messenger; **faire la r. de l'argent/des contributions** to collect the money/contributions
  3 *Culin* recipe; *Pharm* formula; **r. de cuisine** recipe; **livre de recettes** cookery book, recipe book; *Fig* **la r. du succès/bonheur** the recipe for success/happiness, the secret of success/happiness

recevable [rəsəvabl] ADJ *(excuse)* admissible, acceptable; *Com, Ind (marchandises)* fit for acceptance; *Jur (témoignage)* admissible; *Fml* **être r. dans une demande** to be entitled to proceed with a claim

recevant [rəsəvã] ADJ *Can (hospitalier)* hospitable, who likes to entertain

receveur, -euse [rəsəvœr, -øz] N **1** *(d'une lettre, d'une transfusion sanguine)* recipient; *Méd* **r. universel** universal recipient **2** *(des impôts)* collector; **r. des douanes** excise officer; **r. des Finances** district tax collector; **r./ receveuse des Postes** postmaster/postmistress; **r. municipal** = collector of municipal taxes; **r. des contributions directes** tax collector; **r. buraliste** tobacconist **3** *Vieilli* (bus) conductor, *f* (bus) conductress
  NM *Can* **1** *Base-ball* receiver **2** *Am Ftbl (éloigné)* wide receiver; *(rapproché)* tight end; *(inséré)* slotback

RECEVOIR [rəsəvwar] *(prp* **recevant**; *pp* **reçu**; *pr ind* **je reçois, il reçoit, n. recevons, ils reçoivent**; *pr sub* **je reçoive, n. recevions**; *impf* **je recevais**; *p hist* **je reçus**; *fu* **je recevrai**)

> **VT** to receive **1–3, 5, 7** ▪ to get **1, 2, 6, 7** ▪ to deal with **3** ▪ to entertain **4** ▪ to admit **5**

VT 1 *(entrer en possession de) (lettre)* to receive, to get; *(cadeau, conseil, fleurs)* to get, to receive (**de** from); *(prix, récompense)* to get, to be awarded, to receive; *Rel (communion, absolution)* to receive; **r. des nouvelles de qn** *(directement)* to hear from sb, to have news from sb; *(indirectement)* to have news of sb; **j'ai reçu de tes nouvelles par ton père** I had news of you through your father; **j'ai reçu une lettre d'elle** I've had *or* received a letter from her; **nous avons bien reçu votre lettre** we have received *or Com Fml* are in receipt of your letter; **vous avez reçu un appel de Londres** you've had *or* received a call from London; *Com* **reçu pour solde de tout compte** received in full settlement; **r. des ordres de qn** to take orders from sb; **je n'ai de conseils à r. de personne!** I don't need advice from anybody!; **elle ne sait pas r. les compliments** she doesn't know how to take *or* accept compliments; *Com, Admin* **recevez, Monsieur, l'assurance de ma considération distinguée** yours faithfully; *(quand la formule de salutation comprend le nom du destinataire)* yours sincerely; *Rel* **r. la confession de qn** to hear *or* receive sb's confession **2** *(se voir infliger) (blâme)* to receive, to get; *(fessée)* to get, to receive; **il a reçu une balle dans l'épaule** he got a bullet *or* he was shot in the shoulder; **il a reçu le ballon en pleine poitrine** the ball hit him right in the chest, he got the ball right in the chest; **j'ai dû r. un coup** something must have hit me; **il a reçu un coup sur la tête** he got hit on the head, he received a blow to the head; *Fam (il est fou)* he must have got dropped on the head; **r. un choc** to get *or* receive a shock; **laisse-le tranquille, il a reçu un choc** leave him alone, he's had a shock; **r. une blessure (au bras)** to get wounded (in the arm); **la blessure que j'ai reçue (au bras) me fait toujours souffrir** the wound I received *or* got (in the arm) still causes me pain; *Fam* **arrête ou tu vas r. une gifle** stop it or you'll get a slap; *Fam* **arrête ou tu vas r. ma main sur la figure** stop it or you'll feel the back of my hand; *Fam* **qu'est-ce que j'ai reçu quand il est rentré!** he really gave me what for when he got home!; *Fam* **ça ne te ferait pas de mal de r. un coup de pieds aux fesses de temps en temps!** a kick up the backside wouldn't do you any harm from time to time! **3** *(accueillir) (personne)* to receive, to welcome; *(clients)* to deal with; **être mal/bien reçu** to get a poor/good reception; *Iron* **je vais demander une augmentation et je sens que je vais être bien reçu!** I'm going to ask for a rise and I'm sure I'll be in for a warm reception!; **ils vous reçoivent comme un chien**

they treat you like a dog; **r. qn à bras ouverts** to welcome sb with open arms; **je ne peux pas le r. aujourd'hui** I can't see him today; **le projet/la proposition n'a pas été bien reçu(e)** the project/proposal was not well received; **ils ont bien reçu la proposition** they gave the proposal a good reception; **r. la visite de qn** to have a visit from sb; **je pense r. de la visite cet été** I think I'll be having visitors this summer; **tu as reçu la visite d'un monsieur** you had a visit from a gentleman **4** *(inviter) (amis)* to entertain; **r. des amis à dîner** to have friends (round) to dinner; **r. qn à sa table** to receive sb for dinner/lunch; **elle reçoit des pensionnaires** she takes (in) boarders *or* lodgers; **cet hôtel peut r. jusqu'à 200 clients** this hotel can take *or* accommodate up to 200 guests **5** *(admettre)* to receive, to admit; **elle a été reçue à l'Académie française** she was admitted to the Académie Française; *Scol* **élèves reçus en terminale** pupils admitted to the top form; **être reçu à un examen** to pass an exam(ination); **être reçu premier** to be *or* come (out) first *or* top; **incroyable! je suis reçu!** unbelievable! I've passed!; *Naut* **être reçu capitaine** to get one's captain's certificate **6** *(prendre) (pluie, soleil, lumière)* to get; **le Rhône reçoit l'Isère et la Sorgue** the Isère and the Sorgue flow into the Rhone; **la plante ne doit pas r. trop de lumière** the plant shouldn't have *or* get too much light; **r. des radiations** to be exposed to radiation, to receive a dose of radiation **7** *Radio (transmission)* to receive; *(chaîne)* to get; **ce poste ne reçoit pas les radios étrangères** the radio doesn't pick up foreign stations

VI 1 *(donner des réceptions)* to entertain; **aimer r.** to enjoy entertaining; **savoir r.** to be a good host/hostess; **ils reçoivent très peu** they don't do much entertaining, they don't have friends round much *or* often **2** *(consulter)* to be available for consultation; **le docteur ne reçoit que sur rendez-vous** the doctor will only see patients by appointment; **le médecin reçoit à 6 heures** the doctor is available for consultation at 6 o'clock, the doctor's surgery is at 6 o'clock **3** *(se voir offrir)* **mieux vaut donner que r.** it is better to give than to receive

VPR se recevoir *Sport* to land **2** *(s'inviter)* to entertain *or* visit one another, to go to one another's houses

rechange [rəʃãʒ] NM *(vêtements)* change of clothes, spare set of clothes; *Aut* spare; **linge ou vêtements de r.** spare clothes; **trousse de r.** *(d'outils etc)* spare *or* duplicate set; *Aut etc* **pièces de r.** spare parts; **pile de r.** *(pour torche)* spare battery; **solution/politique de r.** alternative solution/policy

rechanger [rəʃãʒe] VT *(conj like* **changer***)* to change again

rechanter [rəʃãte] VT to sing again

rechapage [rəʃapaʒ] NM *(des pneus)* retreading, remoulding

rechaper [rəʃape] VT *(pneu)* to retread, to remould; **pneu rechapé** retread, remould

réchappé, -ée [reʃape] N *Litt (d'un désastre, d'un naufrage etc)* survivor

réchapper [reʃape] VI *(aux* **avoir** *ou* **être***)* **r. de** *(naufrage, accident, maladie etc)* to survive; **il en a** *ou* **est réchappé** he survived; **il n'en réchappera pas** *(de naufrage, accident, maladie)* his chances of survival are nonexistent; **si j'en réchappe** if I get out of this, if I survive; **il ne réchappera pas à ce scandale** his reputation won't survive the scandal; **r. à une crise** to come through *or* survive a crisis

recharge [rəʃarʒ] NF **1** *(pour stylo à bille, briquet, rouge à lèvres etc)* refill; **r. d'encre**

ink refill **2** *(d'une batterie)* recharging; **mettre l'accumulateur en r.** to put the battery on charge **3** *(de téléphone portable)* top-up card

rechargeable [rəʃarʒabl] ADJ *(briquet, vaporisateur de parfum)* refillable; *(pile)* rechargeable; *(arme)* reloadable

rechargement [rəʃarʒəmã] NM **1** *(de briquet, vaporisateur de parfum)* refilling; *(d'un accumulateur)* recharging; *(d'un véhicule, d'un fusil, d'un bateau)* reloading **2** *(d'une route)* remetalling; *(d'une voie ferrée)* reballasting

recharger [rəʃarʒe] VT *(conj like* **charger***)* **1** *(accumulateur)* to recharge; *Fig Fam* **r. ses batteries** *ou* **ses accus** to recharge one's batteries **2** *(camion, fusil, appareil photo)* to reload; *(stylo, briquet, vaporisateur de parfum)* to refill **3** *(route)* to remetal; *(voie ferrée)* to reballast
  VPR se recharger *Ordinat* to reload

réchaud [reʃo] NM **1** stove; **r. à gaz** gas ring; **r. à alcool** spirit stove **2** *(chauffe-plat)* hotplate, plate warmer

réchauffage [reʃofaʒ] NM *(de la nourriture)* reheating, warming up

réchauffé [reʃofe] ADJ **1** *(plat)* reheated, warmed-up, *Péj* rehashed **2** *Fig Fam (plaisanterie)* stale, old
  NM *Fig Fam* **c'est du r.** *(plaisanterie)* that's an old *or* a stale joke; *(nouvelles)* that's stale news *or* old hat; *(politique)* it's the same old thing; *(livre, discours)* it's a rehash; **rien de nouveau dans le journal sur l'affaire, il n'y a que du r.** there's nothing new in the paper about the business, just a rehash of what's been said already

réchauffement [reʃofmã] NM warming (up); **r. de la planète** *ou* **de l'atmosphère** global warming; **un soudain r. de la température** a sudden rise in temperature

réchauffer [reʃofe] VT *(plat)* to reheat, to warm up; *(personne)* to warm up; **ça réchauffe, hein?** it really warms you up *or* gives you a nice warm glow inside, doesn't it?; **on ne réchauffe pas les artichauts** artichokes are no good reheated; *Fig* **r. le cœur à qn** to put new heart into sb; **cela me réchauffe le cœur** it does my heart good, it's heart-warming; **ces paroles m'ont réchauffé le cœur** these were heart-warming words
  VPR se réchauffer *(d'une personne)* to warm up, to get warm (again); **alors, tu t'es réchauffé?** have you warmed up?, are you warm again?; **se r. les pieds** to warm one's feet; **l'atmosphère se réchauffe** the atmosphere is getting warmer *or* warming (up)

réchauffeur [reʃofœr] NM *Tech* heater; **serpentin r.** heating coil

rechausser [rəʃose] VT **1 r. qn** to put sb's shoes/boots on again (for them); **r. ses skis** to put one's skis on again; *(après une longue interruption)* to start skiing again; **ce marchand de chaussures m'a rechaussé de neuf** I got my new shoes in that shop; **il était rechaussé de neuf** he was wearing new shoes **2** *Aut* **r. une voiture** to fit a car with new tyres **3** *(consolider) (structure, mur)* to underpin
  VPR se rechausser to put one's shoes on again; *(acheter de nouvelles chaussures)* to buy (oneself) new shoes

rêche [rɛʃ] ADJ *(surface, vin, matière)* rough; *(cheveux)* coarse; *Fig (personne, attitude)* forbidding

recherche [rəʃerʃ] NF **1** search (**de** for); *Fig Litt, Fml* quest (**de** for); **la r. de la vérité** the search for *or Litt, Fml* after the truth; **la r. des plaisirs** pleasure-seeking, the pursuit of pleasure; **la r. de la gloire/du bonheur** the quest for *or* pursuit of glory/happiness; **ils se sont joints aux recherches pour retrouver l'enfant** they joined in the search *or* hunt for the child; **dans l'affaire Mennesson, la police continue les** *ou* **ses recherches** the police are continuing their enquiry into the Mennesson affair; **les recherches pour retrouver l'otage sont demeurées vaines** the hunt for the hostage has been to no avail; **r. de débouchés** search for markets; **r. d'informations** information search, fact-finding; *Minér* **r. de filons** prospecting; **r. pétrolière** oil prospecting; *Élec* **r. de dérangements** locating of faults; **être à la r. de** *(objet difficile à trouver)* to be looking for; *(objet ou personne qui a disparu)* to be looking *or* searching for, to be in search of; **ils ont fait tout Paris à la r. d'un vase identique** they went round the whole of Paris in search of an identical vase; **j'ai couru à la r. d'un médecin** I ran for *or* to find a doctor; *Naut* **droit de r.** *(en mer)* right of search

2 *(scientifique, universitaire etc)* research *(* **sur** on, into); **faire de la r., être dans la r.** to do research, to be engaged in research; **faire des recherches sur qch** to do research on sth, to research sth; **la r. sur le cancer** cancer research; **r. commerciale** marketing research; **r. et développement** research and development, R&D; **r. documentaire** desk research; **r. expérimentale** experimental research; **laboratoire/équipe de r.** research laboratory/team; **r. mercatique** marketing research; *Mktg* **recherches par panel** panel research; **r. par sondage** survey research; **recherches sur les besoins des consommateurs** consumer research; **r. sur les prix** pricing research; **r. sur le terrain** fieldwork

3 *(effort)* sophistication; **avec r.** with style; **sans r.** *(style)* straightforward, down to earth **4** *Ordinat* find, search; *(de données, d'un fichier)* retrieval; **faire une r.** to do a search; **r. arrière** backward search; **r. avant, r. vers le bas** forward search; **r. booléenne** Boolean search; **r. documentaire** information retrieval; **r. de données** data retrieval; **r. globale** global search; **r. logique** logic seeking; **r. et remplacement** search and replace; **r. et remplacement global** global search and replace; **r. vers le haut** backward search

recherché [rəʃɛrʃe] ADJ **1** *(que l'on recherche) (criminel)* wanted; *(objet)* sought-after, in demand; **être très r.** to be much sought after, to be in great demand; **ce style de fauteuil est très r.** there's a lot of demand for this type of chair; **sa compagnie est très recherchée** he *or* his company is much in demand *or* much sought after **2** *(robe, écriture)* elegant, exquisite; *(style)* refined, elegant; *(discours)* elegantly phrased, well-turned; **d'un travail r.** of exquisite workmanship; **trop r.** *(style)* affected, mannered, *Fml* recherché; *(écriture)* elaborate, fancy

rechercher [rəʃɛrʃe] VT **1** *(objet ou personne qui a disparu)* to look *or* search for; *(causes, raisons etc)* to look *or* search for, to inquire into; *(un emploi)* to look for, to seek; **j'ai laissé ma bicyclette chez Paul, il va falloir que j'aille la r.** I left my bike at Paul's place, I'll have to go and get it back; **je viendrai te r. plus tard** I'll come back to pick you up later; *Ordinat* **r. qch** to search *or* do a search for sth; *Ordinat* **r. et remplacer** to search and replace; *Ordinat* **r. vers le bas/haut** to search forwards/backwards; *Tél etc* **r. un dérangement** to try to locate a fault; **un homme recherché par la police/pour meurtre** a man wanted by the police/for murder; **nous recherchons cette femme, vous la connaissez?** we are attempting to locate *or* find this woman, do you recognize her?; **h. 35 ans recherche j. f. pour sorties** *(dans petite annonce)* male, 35, seeks *or* seeking female for nights out; **r. l'origine d'un mot** to look up the origin of a word

2 *(chercher de nouveau)* to look again for; **il va falloir r. l'information dans tous les dossiers** we'll have to go through all the files again and have another look for the information

3 *(faveurs, perfection)* to look for, to seek; *(gloire, plaisirs, honneurs)* to seek, to be in pursuit of; *(louanges)* to court; **elle recherche la solitude** she's looking for solitude *or* for a place where she can be alone; **r. la difficulté** *(compliquer les choses)* to look for difficulties; *(aimer les défis)* to like a challenge

rechigner [rəʃiɲe] VI *Fam* to grimace, to look sour; **il a rangé sa chambre en rechignant** moaning and groaning, he tidied his bedroom; **faire qch sans r.** to do sth without (making) a fuss; **r. à la besogne** *ou* **au travail** to be unwilling to do it; **r. à faire qch** to make a fuss about doing sth

rechute [rəʃyt] NF**1** *Méd* relapse; **faire une r.** to suffer *or* have a relapse, to have a setback **2** *Écon* slump; **on craint une r. de l'activité économique** there are fears of another slump in economic activity

rechuter [rəʃyte] VI *Méd* to have a relapse

récidivant [residivã] ADJ *Méd (maladie)* recurring, recurrent

récidive [residiv] NF**1** *Jur* repeat offence *or* Am offense; **c'est sa première r.** it's his first repeat offence; **... et depuis il a fait plusieurs récidives ...** and he's had several repeat offences since; **à la première r., tu es renvoyé** do it one more time and you're sacked; **en cas de r., une peine de prison est inévitable** a repeat offence will lead to a mandatory prison sentence **2** *Méd (d'une maladie)* recurrence

récidiver [residive] VI **1** *Jur* to repeat an offence *or* Am offense; **il a récidivé** he has relapsed into crime, *Fam* he's done it again **2** *(d'une maladie)* to recur

récidiviste [residivist] N repeat offender, habitual criminal, *Fml* recidivist

récidivité [residivite] NF *Méd (d'une maladie)* recurrent nature

récif [resif] NM reef; **r. (en) barrière** barrier reef; **r. de corail** *ou* **corallien** coral reef

récipiendaire [resipjɑ̃dɛr] N *Litt (d'honneur, de diplôme)* recipient

récipient [resipjɑ̃] NM container

> Il faut noter que le terme anglais **recipient** est un faux ami. Il signifie **destinataire** ou **bénéficiaire**.

réciprocité [resiprɔsite] NF reciprocity

réciproque [resiprɔk] ADJ **1** *(amour, confiance, tolérance, sentiments etc)* mutual; *(bénéfices, accord, concessions)* reciprocal, mutual; **elle ne veut plus me voir, et c'est r.** she doesn't want to see me again and the feeling is mutual **2** *Gram* reciprocal; *Math (proportion)* reciprocal, inverse; *(en logique), Math (propositions)* converse

NF**1** **rendre la r. à qn** to get one's own back on sb, to get even with sb; **et la r. est vraie** and the reverse is true; **elle le déteste, et la r. est vraie** she hates him and vice versa **2** *(en logique), Math (proposition)* converse; *Math (proportion)* reciprocal

réciproquement [resiprɔkmã] ADV *(mutuellement)* mutually; **et r.** and vice versa

réciproquer [resiprɔke] *Belg* VI **je vous souhaite une bonne année! – je réciproque!** happy New Year! – same to you! VT *(vœux)* to return

récit [resi] NM **1** account; *(histoire)* story; *Littér* narrative; **il nous fit le r. de ses aventures** he gave us an account of his adventures **2** *Mus* solo; **jeux de r.** solo organ

récital, -als [resital] NM recital

récitant, -ante [resitã, -ãt] N **1** *Mus (voix, instrument)* solo **2** *(lecteur)* narrator

récitatif [resitatif] NM *Mus* recitative

récitation [resitasjɔ̃] NF *(action)* recitation, reciting; *Scol (texte)* recitation

réciter [resite] VT *(poème etc)* to recite; **on dirait qu'il récite ses remerciements** his thanks sound rehearsed

reck [rɛk] NM *Suisse* **1** *Sport* horizontal bar **2** *(pente)* steep slope

réclamant, -ante [reklamã, -ãt] N *Jur* claimant; *(en droit civil)* plaintiff

réclamation [reklamasjɔ̃] NF **1** *(plainte)* complaint, objection, protest; **faire une r.** to complain; **r. de client** customer complaint; **pour toute r., veuillez vous adresser au patron** please refer any complaints to the manager; *Tél* **le service des réclamations, les réclamations** complaints *or* service (department); **il y a r.** *(à l'issue d'une course hippique)* a steward's enquiry is taking place **2** *(pour recevoir un dédommagement)* claim; **faire** *ou* **déposer une r.** to make *or* put in a claim; **r. de dommages-intérêts** claim for damages; **prouver le bien-fondé d'une r.** to substantiate a claim; **r. d'indemnité** claim for compensation

réclame [reklam] NF *(publicité)* advertising; *(panneau)* advertisement; *TV, Radio* commercial; **faire de la r. pour qch** to advertise sth; *Fig* **faire de la r. pour qn** to sing sb's praises; *Fig* **cela ne lui fera pas de r.** it's not a very good advertisement for him; **article (en) r.** special offer; **c'était en r.** it was a special offer, *Am* it was on special; **vente r.** sale; **r. lumineuse** illuminated sign

réclamer [reklame] VI to complain; **r. auprès de** to make a claim against; *(se plaindre)* to lodge a complaint with; **r. contre** *(quelque chose)* to protest against, to object to; *(décision)* to appeal against; *Fam* **cet enfant ne cesse de r.** that child's never satisfied

VT **1** *(demander) (livre, cotisation, pourboire, silence)* to ask for; *(droit, allocation)* to claim; *(bien perdu)* to reclaim; **r. de l'argent à qn** to ask sb for money; **l'enfant réclame ses parents** the child is calling for his/her parents; **il va finir par te r. une augmentation de salaire** he'll end up asking you for a pay rise

2 *(exiger) (secours, aide, intervention, réformes etc)* to demand; **il réclame son argent** he wants his money back; **r. des dommages et intérêts** to claim damages; **r. le paiement** to demand payment; **mon client me réclame les épreuves pour mardi** my customer's clamouring to have the proofs back by Tuesday; **les enfants réclament leur dessert** the children are clamouring for *or* demanding their dessert; **Monsieur le Président, je réclame la parole** Mr President, may I say something?; **il me le réclame sans cesse** he keeps nagging me about it; **je ne fais que r. mon dû** I am merely claiming what is mine; **r. qch à cri** to clamour for sth; **r. qn/qch à grands cris** to clamour for sb/sth

3 *(avoir besoin de) (soins, attention)* to require, to need

VPR **se réclamer il se réclame de la droite/du mouvement écologiste** he proclaims to be right-wing/an environmentalist; **elle se réclama du Maire pour se faire nommer** she used the Mayor's name to secure her appointment

> Il faut noter que le verbe anglais **to reclaim** est un faux ami. Il signifie **récupérer**.

reclassement [rəklasmã] NM **1** *(réarrangement)* reordering, rearrangement **2** *(dans une catégorie différente)* reclassifying, reclassification; *(du personnel)* regrading; **r. professionnel** redeployment

reclasser [rəklase] **VT 1** *(réarranger)* to reorder, to rearrange **2** *(dans une catégorie différente)* to reclassify; *(personnel, salaires)* to regrade; *(poste)* to reassign

reclus, -use [rəkly, -yz] **ADJ** *Rel* cloistered
N recluse; *Rel* cloistered monk *or f* nun; *Fig* recluse; **vivre en r.** to live like a hermit, to live the life of a recluse, to be a recluse

réclusion [reklyzjɔ̃] **NF 1** *Jur* imprisonment; **r. criminelle à perpétuité** life imprisonment **2** *(solitude)* seclusion; **il vit dans la r. la plus totale** he lives totally secluded *or* cut off from the world

réclusionnaire [reklyzjɔnɛr] **N** *Jur* long-term prisoner

récognition [rekɔgnisjɔ̃] **NF** *Phil* recognition, identification

recoiffer [rəkwafe] **VT r. qn** to redo sb's hair; *(remettre un chapeau à)* to put sb's hat on again
VPR se recoiffer 1 to redo one's hair **2** *(remettre son chapeau)* to put one's hat on again

recoin [rəkwɛ̃] **NM** nook, recess; **maison pleine de recoins** rambling house, house full of nooks and crannies; **les coins et les recoins** the nooks and crannies; **je l'ai cherché dans les coins et les recoins** *ou* **jusque dans les moindres recoins** I've searched high and low *or* every nook and cranny for it; *Fig* **les recoins de la mémoire** the deepest recesses of the memory

récollection [rekɔlɛksjɔ̃] **NF** *Rel* meditation

recoller [rəkɔle] **VT** *(vase cassé)* to glue *or* stick back together again; *(timbre)* to stick back on; *(enveloppe)* to stick back down; *Fig* **il recolla son front à la vitre glacée** he pressed his forehead back against the frosted windowpane; *Fig Fam* **r. les morceaux** to put the pieces back together again; *Fam* **r. une amende/mauvaise note à qn** to dole out another fine/bad mark to sb
VI *Sport* **r. au peloton** to catch up with the pack
VPR se recoller 1 *(d'un os cassé)* to knit; **ça s'est recollé comme par miracle!** as if by magic, it's back in one piece! **2** *Fam* **ils se sont recollés (ensemble)** they're back together again, they've patched things up

récoltable [rekɔltabl] **ADJ** ready for harvesting

récoltant, -ante [rekɔltɑ̃, -ɑ̃t] **ADJ** apiculteur r. honey producer; **propriétaire** *ou* **viticulteur r.** = winegrower who harvests his own grapes
N mis en bouteille chez le r. estate-bottled

récolte [rekɔlt] **NF 1** *Agr (des cultures, fruits, pommes de terre, miel)* harvesting, gathering; **nous avons fait une bonne/mauvaise r.** we got a good/bad crop; **pendant la r.** during harvesting, at harvest time; **faire la r.** to harvest (the crops); **faire la r. du blé** to harvest the wheat; **partir faire les récoltes** to go harvesting; *Fig Fam* **la r. a été bonne** *(au marché aux puces, chez l'antiquaire etc)* I/we/*etc* came back with a good haul **2** *Bot (de spécimens etc)* collecting, gathering **3** *(produits) (céréales, fruits, pommes de terre)* harvest, crop(s); *(miel)* harvest; **une belle r.** a good harvest *or* crop; **donner une bonne r.** *(d'une terre, une variété de pomme de terre etc)* to give a good crop, to crop well; **rentrer la r.** to get in *or* bring in *or* gather in the harvest *or* the crops; *Fig* **une bonne r. de renseignements** a good crop of information

récolter [rekɔlte] **VT** *(cultures)* to harvest, to gather in, to get in; *Fig Fam (renseignements, documents etc)* to collect, to gather, to garner; **si tu arrives à r. des informations sur ...** if you should happen to come up with any information on ...; **elle a récolté toute** une série de mauvaises notes she got a whole crop *or* series of bad marks; **et finalement, je n'ai récolté que des injures** and in the end, all I got was insults; **il récolte ce qu'il a semé** it's his own fault, he's reaping what he sowed; *Prov* **qui sème le vent récolte la tempête** sow the wind and reap the whirlwind
VPR se récolter *Agr* **ces fraises se récoltent en juin** these strawberries are ready for picking *or* are harvested in June

recombinaison [rəkɔ̃binɛzɔ̃] **NF** *Biol* recombination

recombinant [rəkɔ̃binɑ̃] **ADJ** *Biol* recombinant

recombustion [rəkɔ̃bystjɔ̃] **NF** *(des imbrûlés)* recombustion

recommandable [rəkɔmɑ̃dabl] **ADJ 1** commendable; **en tous points r., r. à tous égards** *(personne)* highly respectable; **le seul restaurant r. du quartier** the only decent restaurant in the area, the only restaurant in the area worth recommending; **peu r.** *(personne)* undesirable; **hôtel peu r.** disreputable hotel **2** *(que l'on conseille)* advisable

recommandation [rəkɔmɑ̃dasjɔ̃] **NF 1** recommendation; **(lettre de) r.** letter of recommendation *or* of introduction; **avez-vous des recommandations?** do you have references?; **je vous mets un mot de r. pour le spécialiste** I'll write you a referral for the specialist **2** *(conseil)* recommendation; **recommandations** advice; **je viens sur la r. d'un de vos clients** I've come on the recommendation of one of your customers, one of your customers recommended you to me; **suivre les recommandations de qn** to follow sb's advice; **maman nous a fait mille recommandations sur la façon de se bien conduire** Mum told us a thousand things to do and not to do **3** *(d'une lettre)* registration

recommandé [rəkɔmɑ̃de] **ADJ** *(lettre)* registered
NM un envoi en r., *Fam* **un r.** a registered letter/parcel; **envoyer qch en r.** to send sth registered (post)

recommander [rəkɔmɑ̃de] **VT 1** *(hôtel, produit, film, employé, médecin etc)* to recommend; **je peux vous la r.** I can recommend her; **est-ce qu'elle est recommandée?** does she have references?; **r. son âme à Dieu** to commend one's soul to God **2** *(conseiller) (discrétion, prudence etc)* to advise, to urge; **r. à qn de faire qch** to advise *or* urge sb to do sth; **je vous recommande de rester** I advise you to stay, my advice is to stay, I recommend that you stay; **r. la prudence à qn** to advise *or* urge sb to be cautious; **je te le recommande fortement** I would strongly advise it; **il est recommandé aux clients de réserver à l'avance** customers are advised to book in advance; **il n'est pas recommandé de boire de l'alcool pendant le traitement** it is inadvisable to drink alcohol during the treatment; **ce n'est pas très recommandé** it's not very advisable, I wouldn't recommend it **3** *(lettre, paquet)* to register **4** *(passer une nouvelle commande)* **r. un café/une bière** to order another coffee/beer
VPR se recommander 1 se r. à Dieu to commend oneself to God **2 se r. de qn** *(pour un emploi)* to give sb *or* use sb's name as a reference; **il se recommande du docteur Martin** he's been referred by Dr Martin **3 se r. par qch** to have sth in one's favour; **elle se recommande par son efficacité** her efficiency is a strong point in her favour; **ce restaurant se recommande par ses poissons** the restaurant is to be recommended for its fish

4 *Suisse (insister)* **je me recommande pour que vous fermiez bien la porte à la clé** I'd just like to remind you to make sure you lock the door

recommencement [rəkɔmɑ̃smɑ̃] **NM** beginning *or* starting again; *(d'un débat, de pourparlers)* reopening; **la vie est un éternel** *ou* **perpétuel r.** life is a constant succession of new beginnings

recommencer [rəkɔmɑ̃se] (**je recommençai(s)**; **n. recommençons**) **VT** *(une tâche, un jeu, un récit etc)* to start *or* begin again, *Fml* to recommence; **r. sa vie** to make a new *or* fresh start (in life), to start life afresh; **r. à faire qch** to start *or* begin to do *or* doing sth again; **tout est à r.** we'll have to start *or* begin all over again; *Fam* we'll have to go back to square one; **si c'était à r., j'accepterais le poste en Martinique** if I could do it all over again, I'd accept the job in Martinique
VI *(d'une personne)* to start *or* begin again, to start afresh, *Am* to start over; *(d'une guerre, de la pluie)* to start (up) again; *(de combats)* to break out again; **ça fait trois fois que je recommence** I've started this three times; **ne recommencez pas!** don't do it again!; **le voilà qui recommence!** he's at it again!; **je vous garantis qu'il ne recommencera pas de sitôt** I can guarantee he won't do that again in a hurry; **qui parle? alors, ça recommence?** who's talking? that chatter's not going to start again, is it?; **l'orage a recommencé en fin de soirée** there was another storm late in the evening; **il recommence à pleuvoir** it's starting to rain again

recommercialiser [rəkɔmɛrsjalize] **VT** to remarket

récompense [rekɔ̃pɑ̃s] **NF** reward; **mille euros de r.** a thousand euro reward; **et en r. elle a reçu ...** and as a reward *or* in reward *or* in return she was given ...; **on ne peut pas les laisser sans r.** they can't go unrewarded; **en r. de vos services** as a reward for your services, in return for your services; **en r. de votre bonté** in return for your kindness, to repay you for your kindness; **c'est une modeste r. pour votre bonté** it's a small recompense *or* return for your kindness; **et c'était là la r. de mes efforts** and that was how you/he/*etc* repaid me, and that was all the thanks I got; **la juste r. de ses crimes** just retribution for his/her crimes

récompenser [rekɔ̃pɑ̃se] **VT** to reward; **r. qn de qch** to reward sb for sth; **r. qn de sa bonté** to repay sb for their kindness; **son travail a été bien récompensé** his/her work was well *or* amply rewarded; *Iron* **me voilà récompensé d'avoir tant travaillé** that's all the thanks I get for working so hard; **film récompensé au Festival de Venise** film that won an award at the Venice Film Festival

recomposer [rəkɔ̃poze] **VT 1** *Chimie (éléments)* to recompose, to recombine **2** *Typ (texte)* to reset **3** *Tél (numéro)* to redial

recomposition [rəkɔ̃pozisjɔ̃] **NF 1** *Chimie* recombining **2** *Typ* resetting **3** *Tél* redialling, *Am* redialing

recompter [rəkɔ̃te] **VT** to recount, to count again

reconcevoir [rəkɔ̃s(ə)vwar] **VT** to redesign

réconciliateur, -trice [rekɔ̃siljatœr, -tris] **N** reconciler

réconciliation [rekɔ̃siljasjɔ̃] **NF** reconciliation; **amener une r. entre deux personnes** to bring about a reconciliation *or* to heal the breach between two people; **en signe de r.** as a sign of reconciliation; **pour sceller notre r.** to show that we've made it up

réconcilier [rekɔ̃silje] **VT** *(personnes, aspects différents d'une personnalité etc)* to reconcile; **r. qn avec ses parents** to reconcile sb with his/her parents, to heal the breach between sb and his/her parents; **ce voyage m'a réconcilié avec la marche** the trip renewed my appetite for walking; **ça m'a réconcilié avec la vie** it renewed my appetite for life, it made life seem worth living again; **la famille s'en trouva réconciliée** it brought the family together again; **réconcilié avec lui-même** at peace with himself

VPR se réconcilier to be or become reconciled; **se r. avec qn** to be reconciled with sb, to make it up or be friends again with sb, to patch things up with sb; **se r. avec soi-même** to be or feel at peace with oneself; **se r. avec la vie** to renew one's appetite for life, to find life worth living again; **se r. avec le sport/son travail** to renew one's appetite for sport/one's job; **c'est ainsi que j'ai pu me r. avec la vie/le sport** that's what made life/sport seem worthwhile again

> Do not confuse with **concilier**.

reconditionner [rəkɔ̃disjɔne] **VT** to repackage

reconductible [rəkɔ̃dyktibl] **ADJ** (contrat, bail) renewable

reconduction [rəkɔ̃dyksjɔ̃] **NF 1** Jur (d'un bail, contrat) renewal; **r. tacite** (d'un accord) tacit renewal **2** Admin, Pol (de budget, mesures, politique etc) continuation; **voter la r. de la grève** to vote for the continuation of the strike or for continued strike action or for the strike to continue

reconduire [rəkɔ̃dɥir] **VT** (conj like conduire) **1 r. qn** (à son hôtel etc) (en voiture) to take or drive sb back; (à pied) to see or walk sb back; (chez lui) (en voiture) to drive or take sb home; (à pied) to see or walk sb home; **r. qn (jusqu'à la porte)** to see or show sb out, to see or walk sb to the door; **r. qn à la frontière** to escort sb back over the border **2** (renouveler) (bail, contrat etc) to renew; Admin, Pol (mesure temporaire, politique, grève) to continue

reconfiguration [rəkɔ̃figyrasjɔ̃] **NF 1** (d'une société) reengineering **2** Ordinat reconfiguration

reconfigurer [rəkɔ̃figyre] **VT** Ordinat to reconfigure

reconfirmation [rəkɔ̃firmasjɔ̃] **NF** reconfirmation

réconfort [rekɔ̃fɔr] **NM** comfort, reassurance; **le r. qu'apporte la religion** the comfort or consolation that religion brings; **le r. procuré par ces paroles** the comfort that these words brought; **avoir besoin de r.** to need cheering up; **paroles de r.** words of comfort, comforting or reassuring words; **vous m'êtes toujours d'un grand r.** you're a great comfort to me

réconfortant [rekɔ̃fɔrtɑ̃] **ADJ 1** (physiquement) (médicament, traitement) tonic **2** (moralement) (personne, attitude) comforting; (paroles, nouvelle) comforting, cheering, cheery; **c'est une idée peu réconfortante** it's not a very comforting idea, there's not much comfort in that idea

réconforter [rekɔ̃fɔrte] **VT 1** (physiquement) to build up; **cette soupe te réconfortera** the soup will help build you or your strength up **2** (moralement) to comfort; **ces paroles l'ont réconforté** these words brought him some comfort; **elle a su nous r. dans ces moments difficiles** she was a great comfort to us in those difficult times; **cela me réconforte de voir que je ne suis pas la seule** it cheers me up or I'm glad to see I'm not the only one

VPR se réconforter to cheer oneself up

reconnaissable [rəkɔnɛsabl] **ADJ** (parfum, odeur, style, allure etc) recognizable (à by, from); **r. entre tous** (style, personne etc) un-mistakable; **c'est difficilement r. sur la photo** it's hardly or scarcely recognizable in the photo, it's hard to recognize in the photo; **il n'est plus r.** he's unrecognizable, you wouldn't recognize or know him, he's changed beyond all recognition

reconnaissance [rəkɔnɛsɑ̃s] **NF 1** (action de reconnaître) recognition; **je porterai un canotier, ce sera notre signe de r.** I'll be wearing a boater, that's how you'll recognize me; **de la main, elle lui fit un signe de r.** she waved to show she'd seen him; Mil **signal de r.** recognition signal

2 (acte formel) (d'une promesse, dette, d'un enfant né hors mariage etc) acknowledgement; (d'un gouvernement) recognition, acknowledgement; (d'une erreur) acknowledgement, admission; **en r. de son courage** in recognition of his courage

3 (gratitude) gratitude; **r. de** ou **pour qch** gratitude or thankfulness for sth; **témoigner de la r. à qn** to show gratitude to sb; **je n'éprouve** ou **je n'ai aucune r. pour eux** I feel no gratitude towards them; **avoir une profonde r. pour qch** to be deeply grateful or thankful for sth; **en r. de votre invitation** in gratitude for your invitation; **avec r.** gratefully; **parler de qch avec r.** to speak of sth with gratitude; Fam **c'est la r. du ventre** that's cupboard love

4 Com note of hand, promissory note; **r. (de dépôt de gage)** pawn ticket

5 Mil reconnaissance, reconnoitring, Fam recce; **détachement/avion de r.** reconnaissance party/aircraft; **faire une r. rapide du village** to do a quick reconnaissance or Fam recce of the village; **être en r.** to be on (a) reconnaissance, to be reconnoitring; **partir en r.** to go off on reconnaissance; Fig Fam **je peux en r.** I'll go and check things out; Fam **j'y suis allé en r.** I went to check it out

6 (d'un terrain, d'un site) inspection, exploration, examination; Min prospecting; (topographie) surveying, charting; **levé de r.** exploratory survey

▸▸ **r. de dette** IOU, promissory note; Ordinat **r. de l'écriture manuscrite** handwriting recognition; Ordinat **r. optique des caractères** optical character recognition, OCR; Ordinat **r. de la parole, r. vocale** speech recognition

reconnaissant [rəkɔnɛsɑ̃] **ADJ** grateful; **être r. à qn de qch/de faire qch** to be grateful to sb for sth/for doing sth; **je vous en suis très r.** I'm very grateful, I'm in your debt; **je vous serais r. de ne plus en parler** I'd thank you not to mention it again, I'd be grateful if you didn't mention it again; Fml **votre fils r.** (dans une lettre) your grateful or loving or devoted son

reconnaître [rəkɔnɛtr] **VT 1** (identifier) (personne, lieu, air) to recognize; **r. qn à sa démarche** to recognize or know or tell sb by his/her walk; **j'ai eu beaucoup de mal à le r.** I hardly knew or recognized him; **je la reconnaîtrais n'importe où** I'd know or recognize her anywhere; **est-ce que vous le reconnaîtriez?** would you know him again?, would you recognize him?; **ils se ressemblent tant qu'on ne peut les r.** they're so alike that you can't tell them apart; **je te reconnais bien là!** that's just like you!, that's you all over!

2 Naut **r. la terre** to sight land

3 (admettre) (vérité, droit, gouvernement) to recognize, to acknowledge; (erreur, faute) to acknowledge, to admit; Jur (enfant) to acknowledge, to own; **r. les qualités de qn** to acknowledge sb's qualities; **tu peux au moins lui r. cette qualité** you could at least acknowledge that or Fam at least give him/her that; **r. qn pour chef** to acknowledge sb as leader; **r. qch comme vrai** to acknowledge

the truth of sth; **reconnu comme (étant) le plus grand chef de France** recognized as the or acknowledged to be the greatest chef in France; **r. qu'on s'est trompé, r. s'être trompé** to admit or acknowledge that one was mistaken; **je suis allée trop vite, je le reconnais** I went too fast, I admit it

4 Mil etc (examiner) (position etc) to reconnoitre, to make a reconnaissance of; (terrain) to explore

5 Min to prospect

VPR se reconnaître 1 (soi-même) to recognize oneself; **je ne me reconnais pas sur cette photo** I don't recognize myself in that photo; **se r. vaincu/coupable** to acknowledge defeat/one's guilt; **elle se reconnaît tout à fait dans son rôle** she recognizes herself in the part

2 (se retrouver) to find one's way about or around; **ce n'est pas facile de se r. dans Tokyo** it's not easy to find your way about or to get your bearings in Tokyo; **je n'arrive plus à m'y r.** I can't find my way around any more; Fig I'm lost, I'm confused; Fig **c'est à ne pas s'y r.** it's all very confusing

3 gaz qui se reconnaît à son odeur gas recognizable by its smell; **un vrai gentleman se reconnaît à ...** you can tell a real gentleman by ...

4 (entre personnes) to recognize or know each other

reconnecter (se) [sərəkɔnɛkte] **VPR** to reconnect

reconquérir [rəkɔ̃kerir] **VT** (conj like conquérir) (province, royaume, pays) to reconquer; (territoire, liberté, droit) to win back, to regain, to recover; (l'estime, l'amitié de qn) to win back, to regain; **r. une femme/un homme** to get or win a woman/man back

reconquête [rəkɔ̃kɛt] **NF** (d'un royaume) reconquest; (d'un droit, de la liberté) recovery, winning back

reconsidérer [rəkɔ̃sidere] **VT** (conj like considérer) to reconsider

reconstituant [rəkɔ̃stitɥɑ̃] **ADJ** Méd tonic; **c'est un aliment r.** it's nourishing
NM pick-me-up, tonic

reconstituer [rəkɔ̃stitɥe] **VT** (armée, gouvernement) to reconstitute; (société, parti) to revive; (bâtiment abîmé, quartier) to restore; (d'un archéologue) (vase, crâne) to piece or put back together; (forces) to build up; (crime) to reconstruct; (faits) to piece together; (fortune) to restore, to build up again; **deux steaks hachés reconstitués** two beef patties; **r. des stocks** to replenish stocks, to restock

reconstitution [rəkɔ̃stitysjɔ̃] **NF** (d'un gouvernement) reconstitution; (d'une société, d'un parti) revival; (d'un bâtiment, d'une danse d'époque etc) restoration; (d'un crime, d'une bataille) reconstruction; Admin **r. de carrière** employment record or history; **r. historique** (spectacle) historical reconstruction; **la r. du squelette/vase sera bientôt complète** the task of putting or piecing the skeleton/vase back together will soon be completed

reconstruction [rəkɔ̃stryksjɔ̃] **NF** (d'une ville), Fig (d'un parti) reconstruction, rebuilding

reconstruire [rəkɔ̃strɥir] **VT** (conj like construire) (édifice, structure) to reconstruct, to rebuild; **r. le monde** to change the world, Fam to put the world to rights; **r. sa vie** to put one's life back together, to rebuild one's life; **essayons de r. notre bonheur passé** let's try to be happy again the way we used to be

reconventionnel, -elle [rəkɔ̃vɑ̃sjɔnɛl] **ADJ** Jur **demande reconventionnelle** counterclaim

reconversion [rəkɔ̃vɛrsjɔ̃] **NF 1** (d'une

usine) conversion; **r. économique** economic restructuring; **r. industrielle** industrial redeployment **2** *(du personnel)* retraining

reconvertir [rəkɔ̃vɛrtir] **VT 1** *(usine)* to convert **2** *(personnel)* to retrain
▪ **VPR se reconvertir** *(se recycler)* to retrain; **se r. dans** *(industrie)* to move into, to diversify into; **se r. dans la publicité** *(d'une personne)* to start a new career in advertising; **ils se sont reconvertis dans le bâtiment** *(d'une entreprise)* they changed over *or* converted to construction work

recopier [rəkɔpje] **VT** *(conj like* **copier***)* **1** *(en double) (document, information etc)* to recopy, to take another copy of; *Ordinat* to recopy; *Ordinat* **r. à l'identique** to replicate **2** *(au propre) (brouillon, devoir, manuscrit)* to copy out, to make a fair *or* clean copy of

record [rəkɔr] **NM** *Sport etc* record; **établir un r.** to set a record; **détenir le r.** to hold the record, to be the record holder; **battre le r.** to break *or* beat the record; **une performance qui bat tous les records** a record-breaking performance; *Fig* **il bat tous les records d'impolitesse, son impolitesse bat tous les records** he takes some beating when it comes to rudeness
▪ **ADJ INV** *(chiffre, vitesse etc)* record; **dans** *ou* **en un temps r.** in record time; **attirer une affluence r.** to draw record crowds

recorder [rəkɔrde] **VT** *(raquette)* to restring

recordman, *pl* **recordmen** [rəkɔr(d)man, -mɛn] **NM** (men's) record holder

recordwoman, *pl* **recordwomen** [rəkɔr(d)-wuman, -mɛn] **NF** (women's) record holder

recors [rəkɔr] **NM** *Jur Arch Fam* bailiff's man; **les r. de la justice** the minions of the law

recouche [rəkuʃ] **NF** *(dans un hôtel)* stay-(over); **liste des clients en r.** stays list

recoucher [rəkuʃe] **VT 1** *(au lit)* **r. qn** to put sb to bed again **2** *(bouteille)* to lay down again
▪ **VI** *Fam* **r. avec qn** to sleep with sb again
▪ **VPR se recoucher** to go back to bed

recoudre [rəkudr] **VT** *(conj like* **coudre***)* to sew again; *(bouton)* to sew on again, to sew back on; *(déchirure, blessure)* to sew *or* stitch up; *Fam* **il a fallu me r.** they had to stitch me up

recoupement [rəkupmɑ̃] **NM** *(de renseignements)* crosschecking; **faire un** *ou* **le r.** to crosscheck, to do a crosscheck; **je l'ai compris par r.** I found out by crosschecking *or* by doing a crosscheck

recouper [rəkupe] **VT 1** *(couper à nouveau) (vêtement)* to recut; **je vous recoupe une tranche de gâteau?** shall I cut you another slice *or* piece of cake? **2** *(vins etc)* to (re)blend **3** *(faire coïncider)* to confirm, to support; **r. des témoignages** to crosscheck testimony **4** *Cartes* to reshuffle
▪ **VPR se recouper** *(de cercles)* to intersect again; *Fig (de témoignages, de résultats)* to tally, to agree

recouponnement [rəkupɔnmɑ̃] **NM** *Bourse* renewal of coupons

recouponner [rəkupɔne] **VT** *Bourse* to renew the coupons of

recourbé [rəkurbe] **ADJ** bent, curved; *(bec)* curved, hooked; **nez r.** hook nose

recourber [rəkurbe] **VT** to bend
▪ **VPR se recourber** to bend, to curve

recourir [rəkurir] **VI** *(conj like* **courir***)* **1** *(courir de nouveau)* to run again; **r. jusque chez soi** to run back home; *Sport* **elle n'a pas recouru depuis les Jeux olympiques** she hasn't run since the Olympic Games **2** *(employer)* **r. à (l'aide de) qn** to appeal to sb for help, to turn to sb; **r. à qch** to use *or* have recourse to sth; **r. à la violence** to resort to violence; **r. à la justice** to take legal proceedings **3** *Jur* **r. en cassation** to appeal

VT *Sport* to rerun, to run again; **je recourrai le marathon l'an prochain** I'll be running in the marathon again next year

recours [rəkur] **NM 1** recourse, resort; **c'est son seul r.** it's his/her only option *or* recourse; **en dernier r.** as a last resort; **c'est sans r.** there's nothing else for it, there's no other option; **avoir r. à qn** to go *or* turn to sb; **avoir r. à un spécialiste/un avocat** to consult *or* see *or* go to a specialist/a lawyer; **avoir r. à** *(la violence)* to resort to; *(une agence immobilière)* to go to, to use **2** *Jur* **r. en cassation** appeal; **r. en grâce** petition for reprieve; **s'assurer contre le r. des tiers** to insure against a third party claim; **r. contentieux** litigation, legal recourse; **r. contre l'endosseur** recourse against the endorser; *Can* **r. collectif** class action

recouvrable [rəkuvrabl] **ADJ** *(dette, facture)* recoverable, collectable; *(impôt)* collectable, collectible

recouvrement¹ [rəkuvrəmɑ̃] **NM 1** *(des dettes, d'une facture)* recovery, collection; *(de l'impôt)* collection; **r. de créances** debt collection; **r. d'impôts** tax collection; **r. du coût total** full cost recovery; **recouvrements outstanding debts 2** *Vieilli (de la santé, des forces etc)* recovery

recouvrement² **NM 1** *(action de recouvrir)* re-covering; *(pour la première fois)* covering; **tôle de r.** covering plate **2** *(fait de chevaucher)* (over)lapping; *(surface recouverte)* overlap; **à r.** lapped, lap-jointed; **en r.** overlapping; **planches à r.** weatherboarding **3** *Tech (ce qui couvre)* cover; *Ordinat* overlay

recouvrer [rəkuvre] **VT 1** *(ses biens, son argent)* to recover, to retrieve, to get back; *(santé, vue)* to recover, to get back; *(forces, liberté)* to regain, to get back; *(courage, enthousiasme)* to get back **2** *(percevoir) (dettes, impôts)* to recover, to collect; **créances à r.** outstanding debts

recouvrir [rəkuvrir] *(conj like* **couvrir***)* **VT 1** *(couvrir de nouveau) (cahier, toit)* to re-cover; *(enfant)* to cover up again
2 *(couvrir complètement)* to cover **(de** in, with**)**
3 *(tapisser)* to cover **(de** with**)**; **fauteuil recouvert de velours** armchair covered in velvet
4 *(masquer) (défauts)*, *Fig (angoisse, égoïsme)* to cover up, to hide
5 *(englober)* to cover
6 *Tech (ardoises etc)* to (over)lap
▪ **VPR se recouvrir** *(du ciel)* to cloud over (again); **le champ s'est recouvert d'eau** the field was covered with *or* in water

recracher [rəkraʃe] **VT** *(bonbon, vin etc)* to spit out; **on lui a fait r. la pièce qu'il avait avalée** they made him bring up the coin he had swallowed
▪ **VI** to spit again

récré [rekre] **NF** *Scol Fam* break, *Am* recess; *(pour les plus jeunes)* playtime; **pendant la r., à la r.** during *or* at break/playtime

récréatif, -ive [rekreatif, -iv] **ADJ** *(activité)* entertaining, amusing; **lecture récréative** light reading; **séance récréative** *(à la maternelle)* playtime

récréation [rekreasjɔ̃] **NF 1** *(détente)* recreation, amusement, relaxation; **le tricot/la télé, c'est ma r.** knitting/watching TV is how I relax, I relax by knitting/watching TV **2** *Scol* recreation, break, *Am* recess; *(pour les plus jeunes)* playtime; **cour de r.** playground; **pendant la r., à la r.** during *or* at break/playtime

recréer [rəkree] **VT** *(conditions, climat, œuvre etc)* to re-create

recrépir [rəkrepir] **VT** *(mur)* to renew the roughcast of

recrépissage [rəkrepisaʒ] **NM** renewal of the roughcast

recreuser [rəkrøze] **VT** *(trou)* to dig again; *Fig (question etc)* to dig deeper *or* go deeper into

récrier (se) [sərekrije] **VPR** *(conj like* **crier***)* *(de mécontents)* to protest, to complain **(contre** about**)**; *(de la meute)* to be in full cry

récriminateur, -trice [rekriminatœr, -tris] **ADJ** recriminatory

récrimination [rekriminasjɔ̃] **NF** recrimination

récriminer [rekrimine] **VI** to make recriminations; **r. contre qn/qch** to make representations about sb/sth

récrire [rekrir] *(conj like* **écrire***)* = **réécrire**

récriture [rekrityr] **NF** rewriting

recroquevillé [rəkrɔkvije] **ADJ 1 r. dans un fauteuil** curled up in an armchair **2** *(feuille, papier etc)* shrivelled, curled up

recroqueviller (se) [sərəkrɔkvije] **VPR 1** *(d'une personne)* to curl up **2** *(d'une feuille)* to shrivel (up), to curl up

recru [rəkry] **ADJ** *Litt* **r. (de fatigue)** tired out, worn out; *Arch* **être r. d'amour** to be replete with love

recrudescence [rəkrydesɑ̃s] **NF** *(du feu, d'une épidémie)* renewed *or* fresh outbreak; *(de la délinquance)* upsurge; **la r. de la violence/des bombardements** the renewed violence/bombing

recrudescent [rəkrydesɑ̃] **ADJ** *Litt* fast-growing

recrue [rəkry] **NF** *(dans un parti, dans une équipe)*, *Mil* recruit; *Can Sport* rookie; **le parti fait de nouvelles recrues** the party is gaining new recruits; **jeune r.** raw recruit

recrutement [rəkrytmɑ̃] **NM** *(de soldats, de personnel etc)* recruiting, recruitment; **nous sommes en plein r.** we are recruiting (staff) at the moment, we are taking on staff at the moment; *Pol* **campagne de r.** recruitment *or* membership drive; **agence de r.** recruiting *or* recruitment agency

recruter [rəkryte] **VT** *(soldats, employés)* to recruit; *(supporters)* to enlist, to recruit **(dans** from**)**; **nous recrutons un secrétaire** we are looking for a secretary, we have a vacancy for a secretary; **notre directeur a été recruté par un chasseur de têtes** our director was headhunted
▪ **VI** to recruit; **r. par voie de concours** to recruit by competition
▪ **VPR se recruter** *(d'employés)* to be recruited **(parmi** from among**)**; *(de supporters)* to be enlisted, to be recruited

recruteur, -euse [rəkrytœr, -øz] **ADJ** *(officier)* recruiting

recta [rɛkta] **ADV** *Fam Vieilli* **payer r.** to pay on the nail; **arriver r.** to arrive punctually *or* on the dot

rectal, -ale, -aux, -ales [rɛktal, -o] **ADJ** *Anat (toucher, température)* rectal; **prendre la température de qn par voie rectale** to take sb's temperature using a rectal thermometer

rectangle [rɛktɑ̃gl] **ADJ** right-angled
▪ **NM** rectangle; *TV* **r. blanc** 'for adults only' sign; *Ordinat* **r. de sélection** selection box

rectangulaire [rɛktɑ̃gylɛr] **ADJ** rectangular; *Math (coordonnées)* right-angled

recteur, -trice [rɛktœr, -tris] **NM** *Rel* rector; *Scol* chief education officer
▪ **ADJ** *Orn* **penne rectrice** tail feather
▪ **NF** *Orn* **rectrice** tail feather

rectificateur [rɛktifikatœr] **NM** *Chimie* rectifier; *Élec* (current) rectifier

rectificatif, -ive [rɛktifikatif, -iv] **ADJ** *(lettre)* of amendment; *(texte, facture)* amended
▪ **NM** correction

rectification [rɛktifikasjɔ̃] **NF 1** *(d'un docu-*

ment, texte) amendment, correction; *(d'un calcul)* correction, adjustment; *(d'une erreur)* rectification, correction; *(d'un compte, instrument)* adjustment; *(d'une courbe, frontière)* adjustment, rectification; *(d'un alignement)* straightening; **je voudrais faire** *ou* **apporter une r.** I'd like to make a correction **2** *Chimie (de l'alcool, du pétrole)* rectifying, redistilling **3** *Élec (du courant)* rectification

rectifier [rɛktifje] **VT 1** *(document, texte)* to amend, to correct; *(calcul)* to correct, to adjust; *(erreur)* to rectify, to correct, to put right; *(prix, instrument)* to adjust; *(compte)* to amend, to adjust; *(frontière, courbe)* to rectify, to adjust; *(alignement)* to straighten; *Mil* **r. l'alignement** to dress the ranks; **r. le tir** *Mil* to adjust the range; *Fig* to take a slightly different tack; **'il est banquier', rectifia-t-elle** 'he's a banker', she corrected him/me/*etc* **2** *Chimie (alcool, pétrole)* to rectify, to redistil **3** *Élec (courant)* to rectify **4** *Arg (tuer)* **r. qn** to bump sb off; **se faire r.** to get bumped off

rectiligne [rɛktiliɲ] **ADJ** *(mouvement)* in a straight line; *(figure)* rectilinear; *(avenue)* straight

rectilinéaire [rɛktilineɛr] **ADJ** *Phot (objectif)* rectilinear

rectitude [rɛktityd] **NF 1** *(d'une ligne)* straightness **2** *Fig (honnêteté)* rectitude, uprightness, integrity; *(d'un jugement, du raisonnement)* correctness, soundness; **agir avec r.** to behave correctly *or* with integrity

recto [rɛkto] **NM** *(d'effet)* face; *(d'une feuille de papier)* front, face, *Spéc* recto; **cinq feuilles r. verso** five sheets written on both sides; **voir au r.** see over; *Typ* **impression r.-verso** double-sided printing

rectorat [rɛktɔra] **NM** *Admin* rectorship, rectorate

rectum [rɛktɔm] **NM** *Anat* rectum; **cancer du r.** rectal cancer, cancer of the rectum

reçu, -ue [rəsy] **ADJ** *(usages)* accepted, recognized; *(opinion)* received; **idées reçues** preconceived ideas; **cela fait partie des usages reçus** it's standard *or* accepted practice **NM** *(pour des marchandises, de l'argent)* receipt; **je vous fais un r.?** would you like a receipt?; **r. d'espèces** cash receipt; **r. libératoire** receipt in full discharge **N** *(à un examen)* successful candidate; **il n'y a que dix reçus** only ten people passed

recueil [rəkœj] **NM** *(de poèmes, chansons, recettes etc)* collection, compilation; *(de lois)* compendium, body; **r. de morceaux choisis** selection, anthology; **r. des données** data collection

recueillement [rəkœjmã] **NM** meditation, contemplation; *(gravité)* gravity; **avec r.** contemplatively; **pensons avec r. à cet homme à qui nous devons tant de choses** let us meditate a little about this man to whom we owe so much

recueilli [rəkœji] **ADJ** meditative, contemplative; *(grave)* grave, sober

recueillir [rəkœjir] *(conj like* **cueillir***)* **VT 1** *(récolter) (argent, fonds)* to collect; *(anecdotes, renseignements, miel etc)* to collect, to gather; *(pour conserver)* to collect, to make a collection of; *(eau de pluie)* to collect, to catch; *(sous-produits)* to recover; *(votes)* to win, to collect; *(louanges)* to win, to attract; *(déposition)* to take; *Journ* **r. le témoignage des passants** to listen to what the passersby have to say; *Journ* **propos recueillis par Daniel Renault** (story by) Daniel Renault; **r. le fruit de ses travaux** to reap the fruit of one's labours; **r. un héritage** to inherit; **r. des données** to collect data **2** *(recevoir)* **r. qn** to take sb in, to give sb a home **VPR se recueillir** to meditate; **se r. sur la tombe d'un ami** to meditate beside a friend's

grave; **se r. pour prier** to gather one's thoughts before praying

recuire [rəkɥir] **VT** *(conj like* **cuire***)* **1 il faut r. ce steak** this steak needs to be cooked longer **2** *(acier)* to anneal, to temper; *(verre)* to anneal

recuisson [rəkɥisõ] **NF** *(de l'acier)* annealing, tempering; *(du verre)* annealing

recuit [rəkɥi] **NM** *(de l'acier)* annealing, tempering; *(du verre)* annealing

recul [rəkyl] **NM 1** *(action) (d'un glacier, d'une armée)* retreat; *(d'un cheval)* backing; *(d'un levier de commande)* backward movement, return; *(d'un canon)* recoil; *(d'un fusil)* recoil, kick; *(baisse) (des valeurs, des exportations)* drop *(de* in); **il eut un brusque mouvement de r.** he recoiled, he started back; **le r. de la mortalité** the downturn *or* decline in the death rate; *Aut* **phare de r.** reversing light **2** *(distance)* **on n'a pas assez de r. dans cette galerie** there's not enough room in this gallery to get a decent look at the pictures; **il faut un certain r. pour juger le tableau** you need to stand back a bit to judge the painting; **manquer de r.** to be too close for a proper view; *Fig* **je manque de r. pour juger** I'm too closely involved *or* too close to be able to judge; *Fig* **considérer la situation avec r.** to consider the situation with detachment; *Fig* **avec le r. (du temps), la situation ne semble pas si désespérée** in retrospect *or* with hindsight *or* looking back (on it), the situation doesn't seem so desperate; *Fig* **tu devrais prendre du r.** you ought to stand back a bit from things; *Fig* **es-tu sûr d'avoir assez de r. pour juger?** are you sure you're objective enough to judge?

reculade [rəkylad] **NF** *(d'une armée)* retreat; *Fig Péj* climbdown

reculé [rəkyle] **ADJ** *(endroit)* remote, distant; *(époque)* remote

reculer [rəkyle] **VI 1** *(aller en arrière) (d'une personne)* to move back, to step back, to draw back; *(d'un glacier, des eaux)* to recede; *Mil* to fall back, to retreat; *(d'une épidémie)* to lose ground; *(du taux de mortalité, natalité, chômage etc)* to decline; *(du cours de Bourse)* to drop; *(d'un fusil, canon)* to recoil; *(d'un automobiliste, d'une voiture)* to reverse; *Ordinat* to backspace; **elle recula de dégoût** she recoiled *or* drew back in disgust; **reculez ou je tire!** back off *or* get back or I'll shoot!; **faire r. un cheval** to back a horse; **la police a fait la foule** the police moved *or* pushed the crowd back; *Fig* **faire r. la maladie** to get the disease under control; **le yen recule par rapport au dollar** the yen is falling against the dollar; **faire r. la pauvreté** to reduce (the level of) poverty; *Fig Fam* **r. pour mieux sauter** to put off the evil day **2** *Fig (renoncer)* to give in; **r. devant des menaces** to give way in the face of threats; **r. devant une obligation** to shirk an obligation; **il ne recule devant rien** nothing daunts him; **elle ne recule devant rien pour le satisfaire** she'll do anything to satisfy him; **comme d'habitude, elle recule devant lui** as usual, she gave in *or* gave way to him; **il est trop tard pour r.** it's too late to draw back *or* pull out; **cela en a fait r. plus d'un** that's put off *or* daunted more than one person; **r. à l'idée de faire qch** to recoil at the idea of doing sth **VT 1** *(chaise)* to move back; *(cheval)* to back; *(voiture)* to back (up), to reverse; *Fig* **r. les frontières de la science** to push *or* roll back the frontiers of science **2** *(remettre) (paiement, décision)* to postpone, to defer, to put off; **r. le moment de décider** to put off (making) a decision **VPR se reculer** to stand *or* step *or* move *or* draw back

reculons (à) [ar(ə)kylõ] **ADV marcher** *ou* **al-**

ler à r. to walk backwards; *Fig* **aller à r.** to go *or* move backwards; **sortir à r.** to back out; *Fig Fam* **aller au travail à r.** to force oneself to go to work

récup [rekyp] **NF** *Fam (abrév* **récupération***)* **1 de la r.** *(des matériaux de récupération)* scrap **2** *(récupération idéologique)* exploitation

récupérable [rekyperabl] **ADJ** *(déchets)* recoverable; **ferraille r.** scrap metal; **les heures supplémentaires sont récupérables** additional time off may be taken in lieu of overtime pay; **ce garçon-là est r./n'est pas r.** there's hope for that boy/that boy's a hopeless case

récupérateur [rekyperatœr] **NM** *Ind* regenerator, recuperator

récupération [rekyperasjõ] **NF 1** *(de dette, livre, vaisseau spatial, TVA etc)* recovery; **la r. des heures supplémentaires** time off in lieu of (overtime pay); **deux jours de r. pour les heures supplémentaires que j'ai faites** two days off to make up for the overtime I've done **2** *Ind (de déchets de fabrication)* recovery, salvage; **r. de chaleur** heat recovery **3** *(de sportif)* recovery **4** *Pol Péj* hijacking; **la r. d'une manifestation par un parti politique** the hijacking of a demonstration by a political party; **c'est de la r.** it's sheer exploitation **5** *Ordinat* **r. de données** data recovery

récupérer [rekypere] *(je récupère, n. récupérons; je récupérerai)* **VT 1** *(objet prêté ou perdu) (livre etc)* to get back, to retrieve, to recover; *(bagages, TVA)* to retrieve, to reclaim; *Ordinat (fichier, données)* to retrieve; *Aviat (boîte noire)* to recover, to retrieve; *Fam (personne)* to collect, to pick up; **elle est passée r. ses affaires** she dropped by to pick up her things; **r. ses forces** to recover (one's strength), to regain one's strength **2** *(recycler) (déchets de fabrication)* to recover, to salvage; *(vieux papiers, canettes etc)* to salvage; *Fig Fam (employé)* to find alternative employment for; *(délinquant)* to rehabilitate; **r. de la ferraille** to collect scrap; **je ne jette rien, je récupère tout** I don't throw anything away, I save everything **3** *Pol Péj (personne, mouvement)* to co-opt, to hijack, to use for one's own ends; *(proposition)* to hijack, to take over; **se faire r.** to be co-opted *or* hijacked **4** *Fin (pertes)* to recoup, to retrieve; *Fin* **r. ses débours** to recoup one's expenditure; *Admin* **r. des heures supplémentaires (en prenant des congés)** to take time off in lieu **VI** *(après une maladie, après un choc)* to recover; **j'ai besoin de r.** *(prendre des vacances)* I need to get my breath back, I need to relax; **j'ai de plus en plus de mal à r.** *(reprendre mon souffle)* it takes me longer and longer to get my breath back

récurage [rekyraʒ] **NM** scouring

récurer [rekyre] **VT** *(casseroles, évier, baignoire etc)* to scour; **poudre/tampon à r.** scouring powder/pad

récurrence [rekyrãs] **NF** recurrence

récurrent [rekyrã] **ADJ** *Anat (nerf, veine)* recurrent; *(thème, son, mot)* recurrent, recurring; *Méd (fièvre)* recurrent; *Math (série)* recurrent; *Ordinat* **processus r.** recursive process

récusable [rekyzabl] **ADJ** *Jur (juré, témoin)* challengeable; *(témoignage)* impugnable; **son témoignage n'est pas r.** it will be impossible to challenge his/her testimony; **c'est une affirmation r.** that statement is open to challenge

récusation [rekyzasjõ] **NF** *(d'une thèse), Jur (d'un témoin)* challenging; *Jur* **r. de juré/d'arbitre** challenge of *or* exception to *or* objection to a juryman/an arbitrator; **r. de témoignage** impugnment of evidence

récuser [rekyze] **vt** *(témoin, juré, arbitre etc)* to challenge, to take exception to, to object to; *(témoignage)* to impugn; *(autorité, thèse)* to challenge
VPR se récuser *Jur* to decline to give an opinion, to disclaim competence

recyclable [rəsiklabl] **ADJ** *(papier, verre etc)* recyclable

recyclage [rəsiklaʒ] **NM 1** *(de matériaux)* recycling; *Aut* **r. des gaz d'échappement** exhaust gas recirculation **2** *Ind (du personnel)* retraining

recycler [rəsikle] **vt 1** *(papier, verre etc)* to recycle **2** *Ind (personnel)* to retrain
VPR se recycler *Ind* to retrain; **se r. en comptabilité** to retrain as an accountant

rédacteur, -trice [redaktœr, -tris] **N 1** *(d'un acte, communiqué)* writer, drafter; *(d'un dictionnaire)* editor, compiler **2** *Journ* editor; **r. en chef** editor-in-chief, (chief) editor; **r. en chef actualités** news editor; **r. en chef adjoint** deputy editor; **r. en chef de nuit** night editor; **r. en chef des affaires financières** financial editor, *Br* City editor; **r. en chef sportif** sports editor; **r. en chef technique** production editor; **r. aux actualités** news editor; **r. d'actualités** news writer; **r. artistique** art editor; **r. juridique** legally responsible editor; **r. politique** political editor; **r. sportif** sports editor; **r. permanent** staff writer; **r. pigiste** freelance writer; **r. publicitaire** copy writer

rédaction [redaksjɔ̃] **NF 1** *(d'un acte, communiqué)* drafting, drawing up, writing; *(d'un article de dictionnaire)* compiling, writing; *(révision)* editing; **la r. de cet article a demandé l'intervention de plusieurs rédacteurs** it took several editors to write the article; **r. de questionnaire** questionnaire design **2** *Journ* editing; *(poste)* editorship; *(personnel)* editorial staff; *(département)* editorial department; **(salle de) r.** editorial office; **note de la r.** editor's note; **secrétaire de r.** subeditor **3** *Scol* essay, composition

rédactionnel, -elle [redaksjɔnεl] **ADJ** *(décision, politique etc)* editorial; **publicité rédactionnelle** advertorial

reddition [redisjɔ̃] **NF 1** *(d'une ville, armée)* surrender; **r. sans conditions** unconditional surrender **2** *Fin (d'un compte)* rendering; **r. de comptes** presentation of accounts for audit, reporting

redécoupage [rədekupaʒ] **NM r. électoral** redrawing of the electoral boundaries; **procéder à** *ou* **effectuer un r. électoral** to redraw the electoral boundaries

redécouverte [rədekuvεrt] **NF** rediscovery

redécouvrir [rədekuvrir] **vt** *(conj like* **couvrir***)* **1** *(auteur, œuvre)* to rediscover **2** *(enfant)* to take the covers off

redéfinir [rədefinir] **vt** *Ordinat (touche)* to redefine

redéfinissable [rədefinisabl] **ADJ** *Ordinat* redefinable

redemander [rəd(ə)mɑ̃de] **vt 1** *(en reposant une question)* to ask again; **r. pourquoi/quand/qui** to ask why/when/who again; **je lui ai redemandé de fermer la porte** I asked him/her again to close the door; **il a dû oublier, il faut le lui r.** he must have forgotten, we'll have to ask him again; **j'ai redemandé qu'il nous écrive un article** I asked again if he would write an article for us; **r. de l'aide à qn** to ask sb again for help
2 *(pour en avoir plus)* **r. de la soupe/des enveloppes** to ask for more soup/envelopes; **r. un litre de vin** to ask for another litre of wine; **je lui ai redemandé un article,** *Fam* **j'ai redemandé qu'il écrive un article** I asked

him for another article, I asked him to write another article; *Fig Fam* **des traducteurs comme ça, on en redemande!** translators like that are much in demand!; **tout le monde en redemande** everybody is clamouring *or* keeps asking for more, they can't get enough of it; *Iron* **elle en redemande** she's still asking for it, she hasn't had enough
3 *(pour récupérer)* **r. qch** to ask for sth back (again); **redemande-le-moi dès que tu en as besoin** ask for it back (again) when you need it, ask me for it when you need it
vi to ask again

redémarrage [rədemaraʒ] **NM 1** *(d'une machine)* starting up again; *Ordinat* reboot, restart; **r. à chaud** warm boot, warm start **2** *(de l'économie, des ventes)* recovery; **attendre le r. de l'économie/des ventes** to wait for the economy/sales to pick up *or* take off again *or* recover

redémarrer [rədemare] **vi** *(d'une voiture)* to start again; *(de l'économie, des ventes)* to recover, to pick up, to take off again; *Ordinat* to reboot; **faire r. une voiture** to start a car again; **faire r. l'économie** to get the economy started again

rédempteur, -trice [redɑ̃ptœr, -tris] **ADJ** redeeming
N redeemer

rédemption [redɑ̃psjɔ̃] **NF** redemption

redéploiement [rədeplwamɑ̃] **NM 1** *Mil (d'une armée)* redeployment **2** *Écon (d'une entreprise, de ressources)* reorganization, restructuring

redéployer [rədeplwaje] **vt 1** *Mil (armée)* to redeploy **2** *Écon (entreprise, ressources)* to reorganize, to restructure
VPR se redéployer *(armée)* to redeploy; *(entreprise)* to reorganize its operations

redescendre [rədesɑ̃dr, -dε-] *(conj like* **descendre***)* **vi** *(du point de vue de qn qui est en haut)* to go down again, to go back down; *(du point de vue de qn qui est en bas)* to come down again, to come back down; *(d'un alpiniste)* to climb back down; *Naut (d'un vent)* to back; **quand tu redescendras, veux-tu …** *(nous sommes au même étage)* when you go down again *or* go back down, will you …; *(je suis à l'étage inférieur)* when you come back down again *or* come back down, will you …; **je suis redescendu en télécabine** *(je viens de le faire)* I came back down by cable car; *(en racontant plus tard)* I went *or* came back down by cable car; **vous pouvez r. par ce sentier-là** you can get back down by that path over there; **r. de voiture** to get out of the car (again)
vt 1 *(apporter) (du point de vue de qn qui est en haut)* to take down again, to take back down; *(du point de vue de qn qui est en bas)* to bring down again, to bring back down; **veux-tu r. la valise?** *(nous sommes au même étage)* will you take the suitcase back down(stairs)?; *(je suis à l'étage inférieur)* will you bring the suitcase back down(stairs)?; **r. des affaires du grenier** to get things back down from the attic
2 *(descendre à nouveau) (escalier, rivière) (du point de vue de qn qui est en haut)* to go down again, to go back down; *(du point de vue de qn qui est en bas)* to come down again, to come back down

redevable [rəd(ə)vabl] **ADJ** **être r. de qch à qn** to be indebted to sb for sth; **je vous suis r. de cent euros** I still owe you a hundred euros; **être r. de l'impôt** to be liable to tax
N person liable for tax

redevance [rəd(ə)vɑ̃s] **NF** *TV* licence fee; *(de téléphone)* rental fee; **r. pétrolière** oil royalty; **redevances d'auteur** author's royalties

redevenir [rədəv(ə)nir] **vi** *(conj like* **devenir***)*

r. jeune to become *or* grow young again; **j'ai l'impression d'être redevenu moi-même** I feel like my old self again; **r. silencieux** to fall silent again; **la situation est redevenue normale** the situation is back to normal; **le temps est redevenu maussade** the weather's turned gloomy again

redevoir [rəd(ə)vwar] **vt** *(conj like* **devoir***)* *(somme d'argent)* to owe a balance of; *Fam* **il me redoit dix euros** he still owes me ten euros

rédhibition [redibisjɔ̃] **NF** *Com* cancellation of sale due to a material defect

rédhibitoire [redibitwar] **ADJ 1** vice **r.** *Com* material defect; *Jur* redhibitory defect **2** **dans ce métier, être petit est r.** being small is a bar to entering the profession; **des conditions de travail rédhibitoires** appalling working conditions; **être d'un égoïsme r.** to be appallingly selfish

rediffuser [rədifyze] **vt** *Radio (émission)* to repeat, to broadcast again; *TV (émission)* to repeat, to show again, to rerun; *(film)* to show again, to rerun

rediffusion [rədifyzjɔ̃] **NF** *Radio (d'une émission)* repeat; *TV, Cin* repeat, rerun

rédiger [rediʒe] **vt** *(* **je rédigeai(s); n. rédigeons***)* **1** *(contrat, lettre etc)* to draw up, to draft, to write; *(article)* to write; *Méd (ordonnance)* to write out; *(bon de commande)* to make out; **savoir r.** to be a good writer, to write well; **être bien/mal rédigé** to be well/badly written **2** *Journ (périodique)* to edit

redimensionnable [rədimɑ̃sjɔnabl] **ADJ** *Ordinat (fenêtre)* resizable

redimensionnement [rədimɑ̃sjɔnmɑ̃] **NM** *Ordinat* resizing

redimensionner [rədimɑ̃sjɔne] **vt** *Ordinat (fenêtre)* to resize

redingote [rədɛ̃gɔt] **NF** *(pour femmes)* fitted coat; *Vieilli (pour hommes)* frock coat

redire [rədir] **vt** *(conj like* **dire***)* **1** to say again, to repeat; **tu redis toujours la même chose** you say the same thing over and over again, you constantly repeat yourself; **pourrais-tu lui r. que …?** could you tell him/her again that …?; **je ne le redirai jamais assez** I can never say it often enough; **elle te l'a dit et redit cent fois!** she's told you time and time again!; **elle ne se l'est pas fait r. deux fois** she didn't need asking twice, she didn't need any persuading; **j'espère qu'elle n'ira pas lui r. ce que je lui ai confié** I hope she won't go and tell him *or* repeat to him what I said to her in confidence **2 trouver à r.** to complain; **trouver à r. à qch** to find fault with *or* to pick holes in sth; *Fam* **il n'y a rien à r. à cela** there's nothing wrong with that

redirection [rədirεksjɔ̃] **NF** *Tél* **r. d'appel** call forwarding, call redirection

rediriger [rədiriʒe] **vt** *Tél* to redirect

rediscuter [rədiskyte] **vt** to have further discussions on, to discuss again

redistribuer [rədistribɥe] **vt** to redistribute, to re-allocate; *Cartes* to redeal

redistribution [rədistribysjɔ̃] **NF** redistribution, re-allocation; *(de personnel)* redeployment

redite [rədit] **NF** *(useless)* repetition

redondance [rədɔ̃dɑ̃s] **NF** *(de style, mot)*, *Ordinat* redundancy; **de nombreuses redondances** a lot of redundancy

redondant [rədɔ̃dɑ̃] **ADJ** *(mot, style, information)*, *Ordinat* redundant

redonner [rədɔne] **vt 1** *(donner de nouveau)* to give again; *Cartes* to redeal; *Théâtre* **on redonne Hamlet** Hamlet is on again; **r. un coup d'œil/un coup de pied à qn** to glance at/kick sb again **2** *(donner davantage de)* to give more of; **tu veux bien m'en r. un peu plus?**

will you give me *or* can I have a bit more? **3** *(pour rendre)* to give back, to return; **r. de l'appétit à qn** to restore sb's appetite, to give sb back his/her appetite; **cela m'a redonné du courage** that put new heart into me *or* restored my courage; **ça m'a redonné envie de voyager** that made me want to travel again; **ce médicament va vous r. des forces** the medicine will give you back your strength *or* will get your strength back; **ces vacances lui ont redonné bonne mine** the holiday put the colour back in his/her cheeks

VI *Litt* **r. dans des excès** to fall back into excess; **r. dans l'exagération** to exaggerate again

redorer [rədɔre] **VT** *Tech* to regild; *(société, image)* to repackage; *Fig* **r. son blason** *(d'un noble qui se remarie)* to restore the family fortunes by marrying money; *(d'une personne) (par un succès etc)* to restore one's reputation

redormir [rədɔrmir] **VI** *(conj like* **dormir***)* to go to sleep again, to go back to sleep; **je n'ai pas pu r.** I couldn't get back to sleep; **je suis allée r. quelques heures** I went to get a few more hours' sleep

redoublant, -ante [rədublɑ̃, -ɑ̃t] **N** *Scol* = pupil who repeats a year

redoublé [rəduble] **ADJ** *Littér (rime)* double; **frapper** *ou* **battre qn à coups redoublés** to thrash sb soundly; **frapper à une porte à coups redoublés** to hammer at a door

redoublement [rədubləmɑ̃] **NM 1** *(de joie, chagrin, violence, douleur etc)* increase; *(d'une tempête)* worsening; **avec un r. de zèle** with renewed *or* redoubled zeal **2** *Ling (d'une syllabe, lettre)* reduplication **3** *Scol* repeating a year *or* class; **dans son cas, le r. n'est pas justifié** there's no need for him to repeat the year

redoubler [rəduble] **VT 1** *(sentiment d'injustice, chagrin)* to add to; *(dose)* to double again, to redouble; *Fam (doubler)* to double; *(film)* to re-voice; **r. ses efforts** to redouble one's efforts; *Scol* **r. une classe** to repeat a year *or* class **2** *(vêtement)* to reline

VI 1 *Scol* to repeat a year *or* *Am* grade **2** *(augmenter) (du chagrin, froid)* to intensify, to increase; **la pluie/le vent redoubla de violence** the rain came down/the wind blew harder than ever, the rain came down/the wind blew twice as hard as before; **r. d'efforts** to redouble one's efforts; **r. de prudence/d'attention/de douceur** to be twice as cautious/attentive/gentle

redoutable [rədutabl] **ADJ** *(personne, adversaire)* formidable; *(ennemi)* formidable, dangerous, *Fml* redoubtable; *(hiver)* fierce; *(odeur)* dreadful; **il fait un froid r.** it's dreadfully cold

redoute [rədut] **NF** *(fortification)* redoubt

redouter [rədute] **VT** *(chose, événement)* to dread, to fear; *(personne)* to be in awe of; **je redoute la journée de lundi** I'm dreading Monday; **ce jour si redouté se passa sans incident notable** the dreaded day passed off without incident; **un prof redouté de tous les élèves** a much-dreaded teacher; **r. d'apprendre qch** to dread hearing sth; **je redoute surtout de devenir aveugle** the thing *or* what I fear *or* dread most is going blind; **elle redoute que tu ne lui en parles** she's terrified that you'll mention it to him/her

redoux [rədu] **NM** *Météo* milder weather; **on attend le r.** we're expecting a return to milder weather

redresse [rədrɛs] **NF** *très Fam* **c'est un type à la r.** he's no soft touch

redressement [rədrɛsmɑ̃] **NM 1** *(d'un objet renversé)* righting, setting up again; *(d'un*

bateau, avion) righting; *(de la tête)* raising; *(des épaules)* straightening **2** *(rectification) (d'un compte, d'une erreur)* rectification, correction; *Compta* adjustment; *(d'un tort)* righting; *Tech (d'une surface)* tru(e)ing; *Écon* **plan de r.** recovery plan; *Vieilli* **maison de r.** ≃ approved school, reformatory **3** *Élec (du courant alternatif)* rectification; **valve de r.** rectifying valve

▶▶ **r. économique** economic recovery; **plan de r. économique** recovery plan; **r. financier** gearing adjustment; *Admin* **r. fiscal** tax adjustment, demand for tax arrears; **r. judiciaire** receivership; **être mis en r. judiciaire** to go into receivership

redresser [rədrɛse] **VT 1** *(objet renversé)* to right, to set upright again; *(bateau)* to right; *(avion)* to right, to straighten up, to lift the nose of **2** *(rectifier) (grief)* to redress, to right; *(erreur, situation)* to rectify, to correct; *(compte)* to adjust; *(bois courbé, tôle cabossée)* to straighten (out); *(surface)* to true; **r. les épaules** to straighten one's shoulders; **r. la tête** to hold up one's head; *(la lever)* to raise *or* lift one's head, to look up; *Fig* **il peut r. la tête maintenant** he can hold his head up now, he can look people in the eye now; **tu n'es pas là pour r. les torts** you're not there to right wrongs; **r. l'équilibre des forces** to redress the balance of power; **pour r. l'économie** in order to bring about an economic recovery; **r. une entreprise** to put a company back on its feet **3** *Élec (courant)* to rectify

VPR se redresser 1 *(d'une personne)* to straighten up, to straighten one's back; *(avec fierté)* to draw oneself up, to hold one's head up; **se r. sur son séant** to sit up straight (again) **2** *(de l'économie, d'un pays, des ventes etc)* to recover

redresseur, -euse [rədrɛsœr, -øz] **N r. de torts** righter of wrongs; *(chevalier), Hum* knight errant; **r. d'entreprise** company doctor

NM *Élec (du courant)* rectifier
ADJ *Élec (appareil)* rectifying

redû [rədy] **NM** balance due

réduc [redyk] **NF** *Fam (abrév* **réduction***)* discount

réducteur, -trice [redyktœr, -tris] **ADJ** *Péj (explication, point de vue etc)* reductive, simplistic; *Chimie* **agent r.** reducing agent; *Tech* **ensemble r.** reduction gear assembly

NM *Chimie* reducing agent; *Tech* reduction gear *or* unit; *Théâtre* **r. d'éclairage** dimmer; **r. de têtes** head shrinker

réductible [redyktibl] **ADJ** *Méd (fracture)* which can be set, *Spéc* reducible; *(dislocation)* *Math (fraction)* reducible

réduction [redyksjɔ̃] **NF 1** *(de prix, salaires, personnel)* reduction, cut (**de** in); *(de dépenses, de la production)* reduction, cutting back (**de** in); *(d'un budget)* cutting back (**de** of); *(de la pression)* reduction, lowering (**de** of); *(d'une pénalité)* reduction (**de** of); *Chir (d'une fraction)* reduction; *(de gravure)* small reproduction; *Fin (d'un capital)* writing down; *Méd (d'une fracture)* setting; *(d'une dislocation)* reduction; *Élec (du voltage)* stepping down; **réductions de salaires/de personnel** reductions *or* cutbacks in wages/staff, wage/staff cuts; **on nous a demandé d'accepter une r. de salaire** we were asked to take a cut in (our) wages; **r. de 60 euros** 60 euros off; **faire une r. de 15%** to give 15% off; **r. de capital** decrease in capital; **r. des impôts** tax cut; **la r. du temps de travail** = reduction of the working week in France from 39 to 35 hours, introduced by the government of Lionel Jospin in 1998 and phased in from 2000 onwards; **carte de r.** discount card; **cette carte donne droit à**

une r. this card entitles the holder to a reduction; **une r. de 15% sur la literie** a 15% reduction on bedding; **faire une r. à qn** to give sb a reduction; **r. des bruits** noise reduction; *Mus* **r. pour piano** *(d'un opéra etc)* short score; **un bateau en r.** a scale model of a ship **2** *(d'une ville)* capture

réduire [redqir] *(prp* **réduisant***; pp* **réduit***; pr ind* **je réduis, il réduit, n. réduisons***; impf* **je réduisais***; p hist* **je réduisis***; fu* **je réduirai***)* **VT** *(montant, vitesse, photographie, dessin), Math (fractions), Culin (sauce)* to reduce; *(prix, taux d'intérêt)* to lower, to bring down; *(dépenses, frais)* to reduce, to cut (down *or* back), to curtail; *(chômage, taux de mortalité, de natalité)* to reduce, to lower, to bring down; *(personnel, salaires)* to reduce, to cut (back); *(texte)* to shorten, to cut; *(pression)* to reduce, to lower, to relieve; *Fin (capital)* to write down; *Élec (voltage)* to step down; *Méd (fracture)* to set, *Spéc* to reduce; *(dislocation)* to reduce; **r. un texte de 200 pages** to shorten a text by 200 pages; **on a nettement réduit les dépenses d'armement** arms spending has been cut right back *or* sharply reduced; **la société réduit progressivement ses opérations en Allemagne** the company is winding down its operations in Germany; *Com, Ind* **r. ses effectifs** to reduce the size of the workforce, to downsize; **r. le personnel** to cut staff, to make staff cutbacks; **billet à prix réduit** cheap *or* cut-price ticket, *Br Fam* concession; **voyager à prix réduit** to travel at reduced rates; **réduit de moitié** half size; *Mus* **r. une partition** to arrange a score for the piano; **r. qch en cendres/poussière** to reduce sth to ashes/dust; **r. des euros en cents/des kilogrammes en grammes** to convert *or* reduce euros to cents/kilograms to grams; **r. qn à la misère/au silence/à la mendicité** to reduce sb to poverty/silence/begging; **r. qn au désespoir** to drive sb to despair; **nous en sommes réduits à ça!** is this what we're *or* we've been reduced to?; **j'en suis réduit à le faire moi-même** I'm reduced to doing it myself

VI *Culin* to reduce; **faire r. un sirop** to reduce a syrup

VPR se réduire 1 se r. à to amount to; **leurs différences se réduisent à peu de choses** their differences don't amount to much; **à quoi se réduit tout cela?** what does it all amount to *or* boil down to? **2** *Culin (d'une sauce)* to reduce; **se r. en poussière** to crumble into dust **3** *Fam Vieilli (faire des économies)* to cut down *or* back

réduit [redqi] **NM** *(petite pièce)* cubbyhole; **elle habite une sorte de r. sale et humide** she lives in a damp and dirty little cubbyhole

réduplication [redyplikasjɔ̃] **NF** *Ling* reduplication

rééchelonnement [reeʃ(ə)lɔnmɑ̃] **NM** *Fin (d'une dette)* rescheduling

rééchelonner [reeʃ(ə)lɔne] **VT** *Fin (dette)* to reschedule

réécrire [reekrir] *(conj like* **écrire***)* **VT** *(rédiger à nouveau) (lettre, texte, annonce etc)* to rewrite; *(devoir etc qui contenait des fautes)* to write (out) again; **j'ai dû lui r. tout son article** I had to rewrite his entire article for him, I had to write his entire article all over again

VI r. à qn to write to sb again, to send sb another letter

réécriture [reekrityr] **NF** *(d'un texte, d'une annonce etc)* rewriting

réédification [reedifikasjɔ̃] **NF** rebuilding, reconstruction

réédifier [reedifje] **VT** *(conj like* **édifier***)* to rebuild, to reconstruct

rééditer [reedite] **VT** *(livre)* to republish, to re-issue; *Fig Fam (exploit)* to give a repeat performance of

réédition [reedisjɔ̃] NF *(d'un livre etc)* re-issue; *Fig Fam* repeat; **c'est une r. de leur dispute de la semaine dernière** it's a repeat *or* rerun of the argument they had last week, it's last week's argument all over again

rééducatif, -ive [reedykatif, -iv] ADJ **thérapie rééducative** occupational therapy

rééducation [reedykasjɔ̃] NF 1 *Méd (de muscles après accident etc)* re-education; *(d'un handicapé, accidenté)* rehabilitation; **r. de la parole** speech therapy; **centre de r. (professionnelle)** rehabilitation centre; **faire de la r.** *(chez un kinésithérapeute)* to have physio(-)therapy *or Am* physical therapy 2 *Psy* re-education; *(de délinquants)* rehabilitation

rééduquer [reedyke] VT *(handicapé, accidenté, délinquant)* to rehabilitate; *Méd (muscle), Psy* to re-educate

réel, -elle [reɛl] ADJ 1 *(avantage, coût, monde), Math (nombre)* real; *(personnage)* real(-life), actual; *(fait)* actual; *Opt (image)* true; **grandeur réelle** actual size; **salaire r.** real salary; **en termes réels** in real terms; **offre réelle** cash offer; **ce film nous rend la personne de Charlie Chaplin plus réelle** this film brings Charlie Chaplin to life 2 *(before noun) (plaisir, sentiment de bonheur etc)* real, great; **connaître enfin un r. sentiment de bonheur** to know real *or* true happiness at last; **prendre un r. plaisir à faire qch** to take real *or* great pleasure in doing sth
▪ NM 1 *Math* real number 2 **le r.** reality

réélection [reelɛksjɔ̃] NF re-election

rééligible [reeliʒibl] ADJ re-eligible

réélire [reelir] VT *(conj like* **élire***)* to re-elect

réellement [reɛlmɑ̃] ADV *(drôle, déçu, incroyable etc)* really; **cela s'est r. passé** it really *or* actually happened; **des choses qui existent r.** things that really *or* actually exist

réembarquer [reɑ̃barke] VT *(passagers)* to re-embark; *(marchandises)* to reload, to re-embark
▪ VI to re-embark, to go back on board
▪ VPR **se réembarquer** to re-embark, to go back on board; *Fig* **se r. dans qch** to get involved in sth again

réembaucher [reɑ̃boʃe] VT **r. qn** to take sb on again, to rehire sb

réémetteur [reemɛtœr] NM *TV, Radio* relay transmitter

réemploi [reɑ̃plwa] NM *(du personnel d'une autre entreprise)* employment

réemployer [reɑ̃plwaje] VT *(ancien employé)* to re-employ, to employ again; *(produit)* to use again

réemprunter [reɑ̃prœ̃te] VT to borrow again

réencoder [reɑ̃kɔde] VT *Ordinat* to recode

réentendre [reɑ̃tɑ̃dr] VT *(disque, cassette etc)* to listen to *or* hear again

réentraînement [reɑ̃trɛnmɑ̃] NM retraining

rééquilibrage [reekilibraʒ] NM *(de pneus)* balancing; **le r. des forces politiques** the restoration of the balance of power; *Pol* **tout faire pour le r. de la gauche** to do everything to restore the balance within the parties of the left

rééquilibrer [reekilibre] VT *(pneus)* to balance; **r. les forces politiques** to restore the balance of power

réescompte [reɛskɔ̃t] NM *Fin* rediscount

réescompter [reɛskɔ̃te] VT *Fin* to rediscount

réessayer [reeseje] VT & VI to retry

réévaluation [reevalɥasjɔ̃] NF revaluation

réévaluer [reevalɥe] VT *(monnaie)* to revalue; *(prix)* to reassess

réexamen [reɛgzamɛ̃] NM *(d'une politique, situation)* re-examination, reappraisal,

reassessment; *(d'une décision)* reconsideration; *(d'un dossier, d'une question, d'un malade)* re-examination

réexaminer [reɛgzamine] VT *(politique, situation)* to re-examine, to reappraise, to reassess; *(décision)* to reconsider; *(dossier, question, malade)* to re-examine, to examine again

réexpédier [reɛkspedje] VT *(conj like* **expédier***)* 1 *(lettres, marchandises)* to send on, to forward, to redirect 2 *(pour rendre)* *(à l'expéditeur)* to send back, to return

réexpédition [reɛkspedisjɔ̃] NF 1 *(d'une lettre, de marchandises)* forwarding, redirection; **frais de r.** fee for redirection; **ordre de r. du courrier** request for mail to be redirected 2 *(à l'expéditeur)* return

réexportation [reɛkspɔrtasjɔ̃] NF *(action)* re-export, re-exportation; **les réexportations** re-exports

réexporter [reɛkspɔrte] VT to re-export

réfaction [refaksjɔ̃] NF *Com, Jur (de biens endommagés ou de qualité inférieure)* allowance, rebate

refaire [rəfɛr] *(conj like* **faire***)* VT 1 *(faire à nouveau) (travail, traduction), Théâtre (scène)* to do (all over) again, to redo, *Am* to do over; *(voyage, robe etc)* to make (all over) again; *(film)* to remake; **j'ai dû r. du riz** I had to make (some) more rice; **tu nous referas du bœuf bourguignon comme l'autre fois?** will you make us some bœuf bourguignon like you did last time?; **r. ses lacets** to tie one's laces again; **r. la conclusion d'une dissertation** to change an essay's conclusion; **on a dépassé le budget, il faut qu'on refasse la fin** *(d'un film)* we've gone over the budget, we'll have to rewrite the ending; **refais le calcul, tu as dû te tromper** do the sum again, you must have made a mistake; **c'est trop serré, il faut r. le pansement** the bandage is too tight, you'll have to redo it; **nous avons refait à pied les vingt kilomètres qui nous séparaient du village** we walked the twenty kilometres back to the village; *Fam* **elle nous a refait sa crise** she gave us another bout of hysterics; *Fam* **tu ne vas pas nous r. ta crise!** you're not going to go into hysterics again!; **tu ne vas pas me r. une scène!** you're not going to start again!; **je refais de la fièvre** my temperature's up again; **c'est à r.** it will have to be done (all over) again; **et si c'était à r.?** and if you had to do it all over again?; **ton éducation est à r.** your education has been sadly neglected!; **r. le monde** to put *or* set the world to rights; **r. sa vie** to make a new life for oneself; **r. sa vie avec qn** to make *or* start a new life with sb; *Tél* **r. le numéro** to redial

2 *(réparer)* to repair, to mend; *(remettre en état) (maison, appartement)* to do up, to redo; **r. la peinture** *ou* **les peintures** to redo *or* do up the paintwork; **r. la décoration d'une maison** to redecorate a house; **r. à neuf** *(moteur)* to recondition; *(appartement, peintures)* to redo completely; *(fauteuil)* to renovate; **r. les talons de ses souliers** to have one's shoes reheeled; **r. l'installation électrique d'une maison** to rewire a house, to redo the wiring in a house; **r. le revêtement de qch** to resurface sth

3 *Fam (personne) (d'un marchand)* to do, to diddle; *(duper)* to fool, to take in; **on vous a refait** you've been had; **on vous a refait de plusieurs centaines d'euros** you've been done *or* diddled out of several hundred euros
▪ VPR **se refaire** 1 **se r. une santé** to recover one's health, to get one's health back; **une soirée comme ça, ça ne se refera pas** a party like that doesn't happen twice *or* only happens once in a lifetime; *Fam* **elle se refait une beauté** she's doing her face again

2 *(se changer)* to change one's ways; **on ne se refait pas** I/you/*etc* can't change the way I am/you are/*etc* (made), a leopard can't change its spots

3 *Fam (financièrement)* to be solvent again; *(au jeu)* to win back the money one has lost; **après mes vacances, j'ai mis trois mois pour me r.** after my holiday it was three months before I was solvent again *or* before I had two pennies to rub together
▪ V IMPERS **il refait soleil** it's sunny again

réfection [refɛksjɔ̃] NF *(réparation) (d'un bâtiment, appartement, d'une maison)* (extensive) repair; **travaux de r.** repair work; **route en r.** road under repair

réfectoire [refɛktwar] NM refectory, dining hall

référé [refere] NM *Jur* summary procedure; **(ordonnance de) r.** provisional order

référence [referɑ̃s] NF 1 reference; *Mktg (produit)* benchmark; **ouvrage/livre de r.** reference work/book; **faire r. à un texte/auteur** to refer to a text/an author; **il n'a pas fait une seule fois r. à notre conversation** he didn't refer to *or* mention our conversation once; **références au bas des pages** footnotes; **r. de page** page reference; *Fam* **ce n'est pas une r.** don't take my/his/*etc* word for it, don't go by what I/he/*etc* say(s); **le film a été primé à Cannes mais ce n'est pas une r.** the film won a prize at Cannes but that's no recommendation 2 *(sur une lettre, sur un document)* reference; **r. à rappeler** in replying please quote, please quote reference; **en r. à** with reference to 3 **références** (employee's) reference, *Vieilli* testimonial; **références exigées** *(sur offre d'emploi)* references required; **une lettre de r.** a reference
▪▪ **références bancaires** bank references; **références commerciales** trade references; *Ordinat* **r. croisée** cross reference; **r. topographique** map reference

référencé [referɑ̃se] ADJ *Com* **être r.** to have a reference number; **votre lettre référencée … your letter reference number …

référencer [referɑ̃se] VT *Ordinat* to reference

référencié [referɑ̃sje] ADJ *(quotation)* with a reference

référendaire [referɑ̃dɛr] ADJ referendum

referendum, référendum [referɛ̃dɔm] NM referendum; **faire un r.** to hold a referendum; **les Français ont décidé par r. de …** the French have decided in a *or* by referendum to …

référent [referɑ̃] NM *Ling* referent

référer [refere] *(je réfère, n. référons; je réfèrerai)* VI **r. à qn d'une question** to refer a matter to sb; **en r. à la cour** to report *or* submit the case to the court; **en r. à son supérieur** to refer to *or* consult one's superior
▪ VPR **se référer** **se r. à qch** to refer to sth; **tout ce qui ne se réfère pas directement à notre affaire** anything that is not directly connected with *or* related to our business; **se r. à** *ou* **s'en r. à qn d'une question** to refer a matter to sb

refermer [rəfɛrme] VT to shut *or* close again; **il referma la porte sur lui** he closed the door behind *or* after him
▪ VPR **se refermer** *(d'une porte)* to close *or* shut (again); *(d'une fleur)* to close up; *(d'une blessure)* to close up, to heal; *Fig* **le piège se referme sur l'espion** the net is closing in around the spy

refiler [rəfile] VT *Fam* **r. qch à qn** *(objet de mauvaise qualité)* to palm sth off on sb, to foist *or* unload sth on sb; *(objet utile)* to pass sth on to sb; **ils vont nous r. les enfants pour le week-end** they're palming the kids off on us *or* dumping the kids on us for the weekend; **il m'a refilé son rhume** he's given me his cold

refinancement [rəfinɑ̃smɑ̃] **NM** *(d'un crédit)* refinancing

refinancer [rəfinɑ̃se] **VT** to refinance

réfléchi [refleʃi] **ADJ 1** *(personne)* thoughtful, reflective; *(action, opinion)* deliberate, considered; **d'un air r.** thoughtfully; **elle est très réfléchie** she doesn't do anything without thinking it over first; **c'est tout r.** that's settled; **tout bien r.** all things considered, after due consideration **2** *Gram (verbe, pronom)* reflexive **SEE GRAMMAR A29–30; B28–9**

réfléchir [refleʃir] **VT 1** *(image)* to reflect; *(lumière, son)* to reflect, to throw back **2 r. que ... + ind** to realize that ...; **il réfléchit que son argent ne suffirait pas** it occurred to him that he wouldn't have enough money **VI** to think; **je réfléchis** I'm thinking; *(avant de décider)* I'm thinking about it; **prends le temps de r.** (take time to) think about it; **donne-moi le temps de r.** give me time to think; **r. à qch** to think about sth, to consider sth, to turn sth over in one's mind; **j'ai beaucoup réfléchi au problème** I've given the problem a great deal of thought; **j'ai réfléchi à ce que vous m'avez dit** I've thought about what you told me; **réfléchissez-y** think about it, think it over; **je demande à r.** I'd like to think about it *or* think it over; **donner à r. à qn** to give sb food for thought, to make sb think twice; **parler sans r.** to speak without thinking *or* hastily

VPR se réfléchir *(d'une image, d'une lumière, de la chaleur, du son etc)* to be reflected

réfléchissant [refleʃisɑ̃] **ADJ** *(miroir, surface)* reflective

réflecteur, -trice [reflɛktœr, -tris] **ADJ** *(miroir, panneau)* reflecting
NM *Aut* reflector; *(miroir)* reflecting mirror; *(télescope)* reflector, reflecting telescope; *TV* **r. parabolique** parabolic reflector

réflectif, -ive [reflɛktif, -iv] **ADJ 1** *(de la réflexion)* reflective **2** *Physiol* reflex

réflectorisé [reflɛktɔrize] **ADJ** *(panneau routier, casque)* reflective

reflet [rəflɛ] **NM** *(dans un miroir, sur l'eau)* reflection; *(de la soie etc)* sheen, shimmer; **r. des eaux** gleam on the waters; **les reflets de la lune sur le lac** the reflection *or* shimmer of the moon on the lake; **chevelure à reflets d'or** hair with glints of gold; **reflets changeants** play of colour; *Fig* **être le r. de qch** to reflect sth; **ce n'est que le r. du temps des colonies** it's a pale reflection of colonial times

refléter [rəflete] (**je reflète, n. reflétons; je refléterai**) **VT** *(lumière, image, Fig (gêne, jalousie, sentiments de qn)* to reflect; **son attitude ne reflète pas ses sentiments** his feelings are not reflected in his attitude
VPR se refléter to be mirrored *or* reflected

refleurir [rəflœrir] **VI** to flower *or* blossom again; *Fig (de l'art, de la littérature, de l'économie etc)* to flourish again
VT *(tombe)* to put fresh flowers on

reflex [reflɛks] **ADJ, NM** *Phot* **(appareil) r.** reflex (camera)

réflexe [reflɛks] **ADJ** *Phys, Physiol* reflex
NM *Physiol* reflex; *(réaction)* reflex, reaction; **r. rotulien** knee reflex *or* jerk; **avoir de bons réflexes** to have good reflexes, to react quickly; **ça a été un r.** it was a reflex (action), it was automatic; **c'est devenu un r.** it's become automatic; **je n'ai pas eu le r. de le lui faire remarquer** I wasn't quick-witted enough to point it out to him/her

réflexif, -ive [reflɛksif, -iv] **ADJ** *Phil, Math* reflexive

réflexion [reflɛksjɔ̃] **NF 1** *(pensée)* reflection, thought; **plongé dans une profonde r.**

deep in thought; **après mûre r.** after much thought; **donner matière à r.** *(d'un film, livre etc)* to provide food for thought; **agir sans r.** to act hastily *or* without thinking; **(toute) r. faite, à la r.** *(finalement)* on reflection; *(après avoir changé d'avis)* on further consideration, on second thoughts; **voilà qui mérite r.** there's food for thought **2** *(remarque)* remark; **elle ne supporte pas qu'on lui fasse la moindre r.** she can't stand the slightest criticism; **faire une r. à qn** to make a remark *or* comment to sb; **on ne m'a jamais fait de r. à ce sujet** nobody's ever made any remarks to me about it *or* remarked on it to me; **s'il te fait la moindre r.** if he says the least little thing to you **3** *Phys (d'une image, de la lumière, du son)* reflection; **angle de r.** angle of reflection; *TV, Cin* **r. parasite** blooming

refluer [rəflye] **VI 1** to flow back; *(de la marée)* to ebb; **le sang lui reflua au visage** the blood surged to his/her cheeks; **la foule a reflué vers la ville** the crowd swept *or* surged back towards the town; **faire r. des gens** to push people back, to make people move back **2** *Fin* **faire r. le dollar/le yen** to keep down the value of the dollar/yen

reflux [rəfly] **NM** *(de la marée)* ebb(ing); *(d'une foule)* surging back

refondation [rəfɔ̃dasjɔ̃] **NF** *(d'un parti politique)* radical reform; **les militants ont réclamé une r. du parti** the militants have called for radical reform of the party

refonder [rəfɔ̃de] **VT** *(parti politique)* to radically reform

refondre [rəfɔ̃dr] **VT 1** *(métal, cloche)* to recast; *(monnaie)* to recoin, to remint **2** *(texte, ouvrage)* to revise, to rewrite, *Fml, Litt* to recast
VI *(de la neige)* to melt again

refonte [rəfɔ̃t] **NF 1** *(du métal)* recasting; *(de la monnaie)* recoinage **2** *(d'un texte)* rewriting, revision

réformable [reformabl] **ADJ** reformable

reformatage [rəformataʒ] **NM** *Ordinat* reformatting

reformater [rəformate] **VT** *Ordinat (page, disque)* to reformat

réformateur, -trice [reformatœr, -tris] **ADJ** *(mesure, initiative)* reforming
N reformer

réformation [reformasjɔ̃] **NF** reformation, reform; *Hist, Rel* **la R.** the Reformation

réforme [reform] **NF 1** *(politique, de l'orthographe, d'un abus, du calendrier etc)* reform; *Hist, Rel* **la R.** the Reformation; **r. constitutionnelle** constitutional reform; **r. électorale** electoral reform; **r. monétaire** monetary reform; **réformes sociales** social reforms **2** *Mil (d'un homme) (pour mauvaise condition physique)* discharge on medical grounds, invaliding out; *(d'une recrue)* rejection; *(de matériel)* scrapping; **r. temporaire** deferment; **commission de r.** special medical board; **matériel en r.** scrapped equipment; *Fam Vieilli* **mettre à la r.** *(objets)* to scrap

réformé, -ée [reforme] **ADJ 1** *Rel* Protestant *(église)* reformed **2** *Mil (exempté)* discharged for unfitness *or* on medical grounds, invalided out; *(recrue)* rejected; *(matériel)* scrapped; **être r. P4** to be rejected/discharged for reasons of mental health
N 1 *Rel* Protestant **2** *Mil* **r. temporaire** deferred recruit

reformer [rəforme] **VT** to form again, to reform; **r. les rangs** to fall into line again
VPR se reformer to re-form

Do not confuse with **réformer**.

réformer [reforme] **VT 1** *(abus, loi etc)* to reform; *Jur (décision)* to reverse **2** *Mil, Naut (homme, officier)* to discharge as unfit *or* on

medical grounds, to invalid out (of the service); *(recrue)* to reject; *(matériel)* to scrap, to condemn; **se faire r.** *(avant l'incorporation)* to be rejected from military service; *(après l'incorporation)* to get oneself discharged

Do not confuse with **reformer**.

réformisme [reformism] **NM** *Pol* reformism

réformiste [reformist] **ADJ, N** reformist

reformulation [rəformylasjɔ̃] **NF** rewording

reformuler [rəformyle] **VT** to reformulate, to reword

refoulé, -ée [rəfule] *Psy* **ADJ** *(sentiments, instincts, pulsions)* repressed; *(personne)* repressed, inhibited
N repressed *or* inhibited person
NM **le retour du r.** a Freudian slip

refoulement [rəfulmɑ̃] **NM 1** *Psy* (unconscious) repression, suppression **2** *Tech (d'une canalisation)* delivery, discharge, output; **soupape de r.** *(d'une pompe)* delivery valve; **tuyau de r.** exhaust pipe **3** *(renvoi)* **il faut instaurer un r. systématique des hooligans** *(à la frontière)* we must start systematically refusing entry to hooligans; **la police tentait d'organiser le r. des supporters** the police were trying to push *or* drive back the supporters

refouler [rəfule] **VT 1** *(faire reculer) (manifestants, foule)* to drive back, to force back, to press back; *Admin (étranger)* to refuse entry to sb, to turn back; *(train)* to back up; **le nombre des étrangers refoulés aux frontières** the number of foreigners turned back at the borders; **on nous a refoulés à l'entrée** we got turned away at the door
2 *(sentiments, colère)* to repress, to suppress, to contain; *(larmes)* to force *or* choke or fight back; *(agressivité, souvenir), Psy (pulsion, instinct)* to repress; *(désirs)* to suppress; **il ne faut pas r. ses sentiments** you mustn't bottle up your feelings
3 *Tech (eau)* to deliver, to discharge; **pompe refoulante** force pump
VI 1 *(de l'égout)* to back up; **la cheminée/la machine à laver refoule** the chimney's not drawing/the washing machine's not draining properly
2 *Vulg (sentir mauvais)* to stink

réfractaire [refraktɛr] **ADJ** rebellious, insubordinate, *Fml* refractory; *Tech, Méd (minerai, maladie)* stubborn, *Spéc* refractory; *(brique, argile)* fireproof, fire; *Hist* **prêtre r.** non-juring priest; **r. à** *Tech* resistant to; *(la loi, des conseils, une proposition)* unwilling *or* loath to accept; **il est r. à l'opéra** opera goes straight over his head; **r. aux acides** acid-proof; **être r. à l'autorité** to reject authority; **elle est r. aux sciences** science is a closed book to her
N rebel; *Mil, Jur* defaulter

réfracter [refrakte] **VT** *(rayons etc)* to refract, to bend

réfracteur, -trice [refraktœr, -tris] **ADJ** refracting
NM refractor

réfraction [refraksjɔ̃] **NF** *(de rayons)* refraction, bending; **indice de r.** index of refraction, refractive index

refrain [rəfrɛ̃] **NM** *(d'une chanson)* chorus, refrain; **chanter de vieux refrains** to sing old songs *or* old ditties; **reprendre le r. en chœur** to sing the chorus; *Fam* **c'est toujours le même r.** it's (always) the same old story *or* thing; *Fam* **change un peu de r.!** change the record! **VOIR GRAMMAIRE A14**

réfrangible [refrɑ̃ʒibl] **ADJ** *Phys* refrangible

refrappe [rəfrap] **NF** *Ordinat* rekeying

refrapper [rəfrape] **VT** *Ordinat* to rekey

refréner [rəfrene] **VT** (**je refrène, n. refré-nons; je refrénerai**) (*sentiments, colère, impatience etc*) to curb, to restrain, to control

réfrigérant [refriʒerɑ̃] **ADJ** (*action, appareil*) refrigerating, cooling; (*produit*) freezing; *Fig* (*accueil, personne*) chilly; **mélange r.** refrigerant

■ **NM** (*mélange*) refrigerant, coolant; (*d'un alambic*) refrigerator, condenser; **r. à cheminée** cooling tower

réfrigérateur [refriʒeratœr] **NM** refrigerator, fridge, *Am* icebox; **conserver au r.** keep refrigerated; **conserver au r. après ouverture** refrigerate after opening; *Fig* **Fam mettre qn au r.** to sideline sb; *Fam* **mettre un projet au r.** to shelve a plan, to put a plan on ice *or* in cold storage; *Fam* **sortir qn du r.** to bring sb in out of the cold; **ils ont sorti le projet du r.** they took the project down off the shelf *or* out of cold storage

réfrigération [refriʒerasjɔ̃] **NF** (*de la viande, de boissons etc*) refrigeration, chilling; **appareils de r.** refrigeration appliances; **r. industrielle** industrial refrigeration

réfrigéré [refriʒere] **ADJ** refrigerated

réfrigérer [refriʒere] **VT** (**je réfrigère, n. réfrigérons; je réfrigérerai**) to refrigerate; **viande réfrigérée** chilled meat; **camion réfrigéré** refrigerated van, reefer; *Fig* **son accueil me réfrigéra** I received a chilly welcome; **ma question l'a réfrigéré** my question met with a chilly response *or* lowered the temperature quite considerably; *Fam* **je suis réfrigérée** I'm freezing

réfringence [refrɛ̃ʒɑ̃s] **NF** *Phys* refringency

réfringent [refrɛ̃ʒɑ̃] **ADJ** *Phys* refringent

refroidi [rəfrwadi] **NM** *Fam* (*cadavre*) stiff

refroidir [rəfrwadir] **VT 1** (*eau*) to cool (down); (*moteur, fluide*) to cool; (*métal*) to quench; **refroidi par (l')air/huile** air-/oil-cooled; **refroidi par eau** water-cooled **2** *Fig* (*amitié, passion, amour etc*) to cool; (*ardeur*) to cool, to quench; (*enthousiasme*) to dampen, to dash, to quench; *Fam* **r. qn** (*d'un accueil, d'une réaction, question*) to dampen sb's enthusiasm **3** *Arg* **r. qn** (*tuer*) to bump sb off, to ice sb

■ **VI** (*d'un liquide ou d'un plat qui devrait être chaud*) to get cold; (*d'un liquide ou d'un plat qui est trop chaud*) to cool down; **laisser r. son thé** (*exprès*) to let one's tea cool down; (*si l'on attend trop*) to let one's tea get cold; **dépêchez-vous! ça va r.!** hurry up! it's getting cold!; **le temps a refroidi** it *or* the weather has got *or* grown colder; *Fam* **tu refroidis!** (*tu devines mal*) you're getting colder!

■ **VPR se refroidir 1 le temps** *ou* **la température se refroidit** it's *or* the weather's getting colder; **la soupe se refroidit** the soup's getting cold **2** *Fig* (*d'une amitié, de relations*) to cool; **nos relations se sont refroidies depuis cette dispute** things have cooled between us since the argument **3** *Méd* to catch a chill

refroidissement [rəfrwadismɑ̃] **NM 1** (*de l'eau, d'un moteur*) cooling; (*du métal*) quenching; *Météo* drop in temperature; **agent de r.** cooling agent, coolant; *Aut* **r. intermédiaire** intercooling; **r. par air** air cooling; **r. par eau** water cooling **2** *Méd* chill **3** *Fig* (*d'une amitié, de relations*) cooling off

refroidisseur [rəfrwadisœr] **NM** cooler, refrigerator unit; *Nucl* cooler, coolant; **système r.** cooling system

refuge [rəfyʒ] **NM 1** refuge, shelter; **(lieu de) r.** place of refuge; **r. anti-bombe** air-raid shelter; **pays r.** country of refuge; **valeur r.** safe investment; **trouver/chercher r.** to find *or* take/seek refuge; *Fig* **le sport/l'alcool est son r.** he takes refuge in sport/alcohol; **Dieu est mon r.** God is my refuge **2** (*en montagne*) (mountain) hut, refuge; (*d'oiseaux*) (bird) sanctuary; (*sur la route*) traffic island

réfugié, -ée [refyʒje] **N** refugee; **r. politique** political refugee

réfugier (se) [sərefyʒje] **VPR** to take refuge, to find shelter, to shelter; **se r. dans le mensonge/le sport** to take refuge in lying/sport

refus [rəfy] **NM** (*d'une invitation, offre*), *Équitation* refusal; (*d'une proposition*) rebuff, rejection; (*d'un candidat, manuscrit, de marchandises*) rejection; **son r. d'obéir** his/her refusal to obey; **essuyer un r.** to meet with a refusal; **se heurter à un r. de la part de qn** to meet with a refusal from sb; **opposer un r. à qn/qch** to turn sb/sth down; **il opposa un r. catégorique à ma proposition** he turned my suggestion down flat; *Fam* **ce n'est pas de r.** I won't say no

▸ ▸ **r. d'acceptation** non-acceptance; **r. d'obéissance** insubordination; *Jur* contempt of court; *Jur* **r. d'obtempérer** obstruction; **r. de paiement** non-payment; (*de traite*) dishonour, *Am* dishonor; *Aut* **r. de priorité** failure to give way *or Am* to yield

> Il faut noter que le terme anglais **refuse** est un faux ami. Il signifie **ordures**.

refuser [rəfyze] **VT 1** (*offre, invitation*) to refuse, to decline, to turn down; (*proposition*) to turn down; (*demande*) to deny; (*marchandises, manuscrit*) to reject; **r. qch à qn** to refuse *or* deny sb sth; **on ne peut rien lui r.** you can't refuse him anything; **on lui refuse jusqu'au droit de voir sa femme** he's even being refused *or* denied the right to see his wife; **se voir r. sa demande** to have one's request turned down *or* denied; **r. toute qualité à qn** to refuse to see any good in sb; **r. sa porte à qn** to refuse to see sb, *Fml* to deny sb admittance; **r. l'obstacle** (*d'un cheval*) to refuse; **r. le combat** to refuse to fight

2 r. qn to turn sb down; *Mil* **r. un homme** to reject a man; **r. du monde** to turn people away; *Scol* **être refusé** (*à un examen*) to fail

■ **VI** to refuse; (*d'un cheval*) to refuse, to ba(u)lk; **r. tout net** to refuse point blank, to give a point-blank refusal; **r. de faire qch** to refuse to do sth; **r. d'accepter un effet** to dishonour a bill by non-acceptance; **r. de payer une traite** to dishonour a bill by non-payment; *Naut* **r. de virer** not to obey the helm; **l'ordinateur refuse de s'allumer** the computer refuses to *or* won't turn on

■ **VPR se refuser cela ne se refuse pas** it's not the kind of thing to pass up; **un petit verre, ça ne se refuse pas** (*en proposant une boisson*) I wouldn't say no to a drink; (*en acceptant une boisson*) you can't say no to a drink; **on ne se refuse rien!, tu ne te refuses rien!** you don't stint yourself!, you don't believe in self-denial!; **se r. à l'évidence** to shut one's eyes to the facts; **se r. à tout commentaire** to refuse *or* decline to comment; **se r. à faire qch** to refuse to do sth; **je me refuse à ce genre de pratique** I refuse to get involved in that kind of thing

réfutable [refytabl] **ADJ** (*argument*) refutable; **c'est difficilement r.** it's hard to refute

réfutation [refytasjɔ̃] **NF** rebuttal, refutation

réfuter [refyte] **VT** to refute, to rebut

refuznik [rəfyznik] **N** refusenik

rég *Mil* (*abrév* **régiment**) Rgt

regagner [rəgaɲe] **VT 1** (*confiance, affection, estime, amitié de qn*) to regain, to win *or* get back; **r. le temps perdu** to make up for lost time; **r. le terrain perdu** to make up lost ground; **r. aux courses l'argent perdu à la Bourse** to win back on the horses the money lost on the Stock Exchange; **c'est en 1999 qu'il s'est mis à r. de l'argent** it was in 1999 that he started earning money again **2** (*en droit*) to get back to; **r. son foyer** to go back *or* return home; **r. sa place** to go back *or* return to one's place; **r. la côte à la nage** to swim back to shore; **r. la capitale en hélicoptère** to go back to the capital by helicopter; **ils purent r. l'Espagne après la mort de Franco** they were able to go back *or* return to Spain after Franco's death; **vous êtes maintenant autorisés à r. vos bureaux** you may now go back to your offices

regain [rəgɛ̃] **NM** (*d'intérêt, activité*) renewal, revival; **un r. d'espoir** renewed hope; **ce r. d'activité/d'intérêt nous a surpris** this renewed activity/interest surprised us; **on constate un r. d'activité sur les marchés boursiers** we can see renewed activity *or* a renewal of activity on the Stock Market; **connaître un r. de vie** to have a new lease of life

régal, -als [regal] **NM** treat; **les marrons glacés, c'est mon r.** I adore marrons glacés, marrons glacés are my favourite treat; **cette tarte aux pommes est un r.** this apple tart is delicious; **c'est un vrai r. de l'écouter** it's a treat *or* a pleasure to listen to him; **c'est un r. pour les yeux** it's a sight for sore eyes

régalade [regalad] **NF** *Fam* **boire à la r.** to pour a drink down one's throat without the bottle touching one's lips

régale [regal] **ADJ** *Chimie* **eau r.** aqua regia

régaler [regale] **VT** (*sol*) to level

régaler [regale] **VT** *Fam* **r. qn** to give sb an excellent meal; **r. qn de qch** to regale sb with sth

■ **VI** *Fam* **c'est moi qui régale** it's on me, (it's) my treat

■ **VPR se régaler on s'est (bien) régalés!** we had an absolute feast!; **se r. de qch** to adore sth; *Fig* **elle se régale avec ses petits-enfants** she's having the time of her life with her grandchildren

regard [rəgar] **NM 1** (*des yeux*) look; (*coup d'œil*) glance; **un r. tendre/amusé/intelligent** a tender/an amused/an intelligent look *or* expression in one's eyes; **r. appuyé** fixed *or* intent gaze *or* look; **ses regards appuyés me dérangent** I don't like the way he looks at me so intently *or* stares at me; **r. de côté** sidelong glance *or* look; **r. vitreux** glassy stare, glazed look; **porter son r. sur qn/qch** to look at sb/sth; **détourner le r.** to look away, to avert one's eyes *or* gaze; **avoir un beau r.** to have beautiful eyes; **nous eûmes un r. complice** we exchanged a knowing look; **avant tout, Lauren Bacall, c'était un r.** the first thing you noticed about Lauren Bacall was the way she looked at you; **je sentis son r. se poser sur moi** I felt him/her looking at me, I felt his/her gaze on me; **tourner son r. vers qn/qch** to turn one's gaze *or* eyes to sb/sth; **jeter un r. à qn** to glance at sb; **jeter** *ou* **lancer un r. à** *ou* **sur qch** to (cast a) glance at sth; **jeter un r. autour de soi** to glance round; **lancer un r. furieux à qn** to glare at sb; **lancer un r. noir à qn** to give sb a black look; **chercher qn du r.** to look round for sb; **interroger qn du r., lancer à qn un r. interrogateur** to give sb a questioning look, to look at sb inquiringly; **j'ai compris au premier r.** I realized at a glance *or* immediately *or* right away; **exposé aux regards** exposed to view; **la jeune fille que l'on avait cachée aux regards des hommes** the young girl who had been kept out of the sight of men; **soustraire qn/qch aux regards de qn** to keep sb/sth out of sb's sight; **à l'abri des regards indiscrets** away from prying eyes; **attirer le(s) regard(s)** to attract attention, to be conspicuous; **elle attirait tous les regards** everyone turns to look at her; **nous attirions des regards très étonnés** we were getting some very strange looks; **sous les regards de la foule** while the crowd looked on; **en r. de**

qch opposite *or* facing sth; *(comparé à)* compared with sth; **texte avec illustration en r.** text with illustration opposite *or* on the opposite page; **au r. de nos livres de comptabilité** on looking at *or* examining our accounts; **au r. de la loi, elle est coupable** she is guilty in the eyes of the law; *Fig* **porter un nouveau r./un r. critique sur qch** to take a fresh/critical look at sth

2 *(ouverture)* *(d'une porte)* peephole; **r. (d'accès ou de visite)** inspection hole; *(d'un égout)* manhole

3 *(contrôle)* *Jur* **droit de r.** right of inspection; **je demande un droit de r. sur tous les textes qui sortent de ce bureau** I demand the right to check all texts leaving this office

---

Il faut noter que le terme anglais **regard** est un faux ami. Il ne correspond jamais au français **regard**.

---

regardant [rəɡardã] ADJ **1** *(avare)* careful with one's money; **être r. à la dépense/sur l'argent que l'on donne** to be careful how one spends one's money/gives one's money away **2** *(exigeant)* **elle n'est pas regardante sur la présentation** she's not concerned *or* bothered about the presentation

REGARDER [rəɡarde]

| VT | to look at **1** ▪ to watch **1** ▪ to consider **2** ▪ to concern **3** |
| VI | to look **1** ▪ to face **2** |

VT **1** *(personne, chose)* to look at; *(émission, film etc)* to watch; **r. qn dans les yeux** to look sb in the eye *or* eyes; **r. qn dans le blanc des yeux** to look sb straight in the eye; **r. qn fixement** to stare at sb; **r. qn avec méfiance** to look at *or* eye sb suspiciously; **regarde où tu marches ou où tu mets les pieds!** look *or* watch where you're going *or* where you're putting your feet!; **r. qn faire qch** to watch sb doing *or* do sth; **elle le regardait partir** she watched him leaving *or* leave; **elle veut être regardée** she wants people to look at her, she wants to attract attention; **r. une définition dans le dictionnaire** to look up a word in the dictionary; *Fam* **regarde voir si ce n'est pas cuit** (check and) see if it's cooked yet; *Fam* **regarde-moi ça!** *(viens voir)* (come and) look at this!; *Fam* **regarde-moi ça, c'est ce que tu appelles du travail fini!** just look at this, that's what you call a job well done!; *Fam* **non, mais tu ne m'as pas regardé!** what do you take me for? **SEE GRAMMAR A41; B35**

2 *(considérer)* *(personne, chose)* to regard, to consider *(comme* as); **r. la vie en face** to face up to life; **r. les choses en face** to face (up to) things; **il faut r. les choses telles qu'elles sont** you've got to see things as they are; **elle regardait cela d'un mauvais œil** she was far from keen on the idea, *Fml, Litt* she took a jaundiced view of it; **ne r. que ses intérêts** to consider only one's own interests

3 *(concerner)* *(personne)* to concern; **cela ne regarde que moi** that's nobody's business but mine; **cela ne vous regarde pas** that doesn't concern you, that's no concern of yours, that's none of your business

VI **1 puis-je r.?** can I look?, can I have a look?; **je regarde seulement, merci** *(dans un magasin)* I'm just looking *or* having a look, thank you; **r. en bas/en arrière/autour de soi** to look down/back/round; **r. vers l'avenir** to look to the future; **r. par ou à la fenêtre** *(du dedans)* to look out of the window; *(du dehors)* to look in (through) the window; **r. par le trou de la serrure** to peep *or* look through the keyhole; **r. dans le dictionnaire** to look in the dictionary; **je ne suis pas sûr de l'orthographe, je vais r. dans le dictionnaire** I'm not sure of the spelling, I'll look it up in the dictionary

2 r. sur *ou* **vers** *(jardin, rue etc)* to look on to, to face

3 r. à qch to pay attention to sth; **sans r. à la dépense** regardless of expense; **je ne regarde pas à vingt euros** I'm not worried about twenty euros; **à y bien r.** on thinking it over; **y bien r.** *ou* **y r. à deux fois avant de faire qch** to think twice before doing sth; **je n'y regarde pas de si près** I'm not as fussy as all that

VPR **se regarder** *(d'une seule personne)* to look at oneself; *(de deux personnes)* to look at each other; **mais regarde-toi donc!** just look at you!; **se r. dans les yeux** to gaze *or* look into each other's eyes; **ils se regardaient en chiens de faïence** they were glaring at each other; **nos deux maisons se regardent** our houses face each other *or* are opposite each other; **ça se regarde dans les deux sens** there are two ways of looking at that; *Fam* **elle ne s'est pas regardée!, elle s'est regardée, elle?** she's got a cheek to talk!, she can talk!

Il faut noter que le verbe anglais **to regard** est un faux ami. Il ne signifie jamais **regarder**.

---

regarnir [rəɡarnir] VT *(garde-manger, étagères)* to restock; **r. une trousse de maquillage** to stock up on make-up; **il faut que je regarnisse mon portefeuille** I must get some money *or* cash

régate [regat] NF *Naut* regatta; **faire de la r.** to race; **faire une r.** to have *or* hold a regatta; **r. à voiles** yacht races; **r. à l'aviron** boat races

régater [regate] VI *Naut* to race

régatier, -ière [regatje, -jɛr] N *Naut* racing yachtsman, *f* racing yachtswoman; *(à l'aviron)* racing oarsman, *f* racing oarswoman

regazonner [rəɡazɔne] VT to returf

regel [rəʒɛl] NM renewed frost

regeler [rəʒ(ə)le] VI *(il regèle; il regèlera)* to freeze again

régence [reʒãs] NF regency; *Hist* **la R.** the Regency *(1715-1723)*
ADJ INV **style R.** Regency (style); **meubles style R.** Regency furniture; *Fam* **elle est très r.** she's very genteel

régénérateur, -trice [reʒeneratœr, -tris] ADJ regenerating, regenerative; *Rel* **eau régénératrice** baptismal water; *Nucl* **pile régénératrice** breeder reactor
NM *Ind* regenerator, regenerating plant *or* furnace

régénération [reʒenerasjɔ̃] NF **1** *(d'une cellule, de la peau etc)* regeneration **2** *Ind* reconditioning; *Nucl* breeding; *Ordinat* **r. de l'écran** screen refresh

régénérer [reʒenere] *(je régénère, n. régénérons; je régénérerai)* VT **1** *Biol (cellule, épiderme)* to regenerate; *Fig (d'une douche, des vacances)* to refresh; **cette discussion/rencontre m'a régénérée** I feel alive again *or* regenerated after that talk/meeting **2** *(catalyseur)* to reactivate
VPR **se régénérer** *Biol (de cellule)* to regenerate (itself); *Fig (de l'enthousiasme, l'intérêt)* to reawaken

régent, -ente [reʒã, -ãt] N **1** *Pol* regent **2** *Fin Anciennement* director **3** *Belg Scol* (secondary) schoolmaster **4 le R.** *(diamant)* the Regent diamond
ADJ **reine régente/prince r.** Queen/Prince Regent

régenter [reʒãte] VT *(personne)* to dictate to; **il veut tout r.** he wants to run everything *or* the show

reggae [rege] NM, ADJ INV reggae; **un chanteur de r.** a reggae singer

régicide [reʒisid] N regicide
NM *(crime)* regicide
ADJ regicidal

régie [reʒi] NF **1** *Admin* management, control; *(d'un domaine)* administration, stewardship; **en r.** in the hands of trustees **2** *(entreprise publique)* public corporation, state-owned company **3** *Hist* **la R.** = collection of taxes by state functionaries, *Br* ≃ Customs and Excise; **employé de la r.** exciseman **4** *Théâtre* management; *Cin* production; *Radio* control room; *TV* control room, gallery; *TV, Cin* **r. de contrôle** video control room; **r. de diffusion** broadcast suite; **r. d'exploitation** control room; **r. de montage** edit suite; **r. mobile** mobile control centre, mobile control room; **r. publicitaire** advertising sales agency, space selling organization; **r. vidéo** video centre
▸ ▸ **r. du dépôt légal** copyright department; *Admin* **r. des impôts indirects** excise (administration), *Br* ≃ Customs and Excise department; *Can* **R. des Loyers** ≃ rental board

regimber [rəʒɛ̃be] VI *(d'une personne)* to jib, to ba(u)lk (**contre** at), to kick (**contre** against); *(d'un cheval)* to kick (**contre** at, against); **il est toujours à r.** he's always protesting about something; **il est inutile de r.** there's no point protesting

régime [reʒim] NM **1** *Pol, Admin* (form *or* system of) government, regime; **le r. féodal** the feudal system; *Hist* **l'Ancien R.** the old regime, the Ancien Régime; **le r. actuel** the present government; **sous le r. de Chirac/Blair** during the Chirac/Blair administration; **la chute du r.** the fall of the regime *or* the government; **r. militaire/parlementaire/totalitaire** military/parliamentary/totalitarian regime

2 *(règlements)* **r. des hôpitaux/des prisons** hospital/prison regulations *or* rules; **le r. du travail** the organization of labour; **nous nous sommes mariés sous le r. de la communauté/de la séparation de biens** our marriage was on the basis of a joint settlement of property/of separate ownership of property; **r. douanier** customs system; **r. électoral** electoral system; **r. de faveur** preferential treatment; **r. fiscal** tax system; *Fin* **r. du forfait** standard assessment system, fixed rate tax assessment system; **r. d'imposition** tax system; *Écon* **r. préférentiel** special arrangements; **r. de protection sociale** social welfare system; *Fin* **r. du réel** full assessment system; *Fin* **r. du réel simplifié** simplified full assessment system; **r. de retraite** pension plan; **r. de retraite par capitalisation** funded pension scheme; *Fin* **r. simplifié** simplified system; *Com* **r. de transit** transit system

3 *Aut* (engine) speed; **à haut r.** at high speed; **à moyen r.** at average speed; *Tech* **r. (nominal)** *(d'une machine, d'un moteur, groupe électrogène)* rating; **r. de marche normal** normal working *or* operating conditions; **charge de r.** rated load; **puissance de r.** normal power; *Aviat, Naut, Aut* **r. de croisière** cruising speed; *Aut* **r. moteur** engine speed; **elle fait trois litres au cent en r. de ville** she does 100 km to three litres in town *or* on an urban cycle; **aller à plein r.** to go full throttle; *Fig* **à ce r., on aura fini dans trois jours** at this rate, we'll be finished in three days; *Élec* **r. de charge** *(d'un accumulateur)* charging rate; **variations de r.** load variations

4 *Géog (d'une rivière etc)* (rate of) flow; **r. climatique** climatic conditions; **r. thermique** temperature pattern

5 *(alimentaire)* diet; **être au r.** to be on a diet, to be dieting; **se mettre au r.** to go on a diet; **je dois faire** *ou* **suivre un r.** I must go on a diet; **mettre qn au r.** to put sb on a diet; **r.**

lacté/sans sel/équilibré/sec milk/salt-free/balanced/alcohol-free diet; **r. amincissant** slimming diet; **r. dissocié** food-combining diet, Hay diet; *Fam* **le r. jockey** a starvation diet; *Méd* **r. hyposodé** low-salt diet, low-sodium diet

6 *Gram* object; **cas r.** objective case; **r. direct/indirect** direct/indirect object

7 *(de bananes)* bunch, stem, hand; *(de dattes)* bunch, stem

régiment [reʒimã] NM *Mil* regiment; *Fig (d'admirateurs, créanciers)* host, swarm; *Fam* **aller au r.** to join the army; **quand j'étais au r.** when I was in the army, when I was doing my military service; **la musique/le drapeau du r.** the regimental band/colours; *Fam* **il y a pour un r.** there's enough for a whole army

régimentaire [reʒimãter] ADJ regimental

région [reʒjõ] NF *(d'un pays)* region, area; *Admin* region; **r. militaire** military district, command; **dans la r. de Nantes** in the Nantes area, in the region of Nantes; **en r.** in the provinces, in provincial areas; **je ne connais pas la r.** I don't know the area; **si jamais tu passes dans la r. ...** if you're ever in the area ...; **les régions polaires** the polar regions; **dans nos régions** in these regions; **la r. parisienne** Paris and its suburbs; **j'habite dans la r. parisienne** I live in the Paris area; *Admin* **la r. Nord-Pas-de-Calais** the Nord-Pas-de-Calais Region; **je suis financé par la R.** I get funding from the region; **r. productrice de coton** cotton-growing area; **r. du vin** wine-producing area; **r. minière** mining area or district; *Anat* **la r. lombaire/du cœur** the lumbar/heart region; *Com* **r. test** test area

régional, -ale, -aux, -ales [reʒjɔnal, -o] ADJ *(expressions, cuisine, développement etc)* regional; *(conseil)* local

NM **1** *Tél* area telephone system **2** *Suisse (train omnibus)* local train

régionalisation [reʒjɔnalizasjõ] NF regionalization

régionaliser [reʒjɔnalize] VT **1** *(décentraliser)* to regionalize **2** *(organiser au niveau régional)* **r. un programme d'investissements** to break down an investment programme by region

régionalisme [reʒjɔnalism] NM regionalism

régionaliste [reʒjɔnalist] ADJ regional

N **1** *(écrivain)* regional writer **2** *Pol* regionalist

régir [reʒir] VT *(d'une loi, d'un principe physique)*, *Gram (cas, nom)* to govern; *(domaine)* to manage; **r. des biens** to manage assets

régisseur [reʒisœr] NM *(d'un domaine)* agent, manager, *Vieilli* steward; *(d'une ferme)* bailiff; *Théâtre* stage manager; *Cin* assistant director; *TV* **r. de plateau** floor manager, FM; **r. de plateau adjoint** assistant floor manager, AFM; **r. général** location manager

registre [reʒistr] NM **1** *(livre)* register, record; *(de comptes)* account book; *(des délibérations)* minute book; *Tech (de machine)* log book; **rapporter un article sur un r.** to post or enter an item in a register; **s'inscrire au r. du commerce** to enter oneself in the trade register; **signer le r.** *(d'un hôtel)* to sign the register; **les registres de l'état civil** the registers of births, marriages and deaths

2 *Mus* register; *(étendue totale)* compass

3 *Typ* register

4 *Tech* regulator lever, throttle (valve)

5 *Ordinat* register

6 *(d'une œuvre)* tone, style; **changer de r.** *(d'un écrivain)* to change one's style; **il choisit ses images dans un r. poétique** he uses poetic images

7 *Ling* register

▸▸ *Ordinat* **r. d'accès mémoire** memory access register; **r. des actionnaires** register of shareholders, shareholders' register; *Tech* **r. d'aérage** ventilation flap; **r. des arrivées** *(d'un hôtel)* arrivals register; **r. de cheminée** *(d'un fourneau, d'une cheminée)* register, damper; **r. des chevaux** stud book; **r. de comptabilité** account book, ledger; **r. des départs** *(d'un hôtel)* departures book; **r. électoral** electoral register; **r. à feuillets rechargeables** loose-leaf register; **r. d'index** index register; *Com* **r. international des marques** international trademark register; **r. de présence** attendance register; **r. des procès-verbaux** minutes book; **r. des salaires** payroll

réglable [reglabl] ADJ adjustable

réglage [regla ʒ] NM **1** *(d'un siège)* adjustment; *(d'un appareil)* adjustment, regulating, setting; *(dispositif)* adjuster; *(d'un chronomètre)* rating; **r. automatique** automatic control; **à r. automatique** self-adjusting; **vis de r.** set screw; **r. de la vitesse** speed control; **r. de distribution** valve timing; *Aut* **r. de pression** pressure setting; **r. des phares** headlamp adjustment; *Aut* **r. programmable** *(des sièges)* memory setting; **r. en hauteur** height adjustment; *Mil* **r. du tir** ranging **2** *Radio, TV* tuning; **réglages** dial readings; **r. de la luminosité** brightness control; *TV, Ordinat* **r. du contraste** contrast control; *TV, Cin* **r. du volume** volume control **3** *(du papier)* ruling

règle [regl] NF **1** *(de conduite, de grammaire etc)*, *Rel (d'un ordre)* rule; **les règles de l'honneur** the code of honour; **les règles de la politesse exigent que ...** courtesy demands that ...; **c'est la première des règles de politesse** it's common courtesy; **les règles du jeu** the rules of the game; *Fig* **c'est la r. du jeu** that's the rule of the game; *Fig* **le gouvernement a encore changé les règles du jeu** the government have moved the goalposts again; **se faire une r. de se coucher de bonne heure** to make it a rule to go to bed early; **en r.** *(passeport, papiers)* in order; **reçu en r.** formal receipt; **bataille en r.** *Mil* battle according to the rules; *Fig* regular set-to; **je suis en r. avec lui** I'm all square with him; **être en r. avec sa conscience** to have a clear conscience; **mettre qch en r.** to sort sth out; **tout est en r.** everything is in order or is correct; **en r. générale** as a general rule; **agir dans les règles** to behave properly, to play by the rules; **jouer selon les règles** to play by the rules; *Fig* **dans ou selon les règles de l'art** by or according to the book; *Fig* **elle fait la bouillabaisse selon les règles de l'art** makes a classic or traditional bouillabaisse; **c'est la r.** that's the rule; **comme c'est la r., comme de r.** as is the rule

2 *(pour tracer des lignes)* ruler; *Tech* rule; *(d'arpenteur)* measuring rod; *Ordinat (sur écran)* ruler line; **r. graduée** ruler; **tirer des traits à la r.** to draw lines with a ruler

3 *Physiol* **règles** period; **avoir ses règles** to have one's period; **règles abondantes** heavy periods; **absence de règles** amenorrhoea

▸▸ *Sport* **r. de l'avantage** advantage rule; **r. à calcul** slide rule; *Compta* **r. du décalage d'un mois** one month in arrears rule; *Typ* **r. d'encadrement** panel rule; **r. d'or** golden rule; *Naut* **règles de route** *(en mer)* rule of the road; *Math* **r. de trois** rule of three

réglé [regle] ADJ **1** *(papier)* ruled; **papier non r.** plain paper **2** *(organisé)* regular, well-ordered, fixed, steady; **vie réglée (comme du papier à musique)** well-ordered life; *Fam* **r. comme du papier à musique** as regular as clockwork; **elle a un emploi du temps r. comme du papier à musique** she has a very strict routine, *Fam* you could set your watch by her **3** *(jeune fille)* who has started having

periods; **elle est mal réglée** she's not very regular

règlement [reglǝmã] NM **1** *(d'un compte)* settlement; *(paiement)* payment; **faire un r. par chèque** to pay by cheque; **pour r. de tout compte** in full settlement; **r. au comptant** payment in cash, cash payment; **en cours de r.** being settled, under discussion **2** *(statut)* regulation(s); *(d'université)* statutes; *(d'une société)* rules; **le r. intérieur** *(d'une école)* school rules; *(d'un bureau)* staff or company regulations; **c'est le r.** that's the rule; **les règlements militaires** army regulations; **règlements douaniers** customs regulations; **règlements et usages** code of practice

▸▸ **r. à l'amiable** amicable settlement; *Fig* **r. de compte(s)** settling of scores; *UE* **r. européen** piece of European legislation; *Jur* **r. judiciaire** compulsory liquidation; **se mettre en r. judiciaire** to go into liquidation or receivership; *Admin* **règlements de police** by(e)-laws

réglementaire [reglǝmãter] ADJ statutory, regulation; **tenue r.** regulation uniform; **ce n'est pas r.** it's against the rules; **faire qch dans le temps r.** to do sth in the prescribed time; **le score était de 0-0 à l'issue du temps r.** the full-time score was nil-nil; **dispositions réglementaires** regulations

réglementariste [reglǝmãtarist] ADJ *(attitude, professeur etc)* pernickety, nit-picking; **un fonctionnaire r.** a civil servant who goes by the book

N nit-picker, pernickety person

réglementation [reglǝmãtasjõ] NF **1** *(action)* regulating, regulation; **r. du trafic des changes** exchange control; **r. douanière** customs regulations; **r. du change** exchange control regulations; **r. du travail** labour legislation; **r. sur l'hygiène** health regulations; **r. sur l'hygiène alimentaire** food hygiene regulations; **r. sur l'hygiène et la sécurité** health and safety regulations; **r. sur la sécurité** safety regulations **2** **la r.** *(règles)* the regulations, the rules

réglementer [reglǝmãte] VT *(ventes, importations)* to regulate, to make rules for; **r. le droit de grève** to control the right to strike

régler [regle] *(je règle, n. réglons; je réglerai)* VT **1** *(papier)* to rule

2 *(mécanisme, montre, siège, boussole)*, *Aut (allumage, freins, ceinture de sécurité)*, *TV (image)* to adjust; *(radio)*, *Aut (moteur)* to tune; **r. sa journée** to plan one's day; **jeune homme, il faut r. ta conduite** young man, it's about time you mended your ways; **r. ses dépenses sur ses revenus** to cut one's coat to suit one's cloth; **les obligations qui règlent des échanges commerciaux** the obligations that govern trade; *Tech, Aut etc* **r. qch avec précision** to fine-tune sth; *Sport* **r. l'allure** to set the pace; **r. son allure sur celle de son compagnon** to adjust one's pace to that of one's companion; *Mil* **r. le tir** to range; **la pendule est bien réglée** the clock keeps good time; **il a réglé sa montre sur la mienne** he set his watch by mine; **r. les livres** to balance the books

3 *(résoudre) (question, dispute)* to settle; **r. ses affaires** to put one's affairs in order; **r. à l'amiable** to settle out of court

4 *(payer) (compte)* to settle; *(facture)* to settle, to pay; *(épicier, femme de ménage, note, loyer etc)* to pay; **est-ce que j'ai réglé tout ce que je vous devais?** are we square?, have I paid you everything I owed you?; **je peux vous r. par chèque?** will you take a cheque?, can I pay by cheque?; **r. au comptant** to pay in cash; **r. le gaz** to pay the gas bill; **r. son compte à qn** *(se venger)* to settle accounts with sb; **je vais lui r. son compte** I'll settle his/her hash or score, I'll sort him/her out; **r. de vieux comptes** to pay off *or* settle old scores

vi to pay; **r. en espèces** to pay (in) cash; **c'est moi qui règle** I'm paying, this is on me

vpr se régler 1 *(d'un mécanisme)* to be adjustable; **son pas finit par se r. sur celui de son compagnon** he finished up walking at the same rhythm as his companion **2** *(se finir)* to be concluded *or* settled; **ça s'est réglé à l'amiable** it was settled amicably

réglette [reglɛt] **NF** small ruler; *Aut (d'une boîte de vitesses)* control rod; *Mktg (sur rayon de magasin)* shelf strip; *Ordinat* **r. de clavier** keyboard template

réglisse [reglis] **NF** *Bot* liquorice

NM OU NF liquorice; **bâton de r.** stick of liquorice; **bonbon à la ou au r.** liquorice-flavoured *or Am* -flavored sweet

réglo [reglo] **ADJ INV** *Fam (contrat, proposition)* kosher; **ça n'est pas très r.** that's a bit dodgy; **elle a été très r.** she played by the rules; **c'est un type très r.** he's as straight as a die *or* as they come, *Am* he's a regular guy; **il n'a pas été très r. avec moi** he wasn't very straight with me

réglure [reglyr] **NF** *(sur ou du papier)* ruling; **r. fine** feint; **à r. fine** feint-ruled

régnant [reɲɑ̃] **ADJ** *(prince, famille)*, *Fig (idéologie)* reigning; *Fig (opinion)* prevailing

règne [rɛɲ] **NM 1** *(d'un roi, d'une reine)*, *Fig (d'un champion, de la démocratie)* reign; **sous le r. de Louis XIV** in the reign of Louis XIV; **c'est le r. de l'argent/de la technologie** money/technology reigns supreme **2** *(végétal, animal)* kingdom

régner [reɲe] **vi** *(je règne, n. régnons; je régnerai)* **1** *(d'un monarque)* to reign, to rule; *Fig (de conditions)* to exist, *Fml* to prevail; *(d'une opinion)* to be prevalent, to hold sway; **r. (pendant) dix ans** to reign *or* rule for ten years; **r. sur un pays** to reign over *or* rule (over) a country; **r. sur l'opinion** to be predominant, to hold sway; **r. en maître sur qch** to reign supreme over sth; **s'efforcer de faire r. la paix** to try to keep the peace; **la police est chargée de faire r. l'ordre** the police are there to keep law and order; **la terreur qu'ils faisaient r. a pris fin** their reign of terror is at an end; **la suspicion qui règne au bureau** the climate of suspicion in the office *or* which pervades the office; **il règne une ambiance très étrange dans la ville** a very strange atmosphere prevails in the town; **il régnait, dans la maison, une atmosphère de paix et de tranquillité** peace and quiet reigned in the house; *Iron* **la confiance règne!** there's trust *or* confidence for you!, confidence reigns supreme!

2 *Vieilli* **une galerie règne le long du bâtiment** a gallery runs *or* extends along the building

regonfler [rəgɔ̃fle] **vt** *(ballon)* to reinflate, to blow up again; *(pneus)* to blow up, to pump up; *Fam* **r. (le moral à) qn** to cheer sb up; *Fam* **je suis regonflé à bloc!** I'm back on form!

vi *(d'une rivière)* to swell, to rise (again); **son pied a regonflé** his/her foot has swollen up again *or* is swollen again

regorger [rəgɔrʒe] **vi** *(je regorgeai(s); n. regorgeons)* **r. de qch** to have an abundance of sth, to abound in sth; **r. de monde** *(d'un train, magasin, d'une pièce)* to be packed (with people), to be packed to overflowing; *(des rues)* to be packed, to be teeming *or* swarming with people; **la ville regorge de musées** the town has an abundance of museums

régresser [regrese] **vi 1** *(diminuer) (de la criminalité, d'une théorie, d'un style)* to decline; *(d'un parti politique)* to lose ground; *(de la douleur)* to improve; *(de la production,*

du chiffre d'affaires) to drop; **j'ai régressé en maths** my maths has deteriorated; **l'industrie textile régresse** the textile industry is in decline **2** *Psy* to regress

régressif, -ive [regresif, -iv] **ADJ** regressive; *(impôt, tarif)* tapering; *Biol* **forme régressive** throwback

régression [regresjɔ̃] **NF 1** regression; *Math* **coefficient de r.** regression coefficient **2** *Biol* retrogression; *Psy* regression; **être en r.** to be regressing **3** *(des affaires, ventes etc)* decline, drop; **être en r.** *(d'une épidémie)* to be on the decline, to be losing ground; *(du chômage, de la production etc)* to be on the decline, to be declining

regret [rəgrɛ] **NM** regret (**de** for); **rongé de regrets** eaten up with regret; **avoir des regrets** to feel regret, to be sorry; **j'avais des regrets de ne l'avoir pas vu davantage** I was sorry not to see more of him, I regretted not seeing more of him; **tu as déjà des regrets?** are you regretting it already?; **exprimer ses regrets** to express one's regret; **exprimer le r. de ne pouvoir être présent** to express regret at not being able to be present; **faire qch à r.** to do sth with regret *or* reluctantly; **j'ai dû le faire à r.** I was reluctant to do it, I did it reluctantly; **... dit-elle avec r.** ... she said with regret *or* regretfully; **nous nous en sommes séparés avec r.** we were sorry to part with it; **je suis parti sans r., c'est sans r. que je suis parti** I left without regret, I had no regrets about leaving; **je n'ai aucun r.** I have no regrets; **je n'ai qu'un r., c'est que ...** my only regret is that ...; **j'ai r. à vous quitter** I'm sorry to leave you; **j'ai le r. ou je suis au r. de vous annoncer que ...** I regret *or* am sorry to inform you that ...; **je suis au r. de ne pouvoir vous répondre favorablement** I regret that I cannot give you a favourable answer; **à mon (grand) r.** (much) to my regret; *Fam* **sans r.?** (you have) no regrets?, you're quite happy about it?; *Fam* **tous mes regrets!** sorry!, my apologies!; **un ton plein de r.** a regretful *or* sorrowful tone of voice; **mourir sans laisser de regrets** to die unmourned; **le r. du pays natal** homesickness; **éprouver le r. du pays natal** to be *or* feel homesick

regrettable [rəgrɛtabl] **ADJ** *(erreur, retard, incident etc)* regrettable, unfortunate; **il est tout à fait r. que vous n'ayez pas été prévenu** it is most unfortunate that you were not informed

regrettablement [rəgrɛtabləmɑ̃] **ADV** *Rare* regrettably

regretter [rəgrɛte] **vt 1** *(sa naïveté, son imprudence etc)* to regret; **vous le regretterez** you'll regret it, you'll be sorry, you'll rue the day; **tu ne le regretteras pas!** you won't regret it!, you won't be sorry!; **je ne regrette rien** I have no regrets; **je regrette le jour où je l'ai rencontré** I rue the day I met him; **il me ferait presque r. ma gentillesse** I'm almost sorry I was so kind to him; **je regrette de vous annoncer que ...** I regret to inform you that ...; **r. d'avoir fait qch** to regret *or* be sorry for having done sth; **je ne regrette pas d'avoir dit cela** I'm not sorry I said it, I don't regret saying it; **je regrette qu'elle soit partie si tôt** I'm sorry that she left so early, I wish she hadn't left so early; **il est à r. que ...** it is to be regretted that ..., it is unfortunate *or* regrettable that ...; **son absence est à r.** his/her absence is unfortunate *or* regrettable *or* is to be regretted; **je regrette!** (I'm) sorry!; **je regrette, je ne pourrai pas y assister** I'm sorry, I won't be able to attend, *Fml* regretfully, I will be unable to attend

2 *(personne, endroit)* to miss; **mourir regretté de tous** to die mourned by all; **il sera regretté de tous** he'll be greatly *or* sorely missed; **r. sa jeunesse/son enfance** to wish

one was young/a child again; **r. son argent** to wish one had one's money back

regrèvement [rəgrɛvmɑ̃] **NM** *Fin* tax increase

regrimper [rəgrɛ̃pe] **vt** *(escalier, pente)* to climb (up) again

vi to climb again; *Fam (de la fièvre)* to go up again; **r. à l'arbre** to climb the tree again

regrossir [rəgrosir] **vi** to put on weight again

regroupement [rəgrupmɑ̃] **NM 1** grouping; *(d'animaux, d'enfants)* rounding up, round-up; *(de sociétés)* amalgamation; *(de comptes)* consolidation; *Mil* regrouping **2** *(groupe)* grouping

regrouper [rəgrupe] **vt** *(personnes)* to gather *or* bring together; *(animaux, enfants)* to round up; *(objets)* to gather *or* put together; *Mil (hommes)* to regroup; *(sections, sociétés)* to merge, to amalgamate; *(comptes)* to consolidate; **les dernières œuvres de Dali ont été regroupées** *(pour cette exposition)* Dali's last paintings have been brought together; **regroupons le parti autour d'une idée-force** let us unite the party around a key idea; **nous avons regroupé nos économies pour lui faire un beau cadeau** we pooled our savings to get him/her a nice present

vpr se regrouper *(de gens)* to gather *or* get together; *Mil (d'hommes)* to regroup; *(de sociétés)* to merge, to amalgamate

régularisation [regylarizasjɔ̃] **NF 1** *(d'une situation, d'un litige)* regularizing, regularization; *Fin (d'un compte, des stocks, charges)* adjustment; *(de papiers d'identité)* putting in order; **ses papiers sont en voie de r.** his/her papers are (in the process of) being put in order **2** *(d'une rivière, d'un mécanisme)* regulation, regulating; **r. de la circulation** traffic control

régulariser [regylarize] **vt 1** *(document)* to put into proper form; *(papiers d'identité)* to put in order; *Fin (compte)* to adjust; **r. une situation** to regularize or *Fam* sort out a situation; **est-ce qu'il va r. la situation?** *(en se mariant)* is he going to make an honest woman out of you/her? **2** *(fleuve, fonctionnement d'une machine)* to regulate; *(circulation)* to regulate, to control

régularité [regylarite] **NF 1** *(de traits, forme, habitudes)* regularity; *(d'un mouvement)* steadiness, evenness, regularity; **faire qch avec une r. infaillible** to do sth with unfailing regularity; **faire preuve de r.** to be reliable; **avec une r. d'horloge** as regular as clockwork **2** *(conformité aux règles) (d'une élection, d'un vote etc)* legality; *Fin* **r. et sincérité des charges** true and fair nature of expenses

régulateur, -trice [regylatœr, -tris] **ADJ** *(mécanisme, hormone etc)* regulating; **soupape régulatrice** governor valve; **le travail est un élément r.** having a job brings a degree of order to your life

NM 1 *(dispositif)* *Tech* regulator; *(d'une horloge)* regulator, governor, balance wheel; *(d'une turbine)* regulator, governor; *(d'une machine à vapeur)* throttle valve, regulator, governor; **r. de marge** margin stop; *Théâtre* **r. d'éclairage de scène** stage dimmer; *Tech* **r. de tension** voltage smoother; *Tech* **r. de vitesse** speed governor **2** *(personne)*, *Rail* controller, *Am* dispatcher; *(de taxis)* dispatcher; **r. aérien** air traffic controller

régulation [regylasjɔ̃] **NF 1** *(action de régler)* *(d'un compas)* regulation, readjustment **2** *(contrôle)* *(de la circulation)*, *Tech (du carburant, de la pression)* control; **r. des naissances** birth control; *Élec* **r. de la tension** voltage regulation *or* control

régulier, -ière[1] [regylje, -jɛr] **ADJ 1** *(service de bus, examens, visites)* regular; *(augmentation, mouvement, progrès)* steady; *(pouls, res-*

piration, coups, revenu) regular, steady; *(vie) (pleine d'habitudes)* ordered; *(morale)* honourable, *Am* honorable; *(résultats)* consistent, steady; *(écriture, couche, pression)* even; *(paroi)* smooth; **avoir un visage r. ou des traits réguliers** to have regular features; **il fit avec le pinceau un trait bien r.** he painted an even line; **son travail n'est pas r.** his/her work isn't consistent or is patchy, he/she doesn't work consistently; **c'est un employé r.** he's a steady worker; **c'est un élève r.** he's a consistent pupil; **se lever et se coucher à heures régulières** to keep regular hours; **être r. dans ses habitudes** to be regular in one's habits; **son humeur régulière** his/her even temper; **d'une humeur régulière** even-tempered; **à intervalles réguliers** at regular intervals

2 *(conforme)* legitimate; *(honnête)* straight, on the level; **ce n'est pas r.** that's not above board; **le coup n'était pas r.** it was a bit of a dirty trick, it was a low blow; **il n'a pas été très r. dans cette affaire** he didn't altogether play by the rules or go by the book; **être r. en affaires** to be an honest person to deal with; **il n'a pas été très r. avec moi** he didn't play fair with me, he wasn't straight with me; **être en situation régulière** to have one's official papers in order; *Gram* **verbe r.** regular verb SEE GRAMMAR A38; B24 ; **quittance régulière** receipt in due form, proper receipt

3 *(soldat, clergé)* regular; **troupes régulières** regular troops, regulars

4 *Can (standard) (format, prix etc)* standard, *surtout Am* regular

N regular (customer); **un r. du bar** a regular (at the bar)

régulière² NF **1** *Vieilli, Hum Fam (épouse)* old lady, *Br* missus; *(petite amie)* steady **2** *Fam* **à la r.** fair and square

régulièrement [regyljɛrmɑ̃] ADV **1** *(avec constance) (aller à un endroit, rendre visite à qn etc)* regularly; *(respirer)* steadily, evenly; *(réparti, étalé)* evenly; **j'entendais des coups frappés r. contre le mur** I heard a steady knocking on the wall; **le son vous fera aller r. à la selle** bran will keep you regular; **elle va r. se plaindre chez le directeur** she regularly goes to the boss to complain **2** *(selon la loi)* legitimately, lawfully; **membres r. désignés** properly or duly elected members; **je ferai en sorte que les choses se passent r.** I'll make sure that things happen as they should

régurgitation [regyrʒitasjɔ̃] NF regurgitation

régurgiter [regyrʒite] VT *(nourriture)* to regurgitate

réhabilitation [reabilitasjɔ̃] NF **1** *(d'un délinquant)* rehabilitation; *(d'une faillite)* discharge; **obtenir la r. de qn** to clear sb's name **2** *(remise en état) (d'un quartier déshérité)* rehabilitation, renovation

réhabilité, -ée [reabilite] N rehabilitated person; *Fin* discharged bankrupt

réhabiliter [reabilite] VT **1** *(délinquant, politicien)* to rehabilitate; *(personne accusée d'un crime, nom de qn)* to clear; *(personne qui a fait faillite)* to discharge; **r. qn dans ses droits** to restore sb's rights **2** *(bâtiment, quartier)* to rehabilitate, to renovate; *(friche industrielle)* to reclaim

VPR **se réhabiliter** to rehabilitate oneself, to restore one's reputation

réhabituer [reabitɥe] VT to reaccustom (**à** to); **r. qn à (faire) qch** to get sb used or accustomed to (doing) sth again

VPR **se réhabituer** **se r. à (faire) qch** to get used or accustomed to (doing) sth again; **on va avoir du mal à se r.** we'll have trouble getting used to it again

rehaussement [rəosmɑ̃] NM *(d'un mur)* raising, heightening; *(d'un tableau sur un mur)* raising; **r. fiscal** tax increase

rehausser [rəose] VT **1** *(mur, bâtiment)* to make higher, to heighten **2** *(faire valoir) (couleur, teint)* to enhance, to set off; *(détail)* to enhance, to accentuate; **r. une veste de jalons** to liven up or brighten up a jacket with braid

réhausseur [reosœr] NM *Aut* child booster cushion

rehaut [rəo] NM *Beaux-Arts (sur un tableau)* highlight

réhydratation [reidratasjɔ̃] NF *Méd* rehydration

réimperméabiliser [reɛ̃pɛrmeabilize] VT *(imperméable)* to reproof

réimplantation [reɛ̃plɑ̃tasjɔ̃] NF **1** *(d'une société, usine)* relocation **2** *Chir* reimplantation; *(d'une dent)* reimplant

réimplanter [reɛ̃plɑ̃te] VT *Chir (une dent)* to reimplant

réimportation [reɛ̃pɔrtasjɔ̃] NF **1** reimport, reimportation **2** *(marchandise)* reimport

réimporter [reɛ̃pɔrte] VT to reimport

réimposer [reɛ̃poze] VT *Fin (produit)* to reintroduce tax on, to retax

réimposition [reɛ̃pozisjɔ̃] NF *Fin* retaxation

réimpression [reɛ̃presjɔ̃] NF **1** *(action)* reprinting; **en cours de r.** *(sur catalogue)* being reprinted, new edition pending; **c'est en cours de r.** it's being reprinted, there's a new edition pending **2** *(livre etc)* reprint

réimprimer [reɛ̃prime] VT to reprint

Reims [rɛ̃s] N Rheims

rein [rɛ̃] NM **1** *Anat* kidney; **r. artificiel** kidney or dialysis machine **2** **reins** *(partie inférieure du dos)* (lower) back; *Litt (taille)* waist; **la chute ou le creux des reins** the small of the back; **douleur ou mal aux reins** backache, lower back pain; **avoir mal aux reins** to have a pain in the small of one's back; **les cheveux lui tombaient jusqu'aux reins** her hair went down to the small of her back; **donner un coup de reins** to heave; **j'ai dû donner un coup de reins pour soulever l'armoire** I had to heave the wardrobe up; *Fam* **se faire un tour de reins** to rick one's back; *Fig* **casser les reins à qn** to ruin or break sb; *Fig* **il a les reins solides** he's tough, he's made of pretty stern stuff; *(financièrement)* he's well-heeled

réincarcération [reɛ̃karserasjɔ̃] NF reimprisonment, *Fml* reincarceration

réincarcérer [reɛ̃karsere] VT to reimprison, *Fml* to reincarcerate

réincarnation [reɛ̃karnasjɔ̃] NF reincarnation

réincarner (se) [sareɛ̃karne] VPR to be reincarnated (**en qn/qch** as sb/sth); **je voudrais me r. en aigle** I want to be reincarnated or come back as an eagle

reine [rɛn] NF **1** *(monarque)*, *Fig* queen; **un port ou un maintien de r.** a queenly or regal bearing; **la r. Anne** Queen Anne; **la r. mère** the Queen Mother; *Fam (belle-mère)* the mother-in-law; *Fam* **je suis la r. des pommes!** what a total idiot I am! **2** *Entom (abeille)* queen (bee) **3** *Échecs* queen **4** *(femme)* **r. de beauté** beauty queen; **la r. du bal** the belle of the ball **5** *Sport* **la petite r.** cycling

reine-claude, pl **reines-claudes** [rɛnklod] NF greengage

reine-des-prés, pl **reines-des-prés** NF *Bot* meadowsweet

reine-marguerite, pl **reines-marguerites** NF *Bot* China aster

reinette [rɛnɛt] NF pippin; **r. grise** russet

réinfecter [reɛ̃fɛkte] VT to reinfect

VPR **se réinfecter** to become reinfected

réinfection [reɛ̃fɛksjɔ̃] NF reinfection

réinitialisation [reinisjalizasjɔ̃] NF *Ordinat* restart; *(de la mémoire)* reinitialization; sim-

ple r. soft reset; **r. totale de la machine** hard reset

réinitialiser [reinisjalize] VT *Ordinat* to reset; *(mémoire)* to reinitialize

réinjecter [reɛ̃ʒɛkte] VT *(liquide)* to reinject; *(argent, fonds)* to reinject, to make a fresh injection of

réinscriptible [reɛ̃skriptibl] ADJ *Ordinat* rewritable

réinscription [reɛ̃skripsjɔ̃] NF registration

réinscrire [reɛ̃skrir] VT *(conj like* **inscrire***)* to re-register

VPR **se réinscrire** to sign up again, to re-register (**à un cours** for a class)

réinsérer [reɛ̃sere] VT *(dans la société etc)* to reintegrate (**dans** into); *Ordinat (bloc)* to reinsert

VPR **se réinsérer** to be reintegrated (**dans** into)

réinsertion [reɛ̃sɛrsjɔ̃] NF reintegration; **r. sociale** rehabilitation

réinstallation [reɛ̃stalasjɔ̃] NF relocation; *Ordinat* reinstallation; **depuis sa r. au premier** since she moved to the first floor; *(pour la deuxième fois)* since she moved back to the first floor

réinstaller [reɛ̃stale] VT *(changer de place)* to move; *(pour la deuxième fois)* to move back; *Ordinat* to reinstall

VPR **se réinstaller** to settle down again; **il s'est réinstallé à Reims** he has moved back to Rheims

réintégration [reɛ̃tegrasjɔ̃] NF **1** *(d'un fonctionnaire etc)* reinstatement; *(dans un parti)* readmission; **r. des démobilisés dans la vie civile** rehabilitation of ex-servicemen (in civilian life) **2** *Jur* **r. de domicile** resumption of residence; **r. du domicile conjugal** restitution of conjugal rights **3** *Fin* add-back

réintégrer [reɛ̃tegre] VT *(conj like* **intégrer***)* **1** **r. qn** *(dans un parti)* to readmit sb; **r. qn (dans ses fonctions)** to reinstate sb **2** **r. son domicile** to return to one's home; *Jur* to resume possession of one's domicile

réintroduction [reɛ̃trɔdyksjɔ̃] NF reintroduction

réintroduire [reɛ̃trɔdɥir] VT *(conj like* **introduire***)* to reintroduce

réinvestir [reɛ̃vɛstir] VT to reinvest

réitératif, -ive [reiteratif, -iv] ADJ reiterative

réitération [reiterasjɔ̃] NF *(d'une demande, promesse)* repetition, reiteration; *(d'une démarche)* repetition

réitérer [reitere] VT *(je réitère, n. réitérons; je réitérerai) (demande, promesse, question)* to repeat, to reiterate; *(démarche)* to repeat

rejaillir [rəʒajir] VI to gush out, to spurt or splash up or out; *Fig* **r. sur qn** *(d'un scandale, du mérite de qn)* to reflect on sb; **tout ceci rejaillit sur moi** it all reflects on me; **sa honte a rejailli sur nous** we suffered disgrace too, the mud stuck to us too

rejaillissement [rəʒajismɑ̃] NM **1** *(d'un liquide)* gushing (out), spurting (up or out) **2** *Fig (de la gloire)* reflection

rejet [rəʒɛ] NM **1** *(action)* throwing out or away; *(de substances toxiques)* dumping; *(terre)* spoil (earth); *Géol* **r. horizontal** heave **2** *(d'une proposition, candidature, personne)*, *Méd (d'une greffe)* rejection; *(d'une requête)* rejection, refusal; *(d'une doctrine)*, *Jur (d'une réclamation, d'un appel)* dismissal; *Fig Fam* **faire un r. de l'école/du sport** to hate school/sports; **ne lui parle pas de sport,** **il fait un r.** don't talk to him about sport, he can't stand it; **un phénomène de r.** rejection; **être victime d'un phénomène de r.** to be rejected; **il a été traumatisé par ces réactions de r.** he was traumatized by this display of rejection **3** *(de plante)* shoot; *(émise par une souche)* sucker **4** *(en poésie)* enjambment

rejeté [rəʒte] ADJ *Journ (article)* on the spike

rejeter [rəʒte] *(conj like* **jeter***)* VT **1** *(relancer, remettre)* (balle, tête) to throw or toss back; *(déchets, gaz toxiques etc)* to release, to discharge; *(de la mer, d'une rivière)* (épaves, poissons etc) to cast up, to wash up; **r. un poisson à l'eau** to throw or toss a fish back; **r. ses cheveux en arrière** to toss one's hair back; **épaves rejetées sur la plage** wreckage cast up or washed up on the beach; **la lave rejetée par le volcan** the lava thrown out or spewed out by the volcano; **la terre rejetée venait s'amonceler derrière eux** the earth which had been dug up was piling up behind them; **les envahisseurs furent rejetés à la mer** the invaders were driven back over the sea; *Fig* **r. le blâme/la responsabilité de qch sur qn d'autre** to shift the blame/the responsibility for sth on to sb else; **en allemand, le verbe est rejeté en fin de phrase** in German, the verb goes to the end of the sentence; **rejette l'idée en fin de paragraphe pour lui donner plus de poids** move this idea to the end of the paragraph in order to give it more weight

2 *(ne pas admettre)* (enfant, conseil), *Méd (greffe)* to reject; *(candidat, candidature)* to turn down, to reject; *(offre, proposition)* to reject, to turn down, to dismiss; *Jur (témoignage)* to disallow; *(doctrine, réclamation, accusation), Jur (pourvoi)* to dismiss; *Journ (un article)* to spike, to kill; **r. un projet de loi** to reject a bill, to throw out or vote out a bill; **elle croit qu'on la rejette** she feels rejected; **ceux que la société rejette** the outcasts of society; **elle rejette toute nourriture** she won't take any food

VPR **se rejeter 1** *(se satisfaire de)* to fall back (**sur** on)

2 *(sauter à nouveau)* to throw oneself again; **se r. en arrière** to jump back; *(d'un cheval)* to shy

3 elles se rejettent la responsabilité de cet échec they're laying the blame for this failure on each other

rejeton [rəʒtɔ̃] NM **1** *(de plante)* shoot, sucker **2** *Fam (progéniture)* offspring; *(enfant)* sprog; **il avait amené ses rejetons avec lui** he'd brought his offspring (with him)

rejoindre [rəʒwɛ̃dr] *(conj like* **joindre***)* VT **1** *(mettre bord à bord)* to join (together); *(lèvres d'une plaie)* to close

2 *(aboutir à)* (d'une rue, rivière) to join (up with), to meet; **la rue rejoint le boulevard cinq cents mètres plus bas** the street joins (up with) the avenue five hundred metres further down; **nous rejoindrons bientôt l'autoroute** we'll soon join (up with) *or Fam* hit the motorway *or Am* freeway

3 *(ressembler à)* to be along the same lines as; **ses propos rejoignent les miens** he echoes what I say; **cela rejoint ce que je disais tout à l'heure** that fits in with what I was saying just now

4 *(retrouver)* (personne) (pour un rendez-vous) to meet; *(rattraper)* to catch up (with); *Mil, Naut (son régiment, son bâtiment)* to (re)join; **le nageur eut du mal à r. le rivage** the swimmer had difficulty reaching the shore

5 *Pol (adhérer à)* to join; **il rejoignit le parti communiste en 1955** he joined the Communist Party in 1955; **elle a fini par rejoindre le parti socialiste** she ended up joining the Socialist Party

VPR **se rejoindre** *(d'amis)* to meet (up); *(de rivières, routes, lignes)* to join (up), to meet (up); **les droites se rejoignent au point P** the straight lines meet at (the point) P

rejouer [rəʒwe] VT *Sport (match, point)* to replay; *(morceau de musique)* to play again; *(pièce de théâtre)* to do again

VI to play again; **on rejoue?** shall we have another game?

réjoui [reʒwi] ADJ joyful; **je voyais à sa mine réjouie que les nouvelles étaient bonnes** I could see from the joyful expression on his/her face or from his/her joyful expression that it was good news; **la mine réjouie, il annonça sa promotion** he delightedly announced his promotion

réjouir [reʒwir] VT *(personne)* to delight, to cheer, to gladden; **toutes ces bonnes nouvelles ne peuvent que nous r.** we can only be glad of all this good news; **cela me réjouit le cœur de l'entendre** it does my heart good or it makes my heart glad or it gladdens my heart to hear it; **r. l'œil** to delight the eye; **savoir qu'il va partir me réjouit** I'm thrilled to know that he's leaving; **cette nouvelle ne me réjouit pas spécialement** I'm less than thrilled to hear the news

VPR **se réjouir 1** to rejoice (**de** at, in), to be glad (**de** of), to be delighted (**de** at); **je me réjouis à la pensée de le revoir** I'm delighted at the thought of seeing him again; **il faut se r. que tout se passe bien** we must be glad that everything is going well; **je me réjouis de te savoir guéri** I'm delighted that you're better **2** *Vieilli (s'amuser)* to enjoy oneself **3** *Suisse* **se réjouir de qch/de faire qch** to look forward to sth/to doing sth

réjouissance [reʒwisɑ̃s] NF rejoicing; **en signe de r.** to mark the occasion; **réjouissances publiques** public festivities; **le programme des réjouissances** the programme of festivities; *Iron* the list of treats in store; *Iron* **quel est le programme des réjouissances?** so what treats have you got in store for me?, what fun things have you got lined up for me to do?

réjouissant [reʒwisɑ̃] ADJ *(nouvelles, perspective etc)* delightful; **cela n'a rien de r.** it's a gloomy prospect; **la nouvelle n'est pas réjouissante** it's not exactly the most cheerful of news

relâche [rəlɑʃ] NF **1** *(arrêt)* respite, rest; **travailler sans r.** to work without a break or a let-up or *Fml* without respite; **elle le répète sans r.** she repeats it continually, she keeps on repeating it; **prendre un peu de r., se donner r.** to have a brief respite; *Théâtre* **il y a r. ce soir** there is no performance this evening; *Théâtre* **faire r.** to be closed; *Théâtre* **r.** *(sur panneau)* closed **2** *(d'une corde)* slackening, loosening **3** *Naut (arrêt)* call; *(port)* port of call; **faire r. dans un port** to call at or put into a port

relâché [rəlɑʃe] ADJ *(corde)* slack, loose; *(mœurs, conduite)* loose, lax

relâchement [rəlɑʃmɑ̃] NM **1** *(d'une corde)* slackening, loosening; *(de la discipline)* relaxation; *(des mœurs)* looseness, laxity, laxness; *(des efforts)* let-up; *(dans le travail)* slacking off; **le r. de l'attention des élèves** the wavering of the pupils' attention; **il y a du r.** people are slacking off **2** *(de prisonniers)* release

relâcher [rəlɑʃe] VT **1** *(corde)* to loosen, to slacken; *(son étreinte, les intestins)* to loosen; *(muscle, discipline, efforts)* to relax; **j'ai relâché mon attention pendant un instant** my attention slackened or wavered for a moment **2** *(prisonnier, oiseau en cage)* to release, to let go; *Fig* **je vous relâche** I'll let you go

VI *Naut* to put into port

VPR **se relâcher** *(de corde)* to slacken; *(d'un lacet)* to come loose; *(d'un employé, de la discipline)* to become slack; *(du zèle)* to flag, to fall off; *(des mœurs)* to grow lax; *(de l'attention)* to slacken, to waver; *(d'une étreinte)* to relax, to loosen; **cet élève s'est relâché** this pupil has slackened off; **se r. dans son tra-**

vail to slacken or ease off; **la discipline s'est un peu trop relâchée ces jours-ci** discipline is a bit too relaxed these days

relais [rəlɛ] NM **1** *(d'ouvriers)* shift; **ouvriers de r.** shift workers; **travail sans r.** unrelieved (spell of) work; **ville-r.** stopover (town); *Sport* **(course de) r.** relay (race); *Sport* **r. 4 fois 100 mètres** 4 x 100-metre relay; **passer le r. à qn** *Sport* to hand over the baton to sb; *Fig* to hand over to sb; **il est temps que je passe le r.** it's time I handed over (control); *Sport* **passage du r.** handover; **prendre le r.** to take over (**de qn** from sb); **l'homéopathie prend le r. de la médecine traditionnelle** homeopathy is taking over from traditional medicine; **tu prendras le r. avec le bébé** you take over with the baby, you have a spell with the baby; *Vieilli* **chevaux de r.** post horses

2 *(auberge) Vieilli* coaching inn, post house; **r.-château** country house hotel; **r. gastronomique** gourmet restaurant; **r. de tourisme** country house hotel; **r. routier** service station (with café); **prochain r. routier: 10 km** *(sur panneau)* ≃ services: 10 km

3 *Tech, Élec* relay; *Radio* **r. de radio-diffusion** relay (broadcasting) station; **r. de télévision** television relay station

4 je leur sers de r. quand ils ont quelque chose à se dire they communicate with each other through me; **le graphiste sert de r. entre le client et l'imprimeur** the graphic artist is the link between the customer and the printer

relais-bébé NM INV baby changing room *(in shopping centre etc)*

relance [rəlɑ̃s] NF **1** *(de l'économie, de la production, des ventes, du commerce)* revival; *(d'un produit)* relaunch; **plan de r.** recovery plan; **des mesures pour la r. de l'économie** measures to revive or boost the economy or to get the economy going again; **r. de la natalité** upturn in the birth rate **2** *Com (d'un client)* follow-up; **lettre de r.** follow-up letter; **r. téléphonique** telephone follow-up **3** *Cartes* raise; **poker sans maximum de r.** poker with no ceiling

relancement [rəlɑ̃smɑ̃] NM **1** *(d'un engin spatial)* relaunch **2** *(d'une machine)* restarting; *(de la production)* boosting; *(d'un produit)* relaunching

relancer [rəlɑ̃se] *(conj like* **lancer***)* VT **1** *(ballon)* to throw again; *(pour le rendre)* to throw back **2** *(économie)* to revive; *(commerce, ventes, production)* to boost; *(moteur)* to restart; *Ordinat (programme)* to rerun; *(logiciel)* to restart; **r. un projet** to relaunch a project **3** *Com (produit)* to relaunch **4 r. qn** *(harceler)* to badger sb, to pester sb; *Com* **r. un débiteur** to chase up a debtor; **r. un client** to follow up or to chase up a customer; **je l'ai relancée plusieurs fois pour qu'elle vienne dîner chez nous** I pestered her several times to come to dinner; **et pourtant, elle continue à lui téléphoner plusieurs fois par semaine pour le r.** and she still badgers him on the telephone several times a week

VI *Cartes etc* to increase the stake, to raise the bid

relaps, -apse [rəlaps] ADJ relapsed; **être laps et r.** to have abandoned the Catholic faith

N relapsed heretic

relater [rəlate] VT *(faits)* to relate, to state

relatif, -ive [rəlatif, -iv] ADJ *(position, valeur, calme, liberté etc), Gram (pronom, proposition)* relative; *Pol* **avoir la majorité relative** to have a relative majority; *Mus* **tons relatifs** related keys; **r. à** relating or related to, connected with; **vivre dans un luxe r.** to live in comparative luxury; **cette notion est très relative** it is a very relative concept; **tout est r.** everything is relative

NM 1 *Gram* relative pronoun `SEE GRAMMAR` `A32–3; B22–3` **2 le r.** the relative

relation [rəlasjɔ̃] **NF 1** *(rapports entre personnes)* relationship; **entamer des relations** *ou* **se mettre** *ou* **entrer en relation(s) avec qn** to enter into a relationship with sb; **avoir** *ou* **entretenir des relations avec qn** to be in touch with sb; **être en r. avec qn** to be in touch *or* in communication with sb; **je vais les mettre en r.** I'll put them in touch (with each other); **avoir de bonnes/mauvaises relations avec qn** to be on good/bad terms with sb, to have a good/bad relationship with sb; **nos relations sont assez tendues** relations between us are rather strained; **nos relations sont très chaleureuses** we are on very good terms (with one another); **relations d'affaires** *ou* **commerciales** business relations; **nos relations sont purement professionnelles** our relationship is purely professional; **être en relation(s) d'amitié avec qn, entretenir des relations amicales avec qn** to be on friendly terms with sb, to have a friendly relationship with sb; **entretenir des relations de bon voisinage avec les pays d'Europe/sa belle-famille** to be on neighbourly *or* good terms with European countries/on good terms with one's in-laws; **les relations humaines** human relationships; **des relations épistolaires** correspondence; **il avait eu une r. épistolaire avec cette femme** he had corresponded with this woman; **relations sociales** labour relations; **les relations culturelles/diplomatiques/internationales** cultural/diplomatic/international relations; **nos relations avec la Hollande** our relations with Holland; **cesser ses relations avec qn/un pays** to break off relations with sb/a country; **les deux pays ont cessé toute r.** the two countries have broken off all relations
2 *(lien entre deux idées, deux faits etc)* relationship, connection; **r. entre la cause et l'effet, r. de cause à effet** relationship between cause and effect; **il n'y a aucune r. entre ces deux faits** the two facts are not related *or* connected; **c'est sans r. avec le sujet** it bears no relation to the subject; **ce n'est pas sans r. avec ce que nous avons dit plus tôt** it is not unconnected with *or* unrelated to what we said earlier; **en r. avec … in relation to …
3 *(d'amour)* relationship; **r. (amoureuse)** love affair; **avoir une r. avec qn** to have a relationship with sb; **elle a eu une r. avec un homme marié** she had an affair with a married man; **avoir des relations sexuelles avec qn** to have (sexual) intercourse with sb
4 *(connaissance)* acquaintance; **r. d'affaires** business acquaintance; **elle a des relations (mondaines)** she is well connected, she has influential friends; **sans relations, on ne peut rien faire** you can't do anything unless you know (the right) people *or* unless you have contacts *or* connections; **faire jouer ses relations** to pull strings; **c'est une r. de travail** he's a colleague
5 *(récit)* account, report; **faire la r. de qch** to give an account of sth
▸▸ *Mktg* **relations clientèle** customer relations; *Pol* **relations extérieures** foreign affairs; **relations presse** press relations; **relations publiques** public relations, PR; **il travaille dans les relations publiques,** *Fam* **il est relations publiques** he's in *or* works in public relations *or* PR

relationnel, -elle [rəlasjɔnɛl] **ADJ** relational; *Ordinat* **base de données relationnelles** relational database

relativement [rəlativmɑ̃] **ADV 1** *(d'une façon relative)* **(rare, fréquent, bien payé etc)** relatively, comparatively **2** *(en relation)* **r. à** relating to, concerning **3** *(en comparaison)* **plus**

petit, r. au premier smaller compared *or* by comparison with the first

relativiser [rəlativize] **VT r. un problème** to put a problem into perspective; **il faut r.** you have to look at things in perspective

relativisme [rəlativism] **NM** *Phil* relativism

relativiste [rəlativist] **ADJ, N** *Phil* relativist

relativité [rəlativite] **NF** relativity; **théorie de la r.** theory of relativity, relativity theory

relaver [rəlave] **VT 1** to wash again

relax [rəlaks] *Fam* **ADJ** *(personne)* laid-back, easy-going; *(soirée, entretien)* laid-back; **fauteuil r.** reclining chair; **baby-r.** baby chair

ADV **on va réviser, mais r., OK?** we'll do some revision, but we'll take it easy, OK?; **vas-y r.** take it easy
INT r. Max! chill out!

relaxant [rəlaksɑ̃] **ADJ** relaxing; **bain r. (aux plantes)** herbal foam bath

relaxation [rəlaksasjɔ̃] **NF** relaxation; **faire de la r.** to practise relaxation; **cours de r.** relaxation class, stress management class

relaxe¹ [rəlaks] **NF** *(d'un accusé)* release, discharge

relaxe² **ADJ** *Fam* = **relax** **ADJ**

relaxer [rəlakse] **VT 1** to relax; **ce bain m'a bien relaxé** I feel really relaxed after my bath **2** *Jur (prisonnier)* to release, to discharge
VPR se relaxer to relax

relayer [rəlɛje] **(je relaie, je relaye, n. relayons; je relaierai, je relayerai) VT 1** *(personne)* to take over from, to relieve **2** *TV, Radio* to relay **3** *(transmettre)* **r. l'information** to relay *or* transmit information
VI *Arch* to relay, to change horses
VPR se relayer to take turns (**pour faire qch** doing sth); *Sport* **les coureurs se relaient tous les cent mètres** the runners take over from each other every hundred metres; **ils se relaient au volant** they take turns at the wheel, they take it in turns to drive; **on se relaie toutes les trois heures** we change over every three hours

relayeur, -euse [rəlɛjœr, -øz] **N** *Sport* relay runner

relecture [rəlɛktyr] **NF** *(d'épreuves)* proofreading; *(d'un livre)* rereading; **faire de la r. en free-lance** to be a freelance proofreader; **la r. de Stendhal m'a pris deux mois** it took me two months to reread Stendhal

relégation [rəlegasjɔ̃] **NF** *Hist, Jur* transportation

reléguer [rəlege] **VT** *(conj like* **léguer***)* **1** *Sport (équipe)*, *Fig* to relegate; **r. un tableau au grenier** to relegate *or* consign a picture to the attic; *Fig* **relégué au second plan** pushed into the background; **mes projets de vacances sont relégués au second plan pour le moment** my holiday plans have been pushed into the background *or* are having to take a back seat for the moment **2** *Hist, Jur (détenu)* to exile, to relegate

relent [rəlɑ̃] **NM** *(odeur)* stale smell; **des relents de graillon** a smell of stale fat; *Fig* **un r. de scandale entoure ce politicien** there is a whiff of scandal about this politician; *Fig* **ces histoires ont un r. de calomnie** these stories smack of slander

relevable [rəlvabl] **ADJ** *(siège, dossier, appuie-tête etc)* adjustable; *Aviat* **train d'atterrissage r.** retractable undercarriage; **accoudoir r.** folding armrest

relevage [rəlvaʒ] **NM** raising, lifting

relevailles [rəlvaj] **NFPL** *Vieilli (d'une femme qui vient d'accoucher)* churching; **faire ses r.** to be churched

relevé [rəlve] **ADJ 1** *(tête)* raised; *(sourcils)* *(après chirurgie esthétique)* lifted; *(manches)* turned up, rolled up; *(col)* turned up; **cha-**

peau r. off-the-face hat; **pantalon à bords relevés** turn-up trousers, turn-ups, *Am* pants with cuffs; *Aut* **virage r.** banked turn **2** *Fig (sentiment)* noble; *(style)* lofty; **dans des milieux plus relevés** in higher circles **3** *(sauce)* highly seasoned; **un plat très/peu r.** a hot *or* spicy/mild dish

NM 1 summary, statement; **r. de consommation (du gaz)** meter reading; **r. de communications téléphoniques** telephone call sheet **2** *(en topographie)* survey; **faire le r. d'un terrain** to plot a piece of land
▸▸ **r. d'achat** purchase report; *Mktg* **r. (d'achat) journalier** diary; **r. de caisse** cash statement; **r. de compte** bank statement, statement of account; **r. de factures** statement of invoices; **r. de fin de mois** end-of-month statement; **r. d'identité bancaire** = document giving details of one's bank account, bank details; **r. d'identité postale** = document giving details of one's post office account; **r. des naissances** table *or* summary of births; **r. de vente** sales report

> ### Relevé d'identité bancaire
> A "RIB" is a small slip of paper with all of a person's bank details. Employers, utility companies and other financial institutions may ask for one to effect standing orders.

relève [rəlɛv] **NF 1** *(des troupes, de la sentinelle)* relief; *Ind (d'une équipe)* changing, changeover; *Mil* **la r. de la garde** the changing of the guard; **(troupes de) r.** relieving troops; **prendre la r. de qn** to take over from sb; *Mil, (au travail)* **to relieve sb,** to take over from sb; **prendre la r.** to take over **2** *(de personnel)* relief (driver/etc)

relèvement [rəlɛvmɑ̃] **NM 1** *(action) (d'un objet renversé)* picking up, righting; *(d'un mur)* raising, heightening; *(des affaires, d'une économie, d'un pays)* recovery, revival; *(des salaires, des tarifs, d'un impôt)* raising, increasing; **contribuer au r. d'un pays/d'une économie** to help a country/an economy recover **2** *(de terrain)*, *Naut* position; *(au compas)* bearing; **r. radio(goniométrique)** radio bearing *or* *Fam* fix; **faire** *ou* **prendre un r.** to take a bearing, to take bearings

RELEVER [rəlve] *(conj like* **lever***)*

> | **VT** to pick up **1** ▪ to collect **2** ▪ to raise **3** ▪ to increase **3** ▪ to turn up **3** ▪ to note **4** ▪ to record **4** ▪ to enhance **5** ▪ to relieve **6**
> | **VI** to be a matter for *(relever de)* **2**
> | **VPR** to get up **1** ▪ to get up again **1** ▪ to lift **1** ▪ to recover **2**

VT 1 *(remettre à la verticale) (objet renversé, personne)* to pick up; *(bateau)* to right; *(mur démoli)* to rebuild; **veuillez r. votre tablette** please fold away your tables; **relevez votre dossier** *(d'avion)* return your seats to an upright position; *(de cabriolet)* pull your seat back up; **r. la tête** to look up, to raise one's head; *Fig* to hold one's head up (again)
2 *(ramasser)*, *Scol (compositions, copies)* to collect, to take in; **r. ses cheveux** to put one's hair up; *Fig* **r. le gant** to take up the gauntlet *or* challenge, to accept the challenge; **r. le défi** to accept *or* take up the challenge
3 *(hausser) (niveau de vie, niveau d'eau)* to raise; *(col)* to turn up; *(manches, bas de pantalon)* to turn up, to roll up; *(voilette)* to raise, to lift; *(jupe)* to lift (up), *Fam* to hoick up; *Tricot (maille)* to pick up; *(navire coulé)* to raise, to refloat; *(salaires, prix)* to increase, to raise; *(notes d'examen)* to put up; **r. les yeux** to look up again (**de** from); **il releva les yeux pour regarder les horaires** he looked up

again at the timetables; **r. l'économie** to revive the economy; **r. une industrie** to revive an industry; **les richesses minières ont permis de r. le pays** mineral wealth contributed to the country's economic revival; *Fam* **cela l'a relevé aux yeux des électeurs** it boosted him in the eyes of the electorate

4 *(noter)* *(contradiction, faux sens etc)* to pick out; *(adresse, numéro de téléphone)* to take down; *(température)* to note, to record; *(traces)* to uncover; *(compte)* to make out; *(compteur)* to read; **r. le gaz** to read the gas meter; **r. des empreintes digitales** *(reporter)* to take fingerprints; **la police n'a pas relevé d'empreintes** the police haven't found any fingerprints; **on n'a relevé aucune preuve contre elle** no evidence has been found against her; **r. l'allusion** to respond, to react, to rise to the bait; **je n'ai pas relevé ce qu'il a dit contre moi** I ignored what he said about me; **il a affirmé l'ignorer et moi, je n'ai pas relevé** he claimed not to know about it and I didn't challenge him

5 *(mettre en valeur)* *(couleur, beauté etc)* to enhance, to heighten, to set off; *(sauce)* to season; *(plat)* to liven *or* perk up; *(histoire)* to liven up, to enliven

6 *(remplacer)* *(troupes, sentinelle)* to relieve; **r. qn** to take sb's place, to take over from sb; **r. la garde** to change the guard

7 *(libérer)* **r. qn d'un vœu** to release sb from a vow; **r. qn de ses fonctions** to relieve sb of his duties

8 *Naut (endroit)* to take the bearings of; *Naut (terre)* to sight; *(d'un arpenteur)* *(terrain)* to survey, to plot; *Math (graphique)* to plot

vi 1 r. de maladie to be recovering from an illness, to be convalescing

2 r. de qn to be answerable *or* responsible to sb, to report to sb; **r. de l'article 7** to come under article 7; **cette affaire ne relève pas de notre département** the matter is not our department's responsibility; **cette affaire relève de la justice** this is a matter for the courts; **son cas relève de la folie** he can be diagnosed as insane; **de telles décisions relèvent d'un manque de responsabilité coupable** decisions like that indicate a culpable lack of responsibility; **tout ce qui relève de la culture étrusque le passionne** everything relating to Etruscan culture fascinates him

vpr se relever 1 *(de son siège)* to get up; *(après être tombé)* to get up, to pick oneself up; *(après avoir été à genoux)* to get up from one's knees; *(du lit)* to get up again, to get out of bed again; *(d'un navire)* to right itself; **l'accoudoir se relève** the armrest lifts up; **aide-le à se r.** *(dans son lit)* help him to sit up; *(debout)* help him up

2 *(d'un pays, d'une économie)* to recover; **se r. d'une maladie** to recover from *or* get over an illness; **il aura du mal à se r. de cette déception** he'll have difficulty recovering from *or* getting over this disappointment; **il ne s'en relèvera pas** he'll never get over it

releveur, -euse [rəlvœr, -øz] **n** *(personne)* meter reader

relief [rəljɛf] **nm 1** *Beaux-Arts, Archit, Géog* relief; *Ordinat* highlight; **mettre en r.** to highlight; **en r.** *Beaux-Arts* in relief; *(caractère)* raised; *(carte)* relief; **cinéma/photographie en r.** stereoscopic cinema/photography; *Fig* **mettre en r., donner du r. à** *(idées, qualité)* to bring out; *(beauté)* to set off, to emphasize; *(taille fine, yeux)* to emphasize, to draw attention to; *(avantage)* to highlight; **mets ce paragraphe en r. en faisant des marges plus larges** make this paragraph stand out by making the margins wider; **l'état de ses finances met en r. son piètre sens de l'économie** the state of his finances emphasizes *or* throws into relief his

lack of financial sense; **sans r.** *(paysage, style)* flat; **r. acoustique** stereophonic sound **2** *Litt* **reliefs** *(d'un repas)* remains; *Fig (de la gloire)* shreds, tatters

> Il faut noter que le nom anglais **relief** signifie le plus souvent **soulagement** ou **aide**, selon le contexte.

relier [rəlje] **vt** *(impf, pr sub* **n. reliions**) **1** *(objets, points, personnes)* to connect, to link, to join (à to); *(idées)* to link together; **le cordon ombilical relie la mère à l'enfant** the umbilical cord attaches *or* connects the mother to the baby; **c'est la seule chose qui les relie** it's the only thing they have in common; **vos idées sont bien/mal reliées entre elles** your ideas are well/badly linked together **2** *(livre)* to bind; **relié en veau** bound in calf, calf-bound

vpr se relier *Ordinat* to link up

relieur, -ieuse [rəljœr, -jøz] **n** (book)binder

religieusement [rəliʒjøzmɑ̃] **adv 1** *(selon la religion)* piously, religiously; **se marier r.** to get married in church, to have a church wedding **2** *(avec révérence)* *(écouter)* reverently; **conservé r. dans un écrin en velours** kept reverently in a velvet case; **il lit l'Humanité r. tous les jours** he reads l'Humanité with reverence every day **3** *(scrupuleusement)* religiously; **elle allait r. à la gym deux fois par semaine** she went to the gym religiously twice a week

religieux, -ieuse [rəliʒjø, -jøz] **adj** *(éducation, communauté, fanatique)* religious; *(musique, art)* sacred; **n'avoir aucun sentiment r.** to have no religious inclinations; **école religieuse** church school; **mariage r.** church wedding; *Fig* **soin r.** religious *or* scrupulous care; **elle prépare ses gâteaux avec un soin r.** she takes (an almost) religious care over her cakes; **conservé avec un soin r. dans du coton** reverently wrapped up in cotton wool; **mettre un soin r. à faire qch** to be religious about doing sth; **silence r.** respectful silence

nm *(moine)* monk, friar

nf religieuse 1 *(nonne)* nun **2** *(gâteau)* cream puff

religion [rəliʒjɔ̃] **nf 1** religion; **avoir de la r.** to be religious; **mourir en r.** to die in the faith; **entrer en r.** to take one's vows; **guerre de r.** war of religion; **la r. chrétienne/juive/bouddhiste** the Christian/Jewish/Buddhist religion *or* faith; **je ne connais pas sa r.** I don't know what religion he is; **est-ce que vous pratiquez une r.?** are you a practising Catholic/Muslim/*etc*? **2** *Fig* religion; **le football est une r. pour certains** football is a religion with some people, some people make a religion out of football; *Arch* **se faire une r. de qch** to make a religion of sth, to make sth a point of conscience; **se faire une r. sur qch** to have made up one's mind about sth

religiosité [rəliʒjozite] **nf** religiousness, *Péj* religiosity

reliquaire [rəliker] **nm** reliquary, shrine

reliquat [rəlika] **nm 1** *(reste)* *(d'argent)* remainder; **r. de compte** account balance; **r. de caisse** cash balance; *Fig Litt* **un r. du passé** a relic of the past **2** *Méd Vieilli (d'une maladie)* aftereffects

relique [rəlik] **nf** *(d'un saint)*, *Fig* relic; **garder qch comme une r.** to treasure sth, to keep sth like a relic; *Litt* **les reliques de sa gloire** the relics *or* remnants of his/her glory

relire [rəlir] *(conj like* **lire**) **vt** *(livre, auteur, ce qu'on a écrit)* to reread, to read (over) again; *(épreuves)* to read; *(vérifier)* to proofread

vpr se relire to read (over) what one has written; **j'ai du mal à me r.** I'm having trouble reading *or* deciphering my own handwriting

reliure [rəljyr] **nf 1** *(activité, art)* bookbinding; **atelier de r.** bindery; **donner un livre à la r.** to send a book for binding *or* to be bound **2** *(couverture)* **r. anglaise** *ou* **en toile** cloth binding; **r. pleine** full leather binding

relocalisation [rələkalizasjɔ̃] **nf** relocation

relogement [rələʒmɑ̃] **nm** rehousing

reloger [rələʒe] **vt** *(conj like* **loger**) to rehouse

relooker [rəluke] *Fam* **vt** to revamp

vpr se relooker to change one's image

relouer [rəlue] **vt 1** *(donner en location)* *(maison etc)* to rent (out) again, *Br* to relet, *Br* to let (out) again (à to) **2** *(prendre en location)* *(maison etc)* to rent again; **nous relouons chaque année le même appartement** we rent *or* take the same flat every year

réluctance [relyktɑ̃s] **nf** *Aut* reluctance

reluire [rəlɥir] **vi** *(conj like* **luire**) *(du parquet, d'un meuble, des chaussures)* to shine, to gleam; *(du métal)* to shine, to gleam, to glitter; **faire r. qch** to polish *or* shine sth (up); **brosse à r.** shoebrush; *Fig Fam* **manier la brosse à r.** to do some soft-soaping *or* buttering-up; **elle sait manier la brosse à r.** she's good at soft-soaping people *or* buttering people up

reluisant [rəlɥizɑ̃] **adj** *(parquet, meuble, chaussures)* shining, gleaming; **r. de propreté** *(sol, parquet, maison etc)* gleaming; *Fig Fam* **ce qu'il a fait n'est pas très r.** *(moralement)* what he did was a bit off; **c'est une perspective peu reluisante** it's hardly a glowing prospect

reluquer [rəlyke] **vt** *Fam (personne, l'argent de qn etc)* to eye; **r. les filles** to eye (up) *or* ogle the girls; **il reluque ta fortune** he's got his eyes on your money, he's only after your money

relutif, -ive [rəlytif, -iv] **adj** *Fin* **avoir un effet r.** to strengthen the equity capital of a company

relution [rəlysjɔ̃] **adj** *Fin* strengthening of equity capital

rem [rem] **nm** *(abrév* **Röntgen equivalent man**) rem

remâcher [rəmɑʃe] **vt** to chew again; *Fig (le passé, une déception)* to brood over *or* about, to chew over

remailler [rəmaje] **vt** *(filet, bas)* to mend; *(pull, chaussette etc)* to darn

remake [rimɛk] **nm** *Cin* remake; **faire un r.** to do a remake

rémanence [remanɑ̃s] **nf** remanence, residual magnetism; *Ordinat (de l'affichage)* afterglow; *Opt* **r. des images visuelles** persistence of vision

rémanent [remanɑ̃] **adj** *(en magnétisme)* *Élec* residual, remanent; *Opt* **image rémanente** after-image

remanger [rəmɑ̃ʒe] **vt** *(conj like* **manger**) to eat again; **j'en ai remangé** I had some more; **je n'en ai jamais remangé** I've never eaten any since *or* again

remaniement [rəmanimɑ̃] **nm 1** *(d'un texte, discours, d'une politique)* reworking, revising, rejigging; **procéder au r. d'un texte** to rework *or* revise *or* rejig a text **2** *(changement)* alteration, modification; **apporter des remaniements à un ouvrage** to make changes to a work; *Pol* **r. ministériel** cabinet reshuffle; **r. du personnel** staff reshuffle

remanier [rəmanje] **vt** *(impf, pr sub* **n. remaniions**) *(texte, discours etc)* to rework, to revise, to rejig; *(équipe)* to make changes in, to reshuffle, to rejig; *Pol (gouvernement)* to reshuffle

remaquiller [rəmakije] **vt r. qn** to make sb up again

VPR se remaquiller *(de nouveau)* to make oneself up again; *(en retouchant)* to touch up one's make-up; **depuis peu, je me remaquille** I've started wearing make-up again recently

remarcher [rəmarʃe] **VI 1** *(d'une personne)* to walk again; **elle ne remarchera plus** she won't walk again **2** *(d'une machine etc)* to work again; **Fam ça a l'air de bien r. entre eux** they seem to have worked things out

remariage [rəmarjaʒ] **NM** remarriage

remarier [rəmarje] **VT r. sa fille** to marry off one's daughter again; **ils espéraient bien r. leur fille** they really hoped to see their daughter married again
VPR se remarier to remarry, to marry or get married again; **se r. avec qn** to remarry sb

remarquable [rəmarkabl] **ADJ** *(changement, résultat, progrès, invention, personne etc)* remarkable; *(événement, livre)* remarkable, noteworthy (**par** for); **les faits remarquables de la semaine** the highlights or outstanding events of the week; **d'un courage r.** remarkably brave; **elle est r. par sa ou de patience/beauté** she is remarkably patient/beautiful; **il est r. qu'il n'ait rien entendu** it's remarkable or strange that he heard nothing

remarquablement [rəmarkabləmã] **ADV** *(bon, mauvais, bien, changer, progresser etc)* remarkably; **danser/cuisiner r.** to dance/cook remarkably well, to be a remarkably good or an outstanding dancer/cook

remarque [rəmark] **NF** *(observation)* remark; **faire une r.** to make or pass a remark; *(critique)* to pass a remark; **cette r. t'était destinée** that was aimed at you, that was a dig at you; **elle a fait la r. que ...** she remarked that ...; **faire la r. de qch** to remark on sth; **je dois lui en faire la r.** I must point it out or remark on it to him; **tu sais, je m'en étais fait la r.** it had crossed my mind, you know; **texte avec remarques** text with notes or comments; **Litt digne de r.** noteworthy

remarqué [rəmarke] **ADJ entrée/absence très remarquée** conspicuous entrance/absence; **discours très r.** speech that attracted considerable attention; **c'est un fait souvent/peu r.** it's a well-known/little-known fact

remarquer [rəmarke] **VT 1** *(constater, voir)* to notice; **r. qn dans la foule** to notice or spot sb in the crowd; **il est entré sans que je le remarque** he came in without me noticing (him); **elle a été remarquée par un réalisateur de télévision** she was spotted or noticed by a television director; **je n'ai pas remarqué son absence** I didn't notice his/her absence, I didn't miss him/her; **je remarque que personne n'en a parlé** I notice or note that no one has spoken about it; **faire r. qch à qn** to point sth out to sb, to call sb's attention to sth; **je te ferai juste r. que tu devais être là à sept heures** you should have been here at seven o'clock, you know; **je vous ferai r. que ...** I'll have you know that ...; **je te ferai r. que c'est encore moi qui ai fait la vaisselle!** just in case you hadn't noticed, it was me that did the dishes again!; **se faire r.** to attract attention, to get noticed; **il est entré sans se faire r.** he came in unobtrusively or without attracting attention, he came in without anybody noticing; **je ne voudrais pas me faire r.** I don't want to attract attention or to make myself conspicuous; **Fam remarque, il n'est pas le seul** he's not the only one, mind (you)
2 *(dire)* to remark, to observe
VPR se remarquer *(d'une tache, d'une cicatrice, d'un sentiment etc)* to show, to be noticeable; **sa déception se remarquait** his/her disappointment showed, he/she was noticeably disappointed; **cela se remarque à**

peine it hardly shows, you hardly notice it; **elle était amoureuse de lui, ça a fini par se r.** she was in love with him and it became obvious; **ça ne se remarquera pas** it won't show, it won't be noticed

> Il faut noter que le verbe anglais **to remark** est un faux ami. Il ne signifie jamais **s'apercevoir de**; il signifie uniquement **faire remarquer**.

remastériser [rəmasterize] **VT** to remaster

remballage [rãbalaʒ] **NM** repacking

remballer [rãbale] **VT** *(marchandises)* to repack, to pack (up) again; *(cadeau)* to wrap (up) again, to rewrap; *Fig Fam* **r. la marchandise** to take out, to clear out; *Fig Fam* **tu peux r. les compliments** you can keep your compliments to yourself

rembarquement [rãbarkəmã] **NM** *(des passagers, des troupes)* re-embarking, re-embarkation; *(de marchandises)* reshipping, reshipment

rembarquer [rãbarke] **VT** *(passagers, troupes)* to re-embark; *(marchandises)* to reship; *(bateau)* to hoist in
VI to re-embark, to go on board again
VPR se rembarquer to re-embark, to go on board again

rembarrer [rãbare] **VT** *Fam* **r. qn** to tell sb where to go, to put sb (firmly) in his/her place; **se faire r.** to get told where to go, to get put (firmly) in one's place

remblai [rãblɛ] **NM** *Constr* **1** *(action)* *(avec de la terre etc)* backfilling; *(pour levée de terre)* embanking, banking (up) **2** *(terre etc)* backfill **3** *(levée de terre)* embankment, bank; **route en r.** (em)banked road

remblayage [rãblɛjaʒ] **NM** = **remblai 1**

remblayer [rãbleje] **VT** (**je remblaie, je remblaye, n. remblayons; je remblaierai, je remblayerai**) *Constr* **1** *(partie effondrée du sol)* to fill (up), to pack **2** *(pour levée de terre)* *(route, voie ferrée)* to embank, to bank (up)

rembobinage [rãbɔbinaʒ] **NM** *(de film etc)* rewinding

rembobiner [rãbɔbine] **VT** *(film, ruban de machine à écrire, cassette)* to rewind
VPR se rembobiner to rewind

remboîtage [rãbwataʒ] **NM** *(d'un livre)* recasing

remboîtement [rãbwatmã] **NM 1** *(d'un livre)* recasing **2** *Chir (d'un os déplacé)* putting back into place, *Spéc* reduction

remboîter [rãbwate] **VT 1** *(livre)* to recase **2** *(pièces etc)* to reassemble, to fit together again **3** *Chir (os déplacé)* to put back into place, *Spéc* to reduce

rembourrage [rãburaʒ] **NM** *(action, matériau)* stuffing

rembourrer [rãbure] **VT** *(chaise, matelas, coussin etc)* to stuff; *(épaulettes)* to pad; **bien rembourré** *(coussin, fauteuil)*, *Fig Fam (personne)* well-padded

remboursable [rãbursabl] **ADJ** *(dépenses, billet)* refundable; *(rente, obligation)* redeemable; *(crédit)* repayable; **les coupons sont remboursables en espèces** coupons are redeemable for cash

remboursement [rãbursəmã] **NM** *(des dépenses)* reimbursement, refund; *(d'une rente, d'une obligation)* redemption; *(d'un crédit)* repayment; **procéder au r. des frais** to refund or reimburse expenses; **obtenir le r. de ses frais de déplacement** to get one's travelling expenses reimbursed or refunded or paid; **r. anticipé** early repayment; **r. garanti** satisfaction or your money back; **r. in fine** bullet repayment; **emprunt de r.** refunding loan; **livraison contre r.** payment or cash on delivery, COD

rembourser [rãburse] **VT** *(dépenses)* to reimburse, to refund; *(achat)* to refund; *(rente, obligation)* to redeem, to pay off; *(crédit, dettes, prêt)* to repay, to pay back; *(coupon)* to redeem; **ce médicament est remboursé à 70%** 70% of the cost of this medicine will be refunded; **est-ce que vous êtes remboursé à 100%?** are you entitled to a full refund?; **r. qn de qch** to reimburse sb for sth; **r. qn de ses frais ou dépenses** to reimburse or refund or pay sb's expenses; **je peux te r. demain?** can I pay you back tomorrow?; **puis-je être remboursé?** *(dans un magasin etc)* can I have or get my money back or a refund?; **je me suis fait r., on m'a remboursé** I got my money back, I got a refund; *Théâtre Fam* **remboursez!** give us our money back!
VPR se rembourser to get one's money back; **elle s'est remboursée dans la caisse** she paid herself back out of the till

rembrunir [rãbrynir] **VT** *Litt (assemblée)* to cast a gloom over
VPR se rembrunir 1 *(d'un visage)* to cloud over; **elle s'est rembrunie** her face darkened, she scowled **2** *Litt (du ciel)* to cloud over, to grow dark

remède [rəmɛd] **NM** *Méd, Fig* remedy, cure (**à, de, contre** for); **c'est un bon r. contre la douleur** it's a good painkiller; **le r. est pire que le mal** the cure is worse than the disease; **r. de bonne femme** old wives' remedy; **r. de cheval** kill-or-cure remedy; **c'est sans r.** it is beyond remedy; **porter r. à qch** to find a remedy or cure for sth; *Prov* **aux grands maux les grands remèdes** desperate times call for desperate measures; *Fig Fam* **c'est un r. contre l'amour** she's/he's/it's a real turn-off

remédier [rəmedje] **VI** *(impf, pr sub n. remédiions)* **r. à** *(erreur, situation)* to remedy, to put right; *(problème)* to remedy, to cure; *(manque)* to remedy; *Méd (maladie)* to cure; *(inconvénient)* to compensate for, to make up for; *(abus)* to right

remembrement [rəmãbrəmã] **NM** *Admin (de terres)* re-allocation, regrouping

remembrer [rəmãbre] **VT** *Admin (terres)* to re-allocate, to regroup

remémorer [rəmemɔre] **VT r. qch à qn** to remind sb of sth
VPR se remémorer se r. qch to remember sth, to recall sth

remerciement [rəmɛrsimã] **NM** remerciements thanks; *(dans un livre)* acknowledgements; **avoir quelques paroles de r.** to say a few words of thanks; **lettre de r.** thank-you letter, letter of thanks; **faire ses remerciements à qn pour qch** to thank sb for sth; **tous mes remerciements à vos parents** (give) my thanks to your parents; **remerciements anticipés** with thanks in advance; **je crois que j'ai droit à un r.** ou **des remerciements** I deserve a thank-you VOIR GRAMMAIRE A10

remercier [rəmɛrsje] **VT** *(impf, pr sub n. remerciions)* **1** *(dire merci à)* to thank (**de, pour** for); **je vous remercie de m'avoir aidé** thank you for helping me; **je remercie Dieu/le ciel de m'avoir épargné la souffrance** I thank God/Heaven for having spared my suffering; **il me remercia d'un sourire** he smiled his thanks, he thanked me with a smile; **remerciez-les bien de ma part** thank them very much for me; **comment vas-tu? – très bien, je te remercie** how are you? – very well, thank you; **(non,) je vous remercie** no thank you; *Iron* **c'est ainsi qu'il nous remercie!** that's how he thanks us!, that's all the thanks we get! **2** *(congédier)* *(employé)* to dismiss; **se faire r.** to be dismissed, *Iron* to be thanked for one's services

réméré [remere] **NM** *Com* repurchase

remettant [rəmɛtã] **NM** *Fin* remitter

remetteur, -euse [rəmɛtœr, -øz] *Fin* ADJ *(banque etc)* remitting

N remitter

REMETTRE [rəmɛtr] *(conj like* **mettre***)*

> VT to put back 1 ▪ to put back on 4 ▪ to add 5 ▪ to deliver 6 ▪ to submit 6 ▪ to hand in 6 ▪ to hand over 6 ▪ to postpone 8 ▪ to put off 8
> VPR to start again 2 ▪ to recover 3 ▪ to rely on *(s'en remettre à)* 4

VT **1** *(replacer)* to put back; **r. qch à sa place** *ou* **en place** to replace sth, to put sth back in its place *or* where it belongs; **n'oublie pas de le r. à sa place** don't forget to put it back (again); *Fig Fam* **r. qn à sa place** to put sb in his/her place; **se faire r. à sa place** to get put in one's place; **r. un os en place** to put a bone back in place, *Spéc* to reduce a bone; *Fam* **r. les idées en place à qn** to bring sb to their senses; *Ftbl* **r. le ballon en jeu** to throw the ball (back) in(to play); *Tennis* **balle à r.** let (ball); **r. un manche à un balai** to put a new handle on a broom; **r. un bouton à un manteau** to sew a button on a coat; **r. une doublure à un habit** to reline a coat; *Fam* **je n'y ai plus jamais remis les pieds** I never set foot in there again; **qu'il ne remette jamais les pieds ici!** I don't want him ever setting foot in here again!; **r. qn sur le trône** to restore sb to the throne; **r. qn sur son chemin** *ou* **sur la bonne voie** to set sb on his/her way *or* on the right path; **r. qch en cause** *ou* **en question** to question sth, to raise questions *or* doubts about sth, to call sth into question; **r. qn en liberté** to set sb free; **on l'a remis en liberté, il a été remis en liberté** he was set free, he was freed *or* released; **r. qn à l'école/en prison** to send sb back to school/prison; **r. un malade à l'hôpital** to readmit a patient to hospital; *Fam* **on ne pourra r. l'eau/le gaz/le téléphone avant demain** we can't connect the water/gas/telephone (up) again until tomorrow; *Ordinat* **r. en forme** *(texte)* to reformat

2 *(rappeler)* to recall, to recollect; **il faut le lui r. en mémoire** he'll have to be reminded of it; *Fml* **je ne vous remets pas** I can't quite place you

3 *(dans un état antérieur)* **r. qn de bonne humeur** to put sb in a good mood again, to bring sb round; **r. à zéro** to reset, to zero; **r. qch en usage** to bring sth back; **r. en ordre** *(dossiers, maison)* to tidy (up); **r. de l'ordre dans sa chambre** to tidy (up) one's bedroom; **r. de l'ordre dans sa vie** to get one's life straightened out; **r. qch en service** to repair sth; **l'ascenseur sera remis en service demain** the lift will be back in service tomorrow; **r. en état** *(auto, machine)* to repair; *(maison)* to restore; **r. à neuf** to do up (like new); **r. en marche** *(moteur, machine)* to restart; **r. le contact** to start the engine again; **r. qn en forme** to get sb back on form; **r. qn sur pied** to restore sb to health, to get sb back on his/her feet again; **r. qn à flot** to put sb back on his/her feet again; *Couture* **r. un vêtement à plat** to alter a garment by unpicking and laying all the pieces out flat before restitching; *Arch Fig* **r. l'esprit de qn** to assuage sb

4 *(mettre de nouveau)* *(vêtement)* to put back on, to put on again; *(chauffage)* to turn *or* put back on *or* on again; *(télévision, radio)* to turn *or* switch back on *or* on again; *(disque, chanson, musique)* to put back on *or* on again; **ne remets pas cette veste demain** don't put that jacket on *or* don't wear that jacket again tomorrow; **nous avons décidé de r. de la moquette dans le salon** we've decided to carpet the living room again

5 *(ajouter)* *(sel, eau)* to add *(dans* to*)*; **je remets quelques pommes de terre** I'll add

some potatoes, I'll put in some more potatoes; **r. de l'argent sur un compte** to pay money into an account; *Fam* **tu devrais r. un peu d'eau à cette plante** you should give that plant a bit more water

6 *(donner)* *(lettre, télégramme, colis etc)* to deliver; *(formulaire)* to send in; *(rapport)* to submit; **r. sa démission** to hand in *or Fml* tender one's resignation; **r. qch en mains propres** to deliver sth in person; **r. qn à la justice** *ou* **entre les mains de la police** to hand *or* turn sb over to the police; **r. son âme à Dieu** to commit one's soul to God; **je remets mon sort entre vos mains** my fate is in your hands; **r. sa charge à qn** to hand over one's duties to sb; **r. une somme à qn** to send *or Fin Fml* to remit a sum to sb; **r. à l'encaissement** to remit for collection; **r. à l'escompte** to remit for discount

7 *(faire grâce de, pardonner)* *(dette)* to cancel; *(peine)* to remit; *(faute)* to pardon, to forgive

8 *(différer)* *(réunion etc)* to postpone, to put off *(à* to, till*)*; **r. une dette** *(à plus tard)* to defer (payment of) a debt; *Jur* **r. une cause à huitaine** to adjourn *or* remand a case for a week; **r. qch à plus tard** to put sth off (till later); *Échecs etc* **partie remise** draw, drawn game; *Fig* **ce n'est que partie remise** we'll do it some other time, there'll be another time for it; **il ne faut jamais r. à plus tard ce qu'on peut faire le jour même** never put off till tomorrow what you can do today; **arrête de r. les choses au lendemain** stop putting things off till tomorrow, stop procrastinating

9 *Fam (recommencer)* **on remet ça?** how about another (one)?; **garçon, remettez-nous ça!** (the) same again!; **il faudra r. ça** we must do it again sometime; **tu ne vas pas r. ça!** you're not going to start that again, are you?

10 *Fam* **en r.** to lay it on (a bit) thick

11 *Belg, Suisse (céder)* to sell; **ils ont remis leur boutique** they gave up their shop

12 *Belg (vomir)* to vomit

13 *Belg (rendre) (monnaie)* **il m'a remis trois euros** he gave me three euros change

VPR **se remettre 1** *(se mettre de nouveau dans un endroit, dans un état)* **se r. au lit** to go back to bed; **se r. en route** to set off again; **le temps se remet (au beau)** the weather is clearing up (again); **se r. en selle** to get back in the saddle; **se r. en cause** *ou* to question oneself; *Fam* **se r. avec qn** to go back to sb again; *Fam* **se r. ensemble** *(époux, amants)* to get back together again

2 *(recommencer)* **se r. au travail** *ou* à travailler to start *or* set to work again; **elle s'est remise à boire** she's (started) drinking again; **se r. au français/au tennis** to take up French/tennis again; **se r. au régime** to go back on one's diet

3 *(d'une maladie, d'un choc)* to recover; **il lui faudra un certain temps pour se r.** it will take her some time to recover *or* to get over it; *Fam* **voyons, remettez-vous!** come on, pull yourself together!; *Fig* **elle ne s'en est pas remise** she couldn't get over it

4 *(se reposer sur)* **s'en r. à qn de qch** to rely on sb for sth; **s'en r. à la discrétion/au jugement de qn** to rely on sb's discretion/judgement; **je m'en remets à vous** I'll leave it to you, it's up to you; **je m'en remets totalement à vous** I have complete confidence *or* faith in you; **je m'en remets à votre avis** I'm leaving the decision entirely to you

---

remeubler [rəmœble] VT *(maison etc)* to refurnish

VPR **se remeubler** to refurnish one's house/flat

remilitarisation [rəmilitarizasjɔ̃] NF remilitarization

remilitariser [rəmilitarize] VT to remilitarize

VPR **se remilitariser** to become remilitarized

réminiscence [reminisɑ̃s] NF **1** *Phil, Psy* reminiscence **2** *(souvenir vague)* vague recollection; **il y a des réminiscences de Mozart dans ce morceau** there are echoes of Mozart in this piece, this piece is reminiscent of Mozart

remise [rəmiz] NF **1** *(dans son lieu ou son état d'origine)* *Ftbl* **r. en jeu** throw-in; *Rugby* **r. en jeu à la touche** line-out; **r. en état** *(d'une maison)* restoration; **r. à neuf** *(d'appareils ménagers, d'une voiture etc)* reconditioning; **r. en ordre** *(de dossiers, d'une maison)* tidying up, putting in order; *Ordinat* **r. en forme** *(de texte)* reformatting; *Ordinat* **r. à blanc** *(d'une disquette)* reformatting; **r. en marche** *(d'un moteur)* restarting; *(d'un projet)* relaunching; **r. en question** doubting, questioning; **ses remises en question continuelles** his/her constant doubts *or* questioning

2 *(fait de donner)* *(d'une lettre, rançon etc)* delivery; **payable contre r. du coupon** payable on presentation of the coupon; **r. des clefs** *(d'un appartement etc)* handing over of the keys; *Scol* **r. des prix** prizegiving

3 *(fait de pardonner)* *(d'une dette, d'un impôt)* cancellation; *(de peine)* reduction; **faire r. d'une dette** to cancel a debt; **bénéficier d'une r. de peine** to be granted a reduction in one's sentence, to have one's sentence reduced

4 *Fin* remittance; **faire une r. (de fonds) à qn** to send sb a remittance; *Com* **r. d'effets** remittance of bills; **r. de fonds** remittance of funds; **r. documentaire** documentary remittance; **r. à vue** demand deposit

5 *(rabais)* discount, reduction, allowance; *(pour paiement anticipé)* settlement discount; **r. sur marchandises** trade discount; **r. de caisse** cash discount, cash rebate; **r. de fidélité au client** loyal-customer discount; **r. pour quantité** quantity discount; **r. promotionnelle** promotional allowance; **r. de marchandisage** merchandising allowance; *Mktg* **r. psychologique** psychological discount; **r. quantitative** bulk discount; **r. saisonnière** seasonal discount; **r. sur les prix** price discount; **faire une r. sur un article** to allow a discount *or* make a reduction on an article; **r. d'usage** trade discount

6 *(appentis)* shed, outhouse; *Rail* engine shed; *(pour carrosses)* coach house; **voiture de (grande) r.** hired car (with chauffeur); **(voiture de) r.** *(carrosse)* hired *or* livery carriage

7 *(ajournement)* postponement; **faire qch sans r.** to do sth without fail; **r. d'une dette** deferment of (payment of) a debt

remiser [rəmize] VT **1** *(voiture, valise, vélo etc)* to put away **2** *Fam (rembarrer)* **r. qn** to put sb in his/her place, to take sb down a peg or two; **se faire r.** to get put in one's place, to get taken down a peg or two

remisier [rəmizje] NM *Bourse* half-commission man, intermediate broker

rémissible [remisibl] ADJ remissible

rémission [remisjɔ̃] NF **1** *(d'un péché, d'une dette)* remission; *Fig* **sans r.** *(travailler)* unremittingly; *(payer, punir qn)* without delay **2** *Méd (d'une maladie)* remission; *(de la douleur)* abatement; *(de la fièvre)* remission, abatement; **être en r.** to be in remission

rémittent [remitɑ̃] ADJ *Méd* remittent

remix [rəmiks] NM *(disque)* remix

remixer [rəmikse] VT *(disque)* to remix

remmailler [rɑ̃maje] VT = **remailler**

remmener [rɑ̃mne] VT *(conj like* **mener***)* *(au point de départ)* to take back; **il fut remmené en prison** he was taken back to prison; **r. un**

enfant au zoo to take a child to the zoo again or back to the zoo; **r. qn en voiture** to drive sb back

remodelage [rəmɔdlaʒ] NM **1** remodelling **2** *(réorganisation)* restructuring

remodeler [rəmɔdle] VT *(conj like* **modeler***)* **1** *(refaçonner)* to remodel **2** *(réorganiser)* to restructure

rémois, -oise [remwa, -waz] ADJ *(population, architecture, école)* of Rheims; *(écrivain)* from Rheims
N **R.** *(natif)* native of Rheims; *(habitant)* inhabitant of Rheims

remontage [rəmɔ̃taʒ] NM **1** *(d'une horloge, montre)* winding up; montre à r. **automatique** self-winding watch **2** *(assemblage) (des pièces d'un mécanisme etc)* reassembly

remontant [rəmɔ̃tɑ̃] ADJ **1** une boisson remontante a tonic, *Fam* a pick-me-up **2** *(rose)* repeat-flowering
NM tonic, *Fam* pick-me-up

remonte [rəmɔ̃t] NF **1** *(d'un poisson qui fraie)* run; *(d'un bateau qui remonte le courant)* ascent **2** *Mil (de la cavalerie)* remounting; **cheval de r.** remount

remontée [rəmɔ̃te] NF **1** *(d'une colline, rivière etc)* ascent; *(d'un sportif), Fin (d'une monnaie), Fig* recovery; *Sport, Fin, Fig* **faire une belle r.** to make a good recovery **2** *Ski* **r. mécanique** ski lift **3** *Min* raising (to the surface)

remonte-pente, *pl* **remonte-pentes** NM T-bar, ski lift, ski tow

remonter [rəmɔ̃te] VI *(aux usu* être, *sometimes* avoir*)* **1** *(dans l'espace) (d'une personne)* to go/come up again, to go/come back up; *(d'une route, ruelle etc)* to rise again, to climb again; *(d'un soutien-gorge, d'une jupe)* to ride up; *(de la marée)* to flow; **je suis remonté lui parler** I went upstairs again or back upstairs to speak to him/her; **je suis remonté pour vous dire que …** I've come back upstairs to tell you that …; **r. dans sa chambre** to go back up to one's room; **r. sur son cheval** to remount one's horse, to get back up on one's horse; **je ne suis jamais remonté sur un cheval depuis** I've never been on a horse again since; **r. (à cheval)** *(après en être descendu)* to remount one's horse, to get back up on one's horse; *(refaire du cheval)* to ride again, to go riding again; **r. à bicyclette** to get back on one's bike, to remount (one's bicycle); **je n'étais pas remontée sur des skis depuis dix ans** I hadn't been on skis for ten years; **r. en voiture** to get back in one's car, to get into one's car again; **r. à la surface** to resurface, to come back up to the surface; **r. vers la source de la rivière** to go upstream; **r. dans l'estime de qn** to go up or rise again in sb's estimation; **r. dans les sondages** to improve one's position or go up in the polls; **r. au classement** to go up in the ranking; *Ftbl* to move up the league or division; *Naut* **r. au** *ou* **dans le vent** to beat up to windward
2 *(dans le temps)* to go back (**à** to); **cette dette remonte à plusieurs années** this debt dates back or goes back several years; **une amitié qui remonte au déluge** a friendship that is as old as the hills
3 *(s'accroître de nouveau) (des actions, d'une monnaie, de la température)* to go up again, to rise again, to climb again; *(d'un baromètre)* to rise again; *Fig Fam* **ses actions remontent** things are looking up for him/her, his/her stock is rising
VT *(aux* avoir*)* **1** *(colline, escaliers etc)* to go/come or climb back up, to go/come or climb up again; **j'ai remonté la colline/l'escalier** *(je suis en bas)* I went or climbed back up the hill/the stairs, I went or climbed up the hill/ stairs again; *(je suis en haut)* I came or

climbed back up the hill/the stairs, I came or climbed up the hill/stairs again; **r. la rue** to go back up the street; **r. la rivière** to go upstream; *(d'un poisson)* to run upstream; **r. une rivière en canoë** to canoe up a river; **r. une pente en canard** to herringbone up a slope; *Fig* **r. la pente** *(financièrement)* to get back on one's feet (again); **il a eu du mal à r. la pente** *(moralement)* he found it difficult to pull himself out of it
2 *(hausser etc) (étagère, poster)* to move up; *(pantalon, jupe)* to pull up, to hitch up; *(pull, manche, chaussettes)* to pull up; *(fermeture à glissière)* to do up, to pull up; *(vitre de voiture)* to close, to wind or roll up; *Min (mineurs, charbon)* to raise; **puisque tu es à la cave, peux-tu r. une bouteille de vin?** since you're in the cellar, can you bring up a bottle of wine?; **peux-tu m'aider à r. cette malle dans la cuisine?** can you help me take this trunk up to the kitchen?; **peux-tu m'aider à r. ma fermeture?** help me with my zip, will you?
3 *Mil (cavalerie)* to remount, to provide fresh mounts for
4 r. une horloge/montre to wind (up) or rewind a clock/watch; **r. le moral à qn** to cheer sb up, to lift or raise sb's spirits; **ça m'a remonté le moral** it cheered me up or made me feel a bit more cheerful or gave me a lift; **un verre de vin vous remontera** a glass of wine will cheer you up or do you good
5 *(assembler) (pièces d'une machine etc)* to put together again, to reassemble
6 *(magasin)* to restock; *(garde-robe)* to replenish
7 *Théâtre (pièce)* to put on again, to revive
VPR **se remonter 1 se r. en vin/café/linge de maison** to stock up on wine/coffee/household linen; **j'ai dû me r. en vêtements** I had to buy a whole new wardrobe **2** *(moralement)* to cheer up, to recover one's spirits; *(physiquement)* to recover one's strength; **j'ai pris un petit whisky pour me r.** I had a small whisky to revive my spirits or cheer me up

remontoir [rəmɔ̃twar] NM *(de montre)* winder

remontrance [rəmɔ̃trɑ̃s] NF remonstrance; **elle ne me fait jamais aucune r.** she never admonishes me; **remontrances** remonstrations, admonishments; **faire des remontrances à qn** to remonstrate with sb, to admonish sb

remontrer [rəmɔ̃tre] VT **1 r. qch** to show sth again **2 en r. à qn** to give sb a lesson or two; **il en remontrerait à ses professeurs** he could teach or show his teachers a thing or two
VPR **se remontrer** to show oneself or one's face again

rémora [remɔra] NM *(poisson)* remora

remordre [rəmɔrdr] VT to bite again
VI **r. à qch** to take another bite of sth; *Fig* to have another go or stab at sth; *Fig Fam* **r. à l'hameçon** to take the bait again, to fall for it again, to be taken in again by the same trick

remords [rəmɔr] NM remorse; **plein de r.** full of or filled with remorse; **avoir du** *ou* **des r.** to feel remorse; **j'ai des r. de l'avoir laissé partir à pied** I feel bad about leaving him to walk; **une pointe de r.** a twinge of remorse; **je n'ai qu'un r.: celui de ne pas le lui avoir dit** my only regret is that I didn't tell him/her; **des r. de conscience** twinges of conscience; **j'ai des r. de conscience** my conscience is troubling or bothering me; **être bourrelé de r.** to be stricken with remorse; **je n'ai aucun r.!** I'm not the slightest bit sorry!

remorquage [rəmɔrkaʒ] NM *(d'une voiture, remorque, péniche etc)* towing; *(d'un train)* pulling, hauling; **barre de r.** tow bar

remorque [rəmɔrk] NF **1** *(traction)* towing;

prendre un navire/une voiture en *ou* **à la r.** to take a ship/a car in tow, to tow a ship/a car; **vous pourriez me prendre en r.?** could you tow me or give me a tow?; **être en** *ou* **à la r.** to be in or on or under tow; **sortir du port à la r.** to be towed out of harbour; *Fig Péj* **être à la r. de qn** to follow where sb leads; *Fam* **il est toujours à la r.** he's always lagging or trailing behind; **croc de r.** tow hook; **timon de r.** tow bar
2 (câble de) r. towline, towrope; *Naut* **donner la r.** to give or pass the tow line
3 *(bateau)* tow, vessel under tow or being towed
4 *(véhicule)* trailer; **r. de plaisance, r. (de) camping** caravan, *Am* (camping) trailer
5 *Rail* **rame r.** slip portion; **voiture r.** slip coach

remorquer [rəmɔrke] VT *(voiture, remorque, péniche etc)* to tow; *(train)* to pull, to haul; **et puis on m'a remorqué jusqu'au garage** and then I was towed or taken in tow to the garage; **le dépanneur a remorqué la voiture** the breakdown man towed the car away; **se faire r.** to get towed; *Fig* **elle remorque toujours un groupe de fans avec elle** she always has a group of fans in tow or following in her wake

remorqueur, -euse [rəmɔrkœr, -øz] ADJ *(bateau etc)* towing; *Rail (machine)* relief
NM tug (boat); *(avion)* towplane

rémoulade [remulad] NF *Culin* **(sauce) r.** rémoulade (sauce) *(mayonnaise sauce with mustard, herbs etc)*; **céleri r.** celeriac in a rémoulade (sauce)

remoulage [rəmulaʒ] NM *(farine)* bran

rémouleur [remulœr] NM knife grinder

remous [rəmu] NM *(d'une rivière)* eddy; *(d'un bateau)* wash, backwash; *(de la marée)* swirl; *Fig (de la foule)* ripple; **il y eut des r. dans la foule** a ripple ran through the crowd; **r. d'eau** whirlpool; *Aviat* **r. d'air** eddy; *Fig* **provoquer des r.** to cause a stir

rempaillage [rɑ̃pajaʒ] NM *(de vieilles chaises)* reseating, rebottoming

rempailler [rɑ̃paje] VT *(vieille chaise)* to reseat, to rebottom

rempailleur, -euse [rɑ̃pajœr, -øz] N upholsterer

rempaqueter [rɑ̃pakte] VT *(conj like* **paqueter***)* to rewrap, to wrap up again

rempart [rɑ̃par] NM rampart; **remparts** walls; **faire un r. de son corps à qn** to shield sb with one's body; *Fig* **le dernier r. de la démocratie** the last bastion of democracy; *Fig* **le r. de nos libertés** the bulwark or bastion of our liberties

rempiéter [rɑ̃pjete] VT (**je rempiète, n. rempiétons; je rempiéterai**) *Constr (mur)* to underpin

rempiler [rɑ̃pile] VT to stack or pile up again
VI *Mil Fam Hum* to re-enlist; **il a rempilé pour cinq ans** he signed up for five more years

remplaçable [rɑ̃plasabl] ADJ replaceable

remplaçant, -ante [rɑ̃plasɑ̃, -ɑ̃t] N *(personne)* substitute, replacement, stand-in; *Sport (dans une équipe)* reserve, substitute, *Fam* sub; *(d'un médecin, d'un pasteur)* locum (tenens); *Scol* supply teacher, *Am* substitute teacher

remplacement [rɑ̃plasmɑ̃] NM **1** replacement, substitution; **le r. du beurre par la margarine** the replacement of butter by margarine, the substitution of margarine for butter; **en r. de qn/qch** in place of sb/ sth, as a replacement or substitute for sb/ sth; **en r. des heures supplémentaires** in lieu of overtime; **assurer** *ou* **faire un r.** to act as a replacement, to stand in, to cover (**de** for); **dactylo qui fait des remplacements** temporary typist, *Fam* temp; *Scol* **je fais des rem-**

placements I do supply teaching, I'm a supply teacher *or Am* a substitute teacher **2 de r.** *(pneu)* spare; *(valeur, pile)* replacement; **produit de r.** substitute

remplacer [rãplase] *(conj like placer)* VT **1** *(succéder à, tenir lieu de) (personne)* to take the place of, to replace, to take over from; *(chose)* to take the place of, to replace; *(temporairement) (personne)* to stand in for, to substitute for, to act as a substitute for; **si je pouvais me faire r.** if I could get somebody to stand in *or* cover for me *or* to take my place; **je la remplace pendant les vacances** I'm standing in *or* filling in (for her) while she's on holiday **2** *(changer) (vieille voiture, pneu etc)* to replace, to renew; *(objet cassé)* to replace; **r. qch par qch d'autre** to replace sth with *or* by sth else, to put sth else in place of sth; **r. le beurre par de la margarine** to replace butter with margarine, to substitute margarine for butter; **r. un mot par un autre** to replace one word with another

VPR **se remplacer** to be replaceable; **cette pièce se remplace facilement** the part is easy to replace; **un ami comme toi, ça ne se remplace pas** friends like you are irreplaceable *or* can't be replaced, friends like you are hard to come by; **une mère, ça ne se remplace pas** there's no substitute for a mother

remplage [rãplaʒ] NM *Archit (d'une fenêtre gothique)* tracery

rempli [rãpli] ADJ full; **visage (bien) r.** full face; **avoir l'estomac bien r.** to have a full stomach; **r. de qch** full of sth, filled with sth; **tout r. de son importance** full of his/her own importance
NM *Couture* tuck

remplir [rãplir] VT **1** to fill (**de** with); *(verre etc)* to fill (up); *(à nouveau)* to refill; *(espace, trou)* to fill in; *(formulaire etc)* to fill in *or* out, to complete; **elle a déjà rempli dix pages** she has already written *or* filled ten pages; **cela a rempli ma journée** it took up my whole day; **cela ne peut r. votre vie entièrement** it can't be the only thing in your life, it can't take up your entire life; **r. qn de joie/colère** to fill sb with joy/anger; **les étrangers remplissaient la ville** the town was filled with *or* full of strangers; **r. l'air de ses cris** to fill the air with one's cries; **comme toujours, il a rempli la salle** as always, he played to a full house *or* he filled the hall; **le corsage est joli mais tu ne le remplis pas** it's a pretty blouse but you're a bit too thin for it **2** *(promesse)* to fulfil, *Am* to fulfill, to carry out; *(condition)* to meet, to satisfy, to fulfil; *(ordre, instructions)* to carry out; *(devoirs, tâche)* to do, to carry out, to perform; *(rôle, contrat)* to fulfil; **r. son office** to do its job

VPR **se remplir** to fill up; **se r. de qch** to fill with sth; **ses yeux se remplirent de larmes** her eyes filled with tears; **la cuve se remplit mal** the tank isn't filling up properly; *Fig* **se r. les poches** to line one's pockets

remplissage [rãplisaʒ] NM **1** *(d'un tonneau, d'un réservoir)* filling (up); *(d'un trou, d'un espace)* filling (in) **2** *(d'un texte)* padding; **faire du r.** to pad

remplisseuse [rãplisøz] NF *Ind* bottle-filling machine

remploi [rãplwa] NM **1** *(réutilisation)* reuse **2** *Fin* reinvestment

remployer [rãplwaje] VT *(conj like employer)* **1** *(réutiliser)* to reuse **2** *Fin (argent)* to reinvest

remplumer (se) [sərãplyme] VPR **1** *(d'un oiseau)* to get new feathers *or* new plumage **2** *Fig Fam (financièrement)* to be in funds again **3** *Fig Fam (grossir)* to put on weight again, to fill out again

rempocher [rãpɔʃe] VT **r. qch** to put sth back in one's pocket

remporter [rãpɔrte] VT **1** *(reprendre)* to take

back *or* away; **le livreur a remporté la commande** the delivery man took the order away (again) *or* took the order back **2** *(gagner) (prix, titre de champion)* to win, to carry off; *(succès)* to achieve; **r. une victoire** to achieve *or* win a victory, *Fam* to chalk up a win; **c'est lui qui remporte l'avantage** he has gained the advantage

rempotage [rãpɔtaʒ] NM repotting

rempoter [rãpɔte] VT *(plante)* to repot

remprunter [rãprɛ̃te] VT to borrow again

remuant [rəmɥã] ADJ *Péj (personne)* overactive, *Fam* hyper; **elle est très remuante** she can't sit still for a minute

remue-ménage [rəmymenaʒ] NM INV commotion, confusion, hubbub; **faire du r.** *(du bruit)* to make a din; **la nouvelle de sa démission a fait un de ces r.!** the news of his/her resignation caused quite a commotion *or* stir!

remue-méninges [rəmymenɛ̃ʒ] NM INV brainstorming; **un r.** a brainstorming session

remuement [rəmymã] NM *Litt* movement

remuer [rəmɥe] VT **1** *(bouger) (d'une personne) (tête, jambes, lèvres etc)* to move; *(oreilles)* to waggle; *(mobilier)* to move, to shift; *(du vent) (feuilles)* to move, to stir; **la queue** *(d'un chien)* to wag its tail; *Fig* **ne pas r. le petit doigt** not to lift a finger **2** *(mélanger) (sauce, café etc)* to stir; *(sol)* to turn up, to turn over; *Fig (de vieux souvenirs, le passé)* to rake up; **r. la salade** to toss the salad; **r. ciel et terre pour faire qch** to move heaven and earth to do sth **3** *(émouvoir)* **r. qn** *ou* **le cœur de qn** to move sb; **cela m'a profondément remué** it moved me deeply, I found it deeply moving

VI *(d'une personne)* to move, to stir; **ne remue pas tout le temps!** don't fidget!, keep still!; **il est petit, ce garçon, mais qu'est-ce qu'il remue!** he may be just a little boy but gosh he's lively *or* he's got a lot of energy!; **dent qui remue** loose tooth; *Fig* **un pays qui remue et qui se prépare à la révolte** a country stirring in preparation for revolt

VPR **se remuer** *(bouger)* to move, to stir; *Fam (être actif)* to have plenty of get up and go; **il a fallu se r. pour obtenir sa signature** we had to go to great lengths *or* to a lot of trouble to get him to sign; **remue-toi un peu!** get a move on!, shift yourself!, get up off your backside!; **on peut dire qu'il se remue, lui!** he's not just sitting back!

rémunérateur, -trice [remyneratœr, -tris] ADJ *(travail etc)* remunerative, profitable, financially rewarding; *(placement)* interest-bearing

rémunération [remynerasjõ] NF payment, remuneration (**de** for); *(salaire)* pay; **r. de capital** interest on capital; **r. à la commission** commission only; **r. de départ** starting salary

rémunératoire [remyneratwar] ADJ *Jur* granted as remuneration *or* payment

rémunérer [remynere] VT (**je rémunère**, n. **rémunérons; je rémunérerai**) *(personne)* to pay, to remunerate; *(travail, services etc)* to pay for; **avoir un emploi rémunéré** to be gainfully employed, to be in gainful employment; **bien/mal rémunéré** well-/poorly *or* badly paid

renâcler [rənakle] VI **1** *(renifler) (d'un animal)* to snort; *(d'une personne)* to sniff, to snort **2** *(rechigner)* to ba(u)lk (**à** at); **r. à la besogne** *ou* **devant le travail** to be workshy; **il a accepté en renâclant** he accepted grudgingly

renaissance [rənɛsãs] NF **1** *Rel* rebirth **2** *Fig (des lettres, des arts etc)* renaissance, revival; **r. du printemps** reappearance of spring; *Beaux-Arts, Littér* **la R.** the Renaissance
ADJ INV **R.** *(art, château etc)* Renaissance

renaissant [rənɛsã] ADJ **1** *(force)* reviving; *(économie, industrie)* reviving, *Fml* renascent; *(passion)* reawakening **2** *(de la Renaissance)* (of the) Renaissance

renaître [rənɛtr] VI *(conj like naître, but pp* **rené** *and compound tenses not in use, and p hist* **je renaquis** *rare)* **1** *Rel* to be born again; **ville qui renaît de ses cendres** town that is rising again from its ashes; **r. à la vie** to come back to life, to take on a new lease of life; **c'est ce qui l'a fait r. à la vie** that's what brought him/her back to life; **r. à la joie/au bonheur** to know what it is to feel joy/happiness again **2** *(réapparaître) (d'une industrie, des arts etc)* to revive; *(de l'espoir)* to revive, to be reborn; *Litt (du printemps, des plantes)* to return, to reappear; *(de la nature)* to reawaken; **faire r. les espérances de qn** to revive sb's hopes, to get sb's hopes up again; **faire r. la confiance** to restore confidence

rénal, -e, -aux, -ales [renal, -o] ADJ *Anat* renal; **calcul r.** kidney stone; **insuffisance rénale** renal insufficiency

renard [rənar] NM **1** *(animal)* fox; **r. argenté** silver fox; **la chasse au r.** fox-hunting; *Fig* **c'est un fin/vieux r.** he's as sly as a fox/he's a sly old devil **2** *(fourrure)* fox *(fur)* **3** *Tech (dans une chaudière, un barrage etc)* leak, fissure

renarde [rənard] NF vixen

renardeau, -eaux [rənardo] NM fox cub

renardière [rənardjɛr] NF **1** *(tanière)* foxhole, *(fox's)* earth **2** *Can (élevage)* fox farm

renauder [rənode] VI *très Fam Vieilli (se plaindre)* to grouse, to grumble

rencaissage [rãkɛsaʒ] NM replanting *(of container-grown plant)*

rencaissement [rãkɛsmã] NM *(d'argent)* putting back (in the till)

rencaisser [rãkɛse] VT **1** *(plante)* to replant **2** *(de l'argent)* to put back in the till

rencard, rencart [rãkar] NM = **rancard**

rencarder [rãkarde] VT = **rancarder**

renchérir [rãʃerir] VT *(rendre plus cher)* to make dearer, to raise the price of; *(prix)* to raise

VI **1** *(augmenter) (des prix, des loyers)* to go up; *(des marchandises)* to go up, to get dearer **2** *(dire ou faire plus qu'un autre)* to go one better (**sur** than); **'un homme fort aimable', renchérit-elle** 'a most likeable man', she added **3** *(aux enchères)* to make a higher bid

renchérissement [rãʃerismã] NM *(de marchandises)* rise *or* increase in price; *(de prix, loyers)* rise, increase (**de** in)

rencogner [rãkɔɲe] *Fam Vieilli* VT to push *or* drive into a corner
VPR **se rencogner** to huddle up

rencontre [rãkõtr] NF **1** *(de personnes)* meeting, encounter; *(de courants)* meeting; *(de routes)* junction; *(entre deux voitures)* collision; *(de circonstances)* conjunction; **faire la r. de qn** to meet sb; **aller à la r. de qn** to go to meet sb; **faire une mauvaise r.** to have an unpleasant encounter; **point de r.** meeting point; **club de rencontres** dating agency; **des rencontres culturelles** cultural festivals *(intended to encourage cultural cross-fertilization)*; *Pol* **r. au sommet** summit (meeting *or* conference) **2** *(d'adversaires)* encounter, meeting; *Sport* match, meeting; *surtout Am* meet; *Boxe* fight; *Vieilli (duel)* duel; *Mil* **une r. avec l'ennemi** a brush *or* skirmish with the enemy **3** **r. de pétrole** strike *or* striking of oil

rencontrer [rãkõtre] VT **1** *(par hasard) (personne)* to meet, to come across, *Fam* to bump *or* run into, *Fml* to encounter; *(thème, plante, arbre)* to come *or* run across, to encounter; *(opposition, difficulté etc)* to encounter, to meet with, to run into, to come

up against; *(obstacle)* to encounter, to come up against; **r. qn par hasard** to run *or* come across sb, *Fam* to bump *or* run into sb; **mon travail m'amène à r. beaucoup de gens** I get to meet a lot of people in my job, my job brings me into contact with a lot of people; **r. l'ennemi** to encounter the enemy; **r. les yeux de qn** to meet sb's eyes; **sa main rencontra quelque chose de froid** his/her hand came up against *or* met something cold; **c'est un ami comme on n'en rencontre plus** he's the sort of friend you don't find any more **2** *(avoir un rendez-vous avec)* to meet; *(disputer un match contre)* to meet, to play against; **je vais le r. ce matin** I'll be meeting him *or Am* meeting with him this morning
VPR se rencontrer 1 *(de gens, de rivières)*, *Sport (d'équipes etc)* to meet; **leurs yeux se rencontrèrent** their eyes met
2 *(se heurter)* to collide, to run into each other **3** *(se trouver)* to occur, to be found **4** *(être d'accord) (de personnes)* to agree; *Hum* **les grands esprits se rencontrent** great minds think alike

rendement [rɑ̃dmɑ̃] **NM 1** *(d'une terre, d'une mine, d'un impôt)* yield; *(d'un investissement)* return, profit, yield; **actions à gros r.** high-yielding shares; **r. réel** inflation-adjusted yield **2** *(de travailleurs)* output; *(d'une usine)* output, production; *(d'un ordinateur)* throughput; **un ouvrier qui a un bon/mauvais r.** a workman whose productivity is good/bad; **travailler à plein r.** *(d'une usine)* to work at full capacity **3** *(d'une machine, d'un moteur)* output, performance, efficiency; **travailler à plein r.** *(d'une machine)* to work at full load; **machine à grand r.** heavy-duty machine; **r. mécanique** mechanical efficiency; **r. thermodynamique** thermodynamic efficiency **4** *Sport* **r. de temps/distance** time/distance handicap

rendez-vous [rɑ̃devu] **NM INV 1** *(rencontre)* appointment; *(d'amoureux)* date, *Hum* rendezvous; *Mil* rendezvous; **votre r. est arrivé** your client/patient/*etc* is here; **donner (un) r. à qn** to arrange to meet sb, to make a date with sb; **prendre r. avec qn/un r. chez le coiffeur** to make an appointment with sb/at the hairdresser's; **j'ai (un) r. à une heure** *(avec un ami)* I'm meeting someone at one o'clock; *(avec un collègue, le médecin, le coiffeur etc)* I have an appointment at *or* for one o'clock; **prendre un r. chez le dentiste** to make an appointment with the dentist; **'ne reçoit que sur r.'** 'by appointment only'; **être en r.** to be in a meeting; **lieu de r.: devant l'église** meet in front of the church; **quel est le lieu du r.?** where are we/they/*etc* meeting?, what's the meeting place?; **le soleil était au r.** the sun was shining **2** *(endroit)* (favourite) meeting place, haunt; **c'est le r. des artistes/musiciens** it's a favourite haunt of artists/musicians
▸▸**r. d'affaires** business meeting *or* appointment; **r. de chasse** meet; **r. citoyen =** short training course due to be introduced following the abolition of the military service in France, emphasizing civic education and defence; **r. social** meeting between employers and unions

rendormir [rɑ̃dɔrmir] *(conj like* **dormir)** **VT** to send to sleep again
VPR se rendormir to fall asleep again, to go (back) (off) to sleep again, to drop (back) off to sleep again

RENDRE [rɑ̃dr]

> **VT** ▪ to give back **1** ▪ to return **1, 2** ▪ to vomit **3** ▪ to surrender **4** ▪ to give out **8** ▪ to render **10** ▪ to make **11**
> **VPR** to go **1** ▪ to surrender **2**
> **VI** to be productive **1** ▪ to vomit **3**

VT 1 *(restituer, rapporter) (objet emprunté ou pris à qn)* to give back, to return; *(argent)* to repay, to pay back; *(achat)* to take back, to return; *(copies, interrogation, cadeau)* to give back, to return; **elle est venue r. le téléviseur** she brought the television back; **il faut lui r. la** *ou* **sa liberté** he must be given his freedom *or* set free; **l'enfant fut rendu à sa famille** the child was handed back to his family; **les soldes ne peuvent être rendus** sale goods are non-returnable; **r. la vie à qn** to bring sb back to life; **r. le repos à qn,** *Litt* **r. qn au repos** to restore sb's peace of mind; **r. la parole à qn** to hand back over to sb; **r. sa parole à qn** to release sb from his commitment; **r. la vue à qn** to restore sb's sight; **cela m'a rendu des forces** it gave me back my strength; **les médecins sont parvenus à lui r. l'usage de sa main** the doctors managed to give him/her back *or* restore the use of his/her hand; **ce médicament m'a rendu le sommeil** this medicine has made me able to sleep again; **il faut r. à César ce qui est à César** *(reconnaître le mérite de qn)* credit where credit's due
2 *(en retour) (compliment)* to return, to repay; **r. une** *or* **son invitation à qn** to invite sb back, to return sb's invitation; **r. un** *ou* **son baiser/coup/coup de pied à qn** to kiss/hit/kick sb back; **r. son salut/sa visite à qn** to return sb's greeting/visit; **r. coup pour coup** to hit back, to give as good as one gets; **r. le bien pour le mal** to return *or Fml* render good for evil; **il ne m'a pas rendu la monnaie** he didn't give me my change; **r. la monnaie d'un billet de cent euros** to give change for a hundred-euro note; *Fig Fam* **r. à qn la monnaie de sa pièce** to get even with sb; **elle l'aime mais il ne le lui rend pas** she loves him but the feeling isn't mutual, she loves him but he doesn't feel the same way about her; **il me déteste et je le lui rends bien** he hates me and the feeling is mutual, he hates me and I feel the same way about him
3 *(vomir) (nourriture, repas etc)* to bring up; **r. du sang par la bouche** to vomit blood
4 *Mil (armes, forteresse etc)* to give up, to surrender; *Fig* **je rends les armes!** I give up!
5 *(générer) Agr* **terre qui ne rend rien** unproductive land; **placement qui rend 10%** investment that brings in *or* yields 10%; **r. un son aigu** to make a high-pitched sound; *Fam* **ça n'a rien rendu** it didn't work out, it didn't come to anything; **j'ai pris un arc-en-ciel en photo mais ça n'a rien rendu** I took a photo of a rainbow but it didn't come out
6 *(livrer)* to deliver; **r. des marchandises à destination** to deliver goods (to their destination); **prix rendu** delivery price
7 *Jur (prononcer) (décret)* to issue, to pronounce; *(jugement)* to deliver; *(verdict)* to bring in, to return; **elle n'a pas encore rendu sa réponse** she hasn't given her answer yet
8 *Culin (de viande, concombre, champignons etc) (jus, eau)* to give out, to release
9 *Sport* **r. du poids/cent mètres** to have a weight/a one-hundred-metre handicap; *Échecs* **r. une pièce** to be a piece behind
10 *(exprimer)* to render, to express; **r. le sens** to convey *or* express the meaning; **c'est un mot difficile à r. en anglais** it's difficult to find an English equivalent for this word; **les couleurs/émotions sont très bien rendues** the colours/emotions are very well portrayed *or* expressed
11 *(+ adj)* **r. qn malade/heureux/intelligent** to make sb ill/happy/intelligent; **r. qch compliqué/simple/ennuyeux** to make sth complicated/simple/boring; **le homard me rend malade** lobster makes me ill; *Fam* **ça me rend malade de voir ces petits enfants dans les orphelinats** it makes me ill *or* sickens me to see those little children in orphanages; **vous me rendez fou!** you're driving me

mad!; **pour te r. les choses plus agréables** to make things more pleasant for you; **r. qn responsable de qch** to hold sb responsible for sth; **elle sait comment faire pour r. un homme amoureux** she knows how to make a man fall in love with her; **r. qn aveugle/sourd/muet** to make sb go blind/deaf/dumb; **le feu l'a rendu aveugle** the fire blinded him, he was blinded in the fire; *Fig* **l'amour l'a rendu aveugle** he was blinded by love; **c'est lui qui a rendu populaire le mythe du bon sauvage** he is responsible for popularizing the myth of the noble savage
12 *(expressions)* **r. hommage à qn** to pay homage to sb; **r. grâce(s) à qn (d'avoir fait qch)** to give thanks to sb (for doing *or* having done sth); **r. service à qn** to do sb a favour; **r. visite à qn** to visit sb; **r. compte de qch** to make a report on sth; **je n'ai pas de comptes à te r.** I don't owe you any explanation; **r. raison de qch** to explain *or* justify sth; **r. la justice** to dispense *or* administer justice; **r. l'âme** *(d'une personne)* to breathe one's last; *Hum (d'une machine)* to give up the ghost; **r. le dernier soupir** to breathe one's last
VPR se rendre 1 *(aller)* **se r. dans un lieu** to go to *or* make one's way to a place; **vous pouvez vous y r. en train/avion/bateau** you can get there by train/plane/boat; **en se rendant au bureau** on the way to the office; **se r. en toute hâte à un endroit** to hurry to a place; **se r. chez qn** to call on sb, to visit sb
2 *(reconnaître défaite, erreur etc)* to surrender, to give (oneself) up; **se r. à la police** *ou* **aux policiers** to give oneself up to the police, to turn oneself in to the police; **se r. à la raison** to see reason, to yield to reason; **se r. compte de qch** to realize sth; **se r. à l'évidence** to face facts; **se r. à l'avis de qn** to come round to sb's way of thinking
3 *(+ adj, + nom) (devenir)* **se r. malade/utile** to make oneself ill/useful; **se r. ridicule** to make a fool of oneself; **il s'est rendu maître de la situation** he took control of the situation
VI 1 *(d'une terre etc)* to be productive; *(de placement)* to yield
2 **le moteur rend bien** the engine runs *or* performs well
3 *(vomir)* to vomit

rendu [rɑ̃dy] **ADJ 1** *(arrivé)* **être r.** to have arrived; **nous voilà rendus à Manchester** here we are in Manchester; **tu seras plus vite r. par le train** you'll get there quicker by train; *Fig Fam* **on n'est pas r.** *(il y a encore beaucoup à faire)* we're not there yet **2** *Vieilli* **r. (de fatigue)** exhausted, tired out **3** **r. à domicile** delivered at domicile; **r. franco bord** delivered free on board; **r. à la frontière** delivered at frontier; **r. droits acquittés/non acquittés** delivery duty paid/unpaid
NM 1 *Beaux-Arts, Ordinat (de sujet)* rendering; **r. exact des couleurs** exact reproduction of colour **2** *Com* returned article, return

rêne [rɛn] **NF** rein; **lâcher les rênes** to loosen the reins, to give a/the horse his head; *Fig (abandonner)* to let go; *Fig* **prendre/tenir les rênes** to take over/hold the reins; **passer les rênes du pouvoir** to hand over the reins (à

renégat, -ate [rənega, -at] **N** renegade, turncoat; *Rel* renegade

renégociation [rənegɔsjasjɔ̃] **NF** renegotiation

renégocier [rənegɔsje] **VT** to renegotiate

reneiger [rəneʒe] **V IMPERS** to snow again

renfermé [rɑ̃fɛrme] **ADJ** *(personne)* uncommunicative, withdrawn
NM odeur de r. musty smell; **sentir le r.** to smell musty

renfermer [rɑ̃fɛrme] **VT 1** *Vieilli (enfermer)* to shut up; *(de nouveau)* to shut up again **2**

(contenir) to contain; **livre qui renferme des idées nouvelles** book that contains new ideas

VPR se renfermer to withdraw into oneself, to shut oneself off from people; **elle se renferma dans un silence d'airain** she withdrew into total silence

renfiler [rɑ̃file] **VT** *(perles etc)* to restring; *(aiguille)* to rethread

renflé [rɑ̃fle] **ADJ** *(pilier)* bulging; *(amphore)* rounded

renflement [rɑ̃fləmɑ̃] **NM** *(d'un pilier etc)* bulge

renfler [rɑ̃fle] **VT r. qch** to make a bulge in sth

VPR se renfler to swell (out), to bulge

renflouage [rɑ̃flua ʒ], **renflouement** [rɑ̃flumɑ̃] **NM** *(d'un bateau échoué)* refloating, floating off; *(d'un bateau coulé)* raising; *Fig (d'une affaire)* refloating

renflouer [rɑ̃flue] **VT** *(bateau échoué)* to float off, to refloat; *(bateau coulé)* to raise; *Fig* **r. une entreprise** to refloat a business, to set a business on its feet again, to bail out a company; *Fig* **r. les caisses de l'État** to swell the government's coffers; *Fig* **ça m'a permis de r. mes caisses pendant un mois** it swelled the coffers *or* kept me going *or* afloat for a month; *Fig* **r. qn** to keep sb afloat (financially)

renfoncement [rɑ̃fɔ̃smɑ̃] **NM 1** *(creux)* *(dans un mur)* recess; *(dans un arbre)* hollow; **r. d'une porte** doorway **2** *Typ (d'une ligne)* indentation

renfoncer [rɑ̃fɔ̃se] *(conj like* **enfoncer***)* **VT 1** *(clou etc)* to drive further in; *(chapeau)* to pull down; *Fig* **je voulais lui r. ses paroles dans la gorge** I wanted to shove the words down his throat **2** *Constr (façade etc)* to recess, to set back; *Typ, Ordinat (ligne, paragraphe)* to indent; *(écriture)* to embolden

VPR se renfoncer *Beaux-Arts (du fond)* to recede

renforçage [rɑ̃fɔrsaʒ] **NM 1** *(d'un mur, d'une couture etc)* strengthening, reinforcing **2** *Phot* intensification

renforcement [rɑ̃fɔrsəmɑ̃] **NM 1** *(d'une poutre etc)* strengthening, reinforcement; *(d'une équipe, armée)* strengthening **2** *Phot* intensification

renforcer [rɑ̃fɔrse] *(conj like* **forcer***)* **VT 1** *(mur, poutre, couture, couverture de livre etc)* to strengthen, to reinforce; *(armée, équipe)* to strengthen; *(sécurité)* to increase, to tighten up **2** *(couleur, éclairage)* to intensify; *(crainte)* to heighten, to intensify; *(impression)* to strengthen, to heighten; *(suspicions, convictions)* to heighten; **r. qn dans une opinion** to confirm sb in an opinion; **tout cela ne fait que r. mes convictions** it just makes me more convinced than ever; **suivre des cours d'anglais renforcé** to do extra English *(more than the normal baccalauréat syllabus demands)*; **faire un henné renforcé** to have an extra-red henna rinse done

VPR se renforcer *(d'un mouvement, de la pression)* to grow stronger, to grow in strength; *(d'une tendance)* to grow, to increase

renfort [rɑ̃fɔr] **NM 1 renforts** *(hommes)* reinforcements; **demander du r.** to ask for help; *(d'un policier, d'un pompier etc)* to ask for backup; **il faut du r. pour finir le projet** we need extra people to finish the project; **des soldats envoyés en r.** reinforcements; **un stagiaire recruté en r.** a trainee recruited to help out; **de r.** backup, extra; **à grand r. d'épingles/de conseils** with the help of lots of pins/advice **2** *(pièce)* reinforcement; *Aut* **r. (anti-impact) latéral** side-impact bar

renfrogné [rɑ̃frɔɲe] **ADJ** *(visage, personne)* frowning, scowling; **avec son air r.** with his scowling look

renfrogner (se) [sərɑ̃frɔɲe] **VPR** to frown, to scowl

rengagé [rɑ̃gaʒe] *Mil* **ADJ** re-enlisted
NM re-enlisted soldier

rengagement [rɑ̃gaʒmɑ̃] **NM** *(du personnel)* re-engagement; *Mil* re-enlistment

rengager [rɑ̃gaʒe] *(conj like* **engager***)* **VT** *(personnel)* to rehire, to take on again; *(combat)* to renew; *(conversation, partie, débat)* to pick up, to start again from where one left off
VI *Mil* to re-enlist
VPR se rengager *Mil* to re-enlist

rengaine [rɑ̃gɛn] **NF** cliché; *(morceau de musique)* tune; **vieille r.** old refrain; *Fam* **c'est toujours la même r.** it's (always) the same old story

rengainer [rɑ̃gɛne] **VT** *(épée)* to sheathe, to put up; *Fig Fam* **r. son compliment** to save one's compliments, to keep one's compliments to oneself

rengorger (se) [sərɑ̃gɔrʒe] **VPR** *(conj like* **engorger***)* *(d'un oiseau)* to strut; *(d'une personne)* to strut, to swagger

reniement [rənimɑ̃] **NM** *(d'un ami etc)* disowning; *(du Christ, de la foi)* denial; *(d'opinions, d'une action etc)* disavowal

renier [rənje] *(conj like* **nier***)* **VT** *(ami, père, racines etc)* to disown; *(le Christ)* to deny; *(foi)* to deny, *Fml* to abjure; *(action, opinion, idée)* to repudiate

VPR se renier to repudiate one's opinions

reniflard [r(ə)niflar] **NM** *Aut* breather

reniflement [rənifləmɑ̃] **NM 1** *(action)* sniffing **2** *(bruit)* sniff

renifler [rənifle] **VI 1** to sniff **2** *Fam (sentir mauvais)* to stink
VT *(fleur)* to sniff (at), to take a sniff at *or* of; *(tabac à priser)* to sniff (up); **il renifla la bonne odeur qui s'échappait de la cuisine** his nose picked up the lovely smell coming from the kitchen; *Fig* **il sait r. une bonne affaire** he's got a (good) nose for a bargain, he's good at sniffing out bargains; **j'ai reniflé le coup** I cottoned on to *or* tumbled to the trick

renifleur, -euse [rəniflœr, -øz] **ADJ** **avion r.** sniffer plane
N sniffer, sniffler

renipper [renipe] *Can* **VT** *(rénover)* *(maison, pièce)* to do up, to renovate
VPR se renipper to smarten oneself up, to smarten up one's appearance

renne [rɛn] **NM** reindeer

renom [rənɔ̃] **NM** *(popularité)* fame, renown; **de r.** famous, renowned; **un restaurant de grand r.** an extremely famous restaurant, a restaurant of great renown; **connaître qn de r.** to know sb by reputation; **en r.** famous, renowned, celebrated

renommé [rənɔme] **ADJ** renowned, famous, celebrated (**pour** for)

renommée [rənɔme] **NF 1** *(popularité)* fame, renown; **connaître qn de r.** to know sb by reputation *or* repute; **être de r. internationale** to be internationally famous; **être de r. mondiale** to be world-famous **2** *Jur* **(preuve par) commune r.** hearsay evidence

renommer [rənɔme] **VT** to reappoint; *Ordinat (fichier)* to rename

renonce [rənɔ̃s] **NF** *Cartes* **1** renounce, inability to follow suit; **avoir une r. à cœur** to be short of hearts **2 fausse r.** revoke; **faire une fausse r.** to revoke

renoncement [rənɔ̃smɑ̃] **NM** renunciation, renouncement (**à** of); **vie de r.** life of renunciation *or* sacrifice

renoncer [rənɔ̃se] (**je renonçai(s);** n. **renon-**

çons) **VI 1 r. à** *(un projet, une carrière)* to abandon, to give *or* throw up; *(des vacances)* to sacrifice, to forgo; *(la couronne, la succession, une réclamation)* to relinquish, to renounce; *(la violence, sa foi)* to renounce; *(le chocolat, la boisson, son indépendance)* to give up; **r. à un droit** to waive *or* relinquish a right; **r. à un voyage** to give up all thoughts of a trip; **r. à la lutte** to give up *or* relinquish the struggle; **r. au monde** to renounce the world; **r. à faire qch** to give up doing sth; *(projet)* to give up *or* drop the idea of doing sth; **je renonce à la convaincre** I've given up trying to convince her; **deux des coureurs ont renoncé** two of the runners dropped out; **j'y renonce!, je renonce!** I give up!; **il est hors de question que j'y renonce** there's no question of me giving up; **r. à qn** *(fiancé)* to let sb go

2 *Cartes* to renounce, to fail to follow suit; *(faire une fausse renonce)* to revoke
VT 1 *Arch (personne)* to disown; *Litt* **r. sa foi** to renounce one's faith
2 *Belg (résilier)* *(bail)* to cancel

renonciation [rənɔ̃sjasjɔ̃] **NF r. à** *(la couronne, une réclamation, la violence etc)* renunciation of; *(à une carrière)* sacrifice *or* renunciation of; *(à un projet)* abandonment of; *(à une lutte)* relinquishment of; *Jur* **r. à un droit** waiver *or* waiving of a right

renoncule [rənɔ̃kyl] **NF** *Bot* ranunculus; *(sauvage)* (wild) buttercup; **fausse r.** lesser celandine

renouée [rənwe] **NF** *Bot* knotgrass, polygonum

renouer [rənwe] **VT 1** *(ruban, lacet etc)* to tie (up) again; *(cravate)* to do up *or* knot again **2** *Fig (conversation, relations)* to renew, to resume; *(amitié)* to renew
VI r. avec qn to make friends with sb again, to make it up with sb; **un auteur qui renoue avec la tradition de la littérature courtoise** an author who is reviving the tradition of courtly literature; **r. avec le succès** to enjoy renewed success

renouveau [rənuvo] **NM 1** *Litt (printemps)* springtide, springtime (of the year) **2** *Fig (renaissance) (religieux, des arts)* revival; **un r. de succès** renewed success; **connaître un r.** to enjoy *or* experience a revival

renouvelable [rənuvlabl] **ADJ 1** *(contrat, énergie etc)* renewable; *(expérience)* repeatable **2** *Pol* **le comité est r. tous les ans** the committee must stand *or Am* run for office each year; **mon mandat est r.** I am eligible to stand *or Am* run (for office) again

renouveler [rənuvle] (**je renouvelle, n. renouvelons; je renouvellerai**) **VT 1** *(stock, équipement, mobilier, garde-robe etc)* to renew, to replace; **r. ses pneus** to get a new set of tyres, to replace one's tyres; **r. l'air d'une salle** to air a room
2 *(équipe, personnel, méthode, style)* to change completely; **une découverte qui renouvelle totalement notre conception du temps** a discovery which radically alters our conception of time
3 *(alliance, contrat, passeport, abonnement, querelle)* to renew; *(promesse, proposition, offre, ordonnance)* to repeat, to renew; *(expérience, exploit, Com (commande))* to repeat; *(usage, tradition, enthousiasme)* to revive; *Com* **r. la commande de qch** to reorder sth; **r. sa demande** to renew *or* repeat one's request; *(pour un emploi)* to apply again, to reapply; **faire r. le prêt d'un livre de bibliothèque** to renew a library book; **r. une traite** to renew a bill of exchange; *Rel* **r. ses vœux** to renew one's vows; **le pays a renouvelé sa confiance au parti au pouvoir** the country has renewed confidence in the governing party; **je vous renouvelle mes re-**

merciements pour votre joli cadeau *(dans une lettre)* thanking you once again for the lovely present

VI r. de zèle to act with renewed zeal

VPR se renouveler 1 *(se reformer) (de l'épiderme)* to be renewed

2 *(se produire)* to recur, to happen again; **que cela ne se renouvelle pas!** don't let it happen again!

3 *(changer)* to change; **il ne se renouvelle pas** it's always the same old thing, he never does anything new; **un artiste qui ne se renouvelle pas** an artist who doesn't bring anything new to his work

4 *(être remplacé)* to be replaced

renouvellement [rənuvɛlmã] **NM 1** *(du stock, de l'équipement)* replacement, renewal; **activer le r. cellulaire** *(d'un produit de beauté)* to encourage the cells to renew themselves **2** *(d'un système)* reform; *(d'une tradition etc)* revival; *(d'une méthode, d'un style)* change **3** *(d'un traité, d'un contrat, d'une offre etc)* renewal

rénovateur, -trice [renɔvatœr, -tris] **ADJ** reforming

N *(personne) (d'une méthode etc)* reformer; *(d'un genre artistique)* reviver

rénovation [renɔvasjɔ̃] **NF 1** *(d'un bâtiment, du mobilier etc)* renovation; **la maison est en (cours de) r.** the house is being renovated *or* is undergoing renovation; **projet/travaux de r.** renovation project/work **2** *Fig (d'une institution)* updating, reform

rénover [renɔve] **VT 1** *(bâtiment, mobilier etc)* to renovate **2** *Fig (genre artistique)* to revive; *(méthode, institution etc)* to update, to reform

renseigné [rãsɛɲe] **ADJ bien/mal r.** well-/ill-informed (**sur** about)

renseignement [rãsɛɲ(ə)mã] **NM** (piece of) information; *Mil etc* (piece of) intelligence; *Tél* **renseignements** directory enquiries, *Am* information; **pour tout r., veuillez appeler ce numéro** for information *or* if you have any queries, please call this number; **pardon Monsieur, c'est pour un r.** excuse me, could you give me some information?; **nous avons beaucoup de mal à obtenir ce r.** we're having a lot of trouble getting the information; **renseignements complémentaires** further information; *Fin* **renseignements de crédit** status *or* credit enquiry; **demander/donner des renseignements sur qn/qch** to ask for/to give (some) information on *or* about sb/sth; **prendre des renseignements sur qn/qch** to make enquiries *or* to enquire about sb/sth; **aller aux renseignements** to go to find out *or* to make enquiries; **bureau de renseignements** information bureau *or* office; **renseignements (techniques)** data; **service de r.** intelligence branch *or* service *or* department; **organes de renseignements et de sécurité** security; **les renseignements généraux** ≃ the security branch of the French police force, *Br* ≃ the Special Branch, *Am* ≃ the FBI; **agent de** *ou* **du r.** (intelligence) agent

renseigner [rãsɛɲe] **VT r. qn** to give sb some information; **on vous a (fort) mal renseigné** you have been (badly) misinformed; **l'office du tourisme nous a très bien/très mal renseignés** the tourist board gave us excellent information/totally the wrong information; **r. qn sur qch** to tell sb about sth, to give sb information *or* inform sb about sth; **r. qn sur un cours/le fonctionnement d'un ordinateur** to tell sb about *or Fam* to fill *or* clue sb in on a course/how a computer works; **être bien renseigné sur qch** to be well informed about sth; **je vais vous r. sur lui** I'll tell you something about him

VPR se renseigner to ask, to make enquiries,

to enquire; *(obtenir des renseignements)* to find out, to get information (**sur** about); **essaie de te r. pour savoir combien coûterait un billet** try to find out how much a ticket would cost

rentabilisation [rãtabilizasjɔ̃] **NF** making profitable; *(de projet, opération)* making cost-effective

rentabiliser [rãtabilize] **VT** *(projet, opération)* to make cost-effective; *(société, placement etc)* to make profitable; **r. des investissements** to obtain a return on investments

VPR se rentabiliser *(d'un projet, d'une opération)* to become cost-effective; *(d'un placement, d'une société)* to become profitable

rentabilité [rãtabilite] **NF** *(d'un projet, d'une opération)* cost-effectiveness; *(d'un placement, d'une société)* profitability; *(d'un investissement)* rate of return; **r. du capital** return on capital; **r. nette d'exploitation** net operating profit

rentable [rãtabl] **ADJ** *(projet, opération)* cost-effective; *(placement, société)* profitable; **ce n'est pas r.** it doesn't pay; **d'accord, si c'est r.** OK, if there's any money in it *or* any money to be made out of it, OK, if it's financially worthwhile; **ses investigations sont peu rentables** his/her investigations aren't proving very profitable; **loyer r./peu r.** economic/uneconomic rent

rente [rãt] **NF 1 rentes** *(revenu)* unearned *or* private income; **vivre de ses rentes** to live off one's private income; **je n'ai qu'un rêve: vivre de mes rentes** I dream of having a private income **2** *(pension)* annuity, pension; **faire une r. à qn** to make sb an (annual) allowance; **on lui a fait une r.** he has been pensioned off **3 rentes** *(de l'État)* (government) stocks *or* funds *or* bonds

▸▸ **r. annuelle** annuity; **r. à paiement différé** deferred annuity; *Fin* **r. de situation** guaranteed income; **r. viagère** life annuity

rentier, -ière [rãtje, -jɛr] **N** person of private means *or* with a private income; **petit r.** person with a small private income; **mener une vie de r.** to lead a life of leisure, to be a lady/gentleman of leisure; **avoir une mentalité de r.** to think one is above earning a living

rentrant, -ante [rãtrã, -ãt] **ADJ 1** *Math* angle **r.** reflex *or* re-entrant angle; *Phot* monture **rentrante** sunken mount **2** *Aviat* train d'atterrissage **r.** retractable undercarriage

N *Cartes* new player, cutter-in

rentré [rãtre] **ADJ 1** *(joues)* hollow, sunken; *(yeux)* sunken **2** *(rire, rage etc)* suppressed

rentre-dedans [rãtdədã] **NM INV** *Fam* **faire du r. à qn** to come on to sb, to chat sb up, *Am* to hit on sb

rentrée [rãtre] **NF 1** *(des vacanciers, des automobilistes etc)* return, return home; *Mus (d'un motif, instrument)* re-entry; **les embouteillages causés par les rentrées sur Paris** the traffic jams caused by Parisians returning home; *Astronaut* **r. atmosphérique** re-entry into the atmosphere

2 *(des tribunaux, des théâtres)* reopening; **r. (parlementaire)** reassembly, reopening (of Parliament); *Scol* **la r. (des classes)/(scolaire)** the beginning of term/the new school year; **on se reverra à la r.!** see you next term!, see you after the holidays!; **la préparation de la r.** preparation for the new term/the new school year; **on s'occupera de cela à la r.** we'll worry about that when the new term starts *or* when term starts again; **le jour de la r.** the first day of (the new) term; **la r.** *(des élèves/des professeurs)* the day the pupils/teachers go back; **la r. sociale** the start of the social calendar; **faire sa r. politique** *(après les vacances)* to resume one's political

activities; *(après une longue absence)* to make one's political comeback; **la r. littéraire** this autumn's new books

3 *(d'argent)* receipt; **rentrées fiscales** tax revenue; **rentrées journalières** daily takings; *Compta* **rentrées et sorties de caisse** cash receipts and payments; **j'attends une r. d'argent** I'm expecting some money; **il n'y a pas assez de rentrées d'argent** there isn't enough money coming in

4 *(de la récolte)* getting in

5 *Ftbl* **r. en touche** throw-in

La rentrée

The time of the year when children go back to school – in September – has considerable cultural significance in France. Coming after the long summer break or "grandes vacances", it is the time when academic, political, social and commercial activity begins again in earnest.

RENTRER [rãtre]

VI to come in **1, 5** ▪ to go in **1** ▪ to come home **2** ▪ to go home **2** ▪ to fit in **4** ▪ to collide with **6**
VT to bring in **1** ▪ to hold back **2**

VI *(aux être)* **1** *(entrer de nouveau)* to re-enter; *(vers le point de référence choisi)* to come in again; *(en s'éloignant du point de référence choisi)* to go in again; **r. dans sa chambre** to go back into one's room; **lorsqu'il rentra en France/à Paris** when he returned to France/Paris; **r. dans son pays** to go back home, to go back to one's own country; *Astronaut* **r. dans l'atmosphère** to re-enter the atmosphere; **r. au port** to return to port, to put back to port; **r. dans les bonnes grâces de qn** to regain favour with sb, to get back into sb's good books; **r. en correspondance avec qn** to resume correspondence with sb; **r. en relation avec qn** to get in touch with *or* contact sb again; **r. dans le droit chemin** to mend one's ways, to turn over a new leaf; **faire r. qn dans le droit chemin** to get sb back on the straight and narrow; **r. en scène** *(d'un acteur)* to come on again

2 *(à la maison)* to return home; *(vers le point de référence)* to come (back) home; *(en s'éloignant du point de référence)* to go (back) home; **r. d'un voyage/de vacances** to come back from a trip/holiday; **elle rentre de Paris** she is just home *or* back from Paris, she has just got home *or* back from Paris; **je serai rentré à cette date** I'll be (back) home by then; **il est rentré très tard** he was very late back, he came home *or* got in very late; **c'est à cette heure-ci que tu rentres?** what kind of time do you call this (to come home at)?; **il est l'heure de r.** it's time we went home, it's time to go home; **nous allons r.** we're going home; **je rentre chez moi** I'm going home; **je l'ai vu en rentrant chez moi** I saw him/it on my way home; **en rentrant de l'école** on my/his/*etc* way home from school; **je rentre de chez ma voisine et il paraît que ...** I've just come (back) from *or* got back from my neighbour's and it seems that ...; **r. dîner** to go home to dinner *or* for dinner; **tu rentreras dîner, ce soir?** will you be home for dinner this evening?; **voilà deux jours qu'elle n'est pas rentrée dormir ici** she hasn't slept here for the past two nights

3 *(reprendre ses occupations) (d'une école, des tribunaux etc)* to reopen; *(du Parlement)* to reassemble, to reopen; *(d'un élève, d'un professeur)* to go back to school; **les enfants rentrent le 15 septembre** the children go back to school *or* school starts again on the 15th of September

4 *(d'objets)* to go in, to fit (in); **cela ne pourra pas r. dans mon sac** it won't go in *or* fit in my bag; **cela rentre mal dans mon sac** there's not enough room for it in my bag; **ça rentre parfaitement dans mon cartable** it's just the right size for my school bag; **j'ai réussi à tout faire r.** I managed to get everything in; **faire r. qch dans sa boîte** to get sth back into its box; **des tubes qui rentrent les uns dans les autres** tubes that fit into one another

5 *(d'argent etc)* to come in; **faire r. ses fonds** to call in one's money; **r. dans ses fonds** to recoup one's investment; **r. dans ses frais** to recover one's expenses

6 *(forme emphatique d'entrer)* to enter, to come/go in; *Cartes* to cut in; **je t'en prie, rentre!** do come in!; **r. dans l'administration** to join the Civil Service, to become a civil servant; **je n'aurais jamais dû r. dans cette boutique** I should never have gone into *or* set foot inside the shop; *Fig* **r. en soi-même** to retire *or* withdraw into oneself; **r. dans un mur** *(d'une voiture)* to collide with *or* smash into *or* plough into a wall; **r. dans un réverbère/qn** *(d'un piéton)* to walk into *or* bang into *or* collide with a lamppost/sb; **ils se sont rentrés en plein dedans** they ran *or* went slap (bang) into each other; *Fam* **elle m'est rentrée dedans** *ou* **dans le chou** she ran into *or* banged into *or* collided with me; **je ne rentre plus dans mon pantalon!** I can't get into my trousers any more!, my trousers don't fit me any more!; **r. dans une catégorie** to fall into a category

7 *Typ* **faire r. une ligne** to indent a line

VT *(aux avoir)* **1** *(le linge, les vaches etc)* to take/bring in; *Naut (cordage)* to heave in, to haul in; *(les couleurs)* to haul down, to strike; *Pêche (filet)* to pull in, to haul in; *Aviat (train d'atterrissage)* to retract, to raise; **veux-tu r. le linge?** *(je suis à la maison)* will you bring the washing in?; *(je suis dans le jardin)* will you take the washing in?; **tu peux r. la voiture dans le garage** you can put the car in the garage; **rentre-le dans son étui maintenant** now put it back in its case; **r. ses griffes** *(d'un chat)* to retract *or* sheathe its claws; *Fig* to draw in one's claws; **rentre ton** *ou* **le ventre!** don't stick your stomach out!; *(tiens-toi droit)* straighten your back!; **r. son pull (dans son pantalon)** to tuck one's sweater in(to one's trousers); **r. la récolte** to get in *or* gather in the harvest; **à l'époque où l'on rentre la moisson** at harvest time

2 *(réprimer)* *(désir, colère)* to repress, to stifle; *(larmes)* to stifle, to hold back; **r. sa déception/sa souffrance** not to let one's disappointment/pain show

VPR se rentrer *Fam* to go home

renumérotation [rənymerɔtasjɔ̃] **NF** *Tél* redial

renuméroter [rənymerɔte] **VI** *Tél* to redial

renversant [rãversã] **ADJ** *Fam (nouvelles, spectacle etc)* astounding, staggering; *(personne)* astounding, amazing; **elle est renversante de bêtise** her stupidity is staggering *or* mind-blowing

renverse [rãvers] **NF 1** *(du courant)* shift, turn; *(du vent)* shift, change **2 tomber** *ou* **partir à la r.** to fall (over) backwards *or* on one's back; **il y a de quoi tomber à la r.** it's staggering *or Fam* mind-boggling

renversé [rãverse] **ADJ 1** *(à l'envers)* *(image)* reversed; *(arche, pyramide)* inverted; **écriture renversée** backhanded writing, writing that slopes backwards **2** *(tombé)* *(chaise, statue, bouteille etc)* overturned, upset **3** *Fam (déconcerté)* staggered

NM *Suisse (café crème)* latte

renversement [rãversəmã] **NM 1** *(de tendances, d'alliances, d'une image)* reversal; *(des opinions)* (dramatic) change *or* shift;

Mus (d'un intervalle, d'un accord) inversion; **r. des valeurs** inversion of values; **r. de situation** reversal of the situation; **quel r. de situation!** how the tables have turned!; **r. des rôles** role reversal; **il y a un r. des rôles entre mère et fille** mother and daughter are switching roles **2** *(de la marée)* turn(ing); *(du vent)* shift(ing), backing; **r. de la vapeur** *(d'une locomotive)* reversing; **attendre le r. de la marée** to wait for the tide to turn **3** *(à l'envers)* turning upside down; **charrette à r.** tip-up cart **4** *(d'un cabinet, ministère)* toppling; *(par la violence)* *(d'un régime, gouvernement)* overthrow

renverser [rãverse] **VT 1** *(tendance, rôles etc)* to reverse; *(lettres d'un mot, proposition)* to invert; **r. la tête** to tip *or* tilt one's head back; **garde-lui la tête renversée** keep his/her head (tilted) back *or* tilted backwards; **r. la marche** to reverse (the engine); *Fig* **r. la vapeur** to change tack; **r. la situation** to reverse the situation

2 *(mettre à l'envers)* *(chaise, vase, assiette)* to turn upside down, to upturn; *(gâteau)* to turn upside down; **'ne pas r.'** 'this side up' **3** *(faire tomber)* *(personne, chaise, vase)* to knock over *or* down; *(verre, seau)* to knock *or* tip over, to overturn, to upset; *(bateau)* to capsize, to overturn; *(liquide)* to spill; *(adversaire)* to knock down; **r. qch d'un coup de pied** to kick sth over; **r. son chargement** *(d'un camion)* to shed its load; **le vent a renversé la table** the wind knocked *or* blew the table over; **être renversé** *ou* **se faire r. par une voiture** to be knocked over *or* down by a car; *Fig* **cela renverse tous mes projets** that disrupts *or* upsets all my plans

4 *Pol (cabinet, ministère)* to bring down, to topple, to vote out of office; *(par la violence)* *(régime, gouvernement)* to overthrow; *Fig (obstacle)* to overcome, to surmount

5 *Fam (bouleverser)* *(personne)* to stagger, to knock sideways; **cela me renverse!** well I'm blowed *or* damned *or* jiggered!; **être renversé par la beauté de qn** to be bowled over by sb's beauty

VI *(de la marée)* to turn

VPR se renverser *(d'une chaise, d'un vase, verre)* to fall over *or* down, to overbalance, to tip over; *(d'un véhicule)* to overturn (**dans** on); *(d'un bateau)* to capsize, to overturn; **se r. sur sa chaise** to lean back on one's chair, to tilt one's chair back

renvoi [rãvwa] **NM 1** *(de marchandises etc)* return, sending back

2 *(des employés)* dismissal, *Br Fam* sacking; *(des troupes)* expulsion; *(d'un élève)* expulsion; **signifier à qn son r.** *(employé)* to inform sb that he has been dismissed *or* sacked; *(élève)* to inform sb that he has been expelled; **au bout de trois avertissements, c'est le r. définitif** *(d'un employé)* after three warnings it's dismissal; *(d'un élève)* after three warnings it's expulsion

3 *(ajournement)* postponement, putting off, deferral; *Jur* adjournment; *Jur* **r. à huitaine** week's adjournment

4 *(à une commission etc)* reference, referral; *Jur (d'une affaire à un autre tribunal)* transfer **5** *Typ, Ordinat (dans un texte, une base de données)* cross-reference; **r. en fin de document** endnote

6 *Tech* **levier de r.** reversing lever; **engrenage de r.** reversing gear

7 *(éructation)* burp, belch; **avoir un r./des renvois** to burp, to belch; **le concombre me donne des renvois** cucumber repeats on me **8** *Sport* clearance; *Tennis etc* return; **et r. de Zidane** Zidane clears (the ball); **... r. de la tête de Petit** ... Petit heads the ball clear

renvoyer [rãvwaje] **VT** *(conj like* **envoyer***)* **1** *(faire retourner)* *(cadeau, lettre etc)* to send back, to return; *(personne)* to send back;

(son) to throw back, to echo; *(chaleur, lumière)* to reflect; **r. à l'expéditeur** to return to sender; **r. qn au lit** to send sb back to bed; *Fig* **r. l'ascenseur** to return the favour; **je le leur ai proposé pour leur r. l'ascenseur** I suggested it to them as a way of returning the favour they had done me; **elle attend que tu lui renvoies l'ascenseur** she expects you to return the favour, *Fam* she feels you owe her one

2 *(faire partir)* *(visiteur)* to send *or* turn away; *Jur (accusé)* to discharge; **r. qn en cour d'assises** to send sb before the Crown Court; **r. des troupes dans leurs foyers** to discharge *or* dismiss troops

3 *(licencier)* *(employé)* to dismiss, *Br Fam* to sack; *(élève)* to expel; **se faire r.** *(du collège)* to get expelled; *(du travail)* to get sacked, to get the sack

4 *(différer)* *(affaire, débat)* to put off, to postpone, to defer; *Jur* **r. une affaire à huitaine** to adjourn a case for a week; *Jur* **r. le prévenu à une autre audience** to remand the accused **5** *(reporter)* *(affaire)* to refer (**à** to); *Ordinat* to cross-refer; *Pol* **r. un projet à une commission** to send a bill to a committee; **les numéros renvoient (le lecteur) aux notes** the numbers refer to the notes; **cet article renvoie à un autre** *(dans un dictionnaire)* this entry is cross-referred to another

6 *Sport (ballon)* to clear; *Tennis etc* to return; **Boli renvoie le ballon de la tête** Boli heads the ball clear

réoccupation [reɔkypasjɔ̃] **NF** *(d'un territoire, d'une usine etc)* reoccupation

réoccuper [reɔkype] **VT** *(territoire, usine etc)* to reoccupy

réorganisateur, -trice [reɔrganizatœr, -tris] **N** reorganizer

réorganisation [reɔrganizasjɔ̃] **NF** reorganization

réorganiser [reɔrganize] **VT** to reorganize **VPR se réorganiser** to be reorganized

réorientation [reɔrjãtasjɔ̃] **NF** reorientation

réorienter [reɔrjãte] **VT** to reorient(ate)

réouverture [reuvertyr] **NF** *(d'un théâtre, magasin, de la frontière etc)* reopening; **r. des débats** resumption of proceedings

repaire [rəper] **NM** *(de lions)*, *Fig (de voleurs)* den, lair; *(de pirates)* nest; *(de criminels)* haunt

repaître [rəpetr] *(prp* **repaissant**; *pp* **repu**; *pr ind* **je repais**, *n.* **repaissons**; *pr sub* **je repaisse***)* **VT** *Litt* **r. ses yeux de qch** to feast one's eyes on sth

VPR se repaître 1 *(d'un animal)* to eat its fill **2** *Fig Litt* **se r. de sang** to wallow in blood; **se r. de chimères** to indulge in vain imaginings; **se r. de commérages** to revel in gossip

répandre [repãdr] **VT 1** *(renverser)* *(sel, liquide etc)* to spill

2 *(parsemer)* *(sable)* to spread, to sprinkle, to scatter; *(liquide)* to pour; *(larmes, sang)* to shed; *(fleurs)* to scatter, to strew; *(lumière)* to shed; *(odeur)* to give off; *(chaleur)* to give *or* throw out; *(rumeur)* to spread (about), to circulate; *(nouvelle)* to spread, to broadcast; *(terreur, usage, doctrine)* to spread; **r. du sable sur le plancher** to sprinkle sand on the floor *or* the floor with sand; **r. du sel sur une tache de vin** to pour salt on a wine stain; **ce poêle répand une douce chaleur dans la maison** the stove spreads a gentle warmth throughout the house; **r. le produit uniformément sur le carrelage** spread the product evenly on the floor; **cette nouvelle répandit la tristesse dans la ville** the news cast a gloom *or* spread gloom throughout the town; **cette nouvelle répandit le bonheur dans toute la maison** the news brought a general air of happiness to the house

3 *(bénéfices etc)* to lavish; *Litt* **alors que le soleil répandait ses bienfaits …** as the sun was pouring out its blessings …

VPR **se répandre 1** *(d'un liquide)* to spill; *(d'une odeur, nouvelle, algue, maladie, de la panique, la fumée)* to spread; *(d'une rumeur, opinion, pratique, d'idées)* to spread, to gain ground; **les métastases se sont répandues dans tout le corps** the tumours have spread throughout the body; **la foule se répandit dans la rue** the crowd spilled into the street; **les touristes se répandent dans la ville** tourists are invading *or* overrunning the town; **l'usage de ce mot s'est répandu** this word is now widely used *or* in wide use

2 se r. en explications to launch forth into explanations; **se r. en excuses** to apologize profusely, to be full of apologies; **se r. en compliments** to be full of compliments, to be very complimentary

3 *Vieilli* **se r. dans le monde** to lead a sociable life

répandu [repɑ̃dy] ADJ **1** *(méthode, préjugé, idée etc)* widespread, prevalent; *(fleur, animal, oiseau)* widespread, common; *(opinion)* widely held; **un objet d'un usage très peu r.** an object that is in limited use **2** *Vieilli (personne)* widely known; **il est très r. dans les milieux politiques** he is extremely well known in political circles

réparabilité [reparabilite] NF repairability

réparable [reparabl] ADJ **1** *(chaussure, machine etc)* repairable; **c'est facilement/difficilement r.** it's easy/difficult to repair; **ce n'est pas r.** it can't be repaired, it's beyond repair **2** *(erreur)* for which amends can be made, *Fml* retrievable; *(perte financière)* which can be made up, *Fml* retrievable; **c'est facilement r.** *(erreur)* it can be easily put right; **c'est difficilement r.** *(erreur)* it won't be easy to put matters right *or* to make amends

reparaître [rəparetr] VI *(conj like paraître; aux often avoir)* *(d'une personne, maladie)* to reappear, to appear again; *(de la lune, du soleil)* to reappear, to appear again, to come out again, to re-emerge

réparateur, -trice [reparatœr, -tris] ADJ *(sommeil)* refreshing; **chirurgie réparatrice** reconstructive surgery

N *(de vélos, d'appareil électroménager)* repairman, f repairwoman; *(d'horloge)* mender

réparation [reparasjɔ̃] NF **1** *(d'une chaussure, d'un vélo, d'une horloge)* repair(ing), mending; *(d'une maison, machine, route etc)* repair(ing); *(d'un bateau)* refit; **les réparations de l'appartement/de la toiture** the repairs to the flat/the roof; **nécessiter des réparations** to need repair; **réparations d'entretien** maintenance; **être en r.** *(d'une route)* to be under repair; *(d'un yacht)* to be under refit, to be refitting; **l'ascenseur/la machine à laver est en r.** the lift/washing machine is being repaired; **route en r.** road up for repairs; **faire des réparations** to make repairs *(sur* to) **2** *(dédommagement)* reparation, amends, redress; *Arch (par les armes)* satisfaction *(by duel)*; **assigner une somme d'argent en r. des dégâts causés** to allocate a sum of money to make good the damage; **en r. d'un tort** to make up for *or Fml* in reparation *or* in atonement for a wrong; **demander r.** to seek redress *(* **de** for); *Ftbl* **coup de pied de r.** penalty kick; *Ftbl* **surface de r.** penalty area

▸▸ *Jur* **r. civile** compensation; *Jur* **r. légale** legal redress; **réparations de guerre** war reparations

réparer [repare] VT **1** *(toit, vélo, machine à laver etc)* to repair, *Fam* to fix; *(chaussure)* to repair, to mend; *(maison)* to repair; *(bateau)*

to refit; *(déchirure, accroc)* to mend; **donner ses chaussures à r.** to take one's shoes to the mender's; **r. ses forces** to get one's strength back, to build up one's strength; **r. le talon d'une chaussure** to re-heel a shoe; **r. ses pertes** to repair *or* make good one's losses; **la maison a besoin d'être réparée** the house is in need of repair *or* needs to be repaired **2** *(remédier à) (méfait)* to make amends for, *Fml* to atone *or* make atonement for; *(erreur)* to put right, to rectify; *(omission)* to make good, to rectify; *(tort)* to redress; *(dommage)* to make good

reparler [rəparle] VI *(après un accident)* to speak *or* talk again; **r. de qch** to speak about sth again; **nous en reparlerons plus tard** we'll talk about *or* discuss it later; **il ne faut plus en r.** it must not be mentioned again; **r. à qn** to speak to sb again; **elle ne lui a pas reparlé depuis** she hasn't spoken (another word) to him/her since; **si je vous surprends à r. ensemble** if I catch you two talking again VPR **se reparler** to speak *or* talk to each other again; **ils se sont remis à se r.** they're talking again, they're on speaking terms

repartie, répartie [rəparti, re-] NF retort, rejoinder; **avoir l'esprit de r., avoir la r. prompte, avoir de la r.** to be good *or* quick at repartee

repartir¹ [rəpartir] VI *(conj like partir, aux être)* *(d'un voyageur, train etc)* to set *or* start off again; *(d'une machine etc)* to start (up) again; **je repars pour Paris** I'm off to Paris again; **r. à zéro** *(dans une tâche)* to start all over *or* from scratch again, to go back to square one; *(dans une relation)* to make a fresh start, to start all over again; **il est reparti d'un éclat de rire** he burst out laughing again; *Fam* **c'est reparti, ils se disputent encore!** they're at it again!, they're off again!; *Fam* **c'est reparti, ils ont encore mis la musique à fond!** there they go again, putting their music on full blast!

> [!NOTE]
> Do not confuse with **répartir**.

repartir², répartir¹ [repartir] VT *(aux avoir)* *(répondre)* to retort, to reply

répartir² [repartir] *(je répartis, n. répartissons)* VT *(partager) (tâches, argent, vivres)* to distribute, to divide (up), to share (out) *(* **entre** among); *(poids, charge, dividende)* to distribute; *(cours, paiements etc)* to spread (out) *(* **sur** over); *(dépenses, responsabilités etc)* to allocate, to apportion; *(impôts)* to assess; *Bourse (titres)* to allot, to allocate; **r. des objets selon leur couleur** to divide objects up by colour; **r. une ville en zones/un pays en régions** to divide a town up into areas/a country up into regions; **charge uniformément répartie** evenly distributed load; **tâche de bien r.** to try to distribute the boxes evenly; **r. les frais** to share the costs; **r. les risques** to share the risks; **r. un produit** to distribute a product; *Fin* **r. une avarie** to adjust an average; *Couture* **r. le surplus du col** to ease the collar (onto the neckband) VPR **se répartir** to split *or* divide (up); **ils se répartissent le travail** they divide *or* split (up) *or* share (out) the work among themselves; **on se répartit les tâches ménagères** we share the housework; **les sommes se répartissent ainsi** the amounts break down as follows

> [!NOTE]
> Do not confuse with **repartir**.

répartiteur [repartitœr] NM **1** *(personne)* distributor; **(commissaire) r.** tax assessor **2** *Aut* proportioner

répartition [repartisjɔ̃] NF *(de la population, du poids, du travail etc)* distribution; *(des dépenses, responsabilités etc)* apportion-

ment, allocation; *(des impôts)* assessment; *Bourse (de titres)* allotment, allocation; *(dividende)* dividend; *(des paiements, cours)* spreading *(* **sur** over); **r. de la population par groupes d'âge** breakdown of the population according to age group; **la r. des richesses est très inégale** the distribution of wealth is very unequal; **la r. des portefeuilles ministériels** the distribution of ministerial posts; **r. des risques** risk spreading; **r. du bénéfice** distribution of profits; **r. du dividende** distribution of the dividend; **r. d'avarie** *(en assurance)* adjustment of average; *Bourse* **première et unique r.** first and final dividend; *Bourse* **dernière r.** final dividend; **r. des votes** voting pattern

repas [rəpa] NM meal; *(d'animal)* feed; **faire trois r. par jour** to have three meals a day; **le bébé fait six r. par jour** the baby has six feeds a day; **ne pas manger entre les r.** don't eat between meals; **r. à 18 h** *(au zoo)* the animals will be fed at 6 p.m., feeding time at 6 p.m.; **r. de noce** ≃ wedding breakfast; **r. chaud** hot meal; **r. d'affaires** business lunch; **r. enfant** children's meal, children's portion; **r. de substitution, substitut de r.** meal replacement; **faire un r.** to have a meal; **r. léger, petit r.** light meal, snack; **aux heures de r.** at meal times; **prendre ses r. chez qn/ chez soi** to have one's meals with sb/to eat at home; **ticket-r., chèque-r.** luncheon voucher, LV

repassage [rəpasaʒ] NM *(des vêtements)* ironing; **faire du r.** to do some ironing; **c'est d'un r. facile** it irons easily, it's easy to iron; **n'exigeant aucun r.** non-iron; **table de r.** ironing board

repasser [rəpase] VI *(aux être)* **1** *(devant qch ou un lieu)* to pass (by) again, to go/come by again; **elle n'est pas là, repassez demain** she's not here, come back tomorrow *or* call again *or* call back tomorrow; **je repasserai le prendre** I'll call *or* come back for it; **r. chez qn** to visit *or* drop in on *or* call on sb again; **je dois r. chez Denise** I have to go over to Denise's again; *Fam* **il peut toujours r.!** he's got another think coming!

2 *Ordinat* to rerun; **faites r. la dernière phrase** *(de bande magnétique)* play back the last sentence; **ce film repasse au Royal** the film is showing again *or* is on again at the Royal; *TV* **ça repassera** it'll be on again, they'll show it again

VT *(aux avoir)* **1** *(franchir) (montagne, frontière)* to go across again, to cross (over) again; *(mer)* to cross again

2 *(répéter) (cassette, disque)* to play again; *(enregistrement)* to play back; *TV, Cin* to show again, to rerun; *(leçon, rôle)* to look over, to go over; **elle nous a repassé le même disque toute la soirée** she played the same record over and over again the entire evening; **r. une annonce** to put an ad in again, to readvertise; **r. qch dans son esprit** to go over sth in one's mind; **r. un examen** to resit *or* retake an exam, to take *or* sit an exam again

3 *(transporter)* to take across again

4 *(donner à nouveau)* to pass; **r. un plat à qn** to pass sb a dish again; **si tu as fini avec le dictionnaire, tu peux me le r.?** if you've finished with the dictionary can I have it back?; *Fam* **r. une fausse pièce à qn** to palm off *or* foist a counterfeit coin on sb

5 *(aiguiser) (couteau, outil)* to sharpen, to grind, to whet; **r. un rasoir sur le cuir** to strop a razor

6 *(avec un fer) (vêtements)* to iron; **fer à r.** iron; **table** *ou* **planche à r.** ironing board

repasseur, -euse [rəpasœr, -øz] NM (knife) grinder

NF **repasseuse** *(personne)* presser; *(machine)* ironing machine

repayer [rəpeje] VT *(conj like payer)* *(facture)*

to pay again; *Fam* **j'ai dû lui r. une veste** I had to pay for another jacket for him/her

repêchage [rəpeʃaʒ] **NM 1** *(dans l'eau)* fishing out **2** *Scol Fig* **épreuve conçue pour permettre le r. des candidats** test designed to give candidates another chance; **épreuve de r.** *Scol (pour les élèves qui ont échoué)* resit; *Sport (pour les coureurs qui suivent le gagnant)* extra heat; *Can (pour sélectionner de jeunes concurrents)* selectors' meeting

repêcher [rəpeʃe] **VT 1** *(retirer de l'eau)* to fish out **2** *Fig (personne en difficulté)* to rescue, to help (out); *Scol* **r. un candidat à l'oral** to let a candidate scrape through at the oral; **se faire r. à l'oral** to scrape through the oral; **ceux qui ont échoué au mois de juillet peuvent être repêchés en octobre** those who failed in July may sit the exam again in October; *Sport* **r. un concurrent** to let a competitor go through

repeindre [rəpɛ̃dr] **VT** *(conj like* **peindre***)* to repaint

repeint [rəpɛ̃] **NM** *Beaux-Arts* touched-up area

repenser [rəpɑ̃se] **VI** to think again (**à** about); **r. à des événements passés** to think back on past events; **quand j'y repense** when I think back (on it); **j'y repenserai** I'll think it over *or* think about it again *or* give it some more thought; **je n'y ai pas repensé** I haven't given it another thought *or* thought about it again
▪ **VT** *(problème, projet, concept etc)* to rethink; **r. la question des transports** to rethink the whole question of transport; **le projet doit être complètement repensé** the plan needs to be completely rethought *or* needs a complete rethink

repentant [rəpɑ̃tɑ̃] **ADJ** repentant, penitent; **d'un air r.** repentantly, penitently

repenti, -ie [rəpɑ̃ti] **ADJ** repentant, penitent; *Vieilli* **fille repentie** reformed prostitute *(who has entered a convent)*
▪ **NF** *Vieilli* **repentie** reformed prostitute *(who has entered a convent)*
▪ **N** *(ancien terroriste)* = former terrorist who now collaborates with the police

repentir¹ [rəpɑ̃tir] **NM** *Rel* repentance, penitence; *Fig* regret; *(d'un tableau)* touching up; *(d'un manuscrit)* correction

repentir² (se) [sərəpɑ̃tir] **VPR** *(prp* se repentant; *pp* repenti; *pr ind* je me repens, il se repent; *pr sub* je me repente; *p hist* je me repentis) *Rel* to repent; **se r. de qch/d'avoir fait qch** to repent (of) sth/doing sth; *Fig* to be sorry for *or* regret sth/doing sth; **je me repens de mon mensonge** I'm sorry I lied; **me repens de lui avoir prêté mon appartement** I'm sorry I loaned him my flat; **elle s'en repentira** she'll be sorry, she'll rue the day

repérage [rəperaʒ] **NM 1** *(action de marquer, jalonnement)* marking off *or* out; *Ordinat* marking, flagging **2** *(action de trouver) (d'un défaut, d'une cible etc)* location, locating; *(d'un avion ennemi)* identification, identifying, *Fam* spotting; *TV, Cin* recce; **r. radio** radio location, radio fix; **faire des repérages avant de faire un film** to check out the location(s) before making a film; **partir en r.** to go to check out the location(s)

répercussion [reperkysjɔ̃] **NF 1** *(du son)* reverberation **2** *Fig* repercussion (**sur** on); **r. de l'impôt** impact of taxation

répercuter [reperkyte] **VT 1** *(son)* to reflect, to reverberate; *(lumière)* to reflect **2** *(ordre, augmentation de prix etc)* to pass on; **r. une augmentation sur les consommateurs** to pass an increase on to the consumer; **r. l'augmentation des salaires sur les prix** to pass the wage increase on to prices
▪ **VPR se répercuter** *(du son)* to reflect, to be

reflected, to reverberate; *(de la lumière)* to reflect, to be reflected; *Fig* to have repercussions (**sur** on)

repère [rəper] **NM** *(point de référence)* reference mark, marker; *(fait exprès)* mark; *(pour s'orienter)* landmark; *(en arpentage)* bench mark; *(balise, jalon)* marker; *Ordinat* marker, flag; *Ordinat* **r. de saisie de commandes** dot prompt; *Tech* **r. de montage/d'ajustage** assembly/line-up mark; **r. de niveau** contour line; **il faut le remplir de liquide jusqu'au r.** you have to fill it with liquid up to the mark; *Fig* **la date de son mariage me sert de r.** I use the date of his/her wedding as a reference point; **point de r.** landmark; *Fig* **tout le monde devrait avoir quelques points de r.** everyone should have some landmarks *or* milestones in their lives; **je manquais de points de r.** I had nothing to go by *or* to guide me

repérer [rəpere] (**je repère**, n. **repérons**; **je repérerai**) **VT 1** *(marquer, jalonner) (terrain, chemin)* to mark off *or* out **2** *(trouver) (défaut, cible, endroit etc)* to locate, to spot; *Fam (robe, coiffeur, personne)* to spot; *TV, Cin (lieu de tournage)* to recce; **r. qn dans la foule** to pick sb out in the crowd; *Courses de chevaux* **r. les gagnants** to pick (out) *or* spot the winners; *Fam* **se faire r.** to attract attention; **attention, tu vas nous faire r. par le prof!** watch out or you'll get us noticed by the teacher!
▪ **VPR se repérer** to get one's bearings, to find one's way about; *Fig* **je n'arrive pas à me r. dans son galimatias** I can't make head (n)or tail of his/her mumbo jumbo

répertoire [repertwar] **NM 1** *(liste)* index, list; *Ordinat* directory; **r. à onglets** thumb index; **r. d'adresses** directory; *(carnet)* address book; *(dans un fichier)* list of adresses; **r. des rues** street directory; **r. des métiers** trade directory; *Ordinat* **r. central** *ou* **principal** main directory; *Ordinat* **r. racine** root directory **2** *Théâtre* repertory; *Mus (de chansons etc)* repertoire; *Fig (de plaisanteries, injures etc)* repertoire; *Théâtre* **pièce de** *ou* **du r.** classic; **le r. classique** the classical repertoire *or* repertory; **il a un r. de trois discours** he has three stock speeches *or* a repertoire of three speeches

répertorier [repertɔrje] **VT** *(impf, pr sub* n. **répertoriions**) *(article, informations)* to list

répéter [repete] (**je répète**, n. **répétons**; **je répéterai**) **VT 1** *(mots, secret, action, expérience)*, *Mus (motif etc)* to repeat; **tu répètes toujours la même chose!** you're constantly repeating yourself!; **r. que ...** to repeat that ...; **je vous répète que ce n'est pas possible!** it's not possible, I tell you!, I repeat, it's not possible!; **répète-moi exactement ce qu'il a dit** tell me (again) exactly what he said; **je t'ai répété cent fois de ne pas le faire** I've told you a hundred times not to do it; **il répète à qui veut l'entendre qu'il a démissionné** he's telling anyone who'll listen that he's resigned; **pourriez-vous me r. votre nom?** could you tell me your name again?; **je ne veux pas avoir à le r.** I don't want to have to say it again *or* to repeat it; **inutile de me le r. deux fois** I don't need to be told twice; **j'ai l'impression de r. toujours le même genre de situations** I feel as if I get involved in the same kind of situation time and time again
2 *(pièce de théâtre, rôle, morceau de musique)* to rehearse; *(leçon)* to learn; **faire r. son rôle à qn** to help sb rehearse his/her lines, to go over sb's lines with him/her; **faire r. ses leçons à un enfant** to go over a child's lessons with him
▪ **VI** *Théâtre, Mus* to rehearse; **faire r. qn** to coach sb, to rehearse sb
▪ **VPR se répéter** *(d'une personne)* to repeat

oneself; *(d'un événement)* to recur, to happen again; *(d'un motif)* to be repeated; **l'histoire se répète** history repeats itself; **les mêmes situations se répètent toujours** the same situations keep recurring

répéteur [repetœr] **NM** *TV, Cin* transmitter; *Aut* **r. de clignotant** repeater lamp

répétiteur, -trice [repetitœr, -tris] **N** *Scol* (private) tutor, coach

répétitif, -ive [repetitif, -iv] **ADJ** repetitive

répétition [repetisjɔ̃] **NF 1** *(d'un mot, d'une action etc)* repetition; *Fig (d'un désastre)* repetition; *Fam* rerun, repeat; *Ordinat* **fonction de r.** repeat function; **fusil à r.** repeating rifle; **montre à r.** repeater (watch); **des laryngites à r.** repeated bouts of laryngitis; **avoir des rhumes à r.** to have one cold after another **2** *Théâtre, Mus* rehearsal; **r. générale** *ou* **en costume** dress rehearsal; **mettre une pièce en r.** to put a play into rehearsal; **nous commençons les répétitions la semaine prochaine** rehearsals start next week, we start rehearsing next week; **r. en studio** studio rehearsal; **r. hors caméra** dry-run; **r. technique** technical run, technical walk-through

repeuplement [rəpœpləmɑ̃] **NM** *(d'un pays etc)* repopulation; *(d'un étang)* restocking; *(d'une forêt)* replanting

repeupler [rəpœple] **VT** *(pays etc)* to repopulate; *(étang)* to restock; *(forêt)* to replant
▪ **VPR se repeupler** *(d'un pays)* to be repopulated; *(d'un étang)* to be restocked; *(d'une forêt)* to be replanted; **la ville se repeuple** the population of the town is increasing again; **la forêt s'est repeuplée d'écureuils** squirrels have returned to the forest, the forest has a squirrel population again

repincer [rəpɛ̃se] **VT** *(conj like* **pincer***)* to pinch again; *Fig Fam* to catch again

repiquage [rəpika3] **NM 1** *Couture* restitching **2** *(de la chaussée)* mending, repairing **3** *(de jeunes plants)* pricking out, planting out **4** *(de bactéries)* subculturing **5** *(d'un disque)* re-recording **6** *Phot* retouching **7** *TV, Cin* overprinting; *(de son)* transfer, dub

repiquer [rəpike] **VT 1** *(percer)* **l'acupuncteur m'a repiqué** the acupuncturist repeated the treatment; *Couture* **r. l'aiguille au même endroit** take the needle back through in the same place
2 *(chaussée)* to mend, to repair
3 *(jeunes plants)* to prick out, to plant out; **plant à r.** bedding plant
4 *(bactéries)* to subculture
5 *(disque, air)* to re-record
6 *Phot* to retouch
7 *Fam (reprendre)* to catch again; **et que je ne te repique pas à faire ça!** don't let me catch you doing that again!
▪ **VI** *Fam* **1 r. au plat** to have a second helping; **r. au truc** to be at it again **2** *(redoubler une classe)* to repeat a year *or Am* grade

répit [repi] **NM** respite, breathing space; *Com* **jours de r.** days of grace; **ne laisser aucun r. à qn** to give sb no rest *or* respite; **la douleur ne lui laisse aucun r.** he is in constant pain, the pain is always there, he has no respite from the pain; **laisser un moment de r. à qn** to give sb a moment's respite; **sans r.** *(travailler)* without a break, continuously; *(harceler qn)* constantly

replacement [rəplasmɑ̃] **NM 1** *(de capitaux)* reinvestment **2 des mesures pour permettre le r. des licenciés** steps to find alternative employment for workers made redundant

replacer [rəplase] *(conj like* **placer***)* **VT 1 r. un objet** *(remettre en place)* to replace an object, to put an object back in its place *or* where it belongs; *Fig* **r. un événement dans son contexte** to look at *or* put an event in context; **il faut r. la scène à l'époque où elle a eu lieu** you have to bear in mind what things were like then **2** *(capitaux)* to reinvest **3** *(licencié)* to find alternative employment *or* a new job for **4** *Can (reconnaître)* to recognize; **je ne l'avais pas vue depuis si longtemps que je n'arrivais pas à la r.** I hadn't seen her for so long that I was unable to recognize her

VPR se replacer *(dans un emploi)* to find (oneself) a new job; **il faut se r. dans l'époque pour comprendre ce qui s'est passé** in order to understand what happened, you have to remember what things were like then *or* you have to think yourself into the mentality of the period

replanter [rəplɑ̃te] **VT** to replant; **r. une forêt en sapins** to replant a forest with firs

replat [rəpla] **NM** *(de versant)* shelf

replâtrage [rəplɑtraʒ] **NM 1** *(d'un mur)* replastering **2** *Fig* patching up; *(réparation)* makeshift repair; **c'est du r.** *(réparation)* it's a bit rough and ready; **ils ont décidé de reprendre la vie commune, à mon avis, c'est du r.** they've decided to move back in together but I think they're just papering over the cracks

replâtrer [rəplɑtre] **VT 1** *(mur)* to replaster **2** *Fig (réparer de façon sommaire)* to patch up

replet, -ète [rəplɛ, -ɛt] **ADJ** *(personne)* podgy, dumpy; *(visage)* chubby; **un petit au visage r.** a chubby-faced little boy

réplétion [replesjɔ̃] **NF** repletion

repleuvoir [rəplœvwar] **V IMPERS** to rain again

repli [rəpli] **NM 1** *(d'un vêtement, de la peau)* fold; **replis du terrain** folds in the land; *Fig* **les plis et les replis du cœur** the innermost recesses of the heart **2** *(d'une rivière)* bend, meander; *(d'une corde, des intestins)* coil; **faire des replis** *(d'une rivière)* to wind, to meander; *(d'un serpent)* to slither **3** *Mil* retreat, withdrawal; *Psy* withdrawal; *Mil* **r. stratégique** strategic withdrawal; **une attitude de r. (sur soi)** a withdrawn attitude **4** *(de monnaie, prix)*, *Bourse* fall

repliable [rəplijabl] **ADJ** folding, fold-up; *(tablette d'avion)* foldaway; *(antenne)* retractable; **couteau à lame r.** knife with a folding blade

repliement [rəplimɑ̃] **NF 1** *Mil* retreat, withdrawal **2** *(sur soi-même)* withdrawal

replier [rəplije] *(conj like* **plier**) **VT 1** *(journal, drap etc)* to fold up; *(lame de couteau)* to fold away; *(bord, coin) (de papier, tissu)* to turn *or* fold down; *(de métal)* to bend down; *(d'une personne) (jambes)* to tuck up; *(d'un oiseau) (ailes)* to fold; **r. les draps** to turn back *or* fold down the sheets; **l'oiseau a replié sa tête sous son aile** the bird tucked its head under its wing **2** *Mil (troupes)* to withdraw, to pull back **VPR se replier 1** *(d'un objet)* to fold up; *(d'un serpent)* to coil up; **la lame se replie dans le manche** the blade folds away into the handle **2 se r. sur soi-même** to withdraw into oneself; **je la trouve trop repliée sur elle-même** I find her too withdrawn **3** *(des troupes)* to retreat, to withdraw **4** *Bourse* to fall back, to drop

réplique [replik] **NF 1** *(réponse)* retort, rejoinder; **lancer une r.** to make a retort; **avoir la r. prompte** *ou* **facile** to be always ready with an answer; **preuve qui ne souffre aucune r.** incontrovertible *or* irrefutable proof; **prouver qch sans r.** to prove sth incontrovertibly *or* irrefutably; **argument sans r.** unanswerable argument; **obéir sans r.** to obey without a word *or* murmur; **la r. ne s'est pas fait attendre** his retort wasn't long in coming; *Fam* **et pas de r.!** don't answer (me) back! **2** *Théâtre* line(s); **apprendre une r.** to learn one's lines; **lancer sa r.** to say one's lines, to come in on cue; **manquer sa r.** to miss one's cue; **donner la r. à un acteur** to play opposite an actor **3** *(copie)* replica; *(sosie)* double; **c'est la r. de sa mère** she's her mother's double

répliquer [replike] **VT** **r. qch à qn** to say sth in answer to sb; **je n'ai pas entendu ce qu'il lui a répliqué** I didn't hear what his reply was *or* what he said to him/her; **'pas de danger!', répliqua-t-il** 'not likely!', he retorted; **que veux-tu r. à ce genre d'arguments?** there's no answer to *or* you can't argue with reasoning like that!

VI *(répondre)* to retort; *(avec impertinence)* to answer back; **r. à qn** to answer sb back; **je ne supporte pas qu'on me réplique** I won't be answered back; **il répliqua par un coup de pied** he answered with a kick; **c'est ainsi qu'il répliquait aux critiques** that was his response to the criticisms

VPR se répliquer to replicate

replonger [rəplɔ̃ʒe] *(conj like* **plonger**) **VT** *(avec force)* to plunge back (**dans** into); *(doucement)* to dip back (**dans** into); *Fig* **cette nouvelle me replongea dans l'angoisse** the news plunged me back into a state of anxiety; *Fig* **le film nous replonge dans l'atmosphère étrange du Berlin des années vingt** the film takes us back into the strange atmosphere of 1920's Berlin

VI to dive (in) again; *Fam (récidiver)* to commit another crime; *Fam (dans l'alcoolisme)* to fall back into; **r. dans l'eau** to dive back into the water

VPR se replonger se r. dans l'étude to become immersed again in study

repolir [rəpɔlir] **VT** to repolish; *Fig (style)* to polish up

répondant, -ante [repɔ̃dɑ̃, -ɑ̃t] **N 1** *(responsable, garant)* surety, security, guarantor; *(d'un questionnaire)* respondent; **être le r. de qn** to stand surety for sb; *Fam* **avoir du r.** to have plenty of money stashed away **2** *Rel (à la messe)* server

répondeur, -euse [repɔ̃dœr, -øz] **ADJ** given to answering back, impertinent

NM r. (téléphonique), r. enregistreur (telephone) answering machine, answerphone

RÉPONDRE [repɔ̃dr]

| **VT** to answer **1** ▪ to reply **1** |
| **VI** to answer **1** ▪ to reply **1** ▪ to answer back **1** ▪ to respond **2** ▪ to write back **1** ▪ to meet *(répondre à)* **3** ▪ to answer for *(répondre de)* **4** |

VT 1 to answer, to reply; *(remarque)* to answer *or* reply with; *(lettre)* to send in reply; **il m'a répondu une sottise** he answered me with something stupid; **essaie de r. quelque chose!** *(pour encourager qn)* try to say something!; *(en s'énervant)* say something!; **r. que ...** to answer *or* reply that ...; *Fml* **il s'est vu r. que ...** he obtained the response that ...; **qu'est-ce qu'elle vous a répondu?** what was her answer *or* reply?, what did she say in reply?; **je n'ai rien répondu** I made no reply, I gave no answer *or* reply; **il répondit n'en rien savoir** he answered *or* replied that he knew nothing about it; **il m'a répondu d'en parler au médecin** he answered *or* replied that I should talk to the doctor about it; **il répond ne pas être au courant** he says he doesn't know; *Pol* **Londres a immédiatement répondu du présent** London immediately signalled its readiness to help

2 *Rel* **r. la messe** to make the responses at Mass

VI 1 to answer, to reply; **r. à** *(personne, lettre, invitation etc)* to answer, to reply to; *(salut)* to return, to acknowledge; *(accusation)* to answer; **pour r. à votre invitation** in answer to your invitation; **elle ne m'a pas encore répondu** she hasn't answered me *or* replied to me yet, I haven't had an answer *or* a reply from her yet; **r. par écrit** to reply in writing, to write back; **r. par un signe de la tête** *(pour dire oui)* to nod in reply, to nod one's reply; *(pour dire non)* to shake one's head in reply; **r. par un haussement d'épaules** to shrug (one's shoulders) in reply; **r. par une mimique** to make a face in reply; **r. par un sourire** to reply with a smile; **est-ce qu'elle a répondu?** *(à la lettre)* has she written back?, did she reply?; *Scol, Mil* **r. à l'appel** to answer the roll *or* to one's name; **r. à un coup de sonnette/au téléphone** to answer the bell/the phone; **laisse, je vais r.!** *(au téléphone, à la porte)* leave it, I'll get it!; *(à une question embarrassante)* leave it, I'll answer it!; **je te défends de me r.!** don't you dare answer me back *or* talk back to me!; **vous devrez r. de plusieurs chefs d'accusation** you'll have to answer several charges; *Tél* **ça ne répond pas** there's no answer; **répondez, s'il vous plaît** *(pour établir un contact radio)* come in, please

2 *(réagir)* *(d'une personne, des freins, d'une voiture)* to respond (à to); **la voiture répond très bien** the car responds very well, the car is very responsive; **r. à l'amour/l'affection de qn** to return sb's love/affection; **on a répondu généreusement à l'appel** the appeal met with a generous response; **le chien répond à son nom** the dog responds *or* answers to his name; **il n'a pas répondu à mon appel** he didn't do what I asked him to

3 *(correspondre)* **r. à** *(besoin)* to meet, to fulfil, *Am* to fulfill; *(but)* to fulfil; *(description)* to fit, to match; *(critères)* to meet; **ne pas r. à l'attente** not to come up to expectations, to fall short of expectations

4 *(être garant de)* **r. de qn/qch** to answer for sb/sth, to be answerable *or* accountable for sb/sth; **répondez-vous d'elle pour ce travail?** will you take responsibility *or* be accountable for her work?; **r. de l'innocence de qn** to answer for sb's innocence; **il va revenir, je vous en réponds** he'll come back, take my word for it, I guarantee he'll come back; **je ne réponds de rien** I'm promising nothing, I'm making no promises

VPR se répondre to answer each other; **les deux parties du livre se répondent** the two parts of the book echo each other

Il faut noter que le verbe anglais **to respond** est un faux ami. Il signifie le plus souvent **réagir**.

répons [repɔ̃] **NM** *Rel* response

réponse [repɔ̃s] **NF 1** answer, reply; **elle a** *ou* **trouve r. à tout** she has an answer for everything, she's never at a loss for an answer; **donner** *ou* **rendre r. à qn** to give sb an answer, to reply to sb; **faire une r. de Normand** to give a non-committal *or* an evasive reply; **argument sans r.** unanswerable argument; **rester sans r.** *(d'une question, une lettre)* to go unanswered; **elle fait toujours les questions et les réponses** she does all the talking; **pour toute r., il éclata en sanglots** his only answer was to burst out sobbing; **il a souri en guise de r.** he answered with a smile; *Fam* **j'ai sonné plusieurs fois, mais pas de r.** I've rung several times, but there's no answer; **en r. à votre lettre** in reply *or* answer to your letter; **bulletin-/carte-r.** reply coupon/card; **r. payée** reply paid; *Jur* **droit de r.** *(dans la presse)* right to reply; *Tél* **r. en retour** answerback; **r. d'attente** holding reply

2 *(réaction)* *(à un appel de fonds, d'aide)*, *Physiol (à un stimulus, d'un moteur, des freins etc)* response; *(à une offre d'emploi)* reply;

Aut **r. à mi-régime** mid-range response

3 *Ordinat* answering; **r. automatique** unattended answering; **temps de r.** response time

4 *Fig (solution)* answer (à to); **je n'ai pas la r. (à ton problème)** I don't have the answer, I don't know what the answer is; **ce problème est resté sans r.** a solution still hasn't been found to the problem

repopulation [rəpɔpylasjɔ̃] NF *(d'une région etc)* repopulation, repopulating

report [rəpɔr] NM **1** *Compta (du total)* carrying forward, bringing forward; *(somme)* amount carried forward, carry forward, carry over; **'r.'** carried forward; **r. de l'exercice précédent** carried forward from the previous financial year; **r. à l'exercice suivant** carried forward to the next financial year; **r. à nouveau** carried forward; **reports et avances sur titres** collateral loans **2** *(de corrections),* *Pol (de voix),* *Phot (transfer);* *Phot* **papier (à) r.** transfer paper **3** *(d'un rendez-vous)* postponement **4** *Radio* plot(ting); **table de r.** plotting board

> Il faut noter que le nom anglais **report** est un faux ami. Il signifie **rapport**.

reportage [rəpɔrtaʒ] NM *Journ, Radio, TV* **1** *(article, émission)* report; **c'est France 2 qui en assurera le r.** France 2 will bring you the report; **r. filmé/télévisé** film/TV report; **r. en direct** live coverage; **r. en exclusivité** scoop, exclusive (report); **r. photographique** photo-reportage; **r. publicitaire** editorial advertisement; *Radio, TV* **r. électronique** electronic news gathering, ENG **2** *(activité)* reporting; **faire du r.** to do some reporting; *(métier)* to be a reporter

reporté [rəpɔrte] ADJ postponed, deferred

reporter¹ [rəpɔrtɛr] NM *Journ, Radio, TV* reporter; **r. photographe** photojournalist; **r.-cameraman** film reporter

reporter² [rəpɔrte] VT **1** *(pour rendre) (objet)* to take back, to return

2 *(transférer) (affection),* *Pol (voix),* *Phot* to transfer (**sur** to)

3 *(dans le temps) (personne)* to take or carry back, to transport; **cela nous reporte à l'époque où ...** that takes us back to the time when ...

4 *(différer)* **r. qch à plus tard** to postpone or *Fml* defer sth, to put sth off until later

5 *Compta (total)* to carry forward, to bring forward, to carry over; **à r.** carried forward; **r. une somme** to carry a sum forward

6 *(transcrire) (notes)* to transfer (**sur** to)

VPR **se reporter 1** *(se référer)* **se r. à** *(un document, une interview)* to refer to; **se r. à ...** *(dans un livre etc)* the reader is referred to ..., see ...

2 **se r. au passé/à la période de l'après-guerre** to look back or think back to the past/to the post-war period

3 *(se déplacer) (de colère, d'une affection),* *Pol (de voix)* to be transferred (**sur** to)

> Il faut noter que le verbe anglais **to report** est un faux ami. Il ne correspond jamais au verbe français **reporter**.

reporteur [rəpɔrtœr] NM reporter

repos [rəpo] NM **1** rest, *Fml* repose; **c'est mon seul r.** it's my only (form of) relaxation; **il vous faut le r. complet** you need a complete rest; **avoir besoin de (prendre du) r.** to need to rest, to need a rest; **chercher le r.** to try to rest; **ces enfants ne lui laissent aucun r.** those children give her no rest; **se donner** *ou* **prendre du r.** to take a rest; **r. compensateur** time off in lieu; *Mil* **r.!** (stand) at ease!; **au r.** at rest; **soldat au r.** soldier standing at ease; **maison de r.** rest home, convalescent home; *(de personnes âgées)* rest home; **cure**

de r. rest cure; **le dimanche est mon unique jour de r.** Sunday is my only day off or day of rest; **après un mois de r.** after a month's rest; **le r. éternel** eternal rest; **terre au r.** fallow land

2 *Tech* **au r.** *(fusil)* at half cock; *(mécanisme)* in neutral (position); *(muscle)* relaxed

3 *Littér (dans un vers)* pause, rest

4 *(quiétude)* peace; **trouver le r.** to relax; **troubler le r. de qn** to disturb sb, to upset sb; **troubler le r. de la nature** to break the stillness, to disturb the quietness; **être en r. au sujet de qn** to feel easy in one's mind about sb; **je n'aurai de r. que lorsque je me serai vengé** I won't rest until I've had my revenge; **laisser qn en r.** to leave sb alone or in peace; **valeur de tout r.** safe investment, gilt-edged security; **vivre avec lui, ce n'est pas de tout r.!** living with him is no bed of roses!

reposant [rəpozɑ̃] ADJ *(vacances, week-end etc)* restful, relaxing; *(sommeil)* refreshing; *(couleur)* soothing

reposé [rəpoze] ADJ **1** *(personne, esprit)* rested, refreshed; **s'éveiller bien r.** to awake refreshed; **elle a le visage vraiment r.** *(après repos, nuit de sommeil)* she looks really rested or refreshed **2** **je le ferai à tête reposée** I'll do it when my mind's clearer; **laissez-moi y réfléchir à tête reposée** give me time to think it over quietly

repose-bras [rəpozbra] NM INV armrest

repose-pied, *pl* **repose-pieds** [rəpozpje] NM *Aut* tread plate; *(d'une moto, d'une chaise)* footrest

repose-poignet, *pl* **repose-poignets** [rəpozpwaɲe] NM wrist rest

reposer [rəpoze] VT **1** *(à sa place)* to put back (down), to replace; **merci de le r. là où tu l'as trouvé** please put it back where you found it; *Mil* **reposez arme!** order arms!

2 *(rectifier la pose de) (moquette)* to re-lay

3 *(détendre)* to rest; **r. sa tête contre l'appui-tête** to lean back against the headrest; **ça le reposera** it'll be a rest for him; **r. l'esprit** *(d'une activité)* to be relaxing; **écouter de la musique me repose l'esprit** listening to music gives my mind a rest; **couleur qui repose les yeux** colour that is restful or soothing to the eyes

4 *(question)* to ask again; **r. un problème** *(au cours d'une réunion)* to bring up a problem again; **je voudrais r. les grandes lignes de notre action** I'd like to outline once again what we'll be doing

VI **1** *(d'une personne)* to rest; *(être étendu)* to lie; **le corps reposait sur son lit de parade** the body was lying in state; **ici repose ...** here lies ...; **qu'elle repose en paix!** may she rest in peace!; *Fam* **ça repose bien, le sauna** a sauna is very relaxing

2 **r. sur** *(rocher etc)* to rest on; *Fig* to be based on; *(dépendre de)* to depend on; **le sort de notre association repose sur lui** the fate of our association rests with him

3 *(d'un liquide)* to settle; *Culin (d'une pâte)* to rest; **faire r. ses chevaux** to rest one's horses; **laisser r. la terre** to let the ground rest or lie fallow

VPR **se reposer 1** *(se relaxer)* to rest, to take a rest; **avoir besoin de se r.** to need to rest, to need a rest; **se r. les yeux/les jambes** to rest one's eyes/legs, to give one's eyes/legs a rest; **j'ai besoin de me r. les yeux** my eyes need a rest; **je pars me r. en Corse** I'm going to Corsica to rest or for a rest; **vous devriez vous r. davantage** you must get more rest, you must rest more

2 *(compter sur)* **se r. sur qn/qch** to rely on sb/sth; **se r. sur qn du soin de qch** to rely on sb to look after sth; **il se repose sur le travail de ses collègues** he relies on or leaves it up to his colleagues to do the work

3 *(d'une question)* to be asked or put again; **il s'est souvent reposé la question** he asked himself the question time after time

repose-tête [rəpoztɛt] NM INV headrest

repositionnement [rəpozisjɔnmɑ̃] NM *Mktg (d'un produit)* repositioning

repositionner [rəpozisjɔne] *Mktg* VT *(produit)* to reposition

VPR **se repositionner se r. à la baisse** to move down-market; **se r. à la hausse** to move up-market

reposoir [rəpozwar] NM *(en plein air)* wayside altar; *(dans l'église)* temporary altar

repourvoir [rəpurvwar] VT *Suisse (poste)* to fill

repoussage [rəpusaʒ] NM embossing, repoussé work

repoussant [rəpusɑ̃] ADJ *(apparence etc)* repulsive, repellent; **d'une laideur repoussante** repulsively ugly

repousse [rəpus] NF *(des cheveux, des plantes, de la pelouse etc)* regrowth, regrowing; **pour activer la r.** to encourage new growth

repoussé [rəpuse] *Tech* ADJ embossed, repoussé

NM embossing, repoussé

repoussement [rəpusmɑ̃] NM *(d'une arme à feu)* recoil, kick

repousse-peaux [rəpuspo] NM INV orange stick

repousser [rəpuse] VT **1** *(objet) (écarter)* to push aside or away; *(en arrière)* to push back; *(volets)* to push or throw back; *(ennemi, attaque)* to repel, to beat or fight off, to beat back; *(les avances de qn)* to repel; *(offre, proposition, idée, demande)* to reject, to turn down; *(conseils)* to reject, to brush aside; **r. qch de la main** to push sth away or aside; **r. qch du pied** to push sth away with one's foot; **r. qn** to push or thrust sb aside; *Fig (rabrouer)* to rebuff sb; **elle a repoussé mes conseils avec mépris** she pooh-poohed my advice

2 *(différer) (événement, rendez-vous etc)* to postpone, to put off (à until); **r. les délais de livraison du travail** to push back the deadline for completion of the work

3 *(dégoûter) (personne)* to be repellent to, to repel; **cette odeur me repousse** I find the smell repellent

4 *(métal, cuir)* to emboss, to work in repoussé

VI *(d'un arbre, d'une plante)* to shoot (up) again, to spring up again; *(des cheveux, de l'herbe, des feuilles)* to grow again; **elle se laisse r. les cheveux** she's letting her hair grow again

repoussoir [rəpuswar] NM **1** *(de manucure)* cuticle pen; *Tech (ciseau)* embossing punch **2** *Fig* foil; **servir de r. à la beauté de qn** to set off sb's beauty, to serve as a foil to sb's beauty **3** *Fam (personne laide)* ugly duckling; **c'est un vrai r.** he/she is really ugly

répréhensible [repreɑ̃sibl] ADJ reprehensible; **de façon r.** *(se conduire, agir)* reprehensibly, in a reprehensible way

REPRENDRE [rəprɑ̃dr] *(conj like* **prendre***)*

VT to retake **1** ▪ to recapture **1** ▪ to have more **2** ▪ to get back **3** ▪ to take back **5** ▪ to resume **6** ▪ to take up again **6** ▪ to repeat **6** ▪ to alter **7** ▪ to correct **7, 8** ▪ to reprimand **8**	
VI to start again **1**	
VPR to recover **1** ▪ to correct oneself **2**	

VT **1** *(ville)* to retake, to recapture; *(fugitif)* to recapture; *(territoire),* *Sport (titre)* to win back, to recapture (**à** from)

2 **r. du pain/vin** to take or have some more

bread/wine; **vous reprendrez bien un peu de thé?** would you like some more tea?

3 *(récupérer) (objet prêté)* to get back; **je suis allé r. mon parapluie** I went to get my umbrella back *or* to recover *or* retrieve my umbrella; **r. ses chaussures chez le cordonnier** to get one's shoes (back) *or* pick up one's shoes from the mender's; **je peux r. ma machine à coudre?** can I have my sewing machine back?; **il est passé r. tous ses meubles** he came and took away all his furniture; **je passerai les r. dans la semaine** I'll come back for them *or* I'll pick them up sometime this week; **je vous reprendrai en passant** I'll pick you up (again) as I go by; **r. sa place** *(s'asseoir)* to take one's seat again; *(dans une entreprise)* to take one's place again; **r. connaissance** to recover *or* regain consciousness, to come to; **r. possession de qch** to regain possession of sth; **r. ses esprits** to collect *or* gather one's thoughts; **r. haleine** to get one's breath back, to recover one's breath; **r. contact avec qn** to get in touch with sb again; **r. contact avec l'actualité** to catch up on the news; **r. goût à la vie** to find life worth living again, to recover one's zest for life; **r. la route** to take to the road again; **r. des forces** to get one's strength back; **r. courage** to summon up one's courage again; **elle reprend espoir** she's starting to hope *or* be hopeful again; **r. la parole** to resume, to go on (talking *or* speaking); **r. les choses/qn en main** to take things/sb in hand again

4 *Fig* **la fièvre l'a repris** he has had another bout of fever; **ça le reprend!** it's starting all over again!; **ça ne va pas te r., tout de même, cette habitude de douter de tout!** you're not going to get back into that habit of doubting everything, are you?; *Fam* **on ne m'y reprendra plus** I won't be had *or* caught again *or* another time; **que je ne vous y reprenne plus!** don't let me catch you at it again!; **et que je ne te reprenne pas à écouter aux portes!** don't let me catch you listening at doors again!

5 *(cadeau, marchandise invendue, article en solde etc)* to take back; *(employé)* to take on again, to re-engage; *(promesse, offre)* to go back on, *Fml* to retract; **les articles ne seront ni repris ni échangés** goods may not be returned or exchanged; **le garagiste me l'a reprise à l'achat de la nouvelle** the man at the garage took it off me in part exchange *or* as a trade-in for the new one

6 *(recommencer) (conversation, fonctions)* to resume, to take up again; *(pourparlers, hostilités, relations)* to reopen, to resume; *Mus (thème)* to restate, to recapitulate; **r. le travail** *(après une grève)* to return to work; *(après une maladie)* to go back to work; **r. son travail** to get back to work, to start work again; **reprenons les faits** let's go over the facts again, let's recapitulate (the facts); **r. les choses au début** to start all over again, to go back to the beginning; **je vais r. toute l'histoire à ses origines** I'll go right back to the beginning *or* to how it all started; **r. son cours** to continue as before, to carry on as before; **r. la lutte/le combat** to continue the *or* carry on the struggle/the fight; *Théâtre* **r. une pièce** to revive a play; **r. un refrain en chœur** to take up a chorus, to join in a chorus; **reprenez après moi ces paroles** repeat these words after me; **'oui', reprit-il** 'yes', he replied

7 *(réparer) (tableau)* to retouch; *(texte)* *(modifier)* to correct; *(refaire)* to redo; *Couture* to alter (**à la taille** at the waist)

8 *(personne) (corriger)* to correct; *(réprimander; Fam* to tell off, *Fml* to reprove (**de** for); **il trouve toujours quelque chose à r.** he always finds something to criticize

VI 1 *(recommencer)* to start *or* begin again;

(de pourparlers, hostilités) to resume, to re-open; *(d'une mode)* to return, to be revived; *(des affaires)* to recover, to pick up (again); **les cours reprennent à quatorze heures** classes start *or* begin again at two o'clock; **le froid a repris** the cold weather has set in again

2 *(d'une plante)* to pick up

VPR se reprendre 1 *(se ressaisir)* to recover, to pull oneself together; **reprends-toi!** pull yourself together!, get a grip on yourself!; **donnez-moi le temps de me r.** give me time to collect myself *or* my thoughts

2 *(se corriger)* to correct oneself *(in speaking)*; *(réciproquement)* to correct each other

3 se r. à faire qch to begin *or* start doing *or* to do sth again

4 s'y r. à plusieurs fois pour faire qch to make several attempts *or* have several goes at doing sth; **j'ai dû m'y r. à trois fois** I had to have three goes at it

repreneur [rəprənœr] **NM** purchaser; *Fin* buyer; **le nom du r. de l'entreprise** the name of the person who took over the company

représailles [rəprezaj] **NFPL** reprisals, retaliation; **par peur des r.** for fear of reprisals; **en r. de qch** in reprisal for sth; **par r.** in reprisal, as a reprisal; **expédition de r.** punitive expedition; **des mesures de r.** reprisals (**contre** against); **user de r.** to take reprisals

représentable [rəprezɑ̃tabl] **ADJ** which can be represented

représentant, -ante [rəprezɑ̃tɑ̃, -ɑ̃t] **N 1** *Pol, Ind* representative; **r. syndical** (trade-)union representative; **la Chambre des représentants** the House of Representatives; **être le r. de l'opinion publique** to represent public opinion; **r. du personnel** employees' representative **2** *Com* **r. (de commerce** *ou* **commercial)** (sales) representative, *Fam* (sales) rep (**en** for); **notre r. au Japon** our agent in Japan; **r. exclusif** sole agent; **r. multicarte** rep for several companies

représentatif, -ive [rəprezɑ̃tatif, -iv] **ADJ** *(échantillon, gouvernement)* representative; *(personne)* typical, representative; **symbole r. du pouvoir** symbol representative *or* re-presenting power; **ceci est tout à fait r. de son état d'esprit** it's quite indicative *or* typical of his state of mind; **voilà des photos, mais elles ne sont pas très représentatives** here are some photos but they don't really give you the right idea

représentation [rəprezɑ̃tasjɔ̃] **NF 1** *Pol, Jur etc* representation; *(représentants)* representatives; *Pol* **r. proportionnelle** proportional representation

2 *Com* representation; *(agence)* agency; **faire de la r., être dans la r.** to be a (sales) representative *or Fam* (sales) rep; **r. exclusive** sole agency

3 *(de concept, de faits, d'objet, en peinture etc)* representation; **c'est sa r. de la situation** that's his/her idea *or* reading of the situation, that's how he/she sees *or* reads the situation; **c'est une r. possible de la situation** that's one possible view *or* reading of the situation; *Psy* **faculté de la r. spatiale** spatial perception

4 *Jur (de documents etc)* production

5 *Théâtre* performance; **troupe en r.** touring company; **droits de r.** performing rights

6 frais de r. entertainment allowance; *Fam* **être en r.** to be trying to impress

représentativité [rəprezɑ̃tativite] **NF** representativeness; **si vous acceptez la r. de notre échantillon** if you accept that our sample is representative

représenter [rəprezɑ̃te] **VT 1** *(présenter de nouveau)* to present again, to re-present; **je voudrais r. ce candidat (au concours)** I

would like to re-enter this candidate (for the exam); **r. une traite à l'acceptation** to re-present a bill for acceptance

2 *Jur (documents etc)* to produce

3 *(figurer)* to represent; **le pronom représente le nom** the pronoun stands for *or* re-places the noun; **on représente souvent Hugo comme un vieil homme barbu** Hugo is often depicted as an old man with a beard; **il représente l'esprit soixante-huitard** he represents *or* typifies the spirit of May 1968; **r. fidèlement/avec réalisme qch** to render sth faithfully/realistically; **il a représenté son modèle avec humour** he has painted his model with great humour; **un croquis qui me représentait à la terrasse d'un café** a sketch of me *or* that showed me sitting outside a cafe; *Théâtre* **la scène représente un patio** the scene is a patio

4 *(être le porte-parole de) (personne, pays, entreprise), Pol (circonscription)* to represent; **se faire r.** to be represented; **il représente la France aux Jeux olympiques** he's representing France in the Olympic Games; **je représente les produits Avon®** I'm an Avon® representative; *Jur* **r. qn en justice** to appear for sb

5 *(correspondre à) (somme, chiffre etc)* to represent; **cela ne représente pas une grosse somme** *ou* **beaucoup pour lui** it's not much to him, it's not a large amount as far as he's concerned; **cela représente une privation financière importante pour eux** that constitutes a major financial sacrifice for them

6 *Théâtre (pièce de théâtre)* to perform, to put on

VI *(en imposer)* **r. (bien)** to impress people, to be impressive; **il ne représente pas au physique** he's not very impressive physically

VPR se représenter 1 se r. à *(examen)* to resit, to sit *or* take again; *(poste, emploi)* to apply for again; **se r. en septembre** to resit in September; **se r. aux élections** to stand for *or Am* to run for election again; *Fam* **se r. au permis de conduire** to take one's driving test again

2 *(d'une occasion)* to arise again; **si ces difficultés se représentent, dis-le moi** let me know if these problems come up again

3 *(s'imaginer)* to imagine; **représentez-vous mon étonnement** (just) imagine my astonishment; **ce n'est pas ainsi que je me le représentais, je me le représentais différemment** that's not how I imagined it

répressif, -ive [represif, -iv] **ADJ** *(loi, parents, tendance etc)* repressive

répression [represjɔ̃] **NF** repression; *(d'une émeute, d'un abus)* suppression; **mesures de r.** repressive measures; **mesures de r. de la fraude fiscale** measures to suppress tax evasion; **r. des fraudes** suppression of fraud; *(service gouvernemental)* consumer protection office

réprimandable [reprimɑ̃dabl] **ADJ** reproachable, blameworthy

réprimande [reprimɑ̃d] **NF** reprimand, rebuke, *Fml* reproof; **faire des réprimandes à qn** to reprimand *or* rebuke sb, *Fml* to reprove sb; **air/ton de r.** reproving look/tone, look/tone of rebuke

réprimander [reprimɑ̃de] **VT** *(personne)* to reprimand, to rebuke, *Fml* to reprove; **se faire r.** to be reprimanded

réprimer [reprime] **VT** *(crime)* to suppress; *(désir, colère, instinct)* to repress, to suppress; *(rire, sanglots, larmes, éternuement)* to suppress, to hold back; *(juron)* to suppress, to smother; *(révolte)* to suppress, to quell, to put down

reprint [rəprint] **NM** *(livre)* reprint

repris [rəpri] **NM r. de justice** ex-prisoner

reprisage [rəprizaʒ] **NM** *(d'un vêtement)* mending; *(de chaussettes)* darning

reprise [rəpriz] **NF 1** *Mil (d'une place forte, ville etc)* retaking, recapture **2** *Com (de marchandises invendues, d'articles en solde etc)* taking back; **nous ne faisons pas de r. des articles en solde** sales goods may not be returned; **r. jusqu'à 5000 euros** part exchange *or* trade-in (allowance) up to 5,000 euros; **r. de l'entreprise par ses salariés** employee buy-out; *Compta* **reprises sur provisions** recovery of provisions, write-back of provisions **3** *(du travail, d'un débat, des essais nucléaires)* resumption; *(des négociations, des pourparlers)* renewal, resumption, reopening; *(des hostilités, de la violence)* renewal, resumption; *(de la mode)* return, revival; *Théâtre (d'une pièce de théâtre)* revival; *Cin (d'un film)* reissue; *Radio, TV* repeat; *TV, Cin (d'un but, essai etc)* replay, rerun; *Ordinat (d'un programme)* restart **4** *(de l'activité)* renewal; *(du froid)* return; *(de la fièvre)* fresh bout; **r. des affaires** business recovery *or* revival; **mouvement de r.** *(dans l'économie)* upward movement; **r. économique** economic recovery, upswing *or* upturn in the economy; **les premiers indices de la r. économique** the first signs of economic recovery **5 r. (de vitesse)** *(d'un moteur)* pick-up, acceleration; **cette voiture a de bonnes reprises** the car accelerates quickly *or* has good acceleration **6** *Boxe* round; *Escrime* bout; *Ftbl (du jeu)* second half; *Équitation* lesson; *(groupe de cavaliers)* riders **7 faire qch à plusieurs reprises** to do sth several times *or* on several occasions; **à trois reprises** three times, on three occasions **8** *Mus* repeat; *(d'un thème, des instruments)* re-entry **9** *Couture (raccord)* darn, mend; **r. perdue** invisible mend **10** *(somme payée à un locataire)* = (money paid for) fixtures and fittings *(paid to outgoing tenant)*

repriser [rəprize] **VT** *(vêtement)* to mend; *(chaussette)* to darn, to mend; **aiguille/coton/œuf à r.** darning needle/cotton/egg *or* mushroom

réprobateur, -trice [reprɔbatœr, -tris] **ADJ** *(air, ton)* reproving; **dire qch d'un ton r.** to say sth reprovingly *or* in a tone of reproof

réprobation [reprɔbasjɔ̃] **NF** reproof; **ton/regard de r.** reproving tone/look, tone/look of reproof

reproche [rəprɔʃ] **NM 1** *(remontrance)* reproach; **un regard plein de r.** a reproachful look, a look of reproach; **regarder qn d'un air plein de r.** to look at sb reproachfully; **faire des reproches à qn** to reproach sb *(pour avoir fait qch* for doing sth); **je ne vous fais pas de reproches** I'm not reproaching *or* blaming you; **ton de r.** tone of reproach, reproachful tone; **sans r.** *(vie, personne)* beyond *or* above reproach, blameless; **le seul r. qu'on puisse faire à ce roman, c'est …** the only criticism one can make about *or* the only thing wrong with the novel is …; **c'est le seul r. que je trouve à lui faire** it's the only criticism I have to make of him **2** *Jur* **r. de témoin** barring of a witness

reprocher [rəprɔʃe] **VT 1** *(blâmer)* to reproach; **r. qch à qn** to blame *or* reproach sb for sth; **r. à qn de faire** to blame *or* reproach sb for doing sth; **r. à qn d'avoir fait qch** to blame *or* reproach sb for doing *or* having done sth; **je ne vous reproche rien** I'm not blaming you for anything; **il n'y a absolument rien à lui r.** he's totally blameless **2** *(critiquer)* *(impatience, négligence)* to criticize; **qu'est-ce que vous reprochez à ce livre?** what have you got against the book?; **on lui reproche sa naissance** they've never

forgiven him his background **3** *Jur (témoin, témoignage)* to bar

VPR se reprocher se r. qch to blame oneself for sth, to reproach oneself with *or* for sth; **je me reproche de lui avoir fait confiance** I blame *or* reproach myself for trusting him; **ils se reprochent (mutuellement) d'avoir pris cette décision** they're blaming each other for the decision

reproducteur, -trice [rəprɔdyktœr, -tris] **ADJ 1** *(organe, cellule etc)* reproductive **2** *(animal)* kept for breeding; *(cheval)* stud **NM** *(animal)* breeder; **reproducteurs** breeding stock, breeders; **r. d'élite** pedigree sire

reproductibilité [rəprɔdyktibilite] **NF** reproducibility

reproductible [rəprɔdyktibl] **ADJ** reproducible

reproductif, -ive [rəprɔdyktif, -iv] **ADJ** reproductive

reproduction [rəprɔdyksjɔ̃] **NF 1** *(génération)* reproduction; **les organes de la r.** the reproductive organs; **animaux élevés en vue de la r.** animals reared for breeding, breeding stock; **r. sexuée/asexuée** sexual/asexual reproduction; **l'époque de la r.** the breeding season **2** *(d'un document, d'une image, du son etc)* reproduction, reproducing; *(image, copie)* reproduction; **cela se prêtera bien à la r.** it will reproduce well; **droits de r.** reproduction rights; **droits de r. en feuilleton** serial *or* serialization rights; **tous droits de r. réservés pour tous pays** all rights of reproduction reserved for all countries; **r. interdite** *(sur disque, cassette)* all rights reserved

reproduire [rəprɔdɥir] *(conj like* **produire)** **VT** *(copier)* *(son, image, tableau, document etc)* to reproduce; *Journ (article)* to reprint; *(imiter)* to imitate, to mimic; **ce tableau a été reproduit à des milliers d'exemplaires** thousands of reproductions have been made of this picture; **tu as reproduit les mêmes erreurs** you've made exactly the same mistakes as before

VPR se reproduire 1 *(des animaux etc)* to breed, to reproduce, to multiply; **ils se reproduisent comme des lapins** they breed like rabbits **2** *(des événements)* to recur, to happen again; **et que cela ne se reproduise plus!** don't let it happen again!

reprogrammable [rəprɔgramabl] **ADJ** *Ordinat (touche)* reprogrammable

reprogrammer [rəprɔgrame] **VT** *Ordinat* to reprogram; **r. une livraison** to reschedule a delivery

reprographie [rəprɔgrafi] **NF** *(de documents)* duplicating, *Spéc* reprography

reprographier [rəprɔgrafje] **VT** *(document)* to duplicate

réprouvé, -ée [repruve] **N** outcast; *Rel* reprobate

réprouver [repruve] **VT 1** *(crime, attitude, méthode, geste)* to condemn **2** *Rel* to damn

reps [rɛps] **NM** *Tex* rep(p)

reptation [rɛptasjɔ̃] **NF** crawling

reptile [rɛptil] **NM** *Zool, Fig Fam* reptile

repu [rəpy] **ADJ** satiated, full; *Fig* **être r. de qch** to have had one's fill of sth

républicain, -aine [repyblikɛ̃, -ɛn] **ADJ, N** republican

républicanisme [repyblikanism] **NM** republicanism

république [repyblik] **NF** *Pol* republic; *Hum* **on est en r.** it's a free country; *Fam* **r. bananière** banana republic; **la R. de Saint-Marin** the Republic of San Marino; **la R. française** the French Republic; **la R. populaire de Chine** the People's Republic of China; *Anciennement* **R. démocratique allemande** Ger-

man Democratic Republic; *Fig* **la r. des lettres** the world of letters

répudiation [repydjasjɔ̃] **NF 1** *(d'une épouse, d'une opinion)* repudiation **2** *Jur (d'une succession, d'une nationalité)* renunciation

répudier [repydje] **VT** *(impf, pr sub n.* répudiions) **1** *(épouse, opinion)* to repudiate **2** *Jur (succession, nationalité)* to renounce, to relinquish

répugnance [repyɲɑ̃s] **NF 1** *(dégoût)* repugnance (**pour** for), aversion (**pour** to), loathing (**pour** of, for); **avoir de la r. pour qn/qch** to loathe sb/sth; **éprouver de la r. à faire qch** to do sth with repugnance *or* loathing; **je me souviens de la r. avec laquelle elle en parlait** I remember her repugnance in talking about it; **avec r.** with repugnance *or* loathing **2** *(réticence)* reluctance, unwillingness; **r. à faire qch** reluctance *or* unwillingness to do sth; **avec r.** reluctantly, unwillingly; **faire qch avec r.** to do sth reluctantly *or* with reluctance, to be reluctant to do sth

répugnant [repyɲɑ̃] **ADJ** *(dégoûtant)* *(personne, odeur)* repulsive, revolting, repugnant; *(lieu)* repulsive, unsavoury; *(acte, comportement)* loathsome, repulsive; **de façon répugnante** disgustingly, repulsively; **il s'est conduit de façon répugnante avec la veuve** he behaved repulsively towards the widow

répugner [repyɲe] **VI 1** *(ressentir du dégoût)* **r. à qch** to feel repelled by sth, to find sth repellent, to feel repugnance for sth; **r. à faire qch** to be reluctant *or* lo(a)th to do sth **2** *(dégoûter)* **r. à qn** to be repugnant *or* repellent to sb; **elle/cette idée me répugne** I find her/the idea quite repugnant *or* repellent, she/the idea is quite repugnant *or* repellent to me **V IMPERS il me répugne de le faire** I am reluctant *or* lo(a)th to do it **VT** *Litt (personne)* to be repugnant to

répulsif, -ive [repylsif, -iv] **ADJ** *Phys, Fig* repulsive

répulsion [repylsjɔ̃] **NF** *Phys, Fig* repulsion; **éprouver de la r. pour qn** to be repelled by sb, to feel repulsion for sb

réputation [repytasjɔ̃] **NF** reputation; **avoir (une) bonne/mauvaise r.** to have a good/bad reputation; **jouir d'une bonne r.** to have a good reputation, to be well spoken of; **se faire une r.** to make a reputation *or* name for oneself; **cela a fait sa r.** it made his/her name; **sa r. de chirurgien** his reputation as a surgeon; **connaître qn de r.** to know sb by reputation *or Fml* repute; **elle a la r. d'être généreuse** she has a reputation for being generous *or* for generosity; **ils ont la r. d'être très chaleureux** they are said *or* reputed to be very kind-hearted; **établissement de mauvaise r.** disreputable establishment; **athlète de r. internationale** world-famous athlete

réputé [repyte] **ADJ** *(expert, restaurant, vin etc)* well-known, famous, renowned (**pour** for); **c'est un écrivain très r. dans son pays** he's a very well-known *or* renowned writer in his country; **r. intelligent** reputed *or* considered to be intelligent; **il est r. ne rien ignorer de cette science** he is reputed to know everything about the science; **malgré ses qualités réputées extraordinaires, il s'est montré incapable de finir à temps** despite his reportedly extraordinary talents, he proved unable to finish on time

réputer [repyte] **VT** *Vieilli* to consider, to think, *Fml* to deem; **on le répute bienveillant** he is considered *or* thought *or* deemed (to be) benevolent

requérant, -ante [rəkerɑ̃, -ɑ̃t] *Jur* **ADJ partie requérante** applicant, claimant **N** applicant, claimant

requérir [rəkerir] VT (conj like **acquérir**) **1** (faveur) to ask for, to seek, Fml to solicit; (la présence ou l'aide de qn) to request; (explication, soin, de la patience, des mains habiles etc) to require, to call for; (l'attention de qn) to demand, to require **2** Hist, Mil r. des civils to conscript civilians (for a public service) **3** Jur (sentence) to call for

requête [rəkɛt] NF **1** (demande) request; Ordinat query; **adresser une r. à qn** to make a request to sb, Fml to petition sb; **à ou sur la r. de qn** at sb's request **2** Jur petition; **r. en cassation** appeal

requiem [rekɥijɛm] NM INV Rel, Mus requiem; **messe de r.** requiem (mass)

requin [rəkɛ̃] NM Zool, Fig shark; **peau de r.** shagreen; **r. de la (haute) finance** financial shark

requinquer [rəkɛ̃ke] Fam VT **r. qn** to pick or perk sb up; **le voilà requinqué** he's (back to) his old self again
▪ **VPR se requinquer** to pick or perk up

requis [rəki] ADJ requisite, required; **les conditions requises** the requirements
▪ NM Hist (civil) labour conscript

réquisition [rekizisjɔ̃] NF **1** Admin (de vivres, de véhicules etc) requisitioning, commandeering; Hist **r. civile** (de personne) conscription for a public service; **mettre en r.** to requisition, to commandeer **2** Jur (plaidoirie) prosecution address

réquisitionner [rekizisjɔne] VT (vivres, véhicules etc) to requisition, to commandeer; Hist (civils) to conscript; Fam **elle nous a réquisitionnés pour faire la vaisselle** she requisitioned or conscripted us to do the washing-up

réquisitoire [rekizitwar] NM Jur prosecution address; Fig indictment (**contre** of)

RER [ɛrəer] NM Rail (abrév **Réseau express régional**) = express rail network serving Paris and its suburbs

re-recording [ririkɔrdiŋ] NM TV, Radio re-recording

RES [ɛrəɛs] NF Fin (abrév **reprise de l'entreprise par ses salariés**) employee buy-out

RESA [reza] NF (abrév **réservation**) = TGV seat reservation ticket

résa [reza] NF (abrév **réservation**) reservation, booking, bkg

resaler [rəsale] VT Culin to put more salt in, to add more salt to

resalir [rəsalir] VT to (get) dirty again
▪ **VPR se resalir** to get oneself dirty again, to dirty oneself again

rescapé, -ée [rɛskape] ADJ (personne) surviving
▪ N (d'un désastre, d'un naufrage etc) survivor

rescinder [rəsɛ̃de] VT Jur to rescind, to annul

rescision [resizjɔ̃] NF Jur rescission, annulment

rescousse [rɛskus] NF **aller/venir à la r. de qn** to go/come to the rescue of sb; **arriver à la r.** to come to the rescue; **appeler qn à la r.** to call on sb for help or assistance, to call sb to the rescue

réseau, -eaux [rezo] NM **1** (de fils etc) network; Archit tracery; Phys, Nucl (de réacteur) lattice; Mil **r. de barbelés** barbed wire entanglement **2** (de routes, de voies ferrées, de rivières etc), Tél network, system; Radio, TV network **3** Fig (d'amis, de contacts etc) network, circle; **r. d'espionnage** spy ring or network; **r. de résistance** resistance network; **un r. de drogue** a drug ring **4** Ordinat network; **mise en r.** networking
▪ ▪ Ordinat **r. en anneau à jeton** token ring network; **r. d'apport** (pour aéroport) feeder network; **r. autoroutier** motorway network;

Ordinat **r. en bus** bus network; **r. câblé** cable(d) network; **r. de commercialisation** marketing network; **r. de communication** communication network; Tél **r. à commutation par paquets** packet-switching network; **r. commuté** switched network; Ordinat **r. connecté en étoile** star network; **r. de distribution** distribution network; Élec **r. de distribution urbain** town mains; Ordinat **r. de données** data network; Rail **Réseau express régional** = suburban train network in Paris; **r. ferroviaire** rail network; **r. informatique** computer network; Tél **r. interurbain** long distance network; Ordinat **r. local** local area network; Ordinat **r. longue distance** wide area network, WAN; Élec **r. national** national grid (system); Ordinat **r. numérique à intégration de services** integrated services digital network; Ordinat **r. de télématique** ou de **communication de données** datacomms network; **r. télévisuel** television network; Tél **r. urbain** local area network; Ordinat **r. d'utilisateurs** user network; Ordinat **r. à valeur ajouté** value-added network, VAN; **r. de vente** sales network

réséda [rezeda] NM Bot reseda; **r. odorant** mignonette
▪ ADJ INV, NM (couleur) reseda, mignonette

réservataire [rezɛrvatɛr] NM (dans un hôtel) party making a reservation

réservation [rezɛrvasjɔ̃] NF **1** (de place, à l'hôtel etc) reservation, booking; **bureau de r.** booking office; **la r. est obligatoire** reservations are necessary; **billet de train avec r.** train ticket with seat reservation; **faire une r.** to make a reservation; **j'ai fait une r. dans un petit hôtel** I booked or reserved a room in a little hotel; **r. d'avion** flight reservation; **r. de groupe** group booking; **r. de place** seat reservation; **r. en bloc** block-booking; **r. ferme** firm reservation or booking; **r. par téléphone** ou **téléphonique** telephone reservation or booking; **r. électronique** electronic reservation **2** Jur reservation; **r. faite de tous mes droits** without prejudice to my rights

réserve [rezɛrv] NF **1** (restriction) reservation; **faire des réserves** to have reservations (**sur** about); **je voudrais faire quelques réserves concernant ce contrat** I would like to express some reservations about the contract; Vieilli **à la r. de ...** except for ...; **sous r. de qch** subject to sth; Jur **sous r.** without prejudice; **donné sous toutes réserves** (horaires de cinéma etc) subject to alteration; **je te le dis, mais sous toutes réserves** I can tell you this, but it will be officially confirmed later; **sans r.** (éloges, admiration) unqualified; (affirmer qch) without reservation

2 (discrétion) reserve; **se tenir** ou **demeurer sur la r.** to refuse to commit oneself; **être sur la r.** to be on one's guard; **son attitude manque de r.** his attitude is lacking in caution or restraint; **parler avec r.** to speak with restraint; **quand il sort de sa r.** when he breaks through his reserve; **il est un peu sorti de sa r.** he was a little less reserved than usual; **je vous rappelle votre devoir de r.** ≃ may I remind you that you have signed the Official Secrets Act

3 (de vivres, d'équipement, d'argent etc) stock, reserve; (de troupes) reserve; Physiol (de l'organisme) reserves, stores (**en** of); Fin reserve; **réserves mondiales** (de pétrole etc) world reserves; **réserves bancaires** bank reserves; **puiser dans les réserves** to draw on the reserves; **en r.** in reserve, set aside; Fin **sans r. de retour** non-returnable, no-return; Com **sans r. de retour** on a sale or return basis; **avoir beaucoup d'énergie en r.** to have great reserves of energy; **mettre qch en r.** to put sth aside or by, to reserve sth; **tenir**

qch **en r.** to keep sth in reserve; **fonds de r.** reserve fund; **vivres de r.** emergency rations, iron rations

4 Mil reserve; **r. de l'armée active** reserve of the regular army; **officier de r.** reserve officer

5 (parc) reserve; (pour gibier) preserve hunting/fishing reserve; **réserves (indiennes)** (Indian) reservation

6 (local) (de magasin) stockroom, storeroom; (de bibliothèque, musée) reserve (collection)

7 TV, Cin **en r.** white-on-black
▪ ▪ Aut **r. d'air** air chest; **r. d'animaux sauvages** safari park; **r. de chasse** hunting reserve; Fin **r. contractuelle** contractual reserve; Fin **r. facultative** optional reserve; **r. de gibier** game reserve; **r. légale** Fin legal reserve; Jur (d'héritage) legal share; **r. liquide** liquid assets, cash reserve; **r. métallique** bullion reserve; **r. naturelle** nature reserve; **r. de pêche** fishing reserve; **r. de prévoyance** contingency reserve; Fin **r. réglementée** regulatory reserve; Fin **réserves statuaires** statutory reserves; **r. zoologique** wild life sanctuary

réservé [rezɛrve] ADJ **1** (chambre, siège etc) reserved, booked; **place réservée aux personnes âgées** seat reserved for the elderly; **salle réservée aux réunions** room reserved or kept for meetings, meeting room **2** Typ **tous droits réservés** all rights reserved **3** (personne, attitude) reserved; **elle a un caractère plutôt r.** she's rather reserved; **avis r.** qualified opinion

réserver [rezɛrve] VT (louer) (chambre, place etc) to reserve, to book; (marchandises, argent etc) to set aside, to put by, to save (**à, pour** for); **r. une place à qn** to keep or save a seat for sb; (d'une agence de voyages etc) to reserve a seat for sb; **je vous ai réservé une place sur le prochain vol** I've booked or reserved a seat for you or I've booked you on the next flight; **place réservée** reserved seat; **r. du bois pour l'hiver** to store wood for the winter; **r. son jugement** to reserve judgement; **r. le meilleur pour la fin** to keep or save the best till last; Journ **r. la une** to hold the front page; **r. une surprise à qn** to have a surprise in store for sb; **nous ignorons le sort qui lui sera réservé** we do not know what fate has in store for him/her; **ils me réservent toujours un excellent accueil** they always welcome me with open arms; **nous attendons de connaître le sort qui nous est réservé** we are waiting to find out what fate has in store for us; Litt **il lui était réservé de grands succès** he was destined for great things; **'chasse/pêche réservée'** 'private hunting/fishing'; Admin Vieilli **quartier réservé** red-light district
▪ VI (au théâtre, à l'hôtel) to book, to reserve, to make a booking or a reservation; (au restaurant) to reserve, to make a reservation; **bonsoir madame, vous avez réservé?** good evening, madam, do you have a reservation?; **j'ai réservé au nom de Roux** I have a reservation in the name of Roux; **pour r., appeler ...** for reservations, call ...
▪ VPR **se réserver se r. le droit de faire qch** to reserve the right to do sth; **je me réserve pour le match de ce soir** I'm saving my strength for this evening's match; **elle s'est réservé une portion du gâteau** she saved a piece of cake for herself; **celui-là, je me le réserve!** I'm keeping that one for myself!; **je préfère me r. pour le dessert** I'd rather save myself or keep my appetite or leave some room for the dessert

réserviste [rezɛrvist] NM Mil reservist

réservoir [rezɛrvwar] NM **1** (bassin) reservoir; **r. de barrage** storage basin **2** (pour poissons) fish pond **3** (cuve) tank; (de toilet-

tes) cistern; **r. à gaz** gasholder, gasometer; **r. à mazout** fuel-oil tank; **r. d'encre** ink reservoir; *Aut* **r. d'essence** petrol *or Am* gas tank; *Aut* **r. d'expansion** expansion tank; *Aut* **r. de lave-glace** windscreen washer reservoir; *(en plastique)* windscreen washer bottle; *Aut* **r. de liquide de frein** brake fluid reservoir; *Aut* **r. en charge** header tank; *Aut* **r. à carburant** fuel tank; *Aut* **r. à dépression** vacuum tank *or* reservoir

résidant [rezidɑ̃] ADJ resident; **r. à** resident *or* living in

résidence [rezidɑ̃s] NF **1** *(séjour)* residence; **certificat de r.** residence permit; **avoir sa r. à Lyon** to be resident *or* to live in Lyons; *Jur* **en r. surveillée** under house arrest **2** *(demeure)* residence, home; *(de diplomate)* residency; **changer de r.** to change one's residence, to move (house) **3** *(immeuble)* block of luxury flats, *Am* luxury apartment building
▸▸**r. hôtelière** apartment hotel; **r. médicalisée (pour personnes âgées)** nursing home; **r. principale** main residence *or* home; **r. secondaire** second home, holiday home, *Am* vacation home; **r. de tourisme** apartment hotel

résident, -ente [rezidɑ̃, -ɑ̃t] N **1** *(diplomate)* resident **2** *(étranger)* (foreign) resident; **tous les résidents français en Grande-Bretagne** all French nationals resident in Great Britain
ADJ *Ordinat* **r. en mémoire** memory-resident

résidentiel, -ielle [rezidɑ̃sjɛl] ADJ residential

résider [rezide] VI **1** *(vivre)* to live, *Fml* to reside *(à, dans, en* in); **dans la ville où l'on réside** in the town where one is resident **2** *Fig* to lie, to reside; **toute la difficulté réside en ceci que …** the whole difficulty rests *or* lies in the fact that …

résidu [rezidy] NM **1** residue; **résidus** *Chimie* residue; *(déchets)* waste; **résidus urbains** town refuse; **résidus de fission** radioactive waste **2** *Math* remainder

résiduaire [rezidɥɛr] ADJ waste; *Ind* **eaux résiduaires** waste water, process water

résiduel, -elle [rezidɥɛl] ADJ residual; *Géog* **relief r.** residual relief

résignation [reziɲasjɔ̃] NF *(soumission)* resignation; **avec r.** *(dire qch)* with resignation, resignedly; *(supporter qch)* with resignation

Il faut noter que le terme anglais **resignation** signifie également **démission**.

résigné [reziɲe] ADJ resigned *(à* to); **je suis r.** I've resigned myself

résigner [reziɲe] VT *Litt (fonction, biens)* to resign, to give up; **r. sa charge** *ou* **ses fonctions** to give up *or* relinquish one's appointment, to resign
VPR **se résigner se r. à qch/à faire qch** to resign oneself to sth/to doing sth; **se r. à une situation** to resign oneself to a situation; **il faut se r.** you have to resign yourself

résiliable [reziljabl] ADJ which may be terminated *or* cancelled *or* annulled

résiliation [reziljasjɔ̃] NF *(d'un contrat)* termination, cancellation, annulment

résilience [reziljɑ̃s] NF resilience

résilient [reziljɑ̃] ADJ resilient

résilier [rezilje] VT *(accord, contrat etc)* to terminate, to cancel, to annul

résille [rezij] NF **1** *(pour cheveux)* snood; **bas r.** fishnet stockings **2** *(de vitrail)* lattice

résine [rezin] NF resin; **r. vinylique** vinyl resin; **r. époxyde** epoxy resin

résiné [rezine] ADJ, NM *(vin)* **(r.)** retsina

résiner [rezine] VT **1** *(enduire de résine)* to coat with resin **2** *(extraire la résine de)* **r. un arbre** to tap a tree *(for resin)*

résineux, -euse [rezinø, -øz] ADJ resinous; *(odeur)* of resin; *(arbre, forêt)* coniferous
NM conifer

résistance [rezistɑ̃s] NF **1** resistance, opposition (à to); *Méd (à un virus etc)*, *Pol* resistance; **n'offrir aucune r.** to put up *or* offer no resistance; **opposer une r. à qn/qch** to resist sb/sth; **je sens une r. de sa part quand j'essaie de lui en parler** I can feel a reluctance on his part to talk about it; **je n'ose pas tirer, je sens comme une petite r.** *(c'est collé)* I don't want to pull, it seems to be stuck; **r. passive** passive resistance; **faire de la r. passive** to engage in passive resistance; *Hist* **la R.** the Resistance (movement)
2 *Phys* resistance; **r. de l'air** air resistance; **r. à l'avancement** drag
3 *Élec* resistance; *(conducteur)* *(d'un appareil)* element; *(composant)* resistor; **unité de r.** unit of resistance
4 *Tech (des matériaux)* resistance, strength, toughness; **r. à la flexion** bending strength; **r. à la traction** tensile strength; **r. au choc** impact resistance; **limite de la r.** yield point; **acier à haute r.** high-resistance *or* high-tensile steel; **tissu qui n'a pas de r.** flimsy material; **r. à l'usure** *(d'un tissu)* ability to stand up to wear and tear, durability
5 *(endurance)* stamina, endurance, staying power; **il a une bonne r. à la fatigue** he doesn't tire easily, he's got good stamina
6 **pièce de r.** *Culin* main course *or* dish, pièce de résistance; *Fig (d'un spectacle etc)* main item (on the programme), pièce de résistance

résistant, -ante [rezistɑ̃, -ɑ̃t] ADJ **1** *(matériau)* hard-wearing, strong, tough; *(couleur)* fast; **r. à -proof; r. à l'acide** acid-proof; **r. à la chaleur** heatproof, heat-resistant; **r. aux chocs** shockproof; **r. à l'usure** hard-wearing **2** *(robuste)* *(personne)* strong, tough, hardy; *(plante)* hardy
N freedom fighter; *Hist* member of the Resistance movement

résister [reziste] VI *(se débattre, s'opposer)* to resist; **il n'a pas résisté à la pneumonie** he succumbed to pneumonia; **je n'ai pas pu r., je les ai achetées** I couldn't resist them so I bought them; **r. à** *(tentation, influence, personne)* to resist; *(attaque)* to hold out against, to resist; *(douleur, pression etc)* to withstand, to stand up to; *(mauvais traitement, fatigue)* to stand up to; *(maladie, épidémie)* to overcome; *(vent, froid)* to withstand; **il n'a pas pu r. au courant** he couldn't fight against the current; **r. à l'analyse** *(d'un argument, d'une explication etc)* to stand up to analysis; *Tech* **r. à la chaleur/aux acides** to be heatproof/acid-proof; **ce pull a bien résisté au lavage** this jumper washed well; **r. au temps, r. à l'épreuve du temps** *(d'une amitié, d'un amour etc)* to stand the test of time; **ces couleurs ne résistent pas** these colours are not fast; *Fig* **on ne peut pas lui r.** he's irresistible, you can refuse him nothing; **personne n'ose lui r.** nobody dares stand up to him/her

résistivité [rezistivite] NF *Élec* resistivity

resituer [rəsitɥe] VT to place; **r. qch dans son contexte** to put *or* place sth in its context

résolu [rezɔly] ADJ *(personne)* determined, resolute; **un air r.** an air of determination; **d'un air r.** determinedly, with an air of determination, resolutely; **elle est (bien) résolue à le faire** she is (quite) determined to do it

résoluble [rezɔlybl] ADJ **1** *(problème)* solvable **2** *Jur (contrat)* which may be terminated *or* cancelled *or* annulled

résolument [rezɔlymɑ̃] ADV determinedly, resolutely; **être r. contre qch** to be resolutely *or* strongly opposed to sth

résolution [rezɔlysjɔ̃] NF **1** *Tech (d'une sub-*

stance, d'un écran de télévision etc) resolution; **écran à haute r.** high-resolution screen **2** *(d'un problème)* solving, *Fml* resolution **3** *Jur (d'un contrat)* termination, cancellation, annulment **4** *(décision)* resolution; **prendre la r. de faire qch** to make a resolution to do sth, to resolve *or* determine to do sth; **ma r. est prise** I've made my decision; *Pol* **prendre une r.** to pass a resolution; **prendre des résolutions** to make resolutions; **mes bonnes résolutions de début d'année** my New Year's resolutions **5** *(détermination) (d'une personne)* determination, single-mindedness, strength of will; **sa r. est remarquable** he is remarkably determined *or* single-minded

résolutoire [rezɔlytwar] ADJ **clause r.** termination clause

résonance [rezonɑ̃s] NF **1** resonance; **la r. est bonne/mauvaise dans cette salle** the acoustics in the hall are good/bad; *Mus* **caisse de r.** sound box; *Méd* **r. magnétique nucléaire** nuclear magnetic resonance, NMR **2** *Fig (effet)* response, echo; **cela n'est pas sans r. sur sa vie affective** it is not without its effects on his/her emotional life; **ce mot prend une r. toute particulière dans ce contexte** in this context, the word has particular connotations

résonateur [rezonatœr] NM *Élec* resonator

résonnant, résonant [rezonɑ̃] ADJ **1** *(voix)* resonant, resounding, sonorous; **r. de cris** resounding *or* echoing *or* resonant with cries **2** *Phys* resonant

résonner [rezone] VI *(d'un son, de pas etc)* to resound, to resonate, to echo; *(d'une voix, d'une pièce)* to echo; **sa voix résonnait dans les haut-parleurs** his/her voice blared out *or* boomed out over the loudspeakers; **ça résonne!** there's an echo!, it echoes!; **faire r. la trompette/le tambour** to sound the trumpet/the drum; **l'air résonnait de leurs cris** the air rang *or* resounded *or* echoed with their cries

résorber [rezɔrbe] VT **1** *Méd* to resorb **2** *(surplus, déficit)* to absorb, to bring down; *(chômage)* to absorb, to curb; *(dettes)* to wipe out, to clear; **r. la crise économique** to solve the economic crisis
VPR **se résorber 1** *Méd* to be resorbed **2** *(d'un surplus, déficit)* to be absorbed, to be brought down; *(du chômage)* to be absorbed *or* curbed

résorption [rezɔrpsjɔ̃] NF **1** *Méd* resorption **2** *(d'un surplus, déficit)* absorption, bringing down; *(du chômage)* absorption, curbing; *(de dettes)* clearing, wiping out

résoudre [rezudr] *(prp* résolvant; *pp* résolu, parfois résous, -oute; *pr ind* je résous, il résout, *n.* résolvons; *impf* je résolvais; *p hist* je résolus; *fu* je résoudrai) VT **1** *(difficulté)* to resolve, to clear up; *(équation, énigme, problème)* to solve; *(question, conflit)* to resolve, to settle; *(crise)* to solve, to resolve **2** *Chimie (transformer)* to break up; **r. qch en qch** to resolve sth into sth, to break up sth into sth **3** *Jur (contrat, accord etc)* to terminate, to cancel, to annul **4** *(décider)* **r. qn à faire qch** to prevail upon *or* persuade *or* induce sb to do sth; **r. de faire qch** to decide *or* make up one's mind to do sth
VPR **se résoudre 1 se r. à faire qch** to decide *or* make up one's mind *or* resolve to do sth; **je ne peux pas me r. à la quitter** I can't bring myself to leave her **2** *Chimie* to resolve itself; **se r. en qch** to resolve into sth, to break up into sth

respect [rɛspɛ] NM respect (**pour** for); **le r. de la nature/des morts** respect for nature/the dead; **inspirer le r.** to inspire respect; **montrer** *ou* **faire preuve de r. pour qn/qch** to show sb/sth (some) respect; **avoir du r. pour qn** to respect sb, to have respect for sb; **il n'a aucun r. pour les autres** he has no respect for other people; **avoir le r. des lois/ des convenances** to respect or have respect for or have regard for the law/the conventions; **son courage suscite le r.** his/her courage commands respect; **parler avec r.** to speak respectfully or with respect; **r. de soi** self-respect; Vieilli **r. humain** fear of other people's judgement (of one's actions); **faire qch par r. pour qn** to do sth out of respect or regard for sb; **manquer de r. envers qn** to be disrespectful to sb, to show sb a lack of respect; **il t'a manqué de r.** he was disrespectful to you, he did not show you any respect; **tenir qn en r.** to fend sb off, to keep sb at a distance; **j'ai réussi à le tenir en r. en le menaçant d'un couteau** I managed to fend him off with a knife; Fig **son autorité naturelle lui permet de tenir en r. les élèves les plus indisciplinés** his/her innate authority enables him to keep the most undisciplined pupils at bay; Fml **sauf le r. que je vous dois, sauf votre r.** with all due respect; **en signe de r.** as a mark of respect; Fml **rendre** ou **présenter ses respects à qn** to pay one's respects to sb; **(je vous présente) mes respects, chère madame** my respects, madam

respectabilité [rεspεktabilite] NF respectability

respectable [rεspεktabl] ADJ **1** (digne de respect) (famille, air, femme etc) respectable **2** (digne de considération) (somme) respectable, fairly large; **un appartement de dimensions respectables** a fair-sized flat; **un nombre r. de spectateurs** a respectable or fairly large or fair number of spectators

respecter [rεspεkte] VT (personne, chose) to respect, to have respect or regard for; (calme d'un endroit, désir ou opinion de qn, limitation de vitesse) to respect; (la loi) to abide by, to obey, to respect; **r. les délais de livraison** to meet delivery schedules; **il ne respecte rien** he has no respect for anything; **faire r. la loi** to enforce the law; **se faire r.** to command respect; **r. le code de la route** to respect or obey or follow the Highway Code; **vous n'avez pas respecté la priorité** you didn't give way

▸ VPR **se respecter** to respect oneself; (réciproque) to respect each other; **comme tout homme qui se respecte** like any self-respecting man; **un professeur qui se respecte ne ferait pas cela** no self-respecting teacher would do that; **il se respecte trop pour faire cela** he has too much self-respect to do that

respectif, -ive [rεspεktif, -iv] ADJ respective

respectivement [rεspεktivmɑ̃] ADV respectively; **ils ont r. deux et trois enfants** they have two and three children respectively

respectueusement [rεspεktɥøzmɑ̃] ADV respectfully

respectueux, -euse [rεspεktɥø, -øz] ADJ respectful (**de** of; **envers** to, towards); **il ne se montre guère r. envers ses parents** he shows little respect for his parents; **d'un ton r.** in a respectful tone, in a tone of respect; **être r. des autres comme de soi** to respect other people as much as one does oneself; **être r. de qch** to respect sth, to show respect for sth; **r. des lois** respectful of the law, law-abiding; **se tenir à distance respectueuse** to keep at a respectful distance; **je vous prie d'agréer, Monsieur, mes salutations respectueuses** (dans une lettre) yours faithfully; (quand la formule de salutation comprend le nom du destinataire) yours sincerely

respirable [rεspirabl] ADJ breathable; Fig **l'atmosphère n'était plus r.** the atmosphere had become oppressive or suffocating

respirateur [rεspiratœr] NM respirator, ventilator

respiration [rεspirasjɔ̃] NF breathing, Spéc respiration; (de plante) respiration; **r. artificielle** artificial respiration; **pratiquer la r. artificielle sur qn** to give sb artificial respiration; Méd **r. contrôlée/assistée** controlled/assisted respiration; **avoir la r. difficile** ou **des difficultés de r.** to have trouble or difficulty breathing; **s'arrêter pour prendre sa r.** to pause for breath; **retenir sa r.** to hold one's breath; Fig **tous retenaient leur r. en attendant le verdict** everyone waited for the verdict with bated breath; **couper la r. à qn** to wind sb; Fig to take sb's breath away, to flabbergast sb

respiratoire [rεspiratwar] ADJ (organe etc) respiratory; (appareil, exercice, problème) breathing; **défaillance r.** respiratory failure; **quotient r.** respiratory quotient; **voies respiratoires** respiratory tract; **troubles respiratoires** breathing or respiratory problems; **difficultés respiratoires** difficulty in breathing

respirer [rεspire] VI (d'une personne, d'un vin, d'une plante) to breathe; **r. longuement** to take or draw a long breath; **r. par le nez/ la bouche** to breathe through the nose/ mouth; Fam **laissez-moi r.!** let me get my breath (back)!, let me catch my breath!; Fam **ouf! je respire!** (de soulagement) thank goodness for that!, that's a load off my mind! ▸ VT **1** to breathe (in), to inhale; **aller r. un peu d'air** to go for a breath of air; **r. une fleur** to smell a flower **2** Fig **r. la vengeance/la paix/ la confiance** to breathe vengeance/peace/ confidence; **r. la santé/l'honnêteté** to radiate health/honesty; **cela respire l'ennui le plus profond** it is profoundly boring

resplendir [rεsplɑ̃dir] VI (d'une personne) to be radiant; (briller) to shine, to glitter, to gleam; **r. de joie/santé** (d'un visage) to be shining with joy/glowing with health; (d'une personne) to radiate joy/health; **sa beauté resplendissait** she was radiantly beautiful

resplendissant [rεsplɑ̃disɑ̃] ADJ (personne, beauté) glowing, radiant; (voiture etc) shining, gleaming; (cuivres) gleaming; **r. de joie/santé** (mine) shining with joy/glowing with health; (personne) radiant with joy/ health; **femme d'une beauté resplendissante** radiantly beautiful woman; **il a une mine resplendissante** he looks wonderfully well

responsabiliser [rεspɔ̃sabilize] VT **r. qn** (le rendre responsable) to give sb a sense of responsibility

responsabilité [rεspɔ̃sabilite] NF responsibility; (légale) liability (**de** for); **r. de l'employeur** employer's liability; **r. du fabricant** manufacturer's liability; **accepter une r.** to take on or assume or accept a responsibility; **élever des enfants est une grande r.** bringing up children is quite a responsibility; **c'est ta r. de répondre au téléphone, pas la mienne** answering the phone is your responsibility, not mine; **avoir la r. de qn/qch** to be responsible for sb/sth; **donner à qn la r. de qch** to give sb responsibility or make sb responsible for sth; **partager la r. d'un projet** to share the responsibility or be jointly responsible for a project; **assumer ses responsabilités** to face up to one's responsibilities; **décliner toute r.** to deny all responsibility; **nous déclinons toute r. pour les objets perdus ou volés** we accept no liability for lost or stolen items; **fuir les responsabilités** to evade or avoid responsibility; **être appelé à de hautes responsabilités** to

be given important responsibilities; **avoir un poste à responsabilités** to have a responsible job; **je cherche un poste à responsabilités** I want a job with responsibilities; **faire qch sous sa (propre) r.** to do sth on one's own responsibility

▸▸ **r. civile** public liability; Fin **être assuré r. civile** to have personal liability insurance; **r. contractuelle** contractual liability; **r. illimitée** unlimited liability; **r. limitée** limited liability; Pol **r. ministérielle** ministerial accountability; **r. patronale** employer's liability; **r. solidaire et indivise** joint and several liability; **r. au tiers** third-party liability; **être assuré r. au tiers** to carry third-party insurance

responsable [rεspɔ̃sabl] ADJ responsible (**de** for); (légalement) liable (**de** for); **elle n'est pas r. de ton échec** she's not responsible or not to blame for your failure; **r. de ses enfants** responsible or answerable for one's children; **le ministre est r. devant** ou **envers les Chambres** the Minister is responsible or answerable or accountable to Parliament; **tenir qn/qch pour r. d'un malheur** to hold sb/sth responsible for a misfortune, to blame sb/sth for a misfortune; **il faut les rendre responsables** they have to be given a sense of responsibility

▸ N **1** (coupable) person responsible (**de** for), culprit; **qui est le r. de cette plaisanterie idiote?** who's responsible or to blame for this silly prank? **2** (personne en charge) person in charge; (dirigeant élu) official; **les responsables du Parti socialiste** Socialist Party officials

▸▸ **r. des achats** buyer; **r. administratif** executive manager; **r. des banquets** banqueting manager; **r. du budget** account executive; **r. client** account manager; **r. des comptes-clients** account executive; **r. des études de marché** market research manager; **r. de la formation** training officer; **r. de groupe** group leader; **r. de magasin** warehouse manager; **r. de marché** market manager; **r. (du) marketing** marketing manager or executive; TV, Cin **r. point** focus puller; **r. politique** political leader; **r. produit** product manager; **r. de projet** project leader; Culin **r. des sauces** (dans un restaurant) sauce chef, saucier; **r. du service commercial** sales and marketing manager; Pol **r. syndical** union leader; **r. de la vente** sales manager; **r. des ventes** sales manager; **r. du vestiaire** cloakroom attendant

resquillage [rεskijaʒ] NM, **resquille** [rεskij] NF (au théâtre etc) sneaking in without paying; (dans l'autobus, le métro etc) fare-dodging; (dans une queue) queue-jumping; **faire de la r.** to dodge paying

resquiller [rεskije] VI (au théâtre, au concert etc) to sneak in without paying; (dans l'autobus, le métro etc) to dodge paying one's fare; (dans une queue) to jump the queue; **entrer dans un cinéma en resquillant** to sneak into a cinema (without paying) ▸ VT **r. une place de théâtre** to sneak into a theatre (without paying); **r. un ticket de métro** to dodge paying one's fare on the metro

resquilleur, -euse [rεskijœr, -øz] N (au théâtre etc) person who has sneaked in without paying; (dans l'autobus, le métro etc) fare-dodger; (dans une queue) queue-jumper

ressac [rəsak] NM Naut undertow

ressaisir [rəsezir] VT (fugitif) to recapture; (biens) to recover (possession of); (pouvoir) to seize again; **la peur l'a ressaisi** fear gripped him again

▸ VPR **se ressaisir** to regain one's self-control, to pull oneself together; **ressaisissez-vous!** pull yourself together!; Scol **se r. au second**

trimestre to improve *or* to make more of an effort in the second term

ressasser [rəsase] **VT** *(en esprit)* to brood over; *(répéter)* to keep coming out with; *(d'un professeur) (cours)* to rehash; **plaisanterie ressassée** (old) chestnut; **un thème ressassé** a hackneyed theme, a theme that's been done to death

ressaut [rəso] **NM** *Archit, Géol (d'une corniche, d'une paroi d'escalade)* projection

ressauter [rəsote] **VI** to jump again; **il n'a jamais ressauté en parachute** he never made another parachute jump

▸ **VT** to jump (over) again

ressemblance [rəsãblãs] **NF** resemblance, likeness; **la r. est grande** there's a great resemblance; **il y a quelques ressemblances entre eux** they resemble each other in a few respects, there are a few points of similarity *or* likeness between them; **il y a une r. frappante entre la mère et la fille** there is a striking resemblance between mother and daughter; **il n'y a aucune r. entre lui et sa sœur** he and his sister do not resemble each other at all; **il y a aussi une r. dans leurs façons de s'exprimer** there is also a similarity in the way they express themselves, they express themselves in a similar way too; **un tableau peint sans aucun souci de r.** a painting done with no concern for rendering a true likeness; *Cin* **toute r. avec des personnes existant ou ayant existé ne peut être que fortuite** any resemblance to persons living or dead is purely coincidental

ressemblant [rəsãblã] **ADJ portrait bien r.** lifelike portrait, good likeness; **elle est très ressemblante** *(sur un portrait)* it is very like her; **ce tableau n'est pas très r.** it's not a very good likeness, it doesn't look much like you/him/*etc*

ressembler [rəsãble] **VI r. à qn** *(physiquement)* to resemble sb, to be like *or* look like sb; *(moralement)* to resemble *or* be like sb; **r. à qch** to resemble *or* be like *or* look like sth; **elle ne ressemble pas beaucoup à ses parents** she doesn't look like *or* resemble her parents very much; **tu ressembles vraiment à ton père, toi!** you're just like your father!; **il te ressemble comme un frère** he's so like you, you'd think he was your brother; **à quoi ressemble-t-elle?** what's she like?, what does she look like?; *Fam* **cela ne ressemble à rien** it looks like nothing on earth; *(ça ne veut rien dire)* it just doesn't make sense; **cela lui ressemble tout à fait!** that's just like him!, that's him all over!; **cela ne lui ressemble pas de se plaindre** it's not like him/her to complain

▸ **VPR se ressembler** to be alike, to resemble each other; **il n'y en a pas deux qui se ressemblent** no two are alike; **les bébés se ressemblent tous** babies all look alike; **ils se ressemblent comme deux gouttes d'eau** they're as like as two peas in a pod; *Prov* **qui se ressemble s'assemble** birds of a feather flock together; **les jours se suivent et ne se ressemblent pas** day follows day and you never know what to expect; **tu ne te ressembles plus!** you're not your usual self!

ressemelage [rəsəmlaʒ] **NM** resoling

ressemeler [rəsəmle] **VT** *(conj like* **semeler***)* *(chaussures)* to resole

ressentiment [rəsãtimã] **NM** resentment (**de** at; **contre** against); **avec r.** resentfully; **éprouver du r.** to feel resentful

ressentir [rəsãtir] *(conj like* **sentir***)* **VT** *(douleur, colère, sympathie, effet, insulte etc)* to feel; *(choc, sensation)* to feel, to experience; **je me demande comment il a pu t. cette trahison** I wonder how he felt about being betrayed like that; **r. de l'affection pour qn** to be fond of sb; **je ne ressens aucune ten-**

dresse pour elle I don't feel any affection for her, I'm not fond of her; **je ne ressens plus rien pour toi** I don't feel anything for you any more; **r. vivement la perte de qn** to feel the loss of sb deeply, to be deeply affected by the loss of sb; **il a durement ressenti les privations** the effects of the hardships he suffered have gone deep

▸ **VPR se ressentir 1 se r. de** to feel the effects of **2** *très Fam* **s'en r. pour qch** to feel fit for sth, to feel up to sth

> Il faut noter que le verbe anglais **to resent** est un faux ami. Il signifie **ne pas aimer du tout**.

resserre [rəser] **NF** *(pour outils)* tool shed; *(pour stocker)* storeroom

resserrement [rəsermã] **NM 1** *(contraction)* *(d'une vallée, route etc)* narrowing; **r. du crédit** credit squeeze, tightening of credit **2** *(d'un nœud, d'un écrou etc)* tightening *Fig (d'une amitié, de liens)* strengthening

resserrer [rəsere] **VT** *(livres sur étagère)* to push closer together; *(nœud, ceinture, pores)* to tighten; *(écrou)* to tighten (up); *Fig (amitié, liens)* to strengthen; *(récit)* to condense; *(discipline)* to tighten (up); *(crédit)* to squeeze, to tighten

▸ **VPR se resserrer 1** *(d'une vallée, route etc)* to narrow, to become narrower; *(des pores)* to tighten **2** *(d'un nœud)* to tighten; *Fig (des liens)* to strengthen, to grow stronger

resservir [rəservir] *(conj like* **servir***)* **VT 1** *(servir de nouveau)* to serve again; **tu ne vas pas nous r. ta quiche d'hier?** you're not going to dish up yesterday's quiche again, are you?; **r. un plat** to serve up a dish again **2** *(servir en plus) (poisson etc)* to serve another helping of; **tu nous ressers un peu de ta quiche?** can we have a bit more of your quiche?

▸ **VI** to be used again; **cette robe pourra r. l'été prochain** the dress will do another summer; **ça peut toujours r.** it might come in handy *or* useful

▸ **VPR se resservir resservez-vous de riz** help yourself to *or* have some more rice *or* another helping of rice; **tu peux te r., si tu veux** you can have some more if you like

ressort [rəsɔr] **NM 1** *(élasticité)* elasticity, springiness; **faire r.** to spring back, to fly back; *Fig* **avoir du r.** to be resilient; **elle ne manque pas de r.** she's resilient

2 *(pièce)* spring; **r. de sommier** bed spring; **r. de montre** watch spring; **r. à boudin** *ou* **en spirale** coil *or* spiral spring; **r. à feuilles** *ou* **à lames** leaf *or* laminated spring; *Aut* **r. d'expansion** expansion *or* expander spring; **r. hélicoïdal** helical *or* coil spring; **r. moteur, grand r.** mainspring; **à r.** spring-loaded; **actionné** *ou* **mû par r.** spring-driven; **suspendu à ressort(s)** *(chariot etc)* sprung; **sans ressort(s)** unsprung

3 *Fig (motivation)* motive; **l'intérêt est un puissant r.** self-interest is a powerful motive *or* driving force

4 *Jur (compétence)* province, scope, competence; *(étendue de juridiction)* jurisdiction; **être du r. de la cour** to be *or* fall within the competence of the court; **cela n'est pas de son r.** that's not his/her responsibility, that doesn't fall within his/her province

5 en dernier r. *Jur* without appeal; *Fig* as a *or* in the last resort

ressortir¹ [rəsɔrtir] *(conj like* **sortir***)* **VI** *(aux être)* **1** *(d'un lieu) (d'une personne)* to come/go out again, to re-emerge; **elle est ressortie** *(je suis à l'intérieur)* she went out again; *(je suis à l'extérieur)* she came/went out of her house again; **je n'ai pas envie de r. ce soir** I don't want to go out again this

evening; **la lame est ressortie ensanglantée** the blade came out covered in blood; **la balle est ressortie par l'épaule** the bullet came out *or* exited through the shoulder

2 *(se détacher)* to stand out; **faire r.** *(couleur)* to bring out, to set off; *(fait, importance de qch)* to emphasize, to accentuate, to stress; *(sens de qch)* to bring out; **pour faire r. tes yeux** to highlight *or* emphasize your eyes; **cela ressort d'autant plus que ...** it stands out all the more since ...

3 *(résulter)* to emerge, to be evident (**de** from); **il en ressort que nous ...** it emerges *or* is evident from this that we ...

▸ **VT** *(aux avoir) (parapluie, vêtements etc)* to get out again; *Fig* **elle ressort toujours le même genre d'histoires** she always comes out with the same old stories; **elle nous a encore ressorti son histoire de ...** she trotted out her story about ...

ressortir² [rəsɔrtir] **VI r. à** to come under the jurisdiction of; *Fig Litt* **concepts qui ressortissent à la géométrie** concepts that belong to geometry *or* that come within the province of geometry

ressortissant, -ante [rəsɔrtisã, -ãt] **ADJ** *Jur* **r. à** under the jurisdiction of

▸ **N** national, citizen; **r. d'un pays de l'Union européenne** EU national

ressouder [rəsude] **VT** to resolder; *(par la soudure autogène)* to reweld

▸ **VPR se ressouder** *(d'un os, d'une fracture)* to knit (again)

ressource [rəsurs] **NF 1** *(habileté)* resourcefulness; **personne de r.** resourceful person, person of resource; **elle a de la r.** she is resourceful; **la situation est grave mais tu n'es pas sans r.** the situation is serious but there are things you can do *or* there are ways out of it

2 *(moyen)* expedient; **avoir mille ressources, être plein de ressources** to be very resourceful; **être à bout de ressources** to have exhausted all one's possibilities; **exploiter les ressources d'une situation/d'un scénario** to exploit the possibilities of a situation/a script; **je n'avais d'autre r. que la fuite** I had no choice but to run away, there was no course open to me but flight; **c'est ma seule r.** it's the only course of action open to me; **en dernière r.** as a last resort

3 ressources *(argent)* resources, means; *(agricoles, pétrolières etc)* resources; **ressources d'appoint** additional sources of income; **ressources financières** financial resources; **les ressources en hommes et en matériel** manpower and material resources; **ressources humaines** human resources; **ressources personnelles** private means

4 *Aviat* flattening out, pull-out

ressourcer (se) [sərəsurse] **VPR** *Fam (revenir aux sources)* to go back to one's roots; *(reprendre des forces morales)* to get back in touch with one's inner self

ressusciter [resysite] **VT 1 r. les morts** to raise *or* resurrect the dead; *Fig* **r. qn** to put new life into sb; **ce vin me ressuscite** this wine is putting new life into me *or* reviving me; **tes larmes ne vont pas le r.** crying won't bring him back (to life) **2** *Fig (querelle, mode, traditions etc)* to revive, to resurrect; *(souvenir, commerce)* to revive

▸ **VI** to revive, to come to life again; *Rel* to rise from the dead; **ressuscité d'entre les morts** risen from the dead, resurrected

> Il faut noter que le verbe anglais **to resuscitate** est un faux ami et ne correspond jamais au français **ressusciter**. Il signifie le plus souvent **ranimer**.

restant [restã] **ADJ 1** remaining, left; **les vingt euros restants** the remaining twenty euros, the twenty euros remaining *or* left (over) **2 poste restante** poste restante, *Am* general delivery

NM remainder, rest; **le r. de sa vie** the rest of one's life; **un r. d'étoffe** a leftover piece of material; *Com* **r. en caisse** cash surplus; **r. d'un compte** balance of an account, account balance

restau [resto] **NM** *Fam* restaurant; **r. U** university canteen *or* refectory

restaurant [restorã] **NM** restaurant; **et si on allait au r. ce soir?** how about eating out *or* going to a restaurant this evening?; **ils vont souvent au r.** they often eat out *or* eat in restaurants; **manger au r.** to eat out ▸▸ **r. gastronomique** gourmet restaurant; **r. libre-service** self-service restaurant; **r. de poissons** seafood restaurant; **r. routier** transport café, *Am* truck stop; **r. self-service** self-service restaurant; **r. de spécialités** speciality restaurant; **r. à thème** theme restaurant; **r. universitaire** university canteen *or* refectory

restaurateur, -trice [restoratœr, -tris] **N 1** *(de bâtiments, de tableaux)* restorer; *Litt (d'un régime, d'une dynastie etc)* restorer **2** *(de restaurant)* restaurateur, restaurant owner/manager

restauration [restorasjɔ̃] **NF 1** *(de bâtiment, d'une dynastie, de finances publiques, discipline etc)* restoration; *Ordinat* restore; **faire de la r. de tableaux** *(comme métier)* to work in art restoration; *Hist* **la R.** the Restoration **2** *(métier)* catering; **la r. collective** institutional catering; **r. rapide** fast food; **chaîne de r. rapide** fast-food chain; **être dans la r.** to be in catering, to work in the catering trade; **r. aérienne** in-flight catering, airline catering **3** *Suisse (restaurant)* restaurant

restaurer [restore] **VT 1** *(rétablir, réparer), Ordinat* to restore; *Fig (discipline, autorité)* to restore, to re-establish **2** *(faire manger)* **r. qn** to give sb something to eat
VPR **se restaurer** *(manger)* to eat something

restauroute [restorut] **NM** *(de route)* roadside restaurant; *(d'autoroute)* motorway *or Am* freeway restaurant

reste [rest] **NM 1** *(de travail, d'argent, de vin etc)* rest, remainder; *Math* remainder; **le r. du temps** the rest of the time; **commence par ceci et je te dirai quoi faire le r. du temps** start with this and I'll tell you what to do for the rest *or* remainder of the time; **le r. (des gens)** the rest, the others; **il y avait un r. de beurre/lait** there was a bit of butter/milk left (over); **accommoder un r. de viande** to use up the leftover meat; **faire un chemisier avec un r. de tissu** to make a shirt out of a remnant of material; **elle a de beaux restes** *(elle est encore belle)* she still has some of her beauty; *(elle travaille encore très bien, c'est encore une très bonne athlète)* she's still on the ball; *Fig* **il n'a pas demandé son r.** he didn't say another word; **partir sans demander son r.** to leave without another word, to leave without further ado; **finis le r.** *(du repas)* finish it off, finish *or* take what's left; **(et) pour le r., on verra plus tard** as for the rest, we'll see about it later; **il sait parler aux clients, mais pour le r., c'est un incapable** he knows how to talk to the customers but otherwise he's quite incapable; **et (tout) le r.** and so on, and so forth; **être** *ou* **demeurer en r.** to be indebted (**avec qn** to sb), to remain under an obligation to sb; *Fig* **pour ne pas être en r.** so as not to be left out; **vous auriez du pain de r.?** do you have any bread left (over)?, do you have any spare bread?, do you have any bread to spare?; **quand j'ai du temps de r.** when I have some spare time *or* time to spare; **avoir de l'argent de r.** to

have more than enough money; **du** *ou* **au r.** besides, moreover

2 restes *(de repas)* leftovers, scraps; *(d'une ancienne ville, d'une fortune etc)* remains; *(d'une armée)* remnant; **restes humains** human remains; *Litt* **restes mortels** mortal remains

RESTER [reste]

to remain **1–3** ▪ to be left **1** ▪ to stay **2, 3** ▪ to keep **3** ▪ to last **4**

VI *(aux* **être)** **1** *(subsister)* to remain, to be left; **les quelques jours qui restent** the few days that are left, the few remaining days; **les cinq euros qui restent** the remaining five euros, the five euros left (over); **dix-neuf divisé par cinq, je pose trois, reste quatre** nineteen divided by five makes three, and four over *or* remainder four; **la vie n'est pas facile pour ceux qui restent** life isn't easy for those left behind

2 *(demeurer)* to stay, to remain; **je pars – non, reste!** I'm going – no, stay!; **il est resté à** *ou* **pour travailler** he stayed (behind) to work; **mon sac a dû r. sur le comptoir** I must have left my bag on the counter; **les mots lui restèrent dans la gorge** the words stuck in his throat; **il restait là à me regarder** he sat/stood there looking at me; **restez où vous êtes** stay where you are; **r. assis** to remain *or* stay seated *or* sitting; **r. debout** to stand; *(ne pas aller se coucher)* to stay up; *(pour attendre)* to wait up; **je ne peux plus r. debout** I can't stay on my feet a minute longer; **je n'en peux plus de r. debout toute la journée** I'm fed up being on my feet all day; **r. au lit** to stay *or* remain in bed; **r. (à) dîner** to stay to *or* for dinner; **qu'est-ce qui reste à faire?** what still has to be done?, what's left to do?; **le plus dur reste à faire** the hardest part remains *or* is still to be done; **r. sur place** to stay where one is, to stay put; *Fam* **j'y suis, j'y reste** here I am and here I stay; *Fam* **y r.** *(mourir)* to kick the bucket, to snuff it; **j'ai bien cru que j'allais y r.** I really thought I'd had it, I really thought my time *or* number was up; **il a bien failli y r.** he nearly didn't make it; **en r. là** to proceed no further; **j'aime autant en r. là** *(dans une conversation, relation)* I'd rather not go any further, I'd rather leave it at that; **restons-en là pour aujourd'hui** let's leave it there *or* at that for today; **les choses en sont restées là** there the matter rested *or* remained; **ne reste donc pas là planté comme un imbécile!** don't just stand there!; **où en sommes-nous restés?** where did we get to?, where did we leave off *or* stop (**de notre lecture** in our reading)?; *TV* **où en es-tu resté?** *(du feuilleton)* what point did you see up to?; **ils en sont restés à l'encre et au papier** *(ils n'utilisent pas encore d'ordinateurs)* they're still stuck in the pen-and-paper era, they haven't progressed beyond the pen-and-paper stage; **que cela reste entre nous** this is strictly between ourselves, this must go no further; **r. sur une impression** to be left with an impression; **cela m'est resté sur l'estomac** *(d'un plat)* it's lying heavy on my stomach; *Fig* it still rankles (with me), *Fam* it still bugs me; *Fig* **cela me reste en travers de la gorge** it still sticks in my throat

3 *(dans un état)* to keep, to stay, to remain; **r. tranquille/calme** to stay *or* keep *or* remain still/calm; **c'est resté collé** it's stuck; **r. en bonne santé** to remain *or* keep in good health, to keep well; **il est resté très en forme** he's kept in very good shape; **je suis resté longtemps fatigué après l'opération** I was tired for a long time after the operation; **la cuisinière est restée allumée** the cooker stayed *or* remained lit; **r. ouvert** *(d'un magasin)* to stay open; **le robinet est resté ouvert toute la journée** the tap was (left) on all day;

la maison est restée ouverte the house wasn't locked up; **r. en bons termes avec qn**, *Fam* **r. bien avec qn** to stay *or* remain on good terms with sb

4 *(durer)* to last, to endure; **le nom lui est resté** the name stayed with him/her, *Fam* the name stuck; **un match qui restera dans les mémoires** a match which will live on in people's memories; **il restera dans l'histoire comme l'un de nos plus grands présidents** he'll live on in history as one of our greatest presidents

5 *Belg* **r. faire qch** *(continuer à faire qch)* to go on *or* continue doing sth

V IMPERS **il me reste cinq euros** I have *or* I've got five euros left; **il me reste à peine de quoi payer le loyer** I barely have enough left to pay the rent; **il ne me reste qu'à vous remercier** it only remains for me to thank you, all that remains is for me to thank you; **(il) reste à savoir s'il a raison** it remains to be seen whether he's right; **il n'en reste pas moins que …** it is nevertheless the case that …; **il ne nous restait plus que cinq cents mètres à parcourir** we only had another five hundred metres to go, we only had five hundred metres left to go; **dis-leur ce qui ne va pas, il en restera toujours quelque chose** tell them what's wrong, some of it is bound to sink in; **que reste-t-il de tes belles promesses?** what remains of your wonderful promises?

restituable [restituabl] **ADJ** *(prêt, somme d'argent)* repayable, returnable; *(dépense)* refundable

restituer [restitɥe] **VT 1** *(reconstituer)* *(inscription, texte)* to restore; **le film restitue parfaitement l'ambiance du Paris d'après-guerre** the film recreates perfectly the atmosphere of post-war Paris **2** *(rendre)* *(marchandises volées etc)* to restore, to return; *(argent, prêt)* to repay, to pay back; **r. de l'argent à qn** to repay sb **3** *(énergie)* to release; *(son)* to reproduce; **cette chaîne restitue un son plus pur** this system gives a better sound, the sound reproduction on this system is better

restitution [restitysjɔ̃] **NF 1** *(reconstitution)* *(d'un texte, d'un monument)* restoration; *(d'une ambiance)* recreation **2** *(fait de rendre)* *(de marchandises volées etc)* return, *Fml* restitution; *(d'argent, prêt)* repayment; **r. d'impôts** tax refund; **r. d'indu** return of payment made in error **3** *(de l'énergie)* release; *(du son)* reproduction

resto [resto] **NM** *Fam* = restau

Restoroute® [restorut] **NM** = restauroute

restreindre [restrɛ̃dr] *(prp* **restreignant;** *pp* **restreint;** *pr ind* **je restreins, il restreint, n. restreignons;** *p hist* **je restreignis;** *fu* **je restreindrai) VT** *(ambition, nombre de personnes etc)* to restrict (**à** to), to curb; *(production, sorties, achats, dépenses)* to cut back (on), to restrict, to limit; *(autorité)* to limit; **une offre restreinte aux abonnés** an offer limited *or* restricted to subscribers; *Fin* **r. le crédit** to restrict credit
VPR **se restreindre 1** *(réduire ses dépenses)* to cut down; **se r. dans ses achats/dépenses** to buy/spend less **2** *(d'un domaine de recherche etc)* to become narrower *or* restricted; **votre choix de montres s'est restreint** you don't have such a large selection of watches as you used to

restreint [restrɛ̃] **ADJ** *(production, nombre de personnes, vocabulaire etc)* restricted, limited (**à** to); *(gamme, service)* limited; *(espace)* confined, limited; *(limites)* narrow; **édition à tirage r.** limited edition

restrictif, -ive [restriktif, -iv] **ADJ** *(terme, clause, pratique etc)* restrictive

restriction [restriksjɔ̃] **NF 1** *(diminution)* restriction; **restrictions budgétaires** budget restrictions **2** *(réserve)* reservation; **faire des restrictions** to express (some) reservations; **restrictions aux exportations** export restrictions; **restrictions gouvernementales** government restrictions; **restrictions journalistiques** reporting restrictions; **r. mentale** mental reservation; **sans r.** *(accord)* unconditional; *(approuver)* unconditionally, unreservedly, without reservation; *Ordinat* **r. d'accès** access restriction

restructuration [rəstryktyrasjɔ̃] NF **1** *(d'une industrie, d'une entreprise)* restructuring **2** *(de dette)* rescheduling

restructurer [rəstryktyre] VT **1** *(industrie, entreprise)* to restructure **2** *(dette)* to reschedule
▸ VPR **se restructurer** to be restructured

resucée [rəsyse] NF *très Fam* **1** *(de vin, de café etc)* drop; **je vous en verse une r.?** would you like a drop more? **2** *Péj (répétition) (d'une pièce de théâtre, d'un livre etc)* rehash

résultant, -ante [rezyltɑ̃, -ɑ̃t] ADJ resultant, resulting, consequent
▸ NF **résultante** consequence, result; *Math* resultant

résultat [rezylta] NM **1** *(de calculs)* result; *(d'une action, d'une enquête etc)* result, outcome; *(d'un traitement)* result, effect; **on arrive à d'excellents résultats avec ce médicament** we're getting excellent results with this drug; **résultats** *(d'examen, de concours)* results; **les résultats de ses recherches** the results of his/her research, his/her findings; **donner des résultats** to give results; **sans r.** without result *or* success; *(expérience)* inconclusive; *(remède)* ineffective; **j'ai essayé de le lui faire comprendre, sans r.** I tried unsuccessfully to make him understand; *Mktg* **résultats antérieurs** past performance; *Mktg* **résultats perçus** perceived performance; **ces révélations eurent pour r. la chute du gouvernement** these revelations led to *or* resulted in the fall of the Government; **ça a eu pour r. de le mettre en colère** it made him angry, he got angry as a result; **attendre le r. des courses** to wait for the racing results; *Fig* to wait and see what happens; *Fam* **r. ou r. des courses: il a été licencié** as a result he was dismissed, the upshot of it all was that he was dismissed
2 *Compta* result, profit *or* loss; **r. brut** gross return; **résultats d'exercice** *ou* **d'exploitation** trading results; **r. courant** profit before tax and extraordinary items; **r. d'exploitation** operating profit or loss; **r. de l'exercice** profit or loss for the financial year; **r. de la période** profit or loss for the financial period; **r. exceptionnel** extraordinary profit or loss; **r. financier** financial profit or loss; **r. net** net return; **résultats prévisionnels** earnings forecast

résulter [rezylte] VI *(used only in the inf, third person and prp; aux often **être**)* to result, to arise (**de** from); **les avantages économiques qui en résultent** the resulting *or Fml* resultant economic benefits; **qu'en a-t-il résulté?** what was the result (of it)?, what came of it?, what was the outcome?; **ce qui résulte de ses propos, c'est que …** what emerges from *or* comes out of what he said is that …; **il en résulte que …** the result of this is that …; **il résulte de cette discussion que …** the outcome *or* result of the discussion is that …

résumé [rezyme] NM summary, résumé; *(d'un article scientifique)* abstract; *(d'un film, d'un livre)* synopsis; *Scol (livre)* study guide; **faire le r. de** *(texte)* to summarize, to give a summary *or* résumé of; *(histoire, situation)* to sum up, to summarize; *Jur* **r. des débats** summing up; **r. managérial** management summary; **en r.** *(en peu de mots)* in short, in brief; *(à tout prendre)* to sum up

résumer [rezyme] VT *(article, idées etc)* to summarize, to give a summary of; *(situation, argumentation, histoire)* to sum up; *Jur* **r. les débats** to sum up; **pour r. les faits** to sum up; **voilà toute l'affaire résumée en un mot** that's the whole thing in a nutshell
▸ VPR **se résumer** *(d'une personne)* to sum up; **pour me r.** to sum up; **voilà à quoi tout cela se résume** that's what it all amounts to *or Fam* boils down to; **tout cela se résume en un seul mot/à peu de choses** it can all be summed up in one word/in a few words

---

Il faut noter que le verbe anglais **to resume** est un faux ami. Il signifie **reprendre, recommencer.**

---

résurgence [rezyrʒɑ̃s] NF *(du racisme, d'une doctrine etc)* resurgence, reappearance; *(d'un courant sous-terrain)* resurgence

résurgent [rezyrʒɑ̃] ADJ *(courant)* resurgent

resurgir [rəsyrʒir] VI to reappear suddenly; **cette idée resurgit dans mon esprit** the idea suddenly came back to me

résurrection [rezyrɛksjɔ̃] NF **1** *Rel* resurrection **2** *Fig (des arts, du passé etc)* resurrection, revival

retable [rətabl] NM reredos, altarpiece

rétabli [retabli] ADJ *(après une maladie)* recovered

rétablir [retablir] VT **1** *(ordre, dynastie, paix etc)* to restore, to bring back; *(communications, relations, réputation)* to restore, to re-establish; **le gaz/l'eau a été rétabli(e)** the gas/water has been reconnected *or* restored *or Fam* is back on; **r. qn** *(d'un traitement etc)* to restore sb to health; **r. sa santé** to recover one's health **2** *(texte, finances)* to restore; **r. les faits** *ou* **la vérité** to set the record straight **3 r. qn (dans ses fonctions)** *(fonctionnaire etc)* to reinstate sb; **r. un officier dans son commandement** to restore an officer to his command; **r. qn dans ses droits** to restore sb's rights
▸ VPR **se rétablir 1** *(après une maladie)* to recover, to get well again; *(après un saut)* to recover **2 l'ordre se rétablit** order is being restored; **le silence s'est rétabli** silence returned **3 se r. dans les bonnes grâces de qn** to get back into sb's good books **4** *Gym* to push oneself up

rétablissement [retablismɑ̃] NM **1** *(de l'ordre, de la paix, d'une dynastie etc)* restoration; *(des communications, des relations)* re-establishment, restoration; *(d'un fonctionnaire etc)* reinstatement; **le r. du téléphone est prévu pour demain** the telephone should be reconnected by tomorrow; **r. de la religion** religious revival **2** *(après une maladie, après un saut)* recovery; **nous vous souhaitons un prompt r.** all our good wishes for a speedy recovery; **faire un mauvais r.** *(après un saut)* to land *or* recover badly **3** *Gym* push-up; **faire un r.** to push oneself up

rétamage [retamaʒ] NM *(d'une casserole etc)* retinning; *(d'un miroir)* resilvering

rétamé [retame] ADJ *Fam (ivre)* canned; *(fatigué)* whacked, dead on one's feet; *(financièrement)* broke

rétamer [retame] VT **1** *(casserole etc)* to retin **2** *(miroir)* to resilver **3** *Fam (enivrer)* to get canned; *(fatiguer)* to wear out; *(au jeu)* to clean out; **se faire r.** *(perdre un match)* to get hammered, to get slaughtered; **je me suis fait r. en anglais** I got a lousy mark in *or Am* I really flunked the English test
▸ VPR **se rétamer** *Fam (tomber)* to tumble; *(échouer)* to fail, *Am* to flunk; **elle s'est rétamée à l'oral** she failed *or Am* she flunked the oral

rétameur [retamœr] NM *(de casserole etc)* tinsmith

retapage [rətapaʒ] NM *Fam (d'une vieille maison, d'une voiture etc)* doing up; *(d'un lit)* straightening

retape [rətap] NF *très Fam* **faire (de) la r.** *(d'une prostituée, d'un représentant)* to tout for business *or* custom; *(d'un parti politique)* to tout for new members

retaper [rətape] VT **1** *Fam (vieille maison, voiture etc)* to do up; *(lit)* to straighten; **r. qn** to pick sb up **2** *(à la machine) (lettre etc)* to retype, to type again
▸ VPR **se retaper** *Fam* **1** *(après une maladie)* to get back on one's feet **2 on se retape une belote?** how about another game of belote?

retapisser [rətapise] VT **1** *(pièce etc)* to repaper; *(fauteuil)* to re-cover, to reupholster **2** *Arg (reconnaître)* to clock

retard [rətar] NM **1** *(dans le temps)* delay; *(de personne attendue)* lateness; **il y aura une heure de r.** there will be an hour's delay; **j'ai une heure de r.** I'm an hour late; **son bébé est né avec cinq jours de r.** her baby was born five days late; **je vous prie de m'excuser pour mon** *ou* **ce r.** please excuse me for being late; **et comment expliquez-vous votre r.?** how do you explain your being late *or* your lateness?; **cinq retards par semestre et c'est la porte** if you're late five times per term you're out; **sans r.** immediately, without delay; **avoir du r.** to be late; **le train a du r.** the train is (running) late; **le train a dix minutes de r.** *ou* **est en r. de dix minutes** the train is ten minutes late; **prendre du r.** to fall behind; *(d'un train)* to be running late; **mettre qn en r.** to make sb late, to delay sb; **arriver en r.** to arrive late; **être en r.** to be late; *(sur un programme)* to be behind; *(d'une horloge, d'une montre)* to be slow; **je suis en r. pour la réunion** I'm late for the meeting; **je suis en r. pour le paiement des remboursements** I'm behind with my repayments; **rattraper** *ou* **combler son r.** to catch up; **combler** *ou* **refaire son r. avec le peloton de tête** *(d'un athlète)* to close the gap with *or* to catch up on the front pack; *Com* **compte en r.** account outstanding *or* overdue; **r. de paiement** delay in payment, late payment
2 *(dans un développement)* backwardness; **le r. dont souffre le pays** the backwardness *or* backward state of the country; **r. mental** backwardness, mental retardation; **ils ont une génération de r.** they're a generation behind; **pays en r. sur les autres** backward country, country lagging behind the others; **cet enfant est en r. pour son âge** this child is backward *or* behind for his age; **élève en r. sur les autres** pupil lagging behind the others; **être en r. de dix ans sur les autres pays industrialisés** to be (lagging) ten years behind other industrialized countries; **en r. sur son temps** behind the times; **cet enfant aura du mal à combler son r.** this child will have trouble catching up; **nous voulons aider les pays en voie de développement à combler leur r.** we want to help developing countries to catch up *or* to close the gap; **être en r. pour** *ou* **dans qch** to be *or* lag behind in sth
3 *Aut* **r. à l'allumage** ignition lag, retarded ignition; *Élec* **r. d'aimantation** magnetic lag
▸ ADJ INV *Pharm (médicament)* slow-release

retardataire [rətardatɛr] ADJ **1** *(qui arrive en retard) (personne)* late **2** *(dans son développement) (pays)* backward; *(enfant)* slow, backward; *(idées, entreprise)* behind the times, out-of-date
▸ N latecomer

retardateur, -trice [rətardatœr, -tris] ADJ retarding; *(tactiques)* delaying
▸ NM *Phot* self-timer

retardé [rətarde] ADJ **1** *(départ)* delayed, late; *(arrivée)* late **2** *(mentalement) (élève)* lagging behind, slow; **enfant r.** backward or retarded child

retardement [rətardəmã] NM delay; Mil **action de r.** delaying action; **bombe à r.** time bomb; Fig **faire qch à r.** to be slow to do or in doing sth; **j'ai compris à r.** I was slow on the uptake; **comprendre une allusion à r.** to be slow in taking or to take a hint

retarder [rətarde] VT **1** (faire arriver en retard) (personne, train etc) to delay, to hold up; **vous êtes sûr que cela ne vous retardera pas?** are you sure that it won't delay you or hold you up?; **les absences répétées retardent les progrès** repeated absences will delay progress; **la tuberculose l'a retardé dans ses études** having tuberculosis has held or kept him back in his studies **2** (différer) (événement, départ, voyage etc) to delay, to postpone, to put off; (paiement) to defer, to delay; **l'intervention du Président a été retardée d'une heure** the President's address has been moved forward one hour; Autr. **l'allumage** to retard the ignition **3** (montre, horloge) to put back (**de** by)

VI **1 l'horloge retarde** the clock is slow; **ma montre retarde** ou Fam **je retarde de dix minutes** my watch is or I'm ten minutes slow; **pendule qui retarde de dix minutes par jour** clock that loses ten minutes a day; **il retarde sur son temps** ou **époque** he's behind the times; Fam **vous retardez** (vous n'êtes pas au courant) you're behind the times **2** Tech to lag

VPR **se retarder** to make oneself late

retâter [rətate] VT **r. qch** to feel sth again

VI Fam **r. de qch** to have another go at sth; **r. de la prison** to do another stretch

reteindre [rətɛ̃dr] VT (conj like teindre) to redye, to dye again

retéléphoner [rətelefɔne] VI to ring or call back or again; **r. à qn** to ring sb up or call sb (up) again, to ring or call sb back

VPR **se retéléphoner** to call each other again, to speak to each other on the phone again; **allez, on se retéléphone demain, d'accord?** talk to you again tomorrow, OK?

retendre [rətɑ̃dr] VT **1** (cordes) to retighten; (raquette) to restring; (piège) to reset **2 r. la main** to hold out one's hand again

RETENIR [rət(ə)nir] (conj like tenir)

VT to hold back **1** ▪ to hold **2** ▪ to withhold **3** ▪ to remember **4** ▪ to book **5** ▪ to restrain **8**
VPR to hold on **1** ▪ to restrain oneself **2**

VT **1** (faire rester) (personne) to hold back, to detain, to delay; (chien) to hold back, to restrain; **je ne vous retiens pas** I mustn't keep you (back), I mustn't hold you back; **ils nous ont retenus trois quarts d'heure** they kept us three quarters of an hour; **r. qn à dîner** to invite sb to stay for dinner; **elle m'a retenu par le bras** she held me back by the arm; **la grippe m'a retenue au lit pendant dix jours** the flu kept me in bed for ten days; **rien ne me retenait en France** there was nothing to keep me in France; **cette question ne nous retiendra pas** this question need not detain us; **r. l'attention de qn** (d'un projet, d'une candidature) to catch sb's attention; **elle a réussi à r. leur attention pendant trois heures** she managed to hold their attention for three hours; **r. la foule** to keep back or hold back or contain the crowd; **r. qn prisonnier/ en otage** to keep or hold sb prisoner/hostage; **r. des marchandises en douane** to hold goods up at customs; Naut **retenu par les glaces** ice-bound

2 (maintenir) to hold in position, to secure, to retain; **r. l'eau** to hold water; (d'une personne) to retain water

3 (garder) (argent) to withhold; (cotisation,

impôt) to deduct (**sur** from); **retenu à la source** deducted at source; **r. 500 euros sur le salaire de qn** to keep back or deduct 500 euros from sb's wages; **la plainte a été retenue contre lui** he was charged; **aucune charge n'a été retenue contre vous** all charges against you have been dropped

4 (se souvenir de) (leçon, nom etc) to remember; **retenez ce numéro** remember or don't forget the number; **je n'ai pas retenu les chiffres** I don't or can't remember the figures; **qu'en avez-vous retenu?** how much of it can you remember?; **je le retiens, ton ami!** I won't forget your friend in a hurry!, I'll remember your friend all right!

5 (réserver) (place, chambre, table etc) to reserve, to book; (chambre d'hôtel) to hold, Spéc to block; (personnel) to engage; **nous pouvons r. une chambre pour vous jusqu'à demain** we can hold a room for you until tomorrow

6 (accepter) (projet, suggestion) to adopt; **deux candidats ont été retenus** (ont réussi) two applicants were successful; (sont admis à l'épreuve suivante) two applicants have been short-listed; **votre candidature n'a pas été retenue** your application was unsuccessful

7 Math **je pose 2 et je retiens 5** put down 2 and carry 5

8 (contrôler) (colère) to restrain, to contain, to curb; (joie, enthousiasme) to restrain, to contain; (larmes) to keep back, to hold back; (cri) to stifle, to smother; (personne) to restrain, to hold back; **la peur/la modestie m'a retenu** fear/modesty held me back; **r. qn de faire qch** to restrain sb or to hold sb back from doing sth; **qu'est-ce qui vous retient?** what's holding you back?; **qu'est-ce qui te retient de le lui dire?** what's stopping or preventing you telling him/her?; **retenez-moi ou je fais un scandale** hold me back or I'm going to make a scene; **r. son souffle** ou **sa respiration** to hold one's breath; **nous retenions notre souffle comme il allait annoncer les résultats** we waited with bated breath for him to announce the results

VPR **se retenir 1 se r. à qch** to hold on to sth; Fig Hum **se r. aux branches** to back-pedal; **c'est ça, retiens-toi aux branches!** that's it, start back-pedalling!

2 (se contenir) to restrain or control or contain oneself; (contrôler un besoin naturel) to hold on; **se r. de faire qch** to stop oneself (from) doing sth, Fml to refrain from doing sth; **je n'ai pas pu me r. de pleurer/rire** I couldn't help crying/laughing; **il faut que tu te retiennes, il n'y a pas de toilettes ici** you're going to have to hold it in, there are no toilets here

3 une comptine qui se retient facilement a counting rhyme that is easy to remember

rétenteur, -trice [retɑ̃tœr, -tris] ADJ (force) retaining; Anat **muscle r.** retentor (muscle)

rétention [retɑ̃sjɔ̃] NF holding back; Méd (d'eau etc) retention; Méd **faire de la r. d'eau** to be retaining water; Méd **r. d'urine** urine retention; **faire de la r. d'information** to hold back or withhold information; Jur **droit de r.** lien (**de** on); Psy **r. sélective** selective retention, selective recall; Jur **r. administrative** = detention of illegal immigrants or of asylum-seekers due to be deported

retentir [rətɑ̃tir] VI **1** to (re)sound, to echo, to ring; (d'un Klaxon®) to sound, to honk; (du tonnerre, du canon) to crash; (d'une alarme) to ring, to sound; (d'un coup de feu, cri) to ring out; **le champ retentit de leurs cris** the field resounded or echoed or rang with their shouts; **la salle retentissait d'acclamations** the hall rang out with applause; **l'explosion retentit dans toute la ville** the explosion was heard right across the city;

leurs cris retentissaient à mes oreilles their cries were ringing in my ears **2** Fig **r. sur** to have an effect or impact on

retentissant [rətɑ̃tisɑ̃] ADJ (voix) resounding, ringing, booming; (succès) resounding; (échec) resounding, dismal; **discours r.** speech that arouses wide interest; **un bruit r.** an earth-shattering noise; **un scandale r.** a sensational scandal

retentissement [rətɑ̃tismɑ̃] NM **1** Litt (bruit) resounding or echoing sound or noise **2** Fig (d'un événement etc) impact, repercussions; **procès qui a eu un grand r.** lawsuit that aroused wide interest or that made a great stir; **cela a eu un grand r. sur sa carrière politique** it had a considerable impact on his political career

retenu [rət(ə)ny] ADJ **1** (réservé) reserved; **s'exprimer de façon retenue** to express oneself in restrained terms, to be restrained **2** Scol **élève r.** pupil in detention; **vous êtes r. samedi matin** you'll do detention or be kept in on Saturday morning

retenue [rət(ə)ny] NF **1** (sur salaire etc) deduction, stoppage; **r. sur salaire** wage deduction; (mensuel) salary deduction; **faire une r. de 5% sur les salaires** to stop or deduct 5% from the wages; **r. à la source** deduction at source; **retenues patronales** employer's contributions; **retenues salariales** wage deductions, employee's contributions

2 Math carry over; **n'oublie pas la r.** don't forget the number you carried over; **n'oublie pas les retenues quand tu fais des additions** don't forget to carry over when you're doing sums

3 Scol detention; **mettre un élève en r.** to keep a pupil in, to give a pupil detention

4 (discrétion) reserve, restraint; **il manque de r. avec les gens** he's a bit too forthcoming with people; **manger avec r.** to eat sparingly; **s'exprimer sans r.** to express oneself without restraint or in unrestrained terms

5 (eau) (dans un barrage) impounded water, reservoir water; **lac de r.** impoundment, dam reservoir; **clapet de r.** back-pressure or non-return valve

6 (barrage) dam

7 (fait de garder) (de biens par la douane) holding

8 Naut (d'un cordage) stay, guy

réticence [retisɑ̃s] NF **1** (hésitation) hesitation, unwillingness; **sans r.** unhesitatingly, without reservation, unreservedly; **après bien des réticences, il a dit oui** after much hesitation, he said yes; **non sans r.** not without reservations **2** (omission) omission

réticent [retisɑ̃] ADJ (hésitant) hesitant, unwilling (**à faire qch** to do sth)

Il faut noter que l'adjectif anglais **reticent** est un faux ami. Il signifie **réservé, discret**.

réticulaire [retikylɛr] ADJ reticular

réticule [retikyl] NM **1** (sac) (small) ladies' handbag **2** Opt reticle, cross wires

réticulé [retikyle] ADJ reticulate(d)

rétif, -ive [retif, -iv] ADJ (cheval) stubborn; (personne) recalcitrant

rétine [retin] NF Anat retina

rétinien, -ienne [retinjɛ̃, -jɛn] ADJ Anat retinal

retirable [rətirabl] ADJ withdrawable; **votre argent est r. à tout moment** you can withdraw money at any time

retirage [rətiraʒ] NM (d'un livre, d'une photo etc) reprinting

retiré [rətire] ADJ **1** (lieu) secluded, remote; (vie) solitary; **vivre r. (de la société)** to live in seclusion, to live a solitary life **2** (à la retraite) retired; **être r. des affaires** to have retired from business

RETIRER [rətire]

VT to take out **1** ▪ to take off **1, 4** ▪ to remove **1, 4** ▪ to withdraw **1, 5** ▪ to extract **3** ▪ to take back **5**
VPR to retire **1, 2** ▪ to withdraw **1** ▪ to subside **3** ▪ to recede **3**

VT 1 (faire sortir) to take out; (aller chercher) to take or get out; (quelque chose d'encastré) to get out; (argent de son compte) to withdraw, to take out (de from); (bagages) to reclaim, to collect (de from); (billet) to collect, to pick up (de from); (bouchon, épine) to pull or get out (de of), to remove (de from); **r. un enfant du collège** to remove a child from school, to take a child away from school; **r. un athlète d'une course** to withdraw an athlete from a race; **r. des pièces de la circulation** to withdraw coins from circulation; **r. des marchandises de la douane** to take goods out of bond, to clear goods; **r. des marchandises de la circulation** to withdraw goods from circulation; **r. du marché** to take off the market, to demarket; **r. progressivement** (produit) to phase out; **r. sa participation d'une société** to sell one's shares in a company, to sell out; **retire tous ces papiers de (sur) la table** get or clear all those papers off the table; **r. les mains de ses poches** to take one's hands out of one's pockets; **on ne lui retirera pas de l'idée qu'il mérite mieux** he won't be persuaded or convinced that he doesn't deserve better

2 (se procurer) **r. un profit de qch** to make a profit out of sth, to profit from sth; Fig to benefit from sth, to profit from sth; **combien en avez-vous retiré?** how much did you get for it?; **quel plaisir peut-il en r.?** what pleasure can he get or derive from it?; **elle dit n'avoir retiré que des ennuis de cet accord** she says she got nothing but trouble out of the agreement

3 (extraire) (huile de schiste etc) to extract
4 (enlever) (gants, lunettes) to take off, to remove; (manteau, pull etc) to take off; **on me retire mon plâtre la semaine prochaine** I'm having the plaster removed or off next week; **r. sa main** to draw back or pull back one's hand; **retire ta main immédiatement ou je crie** get your hand off me immediately or I'll scream; **r. qch à qn** to withdraw sth from sb, to take away sth from sb; **r. son manteau à qn** (pour le déshabiller) to take off sb's coat; (pour le débarrasser) to take sb's coat; **on ne va pas lui r. le droit de garde** they're not going to take the custody of his children away from him; **personne n'a l'intention de te r. ton emploi** no one intends to take your job away from you; **r. le permis de conduire à qn** to disqualify or ban sb from driving, to take away or Fml revoke sb's driving licence; **on lui a retiré le ou son permis** he's been banned (from driving)
5 (revenir sur) (remarque, promesse) to withdraw, to take back; (offre) Jur (plainte) to withdraw; **r. sa candidature** (à une élection) to withdraw one's candidacy; (pour un travail) to withdraw one's application; **je retire ce que j'ai dit** I take it all back, forget what I said
6 (tirer de nouveau) **r. des coups de feu** to fire more shots; **r. une flèche** to shoot another arrow; Typ **r. un livre** to reprint a book
VPR se retirer 1 (s'en aller) to retire, to withdraw; (d'une foule) to move back or away; Mil to retire, to withdraw, to pull out; **se r. d'un consortium** to back or pull out of a consortium; **se r. dans sa chambre** to retire to one's room; **vous pouvez vous y r.** that will be all, you may go; **se r. de la lutte** to retire from the field; **se r. (en faveur de qn)** (d'un candidat) to stand down (in favour of sb)
2 (d'un employé) to retire (**de** from); **se r.**

des affaires to retire from business
3 (des eaux) to subside; (de la mer) to recede; (de la marée) to ebb; **les eaux de la rivière se retirent** the level of the river is dropping

retombée [rətɔ̃be] NF **1** retombées radioactives radioactive fallout **2** Fig (répercussion) retombées repercussions; **l'une des retombées du programme spatial fut la mise au point de nouveaux matériaux** new materials were one of the spin-offs of the space programme; **la grève aura des retombées sur les prix** the strike will have repercussions or a knock-on effect on prices

retomber [rətɔ̃be] VI (aux often être) **1** (tomber de nouveau) to fall (down) again; (de la pluie, des bombes etc), Fig (d'une monnaie) to fall again; **r. dans son fauteuil** to fall back or sink back into one's armchair; **faire r. un store** to let down or pull down a blind; **laisser r. ses bras** to drop one's arms; **r. dans l'erreur** to lapse back into one's old ways; **r. dans le péché** to fall or sink back into one's sinful ways; **r. dans l'oubli** to sink back into obscurity or oblivion; **elle est retombée dans l'anonymat** she faded out of the limelight; **r. dans le désespoir** to fall back into despair; **le pays risque de r. dans la guerre civile** the country may lapse back into a state of civil war; **r. dans le vice** to relapse into vice; **r. en enfance** to lapse into one's second childhood; **r. malade** to fall or become ill again; Fam **r. sur qn** to bump into sb again
2 (tomber) (d'une personne, d'un ballon) to land; **r. sur ses pattes** (d'un chat) to land on its feet; Fig **r. sur ses pieds** ou Fam **ses pattes** to land on one's feet; **r. toujours dans la même situation** always to end up or land in the same situation; **pour éviter que la conversation ne retombe sur le même sujet** to prevent the conversation from coming round to the same subject again; **r. sur qch** (trouver) to come across or stumble on sth; **tu ne retomberas jamais sur une occasion pareille** you'll never come across an opportunity like it again; **le blâme/la responsabilité retombera sur lui** the blame/responsibility will fall on him; **faire r. le blâme sur qn** to put or lay the blame on sb; **tout retombe toujours sur moi!** it's always my fault!, I always get the blame for everything!; Fam **tout ça va me r. dessus** it'll all come back on me
3 (diminuer) (de l'enthousiasme, de l'intérêt) to fall off, to wane; (de l'attention) to fall off, to slacken
4 (des cheveux, des rideaux) to hang (down) (sur over); **ses cheveux lui retombent dans le dos** her hair hangs down her back; **laisser ses cheveux r.** to let or take one's hair down

retordre [rətɔrdr] VT **1** (linge) to wring out again **2** Tex (fil) to twist; Fam **il vous donnera du fil à r.** he'll give you trouble

rétorquer [retɔrke] VT **1 r. que ...** to retort that ... **2** (accusation) to cast back, to hurl back; **r. un argument contre qn** to turn sb's argument against him/her

retors [rətɔr] ADJ **1** Tex (fil, corde) twisted **2** (bec) curved **3** (personne) crafty, wily, devious

rétorsion [retɔrsjɔ̃] NF Jur, Pol retaliation; **mesures de r.** retaliatory measures

retouche [rətuʃ] NF (action) (d'un tableau, d'une photo etc) touching up, retouching; (d'un texte, d'un vêtement) altering; (résultat) (d'un tableau, d'une photo etc) retouch; (d'un texte, d'un vêtement) alteration; **faire des retouches à** (un vêtement) to make alterations to; (un tableau, une photo) to retouch; (un texte) to alter; **il faudra faire une r. dans le dos** it will have to be altered at the back; TV, Cin, Ordinat **r. d'image(s)** image editing

or retouching; TV, Cin **r. numérique** digital retouching

retoucher [rətuʃe] VT (tableau, photo etc) to touch up, to retouch; (texte) to touch up, to alter; (vêtement) to alter, to make alterations to
VI votre article est bien, n'y retouchez pas your article is good, leave it alone or don't change a word of it; **je n'ai jamais retouché à la drogue** I've never touched drugs again

retoucheur, -euse [rətuʃœr, -øz] N **1** Beaux-Arts, Phot retoucher **2** (en confection) alteration hand

RETOUR [rətur] NM **1** (de voyage, après une absence) return; **être de r.** to be back (again); **être de r. de vacances** to be back from holiday; **un journaliste de r. de Paris** a reporter (just) back from Paris; **de r. chez moi, je lui écrivis** I wrote to him when I got home or on my return home; **à mon r.** on my return; **on en parlera à mon r.** we'll talk about it on my return or when I get back; **partir sans espoir de r.** to leave without any hope of returning; **être perdu sans r.** to be irretrievably lost; **point de non-r.** point of no return; **voyage/vol de r.** return journey or trip/flight; **pour le voyage de r., je passerai par Lyon** I'll be coming through Lyons on my way back; **billet aller r.** return ticket, Am round-trip ticket; **coupon de r.** return half; Fam **cheval de r.** (vieux criminel) old offender, old lag; **par r. (du courrier)** by return (of post); **r. à l'envoyeur** return to sender; **le r. de l'hiver/d'une maladie** the return of winter/recurrence of a disease; **faire un r. sur le passé** to look back on the past; **faire un r. sur soi** to take a good hard look at oneself; **r. à la nature/au calme** return to nature/a state of calm; **par un juste r. des choses, celui qui l'a fait a été puni** the one who did it was punished, as was only fair or as was only right and proper; Fam **être sur le r.** (d'une personne) to be past middle age or past one's prime; **beauté sur le r.** beauty on the wane
2 (changement) (de fortune) reversal; **un r. d'opinion** a backlash; **r. de conscience** qualms of conscience
3 course de r. (d'un piston) back stroke; **r. de carburateur** backfire; **avoir des retours à** backfire; **r. automatique de ruban** automatic ribbon reverse; Ordinat **r. d'information** feedback
4 TV, Radio (de son) foldback; Élec **r. à la terre** ou **à la masse** earth connection, earthing, Am grounding; **fil de r.** earth or Am ground wire
5 (de marchandises, de lettre) return; **marchandises de r., retours** returns; **vendu avec faculté de r.** sold on a sale or return basis
6 Tennis **r. de service** return of serve
7 (sur clavier) return; **touche r.** return key; **appuyez sur la touche r.** press return; **r. arrière** backspace
8 (locutions) **payer qn de r.** to repay sb in kind; **payer de r. l'affection de qn** to return sb's affection; **il ne semblait pas payer de r. ma curiosité pour lui** he didn't seem to be as curious about me as I was about him; **en r.** in return (**de** for); **aimer qn en r.** to return sb's love, to love sb back or in return; Sport **match r.** return match
► ► **r. d'âge** (d'une femme) change of life; Cin **r. en arrière** flashback; **faire un r. en arrière** to flash back; **r. de chariot** (de machine à écrire) carriage return; Ordinat **r. chariot obligatoire** hard carriage return; Aut **r. de flamme** blowback; Ordinat **r. ligne** line feed; Ordinat **r. ligne obligatoire** hard return; Aut **r. de manivelle** backfire kick; Fig **il y a eu un r. de manivelle** it backfired; **il faut s'attendre à des retours de manivelle** we'll have to expect a certain amount of backlash; Fin **r. net** net return; Ordinat **r. obligatoire** hard re-

turn; *Mil* **r. offensif** counter attack, counter stroke; *Com* **r. sans frais** return free of charge; **r. sur investissement** return on investment, ROI; **r. sur ventes** return on sales; *Biol* **r. à un type** reversion to type

retourne [rǝturn] NF **1** *(aux cartes)* **la r. est à cœur** hearts are trumps **2** *Fam* **les avoir à la r.** to be bone idle

retournement [rǝturnǝmɑ̃] NM *(de situation)* turnaround, reversal; *(d'opinion)* about-turn (**de** in)

┌────────────────────────┐
│ **RETOURNER** [rǝturne] │
└────────────────────────┘

▪ **VT** to turn inside out **1** ▪ to turn **2** ▪ to turn over **2** ▪ to turn up **2** ▪ to turn round **3** ▪ to return **4**
▪ **VI** to go back **1** ▪ to return **1**
▪ **VPR** to turn over **1** ▪ to turn round **2** ▪ to turn against *(se retourner contre)* **3**

VT 1 *(en mettant la face intérieure à l'extérieur) (parapluie, gant, vêtement)* to turn inside out; **retournez vos poches** turn out your pockets

2 *(verticalement)* to turn over; *(terre)* to turn over *or* up; *(matelas, omelette, steak, foin)* to turn; *(carte)* to turn up; *Fig (idée, projet)* to turn over in one's mind, to mull over; **r. une salade** to toss a salad; **tourner et r. qch** to turn sth over and over *(again)*; *Fig* **r. une question dans tous les sens** to look at *or* consider a question from every angle; *Fam* **on avait retourné tout le bureau pour trouver la lettre** they had turned the office upside down to find the letter; *Fam* **r. qn** *(le bouleverser)* to upset sb

3 *(horizontalement)* to turn round; **r. la tête** to turn one's head, to look round; **il retourna l'arme contre moi et tira** he turned the gun on me and fired; **r. un argument contre qn** to turn an argument against sb; **r. qn contre qn** to turn sb against sb; **r. une situation** to reverse a situation; *Fam* **elle l'a retourné comme un gant** she very quickly got him to change his mind; *Fam* **on le retourne comme un gant** he is easily swayed

4 *(renvoyer, rapporter)* to return; **r. qch à qn** to return sth to sb, to send sth back to sb; *Com* **r. un effet** to return a bill; **r. à l'expéditeur** to return to sender; **r. le compliment** to return the compliment; **je me permets de vous r. le compliment** the same to you

VI *(aux être)* **1** to go back, to return (**à** to); **r. chez soi** to go back home; **je retourne chez ma mère** I'm going back to my mother's; **r. déjeuner chez soi** to go home for lunch; **je ne retournerai pas la voir** I won't go back and see her; **sa fortune retourne à sa famille** his fortune reverts to his family; **r. à l'état sauvage** to revert to the wild; **r. à ses premières amours** to return *or* go back to one's first love

2 de quoi retourne-t-il? *Cartes* what are trumps?; *Fig Fam* what's it all about?, what's up?; **si quelqu'un voulait bien me dire de quoi il retourne!** would someone please tell me what's going on!

VPR se retourner 1 *(d'un dormeur)* to turn over; *(d'une voiture)* to turn *or Fam* flip over; *Fig Fam* **ne pas avoir le temps de se r.** not to have time to draw breath; **laisse-lui le temps de se r.** give him time to sort himself out

2 *(tourner la tête)* to turn *(round)*; **partir sans se r.** to leave without looking back; **on se retourne sur leur passage** they make heads turn, all heads turn when they go by

3 se r. contre qn *(d'une personne)* to turn against sb; *(verbalement)* to round *or* turn on sb; *(d'un chien)* to turn on sb; **cela finira par se r. contre lui** it'll eventually backfire on him

4 s'en r. à un endroit to return to *or* go back to a place; **s'en r. à un endroit/chez soi** to return *or* go back to a place/home

retracer [rǝtrase] VT *(conj like* tracer*)* **1** *(trait)* to draw again, to redraw, to retrace; *(sentier)* to mark out again **2** *Fig (raconter) (événement, vie etc)* to recount

rétractable [retraktabl] ADJ *(antenne)* retractable; *Aut (volant)* collapsible

rétractation [retraktasjɔ̃] NF retraction; *Jur (d'une sentence)* rescinding

rétracter¹ [retrakte] VT *(griffes, antennes)* to retract, to draw in
▪ **VPR se rétracter** *(se contracter) (d'un muscle)* to retract

rétracter² VT *(paroles)* to retract, to withdraw, to take back; *(aveu)* to retract; *Jur (arrêt)* to rescind
▪ **VPR se rétracter** *(se dédire)* to retract

rétracteur [retraktœr] ADJ, NM **(muscle) r.** retractor (muscle)

rétractile [retraktil] ADJ which can be retracted *or* pulled back, *Spéc* retractile; *Aut (volant)* collapsible

rétraction [retraksjɔ̃] NF retraction

retrait [rǝtrɛ] NM **1** *(du ciment etc)* shrinkage, shrinking **2** *(des eaux)* subsiding; *(d'un glacier)* retreat **3** *(d'argent, d'un ordre, d'une candidature, un permis etc)* withdrawal; *(de troupes)* withdrawal, pull-back; *(d'un cheval dans une course)* scratching; **r. des bagages** baggage (re)claim; **r. de marchandises** withdrawal of goods; **r. d'espèces** cash withdrawal; **faire un r.** to withdraw money; **r. automatique** automated withdrawal; **r. du permis de conduire** disqualification from driving, driving ban; **un r. de l'ordre de grève est hors de question** calling off the strike is out of the question **4** *(dans un mur)* recess; **en r.** *(étagères etc)* recessed; **maison en r.** house standing back *or* set back from the road; **en r. de la route** set back from the road; **être/rester en r.** *(d'une personne)* to be/stay in the background **5** *Typ* indent; **mettre en r.** to indent; **en r.** indented; **en r. négatif** hanging; **r. en sommaire** hanging indent; **r. inversé** reverse indent

retraite [rǝtrɛt] NF **1** *Mil etc* retreat, withdrawal; **battre en r.** to retreat, to beat a retreat, to retire; *Fig* to beat a retreat; **battre/sonner la r.** to beat/sound the retreat
2 *(fanfare)* tattoo; **r. aux flambeaux** torchlight tattoo *or* procession
3 *(de la vie active)* retirement; **caisse de r.** superannuation fund, pension fund; **être à la** *ou* **en r.** to be *or* to have retired; *(d'un officier)* to be on the retired list; **militaire en r.** army pensioner; **quand je serai à la r.** when I retire, when I've retired; **un médecin/policier à la r.** a retired doctor/police officer; **prendre sa r.** to retire; **quand j'ai pris ma r.** when I retired, on my retirement; **prendre sa r. anticipée** to take early retirement; **on parle d'une centaine de mises à la r. anticipée** there's talk of making about a hundred people take early retirement; **mettre qn à la r.** to retire sb, to pension sb off
4 *(pension)* retirement pension; **jouir d'une petite r.** to have a small pension; **r. par capitalisation** loanback pension; **r. complémentaire** supplementary pension; **prendre une r. complémentaire** to take out an extra pension scheme
5 maison de r. (pour vieillards) old people's home
6 *(isolement)* retreat; **faire une r.** to go into retreat
7 *(abri)* retreat, refuge; *(de bêtes sauvages)* lair, haunt; *(de voleurs)* hideout
8 *Archit (d'un mur, entre des étages)* offset; *(d'un mur)* recess

retraité, -ée [rǝtrete] ADJ *(à la retraite)* retired; *(officier)* on the retired list
N *(personne du troisième âge)* senior citi-

zen, pensioner, *Br* OAP; **les retraités** retired people, senior citizens

retraitement [rǝtrɛtmɑ̃] NM *(de déchets nucléaires, combustible)* reprocessing; **usine de r.** reprocessing plant

retraiter [rǝtrete] VT **1** *Nucl (déchets, combustible)* to reprocess **2** *Méd (malade)* to treat again

retranchement [rǝtrɑ̃ʃmɑ̃] NM *Mil* entrenchment; *Fig* **forcer qn dans ses (derniers) retranchements** to drive sb to the wall

retrancher [rǝtrɑ̃ʃe] VT **1** *(ôter)* **r. un passage d'un livre** to cut *or* remove a passage from a book; **r. un nombre d'un autre** to take away *or* subtract one number from another; **r. qch sur une somme** to deduct sth from a sum of money; **r. qch à qn** to dock sb sth, to dock sth from sb; **r. un nom d'une liste** to remove *or* delete a name from a list **2** *Mil (position)* to entrench; *Fig* **être retranché** to be entrenched (**derrière ses croyances** in one's beliefs); *Fam* **vivre retranché dans son petit monde** to live in one's own little world *or* a world of one's own
▪ **VPR se retrancher** *Mil* to entrench oneself, to dig in; *Fig* **se r. dans le silence** *ou* **le mutisme** to take refuge in silence; **se r. derrière qn** to hide behind sb

retranscription [rǝtrɑ̃skripsjɔ̃] NF retranscription

retranscrire [rǝtrɑ̃skrir] VT to retranscribe

retransmetteur [rǝtrɑ̃smɛtœr] NM *Radio (appareil)* relay

retransmettre [rǝtrɑ̃smɛtr] VT *(conj like* transmettre*)* to transmit, to broadcast; *(relayer)* to retransmit, to relay

retransmission [rǝtrɑ̃smisjɔ̃] NF transmission, broadcast(ing); *(par relai)* retransmission, relay; **r. en direct de Cardiff** (broadcast *or* relayed) live from Cardiff; **r. en différé de Cardiff** in a recorded relay from Cardiff, recorded live at Cardiff earlier; **la r. du match est prévue pour 14 heures 45** and you can see the match at 2.45 pm

retravailler [rǝtravaje] VT *(discours, texte etc)* to rework, to work on again; *(exercice de gym, muscle)* to work on again; *(argile, pâte etc)* to work again; **votre thèse a besoin d'être retravaillée** your thesis needs reworking
▪ **VI** to go back to work; **après une longue période de chômage, il retravaille enfin** after being unemployed for a long time, he's finally working again

rétréci [retresi] ADJ *(route etc)*, *Fig Péj (esprit, vues)* narrow; *(vêtement)* shrunken

rétrécir [retresir] VT **1** *(rendre plus étroit) (route)* to narrow; *(vêtement)* to take in **2** *(au lavage) (vêtement)* to shrink
▪ **VI** *(de vêtement, de tissu)* to shrink; *Fig* **son univers** *ou* **son horizon a beaucoup rétréci** his world has become much narrower
▪ **VPR se rétrécir** to narrow, to become narrower; **le chemin continue en se rétrécissant** the path gets narrower and narrower

rétrécissement [retresismɑ̃] NM **1** *(action) (d'une route)* narrowing; *(d'un vêtement, un tissu)* shrinking **2** *Méd* narrowing, constriction, *Spéc* stricture **3** *(partie) (d'un tuyau, une route etc)* narrow part

retrempe [rǝtrɑ̃p] NF *(de l'acier)* retempering

retremper [rǝtrɑ̃pe] VT **1** *(linge)* to soak *or* steep again **2** *(acier)* to retemper
▪ **VPR se retremper 1** *(dans l'eau)* to have another quick dip **2** *Fig Fam* **se r. dans un milieu sympathique/le milieu familial** to plunge back into a congenial atmosphere/the family atmosphere

rétribuer [retribɥe] VT *(employé)* to pay; *(travail, service)* to pay for; **travail rétribué**

paid work; **être bien/mal rétribué** to be well/badly paid

rétribution [retribysjɔ̃] NF *(paie) (pour des services)* payment, remuneration; **fonctions sans r.** honorary duties

> Il faut noter que le terme anglais **retribution** est un faux ami. Il signifie **châtiment**.

retriever [retrivœr] NM *(chien)* retriever

rétro [retro] NM **1** *Billard* pull-back, screw-back (stroke) **2** = **rétroviseur 3** *(style)* retro
ADJ INV *(film, robe, mode, musique etc)* retro
ADV **s'habiller r.** to wear retro clothes; **leur appartement est meublé r.** their flat is furnished in retro style

rétroactif, -ive [retroaktif, -iv] ADJ *(loi etc)* retroactive; **augmentation avec effet r. au 1ᵉʳ juillet** increase backdated or retroactive to 1 July

rétroaction [retroaksjɔ̃] NF *Radio, Électron* feedback; **r. acoustique** acoustic feedback; **r. d'une augmentation de salaire** backdating of a rise, making a rise retroactive

rétroactivement [retroaktivmɑ̃] ADV retroactively

rétroactivité [retroaktivite] NF retroactive nature

rétrocéder [retrosede] *(conj like* **céder***)* VT *(revendre)* to resell; *(droit etc)* to cede back, to release back, to retrocede

rétrocession [retrosesjɔ̃] NF *(d'un droit, un don)* releasing back, retrocession

rétroéclairage [retroeklɛraʒ] NM *Ordinat* backlighting

rétroéclairé [retroeklere] ADJ *Ordinat* backlit

rétroflexe [retrofleks] ADJ *Ling* retroflex

rétrofusée [retrofyze] NF retrorocket

rétrogradage [retrogradaʒ] NM *Aut* down-change, downshift, changing down

rétrogradation [retrogradasjɔ̃] NF **1** *Litt (dans un développement)* regression, retro-gression **2** *(d'un sous-officier)* reduction in rank, demotion; *(d'un fonctionnaire)* demotion, downgrading

rétrograde [retrograd] ADJ *(mouvement)* retrograde, backward; *Fig (idée)* reactionary; *Pol (mesure, politique)* retrograde, reaction-ary; *Billard* **effet r.** pull-back, screwback; **phrase r.** palindrome
N *Pol* reactionary

rétrograder [retrograde] VI **1** to move back-wards; *Mil* to fall back, to retreat; *Fig (dans son développement)* to regress, to retro-gress; *Sport* **il a rétrogradé en cinquième po-sition** he's fallen back to fifth place **2** *Aut* to change or shift down; **r. de troisième en se-conde** to change down from third to second
VT *(sous-officier)* to reduce in rank, to de-mote, *Am Fam* to bust; *(fonctionnaire)* to de-mote, to downgrade

rétrogression [retrogresjɔ̃] NF *(mouve-ment)* retrogression

rétropédalage [retropedalaʒ] NM *Cyclisme* back-pedalling

rétropédaler [retropedale] VI *Cyclisme* to back-pedal

rétroprojecteur [retroprɔʒɛktœr] NM over-head projector

rétropropulsion [retroprɔpylsjɔ̃] NF *Astro-naut* reverse thrust

rétrospectif, -ive [retrospɛktif, -iv] ADJ re-trospective; **j'ai eu une peur/jalousie rétros-pective** I was frightened/jealous in retros-pect
NF **rétrospective 1** *Beaux-Arts etc, Fig* re-trospective; *Can Cin* flashback; **une rétros-pective de l'année 1944** a look back at the events of 1944; *Cin* **rétrospective René Clair** René Clair retrospective **2** *Fin* review

rétrospectivement [retrospɛktivmɑ̃] ADV retrospectively, in retrospect; **ça me fait peur r.** it frightens me in retrospect or look-ing back on it

retroussé [retruse] ADJ *(manches)* rolled-up; **nez r.** snub or turned-up or Litt retroussé nose

retroussement [retrusmɑ̃] NM **avec un r. des lèvres** with a curl of the lip

retrousser [retruse] VT *(manches, pantalon)* to turn up, to roll up; *(jupe)* to tuck up; *(lèvres)* to curl (up); *Fig* **r. ses manches** to roll up one's sleeves
VPR **se retrousser** *(d'une femme)* to tuck up one's skirt(s); *(d'une jupe)* to bunch up

retroussis [retrusi] NM *(de vêtement)* turned-back facings; **bottes à r.** topboots

retrouvable [retruvabl] ADJ recoverable, retrievable; **facilement r.** easy to find, easily found

retrouvailles [retruvaj] NFPL reunion

RETROUVER [retruve]

| **VT** to find **1** ▪ to recover **1** ▪ to regain **1** ▪ to get back **1** ▪ to meet up with **2** |
| **VPR** to end up **1** ▪ to find one's way **2** ▪ to meet **3** ▪ to exist **5** |

VT **1** to find again; *(objet perdu)* to find; *(per-sonne)* to track down; *Fig (santé, forces, en-thousiasme etc)* to recover, to regain; *(sa voix)* to get back; *(son appétit)* to get back, to recover; **r. son chemin** to find one's way again; **je n'arrive pas à r. son adresse** I can't find his address; *Prov* **un(e) de perdu(e), dix de retrouvé(e)s** there are (plenty) more fish in the sea; **la clef a été retrouvée, on a retrou-vé la clé** the key has been found; **elle ne parvint jamais à le r.** she never found any trace of him; **la r. après tant d'années, à quoi bon?** what's the point of seeing her again af-ter all this time?; **on retrouve chez lui la cu-riosité de sa grand-mère** he has his grandmother's curiosity; **on ne retrouve plus cet auteur dans son dernier roman** we don't recognize the author in his last novel, the author's last novel is uncharacteristic; **on retrouve souvent cette image dans le ci-néma de Renoir** you often encounter or come across this image in Renoir's films; **tu ne retrouveras jamais une telle occasion** you'll never come across an opportunity like it again; **elle a retrouvé toute sa jeunesse en voyant ce film** the film took her back to her childhood; **tu as retrouvé le sourire** you're looking more cheerful, you've discov-ered how to smile again; **tu as retrouvé la parole** ou *Fam* **ta langue, toi!** you've found your tongue again!

2 *(rejoindre)* **il doit r. ses parents à Venise** he's to join up or meet up with his parents in Venice; **je vous retrouverai devant le ciné-ma** I'll meet you outside the cinema; **je vous retrouve dans une heure au pub** I'll join you at the pub in an hour's time

VPR **se retrouver 1 se r. dans la même posi-tion** to find oneself or to be in the same posi-tion again; **se r. à Paris** to be back in Paris; **je me retrouve donc à Paris** so here I am back in Paris; **finir par se r. au poste/à l'hôpital** to end up in the police station/hospital; *Fam* **tu vas te r. sans un sou** you're going to find yourself without a penny; *Fam* **et c'est comme ça que je me suis retrouvé à travail-ler ici** and that's how I found myself or came to be working here

2 *(retrouver son chemin)* to get or find one's bearings; **elle se retrouve très bien, dans Londres** she can find her way round London without any difficulty; *Fig* **je ne m'y retrouve plus!** I'm hopelessly confused or lost!; *Fam* **vous vous y retrouverez** *(financièrement)*

you'll get your money back soon enough

3 *(entre personnes)* to meet; **nous devons nous r. au restaurant** we're meeting at the restaurant; **ils se retrouvent tous les mardis** they meet every Tuesday, they get together every Tuesday; **nous voulions nous r. seuls pour parler** we wanted to be alone so we could talk; **on se retrouvera!** I'll get even (with you)!, you haven't heard the last of this!; **comme on se retrouve!** fancy meeting you!, it's a small world!

4 *(en soi-même)* to find oneself; **ce couple a besoin de se r.** they need to find each other again as a couple

5 *(exister)* to exist; **ce mot se retrouve dans de nombreuses langues** this word exists or can be found in numerous languages; *Fam* **ça se retrouve, des verres comme ça** glasses like that are easy to find or are easy to come by

rétroversion [retroversjɔ̃] NF *Méd* retro-version

rétrovirus [retrovirys] NM *Méd* retrovirus

rétroviseur [retrovizœr] NM *Aut* **r. (inté-rieur)** (rear-view) mirror; **r. extérieur** wing mirror, *Am* outside mirror; **r. jour/nuit** anti-glare rear-view mirror; **r. à double miroir** split-view mirror; **r. à position nuit** dipping rear-view mirror

rets [rɛ] NM *Litt* net; **prendre qn dans ses r.** to catch sb in one's toils

réuni [reyni] ADJ **1** *(rassemblé)* put together; **plus forts que nous et les Anglais réunis** stronger than us and the English put toge-ther or combined; **il s'est adressé à l'en-semble des élèves réunis** he addressed the assembled schoolchildren; **nous sommes réunis aujourd'hui pour ...** we are gathered together today to ... **2** *Com (laiteries etc)* amalgamated, united

réunification [reynifikasjɔ̃] NF *Pol* reuni-fication

réunifier [reynifje] VT *Pol* to reunify

Réunion [reynjɔ̃] NF Réunion

réunion [reynjɔ̃] NF **1** *(action de rassembler)* *(de deux services)* merger, amalgamation; *(de faits, de renseignements etc)* gathering (together); *(de gens, de famille etc)* bringing together; *(à nouveau)* *(de famille, de parti politique etc)* reunion; *(action de joindre)* joining together; **r. d'une province à la France** union of a province with France; **cette r. de faits** this assemblage of facts; *Math* **r. de deux ensembles** union of two sets **2** *(action de se rassembler)* coming or gather-ing together; **droit de r.** right of assembly; **salle de r.** conference room **3** *(assemblée)* meeting; *(du comité)* session, sitting; *(ré-ception dans un hôtel etc)* function; **le direc-teur est en r.** the manager is in a meeting; **r. de famille** family gathering or get-together; **r. électorale** election meeting; **r. publique** public meeting; **r. d'actionnaires** sharehol-ders' meeting; **r. de comité** committee meet-ing; **r. du conseil** board meeting; **r. du conseil d'administration** board meeting; **r. des créanciers** creditors' meeting; *Mktg* **r. de groupe** *(pour enquête)* group meeting, focus-group session; *Mktg* **r. de remue-méninges** brainstorming session; *Mktg* **r. de représentants** sales meeting; *Pol* **r. au som-met** summit (meeting or conference)

Réunion [reynjɔ̃] NF Réunion

réunionite [reynjɔnit] NF *Fam Hum* mania for meetings, *Hum* meetingitis

réunionnais, -aise [reynjɔnɛ, -ɛz] ADJ of/ from Réunion
N **R.** *(natif)* native of Réunion; *(habitant)* in-habitant of Réunion

réunir [reynir] VT **1** *(rassembler)* *(d'une expo-sition)* *(objets d'art, toiles)* to bring or put to-gether; *(faits, renseignements, documents,* *preuves etc)* to gather (together), to collect; *(somme d'argent, fonds)* to get together, to raise; *(personnes, famille etc)* to bring *or* get together; *(d'un colloque) (scientifiques etc)* to bring together; *(à nouveau) (famille, parti politique etc)* to reunite; *(services, classes)* to combine, to merge; **r. qch à qch** to join sth to sth; **r. une armée** to raise an army; **r. un comité** to convene a committee, to call a committee together **2** *(comporter) (qualités, avantages)* to have, to possess

VPR se réunir 1 *(de personnes)* to meet, to get *or* gather together; *(de routes)* to join up, to meet; **l'assemblée se réunit une fois par semaine** the assembly meets once a week; **se r. autour de qn/qch** to congregate around sb/sth **2** *(de banques etc)* to amalgamate; *(d'églises, d'États etc)* to unite

réussi [reysi] **ADJ** successful; **être r.** *(d'un spectacle, une pièce, un plat)* to be successful *or* a success; *Iron* **c'est r.!, la voilà en larmes!** well done *or* very clever!, she's in tears now!; **mal r.** unsuccessful; **c'est à demi r.** it's partially successful

réussir [reysir] **VI 1** to be successful, to be a success, to succeed; *(d'une plante)* to thrive; **c'est un garçon qui réussira** he's a boy who will do well *or* succeed *or* be successful; **le projet avait mal réussi** the plan had proved a failure; **ce truc-là ne réussira pas** that trick won't work, that trick won't come off; **tout lui réussit** he's successful in everything he does, everything he does turns out well; **r. dans qch** to succeed *or* be successful in sth; **il a réussi dans la vie** he's made a success of things; **une femme d'affaires qui a réussi** a successful businesswoman; **r. à un examen** to pass an examination; *Scol* **r. de justesse** to scrape through, to only just pass; **r. à faire qch** to succeed in doing sth, to manage to do sth; **tu as réussi (à finir/à l'ouvrir)?** did you manage (to finish/open it)?; *Iron* **elle a réussi à déranger tout le monde** she managed to disturb everybody; **ne pas r. à faire qch** not to have any success in doing sth, to fail to do sth; **je n'ai pas réussi à la convaincre** I didn't manage *or* I failed to persuade her, I didn't have any success in persuading her

2 *Fam* **le homard ne me réussit pas** lobster doesn't agree with me

VT *(quelque chose)* to make a success of, to be successful with; **elle réussit (bien) les omelettes** she makes very good omelettes; **c'est ta dissertation qui t'a permis de r. l'examen** it was your essay that got you through the exam; *Fam* **r. son coup** to do the trick, to bring it off; *Iron* **tu as bien réussi ton coup** well done, very clever

réussite [reysit] **NF 1** *(succès)* success; **fêter sa r. à un examen** to celebrate passing an exam *or* getting through an exam; **cette soirée est une belle r.!** the party is a great success!; **l'une des plus belles réussites industrielles françaises** one of France's biggest industrial successes *or* success stories; **r. sociale** social success; **présenter tous les signes de la r.** to show every sign of succeeding *or* of being successful **2** *Cartes* patience, *Am* solitaire; **faire une r.** to play patience

réutilisation [reytilizasjɔ̃] **NF** reuse

réutiliser [reytilize] **VT** to reuse

revaccination [rəvaksinasjɔ̃] **NF** revaccination

revacciner [rəvaksine] **VT** to revaccinate

revaloir [rəvalwar] **VT** *(conj like* valoir*; used chiefly in the* fu*)* **je vous le revaudrai!, je vous revaudrai cela!** *(menace)* I'll get *or* pay you back for that!; *(reconnaissance)* I'll do the same for you some time!

revalorisation [rəvalɔrizasjɔ̃] **NF 1** *(d'une monnaie)* revaluation; *(des salaires, du SMIC, des retraites)* upgrade, upgrading; *(de prix)*

increasing **2** *(d'une image, d'une profession)* upgrade, upgrading; **cela doit aboutir à une r. de la fonction d'enseignant** this should have as an objective an upgrading of the role of the teacher

revaloriser [rəvalɔrize] **VT 1** *(monnaie)* to revalue; *(salaire, SMIC, retraite)* to upgrade, to increase; *(prix)* to increase **2** *(image, profession etc)* to upgrade

revanchard, -arde [rəvɑ̃far, -ard] **ADJ, N** *Pol Péj* revanchist

revanche [rəvɑ̃f] **NF 1** *(vengeance)* revenge; **prendre sa r.** to get one's revenge; **prendre sa r. sur qn** to take one's revenge on sb, to get one's own back on sb, to get even with sb; **je prendrai ma r. un jour** I'll get my revenge *or* get even one day; **vouloir prendre sa r.** to want revenge, to want to get even *or* to get one's own back **2** *Sport* return match *or* game; **je te laisserai prendre ta r. la semaine prochaine** I'll give you your revenge next week **3** *Fig* **en r.** *(en compensation)* in return, in compensation; *(au contraire)* on the other hand; **à charge de r.** on condition that I do the same for you

revanchisme [rəvɑ̃fism] **NM** *Pol* revanchism

revanchiste [rəvɑ̃fist] **ADJ, N** *Pol* revanchist

rêvasser [rɛvase] **VI** to daydream, to let one's mind wander

rêvasserie [rɛvasri] **NF** daydreaming; **rêvasseries** daydreams

rêvasseur, -euse [rɛvasœr, -øz] **ADJ** daydreaming
N (day)dreamer

rêve [rɛv] **NM 1** *(de dormeur)* dream; **faire un r.** to (have a) dream; **voir qch en r.** to see sth in a dream *or* in one's dreams; **ça s'est passé comme dans un r.** it happened as if in a dream; **faites de beaux rêves!** pleasant *or* sweet dreams!; **la psychologie du r.** the psychology of dreams *or* of dreaming **2** *(idéal)* dream; **rêves de gloire/célébrité** dreams of glory/fame; **un r. devenu réalité** a dream come true; **maison/voiture de r.** dream house/car; **la maison de nos rêves** the house of our dreams, our dream house; **avoir une silhouette de r.** to have a gorgeous figure; **c'est le r.!** it's/he's/*etc* a dream *or* everything you ever dreamed of!

rêvé [rɛve] **ADJ** perfect, ideal

revêche [rəvɛʃ] **ADJ 1** *(hargneux)* bad-tempered, cantankerous **2** *Vieilli (vêtement etc)* harsh, rough

réveil [revɛj] **NM 1** waking, awakening; *Fig* awakening; **à mon r., au r.** on waking; **le r. de la nature** the awakening of Nature; **le r. d'un volcan** the renewed rumblings *or* the awakening of a volcano **2** *Mil* reveille; **sonner le r.** to sound reveille **3** *(pendulette)* alarm (clock); **mettre le r.** to set the alarm (à **six heures** for six o'clock); **radio-r.** radio alarm, clock radio; **r. automatique** automatic alarm; **r. de voyage** travel alarm clock; **r. téléphonique** *(dans un hôtel)* wake-up call

réveillé [revɛje] **ADJ** awake; **je suis mal r.** I haven't woken up (properly) yet, I'm still half asleep

réveille-matin [revɛjmatɛ̃] **NM INV** alarm clock

réveiller [revɛje] **VT 1** *(tirer du sommeil)* to wake (up), to (a)waken; **réveillez-moi à sept heures** wake me (up) *or* waken me at seven o'clock; **Docteur, je n'arrive pas à la r.** I can't waken *or* rouse her, Doctor; **un bruit à r. les morts** a noise to wake the dead; *Prov* **ne réveillez pas le chat qui dort** let sleeping dogs lie **2** *Fig (classe ouvrière, pays)* to stir up, to rouse; *(souvenirs)* to awaken, to revive; *(courage, douleur)* to revive; **r. les consciences** to stir people's consciences

VPR se réveiller 1 *(d'un dormeur)* to wake (up), to awake; **se r. d'un sommeil agité** to wake from a troubled sleep; *Fig* **c'est un pays qui est en train de se r.** the country is beginning to stir itself *or* shake itself *or* waken up **2** *(de sentiments)* to be awakened *or* roused *or* stirred (up) **3** *(de la nature, la végétation, l'économie)* to revive

réveillon [revɛjɔ̃] **NM** *(repas)* midnight supper; *(réjouissances)* midnight party *(after midnight Mass on Christmas Eve or New Year's Eve)*

Réveillons

Christmas is traditionally a family celebration. In Catholic families, the "crèche" or miniature nativity scene is decorated and everyone goes to midnight mass on Christmas Eve, after which the long and copious Christmas dinner is served: this includes oysters and, for dessert, the traditional "bûche de Noël" or yule log. The presents under the Christmas tree are opened either on Christmas Eve or on Christmas Day morning. The "réveillon de la Saint-Sylvestre" on New Year's Eve is usually celebrated among friends, either at home or in a restaurant. Champagne is drunk at midnight and everybody embraces and wishes each other a happy New Year. New Year greeting cards can, in theory, be sent up until the end of January.

réveillonner [revɛjɔne] **VI** to see Christmas/the New Year in *(with a midnight supper and party)*

réveillonneur, -euse [revɛjɔnœr, -øz] **N** (Christmas Eve/New Year's Eve) party-goer *or* reveller

révélateur, -trice [revelatœr, -tris] **ADJ** *(signe, attitude, silence etc)* revealing, tell-tale; *(remarque)* revealing, telling; *Chimie (substance)* tracer; **signe r. d'un changement** sign pointing to a change, tell-tale sign of a change; **c'est très r.** it is very revealing; **c'est r. de son manque de confiance en lui** it reveals *or* shows his lack of confidence
NM 1 *(d'une crise etc)* sign, indication **2** *Phot* developer

révélation [revelasjɔ̃] **NF 1** *(action) (d'un secret, d'intentions etc)* revelation, disclosure; *Journ (d'un scandale etc)* exposé **2** *(découverte)* **ce fut une r.!** it was a revelation *or* an eye-opener!; **ce jeune musicien est la r. des années 90** this young musician is the discovery *or* find of the 90s **3** *Rel* revelation; **la r. divine** divine revelation

révélé [revele] **ADJ** *(religion, vérité)* revealed

révéler [revele] (je **révèle**, n. **révélons**; je **révélerai**) **VT 1** *(dévoiler) (secret, intention, projets etc)* to reveal, to disclose; *Journ* **r. ses sources** to reveal one's sources; **il révéla, sans le faire exprès, la vérité** he unwittingly let out the truth; **somme dont le montant n'a pas été révélé** undisclosed amount; **l'enquête révèle que …** the survey reveals that … **2** *(témoigner de) (talent, technique)* to show; *(gentillesse, humour)* to show, to reveal; *(défauts, ignorance, manque de confiance)* to show, to reveal, to betray **3** *Phot* to develop

VPR se révéler 1 *(d'une personne)* to reveal oneself *or* one's character; **se r. difficile** to prove difficult; **il s'est révélé un bon ami** he proved (to be) *or* showed himself (to be) a good friend **2** **cela s'est révélé exact** it turned out *or* proved to be true

revenant, -ante [rəvnɑ̃, -ɑ̃t] **ADJ** *Vieilli (avenant)* pleasing, prepossessing
N ghost; **histoire de revenants** ghost story;

Fam Hum **voilà une revenante!** hello stranger!

revendable [rəvãdabl] **ADJ** resaleable

revendeur, -euse [rəvãdœr, -øz] **N** *Com* retailer; *(d'articles d'occasion)* second-hand dealer; *(de drogue)* dealer

revendicateur, -trice [rəvãdikatœr, -tris] **ADJ** *(discours, lettre etc)* setting forth one's claims *or* demands

N person making demands; **je ne veux pas être mis dans le même sac que tous ces revendicateurs** I don't want to be classed as a troublemaker

revendicatif, -ive [rəvãdikatif, -iv] **ADJ** *(mouvement etc)* protest; **journée revendicative** day of protest

revendication [rəvãdikasjɔ̃] **NF 1** *(action)* claiming **2** *(demande)* demand (**sur** on), claim; **les revendications ouvrières** labour demands; **r. salariale** wage demand, pay claim; **revendications syndicales** union demands; *Jur* **(action en) r.** action for recovery of property

revendiquer [rəvãdike] **VT 1** *(demander)* to claim, to demand; *(droits)* to insist on; *(territoire, succession)* to lay claim to; **r. le droit de faire qch** to claim the right to do sth **2** *(assumer) (responsabilité)* to claim; **l'attentat n'a pas été revendiqué** nobody has claimed responsibility for the attack

revendre [rəvãdr] **VT** *(après achat)* to resell; *(vendre de nouveau)* to sell again; *Fig* **avoir des jouets/des CD à r.** to have more than enough toys/CDs; *Fig* **avoir du temps à r.** to have time to spare; *Fig* **avoir de la bonne humeur à r.** to be extremely good-natured; *Fig* **avoir de l'énergie à r.** to be bubbling over with energy

revenez-y [rəvənezi] **NM INV** *Fam* **ce gâteau a un goût de r.** this cake is very moreish; **ce voyage a un goût de r.** I wouldn't mind doing this trip again

---

REVENIR [rəv(ə)nir]

to come back **1–3** ▪ to return **1, 2** ▪ to recur **1** ▪ to go back to *(revenir à)* **1** ▪ to go back on *(revenir sur)* **1** ▪ to get over *(revenir de)* **5** ▪ to cost *(revenir à)* **7** ▪ to amount to **8**

VI *(conj like* **venir***; aux* **être***)* **1** *(rentrer)* to come back, to return; **il n'était jamais revenu en France** he had never been back to France; **je reviens tout de suite** I'll be back in a minute; **le temps passé ne revient plus** time that is past will never come again; **l'herbe reviendra** the grass will grow again *or* back; **ce nom/sujet revient souvent dans la conversation** this name/subject often turns up *or* crops up in conversation; **c'est un problème qui revient souvent chez les adolescents** it's a problem that often occurs with teenagers, it's a common problem with teenagers; **fête qui revient tous les dix ans** festival that occurs *or* recurs *or* that comes round every ten years; **r. à la hâte** to hurry back; **r. en courant** to come running back, to run back; **r. à ses premières amours** to go back *or* return to one's first love; **vous y reviendrez!** *(à une méthode etc)* you'll go/ come back to it!; **je suis revenu au régime lacté** I've gone back to a milk diet; **r. à la surface** *(d'un sous-marin)* to resurface; **en r. à qch** to come/go back *or* revert to sth; **pour en r. à la question/à ce que je disais** to come back to our subject/to what I was saying; **il n'y a pas à r. là-dessus** there is no going back on it; **r. de** to come back *or* return from; **r. de l'étranger** to come back from abroad; **je l'ai rencontré en revenant de l'église** I met him on my way back from church; **r. sur** *(ses aveux)* to retract; *(une promesse, une déci-*

sion) to go back on; *(son opinion)* to reconsider; *(un sujet)* to bring up again; *(le passé)* to rake up; **r. sur ses pas** to retrace one's steps, to turn back, to backtrack

2 *(de la force, du courage etc)* to return, to come back (**à qn** to sb); **l'appétit devrait lui r.** he should get his appetite back, his appetite should return; **il ne faudrait pas que ces paroles lui reviennent** don't let this get back to him; **la mémoire me revient** my memory is coming back; **c'est un honneur qui vous revient** the honour is yours by rights; **à chacun ce qui lui revient** to each his due

3 cela me revient à la mémoire it's coming back to me; *Fam* **ça me revient maintenant** I have it *or* I've got it now; **votre nom ne me revient pas** your name escapes me *or* has slipped my memory, I can't think of your name

4 *Fam* **il a une tête qui ne me revient pas** there's something about him I don't like; **si ta tête ne lui revient pas ...** if he/she doesn't like the look of you ...

5 r. de sa surprise/d'une maladie to recover from *or* get over one's surprise/an illness; **r. d'une théorie** to abandon a theory; **r. d'une erreur** to realize one's mistake; **je suis revenu de toutes mes illusions** I have lost all my illusions; **je suis revenu, de l'homéopathie!** I've had my fill of homeopathy!; **je n'en reviens pas!** *(étonnement)* I can't get over it!; **r. à la santé** to recover *or* regain one's health; **il revient de loin** *(il a failli mourir)* he has been at death's door; **r. à soi** to recover consciousness, to come round, to come to

6 *Culin* **faire r.** to brown

7 *(d'un prix)* **ça nous est revenu à cent euros par personne** it worked out at a hundred euros each; **ça me revient à deux cents euros par mois** it costs me *or* it works out at two hundred euros a month; **sa maison lui est revenue à plusieurs millions** his house cost him several million; **r. cher** to work out expensive, to cost a lot

8 *Fig* **cela revient au même** it amounts to the same thing, it comes (down) *or Fam* boils down to the same thing; **cela revient à dire que ...** that amounts to saying that ...

VPR se revenir *Litt* **s'en r.** to return, to make one's way back; **comme il s'en revenait de l'école ...** as he was coming *or* was on his way home from school ...

V IMPERS il me revient encore 100 euros I still have 100 euros coming *or* owing to me; **c'est à elle qu'il revient de faire la demande** it's up to her *or* down to her to ask; **il m'est revenu que ...** it has come to my attention that ...

revente [rəvãt] **NF** resale; **objet de r.** second-hand article; **r. à perte** selling at a loss

revenu [rəv(ə)ny] **NM 1** *(d'une personne)* income; *(de l'État)* revenue; *(d'une entreprise)* revenue, income; **avoir un faible r.** to be on a low income; **impôt sur le r.** income tax; **politique des revenus** incomes policy; **à double r.** *(foyer, ménage)* double-income **2** *(d'un investissement, d'un capital)* income, yield

▸ ▸ **revenus accessoires** incidental income; **revenus actuels** current earnings; **r. annuel** annual income; *Mktg* **r. cannibalisé** cannibalized income; **r. cumulé** cumulative revenue; **r. dépensable** spendable income; **r. disponible** disposable income; **r. d'entreprise** corporate income, company earnings; **revenus de l'exportation** export revenue; **r. fictif** notional income; **r. fixe** fixed income; **r. généré par les ventes** sales revenue; **r. imposable** taxable income; **r. minimum d'insertion** income support, *Am* welfare; **r. national brut/net** gross/net national income; **r. personnel disponible** disposable personal income; **r. du travail** earned income

rêver [rɛve] **VI 1** *(d'un dormeur)* to dream; **r. de qn/qch** to dream of *or* have a dream about sb/sth; **on croit r.!** it can't be true!, I can't believe it!; **non, mais je rêve!** I must be dreaming!; *Fig* **j'en rêve la nuit** I dream about it at night **2** *(rêvasser)* to daydream (**à** about), to dream (**à** of); **je ne rêve pas, il l'a bien dit!** I'm not dreaming *or* I'm not imagining things, he did say it! **3** *(souhaiter)* **r. de** to dream of; **r. de faire** to dream of doing; **elle rêve de partir vivre là-bas** she dreams of going to live there, it is her dream to go and live there

VT *(d'un dormeur) (quelque chose)* to dream of; **vous l'avez rêvé!** you must have imagined *or* dreamt it!; **j'ai rêvé que ...** I dreamt (that) ...; **r. sa vie au lieu de la vivre** to dream one's life away; **j'ai rêvé la même chose que toi** I dreamt the same thing as you; *Fig* **r. mariage** to dream of marriage

réverbération [reverberasjɔ̃] **NF** *(de la lumière, de la chaleur)* reflection; *(du son)* reverberation, echo

réverbère [reverbɛr] **NM 1** *(lampe)* street light *or* lamp; *(poteau)* lamppost **2** *(réflecteur)* (heat) reflector

réverbérer [reverbere] **VT** *(il réverbère; il réverbérera) (chaleur, lumière)* to reflect, to throw back; *(son)* to reverberate

reverdir [rəverdir] **VI** to grow *or* turn green again

révérence [reverãs] **NF 1** *(déférence)* reverence (**envers, pour** for); *Fml Vieilli* **r. parler** with all due respect **2 Votre R.** Your Reverence **3** *(salut) (d'un homme)* bow; *(d'une femme)* curtsey; **faire la r. à qn** *(d'un homme)* to bow to sb; *(d'une femme)* to curtsey to sb; *Fig* **tirer sa r.** to leave; *Hum* **je vous tire ma r.** I'm off!; **la société s'est automatisée, alors il a décidé de leur tirer sa r.** when the company automated, he decided to bow out

révérenciel, -ielle [reverãsjɛl] **ADJ** *Litt* **il m'inspire une crainte révérencielle** I stand in awe of him, I find him awe-inspiring

révérencieusement [reverãsjøzmã] **ADV** *Litt* reverently

révérencieux, -ieuse [reverãsjø, -jøz] **ADJ** *Litt* reverent; **peu r.** irreverent

révérend [reverã] *Rel* **ADJ** reverend; **le r. père Martin** Reverend Father Martin; **la révérende mère supérieure** the Reverend Mother Superior

NM reverend; **oui, mon R.** yes, Reverend

révérer [revere] **VT** (**je révère, n. révérons; je révérerai**) to revere

rêverie [rɛvri] **NF** *(activité)* dreaming, reverie, musing; *(moment)* daydream, reverie; *Litt* **elle est toujours plongée** *ou* **perdue dans de vagues rêveries** she's always daydreaming; **être dans une douce r.** to be starry-eyed; **il faut qu'elle cesse ses rêveries** she must stop this daydreaming

revernir [rəvernir] **VT** to revarnish

revers [rəver] **NM 1** *(de pièce, de médaille etc)* reverse (side), back; *(de matériel)* wrong side; *(de page)* other side, back; **r. de la main** back of the hand; *Tennis* **(coup de) r.** backhand (stroke); *Mil* **prendre une position à r.** to capture a position in the rear; *Fig* **c'est le r. de la médaille** that's the other side of the coin **2** *(de manteau)* lapel; *(de chaussette)* turnover; *(de botte)* top; *(de manche)* cuff; **r. de pantalon** trouser turn-up *or Am* pant cuff; **habit à r. de velours** coat faced with velvet *or* with velvet facings; **bottes à r.** top boots **3 r. (de fortune)** reversal (of fortune), setback; **les succès et les r. de la vie** the ups and downs of life

reversement [rəversəmã] **NM** additional payment

reverser [rəvɛrse] **VT 1** *(servir de nouveau)* to pour out again; **je vous reverse un verre?** shall I pour you another glass? **2** *(remettre)* to pour back **3** *Fin (somme)* to transfer (**à**, **sur** to); *(impôt)* to pay

réverser [reverse] **VT** *Typ (texte)* to reverse out

réversibilité [reversibilite] **NF** reversibility; *Jur (d'une pension etc)* revertibility; *Aut (de la direction)* kickback

réversible [reversibl] **ADJ 1** *(processus, vête-ment etc)* reversible; *Fig* **l'histoire n'est pas r.** you can't put the clock back **2** *Jur (pension etc)* revertible

réversion [reversjɔ̃] **NF** *Jur, Biol* reversion

revêtement [rəvɛtmɑ̃] **NM 1** surface, over-lay; *Tech* cladding, sheathing, covering; *(en-duit)* coating; *(à l'intérieur)* lining; *Aviat (du fuselage)* skin; *Menuis* veneer; **r. de sol/mur** floor/wall covering; **câble à r. en caoutchouc** rubber-sheathed *or*-covered cable; **r. calori-fuge** *(d'une chaudière etc)* lagging **2** *Constr (d'un mur)* facing; *(d'un talus)* revetment; *(de chaussée)* surface (material); *(action)* sur-facing

revêtir [rəvɛtir] *(conj like* **vêtir***)* **VT 1** *(habil-ler)* to clothe, to dress; **r. qn de qch** to dress sb in sth; **r. qn d'une robe de cérémonie** to robe sb, to dress sb in a ceremonial robe; *Fig* **r. qn d'une dignité/d'une autorité** to in-vest sb with a dignity/an authority; **pièce re-vêtue de votre signature** document bearing your signature; *Litt* **revêtu de verdure** clo-thed in greenery, verdure-clad **2** *Tech (cou-vrir)* to clad, to sheathe, to cover; *(enduire)* to coat; *(à l'intérieur)* to line (**de** with); *(chau-dière)* to lag; *Constr (mur)* to face; *(chaussée)* to surface; **r. une route de bitume** to tarmac a road; **murs revêtus de boiseries** panelled walls; **route non revêtue** unsurfaced road **3** *(endosser) (uniforme, vêtement de cérémonie etc)* to don, to put on; *Fig* **r. la forme hu-maine/un caractère particulier** to assume human shape/take on a particular charac-ter; **fait qui revêt de l'importance** fact that takes on importance

VPR se revêtir se r. de *(uniforme, vêtement de cérémonie etc)* to don, to put on, to dress oneself in; *(dignité)* to assume

rêveur, -euse [rɛvœr, -øz] **ADJ** dreamy; **ces résultats me laissent r.** these results are be-wildering

N dreamer

rêveusement [revøzmɑ̃] **ADV** dreamily

revient [rəvjɛ̃] **NM (prix de) r.** cost price

revigorant [rəvigɔrɑ̃] **ADJ** *(vent, bain)* invi-gorating; *(boisson)* reviving

revigorer [rəvigɔre] **VT 1** *(d'un vent, un bain)* to invigorate; *(d'une boisson, un aliment)* to revive **2** *(économie)* to boost, to give a boost to; **les subventions ont revigoré l'entreprise** the subsidies gave the company a new lease of life

revirement [rəvirmɑ̃] **NM 1** *Naut* tacking about, going about **2** *(de fortune)* sudden change; *(de sentiments)* (complete) change, about-turn; *(changement d'avis)* about-turn, U-turn, about-face; **r. d'opinion** (sudden) change in public opinion

révisable [revizabl] **ADJ** *Jur (procès)* reviewable

réviser [revize] **VT 1** *(texte, loi etc)* to revise; *(épreuves)* to revise, to check; *(situation, contrat, salaire)* to review; *Ordinat (texte, document etc)* to edit; *Jur (procès)* to review, to reconsider; **r. une estimation à la hausse/ baisse** to revise an estimate upwards/down-wards; **r. son jugement** to revise one's judge-ment; **les salaires doivent être révisés janvier prochain** salaries come up for re-view next January **2** *Scol* to revise; **il faut r.**

you'll/I'll/*etc* have to do some revision **3** *Tech (voiture, moteur etc)* to service

réviseur, -euse [revizœr, -øz] **N** reviser; *Typ (correcteur)* proofreader; *TV, Cin* rewriter, re-write sub; *Fin* **r. (comptable)** auditor; *Fin* **r. externe/interne** external/internal auditor

révision [revizjɔ̃] **NF 1** *(d'un texte, une loi etc)* revision; *(d'une politique, des salaires)* re-view; *Typ* proofreading; *Ordinat* edit; *(activ-ité)* editing; **être en cours de r.** to be under review; **faire l'objet d'une r.** to be reviewed; **les prix peuvent faire l'objet d'une r.** prices are subject to review **2** *Scol* revision, *Am* re-view; **faire des révisions** to revise **3** *(d'un procès)* review, reconsideration, reapprai-sal; *(d'une opinion)* change **4** *Tech (d'une voi-ture, d'un moteur etc)* service, servicing; **la r. des 5000 km** the 5,000 km service

révisionnisme [revizjɔnism] **NM** *Pol* revi-sionism

révisionniste [revizjɔnist] **ADJ, N** *Pol* revi-sionist

revisiter [rəvizite] **VT 1** *(visiter à nouveau)* to revisit **2** *(voir sous un jour nouveau)* to rein-terpret; **r. un auteur/une époque** to reinter-pret a writer/an era; **Racine revisité par le célèbre metteur en scène** a new angle *or* a new take on Racine by the famous director

réviso [revizo] **N** *Pol Fam Péj* revisionist

revisser [rəvise] **VT** to screw back (again)

revitalisant [rəvitalizɑ̃] **ADJ** *(shampooing etc)* revitalizing

revitalisation [rəvitalizasjɔ̃] **NF** *(de la peau, une région)* revitalization

revitaliser [rəvitalize] **VT** *(peau, région etc)* to revitalize

revival [rivajvœl] **NM** revival

revivifier [rəvivifje] **VT** *(impf, pr sub* n. revi-vifiions, v. revivifiiez*)* *(sentiment, souvenir)* to revive

revivre [rəvivr] *(conj like* **vivre***)* **VI** *(recouvrer son énergie)* to revive, to come alive again; **r. dans sa fille/son œuvre** to live on in one's daughter/work; **se sentir r.** to feel revived, to feel alive again; **faire r.** *(personne)* to re-vive, to bring to life again; *(coutume, tradi-tion etc)* to revive

VT *(passé, sa vie)* to relive; *(expérience etc)* to relive, to live through *or* go through again

révocabilité [revɔkabilite] **NF 1** *Jur (d'un contrat etc)* revocability **2** *Admin (d'un fonc-tionnaire)* dismissibility **3** *Pol (d'un élu)* recallability

révocable [revɔkabl] **ADJ 1** *Jur (contrat etc)* revocable; *(crédit)* revocable, callable **2** *Ad-min (fonctionnaire)* dismissible **3** *Pol (élu)* re-callable, subject to recall

révocation [revɔkasjɔ̃] **NF 1** *Jur (d'un testa-ment, un édit, un contrat etc)* revocation; **2** *Admin (d'un fonctionnaire)* removal, dismis-sal **3** *Pol (d'un élu)* recall

révocatoire [revɔkatwar] **ADJ** *Jur* revoca-tory

revoici [rəvwasi] **PRÉP** *Fam* **me r.!** here I am again!, it's me again!; **nous r. à Paris** here we are in Paris again *or* back in Paris; **nous r. à notre point de départ** we're back where we started; **le r. au travail** he's back at work; **la r. qui pleure** she's crying again

revoilà [rəvwala] **PRÉP** *Fam* **= revoici**

revoir[1] [rəvwar] *(conj like* **voir***)* **VT 1** *(voir de nouveau) (quelqu'un, quelque chose)* to see again; *(rencontrer) (quelqu'un)* to see *or* meet again; **je revois encore la maison de mon en-fance** *(en souvenir)* I can see my childhood home again; **je la revois petite** I can see her in my mind's eye when she was little **2** *(exa-miner) (leçon)* to revise, to go over; *(comptes, manuscrit, texte)* to go over *or* look over again; *(épreuves)* to read; **je voudrais r. quel-**

ques points avec toi I'd like to go over a few points with you; **r. à la baisse** to revise downwards; **r. à la hausse** to revise upwards **VPR se revoir 1** *(se rencontrer)* to see each other again, to meet again **2** *(en souvenir)* to see oneself (in one's mind's eye); **je me re-vois petite** I can see myself when I was a little girl

revoir[2] **(au)** [rəvwar] **INT** goodbye

NM INV goodbye; **des au r. sans fin** endless goodbyes; **dis au r. au monsieur** say good-bye to the gentleman; **ce n'est qu'un au r.** it's only au revoir

révoltant [revɔltɑ̃] **ADJ** *(vision, procédure)* revolting, sickening, shocking; *(odeur)* re-volting, sickening; *(comportement)* revolt-ing, outrageous, appalling; *(injustice)* appalling, revolting

révolte [revɔlt] **NF** *(émeute, indignation)* re-volt; *(dans une prison)* riot; **en r.** in revolt (**contre** against); **esprit de r.** spirit of revolt *or* rebellion; **sentiment de r.** feeling of re-volt, rebellious feeling; **mouvement de r.** movement of revolt

révolté, -ée [revɔlte] **ADJ 1** *(indigné)* out-raged, appalled (**de voir** to see) **2** *(en ré-volte)* rebellious; **r. contre** in revolt against

N rebel; **c'est un r. de nature** he's a natural rebel

révolter [revɔlte] **VT 1** *(indigner)* to revolt, to appal, to shock; **de telles pratiques me ré-voltent** I'm appalled by that type of thing; **ça me révolte d'entendre ça!** I'm appalled!, that's appalling! **2** *(inciter à la révolte)* **r. qn** to induce sb to revolt

VPR se révolter to revolt, to rebel (**contre** against); **se r. devant des injustices** to rebel against injustice; **se r. à l'idée que ...** to get indignant at the thought of ...; **ça me donne envie de me r.** I'm tempted to rebel; **le bon sens se révolte contre une telle supposition** common sense revolts against such a supposition

révolu [revɔly] **ADJ** *(jours, époque etc)* past, bygone; **ces jours sont révolus, c'est une époque révolue** those days are gone; **avoir quarante ans révolus** to be over forty years of age; **après trois mois révolus ...** after a full three months ...

révolution [revɔlysjɔ̃] **NF 1** *(rotation) (de la terre, d'une roue)* revolution **2** *Pol etc* revolu-tion; *Hist* **la R.** the French Revolution; **c'est une r. dans la vie du couple** there has been a revolution in sexual relationships; **toute la ville est en r.** the whole town is in revolt *or* up in arms; **faire la r.** to cause a revolution; **il veut faire la r. en introduisant ...** he wants to cause a revolution *or* revolutionize things by introducing ...

▸▸ **r. culturelle** cultural revolution; *Hist* **la R. française** the French Revolution; **r. indus-trielle** industrial revolution; **la R. d'octobre** the October Revolution; **r. de palais** palace revolution; **r. verte** green revolution

révolutionnaire [revɔlysjɔnɛr] **ADJ, N** revolutionary

révolutionnarisme [revɔlysjɔnarism] **NM** revolutionism

révolutionner [revɔlysjɔne] **VT 1** *(transfor-mer) (industrie, théorie, vie familiale etc)* to revolutionize **2** *(mettre en émoi) (village etc)* to cause a stir in

revolver [revɔlvɛr] **NM 1** revolver; *(n'importe quel pistolet)* gun; **r. à six coups** six-shooter **2** *Tech (porte-outils)* **r.** revolving tool holder; **tour (à) r.** turret lathe, capstan lathe

revolvériser [revɔlverize] **VT** *Fam Hum* to gun down

révoquer [revɔke] **VT 1** *(fonctionnaire)* to dismiss, to remove from office **2** *(décret)* to revoke, to repeal, to rescind; *(contrat)* to revoke **3** *Litt* **r. qch en doute** to call sth into question

revoter [rəvɔte] VT *(personne, parti)* to vote again for; **la loi a été revotée** the law has been passed *or* adopted again
VI to vote again

revouloir [rəvulwar] *(conj like* **vouloir)** VT *Fam (quelque chose)* to want again; **en re-veux-tu?** would you like some more?

revoyure (à la) [alarvwajyr] INT *Fam* see you!, bye!

revue [rəvy] NF **1** *(examen)* review; *Mil (des troupes)* review, inspection; *(de caserne-ment)* inspection; **r. de presse** review of the papers *or* the press; **faire la r. des troupes** to review *or* inspect the troops; **passer en r.** *(problèmes, possibilités etc)* to review, to go over; *Mil (troupes)* to review, to inspect; *Fam* **je suis encore de la r.** I'm left high and dry again **2** *(magazine)* magazine; *(scientifique, littéraire)* review, journal; **r. d'entreprise** company *or* in-house magazine; **r. profes-sionnelle** trade journal *or* magazine **3** *Théâ-tre* revue **4** *Fam Vieilli* **nous sommes (des gens) de r.** we'll meet again

révulsé [revylse] ADJ **yeux révulsés** eyes with the whites showing

révulser [revylse] VT **1** *Fam (dégoûter)* to re-volt, to disgust **2** *Méd* to counter-irritate
VPR **se révulser** *(d'un visage)* to contort; **ses yeux se révulsèrent** his/her eyes rolled up

révulsif, -ive [revylsif, -iv] ADJ, NM *Méd* re-vulsive, counter-irritant

révulsion [revylsjɔ̃] NF *Méd* revulsion, counter-irritation; *Fig* revulsion; **éprouver une r. à la vue de qn/qch** to feel revolted at the sight of sb/sth

rewriter [rirajtœr, rərajtœr] NM rewriter, re-write man

rewriter [rirajte, rərajte] VT to rewrite

rewriting [rirajtiŋ, rərajtiŋ] NM rewriting

Reykjavik [rekjavik] N Reykjavik

rez-de-chaussée [redʃose] NM INV **1** *(ni-veau)* ground floor, *Am* first floor; **au r.** on the ground *or Am* first floor **2 (appartement en) r.** ground-floor flat, *Am* first-floor apartment

rez-de-jardin [redʒardɛ̃] NM INV *(niveau)* garden level; **appartement en r.** garden flat *or Am* apartment

RF [ɛrɛf] NF *abrév* **République française**

RFA [ɛrɛfa] NF *Anciennement (abrév* **Répu-blique fédérale d'Allemagne)** FRG

RG [ɛrʒe] NMPL *(abrév* **renseignements géné-raux)** security branch of the French police force, *Br* ≃ Special Branch, *Am* ≃ FBI

rg *abrév* **rive gauche**

Rh NM *Méd (abrév* **facteur Rhésus)** Rh; **Rh-négatif** Rh negative; **Rh-positif** Rh positive

rhabillage [rabijaʒ] NM **1** *(d'une montre)* re-pair, overhaul **2** *(d'un enfant)* dressing again; *(de soi-même)* getting dressed again

rhabiller [rabije] VT **1** *(réparer) (montre)* to repair **2** *(habiller)* **r. qn** to dress sb again, to put sb's clothes on again; *(acheter de nou-veaux vêtements pour)* to buy new clothes for sb; **je n'ai plus rien pour la r.!** I don't have a thing to put on her *or* to dress her in! **3** *Fig (bâtiment, vieille idée etc)* to give a new look to
VPR **se rhabiller** *(mettre ses vêtements)* to put one's clothes on again, to get dressed again; *Fam* **il peut aller se r.** *(d'un athlète)* he might as well give up and go home; *Fam* **va te r.!** get off!; **avec vos 12 000 livres par an vous pou-vez aller vous r.!** you can get lost with your £12,000 a year!, you can take your £12,000 and stuff it!

rhabilleur, -euse [rabijœr, -øz] N *(de mon-tres)* repairer

rhapsode [rapsɔd] NM *Antiq (chanteur)* rhap-sode, rhapsodist

rhapsodie [rapsɔdi] NF rhapsody

rhapsodique [rapsɔdik] ADJ rhapsodic

rhénan, -ane [renã, -an] ADJ *(industrie, économie)* (of/from the) Rhineland
N **R.** Rhinelander

Rhénanie [renani] NF **la R.** the Rhineland; **R.-Palatinat** Rhineland-Palatinate

rhénium [renjɔm] NM *Chimie* rhenium

rhéostat [reɔsta] NM *Élec* rheostat; **r. de dé-marrage** *(d'un moteur électrique)* rheostatic starter

rhésus [rezys] NM **1** *Zool* rhesus monkey **2** *Physiol* **(facteur) r.** rhesus *or* Rh factor; **r. positif/négatif** rhesus *or* Rh positive/nega-tive; **incompatibilité r.** rhesus *or* Rh incom-patibility

rhéteur [retœr] NM **1** *(orateur)* rhetorician **2** *Antiq (professeur)* rhetor

rhétoricien, -ienne [retɔrisjɛ̃, -jɛn] N rhetorician

rhétorique [retɔrik] NF **1** *Littér* rhetoric; **fi-gure de r.** figure of speech **2** *Scol Arch* **(classe de) r.** *Br* ≃ lower sixth form, *Am* ≃ eleventh grade **3** *(emphase)* rhetoric
ADJ *(effet etc)* rhetorical

rhéto-roman, -ane, *pl* **rhéto-romans, -anes** [retɔrɔmɑ̃, -an] ADJ, NM *Ling* Rhaeto-Romanic

Rhin [rɛ̃] NM **le R.** the (river) Rhine

rhinite [rinit] NF *Méd* rhinitis

rhinocéros [rinɔserɔs] NM rhinoceros, *Fam* rhino

rhinologie [rinɔlɔʒi] NF *Méd* rhinology

rhinopharyngé [rinofarɛ̃ʒe], **rhinopha-ryngien, -ienne** [rinofarɛ̃ʒjɛ̃, -jɛn] ADJ *Méd* nose-and-throat, *Spéc* rhinopharyngeal

rhinopharyngite [rinofarɛ̃ʒit] NF *Méd* in-flammation of the nose and throat, *Spéc* rhinopharyngitis

rhinopharynx [rinofarɛ̃ks] NM *Anat* nose and throat, *Spéc* rhinopharynx

rhinoplastie [rinoplasti] NF *Chir* rhino-plasty

rhinoscopie [rinoskɔpi] NF *Méd* rhinoscopy

rhizome [rizom] NM *Bot* rhizome

rhodanien, -ienne [rɔdanjɛ̃, -jɛn] ADJ of the Rhone; *Géog* **couloir r.** Rhone corridor

Rhodes [rɔd] NF Rhodes

Rhodésie [rɔdezi] NF *Anciennement* Rhodesia

rhodésien, -ienne [rɔdezjɛ̃, -jɛn] *Ancien-nement* ADJ Rhodesian
N **R.** Rhodesian

rhodium [rɔdjɔm] NM *Chimie* rhodium

rhododendron [rɔdɔdɛ̃drɔ̃] NM *Bot* rhododendron

rhombique [rɔ̃bik] ADJ rhombic

rhomboïdal, -ale, -aux, -ales [rɔ̃bɔidal, -o] ADJ rhomboid

rhomboïde [rɔ̃bɔid] NM rhomboid

Rhône [ron] NM **le R.** the (river) Rhone

rhubarbe [rybarb] NF rhubarb; **confiture/tarte à la r.** rhubarb jam/tart

rhum [rɔm] NM rum; **r. blanc** white rum

rhumatisant, -ante [rymatizɑ̃, -ɑ̃t] ADJ, N *Méd* rheumatic

rhumatismal, -ale, -aux, -ales [ryma-tismal, -o] ADJ *Méd* rheumatic

rhumatisme [rymatism] NM *Méd* rheuma-tism, *Fam* rheumatics; **avoir des rhumatis-mes** to have rheumatism *or Fam* rheumatics; **être perclus de rhumatismes** to be crippled with rheumatism; **mes rhuma-tismes me font souffrir** my rheumatism is playing me up

▸ ▸ *Méd* **r. articulaire** rheumatic fever; *Méd* **déformant** polyarthritis

rhumatoïde [rymatɔid] ADJ *Méd* rheu-matoid

rhumatologie [rymatɔlɔʒi] NF *Méd* rheu-matology

rhumatologue [rymatɔlɔg] N *Méd* rheu-matologist

rhume [rym] NM *Méd* cold; **gros r.** bad *or* heavy cold; **prendre** *ou* **attraper un r.,** *Fam* **attraper le r.** to catch a cold, to catch cold; **avoir un r.** to have a cold

▸ ▸ **r. de cerveau** head cold; **r. des foins** hay fever

rhumerie [rɔmri] NF rum distillery

ria [rija] NF *Géog* ria

riant [rijɑ̃] ADJ **1** *(visage)* smiling, cheerful; *(yeux)* laughing, merry **2** *Fig (ambiance)* merry, cheerful; *(paysage, campagne)* cheerful, sunny, bright

RIB [rib] NM *Fam (abrév* **relevé d'identité bancaire)** = document giving details of one's bank account, bank details

ribambelle [ribɑ̃bɛl] NF *(d'insultes, de noms etc)* long string; *(de visiteurs)* string, crowd; *Fam* pile; **r. d'enfants** swarm of children

ribaud, -aude [ribo, -od] *Arch Litt* ADJ *(per-sonne)* debauched
N debauchee

riboflavine [riboflavin] NF riboflavin

ribonucléique [ribonykleik] ADJ *(acide)* ribonucleic

ribote [ribɔt] NF *Fam Vieilli* spree; **être en r.** to be tipsy *or* tight

ribouldingue [ribuldɛ̃g] NF *Fam* spree, binge; **faire la r.** to go on a spree *or* binge

ricain, -aine [rikɛ̃, -ɛn] *Fam* ADJ Yank
N **R.** Yank

ricanement [rikanmɑ̃] NM *(rire) (sarcas-tique, de mépris)* sneer, snigger; *(bête)* snig-ger, giggle; **je veux savoir d'où venait ce r.** I want to know who sniggered; **je ne supporte plus tes ricanements** I've had enough of your sniggering/giggling/sneering

ricaner [rikane] VI *(sarcastiquement)* to sneer, to snigger; *(bêtement)* to snigger, to giggle

ricaneur, -euse [rikanœr, -øz] ADJ *(sarcas-tique)* sneering, sniggering; *(bête)* sniggering, giggling; **air r.** sneering look
N *(sarcastique)* sneerer, sniggerer; *(bête)* sniggerer, giggler

Richard [riʃar] N **R. Cœur de Lion** Richard the Lionheart

richard, -arde [riʃar, -ard] N *Fam Péj (per-sonne riche)* **un r.** a moneybags

RICHE [riʃ]

ADJ rich **1–3** ▪ wealthy **1** ▪ elaborate **2** ▪ lush **2** ▪ fertile **2** ▪ rich in *(riche en)* **3** ▪ full of *(riche de)* **4**

ADJ **1** *(fortuné)* rich, wealthy, well-off; **l'un des hommes les plus riches du monde** one of the richest *or* wealthiest men in the world; **les pays riches** (the) rich *or* wealthy countries; **faire un r. mariage** to marry into a wealthy family, *Fam* to marry money; **être r. à millions** to be worth millions; *Fam* **ça fait r.** that looks very grand *or* posh
2 *(qui abonde en qch) (cuisine, fromage, re-pas, aliment)* rich; *(vocabulaire)* extensive; *(style)* elaborate; *(description)* detailed; *(imagination)* vivid, lively; *(végétation)* luxu-riant, lush; *(moisson)* rich, abundant; *(terre)* fertile; *Aut* **mélange r.** rich mixture; **votre analyse est r.** your analysis is full of good things *or* very interesting; **évitez de manger trop r. le soir** don't eat too much rich food in the evening; **une r. nature** a person full of vi-

tality; **il a une très r. personnalité** he's got a lot of personality, he's full of personality; **une r. idée** a splendid idea

3 r. en qch rich in sth; **r. en protéine** rich or high in protein, protein-rich, with a high protein content; **aliment r. en fibres** high-fibre food; **r. en calories** high in calories; **terre r. en minerais** earth rich in minerals; **r. en tableaux/édifices du XIᵉ siècle** with an abundance or wealth of paintings/eleventh-century buildings; **la journée a été r. en événements** it's been an action-packed or exciting day; **mon voyage a été r. en expériences** I learned a lot from my trip, I got a lot out of my trip; **je ne suis pas très r. en produits de beauté** (d'un commerçant) I don't have many cosmetics in stock

4 r. de (espérances etc) full of; **r. de possibilités** (avenir) with lots of potential, full of hope; **livre/expérience r. d'enseignements** very instructive book/experience; **... le cœur gros mais r. de tant d'aventures** heavy-hearted but rejoicing in my/his/etc adventures

N rich or wealthy person; **les riches** the rich, the wealthy; **nouveau r.** nouveau riche; *Péj* **fils ou gosse de riche(s)** rich kid; **tu es vraiment un fils de riche(s)!** you really have no idea how the other half lives, have you?

richelieu, pl **richelieus, richelieux** [riʃəljø] **NM** lace-up (shoe), Oxford (shoe)

richement [riʃmɑ̃] **ADV 1** richly; **pourvoir r. ses enfants** to make abundant provision for one's children; **marier r. sa fille** to marry one's daughter into a wealthy family **2** (luxueusement) (décoré, vêtu, illustré) sumptuously, richly; **être r. logé** to live in sumptuous surroundings

richesse [riʃɛs] **NF 1** (d'une personne, d'un pays) wealth; **la r. publique** public wealth; **vivre dans la r.** to be wealthy; **r. en matières premières** (d'un pays) wealth of raw materials; **le tourisme, c'est la seule r. de la région** tourism is the country's only resource or only source of income; **ce tableau fait la r. du musée** this painting is the prize item in the museum's collection; **richesses** riches, wealth; **voilà toutes mes richesses** this is everything I've got; **musée plein de richesses** gallery full of treasures or valuable objects **2** (du sol, d'un gisement, du vocabulaire) richness; (de la végétation) luxuriance, lushness; (de l'imagination) vividness, liveliness; (d'une description) detailed nature; (de rencontres) abundance

richissime [riʃisim] **ADJ** extremely wealthy, *Fam* loaded

ricin [risɛ̃] **NM** *Bot* castor-oil plant; **huile de r.** castor oil

ricocher [rikɔʃe] **VI** (d'une balle, un caillou) to ricochet (**sur** off); (sur l'eau) to bounce (**sur** off); **faire r. des pierres sur l'eau** = to play (at) ducks and drakes

ricochet [rikɔʃɛ] **NM** (d'une balle) ricochet; (sur l'eau) bounce; **faire des ricochets (sur l'eau)** = to play (at) ducks and drakes; *Fig Fam* **apprendre qch par r.** to hear of sth indirectly or in a roundabout way

ric-rac [rikrak] **ADV** *Fam* **je suis r. ce mois-ci** money's pretty tight this month; **je pense me débrouiller jusqu'à la fin du mois, mais ça va être r.** I think I'll make it to the end of the month but only just; **il a réussi le bac r.** (de justesse) he only just scraped through the bac; **elle m'a remboursé r.** she paid me back to the very last penny

rictus [riktys] **NM** grimace, *Fml* rictus; **prendre/avoir un r.** to grimace

ride [rid] **NF 1** (sur le visage) wrinkle, line; (sur un fruit) wrinkle; **crème anti-rides** anti-ageing cream; **front creusé de rides profon-**

des deeply lined or furrowed brow; *Fig Fam* **cela n'a pas pris une r. en trente ans** it's still just as good as it was thirty years ago **2** (sur l'eau, le sable) ripple; (de sable) ridge

ridé [ride] **ADJ** (visage) wrinkled, lined; (pomme) wrinkled, shrivelled

rideau, -eaux [rido] **NM 1** (d'intérieur) curtain, *Am* drape; **lit garni de rideaux** curtained bed; **rideaux de lit** bed hangings; **tirer les rideaux** to draw the curtains; *Fig Fam* **tirer le r. sur qch** to draw a veil over sth; **on ne peut pas tirer le r. sur le passé** you can't forget the past, you can't put the past behind you **2** *Théâtre* curtain; **r. à huit heures précises** the curtain rises at eight sharp; *Fig Fam* **r.!** let's call it a day!; **allez, r., je ne veux plus en parler!** drop it or that's enough, I don't want to talk about it any more! **3** *Fig* (d'arbres) wall, screen, curtain; (de feu, fumée) wall; (de pluie) curtain **4** (d'un bureau) roll top; **classeur à r.** tambour-door filing cabinet, roll-shutter cabinet

▸ ▸ **r. bonne femme** tie-back curtain; **r. à enrouleur** roller blind; **r. d'entr'acte** act drop; **r. de fer** *Théâtre* safety curtain; (de boutique) metal shutter; *Hist, Pol* Iron Curtain; *TV, Cin* **r. de fond** backdrop; *TV, Cin* **r. de fond scénique** scenic cloth; *Aut* **r. de radiateur** radiator blind or shutter

ridelle [ridɛl] **NF** *Aut* side panel

rider [ride] **VT 1** (front) to wrinkle, to line; (peau, fruit) to wrinkle, to shrivel **2** (eau, sable etc) to ripple
VPR se rider 1 (du front, de la peau) to become wrinkled or lined; (d'une pomme) to shrivel up **2** (de l'eau) to ripple

ridicule [ridikyl] **ADJ** ridiculous, ludicrous (**de faire qch** to do sth); (prix) ridiculously low; **tu es vraiment r. dans cette tenue** you look really ridiculous in that get-up; **se rendre r.** to make a fool of oneself, to make oneself look ridiculous
NM 1 (absurdité) ridiculousness; **c'est d'un r. achevé** it is perfectly ridiculous or the height of absurdity; **tomber dans le r.** to make oneself ridiculous; **se couvrir de r.** to make a fool of oneself, to make oneself look ridiculous, to cover oneself in ridicule **2** (dérision) ridicule; **craindre le r.** to fear ridicule; **tourner qn/qch en r.** to ridicule or make fun of sb/sth, to hold sb/sth up to ridicule **3** (chose ridicule) **les ridicules de notre époque** the absurdities of our time

ridiculement [ridikylmɑ̃] **ADV** ridiculously, ludicrously

ridiculiser [ridikylize] **VT** to ridicule, to make fun of, to hold up to ridicule
VPR se ridiculiser to make oneself look ridiculous, to make a fool of oneself

ridule [ridyl] **NF** (little) wrinkle

RIEN [rjɛ̃] **PRON INDÉF** SEE GRAMMAR B16 **1** (quelque chose) (in questions rien is preferred to quelque chose when a negative answer is expected) anything; **y a-t-il r. de plus triste?** is there anything more depressing?
2 (with ne expressed) nothing, not anything; **r. ne l'intéresse** nothing interests him; **r. ne va plus!** (au casino) rien ne va plus!, no more bets!; **je n'ai r. à faire** I have nothing to do, I don't have anything to do; **il n'y a r. à faire** it can't be helped; *Fam* **r. à faire, ça ne marche pas** it's no good, it's not working; **je n'en sais trop r.** I don't know too much about it; **il n'a plus r.** (plus d'argent) he doesn't have a penny left; (il n'est plus malade) there's nothing wrong or there isn't anything wrong with him now; **tu n'as plus r. à attendre de lui** now you know just or exactly what to expect from him; **il n'y a plus r. à en dire** there is nothing more to be said, there isn't anything more to be said; **je n'ai r. vu** I didn't

see anything, I saw nothing; **je n'ai jamais r. vu d'aussi grand** I've never seen anything quite as big; **il n'a r. mangé depuis hier** he has eaten nothing or he hasn't eaten anything since yesterday; **il ne faut r. lui dire** he mustn't be told anything, he must be told nothing; **on ne peut jamais r. lui dire** you can't say a word or *Fam* open your mouth to him; **personne n'osa r. dire** nobody dared say anything; **n'en dites r.** don't say anything or a word about it, say nothing about it; **il n'y a r. de tel qu'un bon bain chaud** there's nothing like a good hot bath; **je n'ai r. de nouveau à vous dire** I have nothing or I don't have anything new to tell you; **alors, r. de nouveau?** (en attendant des résultats etc) have you heard anything yet?; **sinon? r. de nouveau?** so there's nothing new?, so nothing's been happening?; **r. d'autre** nothing else; **il ne vous fallait r. d'autre?** (is there) anything else?, will that be all?; **elle veut ça et r. d'autre** she wants that and nothing else; **ce n'est r.** it's nothing; **pour elle 10 km à pied, ce n'est r.** she thinks nothing of walking 10 km, a 10 km walk is nothing to her; **ce n'est r. de le dire!** you can say that again!; **ça ne fait r.** it doesn't matter, it makes no difference or *Fam* no odds; **si cela ne vous fait r.** if you don't mind; **comme si de r. n'était** as if nothing had happened; **elle ne ressemble en r. à sa sœur** she's nothing like her sister; *Litt* **il n'en est r.!** such is not the case!; **je n'en ferai r.** I'll do nothing of the kind or sort; **après vous – je n'en ferai r.** after you – not at all or I wouldn't dream of it; **elle n'est r. pour moi** she is or means nothing to me; **elle n'est plus r. pour lui** she doesn't mean anything to him any more; **sa fille n'a r. de lui** his daughter doesn't take after him in any way; **je n'ai r. d'un psychiatre, pourtant!** I'm no psychiatrist!; **la nouvelle perceuse X n'a r. d'une perceuse traditionnelle!** the new X drill is nothing like a traditional drill!; **il n'y était pour r.** he had nothing to do with it or had no hand in it; **je n'y suis pour r.** it's nothing to do with me, I've got nothing to do with it; *Fam* **il ne sait r. de r.** he knows nothing at all or nothing about anything or *Fam* zilch about anything; **que t'a-t-il donné? – r. de r.!** what did he give you? – zilch! or not a sausage! SEE GRAMMAR B62–3

3 (with ne not expressed) **que faites-vous? – r./presque r.** what do you do? – nothing/hardly anything; **elle lit? – jamais r.** does she read? – not a thing; **r. du tout** nothing at all; **c'est tout ou r.** it's all or nothing; **pour r.** for nothing; **avoir qch pour r.** to get sth for (next to) nothing; **parler pour r.** to waste one's breath; **jouer pour r.** to play for fun; **pourquoi demandez-vous cela? – pour r.** why do you ask? – no reason or I just wondered; **se fâcher de r.** to get angry about or for nothing; **merci, monsieur – de r.** thank you – it's a pleasure or you're welcome or (please) don't mention it; **en moins de r.** in less than no time, in no time at all; **une affaire de r. (du tout)** an insignificant matter; *Vieilli Fam* **femme de r.** loose woman; **une petite pièce de r. du tout** a wretched little room; **un homme de r. du tout** a man of no account, a nobody; **un/une r.(-)du(-)tout** a (mere) nobody; **c'est une coupure de r. du tout** it's just a scratch; *Fam* **un moins que r.** (personne) a loser; **pour trois fois r.** (acheter, vendre qch) for next to nothing, for a song; **il possède trois fois r.** he has absolutely nothing; **faire qch comme (un) r.** to do sth easily or without any trouble at all or *Fam* as easy as winking; *Tennis* **quinze à r.** fifteen love SEE GRAMMAR B62–3

4 (the negation is expressed or implied elsewhere in the sentence) **il est inutile de r. dire** you needn't say anything; **avant qu'elle ait r. dit** before she said anything; **sans r. faire**

without doing anything; **sans nous gêner en r.** without troubling us at all *or* in the slightest

5 r. que nothing but, only, merely; **r. que la vérité** nothing but the truth; **je frémis r. que d'y songer** the mere thought (of it) *or* just thinking about it makes me shudder; **r. que pour aller à un bal** for the sake of going *or* just to go to a dance; **r. que pour aller à Paris, ça coûte 60 euros** it costs 60 euros just to go to Paris; **je te le dis, r. qu'à toi** I'm telling you and only you *or* and you alone; **c'est à moi, r. qu'à moi** it's mine, all mine; **r. que cela?** is that all?

6 (*with* ne ... pas) **on ne peut pas vivre de r.** you can't live on nothing; **ce n'est pas r.!** that's something!; **vingt euros de l'heure, ce n'est pas r.!** twenty euros an hour is something at least!; **élever quatre enfants, ce n'est pas r.!** it's quite something raising four kids!

ADV *Arg Vieilli* really, *Br* not half, *Am* real; **elle est r. chic!** she's really smart!, *Br* she isn't half smart!

NM 1 (*bagatelle*) trifle, (mere) nothing; **un r. l'habille** she looks good (dressed) in anything; **un r. suffit pour le fâcher** he gets upset over the least little thing; **se piquer d'un r.** to take offence at nothing *or* the slightest thing; **perdre son temps à des riens** to waste one's time with trifles; **se disputer pour des riens** to argue over nothing; **il court 400 mètres comme un r.** he runs 400 metres just like that *or* with no trouble (at all), running 400 metres is nothing to him

2 un r. de (*un petit peu de*) (just) a little; **un r. d'huile** the merest drop of oil; **en un r. de temps** in no time (at all), in less than no time; **un r. de femme** a tiny little woman

3 un r. (*un peu*) a bit, a trifle, a touch; **il est un r. pénible en ce moment** he's being a bit of a pain at the moment

riesling [risliŋ] NM (*vin*) Riesling

rieur, -euse [rijœr, -øz] ADJ (*air, visage*) cheerful, bright; (*yeux*) laughing, merry; **c'est un garçon très r.** he laughs a lot; **mouette rieuse** black-headed gull

▶ N laugher; **mettre les rieurs de son côté** *ou* **avec soi** to have the last laugh

rififi [rififi] NM *Arg* brawl, free-for-all, punch-up; **il va y avoir du r.** there's going to be trouble *or* a punch-up

riflard [riflar] NM *Fam* (*parapluie*) umbrella, *Br* brolly

riflette [riflɛt] NF *Fam* (*guerre*) war

rift [rift] NM *Géol* rift valley

Riga [riga] N Riga

rigide [riʒid] ADJ **1** (*matériau*) rigid; (*essieu*) fixed; **couverture r.** (*d'un livre*) stiff cover **2** *Fig* (*personne, règlement, système etc*) rigid, inflexible, unbending; **ne sois pas trop r. avec eux** don't be too strict with them

rigidement [riʒidmɑ̃] ADV rigidly

rigidifier [riʒidifje] VT to rigidify, to make rigid

rigidité [riʒidite] NF **1** (*d'un matériau*) rigidity; **r. cadavérique** rigor mortis **2** *Fig* (*d'une personne, d'un règlement, d'un système etc*) rigidity, inflexibility

rigolade [rigɔlad] NF *Fam* **ça n'est pas de la r.** it's no laughing matter *or* no joke; **prendre qch à la r.** to treat sth as a joke, to make a joke out of sth; **j'essaie de le prendre à la r.** I'm trying not to take it too seriously; **ah, la r.!** what a hoot *or* scream!

rigolard, -arde [rigɔlar, -ard] *Fam* ADJ (*personne*) fond of a joke *or* a laugh; **il a toujours un air r.** he's always got a grin on his face, something always seems to be amusing him

▶ N **c'est un r./une rigolarde** he's/she's fond of a joke *or* a laugh

rigole [rigɔl] NF (*caniveau*) channel; (*filet d'eau*) rivulet

rigoler [rigɔle] VI *Fam* **1** (*rire*) to laugh; *Iron* **tu me fais r., tiens!** you make me laugh! **2** (*s'amuser*) to have some fun *or* a laugh, to enjoy oneself **3** (*plaisanter*) to joke (**avec** about); **il ne faut pas r. avec le fisc** you shouldn't mess about with the tax man; **ils rigolent pas avec la sécurité dans cet aéroport** they don't mess about *or* take any chances with security at this airport; **tu rigoles?** are you kidding?, are you joking?

rigolo, -ote [rigɔlo, -ɔt] *Fam* ADJ **1** (*drôle*) funny; **ce n'est pas r.** it's no laughing matter *or* joke; **il est r., ton sac** what a fun bag! **2** (*curieux*) funny, queer, odd

▶ N (*personne amusante, fumiste*) joker, comedian; (*incompétent*) cowboy, joker; **quel petit r. a débranché la prise?** what joker pulled the plug out?

▶ NM *Arg Vieilli* (*revolver*) revolver

rigorisme [rigɔrism] NM strictness

rigoriste [rigɔrist] ADJ (*morale, principe, attitude etc*) strict, rigorous

▶ N strict moralist

rigoureusement [rigurøzmɑ̃] ADV **1** (*strictement*) strictly; **il est r. interdit de marcher sur les pelouses** it is strictly forbidden to walk on the grass; **r. exact** absolutely correct; **suivre r. les consignes** to follow the instructions to the letter; **je l'ai r. vérifié** I checked it thoroughly **2** (*avec dureté*) rigorously, severely, harshly; **être r. opposé à qch** to be rigorously opposed to sth

rigoureux, -euse [rigurø, -øz] ADJ **1** (*dur*) (*punition, mesures, conditions etc*) severe, harsh, rigorous; (*hiver*) hard; (*climat*) harsh **2** (*strict*) strict; (*analyse*) rigorous; (*entraînement*) rigorous, strict; (*discipline*) severe; **observer une neutralité rigoureuse** to observe strict neutrality; **sois plus r.** be more rigorous

rigueur [rigœr] NF **1** (*dureté*) harshness, severity, rigour, *Am* rigor; (*du temps*) harshness, severity; **prendre des mesures de r.** to take rigorous *or* harsh *or* severe measures; **la r. de la loi** the rigour of the law; **les rigueurs de la vie en prison/du climat écossais** the rigours of prison life/the Scottish climate; **un climat de r. économique** a harsh economic climate; **user de r. envers qn** to be severe with *or* hard on sb; **tenir r. à qn** not to forgive sb; **je ne lui en tiens pas r.** I don't hold it against him, I'm not holding a grudge **2** (*du règlement*) strictness; (*d'une analyse*) rigour, *Am* rigor; **manquer de r.** (*d'un style*) to be sloppy; (*d'une personne*) (*dans son travail*) to be sloppy, to lack self-discipline; **manquer de r. dans son analyse** not to be rigorous enough in one's analysis; **apprendre la r.** to learn self-discipline; **être de r.** to be compulsory *or* obligatory; **la cravate est de r.** ties must be worn; **l'habit n'est pas de r.** evening dress is optional; **délai de r.** deadline; **à la r.** (*si nécessaire*) if need be, if really necessary; (*à la limite*) just about, at a pinch

rillettes [rijɛt] NFPL *Culin* potted meat (*made from pork, goose etc*)

rimailler [rimaje] VI *Péj Vieilli* to versify

rimailleur, -euse [rimajœr, -øz] N *Péj Vieilli* versifier, rhymester, poetaster

rimbaldien, -ienne [rɛ̃baldjɛ̃, -jɛn] ADJ **la poésie rimbaldienne** Rimbaud's poetry, the poetry of Rimbaud; **avoir des accents rimbaldiens** to be reminiscent of Rimbaud, to have Rimbaud-like overtones; **ce film a un côté r.** the film has a touch of Rimbaud about it

rime [rim] NF rhyme; **r. pauvre/riche** poor/rich rhyme; **r. féminine/masculine** feminine/masculine rhyme; **rimes croisées** *ou* **alternées** alternate rhymes; **rimes plates** *ou*

suivies couplet rhymes; *Fam* **sans r. ni raison** without rhyme or reason

rimer [rime] VT (*conte etc*) to put into verse, to versify; **poésie rimée** rhyming verse

▶ VI **1** (*d'un mot etc*) to rhyme (**avec** with); *Fam* **à quoi cela rime-t-il?** what's the sense of that?, what sense is there in that?; **cela ne rime à rien** it doesn't make sense, there's no sense in it, there's neither rhyme nor reason in it; **cela ne rimerait à rien** it wouldn't make sense **2** (*faire des vers*) to write verse *or* poetry

rimeur, -euse [rimœr, -øz] N *Péj* rhymer, rhymester

Rimmel® [rimɛl] NM mascara

rinçage [rɛ̃saʒ] NM (*action*) rinsing; (*opération*) rinse; (*pour les cheveux*) (*colour or Am* color) rinse; **cycle de r.** (*d'une machine à laver*) rinse cycle; **produit de r.** (*pour lave-vaisselle*) rinsing agent *or* aid

rince-bouteilles [rɛ̃sbutɛj] NM INV bottle-washing machine

rince-doigts [rɛ̃sdwa] NM INV finger bowl

rincée [rɛ̃se] NF **1** *Fam* (*averse*) downpour; **on a pris une sacrée r. sur le dos** we got soaked through, we were drenched **2** *Arg* (*défaite*) walloping, pounding; *Fam Vieilli* (*coups*) thrashing

rincer [rɛ̃se] (**je rinçai(s); n. rinçons**) VT (*vêtements, vaisselle, cheveux*) to rinse; (*verre, tasse*) to rinse (out); **se faire r.** *Arg* (*au jeu*) to get cleaned out; *Fam* (*par la pluie*) to get soaked (to the skin) *or* drenched

▶ VI *Fam* (*offrir à boire*) to buy the drinks; **c'est moi qui rince!** I'm buying the drinks!, the drinks are on me!; **c'est le patron qui rince!** the drinks are on the house!

▶ VPR **se rincer se r. les mains** to rinse one's hands; **se r. la bouche** to rinse one's mouth (out); *Arg* **se r. le gosier** *ou* **la dalle** (*boire*) to have a drink; *Fam* **se r. l'œil** to get an eyeful

rincette [rɛ̃sɛt] NF *Fam* nip of brandy/*etc* (*put into emptied cup or glass*)

rinceur, -euse [rɛ̃sœr, -øz] N (*personne*) rinser

▶ NF **rinceuse** (*machine*) bottle-washing machine

ring [riŋ] NM *Boxe* ring; **le r.** (*la boxe*) boxing; **monter sur le r.** to go into the ring; (*faire de la boxe*) to take up boxing

ringard¹ [rɛ̃gar] NM (*tisonnier*) poker

ringard², -arde [rɛ̃gar, -ard] *Fam* ADJ **1** (*démodé*) (*personne, chanson*) old-fashioned, *Arg* uncool **2** (*voyant*) (*style, couleur, décor etc*) tacky

▶ N square, nerd

ringardise [rɛ̃gardiz] NF *Fam* tackiness, *Br* naffness; **la déco était d'une r., je te dis pas!** the decor was unbelievably tacky *or Br* naff!

ringuette [rɛ̃gɛt] NF *Can* = type of ice hockey

RIP [ɛrip] NM (*abrév* **relevé d'identité postale**) = document giving details of one's Post Office account

ripage [ripaʒ] NM (*glissement*) slipping; (*de véhicule*) skidding; *Aut* **r. des pneus** tyre scrub

ripaille [ripaj] NF *Fam* feast, blow-out; **faire r.** to have a feast *or* blow-out

ripailler [ripaje] VI *Fam* to feast, to have a (good) blow-out

ripailleur, -euse [ripajœr, -øz] N *Fam* reveller

ripaton [ripatɔ̃] NM *Arg* (*pied*) foot, *Br* plate

riper [ripe] VT (*faire glisser*) (*chargement etc*) to slide along

▶ VI to slip; (*des roues*) to skid; (*d'un chargement*) to shift; *très Fam* (*s'en aller*) to split

Ripolin® [ripɔlɛ̃] NM enamel (paint)

ripoliner [ripɔline] **vт** to enamel, to paint with enamel

riposte [ripɔst] **NF 1** (*réponse*) riposte, retort **2** *Boxe, Escrime (coup)* riposte, counter **3** (*représailles*) counterattack

riposter [ripɔste] **vi 1** (*répondre*) to retort, to riposte **2** *Boxe, Escrime* to riposte, to counter **3** (*user de représailles*) to counterattack, to mount a counterattack; **les annonceurs ont riposté au procès en ...** advertisers responded to the trial by ...

ripou [ripu] *Fam* **ADJ** (*policier*) bent, *Am* bad **NM** bent *or Am* bad cop

riquiqui [rikiki] **ADJ INV** *Fam (tout petit)* teeny-weeny; (*mesquin*) (*portion, cadeau etc*) stingy, mean; (*maillot de bain*) skimpy; **ça fait r.** (*mesquin*) it looks a bit stingy *or* mean

rire¹ [rir] **NM** laughter, laughing; **un r.** a laugh; **il a un gros r.** he has a loud laugh, he guffaws; **il eut un gros r.** he roared with laughter; **éclat de r.** burst of laughter; **des éclats de r.** screams *or* hoots of laughter; **avoir le fou r.** to have a fit of the giggles, to laugh uncontrollably; (*sur scène*) to corpse; **se tenir les côtes de r.** to split one's sides laughing; **provoquer** *ou* **exciter les rires** to cause laughter; **r. moqueur** sneer; **avoir un r. moqueur** to sneer; **il eut un r. d'incrédulité** he laughed incredulously

rire² (*prp* riant; *pp* ri; *pr ind* je ris, n. rions, ils rient; *pr sub* je rie; *p hist* je ris; *fu* je rirai) **vi 1** to laugh; *Prov* **rira bien qui rira le dernier** he who laughs last laughs longest; **r. jaune** to force a laugh, to give a forced laugh; **r. comme un bossu** to laugh like a hyena, to split one's sides laughing; **r. aux éclats** to scream *or* roar with laughter; **éclater de r.** to burst out laughing; **r. bruyamment** to guffaw; **r. en soi-même, r. tout bas** to laugh to oneself, to chuckle; **r. en dedans** to laugh up one's sleeve; **r. bêtement** to giggle, to titter; **dire qch en riant** to say sth laughingly *or* with a laugh; **il a ri (jusqu')aux larmes** he laughed till he cried; **ne pas avoir le cœur à r.** not to be in a laughing mood; **il y a de quoi r.** it's laughable, it's enough to make a horse laugh; **il n'y a pas de quoi r.!** it's no laughing matter!, it's no joke!; **cela nous a souvent fait r.** we've often laughed about it, we've had many a laugh over it; **c'était à mourir** *ou Fam* **à crever de r.** we nearly died laughing; **c'est à mourir de r., cette histoire/cette situation** it's a hysterically funny story/situation; **il nous faisait tordre** *ou* **mourir de r.** he had us splitting our sides; **tu me fais mourir** *ou* **tordre de r.** you crack me up; *Iron* **tu me fais (mourir de) r. avec tes grandes idées** you really make me laugh, you and your big ideas; *Fam* **j'étais mort de r.** I was killing myself laughing; **r. de qn** to laugh at sb, to make fun of sb; **r. d'une histoire** to laugh over *or* at a story; **il rit de vos menaces** he laughs at *or* scoffs at *or* makes light of your threats; **je ris de leurs insultes** I don't care about their insults; **il vaut mieux en r.** it's best to laugh, you might as well laugh; **il prête à r.** he makes himself a laughing stock; **tout cela ne prête guère à r.** it's not exactly funny *or* a laughing matter; **il faut dire que la situation prêtait à r.** admittedly the situation was funny; **vous me faites r.!** you make me laugh!, nonsense!, you must be joking!; **laissez-moi r.!, ne me faites pas r.!** don't make me laugh!

2 (*s'amuser*) to have (some) fun, to have a laugh *or* a few laughs; **vous voulez r.!** you're joking!; **prendre qch en riant** to laugh sth off; **pour r.** for fun, for a laugh *or* a joke; **je te le disais en riant** it was, I was pulling your leg; **non mais sans r.!** no, but seriously!; **sans r., c'est vrai** honestly *or* seriously, it's true; *Fam* **c'était pour r.** it was only for fun; **je l'ai fait histoire de r.** I did it for a laugh *or* a joke *or* for fun

3 *Fig (des yeux)* to dance

VPR se rire se r. de qn to laugh at sb, to make fun of sb; **se r. de qch** to laugh at sth, to make light of sth

ris¹ [ri] **NM** *Litt (rire)* laughter

ris² **NM** *Naut (dans la voile)* reef; **prendre un r.** to take in a reef; **larguer un r.** to shake out a reef

ris³ **NM** *Culin* **r. (de veau)** (calf's) sweetbread

risée [rize] **NF 1** (*moquerie*) mockery, derision; **s'exposer à la r. publique** to expose oneself to public scorn *or* derision **2** (*objet de moquerie*) laughing stock; **nous étions la r. de tous** we were a public laughing stock *or* the butt of everyone's jokes **3** *Naut (brise)* light squall, flurry (of wind)

risette [rizɛt] **NF** (*d'enfant*) (little) laugh, smile; **fais (la) r. à papa!** smile for daddy!, give daddy a smile!

risible [rizibl] **ADJ** (*erreur, conduite, demande etc*) laughable, ridiculous, ludicrous; (*personne*) ridiculous; **la situation n'avait rien de r.** the situation was not at all funny, there was nothing to laugh at in the situation

risiblement [riziblǝmɑ̃] **ADV** ridiculously, ludicrously

risotto [rizɔto] **NM** *Culin* risotto

risque [risk] **NM** risk; **est-ce qu'il y a un r. que cela se produise?** is there any risk of that happening?; **courir un r.** to run a risk; **c'est un r. à courir** it's a risk I/we/*etc* have to take; **courir le r. de qch** to risk sth; **courir le r. de faire qch** to risk doing sth; **prendre un r./des risques** to take a risk *or* chance/risks *or* chances; **j'en prends le r.** I'll take that risk; **groupe à haut r.** high-risk group; **il est parti à ses risques et périls** he went at his own risk; **vous le faites à vos risques et périls** you do it at your own risk, on your head be it; **cela n'est pas sans r.** it is not without its risks *or* dangers; **sans aucun r., sans courir le moindre r.** without (running) any risk; **avoir le goût du r.** to like taking risks *or* chances, to like living dangerously; **au r. de sa vie** at the risk *or* peril of his life; **les risques d'erreur sont moindres** there's less risk *or* chance of making a mistake; **les risques d'aggravation sont importants** there is a significant risk that things will get worse; *Méd* **r. infectieux** risk of infection; **risques de guerre** (*en assurances*) war risks; **au r. de manquer le train** at the risk of missing the train; **c'est un des risques du métier** it's an occupational hazard; **assurance tous risques** comprehensive *or* all-risks insurance; **risques d'incendie/d'inondations** risk of fire/flooding; **cela constitue un r. pour la santé/la sécurité** it's a health/safety hazard; *Fin* **souscrire un r.** to underwrite a risk; *Fin* **r. de change** exchange risk; *Fin* **r. de contrepartie** credit risk; *Fin* **r. de marché** market risk; **r.-pays** country risk

risqué [riske] **ADJ 1** (*dangereux*) (*entreprise etc*) risky, hazardous **2** (*osé*) (*plaisanterie etc*) risqué, *Fam* near the knuckle

risquer [riske] **vт 1** (*mettre en danger*) (*vie, réputation etc*) to risk; **il faut r. le combat** we must risk a battle, we must take a chance and fight; **j'ai risqué ma carrière à cause de toi** I risked my career for you, I put my career on the line for you; **après tout, qu'est-ce que tu risques?** what have you got to lose after all?; *Fig* **r. sa tête** to put one's head on the block; *Prov* **qui ne risque rien n'a rien** nothing ventured, nothing gained; **je ne veux rien r.** I'm not taking any risks *or* any chances; **r. le tout pour le tout** to go for broke; **r. le coup** to risk *or* chance it, to chance one's luck; **r. gros** to play for big stakes; **il risquait de tout perdre** he risked *or* ran the risk of losing everything; **la grève risque de durer**

longtemps the strike may (well) go on for a long time, there's a chance that the strike will go on for a long time; *Fam* **il risque de gagner** he has *or* stands a good chance of winning, he might well win; *Fam* **il ne risque pas de te le dire** fat chance of him telling you **2** (*avancer*) **r. un œil** to peep out; **r. un œil dans une pièce** to peep into a room; **r. sa tête à la fenêtre** to take a hurried look out of the window; **il risqua une main derrière les assiettes** he put a hand gingerly behind the plates

VPR se risquer to take risks/a risk; **je ne m'y risquerais pas** I wouldn't risk it; **se r. à faire qch** to venture to do sth; **se r. dans une maison abandonnée** to venture into an abandoned house

risque-tout [riskǝtu] **N INV** daredevil **ADJ INV** **il est r.** he's a daredevil, he's constantly risking his neck; **un enfant r.** a real little daredevil, a daredevil of a child

rissole [risɔl] **NF** *Culin* rissole

rissoler [risɔle] **vт & vi** *Culin* to brown; **pommes (de terre) rissolées** sauté potatoes

ristourne [risturn] **NF** *Com (rabais)* discount; **faire une r. à qn** to give sb a discount; **r. de droits de douane** customs drawback; **r. de fidélité** regular customer discount *or* rebate; **r. de prime** premium rebate

ristourner [risturne] **vт** (*faire une ristourne de*) to give a discount of; **il nous a ristourné vingt pour cent du prix** he gave us a twenty per cent discount *or* twenty per cent off

ristrette [ristrɛt] **NM** *Suisse (petit café serré)* = very strong small black coffee

Rital, -ale, -als, -ales [rital] **N** *Fam Péj (Italien)* wop, *Br* Eyetie

rite [rit] **NM** rite; *Fig (habitude)* ritual; **les rites de la vie quotidienne** the rituals of everyday life; **rites d'initiation** initiation rites; **rites de passage** *ou* **initiatiques** rites of passage

ritournelle [riturnɛl] **NF** *Mus* ritornello; *Fig Fam* **c'est toujours la même r.** it's (always) the same old story

ritualiser [ritɥalize] **vт** to ritualize, to turn into a ritual

ritualisme [ritɥalism] **NM** *Rel* ritualism

ritualiste [ritɥalist] **ADJ** ritualistic **N** ritualist

rituel, -elle [ritɥɛl] **ADJ** ritual **NM** *Rel, Fig (rites)* ritual; **selon le r.** according to ritual; *Fig* **il a verrouillé les portes selon son r.** he went through his ritual of locking the doors; **r. d'initiation** initiation rites *or* ritual

rituellement [ritɥɛlmɑ̃] **ADV 1** (*habituellement*) invariably; **ils y vont r. chaque année** they go every year without fail **2** (*en sociologie*) according to ritual, ritually

rivage [rivaʒ] **NM** (*de mer, lac*) shore; *Litt (de rivière)* bank

Do not confuse with **rive**.

rival, -ale, -aux, -ales [rival, -o] **ADJ, N** rival; **sans r.** unrivalled, unparalleled; **ce boulanger est sans r. pour ...** there is no one to equal this baker when it comes to ...

rivaliser [rivalize] **vi r. avec qn** to compete *or* vie with sb; **r. d'adresse/de générosité/d'élégance avec qn** to try to outdo sb in skill/generosity/elegance

rivalité [rivalite] **NF** rivalry

rive [riv] **NF** (*de rivière*) bank; (*de lac, de mer*) shore; **la R. gauche** (*de la Seine*) the Left Bank; *Can* **la R. sud** (*du Saint-Laurent*) the South Shore

Do not confuse with **rivage**.

Rive droite, rive gauche
The Right (north) Bank of the Seine is traditionally associated with business and trade, and has a reputation for being more conservative than the Left Bank. The Left (south) Bank includes districts traditionally favoured by artists, students and intellectuals, and has a reputation for being Bohemian and unconventional.

river [rivɛ] VT **1** *(attacher)* to rivet; *Fig* **le matin, je suis rivé au lit** *(je ne peux pas me lever)* I just can't get out of bed in the morning; **il est rivé au lit** *(il refuse de se lever)* he just won't get out of bed; **impossible de bouger, j'étais rivé sur place** I couldn't move, I was rooted to the spot; **être rivé à son bureau** to be glued to *or* stuck at one's desk; **il a les yeux rivés sur elle** he can't take his eyes off her, his eyes are glued to her **2** *Fam* **r. son clou à qn** to shut sb up

riverain, -aine [rivrɛ̃, -ɛn] ADJ *(de rivière)* riverside, waterside; *(de lac) (propriété, propriétaire)* lakeside, waterside; *(de route) (propriété etc)* roadside, bordering (on) the road; **propriétaire r.** owner of lakeside/roadside property
N *(de rivière)* riverside resident; *(de lac)* lakeside resident; **les riverains de cette rue** the people who live in *or* along this street; **'route interdite sauf aux riverains'** 'residents only', 'no entry except for access'

rivet [rivɛ] NM rivet

rivetage [rivtaʒ] NM riveting

riveter [rivte] VT *(pr ind je rivette, n. rivetons)* to rivet

riveteuse [rivtøz] NF riveting machine

rivière [rivjɛr] NF **1** river; **pêche en r.** river fishing **2** *Équitation* water jump **3** *Fig (de lave, boue)* river; **r. de diamants** diamond necklace, *Spéc* diamond rivière

rivoir [rivwar] NM *(marteau)* riveting hammer; *(machine)* riveting machine

rivure [rivyr] NF *(action)* riveting; *(joint)* rivet(ed) joint; *(tête)* rivet head

rixe [riks] NF brawl; **r. au couteau** knife fight

riz [ri] NM rice; **eau/papier de r.** rice water/paper; **poudre de r.** face powder
▸ ▸ **r. blanc** white rice; **r. brun** *ou* **complet** brown rice; **r. créole** boiled rice; **r. au curry** curried rice; **r. décortiqué** husked rice; **r. étuvé** *ou* **incollable** non-stick rice; **r. jaune** *ou* **au safran** saffron rice; **r. au lait** rice pudding; **r. long** long-grain rice; **r. rond** short-grain rice; *(pour le riz au lait)* pudding rice; **r. sauvage** wild rice

riziculteur, -trice [rizikyltœr, -tris] N rice grower

riziculture [rizikyltyr] NF rice growing

rizière [rizjɛr] NF rice field, paddy field

riz-pain-sel NM INV *Mil Arg* commissariat

RMI [ɛrɛmi] NM *abrév* **revenu minimum d'insertion**

RMiste [ɛrɛmist] N *Br* ≃ person on income support, *Am* ≃ person on Welfare

RMN [ɛrɛmɛn] NF *(abrév* **résonance magnétique nucléaire**) NMR

RN [ɛrɛn] NF *abrév* **route nationale**

RNIS [ɛrɛnis] NM *Ordinat (abrév* **réseau numérique à intégration de services)** ISDN; **envoyer qch par RNIS** to ISDN sth, to send sth by ISDN

robe [rɔb] NF **1** *(de femme)* dress **2** *(d'un avocat)* robe, gown; *(d'un prêtre, un cardinal etc)* robe; **les gens de r., la r.** the legal profession **3** *(d'oignon)* skin; *(de fève)* husk; *(d'un cigare)* wrapper (leaf) **4** *(pelage) (de cheval etc)* coat **5** *(du vin)* colour, *Am* color

▸ ▸ **r. de baptême** christening robe; **r. de chambre** dressing gown, *Am* robe; **en r. de chambre** in one's *or* a dressing gown; **pommes de terre en r. de chambre** *ou* **en r. des champs** jacket potatoes, baked potatoes; **r. chasuble** pinafore dress, *Am* jumper; **r. de grossesse** maternity dress; **r. d'intérieur** housecoat; **r. de mariée** wedding dress; **r. du soir** evening gown *or* dress

Il faut noter que le terme anglais **robe** ne désigne jamais un vêtement de femme.

robert [rɔbɛr] NM *très Fam (sein)* tit, boob

robe-tablier, *pl* **robes-tabliers** NF pinafore dress, *Am* jumper

robin [rɔbɛ̃] NM *Péj Vieilli* lawyer

robine [rɔbin] NF *Can Arg* methylated spirits, *Br* meths

robinet [rɔbinɛ] NM *(de l'évier, du lavabo)* tap, *Am* faucet; *(de tonneau)* spigot; **ouvrir/fermer le r.** to turn the tap on/off; **eau du r.** tap water; **r. d'eau froide/chaude** cold-/hot-water tap; *Fig* **c'est un r. d'eau tiède** he drones *or* Br Fam rabbits *or* witters on; **r. mélangeur** mixer tap; **r. du gaz** gas tap; *Tech* **r. d'arrêt** *ou* **de fermeture** stopcock, shut-off *(valve)*; **r. de vidange** *ou* **de purge** drain cock *or* tap; **r. à flotteur** ballcock; *Naut* **r. de prise d'eau à la mer** seacock; *Hum* **problèmes de robinets** sums about filling baths and tanks

robinetterie [rɔbinɛtri] NF *(robinets)* (system of) taps

robineux [rɔbinø] NM *Can Arg* tramp, *Am* hobo

robot [rɔbo] NM *Tech, Fig* robot; **r. (ménager)** food processor; **avion r.** drone

robotique [rɔbɔtik] NF robotics
ADJ robotic

robotisation [rɔbɔtizasjɔ̃] NF automation, roboticization

robotiser [rɔbɔtize] VT *Tech (chaîne de montage etc)* to automate, to roboticize; *Fig* **r. qn** to turn sb into a robot

robre [rɔbr] NM *Cartes* rubber

robusta [rɔbysta] NM *(café)* robusta

robuste [rɔbyst] ADJ *(personne, santé, foi)* robust; *(appétit, confiance en soi)* robust, healthy; *(plante)* hardy; *(bicyclette, machine etc)* sturdy

robustesse [rɔbystɛs] NF *(d'une personne)* robustness; *(d'une plante)* hardiness; *(d'une bicyclette, une machine etc)* sturdiness

ROC [ɛrose] NF *Ordinat (abrév* **reconnaissance optique des caractères)** OCR

roc [rɔk] NM rock; **creusé dans le r.** hollowed out of the rock; **bâti sur le r.** built on rock; *Fig* **bâtir sur du r.** to build on solid foundations; **solide comme un** *ou* **le r.** rock-solid; **Jules, c'est un r.** Jules is as solid as a rock

rocade [rɔkad] NF *(route)* bypass; *Mil* communications line

rocaille [rɔkaj] NF **1** *(arrangement)* **(jardin de) r.** rockery, rock garden **2** *(pierraille)* (loose) stones *or* rocks; **grotte en r.** grotto **3** *(terrain)* stony *or* rocky ground
ADJ INV *Beaux-Arts (style, table etc)* rocaille

rocailleux, -euse [rɔkajø, -øz] ADJ **1** *(pierreux)* stony, rocky **2** *Fig (voix)* harsh, rough

rocambole [rɔkɑ̃bɔl] NF *Bot* Spanish garlic

rocambolesque [rɔkɑ̃bɔlɛsk] ADJ *(aventures, histoire etc)* fantastic, incredible

roche [rɔʃ] NF *(matière, rocher)* rock; *Géol* **roches ignées/sédimentaires/métamorphiques** igneous/sedimentary/metamorphic rocks; **percé dans la r.** drilled in the rock; **r. de fond** bedrock; **eau de r.** clear spring water; *Fig* **clair comme de l'eau de r.** as clear as crystal, crystal-clear

rocher [rɔʃe] NM **1** *(masse de pierre)* rock; *(escarpé)* crag; **r. branlant** rocking stone, logan(stone); **côte hérissée de rochers** rockbound coast; **le R. de Gibraltar** the Rock of Gibraltar, *Fam* the Rock **2** *(paroi)* rock face; **pousser à flanc de r.** to grow out of the bare rock, to cling to the side of the rock; **faire du r.** to go rock climbing **3** *(bouchée de chocolat)* chocolate *(containing nuts)* **4** *(dans l'oreille)* petrous bone

rochet [rɔʃɛ] NM *Tech* ratchet; **roue à r.** ratchet wheel

rocheux, -euse [rɔʃø, -øz] ADJ *(paysage, région)* rocky; **masse/paroi rocheuse** rock mass/face; **les (montagnes) Rocheuses** the Rocky Mountains, the Rockies

rock, rock and roll [rɔk(ɛnrɔl)] *Mus* NM rock (and roll); *(danse)* rock (and roll), jive; **danser le r.** to rock (and roll), to jive; **un groupe/chanteur de r.** a rock group/singer
ADJ INV *(concert, groupe, chanteur etc)* rock

rocker [rɔkœr] N *(musicien)* rock musician; *(enthousiaste)* rock (music) fan

rocking-chair, *pl* **rocking-chairs** [rɔkiŋtʃɛr] NM rocking chair

rococo [rɔkoko] NM *Beaux-Arts* rococo
ADJ INV **1** *Beaux-Arts* rococo **2** *(démodé)* old-fashioned

rodage [rɔdaʒ] NM *(d'un moteur, d'une voiture)* running in; **période de r.** *(d'une structure)* running-in *or* breaking-in period; *Aut* **en r.** running in; **voiture en r.** car that is being run in

rodéo, rodéo [rɔdeo] NM rodeo; **faire du r.** *(métier)* to be a rodeo rider; *(prendre part à un rodéo)* to take part in a rodeo; **finalement, ils se sont livrés à un véritable r. dans les rues du quartier** *(en voiture)* they ended up having a car chase in the streets; **r. de voitures volées** joyriding

roder [rɔde] VT *(moteur, voiture)* to run in; *Fig (entreprise), Théâtre (spectacle)* to get into its stride; *(équipe, structure)* to break in; **être rodé** *(d'une entreprise etc), Théâtre (d'un spectacle)* to be into its stride, to have settled down *or* shaken down; *(d'un employé)* to have got the hang of things
VPR **se roder** *Fam* to break oneself in

rôder [rɔde] VI to prowl, to be on the prowl; **r. dans les rues** to prowl about *or* hang about the streets; **un pauvre chien qui rôde** a poor dog roaming around; *Fig Fam* **il rôde autour de moi depuis quelques jours** he's been hanging around me for a few days

rôdeur, -euse [rɔdœr, -øz] ADJ prowling
N prowler

rodomontade [rɔdɔmɔ̃tad] NF **rodomontade(s)** boasting, bragging; **faire des rodomontades** to boast, to brag

rœsti [røʃti] NMPL *Suisse Culin* rosti, potato cake

Rogations [rɔgasjɔ̃] NFPL *Rel* Rogations

rogatoire [rɔgatwar] ADJ *Jur* rogatory; **commission r.** letters of request, *Spéc* letters rogatory

rogatons [rɔgatɔ̃] NMPL *Fam (de nourriture)* leftovers, scraps

rognage [rɔɲaʒ] NM *(action) (du cuir, du métal etc)* trimming, paring; *Ordinat (d'image)* cropping

rogne [rɔɲ] NF *Fam* bad temper; **être en r.** to be cross **(contre qn** with sb); **mettre qn en r.** to make sb cross; **se mettre** *ou* *Fam* **se ficher en r.** to get angry, to see red

rogner [rɔɲe] VT *(griffes, ongles)* to clip, to trim; *(cuir, métal etc)* to trim, to pare; *Ordinat (image)* to crop; *Fig (de l'inflation) (économies etc)* to eat *or* nibble away at, to whittle away; **r. les tranches d'un livre** to cut *or* trim the edges of a book; *Fig* **les patrons ro-**

gnaient (sur) les salaires the bosses were paring wages to the bone; *Fig* **r. sur les dépenses** to cut down on *or* curtail expenses; *Fig* **r. les ailes à qn** to clip sb's wings

rognon [rɔɲɔ̃] NM *Culin* kidney

rognonner [rɔɲɔne] VI *Fam* to grumble, to grouse

rognures [rɔɲyr] NFPL *(déchets) (de griffes, d'ongles)* clippings; *(de cuir, de métal etc)* trimmings, parings; *(de viande)* scraps

rogomme [rɔgɔm] NM *Fam* **voix de r.** (drunkard's) husky voice

rogue [rɔg] ADJ arrogant, haughty

roi [rwa] NM **1** *(souverain)* king; **le r. Louis XIII** (King) Louis XIII; *Bible* **les Rois mages** the Three Wise Men, the Three Kings, the Magi; **le R.-Soleil** the Sun King; **jour** *ou* **fête des Rois** Twelfth Night; *Rel* Epiphany; **tirer les rois** = to celebrate Twelfth Night; **plat de r.** dish fit for a king; **heureux comme un r.** as happy as a sandboy; *Fig* **le r. n'est pas son cousin** he's got a very high opinion of himself; *Fig* **le choix du r.** a boy followed by a girl **2** *Fig* king; **le r. des animaux** *(lion)* the king of the beasts; **le r. du plastique/des pizzas** the plastics/pizza king; **l'un des rois du pétrole** one of the oil barons; *Hum* **r. de la resquille** *(dans une queue)* champion queue-jumper; *(dans le métro etc)* champion fare-dodger; *(au cinéma, au stade)* champion at sneaking in for nothing; **c'est le r. des imbéciles** he's a prize *or* first-class idiot; *très Fam* **c'est le r. des cons** he's a complete arsehole *or Am* asshole **3** *Cartes, Échecs* king
ADJ INV **bleu r.** royal blue

Tirer les rois

The French traditionally celebrate Epiphany with a round, almond-flavoured pastry ("la galette des Rois") containing a small porcelain figurine ("la fève" – originally a dried bean). The pastry is shared out and the person who finds the "fève" is appointed "king" or "queen" and given a cardboard crown to wear. This tradition is called "tirer les Rois".

roide [rwad], **roideur** [rwadœr], **roidir** [rwadir] *Arch* = **raide, raideur, raidir**

roille [rɔj] NF *Suisse Fam* downpour; **pleuvoir à (la) r.** to bucket down, *Br* to chuck it down

roillé [rɔje] ADJ *Suisse Fam (fou, cinglé)* crazy

roiller [rɔje] VI *Suisse Fam (pleuvoir)* to bucket down, *Br* to chuck it down

roitelet [rwatlɛ] NM **1** *Péj* petty king **2** *(oiseau)* wren; **r. huppé** goldcrest

rôle [rol] NM **1** *Théâtre, Fig* part, role; **r.-titre** title role; **premier r.** leading role, lead; **c'est elle qui a le premier r.** she has the leading role, she is the lead *or* the leading lady; **second r.** supporting part *or* role; **Mme Oldani dans le r. de la Tosca** Mme Oldani as Tosca; **il est toujours excellent dans les rôles de jeune premier** he is always excellent as the romantic lead; **jouer le r. de Macbeth** to play (the part of) Macbeth; **on lui fait jouer le r. d'Ophélia** she's been given the role *or* part of Ophelia, she's been cast as Ophelia; **distribution des rôles** *(action)* casting; *(liste)* cast (list); **répéter/connaître son r.** to learn/ know one's part *or* lines; *Fig* **assigner un r. à qn** to assign a role to sb; *Fam* **jouer un r. secondaire** *(d'une personne)* to play second fiddle; **cet élément joue un r. secondaire dans ...** this element plays a secondary role in ...; **tu as le beau r.** it's easy *or* all right for you, you've got the easy job; **il n'a pas le beau r.** he doesn't have it easy; **les femmes n'ont pas toujours un r. facile** a woman's role

is not always easy, women do not always have it easy; **le r. du médecin** the doctor's role *or* function *or* job; **il avait, en quelque sorte, le r. de confesseur** he acted as a kind of confessor; **le r. du sport dans l'éducation** the role *or* function of sport in education; **un r. de premier plan** a leading role; **jeu de rôles** role playing; **ce n'est pas son r. de te conseiller** it's not his/her job to advise you
2 *(liste)* list, register; **à tour de r.** in turn, by turns, in rotation; **faire qch à tour de r.** to take turns (in) doing sth, to do sth turn and turn about *or* in turns; **nous sommes entrés dans son bureau à tour de r.** we went into his office in turn; **les rôles de l'armée active** the active list; *Naut* **r. de l'équipage** list of the crew, muster roll; *Admin* **r. des impôts** *ou* **d'impôt** assessment book; *Admin* **r. des contributions** tax roll

roller [rɔlœr] NM roller skate

rolleur, -euse [rɔlœr, -øz] N roller skater

rollier [rɔlje] NM *(oiseau)* roller

rollmops [rɔlmɔps] NM INV *Culin* rollmop

roll on-roll off [rɔlɔnrɔlɔf] ADJ INV, NM INV **(navire) r.** roll-on/roll-off ship, RO-RO ship

ROM [rɔm] NF INV *Ordinat* ROM

romain, -aine¹ [rɔmɛ̃, -ɛn] ADJ Roman; **l'Empire r.** the Roman Empire; **l'Église romaine** the Church of Rome; **chiffres romains** Roman numerals; *Typ* **caractère r.** roman character; **en caractères romains** in roman
N **R.** Roman
NM *Typ* roman

romaine² ADJ, NF *(balance)* **r.** steelyard

romaine³ NF *(laitue)* cos (lettuce); *Am* romaine; *Fig Fam* **être bon comme la r.** *(bienveillant)* to be extremely kind; *(destiné à être victime)* to be sure to get it in the neck

roman¹ [rɔmɑ̃] NM **1** *(en prose)* novel; **r. cycle, r.-fleuve** saga, roman fleuve; **sa vie est un véritable r.** his life is like something out of a novel; **le nouveau r.** the antinovel, the nouveau roman **2** *Hist (poème)* romance; **le R. de la Rose** the Romance of the Rose
▸ ▸ **r. d'amour** love story, romance; **r. d'apprentissage** Bildungsroman; **r. de cape et d'épée** swashbuckler; **r. à clés** roman à clef; **r. de gare** airport novel; **r. noir** thriller; **r. policier** detective novel; *Fam* whodunnit

roman² ADJ **1** *Ling* Romance **2** *Archit* Romanesque; *(en Angleterre)* Norman
NM **1** *Ling* Romance **2** *Archit* Romanesque style; *(en Angleterre)* Norman style

Il faut noter que le terme anglais **Roman** est un faux ami. Il signifie **romain**.

romance [rɔmɑ̃s] NF *(chanson)* (sentimental) song, drawing-room ballad

romancer [rɔmɑ̃se] VT *(biographie)* to fictionalize; *(événement, histoire)* to romanticize

romanche [rɔmɑ̃ʃ] ADJ, NM *Ling* Romans(c)h

romancier, -ière [rɔmɑ̃sje, -jɛr] N novelist

romand [rɔmɑ̃] ADJ **la Suisse romande** French(-speaking) Switzerland
NMPL **les Romands** the French(-speaking) Swiss

romanesque [rɔmanɛsk] ADJ **1** *(personnage, aventure etc)* romantic; **un personnage r.** a romantic figure; **une situation r.** a situation worthy of a novel **2** *Littér (technique etc)* novelistic; **l'œuvre r. de Sartre** Sartre's fiction *or* novels

Do not confuse with **romantique**.

roman-feuilleton, *pl* **romans-feuilletons** NM serial

romanichel, -elle [rɔmaniʃɛl] N *Péj* **1** *(tsigane)* gipsy, romany **2** *(vagabond)* tramp, vagrant

romaniser [rɔmanize] VT *Hist* to Romanize

romaniste [rɔmanist] N **1** *Ling* student of the Romance languages **2** *Rel, Jur* Romanist

romano [rɔmano] N *Fam Péj (tsigane)* gippo, *Br* pikey

roman-photo, *pl* **romans-photos** NM photo-story, picture story; *(sentimental)* photo-romance, picture romance

romantique [rɔmɑ̃tik] ADJ **1** *Beaux-Arts, Littér* Romantic **2** *(personne, idées, film etc)* romantic
N **1** *Beaux-Arts, Littér* Romantic(ist) **2** *(sentimental)* romantic

Do not confuse with **romanesque**.

romantisme [rɔmɑ̃tism] NM **1** *Beaux-Arts, Littér* Romanticism **2** *(d'une personne)* romanticism; **ça ne manque pas de r.** it's quite romantic; **paysage plein de r.** romantic countryside

romarin [rɔmarɛ̃] NM *Bot, Culin* rosemary

rombière [rɔ̃bjɛr] NF *Arg* **(vieille) r.** old biddy

Rome [rɔm] N Rome; *Prov* **tous les chemins mènent à R.** all roads lead to Rome

rompre [rɔ̃pr] (**je romps, il rompt, ils rompent**) VT **1** *(casser)* to break; *(en deux parties)* to break in two; *(bâton, fil)* to snap; *(en plusieurs parties)* to break (up); **r. ses digues** *(d'un fleuve etc)* to burst its banks; **r. le silence** to break the silence; **le silence de la nuit était rompu par ...** the silence of the night was shattered by ...; **r. une promesse** to break a promise; **r. le pain** to break bread; *Théâtre* **applaudir à tout r.** to applaud wildly; *Mil* **r. les rangs** to fall out, to dismiss, to break ranks **2** *(interrompre) (conversation, fiançailles, relations diplomatiques, amitié)* to break off; *(contrat), Élec (circuit)* to break; **le charme est rompu** the spell is broken; **cela rompt un peu la monotonie** it helps to break *or* relieve the monotony; **il ne faut pas r. le rythme** keep up the rhythm; **r. le rythme quotidien** to provide a distraction from daily routine; **r. un tête-à-tête** to interrupt a *or* break in on a private conversation; **la France a rompu les relations avec la Chine** France has broken off *or* severed relations with China; **r. l'équilibre** to upset the balance; **r. les chiens** to call off the hounds; *Fig* to change the subject
VI **1** *(casser)* to break; *(d'un bâton, d'un fil)* to break, to snap; *Fig (de deux amants)* to split up, to break it off; **r. avec** *(amant)* to break it off with, to finish with; *(tradition, passé)* to break with; **r. avec sa famille** to break off relations with one's family; **r. avec une habitude** to break (oneself of) a habit **2** *Mil* **r. devant l'ennemi** to break before the enemy **3** *Boxe, Escrime* to break
VPR **se rompre** *(se casser)* to break; *(d'un bâton, d'un fil)* to break, to snap; *(de la glace)* to break (up); *Méd (d'un vaisseau sanguin)* to rupture; **son cœur battait à se r.** his heart was throbbing violently *or* fit to burst; *Fig* **se r. le cou** to break one's neck

rompu [rɔ̃py] ADJ **1** broken; *Méd (vaisseau sanguin)* ruptured; **fiançailles rompues** broken engagement; **chemin r.** road full of potholes; **être r. (de fatigue)** to be worn out *or* tired out; **r. de travail** worn out *or* tired out by work; **couleur rompue** colour with a shot effect **2 r. à** used to; **être r. aux affaires** to be experienced in business

romsteck [rɔmstɛk] NM rump steak

ronce [rɔ̃s] NF **1** *(arbuste)* bramble (bush), blackberry bush; *(branche)* bramble **2** **ronce(s) artificielle(s)** barbed wire **3** *(nœud de certains bois)* **r. de noyer** bur(r) walnut

ronceraie [rɔ̃srɛ] NF bramble patch

ronchon, -onne [rɔ̃ʃɔ̃, -ɔn] *Fam* ADJ grouchy, grumpy
N grumbler, grouser

ronchonnement [rɔ̃ʃɔnmɑ̃] NM *Fam* grumbling, grousing, bellyaching; **j'en ai assez de tes ronchonnements** I've had enough of your grumbling *or* grousing *or* bellyaching

ronchonner [rɔ̃ʃɔne] VI *Fam* to grumble, to grouse, to grouch

ronchonneur, -euse [rɔ̃ʃɔnœr, -øz] ADJ, N *Fam* = ronchon

roncier [rɔ̃sje] NM, **roncière** [rɔ̃sjɛr] NF (thick) bramble bush

rond, ronde [rɔ̃, rɔ̃d] ADJ **1** *(balle, table, nappe etc)* round; *(ventre)* rounded; *(poitrine de femme)* full; *(personne, joues, silhouette)* plump; **écriture ronde** round hand(writing); **avoir le dos r.** to be round-shouldered; **avoir le ventre r.** to have a bit of a stomach; **tuiles rondes** curved *or* rounded tiles; **le ballon r.** (association) football, *Br* soccer; **faire des yeux ronds** to goggle, to gape; **avoir des yeux ronds** to be wide-eyed (with astonishment)
2 *Fig* **voix ronde** full voice; **en chiffres ronds** in round figures; **deux cents euros en chiffres ronds** a round two hundred euros; **compte r.** round sum; *Fam* **homme tout r.** straightforward man; **r. en affaires** businesslike; **être r. en affaires** to be straightforward where business is concerned
3 *Fam (ivre)* wasted, *Br* ratted; **r. comme une queue de pelle** completely wasted *or Br* ratted
ADV **tourner r.** *(d'une roue)* to run true; *(d'un moteur)*, *Fig (d'une entreprise, d'une affaire etc)* to run smoothly; **ça fera 100 euros tout r.** that makes it a hundred euros exactly; **avaler qch tout r.** to swallow sth whole; *Fam* **cela ne tourne pas r.** there's something not right, there's something the matter; *Fam* **elle ne tourne pas r.** there's something up *or* the matter with her
NM **1** *(figure)* circle; **le chat se met en r.** the cat curls (itself) up; **danser/s'asseoir en r.** to dance/sit in a circle *or* a ring; **tourner en r.** to go round in a circle *or* ring; *Fig* to go round in circles; *Fam* **en baver des ronds de chapeau** to be having a helluva time; **il m'en fait baver des ronds de chapeau** he's making my life hell
2 *(rondelle) (de saucisson, carotte)* slice; *(de beurre)* pat; *Fam* **il n'a pas un r.** he hasn't a penny, he hasn't a brass farthing
NF **ronde 1** *(danse)* round (dance); *(chanson)* round, roundelay
2 *Mil etc (visite de surveillance)* round(s); *(de policier)* beat; **faire une/sa ronde** to patrol; *(de policier)* to be on the beat; *Arch* **la ronde de nuit** *(hommes, veille)* the night watch; **chemin de ronde** parapet walk, rampart walk
3 *(écriture)* round hand(writing)
4 *Mus (note)* semibreve, *Am* whole note
5 **à la ronde** around; **visible à dix kilomètres à la ronde** visible for ten kilometres around; **il n'y avait personne à dix kilomètres à la ronde** there was nobody within a radius of ten kilometres; **(faire) passer le vin à la ronde** to pass the wine round, to hand round the wine; **boire à la ronde** to drink in turn
► ► **r. de cuir** *(coussin)* (round leather) chair cushion; *(figure de danse)* **r. de jambe** rond de jambe; *Fam* **faire des ronds de jambe** to bow and scrape; **r. de serviette** napkin ring

rond-de-cuir, *pl* **ronds-de-cuir** NM *Fam Péj* penpusher, clerk

rondeau, -eaux [rɔ̃do] NM **1** *Littér* rondeau **2** *Mus* rondo

ronde-bosse, *pl* **rondes-bosses** NF *Beaux-Arts* sculpture in the round; **en r.** in the round

rondelet, -ette [rɔ̃dlɛ, -ɛt] ADJ *(personne, doigts)* plump, chubby, podgy; **somme rondelette** good (round) sum, tidy sum

rondelle [rɔ̃dɛl] NF **1** *(de carton etc)* disc; *(de citron, de saucisson, de cornichon etc)* slice; *Can* **r. (de hockey)** puck; **couper les légumes en rondelles** to slice the vegetables **2** *(de vis, d'écrou etc)* washer; *Aut* **r. butée** thrust washer; *Aut* **r. de blocage** lock washer

rondement [rɔ̃dmɑ̃] ADV **1** *(promptement)* briskly, promptly, smartly; **mener r. les choses** to make short work of things, to deal with things promptly **2** *(carrément)* bluntly, frankly; **il nous a dit r. qu'il n'était pas d'accord** he told us straight (out) *or* bluntly *or* frankly that he didn't agree

rondeur [rɔ̃dœr] NF **1** roundness; *(d'une personne, des joues etc)* plumpness; **rondeurs** rounded forms *or* lines; *(d'une femme)* curves; **avoir des rondeurs** to be curvy *or* curvaceous **2** *(franchise)* straightforwardness, plain dealing; **avec r.** bluntly, frankly

rondin [rɔ̃dɛ̃] NM log; **cabane en rondins** log cabin; **chemin de rondins** corduroy road

rondo [rɔ̃do] NM *Mus* rondo

rondouillard [rɔ̃dujar] ADJ *Fam (personne)* plump, chubby, podgy

rond-point, *pl* **ronds-points** NM *(sens giratoire)* roundabout, *Am* traffic circle

Ronéo® [rɔneo] NF Roneo®

ronéotyper [rɔneɔtipe] VT to roneo

ronflant [rɔ̃flɑ̃] ADJ *(vent, feu)* roaring; *(moteur)* whirring, purring; *(poêle)* purring; *Fig Péj (titre, promesse, discours, style etc)* high-flown, high-sounding

ronflement [rɔ̃fləmɑ̃] NM **1** *(de dormeur)* snoring **2** *Fig (du vent, d'un feu)* roaring; *(de moteur, machine)* whirring, purring; *(du poêle)* purring

ronfler [rɔ̃fle] VI **1** *(de dormeur)* to snore **2** *Fig (du vent, d'un feu)* to roar; *(d'un moteur)* to whirr, to purr; *(d'un poêle)* to purr; **faire r. le moteur** to rev the engine

ronflette [rɔ̃flɛt] NF *Fam* snooze; **piquer une r.** to have a nap *or* a snooze

ronfleur, -euse [rɔ̃flœr, -øz] N *(personne)* snorer
NM *Tél* buzzer

ronger [rɔ̃ʒe] (je rongeai(s); n. rongeons) VT **1** *(d'une souris etc)* to gnaw (at), to nibble (at); **r. un os** *(d'un chien)* to gnaw (on) a bone; **rongé par les vers** wormeaten **2** *(d'un acide, de la rouille) (métal etc)* to eat away *or* into; *(de la mer) (falaises)* to erode; *Fig* **être rongé de chagrin** to be consumed *or* tormented with grief; **être rongé de remords/par la jalousie/par l'anxiété** to be eaten up with remorse/jealousy/anxiety; **rongé par la maladie** wasted by illness; **rongé par un cancer** riddled with cancer; **c'est quelque chose qui finit par la r.** it's eating away at her
VPR **se ronger 1** to worry, to fret; **se r. de chagrin, se r. le cœur** *ou* **les sangs** to eat one's heart out **2 se r. les ongles** to bite one's nails

rongeur, -euse [rɔ̃ʒœr, -øz] ADJ *(mammifère)* rodent-like
NM rodent

ronron [rɔ̃rɔ̃] NM *Fam (d'un chat)* purr(ing); *(d'un moteur)* purr, purring (noise), whirr, whirring (noise); *(d'un avion, une voix, un discours, de la musique)* drone, droning (noise); *(d'une machine)* whirr, whirring (noise); **faire r.** *(d'un chat)* to purr; *Fig* **le r. de la vie quotidienne** the monotony of everyday life, humdrum routine

ronronnement [rɔ̃rɔnmɑ̃] NM *(d'un chat)* purring; *(d'un moteur)* purr, purring, whirr, whirring, drone; *(d'un avion)* drone, droning (noise); *(d'une machine)* whirr, whirring (noise)

ronronner [rɔ̃rɔne] VI *(d'un chat)* to purr; *(d'un moteur)* to purr, to whirr; *(d'un avion)* to drone; *(d'une machine)* to whirr; *Fig* to be in a rut; **r. de plaisir** to purr with pleasure

room-service [rumsɛrvis] NM room service

roque [rɔk] NM *Échecs* castling; **petit/grand r.** castling on the king's/queen's side

roquefort [rɔkfɔr] NM *(fromage)* Roquefort

roquer [rɔke] VI **1** *Échecs* to castle **2** *(au croquet)* to croquet the ball

roquet [rɔkɛ] NM *Péj (chien)* yapper; *Fam (personne)* little squirt

roquette¹ [rɔkɛt] NF *Bot* rocket

roquette² NF *Mil (projectile)* rocket; **r. antichar** anti-tank rocket

rorqual [rɔrkwal] NM rorqual, finback (whale)

rosace [rozas] NF *Archit* **1** rose (window) **2 r. de plafond** ceiling rose

rosacé [rozase] ADJ *Bot* rose-like, *Spéc* rosaceous

rosaire [rozɛr] NM *Rel* rosary; **dire** *ou* **réciter son r.** to tell one's beads, to say the rosary

rosâtre [rozatr] ADJ pinkish

rosbif [rɔzbif] NM **1** *Culin (rôti)* roast beef; *(à rôtir)* roasting beef **2** *très Fam (terme injurieux) (Britannique)* Brit

rose [roz] NF **1** *(fleur)* rose; **bouton de r.** rosebud; **eau de r.** rosewater; *Fam* **roman à l'eau de r.** soppy love story, soppy romance; **essence de roses** attar *or* otto of roses; **teint de r.** rosy complexion; **frais comme une r.** fresh as a daisy; *Fam* **ça ne sent pas la r.!** it's a bit whiffy!; *Fam* **envoyer qn sur les roses** to send sb packing, to send sb off with a flea in his/her ear; *Prov* **(il n'est) pas de r. sans épines** there's no rose without a thorn **2 bois de r.** rosewood **3** *Archit* rose (window) **4** *(diamant)* rose (diamond), rose-cut diamond
ADJ **1** *(robe etc)* pink; *(teint)* rosy; **des rubans r. pivoine** peony-red ribbons; **tout n'est pas r. dans ce monde** life is not a bed of roses; **ce n'est pas bien r.,** *(certaine histoire-là)* it's a pretty grim story **2** *Fam (socialiste)* left-wing *(relating to the French Socialist Party)*
NM pink; **voir la vie** *ou* **tout en r.** to see everything through rose-coloured glasses *or* spectacles
► ► *Bot* **r. incarnate** damask rose; **r. mousseuse** moss rose; *Géol* **r. des sables** desert rose; **r. sauvage** wild rose, dog rose; *Naut* **r. des vents** compass card

rosé [roze] ADJ pinkish; **vin r.** rosé
NM *(vin)* rosé

roseau, -eaux [rozo] NM reed

rose-croix NM INV Rosicrucian
NF Rosicrucianism

rosée [roze] NF dew; **goutte de r.** dewdrop; *Phys* **point de r.** dew point

roselet [rozlɛ] NM *(fourrure)* ermine

roselier, -ière [rozəlje, -jɛr] ADJ **marais r.** reed marsh
NF **roselière** reed bed

roséole [rozeɔl] NF *Méd* roseola

roser [roze] VT *Litt* **r. qch** to make *or* turn sth pink

roseraie [rozrɛ] NF rose garden

rose-thé, *pl* **roses-thé** NF INV, ADJ INV tea rose

Rosette [rozɛt] N **la pierre de R.** the Rosetta stone

rosette [rozɛt] NF **1** *(nœud)* bow; *(ornement)* rosette **2** *(insigne)* rosette *(esp of the Legion of Honour)*; **recevoir la r.** to be awarded the Legion of Honour **3 r. de Lyon** = sort of slicing sausage

rosicrucien, -ienne [rozikrysjɛ̃, -jɛn] ADJ, N Rosicrucian

rosier [rozje] NM rose tree, rose bush; **r.**

grimpant climbing rose; **r. nain** miniature rose(-bush); **r. sur tige** standard rose; **r. sauvage** briar

rosière [rozjɛr] NF *Hist* = village maiden awarded a wreath of roses for her virtuous conduct; *Fig Hum* **ce n'est pas une r.** she's no angel

rosiériste [rozjerist] N rose grower *or* breeder

rosir [rozir] VT to turn pink
VI **1** *(du ciel)* to go *or* turn pink **2** *(d'émotion)* to blush, to go pink

rosse [rɔs] *Péj* NF **1** *Vieilli (cheval)* hack **2** *Fam (homme)* swine, bastard; *(femme)* bitch
ADJ *Fam (personne, conduite, remarque)* rotten; *(coup)* rotten, dirty

rossée [rɔse] NF *Fam* beating, walloping, pasting

rosser [rɔse] VT *Fam* **r. qn** to beat sb up, to give sb a (good) hiding *or* walloping; **se faire r.** to get a hiding *or* walloping

rosserie [rɔsri] NF *Fam* **1** *(caractère)* rottenness; **il/elle est d'une r.!** he's a bastard/she's a bitch **2** *(mauvaise action)* dirty *or* rotten trick; **faire une r. à qn** to play a dirty *or* rotten trick on sb **3** *(parole)* nasty *or* spiteful remark

rossignol [rɔsiɲɔl] NM **1** *(oiseau)* nightingale **2** *(clef)* skeleton key **3** *Fam (objet)* white elephant; **vieux rossignols** old stock

rossinante [rɔsinãt] NF *Péj Vieilli (cheval)* old worn-out hack

rostre [rɔstr] NM *Antiq (éperon de navire)* rostrum

rot [ro] NM *Fam* belch, burp; *(de bébé)* burp; **faire un r.** to belch, to burp; *(d'un bébé)* to burp; **faire faire son r. à un bébé** to burp a baby

rôt [ro] NM *Arch* roast (meat)

rotarien [rɔtarjɛ̃] NM Rotarian

Rotary [rɔtari] NM Rotary Club

rotatif, -ive [rɔtatif, -iv] ADJ *(pompe, moteur etc)* rotary
NF **rotative** (rotary) press; *Fig* **faire tourner les rotatives** to give the press *or* newspapers something to write about

rotation [rɔtasjɔ̃] NF **1** *Phys, Tech* rotation; *(d'un projectile)* spin; **mouvement de r.** rotating movement; **faire un mouvement de r. sur soi-même** *(de toupie)* to spin; *(de gymnaste)* to spin (round); *(de personne)* to spin round; **corps en r.** rotating body; **pièce à r.** revolving part; **axe de r.** axis of rotation; *Math* **faire faire une r. de 90° à une droite** to rotate a line through an angle of 90° **2** *(de bateau, de bus etc)* rotation; *(du stock, de fonds)* turnover; **par r.** in rotation
▸▸**r. des capitaux** capital turnover; **r. des cultures** crop rotation, rotation of crops; **r. de personnel** *(à des postes différents)* rotation of staff; *(remplacement)* turnover of staff, staff turnover; *Bourse* **r. de portefeuille** churning; **r. des stocks** inventory *or* stock turnover, stock turnaround

rotatoire [rɔtatwar] ADJ **1** *(mouvement)* rotatory; *(force)* rotational **2** *(polarisation)* rotary

rote [rɔt] NF *Belg Fam* anger, rage; **être/se mettre en r.** to be/go mad *or* crazy (**contre qn** at sb); **mettre qn en r.** to make sb hopping mad

roter [rɔte] VI *Fam* to belch, to burp; **faire r. un bébé** to burp a baby

roteuse [rɔtøz] NF *Fam (bouteille de Champagne)* bottle of bubbly *or Br* champers

rôti [roti] NM roast (meat), joint; *(à rôtir)* joint, roast; **r. de porc** *(cuit)* roast pork; *(non cuit)* joint of pork, pork roast; **tranche de r.** slice of roast meat
ADJ roast; **poulet r.** roast chicken; *Fig Fam* **ça**

ne va pas te tomber tout r. dans la bouche it's not going to just fall into your lap

rôtie [roti] NF (slice of) toast

rotin¹ [rɔtɛ̃] NM **1** *Bot* rattan; **sièges en r.** cane *or* rattan chairs **2** *(canne)* rattan walking stick

rotin² NM *Fam Vieilli (sou)* **pas un r.!** not a farthing!; **il n'a plus un r.** he's stone broke *or* stony

rôtir [rotir] VT **1** *(viande, châtaignes)* to roast; *(pain)* to toast **2** *Fam* **le soleil rôtit la colline** the sun is scorching the hillside; **le soleil me rôtissait le dos** my back was getting roasted by the sun
VI *Culin* to roast; **r. au soleil** to toast *or* roast in the sun; *Fam* **on rôtit ici** it's scorching *or* roasting here
VPR **se rôtir** **se r. au soleil** to toast *or* roast in the sun

rôtissage [rotisaʒ] NM roasting

rôtisserie [rotisri] NF **1** *(restaurant)* grill(-room), steakhouse **2** *(boutique)* = shop selling roast meat

rôtisseur, -euse [rotisœr, -øz] N **1** *(restaurateur)* grill-room proprietor; *(cuisinier)* roasting chef **2** *(commerçant)* = seller of roast meat

rôtissoire [rotiswar] NF *Culin* (rotating) spit, rotisserie

rotogravure [rɔtɔɡravyr] NF *Typ* rotogravure

rotonde [rɔtɔ̃d] NF **1** *Archit* rotunda **2** *Rail (circulaire)* engine shed, roundhouse

rotondité [rɔtɔ̃dite] NF **1** *(de la Terre etc)* roundness **2** *(embonpoint)* plumpness; *Fam Hum* **rotondités** *(de femme)* curves

rotor [rɔtɔr] NM *(de dynamo, turbine, hélicoptère)* rotor; *Aut* **r. de distributeur** rotor arm

rottweiler [rɔtvajlœr] NM rottweiler

rotule [rɔtyl] NF **1** *Anat* kneecap, *Spéc* patella; *Fam* **être sur les rotules** to be dead beat *or* on one's last legs **2** *Tech* ball(-and-socket) joint; *Aut* **r. de direction** steering joint; *Aut* **r. d'attelage** *(de caravane)* tow ball

rotulien, -ienne [rɔtyljɛ̃, -jɛn] ADJ *Anat* patellar

roture [rɔtyr] NF *Hist* **1** **terre en r.** land held by a commoner **2** **la r.** *(condition)* the common rank; *(gens)* the commonalty, the commons

roturier, -ière [rɔtyrje, -jɛr] *Hist* ADJ common, of the common people
N commoner

rouage [ruaʒ] NM **1** *(ensemble des roues)* wheels, gear work; **rouage(s) d'une montre** works of a watch, train of wheels of a watch; **r. d'horloge** clockwork; *Fig* **les rouages de l'administration** the workings of government; **organisation aux rouages bien huilés** smooth-running organization **2** *(roue)* (toothed) wheel, cog wheel

rouan, -anne [rwɑ̃, -an] ADJ *(cheval)* roan
NM roan

roubignoles [rubiɲɔl] NFPL *Vulg* balls, bollocks

roublard, -arde [rublar, -ard] *Fam* ADJ *(personne, air)* wily, crafty, cunning; *(ton)* crafty
N wily *or* crafty *or* cunning devil; **un fin r.** an old fox

roublardise [rublardiz] NF *Fam* **1** *(caractère)* cunning, wiliness, craftiness **2** *(acte)* crafty *or* cunning trick

rouble [rubl] NM *(monnaie russe)* rouble

roucoulade [rukulad] NF *(des oiseaux)* cooing; *Fam* **roucoulades** *(des amoureux)* billing and cooing

roucoulement [rukulmɑ̃] NM *(d'un pigeon)* cooing; *Fig (d'amoureux)* billing and cooing

roucouler [rukule] VI *(d'un pigeon)* to coo;

Fig Fam (d'amoureux) to bill and coo
VT *Fam (mots doux, promesses etc)* to coo

roudoudou [rududu] NM *Fam* = type of hard sweet *(licked out of a mould)*

roue [ru] NF wheel; **véhicule à quatre roues** four-wheeled vehicle; **véhicule à quatre roues motrices** four-wheel drive vehicle; **un deux roues** a two-wheeled vehicle, a two-wheeler; *Fig Fam* **être la cinquième r. du carrosse** to be a spare part, *Am* to be the fifth wheel; **avoir l'impression d'être la cinquième r. du carrosse** to feel in the way *or Am* like a fifth wheel; *Fig* **pousser à la r.** to put one's shoulder to the wheel, to lend a helping hand; **sans roues** wheelless, without wheels; *Naut* **la r. du gouvernail** the wheel; **faire la r.** *(d'un paon)* to display, to spread its tail; *(d'un acrobate)* to turn cartwheels/a cartwheel; *Péj (de qn qui parade)* to strut, to swagger; *Naut* **bateau à roues** paddle boat; **la grande r.** the Big Dipper, *Am* the Ferris wheel; *Arch* **condamner un criminel à la r.** to condemn a criminal to the wheel
▸▸ *Tech* **r. de commande** driving wheel; **r. dentée** toothed wheel, cogwheel, gear (wheel); *Tech* **r. à eau** water wheel; **r. d'engrenage** toothed wheel, cogwheel, gear (wheel); **r. à feu** Catherine wheel; *Fig* **la r. de la fortune** the wheel of fortune; **r. hydraulique** hydraulic wheel; *Ordinat* **r. d'impression** print wheel; **r. libre** freewheel; **descendre en r. libre** to coast *or* to freewheel downhill; **r. motrice** driving *or* drive wheel; **r. de moulin** mill wheel; **r. à rayons** spoke wheel; *Aut* **r. de secours** spare wheel; **r. de transmission** driving *or* drive wheel; *Tech* **r. de turbine** turbine wheel, impeller

roué, -ée [rwe] ADJ *Litt (personne)* cunning, sly
N *Litt (roublard)* cunning *or* sly devil
NM *Hist (débauché)* rake, roué

rouelle [rwɛl] NF *(de citron, de carotte etc)* slice; **r. de veau** fillet of veal

rouennais, -aise [rwanɛ, -ɛz] ADJ *(qui vient de Rouen)* from Rouen; *(situé à Rouen)* of Rouen
N **R.** *(natif)* native of Rouen; *(habitant)* inhabitant of Rouen

rouer [rwe] VT **1** *Fam* **r. qn de coups** to beat sb black and blue **2** *Arch (supplicier)* **r. qn** to break sb on the wheel

rouerie [ruri] NF **1** *(acte)* cunning *or* sly trick (**envers** played on) **2** *(caractère)* cunning, slyness

rouet [rwɛ] NM **1** *(de fileuse)* spinning wheel **2** *Tech (de poulie)* sheave; *(de serrure)* scutcheon

rouf [ruf] NM *Naut* deck house

rouflaquettes [ruflakɛt] NFPL *Fam (favoris)* sideboards, sideburns

rouge [ruʒ] ADJ **1** *(manteau, joues, cheveux, viande, vin etc), Pol* red; **fer r.** red-hot iron; **marqué au fer r.** *(animal)* branded; *Fig* **c'est marqué au fer r. dans ma mémoire** it's branded on my memory; **fruits rouges** soft fruit; **r. de colère/d'émotion** red (in the face) with anger/emotion; **être r. de honte** to be red *or* to blush with shame; **être r. comme une tomate** *(d'une personne)* to be as red as a beetroot; **être r. comme une écrevisse** *(brûlé par le soleil)* to be as red as a lobster; **avoir les yeux rouges** to have red eyes, to be red-eyed; *Rel* **le chapeau r.** the cardinal's (red) hat; *Pol* **le drapeau r.** the red flag; **porto r.** ruby port
2 *(inv in compounds)* **des rubans r. cerise** cherry-red ribbons; **r. sang** blood-red; **r. drapeau** pillar-box red; **r. bordeaux** wine-coloured
ADV **se fâcher tout r.** to lose one's temper completely, *Fam* to flip; **voir r.** to see red

NM **1** (couleur) red; **peindre/teindre qch en r.** to paint/dye sth red; **porter le fer au r.** to make the iron red-hot; **le r. lui monte aux joues** he is going red in the face; **Prov r. le soir, espoir** red sky at night, shepherd's delight **2** (cosmétique) rouge; **r. à lèvres, bâton de r.** lipstick; **r. à joues** blusher

3 Fam (signal) **passer au r.** to turn or go red **4** (vin) red wine; **gros r. (qui tache)** coarse red wine

5 Fig **mon compte/le commerce extérieur est dans le r.** my account/foreign trade is in the red

N (communiste) Red

rougeâtre [ruʒɑtr] ADJ reddish

rougeaud, -aude [ruʒo, -od] N red-faced person, person with a red face

ADJ red-faced; **être r.** to have a red face

rouge-gorge, pl **rouges-gorges** NM robin (redbreast)

rougeoiement [ruʒwamɑ̃] NM red glow

rougeole [ruʒɔl] NF Méd measles; **avoir la r.** to have (the) measles VOIR GRAMMAIRE A7

rougeoleux, -euse [ruʒɔlø, -øz] Méd ADJ suffering from (the) measles

N person with measles

rougeoyant [ruʒwajɑ̃] ADJ glowing (red)

rougeoyer [ruʒwaje] VI (il rougeoie; il rougeoiera) **1** (briller) to glow (red) **2** (devenir rouge) to turn red, to redden

rouge-queue, pl **rouges-queues** NM (oiseau) redstart

rouget [ruʒɛ] NM (poisson) red mullet; **r. grondin** gurnard

rougeur [ruʒœr] NF **1** (causée par la chaleur, l'émotion) flush(ing); (causée par la honte, la gêne) blush(ing) **2** Méd (tache) blotch **3** (couleur) redness

rougir [ruʒir] VT **1** (ciel, feuilles etc) to turn red, to redden; **r. son eau** to put a drop of red wine in one's water; **eau rougie** water with a little red wine; Fig **r. ses mains (de sang)** (commettre un crime) to get blood on one's hands **2** **r. le fer au feu** to heat iron in the fire until red-hot; **fer rougi au feu** red-hot iron **3** (visage) to redden

VI **1** (du ciel, des feuillages etc) to turn red, to redden; **faire r. un métal** to heat a metal until it is red-hot **2** (d'une personne) to turn or go red, to flush; (de honte, gêne) to blush, to redden, to turn or go red; **vous devriez r. de dire des choses pareilles!** you should be ashamed to say such things!; **r. jusqu'aux oreilles** to blush to the roots of one's hair; **r. d'un faux pas** to be ashamed of or to blush for a mistake; **r. de qn** to blush for sb; **r. de colère/d'émotion** to flush with anger/emotion; **r. de plaisir** to flush or blush with pleasure; **faire r. qn** to make sb blush

rougissant [ruʒisɑ̃] ADJ **1** (ciel, feuillage, arbre etc) reddening **2** (personne, visage) blushing

rougissement [ruʒismɑ̃] NM **1** (du ciel, feuillage etc) reddening **2** (d'émotion) flushing; (de honte, de gêne) blushing

rouille [ruj] NF **1** rust; **tache de r.** (sur un tissu) rust stain **2** Agr rust, mildew, blight **3** Culin rouille (spicy sauce made with red peppers and garlic)

ADJ INV rust(-coloured)

rouillé [ruje] ADJ **1** (métal, clé, casserole etc) rusty, rusted **2** Fig (français, jeu) rusty; **j'ai les jambes rouillées** my legs are stiff, my legs have seized up; **je suis complètement r.** (physiquement) I've completely seized up; (intellectuellement) I'm completely rusty **3** Agr (plante) mildewed

rouiller [ruje] VT (acier, clé, casserole etc) to rust, to make rusty

VI (d'un métal, d'une serrure etc) to rust (up), to get rusty

VPR **se rouiller 1** (d'un métal, d'une serrure etc) to rust (up), to get rusty **2** Fig Fam **je me rouille** (physiquement) I'm beginning to seize up or get stiff; (intellectuellement) my brain's going; **mon français se rouille** my French is getting rusty

rouillure [rujyr] NF **1** (d'un métal, d'une serrure etc) rustiness **2** Agr (de plantes) rust, blight

roulade [rulad] NF **1** (dans la poussière etc) roll; Gym **r. avant/arrière** forward/backward roll; **faire des roulades** to do rolls **2** Mus roulade **3** Culin rolled and stuffed meat

roulage [rulaʒ] NM **1** (d'une terre labourée, de métal etc) rolling **2** (transport de marchandises) haulage; Aut driving; **entrepreneur de r.** carrier, haulier, Am hauler; **manutention par r.** roll-on, roll-off, ro-ro; **société de r.** haulage company; Vieilli **cheval de r.** cart horse, draught horse **3** Belg (circulation) traffic; **accident de r.** traffic accident

roulant, -ante [rulɑ̃, -ɑ̃t] ADJ **1** (porte) sliding; **pont r.** travelling crane; **table roulante** trolley; **escalier r.** escalator; **tapis** ou **trottoir r.** travelator; **allure roulante** rolling gait; Rail **matériel r.** rolling stock; **personnel r.** train/bus crews, drivers and conductors **2** Com (capital) working; **affaire roulante** going concern; **fonds r.** working capital **3** Fam Vieilli (drôle) (personne, blague, histoire etc) comical

NF Mil Fam **roulante** field kitchen

roulé [rule] ADJ (journal, carte, tapis etc) rolled(-up); Culin rolled; **col r.** roll collar, polo neck, turtle neck; Fam **elle est bien roulée** she has a great figure

NM **1** (viande) rolled joint **2 r. à la confiture** Swiss roll

rouleau, -eaux [rulo] NM **1** Tech roller; Phot roller (squeegee); (d'une matricielle, machine à écrire) platen; **roulements à rouleaux** roller bearings; **r. à mise en plis** (hair) roller; **(store sur) r.** roller blind **2** (bande) (de papier, papier peint, Scotch® etc) roll; (de pellicule) roll, spool; (de fil) coil; (de tabac) twist; (de parchemin) scroll; **r. de réglisse** liquorice roll; Fig Fam **être au bout du r.** (désespéré) to be at the end of one's tether; (près de la mort) to be on one's last legs **3** (vague) billow, roller **4** Sport (saut en hauteur) roll; **r. ventral** straddle; **r. dorsal** Fosbury flop; **r. costal** western roll

▸▸ Tech **r. compresseur** road roller; Fig steamroller; **r. à pâtisserie**, Can, Suisse **r. à pâte** rolling pin; **r. à peinture** paint roller; **r. porte-serviettes** towel-roller; Culin **r. de printemps** spring roll; Tech **r. à vapeur** steamroller

roulé-boulé, pl **roulés-boulés** [rulebule] NM Sport roll (executed tucked up in a ball)

roulée [rule] NF très Fam Vieilli thrashing, beating

roulement [rulmɑ̃] NM **1** (d'une balle etc) rolling; **r. d'yeux** rolling of the eyes **2** Aviat (circulation) taxiing **3** (bruit) (d'un wagon, de la foudre) rumble, rumbling; (de véhicules sur des pierres) rattle; (d'un tambour) rolling; **des roulements de tambour** drum rolls; **un r. de tonnerre** a roll or rumble of thunder **4** Tech (pièce) bearing; **r. à billes** ball bearing; **r. à rouleaux** ou **à galets** roller bearing; Aut **r. de butée** thrust bearing **5** Com **r. de fonds** circulation of capital **6** (rotation) (dans des tâches etc) rotation; **par r.** in rotation; **r. du personnel** staff turnover

ROULER [rule]

VT	to roll **1, 4, 5** ▪ to throw **1** ▪ to swindle **2** ▪ to roll up **3** ▪ to roll out **4**
VI	to roll **1–4** ▪ to go **1** ▪ to travel **1** ▪ to drive **1**
VPR	to roll (about) **1**

VT **1** (pousser, déplacer) (pierre, tonneau, meuble etc) to roll (along); (dés) to throw, to roll; Min (charbon) to haul; **r. les yeux** to roll one's eyes; **r. de gros yeux** to goggle; **r. les hanches** to sway or swing one's hips; Fig Litt **il roulait de sombres projets dans sa tête** he was turning over sombre plans in his mind; Fig Litt **r. de mauvaises/vagues pensées** to think evil/vague thoughts

2 Fam (duper) to do, to swindle; **il m'a roulé de 300 euros** he's done me for or out of three hundred euros; **tu t'es fait r.** you've been done or had; **se faire r. dans la farine** to be made a fool of

3 (enrouler) (carte, tapis, papier, manches) to roll up; (parapluie) to roll up, to furl; (viande, poisson, cigarette) to roll; **r. qn dans une couverture** to roll or wrap sb up in a blanket

4 (passer au rouleau) (court de tennis) to roll; (pâte) to roll out

5 r. les r to roll one's r's

6 Fam **r. une pelle** ou **un palot** ou **un patin à qn** to give sb a French kiss, to French-kiss sb

VI **1** (se déplacer) (d'une balle, une personne qui tombe etc) to roll; (d'une voiture, d'un train) to go, to travel; **r. sur une pente** to roll down a slope; **faire r. qch sur le sol** to roll sth along the ground; **r. (en voiture)** to drive; **nous avons roulé toute la nuit** we drove all night; **nous roulions vite** we were going fast or speeding along; **à quelle vitesse rouliez-vous?** how fast were you travelling?, what speed were you doing?; **cette voiture roule bien/vite** the car gives a smooth ride/is fast or speedy; **cette voiture a peu roulé** the car has a low mileage; Fig **r. pour qn** to serve sb's interests; **ce politicien roule pour le patronat** this politician is on the side of the employers; Aviat **r. sur le sol** to taxi; Fam **ça roule (tout va bien)** everything's fine; Fig **r. sur l'or** to be rolling (in money or in it); Fin **l'argent roule** money is circulating freely; **la conversation roulait sur le sport** the conversation was about sport, we/they/etc were talking about sport; Fam **elle a pas mal roulé dans sa vie** she's knocked about the world a fair bit, she's a bit of a rolling stone; Prov **pierre qui roule n'amasse pas mousse** a rolling stone gathers no moss

2 (du tonnerre) to roll, to rumble; (du tambour) to roll

3 r. des hanches to swing or sway one's hips; **r. des yeux** to roll one's eyes

4 Naut (d'un navire) to roll

VPR **se rouler 1** to roll (about); **se r. par terre** to roll (about) on the floor/on the ground; Fig **se r. (par terre) (rire)** to be convulsed with laughter; **des plaisanteries à se r. par terre** hysterically funny or side-splitting jokes

2 le hérisson se roule en boule ou **sur lui-même** the hedgehog rolls (itself) up into a ball

3 Fam **se r. les pouces, se les r.** to twiddle one's thumbs; **tu vas te les r. encore longtemps?** are you going to sit there twiddling your thumbs or doing sweet FA for much longer?

4 se r. une cigarette to roll a cigarette, to make a roll-up

roulette [rulɛt] NF **1** (de meuble) caster; **à roulettes** (meuble) on casters; Fam **ça marche** ou **va comme sur des roulettes** things are going very smoothly or like clockwork; Aviat **r. de nez/queue** nose/tail wheel **2** Couture tracing wheel, tracer; Culin pastry wheel **3** Fam (de dentiste) drill **4** (jeu) roulette; **r. russe** Russian roulette; **c'est un peu la r. russe, ta proposition** your proposal is a bit dicey or is pretty much of a gamble

rouleur, -euse [rulœr, -øz] NM **1** Arch (vagabond) vagabond **2** Cyclisme **être un bon r.** to be good on the flat **3** *Naut* ship that rolls hea-vily

NF *Entom* **rouleuse** leaf roller

roulier [rulje] **NM** *Naut, Com* ro-ro ship, ro-ro

rouli-roulant, *pl* **roulis-roulants** [rulirulᾶ] **NM** *Can* skateboard

roulis [ruli] **NM** *(d'un bateau)* roll; *(d'un avion, une voiture)* lurch; **mouvement de r.** roll/lurch; **il y a du r.** it's rolling; *Naut* **table à r.** fiddle

roulotte [rulɔt] **NF** *(de bohémiens)* caravan; *(de camping)* caravan, *Am* trailer; *Fam* **vol à la r.** theft from parked cars

roulotté [rulɔte] **ADJ, NM** *Couture* **(ourlet) r.** rolled hem

roulottier [rulɔtje] **NM** *Fam (voleur)* = thief who robs parked cars

roulure [rulyr] **NF** *très Fam (terme injurieux) (prostituée)* whore, *Br Arg* tom

roumain, -aine [rumɛ̃, -ɛn] **ADJ** Romanian, Rumanian

NM *Ling* Romanian, Rumanian

N R. Romanian, Rumanian

Roumanie [rumani] **NF** Romania, Rumania

round [rawnd, rund] **NM** *Boxe* round

roupettes [rupɛt] **NFPL** *très Fam (testicules)* balls, goolies

roupie¹ [rupi] **NF** *(monnaie)* rupee

roupie² **NF** *Fam* **c'est de la r. de sansonnet** it's a load of rubbish; *Arch* **avoir la r.** to have a drippy nose

roupiller [rupije] **VI** *Fam* to sleep, *Br Arg* to kip; *(faire un petit somme)* to have a snooze *or Br Arg* kip, to take a nap; **j'ai roupillé par terre** I kipped *or* crashed on the floor; **je me suis mis à r. dans le train** I crashed out on the train

roupillon [rupijɔ̃] **NM** *Fam* snooze, nap; **faire** *ou* **piquer un r.** to have a snooze *or Br Arg* kip, to take a nap; **un petit r.** a bit of a snooze, *Br Arg* some kip

rouquin, -ine [rukɛ̃, -in] **ADJ** *Fam (personne)* red-haired

N *Fam (personne)* redhead

NM *Arg (vin)* (cheap) red wine

rouscailler [ruskaje] **VI** *Fam (protester)* to grouse, to gripe

rouspétance [ruspetᾶs] **NF** *Fam* moaning (and groaning), grumbling; **pas de r.!** I don't want to hear any moaning and groaning *or* grumbling!

rouspéter [ruspete] **VI** (**je rouspète; je rous-péterai**) *Fam* to moan (and groan), to grumble (**contre** about)

rouspéteur, -euse [ruspetœr, -øz] *Fam* **ADJ** grumpy, grouchy

N moaner, grumbler

roussâtre [rusatr] **ADJ** reddish

rousse [rus] **ADJ, NF** *voir* **roux**

NF *Fam* **la r.** the cops, the pigs

rousserolle [rusrɔl] **NF** *(oiseau)* reed warbler

roussette [rusɛt] **NF 1** *(poisson)* spotted dogfish **2** *(chauve-souris)* flying fox **3** *(grenouille)* common frog

rousseur [rusœr] **NF 1** *(de cheveux)* redness; **tache de r.** freckle; **couvert de taches de r.** freckled **2 rousseurs** *(dans un livre etc)* foxing

roussi [rusi] **NM** **ça sent le r.** there's a smell of (something) burning; *Fig* there's trouble ahead, I smell trouble

roussin [rusɛ̃] **NM** *Hist (cheval)* charger

roussir [rusir] **VT 1** *(cheveux, feuilles)* to turn brown; *Culin (viande, oignons)* to brown **2** *(en brûlant) (linge etc)* to scorch, to singe

VI 1 *(des feuilles, des arbres)* to turn brown *or* russet **2** *Culin* **faire r.** to brown

rouste [rust] **NF** *Fam* thrashing, hammering; **flanquer une rouste à qn** to give sb a thrashing *or* a hammering

roustons [rustɔ̃] **NMPL** *très Fam* balls, nuts, *Br* bollocks

routage [rutaʒ] **NM** *(d'imprimés etc)* (sorting and) routing; *(de navire)* routing; **frais de r.** routing costs

routard, -arde [rutar, -ard] **N** *Fam* backpacker

route [rut] **NF 1** *(voie)* road; **conduite sur r.** driving on the open road; **prendre la r. de Paris** to take the road for *or* to Paris; **r. à double voie** *ou* **r. à deux voies** dual carriageway, *Am* divided highway; **r. à une seule voie** single-track road; **police de la r.** = traffic police, *Am* highway patrol; **par la r.** by road; **les accidents de la r.** road accidents; **l'état des routes** road conditions; **tenir la r.** *Aut* to hold the road; *Fig Fam (d'un argument, une théorie)* to stand up, to hold water; *(d'un projet)* to stand up, to hold together; **barrer la r. à qn** to bar sb's way; *Fig* to stand in sb's way; **un arbre barre la r.** a tree is blocking the road

2 *(itinéraire)* route, way; *Naut* course; *Aviat, Naut (ligne)* route; **connais-tu la r.?** do you know the way?; **après trois heures de r.** after three hours' travelling; *Aut* after three hours on the road; **se tromper de r.** to take the wrong road, to go/come the wrong way; **se mettre en r.** *(d'une personne)* to start out, to set out; *(d'un bateau)* to get under way; **il est en r.** he's on his way; **je n'arrive pas à le joindre, il doit déjà être en r.** I can't reach him, he must already have left; **changer de r.** to change one's route; *Naut* **suivre une r.** to steer a course; *Naut* **faire r. sur Calais** to steer (a course) for Calais, to make for Calais; **navire en r. pour l'étranger** ship outward bound; **faire r. ensemble** *(de passagers)* to travel together; *(de bateaux)* to travel in convoy; **veux-tu faire la r. avec moi?** do you want to come with me?; **faire fausse r.** *(en voiture)* to take the wrong road; *(en bateau)* to stray off course; *Fig (dans un raisonnement)* to be on the wrong tack *or* track; **montrer la r. à qn** to show sb the way; **en cours de r.** en route; **marchandises avariées en cours de r.** goods damaged in transit; **frais de r.** travel(ling) expenses; **je peux te déposer, c'est sur ma r.** I can drop you, it's on my way; **je le trouve toujours sur ma r.** he's always in my way *or* under foot; **en r.!** *(allons)* let's be off!, let's go!, *Fam* let's hit the road!; *(allez)* off you go!; *Fam Hum* **en r., mauvaise troupe!** come on, you lot!; **bonne r.!** have a good trip!

3 *Fig* path; **nos routes se sont déjà croisées** our paths have already crossed; **la r. est toute tracée** your path is marked out *or* mapped out (for you)

4 *(marche)* **mettre en r.** *(moteur)* to start up; *(projet, travaux)* to start up, to get under way; **mise en r.** *(d'une machine, un projet)* start-up; **avoir qch en r.** to be working on sth; *Fam* **j'ai un poulet en r.** I've a chicken cooking; *Fam* **ils ont un bébé en r.** they've got a baby on the way

▸ ▸ **r. aérienne** airway; **r. commerciale** trade route; **r. de contournement** by-pass; **r. départementale** secondary road, *Br* ≃ B-road; **r. des fromages** cheese route; *Naut* **r. de mer** sea route; **r. nationale** main *or* major *or* trunk road, *Br* ≃ A-road, *Am* highway; *Naut* **r. de navigation** (shipping) lane, ocean lane; **r. à péage** toll road, *Am* turnpike; **r. principale** main road; **r. secondaire** *Br* B-road, minor road; **r. terrestre** (over)land route; **r. des vins** wine route

---

Il faut noter que le terme anglais **route** signifie **itinéraire, parcours**.

---

router [rute] **VT** *(imprimés etc)* to (sort and) route

routeur [rutœr] **NM** *Ordinat* router

routier¹, -ière [rutje, -jɛr] **ADJ** *(carte, circulation, sécurité, pont, transports)* road; **police routière** traffic police, *Am* highway patrol; **bicyclette routière** roadster; **locomotive routière** traction engine; **gare routière** bus *or* coach station; **voies routières** highways

NM 1 *(conducteur)* long-distance lorry driver, *Am* teamster, truck driver, trucker **2** *(vélo)* roadster **3** *(cycliste)* road racer **4** *(restaurant)* transport café, *Am* truck stop

NF routière *(voiture)* tourer, touring car

routier² **NM 1 vieux r.** *(homme expérimenté)* old hand (**de** at) **2** *(scout)* rover

routine [rutin] **NF** routine; **pour rompre la r.** to break the routine; **s'enliser dans/sortir de la r.** to get into/out of a rut; **faire qch par r.** to do sth as a matter of routine; **examen/enquête de r.** routine examination/investigation; *Ordinat* **r. d'édition** edit routine; *Ordinat* **r. de césure** hyphenation routine; *Ordinat* **r. de logiciel** software routine

routinier, -ière [rutinje, -jɛr] **ADJ** *(tâches, travail etc)* routine; **être r.** to stick to a routine, to be set in one's ways; **avoir l'esprit r.** *ou* **une mentalité routinière** to hate change, to be a creature of habit

N slave to routine

rouvrir [ruvrir] *(conj like* **ouvrir***)* **VT & VI** to reopen, to open again

VPR se rouvrir to reopen, to open again

roux, rousse [ru, rus] **ADJ** *(feuilles)* russet, reddish-brown; *(cheveux)* red; *(pelage)* reddish-brown; *(vache)* brown; **une petite fille rousse** a little girl with red hair, a little redhead; **chevelure blond r.** sandy hair; *Culin* **beurre r.** brown butter

N *(personne)* red-haired person, redhead; **un grand r.** a tall man with red hair

NM 1 *(couleur)* russet, reddish-brown; **le r. de ses cheveux** his/her red hair **2** *Culin* roux

royal, -ale, -aux, -ales [rwajal, -o] **ADJ** *(palais, résidence, visite etc)* royal; *(digne d'un roi) (cadeau, repas etc)* magnificent, fit for a king; *(salaire)* magnificent, princely; *(mépris, indifférence)* lofty; **prince r.** crown prince; **la famille royale** the royal family, *Fam* the royals; **un membre de la famille royale** a member of the royal family, *Fam* a royal; *Fig* **la voie royale** the high road; *Fam* **il me fiche une paix royale** he's leaving me in peace and quiet

royalement [rwajalmᾶ] **ADV** *(magnifiquement) (payé, traité)* royally; *Fam* **s'amuser r.** to enjoy oneself immensely *or* hugely; *Fam* **je m'en fiche** *ou* **moque r.** I couldn't care less (about it), I don't give a damn

royalisme [rwajalism] **NM** royalism

royaliste [rwajalist] **ADJ** royalist; **être plus r. que le roi** to be more Catholic than the Pope

N royalist

royalties [rwajalti] **NFPL** royalties

royaume [rwajom] **NM** kingdom, realm; *Fig* realm; **le r. des cieux** *ou* **de Dieu** the kingdom of heaven; *Prov* **au r. des aveugles, les borgnes sont rois** in the kingdom of the blind, the one-eyed man is king

Royaume-Uni **NM** **le R.** the United Kingdom

royauté [rwajote] **NF** *(monarchie)* monarchy; *(dignité)* kingship

RP [ɛrpe] **NFPL** *(abrév* **relations publiques***)* PR

RPR [ɛrpeɛr] **NM** *Pol (abrév* **Rassemblement pour la République***)* = right-of-centre political party

RRR [ɛrɛrɛr] *(abrév* **remise, rabais, ristourne***)* discounts and allowances

RSVP [ɛrɛsvepe] (*abrév* **répondez s'il vous plaît**) RSVP

RTL [ɛrteɛl] (*abrév* **Radio-Télé-Luxembourg**) = private broadcasting network based in Luxembourg

RTT [ɛrtete] **NF** (*abrév* **réduction du temps de travail**) = reduction of the working week in France from 39 to 35 hours, introduced by the government of Lionel Jospin in 1998 and phased in from 2000 onwards as part of a drive to create more employment

RU [ry] **NM** *Fam* (*abrév* **restaurant universitaire**) university cafeteria *or Br* canteen *or* refectory

ruade [rɥad] **NF** (*d'un cheval*) lashing out, kick; **allonger** *ou* **décocher** *ou* **lancer une r.** to lash out

Ruanda [rwãda] **NM** Rwanda

ruandais, -aise [rwãdɛ, -ɛz] **ADJ** Rwandan **N R.** Rwandan

ruban [rybã] **NM** ribbon; **attaché avec un r.** (*cheveux*) tied with a ribbon; **r. de chapeau** hatband; **le r. rouge** the red ribbon (*of the Légion d'Honneur*); *Courses de chevaux* **les rubans** the tapes; **mètre à** *ou* **en r.** tape measure, measuring tape

▸▸ **r. d'acier** steel band; **r. adhésif** adhesive *or* sticky tape; **r. encreur** (*de machine à écrire*) inking ribbon; **r. d'impression** print(er) ribbon; *Élec* **r. isolant** insulating tape; **r. de machine à écrire** typewriter ribbon; **r. magnétique** magnetic *or* recording tape; *Ordinat* **r. perforé** punchtape

rubané [rybane] **ADJ** *Biol* striped

rubaner [rybane] **VT 1** (*orner*) to trim with ribbon/ribbons **2** *Élec* (*fil*) to tape

rubanerie [rybanri] **NF** (*fabrication*) ribbon manufacture; (*commerce*) ribbon trade

rubato [rybato] **ADV, NM** *Mus* rubato

rubéole [rybeɔl] **NF** *Méd* German measles, rubella

rubican [rybikã] **ADJ** (*cheval*) roan

rubicond [rybikɔ̃] **ADJ** (*teint*) florid, *Fml* rubicund; **un homme r.** a florid-faced man, a man with a florid face

rubidium [rybidjɔm] **NM** *Chimie* rubidium

rubis [rybi] **NM** ruby; (*de montre, d'horloge*) jewel; **r. de Bohème** rose quartz; **montre montée sur r.** jewelled watch; *Fig Fam* **payer r. sur l'ongle** to pay cash on the nail

rubricard [rybrikar] **NM** *Journ* columnist

rubrique [rybrik] **NF 1** *Journ* (*titre*) heading; (*articles*) (*colonne*) column; (*page*) page; *Fig* **sous la même r.** under the same heading; *Journ* **r. courrier des lecteurs** letters column; **r. d'échos** diary column; **r. mode** fashion feature; **r. nécrologique** deaths column; **r. pratique** advice column; **r. shopping** consumer column **2** (*dans un livre*) imprint

ruche [ryʃ] **NF 1** (*bee*)hive; (*abeilles*) hive; **r. en paille** (*bee-*)skep; *Fig* **r. d'industrie** (*regular*) hive of industry; **à cette heure-ci, la ville est une r.** the town is very busy at this time **2** *Couture* ruche, ruching; **garni de ruches** ruched **3** *Fam* **se piquer la r.** to get wasted *or* trashed *or Br* pissed

ruché [ryʃe] **NM** *Couture* ruche, ruching

ruchée [ryʃe] **NF** (*abeilles*) hive

rucher¹ [ryʃe] **NM** apiary

rucher² **VT** *Couture* to ruche; **une robe ruchée** a ruched dress

rude [ryd] **ADJ 1** (*primitif*) (*personne, manières*) rough, uncouth, unpolished **2** (*au toucher*) (*peau, tissu*) rough; (*au goût*) (*vin*) rough, harsh; (*brosse*) stiff, hard; (*voix*) harsh, grating **3** (*pénible*) (*hiver, climat*) hard, severe, harsh; (*tâche*) stiff, tough; (*coup*) heavy, severe; (*choc*) rude; (*sentier*) steep; (*montée*) stiff, steep; **exercer un r. mé-**

tier to have a demanding job; **être mis à r. épreuve** (*d'une personne*) to be sorely *or* severely tested *or* tried; **il a été à r. école** he was brought up in the school of hard knocks **4** (*sévère*) (*personne*) severe, harsh **5** *Fam* (*remarquable*) **r. appétit** hearty appetite; **un r. gaillard** a stout fellow; **faire une r. gaffe** to put one's foot in it in no uncertain manner

---
Il faut noter que le terme anglais **rude** est un faux ami. Il signifie **grossier**.
---

rudement [rydmã] **ADV 1** (*sévèrement*) (*répondre, traiter qn*) harshly, severely; **être r. éprouvé** to be sorely *or* severely tested *or* tried; **travailler r.** to work hard **2** (*avec violence*) (*frapper, heurter etc*) hard **3** *Fam* (*très*) really, *Am* real; **tu as r. grandi/grossi!** you've got a lot taller!/fatter!; **il est r. plus intelligent que son frère** he's a damn sight more intelligent than his brother; **tu es r. chanceux!** you're a lucky dog!; **tu m'as fait r. mal avec le ballon!** you hurt me something awful with that ball!; **on s'est r. bien amusés à Saint-Tropez!** we had a brilliant time at St-Tropez!

rudesse [rydɛs] **NF 1** (*d'une surface*) roughness; (*d'un style*) roughness, lack of sophistication; (*d'un tissu*) roughness, coarseness; (*d'une voix*) roughness, harshness; (*de la voix*) harshness **2** (*de l'hiver, d'un climat*) severity, harshness; (*d'une tâche, un métier*) toughness **3** (*d'une personne*) severity, harshness; **avec r.** harshly

rudiment [rydimã] **NM 1** (*d'un organe*) rudiment **2 rudiments** (*d'une science*) rudiments; **je ne possède que quelques rudiments de mathématiques** I have only rudimentary mathematics; **avoir des rudiments de chinois** to speak rudimentary Chinese; **comprendre les rudiments de qch** to understand the rudiments of sth, to have a rudimentary grasp of sth; *Litt* **établir les rudiments d'une théorie** to establish the basis of *or* the first principles of a theory

rudimentaire [rydimãtɛr] **ADJ** rudimentary

rudoyer [rydwaje] **VT** (**je rudoie**; **je rudoierai**) to treat roughly *or* harshly

rue¹ [ry] **NF 1** (*voie*) street; **r. principale** main street; **la grande r.** the main street, *Br* the high street; **r. piétonnière** *ou* **piétonne** pedestrian precinct, pedestrianized street; **r. à stationnement interdit** clearway; **descendre dans la r.** (*pour protester etc*) to take to the streets; **manifestation de r.** demonstration; **jouer dans la r.** to play in the street; **pour observer les mouvements de la r.** to watch what is going on in the street; **être/se retrouver à la r.** to be/find oneself out on the street; *Fig* **tu sais que tu n'es pas à la r.** you know you don't have to walk the streets; **mettre/jeter qn à la r.** to put/throw sb out on the street; **courir les rues** to roam *or* walk the streets; **les VTT, ça court les rues** mountain bikes are very common, everybody has a mountain bike these days; **ça ne court pas les rues** (*d'un objet*) you don't find that very often, that's hard to come by; **les experts dans ce domaine ne courent pas les rues** experts in that field aren't exactly ten a penny *or* thick on the ground *or* don't grow on trees; **au coin de la r.** at *or* on the corner; **à tous les coins de r.** on every street corner; **l'homme de la r.** the man in the street **2** *Théâtre* **rues** slips

rue² **NF** *Bot* rue

ruée [rɥe] **NF** rush; **la r. sur** *ou* **vers les plages** the rush to *or* for the seaside; **la r. vers l'or** the gold rush; **il y a eu une r. sur les tickets de loterie** there's been a big run on lottery tickets; **c'est la r.** it's a scramble *or* stampede

ruelle [rɥɛl] **NF 1** (*allée*) lane, alley(way) **2** (*entre le lit et le mur*) = space between the

bed and the wall **3** *Hist* = (part of) room used by ladies to hold salons in the 17th century

ruer [rɥe] **VI** (*d'un cheval etc*) to kick, to lash out

VPR se ruer se r. sur (*quelqu'un*) to rush at, to hurl *or* fling oneself at; (*quelque chose*) to make a rush for, to hurl *or* fling oneself at; **le patron s'est rué sur moi en demandant où était son maudit dossier** the boss charged up to me demanding to know where his damn file was; **les invités se sont rués sur le buffet** the guests rushed towards *or* made a dash for the buffet; **se r. à l'attaque** to throw oneself into the attack; **se r. à la porte** to rush for *or* make a rush for the door

ruf(f)ian [ryfjã] **NM** *Arch* (*proxénète*) procurer

rugby [rygbi] **NM** rugby (football); *Fam* rugger; **r. à treize/quinze** rugby league/union

rugbyman, *pl* **rugbymen** [rygbiman, -mɛn] **NM** rugby player

rugir [ryʒir] **VI** (*d'une personne*) to bellow, to roar (**de** in, with); (*d'un lion, un moteur etc*) to roar; (*du vent, d'une tempête*) to howl **VT** (*insultes etc*) to roar out

rugissant [ryʒisã] **ADJ** (*personne*) bellowing, roaring; (*lion, moteur*) roaring; (*vent, tempête*) howling

rugissement [ryʒismã] **NM** (*d'une personne*) bellow, roar; (*d'un lion, un moteur etc*) roar(ing); (*du vent, d'une tempête*) howl(ing); **pousser des rugissements de colère** to bellow in *or* with anger

rugosité [rygozite] **NF 1** (*caractère*) roughness **2** (*point*) rough spot

rugueux, -euse [rygø, -øz] **ADJ** (*peau, tissu, surface etc*) rough; (*écorce*) rough, gnarled

Ruhr [rur] **NF la R.** the Ruhr

ruine [rɥin] **NF 1** (*écroulement*) (*d'un édifice etc*) ruin; **le château est en r.** the castle is in ruins *or* is a ruin; **un château en r.** a ruined castle; **menacer r.** to threaten to collapse, to be on the verge of collapse; **tomber en r.** to fall into ruin(s), to go to ruin; **maisons qui tombent en r.** tumbledown houses **2** *Fig* (*d'une personne, une société etc*) ruin, downfall; **aller** *ou* **courir à la r.** to be on the road to ruin; **la société est au bord de la r.** the company is on the verge of ruin *or* bankruptcy; **c'est la r. de tous nos espoirs/projets** all our hopes/plans are in ruins, it's the downfall of all our hopes/plans; **cette maison, quelle r.!** this house will be the ruin of me!, this house is ruinously expensive!; **ce sera sa r.** it will be the ruin of him; **l'alcool a fait d'elle une r.** alcohol has been her downfall *or* ruin **3** (*vestige*) ruin; **les ruines de Troie** the ruins of Troy; **leur château est une vieille r.** their castle is an old ruin; *Fig* **se relever de ses ruines** to rise from the ashes

ruiner [rɥine] **VT** *Fin, Fam* to ruin, to bankrupt; *Fig* (*espoirs, projets de qn*) to ruin, to wreck; (*santé*) to ruin; *Fam* **ce n'est pas ça qui va te r.** (*ce n'est pas cher*) it won't ruin you, it won't break the bank; **tu veux me r.!** are you trying to ruin *or* bankrupt me!

VPR se ruiner (*dépenser beaucoup*) to spend a (small) fortune; **je me suis ruinée pour lui acheter cette montre** I spent a small fortune on that watch for him, I just about had to take out a mortgage to buy him that watch; **je ne me suis pas ruiné** I didn't spend much; **je ne veux pas me r.** I don't want to break the bank; **se r. la santé** to ruin one's health

ruineusement [rɥinøzmã] **ADV** ruinously

ruineux, -euse [rɥinø, -øz] **ADJ** ruinously expensive; **dépenses ruineuses** ruinous expenditure; **ce n'est pas r.** it won't ruin you/us/etc, it won't break the bank

ruisseau, -eaux [rɥiso] NM **1** *(cours d'eau)* brook, (small) stream; *Prov* **les petits ruisseaux font les grandes rivières** great oaks from little acorns grow **2** *Fig (de sang, de lave)* stream; *(de larmes)* flood; **il coulait des ruisseaux de lave/de boue/de sang** the lava/mud/blood was flowing in streams **3** *(le long du trottoir)* gutter; *Fig* **ramasser qn dans le r.** to pick sb up out of the gutter; *Fig* **sortir qn du r.** to pull sb out of the gutter; *Fig* **pousser qn au r.** to throw sb into the gutter; *Fig* **tomber dans le r.** to end up in the gutter

ruisselant [rɥislɑ̃] ADJ streaming, dripping (wet) (**de** with); **eaux ruisselantes** running water; *(en filets)* trickling water; **r. de sueur** dripping with sweat; **il était r. de sueur** he was dripping with sweat, the sweat was pouring off him

ruisseler [rɥisle] VI (**il ruisselle**; **il ruissellera**) **1** *(d'un liquide)* to stream, to run; *(en filets)* to trickle; **l'eau ruisselait par la porte** the water was streaming or pouring in/out the door **2** *(d'une surface)* to run, to drip, to stream (**de** with); **le parquet ruisselait** the floor was running with water; **front ruisselant de sueur** forehead dripping or pouring with sweat; **ses joues ruisselaient de larmes** tears were streaming down his/her cheeks, his/her cheeks were streaming with tears; **r. de lumière** to be ablaze with light

ruisselet [rɥislɛ] NM brooklet, rivulet, rill

ruissellement [rɥiselmɑ̃] NM **1** *(de l'eau)* streaming, running; *(en filets)* trickling; *Géog* runoff; **eaux de r.** runoff **2** *(de bijoux, de lumière etc)* shimmer

rumba [rumba] NF *(danse, musique)* rumba

rumen [rymɛn] NM INV *(de ruminant)* rumen

rumeur [rymœr] NF **1** *(bruit confus)* distant murmur; *(de la circulation)* hum; **la r. lointaine de la ville/de l'usine** the distant sound of the city/the factory; **des rumeurs de mécontentement s'élevèrent de la foule** rumblings of discontent rose from the crowd **2** *(on-dit)* rumour, *Am* rumor; **victime de la r. publique, elle dut quitter la ville** a victim of local gossip, she had to leave town; **il démissionna, contraint par la r. publique** he was forced to resign because of rumours going around; **la r. court qu'il est ruiné** rumour has it that or there's a rumour going round that he's ruined; **j'ai entendu des rumeurs selon lesquelles …** I've heard rumours or whispers or a whisper that …

ruminant [rymine] ADJ, NM *Zool* ruminant

rumination [ryminasjɔ̃] NF *Zool* rumination, ruminating

ruminer [rymine] VI *(d'un animal)* to ruminate, to chew the cud
▸ VT **1** *(d'un animal)* to ruminate, to chew **2** *Fig (idée, projet etc)* to ponder, to mull or chew over, to ruminate on

rumsteck [rɔmstɛk] NM rump steak

runabout [rœnabawt] NM *Naut* runabout, speedboat

rune [ryn] NF *Ling* rune

runique [rynik] ADJ runic

rupestre [rypɛstr] ADJ **dessins rupestres** rock drawings; **peintures rupestres** cave paintings; **plantes rupestres** rock plants

rupin, -ine [rypɛ̃, -in] *Fam* ADJ *(riche) (per-*sonne*)* loaded; *(logement)* plush
N **c'est un r.** he's loaded, he's rolling in it; **les rupins** the rich, the well-off

rupiner [rypine] VI *Arg* **r. à un examen** to do well in an exam

rupteur [ryptœr] NM *Élec* contact breaker, circuit breaker; *Aut* **r. (d'allumage)** make-and-break

rupture [ryptyr] NF **1** *(d'une corde, d'une poutre etc)* breaking; *(d'un barrage)* bursting; *(d'un vaisseau sanguin, un ligament)* rupture; *(d'un os)* fracture **2** *(d'une surface etc)* breaking up; *Mil* **obus de r.** armour-piercing shell **3** *Fig (de négociations)* breaking off (**de** of), breakdown (**de** in); *(de relations diplomatiques)* severance, breaking off; *(d'un marché)* calling off; **la r. de ses fiançailles** the breaking off of his/her engagement; *Jur* **r. de contrat/de promesse de mariage** breach of contract/of promise; **r. abusive** *(de contrat)* breach; *Pol* **être en r. avec le parti** to be at odds with or in disagreement with the party; **en r. avec la tradition** in a break with tradition; **il y a eu r. entre eux** they've quarrelled, there's been a split between them, there is a rift between them; **scène de r.** break-up scene; **la r. de la princesse et de son époux** the break-up of the princess and her husband; **lors de leur r.** when they broke up or split up; *Élec* **r. du circuit** breaking of or break in the circuit; **r. de l'alimentation** power outage
▸▸ *Méd* **r. d'anévrisme** ruptured aneurism; *Com* **r. de charge** transhipment of cargo; **r. de stock** stock outage; **ce magasin est en r. de stock** this shop is out of stock

> Il faut noter que le nom anglais **rupture** signifie également **hernie**.

rural, -ale, -aux, -ales [ryral, -o] ADJ *(région)* rural; *(vie)* country, rural; **chemin r.** country lane
N country person; **les ruraux** country people

ruse [ryz] NF ruse, trick; **une r. pour faire qch** a trick for doing sth; **la r.** *(habileté)* cunning; **gagner par la r.** to win by trickery or a trick; **obtenir qch par r.** to obtain sth by a ruse or a trick or by cunning; **r. de guerre** stratagem (of war); *Fig* crafty trick; **c'est une de mes ruses de guerre pour ne pas payer** it's one of my dodges to get out of paying; *Fig* **r. d'Indien** crafty or cunning trick

rusé, -ée [ryze] ADJ cunning, crafty, wily; **r. comme un renard** cunning as a fox
N **c'est une (petite) rusée** she's a crafty or cunning little thing

ruser [ryze] VI to use trickery or cunning

rush [rœʃ] NM **1** *Sport (à la fin d'une course)* sprint, spurt **2** *Fam (de la foule)* rush **3** *Cin* **rushes** rushes, dailies

russe [rys] ADJ Russian
NM *Ling* Russian
N **R.** Russian

Russie [rysi] NF Russia; **R. blanche** White Russia

russification [rysifikasjɔ̃] NF Russification, Russianization

russifier [rysifje] VT *(impf, pr sub n. russifiions)* to Russify, to Russianize

rustaud, -aude [rysto, -od] ADJ uncouth
N *(country)* bumpkin, *Am* hick

rusticité [rystisite] NF **1** rusticity, *Péj* uncouthness **2** *Agr (d'une plante)* hardiness

Rustine® [rystin] NF repair patch *(for mending inner tube of bicycle)*; **mettre une R.** to mend a puncture; **boîte à Rustines**® repair kit

rustique [rystik] ADJ **1** *(manières, vie, maison etc)* rustic; **mobilier r.** rustic(-style) or country-style furniture; **petit pont de bois r.** little rustic bridge **2** *Constr* **ouvrage r.** rustic (stone)work **3** *Agr (plante)* hardy
NM rustic or country look

rustre [rystr] *Péj* ADJ uncouth, oafish
NM oaf, boor, lout

rut [ryt] NM *Zool (de mâle)* rut(ting); *(de femelle)* heat; **en r.** rutting; *(femelle)* in or on heat

rutabaga [rytabaga] NM swede, *Am* rutabaga

ruthénium [rytenjɔm] NM *Chimie* ruthenium

rutilance [rytilɑ̃s] NF gleam; *(rouge)* red glow

rutilant [rytilɑ̃] ADJ gleaming; *(rouge)* glowing red

rutilement [rytilmɑ̃] NM gleam; *(rouge)* red glow

rutiler [rytile] VI to gleam; *(rouge)* to glow red

Rwanda [rwɑ̃da] NM Rwanda

rwandais, -aise [rwɑ̃dɛ, -ɛz] ADJ Rwandan
N R. Rwandan

rythme [ritm] NM *Mus, Littér* rhythm; **r. cardiaque/respiratoire** heart/breathing rate; **le r. de la vie moderne** the tempo or pace of modern life; **il te faudra changer de r.** you'll need to change pace or *Fam* move up/down a gear; **travailler à un r. régulier** to work at a steady rhythm or pace; *Mus* **marquer le r.** to beat time; **suivre le r.** to follow the beat; *Fig* to keep up with the times; **avoir le sens du r.** to have a sense of rhythm; **avoir le r. dans la peau** to have a natural sense of rhythm, to have rhythm; **ce film manque de r.** the film is a bit slow or lacks pace; *Com* **r. des livraisons** delivery rate; **r. de production** rate of production; **à quel r. dois-je te les envoyer?** what rate should I send them to you at?; **au r. de trois par semaine** at the rate of three a week; **à ce r., nous n'aurons pas fini ce soir** at this rate, we won't have finished by this evening; **r. biologique** biorhythm; **les rythmes scolaires** the way in which the school year is organized

rythmé [ritme] ADJ rhythmic, rhythmical

rythmer [ritme] VT *(mouvement, phrase etc)* to put rhythm into, to give rhythm to; **le prof a rythmé la chanson avec une baguette** the teacher tapped out the beat of the song with a stick; **je n'ai pas pu m'empêcher de r. la chanson du pied** I couldn't help tapping my foot to the song

rythmique [ritmik] ADJ rhythmic(al); **section r.** *(dans un orchestre de jazz)* rhythm section
NF rhythmics

S[1], **s** [ɛs] NM *(lettre)* S, s; **faire des s** to zigzag; **la route fait des s sur plusieurs kilomètres** the road zigzags for several kilometres; **en S** S-shaped; **sentier/route en s** winding *or* zigzagging path/road

S[2] **1** *(abrév* **Sud)** S **2** *(abrév* **seconde)** sec

S.A. [ɛsa] NF *(abrév* **Société Anonyme)** plc

sa [sa] ADJ POSS *voir* **son**[1]

Saba [saba] N **la reine de S.** the Queen of Sheba

sabaye [sabɛj] NF *Naut* mooring rope; *(pour remorquer)* towline

sabayon [sabajɔ̃] NM *Culin* zabaglione

sabbat [saba] NM **1** (Jewish) Sabbath; **jour du s.** Sabbath (day); **observer/violer le s.** to keep/break the Sabbath **2** *(assemblée nocturne) (de sorcières)* sabbath; *Litt* **il s'éleva dans la nuit un s. de miaulements et de feulements** a caterwauling sound rent the night air

sabbatique [sabatik] ADJ **1** *Rel (repos)* sabbatical **2** *(d'universitaire) (année, congé)* sabbatical; **prendre un an de congé s., prendre un congé s. d'un an** to take a year's sabbatical, to take a sabbatical year

sabin, -ine [sabɛ̃, -in] *Antiq* ADJ Sabine
N S. Sabine; **l'enlèvement des Sabines** the rape of the Sabine women

sabir [sabir] NM *Ling* lingua franca, *Fam* gibberish; *Fam* **parler dans un drôle de s.** to talk gibberish

sablage [sablaʒ] NM **1** *Ind (de bâtiment)* sandblasting **2** *(de routes)* sanding, gritting

sable[1] [sabl] NM sand; **plage de s.** sandy beach; **dune de s.** sand dune; **tempête de s.** sandstorm; *Naut* **fond de s.** sandy bottom; **bac à s.** *(pour enfants)* sandpit, *Am* sandbox; *Constr* **liant** *ou* **mordant** sharp sand; *Tech* **s. de fer** fine iron filings; *Fig* **bâtir sur du s.** to build on sand; *Fig* **ce fut le grain de s. dans l'engrenage** that threw a spanner in the works; *Fig Fam* **être sur le s.** *(sans travail)* to be out of work *or* a job; *(démuni)* to be down and out; *Fam* **mettre qn sur le s.** to ruin sb
ADJ INV sand-coloured, sandy
▸▸ **sables mouvants** quicksands

sable[2] NM *Hér* sable

sablé [sable] *Culin* ADJ **pâte sablée** sweet shortcrust pastry
NM shortbread (biscuit *or Am* cookie)

sabler [sable] VT **1** *(chemin etc)* to sand; *(route verglacée)* to grit **2** *(bâtiment)* to sandblast **3** *Fam* **s. le champagne** to break open a bottle of champagne

sableuse [sabløz] NF sandblaster, sand jet

sableux, -euse [sablø, -øz] ADJ sandy

sablier [sablije] NM hourglass; *Culin* egg timer

sablière [sablijɛr] NF **1** *(carrière)* sand quarry **2** *(de locomotive)* sand box **3** *Constr etc* (lengthwise) beam, stringer

sablonneux, -euse [sablɔnø, -øz] ADJ sandy

sablonnière [sablɔnjɛr] NF sand quarry

sabord [sabɔr] NM *Naut* porthole; **s. de charge** cargo door; *Fam Vieilli* **mille sabords!** shiver my timbers!

sabordage [sabɔrdaʒ] NM, **sabordement** [sabɔrdəmɑ̃] NM *Naut* scuttling; *Fig (d'entreprise)* scuppering

saborder [sabɔrde] VT *(navire)* to scuttle; *Fig (détruire) (projet, entreprise etc)* to scupper
VPR **se saborder** *Naut* to scuttle one's ship; *Fig (se ruiner)* to bring about one's own downfall; **ce n'est pas possible, il est en train de se s.** *(d'un étudiant, postulant)* it's unbelievable the way he's scuppering his chances

sabot [sabo] NM **1** clog; *Fam* **je vous vois venir avec vos gros sabots** I can see what you're after, I can see you coming a mile off; *Fam* **elle a les deux pieds dans le même s.** she just sits back and waits for things to happen; **elle n'a pas les deux pieds dans le même s.** she doesn't let the grass grow under her feet
2 *Fam Vieilli* old *or* useless article; *(navire)* old tub; *(voiture)* old crock *or* banger; **il joue/chante/danse comme un s.** he can't play/sing/dance to save his life; **elle travaille comme un s.** she makes a botch of everything
3 *(d'un cheval etc)* hoof
4 *Tech (de meuble)* caster socket; **s. d'arrêt** chock; **s. de frein** brake shoe; **s. de Denver** Denver boot, wheel clamp; **mettre un s. de Denver à une voiture** to (wheel-)clamp a car; *Aut* **s. (de pare-chocs)** overrider; *Phot* **s.-contact** hot shoe
5 *(toupie)* (whipping) top
6 *Bot* **s. de Vénus** lady's slipper

sabotage [sabɔtaʒ] NM sabotage; **un s., un acte de s.** an act of sabotage; **l'accident était dû à un s.** the accident was caused by (an act of) sabotage; **le s. d'un plan de paix** the sabotage *or* sabotaging of a peace plan; **c'est du s.!** *(d'un travail)* it's sabotage!

saboter [sabɔte] VT *(voiture, entreprise, plan de paix etc)* to sabotage; *Fam (travail)* to botch (up), to make a mess of

saboteur, -euse [sabɔtœr, -øz] N *(d'une voiture, un train etc)* saboteur; *(d'un travail)* botcher

sabre [sabr] NM sabre, *Am* saber; **s. d'abordage** cutlass; **s. au clair** with drawn sword; *Fig* **le s. et le goupillon** the Army and the Church

sabrer [sabre] VT **1** *Fam (texte)* to make drastic cuts in; *(paragraphe, phrases)* to cut, to axe; **s. tout un passage dans un chapitre** to slash *or* to hack a whole section out of a chapter; **je vais devoir s.** I'll have to do some drastic editing
2 *Fam (noter sévèrement) (étudiant)* to give a lousy mark to; *(recaler)* to flunk
3 *Fam (renvoyer) (employé)* to fire, to sack,
Am to can; **se faire s.** to get the chop *or* sack *or Br* boot
4 *(marquer vigoureusement)* to slash; **la toile avait été sabrée à coups de crayon** great pencil slashes marked the canvas
5 *Fam (bâcler) (travail)* to botch, to bungle
6 *(ouvrir)* **s. le champagne** to break open a bottle of champagne *(originally, using a sabre)*

sabreur [sabrœr] NM swordsman; *Sport* fencer

sac[1] [sak] NM **1** bag; *(plus grand)* sack; **s. de** *ou* **en papier** paper bag *or Am* sack; *(grand)* paper *or Am* grocery bag; **s. en plastique** plastic *or Br Fam* poly bag; **s. à blé** grain sack; **contre trois sacs de blé** for three sacks of wheat; **s. à bandoulière** shoulder bag; **porter un s. en bandoulière** to wear a bag slung over *or* across one's shoulder; **s. à dos, s. de campeur** rucksack, backpack; **partir s. au dos** to set off with one's rucksack on one's back *or* with one's backpack; **s. de sable** *ou* **de terre** sandbag; **course en s.** sack race; *Fam* **un s. de nœuds** *ou* **d'embrouilles** a muddle; **c'est un vrai s. de nœuds, cette histoire** I can't make head (n)or tail of this affair; *Fig* **prendre qn la main dans le s.** to catch sb red-handed; *Boxe* **s. de frappe** *ou Am* **s. de sable** punchbag; **travailler le s.** to practise with the punchbag *or Am* punching bag; *Fam* **habillé comme un s.** dressed like a tramp; *Fam* **je les mets tous dans le même s.** they're as bad as each other, they're all tarred with the same brush; *Fam* **vider son s.** to get it off one's chest; *(avouer)* to come clean; *Fam* **l'affaire est dans le s.** it's in the bag; *Vieilli* **remplir son s.** to fill one's belly; *Arg* **ils ont le s., il y a le s.** they're loaded, they're rolling in it; *Arg* **faire** *ou* **gagner son s.** to make one's pile; *Arg* **épouser le (gros) s.** to marry money
2 *Anciennement Arg* ten francs; **dix sacs** a hundred francs
3 *Anat, Bot* sac
4 *(d'un marsupial)* pouch
5 *Tex (jute)* sackcloth; **sous le s. et la cendre** in sackcloth and ashes
6 *Can Ftbl* quarterback sack
▸▸ **s. de blanchisserie** laundry bag; **s. de couchage** sleeping bag; **s. d'écolier** schoolbag; *Mil* **s. de fantassin** pack, knapsack; **s. à fourrages** nosebag; **s. à main** handbag, *Am* purse; **s. à malices** bag of tricks; *Naut* **s. (de) marin** kitbag; *Mil* **s. à munitions** cartridge pouch; *Vieilli* **s. de nuit** travel *or* overnight bag; *Fam* **s. d'os** bag of bones; **ce n'est plus qu'un s. d'os** he's nothing but skin and bones; **s. à ouvrage** work bag; **s. de plage** beach bag; **s. poubelle** *(petit)* bin liner; *(grand)* bin bag, *Am* garbage bag; **s. à poussière** *(d'un aspirateur)* dust bag; **s. à provisions** shopping bag; *Mil* **s. de soldat** pack, knapsack; *Aviat* **s. à vent** windsock; *Fam* **s. à viande** sleeping bag; *Fam* **s. à vin** boozer, drunk; **s. de voyage** travel *or* overnight bag

sac² NM sacking, pillage; **mettre une ville à s.** to sack or plunder a town; **mettre une maison à s.** to ransack a house; **mise à s. d'une maison** ransacking of a house

saccade [sakad] NF jerk, jolt; **par saccades** in or by fits and starts; **parler par saccades** to speak jerkily or in short bursts, to have a staccato style of delivery

saccadé [sakade] ADJ (mouvement, progression) jerky; (style, voix, débit) jerky, staccato; **respiration saccadée** irregular breathing

saccader [sakade] VT Équitation (cheval) to jerk

saccage [sakaʒ] NM havoc, devastation; **ils se livrèrent à un s. systématique du centre-ville** they engaged in the systematic destruction of the town centre

saccager [sakaʒe] VT (je saccageai(s); n. saccageons) **1** (ville) to wreak havoc in, to devastate; (pour piller) to sack; (maison etc) to ransack; (vandaliser) to vandalize **2** to wreak havoc in, to turn upside down; **ils ont tout saccagé dans la maison** (mis en désordre) they turned the whole house upside down; **les cultures furent saccagées par l'orage** the crops were devastated by the storm

saccageur, -euse [sakaʒœr, -øz] N looter, plunderer

saccharin [sakarɛ̃] ADJ saccharine

saccharine [sakarin] NF Chimie etc saccharin(e)

saccharose [sakaroz] NM Chimie saccharose

sacerdoce [saserdɔs] NM Rel priesthood, ministry; Fig vocation; Fig **l'enseignement est un s.** teaching is a real vocation or calling

sacerdotal, -ale, -aux, -ales [saserdotal, -o] ADJ priestly

sachem [saʃem] NM (chef indien d'Amérique) sachem, sagamore

sachet [saʃɛ] NM **1** (de levure, café instantané, lait en poudre) sachet; **s. de lavande** lavender bag or sachet; **s. de thé** teabag; **thé en sachets** teabags; **je n'achète jamais mon thé en sachets** I never buy teabags; **s. pour garniture périodique** sanitary disposal bag **2** Belg (sac) bag; **s. poubelle** dustbin or Am garbage can liner, bin bag

sachet-cuisson, pl **sachets-cuissons** NM **en s.** boil-in-the-bag

sacoche [sakɔʃ] NF **1** (de vélo etc) saddlebag **2** (besace) bag; (pour ordinateur portable) carrier; **s. du facteur** postman's bag; **s. à outils** tool bag; **s. à courrier** mail bag **3** Belg, Can handbag, Am purse

sacquer [sake] très Fam VT **1** (renvoyer) (personne) to sack; **se faire s.** to be sacked, to get the sack **2** Scol (noter sévèrement) (élève) to mark strictly; **je me suis encore fait s. par le prof!** I got another rotten mark from the teacher! **3** (supporter) **je ne peux pas les s.** I can't stomach them, I hate their guts
VI Scol to be a tough marker

sacral, -ale, -aux, -ales [sakral, -o] ADJ sacred

sacraliser [sakralize] VT to consider sacred; **s. la liberté** to consider freedom to be sacred, to consider freedom as something sacred

sacramentel, -elle [sakramɑ̃tɛl] ADJ Rel sacramental; Fig solemn, binding

sacrant [sakrɑ̃] ADJ Can Arg **au plus s.** as fast as possible

sacre [sakr] NM (d'un roi) coronation; (d'un prêtre) consecration; Fig rite; **recevoir le prix Goncourt, c'est le s. pour un écrivain** being awarded the prix Goncourt is the crowning achievement of a writer's career

sacré¹ [sakre] ADJ **1** Rel (vase, lieu, art, musique etc), Fig sacred; **les ordres sacrés** holy orders; Fig **pour lui, rien n'est s.** nothing is sacred to him; **elle a le feu s.** she is truly inspired; Fam **il lui faut son cigare après le dîner, c'est s.!** he has to have his cigar after dinner, it's sacred! **2** Fam (maudit) damn(ed), bloody; **j'en ai assez de ce s. voisin** I've had enough of that bloody man next door; **il a un s. culot!** he's got a bloody cheek!; **s. nom de Dieu** ou **d'un chien** ou **d'une pipe!** damn and blast it!; **s. Paul, qu'est-ce qu'il va encore inventer?** whatever is that Paul going to come up with next?; **s. Paul, qu'est-ce qu'on ferait sans lui?** good old Paul, what would we do without him?; **il a une sacrée chance** he's damn(ed) or bloody lucky; **elle a eu une sacrée vie** she's had quite a life
NM **le s.** the sacred

sacré² ADJ Anat sacral

Sacré-Cœur [sakrekœr] NM Rel Sacred Heart (of Jesus)

sacredieu [sakrədjø], **sacrebleu** [sakrəblø], **sacredié** [sakrədje] INT Vieilli good God!

sacrement [sakrəmɑ̃] NM Rel sacrament; **le saint S.** the Blessed Sacrament; **recevoir les sacrements** to receive the sacraments; Fig Fam **elle le promène comme le saint S.** she shows it off as if it was the crown jewels

sacrément [sakremɑ̃] ADV Fam damn(ed), bloody; **il fait s. chaud** it's damn(ed) or bloody hot; **elle a s. bien répondu** she gave a damn(ed) or bloody good answer

sacrer [sakre] VT (roi) to crown; (prêtre) to consecrate; **s. qn roi/empereur** to crown sb king/emperor; Fig **il a été sacré meilleur acteur de l'année 2002** he was acclaimed or hailed as the best actor of 2002; **il a été sacré champion de France en 1999** he won the French championship in 1999, he was crowned French champion in 1999
VI Fam Vieilli to curse and swear

sacrifiable [sakrifjabl] ADJ expendable

sacrificateur, -trice [sakrifikatœr, -tris] N sacrificer; **grand s.** (Jewish) High Priest

sacrifice [sakrifis] NM sacrifice; Rel **le saint s.** mass; **ça a dû être un s.** that must have been a sacrifice; **offrir qch en s.** to offer up sth as a sacrifice; **faire à qn le s. de sa vie** to sacrifice one's life for sb; **s'il a réussi, c'est au s. de sa santé** he succeeded, but it was at the cost of his health or it cost him his health; **faire des sacrifices** to make sacrifices; **esprit de s.** spirit of self-sacrifice; **je n'ai pas le goût du s.** I have no desire for self-sacrifice

sacrifier [sakrifje] (impf, pr sub n. sacrifiions, v. sacrifiiez) VT (victime) to sacrifice; (temps, argent, carrière etc) to sacrifice, to give up (à for, to); Com **s. des marchandises** to sell goods at rock-bottom prices; **sacrifié** (prix) rock-bottom; (article) at a rock-bottom price; **il a réussi en sacrifiant sa santé** he succeeded at the cost of his health; **s. sa vie pour son pays** to sacrifice or lay down one's life for one's country; **s. sa vie à une cause** to devote one's (entire) life to a cause
VI **s. aux idoles** to sacrifice to idols; **s. à la mode** to be a slave to fashion
VPR **se sacrifier** to sacrifice oneself (pour for); **se s. pour la bonne cause** to sacrifice oneself in a good cause; **allez, d'accord, je me sacrifie et je vais les chercher à la gare!** OK, I'll be the martyr and pick them up from the station!

sacrilège¹ [sakrilɛʒ] NM sacrilege; **ce serait un s. que de …** it would be sacrilege to …

sacrilège² ADJ (action, pensée etc) sacrilegious
N sacrilegious person

sacristain [sakristɛ̃] NM **1** Rel sacristan **2** Culin = small flaky pastry

sacristi [sakristi] INT Arch good Lord!

sacristie [sakristi] NF Rel sacristy, vestry

sacro-saint [sakrosɛ̃] ADJ sacrosanct; Iron sacrosanct, precious

sacrum [sakrɔm] NM Anat sacrum

sadique [sadik] ADJ sadistic
N sadist

sadisme [sadism] NM sadism

sado-maso [sadomazo] Fam ADJ INV sado-masochistic; **il a des tendances s.** he's into S & M, he has S & M tendencies
N INV sadomasochist; **c'est un s.** he's into S & M

sadomasochisme [sadomazoʃism] NM Psy sadomasochism

sadomasochiste [sadomazoʃist] Psy ADJ sadomasochistic
N sadomasochist

saducéen, -enne [sadyseɛ̃, -ɛn] N Sadducee

safari [safari] NM safari; **en s.** on safari; **s.-photo** photographic safari

safran¹ [safrã] NM **1** Bot saffron, crocus **2** Culin etc saffron
ADJ INV **(jaune) s.** saffron (yellow)

safran² NM Naut rudder blade

safrané [safrane] ADJ saffron(-coloured or Am -colored); Culin (riz) saffron(-flavoured or Am -flavored)

safraner [safrane] VT Culin to flavour or Am flavor with saffron

saga [saga] NF Littér, Fig saga

sagace [sagas] ADJ astute, shrewd

sagacité [sagasite] NF shrewdness, astuteness; **avec s.** shrewdly, astutely; **faire preuve de s.** to be shrewd; **pour une fois, il a fait preuve de s.** for once, he behaved shrewdly

sagaie [sagɛ] NF assegai

sage [saʒ] ADJ **1** (avisé) (politique, personne, décision etc) wise, sensible; **une politique peu s.** an unwise policy, not a very sensible policy; **il serait plus s. de faire ceci** it would be wiser or more sensible to do this **2** (enfant) good, well-behaved; (animal) quiet, docile; (tenue, conduite) sober; (robe) demure; **quand tu seras plus s.** when you're better behaved, once you start behaving yourself; **l'école l'a rendu s.** school has quietened him down; **sois s.!** be good!, behave yourself!; **s. comme une image** as good as gold; **il n'est pas s. du tout, ce petit** that child is very badly behaved; **il porte toujours des tenues très sages** he always dresses very soberly or conservatively; **la mode de cette année est très s.** the demure look is in this year **3** (chaste) good; **j'étais très s. pendant ma jeunesse** I was a very good girl when I was young; **elle n'était pas très s. à cette époque-là!** she was a bit wild then!
NM wise man; Phil sage; **un vieux s.** a wise old man; Pol **comité des sages** committee of wise men

sage-femme, pl **sages-femmes** NF midwife

sagement [saʒmɑ̃] ADV **1** (raisonnablement) wisely, sensibly **2** (tranquillement) quietly

sagesse [saʒɛs] NF **1** (prudence, connaissance) wisdom; **elle a eu la s. de ne pas en parler** she was wise or sensible enough not to mention it; **plein de s.** (remarque) very sensible; (décision) very sensible or wise; **agir avec s.** to act wisely or sensibly; Fig **la voix de la s.** the voice of reason **2** (calme) good behaviour or Am behavior; **la maîtresse lui reproche sa trop grande s.** the teacher says he's too well behaved; **ma grand-mère était d'une s. exemplaire pendant sa**

jeunesse my grandmother was very well-behaved *or* a model of good behaviour when she was a girl; **on le disait d'une très grande s.** he was said to be very well behaved

Sagittaire [saʒiter] NM *Astron, Astrol* **le S.** Sagittarius, the Archer; **être (du signe du) S.** to be (a) Sagittarius *or* (a) Sagittarian

sagou [sagu] NM sago

sagouin [sagwɛ̃] NM **1** *(singe)* squirrel monkey **2** *Fam* slovenly *or* dirty individual; **travailler comme un s.** to be a sloppy worker; **manger comme un s.** to eat like a pig; **vieux s.** revolting old man

Sahara [saara] NM Sahara (Desert)

saharien, -ienne [saarjɛ̃, -jɛn] ADJ Saharan; *(troupes)* desert; **température saharienne** scorching *or* sizzling temperature
N **S.** Saharan
NF **saharienne** safari jacket

Sahel [sael] NM Sahel

sahib [saib] NM sahib

sahraoui, -ie [sarawi] ADJ of the Western Sahara
N **S.** native of the Western Sahara

saignant [sɛɲɑ̃] ADJ **1** *(blessure)* bleeding **2** *Culin (viande)* rare

saignée [seɲe] NF **1** *Méd Arch* blood-letting; *Fig* drain; **la guerre fut une véritable s. pour le pays** the country suffered great losses in the war; *Méd Arch* **faire une s. à qn** to bleed sb; **faire une s. dans un arbre** *(pour récolter du caoutchouc etc)* to tap a tree **2** *Anat (pli)* bend of the arm *or* the knee **3** *(rigole)* (drainage) trench, ditch; *Tech (pour l'huile etc)* groove; *Constr (dans un mur, pour un tuyau, un câble etc)* hole

saignement [sɛɲ(ə)mɑ̃] NM bleeding; **s. de nez** nosebleed; **elle souffre de saignements de nez** she suffers from nosebleeds

saigner [seɲe] VI *(d'une personne, d'une blessure etc)* to bleed; **mon doigt saigne** my finger is bleeding; **je saigne du nez** my nose is bleeding, I have a nosebleed; **elle a tendance à s. du nez** she tends to get nosebleeds; **la chaleur le fait s. du nez** heat makes his nose bleed *or* gives him nosebleeds; *Fig* **c'est une plaie qui saigne encore** it's an open wound, it still rankles; *Fig Litt* **mon cœur saigne, le cœur m'en saigne** it makes my heart bleed; *Fam* **ça va s.** there's going to be trouble
VT *Agr (poulet), Méd Arch (personne)* to bleed; *Fam (tuer à l'arme blanche)* to stab to death; **s. un porc** to stick a pig; **s. à blanc** *(animal)* to bleed white; **s. un arbre** to tap a tree; **s. un fossé** to drain a ditch; *Fig* **s. qn/un pays (à blanc)** to bleed sb/a country white *or* dry
VPR **se saigner** *Fig* **se s. aux quatre membres** *ou* **aux quatre veines** to make enormous sacrifices, to bleed oneself white *or* dry

saigneur [seɲœr] NM **1** *(d'animaux)* slaughterer, slaughterman **2** *(de caoutchouc)* tree tapper, collector of rubber

saillant [sajɑ̃] ADJ *(toit, corniche etc)* projecting, jutting out; *(pommettes)* prominent, high; *(muscles)* bulging; *Fig (trait, caractéristique etc)* striking, outstanding, salient; **angle s.** *(d'une fortification)* salient angle; **les faits saillants de sa vie** the notable *or* noteworthy events of his life; **les faits saillants de l'année** the highlights of the year
NM *Mil* salient

saillie [saji] NF **1** *(partie en avant)* protrusion; *Archit, Constr* projection; **en s.** projecting, jutting out; **s. du mollet** swell of the calf; **faire s.** to project, to jut out **2** *(dans l'élevage) (par un mâle)* covering **3** *Litt* sally, flash of wit

saillir [sajir] VT *(prp saillissant; pp sailli; pr ind je saillis, n. saillissons; fu je saillirai) (dans l'élevage) (femelle)* to cover

VI *(used only in prp* **saillant***; pp* **sailli***; pr ind* **il saille, ils saillent;** *fu* **il saillera***)* to project, to jut out *(***sur** over*)*; **la poutre saille de 25 cm** the beam projects 25 cm

sain, saine [sɛ̃, sɛn] ADJ **1** *(personne, climat, exercice, maison, relations)* healthy; *(cheval, fruit, bois, gestion etc)* sound; *(nourriture)* healthy, wholesome; *(économie, affaire)* healthy, sound; **un esprit s. dans un corps s.** a healthy mind in a healthy body; **s. de corps et d'esprit** sound in mind and body; **s. et sauf** safe and sound **2** *Naut (côte, ancrage)* safe

saindoux [sɛ̃du] NM *Culin* lard

sainement [sɛnmɑ̃] ADV **1** *(salubrement)* healthily **2** *(raisonnablement) (juger)* sensibly

saint, sainte [sɛ̃, sɛ̃t] ADJ **1** *Rel (lieu, guerre etc)* holy; *(personne, vie)* saintly, holy; **la Sainte Église** the Holy Church; **semaine sainte** Holy Week; **le Vendredi s.** Good Friday; **une sainte action** a pious deed; **faire œuvre sainte** to do good works; **la Terre sainte** the Holy Land; **la Sainte Vierge** the Blessed Virgin; **une petite sainte vierge en ivoire** an ivory miniature of the Blessed Virgin; **le s. patron des horlogers** the patron saint of watch-makers; *Fig* **être saisi** *ou* **pris d'une sainte colère/indignation** to be seething with righteous anger/indignation; *Fam* **j'en ai une sainte horreur!** I hate *or* loathe it!; *Fam* **elle ne fait rien de toute la sainte journée** she doesn't do a thing the whole blessed day **2 s. Pierre** St Peter; **sainte Catherine** St Catherine; **l'église S.-Pierre de Rome** St Peter's (church); **la S. Georges** St George's day; *Can Fam* **au mouvement, Sainte Bénite!** get a move on, for Pete's sake!
N *Rel, Fig* saint; **s. d'une ville** patron saint of a town; **il lasserait la patience d'un s.** he would try the patience of a saint; **elle prêche pour son s.** she has an axe to grind; **ne savoir plus à quel s. se vouer** to be at one's wits' end, not to know which way to turn; *Hum* **il vaut mieux s'adresser à Dieu qu'à ses saints** it's best to go right to the top; *Fig Fam* **c'est un petit s.** he's a prig; *Fam* **arrête de faire ton petit s.!** stop being such a prig!; *Rel* **les Saints du dernier jour** the Latter-day Saints
NM **le S. des Saints** the Holy of Holies; *Fig* the inner sanctum; *Hum* the holy of holies, the sanctum sanctorum

saint-bernard [sɛ̃bɛrnar] NM INV *(chien)* St Bernard; *Fam* **c'est un vrai s.** he's a good Samaritan

Saint-Cyr [sɛ̃sir] N Saint-Cyr military academy

saint-cyrien, -ienne, *pl* **saint-cyriens, -iennes** [sɛ̃sirjɛ̃, -jɛn] N cadet training at Saint-Cyr

Saint-Domingue [sɛ̃dɔmɛ̃g] NM Santo Domingo

Sainte-Croix N **l'île S.** Santa Cruz island

Sainte-Hélène N St Helena

Saint-Elme [sɛ̃ɛlm] NM **feu S.** St Elmo's fire

Sainte-Lucie [sɛ̃tlysi] N St Lucia

saintement [sɛ̃tmɑ̃] ADV in a saintly way; **vivre s.** to lead a saintly life, to live like a saint; **mourir s.** to die a saintly death, to die like a saint; **elle s'est toujours conduite très s.** she has always behaved like a saint

sainte-nitouche, *pl* **saintes-nitouches** [sɛ̃tnituʃ] NF *Fam* little hypocrite; **prendre des airs de s.** to look as if butter wouldn't melt in one's mouth; **avec des airs de s.** looking as if butter wouldn't melt in his/her/*etc* mouth

Saint-Esprit [sɛ̃tɛspri] NM **le S.** the Holy Ghost, the Holy Spirit; *Hum* **par l'opération du S.** by magic

sainteté [sɛ̃t(ə)te] NF *(d'une personne)* holi-

ness, saintliness; *(de la loi, d'un serment)* sanctity; *(d'un lieu)* holiness, sanctity; *Rel* **sa S. (le pape)** His Holiness (the Pope)

saint-frusquin [sɛ̃fryskɛ̃] NM *(no pl) Fam* **tout le s.** the whole caboodle; **il s'est pointé avec ses disquettes, ses livres et tout son s.** he turned up with his disks, his books and all the rest of his gear; *Litt* **boire (tout) son s.** to waste one's substance with riotous living

saint-glinglin (à la) [alasɛ̃glɛ̃glɛ̃] ADV *Fam* **jusqu'à la s.** till the cows come home, till doomsday; **on sera payé à la s.** we'll be paid when pigs fly; **repoussé à la s.** postponed indefinitely

Saint-Graal (le) NM *Littér* the (Holy) Grail

saint-honoré, *pl* **saint-honoré(s)** NM Saint-Honoré *(choux pastry ring filled with confectioner's custard)*

Saint-Jean [sɛ̃ʒɑ̃] NF **1 la S.** Midsummer Day **2** *Can* **la Saint-Jean-Baptiste** Saint-Jean-Baptiste Day *(24th of July)*

Saint-Laurent (le) [ləsɛ̃lɔrɑ̃] NM *Géog* the St Lawrence (river); **la Voie maritime du S.** the St Lawrence Seaway

saint-marcellin, *pl* **saint-marcellins** [sɛ̃marsəlɛ̃] NM = type of small, round cheese produced in the Lyons area

Saint-Marin N San Marino

Saint-Martin (la) [lasɛ̃martɛ̃] NF St Martin's day, Martinmas; **l'été de la S.** Indian summer, St Martin's summer

Saint-Michel (la) [lasɛ̃miʃɛl] NF Michaelmas

saint-nectaire, *pl* **saint-nectaires** NM = Saint-Nectaire (cheese)

Saint-Office NM **le S.** *Cathol* the Holy Office; *Hist (l'Inquisition)* the Inquisition

Saint-Père (le) NM *Cathol* the Holy Father

Saint-Pétersbourg [sɛ̃petɛrsbur] N St Petersburg

saint-pierre NM INV *(poisson)* John Dory

Saint-Pierre-et-Miquelon [sɛ̃pjɛremiklɔ̃] N St Pierre and Miquelon

Saint-Siège (le) NM *Cathol* the Holy See

Saint-Simonisme [sɛ̃simɔnism] NM *Écon* Saint-Simonianism, Saint-Simonism

Saint-Sylvestre (la) NF New Year's Eve, *Scot* Hogmanay; **faire la veillée de la S.** to see the New Year in

saisi, -ie [sezi] N *Jur* distrainee

saisie [sezi] NF *(de marchandises de contrebande etc)* seizure; *Jur* seizure, *Spéc* distraint, distress; *(d'une hypothèque)* foreclosure; *Naut* embargo; **s. conservatoire** seizure of goods *(to prevent sale)*; **procès-verbal de s.** warrant (for seizure of property); *Ordinat* **s. de données** data capture, keyboarding; *Ordinat* **s. automatique/manuelle** automatic/manual input

saisie-arrêt, *pl* **saisies-arrêts** NF *Jur* attachment, garnishment

saisie-exécution, *pl* **saisies-exécutions** NF *Jur* distraint *(for sale by court order)*

saisine [sezin] NF *Jur* referral to a court

saisir [sezir] VT **1** *(attraper) (personne, objet)* to take hold of, to grab, to seize; **s. qn par le bras/au collet** to grab *or* catch *or* seize sb by the arm/by the collar; **s. qn à bras-le-corps** to seize *or Fam* grab sb around the waist; **s. l'occasion de faire qch** to seize *or* grasp the opportunity to do sth; **s. un prétexte pour faire qch** to seize on a pretext to do something; **s. la balle au bond** to catch the ball on the rebound; *Fig* to seize the opportunity; **la peur le saisit** fear seized *or* took hold of *or* gripped him; **être saisi d'étonnement** to be startled *or* staggered; **être saisi par le froid/la peur** to be struck by the cold/to

be gripped by *or* overcome by *or* stricken with fear; **être saisi de panique** to be panic-stricken; **l'artiste a bien saisi la ressemblance** the artist has really caught *or* captured the likeness
2 *(comprendre) (vérité, signification donnée par qn)* to grasp, to get; **elle a tout de suite saisi de quoi il s'agissait** she immediately grasped *or* got what it was about; **je n'ai pas saisi son nom** I didn't catch *or* get his/her name
3 *Ordinat (données)* to capture, to keyboard, to key
4 *Jur (navire, biens immobiliers)* to seize, to attach; *(marchandises)* to seize, *Spéc* to distrain upon; **s. une hypothèque** to foreclose on a mortgage
5 *Jur* **s. un tribunal d'une affaire** to refer a matter to a court, to lay a matter before a court; **nous sommes saisis de deux questions** we have two questions before us
6 *Culin (viande)* to seal
7 *Naut (ancres, bateaux)* to stow, to secure
VI *(comprendre)* **je ne saisis pas bien** I don't quite get it; **il saisit vite** he's quick (on the uptake); **alors, tu saisis?** do you get it?
VPR se saisir se s. de qn/qch to seize *or* grab sb/sth, to take hold of sb/sth; **se s. d'un marché** to corner a market

saisissable [sezisabl] **ADJ 1** *(distinction)* perceptible **2** *Jur* distrainable, attachable

saisissant, -ante [sezisɑ̃, -ɑ̃t] **ADJ 1** *(froid)* biting; *(ressemblance)* striking; *(spectacle, scène, paroles)* gripping **2** *Jur (partie)* distraining
N *Jur* distrainer

saisissement [sezismɑ̃] **NM 1** *(sensation de froid)* sudden chill **2** *(émotion)* shock, rush of emotion; **pâle de s.** pale with emotion

saison [sɛzɔ̃] **NF** season; **très tôt en s.** very early in the season; **en cette s.** at this time of year; **en toute(s) saison(s)** all (the) year round; **la s. nouvelle** spring(time); **la mauvaise/la belle s.** the winter/summer months; **moyenne s.** shoulder period; **la s. sèche/des pluies** the dry/rainy season; **la s. des semailles** sowing time; **la haute/basse s.** the high/low season; **faire une bonne/mauvaise s.** to have a good/bad season; **la s. bat son plein** the season is in full swing *or* at its height, it is the height of the season; **le fort de la s.** the busy season *or* time (of the year); **la s. creuse, la morte s.** the off season, the slack season, the low season; **prendre ses vacances à la s. creuse** to take one's holidays off season; **voyager pendant la s. creuse** to travel off season; **la s. touristique** the tourist season; **la s. sportive/de la chasse** the sporting/hunting season; **la s. des amours** the mating season; **la s. des framboises** the raspberry season, the season *or* time for raspberries; **des fraises! mais ce n'est pas la s.!** strawberries! but it isn't the right time of year *or* it isn't the season for them; **être de s.** *(des fruits)* to be in season *or* seasonal; **le pull est de s.** it's the right kind of weather for sweaters; **c'est un temps de s.** it's seasonal weather, it's typical weather for the time of year; **hors de s.** *(légumes etc)* out of season; *Fig* **décidément, ses plaisanteries ne sont pas de s.** his/her jokes are really quite out of place; **faire une s.** *(dans une station thermale)* to take a cure; **cette robe ne me fera pas la s.** this dress won't last me the season; **travailler en s.,** *Fam* **faire les saisons** *(dans les lieux de vacances)* to do seasonal work SEE GRAMMAR A7; A81; B4; B61

saisonnier, -ière [sɛzɔnje, -jɛr] **ADJ** seasonal
N seasonal worker

sajou [saʒu] **NM** *Zool* capuchin (monkey)

saké [sake], **saki**¹ [saki] **NM** *(boisson)* sake, saké, saki

saki² **NM** *Zool* saki (monkey)

salade [salad] **NF 1** *Bot, Culin (plante)* lettuce **2** *(plat)* salad; **faire une s.** to make a salad; **s. verte** green salad; **s. de pommes de terre/de tomates/de riz** potato/tomato/rice salad; **s. composée** mixed salad; **s. niçoise** salade niçoise; **s. russe** Russian salad; **haricots verts en s.** green bean salad; **s. de fruits** fruit salad; *Belg* **s. de blé** lamb's lettuce, corn salad; **3** *Fam (désordre)* mess, shambles; **quelle s.!** what a mess *or* shambles! **4** *Fam* **salades** *(mensonges)* whoppers, fibs; *(absurdités)* nonsense **5** *Fam* **vendre sa s.** to make a pitch, to try to sell an idea

saladier [saladje] **NM** salad bowl

salage [salaʒ] **NM** salting

salaire [salɛr] **NM 1** *(mensuel)* salary, pay; *(hebdomadaire, journalier)* wage(s), pay; *Prov* **toute peine mérite s.** the labourer *or* Am laborer is worthy of his hire VOIR GRAMMAIRE A10-11 **2** *(récompense)* reward, recompense (**de** for); *(punition)* retribution (**de** for); **le s. du péché/de la peur** the wages of sin/of fear
▸ ▸ **s. annuel garanti** annual guaranteed wage/salary; **s. d'appoint** second salary; **s. de base** basic pay, basic wage/salary; **s. brut** gross pay; **s. de départ** starting salary; **s. fixe** fixed salary; **s. fixe plus commission** salary plus commission; **s. à forfait** job wage; **s. horaire** hourly wage; **s. indexé** index-linked pay; **s. indirect** fringe benefits, benefit in kind; **s. légal** legal wage; **s. minimum interprofessionnel de croissance** = guaranteed minimum wage; **s. net** net pay; **s. plafond** maximum wage/salary; **s. plafonné** wage/salary ceiling; **s. réel** real wage/salary, wage/salary in real terms; **s. au rendement** incentive pay; **s. à la tâche** *ou* **aux pièces** piece wage

salaison [salɛzɔ̃] **NF** *(action)* salting; **les salaisons** salted meats

salamalecs [salamalɛk] **NMPL** *Fam* bowing and scraping; **faire des s. à qn** to bow and scrape to sb

salamandre [salamɑ̃dr] **NF 1** *Zool* salamander; **s. aquatique** newt **2** *(poêle)* salamander (stove), slow-burning *or* slow-combustion stove

salami [salami] **NM** salami

salant [salɑ̃] **ADJ** **marais s.** salt marsh

salarial, -iale, -iaux, -iales [salarjal, -jo] **ADJ** wage; *(mensuel)* salary; **masse salariale** wage(s) bill, payroll; **politique salariale** pay *or* wage(s) policy

salariat [salarja] **NM 1** *(état)* wage-earning; **je préfère le s. au travail free-lance** I'd rather be on a salary *or* have a nine-to-five job than do freelance work **2** *(employés)* wage earners

salarié, -ée [salarje] **ADJ 1** *(travailleur) (payé mensuellement)* salaried; *(payé hebdomadairement)* wage-earning **2** *(travail)* paid
N *(payé mensuellement)* salaried employee; *(payé hebdomadairement)* wage earner; **salariés** *(de société)* employees

salarier [salarje] **VT** *(tous les mois)* to pay a salary to; *(toutes les semaines)* to pay a wage to

salaud [salo] *Vulg* **NM** bastard; **alors là mon s., tu m'en bouches un coin!** you've gobsmacked me this time, you old bastard!
ADJ shitty; **un mec s.** a bastard; **ce qu'il est s.!** what a bastard he is!; **il a été très s. avec elle** he was a real bastard to her; **c'est vraiment s. de faire ça** it's a really shitty thing to do

sale [sal] **ADJ 1** *(maison, vaisselle, mains, eau etc)* dirty; *(répugnant)* filthy; *Fig (paroles, histoire)* dirty, filthy, coarse; *Nucl* **bombe s.** dirty bomb; **industrie s.** dirty industry; *très*

Fam **c'était pas s.!** it was pretty good!, it was quite something! **2** *Fam (always before the noun) (méchant) (grippe, situation)* nasty; **s. gosse** little brat; **c'est un s. boulot!** it's a rotten *or* lousy job!; **faire le s. boulot** to do the dirty work; **être dans une s. affaire** to be caught up in a dirty business; **il a une s. tête** *ou* **gueule** *(antipathique)* he looks really nasty; *(malade)* he looks awful; **s. individu, s. type** nasty character, louse; **s. fasciste!** filthy Fascist!; **s. coup** dirty *or* rotten trick; **s. temps** filthy weather; **ah la s. bête!** *(cet animal)* bloody animal!; *(cette personne)* the beast!, the swine!
NM *Fam* **mettre du linge au s.** to put dirty clothes in the wash

salé [sale] **ADJ 1** *(conservé au sel) (poisson, viande etc)* salt; *(additionné de sel) (beurre, amandes etc)* salted; **eau salée** salt water; **le Grand Lac S.** the Great Salt Lake; **le potage est trop s.** the soup is too salty; **prés salés** saltings, salt meadows **2** *Fig (histoire, plaisanterie)* spicy, risqué; *Fam (condamnation)* stiff; *Fam (addition, prix)* steep
NM **le s. et le sucré** savoury food and sweet food; **petit s.** = type of streaky bacon

salement [salmɑ̃] **ADV 1** *(parler, manger, boire)* in a disgusting manner **2** *Fam (blessé, touché, atteint)* (very) badly; **s. difficile/douloureux** damn(ed) *or* Br bloody difficult/painful; **j'ai s. besoin d'argent** I'm badly in need of money; **ça m'aiderait s.** it would be a big *or* great help; **je suis s. fatigué** I'm dog-tired, Br I'm knackered; **elle a s. vieilli** she's aged a hell of a lot; **il est s. amoureux** he's got it bad

saler [sale] **VT 1** *(assaisonner)* to salt, to put salt in, to season with salt **2** *(pour conserver) (bacon etc)* to salt **3** *(route)* to salt **4** *Fam (client)* to rip off, to fleece; **s. la note** to bump up the bill; **on s'est fait s.** *(au restaurant)* we were ripped off *or* done; **il s'est fait s.** *(sanctionné)* he got a stiff *or* tough sentence

saleté [salte] **NF 1** *(d'une personne, d'une rue, de vêtements etc)* dirtiness, filthiness; *(crasse)* dirt, filth; **la maison est d'une s. incroyable** the house is incredibly dirty *or* filthy; **le chat a fait ses saletés par terre** the cat made a mess on the floor **2** *(camelote)* trash, rubbish, junk; **manger des saletés** to eat junk food; **quelle s., cette grippe!** this flu is a real pain *or* nuisance! **3** *(chose obscène)* obscenity; *(remarque)* obscenity, obscene remark; *(blague)* obscene joke; **il m'a dit des saletés** he said dirty *or* filthy things to me **4** *Fam (personne)* bastard; **quelle s.!, il m'a roulé!** the bastard, he's conned me!

saleur, -euse [salœr, -øz] **N** salter

salicoque [salikɔk] **NF** prawn

salicorne [salikɔrn] **NF** *Bot* glasswort, saltwort

salicylate [salisilat] **NM** *Chimie* salicylate

salicylique [salisilik] **ADJ** *Chimie (acide)* salicylic

salière [saljɛr] **NF 1** *Culin* salt cellar **2** *Fam (des clavicules)* salt cellar

saligaud, -aude [saligo, -od] **N** *très Fam (personne sale)* filthy swine, *f* slut; *(ignoble individu)* bastard, *f* bitch

salin, -ine [salɛ̃, -in] **ADJ** *(solution, roches)* saline
NM 1 *(marais)* salt marsh **2** *Chimie, Ind* saline
NF **saline 1** *(entreprise)* salt works **2** *(marais)* salt marsh

salinage [salinaʒ] **NM 1** *(entreprise)* salt works **2** *(solution)* saturated solution of salt; *(concentration)* concentrating of the brine

salinier, -ière [salinje, -jɛr] **ADJ** *(industrie etc)* salt
NM salt producer

salinité [salinite] NF *(de l'eau de mer etc)* salinity, saltness

salique [salik] ADJ *Hist (loi)* Salic

salir [salir] VT *(mains, vêtements etc)* to get or make dirty, to dirty, *Fml* to soil; **attention, ça salit les mains** careful, it gets or makes your hands dirty; **s. sa réputation** to tarnish or sully one's reputation; **s. le nom/la mémoire de qn** to sully or besmirch sb's name/memory; **s. l'idée de l'amour** to debase the idea of love

▶ VPR **se salir** to get dirty; **ça se salit facilement** it's easily dirtied, it dirties easily; *Fig* **elle n'aime pas se s. les mains** she doesn't like to get her hands dirty

salissant [salisɑ̃] ADJ **1** *(travail)* dirty, messy **2** *(tissu, vêtement, moquette etc)* easily soiled; *(couleur)* that shows the dirt

salissure [salisyr] NF dirty mark

salivaire [saliver] ADJ *(glande etc)* salivary

salivation [salivasjɔ̃] NF salivation

salive [saliv] NF saliva; *Fam* **pas la peine de dépenser ta s.** don't waste your breath, save your breath

saliver [salive] VI to salivate; **s. devant qch** to drool at the sight of sth

salle [sal] NF **1** *(pièce)* room; *Sport* **partie en s.** indoor game; **travailler en s.** *(d'un restaurant)* to work in the dining room, to be a member of the dining-room staff; **personnel de s.** *(d'un restaurant)* dining-room staff; **les salles du Louvre** the galleries of the Louvre **2** *Théâtre, Cin (auditorium)* auditorium; *(spectateurs)* audience; **faire s. comble** *ou* **pleine** to have a full house; **toute la s. applaudit** the whole audience applauded; **combien de salles y a-t-il dans ce nouveau cinéma?** how many screens are there in the new cinema?; **sa dernière production sort en s. en septembre** her latest production will be released in September

▶ ▸ **s. d'arrivée** *(à un aéroport)* arrivals lounge; *Cin* **s. d'art et d'essai** art cinema or *Am* movie theater; **s. d'attente** waiting room; **s. de bain(s)** bathroom; **s. de bain(s) particulière** private bathroom, en-suite bathroom; **s. de bal** ballroom; **s. de billard** billiards room, pool room; *Ordinat* **s. blanche** clean room; **s. des chaudières** boiler room; **s. de cinéma** cinema, *Am* movie theater; *Scol* **s. de classe** classroom; *Banque* **s. des coffres** vaults; **s. de composition** *(atelier)* composing room; **s. de conférences** conference room; **s. du conseil** council room or chamber; *Ind etc* boardroom; **s. de contrôle** *(d'un engin spatial)* control room; **s. de contrôle de production** production control room; **s. de cours** lecture room; **s. des dactylos** typing pool; *Ind* **s. de dessin** drawing office; **s. de détente** common room; *TV, Théâtre* green room; *Can* **s. à dîner** dining room; **s. de douches** shower room; **s. d'eau** shower room; **s. d'embarquement** *(d'aéroport)* gate lounge; **s. d'exploitation radar** radar operations room; *Com* **s. d'exposition** showroom; *(pour une foire)* exhibition hall; **s. d'exposition du revendeur** dealer display room; **s. des fêtes** = community hall; *(d'un village)* village hall; *Mil* **s. de garde** guardroom; *Banque* **s. des guichets** banking hall, front office; **s. d'hôpital** (hospital) ward; *Journ* **s. d'impression** publishing room; **s. de jeux** games room; **s. de lecture** *(de bibliothèque)* reading room; **s. des machines** engine room; *Ind* machine room; **s. à manger** dining room; *(meubles)* dining-room suite; **s. de maquillage** make-up room; *Bourse* **s. des marchés** trading floor; **s. de montage** edit suite, cutting room; **s. de musculation** fitness room, gym; **les salles obscures** the movies, *Br* the cinema; *Méd* **s. d'opération** operating theatre or *Am* room; **s. des opéra-**

tions operations room; **s. des pas perdus** *(dans une gare etc)* concourse; *(au Parlement, dans les tribunaux)* lobby; **s. de petit déjeuner** breakfast room; **s. de presse** newsroom; **s. des professeurs** staff room, common room; *Cin* **s. de projection** viewing or projection or screening room; **s. de réception** function room; **s. de rédaction** *(d'un journal)* newsroom; *Cin, TV* **s. de régie** control room; **s. de restaurant** dining room; **s. de réunion** meeting room; **s. de réveil** recovery room; **s. de séjour** living room; **s. de service** orderly rooom; **s. de télévision** TV lounge, television room; **s. du trône** throneroom; **s. des** *ou* **de ventes** saleroom, auction rooms; *Cin* **s. de vision** viewing or projection or screening room; *TV, Cin* **s. de visionnage** looking room

salmigondis [salmigɔ̃di] NM hotchpotch, *Am* hodgepodge

salmis [salmi] NM *Culin* salmi *(game part-cooked by roasting then stewed in a wine sauce)*

salmonella [salmɔnɛla] NF INV, **salmonelle** [salmɔnɛl] NF *Méd* salmonella

salmonellose [salmɔneloz] NF *Méd* salmonellosis, salmonella poisoning

salmoniculteur, -trice [salmɔnikyltœr, -tris] N salmon farmer

salmoniculture [salmɔnikyltyr] NF salmon farming

saloir [salwar] NM **1** *(pour salaisons) (pièce)* salting room; *(bac)* salting tub **2** *Vieilli Fam (salière)* salt pot

Salomon [salɔmɔ̃] N **le roi S.** King Solomon; **les îles S.** the Solomon Islands

salon [salɔ̃] NM **1** *(de maison)* living room, sitting room, *Br* lounge; **petit s.** morning room; **s. réservé** *(dans un hôtel etc)* private room; **jeux de s.** parlour or *Am* parlor games; **s. VIP** VIP lounge; **s. de bridge** card room; *Fig* **un révolutionnaire de s.** an armchair revolutionary **2** *(meuble)* suite **3** *(dans un bateau)* saloon; *(dans un train)* saloon car **4** *Com* **s. de thé** tea room(s), tea shop; **s. de coiffure** hairdressing salon; **s. de beauté** beauty salon **5** *(exposition), Beaux-Arts* exhibition; *(du bateau, des arts ménagers etc)* show; **s.-exposition,** pl **salons-expositions** trade fair; **s. d'exposition du distributeur** distributor display room; **s. professionnel** trade show or fair; **s. spécialisé** specialized trade fair **6** *Hist, Littér* salon; **tenir s.** to hold a salon

▶ ▸ **le S. des Arts ménagers** ≃ the Ideal Home Exhibition; **le S. de l'Automobile** *ou* **de l'auto** the Motor Show; **le S. de l'informatique** = information technology trade fair; **le S. du Livre** the Book Fair; **le S. nautique** the Boat Show

saloon [salun] NM saloon *(in the Wild West)*; **porte de s.** saloon door

salop [salo] NM = **salaud**

salopard [salɔpar] NM *très Fam* bastard

salope [salɔp] *Vulg* ADJ F bitchy; **qu'est-ce qu'elle a été s. avec moi!** she was really bitchy or a real bitch to me!

▶ NF **1** *(femme méprisable)* bitch **2** *(homme méprisable)* bastard; **c'est vraiment une s., ce type!** he's a real bastard, that guy! **3** *(femme de mauvaise vie)* slut

saloper [salɔpe] VT *Fam* **1** *(salir)* to dirty, to mess up **2** *(mal exécuter)* to make a dog's breakfast or *Br* a pig's ear of

saloperie [salɔpri] NF *Vulg* **1** *(camelote)* trash, rubbish, junk; **s. de montre!** what a trashy watch!; **s. de temps!** what filthy weather!; **tu ne vas pas manger cette s.!** you're not going to eat that rubbish or junk!; **cette**

grippe est une s. this flu is a bloody pain in the neck; **il y avait toutes sortes de saloperies par terre** there was a load of trash or crap on the floor **2** *(coup bas)* dirty or rotten trick; **il nous a fait une belle s.** he played a really dirty or rotten trick on us, he really did the dirty on us **3 dire des saloperies** to talk filth, to talk dirty; **elle a encore dit des saloperies sur moi** she made some more bitchy remarks about me

salopette [salɔpɛt] NF dungarees, *Am* overalls

salpêtrage [salpetraʒ] NM **1** *(formation)* manufacture or formation of saltpetre or *Am* saltpeter **2** *(traitement)* treatment with saltpetre or *Am* saltpeter

salpêtre [salpɛtr] NM **1** *Chimie* saltpetre, *Am* saltpeter **2** *(sur les murs)* saltpetre or *Am* saltpeter rot

salpêtrer [salpetre] VT **1** *(sol)* to cover or treat with saltpetre or *Am* saltpeter **2** *(murs)* to rot

salpicon [salpikɔ̃] NM *Culin* salpicon *(diced meat, poultry, vegetables etc in sauce, used as a filling for vol-au-vents etc)*

salpingite [salpɛ̃ʒit] NF *Méd* salpingitis

salsa [salsa] NF *Mus* salsa

salsepareille [salsəparɛj] NF *Bot, Pharm* sarsaparilla

salsifis [salsifi] NM *Bot, Culin* salsify

saltimbanque [saltɛ̃bɑ̃k] N *(de cirque)* circus performer; *(comédien)* entertainer

salto [salto] NM *Gym* salto

salubre [salybr] ADJ *(climat, air, appartement)* healthy, *Fml* salubrious

salubrité [salybrite] NF *(du climat, de l'air, d'un appartement)* healthiness, *Fml* salubriousness; **s. publique** public health

saluer [salɥe] VT **1** *(personne) (en arrivant)* to greet; *(en partant)* to take one's leave of; *(faire la révérence à) (d'un homme)* to bow to; *(d'une femme)* to curts(e)y to; **s. qn (d'un geste) de la main** to wave to sb; **s. qn d'une inclination de la tête** to nod to sb; **il est passé sans me s.** he walked past me without saying hello; **s. qn bien bas** to take one's hat off to sb; *Hum* **au revoir/bonjour, mes amis, je vous salue bien bas** goodbye/hello, my friends, and a very good day to you; *Théâtre* **s. le public** to bow to the audience; **s. qn par un vivat** to greet sb with a cheer; **la loi a été froidement saluée par l'opposition** the bill got a cool reception from the opposition or was coolly received by the opposition; **saluez-le de ma part** give him my regards; *Bible* **Je vous salue, Marie** hail, Mary; **s. qn comme …** to hail sb as …; **je salue en lui notre sauveur** I salute him as our saviour; *Billard* **s. la bille** to miss **2** *Naut* **s. un grain** to reduce sail for a squall

▶ VI **s. en se découvrant** to raise one's hat in greeting; *Mil etc* **s. du drapeau** to lower the colours; *Naut* **s. (du pavillon)** to dip (the flag); **s. de vingt coups** to fire a twenty-gun salute

▶ VPR **se saluer** *(en arrivant)* to greet each other; *(en partant)* to take leave of each other

salure [salyr] NF saltiness

salut [saly] NM **1** *(sauvegarde)* safety; *Rel* salvation; **chercher son s. dans la fuite** to flee for one's life, to seek safety in flight; **travailler à son s.** to work out one's own salvation; **pour le s. de vos âmes** for the salvation of your souls; **l'Armée du S.** the Salvation Army **2** *(salutation)* greeting, *Fml* salutation; **faire** *ou* **adresser un s. à qn** *(de la main)* to wave to sb, to give sb a wave; *(en se découvrant)* to raise one's hat to sb; *Fam* **s. (à tous)!** hello or hi(, everybody)!; *(en partant)* so long (everybody)! **3** *Mil etc* salute; **faire un s. to**

give a salute; **faire le s. militaire** to salute; **s. au drapeau** saluting the colours; *Naut* **s. du pavillon** dipping of the flag **4** *Cathol* Benediction (of the Holy Sacrament)

salutaire [salytɛr] ADJ *(decision, mesure etc)* salutary, beneficial; *(remède)* beneficial; **être s. à qn** to do sb good, to be beneficial to sb; **un goût très s. pour les sports de plein air** a healthy liking for outdoor sports

salutation [salytasjɔ̃] NF salutation, greeting; **Je vous prie d'agréer, Monsieur, l'expression de mes salutations distinguées** yours faithfully; *(quand la formule de salutation comprend le nom du destinataire)* yours sincerely

salutiste [salytist] N Salvationist

Salvador [salvadɔr] NM El Salvador

salvadorien, -ienne [salvadɔrjɛ̃, -jɛn] ADJ Salvadorean
▪ N **S.** Salvadorean

salvateur, -trice [salvatœr, -tris] ADJ *Litt* saving; **la mort salvatrice** the blessed release of death

salve [salv] NF *Mil* salvo, volley; **tirer une s. (d'honneur)** to fire a salute; **s. d'applaudissements** burst of applause

samare [samar] NF *Bot* key

samaritain, -aine [samaritɛ̃, -ɛn] *Bible* ADJ Samaritan
▪ N **S.** Samaritan; **le bon S.** the Good Samaritan; *Fig* **faire le bon S.** to be a Good Samaritan

samba [sãmba] NF samba

samedi [samdi] NM Saturday; **s. prochain/dernier** next/last Saturday; **s. matin** Saturday morning; **s. soir** Saturday night *or* evening; **dans la soirée de s.** on Saturday evening; **dans la nuit de s. (à dimanche)** on Saturday night; **s. 11 mai 2004** Saturday 11 May 2004; **nous sommes s. aujourd'hui** today's Saturday; **je commence s.** I'm starting on Saturday; **il vient le s./tous les samedis** he comes on Saturdays/every Saturday; **un s. sur deux** every second *or* other Saturday; **s. en huit/quinze** a week/fortnight on Saturday; **passer tout son s. à faire qch** to spend one's whole Saturday doing sth SEE GRAMMAR A81; B61

samizdat [samizdat] NM samizdat

Samoa [samɔa] NFPL **les S. occidentales** Western Samoa

samossa [samɔsa] NM *Culin* samosa

samouraï, samurai [samuraj] NM samurai

samovar [samɔvar] NM samovar

sampan(g) [sãpã] NM sampan

sampler¹ [sãplœr] NM *Mus* sampler

sampler² [sãple] VT *Mus* to sample

SAMU [samy] NM *(abrév* **service d'aide médicale d'urgence)** ambulance service; **appelez le S.!** ≃ call an ambulance!; **le S. social** = mobile medical and support service for homeless people

sana [sana] NM *Fam* sanatorium

sanatorium [sanatɔrjɔm] NM sanatorium

sanctificateur, -trice [sãktifikatœr, -tris] ADJ sanctifying
▪ N sanctifier; **le S.** the Holy Ghost

sanctification [sãktifikasjɔ̃] NF sanctification

sanctifier [sãktifje] VT *(impf, pr sub* n. **sanctifiions,** v. **sanctifiiez)** to sanctify, to make holy; **que Ton nom soit sanctifié** hallowed beThy Name

sanction [sãksjɔ̃] NF **1** *(approbation)* sanction, approval **2 s. (pénale)** sanction, penalty; **sanctions diplomatiques** diplomatic sanctions; **sanctions économiques** economic sanctions; *Pol* **prendre des sanctions contre un pays/contre des grévistes** to im-

pose sanctions on a country/take action against strikers; **la s. de la paresse** the price *or* consequence of laziness; **c'est la s. du succès** that's the price of success

sanctionner [sãksjɔne] VT **1** *(approuver)* to sanction, to approve; **sanctionné par l'usage** sanctioned by custom **2** *(punir)* *(faute, personne)* to punish, to penalize

sanctuaire [sãktɥɛr] NM *Rel, Fig* sanctuary; *Pol, Mil* = territory under the nuclear umbrella

sanctuariser [sãktɥarize] NF *(territoire, région)* to sanctuarize

sanctus [sãktys] NM *Rel, Mus* sanctus

sandale [sãdal] NF sandal

sandalette [sãdalɛt] NF (light) sandal

sandow® [sãdo] NM **1** *Gym* chest expander **2** *(pour bagages)* elastic strap *or Am* bungee; *Aviat* catapult

sandre [sãdr] NM OU F pikeperch

sandwich, *pl* **sandwich(e)s** [sãdwi(t)ʃ] NM sandwich; **s. au jambon** ham sandwich; **verre s.** laminated glass; *Fam* **pris en s.** sandwiched (**entre** between)

sandwicherie [sãdwi(t)ʃəri] NF sandwich bar

sang [sã] NM **1** blood; **animaux à s. chaud/froid** warm-blooded/cold-blooded animals; **yeux injectés de s.** bloodshot eyes; **faire couler** *ou* **répandre** *ou* **verser le s.** to shed *or* spill blood; **verser son s. pour la patrie** to shed one's blood for one's country; **pincer/fouetter qn jusqu'au s.** to pinch/whip sb till he/she bleeds *or* till one draws blood; **victoire sans effusion de s.** bloodless victory; **le pays fut mis à feu et à s.** the country was put to fire and sword; **laver un outrage par le s.** to avenge an insult with blood; **écoulement de s.** bleeding, haemorrhage, *Am* hemorrhage; **je n'arrive pas à arrêter le s.** I can't stop the bleeding; **donner son s.** to give blood; **donneur de s.** blood donor; **il était tout en s.** he was covered with blood; *aussi Fig* **avoir du s. sur les mains** to have blood on one's hands; **taché de s.** bloodstained; *Méd Vieilli* **coup de s.** stroke; *Fig Fam* **il a eu un coup de s.** he nearly had a heart attack; *Fig* **avoir le s. chaud** to be hot-blooded; *Fig* **avoir le rythme dans le s.** to have an innate sense of rhythm, to have rhythm; **elle a la musique dans le s.** she has music in her blood; **il a ça dans le s.** it's in his blood; **des êtres de chair et de s.** creatures of flesh and blood; **le s. lui monta au visage** the blood rushed to his face; **cela me glace le s.** it makes my blood run cold; **il n'a pas de s. dans les veines** he's got no guts, he's gutless; *Fam* **avoir du s. de navet** to be spineless, to be a yellow-belly; *Fam* **se faire du mauvais s.** to worry, *Fam* to get all worked up; *Fam* **se ronger les sangs, se faire un s. d'encre** to worry oneself sick; **conte à tourner les sangs** bloodcurdling tale; **mon s. n'a fait qu'un tour** *(de peur)* my heart missed a beat; *(de colère)* I saw red; **dans cette famille, il faudrait un apport de s. frais** the family needs some *or* an infusion of new blood; *très Fam* **bon s. (de bonsoir)!, bon s. de bon Dieu!** damn and blast it!
2 *(race, lignée)* blood; **cheval de s.** blood horse; **cheval pur s.** thoroughbred; **liens du s.** blood ties; **ils ont ça dans le s.** it's in their blood; **son propre s.** one's own flesh and blood; **nous ne sommes pas du même s.** we're not of the same flesh and blood; **droit du s.** birthright
▸▸ **s. bleu** blue blood; **c'est un s. bleu** he has blue blood (in his veins)

sang-froid [sãfrwa] NM INV composure, calm, *Litt* sang-froid; **garder** *ou* **conserver son s.** to keep calm *or* one's head *or Fam* (one's) cool, to maintain one's composure; **perdre son s.**

to lose one's head *or Fam* one's cool, to lose one's composure; **faire qch de s.** to do sth calmly *or* coolly; **tuer qn de s.** to kill sb in cold blood

sanglant [sãglã] ADJ **1** *(blessure, bataille, histoire, mort)* bloody; *(vêtement, mouchoir etc)* bloodstained, bloody **2** *Fig (reproche)* bitter; *(affront)* deadly; *(critique)* scathing

sangle [sãgl] NF strap; *(de selle)* girth; *(de meuble)* webbing; **lit de s.** camp bed

sangler [sãgle] VT *(cheval)* to girth; **sanglé dans son uniforme** buttoned up tight in his uniform
▪ VPR **se sangler** *(dans un vêtement très étroit)* to do oneself up tight

sanglier [sãglije] NM (wild) boar

sanglot [sãglo] NM sob; **éclater en sanglots** to burst out sobbing, to burst into tears; **il pleurait à gros sanglots** he was sobbing his heart out; **avec des sanglots dans la voix** with a sob in one's voice, in a tearful voice

sangloter [sãglɔte] VI to sob

sang-mêlé [sãmele] N INV half-caste

sangria [sãgrija] NF sangria

sangsue [sãsy] NF *Zool, Fig* leech

sanguin, -ine [sãgɛ̃, -in] ADJ **1** *Anat* blood; **groupe/vaisseau s.** blood group/vessel; **produits sanguins** blood products; **transfusion sanguine** blood transfusion; **circulation sanguine** circulation (of the blood) **2** *(tempérament)* impulsive; *(teint, visage)* ruddy **3** **orange sanguine** blood orange
▪ NM **1** *(personne)* fiery person **2** *Bot* dogwood
▪ NF **sanguine 1** *(craie)* red chalk, sanguine **2** *Minér* bloodstone **3** *(orange)* blood orange

> Il faut noter que l'adjectif anglais **sanguine** est un faux ami. Il signifie **optimiste.**
> Do not confuse with **sanguinaire.**

sanguinaire [sãginɛr] ADJ *(homme)* bloodthirsty; *(combat)* bloody

> Do not confuse with **sanguin.**

sanguinolent [sãginɔlã] ADJ **1** *(teinté de sang)* spotted with blood; **sa lèvre sanguinolente** his/her bleeding lip; **une plaie sanguinolente** a wound oozing blood **2** *(rouge)* blood-red

sanie [sani] NF *Méd* pus and blood, *Spéc* sanies

sanitaire [sanitɛr] ADJ **1** *Méd (personnel)* medical, health; *(équipement)* medical; *(mesures)* health; *Mil etc* **voiture s.** ambulance **2** *Constr etc (équipement, installation)* sanitary; **bloc s.** *(dans un camping)* toilet *or* sanitary block; **système s.** sanitation (system)
▪ NM **les sanitaires** *(toilettes)* toilet; *(salle de bains et W.-C.)* bathroom and toilet; **sanitaires privatifs** en-suite *or* private facilities
▪ NF *Mil etc* ambulance

sans [sã] PRÉP **1** *(absence, privation, exclusion)* without; **partez s. moi** go without me; **il est revenu s. argent** *ou* **s. un sou** *ou* **s. le sou** he came back without any money *or* without a penny; **elle arriva s. argent ni bagages** she arrived without any *or* without either money or luggage; **elle est s. emploi depuis deux mois** she's been unemployed *or* without work for two months; **couple s. enfants** childless couple; **pain/régime s. sel** salt-free bread/diet; **faire qch s. faute** to do sth without fail; **demain s. faute** tomorrow without fail; **suffisant, s. plus** adequate but no more (than that); **plaintes s. fin** endless complaints; **se plaindre s. fin** to complain endlessly; **baignade s. danger** safe bathing; **s. parler/travailler** without speaking/working; **s. mot dire, s. dire un mot** without saying a word; **s. hésiter** without hesitating *or* hesitation, unhesitatingly; **cela va s. dire** it goes without saying; **il va s. dire que c'est une réussite** it's a success, needless to say, it goes without saying that it's a success; **s. plus attendre** without further delay, immediately; **non s. difficulté** not without difficulty; *Fml* **vous n'êtes pas s. le connaître** you must know him; *Fml* **tu n'es pas s. savoir que …** you are quite well aware that …; *Fml* **ces questions n'étaient pas s. m'embarrasser** these questions were naturally somewhat embarrassing; *Typ* **s. patte** *ou* **serif** sans serif SEE GRAMMAR A73; B57

2 *(condition)* but for; **s. vous je ne l'aurais jamais fait** but for you *or* if it hadn't been for you, I would never have done it; **s. cela, s. quoi** otherwise; *Fam* **sois sage, s. ça tu seras puni!** be good or (else) you'll be punished!

CONJ s. que + *sub* without + *gerund*; **s. que nous le sachions,** *Rare* **s. que nous ne le sachions** without our knowing, unbeknownst to us; **il ne parlait jamais s. qu'on lui parlât** he never spoke unless he was spoken to

ADV *Fam* **comment ferais-tu s.?** how would you manage without?; **est-ce que tu pourrais vivre s.?** could you live without it/them?; **la télévision, je ne pourrais pas vivre s.** I couldn't live without television

sans-abri [sɑ̃zabri] **N INV** homeless person; **les s.** the homeless

sans-cœur *Fam* **ADJ INV** heartless
N INV heartless person

sanscrit [sɑ̃skri] **ADJ, NM** = **sanskrit**

sans-culotte, *pl* **sans-culottes NM** *Hist* sans culotte *(person with extreme republican sympathies during the French Revolution)*

sans-dessein [sɑ̃desɛ̃] *Can Fam Péj* **ADJ INV** clueless, gormless
N INV clueless person

sans-emploi [sɑ̃zɑ̃plwa] **N INV** unemployed *or* jobless person; **les s.** the unemployed, the jobless; **le nombre des s. augmente** the unemployment *or* jobless figure is rising

sans-façon NM INV *(naturel)* informality
ADJ INV *(naturel)* informal

sans-faute NM INV *Sport* clear round; **accomplir** *ou* **faire un s.** *(d'un cheval)* to have a clear round; *Fig (d'un candidat)* not to put a foot wrong, to turn in a faultless performance

sans-fil NF INV *Vieilli* wireless (telegraphy)
NM INV cordless telephone

sans-gêne *Péj* **NM INV** impudence, brazenness
N INV *(personne)* impudent *or* brazen person
ADJ INV *(personne)* impudent, brazen; **qu'est-ce qu'il est s.!** he's got a cheek!; **des manières s.** brazen ways

sanskrit [sɑ̃skri] **ADJ, NM** *Ling* Sanskrit

sans-le-sou [sɑ̃l(ə)su] **N INV** *Fam* penniless person; **c'est un s.** he doesn't have a penny to his name

sans-logis N INV homeless person; **les s.** the homeless

sansonnet [sɑ̃sɔnɛ] **NM** starling

sans-papiers [sɑ̃papje] **N INV** illegal immigrant *(who does not possess the required work or residence permit)*

sans-parti N INV *Pol* independent member *(of an assembly or a Parliament)*; *(dans un système de parti unique)* non-party member

sans-patrie N INV stateless person

sans-souci ADJ INV carefree, happy-go-lucky

santal, -als [sɑ̃tal] **NM (bois de) s.** sandalwood

santé [sɑ̃te] **NF** health; **être en bonne s.** to be well, to be in good health; **s. de fer** iron constitution; **avoir une bonne/mauvaise s.** to be healthy/unhealthy; **ne pas avoir de s., avoir une s. fragile** *ou* **délicate,** *Fam* **avoir une petite s.** to be in poor health, to be delicate; *Fig Fam* **avoir de la s.** *(avoir de l'audace)* to have a nerve *or Br* a brass neck; **c'est bon/mauvais pour la s.** it's good/bad for your health; *Fam* **comment va la s.?** how's things?, how are you doing?; **perdre/recouvrer la s.** to lose/recover one's health; **elle respire la s.** she looks *or* is the picture of health, she radiates health; **être plein de s.** to be full of life; **absent pour raison de s.** absent for health reasons *or* on medical grounds; **boire à la s. de qn** to drink sb's health; **à votre s.!** your health!, *Fam* cheers!; **buvons à la s. des mariés** let's drink to the married couple; *Suisse Fam* **s.!** *(à vos souhaits)* bless you!; *Admin* **Ministère de la S. et de la Sécurité sociale** *Br* ≃ Department of Social Security, *Am* ≃ Department of Health and Human Services; *Naut* **agent de (la) s.** quarantine officer; **s. publique** public health

santiag [sɑ̃tjag] **NF** *Fam* cowboy boot

santon [sɑ̃tɔ̃] **NM** *(de crèche)* Christmas crib figure

saoudien, -ienne [saudjɛ̃, -jɛn] **ADJ** Saudi (Arabian)
N S. Saudi (Arabian)

saoul [su], **saoulard** [sular], **saouler** [sule] = **soûl, soûlard, soûler**

sapajou [sapaʒu] **NM** *Zool* capuchin (monkey), sapajou

sape [sap] **NF 1** *(d'un mur, d'une tour etc)* undermining; *Mil* sapping; *Fig* **travaux de s.** undermining **2** *(tranchée)* sap, trench **3** *(outil)* mattock **4** *Arg* **sapes** *(vêtements)* gear, togs, *Br* clobber

saper [sape] **VT 1** *Mil etc, Fig* to undermine; **s. le moral de qn** to sap sb's morale **2** *Arg (habiller)* to tog out, to dress; **être bien sapé** to be all togged up
VPR se saper *Arg* to get dressed; *(s'habiller chic)* to get all dressed up

saperlipopette [saperlipopɛt], **saperlotte** [saperlɔt] **INT** *Arch, Hum* gad(zooks)!

sapeur [sapœr] **NM** *Mil* sapper; *Fam* **fumer comme un s.** to smoke like a chimney

sapeur-pompier NM *Admin* fireman, fire fighter; **les sapeurs-pompiers** *(service)* the fire brigade *or Am* department

saphique [safik] **ADJ** Sapphic

saphir [safir] **NM** sapphire

saphisme [safism] **NM** sapphism

sapin [sapɛ̃] **NM 1** *(arbre)* fir (tree); *Com* **(bois de) s.** deal **2** *Fam* **ça sent le s.** that sounds bad, that sounds as if you're heading for an early grave; **il sent le s.** he's done for, he's had it **3** *Can* **se faire passer un s.** *(se faire avoir)* to be taken for a ride

sapine [sapin] **NF 1** *(planche)* deal board **2** *Constr* crane tower **3** *(en viticulture)* deal tub

sapinière [sapinjɛr] **NF** fir plantation

saponaire [saponɛr] **NF** *Bot* soapwort

saponifiant [saponifjɑ̃] *Chimie* **ADJ** saponifying
NM saponifier, saponifying agent

saponification [saponifikasjɔ̃] **NF** saponification

saponifier [saponifje] **VT** *(impf, pr sub* **n. saponifiions, v. saponifiiez)** to saponify

sapristi [sapristi] **INT** *Fam Vieilli, Hum* good heavens!

saprophage [saprofaʒ] **ADJ** *Entom* saprophagous

saprophyte [saprofit] **NM** *Biol* saprophyte

saquebute [sakbyt] **NF** *Hist, Mus* sackbut

saquer [sake] **VT** *Fam* = **sacquer**

sarabande [sarabɑ̃d] **NF** *(danse), Mus* saraband; *Fam (tapage)* racket, row; **ils ont fait la s. toute la nuit** they made a racket *or* row all night long

Sarajevo [sarajevo] **N** Sarajevo

sarbacane [sarbakan] **NF** blowpipe; *(jouet)* peashooter

sarcasme [sarkasm] **NM** sarcasm; *(remarque)* sarcastic remark

sarcastique [sarkastik] **ADJ** sarcastic

sarcastiquement [sarkastikmɑ̃] **ADV** sarcastically

sarcelle [sarsɛl] **NF** teal

sarclage [sarklaʒ] **NM** weeding

sarcler [sarkle] **VT 1** *(jardin, plates-bandes)* to weed; *(sol)* to hoe; *(champ)* to clean **2** *(mauvaises herbes)* to hoe up *or* out

sarclette [sarklɛt] **NF** (weeding) hoe

sarcloir [sarklwar] **NM** (weeding) hoe

sarcome [sarkom] **NM** *Méd* sarcoma; **s. de Kaposi** Kaposi's sarcoma

sarcophage [sarkofaʒ] **NM** *Antiq, Nucl* sarcophagus
NF *Entom* bluebottle

Sardaigne [sardɛɲ] **NF** Sardinia

sarde [sard] **ADJ** Sardinian
N S. Sardinian
NM *Ling* Sardinian

sardine [sardin] **NF 1** *(poisson)* sardine; **sardines à l'huile/à la tomate** sardines in oil/in tomato sauce; *Fam* **serrés comme des sardines** packed together like sardines **2** *Mil Fam* stripe **3** *(de tente)* tent peg

sardinerie [sardinri] **NF** sardine cannery

sardinier, -ière [sardinje, -jɛr] **N** *(pêcheur)* sardine fisher; *(ouvrier)* sardine canner
NM *(filet)* sardine net; *(bateau)* sardine boat

sardonique [sardonik] **ADJ** sardonic

sardonyx [sardoniks] **NF** *Minér* sardonyx

sargasse [sargas] **NF** sargasso, gulfweed; **la mer des Sargasses** the Sargasso Sea

sari [sari] **NM** sari

sarigue [sarig] **NF** opossum, possum

sarin [sarɛ̃] **NM** sarin

SARL [esaɛrɛl] **NF** *(abrév* **société anonyme à responsabilité limitée)** = limited liability company, *Br* ≃ Ltd, *Am* ≃ Inc

sarment [sarmɑ̃] **NM** *(tige)* bine; *(de vigne)* vine shoot

sarmenteux, -euse [sarmɑ̃tø, -øz] **ADJ** *(plante)* climbing

sarong [sarɔ̃] **NM** sarong

saroual [sarwal], **sarouel** [sarwɛl] **NM** = baggy trousers worn by North Africans

sarrasin, -ine [sarazɛ̃, -in] **ADJ** *Hist* Saracen
N *Hist* **S.** Saracen
NM *Agr* buckwheat
NF **sarrasine** portcullis

sarrau [saro] **NM** smock

Sarre [sar] **NF** **la S.** *(région)* Saarland, the Saar; *(rivière)* the Saar

sarriette [sarjɛt] **NF** *Bot, Culin* savory

sarrois, -oise [sarwa, -waz] **ADJ** of/from Saarland *or* the Saar
N S. Saarlander

sas [sɑ(s)] **NM 1** *(crible)* sieve; **passer qch au s.** to sift *or* sieve sth **2** *Tech* lock chamber, coffer **3** *Constr, Naut, Astronaut* airlock

sassafras [sasafra] **NM** *Bot* sassafras

sassage [sasaʒ] **NM, sassement** [sasmɑ̃] **NM 1** *(criblage)* sifting, sieving **2** *(d'un bateau)* passing through a lock

sasser [sase] **VT 1** *(farine, plâtre)* to sift, to sieve; *(grain)* to winnow **2** *(bateau)* to pass through a lock

sasseur, -euse [sasœr, -øz] N sifter

Satan [satã] N Satan

satané [satane] ADJ *Fam* confounded; **s. temps!** what filthy weather!

satanique [satanik] ADJ satanic; *Fig (cruauté, idée, sourire etc)* fiendish

satanisme [satanism] NM satanism

sataniste [satanist] N satanist

satellisation [satelizasjɔ̃] NF **1** *Astronaut (d'un satellite, d'un engin spatial)* putting into orbit; **programme de s.** space programme **2** *Pol (d'un pays, d'une région)* satellization

satelliser [satelize] VT **1** *Astronaut (satellite, engin spatial)* to put into orbit **2** *Pol (pays, région)* to satellize
  VPR se satelliser 1 *Astronaut* to go into orbit **2** *Pol (d'un pays, d'une région)* to become a satellite

satellitaire [sateliter] ADJ *(diffusion, chaîne, téléphone)* satellite; **imagerie s.** satellite pictures

satellite [satelit] NM **1** *Astron* satellite; **s. artificiel** artificial satellite; **s. géostationnaire** geostationary satellite; **s. terrestre/lunaire** earth-orbiting/moon-orbiting satellite; **s. de télécommunications** (tele)communications satellite, *Fam* comsat; **s. météorologique** weather *or* meteorological satellite; *TV* **retransmis par s.** transmitted by satellite; **émission retransmise par s.** satellite broadcast; **télévision par s.** satellite television, *Fam* metsat; **s. de diffusion directe** direct broadcast satellite, DBS; **s. de télédiffusion** broadcast satellite; **s. de télédiffusion directe** direct-broadcast satellite; **s. de télédétection** remote-sensing satellite; **s. météo** weather satellite; **s. terrestre** earth satellite **2** *Pol* satellite; **les satellites du bloc socialiste** the satellite countries of the socialist bloc; *Péj (homme)* satellite, hanger-on **3** *Tech* planet wheel, bevel gear; **engrenage à satellites** (sun-and-)planet gear; *Aut* **s. sur colonne de direction** steering column satellite
  ADJ **1** *Anat* **veines satellites** companion veins **2** *Pol* **pays s.** satellite state; **agglomération s.** satellite town

satiété [sasjete] NF satiety; **manger/boire à s.** to eat/drink one's fill; **répéter qch à s.** to repeat sth ad nauseam

satin [satɛ̃] NM **1** *Tex* satin **2 bois de s.** satinwood **3** *Bot* **s. blanc** honesty

satiné [satine] ADJ *(tissu)* satiny, satin-like; *(cuir, papier)* glazed; *(papier)* calendered; *(peau)* satin-smooth; **peinture satinée** satin-finish paint
  NM satin finish; *(de la peau)* satin smoothness

satiner [satine] VT *(tissu etc)* to give a satin finish to, to satin; *(cuir)* to glaze; *(papier)* to calender

satinette [satinet] NF *Tex (en coton)* sateen; *(en soie et coton)* satinet(te)

satire [satir] NF satire (**contre** on; **de** of); **faire la s. de son époque** to satirize one's times

satirique [satirik] ADJ satirical, satiric

satiriquement [satirikmã] ADV satirically

satiriser [satirize] VT to satirize

satiriste [satirist] N satirist

satisfaction [satisfaksjɔ̃] NF **1** satisfaction; **la s. du travail bien fait** the satisfaction of a job well done; **donner (toute** *ou* **entière) s. à qn** to give sb (complete) satisfaction; **donner s. aux vœux de qn** to satisfy *or* gratify sb's wishes; **avoir la s. de faire qch** to have the satisfaction of doing sth; **nous avons la s. de pouvoir dire que ...** it gives us great satisfaction to be able to say that ...; **j'éprouve une profonde s.** I feel (a) great satisfaction; **à la s. générale** to everyone's satisfaction;

j'ai eu une s. aujourd'hui a good thing happened today; **ils ne m'ont donné que des satisfactions** they've given me nothing but satisfaction; **s. de la clientèle** *ou* **du client** customer satisfaction **2** *(réparation)* satisfaction (**pour, de** for); *Rel* atonement; **donner s. à qn** to give sb satisfaction; **obtenir s.** to obtain satisfaction

satisfaire [satisfɛr] *(conj like* **faire**) VT *(personne, besoin, demandes)* to satisfy; *(curiosité)* to satisfy, to gratify; *(sexuellement)* to satisfy; **s. le désir de qn** *(l'accomplir)* to carry out sb's wish; **s. l'attente de qn** to come up to sb's expectations; *Euph* **s. un besoin naturel** to answer a call of nature, to relieve oneself; **de manière à vous s.** to your satisfaction; **s. sa faim** to satisfy *or* appease one's hunger; **s. une commande** to fulfill an order
  VPR **se satisfaire 1 se s. de peu** to be content with very little, *Péj* to be easily satisfied **2** *(uriner)* to relieve oneself **3** *(sexuellement)* to achieve satisfaction
  VI **1 s. à** *(demande, exigence, condition, besoins)* to satisfy, to meet; *(souhaits)* to satisfy, to fulfil, to carry out; *(règlement, normes de sécurité)* to comply with; *(contrat, obligations)* to fulfil; **s. à son devoir** to carry out *or* fulfil one's duty; **s. à un examen** to pass an exam **2** *Arch* **s. à qn** *(dans un duel)* to give sb satisfaction

satisfaisant [satisfəzã] ADJ *(convenable) (réponse, travail etc)* satisfactory; *(qui contente) (repas, occupation)* satisfying

> Attention: ne pas confondre **satisfying** et **satisfactory** lorsqu'on traduit **satisfaisant**.

satisfait [satisfɛ] ADJ *(heureux)* satisfied; *(suffisant)* satisfied, smug; *(désir, vœu)* fulfilled; *Iron* **vous voilà s.!** well, you asked for it!; **je n'en suis pas s.** I'm not satisfied *or* pleased *or* happy with it; *Com* **j'espère que vous en serez satisfait s.** I trust it will give you complete satisfaction; **s. ou remboursé** satisfaction or your money back, money-back guarantee

satisfecit [satisfesit] NM INV *Litt (approbation)* recognition, credit; *Scol Vieilli* = certificate of satisfactory progress; **décerner un s. à qn** to congratulate sb on a job well done

saton [satɔ̃] NM *Fam* **coup de s.** kick, boot; **donner des coups de s. à qn/dans qch** to boot sb/sth, to give sb/sth a kicking

satonner [satone] VT *Fam* **s. qn/qch** to boot sb/sth, to give sb/sth a kicking

saturable [satyrabl] ADJ saturable

saturant [satyrã] ADJ saturating; **vapeur saturante** saturated vapour

saturateur [satyratœr] NM *Chimie, Ind* saturator; *(humidificateur)* humidifier

saturation [satyrasjɔ̃] NF *aussi Fig* saturation; *(du réseau routier)* gridlock; **arriver à s.** to reach saturation point; *Ordinat (d'une disquette)* to become full; **campagne de s.** *(en publicité)* saturation campaign; **s. du marché** saturation of the market; *TV, Radio* **s. acoustique** popping

saturé [satyre] ADJ *(solution), Fig* saturated; *Ordinat (disque)* full; **l'éponge est saturée d'eau** the sponge is saturated; *Com* **le marché est s.** the market is saturated *or* has reached saturation point; **ville saturée** overcrowded city; **j'en suis s.** I'm sick of it/them; **j'étais s. de soleil** I'd had enough sun

saturer [satyre] VT to saturate (**de** with); *TV, Radio* to overload; *Fig* **on nous sature de publicité** we are swamped with advertising; **le professeur nous sature de travail** the teacher is overloading us with work; **les appels de nos téléspectateurs ont saturé le standard** our viewers' calls have jammed the switchboards

VI **1** *(radio, chaîne hi-fi)* to distort **2** *Fam* **je sature** I've had it up to here

saturnales [satyrnal] NFPL *Antiq, Fig* saturnalia

Saturne [satyrn] N *Myth* Saturn
  NF *Astron* Saturn

saturnie [satyrni] NF emperor moth

saturnien, -ienne [satyrnjɛ̃, -jɛn] ADJ saturnine

saturnin, -ine [satyrnɛ̃, -in] ADJ *Méd* intoxication saturnine lead poisoning

saturnisme [satyrnism] NM *Méd* lead poisoning, *Spéc* saturnism

satyre [satir] NM **1** *Myth, Entom* satyr **2** *Fam (obsédé sexuel)* sex maniac

satyrique [satirik] ADJ *Antiq* satyric

sauce [sos] NF **1** *Culin* sauce; **s. hollandaise/béchamel/béarnaise** hollandaise/béchamel/béarnaise sauce; **s. aux champignons** mushroom sauce; **s. (à) salade** salad dressing; **(r)allonger la s.** to water down the sauce; *Fig Fam* to pad things out; *Fam* **accommoder un même sujet à toutes les sauces** to dish up the same subject in every shape and form; *Fam* **mettre qch à toutes les sauces** to use sth in every way imaginable; *Fig* **à quelle s. sera-t-il mangé?** how shall we deal with him/him? **2** *Beaux-Arts (craie noire)* soft black crayon **3** *Fig Fam (pluie)* **prendre la s.** to get soaked *or* drenched, to get a soaking **4** *Fam* **mettre la s.** to pull out all the stops, to go all out

saucée [sose] NF *Fam (pluie)* downpour; **recevoir une s.** to get soaked *or* drenched, to get a soaking

saucer [sose] VT (**je sauçai(s); n. sauçons**) **1** *(assiette)* to mop up the sauce from **2** *Fam* **se faire s.** to get soaked *or* drenched, to get a soaking

saucette [sosɛt] NF *Can Fam* **faire une s.** to have a quickie; **faire une s. à Québec** to make a quick trip to Quebec City, to pop over to Quebec City

saucier [sosje] NM sauce cook *or* chef

saucière [sosjɛr] NF sauce boat

sauciflard [sosiflar] NM *très Fam* sausage

saucisse [sosis] NF **1** *Culin* sausage; **s. de Francfort** frankfurter; **s. de Strasbourg** knackwurst; **s. de Toulouse** = type of pork sausage; *Fam* **il n'attache pas son chien avec des saucisses** he's tight with his money, he's tight-fisted **2** *Mil Fam* barrage balloon **3** *Fam* **grande s.** beanpole; **s. à pattes** sausage dog

saucisson [sosisɔ̃] NM *Culin* sausage; **s. (sec)** *(salami-type)* sausage; **s. à l'ail** garlic sausage; **s. pur porc** 100% pork sausage; *Fam* **elle est toujours ficelée comme un s.** she's always bulging *or* bursting out of her clothes; *Hum* **s. à pattes** sausage dog

saucissonnage [sosisɔnaʒ] NM *Fam* **1** *(diviser en petites parties)* breaking up; **le désavantage avec cette chaîne, c'est le s. des films par les publicités** a drawback with this channel is the way films are constantly interrupted by commercial breaks **2** *(fait de ficeler)* trussing up

saucissonné [sosisɔne] ADJ *Fam* trussed up; **s. dans son collant/sa robe** poured into her tights/dress

saucissonner [sosisɔne] *Fam* VT *(attacher)* to truss up; *Fig* **film saucissonné de publicités** film broken up by adverts
  VI to picnic, to eat a snack

saucissonneur, -euse [sosisɔnœr, -øz] N *Fam* picnicker

sauf¹, sauve [sof, sov] ADJ *(personne)* safe, unhurt, unharmed; **sain et s.** safe and sound; **avoir la vie sauve** to escape with one's life; **ils lui ont laissé la vie sauve** they spared his life *or* him; **l'honneur est s.** honour is saved; **sa réputation est sauve** his/her reputation is intact *or* saved

sauf[2] PRÉPexcept (for), apart from; **elle n'a rien s. son salaire** she has nothing except (for) *or* apart from *or* but her wages; **il est indemne s. une écorchure au bras** he is unhurt except for *or* apart from a grazed arm; **s. avis contraire, s. contrordre** unless you/I/*etc* hear to the contrary, unless otherwise advised; **s. bonne fin** under usual reserve; **s. indication contraire** unless otherwise stated *or* specified; **s. de rares exceptions** with very few exceptions; **s. accidents, s. imprévu** barring accidents, unless anything unforeseen happens; **s. erreur ou omission** errors and omissions excepted; **s. erreur de ma part, je vous dois encore 500 euros** if I'm not mistaken *or* unless I'm mistaken, I still owe you 500 euros; **s. cas de force majeure** unless anything happens to prevent it; *Jur* except in cases of force majeure; *Litt* **je consens, s. à revenir sur ma décision** I consent, but I reserve the right to reconsider my decision; **s. le respect que je vous dois, s. votre respect** with all due respect; **s. s'il pleut** unless it rains, if it doesn't rain; *Fam* **je n'ai rien fait, s. d'écrire des lettres** I've done nothing except write *or* apart from writing some letters; *Fam* **s. que** + *ind*except that, apart from the fact that

sauf-conduit, *pl* **sauf-conduits** NM safe conduct, pass

sauge [soʒ] NF**1** *Bot, Culin* sage **2** *Bot (plante ornementale)* salvia

saugrenu [sogrəny] ADJ absurd, preposterous

saule [sol] NM willow; **s. pleureur** weeping willow

saumâtre [somatr] ADJ**1** *(goût, eau)* brackish, briny **2** *Fig* bitter; *Fam* **je la trouve s.** I'm not amused *or* impressed, I think it's a bit much

saumon [somɔ̃] NM **1** *(poisson)* salmon; **darne de s.** salmon steak; **s. fumé** smoked salmon, *Am* lox VOIR GRAMMAIRE A12 **2** *Métal (de plomb, d'étain etc)* pig

ADJ INVsalmon-pink; **rose s.** salmon pink

saumoné [somɔne] ADJ **truite saumonée** salmon trout

saumure [somyr] NFbrine

saumuré [somyre] ADJ*(harengs etc)* pickled (in brine)

saumurer [somyre] VTto pickle (in brine)

sauna [sona] NMsauna

saupiquet [sopikɛ] NM *Culin* = spicy stew

saupoudrage [sopudraʒ] NM **1** *Culin* sprinkling, dusting **2** *Fin, Pol (de crédits)* = allocation of small amounts of funding to various beneficiaries

saupoudrer [sopudre] VT**1** *Culin* to dust, to sprinkle (**de** with); **s. des fraises de sucre** to sprinkle *or* dust strawberries with sugar **2** *Fin, Pol* **s. des crédits** = to allocate small amounts of funding to various beneficiaries **3** *Fig Litt (parsemer)* to scatter, to sprinkle (**de** with); **s. un texte de références/de citations** to pepper *or* sprinkle a text with references/quotations

VPR **se saupoudrer se s. les mains de talc** to dust one's hands with talcum powder

saupoudreuse [sopudrøz] NF, **saupoudroir** [sopudrwar] NM *Culin* dredger, caster

saur [sɔr] ADJ M **hareng s.** kipper, smoked herring

saurer [sɔre] VT *(harengs)* to kipper, to smoke; *(poisson, jambon)* to smoke

saurien [sɔrjɛ̃] NM *Zool* saurian

saut [so] NM**1** *(bond)* jump, leap; **faire un s.** to jump, to leap, to take a leap; **la voiture a fait un s. de 50 mètres dans la mer** the car

plunged 50 metres into the sea; *Fig* **faire un s. à Paris/chez le boulanger/en ville** to pop *or Br* nip over to Paris/round to the baker's/into town; **entrer d'un s.** to dash *or* rush in; **au s. du lit** first thing in the morning; **il m'a trouvé au s. du lit** he caught me when I'd only just got up; **faire un s. dans l'inconnu** to take a leap in the dark *or* into the unknown; *Fig* **faire le (grand) s.** *(faire qch de très important)* to take the plunge; *(mourir)* to pass on (to the other side); *Fig* **le héros fit un s. de plusieurs années et se retrouva en l'an 2055** the hero skipped several years and found himself in the year 2055; *Arch* **par sauts et par bonds** in fits and starts; **il n'y a qu'un s. d'ici là** it's only a stone's throw away **2** *Mus* skip

3 *Ordinat* jump; *Typ* **s. de ligne** line break; *Typ* **s. de ligne manuel** hard return; *Typ* **s. de page** page break; *Typ* **s. de page imposé** hard page break

4 *(en élevage)* covering

5 *(de cours d'eau)* waterfall

►►*Natation* **s. de l'ange** swallow dive, *Am* swan dive; *Gym* **s. de carpe** flip; **faire des sauts de carpe** to bounce around; *Natation* **s. carpé** pike; **s. à la corde** skipping; **s. à l'élastique** bungee jumping; *Sport* **s. en hauteur** high jump; *Sport* **s. en longueur** long *or Am* broad jump; **s. en parachute** parachute jump; *(activité)* parachute jumping; **faire du s. en parachute** to go parachute jumping; *Sport* **s. à la perche** pole vault(ing); **s. périlleux** somersault; **s. en ou à skis** ski jump; *(activité)* ski jumping; **faire du s. à skis** to go ski jumping

saut-de-lit NM INV (light) dressing gown

saut-de-loup, *pl* **sauts-de-loup** NM sunken fence, ha-ha

saut-de-mouton, *pl* **sauts-de-mouton** NMflyover, *Am* overpass

saute [sot] NF**s. de vent** change in the wind direction; **sautes de température** sudden changes in temperature; **sautes d'humeur** mood swings

sauté [sote] *Culin* ADJsautéed, sauté

NMsauté; **s. de lièvre** sauté of hare

saute-mouton NM INVleapfrog; **jouer à s.** to play leapfrog

SAUTER [sote] *(aux* **avoir** *)*

VI to jump **1** ▪ to skip **1** ▪ to blow up **2** ▪ to fall **2**	
VT to leap over **1** ▪ to skip **2** ▪ to miss out **2**	

VI **1** *(bondir)* to jump; **s. hors du lit/sur son cheval** to jump *or* leap out of bed/on to one's horse; **s. par la fênetre/du pont** to jump out (of) the window/from the bridge; **s. sur un pied** to hop; **s. à la perche** to pole-vault; **s. à la corde** to skip, *Am* to jump rope; **s. à terre** to jump down; *Équitation* **le cheval refuse de s.** the horse is refusing (the jump *or* fence); *Fam* **et que ça saute!** and make it snappy!, and step on it!, chop! chop!; *Fig* **s. du coq à l'âne** to jump *or* skip from one subject to another; **nous allons s. directement à la page 5** we're going to jump straight to page 5; **s. à la gorge de qn** to pounce *or* jump on sb, to go for sb; *(d'un chien)* to fly at sb *or* at sb's throat; **cela saute aux yeux** it's obvious, it's staring you in the face; **s. au cou de qn** to fling one's arms round sb's neck; **s. au plafond** *(du bouchon de champagne etc)* to hit the ceiling, *(de surprise)* to jump out of one's skin; *(de joie)* to jump for joy, to be overjoyed; *(de colère)* to hit the roof *or* the ceiling; **s. de joie** to jump for joy; **s. sur qn** to pounce on *or* fly at *or* fling oneself at sb; *Fig Fam* to pounce on sb; **s. sur une offre/sur l'occasion** to jump at an offer/at the opportu-

nity; **il faut s. dessus, jamais tu ne trouveras un vélo à ce prix-là** you'll never find another bike at that price, snap it up!

2 *(exploser)* to blow up, to explode; *(d'un bouton)* to come off, to fly off; *Élec (d'un fusible)* to blow, *Fam* to go; *Fig (du gouvernement)* to fall; *(d'une entreprise)* to collapse; *(d'un poste)* to be axed; *Ordinat (d'un réseau)* to crash; **faire s.** *(rocher)* to blast; *(pont etc)* to blow up; *(mine)* to explode; *(chaudière)* to burst; *Fig (projet etc)* to wreck, to ruin; *(gouvernement etc)* to bring down; *(fonctionnaire)* to fire, *Br* to sack; *Culin (pommes de terre)* to sauté; *Culin (crêpe)* to toss; *(serrure)* to force; *(piège)* to spring; **faire s. le bouchon** *(d'une bouteille)* to pop the cork; **j'ai eu du mal à faire s. la partie scellée** I had trouble breaking open the sealed part; *Fam* **faire s. la banque** to break the bank; *Élec* **faire s. les plombs** to blow the fuses; **faire s. un enfant sur ses genoux/en l'air** to bounce a child on one's knees/to throw a child up in the air; **se faire s. la cervelle** to blow one's brains out

VT **1** *(fossé, barrière etc)* to jump (over), to leap over, to clear; *Fig* **s. le pas** to take the plunge

2 *(omettre) (page, ligne etc)* to skip, to miss out; *(repas)* to skip; *Tricot (maille)* to drop; *Scol* **s. une classe** to skip a year; *Fam Vieilli* **je la saute** I'm starving, I'm ravenous

3 *(d'un étalon) (jument)* to cover; *Vulg (femme)* to shag, to screw; **se faire s.** *(d'une femme)* to get laid

sauterelle [sotrɛl] NF**1** *Entom* grasshopper; *(nuisible)* locust; **grande s. d'Orient** locust; **invasion de sauterelles** invasion of locusts **2** *Fig Fam (fille, femme)* chick, *Br* bird; *(fille maigre)* beanpole

sauterie [sotri] NF *Vieilli, Hum* party, *Fam* hop

saute-ruisseau NM INV *Fam Arch* errand boy

sauteur, -euse [sotœr, -øz] ADJ *(insecte etc)* jumping; **scie sauteuse** jigsaw

N**1** *Sport* jumper; **s. en longueur** long jumper; **s. en hauteur** high jumper; **s. à la perche** pole vaulter **2** *Fig Fam (homme sans sérieux)* unreliable sort

NF **sauteuse 1** *(casserole)* frying pan **2** *Arg Vieilli (femme de mœurs légères)* slut

sautillant [sotijɑ̃] ADJ *(rythme, musique)* bouncy; **avancer d'un pas s.** to bounce along

sautillement [sotijmɑ̃] NM hopping *or* skipping (about); **il avançait par sautillements** he was skipping along; *(sur un pied)* he was hopping along

sautiller [sotije] VI *(des oiseaux)* to hop (about); *(des enfants)* to skip *or* hop about; **s. d'un pied sur l'autre** to hop from one foot to the other; **marcher/courir en sautillant** to skip along

sautoir [sotwar] NM **1** *Hér* saltire **2** *(collier)* chain; **s. de perles** string of pearls; **porté en s.** worn round the neck **3** *Sport* jumping area

sauvage [sovaʒ] ADJ **1** *(à l'état de nature) (plante, animal)* wild; **chat s.** wildcat; *Can* **raccoon; lieu s.** wild spot; **la côte ouest est restée très s.** the west coast has remained very wild; **redevenir s.** *(d'un animal apprivoisé)* to revert to the wild; **à l'état s.** wild

2 *Vieilli (peuple, tribu)* savage, primitive; **retourner à la vie s.** to go back to the wild

3 *(violent) (personne, agression)* savage, brutal; *(mœurs)* uncivilized

4 *(peu sociable)* unsociable; *(enfant)* shy

5 *(non autorisé)* unauthorized; **grève s.** wildcat strike; **camping s.** unauthorized camping; **urbanisation s.** uncontrolled urbanization; **immigration s.** illegal immigration; **psychanalyse s.** amateur psychoanalysis

N *(f parfois* **sauvagesse** *)* **1** *Vieilli (indigène)* savage; *Can Péj (Amérindien)* (American) Indian; *Fam Hum* **on n'est pas des sauvages!** we're not savages!; *Fam Hum* **bande de sauvages!** you bunch of savages!

2 *(personne peu sociable)* unsociable person; **c'est un vrai s.** he's a real recluse

sauvagement [sovaʒmã] ADV savagely

sauvageon, -onne [sovaʒɔ̃, -ɔn] NM *(pour greffer)* wild stock

N *(enfant)* little savage

sauvagerie [sovaʒri] NF **1** *(cruauté)* savagery, brutality, barbarity **2** *(insociabilité)* unsociability

sauvagin, -ine [sovaʒɛ̃, -in] ADJ *(goût, odeur)* of wildfowl

NF **chasse à la sauvagine** wildfowling

sauvegarde [sovgard] NF **1** *(protection)* safeguard (**contre** against); **sous la s. de qn** under sb's protection; **la s. des forêts/du patrimoine national** the safeguarding *or* protection of the forests/the nation's heritage **2** *Ordinat* saving, backup; **faire la s. d'un fichier** to save a file; **s. automatique** automatic backup; **s. en ligne** on-line backup; **s. externe** off-line backup; **s. rapide** fast save; **s. sur bande** tape backup; **copie de s.** backup (copy)

sauvegarder [sovgarde] VT **1** *(protéger)* to safeguard (**contre** against) **2** *Ordinat* (*fichier)* to save, to back up; **s. un fichier sur disque** to save a file to disk; **s. automatiquement** to autosave

sauve-qui-peut [sovkipø] NM INV *(débandade)* stampede; *(cri)* every man for himself, run for your life

sauver [sove] VT **1** *(personne)* to save, to rescue (**de** from); *Rel (personne, âme)* to save; **le malade est sauvé** the patient is out of danger; **s. la vie à** *ou* **de qn** to save sb's life; *Fig* **tu me sauves!** you're a lifesaver!; *Fam* **il n'y a que la foi qui sauve!** faith can work miracles!

2 *(préserver) (navire, marchandises)* to salvage; **s. les apparences** to keep up appearances; **s. la face** to save face; *Fig Fam* **s. les meubles** to save *or* salvage something from the wreckage; *Fam* **s. sa peau** *ou* **sa tête** to save one's skin; *Fig* **ce qui le sauve, c'est que ...** his saving grace is that ...; **la fin sauve le film** it's the end that saves *or* rescues the film; **s. la situation** to save the day

VPR **se sauver 1** *(s'échapper)* to escape (**de** from); **sauve qui peut!** every man for himself!, run for your life!

2 *(s'enfuir)* to run away; **se s. à toutes jambes** to take to one's heels, to beat a hasty retreat, *Br Fam* to scarper; *Fam* **il se fait tard, je me sauve** it's getting late, I'm off *or* I must fly; *Fam* **sauve-toi maintenant, tu vas être en retard** be off *or* get going now, you'll be late

3 *(du lait, de préparation culinaire etc)* to boil over

sauvetage [sovtaʒ] NM **1** *(d'un accidenté)* rescue; **s. aérien en mer** air-sea rescue; **il a fait plusieurs sauvetages en mer** he has been involved in several sea rescues; **appareil de s.** life-saving *or* rescue apparatus; **ceinture de s.** life belt; **gilet de s.** life jacket; **bouée de s.** life buoy; **canot** *ou* **embarcation de s.** lifeboat; **échelle de s.** fire escape; *Fig* **le s. d'une entreprise** the rescue of a company **2** *(d'un navire, de marchandises)* salvage

sauveteur [sovtœr] NM rescuer

ADJ M **bateau s.** lifeboat; **chien s.** rescue dog

sauvette (à la) [alasovɛt] ADV *(pour ne pas être vu)* furtively, on the sly; *(à la hâte)* in a hurry *ou* rush; **vendre à la s.** *(illégalement)* to peddle (illicitly) on the streets; **marchand à la s.** (illicit) street vendor

sauveur [sovœr] NM saviour, *Am* savior

SAV [ɛsave] NM *(abrév* **service après-vente)** after-sales service

savamment [savamã] ADV **1** *(avec érudition)* learnedly; **elle expose s. ses connaissances** she presents her knowledge in a learned manner **2** *(en connaissance de cause)* knowingly; **j'en parle s.** I know what I'm talking about **3** *(habilement)* cleverly, skilfully, *Am* skillfully; **elle sait s. convaincre son monde** she's quite adept at convincing people

savane [savan] NF **1** *Géog* savanna(h) **2** *Can (marécage)* swamp

savant, -ante [savã, -ãt] ADJ **1** *(érudit) (personne)* erudite, scholarly; *(bien informé)* knowledgeable (**en** about); *(texte)* scholarly, learned; *(mot, terme)* specialist, technical **2** *(habile)* clever, skilful, *Am* skillful; **s. calcul** clever calculation **3 chien s.** performing dog

N *(scientifique)* scientist; *(érudit)* scholar

savarin [savarɛ̃] NM *Culin* savarin

savate [savat] NF **1** *Fam (pantoufle)* slipper; **être en savates** to be in one's slippers; *Vieilli* **traîner la s.** *(être pauvre)* to be down at heel **2** *Fam (maladroit)* clumsy oaf; **comme une s.** abominably, atrociously **3** *Sport* kick boxing **4** *Tech* sole (plate)

savater [savate] VT *Fam* to kick, to boot

saveur [savœr] NF **1** *(de vin, fruit etc)* taste, flavour, *Am* flavor; **sans s.** tasteless, insipid **2** *Fig (de remarque, récit etc)* spice, pungency

Savoie [savwa] NF Savoy; *Culin* **biscuit de S.** sponge cake

SAVOIR¹ [savwar] *(prp* sachant; *pp* su; *pr ind* je sais, il sait, n. savons, ils savent; *pr sub* je sache, n. sachions, ils sachent; *imp* sache, sachons, sachez; *impf* je savais; *p hist* je sus; *fu* je saurai) VTI **1** *(avoir connaissance de)* to know; **s. qch par cœur** to know sth by heart; **s. l'anglais** to know English; *Litt* **s. le chemin** to know the way; **tu sais la nouvelle?** have you heard the news *ou* the latest?; **je n'en sais rien** I don't know anything about it, I know nothing about it; *(je n'y connais rien)* I don't know; **je n'en sais trop rien** I'm not (very) sure; **en s. trop** to know too much; **qu'est-ce j'en sais?** what do I know?; **comment le saurais-je?** how should I know?; **il paraît que tu as des projets, peut-on s.?** it seems you have plans, may one know what they are?; **tu crois qu'il viendra? – va (donc) s.** do you think he'll come? – who knows?; **saura-t-on jamais?** will we ever know?; **qu'en savez-vous?** what do you know about it?; **il sera peut-être là, qui sait?** perhaps he'll be there, who knows?; *Fam* **est-ce que je sais(, moi)?** I haven't a clue!, don't ask me!; **je ne veux pas (le) s.** I don't want to know; **je voudrais bien s. pourquoi** I'd like to know why, I wonder why; **il n'a rien voulu s.** he wouldn't listen, he didn't want to know; *Litt* **je ne sais** I do not know; **il en sait des choses** *ou* **plus d'une** he knows a thing or two; **reste à s. si ...** it remains to be seen whether *or* if ...; **la question est de s. si elle viendra** the question is whether she will come; **je crois s. qu'il est ici** I understand *or* believe he is here; **faire s. qch à qn** to tell sb sth, to let sb know about sth, to inform sb of sth; **vous auriez dû le lui faire s.** you should have told him, you should have let him know; **je ne suis pas content, et je vais le lui faire s.** I'm not happy and I'll tell him so *or* I'll let him know it; **je le sais par ma sœur** I heard about it from my sister; **(à) s.** that is (to say), namely, i.e.; **pas que je sache** not to my knowledge, not that I know of; **(à ce) que je sache** as *or* so far as I know; **(pour) autant que je sache** as far as I know; **pour autant que je sache, il pourrait très bien être au Canada** he could be in Canada for all I know; **on ne sait jamais** you never know, you never can tell; **si jeunesse savait!** youth is wasted on the young; **si**

j'avais su if I had known, had I known; **des parents que je sais venir de Londres** relatives who I know come from London; **je ne sais (pas) où les trouver** I don't know where to find them; **je ne sais qui de ses amis** some friend or other of his/hers; **elle a mangé je ne sais quoi et ça l'a rendue malade** she's eaten something or other that's made her ill; **je ne sais quelle maladie/quel problème** some illness/problem or other; **il y a je ne sais combien de temps** ages ago, goodness knows how long ago; **des robes, des chapeaux, des gants, que sais-je (encore)?** dresses, hats, gloves, and what have you *or* and goodness knows what else

2 *(être conscient de)* to know; **je ne savais pas cela** I didn't know that, I wasn't aware of that; **je le sais bien!** I know!, I realize that!; **elle est jolie et elle le sait bien** she's pretty, and she knows it *or* and doesn't she know it!; **je ne le savais pas malade** I didn't know he was ill; **ce n'est pas facile, tu sais!** it isn't easy, you know!; **sans le s.** without realizing *or* knowing it, without being aware of it; *Litt (in first person only)* **je ne sache pas qu'on vous ait invité** I am not aware that you have been invited

3 *Litt (connaître) (personne)* to know (of); **je sais un bon horloger** I know (of) a good watchmaker; *Péj* **avec la fille que vous savez** with you know who; *Péj* **c'est encore une lettre de qui vous savez** it's another letter from you know whom

4 *(être certain de)* to know; **il sait ce qu'il veut** he knows what he wants; **ne s. que faire/que dire** not to know *or* to be at a loss what to do/to say; **je ne sais que penser** I don't know what to think; **sachez que ...** be advised that ..., please note that ...; **ne pas s. où se mettre** not to know where to put oneself

5 *(être capable de)* **s. faire qch** to be able to do sth, to know how to do sth; **savez-vous nager?** can you swim?, do you know how to swim?; **s. écouter** to be a good listener; **il faut s. être patient** you have to learn to be patient; **je ne saurais (pas) vous conseiller** I wouldn't know what advice to give you, I wouldn't know how to advise you; **on ne saurait se souvenir de tout** one cannot expect to remember everything; **on ne saurait trop insister sur ce point** this point cannot be emphasized enough; **je sais y aller** I know how to get there; **je crois que je saurai le faire** I think I can manage it; *Fam* **elle sait y faire avec les enfants** she's good with children; *Fam* **s. s'y prendre avec qn** to know how to handle sb; **je ne saurais guère vous le dire** I'm afraid I couldn't really tell you SEE GRAMMAR A58; B40

6 *(locutions)* **un je ne sais quoi de déplaisant** something vaguely unpleasant; **c'est Monsieur/Madame je sais tout** he's/she's a real know-all *or* know-it-all; **arrête de faire ton Monsieur je sais tout** stop being such a know-all *or* know-it-all; **il a des amis, Dieu sait** Lord *ou* God knows, he has plenty of friends; **Dieu sait comment** Lord *ou* God (only) knows how; **Dieu sait si je le lui ai répété** God (only) knows how often I've told him

VPR **se savoir je me savais très malade** I knew I was very ill; **ça se saura vite** it'll soon get out, everyone will know about it soon; **ça se saurait si c'était possible** if it was possible, everyone would know about it

savoir² NM knowledge, learning; **homme d'un grand s.** very knowledgeable *or* learned man, man of great learning

savoir-faire NM INV expertise, know-how

savoir-vivre NM INV savoir-vivre, good manners; **manquer de s.** to have no manners

savon [savɔ̃] NM soap; **(pain de) s.** bar or cake of soap; **s. de toilette** toilet soap; **s. liquide/doux** liquid/mild soap; **s. en paillettes** soap flakes; **pierre de s.** soapstone, Spéc steatite; **tu devrais mettre cette nappe au s.** you should rub the stains on this tablecloth with soap (before putting it into the washing machine); **ça partira avec du s.** it will come off or out with soap, soap will take it off or out; Fam **passer un s. à qn** to give sb a telling-off, to give somebody a roasting ►► **s. à barbe** shaving soap; **s. de Marseille** = household soap, used for washing and laundry

savonnage [savɔnaʒ] NM (de vêtements, mains etc) soaping

savonner [savɔne] VT **1** (mains, vêtement etc) to soap; (en faisant mousser) to lather; **s. le dos à qn** to soap sb's back; Fig **s. la planche à qn** to make things difficult for sb; Fam Vieilli **s. la tête à qn** to give sb a dressing-down; Aut **piste savonnée** skidpan **2** Tech (verre) to rub, to grind
VPR **se savonner** to soap oneself; **se s. les mains** to soap one's hands

savonnerie [savɔnri] NF (usine) soap factory; (fabrication) soap manufacture

savonnette [savɔnɛt] NF bar of (toilet) soap

savonneux, -euse [savɔnø, -øz] ADJ soapy

savourer [savure] VT (plat, moment, vengeance etc) to savour or Am to savor, to relish, to enjoy

savoureusement [savurøzmɑ̃] ADV with relish

savoureux, -euse [savurø, -øz] ADJ (plat) tasty; (vin) full-flavoured, Am full-flavored; Fig (récit, détails) spicy, juicy

savoyard, -arde [savwajar, -ard] ADJ Savoyard
N **S.** Savoyard

Saxe [saks] NF Saxony; **porcelaine de S.** Dresden china

saxe [saks] NM (matière) Dresden china; (objet) piece of Dresden china

saxhorn [saksɔrn] NM Mus saxhorn; **s. basse** euphonium

saxifrage [saksifraʒ] NF saxifrage

saxo [sakso] Fam NM (instrument) sax
N (musicien) sax player

saxon, -onne [saksɔ̃, -ɔn] ADJ Saxon
NM Ling Saxon
N **S.** Saxon

saxophone [saksɔfɔn] NM Mus saxophone

saxophoniste [saksɔfɔnist] N Mus saxophonist

saynète [sɛnɛt] NF Théâtre playlet, comic sketch

SBF [ɛsbeef] NF (abrév Société des bourses françaises) = company which runs the Paris Stock Exchange, Br ≃ LSE, Am ≃ NYSE; **le S.120** = broad-based French stock exchange index

sbire [sbir] NM Péj (homme de main) henchman

SCA [ɛssea] NF (abrév société en commandite par actions) partnership limited by shares

scabieux, -ieuse [skabjø, -jøz] ADJ scabby
NF Bot **scabieuse** scabious

scabreux, -euse [skabrø, -øz] ADJ **1** (indécent) obscene, indecent; Litt scabrous **2** Litt (dangereux) risky, tricky

scalaire¹ [skalɛr] NM (poisson) angel fish

scalaire² ADJ, NM Math scalar

scalène [skalɛn] ADJ Géom, Anat scalene

scalp [skalp] NM (trophée) scalp; (action de scalper) scalping

scalpel [skalpɛl] NM Chir scalpel

scalper [skalpe] VT to scalp

scandale [skɑ̃dal] NM (politique, financier etc) scandal; **faire (un) s., causer un s.** to create or cause a scandal; **il a fait (tout) un s. parce que …** he made a (tremendous) scene or kicked up a (tremendous) fuss because …; **crier au s.** to make or create a great fuss; **au grand s. de ses parents** to the great indignation of his/her parents; **c'est un s.!** it's a scandal!, it's scandalous!

scandaleusement [skɑ̃daløzmɑ̃] ADV scandalously, outrageously; **vivre s.** to lead a scandalous life

scandaleux, -euse [skɑ̃dalø, -øz] ADJ scandalous, outrageous

scandaliser [skɑ̃dalize] VT to scandalize, to shock
VPR **se scandaliser** to be scandalized or shocked (**de** by); **il ne se scandalise de rien** nothing shocks him

scander [skɑ̃de] VT (vers) to scan; (slogan) to chant; Mus (phrase musicale) to mark, to stress

scandinave [skɑ̃dinav] ADJ Scandinavian
N **S.** Scandinavian

Scandinavie [skɑ̃dinavi] NF Scandinavia

scandium [skɑ̃djɔm] NM Chimie scandium

scanner¹ [skanɛr] NM **1** Ordinat scanner; **insérer qch par s., capturer qch au s.** to scan sth in; **passer qch au s.** to scan sth; **s. à main** hand-held scanner; **s. optique** optical scanner; **s. à plat** flatbed scanner **2** Méd scanner; **faire un s.** (d'un médecin) to carry out or do a scan; (d'un patient) to have a scan; **on lui a fait un s.** he was given a scan

scanner² [skane] VT Ordinat to scan

scannérisation [skanerizasjɔ̃] NF Ordinat scanning

scanneur [skanœr] NM Ordinat, TV scanner; Ordinat **s. optique** optical scanner; Ordinat **s. à main** handheld scanner; Ordinat **s. à plat** flatbed scanner

scanographie [skanɔgrafi] NF Méd **1** (science) scanning **2** (cliché) scan

scansion [skɑ̃sjɔ̃] NF Littér scansion, scanning

scaphandre [skafɑ̃dr] NM **1** Naut diving suit; **s. autonome** aqualung, scuba **2** Astronaut space suit

scaphandrier [skafɑ̃drije] NM diver

scaphoïde [skafɔid] ADJ, NM Anat, Biol scaphoid

scapulaire [skapylɛr] NM Rel scapular
ADJ scapular

scarabée [skarabe] NM scarab

scare [skar] NM (poisson) parrot fish, scar

scarificateur [skarifikatœr] NM Agr scarifier; Chir scarificator

scarifier [skarifje] VT (impf, pr sub n. scarifiions, v. scarifiiez) Agr, Chir to scarify

scarlatine [skarlatin] NF Méd scarlet fever, Spéc scarlatina; **avoir la s.** to have scarlet fever

scarole [skarɔl] NF Bot endive

scat [skat] NM Mus scat

scato [skato] ADJ INV Fam dirty; **plaisanterie s.** dirty joke; **humour s.** lavatorial humour

scatologie [skatɔlɔʒi] NF scatology

scatologique [skatɔlɔʒik] ADJ (littérature, plaisanterie) scatological

scatophage [skatɔfaʒ] ADJ (poisson, insecte) scatophagous
NM dung fly, Spéc scatophage

sceau, pl **sceaux** [so] NM seal; **S. de l'État** State seal; **s. privé** private seal; **mettre** ou **apposer son s. à un document** to affix one's seal to or put one's seal on a document; Fig **le s. du génie** the mark or stamp of genius; **sous le s. du secret** under the seal of secrecy; Bot **s. de Salomon** Solomon's seal

scélérat, -ate [selera, -at] Arch, Litt ADJ villainous, wicked
N villain, scoundrel

scellé [sele] ADJ sealed
NM Jur (official) seal; **mettre** ou **apposer/lever les scellés** to put on/remove the seals; **sous scellés** under seal

scellement [sɛlmɑ̃] NM Constr (d'un poteau etc dans la pierre, le béton) bedding, fixing

sceller [sele] VT **1** (document, sac etc) to seal; (ratifier) to ratify, to confirm; **s. un pacte** to set the seal on an agreement **2** Constr to bed, to fix (in); **s. une porte/fenêtre** to seal a door/a window

scénarimage [senarimaʒ] NM story-board

scénario [senarjo] NM Cin, TV scenario; (script) script, screenplay; **s. d'auteur** writer's script; Psy **s. à compléter** story completion; TV, Cin **s.-maquette** storyboard; **s. de répétition** rehearsal script; Fig scenario

scénariser [senarize] VT **1** (écrire le scénario de) to script, write the screenplay for **2** (donner la forme d'un scénario à) to adapt for the screen

scénariste [senarist] N Cin, TV scriptwriter, screenwriter; **s. (de réécriture)** script editor

scène [sɛn] NF **1** Théâtre (plateau) stage; **la s.** (le théâtre) the stage, the theatre or Am the theater; **entrer en s.** (d'un acteur) to appear, to come on; Fig to appear on the scene; **être en s.** (d'un acteur) to be on (stage); **en s. pour le un!** on stage for act one!, beginners please!; **porter qch à la s.** to adapt sth for the stage; **quitter la s.** to retire from the stage or from acting; **faire ses adieux à la s.** to make one's final appearance on stage; Fig **la s. politique/internationale** the political/international scene; Fig **le devant de la s.** the foreground; **occuper le devant de la s.** to hold centre stage; **s. tournante** revolving stage

2 (décor, action) scene; **changement de s.** change of scene; **le tableau représente une s. de chasse** the painting represents a hunting scene; **s. d'intérieur** interior scene; **s. de genre** genre painting; **une s. d'amour** a love scene; **acte II, s. trois** act two, scene three; Fig Hum **il m'a fait la grande s. du II** he put on an Oscar-winning performance; **la s. se passe au Moyen Âge** the action takes place in the Middle Ages, the scene or the action is set in the Middle Ages

3 (événement) scene; **revoir les scènes de sa jeunesse** to revisit the scenes of one's youth; **ce fut une s. pénible** it was a painful scene; **imagine la s.!** imagine or picture the scene!, just imagine or picture it!

4 Fam (dispute) scene; **il m'a fait une s.** he made a scene ►► **s. de ménage** domestic squabble; Psy **s. primitive** primal scene

scénique [senik] ADJ theatrical; **éclairage s.** stage or theatrical lighting; **indications scéniques** stage directions

scéniquement [senikmɑ̃] ADV theatrically

scénographe [senɔgraf] N **1** Beaux-Arts etc scenographer **2** Théâtre stage or theatre designer

scénographie [senɔgrafi] NF **1** Beaux-Arts etc scenography **2** Théâtre stage or theatre design

scepticisme [sɛptisism] NM scepticism, Am skepticism

sceptique [sɛptik] ADJ sceptical, sceptic, Am skeptic(al)
N sceptic, Am skeptic

sceptiquement [sɛptikmɑ̃] ADV Rare sceptically, Am skeptically

sceptre [sɛptr] NM sceptre, Am scepter; Fig **s. de fer** rod of iron

schako [ʃako] NM Mil shako

scheik [ʃɛk] NM sheik

schelem [ʃlɛm] NM *Cartes* slam; **petit/ grand s.** little/grand slam

schéma [ʃema] NM **1** *(graphique) (d'un moteur, d'une structure hiérarchique etc)* diagram, plan **2** *(esquisse) (d'un livre etc)* plan, outline; **s. directeur** master plan; **s. d'entreprise** organization chart; *Ordinat* **s. de clavier** keyboard map; **s. logique** logic diagram

schématique [ʃematik] ADJ **1** *(sous forme de dessin)* diagrammatic **2** *(sous forme de résumé)* schematic, simplified; *Péj* oversimplified

schématiquement [ʃematikmɑ̃] ADV schematically, diagrammatically; *(en gros)* in outline, in a simplified manner; **très s., voici ce que nous vous proposons** in very broad terms *or* very broadly speaking, this is what we propose

schématisation [ʃematizasjɔ̃] NF schematization, *Péj* over-simplification

schématiser [ʃematize] VT to schematize, *Péj* to oversimplify

schématisme [ʃematism] NM *Péj* oversimplification; *Phil* schematism

schème [ʃɛm] NM *Phil, Psy* schema; *Beaux-Arts etc* design

scherzando [skɛrtsando, skɛrdz-] ADV *Mus* scherzando

scherzo [skɛrtso, -dzo] *Mus* NM scherzo
ADV scherzando

schibboleth [ʃibɔlɛt] NM *Rare* shibboleth

schilling [ʃiliŋ] NM *Anciennement (monnaie autrichienne)* schilling

schismatique [ʃismatik] ADJ, N schismatic

schisme [ʃism] NM schism; **faire s.** to break away

schiste [ʃist] NM *Géol* schist, shale

schisteux, -euse [ʃistø, -øz] ADJ *Géol* schistose

schistosomiase [ʃistɔzomjaz] NF *Méd* bilharzia, schistosomiasis

schizogamie [skizɔgami] NF *Biol* schizogenesis

schizoïde [skizɔid] ADJ, N *Psy* schizoid

schizoïdie [skizɔidi] NF *Psy* schizoidism

schizoïdique [skizɔidik] ADJ *Psy* schizoid

schizophrène [skizɔfrɛn] ADJ, N *Psy* schizophrenic

schizophrénie [skizɔfreni] NF *Psy* schizophrenia

schizophrénique [skizɔfrenik] ADJ, N *Psy* schizophrenic

schizothymie [skizɔtimi] NF *Psy* schizothymia

schizothymique [skizɔtimik] ADJ *Psy* schizothymic

schlague [ʃlag] NF *Hist, Mil* flogging; *Fig Fam* **mener qn à la s.** to rule sb with a rod of iron

schlass¹ [ʃlas] ADJ INV *très Fam (épuisé)* knackered, shattered; *(soûl)* pissed, *Br* ratarsed

schlass² NM *très Fam (couteau)* blade

schlinguer [ʃlɛ̃ge] VI *Vulg* to stink, *Br* to pong

schlittage [ʃlitaʒ] NM (timber) sledging

schlitte [ʃlit] NF *(pour transporter le bois)* (timber) sledge

schlitter [ʃlite] VT *(bois)* to sledge

schlof [ʃlɔf] NM *Fam* bed, *Br* pit; **se mettre au s.** to hit the sack *or* the hay *or Am* the rack

schmilblick [ʃmilblik] NM *Fam* **faire avancer le s.** to make progress, to get somewhere; **tout ça, ça fait pas avancer le s.** that's not getting us any further forward

schnaps [ʃnaps] NM schnapps

schnauzer [ʃnawzɛr] NM *(chien)* schnauzer

schnock, schnoque [ʃnɔk] *Fam* ADJ *(fou)* crazy, bonkers; *(bête)* moronic
NM cretin, moron; **un vieux s.** an old fogey; **eh, du s.!** hey, you cretin *or* moron!

schnorchel, schnorkel [ʃnɔrkɛl] NM *(de sous-marin)* snorkel

schnouff [ʃnuf] NF *Arg (drogue)* dope, junk

schofar [ʃɔfar] NM *Rel* shofar, shophar

schuss [ʃus] NM *Ski* schuss; **descendre la piste en s.** *ou* **tout s.** to schuss down the slope

Schweppes® [ʃwɛps] NM tonic

SCI [ɛssei] NF *(abrév* **société de commerce international***)* international trading corporation

sciage [sjaʒ] NM sawing

sciatique [sjatik] ADJ *Anat (nerf)* sciatic
NM sciatic nerve
NF *Méd* sciatica

scie [si] NF **1** *(outil)* saw; **s. à bois** wood saw; **s. à métaux** hacksaw; **s. mécanique** *ou* **à main** hand saw; **s. circulaire** circular saw, *Am* buzz saw; **s. articulée, s. à chaîne(tte)** chain saw; **s. à chantourner** *(manuelle)* bowsaw, turning saw; *(mécanique)* jigsaw, scroll saw; **s. à découper, s. anglaise** *(manuelle)* fret saw; *(mécanique)* jigsaw; **en dents de s.** serrated; *Fig (évolution, progrès)* uneven; *Méd* **bruit de s.** rasping murmur **2** *Mus* **s. musicale** musical saw **3 (poisson) s.** sawfish **4** *Fam Vieilli (personne ennuyeuse)* bore

sciemment [sjamɑ̃] ADV knowingly, on purpose, wittingly

science [sjɑ̃s] NF **1** *(savoir)* knowledge, learning; *Fig* **il croit avoir la s. infuse** you can't tell him anything; **je n'ai pas la s. infuse** I can't be expected to know everything; *Fam* **étaler sa s.** to show off one's knowledge **2** *(domaine spécifique)* science; **la s. n'a pas de patrie** science knows no frontiers; **préparer une licence ès sciences** to be studying for a science degree; **homme de s.** scientist; **s. dure/molle** hard/soft science; **les sciences exactes** *ou* **pures** the exact sciences; **sciences physiques/naturelles/appliquées** physical/natural/applied science; **sciences économiques** economics; **sciences expérimentales** experimental science; **sciences humaines** ≃ social sciences; **les sciences occultes** the occult sciences; **sciences politiques** politics, political science; **sciences sociales** social sciences

science-fiction NF science fiction; **roman/film de s.** science fiction novel/film; *Fig Hum* **c'est de la s.!** it's unbelievable!

Sciences-Po [sjɑ̃spo] NF = grande école for political sciences

scientificité [sjɑ̃tifisite] NF scientific character

scientifique [sjɑ̃tifik] ADJ scientific
N scientist; **ce n'est pas un s.** he's not very scientifically-minded

scientifiquement [sjɑ̃tifikmɑ̃] ADV scientifically

scientisme [sjɑ̃tism] NM **1** *Phil* scientism **2** *Rel* Christian Science

scientiste [sjɑ̃tist] ADJ scientistic
N **1** *Phil* adept of scientism **2** *Rel* **s. chrétien(ne)** Christian Scientist

scientologie [sjɑ̃tɔlɔʒi] NF Scientology®

scientologue [sjɑ̃tɔlɔg] N Scientologist

scier¹ [sje] VT *(pr sub, impf n.* sciions, *v.* sciiez*)* *(bois, métal)* to saw; *(enlever) (branche etc)* to saw off; *Fam* **s. qn** *(étonner)* to dumbfound *or Br Fam* to gobsmack sb; *Fam* **j'étais scié de rire** I was doubled up with laughter; *Suisse Fam* **s. du bois** to snore like a pig

scier² VI *(à l'aviron)* to back water, to back the oars

scierie [siri] NF sawmill

scieur [sjœr] NM sawyer

scieuse [sjøz] NF mechanical saw

scille [sil] NF *Bot* scilla, squill; **s. maritime** sea onion

scinder [sɛ̃de] VT to divide, to split up *(en into)*; *Fin* **s. une société** to break up a company, to split a company
VPR **se scinder** to split up *(en into)*

scinque [sɛ̃k] NM *Zool* skink

scintigramme [sɛ̃tigram] NM *Méd* scintigram

scintigraphie [sɛ̃tigrafi] NF *Méd* scintigraphy

scintillant [sɛ̃tijɑ̃] ADJ *(bijoux, lumières etc)* sparkling, glittering; *(étoile)* twinkling; *(yeux)* sparkling, twinkling; *Fig (esprit, personnalité)* sparkling, scintillating
NM tinsel decoration(s)

scintillation [sɛ̃tijasjɔ̃] NF *Phys, Astron* scintillation

scintillement [sɛ̃tijmɑ̃] NM *(de bijou, lumière etc)* sparkling, glittering; *(d'étoile)* twinkling; *(des yeux)* sparkling; *Cin, TV* flicker(ing), shimmer

scintiller [sɛ̃tije] VI *(d'un bijou, d'une lumière etc)* to sparkle, to glitter; *(d'une étoile)* to twinkle; *(des yeux)* to sparkle; *Électron, TV, Cin* to flicker

scion [sjɔ̃] NM **1** *(pousse)* shoot; *(à greffer)* scion **2** *(d'une canne à pêche)* tip

scirpe [sirp] NM *Bot* bulrush

scissile [sisil] ADJ *Nucl (matériau)* fissionable

scission [sisjɔ̃] NF **1** *Pol etc* split, division; **faire s.** to split away *or* off, to secede; *Fin* **s. d'actifs** divestment of assets, hive-off of assets; **s. d'une entreprise** break-up of a company **2** *Chimie* scission, cleavage; *Nucl* fission, splitting; **s. nucléaire** nuclear fission

scissionniste [sisjɔnist] ADJ, N secessionist

scissipare [sisipar] ADJ *Biol* fissiparous

scissiparité [sisiparite] NF *Biol* schizogenesis, fissiparity

scissure [sisyr] NF *Anat* fissure

sciure [sjyr] NF **s. (de bois)** sawdust; **s. de marbre** marble dust

scléral, -ale, -aux, -ales [skleral, -o] ADJ *Anat* sclerotic

scléreux, -euse [sklerø, -øz] ADJ *Méd* sclerosed

sclérifié [sklerifje] ADJ *Biol (tégument etc)* sclerosed, hardened

sclérodermie [sklerɔdermi] NF *Méd* scleroderma

sclérogène [sklerɔʒɛn] ADJ *Méd* sclerogenic

scléroprotéine [sklerɔprotein] NF scleroprotein

sclérosant [sklerɔzɑ̃] ADJ *Méd* sclerosing; *Fig* ossifying

sclérose [skleroz] NF *Méd* sclerosis; *Fig* ossification; **s. vasculaire** *ou* **des artères** arteriosclerosis, hardening of the arteries; **s. en plaques** multiple sclerosis, MS

sclérosé [skleroze] ADJ *Méd* sclerosed; *Fig* hidebound, fossilized

scléroser [skleroze] VT *Méd* to sclerose
VPR **se scléroser** *Méd* to become sclerotic **2** *Fig* to become fossilized

sclérotique [sklerɔtik] NF *Anat (de l'œil)* sclerotic, sclera

scolaire [skɔlɛr] ADJ **1** *(résultats, réussite)* academic, scholastic; *(réforme, organisation)* educational; **vie s.** school life; **année s.** school *or* academic year; **enfant d'âge s.** child of school age; **frais scolaires** school fees; **livres scolaires** school books, text books **2** *Péj (esprit, mentalité)* bookish;

(style, discours) academic, schoolmasterish; *(peinture)* laboured, *Am* labored

scolairement [skɔlɛrmɑ̃] **ADV** *Péj (réciter, écrire)* in an academic or schoolmasterish way

scolarisable [skɔlarizabl] **ADJ** of school age

scolarisation [skɔlarizasjɔ̃] **NF** prolonga-tion de la s. raising of the school-leaving age; **je suis pour la s. des enfants à partir de l'âge de cinq ans** I'm in favour of children going to or starting school at the age of five; **la s. d'une région** equipping or providing an area with schools; **la s. des enfants** provi-ding education for children; **taux de s.** per-centage of children in full-time education

scolariser [skɔlarize] **VT** s. des enfants to provide education for children; **s. une ré-gion** to equip or provide an area with schools; **enfant scolarisé** child attending school

scolarité [skɔlarite] **NF** s. obligatoire compulsory schooling; **prolongation de la s.** raising of the school-leaving age; **j'ai eu une s. difficile** I had a difficult time at school; **s. à temps partiel** = day-release classes; **cer-tificat de s.** = certificate of attendance *(at school or university)*; **frais de s.** school fees

scolasticat [skɔlastika] **NM** theological training; *(établissement)* theological college

scolastique [skɔlastik] **ADJ** *(philosophie etc)* scholastic
  NM scholastic
  NF scholasticism

scoliaste [skɔljast] **NM** scholiast

scoliose [skɔljoz] **NF** *Méd* scoliosis, lateral curvature of the spine

scolopendre[1] [skɔlɔpɑ̃dr] **NF** *Zool* centi-pede, *Spéc* scolopendrid

scolopendre[2] **NF** *Bot* hart's-tongue, *Spéc* scolopendrium

sconse [skɔ̃s] **NM** skunk; *(fourrure)* skunk (fur)

scoop [skup] **NM 1** *Journ* scoop **2** *Fig Fam* **c'est un s.!** it's hot news!; *Iron* well I never!; **j'ai un s.!** I've got some hot news!; **ce n'est pas un s.!** it's not exactly headline news!

scooter [skutɛr] **NM** (motor) scooter; **s. des mers** jet-ski

scootériste [skuterist] **N** (motor) scooter ri-der, (motor) scooterist

scopie [skɔpi] **NF** *Méd Arg* radioscopy

scopolamine [skɔpɔlamin] **NF** *Chimie, Pharm* scopolamine, hyoscine

scorbut [skɔrbyt] **NM** *Méd* scurvy, *Spéc* scorbutus

scorbutique [skɔrbytik] **ADJ, N** *Méd* scorbutic

score [skɔr] **NM** *Sport* score; **s. électoral** share of the vote; **faire un bon/mauvais s.** to turn in a good/bad performance

scoriacé [skɔrjase] **ADJ** *Métal, Géol etc* slaggy

scorie [skɔri] **NF 1** *Métal* scories slag, cinders, scoria; *(de fer)* (iron) dross; *(de charbon)* clinker **2** *Géol* scories (volcaniques) scoria, volcanic slag **3** *Fig* scories dregs; **débarras-ser une philosophie de ses scories** to rid a philosophy of its dross

scorpène [skɔrpɛn] **NF** scorpion fish

scorpion [skɔrpjɔ̃] **NM 1** *Zool* scorpion; **s. aquatique** ou **d'eau** water scorpion; **s. de mer** scorpion fish **2** *Astron, Astrol* **le S.** Scor-pio; **être (du signe du) S.** to be (a) Scorpio

scorsonère [skɔrsɔnɛr], **scorzonère** [skɔrzɔnɛr] **NF** *Bot* black salsify, *Spéc* scorzonera

Scotch® [skɔtʃ] **NM** self-adhesive tape, *Br* ≃ Sellotape®, *Am* ≃ Scotchtape®

scotch *pl* **scotchs** *ou* **scotches** [skɔtʃ] **NM** scotch (whisky); **un double s.** a double scotch

---

scotché [skɔtʃe] **ADJ** *Fam* **1** *(stupéfait)* je suis resté s. I was staggered or Br gobsmacked **2** **être s. devant la télé** to be glued to theTV

scotcher [skɔtʃe] **VT 1** *(avec du ruban adhé-sif)* to tape, *Br* to sellotape, *Am* to scotch-tape; *Fig Fam* il est toujours scotché devant la télé he's always glued to the television **2** *Fam (stupéfaire)* to flabbergast, to knock sideways; **ça m'a vraiment scotché!** I was stag-gered or Br gobsmacked!

scotch-terrier, *pl* **scotch-terriers NM** Scotch terrier

scottish-terrier, *pl* **scottish-terriers** [skɔtiʃterje] **NM** Scotch terrier

scoumoune [skumun] **NF** *Arg* persistent bad luck; **avoir la s.** to be jinxed

scout [skut] **NM** (boy) scout
  ADJ **groupe/mouvement s.** scout group/movement; *Péj* il a des côtés un peu scouts he's a bit of a boy scout at heart

scoutisme [skutism] **NM** *(activité)* scouting; *(mouvement)* scout movement

SCPI [ɛspei] **NF** *(abrév* **société civile de pla-cement immobilier)** property investment company

Scrabble® [skrabl] **NM** Scrabble®; **jouer au S.** to play Scrabble®

scratch, *pl* **scratches** [skratʃ] *Sp* **NM** *(course)* scratch race; *(joueur)* scratch (player); **par-tir s.** to start (at) scratch
  ADJ **course s.** scratch race; **joueur s.** scratch (player)

scratcher [skratʃe] **VT** *Sport* to scratch
  VPR **se scratcher** *Fam* to go off the road; **il s'est scratché avec la moto de son frère à 150** he went off the road doing 150 on his brother's motorbike

scribe [skrib] **NM** *Antiq* scribe; *Vieilli Péj* pen-pusher

scribouillard, -arde [skribujar, -ard] **N** *Fam Péj* pen-pusher

script[1] [skript] **NM** *Fin* scrip

script[2] **NM 1** *(écriture)* printing; **écrire en s.** to print (one's letters); **écriture s.** printing **2** *Cin* (film) script

scripte [skript] **N** *Cin* continuity man, *f* conti-nuity girl, script girl

script-girl, *pl* **script-girls** [skriptgœrl] **NF** *Cin* continuity girl

scriptural, -ale, -aux, -ales [skriptyral, -o] **ADJ** scriptural; *Banque* **monnaie scriptu-rale** bank money

scrofulaire [skrɔfylɛr] **NF** *Bot* figwort

scrofule [skrɔfyl] **NF** *Méd* scrofula; *Arch* **les scrofules** scrofula; *Arch* the king's evil

scrofuleux, -euse [skrɔfylø, -øz] *Méd* **ADJ** scrofulous
  N scrofulous person

scrotum [skrɔtɔm] **NM** *Anat* scrotum

scrupule [skrypyl] **NM 1** scruple (**sur** about); **sans scrupules** *(adj)* unscrupulous; *(adv)* un-scrupulously; **je n'aurai aucun s. à le lui dire** I'll have no scruples about telling him/her so; **se faire (un) s. de faire qch, avoir des scrupules à faire qch** to have scruples about doing sth; **il ne se fait pas s. d'emprunter à la caisse** he has no scruples about borrowing from the till; **exact jusqu'au s.** scrupulously exact **2** *Arch (unité de poids)* scruple

scrupuleusement [skrypyløzmɑ̃] **ADV** scrupulously

scrupuleux, -euse [skrypylø, -øz] **ADJ** scrupulous (**sur** about); **à faire qch** in doing sth); **peu s.** unscrupulous

scrutateur, -trice [skrytatœr, -tris] **ADJ** *Litt (esprit, regard)* searching
  N *(d'un scrutin)* teller

scruter [skryte] **VT** to examine, to scrutinize; *(horizon, paysage)* to scan

---

scrutin [skrytɛ̃] **NM 1** *(élection)* poll; **s. d'ar-rondissement** = constituency poll; **s. majori-taire** first-past-the-post system; **s. majoritaire uninominal** first-past-the-post system *(voting for a single candidate)*; **s. ma-joritaire plurinominal** first-past-the-post system *(voting for as many candidates/par-ties as there are seats)*; **s. secret** secret vote or ballot; **s. plurinominal** = system of voting for more than one candidate; **s. proportion-nel** ou **de liste** = system of voting by propor-tional representation or by lists; **s. uninominal** = system of voting for a single candidate **2** *(vote)* ballot; **tour de s.** ballot, round (of voting); **il a été élu au premier tour de s.** he was elected in the first round of voting or in the first ballot; **s. de ballotage** second ballot; **dépouiller le s.** to count the votes or ballots **3** *(dans une assemblée)* vo-ting; *Br Parl* division; **procéder au s.** to take the vote; *Br Parl* to divide; **demander le s.** to ask for a count; **projet adopté sans s.** bill passed without a vote

SCS [ɛsseɛs] **NF** *(abrév* **société en comman-dite simple)** limited partnership

SCSI [ɛsseɛsi] **NF** *(abrév* **small computer sys-tems interface)** SCSI; **adresse S.** SCSI ad-dress; **carte S.** SCSI card; **chaîne S.** SCSI chain

SCT [ɛssete] **NM** *(abrév* **syndrome de choc toxique)** TSS

scull [skyl, skœl] **NM** *Sport, Naut* scull; *(acti-vité)* sculling

sculpter [skylte] **VT** to sculpt, to sculpture; *(dans du bois)* to carve (**dans** in, out of); **bois sculpté** carved wood
  VI to sculpt, to (do) sculpture

sculpteur [skyltœr] **NM** sculptor; **femme s.** woman sculptor, sculptress; **s. sur bois** woodcarver

sculptural, -ale, -aux, -ales [skyltyral, -o] **ADJ** *(art)* sculptural; *(silhouette, beauté)* statuesque

sculpture [skyltyr] **NF 1** *(œuvre, art)* sculp-ture; **s. sur bois** woodcarving; **faire de la s.** to sculpt, to (do) sculpture **2** *(d'un pneu)* tread

scutellaire [skytelɛr] **NF** *Bot* skull cap, *Spéc* scutellaria

scythe [sit] **ADJ** Scythian
  N S. Scythian

Scythie [siti] **NF** Scythia

SDF [ɛsdeɛf] **N** *Admin (abrév* **sans domicile fixe)** of no fixed abode; **un S.** a person of no fixed abode; *(sans abri)* a homeless person; **les S.** *(sans abri)* the homeless

SDN [ɛsdeɛn] **NF** *abrév* **Société des Nations**

SE [s(ə)] **PRON (s'** before vowel or mute h) **1** *(réfléchi) (complément direct)* himself; *(sujet féminin)* herself; *(non humain)* itself; *(in-défini)* oneself, *Am* himself; *(pl)* themselves; *(complément indirect)* to himself/herself/it-self/oneself/themselves; **se flatter** to flatter oneself; **il se rase** he's shaving; **elle s'est coupée au doigt** ou **s'est coupé le doigt** she has cut her finger; **il se parle (à lui-même)** he's talking to himself; **il s'est fait mal** he hurt himself; **il se couche tard** he goes to bed late; **fais se laver les mains à cet enfant** make that child wash his hands SEE GRAMMAR A29–30; B28–9

2 *(réciproque) (complément direct)* each other, one another; *(complément indirect)* to each other, to one another; **se nuire (l'un à l'autre)** to hurt each other or one another; **ils/elles se parlent** they talk to each other or one another; **il est dur de se quitter** it is hard to part

3 *(passif)* **cet article se vend partout** this article is sold or is on sale everywhere; **la porte s'est ouverte** the door opened; **ça ne**

se fait pas you don't do that, it's not the done thing; **ça se mange froid** it's eaten cold, you eat it cold

4 *(avec v impers)* **il se peut qu'elle vienne** (it's possible that) she might come; **comment se fait-il que …?** how is it that …?

séance [seɑ̃s] NF **1** *(réunion) (d'une assemblée etc)* sitting, session, meeting; **être en s., tenir s.** to be sitting *or* in session; **la s. s'ouvrira/sera levée à huit heures** the meeting will open/adjourn at eight o'clock; **je déclare la s. ouverte** I declare the meeting open; **en s. publique** at an open meeting; *Jur* in open court; *Bourse* **s. boursière** trading session; **s. de concertation** policy meeting; **s. d'information** briefing (session); **s. plénière** plenary (session); **s. de spiritisme** seance

2 *Cin* performance, showing; **s. à 19h10, film à 19h30** programme 7.10, film starts 7.30; **s. privée** private showing

3 *(période)* session; **faire une longue s. à table** to sit a long time over one's meal; *Méd* **traitement de trois séances** course of three treatments; **s. de travail/d'entraînement** working/training session; **s. de photo** photocall, photo opportunity; **s. de pose** sitting; *Méd* **s. de rééducation** physiotherapy session; *TV* **à la s.** *(film, programme)* pay-per-view **4 s. tenante** straight away, at once **5** *Fam Péj (scène)* performance; **il nous a fait une s. de larmes** he turned on the waterworks

séancier [seɑ̃sje] NM *(parlementaire)* parliamentary reporter

séant [seɑ̃] ADJ *Arch, Litt (flatteur)* becoming (à to); *(convenable)* fitting; **il ne serait pas s. de se contredire** it would not be fitting to contradict each other
▪ NM *Litt, Hum* **se mettre sur son s.** *(au lit etc)* to sit up; **être sur son s.** to be in a sitting position; **tomber sur son s.** to sit down with a bump

seau, *pl* **seaux** [so] NM bucket, pail; *(contenu)* bucket(ful), pail(ful); **s. à glace** *ou* **à rafraîchir** ice bucket; **s. à incendie** fire bucket; **s. à charbon** coal scuttle; **s. à champagne** champagne bucket; *Fam* **il pleut à seaux** it's pouring down, *Br* it's bucketing down

sébacé [sebase] ADJ *(glande)* sebaceous

sébile [sebil] NF (begging) bowl

séborrhée [sebɔre] NF *Méd* seborrhoea, *Am* seborrhea

sébum [sebɔm] NM *Anat* sebum

SEC, SÈCHE [sɛk, sɛʃ]

ADJ dry **1, 3** ▪ dried **1** ▪ lean **2** ▪ sharp **3** ▪ curt **3**	
ADV a lot **1** ▪ sharply **2**	

ADJ **1** *(temps, saison, sol, gorge, peau, vin, toux etc)* dry; *(morue, fruit etc)* dried; *(bois, cigare)* seasoned, matured; **regarder d'un œil s.** to look on dry-eyed; **il avait la gorge sèche** *(il avait soif)* his throat was dry, he was dry *or* parched; *(il avait peur)* his throat was dry; **mettre qn au pain s. et à l'eau** to put sb on bread and water; **mur de pierres sèches** drystone wall; *Aut* **être en panne sèche** to have run out of petrol *or Am* gas; **traverser un torrent à pied s.** to cross a torrent without getting one's feet *or* shoes wet; **s. comme une allumette** bone dry; **ne plus avoir un fil de s.** to be soaked to the skin; **régime s.** *(sans boisson)* alcohol-free diet; **pays secs** *(sans boisson)* dry countries, prohibitionist countries; **perte sèche** dead loss; *Fam* **en cinq s.** in no time at all, in two shakes (of a lamb's tail); *Fam* **je l'ai s.!** *(j'ai soif)* I'm dry *or* parched!; *Fig* am I annoyed!

2 *(maigre) (personne)* spare, lean; *(cheval)* lean; **s. et nerveux** wiry; **s. comme un coup de trique** as thin as a rake

3 *(sans tendresse) (remarque, réponse)* sharp, curt; *(ton)* incisive; *(coup)* sharp; *(cœur)* cold, unfeeling; *(récit, style)* dry, bald; **il est très s. au téléphone** he's very curt on the phone; **casser qch d'un coup s.** to snap sth; **frapper à la porte d'un coup s.** to rap on the door; **arracher un pansement d'un coup s.** to rip a plaster off; **faire un accueil très s. à qn** to give sb a very cool reception
▪ ADV **1 boire s.** *(beaucoup)* to drink a lot, to be a heavy drinker; **il boit toujours son whisky s.** he always drinks his whisky neat *or* straight

2 *(rudement)* hard, sharply; **la voiture a viré très s.** the car swung round sharply; *Aut* **démarrer s.** to shoot off, to tear off; *Fam* **ils ont dérouillé s. pendant la guerre** they went through total hell during the war

3 à s. dry; *(asséché)* dried up; *Fam (sans argent)* hard up, broke; **mettre à s.** *(marais etc)* to drain; *Fig (personne)* to clean out; **nettoyage à s.** dry cleaning; **navire à s.** *ou* **au s.** ship aground *or* high and dry; **filer** *ou* **courir ou fuir à s. (de toile)** *(d'un bateau)* to run under bare poles

4 *Fam* **aussi s.** straight away, right away, at once
▪ NM dryness; **tenir au s.** keep in a dry place
▪ NF *Arg* **sèche** *(cigarette)* fag, *Am* butt

sécable [sekabl] ADJ divisible

SECAM [sekam] ADJ, NM *TV (abrév* **séquentiel couleur à mémoire)** SECAM

sécant, -ante [sekɑ̃, -ɑ̃t] *Math* ADJ *(ligne, surface)* secant, cutting
▪ NF **sécante** secant

sécateur [sekatœr] NM pruning shears, *Br* secateurs

sécession [sesesjɔ̃] NF secession; **faire s.** to secede (**de** from)

sécessionniste [sesesjɔnist] ADJ, N secessionist

séchage [seʃaʒ] NM *(du foin, des vêtements, d'une surface peinte etc)* drying; *(du bois)* seasoning

sèche-cheveux [sɛʃʃəvø] NM INV hair dryer

sèche-linge [sɛʃlɛ̃ʒ] NM INV *(appareil)* tumble dryer; *(armoire)* airing cupboard

sèche-mains [sɛʃmɛ̃] NM INV (hot-air) hand dryer

sèchement [sɛʃmɑ̃] ADV **1** *(avec dureté) (parler, répondre etc)* curtly, sharply; *(taper)* sharply **2** *(sans fioritures) (écrire, traiter un sujet etc)* drily, baldly

sécher [seʃe] *(je sèche, n. séchons; je sécherai)* VT *(vêtements, sol, mains, encre, poisson, etc)* to dry; *(rivière etc)* to dry up; **le vent sèche la peau** wind dries (out) the skin; **s. ses larmes** to dry one's tears; *Fam* **s. un verre** *(le vider)* to drain a glass; *Scol etc Fam* **s. un cours** to skip *or* cut a class
▪ VI **1** *(de vêtements, de sols, de surfaces etc)* to dry; **faire s. du bois** to dry *or* season wood; **faire s. du linge** to dry clothes; **mettre du linge à s.** to put clothes out to dry; **laisser s. les peintures** to leave the paintwork to dry; *Bot, Fig* **s. sur pied** to wilt; *Litt* **s. d'impatience/d'ennui** to be consumed with impatience/boredom **2** *Fam (ne pas aller en classe)* to bunk off, *Am* to play hookey **3** *Fam (ne pas connaître la réponse)* to be stumped; *(ne plus savoir quoi dire)* to dry up
▪ VPR **se sécher** to dry oneself

sécheresse [seʃrɛs, se-] NF **1** *(de l'air, du sol, de la peau, de la gorge etc)* dryness **2** *(absence de pluie)* drought **3** *(des manières etc)* curtness; *(du cœur)* coldness, unfeelingness; *(du style)* dryness, baldness; **parler avec s.** to speak curtly

sécherie [seʃri, se-] NF *(appareil)* drying machine, dryer; *(lieu)* drying area

sécheur [seʃœr] NM *Tech* drying machine, dryer

séchoir [seʃwar] NM **1** *(appareil)* dryer; **s. (à cheveux)** hair dryer; *Ind* **s. à vapeur** steam dryer **2** *(dispositif pliant)* **s. (à linge)** clotheshorse **3** *Tech (lieu)* drying area; **s. à houblon** oast house

second, -onde [səgɔ̃, -ɔ̃d] ADJ **1** second; *Théâtre (rôle)* supporting, minor; **au s. étage** on the second *or Am* third floor; **une seconde fois** a second time; **en s. lieu** in the second place, secondly; **seconde nature** second nature (**chez qn** with sb); **de seconde main** secondhand; **de s. ordre** *ou* **choix** second-rate; *Fam* **ça passe en s.** that comes second, that takes second place; **votre ami est un s. Sherlock Holmes** your friend is another *or* a second Sherlock Holmes; **donner un s. souffle à l'économie** to give a new lease of life to *or* to revitalize the economy; *Sport, Fig* **trouver son s. souffle** to get one's second wind; **le don de seconde vue** the gift of second sight; *Mus* **les seconds violons** the second violins; *Gram* **la seconde personne du singulier** the second person singular; *Rail* **seconde classe** second class; **voyager en seconde classe** to travel second-class; *Jur* **signer en s.** *(d'un notaire)* to countersign; *Sport* **prendre la seconde place** to come second, to take second place; *Phil etc* **causes secondes** second causes; *Bourse* **s. marché** unlisted securities market, USM; *TV, Cin* **s. passage** repeat

2 *Méd* **état s.** *(d'un somnambule)* semi-conscious state; *Fig* **être dans un état s.** to be in a trance *or* a daze

3 *Naut* **commandant** *ou* **officier en s.** executive officer; **commander en s.** to be second in command
▪ NM **1** *(assistant)* principal assistant; *Mil Fam* second in command; *Naut* first mate; *(de duelliste)* second; **s. (de cuisine)** second cook, sous chef; *TV, Cin* **s. assistant** best boy **2** *(étage)* second *or Am* third floor; **habiter au s.** to live on the second *or Am* third floor; **les voisins du s.** the neighbours on the second *or Am* third floor
▪ NF **seconde** *Typ* second proof; *Aut* second (gear); *Aut* **passer en seconde** to change *or* go (up/down) into second; *Rail etc* **voyager en seconde** to travel second-class; **billet de seconde** second-class ticket; *Scol* **(classe de) seconde** ≃ fifth form, *Am* ≃ tenth grade; **élève de seconde** ≃ fifth-former, *Am* ≃ tenth-grader; *Mus* **seconde majeure/mineure** major/minor second
▪ N second; *Sport* **finir bon s.** to finish a good second; **la seconde est française** *(dans une compétition)* the competitor in second place is French; **mon s.** *(enfant)* my second child

secondaire [səgɔ̃dɛr] ADJ **1** *Scol* secondary; **établissement d'enseignement s.** secondary school **2** *(peu important)* secondary; **il faut en parler, mais c'est s.** we must talk about it, but it's of secondary importance; **effets secondaires d'un médicament** side effects of a medicine; *Rail* **voie s.** side track; *Ling* **accent s.** secondary accent, secondary stress; *Mus* **temps s.** off-beat; *Théâtre, Littér* **intrigue s.** sub-plot; **personnage/rôle s.** minor character/part **3** *Écon (secteur)* secondary; *Géol* **l'ère s.** the secondary era
▪ NM **1** *Élec* secondary winding; *Radio (du transformateur)* secondary **2 le s.** *Géol* the secondary era; *Écon* the secondary sector

secondairement [səgɔ̃dɛrmɑ̃] ADV secondarily

seconde [səgɔ̃d] NF *(du temps, d'un arc de cercle, d'un angle)* second; **aiguille des secondes** *(d'une montre)* second hand; **j'en ai pour une s.** I'll only be a second *or* moment;

je reviens dans une s.! I'll be back in a second!, I'll be right back!; **(attendez) une s.!** just a second!, just a moment!; **en un quart** *ou* **une fraction de s., en moins d'une s.** in no time at all

secondement [səɡɔ̃dmɑ̃] ADV secondly, in the second place

seconder [səɡɔ̃de] VT **1** *(personne)* to second, to back up, to support, to assist **2** *(intérêts, projets etc)* to forward, to further, to promote

secoué [səkwe] ADJ *Fam (fou)* off one's nut *or* rocker

secouement [səkumɑ̃] NM shaking

secouer [səkwe] VT **1** *(arbre, tête etc)* to shake; *(coussin, oreiller)* to plump up, to shake up; *(vêtements, tapis)* to shake (out); *(d'un choc, d'une maladie, de nouvelles etc) (personne)* to shake (up); *(du vent) (bateau)* to buffet; **de grands spasmes secouaient son corps tout entier** violent spasms shook his/her whole body; **nous avons été secoués pendant la traversée** we were shaken about during the crossing, we had a rough crossing; **il faut la s.** *(elle est déprimée)* we have to shake her out of it; *Fam* **s. (les puces à) qn** *(réprimander)* to tell sb off; *(pousser à agir)* to shake sb up; **s. qn/qch comme un prunier** to shake sb/sth vigorously
 2 *très Fam* **j'en ai rien à s.** I don't give a damn *or Br* toss
 3 *(se débarrasser de) (poussière, joug etc)* to shake off
 VI **voiture qui secoue** bumpy car; **ça secoue** *(dans un avion/train etc)* it's bumpy; *(dans un bateau)* it's rough
 VPR **se secouer** *(agir)* to shake oneself *or* snap out of it, to pull oneself together

secourable [səkurabl] ADJ helpful, willing to help; **main s.** helping hand; **peu s.** unhelpful

secourir [səkurir] VT *(conj like* **courir***)* to help, to assist, to aid

secourisme [səkurism] NM *Méd* first aid; **brevet de s.** first-aid certificate

secouriste [səkurist] N first-aid worker

secours [səkur] NM help, assistance, aid; *(financier, matériel)* aid; *Mil* relief; **crier au s.** to call for help; **appel au s.** call for help; **au s.!** help!; *Méd* **premiers s.** first aid; **s. en montagne** mountain rescue; **les s. vont arriver** help will arrive; *Mil* relief will arrive; **porter** *ou* **prêter (du) s. à qn** to give sb help *or* assistance, to help *or* assist sb; **demander (du) s.** to ask for help *or* assistance; **aller** *ou* **se porter au s. de qn** to go to sb's assistance; *Mil* **se porter au s. d'un bataillon** to go in support of a battalion; **cela m'a été d'un grand s.** it has been a great help (to me); **puis-je vous être d'aucun s.?** can I be of (some) help *or* (some) assistance?; **sa présence ne m'a été d'aucun s.** his/her presence was of no help (to me); *Ordinat* **de s.** *(copie, fichier etc)* backup; **boîte/trousse de s.** first-aid box/kit; **poste de s.** first-aid post; **caisse de s.** relief fund; **société de s. mutuels** friendly *or Am* benefit society; **sortie** *ou* **porte de s.** emergency exit; *Fig* **c'est sa seule porte de s.** it's his only way out; *Aut* **roue de s.** spare wheel; **éclairage de s.** emergency lighting (system); *Mil* **troupes de s., des s.** relief troops, relieving force; *Rail* **locomotive/train de s.** relief engine/train

secousse [səkus] NF shake; *(cahot)* jolt, bump; *Fig (morale)* shock; **se dégager d'une s.** to jerk *or* wrench *or* shake oneself free; *Fig* **se remettre d'une s.** to recover from a shock; **les secousses que faisait la voiture** the jolting of the car; **sans s.** smoothly; **par secousses** *(avancer)* jerkily; *(respirer)* in gasps; **s. politique** political upheaval; **s. (sismique** *ou* **tellurique)** (earth) tremor; **s. (électrique)** electric shock

secret¹, -ète [səkrɛ, -ɛt] ADJ *(ordres, signal, traité, porte etc)* secret; *(sentiments, pensées)* secret, hidden; *(réservé) (personne)* reticent, reserved; **ses fantasmes les plus secrets** his/her innermost fantasies; **la raison secrète d'un acte** the secret *or* real reason for an action; **la police secrète** the secret police; *Admin* **très secret, ultra-secret** top secret
 NF **secrète 1 la secrète** *(police)* the secret police **2** *Rel (oraison)* secret

secret² NM **1** *(confidence, mystère)* secret; **garder un s.** to keep a secret; **trahir un s.** to betray a secret, to give away a secret; **mettre qn dans le s.** to let sb into *or* in on the secret; **être du s.** *ou* **dans le s.** to be in on the secret, *Fam* to be in the know; **n'avoir point de s. pour qn** *(d'une personne)* to have no secrets from sb; **les ordinateurs n'ont pas de secrets pour elle** computers hold no secrets for her; **ce n'est un s. pour personne** it's no secret; **le s. du bonheur/de la réussite** the secret of happiness/of success; **trouver le s. de qch** to find the secret of sth; **trouver le s. pour faire qch** to find the knack of doing sth; **elle a le s. des soirées réussies** she knows the secret for giving successful parties; **bureau à s.** desk with a secret compartment
 2 *(discrétion)* secrecy; **dire qch à qn sous le sceau du s.** to tell sb sth under pledge of secrecy; **je vous demande le (plus grand) s.** I'm asking you to keep this (strictly) secret; **en s.** *(en cachette)* in secret, secretly; *(intérieurement)* secretly
 3 mettre qn au s. *(l'enfermer)* to put sb in solitary confinement
 ► ► **s. bancaire** banking secrecy; *Rel* **le s. de la confession** the secrecy of the confessional; *Fig* **ce n'est pas un s. d'État!** it's not a state secret!; **s. de fabrication** trade secret; **le s. professionnel** professional secrecy; *Journ* obligation to respect the confidentiality of sources; **abuser du** *ou* **trahir le s. professionnel** to commit a breach of confidence

secrétaire [səkretɛr] N secretary; **s. bilingue/trilingue** bilingual/trilingual secretary; **s. particulier** private secretary; **s. médicale** medical secretary; *(de dentiste)* dentist's secretary; **s. d'État** *(en France)* junior minister; *(en Grande-Bretagne)* Secretary of State; *(aux États-Unis)* State Secretary; **s. d'ambassade** secretary; *Journ* **s. de rédaction** sub-editor, copyreader; **s. de séance** meetings secretary; **s. général** secretary general; *Com* company secretary; **s. général de l'Assemblée** *Br* ≃ Clerk of the House; **s. général de l'ONU** UN Secretary-General; **s. général du Sénat** *Br* ≃ Clerk of the Parliaments; **s. de direction** executive secretary, personal assistant; **s. d'administration** *(fonctionnaire) Br* ≃ assistant principal; **s. de mairie** ≃ town clerk; *(de village)* = mayor's secretarial assistant
 NM **1** *Orn* secretary bird **2** *(meuble)* writing desk, secretaire

secrétariat [səkretarja] NM **1** *(fonction)* secretaryship **2** *(bureau)* secretariat **3** *(métier)* secretarial work **4** *Pol* **s. d'État** *(fonction en France)* post of Junior Minister; *(ministère français)* Junior Minister's Office; *(fonction en Grande-Bretagne)* post of Secretary of State; *(ministère britannique)* Secretary of State's Office; *(fonction aux États-Unis)* post of State Secretary; **s. général de l'ONU** UN Secretary-Generalship

secrètement [səkrɛtmɑ̃] ADV secretly

secréter [sekrete] VT *(il sécrète; il sécrétera) (d'une glande etc)* to secrete; *Fig* **s. l'ennui** to exude boredom

sécréteur, -trice *ou* **-euse** [sekretœr, -tris, -øz] ADJ *(glande etc)* secretory

sécrétion [sekresjɔ̃] NF *Physiol* secretion; **glande à s. externe/interne** exocrine/endocrine gland

sécrétoire [sekretwar] ADJ *Physiol* secretory

sectaire [sɛktɛr] ADJ **1** *(caractérisé par un esprit d'intolérance)* narrow-minded **2** *(relatif aux sectes religieuses)* sectarian, relating to a sect
 N *(personne intolérante)* narrow-minded person

> Il faut noter qu'en anglais britannique, le terme **sectarian** fait le plus souvent référence à l'hostilité et à l'intolérance qui caractérisent les relations entre catholiques et protestants en Irlande du Nord et en Écosse.

sectarisme [sɛktarism] NM sectarianism

> Il faut noter qu'en anglais britannique, le terme **sectarianism** fait le plus souvent référence à l'hostilité et à l'intolérance qui caractérisent les relations entre catholiques et protestants en Irlande du Nord et en Écosse.

secte [sɛkt] NF secte

secteur [sɛktœr] NM **1** *(zone)* area, district; *(d'un magasin)* section; *Mil (de responsabilité, d'attaque etc)* sector, area; **s. français de Berlin** French sector of Berlin; *Com* **s. de vente** sales area; **s. de surveillance** *Radio etc* surveillance sector *or* area; *(de policier)* beat; *Fam* **changer de s.** to move (somewhere else)
 2 *Élec* **s. (de distribution électrique)** mains; **branché sur le s.** plugged into the mains; **ça se branche sur le s.** it runs off the mains; **panne de s.** mains failure
 3 *Écon (d'une activité)* sector; **le s. privé** the private sector; **s. privé à but non lucratif** private nonprofit sector; **le s. public** the public sector; **s. sanitaire** health sector; **s. primaire** primary sector; **s. secondaire** secondary sector; **s. tertiaire** tertiary sector; *Mktg* **s. de la grande distribution** mass distribution sector; *Mktg* **s. de vente** sales territory; **s. industriel** industrial sector; **s. des services** service sector; **s. du marché** market sector, sector of the market; **un s. en expansion** a growth sector; *Fam* **ce n'est pas mon s.** that's not my line
 4 *Astron, Géom, Ordinat* sector; *Tech* sector, quadrant; **graphique à secteurs** pie chart; *Ordinat* **s. d'initialisation** boot sector; *Ordinat* **s. endommagé** bad sector; *Aut etc* **s. de direction** steering sector; *Aut* **s. de frein** handbrake quadrant *or* ratchet; *Naut* **s. dangereux** *(d'un orage)* dangerous quadrant

section [sɛksjɔ̃] NF **1** *(action de couper)* cutting, *Spéc* section; *Vét (de la queue)* docking; **s. des tendons** cutting of the tendons; **l'accident entraîna la s. d'un doigt** a finger was cut off *or* severed in the accident; **la s. du doigt est nécessaire** the finger must be amputated
 2 *(division) (d'un livre, d'un bâtiment etc)*, *Admin (d'un département etc)*, *Biol* section; *(d'un parti politique)* branch; *Mil (de l'infanterie)* platoon; *(de l'artillerie)* section; *Naut (de la flotte)* sub-division; **s. syndicale d'entreprise** union branch; *Mus* **la s. rythmique** the rhythm section; **s. (électorale)** ward; **de vote** ward; *(bureau)* polling station; **chef de s.** *Mil* platoon commander; *Mil, Aviat* flight commander; *Mil, Aviat* **s. de bombardiers** bomber flight
 3 *Géom* section; *(intersection)* intersection; *Archit, Tech (dessin)* section, profile; **point de s.** point of intersection; **ça doit faire cinq centimètres de s.** it must have a section of five centimetres; *Élec* **s. morte** idle coil; *Nucl* **s. efficace** cross section

4 *(d'autoroute)* section; *(sur un trajet de bus etc)* stage; **changement de s.** *Br* ≃ fare stage; *Rail* **s. de block** block section

5 *Scol* = one of the groups into which baccalaureat students are divided, depending on their chosen area of specialization; **il enseigne en s. scientifique** he teaches in the science department; **à l'école, j'étais en s. économique** my main subject at school was economics

sectionnement [sɛksjɔnmɑ̃] **NM 1** *(d'un département, d'une circonscription etc)* division into sections **2** *(coupe)* severing

sectionner [sɛksjɔne] **VT 1** *(fractionner) (service, circonscription etc)* to divide (up) into sections **2** *(couper)* to sever
▶ **VPR se sectionner** *(être coupé)* to be severed

sectionneur [sɛksjɔnœr] **NM** *Élec* disconnecting switch, isolating switch

sectoriel, -ielle [sɛktɔrjɛl] **ADJ** sectorial

sectorisation [sɛktɔrizasjɔ̃] **NF** division into sectors

sectoriser [sɛktɔrize] **VT** to divide into sectors

Sécu [seky] **NF** *Fam abrév* sécurité sociale

séculaire [sekylɛr] **ADJ 1** *(très ancien) (arbre, tradition etc)* centuries-old, age-old **2** *(qui existe depuis un siècle)* a hundred years old; **un arbre plusieurs fois s.** a tree several hundred years old **3** *(événement)* centennial; *Astron* secular; **année s.** last year of the century

> Do not confuse with **séculier**.

sécularisation [sekylarizasjɔ̃] **NF** secularization

séculariser [sekylarize] **VT** to secularize; *(église)* to deconsecrate

séculier, -ière [sekylje, -jɛr] **ADJ** *(clergé, juridiction etc)* secular; *(laïque)* lay; **le bras s.** the secular arm
N secular

> Do not confuse with **séculaire**.

secundo [sɔgɔ̃do, sek-] **ADV** secondly, in the second place

sécurisant [sekyrizɑ̃] **ADJ** reassuring

sécuriser [sekyrize] **VT s. qn** to reassure sb, to make sb feel secure; **s. l'accès à l'ordinateur central** to securitize mainframe access; *Fin* **s. un financement** to guarantee a loan; **s. un paiement** *(sur l'Internet)* to guarantee or ensure the security of a payment

sécurit® [sekyrit] **NM** safety glass

sécuritaire [sekyritɛr] **ADJ mesures sécuritaires** *(pour la protection des informations etc)* security measures; *(pour la protection des personnes)* safety measures; **ce parti tient un discours s.** this party emphasizes law and order

sécurité [sekyrite] **NF 1** *(ordre, stabilité)* security; *(sentiment)* (feeling of) security; **être/se sentir en s.** to be/feel safe or secure; **je veille à sa s.** I'm making sure he's safe; **s. matérielle/affective** material/emotional security; **s. de l'emploi** security of employment, job security
2 *(absence de danger)* safety; **s. de la route** road safety; *Admin* **s. publique** public safety; **s. incendie** fire safety; **s. informatique** computer security; *(des données)* data security; **services de s.** *Mil* security forces; *(dans des manifestations etc)* stewards; *(dans une usine etc)* security officers; **s. intérieure** national security; **s. nationale/internationale** national/international security; **s. sur officier de s.** officer in charge of fire precautions; *Tech, Constr, Ind* **marge de s.** safety margin; **règles de s.** safety rules or code; **dispositif de s.** safety device; **verre de s.** safety

glass, splinterproof glass; *Élec* **éclairage de s.** emergency lighting
3 *(dispositif)* safety catch; **porte munie d'une s.-enfants** door with a childproof lock
▶▶ *Ordinat* **s. des données** data security; **s. routière** road safety; **S. Routière** = road safety organization; *Admin* **S. sociale** Social Security, *Am* Welfare

> **Attention:** ne pas confondre **security** et **safety** lorsqu'on traduit **sécurité**.

Sécurité sociale

The "Sécu", as it is popularly known, was created in 1945 and provides services such as public health benefits, pensions and maternity benefit. These benefits are paid for by obligatory insurance contributions ("cotisations") made by employers ("cotisations patronales") and employees ("cotisations salariales"). Many French people have complementary health insurance provided by a "mutuelle" which guarantees payment of all or part of the expenses not covered by the "Sécurité sociale".

sédatif, -ive [sedatif, -iv] **ADJ, NM** *Méd* sedative

sédation [sedasjɔ̃] **NF** *Méd* sedation

sédentaire [sedɑ̃tɛr] **ADJ** *(occupation, vie, travail, personne)* sedentary; *(population)* settled; *(troupes)* garrison(ed); *(oiseau)* non-migrant

sédentairement [sedɑ̃tɛrmɑ̃] **ADV vivre s.** to live a sedentary life

sédentarisation [sedɑ̃tarizasjɔ̃] **NF** settling

sédentariser [sedɑ̃tarize] **VT** *(population etc)* to settle
▶ **VPR se sédentariser** to settle

sédentarité [sedɑ̃tarite] **NF** sedentary lifestyle

sédiment [sedimɑ̃] **NM** sediment, deposit

sédimentaire [sedimɑ̃tɛr] **ADJ** *Géol etc* sedimentary

sédimentation [sedimɑ̃tasjɔ̃] **NF** sedimentation

séditieux, -ieuse [sedisjø, -jøz] **ADJ** *(discours, écrit, assemblée etc)* seditious; *(troupes, groupe etc)* seditious, rebellious; **tenir des propos s.** to talk treason
N rebel, insurgent

sédition [sedisjɔ̃] **NF** sedition, insurrection

séducteur, -trice [sedyktœr, -tris] **N** seducer, *f* seductress
ADJ seductive

séduction [sedyksjɔ̃] **NF 1** *(action) (physique)* seduction; *(par le charme)* charming **2** *(moyen de séduire)* attraction; **pouvoir de s.** power of attraction; **exercer une s. mystérieuse/irrésistible sur qn** to exercise a mysterious/an irresistible attraction over sb; **la s. des richesses** the lure or attraction of wealth

séduire [sedɥir] *(conj like* **conduire***)* **VT 1** *(sexuellement)* to seduce **2** *(gagner par son charme) (d'une personne)* to charm; *(d'un projet, une proposition etc)* to appeal to; **j'ai été séduite du premier coup** it took my fancy or attracted me or appealed to me right away
VI to charm people

> Il faut noter que le verbe anglais **to seduce** ne signifie pas **charmer**.

séduisant [sedɥizɑ̃] **ADJ** *(idée, proposition etc)* appealing, attractive; *(personne)* attractive

séfarade [sefarad] **ADJ** Sephardic
N Sephardi; **les séfarades** the Sephardim

segment [sɛgmɑ̃] **NM** segment; *Mktg* **s. démographique** demographic segment; *Aut* **s. de frein** brake shoe; *Aut* **frein à segments** segmented brake; *Mktg* **s. de marché** market segment; *Tech* **s. de piston** piston or packing ring; *Aut* **s. primaire** primary or leading shoe; *Aut* **s. secondaire** secondary shoe, trailing shoe

segmentation [sɛgmɑ̃tasjɔ̃] **NF** segmentation, segmenting; *Mktg* **s. démographique** demographic segmentation; *Mktg* **s. du marché** market segmentation; *Mktg* **s. en niches** niching; *Mktg* **s. stratégique** strategic segmentation

segmenter [sɛgmɑ̃te] **VT** to segment, to divide into segments; *Ordinat* to partition, to section, to segment; **s. un marché** to segment a market
▶ **VPR se segmenter** to segment, to split into segments

ségrégation [segregasjɔ̃] **NF** segregation

ségrégationnisme [segregasjɔnism] **NM** *Pol* racial segregation

ségrégationniste [segregasjɔnist] **ADJ, N** *Pol* segregationist

séguedille [segədij] **NF** *(danse, musique)* seguidilla

seiche [sɛʃ] **NF** *(mollusque)* cuttlefish; **os de s.** cuttlebone

séide [seid] **NM** henchman

seigle [sɛgl] **NM** rye; **pain de s.** rye bread

seigneur [sɛɲœr] **NM 1** *(maître)* lord; *(d'un manoir)* lord of the manor, *Br* ≃ squire; *Hist (homme noble)* nobleman, noble; *Hum* **mon s. et maître** my lord and master; **le s. de Sercq** the seigneur of Sark; *(femme)* the dame of Sark; *Hist* **les seigneurs** the nobility; **à tout s. tout honneur** honour where honour is due; **mener une vie de grand s.** to live like a lord; **ne faites pas le grand s.** don't try and lord it over us, stop behaving like the lord of the manor; **en grand s.** in grand style **2** *Rel* **le S.** the Lord; **Notre-S.** our Lord; **le jour du S.** the Lord's day; *Fam* **S.!, S. Dieu!** good Lord!

seigneurial, -iale, -iaux, -iales [sɛɲœrjal, -jo] **ADJ** *(magnifique)* stately, lordly; *Hist (droits, domaine etc)* manorial, seigneurial

seigneurie [sɛɲœri] **NF 1** *Hist (terre, pouvoir)* seigneury; **votre S.** *(titre)* your Lordship; *Iron* **sa S.** his lordship, *Arg* his nibs **2** *Belg (maison de retraite)* retirement home, old people's home

sein [sɛ̃] **NM** *(de femme)* breast; *Litt (d'homme)* breast, bosom; **serrer** ou **presser qn sur son s.** to press sb to one's bosom or heart; **donner le s. à un enfant** to breast-feed a child; **enfant nourri au s.** breast-fed child; **danseuse aux seins nus** topless dancer; **se baigner les seins nus** to swim topless; **le s. de l'Église** the bosom of the Church; **au s. de la famille** in the bosom of the family; **au s. de la commission** within the committee; *Litt* **enfant que j'ai porté dans mon s.** child that I carried in my womb; **le s. de la terre** the bowels of the earth

Seine [sɛn] **NF la S.** the Seine

seine [sɛn] **NF** *Pêche* seine, draw net

seing [sɛ̃] **NM** *Jur* **sous s. privé** under private seal; **acte sous s. privé** private agreement *(without legal certification)*

séisme [seism] **NM** earthquake; *Fig Litt* upheaval

séismique [seismik] **ADJ** seismic

seize [sez] **ADJ INV** sixteen; **Louis S.** Louis the Sixteenth; **numéro s.** number sixteen
NM INV sixteen; **le s. mai** (on) the sixteenth of May, (on) May the sixteenth, *Am* (on) May sixteenth; **habiter au s.** to live at number sixteen

seizième [sɛzjɛm] ADJ sixteenth
N sixteenth; **ils habitent dans le s.** they live in the sixteenth arrondissement *(in Paris)*
NM *(fraction)* sixteenth

Seizième
This term often refers to the upper-class social background, lifestyle, way of dressing etc associated with the sixteenth arrondissement in Paris: "elle est très seizième".

---

séjour [seʒur] NM **1** stay; **carte** *ou* **permis de s.** residence permit; **droit de s.** right of residence *or* abode; **taxe de s.** tourist tax; **s. discompté** bargain break; **s. éducatif** educational trip *or* holiday; **s. linguistique** language-learning trip *or* holiday; **s. de quinze jours** two week(s') *or Br* fortnight's stay; **je te souhaite un bon s. en Grèce** enjoy your stay in Greece **2** *(salle de)* **s.** living room **3** *Litt (lieu)* abode

séjourner [seʒurne] VI *(d'une personne)* to stay; *(de la neige, de l'eau etc)* to lie

sel [sɛl] NM **1** *Chimie, Culin etc* salt; **gros s.** coarse salt; **régime sans s.** salt-free diet; **s. de cuisine** cooking salt; **s. fin** fine salt; **s. marin** sea salt; **s. de céleri** celery salt; *Pharm* **s. d'Angleterre** *ou* **d'Epsom** Epsom salts; **sels de** *ou* **pour le bain** bath salts; **sels** *(à respirer)* (smelling) salts; *Chimie* **s. double** double salt; *Fam* **mettre** *ou* **ajouter son grain de s.** to put *or* stick one's oar in; *Fig* **le s. de la terre** the salt of the earth **2** *Fig (esprit)* piquancy, wit

select, sélect [selɛkt] ADJ *Fam (soirée, clientèle etc)* select; **le monde s.** high society

sélecteur [selɛktœr] NM *Ordinat, Élec etc* selector; *(de motocyclette)* gear(-change) pedal; **s. automatique** automatic switch; *Aut* **s. de vitesses** gear lever

sélectif, -ive [selɛktif, -iv] ADJ selective; *Radio* **récepteur s.** selective receiver; *Ordinat* **en mode s.** in veto mode

sélection [selɛksjɔ̃] NF **1** *(fait de choisir)* selection; **faire** *ou* **opérer une s. parmi ...** to make a selection from among ...; *Mktg* **s. au hasard** random selection; *Biol* **s. naturelle** natural selection; **s. professionnelle** professional recruitment; **épreuve de s.** selection trial; *Sport* **match de s.** trial game; **Gavin Hastings a 51 sélections en équipe nationale** Gavin Hastings has been capped 51 times, Gavin Hastings has 51 caps **2** *(choses choisies)* selection

sélectionné, -ée [selɛksjɔne] ADJ *(joueur, produit etc)* selected; **s. en équipe nationale** capped
N *Sport* selected player

sélectionner [selɛksjɔne] VT **1** *(choisir)* to select **2** *Ordinat (texte)* to block, to select; **s. qch par défaut** to default to sth; **s. et copier** to block and copy

sélectionneur, -euse [selɛksjɔnœr, -øz] N selector

sélectivement [selɛktivmã] ADV selectively

sélectivité [selɛktivite] NF *Radio* selectivity

sélénieux [selenjø] ADJ M *Chimie (acide)* selenious

sélénite [selenit] N *(habitant de la lune)* moon-dweller
ADJ of the moon

sélénium [selenjɔm] NM *Chimie* selenium

sélénographie [selenɔgrafi] NF selenography

sélénographique [selenɔgrafik] ADJ *(carte etc)* selenographic(al)

self [sɛlf] NM *Fam (restaurant)* self-service restaurant

NF *Élec* self-induction; **(bobine de) s.** self-induction coil

self-control [sɛlfkɔ̃trɔl] NM self-control

self-défense NF self-defence, *Am* self-defense

self-inductance, *pl* **self-inductances** NF *Élec* self-inductance

self-induction, *pl* **self-inductions** NF *Élec* self-induction

self-made-man, *pl* **self-made-men** [sɛlfmɛdman, sɛlfmɛdmɛn] NM self-made man

self-service, *pl* **self-services** NM *(restaurant)* self-service restaurant; *(magasin)* self-service shop

selle [sɛl] NF **1** *(de cheval, bicyclette, moto etc)* saddle; **se mettre en s.** to mount; **être bien en s.** to have a good seat; *Fig* to be firmly in the saddle; **aider qn à monter en s.** to help sb into the saddle; *Fig Fam* to give sb a leg up *or* a helping hand; **se remettre en s.** to get back into the saddle; *Fig* to get back in harness; **monter sans s.** to ride bareback **2** *Physiol* stool; **aller à la s.** *(déféquer)* to pass *or* have a motion; **les selles du bébé** the baby's stools *or* motions **3** *Culin* **s. de mouton/d'agneau** saddle of mutton/lamb; **s. de bœuf** baron of beef **4** *(de sculpteur)* turntable

seller [sele] VT *(cheval)* to saddle

sellerie [sɛlri] NF **1** *(selles, métier)* saddlery **2** *(salle)* harness room, tack room **3** *Aut* seating

sellette [sɛlɛt] NF **1** *Fam* **mettre qn/être sur la s.** to put sb/to be in the hot seat **2** *(d'ouvrier de bâtiment)* cradle; *Aut* trailer coupling, fifth wheel **3** *(de sculpteur)* turntable **4** *(de cheval de trait)* saddle

sellier [selje] NM saddler; **façon s.** hand-stitched

selon [s(ə)lɔ̃] PRÉP **1** according to; **s. lui** according to him; **s. moi** in my opinion *or* view, as I see it; **s. facture** as per invoice; **s. vos instructions** in accordance with your instructions, as per your instructions; **s. toute vraisemblance** in all likelihood *or* probability; **s. les cas** on a case by case basis; **varier s. les cas/les saisons** to vary from case to case/season to season; *Fam* **c'est s.** it all depends; **l'Évangile s. saint Jean** the Gospel according to Saint John **2 s. que** + *ind* depending on whether

Seltz [sɛls] NM **eau de S.** soda water, Seltzer (water)

SEM [sɛm] NF *(abrév* **société d'économie mixte)** = company financed by state and private capital

semailles [s(ə)maj] NFPL **1** *(action)* sowing; **(temps des) s.** sowing time **2** *(graines)* seeds

semaine [s(ə)mɛn] NF **1** *(sept jours)* week; **deux fois par s.** twice a week; **s. de cinq jours** five-day week; **s. de trente-cinq heures** thirty-five-hour week; **une s. de vacances** a week's holiday; **fin de s.** *(jeudi, vendredi)* end of the week; *(week-end)* weekend; *Can* **bonne fin de s.!** have a good weekend!, enjoy your weekend!; **je suis de s.** I'm on duty this week *or* for the week; *Scol* **pensionnaire à la s.** weekly boarder; *Fam* **politique à la petite s.** shortsighted policy; **vivre à la petite s.** to live from day to day; *Fam* **la s. des quatre jeudis!** that'll never happen (in a month of Sundays)!; *Com* **la promotion de la s.** this week's special offer; **s. commerciale** week-long special promotion; **jour de s.** weekday; **en s.** during the week, on weekdays
2 *(salaire)* week's pay *or* wages; *(argent de poche)* pocket money (for the week)
3 *Mil etc (tour de service)* week's duty; **officier de s.** duty officer for the week
4 *(bague/bracelet)* seven-band ring/bracelet

▸ ▸ **s. anglaise** five-day week; **faire la s. anglaise** to work a five-day week; **la s. sainte** Holy Week

semainier, -ière [s(ə)menje, -jɛr] N *(personne)* person on duty for the week; *Mil* duty officer for the week
NM **1** *(meuble)* chest of seven drawers **2** *(agenda)* desk diary *(with sections for each day of the week)*

sémantème [semãtɛm] NM *Ling* sémanteme

sémanticien, -ienne [semãtisjɛ̃, -jɛn] N semanticist

sémantique [semãtik] *Ling* ADJ semantic
NF semantics

sémaphore [semafɔr] NM *Rail* semaphore signal; *Naut (à terre)* signal station

semblable [sãblabl] ADJ **1** *(pareil)* similar; **être semblables** to be similar *or* alike; **deux cas tout à fait semblables** two quite similar cases; **triangles semblables** similar triangles; **s. à qch** similar to sth, like sth; **s. à son père** like his/her father; **je n'ai rien dit de s.** I said nothing of the sort, I said no such thing **2** *(tel)* **de semblables projets/propos** such plans/remarks, plans/remarks like that
N **1** *(personne semblable)* **vous et vos semblables** you and people like you, you and your kind *or* sort; **il n'a pas son s. dans l'art occidental** there's no one like him in western art **2** *(être humain)* fellow man *or* creature; **nos semblables** our fellow men, our fellow creatures

semblant [sãblã] NM semblance (**de** of); **elle portait un s. de jupe** she was wearing an apology for a skirt; **montrer un s. de résistance** to make a show of resistance; **opposer un s. d'indignation** to put up a show of indignation; **faire s. de faire qch** to pretend to do sth; **tu fais s.?** are you pretending?; **sans faire s. de rien** without seeming to take any notice; **elle fit s. de rien** she pretended not to notice

sembler [sãble] *(aux* **avoir)** VI to seem; **elle semblait malade** she seemed (to be) ill; **s. être/faire** to seem to be/do; **le vent semble tomber** the wind seems to be dying down
V IMPERS **il me semblait rêver** it seemed to me (that) *or* I thought (that) I was dreaming; **il me semble avoir entendu son nom** I seem to have heard his/her name; **il me semble idiot d'attendre encore plus longtemps** it seems stupid to me to wait any longer; **à ce qu'il me semble** it seems to me; **faites comme bon vous semble(ra)** do as you think best; **il le fera si bon lui semble** he'll do it if he wants to; **il semble que ...** + *ind or sub* it seems that ..., it looks as if ...; **il me semble que ...** + *ind* it seems to me that ...; **me semble-t-il** it seems to me SEE GRAMMAR B29

semé [s(ə)me] ADJ **s. de** scattered with; *(rochers etc)* strewn with; *(fleurs etc)* dotted with; *(diamants etc)* studded with; *(citations etc)* sprinkled with; **s. d'embûches** *ou* **de pièges** full of traps

sème [sɛm] NM *Ling* sememe

semelle [s(ə)mɛl] NF **1** *(d'une chaussure)* sole; *(d'un bas, d'une chaussette)* foot; **s. (intérieure)** insole, inner sole; **chaussures à semelles de caoutchouc/de cuir** rubber-/leather-soled shoes; **remettre une s. à une chaussure** to resole a shoe; **ne pas avancer d'une s.** to make no progress; **il ne reculera pas d'une s.** he won't give an inch; **il ne me quitte pas d'une s.** he's always at my heels; **ce n'est pas de la viande, c'est de la s.!** this isn't meat, it's like shoe leather! **2** *Tech (d'une machine, d'un tour)* bed plate; *(d'une ancre, d'un traîneau)* shoe; **s. de poutre** girder flange **3** *Naut* **s. de dérive** leeboard

semence [s(ə)mãs] NF **1** *Agr* seed; *Physiol* semen; *Fig* **semences** seeds (**de** of); *Agr* **blé de s.** seed corn; **s. de perles** seed pearls; **s. de diamants** diamond sparks **2** *(clou)* tack; **s. de tapissier** upholstery tack

semer [s(ə)me] VT (**je sème, n. semons; je sèmerai**) **1** *(graines, champ)* to sow **2** *(fleurs etc)* to scatter, to strew; *(nouvelles, discorde)* to spread; *Prov* **qui sème le vent récolte la tempête** he who sows the wind shall reap the whirlwind **3** *Fam* **s. qn** *(le distancer)* to shake sb off, to get rid of sb; **s. qch** *(le laisser tomber)* to drop sth, to lose sth

semestre [s(ə)mɛstr] NM **1** *(six mois)* half-year, six months; **le premier s.** the first half of the year **2** *(paiement)* half-yearly *or* six-monthly payment **3** *Scol, Univ* semester

semestriel, -ielle [səmɛstrijɛl] ADJ half-yearly, six-monthly

semestriellement [səmɛstrijɛlmã] ADV half-yearly, every six months; *Scol, Univ* every semester

semeur, -euse [s(ə)mœr, -øz] N *Agr* sower; *Fig (de nouvelles etc)* spreader, *Litt* disseminator; *(de discorde)* sower; *Fam* **semeur de zizanie**, *très Fam* **s. de merde** troublemaker

semi- [səmi] PRÉF semi- (**NOTE** *in the plural of compound words prefixed by* **semi-**, *semi- remains invariable and the following noun or adj takes the pl form*)

semi-automatique ADJ semiautomatic

semi-auxiliaire ADJ *Gram* semiauxiliary

semi-chenillé ADJ, NM **(véhicule) s.** half-track (vehicle)

semi-circulaire ADJ semicircular

semi-conducteur, -trice *Élec* ADJ semiconducting
  NM semiconductor

semi-conserve NF = foodstuff which has a limited life and must be refrigerated

semi-consonne NF semivowel

semi-duplex NM INV half duplex

semi-fini ADJ *Écon (produit)* semifinished

semi-fixe ADJ semifixed

semi-grossiste N retail wholesaler

semi-illettré ADJ semi-illiterate

semi-liberté NF *Jur* partial release; *Fig* state of partial freedom

sémillant [semijã] ADJ *(personne, esprit)* sparkling; *(regard)* bright, engaging

semi-lunaire ADJ half-moon-shaped

semi-mensuel, -elle ADJ *(périodique etc)* bi-monthly, *Br* fortnightly

semi-métal NM *Chimie* metalloid

séminaire [seminer] NM **1** *Univ* seminar; *(conférence)* seminar, conference **2** *Rel* (**grand**) **s.** seminary; **petit s.** secondary school *(staffed by priests)*

séminal, -ale, -aux, -ales [seminal, -o] ADJ *Biol* seminal

séminariste [seminarist] NM *Rel* seminarist

semi-nomade ADJ seminomadic
  N seminomad

semi-nomadisme NM seminomadism

semi-occlusif, -ive ADJ *Ling* semi-occlusive

semi-officiel, -ielle ADJ semiofficial

sémiologie [semjɔlɔʒi] NF *Méd, Ling* semiology

sémiologique [semjɔlɔʒik] ADJ *Méd, Ling* semiological

sémiologue [semjɔlɔg] N *Méd, Ling* semiologist

sémiotique [semjɔtik] ADJ semiotic
  NF semiotics

semi-ouvré ADJ *Écon (produit)* semifinished

semi-perméable ADJ semipermeable

semi-précieux, -ieuse ADJ *(pierre)* semiprecious

semi-présidentiel, -ielle ADJ *Pol* semi-presidential

semi-produit NM semi-manufactured product

semi-professionnel, -elle ADJ semiprofessional

semi-public, -ique ADJ *Jur* semipublic

sémique [semik] ADJ *Ling* semic

semi-remorque NF *(remorque)* semitrailer, *Am Fam* semi
  NM *(poids lourd)* articulated truck *or Br* lorry, *Br Fam* artic

semi-rigide ADJ *(dirigeable)* semirigid

semis [səmi] NM *Agr* **1** *(action)* sowing **2** *(terrain)* seedbed **3** *(jeune plante)* seedling

sémite [semit] ADJ *Semitic*
  N **S.** Semite

sémitique [semitik] ADJ Semitic

sémitisant, -ante [semitizã, -ãt], **sémitiste** [semitist] N Semitist

sémitisme [semitism] NM Semitism

semi-ton NM *Mus* semitone

semi-voyelle NF *Ling* semivowel

semoir [s(ə)mwar] NM *Agr* **1** *(sac)* seed bag **2** *(machine)* sowing machine, seeder

semonce [səmɔ̃s] NF **1** *(réprimande)* reprimand, scolding; **une verte s.** a good telling-off **2** *Naut* **coup de s.** warning shot

semoule [səmul] NF semolina; **sucre s.** caster *or Am* powdered sugar; **s. de blé dur** semolina

sempiternel, -elle [sɛ̃pitɛrnɛl] ADJ never-ending, endless, *Fml* sempiternal

sempiternellement [sɛ̃pitɛrnɛlmã] ADV eternally, endlessly

sénat [sena] NM senate; *(édifice)* senate (house)

> ### Sénat
> The "Sénat" is the upper house of the French Parliament. Its members are elected for a nine-year mandate by the Deputies of the "Assemblée nationale" and certain other government officals. The President of the Senate may deputize for the President of the Republic in the case of incapacity or death. The powers of the Senate are almost as extensive as those of the "Assemblée nationale", although the latter is empowered to override the decisions of the Senate in cases where the two houses disagree.

sénateur [senatœr] NM senator

sénatorial, -iale, -iaux, -iales [senatorjal, -jo] ADJ senatorial
  NFPL **sénatoriales** senatorial elections

séné [sene] NM *Bot, Pharm* senna

sénéchal, -aux [seneʃal, -o] NM *Hist* seneschal

sénéchaussée [seneʃose] NF *Hist (juridiction)* seneschalsy; *(tribunal)* seneschal's court

séneçon [sensɔ̃] NM *Bot* groundsel

Sénégal [senegal] NM Senegal

sénégalais, -aise [senegalɛ, -ɛz] ADJ Senegalese
  N **S.** Senegalese

Sénégambie [senegãbi] NF Senegambia

Sénèque [senɛk] N Seneca

sénescence [senesãs] NF *Biol* senescence, ageing, aging

sénescent [senesã] ADJ *Biol* senescent

sénevé [senve] NM **1** *Bot* mustard **2** *(graine)* mustard seed

sénile [senil] ADJ *Méd, Fam Péj* senile

sénilité [senilite] NF senility

senior [senjɔr] ADJ, N *Sport* senior

senne [sɛn] NF *Pêche* seine, draw net

señorita [senjɔrita] NM cigarillo, whiff

SENS [sãs]

> **sens 1, 3, 4** ▪ meaning **4**
> ▪ direction **5**

NM **1** *(du toucher, de la vue, de la beauté, du rythme etc)* sense; **les cinq s.** the five senses; **le sixième s.** the sixth sense; **s. moral** moral sense, conscience; **avoir le s. de l'humour/ du ridicule/de la famille** to have a sense of humour/of the ridiculous/of family; **avoir le s. des affaires** to have good business sense; **j'ai un très bon s. de l'orientation** I have a very good sense of direction; **s. pratique** practical (common) sense; **il n'a aucun s. pratique** he's completely unpractical, he's not practically minded at all; **reprendre ses s.** to regain consciousness

2 *(sensualité)* **plaisir des s.** sensual pleasures; **éveiller/exciter les s.** to excite/arouse the senses

3 *(jugement)* sense; **s. commun** common sense; **bon s.** good sense; **un homme de bon s.** a sensible man; **tu t'es encore coiffé en dépit du bon s.** what possessed you to do your hair like that?; **agir en dépit du bon s.** to act in a way that defies common sense; **le bon s. veut que …** it stands to reason that …; **gros** *ou* **robuste bon s.** elementary common sense; **à mon s.** to my mind, in my view *or* opinion; **j'abonde dans votre s.** I entirely agree with you; **cela tombe sous le s.** it's perfectly obvious

4 *(signification)* *(d'un mot etc)* meaning, sense; **s. propre/figuré** literal/figurative meaning *or* sense; **au s. propre/figuré** in the literal/figurative sense, literally/figuratively; **au s. ordinaire du mot** in the ordinary meaning *or* sense of the word; **mot à double s.** word with a double meaning; **faire un faux s.** to make a mistranslation; **ça n'a aucun s.** it doesn't make (any) sense; **cela n'a pas de s.** it's crazy, there's no sense to it; **trouver un s. à sa vie** to find a meaning to one's life; **en ce s. que …** in the sense that …

5 *(direction)* direction; **accident sur la voie express dans le s. Brest-Quimper** accident on the Brest-Quimper expressway; **il tenait son livre dans le mauvais s.** he was holding his book the wrong way up; **tu as mis la cassette dans le mauvais s.** you put the tape in the wrong way round; **il a pris l'autoroute dans le mauvais s.** he drove the wrong way up the motorway; **fais demi-tour, on n'est pas dans le bon s.** turn round, we're going the wrong way *or* in the wrong direction; **en s. inverse** in the opposite direction; **dans le s. des aiguilles d'une montre** clockwise; **dans le s. inverse des aiguilles d'une montre** anticlockwise, *Am* counterclockwise; **dans le s. du courant** with the current, with the stream; **dans le s. de la longueur** lengthwise, lengthways; **dans le s. de la largeur** widthwise, breadthwise, across; **tailler dans le s. du bois** to cut in the direction of the grain *or* along the grain; **dans le s. inverse du grain** against *or* across the grain; **courir dans tous les s.** to run in all directions; **s. dessus dessous** [sãdsydsu] upside down, the wrong way up; *(en désordre)* upside down, in a mess, in a state of confusion; **s. devant derrière** back to front, the wrong way round; **dans les deux s.** both ways; *Fig* **ces mesures vont toutes dans le même s.** these measures are all directed at the same object; **son action allait aussi dans ce s.** his/her action was also directed to this end; **le s. de l'histoire** the course of history; **s. de la circulation** direction of the traffic; **rue à double s.** two-way street; **rue en s. unique** one-way street; **s. unique** *(sur panneau)* one-way (street); **s. interdit** *(sur panneau)* no entry; **prendre une rue en s. interdit** to go the wrong way along a street; *Aut* **s. giratoire** roundabout, *Am* traffic circle; *Rail* **voyager dans le s. de la marche** to travel facing the engine; *Math* **s. direct/rétrograde** positive/ negative direction; *Ordinat* **s. de déroulement** flow direction

sensas(s) [sɑ̃sas] ADJ INV *Fam* fantastic, great

sensation [sɑ̃sasjɔ̃] NF **1** *(impression)* feeling; *Physiol* sensation; **une s. de fatigue** a feeling of tiredness, a tired feeling; **avoir la s. que ...** to have a *or* the feeling that ...; **cela donne la s. de ...** it feels like ... **2** *(scandale)* **à s.** *(article, titre)* sensationalist; **presse à s.** gutter press, tabloid press; **roman à s.** sensational novel; **titres à s.** sensationalist headlines; **faire s.** to create a sensation

sensationnel, -elle [sɑ̃sasjɔnɛl] ADJ *(nouvelles, roman etc)* sensational; *Fam (remarquable)* fantastic, great
  NM journaliste à la recherche du s. journalist in search of a sensational story

sensé [sɑ̃se] ADJ *(personne, action, remarque etc)* sensible

senseur [sɑ̃sœr] NM *Électron* sensor, sensing device

sensibilisateur, -trice [sɑ̃sibilizatœr, -tris] ADJ *Phot etc* sensitizing; **lancer une campagne sensibilisatrice pour qch** to launch a campaign to heighten *or* increase public awareness of sth
  NM *Phot* sensitizer
  NF *Biol* **sensibilisatrice** sensitizer

sensibilisation [sɑ̃sibilizasjɔ̃] NF *Phot, Méd* sensitization; *Fig* growing awareness (**à** of); **la s. de l'opinion** *(action)* heightening *or* increasing public awareness; *(résultat)* heightened *or* increased public awareness; **campagne de s. à qch** campaign to heighten *or* increase public awareness of sth

sensibiliser [sɑ̃sibilize] VT *Phot, Méd etc* to sensitize; *Fig* **s. qn à qch** to heighten *or* increase sb's awareness of sth; **s. l'opinion** to heighten *or* increase public awareness (à of)
  VPR se sensibiliser se s. à qch to become aware of sth

sensibilité [sɑ̃sibilite] NF sensitivity; **s. à fleur de peau** hypersensitivity; **avoir une s. à fleur de peau** to be hypersensitive; **enfant d'une grande s.** extremely sensitive child; **la s. romantique/wagnérienne** the Romantic/ Wagnerian sensibility; **avoir de la s.** to be sensitive; *Mktg* **s. aux prix** price sensitivity

sensible [sɑ̃sibl] ADJ **1** *(personne)* sensitive; **cœur s.** tender *or* compassionate heart; **ce programme est déconseillé aux personnes sensibles** this programme is not recommended for people of a sensitive disposition; **s. à** *(ridicule, charme, injustice, douleur etc)* sensitive to; *(influence)* susceptible to; **être s. aux bontés de qn** to appreciate sb's kindness; **peu s.** insensitive; **être peu s. au froid/à la critique** to be impervious to the cold/to criticism; **être s. au froid** to feel the cold, to be sensitive to the cold; *(d'une plante)* to be tender; *Mktg* **s. au prix** price-sensitive; **les plantes sont sensibles à la musique** plants are sensitive to music; **cet enfant est très s. à la musique** this child has a great feeling for music; *Fig* **avoir l'épiderme s.** to be thin-skinned; *Fig* **toucher la note** *ou* **la corde s.** to appeal to the emotions
  2 *(physiquement fragile ou douloureux)* *(pieds etc)* tender; *(dent, peau)* sensitive; **s. au toucher** tender *or* painful to the touch; **toucher qn à un endroit s.** to touch sb on a tender spot; *Fig* **blesser qn au point s.** to tread on sb's corns; *Fig* **vous avez touché un point s.** you've touched on a sore point, you've touched a raw nerve
  3 *(balance, thermomètre, plaque etc)* sensitive; **papier s. à la lumière** light-sensitive paper
  4 *(apte à percevoir)* *Phil* sentient; **avoir l'oreille s.** to have a keen sense of hearing; **ouïe peu s.** dull hearing
  5 *(perceptible)* *(son etc)* perceptible; **le monde s.** the tangible world
  6 *(différence, progrès etc)* noticeable, appreciable; **d'une manière s.** noticeably; **un vide s.** a noticeable gap; **éprouver un plaisir s.** to feel a keen pleasure
  7 *Mus* **la note s.** the leading note

> Il faut noter que l'adjectif anglais **sensible** est un faux ami. Il signifie **sensé**.

sensiblement [sɑ̃sibləmɑ̃] ADV **1** *(notablement)* noticeably, appreciably **2** *(à peu près)* approximately, roughly, more or less

sensiblerie [sɑ̃sibləri] NF *Péj* sentimentality

sensitif, -ive [sɑ̃sitif, -iv] ADJ **1** *Litt* oversensitive **2** *Physiol* sensory
  NF *Bot* **sensitive** sensitive plant, mimosa pudica

sensoriel, -ielle [sɑ̃sɔrjɛl] ADJ sensorial, sensory

sensorimoteur, -trice [sɑ̃sɔrimɔtœr, -tris] ADJ *Méd, Psy* sensorimotor

sensualisme [sɑ̃syalism] NM *Phil* sensualism, sensationalism

sensualiste [sɑ̃syalist] ADJ, N *Phil* sensualist, sensationalist

sensualité [sɑ̃syalite] NF sensuality

sensuel, -elle [sɑ̃syɛl] ADJ *(personne, plaisir etc)* sensual; *(lèvres, voix etc)* sensual, sensuous

sentant [sɑ̃tɑ̃] ADJ sentient

sente [sɑ̃t] NF *(sentier)* (foot)path

sentence [sɑ̃tɑ̃s] NF **1** *(jugement)* sentence **2** *(maxime)* maxim

sentencieusement [sɑ̃tɑ̃sjøzmɑ̃] ADV sententiously

sentencieux, -ieuse [sɑ̃tɑ̃sjø, -jøz] ADJ sententious

senteur, -euse [sɑ̃tœr, -øz] ADJ *Can Péj (indiscret)* nosy, prying
  NF *Litt* scent

senti [sɑ̃ti] ADJ heartfelt
  NM *Phil* sense datum

sentier [sɑ̃tje] NM (foot)path; *Fig* path; **s. pour cavaliers** bridle path; **s. balisé** signposted footpath; **s. de grande randonnée** long-distance footpath; **s. battu** beaten track; *Fig* **sortir des sentiers battus** to venture off the beaten track; *Fig* **sur le s. de la guerre** on the warpath

sentiment [sɑ̃timɑ̃] NM **1** *(sensation)* *(de joie, de soulagement etc)* feeling, sensation; **avoir le s. que ...** to have a *or* the feeling that ...; **privé de s.** *(membre)* devoid of feeling, numb; **il avait le s. de sa mort prochaine** he sensed he would die soon
  2 *(émotion)* feeling; *Mus* **jouer avec s.** to play with feeling; **avoir le s. de la nature** to have a feeling for nature; **avoir le s. de l'honneur/ de la beauté** to have a sense of honour/of the aesthetic; **avoir du s. pour qn** to feel attracted to sb, to be drawn to sb; **ses sentiments vis-à-vis de moi** his/her feelings towards me; **je ne doute pas de ses sentiments pour moi** I have no doubt that he loves me; **faire appel aux bons sentiments de qn** to appeal to sb's finer feelings; **prendre qn par les sentiments** to appeal to sb's softer side; *Fam* **c'est parti d'un bon s.** it was well meant, the intention was good; **faire du s.** to sentimentalize; **je ne fais pas de s. en affaires** I don't let sentiment interfere with business; *allons!* **pas de s.!** come on, don't be sentimental!; **avoir qn au s.** to win sb over by appealing to his/her softer side; **privé de s.** *(personne)* *(sans réaction)* numb; *(insensible)* devoid of feeling; **s. national** sense of nationhood; **je n'ai aucun s. religieux** I'm not the slightest bit religious; **veuillez agréer, Madame, l'expression de mes sentiments distingués** yours faithfully; **veuillez recevoir, Monsieur, l'expression de mes sentiments les meilleurs** yours sincerely
  3 *Litt (opinion)* feeling; **quel est votre s. sur la question?** what is your feeling about the matter?

sentimental, -ale, -aux, -ales [sɑ̃timɑ̃tal, -o] ADJ **1** **vie sentimentale** love life; *Cin, Théâtre etc* **intrigue sentimentale** love affair **2** *(romantique)* *(personne, attachement, chanson etc)* sentimental, *Fam* soppy
  N c'est un s./une sentimentale he's/she's a romantic

sentimentalement [sɑ̃timɑ̃talmɑ̃] ADV sentimentally

sentimentalisme [sɑ̃timɑ̃talism] NM sentimentalism; **faire du s.** to be sentimental

sentimentaliste [sɑ̃timɑ̃talist] ADJ, N sentimentalist

sentimentalité [sɑ̃timɑ̃talite] NF sentimentality

sentine [sɑ̃tin] NF *Naut (d'un navire)* bilge; *Litt* **s. de tous les vices** sink of iniquity

sentinelle [sɑ̃tinɛl] NF *Mil (soldat)* guard, sentry, *Vieilli* sentinel; **nous disposerons des sentinelles le long des quais** we shall be posting guards along the quays; **en s.** on guard, on sentry duty; *Fig* **se mettre en s.** to stand guard, to keep (a) watch

SENTIR [sɑ̃tir] *(prp sentant; pp senti; pr ind je sens, il sent, n. sentons, ils sentent; pr sub je sente; impf je sentais; p hist je sentis; fu je sentirai)*

> **VT** to feel **1, 2** ▪ to be aware of **2** ▪ to be conscious of **2** ▪ to smell **3** ▪ to taste **4** ▪ to smell of **5** ▪ to reek of **5** ▪ to smack of **5**
> **VI** to smell **1, 2**
> **VPR** to feel **2**

VT SEE GRAMMAR A41; B35 **1** *(douleur, faim, froid, joie, peine etc)* to feel; *(par le toucher)* to feel; **je sentais trembler le plancher** I could feel the floor trembling; *Fam* **je sens mes bras/ mes jambes** my arms/legs are aching; **je ne sens plus mes jambes/mes pieds** my legs/ my feet are killing me; *(devenu insensible)* my legs/my feet have gone numb; **je sens l'hiver qui vient** I can feel winter coming; **on ne sent pas la différence** you can't feel the difference; *Fam* **je l'ai senti passer!** *(à propos d'une douleur, d'une facture, d'une réprimande)* I knew all about it!
  2 *(être conscient de) (injure, force, pouvoir etc)* to be conscious of, to feel; *(danger)* to be aware of *or* conscious of; **elle ne sentait pas tout le ridicule de la situation** she wasn't fully aware *or* conscious of the ridiculousness of the situation; **s. grandir son influence** to feel one's influence growing; **je sens que vous avez raison** I have a *or* the feeling that you are right; **ce sont des choses que l'on sent** you can sense *or* feel these things; **il m'a fait s. que ...** he gave me to understand that ...; **fais-lui s. qu'il se trompe** make him understand that he's mistaken; **faire s. son autorité** to make one's authority felt; **l'effet se fera s.** the effect will be felt; **je**

sentis la peur me gagner peu à peu I felt more and more frightened or I felt a growing fear; **je sentis sa colère monter peu à peu** I sensed his/her growing anger; **s. qch de loin** to feel sth coming; **s. qn de loin** to see through sb; **s. la barre** *(d'un navire)* to answer to the helm

3 *(par l'odorat) (odeur, fleur etc)* to smell; **je ne sens rien** I can't smell anything; **faire s. qch à qn** to let sb smell sth; *Fam* **je ne peux pas le s.** *(supporter)* I can't stand (the sight of) him, *Br* I can't stick him; *Fam* **je le sens pas bien, ce mec-là** *(il me déplaît)* I don't take to that guy, there's something about that guy I don't like; *Vieilli Fig* **s. le cadavre** to sense impending disaster

4 *(par le goût)* to taste

5 *(avoir l'odeur de)* to smell of; *(avoir un goût de)* to taste of; **cela sent le brûlé** *(dans une pièce)* there's a smell of burning; *(devant un mets etc)* it smells burnt; **ça sent le bébé/le linge frais** it smells of or there's a smell of babies/clean washing; **ça sent bon le pain frais** there's a delicious smell of fresh bread; **vin qui sent le bouchon** corked wine; **la pièce sent l'humidité** the room smells damp; **la salle sentait le tabac à plein nez** the room reeked of tobacco; *Fig* **ça sentait le piège à plein nez** I/he/*etc* could smell a trap; **il sentait l'acteur à plein nez** he had actor written all over him; *Péj* **ce livre sent l'effort** this book is very laboured; **cet article sent le plagiat** this article smacks of plagiarism; *Fam* **il sent le cadavre** he looks as if he's on his last legs

VI 1 s. bon/mauvais to smell good/bad; **fleurs qui sentent bon** sweet-smelling flowers; **ça sent fort** it has a strong smell

2 *Fam (puer)* to smell; **il sent des pieds** his feet smell, he has smelly feet

VPR se sentir 1 cela se sent it is something that you feel or sense

2 se s. bien/fatigué to feel well/tired; **se s. dix ans de moins** to feel ten years younger; **elle se sentait mourir/revivre** she felt she was dying/coming alive again; **se s. le courage de faire qch** to feel up to doing sth; **je ne m'en sens pas le courage** I don't feel equal or up to it; **tu t'en sens capable?** do you think you can manage it?, do you feel capable of it?

3 il ne se sent pas de joie he is beside himself with joy; *Fam* **ne plus se s.** *(agir comme un fou)* to have taken leave of one's senses; *(agir avec vanité)* to be very full of oneself

4 *Fam (se supporter)* **ils ne peuvent pas se s.** they can't stand (the sight of) each other, *Br* they can't stick each other

---

SEO [ɛsəo] *Compta (abrév sauf erreur ou omission)* E & OE

seoir [swar] **VI** *Litt (used only in prp* **seyant, séant;** *pr ind* **il sied, ils siéent;** *pr sub* **il siée, ils siéent;** *impf* **il seyait, ils seyaient;** *fu* **il siéra, ils siéront)** **s. à** to suit; **cette robe vous sied** that dress suits you or is very becoming **V IMPERS il lui sied de/lui sied mal de ... it** becomes him to/ill becomes him to ...; **comme il sied** as is fitting (**à** for)

Séoul [seul] **N** Seoul

sépale [sepal] **NM** *Bot* sepal

séparable [separabl] **ADJ** separable (**de** from); **deux théories difficilement séparables** two theories which are difficult to separate

séparateur, -trice [separatœr, -tris] **ADJ** separating, separative; *Opt (pouvoir)* resolving

NM *Tech* separator; *Ordinat* delimiter; *Ordinat* **s. de champs** field delimiter or separator; *TV* **s. de faisceau** beam splitter

séparation [separasjɔ̃] **NF 1** separation; **s. d'avec qn** separation from sb; **il n'a pas supporté la s. d'avec son épouse** he could not

bear to be parted or separated from his wife; **s. de la tête et du corps** severance of the head from the body; *Ordinat* **s. automatique des pages** automatic pagination; *Typ* **s. des couleurs** colour separation; **s. quadrichromique** four-colour separation

2 *Jur* **s. de corps** *(entre époux)* legal separation; **s. de fait, s. amiable** voluntary separation; **s. de biens** = marriage settlement under which husband and wife administer their separate properties

3 *Pol* **la s. des pouvoirs** the separation of powers; **s. de l'Église et de l'État** separation of Church and State

4 *(cloison)* partition, division; **mur de s.** dividing wall; **s. en bois** wooden partition; *Fig* boundary, dividing line

séparatisme [separatism] **NM** *Pol* separatism

séparatiste [separatist] **ADJ, N** *Pol* separatist

séparé [separe] **ADJ 1** *(distinct) (notions, chambres etc)* separate **2** *(désuni)* separated; **nous vivons s. l'un de l'autre** we've separated, we live apart; **il vit s. de sa femme** he's separated (from his wife)

séparément [separemã] **ADV** separately

séparer [separe] **VT 1** *(éloigner)* to separate (**de** from); **s. deux combattants** to part or separate two fighters; *Boxe* **séparez!** break!; **personne ne peut nous s.** no one can separate us or come between us; **la guerre sépare les familles** war separates families or keeps families apart; **des milliers de kilomètres nous séparent** we are thousands of miles apart, we are separated by thousands of miles

2 *(partager)* to divide; **le fleuve sépare la ville en deux** the river divides the town in two; **mur qui sépare deux champs** wall separating two fields; **s. une chambre en trois** to divide a room into three; **s. les cheveux en faisant une raie sur le côté** to part one's hair on the side

3 *(diviser)* to divide; **leurs opinions politiques les séparent** their political opinions divide them; **tout les sépare** they are poles apart; **jusqu'à ce que la mort nous sépare** till death do us part

4 *(isoler)* **s. les bons d'avec les mauvais** to separate the good from the bad; **s. la substance active de la substance inerte** to separate the active ingredient from the inert substances; **il faut savoir s. l'amour de la luxure** you must be able to distinguish between love and lust

VPR se séparer *(d'époux)* to separate, to part, *Fam* to split up; *(de la foule, d'une assemblée etc)* to break up, to disperse; *(d'une rivière, d'une route etc)* to divide, to branch off; **nous devons nous s. maintenant** we'll have to say goodbye now; **c'est ici que nos chemins se séparent** this is where we go our separate ways or where our paths diverge; **nous ne nous séparerons jamais** we shall never part; **l'armée se sépara** the army disbanded; **se s. de** ou **d'avec sa femme/son mari** to separate or part from one's wife/one's husband; **elle a dû se s. de son vieux chat/sa voiture** she had to part with her old cat/her car; *Chimie* **se s. à l'état cristallin** *(du sel)* to crystallize out

sépia [sepja] **NF** *(couleur, matière colorante)* sepia; **dessin à la s.** sepia drawing **ADJ INV** sepia

sept [sɛt] **ADJ INV 1** seven; **à s. heures** at seven o'clock; **les S. Merveilles du monde** the Seven Wonders of the World **2** *(dans des séries)* seventh; **page/numéro s.** page/number seven; **Édouard Sept** Edward the Seventh **NM INV** seven; **le s. mai** (on) the seventh of May, (on) May (the) seventh, *Am* (on) May seventh; *Cartes* **le s. de cœur** the seven of hearts; **habiter au s.** to live at number seven

septain [sɛtɛ̃] **NM** *Littér* seven-line stanza

septantaine [sɛptɑ̃tɛn] **NF** *Belg, Suisse* **1** *(quantité)* **une s.** around or about seventy, seventy or so; **une s. de voitures** around or about seventy cars **2** *(âge)* **avoir la s.** to be around or about seventy

septante [sɛptɑ̃t] **ADJ INV** *Belg, Suisse* seventy

NM INV *Bible* **la version des S.** the Septuagint

septantième [sɛptɑ̃tjɛm] *Belg, Suisse* **ADJ** seventieth

N seventieth (one)

septembre [sɛptɑ̃br] **NM** September; **en s., au mois de s.** in September SEE GRAMMAR A81–2; B60–2

septennal, -ale, -aux, -ales [sɛptɛnal, -o] **ADJ** *(période, parlement etc)* seven-year, *Fml* septennial

septennat [sɛptɛna] **NM** *(d'un président etc)* (seven-year) term

septentrion [sɛptɑ̃trijɔ̃] **NM** *Litt* north

septentrional, -ale, -aux, -ales [sɛptɑ̃trijɔnal, -o] **ADJ** northern

septicémie [sɛptisemi] **NF** *Méd* blood poisoning, septicaemia, *Am* septicemia

septicémique [sɛptisemik] **ADJ** *Méd* septicaemic, *Am* septicemic

septième [sɛtjɛm] **ADJ** seventh; **être au s. ciel** to be in seventh heaven; **s. étage** seventh or *Am* eighth floor; **le s. art** the cinema **N** *(personne, objet, événement etc)* seventh; **habiter au s.** to live on the seventh or *Am* eighth floor

NM *(fraction)* seventh; **trois septièmes** three sevenths

NF 1 *Mus* seventh **2** *Scol Anciennement* = top class or *Am* grade of primary school

septièmement [sɛtjɛmmɑ̃] **ADV** seventhly, in the seventh place

septique [sɛptik] **ADJ** septic; **fosse s.** septic tank

septuagénaire [sɛptɥaʒenɛr] **ADJ, N** septuagenarian, seventy-year-old

septuagésime [sɛptɥaʒezim] **NF** *Rel* Septuagesima

septum [sɛptɔm] **NM** *Anat, Bot* septum

septuor [sɛptɥɔr] **NM** *Mus* septet(te)

septuple [sɛptɥpl] **ADJ** sevenfold, *Fml* septuple

NM au s. sevenfold; **le s. de deux** seven times two; **payer le s.** to pay seven times as much

septupler [sɛptɥple] **VTI** to increase sevenfold

sépulcral, -ale, -aux, -ales [sepylkral, -o] **ADJ** sepulchral

sépulcre [sepylkr] **NM** sepulchre; **le saint s.** the Holy Sepulchre; *Fig* **s. blanchi** whited sepulchre

sépulture [sepyltyr] **NF 1** *Litt (inhumation)* burial; **refuser la s. à qn** to refuse burial to sb; **être privé de s.** to be refused burial **2** *(lieu)* burial place; **sépultures militaires** war cemeteries; **violation de s.** desecration of graves

séquelles [sekɛl] **NFPL** *(de maladie, d'accident)* aftereffects; *(de guerre, catastrophe etc)* aftermath; **une des s. de la guerre** one of the consequences or aftereffects of the war

séquençage [sekɑ̃saʒ] **NM** *Biol* sequencing

séquence [sekɑ̃s] **NF** sequence; *Cartes* run; *Ordinat* **s. de caractères** character string, sequence of characters; *Biol* **s. génétique** gene sequence; *Aut* **s. de combustion** firing order; **s. vidéo** video sequence

séquencer [sekɑ̃se] **VT** *(en génétique)* to sequence

séquenceur [sekɑ̃sœr] **NM** *Ordinat* sequencer

séquentiel, -ielle [sekɑ̃sjɛl] ADJ sequential; *Ordinat* accès s. sequential or serial access

séquentiellement [sekɑ̃sjɛlmɑ̃] ADV sequentially

séquestration [sekɛstrasjɔ̃] NF *Jur* **1** *(de biens)* sequestration **2** *(de personne)* illegal confinement

séquestre [sekɛstr] NM *Jur* **1** *(action)* sequestration; *Naut* embargo; **mettre qch sous s.** to sequester or seize sth **2** *(personne)* depository, trustee, administrator

séquestrer [sekɛstre] VT **1** *(biens)* to sequester, to sequestrate; *Naut (navire)* to lay an embargo upon **2 s. qn** to keep sb locked up; *Jur* to confine sb illegally
▪ VPR **se séquestrer** to cut oneself off from the world

séquoia [sekɔja] NM *(arbre)* sequoia

sérac [serak] NM *Géol* serac

sérail [seraj] NM seraglio; *Fig* **c'est normal qu'il soit un financier international, il est né** *ou* **a été élevé dans le s.** it's not surprising he's an international financier, he grew up in that world

séraphin [serafɛ̃] NM seraph VOIR GRAMMAIRE A14

séraphique [serafik] ADJ seraphic

serbe [sɛrb] ADJ Serb, Serbian
N **S.** Serb, Serbian

Serbie [sɛrbi] NF Serbia

serbo-croate [sɛrbɔkrɔat] ADJ Serbo-Croat(ian)
NM *Ling* Serbo-Croat

Sercq [sɛrk] NM Sark

séré [sere] NM *Suisse* fromage frais

serein¹ [sərɛ̃] ADJ *(personne, visage, esprit, jour etc)* serene, calm; *(ciel, nuit)* clear; **jugement s.** calm or impartial judgement

serein² NM evening dew

sereinement [sərɛnmɑ̃] ADV serenely, calmly

sérénade [serenad] NF **1** *Mus* serenade; **donner la s. à qn** to serenade sb **2** *Fam (tapage)* racket; **le bébé nous a fait une drôle de s. toute la nuit** the baby treated us to a demonstration of his vocal power all night; **il nous a fait sa s. habituelle** he treated us to one of his usual scenes

sérénissime [serenisim] ADJ **son Altesse s.** His/Her Most Serene Highness

sérénité [serenite] NF serenity, calmness; **avec s.** serenely, calmly

séreuse¹ [serøz] NF *Anat* serous membrane

séreux, -euse² [serø, -øz] ADJ *Anat, Méd* serous

serf, serve [serf, sɛrv] *Hist* N serf
ADJ **condition serve** serfdom; **terre serve** land in bondage or in villein tenure

serfouette [sɛrfwɛt] NF combined hoe and fork

serge [sɛrʒ] NF *Tex* serge

sergent [sɛrʒɑ̃] NM **1** *Mil* sergeant; **s. fourrier, s. comptable** quartermaster sergeant; **s. instructeur** drill sergeant; *Can* **s. d'armes** sergeant at arms; *Arch* **s. de ville** policeman **2** *Tech* cramp, clamp

sergent-chef, *pl* **sergents-chefs** NM *Mil* staff sergeant

séricicole [serisikɔl] ADJ silkworm-breeding, *Spéc* sericultural

sériciculteur, -trice [serisikyltœr, -tris] N silkworm breeder, *Spéc* sericulturist

sériciculture [serisikyltyr] NF silkworm breeding, *Spéc* sericulture

série [seri] NF VOIR GRAMMAIRE A13 **1** *(d'événements, de changements, de dates etc)* series, succession; *Sport (épreuve)* heat; *Billard*

break; *Billard (de canons)* run; **s. de catastrophes, s. noire** series or catalogue of disasters, run of bad luck; **livre de s. noire** (crime) thriller; **s. de conférences** series or course of lectures; *Radio, TV* **s. (télévisée/radiophonique)** (television/radio) series; *TV* **s. AB** popular television; **s. dramatique** drama series; **s. policière** crime series, *Fam* cop show; *Sport* **s. éliminatoire** qualifying heat

2 *(d'articles de presse, de timbres etc)* series; *(de documents, d'outils etc)* set; *(d'échantillons etc)* range; *Ind, Com (de marchandises)* range, line; *Math, Chimie, Phys, Nucl* series; **s. complète de connaissances** full set of bills of lading; *Admin etc* **s. de prix** *(pour travaux publics etc)* list of charges; **s. de produits** product line; *Fam* **elle en a toute une s.** she has a whole collection of them; **en** *ou* **par série(s)** in series, serially; *Élec* **en s.** in series; **fabrication** *ou* **production en s.** mass production; **fabriquer qch en s.** to mass-produce sth; **chaîne de fabrication en s.** production line; **voiture de s.** standard car; *Com* **fins de séries** ends of lines, oddments, remnants; *(livres invendus)* remainders; **article hors s.** custom-made or custom-built article; **numéro hors s.** *(magazine)* special issue; *Fig* **c'est tout à fait hors s.** it's quite exceptional; **une personnalité hors s.** an exceptional personality

3 *(groupe)* group, category; *Sport* rank; *Boxe* **s. poids plume** featherweight rating; *Cin* **film de s. B** B-movie or film; *Péj* **film de s. Z** real bummer of a film

4 *Scol* specialization; **choisir une s.** to choose a specialization, to decide what one is going to specialize in
ADJ INV *Ordinat* serial

sériel, -ielle [serjɛl] ADJ serial; *Mus* serial, twelve-tone, dodecaphonic

sérier [serje] VT *(impf, pr sub* **n. sériions, v. sériiez)** to arrange (in series), to classify

sérieusement [serjøzmɑ̃] ADV **1** *(avec sérieux)* seriously; *(sincèrement)* seriously, genuinely; **parlez-vous s.?** are you serious?, do you really mean it? **2** *(gravement) (malade, blessé, handicapé)* seriously; **il en a s. besoin** he's seriously in need of it

sérieux, -ieuse [serjø, -jøz] ADJ **1** *(qui ne plaisante pas)* serious; *(sincère) (offre, acheteur etc)* serious, genuine; *(information)* reliable; *(employé, entreprise etc)* responsible, reliable, serious; **des lectures sérieuses** serious reading; *Fam* **s. comme un pape** as solemn as a judge; **êtes-vous s.?** are you serious or in earnest?, do you mean it?; **d'un ton** *ou* **d'un air s.** seriously; **peu s.** *(personne)* unreliable; **voyons, ce n'est pas s.** come on, you're not serious or you don't mean it; **pas s. s'abstenir** *(dans une petite annonce)* genuine replies only; *Com* **client s.** good customer

2 *(important) (maladie, blessure, affaire, situation etc)* serious; **il a fait de s. progrès** he has made good or considerable progress; **si seulement tu avais des raisons sérieuses de refuser** if only you had good reasons to refuse
NM seriousness; **garder son s.** to keep a straight face; **se prendre au s.** to take oneself seriously; **je vous ai pris au s.** I took you seriously, I thought you were serious, I thought you meant it; **on ne peut pas la prendre au s.** you can't take her seriously; **manque de s.** unreliability; **avec s.** seriously
ADV *Fam (sérieusement)* seriously; **ils se sont foutus sur la gueule s.** they seriously went for each other; **s.?** seriously?

serif [serif] NM *Typ* serif

sérigraphie [serigrafi] NF silk-screen printing

sérigraphié [serigrafje] ADJ silk-screen(-printed)

serin, -ine [sərɛ̃, -in] NM *Orn* canary
ADJ INV **jaune s.** canary yellow
ADJ *Fam (personne)* silly, stupid, idiotic
N *Fam (idiot)* nitwit

seriner [sərine] VT **1** *Péj* **s. qch à qn** to go on and on at sb about sth; **s. à qn que ...** to tell sb time after time that ... **2 s. un air à un oiseau** to teach a bird to sing by using a bird organ

seringa(t) [sərɛ̃ga] NM *Bot* seringa

seringue [sərɛ̃g] NF syringe; *Méd* **s. à injections** hypodermic syringe; **s. jetable** disposable syringe; *Aut* **s. à graisse** grease gun

serment [sɛrmɑ̃] NM *(parole solennelle)* oath; *(promesse)* pledge; *(d'amoureux)* vow, pledge; **prêter s.** to take an oath; *(d'un jury)* to be sworn in; **faire prêter s. à qn** to administer the oath to sb; **déclarer sous s.** to state or declare under oath; **déclaration sous s.** sworn statement, statement under oath; **certifier qch sous s.** to declare sth on oath; **violer un s.** to break an oath; **être sous la foi du s.** to be on oath; **faire le s. de faire qch** to swear or vow or pledge to do sth; **faire un faux s.** to commit perjury
▪▪ **s. d'allégeance** oath of allegiance; *Méd* **s. d'Hippocrate** Hippocratic oath; **s. d'ivrogne** empty promise; *Pol* **s. politique** oath of allegiance; *Admin* **s. professionnel** *(des magistrats, des avocats, de la police etc)* oath of office

sermon [sɛrmɔ̃] NM *Rel* sermon (**sur** on); *Fam Péj (remontrance)* sermon, lecture; *Bible* **le S. sur la Montagne** the Sermon on the Mount

sermonner [sɛrmɔne] VT *Fam Péj* **s. qn** to lecture sb, to give sb a lecture or talking-to

sermonneur, -euse [sɛrmɔnœr, -øz] *Fam Péj* ADJ sermonizing
N sermonizer

séroconversion [serɔkɔ̃vɛrsjɔ̃] NF *Méd* seroconversion

sérodiagnostic [serɔdjagnɔstik] NM *Méd* serodiagnosis

sérologie [serɔlɔʒi] NF serology; **faire une s.** to be screened for antibodies

séronégatif, -ive [serɔnegatif, -iv] *Méd* ADJ HIV negative
N person who is HIV negative

séronégativité [serɔnegativite] NF *Méd* the state of being HIV negative; **prouver sa s.** to prove that one is HIV negative

séropo [seropo] ADJ, N *Fam abrév* séropositif

séropositif, -ive [serɔpɔzitif, -iv] *Méd* ADJ HIV positive
N person who is HIV positive; **séropositifs non-évoluteurs** long-term survivors, LTS

séropositivité [serɔpɔzitivite] NF *Méd* the state of being HIV positive; **taux de s.** HIV positive rate; **il a été renvoyé à cause de sa s.** he was dismissed for being HIV positive

sérosité [serozite] NF serous fluid

serpe [sɛrp] NF billhook; **visage taillé à coups de s.** rugged face

serpent [sɛrpɑ̃] NM **1** *(reptile)* snake; *UE, Fin* (currency) snake; *Bible* **le s.** the serpent; **s. à coiffe** *ou* **à lunettes** (Indian) cobra; **s. d'eau** water snake; **s. de mer** *Myth* sea serpent; *(poisson)* pipe fish; *Journ* stock story; **s. à sonnettes** rattlesnake, *Am Fam* rattler; **s. à sonnettes cornu** horned rattlesnake, *Am Fam* sidewinder; **s. de verre** slow-worm; *Fig* **s. de fumée** wreath or coil of smoke; *Écon* **s. monétaire européen** European currency snake; *Journ* **s. de mer** silly-season story **2** *Hist, Mus* serpent

serpentaire [sɛrpɑ̃tɛr] NF **1** *Bot* serpentaria;

s. de Virginie snakeroot **2** *Orn* serpent eater, secretary bird

serpentant [sɛrpɑ̃tɑ̃] ADJ *(courant, route etc)* winding, snaking, meandering

serpenteau, -eaux [sɛrpɑ̃to] NM **1** *Zool* young snake **2** *(fusée volante)* serpent

serpenter [sɛrpɑ̃te] VI *(d'une rivière, d'une route etc)* to wind, to snake, to meander; **le chemin monte/descend en serpentant** the road winds *or* snakes *or* meanders up/down

serpentin, -ine [sɛrpɑ̃tɛ̃, -in] ADJ serpentine
NM **1** *Tech* coil **2** *(ruban pour les fêtes)* paper streamer
NF *Minér* **serpentine** serpentine, ophite

serpette [sɛrpɛt] NF pruning knife

serpillière [sɛrpijɛr] NF floorcloth; **passer la s. dans la cuisine** to mop the kitchen floor

serpolet [sɛrpɔlɛ] NM *Bot* wild thyme

serrage [sɛraʒ] NM *Tech (d'une vis, d'un écrou, d'un nœud etc)* tightening; *(d'un joint)* clamping; **s. des freins** application of the brakes, braking; **vis de s.** set screw, locking screw

serre [sɛr] NF **1** *(construction)* greenhouse; *(qui fait partie d'une maison)* conservatory; **s. chaude** hothouse; **s. de palmiers** palm house; **plante de s.** hothouse plant; **plantes sous s.** plants under glass; *Écol* **effet de s.** greenhouse effect; *Écol* **gaz à effet de s.** greenhouse gas **2** *(action) (des raisins etc)* pressing, squeezing **3** serres *(des oiseaux de proie)* claws, talons

serré [sɛre] ADJ *(bottes, vêtements, nœud, vis etc)* tight; *(texture)* close; *(formation)* dense; *(discussion)* closely argued; *(argumentation)* closely reasoned; *(programme)* tight; *Géog (col)* narrow; **budget s.** tight budget; **surveillance serrée** close supervision; **étude serrée** *(d'un texte)* close *or* intensive study; **style s.** concise style; **on était vraiment serrés dans cette voiture** we were really (tightly) packed in that car; **une robe serrée à la taille** a dress with a fitted waist; **un café noir bien s.** a strong black coffee; **pluie serrée** teeming rain; **deux pages d'une écriture serrée** two closely written pages; **les dents serrées** with clenched teeth; **elle était pâle, les lèvres serrées** she was pale, her lips pressed tightly together; **maisons serrées** houses huddled together; **serrés comme des harengs** *ou* **des sardines** packed like sardines; **rangs serrés** serried *or* closed ranks; **avoir le cœur s.** to be sad at heart, to have a heavy heart; **la gorge serrée** with a lump in one's throat; *Sport* **la partie va être serrée** it's going to be a tight *or* close game; *Sport etc* **arrivée serrée** close finish
ADV **écrire s.** to have cramped handwriting; **tricoter s.** to knit tightly; *Fig* **jouer s.** to play a cautious game, to take no chances

serre-fils NM INV *Élec* wire-retaining screw

serre-frein(s) NM INV *Rail* brakeman

serre-joint(s) NM INV *(outil)* clamp

serre-livres NM INV book end

serrement [sɛrmɑ̃] NM **s. de main** handshake; **avoir un s. de cœur** to feel a pang; **elles se dirent au revoir avec un s. de cœur** they both felt a pang as they said their goodbyes; **il comprit dans un s. de cœur que la maladie serait fatale** his heart sank as he realized the illness was fatal

serre-patte, *pl* **serre-pattes** [sɛrpat] NM *Fam* sergeant

SERRER [sɛre] VT **1** *(saisir, tenir)* to grip, to clasp; *(presser)* to squeeze, to press; **s. la main à** *ou* **de qn** to shake hands with sb, to shake sb's hand; **tenir qch sans s.** to hold sth loosely; **s. qn entre ses bras** to clasp sb in one's arms, to hug sb; **s. qn/qch contre soi** to

hold sb/sth tightly to one; **s. le cou à qn** to wring sb's neck; **cela me serre le cœur** it wrings my heart; **le chagrin lui serrait la gorge** he felt choked with grief
2 *(d'un vêtement, des chaussures etc) (personne)* to be too tight for; **s. les pieds à qn** to pinch sb's feet; **cette jupe me serre (à) la taille** this skirt is too tight round the waist
3 *(nœud, écrou, ceinture etc)* to tighten; *(joint)* to clamp; *(voiles)* to furl, to take in; *(poings)* to clench; **s. les dents** to clench one's teeth; *Fig* to grit one's teeth; **s. les freins** to put on *or* apply the brakes; *Mus* **en serrant** stringendo
4 *(rapprocher)* to close up, to put close together; *Mil, Fig* **s. les rangs** to close ranks; **s. son style** to condense one's style; *Typ* **s. une ligne** to close up a line
5 *(être près de) (personne, chose)* to keep close to; *Naut (côte), Aut (trottoir)* to hug; **s. qn de près** to follow sb closely; *Fig* **s. une femme de près** to be all over a woman; **s. un adversaire dans un coin** to corner an enemy; **s. une question de près** to focus narrowly on a question; **s. le vent** to sail close to the wind
6 *(ranger) Can, Litt* **s. des bijoux dans une cassette** to stow one's jewels in a case
7 *Fam (emprisonner) Br* to nick, to lift, *Am* to bust
VI **serrez à droite!** keep to the right!
VPR **se serrer 1** *(se rapprocher)* to squeeze up *or* together; **se s. les uns contre les autres** to huddle together; **se s. contre qn** to snuggle up to sb; *(pour être protégé)* to cling to sb; **se s. contre un mur** to hug a wall
2 **mon cœur se serra** my heart sank; **ma gorge se serra** I had a lump in my throat; **nous nous serrâmes la main** we shook hands **3** *Fig* **se s. (la ceinture)** to tighten one's belt; *Fam* **s. les coudes** to back one another up, to support one another

serre-tête NM INV **1** *(bandeau)* headband **2** *Sport (bonnet)* cap; *Aviat* helmet

serriculture [sɛrikyltyr] NF hothouse growing

serrure [sɛryr] NF lock; **trou de la s.** keyhole; **s. de capot** bonnet lock; **s. à carte perforée** card-operated lock; **s. électronique** electronic lock, computer-coded lock; **s. magnétique** magnetic lock; **s. de sûreté** safety lock

serrurerie [sɛryrri] NF **1** *(métier)* locksmith's trade; *(magasin)* locksmith's (shop) **2** *(travail, ouvrages)* ironwork, metal work; **s. d'art** ornamental ironwork; **grosse s.** heavy ironwork

serrurier [sɛryrje] NM **1** *(de serrures)* locksmith **2** *(de métaux)* ironsmith

sertir [sɛrtir] VT *(pierre précieuse)* to set; *(cartouche, boîte de conserve etc)* to crimp

sertissage [sɛrtisaʒ] NM *(d'une pierre précieuse)* setting; *(d'une cartouche, d'une boîte de conserve etc)* crimping

sertisseur, -euse [sɛrtisœr, -øz] N *(ouvrier) (de pierres précieuses)* setter; *(de cartouches, de boîtes de conserve etc)* crimper
NM *(appareil) (pour boîtes de conserves etc)* crimper

sertissure [sɛrtisyr] NF *(action, manière) (de pierre précieuse)* setting; *(partie de chaton)* bezel

sérum [serɔm] NM **1** *Physiol, Méd* serum; **s. physiologique** saline solution, saline; **s. sanguin** blood serum; **s. de vérité** truth serum; *Fam* truth drug **2 s. (lactique)** whey

servage [sɛrvaʒ] NM *Hist* serfdom, bondage; *Fig* bondage

serval, -als [sɛrval] NM *Zool* serval

servant, -ante [sɛrvɑ̃, -ɑ̃t] ADJ **frère s.** lay brother; **cavalier** *ou* **chevalier s.** faithful admirer
NM **1** *Mil* gunner **2** *Rel* **s. (de messe)** server

NF **servante 1** *(domestique)* (maid)servant **2** *(table)* side table **3** *Tech* (adjustable) support

serve [sɛrv] ADJ, N *voir* **serf**

serveur, -euse [sɛrvœr, -øz] N **1** *(dans un bar)* barman, *surtout Am* bartender, f barmaid; *(dans un restaurant)* waiter, f waitress **2** *Cartes* dealer **3** *Tennis* server
NM *Ordinat* server; **s. de fichiers** file server; **s. FTP** FTP server; **s. mandataire** proxy server; **s. Minitel®** Minitel® service provider; **s. de réseau** network server; **s. sécurisé** secure server; **s. télématique** bulletin board (system); **s. Web** HTTP server

serviabilité [sɛrvjabilite] NF obligingness, helpfulness

serviable [sɛrvjabl] ADJ obliging, helpful

SERVICE [sɛrvis]

┌──────────────────────────────────────┐
│ service **1–3, 5, 7, 9** ▪ duty **4** │
│ ▪ department **5** ▪ operation **6**   │
│ ▪ favour **8** ▪ sitting **10** ▪ set **11** │
└──────────────────────────────────────┘

NM **1** *(pour un client, un maître)* service; **le s. est désastreux** *(dans ce restaurant)* the service here is appalling; **faire le s.** to serve; **(non) compris** service (not) included; **libre s.** *(dans un magasin etc)* self-service; *Écon* **services** services; **les biens et les services** goods and services; **le secteur des services** the service sector; **société de services** service company; **entrer en s. (chez qn)** to go into (sb's) service, to go into service (with sb); **gens de s.** domestic staff; **être au s. de qn** to be in sb's service; **se passer des services d'un employé** to dispense with an employee's services; **mourir au s. du roi** to die in the king's service; **escalier de s.** backstairs; **porte de s.** tradesmen's entrance; *Admin, Mil* **états de s.** service record; *Com* **s. après vente** after-sales service; **s. clients** customer service; **s. à l'américaine** *(dans un restaurant)* American service; **s. à l'anglaise** *(dans un restaurant)* English service; **s. à la française** *(dans un restaurant)* French service; **s. à la russe** *(dans un restaurant)* Russian service; **s. à l'assiette** *(dans un restaurant)* plate service, American service; **s. au guéridon** *(dans un restaurant)* gueridon service, French service; **s. à table** table service, waiter service, waitress service; **services bancaires** banking services; *Banque* **services de caisse** counter services; **s. dans les chambres** *ou* **en chambre** room service; **services à la clientèle** customer services, customer-support services; **s. du contentieux** *(département)* legal department; *(personnes)* legal experts; *Admin* **s. contractuel** contract service; *Fin* **s. d'un emprunt** servicing a loan; *Fin* **s. des intérêts** interest charges

2 *Mil* **s. militaire (obligatoire)** (compulsory) military service; **faire son s.** to do one's military service; **en s. actif, en activité de s.** on the active list; **service(s) de guerre** active service; **en s. aux armées** on active service; **(in)apte au s.** (un)fit for service; **bon pour le s.** *(jeune appelé)* fit for service; *Fig (appareil)* in working order; **être libéré du s.** to be discharged; **libération du s.** discharge

3 *Tennis* service; **faire un** *ou* **le s.** to serve; **au s., Martin** Martin to serve

4 *(travail)* duty; **s. de jour** day duty; **s. de nuit** night duty; *Naut* night watch; **être de s./ne pas être de s.** to be on/off duty; **à quelle heure prenez-vous/quittez-vous votre s.?** at what time do you go on/off duty?; **avoir dix ans de s. dans une entreprise** to have completed ten years' service with a company; **reprendre du s.** *(personne)* to return to work; *(machine)* to be brought back into operation *or* service; **après des années d'inactivité, le chanteur a repris du s.** after years of silence, the singer has made a comeback; *Mil etc* **mort en s. commandé** killed on active service; **s. de corvée** *Mil* fatigue duty; *Naut* duty; **s. de garde** guard duty; **planton de s.** duty orderly; **tableau de s.** duty chart *or* list *or* roster; **officier/sous-officier de s.** duty/non-commissioned officer; *Fam* **le crétin/pigeon de s.** the usual *or* inevitable cretin/sucker; *Fam* **être s. s.** to be a stickler for rules and regulations

5 *(département)*, *Admin*, *Com* department; *Mil* corps, service; *Méd etc* department, service; **chef de s.** head of department; **correspondance de s.** official correspondence; **s. central** headquarters; **s. clientèle** customer service (department); **s. d'études** research department; **s. de relation avec la clientèle** customer service department; **services commerciaux** marketing services; **services financiers** financial services; **s. informatique** computer department

6 *(d'une machine etc)* operation; **s. à bras** *ou* **manuel** hand *or* manual operation; **en s.** *(machine)* in service, in use, in operation; *(avion, navire)* in commission; **aptitude au s.** serviceability; **en (bon) état de s.**, **propre au s.** in (good) working order, serviceable; **hors (de) s.** *(machine, mécanisme)* out of order; *(canon)* out of action; *(navire)* disabled; **mettre en s.** *(machine etc)* to bring *or* put into service; *(avion, navire)* to bring *or* put into commission; **retirer du s.** to withdraw from service *or* from use; *(avion, navire)* to decommission; **retirer graduellement du s.** to phase out

7 *(transport)* service; **assurer** *ou* **faire le s. entre … et …** to operate between … and …; **s. assuré toute l'année** year-round service; **s. de marchandises** goods *or* freight service; **s. de voyageurs** passenger service

8 *(aide)* favour, *Am* favor, service; **rendre (un) s. à qn** *(d'une personne)* to do sb a favour *or* a service; **si ça peut te rendre s., prends-le** if it's of any use to you, take it; **rendre un bon/un mauvais s. à qn** to do sb a good/a bad turn; **demander un s. à qn** to ask sb a favour; **les services qu'il a rendus à l'enseignement** his services to education; **ce livre m'a rendu grand s.** I found this book very useful; **à votre s.** at your service; **qu'y a-t-il pour votre s.?** what can I do for you?

9 *(en élevage) (d'un étalon)* service

10 *(ensemble de repas)* sitting; *Rail etc* **dernier s. à deux heures** last sitting (for lunch) at two o'clock

11 *(d'ustensiles de cuisine, de linge de table etc)* set; **s. (de table)** *(assiettes etc)* dinner service; *(linge)* set of table linen; **s. à découper** carving knife and fork

INT *Suisse (je vous en prie)* don't mention it!, you're welcome!

NMPL *Suisse* **services** *(couverts)* knifes and forks *(for laying table)*

▸▸**s. des achats** purchasing (department); *(plus grand)* procurement (department); **s. d'action commerciale** marketing department; **s. administratif** administration (department); *Fam* admin; **s. après-vente** aftersales (department); **services autoroutiers** motorway services; **s. babyphone** baby-listening service; *Méd* **s. de cardiologie** cardiology department; **s. des commandes** order department; **s. commercial export** export department; **s. comptable** *ou* **de comptabilité** accounts (department); **s. de conseil** consulting service; **s. consommateurs** customer service (department); *Méd* **s. des contagieux** isolation ward; **s. contrôle qualité, s. de contrôle de qualité** quality control (department); **s. du courrier** mail room; **s. de dépannage** repair service; *Aut* recovery service; *Fin* **s. de la dette** debt servicing; **s. des eaux** = water board; **s. d'écoute** monitoring service; **s. d'étude mer-**

catique marketing research department; **s. de l'expédition** shipping (department); **s. export** export (department); **s. export intégré** integrated export service; **services extérieurs** external services; **s. de facturation** invoicing department; **s. financier** finance (department); **s. de fixation des prix** pricing department; **s. gouvernemental** government agency *or* department; **s. de l'immigration** immigration department; **services industriels** industrial services; **s. informations** enquiries; *Journ* **s. des informations** information service; **s. informatique** EDP-department, computer department; **s. juridique** legal department; **s. lancement** product launch department; *Ordinat* **s. en ligne** on-line service; **s. marketing** marketing department; **s. marketing-vente** sales and marketing department; **s. mercatique** marketing department; **s. d'ordre** *(police)* police contingent; *(dans une manifestation etc)* team of stewards; **s. du personnel** personnel (department); **s. des postes** *ou* **postal** postal service, *surtout Am* mail service; **s. de presse** press office; **s. (de) production** production department; **s. de la prospection** sales and marketing (department), new business department; **s. public** civil service; *TV* public-service broadcasting (network); **s. de la publicité** publicity *or* advertising department; **services publics** (public) utilities; **s. de recherche** research department; **s. de recouvrement** collection department; **Service régional de la police judiciaire** *Br* ≃ regional crime squad; **s. de relations publiques** public relations department; **s. de remorquage et de dépannage** breakdown and recovery service; **s. de renseignements** information office; *Tél* directory enquiries, *Am* information; *Mil* military intelligence (department); *Com* **s. des renseignements commerciaux** status enquiry department; **s. de santé** health services; **services du secteur tertiaire** business services; **services de soutien** support services; **s. de stylique** design department; *(plus grand)* procurement (department); **services supplémentaires** service backup; **s. technique** engineering department, technical branch; *Ordinat* **s. télématique** bulletin board service; *Arg* **s. trois-pièces** wedding tackle; **s. d'urgence** emergency service; **s. vente** *ou* **des ventes** sales department; **s. de voiturier** valet parking

---

Service militaire

Military service (for a period of ten months) used to be compulsory for French men aged between 18 and 26 unless they were declared unfit for service ("réformé"). As an alternative to military service, some chose to work overseas, often in developing countries, as part of a voluntary aid scheme known as "la coopération". However, following the "loi de programmation" 1997–2002, a reform was introduced in order to gradually abolish military service and move towards an exclusively professional army.

---

serviette [sɛrvjɛt] **NF 1 s. (de table)** (table) napkin, serviette; **s. d'enfant** feeder, bib **2** towel; **s. de toilette** hand towel; **s. de plage** beach towel; **s. sans fin** roller towel **3** *(sac)* briefcase

▸▸**s. hygiénique** sanitary towel *or Am* napkin

serviette-éponge, *pl* **serviettes-éponges** **NF** terry towel

servile [sɛrvil] **ADJ** servile; *(imitation, traduction, traducteur)* slavish

servilement [sɛrvilmɑ̃] **ADV** servilely; *(imiter, traduire)* slavishly

servilité [sɛrvilite] **NF** servility; *(d'imitation, de traduction)* slavishness

SERVIR [sɛrvir] *(prp* servant; *pp* servi; *pr ind* je sers, il sert, n. servons; *pr sub* je serve; *impf* je servais; *p hist* je servis; *fu* je servirai)

VI to be useful **1** ▪ to be used for *(servir à)* **2** ▪ to be used as *(servir de)* **3** ▪ to serve **4, 5**
VT to serve **1–4, 6** ▪ to wait on **1**
VPR to help oneself **1** ▪ to be served **2** ▪ to use *(se servir de)* **4**

VI 1 *(être utile)* to be useful *or* of use (**à qn** to sb); **la machine peut encore s.** the machine can still be used *or* is still fit for use; **la voiture peut encore s. quelques années** the car has still got a few years' use left in it; **cela peut s. un de ces jours** it may come in handy *or* be of use one day; **toujours prêt à s.** always ready for use

2 s. à qch/à faire qch *(être destiné à)* to be used for sth/for doing sth; **ne s. à rien** to be (of) no use, to be useless; **je vais le lui dire, mais je sais que ça ne servira à rien** I'm going to tell him but I know it won't do any good *or* it'll be pointless; **ça ne servira pas à grand-chose** that won't be much good *or* much use; **cela ne sert qu'à l'irriter** it only irritates him *or Fml* serves to irritate him; **à quoi cela sert-il?, à quoi ça sert?** what's the good *or* the use *or* the point of that?; **à quoi sert ce truc-là?** what's that gadget (used) for?; **je ne vois pas à quoi sert d'y aller** I don't see the point *or* good of going; **à quoi sert qu'on l'attende?** what's the point *or* use of waiting for him/her?

3 s. de *(d'un objet)* to serve as, to be used as; *(d'une personne)* to act as; **les pupitres servent de tables** the desks serve *or* are used as tables; **s. de prétexte** to serve as a pretext; **elle lui a servi de mère** she has been (like) a mother to him; **tu vas me s. de conseiller** you'll act as *or* be my adviser

4 *Tennis* to serve; *Cartes* **à vous de s.** (it's) your deal

5 *(dans l'armée, dans le gouvernement etc)* to serve (**sous** under); *Mil* **en âge de s.** of military age; **s. à table** to wait at table, *Am* wait (on) table

V IMPERS **il ne sert à rien de pleurer** it's no good *or* use crying, there's no point in crying; **rien ne sert de courir, il faut partir à point** slow and steady wins the race

VT 1 *(consommateur, dîner, poisson etc)* to serve; *(dîneur)* to wait on, to serve; *(client)* to serve, to attend to; **s. qn en marchandises** to supply sb with goods; **s. Dieu/le roi** to serve God/the king; *Vieilli* **Comte de Monte-Cristo, pour vous s.** the Count of Monte-Cristo, at your service; **est-ce qu'on vous sert?** are you being served *or* attended to?; **tout le monde est servi?** has everybody got a drink/something to eat?; *(dans un magasin)* is anybody waiting to be served?; **madame est servie** dinner is served, madam; **vous pouvez nous s., Nestor** you may serve dinner, Nestor; **à s. frais** best (served) chilled; **puis-je vous s. de gratin?** can I serve you with *or* help you to some gratin?; **s. à boire à qn** to give sb a drink *or* something to drink; **nous sommes très bien servis** we have very good domestic help; **on est très bien servi dans ce restaurant** the service in this restaurant is very good; **on n'est jamais si bien servi que par soi-même** if you want something done, do it yourself; *Fam* **en fait de pluie, nous sommes servis** as far as rain goes, we get more than our share; **ce cours d'eau sert le moulin** this stream drives the mill; **s. une rente à qn** to pay an annuity to sb

2 *(aider)* *(personne)* to help, to assist, to be of service to; *(intérêts)* to serve, to further; *(patrie, cause)* to serve; **en quoi puis-je vous s.?** what can I do for you?, how can I help you *or Fml* be of service to you?; **les choses l'ont bien servi** things have worked in his favour; **sa mémoire l'a mal servi** his memory served him badly; **mes études m'ont peu servi** my studies haven't been of much use to me *or* haven't got me anywhere much; **cela m'a peu servi pour obtenir un emploi** that wasn't much use to me in getting a job
3 *Tennis (balle)* to serve
4 *(d'un étalon) (jument)* to serve, to cover
5 *(à la chasse) (animal)* to dispatch
6 *Rel* **s. la messe** to serve at mass
7 *Suisse (utiliser)* to use; **c'est un manteau que je ne sers plus** I don't wear this coat any more
VPR se servir 1 *(d'une personne)* **se s. d'un plat** to help oneself to a dish; **servez-vous!** help yourself!; **je me suis déjà servie deux fois** I've already had two helpings
2 *(d'un plat, d'un vin etc)* to be served; **le champagne se sert frappé** champagne should be *or* is best served chilled
3 *Com* **se s. chez Martin** to shop at Martin's
4 **se s. de qch/qn** *(utiliser)* to use sth/sb; **se s. d'un parapluie comme d'un pare-soleil** to use an umbrella as a sunshade; **il sait se s. de ses poings** he knows how to use his fists, he's good with his fists

serviteur [sɛrvitœr] NM servant; **s. de l'État** civil servant; *Arch* **votre s.** *(dans une lettre)* your obedient servant; *Arch, Hum* **personne ne le sait mieux que votre s.** no one knows it better than yours truly

servitude [sɛrvityd] NF **1** *(asservissement)* servitude; *(contrainte)* constraint; **réduire un pays en s.** to reduce a country to servitude; **la s. de la mode** the tyranny *or* constraints of fashion **2** *Jur* easement; **s. de passage** right of way

servo [sɛrvo] NM *Aut etc* **s. à air comprimé** compressed-air servo

servocommande [sɛrvɔkɔmãd] NF *Aviat, Aut etc* servo(control)

servodirection [sɛrvodirɛksjɔ̃] NF *Aut etc* servo steering, power steering

servofrein [sɛrvofrɛ̃] NM *Aut etc* servobrake, servo-assisted brake

servomécanisme [sɛrvomekanism] NM *Tech* servomechanism, servo system

servomoteur [sɛrvomotœr] NM *Tech* servomotor

ses [se] ADJ POSS *voir* **son¹**

sésame [sezam] NM **1** *Bot* sesame **2** **s., ouvre-toi!** open, sesame!; **ce diplôme lui a servi de s.** the diploma opened doors for him/her

session [sesjɔ̃] NF **1** *Parl, Jur* session, sitting **2** *Univ (examens)* (exam) session; **la s. de juin** the June exams; **il a eu son bac à la deuxième s.** he passed his baccalauréat the second time round *or Br* at the resits; **s. de rattrapage** repeat exams, *Br* resits

sesterce [sɛstɛrs] NM *Antiq (monnaie)* sestertius, sesterce

SET [ɛsœte] NF *Ordinat (abrév* **secure electronic transaction)** SET®

set [sɛt] NM **1** *Tennis* set; **gagner en deux sets** to win in two sets **2 s. (de table)** *(ensemble de napperons)* set of table mats; *(napperon)* table mat

sétacé [setase] ADJ *Biol* bristly, *Spéc* setaceous

setter [setɛr] NM *(chien)* setter; **s. irlandais** Irish setter

seuil [sœj] NM **1** *(entrée)* doorway, threshold; *(dalle etc)* doorstep; *Phys, Psy, Fig* threshold;

---

franchir le s. to cross the threshold; **sur le s.** in the doorway; **un inconnu se tenait sur le s.** there was a stranger standing on the doorstep *or* in the doorway; *Bourse* **s. d'annonce obligatoire** disclosure threshold; **s. d'émissions** *(des gaz d'échappement)* emissions limit; **s. d'imposition** tax threshold; *Écon* **s. de pauvreté** poverty line; **s. de prix** price threshold; *Écon* **s. de rentabilité** break-even point; *Physiol* **s. de sensibilité** threshold of sensitivity *or* of response; *Psy* **s. de la conscience** threshold of consciousness **2** *Géog* **s. continental** continental shelf **3** *(d'une vanne, d'une cale sèche)* sill

SEUL, SEULE [sœl]

ADJ only **1, 3** ▪ alone **2, 3** ▪ by oneself **2** ▪ on one's own **2**
N only one

ADJ SEE GRAMMAR B10 1 *(preceding the noun) (unique)* only, sole; **un s. homme** *(pas plus qu'un)* a single man; *(d'entre tous les autres)* just *or* only one man; **ils se sont tous avancés comme un s. homme** they moved forward as one man; **un s. être vous manque et tout est dépeuplé** there's just one person missing in your life and the entire world seems like a desert; **son s. exécuteur testamentaire** his/her sole executor; **son s. souci** his only *or* sole worry; **c'est la seule chose qui me retient** it's the one *or* the only thing keeping me here; **il ne suffit pas d'un s. exemple** a single example *or* one example alone will not suffice; **il suffit d'une seule fois** once is enough; **mon s. et unique ami/stylo** my one and only friend/pen; **un s. mot, et je pars** one word (from you) and I'll go; **la seule pensée de sa venue m'effraie** the mere *or* very thought of him/her coming frightens me
2 *(following the noun or used predicatively) (séparé des autres)* alone, by oneself, on one's own; **je suis s., tu peux venir** you can come over, I'm on my own; **se sentir très s.** to feel very lonely *or* alone; **tu es trop s.** you're on your own *or* by yourself too much; **être s. au monde** to be alone in the world; **seuls!** alone at last!; **une femme seule** an unattached woman; **il peut marcher tout s. maintenant** he can walk by himself now; **faire cavalier s.** to go it alone; **parler s. à s. à qn** to speak to sb in private, to have a private conversation with sb; **s. (à s.) avec soi-même** alone with one's thoughts; **l'œuvre seule de ...** the sole *or* exclusive work of ...; **j'ai une cachette que moi s. connais** I have a hiding place which no-one else knows about *or Fml* which I alone know; **je l'ai fait tout s. ou à moi s.** I did it (by) myself *or* all on my own *or* single-handed; **cela va tout s.** it's plain sailing, it's straightforward; **cela n'a pas été tout s.** it wasn't all that easy, it wasn't plain sailing; **ça se mange tout s.** it doesn't need anything else; *(se mange facilement)* it's very light; **parler/chanter tout s.** to talk/sing to oneself; *Mus* **passage pour violon s.** passage for unaccompanied *or* solo violin
3 *(following the noun or preceding the article or poss adj) (seulement)* only, alone; **la violence seule ou seule la violence le contraindrait** only violence *or* violence alone *or* nothing short of violence would compel him; **seule la chasse les fait vivre** hunting is their only *or* sole source of food; **s. un expert pourrait nous conseiller** only an expert could advise us; **réservé aux seuls adultes** for adults only; **nous sommes seuls à le savoir** we are the only ones *or* people who know about it

N **un s.** *(pas plus qu'un)* a single person; *(chose)* a single one; *(d'entre tous les autres)* only one person; *(chose)* only one; **le gou-**

---

vernement d'un s. absolute rule; **pas un s.** *(chose)* not (a single) one; *(personne)* not a single person; **vous êtes le s. qui puissiez m'aider** you're the only one *or* person who can help me, *Fml* you alone can help me; **ne t'en fais pas, tu n'es pas le s.!** don't worry, you're not the only one!

Attention: ne pas confondre **alone** et **lonely** lorsqu'on traduit **seul**. Contrairement à l'adjectif **alone**, **lonely** suggère toujours un sentiment de solitude. Par ailleurs **alone** est toujours utilisé comme attribut.

seule [sœl] NF *Com* **s. de change** sola of exchange

seulement [sœlmã] ADV **1** *(juste)* only; **nous sommes s. deux** there are only *or* just two of us; **elle m'a donné s. les plus mûres** she gave me only *or* she only gave me the ripest ones; **je te demande s. un peu de patience** I'm just asking you to be a bit patient; **je viens s. d'arriver/de terminer** I've only just arrived/finished, I've just this minute arrived/finished; **et c'est s. maintenant que tu me le dis!** and you're only telling me about it now!, and you haven't told me before this!; **non s. ..., mais aussi ...** *ou* **mais encore ...** not only ..., but also... VOIR GRAMMAIRE A22
2 *(uniquement)* only, solely, merely; **il y va s. pour vous faire plaisir** he is only going to please you, he is going just *or* merely *or* solely to please you; *Fam* **entrez s.** do come in; *Fam* **essaie s.!** just (you) try!
3 *(même)* even; **sans s. me regarder** without even looking at me, without so much as looking at me; **si s. ...!** if only ...!
4 *(with conj force)* **je viendrais bien, s. ...** I'd like to come, but ... *or* only ...; **elle est gentille, s. elle est un peu sotte** she's kind, but she's a bit silly

sève [sɛv] NF *Bot (d'une plante)* sap; *Fig Litt* vitality, vigour, *Am* vigor; *Bot, Fig* **la s. monte** the sap is rising

sévère [sevɛr] ADJ **1** *(dur)* *(juge, critique, peine, paroles etc)* severe, harsh; *(visage, regard, air)* stern, severe; **climat s.** severe *or* hard climate; **être s. envers** *ou* **pour** *ou* **avec qn/pour les fautes de qn** to be severe *or* hard on sb/on sb's failings; **mener un train s.** to set a gruelling pace **2** *(discipline, principes moraux)* strict, rigid; **morale peu s.** lax morals **3** *(sans ornements) (architecture, style, beauté)* severe **4** *(grave) (pertes, dégâts)* severe, serious
ADV *Fam (gravement)* something rotten; **je déprime s. en ce moment** I'm depressed something rotten at the moment

sévèrement [sevɛrmã] ADV **1** *(durement)* severely, harshly **2** *(strictement)* strictly, rigidly **3** *(gravement)* severely; **s. atteint** severely affected

sévérité [severite] NF **1** *(d'un juge, de mesures, d'une critique, d'une peine etc)* severity, harshness; *(d'un visage, d'un regard)* sternness, severity; *(d'une discipline, d'une éducation)* strictness; **avec s.** with severity, severely **2** *(d'une architecture, du style etc)* severity

sévices [sevis] NMPL brutality, cruelty; **s. (sexuels) à enfant** child abuse

Séville [sevil, sevij] N Seville

sévir [sevir] VI **1** *(agir avec rigueur)* to act ruthlessly; **s. contre qn/qch** to deal ruthlessly with *or Fam* to clamp down on sb/sth **2** *(d'une épidémie, de la guerre etc)* to rage; *(de vandales)* to wreak havoc; **la crise qui sévit actuellement** the present crisis

sevrage [səvraʒ] NM **1** *(de nourrisson)* weaning; *(de drogué)* detoxification; *Méd* **symptômes de s.** withdrawal symptoms **2** *Bot (d'une marcotte, d'un greffon)* separating

sevrer [səvre] **VT** (je sèvre, n. sevrons; je sè-vrerai) **1** (enfant, agneau, drogué etc) to wean; **s. qn de qch** to deprive sb of sth **2** Bot (marcotte, greffon) to separate

sèvres [sevr] **NM** (porcelaine) Sèvres (porcelain)

sexage [seksaʒ] **NM** (de la volaille) sexing

sexagénaire [segzaʒenɛ, seksa-] **ADJ, N** sixty-year-old; Litt sexagenarian

sex-appeal, pl **sex-appeals** [seksapil] **NM** Fam sex appeal

sexe [seks] **NM 1** (classement) sex; **le (beau) s.** the fair sex; **le deuxième s.** the weaker sex; **changer de s.** to have a sex-change; **changement de s.** sex-change operation **2** (parties sexuelles) genitals **3** (sexualité) sex; **problèmes de s.** sexual problems
▸▸ **le s. faible** the weaker sex; **le s. fort** the stronger sex

sexisme [seksism] **NM** sexism; **faire du s.** to be sexist

sexiste [seksist] **ADJ, N** sexist

sexologie [seksɔlɔʒi] **NF** sexology

sexologique [seksɔlɔʒik] **ADJ** sexological

sexologue [seksɔlɔg] **N** sexologist

sex-shop, pl **sex-shops** [seksʃɔp] **NM** sex shop

sextant [sekstɑ̃] **NM** Naut, Math sextant

sextuor [sekstɥɔr] **NM** Mus sextet(te)

sextuple [sekstypl] **ADJ** sixfold, Fml sextuple **NM au s.** sixfold; **le s. de deux** six times two; **payer le s.** to pay six times as much

sextuplé, -ée [sekstyple] **N** sextuplet

sextupler [sekstyple] **VTI** to increase sixfold

sexualisation [seksɥalizasjɔ̃] **NF** sexualization

sexualiser [seksɥalize] **VT** to sexualize

sexualité [seksɥalite] **NF** sexuality

sexué [seksɥe] **ADJ** (plante, animal) sexed; (reproduction) sexual

sexuel, -elle [seksɥɛl] **ADJ** sexual; **vie sexuelle** sex life; **acte s.** sex act; **organes** ou **parties sexuel(le)s** sex organs; **éducation sexuelle** sex education; **rapports sexuels** sexual relations, Fam sex; **nos rapports sexuels se sont détériorés** the sex isn't as good as it used to be; **un obsédé s.** a sex maniac

sexuellement [seksɥɛlmɑ̃] **ADV** sexually; **maladie s. transmissible** sexually transmitted disease; **être attiré s. par qn** to be sexually attracted to sb

sexy [seksi] **ADJ INV** Fam sexy

seyant [sejɑ̃] **ADJ** (vêtement) becoming

Seychelles [seʃɛl] **NFPL les S.** the Seychelles

SF [esef] **NF** Fam (abrév **science fiction**) sci-fi, SF

SFIO [esefio] **NF** (abrév **Section française de l'Internationale ouvrière**) = French Socialist Party 1905–1969

SGAO [esʒeao] **NM** Ordinat (abrév **système de gestion assisté par ordinateur**) computer-assisted management system

SGBD [esʒebede] **NM** Ordinat (abrév **système de gestion de base de données**) DBMS

SGDBR [esʒebedeer] **NM** Ordinat (abrév **système de gestion de bases de données relationnelles**) RDBMS

SGDG [esʒedeʒe] (abrév **sans garantie du gouvernement**) without government guarantee

shah [ʃa] **NM** shah

shake-hand [ʃekɑ̃d] **NM INV** Arch, Hum handshake

shaker [ʃekœr] **NM** cocktail shaker

shakespearien, -ienne [ʃekspirjɛ̃, -jɛn] **ADJ** Shakespearian, Shakespearean

shako [ʃako] **NM** Mil shako

shampoing [ʃɑ̃pwɛ̃] **N** = **shampooing**

shampooiner [ʃɑ̃pwine] **VT** to shampoo

shampooineur, -euse [ʃɑ̃pwinœr, -øz] **N** (employé) shampooer
NF shampooineuse (à moquette) carpet shampooer

shampooing [ʃɑ̃pwɛ̃] **NM 1** (action) shampoo; **faire** ou **donner un s. à qn** to shampoo sb('s hair), to give sb a shampoo **2** (produit) shampoo; **s. sec** dry shampoo; **s. pour cheveux secs/gras** shampoo for dry/greasy hair; **s. antipelliculaire** anti-dandruff shampoo; **s. aux œufs** egg shampoo; **s. à moquettes** carpet shampoo

shampouiner [ʃɑ̃pwine] **VT** to shampoo

shampouineur, -euse [ʃɑ̃pwinœr, -øz] **N** = **shampooineur**

shant(o)ung [ʃɑ̃tuŋ] **NM** Tex shantung

shareware [ʃerwɛr] **NM** Ordinat shareware

sharia [ʃarja] **NF** (loi islamique) sharia

sheik [ʃɛk] **NM** sheik

shekel [ʃekɛl] **NM** shekel

shérif [ʃerif] **NM** sheriff

sherpa [ʃɛrpa] **N** Sherpa

sherry [ʃeri] **NM** sherry

shetland [ʃetlɑ̃d] **NFPL les (îles) S.** the Shetland Islands, the Shetlands
NM Tex Shetland wool; **(pull en) s.** Shetland sweater

shilling [ʃiliŋ] **NM** shilling

shimmy [ʃimi] **NM** Aut shimmy

shinto [ʃɛ̃to], **shintoïsme** [ʃɛ̃tɔism] **NM** Rel Shinto, Shintoism

shintoïste [ʃɛ̃tɔist] **ADJ, N** Rel Shintoist

shipchandler [ʃipʃɑ̃dlœr] **NM** ship's chandler

shit [ʃit] **NM** Fam hash, Br blow, draw

shocking [ʃɔkiŋ] **ADJ INV** Hum, Vieilli shocking

shog(o)un [ʃɔgun] **NM** Hist shogun

shoot [ʃut] **NM 1** Ftbl shot **2** Arg (de drogue) shot; **se faire un s. (d'héroïne)** to give oneself a shot (of heroin), to shoot up (heroin)

shooter [ʃute] **VI** Ftbl to shoot
VT 1 Ftbl **s. un pénalty** to take a penalty (kick) **2** Arg (avec de la drogue) **s. qn** to shoot sb up
VPR se shooter Arg to shoot (up); **se s. à l'héroïne** to shoot (up) heroin

shopping [ʃɔpiŋ] **NM** shopping; **faire du s.** to go shopping

short [ʃɔrt] **NM** (pair of) shorts; **être en s.** to be in shorts, to be wearing shorts VOIR GRAM-MAIRE A10

show [ʃo] **NM** show; **s. aérien** air show

show-biz [ʃobiz] **NM INV** Fam show biz

show-business [ʃobiznɛs] **NM INV** show business

showroom [ʃorum] **NM** showroom

shrapnell [ʃrapnɛl] **NM** Mil shrapnel

shunt [ʃœt] **NM** Élec, Chir shunt

shunter [ʃœte] **VT 1** Élec to shunt **2** TV, Cin to fade

SI¹ [si]

---

if **1–3** ▪ whether **3** ▪ how **4** ▪ what if **5** ▪ what about **5**

CONJ (by elision **s'** before **il, ils**) **1** (hypothèse, condition) if; **je ne sortirai pas s'il pleut** I won't go out if it rains; **s'il n'avait pas plu, nous serions partis** if it hadn't rained we would have gone, Fml had it not rained we would have gone; **si on ne le surveille pas, il s'échappera** he will escape unless he is watched or if he is not watched; **j'aurais été**

soldat, si je n'étais poète I would have been a soldier if I were not a poet, I would have been a soldier were I not a poet; **si j'avais su** if I'd known, had I (but) known; **si tu veux la paix, prépare la guerre** if you want peace, prepare for war; **qui le fera si ce n'est moi?** who'll do it if I don't or unless I do?; **si ce n'était que je l'ai vu moi-même** if I hadn't seen it (for) myself; **un des plus grands, si ce n'est le plus grand** one of the biggest, if not the biggest; **tout va bien, si ce n'est mon dos qui me fait souffrir** everything's fine apart from my sore back or apart from the fact that my back is hurting me; **s'il fait beau et si je suis libre, je sortirai** if it's fine and (if) I'm free, I'll go out; **oui, si on veut** yes, if you like; **un artiste, si on veut** an artist, so to speak; **si je ne m'abuse, si je ne me trompe** if I'm not mistaken; **si j'ose dire** if I may make so bold; **si seulement j'étais à Paris!** if only I were or was in Paris!; Fml **si tant est que ... + sub** provided that ..., so long as ... SEE GRAMMAR A52–3; B34

2 (concession) if; **si je me plains, c'est que j'en ai sujet** if I complain, it's with good reason; **s'il est malheureux et s'il a des ennuis, c'est bien de sa faute** if he is unhappy and in trouble, it is entirely his own fault; **s'il fut sévère, il fut juste** he was fair though severe, he might have been severe but he was fair; **ce fut à peine s'il put distinguer l'heure à sa montre** he could scarcely see the hands of his watch; **c'est tout au plus si l'on peut compter jusqu'à vingt femmes dans la salle** at (the) most there are only about twenty women in the hall; **le père Martin, (un) brave homme s'il en fut** old Martin, a good chap if ever there was one

3 (question indirecte) if, whether; **je me demande si c'est vrai/s'il viendra** I wonder if or whether it's true/he'll come; **je lui ai demandé s'il était marié** I asked him if or whether he was married; Fam **si je connais Paris?** do I know Paris?; Fam **si c'est pas malheureux (de voir ça)!** isn't it just dreadful (to see that)!

4 (combien) how; **pensez si j'étais furieux!** (you can) imagine how angry I was!

5 (supposition) what if, suppose; **et si elle l'apprend?** what if she finds out?, and suppose she finds out?; **si nous changions de sujet?** suppose we change the subject?, how about changing the subject?; **si on faisait une partie de bridge?** what about or how about a game of bridge?

NM **tes si et tes mais** your ifs and buts; **tu mets toujours des si à tout!** you're always iffing and butting; Prov **avec des si, on mettrait Paris dans une bouteille** if ifs and ands were pots and pans there'd be no need for tinkers

---

SI²

---

so **1** ▪ as **2** ▪ so that (si bien que) **4** ▪ yes **6**

ADV 1 (tellement) so; **ne courez pas si vite** don't run so fast; **il est si faible que ...** he is so weak that ...; **un si bon dîner** such a good dinner; **de si bons dîners** such good dinners; **il n'est pas si à plaindre que cela** he is not to be as pitied as all that; **ce n'est pas si facile** it's not so or that easy VOIR GRAMMAIRE A5

2 (= 'aussi' dans une proposition négative) il **n'est pas si beau que vous** he is not as handsome or not so handsome as you

3 **donnez-m'en si peu que vous voudrez** ou **si peu que rien** give me just a (very) little

4 **si bien que ...** so that ..., with the result that ...; **il dépensa sans regarder, si bien qu'en fin de compte il fut ruiné** he spent recklessly, so that or with the result that he was ruined

5 *(concession)* **si … que** + *sub* however; **si jeune qu'il soit** however young he may be, young as he is; **aucun médecin, si habile soit-il** no doctor, however capable (he may be); **si peu que ce soit** however little (it may be)

6 *(réponse à une question négative)* yes; **si fait** yes indeed; **ça ne fait rien – si, ça fait quelque chose** it doesn't matter – yes, it does (matter); **il n'est pas parti? – si/je crois que si** he hasn't gone? – yes, he has/yes, I think he has *or* I think so; **j'ai l'impression qu'il ne pleut pas – il me semble que si** I have the impression it's not raining – it seems to me it is; **tu crois qu'il ne va pas venir? – il m'a assuré que si** do you think he won't come? – he assured me that he would; **mais si, je l'ai vue** I did see her; **il ne s'en remettra pas – que si!** he won't get over it – yes, he will!; **tu ne t'en souviens plus, je pense? – si, si** you probably don't remember, do you? – yes, I do; **vous en voulez? – non merci – mais si!** would you like some? – no, thank you – oh go on! SEE GRAMMAR B64

si³ NM INV *Mus (note)* B; *(en chantant la gamme)* te, ti; **morceau en si** piece in B; **en si bémol** in B flat

Siam [sjam] NM Siam

siamois, -oise [sjamwa, -waz] ADJ Siamese; **chat s.** Siamese cat; **frères s., sœurs siamoises** Siamese twins
▪ N **S.** Siamese
▪ NM **1** *(chat)* Siamese (cat) **2** *Ling* Siamese

siau [sjo] NM *Can Fam* bucket, pail

Sibérie [siberi] NF Siberia

sibérien, -ienne [siberjɛ̃, -jɛn] ADJ Siberian; *Fig* **il fait un froid s.** it's bitterly cold
▪ N **S.** Siberian

sibilance [sibilɑ̃s] NF *Méd* **s. respiratoire** wheezing

sibilant [sibilɑ̃] ADJ *Méd* sibilant, hissing

sibylle [sibil] NF *Antiq* sibyl

sibyllin [sibilɛ̃] ADJ **1** *Antiq* sibylline **2** *Litt (énigmatique)* cryptic, enigmatic

sic [sik] ADV sic

SICAF [sikaf] NF *Fin (abrév société d'investissement à capital fixe)* closed-end investment company

SICAV [sikav] NF *Fin (abrév société d'investissement à capital variable) Br* ≃ unit trust, *Am* ≃ mutual fund; *Bourse* **S. actions** equity-based unit trust; *Bourse* **S. monétaires** money unit trust; *Bourse* **S. obligataire** bond-based unit trust

siccatif, -ive [sikatif, -iv] ADJ, NM siccative

Sicile [sisil] NF Sicily

sicilien, -ienne [sisiljɛ̃, -jɛn] ADJ Sicilian
▪ N **S.** Sicilian

sicle [sikl] NM *Hist (monnaie, poids)* shekel

sida, SIDA [sida] NM *Méd* AIDS, Aids; **avoir le s.** to have AIDS; **s. avéré** full-blown AIDS

sidatique [sidatik] ADJ, N *Péj* = sidéen

side-car, *pl* **side-cars** [sajdkar, sidkar] NM *(habitacle)* sidecar; *(véhicule)* motorcycle and sidecar, *Br* combination

sidéen, -enne [sideɛ̃, -ɛn] *Méd* ADJ suffering from AIDS
▪ N AIDS sufferer

sidéral, -ale, -aux, -ales [sideral, -o] ADJ sidereal

sidérant [siderɑ̃] ADJ *Fam (nouvelles, histoire etc)* staggering

sidéré [sidere] ADJ **1** *Fam* flabbergasted, staggered (**de faire** to do), thunderstruck **2** *Vieilli (par la foudre, par une crise d'apoplexie)* struck down

sidérer [sidere] VT (**il sidère; il sidérera**) **1** *Fam (personne)* to flabbergast, to stagger **2** *Vieilli (de la foudre, d'une crise d'apoplexie etc)* to strike down

sidérose [sideroz] NF **1** *Minér* siderite **2** *Méd* siderosis

sidérurgie [sideryrʒi] NF iron and steel metallurgy; *(industrie)* iron and steel industry

sidérurgique [sideryrʒik] ADJ **industrie s.** iron and steel industry; **usine s.** iron and steel works

sidérurgiste [sideryrʒist] N iron and steel worker

siècle [sjɛkl] NM **1** *(cent ans)* century; **au vingtième s.** in the twentieth century; **cette maison a au moins un s./deux siècles** this house is at least a hundred/two hundred years old; **un lit vieux d'un bon s.** a bed at least a hundred *or* a good hundred years old **2** *(époque)* age; **le s. de Louis XIV, le grand s.** the age of Louis XIV; **le s. des Lumières** the Age of Enlightenment; **notre s.** our age *or* century, the age *or* times we live in; **c'est un homme de son s./d'un autre s.** he's a man of his time(s)/he belongs to another age *or* another century; **vivre dans** *ou* **avec son s.** to be in tune with one's age *or* time(s); **jusqu'à la fin des siècles** to the end of time; *Rel* **pour les siècles des siècles** world without end; *Fam* **il y a un s.** *ou* **ça fait des siècles que je ne vous ai vu** I haven't seen you for ages, it's ages since I saw you **3** *Rel* **le s.** the world, worldly life; **vivre dans le s.** to live in the world

siège [sjɛʒ] NM **1** *(centre)* seat, centre, *Am* center; *(d'une douleur)* seat; **s. administratif** administrative headquarters; *Rel* **s. épiscopal** see; **s. d'exploitation** *(d'une entreprise)* operational headquarters; **s. principal** *(d'une entreprise)* head office; **s. social** *(d'une entreprise)* head office, registered office; **avoir son s. à Londres** *(d'une société etc)* to have its head office *or* headquarters in London, to be headquartered in London
2 *Mil* siege; **mettre le s. devant une ville, faire le s. d'une ville** to lay siege to *or* besiege a town; **lever le s.** to raise the siege; *Fam (partir)* to make tracks; **état de s.** state of siege
3 *(meuble)* seat; *(de cocher)* box; *Parl* seat; *Aut* **s. avant/arrière** front/back seat; *Aut* **s. baquet** bucket seat; *Aut* **s. basculant** tilting seat; **s. de camping** folding chair; **s. chauffant** heated seat; *Aut* **s.-club** armchair; *Aviat* **s. éjectable** ejector seat; *Aut* **s. pour enfant** baby/child seat; **s. inclinable** reclining seat; *Aut* **s. rehausseur** child booster seat; **s. sport** sports seat; **offrir un s. à qn** to offer sb a seat; **prenez un s.** take a seat, do sit down; **s. à pourvoir au conseil d'administration** vacancy on the board
4 *(de chaise, de W.-C., de personne)* seat; **bain de s.** sitz bath, hip bath; *Obst* **(accouchement par le) s.** breech delivery/birth; **le bébé se présente par le s.** the baby is in the breech position
5 *(fonction) Pol* **s. à la Chambre** seat in Parliament; **s. parlementaire** seat in Parliament; *Jur* **s. du juge** the judge's bench; **elle occupe un s. important** she holds an important position
6 *Tech (d'une valve etc)* seating

siéger [sjeʒe] VI (**je siège, n. siégeons; je siégeai(s); je siégerai**) **1 s. à Londres** *(d'une entreprise etc)* to have its head office *or* headquarters in London, to be headquartered in London; **s. au conseil d'administration** to have a seat on the board, to be on the board; **après avoir siégé à Bayeux pendant dix ans** *(d'un évêque)* having held the see of Bayeux for ten years; *Méd, Fig* **c'est là que siège le mal** that is the root of the problem **2** *(d'un tribunal de justice, d'un juge, d'une assemblée etc)* to sit **3 s. à la Chambre/au Parle-**

ment to have a seat *or* to sit in Parliament; *Jur* **s. au tribunal** to be on the bench

sien, sienne [sjɛ̃, sjɛn] PRON POSS *(d'homme etc)* his; *(de femme etc)* hers; *(de bébé, d'animal domestique)* his, hers; *(d'animal, de nation, de chose etc)* its; *(après un sujet indéfini)* one's own; **il te prête le s.** you can borrow his; **tu n'as qu'à prendre la sienne** you can just take his/hers; **de toutes ces solutions, il préfère la sienne** out of those possible solutions, he prefers his own; **elle n'en a pas besoin, elle a la s.** she doesn't need it, she has her own; **je n'en ai pas besoin, j'ai le s.** I don't need it, I've got his/hers; **les deux siens** his/her two, the two *or* both of his/hers; *(en insistant)* his/her own two; **elle t'a laissé deux des siens** she gave you two of hers; **on doit acheter la sienne** everyone must buy their own, *Fml* one must buy one's own; **au total, il y a plus de deux cents drapeaux car chaque pays a le s.** in total there are more than two hundred flags, each country having its own; *très Fam* **le s. de bébé est plus intelligent** his/her baby is more intelligent; *Fam* **à la sienne!** *(en buvant)* let's drink to him/her SEE GRAMMAR A30; B21–2
▪ NM **le s.** *(ce qui lui appartient)* his/hers; **il devrait y mettre du s.** he should do his share
▪ NMPL **les siens** *(sa famille)* his/her family *or Am* folks; *(ses partisans)* his/her followers; *(ses coéquipiers)* his/her teammates; *(après un sujet indéfini)* one's family/followers/team-mates
▪ NFPL **il a encore fait des siennes** he's been up to his old tricks again
▪ ADJ POSS *Litt* his/hers; **un s. cousin** a cousin of his/hers; **il fera siens tes principes** he will adopt your principles as his own; **fera-t-il siennes les félicitations qu'ils m'adresseront?** will he join them in congratulating me?

Sienne [sjɛn] N Siena; *Com* **terre de S. naturelle/brûlée** raw/burnt sienna

sierra [sjera] NF *Géog* sierra

Sierra Leone [sjeraleɔn] NF Sierra Leone

sieste [sjest] NF *(après le repas)* siesta, nap; **faire la s.** to take *or* have a siesta *or* nap

sieur [sjœr] NM **le s. Martin** *Jur, Arch* Mr Martin, *Péj* old Martin

sifflant, -ante [siflɑ̃, -ɑ̃t] ADJ *(bruit)* hissing; *(note)* whistling; *(respiration, toux)* wheezing, wheezy; *(consonne)* sibilant
▪ NF **sifflante 1** *Ling* sibilant **2** *Radio* sibilance

sifflard [siflar] NM *Fam* (salami-type) sausage

sifflement [sifləmɑ̃] NM **1** *(d'une personne, du vent etc)* whistling, whistle; *(d'un serpent, d'une oie, de la vapeur)* hiss(ing); *(du fouet)* swish(ing); *(d'une balle, d'une flèche)* whizz; *(d'un asthmatique)* wheezing; *(de la friture, d'une lampe à arc)* sizzling; **un s.** a whistle/hiss **2** *Théâtre* hiss(ing), boo(ing), cat-call **3 s. d'oreilles** buzzing *or* ringing in the ears

siffler [sifle] VI **1** *(d'une personne, d'un oiseau, d'un train, d'une bouilloire, du vent etc)* to whistle; *(d'un serpent, d'une oie, de la vapeur)* to hiss; *(d'un asthmatique)* to wheeze; *(de la friture, d'une lampe à arc)* to sizzle; *Fam* **ça me siffle dans les oreilles** I've got a buzzing *or* ringing in my ears **2** *(avec un sifflet)* to blow a/the whistle; *Naut* to pipe
▪ VT **1** *(air)* to whistle; *Naut (ordre)* to pipe; *Sport* **s. une faute/la mi-temps** to blow (the whistle) for a foul/for half time **2** *(taxi etc)* to whistle for, to whistle up; *(chien)* to whistle for; *Aut Fam* **je me suis fait s. (par la police)** I've been pulled up (by the police); **s. une fille** to (wolf-)whistle at a girl **3** *Théâtre etc (acteur, pièce etc)* to hiss, to boo **4** *Fam (boire) (verre, bouteille etc)* to knock back

sifflet [siflɛ] **NM 1** *(instrument)* whistle; *Naut* pipe; **coup de s.** blow *or* blast of a/the whistle; *Naut* pipe; **donner un coup de s.** to blow the whistle; **j'ai entendu un coup de s.** I heard a whistle (blowing); **démarrez au coup de s.** start when you hear the whistle *or* when the whistle blows; *Sport* **coup de s. final** final whistle; **s. à vapeur** steam whistle; *Naut* **s. de brume** fog whistle; *Arg* **ça lui a coupé le s.** that shut him up; *Arg* **serrer le s. à qn** to throttle *or* strangle sb; **attaquer en s.** *(de rameur)* to catch a crab **2** *(sifflement)* whistle; *Théâtre etc* hiss, boo, catcall

siffleur, -euse [siflœr, -øz] **N** *(personne)* whistler; *Théâtre* hisser, booer
▪ **NM** *(oiseau)* widgeon
▪ **ADJ** *(oiseau)* whistling; *(serpent)* hissing; *(asthmatique)* wheezy; **canard s.** widgeon

siffleux [siflø] **NM** *Can Zool* groundhog, woodchuck

sifflotement [siflɔtmɑ̃] **NM** whistling (to oneself *or* under one's breath)

siffloter [siflɔte] **VTI** to whistle (to oneself *or* under one's breath)

sigillaire [siʒilɛr] **ADJ anneau s.** signet ring

sigillé [siʒile] **ADJ** *Bot, Cér etc* sigillate(d)

sigisbée [siʒisbe] **NM** *Hum, Litt* gallant

sigle [sigl] **NM** acronym; *(d'une entreprise)* logo

sigma [sigma] **NM** *(lettre grecque)* sigma

signal, -aux [siɲal, -o] **NM 1** *(signe)* signal; *(indice)* sign; *Psy* **réagir à un s.** to react to a signal; **faire des signaux** to signal; **envoyer** *ou* **lancer un s.** to send a signal; **donner le s. de qch** to give the signal for sth; *Fig (d'un événement etc)* to be the signal for sth; **s. de départ** *(d'un train, d'une course etc)* starting signal; **au s., tous se levèrent** on the given signal *or* when the signal was given they all stood up; **le s. d'une crise sociale** the sign of a social crisis **2** *Électron, Radio* signal
▪▪ **s. d'alarme** alarm (signal); **s. d'alerte** warning (signal); *Mil, Aviat* air-raid warning; *Tél* **s. d'appel** call(ing) signal; *Rail* **s. à l'arrêt** signal at danger; *Rail* **s. d'arrêt** danger signal; *Rail* **s. d'arrêt absolu** stop signal; *Rail* **s. avancé** distant (block) signal; **s. d'avertissement** *ou* **avertisseur** warning signal; *Ordinat* **s. d'avertissement de réception** acknowledge; *Ordinat* **s. de baisse de tension des piles** battery low warning; **s. de baisse du toner** toner low warning; **s. à bras** semaphore signal; *Naut* **s. de brume** fog signal; *TV, Cin* **s. caméra** camera cue; **s. de chemin de fer** railway *or Am* railroad signal; **s. de danger** warning sign; **s. de détresse** distress *or* S.O.S. signal; *Rail* **s. à distance** distant (block) signal; *Rail* **s. d'entrée** home signal; *Mil* **s. par fanions** flag signal; *Mil, Aviat etc* **s. de fin d'alerte** all-clear; *Naut, Radio* **s. horaire** time signal; *Ordinat* **s. horodateur** time and date signal; *TV* **s. d'image** picture signal; **s. d'incendie** fire alarm; *Ordinat* **s. d'invitation à transmettre** proceed-to-send signal, *Am* start-dialing signal; **s. lumineux** light signal; *TV, Cin* light cue; *Aut* beacon; *Ordinat* indicator light, warning light; *Admin* **signaux lumineux** traffic lights; **s. optique** visible *or* visual signal; **signaux parasites** clutter; *Naut* **s. à pavillons** flag signal; **s. de priorité** give way sign, *Am* yield sign; *Rail* **s. rapproché** home signal; *Aut* **signaux routiers** *(écriteaux)* road signs; **s. sonore** beep; *(pour avertir)* warning beep; **s. de (sortie)** lecture sense signal; **s. vidéo** video signal; **s. à vue** visible *or* visual signal

signalé [siɲale] **ADJ** *Litt (service, récompense)* signal

signalement [siɲalmɑ̃] **NM 1** *(d'une personne)* description, particulars **2** *Jur* reporting

signaler [siɲale] **VT 1** *(faire remarquer) (erreur, fait etc)* to point out, to indicate (**à qn** to sb); **un sifflement signale que l'eau est à la bonne température** a whistling indicates that the water is at the right temperature; **s. à qn que** to point out to sb that; **s. un livre/un restaurant à qn** to recommend a book/a restaurant to sb; **Libération a signalé cet artiste** Libération drew attention to this artist; **c'est cette première pièce qui l'a signalé au monde du spectacle** it was this first play that brought him to the attention of the theatrical world
2 *(reporter) (retard, changement, vol etc)* to report, to notify (**à qn** to sb); **on nous signale que l'autoroute est bouchée** we have reports that the motorway is blocked, the motorway is reported to be blocked; **rien à s.** nothing to report; *Naut* **date à laquelle un navire a été signalé pour la dernière fois** date when a ship was last contacted *or Spéc* spoken
3 *(par un signal) (train, navire etc)* to signal; *Aviat (piste)* to indicate the position of; **l'entrée de l'autoroute est très mal signalée** the entry onto the motorway is very badly indicated *or* signposted; **c'est signalé par des pancartes lumineuses** it's indicated by illuminated signs
4 *Ordinat (marquer)* to flag up
5 *Vieilli (rendre remarquable)* to make conspicuous
▪ **VPR se signaler** to distinguish oneself (**par** by); **se s. dans les sciences** to have a reputation as a scientist; **se s. à l'attention de qn** to catch sb's eye; *Fam* **se s. par son absence** to be conspicuous by one's absence

signalétique [siɲaletik] **ADJ** *Admin* descriptive *(of a person)*; **fiche s.** *(dans les rapports de police)* description

signaleur [siɲalœr] **NM** *Mil etc* signaller; *Rail* signalman

signalisation [siɲalizasjɔ̃] **NF 1** *Aut (action)* signposting and marking; *(signaux)* signs and markings; **s. routière internationale** international (system of) road signs; **panneau de s.** roadsign; **feux de s.** traffic lights **2** *Rail (action)* installation of signals (**de** on); *(signaux)* signals **3** *Aviat (action)* installation of lights and markings (**de** on)

signaliser [siɲalize] **VT** *Aut (route)* to signpost and mark; *Rail (voie)* to install signals on; *Aviat (piste)* to install lights and markings on

signataire [siɲatɛr] **ADJ, N** signatory

signature [siɲatyr] **NF 1** signature; *(acte)* signing; **s. électronique** *ou* **numérique** digital signature, signature line; **apposer sa s. à un acte** to sign a document; **pour s.** for signature; **document porté à la s. du directeur** document given to the director for his signature; **présenter le courrier à la s.** to present the mail for signature; **avoir la s.** *(pour une entreprise etc)* to be authorized to sign; *Fig* **les plus grandes signatures de la littérature française** the greatest names in French literature; **s. d'un contrat** signing of a contract; **s. légalisée** authenticated signature; **s. par procuration** per pro signature, pp, signature by proxy; **s. sociale** company signature (and stamp) **2** *Typ (lettre, chiffre)* signature; *Journ* by-line

signe [siɲ] **NM 1** *(indice) (de pluie, d'impatience etc)* sign, indication; *(de maladie)* sign; *(d'amitié, d'amour)* sign, mark, token; **il t'a offert des fleurs? c'est un s.** he gave you flowers? that must mean something; **ne donner aucun s. de vie, ne pas donner s. de vie** to show no sign of life; *Fig* **elle ne nous a pas donné s. de vie depuis un mois** we haven't heard from her for a month; **en s. de désapprobation/solidarité** as a sign of dis-

approval/solidarity; **porter du noir en s. de deuil** to wear black as a sign of mourning; **un s. des temps** a sign of the times; **signes extérieurs de richesses** trappings *or* outward signs of wealth; **la réunion a eu lieu sous le s. de la cordialité** cordiality was the keynote of the meeting; **politique conduite sous le s. de la rigueur** policy in which austerity is the keynote; **signes d'usure/de vieillesse** signs of wear/age; **c'est bon/mauvais s.** it's a good/bad sign; **c'est s. que quelque chose ne va pas** it's a sign that there's something wrong
2 *(symbole)* sign, symbol; **s. algébrique** algebraical sign; **s. de classification** number of section or paragraph; **signes de ponctuation** punctuation marks; *Typ* **signes de correction** proof correction marks; *Mus* **signes constitutifs** key signature; **s. du zodiaque** sign of the zodiac; **être né sous le s. du Capricorne/de la Balance/des Poissons** to be born under the sign of Capricorn/Libra/Pisces; **s. de chance** lucky sign; *Typ* **s. différent de** not equals sign; *Typ* **s. dollar** dollar sign; **s. du marché** market signal; *Typ* **s. inférieur à** *ou* **plus petit que** less than sign; *Typ* **s. livre** pound sign; *Typ* **s. moins** minus sign; *Typ* **s. multiplié** multiplication sign; *Typ* **s. plus** plus sign; *Typ* **s. pour cent** percent sign; *Typ* **s. supérieur à** *ou* **plus grand que** greater than sign; *Typ* **s. égal** equals sign
3 *(trait physique) (de personne)* (distinctive) mark; *Admin* **signes particuliers: néant** distinguishing marks: none
4 *(geste)* sign, gesture; **il me faisait des signes** he was making signs *or* he was gesturing to me; **parler par signes** to use sign language; *(d'un sourd)* to use sign language, to sign; **langage par signes** sign language; **apprendre le langage par signes** to learn sign language, to learn how to sign; **s. d'adieu** farewell wave (of the hand); **il me fit un s. d'adieu** he waved me goodbye; **faire s. à qn** to make a sign to sb; *(contacter)* to get in touch with sb; **faire s. à qn de faire qch** to signal to sb to do sth; **je lui ai fait s. de venir** I beckoned him to come over; **il fit s. de se taire** he gave a signal *or* signalled for silence, he made a shushing gesture; **s. de la main** hand signal; **faire s. à qn (de la main) de reculer/de s'écarter/de partir** to wave sb back/aside/away; **faire s. que oui** to nod (in agreement); **faire s. que non** *(de la tête)* to shake one's head; *(du doigt)* to wag one's finger
5 *Rel* **s. de (la) croix** sign of the cross; **faire le s. de la croix** *ou* **un s. de croix** to make the sign of the cross, to cross oneself

signer [siɲe] **VT 1** *(contrat, lettre, tableau etc)* to sign; *Can Sport (joueur)* to sign (up); **s. son nom** to sign one's name; **s. par procuration** to sign by proxy, to pp; *Naut* **s. l'engagement** to sign on; *Fig Fam* **c'est signé** it's easy to guess who did that; *Fig Fam* **c'est signé Paul** it has Paul written all over it, it's just like *or* typical of Paul **2** *Tech (bijoux)* to hallmark
▪ **VI** to sign; **s. de son nom** to sign one's name
▪ **VPR se signer** *Rel* to cross oneself

signet [siɲe] **NM** *aussi Ordinat* bookmark; *Ordinat* **créer un s. sur une page** to bookmark a page

signifiant [siɲifjɑ̃] **ADJ** *Litt (plein de sens)* meaningful
▪ **NM** *Ling* signifier

significatif, -ive [siɲifikatif, -iv] **ADJ** significant; **s. de** indicative of

signification [siɲifikasjɔ̃] **NF 1** *(d'un mot, d'un symbole etc)* meaning, sense; *(d'un événement, d'un fait etc)* significance **2** *Jur (d'une décision)* notification; *(d'un acte judiciaire)* serving

signifié [siɲifje] **NM** *Ling* signified

signifier [siɲifje] **VT** (impf, pr sub n. **signifiions, v. signifiiez**) **1** (vouloir dire) (d'un mot) to mean; (d'une attitude) to mean, to signify; **que signifie ce mot?** what does this word mean?, what is the meaning of this word?; **s. que** (d'une action etc) to show or mean that; **cela ne signifie rien** it doesn't mean anything; **des remarques qui ne signifient rien** meaningless remarks; **qu'est-ce que cela signifie?** (indignation) what is the meaning of this?; **la moindre imprudence signifierait la mort pour eux** the slightest imprudence would mean death for them **2** (notifier) to notify (**qch à qn** sb of sth); **s. son congé à qn** (d'un propriétaire, d'un employé) to give sb notice; Jur **s. un jugement à qn** to notify sb of a decision; Fig **son visage signifiait bien sa douleur** his grief was written on his face for all to see

signofil(e) [siɲofil] **NM** Suisse Aut (clignotant) indicator, Am turn signal; **mettre son s. (à droite/gauche)** to indicate (to the right/left), Am to put on one's turn signal (to turn right/left)

sikh, sikhe [sik] **ADJ** Sikh
N S. Sikh

silence [silɑ̃s] **NM 1** silence; (pause) pause; **il se fit un s. subit** there was a sudden silence; **écrire à qn après un s. de deux ans** to write to sb after a silence of two years; **un s. de mort** a deathly silence or hush; **s. ému** breathless silence; **observer une minute de s.** to observe a minute's silence; **dans le s. de la nuit** in the silence or Litt still of the night; **réduire qn au s.** to reduce sb to silence, to silence sb; **rompre le s.** to break the silence; **garder** ou **observer le s.** to keep silent (**sur** about); **(du) s.!** silence!, be quiet!; **souffrir en s.** to suffer in silence; **passer qch sous s.** to keep quiet about sth, to pass over sth in silence; (par diplomatie) not to mention sth; **la loi du s.** the law of silence (preventing criminals from informing on their fellows); (dans la mafia) omerta; **préparer qch dans le s.** to prepare sth in secrecy; **faire jurer le s. à qn** to swear sb to secrecy; Aviat **cône de s.** cone of silence; Électron **zone de s.** silent zone; **s. radio** Tech radio silence; (silence total) total silence; **j'ai reçu quelques cartes postales peu après mon départ, mais depuis, c'est le s. radio** I got a few postcards shortly after I left, but since then there's been total silence or I haven't heard a word **2** Mus rest

silencieusement [silɑ̃sjøzmɑ̃] **ADV** silently

silencieux, -ieuse [silɑ̃sjø, -jøz] **ADJ** (personne, pas etc) silent; (rue, jardin etc) silent, quiet; (moteur, lave-vaisselle etc) quiet, silent; (soirée) quiet, peaceful; **après la dispute, la reste de la soirée fut s.** (plus personne ne parla) after the quarrel the rest of the evening passed in silence
NM Aut silencer, Am muffler; (d'arme) silencer; Radio squelch

Silène [silɛn] **N** Myth Silenus

silène [silɛn] **NM** Bot campion

siler [sile] **VI** Can **1** (siffler) to whistle; Fig **j'ai les oreilles qui me silent** my ears are ringing **2** (gémir) to whine **3** (respirer avec difficulté) to wheeze

Silésie [silezi] **NF** Silesia

silex [silɛks] **NM INV** (roche) flint; **des s.** (outils, armes) flints

silhouette [silwɛt] **NF** (contours) silhouette, outline; (ligne générale du corps) figure; Mil (cible) figure target; **en s.** silhouetted

silhouetter [silwete] **VT** (dessiner) to outline; Phot to block out
VPR se silhouetter to be silhouetted, to be outlined (**sur** against)

silicate [silikat] **NM** Chimie silicate

silice [silis] **NF** Chimie silica, silicon dioxide; **verre de s., s. fondue** silica (glass)

siliceux, -euse [siliso, -øz] **ADJ** siliceous

silicium [silisjɔm] **NM** Chimie silicon

silicone [silikɔn] **NF** Chimie silicone

siliconer [silikɔne] **VT** to coat with silicone; Hum **elle a les seins siliconés** she's got silicone implants

silicose [silikoz] **NF** Méd silicosis

silicosé [silikoze] **ADJ** Méd silicotic

silique [silik] **NF** Bot siliqua, silique

sillage [sijaʒ] **NM** (d'un navire) wake; Aviat etc slipstream; Aviat **s. aérodynamique** aerodynamic drag; Fig **marcher dans le s. de qn** to follow in sb's wake

sillon [sijɔ̃] **NM 1** Agr furrow; Fig (sur le front) furrow, line; Litt **sillons** (champs) fields, country; Fig **creuser** ou **tracer son s.** to plough or Am plow one's furrow **2** (d'une roue) track; (d'un navire) wake; (d'un projectile) path; **s. de lumière/feu** (d'une fusée etc) streak of light/fire **3** (de disque) groove

sillonner [sijɔne] **VT 1** (creuser) to furrow; (traverser) to cross; **la police sillonne la région** police are combing the area; **les touristes sillonnent le sud de la France** there's a non-stop flow of tourists through the south of France; **flanc de montagne sillonné par les torrents** mountainside grooved or scored by torrents; **forêt sillonnée de nombreux sentiers** forest criss-crossed by many paths; **front sillonné de rides** furrowed brow **2** (d'une lumière, de la foudre etc) (ciel) to streak

silo [silo] **NM** (fosse, tour) silo; **mettre en s.** to silo; **s. à blé** grain silo; **s. à ciment** cement silo; Mil **s. (de lancement)** (launching) silo

silotage [silotaʒ] **NM** Agr etc (action) ensilage

silure [silyr] **NM** (poisson) silurid

silurien, -ienne [silyrjɛ̃, -jɛn] Géol **ADJ** Silurian
NM Silurian; **s. inférieur** Ordovician

SIM [sim] **NM** (abrév **système d'information marketing**) MIS

simagrées [simagre] **NFPL** airs and graces, affectation; **ne fais pas tant de s.** don't make so much fuss

simien, -ienne [simjɛ̃, -jɛn] Zool **ADJ** simian
NMPL simiens simians, Spéc Simiidae

simiesque [simjɛsk] **ADJ** (visage, grimace etc) monkey-like, ape-like, Spéc, Litt simian

similaire [similɛr] **ADJ** similar (**à** to), of the same kind

similairement [similɛrmɑ̃] **ADV** similarly

similarité [similarite] **NF** similarity

simili [simili] **PRÉF** imitation, artificial
NM Fam Vieilli imitation; Phot half-tone; **bijoux en s.** imitation or costume jewellery
NF Fam = **similigravure**

similicuir [similikɥir] **NM** imitation leather, leatherette

similigravure [similigravyr] **NF** half-tone engraving

similitude [similityd] **NF** similarity

simoniaque [simɔnjak] Rel **ADJ** simoniacal
NM simoniac, simonist

simonie [simɔni] **NF** Rel simony

simoun [simun] **NM** Météo simoom, simoon

simple [sɛ̃pl] **ADJ** SEE GRAMMAR B10-11 **1** (direct) (personne) simple, unaffected; (tenue, nourriture, cérémonie etc) simple; **réduit à sa plus s. expression** reduced to its simplest form; **dans le plus s. appareil** (nu) in the altogether, in one's birthday suit
2 (facile) (calcul, méthode etc) simple, easy, straightforward; **c'est bien s., il accepte ou** on part it's quite simple, either he accepts or we go; **c'est s. comme bonjour** it's as easy as pie or as falling off a log
3 (crédule) simple; **s. d'esprit** simple-minded
4 (pur) condamner qn sur un **s. soupçon** to condemn sb on a mere suspicion; **c'est une s. question de temps** it is simply a matter of time; **c'est de la folie pure et s.** it's sheer madness; **c'est la vérité pure et s.** it's the pure and simple truth; **croire qn sur sa s. parole** to believe sb on his/her word alone; **la s. prudence veut que ...** ordinary or elementary prudence demands that ...
5 (commun) ordinary; **un s. particulier** an ordinary citizen; **s. soldat** private (soldier); **s. matelot** ordinary seaman; **je ne suis qu'une s. secrétaire** I'm merely a secretary, I'm just a or a mere secretary; **une s. enveloppe ira parfaitement** an ordinary or a plain envelope will do perfectly
6 (non multiple) (fleur, nœud etc) single; **un cornet s. ou double?** (de glace) one scoop or two?; **un aller s.** a single, Am a one-way ticket; Ordinat **s. densité** single density
7 (non composé), Courses de chevaux **faire un pari s.** to back a horse to win; Gram **passé s.** past historic (tense), simple past; Gram **les temps simples d'un verbe** the simple tenses of a verb SEE GRAMMAR B30; Chimie **corps s.** simple body; Math **équation s.** simple equation
NM 1 Tennis **jouer un s.** to play a singles (match); **s. messieurs/dames** men's/ladies' singles **2 varier du s. au double** to vary by twice as much **3 un s. d'esprit** a simpleton, a simple-minded person
NMPL Bot **simples** medicinal herbs

simplement [sɛ̃pləmɑ̃] **ADV 1** (vivre) simply; **habillé s.** simply or plainly dressed; **elle se maquille s.** she doesn't wear much make-up **2** (avec naturel) simply, naturally, unaffectedly; **le plus s. du monde** without any fuss; **il faut prendre les choses s.** you have to take things as they come **3** (uniquement) simply, just, merely; **purement et s.** purely and simply; **je voulais s. te dire que ...** I simply or just or merely wanted to tell you that ...

simplet, -ette [sɛ̃plɛ, -ɛt] **ADJ** (personne) simple; (idée, théorie, livre etc) simplistic

simplex [sɛ̃plɛks] **NM** Ordinat simplex

simplicité [sɛ̃plisite] **NF 1** (d'une tenue, des manières etc) simplicity; **elle manque de s.** she is pretentious or affected; **la s. de ses manières** his/her lack of affectation, his/her unaffected ways; **elle l'a avoué en toute s.** she admitted it without making a big thing of it; **nous ferons un repas en toute s.** we'll have a very simple meal; **ils se sont mariés en toute s.** they had a very quiet wedding; **venez en toute s.** come as you are; (pour manger) come and take pot luck; **vivre avec s.** to live simply **2** Phys (des atomes etc) elementary nature **3** (facilité) simplicity; **c'est d'une s. enfantine** it's child's play, a child could do it

simplifiable [sɛ̃plifjabl] **ADJ** that can be simplified, capable of simplification; Math (fraction) reducible

simplificateur, -trice [sɛ̃plifikatœr, -tris] **ADJ** (méthode etc) simplifying

simplification [sɛ̃plifikasjɔ̃] **NF** simplification; Math simplification, reduction

simplifier [sɛ̃plifje] (impf, pr sub n. **simplifiions, v. simplifiiez**) **VT** to simplify; Math (fraction) to simplify, to reduce; **cela me simplifie la vie** that simplifies my life, that makes life or things easier for me; **trop s.** to oversimplify
VPR se simplifier to become simpler, to become simplified

simplisme [sɛ̃plism] **NM** simplism

simpliste [sɛ̃plist] *Péj* **ADJ** *(théorie, explication etc)* simplistic; *(esprit)* simplistic, superficial
N simplistic person

simulacre [simylakr] **NM** semblance, show, pretence, *Am* pretense; **s. de résistance** semblance *or* show of resistance; *Mil* **s. de combat** sham fight; **s. de justice** travesty of justice; **son procès ne fut qu'un s.** his/her trial was a travesty of justice *or* a mere mockery

simulateur, -trice [simylatœr, -tris] **N** pretender; *Méd* malingerer; **c'est un habile s.** he's good at pretending *or Fam* faking
NM *Tech* simulator; *Ordinat* **s. de réalité virtuelle** virtual reality simulator; *Aviat* **s. de vol** flight simulator

simulation [simylasjɔ̃] **NF 1** *(action)* simulation, feigning; *Méd* malingering **2** *Aviat, Électron, Ordinat etc* simulation; *Compta (prévision)* forecast; **formation en s. de vol** simulated flight training; **s. par ordinateur** computer simulation

simulé [simyle] **ADJ** *(maladie)* feigned, simulated; *(combat)* sham; *(sentiment, colère, sérieux etc)* feigned, sham, bogus, simulated; *(vente)* bogus; *Tech (situation, conditions etc)* simulated

simuler [simyle] **VT** *(sentiment, colère etc)* to feign, to simulate, to sham; *Tech (situation, conditions, vol etc)* to simulate; **s. une maladie** to pretend to be ill, to feign (an) illness, to malinger; **s. la folie** to pretend to be mad, to feign madness; **la porte simule un rideau** the door is made to look like a curtain

simultané [simyltane] **ADJ** simultaneous

simultanéité [simyltaneite] **NF** simultaneousness, simultaneity

simultanément [simyltanemɑ̃] **ADV** simultaneously

Sinaï [sinai] **NM** Sinai; **le mont S.** Mount Sinai

sinapisé [sinapize] **ADJ** **bain/cataplasme s.** mustard bath/poultice *or* plaster

sinapisme [sinapism] **NM** *Méd* mustard poultice *or* plaster, *Spéc* sinapism

sincère [sɛ̃sɛr] **ADJ 1** *(franc) (personne)* sincere, genuine; *(opinion)* honest, candid; **être s. avec soi-même** to be honest with oneself **2** *(véritable) (joie, amour, effort etc)* genuine, sincere; **ses paroles étaient sincères** he was being sincere, he meant it; **vœux/remerciements sincères** sincere *or* heartfelt wishes/thanks; **agréez mes sincères salutations** yours sincerely **3** *(authentique) (document etc)* genuine, authentic

sincèrement [sɛ̃sɛrmɑ̃] **ADV 1** *(franchement)* sincerely, frankly; **s., je ne crois pas que ce soit une bonne idée** frankly, I don't think it's a good idea **2** *(vraiment) (heureux etc)* genuinely, sincerely

sincérité [sɛ̃serite] **NF 1** *(franchise)* sincerity, frankness; **en toute s.** in all sincerity **2** *(des regrets, de l'amour etc)* sincerity, genuineness; **je ne mets pas en doute la s. de vos paroles** I'm not questioning your sincerity

sinécure [sinekyr] **NF** sinecure; *Fam* **ce n'est pas une s.** it's not exactly a rest cure

sine die [sinedje] **ADV** indefinitely, sine die

sine qua non [sinekwanɔn] **ADJ** *Phil* **condition s.** sine qua non; **c'est la condition s. pour avoir un emploi bien rémunéré** it's essential in order to get a well-paid job, it's a prerequisite for a well-paid job

Singapour [sɛ̃gapur] **NM** Singapore

singapourien, -ienne [sɛ̃gapurjɛ̃, -jɛn] **ADJ** Singaporean
N S. Singaporean

singe [sɛ̃ʒ] **NM 1** *(animal)* monkey; *Fam (imitateur)* mimic; **grand s.** ape; *Fam* **c'est un s., il est laid comme un s.** he's as ugly as sin; **faire le s.** to clown around; **malin/adroit comme un s.** as crafty/clever as a monkey; **payer qn en monnaie de s.** *(en fausse monnaie)* to pay sb with counterfeit money; *(ne pas payer qn)* to make false promises to pay sb; *Prov* **on n'apprend pas à un vieux s. à faire des grimaces** don't teach your grandmother to suck eggs **2** *Culin Arg* **du s.** corned beef **3** *Arg* **le s.** *(patron)* the boss **4** *Ordinat* monkey

singer [sɛ̃ʒe] **VT** (je singeai(s); n. singeons) *(quelqu'un)* to ape, to mimic, *Fam* to take off; *(sentiment)* to feign, *Fam* to fake

singerie [sɛ̃ʒri] **NF 1** singeries *(grimaces, gestes)* antics; **il fait tout le temps des singeries** he's always clowning aound **2** *(imitation)* (grotesque) imitation **3** *(cage)* monkey *or* ape house

single [siŋgəl] **NM 1** *Tennis* singles (game) **2** *Rail* single-berth compartment **3** *(dans un hôtel)* single room

singulariser [sɛ̃gylarize] **VT s. qn** to set sb apart, to make sb stand out (**de** from)
VPR se singulariser to attract attention, to make oneself conspicuous; **il se singularise par sa curiosité** his curiosity sets him apart from the others *or* makes him stand out

singularité [sɛ̃gylarite] **NF 1** *(particularité)* peculiarity; **cette maison a la s. d'être solaire** the house is unusual in that it is solar-heated **2** *(caractère étrange)* strangeness, oddness, peculiarity; **c'est une des singularités de son caractère** it's one of the strange *or* odd things about him; **esprit de s.** desire to be different

singulier, -ière [sɛ̃gylje, -jɛr] **ADJ 1** *Gram* singular **2 combat s.** single combat **3** *(remarquable)* remarkable, *Fml* singular; *(étrange)* strange, odd, peculiar, *Fml* singular; **il est s. qu'il ne soit pas encore arrivé** it is strange *or* odd *or* peculiar that he has not arrived yet
NM *Gram* singular; **au s.** in the singular **VOIR GRAMMAIRE A14–15**

singulièrement [sɛ̃gyljɛrmɑ̃] **ADV 1** *(étrangement)* oddly, strangely, *Fml* singularly **2** *(en particulier)* especially, particularly **3** *(très beaucoup)* remarkably, extremely, *Fml* singularly

sinistre [sinistr] **ADJ 1** *(effrayant) (lieu, atmosphère, personne, expression)* sinister; **c'est s. ici!** it's spooky here! **2** *(déprimant) (paysage)* bleak; *(soirée, repas)* dismal, grim; **on a passé un jour de l'an s.** we spent a dismal *or* a miserable New Year's Day **3** *(emploi intensif)* awful, terrible; **un s. menteur** an awful *or* a terrible liar
NM *(catastrophe)* disaster, catastrophe; *Jur (dommage) (après des dégâts)* damage; *(réclamation)* claim; **bonification pour non-s.** no-claims bonus

sinistré, -ée [sinistre] **ADJ** **population sinistrée** stricken population; **bâtiment s.** damaged building; **région ou zone sinistrée** disaster area
N disaster victim

sinistrement [sinistrəmɑ̃] **ADV** sinisterly

sinistrose [sinistroz] **NF** *Psy* post-traumatic stress disorder; *Fam (mélancolie)* pessimism, gloom; *Fam* **atteint de s.** gloomy, depressed; *Fam* **la s. progresse dans les milieux bourgeois** the middle classes are becoming increasingly pessimistic *or* gloomy

sino- [sino] **PRÉF** Sino-; **s.-japonais** Sino-Japanese

sinologue [sinolog] **N** sinologist, sinologue

sinon [sinɔ̃] **CONJ 1** *(autrement)* otherwise, or else; **donne-moi la clef, s. je me fâche** give me the key otherwise *or* or (else) I'll get angry; **un jus d'orange, s. rien** an orange juice, otherwise nothing, an orange juice or, failing that, nothing **2** *(excepté)* except, but; **il ne fait rien s. manger et boire** he does nothing except *or* but eat and drink; *Vieilli* **s. que** except that **3** *(si ce n'est)* if not; **c'est un des meilleurs, s. le meilleur** it's one of the best, if not the best

sinoque [sinɔk] **ADJ** *Arg (fou)* crackers, crazy

sinuer [sinɥe] **VI** *Litt* to wind, to meander

sinueux, -euse [sinɥø, -øz] **ADJ** *(ligne)* sinuous; *(chemin, courant etc)* winding, meandering; *Fig (raisonnement)* tortuous

sinuosité [sinɥozite] **NF** *(d'un chemin, d'une rivière etc)* bend, curve; *Fig (d'un raisonnement)* tortuousness

sinus ¹ [sinys] **NM** *Anat* sinus

sinus ² **NM** *Math* sine

sinusite [sinyzit] **NF** *Méd* sinusitis; **avoir de la s.** to have sinusitis

sinusoïdal, -ale, -aux, -ales [sinyzɔidal, -o] **ADJ** *Math* sinusoidal

sinusoïde [sinyzɔid] **NF** *Math* sinusoid, sine curve

Sion [sjɔ̃] **N** Zion

sionisme [sjɔnism] **NM** Zionism

sioniste [sjɔnist] **ADJ, N** Zionist

sioux [sju] **ADJ INV** Sioux
N INV S. Sioux; *Fig* **ruses de S.** crafty *or* cunning tricks

siphon [sifɔ̃] **NM 1** *Phys etc (tube)* siphon **2** *(bouteille)* (soda) siphon **3** *Constr etc (d'un évier, d'une canalisation etc)* U-bend, trap **4** *Géol* siphon **5** *Zool* siphon

siphonné [sifɔne] **ADJ** *Fam (fou)* crackers, crazy

siphonner [sifɔne] **VT** to siphon

sire [sir] **NM 1** sir; **beau s.** fair sir; *Péj* **un triste s.** an unsavoury character **2 S.** *(à un souverain)* Sire

sirène [sirɛn] **NF 1** *Myth* siren, mermaid; *Fig (femme)* siren; **chant de s.** siren song **2** *(appareil)* siren; *(d'usine)* hooter, siren; *(de brume)* foghorn; **s. d'alarme** fire alarm; *(en temps de guerre)* air-raid siren

SIRET [siret] **NM N° S.** company registration number

siroc(c)o [sirɔko] **NM** *(vent)* sirocco

sirop [siro] **NM** syrup, (fruit) cordial; *Pharm* syrup; **s. d'érable** maple syrup; **s. de fraise** ≃ strawberry cordial; **s. de menthe** ≃ mint cordial; **s. d'orgeat** barley water; **s. de sucre** golden syrup; **s. contre la toux** cough mixture *or* syrup

siroter [sirɔte] **VT** *Fam (vin, café etc)* to sip

sirupeux, -euse [sirypø, -øz] **ADJ** *(liquide)*, *Péj (musique, ton)* syrupy

sis [si] **ADJ** *Jur, Litt* situated, located; **maison sise rue Saint-Honoré** house situated *or* located in the rue Saint-Honoré

sisal [sizal] **NM** *Bot* sisal

sismal, -ale, -aux, -ales [sismal, -o] **ADJ** **ligne sismale** line of an *or* the earthquake

sismicité [sismisite] **NF** seismicity

sismique [sismik] **ADJ** seismic

sismogramme [sismogram] **NM** seismogram

sismographe [sismograf] **NM** seismograph

sismographie [sismografi] **NF** seismography

sismologie [sismolɔʒi] **NF** seismology

sismomètre [sismomɛtr] **NM** seismometer

Sisyphe [sizif] **N** Sisyphus; **le rocher de S.** the rock of Sisyphus

Sit [sit] **NM** *(abrév* **système interbancaire de télépaiement)** *Br* ≃ CHAPS, *Am* ≃ CHIPS

sitar [sitar] **NM** *Mus* sitar

sitcom [sitkɔm] NM OU F *TV* sitcom, situation comedy

site [sit] NM **1** *(pittoresque)* beauty spot; **s. (touristique)** *(monument etc)* place of interest, tourist attraction; **s. classé** conservation area; **s. historique** historic site **2** *Archéol, Ind (lieu)* site; *Mktg* **s.-témoin** test site **3** *(configuration d'un lieu)* setting, site; **s. d'enfouissement des déchets nucléaires** nuclear dump **4** *Mil etc* **ligne de s.** line of sight **5** *Ordinat* **s. Web** *ou* **Internet** Web site, Internet site; **s. de bavardage** chat room; **s. marchand** e-commerce site

sit-in [sitin] NM INV sit-in; **faire un s.** to have *or* hold a sit-in

sitôt [sito] ADV **1** *(aussitôt)* **s. le soleil couché** *(dans le présent ou le futur)* as soon as the sun sets; *(dans le passé)* as soon as the sun had set; **s. dit s. fait** no sooner said than done; **s. que** + *ind* as soon as; **s. après** immediately after **2** *(with nég)* **vous ne la reverrez pas de s.** it will be some time *or* a good while before you see her again; **je ne reviendrai pas ici de s.** I won't come back here in a hurry

sittelle [sitɛl] NF *(oiseau)* nuthatch

situation [situasjɔ̃] NF **1** *(emplacement) (d'une ville, d'un bâtiment etc)* situation, position, location; *Naut* bearing; **l'hôtel jouit d'une excellente s.** the hotel is excellently situated
   2 *(circonstances)* situation; **s. du marché** market situation; **quelle est votre s. de famille?** what is your marital status?; **quelle est votre s. financière?** what is your financial situation *or* position *or* status?; **je lui ai exposé ma s.** I explained my situation *or* position to him; **être en s. de faire qch** to be in a position to do sth; **se trouver devant une s. de fait** to be faced with a fait accompli; *Fam* **elle est dans une s. intéressante** *(enceinte)* she's in the family way, *Vieilli Euph* she's in an interesting condition; **l'homme de la s.** the right man for the job; **mettre qn en s.** to give sb experience of a real-life situation; *Compta* **s. nette** net worth; **s. de la banque** bank balance; **s. de caisse** cash position *or* balance; **s. de compte** account position *or* balance
   3 *Admin, Mil etc* report, return
   4 *(emploi)* job, position; **il a une belle s.** he has a good position; **se faire une belle s.** to work one's way up into a good position; *Journ* **situations vacantes** (job) vacancies, *Br* situations vacant

situé [situe] ADJ situated, located; **bien/mal s.** well/badly situated *or* located

situer [situe] VT *(maison etc)* to situate, to locate; *Fig (qch dans son contexte)* to place; *Fam* **s. qn** to size sb up; **je situerais plutôt ce groupe dans le courant be-bop** I would describe the band as being more be-bop
   VPR se situer to stand; **je ne sais pas comment il se situe sur ce point** I don't know where he stands on this point; *Théâtre etc* **l'action se situe à Rome en 1516** the action takes place in Rome in 1516; *Pol* **se s. à droite** to be on the right, to be right-wing; **elle se situe plutôt à droite** she's rather to the right

six *(before noun beginning with consonant* [si]; *before noun beginning with vowel sound* [siz]; *otherwise* [sis]) *ADJ INV* **1** six; *Aut* **une s. chevaux** a six-horsepower car; **les s. jours** *(course cycliste)* = six-day cycle race **2** *(dans des séries)* sixth; **page/numéro s.** page/number six; **Charles S.** Charles the Sixth
   NM INV six; **le s. mai** (on) the sixth of May, (on) May the sixth, *Am* (on) May sixth; *Cartes* **le s. de cœur** the six of hearts; **habiter au s.** to live at number six

sixain [sizɛ̃] NM = sizain

six-huit [sisɥit] NM INV *Mus* six-eight time

sixième [sizjɛm] ADJ NUM sixth; **au s. étage** on the sixth *or Am* seventh floor
   N *(personne, objet, événement etc)* sixth (one); **habiter au s.** to live on the sixth *or Am* seventh floor; *Sport etc* **arriver le/la s.** to come (in) sixth
   NM sixth (part); **cinq sixièmes** five sixths
   NF *Scol (enseignement secondaire) Br* ≃ first year of secondary school, *Am* ≃ sixth grade

sixièmement [sizjɛmmɑ̃] ADV in the sixth place, sixthly

six-quatre-deux (à la) [alasiskatdø] ADV *Fam Vieilli* **faire qch à la s.** to do sth in a slapdash manner

sixte [sikst] NF **1** *Mus* sixth **2** *Escrime* sixte

Sixtine [sikstin] ADJ F **la chapelle S.** the Sistine Chapel

sizain [sizɛ̃] NM **1** *Littér* six-line stanza **2** *Cartes* set of six packs *or Am* decks of playing cards

Skaï® [skaj] NM leatherette, imitation leather

skate(-board), *pl* **skate-boards, skates** [skɛtbɔrd] NM skateboard; **faire du s.(-b.)** to skateboard, to go skateboarding

sketch, *pl* **sketches** [skɛtʃ] NM *Théâtre* sketch

ski [ski] NM **1** *(planche)* ski; **descendre à** *ou* **en skis** to ski down; **skis de fond** cross-country skis; **skis paraboliques** parabolic skis, carving skis **2** *(activité)* skiing; **s. alpin** downhill (skiing); **s. de piste** on-piste skiing; **s. de fond, s. de randonnée** cross-country (skiing), langlauf; **faire du s.** to ski; *Fam* **aller au s.** to go skiing; **chaussures de s.** ski boots; **station de s.** ski resort; **vacances de s.** skiing holiday **3** **s. nautique** water-skiing; **faire du s. nautique** to water-ski

skiable [skjabl] ADJ skiable, fit for skiing

ski-bob, *pl* **ski-bobs** [skibɔb] NM skibob

skier [skje] VI to ski

skieur, -euse [skjœr, -øz] N skier; **s. nautique** water-skier; **s. de fond** cross-country *or* langlauf skier; *Mil* **éclaireurs skieurs** ski troops

skif(f) [skif] NM *Naut* skiff

skin(head) [skin(ɛd)] NM skin(head)

skip [skip] NM *Ind* skip

skippé [skipe] ADJ *Naut* **s. par** skippered by

skipper [skipœr] NM *Naut (barreur)* skipper

slacker [slake] VI *Can (relâcher)* to ease up; **s. d'une coche** to ease up a bit

slalom [slalɔm] NM *Ski* slalom; **descente en s.** slalom descent; **s. géant** giant slalom; **s. spécial** special slalom; *Fig* **faire du s. entre les voitures** to dodge in and out among the cars

slalomer [slalɔme] VI *Ski* to slalom; *Fig* to dodge in and out

slalomeur, -euse [slalɔmœr, -øz] N *Ski* slalom skier

slave [slav] ADJ Slav(onic)
   NM *Ling* Slavonic
   N S. Slav

slavisant, -ante [slavizɑ̃, -ɑ̃t], **slaviste** [slavist] N Slavist

sleeping [slipiŋ] NM *Rail Fam Vieilli (wagon)* sleeping car; *(couchette)* berth

slibar(d) [slibar] NM *très Fam* underpants

slip [slip] NM **1** *(d'homme)* briefs, underpants; *(de femme)* briefs, panties, pants; **s. de bain** *(d'homme)* swimming trunks; *(de femme)* bikini bottoms; **s. kangourou** Y-fronts; **s. de soutien (pour sportifs)** athletic support, *Fam* jockstrap VOIR GRAMMAIRE A10 **2** *Naut* slipway

> Il faut noter que le terme anglais **slip** est un faux ami; il ne signifie jamais **culotte**.

sloche [slɔʃ] NF *Can* slush

slogan [slɔgɑ̃] NM *Com, Pol* slogan; **s. publicitaire** advertising slogan

sloop [slup] NM *Naut* sloop; **s. à tape-cul** yawl

sloughi [slugi] NM *(chien)* Saluki

slovaque [slɔvak] ADJ Slovak
   NM *Ling* Slovak
   N S. Slovak

Slovaquie [slɔvaki] NF Slovakia

slovène [slɔvɛn] ADJ Slovene, Slovenian
   NM *Ling* Slovene, Slovenian
   N S. Slovene, Slovenian

Slovénie [slɔveni] NF Slovenia

slow [slo] NM *(danse, musique)* slow dance; **danser un s.** to have a slow dance

SM¹ [ɛsɛm] *(abrév* **Sa Majesté**) HM

SM² [ɛsɛm] *(abrév* **sadomasochisme**) S & M

smala(h) [smala] NF *(de chef arabe)* retinue; *Fam (famille etc)* tribe; *Fam* **toute la s.** the whole tribe

smart [smart] ADJ INV *Fam Vieilli (élégant)* smart

smash [smaʃ] NM *Tennis etc* smash; **faire un s.** to smash the ball

smasher [smaʃe] *Tennis* VT *(balle)* to smash
   VI to smash (the ball)

SME [ɛsɛmə] NM *UE (abrév* **Système monétaire européen**) EMS

smectique [smɛktik] ADJ **argile s.** fuller's earth

SMIC [smic] NM *(abrév* **salaire minimum interprofessionnel de croissance**) = guaranteed minimum wage

smicard, -arde [smikar, -ard] N *Fam* worker on minimum wage, minimum wage earner

smocks [smɔk] NMPL *Couture* smocking

smog [smɔg] NM smog

smoking [smɔkiŋ] NM *(veston)* dinner jacket, *Am* tuxedo, *Fam* tux; *(costume)* dinner *or* evening suit

SMS [ɛsɛmɛs] NM *(abrév* **short message service**) SMS

smurf [smœrf] NM break dance; **danser le s.** to break-dance

snack(-bar), *pl* **snack-bars, snacks** [snak(-bar)] NM *Fam* snack bar

SNC [ɛsɛnse] NF *(abrév* **société en nom collectif**) commercial/industrial partnership

SNCB [ɛsɛnsebe] NF *Belg (abrév* **Société nationale des chemins de fer belges**) = Belgian national railway company

SNCF [ɛsɛnsɛɛf] NF *(abrév* **Société nationale des chemins de fer français**) = French national railway company

snif [snif] INT *Fam* sniff; **s., s. il me l'a pris!** boo-hoo, he's taken it from me!

sniffer [snife] VT *Arg (colle, cocaïne)* to sniff

snob [snɔb] N snob
   ADJ *(inv in f sing) (personne, restaurant etc)* snobbish, snobby; **elle est un peu s.** she's a bit of a snob

snober [snɔbe] VT *(mépriser)* to look down on; *(éviter)* to snub

snobinard, -arde [snɔbinar, -ard] *Fam Péj* ADJ stuck-up, snobbish
   N stuck-up *or* snobbish type

snobisme [snɔbism] NM snobbery, snobbishness; **s. à rebours** inverted snobbery

snowboard [snobɔrd] NM *(sport)* snowboarding; *(planche)* snowboard

snow-boot, *pl* **snow-boots** [snobut] NM snow boot

sobre [sɔbr] ADJ **1** *(personne) (qui n'a pas bu)* sober; *(qui boit ou mange peu)* abstemious; *(repas, vie)* simple; **s. comme un chameau** as sober as a judge **2** **s. de paroles/louanges**

sparing in one's words/praise **3** *(style, lignes, dessin)* sober, restrained

sobrement [sɔbrəmã] ADV **1** *(manger, boire)* in moderation **2** *(s'exprimer)* soberly **3** *(s'habiller etc)* soberly

sobriété [sɔbrijete] NF **1** *(concernant l'alimentation, la boisson)* temperance, sobriety; **manger et boire avec s.** to eat and drink in moderation **2** *(des paroles)* soberness; **s'exprimer avec s.** to speak soberly **3** *(du style)* soberness, sobriety, restraint; *(des lignes)* soberness

sobriquet [sɔbrikɛ] NM nickname

soc [sɔk] NM ploughshare, *Am* plowshare

sociabilité [sɔsjabilite] NF sociability

sociable [sɔsjabl] ADJ sociable; **peu s.** unsociable

social, -ale, -aux, -ales [sɔsjal, -o] ADJ **1** social; **aide sociale** social welfare; *Zool* **animal s.** social animal; **l'homme est un animal s.** man is a social animal; **assistant s.** social worker; **conflit s.** industrial dispute; **couche sociale** social stratum; **l'échelle sociale** the social ladder; **guerre sociale** class war; **œuvres sociales** welfare activities; **l'ordre s.** the social order; **politique sociale** social policy; **réforme sociale** social reform; **science sociale** social science; **vie sociale** social life **2** *Com* **nom s., raison sociale** company name; **capital s.** share capital
▸ NM *Pol* social questions; *Fam* **faire du s.** to do one's good turn for the day

social-chrétien, *pl* **sociaux-chrétiens** ADJ, N *Belg Pol* Christian Socialist

social-démocrate, *pl* **sociaux-démocrates** ADJ, N *Pol* social democrat

social-démocratie, *pl* **social-démocraties** NF *Pol* social democracy

socialement [sɔsjalmã] ADV socially

socialisant, -ante [sɔsjalizã, -ãt] *Pol* ADJ with socialist sympathies *or* tendencies ▸ N socialist sympathizer

socialisation [sɔsjalizasjɔ̃] NF **1** *Écon (du capital, des industries)* socialization, collectivization **2** *(de personne)* socialization

socialiser [sɔsjalize] VT **1** *Écon (biens etc)* to socialize, to collectivize **2** *(personne)* to socialize

socialisme [sɔsjalism] NM socialism; **s. chrétien** Christian socialism; **s. d'État** State socialism

socialiste [sɔsjalist] ADJ, N socialist

socialo [sɔsjalo] ADJ, N *Fam* socialist

social-révolutionnaire, *pl* **sociaux-révolutionnaires** ADJ, N social-revolutionary

sociétaire [sɔsjetɛr] N **1** *(membre)* member **2** *(actionnaire)* *Br* shareholder, *Am* stockholder

SOCIÉTÉ [sɔsjete]

> society **1, 2, 5** ▪ association **2** ▪ company **3, 4** ▪ companionship **4**

NF **1** *(communauté)* society; **dans notre s.** in our society; **ça ne se fait pas dans la bonne s.** that is not done in polite society; **devoirs envers la s.** civic duty; **valeurs de la s.** social values; **vie en s.** life in society; **animaux qui vivent en s.** social animals; **problème de s.** social problem

2 *(association)* society, association; *Sport* club; **s. de secours aux blessés** first-aid association; **s. secrète** secret society

3 *Com, Ind* company, firm; **se monter en s.** to set up in business; **la S. Martin** Martin's

4 *(compagnie)* company, companionship; *Fml* society; **il aime la s.** he likes company; **la s. des personnes de son âge** the company *or Fml* society of people his/her own age

5 *(beau monde) (à la mode)* society; **la**

haute **s.** high society; **femmes de s.** society women; **faire ses débuts dans la s.** to make one's debut in society

6 jeux de s. board games, *Vieilli* parlour *or Am* parlor games

▸▸ **s. d'abondance** affluent society; **s. par actions** joint-stock *or Am* incorporated company; **s. d'affacturage** factoring company; **s. affiliée** affiliated company; **s. anonyme** public limited company, *Am* corporation; **s. d'assurance** insurance company; **s. d'autoroutes** private company which maintains motorways; **s. de Bourse** stockbroker, stockbroking firm; **s. de capital-risque** venture capital company; **s. civile** non-trading company; **s. en commandite** limited partnership; **s. en commandite par actions** partnership limited by shares; **s. en commandite simple** limited partnership; **s. de commerce international** international trading corporation; **s. commerciale** business firm; **s. commune** joint venture; **s. de conseil en investissement** investment consultancy; **s. de conseil en mercatique** marketing consultancy (firm); **s. de consommation** consumer society; **s. de crédit immobilier** *Br* ≃ building society, *Am* ≃ savings and loan company; **s. de crédit mutuel** friendly society; **s. d'économie mixte** semi-public company; **s. d'édition** publishing company *or* firm; **s. d'entrepôts** warehousing company; **s. d'épargne** savings society; **s. d'État** state-owned *or* public company; **s. d'études** research company *or* firm; **s. d'études de marché** market research company *or* firm; **s. d'études mercatiques** marketing research company *or* firm; **s. d'exploitation en commun** joint venture; **s. d'exportation** export company *or* house; **s. fictive** dummy company; **s. fiduciaire** trust company; **s. financière** finance company; **s. de gestion** holding company; **s. immobilière** real-estate company; **s. de location** rental firm; **s. de location de voitures** car hire company; **s. de mercatique** marketing company *or* firm; **s. mère** parent company; **s. multinationale** multinational company *or* corporation, multinational; **s. nationale** state-owned *or* public company; *Hist* **la S. des Nations** the League of Nations; **s. de négoce** trading company; **s. en nom collectif** ≃ general partnership, commercial/industrial partnership; **s. de panels** = market research company specializing in consumer panels; **s. en participation** joint venture; **s. de personnes** partnership; **s. de placement** investment trust; **s. de portage** export management company; **s. à portefeuille** holding company; **s. de prévisions** forecasting firm; **s. de prévoyance** provident society; **s. privée** private company; *TV, Cin* **s. de production** production company; **S. protectrice des animaux** *Br* ≃ RSPCA, *Am* ≃ ASPCA; **s. de radiodiffusion** broadcasting company; **s. à responsabilité limitée** ≃ limited (liability) company; **s. de services** service business; **s. sœur** sister company; *Ordinat* **s. spécialisée dans l'hébergement** host company; **s. de télédiffusion** broadcasting company; **s. de transport** transport company; **s. d'utilité publique** public utility company, *Am* utility; **s. de vente par correspondance** mail order company *or* firm

société-écran, *pl* **sociétés-écrans** NF shield company

socio [sɔsjo] NF *Fam* = **sociologie**

socio- [sɔsjo] PRÉF socio-

socioculturel, -elle [sɔsjokyltyrɛl] ADJ sociocultural; **centre s.** social and cultural centre

sociodrame [sɔsjodram] NM *Psy* sociodrama

socio-économique, *pl* **socio-économiques** ADJ socio-economic

socio-éducatif, -ive, *pl* **socio-éducatifs, socio-éducatives** ADJ socioeducational

sociogramme [sɔsjogram] NM *Psy* sociogram

sociolinguistique [sɔsjolɛ̃gɥistik] ADJ sociolinguistic ▸ NF sociolinguistics

sociologie [sɔsjɔlɔʒi] NF sociology

sociologique [sɔsjɔlɔʒik] ADJ sociological

sociologiquement [sɔsjɔlɔʒikmã] ADV sociologically

sociologue [sɔsjɔlɔg] N sociologist

socioprofessionnel, -elle [sɔsjoprɔfɛsjɔnɛl] ADJ socio-professional

socio-style, *pl* **socio-styles** NM *Mktg* lifestyle

socle [sɔkl] NM **1** *(pour une statue, une colonne)* base, pedestal; *(pour un vase, une horloge)* base; *(pour un appareil)* stand; *(pour un mât etc)* base, socket; *(pour un moteur)* bed plate; *Ordinat* **s. orientable** *ou* **pivotant** *(d'un moniteur)* swivel base **2** *Géol* insular shelf **3** *Constr* **s. de lambris** skirting board, *Am* baseboard **4** *Ordinat* **s. d'extension** expansion socket

socque [sɔk] NM *(sabot)* clog; *Théâtre, Antiq* sock

socquette [sɔkɛt] NF ankle sock, *Am* bobby sock

Socrate [sɔkrat] N Socrates

socratique [sɔkratik] ADJ Socratic

soda [sɔda] NM fizzy drink, *Am* soda (pop); **s. à l'orange** orangeade; **whisky s.** whisky and soda

sodique [sɔdik] ADJ *Chimie* sodic

sodium [sɔdjɔm] NM *Chimie* sodium

Sodome [sɔdɔm] N Sodom

sodomie [sɔdɔmi] NF sodomy, buggery

sodomiser [sɔdɔmize] VT to sodomize, to bugger

sodomite [sɔdɔmit] NM sodomite

sœur [sœr] NF **1** sister; **ma s. cadette/aînée** my younger/older sister; **s. jumelle** twin sister; *Litt* **sœurs d'infortune** sisters in misfortune; *Fam* **et ta s.!** get lost!, mind your own business!; *Fig* **ces deux théories sont sœurs** these two theories go hand in hand; *Fig* **rencontrer l'âme s.** to find a soul mate **2** *Rel* sister, nun; **entrez, ma s.** come in, sister; **bonne s.** nun; **S. Thérèse** Sister Theresa
▸▸ **s. de lait** foster sister

sœurette [sœrɛt] NF *Fam* little sister

sofa [sɔfa] NM sofa, settee

soffite [sɔfit] NM *Archit* soffit

SOFI [sɔfi] NM *(abrév* **système d'ordinateurs pour le fret international)** = computerized system for international freight

Sofia [sɔfja] N Sofia

SOFININDEX [sɔfinɛ̃dɛks] *(abrév* **Société pour le financement des industries exportatrices)** = independent agency providing funding for export industries

SOFRES [sɔfrɛs] NF *(abrév* **Société française d'enquêtes et de sondages)** *Br* ≃ MORI

soft [sɔft] ADJ **1** *Fam (édulcoré) (débat, discussion)* soft **2** *Fam (film, roman)* softporn ▸ NM **1** *Ordinat* software **2** *Fam (genre cinématographique)* soft porn

software [sɔftwɛr] NM *Ordinat* software

soi [swa] PRON PERS *(stressed referring to an indef subject)* **1** *(réflexif ou exprimant la réciprocité) (personne)* oneself, one; *(referring to 'il', 'elle')* himself/herself/itself; **malgré s.** in spite of oneself; **parler de s.** to talk about oneself; **conscience de s.** awareness of self, self-awareness; **confiance en s.** self-confidence; **avoir confiance en s.** to be self-confident; **être sûr de s.** to be sure of oneself; **content/fier de s.** pleased with/proud of oneself; **avoir de l'argent/ses papiers sur s.** to have some money/one's papers on one; **prendre sur s.** to exercise self-control; **prendre qch sur s.** to take sth upon oneself; **chacun pour s.** every man for himself; **chez s.** at home; **rentrer chez s.** to go home; **avoir la loi pour s.** to have the law on one's side; **il n'est plus maître de s.** he is no longer in control of himself; **quand on marche, il faut regarder devant s.** you must keep looking in front of you when you walk; **petits services qu'on se rend entre s.** small mutual favours

2 (emphatic) **se parler à s.-même** to talk to oneself; **rester s.-même** to remain (true to) oneself; **faire tout par s.-même** to do everything oneself; **aimer son prochain comme s.-même** to love one's neighbour as oneself; **on n'est jamais si bien servi que par s.-même** if you want something done, do it yourself

3 (chose, idée) **en s.** in itself, per se; **il va de s. que ...** it goes without saying that ...; *Fam* **ça va de s.!** it goes without saying!, of course!; **ça paraît pourtant aller de s.** it seems obvious

4 *Phil* self; **le sens du s.** the sense of self

5 *Psy* id

6 **il a trouvé en ce camarade un autre s.-même** he's found a soul-mate in this friend

soi-disant [swadizɑ̃] ADJ INV **1** (qui se prétend) (romancier, artiste etc) self-styled, would-be; **une s. comtesse** a self-styled countess **2** (appelé) so-called; **les arts s. libéraux** the so-called liberal arts

ADV supposedly; **il est parti s. pour réfléchir** he's gone, supposedly to think it over; *Fam* **s. qu'il serait parti** he's gone, apparently or so they say

soie [swa] NF **1** *Tex* silk; **s. grège/naturelle/sauvage** raw/natural/wild silk; **robe de s.** silk dress; **papier de s.** tissue paper; **la route de la s.** the silk road **2** (d'un sanglier, d'une chenille etc) bristle; **brosse à cheveux en soies** bristle hairbrush; **couvert de soies** bristly, covered with bristles **3** *Tech* (d'une lame, d'une lime etc) tang

soierie [swari] NF (tissu) silk; (commerce) silk trade

soif [swaf] NF thirst; *Fig* (désir) thirst, craving (**de** for; **de faire** to do); **avoir s.** to be thirsty; **étancher sa s.** to quench one's thirst; **boire à sa s.,** *Fam* **boire jusqu'à plus s.** to drink one's fill; *Fam* **il fait s.** I'd kill for a drink, *Br* I could murder a drink; **cela me donne s.** it makes me thirsty; *Fig* **rester sur sa s.** to remain unsatisfied; **cette émission m'a laissé sur ma s.** the program didn't come up to my expectations or left me unsatisfied; **lire jusqu'à plus s.** to read one's fill; **nous avons ri jusqu'à plus s.** we laughed till we could laugh no more; *Fig* **avoir s. de** to be thirsty or to thirst for; **avoir s. de sang** to be thirsting for blood

soiffard, -arde [swafar, -ard] *Arg* ADJ (personne) boozy
N boozer

soignant [swaɲɑ̃] ADJ *Méd* **aide soignant(e)** nursing auxiliary, auxiliary nurse; **personnel s.** auxiliary nursing staff

soigné [swaɲe] ADJ **1** (personne, apparence) neat, well-groomed; (travail) careful; (repas) carefully prepared; (vêtement) neat, tidy; (style) polished; (cheval) groomed; (mains, ongles, jardin) well-kept; **elle est très soignée (de sa personne)** she is very careful or particular about her appearance; **peu s.** (personne, apparence, tenue, travail) untidy **2** *Fam* **une raclée soignée** a sound thrashing; **un rhume s.** a hell or a stinker of a cold; **l'addition était soignée** the *Br* bill or *Am* check was huge

soigner [swaɲe] VT **1** (maintenir en bon état) (meubles, livre, mains, apparence etc) to look after, to take care of; (apporter du soin à) (travail, repas, détails etc) to take care over; **s. le moindre détail** to take care over every detail; **s. sa ligne** to watch one's figure; **s. son image** to take care of one's image; **s. sa popularité** to nurse one's public; *Fam* **s. l'addition** (dans un restaurant etc) to bump up the bill

2 (maladie) to treat; **on soigne cette maladie avec des antibiotiques** the illness is treated with antibiotics

3 (personne) (d'un hôte, d'une infirmière etc) to look after, to take care of; (d'un médecin) to treat; *Fam* **s. qn aux petits oignons** to give sb first-class treatment; **se faire s.** to be treated; **il faut te faire s.** *Méd* you should have (medical) treatment or see a doctor; *Fam* (tu es fou) you need your head examined; *Fam* **ils nous ont soignés** (dans un restaurant etc) they've ripped us off

VPR **se soigner** (d'une personne) (médicalement) to treat oneself; (faire attention à soi) to take care of or look after oneself; **elle refuse de se s., elle dit que ça va passer tout seul** she won't take anything, she says it'll go away on its own; **cette maladie ne se soigne pas bien** the disease is difficult to treat; **ça se soigne très bien** it's easily treated; *Fam* **ça se soigne!** you need your head examined!

soigneur [swaɲœr] NM *Sport* trainer; *Boxe* second

soigneusement [swaɲøzmɑ̃] ADV carefully

soigneux, -euse [swaɲø, -øz] ADJ careful (**de** with); (propre) (personne, travail etc) tidy, neat

soi-même PRON PERS *voir* **soi, même**

soin [swɛ̃] NM **1** (charge) care; **le s. des enfants** the care of children, looking after children; **c'est à lui que revient le s. des enfants** he's in charge of or looks after or takes care of the children; **les soins du ménage** housekeeping; **avoir** ou **prendre s. de qn/de qch** to look after or take care of sb/sth; **confier qch aux soins de qn** to place sth in sb's care, to entrust sb with sth; **aux (bons) soins de ...** (sur une lettre etc) care of ..., c/o ...; **par les soins de ...** by courtesy of ..., thanks to ...

2 (effort) care; **avoir (grand) s. de faire qch** to take (particular) care to do sth, to make a (particular) point of doing sth; **elle prend grand s. de son jardin/de son apparence** she takes great care of her garden/over her appearance; **il prend peu de s. de sa personne** he is very careless or slovenly about his appearance; **elle a pris s. de lui envoyer tous les documents** she made sure she sent him/her all the documents; **avoir s. que qch ne s'ébruite pas/soit fait** to take care that sth does not leak out/is done; **mettre tous ses soins à faire qch/à ce que qch soit fait** to go to a great deal of trouble or take great pains to do sth/to see that sth is done

3 (tâche) **on lui a confié le s. de les recevoir** he was entrusted with the task or job of receiving them; **je vous laisse le s. de décider** I leave it to you to decide

4 avoir beaucoup de s. to be very tidy or orderly; **avec s.** carefully, with care; **avec beaucoup de s.** very carefully, with great care; **manquer de s.** to be careless; **manque de s.** carelessness; **sans s.** (utilisé adjectivement) careless; (pas propre) untidy; (utilisé adverbialement) carelessly; (pas proprement) untidily

5 soins (attention) care, attention; **soins de beauté** beauty care or treatment; **soins médicaux** medical care; **premiers soins, soins d'urgence** first aid; **rien ne peut remplacer les soins d'une mère** nothing can take the place of a mother; **les soins dont il entoure sa femme/son jardin** the care or attention he lavishes on his wife/his garden; **être aux petits soins pour** ou **avec qn** to fuss over sb, to wait hand and foot on sb; **soins esthétiques** beauty treatment; *Méd* **soins intensifs** intensive care; *Méd* **soins à domicile** home care or nursing; *Méd* **soins palliatifs** terminal care

6 *Arch* (souci) anxiety, worry

soir [swar] NM evening; **ce s.** this evening, tonight; **à ce s.!** see you tonight or this evening!; **le s. tombe** night is falling; *Fig* **le s. de la vie** the evening of one's life; **il fait frais le s.** it's cool in the evening; **que faites-vous le s.?** what do you do in the evening(s)?; **à dix heures du s.** at ten (o'clock) in the evening or at night; **lundi/demain/hier (au) s.** Monday/tomorrow/yesterday evening; **tous les lundis** every Monday evening; **le lendemain s.** the next evening; **la veille au s.** the evening before, the previous evening; **travailler du matin au s.** to work from morning till night; **être du s.** to be a night owl; **journal du s.** evening newspaper; *TV* evening news; **presse du s.** evening newspapers; **robe du s.** evening dress

soirée [sware] NF **1** (durée du soir) evening; **passer la s. chez un ami** to spend the evening at a friend's house; **passer ses soirées à lire** to spend one's evenings reading; **toute la s.** all evening, the whole evening; **les longues soirées d'hiver** the long winter evenings or nights; **en fin de s.** late in the evening, towards the end of the evening; **tard dans la s.** late in the evening; **bonne s.!** have a good evening (out)!, enjoy your evening!; *Fam* **faire une s. télévision** to spend an evening in front of the television; **s. étape** stopover at a hotel; **s. à thème** theme evening; *TV* **s. thématique** themed evening

2 (fête) party; **s. dansante** dance; **s. musicale** musical evening; **tenue de s.** evening dress SEE GRAMMAR B61

3 *Théâtre, Cin etc* (représentation de) s., représentation donnée en s. evening performance; **projecter un film en s.** to show a film in the evening, to have an evening showing of a film

soit [swa] before a vowel or as adv [swat] (third person of pr sub of être) ADV all right!, *Fml* so be it!; **s., tu peux t'en aller** all right then, go

CONJ **1** (supposons) **s. trois multiplié par six** if three is multiplied by six; **s. ABC un triangle** let ABC be a triangle, given a triangle ABC

2 (à savoir) that is to say; **trois objets à dix euros, s. trente euros** three articles at ten euros, that is to say thirty euros

3 s. ... s. ... either ... or ..., whether ... or ...; **s. l'un s. l'autre** (either) one or the other; **j'ai cet article s. en rouge, s. en bleu, s. en vert** I have this item (either) in red, blue or green; **s. tu le fais maintenant ou alors je m'en occupe demain** either you do it now or I'll take care of it tomorrow; **elle va trancher, s. dans un sens, s. dans l'autre** she'll decide (either) one way or the other; **il faut que tu te décides, s. que tu restes, s. que tu partes** you'll have to decide whether you're staying or going; **s. modestie, s. paresse, il n'a jamais rien écrit** whether from modesty or laziness, he has never written anything

soixantaine [swasɑ̃tɛn] NF **1** (nombre) **une s.** about sixty; **une s. de personnes** about sixty people, sixty or so people; **la s. de livres qu'elle a** the sixty (or so) books she has **2** (âge) **la s.** (the age of) sixty; **elle approche de la s.** she's getting on for sixty; **avoir dépassé la s.** to be in one's sixties, to be over sixty

soixante [swasɑ̃t] ADJ INV sixty; **page s.** page sixty; **s. et un** sixty-one; **s. et onze**

seventy-one; **s. et onzième** seventy-first
NM INV sixty; **habiter au s.** to live at number
sixty

soixante-dix ADJ INV, NM INV seventy

soixante-dixième ADJ seventieth
N seventieth
NM (fraction) seventieth (part)

soixante-huitard, -arde [swasɑ̃tɥitar,
-ard] Pol **ADJ** relating to the events of May 1968
N = person involved in the events of May
1968

soixante-neuf [swasɑ̃tnœf] **NM** Fam (position
sexuelle) sixty-nine

soixantième [swasɑ̃tjɛm] **ADJ** sixtieth
N sixtieth
NM (fraction) sixtieth (part)

soja [sɔʒa] **NM** (plante) soya (bean); Culin **lait
de s.** soya milk; **sauce de s.** soy sauce; **germes de s.** bean sprouts

sol[1] [sɔl] **NM 1** (surface de la terre) ground;
(territoire) soil; **le s. natal** one's native soil
or Hum, Litt heath; **au s.** at ground level; **interdit sur le s. français** prohibited on French
soil; Élec **relier un fil au s.** to earth or Am
ground a wire; **conducteur au s.** earthed or
Am grounded conductor; **cloué au s.** Aviat
grounded; Fig rooted to the spot; **position s.**
ground position; Aviat **personnel au s.**
ground staff **2** Géol, Agr (matière) soil; **s. fer-
tile/argileux** fertile/clay soil **3** (plancher)
floor; **revêtement de s.** floor covering; **dormir sur** ou **à même le s.** to sleep on the floor;
Sport **faire de la gymnastique au s.** to do
floor exercises

Attention: ne pas confondre **floor** et
ground lorsqu'on traduit **sol**. Floor désigne toujours le sol à l'intérieur d'un bâtiment, alors que **ground** s'utilise
uniquement pour l'extérieur.

---

sol[2] **NM INV** Mus (note) G; (en chantant la
gamme) so(h), sol; **morceau en s.** piece in G

sol-air ADJ INV (missile) ground-to-air

solaire [sɔlɛr] **ADJ** (chauffage, moteur, four
etc) solar; **cadran s.** sundial; **crème s.** sun lotion; **heure s.** solar time; **maison s.** solar-
heated house; Anat **plexus s.** solar plexus;
système s. solar system; Astron **taches solaires** sunspots; Méd **traitement s.** sunray
treatment

solarisation [sɔlarizasjɔ̃] **NF** solarization

solarium [sɔlarjɔm] **NM 1** Méd (établissment)
(pour bronzer) solarium **2** (terrasse) sun
terrace

soldat, -ate [sɔlda, -at] **NM** soldier; **s. du génie** sapper; **s. de marine** marine; **s. Dubois!**
Private Dubois!; Aviat **s. de 2ᵉ classe/de première classe** aircraftman second-class/first-
class; **s. de 2ᵉ classe, simple s.** private; **les
simples soldats** the rank and file; **se faire s.**
to go into or join the army; Fig **c'est un vrai
petit s.** he's a real trooper
NF soldate (woman or female) soldier; **à la
soldate** in a soldierly or soldier-like way or
fashion
▸▸ **s. des bois** soldier (ant); **s. de fortune**
soldier of fortune; **le S. inconnu** the Unknown Soldier or Warrior; **s. marin** (crustacé)
soldier (crab); **s. de plomb** tin soldier

soldatesque [sɔldatɛsk] Péj **ADJ** (langage,
manières etc) barrackroom
NF army rabble

solde[1] [sɔld] **NF** Mil etc (rémunération) pay;
Mil, Ind **feuille de s.** payroll; **soldes et indemnités** ordinary pay and allowances; **officier
en demi-s.** officer on half pay; **cahier de s.**
ledger; Péj **être à la s. de l'ennemi** to be in
the pay of the enemy; Péj **avoir qn à sa s.** to
have sb in one's pay

solde[2] **NM** Com **1** (somme) balance; **paie-**

ment pour s. payment of balance; **pour s.
(de tout compte)** in (full or final) settlement; **s. actif** credit balance; **s. bancaire, s.
en banque** bank balance; **s. bénéficiaire**
credit balance; **s. en caisse** cash balance; **s.
de compte** balance of account; **s. créditeur**
credit balance, balance in hand; **s. cumulé**
cumulative balance; **s. débiteur** ou **déficitaire** debit balance, balance owed; **s. disponible** available balance; **s. passif** debit
balance
2 soldes (articles) sale goods; (vente au rabais) sale; **courir** ou **faire les soldes** to go
round the sales; **ce magasin fait des soldes**
this shop is having a sale; **saison** ou **période
des soldes** sales season; **s. d'édition** (livre)
remainder; **(en) s.** to clear; **je l'ai acheté en
s.** I got it in or at a sale or the sales; **prix de s.**
bargain prices

solder [sɔlde] **VT 1** Fin (arrêter) (compte) to
balance, to close; (pour acquitter) to settle,
to pay (off); **s. l'arriéré** to make up back payments **2** Com (stock) to sell off, to clear;
(livres) to remainder
VPR se solder 1 Fin **les comptes se soldent
par un bénéfice net de ...** the accounts
show a net profit of ... **2** Fig **se s. par** (échec
etc) to end in; **tout ça va se s. par une catastrophe financière** it's going to end in financial disaster

soldeur, -euse [sɔldœr, -øz] **N** Com discount trader

sole[1] [sɔl] **NF 1** Tech, Métal bed plate **2** Naut
(d'un navire) flat bottom **3** Agr (de l'assolement des cultures) field

sole[2] **NF** (poisson) sole

solécisme [sɔlesism] **NM** Ling solecism

soleil [sɔlɛj] **NM 1** (astre) sun; **lever/coucher
du s.** sunrise/sunset; **se lever avec le s.** to get
up with the sun; **il n'y a rien de nouveau sous
le s.** there is nothing new under the sun; Hist
le Roi S. the Sun King; Couture **plissé s.** sunray pleats
2 (lumière, chaleur) sun, sunshine; **il y a** ou
il fait du s. the sun is shining, it's sunny; **il y
fait un s. de plomb** the sun is scorching hot
there; **se protéger du s.** to protect oneself from the sun; **au (grand) s.** in the
sun(shine); **jour de s.** sunny day; Fam **cette
petite est mon rayon de s.!** that little girl is
my ray of sunshine!; **sans s.** sunless; **coup
de s.** sunburn; (plus fort) touch of sunstroke;
Fam **piquer un s.** to blush; **ôte-toi de mon s.!**
get out of here!; Fig **avoir sa/se faire une
place au s.** to have one's/find oneself a place
in the sun; **avoir des biens** ou **du bien au s.** to
own property
3 Bot sunflower
4 Gym **grand s.** grand circle
5 (feu d'artifice) Catherine wheel, pinwheel
▸▸ **s. de minuit** midnight sun

solennel, -elle [sɔlanɛl] **ADJ 1** (serment, déclaration etc) solemn; (occasion etc) solemn,
formal **2** (ton, silence) solemn, grave; **prendre des airs solennels** to adopt a solemn air
3 Rel **communion solennelle** solemn
communion

solennellement [sɔlanɛlmɑ̃] **ADV** solemnly; (inaugurer etc) formally; **je le jure s.** I solemnly swear

solenniser [sɔlanize] **VT** to solemnize

solennité [sɔlanite] **NF 1** (caractère) solemnity; **avec s.** solemnly **2** (fête) solemn
ceremony

solénoïde [sɔlenɔid] **NM** Élec solenoid

solex® [sɔlɛks] **NM** moped

solfatare [sɔlfatar] **NF** Géol solfatara, sulphur spring

solfège [sɔlfɛʒ] **NM** Mus (tonic) sol-fa, music theory; **apprendre le s.** to learn music
theory; **(livre de) s.** (music) primer

solfier [sɔlfje] **VT** Mus (ton) to sol-fa

solidaire [sɔlidɛr] **ADJ 1** (personnes) **être s.
de qn** to stand by sb, to support sb; **se sentir
s. de qn** to feel a sense of solidarity with sb;
**nous sommes tous solidaires (les uns des
autres)** we all stand or stick together; **dans
leur famille, ils sont très solidaires** they're a
very close-knit family; **ses intérêts sont solidaires des nôtres** his/her interests are
bound up with ours **2** Tech (roue d'engrenage
etc) interdependent; **roue s. d'une autre**
wheel integral with another **3** Jur jointly
liable or responsible (**de** for); **obligation s.**
obligation binding on all parties

solidairement [sɔlidɛrmɑ̃] **ADV** jointly

solidariser [sɔlidarize] **VT 1** Jur to render
jointly liable or responsible **2** Tech **mécanisme à action solidarisée** interlocking gear
VPR se solidariser to make common cause,
to show solidarity (**avec** with)

solidarité [sɔlidarite] **NF 1** (entre personnes)
solidarity; **en signe de s., nous portons ce
badge** we wear this badge as a sign of solidarity; **faire appel à la s. nationale** to call
for national solidarity; **grève de s.** sympathy
strike; **débrayer par s. (avec)** to come out (on
strike) in sympathy (with) **2** Tech (des pièces)
interdependence **3** Jur joint liability or
responsibility

solide [sɔlid] **ADJ 1** (non liquide) (corps, aliment, terre) solid; Math **angle s.** solid angle
2 (résistant) (mur, fondation) solid, strong;
(tissu) strong; (personne) strong, sturdy; (repas) solid, hearty; (appétit) hearty; (preuve)
solid, sound; (raisonnement, éducation)
sound; (amitié) strong; Com (personne)
sound, solvent; (position, affaire) sound,
strong, well-established; **s. sur ses jambes**
steady on one's feet; **peu s.** (personne) weak;
(meuble) flimsy; **solides qualités** solid or
sterling qualities; **garantie s.** solid or reliable guarantee; **ami s.** staunch or reliable
or trusty friend; **de solides liens nous unissent** strong or close ties unite us; **une s. poignée de main** a firm handshake; **avoir la
tête s.** to be level-headed; **il faut avoir les
nerfs solides** you need nerves of steel (**pour
faire qch** to do sth); **j'ai de solides raisons de
croire que ...** I have good or sound reasons
for believing that ...; Fig **être s. au poste** to
be extremely reliable or dependable; Fig **ça
ne repose sur rien de s.** there is no sound or
solid basis for that; **être encore s. (comme
un chêne** ou **un roc)** to be still hale and hearty
NM 1 Géom, Phys solid (body); Géom **s. de
révolution** solid of revolution **2** Fam **ça, c'est
du s.!** that's pretty solid!

solidement [sɔlidmɑ̃] **ADV** (construire etc)
solidly; (attacher, tenir, établir etc) firmly, securely; **homme s. bâti** solidly or sturdily built
man; Fam **elle s'est fait s. reprendre** she got
a good telling-off

solidification [sɔlidifikasjɔ̃] **NF** solidification

solidifier [sɔlidifje] (impf, pr sub n. solidi-
fiions, v. solidifiiez) **VT** to solidify
VPR se solidifier to solidify

solidité [sɔlidite] **NF** solidity; (d'un édifice,
d'un matériau) strength; (d'une société, d'un
jugement) soundness; (d'une amitié)
strength, staunchness; (d'une couleur) fastness; **c'est d'une s. à toute épreuve** it stands
up to anything

soliloque [sɔlilɔk] **NM** soliloquy

soliloquer [sɔlilɔke] **VI** to soliloquize

solin [sɔlɛ̃] **NM** Constr (espace) space; (enduit) plaster filling

solipsisme [sɔlipsism] **NM** Phil solipsism

soliste [sɔlist] **N** soloist

solitaire [sɔlitɛr] **ADJ 1** (qui vit seul) solitary;

(involontairement) (personne) lonely, *Am Fam* lonesome; **passer des vacances solitaires** to spend one's holidays on one's own; **vivre s.** to live a solitary life; **avoir l'humeur s.** to like to be on one's own *or* alone, to like one's own company; **plaisir/vice s.** masturbation/self-abuse **2** *(séparé des autres) (voyageur, arbre, maison etc)* solitary, lone **3** *(désert) (route, lieu etc)* lonely, deserted **4 ver s.** tapeworm

N *(personne)* loner, lone wolf; *(ermite)* hermit, recluse; **en s.** on one's own, alone; *Naut* **croisière en s.** solo cruise

NM 1 *(jeu)* solitaire **2** *(diamant)* solitaire **3** *(sanglier)* rogue boar; *(éléphant)* rogue elephant

solitairement [sɔlitɛrmɑ̃] **ADV** on one's own, alone

solitude [sɔlityd] **NF 1** *(de personne)* solitude; *(involontaire)* loneliness; **rechercher la s.** to seek solitude; **j'aime la s.** I like being alone *or* on my own, I like my own company; **vivre dans la s.** to live alone *or* on one's own **2** *(de lieu)* loneliness; **dans la s. de la nuit/ campagne** in the loneliness *or* solitude of the night/countryside **3** *Litt (endroit)* lonely spot

solive [sɔliv] **NF** *Constr* joist

sollicitation [sɔ(l)lisitasjɔ̃] **NF 1** *(demande)* request; *(avec instance)* entreaty; **céder aux sollicitations de qn** to give in to sb's pleas **2** **les sollicitations de la faim/de l'ambition** gnawing hunger/ambition

solliciter [sɔ(l)lisite] **VT 1** *(entretien, audience etc)* to request; **s. qn (de faire qch)** to appeal to sb (to do sth); **j'ai l'honneur de s. votre bienveillance** I appeal to your kindness; **s. un emploi (de qn)** to apply (to sb) for a job; **s. des voix** to canvass for votes; **ils nous ont souvent sollicités par téléphone** they often made telephone appeals to us; **il est sollicité de toutes parts** he is very much in demand **2** *(attention, regards)* to attract; *(curiosité)* to arouse

solliciteur, -euse [sɔ(l)lisitœr, -øz] **N** petitioner, supplicant (**de** for)

sollicitude [sɔ(l)lisityd] **NF** *(soin)* solicitude; *(inquiétude)* solicitude, concern, anxiety (**pour** for); **ton plein de s.** solicitous *or* concerned tone

solo [sɔlo] **NM** solo; **s. de violon** violin solo; **faire un s.** *(en danse)* to do a solo, to dance a solo; *(en musique)* to do a solo, to play a solo; **jouer en s.** to play solo

ADJ INV solo; **violon s.** solo violin

sol-sol **ADJ INV** *(missile)* ground-to-ground

solstice [sɔlstis] **NM** solstice; **s. d'été/d'hiver** summer/winter solstice

solubiliser [sɔlybilize] **VT s. qch** to make sth soluble

solubilité [sɔlybilite] **NF** *(d'un corps)* solubility

soluble [sɔlybl] **ADJ 1** *(produit)* soluble; **café s.** instant coffee **2** *(problème)* solvable

soluté [sɔlyte] **NM** *Pharm, Chimie* solution, serum

solution [sɔlysjɔ̃] **NF 1** *(de problème, situation, d'équation etc)* solution, answer (**de** to); **s. de paresse** *ou* **de facilité** easy way out; **ce n'est pas une s.!** that's no answer *or* solution! **2** *Chimie, Phys etc (liquide, dissolution)* solution; **sel en s. (dans l'eau)** salt in solution (in water); **s. détergente** cleaning solution *or* fluid **3 s. de continuité** solution of continuity; *Élec etc* break of continuity

▸ ▸ *Hist* **la s. finale** the Final Solution

solutionner [sɔlysjɔne] **VT** *(problème, difficulté)* to solve

solvabilité [sɔlvabilite] **NF** solvency; *(en vue d'un emprunt)* credit rating

---

solvable [sɔlvabl] **ADJ** *(financially)* solvent

> Il faut noter que l'adjectif anglais **solvable** est un faux ami. Il signifie **soluble, résoluble**.

solvant [sɔlvɑ̃] **NM** *Chimie* solvent

soma [sɔma] **NM** *Biol* soma

somali, -ie [sɔmali] **ADJ** Somali

NM *Ling* Somali

N S. Somali; **les Somalis** the Somali(s)

Somalie [sɔmali] **NF** Somalia; *Hist* **S. britannique/italienne** British/Italian Somaliland

somalien, -enne [sɔmaljɛ̃, -ɛn] **ADJ** Somalian

N S. Somalian

somatique [sɔmatik] **ADJ** *Biol, Psy* somatic

somatisation [sɔmatizasjɔ̃] **NF** *Biol, Psy* psychosomatic reaction, *Spéc* somatization

somatiser [sɔmatize] **VT** *Biol, Psy* to react psychosomatically to, *Spéc* to somatize

sombre [sɔ̃br] **ADJ 1** *(foncé) (couleur)* dark; **des robes bleu s.** dark blue dresses **2** *(obscur) (forêt, pièce etc)* dark, dim; *(ciel)* dull, overcast; **il fait s.** *(temps)* it is dull (weather); **il faisait très s. dans la pièce** it was very dark in the room **3** *(triste) (visage, pensées, caractère, avenir etc)* gloomy, *Fml* sombre, *Am* somber; **ils sont fâchés pour une s. histoire d'argent** they quarrelled over some sordid little business of money; **une s. histoire d'assassinat** a sinister tale of murder **4** *Fam* **un s. imbécile** a total imbecile *or* idiot

sombrement [sɔ̃brəmɑ̃] **ADV** *(tristement)* gloomily, sombrely, *Am* somberly; **s'habiller s.** to wear dark clothes

sombrer [sɔ̃bre] **VI** *(d'un navire)* to sink, to founder; *(d'un empire)* to fall, to collapse; *(d'une affaire)* to come to grief, to fail; **s. dans l'alcool/la misère/la folie** to sink into alcoholism/poverty/madness; **il vit s. sa fortune** he saw his fortune swallowed up; **elle vit s. ses espérances** she saw her hopes dashed; **sa raison sombra** he lost his mind *or* his reason; **le bateau a sombré corps et biens** the boat went down with all hands

sombrero [sɔ̃brero] **NM** sombrero

sommaire [sɔ(m)mɛr] **ADJ 1** *(récit)* brief, succinct, concise **2** *(rudimentaire) (repas)* scanty, skimpy; *(examen)* hasty, cursory; **porter une tenue s.** to be scantily *or* skimpily dressed; **faire une toilette s.** to have a quick wash; **avoir des vues sommaires sur qch** to have superficial views on sth **3** *Jur (procédure, exécution)* summary **NM** summary, synopsis

sommairement [sɔ(m)mɛrmɑ̃] **ADV 1** *(expliquer, raconter etc)* briefly, in summary **2** *(de façon rudimentaire)* **vêtu s.** scantily *or* skimpily clad *or* dressed; **l'appartement est s. meublé** the furniture in the flat is very basic, the flat is meagrely furnished; **s. organisé** improvised, hastily organized **3** *Jur (juger)* summarily

sommation[1] [sɔ(m)masjɔ̃] **NF 1** *Jur (injonction)* notice, demand; *(de paraître en justice)* summons; **avoir s. de payer une dette** to receive notice *or* a demand to pay a debt **2** *Mil (de sentinelle)* challenge

sommation[2] **NF** *Math (d'une série)* summation

somme[1] [sɔm] **NF bête de s.** beast of burden; *Fig* drudge; **travailler comme une bête de s.** to work like a slave, to slave away

somme[2] **NF 1** *Math* sum, total; **faire la s. de dix nombres** to add (up) ten numbers; **s. générale/totale** overall total/total sum; **la s. des trois angles d'un triangle** the sum of the three angles of a triangle

2 *(quantité) (d'objets)* number; *(des pertes etc)* amount; **la s. des efforts** the amount of

---

effort; **en s.** *(tout compte fait)* on the whole, all things considered; *(en bref)* in short; **en s., j'ai été plutôt agréablement surpris** on the whole, I was rather pleasantly surprised; **en s. il s'agit d'un travail commercial** in short, it's a sales job; **s. toute** when all is said and done

3 s. (d'argent) sum (of money); **payer la s. de 500 euros** to pay 500 euros; **être mis à l'amende pour la s. de 500 euros** to be fined (a total of) 500 euros; **dépenser des sommes folles** to spend vast sums *or* amounts (of money); **un million! c'est une s.!** a million! that's a lot of money!; **s. due** amount due, total due; **s. nette** net (amount); *Compta* **sommes payables** payables, sums payable

4 *(d'une œuvre)* outline, survey

somme[3] **NM** nap, snooze; **faire un (petit) s.** to have *or* take a nap *or* a snooze, *Fam* to have forty winks

sommeil [sɔmɛj] **NM 1** *(de dormeur)* sleep, *Litt* slumber; **avoir besoin de très peu de s.** to need very little sleep; **s. réparateur/profond** refreshing/deep sleep; **s. de mort** *ou* **de plomb** heavy *or* deep sleep; **dormir d'un s. de plomb** to sleep like a log; **avoir le s. léger/profond** to be a light/a heavy sleeper; **dormir du s. du juste** to sleep the sleep of the just; **chercher le s.** to try to sleep; **faire une cure de s.** to undergo sleep therapy; **j'en perds le s.** I'm losing sleep over it; *Fig* **s. éternel** eternal rest; *Bot* **en s.** (lying) dormant; *Fig* **laisser une affaire en s.** to put a matter aside *or* on the back burner *or* on ice, *Fml* to leave a matter in abeyance; *Zool* **s. hivernal** winter sleep

2 *(somnolence)* sleepiness, drowsiness; **avoir s.** to be *or* feel sleepy *or* drowsy; **ça risque de te donner s.** it might make you sleepy; **le s. me gagne** I'm beginning to fall asleep; **je tombe** *ou* **je meurs de s.** I can't keep awake, I can't keep my eyes open; **maladie du s.** sleeping sickness

▸ ▸ **s. paradoxal** REM sleep

sommeiller [sɔmeje] **VI 1** to doze **2** *Fig* to lie dormant, to be latent (**en qn** in sb)

sommelier [sɔməlje] **NM** cellarman; *(serveur)* wine waiter, sommelier

sommellerie [sɔmɛlri] **NF 1** wine waiter's job **2** *(cave)* wine cellar

sommer[1] [sɔme] **VT** *Math* to sum

sommer[2] **VT** *aussi Jur* to summon (**de faire qch** to do sth); **s. qn de payer** to require sb to pay

sommet [sɔmɛ] **NM** *(d'une montagne, d'une colline)* top, summit, peak; *(d'un arbre, d'un toit, d'une tour, d'une hiérarchie)* top; *(d'un angle, d'une courbe, d'une trajectoire, d'un cône)* vertex; *(d'une vague)* crest; *(d'une arche, de la tête)* crown; *Fig (du pouvoir, de la renommée)* summit, pinnacle, height; *Fig* **atteindre des sommets vertigineux** to reach the dizzy heights; *Fig* **être au s. de l'échelle** to be at the top of the ladder; **atteindre le s. de la gloire/du succès** to reach the height *or* pinnacle of fame/success; *Pol* **conférence** *ou* **réunion** *ou* **rencontre au s.** summit (meeting *or* conference); **un s. franco-américain** a Franco-American summit; *Obst* **présentation d'un bébé par le s.** head presentation of a baby

sommier [sɔmje] **NM 1** *(de lit)* base; **s. à ressorts/lattes** sprung/slatted base **2** *Tech (d'arche)* springer; *(de porte etc)* lintel; *(du sol)* cross beam; *(de pont)* stringer; *(de balance)* beam; *(de machine)* bed **3** *Admin etc* register; *Jur* **sommiers judiciaires** criminal records; **il n'y a rien sur lui au s.** he's got a clean record **4** *Com* cash book

sommier-divan, *pl* **sommiers-divans NM** divan base

sommité [sɔ(m)mite] **NF 1** *Bot* head **2** *Fig*

(personnage) leading figure *or* light; **sommités de l'art** leading figures *or* lights in the art world; **les sommités du monde scientifique** leading experts in the scientific field

somnambule [sɔmnãbyl] ADJ somnambulistic, somnambulant; **il est s.** he's a sleepwalker, he sleepwalks, he walks in his sleep N sleepwalker, *Spéc* somnambulist; **c'est un s.** he's a sleepwalker, he sleepwalks, he walks in his sleep; **travailler/parler comme un s.** to work/speak like a zombie *or Fml* as if in a trance; **ses gestes de s.** his/her zombie-like movements

somnambulisme [sɔmnãbylism] NM sleepwalking, *Spéc* somnambulism; **s. provoqué** hypnotic state

somnifère [sɔmnifɛr] *Méd* ADJ sleep-inducing, soporific; **comprimé s.** sleeping tablet *or* pill
NM sleeping tablet *or* pill

somnolence [sɔmnɔlãs] NF sleepiness, drowsiness, *Litt* somnolence; **ce médicament peut provoquer des états de s.** this medicine may cause drowsiness; **la chaleur nous plonge dans un état de s.** the heat makes us drowsy *or* lethargic

somnolent [sɔmnɔlã] ADJ sleepy, drowsy, *Litt* somnolent

somnoler [sɔmnɔle] VI to doze

somptuaire [sɔ̃ptɥɛr] ADJ **1** *Jur (loi)* sumptuary **2** *Fin* **taxes somptuaires** tax on luxury articles; **dépenses somptuaires** expenditure on luxuries

somptueusement [sɔ̃ptɥøzmã] ADV sumptuously, magnificently

somptueux, -euse [sɔ̃ptɥø, -øz] ADJ sumptuous, magnificent

somptuosité [sɔ̃ptɥozite] NF sumptuousness, magnificence

son¹, sa, ses [sɔ̃, sa, se] ADJ POSS SEE GRAMMAR A30; B21 (**son** *is used instead of* **sa** *before f nouns beginning with a vowel or mute* **h**) *(d'homme etc)* his; *(de femme etc)* her; *(de chose, d'idée, d'animal etc)* its; *(de bébé)* his/her, its; *(d'animal domestique)* its, his/her; *(après un sujet indéfini)* one's; *(après 'tout le monde', 'personne', 'chacun' etc)* their, *Fml* his/her; **s. ami/amie** his/her friend; **s. meilleur ami/sa meilleure amie** his/her best friend; **s. oncle et sa tante** his/her aunt and (his/her) uncle; **s. père et sa mère,** *Litt* **ses père et mère** his/her mother and father; **il a mis s. chapeau et ses gants** he put on his hat and (his) gloves; **un(e) de ses ami(e)s** one of his/her friends, a friend of his/hers; **un professeur de ses amis** a teacher friend of his/hers; **chacun a pris s. sac** *(chacun a un sac)* everybody took their bags; *(le sac de Pierre)* everybody took his bag; **un bébé peut reconnaître sa mère peu de temps après sa naissance** a baby can recognize its mother shortly after it's born; **perdre s. temps** to waste one's time; **ici, on passe s. temps à bavarder** everybody spends their time chatting here; **en Alsace, on prend s. café en même temps que le dessert** in Alsace, they have their coffee along with their desert; *Fam* **elle aura sa chambre à elle** she'll have her own room; *Fam* **s. imbécile de frère** his/her idiot of a brother; *Fam* **s. artiste de mari** her artist husband; *Fam* **alors, tu veux bien le rencontrer, s. artiste?** so, do you want to meet this artist of his/hers?; *Fam* **il a eu s. vendredi** he got Friday off; *Fam* **alors, c'était ça ses vacances de rêve!** so much for his/her dream holiday!

son² NM **1** *(de voix, d'instrument etc)* sound; *(volume)* sound, volume; **baisser/monter le s.** to turn the sound up/down; **le s. profond de la cloche** the deep sound *or* tone of the bell; *Fig* **c'est un autre s. de cloche** that's

(quite) another story; **j'ai entendu plusieurs sons de cloche** I've heard several variants *ou* versions of that story; **s. du tambour/de la trompette** beat of the drum/blare of the trumpet; **danser au s. des accordéons** to dance to the sound of accordions; **annoncer une nouvelle à s. de trompe** to shout a piece of news from the rooftops; *Naut* **s. de sirène** *ou* **de sifflet** siren blast
2 *Phys, Mus* sound; **s. pur** pure tone; **niveau du s.** sound level; **vitesse du s.** speed of sound; *Aviat* **mur du s.** sound barrier; *Cin etc* **enregistrement du s.** sound recording; **prise de s.** sound pick-up; **la prise de s. est bonne** the recording is good; *Cin etc* **ingénieur du s.** sound engineer; **(spectacle) s. et lumière** son et lumière; **s. d'ambiance** ambient sound; *TV* **s. sur image** sound over vision, SOV; **s. numérique** digital sound; **s. stéréo** stereo sound; **s. témoin** cue track; *TV, Radio* **s. de transition** bridging sound; **s. 3D** surround sound

son³ NM *(de grains)* bran; **céréales à base de s.** bran cereal; **pain de s.** bran loaf; **tache de s.** freckle; **poupée de s.** stuffed doll

sonal, -als [sɔnal] NM *Radio, TV* (advertising) jingle

sonar [sɔnar] NM *Naut* sonar

sonate [sɔnat] NF *Mus* sonata; **s. pour violon** violin sonata

sonatine [sɔnatin] NF *Mus* sonatina

sondage [sɔ̃daʒ] NM **1** poll, survey; **s. Gallup** Gallup poll; **faire** *ou* **pratiquer un s.** to carry out a poll; **enquête par s., s. (d'opinion)** opinion poll *or* survey; **faire un s. auprès d'un groupe** to poll a group, to carry out a survey among a group; **s. aléatoire** random sampling; **s. aréolaire** cluster sampling; **sondages de paix** peace feelers; **s. probabiliste** probability survey; **s. par quotas** quotas survey; **s. par téléphone** telephone interviewing
2 *Naut, Aviat etc* sounding, probe; **faire des sondages** to take soundings; **ballon de s.** pilot balloon, sounding balloon
3 *Min* boring; **appareil de s.** drilling rig
4 *Métal* **essai de s.** probe test
5 *Méd (de blessure)* probing

sonde [sɔ̃d] NF **1** *Naut* (sounding) lead, sounding line, plummet; **naviguer à la s.** to navigate by soundings; **être sur la s.** to be in soundings, to have struck soundings
2 *(de pompe, de puits etc)* sounding rod
3 **faire la s.** *(d'une baleine)* to sound
4 *Météo, Aviat* **s. aérienne** sounding balloon; **s. spatiale** space probe; *Aviat* **s. de réservoir** tank probe; **s. à fil chaud** hot-wire anemometer
5 *Méd* probe, tube, catheter; **s. (creuse)** catheter; **nourri à la s.** tube-fed
6 *(à fromage etc)* taster
7 *Min* borer, drill

sondé [sɔ̃de] NM *Mktg* respondent, person polled

sonder [sɔ̃de] VT **1** *Naut* to sound; *Fig (mystère)* to fathom
2 *Aviat, Météo* **s. l'atmosphère** to make soundings in the atmosphere
3 *Min* **s. un terrain** to make borings
4 *(examiner) (fromage)* to taste; *(poutre)* to examine; *(horizon)* to scan; **s. le cœur/les intentions de qn** to sound out sb's heart/intentions; **s. qn** to sound sb out; **je l'ai sondée là-dessus** I sounded her out on the matter; **il la sonda du regard** he looked intently at her; **s. l'opinion** to sound out public opinion, to make a survey of public opinion; **10% de la population sondée** 10% of those polled; *Fig* **s. le terrain** to see how the land lies
5 *Méd (blessure)* to probe; *(patient)* to sound; *(avec une sonde creuse)* to catheterize

VI **1** *(d'une baleine)* to sound
2 *Min* to make borings

sondeur, -euse [sɔ̃dœr, -øz] NM **1** *Naut (personne)* leadsman; *(machine)* sounder **2** *Min (personne)* borer, driller
NF *Min* **sondeuse** borer, drill

songe [sɔ̃ʒ] NM *Litt* dream; **faire un s.** to have a dream; **en s.** in a dream

songe-creux NM INV *Litt* dreamer

songer [sɔ̃ʒe] VI *(je songeai(s); n. songeons)*
1 s. à qch *(penser à)* to think about sth; *(considérer)* to consider sth, to think sth over; **s. à l'avenir** to think about the future; **songez à ce que vous faites!** think about what you're doing!; **il ne faut pas y s.** that's quite out of the question; **on ne peut pas ne pas s. à elle** you can't help but think about her; **s. au mariage** to consider *or* to contemplate marriage; **sans y s.** without thinking; **sans s. à mal** without meaning any harm; **s. à faire qch** to think of doing sth, to contemplate doing sth; **il ne songe qu'à gagner de l'argent** making money is all he thinks about
2 *(imaginer)* to imagine (**que** that); **songez si j'étais furieux** you can imagine how angry I was; **je ne songeais guère que ...** little did I think *or* imagine that ...; **songez donc!** just think!, just imagine!
3 s. à *(se souvenir de)* to remember; **songez à lui** keep *or* bear him in mind, remember him; **songez que ...** remember *or* bear in mind that ...; **je ne songeais pas que ...** I had forgotten that ...; **cela m'a fait s. que ...** that reminded me that ...
4 *Arch (rêver)* to dream

songerie [sɔ̃ʒri] NF *Litt* reverie, daydreaming

songeur, -euse [sɔ̃ʒœr, -øz] ADJ *(rêveur) (personne, nature)* dreamy; *(pensif) (personne)* pensive, thoughtful

sonique [sɔnik] ADJ sonic; **bang s.** sonic boom

sonnaille [sɔnaj] NF (cow)bell

sonnant [sɔnã] ADJ *(horloge)* striking; **arriver à dix heures sonnant(es)** to arrive on the stroke of ten *or* at ten (o'clock) sharp; *Fig* **espèces sonnantes et trébuchantes** hard cash

sonné [sɔne] ADJ **1 il est dix heures sonnées** it's past *or* gone ten; **il a quarante ans (bien) sonnés** he's well over forty, *Fam* he's on the wrong side of forty, he won't see forty again
2 *Boxe etc Fam (groggy)* groggy, punch-drunk; *(fou)* crazy, cracked

sonner [sɔne] VI *(d'une horloge)* to strike; *(de cloches, du téléphone)* to ring; **le glas sonne** the bell is tolling; **s. creux** to sound hollow; *Fig* to ring hollow; **sa réponse a sonné faux** his/her answer did not ring true; **quand elle rit, ça sonne faux** when she laughs it rings false; *Fig* **s. bien/mal** to sound good/bad; **l'italien sonne bien à l'oreille** Italian is a pleasant-sounding language; **adresse qui sonne bien** good address; **faire s. les consonnes** to sound the consonants; **faire s. un mot** to emphasize a word; **faire s. son argent/ses clefs** to jingle one's money/one's keys; *Fam* **il va se faire s.!** he'll catch it!; **six heures sonnèrent** the clock struck six; **midi vient de s.** it has just struck twelve; **le réveil vient de s.** the alarm (clock) has just gone off; **faire s. le réveil à 6 heures** to set the alarm for 6 o'clock; **les vêpres sonnent** the bells are ringing for vespers; **on sonne** there's a ring at the door; **on a sonné** that was the doorbell, there's someone at the door; **j'ai sonné chez eux, mais personne ne m'a répondu** I rang their doorbell, but nobody answered; **s. avant d'entrer** *(sur panneau)* ring before entering; **entrez sans s.** go (straight) in; **s. du clairon** to sound the bugle; **son heure** *ou* **sa dernière heure a sonné** his last hour has come; **la trompette sonne** the trumpet sounds; **les oreilles lui sonnaient** his ears were buzzing

VT 1 *(trompettes etc)* to sound; **s. la cloche** to ring the bell; *Fam* **il va se faire s. les cloches!** he'll catch it!; **horloge qui sonne les heures** clock that strikes the hours; **l'horloge a sonné dix heures** the clock struck ten; **il a sonné deux coups à la porte** he rang the doorbell twice; **s. la messe/l'office** to ring the bell for mass/for church; **s. le dîner** to ring the dinner bell; *Mil* **s. la charge/la retraite** to sound the charge/the retreat **2** *(appeler) (domestique, infirmière etc)* to ring for; *très Fam* **on ne vous a pas sonné, vous!** mind your own business!, nobody asked you! **3** *très Fam (assommer)* **s. qn** to knock sb out **4** *Belg (appeler au téléphone)* to telephone, to call

sonnerie [sɔnri] **NF 1** *(son) (des cloches, du téléphone)* ringing; *(cloches)* (set of) bells *or* chimes; **c'est la s. du téléphone qui m'a réveillé** it was the telephone (ringing) that woke me up **2** *(mécanisme) (d'une horloge)* striking mechanism; *(sonnette)* bell; **pendule à s.** striking clock; **bouton de s.** bell push; **fil à s.** bell wire **3** *Mil (de clairon etc)* call

sonnet [sɔnɛ] **NM** sonnet

sonnette [sɔnɛt] **NF 1** *(de porte)* doorbell; *(clochette)* (small) bell; *(de vélo, pour serviteurs)* bell; **appuyer sur la s.** to ring the bell; **personne ne répondit à mon coup de s.** no one answered the bell; **as-tu entendu la s.?** did you hear the bell?; **cordon de s.** bell pull; **s. d'alarme** alarm bell; **coup de s.** ring **2** *Constr* pile driver **3** **serpent à s.** rattlesnake

sonneur, -euse [sɔnœr, -øz] **N** bellringer; *Fam* **dormir comme un s.** to sleep like a log **NM** *Constr* pile-driver operator

sono [sɔno] **NF** *abrév Fam* = **sonorisation 2, sonorisation 3**

sonore [sɔnɔr] **ADJ 1** *(relatif au son)* sound; **onde s.** soundwave; *Cin* **film s.** sound film; **effets sonores** sound effects; **bande** *ou* **piste s.** sound track; **bip s.** beep; **pollution s.** noise pollution; **église s.** church with good acoustics; **vibrations sonores** acoustic resonance **2** *(voix)* ringing, loud, sonorous; *(cloche)* clear-toned; *(rire)* resounding; *(voûte, couloir etc)* echoing; *Ling* **consonne s.** voiced consonant; **niveau (d'intensité) s.** sound (intensity) level **NF** *Ling* voiced consonant

> Il faut noter que l'adjectif anglais **sonorous** signifie souvent **grandiloquent**.

sonorisation [sɔnɔrizasjɔ̃] **NF 1** *Ling (d'une consonne)* voicing **2** *Cin* addition of the soundtrack **(de** to**), dubbing **3** *(d'une pièce)* fitting of a PA system; *(équipement)* public address system, PA system; *(de discothèque etc)* sound system

sonoriser [sɔnɔrize] **VT 1** *Ling (consonne)* to voice **2** *TV, Cin* to dub; *(présentation)* to add sound to; **s. un film** to add the soundtrack to a film **3 s. une salle** to fit a room with a PA system **VPR se sonoriser** *Ling (de consonne)* to be voiced

sonorité [sɔnɔrite] **NF 1** *(qualité de son)* tone **2** *(résonance)* resonance; *(de salle etc)* acoustics; **ce piano a une belle s.** this piano has a beautiful tone

sonothèque [sɔnɔtɛk] **NF** sound effects *or* audio library

sonotone® [sɔnɔtɔn] **NM** miniature hearing aid

sont [sɔ̃] *voir* **être²**

sopalin® [sɔpalɛ̃] **NM** kitchen paper

sophisme [sɔfism] **NM** sophism

sophiste [sɔfist] **N** sophist

sophistication [sɔfistikasjɔ̃] **NF 1** *(d'une personne, d'un équipement)* sophistication **2** *Vieilli (du vin etc)* adulteration

sophistique [sɔfistik] **ADJ** sophistic(al) **NF** sophistry

sophistiqué [sɔfistike] **ADJ 1** *(personne)* sophisticated; *(équipement etc)* sophisticated, advanced **2** *Vieilli (frelaté) (vin etc)* adulterated

Sophocle [sɔfɔkl] **N** Sophocles

sophrologie [sɔfrɔlɔʒi] **NF** sophrology

sophrologue [sɔfrɔlɔg] **N** sophrologist

soporifique [sɔpɔrifik] **ADJ** *(drogue)* soporific, sleep-inducing; *Fam (ennuyeux)* boring, soporific **NM** *(drogue)* sleeping drug, soporific; *Fam (livre)* boring book, book that sends you to sleep

soprane [sɔpran] **N** *Mus* = **soprano**

sopraniste [sɔpranist] **NM** *Mus* male soprano

soprano [sɔprano] *Mus* **NM** soprano (voice) **N** *(personne)* soprano **ADJ** **saxophone s.** soprano saxophone

sorbe [sɔrb] **NF** *Bot* sorb (apple)

sorbet [sɔrbɛ] **NM** *Culin* sorbet; **s. au cassis** blackcurrant sorbet

sorbetière [sɔrbɛtjɛr] **NF** ice-cream maker

sorbier [sɔrbje] **NM** *Bot* sorb (tree), service (tree)

sorbique [sɔrbik] **ADJ** *Chimie (acide)* sorbic

sorbonnard, -arde [sɔrbɔnar, -ard] *Fam* **N** *(étudiant)* student at the Sorbonne; *(professeur)* teacher at the Sorbonne **ADJ** *Péj* pedantic

sorcellerie [sɔrsɛlri] **NF** witchcraft, sorcery, magic; **c'est de la s.!** it's magic!

sorcier [sɔrsje] **NM** sorcerer, wizard; **il ne faut pas être s. pour faire ça** you don't need to be a genius to do that, that doesn't take much intelligence; *Can Fam* **être en s.** to be fuming, to be hopping mad **ADJ M** *Fam* **ce n'est pas s.** it's simple enough, there's no magic about that

sorcière [sɔrsjɛr] **NF** sorceress, witch; *Fam Péj* **vieille s.** old hag, old witch; **chasse aux sorcières** witch hunt; **cercle** *ou* **rond de sorcières** fairy ring

sordide [sɔrdid] **ADJ 1** *(vêtements)* filthy; *(pièce, quartier etc)* squalid, sordid **2** *(crime, détails, avarice etc)* sordid

sordidement [sɔrdidmɑ̃] **ADV** sordidly; **vivre s.** to live in squalor

sordidité [sɔrdidite] **NF** sordidness

sorgho [sɔrgo] **NM** *Bot* sorghum

Sorlingues [sɔrlɛ̃g] **NFPL** **les S.** the Isles of Scilly, the Scilly Isles

sornettes [sɔrnɛt] **NFPL** twaddle, rubbish

sort [sɔr] **NM 1** *(situation)* **être satisfait de son s.** to be satisfied with one's lot; **faire un s. à** *(choses inutiles, encombrantes)* to dispose of; *Fam (ne rien laisser de) (bouteille, poulet rôti etc)* to polish off, to finish off **2** *(destin)* fate, destiny; **notre s. est décidé** our fate is sealed; **abandonner qn à son triste s.** to abandon sb to his/her fate; **l'artillerie fit le s. de la bataille** the artillery decided the battle; **coup/ironie du s.** stroke/irony of fate; **et alors, ironie du s., qui vois-je en face de moi?** and as fate would have it, who do I see in front of me? him! **3** *(hasard)* chance, fortune; **tirer (qch) au s.** to draw lots (for something); *(jouer à pile ou face)* to toss a coin (for something); **tirer une place au s.** to draw lots for a place; **tirage au s.** drawing of lots; *Ftbl etc* toss; **le s. en est jeté** the die is cast

4 *(magique)* spell, charm; **jeter un s. à qn** to cast a spell on *or* over sb; **conjurer le mauvais s.** to ward off bad luck

sortable [sɔrtabl] **ADJ** *Fam (personne)* presentable; **tu n'es pas s.!** I can't take you anywhere!

sortant, -ante [sɔrtɑ̃, -ɑ̃t] **ADJ** *(numéro à la loterie)* winning; *(membres d'un comité etc)* outgoing, retiring; **élèves sortants** pupils in their last term; *Mil* cadets passing out; **les députés sortants** the outgoing members of parliament **N** **les sortants** those going/coming out

sorte [sɔrt] **NF 1** *(manière)* way; **ne parlez pas de la s.** don't talk like that *or* in that way; **en quelque s.** as it were, in a way; **il sort très peu habillé, de s. qu'il tombe malade** he doesn't dress warmly when he goes out and so he falls ill *or* with the result that he falls ill; **de s. à faire** so as to do; **je lui en ai parlé de s. qu'il ne soit pas pris au dépourvu** I told him about it so that he wouldn't be caught unawares; SEE GRAMMAR B33 **faites en s. que tout soit prêt à temps** see to it that everything is ready in time; **fais en s. de tout préparer à l'avance** try to prepare everything in advance **2** *(genre)* sort, kind; **toute(s) sorte(s) de choses, des choses de toute(s) sorte(s)** all sorts *or* kinds of things; **des gens de toute(s) sorte(s)** all sorts *or* kinds of people; **un homme de la s.** a man of that sort *or* kind; **une s. de ragoût** a *or* some sort *or* kind of stew; **je n'ai rien dit/rien fait de la s.** I said/did no such thing, I said/did nothing of the kind *or* sort VOIR GRAMMAIRE A13

sorteur, -euse [sɔrtœr, -øz] *Belg* **ADJ** *(noceur)* **ils sont très sorteurs** they like to party *or* to live it up **N** *(noceur)* reveller, partygoer **NM** *(videur)* bouncer

sorteux, -euse [sɔrtø, -øz] *Can Fam* **ADJ** *(qui aime sortir)* sociable, who likes going out **N** *(personne sociable)* sociable person

SORTIE [sɔrti]

leaving **1**	▪ exit **1, 5, 12**	▪ way out **12**
▪ publication **2**	▪ release **2**	▪ output **4,**
5	▪ outflow **3, 8**	▪ export **7** ▪ sortie
10	▪ outburst **11**	▪ outlet **13**

NF 1 *(action de quitter un lieu)* going out, coming out, leaving; *Théâtre* exit; **préparer sa s.** to prepare one's exit; **faire une fausse s.** to make a false exit; **c'était ma première s. depuis mon accident** it was the first time I had been out since my accident, it was my first outing after my accident; **à la s. du théâtre/du cinéma** at the end of the performance/of the film; **à la s. des classes** when school comes out; **à (l'heure de) la s. des bureaux** when the offices come out **2** *Com (d'un livre, d'un journal)* publication; *(d'un film, d'un disque)* release; *(d'un modèle)* launch(ing); **s. en salle** *(d'un film)* (cinema) release **3** *(écoulement) (de liquide)* outflow, flowing out; **tuyaux de s.** outlet pipes **4** *Élec, Électron* output **5** *Ordinat* exit; *(information)* output; **s. d'imprimante** printer output; **dispositif de s.** output device; **signal de s.** output signal **6** *Tech (de feuilles de papier d'imprimerie etc)* delivery; **table de s.** delivery table **7** *Com (de marchandises)* export **8** *Fin* **les sorties** *or* the gold withdrawals; **s. de devises/de capitaux** currency/capital outflow **9** *(excursion)* trip, excursion, outing; *(congé)* leave; **organiser une s. entre élèves** to organize a school trip; **priver qn de s.** to stop sb from going out; **faire une s. en mer**

to go for a short sea trip; **jour de s.** day out; **avoir un jour de s. par semaine** to have one free day a week; **nous sommes de s. aujourd'hui** we're going out today; **j'étais de s. mardi** I was out on Tuesday; **quelles sont vos sorties?** where do you go when you go out?; *Naut* **s. à terre** shore leave; **l'année dernière les canots de sauvetage ont fait cinquante sorties** last year the lifeboats went out fifty times

10 *Mil* sally, sortie; **faire une s.** *Ftbl (de gardien de but)* to leave the penalty box

11 *Fam (verbale)* outburst, tirade; **faire une s. à** *ou* **contre qn** to lash out at sb; **je le sais capable de n'importe quelle s. devant eux** I know he's capable of saying anything in front of them

12 *(issue)* exit, way out; **porte de s.** exit door; *Fig* **se ménager une porte de s.** to make sure one has a way out *or* an escape route; **il y a une s. sur la ruelle** there is a way out into the lane; **à la s. de la gare** at the station exit; **par ici la s.** this way out; **s. d'autoroute** motorway exit

13 *(pour l'eau, la vapeur)* outlet

14 *TV, Cin (fin de séquence)* out

▶▶ **s. de bain** bathrobe; *Vieilli* **s. de bal** evening wrap, opera cloak; **sorties de caisse** cash payments; *Ordinat* **s. écran** screen output; **sorties de fonds** outgoings, expenses; *Ordinat* **s. (sur) imprimante** printout; *Ordinat* **s. imprimée** printed output; *Ordinat* **s. jeux** games port; *Ordinat* **s. parallèle** parallel output; **s. de secours** emergency exit; *Ordinat* **s. série** serial output; **sorties de trésorerie** cash outflow *or* outgoings

sortilège [sɔrtilɛʒ] NM spell, charm

SORTIR¹ [sɔrtir] *(prp sortant; pp sorti; pr ind je sors, il sort, n. sortons, ils sortent; pr sub je sorte; impf je sortais; p hist je sortis; fu je sortirai)*

> **VI** to go out **1, 8** ▪ to come out **1, 5** ▪ to leave **1, 5** ▪ to come up **4** ▪ to get out **1, 5** ▪ to stand out **12** ▪ to stick out **12, 13** ▪ to exit **14**
> **VT** to take out **1, 2** ▪ to bring out **3** ▪ to release **3** ▪ to output **5**
> **VPR** to get out of *(se sortir de)*

VI *(aux être)* **1** *(à pied) (aller)* to go out, to leave; *(venir)* to come out, to leave; *(d'un magazine, d'un livre)* to come out, to be published; *(d'un film)* to come out, to be released; **le livre sort chez Gallimard le mois prochain** the book will be published by Gallimard next month; **s. sur le marché** to come onto the market; **je n'arrivais** *ou* **ne parvenais pas à s.** I couldn't get out; *Scol* **est-ce que je peux s.?** may I be excused?; **entrer par une porte et s. par l'autre** to go in one door and out the other; **faire s. qn** *(en promenade etc)* to take sb out; *(mettre à la porte)* to make sb leave, to put sb out; **fais s. les enfants, nous avons à parler** send the children out of the room, we have to talk; **sortez (d'ici)!** get out (of here)!; **je sors d'une mauvaise grippe** I'm just recovering from *or* getting over a bad dose of flu; **s. vainqueur d'un tournoi** to come out on top *or* emerge the winner in a tournament; **tu sors à quelle heure, ce soir?** *(du bureau, du lycée etc)* what time do you finish tonight?; *Fig Fam* **nous ne sommes pas sortis de l'auberge!** we're not out of the wood(s) yet; **cela ne doit pas s. d'ici** *(cela doit rester secret)* it mustn't go any further; *Fam* **d'où sors-tu?** *(tu n'es pas au courant)* what planet have you been on?; *(tu es mal élevé)* where did they find you?; **cela m'est sorti de la mémoire** *ou* **de la tête** it has slipped my mind *or* gone out of my head; **il ne sortira pas grand-chose de tout cela** not much will come of all this; *Ind* **s. de la chaîne de fabrication** to come off the production line;

Théâtre **Macbeth sort** exit Macbeth; *Fin* **s. au tirage** *(d'obligations)* to be drawn; *Scol* **cette question est sortie (à l'examen)** this question came up (in the examination); *Cartes* **le dix de carreau est sorti** the ten of diamonds turned up

2 *(d'un cavalier)* to ride out; *(d'un conducteur, d'un véhicule)* to drive out; *(d'un capitaine de navire)* to sail out; **nous ne sommes pas beaucoup sortis en mer cet été** we didn't get out on the boat much this summer

3 *(avec complément de manière)* **s. en courant/en dansant** to run/dance out; **s. précipitamment** *ou* **à la hâte** *ou* **en toute hâte** to hurry out; **s. furtivement** *ou* **à pas de loup** to steal *or* creep out

4 *(des fleurs)* to come out; *(d'une plante)* to come up, to spring up; **ses dents commencent à s.** *(d'un bébé)* his/her teeth are beginning to come through

5 **s. de** *(quitter) (collège, port, bureau, emploi etc)* to leave; *(voiture)* to get out of; *(enfance, brume, obscurité)* to emerge from; **je sors du collège/de table** I have just left school/the table; **il sort d'ici** he has just left; **je sortais de chez toi quand ...** I was just leaving your house when ...; **je ne savais pas comment le faire s. du bureau** I didn't know how to get him out of the office; **on sortait de l'hiver** winter was just over; **s. de la salle** to go/come out of the room, to leave the room; **s. de son lit** to get out of bed; *Méd* to leave one's bed; *(d'une rivière)* to overflow its banks; *Fig* **s. du bois** *(se révéler tel qu'on est)* to show one's true colours; **il est à peine sorti de l'enfance** he's little more than a child; **s. indemne d'un accident** to come out of an accident unscathed; **sortira-t-elle blanchie de ce scandale?** will she come out of this scandal with her name cleared?; **s. de sa froideur habituelle** to show unusual warmth; **cela lui a permis de s. de soi** it brought him out of himself

6 *Arch, Fam* **s. de faire qch** to have just done sth; *Fam* **merci bien! je sors d'en prendre** no thank you! once is enough

7 *(quitter la maison)* to go out; **Madame Dupont est sortie** Mrs Dupont is out *or* has gone out; **elle est sortie à trois heures** she went out at three o'clock; **il ne sort pas de chez moi** he practically lives at my place; **je ne sors pas de chez moi** I don't go out, I don't leave the house; **tu devrais s. un peu plus** you should get out (of the house) a bit more; **s. faire des courses** to go out shopping; **s. acheter du pain** to go out to buy bread; **s. à cheval/à pied** to go out riding/walking; **faire s. le chien** to let the dog out

8 *(pour s'amuser)* to go out; **ils sortent tous les samedis soir** they go out every Saturday evening; **s. avec qn** *(en amis)* to go out with sb; *(avoir une relation amoureuse avec)* to be going out with sb; **ils sortent ensemble depuis deux ans** they've been going out together *or* with each other for two years; *Fig* **tu n'as pas entendu parler de ce film? mais il faut s. un peu!** you haven't heard of this film? what planet have you been on?

9 **s. de** *(s'écarter de) (son devoir etc)* to swerve *or* deviate from; **s. de son sujet** to deviate *or* wander from one's subject; **cela sort de ma compétence** that doesn't come within my scope; **s. des bornes de la bienséance** to overstep the bounds of decency; **s. d'une règle** to ignore *or* depart from a rule; *(transgresser)* to break a rule; **s. des rails** *(d'un train)* to jump the rails; **la voiture est sortie de la route** the car left the road; *Fig* **il ne sort pas de là, il n'en sort pas** he is sticking to his guns; **ça sort de l'ordinaire** that's out of the ordinary; **s. de cadence** *(d'un danseur)* to be *or* get out of step; *Mus* **s. de mesure** to be *or* get out of time; **s. du ton** to be *or* get out of tune

10 s. de *(échapper à) (difficulté, danger)* to get out of, to extricate oneself from; **aider qn à s. d'une difficulté** to help sb out (of a difficulty); **s. d'affaire** to get out of trouble; **soyez plus précis ou nous n'en sortirons pas** be more precise or we shall never get to the end of it; **j'ai trop à faire, je n'en sors pas** I've too much to do, I shall never get through it *or* to the end of it

11 s. de *(être issu de) (bonne famille etc)* to come from; **ce livre sort de ma plume** this book is one of mine; **s. de l'université** to graduate (from university); **cheval sorti d'un bon haras** horse (that comes) from a good stud *or* stable

12 *(dépasser, être en relief)* to stand out, to stick out, to protrude (**de** from); **yeux qui sortent de la tête** protruding *or* bulging eyes; **les yeux lui sortaient de la tête** his eyes were popping out of his head; **son portefeuille sortait de sa poche** his wallet was sticking out of his pocket

13 *(d'une silhouette sur une photo, d'une pensée, d'une caractéristique etc)* to stand out, to be prominent; **faire s. un trait de caractère/un rôle** to emphasize a characteristic/a part

14 *Ordinat* **s. (d'un système)** to exit (from a system); **s. d'un programme** to exit a program; **s. sans sauvegarder** to exit without saving

VT *(aux avoir)* **1** *(mener dehors) (enfant, chien etc)* to take out; **s. la voiture** to get the car out; **sortez-la!** get her out (of here)!; **cela nous sortira de l'ordinaire** that will make a change; **il faut le s. d'affaire/de ce mauvais pas** I/we'll *etc* have to get him out of this mess/fix

2 *(tirer) (objet)* to take out; **s. les mains de ses poches** to take one's hands out of one's pockets; **et si tu sortais ton bon whisky/tes photos de mariage?** how about getting out your good whisky/your wedding photographs?; **il sortit sa pipe** he brought out *or* took out *or* got out his pipe; **s. ses griffes** to unsheathe its claws; **s. ses cornes** *(d'un escargot)* to put out its horns; **s. un livre de la bibliothèque** to take a book out of the library; *Typ* **s. une ligne** *(dans la marge)* to run out a line

3 *(mettre sur le marché) (livre)* to bring out, to publish; *(journal)* to bring out; *(film, disque)* to bring out, to release; *esp Ordinat* **s. sur le marché** to ship

4 *Fam (raconter)* **il nous en a sorti une bien bonne** he came out with a good one; **tu sais ce qu'il m'a sorti?** do you know what he came out with?; **elle m'a sorti qu'elle y avait pensé avant moi!** she had the cheek to tell me she'd thought of it before me!

5 *Ordinat* to output

VPR se sortir se s. d'une situation difficile to get out of *or* extricate oneself from a difficult situation; **elle aura du mal à se s. de là toute seule** she'll have trouble getting out of that on her own; **le malade s'en sortira** the patient will pull through; **je crois que je ne vais pas m'en s.** I don't think I'll be able to cope *or* manage; **je ne m'en serais jamais sorti sans toi** I'd never have done it *or* managed without you; **tu t'en es bien sorti, pour une première tentative** you did very well considering it was your first attempt

---

sortir² NM **au s. du cinéma** on coming out of the cinema; **au s. de l'école** when they/we/ *etc* come/came out of school; *(pour toujours)* on leaving school; **au s. de la table** at the end of the meal, when we/they/*etc* got up *or* get up from the table; **au s. de l'hiver/de la réunion** at the end of the winter/the meeting

sortir³ VT *(conj like* **finir***) (used only in third* *person) Jur* **cette sentence sortira son plein (et entier) effet** this decision shall have full effect

S.O.S. [ɛsoɛs] **NM** *Aviat, Naut, Fig* SOS; **envoyer** *ou* **lancer un S.** to send (out) an SOS (à to); **S. Amitié** = helpline for people in need of emotional support, *Br* ≃ Samaritans; **S. médecins** emergency medical service; **S.-Racisme** = anti-racist movement

sosie [sɔzi] **NM** *(personne)* double; **on dirait ton s.** he/she is your double; **c'est vraiment le s. de son père** he really is the double of *or* the spitting image of his father

sot, sotte [so, sɔt] **ADJ** *(personne, réponse, projet etc)* silly, stupid, foolish
N fool, idiot; *Hist, Théâtre* fool

> Il faut noter que le nom anglais **sot** est un faux ami. Il signifie **ivrogne**.

sotie [sɔti] **NF** *Hist, Théâtre* (medieval) farce

sot-l'y-laisse [soliles] **NM INV** *Culin (du poulet)* oyster

sotte [sɔt] **ADJ** *voir* **sot**

sottement [sɔtmɑ̃] **ADV** stupidly, foolishly

sottise [sɔtiz] **NF 1** *(stupidité)* stupidity, silliness, foolishness; **cette fille est d'une s. rare** that girl is exceptionally stupid; **je n'ai jamais rencontré une telle s.** I've never met anyone so stupid **2** *(action stupide)* foolish *or* stupid act; *(parole stupide)* foolish *or* stupid remark; **faire des sottises** to do foolish *or* stupid things; *(d'un enfant)* to be naughty; **dire des sottises** to say foolish *or* stupid things, to talk nonsense; **ai-je dit une s.?** have I said something stupid? **3** *Vieilli (parole injurieuse)* offensive remark, insult; **dire des sottises à qn** to abuse sb

sottisier [sɔtizje] **NM** collection of howlers

sou [su] **NM 1 amasser une fortune s. par s.** to scrape a fortune together; **un s. est un s.** every penny counts; **payer s. à s.** to pay in small instalments; **donne un s. au petit** give the lad some coppers; **ne pas avoir** *ou* **être sans le s.** to be penniless; **je n'ai pas le s.** I don't have a penny; *Vieilli* **cela vaut vingt mille euros comme un s.** it's worth a twenty thousand euros if it's worth a penny; **affaire de quatre sous** *Br* twopenny-halfpenny business, *Am* nickel-and-dime business; **il n'est pas ambitieux pour deux sous** *ou* **pour un s.** he hasn't an ounce of ambition, he's not in the least ambitious; **il n'a pas pour deux sous de courage** he hasn't an ounce of courage; **elle n'est pas méchante pour deux sous** *ou* **pour un s.** she hasn't got a nasty bone in her body; *Fam* **s'ennuyer à cent sous de l'heure** to be bored stiff *or* bored out of one's mind; **il est toujours en train de compter ses sous** he watches every last penny, he's always counting every penny; **je te l'achèterais si j'avais des sous** I'd buy it for you if I had the money; **c'est une affaire de gros sous** there's big money involved; **être près de ses sous** to be a penny-pincher; **ils veulent des sous, toujours des sous!** all they want is money for this and money for that!; **appareil** *ou* **machine à sous** slot machine; *(jeu)* one-armed bandit, *Br* fruit machine **2** *Can* (cent) cent **3** *Hist (pièce de cinq centimes)* sou; *Arch* **pièce de cent sous** five-franc piece

souahéli [swaheli], **souahili** [swahili] **ADJ** Swahili
NM *Ling* Swahili

soubassement [subasmɑ̃] **NM 1** *Archit (d'un bâtiment)* base, basement; *Fig* **le s. social** the social substructure **2** *Tech (d'une machine-outil etc)* base (plate) **3** *Géol* bedrock **4** *Aut* sub-frame, under-structure, underbody frame; **s. de châssis** underframe

soubresaut [subrəso] **NM** *(d'un véhicule)* jolt; *(d'une personne)* start, jerk; **avoir un s.** to jump, to give a start

soubrette [subrɛt] **NF** *Théâtre* soubrette, maidservant; *Fam (servante coquette)* soubrette

souche [suʃ] **NF 1** *(d'un arbre)* stump; *(du vin)* stock; *Fam* **rester comme une s.** to be rooted to the spot; **dormir comme une s.** to sleep like a log
2 *(de famille)* founder; **faire s.** to found a line; **il vient de bonne s.** he comes from good stock; **famille de vieille s.** an old family
3 *(d'un virus etc)* strain
4 *Com (de chèques, de tickets etc)* counterfoil, stub; **carnet de tickets à s.** book of tickets with counterfoils
5 *(d'une cheminée)* stack
6 *Ling* root; **mot s.** root word
7 *Belg (ticket de caisse, reçu)* receipt

souci¹ [susi] **NM** *Bot* marigold; **s. d'eau** marsh marigold

souci² **NM 1** *(soin)* concern (**de** for); **avoir le s. de plaire** to be anxious to please; **avoir le s. de la vérité/de l'exactitude** to be meticulously truthful/accurate; **je me suis limité à deux auteurs dans un s. de clarté** I limited myself to two authors in order to keep things clear; **c'est le moindre** *ou* **le dernier** *ou* **le cadet de mes soucis** that's the least of my worries
2 *(inquiétude)* worry, anxiety; **elle doit avoir des soucis** she must have problems; **sans s., libre de soucis** carefree, free from worry *or* anxiety; **cet enfant est un perpétuel s.** this child is a perpetual (source of) worry; *Fam* **il nous fait bien du s.** he worries us a lot, he gives us a lot of worry; **se faire du s.** to worry (**pour qch** about sth); **inutile de te faire du s. pour ça, ce n'est rien** there's no point worrying about it, it's not important; **soucis d'argent** *ou* **financiers** money *or* financial troubles *or* worries; *Fam* **il n'y a pas de soucis!** no worries!

soucier [susje] *(impf, pr sub n.* **souciions,** *v.* **souciiez)* **VT** *Arch (d'une chose) (personne)* to trouble, to worry
VPR se soucier se s. de qn/de qch/de faire qch to worry *or* be concerned about sb/sth/doing sth; **il se soucie toujours des autres** he is always worrying about other people; **ne se s. de rien** not to worry about anything; **pars en vacances et ne te soucie de rien** go on holiday and don't worry about a thing; *Fam* **je m'en soucie comme de l'an quarante** *ou* **de ma première chemise** I don't give a damn (about it)

soucieux, -ieuse [susjø, -jøz] **ADJ 1** *(attentif)* anxious, concerned (**de** about); **être s. de faire qch** to be anxious to do sth; **elle a toujours été soucieuse de ne pas les décevoir** she has always been anxious not to let them down; **peu s.** unconcerned (**de** about); **peu s. de la rencontrer** unconcerned about meeting her **2** *(inquiète)* anxious, worried, concerned; **avoir un air s.** to look anxious *or* worried *or* concerned

soucoupe [sukup] **NF** saucer; *Fig Fam* **elle a ouvert** *ou* **fait des yeux comme des soucoupes** her eyes were as big as saucers
▸▸ **s. volante** flying saucer

soudage [sudaʒ] **NM** soldering; **s. (autogène)** *(de pièces en métal etc)* welding

soudain [sudɛ̃] **ADJ** sudden
ADV suddenly, all of a sudden; **s. elle se mit à hurler** all of a sudden, she started to scream, she suddenly started to scream

soudainement [sudɛnmɑ̃] **ADV** suddenly

soudaineté [sudɛnte] **NF** suddenness

Soudan [sudɑ̃] **NM le S.** the Sudan

soudanais, -aise [sudanɛ, -ɛz] **ADJ** Sudanese
N S. Sudanese

soudant [sudɑ̃] **ADJ** *Métal* **blanc s.** welding heat

soudard [sudar] **NM** *Litt Péj* brutish soldier

soude [sud] **NF 1** *Bot* saltwort, (prickly) glasswort **2** *Chimie, Ind* soda; **(carbonate de) s., cristaux de s., s. ordinaire** washing *or* common soda; **bicarbonate de s.** bicarbonate of soda; **s. caustique** caustic soda

souder [sude] **VT 1** *(avec alliage fusible)* to solder; **s. au cuivre** *ou* **au laiton** to braze; **s. à l'étain** to soft-solder **2** *(autogène)* to weld; **s. à l'arc (électrique)** to arc-weld; **machine à s.** welding machine, welder; **s. par points** to spot-weld **3** *(unir) (os fracturé)* to knit, to join; *Fig (groupes etc)* to unite; **cette épreuve nous a soudés** this hardship united us *or* brought us together
VPR se souder *(des os)* to knit (together), to join; *Fig (d'un groupe)* to unite

soudeur, -euse [sudœr, -øz] **N** *(personne) (employant une pâte sur alliage)* solderer; *(employant la soudure autogène)* welder; **s. par points** spot-welder; **s. au chalumeau** lamp *or* torch welder
NF soudeuse *(machine)* welder, welding machine; **s. par points** spot-welder

soudoyer [sudwaje] **VT** (**je soudoie,** *n.* **soudoyons; je soudoierai**) **1** *Péj (personne)* to bribe; **s. qn pour qu'il fasse qch** to bribe sb into doing sth; **il n'accepterait jamais de se faire s.** he would never accept a bribe; **s. un assassin** to hire a killer **2** *Mil Arch (mercenaire)* to pay

soudure [sudyr] **NF 1** *(opération) (par alliage)* soldering; *(autogène)* welding; **s. au cuivre** *ou* **au laiton** brazing; **s. à l'étain** soft-soldering; **s. par point** spot weld
2 *(lieu)* soldered joint; *(autogène)* weld; **s. à nœud** wipe(d) joint; **sans soudure(s)** seamless; **la s. ne se voit pas du tout** you can't see the join *or* weld at all
3 *(alliage)* solder
4 *(d'os)* join
5 *Écon* **faire la s.** to bridge the gap; *Fig* **faire la s. entre deux directeurs/systèmes** to bridge the gap between two directors/systems; **c'est moi qui fait la s.** I'm filling in (in the meantime); **elle fera la s. entre les deux directeurs** she'll be acting manager

soufflage [suflaʒ] **NM 1** *(de verre)* glass blowing **2** *Métal* blowing

soufflant, -ante [suflɑ̃, -ɑ̃t] **ADJ 1** *Tech* blowing; **machine soufflante** blowing *or* blast engine **2** *Fam (étonnant)* breathtaking
NF Tech soufflante blower, fan; **soufflante de sustentation** *(d'un aéroglisseur)* lift fan; *Aut etc* **soufflante de suralimentation** supercharger

soufflard [suflar] **NM** *Géol* fumarole

souffle [sufl] **NM 1** *(d'air, de vent)* breath, puff; **pas un s. de vent** not a breath of air
2 *(respiration)* breathing; *(de coureur etc)* breath, wind; *(air respiré)* breath; *(air expiré)* blow, puff; **retenir son s.** to hold one's breath; **éteindre une chandelle d'un (seul) s.** to blow out a candle; **on la renverserait d'un s.** you could knock her over with a feather; **couper le s. à qn** to take sb's breath away; **le s. vital** *ou* **de la vie** the breath of life; **être à bout de s.** to be out of breath *or* winded; *Fig* to be unable to go on, *Fam* to have run out of steam; **l'économie est à bout de s.** the economy is running out of steam *or* is on its last legs; **manquer de s., avoir le s. court** to be short of breath *or* short-winded; **reprendre son s.** to get one's breath back; **exhaler son dernier s.** to breathe one's last; **n'avoir plus de s.** to be out of breath; **sa vie ne tient qu'à un s.** his/her life hangs by a

thread; *Fig* **second s. de l'économie** new lease of life for the economy; *Fam* **c'est à vous couper le s.** it's breathtaking; *Fam* **il ne manque pas de s.!** *(culot)* he's got a cheek *or* a nerve! **3** *(d'une explosion)* blast **4** *Aviat (d'hélices)* slipstream, wash **5** *Méd* **(bruit de) s.** murmur; **s. au cœur** *ou* **cardiaque** heart murmur **6** *(force créatrice)* inspiration; **s. poétique** poetic inspiration

soufflé [sufle] **ADJ** *(visage)* puffy, puffed up; *Culin (omelette, pommes de terre etc)* soufflé; *Fam (ahuri)* amazed, taken aback

▪ **NM** *Culin* soufflé; **s. au fromage/au chocolat** cheese/chocolate soufflé; **moule à soufflés** soufflé dish

soufflement [sufləmɑ̃] **NM** blowing

souffler [sufle] **VI 1** *(en expulsant de l'air)* to blow; *(d'un taureau, d'un buffle)* to snort; **s. dans ses doigts** to blow on one's fingers; **si la soupe est trop chaude, souffle!** if the soup's too hot, blow on it!; **s. dans une trompette** to blow a trumpet; *Fig Fam* **tu peux s. dessus!** you haven't a chance!; *Fig Fam* **si tu crois que ça va marcher en soufflant dessus, tu te trompes** if you think it's going to work just like that, you're mistaken; *Fam* **s. dans les bronches à qn** to bawl sb out **2** *(reprendre son souffle)* to get one's breath back; **laisser s. un cheval** to let a horse get its wind, to give a horse a breather; **elle ne nous a pas laissé s.** *(entre deux tâches etc)* she didn't give us time to get our breath back; *(de toute la journée)* she didn't give us time to draw breath *or* to catch our breath **3** *(respirer avec peine)* to pant, to puff; **suant et soufflant** huffing and puffing, puffing and blowing; *Fig Fam* **s. comme un bœuf** to puff and pant **4** *(du vent etc)* to blow; **le vent va s. fort cette nuit** it will be very windy tonight; *Fig* **regarder** *ou* **voir d'où vient** *ou* **de quel côté souffle le vent** to see which way the wind is blowing, to see which way the land lies; *Fig* **un vent de révolte soufflait** there was a spirit of revolt in the air **5** *surtout Scol (à ses camarades)* to prompt; **on ne souffle pas!** no prompting! **6** *(aux dames)* to take; **s. n'est pas jouer** taking a piece doesn't count as a go

▪ **VT 1** *(verre)* to blow; *(ballon etc)* to blow up **2** *(fumée, poussière etc)* to blow (**dans** into); *(orgue)* to blow; *(bougie)* to blow out **3** *(chuchoter)* to whisper (**à qn** to sb); **s. qch à l'oreille de qn** to whisper sth in sb's ear; **ne pas s. (un) mot** not to breathe a word; **s. (son rôle à) un acteur** to prompt an actor; **quelqu'un a dû lui s. l'idée** someone must have given him/her the idea **4** *Fam (prendre)* to pinch (**à qn** from sb); **se faire s. sa place** to have one's seat pinched; **s. un pion** *(aux dames)* to huff a man **5** *(d'une explosion) (bâtiment etc)* to blast **6** *(ahurir)* **s. qn** to amaze sb, to take sb aback; **son culot nous a soufflés** his/her cheek took our breath away

soufflerie [sufləri] **NF 1** *(d'un orgue, d'une forge)* bellows **2** *Ind* blower **3** *Aviat, Phys* wind tunnel; **essais en s.** wind-tunnel tests

soufflet [sufle] **NM 1** *(instrument)* (pair of) bellows VOIR GRAMMAIRE A10 **2 valise à soufflets** expanding suitcase **3** *Rail (entre les voitures)* concertina vestibule **4** *Couture* gusset **5** *Mus (d'un orgue)* swell **6** *Litt (gifle)* slap (in the face); *(insulte)* insult **7** *Aut (ainsi)*

souffleter [sufləte] **VT** (**je soufflette, n. souffletons; je souffletterai**) *Litt Vieilli* **s. qn** *(le gifler)* to slap sb's face; *(l'insulter)* to insult sb

soufflette [suflɛt] **NF** *Belg (ampoule)* blister; *(boursouflure)* swelling

souffleur, -euse [suflœr, -øz] **N s. de verre** glass blower

▪ **NF souffleuse 1** *Can (chasse-neige)* snowblower **2** *Agr (pour les graines etc)* blower container

▪ **N** *Théâtre* prompter

soufflure [suflyr] **NF** *(dans la peinture, le verre, le métal)* blister, bubble; *(dans un pneu)* bulge

souffrance [sufrɑ̃s] **NF 1 en s.** *(travail)* pending; *(candidats)* on the waiting list; *(factures)* overdue, outstanding; *(colis)* held up in transit, awaiting delivery **2** *(douleur)* suffering, pain; **s. physique/morale** physical/mental suffering *or* pain; **rien ne pouvait apaiser ses souffrances** nothing could alleviate his/her suffering

souffrant [sufrɑ̃] **ADJ 1** *(un peu malade)* unwell, poorly; **il a l'air s.** he doesn't look well **2** *Litt (qui souffre)* suffering; **l'humanité souffrante** suffering humanity

souffre-douleur [sufrədulœr] **NM INV** laughing stock, butt (of the joke); **c'est le s. du lycée** he's the laughing stock of the school

souffreteux, -euse [sufrətø, -øz] **ADJ** *(enfant etc)* sickly

souffrir [sufrir] (*prp* **souffrant**; *pp* **souffert**; *pr ind* **je souffre, il souffre, n. souffrons, ils souffrent**; *impf* **je souffrais**; *p hist* **je souffris**; *fu* **je souffrirai**) **VT 1** *(supporter) (douleur, fatigue, froid, perte, insulte etc)* to suffer, to endure; **s. le martyre** to go through torture *or* agonies; **je ne peux pas s. qu'on vienne me déranger** I cannot bear to be disturbed, I cannot stand being disturbed; *Fam* **je ne peux pas s. cet homme/cette odeur** I can't bear *or* stand that man/smell **2** *(permettre)* to permit, to allow; **je ne saurais s. cela** I cannot permit *or* allow that; **souffrez que je vous dise la vérité** allow *or* permit me to tell you the truth; **situation qui ne souffre aucun retard** situation that admits of no delay; **s. l'étalon** *(d'une jument)* to take the stallion

▪ **VI 1** *(physiquement)* to be in pain, to suffer; *(moralement)* to suffer; **mon bras me fait s.** my arm is hurting (me) *or* giving me pain; **il m'a fait s.** *(physiquement, sentimentalement)* he hurt me; **s. du froid/des maux de tête** to suffer from the cold/from headaches; **s. de la jambe** to have trouble with one's leg; **je souffre de le voir si changé** it pains *or* upsets me to see him so changed; **je souffre à marcher** I find walking painful; **avoir cessé de s.** to be out of pain **2** *(pâtir)* to suffer (**de** from); **les vignes ont souffert de la gelée** the vines have suffered from the frost; **nous avons beaucoup souffert de la guerre** we suffered a lot in the war, we were hard hit by the war

▪ **VPR se souffrir** *Fam (se supporter)* **ils ne peuvent pas se s.** they can't stand each other

soufi [sufi] *Rel* **ADJ INV** Sufic

▪ **NM** Sufi

soufisme [sufism] **NM** *Rel* Sufism

soufrage [sufraʒ] **NF** *(des allumettes, des plantes etc)* sulphuring, *Am* sulfuring; *Tex* sulphuration, *Am* sulfuration

soufre [sufr] **NM** sulphur, *Am* sulfur; *Fig* **ces écrits sentent le s.** these writings smack *or* reek of heresy

▪ **ADJ INV s. (jaune)** sulphur *or Am* sulfur yellow

soufré [sufre] **NM** *(papillon)* brimstone

soufrer [sufre] **VT** *(allumettes, plantes etc)* to sulphur, *Am* to sulfur; *Tex* to sulphurate, *Am* to sulfurate

souhait [swɛ] **NM** wish; **faire** *ou* **formuler un s.** to make a wish; **présenter ses souhaits à qn** to offer sb one's good wishes; **présenter**

ses souhaits de bonne année to wish sb a Happy New Year; **à s.** perfectly; **doré/ensoleillé à s.** beautifully golden/sunny; **j'ai fini par trouver une pièce silencieuse à s.** I finally found a room that was as quiet as I could wish; **à vos souhaits!** *(à qn qui éternue)* bless you! SEE GRAMMAR A60; B40

souhaitable [swɛtabl] **ADJ** desirable; **il est s. que ... + sub** it is to be hoped that ...; **ce n'est guère s.** one can hardly wish for that; **il serait s. que ...** it would be desirable if ...

souhaiter [swɛte] **VT** *(succès etc)* to wish for; **je vous souhaite d'être pleinement heureux** I wish you every happiness; **je souhaite qu'on me tienne au courant** I wish to be kept informed; **je souhaite que vous réussissiez, je vous souhaite de réussir** I hope you will succeed; **s. la réussite/bon voyage à qn** to wish sb success/bon voyage; **je vous souhaite une bonne année/un joyeux anniversaire** best wishes for a happy New Year/a happy birthday; **s. bonne chance à qn** to wish sb (good) luck; *Fam Iron* **je vous souhaite bien du plaisir!, je vous en souhaite!** I wish you joy of it!; **cela n'est pas à s.** that is not very desirable; **il est à s. que ... + sub** it is to be hoped that ...; **je ne le souhaite à personne** I wouldn't wish that on anyone

souiller [suje] **VT 1** *(vêtements etc)* to soil, to dirty (**de** with); **vêtements souillés de boue** mudstained clothes **2** *Fig (contaminer)* to taint; **s. ses mains de sang** to stain one's hands with blood **3** *Litt (réputation, souvenir de qn etc)* to tarnish

souillon [sujɔ̃] **NF** *Litt* slut, sloven; *(servante)* slovenly maid

souillure [sujyr] **NF** *(sur un vêtement etc)* stain, *Litt* blot, blemish

souk [suk] **NM 1** *(marché)* souk **2** *Fam (lieu en désordre)* shambles; **c'est le s., dans cette chambre!** what a shambles this bedroom is!; **foutre le s. (dans)** *(mettre en désordre)* to make a mess (of); **il fout le s. en classe** he creates havoc in the classroom

soul [sul] **ADJ INV, NF** *Mus* soul

soûl [su] **ADJ 1** *Fam (ivre)* drunk; **s. comme un Polonais** *ou* **comme un cochon** *ou* **comme une bourrique** drunk as a lord; **s. perdu** blind drunk **2** *Arch (rassasié)* replete, *Litt* **être s. de plaisir/de musique** to have had a surfeit of pleasure/music, to be sated with pleasure/music

▪ **NM** rire/chanter/fumer tout son s. to laugh/sing/smoke to one's heart's content; **manger/boire tout son s.** to eat/drink one's fill *or* to one's heart's content

soulagement [sulaʒmɑ̃] **NM** relief; **éprouver un sentiment de s.** to feel relieved; **son départ sera un s. pour tous** his/her departure will come as a relief to all; **pousser un soupir de s.** to heave a sigh of relief

soulager [sulaʒe] (**je soulageai(s); n. soulageons**) **VT** *(pression, douleur)* to ease, to relieve; *(esprit, chagrin)* to soothe, to comfort; *(quelqu'un)* to relieve; **je vais vous faire une piqûre, ça va vous s.** I'm going to give you an injection which will bring you relief *or* make you feel better; **traitement qui soulage les douleurs** treatment for pain relief; **si ça peut te s., sache que je suis dans la même situation** if it makes you feel any better, I'm in the same situation; **s. les pauvres** to relieve the poor; **je suis soulagé de l'apprendre** I'm relieved to hear it; **on soulage ses maux à les raconter** it is a relief *or* a comfort *or* it helps to talk about one's troubles; **s. une poutre** to ease the strain on a beam; **s. les soupapes** to blow off steam; **cela me soulage l'esprit d'un grand poids** that's a great weight off my mind; *Fam* **s. qn de son portefeuille** to relieve sb of his/her wallet

▪ **VPR se soulager 1** *(en parlant etc)* to ease

one's mind **2** *Fam (satisfaire un besoin naturel)* to relieve oneself

soûlant [sulɑ̃] **ADJ** *Fam (personne)* boring, tiresome

soûlard, -e [sular, -ard], **soûlaud, -e** [sulo, -od] **N** *très Fam* boozer, wino, *Br* piss artist

soûler [sule] **VT** *Fam* **1** *(enivrer)* **s. qn** to get *or* make sb drunk; *Fig (d'un parfum, du succès, d'idées etc)* to go to sb's head **2** *(ennuyer)* **s. qn** to bore sb silly
VPR se soûler *Fam (s'enivrer)* to get drunk; *Arg* **se s. la gueule** to get pissed *or* wasted; *Fig* **se s. de paroles** to get drunk on *or* with the sound of one's own voice

soûlerie [sulri] **NF** *Fam* **1** *(beuverie)* drinking session *or* spree, bender **2** *(ivresse)* drunkenness

soulèvement [sulɛvmɑ̃] **NM** **1** *(de terrain, de l'estomac)* rising, heaving; **s. de cœur** nausea **2** *Géol* upheaval, upthrust **3** *(révolte)* revolt, uprising

soulever [sulve] *(je soulève, n. soulevons; je soulèverai)* **VT** **1** *(charge, malade, couvercle etc)* to lift (up), to raise; **c'est trop lourd, je n'arrive pas à le s.** it's too heavy, I can't lift it; **s. un rideau** to raise a curtain; **la voiture soulevait de la poussière** the car raised *or* threw up dust; *Fig* **cette odeur me soulève le cœur** this smell makes me feel sick *or* turns my stomach
2 *(doutes, question, objection)* to raise, to bring up; **cette question mérite en effet d'être soulevée** this question deserves to be raised *or* brought up
3 *(population en révolte)* to rouse, to stir up
4 *(passion, enthousiasme, indignation)* to excite, to provoke, to arouse; **sa déclaration souleva un tonnerre d'applaudissements** his/her announcement met with thunderous applause
5 *Fam (voler)* to steal, *Fam* to lift
VPR se soulever 1 *(être levé)* to rise; *(de la mer), Fig (de l'estomac)* to heave; **sa jupe se soulevait au moindre souffle de vent** the slightest puff of wind blew her skirt up; **chaque fois que le vent soufflait, le rideau se soulevait légèrement** the curtain moved every time the wind blew; *Fig* **mon cœur se soulève chaque fois que j'y pense** I feel sick every time I think about it
2 *(se lever)* to raise *or* lift oneself up
3 *(se révolter)* to revolt, to rise up

soulier [sulje] **NM** shoe; **souliers de marche** walking shoes; **souliers vernis** patent (leather) shoes; *Fig Fam* **être dans ses petits souliers** to feel awkward

soulignage [suliɲaʒ], **soulignement** [suliɲ(ə)mɑ̃] **NM** underlining

souligné [suliɲe] **NM** underline, underscore; **double s.** double underline; **s. pointillé** with dotted underlining

souligner [suliɲe] **VT** **1** *(d'un trait) (mot, passage etc)* to underline; **s. ses yeux d'un trait de noir** to outline *or* emphasize one's eyes with black eyeliner; **coupe qui souligne la taille** a cut which emphasizes the waist **2** *Fig (mot, fait etc)* to emphasize; *(importance etc)* to underline, to emphasize; **s. que ...** to emphasize that ...

soûlographie [sulografi] **NF** *Fam* drunkenness

soûlon [sulɔ̃] **NM** *Suisse, Can Fam* drunk, drunkard

soûlot, -ote [sulo, -ɔt] **N** *Fam* alky, lush, boozer, *Am* boozehound

soumettre [sumɛtr] *(conj like* **mettre***)* **VT** **1** *(population, pays, passions)* to subdue
2 *(question, demande)* to refer, to submit (**à qn** to sb); **s. ses projets à qn** to submit *or* lay one's plans before sb; **s. un rapport** to submit a report; **s. une lettre à la signature**

to present a letter for signature
3 *(à un examen etc)* to subject (**à** to); **s. qn à une épreuve** to put sb through a test; **être soumis à des règles strictes** to be bound by strict rules; **s. à l'impôt** to subject to tax; **s. les revenus à l'impôt** to make income subject *or* liable to tax; **s. un malade à un régime strict** to put a patient on a strict diet
VPR se soumettre *(obéir)* to submit; **se s. à** *(autorité)* to submit to; *(souhaits)* to comply with; *(loi, décision)* to abide by

soumis [sumi] **ADJ** **1** *(docile)* submissive, obedient **2** *(à une loi, une autorité etc)* subject (**à** to); *(à un impôt)* liable, subject (**à** to); **s. aux droits de douane** subject to customs duty; **non s.** unconquered; *Arch* **fille soumise** registered prostitute

soumission [sumisjɔ̃] **NF** **1** *(à une loi, une autorité etc)* submission (**à** to); **faire (sa) s.** to surrender, to yield **2** *(docilité)* obedience, submissiveness (**à** to) **3** *Com* tender, bid; **faire une s. pour un travail** to tender for a job; *Com* **s. cachetée** sealed bid

soumissionnaire [sumisjɔnɛr] **N** *Com* tenderer

soumissionner [sumisjɔne] **VT** *Com (travail)* to tender for

soupape [supap] **NF** *Tech* valve; *Tech, Fig* **s. de sûreté** safety valve; **s. d'admission** *ou* **d'alimentation** *ou* **d'arrivée** inlet *or* induction *or* intake valve; **s. d'échappement** *ou* **de décharge** outlet *or* exhaust valve; **s. à flotteur** ballcock; *Aut* **soupapes en tête** *ou* **en chandelle** overhead valves; *Aut* **soupapes latérales** *ou* **en chapelle** side valves

soupçon [supsɔ̃] **NM 1** *(suspicion)* suspicion; **s'exposer aux soupçons** to lay oneself open to suspicion; **devenir l'objet des soupçons** to fall under suspicion; **éveiller/endormir les soupçons** to arouse/allay suspicion; **avoir des soupçons sur qn** to have one's suspicions about sb, to be suspicious about sb; **j'en avais le s.!** I thought so *or* as much!, I suspected as much!; **il est au-dessus de tout s.** he is above suspicion; **arrêter qn sur un s.** to arrest sb on suspicion
2 *(idée)* suspicion, idea, notion; **je n'en avais pas le moindre s.** I didn't have the slightest suspicion, I never suspected it for a moment
3 *(faible quantité) (de vinaigre, d'ail etc)* dash, hint; *(de fièvre, de fard, d'ironie etc)* touch; *(de vin)* drop

soupçonnable [supsɔnabl] **ADJ** open to suspicion; **personne difficilement s.** person above suspicion

soupçonner [supsɔne] **VT 1** *(suspecter)* to suspect; **s. qn de qch/d'avoir fait qch** to suspect sb of sth/of having done sth; **je le soupçonne de me cacher qch/de ne pas dire la vérité** I suspect he's hiding something from me/not telling me the truth; **on le soupçonne de meurtre** he is suspected of murder **2** *(deviner)* to suspect; **je ne soupçonnais pas que ...** I had no suspicion *or* no idea that ..., I did not suspect that ...; **je soupçonne de la jalousie dans ses paroles** I suspect (there is some) jealousy in what he says

soupçonneusement [supsɔnøzmɑ̃] **ADV** suspiciously

soupçonneux, -euse [supsɔnø, -øz] **ADJ** suspicious; **d'un air/ton s.** suspiciously

soupe [sup] **NF 1** *Culin* soup; **s. aux pois/à l'oignon** pea/onion soup; *Fig Fam* **cracher dans la s.** to bite the hand that feeds you; *Fam* **gros plein de s.!** fatso!; *Fam* **quand je suis rentré à la maison j'ai encore eu droit à la s. à la grimace** when I got home I got a frosty reception; *Fam* **par ici la bonne s.!** roll up, roll up!; **il monte comme une s. au lait, il est très s. au lait** he flares up very easily, he's always flying off the handle

2 *(repas)* meal; *Fam* **à la s.!** grub's up!; **s. populaire** *(lieu)* soup kitchen **3** *Ski Fam* soft snow **4** *Fam (musique insipide)* supermarket *or* elevator music **5** *Arch (tranche de pain)* sop, soaked slice of bread

soupente [supɑ̃t] **NF** closet, cupboard *(usually under the stairs)*

souper¹ [supe] **NM** VOIR GRAMMAIRE A7 **1** *Belg, Suisse, Can (dîner)* dinner, supper, evening meal **2** *(après le spectacle)* (late) supper

souper² [supe] **VI 1** *Belg, Suisse, Can (dîner)* to have dinner *or* supper *or* one's evening meal; **nous avons soupé de pain et de fromage** we had bread and cheese for supper; *Fig Fam* **j'en ai soupé** I've had enough of it, I'm fed up with it **2** *(après le spectacle)* to have a late supper

soupeser [supəze] **VT** *(je soupèse, n. soupesons; je soupèserai) (objet)* to feel the weight of, to weigh in one's hand; *Fig (problème, argument etc)* to weigh up

soupière [supjɛr] **NF** soup tureen

soupir [supir] **NM 1** sigh; **pousser un s.** to (heave a) sigh; **s. de soulagement/de découragement** sigh of relief/discouragement; **un gros s.** a heavy *or* deep sigh; *Hum* **l'objet de ses soupirs** the object of his affections; **rendre le dernier s.** to breathe one's last **2** *Mus* crotchet *or Am* quarter rest; **demi s.** quaver *or Am* eighth rest; **quart de s.** semiquaver *or Am* sixteenth rest

soupirail, -aux [supiraj, -o] **NM 1** *(de cave)* (cellar) ventilator **2** *(d'appartement en contre-bas)* basement window

soupirant [supirɑ̃] **NM** *Hum* suitor, admirer

soupirer [supire] **VI** to sigh; **en soupirant** with a sigh; **s. après** *ou* **pour qch** to long or yearn for sth

souple [supl] **ADJ** *(branche etc)* supple, flexible; *(corps, danseur etc)* supple, lithe; *(reliure)* limp; *(cuir)* soft, supple; *(cheveux)* manageable; *Fig (système, loi etc)* flexible; *Fig (personne)* flexible, adaptable; **avoir le poignet s.** to have supple wrists; **esprit s.** adaptable *or* versatile mind; *Aut* **moteur s.** flexible engine

souplesse [suplɛs] **NF** *(de branche)* suppleness, flexibility; *(de corps, danseur etc)* suppleness, litheness; *Fig (de système, règle etc)* flexibility; *(de personne)* flexibility, adaptability; *(d'esprit)* adaptability, versatility; **ça n'a pas la s. du cuir** it's not as soft *or* as supple as leather; **en s.** *(travailler, démarrer etc)* smoothly; **transition en s.** smooth transition *(entre* between*)*

souquenille [suknij] **NF** *Vieilli* smock

souquer [suke] *Naut* **VT s. un cordage** to haul a rope taut
VI s. dur *ou* **ferme (sur les avirons)** to pull hard at the oars

source [surs] **NF 1** *(eau)* spring; *(lieu) (d'une rivière)* source; **eau de s.** spring water; **s. d'eau minérale** mineral spring; **s. thermale** hot spring; **le fleuve prend sa s. dans le Massif Central** the river has its source in *or* rises in the Massif Central; *Fig Fam* **ça coule de s.** it's obvious; *(c'est naturel)* it's inevitable *or* natural; **s. jaillissante** gusher; **s. boueuse** mud geyser *or* volcano; *Opt etc* **s. lumineuse** light source; **s. de chaleur** heat source; *Élec* **s. d'énergie** *ou* **d'alimentation** power supply
2 *Fig (du mal, de richesse, d'informations etc)* source; **puiser aux sources** *(dans une étude etc)* to draw on the sources *or* source material; **un retour aux sources** a return to the origins; **s. de revenus** source of revenue; *Fin* **imposé à la s.** taxed at source; **aller à la s. du mal** to get to the root of the evil; **on a appris de s. sûre que ...** we have learned from a

reliable source that …; **informations de s. américaine** information from an American source; **citer ses sources** to cite one's sources; **je le tiens de bonne s.** I have it on good authority *or* from a good source; *Ordinat* **s. de données** data source; *Ordinat* **code s.** source code; **s. nommée** named source; *Ling* **langue s.** source language

sourcier, -ière [sursje, -jɛr] N water diviner, dowser; **baguette de s.** divining *or* dowsing rod

sourcil [sursi(l)] NM eyebrow; **aux sourcils épais** beetle-browed, with bushy eyebrows

sourcilier, -ière [sursilje, -jɛr] ADJ *Anat* superciliary

sourciller [sursije] VI **sans s.** without batting an eyelid, without turning a hair; **elle n'a pas sourcillé** she didn't bat an eyelid *or* turn a hair

sourcilleux, -euse [sursijø, -øz] ADJ **1** *(pointilleux)* fussy, finicky **2** *Litt (hautain)* haughty, supercilious

sourd, sourde [sur, surd] ADJ **1** *(personne)* deaf; **devenir s.** to go deaf; **s. de naissance** deaf from birth; **s. d'une oreille** deaf in one ear; *Fam* **s. comme un pot** deaf as a post; *Fig* **rester s. aux prières de qn** to turn a deaf ear *or* to be deaf to sb's pleas **2** *(teinte, douleur)* dull; *(bruit)* dull, muffled; *(corde)* muted; *(voix)* hollow; *(désir, lutte)* secret; *(hostilité)* veiled; *Ling* **consonne sourde** voiceless consonant

■ N *(personne)* deaf person; **les sourds** the deaf, deaf people; **crier comme un s.** to yell at the top of one's voice; **frapper** *ou* **taper comme un s.** to hit out wildly; **autant vaut parler à un s.** you might as well talk to a brick wall; *Prov* **il n'est pire s. que celui qui ne veut (pas) entendre** there's none so deaf as those who don't want to hear; *Iron* **il vaut mieux entendre ça que d'être s.!** I've heard it all now!; **un dialogue de sourds** a dialogue of the deaf

■ NF *Ling* **sourde** voiceless consonant

sourdement [surdəmɑ̃] ADV **1** *(avec un bruit sourd)* dully, with a dull *or* hollow sound **2** *(en secret)* secretly

sourdine [surdin] NF **1** *Mus* mute; **en s.** softly, quietly; *Fig (en secret)* in secret, on the sly; **violons en s.** muted violins; **mettre une s. à ses plaintes** to tone down one's complaints; *Fig Fam* **mets la s.!** put a sock in it! **2** *Radio etc* damper

sourdingue [surdɛ̃g] *Fam* ADJ deaf
■ N deaf person, cloth-ears

sourd-muet, sourde-muette, *pl* **sourds-muets, sourdes-muettes** ADJ deaf-and-dumb
■ N deaf mute

sourdre [surdr] VI *(used only in third person* **il sourd, ils sourdent** *and in inf; the past tenses are rare) Arch, Litt (de l'eau)* to spring, to rise (up); *Fig (d'une émotion)* to well up

souriant [surjɑ̃] ADJ *(personne)* smiling; *(climat, entourage)* pleasant

souriceau, -eaux [suriso] NM young mouse

souricier [surisje] ADJ M, NM **(chat) s.** mouser

souricière [surisjɛr] NF mousetrap; *Fig (piège)* trap; *(tendu par la police)* police trap

sourire¹ [surir] VI *(conj like* **rire**) **1** to smile (**à qn** at sb); **on peut difficilement en s.** it's hardly a laughing matter; **faire s.** to provoke a smile **2** *(plaire)* to appeal (**à qn** to sb); **cette idée ne lui sourit guère** he's not very keen on the idea, the idea doesn't really appeal to him **3** *(réussir)* **tout lui sourit** he/she makes a success of everything; **la chance lui sourit** fortune smiles on him/her

sourire² NM smile; **large s.** broad smile;

grin; **il s'approcha, le s. aux lèvres** he came up, smiling *or* with a smile (on his lips); **adresser** *ou* **faire un s. à qn** to give sb a smile, to smile at sb; **avoir le s.** to have a smile on one's face; **garder le s.** to keep smiling

souris [suri] NF **1** mouse, *pl* mice; **on aurait entendu trotter une s.** you could have heard a pin drop; **trou de s.** mousehole; *Fig* **il serait bien rentré dans un trou de s.** he would have liked the ground to open up and swallow him **2** *Ordinat* mouse, *pl* mice; **s. à trois boutons** three-button mouse **3** *Arg (femme) Br* bird, *Am* dame **4** *Culin (de l'os de gigot)* knuckle end

■ ADJ INV **(couleur) gris (de) s.** mouse grey *or Am* gray

► ► **s. blanche** white mouse; **s. d'hôtel** *(femlle)* hotel thief; *Ordinat* **s. à infrarouge** infrared *or* cordless mouse; *Ordinat* **s. optique** optical mouse; *Ordinat* **s. sans fil** cordless mouse; *Ordinat* **s. tactile** touchpad mouse

sournois, -oise [surnwa, -waz] ADJ *(personne, méthode)* sly, crafty, underhand; *(regard)* sly, cunning, shifty
■ N sly *or* crafty *or* underhand person

sournoisement [surnwazmɑ̃] ADV slyly

sournoiserie [surnwazri] NF **1** *(caractère)* slyness, craftiness **2** *(acte)* underhand trick

SOUS [su]

under **1–6**	■	underneath **1**
■ beneath **1**	■ on **3, 4**	■ within **7**

PRÉP **1** *(position)* under(neath), beneath; **s'asseoir s. un arbre** to sit down under(neath) *or* beneath a tree; **s. terre** underground, below ground; **nager s. l'eau** to swim underwater; **lettre s. enveloppe** letter in an envelope; **mettre une lettre s. pli scellé** to put a letter in a sealed envelope; **s. le sceau du secret** under pledge of secrecy; **dormir s. la tente** to sleep under canvas; **s. la pluie** in the rain; *Naut* **s. le vent** under the lee; **s. les tropiques** in the tropics; **s. l'équateur** at the equator; *Fig* **s. nos propres yeux** before our very eyes; **elle a été tuée s. les yeux de ses enfants** she was killed in front of her children; **s. cet angle** from that angle *or* point of view; **chercher un mot s. la lettre S** to look up a word under (the letter) S **2** *(cause, action)* **s. le poids de** under the weight of; *Fig* **encore s. le choc elle répondit … still** in shock she replied … **3** *(subordination)* under; **travailler s. les ordres de qn** to work under sb; **étudier s. la direction de qn** to study under sb; **enfant s. la responsabilité du père** child who is the responsibility of his father; **s. contrôle judiciaire** on probation; **accord passé s. conditions** conditional agreement; **s. certaines conditions** on certain conditions; **s. peine de mort** on *or* under pain of death **4** *Méd* **je suis s. antibiotiques depuis dix jours** I've been on antibiotics for ten days; **réaliser une opération s. anesthésie** to perform an operation under anaesthetic; **il est encore s. anesthésie** he's still under the anaesthetic; **mettre qn s. anesthésie** to anaesthetize sb, to put sb under an anaesthetic **5** *(manière)* **s. clef** under lock and key; *Mil* **être appelé s. les armes** to have been called up; *Naut* **s. pavillon anglais** flying the English flag; **naviguer s. pavillon anglais** to sail under the English flag; **connu s. le nom de …** known as *or* by the name of …; **s. des dehors charmants** under a charming exterior; **s. n'importe quel prétexte** on *or* under any pretext **6** *(époque)* under; **s. Louis XIV** under Louis XIV, in the reign of Louis XIV; **s. la IIIᵉ République** during the Third Republic

7 *(avant)* within; **s. trois jours** within three days; **s. huitaine** within the week; **s. peu** shortly, soon

sous- [su] *(before vowel sound* [suz]*)* PRÉF **1** *(subordination, subdivision)* sub-; **s.-catégorie** subcategory **2** *(insuffisance)* under-; **s.-productif** underproductive; **s.-informer** to underinform **3** *(infériorité)* pseudo-; **s.-littérature** pseudo-literature

sous-affréter VT *(conj like* **fréter**) *(navire etc)* to subcharter

sous-aide N junior assistant

sous-alimentation NF malnutrition, undernourishment

sous-alimenté [suzalimɑ̃te] ADJ *(personne)* underfed, under-nourished

sous-bail, *pl* **sous-baux** NM sublease

sous-bibliothécaire N sub-librarian, assistant librarian

sous-bock NM beer mat

sous-bois NM INV **1** undergrowth, underwood; **ils ont retrouvé la bicyclette dans les s.** they found the bicycle in the undergrowth **2** *Beaux-Arts* picture of a forest interior

sous-brigadier NM *(de police)* = deputy sergeant

sous-calibré [sukalibre] ADJ *Mil etc (projectile)* subcalibre

sous-capitalisation [sukapitalizasjɔ̃] NF under-capitalization, underfunding

sous-capitalisé [sukapitalize] ADJ undercapitalized, underfunded

sous-chaîne NF *Ordinat* substring

sous-châssis NM INV *Aut* sub-frame

sous-chef NM **1** *(de bureau)* deputy chief clerk **2** *(d'entreprise)* assistant manager; **s. de gare** deputy stationmaster **3** *Mus* deputy conductor

sous-chemise NF folder

sous-classe NF *Biol* subclass

sous-comité NM subcommittee

sous-commission NF subcommittee

sous-compte NM subsidiary account, sub-account

sous-consommation NF INV *Pol, Écon* underconsumption

sous-continent NM *Géog* subcontinent

sous-contractant NM subcontractor

sous-correction NF *Aut* under-correction

souscoté [sukɔte] ADJ *Fin (action, marché, monnaie)* undervalued

sous-couche NF *(de peinture)* undercoat

souscripteur, -trice [suskriptœr, -tris] N *(de journal etc)* subscriber (**de** to); *(de chèque, d'un effet de commerce etc)* drawer; *(d'un emprunt)* subscriber, underwriter; *(dans les assurances)* policy holder

souscription [suskripsjɔ̃] NF **1** *(à un journal etc)* subscription; **droit de s.** subscription fee **2** *Fin* subscription, application (**à des actions** for shares); *(d'une société)* subscribed capital **3** *(d'une somme d'argent)* subscription, contribution; **lancer une s.** to start a fund; **verser une s.** to pay a subscription **4** *(dans les assurances) (d'une police d'assurance)* taking out

souscrire [suskrir] *(conj like* **écrire**) VT *(abonnement, emprunt, assurance)* to take out; *(garantir) (risque)* to underwrite; *Vieilli (chèque etc)* to sign; *(argent pour une action charitable)* to subscribe; *Fin (actions)* to subscribe for *or* apply for
■ VI **s. à** *(publication etc)* to subscribe to; *Fig (opinion, projet etc)* to subscribe to, to endorse; **je souscris entièrement à votre opinion** I am entirely of your opinion; *Fin* **s. à une émission** to apply for *or* subscribe to an issue; **s. à des actions** to take up shares; **s.**

pour (la somme de) 200 euros to subscribe two hundred euros; **s. pour une œuvre de bienfaisance** to subscribe to a charity

sous-critique ADJ *Phys, Nucl etc* subcritical

sous-cutané ADJ subcutaneous

sous-développé ADJ **1** *Écon (pays etc)* underdeveloped **2** *(usine etc)* underequipped

sous-développement NM *Écon* underdevelopment

sous-diacre NM subdeacon

sous-directeur, -trice N **1** *(de société)* assistant manager; *(plus haut dans la hiérarchie)* assistant director **2** *Scol* deputy head

sous-diviser VT to subdivide

sous-division NF subdivision

sous-document NM *Ordinat* sub-document

sous-dominante NF *Mus* subdominant

sous-dossier NM *Ordinat* subfolder

sous-économe N assistant treasurer *or* bursar

sous-embranchement NF *Biol* subphylum

sous-emploi NM INV *Écon* underemployment

sous-employé ADJ *Écon* underemployed

sous-ensemble NM *Math* subset

sous-entendre VT to imply; **qu'est-ce que tu sous-entends?** what are you implying *or* hinting at?; *Gram* **on sous-entend 'pendant'** 'pendant' is understood; **il est sous-entendu que ...** it is understood that ...

sous-entendu NM implication, *Péj* insinuation

sous-entrepreneur NM *Constr* subcontractor

sous-équipé [suzekipe] ADJ *Écon* underequipped

sous-équipement NM *Écon* underequipment

sous-espace NM *Math* subspace

sous-espèce NF *Biol* subspecies

sous-estimation NF underestimation

sous-estimer VT to underestimate

sous-évaluation NF undervaluation

sous-évaluer VT to undervalue

sous-exposer VT *Phot* to underexpose

sous-exposition NF *Phot* underexposure

sous-famille NF *Biol* subfamily

sous-fifre NM *Fam* underling, dogsbody

sous-garde NF trigger guard

sous-genre NM *Biol* subgenus

sous-gouverneur NM deputy governor, vice-governor

sous-groupe NM *Biol, Math* subgroup

sous-homme NM subhuman

sous-humanité NF *(sous-hommes)* subhuman race; *(état)* subhuman condition

sous-ingénieur NM *Ind etc* assistant engineer

sous-inspecteur, -trice N assistant inspector

sous-jacent [suʒasɑ̃] ADJ underlying

Sous-le-Vent N **les îles S.** the Leeward Islands

sous-lieutenant NM *Mil* second lieutenant; *Naut* sub-lieutenant; *Aviat* **s. (aviateur)** pilot officer, *Am* second lieutenant

sous-locataire N subtenant

sous-location NF **1** *(par le propriétaire)* subletting; *(contrat)* sublease **2** *(par le locataire)* subrenting; *(contrat)* subtenancy

sous-louer VT **1** *(du propriétaire) (maison,*

appartement) to sublet **2** *(du locataire) (maison, appartement)* to subrent

sous-main NM INV desk blotter, blotting pad; *Fig* **en s.** secretly

sous-maître, -maîtresse *Arch* N *Scol* teacher's assistant

　NF **sous-maîtresse** brothel-keeper's assistant

sous-marché NM sub-market

sous-marin ADJ *(navire, volcan etc)* submarine; *(récif)* submerged; **chasse** *ou* **pêche s.** underwater fishing; **masque s.** frogman's mask

　NM **1** submarine; **s. nucléaire** nuclear(-powered) submarine; **s. de poche** pocket submarine **2** *Fam (véhicule de surveillance)* = converted van used for police surveillance

sous-marinier NM submariner

sous-marque NF sub-brand

sous-maxillaire ADJ *Anat (glandes etc)* submaxillary

sous-médiante [sumedjɑ̃t] NF *Mus* supertonic

sous-menu NM *Ordinat* submenu

sous-merde NF *très Fam* nobody, non-entity; **traiter qn comme une s.** to treat sb like shit

Sous-ministre NM *Can Admin* Deputy Minister; **S. adjoint** Assistant Deputy Minister

sous-multiple ADJ, NM *Math* submultiple **(de** of)

sous-nappe NF *(de table)* undercloth

sous-œuvre (en) ADV *Constr* reprise en s. underpinning; **reprendre un bâtiment en s.** to underpin a building

sous-off *(abrév* **sous-officier)** NM *Mil Fam* NCO, non-com

sous-officier NM *Mil* non-commissioned officer

sous-ordre NM **1** *Péj (employé)* subordinate, underling **2** *Biol* suborder

sous-palan (en) ADV *Com, Naut* livraison en s. delivery ready for shipping

sous-payer VT *(conj like* **payer)** to underpay

sous-peuplé ADJ underpopulated

sous-peuplement NM underpopulation

sous-pied NM *(de pantalon)* footstrap

sous-plat [supla] NM *Belg* table mat

sous-positionnement NM *Mktg* under-positioning

sous-préfectoral, -ale, -aux, -ales ADJ subprefectorial

sous-préfecture NF subprefecture

sous-préfet NM *Admin* subprefect

sous-préfète NF *Admin (femme)* sub-prefect

sous-principal, -ale, -aux, -ales NM *Scol* vice-principal

sous-production NF *Écon* underproduction

sous-produit NM *Ind etc* by-product; *Fig* poor imitation

sous-programme NM *Ordinat* subroutine, subprogram

sous-prolétaire N member of the underclass

sous-prolétariat NM underclass

sous-pull NM thin sweater

sous-race NF *Zool* subrace

sous-refroidissement NM *Phys* super-cooling

sous-répertoire NM *Ordinat* subdirectory

sous-représentation NF *Pol* under-representation

sous-représenté ADJ *Pol* under-represented

sous-secrétaire N undersecretary; **s. (d'État)** undersecretary (of state)

sous-secrétariat NM undersecretaryship

sous-seing NM *Jur* private agreement *or* contract

soussigné, -ée [susiɲe] ADJ, N undersigned; **je, s. André Renaud, donne mon autorisation à ...** I, the undersigned, hereby authorize ...

sous-sol NM **1** *Géol* subsoil, substratum **2** *Constr* basement

sous-station NF *Élec* substation

sous-système NM subsystem

sous-tasse NF saucer

sous-tendre VT *Géom* to subtend; *Fig* to underlie; **les principes qui sous-tendent un tel raisonnement** the underlying principles of this argument, the principles that underlie this argument

sous-tension NF *Élec* undervoltage

sous-titrage NM *Cin* subtitling; **le s. est excellent** the subtitles are very good

sous-titre NM *(de livre etc)*, *Cin* subtitle; *Journ* subheading, cross-title

sous-titrer VT *Cin* to subtitle; **film sous-titré en anglais** film with English subtitles

sous-titreur NM subtitler

sous-total, *pl* **sous-totaux** NM subtotal

soustractif, -ive [sustraktif, -iv] ADJ *Math, Phot* subtractive

soustraction [sustraksjɔ̃] NF removal; *Math* subtraction SEE GRAMMAR A77; B59

soustraire [sustrer] *(conj like* **traire)** VT **1** *(enlever) (quelque chose)* to take away, to remove *(à qn* from sb); *Fig (quelqu'un)* to protect, to shield *(à qch* from sth) **2** *Math* to subtract *(de* from)

　VPR **se soustraire** se s. à qch to avoid *or* elude sth; **se s. à une obligation** to back out of an obligation

sous-traitance NF subcontracting; **faire de la s.** to subcontract; **travaux effectués en s.** subcontracted work

sous-traitant NM subcontractor

　ADJ **les entreprises sous-traitantes** the subcontractors, the subcontracting companies

sous-traiter VTI to subcontract

sous-utiliser VT to underutilize

sous-variété NF *Biol* subvariety

sous-ventrière NF bellyband; *(avec selle)* (saddle)girth; *Arg* **manger à s'en faire péter la s.** to stuff oneself stupid

sous-verre NM INV glass mount(ing); *(photo, image)* photograph *or* picture mounted under glass

　NM *Belg, Suisse (dessous-de-verre)* coaster

sous-vêtement NM undergarment; **sous-vêtements** underwear

sous-virage NM *Aut* understeer

sous-virer VI *Aut* to understeer

sous-vireur, -euse ADJ **une voiture sous-vireuse** a car that understeers

soutache [sutaʃ] NF *Couture* braid

soutacher [sutaʃe] VT *Couture* to braid

soutane [sutan] NF cassock, soutane; **prendre la s.** to take (holy) orders; **la s.** *(prêtres)* the cloth

soute [sut] NF *Naut* store (room); *Aviat* hold; *(d'un camion)* load box *or* compartment; **s. à charbon** coal bunker; **s. à munitions** magazine; **s. aux bagages** *Naut* baggage room; *Aviat* baggage compartment *or* hold; **s. à mazout** oil tank; **s. à valeurs** strongroom; *Aviat* **s. à essence** refuelling point; *Aviat* **s. à bombes** bomb bay

soutenable [sutnabl] ADJ **1** *(existence, fardeau etc)* bearable **2** *(opinion, position)* tenable; *(théorie)* tenable, arguable

soutenance [sutnɑ̃s] NF *Univ (de mémoire, de thèse)* viva (voce)

soutènement [sutɛnmɑ̃] NM *Constr* support; **mur de s.** retaining *or* supporting wall

souteneur, -euse [sutnœr, -øz] NM *(proxénète)* pimp

  N *Vieilli (d'un système etc)* defender, upholder

SOUTENIR [sutnir] *(conj like* **tenir***)*

> **VT** to support **1, 3** ▪ to hold up **1** ▪ to sustain **2** ▪ to back up **3** ▪ to maintain **4, 5** ▪ to uphold **4** ▪ to assert **4** ▪ to keep up **5**
> **VPR** to support each other **1**

VT 1 *(tenir debout etc)* to support, to hold up; **piliers qui soutiennent le toit** pillars which support the roof
  2 *(fortifier) (d'un médicament, de l'amour etc)* to sustain, to keep going; **une pareille alimentation ne pourra pas le s. très longtemps** he can't keep going for very long on a diet like that
  3 *(aider) (entreprise, cause, troupes, personne etc)* to back (up), to support; *(personne) (défendre, prendre parti pour)* to back up; **s. les prix/une monnaie** to support prices/a currency; **s. le moral des troupes** to encourage the troops; *Fig* to boost staff *or* team morale; **il a besoin qu'on lui soutienne le moral** his morale needs boosting; **elle m'a soutenu dans l'épreuve** she supported me throughout the ordeal
  4 *(faire valoir) (opinion, théorie etc)* to maintain, to uphold; *(fait)* to assert, to affirm; *Univ (thèse)* to defend; **il soutient que ...** he maintains that ...
  5 *(faire durer) (conversation, vitesse, combat, rang etc)* to keep up, to maintain
  6 *(résister à) (affront, reproche, comparaison etc)* to bear; *(siège, attaque etc)* to hold out against, to stand up to
  VPR se soutenir 1 *(s'entraider)* to support *or* back (up) each other; **ils se soutiennent moralement** they give each other moral support
  2 *(se défendre) (d'une théorie, d'une hypothèse)* to be tenable *or* arguable; **ça se soutient/ne se soutient pas** that's tenable/untenable

soutenu [sutny] ADJ **1** *(attention, effort)* sustained; *(intérêt)* sustained, unflagging, constant; *(rythme, trot, marché)* steady **2** *(style écrit, langage etc)* formal, elevated; **employer un langage s.** to use formal language **3** *(contour)* firm; *(couleur)* deep, strong

souterrain, -aine [sutɛrɛ̃, -ɛn] ADJ **1** *(eau, explosion etc)* underground, subterranean; **passage s.** subway; **chemin de fer s.** underground (railway), *Am* subway **2** *Fig (personne, méthodes)* underhand; *(intentions, menées)* secret
  NM underground passage, tunnel

soutien [sutjɛ̃] NM **1** *(aide)* support; **apporter son s. à** to lend one's support to; **en s.** in support; **s. des prix** price support; *Scol* **cours de s.** remedial class; *Mil* **unité de s.** support unit **2** *(personne, groupe)* support; *Admin* **s. de famille** breadwinner

soutien-gorge, *pl* **soutiens-gorge** NM bra, *Br Fml, Am* brassière; **s. à armatures/d'allaitement** underwired/nursing bra; **je préférerais un s. sans armatures** I'd rather have a bra that wasn't underwired

soutier [sutje] NM **1** *(matelot)* stoker **2** *Fig (personne qui occupe une fonction ingrate)* toiler

soutif [sutif] NM *Fam* bra

soutirage [sutiraʒ] NM *(du vin etc)* racking, decanting

soutirer [sutire] VT **1** *(vin etc)* to rack, to decant **2** *(argent, information, promesse etc)* to extract (**à qn** from sb)

souvenance [suvnɑ̃s] NF *Arch, Litt* recollection; **avoir s. de** to recollect; **je n'en ai pas s.** I have no recollection of it

souvenir[1] [suvnir] *(conj like* **venir***; aux* **être***)*
  V IMPERS *Litt* **il me souvient que ...** I recall *or* remember that ...; **il me souvient d'avoir lu que ...** I recall *or* remember reading *or* having read that ...
  VI **fais-moi s. de lui téléphoner ce soir** remind me to telephone him this evening; **fais-moi s. de l'émission ce soir** don't let me forget *or* remind me about the programme this evening
  VPR **se souvenir se s. de qch/qn** to remember *or* recall sth/sb; **je ne me souviens plus de rien** I can't remember a thing; **nous nous souviendrons de lui** we shall remember him; **je m'en souviens** I remember; **autant que je m'en souviens** *ou* **que je m'en souvienne** as far as I can remember *or* recall; **on s'en souviendra** we won't forget (it); *Iron* **on s'en souviendra de ses 'petites promenades'** we're not likely to forget his 'little walks', we won't forget his 'little walks' in a hurry; **souviens-toi de prendre un pull/de ce que je t'ai dit!** remember *or* don't forget to take a sweater/what I told you! VOIR GRAMMAIRE A44

souvenir[2] NM **1** recollection, memory; **avoir gardé un bon s. de qch** to have a pleasant recollection *or* memory of sth; **je n'en ai pas s.** I have no recollection *or* memory of it; **ce n'est plus qu'un mauvais s.** it's just a bad memory now; **si mes souvenirs sont exacts** if my memory serves me well; **souvenirs de ma jeunesse** memories of my youth; **souvenirs d'enfance** childhood memories; **veuillez me rappeler à son bon s.** please remember me to him/her; **ma mère vous envoie son affectueux s.** my mother sends her love; **en s. de qn** in remembrance of sb; **en s. du passé** for old times' sake
  2 *(objet, cadeau) (d'une personne, d'un lieu)* keepsake, souvenir, memento; *(de touriste)* souvenir; **c'est un s. de ma mère** it's a keepsake from my mother; **magasin de souvenirs** souvenir shop

> Il faut noter que le terme anglais **souvenir** ne s'applique qu'à un objet.

souvent [suvɑ̃] ADV often; **peu s.** not often, seldom, infrequently; **je l'ai vue s. cet hiver** I saw a lot of her this winter; **on en parle s. à la radio** they often talk about it on the radio; **il ne vient pas s. nous voir** he doesn't often come and see us, he seldom comes to see us; **je n'en mange pas s.** I don't eat it/them often; **le plus s.** usually, as often as not, more often than not; **il est malade plus s. qu'à son tour** he has more than his share of illness; *Arg Vieilli* **plus s.!** no fear!, not likely! VOIR GRAMMAIRE A21

souverain, -aine [suvrɛ̃, -ɛn] ADJ *(puissance, prince, état, remède etc)* sovereign; *(bonheur)* supreme; *(mépris)* supreme, lofty; *Jur (tribunal)* supreme; **une femme d'une beauté souveraine** a woman of supreme beauty, a supremely beautiful woman
  N sovereign; **s. absolu** absolute monarch; **s. fantoche** puppet monarch
  NM *Hist (monnaie)* sovereign

souverainement [suvrɛnmɑ̃] ADV **1** *(extrêmement)* supremely, intensely; **il s'en moque s.** he really couldn't care less **2** *Jur* **juger s.** to judge without appeal

souveraineté [suvrɛnte] NF sovereignty

souverainisme [suvrɛnism] NM **1** *(doctrine des défenseurs d'une Europe des nations)* separatism **2** *Can (partisan de l'indépendance du Québec)* (Quebec) separatism

souverainiste [suvrɛnist] ADJ **1** *(favorable à une Europe des nations)* separatist **2** *Can (favorable à l'indépendance du Québec)* (Quebec) separatist
  N **1** *(personne favorable à une Europe des nations)* separatist **2** *Can (personne favorable à l'indépendance du Québec)* (Quebec) separatist

soviet [sɔvjɛt] NM soviet

soviétique [sɔvjetik] ADJ Soviet
  N **S.** Soviet (citizen)

soviétisation [sɔvjetizasjɔ̃] NF sovietization, sovietizing

soviétiser [sɔvjetize] VT to sovietize

soviétologue [sɔvjetɔlɔg] N Sovietologist, expert on Soviet affairs

soya [sɔja] NM soya

soyeux, -euse [swajø, -øz] ADJ silky
  NM *(industriel)* silk merchant

SPA [ɛspea] NF *(abrév* **Société protectrice des animaux)** *Br* ≃ RSPCA, *Am* ≃ ASPCA

spacieusement [spasjøzmɑ̃] ADV *(installé)* spaciously; **ils sont s. logés** their accommodation is very spacious; **ils sont s. installés dans 200 mètres carrés** they have a very spacious 200 square metres

spacieux, -euse [spasjø, -øz] ADJ *(chambre, maison etc)* spacious; *(voiture)* roomy

spadassin [spadasɛ̃] NM **1** *Arch* swordsman **2** *Litt (assassin)* hired assassin

spadice [spadis] NM *Bot* spadix

spaetzli [ʃpɛtsli] NM *Suisse Culin* = small strips of pasta often served with game

spaghetti(s) [spageti] NMPL *Culin* spaghetti; **s. bolognaise/carbonara** spaghetti bolognese/carbonara VOIR GRAMMAIRE A14

spahi [spai] NM *Mil* spahi

spalax [spalaks] NM *Zool* mole rat

spammer [spame] VT *Ordinat* to spam

spamming [spamiŋ] NM *Ordinat* spamming

sparadrap [sparadra] NM (adhesive *or* sticking) plaster, Elastoplast®, *Am* Band-Aid®; **mettre du s. sur une blessure** to put a (sticking) plaster *or* an Elastoplast on a wound

sparages [sparaʒ] NMPL *Can Fam* big *or* expansive gestures; **il parlait en faisant de grands s.** he gestured expansively as he spoke

Sparte [spart] N Sparta

spart(e) [spart] NM *Bot* esparto (grass)

spartiate [sparsjat] ADJ *Hist, Fig* Spartan
  N **S.** *Hist* Spartan; *Fig* **à la s.** in a spartan way; **éduquer un enfant à la s.** to give a child a spartan upbringing
  NF leather sandal

spasme [spasm] NM spasm

spasmodique [spasmɔdik] ADJ *Méd* spasmodic

spasmodiquement [spasmɔdikmɑ̃] ADV *Méd* spasmodically

spasmophilie [spasmɔfili] NF *Méd* spasmophilia

spastique [spastik] ADJ *Méd* spastic

spath [spat] NM *Minér* spar

spatial, -ale, -aux, -ales [spasjal, -o] ADJ **1** spatial; **organisation spatiale** space organization; *Math* **coordonnées spatiales** spatial coordinates; *Électron* **charge spatiale** space charge **2** *Astronaut* space; **engin s.** spacecraft; **voyage s.** space flight; **combinaison spatiale** spacesuit; **guerre spatiale** space warfare; **station spatiale** space station

spatialisation [spasjalizasjɔ̃] NF spatialization

spatialiser [spasjalize] VT **1** *(donner un caractère spatial à)* to spatialize **2** *(lancer)* to send into space

spationef [spasjɔnɛf] NM spaceship, spacecraft

spatio-temporel, -elle [spasjotɑ̃pɔrɛl] ADJ space-time, spatiotemporal

spatule [spatyl] NF 1 spatula; **en s.** spatulate 2 *(de ski)* (ski) tip 3 *(oiseau)* spoonbill

spatulé [spatyle] ADJ spatulate

speaker [spikœr] NM 1 *Radio, TV* announcer; *(qui donne les informations)* newsreader 2 *Pol (en Grande-Bretagne, aux États-Unis)* **le s.** the Speaker

speakerine [spikrin] NF *Radio, TV* (female) announcer; *(qui donne les informations)* (female) newsreader

spécial, -ale, -aux, -ales [spesjal, -o] ADJ 1 *(d'une catégorie particulière)* special, specific, distinctive; **une clé spéciale** a special key; **rien de s.** nothing special; *Journ* **envoyé s.** special correspondent; **édition spéciale** special edition; **privilège s. aux militaires** privilege reserved for *or* restricted to military men; **savon s. peaux grasses** soap for greasy skin 2 *(bizarre)* peculiar, odd; **c'est il est un peu s.** it's/he's rather odd *or* peculiar; **c'est s., il faut aimer** *(d'un plat curieux etc)* not everybody likes it, it's not to everybody's taste
▸ NM *Can* 1 *(plat du jour)* special 2 **en s.** *(en solde)* on special

Il faut noter qu'en anglais l'adjectif **special** ne s'emploie jamais à propos de quelque chose d'inhabituel ou d'étrange.

spécialement [spesjalmɑ̃] ADV (e)specially, particularly; *(exprès)* specially; **pas s.** not especially *or* particularly

spécialisation [spesjalizasjɔ̃] NF specialization

spécialisé [spesjalize] ADJ *(travail, matériaux etc)* specialized; **ouvrier s.** semi-skilled worker; **école/hôpital spécialisé(e)** special school/hospital; **enseignement s.** specialized teaching; **aciers spécialisés** speciality *or Am* specialty steels; **ils sont spécialisés dans les déménagements internationaux** they specialize in international relocations, they're international relocation specialists

spécialiser [spesjalize] VT **s. qn** to make *or* turn sb into a specialist
▸ VPR **se spécialiser se s. dans** *ou* **en qch** to specialize in sth

spécialiste [spesjalist] N specialist (**de, en** in); *Méd* **s. du cœur** heart specialist; *Mktg* **s. produit** product specialist; **s. du vol à voile** gliding specialist *or* expert; *Hum* **c'est un s. des rendez-vous manqués** missing appointments is his speciality, he specializes in missing appointments
▸ ADJ specialist; **médecin s.** specialist (doctor); *Hum* **elle est s. de ce genre de gaffes** she specializes in that sort of blunder

spécialité [spesjalite] NF 1 speciality, *Am* specialty; *Culin* **s. de la maison** speciality of the house; **faire sa s. de qch** to specialize in *or* make a special study of sth; **s. budgétaire** budgetary restriction; **s. médicale** specialized area of medicine; *Hum* **elle sera en retard, c'est sa s.** she'll be late, it's her speciality 2 **spécialités pharmaceutiques** patent medicines

spécieusement [spesjøzmɑ̃] ADV *Litt* speciously

spécieux, -euse [spesjø, -øz] ADJ *Litt* specious

spécification [spesifikasjɔ̃] NF *(action, définition)* specification; **s. de la fonction** job description; **s. du produit** product specification

spécificité [spesifisite] NF *Méd etc* specificity

spécifier [spesifje] VT *(impf, pr sub* n. **spéci-**

fiions, v. spécifiiez) to specify, to state (**que** that); **compte spécifié** detailed *or* itemized account; **nous le lui avions pourtant spécifié par écrit** we had specifically informed him in writing; **je l'avais pourtant bien spécifié** I was quite specific about it

spécifique [spesifik] ADJ specific

spécifiquement [spesifikmɑ̃] ADV specifically

spécimen [spesimɛn] NM specimen; *(livre, fascicule)* specimen *or* sample copy; **page s.** specimen page; **s. gratuit** *(de livre)* presentation copy; **s. de signature** specimen signature

spectacle [spɛktakl] NM 1 *(choses vues)* sight, scene; **au s. de** at the sight of; **se donner en s.** to make an exhibition *or* a spectacle of oneself 2 *Théâtre, Cin etc (représentation)* show; **le s.** *(industrie)* show business; **monter un s.** to put on a show; **s. de variétés** variety show; **s. folklorique** performance of national/regional music/dancing; **s. solo** one-man show; **aller au s.** to go to a show; **salle de s.** hall; *Théâtre* theatre, *Am* theater; *Cin* cinema, *Am* movie theater; *Théâtre* **pièce à grand s.** lavish production; *Cin* **film à grand s.** epic (film)

spectaculaire [spɛktakylɛr] ADJ spectacular

spectateur, -trice [spɛktatœr, -tris] N 1 *(témoin)* spectator, onlooker; *(d'accident)* witness 2 *Sport* spectator; *Théâtre* member of the audience; *Théâtre* **spectateurs** audience

spectral, -ale, -aux, -ales [spɛktral, -o] ADJ 1 *(de fantôme)* ghostly, spectral 2 *Opt* spectral

spectre [spɛktr] NM 1 *(fantôme)* ghost, phantom; *Fig (de la guerre, de la misère etc)* spectre, *Am* specter 2 *Phys etc* spectrum; **s. solaire** solar spectrum; *Pharm* **s. d'action** *(d'un antibiotique)* spectrum

spectrogramme [spɛktrɔgram] NM spectrogram

spectrographe [spɛktrɔgraf] NM spectrograph

spectromètre [spɛktrɔmɛtr] NM spectrometer

spectrométrie [spɛktrɔmetri] NM spectrometry

spectroscope [spɛktrɔskɔp] NM *Opt* spectroscope

spectroscopie [spɛktrɔskɔpi] NF spectroscopy

spéculaire [spekylɛr] ADJ 1 *(minéral)* specular 2 *Méd* **écriture s.** mirror writing

spéculateur, -trice [spekylatœr, -tris] N *Fin* speculator; **s. sur devises** currency speculator; *Bourse* **s. à la baisse** bear; *Bourse* **s. à la hausse** bull; **s. à la journée** day to day trader, scalper; **s. sur plusieurs positions** position trader

spéculatif, -ive [spekylatif, -iv] ADJ *Phil, Fin* speculative
▸ NF **spéculative** *(publicité)* pitch

spéculation [spekylasjɔ̃] NF 1 *Phil* speculation (**sur** on) 2 *Fin* speculation; **s. à la baisse** bear operations; **s. à la hausse** bull operations; **s. immobilière** property speculation

spéculer [spekyle] VI 1 *Phil* to speculate (**sur** on, about) 2 *Fin* to speculate (**sur** in; à for); *Bourse* **s. en Bourse** to speculate on the Stock Market; **s. à la baisse** to go a bear, to be bearish; *Bourse* **s. à la hausse** to go a bull, to be bullish; *Fig* **s. sur qch** to count *or* bank on sth

speculum, spéculum [spekylɔm] NM *Méd* speculum

speech, *pl* **speeches** [spitʃ] NM speech; **il nous a fait tout un s. sur la ponctualité** he gave us a long speech about punctuality

speed [spid] *Fam* ADJ *(nerveux)* hyper
▸ NM *(amphétamine)* speed

speedé [spide] ADJ *Fam* 1 *(hyperactif)* hyped up, hyper 2 *(drogué)* high

speeder [spide] *Fam* VT to rush
▸ VI to get a move on; **je n'aime pas s. le lundi matin** I don't like rushing on Monday mornings; **j'ai speedé toute la journée** I've been running around like a headless chicken all day

spéléologie [speleɔlɔʒi] NF caving, potholing, *Am* spelunking; *(étude)* speleology

spéléologique [speleɔlɔʒik] ADJ speleological

spéléologue [speleɔlɔg] N caver, potholer, *Am* spelunker; *(étudiant)* speleologist

spencer [spɛnsɛr] NM 1 *(d'homme)*, *Naut* monkey jacket; *Mil* mess jacket 2 *(de femme)* short jacket, *Arch* spencer

spermaceti [spɛrmaseti] NM spermaceti

spermatique [spɛrmatik] ADJ *Anat* spermatic

spermatogénèse [spɛrmatɔʒenɛz] NF *Biol* spermatogenesis

spermatozoïde [spɛrmatɔzɔid] NM *Biol* spermatozoon

sperme [spɛrm] NM 1 *Physiol* sperm, semen 2 **s. de baleine** spermaceti

spermicide [spɛrmisid] *Méd* ADJ spermicidal
▸ NM spermicide

spermophile [spɛrmɔfil] NM *Zool* gopher, *Spéc* spermophile

sphaigne [sfɛɲ] NF *Bot* sphagnum (moss), peat moss

sphénoïde [sfenɔid] ADJ, NM *Anat* sphenoid

sphère [sfɛr] NF 1 *Astron* sphere; *Géog* **s. terrestre** globe; **s. céleste** celestial sphere 2 *Fig (d'activité, d'influence etc)* sphere; **la s. des finances** the sphere *or* field of finance, financial circles; **nous ne sommes pas dans les mêmes sphères** we're not in the same field; **les hautes sphères de la politique** the higher reaches *or* realms of politics

sphéricité [sferisite] NF sphericity

sphérique [sferik] ADJ spherical

sphéroïde [sferɔid] NM spheroid

sphéromètre [sferɔmɛtr] NM spherometer

sphincter [sfɛ̃ktɛr] NM *Anat* sphincter

sphinx [sfɛ̃ks] NM 1 *Myth, Fig* sphinx; **sourire de s.** sphinx-like smile 2 *Entom* hawk *or Am* sphinx moth

sphygmomanomètre [sfigmɔmanɔmɛtr] NM *Méd* sphygmo-manometer

spi [spi] NM *Naut Fam* = **spinnaker**

spic [spik] NM *Bot* spike lavender

spider [spidɛr] NM *Aut* dick(e)y, *Am* rumble seat

spin [spin] NM *Nucl* spin

spina-bifida [spinabifida] NM *Méd* spina bifida

spinal, -ale, -aux, -ales [spinal, -o] ADJ *Anat* spinal

spinelle [spinɛl] NM *Minér* spinel

spinnaker [spinakə, -kɛr] NM *Naut* spinnaker

spiral, -ale, -aux, -ales [spiral, -o] ADJ spiral
▸ NM *(de montre)* hair-spring
▸ NF **spirale** spiral, *Spéc* helix; **la spirale inflationniste** the inflationary spiral; **spirale des prix et des salaires** wage and price spiral; **en spirale** *(utilisé adverbialement)* in a spiral, spirally; *(utilisé adjectivement)* spiral; **descendre/monter en spirale** to spiral down/up, to go down/up in a spiral

spirant, -ante [spirɑ̃, -ɑ̃t] *Ling* ADJ spirant
▸ NF **spirante** spirant

spire [spir] **NF** *(d'une spirale)*, Élec *(d'une bobine)* (single) turn; *(d'un coquillage)* whorl

spirée [spire] **NF** *Bot* spiraea

spirille [spirij] **NM** *Biol* spirillum

spirite [spirit] **ADJ, N** spiritualist

spiritisme [spiritism] **NM** spiritualism

spiritualiser [spirityalize] **VT** to spiritualize

spiritualisme [spirityalism] **NM** *Phil* spiritualism

spiritualiste [spirityalist] *Phil* **ADJ** spiritualist(ic)
N spiritualist

spiritualité [spirityalite] **NF** *Phil* spirituality

spirituel, -elle [spirityɛl] **ADJ 1** *Phil, Rel etc* *(être, pouvoir, vie etc)* spiritual; *(musique)* sacred; **père s.** spiritual father **2** *(fin)* *(personne, réponse etc)* witty; *Iron* que c'est s.! very witty *or* droll!
NM **le s.** things spiritual; *(pouvoir)* spiritual power

spirituellement [spirityɛlmɑ̃] **ADV 1** *(de l'esprit)* spiritually **2** *(finement)* wittily

spiritueux, -euse [spiritɥø, -øz] **ADJ** *(boisson)* alcoholic
NM *(liqueur)* spirit

spiroïdal, -ale, -aux, -ales [spiroidal, -o] **ADJ** spiroid

spitant [spitɑ̃] *Belg* **ADJ 1** *(personne)* lively **2** *(gazeux)* **eau spitante** carbonated water

spleen [splin] **NM** *Litt* *(mélancolie)* spleen, melancholy; **avoir le s.** to be melancholic

spleenétique [splinetik] **ADJ** *Litt* splenetic, melancholy

splendeur [splɑ̃dœr] **NF 1** *(somptuosité)* splendour, *Am* splendor, magnificence; *Litt* *(éclat)* radiance, brightness; *(gloire)* splendour, grandeur, glory; **dans toute sa s.** in all his/her/its splendour **2** *(chose)* **splendeurs** splendours, *Am* splendors; **c'est une s.** it's splendid

splendide [splɑ̃did] **ADJ** *(journée, temps)* splendid; *(soleil)* brilliant; *(palais, victoire, repas)* splendid, magnificent; *(personne)* splendid-looking

splendidement [splɑ̃didmɑ̃] **ADV** splendidly

splénectomie [splenɛktɔmi] **NF** *Chir* splenectomy

splénique [splenik] **ADJ** *(artère, maladie)* splenic

spoiler [spɔjlœr] **NM** *Aut* spoiler

spoliateur, -trice [spɔljatœr, -tris] *Litt* **N** despoiler
ADJ *(loi, mesure etc)* spoliatory

spoliation [spɔljasjɔ̃] **NF** *Litt* *(d'une personne)* despoiling, robbing

spolier [spɔlje] **VT** *(impf, pr sub n. spoliions, v. spoliiez)* *Litt* to despoil, to rob (**de** of)

spondée [spɔ̃de] **NM** *Littér* spondee

spondylarthrite [spɔ̃dilartrit] **NF** *Méd* spondylarthritis; **s. ankylosante** ankylosing spondylitis

spondylite [spɔ̃dilit] **NF** *Méd* spondylitis

spongieux, -ieuse [spɔ̃ʒjø, -jøz] **ADJ** spongy

sponsor [spɔ̃sɔr] **NM** sponsor

sponsoring [spɔ̃sɔriŋ] **NM** sponsorship

sponsorisation [spɔ̃sɔrizasjɔ̃] **NF** sponsoring

sponsoriser [spɔ̃sɔrize] **VT** to sponsor

spontané [spɔ̃tane] **ADJ** *(action, personne, combustion), Biol (génération etc)* spontaneous; *(aveux)* unprompted; *(candidature)* unsolicited

spontanéité [spɔ̃taneite] **NF** spontaneity

spontanément [spɔ̃tanemɑ̃] **ADV** spontaneously

---

sporadique [spɔradik] **ADJ** sporadic

sporadiquement [spɔradikmɑ̃] **ADV** sporadically

sporange [spɔrɑ̃ʒ] **NM** *Bot* sporangium, spore case

spore [spɔr] **NF** *Bot* spore

sport [spɔr] **NM** sport; **faire du s.** to do sport; **elle ne pratique aucun s.** she doesn't do any sport; **chaussures/terrain/salle/voiture de s.** sports shoes/ground/arena/car; *Fig Fam* **vous allez voir du s.** now you're going to see some fun; *Fam* **il va y avoir du s.!** there's going to be some fun!
ADJ INV 1 **vêtements s., costume s.** casual clothes; **habillé s.** casually dressed; *Aut* **coupé s.** sports coupé **2** *(personne)* sporting, fair
▸▸ *Fam* **s. en chambre** bedroom sports; **s. de combat** combat sport; **s. d'équipe** team sport; **sports d'hiver** winter sports; **aller aux sports d'hiver** to go skiing; **s. individuel** individual sport; **sports nautiques** water sports

sportif, -ive [spɔrtif, -iv] **ADJ 1** *(résultats, édition, club etc)* sports; **réunion sportive** sports *or* athletics meeting **2** *(fair-play)* *(personne)* sporting, fair; **esprit s.** sporting spirit, sportsmanship **3** *(amateur de sport)* sporty, athletic; **allure sportive** sporty *or* athletic look
N sportsman, *f* sportswoman

sportivement [spɔrtivmɑ̃] **ADV** sportingly, in a sporting spirit; **il prit les choses très s.** he was very sporting about things

sportivité [spɔrtivite] **NF** sportsmanship; **elle eut la s. de ...** she was sporting enough to ...

sport(s)wear [spɔrt(s)wɛr] **NM** sportswear, casual wear
ADJ *(style etc)* casual

sporuler [spɔryle] **VI** *Biol* to sporulate

spot [spɔt] **NM 1** *TV, Électron etc (point)* spot; *Radio* blip **2** *Théâtre (lampe)* spot(light); *TV, Cin* **s. à pinces** clip lamp **3** *Radio, TV* **s. (publicitaire)** commercial, advertisement; **un s. de trente secondes** a thirty-second spot

spouler [spule] **VT** *Ordinat* to spool

spouleur [spulœr] **NM** *Ordinat* spooler; **s. d'imprimante** printer spooler

spoutnik [sputnik] **NM** sputnik

sprat [sprat] **NM** *(poisson)* sprat

spray [sprɛ] **NM** spray, aerosol (spray); **peinture/déodorant en s.** spray(-on) *or* aerosol paint/deodorant

spread [sprɛd] **NM** *Bourse* **s. baissier** bear spread; **s. haussier** bull spread; **s. papillon** butterfly spread

springbok [spriŋbɔk] **NM** springbok

springer [spriŋœr] **NM** *(chien)* springer (spaniel)

sprint [sprint] **NM** *Sport* (final) sprint; *(course)* sprint; *Fam* **piquer un s.** to sprint; **être bon au s.** to have a good sprint finish

sprinter¹ [sprintœr] **NM** *Sport* sprinter

sprinter² [sprinte] **VI** *Sport* to sprint

squale [skwal] **NM** *(roussette)* dogfish; *(requin)* shark

squame [skwam] **NF** *Méd* scale, *Spéc* squama

squameux, -euse [skwamø, -øz] **ADJ** *Méd* scaly, *Spéc* squamous

square [skwar] **NM** *(jardin public)* public garden

squash [skwaʃ] **NM** *Sport* squash; **jouer au s.** to play squash

squat [skwat] **NM** *(action, lieu)* squat

squatter¹ [skwatœr] **NM** squatter

squatter² [skwate], **squatteriser** [skwate-**

---

rize] **VT** *(occuper)* to squat in; *Fam* **il squatte toujours la télécommande quand on regarde un film** he always takes over the remote control when we're watching a film; *Fam* **arrête de s. le joint, fais tourner!** stop bogarting that joint, pass it round!; *Fam* **tous les matins elle squatte la salle de bain pendant une heure** every morning she takes over *or* hogs the bathroom for an hour
VI to squat; *Fam* **ça fait trois semaines qu'il squatte chez moi** he's been squatting *or* camping out at mine for three weeks now

squatteur [skwatœr] **NM** squatter

squaw [skwo] **NF** (Indian) squaw

squeeze [skwiz] **NM** *(au bridge)* squeeze

squelette [skəlɛt] **NM 1** skeleton; **c'est un vrai s.** *ou* **un s. ambulant** he's/she's a bag of bones *or* a walking skeleton **2** *Fig (d'un navire, d'un roman etc)* skeleton, framework; *Typ* rough layout

squelettique [skəletik] **ADJ 1** *Anat* skeletal **2** *(maigre) (personne, bras etc)* skeleton-like; **il est devenu s.** he's turned into a walking skeleton **3** *(réduit) (personnel, armée etc)* skeleton

squille [skij] **NF** *(crustacé)* squill

SRAS [sras] **NM** *(abrév* **syndrome respiratoire aigu sévère)** SARS

Sri Lanka [srilɑ̃ka] **NF** Sri Lanka

sri lankais, -aise [srilɑ̃kɛ, -ɛz] **ADJ** Sri Lankan
N S. Sri Lankan

SRPJ [ɛsɛrpeʒi] **NM** *(abrév* **Service régional de la police judiciaire)** = regional crime unit

SS [ɛsɛs] **NM** *Hist* member of the SS; **les SS** the SS
NF *Admin abrév* **Sécurité sociale**

SSR [ɛsɛsɛr] **NF** *Suisse TV (abrév* **Société suisse de Radiodiffusion et de Télévision**) = French-speaking Swiss broadcasting company

stabilisant [stabilizɑ̃] **NM** *Chimie* stabilizing agent

stabilisateur, -trice [stabilizatœr, -tris] **ADJ** stabilizing; **appareil s.** stabilizing device
NM 1 *(de vélo), Naut* stabilizer; *Aviat* tailplane, *Am* horizontal stabilizer; *(vertical)* fin, *Am* vertical stabilizer **2** *Chimie* stabilizer

stabilisation [stabilizasjɔ̃] **NF** stabilization

stabilisé [stabilize] **ADJ** *Chimie, Écon etc* stabilized; *Biol* balanced

stabiliser [stabilize] **VT** to stabilize, to steady
VPR se stabiliser *(d'une voiture, d'une monnaie)* to stabilize, to steady; *(d'une personne) (dans la vie)* to settle down; **quand la situation se sera stabilisée** once the situation settles down *or* stabilizes

stabilité [stabilite] **NF** stability; **s. des changes** exchange rate stability; **s. des prix** price stability; **s. en courbe** cornering stability

stable [stabl] **ADJ** *(substance, équilibre, échelle, tempérament etc)* stable, steady; *(paix)* stable, lasting

stabulation [stabylasjɔ̃] **NF** *(du bétail)* keeping in sheds; *(des chevaux)* stabling

staccato [stakato] **ADV, NM** *Mus* staccato

stade [stad] **NM 1** *(de sport)* stadium **2** *(étape)* *(d'évolution, de développement, de maladie etc)* stage; *Psy* **s. anal/oral/génital** anal/oral/genital stage **3** *Entom (des chenilles etc)* instar

stadier [stadje] **NM** steward *(at sports stadium)*

staff [staf] **NM 1** *Constr (matériau)* staff **2** *(personnel)* staff; **s. de direction** managerial staff

stage [staʒ] **NM** *(période)* period of instruction *or* training; *(cours)* training course;

stagflation — **stance**

(pédagogique) teaching practice; **s. de formation** training period; **s. professionnel** *ou* **en entreprise** work placement, *Am* internship; **faire un s. de musique/de poterie** *(en vacances)* to do a music/pottery course; **être en s.** to be undergoing training *or* under instruction; **s. de perfectionnement** advanced training course

> Il faut noter que le terme anglais **stage** est un faux ami.

stagflation [stagflasjɔ̃] NF *Écon* stagflation

stagiaire [staʒjɛr] ADJ trainee; **interprète s.** trainee interpreter
  N trainee; *TV, Cin* runner, best boy

stagnant [stagnɑ̃] ADJ *(eau), Fig (ventes etc)* stagnant

stagnation [stagnasjɔ̃] NF *(de l'eau), Fig (des ventes etc)* stagnation; *Fig* **en s.** at a standstill, stagnant

stagner [stagne] VI *(de l'eau), Fig (du commerce etc)* to stagnate

stakhanovisme [stakanɔvism] NM Stakhanovism

stalactite [stalaktit] NF *Géol* stalactite

stalag [stalag] NM stalag

stalagmite [stalagmit] NF *Géol* stalagmite

stalinien, -ienne [stalinjɛ̃, -jɛn] ADJ, N Stalinist

stalinisme [stalinism] NM Stalinism

stalle [stal] NF **1** *(dans une cathédrale)* stall **2** *(dans une étable)* stall, box

stance [stɑ̃s] NF *(strophe)* stanza

stand [stɑ̃d] NM **1** *(dans une course, une exposition etc)* stand, *Am* booth; *(dans une kermesse)* stall; **s. d'exposition** exhibition stand; *Sport, Aut* **les stands de ravitaillement** the pits **2 s. (de tir)** rifle range **3** *(de machine à écrire etc)* stand, rest

standard [stɑ̃dar] NM **1** *(norme)* standard; **s. de vie** standard of living **2** *Tél* switchboard
  ADJ INV standard; *Péj* **sourire s.** fixed smile

standardisation [stɑ̃dardizasjɔ̃] NF standardization

standardiser [stɑ̃dardize] VT to standardize

standardiste [stɑ̃dardist] N *Tél* (switchboard) operator

stand-by [stɑ̃dbaj] *Aviat* ADJ INV stand-by
  NM **ticket/passager en) s.** stand-by (ticket/passenger)

standing [stɑ̃diŋ] NM *Fam* status; *(social)* (social) standing; **avoir un bon s.** to have a good standard of living; **appartement de grand s.** luxury flat *or Am* apartment; **quartier de grand s.** select district

staphylocoque [stafilɔkɔk] NM *(bactérie)* staphylococcus

star [star] NF *(vedette de cinéma, chanteur, sportif etc), Mktg (produit)* star; **faire la s.** to act the star

stariser [starize] VT *Fam* **s. qn** to turn sb into a star

starlette [starlɛt] NF *Cin* starlet

star-system, *pl* **star-systems** [starsistɛm] NM *Cin, Théâtre etc* star system

starter [starter] NM **1** *Sport (qui donne le signal)* starter **2** *Aut* choke; **mettre/enlever le s.** to pull out/push in the choke; **rouler avec le s.** to drive with the choke out

> Il faut noter que le terme anglais **starter** est un faux ami: il ne désigne jamais le dispositif servant à faciliter le démarrage d'un moteur.

starting-block, *pl* **starting-blocks** [startiŋblɔk] NM *Sport* starting block

starting-gate, *pl* **starting-gates** [startiŋgɛt] NM *Courses de chevaux* starting gate

start-up [startœp] NF *Com* start-up

stase [staz] NF *Méd* stasis

station [stasjɔ̃] NF **1** *(position)* position, posture; **s. debout** standing position; **la s. debout lui est déconseillée** he has been advised not to stand for any length of time; **je me fatigue vite en s. debout** standing tires me quickly; **s. horizontale/verticale** horizontal/vertical position; **mise en s.** *(d'un instrument etc)* setting up
  2 *(halte)* stop, pause; **faire une s. à ...** to stop *or* pause at ...; **faire de longues stations devant les magasins** to stop for long periods in front of shops
  3 *Rel (de la Croix)* station
  4 *(lieu d'arrêt) (d'autobus)* (bus) stop; *(de métro)* station; *(de train)* halt; *(de taxis)* (taxi) rank; *Belg (gare)* station
  5 *(lieu de séjour)* resort
  6 *(centre de recherches)* station
  7 *Ordinat (d'un réseau)* station, node
  ▸▸ *Ordinat* **s. d'accueil** docking station; **s. balnéaire** seaside *or* coastal resort; *TV, Radio* **s. de base** base station; *Élec* **s. centrale** power station; **s. climatique** health resort; *Aut* **s. diagnostic** diagnostics bay; **s. émettrice** broadcasting station; *Aut* **s. d'essence** petrol *or Am* gas station; *TV, Radio* **s. généraliste** general-interest station; **s. hydrominérale** spa resort; *Ordinat* **s. individuelle** standalone station; *Aut* **s. de lavage** car wash; **s. météorologique** weather *or* meteorological station; **s. de métro** tube *or* underground *or Am* subway station; **s. de montagne** mountain resort; **s. orbitale** orbiting station; *Pétr* **s. de pompage** pumping station; **s. de radio** radio station; *Ordinat* **s. réseau** network station; *TV, Radio* **s. satellite** satellite station; **s. de ski** winter sports *or* ski resort; **s. spatiale** space station; **s. de sports d'hiver** winter sports *or* ski resort; **s. de télévision** television station; *TV* **s. terrestre** ground *or* earth station; *TV* **s. thématique** themed channel; **s. thermale** spa; **s. de travail** workstation; **s. verte** = well-preserved, picturesque French rural town or village

stationnaire [stasjɔnɛr] ADJ stationary; *(baromètre)* steady; **l'état du malade est s.** the patient('s condition) is stable
  NM *Naut* guardship, station ship

stationné [stasjɔne] ADJ **1** *(véhicule)* parked **2** *Mil* **les troupes stationnées en Allemagne** troops stationed in Germany

stationnement [stasjɔnmɑ̃] NM **1** *(de voitures etc)* parking; **en s.** parked; **parc de s.** car park; **s. interdit** *(sur panneau)* no parking; *(devant la gare etc)* no waiting; **s. gênant** no parking **2** *Can (parking)* car park, *Am* parking lot **3** *Aviat* **aire de s.** apron

stationner [stasjɔne] VI *(d'une voiture, d'un conducteur etc)* to park; **défense de s.** *(sur panneau)* no parking; *(devant la gare etc)* no waiting

station-service, *pl* **stations-service(s)** NF *Aut* service *or* filling *or* petrol *or Am* gas station

statique [statik] ADJ *(électricité, personnage etc)* static
  NF statics

statiquement [statikmɑ̃] ADV statically

statisticien, -ienne [statistisjɛ̃, -jɛn] N statistician

statistique [statistik] ADJ statistical
  NF **1** *(science)* statistics **2** *(donnée)* statistic; **statistiques démographiques** demographics; **statistiques de natalité** birth statistics; **statistiques sociales** social statistics; **statistiques syndicales** trade statistics

statistiquement [statistikmɑ̃] ADV statistically

stator [stator] NM stator

statoréacteur [statoreaktœr] NM *Aviat* ramjet

statuaire [statɥɛr] ADJ *(art, marbre etc)* statuary
  N sculptor, f sculptress
  NF *(art of)* statuary

statue [staty] NF statue; **la s. de la Liberté** the Statue of Liberty; **immobile comme une s.** stock-still; **s. de sel** pillar of salt

statuer [statɥe] VI to give a decision *or* a ruling *(sur on)*

statuette [statɥɛt] NF statuette

statufier [statyfje] VT *(impf, pr sub* **n. statufiions, v. statufiiez)** *Fam (quelqu'un)* to erect a statue to

statu quo [statykwo] NM status quo

stature [statyr] NF stature; **de haute s.** very tall; *Fig* of (great) stature; **elle a une s. de basketteuse** she's very tall; *Fig* **ils ne sont pas de la même s.** they're not in the same league

statut [staty] NM *(état)* status; **avoir un s. privilégié** to have privileged status; **s. social** social status; **s. juridique** *or* **légal** legal status; **avoir le s. de cadre/de fonctionnaire** to have executive/civil servant status; **il réclame le s. de réfugié politique** he is asking for political refugee status
  NMPL **statuts** *(de sociétés, d'associations)* statutes, memorandum and articles of association, *Am* bylaws; **statuts et règlements** rules and regulations

statutaire [statytɛr] ADJ statutory

statutairement [statytɛrmɑ̃] ADV in accordance with the statutes *or* regulations

stayer [stejœr] NM *Cyclisme (derrière une moto)* long-distance cyclist; *Courses de chevaux* stayer

St, Ste *(abrév* **Saint(e))** St

Sté *(abrév* **Société)** Co

steak [stɛk] NM *Culin* steak; **s. tartare** steak tartare; **s. au poivre** peppered steak, steak au poivre; **s. frites** steak and chips

stéarine [stearin] NF *Chimie* stearin

stéarique [stearik] ADJ *Chimie* stearic (acid)

stéatite [steatit] NF *Minér* steatite, soapstone

stéatopyge [steatɔpiʒ] ADJ steatopygic

stéatose [steatoz] NF *Méd* steatosis

steeple [stipl], **steeple-chase,** *pl* **steeple-chases** [stipœlʃɛz] NM *Sport* steeplechase

stèle [stɛl] NF stele

stellage [stelaʒ] NM *Bourse* double option, put and call (option)

stellaire [stelɛr] ADJ *(lumière etc)* stellar
  NF *Bot* starwort

stem(m) [stɛm] NM *Ski* stem turn

stencil [stɛnsil] NM *(à polycopier)* stencil

sténo [steno] NF *(abrév* **sténographie)** shorthand, stenography; **prendre une lettre en s.** to take down a letter in shorthand
  N *(abrév* **sténographe)** stenographer

sténodactylo [stenodaktilo] N shorthand typist, *Am* stenographer
  NF *(abrév* **sténodactylographie)** shorthand typing

sténodactylographie [stenodaktilɔgrafi] NF shorthand typing

sténographe [stenograf] N stenographer, shorthand writer; **s. de presse** press stenographer

sténographie [stenografi] NF shorthand, stenography

sténographier [stenɔgrafje] VT *(pr sub, impf* **n. sténographiions, v. sténographiiez)** **s. une lettre** to take a letter down in shorthand

sténographique [stenɔgrafik] ADJ *(écriture etc)* shorthand

sténopé [stenɔpe] NM pinhole

sténotype [stenɔtip] NF stenotype, stenotyper

sténotyper [stenɔtipe] VT to stenotype

sténotypie [stenɔtipi] NF stenotypy

sténotypiste [stenɔtipist] N stenotypist

stentor [stãtɔr] NM **1 voix de s.** stentorian voice **2** *Zool* stentor

step [stɛp] NM step aerobics

stéphanois, -oise [stefanwa, -waz] ADJ of *or* from Saint-Étienne
▪ N **S.** *(natif)* native of Saint-Étienne; *(habitant)* inhabitant of Saint-Étienne

steppe [stɛp] NF *Géog* steppe

stercoraire [stɛrkɔrɛr] ADJ *Méd* stercoraceous
▪ NM *(oiseau)* skua

stère [stɛr] NM *(unité de mesure)* stere

stéréo [stereo] ADJ INV *(abrév* **stéréophonique**) stereo
▪ NF **1** *(abrév* **stéréophonie**) stereo; **en s.** in stereo; **s. VHF** stereo VHF **2** *(radio)* stereo radio

stéréogramme [stereɔgram] NM *Opt, Phot* stereogram, stereograph

stéréographie [stereɔgrafi] NF *Opt* stereography

stéréométrie [stereɔmetri] NF stereometry

stéréophonie [stereɔfɔni] NF stereophony

stéréophonique [stereɔfɔnik] ADJ stereophonic

stéréoscope [stereɔskɔp] NM *Opt* stereoscope

stéréoscopie [stereɔskɔpi] NF stereoscopy

stéréoscopique [stereɔskɔpik] ADJ stereoscopic

stéréotype [stereotip] NM *Typ, Fig* stereotype

stéréotypé [stereotipe] ADJ *(idées, phrases etc)* stereotype(d)

stéréotypie [stereotipi] NF *Typ, Psy* stereotypy

stérile [steril] ADJ *(homme, femme, animal)* sterile; *(mariage)* childless; *(terre)* sterile, barren, unproductive; *(travail)* unprofitable; *(discussion, efforts etc)* sterile, vain, fruitless; *Méd etc* **instruments stériles** sterile *or* sterilized instruments

stérilement [sterilmã] ADV *(vainement)* fruitlessly

stérilet [sterilɛ] NM *(contraceptif)* coil, IUD; **se faire poser un s.** to have a coil *or* an IUD fitted

stérilisant [sterilizã] ADJ *(agent etc)* sterilizing; *Fig* mind-numbing

stérilisateur [sterilizatœr] NM sterilizer

stérilisation [sterilizasjɔ̃] NF sterilization

stériliser [sterilize] VT *(lait, instrument, personne etc)* to sterilize; *Fig* to stifle, to suffocate

stérilité [sterilite] NF *(d'une personne)* sterility; *(d'une terre)* barrenness; *Fig (d'une discussion, d'efforts etc)* fruitlessness, futility

sterling [stɛrliŋ] ADJ INV sterling; **dix livres s.** ten pounds sterling
▪ NM INV sterling; **payé en s.** paid in sterling

sterne [stɛrn] NF *(oiseau)* tern

sternum [stɛrnɔm] NM *Anat* breastbone, *Spéc* sternum

sternutatoire [stɛrnytatwar] ADJ sternutatory; **poudre s.** sneezing powder

stéroïde [sterɔid] NM *Biol, Méd* steroid; **stéroïdes anabolisants** anabolic steroids

stérol [sterɔl] NM *Chimie, Physiol* sterol

stertoreux, -euse [stɛrtɔrø, -øz] ADJ *Méd (respiration)* stertorous

stéthoscope [stetɔskɔp] NM *Méd* stethoscope

steward [stjuwart, stiwart] NM *Naut* steward; *Aviat* flight *or* cabin attendant

stick [stik] NM **1** *Mil, Sp, Aviat etc* stick; *(de cavalier)* riding whip *or* crop **2** *(de colle etc)* stick; **un s. de rouge à lèvres** a lipstick; **déodorant en s.** stick deodorant **3** *Fam (de marijuana)* (thin) joint *or* spliff

stigmate [stigmat] NM **1** *Méd* mark, stigma; *Fig (du vice etc)* mark **2** *Hist (châtiment)* brand **3** *Hist, Rel* **stigmates** stigmata **4** *Bot, Entom* stigma

stigmatisation [stigmatizasjɔ̃] NF *(condamnation), Rel* stigmatization

stigmatisé, -ée [stigmatize] ADJ stigmatized
▪ N *Hist, Rel* stigmatist, stigmatic

stigmatiser [stigmatize] VT **1** *(condamner) (quelqu'un)* to stigmatize, to condemn **2** *Hist (marquer) (détenu)* to brand

stillation [stilasjɔ̃] NF *(en sciences)* dripping

stim [stim] NF *Mktg (abrév* **stimulation**) incentive, stimulus

stimulant [stimylã] ADJ stimulating; *(résultats)* encouraging
▪ NM **1** *Méd etc* stimulant **2** *Fig* stimulus, spur, incentive; *Mktg* **stimulants** stimuli

stimulateur [stimylatœr] NM *Méd* **s. cardiaque** pacemaker; **on lui a mis un s. cardiaque** he was fitted with a pacemaker

stimulation [stimylasjɔ̃] NF stimulation, incentive, stimulus; **s. de la demande** demand stimulation; **s. financière** cash incentive; **s. à l'achat** incentive to buy; **s. à la consommation** consumer incentive

stimuler [stimyle] VT **1** *(personne)* to stimulate; *(encourager)* to spur on; **il faut le s. sans arrêt** you have to keep prodding him; **cela ne me stimule pas vraiment de travailler avec elle** I don't find working with her very stimulating **2** *(enthousiasme, digestion, économie etc)* to stimulate; *(appétit)* to stimulate, to whet; *(amitié, commerce etc)* to stimulate, to encourage; **s. la demande** to stimulate demand

stimulus [stimylys], *pl* **stimulus** *ou* **stimuli** [stimyli] NM stimulus

stipendiaire [stipãdjɛr], **stipendié, -ée** [stipãdje] *Litt Péj* ADJ *(soldat etc)* hired
▪ N hireling

stipendier [stipãdje] VT *(pr sub, impf n.* **stipendiions,** *v.* **stipendiiez)** *Litt Péj (soldats, politiciens etc)* to hire

stipulation [stipylasjɔ̃] NF stipulation, condition

stipuler [stipyle] VT to stipulate; **il est stipulé dans le contrat que …** it is stipulated in the contract that …

stochastique [stɔkastik] ADJ stochastic

stock [stɔk] NM *Com (des biens)* stock; **stocks** *(en comptabilité)* stock, *Am* inventory; **en s.** in stock; **nous n'avons plus ce modèle en s.** we no longer have this model in stock, this model is out of stock; **rupture de s.** stock outage; **être en rupture de s.** to be out of stock; *Fam* **tout un s., un vrai s.** a whole stock *or* collection; **dans la limite des stocks disponibles** while stocks last, subject to availability; **c'est là qu'elle cache son s. de biscuits** that's where she hides her stock of biscuits; **elle a mis tout son s. de chaussures dans ce tiroir** she put her whole stock of shoes in this drawer; **s. d'alerte** minimum stock level; **stocks excédentaires** surplus stock; **s. final** closing stock; **s. d'ouverture** opening stock; **s. de sécurité** safety stock; **s. stratégique** perpetual inventory; **s. tampon** buffer stock

stockage [stɔkaʒ] NM **1** *(des marchandises)* stocking; *Ordinat* storage; *Ordinat* **s. de données** data storage; *Ordinat* **s. en mémoire tampon** buffering; **s. excessif** overstocking **2** *(en grande quantité)* stockpiling, building up of stocks

stock-car, *pl* **stock-cars** NM *Sport (voiture)* stock car; *(sport)* stock-car racing

stocker [stɔke] VT **1** *(marchandises)* to stock **2** *(en grande quantité)* to stockpile **3** *Ordinat (informations)* to store

stockfish [stɔkfiʃ] NM INV stockfish

Stockholm [stɔkɔlm] N Stockholm

stockiste [stɔkist] N *Com* stockist, *Am* dealer; *Aut* dealer, agent

stoeffer [stufe] VI *Belg (se vanter)* to show off

stoïcien, -ienne [stɔisjɛ̃, -jɛn] ADJ stoical, stoic; *Hist, Phil* Stoic
▪ N stoic; *Hist, Phil* Stoic

stoïcisme [stɔisism] NM stoicism; *Hist, Phil* Stoicism; **avec s.** stoically, with stoicism

stoïque [stɔik] ADJ stoic, stoical
▪ N stoic

stoïquement [stɔikmã] ADV stoically

stolon [stɔlɔ̃] NM *Bot* stolon, runner

stomacal, -ale, -aux, -ales [stɔmakal, -o] ADJ *(spasme etc)* stomach

stomachique [stɔmaʃik] ADJ, NM *Pharm* stomachic

stomatite [stɔmatit] NF *Méd* stomatitis

stomatologie [stɔmatɔlɔʒi] NF stomatology

stomatologiste [stɔmatɔlɔʒist], **stomatologue** [stɔmatɔlɔg] N stomatologist

stomie [stɔmi] NF *Méd* stoma

stop [stɔp] INT stop!; *(dans un télégramme)* stop; **il faut savoir dire s.** you have to learn to say enough is enough; **alors je dis 's.!', j'arrête de travailler avec vous** I'm telling you that's enough, I'm not working with you any more
▪ NM **1** *Aut (feu arrière)* brake light; *(panneau)* stop sign **2** *Fam (abrév* **auto-stop**) hitchhiking; **faire du s.** to hitch(hike); **aller à Paris en s.** to hitch(hike) to Paris

stoppage [stɔpaʒ] NM *Couture (d'un vêtement)* invisible mending

stopper [stɔpe] VT I to stop; **il faut le s. quand il est dans cet état** he has to be stopped when he's in this state
▪ VT *Couture* to repair by invisible mending

stoppeur, -euse [stɔpœr, -øz] N *Fam* **1** *(abrév* **auto-stoppeur**) hitcher, hitchhiker **2** *Sport* fullback

store [stɔr] NM blind; *(devant un magasin)* awning; **s. vénitien** Venetian blind

story-board, *pl* **story-boards** [stɔribɔrd] NM *TV, Cin* storyboard

strabisme [strabism] NM strabismus, squint(ing); **s. convergent/divergent** esotropia *or* convergent strabismus/exotropia *or* divergent strabismus; **yeux atteints d'un léger/fort s.** eyes with a slight/severe squint

stradivarius [stradivarjys] NM *Mus (instrument)* Stradivarius

strangulation [strãgylasjɔ̃] NF strangulation

strapontin [strapɔ̃tɛ̃] NM **1** *Aut, Théâtre etc* folding seat, tip-up seat **2** *Fig (fonction secondaire)* minor role

strasbourgeois, -oise [strazburʒwa, -waz] ADJ of *or* from Strasbourg
▪ N **S.** *(natif)* native of Strasbourg; *(habitant)* inhabitant of Strasbourg

stras(s) [stras] NM *(clinquant)* paste, strass; *Fig* **robe en s.** sequined dress

stratagème [strataʒɛm] NM stratagem

strate [strat] NF *Géol, Fig* stratum, layer

stratège [stratɛʒ] NM strategist

stratégie [strateʒi] NF strategy; **s. commerciale** business strategy; **s. concurrentielle** competitive strategy; *Mktg* **s. de créneau unique** single niching; *Mktg* **s. de créneaux multiples** multiple-niche strategy; **s. électorale** election strategy; *Mktg* **s. d'encerclement** encirclement strategy; **s. de l'entreprise** corporate strategy; **s. globale de l'entreprise** overall business strategy; *Mktg* **s. d'imitation** imitation *or* me-too strategy; *Mktg* **s. de marque** brand strategy; **s. (de) mercatique** game plan, marketing strategy; *Mktg* **s. de niche unique** single-niche strategy; *Mktg* **s. poussée** *ou* **'pousser'** push strategy; *Mktg* **s. du prétendant** challenger strategy; *Mktg* **s. du suiveur** follower strategy; *Mktg* **s. tirée** *ou* **'tirer'** pull strategy

stratégique [strateʒik] ADJ strategic

stratégiquement [strateʒikmã] ADV strategically

stratification [stratifikasjɔ̃] NF stratification; **s. sociale** social stratification

stratifié [stratifje] ADJ stratified; *Tech (papier, tissu etc)* laminated ▪ NM laminate

stratifier [stratifje] VT to stratify

strato-cumulus [stratokymylys] NM INV *Météo* stratocumulus

stratosphère [stratosfɛr] NF *Météo* stratosphere

stratosphérique [stratosferik] ADJ stratospheric

stratus [stratys] NM INV *Météo* stratus

streamer [strimœr] NM *Ordinat* tape streamer

streptocoque [strɛptɔkɔk] NM *(bactérie)* streptococcus

streptomycine [strɛptɔmisin] NF *Méd* streptomycin

stress [strɛs] NM stress; **être en proie au s.** to be under stress; **maladie due au s.** stress-related illness

stressant [strɛsã] ADJ stressful

stresser [strɛse] VT **s. qn** *(d'un travail, d'une activité)* to put sb under stress, *Fam* to stress sb out; **être stressé** to be under stress, *Fam* to be stressed out; **elle/vivre à Paris me stresse** I find her/living in Paris very stressful

stretch® [strɛtʃ] NM *(tissu)* stretch material; **jupe en s.** stretch skirt

striation [strijasjɔ̃] NF striation

strict [strikt] ADJ **1** *(obligation, principes etc)* strict; *(essentiel, minimum)* bare; **au sens s.** in the strict sense; **dans la plus stricte intimité** strictly in private; **c'est la stricte vérité** it's the simple or absolute truth; **c'est son droit le plus s.** it's his absolute right **2** *(personne)* strict *(sur* about); **ils sont très stricts sur la politesse** they're very strict about politeness **3** *(costume, coupe de cheveux)* severe

strictement [striktəmã] ADV **1** *(rigoureusement)* strictly; **s. interdit** *ou* **défendu** strictly forbidden; **s. confidentiel** strictly confidential; **je ne comprends s. rien** I don't understand a (single) thing **2** *(sévèrement) (habillé etc)* severely

striction [striksjɔ̃] NF *Méd* constriction

stricto sensu [striktosɛsy] ADV strictly speaking

strident [stridã] ADJ strident, shrill

stridulation [stridylasjɔ̃] NF stridulation

strie [stri] NF **1** *(sillon)* groove; *(en relief)* ridge; *Anat, Bot, Géol* stria **2** *(de couleur)* streak

strié [strije] ADJ **1** *(sillonné)* grooved; *(en relief)* ridged; *Anat, Bot, Géol* striated **2** *(rayé)* (marbre etc) streaked

strier [strije] VT *(impf, pr sub* n. **striions,** v. **striiez) 1** *(sillonner)* to groove; *(en relief)* to ridge **2** *(rayer)* to streak

string [striŋ] NM *(maillot de bain)* tanga; *(slip)* G-string

stringer [striŋœr] NM *Journ* stringer

stringman [striŋman] NM *Journ* stringer

strioscopie [strijɔskɔpi] NF *Opt* schlieren photography

stripper [stripœr] NM *Chir (instrument)* stripper

stripping [stripiŋ] NM *Méd, Pétr etc* stripping

strip-tease, *pl* **strip-teases** [striptiz] NM striptease; **faire un s.** to do a striptease *or* strip

strip-teaseur [striptizœr] NM male stripper

strip-teaseuse, *pl* **strip-teaseuses** [striptizøz] NF stripper, striptease artist(e)

striure [strijyr] NF striation

stroboscope [strɔbɔskɔp] NM *Opt* stroboscope

stroboscopique [strɔbɔskɔpik] ADJ stroboscopic, strobe

strombolien [strɔ̃bɔljɛ̃] ADJ *Géog* Strombolian

strontium [strɔ̃sjɔm] NM *Chimie* strontium

strophe [strɔf] NF *Littér* stanza

structural, -ale, -aux, -ales [stryktyral, -o] ADJ structural; *Ling* **analyse structurale** structural analysis

structuralement [stryktyralmã] ADV structurally

structuralisme [stryktyralism] NM structuralism

structuraliste [stryktyralist] ADJ, N structuralist

structurant [stryktyrã] ADJ structuring

structuration [stryktyrasjɔ̃] NF structuring

structure [stryktyr] NF structure; **fauteuil à s. métallique** metal-framed armchair ▪▪▪ **s. d'accueil** *(pour minorités)* reception facilities; **s. administrative** administrative structure; *Ordinat* **s. en anneau** ring structure; *Ordinat* **s. arborescente** directory *or* tree structure; *Ordinat* **s. en arbre** tree structure; *Ordinat* **s. de bloc** block structure; *Ordinat* **s. en bus** bus structure; **s. de l'entreprise** company *or* corporate structure; *Ordinat* **s. en étoile** star structure; *Ordinat* **s. de fichier** file structure; **s. hiérarchique** line organization; **s. du marché** market structure; **s. des prix** price structure; **s. des salaires** wage structure

structuré [stryktyre] ADJ structured; *Ordinat* **fichier non s.** flat file

structurel, -elle [stryktyrɛl] ADJ structural; **chômage s.** structural unemployment

structurellement [stryktyrɛlmã] ADV structurally

structurer [stryktyre] VT to structure

strume [strym] NF *Méd, Arch* **1** *(goitre)* goitre **2** *(scrofule)* scrofula

strychnine [striknin] NF *Chimie, Pharm* strychnine

stuc [styk] NM *Constr* stucco; **décoration en s.** stucco decoration

stucage [stykaʒ] NM *Constr* stucco work

stucateur [stykatœr] NM stucco worker

studieusement [stydjøzmã] ADV studiously

studieux, -ieuse [stydjø, -jøz] ADJ *(personne)* studious; *(vacances etc)* study

studio [stydjo] NM **1** *Cin, Phot, TV, Beaux-Arts etc* studio; **tourné en s.** shot in studio **2** *(logement)* studio *or* one-roomed flat, *Am* studio apartment

▪▪ *TV, Radio* **s. d'annonceur** announcer studio; **s. de cinéma** film studio; **s. de danse** dance studio; **s. de doublage** dubbing suite; **s. d'enregistrement** recording *or* sound studio; **s. de peintre** artist's studio; **s. de photographe** photographer's studio; *TV, Cin* **s. de postproduction** postproduction studio; *TV, Cin* **s. de reportage** self-op studio; **s. de télévision** television studio

stupéfaction [stypefaksjɔ̃] NF stupefaction, amazement; **je constate avec s. que ...** I am amazed to note that ...

stupéfait [stypefɛ] ADJ stupefied, stunned, amazed (**de** by)

stupéfiant [stypefjã] ADJ **1** *Méd (substance)* stupefying, *Spéc* stupéfacient **2** *(nouvelles)* astounding, amazing ▪ NM *Méd* drug, narcotic, *Spéc* stupéfacient; **brigade des stupéfiants** drug squad

stupéfier [stypefje] VT *(impf, pr sub* n. **stupéfiions,** v. **stupéfiiez)** to stupefy, to stun, to amaze

stupeur [stypœr] NF **1** *Méd* stupor **2** *(étonnement)* amazement; **muet de s.** dumbfounded; **je constate avec s. que ...** I am amazed to note that ...

stupide [stypid] ADJ **1** *(idiot)* stupid, silly; **c'est s., mais je n'ai pas pu m'empêcher de le lui dire** it was stupid, but I couldn't stop myself telling him; **accident/mort s.** stupid *or* silly accident/death **2** *Litt (stupéfait)* stunned

stupidement [stypidmã] ADV stupidly; **rire s.** to give a stupid laugh; **mourir s.** to die a stupid death; **il m'a regardé faire s.** he stood there like an idiot and watched me

stupidité [stypidite] NF **1** *(caractère)* stupidity, foolishness **2** *(parole, acte)* stupid thing (**to say/do** etc); **dire/faire des stupidités** to say/do stupid things; **répondre par une s.** to give a silly answer

stupre [stypr] NM *Litt* debauchery

stups [styp] NMPL *Fam (abrév* **stupéfiants)** **la Brigade des s., les s.** the Drug Squad

stuquer [styke] VT *Constr* to stucco

style [stil] NM **1** *Littér, Archit, Gram etc* style; **j'ai envie de changer de s.** I want to change my style; **elle a beaucoup de s.** she has a lot of style, she's very stylish; **tourner ses phrases avec s.** to have a stylish turn of phrase; **s. de vie** lifestyle; **ce skieur a un beau s.** this skier has (a) good style; **ce chapeau est tout à fait ton s.** this hat is just your style; *Fam Péj* **ça serait bien son s.!** that would be just like him *or* just his style!; **dans le s. de** in the style of; **une veste un peu dans le s. de la tienne** a jacket in the same sort of style as yours; **meubles de s.** period furniture; **meubles s. Louis XIII/Régence** Louis XIII-/Regency-style furniture

2 *Antiq (pour écrire)* stylus, style

3 *(pour enregistrer un disque)* record cutter; *(d'appareil enregistreur)* (recording) needle

4 *(de cadran solaire)* style, pin, gnomon; *(de baromètre)* hand

5 *Bot* style

stylé[1] [stile] ADJ *Biol* stylate

stylé[2] ADJ *(domestique etc)* trained

styler [stile] VT *(domestique etc)* to train

stylet [stilɛ] NM **1** *(poignard)* stiletto **2** *Chir* stylet, probe **3** *Zool* stylet **4** *Ordinat* **s. lumineux** light pen

stylicien [stilisjɛ̃] NM designer

stylique [stilik] NF design

stylisation [stilizasjɔ̃] NF stylization

styliser [stilize] VT *Beaux-Arts etc* to stylize

stylisme [stilism] NM **1** *Littér* attention to style **2** *Com, Ind* designing

styliste [stilist] N **1** *Littér* stylist **2** *Com, Ind* designer

stylisticien, -ienne [stilistisjɛ̃, -jɛn] N expert in stylistics

stylistique [stilistik] ADJ stylistic
NF stylistics

stylite [stilit] NM *Hist, Rel* stylite

stylo [stilo] NM pen; **s. à encre** *ou* **à plume** fountain pen; **s. bille, s. bic**® ballpoint (pen), *Br* Biro®; *Ordinat* **s. électronique** electronic pen; **s. optique** light pen

stylo-feutre, *pl* **stylos-feutres** NM felt-tip (pen)

stylographe [stilɔgraf] NM *Arch* fountain pen

Stylomine® [stilomin] NM propelling pencil

stylo-surligneur, *pl* **stylo-surligneurs** NM highlighter

styptique [stiptik] ADJ, NM *Méd* styptic

styrax [stiraks] NM *Bot* styrax

styrène [stirɛn] NM *Chimie* styrene

Styx [stiks] NM le S. the Styx

su [sy] PP *voir* savoir[1]
NM au su de to the knowledge of; **au vu et au su de qn** right in front of sb; **elle l'a fait au vu et au su de tout le monde** she did it quite openly *or* for all the world to see

suage[1] [sɥaʒ] NM *(du bois etc)* sweating, oozing

suage[2] NM *(d'un bougeoir, d'un plat en étain etc)* fillet (border)

suaire [sɥɛr] NM **1** *Litt (linceul)* winding sheet, shroud **2** *Rel* **le saint s.** the holy shroud

suant [sɥɑ̃] ADJ **1** *Fam* sweating, sweaty **2** *Arg (ennuyeux)* boring

suave [sɥav] ADJ **1** *(musique, odeur, goût etc)* sweet **2** *Fig (ton, manières)* suave, smooth

Il faut noter que le terme anglais **suave** ne se rapporte pas aux sens et a le plus souvent une connotation péjorative.

suavement [sɥavmɑ̃] ADV *(parler)* suavely

suavité [sɥavite] NF **1** *(d'un parfum, d'une mélodie)* sweetness **2** *(des manières)* suavity

subaigu, -uë [sybegy] ADJ *Méd* subacute

subalpin [sybalpɛ̃] ADJ subalpine

subalterne [sybaltɛrn] ADJ *(officier, position, rôle)* subordinate, minor; *(esprit)* inferior; *(employé)* junior
NM subordinate; *Mil (grade)* subaltern

subaquatique [sybakwatik] ADJ subaquatic, underwater

subatomique [sybatɔmik] ADJ subatomic

subconscient [sybkɔ̃sjɑ̃] ADJ, NM subconscious

subdiviser [sybdivize] VT to subdivide
VPR se subdiviser to be subdivided

subdivision [sybdivizjɔ̃] NF subdivision

subéquatorial, -ale, -aux, -ales [sybekwatɔrjal, -o] ADJ *Géog* subequatorial

subéreux, -euse [syberø, -øz] ADJ *Bot* suberose, corky

subir [sybir] VT *(procès, examen, opération, torture, changement etc)* to undergo; *(mort, violence, conséquences)* to suffer; *(sentence)* to serve; *(influence)* to be under; *(défaite, pertes)* to suffer, to sustain; **s. une majoration** to increase, to rise; **il commence à s. les contrecoups de la crise économique** he's starting to suffer the effects of the economic crisis; **s. qn** to put up with sb; **je ne veux pas avoir à le s. tout le week-end!** I don't want to have to put up with *or* suffer him all weekend!; **faire s. qch à qn** to subject sb to sth

subit [sybi] ADJ *(mort, changement)* sudden, unexpected

subitement [sybitmɑ̃] ADV suddenly, all of a sudden

subito [sybito] ADV *Fam* all of a sudden; *(immédiatement)* at once; **s. presto** at once

subjectif, -ive [sybʒɛktif, -iv] ADJ subjective; *Gram* **cas s.** nominative case

subjectivement [sybʒɛktivmɑ̃] ADV subjectively

subjectivisme [sybʒɛktivism] NM *Phil* subjectivism

subjectivité [sybʒɛktivite] NF subjectivity; **propos pleins de s.** subjective remarks

subjonctif, -ive [sybʒɔ̃ktif, -iv] SEE GRAMMAR A53–4; B32-4 *Gram* ADJ *(mode)* subjunctive
NM subjunctive; **au s.** in the subjunctive

subjugation [sybʒygasjɔ̃] NF subjugation

subjuguer [sybʒyge] VT *(personnes, nation)* to subjugate, to subdue; *(cheval)* to subdue, to master; *Fig (audience, cœurs etc)* to captivate, to enthral

sublimation [syblimasjɔ̃] NF *Chimie, Psy* sublimation

sublimatoire [syblimatwar] ADJ sublimatory

sublime [syblim] ADJ sublime; *Fam* **ça n'a rien de s.** it's nothing to write home about
NM le s. the sublime

sublimé [syblime] ADJ sublimated
NM *Chimie* sublimate

sublimement [syblimmɑ̃] ADV sublimely

sublimer [syblime] VT *Chimie, Psy* to sublimate

subliminaire [sybliminɛr], **subliminal, -ale, -aux, -ales** [sybliminal, -o] ADJ subliminal; **publicité s.** *ou* **subliminale** subliminal advertising

sublimité [syblimite] NF *Litt* sublimeness

sublingual, -ale, -aux, -ales [syblɛ̃gwal, -o] ADJ *Anat (glande etc)* sublingual; *Pharm* **comprimé s.** tablet to be placed under the tongue

submerger [sybmɛrʒe] VT (je **submergeai(s); n. submergeons**) **1** *(pré etc)* to submerge, to flood; *(bateau)* to submerge, to swamp; *(objet)* to submerge; *Fig* **ville submergée par les touristes** town inundated with *or* overrun by tourists **2** *Fig (quelqu'un)* to overwhelm; **être submergé de travail** to be snowed under *or* overwhelmed with work; **depuis que son troisième enfant est né, elle est submergée** she's been snowed under since the birth of her third child

submersible [sybmɛrsibl] ADJ **1** *(bateau)* submersible **2** *Bot (plante)* submerged **3** *(sol)* liable to flooding
NM *Naut* submarine

submersion [sybmɛrsjɔ̃] NF submersion, flooding; **mort par s.** death by drowning

subodorer [sybɔdɔre] VT *Fam (danger, complot etc)* to suspect; **il a subodoré quelque chose** he smelt a rat

subordination [sybɔrdinasjɔ̃] NF subordination; **complément/conjonction de s.** subordinating complement/conjunction

subordonnant [sybɔrdɔnɑ̃] ADJ *Gram (conjonction etc)* subordinating SEE GRAMMAR A74-6; B58

subordonné, -ée [sybɔrdɔne] ADJ **1** *Gram (proposition)* subordinate **2** *(dépendant)* subordinate (à to); **c'est s. aux revenus de l'année précédente** it is subject to the previous year's income
N *(personne)* subordinate
NF *Gram* **subordonnée** subordinate clause

subordonner [sybɔrdɔne] VT to subordinate (à to); *Fig* **s. ses dépenses à ses revenus** to cut one's coat according to one's cloth, to live within one's means; **le service est subordonné au nombre des voyageurs** the service depends on the number of travellers
VPR **se subordonner se s. à qn** to subordinate oneself to sb

subornation [sybɔrnasjɔ̃] NF *Jur* subornation, bribing

suborner [sybɔrne] VT **1** *Jur (témoin)* to suborn, to bribe **2** *Litt (séduire) (femme)* to seduce

suborneur, -euse [sybɔrnœr, -øz] N *Jur (d'un témoin)* suborner, briber
NM *Litt (séducteur)* seducer

subreptice [sybrɛptis] ADJ surreptitious

subrepticement [sybrɛptismɑ̃] ADV surreptitiously

subrogation [sybrɔgasjɔ̃] NF *Jur* subrogation, substitution

subrogé, -ée [sybrɔʒe] ADJ subrogated; *(gardien)* deputy, surrogate
N *Rel, Jur* surrogate, deputy

subroger [sybrɔʒe] VT (je **subrogeai(s); n. subrogeons**) *Jur* to subrogate, to substitute

subséquemment [sypsekamɑ̃, sybs-] ADV *Jur, Litt* subsequently

subséquent [sypsekɑ̃, sybs-] ADJ *Jur, Géog, Litt* subsequent

subside [sypsid, sybz-] NM subsidy, grant; **vivre des subsides de l'État** to live on state grants *or* subsidies

subsidence [sypsidɑ̃s, sybz-] NF *Géol* subsidence

subsidiaire [sypsidjɛr, sybz-] ADJ subsidiary; **question s.** tie-breaker

subsidiairement [sypsidjɛrmɑ̃, sybz-] ADV subsidiarily; **s. à** in addition to

subsidiarité [sypsidjarite, sybz-] NF *UE* subsidiarity

subsistance [sybzistɑ̃s] NF **1** *(survie)* subsistence; **pourvoir à la s. de sa famille** to keep *or* support one's family; **moyen de s.** means of support **2 subsistances** *(vivres)* provisions; *Mil* supplies

subsistant [sybzistɑ̃] ADJ remaining, existing

subsister [sybziste] VI **1** *(d'une chose)* to survive, to remain **2** *(d'une personne)* to live, *Fml* to subsist (**de** on); **moyens de s.** means of support; **cela lui suffit à peine à s.** it's barely enough for him to live on

subsonique [sypsɔnik, sybs-] ADJ *Aviat* subsonic

substance [sypstɑ̃s] NF **1** *(essentiel) (d'un article etc)* substance, gist; **sans s.** *(arguments etc)* insubstantial; **en s.** in substance; **voici en s. de quoi nous avons parlé** this is the gist of what we were talking about **2** *(matière)* substance, matter; **s. étrangère** extraneous substance; **plaie avec perte de s.** wound with loss of tissue; *Anat* **s. grise** grey matter

substantialité [sypstɑ̃sjalite] NF *Phil* substantiality

substantiel, -ielle [sypstɑ̃sjɛl] ADJ substantial

substantiellement [sypstɑ̃sjɛlmɑ̃] ADV substantially

substantif, -ive [sypstɑ̃tif, -iv] *Gram* ADJ nominal
NM noun, substantive

substantifique [sypstɑ̃tifik] ADJ **la s. moelle** *(d'un texte etc)* the essence, the pith

substantivement [sypstɑ̃tivmɑ̃] ADJ *Gram* as a noun, substantively

substantiver [sypstɑ̃tive] *Gram* VT **s. un verbe/un adjectif** to use a verb/an adjective as a noun *or* substantively
VPR **se substantiver** to be used as a noun *or* substantively

substituer [sypstitɥe] VT **1** *(remplacer)* to substitute (à for); **s. un objet à un autre** to substitute one object for another, to replace one object by another **2** *Jur* **s. un héritier** to appoint an heir in succession to another *or* failing another; **s. un héritage** to entail an estate

VPR se substituer se s. à qn/à qch to substitute for sb/sth, to take the place of sb/sth; **tu ne peux tout de même pas te s. à son père!** you can't take the place of his/her father!

substitut [sypstity] NM substitute (**de** for); *Jur* deputy public prosecutor; **un s. de père** a surrogate father; **s. de repas** meal substitute; *Mktg* **s. rapproché** close substitute

substitution [sypstitysjɔ̃] NF **1** (*remplacement*) substitution (**à** for); **son père de s.** his/her surrogate father **2** *Jur* **s. d'enfant** switching round of babies

substrat [sypstra] NM *Géol, Ling, Phil* substratum; *Phot, Biol, Ordinat* substrate

subterfuge [sypterfyʒ] NM subterfuge; **user de s.** to resort to subterfuge

subtil [syptil] ADJ **1** (*fin*) (*plaisanterie, remarque*) subtle; (*esprit, humour etc*) subtle, discerning **2** (*ténu*) (*distinction, différence etc*) subtle, fine **3** *Arch* (*fluide*) tenuous, thin; (*poussière*) fine **4** (*qui pénètre*) (*poison, odeur etc*) pervasive

subtilement [syptilmɑ̃] ADV subtly

subtiliser [syptilize] VT **1** *Fam* (*dérober*) to pinch, *Br* to nick (**à** from); **on lui a subtilisé son portefeuille** he's had his wallet pinched **2** *Arch* (*substance*) to refine
VI (*en raisonnant*) to split hairs, to be oversubtle

subtilité [syptilite] NF **1** (*de l'esprit, d'une manœuvre etc*) subtlety **2** (*d'une distinction*) subtlety, fineness **3** (*d'un argument etc*) subtlety; **les subtilités de la langue** the subtleties of the language

subtropical, -ale, -aux, -ales [syptrɔpikal, -o] ADJ subtropical

suburbain [sybyrbɛ̃] ADJ suburban

subvenir [sybvənir] (*conj like* **venir**; *aux* **avoir**) VI **s. à** (*besoins*) to provide for; (*dépenses*) to meet; **s. aux dépenses de sa famille** to provide for one's family

subvention [sybvɑ̃sjɔ̃] NF subsidy, grant; **subventions en capital** capital grants; **s. aux entreprises** development grant; **recevoir** *ou* **toucher des subventions** to get a subsidy, to be subsidized; **s. d'exploitation** operating subsidy; **s. à l'exportation** export subsidy

subventionner [sybvɑ̃sjɔne] VT (*entreprise, institution etc*) to subsidize, to grant (financial) aid to; **subventionné** (*industrie, théâtre etc*) subsidized; (*école*) maintained, grant-aided

subversif, -ive [sybvɛrsif, -iv] ADJ subversive

subversion [sybvɛrsjɔ̃] NF subversion

subversivement [sybvɛrsivmɑ̃] ADV subversively

subvertir [sybvɛrtir] VT *Litt* to subvert

suc [syk] NM **1** (*de fruit, viande*), *Physiol* juice; *Bot* sap; **s. gastrique** gastric juice **2** *Fig Litt* (*de texte etc*) essence

succédané [syksedane] ADJ, NM *aussi Méd* substitute (**de** for); **s. de café** coffee substitute; *Fig* **un s. de Truffaut** a second-rate Truffaut

succéder [syksede] (**je succède, n. succédons; je succéderai**) VI **s. à qn/qch** to succeed sb/sth, to take over from sb/sth; **un sentiment de pitié succéda à sa rage** his/ her anger gave way to a feeling of pity; **les champs succèdent aux bois** (the) fields give way to woods; **s. au trône** to succeed to the throne; **s. à une fortune** to inherit a fortune
VPR se succéder les révolutions se succédèrent revolution followed revolution, there was a succession of revolutions; **les générations qui se sont succédé** the generations

that followed each other; **les journées se succédaient** day followed day, the days followed each other

succès [syksɛ] NM success; **avoir du s.** to be successful *or* a success; **ne pas avoir de s.** to be unsuccessful; **elle a un grand s. auprès des hommes** she is very successful *or* has great success with men; **se vanter de ses s.** to boast about one's success; **remporter un beau/de grands s.** to have *or* achieve great success; **passer un examen avec s.** to pass an exam; **sans s.** (*utilisé adjectivement*) unsuccessful; (*utilisé adverbialement*) unsuccessfully; **j'ai essayé de le convaincre, mais sans s.** I tried to convince him, but without success *or* I was unsuccessful; **une seconde tentative n'eut pas plus de s.** a second attempt met with no more success *or* was no more successful; **je n'ai pas eu de s. avec ma proposition** I was unsuccessful *or* had no success with my proposal; *Sport* **le plus beau s. de l'équipe** the team's greatest success; **livre à s., s. de librairie** bestseller; **auteur à s.** bestselling author; **chanteur/ acteur à s.** successful singer/actor; **pièce/ chanson à s.** hit play/song; **remporter un** *ou* **avoir grand s.** (*d'une pièce de théâtre etc*) to be a great *or* a huge success; **le public a fait un s. à ce livre/cette pièce/ce film** the book/play/film has been well received (by the public); **s. fou** great success; **s. d'audience** ratings success, *Fam* big *or* smash hit (**auprès de, parmi** with); **les casquettes de baseball ont un s. fou auprès des jeunes** baseball caps are big *or* a big hit with young people

successeur [syksesœr] NM successor (**de** to, **of**)

successif, -ive [syksesif, -iv] ADJ successive

succession [syksesjɔ̃] NF **1** (*série*) (*d'idées, de sons, de jours etc*) succession, series; (*de personnes, d'admirateurs etc*) stream, succession; **s. de catastrophes** series *or* catalogue of disasters **2** (*au trône, au pouvoir etc*) succession (**à** to); **la s. du poste sera assurée par M. Dupont** Mr Dupont will take over the post; **prendre la s. d'une maison de commerce** to take over a business **3** *Jur* (*par héritage*) succession; (*biens*) inheritance; **droits de s.** death duties

successivement [syksesivmɑ̃] ADV successively

succinct [syksɛ̃] ADJ succinct, brief, concise; *Fam* **repas s.** frugal meal; **sois s.** be brief, keep it brief

succinctement [syksɛ̃tmɑ̃] ADV succinctly, briefly; *Fam* (*manger*) frugally

succion [sy(k)sjɔ̃] NF suction; **bruit de s.** sucking noise

succomber [sykɔ̃be] VI **1** (*tomber*) to succumb, to collapse; **s. sous le poids de qch** to collapse under the weight of sth; **s. sous le nombre** to yield to greater numbers; *Fig* **s. sous les soucis/les problèmes financiers** to be overwhelmed by worries/financial problems; **s. devant un adversaire** (*dans un combat*), *Fig* to yield to an opponent **2 s. à** (*peine, tentation etc*) to succumb to, to yield to; (*émotion*) to be overcome by; **j'ai succombé à la fatigue** I succumbed to fatigue **3** (*mourir*) to die, to succumb

succube [sykyb] NM succubus, succuba

succulence [sykylɑ̃s] NF *Litt* succulence

succulent [sykylɑ̃] ADJ (*nourriture*) succulent; *Bot* (*feuille*) fleshy; **plante succulente** succulent

succursale [sykyrsal] NF *Com* branch; **magasin à succursales** chain store

sucer [syse] (**je suçai(s); n. suçons**) VT **1** (*lait, orange, os etc*) to suck; **comprimés à s.** (*sur boîte*) to be sucked; **s. son pouce** to suck

one's thumb; *Vieilli* **s. qch avec le lait** to take sth in with one's mother's milk; *Fig Fam* **s. qn jusqu'au dernier sou** *ou* **jusqu'à la moelle des os** to suck sb dry, to bleed sb white; *Arg* **s. la poire à qn** to French-kiss sb; **ils sont tout le temps à se s. la poire** they're always snogging; *Fam* **il ne suce pas que de la glace** he drinks like a fish **2** *Vulg* (*sexuellement*) **s. qn** (*fellation*) to go down on sb, to give sb head; (*cunnilinctus*) to go down on sb
VPR se sucer 1 se s. les doigts to suck one's fingers; *Arg* **se s. la poire** to snog **2 ces cachets se sucent** these tablets are (meant) to be sucked *or* are for sucking

sucette [sysɛt] NF **1** (*de bébé*) dummy, *Am* pacifier **2** (*confiserie*) lollipop, *Fam* lolly **3** *Fam* **partir en s.** to go down the tubes *or* pan

suceur, -euse [sysœr, -øz] N *Péj* **s. de sang** (*personne*) bloodsucker
NM 1 (*poisson*) sucker, sucking fish **2** (*d'aspirateur*) nozzle
NF suceuse (*drague*) suction dredger

suçon [sysɔ̃] NM *Fam* lovebite, *Am* hickey; **faire un s. à qn** to give sb a lovebite *or Am* hickey

suçoter [sysɔte] VT *Fam* to suck (at)

sucrage [sykraʒ] NM (*du vin*) sugaring

sucrant [sykrɑ̃] ADJ sweetening; **avoir un grand pouvoir s.** to be a strong sweetener; **produit s.** sweetener

sucrase [sykraz] NF *Chimie* sucrase

sucre [sykr] NM **1** (*substance*) sugar; **s. en pains** loaf sugar; **pain de s.** sugar loaf; **montagne en pain de s.** sugar-loaf mountain; **un s. dans mon café** one sugar in my coffee; **vous le prenez avec ou sans s., votre café?** do you take sugar in your coffee or not?; **fruit au s.** fruit sprinkled with sugar; **décorations en s.** sugar decorations; *Fig Fam* **il a été tout s. tout miel** he was all sweetness and light; *Fig* **elle n'est pas en s.!** she's not made of glass!; *Fam* **mon bébé en s.** my sweetie pie; *Fam* **c'est un vrai s.** he's a honey; *Can* **partie de s.** sugaring-off party; *Fam* **casser du s. sur le dos de qn** to bad-mouth sb, *Br* to slag sb off **2** (*monnaie*) sucre
▸▸ **s. de betterave** beet sugar; **s. brut** unrefined sugar; **s. de canne** cane sugar; **s. cristallisé** granulated sugar; **s. de fruit** fructose; **s. glace** icing *or Am* confectioner's sugar; *Chimie* **s. de lait** lactose; **s. en morceaux** lump sugar, sugar lumps; **s. d'orge** barley sugar; *Can* **s. du pays** maple sugar; **s. en poudre** caster sugar; **s. roux** brown sugar; **s. semoule** caster sugar

sucré, -ée [sykre] ADJ **1** (*naturellement*) (*aliment, substance, goût etc*) sweet **2** (*additionné de sucre*) (*à la fabrication*) sweetened; (*café etc*) sugared, sweetened; **boisson non sucrée** unsweetened drink; **eau sucrée** sugar and water; **mon thé est trop s.** my tea is too sweet, there's too much sugar in my tea **3** *Fig* (*paroles, manières, sourire*) sugary; **prendre un ton s.** to speak in a smarmy tone
N faire le/la sucré(e) to be all sweetness and light

sucrer [sykre] VT **1** to sugar, to sweeten; **s. son café** to sugar one's coffee; **je ne sucre pas mes yaourts** I don't put sugar in my yoghurt; *Fig Fam* **s. les fraises** (*trembler*) to shake; (*être gâteux*) to be an old dodderer **2** *Fig Fam* (*supprimer*) (*passage, émission etc*) to cut; **on lui a sucré sa prime** he has had his bonus taken away; **on ne va pas me s. mes vacances!** I'm not going to have my holidays cancelled!
VI (*du miel etc*) to sweeten
VPR se sucrer 1 *Fam* (*prendre du sucre*) to help oneself to sugar **2** *Arg* (*faire des bénéfices*) to line one's pockets

sucrerie [sykrəri] NF **1** (*usine*) sugar refinery

2 sucreries *(friandises)* confectionery, sweets, *surtout Am* candy; **dans votre condition il faut éviter les sucreries** you must avoid eating sweet things in your condition; **aimer les sucreries** to have a sweet tooth **3** *Can (forêt)* maple tree grove

sucrette [sykrɛt] **NF** artificial sweetener

sucrier, -ière [sykrije, -jɛr] **ADJ** sugar; **industrie sucrière** sugar industry
  N *(fabricant)* sugar manufacturer
  NM *(récipient)* sugar bowl *or* basin; **s. verseur** sugar shaker

sud [syd] **NM** *(no pl)* **1** *(point cardinal)* south; **au s., dans le s.** in the south; **où est le s.?** which way is south?; **la partie la plus au s. de l'île** the southernmost part of the island; **le vent vient du s.** it's a south *or* southerly wind, the wind is coming from the south; **un vent du s.** a southerly wind; **le vent du s.** the south wind; **aller au** *ou* **vers le s.** to go south *or* southwards; **les trains qui vont vers le s.** trains going south, southbound trains; **rouler vers le s.** to drive south *or* southwards; **aller droit vers le s.** to head due south; **la cuisine est plein s.** *ou* **exposée au s.** the kitchen faces due south
  2 *(partie d'un pays, d'un continent)* south, southern area *or* regions; *(partie d'une ville)* south; **le s. de l'Italie** southern Italy, the south of Italy; **dans le s. de l'Espagne** in southern Spain, in the south of Spain; **elle habite dans le s.** she lives in the South; **il habite dans le s. de Paris** he lives in the south of Paris; **elle est du s.** she's from the south; **les gens du s.** people who live in the south
  ADJ INV *(côté, face)* south; *(banlieue, partie, région)* southern; **le pôle S.** the South Pole; **le Pacifique S.** South Pacific; **la façade s. d'un immeuble** the south-facing wall of a building; **la chambre est côté s.** the bedroom faces south; **dans la partie s. de la France** in the South of France, in southern France; **suivre la direction s.** to head *or* to go southward

sud-africain, -aine, *pl* **sud-africain(e)s** **ADJ** South African; **la République sud-africaine** the Republic of South Africa
  N S. South African

sud-américain, -aine, *pl* **sud-américain(e)s** **ADJ** South American
  N S. South American

sudation [sydasjɔ̃] **NF** *Méd etc* sudation, sweating

sud-coréen, -enne, *pl* **sud-coréen(ne)s** **ADJ** South Korean
  N S. South Korean

sud-est [sydɛst] **NM INV 1** *(point cardinal)* south-east; **au s. de Paris** south-east of Paris **2** *Géog* **le S. asiatique** South East Asia
  ADJ INV south-east

sudiste [sydist] *Hist* **N** *(de la guerre de Sécession)* Confederate
  ADJ Southern

sudorifère [sydɔrifɛr] **ADJ** = **sudoripare**

sudorifique [sydɔrifik] **ADJ, NM** *Pharm* sudorific

sudoripare [sydɔripar] **ADJ** *Anat* sudoriferous; **glande s.** sweat gland

sud-ouest **NM INV** *(point cardinal)* south-west **2** *(vent)* south-west *or* south-westerly wind
  ADJ INV south-west

Sud-Ouest africain NM *Hist* South West Africa

sud-sud-est NM INV south-south-east
  ADJ INV south-south-east

sud-sud-ouest NM INV south-south-west
  ADJ INV south-south-west

sud-vietnamien, -ienne, *pl* **sud-vietnamien(ne)s** **ADJ** South Vietnamese
  N S. South Vietnamese

Suède [sɥɛd] **NF** Sweden

suédé [sɥede] **ADJ, NM** suede

suédine [sɥedin] **NF** *Tex* suedette

suédois, -oise [sɥedwa, -waz] VOIR GRAMMAIRE A19 **ADJ** Swedish; *Gym* **la gymnastique suédoise** Swedish gymnastics *or* exercises
  NM *Ling* Swedish
  N S. Swede

suée [sɥe] **NF** *Fam (transpiration)* sweat; *(sous l'effet de la peur)* (cold) sweat; **prendre une s.** to get up *or* work up a sweat; **cela m'a donné une sacrée s.** *(d'un travail)* I sweated blood over it; *(d'une expérience effrayante)* it brought me out in a cold sweat; **j'en ai encore des suées** I still break out in a cold sweat when I think about it

suer [sɥe] **VI 1** *(d'une personne)* to sweat; **s. à grosses gouttes** to be pouring with sweat, to be sweating buckets; *Fam* **faire s. qn** *(embêter)* to annoy sb; **ça me fait s. d'aller à cette soirée** it's a drag having to go to that party; **ce que j'ai pu me faire s. pendant les vacances** I was bored stiff during the holidays, the holidays were a real drag; **tu me fais s. à la fin avec tes devoirs!** you're getting on my nerves with your homework!
  2 *(des murs etc)* to ooze
  3 *(travailler)* to labour, *Am* to labor, to sweat; *Fam* **faire s. le burnous** to use sweated labour
  VT to sweat; *Fig (piété, ennui, hypocrisie etc)* to ooze; *Fig* **s. sang et eau** to sweat blood and tears; **cette banlieue sue la tristesse** this suburb positively exudes dreariness

sueur [sɥœr] **NF** sweat; **son visage ruisselait de s.** his/her face was streaming with sweat; **être en s.** to be sweating *or* in a sweat; **avoir des sueurs froides** to be in a cold sweat; **j'en ai encore des sueurs froides, rien que d'y penser** I get in a cold sweat just thinking about it; **à la s. de son front** by the sweat of one's brow; **le fruit de mes sueurs** the fruits of my labour *or Am* labor

Suez [sɥez] **N** Suez; **le canal de S.** the Suez Canal

suffire [syfir] *(prp* **suffisant***; pp* **suffi***; pr ind* **je suffis, n. suffisons, ils suffisent***; pr sub* **je suffise***; impf* **je suffisais***; p hist* **je suffis***; fu* **je suffirai)** **VI** to be enough, to be sufficient; **cela ne me suffit pas (pour vivre)** that is not enough for me (to live on); **votre promesse me suffit** your promise is enough for me; *Prov* **à chaque jour suffit sa peine** sufficient unto the day is the evil thereof; **s. à qch/à faire qch** to be up to sth/to doing sth; **s. à la tâche** to be up to *or* equal to the job; **cela suffit à mes besoins** that's enough for my needs; **je n'y suffis plus** it's too much for me, I can't cope

  VPR se suffire il s'est toujours suffi he has always supported himself *or* earned his own living; **pays qui se suffisent (à eux-mêmes)** self-supporting countries

  V IMPERS il a suffi de quelques mots pour le persuader a few words were enough to persuade him; **il suffit de l'écouter pour …** one only has to *or* one need only listen to him to …; **il suffit qu'il le dise** all he has to do is say so; **ça ne lui suffit pas** that's not enough for him; **il te l'a promis, ça ne te suffit pas?** he's promised you, is that not enough?; **il suffisait que tu passes un coup de téléphone** all you had to do was phone; **ça suffit!, (il) suffit!** that's enough!, that'll do!; **il suffit d'une heure pour …** it only takes an hour to … SEE GRAMMAR B29–30

suffisamment [syfizamɑ̃] **ADV** enough, sufficiently; **agir sans avoir s. réfléchi** to act without sufficient thought; **s. de** enough, sufficient; **j'ai pris s. de temps à le lui expliquer** I took the time to explain it to him/her; **j'ai s. souffert pour savoir**

---

que … I've suffered enough to know that …

suffisance [syfizɑ̃s] **NF 1 avoir s. de** to have sufficient *or* enough; **manger à sa s.** to eat one's fill; **avoir de qch à s.** *ou* **en s.** to have sth in abundance, to have plenty of sth **2** *(vanité)* arrogance, self-importance; **il est d'une s. insupportable** he is unbearably conceited **3** *Arch (capacité)* competence; **homme de s.** competent man

suffisant, -ante [syfizɑ̃, -ɑ̃t] **ADJ 1** sufficient, enough; **c'est plus que s.** that is more than sufficient *or* enough **2** *(vaniteux)* *(air, ton)* self-important, conceited
  N faire le s. to give oneself airs

suffixe [syfiks] **NM** *Gram, Ordinat* suffix

suffixer [syfikse] **VT** *Gram, Ordinat* to suffix, to add a suffix to; **mot suffixé** word with *or* that has a suffix

suffocant [syfɔkɑ̃] **ADJ 1** *(chaleur etc)* suffocating, stifling **2** *Fig (nouvelle, réponse etc)* staggering, astounding

suffocation [syfɔkasjɔ̃] **NF** suffocation; *(crise)* choking fit

suffoquer [syfɔke] **VT 1** *(d'une odeur, de la fumée etc)* to suffocate, to stifle; *Fig (de nouvelles)* to stagger, to astound; **les sanglots la suffoquaient** she was choking with sobs **2** *Arch (tuer)* to suffocate
  VI to suffocate, to choke; **s. de colère/d'indignation** to choke with anger/indignation

suffragant [syfragɑ̃] *Rel* **ADJ** *(évêque)* suffragan
  NM suffragan (bishop)

suffrage [syfraʒ] **NM** *Pol (voix)* vote; *(système)* suffrage; **dix mille suffrages** ten thousand votes; **recueillir de nombreux suffrages** to win numerous votes; **s. universel** universal franchise *or* suffrage, one-man-one-vote; **s. direct/indirect** direct/indirect suffrage; *Fig* **ce nouveau modèle remporte tous les suffrages** this new model wins everyone's approval *or* is universally liked

suffragette [syfraʒɛt] **NF** *Hist, Pol* suffragette

suffusion [syfyzjɔ̃] **NF** *Méd* suffusion

suggérer [syɡʒere] **VT** (**je suggère, n. suggérons; je suggérerai**) to suggest (**à** to); **s. de faire qch** to suggest doing sth; **s. à qn de faire qch** to suggest to sb that he should do sth; **cette expression suggère la lumière/la vitesse** this expression suggests light/speed

suggestibilité [syɡʒɛstibilite] **NF** suggestibility

suggestible [syɡʒɛstibl] **ADJ** suggestible

suggestif, -ive [syɡʒɛstif, -iv] **ADJ 1** *(évocateur)* evocative, suggestive **2** *(érotique)* *(plaisanterie, geste etc)* suggestive; *(tenue, décolleté)* revealing

suggestion [syɡʒɛs(t)jɔ̃] **NF** suggestion; **agir sur la s. de qn** to act on sb's suggestion; **pas la moindre s. de …** not the slightest hint *or* suggestion of … VOIR GRAMMAIRE A59–60

suggestionner [syɡʒɛstjɔne] **VT s. qn** to put an idea *or* ideas into sb's head; **se laisser s.** to allow ideas to be put into one's head (**par** by)

suicidaire [sɥisidɛr] **ADJ** *(tendances, personne)*, *Fig (entreprise etc)* suicidal
  N suicidal person

suicide [sɥisid] **NM** *(acte)* suicide; **tentative de s.** suicide attempt; *Fig* **le s. économique d'un pays** the economic suicide of a country; **s. politique** political suicide; **attentat-s.** suicide attack; **avion-s.** suicide plane

suicidé, -ée [sɥiside] **ADJ** who has committed suicide
  N *(personne)* suicide

suicider (se) [səsɥiside] **VPR** to commit suicide; *Fig* **se s. politiquement** to commit political suicide

suie [sɥi] NF soot

suif [sɥif] NM **1** tallow; **s. de mouton** mutton fat; **chandelle de s.** tallow candle **2** *Arg Vieilli* **recevoir un s.** to get a dressing down; **faire du s.** to kick up a row; **chercher du s.** to be looking for a fight

suifer [sɥife] VT *(cuir etc)* to tallow; *(gond)* to grease

sui generis [sɥiʒeneris] ADJ INV sui generis; *Euph* **odeur s.** *(mauvaise)* distinctive smell

suint [sɥɛ̃] NM *(de laine)* suint

suintant [sɥɛ̃tɑ̃] ADJ *(mur etc)* oozing, dripping; *Méd* running, weeping

suintement [sɥɛ̃tmɑ̃] NM *(de rochers, de mur etc)* oozing, dripping; *(de blessure)* running, weeping

suinter [sɥɛ̃te] VI **1** *(de rocher, de mur etc)* to ooze, to drip **2** *(d'un navire)* to leak; *(d'une blessure)* to run, to weep
VT *(haine etc)* to exude, to ooze

Suisse [sɥis] NF Switzerland; **la S. alémanique/romande/italienne** German-/French-/Italian-speaking Switzerland

suisse [sɥis] ADJ Swiss
N S. Swiss; **les Suisses** the Swiss
NM **1** *Hist, Mil* Swiss mercenary; *(au Vatican)* Swiss guard; *Fam* **manger/boire en s.** to eat/drink on one's own **2** *Rel (en uniforme)* verger **3** **petit s.** petit suisse *(small cream cheese)* **4** *Can Zool* **s. (rayé)** chipmunk

Suissesse [sɥises] NF Swiss (woman)

suite [sɥit] NF **1** *(continuation)* continuation, what follows; *(au restaurant)* next course; **j'ai oublié la s. de la chanson** I've forgotten the rest of the song; **faire s. à** to follow (on from), to be a continuation of; **cette discussion fait s. à ce que nous disions l'autre jour** this discussion follows on from what we said the other day; **le repas qui fit s. à la cérémonie** the meal which followed the ceremony; **(comme) s. à notre lettre d'hier** further to our letter of yesterday; **à la s. de votre demande** further to or with reference to your request; *Com* **donner s. à** *(demande, lettre)* to follow up; *(commande)* to deal with; *(décision)* to give effect to; *Tél* **nous regrettons de ne pouvoir donner s. à votre appel** the number you have dialled has not been recognized; **pour s. à donner** (passed to you) for action; *Com* **sans s.** *(article)* discontinued; **prendre la s. des affaires d'une maison** to take over a business; **à la s. les uns des autres** one after the other; **il a avalé deux gâteaux à la s.** he swallowed two cakes one after the other; **à la s. de cette discussion** following (on) this discussion; **les historiens venus à sa s.** the historians who came after him/her; **les maux que la guerre traîne à sa s.** the evils that war brings in its wake; **se mettre à la s.** to join (the back of) the queue or *Am* the line

2 de s. *(à la suite)* in a row, in succession; **dix heures de s.** ten hours on end; **dix jours de s.** ten days running; **pendant plusieurs semaines de s.** for several weeks at a time or running; **et ainsi de s.** and so on

3 tout de s., *Fam* **de s.** at once, immediately; **je voudrais un café – oui, tout de s. Monsieur** I'd like a coffee – yes (sir), right away; **par la s.** later (on), afterwards

4 *(nouveau roman, film etc)* sequel; *(nouvel épisode)* continuation; *Journ* **s. à la page 30** continued on page 30; **s. et fin** concluded; **la s. au prochain numéro** continued in the next issue; *TV, Cin* **s. à l'américaine** sequel

5 *(de raisonnement)* coherence, consistency; **sans s.** *(paroles, pensées etc)* incoherent, disjointed, disconnected; *(parler)* incoherently, disjointedly; **s. dans les idées** single-mindedness; **elle a de la s. dans les idées!** she's very single-minded; **manquer (d'esprit) de s.** to be inconsistent, to lack consistency

6 *(escorte)* suite; *(d'un monarque etc)* retinue, train

7 *(série) (d'événements etc)* series, succession; *(d'ancêtres)* line; *(d'épreuves)* set; **s. de malheurs** run of misfortunes, chapter of accidents; **dans la s. des siècles** in the course of time or of the centuries

8 *Math* series

9 *Mus* suite

10 *(conséquence)* consequence, result; *(de maladie etc)* aftereffect; **mourir des suites d'une blessure** to die (as the result) of a wound; **par s.** consequently; **par s. de** due to, on account of; **par s. de maladie** due to or owing to illness; **par s. d'une erreur** following or through an error; **par s. de sa blessure** as a result of his/her wound

11 *(dans un hôtel)* suite; **s. de luxe** luxury suite; *(au dernier étage)* penthouse suite; **s. nuptiale** honeymoon or bridal suite; **s. présidentielle** executive suite

12 *(action de poursuivre)* pursuit; **être à la s. de qn** to be in pursuit of sb, *Fam* to be after sb

suivant¹ [sɥivɑ̃] PRÉP **1** *(direction) (ligne etc)* in the direction of, along; **découper s. le pointillé** cut along the dotted line

2 *(selon) (moyens, instructions etc)* according to, in accordance with; **s. son habitude** as is/was his habit or wont; **cela varie s. le jour/la température** it varies from day to day/with the temperature; **s. mon frère** according to my brother, in my brother's opinion; **s. les circonstances** depending on the circumstances; **s. avis** as per advice; **s. connaissement** as per bill of lading; **s. disponibilité** subject to availability; **s. vos instructions** as per your instructions
CONJ **s. que** + *ind* depending on whether, according to whether

suivant², **-ante** [sɥivɑ̃, -ɑ̃t] ADJ *(page, jour etc)* next, following; *(ligne)* next; **le train s. est à 18 heures** the next train is at 6pm; **voir page 6 et suivantes** see page 6 and following or *Fml* et seq; **les trois jours suivants** the next three days; **pas dimanche prochain mais le dimanche s.** not this Sunday but the next (one) or the one after; **notre méthode est la suivante** our method is as follows; **il nous fit part de l'histoire suivante** he told us the following story
N *(prochain)* **le s.**, **la suivante** the next (one); **les suivant(e)s** the next (ones); **au s.!** next (person) please!; *Mktg* **s. immédiat** early follower
NM *(accompagnateur)* attendant
NF *Théâtre* **suivante** attendant

suiveur, -euse [sɥivœr, -øz] NM **1** *(personne sans initiative)* follower *(de* of); *Mktg* follower; *(sur le marché)* market follower **2** *Sport* **les suiveurs** = officials and back-up squads following a cycle race
ADJ **voiture suiveuse** = car following a cycle race

suivi [sɥivi] ADJ **1** *(discours)* connected; *(raisonnement)* sustained, coherent; *(correspondance)* regular; *(travail, effort, qualité, histoire)* consistent; *(ligne de conduite)* steadfast, unwavering; *Com (demande)* steady, persistent; **article s.** stock item **2** *Univ (cours)* well attended, popular; *TV, Radio (émission, feuilleton)* popular; **l'émission a été très suivie** the programme had a large audience or was very popular
NM follow-up; **assurer le s. d'un projet** to follow a project through; **s. de commande** follow-up of an order; *Banque* **s. des risques** risk monitoring; **s. des ventes** sales follow-up

suivisme [sɥivism] NM *Pol etc* follow-the-herd attitude

SUIVRE [sɥivr] *(prp* suivant; *pp* suivi; *pr ind* je suis, il suit, n. suivons, ils suivent; *pr sub* je suive; *impf* je suivais; *p hist* je suivis; *fu* je suivrai)

VT to follow **1, 2, 4–10** ▪ to monitor **1** ▪ to keep an eye on **1** ▪ to understand **2** ▪ to accompany **3** ▪ to watch **5** ▪ to come after **6**	
VI to follow **1, 2** ▪ to keep up **3**	
VPR to follow each other	

VT **1** *(aller derrière)* to follow; **nous sommes suivis** we're being followed; **taxi, suivez cette voiture!** taxi, follow that car!; **partez, je vous suis** you go on, I'll follow (on); **se faire s. dans la rue** to get followed in the street; **s. qn de près** to follow close on sb's heels; *(artiste)* to keep an eye or a close watch on sb; *(patient)* to monitor sb, to keep an eye on sb; **s. qn pas à pas** to follow sb's every step; **elle le suivit des yeux** ou **du regard** she followed him with her eyes; *Fig* **s. son temps** to keep abreast of the times; *Com* **s. une affaire** to follow up business; *Com* **nous n'avons pas suivi cet article** we have discontinued this line; *Tennis etc* **s. la balle** to hit through the ball

2 *(comprendre)* to follow, to understand; **je ne vous suis pas** I don't follow you; **tu me suis toujours?** are you still with me?; **là je ne le suis plus** he's lost me there; **il parle si vite que je ne peux pas le s.** he talks so quickly that I cannot follow him; **s. une conversation dans une langue étrangère** to follow a conversation in a foreign language

3 *(accompagner) (personne)* to accompany; **s. qn dans ses voyages** to accompany sb on his/her travels

4 *(porter son attention sur) (quelque chose)* to follow; **suivez bien ce que je vais dire** pay attention to what I'm about to say

5 *(observer) (progrès, série d'événements etc)* to follow, to watch; **s. les cours de la Bourse** to follow the stock exchange prices; **tu as suivi l'affaire Moulin?** have you been following the Moulin affair?; **s. l'actualité à la télévision/à la radio** to follow events on the television/radio; **c'est une affaire à s.** it's worth keeping an eye on

6 *(venir après) (sans mouvement)* to follow, to come after; **la maison qui suit la nôtre** the house after ours; **le printemps suit l'hiver** spring follows winter; **conjonction suivie du subjonctif** conjunction followed by the subjunctive

7 *(longer) (route)*, *Fig (pensées etc)* to go along, to follow; *Fig* **nous n'avons pas suivi le même chemin** we didn't follow the same path; **s. son chemin** to go on one's way; **je vais s. mon idée** I'll do it my way; **la rivière suit son cours** the river follows its course; *Fig* **la justice suivra son cours** justice will take its course; **laisser les choses s. leur cours** to let things take their course; **la vie suit son cours** life goes on

8 *(obéir à) (mode, exemple, traitement, intuition)* to follow; *(conseil)* to follow, to act upon; *(loi)* to obey, to conform to; *(ligne de conduite)* to follow, to pursue; **s. un régime** to follow or be on a diet; **s. le mouvement** to follow the crowd, to go with the flow; **voici la marche à s.** this is the procedure, this is what you have to do

9 *(être présent à) (série de concerts, de conférences etc)* to attend (regularly); **s. un cours** to follow or take a course (of study)

10 *(en disciple) (personne)* to follow

VI **1** *(venir après)* to follow; **le reste du repas suit** the rest of the meal is coming; **les personnes dont les noms suivent** the following persons; **faire s. une lettre** to forward a letter; **(prière de) faire s.** *(sur une enveloppe)* please forward; **faire s. ses bagages** to have one's luggage sent on; *Typ* **(faire) s.** run on; **à s.** *(à la fin d'un feuilleton)* to be continued **2** *(comprendre)* to follow; *(faire attention)* to pay attention; **pardon, je n'ai pas suivi** sorry, I wasn't paying attention; *Scol* **elle ne suit plus** she can't keep up any more; *(elle rêve)* she doesn't pay attention any more **3** *(aller au même rythme)* to keep up; **j'ai d'excellents projets, mais les finances ne suivent pas** I've got some great plans, but there isn't the funding for them *or* but the funding isn't forthcoming; **tout augmente, mais les salaires ne suivent pas** everything is going up in price, but wages aren't following suit

VPR se suivre to follow each other; **arguments qui se suivent bien** connected *or* coherent arguments; **événements qui se suivent de près** events that follow each other in quick succession

V IMPERS il suit de là que … it follows (from this) that …; **que s'en est-il suivi?** what came of it?; **conditions ainsi qu'il suit** terms as follows

sujet, -ette [syʒɛ, -ɛt] **ADJ 1 s. à** *(exposé à) (maladie etc)* subject to, prone to; **s. à caution** *(nouvelles etc)* unconfirmed; **s. à oublier/mentir** apt *or* liable to forget/given to lying **2** *Jur* **s. à** *(impôts etc)* liable to, subject to **3** *Arch* *(soumis)* dependent

N *(d'un État, d'un souverain)* subject

NM 1 *(cause)* cause, reason, grounds (**de qch** for sth; **de faire** for doing); **un s. de pitié** an object of pity; **s. de querelle** *ou* dispute cause for dispute; **je n'ai pas eu s. de me plaindre** I had no cause *or* reason *or* grounds for complaint; **si je me plains c'est que j'en ai s.** if I complain it's because I have good cause *or* reason; **se mettre en colère sans s.** to lose one's temper without *or* for no good reason *or* cause

2 au s. de qn/de qch about *or* concerning sb/sth; **les choses qu'il m'a racontées à votre s.** the things he told me about you; **elle ne m'a rien dit à ce s.** she said nothing to me about it; **à ce s., je voulais vous dire que …** talking of which, I meant to tell you …; **au s. de votre lettre** with reference to your letter; **éprouver des craintes au s. de qch** to have fears about sth

3 *(question)* *(d'un discours, d'un livre, d'une pièce de théâtre, d'un tableau, d'une discussion etc)* subject (matter), theme; *(d'une conversation)* subject, topic; *Mus (d'une fugue etc)* subject; **nos avis s'accordent sur le s. de la nourriture** we have the same opinions on the subject of food; **changeons de s. (de conversation)** let's change the subject; **quel est le s. du film?** what's the film about?; **un beau s. de roman** a fine subject for a novel; *Scol* **une dissertation hors (du) s., un hors s.** an essay that doesn't deal with the subject; *Ordinat* **hors s.** *(dans un groupe de discussion)* off-topic

4 *Gram* subject; **s. grammatical/logique** grammatical/logical subject `SEE GRAMMAR A78; B18`

5 *Psy, Méd etc (d'une expérience)* subject; *Fam* guinea pig

6 *(individu)* individual; *Vieilli* **mauvais s.** bad lot, ne'er-do-well; *Vieilli* **bon s.** good sort; *Scol* **brillant s.** brilliant pupil

7 *(en horticulture)* stock

8 *(en logique), Ling* subject; **le s. parlant/pensant** the speaker/thinker

sujétion [syʒesjɔ̃] **NF** *Fml* **1** *(servitude)* subjection (**à** to); **s. aux lois** subservience to the laws; **une habitude devient vite une s.** we soon become slaves to a habit **2** *(contrainte)* constraint; **emploi d'une grande s.** job that keeps one tied down; **c'est une vraie s. d'avoir des animaux domestiques** keeping pets really ties one down

sulfamide [sylfamid] **NM** *Chimie* sulphona-mide, *Am* sulfonamide; *Méd* **sulpha** *or Am* **sulfa drug**

sulfatage [sylfataʒ] **NM 1** *Chimie, Ind* sulphating, *Am* sulfating; *Élec (des bornes d'une batterie)* corrosion **2 s. des vignes** treating vines with copper sulphate *or Am* sulfate

sulfate [sylfat] **NM** *Chimie* sulphate, *Am* sulfate

sulfaté [sylfate] **ADJ** *Chimie* sulphated, *Am* sulfated

sulfater [sylfate] **VT** *Agr, Ind* to sulphate, *Am* to sulfate

sulfateuse [sylfatøz] **NF 1** *(pour la vigne)* sulphate *or Am* sulfate sprayer **2** *Arg (mitraillette)* submachine-gun

sulfhydrique [sylfidrik] **ADJ** *Chimie* **acide s.** hydrogen sulphide *or Am* sulfide

sulfite [sylfit] **NM** *Chimie* sulphite, *Am* sulfite

sulfurage [sylfyraʒ] **NM** *Agr etc* sulphurizing, *Am* sulfurizing

sulfuration [sylfyrasjɔ̃] **NF** *Chimie* sulphur(iz)ation, *Am* sulfurization

sulfure [sylfyr] **NM** *Chimie* sulphide, *Am* sulfide; **s. de fer** iron pyrites

sulfuré [sylfyre] **ADJ** *Chimie* sulphuretted, *Am* sulfuretted; **hydrogène s.** hydrogen sulphide *or Am* sulfide, sulphuretted *or Am* sulfuretted hydrogen; *Minér* **fer s.** iron pyrites

sulfurer [sylfyre] **VT** *Agr etc* to sulphurize, *Am* to sulfurize

sulfureux, -euse [sylfyrø, -øz] **ADJ** *Chimie* sulphurous, *Am* sulfurous; *(eau, source)* sulphur, *Am* sulfur; *Fig (écrits, discours)* heretical, *Litt* with a whiff of sulphur; *(charm)* dangerous, hypnotic; **une beauté sulfureuse** a real femme fatale

sulfurique [sylfyrik] **ADJ** *Chimie* sulphuric, *Am* sulfuric

sulfurisé [sylfyrize] **ADJ** sulphurized, *Am* sulfurized; **papier s.** greaseproof paper

sulky, *pl* **sulkies** [sylki] **NM** *Courses de chevaux* sulky

sultan [syltɑ̃] **NM** sultan

sultanat [syltana] **NM** sultanate

sultane [syltan] **NF** *(épouse d'un sultan)* sultana, sultaness

sumac [symak] **NM** *Bot* sumac(h)

sumérien, -ienne [symerjɛ̃, -jɛn] **ADJ** Sumerian

NM *Ling* Sumerian

N S. Sumerian

summum [sɔmɔm] **NM** peak, summit; *Fig (de la gloire, pédanterie etc)* height

sumo [symo] **NM** *(sport)* sumo (wrestling); **lutteur de s.** sumo wrestler

sun-gun [sœngœn] **NM** *TV, Cin* sungun

sunlight [sœnlajt] **NM** *Cin* sun lamp

sunnite [synit] **ADJ, N** *Rel* Sunni

sup [syp] **ADJ INV** *Fam* **heures s.** overtime

super¹ [sypɛr] **ADJ INV** *Fam (bon)* great, terrific, fantastic

INT *Fam* great, terrific

ADV *Fam Br* dead, *Am* real; **un bouquin s. chiant** a *Br* dead *or Am* real boring book; **on s'est s. bien marrés** we had a *Br* fab *or Am* really neat time

NM *Aut (abrév* **supercarburant***)* four-star petrol, *Am* premium gas; **elle marche au s. ou au gasoil?** does it run on four-star or diesel?; **s. plombé** four-star *or Am* premium leaded; **s. sans plomb** four-star *or Am* premium unleaded

super² [sype] **VT** *Naut (d'une pompe)* to suck

VI *(d'une canalisation etc)* to get blocked **2 navire supé** ship stuck in the mud

superbe [sypɛrb] **ADJ 1** *(magnifique, remarquable)* *(bâtiment, temps, spectacle, cheval etc)* superb, magnificent; **il fait des affaires**

superbes he is doing splendid *or* excellent business **2** *(beau)* (very) beautiful

NF *Arch, Litt* pride, haughtiness

superbement [sypɛrbəmɑ̃] **ADV 1** superbly, magnificently **2** *Arch (orgueilleusement)* proudly, haughtily

superbénéfice [sypɛrbenefis] **NM** excess profit

supercagnotte [sypɛrkaɲɔt] **NF** *Fam (de loterie etc)* grand jackpot

supercarburant [sypɛrkarbyrɑ̃] **NM** *Aut* four-star petrol, *Am* premium gasoline

supercherie [sypɛrʃəri] **NF** deception, hoax; **être victime d'une s.** to be the victim of a hoax

superciment [sypɛrsimɑ̃] **NM** *Constr* quick-setting cement

superdividende [sypɛrdividɑ̃d] **NM** super dividend

supérette [sypɛrɛt] **NF** mini-market, (small) supermarket

superfétation [sypɛrfetasjɔ̃] **NF** *Litt (de mots etc)* superfluity

superfétatoire [sypɛrfetatwar] **ADJ** superfluous

superficialité [sypɛrfisjalite] **NF** superficiality

superficie [sypɛrfisi] **NF 1** *(surface)* surface; *Fig* **tout en s.** all on the surface, entirely superficial; **il ne connaît le problème qu'en s.** he has only a superficial knowledge of the problem **2** *(étendue) (d'un champ, d'un triangle etc)* (surface) area; **appartement d'une s. de 100 mètres carrés** apartment with a surface area of 100 square metres

superficiel, -ielle [sypɛrfisjɛl] **ADJ** *(blessure, savoir, réponse, observateur etc)* superficial; *(beauté)* superficial, skin-deep; *(esprit)* superficial, shallow; *Géog* **eau superficielle** surface water; *Phys* **tension superficielle** surface tension

superficiellement [sypɛrfisjɛlmɑ̃] **ADV** superficially; **répondre s.** to give a superficial answer

superfin [sypɛrfɛ̃] **ADJ** *Com* of superior quality

superflu [sypɛrfly] **ADJ 1** *(kilos, poils)* superfluous, unwanted; *(explication, détails etc)* superfluous, unnecessary; *(regrets)* vain, useless **2** *Ordinat* redundant

NM *(caractère)* superfluity; *(ce qui est superflu)* surplus; **il faut savoir distinguer l'essentiel du s.** you have to learn to distinguish what is essential from what is superfluous; **apprendre à se passer du s.** to learn to do without the inessentials; **des vitres électriques, tu ne crois pas que c'est du s.?** don't you think electric windows are a bit of a luxury?

superfluité [sypɛrflyite] **NF** *Litt* superfluity

super-G **NM** *(en ski)* super-G

super-géant **NM** *(en ski)* super-giant slalom

supergéante [sypɛrʒeɑ̃t] **NF** *Astron* super-giant

super(-)grand, *pl* **super(-)grands NM** superpower; **s. de la presse** press baron *or* tycoon

super-huit **ADJ INV, NM INV** *Phot* super-eight

supérieur, -ieure [syperjœr] **ADJ 1** *(plus haut) (étage, membre, province etc)* upper; **cours s. du fleuve** upper reaches of a river; **dans la partie supérieure de la ville** in the upper *or* top part of the town **2** *(d'une valeur plus grande)* superior (**à** to); **s. à la moyenne** above *or* better than average; **être s. en poids/en nombre** to be superior in weight/numbers; **lutter** *ou* **combattre contre des forces supérieures** to fight against superior forces; **se montrer s. aux événements** to rise above events; **être s. à la tâche** to be more than equal to the task; **c'est un esprit s.** he has a superior mind; **d'une intelligence supérieure** of superior *or* higher intelligence; **nommer qn à un emploi s.** to appoint sb to a higher post; **il se croit s. à tout le monde** he thinks he's above everyone else, he thinks he's superior

3 *(dans une hiérarchie)* higher, upper; *Scol (cours)* advanced; *(cadre)* senior; *Mil etc* **un commandement s.** a senior command; **classes supérieures** *(de la société)* upper classes; *Scol* upper forms; **enseignement s.** higher education; **offre supérieure** higher bid; **les animaux supérieurs** the higher animals; *Jur* **cour supérieure** higher court; **la Mère supérieure** the Mother Superior

4 *Com* **de qualité supérieure** of superior quality

5 *(hautain) (manières, ton)* superior, condescending

N 1 *Admin etc* superior; **il est mon s. hiérarchique** he is my superior *or* senior

2 *Rel* superior; **la Supérieure** the Mother Superior

supérieurement [syperjœrmɑ̃] ADV exceptionally

supériorité [syperjɔrite] NF superiority (**de** in); **complexe de s.** superiority complex; **c'est indubitablement une s. que vous avez sur elle** that's definitely one area where you're better than she is; **un air/sourire de s.** a superior air/smile, an air/a smile of superiority; **s. d'âge** seniority; **s. numérique/intellectuelle** numerical/intellectual superiority; **s. sur les marchés mondiaux** command of the world markets; **lutter contre une s. écrasante** to fight against overwhelming odds

superlatif, -ive [syperlatif, -iv] ADJ superlative; *Fig (exagéré)* **faire des louanges superlatives à qn** to praise sb to the skies

NM *Gram* superlative; **s. relatif/absolu** relative/absolute superlative; *Fig* **laid au s.** extremely ugly SEE GRAMMAR A24–7; B11; B13–14

superlativement [syperlativmɑ̃] ADV *Fam* extremely

super-léger, *pl* **super-légers** NM *Boxe (boxeur, catégorie)* light welterweight

superman [syperman], *pl* **supermen** [sypermen] NM *Fam* superman; **jouer les supermen** to act the superman

supermarché [sypermarʃe] NM supermarket

supermarketing [sypermarkɔtiŋ] NM supermarketing

supernova [sypernɔva] NF *Astron* supernova

super(-)ordinateur, *pl* **super(-)ordinateurs** [syperɔrdinatœr] NM supercomputer

superpétrolier [syperpetrolje] NM supertanker

superphosphate [syperfɔsfat] NM *Agr* superphosphate

superposable [syperpozabl] ADJ *(caisses, éléments de rangement)* stacking; *(images etc)* superimposable

superposé [syperpoze] ADJ *(images etc)* superimposed; *Élec, Électron* superposed; **lits superposés** bunk beds

superposer [syperpoze] VT *(boîtes, éléments de rangement)* to stack; *(images etc)* to superimpose (**à** (up)on); *TV etc* to overlay; *Ordinat* **s. une écriture** to overwrite

VPR **se superposer** *(de caisses, chaises etc)* to stack, to be stackable; *(d'images etc)* to be superimposed

superposition [syperpozisjɔ̃] NF *(d'éléments de rangement etc)* stacking; *Géol* superposition; *Phot, Cin, Géom* super-

imposition; *Ordinat* **mode de s. d'écriture** overwrite mode

superproduction [syperprɔdyksjɔ̃] NF *Cin* blockbuster, big-budget film

superprofit [syperprɔfi] NM huge profit

superpuissance [syperpɥisɑ̃s] NF *Pol* superpower

supersonique [sypersɔnik] ADJ supersonic

superstar [syperstar] NF superstar

superstitieusement [syperstisjøzmɑ̃] ADV superstitiously

superstitieux, -euse [syperstisjø, -øz] ADJ superstitious

superstition [syperstisjɔ̃] NF superstition; **avoir la s. du passé** to be overly attached to the past

superstrat [syperstra] NM *Ling* superstratum

superstructure [syperstryktyr] NF superstructure

supertanker [sypertãkœr] NM supertanker

superviser [sypervize] VT to supervise; *Ordinat* to control

superviseur [sypervizœr] NM supervisor; *Ordinat* **s. d'alimentation** power supply controller

supervision [sypervizjɔ̃] NF supervision

superwoman [syperwuman], *pl* **superwomen** [syperwumen] NF *Fam* superwoman

supin [sypɛ̃] NM *Gram* supine

supplanter [syplɑ̃te] VT to supplant, to supersede

suppléance [sypleɑ̃s] NF *(fonction)* temporary *or* supply post; *(action)* temporary replacement; **remplir une s.** to deputize for *or* stand in for someone

suppléant, -ante [sypleɑ̃] N substitute (**de** for), (temporary) replacement; *(de directeur)* deputy; *(professeur) Br* supply teacher, *Am* substitute teacher; *Méd* locum; *Théâtre* understudy

ADJ **1** *(fonctionnaire etc)* acting, temporary; *(juge)* surrogate; **professeur s.** *Br* supply teacher, *Am* substitute teacher **2** *Gram (verbe etc)* substitute

suppléer [syplee] VT *Arch, Litt* **1** *(remplacer) (manque, lacune)* to supply, to make up (for); *(personne)* to deputize for, to stand in for; **une technique qui supplée toutes les autres depuis peu de temps** a technique which has recently replaced all the others; **se faire s.** to be replaced **2** *(ajouter)* to supply

VI **s. à qch** to make up *or* compensate for sth; **s. au vin par le cidre** to eke out the wine with cider

supplément [syplemɑ̃] NM **1** *(surcroît)* **un s. de** *(information, travail etc)* additional, extra; **en s.** extra

2 *(somme)* extra *or* additional charge, surcharge; *Rail* excess fare, supplement, surcharge; **pour réserver sa place, il faut payer un s.** if you want to reserve a seat, you'll have to pay extra; **s. chambre individuelle** single room supplement; **s. d'imposition** additional taxes; **s. de prix** additional *or* extra charge; **je lui ai donné un s. d'argent de poche** I gave him extra pocket money; **nous avons besoin d'un s. d'information** we need additional *or* further information; **s. de solde/travail** extra pay/work; **s. d'imposition** additional tax; *Rail* **train à s. =** train in which an excess fare or a supplement is charged

3 *(livre, magazine etc)* supplement; **le s. du dimanche** the Sunday supplement

4 *(plat de restaurant)* extra (dish)

5 *Math (d'un angle)* supplement

supplémentaire [syplemɑ̃ter] ADJ additional, extra, further; **nous attendons des informations supplémentaires** we are await-

ing further information; *Ind* **une heure s.** an hour's overtime; **tes heures supplémentaires te sont-elles payées?** is your overtime paid?; **faire des heures supplémentaires** to do *or* work overtime; *Rail* **train s.** relief train; *Math* **angles supplémentaires** supplementary angles; *Mus* **lignes supplémentaires** ledger *or* added lines

supplétif, -ive [sypletif, -iv] ADJ, NM *Mil* auxiliary

suppliant [syplijɑ̃] ADJ *(regard etc)* imploring, pleading; **d'un air s.** imploringly

N suppliant, supplicant

supplication [syplikasjɔ̃] NF entreaty, plea; *Rel* supplication

supplice [syplis] NM **1** *(torture)* torture; **s. chinois** Chinese torture; **le s. du fouet** the penalty of the lash; **le dernier s.** capital punishment; **conduire qn au s.** to take sb away to be executed **2** *(tourment)* torment, agony; **le s. de l'attente** the agony of waiting; *Fig* **la goutte est un s.** gout is agony *or* a real torture; **ce genre de situation est pour moi un s.** I find this kind of situation absolute torture; **être au s.** to be in agonies; **mettre qn au s.** to torment *or* torture sb

supplicié, -ée [syplisje] N victim of torture

supplicier [syplisje] VT *(impf, pr sub n. suppliciions, v. suppliciiez)* to torture

supplier [syplije] VT *(impf, pr sub n. suppliions, v. suppliiez)* to beseech, to beg, to implore; **s. qn pour obtenir qch** to beg sb for sth; **s. qn de faire qch** to implore *or* beg sb to do sth; **ne dites rien, je vous en supplie, je vous supplie de ne rien dire** don't say anything, I beg *or* implore you

> Il faut noter que le verbe anglais **to supply** est un faux ami. Il signifie **fournir**.

supplique [syplik] NF petition; **présenter une s. à un fonctionnaire** to petition a civil servant

support [sypɔr] NM **1** *(étai)* support, prop; *Menuis* strut

2 *Hér (d'un écu)* supporter

3 *Tech (pour outils etc)* rest; *(pour une lampe, un tube à essai etc)* stand; *(pour un bloc de papier etc)* holder; *(de photo)* mount; *Archit, Constr (d'une structure, d'une arche etc)* support; *Ordinat* **s. de souris** mouse support

4 *(d'une pièce dans un mécanisme)* bearer, bracket, support

5 *Élec* (electrode) support

6 *Phot, Cin (d'une émulsion)* backing

7 *Fig (média)* medium; *Ordinat* **s. (d'information)** medium, information carrier; **s. de données** data carrier

▸▸ **s. d'affichage** billboard, *Br* hoarding; **s. audiovisuel** audiovisual equipment; **s. de bicyclette** bicycle stand; **s. pour bicyclettes** bicycle rack; **s. magnétique** tape; **s. photographique** photograph; **s. plantaire** arch support; *Com* **s. publicitaire** media vehicle; *Ordinat* **s. de sortie** output medium; *Ordinat* **s. de stockage** storage medium; **s. visuel** visuals

supportable [sypɔrtabl] ADJ **1** *(tolérable) (douleur etc)* bearable; *(comportement)* tolerable; **pas s.** *(douleur etc)* unbearable; *(comportement)* intolerable **2** *(correct)* reasonably good, fair

supporter¹ [sypɔrter] NM *Sport* supporter

SUPPORTER² [sypɔrte]

VT to support **1, 4** ▪ to hold up **1** ▪ to endure **2** ▪ to withstand **2** ▪ to put up with **3** ▪ to stand **3**
VPR to stand each other ▪ to be bearable

VT 1 *(soutenir) (plafond, arche etc)* to sup-

port, to hold up; *Fig (personne, politique, théorie etc)* to support, to back up; *(coût, frais)* to bear; **s. de lourdes responsabilités** to shoulder great responsibilities; **s. les conséquences d'un acte** to bear the consequences of an action

2 *(chaleur, malchance etc)* to endure, to withstand; *(basses températures)* to stand up to; *(alcool)* to take; *Naut (tempête)* to weather; **impossible à s.** intolerable; **son raisonnement ne supporte pas l'examen** his argument doesn't stand up to *or* withstand examination; **il ne supporte plus de se coucher tard** he can't take staying up late any longer

3 *(tolérer) (dureté, injustice, manque de respect etc)* to tolerate, to put up with, to stand; **elle supporte tout de son mari** she puts up with all sorts of things from her husband; **je ne peux pas le s.** I can't stand him; **elle ne supporte pas de voir son fils souffrir** she can't stand seeing her son in pain; **il me ment, et ça, je ne le supporte pas!** he's lying to me, and that's one thing I can't stand!

4 *Sport (équipe, athlète)* to support
VPR se supporter ils ne peuvent pas se s. they can't stand each other; **il faut apprendre à vous s.** you have to learn to put up with *or* tolerate each other; **cela ne peut pas se s.** that is intolerable

supporteur, -trice [sypɔrtœr, -tris] N *Sport* supporter

supposé [sypoze] ADJ **1** *(voleur, auteur etc)* supposed, alleged **2** *(nom etc)* assumed, false; *(testament)* forged

supposer [sypoze] VT **1** *(imaginer)* to suppose, to assume; **l'auteur suppose tout et ne prouve rien** the author assumes everything and proves nothing; **on peut s. qu'elle l'a fait pour lui faire plaisir** we can assume that she did it to make him happy; **en supposant que … + *sub*, à s. que … + *sub*, supposons que … + *sub***suppose *or*supposing that …; **on suppose que … + *indit*** is thought that …; **suppose qu'il revienne** suppose (that) he comes back; **elle lui supposait une grande fortune** she assumed he had a large fortune, she credited him with a large fortune; **tu es supposé le savoir** you are supposed to know it; **on le suppose à Paris, on suppose qu'il est à Paris** he is supposed to be in Paris

2 *(impliquer)* to imply; **cela lui suppose du courage** it implies courage on his/her part; **je peux le faire, mais cela suppose que l'on me donne trois jours de plus** I can do it, provided I get an extra three days

3 *Jur (imposteur)* to put forward; *(faux testament)* to present

VI vous avez supposé juste you guessed right; **tu as raison, je suppose** you are right, I suppose

supposition [sypozisjɔ̃] NF supposition, assumption; **je n'en suis pas sûr, c'est une s.** I'm not sure, I'm only assuming; **si par s. il revenait** supposing (that) he came back; *Fam* **une s. qu'elle soit en retard** supposing she's late VOIR GRAMMAIRE A57

suppositoire [sypozitwar] NM *Méd* suppository

suppôt [sypo] NM henchman; **s. de Satan** *ou* **du diable** fiend

suppression [sypresjɔ̃] NF **1** *(d'une loi, d'un impôt etc)* abolition; *(d'un journal etc)* suppression; *(d'un service d'autobus, d'un train etc)* cancellation; *(d'une difficulté)* removal; *(d'un mot, d'une phrase, d'un paragraphe etc)* deletion; **faire une s. de caractères** to delete characters; **parvenir à la s. des dépenses inutiles** to manage to cut out unnecessary expenditure; **la s. de 500 emplois** the axing *or* loss of 500 jobs; **cela a conduit à la s. du**

service du personnel that led to Personnel being axed *or* getting the axe; **la Commission pour la s. du bruit** the Noise Abatement Commission **2** *Jur (d'un document, d'un fait)* suppression; **s. d'enfant** concealment of birth

supprimable [syprimabl] ADJ suppressible
supprimer [syprime] VT **1** *(loi, impôt etc)* to abolish, to do away with; *(service d'autobus, train, concert etc)* to cancel; *(crédit)* to put an end to, to withdraw; *(mot, phrase, paragraphe)* to delete; *(au montage, texte)* to edit out; *(emploi, service)* to axe; **pour s. les effets de qch** to counteract the effects of sth; **vous n'avez pas été sages, la séance de cinéma est supprimée!** you haven't been good, there's no cinema for you *or* the cinema is out!; **vous devez s. le sucre de votre alimentation** you must cut sugar out of your diet; **l'avion supprime les distances** air travel makes distance irrelevant; **s. un poste** to abolish a position; *Fam* **s. qn** to kill sb, to bump sb off; *Typ* **à s.** delete

2 *Jur (document, fait)* to suppress, to withhold

3 s. qch à qn to deprive sb of sth
VPR se supprimer to commit suicide

Il faut noter que le verbe anglais **to suppress** est un faux ami. Il signifie le plus souvent **réprimer** ou **interdire**.

suppurant [sypyrã] ADJ *Méd* suppurating
suppuration [sypyrasjɔ̃] NF suppuration, discharge

suppurer [sypyre] VI *(d'une blessure, d'une écorchure)* to suppurate

supputation [sypytasjɔ̃] NF calculation, estimation

supputer [sypyte] VT to calculate, to estimate; **s. ses chances** to calculate one's chances

supra [sypra] ADV supra
supra- [sypra] PRÉF supra-

supraconducteur [syprakɔ̃dyktœr] NM *Phys, Élec* superconductor

supraconductivité [syprakɔ̃dyktivite] NF *Phys, Élec* superconductivity

supraliminaire [sypraliminer] ADJ supraliminal

supranational, -ale, -aux, -ales [sypranasjɔnal, -o] ADJ supranational

supranationalisme [sypranasjɔnalism] NM supranationalism

supranationalité [sypranasjɔnalite] NF supranationality

supraterrestre [sypraterestr] ADJ superterrestrial

suprématie [sypremasi] NF supremacy
suprême [syprem] ADJ **1** *(effort, bonheur etc)* supreme; *(degré)* highest; **nous avons eu un plaisir s. à les rencontrer** it gave us immense pleasure to meet them; **un crétin au s. degré** an idiot of the highest degree; **le pouvoir s.** sovereignty **2** *(dernier) (demandes, moments)* last; **s. tentative** final attempt
NM *Culin* supreme; **s. de volaille** chicken supreme

suprêmement [sypremmã] ADV supremely

SUR¹ [syr]

on **1, 5**	upon **1**	over **2, 4**	above **2**	towards **3**	about **5**
out of **8**	by **9, 12**	after **10**	in **11**		

PRÉP SEE GRAMMAR A66-73; B57 **1** on, *Fml* upon; *(avec mouvement)* on (to); **un chapeau s. la tête** with a hat on one's head, wearing a hat; **regarder s. la carte** to look at the map; **il est retombé s. ses pieds** he landed on his feet; **tirage photo s. papier brillant** print on

glossy paper; **je ne suis jamais allé s. un voilier** I've never been on a yacht; **la clef est s. la porte** the key is in the door; **je n'ai pas d'argent s. moi** I don't have any money on me; **tu es tombé s. la tête?** are you mad?; *Fig* **nous étions les uns s. les autres** we were on top of each other, we were all squashed up together; **je suis s. ce dossier depuis deux jours** I've been working on this file for two days

2 *(au-dessus de)* over, above; **les astres s. nos têtes** the stars above our heads; **un pont s. une rivière** a bridge across a river

3 *(vers)* towards; **fenêtre qui donne s. le jardin** window which looks on to the garden; **la police a tiré s. la foule** the police fired on *or* at the crowd; **avancer s. qn** to advance on sb; **s. votre gauche** on *or* to your left; **les trains s. Orléans** the trains for Orleans

4 *(supériorité, ascendant)* **avoir autorité s. qn** to have authority over sb; **elle a une forte influence s. moi** she has great influence over me; **l'emporter s. qn** to beat sb; **avoir des droits s. qn/qch** to have rights over sb/sth

5 *(à propos de)* on, about, concerning; **nous savons beaucoup de choses s. vous** we know a lot about you; **un livre s. l'écologie** a book on *or* about ecology; **s. ce point** on this point; **il pose un regard anxieux s. toute(s) chose(s)** he colours everything with his own anxiety; **tu es toujours en train de pleurer s. ton sort!** you're always feeling sorry for yourself

6 *(temps)* towards, around; **elle va s. ses dix-huit ans** she's coming up for eighteen

7 s. ce, s. quoi whereupon; **s. ce, je vous quitte** and now I must leave you; **s. le coup** immediately, straight away; **s. le coup** *ou* **s. le moment je n'y ai pas pensé** I didn't think about it there and then; **il est s. le départ** he is about to leave; *Fig* **être s. le retour** to be past one's prime

8 *(parmi)* out of; **un professeur s. cinq** one teacher in *or* out of five; **huit s. dix** *(note)* eight out of ten; **une fois s. deux** every other time; **on paie les pompiers s. les fonds de la ville** the firemen are paid out of the municipal funds

9 *(mesure)* by; **huit mètres s. six** eight metres by six; **'virages s. 2 kilomètres'** 'bends for 2 kilometres'; **la frontière s'étend s. 300 kilomètres** the border stretches for 300 kilometres; **ses terres s'étendent s. 100 hectares** his estate extends over *or* covers 100 hectares

10 *(après)* **page s. page** page after page; **j'ai reçu visite s. visite pendant tout l'été** I had visit upon visit *or* one visit after another all summer; **avec lui, c'est reproche s. reproche** with him, it's one criticism after another; **coup s. coup** one after the other, in succession; **il a fait la même erreur deux fois coup s. coup** he made the same mistake twice in a row

11 *(manière)* **s. un ton de reproche** in a reproachful tone, reproachfully; **dire qch s. le ton de la plaisanterie** to say sth jokingly; **ne le prends pas s. ce ton!** don't take it like that!; **ne me parle pas s. ce ton!** don't speak to me in that tone of voice!; *Mus* **chanter qch s. un certain air** to sing sth to a certain tune; **s. le mode mineur** in the minor key

12 *(d'après)* **juger qn s. les apparences** to judge sb by appearances; **s. sa bonne réputation** on the strength of his/her good reputation; **s. une fausse accusation** on a false charge

sur² ADJ *(fruit etc)* sour, tart
sur- [syr] PRÉF over-

sûr [syr] ADJ **1** *(sans danger) (localité, abri, plage etc)* safe; **c'est plus s. s'il t'accompagne** it's safer if he goes with you; **dis-le lui, c'est plus s.** tell him/her, just to be on the safe side; **peu s.** unsafe; **en lieu s.** in a safe place

2 *(digne de confiance) (personne, mémoire)* trustworthy, reliable; *(ami)* trusty, true; *(information, entreprise)* reliable; **savoir qch de source sûre** to learn sth from a reliable source; **avoir le coup d'œil s.** to have a keen eye; **goût s.** discerning taste; **avoir la main sûre/le pied s.** to have a steady hand/to be surefooted; **ne pas avoir le pied s.** to be unsteady on one's feet; **frapper un coup s.** *ou* à **coup s.** to strike an unerring blow; **mettre son argent en mains sûres** to put one's money into safe hands

3 *(certain)* certain, sure; **il l'a oublié, c'est s.** he has forgotten it, that's for certain *or* sure; **c'est une affaire sûre** it's a certainty *or* a sure thing *or Fam* a dead cert; **être s. de réussir** to be sure of success; **être s. de qch** to be sure *or* certain of sth; **je ne suis pas s. de la réussite de ce projet** I'm not sure that this plan will succeed; **je suis s. de lui** I can depend on him; **être s. de son fait** to be positive; **elle n'était pas vraiment sûre de son coup** she wasn't really sure of success; **je suis s. de ce que je te dis** I'm sure about what I'm saying; **s. de soi** self-assured; *Fam* **j'en suis s. et certain** I'm absolutely certain *or* sure of it; **mais oui ça va marcher, c'est s. et certain!** of course it'll work, it's absolutely certain!; **parier à coup s.** to bet on a certainty; **à coup s.** for certain, definitely

  NM jouer au plus s. to play for safety; **le plus s. serait de …** the safest thing would be to … **ADV** *Fam* surely; **s.!** of course!, *Am* sure!; **pas s.!** perhaps not; *Fam* **bien s., pour s.!** of course!, *Am* sure!; *Fam* **bien s.?** you really mean it?; **bien s. que non!** of course not!; **bien s. que je viendrai aussi** of course I'll come too

surabondance [syrabɔ̃dɑ̃s] **NF** overabundance; *Com* glut; **s. de richesses/de détails** wealth of riches/details

surabondant [syrabɔ̃dɑ̃] **ADJ** overabundant

surabonder [syrabɔ̃de] **VI** to be overabundant; **s. de** *ou* **en qch** to have an overabundance of sth

suraccumulation [syrakymylasjɔ̃] **NF s. de capital** over-accumulation of capital

suractivé [syraktive] **ADJ** superactivated

suractivité [syraktivite] **NF** *Physiol* overactivity

surah [syra] **NM** *Tex* syrah

suraigu, -uë [syregy] **ADJ 1** *(voix, son)* high-pitched **2** *Méd (inflammation)* acute

surajouter [syraʒute] **VT** to add (on)
  VPR se surajouter to be added (on)

suralimentation [syralimɑ̃tasjɔ̃] **NF 1** *(de personne)* overfeeding; *Méd* feeding up **2** *Aut (de moteur)* supercharging; **s. par turbocompresseur** turbocharging

suralimenter [syralimɑ̃te] **VT 1** to overfeed; *Méd (personne)* to feed up **2** *(moteur)* to supercharge; **suralimenté** *(moteur)* supercharged; **suralimenté refroidi** charge-cooled

suranné [syrane] **ADJ 1** *(vieilli)* outdated, old-fashioned; **beauté surannée** faded beauty **2** *Arch (qui a expiré) (passeport etc)* expired

surarmement [syrarmɔmɑ̃] **NM** *Mil* excessive arms build-up

surbaissé [syrbese] **ADJ 1** *Archit (arche, voûte)* lowered, depressed **2** *Aut etc (essieu, carrosserie etc)* dropped; *(châssis)* (extra-)low, underslung; **taille surbaissée** *(d'une robe)* drop waist

surbaissement [syrbesmɑ̃] **NM** *Archit* surbasement

surbaisser [syrbese] **VT 1** *Archit (arche, voûte)* to lower, to depress **2** *Aut etc (carrosserie etc)* to drop, to undersling

surbook [syrbuk] **NM** *(d'une chambre d'hô-*

tel, de billets d'avion) overbooking; *(en double)* double booking

surbooker [syrbuke] **VT** to overbook; *(en double)* to double book

surbooking [syrbukiŋ] **NM** overbooking; *(en double)* double booking

surboum [syrbum] **NF** *Fam Vieilli* party; **faire une s.** to have *or* throw a party

surbrillance [syrbrijɑ̃s] **NF** *Typ* highlighting; **apparaître en s.** to be highlighted

surcapacité [syrkapasite] **NF** *Ind etc* overcapacity

surcapitalisation [syrkapitalizasjɔ̃] **NF** overcapitalization

surcapitaliser [syrkapitalize] **VI** to overcapitalize

surcharge [syrʃarʒ] **NF 1** *Tech* overload; *Élec (d'un accumulateur)* overcharge; *Fig* **une s. de travail/de responsabilités/de soucis** extra work/responsibilities/worries; **la s. d'un programme d'études** a heavy syllabus
  2 *(dans un véhicule)* excess load; *(de bagages)* excess weight; **prendre des passagers en s.** to take on excess passengers; **rouler en s.** to drive an overloaded vehicle; *Méd* **s. pondérale** excess weight
  3 *(d'une course de chevaux)* weight handicap
  4 *(à payer)* surcharge
  5 *Typ* correction, alteration; *(dans un contrat etc)* alteration; *(imprimée sur un timbre-poste)* surcharge

surcharger [syrʃarʒe] **VT** (**je surchargeai(s)**; **n. surchargeons**) **1** *(véhicule, cheval, estomac etc)* to overload; *Élec (accumulateur)* to overcharge; *Fig* **s. ses employés de travail** to overwork one's employees; **je suis surchargée de travail depuis deux mois** I've been overburdened with work for two months; **s. d'impôts** to overburden with taxes; *Fin* **s. le marché** to overload the market **2** *Typ (caractères)* to write over with corrections; *(timbre)* to surcharge, to overprint

surchauffe [syrʃof] **NF** *(d'un four, d'un moteur)*, *Fig (de l'économie)* overheating

surchauffer [syrʃofe] **VT 1** *(four etc)* to overheat; **salle surchauffée** overheated room **2** *(vapeur)* to superheat

surchoix [syrʃwa] *Com* **NM** finest quality
  ADJ INV *(produit)* top-quality

surclassement [syrklasmɑ̃] **NM** *(de titre de transport)* upgrade

surclasser [syrklase] **VT** to outclass; *(titre de transport)* to upgrade

surcompensation [syrkɔ̃pɑ̃sasjɔ̃] **NF** *Psy* overcompensation

surcomposé [syrkɔ̃poze] **ADJ** *Gram (temps)* double-compound

surcompression [syrkɔ̃presjɔ̃] **NF** *Tech* supercharging

surcomprimer [syrkɔ̃prime] **VT** *Tech* to supercharge; **moteur surcomprimé** supercharged engine

surconsommation [syrkɔ̃sɔmasjɔ̃] **NF** *Écon* overconsumption

surcontrer [syrkɔ̃tre] **VT** *Cartes* to redouble

sur-correction **NF** *Aut* over-correction

surcouper [syrkupe] **VT** *Cartes* to overtrump

surcoût [syrku] **NM** cost overrun

surcroît [syrkrwa] **NM** **un s. de extra**; **un s. d'effort** an extra effort; **pour donner un s. d'effet à …** to give an added effect to …; **par s., de s.** in addition, moreover; **par s. de besogne** to add to my work; **pour s. de malheur** to make matters worse; **s. de dépenses** additional expenditure

surdéveloppé [syrdevlɔpe] **ADJ** *Écon* highly developed; *(excessivement)* overdeveloped

surdéveloppement [syrdevlɔpmɑ̃] **NM**

Écon high state of development; *(excessif)* overdevelopment

surdimensionné [syrdimɑ̃sjɔne] **ADJ** oversized

surdi-mutité [syrdimytite] **NF** deaf-muteness

surdiplômé [syrdiplome] **ADJ** overqualified

surdité [syrdite] **NF** deafness; **s. musicale** tone deafness

surdon [syrdɔ̃] **NM 1** *(compensation)* = compensation allowable to purchaser for damage to goods **2** *(droit)* = right to non-acceptance of damaged goods

surdosage [syrdozaʒ] **NM** *Méd* overdosage

surdose [syrdoz] **NF** overdose

surdoué, -ée [syrdwe] **N** gifted child
  ADJ exceptionally gifted

sureau, -eaux [syro] **NM** elder (tree); **baie de s.** elderberry

sureffectif [syrefɛktif] **NM** excessive numbers, overmanning; **en s.** surplus; **personnel en s.** excessive (numbers of) staff

surélévation [syrelevasjɔ̃] **NF** *(action)* raising; *(augmentation de hauteur)* increase in height

surélevé [syrelve] **ADJ 1** *(voie ferrée)* elevated **2** *Archit (arche, rez-de-chaussée etc)* raised

surélever [syrelve] **VT** *(conj like* **élever**) *Constr etc* to heighten, to raise; **s. un malade dans son lit** to prop a patient up in his bed

suremballage [syrɑ̃balaʒ] **NM** overpackaging

sûrement [syrmɑ̃] **ADV 1** *(sans doute)* surely; **s.!** certainly!, more than likely!; **s. pas!** certainly not!; **elle est s. tombée en panne** she must have broken down; **il va s. y avoir des changements** there are surely going to be some changes **2** *(de manière confiante)* confidently, with confidence **3** *(sans risque)* safely **4** *(immanquablement)* **frapper s.** to strike with accuracy; **lentement mais s.** slowly but surely

surémission [syremisjɔ̃] **NF** *Fin* overissue

suremploi [syrɑ̃plwa] **NM** overemployment

surenchère [syrɑ̃ʃer] **NF 1** *Com* higher bid, overbid; **faire de la s. sur qn** to outbid sb **2** *Fig* **une s. de violence** an increase in violence; **faire de la s.** to try to go one better than one's rivals, to try to outdo one's rivals; **faire de la s. électorale** to make more extravagant promises to obtain votes

surenchérir [syrɑ̃ʃerir] **VI 1** *Com* to bid higher; *Fig* to try to outdo each other; **s. sur qn** to outbid sb, to bid higher than sb; *Fig* to try to outdo sb *or* go one better than sb **2** *(devenir plus cher)* to rise in price

surenchérisseur [syrɑ̃ʃerisœr] **NM** highest bidder

surencombré [syrɑ̃kɔ̃bre] **ADJ** *(rue etc)* (severely) congested (**de** with)

surencombrement [syrɑ̃kɔ̃brəmɑ̃] **NM** (severe) congestion

surendetté [syrɑ̃dɛte] **ADJ** *Écon* excessively in debt

surendettement [syrɑ̃dɛtmɑ̃] **NM** *Écon* excessive debt (burden), overindebtedness, over-gearing; **courir un risque de s.** to run a risk of getting into excessive debt

surentraînement [syrɑ̃trɛnmɑ̃] **NM** *Sport* overtraining

surentraîner [syrɑ̃trɛne] **VT** *Sport* to overtrain

suréquipement [syrekipmɑ̃] **NM** *Écon* overequipment

suréquiper [syrekipe] **VT** *Écon* to over-equip

surestarie [syrestari] **NF** *Com* demurrage

surestimation [syrɛstimasjɔ̃] **NF** *(de l'importance, la capacité)* overestimation; *(d'une œuvre d'art etc)* overvaluation

surestimer [syrɛstime] **VT 1** *(importance, capacité, nombre, difficulté etc)* to overestimate; *(person)* to overrate, to overestimate **2** *(en valeur) (œuvre d'art etc)* to overvalue **VPR se surestimer** to overrate oneself, to overestimate oneself; **j'ai peur que tu te surestimes si tu penses pouvoir ...** I'm afraid you're being a bit optimistic if you think you can ...

suret, -ette [syrɛ, -ɛt] **ADJ** *(fruit, goût etc)* sour(ish), tart

sûreté [syrte] **NF 1** *(absence de danger)* safety; **lieu de s.** place of safety; **être en s.** to be safe *or* out of harm's way; **mettre qn en (lieu de) s.** *(en prison)* to put sb in prison; *(à l'abri)* to put sb in a safe place *or* out of harm's way; **pour plus de s.** for greater safety; **rasoir/serrure/soupape de s.** safety razor/lock/valve; **épingle de s.** safety pin; *Aut* **à s. intégrée** fail-safe
2 *Pol etc* security; **la s. de l'État** state *or* national security; **la S. (nationale)** = the (French) criminal investigation department, *Br* ≃ the CID, *Am* ≃ the FBI; **agent de la S.** detective
3 *(de la main, du pied)* sureness, steadiness; *(de la vision, du goût, du jugement)* soundness; *(d'un coup)* accuracy; **s. de soi** self-confidence, self-assurance
4 *Com (garantie)* surety, guarantee; **s. en garantie d'une créance** surety for a loan

surévaluation [syrevalɥasjɔ̃] **NF** overvaluation

surévaluer [syrevalɥe] **VT** *(objet, antiquité)* to overvalue; *(efficacité, capacités etc)* to overestimate

surexcitable [syrɛksitabl] **ADJ** overexcitable, easily excited

surexcitation [syrɛksitasjɔ̃] **NF** overexcitement

surexciter [syrɛksite] **VT** to overexcite; **des adolescentes surexcitées** hysterical teenage girls

surexploitation [syrɛksplwatasjɔ̃] **NF** overexploitation

surexploiter [syrɛksplwate] **VT** *(terre, travailleurs etc)* to overexploit

surexposer [syrɛkspoze] **VT** *Phot* to overexpose

surexposition [syrɛkspozisjɔ̃] **NF** *Phot* overexposure

surf [sœrf] **NM** *Sport* **1** *(sport)* surfing; **faire du s.** to go surfing, to surf **2** *(planche)* surfboard

surface [syrfas] **NF 1** surface; **eau de s.** surface water; *Phys* **tension de s.** *(d'un liquide)* surface tension; **bruit de s.** surface noise; **vitesse en s.** *(de sous-marin)* surface speed; **nager en s.** to swim near the surface; **remonter à la s.** to rise to the surface; to surface; **faire s., revenir en s.** *(d'un sous-marin)* to surface; *Fig Fam* **faire s.** *(se réveiller)* to surface; *Fig* **refaire s.** *(après une période difficile)* to get back on one's feet; **en s.** *(de l'eau)* on the surface; *Fig* superficially; **tout en s.** superficial; **il reste à la s. des choses** he doesn't go into things in any depth
2 *Géom* surface; **s. de révolution** *ou* **de rotation** surface of revolution; **s. plane** plane surface
3 *(étendue etc)* (surface) area; **quelle est la s. de l'appartement** how big is the flat?; *Fam* **avoir de la s.** to have influence; **(magasin à) grande s.** hypermarket; **grande s. de bricolage** DIY centre
▸▸ *Ordinat* **s. d'affichage** display area; **s. d'appui** bearing area *or* surface; *Constr* **s. couverte** floor area; *Ordinat* **s. d'enregistre-ment** read-write surface; *Mktg* **s. d'exposition** display space; *Fin* **s. financière** financial situation; **il présente une s. financière suffisante** his financial situation is sound; **s. portante** *ou* **de portée** bearing area *or* surface; *Ftbl* **s. de réparation** penalty area *or* box; **s. au sol** floor area; **s. utile** floor space; **s. de vente** sales area *or* floor; **s. de voilure** sail area

surfaceuse [syrfasøz] **NF** *Tech* surfacer, planing machine

surfacturation [syrfaktyrasjɔ̃] **NF** overbilling

surfaire [syrfɛr] **VT** *(conj like* **faire***)* *Litt* **1** *(marchandises etc)* to overprice **2** *(personne, talent etc)* to overestimate, to overrate

surfait [syrfɛ] **ADJ** *(prix)* excessive; *(personne, réputation etc)* overrated

surfer [sœrfe] **VI** to surf; **s. sur l'Internet** *ou* **le Net** to surf the Net *or* the Internet

surfeur, -euse [sœrfœr, -øz] **N** surfer; **s. des neiges** snowboarder

surfilage [syrfilaʒ] **NM** *Couture* overcasting, oversewing

surfiler [syrfile] **VT 1** *Couture* to overcast, to oversew **2** *Tex (fil)* to give an extra twist to

surfin [syrfɛ̃] **ADJ** *Com (produit)* superior, top-quality

surfrappe [syrfrap] **NF** *Ordinat* double strike, overstrike

surfréquentation [syrfrekɑ̃tasjɔ̃] **NF** *(d'un lieu)* overfrequentation

surgé [syrʒe] **N** *Fam (abrév* **surveillant(e) général(e)***)* head supervisor *(in charge of school discipline)*

surgélateur [syrʒelatœr] **NM** deep-freeze, freezer

surgélation [syrʒelasjɔ̃] **NF** deep *or* quick freezing

surgelé [syrʒele] **ADJ** deep- *or* quick-frozen **NMPL surgelés** frozen foods

surgeler [syrʒele] **VT** *(conj like* **geler***)* to deep- *or* quick-freeze

surgénérateur [syrʒeneratœr] **ADJ, NM** *Nucl (réacteur)* **s.** breeder reactor

surgeon [syrʒɔ̃] **NM** *(de plante)* sucker

surgir [syrʒir] **VI** *(aux* **avoir**, *parfois* **être***)* to appear suddenly; *(d'une plante)* to spring up; *(d'une difficulté)* to crop up; **faire s. de nouveaux problèmes** to create new problems

surgissement [syrʒismɑ̃] **NM** *Litt* sudden appearance

surglacé [syrglase] **ADJ** *(papier)* calendered

surhaussé [syrose] **ADJ** *Archit* raised

surhaussement [syrosmɑ̃] **NM** *Archit* raising; *(différence de hauteur)* increase in height

surhausser [syrose] **VT** *Archit (mur etc)* to raise

surhomme [syrɔm] **NM** superman

surhumain [syrymɛ̃] **ADJ** superhuman

surimi [syrimi] **NM** *Culin* crab stick

surimposer [syrɛ̃poze] **VT** *(par l'impôt)* to overtax

surimposition [syrɛ̃pozisjɔ̃] **NF 1** *(par l'impôt)* overtaxation **2** *Géol* pseudomorphism

surimpression [syrɛ̃presjɔ̃] **NF** *Phot, Cin* superimposition; *Ordinat* overprinting, overstrike; **en s.** superimposed; *Fig* **une foule d'émotions me sont venues en s.** I experienced a whole range of emotions in quick succession

surimprimer [syrɛ̃prime] **VT** *Ordinat* to overprint

surin [syrɛ̃] **NM** *Fam Vieilli* knife, dagger

Surinam(e) [syrinam] **NM** Surinam

surindustrialisation [syrɛ̃dystrijalizasjɔ̃] **NF** overindustrialization

suriner [syrine] **VT** *Fam Vieilli (personne)* to knife

surinfection [syrɛ̃fɛksjɔ̃] **NF** *Méd* secondary infection

surinformation [syrɛ̃fɔrmasjɔ̃] **NF** information overload

surinformé [syrɛ̃fɔrme] **ADJ** overinformed; **les gens sont surinformés** people are bombarded with too much information

surintendance [syrɛ̃tɑ̃dɑ̃s] **NF** *Hist* superintendence

surintendant [syrɛ̃tɑ̃dɑ̃] **NM** *Hist* superintendent

surinvestissement [syrɛ̃vɛstismɑ̃] **NM** *Fin, Psy* overinvestment

surir [syrir] **VI** *(du vin, de la soupe etc)* to turn sour

surjet [syrʒɛ] **NM** *Couture* overcasting, whipping

surjeter [syrʒəte] **VT** *(conj like* **jeter***)* *Couture* to overcast, to whip

sur-le-champ **ADV** at once, immediately

surlendemain [syrlɑ̃dmɛ̃] **NM** **le s.** the day after the next, two days later; **le s. de leur départ** two days after their departure

surligner [syrliɲe] **VT** to highlight

surligneur [syrliɲœr] **NM** highlighter (pen)

surlocation [syrlɔkasjɔ̃] **NF** overbooking, *Am* oversale; *(en double)* double booking

surlouer [syrlwe] **VT** to overbook; *(en double)* to double book

surmarquage [syrmarkaʒ] **NM** overpricing, overcharging

surmarquer [syrmarke] to overprice

surmédiatisation [syrmedjatizasjɔ̃] **NF** excessive media coverage

surmédiatisé [syrmedjatize] **ADJ** *(événement)* that receives/has received too much media coverage

surmédicaliser [syrmedikalize] **VT** to overmedicalize

surmédication [syrmedikasjɔ̃] **NF** overmedication

surmenage [syrmənaʒ] **NM 1** *(état)* overwork, overtiredness; **s. intellectuel** mental strain; **élève en état de s.** overworked pupil **2** *(action)* overworking

surmenant [syrmənɑ̃] **ADJ** *(travail etc)* exhausting

surmené [syrməne] **ADJ** overworked

surmener [syrməne] **VT** *(conj like* **mener***)* *(employés, élèves etc)* to overwork, to work too hard **VPR se surmener** to overwork, to work too hard, *Fam* to overdo it

sur-moi **NM** *(no pl) Psy* superego

surmontable [syrmɔ̃tabl] **ADJ** surmountable

surmonter [syrmɔ̃te] **VT 1** *(être placé sur)* to surmount; **colonne surmontée d'une croix** column surmounted *or* topped by a cross **2** *Fig (obstacle, difficulté)* to overcome, to surmount; *(faim, peine)* to conquer, to get over; *Litt (ennemis)* to overcome **VPR se surmonter** to master *or* control one's feelings

surmortalité [syrmɔrtalite] **NF** excessively high death rate

surmultiplication [syrmyltiplikasjɔ̃] **NF** *Aut* overdrive (system)

surmultiplié, -ée [syrmyltiplije] **ADJ, NF** *Aut* **(vitesse) surmultipliée** overdrive

surnager [syrnaʒe] **VI** (**je surnageai(s)**; **n. surnageons**) **1** to float (on the surface) **2** *Fig* to survive, to remain

surnatalité [syrnatalite] **NF** excessively high birth rate

surnaturel, -elle [syrnatyrɛl] **ADJ** supernatural

NF le s. the supernatural

surnom [syrnɔ̃] **NM** nickname; **on lui a donné le s. de Rick** he was given the nickname of Rick, he was nicknamed Rick

> Il faut noter que le terme anglais **surname** est un faux ami. Il signifie **nom de famille**.

surnombre [syrnɔ̃br] **NM en s.** too many; **les exemplaires/passagers en s.** the excess copies/passengers; **ils étaient en s.** there were too many of them

surnommer [syrnɔme] **VT** to nickname; **s. qn 'le Tigre'** to nickname sb 'The Tiger'

surnuméraire [syrnymerɛr] **ADJ, N** supernumerary

suroffre [syrɔfr] **NF 1** (offre plus avantageuse) better offer or bid **2** (surabondance par rapport à la demande) excess supply

suroît [syrwa] **NM** (vent, chapeau) sou'wester

suroxygéner [syrɔksiʒene] **VT** (je suroxygène, n. suroxygénons; je suroxygénerai) Chimie to superoxygenate

surpaie [syrpɛj, -pɛ] **NF** overpaying, overpayment

surpasser [syrpase] **VT** (espoirs) to surpass, to exceed; (rival) to surpass, to outdo; **dépense qui surpasse mes moyens** expense beyond my means; **s. qn en éclat** to outshine sb; **s. une armée en nombre** to outnumber an army

VPR se surpasser to surpass or excel oneself

surpatte [syrpat] **NF** Fam Vieilli (surprise-party) party

surpaye [syrpɛj, -pɛ] **NF** overpaying, overpayment

surpayer [syrpɛje] **VT** (conj like payer) (personne) to overpay; (quelque chose) to pay too much for

surpeuplé [syrpœple] **ADJ** (pays, région etc) overpopulated; (maison, plage etc) overcrowded

surpeuplement [syrpœpləmɑ̃] **NM** (de pays etc) overpopulation; (de maison, plage etc) overcrowding

surplace [syrplas] **NM** (d'un cycliste avant la course) track stand; **faire du s.** Aut Fam to crawl; (d'un cycliste) to do a track stand; Fig **j'ai l'impression de faire du s. depuis deux ou trois ans** I feel like I've been getting nowhere for the last two or three years

surplis [syrpli] **NM** Rel surplice

surplomb [syrplɔ̃] **NM** overhang; **en s.** overhanging

surplombant [syrplɔ̃bɑ̃] **ADJ** overhanging

surplomber [syrplɔ̃be] **VTI** to overhang

surplus [syrply] **NM** surplus; **le s.** the surplus, what is left (over); **le s. de marchandises** the surplus goods, the goods that are left (over); **payer le s.** to pay the difference; **au s.** besides, what is more; **les s. du gouvernement** government surplus (stock); Fin **s. monétaire** monetary surplus; **s. américain** US army surplus

surpopulation [syrpɔpylasjɔ̃] **NF** overpopulation

surpositionnement [syrpozisjɔnmɑ̃] **NM** Mktg over-positioning

surprenant [syrprɛnɑ̃] **ADJ** surprising, amazing; **chose surprenante** strange to say; **rien de s. si ...** I shouldn't be surprised if ...; **il est s. que vous le sachiez** it is surprising that you should know of it

surprendre [syrprɑ̃dr] (conj like **prendre**) **VT 1** (prendre par surprise) (quelqu'un) to sur-

prise; **aller s. un ami chez lui** to pay a friend a surprise visit; **la nuit nous surprit** night overtook us; **être surpris par la pluie** to be caught in the rain; **s. qn à faire qch** to catch sb (in the act of) doing sth; **s. un voleur en flagrant délit** to catch a thief in the act

2 (découvrir) (lettre, regard) to intercept; (conversation etc) to overhear; **s. le secret de qn** to find out sb's secret

3 (étonner) to surprise, to astonish; **ce qui me surprend, c'est que ...** what surprises or astonishes me is that ...; **cela me surprendrait qu'il revienne** ou **s'il revenait** I should be surprised or astonished if he came back; **ça a l'air de vous s.** you seem surprised; **ce n'est pas pour me s.** it doesn't surprise me in the least

VPR se surprendre se s. à faire qch to find oneself doing sth

surpression [syrpresjɔ̃] **NF** Tech overpressure, excessive pressure

surprime [syrprim] **NF** (d'assurance) extra or additional premium

surpris [syrpri] **ADJ** surprised (**de** at); **je suis s. de te voir ici** I'm surprised to see you here; **je m'arrêtai, s.** I paused in surprise; **s., je les regardais** I watched them in surprise; **s. que** + sub/**si** + ind surprised that/if; **je ne serais pas s. qu'il revienne** ou **s'il revenait** I shouldn't be surprised if he came back

surprise [syrpriz] **NF** (étonnement, cadeau) surprise; **ça m'a fait une s. agréable** it came as a pleasant surprise to me; **à sa grande s.** to his great surprise, much to his surprise; **à la s. générale** to everyone's surprise; **s'emparer d'une ville par s.** ou **par un coup de s.** to capture a town by surprise; **il m'a fait sa demande par s.** he surprised me with his request, he sprang his request on me; **expédition/voyage sans s.** uneventful expedition/journey; **il est bon ce bordeaux? – sans s.** is this Bordeaux good? – nothing special; **craindre une s.** to fear a sudden attack; **quelle bonne s.!** what a pleasant surprise!; **attendez-vous à une drôle de s.** be prepared for a shock; **boîte à s.** Jack-in-the-box; **pochette s.** lucky bag; **grève-s.** lightning strike

surprise-partie, pl **surprises-parties NF** party

surprix [syrpri] **NM** excess price

surproducteur, -trice [syrprɔdyktœr] **ADJ** overproducing

surproduction [syrprɔdyksjɔ̃] **NF** overproduction

surproduire [syrprɔdɥir] **VTI** to overproduce

surprofit [syrprɔfi] **NM** excess profit

surprotection [syrprɔteksjɔ̃] **NF** (d'un enfant) over-protection, coddling

surpuissant [syrpɥisɑ̃] **ADJ** (moteur, pays etc) extremely powerful

surqualifié [syrkalifje] **ADJ** overqualified

surréalisme [syrrealism] **NM** surrealism

surréaliste [syrrealist] **ADJ, N** surrealist

surréel, -elle [syrreɛl] **ADJ** surreal(istic)

NM le s. the surreal

surrégénérateur, -trice [syrreʒeneratœr, -tris] **ADJ, NM** Nucl (réacteur) **s.** breeder reactor

sur-régime NM Aut etc overspeeding

surrénal, -ale, -aux, -ales [syrrenal, -o] **ADJ** Anat (artère, ganglion) suprarenal; (glande) adrenal

surréservation [syrrezɛrvasjɔ̃] **NF** overbooking; (en double) double booking

surréserver [syrrezɛrve] **VT** to overbook; (en double) to double book

sursalaire [syrsalɛr] **NM** bonus

sursaturation [syrsatyrasjɔ̃] **NF 1** Écon oversaturation **2** Phys supersaturation

sursaturé [syrsatyre] **ADJ** Phys (solution) supersaturated; Fig **s. de** overwhelmed with

sursaturer [syrsatyre] **VT 1** Écon to oversaturate **2** Phys to supersaturate

sursaut [syrso] **NM** start, jump; **avoir** ou **faire un s.** to (give a) start, to (give a) jump; **en s.** with a start; **se lever en s.** to jump up with a start; **dans un s. d'énergie** with a (sudden) burst of energy; **un s. de terrorisme** a new outbreak of terrorism

sursauter [syrsote] **VI** to (give a) start, to (give a) jump; **faire s. qn** to startle sb; **s. d'indignation** to leap up in indignation

surseoir [syrswar] **VI** (prp sursoyant; pp sursis; pr ind je sursois, n. sursoyons; pr sub je sursoie; impf je sursoyais; p hist je sursis; fu je surseoirai) Jur **s. à un jugement** to suspend a judgement; **s. à l'exécution d'un condamné** to reprieve a condemned man; **ordonnance de s. (à un jugement)** stay of execution

sursis [syrsi] **NM** Jur (de condamné à mort) stay of execution; Fig reprieve; **condamné à un an de prison avec s.** given a suspended (prison) sentence of one year; Mil **s. d'appel** deferment (of call-up); Fig **mort en s.** condemned man; **s. de paiement** extra time to pay

sursitaire [syrsiter] Mil **ADJ** provisionally exempted

NM provisionally exempted conscript

sursouscription [syrsuskripsjɔ̃] **NF** Fin oversubscription

sursouscrire [syrsuskrir] **VT** Fin to oversubscribe

sursouscrit [syrsuskrit] **ADJ** Fin oversubscribed

surtaux [syrto] **NM** overassessment

surtaxe [syrtaks] **NF 1** surtax, surcharge; (de lettre etc) surcharge; **s. à l'importation** import surcharge **2** (excessive) excessive tax

surtaxer [syrtakse] **VT 1** Admin to surtax, to surcharge **2** (lettre etc) to surcharge

surtension [syrtɑ̃sjɔ̃] **NF** Élec overvoltage

surtitre [syrtitr] **NM** Journ strapline

surtout[1] [syrtu] **ADV** particularly, especially; (avant tout) above all; **ayez s. soin de ...** be especially or particularly careful to ...; **s. n'oubliez pas de ...** do <u>not</u> forget to ...; **non, s. pas!** no, certainly not!; Fam **s. que ...** especially as ...

surtout[2] **NM 1** (sur une table) centrepiece, Am centerpiece **2** Arch (manteau) overcoat

survaleur [syrvalœr] **NF** Compta goodwill

surveillance [syrvɛjɑ̃s] **NF** (contrôle) supervision; Scol invigilation; Mil observation, surveillance; Radio monitoring; (en prenant soin de qn ou qch) watch; **exercer une s. discrète sur qn/qch** to keep a discreet watch on sb/sth; **être sous la s. de la police** to be under police observation or surveillance; Mil **avion/navire de s.** surveillance plane/ship; **s. médicale** medical supervision; **s. électronique** electronic surveillance; Écon **s. des prix** price monitoring

surveillant, -ante [syrvɛjɑ̃, -ɑ̃t] **N** Ind, Admin etc supervisor; (de prison) warder, Am guard; Rail inspector; Scol (d'examen) invigilator; (chargé de la discipline) supervisor

NF Méd **surveillante** head nurse, Br ≃ (ward) sister

> Il faut noter que le terme anglais **surveyor** est un faux ami. Il signifie le plus souvent **expert** ou **géomètre**.

surveiller [syrveje] **VT 1** (contrôler) (travail, employés etc) to supervise; (prix) to monitor;

(machine) to man; *Scol (examen)* to invigilate; *Mil* to observe
2 *(prendre soin de) (personne)* to watch (over); **s. les enfants** to watch (over) *or* keep an eye on the children; **s. la situation de près** to keep a close eye on the situation; **s. son langage** to watch *or* mind one's language; **s. sa ligne** to watch one's figure; *Jur* **en liberté surveillée** on probation
3 *Radio* to monitor
VPR se surveiller to keep a watch on oneself

> Il faut noter que le verbe anglais **to survey** est un faux ami. Il ne signifie jamais **surveiller.**

survendre [syrvãdr] **VT** *Com* to overcharge for

survenir [syrvənir] *(conj like* **venir***; aux* **être)** **VI** *(d'événements)* to happen, to occur; *(d'une crise, d'une difficulté)* to arise; *(d'une personne)* to arrive unexpectedly
V IMPERS s'il ne survient pas de complications if no complications arise *or* occur; **s'il survient un visiteur** if a visitor happens to come

survenue [syrvəny] **NF** *Litt* unexpected arrival

survêt [syrvɛt] **NM** *Fam* = **survêtement**

survêtement [syrvɛtmã] **NM** tracksuit; *(tenue relaxe)* shellsuit

survie [syrvi] **NF** survival; *Rel* afterlife; **croire à la s. de l'homme** to believe in the afterlife; *Astronaut etc* **équipement de s.** life support equipment; **couverture de s.** survival blanket; **une s. de quelques jours, quelques jours de s.** a few more days of life

survirage [syrviraʒ] **NM** *Aut* oversteer
survirer [syrvire] **VI** *Aut* to oversteer
survireur, -euse [syrvirœr, -øz] **ADJ une voiture survireuse** a car that oversteers

survivance [syrvivãs] **NF 1** *(de l'âme)* survival **2** *(vestige) (du passé etc)* survival, relic

survivant, -ante [syrvivã, -ãt] **ADJ** surviving
N survivor

survivre [syrvivr] *(conj like* **vivre***; aux* **avoir)** **VI** to survive; **s. à** *(personne)* to survive, to outlive; *(période, théorie etc)* to outlive; *(accident, maladie etc)* to survive; **va-t-il s.?** will he live *or* survive?
VPR se survivre 1 *(dans ses enfants, son œuvre etc)* to live on **2** *Péj (d'une personne qui est devenu médiocre)* to have had one's day

survol [syrvɔl] **NM 1** *Aviat* **le s. d'un lieu** flying over a place **2** *Fig (d'un problème etc)* cursory glance **(de** at)

survoler [syrvɔle] **VT 1** *Aviat (montagne, localité etc)* to fly over **2** *Ordinat* to browse through **3** *Fig (problème etc)* to get a general view of

survoltage [syrvɔltaʒ] **NM** *Élec* boosting
survolté [syrvɔlte] **ADJ 1** *Élec* boosted **2** *Fam (surexcité)* (over)excited, worked up
survolteur [syrvɔltœr] **NM** *Élec* booster

sus [sy(s)] **ADV 1** *Arch* **courir s. à son adversaire** to rush upon *or* at one's opponent, to charge one's opponent **2 en s. de** *(somme d'argent)* in addition to, over and above
INT *Arch* **s. à l'ennemi!** at them!

susceptibilité [syseptibilite] **NF 1** *(sensibilité)* touchiness, sensitivity; **il est d'une grande s.** he's very touchy *or* sensitive; **ménager la s. de qn** to tread carefully where sb is concerned; **blesser la s. de qn** to wound sb's feelings **2** *(en magnétisme)* susceptibility

susceptible [syseptibl] **ADJ 1** *(qui s'offense facilement)* touchy, sensitive **2 s. de** *(interprétations, critiques etc)* open to, *Fml* susceptible of; **être s. de faire qch** to be liable *or* likely to do sth

susciter [sysite] **VT** *(difficultés, commentaires)* to give rise to; *(étonnement)* to cause; *(hostilité, admiration, intérêt etc)* to arouse; **s. des ennuis à qn** to cause *or* create trouble for sb

suscription [syskripsjɔ̃] **NF** *Admin (sur une lettre)* address

sus-dénommé [sysdenɔme] **ADJ** aforementioned

susdit, -ite [sysdi, -it] **ADJ, N** *Jur* aforesaid, above-mentioned

sus-dominante, *pl* **sus-dominantes NF** *Mus* submediant

susmentionné, -ée [sysmãsjɔne] **ADJ, N** *Jur* above-mentioned, aforesaid

susnommé, -ée [sysnɔme] **ADJ, N** *Jur* above-named

suspect, -e [syspɛ, -ɛkt] **ADJ** *(personne, action etc)* suspicious, suspect; *(idées, preuve etc)* dubious, suspect; **des individus suspects rôdaient autour de la maison** suspicious-looking types were hanging around the house; **une viande tout à fait suspecte** meat which seems decidedly doubtful; **s. de** suspected of, under suspicion of; **cela m'est s.** it looks suspicious *or* suspect to me, I don't like the look of it; **tenir qn pour s.** to be suspicious of sb; **devenir s. (à qn)** to arouse (sb's) suspicion
N suspect

suspecter [syspɛkte] **VT** *(personne)* to suspect **(de qch** of sth; **de faire** of doing); *(bonne foi de qn etc)* to suspect, to question, to doubt; **je le suspecte de ne pas me dire la vérité** I suspect he's not telling me the truth, I suspect him of not telling me the truth

suspendre [syspãdr] **VT 1** *(vêtements, tableau, lampe etc)* to hang (up); *(hamac)* to hang up, to sling; **s. qch à un clou/au mur/à ou par un crochet** to hang sth on *or* from a nail/on the wall/on *or* from a hook
2 *(hostilités, enquête, émission)* to suspend; *(paiement, travail)* to suspend, to stop; *(séance)* to adjourn; **la séance est suspendue** we will now adjourn; **s. le paiement d'un chèque** to stop a cheque; *Ordinat* **s. l'exécution d'un programme** to abort a program; **s. son jugement** to suspend judgement
3 *(fonctionnaire etc)* to suspend
VPR se suspendre to hang **(à** from; **par** by); **il est toujours en train de se s. aux jupes de sa mère** he's very clingy, he never leaves his mother's side

suspendu [syspãdy] **ADJ 1** *(pendu)* hanging, suspended; **s. au plafond** hanging from the ceiling; **s. dans le vide** hanging *or* suspended in mid-air; **les jardins suspendus de Babylone** the hanging gardens of Babylon; **pont s.** suspension bridge; *Aut* **voiture bien suspendue** car with good suspension; *Fig* **enfant toujours s. aux jupes de sa mère** clingy child, child who never leaves his mother's side; **être s. aux lèvres de qn** to be hanging on sb's every word
2 *(arrêté, interrompu)* suspended; *(séance)* adjourned; *Jur (jugement)* postponed
3 *Aut (freins)* inboard

suspens [syspã] **NM 1 en s.** *(personne)* in suspense; *(travail)* unfinished, *Fml* in abeyance; *(affaire etc)* outstanding, *Fml* in abeyance; *(problème)* outstanding, unresolved; *(fumée, poussière etc)* hanging in the air; **tenir qn en s.** to keep sb in suspense **2** *Litt (suspense)* suspense

suspense [syspɛns] **NM** *Cin, Littér etc* suspense; **film à s.** thriller; **je le saurai demain, quel s.!** I'll know tomorrow, the suspense is killing me!

suspensif, -ive [syspãsif, -iv] **ADJ** *Jur (veto etc)* suspensive

suspension [syspãsjɔ̃] **NF 1** *(en haut)* suspension, hanging (up)

2 *Chimie* **en s.** in suspension, suspended; *Méd* **s. buvable** oral suspension
3 *(des hostilités, d'un travail, d'une enquête, d'un paiement etc)* suspension; *(de la circulation)* stoppage; *(de la loi)* abeyance; *(d'une séance)* adjournment; *Mil* **s. d'armes** suspension of fighting; **s. d'un paiement** stopping of a payment; **s. de paiements** moratorium on payment; *Ordinat* **s. d'exécution** *(d'un programme)* abort, aborting; *Gram* **points de s.** suspension points, dots; *Aut* **s. pour un an du permis de conduire** a year's driving ban; *Jur* **arrêt de s.** injunction
4 *(de fonctionnaire etc)* suspension
5 *(lampe)* light pendant, ceiling lamp
6 *Aut* suspension; **s. avant à roues indépendantes** independent front suspension; **s. compound** hydrolastic suspension; **s. hydragas** hydragas suspension; **s. hydraulique** hydraulic suspension; **s. hydro-élastique** hydrolastic suspension; **s. hydropneumatique** hydropneumatic suspension; **s. à roues indépendantes** independent suspension; **s. triangulée** wishbone suspension

suspicieux, -euse [syspisjø, -øz] **ADJ** suspicious

suspicion [syspisjɔ̃] **NF** suspicion; **avoir de la s.** *ou* **des suspicions à l'égard de qn** to have one's suspicions about sb; **s. légitime** reasonable suspicion

sustentateur, -trice [systãtatœr, -tris] *Aviat* **ADJ** *(force etc)* lifting; **effort s.** lift; **surface sustentatrice** aerofoil, *Am* airfoil
NM s. rotatif *(d'un hélicoptère)* rotor

sustentation [systãtasjɔ̃] **NF 1** *Géom* base *ou* **polygone de s.** basis of support **2** *Aviat* lift

sustenter [systãte] **VT** *Arch (nourrir)* to sustain, to nourish
VPR se sustenter *Arch, Hum* to take sustenance, to keep up one's strength

sus-tonique, *pl* **sus-toniques NF** *Mus* supertonic

susurrement [sysyrmã] **NM** *Litt* whispering, murmuring

susurrer [sysyre] **VTI** *Litt* to whisper, to murmur; **s. des mots doux à l'oreille de qn** to whisper sweet nothings in sb's ear

suture [sytyr] **NF** *Anat, Chir* suture; **(point de) s.** stitch

suturer [sytyre] **VT** *Chir* to stitch, to suture

suzerain, -aine [syzrɛ̃, -ɛn] **ADJ, N** suzerain
suzeraineté [syzrɛnte] **NF** suzerainty

svastika [svastika] **NM** swastika

svelte [svɛlt] **ADJ** *(personne, corps etc)* slender, svelte

sveltesse [svɛltɛs] **NF** slenderness, slimness

SVP [ɛsvepe] *(abrév* **s'il vous plaît)** please

swahili [swaili] **ADJ, N** *Ling* Swahili

swap [swap] **NM** *Bourse* swap; **s. d'actifs** asset swap; **s. de change** exchange rate swap; **s. vanilla** vanilla swap

swaper [swape] **VT** *Bourse* to swap

Swaziland [swazilãd] **NM** Swaziland

sweater [switœr, swɛ-] **NM** sweater

sweat-shirt, *pl* **sweat-shirts** [switʃœrt, swɛt-] **NM** sweat shirt

sweepstake [swipstɛk] **NM** *Courses de chevaux* sweepstake

swing [swiŋ] **NM 1** *Boxe, Golf* swing **2** *Mus* swing

swinguer [swiŋge] **VI** *Mus Fam* to swing; **ça swingue, ce soir!** it's really swinging tonight!

sybarite [sibarit] **ADJ, N** sybarite

sybaritique [sibaritik] **ADJ** sybaritic

sybaritisme [sibaritism] **NM** sybaritism

sycomore [sikɔmɔr] **NM** sycamore (tree)

sycophante [sikɔfãt] **NM** informer

syllabaire [silabɛr] **NM** spelling-book

syllabe [silab] NF syllable; **s. ouverte/fermée** open/closed syllable; *Fig* **ne pas prononcer** *ou* **dire une s.** not to say a word; **je n'ai pas pu lui arracher une seule s.** I couldn't get a single word out of him/her

syllabique [silabik] ADJ syllabic

syllogisme [silɔʒism] NM syllogism

syllogistique [silɔʒistik] ADJ syllogistic

sylphe [silf] NM, **sylphide** [silfid] NF sylph; **taille de sylphide** sylphlike waist

sylvestre [silvεstr] ADJ *Bot (arbre etc)* woodland

sylvicole [silvikɔl] ADJ forestry, *Spéc* silvicultural

sylviculteur [silvikyltœr] NM silviculturist

sylviculture [silvikyltyr] NF forestry, *Spéc* silviculture

symbiose [sɛ̃bjoz] NF *Biol* symbiosis; *Fig* **vivre en s. avec qn/la nature** to live in harmony with sb/nature

symbole [sɛ̃bɔl] NM **1** symbol **2** *Rel (formule)* creed

symbolique [sɛ̃bɔlik] ADJ **1** symbolic; *(qui signifie une intention)* (paiement, geste etc) token; **payer** *ou* **verser un euro s. de dommages-intérêts** to pay nominal damages; **il a acheté cette maison un euro s.** he bought this house for a token one euro **2** *Ordinat* symbolic
▪ NF **1** *(science)* symbolics **2** *(système de symboles)* system of symbols **3** **la s. des rêves** the interpretation of dreams

symboliquement [sɛ̃bɔlikmɑ̃] ADV symbolically

symbolisation [sɛ̃bɔlizasjɔ̃] NF symbolization

symboliser [sɛ̃bɔlize] VT to symbolize

symbolisme [sɛ̃bɔlism] NM symbolism; *Littér, Beaux-Arts* Symbolism

symboliste [sɛ̃bɔlist] ADJ, N *Littér, Beaux-Arts* Symbolist

symétrie [simetri] NF *Géom, Fig* symmetry

symétrique [simetrik] ADJ symmetrical **(par rapport à** about); *Électron (circuit)* balanced

symétriquement [simetrikmɑ̃] ADV symmetrically

sympa [sɛ̃pa] ADJ *Fam* = **sympathique**

sympathicectomie [sɛ̃patisεktɔmi], **sympathectomie** [sɛ̃patεktɔmi] NF *Chir* sympathectomy

sympathie [sɛ̃pati] NF **1** *(affinité)* liking; **avoir** *ou* **éprouver de la s. pour qn** to like sb, to have a liking for sb; **je n'ai aucune s. pour ce genre d'individu** I have no sympathy for people like that; **concevoir de la s.** *ou* **se prendre de s. pour qn** to take (a liking) to sb; **sympathies et antipathies** likes and dislikes; **sa gentillesse lui attire toutes les sympathies** her kindness makes her friends wherever she goes
2 *(compassion, condoléances)* sympathy; **croyez à notre s.** our deepest sympathy; **un regard de s.** a look of sympathy, a sympathetic look
3 **idées qui ne sont pas en s.** conflicting ideas

Il faut noter que le terme anglais **sympathy** est un faux ami. Il signifie **compassion**.

sympathique [sɛ̃patik] ADJ **1** *(agréable)* *(personne, personnalité)*, nice, likeable; *(entourages, vacances, soirée etc)* nice, pleasant; **ce n'est pas très s. de sa part** that's not very nice of her; **personnalité peu s.** unattractive personality; **il m'a été tout de suite s.** I took to him at once; **il m'est devenu s.** I came to like him; **Paul est fort s. à ma mère** my mother is very fond of Paul **2** **encre s.** invisible ink **3** *Anat, Physiol etc (nerf etc)* sympathetic
▪ NM *Anat* sympathetic nervous system

Il faut noter que le terme anglais **sympathetic** est un faux ami. Il signifie **compréhensif, compatissant**.

sympathiquement [sɛ̃patikmɑ̃] ADV *(accueillir etc)* in a friendly way, warmly; *(offrir etc)* kindly

sympathisant, -ante [sɛ̃patizɑ̃, -ɑ̃t] ADJ sympathizing
▪ N *Pol etc* sympathizer; **un s. de l'ETA** an ETA sympathizer

sympathiser [sɛ̃patize] VI to get on well (together); **s. avec qn** to get on well with sb; **s. avec une organisation terroriste** to sympathize *or* have sympathies with a terrorist organization

Il faut noter que le verbe anglais **to sympathize** est un faux ami. Il signifie **compatir, se montrer solidaire**.

symphonie [sɛ̃fɔni] NF *Mus, Fig* symphony

symphonique [sɛ̃fɔnik] ADJ *Mus (forme, poème etc)* symphonic; *(orchestre)* symphony

symphoniste [sɛ̃fɔnist] N **1** *(auteur)* symphonist **2** *(musicien)* orchestral player

symphyse [sɛ̃fiz] NF *Anat* symphysis

symposium [sɛ̃pozjɔm] NM symposium
VOIR GRAMMAIRE A13

symptomatique [sɛ̃ptɔmatik] ADJ *Méd, Fig* symptomatic **(de** of)

symptomatiquement [sɛ̃ptɔmatikmɑ̃] ADV symptomatically

symptôme [sɛ̃ptom] NM *Méd, Fig* symptom

synagogue [sinagɔg] NF synagogue

synapse [sinaps] NF **1** *Anat* synapse **2** *Biol* synapsis

synchro [sɛ̃kro] NM *Aut* synchromesh

synchromercatique [sɛ̃krɔmεrkatik] NF synchromarketing

synchrone [sɛ̃kron] ADJ synchronous **(de** with)

synchronie [sɛ̃krɔni] NF *Ling etc* synchrony

synchronique [sɛ̃krɔnik] ADJ synchronic

synchronisateur [sɛ̃krɔnizatœr] NM *Aut* synchromesh

synchronisation [sɛ̃krɔnizasjɔ̃] NF synchronization

synchronisé [sɛ̃krɔnize] ADJ synchronized

synchroniser [sɛ̃krɔnize] VT to synchronize **(avec** with)

synchroniseur, -euse [sɛ̃krɔnizœr, -øz] NM **1** *Élec etc* synchronizer **2** *Aut* synchromesh device
▪ NF *Cin* **synchroniseuse** film synchronizer

synchronisme [sɛ̃krɔnism] NM synchronism; **en s.** in synchronism; **hors de s.** out of synchronism; *Cin Fam* out of sync(h)

synchrotron [sɛ̃krɔtrɔ̃] NM *Nucl* synchrotron

synclinal, -ale, -aux, -ales [sɛ̃klinal, -o] ADJ *Géog* synclinal

syncope [sɛ̃kɔp] NF **1** *Méd* fainting fit, *Spéc* syncope; **tomber en s.** to faint; *Fam* **il a failli avoir** *ou* **faire une s. quand il a entendu son nom** he nearly fainted *or* dropped when he heard his name **2** *Gram* syncope **3** *Mus* syncopation

syncopé [sɛ̃kɔpe] ADJ *Mus* syncopated

syncrétisme [sɛ̃kretism] NM *Phil* syncretism

syndic [sɛ̃dik] NM **1** *Hist* syndic; **s. (de copropriété)** *(dans un immeuble)* property agent; **s. de faillite** = official receiver **2** *Suisse (président de commune)* = high-ranking civic official, similar to a mayor, in certain Swiss cantons

Syndic
A "syndic" is an administrative body which represents the interests of the owners of all the flats in a building, collectively known as the "syndicat de copropriété". The role of the "syndic" is to ensure the upkeep of the building and to organize meetings during which a vote is taken on any repairs, improvements etc, that are deemed necessary. The services of the "syndic" are paid for by the owners of the flats.

syndical, -ale, -aux, -ales [sɛ̃dikal, -o] ADJ *(de salariés, d'ouvriers) (mouvement, leader, revendication etc)* (trade-)union, *Am* labor union

syndicalisation [sɛ̃dikalizasjɔ̃] NF *(action)* unionization; *(appartenance à un syndicat)* (trade) union membership, *Am* labor union membership; **le taux de s. dans l'industrie est en chute libre depuis 20 ans** union membership has been plummeting for the last 20 years

syndicaliser [sɛ̃dikalize] = **syndiquer**

syndicalisme [sɛ̃dikalism] NM trade *or Am* labor unionism; **faire du s.** to be involved in union activities

syndicaliste [sɛ̃dikalist] ADJ *(doctrine, leader etc)* (trade-)union, *Am* labor union
▪ N trade unionist, *Am* labor union member

syndicat [sɛ̃dika] NM **1** *(de salariés, d'ouvriers)* (trade) union, *Am* labor union; **être membre d'un s.** to be a member of *or* be in a (trade) union *or Am* labor union **2** *(d'employeurs)* federation; *(de producteurs, propriétaires)* association; *(de financiers)* syndicate; *Fin* **s. de prise ferme** underwriting syndicate
▪▪▪ **s. de faillite** official receivership; **s. d'initiative** tourist (information) office *or* bureau; **s. ouvrier** trade union; **s. patronal** employers' organization; **s. professionnel** trade *or* professional association, trade body

syndicataire [sɛ̃dikatεr] *Fin* ADJ of a syndicate
▪ N member of a syndicate

syndiqué, -ée [sɛ̃dike] ADJ belonging to a (trade) union *or Am* labor union; **ouvriers syndiqués** union members; **être s.** to be a member of a (trade) union; **ouvriers non syndiqués** non-union workers
▪ N (trade) union member, *Am* labor union member

syndiquer [sɛ̃dike] VT *(travailleurs etc)* to unionize, to form into a (trade) union *or Am* labor union
VPR **se syndiquer** to form a (trade) union *or Am* labor union; *(adhérer à un syndicat)* to join a (trade) union *or Am* labor union

syndrome [sɛ̃drom] NM *Méd, Fig* syndrome; **s. de Down** Down's syndrome; **s. immunodéficitaire acquis** acquired immuno-deficiency syndrome; **s. cervical traumatique** whiplash; **s. prémenstruel** premenstrual syndrome *or* tension

synectique [sinεktik] NF synectics

synérèse [sinerεz] NF *Phys, Ling* synaeresis, *Am* syneresis

synergiciel [sinεrʒisjεl] NM *Ordinat* groupware

synergie [sinεrʒi] NF *Com* synergy

synergisme [sinεrʒism] NM synergism

synesthésie [sinεstezi] NF *Psy* synaesthesia, *Am* synesthesia

syngnathe [sɛ̃gnat] NM pipefish

synode [sinɔd] NM *Rel* synod

synodique [sinɔdik] ADJ **1** *Astron* synodic(al) **2** *Rel* synodal

synonyme [sinɔnim] ADJ synonymous (**de** with); **pour elle, mariage est s. de bonheur** for her, marriage is synonymous with happiness

NM synonym; **dictionnaire de synonymes** thesaurus

synonymie [sinɔnimi] NF synonymy, synonymity

synopse [sinɔps] NF synoptic table of the Gospels

synopsis [sinɔpsis] NF synopsis VOIR GRAMMAIRE A14

synoptique [sinɔptik] ADJ synoptic; **les Évangiles synoptiques** the Synoptic Gospels; **tableau s.** *(scientifique etc)* conspectus

synovial, -iale, -iaux, -iales [sinɔvjal, -jo] ADJ *Anat* synovial

synovie [sinɔvi] NF *Anat, Physiol* synovia; *Méd* **épanchement de s.** water on the knee

synovite [sinɔvit] NF *Méd* synovitis

syntacticien, -ienne [sɛ̃taktisjɛ̃, -jɛn] N *Gram* syntactician

syntactique [sɛ̃taktik] ADJ *Gram* syntactic(al)

syntagmatique [sɛ̃tagmatik] ADJ *Gram* phrasal, syntagmatic

syntagme [sɛ̃tagm] NM *Gram* phrase, syntagm(a)

syntaxe [sɛ̃taks] NF *Gram, Ordinat* syntax; **erreur de s.** syntax error

syntaxique [sɛ̃taksik] ADJ *Gram* syntactic(al); *Ordinat* syntax; **analyseur s.** parser

synthèse [sɛ̃tɛz] NF **1** *(intellectuelle)* synthesis; **faire la s. d'un récit** to summarize the main elements of a story; **avoir l'esprit** *ou* **un esprit de s.** to be able to see the overall picture **2** *Chimie* synthesis; **de s.** synthetic **3** *Électron, Mus* synthesis; **de s.** synthetic

synthétique [sɛ̃tetik] ADJ **1** *(présentation)* all-encompassing; *(bilan)* summary; **esprit s.** ability to see the overall picture; **une vue s. des choses** an overall *or* all-encompassing view of things **2** *Chimie, Tex (tissu, fibres)* synthetic, man-made

NM *Tex* synthetic material; **laver les synthétiques à la main** wash synthetics by hand

synthétiquement [sɛ̃tetikmɑ̃] ADV synthetically; **des faits présentés s.** a contextualized presentation of the facts; **voir les**

choses **s.** to see the overall picture, to see things in context

synthétiser [sɛ̃tetize] VT *Chimie, Ordinat etc* to synthesize

synthétiseur [sɛ̃tetizœr] NM *Électron, Mus* synthesizer; **s. de paroles** *ou* **vocal** speech *or* voice synthesizer

syntonisateur [sɛ̃tɔnizatœr] NM *TV, Radio* tuner

syntoniseur [sɛ̃tɔnizœr] NM *Radio* tuner

syphilis [sifilis] NF *Méd* syphilis

syphilitique [sifilitik] ADJ, N *Méd* syphilitic

Syrie [siri] NF Syria

syrien, -ienne [sirjɛ̃, -jɛn] ADJ Syrian
N S. Syrian

syringe [sirɛ̃ʒ] NF *Archéol* syrinx

sysop [sisɔp] NM *Ordinat (abrév* **Systems Operator***)* SYSOP

systématique [sistematik] ADJ **1** *(automatique)* systematic; *Fam* **c'est s.** it's automatic; **cela m'arrive mais ce n'est pas s.** I have been known to but I don't do it regularly *or* as a matter of course *or* but it's not systematic; **il est dans une position de refus s.** he systematically refuses, he refuses as a matter of course **2** *Péj (dogmatique) (opinions, personne)* dogmatic **3** *(absolu) (soutien)* unconditional

NF systematics

systématiquement [sistematikmɑ̃] ADV systematically

systématisation [sistematizasjɔ̃] NF system(at)ization

systématiser [sistematize] VT to system(at)ize

système [sistɛm] NM **1** *(méthode, moyen etc)* system; **tu connais un s. pour payer moins d'impôts?** do you know a way of paying less tax?; **s. d'éducation/pénitentiaire** education/prison system; **elle agit par s.** once she's made up her mind you can't budge her; **avoir l'esprit de s.** to have a systematic mind, *Péj* to stick to the rules, to go by the book

2 *(de roues, valves etc)* system, set; *(de routes)* system, network; *Physiol* system; *Fam* **il me tape** *ou* **porte sur le s.** he gets on my nerves

3 le s. *(la société etc)* the system; **ne pas entrer dans le s.** not to be part of the system

4 *Ordinat* system

▸▸ *Aut* **s. ABS** ABS system; **s. audio** sound *or* audio system; *Pol* **s. bicaméral** two-chamber system; **s. bipartite** two-party system; *Aut* **s. de climatisation** environmental control system; *Banque* **s. de compensation** clearing system; **s. comptable** accounting system; **s. de contrôle de stocks** stock control system; *Bourse* **s. de criée** open outcry system; **le s. D** resourcefulness; **s. de diffusion de données** broadcast data system; **s. de distribution** distribution system; **s. de distribution intégral** total distribution system; **s. Dolby stéréo** Dolby system; **s. de données par radio** radio data system, RDS; **s. douanier** customs system; *Ordinat* **s. expert** expert system; *Ordinat* **s. d'exploitation** operating system; *Ordinat* **s. d'exploitation de** *ou* **à disques** disk operating system; *Ordinat* **s. d'exploitation réseau** network operating system; **s. fiscal** tax system; *Aut* **s. de freinage ABS** anti-lock braking system; *Ordinat* **s. de gestion de bases de données** database management system; *Ordinat* **s. de gestion de fichiers** file management system; **s. d'information marketing** marketing information system; **s. informatique** computer system; *Mktg* **s. d'intelligence d'entreprise** *ou* **marketing** marketing intelligence system; **s. d'inventaire** inventory method; **s. de marketing vertical** vertical marketing system, VMS; **s. monétaire européen** European monetary system; **s. nerveux** nervous system; *Ordinat* **s. du nom de domaine** domain name system; **s. opératoire** operating system; **s. de participation aux bénéfices** profit-sharing scheme; **s. pileux** hair; **s. de prévoyance** social benefits system; **s. de protection sociale** social welfare system; **s. radio de transmission de données** radio data system; **s. de relance** follow-up system; **s. respiratoire** respiratory system; **s. de retraite** pension scheme; **s. de retraite par répartition** contributory pension plan; *Ordinat* **s. de sauvegarde sur bande** tape backup system; *Ordinat* **s. sentinelle** watchdog system; *Ordinat* **s. serveur** host system; **s. solaire** solar system; *Ordinat* **s. à tour** tower system

systémique [sistemik] ADJ *(insecticide etc)* systemic

systole [sistɔl] NF *Physiol* systole

syzygie [siziʒi] NF *Astron* syzygy; **marées de s.** spring tides

T, t [te] NM INV **1** (*lettre*) T, t **2 t euphonique** *forms a link between verbal endings -a, -e and the pronouns* il, elle, on - va-t-il? ira-t-elle? donne-t-on? SEE GRAMMAR B64 **3 en T** T-shaped; **mettre les bureaux en T** to arrange the desks so that they form a T

t 1 (*abrév* **tonne(s)**) t **2** (*abrév* **tome**) vol.

t' [t] *voir* **te, tu**

ta [ta] ADJ POSS *voir* **ton¹**

tabac¹ [taba] NM **1** *Bot* tobacco (plant); **faire pousser du t.** to grow tobacco
2 (*produit*) tobacco; **prendre du t.** to take snuff; **boîte à t.** snuffbox
3 (bureau de) t. tobacconist's (shop), *Am* tobacco store (*which also sells stamps, phonecards, lottery tickets*); *Fig Fam* **c'est le même t.** it amounts to the same thing; *Fig Fam* **il doit avoir eu des ennuis avec la police ou quelque chose du même t.** he must have had some trouble with the police, or something (like that); *Fam* **faire un t.** to be a big hit; *Fam* **passer qn à t.** to beat sb up, to give sb a hammering
4 *Hist, Admin* **les Tabacs** the Tobacco Department
ADJ INV buff
▸▸ **t. blond** Virginia tobacco; **t. brun** black *or* brown tobacco; **t. à chiquer** chewing tobacco; **t. à fumer** smoking tobacco; **t. à mâcher** chewing tobacco; **t. à priser, t. râpé** snuff

tabac² NM *Fam* **passer qn à t.** (*de la police etc*) to beat sb up; **passage à t.** beating (up); **coup de t.** squall; **nous avons essuyé un sacré coup de t.** we went through a dreadful squall; *Fig Fam* **son spectacle a fait un sacré t.** his show was a huge success *or* a big hit

tabagie [tabaʒi] NF **1** *Fam* = place reeking of stale tobacco smoke; **quelle t., cette chambre!** this room stinks of tobacco! **2** *Can* (*bureau de tabac*) tobacconist's (shop), *Am* tobacco store

tabagique [tabaʒik] ADJ (*intoxication etc*) nicotine

tabagisme [tabaʒism] NM smoking, tobacco addiction; **les effets du t.** the effects of smoking; **la lutte contre le t.** the fight to stop people smoking; **t. passif** passive smoking

tabar(d) [tabar] NM *Hist* (*manteau*) tabard

tabassée [tabase] NF *Fam* beating

tabasser [tabase] *Fam* VT **t. qn** to beat sb up; **se faire t.** to be *or* get beaten up; **il s'est fait t. par son père** his father gave him a thrashing
VPR **se tabasser** to beat each other up

tabatière [tabatjɛr] NF **1** (*boîte*) snuffbox **2** (*lucarne*) (hinged) skylight

tabellion [tabeljɔ̃] NM *Fam Hum* lawyer

tabernacle [tabɛrnakl] NM **1** *Rel* tabernacle **2** *Can Fam* **t.!** damn!

tablar(d) [tablar] NM *Suisse* shelf

tablature [tablatyr] NF *Mus* tablature

table [tabl] NF **1** (*meuble*) table; **t. de cuisine/de salle à manger** kitchen/dining table; **t. roulante** trolley; *Fig* **jouer cartes sur t.** to put one's cards on the table
2 (*tablée, nourriture*) table; **mettre** *ou* **dresser/débarrasser la t.** to lay *or* set/clear the table; **aimer les plaisirs de la t.** to be fond of good food and wine; **avoir une bonne t.** to keep a good table; **la t. est bonne** the food is good; **à t.!** dinner/lunch/*etc* is ready!, *Fam* come and get it!; **être à t.** to be at the table or at dinner/lunch/*etc*; **se mettre à t.** to sit down at the *or Am* to table *or* to dinner/lunch/*etc*, *Arg Fig* to come clean, to spill; **quand est-ce qu'on passe** *ou* **se met à t.?** when are we eating?; **se lever de t.** to leave the table; **réserver une t. dans un restaurant** to book *or* reserve a table in a restaurant; *Rel* **la Sainte T.** the Communion table
3 *Tech* (*d'un marteau, d'une valve etc*) face; (*d'une poutre métallique*) flange
4 *Tél* switchboard
5 *Électron* table, board
6 (*de pierre etc*) slab; (*d'un dolmen*) capstone
7 (*liste*) table
8 *Mus* (*d'un violon etc*) sounding board, belly
▸▸ *Hér* **t. d'attente** field; **t. basse** coffee table; **t. de billard** billiard table; **t. de chevet** bedside *or Am* night table; **t. de cuisson** hob; **t. à découper** carving table; **t. à dessin** drawing board, draughtsman's *or Am* draftsman's table *or* board; *Ordinat* **t. à digitaliser** digitizing pad; *Mktg* **t. d'échantillonnage** sampling tabulation; **t. d'écoute: mettre qn sur t. d'écoute** to tap *or* put a tap on sb's telephone, to wiretap sb; **nous étions sur t. d'écoute** our phone was being tapped; *Ordinat* **t. des fichiers** file allocation table, FAT; **tables frappantes** (*en spiritisme*) table rapping; *Mus* **t. d'harmonie** (*d'un violon etc*) sounding board, belly; **t. d'honneur** (*dans un banquet etc*) top table; **t. d'hôte** table d'hôte; **t. d'intérêts** interest table; **t. de jeu** card table; **t. à langer** changing table; *Bible* **tables de la loi** Tables of the Law; **t. des matières** (table of) contents; **t. de mixage** *TV etc* mixing console; *Radio* sound mixer; **t. de montage** *Journ etc* light table; *TV* editing desk *or* table; **t. de multiplication** multiplication table; **t. des négociations** negotiating table; **s'asseoir à la t. des négociations** to get round the negotiating table; **t. de nuit** bedside *or Am* night table; *Mil* **t. d'officiers** officers' mess; **t. d'opération** operating table; **il a dû repasser sur la t. d'opération** he had to have another operation *or* more surgery; **t. d'orientation** orientation *or* panoramic table; **t. à rallonges** extending table; *Phil* **t. rase** tabula rasa; *Fig* **faire t. rase** to make a clean sweep; *Fig* **faire t. rase (du passé)** to wipe the slate clean; *Fig* **faire t. rase des préjugés** to get rid of one's prejudices; *Ordinat* **t. de recherche** *ou* **de référence** look-up table; **t. à repasser** ironing board; *Pol, Ind* **t. ronde** round-table conference, round table; (*débat*) debate; *TV, Radio* discussion programme; *Littér* **la T. ronde** the Round Table; **t. roulante** tea trolley; *Rail* **t. de roulement** (*d'un rail*) tread; **t. de toilette** washstand; *Ordinat* **t. traçante** plotter; **t. de travail** work table; *Ordinat* **t. de vérité** truth table

tableau, -eaux [tablo] NM **1** (*panneau, support*) board; (*pour les clefs*) key rack *or* board; **t. des publications de mariage** = board where banns are posted; *Scol* **t. (noir)** (black)board; *Scol* **aller au t.** to come out/go out to the board
2 *Beaux-Arts* painting, picture; **un t. de Dürer** a painting by Dürer; **marchand de tableaux** art dealer; **exposition de tableaux** art exhibition, exhibition of paintings; *Fig Fam* **tu imagines le t.!** you can picture *or* imagine the scene!; *Fig* **quel t. vous faites, tous les deux!** look at you two, what a picture!; *Fig* **je vois d'ici le t.!** I can just picture it!; *Fig* **cela faisait un t. charmant/touchant** it was a charming/touching sight *or* scene; *Fig* **de la colline se découvre un magnifique t.** there is a beautiful view from the hill; *Fig* **brosser le t. de la situation** to give a picture of the situation; *Fig* **et pour achever le t.** and to crown it all; *Fam* **vieux t.** (*vieille coquette*) (painted) old hag
3 *Théâtre* scene; **t. vivant** tableau (vivant)
4 (*liste*) list, table; (*graphique*) chart; *Typ* table; *Rail* **t. horaire** timetable; **t. récapitulatif** summary table; *Pharm* **produit de t. A/B/C** A-/B-/C-list product; **mettre sous forme de t.** to tabulate; *Fig Fam* **gagner sur tous les/sur les deux tableaux** to win on all/both counts; **jouer** *ou* **miser sur plusieurs tableaux** to hedge one's bets
5 *Jur* (*d'avocats*) roll; **être rayé** *ou* **se faire rayer du t.** to be struck off the rolls; **se faire inscrire au t.** to be called to the bar
▸▸ **tableaux d'activité économique** economic activity tables; **t. d'affichage** notice *or Am* bulletin board; *Compta* **t. d'amortissement** depreciation schedule; **t. d'avancement** promotions list; **t. d'avancement de commandes** order flowchart; **t. blanc** whiteboard; **t. de bord** *Aut* dashboard, fa(s)cia; *Aviat* instrument panel; *Ordinat* control panel; *Com* management control data; **t. de chasse** (*animaux*), *Fig* (*avions abattus*) bag; *Fig* (*conquêtes*) list of conquests; *Fig* **tu pourras la mettre à ton t. de chasse!** that's another notch on your gun!; **t. à clés** key board *or* rack; *Méd* **t. clinique** clinical picture; **t. de commande** (*d'appareil électroménager*) control panel, panel of switches; *Élec, Tél* **t. commutateur** switchboard, distribution board *or* panel; *Gram* **t. de conjugaison** conjugation table; *Ordinat* **t. de connexions**

plugboard; **t. de contrôle** *Tech* control panel; *Tél* monitoring board; **t. de conversion** conversion table; *Élec, Tél* **t. de distribution** switchboard, distribution board *or* panel; *Élec etc* **t. d'éclairage** lighting panel; *Compta* **t. des emplois et ressources de fonds** statement of sources and applications of funds; **t. de l'état des chambres** *(dans un hôtel)* reception board, room rack; *Compta* **t. de financement** statement of sources and uses of funds, cashflow statement; *(planning)* finance plan; *Scol* **t. d'honneur** = document certifying that a pupil has obtained good marks *or esp Am* grades; **t. de maître** old master; **t. de manœuvre** instrument board *or* panel; **t. d'organisation** organization(al) chart; *Élec* **t. de raccordement** patchboard; **t. récapitulatif** summary table; **t. des réservations** reservations chart; *Compta* **t. de roulement** statement of changes in working capital; *Com* **t. de service** rota; **t. synoptique** synopsis, summary

tableautin [tablotɛ̃] NM *Beaux-Arts* small picture

tablée [table] NF *(personnes à table)* table; **j'ai l'habitude des grandes tablées** I'm used to having a lot of people round the table; **une joyeuse t.** a merry gathering (around a table)

tabler [table] VI **t. sur qch** to count *or* bank on sth

tablette [tablɛt] NF **1** *(d'une étagère etc)* shelf; *(dans un avion)* table; **t. à coulisse** *(d'un bureau)* pull-out flap **2** *Hist* **tablettes** *(pour écrire)* (writing) tablets; *Fig* **écrire qch sur ses tablettes** to make a note of sth **3** *(de chocolat)* bar; *(de chewing-gum)* stick; *Pharm* tablet
▸▸*Aut* **t. arrière** rear parcel shelf, back shelf; *Élec* **t. à bornes** terminal plate; **t. de fenêtre** windowsill; *Ordinat* **t. graphique** graphics tablet; **t. de piano** music rest

tableur [tablœr] NM *Ordinat* spreadsheet; **t. de graphiques** graphics spreadsheet

tablier [tablije] NM **1** *(vêtement)* apron, *Br Fam* pinny; *(d'écolier)* smock; **t. blouse** *(woman's)* overall; *Fig Fam* **rendre son t.** to hand in one's notice; *(d'un domestique)* to give notice **2** *Mil (d'avant-train)* footboard; *(de scooter)* footrest **3** *(de cheminée)* hood **4** *(de magasin etc)* (steel) shutter **5** *(de pont)* deck, road(way); *(de locomotive)* footplate **6** *(de laminoir)* table; *(de tour)* apron; *Ind* **t. sans fin** apron feed **7** *(de forge)* hearth **8** *Aut* apron, valance; **t. de pare-chocs** bumper apron

tabloïd(e) [tablɔid] NM **1** *Journ* tabloid (newspaper) **2** *Pharm* tablet
ADJ **format t.** tabloid format

tabou [tabu] ADJ, NM taboo; **un épisode t. de l'histoire de France** an episode in French history that is never spoken of *or* mentioned; **c'est un sujet t.** that's taboo, that's a taboo subject

taboulé [tabule] NM *Culin* tabbouleh

tabouret [taburɛ] NM stool; *(pour les pieds)* footstool; **t. de bar/piano** bar/piano stool

tabulaire [tabylɛr] ADJ tabular

tabulateur [tabylatœr] NM tab (key); *(de machine à écrire)* tab key, tabulator; **régler les tabulateurs** to set tabs *(à à* t)

tabulation [tabylasjɔ̃] NF tabulation, tabbing; *(colonne)* tab; **poser des tabulations dans** to tab

tabulatrice [tabylatris] NF *(pour cartes perforées)* tabulator

tabuler [tabyle] VT to tabulate, to tab

tac [tak] NM *(bruit)* click; **t. t. t.** *(d'une mitraillette, du pivert)* rat-a-tat; *Fig* **riposter** *ou* **répondre du t. au t.** to answer quick as

lightning; *Fig* **je lui ai répondu du t. au t. que ...** I retorted quick as a flash that ..., I came back quick as lightning that ...

tacet [tasɛt] NM *Mus* tacet

tache [taʃ] NF **1** *(de graisse, de boue, de sang, d'huile etc)* stain; *(de peinture)* blob, splash; *(dans une pierre précieuse)* flaw, blemish; *(dans un fruit)* blemish; *(d'encre)* blot; *(de couleur, lumière)* splash; *Fig (sur la réputation etc)* blot, stain; **faire une/des tache(s)** to make a mess; **tu ne peux donc pas manger sans faire de taches?** can't you eat without making a mess?; **tu es en train de faire des taches sur le canapé/ton pull** you're getting stains on the couch/your sweater; **t. de suie** fleck of soot, smut; *Fig* **sans t.** *(réputation)* spotless; *Fig* **faire t.** *(d'un bibelot, d'une personne etc)* to stick out like a sore thumb; *Fig* **faire t. d'huile** to spread **2** *(sur la peau)* mark; **chien blanc à taches feu** white dog with reddish markings *or* patches *or* spots **3** *Fam (personne)* non-entity, loser, no-hoper; **quelle t. ce mec-là!** what a total non-entity *or* loser *or* no-hoper that guy is!
▸▸**t. de lumière** *Théâtre, Cin* hot spot; *TV* shading; *Anat* **t. de Mariotte** *(à l'œil)* blind spot; **t. de rousseur** freckle; **t. solaire** *ou* **du soleil** sunspot; **t. de vin** strawberry mark

tâche [taʃ] NF task, job; **travail à la t.** *Ind* piece-work; *(intermittent)* jobbing (work); **ouvrier à la t.** *Ind* piece-worker; *(par intermittence)* jobbing workman; **travailler à la t.** to do piece-work; **on n'est pas à la t.!** nobody's timing us!; *Litt* **prendre à t. de faire qch** to undertake to do sth; *Ordinat* **t. d'arrière-plan** *ou* **de fond** background task *or* job

taché [taʃe] ADJ **1** *(vêtement, tissu)* stained; *Biol* spotted; **t. d'encre/de sang/de graisse** ink-/blood-/grease-stained **2** *(fruit)* bruised

tachéomètre [takeɔmɛtr] NM tacheometer, tachymeter

tachéométrie [takeɔmetri] NF tacheometry, tachymetry

tacher [taʃe] VT *(vêtement etc)* to get stains on, to stain; *(réputation etc)* to sully, to tarnish
VI *(de l'encre, du vin etc)* to stain
VPR **se tacher** *(d'une personne)* to get stains on oneself; *(d'un tissu, d'un vêtement etc)* to stain

tâcher [taʃe] VI **t. de faire qch** to try *or* attempt to do sth; **tâchez de ne pas oublier** try not to forget; **tâchons que cela ne se reproduise plus** let's make sure it doesn't happen again

tâcheron [taʃrɔ̃] NM **1** *Péj* skivvy, drudge; **j'en ai assez de faire ce métier de t.!** I've had enough of this drudgery *or* skivvying! **2** *Agr* piece-worker **3** *Constr etc* subcontractor, jobber **4** *Fam* hack

tacheté [taʃte] ADJ *(papier, plumage)* speckled, mottled; *(chat)* tabby; **chat noir t. de blanc** black cat with white spots *or* markings

tacheter [taʃte] VT to spot, to speckle

tacheture [taʃtyr] NF spot, speckle

tachisme [taʃism] NM *Beaux-Arts* tachisme

tachiste [taʃist] ADJ, N *Beaux-Arts* tachiste

tachycardie [takikardi] NF *Méd* tachycardia

tachygraphe [takigraf] NM tachograph

tachymètre [takimɛtr] NM tachometer; *Aut* speedometer

tachymétrie [takimetri] NF tachometry

tachytoscope [takitoskɔp] NM *Mktg* tachistoscope

Tacite [tasit] NM Tacitus

tacite [tasit] ADJ *(consentement, accord, connaissance etc)* tacit; **de façon t.** tacitly; *Jur* **t. reconduction** tacit renewal; *Jur* **renouvelable par t. reconduction** renewable by tacit consent

tacitement [tasitmã] ADV tacitly

taciturne [tasityrn] ADJ taciturn

tacle [takl] NM *Ftbl* tackle; **t. glissé** sliding tackle

tacler [takle] VTI *Ftbl* to tackle

tacot [tako] NM *Fam Péj (voiture)* (old) jalopy, *Br* (old) banger

tact [takt] NM **1** *(délicatesse etc)* tact; **avoir du t.** to be tactful; **être plein de t.** to be very tactful, to be full of tact; **manquer de t.** to be tactless, to lack tact; **avec t.** tactfully, with tact; **sans t.** *(réponse, geste)* tactless; *(répondre, agir)* tactlessly **2** *Vieilli (toucher)* (sense of) touch

tacticien, -ienne [taktisjɛ̃, -jɛn] N tactician

tactile [taktil] ADJ tactile

tactique [taktik] ADJ tactical
NF tactics; **je vais devoir changer de t.** I'm going to have to change my tactics; **une t. nouvelle** new tactics, a new tactic; **ce n'est pas la meilleure t. pour le convaincre** it's not the best way of convincing him

tadjik, -e [tadʒik] ADJ Tadjik
N T. Tadjik

Tadjikistan [tadʒikistã] NM Tadjikistan

tadorne [tadɔrn] NM *Orn* shelduck

tænia [tenja] NM *Méd* tapeworm, *Spéc* taenia, *Am* tenia

taf [taf] NM *Fam (travail)* work; *(tâche, emploi)* job

taffe [taf] NF *Fam (de cigarette)* drag

taffer [tafe] VI *Fam (travailler)* to work

taffetas [tafta] NM **1** *Tex* taffeta **2** *Méd* **t. anglais** *ou* **gommé** sticking plaster, *Am* Band-Aid®

tafiard, -arde [tafjar, -ard] *Belg* ADJ *(vantard)* boastful
N *(vantard)* boaster

tag [tag] NM tag *(piece of graffiti)*

Tage [taʒ] NM le T. the Tagus

tagliatelles [taljatɛl] NFPL *Culin* tagliatelle *(with sing vb)*

taguer [tage] VT & VI to tag

tagueur, -euse [tagœr, -øz] N tagger

Tahiti [taiti] NF Tahiti

tahitien, -ienne [taisjɛ̃, -jɛn] ADJ Tahitian
N T. Tahitian

taïaut [tajo] INT tally-ho!

taie [tɛ] NF **1** **t. (d'oreiller)** pillowcase, pillowslip **2** *Méd* leucoma; *Fig Litt* **avoir une t. sur l'œil** to be blinkered, to have tunnel vision

taïga [tajga] NF *Géog* taiga

taillable [tajabl] ADJ **être t. et corvéable (à merci)** to be a skivvy *or* a drudge; *Hist (d'un serf etc)* to be liable to tallage

taillade [tajad] NF slash, gash; **se faire une t. dans le doigt** to gash one's finger

taillader [tajade] VT to slash, to gash; **se t. le doigt/le menton** to gash one's finger/chin; **se t. les veines** to slash one's wrists; *Couture* **tailladé** slashed

taillandier [tajãdje] NM maker of edge-tools

taillaule [tajol] NF *Suisse Culin* = sweet pastry roll

taille [taj] NF **1** *(hauteur)* *(de personne)* height; **quelle est votre t.?** what height are you?, how tall are you?; **atteindre sa t. adulte** to reach one's full height; **de grande t./t. moyenne** very tall/of medium height; **de petite t.** short
2 *(grandeur)* size; **quelle est votre t.?, quelle t. faites-vous?** *(en vêtement)* what size are you *or* do you take?; **avez-vous la t. en dessus/dessous?** do you have the next size up/down?; **au moins deux tailles en dessous** at least two sizes smaller; **pour les**

tailles exceptionnelles, pour les grandes tailles outsize; de petite t. small; une lettre de la t. d'une affiche a letter the size of a poster, a poster-sized letter; des avocats de la t. du poing avocados the size of your fist; une erreur de belle t. a huge mistake; Ordinat t. de disque dur hard disk size; Ordinat t. de mémoire memory size; Ordinat t. de champ field size; Typ t. de corps body size; Typ t. de fonte font size; Typ t. des caractères type size; t. du papier paper size

3 Fig (mesure) trouver un adversaire à sa t. to meet one's match; trouver un collaborateur à sa t. to find a colleague who is one's equal or who has an equal level of skills; il est de t. à vous battre he is big enough or strong enough to beat you; il n'est pas de t. à être chef he's not cut out to be a leader, he's not the stuff that leaders are made of; je ne suis pas de t. à vous prouver le contraire I'm not in a position to prove you wrong; il n'est pas de t. à lutter contre vous he is no match for you, he stands no chance against you; rien à craindre, il n'est pas de t. have no fear, he's not up to it; un mensonge de t. a whopper; le mensonge était de t. it was a thumping great lie

4 (partie du corps) waist; (de vêtement) waist, waistline; tour de t. waist (measurement); avoir la t. fine to have a trim waist or a good waistline; retrouver une t. fine to get one's waistline back; elle a une t. de guêpe she is wasp-waisted; tu as la t. bien prise dans cette jupe the skirt is a perfect fit at the waist; prendre qn par la t. (d'un bras) to put an arm round sb's waist; (des deux mains) to take sb by the waist, to seize sb round the waist; pantalon à t. haute/basse trousers with a high/low waist(line), high-/low-waisted trousers; pardessus à t. fitted overcoat

5 (action) (de pierre, de pierres précieuses, de vêtements, de cheveux etc) cutting; (d'arbuste) pruning, trimming; (de haie) trimming, clipping; (de roue d'engrenage) milling

6 (tranchant) (d'une épée etc) edge

7 (taillis) jeune t. coppice

8 Min gallery

9 Hist (redevance) tallage

▸▸ t. basse (d'un pneu) low profile; Bourse t. boursière market size; Couture t. normale natural waistline

taillé [tɑje] ADJ bien t. (personne) well-built; bien/mal t. (ongles, moustaches) well-/badly trimmed; (vêtement) well-/badly cut; Fig t. pour commander/pour un métier cut out to be a leader/for a job; cheveux taillés en brosse crew cut; crayon t. en pointe sharp pencil; t. dans le roc carved out out of the rock

taille-crayon, pl taille-crayon(s) NM pencil sharpener

taille-douce, pl tailles-douces NF (technique, estampe) copper-plate engraving

tailler [tɑje] VT **1** (pierre, diamant, herbe, cheveux, bifteck etc) to cut; (arbre) to prune, to trim; (haie, barbe etc) to trim, to clip; (vigne) to dress; (crayon) to sharpen; t. qch en biseau to bevel sth; Fig t. une armée en pièces to cut an army to pieces; Fig Fam t. une bavette to have a chat or Br natter; Fam t. la route (parcourir beaucoup de chemin) to eat up the miles; (partir) to beat it, Br to scarper, Am to book it **2** Couture t. un vêtement to cut out a garment; t. une robe d'après ou sur un patron to cut a dress from a pattern; Fig Fam t. un costard ou une veste à qn to slag sb off; Fam il a failli se faire t. un short en traversant la rue he almost got run over crossing the street

VI Chir to make an incision; t. dans la chair ou dans le vif to cut into the flesh

VPR se tailler **1** (se couper) se t. la barbe to trim one's beard; se t. un chemin à travers

... to carve one's way through ...; Fig se t. un beau succès to be very successful **2** Fam (partir) to beat it, to scram; je me taille! I'm off!

tailleur [tɑjœr] NM **1** (de pierres, de diamants, d'arbres etc) cutter **2** Couture tailor; s'asseoir en t. to sit cross-legged **3** (costume) suit

tailleur-pantalon, pl tailleurs-pantalons NM trouser or Am pant suit

taillis [tɑji] NM copse, coppice; dans les t. in the copse or coppice

ADJ bois t. copsewood, brushwood

tain [tɛ̃] NM (de glace) silvering; refaire le t. d'une glace to resilver a mirror; glace ou miroir sans t. two-way mirror

taire [tɛr] (prp taisant; pp tu; pr ind je tais, il tait, n. taisons, ils taisent; pr sub je taise; impf je taisais; p hist je tus; fu je tairai) VT (quelque chose) to say nothing about, not to mention; (cacher) to suppress, to hush up; une dame dont je tairai le nom a lady who shall be nameless; t. qch à qn to keep or hide or conceal sth from sb

VPR se taire (être silencieux) to be quiet or silent; (cesser de parler) to stop talking, to be or Fml fall silent; (décider de ne rien dire) to keep quiet or silent; (d'un son) to stop, to cease; tu ne vas pas te t. jusqu'à la fin du dîner! you're surely going to open your mouth and say something before the end of the dinner!; tais-toi! be quiet!, Fam shut up!; faire t. (bavard, opposition, critiques) to silence, to reduce to silence, Fam to shut up; (conscience) to silence; (enfant) to keep quiet, Fam to shut up; faire t. sa douleur to stifle one's grief; savoir se t. to know how to keep quiet or to keep one's mouth shut; elle a perdu une occasion de se t. she would have done better to say nothing or to keep her mouth shut

taiseux, -euse [tɛzø, -øz] Belg ADJ (taciturne) taciturn

N (personne taciturne) taciturn person

Taiwan [tajwan] N Taiwan

taiwanais, -aise [tajwanɛ, -ɛz] ADJ Taiwanese

N T. Taiwanese

tajine [taʒin] NM Culin tajine

take-off [tɛkɔf] NM INV Écon takeoff

talc [talk] NM Minér talc; (produit) talc, talcum powder

talé [tale] ADJ (fruit) bruised

talent [talɑ̃] NM **1** (don) talent; son t. de pianiste his talent as a pianist; avoir du t. to be talented; homme/musicien de t. talented man/musician; sans t. untalented; elle n'a aucun t. pour faire la cuisine she has no talent for cooking, she's a hopeless cook; avoir le t. de faire qch to have a knack or gift for doing sth; exploiter ses talents to make use of one's talents (de cuisinier as a cook); faire appel à tous les talents to call in the best talent or brains; éditeur à la recherche de nouveaux talents publisher in search of new talent **2** Antiq (monnaie) talent

talentueusement [talɑ̃tɥøzmɑ̃] ADV with talent

talentueux, -euse [talɑ̃tɥø, -øz] ADJ talented

taler [tale] VT (fruit etc) to bruise

taleth [talɛt] NM Rel tallith

talion [taljɔ̃] NM la loi du t. an eye for an eye (and a tooth for a tooth); appliquer la loi du t. to demand an eye for an eye

talisman [talismɑ̃] NM talisman

talitre [talitr] NM (crustacé) sand flea or hopper

talkie-walkie, pl talkies-walkies [tokiwoki] NM walkie-walkie

talk-show, pl talk-shows [tokʃo] NM TV talk or Br chat show

Tallinn [talin] N Tallinn

Talmud [talmyd] NM Rel le T. the Talmud

talmudique [talmydik] ADJ Talmudic(al)

talmudiste [talmydist] NM Talmudist

taloche [talɔʃ] NF **1** Fam (gifle) clout, cuff **2** Constr (plasterer's) hawk

talocher [talɔʃe] VT Fam (personne) to clout, to cuff

talon [talɔ̃] NM **1** (de pied, de chaussure, de bas etc) heel; marcher sur les talons de qn to tread on sb's heels, to follow close or hard on sb's heels; être toujours sur les talons de qn to dog sb's footsteps; la police est sur ses talons depuis quinze jours the police have been on his heels for two weeks; donner du t. à son cheval to give one's horse the spur; montrer ou tourner les talons to turn on one's heel **2** Tech (d'outil, de mât, de club de golf, de crosse de fusil) heel; Mus (d'archet) heel, nut; (de queue de billard) butt; (de lame d'épée, de baïonnette, de palan, d'essieu) shoulder **3** Cartes stock, reserve, talon **4** (bout) (de pain, de fromage, de jambon etc) heel **5** (de chèque etc) stub, Br counterfoil; t. à retourner reply slip; t. et volant (de chèque) counterfoil and leaf **6** Archit ogee (moulding), talon

▸▸ t. d'Achille Achilles' heel; talons aiguilles stiletto heels; (chaussures) stilettos; talons compensés built-up heels; talons hauts high heels; chaussures à talons hauts high-heeled shoes, high heels; t. minute heel bar; talons plats flat heels; chaussures à talons plats flat-heeled shoes, flats

talonnage [talɔnaʒ] NM Rugby heeling

talonnement [talɔnmɑ̃] NM (de cheval) spurring on; Fig (harcèlement) (de qn) hounding

talonner [talɔne] VT **1** (suivre) (personne) to follow on the heels of, to follow close behind **2** (harceler) (d'une personne) to hound; (de la faim) to dog; être talonné par la mort to be pursued by death; se faire t. par le fisc to be hounded by the tax man, to have the tax man breathing down one's neck **3** (presser du talon) (cheval) to spur on **4** Rugby to heel

VI **1** Naut (d'un navire) to touch, to bump **2** Rugby to heel

talonnette [talɔnɛt] NF **1** (d'une chaussure) counter; (à l'intérieur de la chaussure) heel pad **2** (à l'intérieur d'un pantalon) binding

talonneur [talɔnœr] NM Rugby hooker

talquer [talke] VT to sprinkle with talc or talcum powder

talure [talyr] NF (sur un fruit) bruise

talus [taly] NM **1** (pente) slope; en t. sloping; la voiture est tombée dans le t. the car fell down the slope **2** (construit) embankment, slope, ramp **3** Géol talus, scree

talweg [talvɛg] NM Géog t(h)alweg

tamanoir [tamanwar] NM Zool great anteater, ant bear

tamarin[1] [tamarɛ̃] NM **1** (fruit) tamarind **2** (tamaris) tamarisk

tamarin[2] NM Zool tamarin

tamarinier [tamarinje] NM tamarind (tree)

tamaris [tamaris] NM Bot tamarisk

tambouille [tɑ̃buj] NF Arg **1** (cuisine) cooking; faire la t. to do the cooking **2** (plat etc) grub, nosh; on s'est fait une bonne petite t. we made ourselves some great grub or nosh

tambour [tɑ̃bur] NM **1** (instrument de musique) drum; battre du t. to play the drum, to drum; entendre un bruit de t. to hear the sound of drums; peau de t. drum-head; Fam raisonner comme un t. to talk through one's hat; sans t. ni trompette quietly, without (any) fuss, Fam without a song and dance **2** (personne) drummer **3** Tech (d'une turbine, d'une machine à laver etc), Naut (d'un

cabestan) drum; *Élec (d'une bobine)* cylinder; **freins à t.** drum brakes **4** *(d'église etc)* vestibule; *(tourniquet)* revolving door **5** *(à broder)* (embroidery) frame, tambour **6** *Archit (d'une colonne etc)* drum
▸▸ **t. de basque** tambourine; **t. de câble** cable drum; **t. de frein** brake drum; *Typ* **t. d'impression** print drum; **t. de photocopie** photocopier drum; **t. photosensible** photosensitive drum; *Hist* **t. de ville** town crier

tambourin [tãburɛ̃] NM **1** *(en Provence)* = small drum used in Provençal folk music **2** *(tambour de basque)* tambourine

tambourinage [tãburinaʒ] NM drumming

tambourinaire [tãburinɛr] NM **1** *(musicien)* tambourin player **2** *Hist (annonceur)* town crier

tambourinement [tãburinmã] NM drumming

tambouriner [tãburine] VI *(avec ses doigts, des objets etc)* to drum; **la pluie tambourine sur le toit** the rain is drumming on the roof
VT **1** *(rythme, air etc)* to drum out; *(avec les doigts)* to tap out **2** *(nouvelle)* Arch to announce; *Fam* to shout from the rooftops

tambour-major, *pl* **tambours-majors** NM *Mil* drum major

Tamerlan [tamɛrlã] NM Tamburlaine

tamil, -ile [tamil] ADJ Tamil
NM *Ling* Tamil
N **T.** Tamil

tamis [tami] NM sieve; *(pour le sable etc)* sifter; *(pour les liquides)* strainer; *Ind* riddle, screen; **passer au t.** *(farine etc)* to sieve; *(sable etc)* to sift; *(liquide)* to strain; *Ind* to riddle, to screen; *Fig (témoignage, information, candidats etc)* to sift through

tamisage [tamizaʒ] NM *(de farine etc)* sieving; *(de sable etc)* sifting; *(de liquide)* straining; *Ind* riddling, screening

Tamise [tamiz] NF la **T.** the Thames

tamiser [tamize] VT *(farine etc)* to sieve; *(sable etc)* to sift; *(liquide)* to strain; *Ind* to riddle, to screen; **rideaux qui tamisent la lumière** curtains that filter the light; **lumière tamisée** subdued light
VI *(de la poussière, de la lumière etc)* to filter through

tamoul, -oule [tamul] ADJ Tamil
NM *Ling* Tamil
N **T.** Tamil

tampon [tãpɔ̃] NM **1** *(bouchon)* plug, stopper; *(d'un tonneau)* bung **2** *Constr* wall plug **3** *Méd* swab; *Chir* pad, plug, tampon; *(hygiénique)* tampon *(cachet, instrument)* stamp; *(de la poste)* postmark; **coup de t.** stamp **5** *(pour polir)* pad **6 t. (de choc)** *(de train)* buffer; **coup de t.** collision *(between buffers)*; *Pol* **État/zone t.** buffer state/zone; *Fig Fam* **servir de t. (entre deux personnes)** to act as a buffer (between two people)
▸▸ **t. buvard** blotter; **t. dateur** date stamp; **t. encreur** ink pad; **t. hygiénique** ou **périodique** tampon; **t. à récurer** scourer, scouring pad

tamponnage [tãpɔnaʒ] NM *Chimie* neutralizing

tamponne [tãpɔn] NF *Belg Fam* (drinking) binge; **prendre une t.** to get plastered *or Br* ratted

tamponnement [tãpɔnmã] NM **1** *(bouchage) (de blessure etc)* plugging **2** *(essuyage) (avec un tampon)* swabbing, dabbing **3** *Aut, Rail* collision

tamponner [tãpɔne] VT **1** *(essuyer)* to swab, to dab; *Typ (caractères, plaque de métal)* to ink up **2** *(timbrer) (document etc)* to stamp; **t. une lettre** to frank a letter **3** *(polir) (meuble)* to French-polish **4** *Chimie* to neutralize **5** *(voiture, train etc)* to run into, to collide

with **6** *Vieilli (boucher)* to plug, to stop (up); *Méd (blessure)* to put a wad over, to plug; *Constr (mur)* to plug
VPR **se tamponner 1** *(de voitures, de trains etc)* to run into each other, to collide **2 se t. le front** to mop one's brow; **se t. les yeux** to dab one's eyes; *Arg* **il s'en tamponne (le coquillard)** he doesn't give a damn *or* a monkey's

tamponneur, -euse [tãpɔnœr, -øz] ADJ **autos tamponneuses** Dodgems®, bumper cars

tamponnoir [tãpɔnwar] NM wall drill

tam-tam, *pl* **tam-tams** [tamtam] NM **1** *(tambour)* tom-tom **2** *Fam Péj (tapage)* fuss, ballyhoo; **faire du t. autour de qch** to make a great fuss *or* great ballyhoo about sth **3** *(gong)* gong

tan [tã] NM tan, (tanner's) bark

tancer [tãse] VT (**je tançai(s); n. tançons**) *Litt* to berate, to scold

tanche [tãʃ] NF **1** *(poisson)* tench **2** *Fam (imbécile)* pillock, plonker, *Am* meathead

tandem [tãdɛm] NM **1 chevaux attelés en t.** horses driven tandem **2** *(bicyclette)* tandem **3** *(deux personnes)* twosome, duo; **travailler en t.** to work in tandem; **un t. de comédiens** a comic duo **4** *Tech* **cylindres en t.** tandem cylinders **5** *Ordinat* **central t.** tandem exchange, tandem central office

tandis que [tãdi(s)kə] CONJ **1** *(alors que)* while, whereas **2** *(pendant que)* while, *Fml* whilst

tangage [tãgaʒ] NM *Naut, Aviat* pitching; *Fig* reeling, swaying; **pour supprimer le t. du bateau** to stop the boat pitching

tangara [tãgara] NM *Orn* tanager

tangence [tãʒãs] NF *Géom* tangency; **point de t.** point of contact

tangent, -ente [tãʒã, -ãt] ADJ *Géom* tangential, tangent (**à** to); *Fam* **c'est t.** it's touch and go; **c'était t.** it was touch and go, it was a near thing
NF **tangente** tangent; *Fam* **prendre la tangente** to dodge the question; *(partir)* to slip away

tangentiel, -ielle [tãʒãsjɛl] ADJ *Géom* tangential

tangentiellement [tãʒãsjɛlmã] ADV tangentially

Tanger [tãʒe] N Tangier(s)

tangible [tãʒibl] ADJ tangible

tangiblement [tãʒibləmã] ADV tangibly

tango [tãgo] NM *(danse, musique)* tango; **danser le t.** to tango
ADJ INV *(couleur)* tangerine

tangon [tãgɔ̃] NM *Naut (mobile)* swinging boom; *(de spi)* spinnaker boom

tanguer [tãge] VI *Aviat, Naut* to pitch; *Fig* to reel, to sway

tanière [tanjɛr] NF **1** *(d'animal)* den, lair **2** *(habitation sordide)* hovel **3** *(retraite)* retreat

tanin [tanɛ̃] NM *Chimie, Ind* tannin

tank [tãk] NM *Mil, Naut, Fam (grande voiture)* tank

tanker [tãkɛr] NM *Naut* tanker

tankiste [tãkist] NM *Mil* soldier with a/the tank unit

tannage [tanaʒ] NM *Tech (des peaux)* tanning

tannant [tanã] ADJ **1** *Fam (ennuyeux)* annoying; **il est t.!** he's a drag!; **qu'est-ce que c'est t., ces réunions de famille!** these family get-togethers are a real drag! **2** *Tech* tanning **3** *Can Fam (remuant)* obstreperous, rumbustious

tanne [tan] NF *(sur le cuir)* spot; *(sur le visage)* blackhead

tanné, -ée [tane] ADJ **1** *(peau, visage etc)* weatherbeaten **2** *Can Fam* **être t. (en avoir assez)** to be fed up; **je suis t. à faire le ménage** I'm fed up *or* I've had it up to here doing housework
NM **1** *(couleur)* tan (colour) **2 gants en t.** tan(ned) leather gloves
NF *Fam* **tannée** thrashing, good hiding

tanner [tane] VT **1** *Tech (peaux)* to tan **2** *Arg (ennuyer)* to annoy; *(harceler)* to pester; **elle m'a tanné pour que je le lui dise** she pestered me to tell her **3** *Arg* **t. (le cuir) à un enfant** to thrash a child, to tan a child's hide; **il s'est fait t. le cuir par des voleurs** he was beaten up by thieves

tannerie [tanri] NF *(établissement)* tannery; *(industrie)* tanning

tanneur [tanœr] NM *(de peaux)* tanner

tannin [tanɛ̃] NM *Chimie, Ind* tannin

tannique [tanik] ADJ *Chimie (acide)* tannic

tanrec [tãrɛk] NM *Zool* tenrec

tan-sad, *pl* **tan-sads** [tãsad] NM pillion(-seat)

TANT [tã]

> so much **1** ▪ such **1** ▪ so many **2** ▪ so **3** ▪ as *(en tant que)* **4** ▪ so much the better *(tant mieux)* **6** ▪ as long as *(tant que)* **8**

ADV **1** *(quantité)* so much; **t. de bonté** so much *or* such kindness; **il a t. bu que ...** he has drunk so much that ...; **ce n'est pas la peine de t. vous presser** you needn't be in such a hurry; **elle s'est donné t. de mal** she went to such (a lot of) *or* so much trouble; **pour t. faire** ou **à t. faire** ou *Fam* **t. qu'à faire, j'aimerais autant ...** while I'm at it *or* about it, I would just as soon ...; *Fam* **tu m'en diras t.!** you don't say!, really?; **t. pour cent** so much per cent; **votre lettre du t.** your letter of such and such a date; **il a t. et plus d'argent** he has any amount of money; **ils tiraient t. et plus** they were pulling for all they were worth; **s'inquiéter t. et plus** to be worried to death; **je me suis ennuyé t. et plus** I was bored to tears *or* to death; **t. et si bien que ...** so much so that ...; **j'ai crié t. et t. qu'il est parti** I shouted so much that he went (away); **on a attendu t. et t. que ...** we waited so long that ...; **t. s'en faut** far from it; **un t. soit peu** a little, somewhat; **s'il était un t. soit peu intelligent** if he had any intelligence, if he was the slightest bit intelligent; **si t. est qu'il soit mort** if he really is dead; **il y en a peu, si t. est qu'il y en ait du tout** there is little/there are few, if any

2 *(nombre)* so many; **t. de fois** so many times, so often; **il a des amis t. et plus** he has plenty of friends; **inutile de faire t. d'histoires pour ça** it's pointless to make such a fuss over that

3 *(tellement, à tel point)* so, to such a degree; **il ne peut pas se lever, t. il est malade** he cannot get up, he is so ill; **elle ne parle plus, t. elle a été choquée** the shock was so great that she has stopped speaking; **t. était grande sa discrétion que ...** so great was his discretion that ...; **t. il est vrai que ...** so much so that ...; **elle est t. aimée** she is loved so much; **elle n'est pas t. sotte que naïve** she's not so much stupid as naive; **n'aimer rien t. que ...** to like nothing more than ...; **elle dit n'aimer rien t. que l'automne** she says there is nothing she likes more than the autumn

4 en t. que *(comme)* as; *(dans la mesure où)* in so far as; **je suis Russe en t. que je suis né en Russie** I am a Russian in so far as I was born in Russia; **l'homme en t. qu'il diffère des animaux** man, as distinct from animals; **en t. que vieil ami de votre père** as a very old friend of your father('s)

5 *(quelque)* however; **t. aimable qu'il soit** however pleasant he may be

6 t. mieux so much the better, that's all to the good; **t. mieux pour toi** good for you; **t. pis!** too bad!, it can't be helped!, what a pity!, never mind!; **c'est t. pis** that's just too bad; **t. pis pour toi!** (that's) too bad for you!, that's just too bad!

7 t. que *(autant que)* as much as; **j'ai couru t. que j'ai pu** I ran as hard as I could; *Fam* **il pleut t. qu'il peut** it's raining like anything; **t. aux Indes qu'ailleurs** both in India and elsewhere; **t. les enfants que les adultes** children and adults alike; **un film t. pour les petits que pour les grands** a film for children and adults alike; **t. pour vous que pour moi** for your sake as much as mine, for you as much as for me; **il est sévère t. avec ses enfants qu'avec ses élèves** he is as strict with his children as he is with his pupils; **je suis à l'aise t. avec lui qu'avec elle** I'm at ease with him and her; **t. bien que mal** somehow or other, after a fashion

8 t. que *(aussi longtemps que)* as long as; *(pendant que)* while; **t. que je vivrai** as long as I live; **t. que la vue s'étend** as far as the eye can see; **t. que vous y êtes** while you're about or at it; **rien ne peut être décidé t. qu'il n'a pas donné son avis** nothing can be decided until (such time as) he makes his opinion known SEE GRAMMAR B31–2

9 *Arg* **t. qu'à = quant à,** *voir* **quant à**

Tantale [tɑ̃tal] NM Tantalus

tantale [tɑ̃tal] NM *Chimie* tantalum

tante [tɑ̃t] NF **1** aunt **2** *Vulg Péj (homosexuel)* queer, *Br* poof(ter), *Am* faggot **3** *Arg* **ma t.** *(mont-de-piété)* uncle's, the pawnbroker's (shop)

tantième [tɑ̃tjɛm] NM *Com (de bénéfices etc)* percentage, quota; **t. des administrateurs** directors' fee

tantine [tɑ̃tin] NF *Fam* auntie, aunty

tantinet [tɑ̃tinɛ] NM *Fam* tiny bit; **un t. plus long** a tiny bit or a shade or a fraction longer; **un t. vieillot/ridicule** a tiny bit or a touch or ever so slightly old-fashioned/ridiculous

tantôt [tɑ̃to] ADV **1** *(parfois)* **t. triste, t. gai** now sad, now gay; **t. je suis à Paris, t. à Londres** sometimes I am in Paris, sometimes in London **2** *Arch, Région (bientôt)* soon, presently; *(il y a peu de temps)* just now, a little while ago; **voici t. deux mois qu'il est parti** it will soon be two months since he left **3** *(cet après-midi)* this afternoon; **il pleuvra/il a plu t.** it will rain/it rained this afternoon; **à t.** see you soon

tantouse [tɑ̃tuz] NF *Vulg Péj (homosexuel)* queer, *Br* poof(ter)

tantrique [tɑ̃trik] ADJ Tantric

tantrisme [tɑ̃trism] NM Tantrism

Tanzanie [tɑ̃zani] NF Tanzania

tanzanien, -ienne [tɑ̃zanjɛ̃, -jɛn] ADJ Tanzanian
N T. Tanzanian

Tao [tao] NM Tao

taoïsme, taoïsme [taoism] NM *Rel* Taoism

taoïste, taoïste [taoist] ADJ, N *Rel* Taoist

taon [tɑ̃] NM gadfly, horsefly, cleg

tapage [tapaʒ] NM **1** *(bruit)* din, uproar, *Fam* racket, row; **faire du t.** to kick up a din or racket or row **2** *(publicité)* fuss, ballyhoo; **cette nouvelle a fait du t.** the news caused quite a stir; **faire du t. autour de qch** to make a great fuss or a great ballyhoo or a song and dance about sth; **annoncer qch à grand t.** to announce sth with a lot of ballyhoo
▸▸ *Jur* **t. nocturne: faire du t. nocturne** to create a disturbance

tapageur, -euse [tapaʒœr, -øz] ADJ **1** *(enfant, soirée etc)* noisy, rowdy, raucous **2** *(vê-*

tements, couleur) loud, flashy; *(décoration)* flashy; *(publicité)* blatant

tapageusement [tapaʒøzmɑ̃] ADV *(s'habiller etc)* flashily, loudly

tapant [tapɑ̃] ADJ **à sept heures tapant(es)** on the stroke of seven, at seven o'clock sharp or on the dot

tape [tap] NF slap; **il m'a donné une t. sur l'épaule** he slapped me or gave me a slap on the shoulder; **une petite t. sur la joue** a pat on the cheek

tapé [tape] ADJ **1** *(fruit) (séché)* dried; *(abîmé)* damaged **2** *Arg* **réponse tapée** snappy answer **3** *Fam (fou)* nuts, crazy, cracked

tape-à-l'œil ADJ INV loud, gaudy, flashy
NM INV gaudy or flashy rubbish

tape(-)cul, *pl* **tape(-)culs** NM **1** *(bascule)* seesaw **2** *Naut* jigger (sail) **3** *Fam (véhicule)* rattletrap, boneshaker

tapée [tape] NF *Fam* **une t.** *ou* **des tapées de ...** masses or heaps or loads of ...

taper¹ [tape] VT **1** *(frapper) (enfant)* to hit, to slap; *(cuisse)* to slap; *(table etc)* to bang; *Ordinat* to key; **t. du tambour** to beat the drum; **t. un coup/deux coups à la porte** to knock/knock twice at the door; **t. une lettre (à la machine)** to type a letter; *Ordinat* **tapez entrée ou retour** select enter or return; **t. un air (au piano)** to thump out a tune (on the piano); *Fam* **t. la carte** to play cards

2 *Fam (emprunter)* **t. qch à qn, t. qn de qch** to bum or cadge sth off sb, to hit or *Br* tap sb for sth; **il est encore venu me t.** he came to scrounge off me again; **t. qn de mille euros** to touch or *Br* tap sb for a thousand euros

3 *Fam (atteindre)* **t. le cent/le deux cents** to hit a hundred/two hundred (kilometres an hour)

VI **1** *(frapper)* to bang (**sur** on); **la bôme est venu t. contre le mât** the boom hit the or banged into the mast; *Ordinat* **t. sur une touche** to hit a key; **t. sur le piano** to thump or plonk away on the piano; **t. sur qn** to hit sb; *Fig Fam (critiquer)* to knock sb, to have a go at sb; **t. à la porte** to bang on the door; **t. avec un marteau (contre le mur)** to hammer (the wall); *Fam* **t. sur le ventre à qn** to give sb a dig in the ribs *(as a mark of familiarity)*; **le soleil tapait** the sun was beating down; **le soleil tape dans ma chambre** the sun shines straight into my room; *Fam* **ça tape** *(il fait chaud)* it's scorching; **t. dans** *(nourriture)* to help oneself to, to dig into; *(ses économies, ses réserves)* to break or dig into; *Fam* **t. dans l'œil à qn** to take sb's fancy; **t. dans un ballon** to knock or kick a ball around; **t. du pied** to stamp one's foot; *Mil Fam* **t. sur un objectif** to strafe a target; **t. à côté** to miss the target; *Fig* **alors là, tu as tapé à côté** you're way off beam, *Am* you're way out in left field; **t. à la tête** *(d'un vin)* to go to one's head; **il tape, ce petit vin!** this wine is pretty potent!

2 *(dactylographier)* **t. (à la machine)** to type; **t. au toucher** to touch-type

3 *Vulg (puer)* to stink

VPR **se taper 1** *(se frapper)* to knock each other about; **se t. sur la cuisse** to slap one's thigh; **avec lui, on se tape les cuisses de rire** he makes you split your sides laughing; *Fig* **se t. le derrière par terre** to split one's sides laughing, to fall about laughing; **une situation à se t. le derrière par terre** a hysterically funny situation

2 *très Fam* **se t. qch** *(manger, boire)* to put sth away; *(avoir à supporter)* to let oneself in for sth; **se t. qn** *(sexuellement)* to lay sb; *(avoir à supporter)* to get lumbered with sb; **je me taperais bien une bière** I could murder a beer; **on s'est tapé deux heures d'embouteillages** we got stuck in two hours of traffic jams; **il a fallu que je me tape tout Proust pour l'examen** I had to devour the entire works of Proust for the exam

3 *très Fam (s'en moquer)* **elle s'en tape** she doesn't give a monkey's (**de** about); **si tu savais comme je m'en tape!** I don't give a monkey's!

4 *très Fam (espérer)* **tu peux te t.!** you'll be lucky!, no way!, you can whistle for it!

taper² VT *(boucher) (trou etc)* to plug, to stop up

tapette [tapɛt] NF **1** *(petit marteau)* mallet **2** *(à tapis)* carpet beater; *(à mouches)* fly swatter **3** *(piège)* **t. (à souris)** mousetrap **4** *Arg (langue)* **quelle t.!** what a chatterer or chatterbox!; **il a une fière t.** can he talk! **5** *(petite tape)* (gentle) slap **6** *Vulg (homosexuel)* queer, *Br* poof(ter)

tapeur, -euse [tapœr, -øz] N *Fam* cadger

tapin [tapɛ̃] NM *Arg* **faire le t.** *(se prostituer)* to turn tricks, *surtout Br* to be on the game; **la police a ramassé toutes les filles qui faisaient le t. du côté du port** the police arrested all the girls who were trying to pick up customers on the docks

tapiner [tapine] VI *Arg* to walk the streets, *Br* to be on the game, *Am* to hook

tapineur, -euse [tapinœr, -øz] N *Arg* streetwalker

tapinois (en) [ɑ̃tapinwa] ADV stealthily; **s'approcher en t.** to creep up

tapioca [tapjɔka] NM tapioca; *(soupe)* vegetable soup containing tapioca

tapir¹ [tapir] NM *Zool* tapir

tapir² (se) [sətapir] VPR to crouch; *(se cacher)* to cower, to hide; **maison tapie dans un bois** house nestling in a wood

tapis [tapi] NM **1** *(recouvrant un meuble)* cloth, cover; *Fig* **le t. brûle!** *(au jeu)* put down your stakes!; *Fig* **mettre qch sur le t.** to bring sth up for consideration or for discussion; *Fig* **ce genre de discussion revient toujours sur le t.** this sort of discussion is always coming up

2 *(sur le sol), Fig (de fleurs, neige)* carpet; *(petit)* rug; **t. de haute laine/de laine rase** long-pile/short-pile carpet; **marchand de t.** carpet dealer; **recouvrir le plancher d'un t.** to carpet the floor; **terrain recouvert d'un t. de gazon/de neige** ground carpeted with turf/snow; *Fig* **se prendre les pieds dans le t.** to get into a mess

3 *Boxe etc* canvas; **aller au t.** to go down, to be knocked down; *Fig* **entreprise française mise au t. par la concurrence** French company knocked for six or k.o.'d by the competition; **il est resté au t.** he stayed down, he didn't get up
▸▸ **t. de billiard** billiard cloth; **t. de gym** gym mat; **t. de livraison des bagages** baggage conveyor belt; **t. d'Orient** oriental carpet; **t. de prière** prayer mat; **t. rouge: dérouler le t. rouge pour qn** to roll out the red carpet for sb, to give sb the red carpet treatment; **t. roulant** *Ind etc* conveyor belt; *(pour piétons)* moving walkway, travelator; **t. de salle de bain** bathroom carpet; **t. de selle** saddlecloth; **t. de sol** *(sol de tente)* groundsheet; *(petit matelas)* sleeping mat *(underneath sleeping bag)*; *Ordinat* **t. de souris** mouse mat or pad; **t. de table** table cover; **t. vert** gaming table; *(de conseil)* conference table

tapis-brosse, *pl* **tapis-brosses** NM doormat

tapisser [tapise] VT **1** *(de papier peint) (pièce, appartement etc)* to (wall)paper; **les murs sont tapissés de jaune** the walls are papered in yellow; **mur tapissé d'affiches** wall covered with posters **2** *(de tentures ou tapisseries) (pièce etc)* to cover with hangings or tapestries **3** *(l'intérieur d'une armoire)* to line, to cover (**de** with); **une membrane tapisse l'estomac** the stomach is lined with a membrane; **mur tapissé de lierre** wall covered with ivy, ivy-clad wall

tapisserie [tapisri] **NF 1** *(papier peint)* wallpaper; **refaire toutes les tapisseries d'un appartement** to repaper a flat **2** *(tissage)* tapestry making *or* weaving; **faire de la t.** to make tapestry **3** *(tenture)* tapestry; **chaise en t.** chair upholstered with tapestry, tapestry chair; *Fig* **faire t.** *(dans une soirée dansante etc)* to be a wallflower **4** *(broderie)* **t.** **(au** *ou* **sur canevas)** tapestry *or* crewel work

tapissier, -ière [tapisje, -jɛr] **N 1** *(décorateur)* (interior) decorator **2** *(tisseur)* tapestry maker **3** *(de meubles)* upholsterer

tapocher [tapɔʃe] **VT** *Can Fam (frapper)* to hit; *(battre)* to beat up

tapon [tapɔ̃] **NM** *Vieilli (de tissu, de papier etc)* ball; **en t.** *(vêtements etc)* in a ball, bundled up; *(cheveux)* screwed up into a bun

tapotement [tapɔtmã] **NM** tapping; *(de piano)* plonking

tapoter [tapɔte] **VT** to tap; *(joue d'un enfant etc)* to pat; **t. un air (au piano)** to thump out a tune (on the piano)

VI t. sur *(porte, fenêtre)* to tap on; *(en signe d'énervement)* to drum on

tapuscrit [tapyskri] **NM** typescript

taquet [takɛ] **NM 1** *Menuis etc (support)* angle block; *(cale)* wedge **2** *(butée)* stop; **t. de sûreté** safety stop **3** *(de machine à écrire)* stop; *Ordinat* **t. de tabulation** tab stop; **poser un t. (de tabulateur)** to set a tab(ulator stop) **4** *(d'arpenteur)*, *Agr* (small) picket, peg **5** *Naut* **t. (de tournage)** (belaying) cleat

taquin, -ine [takɛ̃, -in] **ADJ** *(personne, tempérament)* (given to) teasing; *(sourire)* teasing; **elle est un peu taquine** she's a bit of a tease; **elle est très taquine** she's a great one for teasing

N *(personne)* tease(r)

taquiner [takine] **VT 1** *(d'une personne)* to tease; *Fam* **t. le goujon** to do a bit of fishing; *Fam* **t. la muse** to write the odd bit of verse **2** *(de quelque chose)* to bother, to worry; **une pensée qui me revient me t. parfois** a thought that still haunts me sometimes; **j'ai une dent qui me taquine** I've got bother with one of my teeth, one of my teeth is bothering me

taquinerie [takinri] **NF** teasing; **j'en ai assez de tes taquineries** I've had enough of your teasing

tarabiscoté [tarabiskɔte] **ADJ** *(meuble, décor, maison, dessin)* over-elaborate, fussy; *(style)* over-elaborate, convoluted

tarabuster [tarabyste] **VT 1** *(d'une personne)* to pester **2** *(de quelque chose)* to bother, to worry

tarage [taraʒ] **NM** *Com* allowance for tare

tarama [tarama] **NM** *Culin* taramasalata

taratata [taratata] **INT** rubbish!

taraud [taro] **NM** (screw) tap

taraudage [tarodaʒ] **NM** screw cutting, tapping

tarauder [tarode] **VT 1** *Tech (tige, écrou etc)* to tap, to cut, to screw, to thread **2** *(d'un insecte) (bois)* to bore into **3** *Litt Fig (des remords, des scrupules etc) (personne)* to gnaw at

taraudeuse [tarodøz] **NF** *(machine)* tapper, thread cutter

tarbouch(e) [tarbuʃ] **NM** tarboosh

tard [tar] **ADV** late; **plus t.** later, later on; **au plus t.** at the latest; **tôt ou t.** sooner or later; **il est t.** it's late; **il se fait t.** it's getting late; **je ne pensais pas qu'il fût si t.** I didn't think it was so late; **je me suis couché t.** I went to bed late, I was late (in) going to bed; **trop t., il fallait te décider plus vite** (it's) too late, you should have decided sooner; **il se maria t.** he married late (in life); **deux minutes plus**

t. et je manquais le bateau another two minutes and I would have missed the boat; *Prov* **mieux vaut t. que jamais** better late than never; **t. dans la nuit** late at night; **remettre qch à plus t.** to put sth off until later; **je le ferai et pas plus t. que ce soir** I'll do it this very evening; **pas plus t. qu'hier** as recently as yesterday, only yesterday

NM sur le t. *(dans la vie)* late in life

tarder [tarde] **VI** to delay; **pourquoi tarde-t-il?** why is he (taking) so long?; **il ne tardera pas maintenant** he won't be long now; **cela n'a pas tardé** it wasn't long coming; **et cela n'a pas tardé, il s'est cassé le pied** and he broke his ankle before long; **tu vas recevoir une gifle, cela ne va pas t.** you're going to get smacked before long *or* in a minute or two, you've got a smack coming to you; **t. en chemin** to loiter on the way; **t. à faire qch** to take a long time doing sth; **excusez-moi si j'ai tardé à vous répondre** I apologize for not answering sooner; **nous ne tarderons pas à le voir venir** it won't be long before he appears, he'll appear before too long; **nous ne tardâmes pas à avoir de ses nouvelles** it wasn't long before we heard from him, we didn't have to wait too long for news of him; **ça tarde à commencer/venir** it's a long time starting/coming; **sans t.** without delay

V IMPERS il lui tarde de partir/qu'elle revienne he is longing to get away/for her to return

tardif, -ive [tardif, -iv] **ADJ** *(regrets, excuse etc)* belated; *(heure, fruit etc)* late; **c'était un peu t., comme réponse/excuse** the answer/apology was a bit slow in coming

tardivement [tardivmã] **ADV** *(prendre des mesures, s'excuser)* belatedly; *(rentrer, arriver etc)* late; *(se marier, s'établir)* late in life

tare [tar] **NF 1** *(défaut)* defect, flaw; *Méd, Vét* defect; *Hum* **ça n'est pas une t.!** it's not a crime! **2** *Com (pour calculer le poids net)* tare; **faire la t.** to allow for the tare

taré, -ée [tare] **ADJ 1** *Com (fruit etc)* spoilt; *(biens)* damaged **2** *(corrompu) (régime etc)* depraved, corrupt **3** *(dégénéré)* degenerate **4** *Fam (idiot)* crazy; **il faut être t. pour faire cela!** you have to be crazy *or* to have a screw loose to do that!

N *Fam* nutcase, headcase, *Br* nutter

tarentelle [tarɑ̃tɛl] **NF** *(danse, musique)* tarantella

tarentule [tarɑ̃tyl] **NF** *(araignée)* tarantula

tarer [tare] **VT** *Com (emballage etc)* to tare

targette [tarʒɛt] **NF 1** *(verrou)* bolt **2** *Fam* **targettes** *(pieds)* feet, *Br* plates, *Am* dogs; *(chaussures)* shoes

targuer (se) [sətarge] **VPR se t. de qch/de faire qch** to pride oneself on sth/on doing sth; **se t. de ce que ...** to pride oneself on the fact that ...

targui, -ie [targi], *pl* **touareg** [twarɛg] **ADJ** Tuareg

N T. Tuareg

tarière [tarjɛr] **NF 1** *(pour le bois)* auger **2** *(de forage)* drill; *Min* borer **3** *Entom* ovipositor

tarif [tarif] **NM** *(tableau des prix)* tariff, price list; *(prix)* rate; *Fam* **trois mois de prison, c'est le t.** three months' prison is what it'll cost you; **tarifs aériens/ferroviaires** air/rail fares; **t. adulte** adult fare; **t. affaires** business rate; *(transport)* business fare; **t. aller simple** single *or Am* one-way fare; **t.** APEX APEX fare; **t. de base** basic rate; **t. des chambres** room rate; **t. en chambre double** *(dans un hôtel)* double occupancy rate; *Aviat* **t. commun** common rated fare, joint fare; **t. couplage** *(en publicité)* combination rate; **t. dégressif** tapering *or* declining rate; **t. différentiel** differential rate; **t. discriminatoire** price discrimination; **t. du distributeur**

dealer list price; **t. douanier** customs tariff; **t. économique** economy rate; *(d'un voyage)* economy *or* budget fare; **t. étudiant** student rate; *(d'un voyage)* student fare; **t. excursion** excursion fare *or* APEX fare; **t. export** export tariff; **t. famille** family rate; *(d'un voyage)* family fare; **t. de faveur** preferential rate; **t. à forfait** all-in price; **t. forfaitaire** flat rate; *Aviat* **t. hebdomadaire** weekly rate; **t. horaire** hourly rate; **t. intérieur** inland rate; **t. jeune** youth fare; **t. journalier** daily *or* day rate; **t. lettres** letter rate; **t.** *(pour passagers)* full fare; *(pour marchandises etc)* full tariff; *Fam (pour un crime etc)* maximum (penalty); **voyager à plein t./à t. réduit** to travel at full/reduced rate *or* fare; **billet (à) plein t.** full-fare ticket; **t. minimum** minimum charge; **tarifs postaux** postal *or* postage rates; **t. préférentiel** special *or* preferential rate; **t. progressif** increasing rate; **t. promotionnel** promotional rate; *(d'un voyage)* promotional fare; **t. réduit** *Cin* concession; *(d'un voyage)* concession fare; **t. de référence** basing fare; **t. social** reduced train fare for the general public; **t. société** commercial *or* corporate rate; **t. standby** standby fare; **t. syndical** trade union tariff; **t. d'urgence** = first-class rate

tarifaire [tarifɛr] **ADJ** *(lois etc)* tariff; *Com* **politique t.** pricing policy

tarifer [tarife] **VT** *(impôts, prix etc)* to fix the rate for, to set the rate of

tarification [tarifikasjɔ̃] **NF** fixing *or* setting of rates (**de** for), pricing; **t. au coût-plus-marge** mark-up pricing; **t. différentielle** differential pricing; **t. discriminatoire** discriminatory pricing; **t. en fonction de la valeur perçue** perceived value pricing; **t. géographique** geographical pricing

tarin [tarɛ̃] **NM 1** *(oiseau)* siskin **2** *Arg (nez)* beak, *Br* conk

tarir [tarir] **VT** *(source, rivière)* to dry up; *(larmes)* to dry; **la source est tarie** the spring is dry; *Fig* **cela a tari sa créativité** it caused his creativity to dry up

VI 1 *(de l'eau)* to dry up, to run dry; **la source a tari** the spring has dried up **2** *Fig (d'une conversation, de l'inspiration etc)* to dry up; *(de larmes)* to dry; **la discussion n'a pas tari pendant deux heures** the discussion has been flowing freely for two hours; **une fois lancé sur ce sujet, il ne tarit pas** once he's started on the subject he never shuts up *or* stops; **il ne tarit pas sur le sujet** he never stops talking *or* shuts up about the subject; **ne pas t. d'éloges sur qch** to be full of praise for *or* be forever praising sth

VPR se tarir *(d'une rivière, du lait, de l'inspiration etc)* to dry up

tarissement [tarismã] **NM** drying up

tarlatane [tarlatan] **NF** *Tex* tarlatan

tarmacadam [tarmakadam] **NM** *Constr* tarmacadam

tarot [taro] **NM** *Cartes (jeu de)* **tarot(s)** tarot (pack); **faire un t.** *ou* **une partie de t.** to have a game of tarot

Tarse [tars] **N** Tarsus

tarse [tars] **NM** *Anat, Zool* tarsus

tarsien, -ienne [tarsjɛ̃, -jɛn] **ADJ** *Anat (os)* tarsal

tartan [tartɑ̃] **NM** *(tissu)* tartan

tartane [tartan] **NF** *(bateau)* tartan(e), tartana

tartare [tartar] **ADJ 1** *Hist* Tartar **2** *Culin* sauce **t.** tartar(e) sauce; **steak t.** steak tartare

N *Hist* **T.** Tartar

NM *Culin* steak tartare

tarte [tart] **NF 1** *Culin* tart, *Am* (open) pie; **t. aux pommes** apple tart *or Am* pie; *Fig Fam* **ce n'est pas de la t.** it's no picnic **2** *Fam (gifle)* slap

ADJ *Fam* **1** *(ridicule)* ridiculous **2** *(laid)* ugly ►► t. à la crème custard tart; *Fam (envoyée sur qn)* custard pie; *Fam* c'est la t. à la crème des économistes libéraux it's a liberal economist's cliché

tartelette [tartəlɛt] **NF** *Culin* tartlet

tartempion [tartɑ̃pjɔ̃] **NM** *Fam* entreprise T. Company So-and-so; un quelconque t. some guy or other; n'importe quel t. any Tom, Dick or Harry

tartignole [tartiɲɔl] **ADJ** *Fam* ridiculous

tartine [tartin] **NF 1** *(beurrée)* slice of bread and butter; *(pas encore beurrée)* slice of bread; t. de confiture/de miel slice of bread and jam/honey; t. grillée slice *or* piece of toast; faire des tartines to butter (some) bread **2** *Fam (tirade)* long-winded speech; *(article de journal, lettre etc)* screed; pourquoi en mettre toute une t.? why go on *or* bang on about it?

tartiner [tartine] **VT 1** *(beurre, pain)* to spread; t. du pain (de beurre) to butter bread, to spread bread with butter; fromage à t. cheese spread; pâte à t. au chocolat chocolate spread **2** *Fam (écrire)* to churn out; elle a tartiné des pages entières sur ce sujet she has written reams on this subject **3** *Fam (enduire en grande quantité)* t. qn/qch de qch to cover sb/sth in sth

tartir [tartir] **VI** *très Fam* se faire t. to be bored shitless

tartre [tartr] **NM** *(sur les dents, dans les bouteilles etc)* tartar; *(dans une chaudière, une bouilloire)* fur, scale

tartrique [tartrik] **ADJ** *Chimie (acide)* tartaric

tartuf(f)e [tartyf] **NM** (sanctimonious) hypocrite
  ADJ hypocritical

tartuf(f)erie [tartyfri] **NF** hypocrisy

tas [tɑ] **NM 1** *(amas) (de pierres, de feuilles, de bois, de boue etc)* pile, heap; mettre en t. to pile up, to heap up; *Fam* un t. de ferraille *(voiture en mauvais état)* a rusty old heap **2** *(grand nombre, grande quantité)* mass, heap, pile (de of); tout un t. de vieilleries masses *or* heaps *or* a whole pile of old things; un t. de mensonges a pack of lies; *Fam* il y en a des t. (et des t.) there are heaps *or* masses of them; des gens sympas, il n'y en a pas des t. par ici nice people are pretty thin on the ground around here; elle a fait un t. de choses dans sa vie she has done masses of things *or* lots (of things) in her life; des t. de fois heaps *or* lots of times; *Fam* tout un t. de gens a whole gang (of people), a whole load of people; t. d'imbéciles! bunch of idiots! **3** tirer dans le t. to fire into the crowd; sers-toi dans le t. take what you like from that lot; *Fam* dans le t., il doit y en avoir un ou deux que tu connais there must be one or two of that lot that you know **4** *(construction)* building under construction; *(chantier)* building site; être sur le t. to be at work *or* on the job; *Ind etc* formation sur le t. on-the-job training; apprendre sur le t. to learn on the job; grève sur le t. sit-down strike **5** *Fam* un gros t. *(gros individu mou)* a big fat lump; *(grosse fille laide)* a fat old boot ►► *Min* t. de déblais dump; t. de fumier manure heap

Tasmanie [tasmani] **NF** Tasmania

tasmanien, -ienne [tasmanjɛ̃, -jɛn] **ADJ** Tasmanian
  N T. Tasmanian

tassage [tasaʒ] **NM** *Sport (d'un adversaire)* crowding

tasse [tas] **NF 1** cup; je te ressers une t.? would you like another cup?, shall I fill you up again?; t. à café/thé coffee/tea cup; t. de café/thé cup of coffee/tea; t. en métal tin mug **2** boire une *ou* la t. *(en nageant)* to get

a mouthful (of water)

tassé [tase] **ADJ 1** *(serré) (prisonniers, passagers etc)* crammed, packed, squeezed; t. par l'âge shrunk with age **2** *Fam* bien t. *(boisson alcoolique) (avec peu d'eau)* stiff; *(dans un verre bien plein)* large; *(café)* strong; il a 50 ans bien tassés he's 50 at least, he's 50 if he's a day

tasseau, -eaux [taso] **NM** *(pour soutenir une étagère etc)* batten

tassement [tasmɑ̃] **NM 1** *(de terre, de neige etc)* packing (down) **2** *Constr (de fondations etc)* settling, sinking, subsidence **3** *Écon* slowdown (de in)
  ►► *Méd* t. de vertèbres spinal compression

tasser [tase] **VT 1** *(objets)* to cram, to squeeze (dans into); *(personnes)* to cram, to squeeze, to pack (dans into); *(terre, neige etc)* to pack (down), to tamp (down) **2** *Sport (adversaire)* to crowd
  VI *(des plantes)* to grow thick(ly)
  VPR se tasser **1** *(des fondations etc)* to settle, to sink, to subside; *Fig* ça se tassera things will quieten down *or* settle down; il commence à se t. *(se voûter)* he is beginning to shrink (with age) **2** *(se serrer)* to squeeze up

taste-vin [tastəvɛ̃] **NM INV** *(tasse)* wine taster

tata [tata] **NF 1** *Enf* auntie, aunty **2** *très Fam (homosexuel)* queer, *Br* poof(ter)

tatami [tatami] **NM** tatami (mat)

tatane [tatan] **NF** *Fam* shoe

tataner [tatane] **VT** *Fam* t. qn/qch to give sb/ sth a kicking

tatar, -are [tatar] **ADJ** *Hist* Tartar
  NM *Ling* Tartar
  N *Hist* T. Tartar

tâter [tɑte] **VT 1** *(toucher)* to feel; *(fruit)* to feel, to squeeze; t. le pouls à qn to feel sb's pulse; avancer en tâtant to grope one's way forward; t. la porte pour trouver la poignée to feel for the door handle **2** *Fig (sonder)* t. qn to sound sb out; t. l'opinion to sound out opinion; t. le terrain to see how the land lies
  VI 1 *Litt* t. d'un mets to taste a dish **2** t. d'un métier to try one's hand at a trade; *Fam* il a tâté de la prison he's done time; *Litt* t. du chagrin/dégoût to experience sorrow/disgust
  VPR se tâter **1** *(après un choc)* to feel oneself **2** *(hésiter)* to hesitate

tâte-vin [tɑtvɛ̃] **NM INV** *(tasse)* wine taster

tatie [tati] **NF** *Fam* auntie, aunty

tatillon, -onne [tatijɔ̃, -ɔn] **ADJ** finicky, fussy
  N finicky *or* fussy person, *Fam* fusspot

tâtonnant [tɑtɔnɑ̃] **ADJ** *(efforts, geste etc)* tentative, hesitant; *(progrès)* tentative

tâtonnement [tɑtɔnmɑ̃] **NM 1** *(d'aveugle etc)* groping **2** *(essai)* trial and error; les tâtonnements de la science/recherche the tentative progress of science/research; procéder par tâtonnements to proceed by trial and error

tâtonner [tɑtɔne] **VI 1** to grope about; t. pour retrouver la porte to grope about for the door; se diriger en tâtonnant vers qch to grope *or* feel one's way towards sth **2** *Fig* to proceed by trial and error; *(involontairement)* to grope about, to feel one's way

tâtons (à) [atatɔ̃] **ADV** avancer/entrer/sortir à t. to grope *or* feel one's way along/in/out; chercher qch à t. to grope *or* feel for sth; *Fig* les chercheurs avancent à t. the researchers are progressing by trial and error; *(sans la moindre idée)* the researchers are groping their way forward

tatou [tatu] **NM** *Zool* armadillo

tatouage [tatwaʒ] **NM** *(action)* tattooing; *(motif)* tattoo

tatouer [tatwe] **VT** *(motif)* to tattoo; se faire

t. le bras to have one's arm tattooed

tatoueur [tatwœr] **NM** tattooist, tattoo artist

tau [to] **NM INV** *(lettre grecque)* tau

taud [to] **NM** *Naut* rain awning, boat cover

taudis [todi] **NM** slum; leur maison est un vrai t. their house is a real dump

taulard, -arde [tolar, -ard] **N** *Arg* convict; vieux t. old lag

taule [tol] **NF** *Fam* **1** *(prison)* clink, *Br* nick; *Mil Fam* glasshouse; faire de la t. to do time *or* a stretch; sortir de t. to come out of the clink *or Br* the nick; faire dix ans de t. to do a ten-year stretch; après dix ans de t. after ten years inside **2** *(chambre)* room

taulier, -ière [tolje, -jɛr] **N** *Arg (propriétaire)* (hotel) owner; *(gérant)* (hotel) manager

taupe [top] **NF 1** *Zool* mole; myope comme une t. blind as a bat **2** *(fourrure)* moleskin **3** *Scol Fam* = high-level maths class for exceptionally gifted students going on to one of the grandes écoles **4** *Arg Péj* vieille t. *(femme)* old crone *or* hag **5** *(espion)* mole

tauper [tope] **VT** *Suisse Fam* t. qch à qn *(emprunter)* to bum *or* to cadge sth from sb; *(soustraire)* to do *or* to con sb out of sth

taupier [topje] **NM** mole catcher

taupin [topɛ̃] **NM 1** *Scol Fam* = student doing high-level maths class in preparation for one of the grandes écoles **2** *Mil Arch* sapper

taupinière [topinjɛr] **NF** molehill; *(galeries)* mole tunnels

taureau, -eaux [toro] **NM 1** bull; avoir un cou de t. to have a thick neck; course *ou* combat de taureaux bullfight; *Fam* prendre le t. par les cornes to take the bull by the horns; fort comme un t. as strong as an ox **2** *Astron, Astrol* le T. Taurus, the Bull; être (du signe du) T. to be (a) Taurus

taurillon [torijɔ̃] **NM** bull calf

taurin [torɛ̃] **ADJ** jeux taurins bullfights

tauromachie [toromaʃi] **NF** bullfighting, *Spéc* tauromachy

tauromachique [toromaʃik] **ADJ** *(art, règles etc)* of bullfighting

tautologie [totolɔʒi] **NF** tautology; raisonner par t. to argue tautologically

tautologique [totolɔʒik] **ADJ** tautological

taux [to] **NM 1** *(montant) (des salaires, d'impôts etc)* rate **2** *(proportion)* proportion, ratio **3** *(pourcentage)* rate; t. d'un prêt interest rate on a loan; à t. fixe fixed-rate; t. de huit pour cent rate of eight per cent; emprunter à un t. de 7 pour cent to borrow at 7 per cent (interest) **4** *Ordinat* ratio, rate
  ►► t. d'accroissement rate of increase *or* of growth; *Écon* t. d'activité participation rate; t. d'actualisation *Compta* net present value rate, NPV rate; *Ordinat* refresh rate; *Compta* t. d'amortissement rate of depreciation, depreciation rate; *Fin* t. de l'argent au jour le jour overnight rate; t. d'assurance insurance rate; t. d'audience *Radio* ratings; *TV* ratings, viewing figures; t. bancaire bank rate; t. de base bancaire bank base rate; *Compta* t. de capitalisation price/earnings ratio, p/e ratio; t. de change exchange rate, rate of exchange; t. de change à l'achat bank buying rate; t. de change en cours current rate of exchange; t. de change à la vente bank selling rate; t. de change flottant floating exchange rate; t. de chômage unemployment rate; t. de compression *(de moteur)* compression ratio; *Ordinat* compression rate; t. de conversion conversion rate; t. de croissance growth rate, rate of growth; t. d'échange rate of exchange, exchange rate; t. d'écoute *Radio* ratings; *TV* ratings, viewing figures; t. effectif global annual percentage rate, APR; *Banque* t. d'emprunt borrowing rate; t. d'épargne savings rate; t.

d'escompte discount rate; **t. de fréquentation** *(des chambres d'hôtel)* sleeper occupancy; **t. d'imposition** rate of taxation; **t. d'inflation** rate of inflation, inflation rate; **t. interbancaire offert à Paris** Paris Inter-Bank Offer Rate; **t. d'intérêt** interest rate, rate of interest; **t. d'intérêt à court terme/à long terme** short-term/long-term interest rate; *Méd* **t. d'invalidité** degree of disability; *Fin* **t. linéaire** straight-line rate; *Banque* **t. Lombard** Lombard rate; *Bourse* **t. long obligataire** long-term bond rate; **t. de marge** *ou* **de marque** mark-up ratio; **t. minima** minimum rates; **t. de mortalité** death rate; **t. de natalité** birth rate; **t. normal** standard rate; *Mktg* **t. de notoriété** *(d'un produit)* rate of awareness; **t. d'occupation** *(des chambres d'hôtel)* room occupancy, occupancy rate; **t. officiel** official rate; *Pol* **t. de panne** failure rate; **t. de participation** turnout; **t. de participation électorale** voter turnout; **t. de pénétration** *(d'un marché)* penetration rate; *Rail etc* **t. de pente** rate of grade *or* gradient; *Mil* **t. de pertes** casualty rate; **t. plafonné** cap; *Can Banque* **t. préférentiel** prime rate; **t. de prévalence** prevalence rate; **t. privé** market rate; **t. proportionnel** *(d'un crédit)* proportional interest rate, APR; *Ordinat* **t. de rafraîchissement** refresh rate; *Mktg* **t. de réachat** re-buy *or* repurchase rate; *Fin* **t. réduit** reduced rate; *Banque* **t. de référence** reference rate; *Tech, Ind* **t. de rendement** coefficient of efficiency, utilization factor; **t. de rentabilité économique** economic rate of return; *Mktg* **t. de réponse** response rate; *Fin* **t. des repos** repo rate; **t. de rotation** *(des stocks)* turnover rate; **t. des salaires** wage rate; **t. de scolarisation** = percentage of children attending school; **t. de succès** success rate; *Ordinat* **t. de transfert** transfer rate; **t. de TVA** VAT rate, rate of VAT; **t. uniforme** uniform *or* flat rate; *Fin* **t. d'usure** penal rate

tavelé [tavle] ADJ *(visage etc)* spotted, speckled (**de** with); *(fruit)* marked

taveler [tavle] (**il tavelle; il tavellera**) VT *(visage etc)* to spot, to speckle; *(fruit)* to mark **VPR se taveler** *(d'un fruit)* to become marked

tavelure [tavlyr] NF **1** spot, speckle; *(de fruit)* mark **2** *Agr (maladie)* scab

taverne [tavɛrn] NF **1** *(restaurant)* restaurant **2** *Can* beer parlour *or* *Am* parlor, tavern **3** *Arch (auberge)* tavern

tavernier, -ière [tavɛrnje, -jɛr] N *Arch* innkeeper

taxable [taksabl] ADJ taxable

taxateur, -trice [taksatœr, -tris] N taxer, assessor
ADJ *(fonctionnaire etc)* taxing

taxation [taksasjɔ̃] NF **1** *(par l'impôt)* taxation; *(contrôle)* assessment; **t. d'office** special rate of taxation; *Com* **t. au poids** tax on weight; **t. différentielle** differential taxation; **t. à la valeur** tax on value **2** *Tél* **zone de t.** charging area; *Ordinat* **période de t.** charging period **3** *Jur (des dépens)* assessment, calculation

taxe [taks] NF **1** *(impôt)* tax, duty; **toutes taxes comprises** inclusive of tax; **t. sur les chiens** dog tax; **t. locale** local tax; *Théâtre etc* **t. sur les spectacles** entertainment tax **2** *(redevance) (pour un service)* charge; **t. postale** *ou* **des lettres** postage **3** *Jur (des dépens)* calculation, assessment **4** *(prix fixé)* fixed price, official price
► **t. à l'achat** purchase tax; **t. d'aéroport** airport tax; **t. d'apprentissage** = tax paid by businesses to fund training programmes; **t. d'atterrissage** airport landing tax; **t. sur le chiffre d'affaires** sales tax; **t. de départ** *(à l'aéroport)* departure tax; **t. écologique** eco-tax; **t. d'entrée** *(à l'aéroport)* entry tax; **t. à**

l'exportation export tax; **t. foncière** land *or* property tax; **t. forfaitaire** flat rate; **t. d'habitation** council *or* *Am* local tax; **t. sur l'hôtellerie** hotel tax; **t. de luxe** luxury tax; **t. officielle** assessment; **t. parafiscale** indirect *or* excise tax; **t. de port** harbour *or* *Am* harbor dues; **t. professionnelle** = tax paid by businesses and self-employed people; **t. régionale** local tax; **t. sur le revenu** income tax; **t. routière** road tax; **t. sur les salaires** employment tax; **t. de séjour** tourist *or* visitor tax; **t. supplémentaire** surcharge; **t. touristique** tourist tax; **t. à** *ou* **sur la valeur ajoutée** value added tax

taxer [takse] VT **1** *(soumettre à l'impôt) (personne, alcool, cigarettes etc)* to tax; **t. qch à 10%** to put a 10% tax on sth **2** *Tél (appel)* to charge for **3** *Jur (dépens)* to tax **4** *(accuser)* to tax (**de** with), to accuse (**de** of); **la décision du gouvernement a été taxée d'inconscience** the government's decision was described as thoughtless; **se faire t. d'égoïste** to be accused of selfishness *or* being selfish, to be called selfish **5** *Fam (quémander)* **il m'a taxé une cigarette** he cadged a cigarette off me; **t. les autres** to cadge off people **6** *Fam (voler)* to pinch, *Br* to nick; **je me suis fait t. mon cuir par une bande de skins** I got my leather jacket pinched *or* *Br* nicked by a bunch of skinheads

taxi [taksi] NM **1** *(voiture)* taxi (cab), cab; **elle prend souvent le t.** she often takes taxis *or* a taxi; **chauffeur de t.** taxi *or* cab driver; **t. aérien** air taxi, taxiplane; **station de taxis** taxi rank *or* *Am* stand; **t. en maraude** cruising taxi **2** *Fam (chauffeur)* cabby, taxi *or* cab driver

taxidermie [taksidɛrmi] NF taxidermy

taxidermiste [taksidɛrmist] N taxidermist

taxi-girl, *pl* **taxi-girls** NF *(danseuse)* taxi dancer

taximètre [taksimɛtr] NM meter

taxinomie [taksinɔmi] NF *Biol* taxonomy

taxinomique [taksinɔmik] ADJ taxonomic(al)

Taxiphone® [taksifɔn] NM pay phone

taxiway [taksiwɛ] NM *Aviat* taxiway

taxonomie [taksonɔmi] NF *Biol* taxonomy

taylorisation [tɛlɔrizasjɔ̃] NF *Ind* application of time and motion studies

tayloriser [tɛlɔrize] VT *Ind* to apply time and motion studies to

taylorisme [tɛlɔrism] NM *Écon* time and motion studies

TBF [tebeɛf] NM *(abrév* **transferts Banque de France***)* = French automated clearing system

Tbilissi [tbilisi] N Tbilisi

TCA [tesea] NF *(abrév* **taxe sur le chiffre d'affaires***)* sales tax

Tchad [tʃad] NM Chad; **le lac T.** Lake Chad

tchadien, -ienne [tʃadjɛ̃, -jɛn] ADJ Chadian
N **T.** Chadian

tchador [tʃadɔr] NM *(voile)* chador, chuddar

tchadri [tʃadri] NM burka

tchatche [tʃatʃ] NF *Fam* **avoir de la t.** to have the gift of the gab; **tout ça, c'est de la t.** that's just a lot of talk

tchatcher [tʃatʃe] VI *Fam* to chat

tchatcheur, -euse [tʃatʃœr, -øz] N *Fam* smooth talker

tchécoslovaque [tʃekɔslɔvak] *Anciennement* ADJ Czechoslovak, Czechoslovakian
N **T.** Czechoslovak, Czechoslovakian

Tchécoslovaquie [tʃekɔslɔvaki] NF *Anciennement* Czechoslovakia

tchèque [tʃɛk] ADJ Czech; **la République t.** the Czech Republic
NM *Ling* Czech

N **T.** Czech

Tchéquie [tʃeki] NF **la T.** the Czech Republic

tchétchène [tʃetʃɛn] ADJ Chechen
N **T.** Chechen

Tchétchénie [tʃetʃeni] NF Chechnya

tchi [tʃi] *Fam* **que t.** zilch, sweet FA, *Br* bugger all, sod all; **il y comprend que tchi** he doesn't understand a damn *or* *Br* bloody thing

tchin-tchin [tʃintʃin] INT *Fam* cheers!, *Br* chin-chin!

TCI [tesei] NMPL *(abrév* **termes commerciaux internationaux***)* incoterms

TD [tede] NMPL *(abrév* **travaux dirigés***)* tutorial

te, *before a vowel sound or mute h* **t'** [t(ə)]
PRON PERS SEE GRAMMAR A27; B18–19 **1** *(objet direct)* you; **il t'adore** he adores you; **te voilà** there you are **2** *(objet indirect)* (to) you; **il t'a écrit** he wrote to you; **il te l'a dit** he told you so; **ça te servira** it will be of use to you; **je te l'ai donné** I gave you it, I gave it to you; **elle te court après** she's running after you; **si cela te vient à l'esprit** if you should think of it, if it occurs to you; **je vais te le mater, celui-là!** I'll sort him out; **et je te range, et je te fais la cuisine** and I tidy up and I do the cooking **3** *(reflexive)* **tu te fatigues** you are tiring yourself; **tu vas te faire mal** you will hurt yourself; **à quelle heure t'es-tu levé(e)?** what time did you get up (at)?; **va-t'en** go away; **tu te donnes beaucoup de mal** you're going to a lot of trouble; **arrête de te ronger les ongles** stop biting your nails SEE GRAMMAR A29–30; B28–9 **4** *(en s'adressant à Dieu)* You, Thee

té [te] NM **1 en t é** T-shaped; **règle en t é** T-rule **2 (équerre en) t é** T-square

teaser [tizœr] NM *(aguiche)* teaser

tec [tɛk] NF INV *(abrév* **tonne d'équivalent charbon** *)* tce

technicien, -ienne [tɛknisjɛ̃, -jɛn] N technician; **t. du froid** refrigeration engineer; **t. de laboratoire** laboratory technician; **t. de maintenance** maintenance *or* service engineer; *TV etc* **t. du son** sound engineer *or* technician, audio control engineer; **t. de surface** cleaner

technicité [tɛknisite] NF technical nature; **d'une haute t.** highly technical

technico-commercial, -iale, -iaux, -iales [tɛknikokɔmɛrsjal, -jo] ADJ **agent t.** sales engineer; **service t.** technical sales department
N sales engineer

Technicolor® [tɛknikɔlɔr] NM *Cin* Technicolor®; *Fig* **souvenirs en T.** vivid memories

technique [tɛknik] ADJ *(problème, perfection, difficulté, collège etc)* technical; **agent t.** technician; *Aviat, Naut* **escale t.** stopover for technical reasons
NF **1** *(science)* technology; **t. de l'ingénieur** engineering; **t. électrique** electrical engineering **2** *(méthode)* *(d'un artiste, d'un spécialiste etc)* technique; **ce pianiste a une bonne t./manque de t.** this pianist has good technique/lacks technique; *Fam* **tu n'as pas la t.!** you haven't got the knack!; **ce n'est pas la bonne/la seule t.** that's not the right/the only way to go about it; **c'est tout une t.** there's a knack to it; **je crois que je vais devoir changer de t.** I think I'm going to have to change my methods *or* the way I go about things; **c'est sa t.** that's his/her way
NM *(enseignement)* technical *or* vocational training; **élèves du t.** pupils taking technical subjects; **professeurs du t.** teachers of technical subjects

techniquement [tɛknikmɑ̃] ADV technically

techno [tɛknɔ] **ADJ INV, NF** techno

technocrate [tɛknɔkrat] **N** technocrat

technocratie [tɛknɔkrasi] **NF** technocracy

technocratique [tɛknɔkratik] **ADJ** technocratic

technologie [tɛknɔlɔʒi] **NF** technology; **haute t.** high tech(nology); **appareil de haute t.** high-tech apparatus; **t. de pointe** state-of-the-art technology; **technologies nouvelles** new technologies

technologique [tɛknɔlɔʒik] **ADJ** technological

technologiste [tɛknɔlɔʒist], **technologue** [tɛknɔlɔg] **N** technologist

teck [tɛk] **NM** (bois) teak; **bateau en t.** teak boat

teckel [tekɛl] **NM** dachshund; **t. à poil ras** short-haired dachshund

tectonique [tektɔnik] **ADJ** tectonic **NF** tectonics; **t. des plaques** plate tectonics

teddy-bear, pl **teddy-bears** [tedibɛr] **NM** teddy bear

Te Deum [tedeɔm] **NM INV** Mus, Rel Te Deum

tee [ti] **NM** Golf tee

teen-ager, pl **teen-agers** [tinɛdʒœr] **N** teen-ager; **films/vêtements pour teen-agers** teenage films/clothes

tee(-)shirt, pl **tee(-)shirts** [tiʃœrt] **NM** teeshirt

Téflon® [teflɔ̃] **NM** Teflon®; **poêle en T.** Teflon® frying pan

téflonisé [teflɔnize] **ADJ** (poêle à frire etc) Teflon®

TEG [teɔʒe] **NM** Fin (abrév **taux effectif global**) APR

tégument [tegymɑ̃] **NM** Biol (in)tegument

Téhéran [teerɑ̃] **N** Teh(e)ran

teigne [tɛɲ] **NF 1** (papillon) moth; **t. des draps** (clothes) moth **2** (personne méchante) rat, Br nasty piece of work; **méchant** ou **mauvais comme une t.** as nasty as they come **3** Méd ringworm, Spéc tinea

teigneux, -euse [tɛɲø, -øz] **ADJ 1** nasty **2** Méd suffering from ringworm **N 1** Méd ringworm sufferer **2** (personne méchante) rat, Br nasty piece of work

teindre [tɛ̃dr] (prp **teignant**; pp **teint**; pr ind **je teins, il teint, n. teignons**; pr sub **je teigne**; impf **je teignais**; p hist **je teignis**; fu **je teindrai**) **VT 1** (vêtement, cheveux etc) to dye; **t. qch en rouge** to dye sth red; **faire t. une robe** to have a dress dyed **2** (mains etc) to stain **VPR se teindre 1 se t.** (les cheveux) to dye one's hair **2** Litt (se colorer) to be tinged (**de** with)

teint [tɛ̃] **NM 1** Tex (couleur) colour, Am color; **bon t., grand t.** fast colour; **tissu bon** ou **grand t.** colourfast material; Fig **bon t.** (catholique, communiste etc) staunch, Péj dyed-in-the-wool **2** (du visage) complexion; **t. frais/olivâtre/clair** fresh/olive/clear complexion; **je n'ai pas le t. frais ce matin** my skin looks a bit muddy this morning; **au t. jaune** sallow

> Do not confuse with **teinte**.

teinte [tɛ̃t] **NF 1** (couleur nuancée) shade, tint, tone; **plusieurs teintes de bleu** several shades of blue; **teintes chaudes/froides** warm/cold tints **2** Fig (d'ironie, de mélancolie etc) touch, tinge, hint

> Do not confuse with **teint**.

teinter [tɛ̃te] **VT 1** to tint; (lunettes à) **verres teintés** tinted glasses **2** Fig **t.** (légèrement) to tinge (**de** with); **des paroles teintées d'un accent rimbaldien** words reminiscent of Rimbaud **VPR se teinter** (se colorer), Fig to be tinged

(**de** with)

teinture [tɛ̃tyr] **NF 1** (action) (de tissu, des cheveux etc) dyeing; (d'un dessin etc) tinting **2** (produit) dye; **tissu qui prend bien la t.** material that dyes well **3** Fig Litt (connaissance superficielle) (d'anglais etc) smattering; **elle a quelque vague t. de mathématiques** she has a rudimentary knowledge of maths **4** Pharm tincture
▸▸ **t. d'iode** tincture of iodine

teinturerie [tɛ̃tyr(ə)ri] **NF 1** (industrie) dyeing **2** (pressing) (dry) cleaner's

teinturier, -ière [tɛ̃tyrje, -jɛr] **N 1** Ind dyer **2** (qui tient un pressing) (dry) cleaner; **déposer qch chez le t.** to take sth to the cleaner's

tek [tɛk] **NM** (bois) teak

TEL, TELLE [tɛl] SEE GRAMMAR B15

ADJ such **1** ▪ such and such **1** ▪ such as (tel que) **2** ▪ like (tel que) **2, 4**
N so-and-so (un tel/une telle)

ADJ 1 such; **un t. homme** such a man; **une telle conduite est remarquable** such behaviour is remarkable; **avec une telle aide, tu ne peux que réussir** with assistance like that, you can't help succeeding; **il a un t. enthousiasme que ...** he is so enthusiastic that ..., Fml his enthusiasm is such that ...; **t. fut son langage** those were his words; **il n'est pas beau, mais il se prend pour t.** he isn't handsome, but he thinks he is; **de telles choses** such things; **je ne peux pas lui dire de telles choses** I can't say things like that to him; **de telles paroles, de sa part?** he actually said that?; **en t. lieu** in such and such a place; **dans telle et telle rue** in such and such a street; **dans telles et telles conditions** in such and such conditions; **selon que telle ou telle méthode est choisie** depending on whether this or that method is chosen; **inutile de demander si t. ouvrage remplit son but mieux que t. autre** it is useless to ask whether one book achieves its aim better than another; **t. produit n'est pas forcément plus efficace que t. autre** one product is not necessarily any better than another; **dans telles circonstances qu'on le jugera convenable** under such conditions as may be deemed suitable; **sa bonté est telle que ...** he is so kind that ..., Fml so great is his kindness that ...; **elle n'en a pas un besoin t. qu'il faille le lui rendre aujourd'hui** she doesn't need it so badly that we have to give it back to her today; **à t. point** to such an extent; **j'étais inquiet à t. point que je voulais appeler la police** I was worried to the point of wanting to call the police; **il parle de telle sorte que je ne le comprends pas** he speaks in such a way that I don't understand him; **je m'arrangerai de telle sorte qu'elle puisse partir dimanche** I'll arrange things so that or in such a way that she can leave on Sunday; **t. père, t. fils** like father like son; Ordinat **t. écran-t. écrit** WYSIWYG VOIR GRAMMAIRE A5
2 t. que (comme) such as, like; **des gens connus tel(s) qu'Elvis Presley** well-known people such as or like Elvis Presley; **un homme t. que lui** a man like him; **une action telle que la sienne** an action such as his; **une lassitude telle qu'on en éprouve par un jour orageux** the kind of tiredness or Fml a tiredness such as one feels on a stormy day; **une impression telle qu'on en a rarement** the kind of impression that is rare; **la clause telle qu'elle est** the clause as it stands; **voir les hommes/les choses tels qu'ils/telles qu'elles sont** to see men/things as they are; **t. que je connais Jean-Luc, il ne sera pas d'accord!** he won't agree, not if I know Jean-Luc!
3 (il n'y a) **rien de t. qu'un bon cigare** there's

nothing like or you can't beat a good cigar; **il n'est rien de t. que d'être jeune** there's nothing like being young
4 Litt **il allait et venait t.** ou **telle une bête en cage** he paced to and fro like a caged animal
5 t. quel, Fam **t. que** (chose) (just) as it is/was; (personne) (just) as he is/was; **je vous achète la maison telle quelle** I'll buy the house from you (just) as it is or stands or esp Com as is; **j'ai retrouvé la maison telle quelle** I found the house just as I had left it; **il me l'a rendu t. quel** that's how he gave it back to me; **la voiture était couverte de boue, il l'a rendue telle quelle à son père** the car was covered in mud and that was how he gave it back to his father; Fam **elle me l'a dit t. que** she told me straight out, she told me just like that

PRON t. l'en blâmait, t. l'en excusait one would blame him, another would excuse him; Prov **t. est pris qui croyait prendre** it's a case of the biter bit; Prov **t. qui rit vendredi, dimanche pleurera** laugh today, cry tomorrow; **t. ou t. vous dira que ...** some people will tell you that ...; **je serais incapable d'attribuer l'article à t. ou t.** I cannot attribute the article to any particular person **N un t., une telle** so-and-so; **Monsieur un t.** ou **un T.** Mr So-and-so

télé [tele] **NF** Fam **1** (appareil) TV, Br telly; **regarder la t.** to watch TV or the telly; **travailler à la t.** to work in TV; **passer à la t.** (personne) to be or appear on TV; **c'est passé à la t.** it was on TV or telly; **je vais devoir jeter ma vieille t.** I'm going to have to throw out my old TV (set) or telly; **il n'y a rien à la t.** there's nothing on TV **2 la t.** (organisme, technique, émissions) TV; **des émissions de t.** TV programmes; **t. à péage** pay-as-you-view TV

téléachat [teleaʃa] **NM 1** (d'articles présentés à la télévision) teleshopping, home shopping **2** (par l'Internet) on-line shopping; **ce nouveau logiciel améliore la sécurité des téléachats** this new software makes on-line shopping or on-line transactions safer

téléacheteur, -euse [teleaʃtœr, -øz] **N** teleshopper

téléacteur, -trice [teleaktœr, -tris] **N** (en marketing) telemarketer, telesales person

téléaction **NF** telephone marketing

téléassistance [teleasistɑ̃s] **NF** Ordinat remote help

téléavertisseur [teleavertisœr] **NM** Can pager

télébenne [telebɛn] **NF** (dispositif, cabine) cable car

téléboutique® [telebutik] **NF** (de France Télécom) telephone shop

télécabine [telekabin] **NF** (dispositif, cabine) cable car

Télécarte® [telekart] **NF** phonecard

téléchargeable [teleʃarʒabl] **ADJ** Ordinat downloadable

téléchargement [teleʃarʒəmɑ̃] **NM** Ordinat downloading, download; **effectuer un t.** to download

télécharger [teleʃarʒe] **VT** Ordinat to download; (vers un gros ordinateur) to upload

télécinéma [telesinema] **NM** (appareil) telecine

télécommande [telekɔmɑ̃d] **NF** remote control; **t. à infrarouge** infra-red remote control

télécommander [telekɔmɑ̃de] **VT 1** Tech to operate by remote control; **télécommandé** remote-controlled, operated by remote control **2** Fig (complot, soulèvement) to mastermind from a distance; **sa décision était télécommandée par des agents ennemis** his decision was dictated by enemy agents

télécommunication [telekɔmynikasjɔ̃] NF telecommunication; **télécommunications** telecommunications, telecoms; **satellite de t.** telecom(s) satellite

téléconférence [telekɔ̃ferɑ̃s] NF teleconference; **téléconférences** teleconferencing; **la t. est une des méthodes que nous utilisons le plus fréquemment** teleconferencing is one of the methods we use most frequently

téléconseil [telekɔ̃sɛj] NM teleconsulting

télécopie [telekɔpi] NF *(procédé)* fax, facsimile transmission; *(message)* fax; **envoyer qch par t.** to fax sth; **envoyer une t. à qn** to send sb a fax, to fax sb; **numéro de t.** fax number

télécopieur [telekɔpjœr] NM fax (machine)

télécran [telekrɑ̃] NM *(dans un auditorium)* large-sized television screen

tel écran-tel écrit ADJ *Ordinat* WYSIWYG

télédémarchage [teledemarʃaʒ] NM *Mktg* telephone prospecting

télédépannage [teledepanaʒ] NM *Ordinat* remote trouble-shooting

télédétection [teledetɛksjɔ̃] NF remote sensing

télédiffuser [teledifyze] VT to televise, to broadcast

télédiffuseur [teledifyzœr] NM television broadcaster

télédiffusion [teledifyzjɔ̃] NF televising, broadcasting; **T. de France** French broadcasting authority

télédistribution [teledistribysjɔ̃] NF cable television

téléécriture NF *Ordinat* telewriting

téléenseignement NM distance learning

Téléfax® [telefaks] NM fax (machine)

téléférique [teleferik] ADJ *Tech (câble etc)* telpher
    NM *(dispositif, cabine)* cable car

téléfilm [telefilm] NM television film *or* movie, made-for-television movie

télégénique [teleʒenik] ADJ telegenic

télégestion [teleʒɛstjɔ̃] NF *Ordinat* teleprocessing, remote processing

télégramme [telegram] NM telegram, cable, wire

télégraphe [telegraf] NM telegraph

télégraphie [telegrafi] NF telegraphy; *Vieilli* **t. sans fil** wireless (telegraphy)

télégraphier [telegrafje] *(impf, pr sub* **nous télégraphiions, vous télégraphiiez)** VT *(message)* to wire, to cable, to telegraph
    VI **t. à qn** to wire *or* cable sb

télégraphique [telegrafik] ADJ telegraphic; **fil/poteau t.** telegraph wire/pole; **dépêche t.** telegram; **style t.** telegraphic style, *Fam* telegraphese

télégraphiquement [telegrafikmɑ̃] ADV by telegram, by cable, by wire

télégraphiste [telegrafist] N *(technicien)* telegraph operator, telegraphist; **(petit) t.** *(porteur de dépêches)* telegraph boy

téléguidage [telegidaʒ] NM remote control

téléguidé [telegide] ADJ remote-controlled; **engin t.** guided missile; **voiture téléguidée** remote-controlled car

téléguider [telegide] VT **1** *Tech* to operate by remote control **2** *Fig (complot, soulèvement)* to mastermind from a distance; **sa réponse/ décision était téléguidée** his answer/decision was dictated by outside forces

téléimpression [teleɛ̃presjɔ̃] NF teleprinting

téléimprimeur [teleɛ̃primœr] NM teleprinter, *Am* teletypewriter

téléinformatique [teleɛ̃fɔrmatik] ADJ teleprocessing, remote data processing

téléjournaliste [teleʒurnalist] N television journalist

télékinésie [telekinezi] NF telekinesis

télémaintenance [telemɛ̃tnɑ̃s] NF *Astronaut* housekeeping; *Ordinat* remote access

télémanipulateur [telemanipylatœr] NM *Nucl* remote manipulator

Télémaque [telemak] NM *Myth* Telemachus

télémarché [telemarʃe] NM telemarket

télémark [telemark] NM *Ski* telemark

télémarketing [telemarkɔtiŋ, -ketiŋ] NM telemarketing

télématique [telematik] NF data communications, telematics
    ADJ data communications, telecommunications; **par voie t.** using data comms (technology)

télémédecine [telemedsin] NF telemedicine, remote medicine

télémercatique [telemɛrkatik] NF telemarketing

télémessage [telemɛsaʒ] NM *Tél* text message, SMS

télémesure [telemɔzyr] NF *Électron etc* telemetering, telemetry

télémètre [telemɛtr] NM telemeter; *Mil, Phot* rangefinder

télémétrie [telemetri] NF telemetry; *Mil, Phot* range finding

téléobjectif [teleɔbʒɛktif] NM *Phot* telephoto *or* long-focus lens; **photographie au t.** telephotography

téléologie [teleɔlɔʒi] NF *Phil* teleology

téléologique [teleɔlɔʒik] ADJ teleologic(al)

téléostéen [teleɔsteɛ̃] NM *(poisson)* teleost

télépaiement [telepɛmɑ̃] NM telepayment, electronic payment

télépathe [telepat] ADJ telepathic; *Hum* **je ne suis pas t.!** I'm not psychic!
    N telepathist, telepath

télépathie [telepati] NF telepathy

télépathique [telepatik] ADJ telepathic

télépéage [telepeaʒ] NM = toll system using electronic tagging of cars

téléphage [telefaʒ] NM couch potato

téléphérage [teleferaʒ] NM *Tech* telpherage, overhead cable transport

téléphérique [teleferik] ADJ, NM = **téléférique**

téléphone [telefɔn] NM [VOIR GRAMMAIRE A77] *(appareil)* telephone, phone; *(système)* telephone; **(numéro de) t.** (tele)phone number; **donne-moi ton (numéro de) t.** give me your (phone) number; **t. direct** direct dial telephone; **être abonné au t., avoir le t.** to be on the phone, to have a phone; **être au t.** to be on the phone; **coup de t.** (tele)phone call; **donner** *ou* **passer un coup de t.** to make a phone call; **appeler qn au t., donner un coup de t. à qn** to (tele)phone sb, to call sb, *Br* to ring sb (up); **parler à qn au** *ou* **par t.** to speak to sb on the phone; **je l'avais au t. pas plus tard qu'hier** I was on the phone to him/her only yesterday; **apprendre qch par t.** to learn of sth by phone; **demander qch par t.** to phone for sth; **commander qch par t.** to order sth by phone
    ▸▸ *Fam* **t. arabe** grapevine, bush telegraph; *Fam* **par le t. arabe** on the grapevine; **t. bâtiment-terre** ship to shore (tele)phone; **t. à carte** cardphone; **t. cellulaire** cellular phone; **t. avec fonction mains-libres** phone with hands-free facility; **t. mobile** mobile (phone); **t. portable** mobile (phone); **t. public** public telephone; *Pol* **t. rouge** hot line; **t. sans fil** cordless (tele)phone; **t. satellitaire** satellite telephone; **t. de voiture** car phone; **t. WAP** WAP telephone

téléphoner [telefɔne] VT **1** *(nouvelle etc)* to

(tele)phone; **je te téléphonerai tes résultats** I'll call and let you know your results, I'll call you with your results **2** *Sport etc, Fig (coups etc)* to telegraph; *Pol etc* **une manœuvre téléphonée** an obvious manoeuvre; **c'était téléphoné** you could see it coming
    VI to (tele)phone; **je passe tout mon temps à t.** I spend all my time on the phone; **t. à qn** to ring sb (up), to (tele)phone sb, *surtout Am* to call sb; **t. à qn de venir** to (tele)phone for sb
    VPR **se téléphoner** to ring each other (up), to (tele)phone each other, *surtout Am* to call each other (up)

téléphonie [telefɔni] NF telephony; **t. sans fil** wireless telephony, radiotelephony; **la t. mobile** *ou* **portable** mobile phone; **t. sur Internet** Internet telephony

téléphonique [telefɔnik] ADJ *(cabine, appel, ligne, réseau etc)* telephone; **commande t.** order by telephone, telephone order

téléphoniste [telefɔnist] N (telephone) operator, *Br* telephonist

téléphotographie [telefɔtɔgrafi] NF **1** *Tél* phototelegraphy **2** *Phot* telephotography; *(cliché)* telephotograph

télé-poubelle NF *Fam* trash TV

téléprompteur [teleprɔ̃ptœr] NM *TV* Teleprompter®, *Br* Autocue®, *Fam* idiot board

téléprospecteur, -trice [teleprɔspɛktœr, -tris] N telesales operator, telesales person

téléprospection [teleprɔspɛksjɔ̃] NF telemarketing, teleprospecting

téléreportage [teler(ɔ)pɔrtaʒ] NM *(activité)* television reporting; *(commentaire)* television report

téléréunion [telereynjɔ̃] NF teleconference

télescopage [telɛskɔpaʒ] NM *(de trains etc)* telescoping; *Aut* **t. (en série)** pile-up

télescope [telɛskɔp] NM telescope; **t. électronique** electron telescope

télescoper [telɛskɔpe] VT **1** *Aut, Rail (véhicules, train etc)* to crash into **2** *Ling (mots)* to telescope
    VPR **se télescoper 1** *(de véhicules, de trains)* to concertina **2** *Fig (de souvenirs, d'images etc)* to overlap

télescopique [telɛskɔpik] ADJ telescopic

téléscripteur [teleskriptœr] NM teleprinter, *Am* teletypewriter, *Am* teletyper; *Bourse* ticker tape

télésecrétariat [telesɔkretarja] NM remote secretarial services

téléservice [telesɛrvis] NM on-line service

télésiège [telesjɛʒ] NM chair lift

téléski [teleski] NM ski lift *or* tow

télésouffleur [telesuflœr] NM Teleprompter®, video prompter, *Br* Autocue®

téléspectateur, -trice [telespɛktatœr, -tris] N (television) viewer

téléstation [telestasjɔ̃] NF remote station

télésurveillance [telesyrvɛjɑ̃s] NF remote *or* electronic surveillance

Télétel® [teletɛl] NM = computerized information network available through Minitel®

Télétex® [teletɛks] NM *Ordinat* teletex

télétexte [teletɛkst] NM *TV* teletext

téléthèque [teletɛk] NF television film library

téléthon [teletɔ̃] NM telethon

télétraitement [teletrɛtmɑ̃] NM *Ordinat* teleprocessing, remote data processing

télétransmission [teletrɑ̃smisjɔ̃] NF remote *or* data transmission

télétravail [teletravaj] NM telecommuting, teleworking

télétravailler [teletravaje] VI to telecommute

télétravailleur, -euse [teletravajœr, -øz] **N** telecommuter, teleworker

Télétype® [teletip] **NM** Teletype®, teleprinter, *Am* teletype

télévangéliste [televã3elist] **N** televangelist

télévendeur, -euse [televãdœr, -øz] **N** telesales operator

télévente [televãt] **NF** telesales, telephone selling, teleselling; **t. groupée** bus phoning

télévérité [televerite] **NF** realityTV

téléviser [televize] **VT** to televise; **journal télévisé** television news

téléviseur [televizœr] **NM** television *or*TV (set); **t. couleur** colour television (set); **t. grand écran** widescreen television (set)

télévision [televizjõ] **NF 1** *(organisme, technique, émissions)* television,TV; **à la t.** on television; **travailler à la t.** to work in television; **passer à la t.** *(personne)* to go on TV **2** *(poste)* television *or*TV (set); **regarder la t.** to watch television; **écran de t.** television screen **3 (chaîne de) t.** television *or*TV channel
▸▸ **t. à accès conditionnel** conditional-access television; **t. par câble** cable television, *Am* cablecasting; **t. à la carte** pay-per-view TV; **t. en circuit fermé** closed-circuit television, CCTV; **t. commerciale** commercial television; **t. en couleur(s), t. couleur** colour *or Am* color television; **t. à la demande** television on demand; **t. pour enfants** children's television; **t. généraliste** general-interest television channel; **t. haute définition** high-definition television, hi-def television; **t. par Internet** Internet TV; **t. numérique** digital television; **t. numérique terrestre** digital terrestrial television; **t. ouverte** access broadcasting; **t. à péage** *ou* **payante** pay TV; **t. par satellite** satellite television; **t. scolaire** schools *or*educational television, television for schools; **t. de service public** public television

télévisuel, -elle [televizɥɛl] **ADJ**television

télex [teleks] **NM** *(service, message)* telex; **envoyer par t.** to send by telex, to telex

télexer [telekse] **VT** to telex

télexiste [teleksist] **N** telex operator

tellement [tɛlmã] **ADV 1** *(si)* so; *(+ comp)* so much; **elle en parle t. souvent** she talks about it so often; **c'est t. facile** it's so (very) easy; **ce serait t. plus simple** it would be so much simpler; **il est t. sourd qu'il faut crier** he is so deaf that you have to shout; **il en sait déjà t. que ...** he knows so much about it that ...; **ce n'est pas t. beau** it's not all that beautiful; **ça te plaît? – pas t.** do you like it? – not very much *or* not all that much; **je n'ai pas t. envie de le revoir** I'm not all that keen on seeing him again **2** *Fam* **t. de** *(nombre)* so many; *(quantité)* so much; **t. de choses à faire** so many things *or*so much to do; **ça demande t. de courage** it requires so much courage **3** *(tant)* so; **elle ne peut pas se lever, t. elle est malade** she cannot get up, she is so ill

tellure [telyr] **NM** *Chimie* tellurium

tellurique[1] [telyrik] **ADJ** *Chimie (acide)* telluric

tellurique[2] **ADJ** *(courants)* telluric; **secousse t.** earth tremor

téloche [telɔʃ] **NF** *Fam*TV, *Br* telly

tel-tel **ADJ** *Ordinat*WYSIWYG

téméraire [temerɛr] **ADJ** *(personne, entreprise)* rash, reckless; *(jugement, déclaration)* rash

témérairement [temerɛrmã] **ADV** rashly, recklessly

témérité [temerite] **NF** rashness, recklessness

témoignage [temwaɲaʒ] **NM 1** *(attestation)* testimony, evidence; **recueillir des témoignages** to collect evidence; **porter t.** to give evidence; **porter t. en faveur de qn** to give evidence *or*to testify on sb's behalf; **ce livre se contente de porter t. sur l'époque** the book is content to describe the era; **rendre t. de qch** to give evidence about sth; **rendre t. à** *ou* **pour qn** to speak up for sb; *Jur* to testify in sb's favour *or Am* favor; **faux t.** false witness, false evidence; *(délit)* perjury; **faire un faux t.** to commit perjury **2** *(déclaration)* evidence, statement; **d'après son t.** according to his statement; *Fig* **t. des sens** evidence of the senses **3** *(démonstration) (d'amitié, d'admiration etc)* token, sign; **c'est le t. de mon amitié** it's a token of my friendship; **en t. de** as a token *or* sign of **4** *Mktg (publicité)* testimonial advertising

témoigner [temwaɲe] **VI 1**to testify (**en faveur de/contre qn** on behalf of/against sb), to give evidence (**en faveur de/contre qn** for/against sb) **2 t. de** *(montrer) (gratitude, bonne volonté, courage etc)* to show; *(confirmer) (bonne foi etc)* to show, to testify to; **t. d'un goût pour ...** to show *or*display a taste for ...; **t. de l'intérêt à qn/pour qch** to show an interest in sb/sth; **t. du dédain à qn** to show contempt for sb
VT 1 *(attester)* **t. que** to testify that **2** *(montrer) (sentiments, gratitude etc)* to show (**à qn** to sb); **il ne m'a jamais témoigné d'affection/d'amitié** he has never shown me any affection/any signs of friendship; **cela témoigne que/combien ...** that shows that/how much ...; **sa réaction témoigne qu'il s'y attendait** his reaction shows *or*is proof that he was expecting it

témoin [temwɛ̃] **NM 1** *(spectateur)* witness; **être t. de qch** to witness sth, to be a witness to sth; **j'en suis t.** I'm a witness; **ils se sont vus sans t.** they saw each other in private, there were no witnesses present when they saw each other; **mes yeux en sont témoins** I saw it with my own eyes
2 *Jur* witness; **barre des témoins** witness box, *Am* (witness) stand; **à la barre des témoins** in the witness box, *Am* on the stand; **citer qn comme t.** to call sb as a witness; **t. à un mariage** witness at a wedding; **je vous prends tous à t.** I call on you all to witness that ...; **Dieu m'est t. que je n'y suis pour rien** as God is my witness, I had nothing to do with it
3 *(dans un duel)* second
4 *(trace)* evidence; **les témoins d'une civilisation perdue** the evidence of a lost civilization; **t. les coups que j'ai reçus** witness the blows which I received
5 *(borne)* boundary mark
6 *(échantillon)* *Chimie* reference solution; **animal/plante t.** *(dans un essai)* control animal/plant; *Phot* **plaque** *ou* **épreuve t.** pilot print; **denrée t.** basic commodity; **appartement t.** show flat, *Am* model apartment; **voici les bilans de quatre entreprises témoins** here are the balance sheets from four sample companies
7 *Élec, Ind etc* **(lampe) t.** pilot *or* warning light; *Aut* **t. d'alerte de pression d'huile moteur** oil pressure warning light
8 *Sport (dans un relais)* baton
▸▸ *Aut* **t. d'allumage** ignition light; *Jur* **t. assisté** = witness who can be questioned by an examining magistrate without the threat of being placed under investigation; *Aut* **t. de baisse du niveau d'essence** petrol low warning light; *Jur* **t. à charge** witness for the prosecution; *Aut* **t. de charge** *ou* de **contrôle de la batterie** battery charge warning light; *Jur* **t. à décharge** witness for the defence; **t. de frein parking** handbrake-on light; *Rel* **T. de Jéhovah** Jehovah's Witness;

Jur **t. de moralité** character witness; *Jur* **t. oculaire** eyewitness

tempe [tãp] **NF***Anat*temple; **aux tempes grisonnantes** (going) grey at the temples

TEMPÉ [tɛɑ̃mpe] **NM** *Bourse (abrév* **Taux moyen pondéré en euros)** EONIA

tempera (à) [atãpera] *Beaux-Arts* **ADJ** peinture à t. tempera painting
ADV peindre à t. to paint in tempera

tempérament [tãperamã] **NM 1** *(physique)* constitution; **t. de fer** iron constitution; *Fam* **se tuer le t.** to ruin one's health **2** *(moral)* disposition; **être d'un** *ou* **avoir un t. violent** to be of a violent disposition; **c'est un t.** he has character; **avoir du t.** to have character; *(sexuel)* to be highly sexed **3** *Arch (modération)* moderation, restraint **4** *Com* **à t.** by instalments; **vente** *ou* **achat à t.** *Br* hire purchase, *Am* installment plan

tempérance [tãperãs] **NF 1** *(modération)* moderation, temperance; **faire preuve de t.** to show moderation, to be moderate **2** *(sobriété)* temperance; **faire preuve de t.** to drink in moderation; **société de t.** temperance society

tempérant [tãperã] **ADJ** *(personne)* temperate

température [tãperatyr] **NF** *(d'une personne, d'un liquide, d'une région etc)*, *Fig* temperature; **t. du corps humain**temperature of the human body, blood heat; *Méd Fam* **avoir** *ou* **faire de la t.** to have a (high) temperature; *Méd* **feuille de t.** temperature chart; **la méthode des températures** *(de contraception)* the rhythm method; *Phys* **t. d'ébullition** boiling point; **prendre la t. d'un malade** to take a patient's temperature; *Fig* **prendre la t. de l'auditoire** to gauge the temperature of the audience

tempéré [tãpere] **ADJ 1** *(climat)* temperate; *(discours)* moderate; *(style)* restrained, sober **2** *Mus* tempered

tempérer [tãpere] **VT** (**je tempère, n. tempérons; je tempérerai**) *(chaleur)* to moderate; *(passion)* to moderate, to temper

tempête [tãpɛt] **NF** *Météo, Fig (d'applaudissements)* storm; *Fig (d'injures)* storm, hail; **t.** *(sur un baromètre)* stormy; *Fig* **cette mesure va provoquer une t.** the measure will cause a storm of protest; **pendant la t.** during the storm; *Fig* while the storm is raging; *Fig* **une t. dans un verre d'eau** a storm in a teacup *or Am* teapot; *Fig* **nous avons eu droit à une t. d'insultes/de bravos** insults/bravos rained down on us
▸▸ **t. de neige** blizzard, snowstorm; **t. de sable** sandstorm

tempêter [tãpete] **VI** *(d'une personne)* to storm, to rage; **t. contre qn/qch** to rant and rave about sb/sth

tempétueux, -euse [tãpetɥø, -øz] **ADJ** *(vent, mer etc)* stormy, *Fml* tempestuous; *Fig (relations)* tempestuous, stormy; *(accueil)* boisterous, tempestuous; *(vie)* turbulent, stormy

temple [tãpl] **NM** temple; *(protestant)* church; *Fig (de la gastronomie etc)* temple; *Hist* **les chevaliers du T.** the Knights Templar(s)

templier [tãplije] **NM** *Hist* (Knight) Templar

tempo [tɛpo, tãpo] **NM** *Mus, Fig*tempo VOIR GRAMMAIRE A14

temporaire [tãpɔrɛr] **ADJ 1** *(provisoire)* temporary; **agence de travail t.** temporary employment agency; **emploi t.** temporary job; **employé t.** temporary employee, *Fam* temp **2** *Mus* **valeur t. d'une note** time value of a note
N temp

temporairement [tãpɔrɛrmã] **ADV** temporarily

temporal, -ale, -aux, -ales [tɑ̃pɔral, -o] *Anat* **ADJ** *(os, artère)* temporal
NM 1 *(os)* temporal bone **2** *(muscle)* temporal muscle, *Spéc* temporalis
NF temporale temporal (artery)

temporalité [tɑ̃pɔralite] **NF** *Rel, Phil, Gram* temporality

temporel, -elle [tɑ̃pɔrɛl] **ADJ 1** *(terrestre)* temporal, worldly **2** *Gram (proposition etc)* temporal **3** *(qui concerne le temps)* time

temporellement [tɑ̃pɔrɛlmɑ̃] **ADV** temporally

temporisateur, -trice [tɑ̃pɔrizatœr, -tris] **ADJ** temporizing; **ce n'est qu'une tactique temporisatrice de la part du gouvernement** the government is just playing for time with this measure
N *(personne)* **c'est un t.** *(qui attend pour agir)* he doesn't make hasty decisions; *(qui fait traîner les choses)* he's always stalling *or* playing for time
NM *Élec* (automatic) time switch

temporisation [tɑ̃pɔrizasjɔ̃] **NF** playing for time, stalling, *Fml* temporizing

temporiser [tɑ̃pɔrize] **VI** to play for time, to stall, *Fml* to temporize

TEMPS [tɑ̃]

> time **1–7, 13** ▪ weather **8** ▪ tense **9**
> ▪ beat **10** ▪ stroke **12**

NM 1 *(durée)* time; **mettre beaucoup de t. à faire qch** to take a long time doing sth; **mettre peu de t. à faire qch** not to take long to do sth; **tuer le t.** to kill time; **pour passer le t.** to pass the time, to while away the time; **vous avez bien le t., vous avez tout le t.** you've plenty *or* lots of time; **cela prend du t.** it takes *or* requires time; **cela ne prendra pas beaucoup de t.** it won't take long; **en un rien de t.** in no time at all; **prendre (tout) son t.** to take one's time; **prends le t. qu'il faudra** take as much time as you need; **je voudrais prendre un peu de t. pour y réfléchir** I'd like to have some time to think about it; **elle a pris/trouvé le t. de nous l'expliquer** she took/found the time to explain it to us; **donner à qn le t. de faire qch** to give sb time to do sth; **(donnez-moi) le t. de signer** *ou* **que je signe et je suis à vous** just give me time *or* a minute to sign this and I'll be with you; **je trouve le t. long** time is dragging; **nous n'avons pas le t. à présent** we don't have time *or* there's no time now; **nous n'avons que le t. de ...** we just have time to ...; **combien de t. faut-il pour ...?** how long does it take to ...?; **accorder du t. à qn** to give sb time; **vous pourriez m'accorder un peu de t. pour que je vous parle de mon projet?** could you give me a moment or two of your time to talk about my project?; **il n'accorde pas beaucoup de t. à ses enfants** he doesn't have much time for his children, his children don't get much of his time; **gagner du t.** to save *or* gain time; *(temporiser)* to play for time, to stall; **perdre du t.** to waste time; *(à cause d'un imprévu)* to lose time; **tu me fais perdre mon t.** you're wasting my time; **rattraper le t. perdu** to make up for lost time; **dans le cours du t., avec le t.** in (the course of) time, with time; **de t. en t., de t. à autre** now and then, from time to time; **en d'autres t.** at any other time; **en tout t.** at all times; **en même t.** at the same time; **en même t. mère et sœur** both mother and sister, mother and sister at the same time; **travailler à plein t./à t. partiel** *ou* **à mi-t.** to work full-time/part-time, to have a full-time/part-time job; **prendre/se donner du bon t.** to have a good time, to enjoy oneself; *Prov* **le t., c'est de l'argent** time is money; *Myth etc* **le T.** (Father) Time
2 *(moment)* time; **en t. de crise** in a crisis, at a time of crisis; **en t. de guerre/de paix** in wartime/peacetime; **un (certain) t., quelque t.** for a while, for a time; **pendant ce t.** meanwhile, in the meantime; **entre-t. ...** in the meantime ...; **il est arrivé entre-t.** he arrived in the meantime; **après quelque t., au bout d'un certain t.** after a time; **cela ne durera qu'un t.** it won't last for ever; **tout n'a qu'un t.** everything must come to an end; **le t. de la moisson** harvest time; **le t. des cerises** the cherry season; **il y a peu de t.** not long ago, a little while ago, a short time ago; **peu de t. après** shortly *or* a short time *or* not long after; **d'ici quelque t.** soon, shortly, in a short time; **au bout de très peu de t.** in a very short space of time; **tout le t.** all the time; **il est tout le t. en train de se plaindre** he is constantly *or* he keeps complaining; **c'est ce que je lui dis tout le t.** that's what I keep telling him; **faire un t. de galop** to have a short gallop, to gallop for a time *or* a while; **marquer un t.** to pause, to halt
3 faire son t. to serve *or* do one's time; *(d'un détenu)* to serve one's sentence, *Fam* to do one's time; **ce manteau a fait son t.** this coat has had it, *Hum* it's about time this coat was given a decent burial; **cette théorie a fait son t.** this theory is out of date *or* outdated *or* outmoded
4 *Ind* **étude des t. et ordonnancements** time and motion study; *Ordinat* **base de t.** time base
5 *(période, époque)* time(s), days; **les t. préhistoriques** prehistoric times; **les hauts t.** remote antiquity; **en t. normal** usually, normally; **le bon vieux t.** the good old days; **l'Angleterre des t. passés** the England of the past; **les t. sont durs** times are hard; **en ces t. de difficultés économiques** in these times of economic difficulty; **signe des t.** sign of the times; **par les t. qui courent** in this day and age, these days, nowadays; **dans le t.** in the old days; **au t. jadis** in times past, in days gone by, in bygone days; **dans la suite des t.** in the course of time; **en d'autres t., je n'aurais pas hésité** once upon a time I wouldn't have hesitated; **en ce t.-là** at that time, then; **ces t.-ci** these days; **ce fut un grand homme dans son t.** he was a great man in his day *or* time; **elle a eu son t. de beauté** she was a beauty in her day; **du t. ou au t. de Napoléon** in Napoleon's time; **du t. de ma jeunesse, du t. où j'étais jeune** when I was young, in my youth; **il fut un t. où ...** there was a time when ...; **être de son t., vivre avec son t.** to move with the times, to be up to date; **vous n'êtes pas de votre t.** you're behind the times; **être en avance sur son t.** to be ahead of one's time; **de notre t.** in our day *or* time; **il n'en était pas ainsi de mon t.** it wasn't so in my day *or* time; **cela est arrivé de mon t.** it happened in my time; **de tout t.** always
6 *(heure)* **faire qch à t.** to do sth in time; **arriver juste à t.** to arrive just in time *or* in the nick of time; **il est venu t. voulu** *ou* **utile** in due course; **je serai de retour en t. voulu** I'll be back in *or* on time; **il est t. qu'elle descende** it's time she came down; **il est grand t. que ... il est high time *or* about time that ...; **il est** *ou* **serait grand t. que tu te décides** it's high time you made up your mind; **il serait t.!** it's about time!, and about time too!; **il n'est plus t.** it's too late; **il est enfin arrivé, il était t.!** he finally arrived and not before time either!; **il n'était que t.** it was only just in time **VOIR GRAMMAIRE A54**
7 *(occasion)* **il y a un t. pour tout** there's a time for everything; **chaque chose en son t.** all in good time; **en t. et lieu** in the proper time and place; **quand j'aurai le t.** when I have (the) time
8 *Météo* weather; **par tous les t.** in all weathers; **vous sortez par un pareil t.** *ou* **par le t. qu'il fait!** you're going out in weather like this *or* in this weather!; **quel t. fait-il?** what's the weather like?, *Fam* what's the weather doing?; **quelque t. qu'il fasse** whatever the weather (is like); **si le t. le permet** weather permitting; **beau t.** fine weather; **il fait beau/mauvais t.** the weather's fine/bad; *Fam* **il fera beau t. quand je ferai cela** it'll be a long time before I do that; *Naut* **gros t.** heavy weather; **le t. est à la pluie** it looks like rain, we're going to have rain; **prévision du t.** weather forecast; **une robe couleur du t.** a sky-blue dress **SEE GRAMMAR B29**
9 *Gram* tense; **adverbes de t.** adverbs of time **SEE GRAMMAR A39–40; B30–2**
10 *Mus* beat; **mesure à trois t.** three-four time
11 *Mil* **au t.!** as you were!; *Fig* **au t. pour moi!** my mistake!
12 *Tech* **moteur à deux/à quatre t.** two-stroke/four-stroke engine
13 *Sport (d'un coureur etc)* time
▸▸ *Ordinat* **t. d'accès** access time; *Ordinat* **t. d'accès disque** disk access time; *Ordinat* **t. d'adressage** address speed; *TV, Radio* **t. d'antenne** airtime; *Astron* **t. apparent** apparent time; **t. d'arrêt** pause, halt; **t. astronomique** astronomical time; *Ordinat* **t. d'attente** wait state; *Aut* **t. compression** *(d'un moteur)* compression stroke; *Culin* **t. de cuisson** cooking time; *Com* **t. de cycle** business cycle; *Aut* **t. détente** *(d'un moteur)* power stroke; *Ordinat* **t. différé: en t. différé** off-line; **t. d'échauffement** *(d'une machine)* warm-up time; *Ordinat* **t. écoulé** elapsed time; *Ordinat* **t. d'exécution** execution *or* execute time; *Aut* **t. explosion** *(d'un moteur)* power stroke; **t. de fonctionnement** *(d'une machine)* running time; **t. fort: les t. forts de l'actualité/de l'année 2002** the main points of the news/the main events of 2002; **t. d'immobilisation** *(d'une machine)* down time; *Aut* **t. d'immobilité du piston** pis ton dwell; *Ordinat* **t. machine** machine time; *Ordinat* **t. de montée** rise time; **t. mort** *(d'une machine)* idle time *or* period, down time; *Sport* stoppage; **pendant les t. morts** *(dans une période de travail)* when things are quiet; *Aviat* **t. mort au sol** turn-round time; **t. moteur** engine *or* power *or* working stroke; **t. moyen entre deux pannes** *(d'une machine)* mean time between failures, MTBF; **t. moyen local** local mean time; *Élec, Électron* **t. d'ouverture** on period; *Ordinat* **t. partagé** time sharing; *Ordinat* **utilisation (d'un ordinateur) en t. partagé** time sharing; **t. primitifs** *(d'un verbe)* principal parts; *Aut* **t. de réaction** thinking distance; *Ordinat* **t. de recherche** search time; *Ordinat* **t. réel** real time; *Ordinat* **horloge t. réel** real-time clock; *Ordinat* **t. de rémanence** afterglow time; *Ordinat* **t. de réponse** response time; *Ordinat* **t. de sortie** output time; *Ordinat* **t. de traitement** processing time; **t. universel** Greenwich Mean Time; *Tech* **t. à vide** *(d'une machine etc)* off-load period; **t. vrai** true time

tenable [tənabl] **ADJ** *(often with negation)* **1** *Mil etc (position)* tenable, defensible **2** *(situation)* bearable; **par cette chaleur, le bureau n'est pas t.** in this heat the office is unbearable; **ce n'est plus t., je pars** it has become unbearable *or* I can't bear it any longer, I'm leaving

tenace [tənas] **ADJ** *(personne)* tenacious; *(croyance, superstition, préjugé)* stubborn, lingering; *(odeur, parfum)* lingering; *(couleur)* fast; *(volonté, résistance)* dogged, tenacious; *(maladie, douleur, souvenir)* persistent; **espoir t.** fond hope; **tu es t. toi!** you don't give up easily!; **les vieilles habitudes sont tenaces** old habits die hard

tenacement [tənasmɑ̃] **ADV** stubbornly, tenaciously

ténacité [tenasite] NF *(d'une personne)* tenacity, stubbornness; *(d'une odeur)* lingering nature; *(d'une croyance, une superstition, un préjugé)* stubbornness; *(d'une résistance)* doggedness, stubbornness; *(d'une maladie, une douleur)* persistence; **avec t.** stubbornly, doggedly; *(travailler)* doggedly

tenaille [tənɑj] NF VOIR GRAMMAIRE A10 **1** *(pour saisir)* tongs; **t. à vis** hand vice **2 tenailles** *(pour arracher des clous)* pincers; *Mil* **manœuvre en tenailles** pincer movement; **prendre l'ennemi en t.** to trap the enemy in a pincer movement

tenailler [tənɑje] VT *Hist Fig* to torture; **tenaillé par la faim** gnawed by hunger; **tenaillé par le remords** gnawed *or* tortured *or* tormented by remorse

tenancier, -ière [tənɑ̃sje, -jɛr] N **1** *(d'un hôtel, bar etc)* manager; *(d'une maison close, d'un tripot)* keeper **2** *Arch (d'un terrain)* holder **3** *(fermier)* tenant farmer

tenant, -ante [tənɑ̃, -ɑ̃t] ADJ **1 séance tenante** there and then, then and there, on the spot **2 chemise à col t.** shirt with collar attached

▸ N **1** *(partisan)* *(d'une personne, d'une opinion etc)* champion, defender **2** *Sport (d'un titre, d'un prix)* holder

▸ NM **tout d'un (seul) t.** *(propriété)* continuous, all in one block, lying together; *(bloc de pierre)* in one piece; **tenants et aboutissants** *(d'une propriété)* adjacent parts; *Fig (d'une affaire)* ins and outs, full details

tendance [tɑ̃dɑ̃s] NF *(d'une personne)* tendency, inclination; *(de l'opinion, de l'art moderne, du cinéma etc)* trend; *(d'un livre, discours etc)* tenor; **tendance(s) communiste(s)** communist leanings *or* tendencies; **avoir (une) t. à la paresse/le mensonge/l'embonpoint** to be inclined *or* to tend to be lazy/to lie/to put on weight; **avoir (une) t. à faire qch** to be inclined *or* to tend to do sth; **avoir un peu t. à faire qch** to be rather inclined to do sth; **il a facilement t. à s'emporter/mentir/avoir peur** he gets angry/lies/gets scared very easily; **avoir t. à s'enrhumer facilement** to be prone to catching colds; *Bourse* **t. générale à la hausse/baisse** general upward/downward trend; **t. ascensionnelle** upward trend; **t. de l'économie** economic trend; **t. du marché** market trend

▸ ADJ *(à la mode)* trendy; **c'est très t. comme bar** it's a very trendy bar

tendancieusement [tɑ̃dɑ̃sjøzmɑ̃] ADV tendentiously

tendancieux, -ieuse [tɑ̃dɑ̃sjø, -jøz] ADJ bias(s)ed, *Fml* tendentious; *Jur (question)* leading

tender [tɑ̃dɛr] NM *Rail, Naut* tender

tendeur [tɑ̃dœr] NM **1 t. de chaîne** *(de bicyclette)* chain adjuster *or* tightener *or* tensioner; *Aut* **t. de ceinture** seatbelt tensioner; *Aut* **t. de sangle** belt tensioner; *Tech* **t. de courroie** belt tensioner; **t. à vis** turnbuckle **2** *(de machine à coudre)* tension (device) **3 t. pour chaussures** shoe tree **4** *(courroie élastique)* bungee (cord)

tendineux, -euse [tɑ̃dinø, -øz] ADJ *Anat* tendinous; **viande tendineuse** stringy meat

tendinite [tɑ̃dinit] NF *Méd* tendinitis

tendon [tɑ̃dɔ̃] NM *Anat* tendon, sinew; **t. d'Achille** Achilles tendon; **t. du jarret** hamstring

tendre¹ [tɑ̃dr] ADJ **1** *(herbe, mine de crayon, bois, pierre, métal etc)* soft; *(viande, légume)* tender; *(couleur)* delicate, soft; *(peau)* sensitive, tender, soft **2** *(âge, enfance)* early; **dès ma plus t. enfance** from my earliest childhood; **les souvenirs de l'âge t.** early *or* childhood memories **3** *(affectueux) (personne)* loving, affectionate, fond; *(regard, geste)*

loving, affectionate, tender; *(cœur)* tender, soft; **il n'a jamais un geste t. envers sa femme** he never shows his wife any affection; **sois plus t. avec elle** be more loving *or* affectionate towards her; **ne pas être t. (pour** *ou* **avec qn)** to be hard *or* severe (on sb); **elle n'a pas été t. avec lui/le film** she didn't go easy on him/the film; **il a le vin t.** drink makes him sentimental

▸ NM **1** *Arch* **avoir un t. pour qn** to have a soft spot for sb **2** *Culin* **t. de tranche** topside (of beef)

▸ N *(personne)* softhearted person; **c'est un t.** he's softhearted

tendre² VT **1** *(raidir) (corde, corde de violon, ressort etc)* to tighten; *(toile)* to stretch; *(muscles)* to tense; *(arc)* to bend, to draw

2 *(poser) (voile, filet etc)* to spread; *(papier peint, tapisserie)* to hang; *(piège, embuscade, filet)* to set (à for); **t. une pièce de toile de jute** to cover the walls of a room in hessian

3 *(bras, jambe etc)* to stretch out, to hold out; **t. qch à qn** to hold sth out to sb; **t. la main** to hold out *or* stretch out one's hand; *(mendier)* to beg; **pas un ne m'aurait tendu la main!** not one of them would have offered me a hand *or* stretched out a helping hand!; **t. les bras** *(pour accueillir qn)* to stretch one's arms wide, to throw one's arms out; **les bras tendus** with outstretched arms; *Fig* **t. l'oreille** to prick up one's ears; **j'essayais de t. l'oreille pour comprendre ce qu'il disait** I was straining to make out what he was saying; **t. le cou** to crane one's neck

▸ VI **t. à** *ou* **vers la perfection** to try to achieve perfection, to be a perfectionist; **t. à un idéal** to aim at an ideal; **t. vers un résultat** to lead to a result; **t. à sa fin** *(d'une chose)* to be near(ing) its end, to be drawing to a close; *Math* **la valeur de n tend vers zéro** the value of n tends towards zero; **t. à faire qch** to tend to do sth; **les douleurs tendent à disparaître** the pain is starting to go; **cela tendrait à confirmer la première hypothèse** that would tend to confirm the original hypothesis

▸ VPR **se tendre** to become taut; *Fig (des relations)* to become strained; **pas une main ne s'est tendue vers moi** not a hand was stretched out towards me

tendrement [tɑ̃drəmɑ̃] ADV tenderly, lovingly; **ménage t. uni** loving couple

tendresse [tɑ̃drɛs] NF **1** *(affection)* tenderness; **t. maternelle** maternal affection *or* love; **avoir de la t. pour qn** to feel affection for sb, to be fond of sb; **avec t.** tenderly, lovingly; **aimer qn avec t.** to feel great affection for sb **2 tendresses** *(témoignages d'affection)* tokens of affection, caresses; **se dire des tendresses** to exchange sweet nothings; **mille tendresses** *(en fin de lettre)* (with) lots of love, all my love **3 tendresses royalistes** royalist sympathies

tendreté [tɑ̃drəte] NF *(de la viande, fruit)* tenderness

tendron [tɑ̃drɔ̃] NM **1** *Bot* tender shoot **2** *Culin (de veau)* gristle **3** *Fam (jeune fille)* very young and innocent girl

tendu [tɑ̃dy] ADJ **1** *(corde, toile etc)* taut, tight; *(tir)* flat; *Fig (relations, visage)* strained; *Fig (personne, situation, atmosphère, climat politique)* tense; *(estomac)* distended; **t. par la fatigue** tired and strained; *Gym* **corde tendue** tightrope; **chaîne mal tendue** slack chain; **elle a les nerfs tendus en ce moment** she is tense *or* strung up at the moment; **elle est très tendue nerveusement** she's very tense, she's under a lot of nervous strain; *Bourse* **prix tendus** hard *or* firm prices **2** *Ling (son)* strong; *(consonne)* voiceless **3** *(main)* outstretched **4** *(tapissé)* **t. de** *(tapisseries, tissu)* hung with; *(papier peint)* covered with

ténèbres [tenɛbr] NFPL darkness, gloom; *Fig (de l'ignorance, l'inconscient)* depths; **les t. de la nuit** the darkness of the night; **le Prince des T.** the Prince of Darkness

ténébreux, -euse [tenebrø, -øz] ADJ **1** *(obscur) (forêt, prison etc)* gloomy, dark **2** *(mystérieux) (affaire, période de l'histoire etc)* murky; *(style, intentions)* obscure; **un personnage t.** a dark horse

▸ NM **un beau (brun) t.** a tall, dark and handsome man

teneur¹, **-euse** [tənœr, -øz] N **1** *Typ* **t. de copie** copy holder **2 t. de livres** bookkeeper

teneur² NF **1** *(d'un document, d'une lettre etc)* contents; **je vais vous résumer la t. de ses propos** I'll give you the general tenor *or* gist of what he said; **t. d'un contrat** terms of a contract, contractual terms; **t. du marché** market trend *or* maker **2** *Tech, Ind etc (quantité)* content; **t. en eau/or** water/gold content VOIR GRAMMAIRE A10

ténia [tenja] NM *Méd* tapeworm, *Spéc* taenia, *Am* tenia

TENIR [tənir] *(prp* **tenant;** *pp* **tenu;** *pr ind* **je tiens, il tient, n. tenons, v. tenez, ils tiennent;** *pr sub* **je tienne;** *impf* **je tenais;** *p hist* **je tins, n. tînmes, v. tîntes, ils tinrent;** *p sub* **je tinsse;** *fu* **je tiendrai)**

┌─────────────────────────────────┐
│ **VT** to hold **1, 2, 10, 12** ▪ to have **3** ▪ to get **3** ▪ to run **5** ▪ to be in charge of **5** ▪ to keep **6, 10, 12** ▪ to control **9** ▪ to be confined to **11** ▪ to take up **13**
│ **VI** to hold **1, 3, 5** ▪ to hold up **1** ▪ to last **1, 4** ▪ to hold out **3** ▪ to stand fast **3** ▪ to value *(tenir à)* **7** ▪ to be fond of *(tenir à)* **7** ▪ to be keen to do *(tenir à faire)* **7** ▪ to be due to *(tenir à)* **8** ▪ to take after *(tenir de)* **9**
│ **VPR** to stay **1** ▪ to remain **1** ▪ to behave **2** ▪ to hold on **4** ▪ to hang together **5** ▪ to stick to *(s'en tenir à)* **7** ▪ to take place **8**
└─────────────────────────────────┘

VT 1 to hold; **t. qch à la main/sur ses genoux** to hold sth in one's hand/in one's lap; **t. qn par la taille** to hold sb round the waist; **il me tenait par le cou/les épaules** he had his arm round my neck/shoulders; *Fam* **t. un bon rhume** to have a stinking cold; *Fam* **en t. une** *(être ivre)* to be smashed; *Fam* **en t. une couche** *(être bête)* to be thick as two short planks; *Fam* **qu'est-ce qu'il tient!** *(il est ivre)* he's smashed!; *(il est idiot)* what a pillock!; **je tiens mon homme** I've got my man; **t. la solution** to have the solution; *Prov* **un tiens vaut mieux que deux tu l'auras, mieux vaut t. que courir** a bird in the hand is worth two in the bush; **tiens!, tenez!** look!, look here!; **tiens, le voilà qui arrive** there he is now; **tiens, voilà Paul!** there's Paul!; **tenez, mon chien à moi ...** my dog ...; **tenez, c'est ce que me disait encore hier mon médecin** that's just what my doctor was saying to me yesterday; **tenez!** *(ceci est pour vous)* here you are!; **tenez, voilà ce que vous cherchez** here's what you're looking for; **tenez, ôtez-moi cela** here, take this away; **tiens, ça ne m'étonne pas** well, that doesn't surprise me; **tiens, ce n'est pas ce qu'il m'avait dit** that's not what he said to me; *Fin* **t. à bail** to hold a lease on

2 *(contenir)* to hold; *(espace)* to take up; **baril qui tient l'eau** barrel that holds water *or* that is watertight; **t. le coup** to hold out

3 t. qch de *(le recevoir)* to have *or* get sth from; **j'en suis sûr, je le tiens de mon médecin** I'm sure of it, I have it from my doctor *or* my doctor told me; **de qui peut-il t. cela?** who did he get that from?, who told him that?; **il tient sa timidité de sa mère** he gets his shyness from his mother

4 *(stocker) (marchandises etc)* to keep, to stock

5 *(gérer, être responsable de) (boutique, hôtel, école etc)* to keep, to run; *(caisse)* to be in charge of; **Mlle Martin tenait le piano** Miss Martin was at the piano; **t. conseil** *ou* **séance** to meet, to have a meeting; *Fig Hum* **elle tient conseil dans sa boutique** she holds court in her shop; **t. une réunion** to hold a meeting

6 *(parole, promesse)* to keep; **t. un rôle difficile/important** to have a difficult/important role; **j'ignore quel rôle il a pu t. dans cette affaire** I don't know what his role was *or* what role he played in the business

7 *(dire) (discours etc)* to deliver; **t. des propos ambigus** to be ambiguous, to speak ambiguously; **il tient toujours les propos les plus absurdes** he always talks absolute nonsense

8 t. qn en mépris/en grand respect to hold sb in contempt/in great esteem

9 *(maîtriser)* to restrain; *(enfants, cheval)* to control; **t. sa langue** to hold one's tongue; **t. son sérieux** to keep a straight face; **t. qn par le chantage/la pitié** to use blackmail/pity to control sb

10 *(dans une certaine position)* to hold, to keep; *(dans un certain état)* to keep; **cette poutre tient le plafond** that beam holds up the ceiling; **c'est cette colonne qui tient tout le poids** this column takes *or* bears the entire weight; **mon rhume me tient à la maison** my cold is keeping me indoors; **t. son chien en laisse** to keep one's dog on a lead; **il nous a tenus debout pendant deux heures** he kept us standing for two hours; **t. les yeux fermés** to keep one's eyes shut; **t. qch secret** to keep sth (a) secret; **t. qn captif** to keep *or* hold sb prisoner; **t. qch en (bon) état** to keep sth in good condition, to look after sth; **tenez votre gauche/droite** keep to the left/right

11 *(ne pas pouvoir sortir de) (chambre, lit)* to be confined to, to keep to

12 t. la mer *(d'un bateau)* to keep the sea; *(d'une nation)* to rule the seas; **capable/incapable de t. la mer** *(bateau)* seaworthy/unseaworthy; *Aut* **t. la route** to hold the road; **t. son cap** to keep to *or* hold one's course

13 *(occuper) (espace)* to take up, to occupy; **vous tenez trop de place** you're taking up too much room; **la table tient la moitié de la pièce** the table occupies *or* takes up half the room; **t. toute la route** *(d'une voiture, d'un conducteur)* to hog the road; **les soucis/ enfants tiennent trop de place dans ta vie** worries/children take up *or* occupy too much of your life; **le cinéma tient une grande place dans leur vie** cinema plays a large part in their life

14 *(considérer)* **t. qn pour habile** to think sb clever; *Litt* **t. qn comme qch** to consider sb sth; **je vous tiens pour responsable de ce retard** I hold you responsible for the delay; **je le tiens pour vrai** I regard it as (being) true; **tenez cela pour fait** consider it done

VI 1 *(d'un nœud, d'une corde etc)* to hold; *(d'une construction instable etc)* to hold up, to stay up; *(d'une alliance, un projet)* to last; **la corde n'a pas tenu** the rope gave way; **le pansement ne tient pas** the dressing won't stay on; **la colle ne tient pas** the glue's not sticking; **clou qui tient bien** nail that holds well; **ça tient au mur par des clous** it's fixed to the wall with nails; **les manches tiennent par des petites épingles** the sleeves are held together by pins; *Fig* **leur vie ne tient qu'à un fil** their lives are hanging by a thread; *Fam* **il ne tient plus sur ses jambes, il ne tient plus debout** he's ready to drop (with fatigue), he's dead on his feet; **elle ne pouvait t. en place** she couldn't keep still

2 *(border)* **sa terre tient à la mienne** his estate borders on *or* adjoins mine

3 *(résister)* **t. (bon** *ou* **ferme)** to hold out, to stand fast *or* firm; *(d'un câble etc)* to stand the strain, to hold; **tenez bon** *ou* **ferme!** hold *or* hang on!; *Fig* hang in there!; *Fig* **il faut t. bon** you'll/we'll *etc* have to hang in there; **t. bon contre une attaque/des difficultés** to stand firm in the face of an attack/difficulties; **je n'ai pas pu t. une heure** I couldn't stick it out *or* hold out for an hour; **t. debout** *(d'un argument)* to stand up, to hold water; **votre argument ne tient guère** your argument hardly stands up *or* doesn't hold much water; **je n'y tiens plus** I can't stand *or* take it any longer, I can't take any more of this; **n'y tenant plus, elle a tout avoué** unable to stand *or* take it any longer, she confessed everything

4 *(durer) (d'un commerce, le vent, l'amour etc)* to last; **ma mise en plis n'a pas tenu deux jours** my set didn't stay in *or* last two days; *Tex* **couleur qui tient bien** fast colour; **mon offre/mon invitation/le pari tient toujours** my offer/my invitation/the bet still stands; **ça tient toujours pour dimanche?** is it still on for Sunday?

5 *(être contenu)* **voiture où l'on tient à six** car that takes *or* holds six; **on devrait t. à six dans la voiture** there should be room for six of us in the car; **on tient à dix autour de cette table** the table seats ten; **tous ces livres tiendront dans cette caisse** all these books will easily fit *or* go into this box; **ça ne tiendra pas, c'est sûr** it won't go in *or* fit, that's for sure; **tout ça tient en deux mots** all that can be said *or* it can all be put in a couple of words; **son œuvre tient en peu de livres** his work consists of a few books; **ma conclusion tiendra en trois mots** my conclusion can be summed up in three words

6 *Vieilli* **t. pour qn/qch** *(être partisan de)* to be for sb/sth, to be in favour *or Am* favor of sb/sth

7 t. à *(aimer) (liberté, amitié etc)* to value, to prize; *(ami, vase, bague, lieu)* to be fond of; **t. à la vie** to value one's life, to care about living; **cette idée me tient à cœur** the idea is close *or* dear to my heart, I am keen on the idea; **cela nous tenait à cœur** we were keen on it; **t. à faire qch** to be anxious *or* keen to do sth; **je tiens à vous le dire** I am anxious to tell you, I am making a point of telling you; **t. à ce qu'on fasse qch** to be anxious that sth should be done; **je tiens beaucoup à ce qu'il vienne** I am very anxious that he should come *or* for him to come, I very much want him to come; **je tiens à ce que tu le rencontres** I want you *or* I'm keen for you to meet him; **je tiens à ce que tout soit rangé quand je rentre** I want everything to be tidy when I get back; **il faut que ce soit fini demain, j'y tiens** I insist on it; **tu en veux? – je n'y tiens pas** do you want some? – not particularly *or* I'm not bothered; **tu veux le voir? – je n'y tiens pas du tout/particulièrement** do you want to see him? – not in the slightest/particularly; *Fam* **je n'y tiens pas plus que cela** I'm not all that keen on it; **puisque vous y tenez** since you're set *or* keen on it

8 t. à *(venir de)* to be the result of, to be due to; **cela tient à son éducation** that's the result of *or* that's due to his education; **à quoi tient-il?** what's the reason for it?, what is it due to?; **cela tient à ce que vous êtes écossais** that comes of your being Scottish, that's because you're Scottish

9 t. de *(ressembler à) (quelqu'un)* to take after; **cela tient du miracle/du délire/du génie** it's miraculous/mad/ingenious; **tu as vu les prix? – cela tient de la folie!** have you seen the prices? – it's sheer madness!; **cela tient de (la) famille** it runs in the family; **il a de qui t.** it runs in his family; **entre son oncle et son père il a de qui t.!** it's not surprising when you consider his uncle and his father!

V IMPERS il ne tient qu'à vous de le faire it is entirely up to you whether you do it or not; **il ne tient qu'à vous que cela se fasse** it depends entirely on you whether it is done; **s'il ne tenait qu'à moi** if it was just up to me; **qu'à cela ne tienne** never mind, that's not a problem; **s'il ne tient qu'à cela** if that's all, if that's the only problem; **il n'a tenu à rien qu'il ne se noyât** he was within a hair's breadth of drowning

VPR se tenir 1 *(dans un certain état ou lieu, dans une certaine position)* to stay, to remain; **se t. au chaud** to stay *or* keep warm; **tenez-vous là** stay where you are!, don't move!; **tenez-vous droit** *(assis)* sit up straight, sit up; *(debout)* stand up straight; **bien se t.** *(sur sa chaise)* to sit properly; **se t. debout** to be standing, to stand; **se t. auprès de qn** to be standing next to sb; **elle s'est tenue auprès de lui jusqu'à sa dernière heure** she stayed with him till the last

2 *(se comporter)* to behave; **se t. tranquille** to keep quiet; **bien se t.** *(en société, dans un lieu public)* to behave (well); **tiens-toi bien chez ta grand-mère!** behave yourself at your grandmother's!; **il se tient mal à table** he has no table manners; **tu n'as qu'à bien te t.!** you should learn to behave yourself!

3 tenez-vous bien, la voiture a disparu prepare yourself for a shock *or* brace yourself, the car has disappeared; **et alors, tiens-toi bien, il n'était pas là non plus!** well, you won't believe it, but he wasn't there either!

4 se t. (à qch) to hold on (to sth); **tenez-vous bien!** *(dans un autobus etc)* hold tight!; **ils se tenaient par la main** they were holding hands; **ils se tenaient par la taille/les épaules** they had their arms round each other's waist/shoulders; **se t. les côtes de rire** to hold one's sides laughing

5 *(d'un récit, une histoire)* to hang together; **la boisson, la misère, le crime, tout cela se tient** drink, poverty, crime, all these go together; **tous ces problèmes se tiennent** all these problems are interrelated; **ses arguments se tiennent (bien)** his arguments stand up *or* hold water

6 *(se retenir)* **je ne pouvais me t. de rire** I couldn't help laughing

7 s'en t. à *(se borner à) (plaisanteries, généralités, sujets etc)* to confine oneself to, to keep to; *(décision, traité, consignes)* to adhere to, to abide by; *(budget, prix)* to stick to; **s'en t. à ce qu'on a décidé** to stick to *or* abide by what was decided; **je préfère m'en t. là pour aujourd'hui** I prefer to stop there for today; **il ne s'en tint pas là** he didn't stop there *or* at that; **j'espère qu'il ne va pas s'en t. là, qu'il va m'offrir autre chose encore** I hope he'll offer me something else and not stick at that; **tenons-nous-en là** let it go at that; **je ne sais pas à quoi m'en t.** I don't know what to believe

8 *(avoir lieu)* to be held, to take place

9 tiens-le-toi pour dit! *(avertissement)* I'm telling you once and for all *or* for the last time!

10 se t. pour satisfait/content to be satisfied/content

---

tennis [tenis] **NM 1** *(sport)* tennis; **jouer au t.** to play tennis; **t. de table** table tennis **2** **(court de)** tennis court
NF OU NM *(chaussure)* tennis shoe

tennisman, *pl* **tennismen** [tenisman, -mɛn] **NM** tennis player

tenon [tənɔ̃] **NM 1** *Menuis* tenon **2** *(d'une couronne dentaire)* pivot

ténor [tenɔr] **NM 1** *Mus* tenor **2** *Pol, Sp etc* star (performer)
ADJ *Mus* **saxophone t.** tenor saxophone

tenseur [tɑ̃sœr] ADJ M *Anat* muscle t. tensor NM 1 *Anat* tensor 2 *Math* tensor 3 *Tech* = **tendeur**

tensioactif, -ive [tɑ̃sjoaktif, -iv] *Chimie* ADJ *(agent)* surface-active, wetting NM surface-active *or* wetting agent, surfactant

tension [tɑ̃sjɔ̃] NF 1 *(des muscles, d'une corde de violon), Fig (entre personnes etc)* tension; **écrou à t.** tightening nut; *Tech* **t. de courroie** belt tension; **acier à haute t.** high-tensile steel; **t. intellectuelle** mental stress; **état de t. nerveuse** state of nervous tension; **la guerre nous met sous t.** the war is putting us under stress *or* strain 2 *(de vapeur etc)* pressure; *Méd Fam* **avoir** *ou* **faire de la t.** to suffer from *or* have high blood pressure; **prendre la t. de qn** to take sb's blood pressure 3 *Élec, Électron* voltage, tension; **basse/haute t.** low/high voltage *or* tension; **t. nulle** zero voltage *or* potential; **t. de 2000 volts** tension of 2,000 volts; **sans t.** dead; **t. du secteur** supply *or* mains voltage; **t. nominale** nominal voltage; **être sous t.** to be switched on, to be powered up; **mettre sous t.** *(circuit)* to apply the voltage to, to switch on; *(imprimante etc)* to switch on; **fil sous t.** live *or* charged wire; **montage de piles en t.** connection of batteries in series
▸▸*Méd* **t. artérielle** blood pressure; **t. de cisaillement** shear stress; **t. de rupture** breaking strain *or* stress; *Phys* **t. superficielle** surface tension

tensoriel, -ielle [tɑ̃sɔrjɛl] ADJ *Math* tensorial

tentaculaire [tɑ̃takylɛr] ADJ *Zool* tentacular; *Fig (ville)* sprawling; *(société, organisme)* octopus-like

tentacule [tɑ̃takyl] NM *Zool, Fig* tentacle

tentant [tɑ̃tɑ̃] ADJ *(offre, proposition, situation etc)* tempting, attractive; *(repas, plat etc)* tempting, enticing

tentateur, -trice [tɑ̃tatœr, -tris] ADJ tempting NM tempter; *Rel* **le T.** the Tempter NF **tentatrice** temptress

tentation [tɑ̃tasjɔ̃] NF temptation (**de faire qch** to do sth); **succomber à la t.** to give in to *or* to succumb to temptation; **je n'ai pas pu résister à la t. de lui faire la grimace** I couldn't resist the temptation to make a face at him; **ne cède pas à la t. de l'humilier en public** don't give in to temptation and humiliate him in public; **et si vous aviez la t. de nous rejoindre ...** and if you felt tempted to join us ...

tentative [tɑ̃tativ] NF attempt, endeavour, *Am* endeavor, bid; **t. d'évasion** attempt to escape, escape bid; **t. de suicide** suicide attempt *or* bid, attempted suicide; **faire une nouvelle t. de suicide** to make another suicide attempt; **t. d'assassinat** murder attempt, attempted murder; **il a été accusé de t. d'assassinat** he has been charged with attempted murder; **t. de résistance** attempt to resist; **faire une t. de conciliation** to make an attempt at reconciliation, to attempt reconciliation

tente [tɑ̃t] NF 1 tent; **coucher sous la t.** to sleep under canvas; *Fig* **se retirer dans** *ou* **sous sa t.** to sulk in one's corner 2 *Naut* awning
▸▸**t. conique** bell tent; **t. igloo** igloo tent; *Méd* **t. à oxygène** oxygen tent

tenter [tɑ̃te] VT 1 *Bible, Arch (éprouver)* to tempt; *Fig* **t. le diable** to tempt fate; **t. la Providence** to tempt Providence 2 **t. sa chance** to try one's luck; *Fam* **le coup** to give it *or* have a try *or* go 3 *(faire envie à, séduire) (quelqu'un)* to tempt; **cela m'a toujours tenté de partir là-bas** I've always been tempted to go there; **se laisser t.** to let oneself be tempted, to yield to temptation; **tu devrais te lais-**

ser t., laisse-toi t. be a devil; **j'ai envie de me laisser t.** I'm tempted to say yes; **je serais tenté de croire qu'il est responsable, lui aussi** I'm tempted to believe that he is responsible too; **je dois dire que je suis très tenté** I'm very tempted *or* it's very tempting, I must say 4 *(essayer)* to try, to attempt; **t. d'inutiles efforts pour ...** to make useless attempts to ...; **t. une expérience** to try an experiment; **il faut tout t. pour le convaincre** we must try everything to convince him; **t. de faire qch** to try *or* attempt to do sth; **t. de se suicider** to attempt (to commit) suicide, to try to commit suicide, to make a suicide attempt; **t. le tout pour le tout** to go for broke

tenture [tɑ̃tyr] NF 1 *(tapisserie)* hanging; *(de porte)* curtain; *(de cérémonie funèbre)* funeral drape 2 *(ensemble de tapisseries)* hangings

tenu [tɑ̃y] ADJ 1 **bien t.** *(maison, cahier de devoirs, registres, comptes etc)* well kept, tidy; *(jardin etc)* neat, trim; *(enfant)* neatly turned out; **mal t.** *(enfant, jardin etc)* neglected, uncared for; *(maison, cahier de devoirs, registres, comptes etc)* badly kept, untidy 2 **être t. de** *ou* **à faire qch** to be obliged to do sth; **les passants sont tenus de marcher sur le trottoir** pedestrians must walk on the pavement; **le médecin est t. au secret professionnel** the doctor is bound by professional secrecy 3 *Bourse (prix)* firm, hard 4 *(pari)* **t.!** done!, you're on! 5 *Mus (note)* held NM *Ftbl, Boxe* holding

ténu [teny] ADJ *(fil, particule etc)* fine; *(brume)* fine, light; *(voix)* thin, reedy; *(nuance)* subtle, fine; *(lien)* tenuous; *(espoir)* slender, slight, slim

tenue [tɑ̃y] NF 1 *(d'une assemblée etc)* sitting, session; **pendant la t. du conseil/des assises** during the council meeting/the assizes; **t. d'une réunion** holding a meeting 2 *(d'une boutique, d'un hôtel, d'une maison etc)* keeping, running; **s'occuper de la t. de la maison** to look after (the running of) the house 3 *(conduite)* (good) behaviour *or Am* behavior; **Paul, de la t.!** Paul, behave yourself!; **un peu de t.!** (mind your) manners!; **elle manque de t.** she lacks (good) manners, she doesn't know how to behave; **la haute t. de ce périodique** the high standard maintained by this periodical 4 *(maintien)* posture; *Équitation* **bonne/mauvaise t.** good/poor seat 5 *(habillement)* dress, clothes; **changer de t.** to change (one's clothes); **mettre une autre t.** to put on something else; **quelle t.!** what an outfit!; **se mettre en t. de soirée** to wear evening dress; **en grande t.** all dressed up; *Mil* **en dress uniform; **t. de loisirs** *ou* **de tous les jours** casual clothes *or* dress; *Mil etc* **en t.** in uniform; **en t. légère** *(vêtu de façon sommaire)* scantily dressed; *(en vêtements d'été)* in light clothing; **dans une t. débraillée** slovenly dressed; *Fam* **je vais me mettre en t.** I'm going to change; *Fam* **en petite t.** scantily dressed 6 *Mus* holding *or* sustained note 7 *Bourse (des prix)* steadiness, firmness; *(du marché)* tone; **t. de la Bourse** state of the market
▸▸*Aviat* **t. en l'air, t. aéronautique** behaviour in the air; *Compta* **t. de caisse** petty cash management; *Tech* **t. des chaudières** care of the boilers; *Mil etc* **t. civile** plain clothes, civilian clothes, *Fam* civvies; *Mil* **t. de combat** battledress; **t. des comptes** book-keeping; **il est responsable de la t. des comptes** he's responsible for (keeping) the accounts; *Aut* **t. en côte** climbing ability; *Compta* **t. des livres** book-keeping; *Aut* **t. de route** road-holding (qualities); **t. de soirée** evening dress; *Mil* mess dress; **t. des stocks**

stock keeping; **t. de ville** *(de femme)* town clothes; *(d'homme)* lounge suit; *(sur invitation)* semi-formal; **elle était en t. de ville** she was dressed for going out; *Aviat* **t. en vol** attitude of flight

ténuité [tenɥite] NF *(d'un fil, d'une particule etc)* fineness; *(d'une nuance)* subtlety, fineness

tenure [tənyr] NF *Hist, Jur* tenure; *(terre)* holding

TEP [teəpe] NM *(abrév* **terminal électronique de paiement)** electronic payment terminal

tep [teəpe] NF INV *(abrév* **tonne d'équivalent pétrole)** TOE

tequila [tekila] NF tequila

ter [tɛr] ADV *Mus* ter ADJ **numéro 5 t.** *(adresse)* No. 5c

téraoctet [teraɔktɛ] NM *Ordinat* terabyte

tératogène [teratɔʒɛn] ADJ *Méd* teratogenic

tératologie [teratɔlɔʒi] NF teratology

terbium [tɛrbjɔm] NM *Chimie* terbium

tercet [tɛrsɛ] NM *Littér* tercet, triplet

térébenthine [terebɑ̃tin] NF turpentine

térébinthe [terebɛ̃t] NM *Bot* terebinth, turpentine tree

térébrant [terebrɑ̃] ADJ 1 *(insecte etc)* boring, *Spéc* terebrant 2 *Méd (douleur)* piercing; *(ulcération)* deep

Tergal® [tɛrgal] NM *Tex* Terylene®, *Am* Dacron®; **robe en T.** Terylene® *or* Dacron® dress

tergiversations [tɛrʒiversasjɔ̃] NFPL beating about the bush, evasiveness, *Fml* equivocation; **après bien des t.** after a great deal of beating about the bush; **assez de t.!** stop beating about the bush *or* being evasive!

tergiverser [tɛrʒiverse] VI to beat about the bush, to be evasive, to equivocate; **cessons de t.** let's stop beating about the bush

termaillage [tɛrmajaʒ] NM *Écon* leads and lags

terme [tɛrm] NM 1 *(fin) (d'un voyage, un règne etc)* end; **au t. de sa vie** at the end of his life; **toucher à son t.** *(d'un projet)* to be near completion; *(d'une période)* to be nearing an end *or* drawing to a close; **quel est le t. de son mandat?** when does his mandate end?; **mettre un t. à qch** to put an end *or* a stop to sth; **il y a t. à tout** there is an end to everything; **mener qch à bon t.** to bring sth to a successful conclusion, to carry sth through 2 *(date limite)* time (limit), date; **être à t.** *(d'une femme enceinte)* to have reached term; **avant t.** *(accoucher)* prematurely; *(accouchement)* premature; **elle a dépassé le t. de deux semaines** she's two weeks overdue, she's two weeks past her due date; **dans le t. de trois mois** within three months; **t. de rigueur** latest time *or* date; *Bourse* **le t.** the settlement; **marché à t.** forward futures *or* market; **valeurs à t.** securities dealt in for the account; **acheter à t.** *Com* to buy on credit; *Bourse* to buy for the settlement *or* for the account; **à court/long t.** *(projet, engagement, contrat, avance etc)* short-/long-term; *(prévisions)* short-/long-term *or* -range; *Fin (factures)* short-/long-dated; *Fin* **argent à court t.** money at short notice *or* at call; **s'améliorer à court/moyen/long t.** to improve in the short/medium/long term; **voir les choses à long/court t.** to see things in the long/short term, to take a long-/short-term view (of things); **il faut prévoir à long t.** you have to look to the long term; *Fin* **à t. échu** on the due date; **à t. fixe** fixed-term 3 *Jur* **demander un t. de grâce** *(délai)* to ask for time to pay 4 *(versement)* instalment, *Am* installment;

payable en deux termes payable in two instalments

5 (*loyer*) rent; (*jour*) rent day; (*période*) rental period; **j'ai un t. en retard** I'm one payment behind (with my rent)

6 (*mot*) term; **t. de métier, t. technique** technical term; **t. de médecine/de droit** medical/legal term; **employer les termes propres** to use the correct terms; **en d'autres termes** in other words; **pour le dire en d'autres termes** to put it another way; **il ne le disait pas en ces termes, mais ...** he didn't put it in quite those terms or words, but ...; **elle n'a pas ménagé ses termes** she didn't mince her words; **il m'a parlé de vous en très bons termes** he spoke very well or favourably or Am favorably of you; Math **t. d'une progression** term of a progression; **termes d'une équation** terms of an equation

7 termes (*de contrat etc*) terms, terms and conditions

8 termes (*relations*) terms; **être en bons/ mauvais termes avec qn** to be on good or friendly/bad terms with sb; **en quels termes l'a-t-il quittée?** what terms were they on when he left her?; **en quels termes étiez-vous?** how did you get on?

▸▸ **t. de bail** term of lease; **termes commerciaux** commercial terms; **termes commerciaux internationaux** incoterms; **termes d'échange** terms of exchange; *Écon* **termes de l'échange** terms of trade; *Fin* **t. d'échéance** (*d'un effet etc*) maturity date; *Compta* **t. de liquidation** account or settlement period; **t. de livraison** delivery deadline; **termes de paiement** terms of payment; **t. de préavis** notice period; **t. de rigueur** deadline

terminaison [tɛrminɛzɔ̃] NF **1** *Gram* ending; **t. en 'ion'** ending in 'ion' **2** *Jur* (*de procès*) termination **3** *Anat* **t. nerveuse** nerve ending

terminal, -ale, -aux, -ales [tɛrminal, -o] ADJ final; (*à l'extrémité de qch*) terminal; *Méd* (*phase*) terminal; *Méd* **cancer en phase terminale** terminal cancer; **être en phase terminale** (*de malade*) to be terminally ill; **le projet est dans sa phase terminale** the project is in its final stages; *Scol* **classe terminale** final year, *Br* ≃ upper sixth (form), *Am* ≃ twelfth grade; *Ordinat* **marque terminale** end mark

NM **1** *Ordinat* terminal, VDU **2** *Pétr* (pipeline) terminal **3** *Aviat* (*gare*) (air) terminal, terminal (building); **t. d'aérogare** air terminal; **t. urbain** (*d'une ligne aérienne*) city terminal; NF *Scol* **terminale** ≃ upper sixth

▸▸ **t. de consultation** look-up terminal; **t. distant** remote terminal; *Com* **t. électronique de paiement** electronic payment terminal; **t. intelligent** smart terminal; **t. (informatique) interactif** interactive terminal; **t. maritime** shipping terminal; *Com* **t. de paiement en ligne** on-line cash desk terminal; **t. passif** dumb terminal; **t. de pilotage** control terminal; **t. point de vente** point-of-sale terminal

terminateur [tɛrminatœr] NM *Ordinat* terminator

terminer [tɛrmine] VT (*guerre, discours, lettre, repas, réunion etc*) to end, to finish (**par** with); (*affaire*) to end, to settle, to conclude; (*travail*) to complete, to finish (off); **t. ses jours quelque part** to end one's days somewhere; **la phrase qui termine le poème** the phrase that ends the poem; **il faut en t.** we must end or finish; **il faut que j'en termine avec cette histoire** I have to put an end to this; *Ordinat* **t. une session** to log off, to log out

VI to end, to finish; **t. court** to end abruptly, to come to an abrupt ending; *Radio* **terminé!** out!

VPR **se terminer** (*d'une soirée, d'un concert,*

---

des vacances etc) to end (**par** with); (*d'une rue, d'un mot etc*) to end (**par** in); **l'automne se termine** autumn is coming to an end or a close; **la guerre venait de se t.** the war was just over or had just ended; **la veste se termine en pointe** the jacket ends in or comes to a point; **l'année s'est terminée en beauté** the year ended with a flourish

terminologie [tɛrminɔlɔʒi] NF terminology

terminologue [tɛrminɔlɔg] N terminologist

terminus [tɛrminys] NM (*de train, de l'autobus etc*) terminus; **t., tout le monde descend!** all change!

ADJ INV **gare t.** terminus

termite [tɛrmit] NM *Entom* termite, white ant; *Fig* **faire un travail de t.** to work secretly and destructively

termitière [tɛrmitjɛr] NF *Entom* termite nest, termitarium

ternaire [tɛrnɛr] ADJ *Math, Chimie* ternary; *Mus* **mesure t.** triple time

terne [tɛrn] ADJ (*personne, conversation, histoire, soirée, année, teint, métal*) dull; (*personnalité*) colourless; (*vêtements, existence*) dull, drab; (*yeux*) dull, lifeless, lacklustre; (*voix*) dull, flat; (*style*) dull, flat, colourless

ternir [tɛrnir] VT (*métal, Fig* (*réputation, honneur, mémoire*) to tarnish; **la poussière qui ternit le mobilier** the dust that dulls the furniture

VPR **se ternir** (*de métal*), *Fig* (*d'une réputation, d'une mémoire*) to become tarnished

ternissure [tɛrnisyr] NF (*aspect*) (*du métal*) tarnished appearance; (*tache*) tarnished spot

terrafungine [tɛrafɔ̃ʒin] NF *Pharm* oxytetracycline, Terramycin®

terrain [tɛrɛ̃] NM **1** (*étendue*) land; **un t. a** piece or plot of land **2** *Géog etc* ground, terrain; **relief du t.** relief **3** (*sol*) soil, ground; **t. gras** rich soil **4** (*destiné à une activité*) *Ftbl, Rugby* pitch, field; *Golf* course; *Mil* terrain; **aller sur le t.** (*se battre en duel*) to fight a duel; *Ind etc, Fig* **sur le t.** (*travailler, étudier, essayer*) in the field; (*ingénieur, étude, essais*) field; **travaux sur le t.** fieldwork, work in the field; **rester sur le t.** to be killed (*in a duel*); *Fig* (*être battu*) to be defeated; *Mil etc, Fig* **gagner du t.** to gain ground; *Mil etc, Fig* **perdre/céder du t.** to lose/give ground; *Fig* **sonder** ou **tâter le t.** to see how the land lies; *Fig* **être sur son t.** to be on familiar territory or home ground; *Fig* **je ne suis plus sur mon t.** I'm out of my depth; **homme de t.** man with practical experience; *Fig* **préparer le t.** to prepare the ground, to pave the way **5** *Méd* = predisposition to a disease; *Spéc* diathesis; **il y a un t. propice aux angines chez ce patient** this patient is a candidate for angina **6** *Géol* (rock) formation

▸▸ **t. d'atterrissage** landing strip, airstrip; *Aviat* **t. d'aviation** airfield; **t. à bâtir** development site; **terrains à bâtir** development sites, building land; **t. de camping** campsite; **t. de camping-caravaning** camping and caravan site; *Fig* **t. d'entente** common ground; **chercher un t. d'entente** to look for (some) common ground; **t. de jeu** (*pour les sports*) recreation ground, *Br* playing field; (*pour les enfants*) playground; *Mil* **t. de manœuvres** drill or parade ground; **t. de sport** sports ground; **t. vague** waste ground; **entouré de terrains vagues** surrounded by waste ground

terrarium [tɛrarjɔm] NM terrarium

terrasse [tɛras] NF **1** (*levée de terre*) terrace; **jardin en t.** terraced garden; **cultures en terrasses** terrace cultivation **2** (*de café*) **nous étions assis à la t.** we were sitting outside (the café); **les clients en t.** the customers sitting outside; **prix des consommations en**

---

t. price of drinks served outside **3** (*de maison, appartement*) terrace; **(toit en) t.** terrace (roof), flat roof

terrassement [tɛrasmɑ̃] NM **1** (*action*) (*de terre*) banking, digging **2** (*remblai*) earthwork, embankment

terrasser [tɛrase] VT **1** *Agr* (*vignoble etc*) to work the soil of **2** (*abattre*) (*adversaire*) to floor, to fell; *Fig* (*d'une émotion, de la fatigue, d'une nouvelle etc*) to overwhelm, to overcome; (*d'une maladie*) to lay low; **terrassé par le chagrin** prostrate or overcome with grief; **terrassé par une crise cardiaque** felled by a heart attack

terrassier [tɛrasje] NM *Constr* labourer, *Am* laborer, *Br Fam* navvy

TERRE [tɛr]

world **1** ▪ Earth **1** ▪ ground **2** ▪ land **2, 4, 7** ▪ earth **3, 6, 9** ▪ soil **6** ▪ country **8** ▪ clay **10**	

NF **1** (*monde*) world; **la T.** (*planète*) (the) Earth; **la vie sur t.** life on earth; **être encore sur t.** to be still in the land of the living; **elle vient de quitter cette t.** she has just left this world; **revenir sur t.** to come (back) down to earth; **avoir les pieds sur t.** to have one's feet on the ground; **toute la t.** the whole or entire world, everybody

2 (*sol*) ground; (*étendue*) land; **armée de t.** army; **forces de t.** land forces; **pénétrer dans les terres** to go inland; **village dans les terres** inland village; **basses terres** lowlands; **hautes terres** highlands; **tremblement de t.** earthquake; *Aviat* **toucher t.** to touch down, to land; *Fig* **j'ai eu l'impression de ne pas toucher t. depuis deux mois** I feel as if I've been walking on air for two months; **à t., par t.** on the ground; **frapper qn à t.** to strike sb when he is down; **tomber par t., tomber à t.** to fall down; **tout ce que tu tiens dans les mains va tomber par t.** you're going to drop everything you're carrying; *Fam* **ça va tout ficher** ou *très Fam* **foutre par t.** that'll mess or *Fam* screw everything up; **attaquer une ville par t. et par mer** to attack a town by land and sea; **tactique** ou **politique de la t. brûlée** scorched earth policy; **appuyer son oreille contre t.** to put one's ear to the ground; **sous t.** (*ville*) underground; **des galeries creusées sous t.** tunnels dug under the ground; **être sous t.** ou **en t.** ou **à six pieds sous t.** to be in one's grave, *Fam* to be six feet under, to be dead and buried

3 *Élec* earth, *Am* ground; **mettre** ou **relier** ou **raccorder à la t.** (*appareil, prise*) to earth, *Am* to ground

4 (*opposé à mer*) land; **mettre qn à t.** to land sb, to put sb ashore; **descendre à t.** to land, to go ashore; **perdre t.** to lose sight of land; **t. (en vue)!** land ho!; **être à t.** (*d'un navire*) to be aground or ashore

5 t. à t. (*personne*) matter-of-fact, down-to-earth; (*décision, mesures*) practical, down-to-earth; (*préoccupations*) mundane

6 *Agr* (*matière*) soil, earth; **cultiver la t.** to cultivate the soil; **faire son retour à la t.** to go back to the land; **en pleine t.** in the open ground; **chemin de t.** dirt track; **hutte de t.** séchée mud hut; **t. grasse** rich soil; **t. végétale** ou **franche** humus

7 (*propriété*) land; **acheter/vendre une t.** to buy/sell land; **avoir des terres** to have land; **vivre de ses terres** to live off one's land

8 (*territoire*) land, country; **terres étrangères** foreign countries or lands; **terres australes** southern lands; **revenir à la t. natale** to return to one's native soil, to return to the land or country of one's birth; **la nostalgie de la t. natale** homesickness; **avoir la nostalgie de sa t. natale** to be homesick

9 (*élément*) earth

10 *(argile etc)* clay; **pipe en t.** clay pipe; **cruche de** *ou* **en t.** earthenware *or* terracotta jar ►► **t. battue:** *Tennis* **jouer sur t. battue** to play on clay; *Tennis* **jouer bien/mal sur t. battue** to be good/bad on clay, to be a good/bad clay court player; *Tennis* **court en t. battue** clay court; **sol en t. battue** mud floor; **t. de Chine** kaolin; **t. cuite** earthenware, terracotta; *Beaux-Arts* terracotta; *Beaux-Arts* **une t. cuite** a terracotta; **t. ferme** (dry) land, terra firma; *(opposé à l'espace)* earth, terra firma; **la T. de Feu** Tierra del Fuego; **t. d'ombre** umber; **t. de pipe** pipeclay; **t. à poêle** fireclay; **t. à porcelaine** kaolin; **t. à potier** potter's clay; *Chimie* **terres rares** rare earths; **la T. Sainte** the Holy Land; **t. de Sienne** sienna

terreau, -eaux [tɛʀo] **NM** compost

Terre-Neuve **NF** Newfoundland
NM INV **t.** Newfoundland (dog)

terre-neuvien, -ienne, *pl* **terre-neuvien(ne)s** [tɛʀnœvjɛ̃, -jɛn] **ADJ** Newfoundland **N T.** Newfoundlander

terre-neuvier, -ière, *pl* **terre-neuviers, -ières** [tɛʀnœvje, -jɛʀ] **ADJ** *(pêcheur etc)* Newfoundland
NM 1 *(pêcheur)* Newfoundland fisherman **2** *(bateau)* banker, Newfoundland fishing vessel

terre-plein, *pl* **terre-pleins** **NM 1** *Constr* earth platform, raised strip **2** *Aut* **t. central** central reservation, *Am* median strip; **t. circulaire** *(dans un rond-point)* central island

terrer [tɛʀe] **VT 1** *(arbre, plante)* to earth up **2** *(couvrir de terre)* to spread earth over
VPR se terrer *(d'un animal)* to go to earth; *Mil* to entrench oneself, to dig oneself in; *Fig* to go to earth, to hole up; **être terré dans** *(d'un animal)* to have gone to earth in; *Mil* to be entrenched in; *Fig* to have gone to earth in, to be holed up in

terrestre [tɛʀɛstʀ] **ADJ 1** *(plante)* ground; *(animal)* land; **transports terrestres** surface transport; *Mil* **effectifs terrestres** land forces **2** *(magnétisme, attraction)* of the earth; **la croûte t.** the earth's crust **3** *Fig (pensées)* worldly; *(plaisirs)* earthly, worldly; **paradis t.** earthly paradise; **c'est un vrai paradis t.** it's heaven on earth

terreur [tɛʀœʀ] **NF 1** *(effroi)* terror, dread; **fou de t.** wild with fear; **glacé de t.** terror-stricken; **vivre dans la t.** to be terrified *or* in (a state of) terror **2** *(emploi de la violence etc)* terror; **gouverner par la t.** to rule by terror; **faire régner la t.** to instil terror; **semer la t.** to sow terror; **un régime de t.** a reign of terror; *Hist* **la T.** the Reign of Terror **3** *Fig (personne)* *(d'une ville, d'une école etc)* terror; **jouer les terreurs** to play the tough guy

terreux, -euse [tɛʀø, -øz] **ADJ 1** *(goût, odeur)* earthy **2** *(mains)* grubby; *(teint, ciel, gris etc)* muddy; *(visage)* sickly; *(laitue)* gritty

terrible [tɛʀibl] **ADJ 1** *(catastrophe, accident, blessure etc)* terrible, appalling; *(froid, bruit)* dreadful, terrible; *(orage, chaleur)* terrific, terrible; *(temps, caractère)* awful, terrible; **ce n'est qu'une coupure, rien de t.** it's just a cut, nothing serious *or* major; **d'une humeur t.** in an awful *or* a terrible mood; **il est t. quand il s'énerve** he's awful *or* terrible when he loses his temper; **enfant t.** enfant terrible **2** *Fam (formidable) (personne, film, effet etc)* terrific, great; **ce/il n'est pas t.** it's/he's nothing special; **rien de t.** nothing much, nothing to write home about **3** *(impossible)* incredible; **vous êtes t.!** you really are the limit!
ADV *Fam* **ça marche t.!** it's going great!

terriblement [tɛʀibləmɑ̃] **ADV** *(extrêmement)* *(gêné, égoïste)* terribly, dreadfully, awfully

terrien, -ienne [tɛʀjɛ̃, -jɛn] **ADJ 1** *(proprié-*

taire etc) landed **2** *(rural)* country, rural **3** *(de la Terre)* of the Earth
N 1 *(propriétaire)* landowner, landed proprietor **2** *Naut* landlubber **3** *(paysan)* countryman, *f* countrywoman **4** *(habitant de la Terre)* earthling, earthman, *f* earthwoman

terrier [tɛʀje] **NM 1** *(d'un lapin)* burrow, hole; *(d'une taupe)* hole; *(d'un renard)* earth; *(d'un blaireau)* sett **2** *(chien)* terrier

terrifiant [tɛʀifjɑ̃] **ADJ 1** *(effrayant) (description, situation)* terrifying **2** *(extraordinaire)* incredible

terrifier [tɛʀifje] **VT** *(impf, pr sub n.* **terrifiions, v. terrifiiez**) to terrify

terril [tɛʀil] **NM** *Min* slag heap

terrine [tɛʀin] **NF** *Culin (pâté, récipient)* terrine; **t. de canard/de foie de volaille** duck/chicken-liver pâté

terrir [tɛʀiʀ] **VI** *Pêche* **poissons qui terrissent** fish living in coastal waters

territoire [tɛʀitwaʀ] **NM** *(d'un État, d'un oiseau, d'un animal)* territory; *(de juge, d'évêque)* jurisdiction; *(de commune, d'arrondissement etc)* area; **marquer son t.** *(d'un animal, Fig d'une personne)* to mark out one's territory; *Pol* **territoires occupés** occupied territories; **t. d'outre-mer** overseas territory; **aménagement du t.** regional planning *or* development

territorial, -iale, -iaux, -iales [tɛʀitɔʀjal, -jo] **ADJ** *(impôt, eaux)* territorial
NM *Hist, Mil* territorial (soldier)
NF *Hist, Mil* **la territoriale** the territorial army

territorialité [tɛʀitɔʀjalite] **NF** *(d'un impôt)* territoriality

terroir [tɛʀwaʀ] **NM** *Agr* soil; **goût de t.** *(d'un vin)* tang of the soil, native tang; **du t.** *(accent, expression)* local

terrorisant [tɛʀɔʀizɑ̃] **ADJ** *(expérience, souvenir etc)* terrifying

terroriser [tɛʀɔʀize] **VT** *(d'une personne)* to terrorize; *(d'une expérience, d'un souvenir)* to terrify

terrorisme [tɛʀɔʀism] **NM** terrorism; **un acte de t.** an act of terrorism; **t. d'État** government-sponsored terrorism

terroriste [tɛʀɔʀist] **ADJ, N** terrorist

tertiaire [tɛʀsjɛʀ] **ADJ** tertiary; *Écon* **secteur t.** tertiary sector
NM 1 *Écon* tertiary sector **2** *Géol* Tertiary
N *Cathol* tertiary

tertiairisation [tɛʀsjɛʀizasjɔ̃], **tertiarisation** [tɛʀsjaʀizasjɔ̃] **NF** *Écon* tertiarization, growth of the tertiary sector *or* service industries; **la t. de l'économie** the tertiarization of the economy

tertio [tɛʀsjo] **ADV** thirdly

tertre [tɛʀtʀ] **NM** hillock, mound, knoll; *Archéol* **t. funéraire** barrow, tumulus

tes [te] **ADJ POSS** *voir* **ton[1]**

tessiture [tesityʀ] **NF** *Mus (de voix)* range, tessitura; *(d'un instrument)* range

tesson [tesɔ̃] **NM** shard; **t. de bouteille** fragment of broken bottle

test [tɛst] **NM** *(examen)*, *Méd* test **passer/réussir un t.** to take/pass a test; **c'est le t. de sa bonne foi** it is a test of his good faith; **zone/département/semaine t.** test area/department/week; **pendant une période t.** for a trial period; *Méd, Psy, Scol etc* **méthode des tests** testing method; *Mktg* **t. d'acceptabilité auprès des consommateurs** customer-acceptance test; *Mktg* **t. d'acceptation** acceptance test; **t. d'aptitude professionnelle** aptitude test; **t. d'association** association test; **t. aveugle** blind test; *Mktg* **t. de la bande dessinée** *ou* **de la bulle** balloon test; *Aut* **t. de choc** impact test; **t. comparatif** comparative

test; **t. de conformité** compliance test; **tests auprès des consommateurs** consumer testing; *Mktg* **tests d'emballage** package testing; *Mktg* **t. d'enquête** enquiry test; *Mktg* **t. de frustration** balloon test; *Mktg* **t. du lendemain** (day-after) recall test; **t. de marché** market test; *(d'un produit)* test marketing, market test; *Mktg* **t. de média** media test; *Mktg* **t. de mémoire** memory *or* recall test; *Mktg* **tests de nom** name testing; **t. de performance** benchmark *or* performance test; **t. de performance du produit** product performance test; *Mktg* **t. de préférence** preference test; **t. de produit** product test; **tests de produit** product testing; *Mktg* **t. de rappel** recall test; *Mktg* **t. de reconnaissance** recognition test; **t. de Rorschach** Rorschach *or* ink blot test; *Aut* **t. de roulage** road testing; **un t. de roulage** a road test; **t. à sec** dry run; *Mktg* **t. de support** media test; **t. technique** engineering test; *Aut* **t. de tonneaux** roll-over test

Testament [tɛstamɑ̃] **NM** *Bible* **Ancien/Nouveau T.** Old/New Testament

testament [tɛstamɑ̃] **NM 1** *Jur* will, testament; **absence de t.** intestacy; **ceci est mon t.** this is my last will and testament; **tu ne seras pas dans mon t.** you'll be cut out of my will; **elle l'a mis** *ou* **couché sur son t.** she put him in her will; **mourir sans t.** to die intestate; **léguer qch par t.** to leave sth in one's will, to bequeath sth **2** *Fig (artistique, politique)* legacy

testamentaire [tɛstamɑ̃tɛʀ] **ADJ** **disposition t.** clause *or* provision (of a/the will); **exécuteur/exécutrice t.** executor/executrix; **héritier t.** legal heir, heir as established by a/the will; **succession t.** succession as prescribed by a/the will

testateur, -trice [tɛstatœʀ, -tʀis] **N** *Jur* testator, *f* testatrix

tester[1] [tɛste] **VI** *Jur* to make one's will

tester[2] **VT** *(élève, produit etc)* to test; *Mktg* to test, to test-market; **t. sur le marché** to test-market; **t. un questionnaire** to pilot a questionnaire; **testé en laboratoire** laboratory-tested

testiculaire [tɛstikylɛʀ] **ADJ** *Anat* testicular

testicule [tɛstikyl] **NM** *Anat* testicle, *Spéc* testis

testimonial, -iale, -iaux, -iales [tɛstimɔnjal, -jo] **ADJ** *Jur* **preuve testimoniale** evidence of witnesses

testostérone [tɛstɔsteʀɔn] **NF** *Biol, Physiol* testosterone

têt [tɛ] **NM** *Chimie* **t. à gaz** beehive shelf; **t. à rôtir** roasting crucible

tétanie [tetani] **NF** *Méd* spasms, *Spéc* tetany; **accès de t.** fit of spasm; **avoir un accès de t.** to go into spasm

tétanique [tetanik] **Méd** **ADJ** tetanic; **malade t.** person with tetanus
N person with tetanus

tétaniser [tetanize] *Méd* **VT** *(muscle)* to tetanize, to cause tetanus in; *Fig* **tétanisé de peur** paralysed with fear, petrified; **tétanisé de froid** numb with cold
VPR se tétaniser *(d'un muscle)* to become tetanized

tétanos [tetanos, -ɔs] **NM** *Méd (maladie)* tetanus, *Fam* lockjaw; *(contraction de muscle)* tetanus; **vaccin contre le t.** tetanus vaccine

têtard [tɛtaʀ] **NM 1** *Zool* tadpole **2** *Fam (enfant)* kid **3** *(arbre taillé)* pollard

TÊTE [tɛt]

| head **1, 4–10** | hair **2** | face **3** | mind **5** | top **7, 10** | front **10** | in the lead (en tête) **10** |

NF 1 *Anat* head; **de la t. aux pieds** from head

to foot, from top to toe; **dépasser qn d'une t.** to be a head taller than sb; **il a une t. de plus que sa mère** he is a head taller than his mother; **t. nue** bare-headed; **vieillard à t. grise** grey-haired old man; **avoir la grosse t.** to have a big head; *Fig Fam* **une grosse t.** *(intellectuel)* a highbrow, an intellectual; *Fam* **faire une (grosse) t. à qn, faire une t. au carré à qn** to smash sb's face in; *Fam* **c'est une t., ce mec-là** that guy is a bit of a genius or has got brains; **monstre à deux têtes** two-headed monster; **corps sans t.** headless body; **faire t.** *(d'un animal chassé)* to stand at bay; **faire** ou **tenir t. à qn** to stand up to sb; **je t'interdis de me faire** ou **tenir t.!** don't you dare defy me!; **faire** ou **tenir t. au malheur** to bear up in the face of misfortune; *Naut, Fig* **tenir t. à l'orage** to ride out the storm; **les nuages qui flottent sur nos têtes** the clouds overhead; **endetté par-dessus la t.** up to the eyes in debt; **j'en ai par-dessus la t.** I've had it up to here; **je n'en ai pas encore par-dessus la t., mais ça va arriver** I'm not at screaming pitch yet, but I soon will be; **la t. en bas** head down(wards), upside down; *(objet)* upside down; **se laisser pendre la t. en bas** to hang upside down; **marcher la t. haute** to walk with (one's) head held high; *Fig* **je peux à nouveau marcher la t. haute** I can hold my head up again; **la t. la première** head first; **tomber sur la t.** to fall and hit one's head; *Fam* **tu es tombé sur la t.?** have you got a screw loose?; **je ne sais (pas) où donner de la t.** I don't know which way to turn, I don't know whether I'm coming or going; *Fig* **donner t. baissée dans un piège** to rush headlong into a trap; *Vulg* **avoir la t. dans le cul** to be out of it; **par t.,** *Fam* **par t. de pipe** a head; **t. à t. = tête-à-tête; je te le jure sur la t. de mes enfants** I swear on my children's lives; **j'en réponds sur ma t.** I'd stake my life on it; **il y va de votre t.** your life is at stake; **ça va lui en coûter la t.** it is going to cost him his life; **je donnerais ma t. à couper que ...** I'll bet anything you like or I'd stake my life that ...; **signe de t.** nod (of the head); **faire un signe de t. à qn** to nod to sb, to give sb a nod; **mal de t.** headache; **avoir (très) mal à la t.** to have a (bad) headache; **la t. lui tourne, il a la t. qui tourne** his head is spinning; **t. chauve** bald head; **t. ronde** bullet or round head; *Hist* Roundhead; **à t. ronde** bullet- or round-headed; *Ftbl* **faire une t.** to head the ball; **piquer une t.** *(tomber)* to take a header; *Natation* to dive; **je piquerais bien une t.** I'd really like to dive in; *Gym, Mil* **t. (à) droite!** eyes right!; **t. d'une médaille** obverse of a medal; *Arch* **t. ou pile?** heads or tails?

2 *(cheveux)* hair; **une t. rousse/blonde** a redhead/blonde; **se laver la t.** to wash one's hair

3 *(visage)* face; **il a une t. très belle.** he's very good-looking; **elle a une jolie t.** she's pretty; **elle a une bonne t.** she looks nice; **il a une t. vraiment bizarre** he looks very strange, he's very strange-looking; *Arg* **il a une t. de con** he looks like a total prat or *Am* jackass; *Théâtre* **se faire la t. d'un rôle** to make up for a part; *Fam* **faire une t. d'imbécile** to look like an idiot; **je ne sais pas quelle t. il fera** I don't know how he'll take it or react; **il fait une de ces têtes** *(de colère)* he's got a face like thunder; *(de surprise)* he looks stunned or thunderstruck; *(de tristesse)* he looks grief-stricken; **faire sa t. des mauvais jours** to look like thunder; **il me fait une de ces têtes!** he keeps glowering at me!; *Fam* **faire la t.** to be in a huff, to sulk; **faire la t. à qn** to be sulky with sb; *Fam* **faire une t. de six pieds de long** to have a face like a wet weekend; *Fam* **faire sa mauvaise t.** to look like thunder; **faire une t. de circonstance** to look grim; *(hypocritement)* to look suitably upset; **je connais cette t.-là** I know that face; **sa t. ne**

me revient pas I don't like the look of him

4 *(d'un animal, d'un poisson, d'un oiseau etc)* head; **d'une courte t.** *(gagner une course)* by a short head; **têtes** *(de bétail)* head of cattle

5 *(esprit)* mind; *(cerveau)* brains; **il n'a rien dans la t.** he's stupid; **petite t.!** idiot!; **une pareille idée ne me serait jamais passée par la t.** such an idea would never have entered my mind or head; **si une idée te passe par la t., dis-le-moi** let me know if you have any ideas; **se creuser la t.** to rack one's brains; **c'est une femme de t.** she's a capable woman; **elle n'a pas de t.** she's very forgetful; **avoir la t. légère** to be irresponsible or featherbrained; **avoir la t. dure** to be stupid or *Br Fam* thick; *(têtu)* to be pig-headed; **mettre qch dans la t. de qn** to get sth into sb's head; **je me demande qui lui a mis ça dans la t.** I wonder who put that idea in his head; **il s'est mis en t. d'écrire un roman** he's got or taken it into his head to write a novel; **je me suis mis dans la t. qu'il fallait que je déménage** I got it into my head that I had to move; **n'avoir qu'une idée en t.** to have a one-track mind; **quand il a une idée en t.** once he gets an idea in his head; **il n'a que ça en t.** he's got it on the brain, that's all he thinks about; **avoir toutes les informations en t.** to have all the information in one's head; **je n'ai plus son nom en t.** his name has slipped my mind; **ça m'est sorti de la t.** it went clean out of my head or mind; **il a quelque chose en t.** he's planning something, *Fam* he's up to something; **s'endormir des souvenirs plein la t.** to fall asleep with nice memories going through one's head; **des idées plein la t.** full of ideas; **forte t.** *(personne)* strong-minded person; **calculer de t.** to do mental arithmetic; **faire un rapide calcul de t.** to do a quick bit of mental arithmetic; **n'en faire qu'à sa t.** to do exactly as one pleases; **avoir une idée derrière la t.** to have an ulterior motive; *Litt* **idée de derrière la t.** preposterous or ludicrous idea; **où ai-je la t.!** what am I thinking of!; **monter à la t.** to go to sb's head; **garder la t. froide** to stay calm, to keep cool or a cool head; **essaie de garder la t. froide** try to stay calm, *Fam* try not to lose your cool; **est-ce que vous perdez la t.?** have you taken leave of your senses?; **ne perdez pas la t.!** keep or don't lose your head!, keep calm!; **faire perdre la t. à qn** to make sb lose his/her head; **c'était à perdre la t.** it was bewildering; **avoir toute sa t.** to be all there; **il n'a plus toute sa t.** he's not quite all there; **se monter la t.** to imagine things; **ne va pas te monter la t.** don't start imagining things, don't go getting ideas; **j'y penserai à t. reposée** I'll think about it later (when I've got some peace and quiet); *Fam* **prendre la t. à qn** to get up sb's nose, to get on sb's wick, *Am* to tick sb off; *Fam* **quelle prise de t.!** what a pain (in the neck)!

6 *(chef)* *(d'une société, d'un organisme)* head

7 *(du chapitre d'un livre)* top; *Typ* **blanc de t.** margin at the head of a book; **ligne de t.** headline; **t. de lettre** letterhead; *Journ* **article de t.** feature (article), *Am* leading article; *Journ* **t. de colonne** lead (story), top

8 *(de chou, d'ail, d'artichaut)* head; *(d'un arbre)* top, crown; *Anat (du fémur)* apophysis; *(de l'humérus)* head

9 *Tech (d'un violon, d'un mât, d'un marteau, d'un clou etc)* head; *(de fusée)* warhead; **t. inclinable** *(d'une machine-outil, d'un support pour appareil photo ou instrument)* tilting head; *Aut* **soupapes en t.** overhead valves

10 *(d'une procession, d'une colonne, d'une entreprise, d'un régiment etc)* head; *(d'un train)* front; *Sport etc* **prendre la t.** to take the lead; **prendre la t. d'une entreprise** to take over as the head of a company; **être à la t. de** *(une entreprise, une fortune)* to be (at) the head of, to head; *(une conjuration,*

une insurrection) to be the leader of; **être à la t. de la classe** to be (at the) top of the class; **colonne de t.** front column; *Sport* **arriver en t.** to come in first; **être en t.** to be in the lead; **les joueurs en t.** the leaders, the front runners; **marcher en t.** to lead the way; **marcher à la t.** ou **en t. du cortège** to walk at the head of the procession, to lead or head the procession; **arriver en t. du scrutin** to head or come first in the poll; **taxi en t. de file** taxi at the head of the rank; *Rail* **voiture de t.** front carriage or *Am* car; **en t. du train** at the front of the train; **en t. de liste** at the top of the list; **candidats en t. de liste** candidates at the top of or heading the list

▸ ▸ *Théâtre, Cin* **t. d'affiche** top of the bill (de in); **être t. d'affiche** to be top of the bill, to top the bill; *Aut* **t. d'allumeur** distributor cap; **t. de benne** grab head; **t. blonde: nos chères têtes blondes** *(enfants)* our little darlings; **t. brûlée** hothead; **t. de cabestan** drum head; **t. de câble** cable terminal; *TV, Cin* **t. de caméra** camera head; **t. de chapitre** chapter heading; **t. chercheuse** *(d'un missile etc)* homing device; *Fam* **t. à claques: c'est une t. à claques** he just asks for it; *Fam* **t. de cochon: c'est une t. de cochon** he's pig-headed, he's as stubborn as a mule; **t. couronnée** *(souverain)* crowned head; *Aut* **t. de distribution** distributor cap; *Ordinat* **t. d'écriture** writing or write head; *Électron, Ordinat* **t. d'effacement** *(d'un magnétophone etc)* erase head; **t. d'électrode** electrode tip; **t. d'enregistrement, t. enregistreuse** *(d'un ordinateur, d'un magnétophone)* record(ing) head; **t. de flèche** *(d'une grue)* jib head; **t. de fraisage** cutter head, milling head; **t. de fusée** warhead; *Fam* **t. à gifles: c'est une t. à gifles** he just asks for it; *Com* **t. de gondole** end of gondola, aisle end display; **t. d'impression** print head; *Pétr* **t. d'injection** swivel; *Fam* **t. de lard: c'est une t. de lard** he's pig-headed, he's as stubborn as a mule; **t. de lecture** *Cin* sound head; *Ordinat* read(ing) head; *(de magnétophone)* tape reader, play-back head; *(de tourne-disque)* pick-up (head); *Ordinat* **t. de lecture-écriture** read-write head; *Rail etc* **t. de ligne** starting point, terminus; **t. de linotte** bird-brain; **être une t. de linotte** to be bird-brained, to be a bird-brain; *Pol* **t. de liste** leading candidate, *Am* head of the ticket; **t. de lit** bed head; **t. magnétique** magnetic head; **t. de mule: c'est une t. de mule** he's pig-headed, he's as stubborn as a mule; *Vulg* **t. de nœud!** dickhead!, *Am* asshole!; **t. nucléaire** nuclear warhead; *Ordinat* **t. à palpeur** sensor head; **t. de perçage** drill(ing) head; *Fam* **c'est une t. de pioche** he's pig-headed, he's as stubborn as a mule; *Aut* **t. de piston** piston head or crown; *Mil* **t. de pont** bridgehead; **t. porte-foret** drill(ing) head; **t. porte-fraise** cutter head, milling head; **t. porte-outil** tool head; *Tennis* **t. de série** seeded player, seed; **t. sonore** sound head; **t. de Turc** target, butt; **c'est la t. de Turc de toute la classe** the whole class picks on him/her; *Culin* **t. de veau vinaigrette** calf's head in vinaigrette

---

tête-à-queue NM INV *Aut* spin; *Équitation* (sudden) turn; **faire (un) t.** *Aut* to spin or slew round; *(d'un cheval)* to whip round; **la voiture a fait plusieurs t.** the car spun round several times

tête-à-tête NM INV **1** *(à deux)* private interview, tête-à-tête; **en t.** in private; **un dîner en t.** a private dinner; **voir qn en t.** to see sb in private or privately; **en t. avec** alone with **2** *(canapé)* (two-seater) sofa, *surtout Am* love seat **3** *(service)* tea/coffee/breakfast set (for two)

tête-bêche ADV **dormir t.** to sleep head to foot; **ranger des bouteilles t.** to store bottles alternate ways up

tête-de-loup, *pl* **têtes-de-loup NF** ceiling brush

tête de mort, *pl* **têtes de mort NF 1** *(emblème)* death's-head; **pavillon à t.** skull and crossbones (flag), Jolly Roger **2** *Entom* death's-head moth

tête-de-nègre ADJ INV, NM INV dark brown

tétée [tete] **NF 1** *(repas de nourrisson)* feed; **l'heure de la t.** feeding time; **pendant les tétées** during feeds, while feeding; **donner la t. à un enfant** to feed *or Vieilli* suckle a child **2** *(action)* sucking

téter [tete] **VT** (**il tète; il tétera**) **1** *(d'un bébé, d'un petit animal) (lait)* to suck; **t. sa mère** to feed, to suck at one's mother's breast; **donner à t. à un enfant** to feed *or Vieilli* suckle a child **2** *Fam (cigare, pipe, stylo etc)* to suck (on); *(pouce)* to suck
VI *Fam (boire avec excès)* to knock it back, to drink like a fish

tétière [tetjɛr] **NF 1** *(de harnais)* headstall **2** *(de fauteuil)* chairback, *Vieilli* antimacassar

tétine [tetin] **NF 1** *(d'une truie etc)* dug; *(d'une vache)* udder **2** *(d'un biberon)* nipple, teat; **t. (sur anneau)** *(sucette)* comforter, *Br* dummy, *Am* pacifier

téton [tetɔ̃] **NM** *Fam (sein de femme)* boob, tit; *Tech (d'une pièce détachée)* lug; *Tech* **t. de positionnement** spigot, dowel; *Tech* **t. de purge** bleed nipple

tétrachlorure [tetraklɔryr] **NM** *Chimie* tetrachloride; **t. de carbone** carbon tetrachloride

tétracycline [tetrasiklin] **NF** *Pharm* tetracycline

tétraèdre [tetraɛdr] *Géom* **ADJ** tetrahedral
NM tetrahedron

tétraédrique [tetraedrik] **ADJ** *Géom* tetrahedral

tétralogie [tetralɔʒi] **NF** *Littér, Théâtre* tetralogy; *Mus* **la T. (de Wagner)** The Ring, Wagner's Ring

tétramètre [tetramɛtr] **NM** *Littér* tetrameter

tétraphonique [tetrafɔnik] **ADJ** quadrasonic

tétraplégie [tetrapleʒi] **NF** *Méd* tetraplegia, quadriplegia

tétraplégique [tetrapleʒik] **ADJ, N** *Méd* quadriplegic

tétrapode [tetrapɔd] **NM** *Zool* tetrapod

tétrarque [tetrark] **NM** tetrarch

tétras [tetra] **NM** *(oiseau)* grouse; **grand t.** capercaillie; **t.-lyre** black grouse VOIR GRAM-MAIRE A12

tétrasyllabe [tetrasilab], **tétrasyllabique** [tetrasilabik] **ADJ** *Gram* tetrasyllabic; **mot t.** tetrasyllable

têtu, -ue [tety] **ADJ** stubborn, obstinate, *Fam* pig-headed; *Fam* **t. comme un mulet** *ou* **comme une mule** as stubborn *or* obstinate as a mule
N stubborn *or* obstinate person; **c'est un t.!** he's so stubborn *or* obstinate *or Fam* pig-headed!

teuf [tœf] **NF** *Fam* party

teuf-teuf, *pl* **teufs-teufs** [tœftœf] **NM** *Aut Fam (voiture)* jalopy, old banger; *(bruit)* chug-chug

teuton, -onne [tøtɔ̃, -ɔn] **ADJ** Teutonic
NM *Ling* Germanic, Teutonic
N T. Teuton

teutonique [tøtɔnik] **ADJ** Teutonic

texan, -ane [tɛksɑ̃, -an] **ADJ** Texan
N T. Texan

texte [tɛkst] **NM** *(d'un auteur, d'un livre, d'un contrat etc)*, *Ordinat* text; *Mus (d'un opéra)* libretto; *(d'une chanson)* words; *Théâtre (d'un acteur)* lines; *(d'une pièce de théâtre)* script; *Scol (de devoir)* subject; **t. (imprimé)** print,

printed text; **erreur de t.** textual error; **critique des textes** textual criticism; **t. de départ** source text; **t. publicitaire** advertising copy; **gravure hors t.** plate, full-page engraving; **lire Goethe dans le t.** to read Goethe in the original; *Scol* **cahier de textes** homework book *(listing work to be done)*; **textes choisis** selected passages (**de** from)
▸▸ **texte libre: vous avez t. libre pour la rédaction** you can write about anything you like

texteur [tɛkstœr] **NM** *Ordinat* word *or* text processor

textile [tɛkstil] **ADJ** textile
NM 1 textile; **textiles artificiels** synthetic *or* man-made textiles *or* fabrics, synthetics **2** **le t.** *(industrie)* the textile industry, textiles

texto [tɛksto] *Fam* **ADJ** word for word; **il m'a dit t.: 'fous le camp'** 'get the hell out of it'– those were his very words
NM *Tél* text message

textuel, -elle [tɛkstɥɛl] **ADJ 1** *(analyse etc)* textual **2** *(conforme au texte) (traduction)* word-for-word, literal; *Fam* **c'est t.!** those were his/her/their/*etc* very words!; **c'est ce qu'elle a dit, c'est t.!** that's what she said, word for word!

textuellement [tɛkstɥɛlmɑ̃] **ADV** *(conformément au texte) (traduire)* word for word, literally; **je reprends t. ses mots** those were his very words

texture [tɛkstyr] **NF** *(d'une substance, du sol)* texture; *(d'un texte)* structure

texturer [tɛkstyre], **texturiser** [tɛkstyrize] **VT** *Tech* to texturize

TF1 [teɛfœ̃] **NF** *(abrév* **Télévision Française 1)** = French independent television company

TGB [teʒebe] **NF** *(abrév* **très grande bibliothèque)** = the new French national library in the Tolbiac area of Paris

TGV [teʒeve] **NM** *abrév* **train à grande vitesse**

thada [tada] **NM** *(abrév* **trouble d'hyperactivité avec déficit de l'attention)** attention deficit hyperactivity disorder, ADHD

thaï, -ïe [taj] **ADJ** Thai
NM *Ling* Thai
N T. Thai

thaïlandais, -aise [tailɑ̃dɛ, -ɛz] **ADJ** Thai
N T. Thai

Thaïlande [tailɑ̃d] **NF** Thailand

thalamus [talamys] **NM** *Anat* thalamus

thalassémie [talasemi] **NF** *Méd* thalassaemia, *Am* thalassemia

thalassothérapie [talasoterapi] **NF** *Méd* seawater therapy, thalassotherapy

thalidomide [talidɔmid] **NF** *Pharm* thalidomide

thalle [tal] **NM** *Bot* thallus

thallium [taljɔm] **NM** *Chimie* thallium

thalweg [talvɛg] **NM** *Géol* t(h)alweg

thatchérien, -ienne [tatʃerjɛ̃, -jɛn] **ADJ, N** Thatcherite

thatchérisme [tatʃerism] **NM** Thatcherism

thaumaturge [tomatyrʒ] **ADJ** miracle-working, *Spéc* thaumaturgic
NM miracle worker, *Spéc* thaumaturge, thaumaturgist

thé [te] **NM 1** *(boisson, feuilles)* tea; *(arbrisseau)* tea plant; **boire du t.** to drink tea; **faire du t.** to make (some) tea; **et si on se faisait du t.?** how about some tea?; **c'est l'heure du t.** it's tea time; **prendre le t.** to take tea; **t. de Ceylan** Ceylon tea; **t. indien** *ou* **de l'Inde** Indian tea; **t. de Chine** China tea; **t. nature** *ou* **au lait** tea without milk/with milk; **t. au citron** lemon tea; **t. glacé** iced tea; **t. à la menthe** mint tea; **t. en sachet** tea bags; **t. en vrac** loose tea; **négociant en t.** tea merchant **2** *(goûter)* tea party; **t. dansant** tea dance, thé

dansant; **inviter qn pour le t.** to invite sb to *or* for tea **3** **salon de t.** teashop, tearoom(s) **4** *Belg, Suisse (infusion)* herbal tea
ADJ INV **rose t.** tea rose

théâtral, -ale, -aux, -ales [teatral, -o] **ADJ** theatrical; *(effet)* dramatic; *(performance)* stage; *Péj (artificiel)* theatrical, stagy

théâtralement [teatralmɑ̃] **ADV** theatrically

théâtraliser [teatralize] **VT** *Théâtre (roman etc)* to dramatize

théâtralité [teatralite] **NF** theatricality

théâtre [teatr] **NM 1** *(salle)* theatre, *Am* theater; **aller au t.** to go to the theatre **2** *(scène)* stage; **mettre une pièce au t.** to stage *or* put on a play; **adapté pour le t.** adapted for the stage; **se retirer du t.** to give up the stage **3** *(art, métier)* theatre, *Am* theater; **pièce de t.** play; **costumier de t.** theatrical costumier; **faire du t.** to be an actor/actress, to act, to be on the stage; **homme/femme de t.** man/woman of the theatre; **école/cours de t.** drama school/course; **coup de t.** *Théâtre* coup de théâtre; *Fig* dramatic *or* sensational turn of events; *Fig* **sa décision a été un vrai coup de t.** his decision came as a real surprise **4** *(œuvres) (d'un auteur)* plays, dramatic works; *(genre)* theatre, *Am* theater; **le t. anglais** British theatre *or* drama; **t. expérimental** *ou* **off** experimental theatre, fringe (theatre); **écrivains de t.** playwrights **5** *Fig (d'un crime, un accident etc)* scene **6** *(attitude artificielle)* play-acting, histrionics; **tout cela, c'est du t.** it's all an act
▸▸ **t. de boulevard** light comedies; **t. de marionnettes** puppet theatre; **t. d'ombres** shadow theatre; *Mil* **t. d'opérations** theatre of operations; **t. en rond** theatre-in-the-round; **t. de verdure** open-air theatre

théâtreux, -euse [teatrø, -øz] **N** *Fam Péj* would-be actor, *f* would-be actress

thébaïde [tebaid] **NF** *Litt* place of meditation

théier, -ière [teje, -jɛr] **ADJ** *Rare (industrie etc)* tea; *(région)* tea-growing
NM *Bot* tea (plant)
NF théière teapot

théine [tein] **NF** theine, caffeine; **thé sans t.** caffeine-free tea

théisme [teism] **NM** *Rel* theism

théiste [teist] *Rel* **ADJ** theistic
N theist

thématique [tematik] **ADJ** *(catalogue, table, index)* subject; *Mus* thematic
NF *(d'une œuvre, de la littérature contemporaine etc)* themes; **cela entre dans sa t.** it's one of his themes

thème [tɛm] **NM 1** *(sujet) (d'un discours, d'un débat, d'un morceau de musique etc)* theme; **un t. de réflexion** food for thought; **je vous propose un t. de réflexion** here's something you can think about **2** *Scol (traduction)* prose; *Fam* **un fort en t.** a swot **3** *Gram (d'un verbe, d'un nom)* stem **4** *Astrol* **t. (astral)** birth chart; **faire son t. à qn** to draw up sb's birth chart

théocratie [teokrasi] **NF** theocracy

théocratique [teokratik] **ADJ** theocratic

théodicée [teodise] **NF** *Phil* theodicy

théodolite [teodolit] **NM** theodolite

théogonie [teogoni] **NF** theogony, genealogy of the gods

théologal, -ale, -aux, -ales [teologal, -o] **ADJ** **les trois vertus théologales** the three theological virtues

théologie [teoloʒi] **NF** theology; **docteur en t.** doctor of divinity, DD; **faire sa t.** to study theology, to be a divinity student; **cours/études de t.** theology course/studies

théologien, -ienne [teoloʒjɛ̃, -jɛn] **N** theologian

théologique [teɔlɔʒik] **ADJ** theological

théologiquement [teɔlɔʒikmɑ̃] **ADV** theologically

théorbe [teɔrb] **NM** *Hist, Mus* theorbo

théorème [teɔrɛm] **NM** theorem; **le t. de Newton** the binomial theorem

théorétique [teɔretik] *Phil* **ADJ** theoretic(al) **NF** theoretics

théoricien, -ienne [teɔrisjɛ̃, -jɛn] **N** theoretician, theorist

théorie¹ [teɔri] **NF 1** *(doctrine)* theory; **bâtir une t.** to construct a theory; *Math, Ordinat* **t. des probabilités** theory of probability; **t. de la relativité** theory of relativity, relativity theory; **la t. et la pratique** theory and practice; *Mktg* **t. de la décision** decision theory; *Mktg* **t. des jeux** game theory; **en t.** in theory, theoretically; **plus facile en t. qu'en pratique** easier in theory than in practice **2** *Mil* theoretical instruction

théorie² **NF** *Litt (défilé)* procession

théorique [teɔrik] **ADJ** theoretic(al); *Fin* **profits théoriques** paper profits

théoriquement [teɔrikmɑ̃] **ADV** theoretically, in theory

théoriser [teɔrize] **VI** to theorize **VT** to theorize about

théosophe [teɔzɔf] **N** theosophist

théosophie [teɔzɔfi] **NF** theosophy

thérapeute [terapøt] **N** *Méd* therapist

thérapeutique [terapøtik] **ADJ** *(avortement, action, procédé)* therapeutic; **les avancées thérapeutiques sont remarquables dans ce domaine** remarkable medical advances have been made in this field; **acte t.** invasive treatment; **aléa t.** risk attached to treatment; **accident t.** accident in the course of treatment **NF** *(science)* therapeutics; *(traitement)* (course of) treatment, therapy

thérapie [terapi] **NF** *Méd* therapy; *Psy* **t. de groupe** group therapy; **être en t.** to be in therapy; **commencer une t.** to start a course of therapy, to start therapy

thermal, -ale, -aux, -ales [termal, -o] **ADJ** thermal; **eaux thermales** thermal *or* hot springs; **établissement t.** hydropathic establishment, *Br* hydro; **station thermale** spa; **cure thermale** water cure; **faire une cure thermale** to take the waters

thermalisme [termalism] **NM 1** *(thérapie)* hydrotherapy, water cures **2** *(science)* balneology

thermes [term] **NMPL 1** *Méd* thermal baths **2** *Antiq* thermae, public baths

thermicien, -ienne [termisjɛ̃, -jɛn] **N** heat engineer

thermidor [termidɔr] **NM** *Hist* = eleventh month of the French Republican calendar *(July-August)*

thermie [termi] **NF** *Phys* = thermal unit *(1000 kilocalories)*

thermique [termik] **ADJ** *Phys* thermal; *(moteur, écran, traitement)* heat; *Élec* **centrale t.** thermal power station; *Aviat* **courant t.** thermal (current); **papier t.** thermal paper; *Électron* **relais t.** thermorelay; **brise/vent t.** thermal; *Chimie* **analyse t.** thermoanalysis; **science t.** science of heat; *Géog* **régime t.** temperature regime *or* pattern; *Physiol* **sensibilité t.** temperature sense **NM** *Aviat (courant)* thermal **NF** science of heat

thermistance [termistɑ̃s] **NF** *Élec* thermistor

thermisteur [termistœr], **thermistor** [termistɔr] **NM** *Élec* thermistor

thermocautère [termokoter] **NM** *Chir (instrument)* thermocautery

thermochimie [termoʃimi] **NF** thermochemistry

thermocollage [termokɔlaʒ] **NM** heat sealing

thermoconduction [termokɔ̃dyksjɔ̃] **NF** *Phys* heat conduction

thermocontact [termokɔ̃takt] **NM** *Élec* thermal *or* temperature switch

thermocouple [termokupl] **NM** *Élec* thermocouple

thermodynamique [termodinamik] **ADJ** thermodynamic **NF** thermodynamics

thermoélectricité [termoelɛktrisite] **NF** thermoelectricity

thermoélectrique [termoelɛktrik] **ADJ** thermoelectric(al); **pince t.** thermocouple; **couple t.** thermoelectric couple; **pile t.** thermopile

thermoélectronique [termoelɛktrɔnik] **ADJ** thermoelectronic

thermoformage [termofɔrmaʒ] **NM** *Tech* thermoforming

thermogène [termoʒen] **ADJ** *Physiol* heat-producing, *Spéc* thermogenetic

thermographe [termograf] **NM** *Phys* thermograph

thermomagnétisme [termomaɲetism] **NM** *Phys* thermomagnetism

thermomètre [termometr] **NM** thermometer; **t. médical** *ou* **de clinique** clinical thermometer; **t. à maxima et minima** maximum and minimum thermometer; **t. à mercure** mercury thermometer; **le t. monte/baisse** the temperature is rising/falling; *Fig* **le t. de l'opinion** the barometer of public opinion

thermométrie [termometri] **NF** *Phys* thermometry

thermométrique [termometrik] **ADJ** thermometric

thermonucléaire [termonykleer] **ADJ** *Nucl, Mil* thermonuclear

thermopile [termopil] **NF** *Élec* thermopile

thermoplastique [termoplastik] **ADJ, NM** thermoplastic

thermoplongeur [termoplɔ̃ʒœr] **NM** *(portable)* immersion heater

thermopompe [termopɔ̃p] **NF** heat pump

thermopropulsion [termopropylsjɔ̃] **NF** *Aviat* thermopropulsion

thermorégulateur [termoregylatœr] **NM** thermoregulator, thermostat

thermorégulation [termoregylasjɔ̃] **NF** thermoregulation

thermorésistant [termorezistɑ̃] **ADJ** heat-resistant

Thermos® [termos] **NM INV OU NF INV (bouteille) T.** Thermos® (flask *or Am* bottle)

thermoscope [termoskop] **NM** *Phys* thermoscope

thermosphère [termosfer] **NF** thermosphere

thermostat [termosta] **NM** thermostat; **t. 7** *(dans recette)* gas mark 7; **réglage par t.** thermostatic control

thermothérapie [termoterapi] **NF** heat treatment, *Spéc* thermotherapy

thésard, -arde [tezar, -ard] **N** *Univ Fam* PhD student

thésaurisation [tezorizasjɔ̃] **NF** hoarding (of money); *Écon* building up of capital

thésauriser [tezorize] **VTI** to hoard

thésauriseur, -euse [tezorizœr, -øz] **N** *(d'argent)* hoarder

thesaurus [tezorys] **NM** thesaurus

thèse [tez] **NF** VOIR GRAMMAIRE A14 **1** *(doctrine)* thesis, proposition, argument; **il défend la t.**

suivante: ... he argues that ...; *Théâtre* **pièce à t.** problem play, drama of ideas; **roman/littérature à t.** novel/literature of ideas **2** *Univ* thesis *(submitted for degree)*; **soutenir sa t.** to defend one's thesis, to have one's viva (voce) **3** *Phil* thesis; **t., antithèse, synthèse** thesis, antithesis, synthesis

Thésée [teze] **NM** *Myth Br* Theseus

Thessalonique [tesalɔnik] **NF** Thessalonica

thiamine [tjamin] **NF** *Biol, Chimie* thiamin(e), aneurin

thibaude [tibod] **NF** carpet felt, (felt) underlay

thiosulfate [tjɔsylfat] **NM** *Chimie* thiosulphate, *Am* thiosulfate

thio-urée, *pl* **thio-urées** [tjɔyre] **NF** *Chimie* thiourea

thixotropie [tiksɔtrɔpi] **NF** *Chimie, Phys* thixotropy

Thomas [tɔma] **NM saint T. d'Aquin** St Thomas Aquinas

thomas [tɔma] **NM** *Arg Vieilli (pot de chambre)* chamberpot, *Br* jerry

thomisme [tɔmism] **NM** *Rel* Thomism

thomiste [tɔmist] **ADJ, N** *Rel* Thomist

thon [tɔ̃] **NM 1** *(poisson)* tuna, tunny; *Culin* tuna (fish); **la pêche au t.** tuna fishing; **t. au naturel/à l'huile** tuna (fish) in brine/in oil **2** *Fam (femme laide)* dog, *Br* boot, *Am* beast

thonaire [tɔner] **NM** *Pêche* tuna *or* tunny net

thonier [tɔnje] **NM** tuna *or* tunny boat

Thora [tɔra] **NF** *Rel* Torah

thoracique [tɔrasik] **ADJ** *Anat* thoracic; **cage t.** ribcage

thorax [tɔraks] **NM** *Anat* thorax

thorium [tɔrjɔm] **NM** *Chimie* thorium

thoron [tɔrɔ̃] **NM** *Nucl* thoron

Thrace [tras] **NF** Thrace

thrène [tren] **NM** *Antiq* threnody

thriller [srilœr] **NM** *Cin, Littér* thriller

thrips [trips] **NM** *Ent* thrips, *Spéc* thysanopter

thrombine [trɔbin] **NF** *Biol, Chimie* thrombin

thrombose [trɔboz] **NF** *Méd* thrombosis; **t. veineuse profonde** deep-vein thrombosis

thulium [tyljɔm] **NM** *Chimie* thulium

thune [tyn] **NF** *Arg* **1** *(argent)* dough, *Br* dosh; **j'ai pas une t.** I'm stony broke; **gagner de la t.** *ou* **des thunes** to be raking it in, to be making mega bucks **2** *Arch (pièce)* five-franc piece **3** *Suisse (pièce)* Swiss five-franc coin

thuriféraire [tyriferer] **NM 1** *Rel* thurifer, incense bearer **2** *Litt (flatteur)* flatterer

thuya [tyja] **NM** *Bot* thuja, thuya, arbor vitae

thylacine [tilasin] **NM** Tasmanian wolf, *Spéc* thylacine

thym [tɛ̃] **NM** *Bot, Culin* thyme; **t. sauvage** wild thyme

thymus [timys] **NM** *Anat* thymus, thymus gland

thyristor [tiristɔr] **NM** *Élec* thyristor

thyroïde [tirɔid] **ADJ, NF** *Anat* **(glande) t.** thyroid (gland)

thyroïdectomie [tirɔidɛktɔmi] **NF** *Chir* thyroidectomy

thyroïdien, -ienne [tirɔidjɛ̃, -jɛn] **ADJ** *Anat, Méd (hormone, artère, insuffisance etc)* thyroid

thyroïdisme [tirɔidism] **NM** *Méd* thyroidism

thyroïdite [tirɔidit] **NF** *Méd* thyroiditis

thyrotoxicose [tirɔtɔksikoz] **NF** *Méd* Graves' disease

thyrse [tirs] **NM** *Antiq, Bot* thyrsus

tiare [tjar] **NF** *(du pape)* tiara; **coiffer la t.** to become Pope

Tibère [tibɛr] NM Tiberius

Tibet [tibɛ] NM Tibet

tibétain, -aine [tibetɛ̃, -ɛn] ADJ Tibetan ▪ NM *Ling* Tibetan ▪ N **T.** Tibetan

TIBEUR NM *Fin* (*abrév* **Taux interbancaire européen**) EURIBOR

tibia [tibja] NM *Anat, Entom* tibia

tibial, -iale, -iaux, -iales [tibjal, -jo] ADJ *Anat* tibial

Tibre [tibr] NM le **T.** the Tiber

tic [tik] NM **1** *Méd* tic, twitch; **il a un t.** he has a twitch *or* a tic, his face twitches; **t. nerveux** nervous tic *or* twitch; **t. douloureux** facial neuralgia, *Spéc* tic douloureux **2** *Vét* (*de cheval*) vicious habit **3** *Fig* (*habitude*) habit, mannerism; **avoir/prendre le t. de faire qch** to have a/get into the habit of doing sth; **t. de langage** verbal tic *or* mannerism

ticket [tikɛ] NM **1** (*billet*) ticket; **un carnet de tickets de bus** a book of bus tickets **2** *Anciennement Arg* (*billet de dix francs*) ten-franc note; **tu vas en avoir pour deux cents tickets** it'll cost you two thousand francs **3** *Arg* **avoir un t. avec qn** to have made a hit with sb; **j'ai l'impression que tu as un t. avec lui** (*tu lui plais*) I think he likes *or Br* fancies you
▸▸ **t. de caisse** receipt; *Méd* **t. modérateur** = portion of the cost of treatment paid by the insured; *Admin* **t. de pain** bread coupon; *Rail* **t. de quai** platform ticket; **t. de rationnement** ration coupon

ticket-repas, *pl* **tickets-repas** NM *Br* ≃ luncheon voucher, *Am* ≃ meal ticket

Ticket-Restaurant®, *pl* **Tickets-Restaurant** NM *Br* ≃ luncheon voucher, *Am* ≃ meal ticket

tic-tac NM INV (*d'une horloge*) tick-tock, tick, ticking; **faire t.** to tick ▪ INT tick-tock!

tictaquer [tiktake] VI (*d'une horloge*) to tick

tie-break, *pl* **tie-breaks** [tajbrɛk] NM *Tennis* tie break

tiédasse [tjedas] ADJ *Péj* lukewarm, tepid

tiède [tjɛd] ADJ (*agréablement*) (*bain, vent etc*) warm; (*désagréablement*) (*bain, boisson etc*) tepid, lukewarm; *Fig* (*amitié, accueil*) tepid, lukewarm, half-hearted; *Fig* (*foi, défenseur*) half-hearted; *Culin* (*salade*) warm ▪ ADV **il fait t.** (*temps*) it's mild; **je n'aime pas boire t.** I don't like anything that's lukewarm ▪ N half-hearted person

tièdement [tjɛdmɑ̃] ADV half-heartedly, without any great enthusiasm

tiédeur [tjedœr] NF (*agréable*) warmth; (*désagréable*) (*de l'eau*), *Fig* (*d'une amitié, d'un accueil etc*) tepidness, half-heartedness; *Fig* (*d'un défenseur, de la foi*) half-heartedness; **la t. de ses paroles** his unenthusiastic *or* half-hearted words; **avec t.** half-heartedly, without any great enthusiasm

tiédir [tjedir] VI (*devenir plus chaud*) to warm up; (*devenir moins chaud*) to cool down; *Fig* (*d'une amitié, d'une passion etc*) to cool off ▪ VT (*réchauffer*) to take the chill off, to warm (up); (*refroidir*) to cool (down)

tiédissement [tjedismɑ̃] NM (*refroidissement*) cooling (off); (*réchauffement*) warming (up)

tien, tienne [tjɛ̃, tjɛn] PRON POSS **le t., la tienne, les tiens, les tiennes** yours; *Bible, Arch* thine; **tu me prêtes le t.?** can I borrow yours?; **il n'a qu'à prendre la tienne** he can just take yours; **il ressemble au t.** it looks like yours; **tu veux bien me donner du t.?** can I have some of yours?; **de toutes ces solutions, tu préfères la tienne?** out of those possible solutions, do you prefer your own?; **tu n'en as pas besoin, tu as le t.** you don't need

it, you've got your own; **je n'en ai pas besoin, j'ai le t.** I don't need it, I've got yours; **les deux tiens** your two, the two *or* both of yours; (*en insistant*) your own two; **tu lui as laissé deux des tiens** you gave him two of yours; *Fam* **le t. de bébé est plus intelligent** your baby is more intelligent; *Fam* **à la tienne!** (*en buvant*) cheers! SEE GRAMMAR A30; B21-2
▪ NM **le t.** (*ce qui t'appartient*) yours; **ne cherchons pas à distinguer le t. du mien** let's not waste time arguing about who owns what; *Fig* **tu devrais y mettre du t.** (*faire un effort*) you should do your share
▪ NMPL **les tiens** (*ta famille*) your family, *Am* your folks; (*tes partisans*) your followers; (*tes coéquipiers*) your team-mates
▪ NFPL **tu as encore fait des tiennes** you've been up to your old tricks again
▪ ADJ POSS *Litt* **un t. cousin** a cousin of yours; **tu feras tiens ses principes** you will adopt his principles as your own; **feras-tu tiennes les félicitations qu'ils m'adressent?** will you join them in congratulating me?

tiens, tient [tjɛ̃] *voir* tenir

tierce [tjɛrs] NF **1** *Astron, Math* = sixtieth part of a second **2** *Escrime* tierce **3** *Rel* terce, tierce **4** *Mus* third **5** *Typ* final revise, press proof **6** *Cartes* tierce **7** *Ordinat* **t. partie de confiance** trusted third party

tiercé [tjɛrse] ADJ **1** *Courses de chevaux* **pari t.** triple forecast **2** *Hér* tierced, tiercé **3** *rimes tiercées* terza rima **4** *Agr* (*champ*) ploughed *or Am* plowed for the third time ▪ NM *Courses de chevaux* triple forecast; **un beau t.** a good win on the tiercé; **le t. gagnant** the winning combination; **jouer au t.** = to put money on horses

tiercelet [tjɛrs(ə)lɛ] NM tercel, male falcon

tiercer [tjɛrse] VT (**je tierçai(s); n. tierçons**) *Agr* (*champ*) to plough *or Am* plow for the third time

tiers, tierce [tjɛr, tjɛrs] ADJ third; **une tierce personne** a third party; *Jur* **en main tierce** in the hands of a third party; *Méd* **fièvre tierce** tertian fever
▪ NM **1** (*fraction*) third (part); **une remise d'un t.** (*du prix*) a discount of a third, *Fam* a third off; **perdre le t./les deux t. de son argent** to lose a third/two-thirds of one's money **2** (*personne*) third party; *Fam* **le t. et le quart** everybody, anybody; *Fam* **il se moque du t. comme du quart** he doesn't give a damn about anybody or anything; **assurance au t.** third party insurance
▸▸ *Fin* **t. détenteur** third party holder; *Hist* **le T. état** the Third Estate; **le t. monde** *voir* **tiers-monde**; *Admin* **t. payant** = system of direct payment for medical treatment by the insurer; *Fin* **t. porteur** (*d'un effet de commerce*) second endorser; (*d'un effet*) holder in due course; **t. possesseur** third party owner; *Fin* **t. provisionnel** = thrice-yearly income tax payment based on estimated tax due for the previous year

tiers-arbitre, *pl* **tiers-arbitres** NM *Jur* (independent) arbitrator

tiers-monde, *pl* **tiers-mondes** NM *Pol* **le t.** the Third World; **pays du t.** Third World countries

tiers-mondiste, *pl* **tiers-mondistes** [tjɛrmɔ̃dist] *Pol* ADJ Third World ▪ N supporter of the Third World

TIF [tif] NM (*abrév* **transport international ferroviaire**) = international rail transport

tifoso, *pl* **tifosi** [tifozo, -zi] NM fan

tifs, tiffes [tif] NMPL *Arg* hair

TIG [tiʒ] NM (*abrév* **travail d'intérêt général**) ≃ community service

tige [tiʒ] NF **1** (*d'une plante*) stem, stalk; (*d'un arbre*) stem; (**arbre de) haute/basse t.** (tall) standard/half standard; **rosier sur t.** stan-

dard rose **2** *Fig Litt* (*d'une famille*) stock; **faire t.** to found a line **3** *Tech* (*d'une valve*) stem; (*d'une pompe, d'un piston etc*) rod; *Aut* (*sur le volant*) stalk; (*d'un rivet, d'une clé*), *Naut* (*d'une ancre*), *Typ* (*d'une lettre*) shank; *Archit* (*d'une colonne*) shaft; *Mus* (*d'un archet*) stick; (*d'un guéridon*) leg **4** *Tex* (*d'un bas*) leg; (*d'une botte*) leg, upper; **bottes à tiges** top boots **5** *Arg* (*cigarette*) cigarette, cig(gy), *Br* fag
▸▸ *Aut* **t. (de maintien) de capot** bonnet strut; *Typ* **t. à caractères** type bar; *Aut* **t. de crémaillère** rack link; (*de la direction*) control rod; *Aut* **t. de culbuteur** pushrod; *Pétr* **t. de forage** drill(ing) pipe; **t. de frein** brake rod; *Aut* **t. de jauge** dipstick; **t. de paratonnerre** lightning rod; *Aut* **t. de poussée** thrust pin, pushrod; *Aut* **t. poussoir** pushrod; **t. de selle** (*de bicyclette*) saddle pillar; **t. à vis du frein** brake screw

tiglon [tiglɔ̃] NM tigon

tignasse [tiɲas] NF mop

Tigre [tigr] NM le **T.** the Tigris

tigre [tigr] NM *aussi Fig* tiger; **jaloux comme un t.** madly *or* wildly jealous
▸▸ **t. du Bengale** Bengal tiger; **t. royal** Bengal tiger

tigré [tigre] ADJ **1** (*rayé*) striped; **chat t.** tabby (cat) **2** (*tacheté*) spotted (**de** with); **lis t.** tiger lily

tigresse [tigres] NF *aussi Fig* tigress; **jalouse comme une t.** madly *or* wildly jealous

tigron [tigrɔ̃] NM tigon

tilbury [tilbyri] NM (*voiture à cheval*) tilbury, gig

tilde [tild(e)] NM *Typ etc* swung dash; (*espagnol*) tilde

tillac [tijak] NM *Hist, Naut* upper deck

tilleul [tijœl] NM **1** (*arbre*) lime (tree); **en t.** (*coffret, boîte*) limewood **2** (**infusion de) t.** lime-blossom tea ▪ ADJ INV (*couleur*) (**vert) t.** lime green

tilsit [tilsit] NM *Suisse* = hard cheese from the canton of Saint-Gall

tilt [tilt] NM (*au billard électrique*) tilt signal; **faire tilt** to signal the end of the game; *Fig Fam* **ça a fait t.** the penny dropped, it clicked

timbale [tɛ̃bal] NF **1** *Mus* kettledrum; **les timbales** (*dans un orchestre*) the timpani **2** (*gobelet*) (metal) drinking cup; **t. en argent** (*donnée aux enfants baptisés*) silver christening cup; *Fig Fam* **décrocher la t.** to hit the jackpot **3** *Culin* (*moule*) timbale (mould *or Am* mold); (*plat*) timbale; **t. de langouste** lobster timbale

timbalier [tɛ̃balje] NM *Mus* timpanist

timbrage [tɛ̃braʒ] NM (*d'un passeport, d'une lettre etc*) stamping

timbre [tɛ̃br] NM **1** (*vignette*) stamp; **t.(-poste)** (*postage*) stamp; **mettre un t. sur une lettre** to stamp a letter, to put a stamp on a letter; **album de timbres** stamp album **2** (*marque, cachet*) (*sur un document etc*) stamp **3** (*tampon*) stamp **4** *Fin* (*droit*) stamp duty **5** (*sonnette*) bell; **t. de bicyclette** bicycle bell; **t. électrique** electric bell; *Fam Arch* **avoir le t. fêlé** to be cracked *or* daft, to have a screw loose **6** (*son*) (*d'une voix, d'un instrument*) timbre, tone; **voix sans t.** toneless voice; **une voix au t. argentin** a silvery voice **7** *Mus* (*d'un tambour*) snare **8** *Pharm* (*pour traitement médical*) patch
▸▸ **t. de collection** collector's stamp; **t. à date**, **t. dateur** date stamp; **t. à encrage automatique** self-inking stamp; **t. fiscal** excise *or* tax stamp; **t. humide** rubber stamp; *Com* **t. de pesage** weight stamp; **t. de quittance** receipt stamp; **t. sec** embossing press; *Méd* **t. tuberculinique** TB patch

Timbre fiscal
These stamps are sold at most tobacconists and are used to pay fees due for obtaining official documents, such as identity papers, vehicle documents and legal certificates.

timbré [tɛ̃bre] **ADJ 1** *(voix)* sonorous; **voix joliment** *ou* **agréablement timbrée** pleasant voice **2** *Fam (fou)* cracked, crazy **3** *(document, enveloppe etc)* stamped; **une enveloppe timbrée portant vos nom et adresse** a stamped addressed envelope, an sae

timbre-épargne, *pl* **timbres-épargne NM** savings-bank stamp

timbre-poste, *pl* **timbres-poste NM** (postage) stamp

timbre-prime, *pl* **timbres-prime NM** *Com* trading stamp

timbre-quittance, *pl* **timbres-quittances NM** receipt stamp

timbrer [tɛ̃bre] **VT 1** *(avec un tampon) (passeport, document etc)* to stamp; *(lettre, paquet etc)* to postmark; **lettre timbrée de Paris** letter with a Paris postmark, letter postmarked Paris **2** *(coller un timbre sur) (lettre etc)* to stamp, to put *or* stick a stamp/stamps on; **je n'ai pas assez timbré la lettre** I didn't put enough stamps *or* I put insufficient postage on the letter **3 papier timbré au chiffre de qn** paper stamped with sb's arms
VI *Suisse (pointer au chômage)* to sign on

timbre-taxe, *pl* **timbres-taxe NM** postage-due stamp

timide [timid] **ADJ 1** *(personne, sourire, voix, animal etc)* shy, timid; *(embarrassé)* bashful **2** *(timoré) (personne)* timid, timorous; *(critique, protestation, tentative etc)* timid **N** shy person; **c'est un grand t.** he's very shy

timidement [timidmɑ̃] **ADV 1** *(d'une manière gênée)* shyly, timidly, diffidently **2** *(d'une manière timorée)* timidly

timidité [timidite] **NF 1** *(gêne)* shyness, timidity, diffidence **2** *(manque d'audace)* timidity

timing [tajmiŋ] **NM** timing

timon [timɔ̃] **NM 1** *(d'un véhicule tiré par un cheval etc)* shaft, pole; *(d'une charrue)* beam; *Aut* trailing arm **2** *Naut Arch* tiller

timonerie [timɔnri] **NF 1** *Naut* **(kiosque de) t.** wheelhouse, pilot house **2** *Naut (fonction)* (naval) signalling **3** *Aut* steering gear; *(freins)* brake gear

timonier [timɔnje] **NM** *Naut (à la barre)* helmsman, man at the wheel; *(aux signaux)* signalman, wheelhorse, wheeler

Timor [timɔr] **NM** le**T.** *(l'île)* Timor

timorais, -aise [timɔre, -ez] **ADJ** Timorese **N T.** Timorese; **les T.** the Timorese; **T. de l'Est** East Timorese

Timor-Oriental [timɔrɔrjɑ̃tal] **NM** le**T.** East Timor

timoré [timɔre] **ADJ** timorous, fearful; *Rel, Litt (conscience)* overscrupulous

tinctorial, -iale, -iaux, -iales [tɛ̃ktɔrjal, -jo] **ADJ** *(plante, produit)* used in dyeing; *(procédé)* dyeing

tinette [tinɛt] **NF 1** *(baquet)* (sanitary) soil tub **2** *Fam* **tinettes** *(toilettes)* latrines

tins [tɛ̃] **NMPL** *Naut (en cale sèche)* keel blocks

tintamarre [tɛ̃tamar] **NM** *Fam (bruit)* din, racket; **faire du t.** to make a din *or* racket

tintement [tɛ̃t(ə)mɑ̃] **NM 1** *(d'une cloche)* ringing; **t. funèbre** tolling **2** *(de clochettes etc)* tinkling, tinkle; *(de grelots, de clés)* jingling, jingle; *(de pièces)* jingling, jingle,

chink(ing); *(de verres, bouteilles)* chink(ing), clink(ing)
▸▸ **t. d'oreilles** ringing *or* buzzing in the ears, *Spéc* tinnitus; **avoir des tintements d'oreilles** to have a ringing *or* buzzing (noise) in one's ears

tinter [tɛ̃te] **VT** *(cloche)* to ring; **t. la messe** to ring for mass
VI 1 *(d'une cloche)* to ring; *(de clochettes etc)* to tinkle; *(de verres, bouteilles)* to chink, to clink; *(de pièces)* to chink, to jingle; *(de grelots, de clés)* to jingle; **faire t. les verres** to chink *or* clink glasses; **le lustre en cristal tintait doucement** the crystal chandelier was tinkling softly **2** *(des oreilles)* to ring, to buzz; **les oreilles me tintaient** my ears were ringing *or* buzzing; *Fig* **les oreilles ont dû vous t. hier soir** *(on a parlé de vous)* your ears must have been burning last night

tintin [tɛ̃tɛ̃] **INT** *Fam* no way (José)!, nothing doing!; **faire t.** to go without; **tu peux faire t. pour tes places gratuites!** as for your free tickets, forget it *or* no way!

tintinnabuler [tɛ̃tinabyle] **VI** *Litt (des cloches)* to tinkle

Tintoret (le) [lətɛ̃tɔrɛ] **NM** Tintoretto

tintouin [tɛ̃twɛ̃] **NM** *Fam* **1** *(bruit)* din, racket **2** *(souci)* trouble, worry; **se donner du t.** to go to a lot of trouble

TIOP [tiɔp] **NM** *Banque (abrév* **taux interbancaire offert à Paris)** PIBOR

TIP [tip] **NM** *Banque (abrév* **titre interbancaire de paiement)** =payment slip for bills

tiper [tipe] **VT** *Suisse (achat)* to ring up; **est-ce que vous l'avez tipé?** have you counted that?, have you rung that up?

tipi [tipi] **NM** teepee

tip-top [tiptɔp] **ADJ INV 1** *(excellent)* first-rate **2** *Suisse (impeccable)* in tip-top condition, immaculate

tipule [tipyl] **NF** *Entom* crane fly

tique [tik] **NF** *Entom* tick; **collier anti-tiques** tick collar

tiquer [tike] **VI 1** *Fam (d'une personne)* to wince; **il n'a pas tiqué** he didn't turn a hair *or* bat an eyelid **2** *(d'un cheval)* to suck wind, to crib(-bite)

tiqueté [tikte] **ADJ** speckled, mottled, variegated

TIR [tir] **NM** *(abrév* **transport international de marchandises par route)** TIR, international transport of goods by road

tir [tir] **NM 1** *(activité)* shooting
2 *(action de tirer)* firing; *(feu)* fire; **il a un t. précis** he's a good shot *or* marksman; **il a un t. rapide** he shoots quickly; **un t. rasant/plongeant** raking/downward fire; **champ de t.** *(lieu)* firing range; *(d'une arme)* field of fire; **t. au but** precision firing; **t. au fusil** *ou* **à la carabine** rifle shooting; **habileté au t.** marksmanship; **cadence** *ou* **régime** *ou* **vitesse du t.** rate of fire; **allonger/raccourcir le t.** to increase/reduce the range; **t. de batterie** battery fire
3 *Min* blasting
4 *(concours)* shooting match *or* competition
5 *Sport (aux boules)* throw; *Ftbl* **t. (au but)** shot (at goal); *Ftbl* **t. d'angle** corner (kick); **apprendre la technique du t.** *(aux boules)* to learn how to throw; *Ftbl* **faire un t. du pied gauche** to shoot with the left foot
6 *(stand)* rifle range; **t. (forain)** shooting gallery
▸▸ **t. à l'arbalète** crossbow shooting; **t. à l'arc** archery; **tirs amis** friendly fire; **t. d'artillerie** artillery fire; **t. automatique** automatic fire; **arme à t. automatique** automatic weapon; **t. au pigeon (d'argile)** clay pigeon shooting

tirade [tirad] **NF 1** *Péj* tirade **2** *Théâtre* monologue

tirage [tiraʒ] **NM 1** *(de chariots etc)* pulling, hauling; *(de barges)* towing; *(chemin)* towpath; **cordons de t. d'un rideau** curtain pulls; **cheval de t.** draught *or* Am draft horse; *Élec* **interrupteur à t.** pull-and-push switch
2 *Fam (difficultés)* trouble, problems; **il va y avoir du t.** there's going to be trouble; **il y a du t. entre eux** there's friction between them, they don't get on together
3 *Métal* wire drawing; *(de la soie)* spinning
4 *(de rochers)* quarrying, extraction; **t. à la poudre** blasting
5 *(d'un conduit de cheminée)* draught, Am draft; **t. renversé** *ou* **inverti** back draught; *Aut* **carburateur à t. en bas** down-draught carburettor
6 *(de loterie)* drawing; **t. du numéro gagnant** draw for the winning number; **procéder à un t. au sort** to draw lots; **par t. au sort** *(élu etc)* by drawing lots
7 *Typ, Phot etc (action)* printing; *(objet)* print; *(nombre d'exemplaires sortis des presses) (d'un journal)* circulation; *(d'un livre)* print run; *(d'une gravure)* number printed, edition; *(d'un enregistrement)* edition; *Typ* **t. des épreuves** proofing; *Typ* **un mille de t.** (print) run of a thousand; **journal à gros** *ou* **grand t.** paper with a large circulation; **écrivain qui fait de gros tirages** bestselling author; **t. de luxe** de luxe edition; **t. numéroté** numbered edition; **t. à part** offprinting; **édition à t. limité** limited edition; *Typ* **t. héliographique** arc print; *Cin* **t. en surimpression** overprint
8 *Banque etc (d'un chèque, d'une lettre de change)* drawing, emission; *(d'un prêt)* draw down; **t. en blanc** *ou* **en l'air** drawing *or* emission of a dud cheque, *Spéc* kiting; *Compta* **tirages annuels** annual drawings

tiraillement [tirajmɑ̃] **NM 1** *(sur une corde etc)* tugging, pulling **2 tiraillements d'estomac** gnawing of the stomach, pangs of hunger **3** *(friction) (entre deux personnes)* friction, wrangling; *(entre deux choses contradictoires)* conflict (**entre** between); **il y a souvent eu des tiraillements entre eux** there was often friction between them, they often wrangled

tirailler [tiraje] **VT** to pull at, to tug at, to pull about; *Fig* **tiraillé entre deux émotions/ses parents** torn between two opposing feelings/one's parents
VI 1 *Mil* to shoot wildly; *(pour harceler)* to fire in skirmishing order **2 j'ai la peau qui me tiraille** my skin feels tight

tiraillerie [tirajri] **NF 1** *Mil* wild firing **2** *(friction)* wrangling, friction

tirailleur [tirajœr] **NM 1** *Mil* skirmisher, sharpshooter; *Hist* **tirailleurs algériens/sénégalais** native Algerian/Senegalese infantry; **en tirailleurs** in skirmishing order **2** *Journ Fam* freelance (journalist)

Tirana [tirana] **N** Tirana

tirant [tirɑ̃] **NM 1** *(de bourse)* (draw)string **2** *(de botte)* boot strap **3** *Constr (de toit)* tie beam **4** *Tech* stay, brace
▸▸ *Constr etc* **t. d'air** head room; *Naut* **t. d'eau** draught, *Am* draft; **avoir dix pieds de t. d'eau** to draw ten feet of water; **navire à faible t. d'eau** shallow-draught ship; **échelle de t. d'eau** draught marks *or* numbers; **t. de frein** brake rod

tire [tir] **NF 1 voleur à la t.** pickpocket; **vol à la t.** pickpocketing; **le nombre des vols à la t.** the number of cases of pickpocketing **2** *Can (confiserie)* molasses toffee, *Am* molasses candy, taffy; **t. d'érable** maple toffee *or* Am taffy **3** *Fam (voiture)* car, *Br* motor

tiré, -ée [tire] **ADJ 1** *(traits)* drawn, haggard; **il avait les traits tirés** his face was *or* he looked drawn *or* haggard; **aux cheveux tirés** with his/her hair drawn *or* pulled back **2** *Fig*

t. **par les cheveux** far-fetched **3** *Golf* **coup t.** pulled shot, pull **4 broderie à fils tirés** drawn-thread work **5** *Banque* **chèque t. sur qn** cheque drawn on sb; **personne tirée** drawee; **t. par la demande** demand-led

N *Com* drawee

NM 1 (*chasse*) shoot **2** *Typ* **t. à part** offprint, separate

NF tirée *Fam* **1** (*trajet*) long haul; **il y a encore une sacrée tirée** there's still a long way to go **2 une tirée de qch** (*grande quantité*) loads of sth

tire-au-cul NM INV *très Fam* shirker, *Br* skiver

tire-au-flanc NM INV *Fam* shirker, *Br* skiver

tire-botte, *pl* **tire-bottes** NM (*crochet*) boot-hook; (*planchette*) boot-jack

tire-bouchon, *pl* **tire-bouchons** NM **1** (*pour bouteille*) corkscrew; **en t.** (*queue*) curly **2** (*mèche*) corkscrew curl

tire-bouchonné, *pl* **tire-bouchonnés** ADJ (*pantalon*) crumpled; **ses chaussettes étaient tire-bouchonnées** his socks were round his ankles *or* at half-mast

tire-bouchonner [tirbuʃɔne] VT to twiddle **VI** (*chaussettes*) to be at half-mast; (*pantalon*) to be crumpled

tire-bouton, *pl* **tire-boutons** NM *Vieilli* buttonhook

tire-clous NM INV nail puller

tire-d'aile (à) ADV **s'envoler à t.** to fly swiftly away; *Fig* **partir** *ou* **s'éloigner à t.** to fly off; **s'enfuir à t.** to take flight

tirée [tire] NF *Fam* haul, trek; **ça fait une t. d'ici à là-bas** it's a bit of a haul *or* trek from here

tire-fesses NM INV *Fam* T-bar; **monter en t.** to go up by the T-bar, to take the T-bar up

tire-jus NM INV *Vulg* (*mouchoir*) hankie, snot rag

tire-laine NM INV *Vieilli* (*voleur*) footpad

tire-lait NM INV breast pump

tire-larigot (à) [atirlarigo] ADV *Fam* **boire/ manger à t.** to drink/eat one's fill *or* to one's heart's content, to have more than enough to drink/eat; **il y en a à t.** there's loads

tire-ligne, *pl* **tire-lignes** NM drawing pen

tirelire [tirlir] NF **1** (*pour économiser*) bank; *Fig* **il a dû casser sa t.** he had to break into his piggy bank **2** *Fam* (*figure*) mug; (*tête*) nut, bonce; (*ventre*) belly

tire-moelle [tirmwal] NM INV *Vulg* snot-rag

tire-pognon, *pl* **tire-pognons** NM *Fam Vieilli* one-arm(ed) bandit, fruit machine, *Am* slot machine

---

TIRER [tire]

VT to draw **1, 6, 8** ▪ to pull **3, 5** ▪ to print **7** ▪ to fire **9** ▪ to shoot **9** ▪ to let off **10**	
VI to shoot **1** ▪ to pull **2, 6** ▪ to shoot **3** ▪ to throw **3** ▪ to verge on (*tirer sur*) **5**	
VPR to get out of (*se tirer de*) **1** ▪ to be off **3**	

VT 1 (*étendre*) (*fil métallique, câble*) to draw; **t. ses cheveux en arrière** to pull one's hair back; *Fam* **encore une heure à t. d'ici le déjeuner!** still another hour to get through before lunch!; *Arg* **t. cinq ans** (*de prison*) to get five years *or* a five-year stretch

2 (*traire*) (*vache etc*) to milk

3 (*dans une direction*) to pull; (*cordon, sonnette*) to pull (on); (*chaussettes*) to pull up; **t. qn par la manche** to tug at *or* pull (on) sb's sleeve; **t. les cheveux à qn** to pull sb's hair; **je vais te t. les oreilles!** I'll give you what for!; **se faire t. les oreilles** to get told off; **t. la jambe** *ou Fam* **la patte** to limp; (*traîner*) to

lag behind; **t. les rideaux** to draw *or* pull the curtains; **t. le verrou** to shoot the bolt; (*pour ouvrir*) to draw the bolt; **t. qch vers le haut/ bas** to pull sth up/down; **t. qch à soi** to pull sth to *or* towards one; *Fig Fam* **t. la couverture à soi** to want more than one's share; *Fig* **t. un auteur à soi** to put a personal interpretation on an author's words; *Hist* **t. un criminel à quatre (chevaux)** to (hang,) draw and quarter a criminal

4 t. son chapeau à qn to raise *or* lift one's hat to sb; *Fig* **je te tire mon chapeau!** I take my hat off to you!

5 (*extraire*) (*bouchon, portefeuille etc*) to pull (out), to take out (**de** from, of); (*eau, vin, carte, conclusion*) to draw (**de** from); **t. les cartes** to read the cards; **se faire t. les cartes** to have one's cards read *or* one's fortune told; **t. plaisir/satisfaction de qch** to derive pleasure/satisfaction from sth, to get pleasure/satisfaction from *or* out of sth; **je n'en tire aucun(e) plaisir/satisfaction** I don't get any pleasure/satisfaction out of it; **t. vanité de qch** to pride oneself on sth; **d'où tire-t-elle cette certitude?** what makes her so certain?, *Fam* how come she's so sure?; **je n'ai rien pu t. de lui** I couldn't get anything *or* a word out of him; **t. qn d'un mauvais pas** *ou* **d'embarras/de prison** to get sb out of a tight spot *or* a difficulty/of prison; **t. qn de son lit** to drag *or* pull sb out of bed; **je ne vous tire par du lit, au moins?** I didn't get you out of bed, I hope?; **t. qn du sommeil** to drag sb from his/her sleep; **t. qn du doute** to remove sb's doubts; **t. qn de l'erreur** to show sb his/ her mistake; *Fam* **t. de l'argent de qn** to get money out of sb, to extract money from sb; **t. de l'huile des olives** to extract oil from olives; **t. un bénéfice** to take a profit; **ce mot tire son origine de …** this word has its origin(s) in …; **mot tiré du latin** word derived from Latin; **phrase tirée du Cid de Corneille** phrase taken from Corneille's Le Cid; **t. la racine carrée d'un nombre** to extract the square root of a number

6 (*tracer*) (*trait*) to draw; **t. des plans** to draw up *or* prepare plans; *Fig* **to make plans**

7 *Typ* (*gravure, épreuve*) to pull, to print (off), to strike off; (*livre*) to print; **t. un livre à cinq mille exemplaires** to print five thousand copies of a book; **donner le bon à t. d'un volume** to pass a book for press; *Phot* **t. une épreuve d'un cliché** to take a print from a negative; **t. à part** to offprint; *Hum* **se faire t. le portrait** to have one's photograph taken

8 *Com* (*lettre de change, chèque*) to draw (**sur** on); **avez-vous tiré des chèques depuis cette date?** have you written any cheques since then?; **ce chèque a-t-il déjà été tiré?** (*sur mon compte*) has this cheque cleared yet?

9 (*coup de feu, balle, roquette, canon*) to fire; (*flèche*) to shoot; (*feu d'artifice*) to let off; (*lièvre, oiseaux, gibier*) to shoot; **t. un coup de revolver sur qn** to fire *or* shoot at sb with a revolver; **ils se sont fait t. (dessus) comme des lapins** they were shot down like animals; *Vulg* **t. un coup** to get laid, to have a screw *or Br* a shag

10 *Naut* **navire qui tire vingt pieds** ship that draws twenty feet (of water)

VI 1 (*d'un tireur d'élite etc*) to shoot; (*d'une arme à feu*) to go off; **t. à bout portant** to fire at point blank range; **t. à couvert** to fire from cover; **t. à la carabine** to shoot with a rifle; **t. au hasard** to fire at random; **t. dans le dos de qn** to shoot sb in the back; **t. dans le tas** *ou* **la foule** to fire *or* shoot into the crowd; **t. en l'air** to fire into the air; **t. sur qn/qch** to shoot *or* fire at sb/sth

2 (*sur une corde etc*) to pull (**sur** on, at); **j'ai la peau qui tire** my skin feels tight; **t. sur sa pipe/cigarette** to pull *or* draw *or* puff on one's pipe/cigarette

3 *Sport, Ftbl* to shoot; (*aux boules*) to throw; *Ftbl* **t. au but** to shoot at goal

4 *Cartes* **t. pour la donne** to cut for deal

5 *Fig* **bleu tirant sur le vert** blue verging on green; **le jour tire à sa fin** the day is drawing to its close; **nos provisions tirent à leur fin** our stores are running low *or* are giving out; **t. en longueur** to drag; **cela ne tire pas à conséquence** it is of no consequence; **ça pourrait t. à conséquence pour ta carrière** it could have consequences for *or* be important to your career; *Fam* **t. à la ligne** to pad out an article; **t.** *Fam* **au flanc** *ou Vulg* **au cul** to skrive, *Br* to skive; **t. sur la soixantaine** to be getting on for sixty

6 *Aut* **t. sur la gauche/droite** to pull to the left/right; *Naut* **t. au large** to stand out to sea

7 (*d'une cheminée etc*) to draw

8 *Fin* **t. à découvert** to overdraw; **t. à vue** to draw at sight

9 *Suisse* (*thé*) to brew

10 *Belg, Suisse* **ça tire** there's a draught

VPR se tirer 1 se t. d'un mauvais pas to get out of a fix *or* a tight spot; **si tu crois t'en t. comme ça, tu te trompes!** if you think you're going to get out of it like that, you're mistaken!; **vous ne vous en tirerez pas avec cette excuse-là** you won't get away with that excuse; **va-t-elle s'en t.?** is she going to get out of it?; (*d'une maladie, d'un accident*) is she going to make it?, is she going to pull through?; **s'en t. sans aucun mal** to escape uninjured *or* unhurt *or* unscathed; **s'en t. tout juste** to escape by the skin of one's teeth; **on s'en tire, mais c'est juste** we only just manage to make both ends meet, we only just get by

2 *Fam* (*finir*) to come to an end; **ça se tire** it'll soon be over

3 (*partir*) to be off, to make tracks, to beat it; **on se tire?** shall we make tracks?, shall we get out of here?; **moi, je me tire** I'm off; **tire-toi, sale con!** beat it, dickhead!

---

tiret [tirɛ] NM *Typ* (*trait d'union*) hyphen; (*de dialogue*) dash; **ligne de tirets** broken line; *Ordinat* **t. conditionnel/insécable** soft/hard hyphen

tirette [tirɛt] NF **1** (*d'un bureau*) pull-out shelf; (*d'une table*) leaf **2** *Tech* pull handle, pull knob; (*d'un fourneau etc*) flue damper; *Aut etc* (pull-out) knob **3** *Belg* (*fermeture Éclair®*) zip, *Am* zipper

tireur, -euse [tirœr, -øz] N **1** *Com* (*d'un chèque, d'une lettre de change etc*) drawer **2 tireuse de cartes** fortune teller **3** *Phot* printer **4** (*d'arme*) **c'est un bon/mauvais t.** he's a good/bad shot **5** *Escrime Vieilli, Litt* **t. d'armes** fencer **6** (*aux boules*) thrower

NF tireuse 1 *Phot* (*appareil*) printer **2** (*pour remplir les bouteilles*) bottle-filling machine, bottle filler

▸▸ **t. d'élite** marksman, sharpshooter; **t. embusqué** *ou* **isolé** sniper

tiroir [tirwar] NM **1** (*d'une table, armoire etc*) drawer; **fonds de t.** (*petite monnaie*) small change; **râcler ses fonds de t.** to scrape one's pennies together; *Littér* **roman/comédie à tiroir(s)** episodic novel/ play; **nom à tiroir(s)** double-barrelled name **2** *Tech* (*d'une machine à vapeur*) slide, slide valve; **t. à papier** paper tray

tiroir-caisse, *pl* **tiroirs-caisses** NM *Com* till, cash register

tisane [tizan] NF **1** (*infusion*) herb(al) tea; **t. de camomille/menthe/verveine** camomile/ mint/verbena tea **2** *Arg* (*coups*) beating

tisanière [tizanjer] NF teapot (*for herbal tea*)

tison [tizɔ̃] NM **1** (*de bois*) (fire)brand; *Fig* **garder les tisons** to stay by the fire **2 allumette t.** fusee (match)

tisonné [tizɔne] ADJ (*robe d'un cheval*) with black spots

tisonner [tizɔne] VT *(feu)* to poke

tisonnier [tizɔnje] NM poker

tissage [tisaʒ] NM *Tex* **1** *(activité)* weaving; **t. à la main** *ou* **à bras** handloom weaving; **t. mécanique** power-loom weaving **2** *(installation)* cloth mill *or* works

tisser [tise] VT **1** *Tex* to weave; **t. sa toile** *(d'une araignée)* to spin its web **2** *Fig (intrigue)* to weave

VPR **se tisser** *Fig* **l'intrigue qui se tissait autour de cette disparition** the web of intrigue which was being woven around the disappearance

tisserand, -ande [tisrɑ̃, -ɑ̃d] N weaver

tisserin [tisrɛ̃] NM *Orn* weaver(bird)

tisseur, -euse [tisœr, -øz] N weaver

tissu [tisy] NM **1** *Tex* material, fabric, cloth; *Fig* **un t. de mensonges** a tissue of lies; **un t. d'absurdités** one absurdity after another; **c'est un t. de bêtises** it's complete and utter nonsense; **c'est un t. d'incohérences** it's full of inconsistencies **2** *Biol* tissue **3** *Fig* **le t. urbain/social/industriel** the urban/social/industrial fabric

▸▸ *Anat* **t. conjonctif** connective tissue; **t. métallique** wire gauze

> Il faut noter que le terme anglais **tissue** ne signifie jamais **textile**. Il signifie souvent **mouchoir en papier**.

tissu-éponge, *pl* **tissus-éponges** NM *Tex* (terry) towelling; **peignoir en t.** towelling robe; **serviette en t.** terry towel

tissulaire [tisylɛr] ADJ *Biol* (of) tissue

Titan [titɑ̃] NM *Myth, Astron*Titan; **travail de T.** *ou* **t.** Herculean task; **un combat de titans** an epic battle; *Ind* **grue T.** giant crane

titane [titan] NM *Chimie* titanium

titanesque [titanɛsk] ADJ *(entreprise, œuvre etc)* titanic; *(orgueil, force)* colossal

titi [titi] NM *Fam (gavroche)* cheeky urchin

Titien [tisjɛ̃] NM Titian

titillation [titilasjɔ̃] NF titillation

titiller [titije] VT *(chatouiller)*, *Fig* to titillate; **ma curiosité me titillait** I was consumed by curiosity

titisme [titism] NM *Pol* Titoism

titiste [titist] ADJ, N *Pol* Titoist

titrage [titraʒ] NM **1** *Chimie, Ind (d'une solution)* titration, titrating; *(d'un minerai etc)* assaying; *(d'un alcool, d'un vin etc)* determination of the strength **2** *Cin* titling; *Journ* **t. à cheval** spread head

titraille [titraj] NF *Journ* cover-line

TITRE [titr]

- title **1-3, 7, 9, 11** ▪ qualification **4**
- voucher **5** ▪ certificate **6** ▪ claim **7**
- heading **10** ▪ section **11**

NM **1** *(de noblesse, fonction etc)* title; **avoir un t. nobiliaire** to have a title; **porter le t. de duc** to bear the title of duke; **se donner le t. de ...** to call *or* Fml style oneself ...

2 *(qualification)* title; **avoir le t. d'avocat** to have the title of lawyer; **sans t. officiel** without any official status; **professeur en t.** permanent teacher; *Jur* **propriétaire en t.** legal owner; **la maîtresse en t. du roi** the King's acknowledged mistress; **elle ne mérite plus son t. d'amie, le t. d'amie ne lui convient plus** she no longer deserves the title of friend *or* to be called a friend

3 *Sport* title; *Boxe* **combat comptant/ne comptant pas pour le t.** title/non-title fight; **tenant du t.** titleholder; **champion en t.** reigning champion

4 *(diplôme etc)* qualification; **pourvu de tous ses titres** fully qualified

5 *(certificat)* voucher; *Mil* **t. de permission** pass

6 *Fin, Com* security bond, certificate; **titres** stocks and shares, securities, *Am* stock; **titres déposés en nantissement** securities lodged as collateral

7 *(droit)* title, claim, right; **t. juridique à qch** legal claim to sth

8 à t. de as a; **à t. d'office** ex officio; **à t. de précaution** just in case; **à t. d'ami** as a friend; **à t. d'essai** as a trial measure, experimentally; **à t. de faveur** as a favour; **il offre ses services à t. bénévole** he volunteers his services; **à juste t.** rightly; **il s'est mis en colère à juste t.** he got angry and rightly so, he was justifiably angry; **à quel t.?** by what right?, on what grounds?; **au même t.** for the same reason; **à t. gratuit** free of charge; **à ce t.** *(pour cette raison)* therefore; *(en cette qualité)* as such

9 *(de livre, chanson, film etc)* title

10 *(de chapitre, page)* heading; **(page de) t.** title page; **faux t.** half-title; *Journ* **les gros titres** the main headlines; **faire les gros titres** to hit the headlines, to be front page news

11 *(subdivision) (d'une loi etc)* part, section, title

12 *(d'une solution, d'or)* titre, *Am* titer; *(d'un minerai)* grade, content; *(d'une monnaie)* fineness

13 *(du coton, d'un fil de fer)* size, number

▸▸ **t. d'action** share certificate; **t. d'appel** *(publicité)* catch title; *Typ* **t. en bas de page** footer; **t. de civilité** *(dans une lettre)* salutation; *Typ* **t. courant** running head(er) *or* title; **t. de créance** loan note, debt instrument; **titres déposés en nantissement** securities lodged as collateral; **t. d'eau** degree of humidity; **titres émis** issued securities; **titres libérés** fully paid-up securities; **t. nominatif** registered security; **t. d'obligation** loan *or* bond note; **t. participatif** equity loan; **t. de participation** equity investment *or* loan; **titres de placement** marketable securities; **titres en portefeuille** securities (in portfolio); *Fin* **t. au porteur** bearer bond, negotiable instrument; *Jur* **t. de propriété** title deed; *Journ* **t. de rappel** coverline; **t. de rente** government bond; **titres à revenu fixe** fixed income securities; **titres à revenu variable** floating rate securities; **titres à terme** futures; **t. de transport** ticket; *Com* **t. universel de paiement** *(joint à la facture)* payment form, universal payment order

titré [titre] ADJ **1** *(personne)* titled **2** *Chimie (solution)* titrated, standard

titrer [titre] VT **1** *(personne)* to confer a title on; *(livre)* to title, to call **2** *Cin (film)* to title **3** *Chimie, Ind (solution)* to titrate, to standardize; *(minerai etc)* to assay; *(alcool, vin etc)* to determine the strength of **4** *Tex, Tech (coton, fil de fer etc)* to size, to number

titreur, -euse [titrœr, -øz] N *Journ* headline writer

titreuse [titrøz] NF *Cin (appareil)* titler

titrisation [titrizasjɔ̃] NF *Bourse* securitization

titubant [titybɑ̃] ADJ reeling, lurching, staggering

tituber [titybe] VI to reel (about), to lurch, to stagger; **marcher/entrer/sortir en titubant** to stagger *or* lurch along/in/out; **t. de fatigue** to reel *or* stagger *or* totter with exhaustion

titulaire [titylɛr] ADJ *(professeur etc)* with tenure; **devenir t.** to get tenure; **être t. d'un passeport/d'un permis de conduire** to have *or* hold a passport/driving licence

N **1** *(d'un droit, d'un titre, d'un certificat etc)* holder; *(d'un passeport)* holder, bearer; *(d'un office)* holder, occupant, *Admin* incumbent; *Rel (d'une paroisse)* incumbent; **t. d'action** shareholder **2** *Sport* team member; **il a plus de sélections comme remplaçant que comme t.** he has made the squad (as a sub) more often than he has made the team

titularisation [titylarizasjɔ̃] NF **1** *Admin (des fonctionnaires etc)* establishment **2** *Sport* inclusion in the full team

titulariser [titylarize] VT **1** *Admin etc* **t. qn** to confirm sb in his post *or* appointment **2** *Sport* to include in a/the team; **titularisé pour l'équipe de France** capped for France; **quand j'ai été titularisé pour la première fois** the first time I made it into the full team

TJJ [teʒiʒi] NM *Fin (abrév* **taux d'argent au jour le jour**) overnight *or* call rate

TMG [teɛmʒe] NM *(abrév* **temps moyen de Greenwich**) GMT

TNT [teɛnte] NM *(abrév* **trinitrotoluène**) TNT

NF *(abrév* **télévision numérique terrestre**) DTT

toast [tost] NM **1** *(tranche de pain grillé)* piece *or* slice of toast; **t. beurré** piece *or* slice of buttered toast; **des toasts** toast, toasted bread **2** *(hommage)* toast; **porter un t. à qn** to drink *or* propose a toast to sb, to toast sb

toasteur [tostœr] NM toaster

toboggan [tɔbɔgɑ̃] NM **1** *(de piscine)* chute; *(de terrain de jeu etc)* slide; *(dans un parc d'attractions)* helter-skelter; **des enfants qui font du t.** children playing on the slide **2** *Com etc (pour marchandises)* chute **3** *Aut* flyover, *Am* overpass **4** *Can (traîneau)* toboggan; **faire du t.** to go tobogganing; **piste de t.** toboggan run

> Il faut noter que le terme anglais **toboggan** est un faux ami. Il signifie **luge**.

toc [tɔk] INT tap!; **t. t.!** knock knock!; **et t.!** so there!

NM **1** *(à la porte etc)* tap, rap; **j'ai entendu un t. t. à la porte** I heard a tap tap *or* a tapping at the door **2** *Fam (imitation)* **bijoux en t.** imitation *or* paste jewellery; **c'est du t.** it's imitation *or* fake

ADJ INV *Fam* **1** *(faux)* fake; *(de mauvais goût)* tacky, *Br Fam* naff **2** **être un peu t. t.** *(fou)* to be a bit crazy *or* cracked; **il est un peu t. t.** he's not all there

tocante [tɔkɑ̃t] NF *Fam (montre)* watch

tocard, -arde [tɔkar, -ard] *Arg* ADJ worthless, trashy

NM *Courses de chevaux* (rank) outsider

N *Péj (personne)* loser, dead loss

toccata [tɔkata] NF *Mus* toccata

tocsin [tɔksɛ̃] NM alarm bell, *Fml* tocsin; **faire sonner le t.** to sound the alarm (bell) *or* Fml tocsin

tof, toffe [tɔf] ADJ *Belg Fam (excellent)* great, fantastic

toge [tɔʒ] NF **1** *Antiq* toga **2** *Jur, Scol* gown

Togo [tɔgo] NM Togo

togolais [tɔgɔlɛ] ADJ, NM Togolese

tohu-bohu [tɔybɔy] NM INV *(désordre)* chaos, confusion; *(bruit)* hubbub; **dans un t. général** amidst general confusion

toi [twa] PRON PERS **1** you; *Bible, Arch* thou; *(complément direct)* you; *Bible, Arch* thee; **c'est t.** it's you; **c'est t. qui l'as fait** you did it; **ah c'est bien t., ça!** that's typical of you!, that's just like you!; **t. et moi nous irons ensemble** you and I will go together; **il est plus âgé que t.** he is older than you; **il n'aime que t.** he loves only you; **dis-le-lui, t.** you tell him; **avec t.** with you; **ce livre est à t.** this book is yours *or* belongs to you; **à t., je peux le dire** I can tell you; **moi, je reste, et t., tu pars** I'll stay and you go; **t. parti, que vais-je faire?** once you've gone *or* with you gone, what am I going to do? **2** *(reflexive)* **dépêche-t.!** hurry up!; **tais-t.!** be quiet!; **assieds-t.!** sit down!; **maîtrise-t.!** control yourself!

toile [twal] NF **1** cloth; **t. (de lin)** linen; **drap de t.** linen sheet; *Fam* **se mettre dans les toiles** to hit the sack *or* hay; **t. (de coton)** cotton; **pantalon de t.** lightweight trousers; **marchand de t.** draper; **reliure en t.** cloth binding; **sac en t.** canvas bag; **collé sur t.** mounted on canvas **2** *Beaux-Arts (œuvre)* painting, canvas; *(support)* canvas **3** *Naut (voiles)* canvas, sails; **réduire la t.** to reduce sail **4** *(de moulin)* **toiles** sails **5** *Fam (film)* **se faire une t.** to go to the cinema *or Am* movies **6** *Ordinat* **la T.** the Web
▸▸ **t. d'amiante** asbestos; **t. d'araignée** cobweb, spider's web; **t. à bâches** tarpaulin; **t. cirée** American cloth, oilcloth; **nappe en t. cirée** waxed tablecloth; **t. (d')émeri** emery cloth; *Théâtre* **t. de fond** backdrop, backcloth; *Fig* **avec la guerre en t. de fond** with the war as a backdrop, against the backdrop of the war; **t. de Jouy** toile de Jouy; **t. de maître** masterpiece, old master; **t. à matelas** tick, ticking; **t. métallique** wire gauze; **t. de tente** canvas; **t. à voiles** canvas, sailcloth

toilerie [twalri] NF *(commerce)* cotton, linen and hemp industry *or* trade; *(fabrique)* cotton, linen and hemp mill

toilettage [twalɛtaʒ] NM *(d'un animal domestique)* grooming; *Fig* **faire le t. d'un texte** to put the finishing touches to a text

toilette [twalɛt] NF **1** *(action de se laver)* washing, *Litt* toilet; **faire sa t.** to have a wash, to get washed; **être à sa t.** *(se laver)* to be having a wash, to be getting washed; *Vieilli (s'apprêter)* to be making one's toilet; **faire un bout** *ou* **un brin de t.** to have a wash and brush up, to freshen up; *Fig* **faire une t. de chat** to have a cat's lick, to have a lick and a promise; **le chat fait sa t.** the cat is washing *or* grooming itself; **savon de t.** toilet soap **2** **toilettes** *(W.-C.)* toilet, *Am* washroom, *Am* rest room, *Br Fam* loo; *(publiques)* public convenience *or* lavatory; **toilettes pour dames** ladies' toilet *or Am* room; **toilettes pour hommes** gents' toilet, *Am* men's room **3** *(vêtements de femme)* dress, clothes; *(costume)* outfit; **elle porte bien la t.** she looks good in formal clothes; **être en (grande) t.** to be in formal dress, to be formally dressed; **t. de bal** ball dress; **changer de t.** to change one's clothes

toiletter [twalete] VT *(animal domestique)* to groom; *Fig (texte)* to put the finishing touches to
VPR **se toiletter** *Can* to dress up (smartly)

toi-même PRON PERS yourself; *Bible, Arch* thyself; *voir* **même 3**

toise [twaz] NF *(règle)* height gauge; **se mettre sous la t.** to have one's height measured; **passer qn à** *ou* **sous la t.** to measure sb's height

toisé [twaze] NM *Tech* measuring (up), measurement

toiser [twaze] VT **1** *(regarder)* **t. qn** to look *or* eye sb up and down **2** *Vieilli (mesurer)* to measure (the height of)
VPR **se toiser** *(se regarder)* to look each other up and down, to take each other's measure

toison [twazɔ̃] NF *(de mouton)* fleece; *(de lion, de cheval)* mane; *Fig (chevelure)* mane (of hair); *(poils)* fleece, thick body hair; *Myth* **la T. d'or** the Golden Fleece

toit [twa] NM **1** *(de maison, voiture etc)* roof; *Fig (habitation)* home (of one's own); **t. d'ardoises/de tuiles/de chaume** slate/tiled/thatched roof; *Beaux-Arts* **paysage de toits** roofscape; **trouver un t. pour ses enfants** to put a roof over one's children's heads, to find a home for one's children; **sous son t.** under one's (own) roof; **abriter qn sous son t.** to take sb in, to put sb up; **je suis restée plusieurs jours sous leur t.** I stayed with them for several days; **se retrouver sans t.**

to find oneself without a roof over one's head; **habiter sous les toits** to live in a garret; **chambre sous les toits** attic room; *Fig* **publier** *ou* **crier qch sur les toits** to proclaim sth from the rooftops *or* housetops; **double t.** *(de tente)* flysheet; **le t. paternel/familial** the family home; **le t. conjugal** the marital home **2** *Min (d'une mine)* roof, top
▸▸ *Aut* **t. à arceau** en T T-bar roof; *Aut* **t. ouvrant** sun roof; *Aut* **t. ouvrant coulissant** sliding sunroof

toiture [twatyr] NF roofing, roof; **refaire la t.** to repair the roof

tokai, tokay [tɔkɛ] NM *(vin)* Tokay

Tokyo [tɔkjo] N Tokyo

tôle¹ [tol] NF **1** *(matériau)* sheet metal; *(de fer)* sheet iron; **t. d'acier** sheet steel; **t. de cuivre** copper sheeting **2** *(feuille)* metal sheet; *(de fer)* iron sheet; *(d'acier)* steel sheet
▸▸ **t. ondulée** corrugated iron; **toit en t. ondulée** corrugated iron roof

tôle² NF *Arg (prison)* = **taule 1**

tôlée [tole] ADJ F, NF *Ski (neige)* **t.** crusted snow

tolérable [tɔlerabl] ADJ *(supportable) (douleur, situation)* bearable, tolerable; **votre comportement n'est pas t.** your behaviour is unacceptable

tolérance [tɔlerɑ̃s] NF **1** *(compréhension)* tolerance; *Rel* toleration; **faire preuve de t.** to be tolerant; **manquer de t.** to lack tolerance, to be intolerant; *Arch* **maison de t.** licensed brothel; *Pol* **t. zéro** zero tolerance **2** *(concession)* concession; **t. orthographique** acceptable variation in spelling **3** *Tech* tolerance, margin; **t. nulle** zero allowance; **à t. de pannes** fault-tolerant; **t. sur l'épaisseur/la longueur** thickness/length margin; **t. de fonctionnement** operational tolerance; *Électron* **t. de fréquence** frequency tolerance **4** *(à la douane)* **t. (permise)** allowance; **il y a une t. d'un demi-litre** you are allowed to bring in half a litre duty-free **5** *Méd* tolerance; **t. immunitaire** immune tolerance

tolérant, -ante [tɔlerɑ̃, -ɑ̃t] ADJ, N tolerant *(person)*

tolérer [tɔlere] (je **tolère**, n. **tolérons**; je **tolérerai**) VT **1** *(être indulgent pour) (opinions, religions etc)* to tolerate; *(supporter) (personne, situation)* to tolerate, to put up with; **je ne tolère pas qu'on dise ça** I cannot tolerate people saying that (kind of thing) **2** *Méd (médicament)* to tolerate
VPR **se tolérer** to put up with *or* tolerate each other

tôlerie [tolri] NF **1** *(commerce)* sheet-metal trade **2** *(atelier)* sheet-metal workshop; *Aut* body shop **3** *(tôles)* metal sheets *or* plates; *Aut* panels, bodywork

tôlier¹ [tolje] NM **1** *(marchand)* sheet-iron merchant **2** *(ouvrier)* sheet-metal worker; *Aut* panel beater

tôlier², -ière [tolje, -jɛr] N *Arg* = **taulier**

tollé [tɔle] NM (indignant) outcry; **t. général** public outcry

toluène [tɔlɥɛn] NM *Chimie* toluene, methyl benzene

TOM [tɔm] NM *abrév* **territoire d'outre-mer**

tomahawk [tɔmaok] NM tomahawk

tomaison [tɔmɛzɔ̃] NF *Typ* volume numbering

tomate [tɔmat] NF **1** *Bot, Culin* tomato; **sauce t.** tomato sauce; **salade/jus de t.** tomato salad/juice; **concentré de tomates** tomato concentrate *or* purée; *Fam* **être (rouge) comme une t.** to be as red as a beetroot VOIR GRAMMAIRE A12 **2** *Fam (boisson)* pastis with grenadine

tombal, -ale, -aux, -ales [tɔ̃bal, -o] ADJ

pierre tombale tombstone, gravestone; **inscription tombale** tombstone *or* gravestone inscription

tombant [tɔ̃bɑ̃] ADJ **1** **à la nuit tombante** at nightfall **2** *(draperies)* flowing; *(cheveux)* loose; *(branche, oreilles d'un animal, moustache)* drooping; *(épaules)* sloping; **des yeux aux paupières tombantes** hooded eyes

tombe [tɔ̃b] NF **1** *(sépulture)* grave; *(avec un monument)* tomb; **prier sur la t. de qn** to pray at sb's grave(side); **t. collective** mass grave; **être dans la t.** to be dead; **avoir un pied dans la t.** to have one foot in the grave; **suivre qn dans la t.** to follow sb to the grave; **se retourner dans sa t.** to turn in one's grave **2** *(pierre tombale)* tombstone, gravestone

| Do not confuse with **tombeau**. |

tombé [tɔ̃be] ADJ *Rugby* **coup de pied t.** drop kick

tombeau, -eaux [tɔ̃bo] NM tomb; **t. de famille** family vault; **descendre au t.** to go to one's grave; **mettre au t.** to entomb; **mise au t.** entombment; *Fam* **il me mettra** *ou* **conduira au t.** *(il me tuera)* he'll be the death of me; *Fig* **le t.** *(la mort)* the grave; *Fig* **cette pièce est un vrai t.** it's pitch dark in here; *Fig* **à t. ouvert** *(conduire, rouler)* at breakneck speed

| Do not confuse with **tombe**. |

tombée [tɔ̃be] NF **1** **t. du jour** *ou* **de la nuit** nightfall; **à la t. de la nuit** at nightfall **2** *Journ (pour la remise d'un travail)* copy deadline; *(pour la sortie d'une édition)* edition time

tomber¹ [tɔ̃be] NM **1** **au t. du jour** at nightfall **2** *Sport (de lutte)* fall

TOMBER²

VI to fall **1, 2** ▪ to fall out **1** ▪ to fall off **1** ▪ to fall down **1** ▪ to drop **2** ▪ to die down **2** ▪ to knock down *(faire tomber)* **1** ▪ to come across *(tomber sur)* **4** ▪ to fall on *(tomber sur)* **4** ▪ to fall on **5** ▪ to hang down **6**
VT to throw **1** ▪ to take off **2**

VI *(aux* **être***)* **1** *(d'une personne, d'un objet)* to fall (down); *(d'un avion, de feuilles, de la neige etc)*, *Mil (d'une ville)*, *Fig (du gouvernement)* to fall; **le plafond est tombé** the ceiling has come down *or* fallen in; **toutes les feuilles de ma plante sont tombées** all the leaves have dropped off my plant, my plant has lost *or* shed all its leaves; **fruits tombés** windfalls; **les gens tombent comme des mouches** people are dropping like flies; **mes cheveux commencent à t.** I'm beginning to lose my hair, my hair is beginning to fall out; *TV, Radio* **la nouvelle est tombée ce matin et c'est la guerre!** the news came through this morning and it's war!; *Fig* **il faut être tombé bien bas** you have to have sunk pretty low; **t. à l'eau** to fall in (the water); *Fig (d'un projet etc)* to fall through, to come to nothing; **t. à plat** *(échouer) (d'une proposition, une plaisanterie)* to fall flat, *Fam* to go down like a lead balloon; *Fig* **t. de haut** to be dumbfounded; **t. dans un piège** to fall into a trap; *Fig Fam* **t. dans les pommes** to pass out, to faint, to keel over; **t. dans le coma** to lapse into a coma; **t. d'une échelle/du toit/de cheval/de vélo** to fall off a ladder/the roof/one's horse/one's bike; **le livre lui est tombé des mains** the book fell *or* dropped from *or* out of his hands; *Fig* **son dernier roman m'est tombé des mains** his last novel didn't hold my interest; **je tombe de fatigue** *ou* **de sommeil** I'm ready to drop, I'm dead on my feet; **tout tombe en poussière** everything is crumbling to dust; **les bras m'en tombent** I can't believe it; **t. la tête la première** to fall head first, *Fam* to take a header; **t. à la renverse** to fall backwards; **t. sur ses pieds** to fall on one's feet; **t. par terre** *(d'une personne)* to fall; *(d'un objet)* to fall (to the ground); **ce livre m'est tombé sous la main** I came across this book; **comment ce papier a-t-il pu lui t. sous la main?** how could the paper have fallen into his hands?; **ça tombe sous le sens** it stands to reason, it's obvious; **sa décision tombe sous le sens** it stands to reason that he decided as he did; *Math* **t. juste** to come out exactly; **cet argent lui tombe du ciel** the money is a godsend to him; *Naut* **t. sous le vent** to fall off, to fall to leeward; **faire t.** *(d'une personne)* to knock over *or* down; *(du vent)* (table, chaise) to knock over *or* down; *(arbre, barrière), Fig (gouvernement etc)* to bring down, to topple; **laisser t.** *(objet), Fig (projet)* to drop; *Fig Fam* **laisser t. qn** *or* dump sb; *(lui faire faux bond)* to let sb down; *Fig Fam* **laisse t., ça ne vaut pas la peine** forget it, it's not worth it; **se laisser t. dans un fauteuil** to drop *or* sink *or Fam* flop into an armchair

2 *(diminuer)* *(du vent)* to drop, to abate, to subside, to die down; *(des prix, de la fièvre)* to drop, to fall; *(de la colère)* to die down, to abate; *(de la conversation)* to flag; *(de l'enthousiasme, l'intérêt)* to wane, to decline, *Fam* to fizzle out; *(des ventes, du nombre des adhésions)* to drop, to decline; **la nuit** *ou* **le jour tombe** night is falling; **une fois la nuit tombée** after dark; **cela va faire t. la fièvre** this will bring your/his/*etc* temperature down

3 *(indique une transformation)* **t. en disgrâce/en ruine** to fall into disgrace/ruin(s); **t. amoureux,** *Can* **t. en amour** to fall in love (**de qn** with sb); **t. malade** to fall ill; **t. (raide) mort** to drop (down) dead; **t. enceinte** to get pregnant

4 t. sur *(attaquer) Mil (ennemi)* to attack, to fall on; *Fam (personne)* to pitch *or* light into; *(rencontrer) (personne)* to bump into, to come across; *(objet)* to come across *or* upon; **il fallait que ça tombe sur moi!** it had to happen to me!; **et c'est tombé sur lui** and he was chosen, and the choice fell on him; **avec tous les ennuis qui me tombent dessus** with all these worries plaguing me; **si tu savais tout ce qui me tombe dessus** if you only knew all the things I've got on my mind; **il va nous t. sur le dos d'un moment à l'autre** he'll be bursting in on us any moment; **ils nous tombent toujours dessus à l'improviste** they're always dropping in on us

5 *(arriver)* **Noël tombe un jeudi cette année** Christmas falls on *or* is on a Thursday this year; **t. pile** *ou* **à pic** *ou* **à propos** to come at (just) the right moment *or* time; **vous tombez bien** you've come at the right moment, you're just in time; **cet argent/cette invitation tombe vraiment très bien** *ou* **à pic** the money/the invitation has come just at the right time; **cela tombe mal** it's come at the wrong time, it's not a good time; **tu tombes mal** this is not a good time, you've come at the wrong time; **tu tombes mal, j'avais déjà acheté le livre** you picked the wrong thing, I already have the book; **comme ça tombe!** what a coincidence!; *Fam* **ça tombe comme un cheveu sur la soupe** it has come at an awkward moment *or* time

6 *(pendre)* *(de cheveux)* to hang down; *(de draperies)* to fall, to hang (down); *(d'un tissu, d'un vêtement)* to hang; **ses cheveux lui tombent dans le dos** her hair hangs down her back

VT *(aux* avoir*)* **1** *Sport* **t. un adversaire** to throw *or* pull an opponent; *Fam* **t. une femme** to pull a woman

2 *Fam* **t. la veste** to take off one's jacket

V IMPERS il tombe de la pluie/de la grêle it is raining/hailing; **il tombe des grêlons énor-**

mes enormous hailstones are coming down; **qu'est-ce qu'il tombe!** it's really coming down!

tombereau, -eaux [tɔ̃bʀo] **NM 1** *(charrette)* tip-cart; *(contenu)* cartload (**de** of) **2** *(camion)* dumper; **t. à ordures** bin lorry, *Am* garbage truck

tombeur [tɔ̃bœʀ] **NM** *Fam* **1** *(séducteur)* womanizer, *Am* mack **2** *(vainqueur)* **c'est lui le t. du champion du monde** he's the man who defeated the world champion

tombola [tɔ̃bɔla] **NF** raffle, tombola

Tombouctou [tɔ̃buktu] **N** Timbuktu

tome [tɔm] **NM** *(volume)* volume; *(division)* *(d'un livre)* part

tomette [tɔmɛt] **NF** (small red hexagonal) floor tile

tomien, -ienne [tɔmjɛ̃, -jɛn] **ADJ** of/from the French overseas territories

N T. *(natif)* = native of the French overseas territories; *(habitant)* = inhabitant of the French overseas territories

tomme [tɔm] **NF** Tomme, = cheese made in Savoie and Dauphiné

tomographie [tɔmɔgʀafi] **NF** *Méd* tomography

tom-pouce, *pl* **tom-pouces** [tɔmpus] **NM 1** *Fam* dwarf, midget **2** *(petit parapluie)* stumpy umbrella

ton¹, ta, tes [tɔ̃, ta, te] **ADJ POSS** (**ton** *is used instead of* **ta** *before f words beginning with vowel or mute h*) your; *Bible, Arch* thy; **t. ami/amie** your friend; **t. meilleur ami/ta meilleure amie** your best friend; **t. oncle et ta tante** your aunt and (your) uncle; **t. père et ta mère,** *Litt* **tes père et mère** your mother and father; **j'ai mis t. chapeau et tes gants** I put on your hat and (your) gloves; **un(e) de tes ami(e)s** one of your friends, a friend of yours; **un professeur de tes amis** a teacher friend of yours; *Fam* **tu auras ta chambre à toi** you'll have your own room; *Fam* **t. imbécile de frère** your idiot of a brother; *Fam* **t. artiste de mari** your artist husband; *Fam* **alors, je peux le rencontrer, t. artiste?** so, can I meet this artist of yours?; *Fam* **tu as eu t. vendredi** you got Friday off; *Fam* **alors, c'était ça tes vacances de rêve!** so much for your dream holiday! SEE GRAMMAR A30; B21–2

ton² **NM 1** *(qualité de voix)* tone; *(hauteur)* pitch; **parler d'un t. doux/sur un t. amical** to speak gently *or* in a gentle tone/in a friendly tone; **je souhaiterais que tu me parles sur un autre t., je te prie de changer de t.** quand tu me parles don't talk to me in that tone of voice, I don't like your tone; **sur le t. de la plaisanterie** jokingly, in a joking tone of voice; **écrire sur un t. de plaisanterie** to write in a humorous tone *or* style; **si tu le prends sur ce t. …** if that's how you feel …, if you're going to be like that then …; **hausser le t.** to raise one's voice; **parler d'un t. bas** to speak in a low tone; **entre deux tons** in an undertone; *Fam* **faire baisser le t. à qn** to take sb down a peg or two

2 *(goût)* manners; **le bon t.** good form *or* manners; **il est de bon t. de ne pas se faire remarquer** it's the done thing *or* it's good form not to attract attention; **c'est de mauvais t.** it is not the done thing, it is bad form *or* bad manners *or* vulgar; **remarques de bon t.** remarks in good taste

3 *Mus (tonalité)* key; **le t. d'ut** the key of C; **(hauteur du)** t. pitch; **donner le t.** to give the tuning A; *Fig* to set the tone; **sortir du t.** to be out of tune; **se mettre dans le t.** to tune up; *Fig* to blend *or* fit in

4 *Mus (intervalle)* tone et demi-tons tones and semitones; **t. entier** whole tone

5 *Ling* tone; **langue à tons** tonal language

6 *Beaux-Arts, Phot etc (couleur)* tone, shade; **tapis dans le t. des rideaux** carpet toning

(in) with the curtains; **pour que tout l'ameublement soit dans le même t.** so that all the furniture tones in; **peinture/voiture deux tons** two-tone paint/car; *Ordinat* **tons de gris** shades of grey

tonal, -ale, -als, -ales [tɔnal] **ADJ** *Mus* tonal

tonalité [tɔnalite] **NF 1** *Beaux-Arts, Phot, Mus* tonality; *(ton)* key; *(d'instrument, de voix)* *Mus (de morceau), Beaux-Arts (de paysage), Fig (de film, livre)* tone; **j'aime la t. de cet instrument/de sa voix** I like the way the instrument/his voice sounds, I like the timbre of the instrument/his voice **2** *Tél* **t. (continue)** dialling *or Am* dial tone; **t. de réponse** answer tone; **attendez d'avoir la t.** wait for the dialling tone; **t. d'appel** ringing tone; **il n'y a plus de t.** there's no dialling tone, the phone's dead **3** *(de poste de radio etc)* tone

tondeur, -euse [tɔ̃dœʀ, -øz] **N** *(de moutons, drap)* shearer; **t. de moutons** sheepshearer

NF tondeuse 1 *(instrument)* *(de moutons, drap)* shears; *(pour cheveux, pelage)* clippers **2 tondeuse (à gazon)** (lawn) mower; **tondeuse électrique/mécanique** electric/hand mower; **passer la tondeuse à gazon** to mow the lawn, to give the lawn a mow

tondre [tɔ̃dʀ] **VT 1** *(moutons, drap)* to shear; *(animal, haie)* to clip; *(cheveux)* to shave off; *(pelouse)* to mow; **se faire t.** to have all one's hair shaved off; **tu t'es fait t.!** who scalped you? **2** *Fam (dépouiller)* *(personne)* to fleece; *Fig* **il tondrait un œuf** he's a real skinflint *or* scrooge *or Am* tightwad

tondu [tɔ̃dy] **ADJ** *(gazon)* mown; *(chien, haie)* clipped; *(moutons)* shorn; *(cheveux)* shaved off; *(tête)* shaved; **être complètement t.** to have had all one's hair shaved off, to have a shaved head

NM *Rel* monk; *Hist Fam* **le Petit T.** Napoleon (Bonaparte)

toner [tɔnɛʀ] **NM** *(pour imprimante etc)* toner

tong [tɔ̃g] **NF** *(chaussure de plage)* flip-flop, *Am* thong

Tonga [tɔ̃ga] **NFPL les (îles) T.** Tonga

tonicardiaque [tɔnikaʀdjak] *Méd* **ADJ** which stimulates the heart, *Spéc* cardiotonic

NM heart stimulant, *Spéc* cardiotonic

tonicité [tɔnisite] **NF** *Méd (des muscles etc)* tone; *(de l'air marin etc)* bracing *or* tonic effect

tonifiant [tɔnifjɑ̃] **ADJ** *(air, marche etc)* bracing; *(lotion)* tonic

tonifier [tɔnifje] **VT** *(impf, pr sub n.* **tonifiions,** *v.* **tonifiiez)** *(muscles, peau, système nerveux, malade etc)* to tone up; **un bain froid, ça tonifie** a cold bath is bracing *or* invigorating

tonique [tɔnik] **ADJ 1 médicament t.** tonic; **lotion t.** *(pour le visage)* toning lotion, toner **2** *(revigorant)* *(air marin, climat, froid etc)* bracing, invigorating **3** *Ling (accent)* tonic; *(syllabe)* accented, stressed; **l'accent t. tombe sur …** the stress falls on … **4** *Mus* **note t.** tonic, keynote

NM *Méd* tonic; *(pour le visage)* toner, toning lotion

NF *Mus* tonic, keynote

tonitruant [tɔnitʀyɑ̃] **ADJ** *(voix)* like thunder, thundering; **…, dit-il d'une voix tonitruante …,** he thundered

tonitruer [tɔnitʀye] **VI** to thunder

tonka [tɔ̃ka] **NM** *Bot* tonka bean (plant); **fève t.** tonka bean

NF tonka bean

tonnage [tɔnaʒ] **NM** *Naut* **1** *(de navire)* tonnage; **t. brut** gross tonnage; **t. net** register tonnage; *(d'un navire de guerre)* displacement; **t. port en lourd** deadweight tonnage **2** *(d'un port)* tonnage **3** *(droit de)* **t.** (duty based on) tonnage

tonnant [tɔnɑ̃] ADJ thundering; **voix tonnante** voice of thunder, thunderous voice

tonne [tɔn] NF **1** (unité de poids) (metric) ton, tonne (1000 kg); **un camion de 8 tonnes, un 8 tonnes** an 8-ton lorry, an 8-tonner; Fig Fam **des tonnes (et des tonnes) de** tons (and tons) of **2** (récipient) tun, (large) cask
▸▸**t. d'arrimage** measurement ton; **courte t.** short ton (907.185 kg); Naut **t. de déplacement** ton of displacement, displacement ton; **t. d'encombrement** measurement ton; **t. équivalent charbon** ton coal equivalent; **t. équivalent pétrole** ton oil equivalent; **t. forte** long or gross ton (1016.06 kg); Naut **t. de jauge** gross or register ton; **t. kilométrique** ton kilometre or Am kilometer

tonneau, -eaux [tɔno] NM **1** barrel, cask; **mettre du vin en t.** to put wine into barrels or casks; **bière au t.** draught or Am draft beer; Fig **ils sont tous du même t.** they're all the same; Fig **des remarques du même t.** remarks in the same vein; **petit t.** keg; **t. à mortier** mortar mixer; Hist **le t. de Diogène** Diogenes' tub; **t. de fret** freight ton; Fig **c'est le t. des Danaïdes** it's a never-ending task, it's no sooner finished than you have to start all over again; **t. d'arrosage** water cart **2** Naut (unité de volume) ton; **navire de 500 tonneaux** 500-tonner, ship of 500 tons burden **3** Hist (voiture à cheval) governess cart **4** Aviat, Aut roll, roll-over; **faire un t.** Aviat to do a barrel roll; Aviat, Aut (par accident) to flip or roll over; **la voiture a fait trois tonneaux** the car flipped or rolled over three times

tonnelet [tɔnlɛ] NM (small) cask, keg

tonnelier [tɔnəlje] NM cooper

tonnelle [tɔnɛl] NF **1** (charmille) arbour, Am arbor, Br bower **2** Archit barrel or tunnel vault

tonnellerie [tɔnɛlri] NF cooperage

tonner [tɔne] VI **1** (de canons etc) to thunder, to boom **2** (fulminer) to rage (**contre** about), to thunder (**contre** against)
V IMPERS **il tonne** it is thundering; **le chien a peur quand il tonne** the dog is frightened of thunder

tonnerre [tɔnɛr] NM **1** (bruit) thunder; **coup de t.** clap or peal of thunder, thunderclap; Fig bombshell; **roulement de t.** roll of thunder; **sous un t. d'applaudissements** to thunderous applause; **accueilli par un t. d'applaudissements** welcomed by thunderous applause; **voix de t.** voice of or like thunder; **un bruit/fracas de t.** a racket, a din **2** Fam **du t.** (film, personne) wonderful, terrific; **t. (de Dieu ou de Brest)!** heavens above!, good grief!; Vieilli **il fera un marin du t. de Dieu** he'll make a thundering good or a hell of a good sailor

tonométrie [tɔnɔmetri] NF tonometry

tonsure [tɔsyr] NF **1** Rel tonsure **2** Fam (calvitie) bald patch

tonsuré [tɔsyre] Rel ADJ tonsured; **tête tonsurée** shaven head
NM cleric

tonsurer [tɔsyre] VT (clerc) to tonsure

tonte [tɔt] NF **1** (des moutons) shearing; (laine) clip; (saison) shearing time **2** (du gazon) mowing

tontine [tɔtin] NF **1** Jur tontine **2** (pour protéger un arbuste) protective covering

tonton [tɔtɔ] NM Fam uncle; **T. Jules** Uncle Jules; **les tontons Macoute** (en Haïti) the Tonton Macoutes (militia of the Duvalier regime)

tonus [tɔnys] NM **1** Méd (d'un muscle) tone, Spéc tonus, tonicity **2** Fig (énergie) energy, dynamism; **je manque de t.** I don't have any energy; **elle a un sacré t.** she's got an incredible amount of energy, she's incredibly energetic; **un peu de nerf les gars, ça manque de t., tout ça!** put your backs into it, lads, you're like a bunch of old women!; **ce slogan manque de t.** the slogan doesn't have any punch or pizzazz

top [tɔp] NM **1** (son) Radio, TV time signal, cue; **les tops** the pips; **au quatrième t., il sera exactement dix heures** at the fourth stroke, it will be ten o'clock precisely; Électron **t. d'écho** blip, Am pip; Électron **t. de synchronisation** synchronizing signal; **donner le t. départ** to give the starting signal **2** Fam **c'est le t. (du t.)!** it's the best of stuff!, Br it's the business!
ADJ Fam great, Br fab, Am awesome

topaze [tɔpaz] NF topaz

toper [tɔpe] VI Fam to agree (**à qch** to sth); **tope (là)!** done!, agreed!, put it there!

topette [tɔpɛt] NF Région small bottle

topinambour [tɔpinɑ̃bur] NM Bot, Culin Jerusalem artichoke

topique [tɔpik] ADJ **1** Méd (remède) local, topical **2** (argument) apposite, to the point
NM Méd topical or local remedy
NF Phil **la t.** topics

top-modèle, pl **top-modèles** NM supermodel

top niveau NM Fam top level; **être au t.** to be at the top, to be top-notch; **arriver au t.** to get to the top; **des scientifiques au t.** top-level or top-notch scientists

topo [tɔpo] NM Fam **1** Journ article **2** (discours) lecture; (exposé) rundown; **faire le t. de la situation** to give a rundown on the situation; **c'est toujours le même t.** it's always the same old story

topographe [tɔpɔgraf] N topographer

topographie [tɔpɔgrafi] NF **1** (technique, relief) topography **2** (représentation) map, plan

topographique [tɔpɔgrafik] ADJ topographical

topographiquement [tɔpɔgrafikmɑ̃] ADV topographically

topologie [tɔpɔlɔʒi] NF topology

topologique [tɔpɔlɔʒik] ADJ topologic(al)

toponyme [tɔpɔnim] NM place name, Spéc toponym

toponymie [tɔpɔnimi] NF study of place names, Spéc toponymy

toponymique [tɔpɔnimik] ADJ (étude) of place names, Spéc toponymic(al)

top secret ADJ INV top secret

toquade [tɔkad] NF Fam craze (**pour qch** for sth); infatuation (**pour qn** with sb); **avoir une t. pour qn** to be infatuated with sb; **ça lui passera, ce n'est qu'une t.** he'll get over it, it's just a passing fancy

toquante [tɔkɑ̃t] NF Fam (montre) watch

toquard, -arde [tɔkar, -ard] = **tocard**

toque [tɔk] NF **1** (chapeau) (de fourrure) fur hat; (de jockey, juge) cap; **t. (blanche)** (de cuisinier) hat, toque **2** (cuisinier dans un restaurant) chef

toqué, -ée [tɔke] Fam ADJ **1** (fou) crazy, nuts **2** (amoureux) infatuated, madly in love (**de** with) **3** Can (têtu) stubborn, pigheaded
N **1** (fou) nut, Br nutter; **il doit me prendre pour une toquée** he must think I'm nuts **2** Can (personne têtue) **c'est un t.** he's as stubborn as they come

toquer [tɔke] VI Fam (à la porte etc) to knock
VPR **se toquer** Fam **se t. de qn** to fall for sb, to go crazy over sb

Torah [tɔra] NF Rel Torah

torailler [tɔraje] VI Suisse (fumer beaucoup) to smoke like a chimney

torche [tɔrʃ] NF **1** (flambeau) torch; **ils furent transformés en torches vivantes** they were turned into human torches; **procession à la t.** torchlight procession; **t. électrique** (electric) torch, Am flashlight **2** Aviat **parachute en t.** unopened parachute

torché [tɔrʃe] ADJ Fam **1 bien t.** (réponse, devoir, travail etc) pretty good **2** (bâclé) (travail etc) botched

torche-cul NM INV Vulg (papier) toilet paper, Br loo paper; Vulg Péj (texte) (piece of) trash; (journal) rag

torchée [tɔrʃe] NF Arg (coups) (good) beating or thrashing

torcher [tɔrʃe] VT **1** Fam (nettoyer) (assiette) to wipe clean; (derrière d'un enfant, enfant) to wipe **2** Fam (bâcler) (travail etc) to botch, to do in a hurry
VPR **se torcher 1** Arg **se t. (le derrière** ou Vulg **le cul)** to wipe one's backside or Vulg arse or Am ass; Fig **je m'en torche (de tes problèmes)!** I don't give a damn (about your problems)! **2 très fam** (s'enivrer) to get shit-faced or Br pissed or rat-arsed

torchère [tɔrʃɛr] NF (candélabre) candelabra

torchis [tɔrʃi] NM Constr cob, daub

torchon [tɔrʃɔ] NM **1** cloth; (pour essuyer la vaisselle) dish or tea towel; (pour épousseter) duster; **donner un coup de t. à qch** (verre, table) to give sth a wipe; Fig **coup de t.** (querelle) dust-up; (épuration) shake-up; Fam **le t. brûle entre** ou **chez eux** they've had a serious falling out; Fig **il ne faut pas mélanger les torchons et les serviettes** you can't compare apples and oranges **2** Fig Fam (copie peu soignée) mess; (texte sans valeur) trash; (journal) rag
ADJ INV Beaux-Arts **papier t.** torchon paper

torchonner [tɔrʃɔne] VT **1** Fam (travail etc) to botch **2** Belg (passer la serpillière) to mop, to clean (with a floorcloth)

torcol [tɔrkɔl] NM Orn **t. (fourmilier)** wryneck

tordant [tɔrdɑ̃] ADJ Fam screamingly funny, hilarious, side-splitting

tord-boyaux [tɔrbwajo] NM INV Arg Péj (eau-de-vie) rotgut

tordeuse [tɔrdøz] NF Entom (papillon) leaf roller

tordre [tɔrdr] VT (barre de fer) to bend, to twist; (fil de fer, laine etc) to twist; (métal) to buckle; (vêtements etc) (pour essorer) to wring; (cheveux en chignon) to twist; (de la douleur) (visage) to contort, to distort, to twist; **t. le cou à un poulet** / Fam **à qn** to wring a chicken's/sb's neck; **t. le bras à qn** to twist sb's arm; **t. l'estomac à qn** (de la peur etc) to churn up sb's insides; Fam **t. les boyaux à qn** (d'un alcool etc) to rot sb's insides; **t. la bouche** to pull a face, to grimace, to make a wry face; **un rictus de douleur tordait sa bouche** his mouth was twisted or contorted in a grimace of pain; **tordu par la douleur** contorted with pain
VPR **se tordre** (de douleur) to writhe, to twist; (de branches) to become gnarled; **se t. les mains** to wring one's hands; **se t. sur son siège** to squirm in one's seat; **se t. le pied** to twist one's ankle; Fam **se t. (de rire)**, **rire à se t.** to split one's sides laughing; **c'était à se t. de rire, il y avait de quoi se t.** it was a scream, it was hilarious; **il n'y a vraiment pas de quoi se t.** there's really nothing to laugh about; **le film est amusant, mais il n'y a pas de quoi se t.** the film is funny, but not all that funny

tordu, -ue [tɔrdy] ADJ **1** (membres, traits) twisted, distorted; (châssis, couverts etc) bent, buckled; (branche) twisted, gnarled; Arg **avoir la gueule tordue** to be as ugly as sin **2** *(esprit)* warped, twisted; **avoir l'esprit t.** to be warped *or* twisted, to have a warped *or* twisted mind **3** *Fam (fou)* cracked, nutty ▪ N *Fam (fou)* nut, *Br* nutter; **avance eh t.!** move, you stupid bastard!

tore [tɔr] NM *Archit, Géom* torus; *Ordinat* (magnetic) core

toréador [tɔreadɔr] NM toreador, bullfighter

toréer [tɔree] VI to fight (in the bullring)

torero [tɔrero] NM bullfighter, torero

torgnole [tɔrɲɔl] NF *Arg (coup)* clout; **je vais lui filer** *ou* **flanquer une t.** I'll clout *or* land him one; **recevoir** *ou* **prendre une t.** to get clouted

toril [tɔril] NM bull pen

torique [tɔrik] ADJ *Géom, Opt etc* toric

tornade [tɔrnad] NF tornado, *Fam* twister; **entrer comme une t.** to come in like a whirlwind

toron [tɔrɔ̃] NM *(d'une corde)* strand

Toronto [tɔrɔ̃to] N Toronto

torpédo [tɔrpedo] NF *Aut* (open) tourer, *Am* touring car

torpeur [tɔrpœr] NF torpor; **je voulus le faire sortir de sa t.** I tried to rouse him from his torpor

torpide [tɔrpid] ADJ *Méd* torpid

torpillage [tɔrpijaʒ] NM *Naut, Mil, Fig (de négociations, d'un plan de paix)* torpedoing

torpille [tɔrpij] NF VOIR GRAMMAIRE A12 **1** *(poisson)* torpedo (ray), electric ray **2** *Naut, Mil* torpedo; **t. d'avion** aerial torpedo

torpiller [tɔrpije] VT *aussi Fig* to torpedo

torpilleur [tɔrpijœr] NM torpedo boat

torque [tɔrk] NM *(collier)* torque ▪ NF *Tech* coil of wire

torréfacteur [tɔrefaktœr] NM **1** *(appareil)* roaster; **t. à café** coffee roaster **2** *(marchand)* = purveyor of coffee which is roasted on the premises

torréfaction [tɔrefaksjɔ̃] NF *(du café, du tabac)* roasting

torréfier [tɔrefje] VT *(impf, pr sub n. torréfiions, v. torréfiiez) (café, maïs etc)* to roast

torrent [tɔrɑ̃] NM *(cours d'eau)* torrent; *Fig (de larmes, lumière)* flood; *(d'injures)* torrent, barrage, spate; *(de questions)* barrage; **il pleut à torrents** it's raining in torrents, *Fam* it's bucketing down

torrentiel, -ielle [tɔrɑ̃sjɛl] ADJ torrential

torrentueux, -euse [tɔrɑ̃tɥø, -øz] ADJ *Litt (rivière etc)* torrent-like; *Fig (vie etc)* stormy, tempestuous

torride [tɔrid] ADJ *(zone, climat etc)*, *Fig (érotisme)* torrid; *(chaleur)* torrid, scorching; *(été)* scorching (hot); **il fait une chaleur t.** it's scorching; **une journée t.** a scorching (hot) day, a scorcher

torrieu [tɔrjø] INT *Can Fam* hell!

tors [tɔr] ADJ *(fil, jambe)* twisted; *Archit (colonne)* barley-sugar ▪ NM *(torsion) (de corde etc)* twist

torsade [tɔrsad] NF **1** twisted cord; *Tricot* cable; **t. de cheveux** twist *or* coil of hair; *Tricot* **(point) t.** cable stitch; *Tricot* **aiguille à t.** cable needle **2** *Archit* rope *or* cable moulding *or Am* molding

torsadé [tɔrsade] ADJ *(cheveux)* coiled; *Archit* **colonne torsadée** cabled column; *Élec, Tél* **paire torsadée** twisted pair; **raccord t.** twist joint

torsader [tɔrsade] VT **1** *(corde, fil de fer etc)* to twist; *(cheveux)* to twist, to coil **2** *(mettre ensemble)* to twist together

torse [tɔrs] NM *(poitrine)* chest, torso, trunk; *Beaux-Arts* torso; **le t. pris dans une veste très serrée** wearing a very tight jacket; **le t.**

nu stripped to the waist; **se mettre t. nu** to strip to the waist; **bomber le t.** to stick out one's chest; *Fig* to be swollen with pride; **il bombe le t. sous le coup de la fierté** he's puffed up with pride

torseur [tɔrsœr] NM *Phys* torque

torsion [tɔrsjɔ̃] NF twisting; *(des traits, de la bouche)* distortion; *Tech, Phys* torsion; **faire une t. à droite** to twist to the right

tort [tɔr] NM **1** *(faute)* fault; **c'est son seul t.** it's his only fault; **son seul t. a été d'être trop franc** his only mistake was being too frank; **il a eu le t. de ne pas demander de reçu** he made the mistake of not asking for a receipt; **reconnaître ses torts** to acknowledge one's faults; **il a tous les torts** he is entirely to blame, it's all his fault; **c'est un t. de le lui avoir dit** it was wrong *or* a mistake to tell him; **avoir des torts envers qn** to have treated sb badly; **avoir t.** to be wrong *(de faire* to do); **c'est elle qui a t., pas toi** she's the one who's wrong *or* (who's) in the wrong, not you; **il n'est pas d'accord, et il n'a pas t.** he doesn't agree, and he's right (not to); **donner t. à qn** to blame sb, to lay the blame on sb; *(d'un résultat, d'une preuve etc)* to prove sb wrong; **elle donne toujours t. à l'aîné de ses fils** she always blames the elder boy, the elder boy is always in the wrong as far as she's concerned; **être en t.** *ou* **dans son t.** to be in the wrong *or* at fault; **se mettre en t.** *ou* **dans son t.** to put oneself in the wrong; **à t.** wrongly; **à t. ou à raison** rightly or wrongly; **à t. et à travers** at random, without rhyme or reason; **dépenser son argent à t. et travers** to spend one's money thoughtlessly *or* recklessly; **il parle à t. et travers** he talks wildly; *Jur* **prononcer un jugement au t. d'une partie** to find against one of the parties

2 *(dommage)* harm; **un t.** a wrong; **faire du t. à qn** to wrong sb, to do sb wrong; **tu lui as fait beaucoup de t. en l'accusant** you did him/her great wrong in accusing her; **quel t. cela peut-il vous faire?** what harm can it do you?; **cette loi a fait beaucoup de t. aux petits épargnants** this law penalizes the small saver heavily

torticolis [tɔrtikɔli] NM *Méd* stiff neck, *Spéc* torticollis; **avoir/attraper un t.** to have/get a stiff neck

tortillard [tɔrtijar] NM local train

tortillement [tɔrtijmɑ̃] NM wriggling, squirming; *(des hanches)* wiggling

tortiller [tɔrtije] VT *(tordre) (papier, ruban, cheveux etc)* to twist; *(moustache)* to twirl; *(tripoter)* to twiddle (with) ▪ VI **1 t. des hanches** to wiggle one's hips; **marcher en tortillant du postérieur** to walk with a wiggle; **elle avança vers la porte en tortillant du postérieur** she wiggled her way to the door **2** *Fam* **il n'y a pas à t.** it's no good trying to wriggle *or* wiggle out of it ▪ VPR **se tortiller** *(d'un ver, d'une personne sur sa chaise)* to wriggle, to squirm, to wiggle; *(en dansant)* to wriggle about; *(des hanches)* to wiggle

tortillon [tɔrtijɔ̃] NM **1** *(de papier)* twist **2** *(sur la tête) (pour porter une charge)* pad

tortillonner [tɔrtijɔne] VT to twist and turn ▪ VI *Fam* to quibble, to hedge

tortionnaire [tɔrsjɔner] NM torturer ▪ ADJ **policier t.** police torturer

tortore [tɔrtɔr] NF *Fam* cooking; **elle fait de la vachement bonne t.** she makes really great food *or Br* scran

tortorer [tɔrtɔre] VT *Fam (manger)* to wolf down, to gobble up

tortu [tɔrty] ADJ *Litt (nez)* crooked; *(esprit)* warped

tortue [tɔrty] NF **1** *(reptile)* tortoise; *Fig (personne lente)* slowcoach, *Am* slowpoke; **t.**

d'eau douce terrapin; **t. de mer** turtle; **à pas de t.** at a snail's pace **2** *(papillon)* tortoiseshell (butterfly) **3** *Hist, Mil* testudo, tortoise

tortueusement [tɔrtɥøzmɑ̃] ADV tortuously; *(se conduire, manœuvrer etc)* deviously; **la route se déroule t. jusqu'au col** the road winds *or* twists its way (tortuously) up to the col

tortueux, -euse [tɔrtɥø, -øz] ADJ *(rivière)* winding, meandering; *(rue, sentier)* winding, twisting, twisty; *(attitude, personne, esprit, manœuvres)* devious; *(argumentation, discours etc)* tortuous

torturant [tɔrtyrɑ̃] ADJ *(situation, regret, sentiments, pensées etc)* agonizing

torture [tɔrtyr] NF torture; *Fig* torment, torture; **instrument de t.** instrument of torture; **chambre de t.** torture chamber; **victime de la t.** *ou* **de tortures** victim of torture, torture victim; *Fig* **cette séparation est une vraie t. morale pour moi** it's torture being separated; **mettre qn à la t.** to torment *or* torture sb; **je ne souhaite pas vous mettre à la t.** I hate to keep you on tenterhooks; **mettre son esprit à la t.** to rack one's brains

torturer [tɔrtyre] VT *(prisonnier)* to torture; *Fig* to torment **(sur** about); **cette situation la torture** the situation is torture *or* torment for her; **la jalousie le torturait** he was tortured *or* tormented by jealousy, he suffered torments of jealousy ▪ VPR **se torturer** to torture oneself; **se t. l'esprit** to rack one's brains

torve [tɔrv] ADJ *(regard)* grim, menacing

tory [tɔri] ADJ, N Tory

toscan, -ane [tɔskɑ̃, -an] ADJ Tuscan ▪ NM *Ling* Tuscan ▪ N **T.** Tuscan

Toscane [tɔskan] NF Tuscany

tôt [to] ADV **1** *(bientôt, vite)* soon, early; **vous faut-il partir si t.?** must you leave so soon?; **plus t. tu commenceras, plus vite tu auras fini** the sooner you begin, the sooner you'll finish; **vous auriez dû me le dire plus t.** you should have told me sooner *or* earlier *or* before this; **nous n'étions pas plus t. rentrés que ...** we had no sooner returned than ...; **le plus t. sera le mieux** the sooner *or* earlier the better; **le plus t. possible** as soon *or* as early as possible; **revenez au plus t.** come back as soon *or* quick(ly) as possible; **mardi au plus t.** (on) Tuesday at the earliest; *Fam* **c'est pas trop t.!** and about time too!, and not before time either!; **on ne le reverra pas de si t.** we won't see him for a long time; *(il est parti fâché, ruiné etc)* we won't see him again in a hurry; **je ne pensais pas les revoir de si t.** I didn't think I would see them again so soon; **elle a eu t. fait de changer d'avis** she soon changed her mind, it wasn't long before she changed her mind; **t. après** soon after; **t. ou tard** sooner or later

2 *(de bonne heure)* early; **t. dans l'après-midi/dans l'année/dans sa vie** early in the afternoon/in the year/in his life; **il est trop t. pour manger** it's too early to eat; **il est trop t. pour le dire** it's too soon to say, it's early days yet

total, -ale, -aux, -ales [tɔtal, -o] ADJ *(somme, guerre, destruction, éclipse, silence etc)* total; *(obscurité)* total, complete; *(confiance, liberté)* complete; *(hauteur, largeur)* overall; *Méd (hystérectomie)* complete, *Spéc* radical; **c'était une surprise totale** it was a complete surprise; **un échec t.** a complete (and utter) failure ▪ NM total; **le t. de la population** the total population; **faire le t.** to work out the total; **faire le t. de** to add up, to total; **au t.** in all, in total; *(tout compte fait)* all in all; *Compta* **t. des recettes** total receipts; **t. général** grand total; **t. à payer** total payable; *Fam* **et t. to**

sum it all up, in short, in sum; **et t., on l'a renvoyé** and, to cut a long story short, he got the sack; **tu voulais faire ton indépandante, et t., tu es toute seule maintenant** you wanted to be independent, and the sum total of that is that you're all alone now

NF totale 1 *Chir Fam* hysterectomy **2** *Fam (ensemble de problèmes)* **on a eu droit à la totale: verglas, embouteillages, barrages de routiers** black ice, traffic jams, lorry drivers' road blocks, you name it, we had it; **quand il m'a demandée en mariage, il m'a fait la totale** when he proposed to me, he really went all out

totalement [tɔtalmã] **ADV** totally, completely

totalisateur, -trice [tɔtalizatœr, -tris] **ADJ** *(machine)* adding

NM adding machine; *Ordinat* accumulator; *Courses de chevaux* totalizer, *Fam* tote, *Am* pari-mutuel; *Aut* **t. kilométrique journalier** trip recorder

totalisation [tɔtalizasjõ] **NF** totalling, adding up

totaliser [tɔtalize] **VT 1** *(additionner)* to total, to add up **2** *(compter en tout)* to total, to have a total of

totalitaire [tɔtalitɛr] **ADJ** *Pol* totalitarian

totalitarisme [tɔtalitarism] **NM** *Pol* totalitarianism

totalité [tɔtalite] **NF la t. de** all of; **l'entreprise exporte la t. de sa production** the company exports its entire production; **payer qch en t.** to pay sth in full; **la presque t. de** almost *or* virtually all (of); **(pris) dans sa/leur t.** (taken) as a whole; **en t.** in full

totem [tɔtɛm] **NM** totem

totémique [tɔtemik] **ADJ** totemic

totémisme [tɔtemism] **NM** totemism

toto [toto] **NM** *Arg (pou)* louse

toton [tɔtõ] **NM** *(toupie)* teetotum

touareg [twareg] **ADJ** Tuareg

NM *Ling* Tuareg

N T. Tuareg

toubib [tubib] **NM** *Fam* doctor, quack

toucan [tukã] **NM** *(oiseau)* toucan

touchant [tuʃã] **ADJ** *(spectacle, discours, geste etc)* touching, moving; *(reconnaissance)* touching; **d'une manière touchante** touchingly, movingly; **elle est touchante d'humilité** she is touchingly humble

PRÉP *Litt (au sujet de)* touching, concerning, about

touche [tuʃ] **NF 1** *(style) (d'un peintre)* brushwork, style; *(d'un écrivain)* style

2 *(d'un piano, d'un clavier)* key

3 **pierre de t.** touchstone

4 *Billard, Escrime* hit

5 *Pêche* bite, nibble; *Fam* **avoir** *ou* **faire une t. avec qn** to make a hit with sb; **tu as fait une t.!** you've made a hit there!

6 *Sport (ligne)* touchline; *(remise en jeu) Ftbl* throw-in; *Rugby* line-out; *(au hockey)* roll-in; **t. longue** long throw-in; **envoi de t.** kick into touch; **jouer la t.** to take the throw-in; *Rugby* **trouver la t.** to find touch; **sortir en t.** to go into touch; **rester sur la t.** to stay on the sidelines *or* touchlines; *Fig* to stay on the sidelines

7 *Arg (aspect)* appearance, look; **avoir une drôle de t.** to be weird-looking; **t'as vu la t. qu'il a!** get a load of him!

8 *Arg (de drogue etc)* shot, jab

9 *Beaux-Arts (tache de couleur)* touch; *Fig* **une t. romantique** a touch of romance, a romantic touch; **pour apporter une t. locale** for a bit of local colour; **mettre la t. finale à qch** to put the finishing touches to sth; **procéder par petites touches** to proceed step by step

10 *Mus (de violon)* finger board; **touches** *(de guitare etc)* frets

▸▸ *Ordinat* **t. d'alimentation** power-on key; **t. alt** alt (key); **t. d'arrêt de défilement** scroll lock key; **t. à auto-maintien** sticky key; **t. à bascule** toggle key; **t. contrôle** control key; **t. de curseur** cursor key; **t. début** home key; **t. de défilement** scroll key; **t. de déplacement du curseur** cursor movement key; **t. de direction** arrow key; **t. d'échappement** escape key; **t. d'effacement** delete key; **t. d'effacement arrière** backspace delete key; **t. à effleurement** touch-sensitive key; **t. (d')entrée** enter key; **t. d'espacement arrière** backspace key; **t. fin** end key; **t. fléchée** *ou* **(à) flèche** arrow key; **t. flèche vers la droite/la gauche** right/left arrow key; **t. flèche vers le bas/le haut** down/up arrow key; **t. (de) fonction** function key; **t. d'impression d'écran** print screen key; **t. d'insertion** insert key; **t. d'interruption** break key; **t. majuscule** shift key; **t. morte** dead key; **t. multifonction** multifunctional key; **t. numérique** number key; **t. de raccourci** shortcut key; **t. de répétition** repeat-action key; **t. retour** return *or* enter key; **t. de retour arrière** backspace key; **t. de verrouillage des majuscules/du clavier numérique** caps/num(-bers) lock key

touche-à-tout *Fam* **ADJ INV 1 il est t.** *(adulte)* he can't keep his hands off anything; *(bébé)* he's into everything **2** *Fig* **j'ai toujours été un peu t.** I've always dabbled in this and that

N INV 1 c'est un t. *(adulte)* he can't keep his hands off anything; *(bébé)* he's into everything **2** *(personne qui a plusieurs occupations)* dabbler; **il écrit, il peint, c'est un peu un t.** he writes, he paints, he does a bit of everything

touche-pipi **NM** *Fam* **jouer à t.** to play at doctors and nurses

toucher¹ [tuʃe] **NM 1** *(sens, action)* touch; *(qualité)* feel; **sens du t.** sense of touch; **au t.** to the touch *or* feel; **le mur était chaud au t.** the wall was hot to the touch *or* felt hot; **reconnaître qch au t.** to recognize sth by touch *or* by the feel of it **2** *Méd* examination; **t. vaginal** vaginal examination **3** *Mus (d'un pianiste)* touch

TOUCHER²

VT to touch **1, 3, 5** ▪ to hit **1, 2** ▪ to damage **2** ▪ to move **3** ▪ to affect **4** ▪ to reach **7** ▪ to receive **8** ▪ to adjoin **9**
VI to touch **2, 3** ▪ to tamper with **2** ▪ to touch on **3** ▪ to concern **4**
VPR to touch

VT 1 *(du doigt, avec un objet etc) (quelque chose, quelqu'un sur l'épaule etc)* to touch; *Ftbl (balle)* to handle; *(cible), Billard (boule), Escrime (adversaire)* to hit; **t. qch avec des gants** to handle sth with gloves on, to wear gloves when handling sth; **la voiture a failli t. le mur** the car almost hit *or* clipped the wall; *Fam* **touchons du bois!** touch wood!; *Fam* **pas touche!** *(à un enfant)* don't touch!; *Rugby* **t. dans les buts** to touch down

2 *(maison etc) (d'un incendie)* to damage; *(d'une explosion)* to damage, to hit; *(personne) (d'un éclat d'obus etc)* to hit *(à la jambe in the leg)*; **le soldat a été gravement touché** the soldier was seriously injured

3 *(émouvoir)* to move, to touch; **t. qn jusqu'aux larmes** to move sb to tears; **être touché au vif** to be cut *or* stung to the quick

4 *(concerner, affecter)* to concern, to affect; **le chômage touche particulièrement les jeunes** the young are particularly affected *or* hard hit by unemployment

5 *Naut (terre)* to touch; **t. le port** to put in at *or* touch port; **t. le fond** *Naut* to strike, to touch (bottom); *(être à sec)* to be aground; *Fig (déprimer)* to touch (rock) bottom

6 *Min* **t. le pétrole** to strike oil

7 *(contacter)* to get in touch with, to get hold of, to reach; *(d'une lettre)* to reach; **t. qn par téléphone** to reach sb by telephone

8 *(recevoir) (argent)* to get, to receive; *(chèque)* to cash; **t. ses appointements/sa paie** to draw *or* receive one's salary/one's pay; **t. un intérêt** to receive interest; **elle doit bien t. dans les 2 000 euros par mois** she must be making *or* getting about 2,000 euros a month; **je pense t. 500 euros le 15 juin** I think I've got 500 euros coming to me on the 15th of June; **t. le tiercé** = to win the pools, to hit the jackpot

9 *(être tout proche de)* to adjoin; **la bibliothèque touche l'église** the library adjoins the church; **la maison qui touche la nôtre** the house adjoining ours

10 **je lui en toucherai un mot** *ou* **deux mots** I'll mention it to him, I'll speak to him about it

VI 1 t. à un port *(d'un navire)* to put in *or* call at a port, to touch a port

2 t. à *(entrer en contact avec)* to touch; *Fig (en modifiant)* to touch, to meddle with, to tamper with; **palmes qui touchent au plafond** palms that touch *or* reach the ceiling; **t. à terre** to touch the ground; **si tu touches au chat, je te quitte!** if you touch *or* lay a finger on the cat, I'll leave you!; **n'y touchez pas!** (keep your) hands off!; **on ne touche pas!** hands off!; **je n'ai pas touché à l'héroïne/l'alcool depuis** I haven't touched heroin/alcohol since; **il n'avait pas touché à la nourriture** he hadn't touched the food, he had left the food untouched; **t. à ses économies** to touch *or* break into one's savings; *Fig* **avec son air de ne pas y t.** looking as if butter wouldn't melt in his mouth, with an ever so innocent look on his face

3 t. à *(être en contact avec) (quelque chose)* to touch; *(pays)* to border on; *(maison, jardin etc)* to adjoin; *Fig (problème, question)* to touch on; **t. au but** to near one's goal; **l'année/le projet touche à sa fin** the year/the project is drawing to a close *or* nearing its end; **il touche à la quarantaine** he is getting on for *or* nearing forty

4 t. à *(concerner)* to concern; **tout ce qui touche à l'écologie** everything to do with *or* touching on *or* concerning ecology

VPR se toucher *(de lignes etc)* to touch; **nos deux maisons se touchent** our two houses adjoin *or* are adjoining

2 *(se masturber)* to touch oneself

touche-touche (à) **ADV** *Aut* nose-to-tail, bumper to bumper

touchette [tuʃɛt] **NF** *(d'une guitare, d'une mandoline)* fret

toucheur, -euse [tuʃœr, -øz] **N** (cattle) drover

touée [twe] **NF** *Naut* **1** *(câble)* warp, (warping) cable **2** *(longueur)* scope

touer [twe] **VT 1** *Naut (avec point fixe)* to warp **2** *(avec ancre)* to kedge

toueur [twœr] **NM** *Naut* tug

touffe [tuf] **NF 1** *(de cheveux, d'herbe, de poils etc)* tuft; *(de végétation)* clump **2** *Vulg (toison pubienne)* bush, pubes; **une jupe ras la t.** a bum-freezer

touffeur [tufœr] **NF** *Arch, Litt* suffocating heat

touffu [tufy] **ADJ** *(bois, végétation)* thick, dense; *(barbe, cheveux etc)* bushy; *Fig (livre)* dense

touillage [tujaʒ] **NM** *Fam (de liquide)* stirring; *(de salade)* tossing; *(de cartes)* shuffling

touiller [tuje] **VT** *Fam (liquide, soupe etc)* to stir; *(salade)* to toss; *(cartes)* to shuffle

toujours [tuʒur] **ADV 1** *(répétition)* always; **c'est ce que j'ai t. dit, et dirai t.** that's what

I've always said and will keep on saying; **t. plus nombreux** more and more numerous; **influence t. plus étendue** ever-increasing influence; **comme t.** as always, as ever; **optimiste comme t., il …** ever the optimist, he …; **presque t.** almost or nearly always; **un ami de t.** a lifelong friend; **pour t.** for ever; **depuis t.** always; **je t'aime depuis t.** I've always loved you, I've been in love with you for as long as I can remember VOIR GRAMMAIRE A21

2 (encore) still; **il fait t. aussi chaud** it is as hot as ever (it was); **cherchez t.** go on looking; **elle ne le lui a t. pas dit** she still hasn't told him; **alors, il est rentré? – t. pas** he's back then? – not yet

3 (concession) always, anyhow; **je peux t. essayer** I can always or at least try; **essaie/ entrez t.** try/come in anyway; **t. est-il que … the** the fact remains that …, anyhow, …; **elle peut t. attendre!** she'll be lucky!, she'll have a long wait!, in her dreams!; **il peut t. me redemander ma voiture, il ne l'aura pas** he can always ask me for my car again, but he won't get it; **c'est t. ça (de pris)** (at any rate) it's better than nothing, at least it's something; **allez-y t., je vous rejoindrai plus tard** you go on anyhow, I'll catch you up later

---

Attention: ne pas confondre **still** et **always** lorsqu'on traduit **toujours. Still** exprime l'idée de continuité, alors que **always** exprime l'idée de répétition.

---

toulousain, -aine [tuluzɛ̃, -ɛn] ADJ of or from Toulouse

‣ **T.** (natif) native of Toulouse; (habitant) inhabitant of Toulouse

toundra [tundra] NF Géog tundra

toupet [tupɛ] NM **1** (de cheveux) tuft of hair, Br quiff; **(faux) t.** toupee **2** Fam (culot) cheek, nerve; **quel t.!** what a cheek or a nerve!; **il faut un sacré t. pour le faire!** it takes a helluva nerve or cheek!; **avoir du t.** to have a cheek or a nerve; **il a eu le t. de …** he had the cheek or the nerve to …; **elle ne manque pas de t.!** she's got a cheek or a nerve!

toupie [tupi] NF **1** (jouet) (spinning) top **2** Menuis etc moulding or Am molding machine **3** (de meuble) moulded or Am molded foot (Louis XVI style) **4** Fam **vieille t.** (femme) old trout

tour[1] [tur] NF **1** (bâtiment, d'une cathédrale, d'un château etc) tower; (d'habitation) highrise building; Ordinat tower; TV, Cin camera tower; **(immeuble) t., grande t.** tower block, high-rise **2** Fam (personne) hulk **3** Échecs castle, rook

‣ **la t. de Babel** the Tower of Babel; Aviat **t. de contrôle** control tower; **la t. Eiffel** the Eiffel Tower; **t. de forage** derrick, rig; Ind, Chimie **t. de fractionnement** fractionating tower; Fig **t. d'ivoire** ivory tower; **t. de lancement** launch tower; **la t. de Londres** the Tower of London; **t. d'observation** watchtower, observation tower; **la t. (penchée) de Pise** the Leaning Tower of Pisa; **t. de réfrigération** cooling tower; **t. de remplissage** (pour fusée) umbilical tower; **t. de sondage** derrick, rig

TOUR[2]

---

circumference **1** ▪ measurement **1** ▪ turn **2–5, 8, 12** ▪ to go round (faire le tour de) **1** ▪ revolution **5** ▪ stroll **6** ▪ ride **6** ▪ trip **7** ▪ lathe **9** ▪ wheel **10** ▪ round **11** ▪ ballot **13** ▪ trick **14, 15**

NM **1** (circonférence) circumference; (de partie du corps) size, measurement; **arbre qui a deux mètres de t.** tree two metres in circumference, tree with a girth of two metres; **faire**

le t. to go round; **faire tout le t.** to go all the way round; **le chemin fait le t. de la propriété** the path runs right round the estate; Fig **faire le t. de qch** (situation, problème) to review sth; **faire le t. du monde** to go round the world; **faire le t. du monde à la voile/à pied** to sail/walk round the world; **c'est son deuxième t. du monde à la voile** this is the second time he's sailed round the world; Sport **t. de piste** ou **de circuit** lap; **en être au troisième t.** to be on the third lap; **prendre un t. d'avance sur qn** to lap sb; **faire un t. de piste pour s'échauffer** to do a warm-up lap; **faire le t. du cadran** to sleep round the clock; **t. de cou** (mesure) collar size or measurement; Vieilli **quel est votre t. de cou?** what (size) neck are you?; **t. de tête** (mesure) hat size; **t. de taille** (measurement); **quel est votre t. de taille?** what waist are you?; **avoir 75 cm de t. de taille** to have a waist measurement of 75 cm, to measure 75 cm round the waist, to be a 75 cm waist; **perdre cinq centimètres de t. de taille** to lose five centimetres round the waist; **quel est votre t. de hanche?** what hip size are you?

2 Naut (autour de la bitte d'amarrage) turn; **avoir des tours** to have a foul hawse

3 **tours et détours d'un chemin** twists and turns of a road

4 (tournure) (de phrase, d'une situation) turn; **prendre un mauvais t./un t. dramatique** to take a bad/a dramatic turn; **tout cela est en train de prendre un tout autre t. que ce que j'avais prévu** it's all turning out quite differently from what I expected; **cette affaire prend un t. qui ne me plaît guère** this matter is developing in a way I don't like; **donner un autre t. à la conversation** (rendre sérieuse) to raise the tone of the conversation; (rendre légère) to lower the tone of the conversation; **t. d'esprit** turn of mind; Suisse **donner le t.** (maladie) to take a turn for the better; (personne) to wrap up

5 (rotation) (de clé, tournevis, vis) turn; (de roue, moteur) revolution, turn; (de manivelle) turn, swing; **donner un t. de clé à la porte** to turn the key in the door; **fermer qch à double t.** to double-lock sth; Aut **tours de volant** steering wheel turns; (de butée à butée) turns lock to lock; **à t. de bras** (frapper) with all one's might; Fig **vendre/distribuer qch à t. de bras** to sell/distribute loads or masses of sth; **tours par minute, tours/minute** revolutions per minute, Fam revs; **(disque à) 45/33 tours** single/LP

6 (balade) stroll; (à bicyclette, en voiture) ride; **faire un t.** to go for a stroll/ride; **elle aime bien faire un t. en ville** she likes going into town; **faire un t. ou dans le jardin** to have or take a turn or a stroll round the garden; Euph **elle est allée faire un petit t.** she's gone to spend a penny

7 (petit voyage) trip, tour; **ils sont allés faire un t. en Bretagne** they've gone touring in Brittany

8 (de participation) turn; **à qui le t.?** whose turn is it?; **t. de service** spell of duty; **chacun (à) son t.** each in (his) turn; **chacun son t.!** (dans une queue) wait your turn!; **hier c'est moi qui l'ai fait, aujourd'hui c'est toi, chacun son t.!** I did it yesterday, now it's your turn!; **ils s'occupent des enfants chacun leur t.** they look after the children in turn or turn and turn about, they take turns looking after the children; **à t. de rôle** in turns; **nous le faisons à t. de rôle** we do it in turns, we take turns doing it; **les membres assurent la présidence à t. de rôle tous les deux ans** the presidency rotates among members every two years; **t. à t.** by turns, in turn; **s'emporter et se calmer t. à t.** to flare up one moment and calm down the next

9 Tech (machine-outil) (turning) lathe; **fait**

au t. machine-turned; Fam Vieilli (jambe, taille etc) shapely; **atelier des tours** turning shop

10 Cér (potter's) wheel

11 Cartes (manche) round

12 Théâtre etc turn, number

13 Pol **t.** (de scrutin) ballot

14 (sale coup) trick; **faire ou jouer un (mauvais) t. à qn** to play a (nasty) trick on sb, to play sb a (nasty) trick; **mes yeux ont dû me jouer des tours** my eyes must have been playing tricks on me; **cela te jouera des tours** you'll (live to) regret it; Fam **avoir plus d'un t. dans son sac** to have more than one trick up one's sleeve

15 (manipulation) feat; (de prestidigitateur, chien) trick; **t. d'adresse** feat of skill; **t. de cartes** card trick; Fam **en un t. de main** in two minutes flat, in the twinkling of an eye; **je n'ai pas le t. de main** I haven't the knack or hang of it; **c'est un t. à prendre** there's a knack to it

‣ ‣ **t. de chant** song recital; Fam **t. de cochon** lousy or rotten trick; **t. de cou** (ruban) choker; (en fourrure, écharpe) scarf; **t. de force** feat, achievement; **il a réalisé un véritable t. de force en organisant la fête** organizing the festival was quite a feat or an achievement on his part; **T. de France** (cycliste) Tour de France (cycle race); **faire son t. de France** (d'un compagnon) to do one's journeymanship; **t. d'honneur** lap of honour; Fig **t. d'horizon: faire un t. d'horizon** to review matters; **t. de lit** bed valance; **t. de reins: se faire un t. de reins** to strain or rick one's back; Fin **t. de table** backers; **faire un t. de table** (pendant un débat) to go round the table

---

Touraine [turɛn] NF Touraine

tourangeau, -elle, -eaux, -elles [turɑ̃ʒo, -ɛl] ADJ (de la région) of/from Touraine; (de la ville) of/from Tours

‣ **T.** (natif) (de la région/la ville) native of Touraine/Tours; (habitant) (de la région/la ville) inhabitant of Touraine/Tours

tourbe [turb] NF peat, turf

tourbeux, -euse [turbø, -øz] ADJ (sol etc) peaty

tourbière [turbjɛr] NF peat bog

tourbillon [turbijɔ̃] NM **1** (vent) whirlwind; (de poussière, de sable, de cendres, de fumée) swirl, cloud; (de neige) flurry; **monter en tourbillons** (de la poussière, du sable etc) to swirl or whirl up **2** (remous) whirlpool **3** Phys, Astron, Phil vortex VOIR GRAMMAIRE A14 **4** Aut (dans un moteur) rotary or barrel swirl, swirl **5** Fig (des plaisirs etc) whirl; **dans le t. de la vie** in the hurly-burly of life; **le t. de la vie mondaine** the social whirl

tourbillonnaire [turbijɔnɛr] ADJ swirling

tourbillonnant [turbijɔnɑ̃] ADJ (feuilles, jupes etc) whirling

tourbillonnement [turbijɔnmɑ̃] NM whirling

tourbillonner [turbijɔne] VI Fig (d'idées etc) to whirl (round); (de feuilles, d'un danseur) to whirl (round), to spin round and round

tourelle [turɛl] NF **1** Archit turret; **à tourelles** turreted **2** Mil, Naut (gun) turret **3** Opt, Phot **t. à objectifs** lens turret

tourière [turjɛr] ADJ, NF Rel extern

tourillon [turijɔ̃] NM **1** (d'axe) journal; (axe) (wheel) spindle **2** Mil (de canon etc) trunnion **3** (pivot) pivot (pin)

Touring Club de France [turiŋklœbdəfrɑ̃s] NM = French motoring organization

tourismatique [turismatik] NF computerized reservation systems

tourisme [turism] NM tourism; (industrie) tourism, tourist trade; **faire du t.** to do some touring; **office du** *ou* **de t.** tourist office; **agence** *ou* **bureau de t.** travel *or* tourist agency; **centre/ville de t.** tourist centre; **t. de masse** mass tourism

▸▸ **t. d'affaires** business tourism; **t. agricole** agricultural tourism, agritourism; **t. balnéaire** seaside tourism; **t. blanc** winter sports tourism; **t. écologique** eco-tourism; **t. émetteur** outbound tourism; **t. à la ferme** farm tourism; **t. de loisirs** leisure *or* holiday tourism; **t. ludique** leisure tourism; **t. national** national *or* domestic tourism; **t. organisé** package tourism; **t. récepteur** inbound tourism; **t. sexuel** sex tourism; **t. vert** ecotourism, green tourism

touriste [turist] **N** tourist; *Fig Péj* **faire qch en t.** to do sth amateurishly; *Univ etc* **suivre un cours en t.** to do a course in a half-hearted kind of way

ADJ *Naut, Aviat* **classe t.** tourist class

touristique [turistik] **ADJ** *(guide, information, région, ville etc)* tourist; *(menu, prix)* for tourists; *(route)* scenic

tourmaline [turmalin] **NF** *Minér* tourmaline

tourment [turmã] **NM 1** *(douleur)* torture, torment, anguish; **tourments** *(de faim)* pangs; *(de doute, jalousie)* torments **2** *(cause de souci)* torment; **endurer mille tourments** to go through torment, to suffer agonies; **mon fils me donne bien du t.** my son's giving me a lot of worry **3** *Arch, Litt (physique) (d'un prisonnier etc)* torture

tourmente [turmãt] **NF 1** storm; **t. de neige** blizzard; **le vent soufflait en t.** the wind was gusting from all quarters; **nous fûmes pris sous une t. de feu** *(à la guerre)* we were caught in a hail of gunfire **2** *Fig* upheaval

tourmenté [turmãte] **ADJ 1** *(côte)* jagged; *(paysage)* wild **2** *(conscience, visage)* tortured; *(personne, âme)* in torment, tormented **3** *(mer, vie, période)* turbulent; **une époque tourmentée de ma vie** a turbulent time in my life; **nous vivons une époque tourmentée** we are living in troubled times **4** *Beaux-Arts, Archit etc (style)* tortured

tourmenter [turmãte] **VT 1** *(de la jalousie, du doute etc)* to torment, to torture; **le remords/la douleur le tourmente** he is racked with remorse/pain; **tourmenté par la douleur** racked with pain; **être tourmenté par la goutte/ses dents** to suffer agonies with gout/one's teeth **2** *(d'une personne) (personne, chien)* to torment **3** *Arch (physiquement) (prisonnier)* to torture

VPR se tourmenter to worry, to be anxious *or* uneasy; **ne vous tourmentez pas!** don't worry!

tourmentin [turmãtɛ̃] **NM 1** *Naut* storm jib **2** *Orn* petrel

tournage [turnaʒ] **NM 1** *Tech (au tour)* turning **2** *Cér (au tour)* turning, throwing **3** *Naut* belaying **4** *Cin* shooting, filming; **le t. de son nouveau film commence la semaine prochaine** shooting starts on his new film next week; **sur les lieux du t.** on the set; **t. en décor naturel** *ou* **en extérieur** location filming

tournailler [turnaje] **VI** *Fam* to keep wandering round and round, to prowl (around); **elle tournaille autour de moi** she's hovering around me

tournant [turnã] **ADJ 1** *(bibliothèque, scène etc)* revolving; *(fauteuil, siège)* swivel; *(pont)* swing; *Tech (essieu)* live; *(grève)* rotating **2** *(route etc)* winding; *(escalier)* spiral **3** *Mil (mouvement)* encircling

NM 1 *(de route, de rivière)* bend, curve; **la voiture s'est renversée dans un t.** the car overturned on a bend; *Fig Fam* **je l'aurai au t.!** I'll get him yet!; *Fig Fam* **elle t'attend au t.** she's waiting to pounce **2** *Fig (changement) (de sa vie, sa carrière etc)* turning point

(de in); **marquer un t.** to mark a turning point; **cette décision constitue un t. décisif** this decision marked a turning point *or* a watershed; **prendre un nouveau t.** to change direction; **savoir prendre le t.** to know how to adapt, to bend with the wind

tourne [turn] **NF 1** *(du lait)* turning, going sour; *(du vin)* souring **2** *Journ (d'un article sur la page suivante)* continuation

tourné [turne] **ADJ 1** *Tech (au tour)* turned; **bien t.** *(lettre)* nicely worded; *(phrase, réponse, repartie)* well-phrased; **une petite brune bien tournée** a little brunette with a lovely figure; **mal t.** *(lettre)* badly worded; *(phrase, réponse)* badly phrased; **avoir l'esprit mal t.** to have a nasty mind; **une société tournée vers l'avenir** a forward-looking company **2** *(vin, lait etc)* sour **3** *Belg* **être bien/mal t.** to be in a good/bad mood

tourne-à-gauche **NM INV** *(outil)* wrench

tournebouler [turnəbule] **VT** *Fam* **t. qn** *(le bouleverser)* to upset sb

tournebroche [turnəbrɔʃ] **NM** *Culin (appareil)* roasting jack; *Arch (garçon, chien)* turnspit

tourne-disque, *pl* **tourne-disques** **NM** record player

tournedos [turnədo] **NM** *Culin* tournedos, fillet steak

tournée [turne] **NF 1** *(d'inspecteur etc)* round(s); *(de facteur)* round(s), *Am* route; *Théâtre* tour; **pendant la t. du représentant** while the rep is on the road; **faire sa t.** *(d'un facteur, un inspecteur)* to be on *or* doing *or* making one's rounds; *Théâtre* **faire une t. en province** to tour the provinces, to do a provincial tour; *Théâtre* **en t.** on tour, on the road; *Théâtre* **nous passons la plus grande partie de l'année en t.** we spend most of the year touring *or* on tour; **faire la t. des musées** to go round *or* tour *or Fam* do the art galleries; **faire la t. des troquets** to go round the bars, to bar-hop; **faire une t. en Europe** *(d'un chanteur, groupe d'acteurs)* to do a European tour; **faire une t. électorale** *(d'un candidat député)* to canvass a constituency; *(dans une élection présidentielle)* to go on the campaign trail **2** *Fam (consommations)* round (of drinks); **payer une t.** to pay for *or* stand a round (of drinks), to pay for *or* stand drinks all round; **c'est ma t.** it's my round *or Br Fam* shout **3** *Arg (raclée)* beating

▸▸ *Fam* **t. des grands-ducs: faire la t. des grands-ducs** to go out on the town; **Com t. de présentation** road show

tournemain (en un) [ɑ̃nœ̃turnəmɛ̃] **ADV** in an instant, in the twinkling of an eye

tourné-monté, *pl* **tournés-montés** **NM** *TV, Cin* sequential shooting

TOURNER [turne]

| **VT** to turn **1–4, 6, 7** ▪ to stir **1** ▪ to toss **1** ▪ to go round **4** ▪ to make **5** ▪ to shoot **5** ▪ to word **7** |
| **VI** to turn **1–5** ▪ to go round **1** ▪ to revolve **1** ▪ to run **1** ▪ to spin **1** ▪ to shift **3** ▪ to go off **4** |
| **VPR** to turn round **1** |

VT 1 *(roue, clé dans une serrure, la tête, les yeux, son attention, ses pensées etc)* to turn; *Culin (crème)* to stir; *(salade)* to toss; **t. qch autour de qch** to wind sth round sth; **t. le dos à qn/qch** *(action)* to turn one's back on sb/sth, to turn away from sb/sth; *(position)* to have one's back (turned) to sb/sth; **les yeux tournés vers le ciel** with upturned eyes; **t. les talons** *(partir)* to turn on one's heel, to turn and leave; *(s'enfuir)* to take to one's heels; **t. les pieds en dedans/en dehors** to turn one's toes in/out

2 *(changer)* to turn (**en** into); **t. les choses à son profit** to turn things to one's advantage, to capitalize on things; **t. tout en bien/en mal** to put a good/a bad interpretation on everything; **tout t. en reproche/critique** to turn everything into a reproach/a criticism; **t. qch à la plaisanterie** to turn sth into a joke, to laugh sth off; **t. qn/qch en ridicule** to poke fun at *or* make fun of sb/sth, to deride sb/sth; **je n'ai pas envie de me faire t. en ridicule par son frère** I don't want to be made fun of by his brother; **elle essaie de le t. contre son père** she's trying to turn him against his father

3 *(page etc)* to turn (over); *(carte)* to turn up; **t. et retourner qch** *(objet)* to turn sth over and over; **t. et retourner une idée dans sa tête** to go over and over an idea (in one's mind); *Fig* **il faut t. la page** it's time to make a fresh start

4 *(contourner) (coin)* to turn, to go round; *(obstacle)* to get round; *(ennemi)* to outflank, to circumvent; *(difficulté, loi)* to evade, to get round; *Naut* **t. un promontoire** to sail around a headland

5 *Cin (film, documentaire)* to make; *(scène) (cinéaste)* to film, to shoot; **le film a été tourné dans les rues de Paris** the film was shot in the streets of Paris

6 *Fig* **t. la tête à qn** *(du succès, d'une bourse etc)* to turn sb's head, to go to sb's head; *(du vin)* to go to sb's head; **il lui a tourné la tête** he has turned her head; **t. le(s) sang(s) à qn** to make sb's blood run cold; **cela m'a tourné l'estomac** it turned my stomach

7 *Tech (au tour) (objet)* to turn on a lathe; *Cér (pot)* to throw; *Fig (phrase)* to turn; *(compliment)* to word, to turn

VI 1 *(d'une clé)* to turn; *(d'une roue, d'une aiguille d'horloge)* to turn, to go round; *(d'une planète)* to revolve; *(d'une porte)* to swing, to move; *(d'une machine)* to run; *(d'une usine)* to run, to operate; *(d'un moteur)* to turn over; *(d'une toupie)* to spin; **tout tourne autour de lui, la tête lui tourne** he feels giddy, his head is swimming *or* spinning; **je l'ai vu t. autour de ma moto** I saw him hovering round my bike; **le lion tourne dans sa cage** the lion walks *or* paces round and round his cage; *Fig* **elle tourne autour de mon mari** she's sniffing around my husband; **ça devrait t. autour de 3 000 euros/de deux jours de travail** it should cost/take somewhere in the region of *or* something like 3,000 euros/two days; *Fig Fam* **t. autour du pot** to beat about the bush; **tout le poème tourne autour de ce souvenir** the whole poem revolves round this memory; **t. de l'œil** to pass out, to faint; **l'heure tourne** time is passing *or* getting on; *Fam* **il ne tourne pas rond, ça ne tourne pas rond (chez lui)** he's not all there; *Fig Fam* **j'ai l'impression de t. en rond** I feel as if I'm going round in circles; **faire t.** *(clé, roue, bouton de porte)* to turn; *(machine)* to operate; *(moteur)* to keep turning over *or* running; *(entreprise, boutique)* to run; **pour faire t. des usines en difficulté** to provide work for factories in difficulty; **elle fait t. les tables** she does table-turning; **tournez s'il vous plaît** please turn over, PTO

2 *(obliquer)* to turn; **tournez à gauche** turn (to the) left; **ne savoir de quel côté t.** not to know which way to turn, to be at one's wits' end

3 *(changer) (du vent)* to change direction, to shift; *Naut* to come about; **le vent a tourné à l'ouest** the wind has shifted *or* veered to the west; **le temps tourne au froid** it is turning cold; **le temps tourne au beau** the weather is changing *or* taking a turn for the better; **sa chance a tourné** his luck has turned *or* changed

4 *(du lait)* to turn, to go off

5 *(évoluer)* **bien/mal t.** to turn out well/badly; **il a mal tourné** he turned out badly; *Fam* **t. communiste/anarchiste** to turn communist/anarchist; **t. court** *(de négociations, d'une expérience, une discussion)* to stop short, to end abruptly; **cela tournait mal** things were taking a bad turn; **ça tournait mal entre eux** things were going wrong between them; **ça va mal t.** no good will come of it; **portraits qui tournent à la caricature** portraits that are almost *or* that verge on caricatures; **l'affaire tournait au tragique** the matter was taking a tragic turn *or* was turning to tragedy; **t. à la catastrophe** to turn into a catastrophe, to become catastrophic; **son amour a tourné en haine** his love has turned *or* changed to hatred; **t. au vinaigre** *(d'un vin)* to turn acid, to turn to vinegar; **t. à l'aigre** *(du lait)* to go *or* turn sour; *Fig (de relations)* to sour

6 *Cin (de la caméra)* to roll, to turn; **t. dans un film** to act in a film; **silence, on tourne!** quiet please, we're ready to shoot!

V IMPERS *Cartes* **il tourne carreau** the turn-up is diamonds

VPR **se tourner 1** *(se retourner)* to turn round; **se t. vers qn** to turn towards sb; *Fig* **se t. vers qn/la religion** to turn to sb/religion; **se t. et se retourner dans son lit** to toss and turn; **ses yeux se tournèrent vers la porte** his eyes turned to the door; *Fam* **se t. les pouces, se les t.** to twiddle one's thumbs

2 se t. contre qn to turn against sb; **c'est sa femme qui l'a fait se t. contre vous** it was his wife who turned him against you; **se t. du côté du peuple** to side with the people

3 *(changer)* **son amour se tourna en haine** his love turned *or* changed to hate

tournesol [turnəsɔl] NM **1** *Bot* sunflower; **graine/huile de t.** sunflower seed/oil **2** *Chimie* litmus; **papier (de) t.** litmus paper

tournette [turnɛt] NF **1** *(pour couper)* circular glass cutter **2** *Théâtre* revolve

tourneur, -euse [turnœr, -øz] ADJ *(derviche)* whirling

NM *Tech* turner; *Cér* thrower; **t. de vis** screwcutter; **t. sur bois/métaux** wood/metal turner

tournevis [turnəvis] NM screwdriver; **t. cruciforme** cross blade screwdriver; **t. d'électricien** electrician's screwdriver; **t. à choc** impact screwdriver; **t. plat, t. à embout** bit screwdriver; **t. à lame plate** flat blade screwdriver

tournicoter [turnikɔte], **tourniquer** [turnike] VI *Fam* to wander round and round, to prowl; **une idée qui me tournicote dans la tête** an idea that keeps running through my mind

tourniquet [turnikɛ] NM **1** *(barrière)* turnstile; *Mil Arg* **passer au t.** to be court-martialled **2** *Com (présentoir)* (revolving display) stand, spinner **3** *(pour cordages etc)* roller **4** *(sur un volet)* fastener **5** *(de jardin)* sprinkler **6** *Méd* tourniquet

tournis [turni] NM **1** *Vét* staggers **2** *Fam (vertige)* giddiness, dizziness; **avoir le t.** to feel giddy *or* dizzy; **donner le t. à qn** to make sb giddy *or* dizzy

tournoi [turnwa] NM *Hist, Sp, Cartes etc* tournament; **t. d'éloquence** contest of eloquence; **le t. des six nations** the Six Nations tournament

tournoiement [turnwamã] NM **1** whirling; *(d'un objet suspendu)* spinning; *(des oiseaux)* wheeling; *(de l'eau)* eddying, swirling **2** *(vertige)* giddiness, dizziness

tournoyant [turnwajã] ADJ whirling; *(oiseaux)* wheeling; *(eau)* eddying, swirling

tournoyer [turnwaje] VI **(je tournoie, n. tournoyons; je tournoierai)** *(d'objets suspendus ou dans l'eau, de feuilles etc)* to spin

(round and round), to turn round and round, to whirl; *(d'oiseaux)* to wheel; *(de l'eau)* to eddy, to swirl; **descendre en tournoyant** to come whirling down; **faire t. qch** to twirl *or* whirl sth

tournure [turnyr] NF **1** *(direction) (des événements)* turn; **les affaires prennent (une) meilleure/une mauvaise t.** things are taking a turn for the better/the worse; **j'aurais voulu donner une autre t. à l'événement** I wanted things done differently; **donner une t. agréable à la conversation** to steer the conversation to more pleasant topics *(aspect) (d'un objet, d'un édifice etc)* appearance; *(d'une histoire etc)* form; *Vieilli (maintien) (d'une personne)* bearing; **t. (de phrase)** turn of phrase; **t. d'esprit** turn of mind; **je n'ai pas sa t. d'esprit** I don't think the way he does; **prendre t.** to take shape

tournus [turnys] NM *Suisse (rotation des fonctions)* schedule, rota

tour-opérateur, *pl* **tour-opérateurs** NM tour operator

tourte [turt] NF **1** *Culin* pie; **t. aux pommes/à la viande** apple/meat pie **2** *Fam (idiot)* idiot, clot

tourteau, -eaux [turto] NM **1** *Agr* cattle cake **2** *(crustacé)* **t. (dormeur)** edible crab

tourtereau, -eaux [turtəro] NM *(oiseau)* young turtledove

NMPL *Fig* **tourtereaux** *(amoureux)* lovebirds

tourterelle [turtərɛl] NF *(oiseau)* turtledove

tourtière [turtjɛr] NF **1** *(pour tourte)* pie dish; *(pour tarte)* flan dish **2** *Can (tourte)* = (minced) pork pie

tous [tu(s)] ADJ, PRON *voir* **tout**

toussailler [tusaje] VI to have a little cough

Toussaint (la) [latusɛ̃] NF All Saints' Day; **la veille de la T.** Hallowe'en

---

Toussaint

All Saints' Day is a public holiday in France. It is the traditional occasion for a visit to the cemetery to lay flowers (usually chrysanthemums) on the graves of family and loved ones.

---

tousse [tus] NF *Belg (toux)* cough

tousser [tuse] VI *(d'une personne)* to cough; *Fig (d'un moteur)* to cough, to sputter; **il toussa pour m'avertir** he coughed *or* gave a cough to warn me; **t. sèchement** to have a dry cough; **tu tousses?** do you have a cough?

tousseur, -euse [tusœr, -øz] N *Fam* cougher

toussotement [tusɔtmã] NM slight cough; **un discret t.** a discreet cough

toussoter [tusɔte] VI to give a slight cough; **il toussote depuis quelques jours** he's had a slight cough for a few days; **il n'arrête pas de t.** he keeps coughing; **il a toussoté pour m'avertir** he gave a warning cough

tous-temps ADJ INV all-weather

TOUT, TOUTE, *pl* **tous, toutes** [tu, tut, tu, tut] *(when* **tous** *is a pron it is pronounced* [tus]) SEE GRAMMAR A36; B15

| ADJ any **1** ∎ every **1, 4, 5** ∎ all (the) **3, 4** ∎ the whole **3** |
| PRON everything **1** ∎ anything **1** ∎ all *(tous/toutes)* **2** |
| NM the whole **1** ∎ everything **1** ∎ total **3** |
| ADV quite **1** ∎ very **1** ∎ utterly **1** ∎ while *(tout en)* **3** |

ADJ 1 *(n'importe quel)* any, every; **tu peux l'appeler à t. moment** you can call him any time; **t. Français y a droit** any French person

is *or* all French people are entitled to it; **t. travail lui est interdit** he is forbidden to do any work; **t. travail mérite salaire** all work merits payment; **t. autre que vous** anybody but you; **t. autre en aurait fait autant** anybody else would have done the same; **toute liberté d'agir** full liberty to act; **avoir toute liberté de choisir** to be quite free to choose; **j'ai toute raison de croire que ...** I have every reason to believe that ...; **repas servis à toute heure** meals served at any time *or* round the clock

2 *(emploi intensif)* **à la toute dernière minute** at the very last minute; **en t. dernier lieu** last, lastly; **des arbres de toute beauté** most beautiful trees; **à toute vitesse** at full speed; **donner toute satisfaction à qn** to give sb complete *or* full satisfaction; **le nouvel employé nous donne toute satisfaction** the new employee is proving quite satisfactory, we're quite satisfied with the new chap; **c'est t. l'effet que ça te fait?** is that all it means to you?; **pour toute arme il avait une canne** his only weapon was a walking stick; **pour toute réponse il éclata de rire** his only answer was to burst out laughing; **je suis t. à toi** I'm all yours; **il est de toute importance que ...** + *sub* it is of the utmost importance that ...; *Naut* **la barre toute!** hard over!

3 *(complet)* **t. le, toute la** all (the), the whole; **t. le monde** everybody, everyone; **j'ai vu t. Truffaut** I've seen everything of Truffaut's, I've seen all of Truffaut's films; **j'ai lu t. Proust** I've read everything of Proust's, I've read all of *or* the whole of Proust; **elle a t. Ellington dans sa discothèque** she's got everything Ellington ever recorded, she's got all Ellington's records; **t. Paris est en danger** the whole of *or* all Paris is in danger; **t. La Haye se trouvait dans les rues** the whole *or* entire population of The Hague was in the streets; **t. l'univers** the entire *or* whole universe; **toute la famille** the whole *or* entire family, all the family; **t. mon argent** all my money; **t. le jour, toute la journée** the whole *or* entire day, all day (long); **pendant t. l'hiver** throughout the (entire) winter, all through the winter, all winter long; **travailler t. l'été** to work all summer; **t. cet été** this whole summer, all this summer; **t. mars se passa sans nouvelles** the whole of March went by without news; **répéter t. le temps la même chose** to keep on saying the same thing; **au milieu de t. ça ...** in the middle of all this *or* it all ... VOIR GRAMMAIRE A5

4 tous les, toutes les *(la totalité de)* all the; *(chaque)* every; **tous les invités** all the guests; **tous ces livres** all these books; **toutes les femmes du monde te le diraient** any woman in the world would tell you that; **tous les jours** every day; **tous les quarts d'heure** every quarter of an hour; **toutes les fois que ...** whenever ..., each *or* every *or* any time that ...; **les critiques viennent de tous (les) côtés** *ou* **de toutes parts** criticism is coming from all sides *or* quarters; **les fruits arrivent de toutes parts** the fruit comes from everywhere *or Fam* from all over the place; **de toutes (les) couleurs** of every (possible) colour; **champion toutes catégories** overall champion; **meubles tous budgets** furniture to suit all pockets

5 *(avec des nombres)* **tous (les) deux** both; **tous (les) trois/(les) dix** all three/ten; **tous les deux jours** every two days, every other *or* second day; **tous les trois jours** every three days, every third day; **tous les deux ou trois jours** every two or three days; **toutes les cinq minutes** every five minutes; **tous les deux mètres** every two metres; *Fam* **tous les combien?** how often?

6 t. un, toute une a whole, an entire; **t. un quartier de la ville** a whole *or* an entire district of the town; **c'est toute une histoire** it's a long story; *(c'est difficile)* it's quite a job; **pas la peine d'en faire toute une histoire** there's no point in making a big thing *or* a big fuss about it; **il en a fait t. un drame** he made a song and dance about it

PRON **1** everything; **il a t. mangé** he has eaten everything *or* the (whole) lot; **t. est bon** everything is good, it's all good; **t. n'est pas à lire dans son œuvre** not everything he's written is worth reading; **l'argent n'est pas t.** money isn't everything; **mais ce n'est pas t., elle est menteuse aussi** but not only that, she's a liar too; **elle connaît t. de l'affaire** she knows all about it; **il ignore encore t. de notre relation** he still doesn't know anything about our relationship; **ce sera t.?** *(dans un magasin)* will there be anything else?; *Iron* **c'est** *ou* **ce sera t.?** is that all?, anything else while I'm at it?; **je crois que c'est t.** I think that's (about) everything *or Fam* the lot; **ce sera t. pour aujourd'hui** that will be all for today; **c'est t. ou rien** it's all or nothing; *Ordinat* **t.-ou-rien** all-or-nothing; *Fam* **... et t. et t. ...** et cetera, et cetera, ... and all the rest of it; *Prov* **t. est bien qui finit bien** all's well that ends well; **il est capable de t.** he is capable of anything; **elle fera t. pour t'ennuyer/t'aider** she'll do anything (she can) to annoy/help you; **voilà t. ce que je sais** that's all I know; **j'aime t. ce qui est français** I love anything *or* everything French; **je comprends t. ce qu'il dit** I understand everything he says; **t. ce qui vous plaira** whatever you like, anything you like; **c'est t. ce qu'il y a de plus beau/de plus drôle** nothing could be more beautiful/funnier; **t. ce qu'il y a de mieux** nothing but the best; **il mange de t.** he eats anything (and everything); **on trouve de t. à Paris** you find all sorts in Paris; **depuis lors j'ai fait de t.** I've done all sorts of things since then; **j'ai fait un peu de t. dans ce bureau** I've done a bit of everything in this office; *Fam* **il a t. du fonctionnaire** he's the typical *or* complete civil servant; **elle a t. de sa mère** she's just like her mother; **il a t. du garde-champêtre avec son képi** he looks just like a policeman with that cap; **c'est dire** need I say more?; **c'est t. un** it's all one; **homme à t. faire** *(bon en tout)* all-rounder; *(qui touche à tout)* Jack-of-all-trades; *(factotum)* odd-job man; **à t. prendre ...** on the whole ..., all in all ...; *Fam* **drôle/joli comme t.** awfully funny/pretty, as funny/pretty as anything

2 tous [tus], **toutes** all; **tous ont des enfants** they all have children; **leurs amis ont tous des enfants** their friends all have children; **une (bonne) fois pour toutes** once and for all; **venez/approchez tous!** come along/gather round, everybody *or* all of you!; **on ne tiendra pas tous** we won't all fit; **ils sont tous là** they are all there; **vous devez tous accomplir votre devoir** all of you must *or* you must all do your duty; **le meilleur de tous** the best of (them) all, the best of the lot; **il est impossible de les nommer tous** it is impossible to name them all *or* all of them *or* each and every one of them; **on nous en offrit un verre à tous** we were all offered a glass; **il nous a parlé à tous séparément** he spoke to all of us individually; **leur bonheur à tous** the happiness of all of them *or* of them all; **tous à la fois** all at the same time; *Iron* **ne répondez pas tous à la fois!** don't all answer at once!; *Fam* **on l'aimait bien tous** we were all very fond of him; **nous/vous/eux tous** all of us/of you/of them; **combien d'argent ont-ils à eux tous?** how much money do they have between them?

NM **1 le t.** the whole, the lot; **le t. est de réussir** the main thing is to succeed; **jouer le t. pour le t.** to stake *or* gamble everything, *Fam* to go for broke; **former un t.** to form a

whole; *Fam* **ce n'est pas le t. (de rigoler comme ça),** j'ai du travail à faire this is all very well but I've got work to do

2 du t. au t. entirely, completely; **en t.** *(au total)* in all, altogether; **en t. et pour t.** in all, altogether; **(pas) du t.** not at all, not in the slightest; **je ne le connais pas du t.** I don't know him at all *or* in the slightest

3 *Math* (*pl* **touts**) total; **mon t.** *(dans une charade)* my whole

ADV (*before a f adj beginning with a consonant or* **h** *aspirate* **tout** *becomes* **toute**) **1** *(complètement)* quite; **t. nouveau(x), toute(s) nouvelle(s)** brand new; **la toute nouvelle imprimante de chez ...** the very latest printer from ...; **ils sont t. seuls, elles sont toutes seules** they are all alone *or* on their own; **elle était encore toute jeune** she was still quite young; **toute jeune, elle était plus timide que maintenant** when she was very young, she was shyer than she is now; **t. enfant** even as a child, when still a child; **les gens ne sont pas t. bon(s) ou t. mauvais** people are not wholly *or* altogether good or bad; **toute de noir vêtue** (dressed) all in black; **elle était toute honteuse** she was utterly ashamed; **du matériel de t. premier ordre** top-calibre equipment, equipment of the very first order; **une t. autre personne** an entirely *or* a to tally different person; **t. droit** *(se tenir)* bolt upright; *(continuer)* straight on; **parler t. haut/bas** to speak in a normal/low voice; **t. neuf** brand new; **t. nu** stark naked; **t. éveillé** wide awake; **t. endormi** falling asleep, very sleepy; **vêtement t. fait** ready-made garment; **plat t. préparé** ready-made meal; **viande toute cuite** ready-cooked meat; **t. au bout** right at the end, at the very end; **t. près, t. à côté** *(habiter, se trouver)* very close by, just round the corner, a couple of minutes away; **se mettre t. à côté de qn** to stand right alongside sb; **t. là-bas** right over there; **t. contre le mur** right against the wall; **t. en sang/sueur** (all) covered with blood/sweat, bloody/sweaty; **un enfant t. en jambes** a very leggy child; **c'est t. comme chez nous!** it's just like home!; *Fam* **c'est t. comme** it comes to the same thing; **il ne m'a pas raccroché au nez, mais c'était t. comme** he didn't actually hang up on me, but he might as well have; **il est t. à son commerce** he is entirely absorbed in *or* taken up with his business; **t. doux!** gently!

2 t. à fait quite, entirely, altogether; **je suis t. à fait d'accord avec toi** I quite agree with you; *Fam* **oui, t. à fait** *(pour confirmer un fait)* absolutely; **cela me va t. à fait** it suits me perfectly *or* down to the ground; **il lui ressemble t. à fait** he is just like him; *Fam* **il y a t. plein de livres/de neige** there are/is loads of books/of snow; **à t. va** like anything; **t. au plus** at the very most; **t. au moins, t. le moins** at the very least; **t. au moins, c'est ce qu'elle dit** at least that's what she says; **t. à vous** *(dans une lettre)* yours ever

3 t. en parlant/mangeant while speaking/eating; **elle siffle t. en conduisant** she whistles while *or* as she drives; **t. en le disant, je pensais à autre chose** I was thinking of something else while *or* as I was saying it; **elle a accepté, t. en ressentant une certaine jalousie** even though she agreed, she still felt a bit jealous

4 *(aussi)* **t. ignorant qu'il soit** *ou* **qu'il est** however ignorant he is, ignorant though *or* as he is, ignorant though he may be; **t. jeune qu'il soit, il est très capable** young though he is, he's very able, he may be young but he's very able; **t. secrétaire que je suis, j'ai droit au respect** I may only be a secretary but I'm still entitled to some respect; **t. père/toute mère que je suis** although I am a father/a mother, father/mother though I am; **t. aussi joli/intelligent**

just as *or* every bit as pretty/intelligent **5 être t. oreilles** *ou* **toute ouïe** to be all ears; **il était toute crainte et toute haine** he was consumed with fear and hatred; **elle était t. attention** she was all attention; **elle est t. le portrait de sa mère** she is the living *or* spitting image of her mother

▸ ▸ **T.-Paris: le T.-Paris était là** all of Paris *or* anybody who's anybody in Paris was there

tout-à-l'égout NM INV mains drainage; **avoir le t.** to have mains drainage

Toutankhamon [tutākamɔ̃] NM Tutankhamen

toute-épice, *pl* **toutes-épices** NF *Bot, Culin* allspice

toutefois [tutfwa] ADV however; **t., je le garde** I'll keep it however *or* nevertheless

toute-puissance NF **1** *Rel* omnipotence **2** *Pol etc* absolute power

toutes-boîtes [tutbwat] NM INV *Belg* free paper, freesheet

tout-fou, *pl* **tout-fous** *Fam* ADJ M crazy NM idiot, nut

toutim(e) [tutim] NM *Fam* **... et tout le t. ...** et cetera, et cetera, ... and all the rest of it

toutou [tutu] NM *Enf* doggie, bow-wow; **suivre qn comme un t.** to follow sb meekly *or* meek as a lamb *or Am* like a puppy dog

tout-petit, *pl* **tout-petits** NM (tiny) tot, toddler

tout-puissant, toute-puissante, *pl* **tout(es)-puissant(e)s** ADJ *(pays, syndicat, directeur etc)* all-powerful, almighty, omnipotent; *Fig (désir)* overwhelming; *(influence)* enormous NM *Rel* **le T.** the Almighty

tout-terrain ADJ INV **véhicule t.** all-terrain *or* off-road vehicle, ATV; **vélo t.** mountain bike

tout-venant NM INV *Minér* ungraded product; *(houille)* unsorted coal; *Fig* **le t.** *(gens)* everybody and his wife, the ragtag and bobtail; **un livre qui n'est pas accessible au t.** a book that is not accessible to just anybody

toux [tu] NF cough; **une quinte** *ou* **un accès de t.** a coughing fit, a fit of coughing; **t. sèche/grasse** dry/loose cough; **sirop/pastilles pour** *ou* **contre la t.** cough mixture *or* syrup/sweets *or* drops *or* lozenges

township [tawnʃip] NF township

toxémie [tɔksemi] NF *Méd* blood-poisoning, *Spéc* toxaemia, *Am* toxemia

toxicité [tɔksisite] NF toxicity; **coefficient de t.** toxicity rating

toxico [tɔksiko] N *Fam* drug addict

toxicodépendance [tɔksikodepãdãs] NF drug dependence *or* dependency

toxicologie [tɔksikɔlɔʒi] NF toxicology

toxicologique [tɔksikɔlɔʒik] ADJ toxicological

toxicologue [tɔksikɔlɔg] N toxicologist

toxicomane [tɔksikɔman] ADJ addicted to drugs N drug addict

toxicomanie [tɔksikɔmani] NF drug addiction

toxicomanogène [tɔksikɔmanɔʒɛn] ADJ *Méd* addictive

toxicose [tɔksikoz] NF toxicosis

toxine [tɔksin] NF *Physiol* toxin

toxique [tɔksik] ADJ toxic, poisonous; **gaz t.** poison gas NM poison

toxoplasmose [tɔksoplasmoz] NF *Méd* toxoplasmosis

TP [tepe] NMPL *Scol* *(abrév travaux pratiques)* practical work; **avoir un TP de chimie** to have a practical chemistry lesson *or* a chemistry lab

TPC [tepese] NF *Ordinat* (*abrév* **tierce partie de confiance**) TTP

TPIR [tepeiɛr] NM (*abrév*Tribunal pénal international pour le Rwanda) ICTR

TPIY [tepeigrɛk] NM (*abrév*Tribunal pénal international pour l'ex-Yougoslavie) ICTY

tpm [tepeɛm] *Tech* (*abrév* **tours par minute**) rpm

TPV [tepeve] NM (*abrév* **terminal point de vente**) point-of-sale terminal

traboule [trabul] NF *Région* alleyway

trac[1] [trak] NM *Fam* nervousness, fright; *Théâtre* stage fright; **il a le t.** he's nervous; *Théâtre* he's got stage fright; **c'est bon pour le t.** it's good for the nerves; **elle ne sait pas quoi faire contre le t.** she doesn't know how to stop herself getting so nervous

trac[2] NM **tout à t.** out of the blue, without warning

traçage [trasaʒ] NM (*de graphiques etc*) drawing; (*de routes, de jardins etc*) laying out

traçant [trasɑ̃] ADJ **1** *Bot* (*racine*) running, creeping **2** *Mil* (*obus, balle*) tracer **3** *Ordinat* **table traçante** plotter

tracas [traka] NM worry, trouble, bother; **un grand t., bien du t.** a lot of headaches *or* worry *or* trouble *or* bother; **des t.** worry, trouble, bother; **faire du t. à qn** to cause sb trouble *or*bother

tracasser [trakase] VT (*personne*) (*d'un problème etc*) to worry, to bother; (*d'une personne, d'un organisme etc*) to pester, to harass; **avoir l'air tracassé** to look harassed

VPR **se tracasser** to worry (**pour qch** about sth)

tracasserie [trakasri] NF **tracasserie(s)** harassment; **tracasseries administratives** red tape; **en butte aux tracasseries de la police** subjected to police harassment

tracassier, -ière [trakasje, -jɛr] ADJ (*employé, patron etc*) nitpicking, picky
N nitpicker

trace [tras] NF **1** traces (*d'animal*) trail, track, spoor; (*d'une personne*) tracks, trail; (*d'un véhicule*) tracks; **des traces de pas** footprints; **des traces de pneus** tyre tracks; **être sur la t. de qn/qch** to be on the track of sb/ sth; *Fig* **être sur la t. de qn** (*d'un reporter etc*) to dog sb's footsteps; **retrouver la t.** to pick up the scent *or* the trail; **retrouver la t. de qn/de qch** to pick up the trail of sb/sth; **je n'en ai pas vu la t.** I haven't seen hide nor hair of it; **disparaître sans laisser de t.** to disappear without trace; **perdre la t. de qn** to lose trace *or* track of sb; **on ne retrouve aucune t. de cet événement dans les journaux** there is no trace *or* mention of the event in the newspapers; **toute t. de cet événement semble avoir été effacée** all traces of the event seem to have been wiped out; *Fig* **il marche sur** *ou* **il suit les traces de son père** he's following in his father's footsteps; *Fig* **laisser une t. profonde** to leave a deep impression (behind), to leave its mark; **cela a laissé en elle des traces profondes/indélébiles** it affected her deeply *or* made a profound impression on her/left an indelible mark on her; **cette musicienne n'a pas laissé beaucoup de traces** this musician didn't leave much of a mark; *Ski* **faire la t.** to break trail; *Ski* **t. directe** direct descent; *Électron* **t. du spot** trace (*in cathode-ray tube*)

2 (*marque*) mark; **une t. de brûlure/piqûre** a burn/needle mark; **une t. de sang/d'encre** a splash of blood/ink; **une t. de saleté** a dirty mark; **traces de sang/de fatigue** traces of blood/fatigue; **traces de peinture/de doigts** paint/finger marks

3 (*petite quantité*) (*de poison*), *Fig* (*de regret, remords*) trace

4 (*vestige*) (*d'une ancienne civilisation etc*) trace

5 *Géom* (*d'un plan etc*) trace

tracé [trase] NM **1** (*plan*) (*de route, de chemin de fer etc*) route, path, layout; (*de ville*) layout; **t. de ligne** line drawing; **faire le t. de** to plan the layout of **2** (*ligne, contour*) (*de graphique, de côte etc*) line; **suivre le t. du fleuve** to follow the river

tracer [trase] (**je traçai(s); n. traçons**) VT **1** (*dessiner*) (*ligne, plan, dessin etc*) to draw; (*courbe, graphique*) to plot; (*lettre, mot etc*) to write; (*faire le plan de*) (*route, chemin de fer etc*) to map the course of; (*piste, sillon*) to mark out; *Fig* (*ligne d'action*) to map out; **t. les lignes d'un court de tennis** to mark out a tennis court; *Fig* **t. les grandes lignes de qch** to outline sth, to indicate the general outlines of sth; *Fig* **le tableau qu'il nous en a tracé n'est pas des plus reluisants** he didn't exactly paint a very inspiring picture of it **2** (*chemin dans la jungle etc*) to open up; *Fig* **t. le chemin à qn** to lay out a path for sb; *Fig* **son chemin est tout tracé** his path is all laid out *or* mapped out for him **3** *Suisse* (*rayer*) to delete, to cross off

VI **1** (*d'une racine*) to run out, to creep **2** *Arg* (*aller vite*) to move like greased lightning

traceret [trasrɛ] NM (*outil*) scriber, tracing awl

traceur, -euse [trasœr, -øz] NM **1** *Nucl* **t. (radioactif)** tracer **2** *Ordinat* **t. (de courbes)** plotter; **t. à plat** flatbed plotter; **t. à plumes** pen plotter; **t. à tambour** drum plotter
ADJ (*substance, obus, balle*) tracer

trachéal, -ale, -aux, -ales [trakeal, -o] ADJ *Anat* tracheal

trachée [traʃe] NF *Anat, Zool* windpipe, *Spéc* trachea

trachée-artère, *pl* **trachées-artères** NF *Anat, Zool Vieilli* windpipe, *Spéc* trachea

trachéite [trakeit] NF *Méd* tracheitis

trachéo-bronchite [trakeɔbrɔ̃ʃit] NF *Méd* tracheobronchitis

trachéotomie [trakeɔtɔmi] NF *Chir* tracheotomy

trachome [trakom] NM *Méd* trachoma

traçoir [traswar] NM (*outil*) scriber, tracing awl

tract [trakt] NM *Pol* pamphlet, leaflet, tract; *Com etc* leaflet; *Rel* tract

tractable [traktabl] ADJ towable

tractation [traktasjɔ̃] NF *Péj surtout pl* **tractations** dealings, bargaining, negotiations

tracté [trakte] ADJ tractor-drawn

tracter[1] [trakte] VT to tow; **se faire t.** to be towed, to get a tow

tracter[2] VI *Fam* (*distribuer des tracts*) to leaflet

tracteur, -trice [traktœr, -tris] NM tractor; **t. et semi-remorque** articulated vehicle, *Fam* artic; *Aut* **t. routier** tractor; **t. de papier** (*d'une imprimante*) paper tractor; **t. à picots** (*d'une imprimante*) tractor drive
ADJ **1** (*qui remorque*) towing **2** *Géog* **force tractrice** (*d'un courant*) transport capacity

traction [traksjɔ̃] NF **1** *Phys* traction, pulling; *Méd* traction; *Tech* **exercer une t. sur qch** to exercise traction on sth; **effort de t.** pull, *Spéc* tractive effort; **t. magnétique** magnetic pull; **résistance à la t.** tensile strength; *Gym* **faire des tractions** (*en tirant*) to do pull-ups; (*en poussant*) to do press-ups *or Am* push-ups **2** *Aut* **t. avant/arrière** front-wheel/rear-wheel drive

tractopelle [traktɔpɛl] NF backhoe loader

tractoriste [traktɔrist] N tractor driver

tractus [traktys] NM *Anat* tract, system

tradescantia [tradɛskɑ̃sja] NM *Bot* tradescantia

trade-unionisme [trɛdynjɔnism] NM trade unionism

tradition [tradisjɔ̃] NF tradition; **respecter la t.** to respect tradition; **c'est dans la plus pure t. française** it is typically French; **faire qch selon la t.** to do sth in the traditional way; **la t. veut que … + sub** tradition dictates that …; **il existe une longue t. de liens culturels entre ces pays** there is a long history of cultural links between the countries

traditionalisme [tradisjɔnalism] NM tradition-alism

traditionaliste [tradisjɔnalist] ADJ, N traditionalist

traditionnel, -elle [tradisjɔnɛl] ADJ (*fondé sur la tradition*) traditional; (*habituel*) usual, habitual; (*excuse, appareillage etc*) standard, usual; (*plaisanterie*) standing

traditionnellement [tradisjɔnɛlmɑ̃] ADV traditionally, by tradition; **se marier t.** to have a traditional wedding

traducteur, -trice [tradyktœr, -tris] N translator
NM *Ordinat* translator

traduction [tradyksjɔ̃] NF **1** (*action*) translation (**en** into); **la t. n'est pas une discipline facile** translating is not easy; **agence de t.** translation agency; **t. automatique/simultanée** machine/simultaneous translation; **t. assistée par ordinateur** computer assisted translation, machine translation **2** (*texte*) translation; **t. de la Bible en français** the French translation of the Bible; **elle ne lit que des traductions** she only ever reads translations *or* in translation **3** *Ordinat* **t. des informations** data reduction

traduire [traduir] (*prp* **traduisant;** *pp* **traduit;** *pr ind* **je traduis, il traduit, n. traduisons, ils traduisent;** *impf* **je traduisais;** *p hist* **je traduisis;** *fu* **je traduirai**) VT **1** to translate (**de** from; **en** into) **2** *Ordinat* (*carte*) to interpret **3** *Fig* (*exprimer*) (*sentiment, idée etc*) to express, to convey; **vous traduisez mal ma pensée** you're misinterpreting me *or* my thoughts; **cette réaction traduit une grande sensibilité** this reaction is indicative of *or* points to great sensitivity **4** *Jur* **t. qn en justice** to sue *or* prosecute *or* indict sb

VI *Ling* to translate (**de/vers** from/into); **t. mot à mot** to translate word for word

VPR **se traduire 1** *Ling* to be translated; **comment ça se traduit?** how do you translate it? **2** (*avoir pour résultat*) **se t. par qch** to result in sth; **le ralentissement de l'activité économique s'est traduit par de nombreux licenciements** the slowdown in economic activity brought about numerous redundancies; *Fig* **sa douleur se traduisit par des larmes** his grief found expression *or* manifested itself in tears

traduisible [traduizibl] ADJ **1** *Ling* translatable; **ce jeu de mots n'est pas t.** this play on words is untranslatable; **difficilement t.** difficult to translate **2** *Jur* **t. en justice** liable to prosecution

Trafalgar [trafalgar] NM *Fig* **coup de T.** underhand trick

trafic [trafik] NM **1** (*commerce illégal*) traffic; **t. de stupéfiants** *ou* **de drogues/d'armes** drug/arms traffic *or* trafficking; **ils ont mis sur pied un t. d'uranium enrichi** they've set up an arrangement for trafficking in enriched uranium; *Fam* **faire t. de ses charmes** (*d'une prostituée*) to sell one's body; *Fam* **il y a un drôle de t. dans cette boutique** there's something very queer *or* funny going on in that shop; *Fam* **les enfants font un sacré t. avec leurs jouets** the kids are up to *or* involved in some mysterious game with their toys **2** (*circulation*) traffic; **le t. est ralenti sur la nationale 7** traffic is moving slowly on route 7 **3** *Électron* traffic **4** (*de site Internet*) traffic **5** *Vieilli* (*commerce*) trading, trade ▸▸**t. aérien** air traffic; **t. commercial** commercial trade; **t. d'influence** influence peddling; **il a obtenu ce marché grâce à un véritable t. d'influence** he landed the deal thanks to a fair amount of string-pulling; **t. des marchandises** goods traffic; *Ordinat* **t. de réseau** network traffic; **t. routier** road traffic

traficoter [trafikɔte] *Fam* **VI** *Péj* to tinker **VT** (*manigancer*) **je me demande ce qu'il traficote** I wonder what he's up to

trafiquant, -ante [trafikɑ̃, -ɑ̃t] **N** *Péj* trafficker; **t. de** *ou* **en stupéfiants** *ou* **de drogues** drug trafficker; **t. d'armes** arms dealer, gunrunner; **t. du marché noir** black marketeer

trafiquer [trafike] **VI** *Péj* to traffic (**de** in) **VT** *Fam* **1** (*modifier*) (*moteur de voiture, Mobylette® etc*) to tinker with; (*freins, compteur*) to tamper with; (*chèque*) to falsify, to tamper with; (*vin*) to doctor, to tamper with; **t. les comptes** to fiddle the accounts **2** (*manigancer*) **qu'est-ce qu'il trafique?** what's he up to?

trafiqueur, -euse [trafikœr, -øz] **N** *Péj* trafficker (**de, en** in)

tragédie [traʒedi] **NF** *Théâtre, Fig* tragedy; *Fig* **c'est une véritable t.** it's a real tragedy, it's really tragic; *Fam Fig* **ce n'est pas une t.!** it's not the end of the world!

tragédien, -ienne [traʒedjɛ̃, -jɛn] **N** tragic actor, *f* tragic actress, tragedian, *f* tragedienne

tragi-comédie, *pl* **tragi-comédies** [traʒikɔmedi] **NF** *Théâtre, Fig* tragi-comedy

tragi-comique, *pl* **tragi-comiques** [traʒikɔmik] **ADJ** *Théâtre, Fig* tragi-comic

tragique [traʒik] **ADJ** (*auteur, pièce, rôle*), *Fig* (*événement, conséquences etc*) tragic; **... dit-elle d'un accent t.** ... she said in a tragic tone of voice; **ce qu'il y avait de vraiment t., c'est que ...** what was really tragic *or* the real tragedy was that ...; *Littér* **le genre t.** tragedy **NM 1** (*d'un événement*) tragedy, tragic side; **cela tourne au t.** it's turning into a tragedy; *Fig* **prendre qch au t.** to make a tragedy *or* a big thing out of sth **2** *Théâtre* **le t.** tragedy **N** (*auteur*) tragic author, writer of tragedies

tragiquement [traʒikmɑ̃] **ADV** tragically; **finir t.** to end tragically *or* in tragedy

trahir [trair] **VT 1** (*divulguer*) (*secret*) to betray, to reveal, to give away; (*de paroles, silence*) (*gêne, ignorance etc*) to betray, to reveal; (*d'un accent*) (*personne*) to give away; **je fus trahi par les aboiements d'un chien** I was betrayed *or* given away by a dog barking **2** (*cesser d'être fidèle à*) (*personne, pays, confiance, intérêts*) to betray; (*serment, promesse etc*) to break; *Fig* (*de jambes, forces, traducteur*) (*personne, auteur*) to fail; *Fig* **la traduction trahit le texte** the translation fails *or* is not faithful to the text; **son mari la trahit pour une femme plus âgée** her husband is being unfaithful to *or* deceiving her with an older woman; **se sentir trahi** to feel betrayed **3** *Arch* **t. qn/qch à qn** to betray sb/ sth to sb **VPR se trahir** (*d'une personne*) to give oneself away; (*d'un sentiment etc*) to betray itself, to be revealed

trahison [traizɔ̃] **NF 1** (*fait de trahir*) (*d'un ami, de son pays etc*) betrayal **2** (*faute*) treachery; *Pol* treason; **haute t.** high treason; **une t.** an act of treachery

traille [traj] **NF 1** (*câble*) ferry cable **2** (*bac*) ferry

train [trɛ̃] **NM 1** *Rail* train; **je prends le t. de cinq heures** I'm catching the five o'clock

(*train*); **je préfère le t. à la route** I'd rather go by train than by road; **voyager en t.** *ou* **par le t.** to travel by train; **voyage en t.** train journey; **être dans un t.** to be on a train; **monter dans le t.** to get on the train; **prendre le t. en marche** to jump on (a/the train while it's moving); *Fig* to jump *or* climb on the bandwagon; **comme une vache qui regarde passer un t.** like a cow at a five-bar gate **2** *Mil* **le t.** ≃ transport branch of the Army Service Corps **3** (*file*) (*de véhicules, de péniches, d'animaux transhumants etc*) string, line; (*de roues etc*) set; (*de réformes, décrets*) series, string **4** *Arch* (*escorte*) suite, attendants; (*de serviteurs etc*) train **5** (*de cheval*) quarters; (*derrière*) (*de chien*) rump; **t. de derrière/de devant** hindquarters/forequarters **6** *Arg* (*derrière*) (*d'une personne*) backside, rear (end), *Am* butt; **se manier le t.** to get a move on, to shift oneself, *Arg* to get one's arse in gear; **filer le t. à qn** to shadow *or* tail sb **7** (*allure*) pace; **aller bon t.** to go at a good pace; **aller son petit t.** to jog along; **les choses vont leur t.** things are going along as usual; *Vieilli* **dans le t.** up to date; *Fam* **à fond de t.** at top *or* full speed, *Fam* at a rate of knots; **rouler à un t. d'enfer** to go hell for leather; **au t. où il va/où vont les choses** at the rate he's/things are going; **à ce t.-là** at this rate; *Sport* **meneur de t.** pacemaker; **mener le t.** to set the pace; **mener grand t.** to live it up; **avec le salaire que je gagne, je ne risque pas de mener grand t.** I'm not likely to paint the town red on what I make **8 en t.** (*projet, affaire*) under way, in progress; *Fam* **ils ont un petit en t.** they've got a baby on the way, they're expecting; *Fam* **il était un peu en t.** (*ivre*) he'd had a drop (too much); **être en bon t.** to be making good progress; **mettre qch en t.** (*projet etc*) to set sth in train *or* motion, to start sth, to set sth going; (*tricot*) to start sth; **c'est lui qui a tout mis en t.** he got everything started *or* under way; **mise en t.** shakedown; **être en t. de faire qch** to be doing sth; **il était en t. de travailler** he was (busy) working; **elle est toujours en t. de crier** she's always shouting

SEE GRAMMAR B30

9 *Fam* (*tapage*) noise, row; **faire du t., faire un t. de tous les diables** to kick up (a hell of) a row

10 (*humeur*) **être en t.** to be in good spirits *or* in good form; **il n'était pas en t. ce jour-là** he wasn't at his best that day; **être mal en t.** to be out of sorts, to feel unwell; **je ne suis pas en t. pour travailler** I don't feel like working, I'm not in the mood for work; **mettre qn en t.** to get sb into a good mood

11 *Aviat* landing gear, undercarriage ▸▸*Aviat* **t. d'atterrissage** landing gear, undercarriage; **T. Auto et Moto Accompagnées, T. Automobile Accompagnée** *Br* ≃ Motorail, *Am* ≃ AutoTrain; **t. autos-couchettes** car-sleeper train; **t. avant** *Aviat* nose gear *or* wheel; *Aut* front axle (assembly); **t. de bois** timber raft, float; **t. de croisière** luxury train; **t. direct** through train; **t. électrique** electric train; **t. d'engrenages** gear train; **t. express** express (train); *Rail* **t. à grande vitesse** high-speed train; *Vieilli* **t. de maison** style of living; **t. de marchandises** goods *or Am* freight train; **t. militaire** troop train; **t. de neige** = train carrying holidaymakers to ski resorts; **t. omnibus** local *or* slow *or* stopping train; *Phys* **t. d'ondes** wavetrain; **t. postal** mail train; *Tech* **t. de roulement** (*d'un véhicule à roues*) undercarriage; (*d'un véhicule traîné*) suspension and tracks; **t. routier** road train; **t. spatial** space train; **t. supplémentaire** relief train; **t. de vie** lifestyle, way of life; **t. de voyageurs** passenger train

traînage [trɛnaʒ] **NM 1** dragging; *Rail* (*de trains*) haulage; *Rail* (*de péniches*) towing **2** (*transport par traîneaux*) sleigh transport

traînailler [trɛnaje] **VI** *Fam* = **traînasser**

traînant [trɛnɑ̃] **ADJ 1** (*robe etc*) trailing **2** (*lent*) (*voix*) drawling; (*démarche, pas*) shuffling, dragging

traînard, -arde [trɛnar, -ard] **N** *Fam* (*en arrière d'un groupe*) straggler; (*dans son travail*) dawdler, slowcoach, *Am* slowpoke

traînasser [trɛnase] **VI** *Fam* **1** (*errer*) to loaf *or* slouch about *or* around **2** (*être lent*) to dawdle, to drag one's feet; (*n'avoir aucune énergie*) to drag oneself around

train-couchettes **NM** **INV** sleeper

traîne [trɛn] **NF 1** *Naut* **à la t.** in tow; *Fig Fam* **être à la t.** to lag behind **2** (*d'une robe*) train **3** *Pêche* seine (net), drag net **4** *Can* **t. sauvage** toboggan

traîneau, -eaux [trɛno] **NM 1** (*tiré par des chevaux*) sleigh; (*tiré par des chiens*) sledge, *Am* sled; **faire une promenade en t.** to go for a sleigh ride; **chien de t.** sledge dog, husky; **attelage de chiens de t.** dog team **2** *Pêche* seine (net), drag net

traîne-bûches **NM** **INV** *Pêche Fam* bait, *Spéc* caddis worm

traîne-buisson, *pl* **traîne-buissons** **NM** *Orn* dunnock, hedge sparrow

traînée [trɛne] **NF 1** (*de fumée, de sang, de lumière etc*) trail; (*de saleté*) streak; (*de poudre*) train; (*d'un escargot*) trail; *Aviat* vapour *or Am* vapor trail, *Spéc* contrail; *Fig* **se répandre comme une t. de poudre** to spread like wildfire **2** *Phys* (*force*) drag **3** *Arg* (*prostituée*), *Péj* (*femme*) tart

traînement [trɛnmɑ̃] **NM** (*des pieds*) dragging; (*de la voix*) drawling

traîne-misère **N** **INV** *Fam* down-and-out

traîner [trɛne] **VT** (*quelqu'un, quelque chose*) to drag; *Rail* (*wagons etc*) to pull, to haul; (*péniches*) to tow; *Fig* (*sa vie*) to drag out; (*discours, affaire etc*) to spin out, to drag out; (*paroles*) to drawl; **faire t. qch en longueur** to spin *or* drag sth out; **elle traînait cinq enfants après elle** she was trailing *or* dragging five children after her; **elle traîne sa sœur partout** she drags her sister everywhere with her; **t. la jambe** to limp; **t. les pieds** to shuffle; *Fig* to drag one's feet; **elle entra dans la pièce en traînant les pieds** she shuffled into the room; **la perdrix traînait (de) l'aile** the partridge was dragging a wing; **t. qn en prison** to drag sb off to prison; *Fig* **elle traîne un rhume depuis quinze jours** she's had a cold for two weeks that she can't get rid of *or* shake off; *Fig* **t. qn dans la boue** to drag sb *or* sb's name through the mud; *Fam* **il doit bien t. ses guêtres** *ou* **bottes quelque part!** he must be somewhere around!; **j'ai traîné mes bottes dans tous les pays d'Afrique** I've kicked around every country in Africa; **t. son ennui** to be constantly bored

VI 1 (*dans la poussière, la boue etc*) to trail, to drag; **votre robe traîne (par terre)** your dress is trailing

2 (*rester en arrière*) to lag *or* trail (behind); **t. derrière qn** to lag *or* trail behind sb; **une voix qui traîne** a drawling voice

3 (*errer*) (*dans un endroit*) to hang *or* kick *or* knock around *or* about; **t. dans la rue** *ou* **par les rues** to hang *or* kick *or* knock around *or* about the streets; **où est-ce qu'il traîne d'habitude?** where does he usually hang out?; **t. avec qn** to hang about with sb; **il y a un virus qui traîne** there's a virus going around *or* doing the rounds

4 (*être lent*) (*d'une personne*) to dawdle; (*de la conversation*), *Théâtre etc* (*d'une intrigue*) to drag

5 *(en désordre)* to lie *or* kick around *or* about; **laisser t. son argent** to leave one's money lying around *or* about; **tes vêtements traînent partout dans la maison** your clothes are scattered all over the house **6** *(durer longtemps)* *(d'une maladie, d'une conversation etc)* to drag on; **t. en longueur** *(d'un procès etc)* to drag (on); **les choses ne traînent pas avec vous** you're a fast worker, you don't hang about, you don't let the grass grow under your feet; *Fam* **... et que ça ne traîne pas!** ... and don't take forever about it!, ... and be quick about it!; **laisser t. un compte** to leave an account unpaid

VPR se traîner 1 *(d'une personne)* to drag oneself; **il se traînait à peine** he could hardly drag himself along; **il se traîna jusqu'au fossé** he dragged himself *or* crawled to the ditch; **se t. aux pieds de qn** to go on one's knees to sb; **je me suis traîné cette sale grippe tout l'hiver** I've had this rotten cold hanging around all winter; **je me suis traîné ces vieilles chaussures tout l'hiver** I've had to wear *or* put up with these old shoes all winter **2** *(d'une conversation, d'une soirée etc)* to drag on; **les heures se traînent lourdement** time drags, time hangs heavy

traînerie [trɛnri] NF *Can Fam* **1** **ramasse les traîneries dans ta chambre!** *(objets en désordre)* clear away all the junk lying around your bedroom! **2 pas de traînerie!** *(dépêche-toi)* look sharp!, be quick about it!

traîne-savates N INV *Fam* layabout, loafer

traîneux, -euse [trɛnø, -øz] NM *Can Fam* slob

training [trɛniŋ] NM **1** *Sport (entraînement)* training **2** *Psy* **t. autogène** relaxation by autosuggestion **3** *(survêtement)* tracksuit **4** *(chaussure)* trainer

train-poste, *pl* **trains-poste** NM mail train

train-train NM INV *Fam* routine, daily round; **le t. quotidien** the daily routine *or* grind; **rien qui sort du t. des événements ordinaires** nothing out of the ordinary

traire [trɛr] VT *(prp* trayant; *pp* trait; *pr ind* je trais, n. trayons, ils traient; *impf* je trayais; *fu* je trairai; *no p hist)* *(vache, chèvre etc)* to milk; *(lait)* to draw; **machine à t.** milking machine

trait [trɛ] NM **1** *(ligne etc)* stroke, line; *Typ* long dash; **d'un t. de plume** with a stroke of the pen; **signer d'un t. de plume** to sign with a flourish; **t. plein/discontinu** continuous/broken line; **dessin au t.** outline drawing; **copier qch t. pour t.** to copy sth line by line; *Fig* **c'est sa sœur t. pour t.** she is her sister to a T; **gravure au t.** line engraving; **les grands traits de qch** the main features of sth; *Tél* **points et traits** dots and dashes; *Fig* **tirer un t. sur le passé** to forget the past, to draw a line under the past; **tirer un t. sur ses vacances** to say goodbye to one's holidays, to kiss one's holidays goodbye; **j'ai tiré un t. sur lui/notre relation** I've crossed him/our relationship off; **t. de scie** cut(ting) line **2** *(du visage)* feature; **traits réguliers/fins/grossiers** regular/fine/coarse features; **elle avait les traits tirés** she looked drawn, her face was drawn **3** *(caractéristique)* *(d'une personne)* trait; *(d'un écrivain etc)* characteristic touch; **t. de caractère** character trait, trait of character; **c'est l'un de ses traits distinctifs** it's one of his peculiarities *or* distinctive traits **4** *(flèche)* arrow; *Fig* **partir comme un t.** *(d'une personne)* to be off like a shot; *Fig* **les traits de la médisance/la satire** slanders/shafts of satire; *Fig* **un t. mordant/méchant** a sarcastic/nasty remark; *Fig* **envoyer ou lancer un t. à qn** to get a dig in at sb **5 avoir t. à qch** to be connected with sth, to relate to sth; **tout ce qui a t. à la psychana-**lyse everything connected *or* to do with psychoanalysis **6** *(de lumière)* beam, shaft **7** *Mus* fast passage **8** *(de boisson)* gulp, *Litt* draught, *Am* draft; **boire à longs traits** *(bière etc)* to gulp down; **d'un (seul) t.** *(boire qch)* at one gulp, *Fam* at one go, in a oner; *(raconter qch)* without stopping, in one fell swoop; *(lire qch)* without stopping, at a single sitting **9** *(de cordes, de poids)* pulling; **cheval de (gros) t.** (heavy) draught *or Am* draft horse **10** *(d'un harnais)* trace **11** *Échecs etc* **avoir le t.** to have first move **12** *(acte) (de courage)* act, deed; *(de génie)* stroke

▸▸ *Typ* **t. double** double line; *Fig* **t. d'esprit** flash *or* stroke of wit, witticism; *Typ* **t. en pointillé** dotted underline; *Typ* **t. simple** single line; **t. d'union** hyphen; *Fig (entre deux personnes, deux villes etc)* link; *Ordinat* **t. d'union conditionnel** soft hyphen; *Ordinat* **t. d'union insécable** hard hyphen

traitable [trɛtabl] ADJ **1** *Litt (personne)* tractable, accommodating **2** *(sujet etc)* treatable, manageable

traitant [trɛtã] ADJ **1** *(shampoing, crème de beauté etc)* medicated **2 mon médecin t.** my (usual) doctor; **nom du médecin t.** name of the doctor in attendance *or* of the consulting physician

traite [trɛt] NF **1** *(d'une route etc)* stretch; **j'ai fait une longue t.** I've come a long way; **(tout) d'une t., d'une seule t.** in one go; **faire le chemin d'une t.** to do the journey nonstop *or* without stopping *or Fam* in a oner **2** *Fin (billet)* (banker's) draft, bill (of exchange); **présenter une t. à l'acceptation** to present a bill for acceptance **3** *(des vaches)* milking

▸▸ **t. bancaire** bank draft; **t. des Blanches** white slave trade; *Fin* **t. de complaisance** accommodation bill; *Fin* **t. contre acceptation** acceptance bill; *Fin* **t. à courte échéance** short-dated bill; *Fin* **t. à date fixe** time bill; *Fin* **t. documentaire** documentary bill; *Fin* **t. libre** clean bill; *Fin* **t. à longue échéance** long-dated bill; **t. des Noirs** slave trade; *Fin* **t. pro forma** pro forma bill; *Fin* **t. 'sans frais'** bill 'without protest'; *Fin* **t. à terme** term draft; *Fin* **t. à vue** sight draft

traité [trɛte] NM **1** *(ouvrage)* treatise (**de, sur** on) **2** *Pol (accord)* treaty; *UE* **t. d'adhésion** membership treaty; **t. d'alliance** treaty of alliance; **t. de commerce** commercial treaty; *UE* **t. de Maastricht** Maastricht Treaty; **t. de non-prolifération nucléaire** Nuclear Non-Proliferation Treaty; **t. de paix** peace treaty; *UE* **t. sur l'Union européenne** Treaty on European Union

traitement [trɛtmã] NM **1** *(comportement à l'égard de qn)*, *Méd* treatment; *(d'un sujet par un auteur)* treatment, handling; **mauvais t.** ill-treatment, maltreatment; *Méd* **prescrire un t.** to prescribe treatment; **premier t.** initial treatment; **t. chirurgical** surgery; **malade en t.** patient under(going) treatment; **t. de choc/de fond** shock/long-term treatment **2** *Tech (de matières premières)* processing, treatment; *(de l'eau)* treatment; *Constr* **t. superficiel** *(des routes etc)* surfacing; *Ind* **capacité de t.** processing *or* handling capacity **3** *Ordinat* processing; **données en t., capacité ou débit de t.** throughput; **machine à ou de t. de texte** word processor; **logiciel de t. de texte** word processor, word processing software; **unité de t.** task, job **4** *(rémunération)* pay, salary; **t. de base** basic pay *or* salary; **t. fixe** fixed salary; **t. initial** starting salary; **sans t.** *(secrétaire)* honorary; *(magistrat)* unsalaried

▸▸ *Ordinat* **t. automatique de l'information** *ou* **des informations** automatic data pro-cessing; *Com* **t. des commandes** order processing; *Ordinat* **t. différé par lots** batch processing; **t. à distance** teleprocessing; **t. des données** data processing, DP; **t. électronique de l'information** electronic data processing, EDP; **t. de faveur** preferential treatment, red carpet treatment; **t. d'images** image processing; **t. de l'information** *ou* **des informations** data processing, DP, information processing; **t. par lots** batch processing; **t. multitâche** multitasking processing; *Ordinat* **t. en temps réel** real time processing; **t. de texte** word processing, WP; *(logiciel)* word processor, word processing software; *(machine)* word processor; **réaliser qch par t. de texte** to word process sth; *Ordinat* **t. de texte à balises** word processing with embedded visible commands; **t. vectoriel** vector processing

traiter [trɛte] VT **1** *(se conduire envers)* to treat; **t. qn en ami/enfant** to treat sb like *or* as a friend/a child; **t. qn d'égal (à égal)** to treat sb as an *or* one's equal; **t. qn avec douceur** to treat *or* handle sb gently; **t. qn avec condescendance** to be condescending towards sb, to patronize sb; **je ne supporterai pas plus longtemps de me faire t. comme cela!** I won't take much more of being treated like this!, I won't take much more of this treatment!

2 *(qualifier)* to call; **t. qn de lâche** to call sb a coward; **se faire t. de lâche** to be called a coward; **elle l'a traité de tous les noms** she called him all the names under the sun

3 *Méd (patient, maladie)* to treat; **elle se fait t. pour un cancer** she's being treated for cancer, she is having *or* undergoing treatment for cancer; **tu devrais faire t. ça** you ought to get it treated

4 *Tech (matière première, minerai)* to process; *(bois)* to treat; *Agr (vignobles, cultures etc)* to treat, to spray; **oranges non traitées** unsprayed oranges

5 *Ordinat (informations)* to process; **données non traitées** raw data

6 *Litt Vieilli (régaler)* to entertain

7 *Com (marché etc)* to negotiate; *(affaire)* to handle

8 *(s'occuper de)* *(sujet, problème, question etc) (d'un auteur, un artiste, un élève, un article)* to deal with; *(demande d'emploi, dossier de bourse etc)* to process; **l'auteur traite bien le sujet** the author handles the subject well; **comment Paris-Match traite-t-il cet événement?** how does Paris-Match deal with *or* handle *or* cover the event?; **t. une accusation avec mépris** to treat an accusation with scorn

VI 1 *(négocier)* **t. avec** to deal with; *(créanciers)* to negotiate with **2 t. de** *(d'un livre, un écrivain etc)* *(sujet, problème etc)* to deal with

VPR se traiter 1 *(réciproque)* to treat each other; **elles se traitent de tous les noms** they call each other all the names under the sun **2** *(se négocier)* to be dealt with **3** *(d'un sujet, d'un écrivain etc)* to be dealt with; **cela se traite facilement** that can be easily dealt with **4** *(d'une maladie)* to be treated; **cela se traite très bien, maintenant** it can be treated now, there's treatment for it now

traiteur [trɛtœr] NM **1** *Com* caterer **2** *Arch (restaurateur)* restaurateur

traître, traîtresse [trɛtr, trɛtrɛs] ADJ *(personne)* treacherous; *(escalier, crevasse etc)* dangerous, treacherous; *(soleil)* treacherous, strong; *(vin)* deceptively strong; *Fam* **pas un t. mot** not a single word

N **1** traitor, *f* traitress; *Iron, Hum* **ah, le t., il ne nous disait rien!** the sly devil, he didn't tell us!; **être t. à sa patrie** to be a traitor to one's country, to commit treason; **prendre qn en t.** to set out to trap sb, to set a trap for sb; **agir en t.** to be underhanded **2** *Théâtre* **le t.** the villain

traîtreusement [trɛtrøzmɑ̃] ADV *(agir)* treacherously; **se venger t.** to take a traitor's revenge

traîtrise [trɛtriz] NF **1** *(comportement)* treachery, treacherousness **2** *(action)* (piece of) treachery

trajectoire [traʒɛktwar] NF *(d'une étoile, une comète, un avion, un électron, une balle etc)* path, trajectory; *Météo* depression; *Aviat* **t. de vol** flight path; **t. de collision** collision course

trajet [traʒɛ] NM **1** *(voyage)* journey; *(distance)* distance; *(itinéraire)* route; **j'ai fait une partie du t. en avion** I flew part of the way; **faire le t. en voiture** to do the journey by car; **j'ai dû faire le t. à pied** I had to walk all the way; **j'ai dû faire le t. dans l'autre sens pour le chercher** I had to come/go all the way back to get it; **un t. en voiture/autobus** a car/bus journey *or* ride; **il y a bien deux heures de t.** it takes a good two hours; **il a deux heures de t. pour aller au bureau** he has a two-hour journey to the office **2** *(d'une artère, d'un nerf etc)* course; *Mil (d'un projectile)*, *Élec (d'un courant)* path; **t. de papier** *(dans une imprimante)* paper path

tralala [tralala] NM INV *Fam* **en grand t.** *(se marier)* with a lot of fuss; **pas la peine d'en faire tout un t.** there's no point making a great fuss about it; **... et tout le t.** ... et cetera, et cetera, ... and all the rest of it; INT **j'ai gagné, t.!** ha-ha, I've won!

tram [tram] NM *Fam* = **tramway**

tramage [tramaʒ] NM *Ordinat* rastering

tramail, -ails [tramaj] NM *Pêche* trammel (net)

trame [tram] NF **1** *Tex* woof, weft; *Fig (de la vie)* fabric; **usé jusqu'à la t.** *(pull, tapis)* threadbare; *Fig* **la t. du récit** the framework of the story; *Fig* **la t. de l'histoire** the storyline **2** *Anat (complot)* plot, conspiracy **3** *Phot, Typ (écran)* (half-tone) screen **4** *TV* raster; **t. (double)** frame **5** *Typ* **t. de maquette** layout sheet

tramer [trame] VT **1** *Tex, Fig (intrigue d'un roman)* to weave **2** *(combiner) (complot)* to devise, *Fam* to hatch; **je me demande ce qu'il est en train de t.** I wonder what he's up to **3** *Phot* **t. un cliché** to take a negative through a screen
▶ VPR **se tramer il se trame quelque chose** there's something going on, there's something in the wind *or* afoot

traminot [tramino] NM tram *or Am* streetcar worker

tramontane [tramɔ̃tan] NF **1** *(vent)* tramontana **2** *Arch (étoile)* north star; *Fig* **perdre la t.** to lose one's bearings; *(devenir fou)* to go off one's head

tramp [trãp] NM *Naut* tramp (steamer)

trampoline [trãpɔlin] NM *(toile)* trampoline; *(sport)* trampolining; **faire du t.** to go *or* do trampolining

tramway [tramwɛ] NM tram, *Am* streetcar; **voyager en t.** to travel by tram

tranchant [trãʃɑ̃] ADJ **1** *(outil, épée, bord etc)* sharp **2** *Fig (paroles, ton)* trenchant, peremptory, decisive; *(personne)* assertive, peremptory
▷ NM **1** *(d'un couteau, d'une épée etc)* (cutting) edge; *(d'une cale)* thin end; *(de la main)* edge; **à deux tranchants, à double t.** *(épée, couteau etc)* two-edged; *Fig* **argument à double t.** argument that cuts both ways; *Fig* **cette décision est à double t.** the decision is a two-edged sword **2** *(de tanneur)* fleshing knife

tranche [trãʃ] NF **1** *(morceau coupé) (de pain, de melon, de viande etc)* slice; *(de bacon)* rasher; **en tranches** in slices, sliced; **vous le voulez en tranches?** would you like

it sliced?; *Culin* **t. napolitaine** Neapolitan ice (cream); *Culin* **t. grasse** *(morceau de bœuf)* round, top rump; **morceau dans la t.** = piece of topside; *Fam* **s'en payer une t.** to have the time of one's life **2** *(de marbre, de pierre)* slab **3** *(bord, côté) (d'une pièce de monnaie, d'une cale, d'une planche)* edge; *(d'un livre)* (cut) edge; **doré sur t.** *(livre)* with gilt edges, gilt-edged **4** *(série, section) (de chiffres)* group, block; *(d'actions)* block, portion; *(d'un crédit)* instalment, *Am* instalment; *(d'assistance financière internationale)* tranche; *(d'un programme immobilier)* stage, portion; *Rail* **t. de voitures** portion; **t. des salariés moyens** middle-income bracket **5** *Tech (coupe)* section; **t. verticale** vertical section **6** *Ordinat* wafer; **microprocesseur en tranches** bit slice microprocessor
▶▶ **t. d'âge** age bracket *or* group *or* band; *Radio, TV* **t. horaire** (time) slot; **t. d'imposition** tax band *or* bracket; **t. de paiement** instalment, *Am* installment; **t. de prix** price bracket; **t. de revenu** income group; **les gens dans les tranches de revenus les plus élevées** people in the upper income brackets; *Fig* **t. de vie** slice *or* cross-section of life

tranché [trãʃe] ADJ *Fig (couleur, motif etc)* definite, distinct; *(opinion)* definite, clearcut; *(refus)* blunt; **les avis sont très tranchés** opinions are very clear-cut, people are very definite in their opinion

tranchée [trãʃe] NF **1** *(fossé)* trench; *Agr* drain; *Rail* cutting; *Mil* **guerre de tranchées** trench warfare **2** *(dans une forêt)* cutting; **t. garde-feu** firebreak **3** *Méd* **tranchées** colic

tranchée-abri, pl **tranchées-abris** NF *Mil* dugout

tranchefile [trãʃfil] NF *(d'un livre relié)* headband

trancher [trãʃe] VT **1** *(cordage, câble etc)* to cut; *(bras, membre, tête)* to sever; **t. la gorge à qn** to slit *or* cut sb's throat; **t. la tête à qn** to cut off *or* chop off sb's head; **qu'on lui tranche la tête!** off with his/her head! **2** *(discussion)* to cut short; *(question, différend)* to settle (once and for all); *(problème, difficulté)* to resolve, to make short work of; **voilà qui tranche la question!** that settles it!; **tranchons là** let's stop there
▷ VI **1** *(décider)* to decide, to reach a decision; **t. dans le vif** *Chir* to cut into healthy tissue; *Fig* to take drastic measures; **il tranche sur tout** he's always laying down the law **2** *(de couleurs etc)* to contrast strongly (**sur** with), to stand out (**sur** against)
▶ VPR **se trancher se t. le doigt** to sever one's finger

tranchet [trãʃɛ] NM **1** *(de serrurier etc)* anvil cutter **2** *(de tanneur)* paring knife

trancheur, -euse [trãʃœr, -øz] NM *Tech, Min* cutter; *Pêche* cod gutter
▷ NF **trancheuse** stone saw

tranchoir [trãʃwar] NM *(planche)* chopping board

tranquille [trãkil] ADJ **1** *(calme, paisible) (personne, vie etc), Com (marché)* quiet; *(soirée)* still, peaceful, quiet; *(mer)* calm, still, *Litt* tranquil; *(conscience, esprit etc)* easy, untroubled; *(sommeil)* untroubled, peaceful; *(boussole)* steady; *Fam* **un père t.** *(homme, bébé)* a quiet one; **se tenir t.** to keep still; **j'adore cet endroit, je m'y sens vraiment t.** I love this place, I really feel at peace here; **travailler t.** to work in peace; **vous pouvez dormir t.** you can sleep in peace *or* rest easy; **laissez-moi t.** leave me alone *or* in peace, let me be; *Fam* **laisse ce vase t.!** leave that vase alone!; **laisse ça t., je m'en occuperai** don't bother with that, I'll take care of it; **soyez t.** don't worry, set your mind at rest *or* at ease; **soyez t., il reviendra!** he'll come back, don't you worry!; **avec ce**

plan d'épargne/ces chaussures en cuir, je suis t. with this savings plan/these leather shoes I don't need to worry; **elle ne m'a pas rappelé, je ne suis pas t.** she hasn't phoned me back, I'm anxious *or* worried *or* not easy in my mind; **je ne suis pas t. dans cette grande maison** I get nervous in this big house; *Fam* **tu peux être t. que ...** you can be sure that ...; **je n'ai pas la conscience t.** my conscience is bothering me; **moi, j'ai la conscience t.** my conscience is clear; **faire qch la conscience t.** to do sth with a clear conscience
2 *(sans bruit) (ville, quartier)* quiet, peaceful; **est-ce que nous pouvons aller dans un endroit t.?** can we go somewhere quiet?; **se tenir t.** *(ne rien dire)* to keep quiet

tranquillement [trãkilmɑ̃] ADV *(répondre, examiner, travailler etc)* calmly, quietly; *(vivre)* quietly, peacefully; *(dormir)* peacefully; *(partir)* with an easy mind, with a clear conscience, without worrying

tranquillisant [trãkilizɑ̃] ADJ *(nouvelles)* reassuring; *(paroles, voix)* reassuring, soothing, calming; *(effet)* soothing, calming; *Pharm* tranquillizing; *Pharm* **avoir un effet t.** to act as a sedative; **cela n'est pas très t.** that's not very reassuring
▷ NM *Pharm* tranquillizer

tranquilliser [trãkilize] VT **t. qn** to reassure sb, to set sb's mind at rest; **ça te tranquillisera** it will set your mind at rest *or* give you peace of mind
▶ VPR **se tranquilliser** to stop worrying; **tranquillisez-vous** don't worry, set your mind at rest

tranquillité [trãkilite] NF **1** *(calme) (de la mer)* calmness, stillness; *(de la campagne)* stillness, quietness, peace; *(de la nature)* tranquillity; *(du sommeil)* peacefulness; **j'ai besoin de t.** I need some peace and quiet; **c'est un enfant d'une grande t.** he's a very quiet *or* placid child; **t. d'esprit** peace of mind; **troubler la t. publique** to disturb the peace; **en toute t.** without being disturbed; *(sans souci)* with an easy mind, without worrying, with a clear conscience; **je vais pouvoir travailler en toute t.** I'll be able to work in peace (and quiet) **2** *(absence de bruit) (d'une ville)* quietness

tranquillos [trãkilos] ADV *Fam (tranquillement)* **vas-y t., inutile de faire des excès de vitesse** take your time, there's no need to break the speed limit; **ils étaient dans le canapé en train de siroter mon whisky, t.** they were on the sofa sipping away at my whisky, without a care in the world

trans- [trãs, trãz] PRÉF trans-

transaction [trãzaksjɔ̃] NF **1** *Com, Fin* transaction; **transactions** transactions, dealings; **transactions bancaires** bank transactions; **transactions boursières** Stock Exchange transactions; **transactions commerciales** business transactions; *Bourse* **t. au comptant** spot transaction; *Bourse* **t. de clôture** closing trade; *Banque* **t. par carte** card transaction; *Bourse* **transactions hors bourse** after-hours dealings, street dealing; *Bourse* **transactions à terme** futures; *Banque* **t. valeur jour** value today trade **2** *(arrangement)* compromise

transactionnel, -elle [trãzaksjɔnɛl] ADJ **solution transactionnelle** compromise; *Psy* **analyse transactionnelle** transactional analysis

transafricain [trãzafrikɛ̃] ADJ transafrican, cross-Africa

transalpin [trãzalpɛ̃] ADJ transalpine

transaméricain [trãzamerikɛ̃] ADJ transamerican

transat [trãzat] NM *Fam* deck chair

transatlantique [trãzatlãtik] ADJ transatlantic ◆ NM **1** *(paquebot)* (transatlantic) liner **2** *(chaise longue)* deck chair

transbahuter [trãsbayte] *Fam* VT *(affaires, enfants)* to cart, to lug ◆ VPR **se transbahuter** to shift

transbordement [trãsbɔrdəmã] NM *Naut* transhipment; *Rail* transfer

transborder [trãsbɔrde] VT *Naut* to tranship; *Rail (passagers, marchandises)* to transfer

transbordeur, -euse [trãsbɔrdœr] ADJ, NM **(pont) t.** transporter bridge

transcanadien, -ienne [trãskanadjɛ̃, -jɛn] ADJ trans-Canada ◆ NF **la Transcanadienne** *(autoroute)* the Trans-Canada Highway

transcendance [trãsãdãs] NF *Phil, Rel etc* transcendence, transcendency

transcendant [trãsãdã] ADJ **1** *Phil, Rel etc* transcendent; *Fam* **ce/il n'est pas t.** it's/he's not much to write home about, it's/he's nothing great **2** *Math* transcendental

transcendantal, -ale, -aux, -ales [trãsãdãtal, -o] ADJ *Phil* transcendental

transcendantalisme [trãsãdãtalism] NM *Phil* transcendentalism

transcender [trãsãde] VT to transcend ◆ VPR **se transcender** to surpass oneself

transcodage [trãskɔdaʒ] NM *Ordinat* transcribing, transcoding; *TV* standards conversion

transcoder [trãskɔde] VT *Ordinat* to transcribe

transcodeur [trãskɔdœr] NM *TV* transcoder, standards converter; *Ordinat* transcoder

transconteneur [trãskɔ̃t(ə)nœr] NM transcontainer; *(navire)* transcontainer ship

transcontinental, -ale, -aux, -ales [trãskɔ̃tinãtal, -o] ADJ transcontinental

transcriptase [trãskriptaz] NF **t. inverse** *ou* **reverse** reverse transcriptase

transcripteur [trãskriptœr] NM transcriber

transcription [trãskripsjɔ̃] NF **1** *(action)* transcription, transcribing; *(dans un autre alphabet)* transliteration; **t. phonétique** phonetic transcription; **t. génétique** (genetic) transcription **2** *(texte)* transcript; *Mus* transcription; **t. à l'état civil** = certified copy of registry office document

transcrire [trãskrir] VT *(conj like* **écrire**) **1** *(recopier) (manuscrit), Mus (morceau)* to transcribe; **t. une lettre à la machine** to type a letter **2** *Jur (divorce etc)* to register; *Com* to post **3** *(dans un autre alphabet) (texte etc)* to transcribe, to transliterate; **t. un livre en braille** to copy a book in Braille

transculturel, -elle [trãskyltyrɛl] ADJ cross-cultural

transcutané [trãskytane] ADJ transcutaneous

transdermique [trãsdɛrmik] ADJ transdermal; **timbre t.** skin patch, transdermal patch

transdisciplinaire [trãsdisiplinɛr] ADJ interdisciplinary

transducteur [trãsdyktœr] NM *Phys, Électron* transducer

transe [trãs] NF **1** *transes (anxiété)* fear; *Vieilli* **être dans les transes** to be sick with worry, to be out of one's mind with anxiety **2** *(hypnose)* (hypnotic) trance; **en t.** *(médium), Fig (fans)* in a trance; **entrer en t.** to go into a trance; *Fig Fam (se mettre en colère)* to hit the ceiling

transept [trãsɛpt] NM *Archit* transept

transférable [trãsferabl] ADJ transferable

transfèrement [trãsfɛrmã] NM *(de prisonnier etc)* transfer; **t. cellulaire** transfer by police van

transférer [trãsfere] VT (**je transfère, n. transférons; je transférerai**) **1** *(dans un autre lieu) (détenu, siège social etc)* to transfer (**à** to); *Rel (évêque)* to translate; **t. de l'argent d'un compte à un autre** to transfer money from one account to another **2** *(céder) (marchandises etc)* to transfer, to make over, to assign (**à** to); *(propriété)* to convey (**à** to) **3** *Psy (affection etc)* to transfer (**sur** to) **4** *Ordinat (données)* to transfer

transfériste [trãsferist] N *(dans l'industrie du tourisme)* transferist

transfert [trãsfɛr] NM **1** *(d'un prisonnier, d'un siège social), Sport (d'un footballeur etc)* transfer; *(de population)* resettlement (**dans** in) **2** *(cession) (du stock, de droits etc)* transfer, assignment, making over; *(d'un domaine)* conveyance **3** *Psy* transference; **faire un t. sur qn** to use sb as an object of transference; **cela fait partie du t.** it's part of the transference process ► ► **t. d'actions** transfer of shares; *Tél* **t. d'appel** call transfer; **t. de capitaux** transfer of capital, capital transfer; *Banque* **t. par CCP** giro transfer; *Compta* **t. de charges** expense transfer, transfer of charges; *Compta* **t. de créances** assignment of accounts receivable *or* of debts; **t. de devises** currency transfer; *Ordinat* **t. de données** data transfer; *Ordinat* **t. de fichiers** file transfer; **t. de fonds électronique, t. électronique de fonds** electronic funds transfer, EFT

transfiguration [trãsfigyrasjɔ̃] NF transfiguration

transfigurer [trãsfigyre] VT to transfigure

transfiler [trãsfile] VT *Naut* **1** *(voiles etc)* to lace **2** *(cordage)* to snub

transfo [trãsfo] NM *Élec Fam* transformer

transformable [trãsfɔrmabl] ADJ *(canapé, fauteuil etc)* convertible

transformateur, -trice [trãsfɔrmatœr, -tris] *Élec* ADJ transforming; *(station)* transformer ◆ NM transformer

transformation [trãsfɔrmasjɔ̃] NF **1** *(changement)* change; *(radicale)* transformation; *(d'un local)* conversion; **la t. de l'eau en glace** the transformation of water to ice; **acteur à transformations** quick-change artist(e); **industrie de t.** processing industry; *Math* **t. algébrique** algebraic transformation **2** *Élec* **rapport de t.** transformer ratio; *Électron* **t. de signaux** signal transformation **3** *Rugby (d'un essai)* conversion; **faire une t.** to convert (a try)

transformer [trãsfɔrme] VT **1** *(personne, rapports etc)* to change; *(radicalement)* to transform; *(local, maison)* to convert, to remodel; **ils ont transformé l'appartement en l'agrandissant** they've transformed the flat by making it bigger; **cette expérience l'a profondément transformé** the experience has caused a profound change in him *or* has transformed him; **t. en** to turn *or* change *or* transform into; **l'école fut transformée en cinéma** the school was turned *or* converted into a cinema; **la sorcière l'a transformé en souris** the witch turned him into a mouse **2** *Math (équation)* to transform **3** *Rugby (essai)* to convert **4** *Électron* to transform, to map **5** *(en logique) (proposition)* to convert ◆ VPR **se transformer** to be transformed, to change; **tout se transforme** everything changes; **se t. en** to turn into; **se t. en monstre/papillon** to turn *or* change *or* be transformed into a monster/butterfly; **se t. en haine/en cauchemar** to turn into hate/a nightmare

transformisme [trãsfɔrmism] NM *Phil etc* transformism

transformiste [trãsfɔrmist] ADJ *Phil etc* transformist ◆ N *Phil etc* transformist; *(qui s'habille en femme)* drag queen; *(dans cabaret)* drag artist; **spectacle de transformistes** drag show

transfrontalier, -ière [trãsfrɔ̃talje, -jɛr] ADJ cross-border

transfuge [trãsfyʒ] N *Pol, Mil, Fig* defector

transfusé, -ée [trãsfyze] ADJ **sang t.** transfused blood ◆ N **le nombre des transfusés** the number of people receiving (blood) transfusions

transfuser [trãsfyze] VT *(sang)* to transfuse; *(malade)* to give a (blood) transfusion to, to transfuse

transfusion [trãsfyzjɔ̃] NF (blood) transfusion; **faire une t. à un malade** to give a patient a transfusion; **t. sanguine** blood transfusion; **centre de t. sanguine** blood transfusion centre; **t. d'échange** exchange transfusion

transgène [trãsʒɛn] NM transgene

transgenèse [trãsʒənɛz] NF transgenesis

transgénique [trãsʒenik] ADJ transgenic

transgresser [trãsgrese] VT *(règlement, loi)* to infringe, to contravene, *Fml* to transgress; *(interdit)* to infringe; *(ordres)* to disobey

transgresseur [trãsgrescer] NM *Litt* transgressor

transgression [trãsgresjɔ̃] NF *(du règlement, de la loi)* infringement, contravention, *Fml* transgression; *(d'ordres)* disobeying

transhumance [trãzymãs] NF move from/ to summer pastures, *Spéc* transhumance

transhumant [trãzymã] ADJ moving from/ to summer pastures, *Spéc* transhumant

transhumer [trãzyme] VTI to move from/to summer pastures

transi [trãzi] ADJ paralysed (**de peur** with fear); **t. (de froid)** freezing, chilled to the bone; *Iron* **un amoureux t.** a bashful lover

transiger [trãziʒe] VI (**je transigeai(s); n. transigeons**) **1** to compromise (**avec** with; **sur** on); **t. sur ses principes/avec sa conscience** to compromise one's principles/ one's conscience; **je ne transigerai pas avec mon devoir/le règlement** I refuse to compromise *or* I am intransigent when it comes to my duty/the rules; **je ne transigerai pas sur l'honnêteté** I refuse to be anything less than totally honest; **il ne transige pas sur l'honnêteté** he is uncompromisingly honest, he makes no compromises when it comes to a question of honesty **2** *Can (négocier)* to negotiate

Transilvanie [trãsilvani] NF Transylvania

transir [trãzir] VT *(du vent etc)* to chill to the bone; *(de la peur)* to paralyse ◆ VI *Arch (de froid)* to be chilled to the bone; *(de peur)* to be paralysed with fear

transistor [trãzistɔr] NM **1** *Électron (dispositif)* transistor; **à transistors** transistorized; **t. en couche mince** thin film transistor, TFT **2** *(poste de radio)* transistor (radio)

transistorisé [trãzistɔrize] ADJ *Électron* transistorized

transistoriser [trãzistɔrize] VT *Électron* to transistorize

transit [trãzit] NM **1** transit; **en t.** in transit; **passagers en t.** *(dans un aéroport)* passengers in transit, transfer passengers; *Aviat* **salle de t.** transit *or* transfer lounge; *Com* **t. communautaire** Community transit; **marchandises de t.** goods for transit; **maison de t.** forwarding agency **2** *Électron* **t. par bande perforée** tape relay ► ► *Com* **t. douanier** Customs transit; *Méd* **t. intestinal** intestinal transit; **favoriser le t. intestinal** to encourage regular bowel movements; **favorise le t. intestinal** keeps you regular

transitaire [trɑ̃zitɛr] ADJ **pays t.** country of transit; **commerce t.** transit trade NM forwarding agent, freight forwarder; **t. aéroportuaire** airfreight forwarder; **t. portuaire** maritime freight forwarder

transitaire-groupeur, pl **transitaires-groupeurs** [trɑ̃zitɛrgrupœr] NM forwarder and consolidator

transiter [trɑ̃zite] VT (marchandises) to forward
VI (de marchandises, de voyageurs) to (pass in) transit (**par** through); Ordinat (de signaux) to flow

transitif, -ive [trɑ̃zitif, -iv] ADJ Gram, Math transitive; Gram **à la forme transitive** in the transitive

transition [trɑ̃zisjɔ̃] NF transition; TV, Radio **t. musicale** segue; **assurer la t.** to make sure there is no hiatus, to make sure there is a seamless transition; **phase de t.** transition or transitional period; **sans t.** abruptly, Fml without transition; TV, Radio **sans t., nous passons aux nouvelles sportives** and now for something completely different, over to the sports news; Archit **style de t.** transitional style

transitivement [trɑ̃zitivmɑ̃] ADV Gram (employé) transitively, in the transitive

transitivité [trɑ̃zitivite] NF Gram, Math transitivity

transitoire [trɑ̃zitwar] ADJ **1** (fugitif) transitory, transient **2** (provisoire) (période, régime) transitional; (mesure, solution) transitional, temporary

transitoirement [trɑ̃zitwarmɑ̃] ADV (d'une manière fugitive) fleetingly; (d'une manière provisoire) transitionally, temporarily

Transjordanie [trɑ̃ʒɔrdani] NF Hist Transjordan

translation [trɑ̃slasjɔ̃] NF **1** (d'un prisonnier, un tribunal, reliques etc) transfer; Tél (de message) retransmission, relaying **2** Géom, Phys **mouvement de t.** translatory motion **3** Jur **t. de propriété** transfer of property

translittération [trɑ̃sliterasjɔ̃] NF transliteration

translittérer [trɑ̃slitere] VT (texte) to transliterate; (en braille) to copy

translucide [trɑ̃slysid] ADJ translucent

translucidité [trɑ̃slysidite] NF translucence, translucency

transmanche [trɑ̃zmɑ̃ʃ] ADJ INV cross-Channel

transmetteur [trɑ̃zmɛtœr] NM **1** Tél, Ordinat, Biol transmitter **2** Naut **t. d'ordres** (turret) telegraph, transmitter

transmettre [trɑ̃zmɛtr] (conj like **mettre**) VT **1** (lumière, chaleur) to transmit; (message, nouvelle etc) to pass on, to convey; (ordre) to convey, to transmit; (maladie, virus) to pass on, to transmit; (recette, pouvoir magique, don etc) to pass or hand on; (tradition, collier etc) to hand or pass down (**de génération en génération** from generation to generation); (flambeau) to hand over or on; (vérité, énergie) to impart; Tél, Radio (information) to send, to transmit; Radio, TV (émission etc) to broadcast; **t. (par satellite)** to beam; **t. par câble** to cablecast; **qui vous a transmis la nouvelle?** who gave or told you the news?, who passed the news on to you?; **transmettez mon amitié à vos parents** pass on or give or convey my best wishes to your parents **2** Jur (propriété, droit etc) to transfer; (actions etc) to assign; **t. ses pouvoirs à qn** to hand over to sb
VPR **se transmettre** (d'un message, d'une maladie etc) to be passed on

transmigration [trɑ̃zmigrasjɔ̃] NF transmigration

transmigrer [trɑ̃zmigre] VI to transmigrate

transmissible [trɑ̃zmisibl] ADJ **1** (maladie) transmissible, communicable; **sexuellement t.** sexually transmitted **2** Jur (droit, fortune etc) transferable; Fin **t. par endossement** transferable by endorsement

transmission [trɑ̃zmisjɔ̃] NF **1** (de chaleur, lumière), Méd (d'une maladie, d'un virus) transmission; (d'un message, d'un ordre) transmission, passing on; (de la vérité) imparting; (d'une tradition etc) handing down or on; (de caractères génétiques) transmission, handing on; Tél, Radio (d'un message, d'une image etc) transmission, sending; Radio, TV (d'une émission) broadcasting; Radio etc **antenne de t.** transmitting aerial; Com **fiche de t.** routing slip; Ftbl **t. du ballon** passing; **erreur de t.** (d'un message) error in transmission **2** Naut, Mil **les transmissions** signals; **officier de transmissions** signal(s) officer; **centre de transmissions** signal centre **3** Tech gearing; Aut **la t.** the transmission (gear); Tech **t. du mouvement** transmission of movement; Aut power flow **4** Ordinat transmission; **voie de t.** transmission channel; **t. par modem** modem transmission **5** Jur (d'une propriété, d'un droit etc) transfer(ence); (d'actions etc) assignment
▸▸ Aut **t. automatique** automatic transmission; Radio, TV **t. différée** ou **en différé** recorded broadcast or programme; **t. directe** ou **en direct** live broadcast or programme; **t. de données** data transmission or transfer; Fin **t. par endossement** transfer by endorsement; Aut **t. finale** final drive; Tech **t. flexible** flexible shaft(ing); Aut **t. manuelle** manual transmission; Ordinat **t. par modem** modem transmission; **la t. d'un document par modem** the transmission of a document by modem, the modeming of a document; Ordinat **t. de paquets** packet transmission; **t. de pensée** thought transference; Fig **c'est de la t. de pensée!** we/they/etc can read each other's mind!; Admin **t. des pouvoirs** handover; Radio, TV **t. par satellite** satellite broadcast; Aut **t. à variation continue** continuously variable transmission

transmodulation [trɑ̃zmɔdylasjɔ̃] NF Radio etc cross modulation

transmuer [trɑ̃zmɥe] VT to transmute (**en** into)

transmutation [trɑ̃zmytasjɔ̃] NF transmutation (**en** into)

transmuter [trɑ̃zmyte] VT to transmute (**en** into)

transnational, -ale, -aux, -ales [trɑ̃znasjɔnal, -o] ADJ transnational

transocéanien, -ienne [trɑ̃zɔseanjɛ̃, -jɛn], **transocéanique** [trɑ̃zɔseanik] ADJ transoceanic

transpacifique [trɑ̃spasifik] ADJ transpacific

transpalette [trɑ̃spalɛt] NM pallet truck

transparaître [trɑ̃sparɛtr] VI (conj like **paraître**) to show (through); **le doute transparaît sous son calme** doubt is showing (through) beneath his calm; **laisser t. une émotion** to let an emotion show

transparence [trɑ̃sparɑ̃s] NF **1** (d'un tissu, un matériau, un teint), Fig (d'une allusion, une intention) transparency; (d'un parti politique) transparency, openness; **on peut le lire par t.** you can read it by holding it up to the light; **on voit ses jambes par t.** you can see her legs against the light; **on voit mes veines par t.** my veins show through; **t. fiscale** = system of taxing the income of partners in a firm rather than the firm's profits **2** Cin back projection

transparent [trɑ̃sparɑ̃] ADJ (matériau, tissu) transparent; (vêtement) transparent, see-through; Fig (intention, allusion) transparent, clear, obvious; (personne) transparent; **c'était un homme t.** it was easy to read his mind or to know what he was thinking
NM transparency

transpercer [trɑ̃spɛrse] VT (**je transperçai(s); n. transperçons**) (d'une lame, une flèche) to pierce; (d'une balle) to go through, to pierce; (du froid, du vent, de la pluie) (vêtements, chaussures) to go or come through; **t. qn** (d'un coup d'épée) to run sb through (with a sword); **la balle l'a transpercé** the bullet went right through him/it; **le froid/la pluie transperçait les badauds** the passers-by were chilled to the bone/soaked to the skin; **la pluie a transpercé ses vêtements** the rain went or soaked right through his clothes; Fig **t. qn du regard** to give sb a piercing look; Fig **son attitude me transperce le cœur** his attitude is breaking my heart

transpirant [trɑ̃spirɑ̃] ADJ sweating, perspiring

transpiration [trɑ̃spirasjɔ̃] NF **1** (sueur) sweat, perspiration; **humide de t.** (vêtement etc) sweaty; **trempé de t.** soaked in sweat **2** (action) sweating, perspiration; Bot transpiration

transpirer [trɑ̃spire] VI **1** (d'une personne) to sweat, to perspire; **se mettre à t.** to start to sweat, to break into a sweat; **t. des pieds/des aisselles** to have sweaty feet/armpits; **il transpirait à grosses gouttes** he was dripping with sweat, the sweat was pouring off him; Fam **t. sur** (travailler à) to sweat over **2** Bot to transpire **3** Fig (d'un secret, de nouvelles etc) to come to light, to come out

> Il faut noter que le verbe anglais **to transpire** ne signifie jamais **suer**.

transplant [trɑ̃splɑ̃] NM Chir (organe, tissu) transplant

transplantable [trɑ̃splɑ̃tabl] ADJ transplantable

transplantation [trɑ̃splɑ̃tasjɔ̃] NF (d'arbres etc), Fig (de personnes) transplantation, transplanting; Chir transplant; **t. cardiaque/rénale** heart/kidney transplant

transplanté, -ée [trɑ̃splɑ̃te] ADJ (organe) transplanted; **un malade t.** a transplant patient
N **le nombre des transplantés** the number of people receiving transplants; **les transplantés du cœur/du foie** people who have had heart/liver transplants

transplanter [trɑ̃splɑ̃te] VT (arbres etc), Chir (organe), Fig (personnes) to transplant; Chir **t. un cœur/un rein** to perform a heart/kidney transplant (operation)
VPR **se transplanter** (dans un autre milieu) to transplant oneself; **se t. en France/aux États-Unis** to resettle in France/in the United States

transplantoir [trɑ̃splɑ̃twar] NM trowel

transpolaire [trɑ̃spɔlɛr] ADJ transpolar

transpondeur [trɑ̃spɔ̃dœr] NM transponder; **t. satellite** satellite transponder

transport [trɑ̃spɔr] NM **1** (de marchandises, de passagers) transport, Fml carriage; **moyen de t.** means of transport; **avez-vous un moyen de t.?** do you have transport or transportation?; **les transports** transport; **cela permet de faire les transports urgents par avion** this enables urgent freight to be sent by air; **politique des transports** transport policy; **abîmé pendant le t.** damaged in transit; **travailler dans le t.** to work in transport; **capacité de t.** transport capacity; **compagnie de t.** transport company; Com carrying or forwarding company; **entrepreneur de t.** haulage contractor, haulier; **frais de t.** transport costs; Com freight charges, carriage; *Ind* **courroie de t.** conveyor belt; *Mil* **véhicule de t. de personnel** personnel carrier; **avion de t.** transport aircraft; **avion de t. de passagers/de fret** passenger/cargo aircraft; **t. urbain** urban transport VOIR GRAMMAIRE A27

2 *Jur (cession)* **t.(-cession)** *(de biens, de droits etc)* transfer, conveyance

3 *Mil (navire)* transport (ship); *(avion)* transport (plane)

4 *Litt (émotion)* rapture; **transports de joie** transports of joy; **transports de colère** outbursts *or* fits of anger; **avec t., avec transports de joie** rapturously, with rapture

5 *Compta* transfer

▸▸ **t. d'acheminement** transfer transport; **t. aérien** *ou* **par air** air transport; *Com* air freight; **transports aériens** air transport; **t. par canalisations** *(du pétrole)* piping; **t. par chemin de fer** rail transport; **t. civil aérien** civil aviation; **transports en commun** public transport, *Am* mass transit; *Élec* **t. d'énergie** power transmission; **t. ferroviaire** *ou* **par fer** rail transport; **t. fluvial** inland waterway transport; *Élec* **t. de force** high-voltage power transmission; *Jur* **t. de justice** visit to the scene of the accident/crime/*etc*; **t. sur les lieux** visit to the scene of the accident/crime/*etc*; **t. de marchandises** transport of goods; **t. maritime** *ou* **par mer** maritime transport; **transports publics** public transport; **transports routiers** road transport; *Com* road haulage; **t. terrestre** surface transport; *Mil* **t. de troupes** *(navire)* troopship, troop carrier; *(avion)* troop carrier; **t. par voie ferrée** rail transport

transportable [trãsportabl] ADJ transportable; *Méd (patient)* fit to be moved; **le malade est-il t.?** is the patient fit to be moved?, can the patient be moved?

transportation [trãsportasjõ] NF *Jur (penal)* transportation

transporté, -ée [trãsporte] N *Jur* transported convict, transport

ADJ *Fig* carried away, *Litt* transported; **t. de joie** beside oneself with joy, *Litt* transported with joy

transporter [trãsporte] VT **1** *(passagers, troupes etc)* to carry, to transport; *(marchandises)* to transport, to carry, to freight; *Jur (détenu)* to transport; *Fig (d'un film, un roman etc)* to take, to transport; **t. qn à l'hôpital** to take sb to hospital; **le camion transporte des explosifs** the truck is carrying explosives; **t. des marchandises par air/route** to carry *or* transport goods by air/road; *Com* to airfreight/haul goods **2** *Jur (céder) (biens, droits etc)* to transfer (**à** to) **3** *(ravir)* to transport, to carry away; **cette bonne nouvelle l'a transporté** he was overjoyed by the good news; **le nouveau projet ne l'a pas transporté** he was not overjoyed about *or* was less than thrilled with the new project

VPR **se transporter 1** *Jur* **se t. sur les lieux** *(de la police)* to visit the scene of the crime/accident **2** *Com* **se t. mal/facilement** to be difficult/easy to transport; **les fruits se transportent mal** fruit does not travel well **3** *Fig* **se t. (par la pensée) dans un pays lointain** to let one's imagination carry one to a distant country

transporteur, -euse [trãsportœr, -øz] NM **1** *(entrepreneur)* carrier, haulier, haulage contractor, transporter; *Aviat* carrier; **t.-routier** road haulage contractor; **t. international** international carrier; **t. public** public *or* common carrier; **t. routier** road haulier **2** *Ind (appareil)* conveyor; **(chariot) t.** travelling crane *or* platform; **t. élévateur** elevator

ADJ *Ind* **hélice/courroie transporteuse** spiral/belt conveyor

transposable [trãspozabl] ADJ which can

be transposed, transposable; **difficilement t.** difficult to transpose (**dans** to)

transposer [trãspoze] VT *(mots)*, *Mus (morceau)* to transpose; **t. un roman à l'écran** to adapt a novel for the screen

transposition [trãspozisjõ] NF *Anat, Chir, Mus etc* transposition; **t. d'un roman à l'écran** adaptation of a novel for the screen

transputer [trãspytœr] NM *Ordinat* transputer

transpyrénéen, -enne [trãspireneẽ, -ɛn] ADJ transpyrenean

transsaharien, -ienne [trãssaarjẽ, -jɛn] ADJ transsaharan

transsexualisme [trãssɛksɥalism] NM transsexualism

transsexuel, -elle [trãssɛksɥɛl] ADJ, N transsexual

transsibérien, -ienne [trãssiberjẽ, -jɛn] ADJ Trans-Siberian

NM **le T.** the Trans-Siberian Railway

transsubstantiation [trãssypstãsjasjõ] NF *Rel* transubstantiation

Transvaal [trãsval] NM **le T.** the Transvaal

transvasement [trãsvazmã] NM *(de liquide)* decanting

transvaser [trãsvaze] VT *(vin)* to decant (**dans** into); **tu pourrais t. le lait dans la grande jatte?** could you pour the milk into *or* transfer the milk to the big bowl?

VPR **se transvaser** *(de l'eau)* to siphon

transversal, -ale, -aux, -ales [trãsversal, -o] ADJ transverse, transversal; *(coupe, rue etc)* cross; *Constr* **mur t.** partition (wall); *Anat* **muscle t.** transverse (muscle); *Naut* **soutes transversales** cross bunkers; *Géog* **vallée transversale** transverse valley

NF **transversale 1** *Sport (barre)* crossbar; *(passe)* cross **2** *Math* transversal

transversalement [trãsversalmã] ADV *(posé)* crosswise, transversely

transverse [trãsvers] ADJ *Math, Anat etc* transverse

NM *Anat* transverse (muscle)

transvestisme [trãsvɛstism] NM transvestism

transvider [trãsvide] VT to transfer, to decant; **t. qch dans qch** to pour sth into sth, to transfer sth to sth

Transylvanie [trãsilvani] NF Transylvania

trapèze [trapɛz] NM **1** *Géom* trapezium, *Am* trapezoid; **t. rectangle** right-angled trapezium **2** *Anat* trapezius **3** *Gym* trapeze; **t. volant** flying trapeze; **faire du t.** to perform on the trapeze

ADJ *Anat (muscle)* trapezius; *(os)* trapezium

trapéziste [trapezist] N trapeze artist

trapézoïdal, -ale, -aux, -ales [trapezoïdal, -o] ADJ *Géom* trapezial, *Am* trapezoidal

trapézoïde [trapezoïd] ADJ, NM *Anat (os)* **t.** trapezoid

trapillon [trapijõ] NM **1** *(d'une trappe)* catch, bolt **2** *Théâtre (sur le plancher de la scène)* slot

trappage [trapaʒ] NM *Can* trapping

Trappe [trap] NF *Rel* **1** *(monastère)* Trappist monastery **2** *(order)* Trappist order

trappe [trap] NF **1** *(dans le plancher)*, *Théâtre* trap door; *Tech* hatch; **t. de visite** inspection hatch; *Aut* **t. à essence** petrol tank flap; **passer à la t.** *(projet)* to be shelved; *(personne)* to be sacked, to get the push **2** *(piège à animaux)* trap, pitfall

trappeur [trapœr] NM *(d'animaux sauvages)* trapper

trappillon [trapijõ] NM = **trapillon**

trappiste [trapist] NM *Rel* Trappist (monk)

NF *Belg (bière)* beer *(made by Trappist monks)*

trapu [trapy] ADJ **1** *(homme, cheval)* thickset, stocky; *(bâtiment)* squat **2** *Fam (fort) (élève, professeur)* brainy; *(difficile) (problème)* tough, sticky; **être t. en qch** to be a whizz at sth

traquenard [traknar] NM *(piège)* trap

traquer [trake] VT *(gibier, criminel etc)* to hunt; *Fig (de la presse etc)* to hound; **nous le traquerons jusqu'à ce que nous mettions la main dessus** we will hunt *or* track him down; **bête traquée** hunted animal

VI *Fam* to get stage fright

traquet [trakɛ] NM **1** *(battant)* (mill) clapper *or* clack **2** *Orn* **t. (motteux)** wheatear

traqueur [trakœr] NM *(chasseur)* tracker

trauma [troma] NM *Méd, Psy* trauma

traumatique [tromatik] ADJ *Méd, Psy* traumatic

traumatisant [tromatizã] ADJ *Méd, Psy* traumatizing

traumatiser [tromatize] VT *Méd, Psy* to traumatize; **il ne faut pas que ça te traumatise** you mustn't let it traumatize you, you mustn't be traumatized by it

traumatisme [tromatism] NM *Méd, Psy* traumatism, trauma; **t. crânien** head injury, *Spéc* cranial traumatism; **se libérer d'un t. psychologique** to rid oneself of a trauma

traumatologie [tromatoloʒi] NF *Méd* study of trauma, trauma medicine

traumatologiste [tromatoloʒist], **traumatologue** [tromatolog] N *Méd* traumatologist, trauma specialist

---

TRAVAIL, -AUX [travaj, -o]

> work **1, 3–8** ▪ working **1, 2** ▪ job **3, 5** ▪ employment **3** ▪ workplace **4** ▪ labour **9**

NM **1** *(activité)* work; *(de l'imagination, de la mémoire)* working, functioning; **division du t.** division of labour; **se mettre au t.** to get (down) *or* start to work; **allons, au t.!** come on, let's get (down) to work!; **au t., taisez-vous!** be quiet and get on with your work!; **se tuer au t.** to work oneself to death, to kill oneself working; **cesser le t.** *(de grévistes)* to down tools; *(à la fin de la journée)* to stop work, to knock off; **arrêt de t.** *(pour grève)* stoppage; *(pour maladie)* sick leave; **accident du t.** industrial accident; **permis de t.** work permit; **code du t.** labour code; **contrat de t.** work contract, contract of work; **fournir un t. utile** to do useful work; **il a fourni un rude t.** he worked extremely hard, he got through a lot of work; **pendant les heures de t.** during working hours; **à t. égal, salaire égal** equal pay for equal work; **vêtements de t.** working *or* work clothes; **groupe de t.** working group *or* party; **méthode de t.** work method, method of working; *Péj* **ça sent le t.** *(d'un tableau, un poème etc)* it's rather laborious *or* laboured; **séance de t.** *(d'une association etc)* working session; **le monde du t.** the working world, the world of work; **le t. des femmes** women's work; **admission des enfants au t.** employment of children; **ministère du T.** = Department of Employment *or Am* Labor; **Organisation internationale du t.** International Labour Organization; **Bureau international du t.** International Labour Office *(permanent secretariat of the ILO)*; **c'est du t. à la main** it's handmade; **t. à l'aiguille** needlework; **t. au tour** lathe work; **t. du bois/du métal** woodwork/metalwork; **le t. du fer** ironworking; **le t. de l'ivoire/de pierres précieuses** the shaping of ivory/precious stones

2 *Biol (de la digestion)* working; *(du vin)* working, fermenting; *(du bois)* warping; *Tech* **t. à la tension** tension stress; *Tech* **pression de t.** working pressure

3 *(emploi)* work, job, employment; **chercher du t.** to look for work *or* a job; **donner du t. à qn** to give sb work *or* a job; **perdre son t.** to lose one's job; **elle est sans t.** she doesn't have a job, she's out of work *or* unemployed; **ils ne font que leur t.** they're only doing their job; **ça ne fait pas partie de mon t.** that's not part of my job, that's not in my job description; *Myth* **les douze travaux d'Hercule** the twelve labours of Hercules; *Hum* **inspecteur des travaux finis** idler, *Br* skiver *(who arrives after the work has been done)*; **tu te prends pour l'inspecteur des travaux finis?** you skiver!

4 *(lieu)* work, workplace; **il est à son t.** he's at work; **je vais à mon t.** I'm going to work; **je l'ai rencontré au t.** I met him at work; **je vais à mon t. ou au t. à pied** I walk to work

5 *(tâche)* (piece of) work, job; *Ordinat* job; **montre-moi ton t.** show me your work; **elle a fait un t. excellent** she did a first-class job *or* an excellent job of work; **faire des petits travaux** to do odd jobs; **c'est un sacré t. que de nettoyer ces fenêtres** it's quite a job cleaning these windows

6 *(écrit)* work; **travaux** work

7 travaux *(d'aménagement, de réparation)* work; **nous sommes en pleins travaux** we're having work done on the house; *(que nous faisons nous-mêmes)* we're doing work on the house; **attention travaux!** roadworks ahead

8 *(exécution)* work; **un t. bien/mal fait** a good/bad piece of work; **c'est du beau t.** it's a fine piece of work; *Fam Iron* **c'est du beau ou joli t.!** that's really clever that is!, well done!; *(à un élève)* what's this mess *or* rag?; **c'est du t. d'amateur** it's an amateurish piece of work, it's amateurish work

9 *Méd* labour, *Am* labor; **femme en t.** woman in labour; **salle de t.** labour room

▸▸**t. administratif** administrative work, *Fam* admin; *Fig* **t. de bénédictin** intellectually demanding task; **t. de bureau** office work; **t. à la chaîne** assembly line work; **travaux des champs** work in the fields; *Min* **t. à ciel ouvert** opencast mining; **travaux de couture** sewing jobs; *Mil* **travaux de défense** defensive works, outworks; *Univ* **travaux dirigés** *(en lettres)* tutorial; *(en sciences)* practical *or* lab work; **une heure de travaux dirigés de biologie** an hour's biology practical *or* lab; *Jur* **t. disciplinaire** hard labour; **t. à domicile** homework, work done at home, working at home; **t. d'équipe ou en équipes** teamwork; *Jur* **travaux forcés: condamné aux travaux forcés** sentenced to hard labour; **t. intellectuel** intellectual work, brainwork; **t. d'intérêt général** community work; **t. manuel** manual labour; *Scol* **travaux manuels** arts and crafts; **t. mécanique** *Ind* machine work; *Phys* **travaux mécaniques** mechanical energy; **travaux ménagers** housework; **t. à mi-temps** part-time work; *Phys* **t. moteur** mechanical energy; *Ordinat* **t. multitâche** multitasking; **t. au noir** black economy; **t. de nuit** night work; **t. à plein temps** full-time work; **travaux pratiques** *Scol* practical work; *Méd* tutorials; *Admin* **travaux publics** public works; *Ordinat* **t. en réseau** networking; **t. de Romain** Herculean task; **t. par roulement** shift work; **t. à temps partiel** part-time work

travaillé [travaje] ADJ **1** *(fer, bois, pierre)* worked **2** *(style etc)* laboured, *Am* labored **3 jours/heures travaillé(e)s** (number of) days/ hours worked

travailler [travaje] VI **1** *(de personne, cheval, machine), Fig (d'argent)* to work; **t. dur** to work hard; **elle travaille trop** she works too much, she overworks; **aimer t.** to enjoy working; **t. 40 heures par semaine** to work a 40-hour week; **une femme qui travaille** a working woman; **son imagination travaille**

(trop) his imagination is working overtime; **fais t. ton imagination** use your imagination; *Fig* **ça a fait t. les esprits** it made people wonder, people didn't know what to think; *Fam* **t. comme un nègre ou comme quatre ou comme un cheval** to work like a slave *or* a Trojan *or* a dog; *Fam* **t. du chapeau** to have a screw loose; **t. à** *(un roman, un documentaire etc)* to work on; **j'y travaille** I'm working on it; **t. à la perte de qn** *ou* **à perdre qn** to try to ruin sb; **t. à faire qch** to work hard *or* to strive to do sth; **t. à l'aiguille** to do needlework; **t. à la pièce** to do piecework; **t. au noir** to moonlight; **t. contre qn/qch** to work against sb/sth; **t. dans qch** to work in sth; **t. en free-lance** to freelance, to work as a freelance, to do freelance work; **t. pour qn/une société** *(être employé par)* to work for sb/a company; **le temps travaille pour nous** time is on our side; **t. pour soi-même, t. pour** *ou* **à son compte** to be self-employed, to work for oneself; *Fig* **t. pour le roi de Prusse** to work for nothing; **faire t. une machine** to work *or* run a machine; **faire t. son argent** to put one's money to work, to make one's money work for one

2 *(s'entraîner)* *(de sportif, d'acrobate)* to train; *(de musicien)* to practise; *(d'animaux de cirque etc)* to go through their performance

3 *(d'un navire, d'un câble etc)* to strain; *(du vin)* to ferment, to work; *(du bois)* to warp, to shrink; *(des murs)* to crack

VT **1** *(façonner)* *(bois, fer, verre etc)* to work, to fashion, to shape; *Culin (pâte)* to knead; **t. la terre** to work the land; *Tennis* **t. une balle** to spin a ball; **t. un cheval** to work a horse

2 *(étudier)* *(rôle)* to work on, to study; *(sujet)* to work at *or* on; *(texte, auteur)* to study; *(pas de danse)* to work on, to practise; **t. le piano** to practise the piano; **t. son style** to work on *or* polish one's style

3 *(inquiéter)* **ça m'a travaillé toute la journée** it's been preying on my mind all day; **cela ne me travaille pas du tout** I'm not the slightest bit worried *or* concerned; **un désir le travaillait** he was obsessed *or Péj* tormented with a desire; **être travaillé de** *ou* **par la goutte** to be a martyr to gout

4 *Litt (influer sur)* *(quelqu'un, sentiments, opinion publique etc)* to work on

VPR **se travailler** **t. l'esprit** to worry

travailleur, -euse [travajœr, -øz] ADJ hardworking, industrious; **les masses travailleuses** the workers, the working classes

N worker; **bon t.** good *or* hard worker; **t. manuel/intellectuel** manual/non-manual worker; **t. à temps réduit** person on short time; **les travailleurs** the workers, the working people

NF **travailleuse** *(table à ouvrage)* (lady's) work table

▸▸**t. en bâtiment** construction worker; **t. immigré** immigrant worker; **t. indépendant** self-employed worker *or* person; **t. au noir** = worker in the black economy; **t. occasionnel** casual worker; **t. à plein temps** full-time worker; **t. salarié** salaried worker; **t. social** social worker; **t. temporaire** casual worker; **t. à temps partiel** part-time worker

travaillisme [travajism] NM *Pol* (British) socialism, doctrine of the Labour Party

travailliste [travajist] *Pol* N member of the Labour Party; **les travaillistes** the Labour Party, Labour

ADJ *(parti, membre etc)* Labour

travée [trave] NF **1** *Constr, Archit* bay **2** *(de pont)* span; *(séparée)* independent girder **3** *Aviat (d'aile)* rib **4** *(de sièges)* row

traveller's check, traveller's cheque [travlœr(s)ʃɛk] NM traveller's cheque, *Am* traveler's check

travelling [travliŋ] NM *Cin* **1** *(dispositif)* *(pour caméra)* dolly, travelling platform **2** *(déplacement)* tracking; *(plan)* tracking shot; **faire un t.** to dolly; **t. avant/arrière** track in/track out

travelo [travlo] NM *Fam (travesti)* drag queen

travers [travɛr] NM **1 en t.** crosswise; **autobus avec places disposées en t.** bus with seats arranged crosswise; **profil en t.** cross section; **en t. de** across; **se mettre en t. du chemin de qn** to stand in sb's way; **il ne faut pas que des problèmes personnels se mettent en t. du travail** personal problems must not get in the way of work

2 à t. qch, au t. de qch through sth; **prendre à t. (les) champs/bois** to cut through the fields *or* across country/through the woods; **courir à t. la campagne** to run across country; **à t. les siècles** down (through) the centuries; **à t. le monde** throughout the world; *Fig* **elle n'a pas réussi à passer au t.** she didn't manage to escape; **si tu crois passer au t., tu te trompes!** if you think you're going to get away with it, you're mistaken!

3 *Naut* **de t., par le t.** on the beam, abeam; **vent de t.** wind on the beam; **en t. (du navire)** athwart (ships); **collision par le t.** collision broadside on

4 *(locutions)* **marcher de t.** *(d'un ivrogne etc)* to stagger (along); **la machine marche de t.** the machine is not working properly; **tout marche de t. aujourd'hui** everything's going wrong today, nothing's going right today; **tout va de t. entre eux** everything's going wrong between them; **comprendre de t.** to misunderstand; **j'ai encore dû comprendre de t.** I must have misunderstood again *or* got things wrong again; **regarder qn de t.** to look askance *or* sideways at sb; **votre chapeau est de t.** your hat is (on) crooked, *Fam* your hat's all skew-whiff; **il a la bouche/le nez de t.** he's got a crooked mouth/nose; *très Fam* **elle a la gueule de t.** her face is all twisted; **les tableaux étaient accrochés de t.** the pictures were askew *or* crooked *or Fam* skew-whiff; **j'ai avalé de t.** it went down the wrong way; *Fig* **il l'a avalé de t., ta nouvelle!** your news didn't go down very well with him!, he took your news badly!; **il a des idées tout(es) de t.** his ideas are all wrong; **il a répondu de t.** he gave a ridiculous answer; **prendre tout de t.** to take everything the wrong way

5 *(défaut)* failing, shortcoming, fault; *Arch* **t. (d'esprit)** eccentricity

6 *(largeur)* breadth; **un t. de doigt** a finger's breadth

▸▸*Culin* **t. de porc** spare ribs

traversable [travɛrsabl] ADJ *(désert, rivière etc)* that can be crossed

traversant [travɛrsɑ̃] ADJ M *Suisse* **appartement t.** through *Br* flat *or Am* apartment

traverse [travɛrs] NF **1** *(chemin de)* **t.** short cut **2** *(barre de)* **t.** crossbar, crosspiece; *(d'échelle)* rung; *Constr* transom; *Rail* sleeper, *Am* tie; *Aut etc (du châssis)* cross member; *Aut* **t. de suspension avant** front suspension cross member **3** *Litt (obstacle)* setback

traversée [traverse] NF **1** *(de la mer, du désert, d'une rue etc)* crossing; *(d'une ville etc)* going *or* passing through, crossing; *(d'une forêt, une foule etc)* going *or* passing through; **t. de l'Europe en vélo** bike journey across Europe; *Naut* **t. agitée** rough crossing; **faire une bonne t.** to have a good crossing; **faire la t. de Douvres à Calais** to cross from Dover to Calais; **ils ont fait la t. en yacht jusqu'à Cherbourg** they sailed across *or* went over to Cherbourg in a yacht; **faire la t. d'une ville** to go through *or* pass through *or* cross a town; **la t. d'une ville en**

voiture driving through a town **2** *Pol Fig* **t. du désert** time in the wilderness; **il fait sa t. du désert** he has gone into the wilderness

traverser [traverse] VT **1** *(d'une personne) (rue, pont, mer, rivière etc)* to cross, to go across; *(ville, région, pays etc)* to go or to pass through, to cross; *(forêt etc)* to go or to pass through; *(de la pluie, de vin) (pardessus, nappe)* to go (right) through; *Fig (crise, mauvaise période etc)* to go through; **t. la foule** to make one's way or pass through the crowd; **il faut leur apprendre à t. les rues** they'll have to be taught how to cross the street; **c'est une rue difficile à t. aux heures de pointe** it's difficult to get across this street at rush hour; **t. une forêt à cheval/à bicyclette/en auto** to ride/cycle/drive through a forest; **t. la rivière à la nage/en barque** to swim/row across the river; **t. la Manche à la nage** to swim the Channel; **t. l'Europe en vélo** to cross or go across Europe on a bike, to bike across Europe; **t. un désert en avion** to fly across a desert; **pont/route qui traverse la rivière** bridge/road that crosses or goes across the river; **une planche traverse le ruisseau** there is a plank across the stream; **la balle lui traversa le bras** the bullet went through or pierced his arm; **t. les siècles** to come down through the ages; **elle traverse une période heureuse** she's having a spell of happiness; **t. l'esprit** *(d'une idée, d'un doute)* to cross one's mind; **l'idée me traversa l'esprit comme un éclair** the idea flashed through my mind **2** *Arch (contrarier) (quelqu'un, intentions de quelqu'un)* to cross, to thwart

traversier, -ière [traversje, -jɛr] ADJ **rue traversière** cross street; *Mus* **flûte traversière** (transverse) flute
NM *Can (bac)* ferry (boat)

traversin [traversɛ̃] NM **1** *(pour lit)* bolster **2** *Menuis etc* crosspiece **3** *Naut* crosstree

travesti [travesti] ADJ disguised; **bal t.** fancy-dress or costume ball; *Théâtre* **acteur t.** actor playing a female part; **rôle t.** female part (for an actor)
NM **1** *Théâtre (acteur)* actor playing a female part; *(rôle)* female part (for an actor) **2** *(homme habillé en femme)* transvestite **3** *(déguisement)* fancy dress

travestir [travestir] VT **1** *(déguiser) (personne)* to disguise, to dress up **(en** as) **2** *Littér (pièce, poème etc)* to parody, to burlesque; *(auteur)* to parody **3** *(déformer) (vérité, faits, pensée etc)* to distort, to misrepresent; **je ne voudrais pas t. votre pensée, mais …** I don't want to misrepresent you, but …
VPR **se travestir** *(se vêtir en femme/homme)* to dress (up) as a woman/a man; *(pour un bal costumé)* to put on fancy dress

travestisme [travestism] NM transvestism, cross-dressing

travestissement [travestismɑ̃] NM **1** *(action)* disguising, dressing up **2** *(déguisement)* disguise; *Théâtre* **rôle à travestissements** quick-change part **3** *Littér (d'une pièce, un poème etc)* parody **4** *(de la vérité, des faits etc)* travesty **5** *(travestisme)* transvestism

traviole (de) [dətravjɔl] ADV *Fam voir* **travers**

trayeur, -euse [trejœr, -øz] N *(personne)* milker
NF **trayeuse** *(machine)* milking machine

trayon [trejɔ̃] NM *(de vache etc)* dug, teat

trébuchant [trebyʃɑ̃] ADJ *(ivrogne, allure etc)* staggering, stumbling; *(diction)* stumbling, halting

trébucher [trebyʃe] VI to trip, to stumble (**sur** over; **contre** against); **marcher en tré-**

buchant to stumble or stagger along, to walk with a stagger; **faire t. qn** to trip sb up; *Fig* **t. sur les mots étrangers** to stumble or trip over foreign words

trébuchet [trebyʃɛ] NM **1** *(piège)* bird trap **2** *(petite balance)* assay balance

tréfiler [trefile] VT *(métal)* to (wire)draw

trèfle [trɛfl] NM **1** *Bot* clover; **t. blanc** wild white clover; **t. rouge** red clover; **t. à quatre feuilles** four-leaf or four-leaved clover **2** *Archit, Hér (motif)* trefoil; *Aut* **croisement en t.** clover-leaf intersection **3** *Cartes (couleur)* clubs; *(carte)* club; **jouer (du) t.** to play clubs or a club; **as/dix de t.** ace/ten of clubs; **avez-vous du t.?** do you have any clubs? **4** *Fam (argent)* cash, dough, *Br* dosh, *Am* bucks

tréfonds [trefɔ̃] NM *Litt* **au t. de mon cœur/âme** in my heart of hearts/in the depths of my soul; **blessé au t. de son cœur** cut to the quick; **atteint jusqu'au t.** very deeply hurt

treillage [trejaʒ] NM **1** trellis (work), lattice work **2** *(clôture)* trellis fencing; **t. métallique ou en fil de fer** wire fencing

treillager [trejaʒe] VT *(je treillageai(s); n. treillageons) (mur etc)* to trellis; *(fenêtre)* to lattice; **fenêtre treillagée** lattice window

treille [trej] NF **1** *(abri)* vine arbour, trellised vines **2** *(vigne)* (climbing) vine; *Fam* **le jus de la t.** the juice of the grape

treillis [treji] NM **1** *(treillage)* trellis; **t. métallique** wire mesh **2** *Tex* drill, dungaree, (coarse) canvas **3** *Mil* combat uniform

treize [trɛz] ADJ NUM INV thirteen; *Com* **t. à la douzaine** a baker's dozen; *Fam* **j'en ai t. à la douzaine** I've got dozens of them; **le numéro t.** number thirteen; **le t. mai** (on) the thirteenth of May, (on) May the thirteenth, *Am* (on) May thirteenth; **vendredi t.** Friday the thirteenth; **Louis T.** Louis the Thirteenth; *Sport* **jeu ou rugby à t.** Rugby League
NM INV thirteen; **le t. porte malheur** thirteen is unlucky or is an unlucky number; **le t. gagne** number thirteen is the winner; **habiter au t.** to live at number thirteen

treizième [trɛzjɛm] ADJ, N thirteenth
NM *(fraction)* thirteenth
NF *Mus* thirteenth
▸▸ **t. mois** = additional month's salary paid as an annual bonus

treizièmement [trɛzjɛmmɑ̃] ADV in the thirteenth place

trekking [trekiŋ] NM trek; **faire un t.** to go on a trek; **faire du t. en Inde** to go trekking in India

tréma [trema] *Ling* NM diaeresis, *pl* diaereses, *Am* dieresis, *pl* diereses
ADJ INV **e/i t.** e/i diaeresis or *Am* dieresis

tremblant [trɑ̃blɑ̃] ADJ *(genoux, main)* trembling, shaky, quivering; *(lèvres, visage)* trembling, quivering; *(pont)* shaky; *(sol)* quaking; *(lumière)* flickering; *(voix)* shaky, trembling, quavering, *Fml* tremulous; **t. (de peur)** trembling or shaking or quivering with fear; **t. de froid** shivering or trembling or shaking with cold

tremble [trɑ̃bl] NM *Bot* aspen

tremblé [trɑ̃ble] ADJ **1** *(écriture)* shaky; *(ligne)* wavy **2** *(voix)* shaky, trembling, *Fml* tremulous; *Mus (notes)* tremolo

tremblement [trɑ̃bləmɑ̃] NM **1** *(du corps, de la main, d'un pont etc)* trembling, quivering, shaking; *(de lèvres)* trembling, quivering; *(de la voix)* shaking, trembling, quavering **2** *(de peur)* shudder, quiver, tremor; *(de joie, de colère)* quiver; **t. de fièvre** fit of (feverish) shivering; **avoir un t. de froid/d'horreur** to shiver (with cold)/to shudder (in horror); … **dit-il avec un t. dans la voix** … he said with a tremble or a tremor or a quaver in his voice or in a shaky voice; **elle avait des tremblements dans la voix** her voice was shaking

or quavering; **être pris de tremblements** to start to shake; *Fam* **et tout le t.** the works, the whole enchilada, *Br* the full monty; *Fam* **l'église, la robe blanche et tout le t.** the church, the white dress, the whole works **3** *Mus* tremolo
▸▸ **t. de terre** earth tremor; *(plus fort)* earthquake

trembler [trɑ̃ble] VI **1** *(d'une personne) (de peur, d'émotion)* to tremble, to shake, to quiver; *(de froid)* to shiver, to shake; *(de colère)* to shake; *(de la main, des genoux)* to shake, to tremble; *(des lèvres)* to tremble, to quiver; *(de la voix)* to tremble, to shake, to quiver; *(de la terre)* to shake, to quake; *(de la lumière)* to flicker; *(d'une flamme)* to waver; *(d'un pont, un mur, un bâtiment)* to shake; *(des feuilles)* to quiver; **t. comme une feuille** to shake like a leaf; **faire t. les vitres** to make the windows shake or rattle; **faire t. un bâtiment** to rock or shake a building **2** *(avoir peur)* to tremble; **t. de tout son corps** to tremble or shake all over; **t. devant qn** to be terrified of sb, to go in fear (and trembling) of sb; **je tremble de le rencontrer** I tremble or I am terrified at the thought of meeting him; **je tremblais de le réveiller** I was terrified of wakening him; **elle tremble qu'il ne s'en rende compte** she is terrified that he might find out; **t. pour qn** to be frightened or terrified for sb

trembleur [trɑ̃blœr] NM *Élec* trembler, vibrator; *Tél* buzzer

tremblotant [trɑ̃blɔtɑ̃] ADJ *(personne)* trembling (slightly); *(corps)* quivering, shivering; *(sourire, voix)* shaky, tremulous; *(lumière)* flickering

tremblote [trɑ̃blɔt] NF *Fam* **avoir la t.** *(de vieillesse)* to have the shakes; *(de peur)* to have the jitters, to be shaking in one's shoes; *(de froid)* to have the shivers

tremblotement [trɑ̃blɔtmɑ̃] NM *(des mains)* trembling, shaking; *(de la voix)* quavering, trembling, shaking; *(de la lumière)* flickering; **un t. de la voix** a tremble in one's voice; **être pris de tremblotements** to start to shake

trembloter [trɑ̃blɔte] VI *(des mains)* to tremble or shake (slightly); *(de la voix)* to tremble, to quaver, to shake; *(de la lumière)* to flicker; *(des ailes)* to flutter; **j'ai les mains qui tremblotent** my hands are shaky

trémie [tremi] NF **1** *Ind etc (entonnoir)* hopper **2** *(mangeoire) (pour poulets)* feeding box **3** *Constr (pour cheminée)* hearth cavity

trémière [tremjɛr] ADJ *Bot* **rose t.** hollyhock

tremolo [tremolo] NM *Mus* **1** tremolo; *Fig* **avec des trémolos dans la voix** with a quaver or tremor in one's voice, in a shaky voice **2** *(d'un orgue)* tremolo stop

trémoussement [tremusmɑ̃] NM jigging up and down; *(en se dandinant)* wiggling

trémousser (se) [sətremuse] VPR *(d'un enfant)* to jig up and down; *(pour séduire)* to wiggle; **se t. sur sa chaise** to wriggle about on one's chair; **marcher en se trémoussant** to walk with a wiggle; **se t. du derrière** to wiggle one's behind

trempage [trɑ̃paʒ] NM soaking, steeping

trempe [trɑ̃p] NF **1** *(immersion)* soaking, steeping; **mettre qch en t.** to put sth to soak **2** *Métal (traitement)* hardening, quench(-ing); **t. et revenu** quenching and hardening; **acier/atelier de t.** hardening steel/plant; **t. à l'eau/à l'huile** water/oil quenching; **t. par cémentation, t. de ou en surface** case hardening; **bain de t.** hardening or quenching bath **3** *Métal (dureté)* *Fig (qualité)* temper, hardness **4** *Fig (qualité)* calibre; **un homme de sa t.** a man of his calibre; **une intelligence d'une t. exception-**

nelle extremely high intelligence, quite exceptional intelligence **5** *Fam (volée de coups)* hiding, walloping; **si tu continues, je vais te filer une t.** if you don't stop, you'll get a wallop(ing)

ADJ *Can, Suisse (personne, vêtements)* soaked, drenched; *(chaussures, jardin)* waterlogged; **t. de sueur** soaked with sweat

trempé [trɑ̃pe] **ADJ 1** *(mouillé) (personne)* soaked, drenched; *(vêtement)* soaked, saturated, sodden; **être tout t.** to be soaked *or* wet through, to be soaking wet; **t. de larmes** bathed in tears, wet with tears; **t. de sueur** *(personne)* drenched *or* dripping with sweat; *(vêtement)* saturated with sweat; **t. jusqu'aux os** *ou Fam* **comme une soupe** soaked to the skin, wet *or* soaked through **2** *Tech (verre)* hardened; *(acier)* hardened, tempered; *Fig* **bien t.** *(esprit)* resolute; *Sport* with plenty of stamina

tremper [trɑ̃pe] **VT 1** *(mouiller) (dans un liquide)* to soak, to steep; *(plonger) (pain dans la soupe)* to dunk; *(écrevisses, moules, escargots)* to plunge; **se faire t. par la pluie** to get a soaking; **t. un pied dans l'eau** to dip a foot in the water; **t. ses mains dans l'eau** to dabble one's hands in the water; **t. la soupe** to pour the soup on the bread; **t. sa plume dans l'encrier** to dip one's pen in the ink; **t. ses lèvres dans son verre** to put one's lips to one's glass; **j'y ai à peine trempé les lèvres** I've hardly touched it; *Typ* **t. le papier** to wet *or* damp the paper **2** *Métal (acier)* to harden, to quench; *(fonte de fer)* to chill; **t. par induction** to induction harden; *Fig Litt* **cela lui a trempé l'esprit** it put iron in his soul; *Fig* **t. les muscles** to firm up the muscles

VI *(du linge sale, d'une casserole)* to (be in) soak; **faire t. le linge** to soak *or* steep the clothes; **mettre à t.** *(linge, casserole)* to put in soak, to soak; *(lentilles)* to soak; **tes manches trempent dans ton assiette** your sleeves are trailing in your plate; *Fig* **t. dans un complot/une affaire** to be mixed up *or* involved in a plot/an affair; **je refuse de t. là-dedans** I refuse to get mixed up in it

VPR se tremper *(se baigner)* to have a quick dip; **je me suis à peine trempé** I barely got wet, I got out again almost immediately; **se t. les pieds dans l'eau** to go for a paddle

trempette [trɑ̃pɛt] **NF 1 faire t.** *Culin (dans le café, le vin etc)* to dip *or* dunk one's bread/*etc*, *Fam (se baigner)* to have a quick dip; **les enfants font t. dans le bassin** the children are splashing about in the pool **2** *Can Culin* dip

tremplin [trɑ̃plɛ̃] **NM** *Natation, Gym* springboard; *Ski* ski jump; *Fig* springboard, stepping stone

trémulation [tremylasjɔ̃] **NF** *Méd* tremor

trémuler [tremyle] **VI** to tremble
VT t. les doigts to twiddle one's fingers

trench(-coat), *pl* **trench(-coat)s** [trɛnʃ(kɔt)] **NM** trench coat

trentaine [trɑ̃tɛn] **NF 1** *(nombre)* **une t.** about thirty; **une t. de voitures/d'années** about thirty cars/years; **une bonne t. (de)** good thirty; **la t. de livres qu'elle a** the thirty (or so) books she has **2** *(âge)* **la t.** (the age of) thirty; **avoir la t.** to be in one's thirties; **il approche de la t.** he's getting on for thirty

trente [trɑ̃t] **ADJ INV** thirty; **t. jours** thirty days; **le t. juin** (on) the thirtieth of June, (on) June the thirtieth, *Am* (on) June thirtieth; **les années t.** the thirties; *Hist* **la Guerre de T. Ans** the Thirty Years' War; **t. et un** thirty-one; *Cartes (jeu)* trente et un; *Tennis* **t. à** thirty all

NM INV thirty; **je suis payé le t. (de chaque mois)** I'm paid on the thirtieth (of each month); **habiter au t.** to live at number thirty; *Fig* **se mettre sur son t. et un** to get all dressed up; **être sur son t. et un** to

be all dressed up, to be dressed up to the nines

trentenaire [trɑ̃tnɛr] **ADJ 1** *(qui dure trente ans)* thirty-year **2** *(personne)* in his/her thirties; *(bâtiment)* over thirty years old

N person in his/her thirties, *Fam* thirty-something

trente-six *(for rules of pronunciation, see* **six)** **ADJ INV** thirty-six; *Fam (beaucoup)* umpteen; **il n'y a pas t. solutions** there's no getting away from it, there's no two ways about it; **il n'y a pas t. façons de le faire** there aren't umpteen different ways of doing it

NM INV thirty-six; *Fig* **tous les t. du mois** once in a blue moon

trente-sixième **ADJ** *Fig Fam* **être au t. dessous** to be extremely depressed, to be really down in the dumps

trente-trois tours **NM INV** *(disque)* LP

trentième [trɑ̃tjɛm] **ADJ** thirtieth
N INV thirtieth
NM *(fraction)* thirtieth

trépan [trepɑ̃] **NM** *Chir, Tech* trepan

trépanation [trepanasjɔ̃] **NF** *Chir* trepanning

trépaner [trepane] **VT** *Chir* to trepan

trépas [trepɑ] **NM** *Litt* death; **passer de vie à t.** to depart this life

trépassé, -ée [trepase] **N** *Litt* deceased person; **les trépassés** the departed, the deceased; **la fête des Trépassés** All Souls' Day

trépasser [trepase] **VI** *Arch, Litt* to die, to depart this life

> Il faut noter que le verbe anglais **to trespass** est un faux ami. Il ne signifie jamais **mourir**.

trépidant [trepidɑ̃] **ADJ** *(machine, moteur, sol etc)* vibrating; *Fig (vie)* hectic; *(rythme, danse)* lively

trépidation [trepidasjɔ̃] **NF 1** *(d'une machine, d'un moteur, du sol etc)* vibration **2** *Méd* trembling, shaking **3** *Fig (de la vie, d'une ville etc)* bustle, hurly-burly

trépider [trepide] **VI** *(d'une machine, du sol etc)* to vibrate

trépied [trepje] **NM 1** *(support) (d'appareil photo)* tripod; *Culin* trivet **2** *(tabouret)* three-legged stool

trépignement [trepiɲ(ə)mɑ̃] **NM** stamping (of feet); **le bruit des trépignements** the sound of stamping feet

trépigner [trepiɲe] **VI** to stamp (one's feet); **t. de colère/d'enthousiasme/d'impatience** to jump up and down with rage/enthusiasm/impatience; *Fig* **il trépignait à l'idée de partir** he was itching to start

trépointe [trepwɛ̃t] **NF** *(de chaussure)* welt

tréponème [treponɛm] **NM** *Biol* treponema; **t. pâle** treponema pallidum

très [trɛ] ([trɛz] *before vowel or mute* **h**) **ADV** *(différent, inférieur, joli, bien, petit etc)* very; **t. bon** very good; *(généreux)* very *or* most kind; **t. connu** very well-known; **t. estimé** much *or* greatly *or* highly respected; **t. aimé** much *or* greatly liked; **être d'une intelligence t. supérieure à la moyenne** to be of much higher than average intelligence; **t. à la mode** very fashionable, very much in fashion; **un produit t. peu vendu** a product for which there is very little demand; **t. peu utilisé** rarely used; **vivre t. au-dessus de ses moyens** to live way beyond one's means; **elle est t. femme** she is very feminine *or* very much a woman; **être t. réussi** to be very successful, to be a great success; **prendre qch t. au sérieux** to take sth very seriously; **avoir t. faim/soif/peur/chaud/froid** to be very hungry/thirsty/scared/hot/cold; **avoir t. envie de faire qch** to really feel like doing sth; **j'ai**

t. envie de sortir I really feel like going out, I would really like to go out, I would love to go out; **ces robes sont t. portées** these dresses are very fashionable *or* very much in fashion; **un auteur t. lu** a very popular author; **content? – oui, t.!** satisfied? – yes, very!; **ça t'a plu? – non, pas t.** did you like it? – no, not (very) much VOIR GRAMMAIRE A22–3

trésor [trezɔr] **NM 1** *(choses précieuses)* treasure; *Jur* treasure-trove; **trouver un t.** to find treasure; **cette bibliothèque est un véritable t.** this library is a real treasure-trove of information; *Fam* **mon t.** darling; **trésors** treasures; *Fig* **elle a dû dépenser des trésors pour l'acheter** it must have cost her a fortune (to buy); *Fig* **des trésors de** *(patience, générosité, amabilité, imagination etc)* limitless, a wealth of; **t. de guerre** war chest **2** *Rel* (collection of) relics and ornaments **3** *(endroit)* treasure house **4 le T. (public)** *(service)* the Treasury Department; *(finances)* the treasury, public funds; **bons du T.** Treasury bonds **5** *(ensemble) (de documents)* wealth; **ce livre est un t. d'informations** the book is a treasure house *or* a mine of information, the book contains a wealth of information

trésorerie [trezɔrri] **NF 1** *(fonction)* treasurership **2** *(bureau)* accounts department **3** *(fonds)* cashflow, funds, finances; **des problèmes de t.** cashflow problems; **t. nette** net cash position **4** *(gestion)* accounting

trésorier, -ière [trezɔrje, -jɛr] **N** treasurer, financial manager; *Admin* **t.(-payeur) général** *(d'un département)* chief treasurer and paymaster; **commis t.** treasury clerk; **t. de banque** bank treasurer; *Mil* **officier t.** paymaster

tressage [trɛsaʒ] **NM** *(des cheveux)* plaiting, *Am* braiding; *(de la paille)* plaiting; *(d'un panier, d'une guirlande)* weaving

tressaillement [tresajmɑ̃] **NM** *(de surprise, peur, douleur)* start, jump

tressaillir [tresajir] **VI** *(prp* **tressaillant;** *pp* **tressailli;** *pr ind* **je tressaille,** n. **tressaillons,** ils **tressaillent;** *impf* **je tressaillais;** *p hist* **je tressaillis;** *fu* **je tressaillirai)** *(de surprise, peur)* to jump, to start, to give a jump *or* start; *(de joie, d'espoir)* to quiver; *(du cœur)* to flutter; **t. (de douleur)** to flinch

tressautement [tresotmɑ̃] **NM 1** *(de peur, de surprise etc)* start, jump **2** *(secousse)* jolt; **les tressautements des wagons** the jolting of the carriages

tressauter [tresote] **VI 1** *(de peur, de surprise etc)* to start, to jump **2** *(être secoué)* to jolt, to be jolted about

tresse [trɛs] **NF 1** *(de cheveux)* plait, *Am* braid; *(de fil etc)* braid; *Archit (motif)* strap work; **se faire des tresses** to plait *or Am* braid one's hair; **porter des tresses** to have (one's hair in) plaits; **les cheveux noués dans une t.** hair done up in a plait; *Élec* **fil conducteur sous t.** braided conductor wire **2** *Suisse (pain)* plaited loaf

tresser [trese] **VT** *(cheveux)* to plait, *Am* to braid; *(paille, osier etc)* to plait; *(panier, guirlande)* to weave; *Fig* **t. des couronnes à qn** to praise sb to the skies; **je ne veux pas lui t. des couronnes, mais ...** I don't want to praise him unduly, but ...

tréteau, -eaux [treto] **NM 1** *(support)* trestle; **table à tréteaux** trestle table **2** *Théâtre* **les tréteaux** the stage; **monter sur les tréteaux** to go on the stage; *Vieilli, Hum* to tread the boards

treuil [trœj] **NM** *Tech* winch, windlass, winding drum; *(d'ascenseur)* winding gear; **t. à chaîne** chain hoist

treuillage [trœjaʒ] **NM** winching (up)

treuiller [trœje] **VT** to winch (up)

trêve [trɛv] **NF 1** *(amnistie)* truce **2** *Fig*

(pause, arrêt) respite, rest; *Fam* **t. de plaisanteries!** *(il faut se mettre au travail)* that's enough joking or fun!; *(arrête de me raconter des histoires)* joking apart or aside; **t. de plaisanteries, tu comptes vraiment y aller?** joking apart or aside, are you really planning to go?; **il ne me laisse pas de t.** he doesn't give me a moment's peace; **sans t.** unceasingly

▸▸ *Pol Fam* **t. des confiseurs** = lull in political activities between Christmas and New Year

Trèves [trɛv] **N** Trier

tri [tri] **NM** sorting (out); *(de lettres)* sorting; *(de compétences etc)* classifying; *(de candidats etc)* selection; *(de propositions etc)* screening; *Ordinat* sort; **un t. s'impose** I'll/we'll/*etc* have to do some sorting out; **faire le t. de** to sort out; **on ne peut pas tous les garder, il va falloir faire le t.** we can't keep them all, we'll have to sort some out or sort through them; **faire du t. dans ses vêtements/papiers** to sort through or go through one's clothes/papers; **bureau de t.** *(de la Poste)* sorting office; **le (service du) t.** *(d'une entreprise)* the mail room; *Ordinat* **effectuer un t.** to do a sort; *Ordinat* **t. en ordre croissant/décroissant** ascending/reverse or descending sort

▸▸ *Ordinat* **t. alphabétique** alphabetic(al) sort, alphasort; *Mktg* **t. croisé** *(de statistiques)* cross tabulation; *Mktg* **t. à plat** *(de statistiques)* simple tabulation; **t. postal** mail sorting

triacide [triasid] **NM** *Chimie* triacid

triade [trijad] **NF** triad

triage [trijaʒ] **NM 1** *(du charbon, du courrier, de minerai etc)* sorting; *Rail* marshalling; *Rail* **gare de t.** marshalling yard; *Rail* **voie de t.** siding; *Mil* **hôpital de t.** clearing hospital **2** *(en choisissant)* selecting, picking out, sorting

trial, *pl* **trials** [trijal] **NM** *Sport* **1** *(épreuve)* motocross, *Br* (motorcycle) scrambling **2** *(moto)* motocross or *Br* scrambling bike

triangle [trijɑ̃gl] **NM 1** *Géom* triangle; **en t.** *(visage, écharpe etc)* triangular; *Fam* **l'éternel t.** the eternal triangle **2** *Naut (pavillon)* triangular flag **3** *Mus* triangle

▸▸ **t. des Bermudes** Bermuda triangle; **le T. d'or** the Golden Triangle; *Aut* **t. de présignalisation** hazard warning triangle

triangulaire [trijɑ̃gylɛr] **ADJ** *(forme, section, relation)* triangular; *Pol (élection, bataille)* three-cornered

NF *Pol* three-cornered contest or fight

triangulation [trijɑ̃gylasjɔ̃] **NF** *(en arpentage)* triangulation

trianguler [trijɑ̃gyle] **VT** *(en arpentage)* to triangulate

trias [trijɑs] **NM** *Géol (période)* Triassic

triasique [trijazik] **ADJ** *Géol* Triassic

triathlon [triatlɔ̃] **NM** *Sport* triathlon

triathlonien, -ienne [triatlɔnjɛ̃, -jɛn] **N** *Sport* triathlete

triatomique [triatɔmik] **ADJ** *Chimie* triatomic

tribade [tribad] **NF** *Litt, Vieilli* tribade

tribal, -ale, -aux, -ales [tribal, -o] **ADJ** tribal

tribalisme [tribalism] **NM** tribalism

triboélectricité [tribɔelɛktrisite] **NF** triboelectricity

tribord [tribɔr] **NM** *Naut* starboard (side); **à t.** on the starboard side, to starboard

tribu [triby] **NF** *aussi Fig Fam* tribe

tribulations [tribylasjɔ̃] **NFPL** tribulations, troubles; **après toutes sortes de t.** after all kinds of trials and tribulations

tribun [tribœ̃] **NM 1** *Antiq (officier)* tribune **2** *(orateur)* popular orator

tribunal, -aux [tribynal, -o] **NM** VOIR GRAMMAIRE A6–7 *Jur* court (of law); *(bâtiment)* court, *Am* courthouse; *(magistrats)* court; **en plein t.** in open court; **porter une affaire devant les tribunaux** to take a case to court; **prendre la voie des tribunaux** to take legal action, to go to court

▸▸ **t. administratif** = court which deals with internal French civil service matters; **t. arbitral** arbitration tribunal; **t. civil** civil court; **t. de commerce** commercial court; **t. correctionnel** criminal court; **t. criminel** criminal court; **t. pour enfants et adolescents** juvenile court; **t. de grande instance** = court presided over by three judges, authorized to try more serious cases, *Eng* ≃ Crown court; **t. d'instance** = trial court, court of first instance, *Eng* ≃ magistrates' court, *Scot, Am* ≃ district court; **t. judiciaire** court (of law); **t. militaire** military tribunal; **traduire qn devant le t. militaire** to court-martial sb; **passer devant le t. militaire** to be court-martialled; **t. des prud'hommes** industrial tribunal; **t. révolutionnaire** revolutionary tribunal

tribune [tribyn] **NF 1** *(galerie)* gallery; **t. de la presse** press gallery; **t. du public** public gallery **2** *(d'orateur)* rostrum, (speaker's) platform; **avoir l'éloquence de la t.** to be a good public speaker; *Parl* **monter à la t.** to address the House **3** *(débat)* forum, discussion, debate; *Journ* banner headline; **t. libre d'un journal** opinion column of a newspaper; **s'exprimer dans les tribunes d'une émission de radio** to put one's point of view in an open radio programme **4** *Sport* **t. (d'honneur)** (grand)stand **5** *Mus* **t. d'orgues** organ loft

tribut [triby] **NM 1** *Hist (contribution)* tribute, tribute-money; **payer t.** to pay tribute; *Fig* **payer t. à la nature** to pay one's debt to nature; **la France a payé un lourd t. en vies humaines** France paid a heavy cost in human life **2** *Arch, Litt (impôt)* duty, tax

tributaire [tribytɛr] **ADJ 1** *Hist (qui paie tribut)* tributary **2** *(dépendant)* **être t. de** *(produits étrangers etc)* to be dependent or to depend (up)on **3** *Géog* **rivière t.** tributary

tric [trik] **NM** *(au bridge)* odd trick

tricard, -arde [trikar, -ard] *Fam Vieilli* **N** = ex-convict prohibited from entering a certain area

ADJ = prohibited from entering a certain area

tricentenaire [trisɑ̃tnɛr] **NM** tercentenary, tricentennial

ADJ three hundred years old

tricéphale [trisefal] **ADJ** *(monstre)* three-headed

triceps [trisɛps] **ADJ, NM** *Anat* **(muscle) t.** triceps (muscle)

triche [triʃ] **NF** *Fam* cheating; **c'est de la t.!** that's cheating!

tricher [triʃe] **VI** to cheat (**sur** over); *(mentir)* to lie (**sur** about); *(pour dissimuler un défaut)* to cheat a bit, to fiddle it; **t. aux cartes** to cheat at cards/in an exam; **je n'aime pas t. avec les gens** I don't like being dishonest with people

tricherie [triʃri] **NF** cheating; **j'en ai assez de toutes tes tricheries!** I've had enough of your cheating!

tricheur, -euse [triʃœr, -øz] **N** cheat

trichine [trikin] **NF** *(ver)* threadworm, *Spéc* trichina

trichinose [trikinoz] **NF** *Méd* trichinosis

trichloréthylène [triklɔretilɛn] **NM** *Chimie* trichlorethylene

trichrome [trikrom] **ADJ** *(photographie etc)* three-colour or *Am* -color, trichromatic

trichromie [trikrɔmi] **NF** *Phot* three-colour or *Am* -color process

trick [trik] **NM** *(au bridge)* odd trick

tricolore [trikɔlɔr] **ADJ** three-coloured or *Am* -colored; **le drapeau t.** the French flag, the Tricolour, *Am* the Tricolor; *Admin* **feux tricolores** traffic lights or signals; *Sport* **l'équipe t.** the French team

NMPL *Sport* **les tricolores** the French team

tricorne [trikɔrn] **NM** three-cornered hat, tricorn

tricorps [trikɔr] **ADJ** *Aut* notchback

tricot [triko] **NM 1** *(activité)* knitting; **faire du t.** to do some knitting **2** *(ouvrage)* knitting; *Com* knitwear; **j'ai commencé un t.** I've started to knit something **3** *(chandail)* sweater, *Br* jumper; **t. de corps** vest, *Am* undershirt **4** *(tissu)* knitted fabric; **en t.** *(pull, vêtement)* knitted

tricotage [trikɔtaʒ] **NM** knitting

tricoter [trikɔte] **VT 1** to knit; **aiguilles à t.** knitting needles; **machine à t.** knitting machine; **tricoté (à la) main** hand-knitted **2** *Fig (mettre en forme, élaborer)* to work out

VI to knit; **t. à la main/à la machine** to knit by hand/machine; *Arg* **t. des jambes** *ou* **des gambettes** *(s'enfuir)* to take off, to scram; *(pédaler)* to pedal like mad, to go like the clappers

tricoteur, -euse [trikɔtœr, -øz] **N** *(personne)* knitter

NF tricoteuse *(machine)* knitting machine

tricrésylphosphate [trikrezilfɔsfat] **NM** tricresyl phosphate, TCP

trictrac [triktrak] **NM** *(jeu)* backgammon; *(partie)* game of backgammon; *(damier)* backgammon board

tricuspide [trikyspid] **ADJ** *Anat (valve)* tricuspid

tricycle [trisikl] **ADJ** *Aviat (train d'atterrissage)* three-wheeled

NM tricycle; *Fam* trike; **faire du t.** to go tricycling

trident [tridɑ̃] **NM 1** *Myth* trident **2** *Pêche* fish spear **3** *Agr* three-pronged (pitch)fork

tridimensionnel, -elle [tridimɑ̃sjɔnɛl] **ADJ** three-dimensional, 3-D

trièdre [triɛdr] *Géom* **ADJ** trihedral

NM trihedron

triennal, -ale, -aux, -ales [trijenal, -o] **ADJ** *(festival, élection, révision etc)* three-yearly, triennial; *(président etc)* appointed for three years; *(bail, projet etc)*, *Agr (rotation)* three-year

triennat [trijena] **NM** three-year mandate or period of office

trier [trije] *(impf, pr sub* **n. triions, v. triiez***)* **VT 1** *(classer)* *(lettres, minerai etc)*, *Ordinat* to sort; *(garde-robe, informations)* to sort or go through; *(fruits, lentilles)* to pick over; *Rail* to marshall; *Ordinat* **t. par ordre alphabétique** to sort in alphabetical order, to alphasort **2** *(en choisissant)* to sort out, to pick out, to select; **t. à la main** to hand-pick; **trié sur le volet** hand-picked

VPR se trier *Ordinat* to sort

trière [trijɛr] **NF** *Hist, Naut* trireme

trieur, -ieuse [trijœr, -jøz] **N** *(personne)* *(du courrier etc)* sorter

NM *Ind (appareil)* grader

NF trieuse *(machine)* sorter, sorting machine; *Ordinat* sorter; *(logiciel)* sort program

trieur-calibreur, *pl* **trieurs-calibreurs NM** *Ind* grading machine

trifolié [trifɔlje] **ADJ** *Bot* three-leaved, *Spéc* trifoliate

trifouiller [trifuje] *Fam* **VT** *(affaires, papiers etc)* to rummage around in, to go or rake through; *(moteur)* to fiddle with

VI qu'est-ce que tu trifouilles? what are you rummaging or raking around for?; *(qu'est-ce que tu fabriques?)* what are you up to?; **je ne**

sais pas ce que j'ai trifouillé mais ça ne marche plus I don't know what I've done but it's
not working; **t. dans qch** to rummage or rake
around in sth

Trifouillis-les-Oies [trifujilezwa] **N** *Fam =*
fictional name for the archetypal isolated,
dull village

trigémellaire [triʒemelɛr] **ADJ** *(grossesse)*
triple

triglycéride [trigliserid] **NM** triglyceride

trigo [trigo] **NF** *Fam (abrév* **trigonométrie**)
trig

trigonométrie [trigɔnɔmetri] **NF** trigonometry

trigonométrique [trigɔnɔmetrik] **ADJ**
(ligne) trigonometric(al); *(sens)* anticlockwise

trijumeau [triʒymo] **ADJ M, NM** *Anat* **(nerf) t.**
trigeminal nerve

trilatéral, -ale, -aux, -ales [trilateral, -o]
ADJ trilateral

trilingue [trilɛ̃g] **ADJ** *(personne, document
etc)* trilingual

trille [trij] **NM** *(d'un oiseau), Mus* trill; **les trilles des oiseaux** the trilling of the birds

triller [trije] **VTI** *Mus* to trill

trillion [triljɔ̃] **NM** *(10¹⁸)* trillion, *Am*
quintillion VOIR GRAMMAIRE A76

trilobé [trilɔbe] **ADJ 1** *Archit (arche etc)* trefoil
2 *Bot* three-lobed, *Spéc* trilobate

trilobite [trilɔbit] **NM** *(fossile)* trilobite

trilogie [trilɔʒi] **NF** *Littér* trilogy

trimaran [trimarɑ̃] **NM** *Naut* trimaran

trimarder [trimarde] **VI** *Arg* to be on the road

trimardeur [trimardœr] **NM** *Arg* tramp, *Am*
hobo

trimbal(l)age [trɛ̃balaʒ], **trimbal(l)ement**
[trɛ̃balmɑ̃] **NM** *Fam (de paquets etc)* lugging or
carting around; *(d'enfants etc)* trailing
around

trimbal(l)er [trɛ̃bale] *Fam* **VT** *(paquets etc)*
to lug or cart around; *(enfants etc)* to trail
around; **elle trimballe son fils partout** she
trails her son around or drags her son with
her everywhere she goes; *Fam* **qu'est ce
qu'il trimbale!** *(il est bête)* what an idiot (he
is)!, *Br* what a plonker!

VPR se trimballer se t. jusqu'à la gare to trail
or *Am* schlep over to the station; **je ne vais
pas me t. en ville habillé comme ça!** I'm not
going around town dressed like that!; **elle se
trimballe partout avec sa marmaille** she
trails her kids around with her everywhere
she goes, she doesn't go anywhere without
her kids; **elle se trimballe partout dans sa
vieille voiture** she goes everywhere in her
old car

trimer [trime] **VI** *Fam (travailler dur)* to slog
or slave away, to work like a dog; **faire t. qn**
to make sb slog, to keep sb hard at it

trimestre [trimɛstr] **NM 1** *(trois mois)* quarter; *Scol* term, *Am* trimester; **par t.** quarterly;
Scol **payer par t.** to pay every term **2** *(salaire)*
quarter's salary; *(loyer)* quarter's rent; *Scol
(frais)* term fees; *(d'une assurance, une
bourse)* quarterly instalment or payment

trimestriel, -ielle [trimɛstrijɛl] **ADJ** quarterly; *Scol (bulletin)* end-of-term; **fonction
trimestrielle** position lasting for three
months

trimestriellement [trimɛstrijɛlmɑ̃] **ADV**
quarterly; *Scol* once a term

trimoteur [trimɔtœr] **NM** three-engined
plane

tringle [trɛ̃gl] **NF** *(barre)* rod; **t. à rideau** curtain rod; **t. d'escalier** stair rod; *Archit (moulure)* square moulding

tringler [trɛ̃gle] **VT 1** *Tech (avec une ficelle
crayeuse)* to mark with a line **2** *Vulg (sexuel-*

lement) to screw, to lay; **se faire t.** to get
laid

tringlerie [trɛ̃glɛri] **NF** *Aut* linkage

trinitaire [trinitɛr] **ADJ, N** *Rel* Trinitarian

trinité [trinite] **NF 1** *Rel* **la (Sainte) T.** the
(Holy) Trinity; **la T.** *(fête)* Trinity Sunday **2**
(l'île de) la T. Trinidad **3** *(groupe de trois éléments)* trinity

Trinité-et-Tobago [triniteetɔbago] **N** Trinidad and Tobago

trinitrotoluène [trinitrotɔlɥɛn] **NM** trinitrotoluene, TNT

trinôme [trinom] **NM** *Math* trinomial

trinquer [trɛ̃ke] **VI 1** *(porter un toast)* to
clink glasses; **t. à qn/qch** to drink to sb/sth;
t. à la santé de qn to drink a toast to sb; **nous
trinquons à nos cinq ans de mariage** let's
drink to or here's to our five years of marriage **2** *Fam (boire avec excès)* to booze **3**
Fam (subir un désagrément) to suffer, to pay
the cost, to get the worst of it; **les parents di-
vorcent, les enfants trinquent** when parents
get a divorce, it's the children that suffer;
elle fait des bêtises et c'est moi qui trinque
she acts the idiot and I get the blame

trinquet [trɛ̃kɛ] **NM** *Naut* foremast

trinquette [trɛ̃kɛt] **NF** *Naut* storm jib

trio [trijo] **NM** threesome, trio; *Mus* trio

triode [trijɔd] **ADJ, NF** *Électron, Radio* triode

triolet [trijɔlɛ] **NM 1** *Mus* triplet **2** *Littér* triolet

triomphal, -ale, -aux, -ales [trijɔ̃fal, -o]
ADJ *(accueil)* triumphant, triumphal; *(couronne)* of victory; *(élection)* resoundingly
successful; *(geste)* triumphant, of triumph

triomphalement [trijɔ̃falmɑ̃] **ADV** triumphantly; **être accueilli t.** to be received in
triumph or triumphantly

triomphalisme [trijɔ̃falism] **NM** crowing;
sans faire de t., il me semble que ... que while I
don't want to crow, it seems to me that ...

triomphaliste [trijɔ̃falist] **ADJ** *(attitude, air)*
cock-a-hoop; **être t.** to crow
N crower

triomphant [trijɔ̃fɑ̃] **ADJ** *(personne)* triumphant; *(sourire, air, rire)* triumphant, of
triumph; **... dit-il d'un ton t.** ... he said
triumphantly; **il est arrivé t., avec la preuve
qu'il avait raison** he came back cock-a-hoop
with the proof that he was right

triomphateur, -trice [trijɔ̃fatœr, -tris] **ADJ**
triumphant, victorious
N *(vainqueur)* victor, winner
NM *Antiq* conquering hero

triomphe [trijɔ̃f] **NM** triumph (**sur** over); **le
t. de la justice** the triumph of justice; **remporter un t.** to be a resounding success or a
triumph; **c'est le t. de la démocratie/de la
bêtise** it's a triumph for democracy/stupidi-
ty; **faire un t. à qn** to give sb an ovation; **arc
de t.** triumphal arch; **en t.** in triumph; **porter
qn en t.** to carry sb in triumph or shoulder
high; **sourire/cri de t.** smile/shout of
triumph, triumphant smile/shout; **pousser
un cri de t.** to give a shout of triumph, to
shout triumphantly

triompher [trijɔ̃fe] **VI 1** *(l'emporter)* to
triumph, to be triumphant (**de** over); **t. d'une
difficulté** to triumph over or to overcome a
difficulty **2** *(exceller)* to excel (**dans** in);
(avoir un grand succès) to triumph; **la vérité
finit toujours par t.** truth will prevail **3** *(exulter)* to crow

trioxyde [trijɔksid] **NM** *Chimie* trioxide

trip [trip] **NM** *Fam* **1** *(de drogue)* trip; **t. d'acide**
acid trip; **faire un t.** to trip; **être en plein t.** to
be on a trip, to be tripping **2 c'est pas mon t.**
(ça ne m'intéresse pas) it's not my thing or
bag; **le jazz, c'est plutôt son t.** jazz is his
thing or bag; **il est dans son t. écolo** he's on
his environmental kick

tripaille [tripɑj] **NF** *Fam (intestins)* guts

triparti [triparti] **ADJ** tripartite

tripartisme [tripartism] **NM** three-party
government

tripartite [tripartit] **ADJ** tripartite

tripatouillage [tripatujaʒ] **NM** *Fam (de
textes, comptes etc)* tampering or fiddling
with; *(de statistiques)* massaging; **il y a eu t.
des résultats** the results were fiddled

tripatouiller [tripatuje] **VT 1** *(textes)* to
tamper or fiddle with; *(comptes, résultats)* to
fiddle (with); *(statistiques)* to massage **2** *(tripoter) (personne)* to paw, to feel up; *(cheveux
etc)* to play or fiddle with
VI t. dans to be mixed up or involved in

tripatouilleur, -euse [tripatujœr, -øz] **N**
Fam fiddler, tamperer

tripe [trip] **NF 1 tripes** *(d'un animal)* entrails;
Culin tripe; *très Fam (de personne)* guts; *Fam*
une histoire qui vous prend aux tripes a
story that gets you in the guts or right there;
Fam **parler avec ses tripes** to speak from the
heart; *Fam* **dans ce film, elle joue vraiment
avec ses tripes** she gives a powerful performance in this film; *très Fam* **rendre tripes et
boyaux** to spew one's guts out; *Fam* **elle a
des tripes** she's got guts **2** *Fig Fam* **avoir la t.
républicaine** to be a republican through and
through **3** *(de cigare)* core, filling **4 peau en
t.** pelt

triper [tripe] **VI** *Fam* to trip *(after taking
drugs)*

triperie [tripri] **NF 1** *(boutique)* tripe shop **2**
(commerce) tripe trade

tripette [tripɛt] **NF** *Fam* **ça ne vaut pas t., sa
formation/sa chaînette/son conseil** her
training/chain/advice isn't worth a damn

triphasé [trifaze] *Élec* **ADJ** three-phase
NM three-phase current; **installation en t.**
three-phase wiring

triphtongue [triftɔ̃g] **NF** *Ling* triphthong

tripier, -ière [tripje, -jɛr] **N** tripe butcher

triplace [triplas] **ADJ** *Aviat* three-seater

triplan [triplɑ̃] **NM** *Aviat* triplane

triple [tripl] **ADJ 1** triple; *(trois fois plus
grand) (dose)* triple, treble; **t. menton** triple
chin; **t. naissance** triple birth; **en t. exemplaire** in triplicate **2** *(emploi intensif)* **un t.
sot** a prize idiot; **au t. galop** at top or breakneck speed, at a rate of knots; *Fam* **t. buse!**
you stupid nit!
NM le t. three times as much (**de** as); **je l'ai
acheté le t. de toi/de sa valeur** I paid three
times as much as you did/as much as it was
worth; **douze est le t. de quatre** twelve is
three times four
▶▶ *Hist* **la T. Alliance** the Triple Alliance; *Tél* **t.
bande** tri-band, triple band; **t. croche** demisemiquaver, *Am* thirty-second note; *Hist* **la T.
Entente** the Triple Entente; **t. saut** triple
jump, hop, skip and jump

triplé, -ée [triple] **N** triplet
NM *Sport (triple succès)* triple victory;
Courses de chevaux (pari) = bet on the first
three horses in a race

triplement¹ [triplǝmɑ̃] **ADV** *(important)*
trebly, triply; **elle a t. raison** she is right on
three counts

triplement² **NM** trebling, tripling

tripler [triple] **VT** to treble, to triple, to increase threefold; *Scol* **t. une classe** to repeat
a year twice
VI to treble, to triple, to increase threefold

triplette [triplɛt] **NF** *(aux boules)* threesome

Triplex® [tripleks] **NM** *(verre)* laminated
safety glass, *Br* Triplex®

tripode [tripɔd] **ADJ** *Naut (mât)* tripod

Tripoli [tripɔli] **N** Tripoli

triporteur [tripɔrtœr] **NM** delivery tricycle

tripot [tripo] NM gambling den

tripotage [tripɔtaʒ] NM Fam **1** (fraude) fiddling (around) (**de** with); **le t. électoral est monnaie courante** election rigging is common; **tripotages** (magouilles) scheming, dirty tricks, skulduggery; **tripotages électoraux** election rigging; **il y a eu des tripotages** there's been some scheming or fiddling going on **2** (action de toucher) **arrêtez vos tripotages!** stop pawing each other!

tripotée [tripɔte] NF Fam **1** (raclée) hammering **2** (grand nombre) **une t. de** loads of, lots of

tripoter [tripɔte] Fam VI (magouiller) to engage in shady business; **t. dans** to be mixed up or involved in; **t. dans la caisse** to tamper with the cash

VT (toucher à) (appareil) to touch, to mess around or about with; (fruits) to finger, to paw; (parce qu'on est nerveux) (objet, cheveux etc) to fiddle with; **arrête de t. tes boutons** stop fingering or keep your hands off your spots; **t. qn** to paw or grope sb, to touch sb up

VPR **se tripoter** (se masturber) to play with oneself; (de deux personnes) to paw or grope each other, to feel each other up

tripoteur, -euse [tripɔtœr, -øz] N (magouilleur) suspicious character, Arg chancer, m wide boy

ADJ (mains) groping; **il a les mains tripoteuses** he's got wandering hands

triptyque [triptik] NM **1** Beaux-Arts, Littér, Mus triptych **2** Aut, Admin triptyque

trique [trik] NF Fam cudgel, heavy stick; **des coups de t.** cudgel blows; Fig **avoir recours à la t.** to use the big stick; **mener son monde** ou **les gens à la t.** to rule with a rod of iron, to rule by fear; **sec comme une t.** ou **un coup de t.** as thin as a rake; Fig Vulg **avoir la t.** (être en érection) to have a hard-on

triquer [trike] VI Vulg to have a hard-on

triquet [trikɛ] NM (échelle) pair of steps

trirème [trirɛm] NF Hist, Naut trireme

trisaïeul, pl trisaïeuls [trizajœl] NM great-great-grandfather; **trisaïeuls** great-great-grandparents

trisaïeule [trizajœl] NF great-great-grandmother

trisannuel, -elle [trizanɥɛl] ADJ (qui a lieu tous les trois ans) three-yearly, triennial; (qui dure trois ans) three-year

trisection [trisɛksjɔ̃] NF Géom trisection

triso [trizo] N Fam (abrév **trisomique**) spaz, Br mong

trisomie [trizɔmi] NF Méd Down's syndrome, Spéc trisomy; **t. 21** trisomy of chromosome 21; **enfant atteint de t. 21** child with Down's syndrome

trisomique [trizɔmik] Méd ADJ with Down's syndrome; **être t.** to have Down's syndrome N = person with Down's syndrome

trisser (se) [sətrise] VPR Arg (s'enfuir) to scram, to beat it

triste [trist] ADJ **1** (malheureux) (personne) sad; (visage, mine, air) sad, forlorn; (sourire) sad, wan, sorrowful; **c'est vraiment t.** it's really sad to see; **ça me rend t. de te le dire** I am sorry to tell you; **je fus (bien) t. d'apprendre que ...** I was (very) sorry to hear that ...; **tout t.** (very) dejected, in low spirits; **elle a le vin t.** she's not a happy drunk, drink makes her maudlin; **il n'est pas t., son mari!** her husband's a real laugh-a-minute!; **elle n'était pas t., la fête!** it was a terrific or a really fun party!; Iron **tu as vu son gâteau, c'est pas t.!** have you seen that masterpiece of a cake?; Fam **c'était vraiment pas t.** it was really funny **2** (ennuyeux) (vie, temps, pièce etc) dreary,

dismal, depressing; (couleur) dreary, depressing; (campagne) bleak, depressing; (personne) miserable, depressing; **faire t. mine à qn** to give sb an unenthusiastic welcome; **t. à mourir** (gens, ambiance, lieu) thoroughly depressing, dreary

3 (douloureux) (tâche, nouvelle, occasion, épisode) sad, painful; **dans un t. état** in a sorry state; **c'est la t. réalité** that's the way things are; **c'est une t. affaire** it's a sorry or bad business; **(quelle) t. époque!** what terrible times we live in!; **c'est tout de même t.!** it's pretty pathetic!; **c'est quand même t. de voir ça dans notre pays!** it's dreadful to see that type of thing in our own country!

4 Péj (repas, excuse etc) poor, sorry, wretched; (morceau de pain) sad- or sorry-looking

N (personne sombre) gloomy or miserable person; **ce n'est pas un t.** he's a lot of fun

tristement [tristəmã] ADV **1** (avec tristesse) sadly, sorrowfully; **nous avons t. appris la nouvelle** we heard the news with great sadness, we were sad or sorry to hear the news **2** (d'une façon sombre) gloomily; **la maison est t. décorée** the house is decorated in a dreary or depressing fashion **3** (cruellement) sadly; **faire t. défaut** to be sadly lacking; **t. célèbre** notorious

tristesse [tristɛs] NF **1** (d'une personne, d'un événement) sadness; **ressentir de la t.** to feel sad; **un sourire plein de t.** a very sad smile; **avec t.** sadly; **j'ai quitté ce pays avec t.** I was sorry to leave the country **2** (d'une pièce, d'une couleur, d'un décor etc) dreariness; (d'un paysage) bleakness

NFPL **tristesses** (moments) (de la vie etc) sorrows

tristounet, -ette [tristunɛ, -ɛt] ADJ Fam (pièce) dreary, gloomy; (couleur) dreary; (personne, air) gloomy

trisyllabe, trissyllabe [trisilab] NM trisyllable, three-syllable word

trisyllabique, trissyllabique [trisilabik] ADJ trisyllabic, three-syllable

trithérapie [triterapi] NF triple (combination) therapy

tritium [tritjɔm] NM Chimie tritium

triton¹ [tritɔ̃] NM **1** Myth T. Triton **2** (amphibien) triton newt **3** (mollusque) triton, trumpet shell

triton² NM Mus augmented fourth, tritone

trituration [trityrasjɔ̃] NF (broyage) grinding, Spéc trituration

triturer [trityre] VT **1** (broyer) to grind, Spéc to triturate **2** (manier) (son mouchoir etc) to twist up; Fig (l'opinion) to manipulate; **de vieux magazines tout triturés** battered old magazines

VPR **se triturer** Fam **se t. la cervelle** ou **les méninges** to rack one's brains

triumvir [trijɔmvir] NM Antiq triumvir

triumvirat [trijɔmvira] NM Antiq, Pol Fig triumvirate

trivalent [trivalã] ADJ Chimie trivalent

trivalve [trivalv] ADJ Biol trivalvular, trivalve

trivial, -iale, -iaux, -iales [trivjal, -jo] ADJ **1** (vulgaire) (expression, langage, plaisanteries etc) vulgar, coarse **2** (commun) trite, banal, mundane; Math etc (solution) self-evident, obvious

> Il faut noter que l'adjectif anglais **trivial** est un faux ami. Il signifie **anodin, insignifiant.**

trivialement [trivjalmã] ADV (vulgairement) vulgarly, coarsely

trivialité [trivjalite] NF **1** (vulgarité) (d'une expression, une plaisanterie etc) vulgarity, coarseness **2** (caractère commun) (d'une ex-

plication, d'une argumentation) triteness, banality; **tout cela est d'une t.!** it's so banal or trite! **3** (expression) vulgar or coarse expression

tr/mn (abrév **tours par minute**) rpm, rev/min

troc [trɔk] NM exchange (in kind); (système économique) barter; **économie de t.** barter economy; **faire du t.** to barter; **faire le t. d'une chose avec une autre** to exchange or barter or Fam swap one thing for another; **je ne l'ai pas acheté, j'ai fait le t. avec quelqu'un** I didn't buy it, I bartered for it or Fam I did a swap; **faire un t.** to make an exchange or Fam do a swap (**avec qn** with sb)

trochaïque [trɔkaik] ADJ, NM Littér trochaic

trochée [trɔʃe] NM Littér trochee

troène [trɔɛn] NM Bot privet

troglodyte [trɔglɔdit] NM **1** (personne) troglodyte, cave dweller **2** (oiseau) wren

troglodytique [trɔglɔditik] ADJ **habitation t.** cave dwelling

trogne [trɔɲ] NF Fam face, Péj mug; **il a une bonne t.** (d'une personne, d'un bébé) he's got a nice face

trognon [trɔɲɔ̃] NM **1** (de pomme etc) core; (de chou etc) stump; Fig Fam **on s'est fait avoir jusqu'au t.** we were well and truly done **2** Fam (terme d'affection) poppet, sweetie

ADJ INV Fam (mignon) sweet

Troie [trwa] N Troy; **guerre/cheval de T.** Trojan War/horse

troïka [trɔika] NF (traîneau), Pol troika; **t. européenne** European troika

trois [trwa] ([trwaz] before a vowel sound or mute h in the same word group) ADJ INV **1** three; **à t. heures** at three o'clock; **les t. quarts du temps** most of the time; **couper/partager qch en t.** to cut/divide sth into three; Géom **couper** ou **diviser une ligne/un angle en t.** to trisect a line/an angle; **entrer (t.) par t.** to come in in threes or three at a time; **t. par t.** three by three, in threes; **ménage à t.** ménage à trois; **(hôtel) t. étoiles** three-star hotel; **en t. dimensions** in 3D Théâtre **frapper les t. coups** = to announce the beginning of a theatre performance by knocking three times; Mus **à t. temps** in triple or three-four time Fam **haut comme t. pommes** knee-high to a grasshopper **2** (dans des séries) third; **page/numéro t.** page/number three; **Henri T.** Henry the Third **3** (exprimant une approximation) **dans t. minutes** in a couple of minutes; **il n'a pas dit t. mots** he hardly said a word; **deux ou t., t. ou quatre** a few, a handful

NM INV three; **le t. août** (on) the third of August, (on) August the third, Am (on) August third; Cartes **t. de carreau** three of diamonds; **j'habite au t.** I live at number three

3G [trwaʒe] ADJ INV Ordinat, Tél 3G

trois-huit NM INV **1** Mus three-eight time **2** Ind **régime des t.** three-shift working; **faire les t.** to operate three shifts (of eight hours each)

troisième [trwazjɛm] ADJ third; **au t. étage** on the third or Am fourth floor; **de t. ordre** third-rate

N (personne, chose etc) third

NM **1** (fraction) third **2** (étage) third or Am fourth floor; **habiter au t.** to live on the third or Am fourth floor

NF **1** Scol (classe de) t. Br ≃ fourth year of secondary school, Am ≃ eighth grade **2** Aut third (gear); **en t.** in third (gear); **passer la t.** to go (up/down) into third (gear)

▸▸ **t. âge: personnes du t. âge** senior citizens, Am golden agers; Journ **t. de couverture** inside back cover, IBC; Pol **la t. voie** the Third Way

troisièmement [trwazjɛmmɑ̃] ADV thirdly, in the third place

trois-mâts NM INV *Naut* three-masted ship, three-master

trois-pièces NM INV **1** *(appartement)* three-room(ed) flat *or Am* apartment **2** *(costume)* three-piece suit

trois-quarts NM INV **1** *Rugby* three-quarter; **t. aile/centre** wing/centre three-quarter; **t. arrière** three-quarter back **2** *(manteau)* three-quarter-length coat

trois-quatre NM INV *Mus* three-four time

troll [trɔl] NM *Myth* troll

trolley [trɔlɛ] NM **1** *(caténaire)* trolley pole and wheel; **perche de t.** trolley pole **2** *(véhicule)* trolleybus

trolleybus [trɔlɛbys] NM trolleybus

trombe [trɔ̃b] NF **1** *(cyclone)* waterspout **2 t. de vent** whirlwind; **t. d'eau** cloudburst; *Fig Fam* **entrer/sortir en t.** to tear *or* hurtle in/out, to burst in/out (like a whirlwind); **il est passé/parti en t.** he tore *or* hurtled past/off, he went past/left in a cloud of dust

trombine [trɔ̃bin] NF *Arg (visage)* mug

trombinoscope [trɔ̃binɔskɔp] NM *Fam (d'une association, d'un groupe etc)* rogues' gallery

tromblon [trɔ̃blɔ̃] NM *(fusil)* blunderbuss

trombone [trɔ̃bɔn] NM **1** *Mus (instrument)* trombone; *(instrumentiste)* trombone (player), trombonist; **t. à coulisse/à pistons** slide/valve trombone **2** *(agrafe)* paper clip

trompe [trɔ̃p] NF **1** *Mus* horn; **t. de brume/chasse** fog/hunting horn; *Fig* **publier qch à son de t.** to trumpet sth abroad **2** *Zool (d'un animal, d'un insecte)* proboscis; *(d'un éléphant)* trunk **3** *Anat* **t. d'Eustache/de Fallope** Eustachian/Fallopian tube **4** *Archit* pendentive, squinch **5** *Tech* pump; *Métal* blast pump, trompe

trompe-la-mort N INV *Fam (volontaire)* daredevil

trompe-l'œil NM INV **1** *Beaux-Arts* trompe l'œil (painting); **en t.** *(peinture, scène etc)* trompe l'œil; **peindre en t.** to do a trompe l'œil painting, to use trompe l'œil techniques **2** *Fig Péj* bluff, window-dressing

tromper [trɔ̃pe] VT **1** *(abuser)* to deceive, to (deliberately) mislead, to take in; **cela ne trompe personne** nobody's taken in, nobody's fooled; **t. qn sur qn/qch** to deceive *or* mislead sb about sb/sth; **il est incapable de t. qui que ce soit** he is totally incapable of deceit

2 *(être infidèle à)* *(femme, mari)* to deceive, to be unfaithful to, *Fam* to cheat on, to two-time; **il trompe sa femme avec sa secrétaire** he's having an affair with his secretary

3 *(induire en erreur)* to mislead *(sur* as, to); *(decevoir)* *(espoirs de qn)* to disappoint; **son air de s'y connaître m'a trompé** I was misled *or* fooled *or* taken in by the fact that he seemed to know what he was doing; **ne vous laissez pas t.** don't be misled, don't be fooled, don't be taken in; **ça a l'air lourd, mais c'est ce qui vous trompe** it looks heavy, that's what's so misleading; **je ne voulais pas t. son attente** I didn't want to disappoint him; **se laisser t. par les apparences** to be taken in by appearances

4 *(échapper à)* *(contrôle, surveillance, vigilance)* to elude, to escape

5 *Fig (ennui)* to relieve; *(temps)* to while away; **t. la faim** to stave off (one's) hunger

VPR **se tromper 1** *(commettre une erreur)* to be mistaken, to be wrong, to make a mistake; **c'est justement ce en quoi tu te trompes** that's just where you're wrong; **je dois me t.** I must be mistaken, I must be wrong; **j'ai dû me t.** I must have made a mistake; **si/à**

moins que je ne me trompe if I'm not/unless I'm mistaken; **ou je me trompe** or I'm much mistaken; **tout le monde peut se t.** anybody can make a mistake, we all make mistakes; **se t. dans les dates/les proportions** to get the dates/the proportions wrong; **se t. dans son calcul** to get one's sums wrong, *Fml* to be out in one's reckoning; *Tél* **vous devez vous t. de numéro** you must have the wrong number; **je me suis trompé de direction/de maison** I went the wrong way/to the wrong house; **je me suis trompé de Laurent!** I got the wrong Laurent!; **se t. d'heure/de jour** to mistake the time/day, to get the time/day wrong; **je ne m'y trompe pas, du reste** I'm not fooled *or* taken in; **elle ressemble à sa sœur à s'y t.** you can't tell her and her sister apart; **il n'y a pas à s'y t.** there's no mistake about it; **que l'on ne s'y trompe pas** make no mistake about it; **vous m'avez fait me t.** you made me make a mistake; **tu es en train de la faire se t.** you're confusing her **2** *(entre époux)* **se t.** (mutuellement) to be unfaithful to *or Fam* to cheat on each other

tromperie [trɔ̃pri] NF deceit, deception; *(en affaires)* fraud; **j'en ai assez de tes tromperies** I've had enough of your deceit *or* deceitfulness; **il y a t. sur la marchandise** this isn't what it was said to be

trompeter [trɔ̃pete] VT (**je trompette**; **je trompetterai**) *(nouvelles)* to shout from the rooftops

trompette [trɔ̃pɛt] NF **1** *Mus* trumpet; *Mil* **jouer/sonner de la t.** to play/sound the trumpet; **t. de jazz** jazz trumpet; **à la t., Louis Armstrong!** on (the) trumpet, Louis Armstrong!; *Litt* **la t. du jugement dernier** the last trump; *Fig* **nez en t.** turned-up nose **2** *(coquillage)* trumpet shell

  NM trumpet (player), trumpeter

▸▸**t. bouchée** muted trumpet; **t. de cavalerie** bugle

trompette-de-la-mort, pl **trompettes-de-la-mort** NF *(champignon)* horn of plenty

trompettiste [trɔ̃petist] N *Mus* trumpet (player), trumpeter

trompeur, -euse [trɔ̃pœr, -øz] ADJ **1** *(volontairement)* *(personne, paroles etc)* deceitful **2** *(symptôme, apparences etc)* deceptive, misleading; *(publicité)* misleading

  N deceiver, cheat; *Prov* **à t., t. et demi** = cheats never win

trompeusement [trɔ̃pøzmɑ̃] ADV deceptively

tronc [trɔ̃] NM **1** *(d'un arbre, d'un corps)* trunk; **homme-/femme-t.** armless and legless man/woman **2** *(d'une famille)* parent stock **3** *Rel* poor box **4** *Fam* **t. de casser le t.** to strain oneself; **il ne s'est pas cassé le t.** he didn't kill himself, he didn't overexert himself **5** *Math* **t. de cône/pyramide** truncated cone/pyramid

▸▸*Univ etc* **t. commun** core syllabus

troncature [trɔ̃katyr] NF *Ordinat* truncation

tronche [trɔ̃ʃ] NF **1** *Fam (tête)* nut, bonce; *(visage)* mug, kisser; **sa t. ne me revient pas** I don't like the look of him; **il a une sale t.** he's an ugly-looking customer; *Fam* **faire la t.** to sulk **2** *(personne intelligente)* brain, brainy person; **ce mec-là, c'est une t.!** that guy's a real brain *or* so brainy!

troncher [trɔ̃ʃe] VT *Vulg* to fuck, to screw

tronçon [trɔ̃sɔ̃] NM *(de chemin de fer, d'autoroute)* section; *(d'une canalisation)* section, length; *(de phrase, de texte etc)* part, portion; *(d'épée, de lance, de mât etc)* (broken) stump; **t. de bois** log

tronconique [trɔ̃kɔnik] ADJ **segment t.** truncated segment

tronçonnage [trɔ̃sɔnaʒ], **tronçonnement** [trɔ̃sɔnmɑ̃] NM cutting into lengths *or* pieces

tronçonner [trɔ̃sɔne] VT to cut up (into lengths *or* pieces)

tronçonneuse [trɔ̃sɔnøz] NF *(à chaîne)* chain saw; *(circulaire)* circular saw

trône [tron] NM **1** *(de roi, pape etc)* throne; **monter sur le t.** to come to the throne; **placer** *ou* **mettre qn sur le t.** to put sb on the throne **2** *Fam Hum (siège des cabinets)* **être sur le t.** to be on the throne

trôner [trone] VI **1** *(d'un monarque), Fig (d'une personne)* to sit enthroned **2** *(d'objets)* to occupy a place of honour *or Am* honor; **son diplôme trône sur la cheminée** his diploma occupies a place of honour on the mantelpiece; **toutes ses décorations trônaient dans son bureau** all his decorations were prominently displayed in his office **3** *Péj (faire l'important)* to lord it

tronqué [trɔ̃ke] ADJ *(colonne, pyramide)* truncated; *(mât)* stub; *(texte)* cut, truncated

tronquer [trɔ̃ke] VT *(arbre)* to pollard; *Fig (roman, scène etc)* to cut, to shorten, to truncate

trop [tro] ADV **1** *(devant un adj)* too, over-; *(devant un adv)* too; **c'est t. difficile** it's too difficult; **un travail t. difficile** too difficult a job; **t. aimable** [trɔpemabl] too *or* extremely kind; **aliments t. riches** over-rich food; **t. attaché à** too attached to, overfond of; **t. cuit** overcooked; **être t. habillé** to have too many clothes on; **vous n'êtes que t. généreux** you are much too *or* far too *or* overly generous; **t. fatigué** too tired (**pour faire** to do), over-tired; *Litt* **par t. généreux** far too generous; **t. beau pour être vrai** too good to be true; **vous n'êtes pas t. en avance** you're none too early; **je ne me sens pas t. à l'aise** I'm not overly comfortable, I'm none too comfortable; **ça va? – pas t. mal** how are things? – not bad at all *or* not too bad; **ça te plaît/c'est bien fait? – pas t. mal** do you like it/is it good? – it's not bad at all; **c'était t. drôle** it was too funny for words *or* just too funny; **le trou était t. étroit pour qu'un rat entrât par là** the hole was too narrow for a rat to get in by; **c'est t. grand pour qu'on puisse le mettre dans la voiture** it's too big to go in the car; *Fam* **il est vraiment t.!** he's too much! VOIR GRAMMAIRE A5

2 *(avec un verbe)* too much, over-; **t. travailler** to overwork, to work too much *or* too hard; **t. manger** to overeat, to eat too much; **boire t., t. boire** to drink to excess *or* too much; **t. simplifier** to oversimplify; **je ne l'ai que t. dit** I've said it time and time again; **je ne la connais que t.** I know her all *or* only too well; **je l'ai t. aimé** [trɔpeme] I loved him too much; **il n'y tient pas t.** he's not too bothered (about it); *Fam* **ça te plaît? – pas t.** do you like it? – not (very) much; **ne vous y fiez pas t., il ne faut pas t. vous y fier** don't count on it too much; **je ne le croirais pas t.** I wouldn't put too much faith in what he says, I wouldn't be too ready to believe him; **on ne saurait t. le répéter** it cannot be repeated too often; **je ne sais pas t.** I'm not too sure; **je ne sais t. que dire/penser** I hardly know *or* I don't quite know what to say/think

3 *(emploi nominal)* *(quantité)* too much; *(nombre)* too many; **t. de** *(bruit, sel, travail etc)* too much; *(amis, choses, problèmes etc)* too many; **je n'aurai pas t. d'une heure pour le faire** it will take me a good hour; **il a t. d'expérience pour se tromper** he is too experienced to make a mistake; **elle n'a fait preuve que de t. de patience** she has shown far too much patience; **j'ai une carte de t.** *ou* **en t.** I have one card too many; **payer 100 euros de t.** *ou* **en t.** to pay 100 euros too much; **c'est une fois de t.** that's once too often; **quand j'ai du temps de t.** when I have time to spare; **être/se sentir de t.** to be/feel in the way *or* unwelcome *or* de trop; *Fam* **tra-**

vailler de t. to work too hard *or* too much, to overwork; *Fam* **boire de t.** to drink too much, *Fam* to overdo the drink; **t., c'est t.! enough is enough!; c'en est t.!** this really is the limit!; **il allait t. en dire** *ou* **en dire t.** he was going to say too much

trope [trɔp] **NM** *Littér* trope

trophée [trɔfe] **NM** trophy

tropical, -ale, -aux, -ales [trɔpikal, -o] **ADJ** *(plante, climat, température etc)* tropical; *(vêtement)* for wear in the tropics

tropique [trɔpik] **NM** *Astron, Géog (cercle)* tropic; **le t. du Cancer/du Capricorne** the tropic of Cancer/of Capricorn
NMPL les tropiques *(région)* the tropics; **sous les tropiques** in the tropics

tropisme [trɔpism] **NM** *Biol* tropism

troposphère [trɔpɔsfɛr] **NF** *Météo* troposphere

trop-perçu, *pl* **trop-perçus** [trɔpɛrsy] **NM** *Fin (d'impôts)* over-payment, excess payment

trop-plein, *pl* **trop-pleins NM** *(réservoir, excédent)* overflow; **(tuyau de) t.** waste pipe, overflow pipe; **t. d'énergie/de tendresse** overabundance of energy/affection; **laisser déborder le t. de son cœur** to give vent to one's overflowing emotions

troquer [trɔke] **VT 1** *Com* to exchange, to barter **2** *(faire l'échange)* to exchange, *Fam* to swap **(contre qch** for sth**)**

troquet [trɔkɛ] **NM** *Fam* (small) café

trot [tro] **NM** *(de cheval)* trot; **t. assis** sitting trot; **t. enlevé** rising trot, *Am* posting trot; **au petit/grand t.** at a gentle/brisk trot; **prendre le t.** to break into a trot; **aller le t.** *ou* **au t.** to trot; *Fig Fam* **allez-y, et au t.!** go on, and be quick about it!; **t. attelé** harness race; **t. monté** = type of race in which the horse is ridden instead of being harnessed to the sulky; **course de t.** trotting *or* harness race

Trotski [trɔtski] **N** Trotsky

trotskisme, trotskysme [trɔtskism] **NM** Trotskyism

trotskiste, trotskyste [trɔtskist] **ADJ, N** Trotskyist, Trotskyite

trotte [trɔt] **NF** *Fam (longue distance)* (long) stretch; **il y a une bonne t. d'ici au château** it's a good way *or* hike from here to the castle; **tout d'une t.** without stopping

trotte-menu **ADJ INV** **la gent t.** mice

trotter [trɔte] **VI 1** *(d'un cheval, d'un cavalier)* to trot; *(d'une personne)* to trot (around/along); *(d'une souris)* to scamper; **Fam toujours à t.** always on the go; **on entendrait une souris** you could have heard a pin drop; *Fig* **cette chanson me trotte dans la tête** that song keeps running through my head; **ça me trotte dans la tête depuis** I haven't been able to stop thinking about it since

trotteur, -euse [trɔtœr, -øz] **ADJ** **talons trotteurs** flat *or* low heels
N *(cheval)* trotter
NM 1 *(chaussure)* flat(-heeled) *or* low-heeled shoe **2** *(pour bébé)* baby-walker
NF trotteuse 1 *(de montre)* second hand **2** *Can (pour bébés)* babywalker

trottinement [trɔtinmɑ̃] **NM** *(d'une souris)* scampering; *(d'une personne)* trotting about

trottiner [trɔtine] **VI 1** *(de cheval, mule)* to jog-trot **2** *(de souris)* to scamper (around/along), to patter about; *(de personne)* to trot about

trottinette [trɔtinɛt] **NF 1** *(jouet)* scooter; **faire de la t.** to ride one's scooter **2** *Fam (petite voiture)* small car, runabout

trottoir [trɔtwar] **NM** pavement, *Am* sidewalk; *Aut* **heurter le t.** to hit the kerb; **artiste de t.** pavement artist; *Fam* **faire le t.** to walk the streets, to be on the game; **t. roulant**

travelator, moving pavement *or* *Am* sidewalk

trou [tru] **NM 1** *(ouverture)* hole; *(d'aiguille)* eye; **avoir des trous à ses chaussettes** to have holes in one's socks; **t. de clef** *(d'horloge, de montre)* keyhole; **t. de serrure** keyhole; **le t. de la couche d'ozone** the hole in the ozone layer; *Fig* **faire son t.** to find one's niche; *Aviat Arg* **il a fait un t. dans l'eau** he's gone for a Burton; *Fam* **boire comme un t.** to drink like a fish; *Fam* **s'en mettre jusqu'aux trous de nez** to stuff one's face
2 *(dans une haie)*, *Fig (dans un emploi du temps)* gap, opening; *Fig (de mémoire, dans une explication, un CV etc)* gap; *(dans ses économies, son budget)* hole, dent; **j'ai un t. de cinq à sept** I'm free *or* I'm not doing anything between five and seven; **il est parti en laissant un t. de 50 000 euros** he went off leaving us/the company/*etc* 50,000 euros worse off; **j'ai eu un t. (de mémoire)** my mind went blank *or* was a blank; **j'ai un t.** my mind has gone blank *or* is a blank; *Sport* **faire le t.** to break away from the field
3 *Anat Fam* **je n'ai pas les yeux en face des trous** I haven't come to yet, I'm still fast asleep, my brain's still not in gear; *Méd Fam* **t. dans le cœur** hole in the heart
4 *(creusé etc)* hole; *Aut* (pot)hole; **t. de souris** mouse-hole; *Agr* **t. au fumier** manure pit
5 *Fam Péj (village etc)* hole; **elle n'est jamais sortie de son t.** she has never been out of her own backyard; **habiter un petit t. (perdu)** to live at the back of beyond
6 *Golf* hole; **envoyer la balle dans le t.** to hole out; **partie par trous** match play
7 *Arg (tombe)* grave; *(prison)* prison; **on l'a mis dans le t. (au tombeau)** they put him six feet under; **on l'a mis au t. (en prison)** he was sent down
8 *Tech* **t. de graissage** oil hole; **t. d'aération** air vent; *Min* **t. de mine** blast *or* drill hole; *Min, Constr* **t. de sondage** *ou* **de sonde** borehole ▸▸ *Aviat* **t. d'air** air pocket; *Aut* **t. d'alimentation** supply port; *Fam* **t. de balle** arsehole, *Am* asshole; *Naut* **t. du chat** lubber's hole; *Vulg* **t. du cul** arsehole, *Am* asshole; **espèce de t. du cul!** you arsehole *or* *Am* asshole!; *Aut* **t. d'évacuation** drain hole; **t. d'homme** manhole; *Fam* **trous de nez** nostrils; *Fig Fam* **il me sort par les trous de nez** I can't stand the sight of him; *Astron* **t. noir** black hole; *Fig* **c'est le t. noir** I am/he is/*etc* extremely depressed *or* *Fam* really down; **t. normand: faire le t. normand** to have a (glass of) Calvados *(in the middle of a meal)*; *Théâtre* **t. du souffleur** prompter's box

troubadour [trubadur] **NM** *Hist, Littér* troubadour

troublant [trublɑ̃] **ADJ 1** *(qui dérange)* disturbing, unsettling; *(qui déconcerte)* disconcerting **2** *(sensuel)* disturbing, provocative; *(parfum)* heady

trouble¹ [trubl] **ADJ 1** *(liquide, eau)* cloudy; *(lumière, yeux)* dim; *(ciel)* murky, overcast; *(image, photographe)* blurred, fuzzy; **avoir la vue t.** to have blurred vision; **aux yeux troubles** bleary-eyed **2** *(qui manque de clarté) (situation, motivations)* confused, unclear; *(émotion)* mixed, uneasy; *Péj (comportement, affaire etc)* shady, fishy, suspicious; **période t. de l'histoire** murky period of history; **il y a quelque chose de t. dans cette affaire** there's something shady *or* fishy *or* not kosher about this business
ADV **voir t.** to have blurred vision, to see things through a mist *or* haze; **tu ne me reconnais pas? tu vois t.?** is there something wrong with your eyes that you don't recognize me?; **je commence à voir t.** things are beginning to look fuzzy

trouble² [trubl] **NM 1** *(confusion)* confusion, disorder; **jeter le t. dans une famille** to cause

trouble in a family; **c'est une cause de t. dans notre couple** it causes trouble between us, it's a bone of contention between us **2** *(agitation)* agitation, uneasiness; *(gêne)* confusion, embarrassment; *(amoureux)* agitation; **semer** *ou* **jeter le t. dans l'esprit de qn** to perturb sb **3 troubles** (public) disturbances, unrest; **fauteur de troubles** agitator, troublemaker; **période de troubles** period of unrest; **troubles sociaux** social unrest **4** *Méd* **troubles** disorder; **troubles de digestion/de vision/respiratoires** digestive/eye/respiratory disorder *or* *Fam* problems; **troubles affectifs** emotional disturbance **5** *Jur* **t. de jouissance** disturbance of possession

trouble-fête **NM INV** spoilsport, killjoy, party-pooper; **jouer les t.** to be a spoilsport *or* wet blanket, to spoil the fun

troubler [truble] **VT 1** *(liquide)* to make cloudy; *Fig (esprit)* to cloud; *(yeux, horizon)* to dim **2** *(sommeil, silence etc)* to disturb; *(réunion, soirée)* to disrupt; *(opération, projets, activités)* to interfere with, to disrupt; *(progrès)* to impede; *(bonheur)* to spoil, to mar; *(digestion)* to upset; **période troublée par la guerre** period disrupted by war; **un vent léger troubla l'eau** a slight wind ruffled the water; **t. le repos** *ou* **l'ordre public** to create a disturbance; *Jur* to disturb the peace, to create a disturbance; **l'ordre public n'a été nullement troublé** there has been no breach of the peace; **imagination troublée** disturbed imagination **3** *(personne)* to disturb, to make uneasy; *(gêner)* to confuse; **ce qui me trouble dans cette affaire** what bothers *or* disturbs me about this matter **4** *(sensuellement) (personne)* to disturb, to excite, to thrill; *(sens, émotions)* to stir **5** *(émouvoir)* to move **6** *Jur* **t. qn dans la jouissance d'un bien** to disturb sb's enjoyment of possession
VPR se troubler 1 *(du vin etc)* to get cloudy; *(du ciel)* to become overcast; *(d'une vision)* to become blurred; *(de la voix)* to break (with emotion) **2** *(se déconcerter)* to become confused *or* flustered; **sans se t.** *(répondre etc)* unruffled, without turning a hair; **elle se trouble facilement** she is easily flustered, she gets flustered easily

trouée [true] **NF** gap, opening *(de* in*)*; **une t. de ciel bleu** a patch of blue sky

trouer [true] **VT** *(mur etc)* to make a hole/holes in; *(lignes ennemies etc)* to breach; *(vêtement)* to wear *or* make a hole in; *Tech (zinc etc)* to perforate; **avoir les bas troués** to have holes in one's stockings; **être troué** *(de la coque d'un navire)* to be holed; **t. les nuages** *(du soleil)* to break through (the clouds); **des immeubles troués par des bombes** buildings pockmarked with shell holes; *Arg* **se faire t. la peau** to get shot, to be pumped full of lead
VPR se trouer *(d'une chaussette etc)* to get a hole/holes

troufignon [trufiɲɔ̃] **NM** *Arg (anus)* arsehole, *Am* asshole; *(derrière)* arse, *Am* ass

troufion [trufjɔ̃] **NM** *Arg* soldier, private, *Am* grunt

trouillard, -arde [trujar, -ard] *Arg* **ADJ** yellow-bellied, chicken, cowardly; **je n'aime pas les types trouillards** I don't like yellow-bellies *or* cowards
N yellow-belly, chicken, coward

trouille [truj] **NF** *Fam (peur)* **avoir la t.** to be petrified, to be scared stiff; **je n'ai jamais eu une telle t. de ma vie** I've never been so petrified in my life; **au dernier moment, j'ai eu la t.** I got the wind up at the last minute; **donner** *ou* **ficher** *ou* **flanquer la t. à qn** to put the wind up sb; **tu n'as pas la t.!** you've got a nerve!

trouillomètre [trujɔmɛtr] **NM** *Arg* **avoir le t. à zéro** to be scared stiff *or* witless, to be petrified

trouilloter [trujɔte] VI *très Fam* **1** *(avoir peur)* to be scared shitless, to be shit-scared **2** *(sentir mauvais)* to stink, *Br* to pong

troupe [trup] NF **1** *(de personnes)* troop, band, group; *(de brigands etc)* gang, set; *(de scouts)* troop **2** *Théâtre* **t. (de théâtre** *ou de* **comédiens)** company, troupe; **t. d'amateurs** amateur company *or* troupe **3** *(d'éléphants)* herd; *(de lions)* pride; *(d'oiseaux)* flock; **ces animaux vivent en t.** these animals live in herds *or* are gregarious **4** *Mil* troop; **troupes** *(armée)* troops, forces; **officier de t.** regimental officer; **officiers et t.** officers and men *or* and other ranks; *Vieilli* **enfant de t.** army child *or Fam* brat; **cigarettes de t.** army issue cigarettes; *Fam* **en route, mauvaise t.!** come on, let's get moving!

troupeau, -eaux [trupo] NM *(de bétail, de girafes etc)* herd; *(de moutons)* flock; *(d'oies)* gaggle, flock; *(de gens)* flock, *Péj* horde, gaggle, herd

troupier, -ière [trupje, -jɛr] ADJ **comique t.** *(chanson, blague)* music-hall; **du comique t.** music-hall comedy
▪ NM *Mil Fam* private, soldier; **jurer comme un t.** to swear like a trooper, *Br Arg* to eff and blind

troussage [trusaʒ] NM *Culin (de volaille)* trussing

trousse [trus] NF**1** **être aux trousses de qn** to be after *or* chasing sb, to be (hot) on sb's heels; **il avait la police aux trousses** he had the police after him *or* chasing him *or* (hot) on his heels; **comme s'il avait le feu aux trousses** *ou* **le diable à ses trousses** like a bat out of hell **2** *(étui)* kit; *(de médecin)* instrument case; **t. de toilette** toilet *or* sponge bag; **t. d'écolier** pencil case; **t. à ongles** manicure kit; **t. de premiers soins** *ou* **de secours** first-aid kit; **t. à outils** tool kit

troussé [truse] ADJ *Fam* **bien t.** *(objet, compliment)* neat

trousseau, -eaux [truso] NM **1** *(de clés)* bunch **2** *(de fiancée)* trousseau, bottom drawer, *Am* hope chest **3** *(de pensionnaire)* clothes, outfit

trousser [truse] VT**1** *Culin (volaille)* to truss **2** *Fam (faire rapidement) (travail, repas, affaire)* to polish off, to make short work of; **t. un compliment à qn** to pay sb a neat compliment **3** *Vieilli (retrousser) (jupe etc)* to tuck up; *Fam* **t. une fille** to tumble a girl

trousseur [trusœr] NM *Fam Vieilli* **t. de jupons** womanizer, skirt chaser

trouvaille [truvaj] NF **1** *(chose trouvée)* (lucky) find; **une excellente t.** a great find **2** *(bonne idée)* brainwave

TROUVER [truve]

| **VT** to find **1–5** ▪ to come up with **2** ▪ to discover **2, 3** ▪ to come across **3** ▪ to think **4** |
| **VPR** to find oneself **1, 3** ▪ to be **1** ▪ to feel **1** ▪ to happen **2** |

VT 1 *(en cherchant) (personne, objet)* to find; **je ne trouve pas mes clefs** I can't find my keys; **il ne trouve plus ses lunettes** he can't find his glasses, he's lost his glasses; **où est-ce qu'on trouve cela?** where can you get it?; **on le trouve au bar, à cette heure-là** you can find him in the bar at this time; **aller t. qn** to go and see sb; **je n'ai pas trouvé le temps de le faire** I didn't find time to do it, I didn't get round to it; **il n'a pas trouvé les mots pour le dire** he couldn't find the words; *Ordinat* **t. et remplacer** to find and replace; **il trouve du plaisir à lire** he takes *or* finds pleasure in reading, he enjoys reading; **elle trouve un malin plaisir à me faire attendre** she takes malicious pleasure in making me wait; **il va bien t. quelque chose à redire** he's sure to have something to say

2 *(découvrir, inventer) (solution, moyen, compromis, arrangement)* to find, to come up with; *(procédé)* to discover, to invent, to come up with; *(erreur)* to find; **c'est bien trouvé!** good idea!; **exemple bien/mal trouvé** well-/badly chosen example; **je me demande où il est allé t. ça** I wonder where he got that idea from; *Iron* **tu as trouvé ça tout seul?** did you think of that all on your own?

3 t. (par hasard) to find (by chance), to discover, to come upon, to come across; *(idée, méthode)* to hit on; **on l'a trouvé mort** he was found dead; **t. qn en faute** to catch sb out; **t. porte close** to find nobody home; **que je ne te trouve pas en train de fouiller dans mes affaires** don't let me find *or* catch you rummaging about in my things; **bureau des objets trouvés** lost-property office; *Fig* **il a trouvé à qui parler** he has met his match; **il trouva la mort à l'âge de 35 ans/dans un accident de voiture** he died *or Fml* met his death at the age of 35/in a car accident; **il trouva la mort bêtement** he died a stupid death

4 *(juger)* to find; *(penser)* to think; **je la trouve jolie** I think she's pretty, I find *or* consider her pretty; **vous trouvez?** do you think so?; **comment as-tu trouvé ce livre?** how did you find *or* like the book?; **je la trouve mauvaise** *ou* **saumâtre** *(action)* I think it's a bit much *or* a bit thick; **il trouve bon/mauvais de vous en parler** he thinks it's a good/bad idea to talk to you about it; **je trouve mieux de ne pas …** I think it's better not to …; **je lui trouve du charme/mauvaise mine** I think he has charm/looks ill; **je ne trouve aucun intérêt à la refaire** I don't think there's any point in doing it again; **qu'est-ce qu'elle lui trouve?** what does she see in him?; **je trouve que …** I think (that) …; **t. le temps long** to find *or* feel that the time is dragging

5 *(obtenir) (travail, mari, maison etc)* to find, to get; **t. le sommeil** to get to sleep

VPR **se trouver 1** *(dans une situation)* to be, to find oneself; *(d'un objet)* to be; *(sentir)* to feel; **ces plantes se trouvent partout** these plants can be found everywhere; **ça ne se trouve pas partout** you can't get it just anywhere; **je me trouve très bien ici** I'm very comfortable here; **comment vous êtes-vous trouvé de ce traitement?** how did the treatment work?; **à ce moment-là, je me suis trouvé bien bête** at that moment I felt really stupid; **je me trouve trop grosse** I think I'm too fat; **se t. bien de qch/d'avoir fait qch** to feel all the better for sth/for having done sth; **je me trouve mieux** I feel better; **elle se trouve mal** she feels faint

2 *(arriver)* to happen, to turn out; **je me trouve avoir** *ou* **il se trouve que j'ai une heure de libre** I happen to have *or* it so happens *or* it turns out that I have an hour to spare; **la dame se trouva être sa propre femme** the lady turned out to be his own wife; *Fam* **si cela** *ou* **ça se trouve, il est déjà rentré** maybe he's back, with a bit of luck he might be back

3 *(se réaliser)* to find oneself

trouvère [truvɛr] NM *Hist, Littér* trouvère

troyen¹, -enne¹ [trwajɛ̃, -ɛn] ADJ *(de Troie)* Trojan
▪ NT. Trojan

troyen², -enne² ADJ *(de Troyes)* of/from Troyes
▪ NT. *(natif)* native of Troyes; *(habitant)* inhabitant of Troyes

truand, -ande [tryɑ̃, -ɑ̃d] N **1** *Fam (escroc)* crook; *(gangster)* gangster, hood **2** *Arch (mendiant)* beggar

Il faut noter que le terme anglais **truant** est un faux ami. Il désigne un élève qui fait l'école buissonnière.

truander [tryɑ̃de] *Fam* VT *(quelqu'un)* to swindle, to do; *(faire payer trop cher)* to rip off; **se faire t.** to be swindled *or* done; *(payer trop cher)* to get ripped off
▪ VI to cheat (**à un examen** in an exam)

trublion [tryblijɔ̃] NM troublemaker

truc¹ [tryk] NM *Fam* **1** *(moyen)* trick; **il y a un t.!** there's a trick in it!; **un t. pour enlever les taches** a trick for *or* a clever way of removing stains; **connaître les trucs du métier** to know the tricks of the trade; **c'est un t. qu'il faut connaître** there's a trick *or* a knack to it; *Théâtre* **pièce à trucs** play with elaborate stage effects

2 *(personne)* **machin t. (chouette)** thingumajig, what's-his-name, *f* what's-her-name

3 *(chose)* thing; *(machin)* thingumajig, thingummy, thingy; **qu'est-ce que c'est que ce t.-là?** what's that (thingumajig)?; **des trucs comme ça** things like that; **elle a encore acheté des trucs** she's been shopping again; **je voudrais lui offrir un petit t.** I'd like to give him a little something; **il faudrait que tu me dises un t. …** tell me something …

4 **la montagne/la cuisine/le droit, c'est vraiment son t.** he's/she's really into mountain climbing/cooking/the law; **ce n'est pas son t.** it's not his/her thing *or* bag, he's/she's not into that

truc² NM *Rail* truck, *Am* freight car

trucage [trykaʒ] NM **1** *Cin* special effect; **c'est du t.** it's all faked **2** *(d'une photographie)* faking; *(d'un match, une élection etc)* fixing, rigging; *(de comptes)* window-dressing

truchement [tryʃmɑ̃] NM **1** *(intermédiaire)* **par le t. de …** through … **2** *Arch (interprète)* interpreter

trucider [tryside] VT *Fam (tuer)* to bump off; **je vais me faire t. s'il l'apprend** I'm going to end up dead if he finds out

truck [tryk] NM *Rail* truck, *Am* freight car

truckman [trykman] *pl* **truckmen** [trykmɛn] NM *TV, Cin* special effects person *or* engineer

trucmuche [trykmyʃ] NM *Fam* **1** *(chose)* thingumajig, thingummy, thingy **2** **T.** *(personne)* thingumajig, what's-his-name, *f* what's-her-name

truculence [trykylɑ̃s] NF *(pittoresque) (d'un personnage, du langage)* colourfulness, *Am* colorfulness; *(verdeur)* raciness

truculent [trykylɑ̃] ADJ *(pittoresque) (personnage)* colourful, *Am* colorful, larger than life; *(cru) (langage, personnage)* racy

Il faut noter que l'adjectif anglais **truculent** est un faux ami. Il signifie **agressif**.

truelle [tryɛl] NF **1** *(outil)* trowel **2** *Culin* **t. à poisson** fish slice

truffe [tryf] NF **1** *(champignon)* truffle; **omelette aux truffes** truffle omelette **2** *(au chocolat)* truffle **3** *(nez) (d'un chien)* nose; *Fam (d'une personne)* conk **4** *Fam (imbécile)* divvy, *Am* schmuck

truffer [tryfe] VT **1** *Culin (dinde)* to garnish with truffles; **poularde truffée** truffled chicken **2** *Fig* **truffé de** *(balles, fautes, inexactitudes)* riddled with; *(citations)* peppered with

truffier, -ière [tryfje, -jɛr] ADJ *(sol)* truffle(-producing); **chien t.** truffle hound

truie [trɥi] NF sow

truisme [trɥism] NM truism

truite [trɥit] NF trout; **t. de rivière** brown trout; **t. arc-en-ciel** rainbow trout; *Culin* **t.**

meunière = trout sautéed in butter and served with parsley and lemon juice; **t. au bleu** = trout poached in a vinegar-flavoured broth VOIR GRAMMAIRE A12

truité [tɥite] ADJ speckled; *(chien, cheval)* spotted; *(poterie)* crackled

trumeau, -eaux [trymo] NM **1** *Archit* pier **2** *(miroir)* pier glass **3** *Culin* leg of beef **4** *Fam (femme laide)* dog, *Br* boot, *Am* beast

truquage [tryka3] NM = **trucage**

truquer [tryke] VT **1** *(photographie, expérience, données etc)* to fake, to rig; *(match, combat, élection etc)* to fix, to rig; *Fam* **t. les comptes** to cook the books, to window-dress the accounts; **t. les dés** to load the dice **2** *Cin* **scène truquée** scene with special effects **3** *Min (mine, minerai, échantillon)* to salt

truqueur, -euse [trykœr, -øz] N **1** *(qui triche)* cheat **2** *Cin* special effects person *or* engineer

truquiste [trykist] N *Cin* special effects person *or* engineer

trust [trœst] NM *Fin, Com* trust; **t. de l'acier/du pétrole** steel/oil cartel; **t. commercial** commercial monopoly; **t. industriel** industrial monopoly; **t. de valeurs** holding company

truster [trœste] VT **1** *Fin, Com,* to monopolize, to form into a monopoly **2** *Fam (monopoliser)* to monopolize, to hog; **il truste tous les premiers rôles du cinéma français** he gets all the leading roles in French cinema VI *Com* to form a monopoly

tsar [tsar, dzar] NM tsar, czar

tsarévitch [tsarevitʃ, dz-] NM tsarevitch, czarevitch

tsarine [tsarin, dz-] NF tsarina, czarina

tsarisme [tsarism, dz-] NM *Hist* tsarism

tsariste [tsarist, dz-] ADJ, N *Hist* tsarist

tsé-tsé [tsetse] NF INV *Entom* tsetse (fly); *Hum* **tu t'es fait piquer par la mouche t.?** have you got sleeping sickness?

TSF [teɛsɛf] NF *Vieilli (abrév* **télégraphie sans fil)** *(poste de)* **T.** wireless (set)

T-shirt, *pl* **T-shirts** [tiʃœrt] NM T-shirt, tee shirt

tsigane [tsigan] ADJ, N tzigane, Hungarian gypsy

tsunami [tsynami] NM tidal wave, tsunami

TSVP [teɛsvepe] *(abrév* **tournez s'il vous plaît)** PTO

TTC [tetese] *(abrév* **toutes taxes comprises)** inclusive of tax

TU [tey] NM *(abrév* **temps universel)** GMT

tu [ty] PRON PERS **1** you *(usual form of address to relations, close friends, children and animals)*; **tu as raison** you are right; **qui es-tu?** who are you?; **être à tu et à toi** to be very friendly *(avec qn* with sb*)*; **être à tu et à toi avec tout le monde** to be on first-name terms with everybody; **elle lui dit 'tu'** she calls him 'tu'; **crois-tu?** do you think so?; *Arg (elided to* **t'** *before vowel or* **h** *mute)* **qu'est-ce que t'as?** what's up (with you)? SEE GRAMMAR A27; B18; B67 **2** *Rel* thou; *(à Dieu)* Thou; *Bible* **tu ne tueras point** thou shalt not kill

Tuamotu [twamotu] NFPL **les T.** the Tuamotu Archipelago

tuant [tɥɑ̃] ADJ *Fam* **1** *(fatigant) (travail)* killing, back-breaking, exhausting; **elle fait un travail t.** she has an exhausting job **2** *(insupportable)* exasperating; **c'est t., ce bruit** this noise is sending me up the wall; **les enfants sont vraiment tuants aujourd'hui** the kids are being a real pain today

tub [tœb] NM *Vieilli (cuvette)* tub, bath; *(bain)* bath; **prendre un t.** to take *or* have a bath

tuba [tyba] NM **1** *Mus* tuba **2** *(de plongée)* snorkel

tubage [tyba3] NM *Constr, Min, Chir, Vét* tubing

tubaire [tybɛr] ADJ *Méd* tubal

tubard, -arde [tybar, -ard] N *Méd Fam* TB case

tube [tyb] NM **1** *(tuyau)* tube; *(de canalisation)* pipe; *Constr* **bâti en tubes d'acier** tubular-steel-frame; *Fig Fam* **à pleins tubes** at full blast; *Fig Fam* **il déconne à pleins tubes** he's off his rocker; **chaudière à tubes** tubular boiler **2** *(de canon)* barrel **3** *Chir, Vét* tube **4** *Anat* tube, duct **5** *Bot (de la corolle, du calice)* tube **6** *Courses de chevaux Arg (indication)* tip **7** *Fam (chanson, disque)* hit; *Théâtre* (smash) hit, smash; **le t. de l'été** this summer's smash hit **8** *(emballage) (de dentifrice, de peinture etc)* tube; **t. d'aspirine** = packet of aspirin; **t. de rouge à lèvres** (stick of) lipstick; **en t.** in a tube; **acheter de la mayonnaise en t.** to buy a tube of mayonnaise **9** *Élec, Électron* tube

▸▸ **t. d'alimentation** feed pipe; **t. amplificateur** amplifier tube *or* valve; *Anat* **t. bronchique** bronchial tube; *Anat, Phys* **t. capillaire** capillary tube; *Min* **t. carottier** core bar rel; *Électron, Radio* **t. cathodique** cathode-ray tube; **t. de chaudière** boiler tube; **t. de condenseur** *ou* **à condensation** condenser tube; *Anat* **t. digestif** digestive tract, alimentary canal; *Aut* **t. de direction** steering column; *Chimie* **t. pour dosage, t. doseur** measuring tube; *Aut* **t. d'échappement** exhaust pipe; **t. électronique** electron tube; *Chimie* **t. à essai** test tube; **tubes d'exploitation** tubing; **t. à flamme** *(d'un moteur à réaction)* flame tube; **t. fluorescent** fluorescent tube; **t. à gaz** gas-filled tube *or* valve; **t. de graissage** oil duct *or* way; *Élec* **t. guide-fils** *(sur un édifice)* race track, race way; *Naut* **t. lance-torpille(s)** torpedo tube; *Élec* **t. au néon** neon tube; **t. de niveau d'eau** water-gauge column; **t. de Pitot** Pitot tube; **tubes de pompage** tubing; **t. raccord** pipe connection; **t. à vide** vacuum tube *or* valve

tubeless [tyblɛs] ADJ INV *(pneu)* tubeless

tuber [tybe] VT **1** *Constr (puits de mine, puits)* to tube, to case; *(conduit d'air, puits)* to case **2** *Fam (téléphoner à)* **t. qn** to give sb a buzz *or Br* a bell

tubercule [tybɛrkyl] NM **1** *Bot* tuber **2** *Méd* tubercle

tuberculeux, -euse [tybɛrkylø, -øz] ADJ **1** *Bot (racine)* tubercular **2** *Méd* tubercular N tubercular patient, TB case

tuberculine [tybɛrkylin] NF *Méd* tuberculin

tuberculose [tybɛrkyloz] NF *Méd* tuberculosis, TB; **t. pulmonaire** pulmonary tuberculosis

tubéreux, -euse [tyberø, -øz] *Bot* ADJ tuberous NF **tubéreuse** tuberose

tubérosité [tyberɔzite] NF tuberosity

tubulaire [tybylɛr] ADJ tubular

tubulé [tybyle] ADJ *(cornue, fleur)* tubular

tubuleux, -euse [tybylø, -øz] ADJ tubulous

tubulure [tybylyr] NF **1** *Tech (ouverture)* tubulure, pipe(-run), neck; *Aut* manifold; **t. d'alimentation** *ou* **d'admission** intake manifold; *Aut* **t. d'admission** inlet pipe; *Aut* **t. d'échappement** exhaust pipe **2** *(tube)* pipe; *(ensemble de tubes)* piping, pipes

TUC [tyk] NMPL *(abrév* **travaux d'utilité collective)** = community work for unemployed young people N *Fam (employé)* = person doing community work on a 'TUC' scheme

tue-mouches [tymuʃ] NM INV **1** *(champignon)* fly agaric **2** *(tapette)* fly swatter; *(insecticide)* fly spray ADJ INV **papier** *ou* **ruban t.** fly paper

tuer [tɥe] VT **1** *(personne, animal, cultures)* Tennis *(balle)*, *Fig (l'amour)* to kill; **t. qn d'un coup de couteau** *ou* **de poignard** to stab sb to death; **t. qn d'un coup de revolver** to shoot and kill sb (with a revolver); **c'est la solitude/le chagrin qui l'a tué** he died of loneliness/grief; **un coup à t. un bœuf** a blow to fell an ox; **il a reçu une gifle à t. un bœuf** he got an almighty slap, he got a slap that made his ears ring; **la route tue tous les ans** people die on the roads every year; **les tués et les blessés** the dead and wounded; **se faire t.** to get killed; **ils se firent t. en braves** they died like heroes; *Fig* **tu veux te faire t.!** you're asking for it!, you're taking your life in your hands!; *Fig* **cette musique va t. l'ambiance** that music is going to kill the atmosphere stone dead *or* totally destroy the atmosphere; *Fig* **t. le temps** to kill time; *Fig* **l'habitude tue la passion** familiarity breeds contempt; *Fig* **t. qch dans l'œuf** to nip sth in the bud

2 *Fig (épuiser)* **tous ces déplacements m'ont tué** I'm dead *or* done for after all that travelling; **ces escaliers me tuent** these stairs will be the death of me

3 *Fig Fam (révolter)* **ça me tue d'entendre des conneries pareilles!** it really gets me when I hear such nonsense!; **ça m'a tué d'apprendre qu'il se remariait** *(sidéré)* I was staggered to hear that he was getting married again

4 *Fam (être remarquable)* **écoute cette chanson; ça tue!** listen to this song, it's a killer!

VPR **se tuer 1** *(se suicider)* to kill oneself, to commit suicide, *Br Fam* to top oneself **2** *(mourir dans un accident etc)* to die, to get killed **3** *(s'entre-tuer)* to kill one another **4** *Fig* **se t. au travail** *ou* **à travailler/à force de boire** to work/drink oneself to death; **je me tue à vous le dire** I'm sick and tired of *or* sick to death telling you; **c'est ce que je me tue à vous dire** that's what I've been trying to tell you

tuerie [tyri] NF slaughter, butchery

tue-tête (à) [atytɛt] ADV at the top of one's voice

tueur, -euse [tɥœr, -øz] ADJ *(fauves, cellule)* killer N *(assassin)* killer NM *(dans un abattoir)* slaughterman ▸▸ **t. à gages** hired killer *or* assassin; **t. en série** serial killer

tuf [tyf] NM **1** *Géol* **t. volcanique** tuff; *(calcaire)* tufa **2** *Fig Litt* bedrock, foundation

tuile [tɥil] NF **1** *Constr (roof)* tile; **toit en tuiles** tiled roof **2** *Culin* **tuiles aux amandes** almond biscuits **3** *Fam (malchance)* (piece of) bad luck, blow; **il lui est arrivé une (sale) t.** he's had a terrible blow *or* piece of bad luck; **j'ai peur qu'il lui arrive une t.** I'm worried that something will happen to him; **la t.!** what bad *or* rotten luck!

tuilerie [tɥilri] NF **1** *(fabrique)* tile works; *(four)* tile kiln **2 les Tuileries** = a former royal residence in Paris, now the site of the Tuileries gardens, near the Louvre

tulipe [tylip] NF **1** *Bot* tulip **2** *(lampe)* tulip-shaped lamp; *(verre)* tulip glass **3** *Tech (d'une imprimante)* thimble

tulipier [tylipje] NM *Bot* tulip tree

tulle [tyl] NM *Tex* tulle, net (fabric); **t. de soie/de coton** silk/cotton tulle; **robe de t.** tulle dress; *Méd* **t. gras** = material used for dressing burns and wounds

tuméfaction [tymefaksjɔ̃] NF *Méd* swelling, *Spéc* tumefaction

tuméfier [tymefje] VT *(articulations etc)* to cause to swell, *Spéc* to tumefy; **visage tuméfié** swollen face VPR **se tuméfier** to swell (up)

tumescence [tymesɑ̃s] NF swelling, *Spéc* tumescence

tumescent [tymesɑ̃] ADJ swelling, *Spéc* tumescent

tumeur [tymœr] NF *Méd* tumour, *Am* tumor, growth; **t. bénigne/maligne** benign/malignant tumour; **une t. au cerveau** a brain tumour

tumoral, -ale, -aux, -ales [tymɔral, -o] ADJ tumorous, tumoral

tumulaire [tymylɛr] ADJ **pierre t.** tombstone

tumulte [tymylt] NM uproar, commotion, hubbub, *Fml* tumult; *(d'applaudissements)* thunder; *(d'armes)* clash; *(de la politique, des passions)* turmoil; *(des affaires, de la ville)* hustle and bustle; **le t. au sujet de** the uproar *or* commotion about, the furore over; **provoquer un t.** to cause an uproar *or* a commotion; **dans le t.** in an uproar, in confusion; **il y eut des tumultes** there were riots

tumultueusement [tymyltɥøzmɑ̃] ADV tumultuously

tumultueux, -euse [tymyltɥø, -øz] ADJ *(réunion, débat, séance, accueil etc)* noisy, tumultuous; *(rues)* noisy; *(vie, période etc)* tumultuous

tumulus, *pl* **tumulus** *ou* **tumuli** [tymylys, -li] NM barrow, *Spéc* tumulus

tuner [tynœr, tynɛr] NM *Radio* tuner

tungstène [tœ̃kstɛn, tœ̃g-] NM *Métal* tungsten

tungstène-halogène NM tungsten-halogen

tunique [tynik] NF **1** *(vêtement)* tunic **2** *Biol (d'un organe)* tunic, envelope, membrane; *Bot (d'un bulbe)* coat

Tunis [tynis] N Tunis

Tunisie [tynizi] NF Tunisia

tunisien, -ienne [tynizjɛ̃, -jɛn] ADJ Tunisian
  N **T.** Tunisian

tunnel [tynɛl] NM tunnel; **t. routier** road tunnel; **le t. sous la Manche** the Channel Tunnel; *Fig* **voir le bout du t.** to see the light at the end of the tunnel
  ▸▸ *Aviat* **t. aérodynamique** wind tunnel; **t. de publicités** extended commercial break

TUP [typ] NM *(abrév* **titre universel de paiement***)* universal payment order

tuque [tyk] NF *Can* tuque, *Fam* pompom hat, bobble cap

turban [tyrbɑ̃] NM *(coiffure)* turban

turbide [tyrbid] ADJ *(liquide etc)* cloudy, turbid

turbidité [tyrbidite] NF cloudiness, *Fml* turbidity

turbin [tyrbɛ̃] NM *Fam (travail)* grind, slog; *(emploi)* job; **toujours au t.?** still slogging away?

turbine [tyrbin] NF turbine; *(d'une pompe à eau)* impeller; **à t.** turbine-powered; **t. à air** air or wind turbine; **t. à eau, t. hydraulique** water turbine *or* wheel; **t. à gaz/à vapeur** gas/steam turbine; *Tech* **t. centrifuge** centrifugal blower; *Tech* **t. de ventilation** blower; *Tech* **t. moteur** power turbine

turbiner [tyrbine] VI *Arg (travailler)* to slog (away); *Scol* to swot

turbo [tyrbo] ADJ INV turbine-driven, turbo
  NM **1** *Aut* turbo; *Fam* **mettre le t.** to get a move on **2** *Ordinat* turbo
  NF turbo

turboalternateur [tyrbɔaltɛrnatœr] NM *Élec* turbo-alternator

turbocompresseur [tyrbɔkɔ̃prɛsœr] NM *Tech, Aviat* turbocompressor; *Aut* turbo-supercharger, turbocharger

turbodiesel [tyrbɔdjezɛl] NM *(moteur)* turbo diesel
  NF *(voiture)* turbo diesel

turbomarketing NM turbomarketing

turbomoteur [tyrbɔmɔtœr] NM turbomotor, turboshaft engine

turbopompe [tyrbɔpɔ̃p] NF turbo pump, turbine pump

turbopropulseur [tyrbɔprɔpylsœr] NM turboprop(eller); **avion à t.** turboprop aircraft

turboréacteur [tyrbɔreaktœr] NM turbojet (engine)

turbot [tyrbo] NM *(poisson)* turbot

turbotière [tyrbɔtjɛr] NF *Culin (récipient)* fish kettle *(especially for cooking turbot)*

turbotrain [tyrbɔtrɛ̃] NM *Rail* turbotrain

turbulence [tyrbylɑ̃s] NF *Aviat* turbulence; *(d'un enfant)* boisterousness, noisiness; *(de la mer)* storminess, turbulence; *Aviat* **il y aura des turbulences** there will be some turbulence

turbulent [tyrbylɑ̃] ADJ **1** *Vieilli (population)* restless, unruly **2** *(enfant, classe)* boisterous, noisy; *(mer), Fig (relation, période)* stormy, turbulent **3** *Phys* **régime t.** turbulent flow

turc, turque [tyrk] ADJ Turkish; **café t.** Turkish coffee; **être assis à la turque** to be sitting cross-legged; **W.-C.** *ou* **cabinets à la turque** hole in the ground
  NM *Ling* Turkish
  N **T.** Turk; *Pol* **jeune T.** Young Turk; *Fam* **fort comme un T.** as strong as an ox; *Fig* **tête de T.** whipping-boy

turf [tœrf, tyrf] NM **1** *(terrain)* racecourse **2 le t.** *(activité)* racing; **habitué du t.** racegoer **3** *Fam Vieilli (travail)* work; *(lieu de travail)* workplace **4** *Fam Vieilli (prostitution)* prostitution; **faire le t.** to turn tricks, *Br* to be on the game

turfiste [tœrfist, tyr-] N racegoer

turgescence [tyrʒesɑ̃s] NF *Méd, Bot* turgescence

turgescent [tyrʒesɑ̃] ADJ turgescent

turgide [tyrʒid] ADJ *Litt* turgid, swollen

turista [turista] NF *Fam* **la t.** Montezuma's revenge, Delhi belly, Spanish tummy

turkmène [tyrkmɛn] ADJ Turkoman
  NM *Ling* Turkmen
  N **T.** Turkoman

Turkménistan [tyrkmenistɑ̃] NM Turkmenistan

turlupiner [tyrlypine] VT *Fam* to worry, to bother

turlute [tyrlyt] NF *très Fam* blow-job; **faire une t. à qn** to give sb a blow-job, to go down on sb, to give sb head

turluter [tyrlyte] VI *Can Fam* to trill, to sing tra-la-la

turlututu [tyrlytyty] INT *(pour refuser, se moquer gentiment, interrompre)* fiddlesticks!; **t. chapeau pointu!** yah boo, sucks to you!

turne [tyrn] NF **1** *Fam Péj (chambre, maison)* dump, hole **2** *Scol Arg (student's)* room

turnep(s) [tyrnɛp(s)] NM *Agr* kohlrabi

turnover [tœrnɔvœr, -œr] NM turnover

turpitude [tyrpityd] NF **1** *(caractère)* vileness, moral turpitude **2** *(action)* vile act **3** *(parole)* vile remark

turque [tyrk] ADJ F, NF *voir* **turc**

turquerie [tyrk(ə)ri] NF work of art in an Oriental style

Turquie [tyrki] NF Turkey; **tapis de T.** Turkish carpet

turquoise [tyrkwaz] NF *(pierre)* turquoise
  ADJ INV, NM INV *(couleur)* turquoise (blue)

tussor(e) [tysɔr] NM *Tex* tussore (silk)

tutélaire [tytelɛr] ADJ *(divinité)* tutelary; *Jur* **gestion t.** guardianship; **puissance t.** power of guardianship

tutelle [tytɛl] NF **1** *Jur* guardianship; **enfant en t.** child under guardianship; **t. administrative** administrative supervision *(established over mismanaged public body)*; *Pol* **territoires sous t.** trust territories **2** *(protection)* protection; **sous la t. de** *(famille, loi etc)* under the protection of; **prendre qn sous sa t.** to take sb under one's wing

tuteur, -trice [tytœr, -tris] N **1** *Jur* guardian; **t. légal** legal guardian **2** *(protecteur)* protector
  NM *(pour plante)* support, stake; **mettre un t. à une plante** to stake a plant

tutoiement [tytwamɑ̃] NM use of the familiar 'tu' *(instead of the more formal 'vous')*; **le t. est de rigueur** everybody addresses each other as *or* calls each other 'tu'

Tutoiement et vouvoiement

Traditionally, non-native French speakers waited until they were addressed using the informal "tu" form before using it themselves, except when speaking to young children. However in the past twenty or thirty years people in France have become much more casual about using "tu", and it is now commonly used among colleagues in the workplace, while the "vous" form tends to be used when talking to people from an older generation or to hierarchical superiors (see also entries **tu** and **vous**).

tutoyer [tytwaje] *(je* **tutoie***, n.* **tutoyons***; je* **tutoierai***)* VT **1 t. qn** to address sb as 'tu', = to be on familiar terms with sb **2** *Équitation* **t. l'obstacle** to brush against the fence *(without knocking it)* **3** *Fig (être proche de)* to come close to; **il a tutoyé la mort plus d'une fois** he's had more than one brush with death
  VPR **se tutoyer** to address each other as 'tu', = to be on familiar terms (with each other)

tutti [tuti] NM INV *Mus* tutti

tutti frutti [tutifruti] NM INV *(glace)* tutti-frutti

tutti quanti [tutikwɑ̃ti] NMPL **et t.** et cetera, et cetera

tutu [tyty] NM tutu

tuyau, -aux [tɥijo] NM **1** *(canalisation etc)* pipe; *(flexible)* tube; **t. d'eau/de gaz** water/gas pipe; **t. vertical, t. de chute** standpipe; **t. flexible** *ou* **en caoutchouc** rubber tube *or* tubing, **t. acoustique** speaking tube; *Fam Vieilli* **dire qch à qn dans le t. de l'oreille** to whisper sth in sb's ear **2** *(d'une pipe)* stem **3** *(du maïs, de l'herbe etc)* stalk **4** *(pli)* flute, goffer, quill **5** *Fam (conseil)* tip; *(donné à la police, un journaliste)* tip-off; **je vais te filer un t.** I'll give you a tip; **qui est-ce qui t'a donné le t.?** who tipped you off?, who put you on to it?; **un t. percé** a rotten tip; **c'est un t. increvable** it's straight from the horse's mouth; **quelques tuyaux pour économiser l'énergie** a few tips *or* pointers on how to save energy; **avoir des tuyaux** to know the ropes
  ▸▸ **t. d'arrosage** garden hose; **t. de cheminée** (chimney) flue; *Aut* **t. d'échappement** exhaust (pipe), tailpipe; *Aut* **t. d'essence** petrol pipe; **t. d'incendie** fire hose; *Mus* **t. d'orgue** organ pipe; **t. de poêle** stove *or* flue pipe; **en t. de poêle** *(pantalon)* drainpipe; *(chapeau)* stove pipe; *Fam* **la famille t. de poêle** = family whose members have an incestuous relationship; *Aut* **t. de pression** pressure hose; *Aut* **t. de reniflard** breather pipe; *Aut* **t. de trop-plein** overflow pipe

tuyautage [tɥijotaʒ] NM **1** (d'un tissu) fluting, goffering **2** Fam (action de donner des conseils) giving of tips

tuyauter [tɥijote] VT **1** (un tissu) to flute, to goffer; **fer à t.** goffering tongs **2** Fam (conseiller) **t. qn** to give sb a tip; (le mettre au courant) to tip sb off, to put sb in the know (**sur** about)

tuyauterie NF (tuyaux) piping, pipes; Aut **t. de carburant** fuel pipe or line; Aut **t. de frein** brake pipe or line

tuyauteur, -euse [tɥijotœr, -øz] N Fam tipster

tuyère [tɥijɛr] NF Tech, Métal nozzle; Aviat etc **t. d'échappement** jet pipe; **t. de propulsion** thrust nozzle

TV [teve] NF (abrév **télévision**) TV

TVA [tevea] NF (abrév **taxe à la valeur ajoutée**) Br ≃ VAT, Am ≃ sales tax; **exempt de T.** zero-rated; **soumis à la T.** subject to Br VAT or Am sales tax; **T. encaissée** output tax; **T. récupérée** input tax

TVHD [teveaʃde] NF (abrév **télévision haute définition**) HDTV

TVP [tevepe] NF (abrév **thrombose veineuse profonde**) DVT

tweed [twid] NM Tex tweed; **veste de t.** tweed jacket

twin-set, pl **twin-sets** [twinsɛt] NM matching sweater and cardigan, Br twinset

twist [twist] NM (danse) twist

twister [twiste] VI to twist

tympan [tɛ̃pɑ̃] NM **1** Anat eardrum, Spéc tympanum; **bruit à briser** ou **crever** ou **déchirer** ou **rompre les tympans** ear-splitting noise **2** Archit tympanum **3** Tech (mounted on shaft) pinion

tympanal, -ale, -aux, -ales [tɛ̃panal, -o] ADJ, NM Anat (**os**) **t.** tympanic bone

tympanique [tɛ̃panik] ADJ Anat of the ear, Spéc tympanic

tympanon [tɛ̃panɔ̃] NM Mus dulcimer

type [tip] NM **1** (modèle) (de travail, intervention etc) type; (chose ou personne typique) classic example (**de** of); Zool type, Spéc phylum; Biol **genre t.** type genus; **arbre t.** sample tree; **t. de la beauté italienne** typical Italian beauty; **avoir le t. latin/nordique** to have Latin/Nordic looks; **elle est très sensible au t. italien** she really goes for Italian-looking men; **ce n'est pas du tout mon t.** (il ne m'attire pas) he's not at all my type; **c'est tout à fait mon t.** he's just my type (of man) or my sort of man, he's exactly the kind of man I find attractive; **c'est un problème t.** it's a typical problem, it's a standard type of problem; **c'est vraiment l'avare t.** he's a typical miser; **c'est vraiment l'Italienne t.** she's your typical Italian woman, she's typically Italian; **maison t.** show house; **motocyclette t.** motorbike of standard design; **c'est le t. même de la femme d'affaires** she is the classic example of a businesswoman, she is a or the typical businesswoman; **des ennuis techniques (du) t. (de la) panne** breakdown problems VOIR GRAMMAIRE A13

2 Fam (bonhomme) guy, man, Br bloke; **t'es un chic t.!** you're a good sort!; **un sale t.** a bastard; **un pauvre t.** a loser; **pauvre t.!** you're pathetic! **3** Typ type; **t. de caractères** typeface

typé [tipe] ADJ typical; **il est bien** ou **très t.** he has all the characteristic features; **c'est un Portugais mais il n'est pas très t.** he's Portuguese but you wouldn't think so to look at him

typer [tipe] VT Tech to stamp, to mark

typesse [tipɛs] NF Arg Péj Vieilli (femme, fille) female

typhique [tifik] Méd ADJ (du typhus) typhus; (de la typhoïde) typhoid
N typhus/typhoid sufferer

typhoïde [tifɔid] ADJ, NF Méd (**fièvre**) **t.** typhoid (fever)

typhoïdique [tifɔidik] ADJ typhoid, typhoidal; **bacille t.** typhoid bacillus

typhon [tifɔ̃] NM Météo typhoon

typhus [tifys] NM Méd typhus (fever); Vét **t. du chat** (infectious) feline gastroenteritis

typique [tipik] ADJ typical; **il a encore oublié, c'est t.** he's forgotten again, (it's) typical!

typiquement [tipikmɑ̃] ADV typically

typo [tipo] Fam NF = **typographie**
NM = **typographe**

typographe [tipɔgraf] N typographer

typographie [tipɔgrafi] NF (art, procédé) typography, letterpress printing; (présentation d'un texte) typography

typographique [tipɔgrafik] ADJ typographic(al); **erreur t.** typographic(al) error, misprint, Fam typo

typographiquement [tipɔgrafikmɑ̃] ADV typographically

typologie [tipɔlɔʒi] NF typology

typologique [tipɔlɔʒik] ADJ typological

typote [tipɔt] NF Fam = **typographe**

typothèque [tipɔtɛk] NF Ordinat type library

Tyr [tir] N Tyre

tyran [tirɑ̃] NM Pol, Fig tyrant; **se conduire en t.** to act like a tyrant or tyrannically; **arrête de jouer les tyrans** stop acting like a tyrant; **il est le t. de sa famille** he tyrannizes his family

tyranneau, -eaux [tirano] NM Litt petty tyrant

tyrannie [tirani] NF Pol, Fig tyranny; **exercer sa t. sur qn** to tyrannize sb; (frère, sœur) to bully sb

tyrannique [tiranik] ADJ tyrannical; **ne sois pas si t.** don't be such a tyrant; **il est t. avec elle** he bullies her

tyranniquement [tiranikmɑ̃] ADV tyrannically, like a tyrant

tyranniser [tiranize] VT (quelqu'un) to tyrannize; (frère, sœur) to bully

tyrannosaure [tiranozɔr] NM tyrannosaurus

Tyrol [tirɔl] NM **le T.** the Tyrol

tyrolien, -ienne [tirɔljɛ̃, -jɛn] ADJ Tyrolean
N T. Tyrolean, Tyrolese
NF Mus **tyrolienne** Tyrolienne

tzar [tsar, dzar] NM tsar, czar

tzarévitch [tsarevitʃ, dz-] NM tsarevitch, czarevitch

tzarine [tsarin, dz-] NF tsarina, czarina

tzigane [tsigan, dz-] ADJ, N tzigane, Hungarian gypsy

U, u [y] NM **1** *(lettre)* U, u; **fer en U** channel iron; *Géog* **vallée (à profil) en U** U-shaped valley; **tables (disposées) en U** tables arranged in a horseshoe **2** *Univ Fam (abrév universitaire)* **resto U** student refectory; **cité U** student residence, hall(s) of residence

UAS [yaɛs] NF *Com (abrév* **unité d'activité stratégique)** SBU

ubac [ybak] NM = shady side of an Alpine mountain, *Spéc* ubac

ubiquité [ybikɥite] NF ubiquity; **avoir le don d'u.** to have the ability to be in several places at the same time; **je n'ai pas le don d'u.** I can't be in two places at the same time

ubuesque [ybyɛsk] ADJ Ubuesque

UDF [ydeɛf] NF *(abrév* **Union pour la démocratie française)** = right-of-centre French political party

UE [yə] NF *(abrév* **Union européenne)** EU

UEM [yøɛm] NF *(abrév* **Union économique et monétaire)** EMU

UEO [yøo] NF *(abrév* **Union de l'Europe occidentale**) WEU

UER [yøɛr] NF *Univ Anciennement (abrév* **unité d'enseignement et de recherche)** = university department

ufologie [yfɔlɔʒi] NF ufology

UFR [yɛfɛr] NF *Univ (abrév* **unité de formation et de recherche)** = university department

UHF [yaʃɛf] *Radio (abrév* **ultra-haute fréquence)** UHF

UHT [yaʃte] *(abrév* **ultra-haute température)** UHT

ukase [ykɑz] NM *Hist* ukase; *Fig* **u. paternel** paternal fiat

Ukraine [ykrɛn] NF **l'U.** the Ukraine

ukrainien, -ienne [ykrɛnjɛ̃, -jɛn] ADJ Ukrainien
   NM *Ling* Ukranian
   N **U.** Ukranian

ukulélé [jukulele] NM ukulele

ulcération [ylserasjɔ̃] NF *Méd* ulceration

ulcère [ylsɛr] NM ulcer; **avoir un u. à l'estomac** to have a stomach ulcer

ulcéré [ylsere] ADJ **1** *Méd* ulcerated **2** *Fig* **elle en était ulcérée** it rankled with her

ulcérer [ylsere] *(pr ind* il **ulcère**; *fu* il **ulcérera)** VT **1** *Méd* to ulcerate **2** *Fig* **u. qn** to cause resentment in sb, to embitter sb; **sa réaction m'a ulcéré** I resented his reaction, his reaction rankled with me
   VPR **s'ulcérer** *Méd* to ulcerate, to fester

ulcéreux, -euse [ylserø, -øz] ADJ *Méd* ulcerous; *(plaie)* ulcerated, festering

ULM [yɛlɛm] NM INV *Aviat (abrév* **ultraléger motorisé)** microlight

ulmaire [ylmɛr] NF *Bot* meadowsweet

ulnaire [ylnɛr] ADJ *Anat* ulnar

ultérieur [ylterjœr] ADJ later, subsequent (à

to); *(nouvelles, date etc)* later; *(dans le futur)* future; **notre voyage est remis à une date ultérieure** our trip has been postponed; **la parution de ce livre est ultérieure à celle du vôtre** this book came out after yours did

ultérieurement [ylterjœrmɑ̃] ADV later (on), subsequently

ultimatum [yltimatɔm] NM ultimatum; **adresser un u. à un pays** to present a country with an ultimatum

ultime [yltim] ADJ *(paroles, moment, phénomène)* (very) last; *(préparatifs)* final; **l'u. sacrifice** the ultimate sacrifice

ultimo [yltimo] ADV lastly, finally

ultra [yltra] NM *Pol* extremist

ultra-chic ADJ *Fam* ultra-fashionable

ultracompétitif, -ive [yltrakɔ̃petitif, -iv] ADJ *(société, prix)* very highly competitive

ultraconfidentiel, -ielle ADJ top-secret

ultraconservateur, -trice ADJ *Pol* ultra-conservative, far right

ultracourt ADJ *(jupe)* ultra-short, microscopic; *Phys* **ondes ultracourtes** ultra-short waves

ultrafin [yltrafɛ̃] ADJ *(filament, aiguille)* extra-fine

ultra-haute fréquence NF *Phys* ultra-high frequency

ultraléger, -ère [yltraleʒe, -ɛr] ADJ ultralight
   NM microlight
   NF **ultralégère** *(cigarette)* superlight, ultra low

ultralibéralisme [yltraliberalism] NM extreme liberalism

ultramicroscope [yltramikrɔskɔp] NM ultra-microscope

ultramoderne [yltramɔdɛrn] ADJ *(équipement, voiture, intérieur)* ultramodern, state-of-the-art, high-tech; *(appartement)* ultra-modern, high-tech

ultramontain, -aine [yltramɔ̃tɛ̃, -ɛn] ADJ **1** *Rel, Pol* ultramontane **2** *(par rapport à la France)* beyond the Alps
   N *Rel, Pol* ultramontanist

ultraportatif [yltrapɔrtatif] NM notebook computer

ultrarapide [yltrarapid] ADJ *(avion, train, voiture)* ultrafast

ultraroyaliste ADJ, N *Hist* ultraroyalist

ultrasensible ADJ ultra-sensitive; **pellicule/film u.** ultra-sensitive *or* high-speed film; *Fam* **elle est u.** she's hypersensitive

ultrason NM *Phys* ultrasound; **ultrasons** ultrasonic waves; **science des ultrasons** ultrasonics

ultrasonique [yltrasɔnik], **ultrasonore** [yltrasɔnɔr] ADJ ultrasonic, supersonic

ultraviolet, -ette ADJ, NM ultraviolet; **faire une séance d'ultraviolets** to have a sunbed session

ululation [ylylasjɔ̃] NF, **ululement** [ylylmɑ̃] NM ululation; *(des oiseaux de nuit)* hooting

ululer [ylyle] VI to ululate; *(des oiseaux de nuit)* to hoot

Ulysse [ylis] NM Ulysses

UME [yɛmə] NF *(abrév* **Union monétaire européenne)** EMU

UMP [yɛmpe] NF **1** *(abrév* **Union pour la majorité présidentielle)** = former centre-right coalition, now renamed "Union pour un Mouvement Populaire" **2** *(abrév* **Union pour un mouvement populaire)** = centre-right French political party, formed mainly from members from the former RPR party

UMTS [yɛmteɛs] NM *Tél (abrév* **universal mobile telecommunications system)** UMTS

un, une [œ̃, yn] ADJ **1** one; **pourrais-tu me prêter un euro?** could you lend me a euro?; **tu n'aurais pas une pièce d'un euro?** you wouldn't happen to have a one-euro piece?; **deux brioches et un pain** two buns and a loaf (of bread); **il n'en reste qu'un** there's only one left; **il vient un jour sur deux** he comes every other *or* second day; **une personne/une maison sur cent** one person/house in a hundred; **un à un** [œ̃aœ̃], **un par un** one by one, one at a time; **il est une heure** it's one o'clock; **page un(e)** page one, the first page; **numéro un** number one
   2 *(uni)* one; **Dieu est un** God is one; **c'est tout un** [sœtutœ̃] it's the same thing *or* all one *or* all the same; **ils ne font qu'un** *(ils sont très proches)* they are as one; **la maison et l'atelier ne font qu'un** the house and work-shop are one and the same
   N **1** *(chiffre)* one; **un et un** [œ̃eœ̃] **font deux** one and one are two; **un(e), deux, trois, partez!** one, two, three, go!; **il n'a fait ni une ni deux** he didn't hesitate (for a moment); **et d'un(e) tu es toujours en retard, et de deux tu mens** for one thing you're always late, and for another you're lying, one, you're always late, and two, you're lying; *Fam* **en savoir plus d'une** to know a thing or two; *Fam* **il était moins une** it was a close thing *or* a close shave; **heureusement que je suis arrivé, il était moins une** it was lucky I arrived when I did, another minute and it would have been too late
   2 *(première page)* *Journ* **la une** [layn] *(d'un journal)* the front page, page one; **faire la une** *(d'un magazine)* to appear on *or* make the front cover; *(d'un journal)* to make the headlines; *Fig (faire parler de soi)* to make *or* hit the headlines; **la guerre fait la une** the war is front-page news *or* in the headlines; **tu es à la une des journaux** you've made the front page, you're front-page news *or* in the headlines
   PRON one; **un de ces jours** one of these days; **un qui a de la chance** a lucky one, a lucky man; **un qui a de la chance, c'est Pierre, il est parti à la Réunion** Pierre's one of the

lucky ones, he's gone off to Réunion; **en voilà une qui sait ce qu'elle veut!** there's somebody who knows what she wants!; **un que je plains, c'est …** one person I do feel sorry for is …; **il n'y en a pas un qui parle anglais** not one of them speaks English; *Fam* **pas un n'était au courant** not a (single solitary) soul *or* absolutely nobody knew about it; *Fam* **être menteur/hypocrite comme pas un** to be a dreadful liar/hypocrite; *Fam* **il fait du bruit comme pas un** he's unbelievably noisy; *Fam* **il danse comme pas un** he's a great dancer; **(l')un de nous, (l')un d'entre nous** one of us; **ni l'un ni l'autre** neither (of them), neither one nor the other; **ni l'un ni l'autre ne me plaît** I don't like either of them; **l'un dans l'autre** all in all, by and large; **(l')un des danseurs les plus célèbres du monde** one of the most famous dancers in the world; **l'une des voitures les plus vendues d'Europe** one of the biggest-selling cars in Europe; **les uns disent que …** some say that …; **les uns et les autres** people, everybody

ART INDÉF SEE GRAMMAR A5–6; B4–5 (*pl* **des**, *see* **de**) **1** a; *(devant voyelle ou h muet)* an; *(pl some)* **un jour/une pomme/une heure** a day/an apple/an hour; **un père et une mère** a father and mother; **un père de famille** the father of a family; **il est là pour un certain temps** he is here for some time; **cela ne durera qu'un temps** it won't last for long; **venez me voir un lundi** come and see me one Monday *or* some Monday; **cela tombe un mardi** it falls on a Tuesday; **un jour de la semaine dernière** one day last week; *Fam* **un de ces quatre** one of these days; **pour une raison ou pour une autre** for some reason or other

2 *(introduisant un nom propre)* a; *(devant voyelle ou h muet)* an; **c'est une Martin** she's a Martin, she's one of the Martins; **ce sera un Einstein** he'll be another Einstein

3 *(intensif)* **j'ai eu un monde aujourd'hui!** I've had such a lot of visitors today!; **il y a un de ces mondes en ville!** the town is incredibly busy, there are an incredible lot of people in town; **elle parle avec une élégance!** she has such an elegant way of putting things!; **il est d'une bêtise!** he is incredibly *or* so stupid!; **il a fait une de ces têtes!** you should have seen his face!; **elle a poussé un de ces cris** she gave such a shout; **tu m'as fait une peur!** you gave me such a fright!, you did give me a fright!

unanime [ynanim] **ADJ** *(approbation, vote etc)* unanimous; **ils sont unanimes à vous accuser** they are unanimous in accusing you

unanimement [ynanimmɑ̃] **ADV** unanimously

unanimité [ynanimite] **NF** *(d'une réponse, une réaction etc)* unanimity; **à l'u.** unanimously; **faire l'u.** *(d'une proposition, une invitation etc)* to be accepted unanimously

underground [œndœrgrawnd] **ADJ, NM** underground

une [yn] *voir* **un**

UNEF [ynɛf] **NF** *Univ (abrév* **Union nationale des étudiants de France)** = French students' union, *Br* ≃ NUS

Unesco [ynɛsko] **NF** Unesco

unguéal, -ale, -aux, -ales [ɔ̃gɥeal, -o] **ADJ** (of the) nail; **infection unguéale** nail infection, infection of the nail

uni, -ie [yni] **ADJ 1** *(famille, couple etc)* united; **ils sont très unis** they are very close **2** *(sans irrégularité)* *(sol, surface etc)* smooth, level, even; *(mer etc)* smooth, calm, unruffled **3** *(couleur)* plain; *(tissu, robe)* self-coloured, *Am* self-colored

NM *Tex* self-coloured *or Am* self-colored material

NF *Belg, Suisse Fam (abrév* **université)** *Br* uni, *Am* school

uniate [ynjat] **ADJ, N** *Rel* Uniat(e)

Unicef [ynisɛf] **NM OU F** *(abrév* **United Nations International Children's Emergency Fund)** **l'U.** Unicef

unicellulaire [yniselyler] **ADJ** *Biol* unicellular

unicité [ynisite] **NF** *Phil etc* uniqueness

unicolore [ynikɔlɔr] **ADJ** *(tissu etc)* self-coloured, *Am* self-colored, plain

unicorne [ynikɔrn] **NM** *Myth* unicorn
ADJ one-horned, single-horned

unidimensionnel, -elle [ynidimɑ̃sjɔnɛl] **ADJ** one-dimensional

unidirectionnel, -elle [ynidirɛksjɔnɛl] **ADJ** unidirectional

unidose [ynidoz] **NF** single-dose sachet; **ce médicament est disponible en u.** this medicine is available in single-dose sachets

unième [ynjɛm] **ADJ** *(used only in compounds)* **trente et u.** thirty-first

unièmement [ynjɛmmɑ̃] **ADV** *(used only in compounds)* **vingt et u.** in twenty-first place

unificateur, -trice [ynifikatœr, -tris] **ADJ** unifying

unification [ynifikasjɔ̃] **NF** *(d'un pays etc)* unification; *(des crédits)*, *Pol (de la législation)* consolidation; *(des poids et mesures etc)* standardization

unifier [ynifje] **VT** *(impf, pr sub n.* **unifiions**, **v. unifiiez)** *(parti politique, pays etc)* to unify; *(crédits, législation)* to consolidate; *(poids et mesures etc)* to standardize

uniforme [ynifɔrm] **ADJ** *(opinions, expression)* uniform; *(vie)* unchanging; *(allure, surface)* even; *(mouvement)* regular; **taux u.** *(d'un intérêt etc)* flat rate
NM uniform; *Mil* **grand u.** full-dress uniform; **endosser l'u.** to join the forces; **le prestige de l'u.** the appeal of the uniform; **elle est sensible au prestige de l'u.** she has a thing about men in uniform; **quitter l'u.** to leave the service

uniformément [ynifɔrmemɑ̃] **ADV** *(réparti)* uniformly, evenly; *(avancer)* smoothly

uniformisation [ynifɔrmizasjɔ̃] **NF** standardization

uniformiser [ynifɔrmize] **VT** to standardize

uniformité [ynifɔrmite] **NF** *(d'un paysage)* sameness, uniformity; *(des habitudes, coutumes, de la vie etc)* monotony; *(de couleur, teinte)* uniformity

unijambiste [yniʒɑ̃bist] **ADJ** one-legged
N one-legged person

unilatéral, -ale, -aux, -ales [ynilateral, -o] **ADJ** *(décision, désarmement etc)* unilateral; *(contrat, accord)* one-sided; **stationnement u.** parking on one side only

unilatéralisme [ynilateralism] **NM** unilateralism

unilingue [ynilɛ̃g] **ADJ** *(dictionnaire, pays etc)* unilingual, monolingual

uniment [ynimɑ̃] **ADV** evenly; *Litt* **tout u.** *(simplement)* plainly, simply

uninominal, -ale, -aux, -ales [yninɔminal, -o] **ADJ** *Pol* **scrutin u.** voting for a single member *or* for one member only

union [ynjɔ̃] **NF 1** *(alliance)* union; **l'u. du corps et de l'esprit** the union of mind and body **2** *(association)* *(de partis, consommateurs etc)* union, society, association **3** *(mariage)* marriage; **u. conjugale** marriage **4** *(accord, entente)* unity, agreement; *(entre les membres d'une famille, un groupe d'amis)* closeness, unity; **resserrer l'u. entre deux personnes** to strengthen the links *or* bond between two people; *Prov* **l'u. fait la force** unity is strength, strength through unity

▸ **u. douanière** customs union; **u. économique** economic union; **U. économique et**

monétaire Economic and Monetary Union; **U. européenne** European Union; **u. libre** *(pour un couple non marié)* cohabitation; **vivre en u. libre** to live together, *surtout Jur* to cohabit; **u. monétaire** monetary union; **u. monétaire à deux vitesses** two-speed monetary union; **U. nationale des étudiants de France** French National Union of Students; **u. patronale** employers' organization; *Anciennement* **l'U. des républiques socialistes soviétiques** the Union of Soviet Socialist Republics; *Hist* **U. sacrée** = unity of all Frenchmen in the face of the enemy *(called for by Poincaré on the outbreak of the First World War)*; *Anciennement* **l'U. soviétique** the Soviet Union

unionisme [ynjɔnism] **NM** *Pol* unionist movement

unioniste [ynjɔnist] **ADJ, N** unionist

unipare [ynipar] **ADJ** *Biol* uniparous

unipersonnel, -elle [ynipɛrsɔnɛl] **ADJ** *Gram (verbe)* impersonal

unipolaire [ynipɔlɛr] **ADJ** *Élec (interrupteur etc)* unipolar, single-pole; *Biol (cellule, neurone etc)* unipolar

unique [ynik] **ADJ 1** *(seul)* *(fils, tasse)* only; *(parti)* single; *(talent, savoir-faire, occasion, cas)* unique; **d'un même et u. problème** of one and the same problem; **c'est loin d'être un cas u.** it's far from being an isolated case; **il se croit u.** he thinks he's unique; **c'est vendu à un prix u. dans toute la France** it sells for the same price throughout France; **taille u.** one size; **c'est une taille u.** it only comes in the one size; **j'étais enfant u.** I was an only child; **(rue à) sens u.** one-way street; **c'est à sens u.** it's (a) one-way; **voie u.** single lane; **je possède l'exemplaire u.** I have the sole copy; **c'est un exemplaire u.** it's the only copy there is; **c'est une pièce de collection u. au monde** it's the only piece like it in the world; **c'est son u. souci** it's his sole *or* only concern; **c'est son u. sujet de conversation** it's all he ever talks about; **u. en son genre** one of a kind; **ce sont des gens uniques en leur genre** there's nobody like them; **ce fut une soirée u. en son genre** there's never been and there'll never be another party like it; **u. au monde** unlike anything else in the world; **c'est son seul et u. défaut** it's his one and only fault; **je ne ferai qu'une seule et u. critique** I have one and only one criticism to make; **la seule et l'u. Arletty** the one and only Arletty **2** *(incomparable)* unparalleled, unrivalled, unique; *Fam* **il est u.!** he's priceless!

uniquement [ynikmɑ̃] **ADV** just, only; **elle mange u. des légumes** she eats just *or* only vegetables, she eats nothing but vegetables; **je viens u. pour vous voir** I've come just to see you, the only reason I've come is to see you; **vous faites des dictionnaires? – pas u., nous faisons aussi des traductions** you compile dictionaries, don't you? – not just that, we do translations as well

unir [ynir] **VT 1** *(relier)* *(personnes, territoires)* to unite; *(d'un pont, d'une autoroute)* to join, to link; **u. un territoire à un autre** to unite one territory with another; **le tunnel sous la Manche unit Londres à Paris** the Channel Tunnel links London and Paris; **être uni par le mariage à …** to be joined in matrimony *or* marriage to …; **vous voilà unis par les liens du mariage** ≃ I now pronounce you man and wife; **le Père Patrick les unira** Father Patrick will marry them *or* will officiate at their wedding; **l'amitié qui nous a toujours unis** the friendship there has always been between us; **un homme qui unit des qualités de décideur à un sens de l'humour** a man who combines decision-making abilities with a sense of humour **2** *(sol, surface etc)* to smooth, to level

VPR s'unir to join (together), to unite; **s'u. à qn** to join forces with sb; *(se marier)* to marry sb

unisexe [ynisɛks] ADJ *(vêtements etc)* unisex

unisexué [ynisɛksɥe] ADJ *Biol* unisexual

unisson [ynisɔ̃] NM *Mus* unison; **à l'u.** in unison; *Fig* **nos pensées sont à l'u.** we think as one; **les esprits sont à l'u.** everybody feels the same way; **ses idées ne sont pas à l'u. avec celles de la maison** his ideas are not in keeping with the company's

unitaire [yniter] ADJ **1** *(système etc)* unitary; *Com* **prix u.** unit price **2** *Rel* Unitarian N *Rel* Unitarian

unitarien, -ienne [ynitarjɛ̃, -jɛn] ADJ, N *Pol* unitarian; *Rel* Unitarian

unité [ynite] NF **1** *Math etc* unity, unit; *Math* **la colonne des unités** the units column
2 *Com* unit; **10 euros l'u.** 10 euros each; *Com* **prix à l'u.** unit price; **les ventes ont dépassé les 3 000 unités** sales have passed the 3,000 mark
3 *(d'une mesure etc)* unit; **u. de temps/de longueur** unit of time/length; **u. monétaire** unit of currency
4 *(bloc)* unit; **u. d'intervention chirurgicale** field surgical unit; **u. de production** production unit
5 *Mil* unit; **rejoindre son u.** to go back to *or* rejoin one's unit; *Naut* to go back to *or* rejoin one's ship
6 *(caractère de ce qui forme un tout) (d'une nation, une association)* unity; *(de Dieu)* oneness; *(d'un projet, d'une action etc)* unified nature; *(du style etc)* consistency; **cela manque d'u.** *(d'un projet, d'un texte)* it doesn't hang together very well; *Littér* **les trois unités** the three unities
7 *Anciennement Fam (million d'anciens francs)* ten thousand francs
8 *Ordinat* unit; *(de disque)* drive; **u. de bande** tape unit; **u. centrale** central processing unit, CPU; **u. de destination** target drive; **u. de disque** disk drive; **u. de disque dur** hard drive; **u. de disquettes** floppy drive; **u. d'entrée** input device; **u. logique** logical drive; **u. d'origine** source drive; **u. périphérique** peripheral; **u. de sauvegarde** backup drive; **u. de sortie** output device; **u. de stockage** storage device; **u. système** system unit; **u. de traitement** processing unit; **u. de traitement de texte** text processor; **u. de visualisation** visual display unit, VDU ▸ *Com* **u. d'activité stratégique** strategic business unit; **u. administrative** administrative unit; *Com* **u. de chargement** load unit; **u. de choc** shock unit; *Compta* **u. de compte** unit of account; *Pétr* **u. de craquage** cracking unit; *Univ* **u. de formation et de recherche** = university department; *Ling* **u. lexicale** lexeme; *TV, Radio* **u. mobile (de tournage)** OB unit, outside broadcast vehicle; **u. monétaire** monetary unit; **u. de production** production unit; *TV etc* **u. de programme** programme production team; *Mktg* **u. de sondage** sampling unit; **u. de télécommande** remote control unit, RCU; *Bourse* **u. de transaction** lot size; *Univ* **u. de valeur** ≃ credit; *TV etc* **u. de voix hors champ automatique** automatic voice-over unit, ducker

univalent [ynivalɑ̃] ADJ *Chimie* univalent

univers [yniver] NM **1** *Astron* universe; **l'U.** the Universe **2** *Fig* **l'u. mathématique** the field of mathematics; **l'u. du rêve** the world *or* realm of dreams; **le monde de l'argent, ce n'est pas vraiment mon u.** big money isn't really my thing *or* line; **c'est tout son u.** it means everything to him, it's his whole world

universalisation [yniversalizasjɔ̃] NF universalization

universaliser [yniversalize] VT **u. qch** to universalize sth, to make sth universal

universalité [yniversalite] NF *(d'une théorie, une loi, un mythe, une croyance etc)* universal nature, universality

universaux [yniverso] NMPL *Phil* universals

universel, -elle [yniversɛl] ADJ *(paix, jugement, constante etc)* universal; *(réputation, gloire)* worldwide; *(histoire)* of the universe; *(installation)* all-purpose; **l'Exposition universelle** Expo; **suffrage u.** universal suffrage, one man one vote; **élu au suffrage u.** elected by universal suffrage; **savoir u.** all-embracing knowledge; **proposition universelle** universal (proposition); *Tech* **joint u.** universal joint; *Jur* **légataire u.** sole legatee; *Jur* **légataire à titre u.** residuary legatee NM *(en logique)* universal

universellement [yniversɛlmɑ̃] ADV *(connu)* universally, worldwide; **le sida est malheureusement u. répandu** AIDS is unfortunately a worldwide phenomenon

universitaire [yniversiter] ADJ *(ville, études)* university; **honneurs universitaires** academic honours; **cité u.** ≃ student residence, hall(s) of residence; **restaurant u.** student refectory
N **1** *(professeur)* academic **2** *Belg, Suisse (étudiant)* university student; *(diplômé)* graduate

université [yniversite] NF **1** university; **aller à l'u.** to go to university; **u. d'été** summer school; *Pol* **party conference** *(for young members)*; **u. du troisième âge** university of the third age, university for mature students **2 l'U. (de France)** = the teaching profession *(including university staff, schoolteachers, inspectors etc)*

univoque [ynivɔk] ADJ *Ling* univocal; *Math (correspondance)* one-to-one

Untel, Unetelle [œ̃tɛl, yntɛl] N so-and-so, what's-his-name, *f* what's-her-name; **Monsieur U.** Mr So-and-So; **Madame Unetelle** Mrs So-and-So; **les U.** the so-and-sos, what's-their-names

uppercut [yperkyt] NM *Boxe* uppercut; **u. du droit** right uppercut

uranifère [yranifer] ADJ *Géol* uranium-bearing

uranium [yranjɔm] NM uranium

Uranus [yranys] N *(dieu, planète)* Uranus

urbain [yrbɛ̃] ADJ **1** *(de la ville) (développement, voirie, paysage, transport etc)* urban; **la population urbaine** city dwellers; *Tél* **communication urbaine** local call; **vivre en milieu u.** to live in an urban environment **2** *Litt (raffiné)* urbane

urbanisable [yrbanizabl] ADJ suitable for development; **zone difficilement u.** an area which would be difficult to develop

urbanisation [yrbanizasjɔ̃] NF urbanization; **plan d'u.** urban development plan

urbaniser [yrbanize] VT *(zone rurale etc)* to urbanize; **zone urbanisée** built-up area

urbanisme [yrbanism] NM town planning, urban development; **cabinet d'u.** firm of town-planning consultants

urbaniste [yrbanist] ADJ urban; **réglementation u.** municipal bylaws
N town planner; **agence d'urbanistes** firm of town-planning consultants

urbanistique [yrbanistik] ADJ **politique/ projet u.** town-planning *or* urban development policy/project

urbanité [yrbanite] NF *Litt* urbanity; **avec u.** urbanely

urbi et orbi [yrbietɔrbi] ADV urbi et orbi; *Fig* far and wide, to all and sundry; **cela est connu u.** all and sundry know that, *Fam* the world and his wife know that

urée [yre] NF *Chimie* urea

urémie [yremi] NF *Méd* uraemia, *Am* uremia

uretère [yrter] NM *Anat* ureter

urètre [yretr] NM *Anat* urethra

urgence [yrʒɑ̃s] NF **1** *(caractère pressé)* urgency; **ces mesures ont été prises dans l'u.** these measures were taken in a great hurry; **il y a u.** it's a matter of urgency, it's an emergency; **il n'y a aucune u.** there's no rush, it's not an emergency; **y a-t-il u. à ce qu'il parte?** does he have to leave right *or* straight away?; **faire qch en toute u.** to give sth (top) priority, to treat sth as a matter of (top) priority; **en cas d'u.** in an emergency; **mesures d'u.** emergency measures; **état d'u.** state of emergency; **à envoyer/payer d'u.** to be sent/paid immediately; **convoquer d'u. les actionnaires** to call an extraordinary meeting of the shareholders; **il a été appelé d'u.** he received an urgent call
2 *Méd* **une u.** an emergency; **ce n'est pas une u.** it's not urgent, it's not a matter of life and death; **salle des urgences** emergency ward; **transporter qn d'u. à l'hôpital** to rush sb to hospital; **opérer d'u.** to perform an emergency operation; **il fut opéré d'u.** he had an emergency operation

urgent [yrʒɑ̃] ADJ urgent; **rien d'u. ne l'obligeait à sortir** there was nothing urgent forcing him to go out; **cas u.** urgent case, emergency; **affaires urgentes** pressing matters; **il devient u. de trouver une solution** a solution must be found urgently, a solution is urgently required; **avoir un besoin u. de liquidités** to be in urgent need *or* to be urgently in need of cash

urgentiste [yrʒɑ̃tist] N *Méd* emergency doctor

urgentologue [yrʒɑ̃tɔlɔg] N *Can Méd* emergency doctor

urger [yrʒe] VI *Fam* to be urgent; **il n'y a rien qui urge** there's no desperate hurry; **vite, ça urge!** quick, it's urgent!

urinaire [yriner] ADJ *Anat* urinary

urinal, -aux [yrinal, -o] NM *Méd* urinal

urine [yrin] NF urine(s) urine; **évacuer l'u.** to pass water; **analyses d'urines** urine tests

uriner [yrine] VI to urinate, to pass water

urinoir [yrinwar] NM (public) urinal

urique [yrik] ADJ *(acide etc)* uric

urne [yrn] NF **1** *(pour voter)* ballot box; **aller aux urnes** to go to the polls **2** *(vase)* urn

urogénital, -ale, -aux, -ales [yroʒenital, -o] ADJ *Méd* urogenital

urologie [yrɔlɔʒi] NF urology

urologue [yrɔlɔg] N urologist

URSS [yeRess, yrs] NF *Anciennement (abrév* Union des républiques socialistes soviétiques*)* USSR

URSSAF [yrsaf] NF *(abrév* Union de recouvrement des cotisations de Sécurité sociale et d'allocations familiales*)* = organization which collects social security and family allowance payments

ursuline [yrsylin] NF *Rel* Ursuline convent

urticaire [yrtiker] NF *Méd* nettle rash, hives, *Spéc* urticaria; **crise d'u.** attack of hives; **avoir une crise d'u.** to come out *or* break out in hives; *Fig Fam* **donner de l'u. à qn** to irritate sb, to set sb's teeth on edge

urticant [yrtikɑ̃] ADJ stinging

urtication [yrtikasjɔ̃] NF *Méd* stinging

Uruguay [yrygwɛ] NM Uruguay

uruguayen, -enne [yrygwɛjɛ̃, -ɛn] ADJ Uruguayan
N **U.** Uruguayan

urus [yrys] NM *Zool* aurochs

us [ys] NMPL **les us et coutumes d'un pays** the habits and customs of a country

usage [yzaʒ] NM **1** *(utilisation)* use; *Gram* usage; **mot en u.** word in use; **c'est un mot qu'on trouve seulement dans l'u. écrit** the word is found only in written form; **les mots se modifient par l'u.** words are changed by *or* through use; **mot sorti de l'u.** word which has fallen into disuse *or* is no longer in use; **faute d'u.** *(d'un mot)* misuse; **perdre l'u. de la vue/de l'ouïe** to lose one's sight/hearing; **faire u. de qch** *(service, appareil)* to make use of sth, to use sth; **faire u. de la force** to use *or* employ force; **faire bon u. de qch** to make good use of sth, to put sth to good use; **faire mauvais u. de qch** to make bad use of sth, to misuse sth; **avoir l'u. de** to have the use of; **je n'en aurai pas l'u.** I won't be needing it, I won't have any use for it; *Pharm* **à u. externe/interne** for external/internal use; **avoir plusieurs usages** to have various uses; **à l'u. des écoles/des étudiants** for use in schools/by students; **réservé à son u. personnel** reserved for his/her personal use; **à usages multiples** *(équipement etc)* multipurpose; **locaux à u. commercial** business *or* commercial premises; **s'améliorer à l'u.** to improve with use; **tu t'y habitueras à l'u.** you'll get used to it once you start *or* with practice; **d'u. courant** in common *or* everyday use; **c'est un mot d'u. courant** it's a common *or* everyday word; **j'en fais un u. courant** I often use it; **hors d'u.** *(ascenseur)* out of service, out of use; *(usé) (manteau)* worn-out; *(démodé) (mot etc)* obsolete; **faire un u. immodéré de l'alcool** to drink too much *or* to excess; **le bon u.**, *Arch* **le bel u.** correct French

2 *(des vêtements etc)* wear, service; **faire de l'u. ou beaucoup d'u.** to wear well; **ce manteau vous fera de l'u.** you'll get a lot of wear out of this coat; **garanti à l'u.** guaranteed to wear well

3 *Jur* **droit d'u.** (right of) use

4 *(coutume)* custom, practice; **conforme/contraire aux usages** in keeping with/contrary to common practice; **usages locaux** local customs; **c'est l'u.** it's the done thing; **les conditions d'u.** the usual terms; **comme il est d'u. en Algérie** as is customary *or* the custom in Algeria; **selon** *ou* **suivant l'u.** according to custom; **un mariage selon** *ou* **suivant l'u.** a traditional wedding; **il est d'u. de … + inf** it is usual *or* customary to …

5 *(expérience)* practice, experience

usagé [yzaʒe] ADJ *(souliers, manteau, veste)* worn; *(d'occasion)* secondhand; **plaisanteries usagées** tired jokes

usager, -ère [yzaʒe, -ɛr] N *(de quelque chose)* user; **les usagers de la route/du téléphone/du français** road/telephone/French language users; **les usagers du train/du métro** rail travellers/underground users; **les usagers de la poste** post office users *or* customers; **les usagers de la Sécurité sociale** Social Security clients

usant [yzɑ̃] ADJ *(vie, travail)* exhausting, wearing; **il est u.** he wears you out

usé [yze] ADJ *(métal, pierre etc)* worn; *(vêtements)* worn(-out), threadbare; *(corde)* frayed; *(sujet, plaisanterie)* hackneyed, stale; **terre usée** exhausted land; *Ind* **eaux usées** waste water; **je suis u.!** I'm worn-out *or* exhausted!; **u. par l'eau** worn away by water; **u. par le frottement** worn(-out) by rubbing; **u. par les épreuves** careworn; **u. par le temps** timeworn; **u. par le travail** worn-out by work; **c'est une femme usée par les années** the years have told on her, time has taken its toll of her; **c'est u.!** that's an old one!; **argument u. jusqu'à la corde** well-worn *or* threadbare argument

user [yze] VI **u. de** *(persuasion, son influence)* to use; *(termes recherchés)* to use, to make use of; *(violence, ruse)* to use, to resort to; **u.**

de son droit to exercise one's right; **u. de douceur avec qn** to deal gently with sb; **on ne te reprochera jamais de trop u. de patience/calme/compréhension** you can never be too patient/calm/understanding; *Litt* **en u. bien/mal avec qn** to treat sb well/badly

VT **1** *(consommer)* *(énergie, électricité)* to use, to consume; **u. du charbon** to use *or* burn coal; **je ne vais pas u. mon énergie à essayer de te persuader** I'm not going to waste my energy trying to persuade you

2 *(abîmer)* *(vêtements, chaussures)* to wear out; *(santé)* to ruin; **u. un pull aux coudes** to wear out a pullover at the elbows; **elle use trois paires de chaussures par an** she goes through three pairs of shoes in a year; **j'ai usé jusqu'à la corde, ce pull** I've worn this sweater until it's threadbare; **l'érosion use la roche** erosion wears away *or* eats away the rock; *Fig* **cela finit par u. la passion/l'intérêt** in the end it kills off passion/interest; **tu uses tes yeux à lire dans le noir** you'll ruin your eyesight reading in the dark

VPR **s'user** *(de pneus)* to wear out; *(de talons, semelles)* to wear out, to wear down; **ce tissu s'use vite** this material wears (out) quickly; *Fig* **sa résistance finira bien par s'u.** his resistance will wear down *or* break down in the end; *Fig* **ma patience va finir par s'u.** my patience is beginning to wear thin; *Fig* **il s'est usé à ce travail** he's worn himself out with this work; *Fig* **je me suis usé à le lui dire** I'm tired telling him, I've told him till I'm blue in the face; *Fig* **mais c'est ce que je m'use à te dire depuis hier!** that's what I've been trying to tell you since yesterday!

> Il faut noter que le verbe transitif anglais **to use** est un faux ami. Il signifie uniquement **utiliser**, **se servir de**.

usinage [yzinaʒ] NM *Métal* machining
usine [yzin] NF factory, plant; **navire-u.** factory ship; **u. pilote** pilot plant; **u. à gaz** gasworks; **u. à papier** paper mill; **u. de construction automobile** car factory *or* plant; **u. d'armement** arms factory; **u. d'assemblage** assembly plant; **u. de fabrication** manufacturing plant; **u. de montage** assembly plant; **u. de production** production plant; **u. tournevis** screwdriver factory; **ouvrier d'u.** factory worker; *Fig Fam* **ce restaurant est une u.** this restaurant is like a works canteen

usiner [yzine] VT **1** *Métal (moulages etc)* to machine, to tool; *(pièces)* to machine(-finish); **parties usinées** bright parts **2** *(fabriquer)* to manufacture

VI *Fam (travailler dur)* to slog *or* slave away, to be hard at it; **ça usine là-dedans!** they're hard at it in there!

usinier, -ière [yzinje, -jɛr] ADJ *(industrie)* factory; **faubourg u.** industrial suburb

usité [yzite] ADJ in common *or* current use; **mot très u.** very common word; **mot peu u.** little used word

ustensile [ystɑ̃sil] NM implement, tool; **u. de cuisine** kitchen utensil

usuel, -elle [yzɥɛl] ADJ usual, common, ordinary; **l'anglais u.** everyday English; **dénomination usuelle** *(pour une plante etc)* common name

NMPL **usuels** *(dans une bibliothèque)* reference works

usuellement [yzɥɛlmɑ̃] ADV commonly, ordinarily

usufruit [yzyfrɥi] NM *Jur* usufruct, life interest; **laisser qch en u. à qn** *(maison etc)* to leave sb the life tenancy of sth

usufruitier, -ière [yzyfrɥitje, -jɛr] ADJ *Jur* usufructuary

N **1** *Jur* usufructuary **2** *(d'un bien immobilier)* tenant for life

usuraire [yzyrɛr] ADJ *(intérêt etc)* usurious
usure¹ [yzyr] NF *(intérêt)* usury; **pratiquer l'u.** to practise usury; *Fig* **rendre un bienfait avec u.** to repay a service with interest

usure² NF *(de pneu etc)* wear; *(du sol, de roches)* erosion, wearing away; **u. des pneus** tyre wear; **tissu qui résiste à l'u.** material that wears well; **u. par frottement** abrasion; **l'u. normale** normal wear and tear; *Tech* **surface d'u.** wearing surface; **organes sujets à l'u.** *(d'une machine)* wearing parts; **guerre d'u.** war of attrition; *Fig Fam* **je l'aurai à l'u.** I'll wear him down

usurier, -ière [yzyrje, -jɛr] N usurer
usurpateur, -trice [yzyrpatœr, -tris] N usurper

usurpation [yzyrpasjɔ̃] NF *(d'un trône, une réputation, un titre)* usurpation; **u. de pouvoir** usurping *or* usurpation of power

usurper [yzyrpe] VT *(trône, réputation, titre, droits)* to usurp *(sur from)*

VI **u. sur les droits/le domaine de qn** to encroach on sb's rights/territory

ut [yt] NM INV *Mus (note)* C; **ut dièse** C sharp; **clef d'ut** C clef; **clef d'ut quatrième ligne** tenor clef

utérin [yterɛ̃] ADJ uterine; **frères utérins/sœurs utérines** half brothers/sisters (on the mother's side)

utérus [yterys] NM uterus, womb

utile [ytil] ADJ useful; **puis-je vous être u.?** can I do anything (to help)?, can I be of (some) help?; **en quoi puis-je vous être u.?** what can I do for you?, how can I help you?; **si je puis vous être u.** if I can be of any use *or* help *or* service *or* assistance to you; **elle nous a été très u.** she was a lot of help, she was very helpful to us; **elle peut t'être u. un jour** she may be of help *or* useful to you one day; **se rendre u.** to make oneself useful; **tout cela n'était pas très u.** it wasn't much use *or* help, it didn't help much, none of it was very useful *or* helpful; **cela m'a été bien u.** *(cet objet)* it came in very handy, I found it very helpful; *(ce renseignement)* it was very helpful; **est-il u. d'y aller?** is there any use *or* any point in going?; **ce n'est peut-être pas très u. que tout le monde le sache** there's no use in everybody knowing; **il n'était pas u. que tu t'en occupes** there was no point in you dealing with it; **en temps u.** in (good) time, in due course; **prendre toutes dispositions utiles** to make all necessary arrangements; **dictionnaire u. à consulter** useful *or* helpful dictionary to consult

NM **joindre l'u. à l'agréable** to combine *or* mix business with pleasure

utilement [ytilmɑ̃] ADV usefully; **conseiller/renseigner u. qn** to give sb useful *or* helpful advice/information

utilisable [ytilizabl] ADJ usable; *(crédit)* available; **billet u. pour tous les trains** ticket which is valid *or* can be used on all trains; **facilement u.** easy to use

utilisateur, -trice [ytilizatœr, -tris] N user; **u. final** end user; *Mktg* **u. tardif** late adopter

utilisation [ytilizasjɔ̃] NF *(de quelque chose)* use, *surtout Am* utilization; **u. réduite à certaines périodes** use restricted to certain periods; **pour une bonne u. de ce produit, …** in order to make correct use of this product, …

utiliser [ytilize] VT to use, *Fml, Am* to utilize; *(profiter de)* to make use of; *Ordinat* to run; *Ordinat* **il peut être utilisé sur …** it can run on …; **bien u.** *(son temps, ressources, compétences)* to make good use of; *Péj* **avoir l'impression qu'on vous utilise** to have the feeling you're being used

utilitaire [ytilitɛr] ADJ utilitarian; *Aut* **véhicule u.** utility vehicle; *Ordinat* utility; **programme u.** utility (program)

NM *Ordinat* utility; **u. de conversion** conversion utility

utilitarisme [ytilitarism] NM utilitarianism

utilitariste [ytilitarist] ADJ, N utilitarian

utilité [ytilite] NF **1** *(fonction)* usefulness; **être d'une grande u.** to be very useful; **cela m'est d'une grande u.** I find it very useful *or* a lot of help; **cela ne m'est d'aucune u.** it's absolutely no use to me, it's no earthly use to me; **sans u.** useless; **c'est sans u. pour moi** it's of no use to me; **un appareil sans grande u.** an appliance that's not much use; **association d'u. publique** public utility; *(charitable)* registered charity **2** *Écon* utility; **u. collective** collective utility; **u. marginale** marginal utility **3** *Théâtre* **jouer les utilités** to play small *or* bit parts; *Fig* to play second fiddle

utopie [ytɔpi] NF utopia; *Fig Péj* **c'est une u.!** it's nothing but a pipe dream!

utopique [ytɔpik] ADJ utopian

utopisme [ytɔpism] NM Utopianism

utopiste [ytɔpist] N Utopian

utriculaire [ytrikylɛr] NF *Bot* bladderwort

UV¹ [yve] NF INV *Univ abrév* **unité de valeur**

UV² NM INV *(abrév* **ultra-violet)** UV; **se faire faire des UV** to go on a sunbed

uval, -ale, -aux, -ales [yval, -o] ADJ régime u. grape diet

uvulaire [yvylɛr] ADJ uvular

uvule [yvyl] NF *Anat* uvula

V

V, v [ve] NM **1** *(lettre)* V, v; **double v** W, w; **moteur (à cylindres) en V** V (type) engine; *Géog* **vallée (à profil) en V** V-shaped valley; **col en V** V-neck **2** *Fam (abrév* **vitesse**) **à la vitesse grand v** at a rate of knots, at top speed **3** *(abrév* **voir**) see

vacance [vakɑ̃s] NF **1** *(congé)* **vacances** holiday(s), *surtout Am* vacation; *(du Parlement)* recess; **vacances de Pâques/Noël** Easter/Christmas holidays; **vacances d'hiver/d'été** winter/summer holiday; **prendre ses vacances d'été/d'hiver en Écosse** to spend one's summer/winter holiday in Scotland, to go to Scotland for one's summer/winter holiday; **vacances de neige** winter sports holiday; **vacances scolaires** school holidays; **départ/retour de vacances** going away on/coming back from holiday; **attention aux retours de vacances sur la route** watch out for returning holidaymakers on the roads; **les grandes vacances** *Scol* the summer holidays; *Univ* the long vacation; **prendre des vacances** to take a holiday, to go on holiday; **tu as besoin de prendre des vacances** you need a holiday; **prendre ses vacances en août** to take one's holiday in August; **j'ai encore dix jours de vacances à prendre** I still have ten days' holiday to take; **être en vacances** to be on holiday; *(du Parlement)* to be in recess; **partir en vacances** to go away on holiday; **un jour de vacance(s)** a (day's) holiday; **colonie de vacances** holiday camp; **vacances en camping** camping holiday; **vacances en circuit** multi-centre holiday; **vacances judiciaires** *(des tribunaux)* vacation, recess; **vacances studieuses** educational holiday, study holiday; *Fam* **il part? très bien, ça me fera des vacances!** he's going? great, that will be as good as a holiday for me!

2 *(d'un poste)* vacancy; **la v. du pouvoir a eu des conséquences désastreuses** there being no one in power has had disastrous consequences; **il n'y aura pas de v. du pouvoir** there will be a smooth transition of control; **qui assurera les fonctions de président pendant la v. du poste?** who will take over the president's responsibilities during the interregnum?; **pendant la v. du siège** while the seat is empty; **une élection provoquée par la v. du siège** an election made necessary because the seat became vacant

3 *Jur (d'une succession)* abeyance **4** *Litt (de l'esprit)* emptiness

> Il faut noter que le terme anglais **vacancy** ne signifie jamais **congé**.

vacancier, -ière [vakɑ̃sje, -jɛr] N holidaymaker, *Am* vacationer, vacationist; **l'afflux des vacanciers** the influx of holidaymakers

vacant [vakɑ̃] ADJ **1** *(maison etc)* vacant, unoccupied; *(chaire d'université)* vacant; **poste v.** vacancy **2** *Jur* **succession vacante** estate in abeyance **3** *Litt (regard)* vacant; *(mains)* idle

vacarme [vakarm] NM uproar, din, racket; **faire du v.** to create *or* make an uproar, *Fam* to kick up a row

vacataire [vakatɛr] N short-term worker; *(remplaçant)* short-term replacement, stand-in; **c'est une v.** she's on a short-term *or* temporary contract

vacation [vakasjɔ̃] NF **1** *Jur (de juge, d'expert etc)* sitting, session **2** *(dans une vente aux enchères)* day's sale **3** *Jur* **vacations** *(tarif) (d'un avocat etc)* fees; *(arrêt) (des tribunaux)* vacation, recess **4** *(tâche)* session, shift; **être payé à la v.** to be paid by the session *or* shift; **faire des vacations** to work on a short-term basis

vacature [vakatyr] NF *Belg Admin (poste vacant)* vacancy

vaccin [vaksɛ̃] NM vaccine; **v. antivariolique/contre la coqueluche** smallpox/whooping cough vaccine; **plume à v.** vaccine point; **injection du v.** vaccine injection; *Fig* **le meilleur v. contre la paresse** the best antidote to laziness

vaccinable [vaksinabl] ADJ able to be vaccinated *or* inoculated

vaccinal, -ale, -aux, -ales [vaksinal, -o] ADJ vaccine, vaccinal; **complications vaccinales** complications following vaccination; **contamination d'origine vaccinale** contamination originating in a vaccine; **essais vaccinaux** vaccine tests; **préparation vaccinale** vaccine

vaccination [vaksinasjɔ̃] NF vaccination, inoculation; **v. obligatoire** compulsory vaccination; **v. contre la coqueluche** vaccination against whooping cough, whooping cough vaccination; **v. préventive/curative** protective/curative inoculation

vaccine [vaksin] NF **1** *Vét* cowpox, *Spéc* vaccinia **2** *Méd* inoculated cowpox

vacciner [vaksine] VT *Méd* to vaccinate, to inoculate (**contre** against, for); **se faire v.** to get vaccinated *or* inoculated (**contre** against); *Fig* **être vacciné contre les désagréments du métier/les voyages organisés** to be immune to the drawbacks of the job/package holidays; **pas question que je retombe amoureux, je suis vacciné!** there's no way I'm ever falling in love again, I've had enough to last me a lifetime!

vachard [vaʃar] ADJ *Fam* rotten, mean, nasty

vache [vaʃ] NF **1** *(animal)* cow; **lait/fromage de v.** cow's milk/cheese; *Fam* **retrouver le plancher des vaches** to be back on dry land *or* terra firma; *Fam* **parler français comme une v. espagnole** to murder *or* torture the French language; *Fam* **manger de la v. enragée** to have a hard time of it; **coup de pied en v.** stab in the back; **nœud de v.** granny knot; *Prov* **chacun son métier, les vaches seront bien gardées** the cobbler should stick to his

last; *Fam* **il pleut comme v. qui pisse** it's bucketing (down), *très Fam* it's pissing down; *Vét* **la maladie de la v. folle** mad cow disease

2 *Fam (insulte) (homme)* swine, sod; *(femme)* cow, bitch; **quelle v.!** what a swine/bitch!; **ah les vaches, ils sont partis sans moi!** the rotten lot, they left without me!; **regarde-moi cette grosse v.!** look at that fat cow!

3 *Fam (interjection)* **la v., qu'est-ce qu'il fait froid!** God, it's so cold!; **la v., tu as vu avec quelle vitesse ça court!** wow! have you seen the speed it's going at?

4 *Arg* policeman; **les vaches** the cops, the fuzz, the pigs; **mort aux vaches!** kill the pigs! **5** *(cuir)* cowhide; **valise en v.** leather suitcase

ADJ *Fam* rotten, nasty; **elle a été v. avec lui** she was rotten to him

N *Fam* **un v. de mec** a *or* one hell of a guy; **une v. de surprise** a *or* one hell of a surprise

▸▸ **v. à eau** (canvas) water carrier; **v. grasse:** *Fig Fam* **finies, les vaches grasses!** the good days are over!; **notre période de vaches grasses est terminée** we've had our years of plenty; **v. à lait** *Agr* dairy cow; *Fig* milch cow; *Mktg (produit)* cash cow; **j'en ai assez de jouer les vaches à lait!** I'm fed up forking out for everybody!; **v. laitière** dairy cow; **v. maigre:** *Fig Fam* **connaître une période de vaches maigres** to go through a lean period; *Zool* **v. marine** sea cow

vachement [vaʃmɑ̃] ADV *Fam* **c'est v. difficile** it's damned *or* bloody difficult; **c'est v. bien** it's bloody good; **il a v. vieilli** he's got a helluva lot older-looking; **elle a v. changé** she's changed a helluva lot

vacher, -ère [vaʃe, -ɛr] N cowherd, f cowgirl

vacherie [vaʃri] NF *Fam (action)* dirty trick; *(remarque)* nasty remark; **elle lui a fait/dit une v.** she played a dirty trick on him/made a nasty remark to him; **il est d'une v. terrible** he's a really nasty customer, he's rotten to the core; **v. de voiture!** bloody *or* damn car!

vacherin [vaʃrɛ̃] NM *Culin* **1** *(fromage)* vacherin cheese **2 v. (glacé)** = meringue with cream, ice cream and fruit

vachette [vaʃɛt] NF **1** *(animal)* young cow, heifer **2** *(cuir)* calfskin; **sac/chaussures en v.** calfskin bag/shoes

vacillant [vasijɑ̃] ADJ **1** *(table etc)* unsteady, wobbly; *(flamme etc)* flickering; *(main)* unsteady, shaky; *(allure etc)* uncertain, staggering; **v. de fatigue** staggering *or* reeling with tiredness **2** *(esprit etc)* wavering, indecisive, vacillating; *(santé)* failing

vacillation [vasijasjɔ̃] NF, **vacillement** [vasijmɑ̃] NM **1** unsteadiness, shakiness; *(d'une flamme)* flickering; *(d'un lustre)* swaying **2** *(hésitation)* vacillation, shillyshallying

vaciller [vasije] VI **1** *(chanceler)* to be unsteady (on one's feet), to sway; **il vacille sur ses jambes** *(parce qu'il est vieux)* he's shaky on his legs; *(parce qu'il est ivre, blessé)* he's staggering; **tout vacillait autour de moi** everything was swimming around me; **il s'avança en vacillant vers la porte** he staggered towards the door **2** *(d'une flamme, lumière)* to flicker **3** *(hésiter)* to vacillate, to waver **4** *(faiblir)* to falter; **sa raison/santé vacille** his mind/health is failing *or* faltering

va-comme-je-te-pousse (à la) [alavakɔmʃtəpus] ADV *Fam* any old how *or* way

vacuité [vakɥite] NF vacuity, vacuousness; *(de paroles)* emptiness, inanity

vacuole [vakɥɔl] NF *Biol* vacuole

vacuum [vakɥɔm] NM vacuum

vade-mecum [vademekɔm] NM INV handbook, companion, vade-mecum

vadrouille [vadruj] NF **1** *Fam (balade)* ramble, saunter; **partir** *ou* **aller en v.** to roam *or* rove *or* wander about; **ils sont encore partis en v.** they're still out gallivanting; **il est rarement à son bureau, il est toujours en v.** he's hardly ever at his desk, he's always wandering around somewhere **2** *Can* long-handled mop **3** *Naut* (deck) swab

vadrouiller [vadruje] VI *Fam* to roam *or* rove *or* wander about

vadrouilleur, -euse [vadrujœr, -øz] N *Fam* rover, wanderer

va-et-vient [vaevjɛ̃] NM INV **1** *(mouvement)* backward and forward motion; **faire le v. entre** to go to and fro *or* back and forth between; *(d'un bateau)* to go to and fro between, to ply between; **faire le v. entre Paris et Lyon** to go to and fro *or* to shuttle back and forth between Paris and Lyons; **(porte) v.** swing door **2** *(de personnes etc)* coming(s) and going(s), toing(s) and froing(s) **3** *Élec* two-way wiring (system); **(commutateur) v.** two-way switch **4** *Tech* reciprocation

vagabond, -onde [vagabɔ̃, -ɔ̃d] ADJ *(vie etc)* wandering, roving, roaming; *Fig* **avoir l'humeur vagabonde** to have itchy feet ▪ N *Péj* vagrant, tramp; *Litt (voyageur)* wanderer, vagabond; **les vagabonds seront arrêtés** vagrants will be arrested

vagabondage [vagabɔ̃daʒ] NM *(d'un clochard etc)* wandering(s), *Péj* vagrancy; **arrêté pour v.** arrested for vagrancy; **les vagabondages de l'imagination** the wanderings of the imagination; *Admin* **v. spécial** living on immoral earnings

vagabonder [vagabɔ̃de] VI to rove, to roam, to wander (about); *Fig (de ses pensées, son imagination)* to wander, to stray

vagin [vaʒɛ̃] NM vagina

vaginal, -ale, -aux, -ales [vaʒinal, -o] ADJ vaginal

vaginite [vaʒinit] NF *Méd* vaginitis

vagir [vaʒir] VI *(d'un nouveau-né)* to cry, to wail; *(d'un animal)* to squeak, to whimper; *(du lièvre)* to squeal; *(du crocodile)* to bark

vagissant [vaʒisɑ̃] ADJ *(bébé)* crying, wailing; *(animal)* squeaking, whimpering; *(lièvre)* squealing; *(crocodile)* barking

vagissement [vaʒismɑ̃] NM *(d'un bébé)* cry, wail(ing); *(d'un animal)* squeak(ing), whimper(ing); *(d'un lièvre)* squeal(ing); *(d'un crocodile)* bark(ing)

vague¹ [vag] NF **1** *aussi Fig* wave; **une v. a balayé le pont** a wave washed over the deck; **plonger dans les vagues** to dive into the waves; *Fig* **v. d'enthousiasme/de tendresse/de violence/de colère** wave *or* surge of enthusiasm/of tenderness/of violence/of anger; *Fig* **faire des vagues** to make waves, to rock the boat; **être dans le creux de la v.** to be down in the dumps, to be in the doldrums; **v. de vente** sales wave **2** *(ondulations) (de chevelure, de dunes)* wave; *(motif décoratif)* wavy pattern **3** *Littér etc*

nouvelle v. new wave; **les cinéastes (de la) nouvelle v.** film-makers of the new wave, new-wave film-makers

▸▸**v. de chaleur** heatwave; **v. de fond** groundswell; *Fig* groundswell (of opinion); **l'épidémie a frappé le pays telle une v. de fond** the epidemic struck the country like a tidal wave; **v. de froid** cold spell *or* snap

vague² ADJ **1** *(flou, imprécis) (savoir, impression, sentiment, geste etc)* vague; *(souvenir)* vague, dim; **des formes vagues** undefined *or* indistinct shapes; **elle est restée très v. sur ses intentions** she was very vague about her intentions; **j'ai la v. impression que …** I have a vague impression *or* feeling that …; **quelque v. écrivain** some writer or other; **elle dit avoir un v. diplôme en comptabilité** she claims to have some sort *or* kind of diploma in accounting; **regarder qn d'un air v.** to look vacantly at sb **2** *Anat* **nerf v.** vagus (nerve)

▪ NM **1** *(imprécision)* vagueness, indefiniteness; **rester dans le v.** to be vague *or* noncommittal; **reste dans le v.** keep it vague, be as vague as possible; **avoir du v. à l'âme** to be melancholy; **dans un moment de v. à l'âme** in a moment of melancholy **2** *(vide)* space; **fixer les yeux dans le v.** to gaze into space; **regard perdu dans le v.** faraway *or* far-off *or* distant look

vaguelette [vaglɛt] NF wavelet

vaguement [vagmɑ̃] ADV vaguely; **on la reconnaît v. sur la photo** you can just make her out in the photo; **c'est ce que j'ai v. compris** that's what I more or less understood; **répondre v.** to give a vague answer; **je me sentais v. coupable** I felt vaguely guilty, I felt in some vague way that I was to blame

vaguemestre [vagmɛstr] NM *Mil* post orderly; *Naut* postman

vaguer [vage] VI *Litt* to wander, to roam (about); **laisser v. ses pensées** to let one's thoughts wander

vahiné [vaine] NF Tahitian woman

vaillamment [vajamɑ̃] ADV valiantly, bravely

vaillance [vajɑ̃s] NF valour, *Am* valor, bravery, courage; *Mil* gallantry; **supporter une épreuve avec v.** to face an ordeal with courage; **faire preuve de v.** to show courage

vaillant [vajɑ̃] ADJ **1** *(en forme)* **être v.** to be in good health; **je ne me sens pas v.** I feel a bit under the weather **2** **n'avoir pas un sou v.** to be (stony) broke, not to have a penny to one's name **3** *(courageux)* valiant, brave, courageous; *(cœur)* stout; *Mil* gallant

vain [vɛ̃] ADJ **1** *(qui n'aboutit à rien) (démarche, entreprise)* futile; *(efforts)* vain, fruitless, futile; **en v.** in vain, vainly; **j'ai essayé en v. de le convaincre** I tried in vain to convince him; **c'est en v. qu'elle le lui a demandé** she asked him for it in vain, she asked him for it but to no avail **2** *(vide de sens) (plaisirs)* vain, empty; *(promesse)* hollow, empty; *(espoirs)* vain; *(craintes)* groundless, unfounded; *(regrets)* needless; **ce n'étaient pas là de vaines paroles** these were no empty *or* no idle words; **je te dis qu'elle est dangereuse, et ce n'est pas un v. mot!** I tell you she's dangerous, and it's no empty claim *or* and I know what I'm talking about! **3** **vaine pâture** common (land) **4** *Litt (personne)* vain, conceited

vaincre [vɛ̃kr] *(prp* vainquant; *pp* vaincu; *pr ind* je vaincs, il vainc, n. vainquons; *impf* je vainquais; *p hist* je vainquis; *fu* je vaincrai) VT **1** *(l'emporter sur) (adversaire)* to conquer, to defeat, *surtout Litt* to vanquish **2** *Sport etc (concurrent)* to beat; **v. qn aux échecs** to beat sb at chess **3** *Fig (maladie, difficulté etc)* to overcome, to master, to conquer; *(problème, complexes, colère, impulsions, pas-*

sions) to overcome; **v. une résistance** to overcome resistance ▪ VI **il faut v. ou mourir** we must do or die

vaincu, -ue [vɛ̃ky] ADJ beaten, defeated; **être v. d'avance** to be beaten before one starts; **pourquoi partir v. d'avance?** why be so defeatist?; **s'avouer v.** to admit defeat ▪ N defeated man, *f* woman; **attitude/comportement de v.** defeatist attitude/behaviour

vainement [vɛnmɑ̃] ADV vainly, in vain; **je lui en ai v. parlé** I spoke to him about it in vain *or* to no avail

vainqueur [vɛ̃kœr] NM **1** *Sport etc* winner; *Boxe* **être v. par K.O./aux points** to win by a knock-out/on points; **le v. de l'Annapurna** the conqueror of Annapurna; **sortir v. d'une lutte** to emerge the victor of a battle *or* victorious from a battle **2** *Mil* victor, conqueror, *surtout Litt* vanquisher

▪ ADJ M conquering, victorious, *surtout Litt* vanquishing; **air/sourire v.** triumphant look/smile

vair [vɛr] NM vair; **pantoufle de v.** *(dans Cendrillon)* glass slipper

vairon [vɛrɔ̃] ADJ M **avoir les yeux vairons** to have different-coloured eyes

▪ NM *(poisson)* minnow

vaisseau, -eaux [vɛso] NM **1** *Anat, Bot* vessel, canal, duct; **v. sanguin** blood vessel **2** *Archit (d'une église)* nave; *(d'un édifice)* body, hall **3** *Naut Vieilli* ship, vessel; **v. à voiles** sailing vessel; **v. de guerre** warship; **v. amiral** flagship; *Fig* **brûler ses vaisseaux** to burn one's boats **4** *Arch (récipient)* vessel, receptacle

▸▸*Bible* **v. d'élection** chosen vessel; **v. spatial** spaceship

vaisselier [vɛsəlje] NM *(meuble)* dresser

vaisselle [vɛsɛl] NF dishes *pl*, crockery; *(de céramique, de porcelaine)* china; **v. de porcelaine** porcelain, china; **v. plate** (gold/silver) plate; **acheter de la v.** to buy some (china) tableware *or* crockery; **faire** *ou* **laver la v.** to do the washing-up, to do the dishes, *Br* to wash up; *Fam* **je dois finir ma v.** I must finish (the) washing-up *or* the dishes; **machine à laver la v.** dishwasher; **liquide (de) v.** washing-up *or Am* dish-washing liquid; **eau de v.** dishwater; *Fig Fam Péj* **cette bière/soupe, c'est de l'eau de v.** this beer/soup is like dishwater

VAL [val] NM *(abrév* **véhicule automatique léger)** = automatic driverless train

val [val] NM *Géog* (narrow) valley; *(pl* **vals,** *except in the following phrase)* **par monts et par vaux** [vo] up hill and down dale

valable [valabl] ADJ **1** *(valide) (titre, raison, idée)* valid; *(excuse)* valid, legitimate; **billet v. pour deux mois** ticket valid for two months; **votre titre de transport n'est pas v.** your ticket is not valid; **c'est un argument tout à fait v.** it's a perfectly valid *or* acceptable argument; **ce qui est v. pour vous ne l'est pas pour elle** what goes for you doesn't go for her; **promesse toujours v.** promise that still holds good; **ma proposition est toujours v.** my offer still stands **2** *(de qualité) Pol* **pouvoir s'adresser à un interlocuteur v.** to be able to speak to an authorized representative; **devenir un partenaire v. dans l'UE** to become a fully-fledged partner in the EU; **un roman v.** a good novel

> Do not confuse with **valide**.

valablement [valablamɑ̃] ADV validly; **être v. autorisé à qch/à faire qch** to have the necessary authority for sth/to do sth; **c'est ce qu'on lui a v. reproché** this is what he was accused of, and rightly so; **pour pouvoir être à même de traiter v. ce problème** in order to be able to deal with this problem satisfactorily

valdinguer [valdɛ̃ge] **VI** *Fam* to fall flat on one's face; **la bouilloire est allée v. contre le placard** the kettle went flying against the cupboard; **envoyer v. ses affaires** to send everything flying; *Fig* **tout envoyer v.** to pack *or* jack it all in; **envoyer v. qn** to tell sb where to go

Valence [valɑ̃s] **NF 1** *(ville d'Espagne)* Valencia **2** *(ville de France)* Valence

valence [valɑ̃s] **NF** *Chimie* valency, *Am* valence

valenciennes [valɑ̃sjɛn] **NF INV** Valenciennes lace

valériane [valerjan] **NF** *Bot* valerian

valet [valɛ] **NM 1** *Cartes* jack, knave **2** *(domestique)* **v. (de chambre)** manservant; **je ne suis pas ton v.** I'm not your servant *or* slave; *Prov* **tel maître, tel v.** like master, like man **3** *Menuis etc* clamp **4** *(d'un miroir etc)* support, rest, stand **5** *Hist* varlet, page ▸▸*Chasse* **v. de chiens** whipper-in; **v. d'écurie** groom; **v. de ferme** farmhand; **v. de nuit** valet; **v. de pied** footman

valetaille [valtɑj] **NF** *Fam Péj* serfs

valétudinaire [valetydiner] **ADJ, N** *Litt* valetudinarian; **vieillard v.** elderly invalid

---

VALEUR [valœr]

value **1, 2, 4, 5** = worth **1, 2** = meaning **2** = shares **3** = securities **3** = time **4** = equivalent **5** = valour **7**

NF 1 *(prix)* value, worth; **avoir de la v.** to be valuable; **article de v.** article of value, valuable article; **objets de v.** valuables; **de peu de v.** of little value; **sans v.** worthless, of no value; **bijou de grande v.** jewel of great value, very valuable jewel; **d'une v. inestimable** priceless; **des marchandises d'une v. de 5000 euros** goods to the value of 5,000 euros; **v. sentimentale** sentimental value; **il ne cesse de prendre de la v.** it keeps going up in value, its value is constantly increasing

2 *(qualité, mérite)* value, worth; *(importance) (d'un mot)* value; **livre de grande v.** book of considerable merit; **cela n'a pas grande v.** it's not worth much; **renseignements sans v.** worthless information; **ce document n'a aucune v. légale** this document is not legally binding *or* has no standing in law; **tu sais quelle v. j'accorde à ton avis** you know how much I value your opinion; **j'attache beaucoup de v. à la présentation** I set great store by presentation; **votre argument n'est pas sans v.** your argument is not without its merits; **homme de v.** *(doué)* man of real ability, talented man; *(de mérite)* man of merit; **la v. n'attend pas le nombre des années** good is good, no matter how young you are; **estimer qn à sa juste v.** to judge sb at his/her true value *or* worth; **elle n'a pas conscience de sa propre v.** she doesn't fully appreciate her own value *or* worth; **mettre en v.** *(quelque chose)* to show to advantage; *(ses yeux)* to highlight, to bring out; **mettre un mot en v.** to emphasize a word, to give importance to a word; **mettre une terre en v.** to develop a piece of land; **mise en v. d'un terrain** development of a site; **cette couleur ne met pas du tout son bronzage en v.** that colour does nothing to show off her tan; **elle sait se mettre en v.** she knows how to show herself off to the best advantage; **elle était très en v. avec sa robe bleue** her blue dress was very flattering; **c'est là que le terme prend toute sa v.** that's when the term takes on its full meaning; **il faudra cinq ans à ce vin pour prendre toute sa v.** the wine will be at its best five years from now

3 *Bourse* **valeurs (boursières)** securities, shares; **valeurs bancaires** bank shares; **valeurs cotées** *ou* **de Bourse** quoted securities; **valeurs émises** securities issued

4 *Mus (d'une note)* time (value), length; *(de carte)*, *Math (d'une grandeur etc)* value

5 *(équivalent)* equivalent; **ajouter la v. de deux tasses de lait** add the equivalent of two cups of milk

6 *(morale)* value; **valeurs sociales/morales** social/moral values; **jugement de v.** value judgement; **avoir le sens des valeurs** to have a sense of values; **selon son échelle de valeurs** according to his scale of values

7 *Litt (courage)* valour, *Am* valor; **homme de v.** man of courage; **v. militaire** gallantry ▸▸**v. d'achat** purchase value; *Compta* **v. actualisée** present value; *Compta* **v. actuelle** current value; **v. actuelle nette** current net value; *Écon* **v. ajoutée** added value; **à haute v. ajoutée** high value-added; **v. assurable** insurable value; **v. assurée** insured value; **v. de bilan** book value; *Compta* **v. bilantielle** balance-sheet value; **v. en Bourse** stock market value; **v. brute** gross value; **v. en capital** capital assets; *Fin* **v. compensée** cleared value; **v. comptable** book value; **v. comptable nette** net book value; **v. déclarée** declared value; **colis chargé avec v. déclarée cent euros** parcel insured for one hundred euros; **v. en douane** customs value, value for customs purposes; **v. d'échange** exchange value; *Fin* **v. à l'échéance** maturity value; *Fin* **v. à l'encaissement** value for collection; **valeurs immobilières** real property shares; *Compta* **v. d'inventaire** balance sheet value, break-up value; *Banque* **v. jour** same-day value; **v. locative** rental value; **v. marchande** market(able) value; **valeurs mobilières** stocks and shares, transferable securities; **valeurs (mobilières) de placement** marketable securities; **valeurs négociables** marketable securities; **v. nominale** *(d'une obligation)* par value; *(d'une action)* nominal value; **valeurs nominatives** registered securities; *Bourse* **v. non cotée** unlisted security; **v. d'origine** original value; **valeurs passives** liabilities; **v. perçue** perceived value; **valeurs de père de famille** blue chip stock; **valeurs de portefeuille** portfolio securities; **v. de premier ordre** blue chip; **v. de rachat** *(d'une police)* surrender value; **valeurs réalisables** realizable *or* marketable securities; **v. de rendement** *(d'une entreprise)* profitability value; **v. de reprise** trade-in allowance; **v. à la revente** resale value; **valeurs à revenu fixe** fixed income securities; **valeurs à revenu variable** floating rate *or* variable-rate securities; **valeurs du second marché** unlisted securities; **valeurs des sociétés industrielles** industrials; **valeurs spéculatives** *ou* **de spéculation** speculative securities; *Bourse* **v. temporelle** time value; **valeurs à terme** futures; **valeurs de tout repos** gilt-edged securities; **v. d'usage** value as a going concern; **valeurs vedettes** glamour stock; **v. vénale** fair market value

valeureusement [valørøzmɑ̃] **ADV** *Litt* gallantly, bravely, valorously

valeureux, -euse [valørø, -øz] **ADJ** *Litt (dans une bataille)* gallant, valorous

validation [validasjɔ̃] **NF 1** *(d'un titre de transport, d'élections, d'un mariage etc)* validation; *(d'une loi)* ratifying; *(d'un document etc)* authentication **2** *Ordinat* validation

valide [valid] **ADJ 1** *(contrat etc)* valid **2** *(personne)* fit, able-bodied; *(membre)* functioning

---

Il faut noter que l'adjectif anglais **valid** signifie le plus souvent **valable**. Do not confuse with **valable**.

---

validement [validmɑ̃] **ADV** validly

valider [valide] **VT** *(élection, mariage)* to validate; *(contrat etc)* to ratify; *(document)* to authenticate; *Ordinat (option)* to confirm; *(cellule, case etc)* to select; **(faire) v. son titre de transport** *(par un contrôleur)* to have one's ticket stamped; *(dans une machine)* to stamp one's ticket

validité [validite] **NF** *(d'un contrat, d'un passeport, d'une opinion etc)* validity; **durée de v. d'un billet** period of validity of a ticket; **établir la v. d'un testament** to prove a will

valise [valiz] **NF 1** (suit)case; **faire sa v./ses valises** to pack one's bag/one's bags; **la v. diplomatique** the diplomatic bag *or Am* pouch **2** *(sous les yeux)* bag **3** *Can Fam (personne crédule)* dupe, gullible person; *(personne naïve)* simpleton

vallée [vale] **NF** valley; **dans la V. de la Loire/du Rhône** in the Loire/Rhône valley; **v. sèche** *ou* **morte** dried-up valley; **gens de la v.** *(pour les montagnards)* lowlanders; **descendre dans la v.** to go down into the valley; *Litt* **cette v. de larmes** this vale of tears

vallon [valɔ̃] **NM** small valley; *(écossais)* glen

vallonné [valɔne] **ADJ** *(région)* undulating, hilly

vallonnement [valɔnmɑ̃] **NM** undulation

valoche [valɔʃ] **NF** *Fam* case, bag; *Fig Fam* **avoir des valoches sous les yeux** to have bags under one's eyes

---

VALOIR [valwar] (*prp* **valant**; *pp* **valu**; *pr ind* **je vaux, il vaut, n. valons, ils valent**; *pr sub* **je vaille, n. valions, ils vaillent**; *impf* **je valais**; *p hist* **je valus**; *fu* **je vaudrai**)

VI to be worth **1** = to cost **1** = to be equivalent to **2**
VPR to be as good as
VT to earn **1**

VI 1 *(coûter)* to be worth; **une maison qui vaut 50 000 euros** house worth 50,000 euros; **un bijou pareil vaut bien 10 000 euros** a piece of jewellery like that must cost a good 10,000 euros; **ça vaut cher** it's expensive; **ne vaut pas cher** it's cheap *or* inexpensive; **c'est tout ce que ça vaut** that's all it's worth; **ça ne vaut pas plus que ça** it's not worth more than that, that's all it's worth; **ne pas v. grand-chose** not to be worth much; **il ne vaut pas grand-chose, il ne vaut pas cher** he's not much good, he's not up to much; **son explication ne vaut rien** his explanation is worthless *or* useless; **cela ne vaut rien** that's no good; **ce climat ne vous vaut rien** this climate is bad for you *or* doesn't suit you; **les repas lourds ne me valent rien** heavy meals don't agree with me; **prends mon avis pour ce qu'il vaut** take my advice for what it's worth; **cela ne me dit rien qui vaille** that doesn't sound good to me; **rien ne vaut un bon petit déjeuner** there's nothing like a good breakfast; **à v. sur (une somme)** on account of (a sum); **à v. sur qn** on *or* for account of sb; **payer dix euros à v.** to pay ten euros on account

2 *(correspondre à)* to be equivalent to; **un euro vaut cent centimes** a euro is equivalent *or* equal to a hundred centimes; **une livre vaut 2 euros** a pound is worth *or* equivalent to *or* equal to two euros; **c'est une façon qui en vaut une autre** it's as good a way as any (other); **ils se valent tous** there's not much to choose between them, they're all pretty much the same; **ça ne vaut pas ce qui m'est arrivé l'autre jour** that's nothing to what happened to me the other day; **l'un vaut (bien) l'autre** one is (just) as good/bad as the other, there's nothing to choose between them; **il ne vaut pas mieux que son frère** he's no better than his brother; **il ne**

vaut pas son frère he can't compare with his brother, *Fam* he isn't a patch on his brother **3 faire v. qch** to make the most of sth; **monture qui fait v. la pierre** setting that shows off the stone (to (good) advantage); **faire v. ses opinions** to command respect for one's opinions; **faire v. ses droits** to assert one's rights; **faire v. son bon droit** to vindicate one's rights; **faire v. ses raisons** to put forward one's reasons; **j'ai fait v. que ...** I pointed out *or* urged that ...; **pour avoir le poste, il a fait v. ses dix ans d'expérience** to get the job, he stressed his ten years' experience; **faire v. son argent** to invest one's money profitably *or* to good account; **faire v. une terre** to farm an estate

4 *(mériter)* to be worth, to deserve, to merit; **un service en vaut un autre** one good turn deserves another; **le livre vaut d'être lu** the book is worth reading; **cela vaut la peine de faire le voyage, cela vaut le déplacement** it's worth making the journey; **cela ne vaut pas le voyage** it's not worth the journey, it's not worth a special trip; **je viendrai si cela en vaut la peine** I'll come if it's worth (my) while *or* worth the trouble *or* worth it; **cela ne vaut pas la peine de s'y arrêter** there's no point (in) dwelling on it; *Fam* **ça vaut le coup** it's worth a try; *Fam* **ça ne vaut pas le coup** it isn't worth the trouble

vt 1 v. qch à qn to earn sb sth; **cela ne m'a valu que des soucis** all it brought me was trouble; **cette action lui a valu d'être décoré** this act won him a decoration; **qu'est-ce qui me vaut cet honneur?** to what do I owe this honour?

2 vaille que vaille at all costs, come what may

v impers **il vaut mieux** *ou* **il vaudrait mieux rester à la maison** it's *or* it would be better to stay at home; **mieux vaudrait** *ou* **il vaudrait mieux ne pas vous en mêler** you'd better not interfere, it would be better if you didn't interfere; **il vaut mieux qu'il en soit ainsi** it is better that way; **il vaut mieux que vous restiez** you had better stay, it would be better if you stayed; **il vaut mieux** *ou* **mieux vaut partir que de rester** it's better to go than to stay; **ça vaut mieux comme ça** it's better that way; *Prov* **mieux vaut tard que jamais** better late than never; **autant vaut rester ici** we may as well stay here; **choses qu'il vaut autant ne pas rappeler** things best forgotten; **il** *ou* **ça ne vaut pas la peine de les mentionner** they're not worth mentioning; **et ça vaut pour tout le monde** and that goes for everyone **SEE GRAMMAR B30**

vpr se valoir **tous les métiers se valent** one job is as good as another; **ils se valent** one is (just) as good/bad as the other, there's nothing to choose between them; *Fam* **ça se vaut** it's the same either way, it's six of one and half a dozen of the other

valorisant [valɔrizɑ̃] **adj** image-enhancing; **la situation des femmes au foyer n'est guère valorisante** people tend to have a poor opinion of women who work in the home

valorisation [valɔrizasjɔ̃] **nf** *Com, Fin* increase in value; *Compta (d'un inventaire)* valuation; **... ce qui conduira à la v. de vos investissements** ... which will increase *or* enhance the value of your investments; **cela a beaucoup contribué à la v. des femmes au foyer** it did a lot to improve the image of women in the home

valoriser [valɔrize] **vt** *Com, Fin etc* to increase the value of; **v. une région** to develop the economy *or* to increase the value of a region; **v. qn** to improve sb's image *or* standing; **vpr se valoriser** *Com, Fin etc* to increase in value; **région/secteur qui se valorise** region/industry which is going through a period of growth, up-and-coming region/industry

valse [vals] **nf** waltz; **v. de Vienne/Chopin** Viennese/Chopin waltz; **faire un tour de v.** to waltz round the room; *Fig Fam* **la v. du personnel/des ministres** constant changes of staff/the ministerial merry-go-round; *Com* **v. des étiquettes** constant price rises; **v. des prix** spiralling prices; *Fig* **v.-hésitation** pussyfooting, shillyshallying

valser [valse] **vi** to waltz; **la voiture est allée v. contre le mur** the car went careering *or* hurtling into the wall; **faire v. qn** to waltz with sb; *Fig Fam* to keep sb on the hop; *Fig* **faire v. l'argent** to spend money like water; *Fig Fam* **envoyer v. qn** *(le projeter)* to send sb flying; *(le renvoyer)* to send sb packing, to show sb the door; **il m'a envoyé v. contre le mur** he sent me flying into the wall; *Fig Fam* **envoyer v. qch** to send sth flying; **j'ai envie de tout envoyer v.!** I feel like packing it all in *or Br* jacking it all in *or Am* chucking everything

valseur, -euse [valsœr, -øz] **n** *(danseur)* waltzer

    nm *Fam (postérieur)* bum, *Am* fanny

    nfpl **valseuses** *très Fam (testicules)* balls, nuts, *Br* bollocks

valve [valv] **nf** valve; *Tech* **v. d'arrêt** check valve; *Anat* **v. cardiaque** cardiac valve; **v. de chambre à air** tyre valve; *Tech* **v. de compensation** compensating valve; **v. à** *ou* **de dépression** vacuum valve; **v. de gonflage** *(d'un pneu)* tyre valve; *Tech* **v. à inertie** inertia valve; *Tech* **v. modulatrice** modulator valve; *Tech* **v. papillon** butterfly valve; *Tech* **v. de purge** bleed valve; *Électron* **v. redresseuse** rectifying valve

valvulaire [valvylɛr] **adj** valvular

valvule [valvyl] **nf** *Biol* valvule; *Anat* valve, valvule

vamp [vɑ̃p] **nf inv** vamp; **faire la v.** to act the vamp; **prendre des airs de v.** to put on a vampish look

    adj inv vampish; **habillée très v.** dressed very vampishly

vamper [vɑ̃pe] **vt** *Fam* to vamp, to seduce

vampire [vɑ̃pir] **nm 1** *Myth* vampire **2** *Fig Vieilli (personne qui s'enrichit aux dépens d'autrui)* extortionist, bloodsucker; *(assassin)* mass murderer **3** *Zool* vampire bat

vampiriser [vɑ̃pirize] **vt** to dominate (psychologically); **v. un enfant** to dominate a child

vampirisme [vɑ̃pirism] **nm** vampirism

VAN [veaɛn] **nf** *Compta (abrév* **valeur actuelle nette)** NPV, net present value

van¹ [vɑ̃] **nm** *Agr* winnowing basket

van² [van] **nm 1** *(fourgon à chevaux)* horsebox **2** *(camionnette)* van

vanadium [vanadjɔm] **nm** *Chimie* vanadium

vandale [vɑ̃dal] **n** vandal

vandaliser [vɑ̃dalize] **vt** to vandalize

vandalisme [vɑ̃dalism] **nm** vandalism

vandoise [vɑ̃dwaz] **nf** *(poisson)* dace

vanesse [vanɛs] **nf** **v. tortue** tortoiseshell butterfly

vanille [vanij] **nf** vanilla; **gousse de v.** vanilla pod; **glace à la v.** vanilla ice cream; **crème à la v.** vanilla custard

vanillé [vanije] **adj** vanilla(-flavoured *or Am* -flavored); **crème vanillée** vanilla custard; **sucre v.** vanilla sugar

vanillier [vanije] **nm** vanilla plant

vanité [vanite] **nf 1** *(orgueil)* vanity, conceit; **tirer v. de qch** to pride oneself on sth; **elle n'a pas à en tirer v.** it's nothing for her to boast about; **flatter la v. de qn** to flatter sb's vanity; **agir par v.** to act out of vanity **2** *(des plaisirs terrestres etc)* futility, emptiness, hollowness, *Litt* vanity

vaniteusement [vanitøzmɑ̃] **adv** conceitedly

vaniteux, -euse [vanitø, -øz] **adj** vain, conceited

    n c'est un v. he's (very) conceited

vanity-case, *pl* **vanity-cases** [vanitikɛz] **nm** vanity case

vannage [vanaʒ] **nm** *(du grain)* winnowing

vanne¹ [van] **nf 1** *Tech* sluice (gate), floodgate, water gate; **v. de décharge** overflow weir; *Tech* **v. manuelle** manual valve; *Tech, Fig* **ouvrir/mettre les vannes** to open/close the floodgates **2** *Tech etc* valve **3** *Naut* cock

vanne² **nf** *Fam (remarque blessante)* dig, jibe; **lancer** *ou* **faire des vannes** to make snide remarks; **envoyer** *ou* **lancer une v. à qn** to have a dig at sb

vanneau, -eaux [vano] **nm** *(oiseau)* lapwing, peewit; *Culin* **œufs de v.** plovers' eggs

vanner [vane] **vt 1** *Fam (fatiguer)* to wear out, to exhaust; **être (complètement) vanné** to be dead beat *or* all in **2** *(grain)* to winnow

vannerie [vanri] **nf 1** *(activité)* basketmaking, basketry **2** *(objets)* basketwork, wickerwork

vanneur, -euse [vanœr, -øz] **n** winnower

vannier [vanje] **nm** basket worker *or* maker

vantail, -aux [vɑ̃taj, -o] **nm** *(d'une porte, d'un volet, d'une vanne)* leaf; **porte à deux vantaux** folding door

vantard, -arde [vɑ̃tar, -ard] **adj** boasting, boastful, bragging, *Fam* loudmouthed

    n braggart, boaster, *Fam* loudmouth

vantardise [vɑ̃tardiz] **nf** *(caractère)* bragging, boastfulness; *(parole)* boast

vanter [vɑ̃te] **vt** to praise, to speak highly of, *Litt* to vaunt; *Fig* **v. sa marchandise** to blow one's own trumpet; **magazine qui vante les charmes de l'Écosse** magazine which sings the praises of Scotland

    vpr se vanter to boast, to brag; **ce n'est pas pour me v., mais ...** I don't mean to boast, but ...; **il n'y a pas de quoi se v.** there's nothing to boast about; **tu peux t'en vanté!** you kept that quiet *or* under your hat!; **se v. de qch/d'être ...** to pride oneself on sth/on being ...

Vanuatu [vanwatu] **n** Vanuatu

va-nu-pieds [vanypje] **n inv** tramp, beggar; *(enfant)* (street) urchin, ragamuffin

vapes [vap] **nfpl** *Fam* **être dans les v.** to be groggy; *(rêver)* to have one's head in the clouds; **je n'écoutais pas, j'étais dans les v.** I wasn't listening, I was miles away; **tomber dans les v.** to pass out, to faint

vapeur [vapœr] **nf 1 v. (d'eau)** steam, (water) vapour *or Am* vapor; **prendre des bains de v.** to take steam baths; **machine à v.** steam engine; **locomotive à v.** steam locomotive; **bateau à v.** steamer, steamship; **mettre la v.** to put steam on; *Fig* **nous avons dû mettre la v. pour finir à temps** we had to pull out all the stops to finish on time; **navire sous v.** ship under steam; **à toute v.** (at) full steam *or* speed, full steam ahead **2 v. d'essence/d'éther/d'alcool** petrol/ether/alcohol vapour; **flotter dans les vapeurs de l'alcool** to be high on the heady fumes of alcohol **3** *(brume)* haze, vapour **4** *Culin* **cuire des légumes à la v.** to steam vegetables; **faire la cuisine** *ou* **cuisiner à la v.** to steam food **5 vapeurs** *(du vin, d'essence etc)* fumes; *Méd, Arch* vapours; **avoir ses vapeurs** to have (a fit of) the vapours

    nm *Naut* steamer, steamship

vapocraquage [vapokrakaʒ] **nm** *Pétr* steam cracking

vapocraqueur [vapokrakœr] **nm** *Pétr* steam cracking plant

vaporeux, -euse [vapɔrø, -øz] **adj** *(atmo-*

sphère) steamy; *(idées etc)* hazy; *(robe)* flimsy; *Fig* **femme vaporeuse** sylph-like woman

vaporisateur [vapɔrizatœr] NM *(de parfum etc)* spray, atomizer; *Tech* vaporizer; *(de jardinage)* spray(er)

vaporisation [vapɔrizasjɔ̃] NF *(de parfum, engrais etc)* spraying; *Tech* vaporization; *Aut* **v. (du carburant)** (fuel) atomization

vaporiser [vapɔrize] VT **1** *(gazéifier)* to vaporize **2** *(liquide)* to spray; **v. ses cheveux de laque** to spray one's hair with lacquer
VPR **se vaporiser** to become vaporized, to vaporize

vaquer [vake] VI **1 v. à qch** to attend to sth; **v. aux soins du ménage** to see to the housework; **v. à ses affaires** *ou* **occupations** to go about *or* see to one's business **2** *(du Parlement, du tribunal)* to be on vacation *or* in recess, not to be sitting **3** *Vieilli (d'un poste)* to be vacant

varappe [varap] NF rock climbing; **faire de la v.** to rock-climb, to go rock climbing

varapper [varape] VI to rock-climb

varappeur, -euse [varapœr, -øz] N rock climber

varech [varɛk] NM wrack, seaweed, kelp, varec

vareuse [varøz] NF **1** *(de marin)* pea jacket *or* coat, reefer **2** *Mil* tunic **3** *(veste large)* loose-fitting jacket

variabilité [varjabilite] NF **1** *Biol, Gram etc* variability **2** *(de l'humeur, du temps)* changeableness

variable [varjabl] ADJ **1** *Biol, Gram, Math* variable **2** *(humeur etc)* changeable; *(baromètre)* unsteady; *(vitesse)* varying; *(temps)* changeable, unsettled; **être v.** to vary; **c'est très v.** it's very variable, it varies a lot
NM **le baromètre est au v.** the barometer is at change
NF *Math, Ordinat* variable; *Ordinat* **v. de mémoire** memory variable

variance [varjɑ̃s] NF variance

variant [varjɑ̃] NM *Méd* **nouveau v. de la maladie de Creutzfeldt-Jakob** new variant CJD

variante [varjɑ̃t] NF variant, variation

variateur [varjatœr] NM **v. d'intensité** *(d'une lampe électrique)* dimmer switch; **v. de vitesse** speed variator

variation [varjasjɔ̃] NF **1 v. du temps** change in the weather; **v. des températures/des prix** variation in temperature/prices; **v. du compas** compass error; **v. de l'opinion** change of opinion; **variations saisonnières** seasonal variations *or* fluctuations **2** *Mus* variation; **air avec variations** theme and variations

varice [varis] NF *Méd* varicose vein; **avoir des varices** to have varicose veins; **des bas anti-varices** support stockings

varicelle [varisɛl] NF *Méd* chickenpox, *Spéc* varicella; **avoir la v.** to have chickenpox

varié [varje] ADJ *(alimentation, paysage)* varied; *(échantillons)* varying, various; *(vocabulaire)* wide; *(nouvelles)* miscellaneous; *(existence)* varied, chequered; *Mus* **air v.** air with variations; *Phys* **mouvement v.** variable motion; **terrain v.** uneven *or* irregular terrain; *Culin* **hors-d'œuvre variés** selection of starters; **un travail très peu v.** a monotonous job, a job with little variety

varier [varje] *(impf, pr sub* **n. variions, vous variiez)** VT to vary; *(occupations etc)* to vary, to diversify; **v. son alimentation** to vary one's diet; *Fig Iron* **pour v. les plaisirs** by way of a pleasant change
VI to vary, to change; *Fin (des marchés)* to fluctuate; **v. dans ses réponses** to be inconsistent in one's replies; **les auteurs varient**

souvent authors often differ *or* vary; **les prix peuvent v. du simple au double** prices can vary by a factor of two; **leurs opinions varient sur ce point** they differ *or* they don't see eye to eye on this point; **v. de méthode** to vary one's methods

variété [varjete] NF **1** variety (**de** of); *(d'avis etc)* diversity, range; **manquer de v.** to lack variety; **la v. des paysages** the varying nature of the landscapes; **la v. des articles dans un magasin** the variety *or* range of articles in a shop; *Com* **grande v. de rayons** wide range of departments; **donner de la v. au menu** to vary the menu; **apporter de la v. à son alimentation** to vary one's diet **2** *TV* light entertainment, variety; *(musique)* easy listening; **spectacle de variétés** variety show; **émission de variétés** variety show *or* programme; **regarder les variétés à la télévision** to watch variety shows on television **3** *Biol (de fleur etc)* variety

variétoche [varjetɔʃ] NF *Fam* middle-of-the-road music

variole [varjɔl] NF *Méd* smallpox; **avoir la v.** to have smallpox; *Vét* **v. des vaches** cowpox

variolé [varjole] ADJ pockmarked

varioleux, -euse [varjolø, -øz] *Méd* ADJ *(boutons etc)* variolous
N smallpox victim

variqueux, -euse [varikø, -øz] ADJ *(veine etc)* varicose

varlet [varlɛ] NM *Arch* varlet, page

varlope [varlɔp] NF *Menuis* trying plane

Varsovie [varsɔvi] NF Warsaw; **les pays du Pacte de V.** the Warsaw Pact countries

vasculaire [vaskylɛr] ADJ vascular

vascularisation [vaskylarizasjɔ̃] NF *Méd* vascularization

vase¹ [vaz] NM vase; **v. à fleurs** flower vase; **v. à pied** vase with a stem, stemmed vase; **v. en cristal** crystal vase; **vivre en v. clos** to live in isolation *or* a vacuum
▶▶ *Élec, Phys* **vases communicants** communicating vessels; *Fig* **quand lui ça va, moi ça ne va pas, on est comme des vases communicants** when he's OK, I'm not, and vice versa, it's like a see-saw; **v. d'un élément de pile** battery jar; *Aut* **v. d'expansion** expansion tank; **v. de nuit** chamber pot; **v. poreux** porous cell

vase² NF mud, silt, ooze, sludge; **marais plein de v.** muddy swamp; **banc de v.** mudbank

vasectomie [vazɛktɔmi] NF *Chir* vasectomy

vaseline [vazlin] NF Vaseline®, petroleum jelly; *Pharm* **huile de v.** liquid paraffin

vaser [vaze] V IMPERS *Fam* to rain cats and dogs, *Br* to bucket down

vaseux, -euse [vazø, -øz] ADJ **1** *Fam (personne)* off-colour, *Am* off-color; **il a l'air v.** he looks a bit off-colour *or* under the weather; **des idées vaseuses** woolly ideas; **explication vaseuse** confused *or* muddled explanation; **une plaisanterie vaseuse** a pathetic joke **2** *(rivière)* muddy, silty, sludgy

vasistas [vazistɑs] NM fanlight

vasoconstricteur, -trice [vazokɔ̃striktœr, -tris] ADJ, NM *Anat* vasoconstrictor

vasodilatateur, -trice [vazodilatatœr, -tris] ADJ, NM *Anat* vasodilator

vasomoteur, -trice [vazomɔtœr, -tris] ADJ *Anat (nerf)* vasomotor

vasouillard [vazujar] ADJ *Fam (personne)* confused, muddled; **je me sens un peu v. ce matin** I'm not thinking very straight *or* I feel a bit dopey this morning; **il a donné une excuse plutôt vasouillarde** he got a bit bogged down in his apology

vasouiller [vazuje] VI *Fam* to flounder, to stammer and stutter

vasque [vask] NF **1** *(d'une fontaine)* basin **2** *(coupe décorative)* (ornamental) bowl

vassal, -ale, -aux, -ales [vasal, -o] N vassal

vassalité [vasalite] NF, **vasselage** [vaslaʒ] NM vassalage; *Fig (soumission)* vassalage, bondage

vaste [vast] ADJ vast, immense, huge; *Fam (plaisanterie etc)* big, great; **avoir de vastes ambitions** to have great ambitions; **v. étendue** vast *or* broad expanse; **le v. monde** the wide world; **de par le v. monde** the whole world over; **v. érudition** vast *or* comprehensive learning; **c'est une v. fumisterie** it's a complete *or* total farce

vastement [vastəmɑ̃] ADV vastly

va-t-en-guerre [vatɑ̃gɛr] *Péj* N INV war-monger
ADJ INV warmongering

Vatican (le) [ləvatikɑ̃] NM the Vatican

Vaticane [vatikan] ADJ, NF **la (Bibliothèque) V.** the Vatican Library

vaticination [vatisinasjɔ̃] NF *Litt* vaticination

vaticiner [vatisine] VI *Litt* to vaticinate

va-tout [vatu] NM INV *(au jeu)*, *Fig* **jouer son v.** to stake one's all

vaudeville [vodvil] NM **1** *Théâtre (comédie légère)* light comedy; *(avant le XIXᵉ siècle)* light comedy with songs and dances, vaudeville; *Fig* **cette histoire est un vrai v.** this story is a real farce **2** *Vieilli (chanson)* topical *or* satirical song *(with refrain)*

vaudevillesque [vodvilɛsk] ADJ comical, farcical

vaudevilliste [vodvilist] NM *Théâtre* vaudeville writer

vaudois, -oise [vodwa, -waz] ADJ **1** *(du canton de Vaud)* Vaudois, of/from Vaud **2** *Hist, Rel* Waldensian
N **V. 1** Vaudois; *(natif)* native of Vaud; *(habitant)* inhabitant of Vaud **2** *Hist, Rel* Waldensian

vaudou [vodu] NM voodoo
ADJ **culte v.** voodoo cult

vau-l'eau (à) [avolo] ADV downstream, with the stream; *Fig* **tout s'en va à v.** everything's going to rack and ruin *or* to the dogs

vaurien, -ienne [vorjɛ̃, -jɛn] N good-for-nothing, *Fam* layabout, *Br* yob; **petit v.!** you little scamp!, you little rascal!

vautour [votur] NM vulture

vautrer (se) [səvotre] VPR **1** *(d'un cochon)* *(dans la boue)* to wallow; *(d'une personne)* *(dans l'herbe, sur un canapé)* to sprawl; **vautré dans le fauteuil** lolling in the armchair; *Fig* **se v. dans le vice** to wallow *or* revel in vice **2** *Fam (tomber)* to go flying

vauvert [vovɛr] ADJ **c'est au diable v.** it's miles from anywhere, it's out in the wilds *or* a long way away

va-vite (à la) [alavavit] ADV in a rush, in a hurry; **travail fait à la v.** rushed *or* slapdash work

VDQS [vedekyɛs] NM *(abrév* **vin délimité de qualité supérieure)** = label certifying the superior quality of the wine

veau, -eaux [vo] NM **1** *(animal)* calf; *Fam* **pleurer comme un v.** to cry one's eyes out, to blubber VOIR GRAMMAIRE A12 **2** *Culin* veal; **rôti de v.** roast veal; **côtelette de v.** veal cutlet; **tête de v.** calf's head; **gelée de pied de v.** calf's *or* calves' foot jelly **3** *(cuir)* calf leather, calfskin **4** *Fam (personne lourde)* lump; **espèce de gros v.!** you great fat lump! **5** *Fam (voiture au moteur poussif)* hairdrier on wheels
▶▶ **v. gras: tuer le v. gras** to kill the fatted

calf; **v. marin** seal; **v. d'or: adorer le v. d'or** to worship the golden calf

vécés [vese] NMPL *Fam (toilettes) Br* loo, *Am* john

vecteur, -trice [vɛktœr, -tris] ADJ *Math* **rayon v.** radius vector
NM **1** *Math, Méd* vector; *Fig* **v. d'information/de progrès** vehicle for information/for progress **2** *(pour charge nucléaire etc)* vehicle

vectoriel, -ielle [vɛktɔrjɛl] ADJ *Math, Ordinat* vectorial; *Math* **espace v.** vector space; *Ordinat* **police vectorielle** outline font

vectorisation [vɛktɔrizasjɔ̃] NF *Ordinat* **v. d'images** image vectoring

vécu [veky] ADJ **1 choses vécues** things which have been lived through, actual experiences **2** *(pièce, roman)* true to life, founded on fact
NM real-life experience; **le livre m'a intéressé parce que c'était du v.** I found the book interesting because it was based on a real-life experience

vedettariat [vədɛtarja] NM star system

vedette [vədɛt] NF **1** *Théâtre, Cin etc* star; *Mktg (produit)* star; **v. de cinéma** film *or* movie star; **v. de la chanson** singing star; **v. de la télévision** television personality; **v. du barreau/de l'industrie** a big name at the bar/in industry; **une grande v. de la politique** a leading light in politics **2 avoir v. (sur l'affiche)** *(d'un acteur)* to head *or* top the bill, to have star billing; **ce problème a** *ou* **tient la v. depuis longtemps dans ce pays** the problem has long been a major concern in this country; **cette question a la v. dans tous les journaux** this issue is making the headlines in all the newspapers; **être en v.** to be in the limelight, to (have) hit the headlines; **mettre qn/qch en v.** to highlight *or* spotlight sb/sth; **voler la v. à qn** to steal the limelight from sb; **mettre un nom/mot en v.** to highlight *or* emphasize a name/word; **mots en v.** words in bold type **3** *Naut* small motorboat, launch; *(de police etc)* patrol boat **4** *Mil Arch* vedette, mounted sentry; **en v.** on vedette duty
▶ ▶ **v. américaine: passer en v. américaine** to be the warm-up act, to get second billing

védique [vedik] ADJ Vedic

védisme [vedism] NM Vedaism

végétal, -ale, -aux, -ales [veʒetal, -o] ADJ **vie végétale** plant life; **sol v.** humus; **huile végétale** vegetable oil
NM vegetable, plant

végétalien, -ienne [veʒetaljɛ̃, -jɛn] ADJ, N vegan

végétalisme [veʒetalism] NM veganism

végétarien, -ienne [veʒetarjɛ̃, -jɛn] ADJ, N vegetarian

végétarisme [veʒetarism] NM vegetarianism

végétatif, -ive [veʒetatif, -iv] ADJ vegetative; *Fig Péj (existence)* vegetable-like

végétation [veʒetasjɔ̃] NF *(flore)* vegetation
NFPL *Méd* **végétations** vegetations; **végétations (adénoïdes)** adenoids, adenoid growths; **opérer un enfant des végétations** to take out a child's adenoids

végéter [veʒete] VI (**je végète; je végéterai**) **1** *Péj (d'une personne)* to vegetate; **il végète dans ce bureau** he's just vegetating in that office **2** *Arch (d'une plante)* to vegetate, to grow

véhémence [veemɑ̃s] NF *Litt* vehemence; **avec v.** vehemently; **s'exprimer avec v.** to express oneself vehemently *or* passionately

véhément [veemɑ̃] ADJ *Litt* vehement, violent; **un orateur v.** a vehement *or* passionate speaker

véhémentement [veemɑ̃tmɑ̃] ADV *Litt* vehemently

véhiculaire [veikylɛr] ADJ **langue v.** common language, lingua franca

véhicule [veikyl] NM **1** *(moyen de transport)* vehicle; **v. articulé** articulated vehicle, *Fam* artic; **v. à chenilles** tracked *or* tracklaying vehicle; **v. à moteur** motor vehicle; **v. multifonction** *ou* **à usages multiples** multi-purpose vehicle, MPV; **v. de remplacement** courtesy car; **v. de secours** rescue vehicle; **v. de service** company car *(for general use of company staff)*; **v. spatial** spacecraft; **v. spécial pour handicapés** invalid carriage; **v. de tourisme** private vehicle; **v. de transport de marchandises** heavy goods vehicle, HGV; **v. utilitaire** commercial *or* goods vehicle **2** *(moyen de diffusion)* vehicle; **la parole est le v. de la pensée** speech is the vehicle of thought; **le v. du son/de la lumière** the medium *or* the vehicle of sound/light; *Fig* **la radio est un v. de l'information** radio is a vehicle for information *or* is a news medium

véhiculer [veikyle] VT to transport, to convey, to carry; *(émotion)* to convey, to carry

veille [vɛj] NF **1** *(jour qui précède)* preceding day, previous day; **je l'avais vu la v.** I'd seen him the day before; **la v. au soir** the evening before, the previous evening; **la v. de Noël** Christmas Eve; **la v. du jour de l'an** New Year's Eve; **la v. de la bataille** the day before the battle, the eve of the battle; *Fig* **être à la v. de la ruine/d'une guerre** to be on the brink *or* verge of ruin/of a war; **nous étions à la v. de nous séparer** we were on the brink *or* verge of splitting up; **être à la v. de se marier** to be on the point of getting married, to be about to get married; **à la v. de la réunion** just before the meeting; *Fam* **c'est pas demain la v.** that's not going to happen in a hurry; **c'est pas demain la v. qu'ils te proposeront un boulot** they're not going to be offering you a job in a hurry **2** *(absence de sommeil)* wakefulness; **entre la v. et le sommeil** between waking and sleeping **3** *(volontaire)* sitting up, staying up; *(auprès d'un malade)* watching, keeping watch **4** *Mil* (night) watch; *Naut* lookout; *Naut* **homme de v.** lookout (man); *Naut* **chambre de v.** chart house; **ancre de v.** sheet anchor; **prendre la v.** to take one's turn on watch **5** *Ordinat* standby mode; **en (mode) v.** in standby mode

veillée [veje] NF **1** *(soirée) (avec des amis etc)* evening; **pendant les longues veillées d'hiver** during the long winter evenings; **prolonger la v. jusqu'aux petites heures du matin** to stay up until the small hours; **v. au coin du feu** evening spent round the fire; **faire la v. chez qn** to spend the evening at sb's house **2** *(d'un malade)* night nursing; *(d'un mort)* watch, vigil

veiller [veje] VI **1** *(ne pas dormir)* to sit up, to stay up, to keep awake; **je n'ai pas l'habitude de v.** I'm not used to staying up late; **v. tard dans la nuit** to stay up late; **v. auprès d'un malade** to sit up with a sick person **2 v. à qch** to watch over *or* see to sth; **v. aux intérêts de qn** to look after *or* watch over sb's interests; **v. à la besogne** to keep an eye on the work; **v. à ce que qch se fasse** to see (to it) that sth is done; *Fig* **v. au grain** to keep an eye open for trouble **3 v. sur qn** to watch over *or* look after sb, to take care of sb **4** *Mil etc* to watch, to be on (the) lookout
VT *(malade etc)* to sit up with, to watch over; **v. un mort** to keep vigil over a dead body
VPR **se veiller** *Suisse Fam (faire attention)* to be careful

veilleur, -euse [vɛjœr, -øz] NM *Mil etc* lookout
NF **veilleuse 1** *(lampe)* night light; *(sur TV etc)* standby; **mettre la lampe en veilleuse** to dim the light; *Fig* **mettre une entreprise**

en veilleuse to reduce output to a minimum; *Fig* **mettre un projet en veilleuse** to shelve a project, to put a project on the back burner; *Fig Fam* **s'il pouvait la mettre en veilleuse!** I wish he'd cool it *or* put a sock in it!; **mets-la en veilleuse, s'il te plaît!** just put a sock in it, will you! **2** *Aut* sidelight **3** *(sur une cuisinière etc)* pilot light **4** *Bot* meadow saffron
▶ ▶ **v. de nuit** night watchman

veilleuses-codes NFPL *Aut* dim-dip

veinard, -arde [vɛnar, -ard] *Fam* ADJ *(personne)* lucky, *Br Fam* jammy
N lucky devil, *Br Fam* jammy so-and-so; **c'est un v.** he has all the luck; **v.!** lucky *or Br Fam* jammy devil!

veine [vɛn] NF **1** *Anat, Bot etc* vein; *Anat* **v. cave** vena cava; **v. porte** portal vein; **elle menace de s'ouvrir les veines** she's threatening to slash *or* slit *or* cut her wrists; *Fig* **il a du sang dans les veines** he's got guts; **montre-nous si tu as du sang dans les veines!** show us what you're made of!, show us your mettle!, show us whether you're a man or a mouse!
2 *Géol* vein; *(de minerai)* lode; *(de charbon)* seam
3 *(inspiration)* vein; **la v. poétique** the poetic vein; **en v. de plaisanterie** in humorous vein; **être en v. de faire qch** to be in the mood to do sth *or* for doing sth; **être en v. de générosité** to be in a generous mood, to be feeling generous
4 *Fam (chance)* luck; **avoir de la v.** to be in luck, to be lucky; **j'ai eu pas mal de v.** I've had my fair share of luck; **elle n'a pas eu de v.** she's been unlucky; **tu as une v. de pendu** *ou Vulg* **cocu!** you've got the devil's own luck!, you've got the luck of the devil!; **pas de v.!** rotten luck!; **alors là, pas de v., j'étais là avant toi** that's just your rotten luck, I was there before you; **c'est bien ma v.!** just my (rotten) luck!; **quelle v.!** talk about lucky!; **coup de v.** stroke of luck, fluke

veiné [vene] ADJ **1** *Anat* **bras v.** = arm where the veins are very close to the surface **2** *(bois etc)* grained

veiner [vene] VT *(porte etc)* to vein, to grain

veineux, -euse [vɛnø, -øz] ADJ **1** *(système, sang)* venous **2** *(bois etc)* veined, grainy

veinule [venyl] NF *Anat* venule

veinure [venyr] NF *(du bois etc)* graining

vêlage [vɛlaʒ] NM *(d'une vache)* calving

vélaire [velɛr] ADJ, NF *Ling* velar

Velcro® [vɛlkro] NM **(fermeture) V.** Velcro® (fastening); **fermé ou par un V.** fastened with Velcro®, with a Velcro® fastening

vêlement [vɛlmɑ̃] NM = vêlage

vêler [vɛle] VI *(d'une vache)* to calve

velimeux [valimø] *Can Fam* NM **1** *(chanceux)* lucky devil; **le petit v.!** (the) lucky devil! **2** *(intriguant)* crafty devil **3 être fort/riche en v.** to be very strong/rich; **être en v.** to be fuming, to be in a temper

vélin [velɛ̃] NM vellum (parchment); **(papier) v.** vellum (paper)

véliplanchiste [veliplɑ̃ʃist] N windsurfer

velléitaire [veleitɛr] ADJ indecisive
N indecisive person

velléité [veleite] NF vague desire *or* inclination, stray impulse; **faire qch par v.** to do sth on a whim; **j'ai des velléités de changement** I have a vague desire *or* inclination for change; **avoir des velléités de travail** to toy with the idea of work

vélo [velo] NM bicycle, bike; **aller à** *ou* **en v.** to cycle, to ride a bike; **je vais au travail en** *ou* **à v.** I cycle to work, I go to work on my bike, I ride my bike to work; **est-ce que tu sais faire du v.** *ou* **monter à v.?** can you ride a bike?; **aimes-tu faire du v.?** do you like cycling?; **v. de (cyclo-)cross/de piste** cyclo-cross/racing bike; **v. de course** racing cycle, *Fam* racer; **v. d'appartement** exercise bike; **v. tout-terrain** mountain bike; *Fam* **avoir un petit v. dans la tête** to be off one's rocker, to be not all there

vélocipède [velosipɛd] **NM** *Arch* velocipede; *Hum* bike

vélocité [velɔsite] **NF** speed, swiftness; *Tech* velocity; **exercice de v. au piano** five-finger exercise

vélodrome [velodrom] **NM** velodrome

vélomoteur [velomɔtœr] **NM** moped

velours [v(ə)lur] **NM 1** *Tex* velvet; **le v. de ses joues** his/her velvety cheeks; **ce fruit est doux comme du v.** this fruit is as smooth as velvet; **goûte ce vin, c'est du v.** taste this wine, it's sheer velvet; **veste/rideaux en v.** velvet jacket/curtains; **pantalon en v. côtelé** corduroy trousers, cords; *Fig* **jouer sur le v.** to be on velvet; **elle lui fait ses yeux de v.** she is making (sheep's) eyes at him; **la Révolution de v.** the Velvet Revolution; **avoir un regard de v.** to have velvety eyes **2** *(liaison incorrecte)* incorrect liaison *(eg* **j'ai été** [ʒezete]*)*
▸▸ **v. bouclé** uncut velvet; **v. côtelé** *ou* **à côtes** ribbed velvet, corduroy (velvet); **v. de coton** cotton velvet, velveteen; **v. façonné** figured velvet; **v. de laine** velour(s); **v. de soie** silk velvet; **v. uni** plain velvet

velouté [vəlute] **ADJ** *(joues)* velvety, velvet-soft; *(pêche)* velvety, downy; *(vin)* velvety, smooth, mellow
NM 1 *(d'un tissu, des voix etc)* velvetiness, softness; *(d'une pêche etc)* bloom **2** *Culin* cream soup; **v. de champignons** cream of mushroom soup

velouter [vəlute] **VT** *(quelque chose)* to give a velvety appearance to; *(un son)* to soften; *(un goût)* to smooth; *(d'une ombre) (contours)* to soften

velouteux, -euse [vəlutø, -øz] **ADJ** velvety, soft

Velpeau® [vɛlpo] **NM** *Méd* **bande V.** crêpe bandage

velu [vəly] **ADJ** hairy

vélum, velum [velɔm] **NM** awning

Vélux® [velyks] **NM** Velux® window, skylight

venaison [vənɛzɔ̃] **NF** venison

vénal, -ale, -aux, -ales [venal, -o] **ADJ 1** *(privilège, droit etc)* venal, purchasable; *Com* **valeur vénale** market value **2** *Péj (personne)* venal, mercenary, corruptible; *(presse)* corrupt; **l'amour v.** venal love

vénalement [venalmɑ̃] **ADV** venally

vénalité [venalite] **NF** venality

venant [vənɑ̃] **NM à tout v., à tous venants** to all comers, to all and sundry

vendable [vɑ̃dabl] **ADJ** saleable, sellable; **facilement/difficilement v.** easy/difficult to sell

vendange [vɑ̃dɑ̃ʒ] **NF 1** *(temps)* **vendanges** vintage (season); **pendant les vendanges** during the grape-harvesting *or* -picking season **2** *(récolte)* grape gathering *or* picking, wine harvest, grape harvest, vintage; **faire la** *ou* **les vendange(s)** to harvest *or* pick the grapes **3** *(raisin récolté)* grapes (harvested); **une bonne v.** a good vintage

vendanger [vɑ̃dɑ̃ʒe] *(je* **vendangeai(s); n. vendangeons)** **VT** *(raisin)* to harvest, to pick, to gather, to vintage
VI **ils sont partis v. dans le Midi** they went to pick grapes in the South of France

vendangeur, -euse [vɑ̃dɑ̃ʒœr, -øz] **N** grape picker, vintager
NF *Bot* **vendangeuse** aster

vendéen, -enne [vɑ̃deɛ̃, -ɛn] **ADJ** of/from the Vendée
N V. *(natif)* native of the Vendée; *(habitant)* inhabitant of the Vendée

vendémiaire [vɑ̃demjɛr] **NM** *Hist* = first month of the French Republican calendar *(Sep 22nd–Oct 21st)*

vendetta [vɑ̃deta] **NF** vendetta

vendeur, -euse [vɑ̃dœr, -øz] **N** *(dans un magasin)* (sales) assistant, *Am* (sales)clerk; *(non professionnel)* seller; *Bourse* seller; *Jur* vendor; *Fig* **les vendeurs d'évasion** dream merchants, the dream industry; **j'allais vendre ma voiture, mais je ne suis plus v.** I was going to sell my car, but I've decided not to *or* but I've taken it off the market
▸▸ **v. ambulant** travelling salesman; **v. à domicile** door-to-door salesman; **v. export** exporter; **v. de journaux** newspaper seller *or* vendor *or* man; *Mktg* **v. par téléphone** telesales operator; **v-représentant-placier,** *pl* **vendeurs-représentants-placiers** sales representative

vendition [vɑ̃disjɔ̃] **NF** *Belg (vente aux enchères)* auction

vendre [vɑ̃dr] **VT 1** to sell; *(commercialiser)* to market; **v. qch à qn** to sell sb sth, to sell sth to sb; **v. comptant** to sell for cash; **v. à crédit** to sell on credit; *Bourse* **v. à découvert** to sell short, to go a bear; **v. de gré à gré** to sell privately; **v. à perte** to sell at a loss; *Bourse* **v. à terme** to sell forward; **v. qch en gros** to sell sth wholesale; **v. qch au détail** to sell sth retail, to retail sth; **v. moins cher que qn** to undersell sb; **dans ce magasin, ils vendent moins cher que partout ailleurs** this shop undersells everywhere else, this shop is cheaper than anywhere else; **v. chèrement sa vie** to sell one's life dearly; **un objet (à) 50 euros** to sell an object for 50 euros; **maison à v.** house for sale; **l'art de v.** salesmanship; *Écon* **pays qui vend du pétrole/du café** oil-/coffee-selling country; *Fin* **v. des valeurs** to sell stocks and shares; *Fig* **v. de l'évasion** *ou* **du rêve** to sell dreams; **v. son âme au Diable** to sell one's soul to the Devil
2 v. qn *(pour dette)* to sell sb up
3 *(trahir) (quelqu'un, secret)* to betray, to give away
VPR se vendre 1 cela se vend comme des petits pains it's selling like hot cakes **2** to sell oneself; **la société doit mieux se v.** the company has to market itself better; *Péj* **se v. à l'ennemi** to sell oneself *or* to sell out to the enemy

vendredi [vɑ̃drədi] **NM** Friday; **le v. saint** Good Friday *(voir aussi* **samedi)** SEE GRAMMAR A81–2; B61–2

vendu, -ue [vɑ̃dy] **N** traitor
ADJ *(corrompu)* bribed

venelle [vənɛl] **NF** alley

vénéneux, -euse [venenø, -øz] **ADJ** poisonous; **champignon v.** toadstool

Do not confuse with **venimeux**.

vénérable [venerabl] **ADJ** venerable
NM *(d'une loge maçonnique)* worshipful master

vénération [venerasjɔ̃] **NF** veneration, reverence; **avoir de la v. pour qn** to hold sb in veneration, to revere sb

vénérer [venere] **VT** *(je* **vénère, n. vénérons; je vénérerai)** **1** *(admirer)* to venerate, to revere **2** *(saint etc)* to worship

vénerie [venri] **NF** hunting, *Spéc* venery; **petite/grande v.** small game/big game hunting

vénérien, -ienne [venerjɛ̃, -jɛn] **ADJ** *Méd* venereal; **maladie vénérienne** venereal disease, VD

vénérologie [venerɔlɔʒi] **NF** *Méd* venereology

vénérologue [venerɔlɔg] **N** venereologist

veneur [vənœr] **NM** huntsman; *Hist* **le Grand V.** the Master of the Royal Hunt

Vénézuéla [venezɥela] **NM** Venezuela

vénézuélien, -ienne [venezɥeljɛ̃, -jɛn] **ADJ** Venezuelan
N V. Venezuelan

vengeance [vɑ̃ʒɑ̃s] **NF** revenge, vengeance; **esprit de v.** feeling of revenge *or* vengeance; **soif/désir de v.** thirst/desire for revenge, vengefulness; **par v.** out of revenge; **tirer v. d'une injure** to be revenged for an insult; *Prov* **la v. est un plat qui se mange froid** revenge is a dish best eaten cold; **v. sanglante** bloodthirsty revenge; **exercer sa v. sur qn** to have one's revenge *or* vengeance on sb; **crime qui crie v.** crime that cries out for vengeance; *Rel* **v. divine** divine retribution

venger [vɑ̃ʒe] *(je* **vengeai(s); n. vengeons)** **VT** to avenge; **v. qn d'une injure** to avenge sb for an insult
VPR se venger to be revenged, to have *or* get one's revenge; **se v. sur qn (de qch)** to take (one's) revenge on sb (for sth); *Fam* **pas la peine de te v. sur moi!** there's no point in taking it out on me!

vengeur, -eresse [vɑ̃ʒœr, -(ə)rɛs] *Litt* **N** avenger
ADJ avenging, (re)vengeful

véniel, -ielle [venjɛl] **ADJ** *(péché)* venial

venimeux, -euse [vənimø, -øz] **ADJ 1** *(serpent)* venomous, poisonous; *(morsure)* poisonous **2** *Fig* spiteful, malicious

Do not confuse with **vénéneux**.

venin [vənɛ̃] **NM 1** *(d'un serpent etc)* venom, poison **2** *Fig* spite, malice; **jeter** *ou* **cracher son v.** to vent one's spleen

VENIR [v(ə)nir] *(prp* venant; *pp* venu; *pr ind* je viens, il vient, n. venons, ils viennent; *pr sub* je vienne; *impf* je venais; *p hist* je vins, n. vînmes, v. vîntes, ils vinrent; *p sub* je vinsse; *fu* je viendrai; *aux* être)

VI to come **1, 3–5, 7** ▪ to come along **1, 7** ▪ to come from *(venir de)* **1** ▪ to have just done *(venir de faire)* **2** ▪ to come to *(en venir à)* **4** ▪ to reach **5**

VI 1 to come; **il doit v. passer quelques jours chez nous** he's coming to spend a few days with us; **les larmes lui vinrent aux yeux** tears came to his/her eyes; **cela me fait v. l'eau à la bouche** it makes my mouth water; **je viens!** I'm coming!; **je ne ferai qu'aller et v.** I'll come straight back; **je n'ai fait qu'aller et v. entre la maison et le bureau** I just went to and fro *or* back and forth between the house and the office; **il va et vient dans sa chambre** he's pacing up and down (in) his room; **mais venez donc!** do come along!; **il vient d'Amérique** he's from *or* he comes from America; **d'où venez-vous?** *(d'où êtes-vous?)* where do you come *or* Litt hail from?, where are you from?; *(par où êtes-vous passé?)* where have you come from?; **il est venu à** *ou* **vers moi** he came up to me; *Bible* **laissez v. à moi les petits enfants** suffer the little children to come unto me; **il est venu sur moi** he advanced on me (threateningly); **v. au monde** to be born, to come into the world; **l'année qui vient** the coming year, next year; **dans les jours qui viennent** in the coming *or* next few days; **ses succès à v.** his/her future successes; **dans les temps à v.** in the days to come; **faire v. qn** to send for sb, to call sb in, to fetch sb; **faire v. ses robes de Paris** to get one's dresses from Paris; **voir v.**

qn to see sb coming; *Fig* je te vois v. (avec tes gros sabots)! I can see you coming a mile off!; je préfère voir v. I'd rather wait and see; laisser v. les choses to let things take their course; le voici v., le voici qui vient here he comes; être bien/mal venu to be welcome/unwelcome; il serait mal venu de le lui faire remarquer it would be a bit out of place *or Fam* a bit off to point it out to him; *Naut* v. dans le vent to come round; v. sur bâbord/tribord to alter course to port/to starboard; il est venu tomber à mes pieds he fell at my feet; venez me trouver à quatre heures come (round) and see me at four o'clock; viens donc te baigner/te reposer chez nous come (round) to our place for a swim/a rest; je viens vous voir I've come to see you; v. chercher *ou* v. prendre qn/qch to come for sb/sth, to come to collect sb/sth; mot qui vient du latin word which comes *or* is derived from Latin; ce bien lui est venu de famille he/she inherited this property from his family; tout cela vient de ce que ... it all stems from the fact that ...; cela vient du fait que ... this stems from the fact that ...; l'erreur vient de là that's where the error stems from, that explains the mistake; vous y viendrez you'll come round (to it), you'll change your mind

2 (*pr & impf only*) v. de faire qch to have (only) just done sth; il vient/venait de sortir he has/had just gone out SEE GRAMMAR B31

3 (*apparaître, arriver*) to come; le premier exemple venu the first example that comes to mind; le premier crétin venu serait capable de t'en parler any fool could tell you about it; le premier passant venu te le dira the first person you meet *or* anyone will tell you that; *Fam* alors ce steak, ça vient? is my steak coming *or* not?, how much longer do I have to wait for that steak?; alors, tu viens, on y va! are you coming or not? we're off!; les idées ne viennent pas I just can't come up with anything; son nom ne vient pas, j'ai oublié I just can't think of his name; le moment de nous dire au revoir est venu the time has come for us to say goodbye; la pluie ne va pas tarder à v. the rain won't be long in coming; un jour viendra où nous n'aurons plus tous ces problèmes the day will come when we don't have all these problems; il attend que vienne son tour he's waiting for his turn (to come round); il m'est venu des rides he's got wrinkles; il m'est venu des doutes à son sujet I suddenly wasn't so sure about him; il lui est venu une idée géniale he had *or* hit on a brilliant idea; l'idée me vient que ..., il me vient à l'esprit que ..., me vient l'idée que ... the thought comes to my mind *or* it occurs to me that ...; il ne m'est pas venu à l'idée que ... it never entered my head *or* it never occurred to me that ...; il ne me viendrait pas à l'esprit (de penser) que ... it would never occur to me (to think) that ...

4 en v. à qch/à faire qch to come to sth/to the point of doing sth; en v. aux coups *ou* aux mains to come to blows; les choses en sont-elles venues là? have things come to such a point?; je comprends où vous voulez en v. I see what you're getting at *or* driving at; j'en suis venu à votre manière de penser I've come round to your way of thinking; j'en viens à me demander si ... I'm beginning to wonder whether ...; j'en suis venue à perdre toute confiance en lui I've come *or* begun to lose all faith in him

5 (*atteindre*) to attain, to reach; l'eau leur venait aux genoux the water came up to their knees; les cheveux lui viennent aux épaules he has shoulder-length hair; elle lui vient au menton she comes up to his chin

6 v. à faire qch to happen *or* chance to do

sth; si le temps venait à pleuvoir if it happened to rain, if it should rain

7 (*grandir, pousser*) to come on *or* along; bien v. (*d'une plante*) to thrive; (*d'une photo*) to come out well; faire v. du blé to grow wheat; il lui est venu une tumeur he developed a tumour

V IMPERS d'où vient(-il) que ...? how is it that ...?

VPR se venir *Arch, Région* s'en v. to come along

Venise [vəniz] NF Venice; point de V. Venetian lace; carnaval de V. Venice carnival

vénitien, -ienne [venisjɛ̃, -jɛn] ADJ Venetian; store v. Venetian blind

N V. Venetian

vent [vɑ̃] NM **1** wind; le v. du nord/sud the north/south wind; *Naut* v. frais strong breeze; grand v., v. fort high wind, gale; journée de grand v. windy day; coup de v. gust of wind, squall; *Fig* entrer/sortir en coup de v. to dash in/out; elle courait les cheveux au v. she ran with her hair streaming in the wind; à l'abri du v. sheltered from the wind; *Mus* instrument à v. wind instrument; il fait du v. it's windy (weather); le v. tourne the wind is changing; *Fig* the wind is changing, the tide is turning; aller comme le v. to go like the wind; bon v.! God speed!; *Iron* good riddance!; quel bon v. vous amène? what brings you here?, to what do we owe the pleasure?; *Naut* avoir le vent aft *or* dead aft; *Fig* il a le v. en poupe he's on the road to success, he's riding high, he has the wind in his sails; *Fig* avoir du v. dans les voiles to be three sheets in *or* to the wind, to be drunk; *Péj* ce n'est que du v. it's just hot air; *Fig* prendre le v., regarder de quel côté vient le v. to see which way the wind blows, to see how the land lies; tourner à tous les vents to be a weathercock; *Prov* qui sème le v. récolte la tempête he who sows the wind shall reap the whirlwind; ouvert *ou* exposé aux quatre vents exposed to the four winds; *Fam* être dans le v. to be up to date *or* with it; les îles du V. the Windward Islands; *Naut* v. arrière following wind; *Aviat* tail wind; aller v. arrière to sail *or* run before the wind; v. debout head wind; *Aut* v. latéral side wind; contre le v. against the wind, into the wind; *Fig* contre vents et marées come hell or high water; *Naut* sous le v. alee, (to) leeward; avoir bon v. to have a fair wind; *Naut* au v. a-weather, (to) windward; mettre la barre au v. to put the helm up; côté du v. weather side; côté sous le v. lee side

2 (*air*) air; marché/assemblée en plein v. open-air market/meeting; mettre qch au v. to hang sth out to dry

3 (*d'un soufflet, d'une balle*) blast; *Aviat* v. de l'hélice propeller slipstream

4 (*flatulence*) wind, *Am* gas; lâcher un v. to break wind, *Am* to pass gas; avoir des vents to have wind

5 (*à la chasse*) scent; avoir le v. de son gibier to have the wind of one's game; *Fig* avoir v. de qch to get wind of sth

vente [vɑ̃t] NF **1** (*transaction*) sale; (*activité*) selling; réaliser une v. to make a sale; elle est dans la v. she's in sales; la v. de la statue a fait scandale the sale *or* the selling of the statue caused a scandal; nous déménagerons après la v. de la maison we'll move after the house is sold *or* after the sale of the house; *Compta* ventes sales, turnover; acte de v. bill of sale; bureau de v. sales agency; salle des ventes auction rooms, saleroom(s), salesroom; promotion des ventes sales promotion; en v. for sale, on sale; mettre qch en v. to put sth up for sale, to offer sth for sale; médicament en v. libre medicine available over the counter *or* without pre-

scription; en v. dans toutes les bonnes librairies on sale in all good bookshops; (livre) retiré de la v. (book) withdrawn from sale; faire une forte v. (*d'un livre*) to be a best seller **2** *Can* (*soldes*) sale **3** (*action de couper*) (*du bois*) felling; (*clairière*) clearing; jeune(s) vente(s) new undergrowth

▸ ▸ v. à l'amiable sale by private agreement, private sale; *Com* v. à l'arrivée sale at arrival; ventes de base baseline sales, market minimum; v. par catalogue catalogue selling; v. de charité (charity) bazaar; v. (au) comptant cash sale; v. au comptoir over-the-counter sales; v.-conseil sales consultancy; v. en coopération co-operative selling; v. par correspondance mail order (selling); v. à crédit credit sale; (à tempérament) hire purchase, *Am* installment plan; *Bourse* v. à découvert short sale; *Com* v. au départ sale at departure; v. au détail retailing, retail selling; v. directe direct selling; (*une vente*) direct sale; v. directe en B to B back-to-back direct selling; v. à domicile door-to-door selling; v. domiciliaire home party selling; v. électronique on-line selling; v. aux enchères (sale by) auction; v. en l'état sale as seen; ventes export, ventes à l'exportation export sales; v. à froid cold selling; v. en gros wholesaling; v. sans intermédiaire direct selling; v. judiciaire sale by order of the court; v. jumelée twin-pack selling; v. en ligne on-line sales; (*transaction*) on-line selling; v. en magasin counter sales; ventes sur le marché intérieur home sales, domestic sales; v.-marketing sales and marketing; *Bourse* v. nue naked sale; ventes personnelles personal selling; v. porte-à-porte (*activité*) door-to-door selling; ventes de prospection missionary selling; v. publique public sale; v. pyramidale pyramid selling; v. répétée repeat sale; *Mktg* v. par réseau coopté multilevel marketing; v. en semi-gros small wholesale sales; v. spéculative speculative selling; v. par téléphone telephone selling; ventes par téléphone telephone sales, telesales; v. à tempérament hire purchase, *Am* installment plan; *Bourse* v. à terme forward sale; ventes territoriales territorial sales; ventes totales de l'industrie total industry sales

venté [vɑ̃te] ADJ (*région*) windswept, windblown, windy

venter [vɑ̃te] V IMPERS to be windy, to blow; il vente fort it's very windy, it's blowing hard

venteux, -euse [vɑ̃tø, -øz] ADJ (*temps*) windy; (*pays*) windswept

ventilateur [vɑ̃tilatœr] NM ventilator; *Aut* (*soufflante*) blower; *TV, Cin* wind machine; v. rotatif fan; v. électrique electric fan; *Ordinat* v. de refroidissement cooling fan

ventilation [vɑ̃tilasjɔ̃] NF **1** (*aération*) ventilation; mettre la v. (en marche) to switch on the ventilation **2** (*des dépenses etc*) breakdown; la v. des tâches à différents employés the allocation of jobs to various employees **3** *Jur* (*d'un domaine etc*) separate valuation

ventiler [vɑ̃tile] VT **1** (*pièce etc*) to ventilate, to air; mal ventilé poorly *or* badly ventilated, stuffy **2** (*dépenses etc*) to break down; (*crédits, équipements etc*) to allocate; *Com* v. un lot to break bulk **3** *Jur* (*domaine etc*) to value separately

ventilo [vɑ̃tilo] NM *Fam* fan; faire marcher le v. to turn on the fan

ventôse [vɑ̃toz] NM *Hist* = sixth month of the French Republican calendar (*Feb 19th or 21st–March 19th or 21st*)

ventouse [vɑ̃tuz] NF **1** *Méd* cupping glass; poser des ventouses à qn to cup sb **2** *Zool* (*de sangsue etc*) sucker **3** (*de plastique etc*) suction cup *or* disc; fléchettes/cendrier à v. rubber-tipped darts/suction-grip ashtray;

faire v. to adhere by suction; **mine v.** limpet mine; **voiture v.** illegally parked car, abandoned car **4** *(aération)* airhole, vent(hole)

ventral, -ale, -aux, -ales [vɑ̃tral, -o] ADJ ventral; **parachute v.** lap pack (parachute)

ventre [vɑ̃tr] NM **1** *(estomac)* stomach, *Fam* tummy, belly; *(d'animal)* belly, underbelly; *Anat* abdomen; **avoir le v. plein/creux** to have a full stomach, to be full/to have an empty stomach; **danse du v.** belly dance; **faire la danse du v.** to belly dance; **se coucher à plat v.** to lie flat on one's stomach *or Fam* tummy *or* belly; **dormir à plat v.** to sleep (lying) flat on one's stomach *or* (lying) facedown; *Fig* **se mettre à plat v. devant qn** to grovel to sb; *Fig* **passer sur le v. à qn** to trample all over sb; **v. à terre** *(d'un cheval)* at full speed, flat out; **avoir du v.** to have a paunch, to be potbellied; **il commence à prendre** *ou* **avoir du v.** he's starting to get a paunch *or* a belly; **rentrer le v.** to hold one's stomach in; **avoir mal au v.** to have (a) stomach *or Fam* tummy ache; *Fig* **ça fait mal au v. de voir ça** it makes me sick to see that; **ne rien avoir dans le v.** to have nothing in one's stomach; *Fig* to have no guts, to be gutless; **ne bois pas si tu n'as rien dans le v.** don't drink on an empty stomach; **je savais bien qu'il avait quelque chose dans le v.** I knew he had guts; **je voudrais savoir ce qu'elle a dans le v.** I'd like to know what she's up to; *Fam* **donner du cœur au v. à qn** to buck sb up; *Fig* **v. mou** underbelly; *Prov* **v. affamé n'a point d'oreilles** it's no use reasoning with a hungry man; **tu as les yeux plus grands que le v.** your eyes are bigger than your belly **2** *(utérus)* womb; **à cette époque tu étais encore dans le v. de ta mère** you were still in your Mum's tummy then **3** *Tech (d'une bouteille, d'une poutre)* bulge, swell; *(d'une voile)* belly, sag; *(d'un navire)* belly; **faire v.** to bulge (out), to belly out; *(pendre)* to sag **4** *Phys (d'une vague)* antinode, ventral segment; **v. de tension** potential loop, voltage loop **5** *Journ* = centre of the front page of a newspaper

ventrebleu [vɑ̃trəblø] INT *Arch* gadzooks!, zounds!

ventrée [vɑ̃tre] NF *(de nourriture)* bellyful

ventricule [vɑ̃trikyl] NM *Anat* ventricle

ventrière [vɑ̃trijɛr] NF **1** *(harnais)* girth; *(pour hisser un animal)* sling **2** *Constr* purlin

ventriloque [vɑ̃trilɔk] N ventriloquist

ventriloquie [vɑ̃trilɔki] NF ventriloquy, ventriloquism

ventru [vɑ̃try] ADJ **1** *(gros)* potbellied **2** *(colonne)* bulbous; *(voile)* bulging, swelling

venu, -ue¹ [v(ə)ny] ADJ **1** *(bien développé)* well-developed; **plante bien/mal venue** sturdy *or* healthy/stunted *or* unhealthy plant; **photographie bien venue** photograph that has come out well; **enfant mal v.** stunted *or* puny child **2** *(approprié)* **bien v.** appropriate; **mal v.** inappropriate; **je serais mal v. de critiquer** *(je ne suis pas qualifié en la matière)* it's not for me to criticize; *(j'en ai fait autant)* I'm hardly in a position to criticize; **il serait mal v. d'insister** it would be ill-mannered to insist

N **le premier v.** the first to arrive; *(n'importe qui)* anybody; **le premier v. vous le dira** anybody *or* anyone will tell you that; **à la portée du premier v.** easy to use, user-friendly; **ce n'est pas le premier v.** he's not just anybody; **le dernier v.** the last to arrive; **les nouveaux venus/les nouvelles venues** the newcomers

venue² [v(ə)ny] NF **1** *(arrivée)* coming, arrival; *(du printemps etc)* coming, advent, approach; *(d'ordinateurs etc)* advent; *(d'un vol)* approach; *(de l'eau)* rush; **attendre la v. de**

qn to wait for sb to arrive; **c'est ce qui explique ma v.** that's why I'm here; **on ne pouvait pas s'attendre à la v. de la neige** there's no way we could have forecast the snow; **allées et venues** comings and goings; **faire des allées et venues** to come and go; **après de nombreuses allées et venues** after a lot of toing and froing *or* going backwards and forwards **2** *(d'un arbre etc)* growth; **d'une belle v., tout d'une v.** *(arbre)* well-grown; *Fig* **des pages d'une belle v.** beautifully written pages

> Il faut noter que le terme anglais **venue** est un faux ami. Il désigne un lieu où se réunissent des gens.

Vénus [venys] NF *Myth, Astron* Venus; *Bot* **cheveu de V.** maidenhair fern; *Anat* **mont de V.** mons veneris, mound of Venus

vépéciste [vepesist] NM *Com* mail order specialist

vêpres [vɛpr] NFPL *Rel* vespers

ver [vɛr] NM **1** worm; **nu comme un v.** stark naked; *Fam* **tirer les vers du nez à qn** to worm information out of sb **2** *(asticot, larve)* grub, larva; **fruit plein de vers** worm-eaten fruit; **rose rongée de vers** cankered rose; **rongé** *ou* **piqué des vers** worm-eaten; **une histoire pas piquée des vers** one heck of a story

▸▸ **v. blanc** cockchafer grub; **v. du bois** woodworm; **v. de farine** mealworm; **v. luisant** glow worm; **v. des pêcheurs** lug(worm); **v. rongeur** canker(worm); **v. de sable** lug(-worm); **v. à soie** silkworm; *Méd* **v. solitaire** tapeworm; **avoir le v. solitaire** to have a tapeworm; **v. de terre** earthworm; **v. de viande** maggot

véracité [verasite] NF truth, truthfulness, *Fml* veracity

véranda [verɑ̃da] NF veranda(h)

verbal, -ale, -aux, -ales [vɛrbal, -o] ADJ **1** *(promesse)* verbal; **la violence verbale d'une description** the violence of the language used in a description **2** *Gram* verbal; **locution verbale** verbal phrase

verbalement [vɛrbalmɑ̃] ADV verbally, by word of mouth

verbalisation [vɛrbalizasjɔ̃] NF **1** *(expression)* verbalization; **v. des angoisses** putting (one's) anxieties into words **2** *Jur* entry of charge *(by policeman for minor offence)*

verbaliser [vɛrbalize] VI *(d'un policier)* **Madame, je vais devoir v.** I'm going to have to charge you

VT *(exprimer)* to verbalize, to put into words

verbatim [vɛrbatim] ADV *(mot pour mot)* **dire qch v.** to say sth verbatim

NM *(compte rendu mot pour mot)* verbatim account

verbe [vɛrb] NM **1** *Gram* verb; **v. transitif/intransitif** transitive/intransitive verb; **v. composé** compound verb; *(en anglais)* phrasal verb; **v. défectif** defective verb; **v. à particule** *(en anglais)* phrasal verb; **v. pronominal** reflexive verb SEE GRAMMAR A38–66; B24–53 **2** *(langage)* language, word(s); **la magie du v.** the magic of words *or* language; **avoir le v. haut** to speak loudly; *Fig* to be dictatorial **3** *Rel* **le V.** the Word; **le V. s'est fait chair** the Word was made flesh

verbeux, -euse [vɛrbø, -øz] ADJ *(orateur etc)* verbose, long-winded; *(explication etc)* wordy, long-winded, verbose

verbiage [vɛrbjaʒ] NM verbiage; **se lancer dans un v. creux** to launch into a meaningless torrent of words; **tout ce v. ne m'intéresse pas** all this meaningless chatter is of no interest to me

verbosité [vɛrbozite] NF verbosity, wordiness

ver-coquin, *pl* **vers-coquins** NM *(parasite)* vine grub; *Vét* stagger worm

verdâtre [vɛrdɑtr] ADJ greenish

verdeur [vɛrdœr] NF **1** *(d'un fruit, d'un vin)* tartness, acidity **2** *(du langage)* crudeness **3** *(vitalité)* vigour, *Am* vigor, vitality

verdict [vɛrdikt] NM *Jur (du jury)* verdict, finding; **prononcer** *ou* **rendre un v.** to return *or* bring in a verdict; **prononcer** *ou* **rendre un v. pour/contre qn** to find for/against sb; **v. de culpabilité** *ou* **positif/d'acquittement** *ou* **négatif** verdict of 'guilty'/'not guilty'; **attendre le v. du médecin** to await the doctor's verdict

verdier [vɛrdje] NM *(oiseau)* greenfinch

verdir [vɛrdir] VT **v. qch** to make *or* turn sth green

VI *(de végétation etc)* to turn green; *Fig* **v. (de jalousie)** to go *or* turn green with envy; **v. de peur** to go *or* turn white with fear

verdissement [vɛrdismɑ̃] NM turning green

verdoiement [vɛrdwamɑ̃] NM **1** *(action de se couvrir de verdure)* turning green **2** *(des champs)* greenness

verdoyant [vɛrdwajɑ̃] ADJ *(champs, paysage etc)* green, *Litt* verdant; **les champs verdoyants** the lush pasture

verdoyer [vɛrdwaje] VI *(pr ind* **il verdoie;** *fu* **il verdoiera)** *(de végétation etc)* to turn green

verdure [vɛrdyr] NF **1** *(couleur)* greenness **2** *(végétation)* greenery, *Litt* verdure; **rideau de v.** curtain of greenery; **salle de v.** green arbour; **tapis de v.** carpet of green, *Litt* greensward; **théâtre de v.** open-air theatre **3** *Culin (légumes verts)* greens

verdurier, -ière [vɛrdyrje, -ɛr] N *Belg (marchand de légumes)* Br greengrocer, *Am* vegetable seller

véreux, -euse [verø, -øz] ADJ **1** *(fruit)* wormy, maggoty **2** *Péj (affaires)* dubious, shady, *Fam* fishy; **financier v.** shady financier; **dettes véreuses** bad debts; **tremper dans une affaire véreuse** to be involved in a shady business

verge [vɛrʒ] NF **1** *Anat* penis **2** *(baguette)* rod, cane, switch; **(poignée de) verges** birch (rod); **battre de verges un enfant** to birch a child; *Fig* **vous lui donnez des verges pour vous fouetter** you're giving him a stick to beat you with **3** *Naut (d'une ancre)* shank **4** *Bot* **v. d'or** golden rod, Aaron's rod **5** *Can (mesure)* yard

vergé [vɛrʒe] ADJ **1** *Tex* badly dyed, streaky **2** **papier v.** laid paper

NM laid paper

vergeoise [vɛrʒwaz] NF = low-grade beet sugar

verger [vɛrʒe] NM orchard

vergeté [vɛrʒəte] ADJ streaky, streaked; *(peau)* stretchmarked

vergette [vɛrʒɛt] NF small cane, switch

vergeture [vɛrʒətyr] NF **1** stretch mark; **avoir des vergetures** to have stretch marks; **crème contre les vergetures** cream to prevent stretch marks **2** *(causée par un fouet etc)* weal, red mark

vergeure [vɛrʒyr] NF *(sur papier vergé)* wire mark

verglacé [vɛrglase] ADJ *(route)* icy; *Can* **pluie verglacée** freezing rain

verglas [vɛrgla] NM *(sur la route)* (black) ice, *Am* glaze; **il y a du v.** it's icy *or* slippery

vergogne [vɛrgɔɲ] NF **sans v.** *(emploi adjectival)* shameless; *(emploi adverbial)* shamelessly

vergue [vɛrg] NF *Naut* yard; **grande v.** main yard; **v. de misaine** foretop yard; **v. de hunier** topsail yard; **bout de v.** yard-arm

véridique [veridik] ADJ truthful, *Litt* veracious; **informations véridiques** accurate information

véridiquement [veridikmɑ̃] **ADV** truthfully, *Litt* veraciously

vérifiable [verifjabl] **ADJ** verifiable; *(déclaration etc)* that can be checked

vérificateur, -trice [verifikatœr, -tris] **N** *(personne)* inspector, examiner, checker; **v. de comptes** auditor
NM *Ordinat* **v. orthographique** spellchecker
ADJ appareil v. testing machine; **instrument v.** gauge, calipers

vérification [verifikasjɔ̃] **NF** *(de déclarations etc)* checking, verification; *(du travail etc)* inspection, examination, checking; *(des votes)* checking; *(d'un pronostic, d'une réservation)* confirmation; *Aut etc* **v. sur place** spot check; **v. de comptes** *ou* **d'écritures** audit(ing) of accounts; **v. fiscale** tax audit; *Ordinat* **v. antivirale** antiviral check; *Ordinat* **v. d'erreurs** error checking; **v. orthographique** spellcheck; *Compta* **v. à rebours** audit trail

vérifier [verifje] *(impf, pr sub* **n. vérifiions, vous vérifiiez)* **VT** *(votes, un calcul, l'heure du train etc)* to check; *(travail etc)* to inspect, to examine, to check; *(déclaration)* to verify, to check, to confirm; *(mécanismes etc)* to overhaul; *(comptes)* to audit; **il doit être là, je vais v.** he must be there, I'll check *or* make sure; **vérifié et revérifié** checked and double-checked; **v. des références** to take up references; **v. que tous les robinets sont fermés** to check that all the taps have been turned off; **v. si qch est vrai** to check whether sth is true
VPR se vérifier *(d'une affirmation etc)* to prove correct, to be confirmed; **mes soupçons se sont vérifiés par la suite** my suspicions were subsequently confirmed; **mon pronostic s'est vérifié** what I predicted came true

vérin [verɛ̃] **NM** *Tech* jack; **v. hydraulique/pneumatique** hydraulic/pneumatic jack; **v. à cliquet** ratchet jack; **v. à gaz** gas strut; **v. à vis** screw jack

véritable [veritabl] **ADJ 1** *(histoire etc)* true; **ce n'est pas son nom v.** that's not his real name; **se montrer sous son v. jour** to show one's true colours, to show oneself in one's true light **2** *(réel)* real, genuine, *Fml* veritable; **en soie/ivoire v.** made of real *or* genuine silk/ivory; **un v. ami** a real *or* genuine *or* true friend; **c'est un v. coquin** he's a downright *or* an absolute *or* an out-and-out rogue; **c'est un v. épouvantail** he's a perfect *or* an absolute fright; **c'était une v. surprise** it was a real surprise

véritablement [veritabləmɑ̃] **ADV 1** *(conformément à la vérité)* truly, *Fml* veritably **2** *(réellement)* really, genuinely; **nous nous sommes v. compris** we understood each other perfectly; **je ne le crois pas v. fait pour ce genre de travail** I don't think he's really cut out for this kind of work

vérité [verite] **NF 1** *(d'une déclaration etc)* truth, *Fml* verity; **respect de la v. historique** respect for historical fact; **c'est une v. éternelle** it's an eternal truth; **dire la v.** to tell *or* speak the truth; **la v. sort de la bouche des enfants** out of the mouths of babes and sucklings; **la v. finit toujours par se découvrir** truth will out; **récit conforme à la v.** true *or* factual account; **à la v.** to tell the truth, as a matter of fact; **en v.** really, actually; **heure de v.** moment of truth; *Jur* **la v., toute la v., rien que la v.** the truth, the whole truth and nothing but the truth; **c'est la v.** it's true, it's a fact; *Fam* **c'est la v. vraie** it's an actual fact, it's the honest truth, *Fam* it's gospel; **la v. d'un personnage** the trueness to life of a character; *Cin* **cinéma-v.** cinéma vérité; **dire à qn (tou-**

tes**) ses vérités** *ou* **ses quatre vérités** to tell sb a few home truths **2** *(sincérité)* sincerity, truthfulness; **accent/intonation de v.** truthful note/tone; **air/accent de v.** ring of truth

verjus [vɛrʒy] **NM** verjuice

verlan [vɛrlɑ̃] **NM** *Ling* back slang; **parler en v.** to speak in back slang

---

Verlan

This form of slang, mostly used among young French people, particularly in the impoverished areas of large cities, involves inverting the syllables of words and making any spelling changes necessary to facilitate pronunciation. The word "verlan" is itself the inverted form of "l'envers" meaning "the other way round". Some "verlan" terms are used or understood by a great many speakers, eg "laisse béton!" ("laisse tomber!" = "forget it!"), "ripou" ("pourri", used to refer to corrupt policemen), "meuf" ("femme") and "beur" ("arabe"). It is, however, an extremely generative form of slang and new words are constantly being made up.

---

vermeil, -eille [vɛrmɛj] **ADJ** vermilion, bright red; *(lèvres)* ruby(-red), bright red; *(joues)* rosy, bright red
NM silver gilt

vermicelle [vɛrmisɛl] **NM** *Culin* vermicelli, noodles; **v. chinois** Chinese noodles; **soupe aux vermicelles** noodle soup

vermiculaire [vɛrmikylɛr] **ADJ** worm-shaped, *Spéc* vermicular; *Anat* **appendice v.** vermiform appendix

vermiculé [vɛrmikyle] **ADJ 1** *Archit (maçonnerie etc)* vermiculated **2** *(boîtier de montre etc)* engine-turned **3** *Biol (taches)* vermiculate

vermiculure [vɛrmikylyr] **NF** *Archit etc* vermiculation

vermiforme [vɛrmifɔrm] **ADJ** worm-like, *Spéc* vermiform

vermifuge [vɛrmifyʒ] **ADJ, NM** *Pharm* vermifuge; **(poudre) v.** worming powder

vermillon [vɛrmijɔ̃] **NM 1** *(couleur)* vermilion **2** *(poudre)* vermilion, cinnabar
ADJ INV vermilion, bright red

vermine [vɛrmin] **NF 1** vermin; **couvert** *ou* **grouillant de v.** verminous, crawling with vermin VOIR GRAMMAIRE A11 **2** *Fig Péj* fréquenté par la v. frequented by lowlife characters *or* members of the underworld; **quelle v.!** what a rat!; *(ces gens-là)* scum!

vermisseau, -eaux [vɛrmiso] **NM** small (earth)worm

vermoulu [vɛrmuly] **ADJ** *(bois etc)* worm-eaten; *Fig* decrepit; **des institutions/diplômes/universités vermoulu(e)s** antiquated institutions/diplomas/universities

vermoulure [vɛrmulyr] **NF 1** *(dans le bois)* wormhole **2** *(poussière) (causée par des vers)* worm dust

vermout(h) [vɛrmut] **NM** vermouth

vernaculaire [vɛrnakylɛr] **ADJ** vernacular; **la langue v.** the vernacular; **nom v.** vernacular *or* common name

vernal, -ale, -aux, -ales [vɛrnal, -o] **ADJ** vernal

verni [vɛrni] **ADJ 1** varnished; *(acajou)* French-polished; **parquet v.** varnished *or* polished floor; **cuir v.** patent leather; **chaussures vernies** patent(-leather) shoes **2** *Fam* **être v.** *(chanceux)* to be lucky *or* *Br Fam* jammy **3** *Cér (carreau etc)* glazed, vitrified

vernier [vɛrnje] **NM** vernier, sliding gauge

vernir [vɛrnir] **VT 1** *(tableau, bois etc)* to varnish; *(acajou)* to French-polish; *(cuir)* to japan; **v. au tampon** to French-polish **2** *Cér* to glaze

vernis [vɛrni] **NM 1** varnish; **v. à bois** (wood) varnish; **v. à ongles** nail varnish *or* polish; **se mettre du v. à ongles** to varnish *or* paint one's nails; **v. à l'alcool** spirit varnish; **v. à l'essence** turpentine varnish; **v. cellulosique** cellulose varnish; **v. japonais** japan; **v. au tampon** French polish; *Cér* **v. (luisant)** glaze; **v. de plomb** lead glaze **2** *Fig* veneer; **dès qu'on gratte le v.** as soon as you scratch the surface; **ce n'est qu'un v.** it's just a veneer; **v. de politesse** veneer of politeness; **un v. de savoir** a smattering of knowledge **3** *Bot* **v. du Japon** varnish tree, lacquer tree, tree of heaven

vernissage [vɛrnisaʒ] **NM 1** varnishing; *Cér* glazing **2** *(d'une exposition)* private view(ing)

vernissé [vɛrnise] **ADJ 1** *Cér* glazed **2** *(brillant)* glossy

vernisser [vɛrnise] **VT** *(poterie)* to glaze

vernisseur, -euse [vɛrnisœr, -øz] **N 1** *(de bois etc)* varnisher; **v. au tampon** French polisher **2** *Cér* glazer

vérole [verɔl] **NF** *Méd* **1 petite v.** smallpox; **avoir la petite v.** to have smallpox **2** *Arg* syphilis, *Fam* pox

vérolé [verɔle] **ADJ** *Arg* syphilitic; **il est v.** he's got the pox

véronal [verɔnal] **NM** *Pharm* Veronal, barbitone

véronique [verɔnik] **NF** *Bot* speedwell, veronica

verrat [vera] **NM** boar

verre [vɛr] **NM 1** *(matière)* glass; **laine de v.** glass wool; **papier de v.** glasspaper, sandpaper; **passer qch au papier de v.** to sand(-paper) sth; **coton de v.** fibreglass, *Am* fiberglass, glass fibre; **articles de v.** glassware; **œil de v.** glass eye; **peintre sur v.** artist in stained glass; **sous v.** under glass; **gravure sous v.** glass-mounted engraving; **se casser** *ou* **se briser comme du v.** to be as brittle as glass
2 *(récipient)* glass; **lever son v. à qn** to raise one's glass to sb
3 *(contenu)* glass(ful); **il me suffit d'un v. (d'alcool) pour que je devienne ivre** it only takes one drink to get me drunk; **je n'ai bu qu'un v. ce soir** I've only had one drink this evening; **v. de vin** glass of wine; *Fam* **boire un petit v.** *(d'alcool)* to have a drink; **prendre un v.** to have a drink; **il a pris** *ou* **bu un v. de trop, il a un v. dans le nez** he's had one too many, he's had a drop too much; **tempête dans un v. d'eau** storm in a teacup *or Am* teapot
4 *(objet en verre)* glass; *(de lunettes)* lens
▸▸ **v. armé** wire(d) glass; **v. blanc** white glass; **v. à boire** glass; **v. à champagne** champagne glass; **v. coloré** stained glass; **verres de contact** contact lenses, *Fam* contacts; **verres dalles** pavement lights; **v. à dents** tooth glass; **v. dépoli** frosted glass; **v. à eau** tumbler, water glass; **v. feuilleté** laminated glass; **v. filé** spun glass; **verres fumés** tinted lenses; **v. à glaces** plate glass; **v. gradué** measuring jug; **v. grillagé** wire(d) glass; **v. grossissant** magnifying glass; **v. à liqueur** liqueur glass; **v. de montre** watch glass; **v. moulé** pressed glass; **v. à moutarde** = empty mustard jar used as glass; **v. pare-balles** bulletproof glass; **v. à pied** stemmed glass; **v. de sécurité** safety glass; **v. soluble** water glass; **v. trempé** toughened glass; **v. à vin** wineglass; **v. à vitres** window glass; **v. de vitrine** windowpane; **v. à whisky** whisky glass

verrée [vɛre] NF *Suisse (tournée)* round (of drinks); *(rencontre)* drinks party

verrerie [vɛr(ə)ri] NF **1** *(fabrication)* glass-making **2** *(atelier)* glassworks **3** *(marchandise)* glassware

verrier [vɛrje] NM **1** *(artisan)* glass-maker, glass-worker; *(souffleur)* glass-blower **2** *(casier)* glass rack
  ADJ M **peintre v.** artist in stained glass

verrière [vɛrjɛr] NF **1** *(d'une gare etc)* glass roof; *(paroi vitrée)* glass wall **2** *(pour protéger un tableau etc)* glass casing **3** *(vitre)* stained or glass window **4** *Aviat* canopy

verroterie [vɛrɔtri] NF *(bijoux)* glass jewellery; **collier de v.** string of glass beads, glass necklace; **ce n'est que de la v.** they are only glass trinkets

verrou [vɛru] NM **1** bolt; **fermer une porte au v.** to bolt a door; **mettre** *ou* **tirer le v.** *(pour fermer une porte)* to bolt the door; **s'enfermer au v.** to bolt oneself in; **tirer le(s) verrou(s)** *(ouvrir)* to unbolt the door **2** *Fam* **verrous** *(prison)* prison, *Br Fam* nick; **il est sous les verrous depuis 5 ans** he's been inside *or* behind bars *or* in the nick for 5 years; **il a fini sa vie sous les verrous** he ended his days behind bars; **mettre qn sous les verrous** to put sb inside, to put sb behind bars, *Br* to send sb down **3** *(d'une arme à feu)* bolt

verrouillage [vɛrujaʒ] NM bolting, locking; *(mécanisme)* locking mechanism; **une voiture à v. automatique** a car with central locking; *Aut* **v. central** *ou* **centralisé des portes** central door locking; *Aut* **v. centralisé à télécommande** remote central locking; *Aut* **v. du volant** steering lock; *Aut* **v. sécurité enfant** child-proof lock; *Aut* **v. à distance** remote control locking; *Ordinat* **v. des fichiers** file lock; *Ordinat* **v. du clavier numérique** numbers lock; *Ordinat* **v. en lecture seule** read-only lock; *Ordinat* **v. en majuscule(s)** caps lock

verrouiller [vɛruje] VT **1** *(porte)* to bolt; *Ordinat (capitales)* to lock on; **v. en écriture** *(fichier)* to lock; **verrouillé en majuscule(s)** *(clavier)* with caps lock on; **v. qn** to bolt sb in, to lock sb in **2** *Mil (ouverture)* to lock; *(passage, brèche)* to block **3** *(contrôler) (système, équipe)* to control; **avant d'envoyer le contrat, assure-toi que tout est verrouillé** before you send off the contract, make sure that everything is in order
  VPR **se verrouiller** to bolt oneself in; **je me suis verrouillée chez moi** I bolted *or* locked myself in

verrue [vɛry] NF wart; *(surtout au pied)* verruca; *Fig* **ce musée est une v. dans la ville** this museum is a real eyesore in the town, this museum is a carbuncle on the face of the town

verruqueux, -euse [vɛrykø, -øz] ADJ warty

vers¹ [vɛr] NM *(poétique)* verse, line; **v. alexandrins** alexandrine verse; **v. blancs** blank verse; **v. libres** free verse; **écrire** *ou* **faire des v.** to write verse *or* poetry; **c'est en v.** it's in verse; **morceau en v.** piece of verse *or* poetry

vers² PRÉP **1** *(dans l'espace)* toward(s); **façade qui regarde v. la forêt** façade facing the forest; **notre chambre regarde v. le nord** our bedroom faces north *or* is north-facing; **le lieu v. où nous allons** the place we're heading for *or* toward(s) *or* to; **un pas v. la démocratie** a step towards democracy; **habiter v. Pau** to live near *or* in the neighbourhood *or* Am neighborhood of Pau **2** *(dans le temps)* toward(s); *(autour de)* about; **v. la fin du siècle/de sa vie** towards the end of the century/his life; **venez v. (les) trois heures** come (at) about three (o'clock)

versaillais, -aise [vɛrsaje, -ɛz] ADJ of/from Versailles
  N V. inhabitant of Versailles

versant [vɛrsɑ̃] NM *(d'une montagne)* slope, side; *(d'un canal etc)* bank; *Fig* side; **v. de colline** hillside; *Fig* **il s'intéresse au v. politique de cette affaire** he's interested in the political aspect *or* side of the story

versatile [vɛrsatil] ADJ **1** *(disposition etc)* changeable, fickle **2** *Biol* versatile

> Il faut noter que l'adjectif anglais **versatile** est un faux ami. Il signifie **polyvalent**.

versatilité [vɛrsatilite] NF **1** changeability, fickleness **2** *Biol* versatility

verse [vɛrs] NF **1** *(des cultures dans le vent etc)* laying, beating down **2 à v.** in torrents; **il pleut à v.** it's pouring (down)

versé [vɛrse] ADJ *(dans une matière)* conversant (**dans** with); *(qui a de l'expérience)* experienced, practised (**dans** in); **très v. dans la littérature tchèque** well-versed in *or* very conversant with Czech literature

Verseau [vɛrso] NM *Astron, Astrol* **le V.** Aquarius, the Water Carrier; **être (du signe du) V.** to be (an) Aquarius *or* an Aquarian

versement [vɛrsəmɑ̃] NM payment; **v. à la commande** down payment; **versements échelonnés** staggered payments; **en plusieurs versements, par versements échelonnés** by *or* in instalments *or* Am install ments; **premier v.** down payment; *Banque* **bulletin de v.** paying-in *or* Am deposit slip; **v. d'espèces** cash deposit

verser [vɛrse] VT **1** *(liquide etc)* to pour (out); **v. du vin dans une cruche** to pour wine into a jug; **tu me verses un peu d'eau, s'il te plaît?** will you pour me some water, please?; **v. à boire à qn** to pour sb a drink, to pour a drink for sb
  2 *(renverser) (véhicule)* to overturn; *(du vent) (cultures)* to lay, to beat down
  3 *(larmes, lumière)* to shed; *(sang)* to spill, to shed; **v. son sang** to shed *or* spill one's blood; **prêt à v. son sang pour défendre ses idées** willing to fight for one's ideas
  4 *(argent)* to pay (in); *(sur un compte)* to deposit; **v. qch au crédit de qn** to credit sb with sth; **v. un acompte** to make a down payment; **on doit me v. un peu d'argent à la fin du mois** I should receive a little money at the end of the month; **v. de l'argent sur son compte** to pay money into one's account; **capitaux versés** paid-up capital; *Bourse* **v. un premium** to pay a premium
  5 *Jur etc* **v. un document au dossier** to add a document to the file
  6 *Mil* **v. des hommes à un régiment/dans une armée** to draft *or* assign *or* transfer men to a regiment/to an army
  7 *Mil (provisions)* to issue
  VI **1** *(d'un véhicule)* to overturn; *(des cultures)* to be beaten down, to be laid flat; **sa voiture est allée v. dans le ravin** his car tipped over into the ravine **2** *Fig* **il verse dans l'orgueil/la violence/le snobisme** he tends to be conceited/violent/snobbish

verset [vɛrsɛ] NM *(de la Bible etc)* verse

verseur, -euse [vɛrsœr, -øz] N *(personne)* pourer
  NM *Min* tipper
  NF **verseuse** *(de cafetière)* jug, (coffee) pot
  ADJ **bec v.** spout

versicolore [vɛrsikɔlɔr] ADJ particoloured, *Am* particolored, variegated

versificateur [vɛrsifikatœr] NM versifier

versification [vɛrsifikasjɔ̃] NF versification

versifier [vɛrsifje] *(impf, pr sub n.* **versifiions, vous versifiiez)** *Littér* VI to write verse
  VT **v. de la prose** to put prose into verse

version [vɛrsjɔ̃] NF **1** *(vers la langue mère)* translation; *Scol* unseen (translation); **v. latine** Latin translation, translation from Latin; **faire une v. vers le français** to translate into French; **v. anglaise/espagnole (vers le français)** translation from English/Spanish (into French); **thème et v.** prose and translation **2** *Cin* **v. originale** = version in the original language; **en v. originale** in the original language; **en v. originale sous-titrée** with subtitles; **v. française (doublée)** French version; **en v. française** dubbed in French; **film américain en v. française** American film dubbed into French **3** *Littér (d'un texte)* version **4** *(d'un événement)* version, account; **elle m'a raconté sa v. de l'histoire** she told me her version of the story; **chacun a sa v. des faits** everyone has their own version of the facts **5** *Ordinat* **v. bêta** beta version; **v. brouillon** draft version
  ▶▶ *Aut* **v. bâchée** soft-top; **v. nationale** *(d'un produit)* country version

verso [vɛrso] NM *(d'une feuille de papier)* verso, back, reverse; **voir au v.** see over(leaf); **l'adresse est au v.** the address is overleaf *or* on the back

versoir [vɛrswar] NM *Agr (d'une charrue)* mouldboard, *Am* moldboard

vert, verte [vɛr, vɛrt] ADJ **1** green; **légumes verts** green vegetables, *Fam* greens; **plantes vertes** house *or* pot plants; *Aut etc* **feu v.** green light; **attendre le feu v.** to wait for the green light; *Fig* **donner son feu v.** to give the green light (à for); **v. de peur** white with fear; **v. de jalousie** green with envy; **être v. de rage** to be livid (with rage)
  2 *(écologique)* green; **produit v.** green *or* environmentally friendly product; **candidat v.** green candidate
  3 *(agricole)* green; **pouvoir v.** power of the farming lobby; **l'Europe verte** European agriculture; **encourager les vacances vertes** to encourage holidays in the country; **partir en classe verte** to go on a school trip to the country-side; **la ceinture verte qui entoure Paris** the green belt around Paris
  4 *(bois)* green; *(fruit)* unripe; *(vin)* too young; **ce vin est encore v.** this wine isn't ready for drinking yet; **chêne v.** holm oak, ilex; **cuir v.** rawhide
  5 *Tél* **téléphone v.** *Br* ≃ Freefone®, *Can* ≃ Zenith, *Am* ≃ 800 number
  6 *(vieillard)* spry, sprightly
  7 *(histoire etc)* spicy, risqué; **dans un langage un peu v.** in rather risqué language
  8 langue verte slang
  9 *Vieilli (réprimande etc)* sharp, tart
  NM **1** *(couleur)* green; **v. profond/vif** deep/bright green **2 mettre un cheval au v.** to put a horse out to pasture *or* to grass; *Fam* **se mettre au v.** to go to the country to recuperate; *(pour se cacher)* to hide out *or* lie low *or* hole up in the country; **cet été, je me mets au v. et je lis** I'm going to spend this summer tucked away in the countryside reading **3** *Pol* **V.** Green; **la montée des Verts** the rise of the Greens
  NFPL *Fam* **en dire de vertes** to tell spicy *or* risqué stories; **il en a vu des vertes et des pas mûres** he's been through a lot
  ▶▶ **v. amande** almond green; **v. bouteille** bottle green; **v. cendre** sage green; **v. de chrome** chrome green; **v. d'eau** sea green; **v. émeraude** emerald green; **v. olive** olive green; **v. pomme** apple green; **v. tendre** soft green

vert-de-gris NM INV verdigris
  ADJ grey(ish)-green

vert-de-grisé, *pl* **vert-de-grisé(e)s** [vɛrdə-grize] ADJ coated with verdigris

vertébral, -ale, -aux, -ales [vɛrtebral, -o] ADJ *Anat* vertebral; **colonne vertébrale** spinal *or* vertebral column, spine, backbone

vertèbre [vɛrtɛbr] NF *Anat* vertebra; **v. cervicale/dorsale/lombaire** cervical/dorsal/lumbar vertebra; **se déplacer une v.** to slip a disc

vertébré [vɛrtebre] ADJ, NM *Zool* vertebrate

vertement [vɛrtəmã] ADV **réprimander v. qn** to reprimand sb sharply or severely, *Fam* to give sb a good telling off or ticking off; **il le tança v.** he gave him a good dressing-down; **répondre v. à qn** to answer sb sharply, to give sb a sharp reply

vertical, -ale, -aux, -ales [vɛrtikal, -o] ADJ vertical, upright; *(organisation, structuration)* vertical; **en position verticale** *(objet)* in a vertical position, upright; *(personne)* in a standing position; **elle se sent mal en station verticale** she doesn't feel well when she stands up; **éclairage v.** overhead lighting; *Ordinat* **boîtier v.** tower; *Écon* **concentration verticale** vertical integration ▪ NF **verticale** vertical; *Tech* plumb-line; **à la verticale** vertically; *(monter)* vertically, straight up; *(tomber, descendre)* vertically, straight down; **la falaise tombe à la verticale dans la mer** there is a sheer drop from the cliff to the sea; **falaise à la verticale** sheer cliff

verticalement [vɛrtikalmã] ADV vertically; *(avec mouvement vers le haut)* straight up; *(avec mouvement vers le bas)* straight down; *(dans les mots croisés)* down

verticalité [vɛrtikalite] NF verticality

verticille [vɛrtisil] NM *Bot* whorl

vertige [vɛrtiʒ] NM vertigo, fear of heights; *(étourdissement)* dizziness, giddiness, dizzy spell; **cela me donne le v.** it gives me vertigo, it makes me feel dizzy or giddy, it makes my head swim; **des salaires à vous donner le v.** salaries that make your head spin; **je n'ai pas le v.** I'm not scared of heights; **avoir facilement le v.** to have a bad head for heights; **avoir des vertiges** to get dizzy or giddy, to have fits of giddiness, to have dizzy spells; *Fig* **les vertiges du succès** the feeling of intoxication that success brings

vertigineusement [vɛrtiʒinøzmã] ADV dizzily, *Fml* vertiginously; **une route v. escarpée** a breathtakingly steep road

vertigineux, -euse [vɛrtiʒinø, -øz] ADJ *(hauteur etc)* dizzy, giddy; *(vitesse)* breakneck, breathtaking; *(somme)* staggering; **hausse vertigineuse des prix** staggering increase in prices

vertigo [vɛrtigo] NM *Vét* (blind) staggers

vertiport [vɛrtipɔr] NM *Aviat* heliport

vertu [vɛrty] NF **1** *(de remède etc)* quality, property, virtue; **v. sédative/calmante** sedative/calming property; **plantes aux vertus curatives** plants that have healing properties; **en v. de** by virtue of; *Jur* in pursuance of; **en v. de quoi est-il intervenu?** what gave him the right to intervene?; **et en v. de ce contrat, vous nous devez ...** under the terms of this contract, you owe us ...; **vous avez signé ce contrat, en v. de quoi vous nous devez une certaine prestation** you signed this contract, under the terms of which or in accordance with which you owe us a certain sum of money; **en v. de cet arrangement** under (the terms of) this agreement
  2 *(morale)* virtue; **faire de nécessité v.** to make a virtue (out) of necessity; **l'honnêteté est une v.** honesty is a virtue; **il a de la v. à la supporter** I admire his courage in putting up with her; **je n'ai aucune v. à ne pas fumer, je n'aime pas ça** I can't claim any credit for not smoking or *Fml* there is nothing admirable in my not smoking, I just don't like it; **elle le pare de toutes les vertus** she's forever singing his praises; **femme de petite v.** woman of easy virtue

vertueusement [vɛrtyøzmã] ADV virtuously

vertueux, -euse [vɛrtyø, -øz] ADJ virtuous; **intentions vertueuses** honourable intentions; *Arch* **femme vertueuse** virtuous or chaste woman

vertugadin [vɛrtygadɛ̃] NM *Hist* farthingale

verve [vɛrv] NF verve, vigour, *Am* vigor, *Fam* go; **être en v.** to be in top form; **jouer avec v.** to give a spirited performance

verveine [vɛrvɛn] NF *Bot* vervain, verbena; **(tisane de) v.** verbena tea; **(liqueur de) v.** = verbena flavoured liqueur

verveux¹, -euse [vɛrvø, -øz] ADJ *Litt* animated, lively, spirited

verveux² NM *(filet)* hoop net

vesce [vɛs] NF *Bot* vetch, tare

vésical, -ale, -aux, -ales [vezikal, -o] ADJ *Anat* vesical

vésicant [vezikã] ADJ, NM *Méd* vesicatory; **gaz v.** blister gas

vésicatoire [vezikatwar] ADJ, NM *Méd* vesicatory; **appliquer un v. à qn** to blister sb

vésicule [vezikyl] NF **1** *Anat* vesicle; *Bot* air cell; *Anat* **v. biliaire** gall bladder **2** *(sur la peau)* blister

vespasienne [vɛspazjɛn] NF street urinal

vespéral, -ale, -aux, -ales [vɛsperal, -o] ADJ evening

vesse-de-loup, *pl* **vesses-de-loup** [vɛsdəlu] NF puffball

vessie [vesi] NF *Anat etc* bladder; **v. natatoire** *(de poisson)* air bladder, swim bladder; *Méd* **v. à** ou **de glace** ice bag or pack; *Fig* **prendre des vessies pour des lanternes** to believe that the moon is made of green cheese

vestale [vɛstal] NF *Antiq* vestal (virgin)

veste [vɛst] NF jacket; **v. d'intérieur** smoking jacket; **v. croisée** double-breasted jacket; *Fam* **tomber la v.** to take off one's jacket; *Fig* **retourner sa v.** to be a turncoat; *Fig Fam* **ramasser** ou **prendre une v.** *(échouer)* to come unstuck; *(être rejeté)* to get turned down, *Br* to get a knockback

> Il faut noter que le terme anglais **vest** est un faux ami. Il signifie **maillot de corps** en anglais britannique et **gilet** en anglais américain.

vestiaire [vɛstjɛr] NM **1** *(dans un théâtre etc)* cloakroom; *Sport etc* changing room, locker room; *Jur* robing room; *Théâtre Fam* **au v.!** off! off! **2** *(vêtements)* **renouveler son v.** to renew one's wardrobe; *Fam* **mon v., s'il vous plaît** could I have my coat/hat and coat, please?; **récupérer son v.** to collect one's things from the cloakroom; *Fig* **laisser sa fierté/ses principes au v.** to forget one's pride/principles **3** *(meuble) (dans une usine etc)* locker

vestibule [vɛstibyl] NM vestibule, (entrance) hall, lobby

vestige [vɛstiʒ] NM *(d'anciennes habitations etc)* vestige, trace; **derniers vestiges de ...** last remnants of ...; **vestiges du passé** relics of the past

vestimentaire [vɛstimãtɛr] ADJ *(commerce)* clothing; **détails vestimentaires** accessories

veston [vɛstɔ̃] NM *(d'homme)* jacket; *Naut* monkey jacket; **complet v.** lounge suit

Vésuve [vezyv] NM Vesuvius

vêtement [vɛtmã] NM garment, article or item of clothing; **vêtements** clothes, clothing; **mon budget vêtements** my clothes or clothing budget; **industrie du v.** clothing or *Fam* rag trade; **tissus pour vêtements** dress material; **mettre ses vêtements du dimanche** to put on one's Sunday best; **vête-**ments de plage/de pluie beachwear/rainwear; *Rel* **vêtements sacerdotaux** vestments; **tu devrais mettre** ou **passer un v.** you should put something on

vétéran [veterã] NM *Mil etc* veteran, old campaigner; *Sport* veteran; *Fig* old hand; *Pol* elder statesman

vétérinaire [veterinɛr] ADJ veterinary ▪ N vet, *Br Fml* veterinary surgeon, *Am* veterinarian

vétille [vetij] NF (mere) trifle, triviality; **vétilles** trivia; **se disputer pour des vétilles** to argue over trivialities or trivial details

vétilleux, -euse [vetijø, -øz] ADJ *Litt* captious

vêtir [vetir] *(prp* **vêtant**; *pp* **vêtu**; *pr ind* **je vêts, n. vêtons**; *impf* **je vêtais**; *p hist* **je vêtis**; *fu* **je vêtirai)** VT *(quelqu'un)* to clothe, to dress (**de** in); **tout de noir vêtu** dressed or *Fml* clad all in black ▪ VPR **se vêtir** to dress (oneself) (**de** in)

vétiver [vetivɛr] NM vetiver

veto [veto] NM veto; **opposer son v. à qch** to veto sth, to exercise one's veto over sth; **mettre son v. à qch** to veto sth; **droit de v.** right of veto

véto [veto] N *Fam (abrév* **vétérinaire)** vet, *Am* veterinarian

vêtu [vety] ADJ dressed; **v. de blanc/de lin** dressed in white/in linen; **être u. chaudement** ou **chaudement v.** to be warmly dressed; **professeurs vêtus de leurs toges** professors wearing or in their gowns; **à demi-v.** half-dressed; *Litt* **mur v. de lierre** ivy-clad wall, wall covered in ivy

vétuste [vetyst] ADJ decayed, decrepit

vétusté [vetyste] NF decay, decrepitude

veuf, veuve [vœf, vœv] ADJ *(homme, femme)* widowed; *Fig* **v. de qch** bereft of sth ▪ N widower, f widow ▪ NF **veuve 1** *Typ* widow **2** *Fam Arch* **la Veuve** the guillotine **3** *très Fam* **la veuve Poignet** masturbation; **fréquenter la veuve Poignet** to bang or *Br* bash the bishop

veule [vøl] ADJ *(personne etc)* weak, feeble; **un air v.** a listless look

veulerie [vølri] NF inertia, listlessness

veuvage [vœvaʒ] NM widowhood

vexant [vɛksã] ADJ **1** *(remarque, personne etc)* hurtful **2** *Vieilli (contrariant)* vexing, provoking, annoying; **nous nous sommes manquées de peu, c'est v.!** how annoying that we just missed each other!

vexation [vɛksasjɔ̃] NF **1** *(humiliation)* mortification; **essuyer** ou **subir des vexations** to be snubbed or put down; **elle ne supporte pas les vexations** she can't stand being snubbed or put down; **être en proie aux vexations de qn** to be constantly being snubbed or put down by sb **2** *Vieilli (mauvais traitement)* vexation

vexatoire [vɛksatwar] ADJ vexatious

vexer [vɛkse] VT **v. qn** to hurt sb or sb's feelings ▪ VPR **se vexer** to get upset or offended; **elle se vexe facilement** she gets upset very easily, she's easily offended; **se v. de qch** to feel hurt or to be upset by sth; **il se vexe de tout/pour un rien** he gets upset over everything/the slightest thing

> Il faut noter que le verbe anglais **to vex** est un faux ami. Il signifie **fâcher, chagriner.**

VF [veɛf] NF *(abrév* **version française)** French version

VHF [veaʃɛf] NF VHF

VHS [veaɛs] NM *(abrév* **video home system)** VHS

VI [vei] NF *Compta (abrév* **valeur d'in-**

ventaire) balance sheet value, break-up value

via [vja] PRÉP via, by way of; **Paris, v. Calais** Paris, via Calais

viabilisé [vjabilize] ADJ *Admin* **terrain v.** serviced site, site with services

viabiliser [vjabilize] VT to service; **v. un terrain** to service a site; **v. une entreprise** to make a business viable

viabilité¹ [vjabilite] NF *(d'un fœtus)* viability, survival potential; *(d'un projet etc)* viability

viabilité² NF1 *(de chemin etc)* practicability **2** *Constr (d'un site de construction)* development

viable [vjabl] ADJ *(fœtus, projet etc)* viable

viaduc [vjadyk] NM viaduct

viager, -ère [vjaʒe, -ɛr] ADJ (for) life; **rente viagère** life annuity
NM life interest; **placer son argent en v.** to invest one's money in *or* to buy an annuity; **acheter une propriété en v.** = to acquire a property by paying predetermined instalments until the death of the owner(s)

viande [vjɑ̃d] NF **1** meat; **v. de boucherie** butcher meat, fresh meat; **v. blanche/rouge** white/red meat; **jus de v.** meat juices, gravy; **v. hachée** minced *or Am* ground meat, *Br* mince; **v. de cheval** horsemeat, horseflesh **2** *Arg* **amène ta v.!** come on, move your carcass!; **il y a de la v. soûle dans les rues** the streets are full of drunken bodies; **de la v. froide** *(un cadavre)* a stiff; *(des cadavres)* stiffs

viander (se) [səvjɑ̃de] VPR *Fam* to get smashed up; **ils se sont viandés contre un mur** they smashed into a wall

viatique [vjatik] NM1 *Vieilli (argent)* money; *(provisions)* provisions for a journey; **on lui a donné un v. de 200 livres pour son voyage** we gave him £200 for his trip; *Fig Litt* **il n'a que le diplôme pour v.** this diploma is his sole asset; **j'avais pour seul v. cette lettre de recommandation** this letter was all I had to recommend me **2** *Rel* last sacrament

vibrant [vibrɑ̃] ADJ **1** *(corde etc)* vibrating; **consonne vibrante** vibrant consonant **2** *(voix)* resonant, vibrant; *(discours)* rousing, stirring; *(personnalité etc)* vibrant; **v. et réceptif** *(personne)* eager and receptive; **c'est une nature vibrante** he is very sensitive *or* highly strung

vibraphone [vibrafɔn] NM *Mus* vibraphone

vibraphoniste [vibrafɔnist] N *Mus* vibraphone player

vibrateur [vibratœr] NM vibrator

vibration [vibrasjɔ̃] NF **1** vibration; *(de la voix)* resonance; *Phys* **v. de la lumière** vibration of light **2** *Tél (de téléphone portable)* vibrating alert

vibrato [vibrato] NM *Mus* vibrato

vibratoire [vibratwar] ADJ vibratory

vibrer [vibre] VI to vibrate; *Fig* **v. d'enthousiasme** to be quivering with excitement; *Fig* **faire v. le cœur de qn** to make sb's heart pound; *Fig* **c'est la seule chose qui le fait v.** it's the only thing that gets him going

vibreur [vibrœr] NM *Tech* vibrator; *(d'une sonnette)* buzzer

vibrion [vibrijɔ̃] NM **1** *(bactérie)* vibrio(n); *Méd* **v. septique** gas bacillus **2** *(personne agitée)* fidget

vibromasseur [vibromasœr] NM *(électrique)* (*pour massage*) vibrator

vicaire [vikɛr] NM *Rel* **1 v. apostolique** vicar apostolic; **grand v., v. général** vicar-general **2** *Rel (dans l'église anglicane)* curate; *Cathol* (assistant) priest

vicariat [vikarja] NM *Rel* curacy

vice [vis] NM **1** *(défaut moral)* vice; **il a tous**

les vices he has all the vices; **il a le v. de la boisson** drinking is his vice; *Fig* **mais c'est un v.!** it's an obsession!, he/she/they *etc* is/are totally obsessed! **2** *(défaut)* fault, defect, flaw **3** *(corruption etc)* vice; **vivre dans le v.** to lead a life of vice
▸▸ *Com* **v. apparent** obvious defect; **v. caché** hidden *or* latent defect; *Vét etc* **v. de conformation** (congenital) malformation, physical defect; **v. de construction** structural fault *or* defect *or* flaw; **v. de fabrication** manufacturing defect; *Jur* **v. de forme** legal technicality; *(dans un contrat etc)* flaw; *Com* **v. inhérent** inherent vice; **v. contre nature** unnatural vice; **v. de prononciation** faulty pronunciation; **v. propre** inherent defect; *Com* **v. rédhibitoire** material defect; **v. solitaire** masturbation, self-abuse

vice-amiral, *pl* **vice-amiraux** NM vice admiral

vice-chancelier, *pl* **vice-chanceliers** NM vice chancellor

vice-consul, *pl* **vice-consuls** NM vice-consul

vice-consulat, *pl* **vice-consulats** NM vice-consulate

vice-gérant, -ante, *pl* **vice-gérant(e)s** N deputy manager

vicelard, -arde [visəlar, -ard] *Fam* ADJ1 *(dépravé)* dirty **2** *(perfide)* vicious
N lecher, pervert; **un vieux v.** a dirty old man; **c'est une petite vicelarde!** she's a little tramp!

vicennal, -ale, -aux, -ales [visenal, -o] ADJ *(qui dure vingt ans)* twenty-year, *Fml* vicennial; *(qui a lieu tous les vingt ans)* occurring every twenty years, *Fml* vicennial

vice-présidence, *pl* **vice-présidences** NF *(d'État, d'organisation)* vice-presidency; *(d'entreprise)* vice-chairmanship

vice-président, -ente, *pl* **vice-président(e)s** N *(d'État, d'organisation)* vice-president; *(d'entreprise)* vice-chairman

vice-roi, *pl* **vice-rois** NM viceroy

vice versa [vis(e)vɛrsa] ADV vice versa

vichy [viʃi] NM **1** *Tex* gingham; **jupe en v. rouge et blanc** red and white checked cotton skirt, red and white gingham skirt **2** *(eau minérale)* vichy water; **v. fraise** = strawberry syrup in vichy water **3** *V.* Vichy; *Hist* **la France de V.** Vichy France

viciateur, -trice [visjatœr, -tris] ADJ contaminating, *Fml* vitiating

viciation [visjasjɔ̃] NF *(de principes, moraux etc)* corruption, *Fml* vitiation; *(de l'air etc)* pollution, contamination; *(du sang)* thinness; *Jur (d'un contrat)* invalidation, vitiation

vicié [visje] ADJ corrupt, *Fml* vitiated; *(sang)* poor, thin; **air v.** *(par des émanations)* stale *or* foul air

vicier [visje] VT *(impf, pr sub* **n. viciions, vous viciiez)** **1** to corrupt, *Fml* to vitiate; *(air)* to pollute, to contaminate; *Fig (jugement, goût)* to corrupt **2** *Jur (contrat)* to invalidate, to vitiate

vicieusement [visjøzmɑ̃] ADV **1** *(avec dépravation)* lecherously **2** *(perfidement)* viciously

vicieux, -ieuse [visjø, -jøz] ADJ **1** *(corrompu) (personne)* depraved **2** *(perfide) (personne, coup)* underhand, sly; **cercle v.** vicious circle **3** *(incorrecte) (prononciation)* wrong, incorrect **4** *(rétif) (cheval)* bad-tempered

---

Il faut noter que l'adjectif anglais **vicious** est un faux ami. Il signifie **méchant, agressif**.

---

vicinal, -ale, -aux, -ales [visinal, -o] ADJ **chemin v.** local road

NM *Belg (tramway de banlieue)* suburban tram

vicissitude [visisityd] NF vicissitude; **les vicissitudes de la vie** *ou* **de l'existence** the ups and downs *or* trials and tribulations of life

vicomte, -esse [vikɔ̃t, -ɛs] N viscount, *f* viscountess

vicomté [vikɔ̃te] NF **1** *(titre)* viscountcy **2** *(terrain)* viscounty

victime [viktim] NF1 victim; **les victimes du désastre/de la guerre** the victims *or* casualties of the disaster/of war; **les victimes de la route** road accident victims; **être (la) v. d'un système d'imposition** to be badly hit by a system of taxation; **être (la) v. d'une illusion/d'un malentendu** to labour *or Am* labor under an illusion/a misconception; **j'ai été (la) v. d'un escroc** I've been had by a conman; **se prendre pour une v.** to think oneself a victim, to feel victimized; **j'ai dû être v. d'une hallucination** I must have been hallucinating; **être v. de la fourberie/négligence de qn** to be the victim of sb's deceit/negligence **2** *(de sacrifice)* victim

victimologie [viktimɔlɔʒi] NF victimology

victoire [viktwar] NF **1** victory; *Sport* win, victory; **remporter la v.** to gain a victory **(sur** over), to carry *or* win the day; **remporter une v. sur soi-même** to triumph over oneself; **chanter** *ou* **crier v.** to claim victory; **v. à la Pyrrhus** Pyrrhic victory **2** *(déesse)* **V.** Victory, Victoria

Victoria [viktɔrja] NF **1 la reine V.** Queen Victoria **2 v.** *(voiture)* victoria

victorien, -ienne [viktɔrjɛ̃, -jɛn] ADJ Victorian

victorieusement [viktɔrjøzmɑ̃] ADV victoriously

victorieux, -ieuse [viktɔrjø, -jøz] ADJ victorious; *(air, sourire etc)* triumphant; *Sport* **sortir v. d'une épreuve/d'un match** to emerge the winner of a heat/a match; **être v.** to win (the day), to be victorious

victuailles [viktɥaj] NFPL *Vieilli* food, provisions, *Fml* victuals

vidage [vidaʒ] NM **1** *(de poissons)* gutting, cleaning; *(de volailles)* drawing **2** *Fam (d'un bar etc)* throwing out, chucking out **3** *Ordinat* dump

vidange [vidɑ̃ʒ] NF1 *Aut* oil change; **faire la v.** to change the oil; **v.-graissage** oil change and lubrication; **bouchon de v.** sump plug; *(de radiateur)* draining plug; **robinet de v.** draincock; **tuyau de v.** waste pipe; **tonneau en v.** broached cask **2** *(d'un carter à huile, d'une fosse d'aisances etc)* draining, emptying; *(d'une chaudière)* blowing off **3** *Belg (bouteille vide consignée)* returnable empty
NFPL **vidanges** sewage

vidanger [vidɑ̃ʒe] VT **(je vidangeai(s); n. vidangeons)** *(fosse d'aisances, radiateur, carter à huile etc)* to empty, to drain; *(chaudière)* to blow off; *(huile, eaux résidentielles)* to empty out, to drain off

vidangeur [vidɑ̃ʒœr] NM **1** *(de fosses septiques)* cesspit clearer *or* emptier **2** *Can Fam (éboueur)* dustman, *Am* garbage collector

vide [vid] ADJ *(verre, pièce etc)* empty; *(case dans un document etc)* blank; *(siège, place)* empty, unoccupied, vacant; **la ville est v. de ses habitants** the town is empty (of its inhabitants); **l'appartement est encore très v.** *(peu meublé)* the flat is still very bare; **bouteilles vides** empty bottles, *Fam* empties; **arriver les mains vides** to arrive empty-handed; **je suis rentré de vacances les poches vides** I came back from holiday penniless; **avoir l'estomac v.** to have an empty stomach; **j'ai l'estomac v.** my stomach is empty; **j'ai la tête v.** my mind's a blank; **ma vie est v.** my life is empty; **v. de sens** devoid of meaning, meaningless; **phrases vides** empty *or* meaningless words; **avoir le regard v.** to have a blank look; *Com* **v. en retour** empty on return

NM empty space, gap; *(dans un document)* blank; *Phys* vacuum; *Fig (néant)* emptiness, void; *(dans un emploi du temps)* gap; **combler les vides** to fill (up) the gaps; *Fig* **son départ laisse un v.** his departure has left a gap *or* void; **faire le v.** to create a vacuum; **la nature a horreur du v.** nature abhors a vacuum; *Fig* **il faut faire le v.** *(tout oublier)* you'll have to put it out of your mind; *Fig* **ça me permet de faire le v.** it helps me (to) switch off *or* blank everything out; **faire le v. autour de qn** to isolate sb completely, to leave sb on his/her own; **nettoyage par le v.** vacuum cleaning; *Fig* **faire le nettoyage par le v.** to throw everything out, to get rid of everything, *Fam* to gut the place; **le v. dans sa vie** the void in his life; **taper dans le v.** to (hit out and) miss the mark; **se jeter dans/regarder dans le v.** to jump into/stare into space; **avoir peur du v.** to be afraid of *or* to have no head for heights; **j'étais attiré par le v.** I felt an urge to jump; **Fig parler dans le v.** to talk to a brick wall; **à v.** *(batterie)* discharged; **camion revenant à v.** truck returning empty; **poids à v.** unladen weight; **marcher à v.** *(d'une machine)* to run light *or* without load; **le train est parti à v.** the train left empty; **le mécanisme tourne à v.** the engine is ticking over; *Mus* **corde à v.** open string; **emballé sous v.** vacuum-packed

▶▶**v. juridique** legal loophole; **v. sanitaire** crawl space

vidé [vide] **ADJ 1** *(poisson)* gutted; *(volaille)* drawn **2** *Fam (personne)* tired out, worn out, all in, dead beat; **c'est un homme v.** he's played out

vidéaste [videast] **N** video maker

vide-greniers **NM INV** second-hand goods sale, *Am* yard sale

vidéo [video] **ADJ INV** video; **caméra/cassette v.** video camera/cassette

NF INV *(média)* video; *(cassette)* video(-tape); **la dernière v. de Madonna** Madonna's latest video; **faire de la v.** *(d'un artiste)* to make videos; **v. à la demande** video-on-demand, VOD; **v. d'entreprise** *ou* **institutionnelle** corporate video; **v. fixe** video still; **v. interactive** interactive video; *Ordinat* **v. inversée** reverse video; **v. numérique** digital video; **v. promotionnelle** promotional video

vidéoachat [videoaʃa] **NM** videoshopping

vidéocassette [videokaset] **NF** videocassette

vidéoclip [videoklip] **NM** *TV (d'un groupe de rock etc)* video

vidéoclub [videoklœb] **NM** videoclub

vidéocommunication [videokɔmynikasjɔ̃] **NF** *Électron* video communication

vidéocomposite [videokɔ̃pozit] **ADJ** *Électron* **signal v.** videocomposite signal

vidéoconférence [videokɔ̃ferɑ̃s] **NF** video conference; *(concept)* video conferencing

vidéodiagnostic [videodjagnɔstik] **NM** *Méd* videodiagnostics

vidéodisque [videodisk] **NM** *Électron* videodisc, *surtout Am* videodisk

vidéofréquence [videofrekɑ̃s] **NF** *Radio* video frequency

vidéogramme [videogram] **NM** videogram

vidéographie [videografi] **NF** *Électron* = videotex; **v. diffusée** ≃ Teletext®; **v. interactive** ≃ Videotex®, Viewdata®

vidéographique [videografik] **ADJ** videographic

vidéolecteur [videolɛktœr] **NM** video player

vidéophone [videofɔn] **NM** *Électron* videophone

vidéoquestionnaire [videokɛstjɔnɛr] **NM** *(par Minitel®)* video-questionnaire

vide-ordures **NM INV** rubbish chute

vidéotex [videotɛks] **NM** *Ordinat* Videotex®, Viewdata®; **v. diffusé** teletext

vidéothèque [videotɛk] **NF** video library; *(personnelle)* video collection

vidéotransmission [videotrɑ̃smisjɔ̃] **NF** video transmission *or* broadcasting

vidéovente [videovɑ̃t] **NF** video-selling

vide-poches **NM INV 1** *(de voiture)* storage tray; *(dans la porte)* door pocket, map pocket **2** *(de table)* (dressing table) tidy

vide-pomme, *pl* **vide-pommes** **NM** apple corer

vider [vide] **VT 1** to empty; *(pièce, tiroir)* to empty, to clear out; *(tonneau, verre, étang etc)* to empty, to drain; *(chaudière)* to blow off; *(œuf)* to blow; *Ordinat* **v. l'écran** to clear the screen; *Ordinat* **v. la corbeille** to empty the wastebasket *or Am* the trash; **videz vos verres!** drink up!; **v. les lieux** to vacate the premises; **le juge a ordonné de faire v. la salle** the judge ordered the court (to be) cleared; **v. une chambre de ses meubles** to clear the furniture from a room; **la chaleur a vidé la ville de ses habitants** the heat has emptied the town (of its inhabitants); *Fam* **v. qn** *(l'épuiser)* to drain sb (of energy), to exhaust sb, to wear sb out; **partir en vidant la caisse** to make off with the takings; **v. les poches de qn** to empty sb's pockets; *(d'un voleur)* to pick sb's pockets; *Fam* **v. son sac** to get it off one's chest; **v. son cœur** to pour out one's feelings

2 *Fam (quelqu'un) (d'un bar etc)* to throw out; *(d'un travail)* to sack; *Équitation (cavalier)* to throw; *Équitation* **v. les arçons** *ou* **les étriers** to be thrown (from one's horse); **se faire v.** *(de son cheval)* to be thrown; *Fam (d'une pièce)* to be sent out; *(d'un bar etc)* to be chucked *or* thrown out; *(d'un collège)* to be expelled; *(être renvoyé)* to get the sack

3 *(carcasse)* to eviscerate; *(poisson)* to gut, to clean; *(volaille)* to draw; *(pomme)* to core; *(fruit)* to stone, *surtout Am* to pit

4 *(question, querelle)* to settle

VPR se vider to empty; **la baignoire est en train de se v.** the bath is emptying out, the bathwater is draining away; **ce réservoir se vide dans le lac** this tank drains *or* empties into the lake; **se v. de son sang** to bleed to death; **la locution s'est peu à peu vidée de son sens** the expression has gradually lost its meaning

vide-tasses **NM INV** slop basin

videur, -euse [vidœr, -øz] **N** *(dans un club etc)* bouncer

viduité [vidɥite] **NF** *Jur* widowhood; **délai de v.** minimum legal period of widowhood

vie [vi] **NF** VOIR GRAMMAIRE A12 **1** *(principe vital)* life; **v. végétative/animale** plant/animal life; **être en v.** to be alive; **donner la v. à un enfant** to give birth to a child; **perdre la v.** to lose one's life; **avoir la v. dure** *(de mauvaise herbe, personne)* to be tough (as old boots), to be hard to kill *or* to get rid of; *(de superstitions, préjugés etc)* to be hard to kill off *or* to get rid of; **on peut dire que tu as la v. dure, toi!** it takes a lot to kill you!; **il est entre la v. et la mort** he is (hovering) between life and death; **question de v. ou de mort** matter of life and death; **il y va de sa v.** his life is at stake; **je lui dois la v.** I owe him my life; **sauver la v. à qn** to save sb's life; *Fig* **tu me sauves la v.!** you're a life-saver!; **ramener qn à la v.** to bring sb back to life; *Fig* **revenir à la v.** to come back to life, to be back in the land of the living; **donner de la v. à une conversation/une réunion** to liven up *or* enliven *or* animate a conversation/a meeting; **elle dé-**

borde de v., elle est pleine de v. she's full of life, she's very lively; **la v. des idées/des volcans** the evolution of ideas/volcanoes; **sans v.** lifeless

2 *(existence considérée dans sa durée)* life, lifetime; **espérance de v.** life expectancy; **pour la v.** for life; **une fois dans la v.** once in a lifetime; **plus tard dans la v.** later (on) in life; **de toute ma v. je n'ai jamais entendu chose pareille!** I've never heard such a thing in all my life!; **jamais de la v.!** never!, not on your life!, no way!; **pension à v., pension la v. durant** life pension; **nommé à v.** appointed for life

3 *(biographie)* biography, life story; *Fam* **tu nous racontes ta v.!** we don't want your life story!

4 *(façon de vivre)* existence, way of life, lifestyle; **ainsi va la v.!, c'est la v.!** that's life!, such is life!; **je connais la v.** I've seen something of life; **regarder la v. en face** to look life in the face; **avoir une v. sédentaire** to have a sedentary lifestyle *or* (way of) life; **changer de v.** to change one's (way of) life; *(faire amende honorable)* to mend one's ways, to turn over a new leaf; **elle veut mener sa v. comme elle l'entend** she wants to lead her life as she sees fit; **rendre la v. dure à qn** to make life hard *or* a misery for sb; **avoir une v. dure** to have a hard life; **mener une v. de patachon** *ou* **de bâton de chaise** to lead a wild *or* riotous life, to live it up; **la v. à l'américaine** the American way of life; **la v. nocturne** nightlife; **femme de mauvaise v.** loose woman; *Fam Vieilli* **faire la v.** to lead a riotous life; **faire toute une v.** to kick up a fuss *or* a row

5 *Écon* living, livelihood; **la v. est très chère dans ces pays** the cost of living is very high in these countries; **niveau de v.** standard of living; **coût de la v.** cost of living; **indemnité de v. chère** *ou* **de cherté de v.** cost of living allowance; **gagner sa v.** to earn one's living *or* crust; **elle gagne bien/mal sa v.** she earns/doesn't earn a good living *or* wage; **comment gagne-t-elle sa v.?** what does she do for a living?, how does she earn a living?

vieil, vieille *voir* **vieux**

vieillard [vjejar] **NM** old man; **les vieillards** old people, the elderly, the aged; **hospice de vieillards** old people's *or Fam* old folk's home

vieillerie [vjejri] **NF** **vieilleries** old(-fashioned) *or* out-of-date things; *(idées)* old(-fashioned) *or* out-of-date *or* outdated ideas

vieillesse [vjejes] **NF** old age; **bâton de v.** support *or* prop of old age; **ma fille est mon bâton de v.** my daughter gives me support in my old age; **la v.** *(vieillards)* old people, the elderly, the aged; **aide à la v.** help for the aged

vieilli [vjeji] **ADJ 1** *(mot etc)* obsolescent; *(style etc)* old-fashioned, out-of-date **2** *(vieux)* (grown) old, aged

vieillir [vjejir] **VI 1** to grow old, to age; **vous n'avez pas vieilli, vous êtes toujours le même!** you haven't aged *or* got any older, you're still the same!; **il a vieilli, il est vieilli** he looks older, he's aged **2** *(d'un usage, d'un mot)* to become obsolete *or* antiquated *or* out of date; **ce mot a vieilli** this word is obsolescent; **cette chanson/construction n'a pas vieilli** this song/building has stood the test of time *or* hasn't dated; **la pièce a beaucoup vieilli** the play seems very dated **3** *(d'un fromage, d'un vin)* to mature

VT 1 v. qn *(du maquillage, d'une coupe de cheveux)* to make sb look old(er), to age sb; *(adolescent)* to make sb look older; **tu me vieillis!** I'm not that old! **2** *(meubles)* to distress; **pour v. un peu la photo** to age the photo a little

VPR se vieillir 1 *(par l'apparence)* to make

oneself look old(er) **2** *(en mentant)* to pretend to be older (than one is)

vieillissant [vjejisɑ̃] ADJ *(personne, édifice)* ageing; *(institution, style)* which is becoming outdated

vieillissement [vjejismɑ̃] NM **1** ageing, growing old; **ralentir le v. de la peau** to slow down the ageing process of the skin; **crème contre le v. de la peau** anti-ageing cream; **v. général de la population** general ageing of the population **2** *(d'un mot etc)* becoming obsolete, obsolescence **3** *(d'un fromage, d'un vin etc)* ageing, maturing **4** *(de meubles)* distressing; *(d'une photo, d'un cadre en bois etc)* ageing

vieillot, -otte [vjejo, -ɔt] ADJ antiquated, old-fashioned

vielle [vjɛl] NF *Mus* hurdy-gurdy

Vienne [vjɛn] NF Vienna

viennois, -oise [vjenwa, -waz] ADJ Viennese; **pain v.** Viennese bread; **un pain v.** a Vienna loaf
▪ N **V.** Viennese

vierge [vjɛrʒ] NF **1** virgin; *Fam* **jouer les vierges effarouchées** to go all squeamish; **la (Sainte) V.** the Blessed Virgin (Mary); **la V. Marie** the Virgin Mary; **chapelle de la V.** Lady chapel; *Beaux-Arts* **une V. à l'enfant** a Madonna and child **2** *Astron, Astrol* **la V.** Virgo; **être (du signe de la) V.** to be (a) Virgo
▪ ADJ **1** *(personne)* virgin, virginal; *(sol, forêt, huile etc)* virgin; **laine v.** virgin wool, pure new wool **2** *(page, cassette etc)* blank; *(blanc etc)* pure; *Phot (plaque)* unexposed; *Ordinat (ligne, espace)* blank; *(disquette)* blank, unformatted; **cahier v.** new *or* blank jotter; **réputation v.** untarnished reputation

Viêt-cong [vjɛtkɔ̃g] NM Vietcong, Viet Cong

Vietnam, Viêt Nam [vjɛtnam] NM Vietnam

vietnamien, -ienne [vjɛtnamjɛ̃, -jɛn] ADJ Vietnamese
▪ NM *Ling* Vietnamese
▪ N **V.** Vietnamese

vieux, vieil, vieille [vjø, vjɛj] ADJ *(the form vieil is used before masc nouns beginning with a vowel or h mute, but vieux also occurs in this position)* **1** *(personne)* old; **se faire v.** to be getting old, to be getting on (in years); **il est plus v. que moi** he's older than me; **moins v. que lui** younger than him; **vivre v.** to live to a ripe old age; **se sentir v.** to feel old; **il n'est pas bien v.** he's not very old, he's still young; **pour ses v. jours** for one's old age
VOIR GRAMMAIRE A17
2 *(amitié etc)* old, longstanding; **un vieil ami** an old friend, a friend of long standing; **il est v. dans ce métier** he's an old hand at this job; *Fam* **v. crétin!** old fool!; *Fam* **salut vieille noix** *ou* **branche!** hullo, old stick!; **c'est un v. marin** he's an old salt; **c'est un homme/une femme de la vieille école** he's/she's one of the old school **3** *(objet) (bâtiment etc)* old, ancient; *(pain, information etc)* old, stale; *(chapeau etc)* old, worn, shabby; **v. papiers** waste paper; **mes vieilles mains tremblent** my old hands are shaking; **elle ne va pas faire de v. os** she won't make old bones, she won't live long; *Fig* **je ne vais pas faire de v.** I'm not going to hang around here for long; **c'est v. comme Hérode** *ou* **le Pont-Neuf** *ou* **le monde** it's as old as the hills, it goes back to the year dot; **il est très vieille France** he's very much one of the old school; **c'est une vieille histoire** it's an old story; **elle est vieille, celle-là!** that's a real oldie *or* an old one!
4 *inv* **v. jeu** old-fashioned, antiquated, out of date; **ça, c'est v. jeu** that's old hat; **s'habiller/être v. jeu** to be old-fashioned in one's dress/to be old-fashioned; **des rubans vieil** *or* **v. rose** old-gold/old-rose ribbons

ADV **elle s'habille plus v. que son âge** she dresses too old for *or* older than her age; **elle fait moins v. que ça** she looks younger than that; **elle fait plus v. que son âge** she looks older than she really is
▪ N **un v.** an old man; **une vieille** an old woman; **un v. de la vieille** one of the old brigade, an old hand; **les v.** old people, the old *or* elderly *or* aged; *Fam* **mes v.** my parents *or Fam* folks; **mon v.** *(père)* my old man; *(mon ami)* mate, pal, chum; **ma vieille** *(mère)* my old lady; **comment ça va ma vieille?** *(à une amie)* how are you?; **viens, ma vieille!** come on, old girl!; **alors là, mon v., ce n'est pas mon problème** that's not my problem, mate *or* pal
▪ NM *Fam* **faire du neuf avec du v.** to make do and mend; **prendre un coup de v.** to age, to look (a lot) older; **j'ai l'impression d'avoir pris un coup de v.** I suddenly feel a lot older
▪ NF **vieille** *(poisson)* wrasse, seawife
▶▶ **v. beau** ageing Adonis, old roué; **vieille fille,** *Belg* **vieille jeune fille** old maid, spinster; **rester vieille fille** to remain single *or* a spinster; **v. garçon,** *Belg* **v. jeune homme** bachelor; **rester v. garçon** to remain single *or* a bachelor

Il faut noter qu'en anglais l'expression **old boy** ne désigne pas un vieux garçon mais un ancien élève d'un établissement scolaire privé.

vif, vive [vif, viv] ADJ **1** *(en vie)* alive, living; **être brûlé v.** to be burnt alive; **prendre de vive force** to take by storm *or* by force; **de vive voix** by word of mouth, *Litt* viva voce; **il l'a dit de vive voix** he said it himself; **haie vive** quickset hedge; **eau vive** running water, spring water; **marée de vive eau** spring tide; **chaux vive** quicklime; *Ordinat* **mémoire vive** random access memory, RAM
2 *(action, discussion etc)* lively, animated, brisk; *(personne)* vivacious, lively, animated; **vive allure, allure vive** brisk pace; **elle a été un peu vive et il est blessé** she was a bit sharp *or* curt *or* abrupt with him and hurt his feelings; **être v., avoir l'humeur un peu vive** to be quick-tempered; **il y avait un échange de paroles vives** there was a sharp exchange of words; **v. à répondre** quick to answer *or* reply, quick in answering; **avec mes plus vives félicitations** with my warmest *or* most heartfelt congratulations; **une flambée vive brûlait dans la cheminée** a fire was blazing away merrily in the hearth; **cheval v.** high-spirited horse
3 *(vent, réprimande etc)* sharp; *(douleur etc)* acute, sharp; **l'air est v.** there's a nip in the air; **l'air v. de la montagne** the sharp *or* bracing mountain air; **arête vive** sharp edge
4 *(esprit etc)* keen, quick; *(imagination etc)* vivid; *Euph* **il n'est pas très v.** he's not very bright *or* quick(-witted); **v. plaisir** keen *or* great pleasure; **éprouver un v. plaisir à faire qch** to take great pleasure in doing sth; **vive satisfaction** keen *or* great satisfaction; **écouter avec un v. intérêt** to listen with keen *or* deep *or* great interest
5 *(couleur)* bright, vivid, intense
▪ NM **1** **peindre sur le v.** to paint from life; *Fig* **être pris sur le v.** to be caught red-handed *or* in the act; *Fig* **une photo prise sur le v.** an action shot *or* photo **2** **blessé** *ou* **piqué au v.** cut *or* stung to the quick; **plaie à v.** open wound; **j'ai les nerfs à v.** my nerves are on edge; **entrer dans le v. de la question** to get to the heart of the matter; **couper** *ou* **trancher dans le v.** to take drastic measures **3** **pêcher au v.** to fish with live bait **4** *Jur* **living person; donation entre vifs** donation inter vivos

vif-argent NM INV **1** **il a du v. dans les vei-**

nes, **c'est du v.** he's never still (for a minute) **2** *Chimie, Arch* quicksilver, mercury

vigie [viʒi] NF **1** *(garde, gardien)* lookout (man); **être de v.** *ou* **en v.** to be on the lookout **2** *(poste)* watchtower; *Rail (sur wagon)* (observation) box; *Rail* **v. de signaux** signal cabin; *Rail* **v. de frein** brake cabin

vigilance [viʒilɑ̃s] NF vigilance, watchfulness; **avec v.** vigilantly; **surprendre la v. de qn** to catch sb napping; **redoubler de v.** to increase one's vigilance

vigilant [viʒilɑ̃] ADJ vigilant, watchful, alert

vigile [viʒil] NF *Rel (d'une fête)* vigil

vigile [viʒil] NM *(veilleur de nuit)* night watchman; *(gardien)* security guard

Il faut noter que le terme anglais **vigil** est un faux ami. Il ne signifie jamais **gardien**.

vigne [viɲ] NF **1** *(arbre)* vine; **feuille de v.** vine leaf **2** *(terrain planté)* vineyard; *Fig* **être dans les vignes du Seigneur** to be drunk, to be in one's cups **3** *Bot* **v. vierge** Virginia creeper

Do not confuse with **vignoble**.

vigneau, -eaux [viɲo] NM *(mollusque)* periwinkle

vigneron, -onne [viɲ(ə)rɔ̃, -ɔn] N wine grower

vignette [viɲɛt] NF **1** *Méd* label *(showing details of cost etc of medication, which has to be attached to the 'feuille de maladie' in order to qualify for a refund)*; *Aut Anciennement* **la v.** **(automobile)** the (road) tax disc; **v. d'assurance** insurance disc; **tu as pensé à acheter la v.?** did you remember to pay the road tax? **2** *Beaux-Arts, Typ* vignette **3** *Ordinat* thumbnail

vignettiste [viɲetist] N *Beaux-Arts, Typ* vignettist

vignoble [viɲɔbl] NM vineyard
▪ ADJ **région v.** wine(-growing) region

Do not confuse with **vigne**.

vignot [viɲo] NM *(mollusque)* periwinkle

vigogne [vigɔɲ] NF *Zool, Tex* vicuña, vicuna

vigoureusement [vigurøzmɑ̃] ADV vigorously

vigoureux, -euse [vigurø, -øz] ADJ *(personne, animal)* vigorous, robust; *(plante, arbre)* sturdy, robust; **elle est encore vigoureuse pour son âge** she's still hale and hearty for her age; **coup v.** powerful blow; **opposer une résistance vigoureuse à** *(projet, réforme)* to put up strong opposition to; **elle a opposé une résistance vigoureuse à son assaillant** she put up a strong fight, she tried to fight her attacker off

vigousse [vigus] ADJ *Suisse Fam (personne)* lively, bouncy; *(plante)* sturdy; **être v.** to be full of beans

vigueur [vigœr] NF **1** *(d'une personne, d'un animal, d'un style)* vigour, *Am* vigor, robustness; *(d'une plante, d'un arbre)* sturdiness, robustness; **donner de la v. à qn** to invigorate sb, to brace *or* perk sb up; **sans v.** *(personne)* exhausted, washed out; *(style etc)* flat, lifeless; **avec v.** vigorously **2** **en v.** *(décret etc)* in force, in effect; **entrer en v.** to come into force *or* effect *or* operation; **cesser d'être en v.** to lapse; **mettre un règlement en v.** to enforce a regulation

VIH [veiaʃ] NM *(abrév* **virus de l'immunodéficience humaine**) HIV; **V. positif** HIV positive

viking [vikiŋ] *Hist* ADJ Viking
▪ N **V.** Viking

vil [vil] ADJ **1** **vendre qch à v. prix** to sell sth at a low price, *Fam* to sell sth dirt cheap; **je l'ai acheté à v. prix** I bought it for next to nothing

2 *Litt, Arch (personne, motif etc)* vile, base; *Arch (origine, condition etc)* lowly; **vile calomnie** foul calumny **3** *(métal)* base

vilain, -aine [vilɛ̃, -ɛn] **N 1** *Fam* oh, le **v./la vilaine!** *(à un enfant)* you little villain!, you naughty boy/girl! **2** *Hist* villain, villein

NM *Fam* **il va y avoir du v.** there's going to be trouble; **tourner au v.** to turn nasty

ADJ 1 *(déplaisant)* nasty, bad, unpleasant; *(rhume)* nasty; **ne dis pas ces vilains mots** don't say those bad words; **tu es un v. petit garçon** you are a naughty little boy; *Fam* **c'est un v. monsieur** he's a nasty piece of work; **ce sont de vilaines gens** they're a bad *or* nasty lot; **v. tour** mean *or* dirty trick; **c'est une vilaine histoire** it's not a nice story, it's an ugly story; **une vilaine blessure** a nasty *or* an ugly wound **2** *(qui offense la vue) (chapeau, rue etc)* ugly; **elle n'est pas vilaine** she's not bad looking, she's not what you'd call ugly

vilainement [vilɛnmɑ̃] **ADV** in an unpleasant *or* a nasty way

vilebrequin [vilbrəkɛ̃] **NM 1** *(outil)* (bit) brace, brace and bit; **v. à cliquet** ratchet brace **2** *(dans moteur)* crankshaft

vilement [vilmɑ̃] **ADV** *Vieilli* vilely, basely

vilenie [vileni] **NF** *Litt* **1** *(caractère)* vileness, baseness **2** *(action)* mean *or* vile *or* low action, foul deed

villa [villa] **NF 1** villa, detached house **2** *Antiq* villa

village [vilaʒ] **NM** village; **il est bien de son v.** you can tell that he comes from the country; **v. de vacances, v.-vacances** holiday village; **v. de pêcheurs** fishing village; **le v. mondial** *ou* **planétaire** the global village

villageois, -oise [vilaʒwa, -waz] **N** villager; *(campagnard)* countryman, *f* countrywoman

ADJ rustic; **traditions villageoises** country *or* village customs

ville [vil] **NF** SEE GRAMMAR B7 town; *(plus grande)* city; **grande v.** city; **centre-v.** town centre, *Am* downtown; *(d'une ville plus grande)* city centre, *Am* downtown; **la seconde v. de France** France's second city; **gens de la v.** townspeople, townsfolk, city dwellers, *Fam* townies; **toute la v. ne parle plus que de lui** the whole town's talking about him, he's the talk of the town; **en v.** in (the) town; *(au centre-ville)* in the town/city centre, *Am* downtown; *(sur enveloppe)* local; **dîner en v.** to dine out; **aller à la v.** to go into town, *Am* to go downtown; **habiter à la v.** to live in a town *(as opposed to the country)*; **tenue de v.** town clothes; *(sur une invitation)* lounge suit; **financé par la v.** financed by the local authority; **hôtel de v.** town hall, *Am* city hall

▸▸**v. champignon** boom town; **v.-dortoir,** *pl* **villes-dortoirs** dormitory town; **v. d'eaux** spa (town); **la V. éternelle** the Eternal City; **v. fortifiée** fortified town; **la V. lumière** the City of Lights; **v. nouvelle** new town; **v. ouverte** unfortified town; **v. sainte** centre of pilgrimage, holy city; **v. satellite** satellite town; *Mktg* **v.-test,** *pl* **villes-test** test city; **v. thermale** spa town

villégiature [vileʒjatyr] **NF 1** holiday, *Am* vacation; **être en v.** to be on holiday *or* vacation; **ils partent tous les ans en v. à Capbreton** they go on holiday every year to Capbreton **2** *(lieu)* (holiday) resort

villeux, -euse [vilø, -øz] **ADJ** *Biol* hairy, *Spéc* villous

villosité [vilozite] **NF 1** hairiness **2** *Anat etc* villosity, villus

Vilnius [vilnjys] **N** Vilnius

vin [vɛ̃] **NM** wine; **les grands vins** vintage wines; **v. de Bordeaux** Bordeaux; **v. du Rhin** hock; **v. de Bourgogne** burgundy; **v. blanc/rouge/rosé** white/red/rosé wine; **v. mousseux** sparkling wine; **marchand de v.** (retail) wine merchant; **négociant en vins** (wholesale) wine merchant; **offrir un v. d'honneur à qn** to hold a reception in honour *or Am* honor of sb; **être pris de v.** to be the worse for drink; *Fam* **cuver son v.** to sleep it off; **avoir le v. gai/triste** to be/not to be a happy drunk; **entre deux vins** tipsy, merry; *Prov* **quand le v. est tiré, il faut le boire** there's no turning back now, you've made your bed and you must lie in it; **mettre de l'eau dans son v.** to water (down) one's wine; *Fig (modérer ses exigences)* to back off a bit; *(faire preuve de mesure)* to come down a peg or two

▸▸**v. d'appellation contrôlée** = wine of guaranteed vintage; **v. du cru** regional wine *(not from recognized vineyard)*; **v. cuit** fortified wine; **v. délimité de qualité contrôlée** medium quality wine; **v. de fruits** fruit wine; *Rel* **v. de messe** altar *or* communion wine; **v. ordinaire** table wine, *Br Fam* plonk; **v. de paille** straw wine; **v. de pays** regional wine; **v. de table** table wine

vinaigre [vinɛgr] **NM 1** vinegar; **v. blanc** distilled vinegar; **v. d'alcool** vinegar made from alcohol; **v. de vin** wine vinegar; **v. à l'estragon** tarragon vinegar; *Prov* **on ne prend pas les mouches avec du v.** you catch more flies with honey than vinegar **2** *(au jeu)* **sauter au v.** to jump (over) the skipping rope quickly, to skip quickly **3** *Fig Fam* **faire v.** to hurry, to get a move on; **tourner au v.** to turn sour

vinaigrer [vinɛgre] **VT** to season with vinegar

vinaigrerie [vinɛgrəri] **NF** *(fabrique)* vinegar factory; *(fabrication)* vinegar making

vinaigrette [vinɛgrɛt] **NF** *Culin* vinaigrette, French dressing; **poireaux v.** leeks (in) vinaigrette

vinaigrier [vinɛgrije] **NM 1** *(flacon)* vinegar bottle; **huilier-v.** oil and vinegar cruet **2** *(fabricant)* vinegar manufacturer

vinasse [vinas] **NF** *Fam* (cheap and nasty) wine, *Br* plonk

vindicatif, -ive [vɛ̃dikatif, -iv] **ADJ** vindictive

vindicte [vɛ̃dikt] **NF** *Jur (d'un crime)* prosecution; **v. publique** vindication of public morality; *Litt* **désigner qn à la v. publique** to expose sb to public condemnation

vineux, -euse [vinø, -øz] **ADJ 1** *Spéc (vin)* full-bodied **2** *(goût)* winy, *Fml* vinous; *(pêche etc)* wine-flavoured *or Am* -flavored; **odeur vineuse** winy smell, smell of wine; **haleine vineuse** breath smelling of wine **3** *(couleur)* wine-coloured *or Am* -colored; *Fam* **nez v.** ruby *or* winy nose, drinker's nose

vingt [vɛ̃] **ADJ INV** twenty; **v. et un** [vɛ̃teœ̃] twenty-one; **v.-deux** [vɛ̃tdø] twenty-two; *Arg* **v.-deux!** watch it!, look out!; **le v. juin** [ləvɛ̃ʒɥɛ̃] (on) the twentieth of June, (on) June (the) twentieth; **ouvert v.-quatre heures sur v.-quatre** open all day *or* round the clock, open twenty-four hours (a day); **les années v.** the twenties; **il n'a pas encore v. ans** he's not yet twenty, he's still in his teens; **je n'ai plus mon cœur de v. ans** I'm not as young as I was; **les moins de v. ans** teenagers; **je te l'ai dit v. fois** I've told you a hundred times *or* time and time again; **quatre-vingts** eighty; **quatre-v.-deux** eighty-two

SEE GRAMMAR B58–9

NM INV twenty; **je suis payée le v. de chaque mois** I'm paid on the twentieth of the month; *Cartes* **v.-et-un** pontoon, *Am* blackjack; *Am* twenty-one; **habiter au v. de l'avenue** to live at number twenty in the avenue

vingtaine [vɛ̃tɛn] **NF** **une v.** (about) twenty, a score; **une v. de personnes** twenty or so

people; **d'une v. d'années** about twenty years old SEE GRAMMAR A12–13; B59

vingtième [vɛ̃tjɛm] **ADJ** twentieth

N twentieth

NM *(fraction)* twentieth (part)

vingtièmement [vɛ̃tjɛmmɑ̃] **ADV** in (the) twentieth place

vinicole [vinikɔl] **ADJ** *(région etc)* wine(-growing)

vinifère [vinifɛr] **ADJ** *(sol etc)* wine-producing

Vintimille [vɛ̃timij] **N** Ventimiglia

vinyle [vinil] **NM** *Chimie* vinyl; *Fam (disque)* record; **c'est sorti sur v.** it came out on vinyl; **il rachète tous les vieux vinyles qu'il trouve** he buys all the old records he can find

vioc [vjɔk] **N** *Fam* old fart; **les** *ou* **mes viocs rentrent demain** the *or* my old dears come back tomorrow

viol [vjɔl] **NM 1** rape; **au v.! au v.!** rape! rape!; **v. collectif** gang rape *or Fam* bang **2** *(d'un sanctuaire, du règlement, des lois etc)* violation

violacé, -ée [vjɔlase] **ADJ** purplish-blue; **un rouge v.** a purplish red; **prendre un teint v.** *(à cause du froid)* to go blue; **son nez a pris une couleur violacée** his nose has gone a purplish colour

NFPL *Bot* **violacées** Violaceae

violacer [vjɔlase] *(je viola çai(s); n. viola çons)* **VT** **v. qch** to turn sth blue *or* purplish

VPR se violacer to turn blue *or* purplish; **sous l'effet du froid, la peau se violace** the skin turns blue *or* purple with cold

violateur, -trice [vjɔlatœr, -tris] **N** violator; *(de lois etc)* transgressor

violation [vjɔlasjɔ̃] **NF** *(de la loi etc)* violation, infringement, transgression, breach; *(d'une tombe)* desecration; **v. des règles** breaking of rules; **agir en v. d'une règle** to act in contravention of a rule

▸▸**v. de domicile** illegal entry; **v. de sépulture** desecration of graves

violâtre [vjɔlatr] **ADJ** purplish

viole [vjɔl] **NF** *Mus* viol; **v. d'amour** viol(a) d'amore; **v. de gambe** viola da gamba, bass viol

violemment [vjɔlamɑ̃] **ADV** violently; **elle le déteste v.** she hates him intensely; **il me dégoûtait v.** I found him deeply offensive

violence [vjɔlɑ̃s] **NF** violence, force; *(d'une confrontation etc)* fierceness; **obtenir qch par la v.** to obtain sth by violent means; **la v. des sentiments** the intensity of feeling; **faire v. à qn** to do violence to sb; **j'ai dû me faire v. pour me lever tôt** I had to force myself to get up early; *Hum* **je vais devoir me faire une douce v.** I'm going to have to force myself, I'm really going to have to make an effort; **faire v. à un texte** to distort a text; **subir des violences physiques/morales** to suffer *or* be subjected to physical violence/mental cruelty; *Vieilli* **faire v. à une femme** to violate *or* rape a woman; **v. conjugale** marital violence

violent, -ente [vjɔlɑ̃, -ɑ̃t] **ADJ** violent; *(vent)* high, fierce; *(échanges verbaux)* fierce, violent; *(mesures etc)* drastic; *(odeur)* pungent; **faire un effort v.** to make a huge *or* strenuous effort; **un v. orage éclata** a violent *or* raging storm broke out; **mourir de mort violente** to die a violent death; **choc très v.** tremendous impact; **une violente opposition** violent opposition; *Fam* **c'est un peu v.!** it really is too much!, that really is going too far!

N violent person

violenter [vjɔlɑ̃te] **VT 1** *(femme)* to rape **2** *Litt (nature)* to tamper with; *(morale)* to do violence to; *(texte)* to distort

violer [vjɔle] **VT 1** *(femme)* to rape; **se faire v.** to be raped **2** *(transgresser) (trêve, loi)* to violate, to break; *(loi)* to transgress, to infringe; *(traité, confiance)* to break; **v. un secret** to divulge a secret; **v. une sépulture** to desecrate a grave; **v. le domicile de qn** to break into sb's house; **v. les consciences** to violate people's consciences

violet, -ette 1 [vjɔlɛ, -ɛt] **ADJ** purple, violet; **mains violettes de froid** hands blue with the cold

NM *(couleur)* purple, violet

violette 2 [vjɔlɛt] **NF** *Bot* violet; **v. de Parme** Parma violet

violeur [vjɔlœr] **NM** rapist

violier [vjɔlje] **NM** *Bot* stock; **v. jaune** wallflower

violine [vjɔlin] **ADJ** dark *or* deep purple

violon [vjɔlɔ̃] **NM 1** *Mus (instrument)* violin, *Fam* fiddle; **jouer du v.** to play the violin; *Fam* **accordez vos violons** make sure you tell the same story, make sure you get your stories straight; **c'est son v. d'Ingres** it's his hobby **2** *(musicien)* violin (player); **premier v.** *(dans un orchestre)* first violin, leader; *Fig* **payer les violons (du bal)** to pay the piper **3** *Arg* **le v.** the cells, the lockup; **au v.** in the lockup; **passer la nuit au v.** to spend the night in the cells **4** *Tech* **(poulie à) v.** fiddle block **5** *Naut* **violons de mer** *(contre le roulis)* fiddles

violoncelle [vjɔlɔ̃sɛl] **NM** *Mus* **1** *(instrument)* cello, *Fml* violoncello; **jouer du v.** to play the cello **2** *(musicien)* cello (player), cellist

violoncelliste [vjɔlɔ̃selist] **N** cellist

violoneux [vjɔlɔnø] **NM** fiddler, *Péj* second-rate *or Am* two-bit violinist

violoniste [vjɔlɔnist] **N** violinist, violin player

vioque [vjɔk] **N** = **vioc**

viorne [vjɔrn] **NF** *Bot* viburnum

VIP [veipe, viajpi] **NM** *Fam* VIP

vipère [viper] **NF** viper, adder; *Fig (personne)* viper; **c'est une v., je préfère ne pas la rencontrer** she's really spiteful, I'd rather not meet her; **v. aspic** asp; **v. heurtante** puff adder; *Fig* **c'est une langue de v.** she's got a nasty tongue; *Fig* **nid de vipères** nest of vipers, snake pit

vipereau, -eaux [vipro] **NM** young viper

vipérin, -ine [viperɛ̃, -in] **ADJ** viperine; **NF vipérine 1** *Bot* viper's bugloss **2** *(reptile)* viperine snake

virage [viraʒ] **NM 1** *(mouvement)* turn, turning (round); *(d'une grue etc)* turning *or* swinging round; *Naut* tacking, going about; *Aviat* **v. (incliné)**, **v. sur l'aile** bank(ing); **angle de v.** angle of bank; **le skieur fait des virages** the skier is making turns **2** *(tournant) (sur la route)* (sharp) turn, bend, corner; **v. sans visibilité** blind corner; **v. en épingle à cheveux** hairpin bend; **v. à la corde** sharp turn; **v. relevé** banked corner; **virages sur 5 km** *(sur panneau)* bends for 5 km; **prendre ou aborder un v.** to take a bend, to corner **3** *(d'une piste de vitesse)* banked corner, bank **4** *(changement)* change (in direction); **le parti amorce ou prend un v.** the party is changing direction *or* shifting ground; **un v. net dans la vie politique du pays** a U-turn in the political life of the country **5** *Chimie* changing of colour *or Am* color; **v. au rouge** turning red **6** *Phot (des épreuves)* toning

virago [virago] **NF** virago, termagant; **c'est une vraie v.** she's a real shrew

viral, -ale, -aux, -ales [viral, -o] **ADJ** *Méd* viral

virée [vire] **NF** *Fam (en voiture etc)* trip, run, outing; *(dans les cafés, pubs)* pub crawl, *Am* bar hop; **faire une v.** *(en voiture etc)* to go for

an outing *or* a run; *(dans les cafés, pubs)* to go on a pub crawl, *Am* to bar hop

virelai [virlɛ] **NM** *Littér* virelay

virement [virmɑ̃] **NM 1** *Banque* (credit) transfer; **v. automatique** automatic transfer; **v. bancaire** bank transfer; **banque de v.** clearing bank; **v. par courrier** mail transfer; **v. de fonds** = transfer (often illegal) of funds from one article of the budget to another; **v. interbancaire** interbank transfer; **v. postal** post office transfer; **v. SWIFT** SWIFT transfer; **v. télégraphique** cable transfer; **v. par télex** telex transfer **2** *Naut* **v. de bord** tacking, going about

virer [vire] **VI 1** *(tourner) (du vent)* to veer; *Aut etc* to take a bend *or* a corner, to corner; *Aviat* to bank; *(d'une grue etc)* to turn round, to swing round; *Aut* **v. court** to corner sharply; *Aut* **v. sur place** to turn in one's own length; **la discussion a viré à l'aigre** the discussion took an acrimonious turn; *Naut* **v. de bord** to tack, to go about; *(d'un bateau à vapeur)* to turn; *Naut* **paré à v.!** ready about! **2** *(changer d'aspect)* to change colour *or Am* color; *Phot (d'une épreuve)* to tone; **encre qui vire au noir en séchant** ink that dries black; **la couleur est en train de v.** the colour is changing; **le rouge a viré à l'orange** the red has turned *or* changed to orange; **cutiréaction qui vire** skin test which comes up positive; *Fam* **v. homo** to turn gay; **v. voyou** to become *or* turn into a thug

VT 1 *Banque (somme)* to transfer; *(chèques etc)* to clear; **je lui vire 200 euros tous les mois sur son compte** I transfer 200 euros into his/her account every month

2 *Phot (épreuve)* to tone

3 *Fam* **v. qn** to throw *or* kick *or* chuck sb out; **se faire v.** *(d'un travail)* to get sacked *or* fired; *(d'un bar etc)* to get thrown *or* kicked *or* chucked out; **il faudrait v. ces étagères** we should throw *or* chuck these shelves out, we should get rid of these shelves

VPR se virer *Fam* **vire-toi!** move!

vireux, -euse [virø, -øz] **ADJ** poisonous, noxious

virevolte [virvɔlt] **NF 1** *(changement)* U-turn, volte-face; **v. de la fortune** sudden change of fortune; **je m'attends à une v. de sa part** I expect he'll change his mind; **une de ses inévitables virevoltes** one of his inevitable U-turns *or* about-turns **2** *Équitation Arch (d'un cheval)* quick circling **3** *(d'un danseur etc)* half-turn

virevolter [virvɔlte] **VI** *(d'un cheval)* to circle; *(d'une personne)* to spin round; *Fig* to make a U-turn

Virgile [virʒil] **NM** *Littér* Virgil, Vergil

virginal, -ale, -aux, -ales [virʒinal, -o] **ADJ** virginal; **blanc v.** pure *or* virginal white; **NM** *Mus* virginal, (pair of) virginals

Virginie [virʒini] **NF** Virginia

virginité [virʒinite] **NF** virginity; **perdre sa v.** to lose one's virginity; *Fig* **se refaire une v.** to restore one's image

virgule [virgyl] **NF 1** *Gram* comma; **point v.** semicolon; *Fig* **sans changer une v.** without changing a single thing *or* an iota; **c'est ce qu'il a dit à la v. près** that's word for word what he said **2** *Math* decimal point; **trois v. cinq (3,5)** three point five (3.5); *Ordinat* **v. fixe** fixed point; *Ordinat* **v. flottante** floating point; **arithmétique à v. flottante** floating point arithmetic

viril [viril] **ADJ 1** *(sexe etc)* male; *Anat* **membre v.** male member *or* organ; *Antiq* **toge virile** toga virilis **2** *(action etc)* manly; **allure/démarche virile** *(pour une femme)* masculine appearance/walk; **l'âge v.** manhood; **qualité virile** male characteristic

virilement [virilmɑ̃] **ADV** like a man, in a manly way

virilisant [virilizɑ̃] **ADJ** *Méd (substance)* which gives male characteristics

viriliser [virilize] **VT 1** *(rendre viril)* to make more virile *or* manly; *(forme etc)* to make appear masculine **2** *Biol (organisme etc)* to give male characteristics to

virilité [virilite] **NF** virility, manhood; **se sentir menacé/attaqué dans sa v.** to feel that one's manhood is being threatened/attacked

virole [virɔl] **NF** *(d'une canne, d'un couteau, d'un parapluie)* ferrule; *Tech* collar, hoop, sleeve

viroler [virɔle] **VT** *(manche d'outil etc)* to fit with a ferrule

virologie [virɔlɔʒi] **NF** *Méd* virology

virologiste [virɔlɔʒist], **virologue** [virɔlɔg] **N** *Méd* virologist

virose [virɔz] **NF** *Méd* virus disease, virosis

virtualité [virtɥalite] **NF** potentiality

virtuel, -elle [virtɥɛl] **ADJ** potential; *Opt, Phil, Ordinat (image etc)* virtual

virtuellement [virtɥɛlmɑ̃] **ADV 1** *(potentiellement)* potentially **2** *(pour ainsi dire)* virtually, to all intents and purposes

> Il faut noter que l'adverbe anglais **virtually** ne s'emploie jamais dans le sens de **potentiellement**.

virtuose [virtɥoz] **N** virtuoso; **c'est un v. du violon** he's a violin virtuoso VOIR GRAMMAIRE A14

virtuosité [virtɥozite] **NF** virtuosity

virulence [virylɑ̃s] **NF** *(d'un poison etc)* virulence; *(d'une satire, de paroles)* viciousness, venom

virulent [virylɑ̃] **ADJ** *(poison)* virulent; *Fig (satire, critique)* virulent, scathing; *(paroles)* scathing; **faire une critique virulente de qch** to criticize sth venomously; **diatribe virulente** scathing attack

virure [viryr] **NF** *Naut* strake

virus [virys] **NM** VOIR GRAMMAIRE A14 **1** *Méd* virus; **maladie à v.** viral disease; **le v. de la grippe** the influenza virus; **v. d'immunodéficience humaine** human immunodeficiency virus; *Fam* **il y a un v. qui traîne ou dans l'air** there's a virus going around; *Fam* **avoir le v. du ski** to have been bitten by the skiing bug **2** *Ordinat* virus; **désactiver un v.** to disable a virus

vis [vis] **NF** screw; **v. d'arrêt** *ou* **de blocage** stop screw; **v. à bois** wood screw; **v. à métaux** metal screw; **v. à tête cylindrique** cheese-head(ed) screw; **v. à tête fraisée** countersunk (head) screw; **v. à tête ronde** roundhead(ed) screw; **v. à oreilles** *ou* **à ailettes** wing screw; **v. autotaraudeuse** self-tapping screw; **v. à droite/à gauche** right-handed/left-handed screw *or* thread; **v. de purge** bleeder screw, bleed screw; **v. de réglage** adjuster screw, adjusting screw; **v. hexagonale** hexagon screw; **v. à pointe ronde** ball-ended screw; **v. sans fin** endless screw, worm (screw); *Tech* **v. d'Archimède** Archimedean screw; *Ind* **v. de transport** spiral conveyor; *Aut* **v. platinées** (contact) points; **tige à v.** screwed *or* threaded rod; **escalier à v.** spiral staircase; *Fig* **serrer la v. à qn** to be very hard *or* crack down on sb; *Fig* **il va falloir donner un tour de v.** things will have to start tightening up

visa [viza] **NM 1** *(pour passeport)* visa; **demander/obtenir un v.** to apply for/obtain a visa; **apposer un v. à un passeport** to stamp *or* visa a passport; **v. d'entrée** entry visa; **v. de sortie** exit visa **2** *(signature) (sur un document etc)* signature; *(paraphe) (d'un supé-*

rieur etc) initials; *(sceau) (sur un document)* stamp; *Cin* **v. de censure** censor's certificate; **v. d'exploitation** exploitation licence

visage [vizaʒ] NM face; **homme au v. agréable** pleasant-faced man; **soins du v.** (facial) skin care; **cela se lisait sur son v.** you could see it in his face, it was obvious; **frapper qn au v.** to hit sb in the face; **v. ouvert** open *or* honest face; **il a un v. d'enfant** he's baby-faced, he's a baby-face; **elle a changé de v.** her face *or* expression changed; **cette région a changé de v.** the area has had a face-lift; **à deux visages** two-faced; **il a deux visages** he's two-faced; **avoir bon v.** to look well; **faire bon v.** to put a brave face on things; **faire bon v. à qn** to be outwardly friendly to sb; **sans v.** faceless; **vrai v.** true face *or* nature; **l'Europe sous son vrai v.** the true face of Europe; **présenter un pays sous un autre** *ou* **nouveau v.** to present a country in a new light; **à v. découvert** *(ouvertement)* openly; **socialisme à v. humain** socialism with a human face; **je n'arrive pas à mettre un nom sur ce v.** I can't put a name to that face; **un v. ami** a friendly face; **il y a des visages qui frappent** some faces are very striking; **rencontrer de nouveaux visages** to meet new faces; **il y avait des visages connus** there were some familiar faces; **cela a donné un nouveau v. à notre pays** that has shown our country in a new light; **visages pâles** palefaces

visagiste [vizaʒist] N beautician

vis-à-vis [vizavi] PRÉP **1** *(en face)* **v. de qn/ qch** opposite *or* facing sb/sth **2** *(envers)* **v. de qn/qch** towards *or* in relation to *or* vis-à-vis sb/sth; **ses sentiments v. de moi** his feelings towards me; **être sincère v. de soi-même** to be truthful with oneself **3** *(par rapport à, comparé à)* **v. d'elle, je ne suis pas intéressante** compared with *or* next to her, I'm not interesting
▷ NM **1** *(à une table etc)* person opposite; *Cartes* partner; *(entretien)* tête-à-tête, meeting; **mon v.** the person sitting opposite me; **un long v.** a long tête-à-tête; **faire v.** *ou* **être en v. à qn** to be/stand/sit opposite sb, to face sb; **nous avons le lac pour v.** we look out on to *or* face the lake **2** *(meuble)* vis-à-vis, tête-à-tête, S-shaped couch

viscéral, -ale, -aux, -ales [viseral, -o] ADJ **1** *Anat* visceral **2** *Fig (haine)* deep, deeply ingrained; *(peur)* gut-wrenching; *(pensées etc)* innermost; *(réaction)* gut; *(répulsion)* instinctive

viscères [viser] NMPL *Anat* viscera, internal organs

viscose [viskoz] NF *Chimie, Ind* viscose; **robe en v.** viscose dress

viscosité [viskozite] NF viscosity, stickiness

visée [vize] NF **1** aim; *Mil etc* aiming, sighting; **ligne de v.** line of sight; **point de v.** target **2** *Fig* visées aims, designs; **avoir de grandes visées** *ou* **des visées ambitieuses** to have big *or* ambitious plans, to have great ambitions, to aim high; **il a des visées sur ce poste** he has designs on this job

viser[1] [vize] VT **1** *(avec une arme)* to aim *or* take aim at; *Fig (d'une remarque, accusation)* to be aimed *or* directed at; *Fig (ambitionner)* to have one's eyes on, to set one's sights on; *Com (clientèle, public)* to target; **qui visais-tu par cette remarque?** who was your remark aimed *or* directed at?; **je ne vise personne** I'm not alluding *or* referring to anybody in particular; **je sais très bien que cela me vise** I know very well that's directed at me; *Golf* **v. la balle** to address the ball; **il vise ce poste depuis longtemps** he's had his eye on this job for a long time
2 *(concerner)* to relate to; **les denrées alimentaires ne sont pas visées par ce décret** articles of food are not affected by this order **3** *Arg (regarder)* to (have a) look at; **vise un peu la fille!** have a look at her!, get a load of her!
▷ VI *Fig* to aim, to take aim *(à* at, for*)*; **v. à un but précis** to have a specific purpose; **v. à faire qch** to aim at doing sth *or* to do sth; **v. haut** to aim high; **v. juste** to aim straight; **tu as visé juste en lui disant cela!** you didn't miss the mark when you said that to him!; *Fig* **v. plus haut** to aim higher, to set one's sights higher

viser[2] VT *Admin (passeport)* to visa; *(document) (signer)* to countersign; *(apposer ses initiales à)* to initial; *(apposer un sceau à)* to stamp; *Compta* **v. des livres de commerce** to certify the books; *Fin* **v. un effet** to stamp a bill

viseur [vizœr] NM *Phot* viewfinder; *(d'un instrument de contrôle etc)* eyepiece, sighting tube; *Aviat* **v. de lancement** bomb sight(s)

visibilité [vizibilite] NF visibility; **la v. est très réduite par le brouillard** visibility has been greatly reduced by the fog; **v. nulle** zero visibility; **bonne/mauvaise v.** good/ poor visibility; *Aviat* **vol sans v.** instrument flying; **virage sans v.** blind turn; *Aut* **v. de trois-quarts** three-quarter vision; *Aut* **v. panoramique** all-round visibility

visible [vizibl] ADJ **1** visible; **v. à l'œil nu/au microscope** visible to the naked eye/under a microscope; **c'est à peine v.** it's scarcely visible, you can hardly see it; **très v.** highly visible, conspicuous; **il n'y avait personne de v.** there was nobody in sight; **elle est jalouse, c'est v.** it's obvious that she's jealous; **il est v. que …** it's obvious *or* clear that … **2** *(à qui l'on peut rendre visite)* ready to receive company; **je ne suis pas v.** I am not at home, I am not in; **je ne serai pas v. avant trois heures** I can't see anybody before three o'clock; *Fam* **n'entre pas, je ne suis pas v.** don't come in, I'm not decent; **cette collection n'est pas v.** this collection is not open to the public

visiblement [vizibləmã] ADV visibly; **v., il était contrarié** he was visibly *or* obviously *or* clearly annoyed

visière [vizjɛr] NF *(d'une casquette)* peak; *(pour protéger les yeux)* eyeshade; *(d'un casque)* visor; **mettre sa main en v.** to shade one's eyes with one's hand; *Litt* **rompre en v. à** *ou* **avec qn** *(se quereller)* to quarrel openly with sb; *(être d'avis contraire)* to have a diametrically opposite view to sb

visioconférence [vizjokɔ̃ferɑ̃s] NF videoconference; **visioconférences** *(concept)* videoconferencing

vision [vizjɔ̃] NF **1** *(sens)* (eye)sight; *(vue)* sight, view; **trouble de la v.** eye trouble; **défaut de la v.** visual defect; **v. momentanée de qch** momentary glimpse of sth; **nous n'avons pas la même v. des choses** we don't see things the same way; **nous partageons la même v. du monde/des choses/de la vie** we see *or* view the world/things/life in the same way; **cela m'a donné une nouvelle v. du problème** that gave me a new perspective on the problem; **v. réaliste/simpliste** realistic/simplistic view **2** *(d'un poète etc)* vision, imagination **3** *(hallucination)* vision; **avoir des visions** *(hallucinations)* to have visions *or* hallucinations, to see things; *Fam (rêver)* to fantasize

visionnaire [vizjɔnɛr] ADJ visionary
▷ N visionary, dreamer

visionnement [vizjɔnmã] NM *TV, Cin* screening; **v. préalable** preview

visionner [vizjɔne] VT *Cin* to screen; *(pour analyser)* to view

visionneuse [vizjɔnøz] NF *Cin, Phot* viewer

Visiopass® [vizjopas] NM *TV* = decoding card for French pay channels

visiophone [vizjɔfɔn] NM videophone, viewphone

visiophonie [vizjɔfɔni] NF video teleconferencing

visitandine [vizitɑ̃din] NF *Cathol* nun of the Order of the Visitation

Visitation [vizitasjɔ̃] NF *Rel (de la Sainte Vierge à sainte Élisabeth)* Visitation

visite [vizit] NF **1** *(à une personne)* visit, (social) call; *(d'un lieu touristique)* visit; *(visiteur)* visitor, caller; **j'aime bien avoir des visites** I like having visitors *or* guests; **faire une v.** *ou* **rendre v. à** to visit sb, to call on sb, to pay sb a visit *or* a call; **rendre une v.** *ou* **sa v. à qn** to return sb's visit *or* call; **il nous fait une petite v. tous les soirs** he drops in on us every evening; **être en v. chez qn** to be visiting sb *or* on a visit to sb; **nous avons eu la v. de Marc** Marc called in to see us; **recevoir la v. d'un représentant de commerce** to be called on by a representative; **v. de politesse** courtesy call, duty call; **v. officielle** official visit; **carte de v.** visiting card; *Sport* **équipe en v.** visiting team; **heures de v.** *(à l'hôpital etc)* visiting hours; **nous attendons des visites** *ou* **de la v.** we're expecting visitors *or* guests; **visites à domicile** *(d'un médecin)* house calls; **le docteur ne fait pas de visites** the doctor doesn't make house calls; *Jur* **droit de v.** *(de parents)* right of access
2 *(inspection)* *(d'un bâtiment, d'un navire)* inspection, examination, survey; *Méd* (medical) examination; **faire la v.** to go on one's round of inspection; *Mil etc* **passer la v.** to come before the medical officer *or* the medical board; *Mil* **v. des malades** sick parade; *Rel* **v. pastorale** *ou* **de l'évêque** pastoral visit, visitation *(by bishop)*; **trou de v.** *(d'un égout etc)* inspection hole, manhole; *Naut* **droit de v.** right of search; **v. de douane** customs examination
▷ ▷ **v. d'affaires** business call; **v. éclair** flying visit; *Com* **v. à froid** cold call; **v. guidée** guided tour; *(d'une ville)* sightseeing tour; **v. médicale: passer (à) une v. médicale** to have a medical examination; **v. pédagogique** educational visit; *Com* **v. de relance** follow-up visit

visiter [vizite] VT **1** *(de touristes)* to visit; **v. une cathédrale** to visit *or* tour a cathedral; **on nous a fait v. l'usine** we were shown round *or* over the factory, we were given a tour of the factory; *Ordinat* **v. un site Internet** to visit a Web site **2** *(inspecter) (bâtiment, mécanismes etc)* to inspect, to examine, to survey; *(maison à vendre)* to view, to go over; *(de la police etc) (maison etc)* to search; *(bagages)* to inspect, to examine; **quelqu'un est venu v. mon bureau en mon absence** someone has gone through my office during my absence; **je vais te faire v. les lieux/la maison** I'll show you round the premises/ the house **3** *(personne malade, patient etc)* to visit; *Com (client)* to call on
▷ VPR **se visiter** to be open to visitors

visiteur, -euse [vizitœr, -øz] N **1** *(touriste)* *(dans un musée etc)* visitor; **ouvert aux visiteurs à partir de quinze heures** open to visitors *or* to the public from three p.m. **2** *(hôte etc)* visitor, caller; *(dans une prison)* visitor; **recevoir des visiteurs** to receive visitors *or* guests; **nous avons eu de nombreux visiteurs** we had a large number of visitors; **infirmière visiteuse** community *or* district nurse; *(pour les nouveau-nés)* health visitor; *Sport* **les visiteurs** the visitors, the visiting team; *Com* **v. en soies** representative *or* traveller in silks **3** *(inspecteur)* inspector; **v. des douanes** customs officer
▷ ▷ **v. médical** medical representative; **visiteuse scolaire** *ou* **sociale** = social worker who specializes in visiting schools in the interests of child welfare

vison [vizɔ̃] NM **1** *(animal)* (American) mink **2** *(fourrure)* mink; *Fam (manteau)* mink coat

visonnière [vizɔnjɛr] NF *Can* mink farm

visqueux, -euse [viskø, -øz] ADJ sticky, viscous; *(huile)* thick, viscous; *(sécrétion etc)* slimy; *Fig* **sourire v.** smarmy smile

vissage [visaʒ] NM *(d'une vis)* screwing in; *(du couvercle d'un pot)* screwing on; *(d'une planche à un support)* screwing down; *(en serrant fort)* screwing up

vissé [vise] ADJ *Fam* **être bien v.** *(de bonne humeur)* to be in a good mood; **être mal v.** *(de mauvaise humeur)* to be in a foul mood

visser [vise] VT **1** *(une vis)* to screw in; *(couvercle d'un pot)* to screw on; *(planche à un support)* to screw down; *(en serrant fort)* to screw up; **v. un écrou à bloc** to screw a nut tight; *Fam* **être vissé sur sa chaise** to be glued to one's chair **2** *Fam* **v. qn** to treat sb severely, to be very hard or crack down on sb ▸VPR **se visser** to screw on; **le couvercle se visse facilement/mal** the lid screws on easily/doesn't screw on properly; **la lance se visse au bout du tuyau** the nozzle screws on to the end of the hose

visualisation [vizɥalizasjɔ̃] NF visualization; *Ordinat* **console** *ou* **unité** *ou* **écran de v.** (visual) display unit; *Ordinat* **v. de la page à l'écran** page preview; **v. de vidéo** video playback

visualiser [vizɥalize] VT *(imaginer)* to visualize; *(rendre visible) (quelque chose)* to make visible to the eye; *Ordinat* to display

visualiseur [vizɥalizœr] NM *Ordinat* viewer

visuel, -elle [vizɥɛl] ADJ visual; **champ v.** field of vision ▪ NM **1** *Ordinat* visual display unit, VDU **2** *(d'une affiche etc)* artwork **3** *(publicité)* visual ▪N visual person

visuellement [vizɥɛlmɑ̃] ADV visually

vit [vi] NM *Vieilli, Litt (verge)* member

vital, -ale, -aux, -ales [vital, -o] ADJ *(relatif à la vie) (énergie, force)* vital **2** *(indispensable à la vie)* vital; **centres vitaux** vital organs; *Fig* **centre v.** nerve centre **3** *(capital) (problème, question)* vital; *Fam* **il faut que tu viennes, c'est v.!** you must come, it's vital!, you absolutely must come!

vitalisme [vitalism] NM *Biol* vitalism

vitalité [vitalite] NF vitality

vitamine [vitamin] NF *Biol, Chimie* vitamin; **v. A/B12** vitamin A/B12; **alimentation riche/pauvre en vitamines** food with a high/low vitamin content, food that is high/low in vitamins; **enfant qui manque de vitamines** child with a vitamin deficiency; **as-tu pris tes vitamines?** have you taken your vitamins?

vitaminé [vitamine] ADJ enriched with vitamins, vitamin- enriched

vitaminique [vitaminik] ADJ *Méd* **carence v.** vitamin deficiency

vite [vit] ADV quickly, fast; **viens v. nous retrouver au bord de la mer!** come and join us at the seaside soon!; **lève-toi v., on sonne!** get up quick, there's someone at the door!; **je vais v. faire une course** I'm going to do one quick errand; **plus v.!** faster!; *Naut* increase speed!; **roule moins v.** don't drive so fast, drive more slowly; **le temps passe v.** time goes quickly, time flies; **manger trop v.** to eat too fast or too quickly; **tu as parlé trop v.** you spoke too soon; **ne va pas si v.!** *(en voiture)* not so fast!, slow down a bit!; **vous allez v. en besogne** you're a fast or quick worker, that's fast or quick work; **ça ne va pas v.** it's slow work; **vous serez v. guéri** you'll be better soon; **(faites) v.!** quick!, hurry up!, be quick (about it)!; **allons, et plus v. que cela!** now then, get a move on!; **au**

plus v. as quickly as possible; **je me suis v. rendu compte que …** I soon or quickly or swiftly realized that …; **avoir v. fait de faire qch** to be quick (about) doing sth; **tu auras v. fait de t'en apercevoir** you'll soon realize; **il eut v. fait de s'habiller** he was dressed in no time; *Fam* **on a tout rangé v. fait (bien fait)** we tidied everything away in no time; **on a v. fait de dire …** it's easy to say …

▪ADJ *Sport (voitures etc)* fast, quick

vitellus [vitelys] NM *Biol* vitellus, yolk

vitesse [vites] NF **1** speed, quickness; **à quelle v. allait-il?** how fast was he going?; **à la v. de …** at the rate of …; *Aut* at a speed of …; **à la v. de deux pages par jour** at the rate of two pages per day; **médecine/sécurité sociale à deux vitesses** two-tier medical/social security system; **une Europe à deux vitesses** a two-speed Europe; **v. folle** breakneck speed; **rouler à une v. folle** to drive at breakneck speed; **faire de la v.** to move or go quickly or at (high) speed, to speed along; *Aut etc* **excès de v.** exceeding or breaking the speed limit, speeding; **elle a été arrêtée pour excès de v.** she was arrested for speeding; *Aut* **limitation de v.** speed limit; *Fam* **en v.** quickly, at speed; **fais vors, et en v.!** get out pronto or now!; **partir en v.** to rush away or off; **un petit mot en v. pour vous dire …** just a quick line to let you know …; **lutter de v. avec qn** to race sb; **gagner** *ou* **prendre qn de v.** to outrun or outstrip sb; *(l'anticiper)* to steal a march on sb; **prendre de la v.** to pick up or gather or increase speed; *Pol* **ce parti est en perte de v.** the party is losing ground or popularity; *Aviat* **se mettre en perte de v.** to stall; *Aut etc* **compteur** *ou* **indicateur de v.** speedometer; **aller à toute v.** to go at full or top speed, to rush along; *Naut* **en avant à toute v.** full speed ahead; *Rail Arch* **grande/petite v.** fast/slow goods service; **train à grande v.** high-speed train

2 *Phys* velocity; **v. initiale** initial velocity; *(en ballistique)* muzzle speed or velocity; **v. du son** speed of sound; **v. acquise** impetus, momentum

3 *Aut* gear; **changer de v.** to change gear; **boîte de vitesses** gearbox; **passer en deuxième v.** to go or move into second (gear); **v. avant** forward gear; **v. inférieure** bottom gear, bottom; **v. supérieure** top gear, top; **vitesses synchronisées** synchromesh gears; *Fig Fam* **filer en quatrième v.** to disappear at top speed; *Fig* **il faut t'en occuper, et en quatrième v.** you'll have to take care of it without delay

▸▸*Ordinat* **v. d'affichage** display speed; *Ordinat* **v. de calcul** processing or computing speed; *Ordinat* **v. de clignotement** blink rate; **v. de croisière** *(d'un navire, d'un avion, d'une voiture)* cruising speed; **trouver sa v. de croisière** *(d'un navire etc)* to reach cruising speed; *Fig* to get into the swing of things; *Ordinat* **v. d'écriture** write speed; *Ordinat* **v. d'exécution** execution speed; **v. de frappe** typing speed; *surtout Ordinat* keying speed; **v. de frappe à la minute/l'heure** keystrokes per minute/hour; **v. d'impression** print speed; *Aut* **v. de pointe** top speed; *Ordinat* **v. du processeur** processor speed; *Com* **v. de rotation des stocks** inventory turnover rate; *Physiol* **v. de sédimentation** erythrocyte sedimentation rate; *Ordinat* **v. de traitement** processing speed

viticole [vitikɔl] ADJ *(région etc)* wine-producing, wine-growing; **industrie v.** wine industry

viticulteur, -trice [vitikyltœr, -tris] N vine grower, wine grower

viticulture [vitikyltyr] NF vine growing, wine growing, *Spéc* viticulture

vitiligo [vitiligo] NM *Méd* vitiligo, leucoderma

vitrage [vitraʒ] NM **1** *(d'une serre etc)* glazing; **double v.** double-glazing; **fenêtre à double v.** double-glazed window **2** *(d'un bâtiment etc)* windows **3** *(cloison)* glass partition **4** *(rideau)* net curtain

vitrail, -aux [vitraj, -o] NM leaded-glass window; *(coloré)* stained-glass window; **l'art du v.** the art of making stained-glass windows or stained glass; **les vitraux sont superbes** the stained-glass windows are superb, the stained glass is superb

vitre [vitr] NF window(pane), pane (of glass); **produit pour les vitres** glass- or window-cleaning product; **faire les vitres** to clean the windows; *Fam* **casser les vitres** to get angry, to kick up a fuss; *Fam* **ça ne casse pas les vitres** it's pretty ordinary or run-of-the-mill, it's nothing to write home about

vitré [vitre] ADJ **1** *(porte etc)* glazed; **baie vitrée** picture window; **bibliothèque vitrée** glass-fronted bookcase; **porte vitrée** glass door **2** *(substance etc)* vitreous, glassy; **humeur vitrée** vitreous humour

vitrer [vitre] VT *(fenêtre etc)* to glaze

vitrerie [vitrəri] NF glaziery; *(industrie)* glass industry

vitreux, -euse [vitrø, -øz] ADJ *(amas, roche etc)* vitreous; *(apparence etc)* glassy; *(yeux etc)* glazed; **regard v.** glassy stare, glazed look; **porcelaine vitreuse** vitreous china

vitrier [vitrije] NM glazier; *Fam* **ton père n'est pas v.!** I can't see through you, you know!

vitrification [vitrifikasjɔ̃] NF vitrification; *(du parquet)* varnishing, sealing

vitrifier [vitrifje] VT *(impf, pr sub n. vitrifiions, vous vitrifiiez) (sable etc)* to vitrify; **brique vitrifiée** glazed brick; **v. un parquet** to varnish or seal a parquet floor

vitrine [vitrin] NF **1** *(devanture)* shop window; **faire une v.** to do or dress a window; **refaire la v.** to change the window display; **articles en v.** articles (on show) in the window; **mettre des marchandises en v.** to display goods in the window; **regarder** *ou* **lécher les vitrines** to go window-shopping; **Paris est la v. de la France** Paris is the showcase of France **2** *(de musée)* glass case, cabinet, showcase; *(armoire)* display cabinet; **v. d'exposition** display cabinet

vitriol [vitrijɔl] NM **1** *Chimie Arch* vitriol; **(huile de) v.** oil of vitriol; *Fig* **au v.** *(critique, pamphlet etc)* vitriolic **2** *Fam (mauvais vin)* cheap wine, *Br* plonk; *(mauvais alcool)* gutrot

vitriolage [vitrijɔlaʒ] NM *(sur quelqu'un)* vitriol throwing

vitrioler [vitrijɔle] VT *(quelqu'un)* to throw vitriol at; **se faire v.** to be the victim of an acid attack

vitrioleur, -euse [vitrijɔlœr, -øz] N vitriol thrower

vitrocéramique [vitroseramik] ADJ ceramic; **plaque v.** ceramic hob

vitupération [vityperasjɔ̃] NF *Litt* vituperation

vitupérer [vitypere] (**je vitupère, n. vitupérons; je vitupérerai**) VT *Litt (quelqu'un, quelque chose)* to abuse ▪VI to protest, to storm, *Litt* to vituperate (**contre qn/qch** against sb/sth); **elle passe son temps à v. contre les transports en commun** she spends her time ranting and raving about public transport

vivable [vivabl] ADJ *Fam (personne)* livable with; *(maison etc)* livable (in); **cette situation n'est plus v.** this situation is intolerable; **il n'est pas v.** he's just impossible (to live with)

vivace¹ [vivas] ADJ *(résistant)* long-lived;

Biol hardy, robust; *Bot* perennial; *Fig (haine etc)* undying, inveterate; *Fig* **souvenirs encore vivaces** memories that are still fresh; *Bot* **pois v.** everlasting pea

vivace² [vivatʃe] ADJ INV, ADV *Mus* vivace

vivacité [vivasite] NF **1** vivacity, vivaciousness, liveliness; *(enthousiasme)* keenness; *(rapidité)* briskness, quickness; **v. d'esprit** quick-wittedness; *(humour)* sparkling wit; **avoir de la v.** to be vivacious *or* full of life; *(malgré son âge)* to be sprightly; **une femme âgée pleine de v.** a sprightly old woman; **avec v.** vivaciously **2** *(d'un sentiment)* acuteness; *(d'une discussion)* heat; *(d'une passion)* fire, intensity **3** *(d'un tempérament)* hastiness; **avec v.** hastily

vivandier, -ière [vivɑ̃dje, -jɛr] N *Arch* sutler, f vivandière

vivant [vivɑ̃] ADJ **1** *(doué de vie)* living; **un organisme/être v.** a living organism/being **2** *(en vie)* alive; **il est encore v.** he is still alive; **être enterré v.** to be buried alive; *Vieilli Fig* **s'enterrer v.** to bury oneself away; **portrait v.** lifelike portrait; **être le portrait v. de qn** to be the living *or* spitting image of sb; **langue vivante** modern language; *Fam* **c'est une bibliothèque vivante** he's a walking encyclop(a)edia; *Théâtre* **tableau v.** tableau (vivant)

3 *(plein de vie) (rue, scène, conversation etc)* lively, animated; *(enfant)* lively; **description/récit vivant(e)** lively description/account; **il a laissé en nous un souvenir très v.** he left us with a very vivid memory of him

NM **1** *(personne)* living being; **les vivants et les morts** the living and the dead; **bon v.** man who enjoys (the pleasures of) life, bon vivant **2 de son v.** during his lifetime, in his day; **du v. de votre père** when your father was alive, in your father's (life)time

Attention: lorsqu'on traduit l'adjectif **vivant**, il faut noter que les termes **alive** et **living** ne sont pas interchangeables. **Alive** signifie **en vie** et s'utilise uniquement comme attribut, alors que **living** signifie **doué de vie** et s'utilise comme épithète.

vivarium [vivarjɔm] NM vivarium

vivat [viva] INT *Arch* hurrah!, bravo!
     NMPL **vivats** *(d'un public etc)* cheers

vive [viv] NF *(poisson)* weever, stingfish

vivement [vivmɑ̃] ADV **1** *(rapidement)* briskly, quickly; **se tourner v.** to turn round quickly **2** *(durement)* sharply; *Fam* **réprimander v. qn** to give sb a sharp rebuke, to rebuke sb sharply; **répondre v.** to answer sharply *or* brusquely **3** *(intensément)* keenly, deeply, acutely; *(éclairé)* brightly; *(coloré)* vividly; **s'intéresser v. à qch** to take a keen interest in sth; **remercier qn v.** to thank sb warmly; **être v. ému** to be deeply moved; **contraster v. avec** to contrast sharply with **4** *(marque l'impatience)* **v. les vacances!** roll on the holidays!; **v. qu'il parte!** I'll be glad when he's gone!, he can't leave soon enough!

viveur [vivœr] NM *Péj* pleasure seeker, *Fam* fast liver

vivier [vivje] NM fishpond; *(dans un restaurant)* fish tank; *(de bateau)* fish well; *Fig* breeding ground (**de** for)

vivifiant [vivifjɑ̃] ADJ enlivening; *(air, climat etc)* invigorating, bracing

vivifier [vivifje] VT *(impf, pr sub* n. **vivifiions, vous vivifiiez)** to enliven, to (re)vitalize; *(de l'air etc)* to invigorate; **v. l'industrie d'un pays** to revive *or* give fresh life to a country's industry

vivipare [vivipar] ADJ *Biol* viviparous

viviparité [viviparite] NF *Biol* viviparity

vivisection [visiseksjɔ̃] NF vivisection; **ligue contre la v.** anti-vivisection league

---

vivoir [vivwar] NM *Can* living room

vivoter [vivɔte] VI to (just) get by; **j'avais à peine de quoi v. avec ce salaire** I could hardly keep body and soul together on that salary; **usine qui vivote** factory that is just managing to keep going *or* is just keeping its head above water

vivre¹ [vivr] NM **1 vivres** provisions, supplies; *Mil* rations; **vivres de réserve** iron rations; **couper les vivres à qn** to stop sb's allowance **2** *Arch* food; **le v. et le couvert** bed and board, board and lodging

vivre² *(prp* vivant; *pp* vécu; *pr ind* je vis, il vit, n. vivons, ils vivent; *pr sub* je vive; *impf* je vivais; *p hist* je vécus; *fu* je vivrai) VI **1** to live, to be alive; **v. au vingt et unième siècle** to live in the twenty-first century; **elle vit encore** she's still alive; **v. longtemps** to live a long time; **v. vieux** to live to a ripe old age; **cesser de v.** to die; **le Front populaire a vécu** the Popular Front has had its day *or* is finished; *Fam* **ma pauvre vieille télé a vécu** my poor old telly is on its last legs; **ne v. que pour son travail** to live (only) for one's work; **raison de v.** reason for living; **être las de v.** to be tired of living *or* of life; **vive le roi!** long live the King!; **vive l'armée!** three cheers for the army!; **vive les vacances!** three cheers *or* hurray for the holidays!; *Mil etc* **qui vive?** who goes there?; **ne rencontrer âme qui vive** to meet no one *or* not a living soul; *Prov* **qui vivra verra** time will tell; **ouvrage qui vivra** work that will endure; **traditions qui vivent encore** traditions that are still alive

2 *(d'une certaine façon)* to live; **v. à Paris/en province/à la campagne/à l'étranger** to live in Paris/in the provinces/in the country/ abroad *or* overseas; **il a beaucoup vécu** *(d'une personne)* he's seen life; *Fam* **v. pleinement** to live life to the full; **v. en honnête homme** to lead an honest life; **v. avec qn** to live with sb; **être facile à v.** to be easy to live with *or* to get on with; **savoir v.** to know how to behave, to be well-bred; **v. heureux** to live happily; *Prov* **pour v. heureux, vivons cachés** = the happiest people are those who keep themselves to themselves; **v. dans le présent/au jour le jour** to live in the present/one day at a time; **apprendre à v. à qn** to teach sb good *or* better manners; *Fam* **je vais t'apprendre à v.!** I'll teach you some manners!; **se laisser v.** to take life easily *or* as it comes; **il fait bon v. ici** life is pleasant here; **le plaisir de v.** the joy of living; **prendre le temps de v.** to take the time to enjoy life

3 *(économiquement)* to live; **on vivait bien juste** we could just manage *or* just rub along; **v. bien** to live in comfort, to live well; **travailler pour v.** to work for a living; **il fait cher v. ici** life *or* living is expensive here, the cost of living is high here; **faire v. sa famille** to support *or* keep one's family; **v. au jour le jour** *(avec ce qu'on a)* to live from hand to mouth *or* from day to day; **v. de poisson** to live on fish; **v. de sa plume/de ses rentes** to live by one's pen/on one's (private) income; **v. d'amour et d'eau fraîche** to live on fresh air, to live on love alone; **v. d'espérances** to live on hope; **l'espoir fait v.** where there's life there's hope; *Iron* what a hope!, you're/he's/*etc* optimistic!; **de quoi vit-il?** what does he live on?; *(que fait-il dans la vie?)* what does he do for a living?; **avoir de quoi v.** to have enough to live on; **ils n'ont que de quoi v.** they've just enough to live on
     VT **v. sa vie** to live one's (own) life; **les événements que nous avons vécus** the events we experienced *or* lived through; **elle a vécu la guerre** she lived through *or* went through the war; **v. des moments difficiles** to be going through *or* having *or* experiencing a difficult time; **v. une expérience unique/ inoubliable** to go through *or* have a unique/

---

an unforgettable experience; **v. une passion** to live out a passion; **v. sa foi** to live one's faith
     VPR **se vivre** **la maladie se vit mal quand on est seul** it's difficult being ill when you're on your own

vivrier, -ière [vivrije, -jɛr] ADJ **cultures vivrières** food crops

vizir [vizir] NM vizier

v'là [vla] PRÉP *Fam (abrév* **voilà)** **v. mon frère** here comes my brother; **et juste à ce moment-là, v. t-y pas qu'il se met à pleuvoir!** and just then, would you believe it, it starts raining!

vlan, v'lan [vlɑ̃] INT slap(-bang)!, whack!, wham!; **et v.! il est tombé!** and bang! he fell over!

vlimeux [vlimø] NM *Can Arg* **1** *(chanceux)* lucky devil; **le petit v.!** (the) lucky devil! **2** *(intrigant)* crafty devil

VMP [veempe] NFPL *Fin (abrév* **valeurs mobilières de placement)** marketable securities

VO [veo] NF *Cin (abrév* **version originale)** original (language) version; **voir un film en VO** to see a film in the original (language) version; **la VO est meilleure que la version doublée** the original version is better than the dubbed one

vocable [vɔkabl] NM **1** *(mot)* word, *Spéc* vocable **2** *Rel (d'un saint)* name, patronage; **église sous le v. de saint Pierre** church dedicated to Saint Peter

vocabulaire [vɔkabylɛr] NM **1** *(liste)* vocabulary, word list; **un v. (de termes) de chimie** a vocabulary of chemistry terms **2** *(d'une personne etc)* vocabulary; **enrichir son v.** to enlarge one's vocabulary; **le v. d'un enfant de six ans** the vocabulary of a six-year-old (child); **ce mot n'est pas dans mon v.** it's not a word that I use; *Péj* **quel v.!** what language!; **supprime ce mot de ton v.** stop using that word **3** *(jargon)* vocabulary; **v. administratif/juridique/technique** administrative/legal/technical vocabulary; **employer le v. à la mode** to use all the in words; **un junkie, pour employer le v. à la mode** a junkie, to use the in *or* fashionable word

vocal, -ale, -aux, -ales [vɔkal, -o] ADJ vocal

vocalement [vɔkalmɑ̃] ADV vocally

vocalique [vɔkalik] ADJ *Ling* vocalic; **son v.** vocalic *or* vowel sound

vocalisation [vɔkalizasjɔ̃] NF *Ling, Mus* vocalization

vocalise [vɔkaliz] NF *Mus* exercise in vocalization; **faire des vocalises** to do singing exercises

vocaliser [vɔkalize] VT *(mélodie, consonne)* to vocalize
     VPR **se vocaliser** to become vocalized

vocalisme [vɔkalism] NM *Ling, Mus* vocalism

vocatif [vɔkatif] NM *Gram* vocative (case); **au v.** in the vocative (case)

vocation [vɔkasjɔ̃] NF **1** *(goût)* vocation, calling; **pour ce genre de métier, il faut avoir la v.** you have to have a vocation for this kind of job; **manquer/suivre sa v.** to miss/follow one's vocation; **avoir la v. du professorat** to have a vocation for teaching, *Fam* to be cut out for teaching; **avoir la v. du commerce** to have an aptitude for business; *Fam* **il faut avoir la v.** you really need to be dedicated; **faire qch par v.** to do sth as a labour of love; **la v. industrielle de l'Allemagne** Germany's long industrial tradition; **région à v. agricole/industrielle** agricultural/industrial region **2** *(religieuse)* vocation, call; **je ne me sens pas la v. de la prêtrise** I feel no call to the Church *or* no calling for the Church

vociférateur, -trice [vɔsiferatœr, -tris] **N** *Litt* vociferator

vocifération [vɔsiferasjɔ̃] **NF** outcry, *Fml* vociferation; **vociférations** shouts, yells; **pousser des vociférations** to shout and bawl

vociférer [vɔsifere] (*pr ind* **je vocifère,** n. **vociférons;** *fu* **je vociférerai**) **VI** to shout, to yell, to bawl, *Fml* to vociferate (**contre** about)

VT v. des injures to shout *or* hurl insults (**contre** at)

vodka [vɔdka] **NF** vodka; **v. orange** (*verre*) vodka and orange

vœu, -x [vø] **NM 1** (*souhait*) wish; **faire un v.** to make a wish, to wish; **si je n'avais qu'un v. à faire, ce serait celui de ...** if I could have just one wish, it would be to ...; **émettre un v.** to express a wish *or* a desire; **former le v. que qch se réalise** to express a *or* the wish that sth should be done; **le Premier ministre a formé** *ou* **émis le v. que la loi soit modifiée** the Prime Minister expressed the wish that the law should be changed; **je fais des vœux pour qu'il ne pleuve pas dimanche** I'm praying it won't rain on Sunday; **tous mes/nos vœux, avec mes/nos meilleurs vœux** best wishes, with all good wishes; **tous mes vœux de bonheur** best wishes for your future happiness; **vœux de bonne** *ou* **de nouvelle année** New Year greetings; **le Président a adressé ses vœux à la nation** the President made his New Year address to the nation; **envoyer ses vœux à qn** to send sb one's best wishes; **carte de vœux** greetings card

2 (*promesse*) vow; **j'ai fait le v. de ne plus y retourner** I vowed never to go back (there again); **il a fait le v. de se venger** he vowed revenge; *Rel* **faire v. de pauvreté** to take a vow of poverty; **prononcer ses vœux** to take one's vows; **les vœux de baptême** the baptismal vows

▸▸ **v. pieux** pious hope

vogue [vɔg] **NF** fashion, vogue; **c'était la v. des cheveux courts** short hair was in fashion, it was the fashion to have short hair; **c'est la grande v.** it's all the rage; **en v.** fashionable, in vogue; **musique/artiste en v.** fashionable music/artist; **connaître une v.,** **être en v.** to be popular *or* fashionable, to be in fashion *or* in vogue; **les jupes longues sont à nouveau en v.** long skirts are back in fashion; **entrer en v.** to come into vogue *or* fashion, to come in

voguer [vɔge] **VI** *Litt* to sail; **les nuages voguant dans le ciel** the clouds sailing *or* floating by, the drifting clouds; **vogue la galère!** come what may!

voici [vwasi] **PRÉP 1** here is/are; **v. Henri** here's Henri; **v. mes neveux** (*en les présentant*) these are my nephews; (*ils arrivent*) here are my nephews; **me/les v.** here I am/they are; **ah te v. donc!** there you are!; **nous v. arrivés!** here we are!; **vous v. installés** here you are, all settled in; **nous v. à Paris** here we are in Paris; **nous v. riches!** we're rich!; **du pain? en v.** bread? here's some *or* here you are; **en v. une qui sera plus à ta taille** here's one which will be more your size; **la v. qui vient** here she comes, that's her (coming) now; **la v. qui recommence à pleurer** she's starting to cry again, that's her starting to cry again; **v. qu'il se met à pleuvoir** that's the rain on; *Litt* **v. venir Jeanne** here comes Jeanne; **mon ami que v. vous le dira** my friend here will tell you; **Monsieur/l'objet que v.** this gentleman/object; **la petite histoire que v.** the following little story; **v. de dont il s'agit** this is *or* here's what it's all about; **v. ce qu'il m'a dit** this is *or* here's what he told me; **v. comment**

je vois les choses this is *or* here's how I see things; **je le ferai et v. comment** I'll do it and here's how, *Fml* I shall do it in the following manner; **v. pourquoi** this is why; **et v. pour toi** and this is for you; **v. Noël!** Christmas is here!

2 (*il y a*) **je l'ai vu v. trois ans** I saw him three years ago; **v. deux mois que je ne l'ai pas vue** I haven't seen her for two months; **v. trois mois que j'habite ici** I have been living here for (the last) three months

voie [vwa] **NF 1** (*chemin*) way, road; (*non construit*) track; (*itinérant*) route; *Admin, Aut* traffic lane; **v. publique** public thoroughfare, public highway; **v. privée** private road; **route à quatre voies** four-lane road *or Am* highway; *Fig* **être par voies et par chemins** to be always on the move; **v. de communication** road, thoroughfare; (*avion, bateau, train*) means of transport; **grande v. de communication** main artery, arterial road; **la V. maritime du Saint-Laurent** the St Lawrence Seaway; **par v. de terre** by land, overland; **par v. de mer** by sea; **par la v. des airs** by air; *Fig* **la v. est libre** the coast is clear

2 (*à la chasse*) **voies** (*du gibier*) tracks; (*d'un daim etc*) slot; **mettre les chiens sur la v.** to put the dogs on the scent; *Fig* **mettre qn sur la v.** to put sb on the right track; **être sur la bonne v.** to be on the right track

3 *Rail* **v. ferrée** railway *or Am* railroad (track *or* line); **v. de service** *ou* **de garage** siding; *Fig* **mettre un projet sur une v. de garage** to shelve a plan; **mettre** *ou* **ranger qn sur une v. de garage** to put sb on the sidelines, *surtout Am* to sideline sb; **on l'a mis sur une v. de garage** he's been sidelined; **v. impaire, v. descendante** down line; **v. paire, v. montante** up line; **ligne à une v./à deux voies** single-/double-track line; **v. étroite** narrow-gauge line; **sur quelle v. arrive le train?** what platform *or Am* track does the train come in at?

4 *Ordinat* **v. d'accès** path; **v. bidirectionnelle simultanée** full duplex; **v. d'entrée** input channel; **v. de transmission de données** data link

5 (*moyen*) way; **voies et moyens** ways and means; **préparer la v.** to prepare *or* pave the way; **il finira par trouver sa v.** he'll find his way in the end; **avoir sa v. toute tracée** to have one's way marked out *or* mapped out; **la v. des armes** recourse to arms; **par la v. diplomatique** through diplomatic channels; **par v. hiérarchique** through official channels; **suivre** *ou* **prendre la v. hiérarchique** to go through official channels; **la v. la plus simple/rapide** the easiest/quickest way; **une v. dangereuse** a dangerous course; **les voies de Dieu** the ways of God; **la v. étroite** the straight and narrow; **en v. d'achèvement** nearing completion; **en v. de construction** under construction; **en v. de formation** in the process of formation; **un pays en v. de développement** a developing country; **en v. de réparation** under *or* undergoing repair; **il est en v. de guérir** *ou* **de guérison** he's on the mend, he's recovering; **être en v. de faire qch** to be (well) on the way to doing sth; **être en (bonne) v. de réussir** to be (well) on the way *or* road to success; **être en bonne v. de guérir** to be well on the road *or* way to recovery; **être en bonne v.** to be on the right track; **affaire en bonne v.** business that is going well; *Jur* **voies de droit** recourse to legal proceedings; *Jur* **voies de fait** assault and battery; **en venir aux voies de fait** to come to blows, to exchange blows; *Chimie etc* **v. sèche/humide** dry/wet process; **essai par la v. sèche** dry test

6 (*des roues d'un véhicule*) gauge; (*d'un outil*) kerf, clearance; (*d'une scie*) set; **donner de la v. à une scie** to set a saw

7 *Anat* passage, duct; **les voies digestives** the digestive tract(s); **par v. buccale** orally

▸▸ *Aut* **v. d'accélération** acceleration lane; *Min* **v. d'aérage** airway; *Aut* **v. de décélération** deceleration lane, exit lane; **v. de dégagement** filter lane; *Naut* **v. d'eau** leak; **faire une v. d'eau** to spring a leak; **v. express** expressway; **v. express urbaine** urban expressway; **v. fluviale** waterway; *Astron* **la V. lactée** the Milky Way; **v. navigable** waterway; **v. rapide** expressway; **v. rapide urbaine** urban expressway; **v. romaine** Roman road; **v. sans issue** dead end, cul-de-sac; **v. pour véhicules lents** crawler lane

voilà [vwala] **PRÉP 1** there is/are; **v. Henri** (*qu'on cherche*) there's Henri; (*qui arrive*) here comes Henri; (*dont je te parlais*) that's Henri; **v. Paul et Henri** (*en les présentant*) this is Paul and this is Henri; (*sur une photo*) this is Paul and this *or* that is Henri; **la/les v.** there she is/they are; **les v. qui arrivent** there they are (now); **la v. rassurée** she's calmed down now; **comme te v. changé** you've changed so much, how you've changed; *Fam* **nous v. frais** *ou* **beaux!** now we're in a fix *or* mess!; **la pendule que v.** that clock (there); **la petite histoire que v.** the following little story; **v. où il demeure** that's where he lives; **v. où je voulais en venir** that's what I was getting *or* driving at; **en v. assez!** that's enough!, that will do!; **j'attends depuis deux heures, en v. assez, je pars!** I've been waiting for two hours and I've had enough, I'm leaving!; **en v. une idée!** (*bizarre*) what a ridiculous idea!; (*excellente*) now there's an idea!; **en v. une jolie fille!** now there's a pretty girl!; **en v. de la reconnaissance!** there's gratitude for you!; **en v. un qui fera son chemin!** there's a man who will get on!; **en v. une qui sait ce qu'elle veut** there's someone who knows what she wants; **en v. pour cent euros** there's a hundred euros' worth; **tu n'en as pas assez? en v.** don't you have enough? here *or* there you are *or Am* there you go; **v. tout** that's all; **elle était déçue, v. (tout)** she was disappointed, that's all; **v. ce qui rend la situation difficile** that's what makes the situation difficult; **v. ce que c'est que de mentir à ses parents/d'être trop honnête** that's what happens *or* that's what you get when you lie to your parents/when you're too honest; **v. le hic** there's *or* that's the snag *or* the rub; **le v. qui entre, v. qu'il entre** there he is coming in; **v. (ce) qui s'appelle danser!/un homme!** now that's what I call dancing!/a man!; **v. qui est curieux!** that's curious!; **v. ce qu'il m'a dit** that's what he told me; **v. comme elle est!, la v. bien!** that's just like her!; **v. qu'il se remarie** and now he's getting married again; **v.!** there you are!; **et v.!** and that's that!; **v., monsieur!** (*dans un restaurant*) coming, sir!

2 (*voici*) **me v.!** here I am!; **le v.!** here he is!, here he comes!; **nous v. arrivés** we're here, here we are; **nous y v. enfin!** (*dans un endroit*) here we are at last!; **je l'avoue, j'étais jaloux – nous y v.!** I admit it, I was jealous – now the truth's coming out!

3 (*il y a*) **en juin v. trois ans** three years ago in June; **v. dix ans que je le connais** I've known him (for) ten years; **v. trois ans que je n'y suis pas retournée** I haven't been back there for three years

voilage [vwalaʒ] **NM 1** (*sur un chapeau etc*) net **2 voilages** (*rideau*) net curtains

voile¹ [vwal] **NF** sail; **v. carrée** square sail; **déployer** *ou* **établir une v.** to set a sail; **bateau à voiles** sailing boat; **aller à la v.** to sail; **vaisseau sous voile(s)** ship under sail *or* canvas; **mettre à la v.** to set sail; **faire v. sur Alger** to sail to *or* head for Algiers; **faire force de voiles** to crowd on *or* cram on all sail; **toutes voiles dehors** in full sail, all sail(s) set; **mettre toutes voiles dehors** to put on full sail *or* canvas; *Fig* to go at full tilt, to pull out all the stops; **faire de la v.** to sail; *Fam* **mettre les voiles** *(partir)* to scram, to do a bunk; *Fam* **marcher à v. et à vapeur** *(être bisexuel)* to swing both ways

voile ² **NM 1** veil; **v. de mariée** marriage *or* bridal veil; **les femmes qui portent le v.** women who wear the veil; *Rel* **prendre le v.** to take the veil **2** *(devant les yeux)* film, mist; **un v. de fumée/de brouillard** a veil of smoke/fog; *Fam* **jeter un v. sur qch** to cast *or* draw a veil over sth; *Méd* **avoir un v. au poumon** to have a shadow on one's lung; *Méd Fam* **v. noir** blackout; **v. de larmes** blur of tears **3** *Tex* voile **4** *Anat* **v. du palais** soft palate, velum **5** *Phot (sur un négatif)* fog **6** *Aut (flanc de roue)* spider

voilé [vwale] **ADJ 1** *(lumière)* veiled, dim; *(sens)* veiled, obscure; *(tambour)* muffled; *(voix)* husky; *Phot (épreuve)* fogged; **le ciel est v.** it's hazy; **femme voilée** woman wearing the veil; **des yeux voilés de larmes** eyes dimmed *or* blurred with tears; **en termes voilés/peu voilés** in veiled/thinly veiled terms **2** *(roue, tige etc)* buckled, out of true

voiler [vwale] **VT 1** to veil; *(lumière, soleil)* to dim; *(ciel)* to cover, to veil; *(son, tambour etc)* to muffle; *Phot (épreuve, plaque)* to fog; *Fig (trouble, émotion etc)* to hide, to conceal; **v. une statue/sa nudité** to cover a statue/one's nakedness **2** *(roue etc)* to buckle **3** *Naut (navire)* to rig with sails
VPR se voiler 1 se v. (le visage) to wear a veil; **les femmes doivent se v.** women must wear the veil; *Fig* **se v. la face** to hide *or* bury one's head in the sand; **sa voix se voile (d'émotion)** his voice is husky (with emotion) **2** *(du ciel etc)* to become overcast, to cloud over; *(des yeux)* to mist over; **le soleil était en train de se v.** the sun was becoming hazy **3** *(d'une roue etc)* to buckle

voilerie [vwalri] **NF** *Naut* sail loft

voilette [vwalɛt] **NF** *(hat)* veil

voilier [vwalje] **NM 1** *Naut (de plaisance)* yacht; **faire du v.** to go yachting; **un v. de 15 mètres** a 15-metre yacht **2 navire bon/mauvais v.** good/bad sailer **3** *(fabricant)* sailmaker; **maître v.** master sailmaker **4** *(oiseau)* **grand v.** long-flight bird

voilure ¹ [vwalyr] **NF 1** *(d'un navire)* sails; **réduire la v.** to shorten *or* reduce sail **2** *Aviat* wing(s), flying surface, aerofoil, *Am* airfoil; **appareil à v. fixe/tournante** fixed/rotary wing aircraft

voilure ² **NF** *(du métal, d'une roue)* buckling

voir [vwar] *(prp* voyant; *pp* vu; *pr ind* je vois, il voit, n. voyons, ils voient; *pr sub* je voie; *impf* je voyais; *p hist* je vis; *fu* je verrai) **VT 1** *(quelqu'un, quelque chose)* to see; *Naut (navire)* to sight; **je l'ai vu de mes (propres) yeux**, *Fam* **je l'ai vu comme je te vois** I saw it with my own eyes; **v. la mort de près** to stare death in the face; **il n'y a rien à v.** there's nothing to see *or* to be seen; **hôtel vu de face** front view of the hotel; *Archit* front elevation of a hotel; **bâtiment vu de côté/par la gauche** side/left-hand view of the building; *Archit* side elevation of a building; **(détail) vu de près** close-up (detail); **ce lieu a vu la fin de la guerre d'Indépendance** this spot saw the end of the War of Independence; *Fam* **on aura tout vu!** now we've seen everything!, wonders will never cease!; **j'en ai vu d'autres!** I've seen *or* been through worse!; **il faut le v. pour le croire** it has to be seen to be believed; **j'aimerais (bien) t'y v.!** I'd like to see you do it *or* try!; **c'est à v.** *(film, exposition etc)* it's worth seeing; **c'est encore à v.** that remains to be seen; **je le vois qui arrive** I can see him coming; **à le v., on dirait ...** by the look of him *or* to judge by his looks, one

would say ...; **on voit son jupon** her slip is showing; **mon fils, voyez-vous, est mort** my son is dead, you see; **v. page 23/ci-après** see page 23/below; *Litt* **que vois-je?** what is this (that I see)?; **faire v. qch à qn** to show sth to sb, to show sb sth; **il ne veut pas me faire v. son livre** he won't show me his book; **laisser v. qch à qn** to let sb see sth; **laisser v. son ignorance** to show *or* reveal *or* betray one's ignorance
2 *(+ inf)* **v. venir qn** to see sb coming; **je l'ai vu tomber** I saw him fall; **quels acteurs avez-vous vus jouer ce rôle?** what actors have you seen in this part?; **quelles pièces avez-vous vu jouer?** what plays have you seen?; **v. faire qch** to see sth done; **elle a vu construire la tour Eiffel** she saw the Eiffel Tower being built; **je l'ai vu faire ses pitreries** I saw him clowning around ◼️SEE GRAMMAR A41; B35
3 *(pour une visite)* *(quelqu'un, quelque chose)* to visit; **aller v. qn** to go to see sb, to go and see sb; **tu devrais aller v. un médecin/un avocat** you should go and see a doctor/a lawyer; **venez me v. quand vous serez à Paris** come and see me when you're in Paris; **nous avons vu les musées** we visited the museums; **je n'ai jamais vu Venise** I've never seen Venice; **v. du pays** to travel; **elle en a vu, du pays** she has travelled a lot *or* seen a lot of the world
4 *(fréquenter)* to see; **il ne voit (jamais) personne** he never sees anyone; **nous le voyons beaucoup** we see a lot of him; **on ne vous voit plus!** you're quite a stranger!; **nous ne les voyons plus** we don't see them any more; **je ne peux pas le v. (en peinture)** I can't stand (the sight of) him; **allez, file maintenant, je t'ai assez vu!** clear off, I've seen enough of you!
5 *(comprendre)* to see, to understand; **je vois où vous voulez en venir** I see *or* understand what you're driving at; **ah oui, je vois** oh yes, I see; **on voit bien qu'il est incompétent/jeune/innocent** you can see *or* it's obvious that he's incompetent/young/innocent; **je vois que vous m'avez attendu** I see you've waited for me; *Fam* **ni vu, ni connu** without anyone being any the wiser for it; **j'emprunte leur voiture pendant qu'ils sont partis, ni vu ni connu!** I'm borrowing their car while they're away, they'll be none the wiser!; **OK? c'est tout vu!** that's all there is to it!; **comment voyez-vous l'avenir?** how do you see *or* view the future?
6 *(observer)* *(quelque chose)* to see, to notice, to observe; **je vois que vous avez compris** I see you have understood; **à ce que je vois** from what I can see; **vous voyez ça d'ici** you can guess what it was/is/would be like; **je vois ça d'ici** I can see it coming; **je vois la scène comme si j'y étais** I can picture the scene as if I were there
7 *(examiner, étudier)* *(quelque chose)* to look after, to see to, to see about; **v. une affaire à fond** to look into *or* examine a matter thoroughly; **vu et approuvé** seen and approved; **elle a vu le dossier de la première à la dernière page** she studied *or* examined the dossier from beginning to end; **c'est que nous verrons!** we shall see!, that remains to be seen!; *Fam* **va-t'en v. si j'y suis!** get lost!, clear out!, scram!; **il n'a rien à v. là-dedans** *ou* **à y v.** it's nothing to do with him, it's no business *or* concern of his, it's none of his business; *(il n'y est pour rien)* he's got nothing to do with it; **cela n'a rien à v. avec l'affaire** that's beside the point, that has nothing to do with it; **ceci est à v., c'est à v.** it remains to be seen; **juste pour v. si ça marche** just to see if it works
8 *(voir à + inf)* **il va v. à nous loger** he'll see that we have somewhere to stay, he'll take care of our accommodation; **il faudrait v. à**

vous dépêcher! you'd better hurry up!; *Fam* **il faudrait v. à v.!** just you try!
9 *(voir que + sub)* **c'est à vous de v. que rien ne nous manque** it's up to you to see that we have everything we need
10 *(considérer)* *(qch d'une certaine façon)* to see, to look at, to consider, to regard; **je ne le vois pas marié** I can't see *or* imagine *or* picture him married; **je te verrais bien instituteur** I can just see *or* picture you as a teacher; **elle voit en lui un père/un ami** she looks on him as a father/a friend; **elle a tendance à v. tout en noir** she tends to look on the gloomy side of things; **v. la vie en rose** to see life through rose-coloured spectacles; **sa façon de v. les choses** his/her way of looking at things, his/her outlook; **v. les choses telles qu'elles sont** to see things as they are; **je ne vois pas cela comme ça** I don't see *or* look at it like that; **ce n'est pas ainsi que je vois les choses** that's not how I see things; **elle y voit un seul inconvénient** she can see only one drawback; **je ne vois pas où est le problème/la difficulté** I don't see what the problem/difficulty is; **si tu n'y vois pas d'inconvénients** if that's all right *or* OK with you; **c'est un café où il faut se faire v.** it's the café to go to *or* to be seen in; *Fam* **va te faire v., patate!** the same to you!; **il peut aller se faire v., qu'il aille se faire v.** he can go to hell; **se faire bien v. de qn** to gain sb's favour, to get into sb's good books; **se faire mal v. de qn** to get into sb's bad books; **être bien vu de tous** to be highly esteemed *or* well thought of by everyone; **elle est mal vue de tous** everyone has a low opinion of her; **c'est plutôt mal vu dans ce milieu** it's rather frowned on in these circles
VI to see; **elle ne voit plus** she can't see any more; **v. double** to see double; **v. clair** to see clearly; **tu ne vois pas clair?** are you not seeing straight?; *Fig* **je commence à y v. plus clair** I'm starting to get the picture; **v. mal** to have poor eyesight; **v. loin** to be farsighted; **il ne voit pas plus loin que le bout de son nez** he can't see any further than the end of his nose; *Fig* **v. grand** to think big; **v. c'est croire** seeing is believing; **je n'y vois plus** I can't see any more; **on n'y voit rien** *(il fait noir)* you can't see a thing; **v. rouge** to see red; **voyez vous-même!** see for yourself!; **voyez un peu l'état dans lequel il se trouve!** just look at the state he's in!; **faites v.!** let me see (it)!, let's have a look!; **en faire v. (de toutes les couleurs) à qn** to make sb's life a misery; *(le faire tourner en bourrique)* to lead sb a merry dance; *Fam* **voyons v.** let's see, let's have a look; **alors, voyons v., il faut commencer par ...** now, let's see *or* let me see, you have to start by ...; **montrez v.** just let me see it!; **dites v. ...** tell me ...; **essayez v.** just have a try; *(menace)* just you try it!; **regardez v.** just have a look; **regarde v. si elle n'est pas réveillée** have a look and see if she's woken up; **faire qch seulement pour v.** to do sth to see what happens *or* just as an experiment; **tu peux toujours essayer pour v.** you can always try just to see; **eh bien, je verrai** well, I'll see *or* think about it; **voyons!** *(pour examiner une question)* let's see!; *(pour exprimer une désapprobation)* come (on) now!, come!
VPR se voir 1 *(d'un phénomène, d'un objet)* to be seen; **monument qui se voit de loin** monument that can be seen *or* that is visible from a distance; **ça se voit que j'ai pleuré?** can you tell I've been crying?; **cela se voit tous les jours** you see things like that all the time, that kind of thing happens every day; **cela ne se voit pas tous les jours** it's not something you see every day; **ça se voit** that's obvious; *Fam* **cela se voit comme le nez au milieu de la figure** it's as plain as the nose on your face **2** *(d'une personne dans un*

miroir etc) to see oneself; *(de deux personnes)* to see each other; **je n'aime pas me v. en photo** I don't like looking at photos of myself; **elle ne se voit pas du tout avec des enfants** she just can't see herself with children; **il se voyait déjà perdu** he already imagined himself lost

voire [vwar] ADV indeed; **v. (même)** and even; *(alternativement)* or even; **j'en suis ahuri, v. révolté** I'm astounded, indeed disgusted; **elle est méticuleuse, v. maniaque** she's meticulous, obsessive even

voirie [vwari] NF **1** *Admin* = administration of public thoroughfares; **service de v.** roads department; **travaux de v.** road works; **employé de la v.** street sweeper **2** *(routes etc)* road system; **la grande v.** the main roads **3** *Vieilli (décharge)* refuse dump; **jeter les ordures à la v.** to dump the rubbish

voisin, -ine [vwazɛ̃, -in] ADJ neighbouring, *Am* neighboring; *(mitoyen)* bordering (**de** on); **une rue voisine des champs Élysées** a street adjoining the Champs Élysées; **la chambre voisine** the next room; **deux maisons voisines** two houses next to each other, two adjoining houses; **il habite dans la maison voisine** he lives (in the house) next door; **pays voisins** neighbouring countries; **cela aura lieu à une date voisine de la rentrée** it'll be sometime around the start of the new term; **les années voisines de 1990** the years around 1990; *Biol* **espèces voisines** closely allied *or* related species; **être v. de qn/qch** to be next to sb/sth; *Fig* **émotion voisine de la terreur** emotion akin to *or* bordering on terror; **des expériences très voisines** very similar experiences; **v. de la mort** at death's door

N neighbour, *Am* neighbor; **v. d'à côté/de porte/de palier** next-door neighbour; **les voisins du dessus/dessous** the upstairs/downstairs neighbours, the people upstairs/downstairs; **mon v. de table** the person I was sitting next to (at table), my neighbour at table; **dire du mal de son v.** to speak ill of one's neighbour; **agir en bon v.** to act in a neighbourly *or Am* neighborly way

voisinage [vwazinaʒ] NM **1** *(proximité)* vicinity, proximity, nearness; **apprécier le v. de la nature** to enjoy the proximity *or* closeness of nature; **les maisons dans le v. des montagnes** the houses in the vicinity of *or* near the mountains; **le v. de la gare est un avantage** proximity *or* being close to the station is an advantage **2** *(entourage)* vicinity, neighbourhood, *Am* neighborhood; **il n'y avait personne dans le v.** there was nobody in the vicinity, there was nobody about; **relations de bon v.** (good) neighbourliness *or Am* neighborliness; **être en bon v. avec qn**, **entretenir des relations de bon v. avec qn** to be on good terms with sb

voisiner [vwazine] VI **1** *Litt* to visit one's neighbours *or Am* neighbors; **à Paris on voisine peu** in Paris you don't see much of your neighbours **2** **v. avec qch** to be (placed) side by side with sth; *(être mitoyen de qch)* to adjoin sth

voiturage [vwatyraʒ] NM *(de marchandises etc)* carriage, conveyance, cartage

voiture [vwatyr] NF **1** *Aut* car, *Am* automobile, *Br Fam* motor; **location de voitures** car hire *or* rental; **prendre sa v.** to take the car; **aller à Paris en v.** to go to Paris by car; **petite v.** invalid carriage; **v. à combustible mixte** dual-fuel car; **v. de compétition** competition car; **v. de course** racing car; **v. de démonstration** demo model, demonstrator; **à double commande** dual-controlled car; **v. familiale** family car; **v. de fonction** company car; **v. d'infirme** invalid carriage; **v. de livraison** delivery van; **v. de location** rental *or Br*

hired car; **v. de maître** chauffeur-driven car; **v. de marchandises** goods van; **v. d'occasion** used car, second-hand car; **v. radio** radio car; *TV, Radio* **v. de reportage** remote van; **v. de série** production car; **v. de société** company car; **v. de sport** *ou* **sportive** sports car; **v. de tourisme** private *or* touring car **2** *Rail* coach, carriage, *Am* car; **v. fumeurs** smoking carriage, smoker; **v. non fumeurs** no-smoking carriage, non-smoker; **en v.!** take your seats!, all aboard! **3** *Arch (mode de transport)* conveyance, transport **4** *Com* **lettre de v.** waybill, consignment note **5** *(tiré par des chevaux)* (horse-drawn) vehicle; *(pour passagers)* carriage, coach; *(pour des marchandises)* cart; **v. à deux chevaux** carriage and pair; **v. de place** hackney (carriage *or* cab)

▶▶ **v. à bras** barrow, handcart; **v. d'enfant** pram, *Am* baby carriage; *Vieilli* **v. de malade** bathchair

voiture-bar, *pl* **voitures-bars** NF *Rail* buffet car, refreshment car

voiture-couchette, *pl* **voitures-couchettes** NF *Rail* couchette car

voiturée [vwatyre] NF *Vieilli (de passagers)* carriageful; *(de marchandises etc)* cartload

voiture-école, *pl* **voitures-école** NF driving school car

voiture-lit, *pl* **voitures-lits** NF *Rail* sleeping car, sleeper

voiturer [vwatyre] VT *Vieilli (marchandises etc)* to convey, to transport, to carry, to cart; *Fam* **je vais te v.** I'll drive you

voiture-restaurant, *pl* **voitures-restaurants** NF *Rail* restaurant car, dining car

voiture-salon, *pl* **voitures-salon** NF *Rail* saloon *or Am* parlor car

voiturette [vwatyret] NF trap; *Aut* small car

voiturier [vwatyrje] NM *Jur Arch* carrier, carter; *(dans un hôtel etc)* parking valet; **service de v.** valet parking

voix [vwa] NF **1** voice; **'arrêtez', dit une v.** 'stop', said a voice; **avoir une belle v.** *(en chantant)* to have a fine voice; *(en parlant)* to have a pleasant voice; **avoir une v. grave/chaude** to have a deep/warm voice; **entendre des v.** to hear voices; **parler à v. haute** *ou* **à haute v.** to speak in a loud voice; *(clairement)* to speak aloud, to speak out loud; **parler à v. basse** to speak in a low voice *or* under one's breath *or* in an undertone; **faire la grosse v.** to speak sternly *or* in a severe tone; **élever la v.** to speak up; *(se mettre en colère)* to raise one's voice; **rester sans v.** to remain speechless; **de vive v.** by word of mouth, viva voce; **il me l'a appris de vive v.** he informed me himself; **la v. de la conscience** the voice *or* the dictates of conscience; *Fig* **la v. de la nature** the call of nature; **la v. du peuple** the voice of the people, public opinion, vox populi; **d'une commune v.** by common consent, with one voice; **à portée de (la) v.** within earshot; **hors de portée de (la) v.** out of hearing, out of earshot; **donner de la v.** *(des chiens)* to bark; *(d'un limier)* to give tongue, to bay; *Fig* **donner de la v. contre qch** *(protester)* to protest vehemently against sth; *Mus* **v. de basse/de ténor** bass/tenor voice; **v. de poitrine** chest voice; **v. de tête** head voice; **v. de fausset** falsetto (voice); **v. claire/gaie/enjouée** clear/cheerful/lively voice; **chanter à plusieurs v.** to sing in parts; **je ne suis pas en v.** I'm not in good voice

2 *Pol* vote; **donner sa v. à qn** to vote for sb; **élu à la majorité des v.** elected by a majority; **mettre une question aux v.** to put a question to the vote; **avoir v. consultative/délibérative** to have a consultative role/voting

rights; *Fig* **avoir v. au chapitre** to have a say in the matter; **v. prépondérante** casting vote **3** *Gram* voice; **à la v. active/passive** in the active voice/in the passive (voice) SEE GRAMMAR A40; B39

▶▶ *TV, Cin* **v. dans le champ** in-frame voice; *TV, Cin* **v. hors champ** VO, voiceover; **v. humaine** *(d'un orgue)* vox humana; *TV, Cin* **v. in** voice in; *TV, Cin* **v. off** voiceover; **commentaire en v. off** voiceover commentary; *Cin* **v. en surimpression** voiceover

vol¹ [vɔl] NM **1** flight; **prendre son v.** *(d'un oiseau)* to take wing, to take off; *Fig (prendre son essor)* to take off; **tirer un oiseau au v.** to shoot a bird on the wing; *Fig* **saisir l'occasion au v.** to grasp *or* leap at the opportunity; **à v. d'oiseau** as the crow flies; **à v. d'oiseau, il y a cinq kilomètres** it's five kilometres as the crow flies; **de haut v.** *(personne, collaborateur etc)* high-flying; **un escroc de haut v.** a big-time crook; **oiseau de haut v.** high-flying bird

2 *Aviat* flight; **heures de v.** flying time; **à trois heures de v. de Paris** three hours' flying time from Paris; **il a près de mille heures de v.** he has nearly one thousand flying hours; *Fig Fam* **elle a pas mal d'heures de v.** *(elle n'est plus de la première jeunesse)* she's no spring chicken; **numéro de v.** flight number; **v. 944 pour Glasgow** flight 944 to Glasgow; **tous les vols sont annulés** all flights are cancelled; **avion en v.** aircraft in flight; **v. de nuit** night flying; **v. 'sec'** flight only; **v. aller-retour** return flight, *Am* round-trip flight; **v. charter** charter flight; **v. d'apport** feeder flight; **v. de correspondance** connecting flight; **v. direct** direct flight; **v. avec escale** flight with stopover; **v. habité** manned flight; **v. intérieur** domestic flight, internal flight; **v. libre** hang-gliding; **faire du v. libre** to hang-glide, to go hang-gliding; **v. moyen-courrier** medium-haul flight; **v. nolisé** charter flight; **v. régulier** regular flight, scheduled flight; **v. plané** gliding flight; **descendre en v. plané** to glide down; *Fam* **il a fait un de ces vols planés!** he went flying!; **v. à voile** gliding; **faire du v. à voile** to glide, to go gliding

3 *(nuée d'oiseaux)* flock, flight; *(de perdrix, tétras)* covey; *(de criquets)* swarm **4** *Arch* **(chasse au) v.** hawking

vol² NM theft, stealing, robbery; **commettre un v.** to commit a theft *or* robbery; **v. de grand chemin** highway robbery; *Fam* **c'est du v.!** it's a rip-off!, it's daylight robbery!

▶▶ **v. à l'américaine** confidence trick; **v. avec effraction** breaking and entering, housebreaking; **v. à l'étalage** shoplifting; **v. à main armée** armed robbery; **v. à la portière** = act of theft whereby the thief opens the door of a stationary vehicle and steals any valuable item before the driver has time to react; *Jur* **v. qualifié** aggravated theft, robbery; **v. à la tire** pickpocketing; **être victime d'un v. à la tire** to have one's pocket picked

volage [vɔlaʒ] ADJ fickle, inconstant, flighty

volaille [vɔlaj] NF **1** poultry; **une v.** a fowl; **marchand de volailles** poulterer VOIR GRAMMAIRE A12 **2** *Culin* poultry; **foies de v.** chicken livers

volailler [vɔlaje] NM poulterer

volant [vɔlɑ̃] ADJ **1** flying; *(rubans etc)* fluttering; **objet v. non identifié** unidentified flying object; *Fam* **soucoupe volante** flying saucer; **poisson v.** flying fish; *Aviat* **personnel v.** flight crew; *Mil* **air crew**; **Naut escadre volante** flying squadron **2** *(câble etc)* loose; *(mur etc)* movable; **feuille volante** *(de papier)* loose leaf; **table volante** occasional table; *Constr* **pont v.** flying bridge; **camp v.** temporary camp

NM **1** *Aut* (steering) wheel; **prendre le v.** to take the wheel; **un violent coup de v.** a violent turn of the wheel; **les fous du v.** reckless drivers, roadhogs; **un as du v.** a crack (racing) driver; **v. inclinable** tilt steering wheel; **v. sport** sports steering wheel; **v. télescopique** telescoping wheel **2** (de badminton) shuttlecock; **jeu de v.** (game of) battledore and shuttlecock **3** Couture flounce; (panneau) shaped panel; **volants froncés** gathered flounces; **jupe à volants** flounced skirt **4** (d'horloge) fly **5** (de moteur etc) handwheel **6** Fin, Écon reserve; **v. de sécurité** reserve fund; **v. de trésorerie** cash reserve **7** (d'un carnet de tickets) **talon et v.** counterfoil and leaf

volatil [vɔlatil] ADJ volatile

volatile [vɔlatil] NM Hum winged creature, bird

volatilisable [vɔlatilizabl] ADJ volatilizable

volatilisation [vɔlatilizasjɔ̃] NF volatilization

volatiliser [vɔlatilize] VT **1** Chimie to volatilize **2** (faire disparaître) to make disappear; **on lui a volatilisé sa montre** he's had his watch pinched or nicked
VPR **se volatiliser 1** Chimie to volatilize **2** (disparaître) to vanish (into thin air)

volatilité [vɔlatilite] NF volatility

vol-au-vent NM INV Culin vol-au-vent

volcan [vɔlkɑ̃] NM VOIR GRAMMAIRE A12 **1** volcano; **v. actif/dormant/éteint** active/dormant/extinct volcano; **v. en activité** active volcano **2** Fig (personne) fiery or impetuous person; (situation) volcano; **c'est un vrai v.** he's/she's really fiery or a real spitfire; **danser sur un v.** to be sitting on a powder keg or a time bomb; **son imagination est un v.** he/she has a vivid imagination

volcanique [vɔlkanik] ADJ (roche etc) volcanic; Fig (passion) fiery, ardent; (imagination) vivid; (tempérament, caractère) fiery, impetuous

volcanologie [vɔlkanɔlɔʒi] NF vulcanology

volcanologue [vɔlkanɔlɔg] N vulcanologist

vole [vɔl] NF Cartes vole, all the tricks

volée [vɔle] NF **1** (d'un oiseau, d'un projectile etc) flight; Tennis volley; **prendre sa v.** to take wing; Fig to take off; **tirer à toute v.** to fire a gun at maximum elevation; **lancer qch à toute v.** to hurl sth, to send sth flying; **coup de v.** Rugby punt; Ftbl volley; Tennis volley; **une balle à la v.** to volley a return; Tennis **v. amortie** drop volley; **attraper une balle à la v.** to catch a ball in mid air; Fig **saisir une allusion à la v.** to catch an allusion promptly or instantly; **Agr semer à la v.** to broadcast **2** (de corbeaux etc) flock, flight; (de perdrix) covey; (de filles) band, bevy; (d'écoliers, d'enfants) swarm, crowd **3** (niveau social) rank, standing; **de haute v.** (personne) high-class, top-flight; (par ses aptitudes) high-flying; **un escroc de haute v.** a big-time crook **4** (de missiles) volley; (de coups) shower; **recevoir une bonne v.** to get a sound thrashing; **sonner à toute v.** to set all the bells ringing; (des cloches) to ring a full peal, to be in full peal **5 v. d'escalier** flight of stairs **6** Tech (d'une grue) jib **7** Suisse (promotion) **on est de la même v.** we were in the same year

voler¹ [vɔle] VI **1** (dans les airs) to fly; **nous volons à une vitesse de …** we are flying at a speed of …; Fig **v. de ses propres ailes** to stand on one's own two feet, to fend for oneself; **on aurait entendu v. une mouche** you could have heard a pin drop; **la fenêtre a volé en éclats** the window smashed into pieces or smithereens; **tous nos espoirs ont volé en éclats** all our hopes went up in smoke; **faire v. un cerf-volant** to fly a kite; Fig Fam **elle lui a volé dans les plumes** she went for him, she flew at him **2** Litt to travel fast, to move with speed; **v. au secours de qn** to fly to sb's aid

voler² VT **1** (dérober) to steal; **v. qch à qn** to steal sth from sb, to rob sb of sth; **elle lui a volé cette idée** she stole the idea from him; **on m'a volé ma montre, je me suis fait v. ma montre** someone has stolen my watch, I've had my watch stolen; **je me suis tout fait v.** I've been robbed of everything, I've had everything stolen; Prov **qui vole un œuf vole un bœuf** that's how it all starts; Fam **il ne l'a pas volé** it serves him right; **il se repose un peu maintenant, il ne l'a pas volé** he's having a well-deserved or well-earned rest now, he's having a rest now, and he's earned it **2** (dépouiller) to rob; (rouler) to swindle, to cheat; **on s'est fait v.** (dans ce restaurant) we were ripped off, we were really stung

> Attention: ne pas confondre **to steal** et **to rob** lorsque l'on traduit le verbe **voler**. **To steal** signifie **dérober** (quelque chose), alors que **to rob** signifie **dévaliser** (quelqu'un, un lieu).

volet [vɔlɛ] NM **1** (de fenêtre, de magasin) shutter; **ouvrir/fermer les volets** to open/close the shutters; **mettre/enlever les volets** to put up/take down the shutters **2** (section) (d'un triptyque) panel; (de permis de conduire, d'un dépliant) page; (d'une facture, d'un formulaire) portion; (de chèque) tear-off portion; (sur lumière) flap; (d'une vidéo) wipe; (d'une étude, d'un livre) section; Fig (d'un plan, d'une enquête) stage, part; UE **le v. social** the social chapter **3** Aviat flap; **sortir/rentrer les volets** to lower/raise flaps **4** (d'une roue à eau) paddle; (de carburateur) throttle valve, butterfly valve

voleter [vɔlte] VI (**il volette; il volettera**) (d'un oiseau) to flutter; **v. d'arbre en arbre** to flit from tree to tree

voleur, -euse [vɔlœr, -øz] N thief, pl thieves, robber; (cambrioleur) burglar; **cet épicier est un v.** that grocer's a crook or swindler; **au v.!** stop thief!; **v. d'idées** stealer of ideas, plagiarist; **v. de moutons** sheep stealer
ADJ thieving, thievish; Fml (commerçant etc) rapacious; (enfant) pilfering; **elle est voleuse comme une pie** she has sticky fingers
▸▸ **v. d'enfants** kidnapper; **v. à l'étalage** shoplifter; Hist **v. de grand chemin** highwayman, footpad; **v. à la tire** pickpocket

Volga [vɔlga] NF **la V.** the Volga

volière [vɔljɛr] NF aviary; Fig **cette classe est une vraie v.!** this class is like a zoo!

volige [vɔliʒ] NF Constr scantling, batten; (pour tuiles) slate lath; **caisse en voliges** crate

voligeage [vɔliʒaʒ] NM Constr battening; (pour tuiles) lathing

voliger [vɔliʒe] VT (**je voligeai(s); n. voligeons**) Constr to batten; (pour tuiles) to lath

volis [vɔli] NM broken tree top

volitif, -ive [vɔlitif, -iv] ADJ volitional

volition [vɔlisjɔ̃] NF volition

volley [vɔlɛ] NM Fam (abrév **volley-ball**) volleyball; **v. de plage** beach volleyball

volley-ball [vɔlɛbol] NM Sport volleyball; **jouer au v.** to play volleyball

volleyeur, -euse [vɔlɛjœr, -øz] N Sport **1** volleyball player **2** Tennis volleyer

volontaire [vɔlɔ̃tɛr] ADJ **1** (délibéré) (action) voluntary; **homicide v.** wilful murder, voluntary homicide; **acte v.** wilful act; **contribution v.** voluntary donation; Mil **engagé v.** volunteer **2** (personne) self-willed, wilful, headstrong, obstinate; **menton v.** firm or determined chin
N volunteer

volontairement [vɔlɔ̃tɛrmɑ̃] ADV **1** voluntarily, willingly **2** (délibérément) deliberately, intentionally

volontariat [vɔlɔ̃tarja] NM Mil etc voluntary service; **faire du v.** to do voluntary service

volontarisme [vɔlɔ̃tarism] NM **1** resoluteness, aggressiveness; **faire preuve de davantage de v.** to be more aggressive **2** Phil voluntarism

volontariste [vɔlɔ̃tarist] ADJ **1** (politique, attitude) aggressive **2** Phil voluntaristic, voluntarist

volonté [vɔlɔ̃te] NF **1** (faculté de décision) will; **la v. de vaincre/de puissance** the will to win/for power; **v. de fer** will of iron, iron will; **avoir une v. de fer** to be iron-willed, to have a will of iron or an iron will; **circonstances indépendantes de notre v.** circumstances beyond our control; **par un effort de la v.** by an effort of will; **de sa propre v.** of one's own accord, spontaneously; **manque de v.** lack of will(power); **ne pas avoir de v.** to have no will of one's own, to have no willpower; **elle n'a aucune v.** she has no willpower; **avec la meilleure v. du monde** with the best will in the world; **arriver à qch à coups ou à force de v.** to achieve sth by sheer willpower; **bonne v.** willingness; **faire preuve de bonne v.** to show willing(ness); **personne de bonne v.** willing person; **homme de bonne v.** (pour une entreprise dangereuse etc) volunteer; **mauvaise v.** unwillingness; **faire preuve de mauvaise v.** to show unwillingness, to be grudging; **personne de mauvaise v.** unwilling or grudging person; **elle montre toujours de la bonne v.** she always shows willing; **faire qch de bonne/mauvaise v.** to do sth willingly/unwillingly or with good/bad grace; **elle y met de la mauvaise v.** she's doing it with very bad grace; **en faire à sa v.** to have one's own way; **à v.** at will; **dessert à v.** as much dessert as you like, unlimited dessert; Culin **ajouter du sucre à v.** add sugar to taste; Fin **billet payable à v.** promissory note payable on demand; Mil **feu à v.** fire at will
2 (souhait) wish; **accomplir la v. de qn** to carry out sb's wish; **faire qch contre la v. de qn** to do sth against sb's will; **les dernières volontés de qn** (document) sb's last will and testament; (vœux) sb's last wishes; **dire sa v. de réussir/progresser** to express a wish to succeed/advance; **il fait ses quatre volontés** he does just what he pleases; **elle lui fait faire ses quatre volontés** she can twist him round her little finger

volontiers [vɔlɔ̃tje] ADV **1** (avec plaisir) willingly, gladly, with pleasure; **très v.** I'd be glad to, I'd love to; **prenez du vin – oui, très v.** have some wine – I'd love some; **je prendrais un verre de vin** I could do with or I'd love a glass of wine; **il cause v.** he is fond of talking; **elle en parle v.** she will happily talk about it; **vous venez? – (oui,) v.** are you coming? – yes, I'd love to; **je le ferai le plus v. du monde** I'll be absolutely delighted or it'll give me the greatest pleasure to do so **2** (facilement) readily; **on croit v. que …** we are apt to think that …

volt [vɔlt] NM Élec volt

voltage [vɔltaʒ] NM Élec voltage

voltaïque [vɔltaik] ADJ Élec (cellule, pile) voltaic

voltaire [vɔltɛr] NM Voltaire chair

voltairien, -ienne [vɔltɛrjɛ̃, -jɛn] ADJ, N Voltairian

voltamètre [vɔltametr] NM Élec voltameter

voltampère [vɔltɑ̃pɛr] NM Élec voltampere

volte [vɔlt] NF **1** Équitation, Escrime volt **2** Naut (changement de cap) turn

volte-face [vɔlt(ə)fas] NF INV **1** about-turn, Am about-face; **faire v.** to turn round **2** Fig about-turn, U-turn, Litt volte-face, Am about-face; **faire v.** to do a U-turn *or* an about-turn *or Am* about-face

volter [vɔlte] **VI** *Équitation* **faire v. un cheval** to make a horse circle

voltige [vɔltiʒ] **NF** *(au cirque)*, *Équitation* acrobatics; *(sur trapèze)* flying-trapeze exercises; *Aviat* aerobatics; *Équitation* **haute v.** trick riding; *Aviat* **pilote de v.** stunt pilot; *Fig* **c'est de la haute v. intellectuelle** it's intellectual acrobatics *or* gymnastics

voltiger [vɔltiʒe] **VI** *(je voltigeai(s); n. volti- geons)* **1** *(sur trapèze)* to do acrobatics, to perform on the flying trapeze; *(sur cheval)* to do acrobatics, to perform on horseback **2** *(d'un oiseau, d'un insecte)* to fly about, to flutter (about); *(d'un rideau, d'un drapeau etc)* to flutter, to flap

voltigeur, -euse [vɔltiʒœr, -øz] **N** *(au cir- que)* acrobat; *(sur trapèze)* trapeze artist; *(sur cheval)* performer on horseback
NM *Mil Arch* light infantryman, rifleman

voltmètre [vɔltmetr] **NM** *Élec* voltmeter

volubile [vɔlybil] **ADJ 1** *Bot* voluble; *(tige)* twining **2** *(personne)* voluble

volubilis [vɔlybilis] **NM** *Bot* convolvulus; **v. des jardins** morning glory

volubilité [vɔlybilite] **NF** volubility; **parler avec v.** to be a voluble talker, to talk volubly

volucompteur [vɔlykɔ̃tœr] **NM** volume indicator

volume [vɔlym] **NM 1** *(livre)* volume; **il fau- drait des volumes pour raconter ...** it would take volumes to relate ... **2** *(d'un solide, d'un fluide)* volume, bulk, mass; **v. excessif** *(d'un paquet etc)* bulkiness; **v. d'achat** purchase volume; **v. des affaires** volume of business; **v. annuel de production** annual (volume of) production; **le v. des échanges commer- ciaux** the volume of trade; *Com* **v. de point mort** break-even quantity; **v. des ventes** sales volume, volume of sales; *Naut* **chargé en v.** laden in bulk; **faire du v.** *(d'une chose)* to take up a lot of space; *Fam (d'une per- sonne)* to show off, to throw one's weight about **3** *(du son, de la voix)* volume; **baisser/ monter le v.** to turn the sound *or* volume down/up; **v. sonore** sound level **4** *(de réser- voirs etc)* capacity

volumétrique [vɔlymetrik] **ADJ** volumetric

volumineux, -euse [vɔlyminø, -øz] **ADJ** voluminous, bulky, large; **très peu v.** taking up little space; **dossier v.** bulky file

volupté [vɔlypte] **NF** *(sensual)* pleasure *or* delight; **toutes les voluptés** every plea- surable sensation; **la v. de la revanche ac- complie** the sweet taste of revenge; **avec v.** with (sensual) delight

voluptueusement [vɔlyptɥøzmɑ̃] **ADV** voluptuously

voluptueux, -euse [vɔlyptɥø, -øz] **ADJ** vo- luptuous
N voluptuary, sensualist

volute [vɔlyt] **NF 1** *Archit etc* helix; *(d'un vio- lon)* scroll; *(de fumée)* curl, spiral, wreath; **la fumée s'élève en v.** the smoke is spiralling upwards; **ressort en v.** helical spring **2** *(de coquillage)* whorl

vomer [vɔmer] **NM** *Anat* vomer

vomi [vɔmi] **NM** vomit, *Fam* sick

vomique [vɔmik] **ADJ** *Bot, Pharm* **noix v.** nux vomica

vomiquier [vɔmikje] **NM** *Bot* nux vomica (tree)

vomir [vɔmir] **VT 1** *(nourriture)* to vomit, to bring up, to spew up **2** *(d'une cheminée, d'un volcan etc)* *(fumée, flammes etc)* to belch forth, to spew out; **v. des insultes** *ou* **des injures sur qn** to heap insults *or* abuse on sb **3** *Fig (quelqu'un)* to loathe, *Fml* to abhor
VI to be sick, *Fam* to throw up; **avoir envie de v.** to feel sick *or Am* nauseous; **c'est à (faire) v.** it's enough to make you sick; **une odeur à vous faire v.** a nauseating smell

vomissement [vɔmismɑ̃] **NM 1** *(action)* vo- miting; **il fut pris de vomissements** he star- ted vomiting *or* to vomit **2** *(matière)* vomit, *Fam* sick

vomissure [vɔmisyr] **NF** vomit, *Fam* sick

vomitif, -ive [vɔmitif, -iv] **ADJ, NM** *Méd* emetic, vomitory

vorace [vɔras] **ADJ** voracious; *(appétit)* vor- acious, ravenous; **se sentir d'un appétit v.** to feel ravenously hungry; **plante v.** heavy feeder

voracement [vɔrasmɑ̃] **ADV** voraciously

voracité [vɔrasite] **NF** voracity, voracious- ness

vortex [vɔrteks] **NM** vortex

vos [vo] **ADJ POSS** *voir* **votre**

Vosges [voʒ] **NFPL les V.** the Vosges

vosgien, -ienne [voʒjɛ̃, -jɛn] **ADJ** *(of/from the)* Vosges
N V. *(natif)* native of the Vosges; *(habitant)* inhabitant of the Vosges

votant, -ante [vɔtɑ̃, -ɑ̃t] **N** voter

votation [vɔtasjɔ̃] **NF** *Suisse (élection)* vote

vote [vɔt] **NM 1** vote; *(action)* voting, ballot(- ing), poll; *Parl* **v. d'une loi** passing of a bill; **provoquer un v.** to challenge a division; **droit de v.** right to vote, franchise; **accorder le droit de v. aux femmes** to give women the vote; **prendre part au v.** to go to the polls, to vote; **bulletin de v.** ballot paper; **section de v.** polling district *or* station; **v. blanc** blank ballot paper; **v. à bulletin secret** secret bal- lot; **v. de confiance** vote of confidence; **v. par correspondance** postal vote *or* ballot, *Am* absentee ballot; **v. défavorable** no vote; **v. de défiance** vote of no confidence; **v. di- rect/indirect** direct/indirect vote; **v. libre** free vote; **v. à main levée** vote by (a) show of hands; **v. majoritaire** majority vote; **v. nul** spoilt ballot paper; **v. obligatoire** compul- sory vote; **v. pondéré** weighted vote; **v. pré- férentiel** preferential voting; **v. par pro- curation** vote by proxy, proxy (vote); **v. de protestation** protest vote; **v. utile** tactical vote

voter [vɔte] **VI** to vote; **v. à droite/à gauche/ au centre** to vote for the right/left/centre; **v. communiste** to vote communist; **v. à main levée** to vote by (a) show of hands; **v. par procuration** to vote by proxy; **v. pour/contre un projet de loi** to vote for/against a bill; **v. (pour) Thomas!** vote for Thomas!; **v. utile** to vote tactically
VT 1 *Parl (loi)* to pass, to carry; **v. une propo- sition** to vote in favour of a proposal **2** *(crédit etc)* to vote; **v. des remerciements à qn** to of- fer sb a vote of thanks

votif, -ive [vɔtif, -iv] **ADJ** *(offrande, messe)* votive

votre, *pl* **vos** [vɔtr, vo] **ADJ POSS** SEE GRAMMAR A30; B21-2 **1** your; **v. oncle et v. tante** your aunt and (your) uncle; **v. père et v. mère**, *Litt* **vos père et mère** your mother and father; **j'ai mis v. chapeau et vos gants** I put on your hat and (your) gloves; **mettez v. chapeau et vos gants** *(à une personne)* put on your hat and gloves; *(à plusieurs personnes)* put on your hats and gloves; **un(e) de vos ami(e)s** one of your friends, a friend of yours; **un profes- seur de vos amis** a teacher friend of yours; *Fam* **vous aurez v. chambre à vous** *(chacun aura sa chambre)* you will have your own rooms; *Fam* **v. imbécile de frère** your idiot of a brother; *Fam* **v. artiste de mari** your ar- tist husband; *Fam* **vous avez v. vendredi** you've got Friday off; *Fam* **alors, c'était ça vos vacances de rêve!** so much for your dream holiday! **2** *(pour s'adresser à qn)* **V. Al- tesse** Your Highness; **V. Majesté** Your Majesty

vôtre [votr] **PRON POSS le v./la v./les vôtres** yours; **vous me prêtez le v.?** can I borrow yours?; **il ressemble au v.** it looks like yours; **vous voulez bien nous donner du v.?** can we have some of yours?; **de toutes ces solu- tions, préférez-vous la v.?** out of those pos- sible solutions, do you prefer yours *or* your own?; **vous n'en avez pas besoin, vous avez le v.** you don't need it, you've got your own; **les deux vôtres** your two, the two *or* both of yours; *(en insistant)* your own two; **vous lui avez laissé deux des vôtres** you gave him two of yours; *(vous lui en avez sacrifié deux)* you gave him two of your own; *très Fam* **le v. de bébé est plus intelligent!** your baby is more intelligent; *Fam* **à la v.!** *(en buvant)* cheers!; *Fam* **à la bonne v.!** good health! SEE GRAMMAR A30; B21
NM le v. *(ce qui vous appartient)* yours; **vous devriez y mettre du v.** you should do your share
NMPL les vôtres *(votre famille)* your family, *Am* your folks; *(vos partisans)* your fol- lowers; *(vos coéquipiers)* your team-mates; **je serai des vôtres ce soir** I'll be with you *or* joining you tonight; **je bois à vous et aux vô- tres** I drink to you and yours
ADJ POSS *Litt* **un v. cousin** a cousin of yours; **vous ferez v. nos principes** you will adopt our principles as your own; **ferez-vous vô- tres les félicitations qu'ils nous adressent** will you join them in congratulating us?; **bien sincèrement v.** with kindest regards; **amicalement v.** best wishes

vouer [vwe] **VT** to dedicate, to consecrate; **v. obéissance au roi** to pledge allegiance to the king; **toute l'affection que nous lui avons vouée** all the affection we gave him; **v. sa vie à l'étude** to devote *or* dedicate *or* give up one's life to study; **voué à l'échec** doomed to failure
VPR se vouer se v. à l'étude to devote oneself to study; *Fam* **il ne sait (pas) à quel saint se v.** he's at his wits' end, he doesn't know which way to turn

vouloir [vulwar] **NM** will; **bon/mauvais v.** goodwill/ill will (**pour, envers** towards); **cela dépendra de son bon v.** it will depend on how he feels

VOULOIR [2] *(prp* **voulant**; *pp* **voulu**; *pr ind* **je veux, il veut, n. voulons, ils veulent**; *pr sub* **je veuille, n. voulions, ils veuillent**; *imp* **voulez**, *otherwise* **veuille, veuillez**; *impf* **je voulais**; *p hist* **je voulus**; *fu* **je voudrai**)*

| **VT** to want **1**, **3** ▪ to wish **1**, **3** ▪ to bear somebody a grudge *(en vouloir à qn)* **1** ▪ to require **3** ▪ to demand **3** ▪ to intend **3** ▪ to mean **3** ▪ to be willing *(vouloir bien)* **4** ▪ to admit **6** ▪ to require **8** |
| **VPR** to try to be **1** |

VT SEE GRAMMAR B40 **1** *(désirer)* *(quelque chose)* to want, *Fml* to wish (for), to desire; **v. la paix/la guerre** to want peace/war; **elle sait ce qu'elle veut** she knows what she wants, she knows her own mind, she has a mind of her own; **faites comme vous vou- drez** do as you please *or* like *or* wish; **c'est comme vous voudrez** just as you like; **vous le ferez, je le veux!** you shall do it!; **qu'il le veuille ou non** whether he likes it or not; **je ne le veux pas!** I will not have it!; **que voulez- vous?, qu'est-ce que vous voulez?** what do you want?; *(qu'est-ce que vous croyez?)* what do you expect?; **que voulez-vous que j'y fasse?** what do you want me to do about it?; **il veut tout faire par lui-même, que voulez- vous!** he wants to do everything by himself, what can you do!; **tu n'écoutes jamais ce**

qu'on te dit, que veux-tu! you never listen to what people tell you, what can you expect?; **v. qch de qn** to want sth from sb; **que lui vou-lez-vous?** what do you want from him?; *(pourquoi le cherchez-vous?)* what do you want him for?; **combien en voulez-vous?** how much are you asking *or* do you want for it?; **voulez-vous du thé?** would you like some tea?; **v. de qch** to want (some of) sth; **je ne veux pas de cela** I'll have none of that; **je ne veux pas de ça chez moi** I won't have that in my house; **ils ne veulent pas de moi** they don't want me; **en voulez-vous?** do you want any?, will you have some?, would you like some?; **ils ont de l'argent en veux-tu, en voilà** they're not short of money, they've got money to spare; **v. qn pour roi** to want sb for (a) king *or* as king; **je te veux heureux** I want you to be happy; **v. du bien à qn** to wish sb well; **je ne lui veux pas de mal** I mean him/ her no harm; **en v.** to be very determined *or* ambitious; **en v. à qn** to bear sb a grudge; **à qui en voulez-vous?** what's the trouble now?; **pourquoi lui en veux-tu?** what have you got against him/her?; **tu ne m'en veux pas, au moins?** I hope you don't hold it against me; **ils en veulent à mon argent** they're after my money; **ne m'en veuillez pas** don't be cross with me, don't hold it against me; **en v. à qn de qch/d'avoir fait qch** to have *or* hold *or* bear a grudge against sb for sth/for doing sth

2 *(avec force)* to will; **ce que Dieu veut** the will of God; **ce que femme veut, Dieu le veut** when a woman's made up her mind, that's it; **Dieu le veuille!** please God!; **vous l'avez voulu!** you have only yourself to blame!

3 v. + inf *(expressed or understood)*, **v. que + sub;** *(exiger)* to require, to demand, to will; *(avoir envie de)* to want, to wish; *(essayer de)* (faire qch) to try to; *(avoir l'intention de)* to intend, to mean; **elle veut que nous venions tous** she wants us all to come; **je dire** to mean; **je me demande ce que veut dire ce mot** I wonder what this word means; **ça ne veut rien dire, tout ça** that doesn't mean a thing; **mais qu'est-ce que ça veut dire, cette absence?** what's the meaning of this absence?; **le sort voulut qu'il mourût** fate willed *or* ordained that he should die; **le mauvais sort voulut qu'il arrivât trop tard** as ill luck would have it, he arrived too late; **je veux être obéi!** I intend *or* mean to be obeyed!, I will be obeyed!; **v. absolument** *ou* **à toute force faire qch** to insist on doing sth, to be determined to do sth; **elle veut absolument y être demain** she is determined to be *or* is set on being there tomorrow; **je veux absolument que vous veniez** I insist on your coming; **le moteur ne veut pas démarrer** the engine won't start; **il voulait me frapper** he wanted to hit me; **elle voulut me frapper** she made as if to strike me; **quand j'ai voulu l'embrasser** when I tried to kiss him/her; **elle ne voulait pas s'en aller** she didn't want to go; **mais tu ne veux pas nous laisser un peu tranquilles!** will you (just) leave us alone!; **je fais de lui ce que je veux** I can do as I like with him; **j'aurais tant voulu le voir** I should so much like to have seen him; **j'aurais voulu y rester toujours** I would *or* could have stayed there for ever; **je voudrais bien être à votre place** I wish I were in your place; **je voudrais bien qu'on me le demande, à moi** I wish they'd ask me; **voulez-vous prendre une douche?** would you like to take a shower?; **voulez-vous que j'ouvre la fenêtre?** shall I *or* should I open the window?, would you like me to *or* do you want me to open the window?; **je veux que vous sachiez que ...** I should like you to know that …; **j'aurais voulu qu'elle le sache** I wish she had been told; **je voudrais le voir me parler sur ce ton** I'd like to see him speak to me in

that tone of voice; **je veux que vous soyez heureux** I want you to be happy; **je veux que les choses marchent pour vous** I want things to work out for you; **que voulez-vous que je fasse?** what do you expect *or* want me to do?; **rentrons, voulez-vous?** let's go in, shall we?; **nous n'avons jamais su ce qu'elle voulait faire** we never knew what she meant to do; **faire qch sans le v.** to do sth unintentionally *or* without meaning to *or* without meaning it; **si je t'ai blessé, c'est vraiment sans le v.** if I hurt you, it really was unintentional *or* I really didn't mean to

4 v. (bien) faire qch to consent *or* be willing to do sth; **oui, je veux bien** yes, with pleasure; **je veux bien que vous veniez** I'm quite willing for you to come; **voulez-vous bien attendre un instant?** would you (please) wait *or* would you care to wait a moment?; **veuil-lez (bien) vous asseoir** please sit down; *(plus poli)* do (please) sit down, won't you sit down?; **voulez-vous faire moins de bruit?** would you mind making less noise!, will you please make less noise!; **veuillez agréer, Madame, l'expression de mes senti-ments distingués/dévoués** yours sincerely; **je veux bien attendre** I'm quite happy *or* quite willing to wait; **si vous voulez** if you like, *Fml* if you wish; **je viens quand je veux** I come when I choose *or* like *or* please; **si vous (le) voulez bien** if you don't mind

5 *(bien used as an intensive)* **voulez-vous bien vous taire!** will you be quiet!, *Fam* do shut up!

6 *(admettre)* (quelque chose, dans une argu-mentation) to admit, to allow; **vous n'avez rien à vous reprocher, je le veux bien, mais ...** you are in no way to blame, I am ready to admit *or* I grant you, but …; **je veux bien, mais ...** I understand, but …, fair enough, but …

7 *(soutenir)* to be convinced, to maintain; **il veut absolument que je me sois trompé** he insists that I was mistaken

8 *(d'une chose)* (quelque chose) to require, to need, to demand; **la vigne veut un terrain crayeux** vines need *or* require a chalky soil; **ce verbe veut l'accusatif** this verb takes the accusative

vi to want; **il ne suffit pas de v.** it's not enough just to want something; *Prov* **v., c'est pouvoir** where there's a will there's a way; *Fam* **je veux!** *(je suis entièrement d'accord)* you bet!, and how!

VPR se vouloir 1 elle se veut différente she likes to think she's different; **il se voulait ras-surant** he was trying to be reassuring

2 s'en v. to be angry *or* annoyed with one-self (**de qch** about sth); **je m'en veux énor-mément de lui avoir fait de la peine** I feel really bad about hurting him/her

---

voulu [vuly] **ADJ 1** *(formalités etc)* required, requisite; **cela se fera à l'heure voulue** it will be done in due course; **en temps v.** in due course, eventually **2** *(délibéré)* deliberate, intentional; **c'était v. de sa part** he/she did it deliberately *or* intentionally

[vu] **PRON PERS** SEE GRAMMAR A27; B18–19; B67 **1** *(sujet)* you; **v. et votre femme** you and your wife; **v. deux** you two, the two of you, you both, both of you; **v. tous** you all, all of you; **v. autres Anglais** you English; **c'est v. qui êtes arrivé le premier/arrivés les premiers** it was you who arrived first, you arrived first; **c'était v.-même qui me l'avez dit** you told me so yourself; **v., v. avez raison, v. avez raison, v.** you're the one who's right

2 *(objet)* you; *(objet indirect)* to you; **il ne v. connaît pas** he doesn't know you; **je v. en ai parlé** I've spoken to you about it; **c'est à v. que je parle** it's you I'm talking to; **c'est à v. que je pensais** it's you I was thinking about; **c'est à v. de jouer** it's your turn (to play); **ces**

gants sont à v. these gloves are yours; **c'est un ami à v.** it's a friend of yours; **voilà une photo de v.** here's a photo of you; **j'ai con-fiance en v.** I trust you

3 *(réfléchi)* **v. êtes-v. bien amusé(e)/amu-sé(e)s?** did you enjoy yourself/yourselves?; **v. allez v. faire du mal** you're going to hurt yourself/yourselves; **taisez-v.!** be quiet!; **v. les avez rassemblés autour de v.** you ga-thered them round you; **v. ne pensez qu'à v.(-même)** you think only of yourself; **v. le dites/le savez v.-même** you say so/know yourself SEE GRAMMAR A29–30; B28–9

4 *(réciproque)* **est-ce que v. v. connaissez?** do you know each other *or* one another?

5 *(pour remplacer on)* you, one; *Fml* **c'est désagréable quand on ne v. reconnaît pas** it's annoying when people don't recognize you

vous-même(s) **PRON PERS** yourself, *pl* yourselves; *voir* **vous**, **même**

vousoiement [vuzwamɑ̃] **NM** *Suisse* (vou-voiement) = 'vous' form of address

vousoyer [vuzwaje] *Suisse* **VT** (vouvoyer) to address as 'vous'; **les parents se faisaient v. par leurs enfants** the children addressed their parents as 'vous'
▸ **VPR se vousoyer** to address each other as 'vous'

vousseau, -eaux [vuso], **voussoir** [vuswar] **NM** *Archit* voussoir, archstone

voussure [vusyr] **NF** *Archit (d'une arche)* curve, arch moulding

voûte [vut] **NF** *Archit* vault, arch; **v. d'arête** groined vault; **v. en berceau** barrel vault; **v. d'ogives** ribbed vault; **v. en plein cintre** semicircular vault; **voûte(s) en éventail** fan vaulting; **en v.** vaulted
▸▸ *Litt* **la v. céleste** the vault *or* canopy of heaven; **v. crânienne** dome of the skull; **v. du palais, v. palatine** roof of the mouth; **v. plantaire** arch (of the foot)

voûté [vute] **ADJ** *(toit etc)* vaulted, arched; *(personne)* stooping, round-shouldered; *(dos)* bent; **j'ai toujours eu le dos v.** I've al-ways had a stoop

voûter [vute] **VT** *(toit etc)* to arch, to vault; **l'âge a voûté son dos** age has bowed his back *or* made him stoop
VPR se voûter to become bent *or* bowed *or* round-shouldered, to begin to stoop

vouvoiement [vuvwamɑ̃] **NM** = addressing people as 'vous' *(as opposed to 'tu')*; **le v. est de rigueur au bureau** people must address each other as 'vous' in the office

vouvoyer [vuvwaje] **VT** *(pr ind* **je vouvoie, n. vouvoyons;** *fu* **je vouvoierai)** *(quelqu'un)* to say 'vous' to, to address as 'vous' *(as op-posed to 'tu')*

voyage [vwajaʒ] **NM** journey, trip; *(circuit)* tour; **v. en chemin de fer** rail(way) journey; **v. (sur mer)** (sea) voyage; **v. (touristique) ac-compagné** conducted *or* guided tour; *(ex-cursion)* escorted tour; **il ne sera pas du v.** he won't be making the journey; **aimer les voyages** to be fond of travel *or* of travelling; **livre de v.** travel book; **récit de v.** travel story; *Radio* travelogue; **v. autour du monde** world tour, round-the-world trip; **faire un v. autour du monde** to go round the world, to go on a world tour *or* on a round-the-world trip; **les gens du v.** travelling people, travel-lers; **elle est en v.** she is travelling; **est-il tou-jours en v.?** is he still away, is he still on his travels?; **partir en v.** to set off on a journey; **bateau engagé au v.** ship hired by the run; **frais de v.** travelling expenses; **compagnon de v.** travelling companion; *(dans voiture etc)* fellow passenger; **bon v.!** have a good trip!; **ça va t'obliger à faire deux voyages** that way you'll need to make two trips; **je**

n'aurai pas fait le v. pour rien I won't have made the trip for nothing, it won't have been a wasted journey; *Litt* faire le grand v. to go on one's last journey

▸▸v. d'affaires business trip; être en v. d'affaires to be away on business; partir en v. d'affaires to go (off) on business trip; v. aller outward trip; v. aller et retour round trip; v. en au-journey; v. en trip; voyages en autocar coach tour; voyages en avion air travel; v. d'études study trip; (d'encouragement) familiarization tour; v. de familiarisation familiarization trip; v. à forfait inclusive tour, package tour, all-expense tour, all-in tour; v. d'information fact-finding mission *or* tour; voyages en mer sea travel; v. de noces honeymoon; nous sommes partis en v. de noces en Guadeloupe we went to Guadeloupe on *or* for our honeymoon; v. organisé package holiday *or* tour, inclusive tour; v. de presse press trip; v. professionnel business trip; voyages professionnels business travel; v. retour return journey; v. scolaire school trip; v. de stimulation incentive trip *or* tour

voyager [vwajaʒe] **vi** (**je voyageai(s); n. voyageons**) **1** to travel; **v. par mer/par chemin de fer** to travel by sea/by rail; **v. pour affaires** to travel on business **2** *Com* to travel, *Fam* to be on the road; **v. pour les vins** to travel in wine **3** *(de marchandises etc)* to be transported; **vin qui ne peut pas v.** wine that does not travel; **ce produit voyage très bien** this product travels very well

voyageur, -euse [vwajaʒœr, -øz] **N 1** traveller, *Am* traveler; *(en train etc)* passenger; *(en taxi)* fare **2** *(aventurier)* voyager, explorer **3 v. de commerce, v. représentant placier** (commercial) traveller, travelling salesman, rep; **v. d'affaires** business traveller
■ **ADJ 1** *(qui voyage souvent)* travelling; **commis v.** commercial traveller **2 pigeon v.** carrier pigeon, homing pigeon

voyagiste [vwajaʒist] **N** tour operator; *(grossiste)* tour wholesaler

voyance [vwajãs] **NF** clairvoyance

voyant, -ante [vwajã, -ãt] **ADJ** *(couleur)* gaudy, loud, garish; *(monument etc)* showy, conspicuous
■ **N 1** *(contraire d'aveugle)* sighted person; **les voyants** the sighted **2** *(qui perçoit le sens caché des choses)* seer, prophet
■ **NM 1** *(signal)* *(indicateur)* signal; *(pour arpenteur)* *(plaque de nivellement)* sighting board, slide vane, sight; *Naut (d'un bateau-phare)* sphere **2** *(d'un instrument scientifique)* sighting slit, aperture **3** *Aut* **v.** *(lumineux)* warning light; **v. d'huile/d'essence** oil/petrol indicator light; **v. de baisse de tension des piles** 'battery low' warning light; **v. de charge** battery charge warning light; **v. de frein à main** 'handbrake on' light; **v. de marche** activation light
■ **NF voyante** clairvoyant; **voyante extra-lucide** clairvoyant

voyelle [vwajɛl] **NF** *Ling* vowel

voyeur, -euse [vwajœr, -øz] **N** voyeur, *f* voyeuse, *m* Peeping Tom

voyeurisme [vwajœrism] **NM** *Psy* voyeurism

voyou [vwaju] **NM** *(délinquant)* (young) lout, hooligan, *Br* yob(bo); *(enfant)* (cheeky) street urchin, guttersnipe
■ **ADJ** *(often inv in f, sometimes* **voyoute**) crude, loutish

VPC [vepese] **NF** *(abrév* **vente par correspondance**) mail order (selling)

vrac (en) [ãvrak] **ADV 1** *(sans emballage)* loose; **charger en v.** to load in bulk; **marchandises en v.** *(non emballées)* loose goods; **vendu en v.** sold loose **2** *(en désordre)* higgledy-piggledy, in a jumble; **outils jetés**

en v. sur le plancher tools thrown higgledy-piggledy on the floor; **tout est posé en v. sur ma table** everything is lying higgledy-piggledy *or* in a jumble *or* jumbled together on my table; **elle a déposé ses affaires en v. sur la table** she dumped her things on the table

vrai, -aie [vrɛ] **ADJ** SEE GRAMMAR B10 **1** *(indéniable)* true; **c'est (bien) v.!** it's true!, that's right!; **elle est gentille, c'est v., mais pas très fine** she's nice, I agree, but she's not very bright; *Fam* **c'est pas v.!** I don't believe it! **2** *(réel)* *(ami)* true, genuine; *(diamant)* real, genuine; *(tableau, antiquité)* genuine; *(déception, raison)* real; **elle a eu une vraie déception/colère** she was really disappointed *or* angry; **le v. Dieu** the true God; **il a été un v. père pour moi** he was like a father to me; **un v. Anglais d'Angleterre** an Englishman born and bred, a real Englishman; **couleurs vraies** lifelike *or* realistic colours; **un homme v.** a genuine man **3** *(véritable)* real, downright, regular; **c'est un v. clown** he's a real clown; **c'est une vraie menteuse** she's a real *or* a downright liar
■ **ADV** truly, really, indeed; **faire v.** to write/paint/*etc* realistically; **ces détails/descriptions font tout à fait v.** these details/descriptions are very lifelike *or* realistic; **tu m'aimes, pas v.?** you do love me, don't you?; **v. de v.!** really and truly!; **pas v.?** I'm right, aren't I?, isn't that so?; **toi aussi, tu le penses, pas v.?** you think so too, don't you *or* right?
■ **NM distinguer le v. du faux** to distinguish truth from falsehood; **être dans le v.** to be right; **il y a du v. là-dedans** there's some truth in it; **dire v.** to tell the truth; **à v. dire, à dire v.** as a matter of fact, to tell the truth; *Fam* **pour de v.** really, seriously, *surtout Am* for real; **elle ne le disait pas pour de v.** she wasn't (being) serious, she didn't (really) mean it; **on ne jouait pas pour de v.** we weren't playing for real *or* seriously; **c'est pour de v.** I'm serious, I (really) mean it; **c'est pour de v. cette fois** this time it's serious *or* for real
■ **N un homme, un v.** a real man; **c'est une infirmière, une vraie** she's a nurse, the real thing *or* the genuine article

vraiment [vrɛmã] **ADV** really; **vous êtes v. trop bon** you are really too kind; **je ne sais pas v. ce que je vais faire** I don't really know what I'm going to do; **je ne savais v. pas quoi faire** I really didn't know what to do; **v.?** really?; **ils voyagent v. beaucoup** they really travel a lot; **oui, v.** yes, indeed; **non merci, v.** no thank you, really

vraisemblable [vrɛsɑ̃blabl] **ADJ** probable, likely; *(crédible)* credible; *(plausible)* plausible; **il n'est pas v. que** + *subit* is hardly likely that; **excuse peu v.** implausible *or* unconvincing excuse
■ **NM le v.** what is probable *or* likely

vraisemblablement [vrɛsɑ̃blabləmã] **ADV** probably, very likely; **nous devrions v. arriver vers 16 heures** we should probably arrive around 4 p.m.

vraisemblance [vrɛsɑ̃blãs] **NF** probability, likelihood; **selon toute v.** in all probability

vraquier [vrakje] **NM** bulk carrier

VRC [veɛrse] **NF** *Mktg (abrév* **vente par réseau coopté**) MLM, multilevel marketing

V/Réf *(abrév* **votre référence**) your ref

vrillage [vrijaʒ] **NM** *Aut (de la transmission)* wind-up

vrille [vrij] **NF 1** *Bot* tendril **2** *(outil)* gimlet, borer, piercer; **yeux percés en v.** gimlet eyes, beady eyes **3** *Aviat* spin; **descente en v.** spinning dive; **faire la v., se mettre en v., tomber en v.** to go into a spin; **monter en v.** to corkscrew up; **à plat** flat spin; **v. serrée** steep spin; **v. sur le dos** inverted spin **4** *Fig Fam* **partir en v.** to go down the tubes *or* pan

vrillé [vrije] **ADJ 1** *(percé)* bored into, pierced into **2** *(corde)* twisted, kinked **3** *Bot* with tendrils, tendrilled

vrillée [vrije] **NF** *Bot Fam* bindweed

vriller [vrije] **VT** *(avec une vrille)* to bore
■ **VI 1** *(d'un avion etc)* to spiral, to spin (up/down) **2** *(d'une corde, d'un fil)* to twist, to kink

vrillette [vrijɛt] **NF** deathwatch (beetle)

vrombir [vrɔ̃bir] **VI** *(des mouches etc)* to buzz; *(d'un avion, d'une toupie etc)* to hum; *(d'un moteur)* to roar

vrombissement [vrɔ̃bismã] **NM** *(d'insectes)* buzz(ing); *(d'un avion, d'une toupie etc)* hum(ming); *(d'un moteur)* roar(ing)

VRP [veerpe] **NM** *(abrév* **voyageur représentant placier**) sales representative, *Fam* rep; **V. multicarte** freelance rep

VSN [veesen] **NM** *(abrév* **volontaire du service national**) = recruit who chooses to carry out his national service by doing voluntary service overseas

VTC [vetese] **NM** *(abrév* **vélo tout chemin**) hybrid bike

VTT [vetete] **NM** *(abrév* **vélo tout-terrain**) mountain bike

vu [vy] **NM 1 au vu de tous** openly, publicly; **au vu et au su de tous** openly and publicly; **c'est du déjà vu** that's nothing new; *Com* **sur le vu de la facture** on sight of the invoice **2** *Jur (d'un décret)* preamble
■ **PRÉP** in view of, considering, seeing; **vu la chaleur, je voyagerai de nuit** in view of *or* because of the heat, I'll travel by night; *Fam* **vu que ... +** *ind* seeing that ...; **vu qu'on te l'a déjà expliqué plusieurs fois** seeing that it's already been explained to you several times

vue [vy] **NF 1** *(faculté de voir)* (eye)sight; **avoir des troubles de la v.** to have eye trouble; **perdre la v.** to lose one's sight; **avoir la v. courte** *ou* **basse** to be shortsighted; **avoir une bonne v.** to have good eyesight; **jeter** *ou* **porter la v. sur qch** to take a look at sth; **connaître qn de v.** to know sb by sight; **perdre qn de v.** to lose sight of sb; *(perdre contact)* to lose touch with sb; **nous nous sommes perdus de v. depuis cette période** since then, we've lost touch with each other; **à perte de v.** as far as the eye can see; **parler à perte de v.** to talk endlessly, to keep on talking; **personnes les plus en v.** people most in the public eye; **une personnalité en v.** a prominent *or* conspicuous personality; **mettre qch (bien) en v.** to display sth (conspicuously); *Fam* **en mettre plein la v. à qn** to impress *or* dazzle sb; **faire qch à la v. de tous** to do sth in sight *or* in full view of everybody; **se tenir hors de v.** to keep out of sight; *Fam* **à v. de nez** at a rough guess *or* estimate; **à v. d'œil** visibly; *Aviat, Naut* **navigation à v.** visual navigation; *Aviat* **voler à v.** to fly visually

2 *(d'extra-lucide)* **seconde v.** second sight

3 *(opinion)* view; **échange de vues** exchange of views; **c'est une v. de l'esprit** that's a very theoretical point of view

4 à la v. de qn/qch at the sight of sb/sth; **à la v. du chien, elle se mit à paniquer** at the sight of *or* when she saw the dog, she began to panic; **à première v.** at first sight; *Fin* **à v.** at sight; *Com* **payable à v.** payable at sight; *Mus* **jouer un morceau à v.** to play a piece at sight; **à v.** *ou* **en v. de terre** (with)in sight of land

5 *(panorama)* view, outlook; **chambre qui a v. sur le jardin** room that looks out on(to) the garden; **je voudrais une chambre avec v., s'il vous plaît** I'd like a room with a view, please; **vues de Paris** views of Paris; **v. aérienne** aerial view; *Phot* **v. fixe** slide; *Aut* **v. panoramique** all-round view; **v. de face/de côté** *(d'objet, de personne)* front/side view;

v. en coupe cross section
6 *Jur (d'une maison)* window, light; **droit de vues** ancient lights; **condamner les vues** to block up the windows
7 *(intention)* intention, purpose, design; **avoir des vues sur qn/qch** to have plans for *or* designs on sb/sth; **elle a des vues sur mon frère** she has designs on my brother; **avoir qch en v.** to have sth in view *or* in mind; **je crois qu'il a déjà quelqu'un en v.** I think he's already got someone in mind; **en v. de** with a view to; **travailler en v. de l'avenir** to work with an eye to the future
8 *Can Fam* **les vues** *(le cinéma)* the cinema *or Am* movies; **aller aux (petites) vues** to go to the cinema *or Am* movies

Vulcain [vylkɛ̃] NM **1** *Myth, Astron* Vulcan **2** *Entom* **v.** red admiral (butterfly)

vulcanisation [vylkanizasjɔ̃] NF *Ind* vulcanization

vulcaniser [vylkanize] VT *Ind (caoutchouc)* to vulcanize

vulgaire [vylgɛr] ADJ **1** *Péj* vulgar, common; **tenue v.** tarty *or* common outfit; **plaisanterie**

v. vulgar joke; **cela la rend v.** it makes her look common **2** *(courant)* *(communes etc)* common, everyday; **l'opinion v.** the common *or* general opinion; **langue v.** vernacular; **le latin v.** vulgar Latin; **nom v.** **(d'une plante)** common name (for a plant); **expression v.** common *or* widely used expression **3** *Péj* **un v. poste de radio** a very ordinary *or* a common-or-garden radio
▸ NM **1 le v.** *(les gens)* the common people *or* herd **2 donner dans le v.** to be vulgar; **tomber dans le v.** to lapse into vulgarity

vulgairement [vylgɛrmɑ̃] ADV **1** *Péj* vulgarly; **parler v.** to be vulgar in one's speech; **s'habiller/se conduire v.** to dress/behave vulgarly *or* tastelessly **2** *(en général)* generally, commonly; **la fleur v. appelée bouton d'or** the flower commonly called the buttercup

vulgarisateur, -trice [vylgarizatœr, -tris] N popularizer

vulgarisation [vylgarizasjɔ̃] NF *(d'un savoir)* popularization; **ouvrage de v.** popular work

vulgariser [vylgarize] VT *(connaissance)* to popularize

vulgarisme [vylgarism] NM vulgarism

vulgarité [vylgarite] NF vulgarity

vulgate [vylgat] NF **1** *Rel* **la V.** the Vulgate (version of the Bible) **2** *Fig* popular ideology; **la v. marxiste** popular Marxist ideology

vulgos [vylgos] ADJ INV *Fam* common, vulgar

vulgum pecus [vylgɔmpekys] NM *Fam* the hoi polloi, the rabble

vulnérabilité [vylnerabilite] NF vulnerability

vulnérable [vylnerabl] ADJ vulnerable

vulnéraire [vylnerɛr] NF *Bot* kidney vetch, lady's finger, woundwort

vulpin [vylpɛ̃] NM *Bot* foxtail (grass)

vulvaire [vylvɛr] ADJ *Anat* vulvar

vulve [vylv] NF *Anat* vulva

vumètre [vymɛtr] NM *Radio* VU meter, volume meter

W¹, w [dublave] NM INV *(lettre)* W, w

W² *Élec (abrév* **watt**) w

W3 NM *Ordinat (abrév* **World Wide Web)** WWW

wagnérien, -ienne [vagnerjɛ̃, -jɛn] ADJ, N *Mus* Wagnerian

wagon [vagɔ̃] NM *Rail* **1** *(véhicule) (de passagers)* carriage, coach, *Am* car; *(de marchandises)* truck, wagon, *Am* car; **w. de marchandises** goods van; **monter en w.** to get into *or* onto *or* to board the train; **w. à bagages** luggage van, *Am* baggage car; **w. à bestiaux** cattle truck, *Am* stock car; **w. frigorifique** refrigerated van **2** *(contenu)* truckload, wagonload, *Am* carload (**de** of)

wagon-bar, *pl* **wagons-bars** NM *Rail* buffet car

wagon-citerne, *pl* **wagons-citernes** NM *Rail* tank wagon *or Am* car

wagon-foudre, *pl* **wagons-foudres** NM *Rail* tank wagon *or Am* car

wagon-lit, *pl* **wagons-lits** NM *Rail* sleeping car, sleeper; **voyager en w.** to take a sleeper

wagonnet [vagɔnɛ] NM tip truck

wagonnier [vagɔnje] NM *Rail* truck *or Am* car shunter

wagon-poste, *pl* **wagons-poste** NM *Rail* mail van *or Am* car

wagon-réservoir, *pl* **wagons-réservoirs** NM *Rail* tank wagon *or Am* car

wagon-restaurant, *pl* **wagons-restaurants** NM *Rail* dining *or* buffet car, *Br* restaurant car

wahhabite [waabit] ADJ, N Wahhabi

Walhalla [valala] NM *Myth* Valhalla

Walkman® [wɔkman] NM Walkman®, personal stereo

walk-over [wɔlkɔvœr] NM INV *Sport, Courses de chevaux* walkover

Walkyrie [valkiri] NF *Myth* Valkyrie, Walkyrie; *Hum Fig* **une w.** an Amazon

wallaby, *pl* **wallabies** [walabi] NM wallaby

wallingant, -ante [walɛ̃gɑ̃, -ɑ̃t] N *Péj* Walloon separatist

Wallis-et-Futuna [walisefutuna] N Wallis and Futuna Islands

wallon, -onne [walɔ̃, -ɔn] ADJ Walloon
NM *Ling* Walloon
N **W.** Walloon

Wallonie [walɔni] NF **la W.** Wallonia *(the south and south-east regions of Belgium, where French and Walloon are spoken)*

WAP [wap] NM *Tél (abrév* **wireless applications protocol)** WAP; **W. lock** WAP lock

wapiti [wapiti] NM *Zool* wapiti, American elk

warrant [warãt, va-] NM *Com, Jur* (warehouse) warrant, warehouse receipt; **w. en marchandises** produce warrant; *Com* **w. cédule** warrant

warrantage [warɑ̃taʒ, va-] NM *Com* securing goods by warrant

warranté [warɑ̃te, va-] ADJ **marchandises warrantées** goods covered by a warehouse warrant

warranter [warɑ̃te, va-] VT *Com* to secure by warrant, to warrant

wasserette [wasrɛt] NF *Belg (laverie automatique)* launderette, *Am* laundromat

wassingue [wasɛ̃g] NF *(dans le nord de la France)* floorcloth

water-closet, *pl* **water-closets** [watɛrklɔzɛt] NM lavatory, toilet

watergang [watɛrgɑ̃g] NM *(dans le nord de la France, en Belgique)* polder channel

wateringue [watarɛ̃g] NF *Tech (dans le nord de la France, en Belgique)* draining works

water-polo [watɛrpolo] NM *Sport* water polo

waterproof [watɛrpruf] ADJ INV waterproof

waters [watɛr, va-] NMPL lavatory, toilet; **où sont les w.?** where is the lavatory *or* toilet?

watt [wat] NM *Élec* watt

wattheure [watœr] NM *Élec* watt-hour

wattman, *pl* **wattmen** [watman, -mɛn] NM *Vieilli (d'un tramway électrique)* driver

wattmètre [watmɛtr] NM *Élec* wattmeter

W.-C. [vese, dublavese] NMPL lavatory, toilet

Web [wɛb] NM INV *Ordinat* **le W.** the Web

webcam [wɛbkam] NF *Ordinat* Web cam

webmestre [wɛbmɛstr] NM *Ordinat* Web master

webzine [wɛbzin] NM *Ordinat* webzine

week-end, *pl* **week-ends** [wikɛnd] NM weekend; **partir en w.** to go away for the weekend

western [wɛstɛrn] NM *Cin* western; **w.-spaghetti** spaghetti western

Westphalie [vɛs(t)fali] NF Westphalia

wharf [warf] NM wharf

whig [wig] ADJ, NM *Hist* Whig

whisky, *pl* **whiskies** [wiski] NM whisky; *(irlandais, américain)* whiskey; **un w.-coca** a whisky and Coke®; **verre à w.** whisky glass

whist [wist] NM whist; **w. de Gand** solo (whist)

white-spirit, *pl* **white-spirits** [wajtspirit] NM white spirit

wigwam [wigwam] NM wigwam

Williamine® [wiljamin] NF *Suisse* = pear brandy made from Williams pears

william(s) [wiljam(s)] NF Williams pear; **poire-w.** Williams pear

winch [wintʃ] NM *Naut* winch

winchester [winʃɛstɛr] NF Winchester (rifle)

Windsurf® [windsœrf] NM *(marque de planche à voile)* Windsurfer®

windsurfiste [windsœrfist] N windsurfer

wishbone [wiʃbon] NM *(de planche à voile)* wishbone boom

wisigoth, -othe [vizigo, -ɔt] *Hist* ADJ Visigothic
N **W.** Visigoth

wolfram [vɔlfram] NM *Minér* wolfram

wolof [wɔlɔf] ADJ, NM *Ling* Wolof

wombat [wɔ̃ba] NM wombat

won [wɔn] NM *(monnaie)* won

woofer [wufœr] NM *(haut-parleur)* woofer

World Wide Web [wœrldwajdwɛb] NM *Ordinat* **le W.** the World Wide Web

wurtembergeois, -oise [vyrtɛ̃berʒwa, -waz] ADJ of/from Würtemberg
N **W.** Würtemberger

WWW, W3 NM *Ordinat (abrév* **World Wide Web)** WWW

wysiwyg [wiziwig] ADJ, NM *Ordinat* WYSIWYG

X, x [iks] NM INV **1** *(lettre)* X, x **2** *(nombre inconnu, personne inconnue)* X, x; **Monsieur X** Mr X; **je vous l'ai dit x fois** I've told you umpteen times *or* a thousand times; **dans x années** in X number of years; **plainte contre X** suit against person or persons unknown **3** *Méd* **rayons X** X-rays **4** *Univ Fam* **l'X** the École polytechnique; **un X** a student at the École polytechnique **5** *Cin* **film classé X** adults-only *or* X-rated film **6** *Jur* **accoucher sous X** to give birth anonymously; **naître sous X** to be born to an unidentified mother **7** *Fam (ecstasy)* X, E

xanthome [gzātom] NM *Méd* fatty lump, *Spéc* xanthoma

xanthophylle [gzātɔfil] NF *Bot* xanthophyll

xénon [gzenɔ̃] NM *Chimie* xenon

xénophobe [gzenɔfɔb] ADJ xenophobic N xenophobe

xénophobie [gzenɔfɔbi] NF xenophobia

Xénophon [gzenɔfɔ̃] NM Xenophon

xérès [keres, gzeres] NM *(vin)* sherry N **X.** *(ville)* Jerez

xérophile [gzerɔfil] ADJ *Bot* xerophilous

xérophyte [gzerɔfit] NF *Bot* xerophyte

Xerxès [gzerses] NM Xerxes

xiphoïde [gzifɔid] ADJ *Anat* **appendice x.** xiphoid process

xiphophore [gzifɔfɔr] NM *(poisson)* swordtail

xylène [gzilen] NM *Chimie* xylene

xylographe [gzilɔgraf] N wood-engraver, *Spéc* xylographer

xylographie [gzilɔgrafi] NF **1** *(technique)* wood-engraving, *Spéc* xylography **2** *(gravure)* woodcut, *Spéc* xylograph

xylophage [gzilɔfaʒ] *Zool* ADJ wood-eating NM wood-eater

xylophone [gsilɔfɔn, gz-] NM *Mus* xylophone

xylophoniste [gzilɔfɔnist] N xylophone player

Y, y ¹ [igrek] NM INV *(lettre)* Y, y

y ² [i] SEE GRAMMAR B20 ADV *(lieu)* there; **est-il à Paris? – oui, il y est** is he in Paris? – yes, he is (there); **je ne m'y sentais pas très bien, dans cette ville** I didn't feel very happy in that town; **j'y suis, j'y reste!** here I am and here I stay!; **je n'y suis pour personne** I'm not at home to anybody; *Fam* **ah, j'y suis!** ah, now I've got *or* I get it; **excusez-moi, je n'y étais pas du tout** I'm sorry, I didn't get that at all; **vous n'y êtes pas du tout** you're way off the mark; **pendant que vous y êtes** while you're at *or* about it; *Iron* **non mais fouille dans mes affaires pendant que tu y es!** just rummage through my things, why don't you!

PRON INV **1 j'y pense sans cesse** I think about it constantly; **l'aider? tu n'y penses pas!** help him? what are you thinking of?; **vous y avez tout intérêt** you'd be well advised to; **je n'y comprends rien** I can't make head nor tail of it; **tu as l'air de t'y connaître en informatique** you seem to know quite a bit about computers *or* what you're doing when it comes to computers; **je ne m'y connais pas du tout** I don't know the slightest thing about it/them; **tu peux lui faire confiance, il s'y connaît** you can trust him, he knows what he's doing; **j'y gagnerai** I'll gain by it; **n'y compte pas** don't count on it; **je m'y attendais** I expected as much; **ça, on pouvait s'y attendre** it was to be expected; **venez nous voir – je n'y manquerai pas** come and see us – I certainly shall *or* I'll do that

2 *(standing for person just mentioned)* **pensez-vous encore à lui? – oui, j'y pense sans cesse** do you still think of him? – yes I do, all the time; **les femmes? je n'y comprends rien** women? I don't understand them

3 *(indeterminate uses)* **je vous y prends!** caught you!; **ça y est, on peut manger/elle est prête** OK, we can eat/she's ready; **ça y est, j'ai une idée!** I've had an idea!; **alors ça y est, tu as fini?** have you finished?; **ça y est, la vitre est cassée!** I knew it, they've broken the window!; **ça y est, j'ai trouvé!** *(solution)* I've got it!; **ça y est enfin, je l'ai retrouvé!** I've found it at last!; **j'y suis pour un tiers** I'm in for a third; **elle n'y est pour rien** she's got nothing to do with it; **il y est pour quelque chose** he's got a hand in it, he's got something to do with it; **il doit y être pour une bonne part** *(dans une décision)* he must have had a lot to do with it; **j'ai tout mangé, y compris les légumes** I've eaten everything, including the vegetables

4 *(imperative form preceding y takes s for liaison)* **vas-y** [vazi] go there; *(agis)* go on!, get on with it!; **penses-y** [pãszi] think about it

y ³ PRON PERS *Fam* = **il**

***yacht** [jɔt] NM yacht; **croisière en y.** yachting cruise; **y. de croisière** cabin cruiser

***yacht-club,** *pl* **yacht-clubs** NM yacht club

***yachting** [jɔtiŋ] NM yachting; **faire du y.** to go yachting

***yacht(s)man,** *pl* **yacht(s)men** [jɔtman, -mɛn] NM yachtsman

***ya(c)k** [jak] NM *Zool* yak

***yang** [jãg] NM yang

***yankee** [jãki] ADJ Yankee
  N **Y.** Yankee

***yaourt** [jaur(t)] NM yog(h)urt; **y. nature/aux fruits/aromatisé** plain/fruit/flavoured *or Am* flavored yog(h)urt; **y. maigre** low-fat yog(h)urt

***yaourtière** [jaurtjɛr] NF *(appareil)* yog(h)urt maker

***yatagan** [jatagã] NM *(sabre)* yataghan

***yearling** [jœrliŋ] NM yearling (colt)

***Yémen** [jemen] NM Yemen

***yéménite** [jemenit] ADJ Yemeni
  N **Y.** Yemeni

***yen** [jɛn] NM *(monnaie japonaise)* yen

***yeti** [jeti] NM yeti

yeuse [jøz] NF *Bot* ilex, holm-oak, holly-oak

yeux [jø] NMPL *voir* œil

***yé-yé** [jeje] *Vieilli* ADJ INV *(chanteur, groupe)* (60s style) pop; *(style, mode)* 60s
  N INV pop fan

***yiddish** [jidiʃ] ADJ INV, NM Yiddish

***yi-king** [jikiŋ] NM I Ching

***yin** [jin] NM yin

***yoga** [jɔga] NM yoga; **faire du y.** to do yoga; **cours/prof/posture de y.** yoga class/teacher/position

***yoghourt** [jogurt] NM = **yaourt**

***yogi** [jɔgi] NM yogi

***yogourt** [jogurt] NM = **yaourt**

***yole** [jɔl] NF *Naut* gig, skiff

***Yom Kippour** [jɔmkipur] NM *Rel* Yom Kippur

***yorkshire** [jɔrkʃœr] NM Yorkshire terrier

***yougoslave** [jugɔslav] *Anciennement* ADJ Yugoslav, Yugoslavian
  N **Y.** Yugoslav, Yugoslavian

***Yougoslavie** [jugɔslavi] NF *Anciennement* Yugoslavia; **l'ex-Y.** the former Yugoslavia

***youp** [jup] INT hup!

***youpala** [jupala] NM baby bouncer

youpi [jupi] INT yippee!

***youpin, -ine** [jupɛ̃, -in] N *Fam (terme injurieux) (juif)* Yid, *Am* hebe

***youyou** [juju] NM *Naut* dinghy

***Yo-Yo**® [jojo] NM INV yo-yo

yoyoter [jɔjɔte] VI *Fam* **1** *(mal fonctionner)* to be on the blink, *Am* to be on the fritz **2** *(déraisonner)* to have a screw *or Br* a slate loose, to be off one's trolley

ypérite [iperit] NF *Mil* mustard gas, *Spéc* yperite

ypréau, -aux [ipreo] NM *Bot* **1** *(orme)* wych-elm **2** *(peuplier blanc)* white poplar

ytterbium [iterbjɔm] NM *Chimie* ytterbium

yttrium [itrijɔm] NM *Chimie* yttrium

***yuan** [juan] NM yuan

***yucca** [juka] NM *Bot* yucca

***Yukon** [jukɔ̃] NM **le Y.** the Yukon

***yuppie** [jœpi, jupi] N yuppie

An asterisk before a noun indicates that the definite article is **le** *or* **la**, *not* **l'**

Z, z [zɛd] NM INV *(lettre)* Z, z

ZAC [zak] NF *abrév* zone d'aménagement concerté

Zacharie [zakari] NM *(prophète)* Zechariah; *(père de saint Jean-Baptiste)* Zachariah

ZAD [zad] NF *abrév* zone d'aménagement différé

Zagreb [zagrɛb] N Zagreb

Zaïre [zair] NM Zaire

zaïrois, -oise [zairwa, -waz] ADJ Zairean ▸ N Z. Zairean

zakouski [zakuski] NMPL *Culin* zak(o)uski *(mixture of Russian hors d'oeuvres served with drinks)*

Zambèze [zãbɛz] NM le Z. the Zambezi

Zambie [zãbi] NF *Géog* Zambia

zambien, -ienne [zãbjɛ̃, -jɛn] ADJ Zambian ▸ N Z. Zambian

zanzi [zãzi] NM = zanzibar

Zanzibar [zãzibar] NM Zanzibar

zanzibar [zãzibar] NM = sort of dice game *(played for drinks)*

zapper [zape] VI *TV* to zap, to channel-hop, to channel-surf ▸ VT *Fam (supprimer)* to scrap, to scratch

zappette [zapɛt] NF *Fam* remote (control)

zappeur [zapœr] NM (compulsive) channel-hopper *or* channel-surfer

zapping [zapiŋ] NM le z. channel-hopping, channel-surfing; **faire du z.** to channel-hop, to channel-surf

Zarathoustra [zaratustra] NM Zarathustra

zarbi [zarbi] ADJ *Fam* strange, weird, odd

zazou, -oue [zazu] *Fam Vieilli* ADJ hep; **il a des côtés zazous** he's a bit of a hepcat ▸ N hepcat

zèbre [zɛbr] NM **1** *Zool* zebra; *Fam* **courir comme un z.** to run like the wind **2** *Fam (individu)* character, guy; *Br* bod; **quel drôle de z.!** he's quite something, that guy!

zébré [zebre] ADJ striped (**de** with), stripy; **un mur z. d'ombre et de lumière** a wall with stripes of *or* striped with shadow and light

zébrer [zebre] VT (**je zèbre; je zébrerai**) to stripe, to streak; **un ciel d'orage zébré par les éclairs** a stormy sky streaked with lightning

zébrure [zebryr] NF *(dessin régulier)* stripe; *(dessin irrégulier)* streak; *(cicatrice)* weal; **les zébrures du tigre** the tiger's stripes

zébu [zeby] NM *Zool* zebu, humped ox

zée [ze] NM *(poisson)* John Dory

zef [zɛf] NM *Fam* wind

Zélande [zelãd] NF Zealand

zélateur, -trice [zelatœr, -tris] N zealot, zealous supporter; **les zélateurs du socialisme** Socialist zealots

zèle [zɛl] NM zeal, ardour, *Am* ardor (**pour**

for); **avec z.** zealously; **faire du z.** to be over-zealous, to overdo it; **excès de z.** overzealousness; **faire preuve d'un excès de z.** to be overzealous; **faux z.** misguided zeal; **grève du z.** work-to-rule; **pas de z.!** don't overdo it!

zélé, -ée [zele] ADJ *(personne)* zealous; **peu z.** lacking in zeal, not very zealous ▸ N zealous person

zélote [zelot] NM *Hist* Zealot ▸ N *Péj (personne animée d'un zèle fanatique)* zealot

zen [zɛn] NM Zen ▸ ADJ INV **1** *(relatif au zen)* Zen **2** *Fam (serein)* être/rester z. to be/stay cool

zénith [zenit] NM *Astron, Fig* zenith; *Astron, Fig* **être à son z.** to have reached its/one's zenith; **il était au z. de sa gloire quand ...** he was at the height of his fame when ...

zénithal, -ale, -aux, -ales [zenital, -o] ADJ *Astron* zenithal

Zénon [zenɔ̃] NM Zeno

zéolit(h)e [zeolit] NF *Minér* zeolite

ZEP [zɛp] NF **1** *(abrév zone d'éducation prioritaire)* = area targeted for special help in education **2** *(abrév zone d'environnement protégé)* = environmentally protected zone

zeph [zɛf] NM *Fam* wind

zéphyr [zefir] NM **1** *Litt (vent)* zephyr, balmy breeze **2** *Tex* zephyr (cotton)

zeppelin [zeplɛ̃] NM zeppelin

zéro [zero] NM VOIR GRAMMAIRE A77 **1** *(chiffre)* *Tél, Scol* zero, *Br* nought; *Scol* **ça mérite un z. de conduite** that deserves a zero for behaviour; *Scol* **elle lui a mis un z. pointé** she gave him zero; *Fig* **alors, là, z. pointé, tout le monde sait ça!** God you're ignorant, everybody knows that!; *Fam* **il est bien gentil, mais pour le travail, z.!** he's nice enough, but when it comes to work he's a dead loss; *Fam* **c'est un z.** *(personne)* he's a nonentity; *Sport* **trois à z.** three nil; *Tennis* **quinze à z.** fifteen love; *Pol* **option z.** zero option **2** *(d'échelle de graduation)* zero; *Élec (sur cuisinière électrique etc)* 'off'; **point z.** *Phys* zero (degrees); *Mil* degree zero; **à z.** zeroed; **remettre à z.** to zero; *Fam* **être** *ou* **avoir le moral à z.** to be feeling down (in the dumps) *or* thoroughly depressed; *très Fam* **les avoir à z.** to be scared stiff *or* witless; **avoir la boule à z.** to have a shaved head; **partir de z.** *(dans un projet)* to start from scratch; *(dans sa carrière)* to start from nothing; **il faut tout reprendre à z.** you'll/we'll/*etc* have to start all over again *or* start again from scratch ▸ ADJ INV **z. faute** no mistakes; **z. heure cinq** five past twelve (midnight); **z. degré Celsius** zero degrees Celsius; **z. défaut** zero defect

zérotage [zerotaʒ] NM *(d'un thermomètre)* calibration, fixing of the zero point

zest [zɛst] NM *Arch* **être entre le zist et le z.** to be neither one thing nor the other, to be be-

twixt and between; *(hésiter)* to shillyshally, to waver

zeste [zɛst] NM *Culin (d'agrumes)* peel, zest; **un z. de citron** a piece of lemon peel; **z. confit, z. d'Italie** candied peel; *Fig* **un z. d'accent** a touch *or* a bit of an accent; *Fig* **un z. d'ironie/d'humour/de cynisme** a touch *or* note of irony/humour/cynicism

zêta [dzeta] NM *(lettre grecque)* zeta

zeugma [zøgma], **zeugme** [zøgm] NM *Littér* zeugma

zézaiement [zezemã] NM lisping, lisp; **souffrir de z.** to have a lisp

zézayer [zezeje] VI (**je zézaie, je zézaye, n. zézayons; je zézaierai, je zézayerai**) to lisp

ZI [zedi] NF *abrév* zone industrielle

zibeline [ziblin] NF **1** *Zool* **(martre) z.** sable **2** *(fourrure)* sable (fur)

zievereer [zivərer] NM *Belg Fam Hum (radoteur)* drivelling fool

zieuter [zjøte] VT *Fam* = zyeuter

ZIF [zif] NF *abrév* zone d'intervention foncière

zig [zig] NM *Fam* guy, *Br* bloke; **un bon z.** a decent type, a good sort; **c'est un drôle de z.** he's a queer customer

ziggourat [zigurat] NF *Archéol* ziggurat

zigomar [zigomar], **zigoto** [zigoto] NM *Fam* **c'est un drôle de z.!** he's a weird one!; **faire le zigoto** to act the fool, to clown around

zigouiller [ziguje] VT *Fam (tuer)* to do in; **se faire z.** to get done in

zigue [zig] NM *Fam* = zig

zigzag [zigzag] NM zigzag; **en z.** *(chemin, tranchée)* zigzag; *(éclair)* forked; **faire des zigzags** *(d'une route, une voiture)* to zigzag; *(d'une personne ivre etc)* to stagger *or* zigzag along; *Naut* **faire route en z.** to steer a zigzag course; **rivets disposés en z.** staggered rivets

zigzaguer [zigzage] VI to zigzag; *(d'une personne ivre etc)* to stagger *or* zigzag along

Zimbabwe [zimbabwe] NM Zimbabwe

zimbabwéen, -enne [zimbabweɛ̃, -ɛn] ADJ Zimbabwean ▸ N Z. Zimbabwean

zinc [zɛ̃g] NM **1** *(métal)* zinc; **pommade à l'oxyde de z.** zinc ointment **2** *Fam (comptoir)* counter, bar; **prendre un verre sur le z.** to have a drink at the counter *or* bar **3** *Fam (avion)* plane

zingage [zɛ̃gaʒ] NM **1** *(du toit etc)* covering with zinc **2** *Métal (de l'acier)* galvanizing

zingaro [dzingaro], *pl* **zingari** [dzingari] NM *Arch* gipsy

zinguer [zɛ̃ge] VT **1** *(toit)* to cover with zinc **2** *Métal (acier)* to galvanize

zingueur [zɛ̃gœr] NM *Métal* zinc worker; **plombier z.** plumber and zinc worker

zinnia [zinja] NM *Bot* zinnia

zinzin [zɛ̃zɛ̃] *Fam* ADJ *(Fon)* loopy, cracked; **elle est devenue complètement z.** she's gone completely off her rocker
NM **1** *(truc)* thingumajig, thingummy, whatsit **2** *Fin* institutional investor

zinzolin [zɛ̃zɔlɛ̃] ADJ, NM reddish purple

Zip® [zip] NM zip

zippé [zipe] ADJ *(jupe)* with a zip; **robe zippée dans le dos** dress that zips up at the back

zipper [zipe] VT *Ordinat* to zip

zircon [zirkɔ̃] NM *Minér* zircon

zirconium [zirkɔnjɔm] NM zirconium

zist [zist] NM *voir* zest

zizanie [zizani] NF **1** *(entre les gens)* ill feeling; **semer la z. dans la famille** to cause trouble in the family; **il aime mettre la z. dans les ménages** he loves stirring things up in other people's households **2** *Bible (ivraie)* tare

zizi [zizi] NM *Enf (pénis)* thing(y), *Br* willy

zizique [zizik] NF *Fam* music, sounds, tunes

zloty [zlɔti] NM *(monnaie polonaise)* zloty

zob [zɔb] NM *Vulg* dick, knob

zoccoli(s) [zɔkoli] NMPL *Suisse (sabots)* clogs

Zodiac® [zɔdjak] NM dinghy

zodiacal, -ale, -aux, -ales [zɔdjakal, -o] ADJ *(lumière, étoile)* zodiacal; **signes zodiacaux** signs of the zodiac

zodiaque [zɔdjak] NM **le z.** the zodiac; **signe du z.** sign of the zodiac

zombi(e) [zɔ̃bi] NM *(revenant)*, *Fig Fam* zombie

zona [zona] NM *Méd* shingles, *Spéc* (herpes) zoster, zona; **avoir un z.** to have shingles
VOIR GRAMMAIRE A10

zonage [zonaʒ] NM *(en urbanisme)* zoning

zonal, -ale, -aux, -ales [zonal, -o] ADJ zonal

zonard, -arde [zonar, -ard] N *Fam (marginal)* drop-out

zone [zon] NF *Géom* zone; **la z. du zodiaque** (the belt of) the zodiac; *Géog* **z. tempérée** temperate zone; **z. des alizés** trade-wind belt; **z. houillère** coal belt; *Météo* **z. de dépression** trough (of low pressure); **z. de haute pression** area of high pressure; **z. dangereuse** danger zone; **z. interdite** prohibited *or* restricted area; **z. fumeurs/non fumeurs** smoking/no-smoking area; **de seconde z.** second-rate; **la z.** *(bidonville)* the slum area *(on outskirts of city)*, *Fam Péj* **c'est la z.!** it's the pits!; **c'est vraiment la z. dans ce bureau** this office looks like a tip
▸▸ *Ordinat* **z. adresse** location box; *Ordinat* **z. d'affichage** display area, viewable area; **z. d'aménagement concerté** = area developed through cooperation between public and private sectors; **z. d'aménagement différé** = area designated for future development; *Ordinat* **z. d'amorçage** boot sector; **z. des armées** war zone, zone of operations; *Aut* **z. bleue** me-

ter zone, restricted parking zone; **z. de chalandise** shop site; *Aut* **z. de choc** impact zone; **z. commerciale** retail park; **z. de couverture** *(d'un satellite)* area of coverage; *Aut* **z. de déformation** crumple zone; **z. de dégradé** *(d'un satellite)* shadow area; **z. démilitarisée** demilitarized zone; *Ordinat* **z. de dialogue** dialog(ue) box; **z. dollar** dollar area; *Ordinat* **z. dynamique** hot spot; *Aut* **z. d'écrasement** crush zone; *Ordinat* **z. d'écriture** write area; **z. d'éducation prioritaire** = area targeted for special help in education; *Ordinat* **z. d'état** status box; **z. euro** euro zone; **z. franc** franc area; *Écon* **z. franche** free zone; *Com* **z. franchise** duty free zone; **z. frontière** frontier zone; **z. industrielle** industrial estate *or* park; **z. d'influence** sphere of influence; **z. d'intervention foncière** = area designated for possible development; *Hist* **z. libre** unoccupied France; **z. de libre-échange** free-trade area; **z. monétaire** monetary area; *Hist* **z. occupée** occupied France; **z. d'ombre** *Fig* grey area; *(d'un satellite)* shadow area; **z. postale** postal area; *Aut* **z. rouge** *(du compte-tours)* red zone; **z. sous douane** customs zone; **z. de stationnement** parking zone; **z. de stationnement contrôlé** *ou* **réglementé** controlled parking zone; **z. sterling** sterling area; *Ordinat* **z. tampon (en mémoire)** (memory) buffer; *Mktg* **z.-test** test area; *Ordinat* **z. de travail** work area; **z. à urbaniser en priorité** priority development area; **z. verte** green belt; *Aut* **z. de vision** zone of vision

---

Zone
The Paris area is divided into fare zones for public transport. Zones 1 and 2 cover metropolitan Paris and certain areas of the nearby suburbs. The remaining zones cover the outer suburbs: "j'habite en zone 3", "une carte orange quatre zones". France is divided into three "zones" (A, B and C), the schools in the different zones taking their mid-term breaks and Easter holidays at different times to avoid swamping the public transport system and tourist infrastructure.

---

zoné [zone] ADJ *Minér* zoned, zonate

zoner [zone] *Fam* VI *(traîner)* to hang around, to bum around
VT *(faire)* **qu'est-ce que tu zones?** what are you up to?
VPR **se zoner** to hit the sack *or* hay *or Am* rack

zoo [zo, zoo] NM zoo

zoolâtrie [zɔɔlɑtri] NF zoolatry

zoologie [zɔɔlɔʒi] NF zoology

zoologique [zɔɔlɔʒik] ADJ zoological; **jardin** *ou* **parc z.** zoo, zoological garden(s)

zoologiste [zɔɔlɔʒist], **zoologue** [zɔɔlɔg] N zoologist

zoom [zum] NM *Cin (effet)* zoom; *(objectif)* zoom (lens); **faire un z.** to zoom in; **faire un z. sur qn/qch** to zoom in on sb/sth; **z. arrière** zoom-out; **faire un z. arrière** to zoom out; **z. avant** zoom-in; **faire un z. avant** to zoom in (sur on)

zoomer [zume] VI *Cin Fam* to zoom; **z. sur qn/qch** to zoom in on sb/sth

zoomorphe [zɔɔmɔrf], **zoomorphique** [zɔɔmɔrfik] ADJ zoomorphic

zoophilie [zɔɔfili] NF bestiality

zooplancton [zɔɔplãktɔ̃] NM zooplankton

zoospore [zɔɔspɔr] NF *Biol* zoospore

zootechnie [zɔɔtɛkni] NF = science of animal domestication and breeding, *Spéc* zootechnics

Zoroastre [zɔrɔastr] NM Zoroaster, Zarathustra

zoroastrien, -ienne [zɔrɔastrijɛ̃, -jɛn] ADJ, N Zoroastrian

zoroastrisme [zɔrɔastrism] NM Zoroastrianism

zostère [zɔstɛr] NF *Bot* eel grass, zostera

zou [zu] INT *Fam* **(allez) z.!** off with you!, off you go!; **allez z., tout le monde dehors!** come on, everybody outside!

zouave [zwav] NM *Mil* Zouave; *Fam (pitre)* fool, clown; **faire le z.** to play the fool, to fool *or* clown about

zouk [zuk] NM *Mus* = type of Caribbean music

zoulou, -oue [zulu] ADJ Zulu
N **Z.** Zulu

Zoulouland [zululãd] NM Zululand

zozo [zozo] NM *Fam* nitwit, *Br* twit

zozoter [zɔzɔte] VI *Fam* to lisp

ZUP [zyp] NF *abrév* **zone à urbaniser par priorité**

Zurich [zyrik] N Zurich

zut [zyt] INT *Fam* damn!, blast!; **et puis z., si tu n'es pas content, c'est pareil!** and if you don't like it, tough! *or* hard cheese!; **et puis z.! tant pis, on y va sans lui!** what the hell! let's go without him!; **avoir un œil qui dit z. à l'autre** to squint, to be cross-eyed

zwanze [zwɑ̃z] N *Belg Fam* joke; **faire la z.** to live it up, to party; **mettre de la z.** to liven things up

zwieback [tsɥibak] NM *Suisse (biscotte)* = piece of toasted bread sold in packets and often eaten for breakfast, *Am* zwieback

zyeuter [zjøte] VT *Arg (jeter un coup d'œil à)* to have a look *or Br* a dekko at; *(observer, regarder avec insistance)* to eye up

zygomatique [zigɔmatik] ADJ *Anat* zygomatic

zygomorphe [zigɔmɔrf] ADJ *Bot* zygomorphous, zygomorphic

zygote [zigɔt] NM *Biol* zygote

zymase [zimaz] NF *Chimie* zymase

Labels and abbreviations used in the text

Term	Abbreviation	Equivalent
abbreviation	ABBR, ABRÉV	abréviation
accountancy	Acct	comptabilité
adjective	ADJ	adjectif
administration	Admin	administration
adverb	ADV	adverbe
agriculture	Agr	agriculture
American English	Am	anglais américain
anatomy	Anat	anatomie
antiquity	Antiq	antiquité
approximately	approx	approximativement
archaic, obsolete	Arch	archaïque
archaeology	Archeol, Archéol	archéologie
architecture	Archit	architecture
slang	Arg	argot
article	ART	article
	Art	beaux-arts
astrology	Astrol	astrologie
astronomy	Astron	astronomie
space travel	Astronaut	astronautique
Australian English	Austr	anglais d'Australie
cars, motoring	Aut	automobiles, circulation routière
auxiliary	AUX	auxiliaire
aviation	Aviat	aviation
	Banking, Banque	
art	Beaux-Arts	
Belgian French	Belg	français de Belgique
	Billiards, Billard	
biology	Biol	biologie
botany	Bot	botanique
	Bowling, Boules	
Stock Exchange	Bourse	
	Boxing, Boxe	
British English	Br	anglais britannique
Canadian French	Can	français du Canada
	Cards, Cartes	
carpentry	Carp	menuiserie
catholicism	Cathol	catholicisme
ceramics	Cer, Cér	céramique
chemistry	Chem, Chimie	chimie
	Chess	échecs
surgery	Chir	chirurgie
Church of England	Church of Eng	Église anglicane
cinema, films	Cin	cinéma, films
commerce	Com	commerce
comparative	comp	comparatif
accountancy	Compta	comptabilité
computing	Comput	ordinateurs, informatique
conditional	cond	conditionnel
conjunction	conj	conjonction
conjugated like	conj like	se conjugue comme
building industry	Constr	construction
horseracing	Courses de chevaux	
sewing	Couture	
cricket	Cr	cricket
cookery	Culin	cuisine
	Cycling, Cyclisme	
definite	DEF, DÉF	défini
demonstrative	DEM, DÉM	démonstratif
dialect	Dial	dialecte
diminutive	dimin	diminutif
chess	Échecs	
ecology	Ecol, Écol	écologie
economics	Econ, Écon	économie
for example	eg	par exemple
Church of England	Église anglicane	
electricity	Elec, Élec	électricité
electronics	Electron, Électron	électronique
children's language	Enf	langage des enfants
English	Eng	anglais
entomology	Entom	entomologie
horseriding	Équitation	
fencing	Escrime	
especially	esp	surtout
et cetera	etc	et cetera
European Union	EU	Union européenne
euphemism	Euph	euphémisme
feminine	f	féminin
familiar, colloquial	Fam	familier
football	Ftbl	football
	Fencing	escrime
figurative use	Fig	sens figuré
finance	Fin	finance
	Fishing	pêche
formal use	Fml	language formel
	Formerly	anciennement
feminine plural	fpl	féminin pluriel
French	Fr	français
future tense	fu	futur
geography	Geog, Géog	géographie
geology	Geol, Géol	géologie
geometry	Geom, Géom	géométrie
grammar	Gram	grammaire
gymnastics	Gym	gymnastique
heraldry	Her, Hér	héraldique
history	Hist	histoire
	Horseracing	courses de chevaux
	Horseriding	équitation
humorous	Hum	humoristique
imperative	imp	impératif
impersonal	IMPERS	impersonnel
imperfect	impf	imparfait
indicative	ind	indicatif
industry	Ind	industrie
indefinite	INDEF, INDÉF	indéfini
infinitive	inf	infinitif
interjection	INT	interjection
interrogative	INTERR	interrogatif
invariable	INV	invariable
Irish English	Ir	anglais d'Irlande
ironic	Iron	ironique
journalism, press	Journ	journalisme, presse
law, legal	Jur	juridique, droit
	Knitting	tricot
	Law	juridique, droit
linguistics	Ling	linguistique
literary use	Lit, Litt	usage littéraire
literature	Liter, Littér	littérature
masculine	m	masculin